P9-CAM-955

PASSENGER ARRIVALS

at the

Port of New York

1820–1829

Bentley, Elizabeth Petty

PASSENGER ARRIVALS

at the

PORT OF NEW YORK

1820–1829

Transcribed by
ELIZABETH P. BENTLEY

Baltimore
GENEALOGICAL PUBLISHING CO., INC.
1999

Flagstaff Public Library
Flagstaff, Arizona

Copyright © 1999
Genealogical Publishing Co., Inc.
Baltimore, Maryland
All rights reserved. No part of this publication
may be reproduced, in any form or by any means,
including electronic reproduction or reproduction
via the Internet, except by permission of the publisher.
Library of Congress Catalogue Card Number 98-75654
International Standard Book Number 0-8063-1610-1
Made in the United States of America

9er.
729.37471
4771 P
B v.1

INTRODUCTION

The National Archives has preserved the passenger lists of over 6,000 ships, which brought more than 85,000 individuals to New York City from 1820 through 1829. This, unfortunately, does not represent all the ships that arrived. Those months which are wholly without surviving lists are noted below, and one can only assume that some smaller, undetected gaps exist in other months as well. The volume of arrivals seems to follow a seasonal pattern, so the chart showing the number of ships arriving in each month compared to the whole year and to the same month of the previous year may be of some use in determining whether a given month has fewer arrivals than would seem normal. The growing volume of arrivals over the years is an indication of both increasing traffic and increasing compliance with the new law requiring submission of passenger lists.

The ship carrying the largest number of passengers during this period was the *Marchioness*, which arrived May 13, 1828 from Liverpool. Some interesting passengers in these records are General Lafayette and his son, George Washington Lafayette, on the *Cadmus*, arriving in New York from Havre on August 17, 1824, presumably when the General visited the states to celebrate the 50th anniversary of the Revolution. Jerome Napoleon Bonaparte, son of Jerome Bonaparte, brother of Napoleon I, and Betsy Patterson of Baltimore, is enumerated in 1827. And in 1829, Henry Longfellow, a merchant, is listed as aged 22, which is compatible with his being the American poet, Henry Wadsworth Longfellow (1827–1882).

The microfilm version of the records presented some challenges to interpretation in that the frames were unevenly exposed, sometimes being so light or dark as to be virtually unreadable, especially along the edges. These gaps are indicated in the text by an ellipsis, as are those spots in which the original appears to be torn away or blotted out. Many of the lists appear to be in the same handwriting and on a standardized form, indicating that the lists were recopied, probably by the collector of customs, to whom the lists were delivered. Several lists in August 1829 are preserved in two different versions, one of which shows considerable redaction, such as changing various states of destination to uniformly read "United States," which may mean that other lists have received similar treatment, whether or not they are actually stamped "[COPY]" on the typed or handwritten sheet that precedes each list. This header frame gives the name of the vessel, the port of embarkation (usually only on the typed sheet), the date of arrival, and a ship number. The typed information is sometimes at variance with the handwritten information on the list itself, and even the handwritten information varies, especially the signature of the master at the bottom of the list, compared with his name as it is written in blanks at the head of the form: "I, _____ [master's name] do solemnly, sincerely, and truly _____ [swear or affirm] that the following List or Manifest of Passengers, subscribed with my name, and now delivered by me to the Collector of the Customs for the District of New-York, contains, to the best of my knowledge and belief, a just and true account of all the Passengers received on board the _____ [ship name] whereof I am Master, from _____ [port of embarkation] So help me God. _____ [Sworn or Affirmed] to the _____ [day and month] 18_____ [year], before me, _____ [collector of customs] _____ [master's signature] List or Manifest of all the PASSENGERS taken on board the _____ [ship name] whereof _____ [master's name] is Master, from _____ [port of embarkation] burthen _____ [number] tons.

The numbering of the ships begins anew each year, and this consecutive number is included in the list of ships in this volume, preceded by the last two digits of the year; for example: 20-123 means the 123rd ship to arrive in 1820. As noted below, a few lists were inserted into the order with an "A" or "B" after the duplicate number.

Some non-standard manifest forms include, instead of "the country to which they severally belong" and "the country in which they intend to become inhabitants," three columns, namely, "place of nativity," "last place of settlement," and "allegiance." Also, ditto marks are somewhat inconsistent: often written out "ditto" or "do," or with a mark ("), or with a horizontal line that includes a little wiggle that is presumably intended to be a ditto mark, or with brackets, or with a vertical line extending over several entries or down the length of an entire page. These marks, however, especially in the age column, are often used simply as place holders, without reference to any previous data, and the wiggly line, in practice, is often indistinguishable from a straight line that generally means "none" or "not applicable," but which I've transcribed as if there were no data in that area. Thus, when no occupation, sex or place is listed, it might actually be the same as a previous entry, or, on the other hand, a stray mark may have been interpreted as a ditto. Very often a whole family will be bracketed or have ditto marks of some sort in the occupation column, resulting in such incongruities as a month-old Blacksmith. A wide range of occupations are listed, and their typically eccentric spelling has been reproduced. Occupations range from nondescript "Labourers and Servants" for everyone on the ship to detailed information regarding relationships, to some curiosities such as "Child Maker" or "Anything." Where surnames were not indicated by ditto marks, it was not uncommon to find variant spellings within what appeared to be a family group. For instance: Catherine Halerine, David Hallerin, Martin Halerin, and Jane Harlerin. Where I thought it was useful, I've included names that were crossed out in the original. Some of these individuals may have, in fact, died on the voyage, even though a column for that information is available on the form. Some extraneous information is included in this index through the use of notes, but much information has been excluded, such as passage in cabin or steerage, complexion, color of hair and eyes, stature, and baggage.

I would like to express my thanks to Dr. Michael Tepper, the general editor and originator of this project, and to my family, who had to put up with my nighttime microfilm viewing in total darkness.

NATIONAL ARCHIVES MICROFILM #237

Roll 1: 20-001 (7 Jan)   – 20-362 (30 Dec)
           21-001 (2 Apr)   – 21-145 (30 Jun)

Roll 2: 21-146 (2 Jul)   – 21-442 (31 Dec)
           22-001 (2 Jan)   – 22-204 (17 May)

Roll 3: 22-205 (18 May) – 22-614 (31 Dec)
           23-001 (3 Jan)   – 23-098 (26 Mar)

Roll 4: 23-099 (3 Apr)   – 23-599 (17 Nov)

Roll 5: 23-600 (18 Nov) – 23-657 (31 Dec)
           24-001 (2 Jan)   – 24-445 (11 Aug)

Roll 6: 24-446 (12 Aug) – 24-744 (30 Dec)
           25-001 (3 Jan)   – 25-229 (30 Apr)

Roll 7: 25-230 (2 May) – 25-737 (29 Dec)

Roll 8: 26-001 (2 Jan)   – 26-514 (31 Aug)

Roll 9: 26-515 (2 Sep) – 26-739 (27 Dec)
           27-001 (2 Jan)   – 27-313 (30 May)

Roll 10: 27-314 (1 Jun)   – 27-763 (16 Nov)

Roll 11: 27-764 (21 Nov) – 27-869 (31 Dec)
           28-001 (2 Jan)   – 28-345 (30 Jun)

Roll 12: 28-346 (1 Jul)   – 28-721 (30 Dec)
           29-001 (2 Jan)   – 29-069 (28 Feb)

Roll 13: 29-070 (4 Mar) – 29-343 (31 Oct)

PASSENGER ARRIVALS

at the

Port of New York

1820–1829

PASSENGER ARRIVALS AT THE PORT OF NEW YORK

NAMES OF PASSENGERS	AGE	SEX	OCCUPATIONS	COUNTRY TO WHICH THEY BELONG	COUNTRY THEY INTEND TO INHABIT	SHIPS/DATES OF ARRIVAL	
AARONS, Aaron	17	M	Merchant	England	England	Tontine	1 Jun 1826
Abigal	35	F		England	England	Tontine	1 Jun 1826
Alexander	3	M		England	England	Tontine	1 Jun 1826
Flora	21	F		England	England	Tontine	1 Jun 1826
George	12	M		England	England	Tontine	1 Jun 1826
Henry	5	M		England	England	Tontine	1 Jun 1826
Jacob	44	M	Merchant	England	England	Tontine	1 Jun 1826
Julia	8	F		England	England	Tontine	1 Jun 1826
AARRANDER, Chas.	28	M	Planter	U. States	U. States	Pedlar	18 Nov 1824
ABADIE, Victor, Mr.	23	M	Gentleman	United States	United States	Montano	18 Dec 1827
ABASIAL, S.	14	M	Student	Spain		Dionisio	30 Oct 1827
ABBAH, Fred	20	M	Gent	England	U. States	Charlemagne	19 Sep 1828
ABBERS, J. H.	30	M	Merchant	Germany	U. States	Bayard	5 Sep 1828
ABBOT, Alfred	35	M	Gent	U. States	U. States	Charlemagne	19 Sep 1828
Amelia	14	F	Gent	U. States	U. States	Charlemagne	19 Sep 1828
Clarah	6	F	Gent	U. States	U. States	Charlemagne	19 Sep 1828
Edvard	2	M	Gent	U. States	U. States	Charlemagne	19 Sep 1828
George	4	M	Gent	U. States	U. States	Charlemagne	19 Sep 1828
Henry	24	M	Shoemaker	England	Boston	Curler	7 Jul 1827
Henry	48	M	Gent	U. States	U. States	Charlemagne	19 Sep 1828
Jams	3	M	Gent	U. States	U. States	Charlemagne	19 Sep 1828
John	20	M	Servant	England	Mexico	Jupiter	27 Jun 1828
Mariah	10	F	Gent	U. States	U. States	Charlemagne	19 Sep 1828
Maryan	48	M	Gent	U. States	U. States	Charlemagne	19 Sep 1828
Thomas	23	M	Labourer	England	America	William	21 Sep 1821
William	36 6/12	M	Engineer	England	U. States	Mary Ann	2 Jan 1829
William G.	64	M	Joiner	England	America	Britannia	22 Jul 1829
ABBOTDAY, Samuel	31	M	Farmer	England	America	Britannia	22 Jul 1829
ABBOTT, Aaron	38	M	Farmer	England	Upper Canada	Comet	6 Mar 1823
Ann	50	F	Family [of James]	England	Upper Canada	Comet	6 Mar 1823
Anna	9	F	Family [of Aaron]	England	Upper Canada	Comet	6 Mar 1823
Ele..., Miss	7	F	Carpenter	England	U.S.	Acasta	11 May 1827
Elizabeth	7	F	Family [of Aaron]	England	Upper Canada	Comet	6 Mar 1823
Esther	5	F	Family [of Aaron]	England	Upper Canada	Comet	6 Mar 1823
George	35	M	Shoemaker	England	Upper Canada	Comet	6 Mar 1823
Hebzeabah	33			England	America	Britannia	22 Jul 1829
Isaac	29	M	...	...	...	Braganza	8 Aug 1825
J.	33	M	builder	England	America	Britannia	22 Jul 1829
J. S. A.	10	M			United States	Trent	1 Oct 1823
James	1 6/12	M		U. States	Philidelphia	Jupiter	19 Oct 1826
James	3	M	Family [of Aaron]	England	Upper Canada	Comet	6 Mar 1823
James	19		United States Officer	Charleston, S.C.	New York	Hiram	10 Nov 1824
James	40	M	Shoemaker	England	Upper Canada	Comet	6 Mar 1823
Jane, Mrs.	30	F	Lady	U. States	Philidelphia	Jupiter	19 Oct 1826
John	21	M	Servant	England	Canada	York	8 Aug 1829
John F.	4 6/12	M		U. States	Philidelphia	Jupiter	19 Oct 1826
Joseph	26		Cabinet Maker	London	England	London	13 Dec 1822
Martha	39	F	Family [of Aaron]	England	Upper Canada	Comet	6 Mar 1823
Mary	63	F		England	America	Britannia	22 Jul 1829
Mary J., Miss	6	F		U. States	Philidelphia	Jupiter	19 Oct 1826
Rebecca	17	F	Family [of James]	England	Upper Canada	Comet	6 Mar 1823
Robert	35	M	Doctor	U. States	U. States	Chase	24 Jul 1823
Robert, Doctor	34	M	Doctor	U. States	Philidelphia	Jupiter	19 Oct 1826
Robert O.	3	M		U. States	Philidelphia	Jupiter	19 Oct 1826
S.	34	M	Planter	England	U. States	Elias Burger	30 Nov 1822
Saml.	37	M	Mercht.	United States	United States	Importer	21 May 1821
Saml.	38	M	Merchant	St. Croix	St. Thomas	Four Sons	8 Dec 1827
Saml.	54	M	Planter	St. Croix	St. Croix	Elias Burger	21 Aug 1823
Samuel	60	M	Gentleman	St. Croix	U. States	Carlo	30 Jul 1827
Susan	26	F	Se[r]vant	United States	United States	Sylvester Healy	17 Oct 1825
Thomas	10	M	Family [of Aaron]	England	Upper Canada	Comet	6 Mar 1823
William	12	M	Family [of James]	England	Upper Canada	Comet	6 Mar 1823

NAMES OF PASSENGERS	AGE	SEX	OCCUPATIONS	COUNTRY TO WHICH THEY BELONG	COUNTRY THEY INTEND TO INHABIT	SHIPS/DATES OF ARRIVAL	
ABBOTT (cont'd)							
William	12	M	Family [of Aaron]	England	Upper Canada	Comet	6 Mar 1823
ABEEL, Alfred, Mr.	22	M	...	U.S.	U.S.	Cadmus	11 Jul 1827
David	25		Professional	New York	United States	General Marion	18 Jul 1829
ABEILLE, A., Dr.	24		M.D.	New York		Antelope	22 Dec 1820
F.	25	M	Doctor	France	U. States	Union	13 May 1823
Francis	30	M	Merchant	Porto Rico	Porto Rico	Eliza	10 Jul 1827
ABEL, Ann	4 6/12	F		Great Britain	New York	Thames	16 May 1821
Charles	1 8/12	M		Great Britain	New York	Thames	16 May 1821
Elizabeth	33 3/12	F		Great Britain	New York	Thames	16 May 1821
George	6 1/12	M		Great Britain	New York	Thames	16 May 1821
James	36 2/12	M	Coach brass founder	Great Britain	New York	Thames	16 May 1821
Jas.	48	M	Butcher	Gt. Brittain	United States	Balaena	9 Oct 1823
Mary	38	F	None	Gt. Brittain	United States	Balaena	9 Oct 1823
ABELL, Robert A.	34 5/12	M	Vice President of Bardstown's College	America	America	Henry	17 May 1828
ABELLE, Joseph	40	M	Merchant	Spain	Spain	Brown	15 Nov 1825
ABENDSCHEIN, G. P.	24	M	Weaver	Germany	U. States	Minerva	9 Jan 1827
ABENETHER, Ellinor	25	F	Servant	Ireland	U. States	Nancy	13 Dec 1822
ABEO, Juan	40	M	Merchant	Spain	U. States	Albany Packet	23 Mar 1827
ABEONA, Michael	25	M	Labourer	Gt. Britain	U. States	Sarah G.	14 Apr 1828
ABERCROMBY,							
Catherine	4	F	Child	Ireland	United States	St. Michaels	23 Dec 1826
Frances	2	F	Child	Ireland	United States	St. Michaels	23 Dec 1826
Margaret	7	F	Child	Ireland	United States	St. Michaels	23 Dec 1826
Mary	35	F	Wife	Ireland	United States	St. Michaels	23 Dec 1826
Roger	10	M	Child	Ireland	United States	St. Michaels	23 Dec 1826
ABERHOF, Geralo	13	M	None	Spain	U. States	Brown	7 Jul 1826
Mariano	21	M	Planter	Spain	U. States	Brown	7 Jul 1826
ABERNATHEY, Mary	20	F		Irereland	America	Carolina Ann	20 Jun 1825
ABERSOL,							
Catharan	20 5/12	F	Farmer	Switzerland	U. States	France	26 Jun 1828
Christian	13 4/12	F	Farmer	Switzerland	U. States	France	26 Jun 1828
Christian	41 3/12	F	Farmer	Switzerland	U. States	France	26 Jun 1828
Jason	46 21/12	F	Farmer	Switzerland	U. States	France	26 Jun 1828
John	22 4/12	F	Farmer	Switzerland	U. States	France	26 Jun 1828
Joseph	9 5/12	M	Farmer	Switzerland	U. States	France	26 Jun 1828
Susan	6 2/12	F	Farmer	Switzerland	U. States	France	26 Jun 1828
ABERSTON, Thos.	20	M	Turner	Great Britain	New York	Dublin	21 Dec 1824
ABETS, Claus	24	M	Labourer	Germany	United States	Constitution	2 Aug 1826
ABIEL, Chas.	27	M	Teacher	France	U. States	Diana	17 Jul 1821
ABIELLE, D. J. A.	24	M	Doctor	U. States	U. States	Ann Eliza Jane	6 Sep 1822
Francis	24	M	Merchant	U. States	U. States	Arrington	9 Oct 1826
Frs.	43 4/12	M	Merchant	Philadelphia	U. States	Rover	22 Dec 1824
Jno. A.	23	M	Merchant	France	U. States	Union	13 May 1823
Mary	19	F		U. States	U. States	Arrington	9 Oct 1826
ABLE, Saml.	22	M	Instrument maker	England	U. States	Pacific	17 Jun 1828
ABRAHAM, Alicia	28	F		France	U. States	Great Britain	6 Sep 1828
Catharine	5 6/12	F	Child	England	United States	Maria	29 Sep 1823
Catharine	34	F		England	United States	Maria	29 Sep 1823
Cathr.	4	F		France	U. States	Great Britain	6 Sep 1828
George	1	M	Child	England	United States	Maria	29 Sep 1823
Isaac	16	M		St. Croix	U. States	South Carolina Packet	26 Jul 1824
James	47	M	Carpenter	England	United States	Maria	12 May 1823
R. F.	2	M		France	U. States	Great Britain	6 Sep 1828
Richard	28	F	Artist	France	U. States	Great Britain	6 Sep 1828
ABRAHAMS, —	26	M	Mariner	U. States	U. States	La Grange	19 Apr 1826
Catharine	20	F		Wales	U. States	Mary Stewart	12 May 1827
Ellis	40	M	Tailor	Wales	U. States	Mary Stewart	12 May 1827
Jane	5	F		Wales	U. States	Mary Stewart	12 May 1827
John	10	M		Wales	U. States	Mary Stewart	12 May 1827
Rowland	12	M		Wales	U. States	Mary Stewart	12 May 1827
ABRAMS, Jno.	31	M	Merchant	Philada.	U. States	Alfred	17 Sep 1822
John	25	M	Merchant	Great Britian	United States	Columbia	17 Apr 1827
Wm.	40	M	Merchant	L'pool	Canada	James Cropper	4 Feb 1824

NAMES OF PASSENGERS	AGE	SEX	OCCUPATIONS	COUNTRY TO WHICH THEY BELONG	COUNTRY THEY INTEND TO INHABIT	SHIPS/DATES OF ARRIVAL	
ABRANTZ, H., Mrs.	28	F	Lady	France	Havana	Robert Fulton	22 May 1824
Lewis R.	34	M	Merchant	France	Havana	Robert Fulton	22 May 1824
ABREO, Juan	40	M	Mercht.	Spain	Spain	Albany Packet	14 Nov 1826
ABREW, Francis, Don	21	M	Merchant	Spain	Spain	Jas. Monroe	9 Jun 1826
ABRILLE, Ed.	24	M	Mariner	America	U. States	Ambuscade	11 Jul 1821
ABRIO, Gracio da Santis	26	M	Merchant	Madeira	Madeira	Uniao	19 Aug 1829
ABSTROP, —, Mr.	28	M	Mercht.	Spain	Spain	Fabius	19 Mar 1825
ABTHORP, C. W.	31	M	Merchant	United States	U. States	Amos Palmer	29 Sep 1827
ABTJEAN, Elizabeth	22	F		Brattain		L'Esperance	6 Sep 1828
Elizabeth	57	F		Brattain		L'Esperance	6 Sep 1828
Jacob	56	M	Carpenter	Brattain		L'Esperance	6 Sep 1828
Maria	20	F		Brattain		L'Esperance	6 Sep 1828
ABUDANO, —, Mrs.	34	F				Manchester Packet	21 Aug 1823
Catharine	3	F				Manchester Packet	21 Aug 1823
ABZON, Jose D., Don	66	M	Merchant	Spain	Spain	Jas. Monroe	9 Jun 1826
ACHERE, Ann	22	F		Ireland	United States	St. John	5 Oct 1829
Charles A.	29	M		China	United States	St. John	5 Oct 1829
Xery	2	F		Ireland	United States	St. John	5 Oct 1829
ACHERMAN, George		M	Consular agent of the U. States at Guatemala	United States		Joseph	20 Jul 1829
ACKER, Louis	43	M	Apothecary	France		Nimrod	21 Sep 1820
ACKERLY, James	13	M		Great Britain	U. States	United States	8 Sep 1827
Joseph	28	M	Weaver	England	United States	Roman	12 Jun 1826
ACKERMAN, Geo.	23	M	Mariner	Great Britain	U. States	Emma	25 Feb 1826
ACKERS, Mary E.	20	F	None	Gt. Britan	Gt. Britan	Canada	8 Jun 1826
Thos., Mr.	22	M	Gentlm.	England	England	Helen	17 Dec 1827
William	42	M	Merchant	Gt. Britan	Gt. Britan	Canada	8 Jun 1826
William	45	M	Merchant	England	So. America	Endymeon	20 Aug 1822
ACLAND, Gideon	29	M	Gentleman	England	Upper Canada	Camillus	29 Jan 1829
ACOS, Anger	50	M	...	...	United States	Abeona	26 Jun 1824
ACOSTA, Joaquim	27	M	A...	Colombia	Colombia	Bunker Hill	10 Dec 1825
ACOSTER, Juan	55	M	Merchant	Matanzas	U. States	Orono	21 May 1827
ACROID, Titus	35		Farmer	Great Britain		John Dickinson	5 Apr 1821
ACTON, Robert Graham	19 1/12	M	Surgeon	Ireland	United States	Wilson	27 Jun 1826
ADAIN, Wm.	21		Farmer	Great Britain	United States	Camillus	12 Sep 1827
ADAIR, Anne	3	F	Farmer	Ireland	America	Superior	12 Jun 1824
Cath.	23	F	Wife	Ireland	United States	Louisa	18 Apr 1827
Eliza	1	F	Farmer	Ireland	America	Superior	12 Jun 1824
H.	22		Farmer	Ireland	United States	Courier	16 May 1825
Margaret	5	F	Farmer	Ireland	America	Superior	12 Jun 1824
Martha	20	F		Ireland	United States	Dublin Packet	3 May 1823
Mary	34	F	Farmer	Ireland	America	Superior	12 Jun 1824
Robert	35	M	Farmer	Ireland	America	Superior	12 Jun 1824
Thos.	19	M				Ann Maria	29 Nov 1821
Thos. B.	22 10/12	M	Gent.	America	America	Napoleon	26 May 1828
Wm.	5/12	M	Son	Ireland	United States	Louisa	18 Apr 1827
Wm.	27	M	Jeweler	Ireland	New York	Louisa	18 Apr 1827
ADAM, Andrew	25	M	Laborer	Scotland	United States	Tom	2 Jul 1827
John	3	M	None	Scotland	United States	Mary & Susan	5 Aug 1828
John	30 6/12	M	Merchant	Hondurass	Hondurass	Calais Packet	6 Nov 1828
John	31	M				Czar	29 Aug 1829
John J.	20		Doctor	b. Paisley, last of N. York	N. York	Peru	30 May 1828
Lilly, Mrs.	29	F	None	Scotland	United States	Mary & Susan	5 Aug 1828
Thomas	20	M	Labourer	England	U. States	Ayrshire	12 May 1828
William	42	M		Scotland	United States	Camillus	9 May 1827
ADAMS, —, Mrs.					New York	Hero	19 May 1828
—, one childe	20/12					Eunice	13 Dec 1827
—, one childe	3					Eunice	13 Dec 1827
A.	40	M		Ireland	U. States	Greenhow	10 Mar 1823
Abrm.	21	M		England	America	Ann	3 Jul 1820
Adam	3	M	None	Great Britain	United States	Mary & Harriet	3 Jul 1829
Adele	6	F	Shoemaker	France		Antioch	18 Aug 1829
Alexander	20 6/12	M	Clark	Scotland	U. States	Josephine	23 Jan 1829
Alexander	25	M	Merchant	America	America	Pacific	13 Jan 1827

NAMES OF PASSENGERS	AGE	SEX	OCCUPATIONS	COUNTRY TO WHICH THEY BELONG	COUNTRY THEY INTEND TO INHABIT	SHIPS/DATES OF ARRIVAL	
ADAMS (cont'd)							
Alexr., Jr.	2	M		America	America	Pacific	13 Jan 1827
Andw.	2	M			New York	Hero	19 May 1828
Ann	18	F	None	Halifax	U. States	Loire	7 Jul 1827
Ann	22	F	Lady	United States	United States	Hopes Delight	22 Jul 1829
Ann	38	F		U. States	U. States	Alciope	6 Jul 1822
Benj.	16	M	Shoemaker	England		Marchioness	13 May 1828
Benjamin	52	M	Merchant	Wales	United States of America	Orozimbo	11 Aug 1823
Bennet	42	M	Carpenter	England	U.S.A.	Hudson	21 Aug 1829
Catharine	21	F	None	England	United States	Montgomery	6 Mar 1829
Charlotte	8	F				Charlotte Corday	15 Aug 1820
Daniel	30	M	Mason	Ireland	United States	Montgomery	6 Mar 1829
David	40		Merchant	U. States	U. States	Nancy	11 Sep 1820
Edward	37	M	Mechanic	England	Canada	Hogarth	12 Oct 1829
Elisabeth	24	F	Lady	Scotland	New York	Eunice	13 Dec 1827
Eliza	27	F	None	Scotland	United States	Aspasia	5 Sep 1827
Elizabeth	12	F	...	England	United States	Milton	20 Oct 1827
Elizabeth	22	F		Switzerland	U. States	Robert Edward	2 Nov 1827
Elizth.	11	F	None	Great Britain	United States	Mary & Harriet	3 Jul 1829
Ellen	7	F	None	Great Britain	United States	Mary & Harriet	3 Jul 1829
Ellen	8	F	Child	St. Johns, N.B.	St. Johns, N.B.	Sarah G	11 Sep 1827
Ellen	10	F		Great Briton	Canada	Brighton	12 Jun 1826
Emma	2	F	...	England	United States	Milton	20 Oct 1827
F.	30	M	Merchant	United States	U. States	Blue Ey'd Mary	26 Jun 1823
Florence	36	F	Shoemaker	France		Antioch	18 Aug 1829
Frans.		M		U. States	U. States	Corsair	1 Sep 1821
Frans.	30	M	Merchant	U. States	U. States	Perseverance	11 Jun 1824
G. F.	33	M	Mariner	Puston	U. States	Ann	21 May 1824
Geo.	6	M		England	U.S. America	Magnet	17 Aug 1825
Geo.	17	M	Farmer	Great Britain	United States	Grecian	24 Sep 1828
George	10	M		Ireland	United States	General Putnam	20 Jun 1825
George	25	M	...	Great Britain	United States	Baltic	24 Dec 1824
George	28	M	U.S. Navy	U. States	U. States	Ardelle	27 Nov 1826
George	28	M	Comissary	England	United States	McFingal	9 Dec 1826
H.	17	M		Ireland	U. States	Greenhow	10 Mar 1823
Hanah	30	F	...	Ireland	United States	General Putnam	20 Jun 1825
Harlan	1	M		America	America	Pacific	13 Jan 1827
Humel	36	M	Shoemaker	France		Antioch	18 Aug 1829
Isabella	8	F		Ireland	United States	General Putnam	20 Jun 1825
Isabelle	31	F	None	England	United States	Trident	18 Jul 1827
J.	26	M	Mariner	Germany	United States	Howard	15 Jun 1825
J.	52	M	Mariner	U. States	U. States	Matilda	23 May 1826
J. A.	28	M	Portor	...	United States	Howard	14 May 1825
J. N.	12	F	Spinster	U.S.	U.S.	Emma	24 Jun 1825
James	6	M		Ireland	United States	General Putnam	20 Jun 1825
James	19 8/12	M	Baker	Scotland	United States	Mobile	21 Aug 1827
James	22	M	Merchant	United States	United States	Romulus	3 Dec 1827
James	25	M	Pattern Painter	England		Fame	9 Dec 1826
James	31	M	Spinner	Scotland	United States	Aspasia	5 Sep 1827
James	32	M	Grocer	Ireland	United States of America	Marion	25 Nov 1825
James	40	M	Merchant	U.N.S.	U. States	Merchant	22 Oct 1821
Jane	9	F	...	England	United States	Milton	20 Oct 1827
Jane	9	F	None	Great Britain	United States	Mary & Harriet	3 Jul 1829
Jane	18	F	Spinster	Ireland	United States	Trident	17 May 1825
Jane	19	F	Spinster	Ireland	U. States	Josephine	7 May 1827
Jane	23	F	None	England	U.S.A.	Lima	6 Dec 1826
Jane	24		Spinster	Ireland	United States	Courier	15 Oct 1827
Jane	35	F	Lady	St. Johns, N.B.	St. Johns, N.B.	Sarah G	11 Sep 1827
Jane	38	F	None	Great Britain	United States	Mary & Harriet	3 Jul 1829
Janet	4	F			New York	Hero	19 May 1828
Jean	55	F	Wife	Scotland	United States	Tom	2 Jul 1827
Jeanette	1	F	None	England	United States	Trident	18 Jul 1827
Jno.	13	M		Ireland	U. States	Greenhow	10 Mar 1823
John	8/12	M			New York	Hero	19 May 1828
John	1 3/12	M		Great Briton	Canada	Brighton	12 Jun 1826
John	6	M	None	England	United States	Trident	18 Jul 1827
John	15	M	...	England	United States	Milton	20 Oct 1827

NAMES OF PASSENGERS	AGE	SEX	OCCUPATIONS	COUNTRY TO WHICH THEY BELONG	COUNTRY THEY INTEND TO INHABIT	SHIPS/DATES OF ARRIVAL	
ADAMS (cont'd)							
John	20	M	Gentleman	U. States	U. States America	Purrington	22 Jan 1825
John	21		Merchant	United States	United States	Selina	18 Jul 1822
John	22	M	Clerk	U. States	U. States	Hippomenes	23 Jun 1823
John	22	M	Merchant			Sarah G.	20 Jul 1827
John	24	M	Gentleman	Great Britian	United States	Silvanus Jenkins	6 Apr 1826
John	24	M	Mercht.	England	U.S.A.	Lima	6 Dec 1826
John	25	M	Engineer	U. States	U. States	Clio	8 Apr 1828
John	30	M	Laborer	Ireland	United States	Trio	13 Jun 1827
John	35	M	...	England	United States	Milton	20 Oct 1827
John	37 4/12	M	Gentleman	Great Briton	Canada	Brighton	12 Jun 1826
John	42	M	Lady	St. Johns		Charlotte Corday	15 Aug 1820
John	42	M	Pattern Man	...	United States	Minerva	30 Oct 1827
John, Mr.	25	M	Merchant	England	U. States	Emily	25 Aug 1827
John S.	22		Labourer	Ireland	United States	Courier	15 Oct 1827
John Tyng	23	M	Gent.	U.S. America	U. States	William Thompson	25 Aug 1828
John W.	28		Labourer	Ireland	United States	Courier	15 Oct 1827
Joseph	9	M	None	England	United States	Trident	18 Jul 1827
Joseph	28	M	Ship Master	U. States	U. States	Plant	18 Sep 1827
Josephine	5	F	Shoemaker	France		Antioch	18 Aug 1829
Julius	45	M	Servant	Haity	Haity	Hope Return	6 Jun 1823
L. H.	2	F	Spinster	U.S.	U.S.	Emma	24 Jun 1825
M. R.	8	F	Spinster	U.S.	U.S.	Emma	24 Jun 1825
M. R.	35	F	Lady	U.S.	U.S.	Emma	24 Jun 1825
Margt.	12	F		Ireland	United States	General Putnam	20 Jun 1825
Maria	1 4/12	F		England	U.S.A.	Hudson	21 Aug 1829
Maria	22	F	Lady	Great Britian	United States	Silvanus Jenkins	6 Apr 1826
Maria	36	F		England	U.S.A.	Hudson	21 Aug 1829
Mary	...	F	Spinster	Ireland	United States	General Putnam	20 Jun 1825
Mary	3	F	...	England	United States	Milton	20 Oct 1827
Mary	19	F		England	United States	McFingal	9 Dec 1826
Mary	22	F		America	America	Pacific	13 Jan 1827
Mary	25	F		Ireland	United States	Trio	13 Jun 1827
Mary	33 5/12	F		Great Briton	Canada	Brighton	12 Jun 1826
Nancy	8	F	None	Scotland	United States	Aspasia	5 Sep 1827
Priscilla	35	F		England	U.S. America	Magnet	17 Aug 1825
R.	20		Labourer	Halifax	U. States	Edwin	26 Sep 1828
R.	46	M	Gentleman	U. States America	U. States America	Purrington	22 Jan 1825
R.	50	M	Farmer	Ireland	U. States	Greenhow	10 Mar 1823
Rebecca	6	F		England	U.S.A.	Hudson	21 Aug 1829
Robert	4	M		Ireland	United States	General Putnam	20 Jun 1825
Robert	17		Labourer	England	United States	Corinthian	7 Jul 1829
Robt.	6	M	None	Scotland	United States	Aspasia	5 Sep 1827
Robt.	22	M	Labourer	Ireland	United States	Henry Kneeland	7 Jun 1828
Sally	4	F		Ireland	United States	Trio	13 Jun 1827
Saml.	9	M				Charlotte Corday	15 Aug 1820
Samuel	4	M	Shoemaker	France		Antioch	18 Aug 1829
Samuel	27	M	Gentleman	Ireland	United States	Romulus	24 Jun 1826
Samuel	43	M	Labourer	Ireland	U. States	Josephine	30 Aug 1828
Sarah	2	F		England	U.S. America	Magnet	17 Aug 1825
Sarah	6	F	...	England	United States	Milton	20 Oct 1827
Sarah	37	F	...	England	United States	Milton	20 Oct 1827
Sarah	65	F	Lady	St. John	St. John	Ann Maria	5 May 1824
Thomas	22	M	Labourer	G. Britain	United States	Louisa	14 Jun 1825
Thos.	27	M	Farmer	Switzerland	U. States	Robert Edward	2 Nov 1827
Thos.	36	M	Farmer	Great Britain	United States	Mary & Harriet	3 Jul 1829
Titus	47	M	Merchant	Gt. Britain	U. States	Napolean	26 Sep 1828
William	13	M	None	Great Britain	United States	Mary & Harriet	3 Jul 1829
William	19	M	Merchant	England	England	James Cropper	16 Oct 1826
William	23	M	family [of George D. Tucker]	Turks Island	U. States	Gold Hunter	24 Oct 1829
William	25	M	Seaman	Liverpool	United States	Genl. Marion	4 Jun 1828
William	31	M	Bachelor	G.B.	G.B.	George Canning	26 Aug 1829
William, Jr.	25	M	Merchant	U. Kingdom, G. Britain & Ireland	New York	James Cropper	21 Oct 1825
William A.	6	M		New York	U. States	Zephyr	18 May 1825

NAMES OF PASSENGERS	AGE	SEX	OCCUPATIONS	COUNTRY TO WHICH THEY BELONG	COUNTRY THEY INTEND TO INHABIT	SHIPS/DATES OF ARRIVAL	
ADAMS (cont'd)							
Wm.	2	M	None	Scotland	United States	Aspasia	5 Sep 1827
Wm.	23	M	Merchant	England	U. States	Panthea	5 Oct 1822
Wm.	3...	M	Farmer	Ireland	United States	General Putnam	20 Jun 1825
Wm.	30	M	Merchant	G. Brittain	England	Abigail	25 Feb 1826
Wm.	60	M	Laborer	Scotland	United States	Tom	2 Jul 1827
ADAMSON, James	23	M		Ireland	United States	William Byrnes	6 Apr 1826
Marey	16	F	Farmer	England	United States	Florida	1 Sep 1823
ADCOCK, Edward	24	M	Merchant	England	U.N. States	Corinthian	1 Sep 1823
ADDAMES, Jon	30	M	Trader	G. Brittan	U. States	Henry	24 Oct 1828
William	25	M	F. Dresser	Ireland	New York	Trusty	12 Sep 1828
ADDAMS, —, Mr.	26	M		U. States	U. States	Zephyr	2 Oct 1826
—, Mrs.	26	F		U. States	U. States	Zephyr	2 Oct 1826
Alfred	13	M				Hudson	23 Jul 1828
John	45	M	Sherriff			Hudson	23 Jul 1828
Joseph	27 3/12	M	Atn. at Law	U. States	U. States	France	26 Jun 1828
Sam.	1	M	D. Maker	Ireland	N. York	Trusty	12 Sep 1828
Susan	17	F	Servant	Ireland	N. York	Trusty	12 Sep 1828
Tho.	38	M	None	Ilan...	U. States	Electra	7 Jul 1828
ADDAMSON, John	30	M	Merchant	Great Britian	United States	Diamond	8 Nov 1824
ADDENS, Wm.	40	M	Accountant	England	U. States	Fifeshire	25 Sep 1827
ADDICKS, Barbara Catharine Caroline Regina Fitzgerald O'Sullivan, Miss	10	F	None	U. States	U. States	Conveyance	9 Feb 1825
Barbara O'Sullivan, Mrs.	40	F	None	U. States	U. States	Conveyance	9 Feb 1825
ADDISON, ...ances	15	F		Gt. Britain	U. States	Maria	22 May 1822
Elizabeth	21	F		Great Britain	U.S. of America	Gratitude	3 Oct 1829
John	23	M	Farmer	Great Britain	U.S. of America	Gratitude	3 Oct 1829
Thomas	23	M	Grocer	Gt. Britain	U. States	Maria	22 May 1822
William	23	M	Physician	U.S.	U.S.	Howard	4 May 1827
ADDOMS, Isabela	18	F	Spinster	Ireland	United States	Fabius	4 Jun 1828
Joseph	65	M	Farmer	Ireland	United States	Fabius	4 Jun 1828
Margret	55	F		Ireland	United States	Fabius	4 Jun 1828
Matha	30	F		Ireland	United States	Fabius	4 Jun 1828
ADDS, Elizth.	4	F	None	Great Brittain	New York	Albion	11 Jun 1821
Geo.	28	M	Joiner	Great Brittain	New York	Albion	11 Jun 1821
Mary	27	F	None	Great Brittain	New York	Albion	11 Jun 1821
Mary, Jr.	6	F	None	Great Brittain	New York	Albion	11 Jun 1821
ADDUM, John	48	M	Merchant	United States of America	United States	Virginia	24 Jul 1821
ADERSBACH, Gerard	33	M	Surgeon	Prussia	United States	Talma	12 Oct 1826
ADERTON, Thos.	40	M	Mariner			Hector	11 Sep 1820
ADIE, ...	23	M	Merchant	Scotland	New York	Joseph Hume	26 Oct 1829
ADLAM, Joseph	35	M	Joiner	England	U.S.	Acasta	11 May 1827
ADLETON, Catharn	40	F	Spinster	Ireland	U. States	Meteor	19 Jul 1828
Margaret	21	F	Spinster	Ireland	U. States	Meteor	19 Jul 1828
ADLEY, Ane	23	F		G. Britain	U. States	Mary & Harriot	8 Sep 1828
James	28	M	Farmer	G. Britain	U. States	Mary & Harriot	8 Sep 1828
John	26	M	Farmer	Ireland	United States	Leonidas	3 Aug 1825
Margaret	30	F		Ireland	United States	Leonidas	3 Aug 1825
ADOLPHE, B. J.	25	M	Manufacturer	England	U. States	York	12 Jul 1825
ADOLPHO, Theadore	22	M	Merchant	France	France	Dromo	4 May 1827
ADOLPHUS, Mary	34	F		England	New York	Hudson	20 Nov 1828
Nathaniel	23	M	Glass Cutter	England	New York	Hudson	20 Nov 1828
ADOLTO, Angullo G.	15	M	Farmer	Geneva	U.S. America	New Hampshire	28 Sep 1826
ADOM, John	28	M	Black Smith	England	America	England	23 Jun 1828
ADOMS, Jane	30	F		St. Johns	St. John, N.B.	Brothers	17 Oct 1823
John	30	M	Mechanic	Halifax	St. John, N.B.	Brothers	17 Oct 1823
ADRONE, Bordeaux	50	M	Gentleman	Holland	Holland	Governor Von Schollen	7 Nov 1827
AEKIN, —, Mrs.	38	F		New York	New York	Mary	1 Nov 1824
Geo.	6	M		Ireland	U. States	Balaena	29 Apr 1825
Hannah	8	F		Ireland	U. States	Balaena	29 Apr 1825
Robt.	30	M	Physician	Ireland	U. States	Balaena	29 Apr 1825
Sarah	30	F		Ireland	U. States	Balaena	29 Apr 1825
AERAGORD, Jos. M.	14	M		Cuba	Spain	Transit	13 Nov 1823
AEROTT, David	24	M	Merchant	United States		London	29 Apr 1824

NAMES OF PASSENGERS	AGE	SEX	OCCUPATIONS	COUNTRY TO WHICH THEY BELONG	COUNTRY THEY INTEND TO INHABIT	SHIPS/DATES OF ARRIVAL	
AEROZ, F.	27	M	Merchant	Spain	Spain	Carpenter	3 Sep 1821
AFER, Anna	28	F		Switzerland	U. States	Romulus	24 Sep 1828
Christian	16	M		Switzerland	U. States	Romulus	24 Sep 1828
Joshua	19	M		Switzerland	U. States	Romulus	24 Sep 1828
Mary	58	F		Switzerland	U. States	Romulus	24 Sep 1828
AFFLECK, Henry	40	M	Joiner	Scotland	United States	Culloden	17 May 1828
AFFLICK, Heny	40	M	Carpenter	England	United States	Siroc	31 Oct 1829
AFFOLTER, Benoist	28	M	Joiner	Switzerland	Switzerland	Sully	15 Jul 1829
AFLECK, Dorethy	12	F		Scotland	United States	Culloden	17 May 1828
Dorethy	38	F		Scotland	United States	Culloden	17 May 1828
Henry	4	M		Scotland	United States	Culloden	17 May 1828
John	10	M		Scotland	United States	Culloden	17 May 1828
William	8	M		Scotland	United States	Culloden	17 May 1828
AGALA, Genl.	55	M	...il...	Canada	Canada	Julia	28 Jul 1824
AGAN, Ellen	30	F	None	Ireland	United States of America	Jubilee	12 May 1828
James	24	M	Merchant	Spain	Spain	Nile	24 Aug 1821
AGAR, Julia	25		Milliner	French	America	Romulus	15 May 1828
AGASCOT, Francis	22	M	Merchant	Philadelphia	Philadelphia	Independence	25 Oct 1828
AGASSEY, A.	26	M	Merchant	England	England	John Wells	14 Oct 1823
AGEA, J. M.	25	M	Merchant	France	France	Eliza	28 Apr 1827
AGERON, John	26	M	Farmer	England	United States	Ganges	10 May 1828
Laura D.	23	F	None	Paris	U. States	Bayard	18 Jul 1823
AGESTARAN, J.	48	M	Merchant	Spain	U. States	Dromo	22 May 1826
AGESTRAN, L.	28	F	No	Spain	U. States	Dromo	22 May 1826
AGG, John	36	M	Gentleman			Hector	11 Sep 1820
AGIN, Brid	3	F		Ireland	United States	Potomac	28 Sep 1827
Martha	30	F		Ireland	United States	Potomac	28 Sep 1827
Michal	24	M	Joiner		New York	Governor Clinton	3 Jul 1827
William	35	M	Labourer	Ireland	United States	Potomac	28 Sep 1827
AGNESS, Wm.	3	M	Farmer	New Brunswick	Canada	Susan Morton	17 Jun 1823
AGNEW, Andrew	25	M	Farmer	Ireland	U. States	Sabina	29 Apr 1825
Catherine	22	F	Spinster	Ireland	United States America	Gem	16 Jun 1824
Cornelius	21	M	Merchant	United States	United States	Helen	7 Feb 1820
Isabella	30	F	Spinster	Ireland	United States America	Gem	16 Jun 1824
John	21	M	Farmer	Ireland	United States America	Gem	16 Jun 1824
John	24	M	Merchant	St. John, N.B.	St. John, N.B.	Ann Maria	1 Apr 1826
Martha	...	F	Spinster	Ireland	United States America	Gem	16 Jun 1824
Martha	20	F	Spinster	Ireland	United States America	Gem	16 Jun 1824
AGNOIS, Antoniette	32	F	Child Maker	Spain	U. States	France	14 Mar 1828
AGNUS, Wm.	30	M	Farmer	Scotland	United States	Minerva	29 Oct 1822
AGRY, Thos.	34	M	Merchant	U. States	U. States	Diana	12 Apr 1825
AGUSTINA, J.	21	M	Merchant	Curacoa	U. States	Milo	23 Dec 1824
AH...AN, Robt.	20	M	Labourer	Lancaster	Lancaster	Howard Douglass	11 May 1827
AHEARN, Tim	30			Ireland	U.S.	Union	20 Aug 1827
AHERENS, Henry	45	M	Merchant	U. States	U. States	Roman	1 Dec 1828
AHERN, Abigal	25	F	Spinster	Ireland	United States	Diana	1 May 1826
Elizabeth	14	F	Spinster	Ireland	United States	Diana	1 May 1826
Ellen	16	F	Spinster	Ireland	United States	Diana	1 May 1826
Maurice	40	M	Farmer	Ireland	United States	Diana	1 May 1826
Micheal	11	M	None	Ireland	United States	Diana	1 May 1826
Thos.	7	M	None	Ireland	United States	Diana	1 May 1826
AHERR, Daniel	2 6/12		Farmer & Labourer	Great Britain & Ireland	United States of North America	Trio	8 Feb 1827
Grace	46		Farmer & Labourer	Great Britain & Ireland		United States of North America	Trio 8 Feb 1827
Honora	5		Farmer & Labourer	Great Britain & Ireland		United States of North America	Trio 8 Feb 1827
Michael	45		Farmer & Labourer	Great Britain & Ireland		United States of North America	Trio 8 Feb 1827
AHILLE, Binry	30	M		G. Britan	U. States	William Neilson 26 Jul 1828	
Briget	2	M		G. Britan	U. States	William Neilson 26 Jul 1828	

NAMES OF PASSENGERS	AGE	SEX	OCCUPATIONS	COUNTRY TO WHICH THEY BELONG	COUNTRY THEY INTEND TO INHABIT	SHIPS/DATES OF ARRIVAL	
AHILLE (cont'd)							
Sally	28	M		G. Britan	U. States	William Neilson	26 Jul 1828
AHRENFELD, L. J.	22	M	Merchant	Lubeck	New York	Maria Elizabeth	18 Jun 1827
AIGIN, Ann	20 9/12	F		Ireland	U.S. of America	Douglass	6 Jul 1829
Robert	1 9/12	M		Ireland	U.S. of America	Douglass	6 Jul 1829
AIKEN, Mary	21	F		Ireland	U.S. of America	Douglass	6 Jul 1829
William, Jr.	23	M	Gentleman	Charleston, S.C.	Charleston, S.C.	New York	31 Jul 1829
Wm.	13	M		G. Britain	U. States	Camillus	8 Sep 1828
AIKENS, Elizabeth	22	F		U. States		Leader	28 Mar 1822
Jane	14	F		U. States		Leader	28 Mar 1822
AIKIN, B.	40	M	Citizen	U. States	U. States	Sall & Hope	12 Jul 1820
Catharine	25	F	None	Great Britain	United States of America	Comet	9 Aug 1822
David	3	M		England	United States	Peru	23 May 1827
Ellen	5	F		England	United States	Peru	23 May 1827
Ellen	31	F		England	United States	Peru	23 May 1827
James	31	M	Wheelwright	England	United States	Peru	23 May 1827
Jas.	22			Scotland		Anacreon	7 Sep 1827
John	7	M		England	United States	Peru	23 May 1827
Patrick	30	M	Farmer	Great Britain	United States of America	Comet	9 Aug 1822
AIKINS, —, Master	13	M	Navy	U. States	U. States	Good Friends	20 May 1825
—, Miss	11	F		U. States	U. States	Good Friends	20 May 1825
Henry	2	M				Amity	11 Sep 1820
Jane	23	F				Amity	11 Sep 1820
Joshua	35	M	Merchant			Amity	11 Sep 1820
Wm.	21	M	Labourer	Ireland	U. States	Union	10 Mar 1823
AILY, Margaret	1	F	Child	Ireland	N. York	Trusty	12 Sep 1828
AIMELIA, John	28	M	Physician	United States	United States	Paris	10 Sep 1823
AIMSBURG, Andrew	30	M	U.S. Agent	U. States	U. States	Bunker Hill	25 Jun 1827
AINENBOIL, Hannah	19	F	Spinster	Ireland	United States	Sarah Ann	18 Nov 1826
AINETES, Felix	53	M	Merchant	Sardenia	America	Exchange	25 Feb 1822
AINS, George	21	M	Tobacconist	U.S.	U.S.	Pactolus	19 Aug 1823
AINSEN, Thomas	40	M	Weaver	England	United States	Delta	24 Oct 1829
AINSLEY, Charles P.	17	M	Army	G. Bt.	G. Bt.	Canada	13 Oct 1825
George	8	M	Farmer	Scotland	U. States	Camillus	17 Sep 1823
Hugh G.	5	M	Farmer	Scotland	U. States	Camillus	17 Sep 1823
Janet	9	F	Farmer	Scotland	U. States	Camillus	17 Sep 1823
Janet	30	F	Farmer	Scotland	U. States	Camillus	17 Sep 1823
Marry	1	F		Scotland	U. States	Camillus	17 Sep 1823
Waller	20	M	Surgeon	Britain	America	Camillus	9 Oct 1820
William	6	M	Farmer	Scotland	U. States	Camillus	17 Sep 1823
AINSLIE, Hugh	30	M	Farmer	Great Britain	United States	Nestor in Liverpool	29 Jul 1822
AINSWORTH, Catharine	3	F	None	England	United States	Dalhouse Castle	6 Sep 1827
James	...	...	...	...	...	Pioneer	21 Jun 1825
John	44		...	England	United States	Alexander Mansfield	23 Nov 1824
Wm.	15			England	United States	Alexander Mansfield	23 Nov 1824
AINWORTHY, Henry	16	M	Merchant	Yorkshire	New York, U.S.	New York	14 Mar 1828
AIREY, Richard	27	M	Mason	England	New York	Lima	5 Aug 1829
Richard	27	M	Mason	England	U. States	Lima	5 Aug 1829
AIR HART, Fredrick	45	M	Butcher	Germany	United States	Samuel Robertson	8 Aug 1828
George	14	M		Germany	United States	Samuel Robertson	8 Aug 1828
AIRLEE, C.	6	F		Scotland	U. States	Superior	25 Sep 1828
D.	1	M		Scotland	U. States	Superior	25 Sep 1828
Edward	30	M	Labourer	Scotland	U. States	Superior	25 Sep 1828
Mell	27	F		Scotland	U. States	Superior	25 Sep 1828
Wm.	4	M		Scotland	U. States	Superior	25 Sep 1828
AIRLEY, Thomas	18	M	Farmer	Ireland	U.S.A.	Dalhouse Castle	21 Aug 1829
AIRLY, Marg A., Jur.	6	F	Child	Ireland	N. York	Trusty	12 Sep 1828
Mary	19	F	Servant	Ireland	N. York	Trusty	12 Sep 1828
Mary	36	F	D. Maker	Ireland	N. York	Trusty	12 Sep 1828
Mary	52	F	Servant	Ireland	N. York	Trusty	12 Sep 1828
AIRTHENBUCK, Thos.	19	M		Ireland	U. States	Alex Mansfield	1 Jun 1822
AITCHINSON, George	38	M	Farmer	Scotland	United States	Margaret Bogle	11 Jun 1824

NAMES OF PASSENGERS	AGE	SEX	OCCUPATIONS	COUNTRY TO WHICH THEY BELONG	COUNTRY THEY INTEND TO INHABIT	SHIPS/DATES OF ARRIVAL	
AITCHISON, Walter	25	M	Merchant	Scotland	United States	Friends	13 Mar 1824
William	26		Taylor	Leeds	England	London	13 Dec 1822
AITKEN, James	23	M	Clerk	Great Britain	United States	Natchez	17 Aug 1822
AIVARCO, Manuel							
Joseph, Jr.	15	M		Brazil	Brazil	America	16 May 1827
AKELY, John J.	25	M	Merchant	Great Brittain	Great Britain	Loire	12 Dec 1820
AKIN, —, Mr.	50	M	Merchant	Havana	Spain	Fair American	24 Dec 1821
Eliza	7	F		New York	New York	Mary	1 Nov 1824
George	8	M		G. Britain	U. States	Eliza	9 May 1827
James	39	M	Weaver	G. Britain	U. States	Eliza	9 May 1827
Jennett	40	F		G. Britain	U. States	Eliza	9 May 1827
John	6	M		G. Britain	U. States	Eliza	9 May 1827
Jos.	4	M		New York	New York	Mary	1 Nov 1824
L. S., Mrs.	23	F	Catpn.'s Wife	U. States	U. States	Elbe	13 Jun 1827
Sarah	20	F	Capt. Wife		U. States	Xenophon	30 Oct 1824
Sarah	23	F	Wife of Capt.	United States	United States	Elbe	30 Sep 1826
AKINS, Thos.	14	M	Labourer	Ireland	U. States	Sabina	29 Apr 1825
AKRIGG, Elizabeth	6/12	F	None	England	Pennsylvania	Indian Chief	16 Aug 1822
Elizabeth	57	F	None	England	Pennsylvania	Indian Chief	16 Aug 1822
George	3	M	None	England	Pennsylvania	Indian Chief	16 Aug 1822
Michael	45	M	Farmer	England	Pennsylvania	Indian Chief	16 Aug 1822
Robert	5	M	None	England	Pennsylvania	Indian Chief	16 Aug 1822
ALAGNER, H.	25	M	Labourer	Holland	Holland	Hudson	13 Jan 1827
ALAIN, Stanislaus	27		Gentleman	France		Bayard	10 Sep 1827
ALAMBA, B.	7	M		G. Britain		Caravan	8 Sep 1828
M.	30	M		G. Britain		Caravan	8 Sep 1828
ALANE, Parresco	27	M	Mercht.	Havama	United States	Brown	26 Apr 1826
ALAUX, George	45	M	Merchant	France	United States	Lewis	30 May 1823
ALAX, M.	52	M	Merchant	Mexico	U. States	Laveria	23 Jul 1828
ALBAIN, Adolph	33	M	military officer	France	South America	Cortes	16 Jul 1827
ALBARET, —	35	M	Merchant	Hayti		Ranger	29 Jul 1828
ALBASO, J.	22	M	Merchant	Spain	Spain	Franklin	27 May 1825
ALBE, John	15	M	Student	America	America	Commodore Chauncy	19 Jan 1826
ALBERHART, Christian	25	M	Weaver	Swiss	U. States	Montano	23 Apr 1825
ALBERLAIN, Charles	23	M	Servant	Swiss	U. States	Comet	28 Jul 1825
John Jacob	30	M	Servant	Swiss	U. States	Comet	28 Jul 1825
ALBERS, Jno. H.	26	M	Merchant	Denmark	U. States	Cumberland	10 Nov 1823
R.	24	M	Merchant	Hamburg	U. States	Ysdva	11 Sep 1828
ALBERT, —, Mr.			Servant	Philadelphia	United States	Henrietta	18 Aug 1829
Lewis	29	M	Merchant	Switzerland	U. States	Nancy	7 Sep 1824
Simon	18	M	Seaman	Norwich	United States	Venus	8 Sep 1820
ALBERTI, William	18	M	...	Great Brittain	Quebec	Albion	11 Jun 1821
ALBERTSON,							
Robert	25 2/12	M	...	England	America, U.S.	Illinois	3 Jun 1822
ALBIE, P. J.	26	M	Merchant	U. States	U. States	Rehoboth	10 Apr 1828
ALBION, Catherine	10	F	Spinster	Switzerland	United States	Andes	5 May 1828
George	40	M	Farmer	Switzerland	United States	Andes	5 May 1828
Jacob	13	M	Farmer	Switzerland	United States	Andes	5 May 1828
Margaret	20	F	Spinster	Switzerland	United States	Andes	5 May 1828
Salina	8	F	Spinster	Switzerland	United States	Andes	5 May 1828
Salina	40	F	Spinster	Switzerland	United States	Andes	5 May 1828
ALBIS, Anna	21	M	Sugar Baker	Germany	U. States	Condstitution	21 Mar 1825
ALBO, J.	29	M	Merchant	Mexico	U. States	Ranger	2 Jul 1827
ALBORDE, Francis	18	M	Student	Spain	U. States	Altamira	31 Jan 1828
ALBOT, Charles, Mr.	43	M	Gentlm.	England	England	Helen	17 Dec 1827
ALBRECHT, Carel Christ	17	M	B...ker	Germany	America	Falcon	28 Aug 1828
Christanna	44	F	Farmer	Wortenberg	Lancaster	Louisa	6 Oct 1828
Christina Catharine	12	F	Farmer	Wortenberg	Lancaster	Louisa	6 Oct 1828
Johan Andrew	45	M	Farmer	Wortenberg	Lancaster	Louisa	6 Oct 1828
Johann Matthew	11	M	Farmer	Wortenberg	Lancaster	Louisa	6 Oct 1828
Ora		M	None	United States	United States	United States	18 Sep 1826
Rosina Catharina	13	F	Farmer	Wortenberg	Lancaster	Louisa	6 Oct 1828
ALBUZE, Philippe	40	M	Doct. Medicine	Netherlands	Netherlands	General Paez	3 Aug 1829
ALCALA, Thos. Torenzo	53	M	Clergyman	Spain	Spain	Wallace	18 May 1825
ALCANTARA, —, Master	7	M		Havana	Havana	General Brown	10 Dec 1823
—, Mrs.	33	F		Havana	Havana	General Brown	10 Dec 1823
A., Master	5	M				General Brown	10 Dec 1823
P.	34	M	Lawyer	Havana	Havana	General Brown	10 Dec 1823

NAMES OF PASSENGERS	AGE	SEX	OCCUPATIONS	COUNTRY TO WHICH THEY BELONG	COUNTRY THEY INTEND TO INHABIT	SHIPS/DATES OF ARRIVAL	
ALCOCK, Charles	15	M	Farmer	England	United States	Siroc	31 Oct 1829
James	20	M	Mechanic	England	New York	Lewis	29 Oct 1825
John	20	M		Great Brit.	Ohio	Gov. Griswald	3 Jul 1820
John	22	M	Farmer	England	United States	Siroc	31 Oct 1829
ALDAMA, —, Mr.	25	M	Merchant	France	U. States	Hiram	17 Jun 1826
ALDAY, John	26	M	Merchant	Jamaica	Jamaica	Eliza Ann	2 May 1826
ALDEN, Sarah	48	F	None	England	United States	Jubilee	1 Oct 1828
ALDER, John	35	M	Merchant	U. States	U. States	Columbia	7 Sep 1827
ALDERA, Raymond	15	M	Servant	Campeachy	Campeachy	Margaret Wright	20 May 1825
ALDERETE, Coneteblation	21		Gentleman	Spain	Spain	Florida	1 Dec 1828
ALDERMAN, B.	4	M		England	Philada.	Galaxy	10 Jun 1824
E. H.	33	M	Mechanic	England	Philada.	Galaxy	10 Jun 1824
Edw.	3	M		England	Philada.	Galaxy	10 Jun 1824
Eliza.	2	F		England	Philada.	Galaxy	10 Jun 1824
Fanny	38		Farmer	Germany	United States	Corinthian	30 May 1828
Jacob	37		Farmer	Germany	United States	Corinthian	30 May 1828
Margaret	28	F		England	Philada.	Galaxy	10 Jun 1824
ALDERSON, John	38	M	Merchant	England	So. America	Endymeon	20 Aug 1822
W.	35	M	Merchant	England	U. States	Edgar	23 Nov 1824
William	40		Merchant	England	United States	Florida	11 Mar 1829
ALDINGTON, —, Mrs.	72	F	Lady	England	United States	New York	14 Jul 1827
ALDRED, David	23	M	...	Great Britain	Taunton, Mass.	Hesperus	13 Oct 1825
Hannah	23	F	...	Great Britain	Taunton, Mass.	Hesperus	13 Oct 1825
William	3/12	M	...	Great Britain	Taunton, Mass.	Hesperus	13 Oct 1825
ALDRERTE, Gabriel Pawz	21		Gentleman	Spain	Spain	Florida	1 Dec 1828
ALDRICH, —, Mr.	34	M	Mariner	U. States	U. States	Laura Ann	10 Sep 1821
ALDRIDGE, Charlotte	29	F		Great Britain	Philadelphia	Zodiac	14 Jun 1822
John	23	M	Farmer	Great Britain	Philadelphia	Zodiac	14 Jun 1822
Mary	53	F	None			Importer	30 Oct 1820
Phoebe	22	F	None			Importer	30 Oct 1820
Robt.	22	M	Farmer	Steers	Yorkshire	Howard Douglass	11 May 1827
ALEER, A. W.	26	M	Farmer	Ireland	U. States	Dickinson	30 Jul 1825
ALEHURST, Saml.	25	M	Farmer	Great Britain	United States	Mary & Harriet	3 Jul 1829
ALEMSLEY, Louisa	22	M		England		Edward Quesnel	17 Nov 1828
ALENES, Deedrick	25		Mason	Germany	U. States	Columbia	7 May 1828
ALENNETHA, Benjamin	40	M	Gentleman	Scotland	Scotland	Athenian	8 Jul 1828
ALEO, Salvadore	34	M	Merchant	Sicily	U. States	Pilgrim	27 Mar 1827
ALERNACH, Jacob	17	M	Brewer	Hesse	United States	Constitution	2 Aug 1826
ALES, Dominick	57	M	Planter	Italy	U. States	Circassian	3 Jun 1826
ALESANDER, Andrew	38	M	Smith	England	New York	America	1 Aug 1828
ALEXANDER, —	30	M	Grocer	Hayti		Ranger	29 Jul 1828
—, Miss	20	F				Czar	29 Aug 1829
—, Mr.	40	M	Merchant	France	United States	Marmione	20 Nov 1821
Alfred	42	M	Gentleman	Philadelphia	Philadelphia	Inspector	26 May 1828
Alfred, Jr.	2	M	Boy	Philadelphia	Philadelphia	Inspector	26 May 1828
Amelia	24	F	Spinster	Jamaica	U. States	Sanford William	26 Jul 1824
Belinda	22	F	Spinster	Jamaica	U. States	Sanford William	26 Jul 1824
Booth	7	M	None	Ireland	United States	Catharine	22 Jul 1825
Catherine	48	F	Spinster	G. Britain	New York	Prince Madore	28 Aug 1820
Elisabeth	5	F	None	Ireland	United States	Catharine	22 Jul 1825
Frances	14	F	Spinster	Jamaica	U. States	Sanford William	26 Jul 1824
George	26	M	Farmer	Great Brittain	United States	United States	16 Feb 1827
J. S.	30	M	Merchant	France	France	Jane	3 Sep 1827
Jacob	25	M	Merchant	England	United States	New York	14 Jul 1827
James	44		Farmer	Belfast	Ireland	Carolina Ann	21 May 1823
Jane	22	F	Spinster	Gt. Britain	New York	Columbia	3 Apr 1826
Jane	22	F		England	U. States	Lady Hunter	8 Aug 1826
Jeanette	20	M	Shoemaker	Germany	United States	Wm. Osborne	16 Sep 1828
Jno.	19	M	Merchant	Madeira	U. States	Albion	11 Dec 1828
John	17	M	Farmer	Ireland	U. States	Josephine	7 May 1827
John	32	M	Farmer	Ireland	United States	Catharine	22 Jul 1825
John	50	M	N Farmer	G. Britain	New York	Prince Madore	28 Aug 1820
John, Jur.	12	M	None	Ireland	United States	Catharine	22 Jul 1825
John H.	45	M	Merchant	Hayti		Nestor	20 Oct 1827
Jos.	25		Merchant	New York	United States	Robert Burns	18 Jun 1821
Joseph	30	M	Laborer	Great Britain	United States	John Jay	8 May 1828

NAMES OF PASSENGERS	AGE	SEX	OCCUPATIONS	COUNTRY TO WHICH THEY BELONG	COUNTRY THEY INTEND TO INHABIT	SHIPS/DATES OF ARRIVAL	
ALEXANDER (cont'd)							
Julia	17	F	Spinster	Jamaica	U. States	Sanford William	26 Jul 1824
Lewis	20	M	None	England	United States	Silas Richards	3 Apr 1826
Lousia	24	M	Acoun...	G. Brittan	U. States	Henry	24 Oct 1828
M. L.	29	M	Merchant	France	U. States	Dawn	8 Jun 1827
Margaret	24 8/12	F	Wife	G. Brittian	United States	Louisa	14 Jun 1825
Marther	6/12			England	U. States	Corinthian	8 Oct 1828
Mary	10	F	None	Ireland	United States	Catharine	22 Jul 1825
Mary	28	F	Wife	G. Brittan	U. States	Henry	24 Oct 1828
Mary	40	F	Lady	Philadelphia	Philadelphia	Inspector	26 May 1828
Matthew	32	M	Farmer	Scotland	United States	Friends	13 Mar 1824
R.	20	M	Cord Wainer	Ireland	United States	Samuel Robertson	9 Apr 1828
Rebecca	21	F	None	Great Britain	New York	Superior	5 Sep 1827
Robert	18		Writer			Rufus King	7 Aug 1820
Robt.	21	M	Clerk	England	New York	Eliza	8 Mar 1827
Saml.	19	M	Sadler			John Dickinson	14 Sep 1820
Samuel	2	M	None	Ireland	United States	Catharine	22 Jul 1825
Samuel	22			England	U. States	Corinthian	8 Oct 1828
Sarah	25			England	U. States	Corinthian	8 Oct 1828
Sarah	38	F	Spinster	Ireland	United States	Catharine	22 Jul 1825
Sarah	52	F	Weaver	Jamaica	U. States	Sanford William	26 Jul 1824
Thos.	27	M	Joiner	Ireland	Und. Stts of America	Alexander Mansfield	18 Aug 1826
Violet	18	F	Milliner	Ireland	New York	Louisa	20 Jul 1826
William	13	M	None	Ireland	United States	Catharine	22 Jul 1825
William	23	M	Labourer	Great Britan	United States	Clematis	8 May 1827
William	25	M	Merchant	United States	United States	Friends	13 Mar 1824
ALEXANDRE, Thecaul	32 6/12	M	Servant	Itally	Itally	France	28 Mar 1829
ALEXANDRINA, Dorothea	35	F	Spinster	Portugeese	United States	Mary Elizabeth	15 Oct 1829
ALEXIS, F.	10	M	Student	France	U.S.	Cadmus	20 Dec 1824
M. F.	35	F		Hatien	Hayti	Fair American	25 Jul 1822
ALEXS, Susan	36	F	Servant	St. Croix	U. States	Chase	2 Oct 1826
ALEZER, J.	26	M	Servant	Columbi	U. States	Laveria	23 Jul 1828
ALFAIN, George	18	M	Cabinet Maker	France	U. States	Sully	24 Oct 1828
ALFARO, E.	18	M	Merchant	Spain	America	Port Captain	6 Dec 1825
ALFARRA, A. G.	14	M	No	Campeache	U. States	Doris	22 May 1826
ALFONSO, D.	25	M	Merchant	Mexico	U. States	Prince Edward	5 Jul 1825
ALFORD, Chas.	40	M	Mechanic	United States	United States	Edgar	4 Jan 1826
Consider	45	M	Gentleman	United States	United States	Concordia	25 Aug 1827
Consider	46	M	Merchant	U.S.A.	U.S.A.	Silas Richards	7 Mar 1827
Elizabeth	32	F		United States	United States	Concordia	25 Aug 1827
ALGATE, D. C.	25	M	Merchant	Bermuda	Bermuda	Alpha	15 Jul 1823
Daniel ...	28	M	Merchant	Ireland	Bermuda	Triton	24 Oct 1826
George	18	M	Merchant	United States	United States	Uniao	19 Aug 1829
Rd.	23	M	Mechanic	Bermuda	U. States	Alpha	28 May 1823
ALGOE, May	32	F	Labourer	Ireland	U. States	Virginia	20 Jun 1825
Thomas	42	M	Labourer	Ireland	U. States	Virginia	20 Jun 1825
ALGOLO, J.	31	M		Mexico	U. States	Laveria	23 Jul 1828
ALI..., Joseph	45	M	Merchant	Spain	Spain	Commodore Chauncy	19 Jan 1826
ALISON, Agnes	24	F		Scotland	United States	Camillus	9 May 1827
Fredrick	9	M		Scotland	United States	Camillus	9 May 1827
James	39	M	Weaver	Ireland	United States	Carolina Ann	11 Dec 1826
Jane	23	F		Scotland	United States	Camillus	9 May 1827
Raschele	17	F		Scotland	United States	Camillus	9 May 1827
William	38	M		Scotland	United States	Camillus	9 May 1827
ALIVIN, Mary Ann	18	F	Lady	Ireland	United States	Ann Maria	28 Jan 1828
ALIXANA, Cesarrio	18	M	Servant	Mexico	Mexico	Virginia	8 Mar 1828
ALKER, Adele	20	F	Girl	France	New York	Lewis	29 Oct 1825
Adolphus	15	M	Boy	France	New York	Lewis	29 Oct 1825
Archangel	46	F	Wife	France	New York	Lewis	29 Oct 1825
Felicia	7	F	Girl	France	New York	Lewis	29 Oct 1825
Henry	5	M	Boy	France	New York	Lewis	29 Oct 1825
Loussa	12	F	Girl	France	New York	Lewis	29 Oct 1825
Nicholas	51	M	Mechanic	France	New York	Lewis	29 Oct 1825
Sophia	25	F	Girl	France	New York	Lewis	29 Oct 1825

NAMES OF PASSENGERS	AGE	SEX	OCCUPATIONS	COUNTRY TO WHICH THEY BELONG	COUNTRY THEY INTEND TO INHABIT	SHIPS/DATES OF ARRIVAL	
ALKER (cont'd)							
Virginia	18	F	Girl	France	New York	Lewis	29 Oct 1825
ALL..., Jane	23	F	Spinster	Ireland	U. States	Josephine	7 May 1827
ALLADAY, Fras.	17	F				Cassack	25 Jul 1820
ALLAIN, —, Mrs.	20	F	Wife	France	United States	Bayard	13 Nov 1823
Edwaner	3	M	Labourer	G. Britan	U. States	William Neilson	26 Jul 1828
James	1	M		G. Britan	U. States	William Neilson	26 Jul 1828
James	24	M	Merchant	France	United States	Bayard	13 Nov 1823
Joseph	5	M	Nothing	G. Britan	U. States	William Neilson	26 Jul 1828
Wm.	7	M	Nothing	G. Britan	U. States	William Neilson	26 Jul 1828
ALLAN, Alex	12	M		Gt. Brittain	U. States	Robert Fulton	1 Nov 1822
Ann	13	F		Maryland	New York	Brighton	14 Oct 1824
Elizabeth	13	F		Canada	Canada	Brighton	20 Aug 1825
Elizabeth	33	F	None	Canada	Canada	Brighton	20 Aug 1825
Elizth.	24	F				Splendid	14 Aug 1829
James	2	M	None	Scotland	United States	Camillus	27 Oct 1829
James	27	M	Carpenter	Great Britain	Mexico	Corinthian	27 Apr 1824
Jane	35	F		Gt. Brittain	U. States	Robert Fulton	1 Nov 1822
Janet	4	F	None	Scotland	United States	Camillus	27 Oct 1829
Jean	20		Spinster	Scotland	United States	Camillus	3 May 1828
John	21	M	Miner	England	England	Virginia	8 Mar 1828
John	35	M	Instrument Maker	Maryland	New York	Brighton	14 Oct 1824
John	50	M	Merchant	Canada	Canada	Brighton	20 Aug 1825
John, Revd.	32	M	Clergyman	U. States	U. States	James Monroe	18 Apr 1821
Joseph	6	M	None	Scotland	United States	Camillus	27 Oct 1829
Joseph	24	M	F...	Scotland	United States	Camillus	27 Oct 1829
Libby	3/12	M		Canada	Canada	Brighton	20 Aug 1825
Margaret	30	F		Maryland	New York	Brighton	14 Oct 1824
Richd.	39	M	Miner	England	U.S. States	Splendid	14 Aug 1829
Robt.			Child	Scotland	United States	Camillus	3 May 1828
Robt.	25	M	Servant	Ireland	U. States	Henrietta	7 Jul 1825
ALLANTON, Robert	50	M	Farmer	England	United States	Herald	29 Oct 1825
ALLCOUD, A.	18	M		France & Switzerland	U. States	Bayard	14 Jul 1826
ALLDAY, John	23	M	Merchant	Jamaica	U. States	Hal	7 Jun 1824
ALLEK, Henly	24	M	Blacksmith	Ireland	United States	Trident	18 Jul 1827
ALLEN, —,							
Lady [of Heman], & Servant	35			U.S.	U.S.	Brilliant	28 Jan 1828
—, Mrs.	35	F		England	U. States	Venus	4 Oct 1824
—, Mrs.	68	F		Scotland	U. States	Aurora	18 Sep 1821
A.	35	M	Mariner	U.S.	U.S.	Andrew Jackson	9 Oct 1820
A. B.	21	M	Merchant	America	America	Wm. Tell	9 Jan 1827
Alexander	4	M		Ireland	United States	Magnet	16 May 1823
Alexander	13	M	None	Great Britian	United States	Silvanus Jenkins	6 Apr 1826
Alexander	40	M	Bookeeper	Great Britian	United States	Silvanus Jenkins	6 Apr 1826
Alfred	35	M	Merchant	United States	United States	Eliza	31 Jul 1826
Alice	12	F	Spinster	Ireland	United States America	Wilson	4 Oct 1827
Amelia, Mrs.	20	F		England	U. States	Hudson	10 Nov 1825
Ann	25	F	Spinster	Ireland	United States America	Wilson	4 Oct 1827
Ann	26	F		Great Brittain	U. States	Atticus	25 Apr 1822
Ann	30	M		Ireland	United States	Magnet	16 May 1823
Benjamin, Mr.	28	M		New Rochelle	U. States	Hudson	10 Nov 1825
Betty	14	F		Ireland	United States	Commerce	13 Jun 1828
C. B.	27	M	Merchant	U. States	U. States	Angenora	12 May 1826
Charles	21	M	Cotton Spinner	Ireland	America	Franklin	13 Aug 1827
Charles	30					Prometheus	30 Aug 1828
Charles B.	23	M	Merchant	U. States	U. States	Dart	5 Apr 1822
Charlotte	25	F	None	Scotland	U. States	Camillus	27 Jun 1826
Cosmo	17	M	Apprentice to Coach Maker [Nicholas Lair...]	United States	United States	Dromo	9 Oct 1828
D. R.	11	M	None	U. States	U. States	Othello	11 Jul 1825
David	5 3/12	M		U.S.A.	U.S.A.	Silas Richards	27 Oct 1826
David	14		Son	United States		New Orleans	27 Feb 1829
David	19	M	Servant	Great Britain	U.S. of America	Canada	1 Oct 1827
David R.	13	M	Mariner	U.S. of America		Brilliant	28 Jan 1828

NAMES OF PASSENGERS	AGE	SEX	OCCUPATIONS	COUNTRY TO WHICH THEY BELONG	COUNTRY THEY INTEND TO INHABIT	SHIPS/DATES OF ARRIVAL	
ALLEN (cont'd)							
Dd.	40	M	Merchant	America	U. States	Falcon	12 Oct 1822
E..., ...	11	M	None	...ia	United States	Martha	22 Jul 1820
Edward	19	M	Gentleman	Gt. Britain		Corinthian	27 Oct 1829
Edward, Jr.	25	M	Merchant	America	America	Cincinnatus	19 Oct 1826
Eliza	7	F		U. States	U. States	Prince Leopold	2 Jul 1821
Eliza	19		Spinster	Ireland	United States	Fabius	18 Mar 1829
Eliza	19 2/12	F		U.S.A.	U.S.A.	Silas Richards	27 Oct 1826
Elizabeth	6	F		England	U.S. America	Cortes	19 May 1826
Elizabeth	25	F		Gt. Brittain	United States	Cortes	11 Aug 1823
Elizabeth	50 2/12	F	Farmer	England	United States	Young Phoenix	26 Jul 1824
Ellen	21	M	Servant	Ireland	America	Carolina Ann	7 Aug 1826
Esther	50	F		U. States	U. States	Prince Leopold	2 Jul 1821
Frances	38	F	None	...ia	United States	Martha	22 Jul 1820
Frederick	9 1/12	M	Farmer	England	United States	Young Phoenix	26 Jul 1824
Geo.	5	M	...	...	United States	Minerva	30 Oct 1827
George	22	M	Tin Smith	Great Britain	United States	Colossus	5 Jun 1827
George	24	M	None	England	United States	Mary & Harriet	9 Mar 1829
George W.	12 6/12	M	Boy	Connecticut	Connecticut	Potosi	28 May 1825
Hannah	26	F	...	...	United States	Minerva	30 Oct 1827
Hannah	30	F	Servant	Great Britan	Canada	Canada	2 Jun 1824
Hannah	64	F	...	...	United States	Minerva	30 Oct 1827
Harriet	3	F	...	...	United States	Minerva	30 Oct 1827
Harriet	6	F		England	U.S. America	Cortes	19 May 1826
Harriet	35	F		England	U.S. America	Cortes	19 May 1826
Heman, Hon., late minister plenipotentiary to Chili	45			U.S.	U.S.	Brilliant	28 Jan 1828
Henry	15	M	Clerk	U. States of America	U.S. of America	Friends	25 Sep 1823
Henry	16	M	Farmer	England	United States	Young Phoenix	26 Jul 1824
Henry	32	M	None	Ireland	United States	Magnet	16 May 1823
Herbert	22	M	Merchant	Nova Scotia		Elba	14 Jun 1828
Horatio	26	M	Merchant	United States	U. States	New York	19 Nov 1828
Ichabod		M	Mariner, Supercargo	U. States	U. States	Mary	7 Jun 1821
Ichabod	30	M	Mariner	U. States	U. States	Mary	29 Feb 1820
Ichabod	35	M	Merchant	U. States	U. States	Jasper	24 Feb 1826
Isabella	2	F		Great Brittain	U. States	Atticus	25 Apr 1822
J.	35	M	Mariner	U. States	U. States	Cherub	20 Sep 1824
James	6	M		Ireland	United States	Magnet	16 May 1823
James	9	M		Ireland	United States	Magnet	16 May 1823
James	18	M	...	...	...	Laurel	16 Nov 1824
James	20 3/12	M	Farmer	England	United States	Young Phoenix	26 Jul 1824
James	21	M	Merchant	Boston	U. States	Day	16 Aug 1826
James	30	M	Shoemaker	England	United States	Robert Edwards	3 Oct 1829
James	32	M	Mercht.	U. States	U. States	Octavia	26 Jul 1824
James	36	M	Teacher	Scotland	U. States	Camillus	27 Jun 1826
James	43		Mariner	United States		New Orleans	27 Feb 1829
James, Capt., Junr.	39	M	Mariner	U.S. of America		Brilliant	28 Jan 1828
James, 3d	43	M	Sea Captain	Connecticut	Connecticut	Potosi	28 May 1825
James W.	56	M	Mariner	U. States	U. States	Commerce	6 Feb 1824
Jane	10	F		Gt. Brittain	U. States	Robert Fulton	1 Nov 1822
Jane	14 2/12	F	Farmer	England	United States	Young Phoenix	26 Jul 1824
Jno.	23	M	Merchant	U. States	U. States	Blooming Rose	14 Jul 1821
John	3	M		Ireland	United States	Magnet	16 May 1823
John	12	M	None	Great Britian	United States	Silvanus Jenkins	6 Apr 1826
John	13	M	Gunsmith	England	New York	Brighton	19 Aug 1829
John	13	M	Gunsmith			Brighton	19 Aug 1829
John	20	M	Servant	Ireland	America	Carolina Ann	7 Aug 1826
John	24	M	Farmer	Ireland	United States	Henry Kneeland	7 Jun 1828
John	26	M	Seafaring	Maryland	U. States	Gervis	18 Aug 1823
John	30	M	Gentleman	Ireland	United States	Dublin Packet	24 Sep 1823
John	36	M	Farmer	Ireland	United States	Diana	1 May 1826
John	38	M	Labourer	Ireland	United States	Mary & Harriet	9 Mar 1829
John	40	M	Merchant	Great Britain	United States	Martha	22 Jul 1820
Jos.	22	M	Merchant	N. York	N. York	Ben Alam	24 Jul 1826
Joseph	14	M	Gunsmith	England	New York	Brighton	19 Aug 1829

NAMES OF PASSENGERS	AGE	SEX	OCCUPATIONS	COUNTRY TO WHICH THEY BELONG	COUNTRY THEY INTEND TO INHABIT	SHIPS/DATES OF ARRIVAL	
ALLEN (cont'd)							
Joseph	53	M	Gunsmith	England	New York	Brighton	19 Aug 1829
Leymoin	28	M	Merchant	U. States	U. States	York	10 Dec 1825
Lydia	38	F		U. States	U. States	Prince Leopold	2 Jul 1821
Margaret	22	F	None	Ireland	United States of America	Jubilee	12 May 1828
Maria	40	F	Spinster	Scotland	United States	Tom	2 Jul 1827
Marria	19	F	Lady	England	America	Criterion	27 Oct 1821
Mary	1	F	...	...	United States	Minerva	30 Oct 1827
Mary, Miss	18	F	Lady	U.S. Am.	U.S. Am.	Henry IV	5 Feb 1827
Mary Ann	20	F	Spinster	Ireland	United States	Antioch	21 Sep 1827
Mary Jane	8	F		Ireland	United States	Magnet	16 May 1823
Matilda	12 1/12	F	Farmer	England	United States	Young Phoenix	26 Jul 1824
Micheal	45 1/12	M	Merchant	U.S.A.	U.S.A.	Silas Richards	27 Oct 1826
N.	32	M	Merchant	American	Deliwar	Bolivar	10 Aug 1827
Nicholas	26	M	Seaman	England	England	Mentor	9 Apr 1822
Phillip	32	M	Printer	England	N. York	France	29 Nov 1827
Piere	21	M	Labourer	Gt. Brittan		L'Esperance	6 Sep 1828
R. F.	34	M	Merchant	U. States	U. States	Cincinnatus	24 May 1821
Rebecce	13	F	Spinster	Ireland	United States America	Wilson	4 Oct 1827
Richard	29	M	Farmer	England	U. States	Acasta	21 Oct 1825
Robert	18		Tailor	Ireland	United States	Courier	15 Oct 1827
Robert	28	M	Farmer	Ireland	New York	Carolina Ann	15 Oct 1824
Robert	28		Labourer	Ireland	United States	Fabius	18 Mar 1829
Robr.	27	M	Engineer	Great Britain	United States	Colossus	5 Jun 1827
Robt.	48	M	Labourer	England	U. States	Comet	23 Aug 1828
Sarah	19	F	Servant	Ireland	New York	Atlantic	8 May 1828
Sarah	20	F	family of [Margaret]	U. Kingdom of Great Britain	United States of Amer.	Cambria	7 May 1828
Sarah	23 7/12	F		U.S.A.	U.S.A.	Silas Richards	27 Oct 1826
Sarah	31 3/12	F	Lady	U.S. America	U.S. America	Erie	19 Oct 1829
Sarah Ann	11	F		Ireland	United States	Magnet	16 May 1823
Susan	24	F	None	America	America	Braganza	8 Aug 1825
T. C.	45	M	Merch.	Spain		David Moffitt	7 Oct 1822
Telora	4	F		England	U.S. America	Cortes	19 May 1826
Thomas	27	M	Labourer	Ireland	United States	Catharine	22 Jul 1825
Thomas	35	M	Farmer	England	Massachusetts	Indian Chief	19 Jun 1823
Thomas	62	M	Farmer	United States	United States	Friends	21 Oct 1825
Ths.	2	M		Ireland	United States	Magnet	16 May 1823
W. H.	24	M	Marinor	U. States	New York	London Packet	5 Jan 1829
William	12	M		Ireland	United States	Antioch	21 Sep 1827
William	17	M	Seaman	Swizerland		Antioch	18 Aug 1829
William	18	M	Mariner	U. States	U. States	Fourth of July	19 Oct 1824
William	18	M	Gunsmith	England	New York	Brighton	19 Aug 1829
William	30	M	Cabinet or Joiner	England	U. States	George Canning	13 Jun 1826
William H.	27	M	Attorney	United States	United States	Ann	24 Sep 1822
Wm.	18	M	Merchant	United States	United States	Three Brothers	22 Mar 1825
Wm.	24	M	Merchant	Philad.	U. States	Velocipede	16 Dec 1824
Wm.	27	M	...	...	United States	Minerva	30 Oct 1827
Wm.	27	M	Butcher	England	United States	Essex	23 May 1828
Wm.	28	M		Great Brittain	U. States	Atticus	25 Apr 1822
Wm.	30	M	Saddler	England	U.S. America	Cortes	19 May 1826
Wm.	65	M	...	...	United States	Minerva	30 Oct 1827
Wm., Jr.	10	M		England	U.S. America	Cortes	19 May 1826
Zacharia	30	M	Merchant	U. States	U. States	Canada	13 Oct 1825
ALLENBURG, G. G. A.	32	M	Blacksmith	Bremen	Bremen	Germania	15 Jun 1825
ALLENDO, Antonio	34	M	Merchant	Gutamala	Spain	Swan	23 Jun 1823
ALLENT, Hieronimus	25	M	Taylor	Baden	United States	Jason	3 Nov 1828
ALLESO, J.	23	M	Servant	France	France	Eliza	28 Apr 1827
ALLEXANDER, James	1	M	Clerk	...	United States	Minerva	30 Oct 1829
ALLEYNE, Benj.	28	M	Merchant	Barbadoes	Great Britain	Only Daughter	26 Apr 1826
John	30	M	Merchant	Barbados	Supposition is he will return	Superb	7 Jul 1823
John	32	M	Merchant	Barbadoes	Great Britain	Only Daughter	26 Apr 1826
ALLGOOD, Jno.	44	M	Plater	U. States	Great Britain	Thompson	26 Apr 1828
Mary A.	17	F		U. States	Great Britain	Thompson	26 Apr 1828
Sarah	43	F		U. States	Great Britain	Thompson	26 Apr 1828

NAMES OF PASSENGERS	AGE	SEX	OCCUPATIONS	COUNTRY TO WHICH THEY BELONG	COUNTRY THEY INTEND TO INHABIT	SHIPS/DATES OF ARRIVAL	
ALLIAUME, —,							
Sergeant	28	M	Planter	Gaudaloupe	U. States	Eliza	3 Jul 1820
Sergeant, Madam	19	F	Planter	Gaudaloupe	U. States	Eliza	3 Jul 1820
ALLIER, John P.	37	M	Merchant	France		Samuel	25 Apr 1828
ALLINSON, A.	20	M	Farmer	Great Britain	United States	Ann Maria	12 Jul 1821
Adam	56	M	Farmer	Great Britain	United States	Ann Maria	12 Jul 1821
Mary	53	F	None	Great Britain	United States	Ann Maria	12 Jul 1821
Saml.	23	M	Merchant	England	United States	Columbia	16 Jan 1829
Saml.	35	M	Merchant	U. States	U. States	Marcellus	26 Feb 1824
Samuel, Mr.	40		Merchant	U.S. of America	U.S. America	Mary	10 Mar 1826
ALLIS, Alexander	21	M	Tailor	Scotland	United States	Mary & Susan	5 Aug 1828
ALLISON, Hugh	24	M	Farmer	America	America	Minerva	8 Oct 1824
Jas.	26	M	Farmer	Ireland	United States	Trident	16 May 1826
John	3	M	None	Great Britain	United States	Mary & Harriet	3 Jul 1829
John	27	M	Labourer	Great Britain		Moro Castle	6 Jul 1827
John	45	M	Weaver	England	Upper Canada	Lima	5 Aug 1829
Joseph	27	M	Farmer	Great Britian	United States	Andes	19 Aug 1829
Marion	50	F	Widow	Scotland	United States	Tom	2 Jul 1827
William	30	M	Mechanic	Great Britain	United States	Mary & Harriet	3 Jul 1829
ALLKENNEDY,							
Alexander	18	M	Weaver	Scotland	America	John Adams	2 Aug 1827
Christian	20	F		Scotland	America	John Adams	2 Aug 1827
John	26	M	Weaver	Scotland	America	John Adams	2 Aug 1827
ALLOU, Emil	10	M		France	United States	Helen Mar	29 Jun 1827
John Charles	39	M	Merchant	France	United States	Helen Mar	29 Jun 1827
Julius	7	M		France	United States	Helen Mar	29 Jun 1827
M. L.	69	F		United States	United States	Helen Mar	29 Jun 1827
ALLPORT, James	32	M	Merchant	Great Britain		Manhattan	7 Nov 1827
ALLSIP, Mary	20	F	...	Ireland	United States	Carolina Ann	24 Oct 1825
ALLSTON, Fras.	19	F	None	England	United States	Dalhouse Castle	6 Sep 1827
William D.	40	M	Merchant	South Caroline	United States	Jane	17 Jul 1821
ALLWARE, Michael	24	M	Taylor	Baden	United States	Jason	3 Nov 1828
ALLWER, Elizth.	20	F	Servant	Ireland	U. States of America	Courier	17 Mar 1827
ALLWORTH, Sofia	28	F	Perfumer	England	U.S. America	Criterion	27 Oct 1821
ALLY, Jas.	22	M	Hatter	England	United States	Loire	26 May 1828
ALLYN, Eliza, Mrs.	40	F	Lady	England	Barbadoes	Jupiter	27 Jun 1828
James M.	40	M	Gentleman	England	Barbadoes	Jupiter	27 Jun 1828
ALLYSON, S. M.	35	M	Merchant	G. Britain		Hope & Polly	17 Aug 1827
ALMEDIA, Jno. A.	40	M	Merchant	U. States	U. States	Trimmer	21 Jul 1825
J.	42	M	Mariner	Brazil	Brazil	Atlas	24 Jun 1828
Jas.	20	M	Mariner	U. States	U. States	Fair American	26 Jul 1825
ALMELL, Michl.	26		Labourer	Ireland	America	Sarah	18 Aug 1829
ALMINGER, Louisa	26	F	Maid Servant	France	United States	Helen	5 Sep 1828
ALMY, Peleg	43	M	Mariner	U. States	U. States	Newport	16 Feb 1824
ALNWICK, Ann	31	F	None	G. Britain	U. States	James Monroe	18 Apr 1821
Mary Jane	6	F	None	G. Britain	U. States	James Monroe	18 Apr 1821
ALOISI, Burnardo	26	M	Linguest	Italy	United States	Friends	13 Mar 1824
ALONZA, Loper	20		Merchant	U. States	U. States	Eliza Pigott	25 Sep 1820
ALONZO, ...	27		Merchant	Mexico	Mexico	Brown	11 Jun 1827
ALOOS, Antonis J.	32		Mariner	Spain	Spain	Maria	20 Jul 1820
ALOY, ...quin		F		Spain	U. States	Madison	22 May 1822
ALPHONSO, Josea	14	M	Planter	Spain	Havana	Robert Fulton	22 May 1824
Silvesto	22	M	Planter	Spain	Havana	Robert Fulton	22 May 1824
ALPIN, A. B.	29	M	Merchant	Philadelphia	U. States	John Wells	8 Sep 1897
ALPS, James	19	M	Farmer	England	U. States	Cincinnatus	24 May 1821
ALREA, Carlos	34	M	Gentn.	So. America	U. States	Pacific	11 Sep 1824
ALSEDO, S.	25	M	Soldier	Spain	Spain	Prince Edward	22 Jul 1824
ALSEY, Samuel	31		Merchant	Baltimore	United States	London	13 Dec 1822
ALSOLA, S. Gracio	37	M	Merchant	Spain	London	Charles	5 Mar 1824
ALSOP, Jos. W.	48	M	Mercht.	U. States	U. States	Condor	22 Aug 1822
Joseph H.	50	M	Merchant	United States	United States	Ludwig	10 Aug 1825
Paul	40	M	Merchant	France	New York	Enterprize	3 Nov 1824
Rd.	34	M	Merchant	U. States	U. States	Franklin	26 May 1825
ALSTON, Margt.	3	F		Newmills, Louden [Parish], Dumbarton			
*going to her friends				[County]	New York	Hero	19 May 1828
Marian	25	F		Newmills, Louden [Parish], Dumbarton			
*going to her friends				[County]	New York	Hero	19 May 1828

NAMES OF PASSENGERS	AGE	SEX	OCCUPATIONS	COUNTRY TO WHICH THEY BELONG	COUNTRY THEY INTEND TO INHABIT	SHIPS/DATES OF ARRIVAL	
ALSWORTH, John	48	M	Farmer	England	America	Dublin Packet	9 Oct 1820
ALTER, Jno.	21			England		Anacreon	7 Sep 1827
ALTERBURY, B.	28	M	Merchant	N. York	U. States	Rising States	23 Apr 1825
ALTERMANN, Adam	10	M	Farmer	Swizerland		Antioch	18 Aug 1829
André	63	M	Farmer	Swizerland		Antioch	18 Aug 1829
Catherine	8	F	Farmer	Swizerland		Antioch	18 Aug 1829
Catherine	50	F	Farmer	Swizerland		Antioch	18 Aug 1829
ALTHON, Richard B.	28 5/12	M	Machanick	America	America	France	28 Mar 1829
ALTON, Harriet Matilda	30	F		G. Britian	G. Britian	Industry	14 Feb 1826
Jacob	28 3/12	M	Farmer	Switzerland	U. States	France	26 Jun 1828
ALVA, —, Mr.	45	M	Merchant	Havana	Havana	Milo	15 May 1824
ALVAAREZ, Manuel	27	M	Merchant	Spain	Vera Cruz	Droma	25 Mar 1826
ALVARADO, John Antony	30	M	Gent.	Central America	U. States	William Thompson	25 Aug 1828
ALVARES Y SAGARTIQUI, Jose, Don	30	M	Merchant	Mexico	Tampico, Mexico	Nancy	15 Apr 1824
ALVAREZ, F.	35	M		Spain		Apollo	11 Jun 1828
ALVARTY, Anthony	55	M	Planter	Porto Rico	U. States	Olympia	19 Jun 1828
Saint	8	M		Porto Rico	U. States	Olympia	19 Jun 1828
ALVEN, Manuel Almeda de Couhinho	26	M	Planter	Brazil	Brazil	Isabella	1 Aug 1829
ALVERADO, Jose, Don	30	M	Merchant	Spain	Mexico	Nancy	1 Oct 1824
ALVERID, Jose						Dromo	14 Aug 1829
ALVERTA, —, Mrs.	25	F			United States	Alfred	8 Jul 1822
R.	26	M	Merchant	France	United States	Alfred	8 Jul 1822
ALVES, John	44	M	Merchant	Gt. Britain	United States	Seeds	29 Sep 1824
ALWORTH, Catherine	25	F		Limerick	N. York	Thomas & William	25 May 1827
Edward	25	M	Mason	Limerick	N. York	Thomas & William	25 May 1827
Joseph	2	M		Limerick	N. York	Thomas & William	25 May 1827
ALZEAR, Francisco	28	M	Merchant	U. States	U. States	Burdett	11 Oct 1827
ALZINE, Francis	30	M	Merchant	Havana	Havana	Nile	18 Oct 1828
ALZOLA, Y.	30	M	Merchant	New York	U. States	Alfred	23 Oct 1826
AMACH, Cathrin	40	F		Great Britain	U. States	Lady Hunter	28 May 1823
AMACHEN, Elizabeth	9	F		Switzerland	Switzerland	Edward Quesnel	3 Jul 1829
Gottlieb	2	M		Switzerland	Switzerland	Edward Quesnel	3 Jul 1829
John	12	M		Switzerland	Switzerland	Edward Quesnel	3 Jul 1829
John	51	M		Switzerland	Switzerland	Edward Quesnel	3 Jul 1829
Maria	42	F		Switzerland	Switzerland	Edward Quesnel	3 Jul 1829
Marianna	5	F		Switzerland	Switzerland	Edward Quesnel	3 Jul 1829
AMADA, Anthony	35	M	Merchant	U. States	U.S.	Fair American	9 May 1825
AMADO, H.	32	M	Merchant	N. Orleans	U. States	Greek	3 Mar 1825
AMADU, —, Mr.	23	M	Merchant	France	U. States	Henry	8 Jun 1824
AMALRIE, Anto. Jacqs. Scipion	26	M	Merchant	France	New York	Cadmus	19 Aug 1823
AMANDE, Caroline	5/12	F				Howard	4 May 1827
Catherine	30	F		Saxony		Howard	4 May 1827
Charles Henry	32	M	Mechanic	Saxony	U.S.	Howard	4 May 1827
AMANN, Cathr.	9	F		Brattain		L'Esperance	6 Sep 1828
Elizabeth	17	F		Brattain		L'Esperance	6 Sep 1828
Joseph	7	M		Brattain		L'Esperance	6 Sep 1828
Joseph	44	M	Carpenter	Brattain		L'Esperance	6 Sep 1828
Magdelene	14	F		Brattain		L'Esperance	6 Sep 1828
Mgdelene	40	F		Brattain		L'Esperance	6 Sep 1828
Utillia	4 2/12	F		Brattain		L'Esperance	6 Sep 1828
AMBERG, Jacob	31	M	Labourer	Manchen, Bayern	Pennsylvania, U.S.	Europa	6 Oct 1828
John	34	M	Merchant	United States	Citizen of East Town	Europa	6 Oct 1828
AMBLER, Jn. J.	23	M	Planter	United States	United States	Howard	19 May 1826
AMBOUS, Addelee	40	F	Mason	Ireland		Quatre Freres	29 Jul 1828
John	44	M	Mason	Ireland		Quatre Freres	29 Jul 1828
AMBROIS, Amant	4	M	Mason	Ireland		Quatre Freres	29 Jul 1828
Elisa	3/12	F	Mason	Ireland		Quatre Freres	29 Jul 1828
Hulebert	3	M	Mason	Ireland		Quatre Freres	29 Jul 1828

NAMES OF PASSENGERS	AGE	SEX	OCCUPATIONS	COUNTRY TO WHICH THEY BELONG	COUNTRY THEY INTEND TO INHABIT	SHIPS/DATES OF ARRIVAL	
AMBROIS (cont'd)							
John	7	M	Mason	Ireland		Quatre Freres	29 Jul 1828
Joseph	9	M	Mason	Ireland		Quatre Freres	29 Jul 1828
AMCOT, P. T.	21	M	Mechanic	France	U. States	Bayard	25 Apr 1828
AMEDY, John B.	30	M	Mariner	Massachusetts	Massachusetts	Brighton	14 Oct 1824
AMES, Amos	30	M	Seaman	United States	United States	Four Sons	1 Sep 1827
Francis	3	M	Child	Ireland	U. States	Courier	17 Mar 1828
John	22	M	Labourer	Great Britain	United States	Blakely	29 Sep 1826
Margeret	24 6/12	F	Matron	Ireland	U. States	Courier	17 Mar 1828
P. F.	25	M	Doctor	United States	United States	Howard	27 Sep 1826
AMESTRY, Lewis	18	M		Columbian Republic	Columbian Republic	Meta	5 Jun 1824
AMEWORTH, David, Rev.	58	M	Minister of Gospel	Grate Britain	...	Courier	14 Jun 1825
AMIDON, Philip	19	M	Student	Providence	U. States	Beaver	16 Mar 1824
S.	14	M	Merchant	Columbia	Columbia	Franklin	27 May 1825
AMIES, James Amsons	39	M	Merchant	Great Britan	United States	Silvanus Jenkins	10 Mar 1827
AMILY, P.	21	M	Merchant	U. States	U. States	Brown	29 Apr 1825
AMININAC, Matthew	58	M	Mechanic	United States	United States	Rapid	24 Oct 1823
AMISITO, Jos.	11	M	School Boy	Columbia	U. States	Exchange	26 Jul 1824
AMISTRY, Jno.	30	M	Mariner	U.S.	U.S.	Bruce	21 Nov 1827
AMLEY, John D.	25	M	Mercht.	Great Britain	Great Britan	Nancy	13 Dec 1822
AMMIDON, Philip	42	M	Merchant	America	America	Cortes	16 Jul 1827
AMMON, William	23	M	Carpenter	Ireland	United States	Fabius	31 Jul 1829
AMNER, Thomas	30	M	Merchant	England	England	Birmingham	16 Jun 1828
AMORY, J. H.	25	M	Merchant	U. States	U. States	Othello	11 Jul 1825
Jona., Jur.	22	M	Merchant	U. States	U. States	Canada	6 Jun 1825
AMOS, Alexr.	20		Farmer	Great Britain	United States	Camillus	12 Sep 1827
Geo. T.	50	M	Merchant	Germany	U. States	Franklin	6 May 1828
George	27	M	Tanner	U. States	U. States	Topaz	28 May 1827
Jose Domingo	31	M	Merchant	Colombia	Colombia	Tampico	29 Apr 1826
AMOSSA, Joaquim	19	M	Carpenter			Atlanta	20 May 1822
AMPHLET, Catherine	50	F		England	United States	St. John	5 Oct 1829
Eliza	15	F		England	United States	St. John	5 Oct 1829
George	12	M		England	United States	St. John	5 Oct 1829
Jno.	50	M	Confectioner	England	United States	St. John	5 Oct 1829
John	26	M	Cabinet Maker	England	United States	St. John	5 Oct 1829
AMSTEN, Anna	5	F	Farmer	France	U. States	Lewis	6 Jul 1825
Casper	18	M	Farmer	France	U. States	Lewis	6 Jul 1825
John	23	M	Farmer	France	U. States	Lewis	6 Jul 1825
John	54	M	Farmer	France	U. States	Lewis	6 Jul 1825
Margt.	8	F	Farmer	France	U. States	Lewis	6 Jul 1825
Peter	26	M	Farmer	France	U. States	Lewis	6 Jul 1825
AMSTRUTZ, Annah	25		...	France	U. States	Elizabeth	9 Jul 1825
Christian	22		...	France	U. States	Elizabeth	9 Jul 1825
AMZLEN, Jacob B.	26 6/12	M	Seaman	Switzerland	United States of America	Criterion	13 Oct 1825
ANAGUY, Wm.	38	M	Missionary	Great Brittan	United States	Euphrates	12 Mar 1824
ANBLING, Lemuel	24	M	Merchant	America	America	Soto	1 Aug 1829
ANBRIDGE, John	22	M		England	New York	Cincinnatus	5 Dec 1825
ANCE, Adaline	36	F		Germany	United States	Samuel Robertson	8 Aug 1828
Barbara	5	F		Germany	United States	Samuel Robertson	8 Aug 1828
Catherine	3	F		Germany	United States	Samuel Robertson	8 Aug 1828
Catherine	85	F		Germany	United States	Samuel Robertson	8 Aug 1828
Pumtian	28	M	Weaver	Germany	United States	Samuel Robertson	8 Aug 1828
Simon	55	M	Weaver	Germany	United States	Samuel Robertson	8 Aug 1828
ANCELL, Henry	20 6/12	M	Surgeon	England	U. States	Sceptre	24 Jul 1822
ANCIOLA, Antonia	29	M	Merchant	Spain	Spain	Frances	21 Mar 1827
ANCOT, J. R.	50	M	Mechanic	France	U. States	Bayard	25 Apr 1828
ANDARIESE, Edward	21	M	Clerk	United States		Sarah	16 May 1828
ANDENSE, James	30	M	Merchant	U. States	U. States	Eliza	20 Nov 1828
ANDEREEG, John	18	M	Butcher	Brattain		L'Esperance	6 Sep 1828
ANDERS, Jno.	38	M	Mechanic	Connecticutt	U. States	Mary	7 Apr 1823
John. Danl.	56	M	Bishop	Germany	Pensilvania	Maria Elizabeth	24 Mar 1828

NAMES OF PASSENGERS	AGE	SEX	OCCUPATIONS	COUNTRY TO WHICH THEY BELONG	COUNTRY THEY INTEND TO INHABIT	SHIPS/DATES OF ARRIVAL	
ANDERSEN, Ernestine	46	F		Germany	Pensilvania	Maria Elizabeth	24 Mar 1828
ANDERSON, —	25	M	Store keeper	England	U.S.	James & Margaret	4 Aug 1823
—	29	M		Scotland	U.S.	Curler	19 Jul 1828
—	30	M	Merchant	England		Marchioness	13 May 1828
—, Master	12	M		Halifax	some to return & the others to Canada	Albert	14 May 1822
—, Mrs.	28	F		Halifax	some to return & the others to Canada	Albert	14 May 1822
—, Mrs.	28	F	Merchant	Eastport	U. States	Franklin	24 May 1825
A.	30	M	Labourer	England	United States	Loire	4 Oct 1824
Abraham	45	M	Black	United States	United States	Falcon	1 May 1824
Alexander	13	M	Child	Ireland	New York	Louisa	20 Jul 1826
Alexr.	25	M	Farmer	Ireland	U. States	Nancy	29 Nov 1821
Anders	28	M	Farmer	Norway	United States	Salem	31 Aug 1829
Ann	4	F		G. Britain	U. States	Camillus	8 Sep 1828
Ann	35	F		Ireland	U. States	Alex Mansfield	1 Jun 1822
Ann G.	2	F	None	United States	United States	William Bayard	17 May 1825
Anna Winsloe	23	F	None	Gt. Brittain	Canada	York	6 Dec 1826
Anne	23	F	Child	Ireland	New York	Louisa	20 Jul 1826
Anne	35	F		Massachusetts	United States	Meteor	19 Aug 1829
Arthur	21	M	Laborer	Ireland	United States	Mary	1 Jul 1829
Benjamin	19	M	Servant	New York	U.S.A.	Brighton	21 Jan 1826
Caroline	7	F		U. States	U. States	Robt. Reade	12 Apr 1825
Cath.	50	F		Pennsylvania	U. States	Enterprize	14 Jul 1823
Catharina	6/12	F		Scotland	United States	Scotsman	22 Aug 1828
Catharine	15	F	Farmer	Scotland	United States	Minerva	29 Oct 1822
Catharine	30	F		Scotland	United States	Scotsman	22 Aug 1828
Charles	26	M	Farmer	Great Brittain	U. States	William Byrnes	23 Jul 1824
Charles	32	M	Baker	Scotland	United States	Commerce	17 Jul 1823
Christian	20	F		Great Britian	United States	Brok	29 Aug 1823
Christian, Mrs.	29	F		Great Britain	Canada	Florida	2 Oct 1828
Christopher	17	M		Lincolnshire	U. States	Atlantic	13 Jul 1824
David	...	M	Merchant	Scotland	New York	Amity	13 Sep 1821
David	3	M		Scotland	United States	Scotsman	22 Aug 1828
David	18	M	Farmer	Scotland	United States	Minerva	29 Oct 1822
David	22		Merchant	G. Britain	America	Spring	12 Oct 1821
David	36	M	Mariner	United States	U. States	South Carolina Packet	5 Nov 1821
David	51	M	Merchant	New York	New York	Silvanus Jenkins	24 Jul 1828
Diana	27	F	Spinstress	Ireland	New York	Louisa	20 Jul 1826
E.	23	M	Mariner	United States	United States	Chili	9 Jan 1829
Edwd.	25	M	Labourer	U. States	U. States	Robt. Reade	12 Apr 1825
Elisabeth	6	F	None	United States	United States	William Bayard	17 May 1825
Elizabell	22 3/12	F	Dress Maker	Ireland	U. States	Fabius	22 Sep 1828
Elizabeth	12	F		Lincolnshire	U. States	Atlantic	13 Jul 1824
Elizabeth	12	F		Halifax	New York	Hope & Esther	25 Aug 1827
Elizabeth	44	F		Lincolnshire	U. States	Atlantic	13 Jul 1824
Elizth.	20	F	F...	...	...	Diamond	27 Jul 1824
Frances	60	F		England	United States	William Byrnes	1 Dec 1824
George	7	M		Lincolnshire	U. States	Atlantic	13 Jul 1824
George	68	M	Merchant	United States	U. States	Splendid	1 Jul 1829
George C.	6	M	Child of [Mrs. Christian]			Florida	2 Oct 1828
Gillis, Mrs.	29	F		G. Britain	U. States	Eliza	9 May 1827
Henry	14	M		Halifax	New York	Hope & Esther	25 Aug 1827
Henry K.	6/12	M	Child	United States	United States	Henry Kneeland	7 Jun 1828
Hugh	38		Weaver	Great Britain	United States	Camillus	12 Sep 1827
Isabella	16	F		Halifax	New York	Hope & Esther	25 Aug 1827
Isabella	40	F		Halifax	New York	Hope & Esther	25 Aug 1827
Isabella	50	F	Wife	Ireland	New York	Louisa	20 Jul 1826
Isabella	60 6/12	F	Spinster	Ireland	U. States	Fabius	22 Sep 1828
J.	40	M	Merchant	Virginia	U. States	Leonora	25 May 1826
J., Mrs.	26	F		G. Britain	U. States	Camillus	8 Sep 1828
Jacob	30	M	Merchant	Scotland	U. States	Mary Ann	27 Sep 1822
James	5	M	Farmer	Scotland	United States	Minerva	29 Oct 1822
James	19		Manufacturer	Gospoort	Great Britain	Ann	27 Nov 1820

NAMES OF PASSENGERS	AGE	SEX	OCCUPATIONS	COUNTRY TO WHICH THEY BELONG	COUNTRY THEY INTEND TO INHABIT	SHIPS/DATES OF ARRIVAL	
ANDERSON (cont'd)							
James	19	M	Taylor	Halifax	New York	Hope & Esther	25 Aug 1827
James	20		Tailor	U. States	United States	Cambria	19 Oct 1829
James	22	M	Farmer	G. Britain	U. States	Perseverance	9 Jun 1827
James	22	M	Silver Smith	Scotland	Unt. States	Robert Fulton	14 Mar 1827
James	24	M	Merchant	Ireland	New York	Louisa	20 Jul 1826
James	25		Farmer			Amphion	31 May 1824
James	25	M	Joiner	Great Britain	United States	Colossus	5 Jun 1827
James	26	M	Merchant	England	U. States	Amity	23 Sep 1823
James	29	M	Farmer	Scotland	United States	Minerva	29 Oct 1822
James	30	M	Shop Keeper	Great Brittain	U. States	William Byrnes	23 Jul 1824
James	33	M	Merchant	Gt. Brittain	United States	Cortes	23 Mar 1824
James	35	M	E...mm...	United States	United States	Wanderer	31 Aug 1829
James	38	M	Farmer	Scotland	U. States	Roger Stewart	9 Jun 1828
James W.	39	M	Physician	United States	United States	Centurion	22 Dec 1828
Jane	21	F	Shop Keeper	Great Brittain	U. States	William Byrnes	23 Jul 1824
Jane	28	F	Child	Ireland	New York	Louisa	20 Jul 1826
Jane	55	F	Labourer	Ireland	U. States	Two Marys	20 Apr 1825
Janet	4	F		G. Britain	U. States	Camillus	8 Sep 1828
Janet	4	F	Child of [Mrs. Christian]			Florida	2 Oct 1828
Janet	6		Family [of Hugh]	Great Britain	United States	Camillus	12 Sep 1827
Jas.	18	M	Taylor	England	S.C.	Hope & Esther	19 Aug 1824
Jas.	25	M	Labourer	Ireland	U. States	Two Marys	20 Apr 1825
Jas.	35	M	Merchant	U. States	U. States	York	10 Dec 1825
Jas.	35	M	Labourer	G. Britain	U. States	Eliza	9 May 1827
Jean	30	F	Milliner	Scotland	United States	Louisiana	3 Nov 1827
Jean F.	30	M	Cooper	Wertemburg	America, U.N.S.	Great Britain	3 Aug 1829
Jemima	10	F		Lincolnshire	U. States	Atlantic	13 Jul 1824
Jesse	25	M	C...	...	...	Diamond	27 Jul 1824
Jno.	34	M	Merchant	Eastport	U. States	Franklin	24 May 1825
Jno.	35	M	Mariner	Portugal	U. States	Sea Flower	16 Jul 1821
John	4	M		Halifax	New York	Hope & Esther	25 Aug 1827
John	21	M	Merchant	Gt. Britain	Gt. Britain	Canada	4 Oct 1824
John	21	M	Labourer	Scotland	United States	Mary & Susan	5 Aug 1828
John	22	M	Farmer	Ireland	U. States	Nancy	29 Nov 1821
John	22	M	Child	Ireland	New York	Louisa	20 Jul 1826
John	30	M	None	England	U. States	Montgomery	18 Oct 1828
John	40	M	Farmer	Ireland	U. States	Dickinson	30 Jul 1825
John	43	M	Merchant	England	United States	New York	14 Jul 1827
John	65	M	Miner	Great Britain	United States	Colossus	5 Jun 1827
John, Mr.	35 4/12	M	Merchant	Boston	United States	Bethlehem	18 Oct 1828
John Richard	7	M	Child of [Mrs. Christian]			Florida	2 Oct 1828
L.	25	M	Merchant	U. States	U. States	Weymouth	16 Feb 1825
L. A.	4	M	None	United States	United States	William Bayard	17 May 1825
Magr.	10		Family [of Hugh]	Great Britain	United States	Camillus	12 Sep 1827
Margaret	6	F		Halifax	New York	Hope & Esther	25 Aug 1827
Margaret	8		Family [of Hugh]	Great Britain	United States	Camillus	12 Sep 1827
Margaret	9	F	Farmer	Scotland	United States	Minerva	29 Oct 1822
Margaret	27		Wife, Going to her husband	Scotland	United States	Camillus	3 May 1828
Margaret	38	F	Farmer	Scotland	United States	Minerva	29 Oct 1822
Margret	20	F	None	Scotland	United States	Washington	2 Oct 1828
Margt.	1	F	Labourer	Ireland	U. States	Two Marys	20 Apr 1825
Margt.	8			Scotland	United States	Camillus	3 May 1828
Margt.	30		Family [of Hugh]	Great Britain	United States	Camillus	12 Sep 1827
Marion	50	M	Labourer	Argyle (Tedland) Scotland	United States	Jean Hastie	27 Jul 1829
Mary	2			Scotland	United States	Camillus	3 May 1828
Mary	6	F	Farmer	Scotland	United States	Minerva	29 Oct 1822
Mary	6	F		G. Britain	U. States	Camillus	8 Sep 1828
Mary	6	F		Massachusetts	United States	Meteor	19 Aug 1829
Mary	21	F	Seamstress	Ireland	New York	Louisa	20 Jul 1826
Mary	22	F	None	Scotland	New York	Margaret	18 May 1825
Mary	26	F		Jamaica	U. States	Nile	15 Aug 1823
Mary	28	F	None	Gt. Britain	United States	Importer	21 May 1821
Mary Ann	25	F		G. Britain	United States	Sarah G.	15 May 1828
Matilda	35	F	None	United States	United States	Hannibal	12 Oct 1829

NAMES OF PASSENGERS	AGE	SEX	OCCUPATIONS	COUNTRY TO WHICH THEY BELONG	COUNTRY THEY INTEND TO INHABIT	SHIPS/DATES OF ARRIVAL	
ANDERSON (cont'd)							
Michael	32	M		Great Britian	United States	Mount Vernon	19 May 1823
Michael	36	M	Mariner	United States	United States	Roxana	30 Apr 1823
Peter	24	M	Labourer	Scotland	United States	Tom	2 Jul 1827
R.	27	M	Mariner	U.S.	U.S.	Hesperus	13 Mar 1825
R. C.	37	M	Gentleman	United States	United States	William Bayard	17 May 1825
R. H.	22	M	Gentleman	America	America	Brittania	17 Jul 1828
Richardson	15	M		Lincolnshire	U. States	Atlantic	13 Jul 1824
Rob.	36	M	Farmer	Ireland	U. States	Frances Henrietta	19 Feb 1823
Robert	9			Scotland	United States	Camillus	3 May 1828
Robert	14	M	Labourer	Gt. Britain	U. States	Frances Henrietta	18 Apr 1825
Robert	16	M	Child	Ireland	New York	Louisa	20 Jul 1826
Robert	21	M	Laborer	Ireland	United States	Ann Maria	18 Dec 1827
Robert	22	M	Blacksmith	Scotland	United States	Mary & Susan	5 Aug 1828
Robert	24	M	Farmer	Ireland	New York	Carolina Ann	15 Oct 1824
Robert	24	M	Musician U.S.N.	United States	United States	India	24 Mar 1826
Robert	24	M	Gold Smith	Scotland	New York	Eunice	13 Dec 1827
Robert	28	M	Stone Cutter	Scotland	United States	Scotsman	22 Aug 1828
Robert	36	M	None	United States	United States	Hannibal	12 Oct 1829
Robt.	21	M	Cabinet Maker	Gt. Britain	United States	Importer	21 May 1821
Robt.	65 7/12	M		Ireland	U. States	Fabius	22 Sep 1828
Ruth	23	F		Ireland	New York	Carolina Ann	15 Oct 1824
S., Mrs.	23	F	Lady	U. States	U. States	Mary Ann	13 Jul 1826
Sally	30 2/12	F	Lady	Boston	United States	Bethlehem	18 Oct 1828
Samuel	21		Laborer	Ireland	G. Britain	Robert Burns	14 Jun 1824
Sarah	21	F	Child	Ireland	New York	Louisa	20 Jul 1826
Sarah	27	F	None	Great Britain	United States	Roman	19 Dec 1825
Susannah	32	F	Weaver	Great Britian	U. States	St. Michael	3 Jan 1825
Thomas	50	M	Servant	Great Britain	United States	Fenwick	16 Aug 1826
Thomas D.	37 9/12	M	Consul	United States	United States	Potomac	29 Oct 1828
Thos.	20	M	Surgeon	Great Britain	United States	Ann Maria	23 Oct 1820
Thos.	30	M	Farmer	Killinchey	United States	Carolina Ann	11 Jun 1824
Thos.	32	M	Farmer	Scotland	New York	Margaret	18 May 1825
Thos. R.	30	M	...ler	Scotland	America	Camillus	12 Sep 1822
Violet	12	F	Spinster	Gt. Britain	U. States	Frances Henrietta	18 Apr 1825
William	19	M	Laborer	Ireland	United States	Mary	1 Jul 1829
William	20	M	Labourer	Ireland	United States	Henry Kneeland	7 Jun 1828
William	22	M	Weaver	Ireland	United States	Hannah Eliza	6 Jun 1826
William	47	M	Farmer	Lincolnshire	U. States	Atlantic	13 Jul 1824
William	55	M	Merchant	Ireland	New York	Louisa	20 Jul 1826
Wm.	6			Scotland	United States	Camillus	3 May 1828
Wm.	20	M	Labourer	Ireland	U.S.	Lady Hunter	10 Jul 1826
Wm.	20	M	Dyer	Scotland	United States	Washington	2 Oct 1828
Wm.	21	M	Machine Maker	Ireland	U. States	Fabius	22 Sep 1828
Wm. C.	37	M	Military	Great Britain	Canada	Florida	2 Oct 1828
ANDERSONE, Sally	18	F	Servant	Ireland	United States	Sarah G.	15 May 1828
ANDERTIN, John	39	M	Farmer	Great Britain	United States	Atlantic	28 May 1827
Mary	30	F	None	Great Britain	United States	Atlantic	28 May 1827
Nancy	6	F	None	Great Britain	United States	Atlantic	28 May 1827
Percy	4	F	None	Great Britain	United States	Atlantic	28 May 1827
ANDERTON, John	30	...	...	U.N. States	United States of America	Criterion	27 Jun 1827
ANDERVENT, Jos.	35	M	Blacksmith	Switzerland	U. States	Criterion	16 May 1825
ANDEWS, Mary, Mrs.	21	F		England		Hudson	23 Jul 1828
ANDOE, John	28	M	Store Keeper	United States		Robert Fulton	8 Mar 1823
ANDOIN, Jean	33	M	M.D.	France	France	New York	5 Jul 1826
ANDRAE, William	23	M	Merchant	Germany	in the U.N.S.	Martha	15 Oct 1825
ANDRE, —	25	M	Cooper	Gt. Brittan		L'Esperance	6 Sep 1828
J. M.	25	M		Spain	Spain	Fabius	3 Jun 1825
Jane	10	F	Labourer	Wales	U. States	Franklin	28 Jun 1825
ANDRÉ, —, Miss	20	F		Holland	United States	Alexander	2 Oct 1829
D., Mr.	27	M		Spain		François I	19 Nov 1828
ANDREUS, Edward	47	M	Gentn.	England	U.S.A.	Lima	6 Dec 1826
Willm.	48	M	Gentn.	England	U.S.A.	Lima	6 Dec 1826
ANDREW, Ann	24	F		England	United States	Nimrod	31 Jul 1828
Arthur	28	M	Surgeon	England	United States	Nimrod	31 Jul 1828

NAMES OF PASSENGERS	AGE	SEX	OCCUPATIONS	COUNTRY TO WHICH THEY BELONG	COUNTRY THEY INTEND TO INHABIT	SHIPS/DATES OF ARRIVAL	
ANDREW (cont'd)							
F.	30	M	Merchant	Great Britain	United States	Washington	3 Sep 1827
Humphry	25	M	Turner	Great Britain	United States	Samuel Wright	12 Oct 1829
James	28	M	Merchant	Glasgow	U. States	Duchess of Gloucester	1 Dec 1823
Janet	20	F		Scotland	U. States	Camillus	29 Jan 1829
John	22	M	Jeweller	Great Britain	United States	Washington	3 Sep 1827
John	25	M	Labourer	England	U. States	Ayrshire	12 May 1828
John	32	M	Merchant	America	America	Minerva	8 Oct 1824
Michael	23	M	Farmer	Gt. Britain	U. States	Diana	28 Apr 1828
Richard	22	M	Labourer	England	U. States	Ayrshire	12 May 1828
William	26	M	Bricklayer	Ireland	United States	Andes	2 Oct 1828
Wm.	24	M	Labourer	England	U. States	Ayrshire	12 May 1828
ANDREWS, —, Mr.	23	M	Mechanic	U. States	U. States	Rebecca	27 May 1823
A.	19	M	Merchant	Norfolk	U. States	Three Brothers	27 Apr 1825
A.	40 3/12	M	Merchant	England	England	Leeds	6 Feb 1826
Adeline, Miss	22		Merchant	America	New York	Hopes Return	6 Sep 1823
Agnes	3	F	None	Great Britain	United States	Colossus	5 Jun 1827
Alexr.	10	M	None	Great Britain	United States	Colossus	5 Jun 1827
Allen	10	F	None	Ireland	U. States	Franklin	7 Jul 1828
Ann	40	F		Gt. Britain	United States	Penelope	9 Sep 1828
C., Miss	20	F	None	Gt. Britain	Canada	Corks	3 Aug 1824
Chester	20	M	Merchant	New York, America	U.S.A.	Orozimbo	19 Oct 1822
D., Mrs.	34	F	None	United States	New York	Cortes	7 Jul 1821
David	48	M	Merchant	United States	New York	Cortes	7 Jul 1821
E.	35	M	Merchant	U. States	U. States	Hiram	10 Dec 1825
Edmund	35	M	Merchant	America	United States	Cambridge	19 Sep 1828
Elizabeth	15	F	Merchant	United States	United States	Stephania	22 Apr 1822
Elizabeth	18			England	Philadelphia	Xenophon	25 Jul 1826
Elizabeth	43			England	Philadelphia	Xenophon	25 Jul 1826
G.	36		Merchant	Liverpool	England	Almira	15 Jul 1822
Hannah	12	F	None	Ireland	U. States	Franklin	7 Jul 1828
Henry	9	M				Stephania	22 Apr 1822
Henry	26	M	Bookseller	England	United States	Cambria	3 Jul 1829
Hugh	43	M	Weaver	Great Britain	United States	Colossus	5 Jun 1827
J.	25	M	Labourer	Great Britain	United States	Sarah Ralston	27 Jan 1827
J.	29	M	Doctor	U. States	U. States	Signal	3 Jan 1826
J. H.	58	M	Merchant	G. Brittain	U. States	Canada	6 Jun 1825
James	16	M	Labourer	Gt. Britain	U. States	Frances Henrietta	18 Apr 1825
James	28	M	Labourer	Gt. Britain	U. States	Frances Henrietta	18 Apr 1825
Jane	23	F	None	Scotland	U. States	Dalhouse	23 Mar 1829
Jane	50	F	Spinster	Gt. Britain	U. States	Frances Henrietta	18 Apr 1825
Jas.	22	M	Baker	Scotland	U. States	Dalhouse	23 Mar 1829
Jno.	20		Merchant	...eter...	U. States	Rebecca	16 Oct 1826
Jno.	24		Mercht.	England	U. States	New York	30 Oct 1827
Jno. P.	22		Supercargo	U.S.	U.S.	Rebecca	20 Dec 1827
John		M	Chiefly farmers		United States	Factor	8 Jul 1829
John	10	M				Stephania	22 Apr 1822
John	18	M	Weaver	Gt. Britain	U. States	Frances Henrietta	18 Apr 1825
John	20	M	Tinman	Scotland	United States	Alexander Mansfield	16 Sep 1823
John	23	M	Mariner	America	United States of America	Two Marys	12 Feb 1820
John	28	M	Hatter	England	United States	Eliza Grant	6 Oct 1828
John	40	M	Stenographer	Ireland	New York	Thames	6 Oct 1820
John	50	M	Labourer	Gt. Britain	U. States	Frances Henrietta	18 Apr 1825
John N.	25	M	Merchant	New York, America	U.S.A.	Orozimbo	19 Oct 1822
Johnson	20	M	...	Ireland	United States	General Putnam	20 Jun 1825
Jonah	40	F	None	Ireland	U. States	Franklin	7 Jul 1828
M.	23	M	Engenerer	Gt. Britain	New York	Leeds	7 Nov 1828
Margaret	15	F	Spinster	Gt. Britain	U. States	Frances Henrietta	18 Apr 1825

NAMES OF PASSENGERS	AGE	SEX	OCCUPATIONS	COUNTRY TO WHICH THEY BELONG	COUNTRY THEY INTEND TO INHABIT	SHIPS/DATES OF ARRIVAL	
ANDREWS (cont'd)							
Margaret	36	F	Merchant	United States	United States	Stephania	22 Apr 1822
Mary	3	F				Stephania	22 Apr 1822
Mary	25	F	None	Scotland	U. States	Dalhouse	23 Mar 1829
Mary	40	F	None	Great Britain	United States	Colossus	5 Jun 1827
Mary O.	13			New York	New York	Braganza	9 Oct 1820
Nancy	8	F	None	Ireland	U. States	Franklin	7 Jul 1828
Nancy	14	F				Stephania	22 Apr 1822
Otis	30	M	Farmer	Hamburg	U. States	Martha	4 Sep 1828
Owen	15		Stone Mason	England	United States	Corinthian	7 Jul 1829
Pedro	20	M	Seaman	Spain	Spain	Fabius	2 Oct 1826
Richard	48	M	Turner	England	United States	Andes	2 Oct 1828
Robert	22	M	...t	...	United States	Montano	8 May 1827
Robert	28	M	Miller & Baker	England	United States	Andes	2 Oct 1828
Robert	47	M	Merchant	United States	United States	Stephania	22 Apr 1822
S. B.	23	M	Merchant	New York	New York	Emeline	14 Dec 1827
Thomas	20	M	Gentleman	United States	United States	Empress	22 Dec 1828
Thomas	27	M	Labourer	Ireland	United States	Robert Fulton	24 Jul 1826
Thos. F., Mr.	24		Physician	Norfolk, Va./ London	Norfolk, Va.	Venus	12 Apr 1821
W. H.	30	M		U. States	U. States	Admittance	17 May 1826
William	28	M	Cordwainer	England	Pennsylvania	Governor Fenner	23 Jul 1829
Wm.		M	Chiefly farmers		United States	Factor	8 Jul 1829
Wm.	13	M	None	Scotland	U. States	Dalhouse	23 Mar 1829
Wm.	18	M	Labourer	Gt. Britain	U. States	Frances Henrietta	18 Apr 1825
ANDREZ, Archebald	27	M	Farmer	Scotland	United States	Commerce	17 Jul 1823
ANDRICI, F.	17	M		Spain	Spain	Sabina	5 May 1826
ANDRIO, A.	35	F		St. Domingo	U. States	Diana	1 Jun 1822
ANDUAGO, D., Chanceller	35		Minister to U.S.	Spain	Washington City	Albion	11 Oct 1821
ANGE, Louise		F	Wife of [Engel dit Ange]	Switzerland	United States	Aurora	11 Dec 1824
ANGEL, Frs.	52	M	Merchant	Spain	Spain	Packet	10 Jul 1823
Richard	19		Druggist	England	United States	Caspian	12 Jul 1821
Robert	38	M	Spinner	England	United States	Siroc	31 Oct 1829
ANGELL, J. K.	27	M	Merchant	Rhode Island	U. States	William Thompson	6 Sep 1822
Jas. K.	25	M	Merchant	United States	U. States	Ann Maria	23 Oct 1820
ANGELLA, Ed.	10	M	Miner	New York	U. States	Frances	7 Aug 1826
M.	44	F	Merchant	France	U. States	Frances	7 Aug 1826
ANGER, Joseph	32	M	Merchant	Gt. Britain	United States	Meteor	19 Aug 1829
ANGERD, H.	69	M	Slingman	Havre	Montreale	Edward Bonaffe	23 Jul 1828
ANGERER, M.	40	M	Farmer	Swizerland		Antioch	18 Aug 1829
Marguerite	36	F	Farmer	Swizerland		Antioch	18 Aug 1829
Michel	7	M	Farmer	Swizerland		Antioch	18 Aug 1829
ANGERMEIER, Mather	15	M	Farmer	Germany	Maryland	James Noble	27 Aug 1827
ANGLADE, Andre, Mr.	34	M	Gentleman	France	U. States	Pocahontas	11 Aug 1829
ANGLAS, Margaret, Miss	6	F	Child	U. States	U.S.	Lewis	29 Oct 1825
ANGLES, Chls.	23	M	...	Germany	U. States	York	10 Dec 1825
John	32	M	...	Germany	U. States	York	10 Dec 1825
ANGOS, Ann	30	F	Spinner	Scotland	United States	Washington	2 Oct 1828
Jane	2	F	Spinner	Scotland	United States	Washington	2 Oct 1828
John	30	M	Spinner	Scotland	United States	Washington	2 Oct 1828
Mary	5	F	Spinner	Scotland	United States	Washington	2 Oct 1828
ANGRADA, P.	26	M	Merchant	Spain	Havana	Bellona	3 May 1826
ANGUARA, Paul	24	M	Merchant	Spain	United States	Saluda	14 May 1827
ANGUERO, Jose Maria	18	M	Mechanic	Havana	U. States	Courier	9 Feb 1829
ANGUS, Dan.	20	M	Painter	Scotland	U. States	Joseph	3 Oct 1820
G. P.	20	F		Scotland	America	Camillus	12 Sep 1822
Jean	14	F		Glasgow, St. James [Parish], Lanark [County]	New York	Hero	19 May 1828
*going to her friends							
John	28	M	Merchant	Philada.	U. States	Natchez	10 Apr 1823

NAMES OF PASSENGERS	AGE	SEX	OCCUPATIONS	COUNTRY TO WHICH THEY BELONG	COUNTRY THEY INTEND TO INHABIT	SHIPS/DATES OF ARRIVAL	
ANGUS (cont'd)							
Rt.	10	M		Glasgow, St. James [Parish], Lanark [County]	New York	Hero	19 May 1828
ANIAS, Jos.	29	M	Mechanic	Gt. Brittain	U. States	Robert Fulton	1 Nov 1822
ANJARINE, Caleb S.	27		Farmer	New York	New York	Xenophon	25 Jul 1826
ANNAHAN, Margaret	52	F		...	America	Columbia	6 Oct 1825
Patrick	54	M	...	...	America	Columbia	6 Oct 1825
ANNAN, Dorcas	24	F	Servant	Ireland	America	Carolina Ann	7 Aug 1826
ANNER, Peter	36	M	Mariner	American	United States	American Frederick	26 Oct 1820
ANNINOTT, Wm.	26	M	Farmer	G. Britain	U. States	Mary & Harriot	8 Sep 1828
ANNO, Francis	30	M	Merchant	U. States	U. States	Prince Edward	25 Feb 1822
ANNOUR, L.	...5	M	Merchant	France	France	Hiram	8 Jul 1828
ANNUS, Ann	24	F	None	Great Britain	United States	Magnet	19 Aug 1822
James	25	M	None	Great Britain	United States	Magnet	19 Aug 1822
ANOLLE, Robert	29	M	Merchant	England	U. States	William Thompson	17 Dec 1827
ANON, James	22	M		U. States	U. States	Wanderer	30 Oct 1828
ANOTT, Robert	24	M	Merchant	Gt. Britain	Gt. Britain	Canada	4 Oct 1824
ANREN, Benjn., Mr.	28		Merchant	England	G.B.	Pacific	24 May 1824
ANROT, Jno.	21	M	Farmer	Scotland	U. States	Aurora	18 Sep 1821
ANSCOMB, Allen	39	M	Weaver	England	United States	New Packet	7 Aug 1826
Ann	3/12	F	None	England	United States	New Packet	7 Aug 1826
Hannah	4	F	None	England	United States	New Packet	7 Aug 1826
Jane	31	F	None	England	United States	New Packet	7 Aug 1826
John	10	M	None	England	United States	New Packet	7 Aug 1826
Thos.	8	M	None	England	United States	New Packet	7 Aug 1826
ANSCOMBE, Jas., Mr.	26	M	Farmer	England	U. States	Acasta	12 May 1825
John, Mr.	31	M	Farmer	England	U. States	Acasta	12 May 1825
Thos., Mr.	22	M	Farmer	England	U. States	Acasta	12 May 1825
ANSEL, Benj., Mr.	33	M	Merchant	Great Britain	Great Britain	Roman	10 May 1828
ANSELL, Thos.	32	M	Poet	G. Britain	Canada	Columbia	7 Sep 1827
ANSELM, Ann	18	F	None	Great Brittan	U. States	Gem	26 Jul 1827
ANSLEY, —, Mr.	40	M	Mariner	N. York	U. States	Franklin	27 Aug 1822
Mary	60	F	Lady	United States	United States	Hanford	9 Oct 1829
Thomas	26	M	Merchant	Nova Scotia	U. States	General Pulman	3 Jun 1828
ANSLY, T. D.	26	M	Merchant	Newbrunsick	Newbrunsick	Nancy	23 Oct 1823
ANSTENICK, Ann	22	F			U. States	William	2 May 1821
ANSTIA, Moses	28	M	Merchant	England	United States	Acasta	12 Dec 1823
ANSTICE, Judith	30	F		United States	United States	Britannia	29 Oct 1829
Moses	32	M	Merchant	England	United States of America	Hamilton	13 Nov 1827
Thos.	32	M	Merchant	United States	United States	Britannia	29 Oct 1829
ANTELL, Ben	31	M	Weaver	G.B.	Connecticut	Eliza Grant	29 Aug 1829
William	19	M	Mault Maker	G.B.	Connecticut	Eliza Grant	29 Aug 1829
ANTELO, Mariquira, Miss	23	F	None	Havama	United States	Brown	26 Apr 1826
ANTERIM, P.	28	M	Mariner (Capt.)	United States	United States	India	24 Mar 1826
ANTHEAMNE, M.	3	F		France	United States	Howard	20 Aug 1827
Mae.	25	F		France	United States	Howard	20 Aug 1827
P.	33	M	Professor of Languages	France	United States	Howard	20 Aug 1827
Sophie	6	F		France	United States	Howard	20 Aug 1827
ANTHONY, Alexander	...	...	...	...	...	St. Michael	22 Sep 1824
B.	44	M	Merchant	Spain	U.States	Sally	16 Apr 1821
Brarbe	24	F	None	France	U. States	Sully	25 Jun 1828
Francis	26	M	Labourer	Ireland	U. States	Lady Hunter	18 Jul 1825
James						Aria	16 Jan 1829
*American Seaman sent home by the U.S. Consul at St. Barts							
Joseph	30	M	Mariner	U. States	U.S.	Ambuscade	14 Mar 1820
Julie	30	M	None	Ireland	U. States	Franklin	7 Jul 1828
Peter	28	M	Farmer	France	U. States	Sully	25 Jun 1828
ANTILL, Benjm.	31	M	Weaver	Great Britain		Eliza Grant	29 Aug 1829
William	19	M	Cloath Maker	Great Britain		Eliza Grant	29 Aug 1829
ANTIN, Anne	28	F	None	Scotland	United States	Jubilee	12 May 1828
Anne, Jr.	1 6/12	F	None	Scotland	United States	Jubilee	12 May 1828

NAMES OF PASSENGERS	AGE	SEX	OCCUPATIONS	COUNTRY TO WHICH THEY BELONG	COUNTRY THEY INTEND TO INHABIT	SHIPS/DATES OF ARRIVAL	
ANTIOCUS, E.	28	M	Mercht.	Italy	Italy	Britannia	5 Nov 1828
ANTOIN, Felix	19	M	Merct.	France	U.S.	Stephania	15 Aug 1825
ANTOINE, Caroline	1	F	Farmer	Alsace in the Department of Upper and lower Rhine	United States	Carolina Augusta	16 May 1828
Mary	37	F	Farmer	Alsace in the Department of Upper and lower Rhine	United States	Carolina Augusta	16 May 1828
Peter	41	M	Farmer	Alsace in the Department of Upper and lower Rhine	United States	Carolina Augusta	16 May 1828
ANTONIA, —	32	M	Servant	Portugal	belonging to the Portuguese Legation	Alexander	18 Mar 1822
Frans.	22	M	Servant	Spain	U. States	Industry	3 May 1823
G.	12	M	Servant	Aquin	U. States	Sarah Ann	25 Jun 1822
Jack	22	M	Servant	Aquin	U. States	Sarah Ann	25 Jun 1822
ANTONIC, Catherine	29	F		Switzerland	U.S.	Francois I	8 Aug 1829
Henry	2	M		Switzerland	U.S.	Francois I	8 Aug 1829
Henry	29	M	Farmer	Switzerland	U.S.	Francois I	8 Aug 1829
Jacob	5	M		Switzerland	U.S.	Francois I	8 Aug 1829
Jonas	7	M		Switzerland	U.S.	Francois I	8 Aug 1829
ANTONIE, Jos.	45	M	Servant	N. Orleans	U. States	Parthian	10 May 1824
ANTONIO, Jno.	18	M	Merchant	Havana	Havana	New Packet	12 Dec 1825
Jose	40	M	Servant	Havana	Boston, Mass.	Rubicon	22 May 1826
Joseph	28	M	Gentleman	Portugal	Biganairs	Mary	26 Sep 1820
Lorenzo L.	49	M	Merchant	Spain	U. States	Altamira	31 Jan 1828
Peter	30	M	Servant	Para	Para	Director	20 Sep 1824
ANTONY, Anna Maria	11 6/12	F		Germany	United States	Samuel Robertson	8 Aug 1828
Frane	30	M	Farmer	Germany	United States	Samuel Robertson	8 Aug 1828
Frona	28	F		Germany	United States	Samuel Robertson	8 Aug 1828
ANTREMONT, Augustus	35	M	Planter	U. States	U.S.	Bayard	10 Nov 1824
ANULLEY, Patk.	25	M	Labourer	Ireland		Robert Fulton	4 Jun 1828
AORAN, Mary	26	F	Spinster	Great Britain	United States	Wilson	26 Feb 1824
Patrick	6	M	Child	Great Britain	United States	Wilson	26 Feb 1824
AP.., —	56	F		Switzerland	United States	Elbe	2 Aug 1822
APARICCIO, Juan	50	M	Artist	Spain	U.S.	Radius	27 Apr 1824
APES, Abraham	20	M	Miller	England	United States	Euphrates	18 Aug 1827
David	3	M	Miller	England	United States	Euphrates	18 Aug 1827
Hamah	28	F	Miller	England	United States	Euphrates	18 Aug 1827
Jnes	5	M	Miller	England	United States	Euphrates	18 Aug 1827
Sarah	8	F	Miller	England	United States	Euphrates	18 Aug 1827
APPLEBY, E.	65			Ireland	U. States	Schuylkill	22 Aug 1825
Jas.	30		Farmer	Ireland	U. States	Schuylkill	22 Aug 1825
P.	14		Farmer	Ireland	U. States	Schuylkill	22 Aug 1825
P.	20		Farmer	Ireland	U. States	Schuylkill	22 Aug 1825
APPLEGARTH, —, Mr.	25	F		Great Britian	United States	Columbia	17 Apr 1827
APPLETON, Ann	38	F		England	U. States	Cincinnatus	24 May 1821
E.	37	M	Physician	England	U. States	Cincinnatus	24 May 1821
John James	33	M	Secretary of Laguara to U. States	U. States	U. States	Florida	7 Feb 1825
Lydia	4	F		England	U. States	Cincinnatus	24 May 1821
Mary Ann	10	F		England	U. States	Cincinnatus	24 May 1821
Matilda	5	F		England	U. States	Cincinnatus	24 May 1821
Pricilla	3	F		England	U. States	Cincinnatus	24 May 1821
Susannah	2	F		England	U. States	Cincinnatus	24 May 1821
APPLEYARD, James	37	M	Weaver			Eliza Jane	12 Sep 1820
APSIL, Peter, Mr.	23	M	Joiner	France	United States	Montano	18 Dec 1827
APSLEY, —, Child	1 2/12	F				Pilgrim	24 Nov 1820
—, wife [Andrew]	22	F				Pilgrim	24 Nov 1820
Andrew	25	M	Labourer	Ireland	America	Pilgrim	24 Nov 1820

NAMES OF PASSENGERS	AGE	SEX	OCCUPATIONS	COUNTRY TO WHICH THEY BELONG	COUNTRY THEY INTEND TO INHABIT	SHIPS/DATES OF ARRIVAL	
AQUILLIRA, Lewis	44	M	Gentn.	Spain	Spain	Fabius	2 Oct 1826
AQUINERE, John	32					Apollo	11 Jun 1828
AQUIRRE, Antonio	10	M	None	Cuba	U. States	Brown	8 Aug 1825
ARACHIBOLD, Margt.	19	M		Gt. Britain	U. States	St. George	20 Sep 1828
ARAGOR, Jera	32	M	Merch.	Spain	United States	Rapid	24 Oct 1823
ARAIYO, Manuel	28	M	Merchant	Spain	U. States	Eliza	20 Aug 1824
ARANDALE, Alfred	1	M	Carpenter	England	United States	Cincinnatus	21 Nov 1821
Charles	9	M	Carpenter	England	United States	Cincinnatus	21 Nov 1821
Elizabeth	41	F		England	United States	Cincinnatus	21 Nov 1821
Frederick	7	M	Carpenter	England	United States	Cincinnatus	21 Nov 1821
Harriett	4	F		England	United States	Cincinnatus	21 Nov 1821
Thomas	11	M	Carpenter	England	United States	Cincinnatus	21 Nov 1821
Walter	41	M	Carpenter	England	United States	Cincinnatus	21 Nov 1821
ARANGO, Antonio	29	M	Servant	Russia	Russia	New York	11 Mar 1823
Jesse A.	23	M	Advocate	Cuba	Spain	Jane	29 Jul 1823
ARANGS, Antonio	34	M	Servant	France	N. York	France	29 Nov 1827
ARANGUEREN, Casitan	21	M	Merchant	South America	South America	Pioneer	28 Jun 1827
ARANGUREN, A.	35	M	Merchant	La Gueira	U. States	Herald	6 Feb 1824
ARANNIS, Esedore	25	M	Merchant	Cuba	Cuba	Richmond Packet	23 Feb 1827
ARARAS, F. Fernandes	23	M	Merchant	Spain	Spain	Victory	8 Oct 1821
ARARGO, J. A.	35	M	Gentleman	Havanna	Different	Tampico	11 Jul 1826
ARBELO, Rafael	14	M	Merchant	Columbia	U. States	Tampico	19 Oct 1826
ARBUCKLE, James	33		Minister	England	America	Thames	25 Oct 1821
Thos.	22	M	Engineer	America	U. States	Camillus	29 Jan 1829
ARBUTHNOT, John	32	M	Soldier	England	U.S.	Panthea	13 Nov 1823
ARCADIE, José	35	M	Servant	Manilla	Mexico	Virginia	9 Feb 1829
ARCANIO, Thomas	4	M	None	Spain	U. States	St. Croix	31 Jul 1827
ARCH, James	19	M	Blacksmith	U. States	U. States	Adno	21 Apr 1827
ARCHAMBAULT, Louis E. E.	23	M	None	Canada	New York	Sully	11 Mar 1829
ARCHBOLD, Elizabeth	4	F	None	Great Britan	U. States	Canada	2 Jun 1824
John	30	M	Butcher	Great Britan	U. States	Canada	2 Jun 1824
John	34	M	Butcher	G. Bt.	U. States	Canada	13 Feb 1826
William	42	M	Labourrer	Great Britan	U. States	Ann Marria	6 Aug 1823
ARCHBORD, Lawerence	23	M	Farmer	Great Britain	United States	Ocean	27 Jul 1825
Margaret	26	F	None	Great Britain	United States	Ocean	27 Jul 1825
ARCHDALE, Ann	1	F	Labourer	England	U. States	Ayrshire	12 May 1828
Asabell	6	F	Labourer	England	U. States	Ayrshire	12 May 1828
Asen	21	M	Labourer	England	U. States	Ayrshire	12 May 1828
Mary	14	F	Labourer	England	U. States	Ayrshire	12 May 1828
T.	24	M	Hatter	England	U.S.	York	1 Dec 1827
Wm.	3	M	Labourer	England	U. States	Ayrshire	12 May 1828
ARCHDEACON, Esther	20		None	England	...	James Cropper	28 Jun 1824
Mirran	20			Ireland	U.S.	Union	20 Aug 1827
ARCHEHBOLD, Ann	36	M	None	G. Bt.	U. States	Canada	13 Feb 1826
ARCHER, Ann	28	F	Servant	U. States	U. States	Lewis	10 Sep 1823
David	25		Ploughman			Zamoa	5 Nov 1828
Elizabeth	50	F		England	U. States	Cincinnatus	24 May 1821
John	26	M	Laborer	Scotland	United States	Camillus	27 Oct 1829
S. W.	21	M	Merchant	U. States	U. States	Superior	16 Apr 1827
Sarah	10	F		England	U. States	Cincinnatus	24 May 1821
Thomas	32	M	Gentleman	England	United States	Montano	27 Aug 1827
William	15	M	Servant	Ireland	America	Carolina Ann	7 Aug 1826
Willm.	40	M	Carpenter	England	U.S.A.	Lima	6 Dec 1826
ARCHIBALD, —	1 6/12					Cadmus	18 Aug 1828
—, Mrs.	22	F				Cadmus	18 Aug 1828
J. N.	25	M	Merchant	Ponce	U. States	Commodore Porter	8 Sep 1823
Josiah	34	M	Merchant			Cadmus	18 Aug 1828
ARCHIBOLD, James	20	M	Merchant	Ireland	New York	Vigilant	6 May 1822
John	20	M		G. Britain	U. States	George Clinton	10 Sep 1828
Thos.	20	M	Farmer	Ireland	United States	Aurora	27 Apr 1825
ARCKLER, Jacob	55	M	Merchant	France	U. States	France	14 Mar 1828
ARCOS, —, Junr.	12	M	School Boy	Spain	Spain	Commodore Perry	24 Nov 1820
A. M.	45	M	Merchant	Havana	U. States	Greek	17 May 1825
Angel Martin	44	M	Merchant	Spain	United States	Huntress	25 Mar 1822

NAMES OF PASSENGERS	AGE	SEX	OCCUPATIONS	COUNTRY TO WHICH THEY BELONG	COUNTRY THEY INTEND TO INHABIT	SHIPS/DATES OF ARRIVAL	
ARCOS (cont'd)							
D. Angel	39	M	Merchant	Spain	Spain	Commodore Perry	24 Nov 1820
Martin	40	M	Mercht.	Spain	U. States	Abeona	5 Jul 1822
S. M.	21	M	Merchant	Havan	U. States	Greek	3 Mar 1825
ARCOZ, A. M.	49	M	Merchant	Spain	U. States	Neptune	25 Jan 1823
ARDACRE, Wm.	24	M	Hatter	England	America	Two Marys	24 Sep 1827
ARDAGH, Elizabeth	26	F	Servant	Ireland	United States	Wilson	27 Jun 1826
ARDEN, A., Miss	55	F		U. States	U. States	Chase	9 May 1823
A., Miss	70	F	Spinster	New York	U. States	Chase	29 Apr 1825
ARDING, —, Mr.	36	M	Farmer	Gt. Britain	U. States	Constitution	19 Jul 1825
—, Mrs.	29	F	Farmer	Gt. Britain	U. States	Constitution	19 Jul 1825
ARDMAN, Saml.	34	M	Weaver	England	America	Two Marys	24 Sep 1827
ARDUR, George	20	M	Labourer	Great Britain	United States	Frances Henrietta	17 Sep 1827
AREANS, Francisco	28	M	Merchant	Spain	United states	Prince Edward	22 Jul 1824
AREAS, Antony M.	23	M	Merchant	Spain	United States	Saluda	14 May 1827
AREGHINI, J.	30	M	Merchant	Leghorn	U. States	Emblem	14 May 1827
AREGUS, James	25	M	Baker	G. Britain	U. States	George Clinton	10 Sep 1828
ARENA, Joaquin	22	M	Servant	Spain	Mexico	Virginia	9 Feb 1829
ARENAL, F.	27	M	Merchant	Spain	United States	Prince Edward	1 Apr 1825
ARENAS, Francisco	26	M	Merchant	Guatemala	U. States	Emma	15 Dec 1824
Francisco	27	M	Merchant	Spain	Vera Cruz	Droma	25 Mar 1826
ARENDS, Francis	23	M	Marchant	Havana	Spain	Commodore Perry	9 Apr 1821
ARENO, Frs.	32	M	Merchant	Havana	U. States	Fair American	6 Feb 1823
ARENZA, Franz	25	M	Merchant	German	U. States	Dawn	8 Jun 1827
ARES, Frans.	20	M	Merchant	Mexico	Mexico	Washington	29 Apr 1826
ARGENO, —, Mrs.		F		U. States	U. States	Neptune	18 Jul 1822
A.		M		U. States	U. States	Neptune	18 Jul 1822
ARGENTE, Manuel	26	M	Merchant	Spain	Havana	Liberty	31 Jan 1826
ARGIZE, Alexandria	6			Spain	U. States	Mary Ann	30 Aug 1824
Anna	30	M		Spain	U. States	Mary Ann	30 Aug 1824
Hanouin	2 5/12			Spain	U. States	Mary Ann	30 Aug 1824
Parmine	4			Spain	U. States	Mary Ann	30 Aug 1824
ARGOS, —	21	M	Gentleman	Spain		China	17 Feb 1824
ARGUILLOUS, —	3/12	F		Spain	Spain	Mary Betsey	10 Dec 1821
Francisca	19 5/12	F		Spain	Spain	Mary Betsey	10 Dec 1821
Jose Maria	34 6/12	M	Soldier	Spain	Spain	Mary Betsey	10 Dec 1821
ARGUO, Juan	13	M		So. America	U. States	Eclipse	10 Jun 1823
ARGUR, R.	42	M	Mariner	U. States	U. States	Hiram	25 Jul 1828
ARGYLE, John	35	M	Farmer	England	U. States	Montgomery	18 Oct 1828
ARIAS, Cratoval	13	M		Spain	U. States	Independence	2 Sep 1824
ARIEL, Peggy	27	M	Labourer	G. Britain	U. States	Hanford	18 Sep 1828
Sarah	2	F		G. Britain	U. States	Hanford	18 Sep 1828
ARIEN, Pegy	3	M	Labourer	G. Britain	U. States	Hanford	18 Sep 1828
ARIGHINI, G.	26	M	Merchant	Leghorn	U. States	Pedler	9 Jan 1827
ARISON, E.	10	F		Great Brittain	United States	Sarah Ralston	27 Jan 1827
J.	8	F		Great Brittain	United States	Sarah Ralston	27 Jan 1827
J.	17	M	Shoemaker	Great Brittain	United States	Sarah Ralston	27 Jan 1827
Joseph	17	M		Great Brittain	United States	Sarah Ralston	27 Jan 1827
ARISPALTES, G.	36	M	Gentleman	Naples	U. States	Ospray	11 Apr 1825
ARISTIZABLE, D.	45	M	Merchant	Spain	U. States	Amphion	24 Aug 1821
ARKLE, Robert	19	M	Joiner	England	United States	Paul Jones	14 Oct 1829
ARLINS, Patrick	20	M	Servant	Ireland	United States	Sylvester Healy	19 Aug 1825
ARMADILLA, J.	40	M	Merchant	France	U. States	Ranger	2 Jul 1827
ARMANT, Ame	7	F		Scotland	United States	Camillus	27 Oct 1829
Cathrin	2	F		Scotland	United States	Camillus	27 Oct 1829
*died on passage							
Ellen	9	F		Scotland	United States	Camillus	27 Oct 1829
Isabella	4	F		Scotland	United States	Camillus	27 Oct 1829
Issabella	30	F		Scotland	United States	Camillus	27 Oct 1829
John	12	M		Scotland	United States	Camillus	27 Oct 1829
ARMARET, Ellen	7	F	None	England	America	Two Marys	24 Sep 1827
Mary	30	F	None	England	America	Two Marys	24 Sep 1827
Peter	5	M	None	England	America	Two Marys	24 Sep 1827
Ralph	4	M	None	England	America	Two Marys	24 Sep 1827
Thos.	0 6/12	M	None	England	America	Two Marys	24 Sep 1827

NAMES OF PASSENGERS	AGE	SEX	OCCUPATIONS	COUNTRY TO WHICH THEY BELONG	COUNTRY THEY INTEND TO INHABIT	SHIPS/DATES OF ARRIVAL	
ARME, G.	44	M	Farmer	Germany	United States	Lydia	18 Jun 1828
ARMENTEROS, Z.	15	M		Cuba	Spain	Transit	13 Nov 1823
ARMENTEWS, Fran.,							
Genl.	40	M	... Officer	Cuba	Cuba	James Cropper	2 Aug 1827
ARMESTRONG, Thos.	60	M	Farmer	England	U. States	Commerce	2 Oct 1823
ARMETAGE, Elizabeth	29	F		England	U.N. States	Helen	17 Dec 1827
Thos.	35	M	Merchant	England	U.N. States	Helen	17 Dec 1827
ARMIN, Francis	30	M	Farmer	Great Britain	United States	Atlantic	28 May 1827
ARMISTAGE, Wm.	33	M	Clothier	England	Alexandria, U.S.	Roman	17 Oct 1826
ARMITAGE, Ann	26	F		Great Britain	United States	John Jay	8 May 1828
John	33	M	Tin Plate ...ker	England	America	John Adams	2 Aug 1827
ARMOND, Michael	25	M	Labourer	Ireland	United States	Combine	4 Jun 1825
ARMORER, Paul	22		Labourer	Ireland	England	Emulous	26 Jul 1821
ARMOUR, Ann	13	F	Spinster	Ireland	United States	Robert Fulton	24 Jul 1826
J. C.	35		Merchant	Savannah	U. States	Brown	11 Jun 1827
John	34	M	Farmer	..., ..., Ireland	Brookline	New Orleans	24 Aug 1827
L.	45	M	Merchant	France	France	Hiram	8 Jul 1829
ARMSTEAD, John	23		Labourer	Huddersfield, England	Great Britain	Franklin	22 Jun 1827
ARMSTED, John	41	M	Farmer			Evergreen	28 Jul 1820
Wm.	45	M	Farmer			Evergreen	28 Jul 1820
ARMSTRONG, —,							
Madam	19	F		England	United States	Henry	9 Jun 1826
A.	50	M	U.S. Cons. Agent	United States	United States	Mazzinghi	31 Mar 1826
Alexr.	27	M	Farmer	Ireland	United States	Asia	29 Jul 1829
Anda.	32	M	Farmer	Ireland	U. States	Xenophon	13 Jun 1823
Andrew	20	M	...	Great Britain	United States	Friends	13 Jun 1825
Ann	20	F	Servant	Ireland	United States	Sylvester Healy	17 Oct 1825
Ann	28	F	Spinster	Ireland	United States	Sarah G	19 Jun 1827
Anne	16	F	Servant	Ireland, Great Britain	U.S. of America	Dublin	21 Feb 1826
Betty	8	F		Scotland	U. States	Silas Richards	29 Oct 1828
Caroline	8	F	None	Scotland	New York	America	1 Aug 1828
Catharine	14	F		Scotland	U. States	Silas Richards	29 Oct 1828
Catherine	18	F	Laborer or Spinster	Ireland	United States	Sarah G	11 Sep 1827
Catherine	30	F		Ireland	United States	Romulus	24 Jun 1826
Christian	24	M	...	Great Britain	United States	Friends	13 Jun 1825
Christian	30	M	Gentleman	Ireland	New York	Betsy	4 Sep 1820
Christopher	17	M				Imperial	19 Jul 1820
Danl.	25		Mariner	Baltimore	Baltimore	Albion	5 Feb 1822
Easter	18	M	Lady	Ireland	U. States	Sarah G	7 May 1827
Ed.	55	M	Planter	Ireland	on a Visit	Catharine	3 Sep 1821
Edward	6/12	M		France	United States	Henry	9 Jun 1826
Edwd.	10	M	Labourer	Ireland, Great Britain	U.S. of America	Dublin	21 Feb 1826
Elisabeth	8	F		Great Britian	United States	Andes	19 Aug 1829
Eliza	60	F		U. States	U. States	United States	11 Sep 1828
Ellen	10	F	None	Scotland	New York	America	1 Aug 1828
Ester	1/2	...		Ireland	United States	Lincoln	10 Dec 1823
Fanny, or Johnston	7	F	child of A. Armstrong	Ireland	United States	Asia	29 Jul 1829
Frances	11	F		Scotland	U. States	Silas Richards	29 Oct 1828
Francis	19	M	Schoolmaster	Great Brittain	N. York	Leonidas	24 Jul 1824
Francis	25	M	Merchant	Scotland	Scotland	Agness	7 Jan 1828
Geo.		M	Merchant	St. Croix	Denmark	Catharine	23 Jun 1821
George	6	M	None	Scotland	New York	America	1 Aug 1828
George	18	M	Labourer	Ireland	New York	Louisa	20 Jul 1826
George	30	M	Joiner	Scotland	New York	America	1 Aug 1828
Hugh	17	M	Labourer	Ireland	United States	Meteor	26 Jun 1827
Isabella	23	F		Ireland	U.S.	Oliver Wolcott	3 Nov 1827
J.	27	F	None	Gt. Britain	U. States	Isaac Hicks	18 Apr 1825
J. D.	22		Merchant	U. States		New York	18 Jul 1828
James	3	...	...	Ireland	United States	Carolina Ann	24 Oct 1825
James	6	M		Ireland	United States	Lincoln	10 Dec 1823
James	7	M	Laborer or Spinster	Ireland	United States	Sarah G	11 Sep 1827
James	30	M	Engineer	Great Britain	United States	Meridian	2 Jul 1827
James	52	M	Labourer	G. Britain	U. States	Leavitts	25 Aug 1828
James C.	23	M	Farmer	Ireland	U. States	Adno	5 Jul 1828

NAMES OF PASSENGERS	AGE	SEX	OCCUPATIONS	COUNTRY TO WHICH THEY BELONG	COUNTRY THEY INTEND TO INHABIT	SHIPS/DATES OF ARRIVAL	
ARMSTRONG (cont'd)							
Jane	3/12	F	child of A. Armstrong	Ireland	United States	Asia	29 Jul 1829
Jane	2	F	Child	Ireland	United States	Sylvester Healy	17 Oct 1825
Jane	3	F	None	Great Brittan	United States	America	24 Jul 1827
Jane	18	F	Farmer	England	U. States	Commerce	2 Oct 1823
Jane	24	F	his wife	Ireland	United States	Asia	29 Jul 1829
Jane	34		Servant	St. Croix	United States	Emelia	10 Dec 1827
Jane	40	F	Laborer or Spinster	Ireland	United States	Sarah G	11 Sep 1827
Janet	24	F		Ireland	United States	Lincoln	10 Dec 1823
Janis	6/12	M	None	Great Brittan	United States	America	24 Jul 1827
Jas.	18	M	Farmer			Commerce	22 Jun 1825
Jas.	22	M	Farmer	Great Brittan	United States	America	24 Jul 1827
Jas.	28	M	Farmer	Great Britain	United States	William Dawson	18 Jun 1827
Jasper	33	M	Farrier	England	United States	Delta	24 Oct 1829
Jessie D.	25	M	Master Mariner	Canada	U. States	James Monroe	18 Apr 1821
Jno.	24	M	Weaver	Tyrone	Ireland	Carolina Ann	11 Jun 1824
Jno.	34	M	Farmer	Great Britain	U. States	Yamacraw	4 Sep 1822
Jno.	45	M	Labourer	Great Britain	U. States	Morning Star	9 Nov 1824
John	4	M	Laborer or Spinster	Ireland	United States	Sarah G	11 Sep 1827
John	4	M	None	Scotland	New York	America	1 Aug 1828
John	1...	M	Labourer	Ireland	United States	Robert Fulton	24 Jul 1826
John	25	M	Farmer	Great Brittan	United States	Andes	19 Aug 1829
John	28	M	Laborer	Ireland	United States	Sylvester Healy	17 Oct 1825
John	37	M	Preacher	Great Brittan	G. Britain	Horizon	26 Apr 1824
John	43	M	Ga...er	Scotland	U. States	Isabella	21 May 1825
Josan	19	M	Labourer	Ireland	United States	Robert Fulton	24 Jul 1826
Joseph	66	M	Farmer	England	United States	Justina	5 Aug 1823
Letis	3	F	Laborer or Spinster	Ireland	United States	Sarah G	11 Sep 1827
Margaret	7	...	...	Ireland	United States	Carolina Ann	24 Oct 1825
Margaret	13	F		Scotland	U. States	Silas Richards	29 Oct 1828
Margaret	50	M				Imperial	19 Jul 1820
Margeret	25	F	Matron	Ireland	U. States	Josephine	30 Aug 1828
Margeret	50	F	Matron	Ireland	United States	Robert Fulton	24 Jul 1826
Mary	3	F		Ireland	United States	Romulus	24 Jun 1826
Mary	10	F	Laborer or Spinster	Ireland	United States	Sarah G	11 Sep 1827
Mary	12	F		Scotland	U. States	Silas Richards	29 Oct 1828
Mary	26	F	Wife	Scotlandd	United States	Meteor	27 Sep 1826
Mary	28	F		Scotland	U. States	Isabella	21 May 1825
Mary	33	F	None	Scotland	New York	America	1 Aug 1828
Mary Ann	8/12	F	None	Scotland	New York	America	1 Aug 1828
Mary Jane	24	F		Great Britain	United States	Meridian	2 Jul 1827
Owen	56	M	Farmer	Ireland	America	Mary	29 May 1827
Patrick	20	M	Farmer	G.B.	U.S.A.	Silas Richard	30 Jun 1828
Rebecca	25	F		U. States	U. States	United States	11 Sep 1828
Rob., Jr.	23	M	Labourer	Ireland	U. States	Olive Branch	30 Oct 1823
Robert	5	M	child of A. Armstrong	Ireland	United States	Asia	29 Jul 1829
Robert	13	M	Farmer	Ireland	United States	Fabius	4 Jun 1828
Robert	34	M	Farmer	Ireland	United States	Romulus	24 Jun 1826
Robert	50	M				Imperial	19 Jul 1820
Robt.	3			Ireland	United States	Lincoln	10 Dec 1823
Robt.	26	M	Farmer	U. States	U. States	United States	11 Sep 1828
Robt.	66	M	Farmer	U. States	U. States	United States	11 Sep 1828
Robt., Junr.	19	M				Imperial	19 Jul 1820
Saml.	35	M	Farmer	Gt. Brittain	United States	Cortes	5 Aug 1822
Sarah	19	F	Servant	Ireland, Great Britain	U.S. of America	Dublin	21 Feb 1826
Sarah	22	M		Great Brittan	United States	Andes	19 Aug 1829
Sidney, or Johnston	16	F	Spinster	Ireland	United States	Asia	29 Jul 1829
Thomas	14	M		Scotland	U. States	Silas Richards	29 Oct 1828
Thomas	23	M	Merchant	France	United States	Henry	9 Jun 1826
Thomas	40	M	Planter	St. Croix	St. Croix	Condor	4 Dec 1828
Thos.	22	M				Imperial	19 Jul 1820
Thos. Wm.	24	M	Clergyman	America	America	Hector	20 Sep 1821
William			child of A. Armstrong	Ireland	United States	Asia	29 Jul 1829
William	20	M	Weaver	Ireland	United States	Carolina Ann	14 May 1827
William	22	M	Labourer	Ireland	United States	Robert Fulton	24 Jul 1826

NAMES OF PASSENGERS	A G E	S E X	OCCUPATIONS	COUNTRY TO WHICH THEY BELONG	COUNTRY THEY INTEND TO INHABIT	SHIPS/DATES OF ARRIVAL	
ARMSTRONG (cont'd)							
William	23	M	Farmer	England	United States	Justina	5 Aug 1823
William	23	M	Labourer	Ireland	United States	Catharine	22 Jul 1825
William	24	M	Weaver	U. States	U. States	United States	11 Sep 1828
William	40	M	Weaver	England		Fame	9 Dec 1826
Willm.	20	M	Labourer	St. John, N.B.	St. John, N.B.	St. Michael	28 Feb 1826
Wm.	2	M	None	Great Brittan	United States	America	24 Jul 1827
Wm.	14	M		Scotland	U. States	Silas Richards	29 Oct 1828
Wm.	18	M	Labourer	Ireland,			
				Great Britain	U.S. of America	Dublin	21 Feb 1826
Wm.	24	M				Imperial	19 Jul 1820
Wm.	27	M		Ireland	United States	Lincoln	10 Dec 1823
Wm.	45	M	Farmer	U. States	U. States	St. Croix	13 Sep 1827
Wm., Dr.	42	M	Physician	England	Boston, U.S.	Leeds	7 Nov 1828
ARNAIT, Y.	28	M	Merchant	Spain	Spain	Richmond	
						Packet	30 Oct 1827
ARNESBROUG,	54	F		Ireland	U. States	Frances	
Elizabeth						Henrietta	19 Feb 1823
ARNETT, Colin	9		None	Phila.	Philadelphia	Albion	11 Oct 1821
Corn.	12		None	Phila.	Philadelphia	Albion	11 Oct 1821
James	44		Merchant	Scotland	Philadelphia	Albion	11 Oct 1821
ARNO, James	45	M	Merchant	New York	New York	Curlew	1 Mar 1824
James	46	M	Merchant	America		If	12 Oct 1820
James	48	M	Merchant	Citizen of			
				U. States	U. States	Packet	20 Feb 1823
James	52	M	Merchant	U.N. States	U.N. States	Exchange	13 Mar 1827
ARNOLD (see Ornold)							
Edward	26	M	Carpenter	Ireland	U. States	Belville	5 Jul 1827
Elias	23	M	Merchant	America	America	Abeona	17 May 1825
Eliza, Miss	21	F	Lady	Ireland	United States	Dublin Packet	9 Jul 1827
Fredrick	24	M	Cabinet Maker	France	U. States	Sully	25 Jun 1828
Goseph	18	M	Officer	U.S. America		Phoebe Ann	27 Dec 1825
Horatis N.	23	M	Minister	Great Britain	Great Britain	Nancy	13 Dec 1822
J. C., Dr.	24	M				Henri IV	17 May 1828
Job	24	M	Blacksmith	United States		Mentor	23 May 1821
John	22	M	Mariner	U. States	U. States	Atlas	24 Jun 1828
John	30	M				Cassack	25 Jul 1820
Jos.	23	M	...	Germany	U. States	York	10 Dec 1825
Maria, Miss	13	F	Lady	Ireland	United States	Dublin Packet	9 Jul 1827
Mary, Mrs.	45	F	Lady	Ireland	United States	Dublin Packet	9 Jul 1827
Peter	28	M	Labourer	England	United States	Dalhouse Castle	8 May 1827
Philip	19	M	Labour			Seine	10 Jun 1822
Richard	40	M				Cassack	25 Jul 1820
Richd. G.	23	M	Merchant	United States	U. States	Ann Maria	23 Oct 1820
William	35 6/12	M	Merchant	Great Briton	United States	Erin	26 May 1821
ARNOTT, Benj.	20	M	Shoemaker	England		Marchioness	13 May 1828
Hannah	19	F	None	England		Marchioness	13 May 1828
ARNSTALL, Anna	27	F	Agriculture	Bavaria	United States	Henri IV	14 Oct 1829
Catrine	12	F	Agriculture	Bavaria	United States	Henri IV	14 Oct 1829
Elizabeth	45	F	Agriculture	Bavaria	United States	Henri IV	14 Oct 1829
Eve	9	F	Agriculture	Bavaria	United States	Henri IV	14 Oct 1829
Joe	50	M	Agriculture	Bavaria	United States	Henri IV	14 Oct 1829
Marguerite	3	F	Agriculture	Bavaria	United States	Henri IV	14 Oct 1829
Maria	17	F	Agriculture	Bavaria	United States	Henri IV	14 Oct 1829
Peter	8	M	Agriculture	Bavaria	United States	Henri IV	14 Oct 1829
Tawin	6	M	Agriculture	Bavaria	United States	Henri IV	14 Oct 1829
ARO, Manual	38	M	Merchant	Spain	Spain	Sciot	12 Mar 1828
ARONOZ, —, Mrs.	40	F		Spain	U. States	Sarah	14 Mar 1825
L.	40	M	Merchant	Spain	U. States	Sarah	14 Mar 1825
AROON, Isaac	36	M	Tailor	England	U.S. America	Ganges	15 Dec 1826
Sophia	31	F		England	U.S. America	Ganges	15 Dec 1826
AROSSAMENA, James	14	M	Student	Panama	New York	Tampico	10 Feb 1829
Paul	16	M	Student	Panama	New York	Tampico	10 Feb 1829
AROXARENA, Rennon	28	M	Merch.	Spain	United States	Rapid	24 Oct 1823
AROZARENAS, Peter,							
Mr.	28		Gentleman	Cuba	Cuba	Meteor	25 Aug 1823
AROZASINA, Leander	30	M	Gent.	Spain	Havana	Robert Fulton	22 May 1824
ARPERO, Juan	48	M	Mercht.	Spain	U.S.	Emma	24 Jun 1825
ARQULAR, John	35	M	Merchant	U. States	U. States	Hope Return	9 Oct 1827

NAMES OF PASSENGERS	AGE	SEX	OCCUPATIONS	COUNTRY TO WHICH THEY BELONG	COUNTRY THEY INTEND TO INHABIT	SHIPS/DATES OF ARRIVAL	
ARRATT, David	21	M	Merchant	Great Britian	U. States	Orbit	29 Apr 1822
Isabella	35	F			U. States	Silas Richards	29 Oct 1828
ARREDANO, P.	12	M	Merchant	Florida		James Monroe	3 Jul 1824
ARREDONA, F.	19	M	Merchant	Havana	United States	James Monroe	3 Jul 1824
ARROTT, Colin	25	M	Merchant	Demarra	Great Britton	William	11 May 1821
Isabella	29	F	None	Manchester	Manchester	New York	14 Nov 1826
William	29	M	Merchant	Manchester	Manchester	New York	14 Nov 1826
ARROYA, Jose, Don	22	M	Attached to the Mexican Legation	Mexico	United States	Mercid	21 Oct 1824
ARROYO DE LAMOTE,							
Francisco	11	M	for Schooling	Spain	Porto Rico	Ann	26 May 1824
Jose	9	M	for Schooling	Spain	Porto Rico	Ann	26 May 1824
ARSENIEW, D.	40	M	Gentleman	Russia	U. States	Pocahontas	28 Jun 1824
ARSOTT, Robt.	21	M		England	England	Amity	31 May 1822
ARSTINGSTALL,							
Dorothy	15					Agricola	1 Jul 1820
Francis	5					Agricola	1 Jul 1820
George	29					Agricola	1 Jul 1820
Henry	9					Agricola	1 Jul 1820
Mary	7					Agricola	1 Jul 1820
Thos.	19					Agricola	1 Jul 1820
Wm. O.	13					Agricola	1 Jul 1820
ARSTOP, C. M.	48	M	Collector of Customs	St. Croix	St. Croix	Excel	26 Apr 1827
ARTEASE, B.	30	M	Merchant	Mexico	Mexico	Climax	24 Oct 1829
ARTEZ, P.	27	M	Merchant	France	U. States	Circassian	26 Jun 1823
ARTH..., John	24			Germany	Germany	London	16 Aug 1824
ARTHER, James	37	M	Labourer	Scotland	United States	Samuel Robertson	9 May 1827
Robert	16	M	Labourer	Scotland	United States	Samuel Robertson	9 May 1827
ARTHUR, Andrew	32	M	Weaver	Paseley, Paisley, Scotland	U. States	New Orleans	24 Aug 1827
Catharine	1			Scotland	United States	Camillus	3 May 1828
Catharine	24	F	Spinster	Ireland	United States	Catharine	22 Jul 1825
David	29		Weaver	Scotland	United States	Camillus	3 May 1828
Edward	28	M	Labourer	Scotland	United States	Mary & Susan	5 Aug 1828
Elizabeth	...	...	...	...	...	Pioneer	21 Jun 1825
Elizabeth	25		Seamster	Scotland	United States	Camillus	3 May 1828
Ellen	24	F	None	Wales	United States	Orozimbo	11 Aug 1823
J. D.	23		Labourer	Halifax	U. States	Edwin	26 Sep 1828
Jane	21	F	Spinster	Ireland	United States	Catharine	22 Jul 1825
Jas.	24	M	Land Surveyor	Ireland	New York	Carolina Ann	15 Oct 1824
John	15	...	...	...	...	Pioneer	21 Jun 1825
Jonathan	13	...	...	...	...	Pioneer	21 Jun 1825
Margaret	50	F	Spinster	Ireland	United States	Catharine	22 Jul 1825
Mary	4			Scotland	United States	Camillus	3 May 1828
Mary	17	F	Labourer	Ireland	United States	General Putnam	20 Jun 1825
Peter	4...	...	...	...	...	Pioneer	21 Jun 1825
Robert	20	M	Farmer	England	United States	John Dickinson	30 Sep 1823
Sarah	11	...	...	...	...	Pioneer	21 Jun 1825
Sh...	1	...	...	...	...	Pioneer	21 Jun 1825
Thomas	21	M	Labourer	Ireland	United States	Catharine	22 Jul 1825
William	19	M	Weaver	Ireland	United States	Catharine	22 Jul 1825
Wm.	2	M	Labourer	Ireland	United States	General Putnam	20 Jun 1825
Wm.	28	M	Labourer	Ireland	United States	General Putnam	20 Jun 1825
ARTICHEARE, A. J.	26	M	Merchant	United States	U. States	Havana Packet	27 Jul 1827
ARTIS, John S.	27	M	Carpenter	America	America	Telegraph	18 May 1827
ARTLEY, Jno.	23	M	Painter	Great Britain	United States	Atlantic	28 May 1827
ARTOCHEN, Antiona	19	M	Marchant	Spain	America	Abby Jones	21 Oct 1824
ARTOLA, Joseph, Mr.	22	M	Merchant	Spain	Spain	Burdett	7 Dec 1827
ARTWISLE, Martha	30	F	None	England	United States	Trident	18 Jul 1827
ARUNDEL, Walter	16 2/12	M	Shopman	Great Britain	New York	Thames	16 May 1821
ARVIN, Jane	6/12	F	Child	Ireland	United States	Ann Maria	28 Jan 1828
ARYENO, Luis	40	M	Mariner	U. States America	U.S. America	George	17 Jul 1823
ARZENO, L.	40	M	Mariner	U. States	U.S.	Ambuscade	14 Mar 1820
ASANSULO, Ygnacio	15	M	Educated	Mexico	United States	General Warren	8 Jul 1829

NAMES OF PASSENGERS	AGE	SEX	OCCUPATIONS	COUNTRY TO WHICH THEY BELONG	COUNTRY THEY INTEND TO INHABIT	SHIPS/DATES OF ARRIVAL	
ASBERRY, John	20	M	Weaver	England	United States	Lord Wellington	14 Nov 1827
ASBON, Ann	24	F	None	Great Britan	Great Britan	United States	21 May 1827
ASBOURNE, Hannah	24	F	None	England		Marchioness	13 May 1828
ASCERATO, J.	18	M	Servant	Mexico	Mexico	Savannah	24 Apr 1828
ASCHCROFT, Michael	35	M	Inn Keeper	England	United States	Maria	12 May 1823
Sarah	30	F		England	United States	Maria	12 May 1823
ASCHPACH, Elisabeth	51	F		Germany	Washington	Orient	25 Nov 1825
Johan	56			Germany	Washington	Orient	25 Nov 1825
ASEABO, Uselurno	30	M	Merchant	Spain	Havana	Robert Fulton	22 May 1824
ASH, Joseph M.	27	M	Merchant	United States	United States	Orozimbo	28 Jun 1827
Moris	22	M		York, Great Britain		Casanda	5 Sep 1827
Thos.	18	M	...	Ireland	United States	General Putnam	20 Jun 1825
W.		M	Merchant			Sally	26 Jun 1822
William	34	M	Baker	Ireland	United States	Herald	29 Oct 1825
ASHBURN, Catharine	25	F		United States		Exploit	18 Jun 1827
ASHBURNE, ...	7	M		Great Britian	United States	London	24 Jun 1823
...	9	F		Great Britian	United States	London	24 Jun 1823
...	11	F		Great Britian	United States	London	24 Jun 1823
...	16	F		Great Britian	United States	London	24 Jun 1823
...	49	M	Gentl.	Great Britian	United States	London	24 Jun 1823
ASHBURNER, Coke	46 2/12	M	Gentleman	Great Britain	United States	Venus	8 Sep 1820
ASHBY, Wm.	25	M	...	...	...	Antioch	8 Oct 1827
ASHCOFT, Barber	23	F	Lady	Ireland	United States	Borneo	2 Oct 1827
James	27	M	Weaver	Ireland	United States	Borneo	2 Oct 1827
Richd.	3	M	boy, Child	Ireland	United States	Borneo	2 Oct 1827
ASHCOTT, Ann	17	F		Great Britain	U. States	Silas Richards	27 Jun 1827
ASHCROFT, Elizabeth	30	F	None	England	United States	Trident	18 Jul 1827
James	3	M	None	England	United States	Trident	18 Jul 1827
ASHE, Elizabeth	26	F		England	U. States	Pleiades	9 Oct 1829
ASHENHRUST, A. M.	25	M	Merchant	Great Britain	United States	Atlantic	8 Dec 1827
Chas.	22	M	Writer	Ireland	United States	Carolina Ann	11 Dec 1826
ASHER, Jane	18	F	Wife	Ireland	United States	Ann Maria	4 Oct 1824
William	20	M	Labourer	Ireland	United States	Ann Maria	4 Oct 1824
ASHFELD, Ephriham	19	M	Farmer	Great Britian	United States	Andes	19 Aug 1829
ASHFORD, H.	28	F	None	New York	U. States	Sarah	1 Aug 1827
ASHFORTH, Miles	21	M	Merchant	G. Britain	G. Britain	James Monroe	8 Aug 1820
ASHLEY, Camilla	40	F	Servant	England	England	Tontine	1 Jun 1826
Catharine	18	F			United States	William	5 Oct 1822
Catharine	50	F			United States	William	5 Oct 1822
Da...	...			...	England	Great Britain	7 May 1827
Ebenezer	10	M			United States	William	5 Oct 1822
Ebenezer	44	M	Cabinetmaker	England	United States	William	5 Oct 1822
George	14	M			United States	William	5 Oct 1822
John	4			...	England	Great Britain	7 May 1827
John	33		Carpenter	...	England	Great Britain	7 May 1827
Mary	16	F			United States	William	5 Oct 1822
Nicholas	12	M			United States	William	5 Oct 1822
Sarah	33			...	England	Great Britain	7 May 1827
Soph...	6			...	England	Great Britain	7 May 1827
Thomas	...			...	England	Great Britain	7 May 1827
William	20		Labourer	Gil...	England	Great Britain	7 May 1827
ASHON, Betty	21	F	None	Great Britain	United States	Penelope	11 Jun 1827
Jno.	26	M	Weaver	Great Britain	United States	Penelope	11 Jun 1827
Margret	2	F	None	Great Britain	United States	Penelope	11 Jun 1827
ASHPOLE, ...	1	F	None	Great Britain	United States	Dalhouse Castle	21 Aug 1829
...	3	M	None	Great Britain	United States	Dalhouse Castle	21 Aug 1829
...	28	M	Butcher	Great Britain	United States	Dalhouse Castle	21 Aug 1829
Catherine	1	F	None	Great Britain	U.S.A.	Dalhouse Castle	21 Aug 1829
George	28	M	Butcher	Great Britain	U.S.A.	Dalhouse Castle	21 Aug 1829
Susan	24	F	None	Great Britain	U.S.A.	Dalhouse Castle	21 Aug 1829
William	3	M	None	Great Britain	U.S.A.	Dalhouse Castle	21 Aug 1829
ASHTON, Adam	25	M	Merchant	England	U. States	Florida	16 May 1827
Adam	26	M	Merchant	G.B.	G.B.	George Canning	26 Aug 1829
Amelia	12	F	None	Great Brittan	United States	America	24 Jul 1827
Betsey	4	F	None	Great Brittan	United States	America	24 Jul 1827
Betty	30	F		England	United States	Yobah	26 Sep 1827
Caroline	8	F	None	Great Brittan	United States	America	24 Jul 1827

NAMES OF PASSENGERS	AGE	SEX	OCCUPATIONS	COUNTRY TO WHICH THEY BELONG	COUNTRY THEY INTEND TO INHABIT	SHIPS/DATES OF ARRIVAL	
ASHTON (cont'd)							
Caroline	13	F	None	Haddersfield		Aurora	8 Jun 1827
Edward	1 6/12	M	Farmer	England	United States	London	21 May 1828
Edward	2	M	None	Great Brittan	United States	America	24 Jul 1827
Edward	21		Glass Cutter	England	Alexandria, U.S.	Roman	17 Oct 1826
Elizabeth	10	F	None	Haddersfield		Aurora	8 Jun 1827
Elizabeth	44	F		England	United States	Silas Richards	3 Apr 1826
Ellen	6	F	None	Great Brittan	United States	America	24 Jul 1827
George	24	M	Gentleman	Gt. Britain		Corinthian	27 Oct 1829
Hezekiah	26	M	Gardner	Haddersfield		Aurora	8 Jun 1827
Isabella	24	F		Scotland	United States	Camillus	27 Oct 1829
Jane	5	F		England	United States	Yobah	26 Sep 1827
John	3	M		England	United States	Yobah	26 Sep 1827
John	7	M	None	Haddersfield		Aurora	8 Jun 1827
John	14	M	None	Great Brittan	United States	America	24 Jul 1827
John	43	M	Weaver	England	United States	Silas Richards	3 Apr 1826
Joseph	10	M	Spinner	Gt. Britain	U.S. America	James Cropper	2 Aug 1827
Martha	27	F	None	England	United States	London	21 May 1828
Peter	1	M		Scotland	United States	Camillus	27 Oct 1829
Robert	2	M		Scotland	United States	Camillus	27 Oct 1829
Sabina	1	F	None	Great Brittan	United States	America	24 Jul 1827
Sarah	10	F	None	Great Brittan	United States	America	24 Jul 1827
Sarah	35	F	None	Haddersfield		Aurora	8 Jun 1827
Selina	3	F	None	England	United States	London	21 May 1828
Susan	36	F	None	Great Brittan	United States	America	24 Jul 1827
Thomas	6	M		England	United States	Yobah	26 Sep 1827
Wm.	4	M	None	Haddersfield		Aurora	8 Jun 1827
Wm.	23	M	Whitesmith	Great Britain	United States	Ganges	26 Oct 1826
ASHWICK, Ann	36	F		England	United States	Copernicus	3 Aug 1829
Edward	2 6/12	M		England	United States	Copernicus	3 Aug 1829
Geo.	38	M	Musician	England	United States	Copernicus	3 Aug 1829
ASHWORTH, B.	17	F	Spinster	Great Britain	United States	Washington	3 Sep 1827
Eliza	5	F		England	United States	Hannibal	25 Sep 1827
James	18	M	Merchant	Gt. Britain		Silas Richards	20 Jun 1826
James	29	M	Weaver	Great Brittain	United States	Robert Fulton	13 Mar 1827
Johanna	21	F		England	United States	Hannibal	25 Sep 1827
John	22	M	Weaver	Great Britain	United States	Washington	3 Sep 1827
John	40	M	Servant	England	United States	Cambria	3 Jul 1829
Joseph	34	M	Hatter	England	America	Two Marys	24 Sep 1827
Mary	47	F	Widow	Great Britain	United States	Washington	3 Sep 1827
Mary	54	F	None	Perien [?]		Governor Clinton	3 Jul 1827
Miles	21	M	Merchant	G. Britain	U. States	James Monroe	18 Apr 1821
Miles	23	M	Merchant	Great Britan	Great Britan	Columbia	11 Aug 1823
Nancy	4	F	Hatter	England	America	Two Marys	24 Sep 1827
Q.	2	F		England	United States	Hannibal	25 Sep 1827
Richard	26	M	Blacksmith	Great Brittain	United States	Nimrod	9 Jan 1827
Richard	35	M	Printer	Lancashire, England	United States	Aurelia	7 Jun 1826
Robert	8	M	Hatter	England	America	Two Marys	24 Sep 1827
Saml.	2	M	Hatter	England	America	Two Marys	24 Sep 1827
Saml.	30	M	Hatter	England	America	Two Marys	24 Sep 1827
Sarah	29	F	Hatter	England	America	Two Marys	24 Sep 1827
Seragh	11	F	None	Perien [?]		Governor Clinton	3 Jul 1827
Thomas	7	M		Great Britain	United States	Washington	3 Sep 1827
Thos.	29	M	Mechanic	Great Britain	United States	Mary & Harriet	3 Jul 1829
ASHWORTHY, Allice	23	F	None	England	United States	Jubilee	1 Oct 1828
ASKEN, Emma	10/12	F	None	England	United States	London	21 May 1828
Jno.	26		Laborer	Great Britain	United States	Comet	9 Aug 1822
Mary	6	F	None	England	United States	London	21 May 1828
Mary	37	F	None	England	United States	London	21 May 1828
Sarah	9	F	None	England	United States	London	21 May 1828
Thomas	4	M	None	England	United States	London	21 May 1828
Thomas	36	M	Turner	England	United States	London	21 May 1828
William	7	M	None	England	United States	London	21 May 1828
ASKEW, John	30	M	Farmer	England	United States	Silas Richards	3 Apr 1826
ASKIN, Ann	2	F	Child	Great Britain	United States	Wanderer	11 Jul 1826
Arn	16	F	Spinster	Great Britain	United States	Wanderer	11 Jul 1826

NAMES OF PASSENGERS	AGE	SEX	OCCUPATIONS	COUNTRY TO WHICH THEY BELONG	COUNTRY THEY INTEND TO INHABIT	SHIPS/DATES OF ARRIVAL	
ASKIN (cont'd)							
Betsey	28	F	Spinster	Great Britain	United States	Wanderer	11 Jul 1826
Geo.	19	M	Farmer	Great Britain	United States	Wanderer	11 Jul 1826
John	3	M	Child	Great Britain	United States	Wanderer	11 Jul 1826
John	21	M	Farmer	Great Britain	United States	Wanderer	11 Jul 1826
John	66	M	Farmer	Great Britain	United States	Wanderer	11 Jul 1826
Mary	5	F	Child	Great Britain	United States	Wanderer	11 Jul 1826
Thomas	13	M	...t...ller	Great Britain	United States	Wanderer	11 Jul 1826
ASKNE, Henry	23	M	Cordwainer	Gt. Brittain	United States	Horizon	8 Aug 1823
ASLER, Geo.	45	M	Merchant	New York	U. States	Pacific	20 Aug 1825
Geo. P.	14	M		New York	U. States	Pacific	20 Aug 1825
Sarah, Mrs.	37	F		New York	U. States	Pacific	20 Aug 1825
ASPARIO, John	48	M	Merchant	Spain	Spain	Commodore Chauncy	19 Jan 1826
ASPARO, John	42	M	Merchant	N. York	U. States	Dromo	13 Nov 1827
ASPDEN, Thos.	48	M	Joiner	England	America	Birmingham	16 Oct 1826
ASPENAL, Isaac	41	M	Weaver	England	U.S.A.	Lima	6 Dec 1826
Mary	6	F	None	England	U.S.A.	Lima	6 Dec 1826
ASPENALL, Stephen	24	M	Dealer	England	United States	Dalhouse Castle	8 May 1827
ASPINALL, Dorothy	27	F	None	Great Britain	United States	Ganges	26 Oct 1826
Dyson	23	M	Dresser	Great Britain	United States	Ganges	26 Oct 1826
Elizabeth	21	F	None	Great Britain	United States	Ganges	26 Oct 1826
Francis	16	M	Dresser	Great Britain	United States	Ganges	26 Oct 1826
Francis	53	M	Dresser	Great Britain	United States	Ganges	26 Oct 1826
George	18	M	Dresser	Great Britain	United States	Ganges	26 Oct 1826
John	23	M	Blacksmith	Ireland	U. States	Henry Kneeland	27 Jul 1825
Robert	24	M	Dresser	Great Britain	United States	Ganges	26 Oct 1826
Robert	57	M	Dresser	Great Britain	United States	Ganges	26 Oct 1826
Sarah	26	F	None	Great Britain	United States	Ganges	26 Oct 1826
Wm.	18	M	Dresser	Great Britain	United States	Ganges	26 Oct 1826
ASSELIN, A.	17	M	Merchant	Havana	U. States	Mary Joan	2 Dec 1822
ASSELL, Frederick	44	M	Cooper	Germany	United States	Samuel Robertson	8 Aug 1828
ASSER, Sam.	32	M	Merchant	Aquin	U. States	Sarah Ann	25 Jun 1822
ASSOLA, B.	5	M		Spain	Spain	Sabina	5 May 1826
ASSY, Mary	16	F	None	England	United States	India	8 Jun 1827
AST, Thomas	38	M	Mason	Ireland	United States	Nancy	16 Aug 1824
ASTBURY, Robert	35	M	Mechanic	England	U.S.	Trimmer	28 Nov 1826
ASTEN, John	40	M	Shoe Maker	England	America	England	23 Jun 1828
ASTER, Wm. B.	35	M	Merchant	U.S.	U.S.	Francois I	8 Aug 1829
ASTLO, Hannah	40	F	Lady	Saint John	St. John	Nancy	11 Apr 1822
James	18	M	Merchant	Saint John	St. John	Nancy	11 Apr 1822
ASTON, William	46	M	Clerck	Great Brittan	United States	America	24 Jul 1827
ASTOR, Eliza	10	F	Merchant	United States		Cincinnatus	29 Apr 1822
Hugh	36	M	Carpenter	England	United States	India	8 Jun 1827
John Jacob	59	M	Merchant	United States		Cincinnatus	29 Apr 1822
John Jacob	65	M	Merchant	U. States	U. States	Danube	11 Apr 1826
Samuel	22	M	Farmer	Huddlesfield	United States	Dalhousie Castle	27 Jul 1826
ASWORTH, Eliza	13	F	None		Perien [?]	Governor Clinton	3 Jul 1827
ATCHESAN, Mary	25	F				Catherine	19 Aug 1825
ATCHISAN, Elizabeth	22	F				Catherine	19 Aug 1825
John	30	M	...			Catherine	19 Aug 1825
ATCHISON, Andrew	38	M	Merchant	Glasgow	U. States	Duchess of Gloucester	1 Dec 1823
ATHARN, Samuel	42	M	None	Great Britain	United States	Eliza Barker	3 Jul 1826
ATHEAN, Timothy	20	M	Labourer	England	U. States	Hope & Esther	10 Jul 1827
ATHERSTONE, Ann	24	F	Wife	England	U.N. States	Corinthian	1 Sep 1823
Francis	9/12	M	Child	England	U.N. States	Corinthian	1 Sep 1823
Oliver	21	M	Gentleman	Great Briton	United States	Orion	18 Jun 1821
ATHERTON, John	30	M	Labourer	England	U. States	Comet	23 Aug 1828
Mary	30	F	Labourer	England	U. States	Comet	23 Aug 1828
Mary Ann	2	F	Labourer	England	U. States	Comet	23 Aug 1828
ATJOE, Eliza	10 10/12	F		Ireland	U.S. of America	Douglass	6 Jul 1829
ATKERSON, Wm.	26	M	Seaman	U. States		Mary	10 Aug 1820
ATKIN, A.	27	M	Merchant	Scotland	U. States	Superior	25 Sep 1826
Agnes	60	F		Scotland	United States	Camillus	27 Oct 1829
Alex	60	M	Tailor	Scotland	United States	Camillus	27 Oct 1829
Ann	12	F		Scotland	United States	Camillus	27 Oct 1829

NAMES OF PASSENGERS	AGE	SEX	OCCUPATIONS	COUNTRY TO WHICH THEY BELONG	COUNTRY THEY INTEND TO INHABIT	SHIPS/DATES OF ARRIVAL	
ATKIN (cont'd)							
Janet	22	F		Scotland	United States	Camillus	27 Oct 1829
John	24	M	Merchant	Great Britain	America	Washington	2 Oct 1828
Robt.	17	M	Brass founder	Great Britain	United States	Colossus	5 Jun 1827
ATKINS, Agnes	25	M	Farmer	Ireland	America	William	21 May 1825
Ann	27	F	Wife [of Thos.]	England	America	Ann	23 Jul 1821
Hanner, Miss	30	F	Lady	United States	U.S.	Acasta	11 May 1827
John	32	M	Mariner	England	Newyork	Cortes	16 Jul 1827
John	38		Hat Maker	England	United States	Corinthian	7 Jul 1829
Mark, Mr.	30	M	Gentelman	England	U. States	Acasta	11 Dec 1826
Mary	32	F		England	Newyork	Cortes	16 Jul 1827
T. G.	35	M	Merchant	U.S.	U.S.	New England	29 Jan 1828
Thomas	22	M	Farmer, Labourer or Spinster	Ireland	U. States	Meteor	4 Oct 1827
Thomas N., Mr.	17	M		Barbadoes		Douglass	8 May 1826
Thos.	39	M	Farmer	England	America	Ann	23 Jul 1821
ATKINSON, Ann	10	F		England	U.S.A.	Robin Hood	6 May 1828
Ann	19			England	England	Thames	25 Oct 1821
Ann	28	F	None	England		Exchange	11 Jul 1823
Ann F.	24	F		England	U. States	York	12 Jul 1825
Anna	6	F	None	England	U. States	Hamlet	16 Aug 1820
B.	20	M		Gt. Britain	United States	John & Elizabeth	25 Sep 1827
B.	60	M		Gt. Britain	United States	John & Elizabeth	25 Sep 1827
Benja.	59	M	Weaver	..., Glasgow, Scotland	U. States	New Orleans	24 Aug 1827
Benjamin	27	M	Joiner	England	United States	Jubilee	4 Mar 1829
Charles	20	M	Farmer	Great Britain	United States	Robert Fulton	27 Jun 1822
Charles	27	M	Lieutenant marines	England		Exchange	11 Jul 1823
Chs.	23	M		Gt. Britain	United States	John & Elizabeth	25 Sep 1827
Edward		M	Surveyor	Ireland	New York	Carolina Ann	15 Oct 1824
Edward	30	M	...	St. Johns, N.B.	United States	Henrietta	17 Aug 1825
Eliza	8	F		England	U. States	Birmingham	16 Jun 1828
Elizabeth	5	F				Hector	11 Sep 1820
Ellen	2	F	None	England	U. States	Hamlet	16 Aug 1820
Faithy	35	F				Hector	11 Sep 1820
Francis	19	M	Farmer	Scotland	United States	Orozimbo	11 Aug 1823
Frank	4	M	None	England	U. States	Hamlet	16 Aug 1820
Geo.	1	M		Gt. Britain	United States	John & Elizabeth	25 Sep 1827
Hardwood	31	M	Merchant	G. Britan	U. States	Geo. Canning	2 Sep 1828
Hen.	22	M	Merchant	Great Britain	United States	Mary & Harriet	3 Jul 1829
Henry	15	M	Gentleman	Great Britian	United States	Isaac Hicks	13 Jan 1826
Henry	18	M	Manufacturer	Great Britain	United States	Atlantic	8 Dec 1827
Henry	19	M	Merchant	Great Britain	United States	Isaac Hicks	27 Sep 1826
Henry	33	M	Merchant	England	Quebec	Robert Edwards	3 Oct 1829
James	19	M	Farmer	Great Britaian	United States	Margaret Ann	3 Apr 1822
Jas. B.	23	M	Merchant	Baltimore	U. States	Commodore Porter	8 Sep 1823
Jereh.	55	M	Farmer	Scotland	United States	Orozimbo	11 Aug 1823
Joeph	50	M	Dyer	Great Britain	United States	Samuel Wright	12 Oct 1829
John	9	M				Hector	11 Sep 1820
John	25	M	Sawyer	Great Britain	U.S. America	Chili	7 Jul 1827
John	28	M	Farmer	Great Britaian	United States	Margaret Ann	3 Apr 1822
John	30		Farmer			Splendid	14 Aug 1829
John	45	M	Farmer	England	U.S.A.	Robin Hood	6 May 1828
John	57	M	Farmer			Hector	11 Sep 1820
John	57	M	Farmer		New York	Governor Clinton	3 Jul 1827
Joseph	18	M				Hector	11 Sep 1820
Joseph	30	M	Taylor	England	U. States	Hamlet	16 Aug 1820
Joseph	45 3/12	M	Farmer	England	U.S. America	Illinois	16 Oct 1822
Lydia	20	F		Gt. Britain	United States	John & Elizabeth	25 Sep 1827
Martha	18	F	None	Scotland	United States	Orozimbo	11 Aug 1823
Mary	4	F		England	U.S.A.	Robin Hood	6 May 1828
Mary	7	F				Hector	11 Sep 1820
Mary	10	F		England	U. States	Birmingham	16 Jun 1828

NAMES OF PASSENGERS	AGE	SEX	OCCUPATIONS	COUNTRY TO WHICH THEY BELONG	COUNTRY THEY INTEND TO INHABIT	SHIPS/DATES OF ARRIVAL	
ATKINSON (cont'd)							
Mary	33	F		England	U.S.A.	Robin Hood	6 May 1828
Mary	33	F		England	U. States	Birmingham	16 Jun 1828
Richard	30		Mercht.	England	England	Thames	25 Oct 1821
Robert	6/12	M		England		Exchange	11 Jul 1823
Robert	22	M	Labourer	England	U. States	Hamlet	16 Aug 1820
Robt.	33	M		England	U. States	Birmingham	16 Jun 1828
Saml.	9	M	None	England	U. States	Hamlet	16 Aug 1820
Samuel	24	M	Farmer	Great Britan	United States	Clematis	8 May 1827
Sarah	29	F	None	England	U. States	Hamlet	16 Aug 1820
Sarah	30			England	United States	Hugh Johnson	11 Jun 1828
Sarah	30			England	United States	Hugh Johnson	11 Jun 1828
Sarah	54	F		England	New York	Hector	11 Sep 1820
Sarah	71	F		England	U.S.A.	Robin Hood	6 May 1828
Thomas	30		Upholster	England	U. States	Euphrates	8 Aug 1820
Thos.	18			England	United States	Hugh Johnson	11 Jun 1828
William	19 5/12	M	...	England	America, U.S.	Illinois	3 Jun 1822
Wm.	20	M	Merchant	Great Britain	Canada	Canada	20 Jun 1823
Wm.	30	M	Gentleman	England	America	Criterion	27 Oct 1821
Wm.	30	M	Mason	England	United States	Hannibal	25 Sep 1827
Wm.	36	M	Farmer			Hector	11 Sep 1820
Wm.	36	M	Mariner	U. States	U. States	John London	20 Jan 1823
Wm.	36	M		England	U. States	Birmingham	16 Jun 1828
Wm.	37	M	Mariner	U. States	U. States	Telegraph	14 Jun 1828
Wm.	40	M	Merchant	England	England	John Wills	21 May 1824
ATKISON, Patric	18			Longford	Boston	Peru	30 May 1828
ATLEY, Wm.	18	M	Servant	G. Britton	U. States	Sully	25 Jun 1828
ATSOP, Jos. W.	55	M	Merchant	United States	United States	Thetis	17 Aug 1824
ATTERBUREY,							
John	29 6/12	M	Brickmaker	England	U. States	Mary Ann	2 Jan 1829
ATTERBURY,							
Benjamin	30	M	Merchant	N. York	N. York		
Benjn.	28	M	Merchant	U. States	New York	Exchange	1 May 1824
ATTIES, David	55	M	Merchant	Morroco	Isd. Jamaci	Hope Mary Ann	21 Aug 1824
ATTIESK, Edbert	40	M		Holland	United States	William	12 Aug 1826
ATTRIDGE, Mary	19	F	Servant	Ireland	United States	William Byrnes	15 Aug 1826
ATTWOOD, Wm. A.	21	M	Merchant	Bermuda		Trio	31 Oct 1827
ATWOOD, Anthony, Jur.	21	M	Merchant	Bermuda	Bermuda	Mary	3 Aug 1825
Joseph	50	M	Mariner	U. States	United States	Magnet	10 Jul 1820
Nelson	22	M	Mechanic	U. States	U. States	Eclipse	26 Feb 1827
AUBERT, J. B.	22	M	Merchant	U. States	U. States	Hannah & Rebecca	12 Jun 1824
Lewis	18	M	Servent	France	U. States	New England	11 Sep 1828
AUBIN, Nicholas	17 4/12	M	Merchant	France	America	Britannia	20 Jun 1827
AUBURRY, William	24	M	Farmer	Wales South	U. States	Erie	19 Oct 1829
AUCHELUS, E. E.	27	M	Merchant	Germany	United States	Oglethorpe	8 Jul 1824
T. C.	28	M	Merchant	Germany	United States	Columbus	25 Jun 1825
AUCHINLUK, Mary	40			Ireland	United States	Columbus	25 Jun 1825
AUCHMUTY, R. T., Mr.	28	M	Gentlm.	United States	U.S.	Alexander Mansfield	9 Nov 1822
AUCHNATTY, Susan	17	F	None	Ireland	United States	Pacific	22 May 1826
AUDAIN, Johanna	38	F		S. Eustatia	England	Jubilee	4 Mar 1829
John, Revd.	60	M	Clergyman	St. Thomas	England	Chase	29 June 1821
AUDEBERT, D. L.	49	M	Merchant	France	France	Chase	29 June 1821
AUEL, M.	22	M	None	London	United States	Frances	7 Aug 1826
AUGER, G.	40	M	Shipmaster	U. States	U. States	Dalhousie Castle	27 Jul 1826
AUGESTEIAN, —	11	M	Merchant		U. States	Gertrude	13 Nov 1826
AUGHLEY, David	21	M	Weaver	Ireland	United States	Anne	20 Jun 1828
Eliza	21	F	Wife	Ireland	United States	Meteor	27 Sep 1826
AUGLOUR, N. L.	25	M	Merchant	France	United States	Meteor	27 Sep 1826
AUGUR, Wm.	28	M	Labourer	Great Britain	U. States	Elizabeth	22 May 1822
AUGUST, Broocks	4	M				Balance	19 Jun 1824
Guogue, Mr.	34	M	Tanner	France	United States	Eliza Jane	12 Sep 1820
L.	25	M	Mariner	N. Orleans	United States	Martha	20 May 1825
Robert	9	M				Levant	15 Aug 1823
Robert	50	M	Farmer	England	U. States	Eliza Jane	12 Sep 1820
Sarah	38	F		England	U. States	Eliza Jane	12 Sep 1820
AUGUSTINE, Adelle	38	F	None	Spain	United States	Eliza Jane	12 Sep 1820
Alsene	5	F	Child	France	U. States	Honor & Amey	15 Mar 1823
						Sally	14 May 1821

NAMES OF PASSENGERS	AGE	SEX	OCCUPATIONS	COUNTRY TO WHICH THEY BELONG	COUNTRY THEY INTEND TO INHABIT	SHIPS/DATES OF ARRIVAL
AUGUSTINE (cont'd)						
Aniele	5	M	None	Spain	United States	Honor & Amey 15 Mar 1823
Augustus	6/12	M	None	Spain	United States	Honor & Amey 15 Mar 1823
Catelina	23	F	None	Spain	United States	Honor & Amey 15 Mar 1823
Chris.	7	M	None	Spain	United States	Honor & Amey 15 Mar 1823
Delphine	33	F	Lady	France	U. States	Sally 14 May 1821
John	45	M	Merchant	Spain	Porto Rico	Otter 5 Aug 1822
John	46	M	Merchant	Italy	United States	Honor & Amey 15 Mar 1823
Josephine	8	F		Spain	Porto Rico	Otter 5 Aug 1822
Theodore	2	M	None	Spain	United States	Honor & Amey 15 Mar 1823
AUGUSTYNONSTIE,						
Adam	27	M	Servant	Poland	Poland	Corinthian 2 Sep 1824
AUJAL, M.	18	M	Gentleman	France	U. States	Six Brothers 6 Jul 1824
AUL, Robert	28	M	Weaver	Scotland	N. York	Mexico 19 Mar 1828
AULD, Andrew	26	M	Tinman	Great Britain	United States	Courier 26 Jun 1827
Robert Ogilvie	19	M	Secretary	Great Britain	Mexico	Corinthian 27 Apr 1824
S.	11	M	Servant	Ireland	United States	Josephine 30 Apr 1828
AULIER, August	29	M	Merchant	France	France	Emigrant 15 May 1826
AULY, Patrick	18	M	Labourer	Great Britain	United States	Roman 10 May 1828
AUMAN, V. G.	24	M	Clerk	Russia		Nimrod 21 Sep 1820
AUPOIX, L.	22	M	Merchant	N. York	U. States	Panther 9 Jul 1825
AURDAN, E. V.	60	M	Caulker	France	U. States	Day 16 Aug 1826
AUREN, Catherin	22	F	Child	Ireland	N. York	Trusty 12 Sep 1828
E.	20	F	Child	Ireland	N. York	Trusty 12 Sep 1828
M.	16	F	Child	Ireland	N. York	Trusty 12 Sep 1828
AURTEA, Antonio	20	M	Musician	Spain	Havana	Stephania 26 Apr 1824
AUSCOMB, Abraham	6	M		England	Gt. Britain	Electra 4 Sep 1827
Allen	18	M	Mason	England	Gt. Britain	Electra 4 Sep 1827
Allen	65	M	Weaver	England	Gt. Britain	Electra 4 Sep 1827
Ewd.	19	M	Shoe Maker	England	Gt. Britain	Electra 4 Sep 1827
Hannah	46	F		England	Gt. Britain	Electra 4 Sep 1827
James	16	M	Farmer	England	Gt. Britain	Electra 4 Sep 1827
John	8	M		England	Gt. Britain	Electra 4 Sep 1827
Susan	11	F	Spinster	England	Gt. Britain	Electra 4 Sep 1827
Wm.	45	M	Sta...er	England	Gt. Britain	Electra 4 Sep 1827
AUSELL, Ann	40	F	None	Great Britain		Olive Branch 9 Oct 1829
AUSLEY, Celina	14	F		England	U. States	Pacific 20 Aug 1825
Jno. L.	26	M	Mercht.	England	U. States	Pacific 20 Aug 1825
AUSPECK, P.	28	M	Merchant	U. States	U. States	Elias Burger 30 Nov 1822
AUSTED, Robert	14	M	None	England		Edward Quesnel 13 Mar 1828
AUSTICH, Ann	2/12	F	None	Leeds	United States	Dalhousie Castle 27 Jul 1826
Elizabeth	6	F	None	Leeds	United States	Dalhousie Castle 27 Jul 1826
John	12	F	None	Leeds	United States	Dalhousie Castle 27 Jul 1826
Lydia	8	F	None	Leeds	United States	Dalhousie Castle 27 Jul 1826
Mary	2	F	None	Leeds	United States	Dalhousie Castle 27 Jul 1826
Mary	40	F	None	Leeds	United States	Dalhousie Castle 27 Jul 1826
Sarah	10	F	None	Leeds	United States	Dalhousie Castle 27 Jul 1826
AUSTICK, Saml.	32	M	Butcher	Great Britain	United States	Wyton 12 May 1821
Samuel	34	M	Manufacture	England	U. States	York 4 Apr 1826
AUSTIN, —, Mr.	26	M	Merchant	U. States	U. States	Nymph 17 Jan 1822
*died on the passage				Philada.	Philada.	Panther 21 Oct 1826
Alexr.	26	M	Merchant	England	Pittsburgh	Orozimbo 8 Jun 1822
Ambrose	19	M	None	England	United States	Corinthian 30 May 1828
Ann	25		Labourer	England	United States	France 6 Oct 1828
Benjamin	5	M	Mechanic	England	U. States	Criterion at London 10 May 1821
Charles	3	M		England		Criterion at London 10 May 1821
Charles	34	M	Farmer	England	U. States	London 6 Feb 1829
Charlotte	22 2/12	F	Domestic	England	United States	Orozimbo 8 Jun 1822
Charlotte	22 6/12	F	None	England	Pittsburgh	William Smith 9 May 1822
D.	45	M	Merchant	N. York	U. States	America 16 May 1827
Edward	25	M	Farmer	America	United States	Sarah 18 Aug 1829
Edward	29	M	Labourer	England	America	France 6 Oct 1828
Elisabeth	10 4/12	F	Mechanic	England	United States	France 6 Oct 1828
Elisabeth	30 2/12	F	Mechanic	England	United States	William Neilson 26 Jul 1828
Eliza	14	F				William Neilson 26 Jul 1828
Elizabeth	30	F				Margarett Scott 22 Aug 1827
Ellen	30	F	Merchant	Scotland	United States	

NAMES OF PASSENGERS	AGE	SEX	OCCUPATIONS	COUNTRY TO WHICH THEY BELONG	COUNTRY THEY INTEND TO INHABIT	SHIPS/DATES OF ARRIVAL	
AUSTIN (cont'd)							
Emilly	8	F	Labourer	England	America	Sarah	18 Aug 1829
Emilly	26	F	Labourer	England	America	Sarah	18 Aug 1829
Enilini	12	F				William Neilson	26 Jul 1828
Geo.	10/12			Hartford	England	Hudson	14 Jun 1827
Hannah	28	F	Farmer	England	Albany, N.Y.	Chelsea	16 May 1828
Henry	5	M	Child	U. States	U. States	Wallace	12 Apr 1824
Henry	35	M	Mariner	U. States	U. States	Jane	15 Oct 1821
J.	50		None	Suffolk	England	Elizabeth	8 Dec 1821
James	23	M	Clerk	England	United States	William & Henry	19 Jul 1822
James	25	M	Farmer	English	United States	Patriots Eagle	30 Oct 1829
James	35	M	Planter	England	Jamaica	Peace	27 Dec 1824
Jno.	32	M	Merchant	Scotland	United States	Margarett Scott	22 Aug 1827
John	9 3/12	M	Mechanic	England	United States	France	6 Oct 1828
John	28		Labourer	England	United States	Corinthian	30 May 1828
Jonathan	52	M	Merchant	Great Britan	United States	Clematis	8 May 1827
Joseph	24	M	Weaver	England	United States	Jubilee	4 Mar 1829
Letitia	17	F				Silas Richards	20 Jun 1826
Lydia	30			Hartford	England	Hudson	14 Jun 1827
Margarett	1	F	Labourer	England	America	Sarah	18 Aug 1829
Mariah	13	F				William Neilson	26 Jul 1828
Mary	26			England	U.S. America	Constitution	18 Jun 1827
Mary Ann	3			Hartford	England	Hudson	14 Jun 1827
Mary Ann	7	F	Labourer	England	America	Sarah	18 Aug 1829
Mary Ann	7 1/12	F	Mechanic	England	United States	France	6 Oct 1828
Naoma	9	F	Farmer	England	Albany, N.Y.	Chelsea	16 May 1828
Nathaniel B.	30 4/12	M	Farmer	England	America	Euphrates	26 Jun 1821
Richard	5	M	Farmer	England	Albany, N.Y.	Chelsea	16 May 1828
Richard, & family	35	M	Farmer	England	Albany, N.Y.	Chelsea	16 May 1828
Rodrick	68 5/12	M	Merchant	America	America	France	28 Mar 1829
Samuel	1 6/12	M	Mechanic	England	United States	France	6 Oct 1828
Samuel	38 6/12	M	Mechanic	England	United States	France	6 Oct 1828
Sarah	11	F	Farmer	England	Albany, N.Y.	Chelsea	16 May 1828
Sarah	33	F		England	U. States	Criterion at London	10 May 1821
Susan	7	F		England	U. States	Criterion at London	10 May 1821
Susannah	60	F	None	England	Pittsburgh	Orozimbo	8 Jun 1822
Thomas	6	M		England	U. States	Criterion at London	10 May 1821
Thomas	18	M	Gentn.	Gt. Britain		Silas Richards	20 Jun 1826
Thomas	28		Labourer	England	U.S. America	Constitution	18 Jun 1827
William	3 2/12	M	Mechanic	England	United States	France	6 Oct 1828
Wilson H.	28		B... ...	Kent	England	Hudson	14 Jun 1827
AUSTRADT, Adam	9	M	Agriculture	Bavaria	United States	Henri IV	14 Oct 1829
Adam	46	M	Agriculture	Bavaria	United States	Henri IV	14 Oct 1829
Catherine	16	F	Agriculture	Bavaria	United States	Henri IV	14 Oct 1829
Elizabeth	38	F	Agriculture	Bavaria	United States	Henri IV	14 Oct 1829
Elizabeth	44	F	Agriculture	Bavaria	United States	Henri IV	14 Oct 1829
Eve	15	F	Agriculture	Bavaria	United States	Henri IV	14 Oct 1829
Mathew	8	M	Agriculture	Bavaria	United States	Henri IV	14 Oct 1829
Peter	10	M	Agriculture	Bavaria	United States	Henri IV	14 Oct 1829
Peter	38	M	Agriculture	Bavaria	United States	Henri IV	14 Oct 1829
AUTCHINGHAM,							
Andrew	7	M	Child	Ireland	U. States	Meteor	19 Jul 1828
John	14	M	Child	Ireland	U. States	Meteor	19 Jul 1828
Mary	10	F	Child	Ireland	U. States	Meteor	19 Jul 1828
Mary	40	F	Wife	Ireland	U. States	Meteor	19 Jul 1828
Susan	15	F	Spinster	Ireland	U. States	Meteor	19 Jul 1828
AUTCLIFF, James	38	M	Stone Mason	England	United States	Hamilton	13 Nov 1827
AUTH, Saml.	47		Finder	England	America	Florida	14 Oct 1829
AUTRE, Paul	28	M	Mercht.	France	France	Savannah	10 Jan 1828
AUTTER, Georg	54	M	Farmer	Ireland		Quatre Freres	29 Jul 1828
AUZE, Jos.	41	M	Merchant	...	U. States	Desdemona	21 Oct 1825
AVAERNIER, Fraser	26	M	Servant	France	U. States	Danube	11 Apr 1826
AVEN, —, child of Eliza	2	F	Farmer	France	United States	Globe	30 Aug 1828
—, wife of P.	48	F	Farmer	France	United States	Globe	30 Aug 1828
Catherine	11	F	Farmer	France	United States	Globe	30 Aug 1828

NAMES OF PASSENGERS	AGE	SEX	OCCUPATIONS	COUNTRY TO WHICH THEY BELONG	COUNTRY THEY INTEND TO INHABIT	SHIPS/DATES OF ARRIVAL	
AVEN (cont'd)							
Eliza	22	F	Farmer	France	United States	Globe	30 Aug 1828
Jacob	8	M	Farmer	France	United States	Globe	30 Aug 1828
Peter	10	M	Farmer	France	United States	Globe	30 Aug 1828
Philip	48	M	Farmer	France	United States	Globe	30 Aug 1828
AVEREL, —, Mr.	36	M	Mariner	N. York	N. York	Fanny	20 Mar 1820
AVERRY, John	40	M	Merchant	United States	United States	Brighton	11 Mar 1825
AVERY, Chs.	37	M	Mariner	U. States	U. States	Leeds	16 Apr 1825
Geo.	28	M	Farmer	England	U. States	William	17 Jun 1823
Wm.	24	M	Farmer	England	U. States	Hercules	6 Jul 1827
Wm. D.	29	M	Merchant	U. States	U. States	Canada	2 Jun 1824
AVES, John	23	M	Sugar Baker	Prussia	United States	Richmond	4 Aug 1826
AVIGNON, John Pierre	64	M	...	...	New York	Curlew	28 Jun 1824
AVINSON, Peter	22	M	... Maker	Great Britain	N. York	Josephine	10 Dec 1825
AVISON, Esther	22	F	Shoemaker	England	U. States	York	13 Aug 1827
John	22	M	Shoemaker	England	U. States	York	13 Aug 1827
John	49	M	Shoemaker	Great Britain	U. St.	Manchester	7 Dec 1826
AWERSHAP, E., Mrs.	27	F	None	St. Croix	U. States	Chase	2 Oct 1826
M. J., Miss	7	F	None	St. Croix	U. States	Chase	2 Oct 1826
M. L., Miss	3	F	None	St. Croix	U. States	Chase	2 Oct 1826
AWHONG, —	40	M	Servant	China	China	Venus	4 Oct 1824
AXEN, Samuel	26	M	Turner	England	America	Plutarch	18 Jul 1826
AXLUS, Joseph	45	M		G. Britain	Great Britain	Thompson	26 Apr 1828
AXON, Aron	13	F	Child	Manchester	United States	Nile	17 May 1827
Elizabeth	32	F	Joiner	Manchester	United States	Nile	17 May 1827
George	36	M	Joiner	Manchester	United States	Nile	17 May 1827
AXTELL, Charles	25	M	Carpenter	New York	New York	Brighton	14 Oct 1824
Thomas	28	M	Carpenter	New York	New York	Brighton	14 Oct 1824
AYALLS, J., Mr.	28	M	Officer	S. America	S. America	Henri IV	14 Sep 1827
AYCINENA, Pedro	25	M	Merchant	Guatemala	Guatemala	Favorite	9 Oct 1823
AYER, Francis	22	M	Labourer	Scotland	U. States	Czar	29 Aug 1829
AYERS, Mary	36	F		England	U. States	Electra	7 Jul 1828
Michal	40	M		England	U. States	Electra	7 Jul 1828
Robert	24		Farmer			Rufus King	7 Aug 1820
AYERSABAL, John	21	M		Spain		Leander	18 May 1827
AYFE, Magnet	22	F	Spinster	G. Britain	U. States	Hynd	12 Jul 1820
AYLWARD, Thomas	26	M	Labourer	Ireland	United States	Combine	4 Jun 1825
AYMAR, Elizabeth	1	F	Dyer	England	United States	Amelia	20 Aug 1829
James	28	M	Dyer	England	United States	Amelia	20 Aug 1829
John Q.	20	M	Merchant	U. States	U. States of America	Junius	5 Jul 1820
John W. H.	21	M	Merchant	U. States	U. States	Wm. Howland	30 Aug 1820
M.	60	F	Merchant	N. York	U. States	Infant	10 Jul 1821
Peter	30	M	Dyer	England	United States	Columbia	16 Jan 1829
Phoebe	25	F	Dyer	England	United States	Amelia	20 Aug 1829
Sarah	4	F	Dyer	England	United States	Amelia	20 Aug 1829
William	3	M	Dyer	England	United States	Amelia	20 Aug 1829
AYMERICH, Josephne	34	F	Lady	Spain	Havana	Henry	11 Oct 1825
Rosa	14	F	Lady	Spain	Havana	Henry	11 Oct 1825
AYOLA, Alfonso, Dr.	20	M	Merchant	Havana	U. States	Senica	17 Mar 1824
AYOLO, R., Lieu. Col.	30	M	Army	America	America	Medina	4 Sep 1828
AYRES, Geo.	24	M	Farmer	Great Britain	U. States	United States	8 Sep 1827
Henry	30	M	m...	...	U. States	Julia	20 Dec 1825
Jno.	40	M	Merchant	U. States	United States	Alfred	3 Jun 1826
L.	21	M		Great Britain	U. States	United States	8 Sep 1827
Lorenzo	19		Gentleman	Columbia	Columbia	Triumph	23 Jul 1829
AZPEIRSIN, F. D.	47	M	Merchant	Spain	Spain	General Paez	30 Jun 1827
B..., Elizabeth	27	F		Great Britian	United States	Robert Quayle	29 Jul 1822
Patience	20	F		Great Britain	United States	Orozimbo	7 Nov 1826
Patt	...	M	Farmer	Queen County, Corkley, Ireland	N. York	New Orleans	24 Aug 1827
Polly	24	F	Servant	Denmark	Denmark	Gleaner	31 Jul 1821
Robert	31	M	Labourer	Scotland	United States	Samuel Robertson	9 May 1827
Samel.	28	M	Gentleman	Great Brittain	G. Brittain	Gleaner	31 Jul 1821
B...CK, Susan	23	F		Switzerland	United States	Elbe	2 Aug 1822
B...ES..., Thos.	30	M	Labourer	England	United States	Alicia	9 May 1827
B...G..., Wm.	27	M	...	England	U. States	Unity	27 Mar 1827

NAMES OF PASSENGERS	AGE	SEX	OCCUPATIONS	COUNTRY TO WHICH THEY BELONG	COUNTRY THEY INTEND TO INHABIT	SHIPS/DATES OF ARRIVAL	
B...GHTY, Catherine	...	F	Spinster	Ireland	Unt. St. America	Wilson	21 May 1827
B...ING, Francis J.	25	M	...	Gt. Britain	United States	Crisis	13 Nov 1824
B...SILLE, Balfour	21	M	Mason	Scotland	United States	Culloden	17 May 1828
B...SS, ...	28	M	Clerk			Robert Burns	13 Jul 1820
B...TT, Richard	19	M	Officer	England	U. States	Hiram	17 Jun 1826
BA...CLOUGH, Thomas	33	M	Merchant	Great Britain	United States	John Wells	18 Sep 1826
BA...T, Thomas	...	M	...	Great Britain	Canada	James Monroe	5 Apr 1820
BABAD, Henry	26	M	Merchant	Philadelphia	Philadelphia	Jas. Monroe	11 Aug 1823
BABARA, T.	23	M	Merchant	Spain	U. States	Dromo	22 May 1826
BABAS, Henry	24	M	Merchant	France	France	Orozimbo	21 May 1821
BABB, William	40	M	Weaver	Great Britain	United States America	Spartan	25 Jul 1821
BABCOCK, —, Mrs.	35	F		U.S.	U.S.	Envoy	4 Jan 1826
Amos	34	M	Planter	W. Indies	U. States	Elias Burger	12 Sep 1822
Bradford	44	M	Seaman	N. York	N. York	St. Helena	18 Feb 1823
*Invalid from the U.S. Ship Cayenne, to be received in the Maine Hospital							
Cath.	27	F		W. Indies	U. States	Elias Burger	12 Sep 1822
J. C., Mr.	24	M		U. States	U. States	Chase	9 May 1823
James	34	M	Merchant	U. States	U. States	Frederick	28 Jul 1823
James	36	M	Merchant	American	U. States	Frederick	27 Jan 1823
M., Miss	19	F	Merchant	U. States	U. States	Chase	9 May 1823
Margaret	20	F	Spinster	New York	U. States	Chase	29 Apr 1825
Mary	15	F	Spinster	New York	U. States	Chase	29 Apr 1825
BABSTIER, Jos.	34	M	Merchant	...	U. States	Chase	29 June 1821
BACCHUS, Edward	22	M		Great Brittian	United States	Carolina Augusta	2 Dec 1828
BACCUS, E.	23	M	Merchant	U. States	U. States	Betsey	6 May 1826
BACELY, Catherine	22	F	Agriculturist	France	U.S.	Helen	3 May 1828
BACH, Alexr.	35	M	Teacher	G. Britain	U. States	Camillus	8 Sep 1828
Jas. Brown	21	M		United States		Corinthian	27 Oct 1829
Johann Karls	12	M		Germany	America	Falcon	28 Aug 1828
Louisa	42	F		Germany	America	Falcon	28 Aug 1828
BACHAR, Michael	35	M	Farmer	Ireland	America	Farmer	15 Nov 1823
BACHE, T.	21	M	Mariner	Germany	United States	Howard	15 Jun 1825
BACHELIEN, Thomas	50	M	Merchant	France	U. States	Peter Remsen	30 Jun 1828
BACHER, Balzer	1	M	Farmer	Germany	United States	Oxford	14 Aug 1828
Chatar	2	M	Farmer	Germany	United States	Oxford	14 Aug 1828
Georges	3	M	Farmer	Germany	United States	Oxford	14 Aug 1828
Madelaine	8	F	Farmer	Germany	United States	Oxford	14 Aug 1828
Madelaine	33	F	Farmer	Germany	United States	Oxford	14 Aug 1828
Michel	7	M	Farmer	Germany	United States	Oxford	14 Aug 1828
Michel	33	M	Farmer	Germany	United States	Oxford	14 Aug 1828
BACHLER, J.	40	M	Farmer	...	United States	Howard	14 May 1825
BACK, Ann	23 10/12	F		Ireland	America	Carolina Ann	7 Apr 1826
Henry	26	M	Sugar Baker	Ireland	U. States	Frederick	2 Apr 1828
James	27	M	Merchant	N...	Russia	Bayard	30 Oct 1820
Willm.	18 3/12	M		Ireland	America	Carolina Ann	7 Apr 1826
BACKANON, Wm.	26	M	Farmer	Ireland	United States	Nancy	16 Jul 1824
BACKER, Charlot	1/2	F	Barbour	Germany	United States	Virginia	31 May 1828
Elisabeth	6	F	Barbour	Germany	United States	Virginia	31 May 1828
Jacob	9	M	Barbour	Germany	United States	Virginia	31 May 1828
Louice	10	M	Barbour	Germany	United States	Virginia	31 May 1828
Mareh	45	F	Barbour	Germany	United States	Virginia	31 May 1828
Peater	7 1/2	M	Barbour	Germany	United States	Virginia	31 May 1828
Pheobus	47	M	Barbour	Germany	United States	Virginia	31 May 1828
BACKHOUSE, C. T.	25	M	...ler	U. States	U. States	Indian Queen	5 Dec 1825
Gustan	22	M	Merchant	Alaenburg		Constitution	20 Jun 1828
M.	22	F		Alaenburg		Constitution	20 Jun 1828
BACKIN, C.	6	F	Gent	French	Switzerland	Charlemagne	19 Sep 1828
C.	10	F	Gent	French	Switzerland	Charlemagne	19 Sep 1828
D.	9	F	Gent	French	Switzerland	Charlemagne	19 Sep 1828
Do. [ditto: C.?]	4	F	Gent	French	Switzerland	Charlemagne	19 Sep 1828
G.	38	M	Gent	French	Switzerland	Charlemagne	19 Sep 1828
John	32	M	Gent	French	Switzerland	Charlemagne	19 Sep 1828
BACKKON, James	10	M	None	Great Britan	United States	Bolivar	21 May 1827
Richard	38	M	Labourer	Great Britan	United States	Bolivar	21 May 1827
William	21	M	None	Great Britan	United States	Bolivar	21 May 1827
BACKMAN, Claus	21 6/12	M	Sugar baker	Hanover	New York	Thames	16 May 1821
Madelina	28	F	Servant	Wirtemberg	America, U.N.S.	Great Britain	3 Aug 1829

NAMES OF PASSENGERS	AGE	SEX	OCCUPATIONS	COUNTRY TO WHICH THEY BELONG	COUNTRY THEY INTEND TO INHABIT	SHIPS/DATES OF ARRIVAL	
BACKSBY, John H.	30	M	Farmer			Splendid	14 Aug 1829
BACKSHAW, Jno.	40	M	Shoemaker	Great Britain	United States	Penelope	11 Jun 1827
BACKSONDALE, David	13			Bl...	England	Great Britain	7 May 1827
Hannah	...			Bl...	England	Great Britain	7 May 1827
John	...		Farmer	Bl...	England	Great Britain	7 May 1827
John	16			Bl...	England	Great Britain	7 May 1827
Martha	...			Bl...	England	Great Britain	7 May 1827
Phebe	9			Bl...	England	Great Britain	7 May 1827
Saml.	1...			Bl...	England	Great Britain	7 May 1827
William	18			Bl...	England	Great Britain	7 May 1827
Willm.	...		... Maker	Bl...	England	Great Britain	7 May 1827
BACKUS, T.	40	M	Merchant	U. States	U. States	Emeline	12 Sep 1823
Thomas	38	M	Merchant	U. States	U. States	Traveller	24 Sep 1822
Thos.	37	M	Merchant	U. States	U. States	Prudence	8 Apr 1822
Thos.	37	M	Mariner	U. States	U. States	Eliza Jane	23 Aug 1824
Thos.	45	M	Mariner	U. States	U. States	Nancy	21 Jul 1825
BACKWOOD, William	40	M	Baker	St. John, N.B.	St. John, N.B.	St. Michaels	24 Mar 1825
BACLER, Frederick	29	M	Agriculturist	France	U.S.	Helen	3 May 1828
BACOCK, James	24	M	Labourer	Ireland	United States	Jubilee	13 Jul 1829
BACON, Ebenezer	29	M	Mariner	U. States	U. States	Pulaski	12 May 1826
Ebenr.	28	M	Mariner	U. States	United States	Emelie	6 Nov 1824
James	4	M	None	England	United States	Jubilee	1 Oct 1828
Philip	38	M	Carpenter	England		Brighton	19 Aug 1829
Phillipp	38	M	Carpenter	G. Brittain	U. States	Cincinnatus	2 Oct 1822
Sophia	11		None	England	New Jersey	Albion	11 Oct 1821
William	24	M	Joiner	England	United States	Danube	13 Jul 1827
Win	9		None	England	New Jersey	Albion	11 Oct 1821
BACOT, Henry H.	47	M	Gentleman	U. States	S. Carolina	Sully	30 Oct 1827
BACQUE, John	68	M	Merchant	U. States	U. States	Transit	21 Apr 1821
BADAL, M., Miss	23		None	Clermont	Bardslow, N.C.	Manchester	30 May 1821
BADDELEY, Fredk.	26	M	Military	G. Brittain	Canada	Hercules	24 Oct 1821
BADDEN, Ellen	24	F	Spinster	Ireland	United States	Robert Fulton	10 Aug 1827
BADDY, Alice	5	F	None	Great Britain	United States	Eliza Barker	3 Jul 1826
Catherine	15	F	None	Great Britain	United States	Eliza Barker	3 Jul 1826
Joseph	46	M	Joiner	Great Britain	United States	Eliza Barker	3 Jul 1826
Mary	46	F	None	Great Britain	United States	Eliza Barker	3 Jul 1826
Michael	17	M	None	Great Britain	United States	Eliza Barker	3 Jul 1826
Valentine	3	M	None	Great Britain	United States	Eliza Barker	3 Jul 1826
BADEN, Easter	28	F	Servant	England	United States of Am.	Helen	17 Dec 1827
James	21	M	Merchant	Spain	Cuba	Britannia	5 Nov 1828
BADER, Adam	14	M	Saddler	Germany	America	Falcon	28 Aug 1828
BADGE, David	30	M	Merchant	U.S. America	U.S. America	James Cropper	23 Mar 1827
BADGER, David S.	28	M	Merchant	United States	United States	York	31 Mar 1828
J.	35	M	Mariner	U. States	U. States	Courier	9 Feb 1829
Jos.	45	M	Merchant	U. States	U. States	Albion	11 Dec 1828
Joseph	28	M	Master	United States	New York	Cortes	7 Jul 1821
BADGES, W.	26	M	Labourer	Ireland	U. States	Bellville	14 May 1827
BADISTA, Jori	40	M	Military	Spain	Spain	Paquebot Bordeaux	25 May 1828
BADONA, Gasper	30	M	Piano Forte	Italy	U. States	Howard	21 May 1827
BADY, Hugh	19	M		Ireland	United States	William Byrnes	6 Apr 1826
BAEDER, Gottfried	32	M	Farmer	Germany	America	Falcon	28 Aug 1828
BAELLIE, John T.	28	M	Gentleman	England	Mexico	Jupiter	27 Jun 1828
BAELLING, H.	22	M	Baker	Germany	U. States	Howard	11 Mar 1823
BAFFIN, Mary	23	F	None	Ireland	U.S. of America	Hamilton	18 Jul 1827
BAGARD, —, Supercargo	27	M	Merchant	Martinique	Martinique	La Gratitude	25 Jan 1820
BAGG, William	25	M	Labourer	Argyle (Tedland) Scotland	United States	Jean Hastie	27 Jul 1829
BAGGELY, John	42	M	...	...	...	Braganza	8 Aug 1825
BAGGLÉ, Eliza	1/12	F		France	U. States	Edward Quesnel	4 Aug 1828
*born at Sea							
Godfrey	8	M		France	U. States	Edward Quesnel	4 Aug 1828
Louisa	3	F		France	U. States	Edward Quesnel	4 Aug 1828
Mary E.	5	F		France	U. States	Edward Quesnel	4 Aug 1828
Mary E.	31	F		France	U. States	Edward Quesnel	4 Aug 1828
Solomon	40	M	Carpenter	France	U. States	Edward Quesnel	4 Aug 1828
BAGGLEY, Elizabeth	42	F	...	...	...	Braganza	8 Aug 1825
Seth	10	M	...	...	...	Braganza	8 Aug 1825
William	3	M	...	...	...	Braganza	8 Aug 1825

NAMES OF PASSENGERS	AGE	SEX	OCCUPATIONS	COUNTRY TO WHICH THEY BELONG	COUNTRY THEY INTEND TO INHABIT	SHIPS/DATES OF ARRIVAL	
BAGGLY, Elizabeth	8	F	...	...	...	Braganza	8 Aug 1825
John	14	M	...	...	...	Braganza	8 Aug 1825
Joseph	6	M	...	...	...	Braganza	8 Aug 1825
Rebecca	12	F	...	...	...	Braganza	8 Aug 1825
Sarah	12	F	...	...	...	Braganza	8 Aug 1825
BAGGOTT, Eliza	4	F	None	Great Britain	United States	Isaac Hicks	27 Sep 1826
John	31	M	Glassmaker	Great Britain	United States	Isaac Hicks	27 Sep 1826
Joseph	7	M	None	Great Britain	United States	Isaac Hicks	27 Sep 1826
Joseph	22	M	Glassmaker	Great Britain	United States	Isaac Hicks	27 Sep 1826
Leonora	18	F	None	Great Britain	United States	Isaac Hicks	27 Sep 1826
Samuel	25	M	Glassmaker	Great Britain	United States	Isaac Hicks	27 Sep 1826
Thomas	9 6/12	M	None	Great Britain	United States	Isaac Hicks	27 Sep 1826
BAGLAND, Jane	10			Ireland	Philidelphia	General Marion	21 Nov 1828
May	30			Ireland	Philidelphia	General Marion	21 Nov 1828
BAGLEE, Lewis	28	M	Farmer	...	United States	Antioch	8 Oct 1827
BAGLEY, John, Mast.	2	M	Labourer	England	U.S.	Acasta	11 May 1827
John, Mr.	35	M	Labourer	England	U.S.	Acasta	11 May 1827
BAGLY, Elizabeth	4	F		England	United States	Dalhouse Castle	26 Dec 1827
Isabella	5	F		England	United States	Dalhouse Castle	26 Dec 1827
Jane	26	F		England	United States	Dalhouse Castle	26 Dec 1827
Margrt., Mrs.	34	F	Labourer	England	U.S.	Acasta	11 May 1827
Mary	3	F		England	United States	Dalhouse Castle	26 Dec 1827
Michael, Mast.	1	M	Labourer	England	U.S.	Acasta	11 May 1827
Thomas	2	M		England	United States	Dalhouse Castle	26 Dec 1827
BAGMAN, Wm.	38	M	Mariner	N. York	U. States	Franklin	27 Aug 1822
BAGNAL, Michael	20	M	Surgeon's Clerk	U. Kingdom Great Britain	United States	Cambria	7 May 1828
BAGNALL, Ann	46	F	Farmer	Great Britain	New York	Eliza Grant	29 Aug 1829
George	21	M	Farmer	Great Britain	New York	Eliza Grant	29 Aug 1829
Jane	7	F	Farmer	Great Britain	New York	Eliza Grant	29 Aug 1829
Mary	17	F	Farmer	Great Britain	New York	Eliza Grant	29 Aug 1829
Sarah Ann	13	F	Farmer	Great Britain	New York	Eliza Grant	29 Aug 1829
Thomas	3	M	Farmer	Great Britain	New York	Eliza Grant	29 Aug 1829
Thomas	43	M	Farmer	Great Britain	New York	Eliza Grant	29 Aug 1829
William	18	M	Farmer	Great Britain	New York	Eliza Grant	29 Aug 1829
BAGNELL, Isaac	30	M	Millman	Great Britain	United States	Isaac Hicks	10 Jul 1827
BAGOTT, Clara	14	F	None	England		Manhattan	22 May 1827
Elizabeth	23	F	None	England		Manhattan	22 May 1827
Esther	16	F	None	England		Manhattan	22 May 1827
Maria	2	F	None	England		Manhattan	22 May 1827
Sarah	6	F	None	England		Manhattan	22 May 1827
Sarah	9	F	None	England		Manhattan	22 May 1827
BAGRETTE, Pedro							
Celestino	50 3/12	M	Officer Army	Mexican	New York	Leonidas	22 Jan 1829
Wm. Hoza, (son)	5 6/12	M		Mexican	New York	Leonidas	22 Jan 1829
BAGSHAW, George	3	M	None	England	U. States	Montgomery	18 Oct 1828
Harriet	1	F	None	England	U. States	Montgomery	18 Oct 1828
Harriet	23	F	None	England	U. States	Montgomery	18 Oct 1828
Maria	3	F	None	England	U. States	Montgomery	18 Oct 1828
Sarah	28	F	None	England	United States	Jubilee	12 May 1828
Thomas	34	M	Merchant	England	United States	Jubilee	12 May 1828
BAGWILL, John	40	M	Farmer	England	Upper Canada	Manhattan	11 Oct 1824
BAHAN, Margaret				Ireland	England	General Starke	17 Jul 1827
Mary Anne				Ireland	England	General Starke	17 Jul 1827
BAHMANN, J. A.	40	M	Servant	Prussia	Prussia	Columbia	10 Mar 1824
BAI, Francis	32	M	Brewer	France	U.S.	Helen	3 May 1828
Johann Gorge	30	M	Weaver	Germany	America	Falcon	28 Aug 1828
BAIER, Johannes	31	M	Smith	Germany	America	Falcon	28 Aug 1828
BAIL, Mary	27	F	Lady	Ireland	United States	Belleville	13 Oct 1827
Pat	26	M	Weaver	St. Johns, N.B.	United States	Antioch	21 Sep 1827
Patrick	40	M	Labourer	Ireland	United States	Belleville	13 Oct 1827
BAILAS, Janet	35	F	Spintres	U. States	U. States	Servant	30 Aug 1820
BAILEN, John	25	M	Stone Cutter	Scotland	U. States	Hopes Delight	29 Nov 1827
BAILER, John Francis	21	M	Merchant	Prusia	U. States	Franklin	3 Jul 1820
BAILEY, —, Mr.	30	M	Farmer	Great Britian	U.S.	Robert Edwards	11 Nov 1822
A.	21	M		G. Britain	U. States	St. George	7 Jun 1828
Alexr.	27	M	Carpenter	Ireland	United States	Commerce	13 Jun 1828
Ann	28	F		Great Britain	United States	John Jay	8 May 1828
Ar.	24	M	Dentist	Great Britain	United States	Cortes	11 Dec 1822

NAMES OF PASSENGERS	AGE	SEX	OCCUPATIONS	COUNTRY TO WHICH THEY BELONG	COUNTRY THEY INTEND TO INHABIT	SHIPS/DATES OF ARRIVAL	
BAILEY (cont'd)							
Augustus	1 3/12	M		New Haven	New Haven	William	17 Dec 1823
B.	22	M	Weaver	England	United States	Topaz	14 Aug 1826
B. C.	20	M	Ship Master	United States	United States	Franklin	11 Oct 1827
Catharine	19		Spinster	Ireland	United States	Robert Burns	18 Jun 1821
Charllotte	25	F				Acosta	28 Jul 1823
Charlotte	1	M		England	America	Sarah	18 Aug 1829
Charlotte	18	F		Rhode Island	U. States	Prize	23 Mar 1824
Clarissa	22	F		New Haven	New Haven	William	17 Dec 1823
Daniel	...	M	Joiner	Great Britain	New York	Superior	5 Sep 1827
Eliz.	3 2/12	F	his Daughter [Robt. Nalder]	Great Britain	New York	Venus	8 Sep 1820
Eliza	20		Spinster	Ireland	United States	Robert Burns	18 Jun 1821
Fanny	1	F				Acosta	28 Jul 1823
Francis	2	M		New Haven	New Haven	William	17 Dec 1823
Geo.	20	M	Chemist	Paris	United States	Columbia	16 Jan 1829
George	4	M				Acosta	28 Jul 1823
J. G.	25	M	Merchant	U. States	U. States	Prudence	11 Jun 1825
James	13	M		G. Britain	U. States	St. George	7 Jun 1828
James	22	M	Tailor	Scotland	United States	Tom	2 Jul 1827
James	23	M	Clerk	N. York	U. States	Hope	17 Apr 1824
James	24	M	None	Cuba	United States	Ariel	30 Jun 1828
James	33	M	Mariner	U. States	U. States	Dollar	29 Aug 1825
Jno.	24	M	Wire drawer	Great Britain	New York	Superior	5 Sep 1827
Jno. G.	24	M	Merchant	U. States	U. States	Velocipede	26 Jun 1823
John	4	M		England	America	Sarah	18 Aug 1829
John	22	M	Mariner	U. States	U. States	Enterprize	24 Mar 1823
John	23	M	Yeoman	G. Brittain	U. States	Cincinatus	2 Oct 1822
John	24	M	Mariner	U. States	U. States	John Dickinson	16 Feb 1825
John	26	M	Mechanic	Halifax	Halifax	New York	31 Jul 1829
John G.	28 7/12	M	Merchant	New York	New York	Ann Maria	19 Jul 1826
John G., Esqr.	26	M	Merchant	U.S. America	U. States	St. Thomas	24 May 1824
Joseph		M		England	United States	Cambria	16 Aug 1827
Joseph	5	M		England	America	Sarah	18 Aug 1829
Joseph	1...	M	...	Ireland	United States	Lima	19 Jun 1824
Joseph	12	M	Mechanic	Halifax	Halifax	New York	31 Jul 1829
Joseph	25	M	Carpenter	Ireland	United States	Commerce	13 Jun 1828
Joseph	26	M	Farmer	England	United States	Cambria	16 Aug 1827
Lucia C.	22	F	Merchant	Newport	U. States	Chase	12 May 1826
M., Miss	18	F		N. York	U. States	Star	4 Oct 1826
Margaret	23	F		England	United States	Ganges	10 May 1828
Martin	45	M	Slaymaker	England	United States	William	4 Oct 1822
Mary	3	F	child	Ireland	Pennsylvania	Susquehanna	9 Jan 1824
Michal	5	M	child	Ireland	Pennsylvania	Susquehanna	9 Jan 1824
Moses	35	M	Farmer	Ireland	United States	Independence	10 Oct 1821
Mosses	30	M	Accountant	Ireland	United States	Trident	17 May 1825
Philip	6	M		England	United States	William	4 Oct 1822
Philip	50	M	None	England	United States	William	4 Oct 1822
Richard A.	24	M	Painter	England	United States	William	4 Oct 1822
Robt.	3	M		England	United States	Ganges	10 May 1828
Robt.	30	M	Servant	Switzerland	U. States	Robert Edward	2 Nov 1827
Robt. Nalder	40 3/12	M	Accomptant	Great Britain	New York	Venus	8 Sep 1820
Sam	17	M	Servant	Great Britain	Great Britain	Harriet	11 Jan 1820
Samuel	35	M	Servant	United States	United States	Cortes	19 Nov 1821
Sarah	30	F	no buisniss	England	America	Sarah	18 Aug 1829
Sarah	40	F		England	Cincinati	Hudson	20 Nov 1828
Sarah	42	M	his Wife [Robt. Nalder]	Great Britain	New York	Venus	8 Sep 1820
Sarah, Jr.	6 5/12	F	his Daughter [Robt. Nalder]	Great Britain	New York	Venus	8 Sep 1820
Sophrenia, Mrs.	19	F		U.S. America	U. States	St. Thomas	24 May 1824
Stephen	45	M	Mercht.	Hayti	Hayti	New York	20 Jun 1825
Thomas	4	M		England	United States	William	4 Oct 1822
Thomas	58	M	Gentleman	England	New York	Brighton	24 Aug 1827
William	3	M				Acosta	28 Jul 1823
William	6	M		England	America	Sarah	18 Aug 1829
Winnifed	2	F		England	United States	Cambria	16 Aug 1827
Winnifed	25	F		England	United States	Cambria	16 Aug 1827
Wm.	...4	M	Joiner	Great Britain	New York	Superior	5 Sep 1827

NAMES OF PASSENGERS	AGE	SEX	OCCUPATIONS	COUNTRY TO WHICH THEY BELONG	COUNTRY THEY INTEND TO INHABIT	SHIPS/DATES OF ARRIVAL	
BAILEY (cont'd)							
Wm.	26	M	Shoemaker			Lady of the Lake	23 Aug 1828
BAILIE, Ann	28		Spinster	Ireland	United States	Courier	15 Oct 1827
Mary	19	F	Daughter	Ireland	New York	Louisa	20 Jul 1826
Patk.	34		Millwright	Ireland	United States	Courier	15 Oct 1827
Peter	30	M	Carpenter	U. States	U. States	Palestine	1 May 1821
William	50	M	Merchant	American		Dublin Packet	30 Apr 1821
BAILLAT, John Jaques	27	M	Mason	Swiss	United States	Elizabeth	4 Sep 1826
BAILLENT, —, Madame		F	Domestic	France	United States	Mazzinghi	31 Mar 1826
Charles		M	Domestic	France	United States	Mazzinghi	31 Mar 1826
BAILLERT, —, Mrs.	24	F		France	U. States	Dawn	9 Dec 1826
Chs. D.	28	M	Merchant	France	U. States	Dawn	9 Dec 1826
BAILLICAL, Nicholas	26	M	Farmer	Germany	U. States	Bayard	16 May 1827
Sophia	18	F	Farmer	Germany	U. States	Bayard	16 May 1827
BAILLIO, Hippollite	28	M	Merchant	Haytie	U. States	Belle Victorie	18 Oct 1827
BAILLY, Richard	23		Farmer	U. States	U. States	Venus	4 Oct 1821
Wm. C.	21	M	Merchant	England	U. States	Criterion at London	10 May 1821
BAILY, Ann	4	F		Ireland	United S.	Hanford	19 Aug 1828
David	3/12	M		Ireland	United S.	Hanford	19 Aug 1828
Jane	28	F		Ireland	United S.	Hanford	19 Aug 1828
Margaret	62	F	...	Ireland	United States	Lima	19 Jun 1824
Mary	5	F	Seamstress	Ireland	U. States	Atlantic	19 Aug 1825
Mary	18	F		Bluenase	United S.	Hanford	19 Aug 1828
Mary	22	F				Susquehanna	9 Jan 1824
Michal	24	M	Farmer	Ireland	Pennsylvania	Susquehanna	9 Jan 1824
Robert	18	M	None	United States	U. States	Seine	20 Dec 1825
Sarah	31	F	Seamstress	Ireland	U. States	Atlantic	19 Aug 1825
William	3	M		Ireland	United S.	Hanford	19 Aug 1828
William	32	M	Joiner	Ireland	United S.	Hanford	19 Aug 1828
BAIN, Jno. H.	21	M	Gentleman	France	U. States	Brandt	8 Nov 1828
BAINARD, F.	50	M	Merchant	France	France	Pacification	30 Jun 1823
BAINES, Martin	28	M	Labourer	G. Britain	U. States	Leavitts	25 Aug 1828
BAINETA, A. E.	27	M	Gentleman	Italy	S. America	Bengal	14 Jul 1825
BAIR, L. P.	30	M	Mercht.	France	U. States	Mary	28 Feb 1822
BAIRD, A. E.	20	F		Ireland	New York	Orozimbo	2 Oct 1824
Alexr.	2	M	Child	Scotland	United States	Tom	2 Jul 1827
Ananser	19	M	Farmer	England	United States	Panthia	7 Feb 1822
David	18	M	Cabinet Maker	Ireland	United States	Henry Kneeland	7 Jun 1828
Hanson	11	M	Boy	Ireland	United States	Dublin Packet	6 Dec 1827
Helen	66	F		Scotland	United States	Samuel Robertson	5 Oct 1827
James	22	M	Laborer	Scotland	America	Camillus	12 Sep 1822
James	65	M	Labourer	Scotland	United States	Samuel Robertson	5 Oct 1827
Jane	20	F		Gt. Britain		Dalhouse Castle	13 May 1828
Jas.	60	M	Merchant		U. States	Margaret	3 Jun 1822
Jean	24	F	Wife	Scotland	United States	Tom	2 Jul 1827
Margaret	38	F		Scotland	United States	Broke	16 Jul 1829
Thomas	12	M	Boy	Ireland	United States	Dublin Packet	22 Aug 1829
Thomas	30	M	Mariner	Scotland	U.S. of America	Camillus	16 Apr 1822
Washington	25	M	Merchant	Ireland	New York	Orozimbo	2 Oct 1824
Wm.	4	M	Child	Scotland	United States	Tom	2 Jul 1827
Wm. Brown	27	M	Currier	Scotland	United States	Tom	2 Jul 1827
BAIRE, John A.	19	M	Merchant	U. States	U. States	Marmion	30 Apr 1828
BAIREA, John	45	M	Merchant	America	U. States	Transit	11 Oct 1822
BAIRETTO, Frans.	60	M	Merchant	U. States	U. States	Hopes Delight	6 Aug 1823
BAIRRA, W.	38	M	Merchant	France	U. States	Fortune	23 Nov 1821
BAIRRE, Jno.	45	M	Merchant	U. States	U. States	Julia	1 Feb 1827
BAISBOROUGH, Robert	30	M	bolster	England	United States	Phenix	11 Oct 1825
BAITSON, John	20	M	Labourer	Great Britain	United States	William Dawson	18 Jun 1827
BAITT, Jacque	12	M		Switzerland	U.S.	C. Amelia	30 Jun 1828
BAIZ, Jos.	42	M	Merchant	France	U. States [crossed out]	Commerce	8 Aug 1822
Jos.	47	M	Merchant	France	Porto Rico	Concordia	8 Nov 1822
BAKER, —	24	F	Farmer	Great Britian	United States	Columbia	17 Apr 1827
—	45	M	Gentleman	England	U. States	Imperial	10 Dec 1821
—, Mrs.	46	F	Servant	St. Croix	U. States	Martha	13 Jul 1826

NAMES OF PASSENGERS	AGE	SEX	OCCUPATIONS	COUNTRY TO WHICH THEY BELONG	COUNTRY THEY INTEND TO INHABIT	SHIPS/DATES OF ARRIVAL
BAKER (cont'd)						
Amos	35	M	Farmer	England	U. States	Congress 21 Nov 1823
Ann	28					Xenophon 25 Jul 1826
Arthur	3	M	None	France	U. States	New York 11 Jul 1823
Arthur	32	M	Taylor	France	U. States	New York 11 Jul 1823
B. D.	27	M	Merchant	U. States	U. States	Trent 23 Jan 1829
Bartel	30	M	Carpenter	Great Britain	United States	Fame 26 May 1828
Betsey	8	F		P. Amboy	U. States	General Paez 30 Jun 1827
C.	40	M		Great Britain		Caravan 8 Sep 1828
Catherine	18	F	Servant	Germany	United States	Wm. Osborne 16 Sep 1828
Catherine	27	F		Germany	United States	Samuel Robertson 8 Aug 1828
Ch.	23			France	United States	New England 29 Aug 1828
Charles	25	M	Brazier	England	United States	Cambria 8 Oct 1828
Charlotte	36	F	Lady	U.S.A.	Baltimore	William 26 Apr 1823
Chas. L.	45	M	Gentleman	New Orleans	New Orleans	Mary Livingston 2 Nov 1826
Crauncy	29	M	Merchant	N. York	N. York	Indian Queen 10 May 1825
E., Mrs.	31	F		London	Engld.	Criterion 9 Aug 1826
Edward	23	M	Cordwainer	Gt. Britain	United States	Robert Edwards 1 Jun 1826
Edward	28	M	Merchant	Dutch	United States	Ann 11 Sep 1827
Edwin	6	M	None	Honduras	Great Britain	Penobscot Packet 4 May 1826
Eliza	8	M		Great Britain		Caravan 8 Sep 1828
Eliza	19	F	Servant	England	U. States	Pacific 5 Sep 1827
Emily L.	4	F	Medical	England	U.S.	Panthea 22 Jul 1826
F. C.	22	M	D.M.	U. States	U. States	Cadmus 9 Apr 1825
Frances Elizabeth	28	F	None	Honduras	Great Britain	Penobscot Packet 4 May 1826
G.	25	M	Merchant	Prusia	Uncertain	Ocean 30 Jun 1821
Geo.	26	M	Merchant	Great Britain	United States	Grecian 24 Sep 1828
George L.	29	M	Farmer	United States	United States	Martha 30 Jun 1823
Grace	25	F	None	England	United States	St. George 25 Aug 1829
Grace	25	F		England	United States	St. George 25 Aug 1829
Hannah	30	F		Great Britain	U. States	Silas Richards 27 Jun 1827
Harriet	22	F	Servant	England	U.S.A.	Hudson 21 Aug 1829
Harriet	28	F	None	France	U. States	New York 11 Jul 1823
Hathway St. John	37	M	...	Gt. Britain	United States	Crisis 13 Nov 1824
Henrietta	45	F	None	England	United States	Colossus 26 Aug 1828
Idelade, Miss	23	F	None	Gt. Britain	United States	Crisis 13 Nov 1824
J.	6	M		Great Britain		Caravan 8 Sep 1828
J., Mr.	35	M	Mercht.	Gt. Brittian	Gt. Brittian	Manchester 24 Aug 1827
J. A.	59	M	Farmer	Great Britain		Caravan 8 Sep 1828
James	16	M		England	United States	Exchange 18 Nov 1822
James	36	M	Merchant	U. States	U. States	Kanhawa 16 Apr 1823
Jaquel	24	M	Farmer	Switzerland	United States	Andes 5 May 1828
Jno.	20	M	Servant	U. States	U. States	Hamlet 31 Jan 1825
Jno.	57	M	Sailor	England	U. States	Marmion 29 Sep 1823
Jno. G.	29	M	Mercht.	Prussia	U. States	London 13 Sep 1824
John	16	M		France	U. States	Edward Quesnel 4 Aug 1828
John	19		Farmer	England	S. New York	Xenophon 25 Jul 1826
John	22	M	Carpenter	England	New York	Brighton 29 Aug 1828
John L.	2	M	Medical	England	U.S.	Panthea 22 Jul 1826
John M.	37	M	Mariner	United States	United States	Euphrates 12 Mar 1824
John S.	37	M	Mariner	Philada.	U. States	MacDonough 28 Dec 1821
Louisa	30	F	Medical	England	U.S.	Panthea 22 Jul 1826
M.	11	M		Great Britain		Caravan 8 Sep 1828
M.	44	F		Great Britain		Caravan 8 Sep 1828
Margret	10	F	Servant	Germany	United States	Wm. Osborne 16 Sep 1828
Maria	22	M		Prussia	U. States	London 13 Sep 1824
Martha	50	F		England	U. States	Marmion 29 Sep 1823
Mary	2					Xenophon 25 Jul 1826
Mary	25	F	Labourer	Ireland	United States	William & Henry 19 Jul 1822
Mary	25	F		Great Britain	United States	Grecian 24 Sep 1828
Mary Ann	17/12	F	None	France	U. States	New York 11 Jul 1823
Matthew			Distressed Seaman	Falmouth, Mass.	U. States	Mary & Eliza 2 Jul 1829
P.	4	M		Great Britain		Caravan 8 Sep 1828
P. W.				Great Britain		Day 14 Jun 1822
Peter	45	M	Wheelwright	Great Britain		Caravan 8 Sep 1828

NAMES OF PASSENGERS	AGE	SEX	OCCUPATIONS	COUNTRY TO WHICH THEY BELONG	COUNTRY THEY INTEND TO INHABIT	SHIPS/DATES OF ARRIVAL	
BAKER (cont'd)							
Philip	33	M	Merchant	England	England	Louisiana	20 Sep 1822
Samuel	30	M	Mariner	Philadelphia	U. States	Marcellus	24 Dec 1824
Samuel F.	7	M	None	England	United States	St. George	25 Aug 1829
Samuel F.	7	F		England	United States	St. George	25 Aug 1829
Seth	30	M	Mariner	U. States	U. States	Howard	11 Apr 1826
Stephen	4					Xenophon	25 Jul 1826
Stephen	29		Farmer	England	S. New York	Xenophon	25 Jul 1826
Thomas	18	M	Laborer	Great Britain	United States	Hanford	9 Oct 1829
Thomas	19	M	Book keeper	England	U.N. States	Jane	7 Oct 1826
Thomas	28	M	Labourer	Ireland	United States	William & Henry	19 Jul 1822
Thomas	36	M	Farmer	England	United States	Exchange	18 Nov 1822
Thomas	45	M	Ship Master	U. States	U. States	Porcia	28 May 1827
Thos.	31	M	None	Great Britain	United States	Comet	9 Aug 1822
Thos.	50	M	Sevt.	Jamaica	U. States	Plandome	12 Aug 1826
William	3/12					Xenophon	25 Jul 1826
William	19	M	Mariner	Great Britain	Great Britain	Protection	6 Nov 1826
William	23	M	Labourer	Ireland	U. States	William & John	10 Jul 1824
William	25	M	Bricklayer	Great Britain	U.S. of America	Gratitude	3 Oct 1829
Winkey	28		None	Great Britain	United States	Comet	9 Aug 1822
Wm.	22	M	Shoemaker	Great Britain	United States	William Dawson	18 Jun 1827
Wm.	30 5/12	M	Labourer	Ireland	America	Rising States	7 Jul 1828
Wm.	31	M	Medical	England	U.S.	Panthea	22 Jul 1826
Wm.	44	M	Farmer	Ireland	U. States	Howard	25 Jul 1823
Wm. L.	6	M	Medical	England	U.S.	Panthea	22 Jul 1826
Wm. W.	30	M	Merchant	U. States	U. States	Napolean	26 Sep 1828
BAKERSICKLE, Henry	27		Sugar Baker	Germany	U.S. of America	Mary	21 Sep 1821
BAKUM, H.	21	M	Professor	Prussian	U. States	Minerva	18 Oct 1828
BALAGNER, M.	28	M	Mercht.	Spain	Spain	Richmond Packet	11 Jul 1827
BALANO, J.	18	M	Gentleman	Spain	U. States for a time	Lucy Ann	17 Apr 1822
BALAY, Caulette	38	F		France	France	Edward Quesnel	3 Jul 1829
Claude J.	40	M		France	France	Edward Quesnel	3 Jul 1829
Delpina	9 6/12	F		France	France	Edward Quesnel	3 Jul 1829
Eleonore	12	F		France	France	Edward Quesnel	3 Jul 1829
Francois	16	M		France	France	Edward Quesnel	3 Jul 1829
Francoise	16	F		France	France	Edward Quesnel	3 Jul 1829
Pierre	11	M		France	France	Edward Quesnel	3 Jul 1829
BALCH, Justin, Mr.	41	M	Ship Master	United States	United States	Maria	29 Sep 1823
BALCK, Michael	26	M	Merchant	Russia	Unknown	Mercury	2 Feb 1825
BALCOUR, Ls.	38	M	Planter	France	France	James Monroe	24 Feb 1826
BALDER, Bartolo	10	M		Cuba	U. States	Zephyr	18 May 1825
BALDERON, Thomas	30	M	Merchant	Barbados	Supposition is he will return	Superb	7 Jul 1823
BALDEZ, Jno. Jas.	23	M	Merchant	N. Orleans	U. States	Hope Return	13 Jan 1826
BALDOCK, Harpe	27	F		G. Britain	New York	Brighton	26 Mar 1827
James	1	M		G. Britain	New York	Brighton	26 Mar 1827
James	31	M		G. Britain	New York	Brighton	26 Mar 1827
John	2	M		G. Britain	New York	Brighton	26 Mar 1827
Richd.	35	M	Merchant	England	U. States	Remittance	18 Feb 1825
BALDWIN, —, Mrs.	30	F		N. York	U. States	Enterprize	27 Feb 1826
—, Mrs.	30	F		U. States	U. States	Lark	11 Jun 1828
...a...	25	M	Farmer	England	America	Thames	27 May 1822
Alfred	1	M				Hudson	23 Jul 1828
Ann	34	F		Great Britain	United States	Ganges	8 Jul 1820
Anna Maria	17	F	None	Great Britain		Roman	19 Dec 1825
Anna Maria	48	F	None	Great Britain		Roman	19 Dec 1825
Augustus	14	M	None	Great Britain		Roman	19 Dec 1825
Benjamin	17	M	Farmer	Great Britain	United States	Ganges	8 Jul 1820
Bun	6	M				Hudson	23 Jul 1828
Caroline	4	F				Hudson	23 Jul 1828
Edw.	36	M	Merchant	N. York	U. States	Pocahontas	18 May 1825
Edward	17	M	None	...	U. States	Columbia	7 Jul 1824
Edwin	35	M	Merchant	New York	U. States	Velocipede	16 Dec 1824
Elizabeth	13	F		Great Britain	United States	Ganges	8 Jul 1820
Ellen	3	F				Hudson	23 Jul 1828
Geo.	14	M		U. States	U. States	Rodman	9 Mar 1826
Henry	45	M	Gentleman	Great Britain		Roman	19 Dec 1825

NAMES OF PASSENGERS	AGE	SEX	OCCUPATIONS	COUNTRY TO WHICH THEY BELONG	COUNTRY THEY INTEND TO INHABIT	SHIPS/DATES OF ARRIVAL	
BALDWIN (cont'd)							
Jane	8	F		Great Britain	United States	Ganges	8 Jul 1820
John	6	M		Great Britain	United States	Ganges	8 Jul 1820
John	38	M	Colonel	Ireland	U. States	Courier	31 Jul 1828
John G.	8	M				Hudson	23 Jul 1828
Joseph	34	M	Tailor	England	United States	Lord Wellington	14 Nov 1827
L.	43	M	Engineer	U. States	U. States	Canada	2 Jun 1824
Mar	10	F				Hudson	23 Jul 1828
Mary		F	Infant	Great Britain	United States	Ganges	8 Jul 1820
Mary Ann	8	F		Great Britain	United States	Ganges	8 Jul 1820
Pearson	41	M	Mariner	United States	United States	Florida	23 Aug 1825
Richard	38	M	Farmer	Great Britain	United States	Ganges	8 Jul 1820
Robert R.	15	M	None	Great Britain		Roman	19 Dec 1825
S.	16	F		U. States	U. States	Lark	11 Jun 1828
Saml. P.	19	M	Merchant	U. States	U. States	Hesper	16 Jun 1828
Sarah	10	F		Great Britain	United States	Ganges	8 Jul 1820
Sarah	37	F				Hudson	23 Jul 1828
Susan	14	F				Hudson	23 Jul 1828
Thos.	12	M				Hudson	23 Jul 1828
Thos.	37	M	Merchant	Great Britain	Barbadoes	Spartan	5 May 1826
Thos.	37	M	Carpenter			Hudson	23 Jul 1828
William	36	M	Merchant	U. States	U. States	Lark	11 Jun 1828
Wm.	14	M		U. States	U. States	Lark	11 Jun 1828
Wm.	26		Labourer	Ireland	United States	Geo. Canning	5 Jun 1828
Wm. H.	32	M	Merchant	England	U. States	Cato	9 Aug 1823
BALDY, J. P.	30	M	Gentleman	England	U. States	Milton	20 Aug 1827
BALEQUER, Mateo	27	M	Merchant	Cuba	Cuba	Richmond Packet	25 Feb 1826
BALES, Catherine	24	F	None	Ireland	United States	Diana	1 May 1826
BALESTEER, Maria T.	24	F	Lady	U. States	U. States	Horace	23 Jun 1827
BALESTIER, Joseph	28		Merchant	...	U. States	South Carolina Packet	17 May 1827
William T.	22	M	Merchant	U.S.A.	U. States	Edward Quesnel	17 Mar 1829
BALEY, Wm.	26	M		Ireland	United States	John & Adam	21 Sep 1822
BALFE, Lucas, Mr.	36	M	Merchant	U.S.	U.S.	Hesper	2 May 1826
BALFOUR, John	21	M	Merchant	Great Britain	Great Britain	Martha	25 Nov 1820
BALGER, Catherine	32	F	Wife	Ireland	United States	Dublin Packet	9 Jul 1827
BALGUAD, Joseph	36	M	Miller	France	United States	Le Voltaire	19 Jul 1828
BALIE, Jane	3 6/12	F	Child	Ireland	United States	Fabius	31 Jul 1829
Wallace	20	M	Weaver	Ireland	United States	Commerce	13 Jun 1828
BALIOL, Thomas	25	M	Glass Blower	England	United States	Justina	5 Aug 1823
BALL, —	30	M	Merchant	England	England	Ductile	12 May 1826
Ann	30	F	None	Great Britain	New York	Superior	5 Sep 1827
Ann C.	6	F	None	Great Britain	New York	Superior	5 Sep 1827
Danl. C.	8	M	None	Great Britain	New York	Superior	5 Sep 1827
Eleanor	32	F	None	England		Manhattan	22 May 1827
James	3	M		Great Brittan	United States	Lewis	13 Jan 1827
James	17	M	Gentleman	U. States	U. States	Congress	21 Nov 1823
James	32	M	Merchant	U. States	U. States	Emblem	14 May 1827
Jas.	44	M	Merchant	England	England	Acasta	15 Jul 1822
Jno.	10	M	Merchant	Teneriffe	Spain	Louisiana	20 Sep 1822
John						Venus	12 Apr 1821
John	20		Saddler	England	United States	Hudson	5 Apr 1826
Lydia	20	F	None	England		Manhattan	22 May 1827
Mary	30	F		Great Brittan	United States	Lewis	13 Jan 1827
Mary	50	F		U. States	U. States	Brothers	1 Sep 1824
Samuel	29	M	Cordwainer	Great Britain	New York	Superior	5 Sep 1827
Thomas	36	M		Great Brittan	United States	Lewis	13 Jan 1827
Thomas	49	M	Carpenter	England	America	Cincinnatus	22 May 1826
Thos.	36	M	Farmer	Ireland	New York	Margaret	18 May 1825
William	21	M	Glass Cutter	England	United States	Andes	2 Oct 1828
Wm.	21	M		St. Johns	U. States	Wanderer	30 Oct 1828
Wm.	35	M	Merchant	Philadelphia	U. States	Franklin	27 May 1825
BALLA, Anthony	37	M	Mechanic	Switzerland	U. States	Thomas	3 Sep 1822
BALLAGH, John	25	M	Farmer	Ireland	United States	Lord Wellington	14 Nov 1827
BALLANTINE, —, Mrs.	26	F		G. Britain	U. States	Camillus	8 Sep 1828
Catherine	12	F	None	Scotland		Criterion	27 Oct 1820
Henery	17/12	M		Ireland	United States	Carolina Ann	14 May 1827
Isabella	17	F	None	Scotland		Criterion	27 Oct 1820

NAMES OF PASSENGERS	AGE	SEX	OCCUPATIONS	COUNTRY TO WHICH THEY BELONG	COUNTRY THEY INTEND TO INHABIT	SHIPS/DATES OF ARRIVAL
BALLANTINE (cont'd)						
James	24	M	Farmer	Scotland	Pennsylvania	Governor Fenner 23 Jul 1829
Jane	30	F	House Keeper	Ireland	United States	Carolina Ann 14 May 1827
Jane	38	F	None	Scotland		Criterion 27 Oct 1820
Jean	9	F	None	Scotland		Criterion 27 Oct 1820
John	1 2/12	M	None	Scotland		Criterion 27 Oct 1820
Merrion	15	F	None	Scotland		Criterion 27 Oct 1820
Nancy	14	F	None	Scotland		Criterion 27 Oct 1820
Richard	6	M	None	Scotland		Criterion 27 Oct 1820
Robt.	32	M	Store Keeper	G. Britain	U. States	Camillus 8 Sep 1828
Rosanna	4	F	None	Scotland		Criterion 27 Oct 1820
Thomas	18	M	Bootmaker	Ireland	United States	Carolina Ann 14 May 1827
Thos.	34	M	Farmer	Gt. Britain	United States	Pacific 22 May 1826
William	9	M	None	Scotland		Criterion 27 Oct 1820
William, R. Revd.	50	M	Minister of the Gospel	Scotland	United States	Criterion 27 Oct 1820
Wm.	32	M	Joiner	Scotland	United States	Camillus 27 Oct 1829
BALLARD, Saml.	22	M	Clerk	Ireland	U. States	Lukey 12 Jun 1822
BALLENTINE, Margaret	18	F	None	Scotland		Criterion 27 Oct 1820
BALLERE, F. A.	18	M	Clerk	France		Deux Ernest 11 Dec 1828
BALLETT, P. B.	23	M	Merchant	Philadelphia	U. States	Alexander 18 Mar 1822
BALLEY, A., Miss	23	F		U. States	United States	Henri IV 14 Sep 1827
BALLINA, Charles, Don	28	M	Attached to the Columbian Legation	Columbia	United States	Mercid 21 Oct 1824
BALLINGALE, Cathr.	26	F	None	Glasgow	Glasgow	Howard Douglass 11 May 1827
Isabela	24	F	None	Glasgow	Glasgow	Howard Douglass 11 May 1827
BALLINGER, Peter	22	M	...	...	N. York	Josephine 10 Dec 1825
BALLISTIER, J.	35	M	Mercht.	Boston	U. States	Leno 21 May 1822
BALLOCH, Alexr.	23	M	Gentleman	Great Britain	Great Britain	Agenora 3 Oct 1826
BALLS, James	20	M	Miller	England	United States	Ariadne 7 May 1821
Ths. L.	21	M	Merchant	U. States	U. States	Cadmus 3 Sep 1827
BALMER, Wm.	40	M	Farmer	Great Britain	U. States	Cadmus 26 Oct 1821
BALOW, Wm.	30	M	Farmer	G. Britain	U. States	Freak 9 Jun 1828
BALRIGER, —, his Wife & two children	52	M		Swisse	United States	Deux Ernest 29 Dec 1827
*landed at Lewiston, Delw.						
BALSHAN, Peter	21	M	Joiner	G. Brittian	U. States	Pacific 19 Oct 1829
BALSIGER, —	52			Suisse		Deux Ernest 29 Dec 1827
*son épouse & 2 enfans [his wife and two children]						
BALTAN, Ann, Mrs.	36			United States	U. States	South Carolina Packet 30 May 1825
BALTON, John	23	M	Merchant	U. States	U. States	Swift 28 Jan 1828
BALY, Isabeller	11	F			United States	William 5 Oct 1822
Jacob	9	M			United States	William 5 Oct 1822
Jaine	5	F			United States	William 5 Oct 1822
Jane	43	F			United States	William 5 Oct 1822
Joseph	7	M			United States	William 5 Oct 1822
Mary	15	F			United States	William 5 Oct 1822
Robt.	45	M	Farmer	England	United States	William 5 Oct 1822
William	13	M			United States	William 5 Oct 1822
BALZA, Jaques	24	M		Swisse	United States	Deux Ernest 29 Dec 1827
*landed at Lewiston, Delw.						
BAMBER, John	12	M	None	Chorley	L. Shire	Howard Douglass 11 May 1827
Margt.	3	F	None	Chorley	L. Shire	Howard Douglass 11 May 1827
Mary	7	F	None	Chorley	L. Shire	Howard Douglass 11 May 1827
Mary	33	F	None	Chorley	L. Shire	Howard Douglass 11 May 1827
Robt.	34	M	Farmer	Chorley	L. Shire	Howard Douglass 11 May 1827
Wm.	5	M	None	Chorley	L. Shire	Howard Douglass 11 May 1827
BAMFIRD, Jas.	15	M	Mariner	U. States	U. States	Florida 25 Apr 1825
BAMFORD, James	32	M	Joiner	Hadderfield		Aurora 8 Jun 1827

NAMES OF PASSENGERS	AGE	SEX	OCCUPATIONS	COUNTRY TO WHICH THEY BELONG	COUNTRY THEY INTEND TO INHABIT	SHIPS	DATES OF ARRIVAL
BAMFORD (cont'd)							
John	52		Woollen Weaver	Haddersfield		Aurora	8 Jun 1827
Samuel	24	M	Baker	Great Britain	United States	Illinois	9 Oct 1820
BAMINGER, Edward	21	M	Gentleman	America	America	Cincinnatus	19 Oct 1826
BAMMAN, John	25	M	Laborer	Germany	U. States	Hannibal	12 Oct 1829
BANABENO, E. A.	27	M	Gentleman	U. States	U. States	Don Quixotte	27 Jun 1827
BANAGHAN, Owen	21	M	Labourer	Ireland		Marchioness	13 May 1828
BANCALARI, Charlotte	32	F		Italy	U. States	Pedler	18 Nov 1825
BANCEL, A. F. E.	25	M	Merchant	France	France	Frances	19 Jun 1826
BANCKS, Abel	25		Merchant	U. States		Nancy	11 Sep 1820
BANCROFT, Geo.	21	M	Student of Theology	... U.S.A.	United States	Belle	3 Aug 1822
BAND, Ann	7	F		England	United States	Maria	12 May 1823
Betsy	26	F		England	United States	Maria	12 May 1823
Charles	2	M		England	United States	Maria	12 May 1823
Maria	6/12	F		England	United States	Maria	12 May 1823
Robert	5	M		England	United States	Maria	12 May 1823
BANDAERET, —, Mrs.	20	F		Switzerland	U. States	Desdemonia	9 Jun 1825
BANDAN, Stephen	60	M	Slingman	Havre	Montreale	Edward Bonaffe	23 Jul 1828
BANDAW, Joseph	25	M	Baker	France	U. States	Rival	25 May 1826
BANDE, Stephen	33	M	Merchant	U. States	U. States	Lady Tompkins	13 Apr 1824
BANDELI, Ed., Mr.	29 6/12	M	None	Switzerland	United States	Alexander	2 Oct 1829
BANDENER, W.	42	M	Speculator	U. States	U. States	Weymouth	3 Apr 1821
BANDER, James	30	M	Mercht.	United States	United States	Nestor	14 Nov 1823
BANDI, Jacob	14	M	Farmer	Switzerland	U. States	Sully	15 Jul 1829
BANDO, Agostine	25	M	Mariner	Genoa	South America	Packet	24 Mar 1824
BANDON, Antonio	22	M	Gentleman	Spain	Mexico	William	12 Aug 1826
BANE, Alexr. [crossed out]	19	M	Dyer	England	U. States	Thomas Ritchie	2 Jul 1827
Mary	15	F	Spinster	Ireland	United States	Robert Fulton	10 Aug 1827
BANGELY, James	48	M	Merchant	Leiden	N. York	Manhattan	21 May 1821
BANGER, Jane	45	F		Great Britain	U. States	Columbia	22 Sep 1828
BANGHER, Jno.	21	M	None	Great Britain	United States	Penelope	11 Jun 1827
BANGO, Esteran	28	M	Merchant	U. States	U. States	Lady Tompkins	13 Apr 1824
BANHAN, Richd.	26	M	Carpenter	England	United States	Essex	23 May 1828
BANISTER, John	21	M	Merchant	Great Britain	U. States	William Thompson	29 Jan 1823
BANJANDER, Clement	29	M	Farmer	France	United States	Henri IV	2 Oct 1828
BANK, Ann	47	F		England	United States	William Byrnes	6 Apr 1826
Jno.	26	M	Clerk	U. States	U. States	Porcia	28 May 1827
Richard	40	M	Gardner	Great Britian	United States	Isaac Hicks	22 May 1826
BANKER, David M.	38	M	Mariner	U. States	United States	Pomona	19 Feb 1827
BANKES, William	42	M	Merct.	Great Britain	G. Brittain	Cadmus	7 Jun 1824
BANKHEAD, Charles	27		Secry. British Legation Wash.	England		Hudson	5 Apr 1826
						Hudson	5 Apr 1826
Maria	20					Cassack	25 Jul 1820
BANKS, —, Miss	11	F				Olive Branch	30 Oct 1823
—, Mrs.	39	F		Ireland	U. States	Cassack	25 Jul 1820
—, Mrs.	48	F				Eliza	9 May 1827
Alexander	24	M	Scrivener	G. Britain	U. States	Superb	18 Jul 1820
Ann	8	F				Sarah	9 Nov 1820
Ann	30	F			United States	Isaac Hicks	22 May 1826
Daniel	26	M	Shoe Maker	Great Britian	United States	Eliza Grant	29 Aug 1829
Elizabeth	1	F	Farmer	Great Britain	New York	Eliza Grant	29 Aug 1829
Elizabeth	1	F	Farmer	Great Britain	U. States	Eliza Grant	29 Aug 1829
Elizabeth	40	F	Farmer	Great Britain	New York	Eliza Grant	29 Aug 1829
Elizabeth	40	F	Farmer	Great Britain	U. States	Criterion	27 Oct 1821
Emma	21	F	Lady	England	U.S. America	Elizabeth	22 May 1822
F. A.	23	M	Merchant	Spain	United States	William	28 Nov 1823
Frs.	27	M	Taylor	England	U. States	Aurora	14 Oct 1824
Geo.	35	M	Merchant	Baltimore	Baltimore	Lady of the Lake	23 Aug 1828
James	2	M					
*left ship							
James	24		Farmer	Ireland	U. States	Xenophon	28 May 1822
James	40	M	Farmer	Great Britain	New York	Eliza Grant	29 Aug 1829
James	40	M	Farmer	Great Britain	U. States	Eliza Grant	29 Aug 1829
James	47	M	Farmer	Great Britain	Great Britain	Ann	24 Sep 1822
Jane	12	F			United States	Sarah	9 Nov 1820
Jane	24	F	Servant	England	America	Birmingham	16 Oct 1826

48

NAMES OF PASSENGERS	AGE	SEX	OCCUPATIONS	COUNTRY TO WHICH THEY BELONG	COUNTRY THEY INTEND TO INHABIT	SHIPS/DATES OF ARRIVAL
BANKS (cont'd)						
Jas.	10	M			United States	Sarah 9 Nov 1820
Joanna	33	F	None	U. States	U. States	Henry 24 Nov 1828
John	18/12	M			United States	Sarah 9 Nov 1820
John	10	M		Ireland	U. States	Olive Branch 30 Oct 1823
John	22	M	Labourer	Scotland	United States	Mary & Susan 5 Aug 1828
John	28	M	...	Ireland	U.S. of America	Hamilton 18 Jul 1827
John	35	M	Brick Layer	Ireland	America	Rising States 7 Jul 1828
Margt.	9	F			United States	Sarah 9 Nov 1820
Mary	6	F				Superb 18 Jul 1820
Mary	26	F				Lady of the Lake 23 Aug 1828
*left ship						
Mary	30	F				Superb 18 Jul 1820
Mary Jane	7	F	None	U. States	U. States	Henry 24 Nov 1828
Matt...	6	M			United States	Sarah 9 Nov 1820
Philepena	5	F	None	U. States	U. States	Henry 24 Nov 1828
R. H., Captn.	28	M	Mariner	U.S.	U.S.	Hesperus 13 Mar 1826
Samuel	19	M		England	United States	William Byrnes 6 Apr 1826
Samuel	65	M	Farmer	Great Britain	New York	Eliza Grant 29 Aug 1829
Samuel	65	M	Farmer	Great Britain	U. States	Eliza Grant 29 Aug 1829
Stephon	35	M	Weelwright	None	U. States	Manhattan 21 May 1821
Thomas	27	M				Lady of the Lake 23 Aug 1828
*left ship						
Thomas	37	M	Farmer	England	United States	William & Henry 19 Jul 1822
Thos.	35	M	Farmer		United States	Sarah 9 Nov 1820
William	5	M	Farmer	Great Britain	New York	Eliza Grant 29 Aug 1829
William	5	M	Farmer	Great Britain	U. States	Eliza Grant 29 Aug 1829
William	32	M	...maker	G. Britain	Boston	Brighton 26 Mar 1827
Wm.	47	M		England	United States	William Byrnes 6 Apr 1826
BANNAN, Edward	30	M	Farmer	Great Brittan	U. States	John & Elizabeth 11 Dec 1826
BANNER, Fredric	27	M	Conditor	Germany	Pensylvania	James Noble 27 Aug 1827
Mary	27	F	Matron	Ireland	United States	Robert Fulton 10 Aug 1827
William	22	M	Labourer	Ireland	United States	Robert Fulton 10 Aug 1827
BANNERMAN,						
Anna, Miss	27	F		Ireland	United States	Alex. Mansfield 17 May 1823
Eliza, Miss	30	F		Ireland	United States	Alex. Mansfield 17 May 1823
BANNISTER, David	...	M	Mechanic	Great Brittan	Great Brittan	Tuscarora 26 Jan 1827
Edward	25		Sawyer	England	United States	Hudson 5 Apr 1826
Eliza	18 6/12	F	a Lady	United States	U. States	George Canning 13 Jun 1826
G.	24	M	Cabinet Maker	G. Brittain	U. States	Rengal 9 Oct 1822
George	19 6/12	M	Gentleman	United States	U. States	George Canning 13 Jun 1826
John	19	M	Land Surveyor	G. Brittian	U. States	Pacific 19 Oct 1829
Joseph	...	M	Mechanic	Great Brittan	Great Brittan	Tuscarora 26 Jan 1827
Thomas	44	M	Merchant	England	U. States	Edward Bonnaffe 4 May 1827
Thos.	48	M	Land Surveyor	G. Brittian	U. States	Pacific 19 Oct 1829
William	30	M	Laborer	Great Brittan	U. States	Gem 26 Jul 1827
BANNON, E.	26	M	Labourer	Great Brittain	United States	Sarah Ralston 27 Jan 1827
Pat	20	M	Labourer	Great Britain	United States	William Dawson 18 Jun 1827
BANNOT, L.	36	M	Merchant	France	U. States	Henry 24 Apr 1821
BANNTER, Edward	21	M	Farmer	England	U. States	Cincinnatus 24 May 1821
BANSHAW, James	30	M	Farmer	Ireland	U. States	Howard Douglass 29 Jan 1828
BANSLEY, Gosselin	35	M	Baker	France	France	Sully 15 Jul 1829
John	24	M	Farmer	France	France	Sully 15 Jul 1829
BANSON, Thomas	30	M	None	England	U. States	Montgomery 18 Oct 1828
BANTARD, Joseph	24	M	Mercht.	France	France	Stephania 13 Sep 1821
BANTER, Robert	34	M	Clergyman	United States	United States	York 6 Dec 1826
BANTLY, Alley	21	M	Spinster	Ireland	U. States	Meteor 19 Jul 1828
Biddy	6	F	Child	Ireland	U. States	Meteor 19 Jul 1828
Rose	3	F	Child	Ireland	U. States	Meteor 19 Jul 1828
Winolen	34	F	Wife	Ireland	U. States	Meteor 19 Jul 1828
BANTON, Alonzo	26	M	Merchant	Spain	Havana	Eliza Pigott 23 Mar 1824
BAÑULES, Francis	40	M	Servant	Spain	Mexico	Virginia 9 Feb 1829
BANYON, William	22	M	Joiner	Scotland	America	John Adams 2 Aug 1827

NAMES OF PASSENGERS	AGE	SEX	OCCUPATIONS	COUNTRY TO WHICH THEY BELONG	COUNTRY THEY INTEND TO INHABIT	SHIPS/DATES OF ARRIVAL	
BAPPENGER, Jos.	20	M	Merchant	Germany	St. Domingo	Minerva	1 Sep 1824
BAPTIS, John	40	M	Docker	New Jersey	New Jersey	Annah	17 Dec 1823
BAPTIST, John	22 ...	M	...	France	United States	Criterion	13 Oct 1825
Wm. D.	28	M	Merchant	U. States	U. States	Patty & Sally	29 Apr 1822
BAPTISTE, C.	4	M	Farmer	Switzerland	U. States	Alfred	8 Jul 1828
J.	2	M	Farmer	Switzerland	U. States	Alfred	8 Jul 1828
J.	37	M	Merchant	Spain	U. States	Ysdva	11 Sep 1828
Jean	24	M	Labourer	Italy	U. States	Fortune	31 Jul 1824
M. J.	48	M	School Master	France	United States	New England	29 Aug 1828
BAQUIME, Alexander	24	M	Merchant	France	America	Henry	18 Oct 1826
BAR, Barbara	38	F	Family [of Joseph]	France	America	La Grange	7 Aug 1828
Gertrude	4	F	Family [of Joseph]	France	America	La Grange	7 Aug 1828
Joseph	15	M	Family [of Joseph]	France	America	La Grange	7 Aug 1828
Joseph	45	M	Farmer	France	America	La Grange	7 Aug 1828
Maria	12	F	Family [of Joseph]	France	America	La Grange	7 Aug 1828
Rosina	6	F	Family [of Joseph]	France	America	La Grange	7 Aug 1828
Theresa	9	F	Family [of Joseph]	France	America	La Grange	7 Aug 1828
BARALY, M. L.	40	F		St. Domingo	U. States	Dromo	24 Jul 1826
BARAN, Catharine	2	F	None	Ireland	New York	Concordia	12 Oct 1826
Mary	20	F	None	Ireland	New York	Concordia	12 Oct 1826
Pat.	24	M	Black Smith	Ireland	New York	Concordia	12 Oct 1826
BARASS, Jos. W.	40	M	Mariner	Spain	Spain	Mechanic	14 Jul 1821
BARBA, René A.	24	M	Physician	France	France	Stephania	13 Sep 1821
BARBANT, —, Mr.	30	M	Merchant	France	U. States	Othello	31 Aug 1824
BARBARA, Ann	25	F		Baltimore	U. States	Pulaski Andrews	13 Sep 1826
Maria	18	F		Germany	U. States	Isabella	10 Aug 1829
BARBER, —, Mrs.	50	F		England	America	Birmingham	16 Oct 1826
Alfred	24	M	Merchant	Gt. Britian	United States	Cortes	11 Dec 1822
Annette	14	F		New York	New York	Hope	7 Oct 1825
Catharine	26	F		Ireland	United States	William & George	14 May 1828
Christopher	19	M	Farmer	St. Johns	U. States	Wanderer	30 Oct 1828
Cynthia	9	F		New York	New York	Hope	7 Oct 1825
David	21	M	Baker	Scotland	New York	Governor Fenner	23 Jul 1829
Eliza	10	F		Great Britain	United States	Thames	16 May 1821
Eliza	22	F		Ireland	U. States	Alex Mansfield	1 Jun 1822
Eliza	30	F		Ireland	United States	Commerce	13 Jun 1828
Elizabeth	1	F	None	England	America	Hannibal	28 May 1827
Elizabeth	36	F	None	England	America	Hannibal	28 May 1827
Hannah	8	F		St. Johns	U. States	Wanderer	30 Oct 1828
Jabez	22	M	Farmer	Brewnsley		Colossus	27 Mar 1828
John	3	M	None	England	America	Hannibal	28 May 1827
John	16	M	Farmer	St. Johns	U. States	Wanderer	30 Oct 1828
John	24	M		England	New York	Cincinnatus	5 Dec 1825
John	32	M	Surgeon	London	England	Flora	3 May 1825
John	34	M	Iron Founder	Ashton	U. States	Milton	21 May 1827
Jonathan	37 1/12	M	Physician	Great Britain	United States	Thames	16 May 1821
Jonathan, Jr.	4 3/12	M		Great Britain	United States	Thames	16 May 1821
Joseph	22	M	Merchant	Derby		Leeds	26 Sep 1828
Joseph	23	M	Gentleman	Great Britain	U. States	Silas Richards	27 Jun 1827
Lewis	30	M	Seaman	Spain	Spain	Hesper	21 Sep 1827
Marey	6	F	None	England	America	Hannibal	28 May 1827
Martha	28	F		Ireland	United States	William & George	14 May 1828
Mary	8 5/12	F		Great Britain	United States	Thames	16 May 1821
Mary	38	F		St. Johns	U. States	Wanderer	30 Oct 1828
Mary Jane	10	F		St. Johns	U. States	Wanderer	30 Oct 1828
Sarah	32	F	Servt.	U. States	U.S.	Bayard	10 Nov 1824
Thos.	28	M	Farmer	Ireland	U. States	Alex Mansfield	1 Jun 1822
Viletta	26	F		Great Britain	U. States	Silas Richards	27 Jun 1827
Wm.	17	M		New York	New York	Hope	7 Oct 1825
Wm.	50	M	Merchant	Great Britain	Great Britain	Martha	25 Nov 1820
BARBERY, Joseph	26		Planter	France		Bayard	10 Sep 1827
BARBETION,							
P. B. G. Lafons, Mr.	19	M	Gent.	France		Henri IV	7 May 1827
BARBIER, A.	55	M	Merchant	France	U. States	Howard	27 Feb 1824
Alphonse V.	26	M		France	U. States	Lewis	16 Mar 1826
Eliz.	46	F	...	F...	U.S. America	Columbia	26 Nov 1825

NAMES OF PASSENGERS	AGE	SEX	OCCUPATIONS	COUNTRY TO WHICH THEY BELONG	COUNTRY THEY INTEND TO INHABIT	SHIPS/DATES OF ARRIVAL	
BARBIER (cont'd)							
Henry	27	M	Premier Dyer	France	America	Eliza	20 Mar 1824
Peter	8	M	Child	France	America	Henry	15 Feb 1826
Peter	41	M	Curriest	France	America	Henry	15 Feb 1826
BARBONER, James	25	M	Taylor	Scotland	U. States	Roger Stewart	9 Jun 1828
BARBOUR, F. C.	18	F		United States	United States	Britannia	29 Oct 1829
Jas.	25	M	Bentleman	United States	United States	Britannia	29 Oct 1829
Jas., Senr.	54	M	Gentleman	United States	United States	Britannia	29 Oct 1829
John	35	M	Merchant	United States	Groton	Dime	15 Mar 1820
John J.	29	M	Gentleman	U. States	U.S.	Bayard	10 Nov 1824
Johnston	8	M		United States	United States	Britannia	29 Oct 1829
Lucy	53	F		United States	United States	Britannia	29 Oct 1829
BARBY, Henry F.	28	M	Merchant	Switzerland	U. States	Marmion	29 Sep 1823
BARCAIZTEQUI, Xavier	29	M	Merchant	Spain	Spain	Virginia	9 Feb 1829
BARCARD, J. J.	25	M	Weaver	Switzerland	U. States	Seine	30 Aug 1824
BARCCANNA, Anthony	30	M	Planter	Spain	U. States	Leo	7 Jun 1827
BARCETT, John	14	M	Miner	England	England	Virginia	8 Mar 1828
BARCHARD, Wm.	30	M	Farmer	Great Britain	United States	Diana	6 Jul 1829
BARCLAY, Ann	26	F	Wife	Scotland	United States	Tom	2 Jul 1827
Arthur	28	M	Miller	Scotland	United States	Tom	2 Jul 1827
Eliz.	4	F	Child	Scotland	United States	Tom	2 Jul 1827
Eliza	13	M	Spinster	Ireland	United States	Fabius	4 Jun 1828
Eliza	45	M	Laborer	Ireland	United States	Fabius	4 Jun 1828
George	32	M	Merchant	United States	United States	London	24 Jun 1823
Henry	30	M	Merchant	U. States	U. States	Olive Branch	16 Aug 1826
Hugh	24	M	Farmer	Scotland	America	Camillus	12 Sep 1822
James	19	M	Laborer	Ireland	United States	Fabius	4 Jun 1828
James	20	M	Miller	Scotland	United States	Tom	2 Jul 1827
Jane	15	M	Spinster	Ireland	United States	Fabius	4 Jun 1828
Jean	2	F	Child	Scotland	United States	Tom	2 Jul 1827
John	6	M	Child	Scotland	United States	Tom	2 Jul 1827
John, Revd.	26		Clergyman	Gt. Britan	Canada	James Monroe	11 Dec 1821
Margaret	14	F		England	United States	McFingal	9 Dec 1826
Matil...	30	F		United States	United States	London	24 Jun 1823
BARCROFT, John	25		Merchant	United States	United States	Carolina Ann	12 Sep 1823
BARD, John	20	M	Labourer	Ireland		Robert Fulton	4 Jun 1828
Rachael	18	F		Ireland	U. States	Nancy	10 Jul 1822
Thomas	28	M	Farmer	Ireland	U. States	Nancy	10 Jul 1822
BARDAY, James	10	M	child [of Mary]	G. Britain	United States	Louisa	14 Jun 1825
Mary	36 3/12	F	going to her Husband	G. Britain	United States	Louisa	14 Jun 1825
William	9	M	child [of Mary]	G. Britain	United States	Louisa	14 Jun 1825
BARDCOM, Job	40	M	Founder			Plato	31 Oct 1829
BARDEN, Ann	28	F	None	England	United States	Aurelia	7 Jun 1826
Jeremiah	25	M	shoemaker	Ireland	America	William	21 May 1825
John	33	M	Farmer	England	United States	Aurelia	7 Jun 1826
Thomas	22	M	Farmer	England	In the Country	Chelsea	16 May 1828
BARDILLE, Frederick, Doct.	23	M	Clergiman	Germany	U. States	Acasta	11 Dec 1826
BARDOTTE, J., Mr.	32	M	Merchant	America	America	Osprey	22 Nov 1824
BARDS, James	22	M	Labourer	Ireland	Canada	Ann Maria	7 Sep 1827
BARDSLEY, James	17	M	Mechanic	England	Canada	Hogarth	12 Oct 1829
BARDWELL, Seth	38	M	Merchant	U. States	U. States	Governor Clinton	3 Feb 1829
BARDY, Etienne M.	21	M	Prof. of Medicin	England	Quebec	Cadmus	27 Aug 1822
BARENDS, —, Mrs.	37 1/12			Hamburg		Ann Maria	28 Mar 1822
BARENS, Jos.	40	M	Merchant	Spain	Havana	Liberty	31 Jan 1826
BAREO, Josa	40	M	Merchant	Very Cruz	Very Cruz	Mary Jane	7 Jan 1829
BARET, D.	40	F		G. Britain	U. States	Robt. Edwards	4 Sep 1828
Dorcas	8	M		G. Britain	U. States	Robt. Edwards	4 Sep 1828
Fred	5	M		G. Britain	U. States	Robt. Edwards	4 Sep 1828
Geo.	12	M		G. Britain	U. States	Robt. Edwards	4 Sep 1828
James	10	M		G. Britain	U. States	Robt. Edwards	4 Sep 1828
Martin	1	M		G. Britain	U. States	Robt. Edwards	4 Sep 1828
R.	11	F		G. Britain	U. States	Robt. Edwards	4 Sep 1828
R.	13	M		G. Britain	U. States	Robt. Edwards	4 Sep 1828
R.	36	M	Farmer	G. Britain	U. States	Robt. Edwards	4 Sep 1828
Stephen	2	M		G. Britain	U. States	Robt. Edwards	4 Sep 1828

NAMES OF PASSENGERS	AGE	SEX	OCCUPATIONS	COUNTRY TO WHICH THEY BELONG	COUNTRY THEY INTEND TO INHABIT	SHIPS/DATES OF ARRIVAL	
BARFOOT, Mary	8	F		England	America	Ann	3 Jul 1820
BARFORD, E.	34	M	Farmer	U. States	U. States	Edward Quesnel	3 Sep 1826
BARGAN, John	25	M	Gardner	Ireland	U. States	Hope & Esther	22 Jul 1825
Thos.	24	M	Labourer	Ireland	U. States	Hope & Esther	22 Jul 1825
Mary	22	F		Ireland	Pennsylvania	Susquehanna	9 Jan 1824
BARGUEZ, P.	24	M	Merchant	Spain	Columbia	Don Quixote	15 Apr 1825
BARIGE, —, Miss	19	F		Amsterdam	U. States	Martha	8 Jun 1824
—, Mrs.	59	F		Amsterdam	U. States	Martha	8 Jun 1824
BARINARD, Jos.	23	M	Mechanic	France	U. States	Charles	11 Jul 1823
BARING, Francis, Mr.	21	M	Merchant	Great Britain	Great Britain	Nestor	3 Nov 1820
John	25	M	Mercht.	Gt. Brittian	United States	Nestor	14 Nov 1823
Thomas	29	M	Merchant	England	England	Britannia	5 Nov 1828
BARINGER, Thon	27	M	Butsker	Germany	Maryland	Orient	25 Nov 1825
BARINGTON, Hannah	12	F		Great Britain		London	29 Apr 1824
BARK, James	21	M	Smith	England	New York	Lima	5 Aug 1829
James	21	M	Smith	England	U. States	Lima	5 Aug 1829
BARKER, —	21	M	Pastry Cook	England	United States should they approve of it	Robert Edwards	20 Jan 1829
—	24	M	Merchant	U. States	U. States	Imperial	10 Dec 1821
—, Mrs.	44	F	Priestess	France	U.S.	Edward Quesnel	31 Jul 1827
Ann	4	F		Great Brittian	United States	Carolina Augusta	2 Dec 1828
Ann	25	F				Lady of the Lake	23 Aug 1828
Archibald	30	M	Spinner	Great Britan	United States	Clematis	8 May 1827
Charlotta	21	F	Spinster	England	England	Venus	15 Apr 1822
Daniel	8			County of Cumberland	Utica	Peru	30 May 1828
Daniel	24	M	Servt.	Germany	United States	Cadmus	9 Dec 1825
Elijah	26	M	Mechanic	St. John, N.B.	St. John, N.B.	St. Michael	28 Feb 1826
Elizabeth	10			County of Cumberland	Utica	Peru	30 May 1828
Elizabeth	39	F		G. Britain	U.S. America	Cincinnatus	31 Oct 1820
Ellen	17	F	Spinster	Ireland	United States	Diana	1 May 1826
Emma	4	F				Lady of the Lake	23 Aug 1828
Francis	1	F		Great Brittian	United States	Carolina Augusta	2 Dec 1828
Frederick	21	M	None	England	U. States	Criterion	20 Nov 1823
George	29	M	Farmer	Great Britan	Great Britan	United States	21 May 1827
Hannah	34			County of Cumberland	Utica	Peru	30 May 1828
James	20	M	Master	U. States	United States	William Howland	5 Jul 1821
James	27	M	V. Consul H.B.M.	Great Britain	Great Britain	Silas Richards	27 Jun 1827
John	27	M	Butcher	Great Britain	U. States	Eliza Barker	13 May 1824
John	30	M		Great Brittian	United States	Carolina Augusta	2 Dec 1828
John	45	M	Farmer	Yorkshire	Ohio	Curler	7 Jul 1827
John E.	21	M	Gentleman	United States	U. States	Bunker Hill	12 Aug 1828
Jonathan	9	M	Farmer	Yorkshire	Ohio	Curler	7 Jul 1827
Joseph	25	M	Labourer	Ireland	United States	Jubilee	1 Oct 1828
Joshua	15	M	Print Seller	Great Britain	United States	Unity	20 Oct 1829
Mary	22			England	Charleston	Xenophon	25 Jul 1826
Mathew	41	M	Print Seller	Great Britain	United States	Väÿty	20 PŒ †1829
Matthew	25	M	Stone Cutter	Scotland	Scotland	Sarah G.	28 Nov 1827
May	6	F		Great Brittian	United States	Carolina Augusta	2 Dec 1828
Nancy	23	F	Matron	Ireland	U. States	Courier	17 Mar 1828
P.	6	F	Farmer	Switzerland	U. States	Alfred	8 Jul 1828
Peter	22	M	Stone Cutter	Scotland	Scotland	Sarah G.	28 Nov 1827
Peter	50	M	Gentleman	U. States	U. States	Robt. Reade	12 Apr 1825
Richard	22		Wever	County of Cumberland	Utica	Peru	30 May 1828
Saml.	19		Seaman	United States		Cynosure	4 Mar 1828

*Consul's man, put on bord by the american Consil at St. Michal's Belonging to the brig Emeline of Portland Was Rackt on the 25 of Dec 1827 in the Harber of St. Michals

| Sarah | 30 | F | | Great Brittian | United States | Carolina Augusta | 2 Dec 1828 |

NAMES OF PASSENGERS	A G E	S E X	OCCUPATIONS	COUNTRY TO WHICH THEY BELONG	COUNTRY THEY INTEND TO INHABIT	SHIPS/DATES OF ARRIVAL	
BARKER (cont'd)							
Thomas	26	M	Barber			Lady of the Lake	23 Aug 1828
William	26	M		Great Brittian	United States	Carolina Augusta	2 Dec 1828
Wm.	6			County of Cumberland	Utica	Peru	30 May 1828
Wm.,	39	M	Carpenter	G. Britain	U.S. America	Cincinnatus	31 Oct 1820
Wm., Jr.	39	M		G. Britain	U.S. America	Cincinnatus	31 Oct 1820
Wm. H.	20	M	Merchant	America	America	Wm. Tell	22 Sep 1828
BARKES, Wm.	38	M	Merchant	England	U. States	Nymph	17 Jan 1822
BARKHILL, Jane	25	F	Spinster	Ireland	U. States	William & John	10 Jul 1824
BARKLEY, ...ay	23	M				Hesperus	2 Nov 1820
Joseph	20	M	Clothier	England	United States	Herald	29 Oct 1825
Sarah	19			Ireland	Great Britain	Robert Burns	14 Jun 1824
Thomas	70	M	Gentleman	New York	U. States	William Thompson	6 Sep 1822
BARKSDALE, —, Mr.	45	M	Merchant	U. States	U. States	Columbia	7 Sep 1827
BARLEY, John	9	M		Great Britain	United States	Baltic	24 Dec 1824
Mary	11	F		Great Britain	United States	Baltic	24 Dec 1824
Thomas	18	M	... maker	Great Britain	United States	Baltic	24 Dec 1824
BARLING, Anna	4 1/12	F	Farmer	England	United States	Young Phoenix	26 Jul 1824
Caroline	24	F		England	U.S.A.	Hudson	21 Aug 1829
Emma	5		his Daughter			Cambria	19 Oct 1829
Fanny	3		his Daughter			Cambria	19 Oct 1829
Jacob	32	M	Labourer	England	United States	Maria	12 May 1823
James	29	M	Labourer	England	United States	Maria	12 May 1823
James	33		Farmer	Ireland	United States	Cambria	19 Oct 1829
John	1 6/12	M	Farmer	England	United States	Young Phoenix	26 Jul 1824
John	30	M	Druggist	England	U.S.A.	Hudson	21 Aug 1829
John	35 4/12	M	Farmer	England	United States	Young Phoenix	26 Jul 1824
Mary	20		his Wife			Cambria	19 Oct 1829
Mary	35	F	Farmer	England	United States	Young Phoenix	26 Jul 1824
Stephen	25	M	Labourer	England	United States	Maria	12 May 1823
BARLOW, —, Mrs.	28	F	None	U.K. Gt. Britain	U.S. America	James Cropper	29 Nov 1827
—, Mrs.	30	F	Spinster	England	U. States	Moro	20 Oct 1826
Aneta	6		Planter	United States		Bayard	10 Sep 1827
Ann	12	F	None	England	United States	Trident	18 Jul 1827
Catherin	20	F		Great Britain	United States	Lady Hunter	26 Nov 1823
Elizabet	6	F	Spinster	England	U. States	Moro	20 Oct 1826
Elizabeth	10	F	None	England	United States	Trident	18 Jul 1827
Elizabeth	40	F	None	England	United States	Trident	18 Jul 1827
Emma	9		Planter	United States		Bayard	10 Sep 1827
Francis	28		Planter	United States		Bayard	10 Sep 1827
Hy.	19	M	Mariner	U. States	U. States	Florida	25 Apr 1825
James	1	M	None	England	United States	Trident	18 Jul 1827
James	23	M	Farmer	G. Britain	U. States	Freak	9 Jun 1828
John	13	M	None	England	United States	Trident	18 Jul 1827
John	42	M	Clergyman	England	U. States	William Prince	13 Dec 1827
Joseph	6	M	None	U.K. Gt. Britain	U.S. America	James Cropper	29 Nov 1827
Mary	5	F	None	England	United States	Trident	18 Jul 1827
Mary	11	F	Spinster	England	U. States	Moro	20 Oct 1826
Mary Anne	3	F	None	U.K. Gt. Britain	U.S. America	James Cropper	29 Nov 1827
Nicholas	2	M	None	U.K. Gt. Britain	U.S. America	James Cropper	29 Nov 1827
Samuel	3	M	None	England	United States	Trident	18 Jul 1827
Thos.	32		Planter	United States		Bayard	10 Sep 1827
William	8	M	None	England	United States	Trident	18 Jul 1827
BARMON, Francis	21	M	Labourer	Ireland	United States	William & George	14 May 1828
BARMOND, F.	50	M	Merchant	Port au Prince	France	Artibonite	9 Sep 1826
BARN, Hardich	42	M	Gent	French	Switzerland	Charlemagne	19 Sep 1828
BARNABEU, Chevel	57	M	Consul Gen. of Spain ne... U. States	Spain	United States	Henri IV	14 Oct 1829
Clara	50	F		Spain	United States	Henri IV	14 Oct 1829
Isabell	27	F		Spain	United States	Henri IV	14 Oct 1829
Jane	18	F		Spain	United States	Henri IV	14 Oct 1829
BARNADIN, Peter, Mr.	30	M	Merchant	France	United States	Jane	9 Jul 1821
BARNAN, Catherine	25			Ireland	New York	General Marion	21 Nov 1828

NAMES OF PASSENGERS	AGE	SEX	OCCUPATIONS	COUNTRY TO WHICH THEY BELONG	COUNTRY THEY INTEND TO INHABIT	SHIPS/DATES OF ARRIVAL	
BARNAN (cont'd)							
Thos.	35		Farmer	Ireland	New York	General Marion	21 Nov 1828
BARNARD, ...au...	5		Ladies and Gentlemen	England	United States	Corinthian	7 Jul 1829
Antoine	2 6/12	M		France	U. States	Leonarde	29 Aug 1828
Benjamin	40	M	Mariner	United States	Newyork	Dime	15 Mar 1820
Betsey	4	F		Great Britain	United States	Roanoak	19 Sep 1827
C.	32	F	Servant	England	unknown	Robert Edwards	4 Jun 1824
Cath.	13	F		France	U. States	Leonarde	29 Aug 1828
Cath. K.	40	F		France	U. States	Leonarde	29 Aug 1828
David	7		Ladies and Gentlemen	England	United States	Corinthian	7 Jul 1829
Edward	11		Ladies and Gentlemen	England	United States	Corinthian	7 Jul 1829
Eliz.	21	F	Weaver	France	U. States	C. Amelia	30 Jun 1828
Eliza	21	M	Farmer	Ireland	U. States	Gem	28 Dec 1824
Elizabeth	6	F	Farmer	France	U. States	C. Amelia	30 Jun 1828
Francoise	8	M		France	U. States	Leonarde	29 Aug 1828
George, Mr.	31	M	Architect	England	United States	Maria	29 Sep 1823
Henry	4	M	Farmer	Ireland	U. States	Gem	28 Dec 1824
Henry	13		Ladies and Gentlemen	England	United States	Corinthian	7 Jul 1829
James	13	M	None	Great Britain	United States	Hannibal	12 Oct 1829
James	24	M				Lady of the Lake	23 Aug 1828
*left ship							
Jno.	24	M	Mariner	U. States	U. States	Venus	12 Oct 1824
Jno. R.	36	M	Merchant	St. Domingo	St. Domingo	John Wells	14 Oct 1823
Jno. S.	22	M	Mercht.	U. States	U. States	Mary	23 Jul 1822
John	26	M	Mechanic	N. York	U. States	St. Michaels	21 Apr 1824
Joseph	14	M		France	U. States	Leonarde	29 Aug 1828
Leon	8/12	M		France	U. States	Leonarde	29 Aug 1828
Leon	40	M	Shoe Maker	France	U. States	Leonarde	29 Aug 1828
Levi	39	M	Comb Maker	United States	Boston	Patriot	13 Aug 1828
Marie	18	F		France	U. States	Leonarde	29 Aug 1828
Mary Ann	2	F		Ireland	U. States	Gem	28 Dec 1824
Mary Ann	28	F	None	Great Britain	Great Britain	Columbia	24 Dec 1822
Michael	9	M		Ireland	United States	Gem	16 Jun 1824
Pierre	5	M		France	U. States	Leonarde	29 Aug 1828
Rachael	54	F		England	Cincinati	Hudson	20 Nov 1828
Sarah	42		Spinster	England	United States	Courier	15 Oct 1827
Sarah	45		Ladies and Gentlemen	England	United States	Corinthian	7 Jul 1829
Soloman	22	M	Mechanic	England	U. States	Neptune	19 Nov 1828
Thomas	40	M	Gentleman	England		Courier	29 Jun 1827
Thomas	40	M	None	Great Britain	United States	Hannibal	12 Oct 1829
Thos.	30	M	Mechanic	United States	United States	Ann Maria	23 Oct 1820
Willm.	32	F	Weaver	England	United States	Helen	17 Dec 1827
Wm.	42	M	Merchant	Great Britain	Great Britain	Pacific	7 May 1827
BARNEBE, Joseph	28	M	Mariner	Great Britain	Great Britain	Cuba	25 Feb 1822
BARNEDUE, Peter	34	M	Merchant	France	U. States	Leontine	18 Mar 1825
BARNES, —, Mr.	22	M	Clerk	U. States	U. States	Rebecca	22 Mar 1823
Agnes	...			York County	Ohio	Peru	30 May 1828
Ann	22	F	Lady	Denmark	U. States	Catherine	3 Jul 1820
Ann	34	F		England	Albany	Cortes	16 Jul 1827
Anna, Mrs.	22	F	Lady	St. Croix	New York	Clarice	15 Jun 1825
Charlett M.	5	F		England	United States	Nimrod	30 Aug 1824
Charlotte	9	F		U. States	U. States	Caledonia	10 Sep 1828
Eles	33			York County	Ohio	Peru	30 May 1828
Eliza	15	F	None	Bary...		Aurora	8 Jun 1827
Elizabeth	9			York County	Ohio	Peru	30 May 1828
Ellen	5			York County	Ohio	Peru	30 May 1828
George	1	M		Denmark	U. States	Catherine	3 Jul 1820
Harriet	21			Postora, Eng.	England	Hudson	18 Jun 1825
*Officers, Seamen and Passengers belonging to the Ship Jane of Boston and taken from on board the Schooner Olive of St. Johns , N.B. on the 4th June 1825, Lat. 41.30, Long 53.19, which ship foundered on the 31st ultimo in Lat. 41.44 Long 52.							
Henry		M	Merchant	America	America	Gertrude	8 Aug 1821
Henry	17	M	Clerk	U.S.	U.S.	Agenora	28 Jan 1826
Henry	23	M	Painter	Great Britain	United States	William Dawson	18 Jun 1827

NAMES OF PASSENGERS	AGE	SEX	OCCUPATIONS	COUNTRY TO WHICH THEY BELONG	COUNTRY THEY INTEND TO INHABIT	SHIPS/DATES OF ARRIVAL	
BARNES (cont'd)							
James	...5		Supercargo	U. States	U. States	Almira	5 Nov 1827
James	7	M	None	England	United States	London	21 May 1828
James	18	M	Calico Printer	England	America	Hercules	2 Nov 1825
James	28	M	Labourer	Ireland	United States	Concordia	25 Aug 1827
James	60	M	Carpenter	England	Newyork	Cortes	16 Jul 1827
Jane	1/2	F		G. Britain	U. States	Leavitts	25 Aug 1828
Jane	1			York County	Ohio	Peru	30 May 1828
Jane	17	F	Lady	Denmark	U. States	Catherine	3 Jul 1820
John	4	M	Child	Ireland	United States	Ann Maria	4 Oct 1824
John	5	M	None	England	United States	London	21 May 1828
John	40	M	Comedian	England	United States	Nimrod	30 Aug 1824
John	48			York County	Ohio	Peru	30 May 1828
Jos.	19	M	Labourer	England	United States	Dalhouse Castle	8 May 1827
Joseph	38	M	Weaver	Gt. Britain	United States	Silas Richards	20 Jun 1826
Joseph	50	M	Brewer	England	U. States	Trident	8 Mar 1824
Lacy	23	M	Labourer	Gt. Britain	U. States	Isaac Hicks	18 Apr 1825
Margret	7			York County	Ohio	Peru	30 May 1828
Mary	11	F	Spinster	England	U. States	Trident	8 Mar 1824
Mary	19	F		England	Albany	Cortes	16 Jul 1827
Mary	24	F		G. Britain	U. States	Leavitts	25 Aug 1828
Mary	29	F	None	Ireland	United States	Ann Maria	4 Oct 1824
Mary	31	F	Lady	England	United States	Nimrod	30 Aug 1824
Mary	36	F		U. States	U. States	Caledonia	10 Sep 1828
O. Eliza	2/12	F	Child	St. Croix	New York	Clarice	15 Jun 1825
Perigrine	40	M	Gentleman	U. States	U. States	Sally Ann	6 Nov 1824
Saml.	27		White Smith	Postora, Eng.	England	Hudson	18 Jun 1825

*Officers, Seamen and Passengers belonging to the Ship Jane of Boston and taken from on board the Schooner Olive of St. Johns , N.B. on the 4th June 1825, Lat. 41.30, Long 53.19, which ship foundered on the 31st ultimo in Lat. 41.44 Long 52.

NAMES OF PASSENGERS	AGE	SEX	OCCUPATIONS	COUNTRY TO WHICH THEY BELONG	COUNTRY THEY INTEND TO INHABIT	SHIPS/DATES OF ARRIVAL	
Sarah	27	F	None	England	United States	London	21 May 1828
Sarah	65	F		England	Newyork	Cortes	16 Jul 1827
Seth	22	M	Gentleman	Denmark	U. States	Catherine	3 Jul 1820
Tarence	20	M	Labourer	Ireland	United States	Ann Maria	4 Oct 1824
Thomas	2	M	Child	Ireland	United States	Ann Maria	4 Oct 1824
Thomas	22	M	Laborer	England	United States	London	21 May 1828
Thos.	45	M	Labourer	Haslenden	Haslenden	Howard Douglass	11 May 1827
Thos., Junr.	16	M	Labourer	Haslenden	Haslenden	Howard Douglass	11 May 1827
Walter	5	M	None	England	United States	London	21 May 1828
William	29	M	Ship Master	U. States	U. States	Hiram	4 Jun 1824
Wm.	41	M	Shepherd	England	U.S. States	Splendid	14 Aug 1829
BARNESFORTH, Elizabeth	29			England	United States	Thomas Dickason	5 Jun 1827
Samuel	25		School Master	England	United States	Thomas Dickason	5 Jun 1827
BARNET, James	24	M	Gentleman	England	United States	Siroc	31 Oct 1829
Jno.	22	M	Tanner	Argyle (Tedland) Scotland	United States	Jean Hastie	27 Jul 1829
Jos. P.	25	M	Ship Master	Baltimore	U. States	Camille	1 Nov 1826
Wm. A. J.	21	M	Gent.	U. States	U. States	Cadmus	28 May 1821
BARNETT, Alexr.	30	M	Farmer	Ireland	United States	Henry Kneeland	7 Jun 1828
Amelia	16		Servant	England	Boston	Xenophon	25 Jul 1826
Ewd.	19	M	Cleark	Ireland	United States	Henry Kneeland	7 Jun 1828
Geo.	22	M	U.S. Mariner	U. States	U. States	Enterprize	9 Aug 1825
James	21	M	Labourer	Grt. Britain	United States	Robert Fulton	8 Oct 1828
Jno.	27	M	Farmer	Ireland	America	Mary	29 May 1827
Samuel	21	M	Joiner	Gt. Britain	U.S. America	Canada	30 Jan 1829
BARNEY, Gavet	19	M	...	G. Britain	U. States	York	10 Dec 1825
George	35	M	...b...	...shire	U. States	Panthea	24 Mar 1825
James	30	M	Labourer	Ireland	Ireland	Sarah G.	28 Nov 1827
James	40	M	Merchant	England	U. States	Pacific	5 Sep 1827
James	46	M	Merchant	England	New York	William Byrnes	14 Apr 1824
Jarvis	26	M	Sailor	American	America	Meteor	19 Aug 1825
John	31	M	Merchant	New Port		Felix	10 Sep 1824
John	35	M		Spain	Spain	Dollar	29 Aug 1825
Josha.	19	M	Navy	U. States	U. States	Helen	20 Jan 1825
Mary	45					Cincinnatus	29 Apr 1822
R.	33	M	Gentleman	United States	United States	Britannia	29 Oct 1829

NAMES OF PASSENGERS	AGE	SEX	OCCUPATIONS	COUNTRY TO WHICH THEY BELONG	COUNTRY THEY INTEND TO INHABIT	SHIPS/DATES OF ARRIVAL	
BARNEY (cont'd)							
S.	21	F		United States	United States	Britannia	29 Oct 1829
Susan	29	F		United States	United States	Britannia	29 Oct 1829
W. F.	33	M	Merchant	U. States	U. States	Dromo	19 Jul 1827
BARNFETHER, Wm.	36	M	Farmer	England	United States	Essex	23 May 1828
BARNFIELD, Elizabeth	52	F	Sempstress	Ireland	New York	Brighton	24 Aug 1827
BARNHILL, Jos.	21		Farmer	Ireland		Westmoreland	1 Aug 1826
BARNIS, J.	40	M	Merchant	Spain	U. States	Native	15 Apr 1826
BARNS, Cathrine	2	F		Scotland	United States	Camillus	9 May 1827
Ellen	20	F	Spinster	Ireland	United States	Trident	16 May 1826
Henry	23	M	Sugar Baker	Prussia	United States	Richmond	4 Aug 1826
Jas.	40	M	Weaver	Great Britian	U. States	Henry Kneedland	7 Aug 1826
John	40	M	Farmer	Ireland	U. States	Beaver	27 Oct 1828
Jonan.	6	M	None	Great Britian	U. States	Henry Kneedland	7 Aug 1826
M.	45	M	Merchant	France	U. States	Huntress	30 Jun 1824
Martha	42	F	Laborer	Great Britian	U. States	Henry Kneedland	7 Aug 1826
Richard	49	M	Engraver	Great Britain	U.S.A.	Silas Richards	28 Jun 1825
BARNSHALL, John	35	M	Laborer	England	United States	Delta	24 Oct 1829
BARNSLEY, Godfrey	22	M	Merchant	Great Britain, Ireland	New York	Britannia	3 Nov 1827
BARNUM, Benger	28	M	Mechantile	Vermont	U. States	Alexander	1 May 1826
BARNY, Mary	8	F	...	G. Brittain	U. States	York	10 Dec 1825
BARNYNE, Archibald	17	M		Scotland	United States	William Byrnes	11 Dec 1827
Robert	26	M		Scotland	United States	William Byrnes	11 Dec 1827
BARODY, Hosea	20	M	Merchant	Spain	Spain	Virginia	26 May 1828
BARON, John	26	M	Taylor	G. Britain	U. States	America	17 Oct 1825
Philip	38	M	Carpenter	England	New York	Brighton	19 Aug 1829
BARR, Allen	4	M	None	Great Britain	United States	Manchester	12 Aug 1829
Ann	14	F	None	Great Britain	United States	Manchester	12 Aug 1829
Barbary	38	F	None	Great Britain	United States	Manchester	12 Aug 1829
Bridget	44	F	Spinster	Ireland	United States	Robert Fulton	10 Aug 1827
Charles	24		Farmer			Rufus King	7 Aug 1820
Charles	28	M	Merchant	Baltimore	Baltimore	New York	31 Jul 1829
Daniel	18	M	Labourer	Ireland	United States	Gem	16 Jun 1824
Elizabeth	27	F		Ireland	United States	Carolina Ann	11 Dec 1826
Henry	28	M	Mariner	U. States	U. States	White Oak	5 Apr 1828
Henry	60	M	Merchant	U. States	U. States	Jane Ann	19 Aug 1822
J. P.	30	M	Merchant	England	Vera Cruz	Droma	25 Mar 1826
James	15	M	Weaver	Great Britain	United States	Roanoak	19 Sep 1827
James	25 4/12	M	Spinner	Great Britain	United States	Amity	1 Dec 1826
James	40	M	Mill Wright	Scotland	America	Camillus	12 Sep 1822
Jane	11	F	None	Great Britain	United States	Manchester	12 Aug 1829
Jean	18 6/12	F	Spinner	Great Britain	United States	Amity	1 Dec 1826
John	9	M	None	Great Britain	United States	Manchester	12 Aug 1829
John	22	M	Weaver	Great Britain	United States	Roanoak	19 Sep 1827
John	25 2/12	M	Stone Mason	Ireland	America	Carolina Ann	7 Apr 1826
John	28	M	Weaver	Ireland	United States	Carolina Ann	11 Dec 1826
John	45	M	Weaver	Great Britain	United States	Roanoak	19 Sep 1827
Margarett	29	F		Baltimore	Baltimore	New York	31 Jul 1829
Neill	66	M	Cooper	Ireland	United States	Robert Fulton	10 Aug 1827
Robert	2	M	None	Great Britain	United States	Manchester	12 Aug 1829
Robert	24	M	Boy	Ireland	New York	General Jackson	31 Oct 1820
Robert	37	M	Shipmaster	U. States	U. States	Mary Livingston	6 Dec 1827
Thomas	7	M	None	Great Britain	United States	Manchester	12 Aug 1829
William H.	7_/12	M		Ireland	United States	Carolina Ann	11 Dec 1826
BARRACLOUGH,							
Deborah	27	F	None	Gt. Britain	U. States	Importer	15 Sep 1821
Fs.	40	M		England	U. States	William Barker	29 Aug 1823
Thomas	17	M	Merchant	Gt. Britain	U. States	Importer	15 Sep 1821
Wm.	30	M	Merchant	Great Britain	United States	Florida	2 Sep 1822
Wm.	32	M		England	United States	Hannibal	6 Sep 1824
BARRADO, G.	24	M	Merchant	Spain	Spain	Native	8 Feb 1826
W.	30	M	Merchant	Spain	Spain	Native	8 Feb 1826
BARRADOUCH, Thos.	19	M	Merchant	England	England	John Wells	14 Oct 1823
BARRADRE,							
Augustine, Don	18	M				Mercid	21 Oct 1824

NAMES OF PASSENGERS	AGE	SEX	OCCUPATIONS	COUNTRY TO WHICH THEY BELONG	COUNTRY THEY INTEND TO INHABIT	SHIPS/DATES OF ARRIVAL	
BARRAGAN, Michael		M		Mexico		Joseph	20 Jul 1829
BARRCLOUGH, Frank	34	M	Shoemaker	Great Britain	United States	Spartan	25 Jul 1821
BARRDWELL, Robet	22	M	Farmer	G. Britain	U. States	George Clinton	10 Sep 1828
BARRE, J. P.	27	M	Merchant	France		Howard	17 Oct 1822
J. P.	33	M	Merchant	France	U. States	Laveria	23 Jul 1828
J. P.	36	M	Merchant	France		Lucy Ann	5 Oct 1825
L. P.	27	M	Merchant	France	France	Mary	23 Dec 1821
Lewis P.	34	M	Merchant	France	U. States	Merope	6 Dec 1825
BARREL, Joseph	25	M	Gentleman	U. States	U. States	Chase	17 Jan 1825
BARRELL, John C.	30	M	Merchant	U. States	U. States	Cincinnatus	24 May 1821
BARRELT, —, Master		M	Merchant	Maracaybo	South America	Exchange	11 Oct 1824
—, Mr.		M	Merchant	Maracaybo	South America	Exchange	11 Oct 1824
BARREMISTER, Hans	18	M	f...	Germany	New York	Constitution	20 Aug 1825
BARRESDALE, Sarah	42	F	F...	...	...	Diamond	27 Jul 1824
Wm.	43	M	Ca...	...	...	Diamond	27 Jul 1824
BARRET, Allen	25	M	None	U. States	U. States	Golden Age	19 Dec 1827
E., Miss	12	F	Schoolar	S. Croix	U. States	Jupiter	29 Jun 1825
John	20		Labourer	Cork	Gt. Britain	Enterprize	19 Feb 1822
Wm.	40	M	Merchant	S. Croix	S. Croix	Jupiter	29 Jun 1825
BARRETT, —	22			Ireland	U.S.	Union	20 Aug 1827
A., Miss	18	F	Merchant	England	U. States	Pacific	16 Apr 1825
Ann	15	F	None	Ireland	U.S.A.	Dalhouse Castle	21 Aug 1829
Ann	15	F	None	Ireland	United States	Dalhouse Castle	21 Aug 1829
Ann	17	F	Spinster	Great Britain	United States	Magnet	28 Jun 1821
Catharine	22	F	Labourer	Ireland	U.S.A.	Dalhouse Castle	21 Aug 1829
Cathr.	22	F	None	Ireland	United States	Dalhouse Castle	21 Aug 1829
James	20	F		Ireland	United States	Geo. Canning	5 Jun 1828
James	29	M	C. Printer	England	United States	Amelia	20 Aug 1829
Jane	9	F	None	Great Britain	United States	Magnet	28 Jun 1821
Jane	17	F	None	Ireland	United States	Dalhouse Castle	21 Aug 1829
John	14	M	None	Great Britain	United States	Magnet	28 Jun 1821
John	20	M	Labourer	Ireland	U.S.A.	Dalhouse Castle	21 Aug 1829
John	20	M	Labourer	Ireland	United States	Dalhouse Castle	21 Aug 1829
John	22	M		Ireland	U. States	Howard	25 Jul 1823
John	23	M	Farmer	England	United States	Manhattan	22 May 1827
John	23			Ireland	U.S.	Union	20 Aug 1827
John	23	M	Farmer	Great Britian	United States	Andes	19 Aug 1829
John	29	M	Farmer	Great Britain	United States	Diana	6 Jul 1829
Jone	17	F	None	Ireland	U.S.A.	Dalhouse Castle	21 Aug 1829
Joseph	7	M	None	Great Britain	United States	Magnet	28 Jun 1821
Mary	18	F	None	Ireland	U.S.A.	Dalhouse Castle	21 Aug 1829
Mary	18	F	None	Ireland	United States	Dalhouse Castle	21 Aug 1829
Mary	20			Ireland	United States	Geo. Canning	5 Jun 1828
Mary	23	F		Great Britian	United States	Andes	19 Aug 1829
Mary	25	F	Seamstress	Ireland	United States	Hope & Esther	27 Jul 1829
Mary	39	F	Spinster	Great Britain	United States	Magnet	28 Jun 1821
Robt.	32	M	Hatter	Gt. Britain	U. States	Panthia	13 Nov 1824
Saml.	27 2/12	M	Looking Glass Manufacturer	England	United States	Robert Edwards	3 Oct 1829
Saml.	37	M	Surgeon	England	U. States	Hudson	8 Oct 1827
Saml. H.	5	M		England	U. States	Hudson	8 Oct 1827
Thomas	4	M	None	Great Britain	United States	Magnet	28 Jun 1821
Thomas	16	M	Labourer	Ireland	U.S.A.	Dalhouse Castle	21 Aug 1829
Thomas	42	M	Farmer	Great Britain	United States	Magnet	28 Jun 1821
Thos.	16	M	Labourer	Ireland	United States	Dalhouse Castle	21 Aug 1829
Thos.	22	M		Ireland	U. States	Howard	25 Jul 1823
Wm.	11	M	None	Great Britain	United States	Magnet	28 Jun 1821
BARRETTO, H. C.		M	Merchant	N. York	U. States	Charleston Packet	26 May 1824
Nichs.	34	M	Merchant	Spain	U. States	New York	8 Mar 1825
BARREW, Cathr.	35	M	Merchant	U. States	U. States	Fabius	30 Aug 1827
BARREY, William	20	M	Servant	Denmark	Denmark	Jupiter	29 Aug 1828
BARRIBAL, William	27	M	Book binder	United States	United States	Hannibal	12 Oct 1829
BARRIE, Bernard	16	M	Merchant	Naturalized Citzn. of U.S.	Cuba	Robert Fulton	22 May 1824
Jno.	45	M	Merchant	U.S.	U.S.	Marcia	5 Jul 1823
John	40	M	Merchant	U. States	U. States	John	15 Sep 1827
John	44	M	Merchant	Cuba	U. States	James Monroe	8 Sep 1824

NAMES OF PASSENGERS	AGE	SEX	OCCUPATIONS	COUNTRY TO WHICH THEY BELONG	COUNTRY THEY INTEND TO INHABIT	SHIPS/DATES OF ARRIVAL	
BARRIE (cont'd)							
John	45	M	Merchant	Naturalized Citzn. of U.S.	Cuba	Robert Fulton	22 May 1824
BARRIERE, Jae, Miss	19	F	Lady	U.S.	U.S.	Montano	24 Jun 1823
BARRIERI, P.	50	M	Merchant	United States	United States	Joseph	11 Jul 1821
BARRIERO, Joseph	30	M	Merchant	Spain	Spain	Neptune	22 Oct 1822
BARRIS, Samuel	22		Cooper	France	U. States	Sall & Hope	12 Jul 1820
BARRISTER, Elizabeth	22	F	Laborer or Spinster	Ireland	United States	Sarah G.	15 Aug 1827
BARRLETT, Chas. L.	25	M	Merchant	U. States	U. States	General Jackson	15 Jan 1829
BARRON, Allice	1	F	None	Dublin	Dublin	Howard Douglass	11 May 1827
Benj.	21	M	Baker	Great Britain	United States	William Dawson	18 Jun 1827
Christ.	36	M	Farmer		Yorkshire	Howard Douglass	11 May 1827
George	16	M		Great Britain		Robert Fulton	8 Mar 1823
John	24 6/12	M	Weaver	Ireland	U. States	Courier	17 Mar 1828
John	26	M	Watchmaker	Great Britain	United States	Dapper	21 Aug 1828
Mary	26	F	None	Dublin	Dublin	Howard Douglass	11 May 1827
Nichs.	31	M	Farmer	Dublin	Dublin	Howard Douglass	11 May 1827
Pat	3	M	None	Dublin	Dublin	Howard Douglass	11 May 1827
S.	19	M	Navy	America	U. States	Catharine Rogers	6 Oct 1823
Willm.	10	M	Farmer		Yorkshire	Howard Douglass	11 May 1827
BARROR, Jas. Leather	26			England		Anacreon	7 Sep 1827
BARROS, Manuel	29		Secretary to the Legation of Spain	Cadiz	Spain	William Thompson	13 May 1823
BARROW, A.	28	M	Merchant	Great Britain	Great Britain	John Jay	8 May 1828
Ann	7	F		England	United States	William Byrnes	11 Dec 1827
Ann	32	F		England	United States	William Byrnes	11 Dec 1827
Daniel	4	M	Farmer	Alsace in the Department of Upper and lower Rhine	United States	Carolina Augusta	16 May 1828
Daniel	28	M	Farmer	Alsace in the Department of Upper and lower Rhine	United States	Carolina Augusta	16 May 1828
Dodgson	22	M	Draper	Great Britain	United States	Robert Fulton	27 Jun 1822
Edwd.	27	M	Farmer	Younghall, Great Britain	United States	Union	24 Sep 1823
Ellen	9	F		England	United States	William Byrnes	11 Dec 1827
Geo. C.	22	M	Merchant	Barbadoes	Barbadoes	Rose in Bloom	4 Apr 1826
George	6	M	Farmer	Alsace in the Department of Upper and lower Rhine	United States	Carolina Augusta	16 May 1828
Hery	2	M	Farmer	Alsace in the Department of Upper and lower Rhine	United States	Carolina Augusta	16 May 1828
Jno.	30	M	Merchant	Cuba	U. States	Ladies Delight	9 Aug 1823
John F., Mr.	23	M	Merchant	Gt. Britain	Gt. Britain	Pacific	22 May 1826
Jos. B.	21	M	Merchant	Barbadoes	Barbadoes	Rose in Bloom	4 Apr 1826
L.	25	M	Merchant	Great Britain	New York	Auritz	20 May 1823
Margaret	36	F		England	United States	Copernicus	3 Aug 1829
Philip	1	M	Farmer	Alsace in the Department of Upper and lower Rhine	United States	Carolina Augusta	16 May 1828
Rachel	11	F		England	United States	Copernicus	3 Aug 1829
Sophia	28	F	Farmer	Alsace in the Department of Upper and lower Rhine	United States	Carolina Augusta	16 May 1828

NAMES OF PASSENGERS	AGE	SEX	OCCUPATIONS	COUNTRY TO WHICH THEY BELONG	COUNTRY THEY INTEND TO INHABIT	SHIPS/DATES OF ARRIVAL	
BARROW (cont'd)							
Thos.	23	M	Morocco dresser	U. States	United States	Crisis	6 Apr 1825
Tom	19	M	Currier	Ireland	U.S.A.	Dalhouse Castle	21 Aug 1829
Tom	19	M	Currier	Ireland	United States	Dalhouse Castle	21 Aug 1829
William	46	M	Silk Weaver	England	United States	Copernicus	3 Aug 1829
BARROWS, John	27	M	Labourer	Ireland	Ireland	Sarah G.	28 Nov 1827
William	20	M	Farmer	Great Brittain	U. States America	James Cropper	23 Mar 1827
BARRURO, Geronimo,							
Don	24	M	Merchant	Spain		Prince Edward	18 Dec 1826
BARRY, Anne Jane	20	F	Farmer	Ireland	America	Superior	12 Jun 1824
Catherine	14	F		Ireland	United States	Trio	2 Oct 1828
Charles	31	M	Farmer	Ireland	America	Superior	12 Jun 1824
David	8	M	None	Ireland	N. York	Josephine	10 Dec 1825
David	21	M	Farmer	Ireland	America	William	21 May 1825
David	22		Labourer	Ireland	United States	Geo. Canning	5 Jun 1828
David	23	M		Ireland	United States	William Byrnes	15 Aug 1826
Edward	34	M	Merchant	Ireland	United States	Dublin Packet	29 Jun 1825
Elen	24	F	Farmer	England	America	Cincinnatus	19 Oct 1826
Elisabeth	3	F	None	England	America	Cincinnatus	19 Oct 1826
Eliza	13	F	None	England	America	Cincinnatus	19 Oct 1826
Eliza	21	F	Wife	Ireland	U.S. of America	Meteor	19 Mar 1828
Eliza, Mrs.	28	F	Lady	England	U. States	Acasta	11 Dec 1826
Elizabeth	2	F	Farmer	Ireland	America	Superior	12 Jun 1824
Elizabeth	54	F	Farmer	England	America	Cincinnatus	19 Oct 1826
Ellen	27		Farmer	Ireland	U. States	Schuylkill	22 Aug 1825
Esther	8	F	None	G. Britain	U. States	Courier	16 Aug 1824
Francis	1/12	F	None	England	America	Cincinnatus	19 Oct 1826
Francis	24	M	None	Great Britain	United States	Eliza Barker	3 Jul 1826
G. R.	30	M	Merchant	English	Port au Prince	William	28 Feb 1826
G. R.	30	M	Merchant	Hayty	U. States	Belle Victoire	10 Oct 1828
Garret	5	M	Labourer	Ireland	United States	Trio	2 Oct 1828
Helen	28	F	None	England	New York	Brighton	29 Aug 1828
Honora	5	F				Robert Fulton	8 Mar 1823
J. M.	26	F	Spinster	U. States	U. States	Hibernia	24 Aug 1820
James	10	M	None	England	America	Cincinnatus	19 Oct 1826
James	17	M	Laborer	Gt. Britain		Dalhouse Castle	13 May 1828
James	21	M	Gentleman	England	America	Cincinnatus	19 Oct 1826
James	25	M	Mechanic	Great Britain		Birmingham	11 Oct 1828
James	40	M	Farmer	Ireland	N. York	Josephine	10 Dec 1825
Jane	1	F	Farmer	Ireland	America	Superior	12 Jun 1824
Jas.	29	M		Ireland	America	Liverpool	31 Aug 1827
Jno. M.	28	M	Merchant	England	U. States	Carpenter	3 Sep 1821
Jno. M.	32	M	Merchant	U. States	U. States	Georgetown Packet	6 Nov 1822
Johanna	22	F	Seamstress	Great Britain	United States	Henrietta	19 Oct 1825
John	4/12	M	Child	Ireland	U.S. of America	Meteor	19 Mar 1828
John	18	M	None	England	America	Cincinnatus	19 Oct 1826
John	25	M		Ireland	U. States	Howard	25 Jul 1823
John	28	M	Laborer	Ireland	United States	St. Michaels	18 Jul 1826
John	28	M	Carpenter	England	New York	Brighton	29 Aug 1828
John	31	M	Labourer	Ireland	U. States	Albion	11 May 1827
John	32	M	Labourer	Great Britain	U. States	Princess Charlotte	6 Sep 1828
John, Jr.	10					Robert Fulton	8 Mar 1823
John M.	36	M	Merchant	U. States	U. States	Prince Edward	29 Jul 1823
Joseph	7	M		Halifax, N.S.	United States	Hannah Eliza	23 Sep 1826
Joseph	26	M	Farmer	Great Britain	United States	Birmingham	15 Jun 1827
July	10	F	None	Ireland	N. York	Josephine	10 Dec 1825
July	35	F	None	Ireland	N. York	Josephine	10 Dec 1825
Luke	30	M	Priest	Ireland	U.S.	Panthea	13 Nov 1823
Mary	7	F		Ireland	United States	Trio	2 Oct 1828
Mary	18	F	Sevt.	Sligo	New York	Susquehana	27 Jun 1823
Mary	20	F	None	England	America	Cincinnatus	19 Oct 1826
Mary	23	F	None	England	New York	Brighton	29 Aug 1828
Mary	29	F		Ireland	United States	Trio	2 Oct 1828
Mary, Mrs.	38	F	None	G. Britain	U. States	Courier	16 Aug 1824
Mary Ann	30	F				Robert Fulton	8 Mar 1823
Moses	16	M	None	England	America	Cincinnatus	19 Oct 1826
Nancy	17	F	Seamstress	Great Britain	United States	Henrietta	19 Oct 1825

NAMES OF PASSENGERS	AGE	SEX	OCCUPATIONS	COUNTRY TO WHICH THEY BELONG	COUNTRY THEY INTEND TO INHABIT	SHIPS/DATES OF ARRIVAL	
BARRY (cont'd)							
Norry	20	F		Ireland	America	Liverpool	31 Aug 1827
Pat	24	M	Labourer	Ireland	Unt. St. America	Wilson	21 May 1827
Patrick	20	M	Laborer	Gt. Britain		Dalhouse Castle	13 May 1828
Peter	26	M	Laborer	Ireland	United States	St. Michaels	18 Jul 1826
Redmund	25		Labourer	Ireland	United States	Geo. Canning	5 Jun 1828
Richard	26	M		Ireland	United States	John & Adam	21 Sep 1822
Rob.	40	M	Merchant	Ireland	U. States	Mary Ann	27 Sep 1822
Robert	1					Robert Fulton	8 Mar 1823
S. J. W.	20	M	Merchant	Nova Scotia	U. States	Harriet	16 Mar 1824
Samuel	23	M	Weaver	Ireland	U.S. of America	Meteor	19 Mar 1828
Sarah	30	F		Halifax, N.S.	United States	Hannah Eliza	23 Sep 1826
Thomas	12	M	None	G. Britain	U. States	Courier	16 Aug 1824
Thomas	29	M	Farmer	Ireland	America	William	21 May 1825
Thomas	30	M				Trio	5 May 1828
Thomas	52	M	Farmer	England	America	Cincinnatus	19 Oct 1826
Thomas, Mr.	30	M	Gentelman	England	U. States	Acasta	11 Dec 1826
William	23	M		U. States	U. States	Hibernia	24 Aug 1820
William	28	M	Carpenter	Halifax, N.S.	United States	Hannah Eliza	23 Sep 1826
Wm.	20	M	Labourer	G. Britain	U. States	St. George	7 Jun 1828
BARS, Dorthan	18	F	Gent	French	Switzerland	Charlemagne	19 Sep 1828
George	10	M	Gent	French	Switzerland	Charlemagne	19 Sep 1828
Magdalen	16	F	Gent	French	Switzerland	Charlemagne	19 Sep 1828
Margaret	40	F	Gent	French	Switzerland	Charlemagne	19 Sep 1828
BARSLEY, Robt.	24	M	Farmer	Great Brittian		Merchant	22 Apr 1822
BARSON, George	1 8/12	M	Farmer	Switzerland	America	Henry	17 May 1828
Jacob	2 4/12	M	Farmer	Switzerland	America	Henry	17 May 1828
Jacob	30 5/12	M	Farmer	Switzerland	America	Henry	17 May 1828
Mary	5 9/12	F	Farmer	Switzerland	America	Henry	17 May 1828
Mary	31 7/12	F	Farmer	Switzerland	America	Henry	17 May 1828
BARSTOW, Benj.	25	M	Merchant	U.S.	U.S.	Minerva	3 Dec 1821
Ed.	22	M	Doctor	Bermuda	Bermuda	Emblem	25 Oct 1825
Elizabeth	16	F		G. Britain	U. States	Armadello	22 Jun 1827
Hannah	12	F		G. Britain	U. States	Armadello	22 Jun 1827
John	13	M		G. Britain	U. States	Armadello	22 Jun 1827
Maria	9	F		G. Britain	U. States	Armadello	22 Jun 1827
Mary	48	F		G. Britain	U. States	Armadello	22 Jun 1827
Richard	17	M	Blacksmith	G. Britain	U. States	Armadello	22 Jun 1827
Richard	48	M	Farmer	G. Britain	U. States	Armadello	22 Jun 1827
Wm. C., Capt.	29	M	Mariner	U. States	U. States	Artibonite	3 Jul 1826
BARTALOZE, Eliza	25	F		Jamaica	Jamaica	Tontine	25 Sep 1826
Magdalen	40	F		Jamaica	Jamaica	Tontine	25 Sep 1826
BARTELAUS, W. L.	34	M	Merchant	Hanover	U. States	Minerva	9 Jan 1827
BARTER, John	30	M	Gunsmith	England	U.N. States	Earl of Liverpool	20 Aug 1825
Mary	47	F		England	U.N. States	Earl of Liverpool	20 Aug 1825
William	47	M		England	U.N. States	Earl of Liverpool	20 Aug 1825
BARTH, Joe	38	M	Weaver	Germany	United States	Helen	5 Sep 1828
BARTHELON, —, Mrs.	22	M		Spain	St. Domingo	Sampson	5 Oct 1825
Evelina	3	F		Spain	St. Domingo	Sampson	5 Oct 1825
John	7	M		Spain	St. Domingo	Sampson	5 Oct 1825
Manuel	21	M	Merchant	Spain	St. Domingo	Sampson	5 Oct 1825
Thomas	5	M		Spain	St. Domingo	Sampson	5 Oct 1825
BARTIN, Ann	12	F		Great Britain	United States	Atlantic	28 May 1827
Betsty	10	F		Great Britain	United States	Atlantic	28 May 1827
Martha	7	F		Great Britain	United States	Atlantic	28 May 1827
Mary	11	F		Great Britain	United States	Atlantic	28 May 1827
BARTLES, John, Jr.	32	M	Gentleman	England	U. States	Milton	20 Aug 1827
BARTLESQES,							
M., Black	40	F	Servant	St. Croix	St. Croix	Commerce	13 Nov 1823
BARTLETT, Charles F.	25	M	Merchant	Boston	Massachusetts	Constitution	9 Dec 1824
Chas. F., Mr.	44	M	Merchant	Massa.	Boston	South America	29 Aug 1826
Edwd.	58	M	Gentleman	G. Brittain	U. States	Hope & Esther	26 Nov 1822
Elisha	22	M	...	...	America	Robin Hood	20 Jul 1827
Emma	5	F	Child			Seine	10 Jun 1822
Fred.	1	M	Child			Seine	10 Jun 1822
Hester	30	F	Lady			Seine	10 Jun 1822

NAMES OF PASSENGERS	AGE	SEX	OCCUPATIONS	COUNTRY TO WHICH THEY BELONG	COUNTRY THEY INTEND TO INHABIT	SHIPS/DATES OF ARRIVAL	
BARRY (cont'd)							
Isaac	26		Shoemaker	France	U. States	Elizabeth	9 Jul 1825
Jane	3	F	Child			Seine	10 Jun 1822
John	34	M	Farmer			Seine	10 Jun 1822
Josha.	45	M	Mariner	Thomastown	U. States	Ruby	10 Apr 1823
Mariah	9	F	Child			Seine	10 Jun 1822
Mary Ann	7	F	Child			Seine	10 Jun 1822
T.	19	M	None	Halifax	England	Loire	7 Jun 1827
BARTLETTE, —, Mrs.	40	F		St. Croix	United States	Carlo	28 Jun 1826
BARTLEY, Allexander	26	M	...	...	United States	Hanford	17 Oct 1828
Ann	22	F	Spinster	Ireland	United States	Robert Fulton	24 Jul 1826
William	16	M	Labourer	Ireland	United States	Robert Fulton	24 Jul 1826
BARTLIN, John	19		Clerk	England	America	Sarah	18 Aug 1829
BARTLING, Charles	36	M	Mariner	Ireland	U. States	Globe	14 Jul 1821
BARTNIN, Ann M.	10	F	Gent	French	Switzerland	Charlemagne	19 Sep 1828
Dorthea	14	F	Gent	French	Switzerland	Charlemagne	19 Sep 1828
Jacob	16	M	Gent	French	Switzerland	Charlemagne	19 Sep 1828
Peter	16	M	Gent	French	Switzerland	Charlemagne	19 Sep 1828
Shrine	40	M	Gent	French	Switzerland	Charlemagne	19 Sep 1828
BARTOL, William	18	M	Gentleman	United States	United States	Astrea	20 Aug 1825
BARTON, —, Mrs.	27	F		Scotland	U. States	Dale	14 Mar 1828
—, Mrs.	35	F	Lady	England	Antigua	Illuminator	26 Jul 1825
C.	24	M	Lawyer	Philad.	U. States	Stephania	18 Dec 1824
David	33	M	Farmer	Scotland	U. States	Dale	14 Mar 1828
Edward	4	M		Ireland	Pensylvania	Eliza Grant	29 Aug 1829
Elizabeth, Mrs.	30	F	None	G. Britain	U. States	Courier	16 Aug 1824
F.	5	M		England	America	Birmingham	16 Oct 1826
G. G.	6	M		England	Antigua	Illuminator	26 Jul 1825
George	15	M		Ireland	Pensylvania	Eliza Grant	29 Aug 1829
George	28	M	Seaman	United States	United States	Ceres	13 Dec 1827
George	29	M	None	England	America	Britannia	23 Mar 1829
Hannah	21	F		Ireland	Pensylvania	Eliza Grant	29 Aug 1829
Jas. H.	41	M	Gentleman	England	Antigua	Illuminator	26 Jul 1825
John	19	M		Ireland	Pensylvania	Eliza Grant	29 Aug 1829
John	35	M	Gentleman	England		Baltic	21 Apr 1827
John	40	M	Merchant	England		Carolina Ann	7 Apr 1826
Joseph	13	M		Ireland	Pensylvania	Eliza Grant	29 Aug 1829
Joseph	30	M	Mechanic	England	United States	Columbia	16 Jan 1829
Maria	9	F		Ireland	Pensylvania	Eliza Grant	29 Aug 1829
Mary	1 4/12	F	None	G. Britain	U. States	Courier	16 Aug 1824
Mary	41	F		Ireland	Pensylvania	Eliza Grant	29 Aug 1829
Mary	53	M	Lady	New York	Canada	Belleville	29 Aug 1827
R.	38	M	Grinder	England	America	Birmingham	16 Oct 1826
Richard	10	M	Labourer	New Brunswick	Canada	Belleville	29 Aug 1827
Sarah	17	F		Ireland	Pensylvania	Eliza Grant	29 Aug 1829
Stephen	12	M	Boy	New Brunswick	Canada	Belleville	29 Aug 1827
Thomas	11	M		Ireland	Pensylvania	Eliza Grant	29 Aug 1829
William	14	M	Labourer	New Brunswick	Canada	Belleville	29 Aug 1827
Wm.	3	M	None	G. Britain	U. States	Courier	16 Aug 1824
Wm.	27	M	Labourer	Ireland	United States	Hope	12 Jun 1828
Wm.	30	M	Farmer	Scotland	U. States of America	Dale	14 Mar 1828
BARTOW, Samuel	25	M	Seaman	New York	New York	Mary & Elizabeth	7 Sep 1824
BARTROP, Lucy	20			England	United States	Hugh Johnson	11 Jun 1828
BARY, Mary	8	F				Robert Fulton	8 Mar 1823
BARZELL, —	30	M	Merchant	Guadaloupe		Industry	11 Jun 1821
BASADRE, Ignacio, Don	28	M	Attached to the Columbian Legation	Columbia	United States	Mercid	21 Oct 1824
BASCHEN, C.	24	M	Sugar Baker	Germany	U. States	Constitution	25 Jul 1823
BASCHY, Rudolph	56	M	Framer	Switzerland	Ohio	Danube	20 Jul 1826
BASCOM, Thomas R.	31	M	Gentleman	Barbadoes	Barbadoes	Falcon	4 Jun 1825
BASCOME, D.	40	M	Salt Raker	Bermuda	U. States	Mohawk	15 Nov 1821
Nathaniel	50	M	Merchant	Gt. Britain	United States	Neptune	24 May 1824
BASDEN, Jane	49	F	Lady	Curracoa	U. States	Charleston	10 May 1825
BASGNER, —, Mr.	25	M	Merchant	Havana	Havana	Milo	15 May 1824
BASHAM, George, Master	17	M	Farmer	England	U. States	Acasta	21 Oct 1825
Hannah, Miss	19	F	Farmer	England	U. States	Acasta	21 Oct 1825
Hannah, Mrs.	42	F	Farmer	England	U. States	Acasta	21 Oct 1825

NAMES OF PASSENGERS	AGE	SEX	OCCUPATIONS	COUNTRY TO WHICH THEY BELONG	COUNTRY THEY INTEND TO INHABIT	SHIPS/DATES OF ARRIVAL	
BASHAM (cont'd)							
James, Master	13	M	Farmer	England	U. States	Acasta	21 Oct 1825
John, Master	11	M	Farmer	England	U. States	Acasta	21 Oct 1825
Michael, Master	15	M	Farmer	England	U. States	Acasta	21 Oct 1825
William, Master	9	M	Farmer	England	U. States	Acasta	21 Oct 1825
BASHFORD, David	23	M	Brass founder	England	United States	Aurora	9 Jul 1827
BASHIN, Peter	34	M	Laborer	Germany	U. States	Hannibal	12 Oct 1829
BASKMAN, Sarah	26	F		Great Britain	U. States	Albert	1 Apr 1822
BASLE, James	24	M	Servant	Ireland	St. Johns	Nancy	3 Apr 1824
BASNIAN, —	22	M	Merct.	France	U.S.	Stephania	15 Aug 1825
BASON, Ann	5		Carpenter	England	United States	Corinthian	7 Jul 1829
BASQNER, —, Master	17	M	Merchant	Havana	Havana	Milo	15 May 1824
BASQUIN, E. J.	25	M	Merchant	Spain	U. States	Anne	20 Jun 1828
BASS, A. W.	30	M	None	Columbia	U. States	Theresa	10 Dec 1825
Eliza	25		Wife			Cambria	19 Oct 1829
James	50	M	Weaver	England		Marchioness	13 May 1828
Jane	1		his Daughter			Cambria	19 Oct 1829
Mexerno	14	M	Merchant	Florada	U. States	Annah	7 May 1825
P.	29	M	Merchant	U. States	U. States	Centurion	20 Aug 1828
Robert	32		Silk Weaver	Ireland	United States	Cambria	19 Oct 1829
Sarah	12		his Daughter			Cambria	19 Oct 1829
BASSET, William	25		Farmer	England	England	Hudson	4 Sep 1823
BASSETT, —, Mrs.	25	F			U. States	Congress	21 Nov 1823
Elias	25	M	Farmer	England	United States	Mary & Harriet	9 Mar 1829
F. C.	35	M	Mariner	Connecticut	United States	Hammond	9 Feb 1820
Fanny	25	F	Farmer	England	United States	Mary & Harriet	9 Mar 1829
Henry	1 6/12	M			U. States	Congress	21 Nov 1823
Jane		F		England	U. States	Milton	6 Dec 1825
William	2	M	None	England	United States	Mary & Harriet	9 Mar 1829
Wm.	30	M	Farmer	England	U. States	Congress	21 Nov 1823
BASSIEUX, John M.	45	M	Dancing Master	France	U.S. America	Gibraltar	12 Oct 1829
BASSORA, Jos.	24	M	Merchant	Spain	Spain	Ann	26 Feb 1825
BAST, Alice	1	F		Manchester	Lancaster	Howard Douglass	11 May 1827
Ann	3	F		Manchester	Lancaster	Howard Douglass	11 May 1827
Elizabeth	22	F		Manchester	Lancaster	Howard Douglass	11 May 1827
BASTABLE, Arthur	52		Merchant	Ireland	England	London	16 Aug 1824
Avasia	16			Ireland		London	16 Aug 1824
*Died 15th July							
William	16			England	England	Hudson	4 Sep 1823
BASTELL, Chas.	12	M	Schoolar	S. Croix	U. States	Jupiter	29 Jun 1825
BASTIAN, —, Mrs.	35	F	Hairdresser	Italy	U. States	Ariadne	15 Apr 1822
Barbery	4	F	Farmer	France	United States	Crescent	12 Jul 1827
Elizabeth	34	F	Farmer	France	United States	Crescent	12 Jul 1827
Gerry	7	M	Farmer	France	United States	Crescent	12 Jul 1827
Gerry	32	M	Farmer	France	United States	Crescent	12 Jul 1827
Jacob	9	M	Farmer	France	United States	Crescent	12 Jul 1827
Jno. F.	38	M	Merchant	New Haven	New Haven	Native	30 Jun 1826
Peter	35	M	Hairdresser	Italy	U. States	Ariadne	15 Apr 1822
BASTIEN, Johanna	32	F	None	Nassau, N.P.	U. States	Brown	8 Aug 1825
P. F.	28	F	None	Nassau, N.P.	U. States	Brown	8 Aug 1825
Theodore	4	M	None	Nassau, N.P.	U. States	Brown	8 Aug 1825
Wihelmina	5	F	None	Nassau, N.P.	U. States	Brown	8 Aug 1825
Wm.	8	M	None	Nassau, N.P.	U. States	Brown	8 Aug 1825
BASTINA, Alexander	24		Merchant	Germany	New York	Xenophon	25 Jul 1826
BASTINO, John	22	M	Music Grinder	Genoa		Olive Branch	9 Oct 1829
Sylvestus	24	M	Music Grinder	Genoa		Olive Branch	9 Oct 1829
BASTOCK, Ann	4	F		England	America	Thames	27 May 1822
Chas.	38		Merchant	Germany	U. States America	Maria	22 May 1822
Hannah	8	F		England	America	Thames	27 May 1822
John	44	M	Farmer	England	America	Thames	27 May 1822
Mary	13	M		England	America	Thames	27 May 1822
Mary	37	F		England	America	Thames	27 May 1822
Richard	infant	F		England	America	Thames	27 May 1822
William	15	M		England	America	Thames	27 May 1822
BASTON, Isac	27	M	Mariner	U. States	U. States	Pedler	27 May 1825
William	28	M	Instrument Maker	Great Britain	U. States	Ganges	21 Jun 1827

NAMES OF PASSENGERS	AGE	SEX	OCCUPATIONS	COUNTRY TO WHICH THEY BELONG	COUNTRY THEY INTEND TO INHABIT	SHIPS/DATES OF ARRIVAL	
BASTOUL, Peter Sernin	28	M	Taylor	France	United States	Montano	29 Apr 1826
BATAILLE, G.	24	M	Servant	Russia	Russia	New York	11 Mar 1823
Peter	46	M	Merchant	France		Edward Quesnel	17 Nov 1828
BATAMAN, Calvin	23	M	Mariner	Boston	Boston	St. Helena	18 Feb 1823
*Invalid from the U.S. Ship Cayenne, to be received in the Maine Hospital							
BATANCOURT,							
Justo Josef	53	M		Spain	Spain	Wallace	18 May 1825
BATBY, J.	18	M	Turner	France	United States	Joseph	11 Jul 1821
J.	40	F		France	United States	Joseph	11 Jul 1821
BATBY, James	20	M	Labourer	Great Brittain	United States	Active	12 Sep 1828
BATCHELER, Clarissa	32	F	Lady	England	United States	Richmond	4 Aug 1826
Margarett	1	F		England	United States	Richmond	4 Aug 1826
Mary Ann	10	F		England	United States	Richmond	4 Aug 1826
William	38	M	Merchant	United States	United States	Cambria	7 May 1828
BATCHELET, M.	40	M		France & Switzerland	U. States	Bayard	14 Jul 1826
BATCHELOR, Eliza C.	8	F		England	United States	Richmond	4 Aug 1826
James	6	M		England	United States	Richmond	4 Aug 1826
Mathew	25	M	Weaver	Great Britain	United States	Unity	20 Oct 1829
Wm. C.	16	M	Clerk	England	United States	Cambria	8 Oct 1828
BATCHLET, —	4/12	F		France & Switzerland	U. States	Bayard	14 Jul 1826
J.	18	F		France & Switzerland	U. States	Bayard	14 Jul 1826
J.	20	F		France & Switzerland	U. States	Bayard	14 Jul 1826
M.	30	F		France & Switzerland	U. States	Bayard	14 Jul 1826
BATE, Betsy	5	F		England	America	Plutarch	18 Jul 1826
Charles	27	M	Servant	Germany	N. York	France	29 Nov 1827
Christopher	27	M	Merchant	Hayti	U. States	Curlew	16 Jun 1823
Henry	2	M		England	America	Plutarch	18 Jul 1826
Henry	49	M	Farmer	England	America	Plutarch	18 Jul 1826
Mary	34	F		England	America	Plutarch	18 Jul 1826
BATELER, R., Lt. Col.	35	M	Lt.	England	America	Silas Richard	24 Oct 1829
BATEMAN, John	5	M		England	Newyork	Cortes	16 Jul 1827
Jos.	27	M	Engineer	London	U. States	Plato	18 Apr 1826
Mary	25	F		England	Newyork	Cortes	16 Jul 1827
BATES, ...	35	M	Merchant	Great Britain	United States	John Wells	18 Sep 1826
Ann	3	F		Great Britain	U. States	Ann Marria	6 Aug 1823
Ann	30	M	Weaver			Hercules	25 Sep 1820
Benjamin	6	M		England	U. States	Trident	1 Dec 1824
Betsey	4	F				Hercules	25 Sep 1820
Charles	5	M				Hercules	25 Sep 1820
Daniel	7	M		England	U. States	Trident	1 Dec 1824
Eliza	17	F	Spinster	Ireland	United States	Trident	17 May 1825
Eliza	30	F		G. Britain	U. States	Nimrod	31 Jul 1828
Eliza	44	F	None	Great Britain	U. States	Ann Marria	6 Aug 1823
Eliza A. S.	6			U. States	U. States	Silvanus Jenkins	30 Nov 1827
Elizabeth	20	F		England	America	Thames	27 May 1822
Emma	4	F		England	U. States	Trident	1 Dec 1824
George	14		None	Great Brittain	Great Brittain	Commerce	14 Mar 1823
George	83	M		England	America	Thames	27 May 1822
J. D.	25	M	Merchant	U. States	U. States	Emma	26 May 1827
James	3	M		G. Britain	U. States	Nimrod	31 Jul 1828
James	9	M				Hercules	25 Sep 1820
James	12	M		Great Britain	U. States	Ann Marria	6 Aug 1823
James	20	M	Labourer	Gt. Britain	U. States	Panthea	21 Jul 1825
James	23	M	Iron Roller	Gt. Britain	U.S. America	James Cropper	14 Mar 1828
James	28	M	Farmer	Ireland	U. States	Vermont	19 Mar 1827
James	40		Joiner	Great Brittain	Great Brittain	Commerce	14 Mar 1823
Jane	1	F		England	U. States	Cincinnatus	24 May 1821
Jno.	23	M	Joiner	England	United States	Nancy Henrietta	3 Nov 1828
Jno. D.	22	M	Merchant	U.S.	U.S.	Minerva	3 Dec 1821
Joel	4	M		G. Britain	U. States	Nimrod	31 Jul 1828
John	9	M		England	U. States	Trident	1 Dec 1824
John	12	M				Hercules	25 Sep 1820
John	13	M	Boy	Mexico	United States	Saluda	14 May 1827
John	21	M	Sawyer	England	U. States	Cincinnatus	24 May 1821

NAMES OF PASSENGERS	AGE	SEX	OCCUPATIONS	COUNTRY TO WHICH THEY BELONG	COUNTRY THEY INTEND TO INHABIT	SHIPS/DATES OF ARRIVAL	
BATES (cont'd)							
John	33		...ker	London, England	America	Frances Henrietta	31 May 1824
John	40	M	Seaman	U. States	United States	Brilliant	24 Sep 1827
John Douglas	23 5/12	M	Merchant	Boston	Boston	Florida	13 Jan 1827
Joseph	13	M		England	U. States	Trident	1 Dec 1824
Joseph	29			England		Anacreon	7 Sep 1827
Joseph	40	M	Farmer	G.B.	U.S.	Silvanus Jenkins	27 Jul 1829
Joshua	37	M	Merchant	U. States	U. States	Silvanus Jenkins	30 Nov 1827
Lucretia	33			U. States	U. States	Silvanus Jenkins	30 Nov 1827
Mary	34	F	Spinster	England	U. States	Trident	1 Dec 1824
Nathan	24		Sawyer	England	United States	Hudson	5 Apr 1826
Peter	30	M	Tailor	G. Brittain	America	Robin Hood	20 Jul 1827
R.	20	M	Merchant	America	America	Nancy	18 Aug 1821
Richard	7/12	M		England	U. States	Trident	1 Dec 1824
Samuel	24	M	Shoemaker	G. Britain	U. States	St. George	16 Jan 1829
Sarah	3	F		England	U. States	Cincinnatus	24 May 1821
Sarah	29		None	Prince George County, U.S.	America	Frances Henrietta	31 May 1824
Sarrah	infant	F		England	America	Thames	27 May 1822
Selina	11	F		England	U. States	Trident	1 Dec 1824
Siemon	2 1/12	M		England	U. States	Trident	1 Dec 1824
Susana	5	F		G. Britain	U. States	Nimrod	31 Jul 1828
Susannah	24	F		England	U. States	Cincinnatus	24 May 1821
Thomas	44	M		Great Britain	U. States	Ann Marria	6 Aug 1823
Thos.	43	M	Farmer	England	America	Erin	7 Nov 1821
Walter	40	M	Merchant	St. John, N.B.	St. John, N.B.	Nancy	2 May 1823
William	26	M	Sawyer	England	U. States	Cincinnatus	24 May 1821
William	31		Joiner	Great Brittain	Great Brittain	Commerce	14 Mar 1823
Willm.	18	M	Clerk	Ireland	United States	Dublin Packet	22 Apr 1822
Wm.	14	M		England	U. States	Trident	1 Dec 1824
Wm. R. Gray	12		Merchant	U. States	U. States	Silvanus Jenkins	30 Nov 1827
BATESON, Thomas	22	M	Joiner	England	United States	Lord Wellington	14 Nov 1827
BATEY, James	21	M	Laborer	Ireland	United States	Ann Maria	18 Dec 1827
James	22	M	Weaver	Ireland	United States	Commerce	13 Jun 1828
Sarah	20	F		Ireland	United States	Commerce	13 Jun 1828
BATH, —, Mrs.	40	F	Spinster	Somersetshire	United States	Bolivar	14 Sep 1826
Geo.	13	M	None	Somersetshire	United States	Bolivar	14 Sep 1826
John	30	M	Labourer	Drajheder	United States	Dalhousie Castle	27 Jul 1826
BATHELET, Benjamin	24	M	Dr. of Medicin	Great Britan	Great Britan	Columbia	11 Aug 1823
BATIEST, L.	40	M	Servant	France	France	Caravan	1 May 1824
BATISTER, Juann	47	M	Sailor	Portugal	Portugal	Jeune Antoinette	31 Oct 1829
Manuel	12	M	Sailor	Portugal	Portugal	Jeune Antoinette	31 Oct 1829
BATLEAF, Betsey	19	F		England	U. States	Panthea	22 Nov 1826
BATLIE, Peter	42	M	Merchant	France	France	Dromo	4 May 1827
BATONER, David	36	M	Merchant	U. States	U. States	Zephyr	2 Oct 1826
BATRE, Charles	30 8/12	M	Merchant	United States	United States	Cadmus	9 Dec 1825
BATREL, Thos.	14	M		United States	U. States	Splendid	1 Jul 1829
BATRES, Joses Peres	25	M	Gentleman	Spain	United States	Liberty	7 Aug 1821
BATSET, Hy. Geo.	23	M	Shoe Maker	Switzerland	U.S.	C. Amelia	30 Jun 1828
Piere	30	M	Weelwright	Switzerland	U.S.	C. Amelia	30 Jun 1828
BATSON, Frs.	23		Waiter	England	U.S. of America	Mary	21 Sep 1821
BATSOW, Josiah	25	M	Farmer	Great Britain	United States	Mary & Harriet	3 Jul 1829
Maria	20	F	None	Great Britain	United States	Mary & Harriet	3 Jul 1829
BATT, Flora	40	F	Farmer	France	U. States	Edward Quesnel	4 Aug 1828
George	24		Farmer	England	United States	Corinthian	30 May 1828
John	40	M	Farmer	France	U. States	Edward Quesnel	4 Aug 1828
Magdalina	18	F	Farmer	France	U. States	Edward Quesnel	4 Aug 1828
Theresa	20	F	Farmer	France	U. States	Edward Quesnel	4 Aug 1828
Walter	35		Farmer	England	United States	Mary	15 Jul 1822
Xavia	21	F	Farmer	France	U. States	Edward Quesnel	4 Aug 1828
BATTAILE, Theresa	31			Normandy	Havanna	Venus	4 Oct 1821
BATTE, A.	13	M	Gent	French	Switzerland	Charlemagne	19 Sep 1828
A.	18	M	Gent	French	Switzerland	Charlemagne	19 Sep 1828
A.	32	M	Gent	French	Switzerland	Charlemagne	19 Sep 1828
Ann	22	M	Gent	French	Switzerland	Charlemagne	19 Sep 1828
C.	42	F	Gent	French	Switzerland	Charlemagne	19 Sep 1828
J.	30	F	Gent	French	Switzerland	Charlemagne	19 Sep 1828
J. B.	15	M	Gent	French	Switzerland	Charlemagne	19 Sep 1828

NAMES OF PASSENGERS	AGE	SEX	OCCUPATIONS	COUNTRY TO WHICH THEY BELONG	COUNTRY THEY INTEND TO INHABIT	SHIPS/DATES OF ARRIVAL	
BATTE (cont'd)							
M.	12	F	Gent	French	Switzerland	Charlemagne	19 Sep 1828
M.	14	F	Gent	French	Switzerland	Charlemagne	19 Sep 1828
M.	39	F	Gent	French	Switzerland	Charlemagne	19 Sep 1828
S.	20	F	Gent	French	Switzerland	Charlemagne	19 Sep 1828
BATTEEN, B.	35	M	Farmer	Great Britain	United States	Isaac Hicks	6 Dec 1827
BATTEN, Thomas	14	M		G. Britain	G. Britain	Brittania	17 Jul 1828
Wm.	12	M	Shoemaker	England	United States	Euphrates	12 May 1823
BATTERBY, Francis	22	M	Weaver	Ireland	America	Wilson	16 May 1825
BATTERHILL, Ann	1	F		England	United States	Yobah	26 Sep 1827
James	6	M		England	United States	Yobah	26 Sep 1827
Susan	30	F		England	United States	Yobah	26 Sep 1827
BATTERLY, Margaret	6/12	F	None	Ireland	New York	America	1 Aug 1828
Margaret	26	F	None	Ireland	New York	America	1 Aug 1828
BATTERSBY, Thomas	21	M	Weaver	Ireland	America	Wilson	16 May 1825
BATTERSON,							
Thomas	20 9/12	M	Shoe Maker	England	America	Minerva	15 Jun 1825
BATTIE, Ann	60		Farmer	Halifax	U. States	Edwin	26 Sep 1828
James	19	M	Stone Cutter	Great Britain	United States	Brutus	6 May 1828
BATTISTE, Catherine	16	F	Family [of John]	France	America	La Grange	7 Aug 1828
Francis	14	F	Family [of John]	France	America	La Grange	7 Aug 1828
John	40	M	Farmer	France	America	La Grange	7 Aug 1828
Luisa	2	F	Family [of John]	France	America	La Grange	7 Aug 1828
Maria	8	F	Family [of John]	France	America	La Grange	7 Aug 1828
Maria	40	F	Family [of John]	France	America	La Grange	7 Aug 1828
BATTLE, Michael	19	M	Tailor	Ireland	Und. Stts of America	Alexander Mansfield	18 Aug 1826
BATTON, Joseph	43	M	Clothier	England	Alexandria, U.S.	Roman	17 Oct 1826
BATY, Elizabeth	40	F		Ireland	U. States	Lewis	17 Sep 1821
Jno.	39	M	None	Great Britain	United States	Comet	9 Aug 1822
Thos.	10	M		Ireland	U. States	Lewis	17 Sep 1821
BATYEL, Robt.	22	M	Farmer	Ireland	Ohio	Commerce	24 Sep 1823
BAU, Adam F.	20	M	Mason	France	United States	New England	29 Aug 1828
BAUBARD, J.	19	M	Tailor	Guadaloupe	Guadaloupe	Orra Maria	18 Oct 1823
BAUER, Adam	11	M	Child	Germany	New York	Lewis	29 Oct 1825
Angelique	10	F	One Family [Pierre]	France	United States	Henri IV	2 Oct 1828
Antoine	8	M	One Family [Pierre]	France	United States	Henri IV	2 Oct 1828
Barbara	1	F		France	America, U.N.S.	Great Britain	3 Aug 1829
Barbara	30	F		France	America, U.N.S.	Great Britain	3 Aug 1829
Catharine	31	F	Wife	Germany	New York	Lewis	29 Oct 1825
Catherine	58	F	his Wife [Frederick]	Germany	United States	Helen	5 Sep 1828
Cathrene	10	F	One Family [Pierre]	France	United States	Henri IV	2 Oct 1828
Christian	4	M	Child	Germany	New York	Lewis	29 Oct 1825
Conrad	28	M	there child [Frederick & Catherine]	Germany	United States	Helen	5 Sep 1828
Elizabeth	17	F	there child [Frederick & Catherine]	Germany	United States	Helen	5 Sep 1828
Ernestine	15	M		France	U. States	Edward Bopnnaffe	30 Jul 1829
Francoise	36	M	Waiter	France	U. States	Leonarde	29 Aug 1828
Francoise	42	M	One Family [Pierre]	France	United States	Henri IV	2 Oct 1828
Frederica	37	F		France	U. States	Edward Bopnnaffe	30 Jul 1829
Frederick	9	M		France	U. States	Edward Bopnnaffe	30 Jul 1829
Frederick	60	M	Farmer	Germany	United States	Helen	5 Sep 1828
Fredk.	45	M	Gent	Denmark	U. States	Chase	5 Oct 1824
George	38	M	Mechanic	Germany	New York	Lewis	29 Oct 1825
Gustave	16	M		France	U. States	Edward Bopnnaffe	30 Jul 1829
Henri	27	M	Miller	France	America, U.N.S.	Great Britain	3 Aug 1829
James	14	M	there child [Frederick & Catherine]	Germany	United States	Helen	5 Sep 1828
Jean Batiste	2	M	One Family [Pierre]	France	United States	Henri IV	2 Oct 1828
Johan Adam	45	M	Miller	Germany	U. States	Three Brothers	21 Mar 1825
Johannes	18	M	Baker	Germany	U. States	Three Brothers	21 Mar 1825

NAMES OF PASSENGERS	AGE	SEX	OCCUPATIONS	COUNTRY TO WHICH THEY BELONG	COUNTRY THEY INTEND TO INHABIT	SHIPS/DATES OF ARRIVAL	
BAUER (cont'd)							
John	7	M	Child	Germany	New York	Lewis	29 Oct 1825
Kraff	17	M		France	U. States	Edward Bopnnaffe	30 Jul 1829
Mary	17	F	One Family [Pierre]	France	United States	Henri IV	2 Oct 1828
Peter	12	M	One Family [Pierre]	France	United States	Henri IV	2 Oct 1828
Philip	42	M	Laborer	France	U. States	Edward Bopnnaffe	30 Jul 1829
Pierre	54	M	Farmer	France	United States	Henri IV	2 Oct 1828
Veronique	44	F	One Family [Pierre]	France	United States	Henri IV	2 Oct 1828
BAULDERY, Felix	14		Planter	France		Bayard	10 Sep 1827
Julian	18		Planter	France		Bayard	10 Sep 1827
Louise	18		Planter	France		Bayard	10 Sep 1827
BAULIOT, Perre	25	M	Clerk	France		Pallas	14 Jun 1828
BAULLET, Julius	4	M	(Boy)	U. States	U. States	Mary	14 Nov 1822
BAUM, Fredk.	20 6/12	M	Gentleman	Germany	U. States	Minerva	9 Feb 1829
BAUMAN, Elizabeth	3	F		Swiss	United States	Iris	21 Sep 1821
Elizth.	23	F	Merchant	Switzerland	United States	Factor	1 Sep 1823
Petrus	26	M	Farmer	Swiss	United States	Iris	21 Sep 1821
Susannah	24	F		Swiss	United States	Iris	21 Sep 1821
BAUMINE, M.		F		France	United States	Catharine	10 Sep 1827
BAUMY, Lewis	44	M	Fringe Maker	France		Edward Quesnel	17 Nov 1828
BAUR, Augusta	1	M		Brattain		L'Esperance	6 Sep 1828
Cathr.	9	F		Brattain		L'Esperance	6 Sep 1828
Conrad	28	M	Tanner	Swiss	United States	Elizabeth	4 Sep 1826
Johan Nepomuck	24	M	Merchant	Mösskirch	Germany	Bayard	30 Oct 1820
Joseph	6	M		Brattain		L'Esperance	6 Sep 1828
Joseph	32	M	Shoemaker	Brattain		L'Esperance	6 Sep 1828
Margt.	10	F		Brattain		L'Esperance	6 Sep 1828
Margt.	29	F		Brattain		L'Esperance	6 Sep 1828
Susanna	30	F	Wife	Swiss	United States	Elizabeth	4 Sep 1826
BAUVIER, M.	30	M	Gentleman	Spain	Porto Rico	Edward Quesnel	15 May 1826
BAVERS, James	22	M	Farmer	England	Ut. States	Courier	13 Jul 1826
BAVIN, John	39	M	Labourer	England	United States	Alexander Mansfield	16 Sep 1823
*Died Sept. 2d, 1823							
BAVIS, William	28	M	Farmer	C. Armannar [Armagh or Farmanagh?]	Boston	Nile	18 Aug 1829
BAVRIRAS, Juan	32	M	Marchant	Nassau	New Providence	Sea Flower	24 Jun 1824
BAWFIELD, ...	30	M	Miner	Great Briton	U. States	Leontine	10 Jul 1826
BAWITTA, J.	22	M	Merchant	Spain	Havana	Robert Fulton	11 Jan 1825
BAWMAR, —,							
child of Mrs. Bawmar	2	M		Guadaloupe	U. States	Turner	8 Jun 1824
—, child of Mrs. Bawmar	5	F		Guadaloupe	U. States	Turner	8 Jun 1824
—, Mrs.	40	F	Lady	Guadaloupe	U. States	Turner	8 Jun 1824
BAXTER, —,							
2 children	2, etc.			England	Canada	Thames	6 Oct 1820
B. C.	25	M	Merchant	Connecticutt	U. States	Spermo	12 Aug 1826
Benjn.	20	M	Baker	Utica, U.S., of British Parents	Utica	Aldebaron	21 Jan 1826
Benjn.	24	M		Great Brittan	U.S.	Florida	17 May 1825
David	25	M	Weaver	Ireland	United States	Josephine	30 Apr 1828
G.	23	M	Merchant	United States	United States	Orion	1 Feb 1820
George	9	M		Gt. Britain	U. States	Diana	28 Apr 1828
Henry	32	M	Mason	Gt. Britain	U. States	Diana	28 Apr 1828
Jam...	61	F	Wife of William	England	United States	Aurelia	7 Jun 1826
Jane	28	F	None	N. York	U. States	Sarah G	7 May 1827
Jas.	40			Great Britain	U. States America	Maria	22 May 1822
John	19	M	Farmer	Scotland	Alibama	Indian Chief	19 Jun 1823
John	24	M	Labourer	G. Britain	U. States	St. George	7 Jun 1828
John	50	M	Labourer	Great Britain	United States	Blakely	29 Sep 1826
Joseph	2	M		Gt. Britain	U. States	Diana	28 Apr 1828
Josephine	33	F	Spinster	U. States	U. States	Chase	20 Jul 1826
Maria, Mrs.	25	F		England	Canada	Thames	6 Oct 1820
Mary	30	F		Gt. Britain	U. States	Diana	28 Apr 1828
Mary Ann	22	F	daughter [of William]	England	United States	Aurelia	7 Jun 1826

NAMES OF PASSENGERS	AGE	SEX	OCCUPATIONS	COUNTRY TO WHICH THEY BELONG	COUNTRY THEY INTEND TO INHABIT	SHIPS/DATES OF ARRIVAL	
BAXTER (cont'd)							
Patrick	19	M	Laborer	Ireland	United States	Weser	29 Jul 1823
Richard	24	M	Baker	Utica, U.S., of British Parents	Utica	Aldebaron	21 Jan 1826
Sophronia	25	F		America	America	Clio	1 Dec 1823
Timothy	30	M	Merchant	U. States	U. States	Hudson	13 Jan 1827
Timothy, Mr.	33	M	Gentleman	England	Canada	Thames	6 Oct 1820
William	7	M		Gt. Britain	U. States	Diana	28 Apr 1828
William	20	M	Clerk	England	Pennsylvania	Governor Fenner	23 Jul 1829
William	64	M	Gardiner	England	United States	Aurelia	7 Jun 1826
BAXTON, Joshua	26	M	Cabinet Maker	United States	United States	Pilot	27 Feb 1826
BAYAND, —	35	M	Merchant	France	United States	Sisters	24 Jan 1820
BAYARD, A.	20	M	Merchant	France	U. States	Seine	16 Jun 1826
E.	20	F	None	U. States	United States	Marmione	20 Nov 1821
R.	27	M	Merchant	U. States	United States	Marmione	20 Nov 1821
Samuel	20	M	Doctor	Great Britain	Great Britan	Nancy	13 Dec 1822
Wm.	9/12	M	None	U. States	United States	Marmione	20 Nov 1821
BAYBEY, Joseph	2...	M	Laborer	Irland	United States	Nancy	28 Oct 1822
BAYER, Goldsborough							
Le Rey	23	M		United States		Britannia	20 Jun 1827
Jacobine	24	M	Butcher	Bardin	U. States	Bayard	5 Sep 1828
Joseph	25	M	Cabinet Maker	Bardin	U. States	Bayard	5 Sep 1828
Peter	42	M	Merchant	France	U. States	Ann Maria	11 May 1822
Robert	32	M	Farmer	Great Britain	United States	Corinthian	2 Sep 1824
BAYFIELD, Henry, Capt.	38	M	Royal Navy	England	Canada	Brighton	24 Aug 1827
BAYGAIN, Joseph	25	M	Merchant	France	U.S.	Bayard	10 Nov 1824
BAYHUE, Edward	45		Mason	Birmingham, Eng./Birmingham, Eng.	New York	Venus	12 Apr 1821
Margaret, Mrs.	46			F.../Birmingham, Eng.	New York	Venus	12 Apr 1821
BAYLE, Eliza	27	F	Wife	Great Britain	United States	Washington	3 Sep 1827
James	22		Farmer	Ireland		Westmoreland	1 Aug 1826
Philip	26	M	Labourer	England	U. States	Ayrshire	12 May 1828
BAYLES, Ann	3	F		London	U. States	Robert Fulton	9 Feb 1822
Charles	36	M	Farmer	Great Britain	United States	Robert Fulton	22 Oct 1821
Sarah	35	F		Stratfordshire	U. States	Robert Fulton	9 Feb 1822
BAYLEY, Ann	15	F	None	Great Britain	United States	Isaac Hicks	22 Aug 1828
Ann	42	F	None	Great Britain	United States	Isaac Hicks	22 Aug 1828
Barnard	30	M	Merchant	London	U. States	New York	15 Nov 1823
Benjamin	11	M	None	Great Britain	United States	Isaac Hicks	22 Aug 1828
E.	7	F	Child	Great Britain	United States	Washington	3 Sep 1827
Elizabeth	16	F	None	Great Britain	United States	Isaac Hicks	22 Aug 1828
Francis	31	M	Mariner	Great Britain	United States	Washington	3 Sep 1827
Hannah	9	F	None	Great Britain	United States	Isaac Hicks	22 Aug 1828
J.	38	M	Joiner	Gt. Britan	U. States	Sarah Skeafe	10 Sep 1827
John	18	M	Clerk	Ireland	United States	Dublin Packet	22 Aug 1829
John	20	M	Farmer	Great Britain	United States	Isaac Hicks	22 Aug 1828
John	51	M	Farmer	Great Britain	United States	Isaac Hicks	22 Aug 1828
Joseph	9	M	None	Great Britain	United States	Isaac Hicks	22 Aug 1828
Mary	5	F	Child	Great Britain	United States	Washington	3 Sep 1827
Mary	13	F	None	Great Britain	United States	Isaac Hicks	22 Aug 1828
Richd.	50	M	Merchant	America	U. States	William Byrnes	17 Jul 1825
Robert	19	M	Merchant	Newberry Port	Newberry Port	Francis Jarvis	30 Aug 1826
Samuel	23	M	Weaver	C. Tirone	Ohione	Nile	18 Aug 1829
Sarah	5	F	None	Great Britain	United States	Isaac Hicks	22 Aug 1828
Wm.	13	M		Gt. Britan	U. States	Sarah Skeafe	10 Sep 1827
BAYLIES, Edmund	30	M	Merchant	United States	United States	James Monroe	14 Dec 1820
Francis	24	M	Merchant	U. States	U. States	Mora	30 Apr 1827
Wm.	20	M	...	G. Britain	U. States	Cosmo	15 May 1827
BAYLLEIN, Patt	25	M	Weaver	Ireland	America	Plutarch	18 Jul 1826
BAYLLENS Y SOVORE,							
Juan	38	M	Gentn.	Spain	Spain	Fabius	2 Oct 1826
BAYLON, Mary	20	M	Shoemaker	G. Britain	U. States	America	17 Oct 1825
BAYLOR, Michael	25	M	Gardner	G. Britain	U. States	America	17 Oct 1825
BAYMAN, Wm.	36	M	Mariner	Bermuda	Bermuda	Eclipse	14 Feb 1820
BAYNALL, Ann	46	F	Farmer	Great Britain	U. States	Eliza Grant	29 Aug 1829
George	21	M	Farmer	Great Britain	U. States	Eliza Grant	29 Aug 1829
Jane	7	F	Farmer	Great Britain	U. States	Eliza Grant	29 Aug 1829

NAMES OF PASSENGERS	AGE	SEX	OCCUPATIONS	COUNTRY TO WHICH THEY BELONG	COUNTRY THEY INTEND TO INHABIT	SHIPS/DATES OF ARRIVAL	
BAYNALL (cont'd)							
Mary	17	F	Farmer	Great Britain	U. States	Eliza Grant	29 Aug 1829
Sarah Ann	13	F	Farmer	Great Britain	U. States	Eliza Grant	29 Aug 1829
Thomas	3	M	Farmer	Great Britain	U. States	Eliza Grant	29 Aug 1829
Thomas	43	M	Farmer	Great Britain	U. States	Eliza Grant	29 Aug 1829
William	18	M	Farmer	Great Britain	U. States	Eliza Grant	29 Aug 1829
BAYNES, Alice	11/12	F	None	England	Pennsylvania	Indian Chief	16 Aug 1822
B.	27	M	Farmer	England	U. States	Orazimbo	7 Jan 1821
Bizan	4	M	None	England	Pennsylvania	Indian Chief	16 Aug 1822
Elizabeth	11	F	None	England	Pennsylvania	Indian Chief	16 Aug 1822
Elizabeth	46	F	None	England	Pennsylvania	Indian Chief	16 Aug 1822
Fanny	14	F	None	England	Pennsylvania	Indian Chief	16 Aug 1822
Hannah	18	F	None	England	Pennsylvania	Indian Chief	16 Aug 1822
Hy. J.	36	M	Domestic	England	U. States	James Cropper	10 Jun 1823
James	46	M	Farmer	England	Pennsylvania	Indian Chief	16 Aug 1822
John	16	M	None	England	Pennsylvania	Indian Chief	16 Aug 1822
John, Inf.		M		Great Britain	United States	Mary Howland	19 Jul 1827
Mary	9	F	None	England	Pennsylvania	Indian Chief	16 Aug 1822
Mary	23	F		Great Britain	United States	Mary Howland	19 Jul 1827
Miriam	6	F	None	England	Pennsylvania	Indian Chief	16 Aug 1822
Thomas	2	M		Great Britain	United States	Mary Howland	19 Jul 1827
Thomas	13	M	None	England	Pennsylvania	Indian Chief	16 Aug 1822
BAYNOR, John	24	M	Merchant	Leiden	N. York	Manhattan	21 May 1821
BAYRA, Chas.	26	M	Farmer	Ireland	England	Josephine	8 Jan 1827
BAYS, Frederick	25	M	Dye Sinker	Great Britain	U. States	Robert Fulton	3 Dec 1827
John	18 11/12	M	Weaver	G. Britain	United States	Louisa	14 Jun 1825
BAYWEH, Hannah	6	F		England	U. States	Oglethorpe	9 Nov 1824
Hannah	46	F		England	U. States	Oglethorpe	9 Nov 1824
BAYWEN, Joseph	50	M	Farmer	England	U. States	Oglethorpe	9 Nov 1824
BAZIRE, S.	28	F	Min	France		Antioch	18 Aug 1829
BE..., Barbara	29	F		Switzerland	United States	Elbe	2 Aug 1822
BE...ENOR, Stephen	22	M	Farmer	England	U. States	Hercules	6 Jul 1827
BEACH, H. C.	29	M	Mercht.	U.S.	U.S.	Edward Quesnel	21 Apr 1827
M. G.	10	M				Lady of the Lake	23 Aug 1828
Mary	31	F				Lady of the Lake	23 Aug 1828
Susan	8	F				Lady of the Lake	23 Aug 1828
William	39	M	Mariner	U.S. America		Ospray	30 Jul 1827
William	45	M	Mariner	U. States	United States	Fox	9 Mar 1829
BEACHAM, ...	33	F	Carpenter	United States	United States	Globe	30 Aug 1828
...l...dies	6	M		United States	United States	Globe	30 Aug 1828
Catharine	30	F		United States	United States	Globe	30 Aug 1828
George	8	M		United States	United States	Globe	30 Aug 1828
Michael	4	M		United States	United States	Globe	30 Aug 1828
BEACHIN, Chars.	32	M	Farmer	England	U. States	Emily	25 Aug 1827
George	5	M		England	U. States	Emily	25 Aug 1827
Harriot	3	F		England	U. States	Emily	25 Aug 1827
Jesse	18/12	M		England	U. States	Emily	25 Aug 1827
Sarah	9	F		England	U. States	Emily	25 Aug 1827
Sarah, Mrs.	26	F		England	U. States	Emily	25 Aug 1827
BEACOOK, John	29	M	Teacher	Great Brittain	United States	Cortes	18 Oct 1820
BEADIN, James	33	M	Labourer	G. Britain	U. States	Hanford	18 Sep 1828
BEADS,							
Joze Sanchez, Don	25	M	... in Spanish ...	Spain	Spain	James Monroe	5 Apr 1820
BEAK, Coffur	4	F		United	U. States	Sarah G	30 Jun 1828
Henry	6	F		United	U. States	Sarah G	30 Jun 1828
Joseph	1	M		United	U. States	Sarah G	30 Jun 1828
Mary	8	F		United	U. States	Sarah G	30 Jun 1828
Mary Jane		F		Ireland	U. States	Sarah G	30 Jun 1828
BEAK..., Barbara	37	F	his wife [Heny]	France	United States	Helen	5 Sep 1828
Elizabeth	8	F	there child [Heny & Barbara]	France	United States	Helen	5 Sep 1828
George	1	M	there child [Heny & Barbara]	France	United States	Helen	5 Sep 1828
Henry	4	M	there child [Heny & Barbara]	France	United States	Helen	5 Sep 1828
Heny	...	M	Black...th	France, Calsaic	United States	Helen	5 Sep 1828

NAMES OF PASSENGERS	AGE	SEX	OCCUPATIONS	COUNTRY TO WHICH THEY BELONG	COUNTRY THEY INTEND TO INHABIT	SHIPS/DATES OF ARRIVAL	
BEAK... (cont'd)							
Magdelene	6	F	there child [Heny & Barbara]	France	United States	Helen	5 Sep 1828
BEAL, John	42	M	Carpenter	England	New York	Governor Fenner	23 Jul 1829
Joshua	30	M	Brewer	England	United States	Nancy Henrietta	3 Nov 1828
Stephen	26	M	Labourer	Great Britain	United States	Juno	5 Oct 1822
Thomas J.			Distressed Seaman	Virginia	U. States	Mary & Eliza	2 Jul 1829
Wm.	29	M	Farmer	Gt. Britain	United States	Europa	20 Apr 1825
BEALBY, Esther	60	F	None	England	Pittsburgh	Orozimbo	8 Jun 1822
BEALE, David	11	M	None	England	United States	Colossus	26 Aug 1828
Elizabeth	39	F	None	England	United States	Colossus	26 Aug 1828
Elizabeth	72	F	None	England	United States	Colossus	26 Aug 1828
Emma	7	F	None	England	United States	Colossus	26 Aug 1828
Hannah	9	F	None	England	United States	Colossus	26 Aug 1828
Hashia	14	M	None	England	United States	Colossus	26 Aug 1828
Jabez M.	1 9/12	M	None	England	United States	Colossus	26 Aug 1828
John	24	M	Merchant	Eastport	United States	Champion	3 Nov 1827
Sophia	8	F	None	England	United States	Colossus	26 Aug 1828
Thomas	43	M	Farmer	England	United States	Colossus	26 Aug 1828
Thomas A.	4	M	None	England	United States	Colossus	26 Aug 1828
BEALLIO, Heppolite	29	M	Merchant	Hayti	return to Haity	Vernon	17 Dec 1828
BEALY, Argadon	4	F		Germany	United States	Samuel Robertson	8 Aug 1828
John Batias	5/12	M		Germany	United States	Samuel Robertson	8 Aug 1828
Joseph	10	M		Germany	United States	Samuel Robertson	8 Aug 1828
Marion	40	F		Germany	United States	Samuel Robertson	8 Aug 1828
Martin	12	M		Germany	United States	Samuel Robertson	8 Aug 1828
Martin	40	M		Germany	United States	Samuel Robertson	8 Aug 1828
Patrik	20/12	M		Great Britain	U. States	Lady Hunter	28 May 1823
Saml.	23			England	U.N. States	Helen	17 Dec 1827
BEAM, Christopher	28	M	Butcher	Germany	United States	Ohio	10 Jul 1820
BEAMISH, Francis	25	M	Farmer	Ireland	U.S. America	Traveller	10 Sep 1827
Mary	22	F		Ireland	U.S. America	Traveller	10 Sep 1827
Samuel	7/12			Ireland	U.S. America	Traveller	10 Sep 1827
BEAN, Dennis	24	M	Cordwinder	Ireland	America	John Adams	2 Aug 1827
Francis	27	M	Stone Layer	Scotland	United States	Indus	5 Sep 1827
Mary	20	F		Ireland	America	John Adams	2 Aug 1827
Patrick	30	M	Gardner	Ireland	America	John Adams	2 Aug 1827
Reuben	28	M	Baker	Gt. Britain	United States	Robert Edwards	1 Jun 1826
Sarah	28	F		Gt. Britain	United States	Robert Edwards	1 Jun 1826
BEANE, P.	30	M	Merchant	W. Indis	W. Indis	Hiram	8 Jul 1828
BEANES, Edmond	11	M	Servant	England	U. States	Manhattan	12 Jun 1824
BEANEY, Eliza	13					Cincinnatus	29 Apr 1822
Eliza	16					Cincinnatus	29 Apr 1822
Elvina	9					Cincinnatus	29 Apr 1822
Harriot	11					Cincinnatus	29 Apr 1822
James	7					Cincinnatus	29 Apr 1822
Samuel	15					Cincinnatus	29 Apr 1822
BEANY, Samuel	18		Farmer	England	England	London	16 Aug 1824
BEAR, Mary	40	F	None	Bermuda	U. States	Orlando	28 Sep 1826
Wm.	40			England	U. States	Corinthian	8 Oct 1828
BEARCROFT, James	30	M		Great Britain	U. States	Ann Marria	6 Aug 1823
Jane	21	F		Great Britain	U. States	Ann Marria	6 Aug 1823
BEARD, Alexander	6	M	Shoe Maker	England	America	William	21 Sep 1821
James	2	M	Shoe Maker	England	America	William	21 Sep 1821
James	30	M	Mariner	U. States	U. States	Bordeaux	12 Apr 1822
Jane		F	Shoe Maker	England	America	William	21 Sep 1821
Jane	34	F	Shoe Maker	England	America	William	21 Sep 1821
John	...3	M	Labourer	Ireland	United States	Meteor	26 Jun 1827
John	4	M	Shoe Maker	England	America	William	21 Sep 1821
Mat.	20	M	Farmer	Limerick	N. York	Thomas & William	25 May 1827
Wm.	22	M	Student	United States	United States	Sarah G	11 Sep 1827
Wm.	23	M	Farmer	Ireland	U. States	Edward	15 Jul 1825

NAMES OF PASSENGERS	AGE	SEX	OCCUPATIONS	COUNTRY TO WHICH THEY BELONG	COUNTRY THEY INTEND TO INHABIT	SHIPS/DATES OF ARRIVAL	
BEARDE, William, Jur.	14	M	Student	United States	United States	Sarah G	11 Sep 1827
BEARMAN, Margt.	32	F		Germany	United States	Belmont	30 Aug 1828
Martin	35	M	Sugar boiler	Germany	United States	Belmont	30 Aug 1828
BEARNUTT, Saml., Mr.	61	M	Cordwiner	Connecticut	New haven	South America	29 Aug 1826
BEARSONN, Robert	32			b. Carghuo, last of Westmoreland	Ohio	Peru	30 May 1828
BEARTOWN, Cathr.	49	F		Nova Scotia	U. States	Wanderer	1 Sep 1828
Charles	10	M		New Haven	U. States	Wanderer	1 Sep 1828
Philip	48	M	Farmer	Nova Scotia	U. States	Wanderer	1 Sep 1828
BEASDALER, W.	22	M	Merchant	N. York	U. States	Lyon	5 Jul 1825
BEASLY, Gollial	19	M		Germany	U. States	Rook	25 Jul 1827
J.	21	M	Shoemaker	Germany	U. States	Rook	25 Jul 1827
BEASON, John	32	M	Manufacturer	Scotland	United States	Shakespeare	24 Jul 1828
Mary	28	F		Scotland	United States	Shakespeare	24 Jul 1828
BEATIE, Janmes	30	M	Laborer or Spinster	Ireland	United States	Frances Miller	27 Jul 1827
BEATON, George	24	M	Farmer	Scotland	U.S. of America	Friends	10 May .1823
Janett	26	F		Scotland	U.S. of America	Friends	10 May 1823
BEATTEE, Francis	44	M	Mercht.	G. Britain	Canada	Adrianna	5 Sep 1823
BEATTERY, Ann	38	F		Great Britain	U. States	Lady Hunter	28 May 1823
Cathrin	8	F		Great Britain	U. States	Lady Hunter	28 May 1823
John	5	M		Great Britain	U. States	Lady Hunter	28 May 1823
BEATTIE, Hugh	26 1/12	M	Surgeon	Demerara	United States	Visitor	21 Jul 1823
James	22	M	Tailor	Scotland	United States	Tom	2 Jul 1827
BEATTY, Alexander	60	M	Farmer	Ireland	U. States	Henry Kneeland	27 Jul 1825
Alexander, Jr.	11	M	None	Ireland	U. States	Henry Kneeland	27 Jul 1825
Alexr.	21	M	Blacksmith	Ireland	U. States of America	Courier	17 Mar 1827
Andrew	1	M		Great Britain	United States	Meridian	2 Jul 1827
Ann	3	F		Great Britain	United States	Meridian	2 Jul 1827
Ann	13	F	None	Ireland	U. States	Henry Kneeland	27 Jul 1825
Charlotte	6	F		Great Britain	United States	Meridian	2 Jul 1827
Elisabeth	40	F	Servant	Ireland	U.States	Nancy	31 May 1823
Elisabeth	50	F	None	Ireland	U. States	Henry Kneeland	27 Jul 1825
Gordon	1 1/2	M		Great Britain	United States	Meridian	2 Jul 1827
Jane	24	F		Great Britain	United States	Meridian	2 Jul 1827
Jane	29	F		Great Britain	United States	Meridian	2 Jul 1827
Jno.	21	M	Lawyer	U. States	U. States	Eliza	26 Jul 1825
John	10	M		Great Britain	United States	Meridian	2 Jul 1827
John	23		Farmer			Amphion	31 May 1824
Joseph	4	F		Great Britain	United States	Meridian	2 Jul 1827
Maria	20	F		England	United States	Dalhouse Castle	8 May 1827
Mary	5	F		Great Britain	United States	Meridian	2 Jul 1827
Richard	30	M	Weaver	Great Britain	United States	Colossus	5 Jun 1827
Robert	17	M	None	Ireland	U. States	Henry Kneeland	27 Jul 1825
Robert	31	M	Farmer	Great Britain	United States	Meridian	2 Jul 1827
Thomas	18	M	None	Ireland	U. States	Henry Kneeland	27 Jul 1825
Wm.	28	M	Labourer	G. Britain	U. States	St. George	7 Jun 1828
BEATY, Anne	19	F		Ireland	United States	Meteor	27 Sep 1826
Bridget	30	F		Ireland	United States	Nancy R. Crowell	21 Sep 1822
David	23	M	Hatter	Ireland	America States	Beaver	18 Aug 1827
Elisbath	38	F	Spinster	Ireland	United States	Fabius	31 Jul 1829
Eliza	12	F		Ireland	United States	Meteor	27 Sep 1826
Geo.	37	M	Farmer	Great Britain	U. States	Yamacraw	4 Sep 1822
James	23	M	Soap Boiler	Ireland	U. States	Josephine	30 Aug 1828
Jane	22	F		Ireland	United States	Meteor	27 Sep 1826
Jas.	17	M	Farmer			Commerce	22 Jun 1825
John	9	M		Ireland	United States	Meteor	27 Sep 1826
John	24	M	Labourer	Ireland	United States	Robert Fulton	10 Aug 1827
John	42	M	Labourer	Ireland	United States	Fabius	31 Jul 1829
Joshua	24	M	Labourer	G. Britain	U. States	London	23 Sep 1828
Josiah	14	M	Farmer	Ireland	United States	Meteor	27 Sep 1826
Margaret	24	F	Spinster	Ireland	United States	Dublin Packet	29 Jun 1825
Margeret	17	F	Spinster	Ireland	United States	Robert Fulton	10 Aug 1827
Maria	21	F		Ireland	United States	Meteor	27 Sep 1826
Martha	50	F	Wife	Ireland	United States	Meteor	27 Sep 1826
Rebeca	25	F		Ireland	America States	Beaver	18 Aug 1827
Robert	19 6/12	M	Weaver	Ireland	U. States	Courier	17 Mar 1828
Robert	55	M	Farmer	Ireland	United States	Meteor	27 Sep 1826

NAMES OF PASSENGERS	AGE	SEX	OCCUPATIONS	COUNTRY TO WHICH THEY BELONG	COUNTRY THEY INTEND TO INHABIT	SHIPS/DATES OF ARRIVAL	
BEATY (cont'd)							
Rowland	19	M	Labourer	Ireland	United States	Robert Fulton	10 Aug 1827
Thomas	18	M	Farmer	Ireland	United States	Dublin Packet	13 Oct 1828
BEAU, Luaque	22		Boucher [butcher]	Suisse		Deux Ernest	29 Dec 1827
BEAUBIEN, Derevier	36	M	Mercht.	America	America	Henry	11 Oct 1825
BEAUBIER, Piere	31	M	Physician	Canada	U. States	Edward Bonaffe	11 Dec 1827
BEAUCHAMP, T., Col.	40	M	Merchant	Switzerland	U. States	Laveria	23 Jul 1828
BEAUCHET, J.	26	F		Holland	U. States	Talma	23 Sep 1828
BEAUCKAMON, E.	10	F	Spinster	Ireland		Robert Fulton	4 Jun 1828
BEAUDE, P.	25	M	Jeweller	France	U. States	Montano	2 Sep 1828
BEAUERMEL,							
Michel Dean Marie	27	M	Clerk	France	United States	Montano	8 May 1827
BEAUFIA, Francis	22 9/12	M	Merchant	Hayti	return to Haity	Vernon	17 Dec 1828
BEAUFILS, P.	24 10/12	M	Merchant	France	U. States	Jaine Louis	24 Aug 1820
BEAUFOY, Mart.	30	M	Mariner	Great Britain	U. States	Emma	25 Feb 1826
BEAUMENT, Nelson	23	M	Silk Dyer	Great Britain	United States	Samuel Wright	12 Oct 1829
BEAUMON, Darby	12	M	Farmer	Great Britain	United States	Frances Henrietta	17 Sep 1827
Francis	2	M	Farmer	Great Britain	United States	Frances Henrietta	17 Sep 1827
James	8	M	Farmer	Great Britain	United States	Frances Henrietta	17 Sep 1827
James	41	M	Farmer	Great Britain	United States	Frances Henrietta	17 Sep 1827
Jane	12	F	Spinster	..., ..., England	Philadelphia	New Orleans	24 Aug 1827
Johanna	4	M	Farmer	Great Britain	United States	Frances Henrietta	17 Sep 1827
Martha	9	F	Spinster	..., ..., England	Philadelphia	New Orleans	24 Aug 1827
Martha	35	F	Spinster	..., ..., England	Philadelphia	New Orleans	24 Aug 1827
Mary	13	F	Farmer	Great Britain	United States	Frances Henrietta	17 Sep 1827
N.	6	M	Farmer	Great Britain	United States	Frances Henrietta	17 Sep 1827
Rhody	10	M	Farmer	Great Britain	United States	Frances Henrietta	17 Sep 1827
Sarah	40	F		Great Britain	United States	Frances Henrietta	17 Sep 1827
BEAUMONT, Aethins	38	M	Farmer	England	America	Britannia	22 Jul 1829
Ann	31	F		U. States	United States	Crisis	6 Apr 1825
Enoch	20	M	Manufacturer	England	America	Meteor	22 Apr 1822
James	42	M	Manufacturer	Great Britain	United States	Ann	24 Sep 1822
Joseph	7	M		England	America	Britannia	22 Jul 1829
Saml.	42	M	Carpenter	U. States	United States	Crisis	6 Apr 1825
William H.	6	M		England	America	Britannia	22 Jul 1829
BEAUPRIS, P.	28	M	Clergyman	France		Antioch	18 Aug 1829
BEAVER, Geo.	44	M	Agriculture	Wirtemburg	United States	Henri IV	14 Oct 1829
BEBE, Abraham	21 4/12	M	distressed seaman	Philadelphia	United States	Florida	27 Aug 1825
BEBEAR, Barbary M.	40	F		France	U.S. America	Huntress	6 Sep 1827
Caroline	5	F		France	U.S. America	Huntress	6 Sep 1827
Cattle	11 1/12	...oth		France	U.S. America	Huntress	6 Sep 1827
Christian	2	F		France	U.S. America	Huntress	6 Sep 1827
Jerry	9	M		France	U.S. America	Huntress	6 Sep 1827
Peter	45	M	Farmer	France	U.S. America	Huntress	6 Sep 1827
Philip	21	M		France	U.S. America	Huntress	6 Sep 1827
Sophia	15	F		France	U.S. America	Huntress	6 Sep 1827
BEBURI, Christina F.	27	F		Germany	America	Falcon	28 Aug 1828
BECAN, Joseph	39	M	Farmer	Great Briton	New York	Brighton	12 Jun 1826
BECAR, Auguste	30	M	Merchant	France	United States	Montano	27 Aug 1827
Jos.	18	M	Merchant	France	America	Liverpool Packet	23 Mar 1822
Noel P.	24	M	Merchant	U. States	New York	Sully	30 Oct 1827
P. J.	27	M	Merchant	France	America	Liverpool Packet	23 Mar 1822
BECEINE, John	23	M	Clouthier	France	United States	Virginia	31 May 1828
BECENTER, José	10	M	Boy	Cuba	Cuba	Franklin	14 Jul 1827
BECGX, Stephen	26	M	Merchant	France	United States	Stephania	3 Oct 1822
BECHAN, Hugh	19	M	Tailor	Ireland	United States	Trident	16 May 1826
BECHER, André	20	M		France	U. States	Edward Bopnnaffe	30 Jul 1829

NAMES OF PASSENGERS	AGE	SEX	OCCUPATIONS	COUNTRY TO WHICH THEY BELONG	COUNTRY THEY INTEND TO INHABIT	SHIPS/DATES OF ARRIVAL	
BECHER (cont'd)							
André	40	M	Farmer	France	U. States	Edward Bopnnaffe	30 Jul 1829
Anna	9	F		France	U. States	Edward Bopnnaffe	30 Jul 1829
Barbara	29	F		France	U. States	Edward Bopnnaffe	30 Jul 1829
BECHLER, August	19	M	Manufacturer	Germany	United States	Henri IV	14 Oct 1829
Calle	12	M	Manufacturer	Germany	United States	Henri IV	14 Oct 1829
Christoph	48	M	Manufacturer	Germany	United States	Henri IV	14 Oct 1829
Jno.	18	M	Gold Smith	Germany	United States	Henri IV	14 Oct 1829
BECHOLDIN, Catherine	27	F	Farmer	Germany	United States	Oxford	14 Aug 1828
Madelaine	30	F	Farmer	Germany	United States	Oxford	14 Aug 1828
BECHTLER, Christopher	30	M	Instrument Maker	Switzerland	U. States	Don Quixote	25 Oct 1828
BECK, —, Mrs.	30	F		France	United States	Burdett	30 Apr 1828
Adam	37	M	Farmer	Great Britain	United States	Ann Maria	12 Jul 1821
Alexr.	19	M	Baker	Ireland	United States	Champion	3 Nov 1827
Ann	5	F	None	Great Britain	United States	Ann Maria	12 Jul 1821
Catharine	20	F	Lady	U. States	U. States	Nancy	19 Oct 1821
Catherine	3	F		Germany	Missouri	Isabella	15 Sep 1828
Frances	28	F		Germany	Missouri	Isabella	15 Sep 1828
Harvey	23	M	Mercht.	Phila.	Phila.	Canada	1 Nov 1823
J. D.	30	M	Farmer	France	U. States	Montano	2 Sep 1828
James	30	M	Labourer or Spinster	Ireland	United States	Champion	3 Nov 1827
Jams.	53	M	Farmer	Great Britain	United States	Ann Maria	12 Jul 1821
John	28	M	Farmer	Germany	Missouri	Isabella	15 Sep 1828
Karl	27	M	Professor	Germany		Cadmus	20 Dec 1824
Margaret	32	F	Labourer or Spinster	Ireland	United States	Champion	3 Nov 1827
Maria	1	F		Germany	Missouri	Isabella	15 Sep 1828
Mary Jane	9	F	Labourer or Spinster	Ireland	United States	Champion	3 Nov 1827
Metcalf	9	M	None	Great Britain	United States	Ann Maria	12 Jul 1821
Moses	38	M	Farmer	Great Britain	United States	Ann Maria	12 Jul 1821
Rosa	7	F		Germany	Missouri	Isabella	15 Sep 1828
Sun	17	F	Lady	United States	United States	Sarah	31 Oct 1829
Thos.	30		Farmer	Great Britain	U. States	Columbia	7 May 1828
Wm.	11	M	Labourer or Spinster	Ireland	United States	Champion	3 Nov 1827
BECKE, John	23	M	Farmer	England	America	Hercules	10 Apr 1823
BECKER, Anna Maria	10	F		Baden	United States	Jason	3 Nov 1828
Anna Maria	37	F		Baden	United States	Jason	3 Nov 1828
Barbara	9 2/12	F		France	America, U.N.S.	Great Britain	3 Aug 1829
Carl	16	M		France	United States	New England	29 Aug 1828
Dorothy	40 10/12	F		United States		Conveyance	6 Jun 1826
Edmund	20	M	Merchant	Germany	U. States	Edward Quesnel	4 Aug 1828
Elisabethe	15	F		Baden	United States	Jason	3 Nov 1828
Elizabeth	15	F		France	America, U.N.S.	Great Britain	3 Aug 1829
Ernest	7	M		France	United States	New England	29 Aug 1828
Frederick	21	M	Cooper	France	United States	New England	29 Aug 1828
George	40	M	Farmer	France	United States	New England	29 Aug 1828
George Died.	40	M	Shoemaker	Wurtemburg	United States	Jason	3 Nov 1828
Hans	21	M	Dyer	Germany	U.S.A.	Robert Wilson	2 Dec 1828
Jacob	15	M		France	United States	New England	29 Aug 1828
Jacob	38	M		France	United States	New England	29 Aug 1828
Jacob Frederick	8	M		Baden	United States	Jason	3 Nov 1828
M.	50	M	Farmer	France	America, U.N.S.	Great Britain	3 Aug 1829
Magdalena	2	F		Baden	United States	Jason	3 Nov 1828
Magdelina	9	F		France	United States	New England	29 Aug 1828
Marguerita	51	F		France	America, U.N.S.	Great Britain	3 Aug 1829
Martha	11	M		France	America, U.N.S.	Great Britain	3 Aug 1829
Michael	6 6/12	M		Baden	United States	Jason	3 Nov 1828
Michael	11	M		France	United States	New England	29 Aug 1828
Philip	48	M	Saddler	Hamburg		Caesar	24 Aug 1829
Susana	13	F		France	United States	New England	29 Aug 1828
BECKET, Aquila	22 1/12	F	Lady	Gt. Britain	U. States	Maria	22 May 1822
William	40	M	Labourer	Great Britain	United States	Robert	15 Jul 1822
BECKETT, William	24	M	Labourer	England	U. States	Montgomery	18 Oct 1828
BECKLEY, James	29	M	pudler		uncertain	Mount Vernon	29 Aug 1828

NAMES OF PASSENGERS	AGE	SEX	OCCUPATIONS	COUNTRY TO WHICH THEY BELONG	COUNTRY THEY INTEND TO INHABIT	SHIPS/DATES OF ARRIVAL	
BECKMAN, Daniel	44	M	...	Baden	United States	Wade	29 Aug 1825
Joseph	10	M	...	Baden	United States	Wade	29 Aug 1825
Magdalina	5	F	...	Baden	United States	Wade	29 Aug 1825
Salomon	2	M	...	Baden	United States	Wade	29 Aug 1825
Tekla	12	F	...	Baden	United States	Wade	29 Aug 1825
BECKWITH, H.	35		Cooper	U. States		Maria	23 Aug 1824
Horace	26	M	Hartford	U. States		George	25 Sep 1820
Horace	27	M	Merchant	U. States	U. States	Traveller	24 Sep 1822
BECKWORTH, Geo.	26	M	Farmer	England	U. States	Mentor	5 Jul 1825
BECTEAUR, John	26	M	Farmer	Great Britian	United States	Andes	19 Aug 1829
BEDFORD, Francis	19	M	Weaver	England		Manhattan	22 May 1827
George	6/12	M		England	United States	St. John	5 Oct 1829
Hariot	9	F	None	England	United States	Jubilee	1 Oct 1828
Henery	4	M	None	England	United States	Jubilee	1 Oct 1828
Henry	44	M	Farmer	England	United States	Curler	3 Mar 1828
James	12	M	None	England	United States	Jubilee	1 Oct 1828
James	22	M	Gold Smith	G. Britain	New York	Hesperus	13 Oct 1825
Jno.	35	M	Farmer	England	U. States	Thomas Ritchie	2 Jul 1827
John	19	M	None	England	United States	Jubilee	1 Oct 1828
Jonas	7	M	None	England	United States	Jubilee	1 Oct 1828
Mary	5	F		England	United States	St. John	5 Oct 1829
Mary	28	F		England	United States	St. John	5 Oct 1829
Richard	15	M	None	England	United States	Jubilee	1 Oct 1828
Sarah	4	F		England	United States	St. John	5 Oct 1829
Sarah	40	F	None	England	United States	Jubilee	1 Oct 1828
William	2	M		England	United States	St. John	5 Oct 1829
William	32	M	Taylor	England	United States	St. John	5 Oct 1829
BEDINTON, Pat	29 3/12		Labourer	Ireland	Albany, N.York	Marcella	18 May 1827
BEDLOW, —, Mrs.		F		St. Croix		Virginia	12 Jul 1820
Alice				St. Croix		Virginia	12 Jul 1820
James		M		St. Croix		Virginia	12 Jul 1820
James, Jur.		M		St. Croix		Virginia	12 Jul 1820
Jaml.		M		St. Croix		Virginia	12 Jul 1820
Jane		F		St. Croix		Virginia	12 Jul 1820
Julia				St. Croix		Virginia	12 Jul 1820
BEDMY, Sophy	14		Child	England	England	London	16 Aug 1824
BEDOIT, Victoire			Servant	France	U.S.	Sully	26 Oct 1829
BEDRAND, Francis	16	M	Book Binder	France	United States	American	27 Aug 1827
Jacob	18	M	Book Binder	France	United States	American	27 Aug 1827
Justiania	2	F	Book Binder	France	United States	American	27 Aug 1827
Maria	45	F	Book Binder	France	United States	American	27 Aug 1827
Silvester	45	F	Book Binder	France	United States	American	27 Aug 1827
Simon	20	M	Book Binder	France	United States	American	27 Aug 1827
BEE, Mary, & Child	26	F	Labourer	England	United States	Brilliant	24 Sep 1827
BEEBE, J.	23	M	Servant	U. States	U. States	Planter	17 Jul 1826
Solomon	59 3/12	M	Farmer	U. States	U. States	Josephine	7 May 1827
BEECH, George	33	M	Farmer	Great Britan	United States	Clematis	8 May 1827
Hester	27	F	None	England	United States	London	21 May 1828
William	28	M	Laborer	England	United States	London	21 May 1828
BEECHER, Thos.	17	M		G. Britain	U. States	St. George	7 Jun 1828
BEELER, W.	33	M	Farmer	Great Britain	United States	Grecian	24 Sep 1828
BEELY, Ann	13	F	None	Great Britain	United States	Comet	9 Aug 1822
Ann	53	F	None	Great Britain	United States	Comet	9 Aug 1822
Eliza	24	F	None	Great Britain	United States	Comet	9 Aug 1822
Jacob	17	M	Farmer	Great Britain	United States	Comet	9 Aug 1822
James	22	M	Farmer	Great Britain	United States	Comet	9 Aug 1822
Jno.	11	M	None	Great Britain	United States	Comet	9 Aug 1822
John	52		Farmer	Great Britain	United States	Comet	9 Aug 1822
Robert	15	M	Farmer	Great Britain	United States	Comet	9 Aug 1822
BEEN, Mary Ann, Mrs.	35	F	Lady	U.S.	U.S.	Athenian	14 Oct 1828
BEENEY, Maria	1 9/12	F		England	America	Criterion	27 Oct 1821
Sarah	6/12	F		England	America	Criterion	27 Oct 1821
Sarah	22	F		England	America	Criterion	27 Oct 1821
Wm.	27	M	Miller	England	America	Criterion	27 Oct 1821
BEER, Anna	10	F		Germany	United States	Origon	8 Jun 1824
Catharine	6	F		Germany	United States	Origon	8 Jun 1824
Chris.	50	M	Farmer	Germany	United States	Origon	8 Jun 1824
Christien	22	M	Weaver	Switzerland	United States	Thetis	5 Jul 1821
Eliza	4	F	None	Great Britain	United States	Richmond	18 Feb 1820

NAMES OF PASSENGERS	AGE	SEX	OCCUPATIONS	COUNTRY TO WHICH THEY BELONG	COUNTRY THEY INTEND TO INHABIT	SHIPS/DATES OF ARRIVAL	
BEER (cont'd)							
Hannah	36	F	None	Great Britain	United States	Richmond	18 Feb 1820
Henry	3	M	None	Great Britain	United States	Richmond	18 Feb 1820
Henry	57	M	Farmer	England	U. States	Lewis	1 Jul 1820
Mary	8	F	None	Great Britain	United States	Richmond	18 Feb 1820
Mary	60	F	Unknown	Great Britain	United States	Richmond	18 Feb 1820
Peter	6	M		Germany	United States	Origon	8 Jun 1824
Richard	10	M	None	Great Britain	United States	Richmond	18 Feb 1820
Thomas	1 6/12	M	None	Great Britain	United States	Richmond	18 Feb 1820
Thomas	35	M	Farmer	Great Britain	United States	Richmond	18 Feb 1820
BEERS, Rizza	16	M	Farmer	America	U. States	Lewis	1 Jul 1820
BEESLY, John	25	M	Labourer		United States	Eliza Grant	6 Oct 1828
BEEVOUER, Stephn.	23	M	Merchant	France	Mexico	Desdemona	21 Oct 1825
BEFFINGER, Mary	55	F	Farmer	France	U. States	Lewis	6 Jul 1825
BEGG, Ann	35	F	None	Ireland	United States	Dalhouse Castle	8 May 1827
David	19	M	Farmer	Scotland	U. States	Superior	25 Sep 1828
E.	21	F		Scotland	U. States	Superior	25 Sep 1828
Joseph	35	M	Labourer	Ireland	United States	Dalhouse Castle	8 May 1827
BEGH, Francis	25	M	None	Prussia	Prussia	Canada	13 Oct 1825
BEGLAN, Wm.	30	M	Labourer	Ireland	United States	Hannah Eliza	23 Sep 1826
BEGLEY, Hugh	22	M	Farmer	Ireland	United States	Asia	29 Jul 1829
BEGLIN, Julia	16	F	Spinster	Ireland	U. States	Erin	5 Jul 1820
BEGNON, Even	36		None	United States	United States	James Monroe	11 Dec 1821
BEHA, Barnard	30	M	Clockmaker	Baden	United States	Acasta	15 Jul 1822
BEHANT, Thos.	19	M	Laborer	Guersey	New York	Comet	19 Oct 1826
BEHR, Charles	26	M	Merchant	Switzerland	United States	Howard	14 May 1825
Charles	27	M	Merchant	Germany	New York	Sully	4 Mar 1828
Chas.	23	M	Merchant	Germany	United States	Don Quixote	7 May 1824
Jas. B.	22	M	Merchant	U. States	U. States	Harriet	20 Oct 1824
BEIKLE, Richard		M	Miner	England		Iris	7 Dec 1827
*died on the passage							
BEILEY, Bernd.	23	M	Farmer	England	U. States	Thomas Ritchie	2 Jul 1827
BEIMLER, Ard.	55	M	Coachmaker	United States	U. States	Constitution	15 Nov 1822
BEISSER, Cristian	25	M	Labourer	France	America, U.N.S.	Great Britain	3 Aug 1829
BEKARD (see Bekart)							
Oto	9/12	M	Child of Jos. Bekard (Bekart)			Romulus	24 Sep 1828
*Died on the Voyage							
BEKART (see Bekard)							
B.	3	F		Switzerland	U. States	Romulus	24 Sep 1828
Hance	10	M		Switzerland	U. States	Romulus	24 Sep 1828
Jos.	6	M		Switzerland	U. States	Romulus	24 Sep 1828
Joseph (Bekard)	44	M	Copper Smith	Switzerland	U. States	Romulus	24 Sep 1828
Madelina	38	F		Switzerland	U. States	Romulus	24 Sep 1828
Nina	7	M		Switzerland	U. States	Romulus	24 Sep 1828
BEKENSTAFF, C.	20	M	Farmer	U. States	U. States	United States	11 Sep 1828
BEKKER, Carl	26	M	Butcher	Switzerland	U. States	Hewes	30 Oct 1829
BEKLE, Catherine	26	F		Wertemberg	Wertemberg	Edward Quesnel	3 Jul 1829
John	5	M		Wertemberg	Wertemberg	Edward Quesnel	3 Jul 1829
John	27	M	Carpenter	Wertemberg	Wertemberg	Edward Quesnel	3 Jul 1829
BEKMANN, Luis	24	M	Laborer	Hannover	U.N. States of America	Constitution	7 Dec 1827
BEKOFSKY, Austin	25			Kingdom of Hanover	U. States	Princess Louise	10 Mar 1825
BEKRAN, N.	12	M	Military	Valancia, Spain	N. York	Brown	12 Oct 1824
*to Compleat his Education							
BELA, Barth.	42	M	Merchant	U. States	U. States	Factor	9 Mar 1829
BELAMS, Elizabeth	11	F				Charlotte Corday	15 Aug 1820
BELAMY, A.	37	M	Mercht.	Spain	U. States	Fair American	16 Oct 1822
A.	40	M	Mercht.	America	U. States	Ambuscade	5 Jul 1822
Ann	19	F		Ireland	America	Liverpool	31 Aug 1827
Cathr.	16			Ireland	America	Liverpool	31 Aug 1827
Mary	10			Ireland	America	Liverpool	31 Aug 1827
BELANY, Anthony	36	M	Merchant	United States	United States	Charleston Packet	25 Jul 1821
Anthony	38	M	Merchant	U.S. of America	U.S. of America	Harmony	20 Nov 1820
Chas.	30	M	Merchant	Spain	U. States	Pedler	16 Feb 1824
BELARBRE, Lambert	18	M	Student	Guadaloupe	France	Jane	24 May 1828
BELAY, Margarette	23	F				Henri IV	17 May 1828

NAMES OF PASSENGERS	AGE	SEX	OCCUPATIONS	COUNTRY TO WHICH THEY BELONG	COUNTRY THEY INTEND TO INHABIT	SHIPS/DATES OF ARRIVAL	
BELAY (cont'd)							
Mary	17	F				Henri IV	17 May 1828
Piere	53	M	Shoe Maker			Henri IV	17 May 1828
Susan	10	F				Henri IV	17 May 1828
Susan	30	F				Henri IV	17 May 1828
BELCHER, Charles	21	M	Mechanic	Great Britain	United States	Orozimbo	31 May 1824
George	24	M	Mariner	America		Samuel	23 Aug 1824
Martha	20	F	None	England	England	Nestor	20 Nov 1821
P. B.	19	M		U. States	Alexandria	William	22 Jul 1820
W.	22	M	Rule Maker	England	England	Nestor	20 Nov 1821
BELDORE, T.	31	M	Merchant	Spain	U. States	Georgiana	25 Jun 1824
BELE, Wm.	20	M	Engineer	Scotland		Marchioness	13 May 1828
BELEARE, Robert	22	M	Printer	United States	United States	Brighton	9 Dec 1828
BELER, Johannes	24	M	Weaver	Germany	U. States	Isabella	10 Aug 1829
BELETE, Mus.	55	M	Merchant	Spain	Spain	Claudio	16 Oct 1827
BELEY, George	28	M	Merchant	England	England	Cadmus	14 Oct 1824
BELGAM, —, Mons.	22	M	Printer	Sandimngo	to return to St. Domingo	Huntress	27 Sep 1821
BELIA, Lawrence	30	M	Weaver	Ireland	America	Farmer	4 Aug 1825
Rebecca	21	F		Ireland	America	Farmer	4 Aug 1825
BELJEAN, Francis	31		Mechanic	France	U. States	Parachute	14 May 1828
BELKNAP, Andw. E.	40	M	Merchant	U. States	U. States	Acasta	27 Aug 1821
BELL, Abraham	25	M	Carpenter	United States	United States	Ann Maria	23 Jan 1826
Allisin	4	F	None	Scotland	U. States	Camillus	27 Jul 1825
Ann	5	F		Scotland	United States	Shakespeare	24 Jul 1828
Anne	22	F	...	Ireland	United States	General Putnam	20 Jun 1825
Anne	26	F	Spinster	Ireland	America	Superior	12 Jun 1824
C.	27	M	Mariner	U. States	U. States	Villard de Cayes	10 Apr 1827
Caroline	18	F	Servant	United States	United States	Only Daughter	29 Apr 1825
Catharine	20		Seamster	Scotland	United States	Camillus	3 May 1828
Catharine	22			Ireland	Great Britain	Robert Burns	14 Jun 1824
Cathe.	18	F	Servant	G. Britain	U. States	Sarah G	5 Jun 1828
Christian	50	M	Farmer	Great Britain	U. States	Yamacraw	4 Sep 1822
Eliza	20	F	Farmer	Ireland	U. States	Dickinson	30 Jul 1825
Eliza	25	F	Servant	Richmond	United States	Astrea	16 Nov 1825
Elizth.	60	F	None	Great Britain	United States	Mary & Harriet	3 Jul 1829
Ellen	21	F	Mantua Maker	Ireland	New York	Atlantic	8 May 1828
Ellisius	45	F	None	Scotland	U. States	Camillus	27 Jul 1825
Ewd.	26	M	Jeweller	G. Britain	U. States	Camillus	8 Sep 1828
Geo. B.	22	M	Merchant	England	U. States	New York	11 Jul 1823
George	24	M	Merchant	United States	United States	Zamoa	5 Nov 1828
Graham	5	M	Child	Richmond	United States	Astrea	16 Nov 1825
Henry	74	M	Seaman	U. States	U. States	Electra	28 Apr 1827
Jacob	16	M	Joiner	Great Britain	United States	Washington	3 Sep 1827
Jacob	63	M	Joiner	Great Britain	United States	Washington	3 Sep 1827
James	6	M	None	Ireland	U. States	John Dickinson	14 Sep 1820
James	6	M		Scotland	United States	Shakespeare	24 Jul 1828
James	10	M	None	Scotland	U. States	Camillus	27 Jul 1825
James	16	F	Servant	Ireland	United States	Josephine	30 Apr 1828
James	20	M	Servant	Ireland	America	Carolina Ann	7 Aug 1826
James	24	M	Cotton Printer	Ireland	America	Josephine	8 Dec 1827
James	30	M	Servant	G. Britain	U. States	Sarah G	5 Jun 1828
James	54	M	Farmer	Ireland	United States	Robert Fulton	22 Oct 1821
James A.	21	M	Merchant	Great Britain	United States	Juno	5 Oct 1822
James G.	20 1/12	M		Ireland		Carolina Ann	7 Apr 1826
Jane	8	F	None	Scotland	U. States	Camillus	27 Jul 1825
Janet	28	F		Scotland	United States	Shakespeare	24 Jul 1828
Jennet	20	F	None	Great Britain	United States	Courier	26 Jun 1827
John	1			Ireland	Great Britain	Robert Burns	14 Jun 1824
John	14	M		Great Britain	United States	Washington	3 Sep 1827
John	22	M	Labourer	Ireland	United States	Lord Wellington	28 May 1827
John	23	M	Surgeon	Ireland	United States	Princess Charlotte	26 Apr 1827
John	24		Merchant	St. John	U. States	Lady Hunter	5 Jul 1823
John	25	M	Merchant	England	America	Friends	28 Sep 1822
John	27 5/12	M	Jeweller	Ireland	U. States	Fabius	22 Sep 1828
John	32	M	Merchant	U. States	U. States	Cannon	21 Jul 1824
John	35	M	Weaver	Scotland	United States	Shakespeare	24 Jul 1828
John D.	21	M	Servant	Ireland	United States	Wanderer	31 Aug 1829

NAMES OF PASSENGERS	AGE	SEX	OCCUPATIONS	COUNTRY TO WHICH THEY BELONG	COUNTRY THEY INTEND TO INHABIT	SHIPS/DATES OF ARRIVAL	
BELL (cont'd)							
Kirah	8/12			St. John	U. States	Lady Hunter	5 Jul 1823
M.	1 1/2	F		G. Britain	U. States	London	23 Sep 1828
*Died on the Passage							
Margaret	34	F	going to her husband	Scotland	America	Camillus	12 Sep 1822
Margt.	0 4/12	F		Scotland	United States	Shakespeare	24 Jul 1828
Margt.	21	F		Ireland	United States	Sarah G.	15 May 1828
Mary	21	F	going to her husband	Britain	America	Camillus	9 Oct 1820
Mary	56	F	Wife	Great Britain	United States	Washington	3 Sep 1827
Mary Ann	2	F	Child	Britain	America	Camillus	9 Oct 1820
Matilda	20	F		Ireland	America	Carolina Ann	7 Apr 1826
Olrie	18	M	Weaver	Switzerland	United States	Thetis	5 Jul 1821
Peter	27	M	Gentleman	England	Canada	Hercules	21 Nov 1822
Pettitt	65	F	Spinster	Ireland	United States	Fabius	31 Jul 1829
Pettitt, Jr.	17	F	Spinster	Ireland	United States	Fabius	31 Jul 1829
R.	28	M	Merchant	Ireland	United States	Florida	14 Sep 1827
Rebecca	25	F	Spinster	Ireland	United States	Fabius	31 Jul 1829
Richd.	22	M	Shoe Maker	Ireland	U. States	Sarah G	30 Jun 1828
Robert	25		Weaver	Ireland	Great Britain	Robert Burns	14 Jun 1824
Robert	26	M	Engineer	Great Britain	United States	Courier	26 Jun 1827
Robert	29	M	Taylor	England	United States	Eliza Grant	7 Jun 1827
Robert, Senr.	28	M	Weaver	Ireland	United States	Carolina Ann	11 Dec 1826
Robt.		M	None	Great Britain	United States	Ann Maria	12 Jul 1821
Robt.	27	M	Hosier	Ireland	United States	Fabius	31 Jul 1829
Robt., Junr.	6	M		Ireland	United States	Carolina Ann	11 Dec 1826
Rosa	20	F	Spinster	Ireland	U.S. of America	Meteor	19 Mar 1828
Sarah	15	F		Ireland	America	Carolina Ann	7 Aug 1826
Sarah	20			St. John	U. States	Lady Hunter	5 Jul 1823
Thomas	12	M	None	Scotland	U. States	Camillus	27 Jul 1825
Thomas	26	M	Farmer	Ireland	America	Farmer	4 Aug 1825
Thomas	30		Merchant	U. States	U. States	Swan	29 May 1821
Thomas	45	M	Gardiner	Scotland	U. States	Camillus	27 Jul 1825
Thomas	50	M	Labourer	Bally Kenon	United States	Minerva	30 Oct 1829
Thomas	60	M	Weaver	Ireland	New York	Trusty	12 Sep 1828
Thoms.	26	M	Merchant	England	U. States	Endymion	12 Mar 1822
Thos.	22	M	Farmer	England	United States	Robert Edwards	1 Jun 1826
Thos.	28	M	Merchant	England	U. States	Endymion	22 May 1822
William	7	M		Ireland	United States	Carolina Ann	11 Dec 1826
William	18	M	Labourer	Ireland	U.S.	Lady Hunter	10 Jul 1826
William	30		Weaver	England	United States	Thomas Dickason	5 Jun 1827
William	33	M	Merchant	England	New Orleans	William Byrnes	11 Dec 1827
Wm.	2			St. John	U. States	Lady Hunter	5 Jul 1823
Wm.	14		Boy	Ireland	United States	Courier	15 Oct 1827
Wm.	21	M	Merchant	Belfast	New York	Anthusa	24 Aug 1825
Wm.	24	M	Carpenter	..., Manchester, England	U. States	New Orleans	24 Aug 1827
Wm.	25	M	...	Ireland	United States	General Putnam	20 Jun 1825
BELLAH, Robt.	20	M	Labourer	Europe	United States	Aspasia	5 Sep 1827
Wm.	33	M	Baker	Europe	United States	Aspasia	5 Sep 1827
BELLAME, E.	20	M	Farmer	England	U. States	Acasta	12 May 1825
BELLAMIN, D.	30	M	Merchant	St. Domingo	U. States	Fair Play	22 Feb 1823
BELLAMY, Ann	18	F	Servant	Ireland	United States	Trio	31 Oct 1827
J. M.	42		Farmer	England	England	Hudson	4 Sep 1823
Joseph, Mastr.	14	M		G.B.	U.S.	London	19 Dec 1823
*Family of Mr. Bellamy, a farmer from England, now in N. York							
Louisa, Miss	12	F		G.B.	U.S.	London	19 Dec 1823
*Family of Mr. Bellamy, a farmer from England, now in N. York							
Mary Ann, Miss	16	F		G.B.	U.S.	London	19 Dec 1823
*Family of Mr. Bellamy, a farmer from England, now in N. York							
Mary Ann, Mrs.	40	F		G.B.	U.S.	London	19 Dec 1823
*Family of Mr. Bellamy, a farmer from England, now in N. York							
Sarah, Miss	18	F		G.B.	U.S.	London	19 Dec 1823
*Family of Mr. Bellamy, a farmer from England, now in N. York							
Thomas	10	M		G.B.	U.S.	London	19 Dec 1823
*Family of Mr. Bellamy, a farmer from England, now in N. York							

NAMES OF PASSENGERS	AGE	SEX	OCCUPATIONS	COUNTRY TO WHICH THEY BELONG	COUNTRY THEY INTEND TO INHABIT	SHIPS/DATES OF ARRIVAL	
BELLAMY (cont'd)							
Willm., Mastr.	8	M		G.B.	U.S.	London	19 Dec 1823
*Family of Mr. Bellamy, a farmer from England, now in N. York							
BELLAN, F.	11	M		Hayti	U. States	Larch	18 Jul 1828
J.	9	M		Hayti	U. States	Larch	18 Jul 1828
J. A.	40	M	Merchant	Hayti	U. States	Larch	18 Jul 1828
Pascel	50	M	Merchant	France	France	Arthenian	28 Apr 1827
BELLANGER, Marie, Mr.	40	M	Merchant	France	France	Cadmus	11 Jul 1827
BELLCHARE, Jno.	9 2/12	M		U. States	U. States	Circassian	26 Jun 1823
BELLE, Catharine	26	F	Farmer	N. Brunswick	New Brunswick	Abigale	9 Aug 1821
S.	36	M	Farmer	N. Brunswick	New Brunswick	Abigale	9 Aug 1821
Stien A.	42	M	Attorney	Denmark	U. States	Chase	5 Oct 1824
BELLEVOCHE, John	19	M	Mercht.	Germany	U. States	Catherine	4 Sep 1824
BELLEVUE, Adele	18	F	Mulatto	Martinico	United States	Falcon	1 May 1824
Anna	12	F	Mulatto	Martinico	United States	Falcon	1 May 1824
BELLIC, A.	27		Merchant	France	New Orleans	Albion	11 Oct 1821
BELLINGHAM, William	26	M	Mariner	Jersey in Europe	England	Rebecca Ann	22 Jul 1820
BELLIS, Felix, Don	33	M	Merchant	France	U. States	Dawn	8 Jun 1827
James	22	M	Merct.	Ireland	U. States	Josephine	7 May 1827
BELLO, A. H.	31	M	Mercht.	Teneriffe		Marcella	15 Mar 1827
BELLOT, Isaac	45	M	Cotton Manufacturer	England	New York	Curler	7 Jul 1827
BELLSBUROUGH, Yates	23	M	Farmer	England	U. States	Amity	23 Sep 1823
BELLUN, —, Mr.	27	M	None	Holland	United States	Alexander	2 Oct 1829
BELON, J. J., Mr.	41	M		France		Henri IV	17 May 1828
BELT, T. W.	29	M	Merchant	U. States	U. States	Lewis	20 Feb 1824
BELTRAN, A.	26	M	Merchant	N. York	U. States	Caravan	1 May 1824
BELTRAND, Antonio	30	M	Mercht.	Spain	U. States	Packet	6 Aug 1822
BEMAN, Wm.	28	M	Farmer	England	U. States	Auritz	20 May 1823
BEMION, John U.	25	M	Labourer	France	United States	Helen	5 Sep 1828
BENARD, —, Mr.	38	M	Merchant	France	America	Henry	19 Jun 1825
Mary	24	F	None	France	St. Comingo	Euphrates	8 Aug 1820
BENBEETHY, Isaac	28	M	Miner	Great Britain	Mexico	Corinthian	27 Apr 1824
BENBRIDGE, Matthew	23	M	Shoe Maker	Halifax	...	Hunter	19 May 1823
BEND, Wm.	21	M	Carpenter	United States	United States	Deborah	3 Jul 1824
Wm. B.	31	M	Merchant	U.S. of America	U.S. of America	Canada	1 Oct 1827
BENDER, Fred., Mr.	16	M		England	United States	Cosmo	26 Aug 1829
Robert	24	M	Carpenter	England	United States	Cosmo	26 Aug 1829
Thos., Mr.	38	M	Mercht.	England	United States	Cosmo	26 Aug 1829
BENDICK, Ann	30	F	Lady	Philadelphia	Philadelphia	Inspector	26 May 1828
Ann, Jr.	6	F	Girl	Philadelphia	Philadelphia	Inspector	26 May 1828
Betsey	4	F	Girl	Philadelphia	Philadelphia	Inspector	26 May 1828
Ephraim	33	M	Gentleman	Philadelphia	Philadelphia	Inspector	26 May 1828
John	8	M	Baoy	Philadelphia	Philadelphia	Inspector	26 May 1828
BENDIN, Mary	20	M	Labourer	England	U. States	Ayrshire	12 May 1828
BENEDICK, James S.	20	M	Merchant	United States	St. Johns	Nancy	3 Apr 1824
BENEDICT, C.	20	M		Columbia	U. States	Medina	23 Apr 1828
C.	50	M	Merchant	Columbia	U. States	Medina	23 Apr 1828
J.	13	M	No	Campeache	U. States	Doris	22 May 1826
Lewis	18	M	Merchant	U. States	U. States	St. Michael	27 Mar 1827
BENELED, Henry	26	M	Mariner	Portsmith		Robert Edwards	8 Nov 1825
BENESS, Robt.	24	M	Labourer	U. States	U. States	United States	11 Sep 1828
Wm.	22	M	Labourer	U. States	U. States	United States	11 Sep 1828
BENET, Auguste	20 8/12	M	Merchant	France	Island of Gaudaloupe	Woodroop Sims	19 Oct 1829
BENGEL, Adam	29	M	Agriculture	Bavaria	United States	Henri IV	14 Oct 1829
BENGER, Michael, Mr.	27	M	Farmer	Grate Britain	...	Courier	14 Jun 1825
BENGILT, J.	14	M	Gent	French	Switzerland	Charlemagne	19 Sep 1828
M.	16	F	Gent	French	Switzerland	Charlemagne	19 Sep 1828
M.	45	F	Gent	French	Switzerland	Charlemagne	19 Sep 1828
P.	50	M	Gent	French	Switzerland	Charlemagne	19 Sep 1828
P. B.	20	M	Gent	French	Switzerland	Charlemagne	19 Sep 1828
BENHALL, Bridget	40	F		G.B.	New York	Eliza Grant	29 Aug 1829
Bridget	40	F		Great Britain		Eliza Grant	29 Aug 1829
Martha	3	F		G.B.	New York	Eliza Grant	29 Aug 1829
Martha	3	F		Great Britain		Eliza Grant	29 Aug 1829
Mary	5	F		G.B.	New York	Eliza Grant	29 Aug 1829
Mary	5	F		Great Britain		Eliza Grant	29 Aug 1829
Nancy	11	F		G.B.	New York	Eliza Grant	29 Aug 1829
Nancy	11	F		Great Britain		Eliza Grant	29 Aug 1829

NAMES OF PASSENGERS	AGE	SEX	OCCUPATIONS	COUNTRY TO WHICH THEY BELONG	COUNTRY THEY INTEND TO INHABIT	SHIPS/DATES OF ARRIVAL	
BENHALL (cont'd)							
Ruth	9	F		G.B.	New York	Eliza Grant	29 Aug 1829
Ruth	9	F		Great Britain		Eliza Grant	29 Aug 1829
BENHAM, Alfred	1 1/2	M		England	Gt. Britain	Electra	4 Sep 1827
Charlotte	2	F		England	America	Leeds	2 Aug 1828
Fanny	4	F		England	America	Leeds	2 Aug 1828
Mary A.	33	F		England	America	Leeds	2 Aug 1828
Sarah	6	F		England	Gt. Britain	Electra	4 Sep 1827
Wm.	29	M	Farmer	England	Gt. Britain	Electra	4 Sep 1827
BENHAN, Nelson	21	M		U. States	U. States	Alfred	26 Apr 1828
BENINGER, Anna	32	F	Wife	Germany	United States	Elizabeth	4 Sep 1826
Jacques	6 9/12	M	Son	Germany	United States	Elizabeth	4 Sep 1826
Madelina	2	F	Daughter	Germany	United States	Elizabeth	4 Sep 1826
Maria	4	F	Daughter	Germany	United States	Elizabeth	4 Sep 1826
BENINGTON, John	...	M	Merchant	England	Philadelphia	Amity	13 Sep 1821
BENIT, Mary	17	F		France	U. States	Edward Bonaffe	23 Jul 1828
BENJAMIN, Anne	6	F		Llannstyn	United States	Marquis of Anglesea	8 Jun 1827
B. H.	5	M		Demerara	U. States	South Carolina	2 Aug 1822
Benjn.	9	M		Llannstyn	United States	Marquis of Anglesea	8 Jun 1827
E.	40	F		Great Britain	United States	Saml. Wight	6 Sep 1827
Evan	39	M	Labourer	Llannstyn	United States	Marquis of Anglesea	8 Jun 1827
F. A.	29	M	Musician	Prussia		Constitution	20 Jun 1828
Henry B.	23	M	Mariner	U. States	United States	Pionier	4 Mar 1828
J.	31	M	Painter	Jacmel	New Orleans	Hero	5 Jul 1828
Mary	2	F		Llannstyn	United States	Marquis of Anglesea	8 Jun 1827
Mary	47	F		Llannstyn	United States	Marquis of Anglesea	8 Jun 1827
Mary J.	40	F		Barbadoes	U. States	South Carolina	2 Aug 1822
Park	53	M	Merchant	Connecticutt	U. States	South Carolina	2 Aug 1822
Susan M.	7	F		Demerara	U. States	South Carolina	2 Aug 1822
BENJAUR, E.	22	M	Goldsmith	U. States	U. States	Charles Hays	28 Mar 1825
BENKARD, James	24	M	...	Germany	U. States	Columbia	7 Jul 1824
BENN, Edvard	23		Attorny			Caroline	10 Mar 1828
BENNAGE, —	28	M	Mariner	U. States	U. States	Artibonite	31 Jan 1827
BENNEFOUX, L.	36	M	Merchant	France	United States	Aurora	11 Dec 1824
BENNER, —, Miss	1	M	Merchant	U. States	U. States	Zephyr	2 Oct 1826
—, Miss	4	M	Merchant	U. States	U. States	Zephyr	2 Oct 1826
Thos.	17	M	Labourer	Great Britain	United States	Atlantic	28 May 1827
BENNET, —, Capt.	25	M	Mariner	Baltimore	Baltimore	Leif	6 Sep 1824
A.	20	F		U. States	U. States	Southern Trader	23 Apr 1823
Ann	10	F		England	New York	William	2 Sep 1822
Bridget	21	F	Farmer	Ireland		Manhattan	20 Jun 1826
Catherine	25	F	Spinster	Ireland	United States	Dublin Packet	9 Jul 1827
Eliz.	18	F		England	New York	William	2 Sep 1822
H. L.	22	M	Merchant	U.S. America		Robert Read	25 Aug 1824
Hester	6	F		England	New York	William	2 Sep 1822
Hester	38	F		England	New York	William	2 Sep 1822
Janet	19	F		Scotland	U. States	Percival	16 May 1821
Jno.	36	M	Glassmaker	England	U. States	Pierson	26 Apr 1822
Jno., Jr.	15	M	Glassmaker	England	U. States	Pierson	26 Apr 1822
John	13	M	Farmer	Ireland	America	John Adams	2 Aug 1827
John	24 3/12	M	Spinner	Great Britain	America	Hannibal	12 Oct 1826
Margret	23	F	None	Great Britain	America	Hannibal	12 Oct 1826
Noble	24	M		Great Britain	New York	Philetus	21 Jul 1827
Paulina	3	F		England	New York	William	2 Sep 1822
Peter	23	M	Farmer	Ireland	United States	Dublin Packet	9 Jul 1827
Phillip	34	M	Cabinet Maker	England	United States	Warrior	6 Oct 1828
Phillip	34		Mercht.	England	United States	Cosmo	26 Aug 1829
Rachel	4	F		England	New York	William	2 Sep 1822
Richard	16	M	Farmer	Ireland	America	John Adams	2 Aug 1827
Robert	40	M	Farmer	Ireland	America	John Adams	2 Aug 1827
Robert, Jr.	6	M	Farmer	Ireland	America	John Adams	2 Aug 1827
Thomas	9	F		England	New York	William	2 Sep 1822
BENNETS, Robert	55	M	Farmer	U. States	U. States	Teio	5 Jun 1826

NAMES OF PASSENGERS	AGE	SEX	OCCUPATIONS	COUNTRY TO WHICH THEY BELONG	COUNTRY THEY INTEND TO INHABIT	SHIPS/DATES OF ARRIVAL	
BENNETT, Ann	23	F	Taylor	Great Britian	United States	Princess Charlotte	6 Sep 1828
Ann	52	F	None	England		Marchioness	13 May 1828
Ann, Mrs.	55	F	Lady	Great Britain	England	Jay	18 Apr 1823
E.	24	F		G. Britain	U. States	London	23 Sep 1828
Edward	6	M	Farmer	England	United States	Oxford	14 Aug 1828
Edward	25	M	Merchant	England	England	Medina	23 Apr 1828
Elisabeth	4	F	Farmer	England	United States	Oxford	14 Aug 1828
Eliza R.	20	F		U. States	U. States	Hudson	8 Oct 1827
Fanny	9	F	Farmer	England	United States	Oxford	14 Aug 1828
Geo.	21	M	Miner	U. States	U. States	Martha	20 Jun 1825
George	23	M	Merchant	Great Britian	U. States	Orbit	29 Apr 1822
Humphry	22	M	Laborer	Ireland	United States	Trio	13 Jun 1827
J.	42	M		Great Britton	U. State	Earl of Liverpool	16 Aug 1826
James	17	M	Labourer	England	U. States	Brighton	14 Apr 1828
James	18		None	...ss..	...	James Cropper	28 Jun 1824
James	31	M	Physician	New York, U.S.	United States	Union	24 Sep 1823
Janne	36	F	Farmer	England	United States	Oxford	14 Aug 1828
Jno.	16		Seaman	Boston		Hudson	18 Jun 1825

*Officers, Seamen and Passengers belonging to the Ship Jane of Boston and taken from on board the Schooner Olive of St. Johns , N.B. on the 4th June 1825, Lat. 41.30, Long 53.19, which ship foundered on the 31st ultimo in Lat. 41.44 Long 52.

NAMES OF PASSENGERS	AGE	SEX	OCCUPATIONS	COUNTRY TO WHICH THEY BELONG	COUNTRY THEY INTEND TO INHABIT	SHIPS/DATES OF ARRIVAL	
John	7	M	Farmer	England	United States	Oxford	14 Aug 1828
John	26	M	Joiner	England	United States	William & Henry	19 Jul 1822
John	30	M	Farmer	Great Britian	United States	Columbia	17 Apr 1827
John	33	M	Labourer	G.B.	New York	Eliza Grant	29 Aug 1829
John	33	M	Labourer	Great Britain		Eliza Grant	29 Aug 1829
John	36	M	Labourer	Great Britian	United States	Princess Charlotte	6 Sep 1828
John	38	M	Labourer	Great Britian	United States	Princess Charlotte	6 Sep 1828
Lucy	12	F	Farmer	England	United States	Oxford	14 Aug 1828
Maranner	4	F	Farmer	England	United States	Oxford	14 Aug 1828
Martin	30	M	Miller	Germany	Missouri	Isabella	15 Sep 1828
Mary	19	F		England	United States	William & Henry	19 Jul 1822
Mary	37	F	Taylor	Great Britian	United States	Princess Charlotte	6 Sep 1828
Nancy	26	F	Lady	United States	U.S.	Panthea	13 Mar 1823
Nancy	27	F		America	America	Panthea	5 Oct 1822
Presille	11	F	Farmer	England	United States	Oxford	14 Aug 1828
R.	29	M	Mariner	Baltimore	U. States	Ann Maria	11 Jun 1828
Rob.	17	M	Glassmaker	England	U. States	Pierson	26 Apr 1822
Robert	28	M	Farmer	England	New York	Robert Edwards	17 Mar 1828
Samuel	36	M	Seaman	Spain	U. States	Factor	9 Mar 1829
Thomas	3	M	Farmer	England	United States	Oxford	14 Aug 1828
Thos.	24	M	Farmer	Ireland	U. States	Edward	15 Jul 1825
Thos. Ruby	40	M	Labourer	Great Britain	United States	Orbit	23 Oct 1826
William	14	M	Farmer	England	United States	Oxford	14 Aug 1828
Wm.	30	M	Seaman	New York	New York	Charleston	1 Jun 1826
BENNIER, Eleaz.	20	M	Bricklayer	Great Britain	United States	Colossus	5 Jun 1827
BENNIJER, Mary, Mrs.	60		Servant	United States	United States	Acasta	16 Aug 1826
BENNINGER, Jacob	33	M	Tailor	Germany	United States	Elizabeth	4 Sep 1826
BENNINGTON, G.	50	M	Labourer	England	U. States	Comet	23 Aug 1828
Henry		M	Merchant	Great Brittan	Great Brittain	Florida	17 May 1825
Mary	40	F	Labourer	England	U. States	Comet	23 Aug 1828
BENNIT, James	35	M	Labourer	Ireland		Marchioness	13 May 1828
James	60	M	None	Ireland	U. States	Union	3 Jun 1822
John	25	M	Carpenter	England	U.S.	Acasta	11 May 1827
Margaret	56	F	None	Ireland	U. States	Union	3 Jun 1822
Mary	25	F	None	Ireland	U. States	Union	3 Jun 1822
Sarah, Mrs.	24	F	Carpenter	England	U.S.	Acasta	11 May 1827
BENNITT, Thomas	17	M	Merchant	United States	United States	Florida	2 Sep 1822
BENNON, Bints	28 3/12	M	Joiner	France	U. States	France	26 Jun 1828
G.	28	M	Merchant	U. States	U. States	Marcellus	26 Feb 1824
BENNY, Anthony	48		Mines	England	England	Triumph	23 Jul 1829
Bridgett, Mrs.	19	F	Lady	Nova Scotia	United States	Washington	23 Dec 1828
BENODE, Frs.	48	M	Gent	French	Switzerland	Charlemagne	19 Sep 1828

NAMES OF PASSENGERS	AGE	SEX	OCCUPATIONS	COUNTRY TO WHICH THEY BELONG	COUNTRY THEY INTEND TO INHABIT	SHIPS/DATES OF ARRIVAL	
BENOFENOLE, Vincent	37	M	Merchant	Italy	Lpool [Liverpool]	Niagara	4 Sep 1824
BENOIT, —, Mrs.	30	F		U. States	U. States	Fair Play	16 Dec 1823
A.	18	F		France	U. States	Cadmus	28 May 1821
A., Miss	21	F		France	U. States	Cadmus	28 May 1821
Francis	22	M	Merchant	France		Charlemagne	16 Jan 1829
Frs.	30	M	Mariner	France	U. States	John London	1 Oct 1822
H. F.	21	M	Clerk	France	U. States	Cadmus	28 May 1821
Henry	9	M		U. States	U. States	Fair Play	16 Dec 1823
Jacob	22	M	Farmer			Nimrod	21 Sep 1820
Lewis	7	M		U. States	U. States	Fair Play	16 Dec 1823
Lewis	30	M	Musician	U. States	U. States	Fair Play	16 Dec 1823
BENS, Buckley	28	M		Great Britain	U. States	Corinthian	2 Sep 1824
BENSCH, Catharine	45	F		France	U. States	Edward Quesnel	4 Aug 1828
Catheran	19	F		France	U. States	Edward Quesnel	4 Aug 1828
Phillip	18	M		France	U. States	Edward Quesnel	4 Aug 1828
Randolph	55	M	Farmer	France	U. States	Edward Quesnel	4 Aug 1828
Soloman	9	M		France	U. States	Edward Quesnel	4 Aug 1828
BENSCHERY, N.	17	F		France & Switzerland	U. States	Bayard	14 Jul 1826
BENSEMANN, John F.			Merchant	America	U. States	Princess Louise	10 Mar 1825
BENSLEY, Alexander	20	M	...dler	Switzerland	U. States	Edward Bonnaffe	4 May 1827
John	28	M	Farmer	Ireland	U. States	Josephine	7 May 1827
Margaret	24	F	Spinster	Ireland	U. States	Josephine	7 May 1827
Mary	54	F	Matron	Ireland	U. States	Josephine	7 May 1827
William	20	M	Farmer	Ireland	U. States	Josephine	7 May 1827
William	60	M	Farmer	Ireland	U. States	Josephine	7 May 1827
BENSON, C.	17	M	Gentleman	New York	U. States	Columbia	12 Sep 1827
Catherine	23	F	Spinster	Ireland	United States	Trident	17 May 1825
Ellen	21	F	Spinster	Ireland	United States	Trident	17 May 1825
James	24	M	Laborer	Ireland	United States	St. Michaels	12 Jun 1826
John	20	M	Surveyor	England	America	John Adams	2 Aug 1827
John	32	M				Betsey	17 Aug 1820
John	49	M	Farmer	U. States		New York	18 Jul 1828
Joseph	25	M	Perfumer	England	United States	Roman	12 Jun 1826
Margt.	67	F	Widow	Ireland	United States	Trident	17 May 1825
Mary Ann	24	F		United States	New York	Nassau	19 Aug 1823
Patrick	19	M	Farmer	Ireland	United States	Lima	19 Jun 1824
Ricd.	30	M	Farmer	England	U. States	Auritz	20 May 1823
Sarah	22	F	Spinster	Ireland	United States	Fabius	31 Jul 1829
Thos.	24		...	France	U. States	Elizabeth	9 Jul 1825
William	24	M	Farmer	Great Britain	United States	Illinois	9 Oct 1820
Wm.	13	M	Merchant	Spain	U. States	Abeona	11 Sep 1828
BENST, J.	20	M	Farmer	Gt. Britain	U. States	Columbia	7 Sep 1827
BENSTEIN, Lorenz	25		Merchant	Germany		Amazon	7 Jul 1820
BENT, Jane	5	F	Farmer	Gt. Britain	United States	Europa	20 Apr 1825
John	6/12	M	Farmer	Gt. Britain	United States	Europa	20 Apr 1825
Luke	24	M	Surgeon	Massachusetts	Monteral	Eunice	8 Jan 1825
Mary	2	F	Farmer	Gt. Britain	United States	Europa	20 Apr 1825
Mary	26	F	Farmer	Gt. Britain	United States	Europa	20 Apr 1825
Wm.	30	M	Merchant	G. Britain	U. States	St. George	7 Jun 1828
Wm.	34	M	Farmer	Gt. Britain	United States	Europa	20 Apr 1825
Wm., Jr.	4	M	Farmer	Gt. Britain	United States	Europa	20 Apr 1825
BENTEGEUT, Ignis.	46	M	Planter	Guadaloupe		Alexander	18 Aug 1828
BENTES, Catherine	11	F		Switzerland	U.S.	Francois I	8 Aug 1829
Christiana	1	F		Switzerland	U.S.	Francois I	8 Aug 1829
John	7	M		Switzerland	U.S.	Francois I	8 Aug 1829
Ludwic	40	M	Weaver	Switzerland	U.S.	Francois I	8 Aug 1829
Magdalen	5	F		Switzerland	U.S.	Francois I	8 Aug 1829
Magdalen	40	F		Switzerland	U.S.	Francois I	8 Aug 1829
BENTIJAC, Caroline, Mrs.	15	F		U.S. of America	U.S. of America	Canada	1 Oct 1827
John	27	M	Merchant	France	U.S. of America	Canada	1 Oct 1827
BENTLEY, —	32	M	Farmer	England	U. States	Imperial	10 Dec 1821
—, Mrs.	28	F	Lady	England	U. States	Imperial	10 Dec 1821
Betsey	5	F		England	U. States	Imperial	10 Dec 1821
Elizabeth	22	F	Wife	England	United States	Trident	30 Sep 1826
Elizabeth	39	F				Governor Fenner	23 Jul 1829
F. J.	25 2/12	M	Merchant	U. States	United States	Young Phoenix	26 Jul 1824
George	5	M	Child	Manchester	United States	Nile	17 May 1827

NAMES OF PASSENGERS	AGE	SEX	OCCUPATIONS	COUNTRY TO WHICH THEY BELONG	COUNTRY THEY INTEND TO INHABIT	SHIPS/DATES OF ARRIVAL
BENTLEY (cont'd)						
James	2	M				Governor Fenner 23 Jul 1829
John	1	M		England	U. States	Imperial 10 Dec 1821
John	5	M				Governor Fenner 23 Jul 1829
John	26	M	Calico Printer	England	United States	Trident 30 Sep 1826
Joseph	2	M	Child	Manchester	United States	Nile 17 May 1827
Joseph	8	M				Governor Fenner 23 Jul 1829
Joseph	34	M	Wheelwright	England	New York	Governor Fenner 23 Jul 1829
Richard	8	M		England	U. States	Imperial 10 Dec 1821
Thomas	12	M				Governor Fenner 23 Jul 1829
Thos.	22	M		Ireland	U. States	Fame 15 Nov 1826
William	10	M				Governor Fenner 23 Jul 1829
BENTLY, Alice	9	F	None	England	U. States	Montgomery 18 Oct 1828
Ann	5	F	None	England	U. States	Montgomery 18 Oct 1828
Catherine	24	F	Wife	Manchester	United States	Nile 17 May 1827
Elizabeth	7	F	None	England	U. States	Montgomery 18 Oct 1828
Elizabeth	32	F	None	England	U. States	Montgomery 18 Oct 1828
James	27	M	Craser	Manchester	United States	Nile 17 May 1827
James	36	M	Millright	England	U. States	Montgomery 18 Oct 1828
John	13	M	None	England	U. States	Montgomery 18 Oct 1828
Mary	12	F	None	England	U. States	Montgomery 18 Oct 1828
Samuel	2	M	None	England	U. States	Montgomery 18 Oct 1828
Wm.	28	M	Farmer	Great Britain	United States	Frances Henrietta 17 Sep 1827
BENTOE, Thos.	46	M	Farmer	G. Britain	U.S. America	Cincinnatus 31 Oct 1820
BENTOFFER, Miles	30	M		G. Britain	U. States	Mary & Harriot 8 Sep 1828
BENTON, Catharine	25	F		Scotland	United States	Belmont 30 Aug 1828
David	29		Plaisterer	Scotland	United States	Camillus 3 May 1828
Edwin	3	M		England	America	Birmingham 16 Oct 1826
Flora	20	F		Scotland	United States	Belmont 30 Aug 1828
Flora	30	F		Scotland	United States	Belmont 30 Aug 1828
Geo.	23	M	Laborer	Scotland	U. States	Magnet 22 Aug 1822
Hugh	21	M	Weaver			Hercules 25 Sep 1820
Jane	25	F	wife to Laborer [Peter]	Scotland	U. States	Magnet 22 Aug 1822
John	19		Plaisterer	Scotland	United States	Camillus 3 May 1828
John	32	M	Farmer	Scotland	United States	Belmont 30 Aug 1828
John	63	M	Merchant			Hercules 25 Sep 1820
Malcolm	30	M		Scotland	United States	Belmont 30 Aug 1828
Nanty	30	F		Scotland	United States	Belmont 30 Aug 1828
Neil	32	M		Scotland	United States	Belmont 30 Aug 1828
Pat	22	M	Labourer	Ireland	United States	Wilson 6 Jun 1828
Peter	30	M	Laborer	Scotland	U. States	Magnet 22 Aug 1822
Rafael	26	M	Merchant	Spain	Spain	Dromo 5 Oct 1829
Saml.	14	M	Servant			Hercules 25 Sep 1820
Wm.	25	M	Labourer	G. Britain	U. States	St. George 7 Jun 1828
BENTS, James	18	M	Student	St. John, N.B.	St. John, N.B.	St. Michaels 27 Nov 1824
BENVAGNAN, Amelie	20	F	Servant	Switzerland	Massachusetts	Stephania 28 Jul 1823
Jeannette	28	F	Servant	Switzerland	Massachusetts	Stephania 28 Jul 1823
BEONPLAND, Phoebe	15	F	Domestic	Point Petre, Guadaloupe	United States	General Macombe 17 Jul 1827
V. T. K.	36	M	Planter	Point Petre, Guadaloupe	United States	General Macombe 17 Jul 1827
BEOUZRING, George	19	M		Scotland	U. States	Phocion 8 May 1824
BEPEN, M.	28	M	Blacksmith	France	U. States	Edwd. Quesnel 30 Apr 1825
BEQUIT, C.	24	M	Merchant	France	U. States	Circassian 26 Jun 1823
BERA, Robert L.	37	M	Merchant	U.S.	U.S.	Edward Quesnel 3 Jul 1829
BERART, James	30	F	Spinstress	Great Britain	United States	Roanoak 19 Sep 1827
BERAULT, Charles, Mrs.	30	F	None	U. States	U. States	Bayard 9 Jul 1824
Lora, Miss	15	F	None	U. States	U. States	Bayard 9 Jul 1824
BERBECK, —, Mr.	50	M	Planter	Barbadoes	Barbadoes	William & Nancy 5 Jun 1823
Christopher	21	M		Ireland	U. States	Fame 15 Nov 1826
BERCHAUD, Catharine	6	F	Farmer	Switzerland	United States	Olympia 12 Aug 1828
Catharine	36	F	Farmer	Switzerland	United States	Olympia 12 Aug 1828
Margaret	10	F	Farmer	Switzerland	United States	Olympia 12 Aug 1828
Michel	7	M	Farmer	Switzerland	United States	Olympia 12 Aug 1828
Pierre	36	M	Farmer	Switzerland	United States	Olympia 12 Aug 1828
BERCIER, Lambert	45	M	Merchant	New York	France	Jane 24 May 1828

NAMES OF PASSENGERS	AGE	SEX	OCCUPATIONS	COUNTRY TO WHICH THEY BELONG	COUNTRY THEY INTEND TO INHABIT	SHIPS/DATES OF ARRIVAL	
BERDANSER,							
Christopher	43	M	Farmer	Holland	U. States	Don Quixote	25 Oct 1828
BERDERE, Lambert	41	M	Merchant	Gaudaloupe	U. States	Henry	26 May 1823
Ursule	57	F		St. Eustatia	U. States	Henry	26 May 1823
BEREENGER, Joseph	62	M	Merchant	France	United States	Reaper	31 Aug 1826
BERGAMI, Jas.	30	M	Labourer	England	U. States	Mary	24 Jun 1824
BERGAN, Jno.	24	M	Labourer	Ireland	United States	Essex	23 May 1828
Mathew	30	M	...	Ireland	United States	Carolina Ann	24 Oct 1825
Patrick	17	M	...	Ireland	United States	Carolina Ann	24 Oct 1825
Patrick	23 4/12	M	Labourer	Ireland	United States	Wilson	22 Jun 1824
BERGDOLF, Adam	87	M	Tailor	Germany	United States	Martha	30 Jun 1823
BERGE, J.	36	M	Merchant	France	United States	Joseph	11 Jul 1821
BERGEN, Ambrosius	20	M		Germany	Cincinatti	Isabella	15 Sep 1828
Augustine	12	F		Germany	Cincinatti	Isabella	15 Sep 1828
Catharine	19	F	Servant	Ireland	United States	Wilson	27 Jun 1826
Elizabeth	16	F		Germany	Cincinatti	Isabella	15 Sep 1828
Elizabeth	31	F		Germany	Cincinatti	Isabella	15 Sep 1828
Grecian	19	M		Germany	Cincinatti	Isabella	15 Sep 1828
James	40	M	Farmer	G. Britain	U. States	George Clinton	10 Sep 1828
John, Mr.	27	M	Farmer	Grate Britain	...	Courier	14 Jun 1825
Marian	47	F		Germany	Cincinatti	Isabella	15 Sep 1828
Martin	21	M	Gentleman	Ireland	United States	Erin	25 Dec 1820
Michael	53	M	Farmer	Germany	Cincinatti	Isabella	15 Sep 1828
Michel	20	M	Labourer	England	America	William	21 Sep 1821
Rosina	21	F		Germany	Cincinatti	Isabella	15 Sep 1828
Sebastain	10	M		Germany	Cincinatti	Isabella	15 Sep 1828
Vincentt	24	F		Germany	Cincinatti	Isabella	15 Sep 1828
Willm.	20	M	Labourer	Ireland	United States	Wilson	27 Jun 1826
BERGENT, Jno.	30	M	Merchant	Spain	United States	Burdett	30 Apr 1828
BERGER, —, Mrs.	22	F			U. States	Hiram	17 Jun 1826
Antonn	37	M	Merchant	France	U. States	America	22 Sep 1826
Charles	23	M	Farmer	France	United States	Virginia	31 May 1828
F. B.	27	M	Carpenter	Charleston	U. States	Robt. Y. Hayne	27 Jun 1825
H.	28	M	Merchant	Germany	U. States	Hiram	17 Jun 1826
BERGERON, U.	41	M	M	Hayti	Hayti	Pacification	30 Jun 1823
BERGIN, M.	18	M		G. Britain	U. States	George Clinton	10 Sep 1828
BERGMAN, Mariah	26	F	Servant	Switzerland	U. States	Bayard	5 Sep 1828
BERGSTEDT, Joh.	20	M	Joiner	Altona	Charleston	Maria Elizabeth	18 Jun 1827
BERICK, John	30		Blacksmith	Germany	Germany	London	16 Aug 1824
BERK, A. G.	10	M	Merchant	U. States	United States	Burdett	30 Apr 1828
C. D.	8	F		U. States	United States	Burdett	30 Apr 1828
Elizabeth	4	F		Great Britain	United States	Diana	30 Oct 1827
John	29	M	Shoemaker	Great Britain	United States	Diana	30 Oct 1827
Mary Ann	5	F		Great Britain	United States	Diana	30 Oct 1827
Millisent	30	F		Great Britain	United States	Diana	30 Oct 1827
BERKAWIG, Micheal	21	M	Merchant	Great Britian	U. States	Pallas	17 Aug 1824
BERKE, Jno.	21	M	Farmer	Ireland	America	Mary	29 May 1827
BERKENBUSH, Chs.							
Hens. Chr.	32	M	Silver Smith	Germany	U. States	Acasta	28 Jan 1823
BERKETT, James	48	M	Mariner	Ireland	U. States	Howard	25 Jul 1823
BERKINS, James	35	M	Merchant	Boston, U.S.		Robert Edwards	8 Nov 1825
BERKLER, George	22	M	Butcher			Henri IV	17 May 1828
BERLER, Piere	25	M	Mackanic			Henri IV	17 May 1828
BERLOCHER, J. C.	20	M	Merchant	France	U. States	Don Quixote	20 Mar 1827
BERMAN, —, Mrs.	20	F		U. States	U. States	Zephyr	2 Oct 1826
Bidget	26	F				Ocean	17 Aug 1820
BERMAND, S.	28	M	Merchant	France	France	Eliza	28 Apr 1827
BERNAL, John	25		...	France	France	Bogota	25 Oct 1827
BERNARD, —	21	M	Merchant	Ireland	United States	Deux Ernest	29 Dec 1827
*landed in N. York							
—	21		Rontier	Irlande [Ireland]		Deux Ernest	29 Dec 1827
—, Mr.	40	M	Merchant	Isle of Man	Isle of Man	Wilhelmina	31 May 1824
—, Mrs.	26	F			U. States	Ann Maria	11 May 1822
Ann	4	F		United States	United States	Globe	30 Aug 1828
Ann	29	F	Seamstress	United States	United States	Globe	30 Aug 1828
Benjamin	27	M	Farmer	England	Canada	Brighton	14 Oct 1824
Catharine	6	F		United States	United States	Globe	30 Aug 1828
Chas.	51	M				Henri IV	17 May 1828
Eve	2	F		United States	United States	Globe	30 Aug 1828

NAMES OF PASSENGERS	AGE	SEX	OCCUPATIONS	COUNTRY TO WHICH THEY BELONG	COUNTRY THEY INTEND TO INHABIT	SHIPS/DATES OF ARRIVAL	
BERNARD (cont'd)							
Fredk.	12		Boy	England	United States	Courier	15 Oct 1827
J. R.	27	M	Merchant	England	England	Pacific	17 Jun 1828
J. R.	31	M	Merchant	Prusia	U. States	Ann Maria	11 May 1822
James	12	M		Great Britain	United States	Roanoak	19 Sep 1827
John	8	M		Great Britain	United States	Roanoak	19 Sep 1827
John P.	2	M				Henri IV	17 May 1828
John R.	40	M	Merchant	Port au Prince	England	Nature	17 Aug 1824
Margarette	43	F				Henri IV	17 May 1828
Michael	8	M		United States	United States	Globe	30 Aug 1828
Octs.	2		Child	England	United States	Courier	15 Oct 1827
Paul	30	M	Hairdresser	France	U. States	Ariadne	15 Apr 1822
Peter F.	27	M	Merchant	England	U. States	Sully	24 Oct 1828
Sopha.	6	F				Henri IV	17 May 1828
Thos.	14		Boy	England	United States	Courier	15 Oct 1827
BERNARDO, Stower	40	M	Seaman	Spain	Spain	Fabius	2 Oct 1826
BERNART, David	50	M	Farmer	Great Britain	United States	Roanoak	19 Sep 1827
BERNEL, Mariah	24	F	Spinster	Ireland	U. States	Meteor	19 Jul 1828
BERNHARD, Philip	20	M	Merchant	Hamburg	United States	Howard	6 Jul 1829
BERNIAND, Louis	22	M	Clerk	U. States	U. States	Dionesio	28 Jan 1828
BERNLEY, Thomas	35	M	Machine Maker	Great Britain	United States	Orbit	23 Oct 1826
BERNS, Ann	25	F		Ireland	U. States	Nancy	16 Aug 1822
Herman	26		Sugar boiler	Germany	Germany	Hudson	18 Jun 1825
BERNTEN, Sarah	17	F	Servant	Ireland	United States	Louisa	16 Mar 1826
BERON, George	18	M	Laborer	England	New York	Indian Chief	16 Aug 1822
BERRA, Henry	20	M	Mercht.	Spain	U.S.	Emma	24 Jun 1825
BERRI, Alexander	41	M	Farmer	England	America	Hercules	2 Nov 1825
BERRIER, Maria							
Catherine	40	F	Teacher	Switzerland	United States	Thetis	5 Jul 1821
BERRINGTON, William	25	M	Seaman	Great Brittan		Voltigeuse	4 Oct 1827
BERRY, Alexr.	31	M	Mason	G. Britain	U. States	Wanderer	23 Jun 1828
Cathn.	18	F	Servant	Ireland	United States	Wilson	27 Jun 1826
Chls.	20	M	Merchant	U. States	U. States	York	10 Dec 1825
David	25	M	Gardner	Yorkshire	United States	Dalhousie Castle	27 Jul 1826
Francis	2			Great Britain	U. States	Columbia	7 May 1828
Francis	15	M	None	Breeton	United States	Dalhousie Castle	27 Jul 1826
Gavin	21	M		Scotland	United States	Camillus	9 May 1827
George	28	M	Merchant	Westmoreland	America	Hannibal	4 Apr 1823
Hanah	5	F	None	G. Britain	U. States	Courier	16 Aug 1824
Hannah	40	F	None	Great Brittain	U. States	Louisa	11 Jun 1824
Hanny	40	F		England	United States	Curler	3 Mar 1828
James	30		Mason	Great Britain	U. States	Columbia	7 May 1828
James	30	M	Farmer	G. Britain	U. States	Wanderer	23 Jun 1828
Jno.	25	M	Farmer	Great Britain	U.S. of America	Gratitude	3 Oct 1829
John	31	M	Stone Mason	England	U.S.A.	Lima	6 Dec 1826
John	40	M	Baker	England	Phila.	Florida	28 Apr 1823
Mackbeth	24	F	None	England	United States	Jubilee	1 Oct 1828
Mary	1	F	None	England	United States	Jubilee	1 Oct 1828
Mary	16	F	Wife	England	U. States	Corinthian	20 Apr 1825
Mary	18	F		G. Britain	U. States	Sarah G	5 Jun 1828
Mary	20	F		G. Britain	U. States	Wanderer	23 Jun 1828
Mary	22			Great Britain	U. States	Columbia	7 May 1828
Paul	55	M	Farmer	Maryland	U. States	Topaz	23 Feb 1827
Peter	47	M	Farmer	England	U. States	Acasta	28 Jan 1823
Richard	25		Mason	Great Britain	U. States	Columbia	7 May 1828
Richd.	26	M	Carpenter	Bristol, Maine	U. States	Mercator	27 Aug 1821
Thomas	35	M	Umbrella Maker	Great Britain	U. States	Great Britain	18 Mar 1828
Thos.	1			Great Britain	U. States	Columbia	7 May 1828
W.	70	M	Farmer	England	U. States	Corinthian	20 Apr 1825
Wm.	6/12			Great Britain	U. States	Columbia	7 May 1828
BERRYANN, Ann	24	F	Wife	United States	U. States	Hanford	29 Dec 1828
Henry	26	M	Farmer	United States	U. States	Hanford	29 Dec 1828
BERSLAW, Ann	3	F		G. Britain	U. States	George Clinton	10 Sep 1828
Jane	5	F		G. Britain	U. States	George Clinton	10 Sep 1828
M.	1	M		G. Britain	U. States	George Clinton	10 Sep 1828
May	25	F		G. Britain	U. States	George Clinton	10 Sep 1828
BERSOM, Ann	51	F	Confection	Great Britian	United States	Andes	19 Aug 1829
Francis	21	M	Confection	Great Britian	United States	Andes	19 Aug 1829
James	51	M	Confection	Great Britian	United States	Andes	19 Aug 1829

NAMES OF PASSENGERS	AGE	SEX	OCCUPATIONS	COUNTRY TO WHICH THEY BELONG	COUNTRY THEY INTEND TO INHABIT	SHIPS/DATES OF ARRIVAL	
BERT, Francis	44	M	Mercht.	France	U.S.	Cadmus	20 Dec 1824
BERTAUX, Nicholas			Baker	France	U.S.	Sully	26 Oct 1829
BERTHELS, Nathaniel	22	M	Plaisterer	Liverpool	Washington	Curler	7 Jul 1827
BERTHENEY, C.	35	M	Gentleman	France	France	Ohio	18 Jul 1821
BERTHLETT, Augustus	33	M		G. Brittain	U. States	Cincinnatus	2 Oct 1822
BERTHOL, B.	7	F		Switzerland	U. States	Romulus	24 Sep 1828
Cath.	3	F		Switzerland	U. States	Romulus	24 Sep 1828
J.	43	M	Weaver	Switzerland	U. States	Romulus	24 Sep 1828
John	11	M		Switzerland	U. States	Romulus	24 Sep 1828
Jos.	9	M		Switzerland	U. States	Romulus	24 Sep 1828
M.	0 3/12	F		Switzerland	U. States	Romulus	24 Sep 1828
Mary	6	F		Switzerland	U. States	Romulus	24 Sep 1828
Mary	38	M		Switzerland	U. States	Romulus	24 Sep 1828
S.	8	M		Switzerland	U. States	Romulus	24 Sep 1828
BERTLEDGE, Robert	28	M	Merchant	United States	United States	Florida	11 May 1822
BERTON, Joseph	18	M	Black Smith	France	United States	Virginia	31 May 1828
BERTOSSI, Jacob M.	24	M	Merchant	Brazil	Brazil	Protection	26 Oct 1827
BERTRAM, A.	28	M	Merchant	United States	U. States	Havana Packet	27 Jul 1827
David	25	M	Farmer	Scotland	United States	Camillus	9 May 1827
BERTRAND, A.	28	M	Merchant	France	U. States	New Packet	5 May 1823
A.	30	M	Merchant	Spain	Spain	Sarah Ann	8 May 1822
Entreal, sue fils [his son?]	12	M	Merchant	Spain	Spain	Sarah Ann	8 May 1822
Jaques	75 4/12	M	Gentlman.	France	France	France	28 Mar 1829
Jenny	20	F	Attendant	France	America	Lima	11 Dec 1823
Jno.	34	M	Merchant	France	U. States	Frances Ann	27 Aug 1821
Virginia	7 5/12	F		France	France	France	28 Mar 1829
BERTRIN, Joseph	23	M	Merchant	Guadaloupe	Guadaloupe	Leo	2 Oct 1822
BERVEREIR, Jas. M.	30	M	Merchant	Spain	Spain	Admittance	22 Sep 1823
BERWICK, John	45	M	Merchant	England	America	Panthea	18 Jul 1823
BES..., John	30	M	Weaver	Switzerland	United States	Elbe	2 Aug 1822
BESANSON, Agath	17	M		Native of Switzerland	United States	Canaris	30 Jun 1827
Anthony	52	M	Shoemaker	Native of Switzerland	United States	Canaris	30 Jun 1827
Augest	7	M		Native of Switzerland	United States	Canaris	30 Jun 1827
Francis	11	M		Native of Switzerland	United States	Canaris	30 Jun 1827
Francis	40	M		Native of Switzerland	United States	Canaris	30 Jun 1827
Frank	9	M		Native of Switzerland	United States	Canaris	30 Jun 1827
James	2	M		Native of Switzerland	United States	Canaris	30 Jun 1827
James	19	M		Native of Switzerland	United States	Canaris	30 Jun 1827
Joseph	5	M		Native of Switzerland	United States	Canaris	30 Jun 1827
BESE..., Elizabeth	22	F		Switzerland	United States	Elbe	2 Aug 1822
Frances	20	F		Switzerland	United States	Elbe	2 Aug 1822
Mary	28	F		Switzerland	United States	Elbe	2 Aug 1822
BESEGER, Christian	52	M	Wheaver	Switzerland	United States	Elbe	2 Aug 1822
BESHEL, W. T. C.	18	M	Mariner	Gt. Britain	U. States	Fourth of July	13 Jul 1825
BESSAY, Mary	17	F	Lady	United States	United States	Ariadne	25 Jul 1822
BESSE, John L.	18	M	Merchant	France	United States	Maria Theresa	13 Apr 1822
BESSINGER, Cons. Ad.	23	M	...	Wirtemburg	United States	Wade	29 Aug 1825
BESSON, Louis, Mr.	30	M	Mercht.	Pennsylvania	Pennsylvania	Cadmus	16 Aug 1826
BEST, David	24	M	Labourer	Gt. Britain	U. States	Maria	22 May 1822
Eliza	23	F		Gt. Britain		Maria	22 May 1822
Henry	32	M	Farmer	Great Brittan	United States	Hanford	3 Aug 1829
Jane	26	F		England	United States	Essex	23 May 1828
Richd.	30	M	Carter	Ireland	United States	Essex	23 May 1828
BESTON, Thos.	19	M	Labourer	Great Britain	United States	Mary & Harriet	3 Jul 1829
BESWICK, John W.	24	M	Gentleman	Great Britain	United States	Albion	18 Feb 1823
Wright	27	M	Spinster	Great Brittain		Corinthian	9 Jan 1827
BETCHIE, William	55	M	Labourer	Scotland	United States	Samuel Robertson	9 May 1827
BETERKEN, John	30	M	Farmer	Great Brittan	U.S.	Emulous	29 Jun 1827

NAMES OF PASSENGERS	AGE	SEX	OCCUPATIONS	COUNTRY TO WHICH THEY BELONG	COUNTRY THEY INTEND TO INHABIT	SHIPS/DATES OF ARRIVAL	
BETERLO, Andrew	19	M	Merchant	Spain	U. States	Union	21 Jul 1825
BETHEL, Wm. H.	22	M	Mercht.	Great Britan	Great Britan	Ann Howard	4 Aug 1829
BETHUIN, Harman	30	M	Merchant	Canada	Canada	John Wells	16 May 1825
BETHUNE, Angus	37	M	Merchant	Canada	Great Brittan	Amity	11 May 1821
Diver	49	M	Merchant	Great Britain	United States	Nestor	3 Nov 1820
Lucy	34	F	Servant	United States	United States	James Monroe	14 Dec 1820
N.	33	M		Great Britain	Canada	James Monroe	25 Apr 1822
Norman	34	M	Merchant	Gt. Brittain	Canada	Leeds	19 May 1823
BETLAND, Charles	37	M	Mariner	England	England	Enterprize	14 Oct 1828
BETMAN, Elizabeth	29	F	Milliner	Great Britain	United States	India	5 Sep 1827
BETON, Ann	18	F	Servant	Ireland	United States	St. Michaels	18 Jul 1826
BETREE, Batria	1	M		Switzerland	U.S. America	Huntress	6 Sep 1827
J. P.	32	M	Blacksmith	Switzerland	U.S. America	Huntress	6 Sep 1827
John P.	4	M		Switzerland	U.S. America	Huntress	6 Sep 1827
Maria	30	F		Switzerland	U.S. America	Huntress	6 Sep 1827
Marian	3	F		Switzerland	U.S. America	Huntress	6 Sep 1827
BETRUE, Joseph	6	M		Switzerland	U.S. America	Huntress	6 Sep 1827
BETTERTON, Ann	35	F		U. States	U. States	Magnet	29 Sep 1823
BETTETTE, —, Miss	14	F		St. Croix	United States	Carlo	28 Jun 1826
—, Miss	16	F		St. Croix	United States	Carlo	28 Jun 1826
—, Miss	18	F		St. Croix	United States	Carlo	28 Jun 1826
BETTLE, Lot	20	M	Merchant	Germany	U. States	James M	15 Sep 1828
BETTS, Barben	5	F		Switzerland	U.S.	C. Amelia	30 Jun 1828
Catherine	12	F		Switzerland	U.S.	C. Amelia	30 Jun 1828
Eliz.	6	F		Switzerland	U.S.	C. Amelia	30 Jun 1828
Jane	22	F	Child	Ireland	N. York	Trusty	12 Sep 1828
Jean	28	M		Switzerland	U.S.	C. Amelia	30 Jun 1828
Madeline	8	F		Switzerland	U.S.	C. Amelia	30 Jun 1828
Mary		F		U. States	U. States	Governor Griswold	18 Jun 1821
Nicholas	12	M		Switzerland	U.S.	C. Amelia	30 Jun 1828
Saml.	25	M	Farmer	G. Britain	U. States	Nimrod	31 Jul 1828
Thomas	46	M	Mariner	U. States	U. States	New Packet	27 Apr 1822
William	23	M	...	United States	United States	Ludwig	10 Aug 1825
William	33	M	Mercht.	Great Britain	United States	Samuel Wright	12 Oct 1829
BETY, George F., 1st	25	M	Farmer or Mechanic	France	U.S.	Edward Quesnel	31 Jul 1827
George F., 2d.	17	M	Farmer or Mechanic	France	U.S.	Edward Quesnel	31 Jul 1827
John P.	17	M	Farmer or Mechanic	France	U.S.	Edward Quesnel	31 Jul 1827
BEUCHE, Carles H.	40	M	Shepherd	Bremen	Bremen	Francis	4 May 1826
BEUFLAND, —	36	M	Planter	Gaudiloupe	Gaudiloupe	Nancy	29 May 1826
—, Master	6/12	M	Child	Gaudiloupe	Gaudiloupe	Nancy	29 May 1826
—, Master	4	M	Child	Gaudiloupe	Gaudiloupe	Nancy	29 May 1826
—, Master	5	M	Child	Gaudiloupe	Gaudiloupe	Nancy	29 May 1826
—, Miss	2	F	Child	Gaudiloupe	Gaudiloupe	Nancy	29 May 1826
—, Mrs.	34	F	Lady	Gaudiloupe	Gaudiloupe	Nancy	29 May 1826
BEUFOY, M.	22	M	Gentleman	England	England	Eliza	28 Apr 1827
BEUTERMAN, G. W. C.	4	M		England	U. States	Trident	1 Dec 1824
BEUTIER, Mark A.	21	M	Gentleman	France	United States	Montano	27 Aug 1827
BEUTSAKER, Jh.	25			Suisse		Deux Ernest	29 Dec 1827
BEVER, Catharin	25	F	Servant	France	America, U.N.S.	Great Britain	3 Aug 1829
S. P., Mr.	36	M	Mercht.	Holland	United States	Nestor	25 Jul 1823
BEVEREDGE, Jno.	30	M	Labourer	Argyle (Tedland) Scotland	United States	Jean Hastie	27 Jul 1829
BEVERHANDT, Peter	35	M	Merchant	Havana	U. States	Hesper	28 Dec 1825
BEVERIDGE,							
Anna Maria	19	F	Lady	Maryland	America	Orbit	1 Sep 1823
Isabella	13	F	Child	Scotland	United States	Tom	2 Jul 1827
Isabella	54	F	Wife	Scotland	United States	Tom	2 Jul 1827
Mary	32	F	Widow	Scotland	United States	Tom	2 Jul 1827
Peter	33	M	Bookseller	Scotland	United States	Tom	2 Jul 1827
Robert	5	M	Child	Scotland	United States	Tom	2 Jul 1827
Robert	29	M	Merchant	Maryland	America	Orbit	1 Sep 1823
William, Mr.	17	M	Merchant	Scotland	New York	Hannibal	28 Apr 1824
BEVEY, George	29	M	Weaver	Great Britain	United States	Corinthian	2 Sep 1824
John	15	M	Weaver	Great Britain	United States	Corinthian	2 Sep 1824
William	70	M	Weaver	Great Britain	United States	Corinthian	2 Sep 1824
William, Jr.	19	M	Weaver	Great Britain	United States	Corinthian	2 Sep 1824
BEVIN, Christian	10			France	U. States	Parachute	14 May 1828
Margaret	50			France	U. States	Parachute	14 May 1828

NAMES OF PASSENGERS	AGE	SEX	OCCUPATIONS	COUNTRY TO WHICH THEY BELONG	COUNTRY THEY INTEND TO INHABIT	SHIPS/DATES OF ARRIVAL	
BEVIN (cont'd)							
Nicholas	11			France	U. States	Parachute	14 May 1828
Peter	20			France	U. States	Parachute	14 May 1828
Philip	18			France	U. States	Parachute	14 May 1828
Sophia	24			France	U. States	Parachute	14 May 1828
BEVOIN, William	35	M	Labourer	England	United States	Maria	29 Sep 1823
BEVRAGE, William	35	M	Taylor	Scotland	United States	Hope	5 Dec 1827
BEWDELIN, T.	52	M	Gentleman	G. Britain	U. States	Canada	19 Sep 1828
BEYER, Barbara	10	F	None	France	U. States	Sully	25 Jun 1828
Jacob	6 6/12	M	None	France	U. States	Sully	25 Jun 1828
Margaret	5	F	None	France	U. States	Sully	25 Jun 1828
Philip	8	M	None	France	U. States	Sully	25 Jun 1828
Philip	45	M	Farmer	France	U. States	Sully	25 Jun 1828
BEYLARD, C.	7	M		U.S.	U.S.	Francois I	8 Aug 1829
E.	24	F		U.S.	U.S.	Francois I	8 Aug 1829
J.	34	M	Merchant	U.S.	U.S.	Francois I	8 Aug 1829
BEZEAU, Adaline	12	F		U.S.A.	Philadelphia	Huntress	11 Dec 1821
Cornellia	5	F		U.S.A.	Philadelphia	Huntress	11 Dec 1821
Hetty, Mrs.	30	F		U.S. of America	Philadelphia	Huntress	11 Dec 1821
William	4/12	M		U.S.A.	Philadelphia	Huntress	11 Dec 1821
BEZLEER, John	28	M	Weaver	Switzerland	United States	Elbe	2 Aug 1822
BIAS, Timothy C.	24	M	Merchant	St. Johns	St. Johns	Nancy	3 Apr 1824
BICHEL, Glaude	42	M	Farmer	France	U. States	C. Amelia	30 Jun 1828
BICHET, Jos. P.	13	M	Farmer	France	U. States	C. Amelia	30 Jun 1828
Maria F.	9	F	Farmer	France	U. States	C. Amelia	30 Jun 1828
V. de Rose	7	F	Farmer	France	U. States	C. Amelia	30 Jun 1828
BICKER, Martin	58	M	Merchant	U.S. America	U.S. America	Gallego	13 Mar 1829
Nichs.	41	M	Mariner	N. York	U. States	Anna Elizabeth	15 Feb 1823
BICKERSTOFF, —, Mr.	22	M	Gentleman	Dublin	U. States	Hibernia	26 Oct 1826
BICKETT, James	19	M	Farmer	Ireland	America	Dublin Packet	9 Oct 1820
BICKLEMAN, And.	30	M	Agriculture	Wirtemburg	United States	Henri IV	14 Oct 1829
Ann	26	F	Agriculture	Wirtemburg	United States	Henri IV	14 Oct 1829
Christine	6	F	Agriculture	Wirtemburg	United States	Henri IV	14 Oct 1829
Johanns	1	M	Agriculture	Wirtemburg	United States	Henri IV	14 Oct 1829
Rosane	3	F	Agriculture	Wirtemburg	United States	Henri IV	14 Oct 1829
BICKLER, Francois	26	M	Farmer	Switzerland	U. States	La Urania	3 Jul 1828
BICKMAS, Adam	24	M	Merchant	U. States	U. States	Greyhound	29 Sep 1820
BICKVESTUFF, —	22	F	Spinster	Ireland	United States	Thomas	13 Dec 1827
BIDDLE, Samuel	24	M	M...	Great Britain	U. States	Panthea	24 Mar 1825
Thos.	27		Farmer	England	United States	Hugh Johnson	11 Jun 1828
BIDDY, Mary	20	F	Spinster	G. Britain	U. States	St. George	7 Jun 1828
Patrick	25	M		G. Britain	U. States	Mary & Harriot	8 Sep 1828
BIDEAUX, Celestine	5	F		France	U. States	Leonarde	29 Aug 1828
Marianne P.	32	F		France	U. States	Leonarde	29 Aug 1828
Rose	8	F		France	U. States	Leonarde	29 Aug 1828
Therese	1 9/12	F		France	U. States	Leonarde	29 Aug 1828
Xayar	36	M	Weaver	France	U. States	Leonarde	29 Aug 1828
BIDEL, P.	29	M	Butcher	Germany	United States	Howard	15 Jun 1825
BIDEN, Edmund	15	M		G. Brittain	U. States	Cincinnatus	2 Oct 1822
Eliza	13	F		G. Brittain	U. States	Cincinnatus	2 Oct 1822
Georgeanna	11	F		G. Brittain	U. States	Cincinnatus	2 Oct 1822
John	17	M		G. Brittain	U. States	Cincinnatus	2 Oct 1822
John	38	M	Carpenter	G. Brittain	U. States	Cincinnatus	2 Oct 1822
Mary	9	F		G. Brittain	U. States	Cincinnatus	2 Oct 1822
Sarah	39	F		G. Brittain	U. States	Cincinnatus	2 Oct 1822
BIDLIN, Thomas	27	M	Labourer	Ireland	America	Dewitt Clinton	27 Jul 1824
BIDSTRA, Harmon Enul	H.22		Gentleman	Denmark	U. States	Solon	7 Aug 1820
BIDWELL, John	21					Aurora	8 Jun 1827
Z.	25		Mechanic	United States	U.N. States	James	27 May 1824
BIÉ, Paul	23	M	None	France	U. States	Sully	15 Jul 1829
BIEDENFELT, Herman	25	M	on Bussiness	Germany	United States	Martha	30 Jun 1823
BIEMAN'S, M.	51	M	Mercht.	Holland	U. States	Howard	13 Feb 1829
BIERMAN, Charles	24	M	Merchant	Ireland	United States	William Byrnes	15 Aug 1826
BIERTWIPPLE, Phillip	25	M	Servant	Gt. Britian	United States	Nestor	16 Aug 1824
BIGATT, Anne	24			St. Croix	United States	Emelia	10 Dec 1827
BIGELOW, Joseph	35	M	Gentleman	U. States	U. States	Jupiter	26 Dec 1827
BIGG, Caroline	5 2/12	F	Farmer	England	United States	Young Phoenix	26 Jul 1824
George	22	M	Merchant	England	United States	Herald	29 Oct 1825
Harriet	6	F	Farmer	England	United States	Young Phoenix	26 Jul 1824

NAMES OF PASSENGERS	AGE	SEX	OCCUPATIONS	COUNTRY TO WHICH THEY BELONG	COUNTRY THEY INTEND TO INHABIT	SHIPS/DATES OF ARRIVAL	
BIGG (cont'd)							
Mary	8 5/12	F	Farmer	England	United States	Young Phoenix	26 Jul 1824
Mary	20	F	Farmer	England	United States	Young Phoenix	26 Jul 1824
Peggy	7 3/12	F	Farmer	England	United States	Young Phoenix	26 Jul 1824
Thomas	1 4/12	M	Farmer	England	United States	Young Phoenix	26 Jul 1824
Wm.	3 1/12	M	Farmer	England	United States	Young Phoenix	26 Jul 1824
BIGGAM, Agnes	22	F				John Dickinson	14 Sep 1820
BIGGER, Betty	3	F	Child	Scotland	America	Concord	4 Jun 1821
Isabella	7	F	Child	Scotland	America	Concord	4 Jun 1821
James	20	M	Labourer	Ireland	America	Franklin	13 Aug 1827
Jane	9	F	Child	Scotland	America	Concord	4 Jun 1821
Jenett	5	F	Child	Scotland	America	Concord	4 Jun 1821
Margarett	21	F		Ireland	America	Franklin	13 Aug 1827
Margret	11	F	Child	Scotland	America	Concord	4 Jun 1821
Margret	36	F	Spinster	Scotland	America	Concord	4 Jun 1821
Robert	13	M	Child	Scotland	America	Concord	4 Jun 1821
Robert	36	M	Farmer	Scotland	America	Concord	4 Jun 1821
Walter	40	M	Farmer	Scotland	America	Concord	4 Jun 1821
BIGGET, Maxwell	22	M	Farmer	Ireland	United States	Trident	16 May 1826
BIGGHIM, Alexander	35	M	Tailor	Ireland		Marchioness	13 May 1828
Jane	3	F	None	Ireland		Marchioness	13 May 1828
Jane	28	F	None	Ireland		Marchioness	13 May 1828
BIGGOTT, Wm.	5	M		St. Croix	St. Croix	Carlo	19 Apr 1828
BIGGS, —, Mrs.	28	F		Great Britian	United States	Columbia	17 Apr 1827
George	23		Copper Refiner	Great Britian	Upper Canada	Nile	30 Apr 1827
George	29	M	Weaver	Manchester	United States	Nile	17 May 1827
Saml.	56	M	Mechanic	England	United States	Concordia	25 Aug 1827
Susan	10	F	Labourer	England	U. States	Ayrshire	12 May 1828
Thomas	25	M	Labourer	England	U. States	Ayrshire	12 May 1828
William	21 2/12	M	Millwright	Scotland	United States	Mobile	21 Aug 1827
BIGLAND, Patrick	26	M	Farmer	Ireland	United States	Dublin Packet	28 Apr 1824
BIGLIN, D., Revd.	34		D.D.	U. States	United States	Henri IV	14 Sep 1827
BIGLOR, Frederick	10	M	Servant	U. States	U. States	Manchester Packet	5 Dec 1826
BIGNALL, Mary	20	F		Great Brittian	United States	Carolina Augusta	2 Dec 1828
BIGOR, Ann	23 5/12	F		Denmark	U.S.A.	Silas Richards	27 Oct 1826
BIGSBY, Jeremiah J.	30	M	None	Grat Britan	Cannada	Columbia	7 Apr 1823
BIGSEROUX, John	34	M	Merchant	St. Domingo	St. Domingo	Fair Play	9 Sep 1823
BILBOW, Charles	14	M	Farmer	Pep...	U.S. America	Superior	18 Jun 1825
David	55	M	Farmer	Pep...	U.S. America	Superior	18 Jun 1825
Margaret	44	F	Farmer	Pep...	U.S. America	Superior	18 Jun 1825
BILEY, George	...	M	Merchant	England	Lower Canada	Amity	13 Sep 1821
BILL, Edward		M	Merchant	N. York	U. States	Antelope	17 Nov 1823
John	32	M	Merchant	Great Britain	U. States	William Thompson	24 Aug 1827
Thos.	38	M	Merchant	U. States	U. States	Prince Edward	23 Dec 1823
Walter	25	M	Farmer	Cookstown	Aug Co.	Favourite	8 Oct 1823
BILLALY, L.	36	M	Merchant	Rhode Island	U. States	Betsey Ann	15 Oct 1821
BILLAMY, —, Revd.	30	M	Revd.	France	U. States	Othello	31 Aug 1824
BILLANY, John	25	M	Farmer	Ireland	United States	Aurelia	7 Jun 1826
BILLARDES, G.	30	M	Soldier	Spain	Spain	Prince Edward	22 Jul 1824
BILLCO, Lorenzo Jose	36 2/12	M	Shipmaster	Portugal	Havana	Margaret	22 Jun 1821
BILLEARY, Henry	9	M	Farmer	Gt. Brittian	Gt. Brittian	Manchester	21 Apr 1827
BILLEY, Felix	27	M	Merchant	France	United States	Montano	27 Aug 1827
BILLIN, J.	45	M	Merchant	St. Domingo	St. Domingo	Enterprize	19 Aug 1825
Maria	12	F	Daughter	St. Domingo	St. Domingo	Enterprize	19 Aug 1825
BILLING, John	32	M		England	United States	Hercules	25 Jan 1820
Robert	22	M	Laborer	St. Johns	G. Briten	Nancey	13 May 1822
BILLINGHURST,							
Farncomb	25	M	Farmer	England	U. States	Cincinnatus	24 May 1821
Harriet	26	F		England	U. States	Cincinnatus	24 May 1821
BILLINGS, Noyes	27	M	Merchant	United States	United States	Bayard	13 Nov 1823
W. W.	21		Gentn.	United States	United States	Othello	6 Nov 1823
Wm. W.	20	M	Merchant	U. States	U. States	Sarah Herrick	15 Apr 1823
BILLSEN, Edward	3	M	None	Gt. Britain	United States	Eliza Barker	11 Jan 1826
Robt.	39	M	Labourer	Gt. Britain	United States	Eliza Barker	11 Jan 1826
Samuel	5	M	None	Gt. Britain	United States	Eliza Barker	11 Jan 1826

NAMES OF PASSENGERS	AGE	SEX	OCCUPATIONS	COUNTRY TO WHICH THEY BELONG	COUNTRY THEY INTEND TO INHABIT	SHIPS/DATES OF ARRIVAL	
BILLSEN (cont'd)							
Susan	34	F	None	Gt. Britain	United States	Eliza Barker	11 Jan 1826
BILLY, Francisco	20	M	Mercht.	Omoa	Omoa	Savannah	22 May 1827
Samuel	30	M	Merchant	U.S.	U.S.	Abeona	12 Mar 1825
BILOBORROW, James	29	M	Distiller	England	America	Manhattan	21 Sep 1822
Robt.	27	M	Distiller	England	America	Manhattan	21 Sep 1822
BILOT, Jean	22	M	Farmer	Germany	United States	Oxford	14 Aug 1828
BILSBARROW, Allen	34	M	None	England	United States	Trident	18 Jul 1827
Ann	34	M	None	England	United States	Trident	18 Jul 1827
Deliverance	12	F	None	England	United States	Trident	18 Jul 1827
Faith	14	F	None	England	United States	Trident	18 Jul 1827
John	50	M	None	England	United States	Trident	18 Jul 1827
Lazarus	16	M	None	England	United States	Trident	18 Jul 1827
Mary	10	F	None	England	United States	Trident	18 Jul 1827
Plinn	21	M	None	England	United States	Trident	18 Jul 1827
BILSBARY, Abner	21	M	Bk. Smith	Gt. Britain	United States	Meteor	19 Aug 1829
BILSBOROUGH, Charles	17	M	Farmer	Great Britain	United States	John Wells	18 Sep 1826
Jasper	38	M	Merchant	England	England	James Cropper	10 Feb 1823
Thomas	22	M	Farmer	Great Britain	United States	John Wells	18 Sep 1826
BILTRAN, Anthony	27	M	Merchant	Spain	Mexico	Eliza	14 Mar 1825
BINAR, Constarn	13	M	None	France	New York	Billow	1 Jun 1826
BINDER, Fanny, Mrs.	22	F	None	U. States	U. States	John Laird	16 Jun 1827
BINDLEY, Charlotte	40		Lady	England	United States	Corinthian	30 May 1828
Edgar	12		Gentleman	England	United States	Corinthian	30 May 1828
Edward	11		Gentleman	England	United States	Corinthian	30 May 1828
Frederick	13		Gentleman	England	United States	Corinthian	30 May 1828
Thomas	50		Gentleman	England	United States	Corinthian	30 May 1828
BINELL, Henry	42	M	Farmer	Ireland	United States	Friends	21 Oct 1825
BINGAY, Thomas H.	33	M	Shipmaster	Great Britain		Howard	4 Feb 1826
BINGELSBERGEN, Jacob	19	M	Mason	Germany	Maryland	Orient	25 Nov 1825
BINGHAM, David	31	M	Labourer	Ireland	United States	Fabius	31 Jul 1829
Elisbath	1	F	Child	Ireland	United States	Fabius	31 Jul 1829
J.	30	M	Enginer	New York	New York	Richard Meade	27 Apr 1822
James	31	M	Leather Dyer	G.B.	U.S.	London	19 Dec 1823
Pam				Ireland	United States	Fabius	31 Jul 1829
William	19	M	None	U. N. States	U. N. States	Nestor	3 Nov 1820
BINGLEY, Mark	45	M	Servant	England	United States	William Thompson	19 Aug 1829
BINGLY, George	26	M	Merchant	Great Britain	United States	Martha	3 May 1821
BINLEY, Eliza	13			England		Anacreon	7 Sep 1827
Jno.	18	M	Joiner	England	United States	Essex	23 May 1828
Jno.	42			England		Anacreon	7 Sep 1827
Job	3			England		Anacreon	7 Sep 1827
John	16			England		Anacreon	7 Sep 1827
Kiskell	6	F		England		Anacreon	7 Sep 1827
Lear	9	F		England		Anacreon	7 Sep 1827
Nomiah	5	M		England		Anacreon	7 Sep 1827
Rachel	4			England		Anacreon	7 Sep 1827
Ruth	11			England		Anacreon	7 Sep 1827
Sarah	1			England		Anacreon	7 Sep 1827
Sarah	39			England		Anacreon	7 Sep 1827
BINLIN, Francis	29	M	Carpenter	France	U. States	Edward Bonaffe	23 Jul 1828
Jacob	37	M	Farmer	France	U. States	Edward Bonaffe	23 Jul 1828
BINN, Patrick	22	M	Taylor	Ireland	United States	Fabius	31 Jul 1829
BINNEY, Stephen	27	M	Merchant	Halifax, N.S.	Halifax	Nestor in Liverpool	29 Jul 1822
W. J.	39	M	Mechanic	Barbadoes	Barbadoes	Sudan	6 Aug 1823
BINNS, ...	16/12	F	None	Leicester		Aurora	8 Jun 1827
Ann	23	F	None	Leicester		Aurora	8 Jun 1827
George	6	M	Weaver	Edgeworth		Aurora	8 Jun 1827
John	13	M	Cloth dresser	Great Britain	United States	Birmingham	15 Jun 1827
John	60	M	Clogger	Crawst...		Aurora	8 Jun 1827
BINOIT, J.	20	M	Merchant	Switzerland		Howard	17 Oct 1824
BINSLEY, John	28		Labourer	England	United States	Hugh Johnson	11 Jun 1828
Margt.	26			England	United States	Hugh Johnson	11 Jun 1828
BINTHAL, Wm. H.	38	M	Mariner	U. States	U. States	Mary Ann	13 Jun 1821
BINTON, L. F.	54	M	Merchant	England	England	Amity	31 May 1822
BIRAN, George	32	M	Servant	Great Britain	United States	Ann	24 Sep 1822
BIRBECK, Margaret	22	F	Miner	Great Britian	United States	Andes	19 Aug 1829

NAMES OF PASSENGERS	AGE	SEX	OCCUPATIONS	COUNTRY TO WHICH THEY BELONG	COUNTRY THEY INTEND TO INHABIT	SHIPS/DATES OF ARRIVAL	
BIRBECK (cont'd)							
Thomas	28	M	Miner	Great Britian	United States	Andes	19 Aug 1829
William	23	M	Miner	Great Britian	United States	Andes	19 Aug 1829
BIRCASS, B.	35	M	Mariner	France	U. States	Emeline	5 Jul 1823
BIRCH, Alice	6	F	Child	Great Britain	United States	Washington	3 Sep 1827
Ann	8	F	Child	Great Britain	United States	Washington	3 Sep 1827
Carol...a	18 6/12	F	Spinster	Ireland	U. States	Josephine	30 Aug 1828
David	4	M	Labourer	Ireland	U. States	Josephine	30 Aug 1828
Edward	6	M	Farmer	Great Britain	United States	Columbia	17 Apr 1827
Elias	38	M	Spinner	England	United States	Trident	31 Mar 1827
Fanny	8	F	Farmer	Great Britain	United States	Columbia	17 Apr 1827
Frances	23	F	None	England	United States	Roman	12 Jun 1826
George	26	M	Blacksmith	England	United States	Roman	12 Jun 1826
Hannah	16	F	None	England	United States	Trident	31 Mar 1827
James	13	M	Labourer	Ireland	U. States	Josephine	30 Aug 1828
John	9	M	Labourer	Ireland	U. States	Josephine	30 Aug 1828
John	23	M	Weaver	England	United States	Trident	31 Mar 1827
John	30	M	Carpenter	England	United States	Roman	12 Jun 1826
Margaret	16	F	Spinster	Ireland	U. States	Josephine	30 Aug 1828
Martha	3	F	Child	Great Britain	United States	Washington	3 Sep 1827
Mary	33	F	None	England	United States	Trident	31 Mar 1827
Mary Ann	10	F	Farmer	Great Britain	United States	Columbia	17 Apr 1827
Richard	22	M	Merchant	England	U. States America	Cambria	2 Jul 1821
Saml.	29	M	Labourer	England	United States of Am.	Helen	17 Dec 1827
Sarah	30	F	Farmer	Great Britain	United States	Columbia	17 Apr 1827
Sarah	31	F	wife	Great Britain	United States	Washington	3 Sep 1827
Thos.	9	M	Farmer	Great Britain	United States	Columbia	17 Apr 1827
Thos.	31	M	Blacksmith	Great Britain	United States	Washington	3 Sep 1827
Wm.	3	M	Farmer	Great Britian	United States	Columbia	17 Apr 1827
BIRCHALL, John	32		Farmer	Great Briton	United States	Orion	18 Jun 1821
BIRCHAM, John	29	M	Farmer	Great Britaian	United States	Margaret Ann	3 Apr 1822
Richd.	20	M	Farmer	Great Britaian	United States	Margaret Ann	3 Apr 1822
BIRCHARD, Harvey	28	M	Mechanic	U. States	U. States	Edward Quesnel	4 Aug 1828
Jno.	12	M	Apprentice	N. York	N. York	Emily	2 Jun 1824
BIRCKHEAD, —, Mrs.	28	F		U. States	U. States	Native	29 Apr 1825
Hy.	1	M		U. States	U. States	Native	29 Apr 1825
K.	8	M		U. States	U. States	Native	29 Apr 1825
Margt.	13	F		U. States	U. States	Native	29 Apr 1825
Maria	5	F		U. States	U. States	Native	29 Apr 1825
BIRD, —, Mrs.	33	F		England	England	Loyalist	17 Oct 1829
Ann	20	F		Ireland	U. States	Howard Douglass	29 Jan 1828
Anthony	27	M	Mariner	United States	United States	Cambria	16 Aug 1827
Bridget, Mrs.	26			Liverpool		Mount Vernon	18 Oct 1822
Catharine	4	F		England	United States	Amelia	20 Aug 1829
Catharine	24	F		England	United States	Amelia	20 Aug 1829
Charles	43	M	Merchant	United States	United States	Cortes	10 Apr 1822
Clarence	24	M	Merchant	Gt. Britan	Gt. Britan	Canada	8 Jun 1826
E.	52	F		Great Britain	U. States	United States	8 Sep 1827
Eliza	7	F		G. Britain		Caravan	8 Sep 1828
Geo.	18	M	Farmer	Great Britain	United States	Ann Maria	12 Jul 1821
Gertrude	9	F		G. Britain		Caravan	8 Sep 1828
Isaac	36	M	Farmer	Great Britain	U. States	United States	8 Sep 1827
James	5	M		Great Britian	United States	Andes	19 Aug 1829
James	22	M	Mason	Great Britain	U. States	United States	8 Sep 1827
James	25	M	Labourer	England	U. States	William	28 Nov 1823
James	26	M	...	Great Britain	N. York	Josephine	10 Dec 1825
Jane	10	F		Great Britain	U. States	United States	8 Sep 1827
Jane	13	F		Great Britain	U. States	United States	8 Sep 1827
Jane	26	F		Great Britain	United States	Andes	19 Aug 1829
Jas.	48	M	Merchant	England	Canada	James Monroe	29 Apr 1823
John	1	M		Great Britian	United States	Andes	19 Aug 1829
John	14	M		G. Britain		Caravan	8 Sep 1828
John	22	M	Sawyer	Ireland	U. States	Josephine	30 Aug 1828
John	24	M	Taylor	Ireland	U. States	Howard Douglass	29 Jan 1828
John	30	M	Farmer	Great Britian	United States	Andes	19 Aug 1829
John	35		Shoemaker	Gloucester	Utica	Peru	30 May 1828
John D.	23	M	Mariner	United States	Philadelphia	Hope	2 Jul 1824

NAMES OF PASSENGERS	AGE	SEX	OCCUPATIONS	COUNTRY TO WHICH THEY BELONG	COUNTRY THEY INTEND TO INHABIT	SHIPS/DATES OF ARRIVAL	
BIRD (cont'd)							
Jos.	9	M		G. Britain		Caravan	8 Sep 1828
L.	18	M	Farmer	Great Britain	U. States	United States	8 Sep 1827
Margaret	3	F		Great Britian	United States	Andes	19 Aug 1829
Martin	5	M		G. Britain		Caravan	8 Sep 1828
Mary	6	F		Great Britain	U. States	United States	8 Sep 1827
Mary	6	F		England	United States	Amelia	20 Aug 1829
Mary	15	F		Gt. Britain	United States	Silas Richards	20 Jun 1826
Mary	25	F	None	Great Britain	N. York	Josephine	10 Dec 1825
Mary Ann	3	F		G. Britain		Caravan	8 Sep 1828
Michael	12	M		G. Britain		Caravan	8 Sep 1828
Nicholas	26	M	Labourer			Evergreen	28 Jul 1820
Richard	32		Merchant	England	England	Napoleon	10 Jan 1828
Robert	11	M	None	England	New York	America	1 Aug 1828
Sarah	29	F	None	Great Britain		Olive Branch	9 Oct 1829
Sarah, Jr.	2 6/12	F	None	Great Britain		Olive Branch	9 Oct 1829
Stephen	20		Labourer	England	United States	Corinthian	7 Jul 1829
Thomas	32	M	Farmer	Ireland	United States	Lord Strangford	20 Jun 1824
William	24	M	Shoe Maker	Great Britain		Olive Branch	9 Oct 1829
William, Jr.	6/12	F	None	Great Britain		Olive Branch	9 Oct 1829
William, Junr.	19	M	Farmer	Ireland	America	Fairy	8 Aug 1821
William, Senr.	22	M	Farmer	Ireland	America	Fairy	8 Aug 1821
Wm. S.	27	M	Merchant	United States	U. States	Pacific	5 Sep 1827
BIRDSALL, George	19	M	Shoemaker	Great Britain	United States	James Monroe	27 Jul 1821
Jas.	68	M	Labourer	Great Britain		Moro Castle	6 Jul 1827
BIRDSELL, John	28	M	Farmer	New Brunswick	United States	Hanford	19 Aug 1828
Samuel	23	M	Farmer	New Brunswick	United States	Hanford	19 Aug 1828
BIRLE, ...	2	F				New York Packet	19 Aug 1820
Anna, his wife	30	F				New York Packet	19 Aug 1820
Elizabeth	6	F				New York Packet	19 Aug 1820
Henry	32	M	Farmer			New York Packet	19 Aug 1820
Salome	6/12	F				New York Packet	19 Aug 1820
BIRM, Edward	27 3/12	M	Tailor	Ireland	United States	Atlantic	21 Jul 1827
BIRMINGHAM, Ann	8	F		Ireland	New York	Phoenix	29 Apr 1826
Ann	15	F	Spinster	Ireland	United States	Dublin Packet	22 Aug 1829
Bridget	15	F		Ireland	New York	Phoenix	29 Apr 1826
Catherine	27	F	None	Ireland	United States	Trident	18 Jul 1827
Honarah	12	F		Ireland	New York	Phoenix	29 Apr 1826
Julia	1	F	Labourer	England	U. States	Hope & Esther	10 Jul 1827
K.				Ireland	U. States	Fabius	22 Sep 1828
Magaret	10	F		Ireland	New York	Phoenix	29 Apr 1826
Margaret	20	F	Labourer	England	U. States	Hope & Esther	10 Jul 1827
Mary W.	50	F		Ireland	New York	Phoenix	29 Apr 1826
Michael	19	M	Labourer	Ireland	New York	Phoenix	29 Apr 1826
Thomas	34	M	Cooper	Ireland	United States	Trident	18 Jul 1827
Thos.	30	M	Labourer			Lady of the Lake	23 Aug 1828
Timothy	18	M		Limerick	N. York	Thomas & William	25 May 1827
BIRNE, John	29		Coach Trimmer	England	United States	Caspian	12 Jul 1821
BIRNER, Owen	24	M	Labourer	Great Brittan	United States	Hanford	3 Aug 1829
BIRNEY, Richard	25	M	Merchant	Ireland	United States	Dublin Packet	3 May 1823
BIRNIE, Charles	21	M	Butcher	U. States	U. States	Robt. Edwards	4 Sep 1828
George	36	M	Farmer	Scotland	United States	Shakespeare	24 Jul 1828
BIRON, Geo. S.	26	M		England	United States	Amelia	20 Aug 1829
Margaret	20	F		England	United States	Amelia	20 Aug 1829
BIRSTAMANTE, José Ma.	19	M		Mexico	Mexico	Virginia	9 Feb 1829
BIRTSWHISTLE, Ann	1	F		England	U. States	Alex Mansfield	27 Aug 1825
John	26	M	Printer	England	U. States	Alex Mansfield	27 Aug 1825
Mary	28	F		England	U. States	Alex Mansfield	27 Aug 1825
BISBEE, George	26	M	Merchant	U. States	New York	Diamond	13 Nov 1823
BISCHEL, Jacob	19	M	Weaver	Switzerland	United States	Thetis	5 Jul 1821
BISCHOFF, Ann	22	F	None	England	United States	Jubilee	13 Jul 1829

NAMES OF PASSENGERS	AGE	SEX	OCCUPATIONS	COUNTRY TO WHICH THEY BELONG	COUNTRY THEY INTEND TO INHABIT	SHIPS/DATES OF ARRIVAL	
BISCHOFF (cont'd)							
Francis	1	M	None	England	United States	Jubilee	13 Jul 1829
Joseph	21	M	Farmer	England	United States	Jubilee	13 Jul 1829
BISET, David	24	M	Farmer	Scotland	U.S. of America	Friends	10 May 1823
BISHOP, Ann	9 3/12	F	Family [of Samuel]	G. Brittian	United States	Louisa	14 Jun 1825
Ann	27	F	Labourer	England	England	Sir James Kempt	10 Dec 1827
Archabold	5 2/12	M	Family [of Samuel]	G. Brittian	United States	Louisa	14 Jun 1825
Christopher	31	M	Brick Layer	Hampt Shire	America, New York	Washington	3 Mar 1828
Chs.	5	M		U. States	U. States	Silvia	10 Sep 1827
David	12	M	Family [of Samuel]	G. Brittian	United States	Louisa	14 Jun 1825
Edward D.	34	M	Merchant	England	Canada	Silas Richards	3 Apr 1826
Edwd. G.	2	M		England	U. States	Cincinnatus	24 May 1821
Elizabeth	6	F		England	U. States	Cincinnatus	24 May 1821
Flora	9 3/12	F	Family [of Samuel]	G. Brittian	United States	Louisa	14 Jun 1825
Gor	13	M	None	England	U. States	Hercules	6 Jul 1827
James	19	M	Farmer	England	United States	Cambria	3 Jul 1829
James	20	M	Seaman	Boston	U. States	Rebecca & Sally	7 Oct 1823
James	38	M	B. N. Service	England	West Indies	Soto	11 Nov 1828
Jane	3	F	None	Ireland	United States	Jubilee	13 Jul 1829
Jane	10 1/12	F	Family [of Samuel]	G. Brittian	United States	Louisa	14 Jun 1825
Jno.	6	M	Labourer	England	England	Sir James Kempt	10 Dec 1827
John	6	M	None	Hampt Shire	America, New York	Washington	3 Mar 1828
John	11	M		U. States	U. States	Silvia	10 Sep 1827
John	39	M	Brick Layer	Handover	America, New York	Washington	3 Mar 1828
Jos.	5	M	None	England	U. States	Hercules	6 Jul 1827
Joseph	1	F	None	Ireland	United States	Jubilee	13 Jul 1829
Mark	23	M	Farmer	England	U.S. America	Majestic	24 Mar 1828
Mary	6	F	Family [of Samuel]	G. Brittian	United States	Louisa	14 Jun 1825
Mary	8	F		U. States	U. States	Silvia	10 Sep 1827
Mary	26	F	None	Ireland	United States	Jubilee	13 Jul 1829
Mary	30	F		U. States	U. States	Silvia	10 Sep 1827
Mary	38					Cincinnatus	29 Apr 1822
Nancy	38	F	Family [of Samuel]	G. Brittian	United States	Louisa	14 Jun 1825
Nathaniel	44	M	Labourer	U. States	U. States	Robt. Reade	12 Apr 1825
Richd.	4	M	None	England	U. States	Hercules	6 Jul 1827
Robert	29	M	Carpenter	Great Briton	New York	Brighton	12 Jun 1826
Robert	30	M	Farmer	Ireland	United States	Jubilee	13 Jul 1829
Samuel	28 2/12	M	Farmer	G. Brittian	United States	Louisa	14 Jun 1825
Sopher	36	F	None	England	U. States	Hercules	6 Jul 1827
Stephen	9	M	Labourer	Bristol	U. States	Latona	7 Jul 1827
Stephen	36	M	Farmer	England	U. States	Hercules	6 Jul 1827
Thomas	14	M	Merchant	England	U. States	Cincinnatus	24 May 1821
Thomas	21	M	Farmer	England	United States	Cambria	3 Jul 1829
Thomas	23	M	Clerk	Ireland	United States	Dublin Packet	22 Oct 1821
William	19 2/12	M	Farmer	Ireland	America	Farmer	3 May 1824
Wm.	7	M		U. States	U. States	Silvia	10 Sep 1827
Wm.	25	M	Merchant	Barbados, U.S.	West Indies	Spartan	24 Jul 1826
Wm.	37	M	Taylor	England	United States	Ann Maria	26 Apr 1822
Wm.	40	M	Labourer	Bristol	U. States	Latona	7 Jul 1827
Wm. B.	26	M	Gentleman	Barbadoes	Barbadoes	Falcon	4 Jun 1825
BISHUP, J.	24	M	Blacksmith	United States	U.S.	Frances	15 Jun 1825
BISHWIGTON, George	19	M		Great Brittain	United States	Active	12 Sep 1828
*Died on the Passage							
BISILION, Claude	33	M	Watchmaker	Suisse	United States	Montano	5 May 1828
BISKETT, Henry	30	M	Merchant	Great Britain	United States	Cortes	19 Nov 1821
BISLAND, Adam	28	M	Dyer	Scotland	United States	Broke	16 Jul 1829
Agnes	26	F		Scotland	United States	Broke	16 Jul 1829
James	6/12	M		Scotland	United States	Broke	16 Jul 1829
Jane	2	F		Scotland	United States	Broke	16 Jul 1829
Mary	20	F		Scotland	United States	Broke	16 Jul 1829
Willm.	20	M		Scotland	United States	Broke	16 Jul 1829
BISLET, Timo.	18	M	Sadler	G. Britain	U. States	Mary & Harriot	8 Sep 1828
BISOARD, Geor.	20	M	Waiter	Switzerland	U.S.	C. Amelia	30 Jun 1828
BISOSE, Eugenio		M	Merchant	Spain	Mexico	Virginia	9 Feb 1829
*the 28th Jan [died on the voyage]							
BISOSO, Luys	38	M	Farmer	Spain	Spain	Sciot	12 Mar 1828
BISSELL, Mary Ann	10	F	Spinstress	England	U. States	Ann	29 Jan 1820
Sarah	8	F	Spinstress	England	U. States	Ann	29 Jan 1820
BISSETT, —, Mrs.	34	F		N. Carolina	U. States	Agenora	10 Apr 1823

NAMES OF PASSENGERS	A G E	S E X	OCCUPATIONS	COUNTRY TO WHICH THEY BELONG	COUNTRY THEY INTEND TO INHABIT	SHIPS/DATES OF ARRIVAL	
BISSETT (cont'd)							
Charles	40	M	Mariner	N. Carolina	U. States	Agenora	10 Apr 1823
Chas.	45	M	Mariner	U. States	U. States	Prospect	4 Apr 1822
BISSEX, James	16	M	Cordwainer	England	America	Criterion	27 Oct 1821
BITCHERNELL, R.	14		Weaver	Cork	Philadelphia	Schuylkill	22 Aug 1825
BITHELOT, Amiable	46	M	Attorney	Great Britan	Great Britan	Columbia	11 Aug 1823
BITTEL, J.	52	M	Mason	Switzerland	U. States	La Urania	3 Jul 1828
J. G.	60	F		Switzerland	U. States	La Urania	3 Jul 1828
BITTELL, Antoine	5	M		Switzerland	U. States	La Urania	3 Jul 1828
Cathr.	50	F		Switzerland	U. States	La Urania	3 Jul 1828
Jaque	32	M	Mason	Switzerland	U. States	La Urania	3 Jul 1828
Jos.	11	M		Switzerland	U. States	La Urania	3 Jul 1828
Jos.	54	M	Mason	Switzerland	U. States	La Urania	3 Jul 1828
Louis	3	M		Switzerland	U. States	La Urania	3 Jul 1828
M.	7	F		Switzerland	U. States	La Urania	3 Jul 1828
R. C.	32	F		Switzerland	U. States	La Urania	3 Jul 1828
BITTENCON, J. R.	25	M	Gentleman	Cuba	United States	Polly & Sophia	13 Sep 1821
Paul	14	M	Gentleman	Cuba	United States	Polly & Sophia	13 Sep 1821
BITTLER, James	3/12	M		Great B.	U. States	William Neilson	26 Jul 1828
John	32	M		Great B.	U. States	William Neilson	26 Jul 1828
Mary	20			Ireland	United States	John Dickinson	28 Jun 1822
Mary	28	F		Great B.	U. States	William Neilson	26 Jul 1828
Thomas	3/12	M		Great B.	U. States	William Neilson	26 Jul 1828
BITTLES, Mary	50	F		Ireland	United States	Alex. Mansfield	17 May 1823
Schovil	26 2/12	M	Labourer	Ireland	United States	Atlantic	16 Dec 1825
BITTMAN, Susana	27	F		France	United States	New England	29 Aug 1828
BIVEN, Jonathan	17	M	Farmer	Ireland	Canada	Amelia	20 Aug 1829
BIZONARD, Thos.	32	M	Gent.	France	U. States	Cadmus	28 May 1821
BIZSUARD, Anne	22	F	Servt.	France	France	Lewis	29 Oct 1825
BL..., Edward	30	M	Minister	Great Britian	United States	Robert Quayle	29 Jul 1822
BL...UM, Ann	22	F	Servant	Ireland	United States	Trident	30 Sep 1826
BLACHE, Martin	31	M	Merchant	U. States	U. States	Sully	24 Oct 1828
BLACK, ...o...	23	M	Weaver	Ireland	U. States	Josephine	7 May 1827
A.	27	M	Merchant	U. States		Cordelia	8 Sep 1820
Abigail	12	F		St. Johns, N.B.	United States	Henrietta	17 Aug 1825
Agness	1 1/2	F	None	Ireland	U. States	Josephine	27 Jul 1825
Agness	22	F	None	Scotland	U. States	Camillus	27 Jul 1825
Alexander	22	M	Blacksmith	Ireland	U. States	Josephine	30 Aug 1828
Alexr.	14	M		St. Johns, N.B.	United States	Henrietta	17 Aug 1825
Alexr. McG.	20	M	Gentleman	America	America	Hector	20 Sep 1821
Alix	7	M	Farmer	Scotland	U. States	Roger Stewart	9 Jun 1828
Andrew	40	M	Farmer	St. John, N.B.	United States	Nancy	18 Oct 1824
Ann	9	F	Farmer	Scotland	U. States	Roger Stewart	9 Jun 1828
Ann	27	F	Matron	Ireland	U. States	Josephine	30 Aug 1828
Betsey	12	M	Farmer	Great Britain	U. States	Yamacraw	4 Sep 1822
Daniel	19	M		St. Johns, N.B.	United States	Henrietta	17 Aug 1825
Danl.	3	M	Weaver	Scotland	U. States	Roger Stewart	9 Jun 1828
David	15	M	Farmer	Great Britain	U. States	Yamacraw	4 Sep 1822
Eliza	2	F		St. Johns, N.B.	United States	Henrietta	17 Aug 1825
Gavin	11	M	None	Scotland	United States	Friends	7 Jul 1827
Geo.	24	M	Merchant	U. States	U. States	Lewis	20 Feb 1824
Geo.	24	M	Merchant	New York	U. States	Natchez	7 Feb 1825
Geo.	35	M	Merchant	England	Long Island, State of New York	Native	11 Sep 1821

*Died at the Quarantine ground, N.B.

NAMES OF PASSENGERS	A G E	S E X	OCCUPATIONS	COUNTRY TO WHICH THEY BELONG	COUNTRY THEY INTEND TO INHABIT	SHIPS/DATES OF ARRIVAL	
Giles	10	M		St. Johns, N.B.	United States	Henrietta	17 Aug 1825
H.	36	M	Merchant	England	gone to France	Diana	9 Aug 1823
Helen	40	F				Hector	11 Sep 1820
Hugh	8	M		St. Johns, N.B.	United States	Henrietta	17 Aug 1825
J. J.	26	M	Merchant	United States	United States	Zamoa	5 Nov 1828
Jame	29	M	Grocer	Ireland	New York	Orozimbo	2 Oct 1824
James	18	M	Merchant	Scotland	New York	Joseph Hume	26 Oct 1829
James	48	M	Merchant	United States	New York	Britannia	3 Nov 1827
Jane	4	F		Ireland	U. States	Nancy	16 Aug 1822
Janet	13	F	Spinster	Scotland	United States	Friends	7 Jul 1827
Jas.	21	M	Merchant	Canada	Quebec	Acasta	14 Jun 1824
Jean	6/12	F	Joiner	Scotland	U. States	Roger Stewart	9 Jun 1828
Jean	20	F		Ireland	U. States	Nancy	16 Aug 1822
Jean	24	M	Mason	Scotland	U. States	Roger Stewart	9 Jun 1828

NAMES OF PASSENGERS	AGE	SEX	OCCUPATIONS	COUNTRY TO WHICH THEY BELONG	COUNTRY THEY INTEND TO INHABIT	SHIPS/DATES OF ARRIVAL	
BLACK (cont'd)							
Jean	32	F	Farmer	Scotland	U. States	Roger Stewart	9 Jun 1828
Jenny	28	F	Servant	U.S.	U.S.	Montano	24 Jun 1823
Jno.	18	M	Farmer	Great Britain	U. States	Yamacraw	4 Sep 1822
John	23	M		Ireland	United States	William & George	14 May 1828
John	25	M		Ireland	U. States	Nancy	16 Aug 1822
John	25	M	Farmer	England	U.S.	Pacific	24 Oct 1828
John	32	M		U. States	U. States	Hector	11 Sep 1820
John	34	M	Husband Man	Ireland	United States	Neury	27 Jan 1827
John, Mr.	45	M	Gentn.	England	American	Acasta	3 Apr 1826
Margaret	9	F		St. Johns, N.B.	United States	Henrietta	17 Aug 1825
Margaret	48	F	Farmer	Great Britain	U. States	Yamacraw	4 Sep 1822
Mary	16	F		St. Johns, N.B.	United States	Henrietta	17 Aug 1825
Mary	35	F	Seamstress	St. Johns, N.B.	United States	Henrietta	17 Aug 1825
Mary	55	F	Spinster	Scotland	United States	Friends	7 Jul 1827
Mary	59 3/12	F	None	United States	United States	Manchester	12 Aug 1829
Mary A.	20	F	Servant	W. Indies	U. States	Elisa	1 May 1821
Matthew	20	M	Labourer	Scotland	United States	Friends	7 Jul 1827
Maurice	26	M	Farmer	Ireland		Quatre Freres	29 Jul 1828
Paul	...	M	...	Ireland	United States	General Putnam	20 Jun 1825
Peter	39	M	Servant	U.S.	U.S.	Montano	24 Jun 1823
Phebe	5	F		St. Johns, N.B.	United States	Henrietta	17 Aug 1825
Rebecca	1	F		St. Johns, N.B.	United States	Henrietta	17 Aug 1825
Rebecca	27	F		Ireland	United States	Aurora	9 Jul 1827
Robert	24	M	Labourer	Scotland	United States	Friends	7 Jul 1827
Robert	25	M	Farmer			Importer	30 Oct 1820
Robert	25	M	Seaman	Great Britain	United States	Martha	25 Nov 1820
Robert	60	M	Labourer	Scotland	United States	Friends	7 Jul 1827
S.	40	M	Merchant	Scotland	Canada	James Monroe	29 Apr 1823
Thomas	12	M	Farmer	Great Britain	U. States	Yamacraw	4 Sep 1822
Thomas	20	M	Surgeon	Ireland	United States	Lord Wellington	28 May 1827
Thomas	25	M	Laborer or Spinster	Ireland	United States	Sarah G.	15 Aug 1827
W.	36	M	Mason	Scotland	U. States	Roger Stewart	9 Jun 1828
W. M.	29	M	...	...	U.S. America	Columbia	26 Nov 1825
William	3 6/12	M	Child	Ireland	U. States	Josephine	30 Aug 1828
William	24	M	Labourer	Scotland	United States	Mary & Susan	5 Aug 1828
William	32	M	Labourer	Scotland	United States	Samuel Robertson	5 Oct 1827
Wm.	13	M	Farmer	Great Britain	U. States	Yamacraw	4 Sep 1822
Wm.	18	M	Labourer	Ireland	United States	Henry Kneeland	7 Jun 1828
Wm.	23		Weaver	Ireland	United States	John Dickinson	28 Jun 1822
BLACKALL, Elizabeth	20	F	None	England	United States	Euphrates	12 May 1823
Henry	18	M	Wheelwright	England	United States	Euphrates	12 May 1823
Mary	55	F	None	England	United States	Euphrates	12 May 1823
Peter	36	M	No	England	United States	Euphrates	12 May 1823
Thos.	53	M	Farmer	England	United States	Euphrates	12 May 1823
Wm.	55	M	Farmer	America	United States	Euphrates	12 May 1823
BLACKBERN, Mary	17	F	None	England	United States	Florida	11 May 1822
Phoebe	30	F	None	England	United States	Florida	11 May 1822
BLACKBORN, Ellen	17	F		England	U. States	Panthea	22 Nov 1826
Hannah	26	F		England	U. States	Panthea	22 Nov 1826
Mary Ann	2	F		England	U. States	Panthea	22 Nov 1826
BLACKBROUGH, Thos.	20	M	Servant to Mr. Froste	Great Britain	United States	Robert Fulton	27 Jun 1822
BLACKBURN, Buckley	20	M	Woolen Manufa.	England	America	Hannibal	28 May 1827
Francis	13	M	None	Gt. Britain	United States	Corks	3 Aug 1824
George	23	M	Clark	G. Brittian	U. States	Pacific	19 Oct 1829
Henry	21	M	Clothier	Great Britain	United States	Colossus	1 Nov 1826
Henry	63	M	Woolen Manufa.	England	America	Hannibal	28 May 1827
James	25 8/12	M	Weaver	Great Britain	Long Island	Venus	8 Sep 1820
James	33	M	Merchant	England	United States	Justina	5 Aug 1823
John	43	M	Clerk	United States	United States	Importer	21 May 1821
John	56	M		G. Britain	United States	United States	11 Sep 1828
Jos.	6	M	Child	England	United States	Ganges	20 Aug 1825
Kitty	63	F	None	England	America	Hannibal	28 May 1827
M.	26	F	Lady	England	United States	Ganges	20 Aug 1825
Marey A.	24	F	None	England	America	Hannibal	28 May 1827
Mary Ann	26	F	None	England	U. States	New York	4 Nov 1824

NAMES OF PASSENGERS	AGE	SEX	OCCUPATIONS	COUNTRY TO WHICH THEY BELONG	COUNTRY THEY INTEND TO INHABIT	SHIPS/DATES OF ARRIVAL	
BLACKBURN (cont'd)							
O.	26	M	Farmer			Hercules	25 Sep 1820
Robon	10	M	None	England	United States	Florida	11 May 1822
Robona	17	F	None	Great Britain	United States	Florida	2 Sep 1822
Sarah	20	F	None	Great Britain	United States	Florida	2 Sep 1822
Sarah	40	F	None	Gt. Britain	United States	Corks	3 Aug 1824
Thomas	35	M	Dyer	Great Britan	United States	Hamilton	19 Mar 1827
Thos.	21	M	Woolen Manufa.	England	America	Hannibal	28 May 1827
Thos.	25	M	Mechanic	England	U.S.	Panthea	22 Jul 1826
Thos.	29	M	Farmer			Manhattan	25 Dec 1820
William	19	M	Weaver	Great Britain	Long Island	Venus	8 Sep 1820
BLACKER, Jas.	25	M	Cabinet Maker	Scotland	America	John Adams	2 Aug 1827
BLACKERARD, Wm.	36	M	Merchant	Scotland		London	29 Apr 1824
BLACKFORD,							
Francis	28 9/12	M	Merchant	United States	United States of A.	New York	3 Apr 1826
BLACKHAM, John	23	M	Farmer	Ireland	United States	Romulus	24 Jun 1826
BLACKHURD, John	48	M	Farmer	Gt. Brittian	Gt. Brittian	Manchester	21 Apr 1827
BLACKHURST, James	20	M	Taylor	England	United States	Marion	25 Nov 1825
Mary	35	F	None	Great Britain	United States	Manchester	12 Aug 1829
Peter	28	M	Joiner	England	United States	Marion	25 Nov 1825
BLACKINEER, James	37	M	Weaver	England	New York	Colossus	2 Oct 1827
BLACKLER, William	17	M	Gentleman	United States	United States	Collector	6 Oct 1820
BLACKLOCK, Geo.	8	M	Farmer	England	U. States	Montano	23 Apr 1825
Hy.	34	M	Farmer	England	U. States	Montano	23 Apr 1825
Hy., Jr.	11	M	Farmer	England	U. States	Montano	23 Apr 1825
BLACKMAN, James	19	M	Labourer	Great Britan	United States	Clematis	8 May 1827
Jno.	43	M	Labourer	England	United States	Nancy Henrietta	3 Nov 1828
John	35	M	Servant	United States	United States	Cortex	4 Dec 1824
William	30	M	Wheelwright	Great Britain	United States	Unity	20 Oct 1829
William	63	M	Yeoman	England	New York	Cincinnatus	5 Dec 1825
BLACKSADE, Richard	23	M		Great Brit.	Ohio	Gov. Griswald	3 Jul 1820
BLACKSHAW, Israel	23	M	Mechanic	Great Britain	United States	Mary & Harriet	3 Jul 1829
BLACKSLEE, Henry	32	M	Merchant	St. John, N.B.	St. John, N.B.	St. Michaels	25 Nov 1825
BLACKSONDALE,							
Phebe	48			Bl...	England	Great Britain	7 May 1827
BLACKSTOCK, David	34	M	Joiner	England	United States	Trident	30 Sep 1826
George	3	M	Child	England	United States	Trident	30 Sep 1826
Hannah	27	F	Wife	England	United States	Trident	30 Sep 1826
Mary Ann	1	F	Child	England	United States	Trident	30 Sep 1826
William	4	M	Child	England	United States	Trident	30 Sep 1826
BLACKWELL,							
Francis	23 1/12	M	Chemist & Drugist	Ireland	U.S. American	Criterion	7 Jul 1824
James	21	M	Mason	Great Britain	United States	John	6 Oct 1820
BLACKWOOD, ...m.	35		Merchant	Ayrshire	Great Britain	William Thompson	13 May 1823
M.	34	M		Great Britain	Canada	James Monroe	25 Apr 1822
William	32	M	Merchant	Scotland	Great Brittan	Amity	11 May 1821
Wm.	40	M	Merchant	Canada	Canada	John Wells	16 May 1825
BLADDEN, Ann	22	F	Spinster	Ireland	United States	Emily	28 Aug 1829
BLADDER, Catharine	19	F		Great Brittain	United States	United States	16 Feb 1827
BLADES, R.	37	M	Labourer	England	America	Two Marys	24 Sep 1827
BLAGLY, Wm.	17	M	Clerk	England	N. York	Salem	15 Mar 1828
BLAIN, Geo.	1	M		G. Britain	U. States	London	23 Sep 1828
Joseph	23	M	Merchant	Carlisle, G.B.	New York, U.S.	New York	14 Mar 1828
Wm.	18	M	Weaver	Great Britain	United States	Kate	2 Oct 1821
BLAINE, S.	36	M	Mariner	American	U. States	Sarah Ann	5 Aug 1820
BLAIR, Agnes	1	F		Scotland	United States	Camillus	27 Oct 1829
Agnes	3	F	None	Great Britain	United States	Colossus	5 Jun 1827
Agnes	24	F	None	Great Britain	United States	Colossus	5 Jun 1827
Agnes	24	F		Scotland	United States	Camillus	27 Oct 1829
Agness	25	F		Scotland	U.S. of America	Friends	10 May 1823
David	3	M	Son	Scotland	America	Camillus	12 Sep 1822
David	20	M	Farmer	Great Britain	United States	Elizabeth & Mary	20 Mar 1828
David	23	M	Farmer	Mi...ter Russia	United States	Henry Clay	25 Apr 1822
Eliza	40	F	Farmer	Ireland	U. States	Champion	26 Jul 1827
George	55	M	Mariner	U. States	U. States	Factor	2 Apr 1824
Jacob	23	M	Butcher	Witemburg	U. States	Comet	28 Jul 1825
James	10	M	Son	Scotland	America	Camillus	12 Sep 1822

NAMES OF PASSENGERS	AGE	SEX	OCCUPATIONS	COUNTRY TO WHICH THEY BELONG	COUNTRY THEY INTEND TO INHABIT	SHIPS/DATES OF ARRIVAL	
BLAIR (cont'd)							
James	23	M	... maker	England	United States	Richmond	4 Aug 1826
Jane	30	F	going to her husband	Scotland	America	Camillus	12 Sep 1822
Janet	40	F	Spinster	Glasgow	United States	Henry Clay	25 Apr 1822
Jas.	30	M	Merchant	U. States	U. States	Govr. Von Scholten	23 Apr 1825
Jno.	21	M	Farmers and Mechanics	Ireland	America	Constitution	1 Oct 1825
Jno.	29	M	Farmer	England	U. States	New England	12 Apr 1825
John	21	M	Farmer	Mi...ter Russia	United States	Henry Clay	25 Apr 1822
John	24	M	Cabinet Maker	Scotland	United States	Lord Wellington	14 Nov 1827
John	30	M	Merchant	Great Britain	United States	Courier	26 Jun 1827
John	33	M	Labourer	G. Britain	U. States	Leavitts	25 Aug 1828
Lindsay	15	M	Farmer	Ireland	U. States	Champion	26 Jul 1827
Margaret	2	F	Farmer	Ireland	U. States	Champion	26 Jul 1827
Maria	10	F	Daughter	Scotland	America	Camillus	12 Sep 1822
Maria	28	F		G. Britain	U. States	Leavitts	25 Aug 1828
Mary	7	F	Daughter	Scotland	America	Camillus	12 Sep 1822
Robert	25	M	Shoemaker	Scotland	United States	Camillus	27 Oct 1829
Thomas	19	M	Farmer	Great Britain	United States	Elizabeth & Mary	20 Mar 1828
William	5		Weaver	Scotland	United States	Camillus	3 May 1828
Wm.	1	M	Son	Scotland	America	Camillus	12 Sep 1822
Wm.	35	M	Farmer	G. Britain	New York	Missouri	10 Apr 1821
BLAIS, John	25	M	Farmer	Ireland	U. States	Dickinson	30 Jul 1825
BLAKE, Alfred	5	M	Cloth Dreper	England	United States	Maria	12 May 1823
Betty	30	F	None	Great Britain	United States	Fidelity	16 Oct 1820
Catharine	5			Cork	Gt. Britain	Enterprize	19 Feb 1822
Catherine	21	F		Ireland	America	Wilson	27 Nov 1826
Edmund	10	M	None	Great Britain	United States	Fidelity	16 Oct 1820
Eliza	2	F				Acosta	28 Jul 1823
Elizabeth	16	F	Cloth Dreper	England	United States	Maria	12 May 1823
Elizabeth	43	F				Acosta	28 Jul 1823
Ellen	35			Cork	Gt. Britain	Enterprize	19 Feb 1822
George	3	M	None	Great Britain	United States	Fidelity	16 Oct 1820
George	8	M				Acosta	28 Jul 1823
Isabella	20	F	Spinster	Ireland	U. States	Hector	18 Apr 1825
J. W.	21	M	Merchant	Boston	Boston	Sea Island	3 Jan 1826
James	10	M	Cloth Dreper	England	United States	Maria	12 May 1823
James	33	M	Farmer	Great Britten	America	Cortes	6 Mar 1827
Janes	35	M	Lavourer			Hudson	23 Jul 1828
John	16	M	Gardner	Scotland	U. States	Camillus	17 Sep 1823
John	26	M	Farmer	Great Britten	America	Cortes	6 Mar 1827
John	38		Carpenter	United States	United States	Iris	26 Jun 1821
John	4...	M	Farmer	G. Britain	New York	Brighton	26 Mar 1827
John	40		Merchant	Great Britain		John Dickinson	5 Apr 1821
John G.	21	M	Merchant	Halifax	United States	Potomac	28 Sep 1827
Jos.	40	M	Clothier	G. Britain	Canada	Cosmo	25 Nov 1826
Jos. W.	19	M	Merchant	Massachusetts	U. States	Sea Island	2 Jul 1825
Louisa	12	F				Acosta	28 Jul 1823
Mary	3			Cork	Gt. Britain	Enterprize	19 Feb 1822
Mary	7	F	Cloth Dreper	England	United States	Maria	12 May 1823
Mary	14	F	None	Gt. Brittain	United States	Balaena	9 Oct 1823
Mary	24	F	None	Longford	United States	Solon	21 Jun 1824
Mary Ann	16	F				Acosta	28 Jul 1823
Michael	10			Cork	Gt. Britain	Enterprize	19 Feb 1822
Nat.	25	M	Merchant	U. States	U. States	Arthenian	28 Apr 1827
Peter	26	M	Labourer	Longford	United States	Solon	21 Jun 1824
Saml. P.	23	M	Merchant	United States	U. States	Pacific	5 Sep 1827
Sarah	32	F	Cloth Dreper	England	United States	Maria	12 May 1823
Walter	23	M	Gentleman	England	U.N. States	Robert Edwards	20 Jan 1829
William	6/12	M	None	Great Britain	United States	Fidelity	16 Oct 1820
William	3	M	Cloth Dreper	England	United States	Maria	12 May 1823
William	7			Cork	Gt. Britain	Enterprize	19 Feb 1822
William	30	M	Farmer	Great Britain	United States	Fidelity	16 Oct 1820
William	38	M	Cloth Dreper	England	United States	Maria	12 May 1823
William	45	M	Gardner	England	United States	Acosta	28 Jul 1823
Wm.	20	M	Clerk	England	U. States	Charlotte	19 Feb 1822

NAMES OF PASSENGERS	AGE	SEX	OCCUPATIONS	COUNTRY TO WHICH THEY BELONG	COUNTRY THEY INTEND TO INHABIT	SHIPS/DATES OF ARRIVAL	
BLAKE (cont'd)							
Wm. R.	21	M	Comedian	Halifax	G. Brittain	Nile	22 Nov 1823
BLAKELEY,							
Reuben	24 6/12	M	Mechanic	England	United States	John Wells	22 May 1826
Thomas	31	M	Merchant	Wakefield, England	Great Britain	James Cropper	7 Oct 1823
BLAKELY, Alexr.	15	M		New York	New York	Carolina Ann	15 Oct 1824
John	30	M	Laborer	England	United States	London	21 May 1828
Michael	39	M	Farmer	Ireland	America	William	21 May 1825
Thos.	28	M	Mercht.	G. Britain		Ann Maria	3 Jul 1820
Timothy	30	M	Farmer	Ireland	America	William	21 May 1825
BLAKEY, James	40	M	Gentleman	England	United States	Robert Edwards	3 Oct 1829
Mary	40	F	Wife	England	United States	Robert Edwards	3 Oct 1829
BLAKLY, Richard	17	M	Labourer	Great Britain	Cannada	Columbia	1 Dec 1823
BLANC, Eugene	26	M	Gentleman	France	U. States	Bayard	8 Mar 1825
Jean Anto. Jules	30	M	Proprietor	France	United States	Henry	9 Jun 1826
Jean Frans. Xavier	33	M	Proprietor	France	United States	Henry	9 Jun 1826
Jean Pierre	67	M	Proprietor	France	United States	Henry	9 Jun 1826
Jeanne, Madam	57	F		France	United States	Henry	9 Jun 1826
Jules	32	M	Gentleman	France	U. States	Bayard	8 Mar 1825
Savern	26	M	None	United States	United States	Columbia	9 Aug 1822
Virginia, Mademoiselle	23	F		France	United States	Henry	9 Jun 1826
BLANCA, A.	19	M	Merchant	France	U. States	Desdemona	21 Oct 1825
Anastasa	33	F		France	U. States	Desdemona	21 Oct 1825
O.	16	M	Merchant	France	U. States	Desdemona	21 Oct 1825
BLANCE, B.	22	M		Spain	France & Spain	Native	24 Aug 1825
BLANCHARD, Anna	26	F	Framer	Switserland	Ohio	Danube	20 Jul 1826
Elizabeth	25	F		England	United States	William & Henry	19 Jul 1822
Francis	27	F	Dress Maker	England	U.S.	Maria Caroline	12 Jul 1820
G.	47	M	Cultivator	France	U. States	Lewis	6 Jul 1825
Henry	12	F	Cultivator	France	U. States	Lewis	6 Jul 1825
Jno. P.	65	M	Cultivator	France	U. States	Lewis	6 Jul 1825
Margt.	19	F	Cultivator	France	U. States	Lewis	6 Jul 1825
Martha	1	F		England	United States	William & Henry	19 Jul 1822
William	27	M	Farmer	England	United States	William & Henry	19 Jul 1822
Wm.	25	M	Mechanic	England	U.S.	Maria Caroline	12 Jul 1820
BLANCHEL, A.	32	M	Merchant	N. Orleans	U. States	Annah	7 May 1825
BLANCHET, F. A.	27	M	Gentleman	Hayti	Hayti	Artibonite	31 Jan 1827
Lois A., Mr.	28	M	Lawyer	France	France	Acasta	12 May 1825
Louis A.	30	M	Merchant	Hayti	Hayti	Artibonite	3 Jul 1826
T. N.	25	M	Merchant	New York	U. States	Fancy	28 Apr 1824
Thomas, Mr.	26	M	Merchant	France	France	Acasta	12 May 1825
BLANCHETT, T. A.	26	M	Merchant	Port au Prince	Port au Prince	Cadmus	14 Apr 1826
BLANCHFLOWER,							
Mary	25	F		Great Britain	United States	Britannia	29 Oct 1829
BLANCO, B.	30	M	Merchant	Spain	U. States	Superion	30 Apr 1825
B.	40	M	Merchant	Boston		James Monroe	3 Jul 1824
Bartholomew	25	M	Merchant	Spain	Havana	James Monroe	21 Apr 1824
L.	30	M	Merchant	Spain	Spain	Panther	18 Jun 1828
M.	28	M	Merchant	Spain	U. States	Mary Livingston	26 Jul 1824
R.		M	Merchant	Spain	U. States	Lady Tompkins	31 Jan 1824
BLAND, John	26	M	Millwright	Great Britian	United States	Isaac Hicks	22 May 1826
BLANDAIRE, Gregory	22	M	None	United States	United States	Pacific	24 Oct 1828
BLANDE, B.	25	M	Merchant	France	New York	Nancy	17 Nov 1823
BLANDER, Jos.	52	M	Merchant	England	United States	Lewis	30 May 1823
BLANDIN, —, Mr.	31	M	Merchant	Spain	Cuba	Constitution	8 Sep 1823
BLANDY, Robt.	24	M	Merchant	Great Britian	United States	Columbia	17 Apr 1827
BLANE, Emile	25	M	Travling	France	Not Known	Desdemonia	11 Feb 1825
Francois	27		Farmer	France	U. States	Parachute	14 May 1828
BLANEY, Charles	18 6/12	M		Ireland	America	Carolina Ann	7 Apr 1826
Danl.	17 1/12	M		Ireland	America	Carolina Ann	7 Apr 1826
Geo.	26	M	Army	U. States	U. States	Chase	6 Jun 1822
Mary	13 10/12	F		Ireland	America	Carolina Ann	7 Apr 1826
Mary	20 1/12	F		Ireland	America	Carolina Ann	7 Apr 1826
Michl.	24	M	Weaver	Ireland	America	Carolina Ann	7 Apr 1826
BLANGO, Domingun	40	M	Planter	France	Havana	Orvis	20 Apr 1824

NAMES OF PASSENGERS	AGE	SEX	OCCUPATIONS	COUNTRY TO WHICH THEY BELONG	COUNTRY THEY INTEND TO INHABIT	SHIPS/DATES OF ARRIVAL
BLANKO, B.	22	M	Mercht.	Spain	U. States	Lady Tompkins 9 Feb 1825
BLANY, Ed.	25	M	Farmer	Ireland	U. States	Frances Henrietta 19 Feb 1823
Geo.	42	M	Farmer	Ireland	U. States	Frances Henrietta 19 Feb 1823
Margaret	20	F	Merchant		U. States	Chase 6 Jun 1822
Mary	20	F		Ireland	U. States	Frances Henrietta 19 Feb 1823
Rebecca	18	F		Ireland	U. States	Frances Henrietta 19 Feb 1823
BLARNEY, Mary	55	F	Spinster	Grt. Britain	United States	Robert Fulton 8 Oct 1828
Mary Ann	12	F	Spinster	Grt. Britain	United States	Robert Fulton 8 Oct 1828
Owen	14	M	Labourer	Grt. Britain	United States	Robert Fulton 8 Oct 1828
BLASCO, Ramond	20	M	Merchant	Spain	Havana	Robert Fulton 22 May 1824
BLASS, J.	26	M	Merchant	Baltimore	U. States	Nestor 7 Jan 1825
BLATHWICK, Joseph	18	M	Machinist	England	Rhode Island	Governor Fenner 23 Jul 1829
BLATNER, M.	18	M	Turner	France	United States	La Flora 30 Jun 1828
BLEASDALE, Ann	4	F	Mechanic	Great Britain	United States	Thomas Dickason 31 Jul 1829
Elizabeth	5 6/12	F	Mechanic	Great Britain	United States	Thomas Dickason 31 Jul 1829
John	1 6/12	M	Mechanic	Great Britain	United States	Thomas Dickason 31 Jul 1829
Richard	33	M	Mechanic	Great Britain	United States	Thomas Dickason 31 Jul 1829
Sarah	32	F	Mechanic	Great Britain	United States	Thomas Dickason 31 Jul 1829
Thomas	10	M	Mechanic	Great Britain	United States	Thomas Dickason 31 Jul 1829
BLEAT, Ellen	25	F		Ireland	United States	Curler 3 Mar 1828
BLEE, James	27	M	Weaver	Ireland	U. States	Ann Maria 5 Aug 1824
BLEECHER, James	24	M	Merchant	U. States	U. States	Ardell 7 Jul 1827
BLEECKER, George W.	20	M	Gentleman	Denmark	U. States	Catherine 3 Jul 1820
BLEITH, Barbara, (his daughter [Jacob])	36	F		Germany	Pensylvania	James Noble 27 Aug 1827
Barbara, (his grand-daughter [Jacob])	9	F		Germany	Pensylvania	James Noble 27 Aug 1827
Jacob	66	M	Cooper	Germany	Pensylvania	James Noble 27 Aug 1827
Katherine, (his daughter [Jacob])	38	F		Germany	Pensylvania	James Noble 27 Aug 1827
BLENDERMANN, Gerd	22	M	Blacksmith	Hannover	New York	Constitution 12 Jul 1827
John	23	M	Sugar Baker	Germany	U. States	Hudson 10 Nov 1825
BLENKERSOP, —, Mrs.	50	F		England	U. States	Elizabeth 12 Aug 1824
John	10	M		England	U. States	Elizabeth 12 Aug 1824
Joseph	15	M		England	U. States	Elizabeth 12 Aug 1824
Peter	17	M		England	U. States	Elizabeth 12 Aug 1824
Rosetta	12	F		England	U. States	Elizabeth 12 Aug 1824
William	8	M		England	U. States	Elizabeth 12 Aug 1824
BLENNER, Irenziska	41	F		France	United States	New England 29 Aug 1828
BLENNY, B.	54	F	Spinster	Ireland		Robert Fulton 4 Jun 1828
BLENON, Charlotte, Miss	24	F	Lady	France	U. States	Lewis 11 Nov 1824
BLENSDIN, Manuel, Esq.	28	M	Merchant	France	Mexico	Potomac 25 Jul 1829
BLESSINGTON, Bidy	19	F	None	Gt. Britain	U. States	Isaac Hicks 18 Apr 1825
Charles	29	M	Labourer	Ireland	America	Josephine 8 Dec 1827
Jas.	20	M	Labourer	Gt. Britain	U. States	Isaac Hicks 18 Apr 1825
BLEUTERMAN, —, Doctr.	20	M	Professor of Letralea [?]	Germany	U. States	Trident 1 Dec 1824
Eliza	29	F		England	U. States	Trident 1 Dec 1824
BLEWET, Thomas	23	M	Farmer	G. Britian	U. States	Leader 14 Apr 1826
BLEY, Barbara	57	F	Farmer	France	France	Sully 15 Jul 1829
Catharine	26	F	Farmer	France	France	Sully 15 Jul 1829
Catharine, Jr.	11	F	Farmer	France	France	Sully 15 Jul 1829
Christian	20	M	Farmer	France	France	Sully 15 Jul 1829
Daniel	16	M	Farmer	France	France	Sully 15 Jul 1829
George	23	M	Farmer	France	France	Sully 15 Jul 1829
George, Jr.	12	M	Farmer	France	France	Sully 15 Jul 1829
Madalina	36	F	Farmer	France	France	Sully 15 Jul 1829

NAMES OF PASSENGERS	AGE	SEX	OCCUPATIONS	COUNTRY TO WHICH THEY BELONG	COUNTRY THEY INTEND TO INHABIT	SHIPS/DATES OF ARRIVAL	
BLEY (cont'd)							
Michael	58	M	Farmer	France	France	Sully	15 Jul 1829
Michael, Jr.	30	M	Farmer	France	France	Sully	15 Jul 1829
BLGBORNE, John	25	M	Merchant	England	United States	Hannibal	25 Sep 1827
BLIGHT, M. P.	24	M	Merchant	U. States	U. States	Superior	16 Apr 1827
Thos.	33		Gentleman	England	England	Hudson	14 Jun 1827
BLILOCK, Janet	19	F	Baker	Argyle (Tedland) Scotland	United States	Jean Hastie	27 Jul 1829
Jno.	22	M	Baker	Argyle (Tedland) Scotland	United States	Jean Hastie	27 Jul 1829
BLINCON, George	22	M	Weaver	England		Eliza Jane	12 Sep 1820
BLINE, Jacob						Olympia	12 Aug 1828

*After having been at Sea a Number of Days was ascertaining the quantity of Baggage to report found the under mentioned persons had secreted themselves away notwithstanding our searach with the Gendearmes at the of leaving the port

NAMES OF PASSENGERS	AGE	SEX	OCCUPATIONS	COUNTRY TO WHICH THEY BELONG	COUNTRY THEY INTEND TO INHABIT	SHIPS/DATES OF ARRIVAL	
BLINKHORN, Ann	5	F	Farmer	Novascotia	Canada	Pedlar	2 Sep 1823
Ann	54	F	Farmer	Yorkshire	Canada	Pedlar	2 Sep 1823
B., Mr.	57	M	Farmer	Yorkshire	Canada	Pedlar	2 Sep 1823
Elenor	20	F	Farmer	Novascotia	Canada	Pedlar	2 Sep 1823
Esther	49	F	Farmer	Yorkshire	Canada	Pedlar	2 Sep 1823
Grace	23	F	Farmer	Novascotia	Canada	Pedlar	2 Sep 1823
Jonah	18	M	Farmer	Novascotia	Canada	Pedlar	2 Sep 1823
Peter	25	M	Farmer	Cumberland	Canada	Pedlar	2 Sep 1823
Wm.	2	M	Farmer	Novascotia	Canada	Pedlar	2 Sep 1823
BLINNARHASSET, H.	22	M	Gentleman	U. States	U. States	Abigail	24 Mar 1825
BLINSCHBACK, Gotthel	39	M	Farmer	Germany	Ohio	James Noble	27 Aug 1827
BLISLE, Jacob Fredk.	22	M	Farmer	Germany	America	Falcon	28 Aug 1828
BLISS, Rosa	16	F		England		Ann	17 May 1822
Saml.	14	M		England		Ann	17 May 1822
BLIZARD, Magdelana	30	F	Servant	England, Antigua	England	Fanny	8 May 1824
BLODGET, James	26	M	Merchant	United States	United States	Cyno	8 Dec 1827
Mary	32	F	None	Gibraltar	Gibraltar	New York	14 Nov 1826
Saml. C.	40	M	Merchant	Gibraltar	Gibraltar	New York	14 Nov 1826
BLODSON, M., Miss	15	F		U. States	U. States	New England	4 Jun 1828
BLOESLY, Ann	2	F		Switzerland	Ohio	Eugenie	20 Aug 1827
Christian	30	M		Switzerland	Ohio	Eugenie	20 Aug 1827
Elizabeth	40	F		Switzerland	Ohio	Eugenie	20 Aug 1827
Randolf	5	M		Switzerland	Ohio	Eugenie	20 Aug 1827
BLOIS, Joseph	...	M	Labourer	Ireland	United States	Robert Fulton	10 Aug 1827
BLOKZEIL, H.	28	M	Mariner	Holland	U. States	Prince Edward	23 Dec 1823
BLONADETTE, Joseph	22	M	Mussician	Geneva	U.S. America	New Hampshire	28 Sep 1826
BLONCK, Johannes	22	M	Shoemaker	Holland	America, U.N.S.	Great Britain	3 Aug 1829
BLONDEL, Charles	6	M	Boy	Great Briton	United States	Erin	26 May 1821
Elizabeth	38 5/12	F	Lady	Great Briton	United States	Erin	26 May 1821
Jacob	3	M	Boy	Great Briton	United States	Erin	26 May 1821
James	12	M	Boy	Great Briton	United States	Erin	26 May 1821
Joseph	1	M	Infant	Great Briton	United States	Erin	26 May 1821
Joshua	9	M	Boy	Great Briton	United States	Erin	26 May 1821
Peter	44 7/12	M	Merchant	Great Briton	United States	Erin	26 May 1821
Susannah	14	F	Girl	Great Briton	United States	Erin	26 May 1821
William	16 6/12	M	Boy	Great Briton	United States	Erin	26 May 1821
BLONDELLE, —, Miss	30	F		France	U. States	Danube	21 Nov 1826
John	37	M	Farmer	France	U. States	Danube	21 Nov 1826
Susan	2	F		France	U. States	Danube	21 Nov 1826
Theodore	4	M		France	U. States	Danube	21 Nov 1826
BLONGRINT, Ann S.	40	F	None	Stockholm	U. States	Roanoake	12 Oct 1826
BLOO...ALL, Edmund	...			Bolton	England	Great Britain	7 May 1827
Mary	...			Bolton	England	Great Britain	7 May 1827
BLOOD, —, Mrs.	28	F	Lady	Saint John	St. John	Nancy	11 Apr 1822
Charles	8	M	Child	Saint John	St. John	Nancy	11 Apr 1822
Eliza	13	F	Lady	Ireland	United States	Dublin Packet	22 Apr 1822
Harriet	26	F		United States	United States	Canada	20 Jun 1823
Joseph Harris	2	M		United States	United States	Canada	20 Jun 1823
Rebecca, Mrs.	30	F		New Brunswick	U. States	Lady Hunter	14 Mar 1826
BLOODER, Caroline	28	F	One Family [Christian]	France	United States	Henri IV	2 Oct 1828
Christian	26	M	Gardner	France	United States	Henri IV	2 Oct 1828
Louis	6/12	F	One Family [Christian]	France	United States	Henri IV	2 Oct 1828

NAMES OF PASSENGERS	AGE	SEX	OCCUPATIONS	COUNTRY TO WHICH THEY BELONG	COUNTRY THEY INTEND TO INHABIT	SHIPS/DATES OF ARRIVAL	
BLOODGOOD, H. S.	23	M	Merchant	N. York	N. York	Thetis	14 Feb 1824
H. S.	29	M	Merchant	U. States	U. States	Commerce	27 May 1822
Thom	22	M	Merchant	U. States	U. States	Maria	2 Apr 1827
BLOOM, Ann	23	F		England	New York	Chelsea	16 May 1828
BLOOMBURGH, Edward	23	M	Doctor	Emden	New York	Hesperus	2 Nov 1820
BLOOMFIELD, Henry	32	M	Builder	Gt. Britain	U. States	Panthia	13 Nov 1824
John	20	M	Wever	Ireland	United States	Fabius	4 Jun 1828
BLOOMITZ, Elizabeth	10	F				Hector	11 Sep 1820
BLOTTLOR, Ana	24	F		Switzerland	United States	Elizabeth	27 Jul 1824
Barbara	32	F		Switzerland	United States	Elizabeth	27 Jul 1824
Christian	4	M		Switzerland	United States	Elizabeth	27 Jul 1824
Eliza	2	F		Switzerland	United States	Elizabeth	27 Jul 1824
Frederick	6/12	M		Switzerland	United States	Elizabeth	27 Jul 1824
Jacob	26	M	Mechanic, maker of handsom	Switzerland	United States	Elizabeth	27 Jul 1824
Jacob	51	M	Mechanic, maker of handsom	Switzerland	United States	Elizabeth	27 Jul 1824
Johanes	8	M		Switzerland	United States	Elizabeth	27 Jul 1824
Maria	6	F		Switzerland	United States	Elizabeth	27 Jul 1824
BLOUNT, Ann	6	F	None	Great Britain	United States	Richmond	18 Feb 1820
Benjamin	1	M	None	Great Britain	United States	Richmond	18 Feb 1820
Eliza	4	F	None	Great Britain	United States	Richmond	18 Feb 1820
Job	2	M	None	Great Britain	United States	Richmond	18 Feb 1820
BLOWEN, Mary	30	F	Labourer	Gt. Britain	U. States	Panthea	21 Jul 1825
BLOWER, Harry	5	M		Great Brit.	Ohio	Gov. Griswald	3 Jul 1820
Heiclith	30	F		Great Brit.	Ohio	Gov. Griswald	3 Jul 1820
Henry	31	M	Labourer	Great Brit.	Ohio	Gov. Griswald	3 Jul 1820
Jane	7	F		Great Brit.	Ohio	Gov. Griswald	3 Jul 1820
Thomas	3	M		Great Brit.	Ohio	Gov. Griswald	3 Jul 1820
William	1	M		Great Brit.	Ohio	Gov. Griswald	3 Jul 1820
BLOXAN, Ann	28	F		England	United States	Delta	24 Oct 1829
BLUCKER, W.	18	M	Mariner	America	U. States	Ambuscade	11 Jul 1821
BLUCKLEE, Rosanna	18	F	Servant	Ireland	United States	St. Michaels	24 Mar 1825
BLUDS, W. H.	14	M	Servant	U.S.A.	U.S.A.	Noble	5 Nov 1828
BLUM, Wm. N.	22	M		G. Brittain	U. States	Cincinnatus	2 Oct 1822
BLUMDELL, John	24	M	Farmer	Derbyshire	U. States	Manhattan	21 May 1821
BLUME, Elizabeth	65	F	Farmer	France	U. States	Lewis	6 Jul 1825
BLUMENTHAL, Charles, Junr.	19	M	Teacher	Hamburg	United States	Howard	6 Jul 1829
BLUNC, George	22	M	Weaver	Germany	Pensylvania	Isabella	15 Sep 1828
BLUNDEN, Harriot	2	F		England	U. States	Cincinnatus	24 May 1821
John	28	M	Farmer	England	U. States	Cincinnatus	24 May 1821
Marion	3	F		England	U. States	Cincinnatus	24 May 1821
Mary	27	F		England	U. States	Cincinnatus	24 May 1821
Walter John	Infant	M		England	U. States	Cincinnatus	24 May 1821
BLUNT, Ann	6/12	F	Miner	Great Britain	United States	Thomas Dickason	31 Jul 1829
Ann	26	F	Miner	Great Britain	United States	Thomas Dickason	31 Jul 1829
Betsy	30	F	Labourer	Ireland	United States	Margarett Scott	22 Aug 1827
Edmund	27	M	Surveyor	United States	United States	Mary Livingston	7 Jan 1826
Edward	24	M	Miner	Great Britain	United States	Thomas Dickason	31 Jul 1829
Edwd.	4	M	Labourer	Ireland	United States	Margarett Scott	22 Aug 1827
Hannah	10	F	None	Great Britain	United States	Richmond	18 Feb 1820
Joseph	40	M	Farmer	Great Britain	United States	Richmond	18 Feb 1820
Mary	1	F	Labourer	Ireland	United States	Margarett Scott	22 Aug 1827
Mary	10	F	None	Great Britain	United States	Richmond	18 Feb 1820
Melliant	11	M	None	Great Britain	United States	Richmond	18 Feb 1820
N. B.	23	M	Counsellor	United States	United States	John Jay	8 May 1828
Peter	2	M	Labourer	Ireland	United States	Margarett Scott	22 Aug 1827
Phoebe	13	F	None	Great Britain	United States	Richmond	18 Feb 1820
Samuel	12	M	None	Great Britain	United States	Richmond	18 Feb 1820
Sarah	19	F	None	Great Britain	United States	Richmond	18 Feb 1820
Sarah	40	F	None	Great Britain	United States	Richmond	18 Feb 1820
Thomas	3	M	Miner	Great Britain	United States	Thomas Dickason	31 Jul 1829
Thos.	35	M	Labourer	Ireland	United States	Margarett Scott	22 Aug 1827
William	15	M	None	Great Britain	United States	Richmond	18 Feb 1820

NAMES OF PASSENGERS	AGE	SEX	OCCUPATIONS	COUNTRY TO WHICH THEY BELONG	COUNTRY THEY INTEND TO INHABIT	SHIPS/DATES OF ARRIVAL	
BLUSHNER, J. H.	29	M	Butcher	Switzerland	United States	India	4 Aug 1826
BLYTH, Elijah H.	17	F	None	England	United States	Great Britain	5 Sep 1827
George	25	M	Weaver	Scotland	New York	Joseph Hume	26 Oct 1829
James	64	M	Farmer	England	U. States	Birmingham	16 Jun 1828
John	25	M	Farmer	England	U. States	Birmingham	16 Jun 1828
Margaret	16	F	None	Great Britain	United States	Friends	13 Jun 1825
Mary	30	F		England	U. States	Birmingham	16 Jun 1828
Mary	64	F		England	U. States	Birmingham	16 Jun 1828
Mary Ann	2	F		England	U. States	Birmingham	16 Jun 1828
Walter	20	M	Mason			Lady of the Lake	23 Aug 1828
Wm.	28	M	Merchant	Gt. Britain	New York	Betsey	18 Apr 1822
BLYTHE, George	27	M	Gentleman	England	Canada	Hercules	21 Nov 1822
BOAEN, Ellen	22			Ireland	America	Liverpool	31 Aug 1827
BOAG, Arcilla, Miss	16	F	Lady	England	United States	Florida	26 Sep 1826
BOAGE, Samuel	21	M	Bookkeeper	Great Britain	United States	Columbia	1 Dec 1823
BOARDMAN, E.	35	M	U.S. Army	U. States	U. States	Weymouth	3 Apr 1821
Farnworth	3...		Weaver	Bolton	England	Great Britain	7 May 1827
John	21	M	Moulder	England	U.S. America	New Hampshire	28 Sep 1826
John	38 6/12	M	...	England	U.S. American	Criterion	7 Jul 1824
Joseph	40	M	Weaver	England	United States	Delta	24 Oct 1829
William	14	M	None	England	United States	Trident	18 Jul 1827
Wm.	24	M	Turner	Great Britain		Moro Castle	6 Jul 1827
Wm.	27	M	Lawyer	British ...	American States	Loyalty	9 Sep 1822
Wm. B.	25	M	Mercht.	U. States	U. States	Rambler	12 Feb 1822
BOARDNAVE, Wm.	40	M	Merchant	America	America	Mercator	21 Feb 1820
BOARMAN, Charles	29 9/12	M	U.S. Navy	United States	United States	Potomac	29 Oct 1828
BOARONDALE, John	23	M	Merchant	England	U. States	St. George	16 Jan 1829
BOARTSCHEER, Wm.	52	M	Mariner	Baltimore	U. States	Fair Play	22 Feb 1823
BOARUM, Wm.	24	M	Officer	U. States	U. States	Rosalie	22 Aug 1820
BOASAND, Chas.	36	M		Spain	U. States	Thankfull Winslow	23 Aug 1826
BOATY, Margaret	17	F	Spinster	Ireland	United States	Fabius	31 Jul 1829
BOAUMONT, Lydia	1	F	None	Great Britain	United States	Cortes	18 Oct 1820
Sarah	25	F	None	Great Britain	United States	Cortes	18 Oct 1820
Walter	4	M	None	Great Britain	United States	Cortes	18 Oct 1820
BOBB, Peter	29	M	Merchant	Philadelphia	United States	New York	14 Jul 1827
BOBET, John	28	M	Merchant	France	U. States	Frances	27 Dec 1826
BOCHE, Ferdinand	22 4/12	M	Farmer	France	U.S. America	Erie	19 Oct 1829
BOCHOF, Janet	20	F	None	Great Britain	United States	Colossus	5 Jun 1827
John	21	M	Weaver	Great Britain	United States	Colossus	5 Jun 1827
BOCK, ...maria	10	F		England	America	Alexander Mansfield	16 Nov 1821
Eliza	1 9/12	F		England	America	Alexander Mansfield	16 Nov 1821
George Albert	6 6/12	M		England	America	Alexander Mansfield	16 Nov 1821
Lucy	3 7/12	F		England	America	Alexander Mansfield	16 Nov 1821
Lucy	30	F	Housekeeper	England	America	Alexander Mansfield	16 Nov 1821
BOCKLIS, Thos. R.	30	M		Ireland	U. States	Nancy	10 Jul 1822
BODA, Stephen	35	M	Merchant	France	Havana	Lady Tompkins	10 Nov 1823
BODDINGTON, Emily	1 1/12	F	Daughter	England	United States	Robert Edwards	3 Oct 1829
Letha	40	F	Wife	England	United States	Robert Edwards	3 Oct 1829
Richard	40	M	Taylor	England	United States	Robert Edwards	3 Oct 1829
BODE, Frederich	25	M	Farmer	Brunwick	United States	Pioneer	28 Jun 1827
Henry	23	M	Farmer	Brunwick	United States	Pioneer	28 Jun 1827
BODEAU, Maria Joseph	32	F	Gardner	France	United States	American	27 Aug 1827
BODEL, Charles	22		Merchant	Switzerland	...	James Cropper	28 Jun 1824
BODEN, James	25		...	Ireland	United States	Alexander Mansfield	23 Nov 1824
Mary	24			Ireland	United States	Alexander Mansfield	23 Nov 1824
BODENHOFER,							
Christina Rosina	30	F		Germany	America	Falcon	28 Aug 1828
Johann Jacob	58	M	Farmer	Germany	America	Falcon	28 Aug 1828
BODERS, Martin	23	M	Labourer	Hanover		Constitution	20 Jun 1828
BODIE, Conrite	51	M	Farmer	Germany	United States	Quito	16 Jun 1826

NAMES OF PASSENGERS	AGE	SEX	OCCUPATIONS	COUNTRY TO WHICH THEY BELONG	COUNTRY THEY INTEND TO INHABIT	SHIPS/DATES OF ARRIVAL	
BODIE (cont'd)							
Dorothie	12	F	daughter of [Conrite]	Germany	United States	Quito	16 Jun 1826
Rebecca	41	F	Wife of [Conrite]	Germany	United States	Quito	16 Jun 1826
BODKIN, Thomas	33	M	Farmer	England	United States	Jubilee	1 Oct 1828
BODLET, Amidee	20	M	Mechanic	France	New York	Lewis	29 Oct 1825
BODMAN, Andrew	18	M		Switzerland	U. States	Romulus	24 Sep 1828
C. F.	0 6/12	M		Switzerland	U. States	Romulus	24 Sep 1828
Caroline	35	F		Switzerland	U. States	Romulus	24 Sep 1828
Christine	16	F		Switzerland	U. States	Romulus	24 Sep 1828
Elizabeth	10	F		Switzerland	U. States	Romulus	24 Sep 1828
G. F.	3	M		Switzerland	U. States	Romulus	24 Sep 1828
Jacob F.	6	M		Switzerland	U. States	Romulus	24 Sep 1828
John F.	21	M		Switzerland	U. States	Romulus	24 Sep 1828
Philip	8	M		Switzerland	U. States	Romulus	24 Sep 1828
Philip F.	47	M		Switzerland	U. States	Romulus	24 Sep 1828
BODRAM, Corneals	22	M	Doctor	Newbrunsick	Newbrunsick	Nancy	23 Oct 1823
BOECKLY, Jacob	13	M	Servant	Wittenburg	U. States	Comet	28 Jul 1825
Kitty	20	F	Servant	Wittenburg	U. States	Comet	28 Jul 1825
BOEFOE, John	35	M	Gentleman	Nassau	U.States	Venus	28 Jun 1825
BÖEL, Paul	13	M		Germany	U. States	Cadmus	28 May 1821
BOELL, C.	...	M	Merchant	France	France	Howard	27 Sep 1826
BOERNDER, A.	23	M	Shepherd	Germany	U. States	Minerva	9 Jan 1827
BOEUF, Maria Rose	25	F	None	France	U. States	Howard	21 Aug 1826
Therese Adelaide	60	F	None	France	U. States	Howard	21 Aug 1826
BOGAN, Biddy	22	F	Spinster	Ireland	United States	Catharine	22 Jul 1825
Own	25 6/12	M	Labourer	Ireland	United States	Robert Fulton	24 Jul 1826
Rosannah	24	F	Farmer	Great Britain	United States	Wanderer	14 May 1828
BOGARDUS, N.	26	M	Horseman	N. York	U. States	Hero	17 May 1825
BOGARONE, Robert	32	M	Carpenter	New York	United States	St. Michaels	12 Apr 1826
BOGARTH, J.	29	M	None	U. States	U. States	Golden Age	19 Dec 1827
BOGEL, Cathr.	22	F		Ireland	U. States	Sarah G	7 May 1827
Eliz.	30	F		Ireland	U. States	Sarah G	7 May 1827
BOGEN, Dorothia	1	F		Germany	U.S.	Stephania	27 Nov 1826
E.	19	F	Farmer	Germany	America	Howard	27 Sep 1826
G.	16	M	Farmer	Germany	America	Howard	27 Sep 1826
G. P.	17	M	Farmer	Germany	America	Howard	27 Sep 1826
Jacob	47		Farmer	Germany	Baltimore	Don Quixote	19 Aug 1825
Louiza	42	M		Germany	U.S.	Stephania	27 Nov 1826
M.	6	F	Farmer	Germany	America	Howard	27 Sep 1826
Magdalena	13	F		Germany	U.S.	Stephania	27 Nov 1826
Sophia	10	F		Germany	U.S.	Stephania	27 Nov 1826
BOGERT, James	28	M	Laborer	Ireland	United States	St. Michaels	23 Dec 1826
Jas. L.	30	M	Merchant	U. States	U. States	William & Henry	27 Mar 1827
BOGGS, James	31	M	Mason	Ireland	U. States of America	Courier	17 Mar 1827
James, Jr.	...	...	...	Ireland	U. States of America	Courier	17 Mar 1827
John	20	M	Labourer	Ireland	United States	William & George	14 May 1828
Rhoda, Mrs.	53	F		U. States	U. States	Packet	4 Nov 1822
Sarah, Mrs.	23	F		U. States	U. States	Packet	4 Nov 1822
William Fountain	1 8/12	M		U. States	U. States	Packet	4 Nov 1822
Wm.	24		Farmer	Ireland	United States	Robert Burns	18 Jun 1821
BOGIERE, —, Mr.	16	M	Student	Columbia	U. States	General Paez	21 Jun 1826
BOGLE, James	22	M	Labourer	Ireland	United States	Hope	12 Jun 1828
Peter	31	M				Hanford	17 Jul 1828
BOGLOGETT, D. G.	23	M	Merchant	Carthegena		Leonardas	30 Oct 1822
BOGMAN, William	36	M	Captain	United States	United States	Trident	30 Sep 1826
BOGNELL, Charles	7	M	Farmer	England	U. States	Franklin	7 Jul 1828
George	5	M	Farmer	England	U. States	Franklin	7 Jul 1828
George	38	M	Farmer	England	U. States	Franklin	7 Jul 1828
Mary	2 6/12	F	Farmer	England	U. States	Franklin	7 Jul 1828
Sidney	26	F	Farmer	England	U. States	Franklin	7 Jul 1828
BOGS, John	25		Farmer			Mount Vernon	26 Aug 1820
BOGSHAW, Edward	50	M	Farmer	Great Britan	United States	Silvanus Jenkins	10 Mar 1827
Edward, Jr.	22	M	Farmer	Great Britan	United States	Silvanus Jenkins	10 Mar 1827
BOGUE, William	33	M	Farmer	Ireland	United States	Meteor	27 Sep 1826
BOGURT, Nicholas	30	M	Seaman	New York	New York	Mary & Elizabeth	7 Sep 1824

NAMES OF PASSENGERS	AGE	SEX	OCCUPATIONS	COUNTRY TO WHICH THEY BELONG	COUNTRY THEY INTEND TO INHABIT	SHIPS/DATES OF ARRIVAL	
BOHAIN, James	29	M	Butcher	England	United States	Siroc	31 Oct 1829
BOHALL, Andrew	5	M		Ireland	United States	Thompson	12 Sep 1827
Biddy	6	F		Ireland	United States	Thompson	12 Sep 1827
James	4	M		Ireland	United States	Thompson	12 Sep 1827
Mary	30	F		Ireland	United States	Thompson	12 Sep 1827
Peter	1	M		Ireland	United States	Thompson	12 Sep 1827
*Died Sept. 4th 1827							
Peter	30	M		Ireland	United States	Thompson	12 Sep 1827
Repy	3	F		Ireland	United States	Thompson	12 Sep 1827
BOHAN, —, Mrs.	24	F	Spinster	Ireland	United States	Abigail	25 Jun 1822
James	26	M	Farmer	Ireland	United States	Abigail	25 Jun 1822
BOHIN, Francoise	10	F				Henri IV	17 May 1828
Francoise	35	F				Henri IV	17 May 1828
Jaque	35	M				Henri IV	17 May 1828
BOHL, —, Mrs.	36	F		Bavaria		François I	19 Nov 1828
Adam	7	M		Bavaria		François I	19 Nov 1828
Adam	9 6/12	M		Bavaria		François I	19 Nov 1828
Adam	38	M	Farmer	Bavaria		François I	19 Nov 1828
Anna Barbara	9	F		Bavaria		François I	19 Nov 1828
Catharina	2	F		Bavaria		François I	19 Nov 1828
Elizabeth Derbecker	28	F		Bavaria		François I	19 Nov 1828
Eva	6	F		Bavaria		François I	19 Nov 1828
Eva Catharine	34	F		Bavaria		François I	19 Nov 1828
Friedrich	8	M		Bavaria		François I	19 Nov 1828
George	3	M		Bavaria		François I	19 Nov 1828
George	8	M		Bavaria		François I	19 Nov 1828
George	31	M	Farmer	Bavaria		François I	19 Nov 1828
Heinrich	9 3/12	M		Bavaria		François I	19 Nov 1828
Jacob	34	M	Tailor	Bavaria		François I	19 Nov 1828
Maria Elizabeth	5	F		Bavaria		François I	19 Nov 1828
Salomea	3/12	F		Bavaria		François I	19 Nov 1828
Salomea	4	F		Bavaria		François I	19 Nov 1828
BOHLEN, Joh.	33	M	Sugar Baker	Germany	U. States	Constitution	21 Jun 1824
BOHMER, John C.	34	M	Merchant	Germany	U. States	Canada	4 Oct 1824
BOHRINGER, Catharine	5	F		Wertemburg	America, U.N.S.	Great Britain	3 Aug 1829
Catharine	34	F		Wertemburg	America, U.N.S.	Great Britain	3 Aug 1829
George	38	M	Weaver	Wertemburg	America, U.N.S.	Great Britain	3 Aug 1829
Jacob	8	M		Wertemburg	America, U.N.S.	Great Britain	3 Aug 1829
Jacobina	...	F		Wertemburg	America, U.N.S.	Great Britain	3 Aug 1829
Loderick	4	M		Wertemburg	America, U.N.S.	Great Britain	3 Aug 1829
BOID, Dorcas	18	F		U. States	U. States	Lewis	17 Sep 1821
Jas.	24	M	Shoemaker	U. States	U. States	Lewis	17 Sep 1821
John	33	M	Weaver	Ireland	New York	Washington	3 Mar 1828
BOIDE, Margaret	16	F		U. States	U. States	Lewis	17 Sep 1821
BOILL, C. W.	18	M	Merchant	France	U. States	Quesnel	6 Sep 1824
BOIS, Louis Petit	27	M	...	...	New York	Curlew	28 Jun 1824
BOISAUBOA, Lewis	25		Merchant	...		Little John	4 Nov 1820
BOISENGER, Catharine	40		Farmer	France	U. States	Elizabeth	9 Jul 1825
Elizabeth	4		Farmer	France	U. States	Elizabeth	9 Jul 1825
BOISGERARD, Edward	21	M	Merchant	Charleston	U.S.	Bayard	30 Oct 1820
BOISGERART, ...	24	M	Merchant	United States	United States	Bayard	13 Nov 1823
BOISONNET, Ls.	27	M		Jacqumel	Rebulic of Hayti	Renuniero	3 Jan 1822
BOISSERE, Agustus, Esqr.	27	M	Gent. Man	France	U. States	Don Quixotte	17 Jan 1825
BOIT, —, Mrs.	30					Olympia	2 Sep 1823
Angeleth	12					Olympia	2 Sep 1823
Henery	35			United States	Boston	Olympia	2 Sep 1823
William	9					Olympia	2 Sep 1823
BOITOT, Benjamin	24	M	Carpenter	France	United States	Henri IV	2 Oct 1828
BOKA, Peater	28	M	Farmer	Germany	United States	Virginia	31 May 1828
BOKINS, Caroline	7	F		United States	United States of Am.	Constitution	6 Jul 1829
Hanna	10	F		United States	United States of Am.	Constitution	6 Jul 1829
Louisa	42	F		United States	United States of Am.	Constitution	6 Jul 1829
V.	58	M	Hatter	United States	United States of Am.	Constitution	6 Jul 1829
BOLANCUL, P.	28	M	Merchant	Spain	Spain	Richmond Packet	30 Oct 1827
BOLAND, Darley	43	M	Farmer	Ireland	Philadelphia	Virginia	7 May 1824
E.	28		Farmer	Limerick	Baltimore	Schuylkill	22 Aug 1825
Louis	25	M	Servant	France	U. States	Sully	15 Jul 1829
Thomas	45	M	Farmer	Ireland	Philadelphia	Virginia	7 May 1824

NAMES OF PASSENGERS	AGE	SEX	OCCUPATIONS	COUNTRY TO WHICH THEY BELONG	COUNTRY THEY INTEND TO INHABIT	SHIPS/DATES OF ARRIVAL	
BOLAND (cont'd)							
Wm.	4...			Ireland	U.S.	Union	20 Aug 1827
BOLARD, Abraham	...			Gil...	England	Great Britain	7 May 1827
Ann	...			Gil...	England	Great Britain	7 May 1827
Benjn.	29		Carpenter	Gil...	England	Great Britain	7 May 1827
Flora	7			Gil...	England	Great Britain	7 May 1827
Gormly	...			Gil...	England	Great Britain	7 May 1827
Sarah	31			Gil...	England	Great Britain	7 May 1827
BOLAST, Mary	23	F	Farmer	Ireland	America	Farmer	4 Aug 1825
BOLAVER, Josefa							
de Clemente	17	F		Curaccas	South America	Virginia Packet	1 Jun 1822
Pablode Clemente	16	M		Curaccas	South America	Virginia Packet	1 Jun 1822
BOLDERICH, Elisabeth	24	F	Carpenter	Netherlands	Philadelphia	Louisa	6 Oct 1828
BOLDES, B.	20	M	Merchant	Mexico	Mexico	Washington	29 Apr 1826
BOLDICH, Richard	38	M	Hostler	U. States	U. States	Pedler	27 May 1825
BOLDORA, B.	47	M	Seaman	Spain	U. States	Income	12 Mar 1822
BOLE, Ann	21	F	None	Gt. Brittain	United States	Balaena	24 Aug 1825
Ann	60	F	None	Gt. Brittain	United States	Balaena	24 Aug 1825
BOLEN, —, Mrs., & Son	32	F		... U.S.A.	United States	Belle	3 Aug 1822
BOLENS, Ann	19	F		Greenwich	U. States	Plato	18 Apr 1826
BOLETE, Jose	40	M	Merchant	Spain	Spain	Claudio	16 Oct 1827
BOLF, Matthew	20	M	Farmer	Great Britain	United States	Frances Henrietta	17 Sep 1827
BOLIDARSON,							
Jno. B. Mison	32	M	Spoonmaker	Holland	U. States	Xenophon	15 Sep 1820
BOLILGER, Jean	24			Suisse		Deux Ernest	29 Dec 1827
BOLIND, Edmond	32	M	Tailor	Ireland	U. States	Combine	30 Nov 1825
BOLIVAR, F.	12	M	Merchant	Spain	United States	Sally	26 Jun 1822
Maria Antonia	37	F		Curaccas	South America	Virginia Packet	1 Jun 1822
BOLLANA, Henry	40	M	None	England	U. States	Criterion	20 Nov 1823
BOLLAP, Elizabeth	18	F		England	New York	Corinthian	5 May 1827
Joseph	9	M		England	New York	Corinthian	5 May 1827
Sarah	40	F		England	New York	Corinthian	5 May 1827
BOLLBENLY, James	25	M	Merchant	England	U. States	America	30 Sep 1822
BOLLERMANN, Anth.	26	M	Merchant	France	United States	Stephania	27 Nov 1826
BOLLES, Wm., Jr.	15	M	Farmer	Great Britain	United States	Exertion	17 Jul 1829
BOLLEWINKLE, Jasper	30	M	Sugar Baker	England	New York	Cortes	23 Nov 1827
BOLLIE, Juan	25	M	Merchant	Spain	U. States	Lucy Ann	4 Sep 1822
BOLLINGALL, Wm.	26	M	Mechanic	Great Britain	Great Britain	Hercules	6 Oct 1828
BOLLIS, Wm.	40	M	Farmer	Great Britain	United States	Exertion	17 Jul 1829
BOLLMANN,							
Caroline, Miss	23			Philadelphia	United States	London	13 Dec 1822
Elizh., Miss	21			Philadelphia	United States	London	13 Dec 1822
BOLLS, Caroline	3	F	Farmer	England	United States	Essex	23 May 1828
Edwd.	2	M	Farmer	England	United States	Essex	23 May 1828
Jemima	1	M	Farmer	England	United States	Essex	23 May 1828
Penniah	24	F	Farmer	England	United States	Essex	23 May 1828
Wm.	26	M	Farmer	England	United States	Essex	23 May 1828
BOLLY, Edward	1	M	None	Ireland	United States	Catharine	22 Jul 1825
Mary	25	F	Spinster	Ireland	United States	Catharine	22 Jul 1825
BOLOMLEY, Jonathan	20	M	Farmer	England	America	Plutarch	18 Jul 1826
BOLT, Benjamin	24	M	Butcher	England	America	Britannia	22 Jul 1829
BOLTER, —, Miss	4	F		Barbadoes	Barbadoes	Azores	2 Jun 1824
BOLTON, —	25	M		England		Amity	11 May 1821
—, Mr.	42	M	Merchant	England	Barbadoes	Celia	15 Oct 1825
—, Mrs.	35	F	Lady	England	U.S.	James & Margaret	4 Aug 1823
Ann	6	F	None	Great Brittain	Savannah	Albion	11 Jun 1821
Ann	27	F	None	Great Brittain	Savannah	Albion	11 Jun 1821
Ann	30	F	None	Gt. Britain	Canada	New York	5 Jul 1826
Daniel	35	M	British Army	Gt. Britain	Canada	New York	5 Jul 1826
Darcey	28	M	Gentleman	Great Briton	Canada	Brighton	12 Jun 1826
Elizabeth	5	F		Great Britian	United States	Robert Quayle	29 Jul 1822
Henry	32	M	Manufacturer	England	U. States	Hudson	8 Oct 1827
Henry	38	M	S. General	Up. Canada	Up. Canada	Columbia	31 Jul 1826
James	26	M	Mechanic	Scotland	U. States of America	Dale	14 Mar 1828
James	27	M	...	Great Britian	United States	Robert Quayle	29 Jul 1822
James	28	M	Gentleman			Helen	4 Aug 1829
James	29	M		Great Britian	United States	Robert Quayle	29 Jul 1822

NAMES OF PASSENGERS	AGE	SEX	OCCUPATIONS	COUNTRY TO WHICH THEY BELONG	COUNTRY THEY INTEND TO INHABIT	SHIPS/DATES OF ARRIVAL	
BOLTON (cont'd)							
James	30		Merchant	England	United States	Mary	15 Jul 1822
John	2	M		Great Britian	United States	Robert Quayle	29 Jul 1822
John	4	M	None	Great Brittain	Savannah	Albion	11 Jun 1821
John Lawrence	1/2	M	None	Gt. Britain	Canada	New York	5 Jul 1826
Joseph	7	M	child	England	U.S.	James & Margaret	4 Aug 1823
Joseph	18	M	Clerk	Great Britain	United States	Grecian	24 Sep 1828
Joseph	22	M		England	United States	William Byrnes	11 Dec 1827
Margaret	5	F	Servant	Ireland	New York	Louisa	20 Jul 1826
Mary	6/12	F	None	Great Brittain	Savannah	Albion	11 Jun 1821
Mary	30	F		Great Britian	United States	Robert Quayle	29 Jul 1822
Mary	35	F	Seamstres	G. Brittain	America	Atlantic	11 Oct 1822
Robert	21	M	Merchant	England	England	Britannia	5 Nov 1828
Robert	30	M		United States	Savannah	Albion	11 Jun 1821
Robert, Jr.	7	M	None	Great Brittain	Savannah	Albion	11 Jun 1821
Robt.	23	M	Farmer	Ireland	U.S. America	Columbia	31 Jul 1826
Thomas	26	F	Carpenter	England	U.S. States	Splendid	14 Aug 1829
William	5	M	child	England	U.S.	James & Margaret	4 Aug 1823
Winffee	2	M	None	Great Brittain	Savannah	Albion	11 Jun 1821
Wm.	22	F	Sawyer	England	U.S. States	Splendid	14 Aug 1829
Wm.	24	M	Turner	England	United States	Trident	31 Mar 1827
Wm.	24	M	Weaver	England	U. States	Thomas Ritchie	2 Jul 1827
Wm. J...	5	M	None	Great Brittain	Savannah	Albion	11 Jun 1821
BOLUS, Thos.	22	M	Mechanic	Greenwich	U. States	Plato	18 Apr 1826
BOMER, Wm.	16	M		Ireland	United States	Florida	14 Sep 1827
BOMERS, Jas.	27	M	Merchant	Germany	Philada.	Almira	6 Feb 1826
BOMESHER, J.	24	M	Merchant	Germany	Philadelphia	Cotton Plant	15 Nov 1823
W.	26	M	Merchant	Germany	Philadelphia	Cotton Plant	15 Nov 1823
BOMINICK, Jose	45	M	Merchant	Spain	Spain	Claudio	16 Oct 1827
BOMMFOUX, L.	31	M	Merchant	France		Howard	17 Oct 1822
BONADALE, Wm.	33	M	Merchant	England	U. States	John Wells	8 Sep 1897
BONADEAU, Peter	31	M	Merchant	Philad.	Philadelphia	E. D. Douglass	12 Apr 1824
BONAPARTE, Jerome Napoleon	22	M	Gentleman	U. States	U. States	William Byrnes	23 Aug 1827
BONAPORTE, Charles	20	M		Roma	Philadelphia	Falcon	10 Sep 1823
Lenoïsa	20	F		Roma	Philadelphia	Falcon	10 Sep 1823
BONASSET, Antony	47	M	Merchant	U. States	United States	Seine	7 Dec 1821
BONAUFAUX, L.	37	M	Merchant	France	N. York	Queen Mab	20 Nov 1826
BOND, Charles	23	M	Merchant	England	United States	Cincinnatus	21 Nov 1821
Christian	1			Scotland	United States	Camillus	3 May 1828
D.	34	M	Consul	U.S.	U.S.	Porcia	4 Jan 1828
F., Mrs.	18	F		England	United States	Cincinnatus	21 Nov 1821
Geo.	20	M	Merchant	U. States	U. States	Silvia	10 Sep 1827
George	38	M	Merchant	U.S. America	U.S. America	Columbia	15 Nov 1826
Helen	22		Wife, going to her husband	Scotland	United States	Camillus	3 May 1828
Hugh	3			Scotland	United States	Camillus	3 May 1828
James	28	M	...	G. Brittain	America	Robin Hood	20 Jul 1827
John	32	M	Miner	England	England	Virginia	8 Mar 1828
Th. J.	33	M	Mercht.	United States	United States	Panthea	11 Nov 1825
BONDELY, —, Mrs.	18	F		Switzerland	United States	Alexander	2 Oct 1829
BONE, Adolpheus A.	18	M		U. States	U. States	Florida	2 Jun 1828
Eliza	40	F		Ireland	United States	Hannibal	25 Sep 1827
John	10	M		Ireland	United States	Hannibal	25 Sep 1827
M.	6	M		Ireland	United States	Hannibal	25 Sep 1827
Michl.	31	M	Minister	Ireland	United States	Hannibal	25 Sep 1827
Patrick	8	M		Ireland	United States	Hannibal	25 Sep 1827
BONEALL, Erastas	20	M	Carver & Gilder	Great Britain	U.S. of America	Gratitude	3 Oct 1829
BONEFA, C.	20	M	Gentleman	Bordeaux	U. States	Robert Lenox	6 Jun 1821
BONELLY, J.	29	M	Farmer	France	U.S.	Stephania	15 Aug 1825
BONEMON, John P.	25	M	Teacher	Switzerland	U.S. America	Huntress	6 Sep 1827
BONER, Charles	40		Farmer			Rufus King	7 Aug 1820
Janer	34		Housewife			Rufus King	7 Aug 1820
Margaret	19	F	going to her Brother	G. Brittian	United States	Louisa	14 Jun 1825
Robert	24	M	Farmer	G. Brittian	United States	Louisa	14 Jun 1825
BONES, Ann	6	F	Farmer	England	In the Country	Chelsea	16 May 1828
Elizabeth	37 6/12	F	Farmer	England	In the Country	Chelsea	16 May 1828

NAMES OF PASSENGERS	AGE	SEX	OCCUPATIONS	COUNTRY TO WHICH THEY BELONG	COUNTRY THEY INTEND TO INHABIT	SHIPS/DATES OF ARRIVAL	
BONES (cont'd)							
James, & family	36	M	Farmer	England	In the Country	Chelsea	16 May 1828
John	4	M	Farmer	England	In the Country	Chelsea	16 May 1828
Thomas	2	M	Farmer	England	In the Country	Chelsea	16 May 1828
BONET, Eliza	1/2	F	Child	Ireland	United States	Borneo	2 Oct 1827
Jane	7	F	Child	Ireland	United States	Borneo	2 Oct 1827
BONEY, William	14 7/12	M	Labourer	Ireland	America	Enterprize	29 Jun 1827
BONFREY, Watson	24	M	Farmer	Great Britain	U. States	Ann Marria	6 Aug 1823
BONGLESS, Catherine							
Donafort	23 7/12	F	Farmer	Switzerland	America	Henry	17 May 1828
BONHAM, E.	22	M	Seaman	U.S.	U.S.	Enterprise	18 Sep 1820
BONIFACE, Chas.	7	M	...	Switzerland	U. States	Robert Edward	2 Nov 1827
Fredk.	5	M	...	Switzerland	U. States	Robert Edward	2 Nov 1827
Geo. G.	1	M	...	Switzerland	U. States	Robert Edward	2 Nov 1827
Jas.	32	M	...ler	Switzerland	U. States	Robert Edward	2 Nov 1827
Mary	30	F	...	Switzerland	U. States	Robert Edward	2 Nov 1827
BONKEY, Francis	30	M	Farmer	Gt. Britain	United States	Penelope	9 Sep 1828
BONNAFFE, Mark	19	M	Student	Bordeaux	U. States	Smyrna	30 Apr 1825
BONNAGGOR, J.	24	M	Sugar Baker	Holland	U. States	United States	7 Jul 1827
BONNEFORER, L.	35	M	Merchant	France	United States	Marmione	20 Nov 1821
BONNEFOUX,							
Laurant	36 3/12	M	...	...	U.S. America	Edward	28 Oct 1825
BONNEN, Catharine	24 0/12	F	Lady	Ireland	United States	Lunar	5 May 1828
BONNER, A.	48	M	Merchant	U. States	U. States	Seneca	7 Nov 1825
Alex	36	M	Merchant	New York	New York	Hesperus	2 Nov 1820
Alexr.	35	M	Mercht.	U. States	N. York	Favourite	8 Oct 1823
Charles	5		Boy			Rufus King	7 Aug 1820
David	7		Boy			Rufus King	7 Aug 1820
Hamilton	13		Boy			Rufus King	7 Aug 1820
James	12	M		U. States	U. States	Seneca	7 Nov 1825
John	21		Labourer	Ireland	Great Britain	Robert Burns	14 Jun 1824
John James	11		Boy			Rufus King	7 Aug 1820
L.	16	M	L. Maker	Holland	U. States	Edward Bonaffe	23 Jul 1828
Mary	34		Spinster			Rufus King	7 Aug 1820
May	2	F	Child	Ireland	U. States	William & John	10 Jul 1824
Michael	26	M	Labourer	Ireland	United States	William & George	14 May 1828
Miles	40	M	Farmer	Ireland	U. States	William & John	10 Jul 1824
Sally	1	F	Child	Ireland	U. States	William & John	10 Jul 1824
Sarah	25	F	wife to [Miles]	Ireland	U. States	William & John	10 Jul 1824
William	7/12		Boy			Rufus King	7 Aug 1820
BONNET, Anne, Mrs.	50	F	Wife	France	France	Lewis	29 Oct 1825
Eutienne	23	M	Watch Maker	Switzerland	Curacoa	Bayard	15 Feb 1827
Francois	19	M	Watch Maker	Switzerland	Curacoa	Bayard	15 Feb 1827
BONNETT, —, Mrs.	62	F				Betsey	17 Aug 1820
Ann	23	F				Betsey	17 Aug 1820
Betsey	10	F	Child	Ireland	United States	Ann Maria	3 Jul 1827
Cassena	16	F	Lady	St. John, N.B.	United States	Sylvester Healy	17 Oct 1825
James	13	M	Child	Ireland	United States	Ann Maria	3 Jul 1827
James	34	M	Surgeon			Betsey	17 Aug 1820
Jane	3	F	Child	Ireland	United States	Ann Maria	3 Jul 1827
Jane	21	F				Betsey	17 Aug 1820
John	1	M	Child	Ireland	United States	Ann Maria	3 Jul 1827
Mary	18	F	Lady	Newbrunsick	Newbrunsick	Nancy	23 Oct 1823
Mary	18	F	Lady	St. John, N.B.	United States	Sylvester Healy	17 Oct 1825
Mary	18		Farmer	Halifax	U. States	Edwin	26 Sep 1828
Mary	19	F	Child	Ireland	United States	Ann Maria	3 Jul 1827
Nancy	49	F	Wife	Ireland	United States	Ann Maria	3 Jul 1827
Rachel	22	F	Lady	Newbrunsick	Newbrunsick	Nancy	23 Oct 1823
Rachel	22		Farmer	Halifax	U. States	Edwin	26 Sep 1828
Samuel	17	M	Child	Ireland	United States	Ann Maria	3 Jul 1827
Thomas	50	M	Laborer	Ireland	United States	Ann Maria	3 Jul 1827
BONNEY, Michl.	21	M	Farmer	Ireland	United States	Trident	17 May 1825
BONNICH, G.	19	F	Milliner	Malta	U. States	Fortune	28 Jul 1825
BONNIOT, James M.	25 6/12	M	Student in Bardstown's College	Savoy	America	Henry	17 May 1828
BONNIT, Abraham	23	M	Malster			Hector	11 Sep 1820
BONNMER, Lewis, Mr.	30	M	Gent.	England	U. States	Acasta	11 Dec 1826

NAMES OF PASSENGERS	AGE	SEX	OCCUPATIONS	COUNTRY TO WHICH THEY BELONG	COUNTRY THEY INTEND TO INHABIT	SHIPS/DATES OF ARRIVAL	
BONNY, Elizabeth	60	F	Woman	Ireland	United States	Dublin Packet	6 Dec 1827
BONSAL, Jos.	60	M	Miner	G. Brittain	U. States	Pacific	23 Jan 1826
BONSALL, Saml.	24	M	Miner	G. Brittain	U. States	Pacific	23 Jan 1826
BONSAN, Caroline, Miss	14	F	Lady	Ireland	America	Dublin Packet	9 Oct 1820
Maria, Mrs.	40	F	Lady	Ireland	America	Dublin Packet	9 Oct 1820
BONSDAY, Jean Danl.	22	M	Watch Maker	Switzerland	U. States	Little William	16 Jun 1821
BONSER, Ann	39	F		Great Britan	United States	Delaware	20 Aug 1829
Ann, Jr.	10	F		Great Britan	United States	Delaware	20 Aug 1829
George	6	M		Great Britan	United States	Delaware	20 Aug 1829
Henry	1	M		Great Britan	United States	Delaware	20 Aug 1829
Matilda	8	F		Great Britan	United States	Delaware	20 Aug 1829
Phebe	4	F		Great Britan	United States	Delaware	20 Aug 1829
Thomas	14	M		Great Britan	United States	Delaware	20 Aug 1829
William	12	M		Great Britan	United States	Delaware	20 Aug 1829
BONSNELL, Elen	1	F	Cooper	England	U. States	York	7 Aug 1828
Jane	25	F	Cooper	England	U. States	York	7 Aug 1828
Joseph	28	M	Cooper	England	U. States	York	7 Aug 1828
BONTON, Thomas	27	M	Labourer	Ireland	U. States	Nancy	1 Sep 1823
BONVALLET, Eugene	21	M		France	United States	Alexander	20 Aug 1828
BONY, Ellen	29	F	Spinster	Ireland	United States	Dublin Packet	28 Apr 1824
Mary	1	F	Child	Ireland	United States	Dublin Packet	28 Apr 1824
William	24	M	Farmer	Ireland	United States	Dublin Packet	28 Apr 1824
BOO, Antonio	32	M	Merchant	U. States	U. States	Ardell	7 Jul 1827
Saletien	30	F	None	U. States	U. States	Ardell	7 Jul 1827
BOODY, Ann, his wife [James]	27	F	Housekeeper	Ireland	United States	Andes	2 Oct 1828
Maria, their daughter [James & Ann]	12	F	Spinster	Ireland	United States	Andes	2 Oct 1828
BOOL, Chas. A.	19	M	Super Cargo	U. States	U. States	Laurel	29 Aug 1826
J.	20	M	Servant	Mexico	U. States	Laveria	23 Jul 1828
BOOM, Charlotte	11	F		G. Britain	U. States	Robt. Edwards	4 Sep 1828
Emily	7	F		G. Britain	U. States	Robt. Edwards	4 Sep 1828
Geo.	6	M		G. Britain	U. States	Robt. Edwards	4 Sep 1828
Geo.	33	M	Taylor	G. Britain	U. States	Robt. Edwards	4 Sep 1828
Hamah	2	F		G. Britain	U. States	Robt. Edwards	4 Sep 1828
Harriet	32	F		G. Britain	U. States	Robt. Edwards	4 Sep 1828
Lydia	9	M		G. Britain	U. States	Robt. Edwards	4 Sep 1828
Mark	4	M		G. Britain	U. States	Robt. Edwards	4 Sep 1828
BOON, Ann	22			England	Canada	Venus	4 Oct 1821
Mary	24	F		England	America	Two Marys	24 Sep 1827
R.	27	M	Spinner	England	America	Two Marys	24 Sep 1827
BOONE, Jane	24	F		Gt. Britain		Dalhouse Castle	13 May 1828
Rebecca	22	F		Gt. Britain		Dalhouse Castle	13 May 1828
William R.	27	M	Merchant	America	U. States	Governor Lincoln	10 Jul 1827
*Died on the Voyage							
BOORMAN, Robt.	38	M	Gentleman	United States	United States	Robert Edwards	3 Oct 1829
Sarah Ann	22	F	Wife	United States	United States	Robert Edwards	3 Oct 1829
Thoms.	26	M	Miner	England	U.S. States	Splendid	14 Aug 1829
Thos.	20	M	Farmer	England	U. States	Acasta	12 May 1825
BOORNIAN, Francis	25	M	Mechanic	U.S.	U.S.	Aginoria	16 Apr 1821
BOOT, Wm., Mr.	25	M	Merchant	United States	United States	Manchester	8 Dec 1827
BOOTH, —, Mrs.		M		G. Britain	U. States	Canada	19 Sep 1828
—, Mrs.	30	M		G. Britain	U. States	Canada	19 Sep 1828
...	47	F	Carpenter	England	U. States	Electra	7 Jul 1828
Abel	26	M	Farmer	Ireland	America	Minerva	31 May 1824
Alfred	9			Manchester		Mount Vernon	18 Oct 1822
Alice	26	F		Great Britain	United States	Mary	11 Jul 1820
Andrew	4	M	Farmer	...	America	Farmer	4 Aug 1825
Ann	13	F	Carpenter	England	U. States	Electra	7 Jul 1828
Ann	26	F		Great Britain	United States	Mary	11 Jul 1820
Ann Maria Smith	27	F	...	...	...	Braganza	8 Aug 1825
Benjamin	40	M	Printer	England	Philadelphia	Curler	7 Jul 1827
Betty	1	F		Great Britain	United States	Mary	11 Jul 1820
Betty	59	F		Great Britain	United States	Mary	11 Jul 1820
Daniel	4	M	Carpenter	England	U. States	Electra	7 Jul 1828
Edward	22	M		Great Britain	United States	Mary	11 Jul 1820
Edwd.	25	M	Labourer	Ireland		Fame	9 Dec 1826
Elisa	10/12	F	None	England	U.S. States	Solon	25 Nov 1824

NAMES OF PASSENGERS	AGE	SEX	OCCUPATIONS	COUNTRY TO WHICH THEY BELONG	COUNTRY THEY INTEND TO INHABIT	SHIPS/DATES OF ARRIVAL	
BOOTH (cont'd)							
Eliza	7			York Shire (Yorkshire)	Utica	Peru	30 May 1828
Eliza	14			Manchester		Mount Vernon	18 Oct 1822
Elizabeth	1 1/2	F		England	England	William Byrnes	14 Apr 1824
Elizabeth	30	F		Gt. Britain	United States	Meteor	19 Aug 1829
Elizabeth	38	F		Gt. Britain		Dalhouse Castle	13 May 1828
Geo.	45	M	Mechanic	Havana	Spain	Hesper	21 Sep 1827
George	2	M	Carpenter	England	U. States	Electra	7 Jul 1828
George	40	M	Merchant	New Brunswick	United States	Edwin	27 Oct 1828
Hy.	24	M	Farmer	United States	United States	Euphrates	2 Sep 1823
Imas	25	M	Printer	England	U.S. States	Solon	25 Nov 1824
Isach	21	M	Weaver	England	United States	Cambria	16 Aug 1827
J.	38	M	Printer	Great Britain	United States	Isaac Hicks	6 Dec 1827
James	5	M		Gt. Britain		Dalhouse Castle	13 May 1828
James	20	F	None	England	United States	Trident	18 Jul 1827
James	22	M	Farmer	England	New York	Chelsea	16 May 1828
Jaques	27	M		France		Pallas	14 Jun 1828
Jas.	21	M	Spinner	Great Britain	United States	Penelope	11 Jun 1827
Jas.	33	M	Labourer	Great Britain	United States	Atlantic	28 May 1827
Jeremiah	18		Letterpress Printer	Manchester		Mount Vernon	18 Oct 1822
Jno.	31	M	Labourer	Great Britain	United States	Atlantic	28 May 1827
John	6	M	Carpenter	England	U. States	Electra	7 Jul 1828
John	22	M	Weaver	England		Manhattan	22 May 1827
John	23	M		Great Brittain	United States	Sarah Ralston	27 Jan 1827
John	24	M	Grocer	Great Brittan	U. States	John & Elizabeth	11 Dec 1826
John	26	M	Weaver	England	United States	Dalhouse Castle	6 Sep 1827
John	27	M		Great Britain	United States	Mary	11 Jul 1820
John	27		Weaver	Rochdale, England	Great Britain	Franklin	22 Jun 1827
John	28	M	Labourer	England		Britannia	20 Jun 1827
John	29	M	Farmer	England	England	William Byrnes	14 Apr 1824
John	36	M	Weaver	England	United States	Aurelia	7 Jun 1826
Jonas	27	M	...	Great Britain	United States	Atlantic	28 May 1827
Jonas	52		Letterpress Printer	Manchester		Mount Vernon	18 Oct 1822
Joseph	17	M	Carpenter	England	U. States	Electra	7 Jul 1828
Lucretia	30	F		London	New York	Ann Maria	24 Feb 1824
Luke	23					Splendid	14 Aug 1829
M.	33	F		Great Britain	United States	Isaac Hicks	6 Dec 1827
Martha	10	F	Carpenter	England	U. States	Electra	7 Jul 1828
Mary	2	F	None	England	U.S. States	Solon	25 Nov 1824
Mary	24	F	None	England	U.S. States	Solon	25 Nov 1824
Mary	26	F	Farmer	England	England	William Byrnes	14 Apr 1824
Nathaniel	8	M		Gt. Britain		Dalhouse Castle	13 May 1828
Obadiah	28	M	...	Ireland	United States	Colossus	30 May 1825
Pheebe	50			York Shire (Yorkshire)	Utica	Peru	30 May 1828
Robert	25	M	Mechanic	Scotland	United States	Concordia	25 Aug 1827
Robert	38	M	Grocer	London	New York	Ann Maria	24 Feb 1824
Robert	42	M	Farmer	England	United States	Amelia	20 Aug 1829
Samuel	7			Manchester		Mount Vernon	18 Oct 1822
Sarah	4	F	None	England	U.S. States	Solon	25 Nov 1824
Sarah	26	F	Farmer	...	America	Farmer	4 Aug 1825
Sarah	50			Manchester		Mount Vernon	18 Oct 1822
Thomas	7	M		Gt. Britain		Dalhouse Castle	13 May 1828
Thomas	50		Weaver	York Shire (Yorkshire)	Utica	Peru	30 May 1828
Thos.	30	M		G. Britain	U. States	Canada	19 Sep 1828
Thos.	49	M	Carpenter	England	U. States	Electra	7 Jul 1828
William	20		Gentn.	England	United States	Corinthian	30 May 1828
William	25	M	Labourer	England	United States	Andes	2 Oct 1828
William	35	M	Mason	Gt. Britain	United States	Meteor	19 Aug 1829
William	59	M	Farmer	Great Britain	United States	Mary	11 Jul 1820
Wm.	45	M	Carpenter	England	U. States	Electra	7 Jul 1828
BOOTHBY, Wm.	24	M	Watchmaker	Great Britain	United States	Ann	22 Dec 1821
BOOTHE, James	34	M	Clothier	England	United States	Aurora	9 Jul 1827
Peter D.	19	M	Student	U. States	United States	Peruvian	13 May 1823
BOOTHMAN, John	27	M	Grocer	Great Britain	United States	Luella	15 Jun 1825

NAMES OF PASSENGERS	AGE	SEX	OCCUPATIONS	COUNTRY TO WHICH THEY BELONG	COUNTRY THEY INTEND TO INHABIT	SHIPS/DATES OF ARRIVAL	
BOOTHROY, Sarah	21		None	Great Britain	United States	Roman	10 Sep 1827
BOOTHROYD, Anna	2	F		Great Britain	United States	John Wells	18 Sep 1826
Elizabeth	16	F		Great Britain	United States	John Wells	18 Sep 1826
Elizabeth	51	F		Great Britain	United States	John Wells	18 Sep 1826
John	34	M	Tailor	England	United States	Lord Wellington	14 Nov 1827
John Thomas	5/12	M		Great Britain	United States	John Wells	18 Sep 1826
Joseph	30	M	Clothier	Great Britain	United States	John Wells	18 Sep 1826
Joseph	61	M		England	United States	William Byrnes	6 Apr 1826
Mary	26	F		Great Britain	United States	John Wells	18 Sep 1826
Ricd.	20	M		England	United States	William Byrnes	6 Apr 1826
Samuel	13	M		Great Britain	United States	John Wells	18 Sep 1826
BOOTS, Ann	23			England	England	Hudson	4 Sep 1823
Henry	24		Farmer	England	England	Hudson	4 Sep 1823
John	20	M	Farmer	England	America	Sarah	18 Aug 1829
Mary Ann	1			England	England	Hudson	4 Sep 1823
Silvia	28	F	Farmer	England	America	Sarah	18 Aug 1829
BOPP, Alexander	30	M	Merchant	England	England	Virginia	26 May 1828
BOPUCHER, Ann	1	F		France	U. States	Superb	9 Jul 1821
BORA, Wm.	25	M	Cotton Spinner	Gt. Brittain	U. States	Catharine	7 Feb 1826
BORAN, James	38	M	Labourer	England	U. States	Comet	23 Aug 1828
BORAS, Jos.	40	M	Merchant	Spain	U. States	Prince Edward	3 Apr 1826
BORCHERS, L.	26	M	Merchant	France	U. States	Harriet	3 Sep 1823
BORDAMAN, Anna	32	F	Farmer	Holland	U. States	Don Quixote	25 Oct 1828
Charles	0 3/12	M	Farmer	Holland	U. States	Don Quixote	25 Oct 1828
BORDAMAR, Christopher	8	M	Farmer	Holland	U. States	Don Quixote	25 Oct 1828
Jacob	7	M	Farmer	Holland	U. States	Don Quixote	25 Oct 1828
Jacobina	9	F	Farmer	Holland	U. States	Don Quixote	25 Oct 1828
Louiza	4	M	Farmer	Holland	U. States	Don Quixote	25 Oct 1828
BORDAS, Adeline	22	F		France	U. States	Lewis	6 Jul 1825
BORDEN, Ann	21	F		G. Brittian	United States	Louisa	14 Jun 1825
Hugh	11	M		G. Brittian	United States	Louisa	14 Jun 1825
Sarah	13	F		G. Brittian	United States	Louisa	14 Jun 1825
Susannah	16 3/12	F		G. Brittian	United States	Louisa	14 Jun 1825
*Died							
BORDENLY, —, Mrs.	41	F	Farmer	Switzerland	U. States	Seine	30 Aug 1824
B.	12	M	Farmer	Switzerland	U. States	Seine	30 Aug 1824
C.	1	M	Farmer	Switzerland	U. States	Seine	30 Aug 1824
Francis	42	M	Farmer	Switzerland	U. States	Seine	30 Aug 1824
J.	6	M	Farmer	Switzerland	U. States	Seine	30 Aug 1824
BORDEZET, J.	23	M	Merchant	U. States	U. States	Cadmus	28 May 1821
BORDIE, Antonie	23 3/12	M	Farmer	Switzerland	United States	France	6 Oct 1828
Henry	88 7/12	M	Farmer	Switzerland	United States	France	6 Oct 1828
Joseph	28 1/12	M	Farmer	Switzerland	United States	France	6 Oct 1828
Mary	18 2/12	F	Farmer	Switzerland	United States	France	6 Oct 1828
Mary	60 4/12	F	Farmer	Switzerland	United States	France	6 Oct 1828
BORDINOW, Wm.	40	M	Merchant	Port au Prince	U. States	Nile	11 Jul 1822
BORDMAN, Joseph J.	3	M	None	U. States	U. States	Olive Branch	28 Aug 1828
Mary J.	1	F	None	U. States	U. States	Olive Branch	28 Aug 1828
BOREAS ARES, A.	25	M	Merchant	Cuba	U. States	Caroline	9 May 1822
BOREAU, Philater	28	M	Merchant	France	U.S.	Edward Bonnaffe	20 Jun 1825
BOREL, Francis	32 4/12	M	Merchant	France	France	France	28 Mar 1829
BORELAND, Jas.	25	M	Farmer	Omagh	N. York	Favourite	8 Oct 1823
Robt.	24	M	Labourer	Ireland	United States	Fabius	31 Jul 1829
BOREN, John	20	M	Laborer	Ireland	United States	Sarah Ann	18 Nov 1826
BORER, John	33	M	Farmer	England	Ohio	Thames	6 Oct 1820
BORFED, George, Master	21	M	Gentn.	England	U. States	Acasta	3 Apr 1826
BORFEDE, Emily, Miss	2	F	Gentn.	England	U. States	Acasta	3 Apr 1826
James, Master	14	M	Gentn.	England	U. States	Acasta	3 Apr 1826
BORFELD, Harriot, Miss	23	F	Gentn.	England	U. States	Acasta	3 Apr 1826
BORFIELD, Lydia, Mrs.	42	F	Gentn.	England	U. States	Acasta	3 Apr 1826
BORG, Alex	23	M	Farmer	G. Brittan	U. States	Trafalgar	4 Jun 1822
George	28	M	Farmer	Switzerland	United States	Andes	5 May 1828
Wm. S.	26	M	Merchant	Gt. Britain	United States	Seeds	29 Sep 1824
BORGLE, Felten	26	M	Farmer	France	U. States	Edward Bonaffe	23 Jul 1828
BORILLY, —, Mrs.	29	F		France	U.S.	Stephania	15 Aug 1825
BORK, Elisa	18	F		Ireland	United States	Nancy R. Crowell	21 Sep 1822
BORNASLER, I.	40	M	Merchant	Great Britan	United States	Bolivar	21 May 1827

108

NAMES OF PASSENGERS	AGE	SEX	OCCUPATIONS	COUNTRY TO WHICH THEY BELONG	COUNTRY THEY INTEND TO INHABIT	SHIPS/DATES OF ARRIVAL	
BORNE, Andrew	30	M	Labourer			Catherine	19 Aug 1825
Lewis P.	35		Merchant	America	New York	Cicero	18 Aug 1829
BORNER, Honour	26	F	None	France	U. States	Sully	25 Jun 1828
John S.	30	M	Merchant	U. States	U. States	Clarice	11 Apr 1827
Mary	27	F	None	France	U. States	Sully	25 Jun 1828
BORNES, Chas.	36	M	Merchant	America	America	Brittannia	28 Feb 1827
BORNETT, B. F.	28	M	Merchant	United States	St. John, N.B.	Sylvester Healy	14 Jun 1825
BORNOVEL, Catharin	35	F	Farmer	France		Pallas	14 Jun 1828
Jear P.	33	F		France		Pallas	14 Jun 1828
Perre	8	M	Farmer	France		Pallas	14 Jun 1828
BORNOVER, Berre	35	M	Farmer	France		Pallas	14 Jun 1828
Lousia	2	F	Farmer	France		Pallas	14 Jun 1828
Susan	4	F	Farmer	France		Pallas	14 Jun 1828
BOROSS, Carolina	13	F				Washington	16 Sep 1820
BORRAS, Rafael	22	M	Gentleman	Mexico	U. States	Sally Ann	6 Nov 1824
BORREAU, R. L.	28	M	Merchant	Mexico	Mexico	Claudio	16 Oct 1827
BORRELLE, D. F.	41	M	Merchant	Switzerland	Switzerland	Argus	3 Oct 1825
BORRES, Joseph	39	M	Mariner	N. York	U. States	Shepherdess	15 Jul 1824
BORRETT, Bridget	8	F		England	Pittsburg	Hudson	20 Nov 1828
Bridget	37	F		England	Pittsburg	Hudson	20 Nov 1828
Daniel	16	M		England	Pittsburg	Hudson	20 Nov 1828
Daniel	40	M	Farmer	England	Pittsburg	Hudson	20 Nov 1828
Edward	12	M		England	Pittsburg	Hudson	20 Nov 1828
Frances	39	F		England	Pittsburg	Hudson	20 Nov 1828
Henry	14	M		England	Pittsburg	Hudson	20 Nov 1828
Jane	2	F		England	Pittsburg	Hudson	20 Nov 1828
John	11	M		England	Pittsburg	Hudson	20 Nov 1828
Rebecca	4	F		England	Pittsburg	Hudson	20 Nov 1828
Susan	6	F		England	Pittsburg	Hudson	20 Nov 1828
William	14	M		England	Pittsburg	Hudson	20 Nov 1828
BORRIE, Wm.	40	M	Merchant	U. States	U. States	Rachel	14 Mar 1825
BORRIES, H. Hermann	23	M	Baker	Germany	U. States	Constitution	21 Jun 1824
BORROUGHS, John M.	40	M	Merchant	N. York	N. York	Mary	12 Jul 1824
BORROW, August	3	M		France	U.S. America	Huntress	6 Sep 1827
Jacob	5	M		France	U.S. America	Huntress	6 Sep 1827
John Peter	36	M		France	U.S. America	Huntress	6 Sep 1827
Lorans	39	M		France	U.S. America	Huntress	6 Sep 1827
Maria	1	F		France	U.S. America	Huntress	6 Sep 1827
Maria A. T.	30	F		France	U.S. America	Huntress	6 Sep 1827
BORSA, Mary, Miss	43	F		St. Domingo	United States	Paquet des Cayes	26 May 1828
BORSAN, Charles	25	M	Merchant	England	U. States	Emulous	22 Aug 1828
BORSMINSSON, C. C., Mr.	45	M	Gentleman	Denmark	U. States	Chase	2 Oct 1826
BORTOLI, Diego	50	M	Merchant	G. Brittain	U. States	Dolphin	15 Apr 1822
BORUCK, J.	26	M	Merchant	United States	United States	Silas Richards	9 Mar 1829
BORUSS, Charles W. W.	19	M	Mercht.	Danmark	U. States	Matteawan	1 Aug 1827
BOS..., Eliza	18	F				William Neilson	26 Jul 1828
Margaret	...0	F				William Neilson	26 Jul 1828
Margaret	16	F				William Neilson	26 Jul 1828
Wm.	14	M				William Neilson	26 Jul 1828
BOSE, Died.	34	M	Sugar Baker	Germany	U. States	Constitution	21 Jun 1824
BOSEGAR, Anna	50	F	Framer	Switzerland	Ohio	Danube	20 Jul 1826
Elizabath	20	F	Framer	Switzerland	Ohio	Danube	20 Jul 1826
Simon	48	M	Framer	Switzerland	Ohio	Danube	20 Jul 1826
BOSEGER, Christian	17	M	Framer	Switzerland	Ohio	Danube	20 Jul 1826
Peter	13	M	Framer	Switzerland	Ohio	Danube	20 Jul 1826
Simeon	11	M	Framer	Switzerland	Ohio	Danube	20 Jul 1826
BOSEKER, —, Mr.	32	M	Merchant	Germany	U. States	Orion	8 Oct 1823
BOSELL, William, Esq.	27	M	Gentleman	Great Britain	America	Lady Gallatin	21 Jun 1820
BOSHER, Imez.	27	M	baker	Germany	New York	Constitution	20 Aug 1825
BOSITH, John	28	M	Miner	England	England	Virginia	26 May 1828
BOSKETER, John	25	M	Farmer	England	America	Josephine	8 Jan 1827
BOSLEY, Isiah	20	M	Tailor	Manchester	United States	Aurelia	7 Jun 1826
BOSQUES, Felix	24	M	Merchant	Italy	Italy	New York	6 Jul 1829
BOSS, —, Mrs.	33	F		U. States	U. States	Ann Elizabeth	6 Oct 1824
Christiana	4	F		U. States	U. States	Ann Elizabeth	6 Oct 1824
John T.	39	M	Mariner	U. States	U. States	Virginia	30 Oct 1828
Wm.	7	M		U. States	U. States	Ann Elizabeth	6 Oct 1824
BOSSER, Bridget	15	F	Spinster	Ireland	United States	Robert Fulton	24 Jul 1826

NAMES OF PASSENGERS	AGE	SEX	OCCUPATIONS	COUNTRY TO WHICH THEY BELONG	COUNTRY THEY INTEND TO INHABIT	SHIPS/DATES OF ARRIVAL
BOSSET, George	30	M	Merchant	Switzerland	U. States	Edward Quesnel 4 Aug 1828
BOSSEX, Felix	25	M	Merchant	U. States		Fanny 14 Mar 1820
BOSTICK, Wm. L.	9	M	Labourer	Bermuda	U. States	Wormontogus 17 May 1822
BOSTON, Abm.	36	M	Servant	United States	United States	Cortes 7 Dec 1825
BOSTRICK, Wm.	23	M	Labourer	Gt. Britain	U. States	Panthea 21 Jul 1825
BOSWELL, Henry	30	M	Millman		uncertain	Mount Vernon 29 Aug 1828
Mary	25	F	Servant	England	New York	James Cropper 12 Jul 1822
Thomas H., Mr.	22	M	Merchant	U. States	U. States	Hudson 10 Nov 1825
BOSWICK, John	20	M	Weaver	England	United States	Jubilee 4 Mar 1829
BOTHEN, Mary	20	F	Dress Maker	Ireland	Canada	Ann Maria 7 Sep 1827
BOTHGATE, Wm.	22	M	Baker	Scotland	America	Maine 16 Jul 1821
BOTHROY, Michael	22		Clothier	Great Britain	United States	Roman 10 Sep 1827
BOTILGER, Jean	24	M		Swisse	United States	Deux Ernest 29 Dec 1827
*landed at Lewiston, Delw.						
BOTNER, Jacob	23	M	Farmer	Swis	United States	Iris 21 Sep 1821
BOTREL, Mary	50	F		United States	U. States	Splendid 1 Jul 1829
BOTT, —	1			England	United States	Hugh Johnson 11 Jun 1828
—	26			England	United States	Hugh Johnson 11 Jun 1828
—	26			England	United States	Hugh Johnson 11 Jun 1828
—	28			England	United States	Hugh Johnson 11 Jun 1828
—	32			England	United States	Hugh Johnson 11 Jun 1828
Christopher	23	M	Sugar Baker	Germany		Helen 4 Aug 1829
M.	32			England	United States	Hugh Johnson 11 Jun 1828
Wm.	37			England	United States	Hugh Johnson 11 Jun 1828
BOTTEMLY, John	20		Hatter	Rochester, England	Great Britain	Franklin 22 Jun 1827
BOTTLE, Alfred	19	M	Carpenter	England	U. States	Electra 7 Jul 1828
Ann	1...	F		G. Britain	New York	Brighton 26 Mar 1827
Charlotte	...	F		G. Britain	New York	Brighton 26 Mar 1827
Elisabeth	16	F		G. Britain	New York	Brighton 26 Mar 1827
Elizabeth	30	F	Carpenter	England	U. States	Electra 7 Jul 1828
George	2...	M		G. Britain	New York	Brighton 26 Mar 1827
John	5	M	Carpenter	England	U. States	Electra 7 Jul 1828
John	35	M	Carpenter	England	U. States	Electra 7 Jul 1828
John	5...	M	...	G. Britain	New York	Brighton 26 Mar 1827
Mary	1...	F		G. Britain	New York	Brighton 26 Mar 1827
Mary	48	F		G. Britain	New York	Brighton 26 Mar 1827
Wm.	1 6/12	M	Carpenter	England	U. States	Electra 7 Jul 1828
BOTTOMLEY, Fletcher	19	M	Labourer	Ashert...h..., L...f...d		Aurora 8 Jun 1827
Hannah	23	F	None	Ireland	United States	Mary & Harriet 3 Jul 1829
James	33	M	Merchant	England	United States	Concordia 25 Aug 1827
John	3	M	None	Ireland	United States	Mary & Harriet 3 Jul 1829
Thomas	22	M	Mason	England	New York	Curler 7 Jul 1827
Wm.	18	M	Merchant	England	United States	John Wells 22 May 1826
BOTTOMLY, Moses	22	M	Merchant	Great Britain	United States	Corinthian 2 Sep 1824
Nat.	29	M	...	G. Britain	U. States	New England 28 Sep 1824
BOTTOMY, William	32	M	Gun Smith	England	U. States	Acasta 28 Jan 1823
BOTTONWORTH, E.	37	M	Farmer	Great Britton	U. State	Earl of Liverpool 16 Aug 1826
BOTTS, D.	28	M	Merchant	Italy	Italy	Buck 24 Jul 1821
BOUBIERS, F.	21	M	Merchant	France	France	Eliza 28 Apr 1827
BOUCHAND, J.	23	M	Gentleman	Netherlands	Netherlands	Jasper 22 Sep 1827
BOUCHER, Ann, Mrs.	30	F	Lady	France	U. States	Superb 9 Jul 1821
Charles	30	M	One Family [Isaac]	France	United States	Henri IV 2 Oct 1828
Isaac	32	M	Baker	France	United States	Henri IV 2 Oct 1828
Peter	35	M	Merchant	France	U. States	Superb 9 Jul 1821
Peter A.	6	M		France	U. States	Superb 9 Jul 1821
Theresa	24	F	One Family [Isaac]	France	United States	Henri IV 2 Oct 1828
BOUCHETTE, John	19	M	Merchant	Canada		Cincinnatus 29 Apr 1822
John	22	M	None	Canada	Canada	Cincinnatus 16 Apr 1824
BOUDA, Eliza Ann	21	F	Merchant	U. States	U. States	Dromo 4 May 1827
Stephan	32	M	Merchant	U. States	U. States	Dromo 4 May 1827
Stephan, Jr.	9/12	M	Merchant	U. States	U. States	Dromo 4 May 1827
BOUDELLE, Adam	39	M	Waiter	Bavarian	United States	American 27 Aug 1827
Catharine	31	M	Waiter	Bavarian	United States	American 27 Aug 1827
Elisabeth	7	F	Spinster	Bavarian	United States	American 27 Aug 1827
Epha	1 6/12	F		Bavarian	United States	American 27 Aug 1827
Henry	5	F		Bavarian	United States	American 27 Aug 1827

NAMES OF PASSENGERS	AGE	SEX	OCCUPATIONS	COUNTRY TO WHICH THEY BELONG	COUNTRY THEY INTEND TO INHABIT	SHIPS/DATES OF ARRIVAL	
BOUDER, J.	25	M		France & Switzerland			
BOUDIN, S.	28	M	Merchant	France	U. States	Bayard	14 Jul 1826
BOUDWAY, P.	12	M	Merchant	Philadelphia	U. States	Arrington	14 Nov 1825
BOUEF, Joseph Francis	19	M	None	France	U. States	Betsey	31 Jul 1826
BOUER, Emma	3	F	None	England	United States	Howard	21 Aug 1826
Frederick		M	Chemist			John Wells	11 May 1827
Joseph	5	M	None			Frederick	18 Feb 1822
Sarah	28	F	None	England	United States	John Wells	11 May 1827
William	1	M	None	England	United States	John Wells	11 May 1827
BOUGET, P.	18	M	Merchant	England	United States	John Wells	11 May 1827
BOUGH, John	20	M	Mechanic	France	U. States	Waldo	19 Aug 1826
Mary	20		Servant/Maid	Great Britain	United States	Florida	2 Oct 1828
BOUGHAN, Joseph	22	M	Lab.	England	England	William	2 Sep 1822
				Rathangar	K. Co.	Howard	
Mary	22	F	None			Douglass	11 May 1827
				Rathangar	K. Co.	Howard	
BOUGHARTY, Edward	24		Farmer			Douglass	11 May 1827
BOULAND, —, Mrs.	25	F		New York	United States	Rufus King	7 Aug 1820
S. V.	35	M	Merchant	New York	United States	Montano	2 Sep 1824
BOULER, J.	20	M		France	U. States	Montano	2 Sep 1824
BOULET, —, Child	4	M	None	U. States	U. States	Edward Quesnel	3 Sep 1826
—, Mrs.	29	F	None	U. States	U. States	Catherine	27 Sep 1820
BOULSTON, Joseph	16	M	Labourer	Ireland	South America	Catherine	27 Sep 1820
BOULTON, Elizabeth	23	F	Lady	England	Upper Canada	Robert Fulton	24 Jul 1826
George T.	26 6/12	M	Barrister at Law	England	Upper Canada	Nimrod	28 Apr 1824
Giles	78	M	Gentleman	Great Britain	United States	Nimrod	28 Apr 1824
John	39	M	Sawyer	Great Britain	New York	Orbit	29 Aug 1821
Joseph	33	M	Gentleman	Great Britain	United States	Superior	5 Sep 1827
Sarah	16	F	Female	Great Britain	United States	Orbit	29 Aug 1821
BOUNAIN, Wm.	24	M	Miner	England	England	Orbit	29 Aug 1821
BOUNER, Arendina, Vrouw (wife [Gerrit des Ruelles])	31	F		Middlecharnas	United States	Eliza	31 Jul 1826
BOURCARD, Emma	21	F	None	United States	United States	Juffraw Johanna	16 Oct 1821
BOURDE, Isaac	33	M	Mechanic	United States	U. States	Isaac Hicks	22 Aug 1829
Louis	34	M	Mechanic	Spain	U. States	Thankfull Winslow	23 Aug 1826
BOURDILLIAT, Ph.	36	M	Merchant	France	U. States	Thankfull Winslow	23 Aug 1826
BOURDLOES, J.	20	M	Merchant	France	United States	Sully	24 Oct 1828
BOURDMAN, J.	35	M	Lawyer	U. States	U. States	Elizabeth	22 May 1822
Samuel	28	F	None	U. States	U. States	Olive Branch	28 Aug 1828
BOURDOES, H.	45	M	Merchant	France	United States	Olive Branch	28 Aug 1828
J.	6	M	Merchant	France	United States	Elizabeth	22 May 1822
BOURE, Charlotte	52	F	Wife	Swiss	U. States	Elizabeth	22 May 1822
Edward	7	M	Son	Swiss	U. States	Comet	28 Jul 1825
Ferdinand	5	M	Son	Swiss	U. States	Comet	28 Jul 1825
Frederick	17	M	Son	Swiss	U. States	Comet	28 Jul 1825
Nicholas	44	M	Farmer	Swiss	U. States	Comet	28 Jul 1825
Rose	14	F	Daughter	Swiss	U. States	Comet	28 Jul 1825
BOURES, M.	30	M	Farmer	France	U. States	Comet	28 Jul 1825
BOURGAUX, W. A.	27	M	Mercht.	France	Savannah	Bayard	25 Apr 1828
BOURGEOIS,						Lewis	29 Oct 1825
Marie Ann B.	62	F		France	U. States	Leonarde	29 Aug 1828
Michel	64	M	Cabinet Maker	France	U. States	Leonarde	29 Aug 1828
BOURGERE, —, Madme.	20	F	None	France	New Orleans	Brighton	16 Nov 1826
Charles	26	M	Lawyer	France	New Orleans	Brighton	16 Nov 1826
BOURGERMEISTER, Madalina	44	F		France	United States	New England	29 Aug 1828
BOURGES, John	29	M	Farmer	England	U. States	Hercules	6 Jul 1827
BOURGUIGNO, Lous	30	M		France	France	Caledonia	10 Sep 1828
BOURK, Houra	16	F	None	Great Brittan	U. States	John & Elizabeth	11 Dec 1826
Michal	36	M	Farmer	Ireland	Philadelphia	Virginia	7 May 1824
BOURLIN, Charles	20	M	...t...	...land	Havana	Stephania	29 Nov 1825
BOURNAN, George	22	M	Farmer	G. Britain	U.S.A.	Silas Richards	29 Oct 1827
BOURNE, Anne	50	M	Mariner	U. States	U. States	Belvidere	31 Jul 1822
Antonio	36	M	Engineeer	England	U. States	Emma	15 Dec 1824
B. F.	30	M	U.S. Navy	U. States	U. States	Henry	27 Mar 1820

NAMES OF PASSENGERS	AGE	SEX	OCCUPATIONS	COUNTRY TO WHICH THEY BELONG	COUNTRY THEY INTEND TO INHABIT	SHIPS/DATES OF ARRIVAL	
BOURNE (cont'd)							
Geo. L.	23	M	Merchant	France	U. States	Canton	17 Aug 1824
James	22	M	Butler	Ireland	United States	Dalhouse Castle	6 Sep 1827
Jemima	26	F	Farmer	Great Britan	United States	Clematis	8 May 1827
John	50	M	Carpenter	N. York	U. States	James Monroe	21 Apr 1824
Joseph	22	M	Pottery Maker	Staffordshire	New York	New York	31 Jul 1829
Mary Ann	2	F		Great Britan	United States	Clematis	8 May 1827
Richard	7/12	M		Great Britan	United States	Clematis	8 May 1827
Richard	32	M	Farmer	Great Britan	United States	Clematis	8 May 1827
Sarah	4	F	Farmer	Great Britan	United States	Clematis	8 May 1827
Thomas, Mr.	36	M	Merchant	New York	New York	Governor Fenner	23 Jul 1829
Wm. N.	27	M	Merchant	U. States	U. States	Leeds	24 Sep 1827
BOURQUIN, Anatan	16	M	Weaver	France	U. States	Bayard	16 May 1827
Francis	5	M	Farmer	France	U. States	Bayard	16 May 1827
Jaquel	26	M	Farmer	France	U. States	Bayard	16 May 1827
Joseph	1	M	Weaver	France	U. States	Bayard	16 May 1827
Joseph	3	M	Farmer	France	U. States	Bayard	16 May 1827
Joseph	27	M	Weaver	France	U. States	Bayard	16 May 1827
Maria	1	M	Farmer	France	U. States	Bayard	16 May 1827
Mary A.	27	F	Weaver	France	U. States	Bayard	16 May 1827
Mary R.	22	F	Farmer	France	U. States	Bayard	16 May 1827
Peter	3	M	Weaver	France	U. States	Bayard	16 May 1827
BOURQUINE, ...hame	7		Watch Maker	Somwiller	Switzerland	Ann	27 Nov 1820
Adelaide	16		Watch Maker	Somwiller	Switzerland	Ann	27 Nov 1820
David	42		Watch Maker	Somwiller	Switzerland	Ann	27 Nov 1820
Eliza	10		Watch Maker	Somwiller	Switzerland	Ann	27 Nov 1820
Felicien	18		Watch Maker	Somwiller	Switzerland	Ann	27 Nov 1820
Justine	32		Watch Maker	Somwiller	Switzerland	Ann	27 Nov 1820
Louis	9		Watch Maker	Somwiller	Switzerland	Ann	27 Nov 1820
Marrianne	30		Watch Maker	Somwiller	Switzerland	Ann	27 Nov 1820
P...l...a	6		Watch Maker	Somwiller	Switzerland	Ann	27 Nov 1820
Tralane	3		Watch Maker	Somwiller	Switzerland	Ann	27 Nov 1820
BOURTON, Anne	29	F				Governor Fenner	23 Jul 1829
John	3	F				Governor Fenner	23 Jul 1829
Jonas	29	M	Farmer	England	New York	Governor Fenner	23 Jul 1829
Susannah	5/12	F				Governor Fenner	23 Jul 1829
BOURY, Joseph	28	M		France	United States	Henri IV	2 Oct 1828
BOUSAUBIN, Edward	23	M	Lawyer	New Jersey	United States	Henri IV	2 Oct 1828
BOUSIA, John	60	M	Minister of Gospel	Scotland	United States	Minerva	29 Oct 1822
BOUSIERE, Daniel	27	M	Merchant	U. States	U. States	Peruvian	13 May 1823
BOUSQUET, C.	18	M	Merchant	France	U. States	Edward Quesnel	15 May 1826
John	24	M	Merchant	U. States	U. States	Bayard	9 Jul 1824
BOUTARA, Joseph	26	M	Merchant	England	U.S.	Maria Caroline	12 Jul 1820
BOUTERGE, —, Mr.	22	M	Merchant	France	U. States	William & Ezra	18 Oct 1824
BOUTIN, L.	30	M	Merchant	Norfolk	U. States	William	23 Jun 1821
BOUTON, Thos.	48	M	Farmer	England	England	Ann Maria	26 Apr 1822
BOUTONNET, Jean B.	31	M	Medeern [?]	Guadaloupe		Alexander	18 Aug 1828
BOUVAIRD, James	49		Merchant	United States	United States	Robert Burns	30 May 1823
BOUVIER, Frs.	17	M		Matanzes	Matanzes	Blue Ey'd Mary	23 Oct 1823
BOVEE, J.						Paquet des Cayes	16 Aug 1828
*Died on the Voyage							
BOVEN, A.	0 6/12	M	Sailor	America	U. States	Robt. Edwards	4 Sep 1828
BOVIE, Jacob	2...	M	Mechanic	United States	United States	Decature	17 Mar 1820
BOVSACK, Blasick	28	M		Switzerland	U.S. America	Huntress	6 Sep 1827
BOW, William	28	M	Farmer	Ireland	Virginia	Curler	7 Jul 1827
BOWAN, Edward	24	M	Farmer	England	U.S. America	Cortes	19 May 1826
John	54		Merchant	United States	United States	William Byrnes	25 Aug 1828
BOWARS, Charles	9	M		England	Pittsburg	Curler	7 Jul 1827
William	41	M	Millwright	England	Pittsburg	Curler	7 Jul 1827
BOWAS, John	32	M	Farmer	Great Britain		Dalmannock	24 Ocg 1826
BOWBOTTOM, Elizth.	46	F	Farmer	England	United States	Florida	1 Sep 1823
Jane	4	F	Farmer	England	United States	Florida	1 Sep 1823
BOWDEN, Able	24	M	Hatter	England	United States	Lord Wellington	14 Nov 1827
Alexr.	24	M	Farmer	Ireland	New York	Globe	3 Dec 1821
Andrew	54	M	Farmer	Ireland	New York	Louisa	20 Jul 1826
Elizabeth	18	F	Spinster	Ireland	U. States	Josephine	7 May 1827
Henrietta	22	F		England	United States	Lord Wellington	14 Nov 1827
James	6	M		England	United States	Lord Wellington	14 Nov 1827

NAMES OF PASSENGERS	AGE	SEX	OCCUPATIONS	COUNTRY TO WHICH THEY BELONG	COUNTRY THEY INTEND TO INHABIT	SHIPS/DATES OF ARRIVAL	
BOWDEN (cont'd)							
Jas.	29	M	Gentleman	England		New York Packet	20 Mar 1824
Johanna	7	F		Ireland	America	William	21 May 1825
John	4	M		England	United States	Lord Wellington	14 Nov 1827
Lawrence	64	M	Labourer	Ireland	U. States	Josephine	7 May 1827
Margret	45 0/12	F	Wife	Ireland	New York	Globe	3 Dec 1821
Mary	12	F		Ireland	America	William	21 May 1825
Mary	24	F		England	United States	Lord Wellington	14 Nov 1827
Samuel	2	M		England	United States	Lord Wellington	14 Nov 1827
W.	19	M	None	U. States	United States	Prince Edward	1 Apr 1825
William	10	M		Ireland	America	William	21 May 1825
William	56 4/12	M	Farmer	Ireland	New York	Globe	3 Dec 1821
BOWDOIN, Temple	46	M	None	England	U. States	New York	11 Jul 1823
BOWE, John	17	M	Labourer	England	U. States	Hope & Esther	10 Jul 1827
BOWEN, Charles		F		Ireland	America	Carolina Ann	7 Aug 1826
Chas.	71	M		England		Ann	17 May 1822
George	40	M	Merchant	U. States	U. States	Pacific	19 Oct 1829
Jane	14	F		U. States	U. States	Corinthian	2 Sep 1824
John	34	M	Farmer	England	United States	Lord Wellington	14 Nov 1827
John	51	M	Merchant	Great Britan	United States	Columbia	11 Aug 1823
John	52	M	Merchant	U. States	U. States	Corinthian	2 Sep 1824
John	6...	M	Merchant	New York	New York	Amity	13 Sep 1821
John S.	16	M	Merchant	United States of Am.	United States of Amer.	Cambria	7 May 1828
Joseph	30	M	Priest	England	Great Britain	Asaph	23 Mar 1827
Mary	20					Trio	5 May 1828
Mary	30	F		England	United States	Lord Wellington	14 Nov 1827
William	35	M	Farmer	Ireland	U.S.A.	Silas Richards	28 Jun 1825
Wm. J.	20	M	Merchant			Willmot	21 Jul 1820
BOWER, —	3	F		Dublin	U. States	Hibernia	26 Oct 1826
—, Mr.	22	F		Dublin	U. States	Hibernia	26 Oct 1826
—, Mr.	24	M	Gentleman	Dublin	U. States	Hibernia	26 Oct 1826
Ann	15	F	Farmer, Labourer or Spinster	Ireland	U. States	Meteor	4 Oct 1827
Archd.	30	M	Labourer	Scotland	United States	Samuel Robertson	9 May 1827
Charles	8	M	Farmer, Labourer or Spinster	Ireland	U. States	Meteor	4 Oct 1827
Christian	3 6/12	M		Germany	U. States	Isabella	10 Aug 1829
Edward	26	M	Coachman	Ireland	United States	Hopes Delight	29 Nov 1827
Eve	60	F	None	United States	United States	Crisis	13 Nov 1824
Frank	58	M	Butcher	United States	United States	Crisis	13 Nov 1824
Hendrick	2	M		Germany	U. States	Isabella	10 Aug 1829
James, Mr.	18	M	Royal Navy	England	Canada	Brighton	24 Aug 1827
John	12	M	Farmer, Labourer or Spinster	Ireland	U. States	Meteor	4 Oct 1827
John	27	M	Labourer	...	...	Frances Henrietta	30 Jun 1827
John	29	M	Blacksmith	Great Britain	U.S. of America	Gratitude	3 Oct 1829
John P.	35	M	Gentl.	Cherty fred. Kings Co.	Canada	Aldebaron	21 Jan 1826
Joseph	30	M	Manufactioner	Germany	U. States	Isabella	10 Aug 1829
Margaret	30	F		Germany	U. States	Isabella	10 Aug 1829
Margarete	6/12	F		Germany	U. States	Isabella	10 Aug 1829
Mary	6	F	Farmer, Labourer or Spinster	Ireland	U. States	Meteor	4 Oct 1827
Mary	34	F		Great Britain	U.S. of America	Gratitude	3 Oct 1829
Matilda	10	F	Farmer, Labourer or Spinster	Ireland	U. States	Meteor	4 Oct 1827
Mr.	30	F	Spinster	Ireland	America	Mary	29 May 1827
R.	25	M	Farmer	U. States	U. States	United States	11 Sep 1828
Rose	40	F	Farmer, Labourer or Spinster	Ireland	U. States	Meteor	4 Oct 1827
Walter	24	M	Farmer	England	United States	Herald	29 Oct 1825
William	17	M	Farmer, Labourer or Spinster	Ireland	U. States	Meteor	4 Oct 1827
Wm.	29	M	Clouthier	Ireland	Ut. States	Courier	13 Jul 1826

NAMES OF PASSENGERS	AGE	SEX	OCCUPATIONS	COUNTRY TO WHICH THEY BELONG	COUNTRY THEY INTEND TO INHABIT	SHIPS/DATES OF ARRIVAL
BOWERS, —, Mrs.	35	M	Dealer in Horses	Barbadoes	Barbadoes	William & Nancy 5 Jun 1823
...	26	M	Blacksmith	Great Britain	United States	Atlantic 28 May 1827
John	42 3/12	M	Merchant	U.S.A.	U.S.A.	Silas Richards 27 Oct 1826
John, Junr.	54 2/12	M	Merchant	U.S.A.	U.S.A.	Silas Richards 27 Oct 1826
W. R.	25	M	Merchant	France	France	Eliza 28 Apr 1827
Wm.	40	M	Merchant	Greenwich Kent, England	Gt. Britain	Orozimbo 19 Oct 1822
BOWERY, John	27	M	Farmer	Great Brittan	U. States	John & Elizabeth 11 Dec 1826
BOWES, James	30	M	Merchant	St. Johns	U. States	Sarah G 7 May 1827
Jane, Mrs.	35	F	Lady	England	Canada	Brighton 24 Aug 1827
BOWHEY, Amelia	2	F	Child [of George]	England	U. States	New Packet 15 Nov 1828
George	41	M	Baker	England	U. States	New Packet 15 Nov 1828
James	13	M	Child [of George]	England	U. States	New Packet 15 Nov 1828
Mary	38	F	Wife [of George]	England	U. States	New Packet 15 Nov 1828
Matilda	15	F	Child [of George]	England	U. States	New Packet 15 Nov 1828
BOWIE, E.	19	F		Great Britain	United States	Aspasia 16 Jul 1828
James D.	32	M	Gentleman	Colombia	Colombia	Robert Y. Hayne 21 Aug 1828
James D.	34	M	Merchant	Colombia	Colombia	Ned 1 Oct 1829
John H.	21	M	Currier	Great Brittain	U. States	Florenzo 20 Mar 1827
M.	52	F		Great Britain	United States	Aspasia 16 Jul 1828
BOWING, Isabella	6/12	F	None	G. Britain	U. States	James Monroe 18 Apr 1821
Mary	21	F	None	G. Britain	U. States	James Monroe 18 Apr 1821
Samuel	3	M	None	G. Britain	U. States	James Monroe 18 Apr 1821
BOWLAN, Jas.	22	M	Butcher	Co. La...gford	La...gford	Howard Douglass 11 May 1827
Tobias	20	M	Labourer	Co. La...gford	La...gford	Howard Douglass 11 May 1827
BOWLAND, Robert	20	M	Farmer	Wales	America	Hercules 2 Nov 1825
BOWLEN, John	13	M	None	England		Marchioness 13 May 1828
BOWLER, Harry	1/2	M		England	Newyork	Cortes 16 Jul 1827
John	22	M	Merchant	England	Newyork	Cortes 16 Jul 1827
Mary	23	F		England	Newyork	Cortes 16 Jul 1827
Mary	62	F	Servant	United States	United States	Only Daughter 29 Apr 1825
BOWLES, Elizabeth	30	F		Bermuda		Lancatter 5 Jul 1820
William	25		Merchant	Boston (U.S.)	Boston	Don Quixote 19 Aug 1825
BOWLEY, E.	43	M	Plain Maker	G. Britan	U. States	Geo. Canning 2 Sep 1828
BOWLING, Edward	33	M	Merchant	U. States	U. States	Transit 21 Apr 1821
Pat	28	M	Labourer	England	U. States	Thomas Ritchie 2 Jul 1827
BOWMAN, Alexr.	9	M	Farmer	Scotland	United States	Statird 26 Aug 1823
Benja.	30		Farmer	Ulcombe	England	Packet 27 Aug 1822
Edwin	6		Child	Sutton	England	Packet 27 Aug 1822
Eliza	1 6/12	F		St. Johns	St. Johns	Silvanus Jenkins 24 Jul 1828
Elizabeth	50			b. Westmoreland, last of Ohio	Ohio	Peru 30 May 1828
Isaac	53		Cabinet Worker	b. Westmoreland, last of Ohio	Ohio	Peru 30 May 1828
James	45	M	Farmer	Scotland	United States	Statird 26 Aug 1823
Jane	45	F	Wife	Scotland	United States	Statird 26 Aug 1823
Jas., Jr.	20	M	Farmer	Scotland	United States	Statird 26 Aug 1823
Joseph	Infant					Packet 27 Aug 1822
Mary Ann	4		Child	Sutton	England	Packet 27 Aug 1822
S. S.	24	M	Merchant	Boston	U. States	Franklin 27 May 1825
Saml.	25	M	Merchant	Boston	Boston	William Bayard 24 Jan 1825
Samuel S.	23	M	Gentleman	United States	United States	Empress 22 Dec 1828
Sarah	26			Smartin	England	Packet 27 Aug 1822
Sarah	40	F		United States	United States	Seine 21 Oct 1822
Wm.	30	M	G.	St. Johns	St. Johns	Silvanus Jenkins 24 Jul 1828
BOWMOTT, W.	35	M	Manufacture	England	U. States	Favourite 2 Sep 1822
BOWN, Wm. N.	29	M	Merchant	U. States	U. States	Canada 4 Oct 1824
BOWNAR, Catherine	20	F	His Wife [John]	Ireland	United States	Asia 29 Jul 1829
James [crossed out]	3/12	M	Farmer	Ireland	United States	Asia 29 Jul 1829
Jas.			Their Child [John & Catherine]	Ireland	United States	Asia 29 Jul 1829
John	60	M	Farmer	Ireland	United States	Asia 29 Jul 1829
BOWNE, A. G.	35	M	Merchant	England	Mexico	Canada 14 Feb 1824
Mary	38	F	Spinner	England	U. States	Panthea 22 Nov 1826
Richard	2	M	Spinner	England	U. States	Panthea 22 Nov 1826

NAMES OF PASSENGERS	AGE	SEX	OCCUPATIONS	COUNTRY TO WHICH THEY BELONG	COUNTRY THEY INTEND TO INHABIT	SHIPS/DATES OF ARRIVAL	
BOWNE (cont'd)							
Thomas	19	M	Spinner	England	U. States	Panthea	22 Nov 1826
Wm.	2	M	Spinner	England	U. States	Panthea	22 Nov 1826
Wm.	27	M	Cotton Manufacturer	Ireland	U. States	Albion	11 May 1827
BOWNELL, Paul	30	M	Iron Roller	Gt. Britain	U.S. America	James Cropper	14 Mar 1828
BOWRNE, M.	25	F		U. States	United States	Burdett	30 Apr 1828
BOWSEN, Edwd.	17	M	Labourer	Great Britain		Moro Castle	6 Jul 1827
BOWYET, Charles	26	M	Merchant	Holland	Holland	Orbit	31 Dec 1823
BOX, James	35	M	Joiner	England	England	Virginia	8 Mar 1828
Wm.	28	M	Farmer	Great Britain	United States	Ann Maria	12 Jul 1821
BOXALL, Elizabeth	7			Great Brit.	U. States	Columbia	7 May 1828
Sarah	35			Great Brit.	U. States	Columbia	7 May 1828
BOXBOROUGH, Wm.	21	M	...	Ireland	United States	General Putnam	20 Jun 1825
George	23	M	Labourer	Ireland	United States	Robert Fulton	24 Jul 1826
BOYCE, —, Mrs.	70	M			U. States America	Cambria	2 Jul 1821
Ann	15	F	Spinster	Ireland	U. States	Erin	5 Jul 1820
Ann	47	F	Spinster	Ireland	U. States	Erin	5 Jul 1820
B. A.	19	F		Gt. Britain	United States	Penelope	9 Sep 1828
Catharin	22	F	Labourer	Ireland	United States	Hope	12 Jun 1828
George [crossed out]	34	M	Farmer	...	U. States	New Orleans	24 Aug 1827
*Cabin Passenger							
James	21 5/12	M	Merchant	Great Briton	United States	Erin	26 May 1821
Margaret	24	F	Spinster	Ireland	United States	Dublin Packet	22 Aug 1829
Matthew	26	M	Farmer	Ireland	U. States	William & John	10 Jul 1824
Sam	21	M	Weaver	Gt. Britain	United States	Penelope	9 Sep 1828
Sheba [crossed out]	30	F	Wife	...	U. States	New Orleans	24 Aug 1827
*Cabin Passenger							
BOYCH, John	26	M	Engineer	England	United States	Baltic	21 Apr 1827
BOYD, —	1	F		U. States	Spain	Fabius	3 Jun 1825
—	2	M		U. States	Spain	Fabius	3 Jun 1825
—	3	M		U. States	Spain	Fabius	3 Jun 1825
—	4	M		U. States	Spain	Fabius	3 Jun 1825
—, Mrs.	25	F		U. States	Spain	Fabius	3 Jun 1825
A.	36	M	Mariner	U. States	U. States	Abigail	24 Mar 1825
Anna	27	F		Co. L...	United States	Java	9 Jul 1827
Auraba, Mrs., & Infant	32	F		United States	U. States	Greyhound	19 Aug 1820
Barkhead	16	M	Farmer	Ireland	United States	Gem	16 Jun 1824
Catherine	26	F	None	Great Britain	United States	Mary & Harriet	3 Jul 1829
Christopher	19	M	Weaver	Ireland	United States	Princess Charlotte	26 Apr 1827
Daniel	31 6/12	M	Farmer	Ireland	United States	Louisa	27 Nov 1826
David	26	M	Farmer	Ireland	America	Superior	12 Jun 1824
David	40	M	Labourer	Ireland	United States	Lord Wellington	28 May 1827
Edward	30	M	Merchant	St. John, N.B.	St. John, N.B.	St. Michael	24 Jun 1824
Eliza	7 2/12	F	Daughter	Ireland	United States	Louisa	27 Nov 1826
Eliza	9	F	None	Ireland	United States	Lord Wellington	28 May 1827
Eliza	10	F	Servant	Ireland	United States	Carolina Ann	14 May 1827
Eliza	18	F	Farmer	Ireland	U. States	Francis	6 Sep 1827
Elizabeth	26	F	Farmer, Labourer or Spinster	Ireland	U. States	Meteor	4 Oct 1827
Elizabeth	29 3/12	F	Wife	Ireland	United States	Louisa	27 Nov 1826
Elizabeth	53	F	Spinster	Ireland	United States	Gem	16 Jun 1824
Ellinor	25	F		Ireland	United States	Princess Charlotte	26 Apr 1827
F.	22	M	Labourer	Ireland	United States	Josephine	30 Apr 1828
Fanny	20	F	Farmer	Ireland	U. States	Francis	6 Sep 1827
Fanny	40	F		U. States	U. States	Robert Fulton	1 Nov 1822
Francis	38 4/12	M	Gentleman	England	England	Leeds	29 May 1824
Henry Hall	25	M	Merchant	Ireland	United States	Dublin Packet	30 Apr 1821
Herritt	28	M	Laborer	Ireland	United States	Sarah G	19 Jun 1827
Hugh	63	M	Farmer	Ireland	United States	Gem	16 Jun 1824
Isabella	24	F	Farmer	Ireland	U. States	Francis	6 Sep 1827
James	20	M	Doctor	Ireland	Virginia	Curler	7 Jul 1827
James	21	M	Super Cargo	Washington	U. States	Cynthia	16 Feb 1824
James	24 1/12	M	Farmer	Ireland	United States	Atlantic	21 Jul 1827
James	52	M	General in Russian service	Russia	U. States	Balance	28 Sep 1822
James K.	25	M	...	U.S. America	U. States	Victory	21 Jun 1824

NAMES OF PASSENGERS	AGE	SEX	OCCUPATIONS	COUNTRY TO WHICH THEY BELONG	COUNTRY THEY INTEND TO INHABIT	SHIPS/DATES OF ARRIVAL	
BOYD (cont'd)							
Jane	1/2	F	Farmer, Labourer or Spinster	Ireland	U. States	Meteor	4 Oct 1827
Jane	9	F	Daughter	Ireland	United States	Louisa	27 Nov 1826
Jno. H.	30	M	Merchant	Spain	Spain	Fabius	3 Jun 1825
John	1	M	Child	Ireland	United States	Sarah G	19 Jun 1827
John	19 8/12	M		Ireland	America	Carolina Ann	7 Apr 1826
John	24 10/12	M	Weaver	Ireland	United States	Atlantic	21 Jul 1827
John	27	M	Baker	... ock	United States	Rambler	17 Feb 1820
John	28	M	Labourer	England	United States	Nimrod	31 Jul 1828
John J.	29	M	Merchant	New York	U.S.	Bayard	30 Oct 1820
Margaret	3	F	None	Ireland	United States	Lord Wellington	28 May 1827
Margt.	20	F	Spinster	Ireland	United States	Gem	16 Jun 1824
Mary	11 4/12	F	Daughter	Ireland	United States	Louisa	27 Nov 1826
Mary	20	F	Spinner	Great Britain	United States	Atlantic	8 Dec 1827
Mary	20	F		England	U. States	Emulous	22 Aug 1828
Mary	22	F	Spinster	Ireland	United States	Gem	16 Jun 1824
Mary	35	F	None	Ireland	United States	Lord Wellington	28 May 1827
Mary Ann	9	F		Irereland	America	Carolina Ann	20 Jun 1825
Mary Ann	28	F		Ireland	United States	Princess Charlotte	26 Apr 1827
Mary J.	7	F	Servant	Ireland	United States	Carolina Ann	14 May 1827
Mathew	25	M	Cabinet maker	England	U. States	Emulous	22 Aug 1828
Matilda	9/12	F	None	Ireland	United States	Lord Wellington	28 May 1827
Matthew	5	M	None	Ireland	United States	Lord Wellington	28 May 1827
Nancy		F	Chiefly farmers		United States	Factor	8 Jul 1829
Nancy	28	F	House Keeper	Irereland	America	Carolina Ann	20 Jun 1825
Rob.	14	M	Servant	G. Britain	U. States	Diligence	29 Jul 1823
Robert	3	M	Farmer, Labourer or Spinster	Ireland	U. States	Meteor	4 Oct 1827
Robert	6	M	None	Ireland	United States	Lord Wellington	28 May 1827
Robert	7 3/12	M		Irereland	America	Carolina Ann	20 Jun 1825
Robert	25	M	Labourer	Ireland	United States	Meteor	26 Jun 1827
Robt.	24	M	Farmer	Ireland	United States	Gem	16 Jun 1824
S.	24	M	Physician	U.S.	U.S.	Francois I	8 Aug 1829
Saml.	22	M		Ireland	America	Carolina Ann	7 Apr 1826
Sarah	6	F	Child	Ireland	United States	Sarah G	19 Jun 1827
Sarah Ann	1 1/12	F	Daughter	Ireland	United States	Louisa	27 Nov 1826
Thomas	5	M		Ireland	United States	Carolina Ann	14 May 1827
Thomas	23	M	Farmer	Ireland	United States	Trident	17 May 1825
Thomas	30	M	Laborer	Ireland	United States	Sarah G	19 Jun 1827
Thos.	22	M	Merchant	American	U. States	Neptune	25 Jan 1823
William	2	M	Child	Ireland	United States	Sarah G	19 Jun 1827
William	20	M	Laborer	Ireland	U. States	Albion	9 Aug 1826
William	22	M	Farmer	Scotland	U.S. of America	Friends	10 May 1823
William	22	M	Carpenter	Ireland	United States	Carolina Ann	14 May 1827
William	24	M	Hatter	Ireland	Virginia	Curler	7 Jul 1827
William	27	M	Merchant	Scotland	United States	Camillus	27 Oct 1829
Wm.	2 6/12	M	Son	Ireland	United States	Louisa	27 Nov 1826
BOYDE, James	30	M	Farmer	England	United States	Copernicus	3 Aug 1829
Robt.	22	M	Labourer	Ireland	United States	Fabius	31 Jul 1829
BOYER, ...	...0	M	...	...	...	Antioch	8 Oct 1827
Daniel	39	M	Weaver	Great Brittan	U. States	John & Elizabeth	11 Dec 1826
David	8	M		England	United States	Essex	23 May 1828
David	33	M	Tin Plate Worker	England	United States	Acasta	25 Sep 1827
Elizabeth	13	F	...	...	...	Antioch	8 Oct 1827
Geo.	10	M		England	United States	Essex	23 May 1828
Henry	25	M	Merchant	Ireland	U. States	Wave	28 Dec 1821
Jane	50	F	Labourer	England	United States	Essex	23 May 1828
Jno.	18	M	Farmer	England	United States	Essex	23 May 1828
Jos. S.			Distressed Seaman	New York	U. States	Mary & Eliza	2 Jul 1829
Joseph S.	20	M	Mariner	U. States	U. States	Tipporah	22 Dec 1828
Kenneth	21	M	...	...	...	Antioch	8 Oct 1827
Louisa	17	F	Servant	Boston	U. States	Circassian	3 Jun 1826
Mary	12	F		England	United States	Essex	23 May 1828
Oliver	50	M	...	...	...	Antioch	8 Oct 1827
Tho.	13	M		England	United States	Essex	23 May 1828

NAMES OF PASSENGERS	AGE	SEX	OCCUPATIONS	COUNTRY TO WHICH THEY BELONG	COUNTRY THEY INTEND TO INHABIT	SHIPS/DATES OF ARRIVAL	
BOYES, John	20 9/12	M	Weaver	Ireland	America	Carolina Ann	7 Apr 1826
William	36	M	Mill Right	C. Armannar [Armagh or Farmanagh?]	N. York	Nile	18 Aug 1829
BOYL, Chals.	48	M	Gentleman	U. States	U.S.	Gleaner	31 Jul 1821
Edward	18	M	Glass Cutter	Scotland	United States	Orion	15 Jan 1827
BOYLAN, James	30	M	Gentleman	Ireland	United States	Dublin Packet	13 Oct 1828
John	21	M	Farmer	Wexford		Mount Vernon	7 Jun 1824
Peter	20	M	Tailor	Ireland	New York	Atlantic	6 Oct 1828
BOYLAND, Ann	48	F	Labourer	Ireland	United States	Essex	23 May 1828
Judy	40	F	Labourer	Ireland	United States	Essex	23 May 1828
Owen	17	M	Labourer	Ireland	United States	Essex	23 May 1828
Pat	11	M	Labourer	Ireland	United States	Essex	23 May 1828
Peter	9	M	Labourer	Ireland	United States	Essex	23 May 1828
Peter	26	M	Labourer	Ireland	United States	Essex	23 May 1828
Peter	30	M	Labourer	Ireland	United States	Essex	23 May 1828
Thos.	12	M	Labourer	Ireland	United States	Essex	23 May 1828
BOYLE, Ann	18	F		Ireland	U. States	Virginia	20 Jun 1825
B.	17	M		Great Britain	United States	Aspasia	16 Jul 1828
Bridget	35	F		Ireland	U. States	Alexander	28 Jul 1821
Catherine	8	F	...	Ireland	United States	Lima	19 Jun 1824
Catherine	12	F	Girl	Ireland	United States	Trident	17 May 1825
Catherine	24	F	None	Gt. Brittain	United States	York	6 Dec 1826
Catherine	30	F	Spinster	Ireland	Unt. St. America	Wilson	21 May 1827
Cathrine	52	F	None	England	United States	India	8 Jun 1827
Daniel	3	M		Ireland	United States	Concordia	25 Aug 1827
Daniel	24	M	Labourer	Ireland	United States	Josephine	30 Apr 1828
Danl.	20	M	Labourer	Ireland		Robert Fulton	4 Jun 1828
Edward	20	M	Labourer	Ireland	United States	Asia	29 Jul 1829
Edward	23	M	Labourer			Ocean	17 Aug 1820
Edward	23 6/12	M	Farmer	Ireland	U. States	Virginia	20 Jun 1825
Edward	25	M	Labourer	Great Britain	United States	India	5 Sep 1827
Edward	29	M	Labourer	England	U. States	Comet	23 Aug 1828
Edward	33	M	Tailor		New York	Governor Clinton	3 Jul 1827
Edward	41	M	Mechanic	Ireland	United States	Concordia	25 Aug 1827
Elenor	28	F	...	Ireland	United States	Lima	19 Jun 1824
Elizabeth	23		Servant	Great Britain	United States	Camillus	12 Sep 1827
Elizabeth	31	F		Ireland	United States	Concordia	25 Aug 1827
Ellenor	50	M	Labourer	England	U. States	Comet	23 Aug 1828
Fanny	25	F	Spinster	Ireland	United States	Trident	17 May 1825
Francis	30	M	Labourer	Sligo	U. States	Panthea	8 Apr 1826
George	6/12	M		Ireland	United States	Concordia	25 Aug 1827
George	18	M	Farmer	Ireland	United States	Trident	17 May 1825
Henry	48	M	Stone Dresser	Holland	New York	Thames	6 Oct 1820
James	20	M		Ireland	United States	William & George	14 May 1828
James	22	M	Labourer	Ireland	Rhode Island	Governor Fenner	23 Jul 1829
James	27	M	Farmer	Ireland	United States	Trident	17 May 1825
James	30	M	Servant	Great Britain	U.S. of Ama.	Robert Fulton	16 Aug 1824
James	30	M	Joiner	U. States	U. States	United States	11 Sep 1828
Jane	10	F	Girl	Ireland	United States	Trident	17 May 1825
John	19	M	Weaver	Scotland	United States	Lunar	5 May 1828
John	19	M	Labourer	Ireland		Robert Fulton	4 Jun 1828
John	24	M	Labourer	Ireland	U. States	Hanford	29 Dec 1828
John	30	M	Horseler	U. States	U. States	Ribicon	13 Mar 1826
John, Mr.	27		Lady	England	United States	Acasta	16 Aug 1826
John P., Mr.	29		Gentleman	England	United States	Acasta	16 Aug 1826
Joseph B.	25	M	None	England	U.S. America	Samuel Wright	9 Jan 1829
Lewis	23	M	Joiner	Co. Fermanagh	United States	Dalhousie Castle	27 Jul 1826
Louisa, Miss	2		Child	England	United States	Acasta	16 Aug 1826
Margaret	22	F	Servant	Ireland	U.States	Nancy	31 May 1823
Margeret	30	F	Matron	Ireland	United States	Robert Fulton	24 Jul 1826
Mary	1/12	F	their child [Edward & Susan]	Ireland	United States	Asia	29 Jul 1829
Mary	16	M	Labourer	England	U. States	Comet	23 Aug 1828
Mary	21	F	Spinster	Ireland	United States	Wilson	6 Jun 1828
Mary Ann	5	F		Ireland	United States	Concordia	25 Aug 1827
Mathew	32	M	Carpenter	Ireland	United States	Dalhouse Castle	6 Sep 1827
Michael	40	M	Joiner	U. States	U. States	United States	11 Sep 1828

117

NAMES OF PASSENGERS	AGE	SEX	OCCUPATIONS	COUNTRY TO WHICH THEY BELONG	COUNTRY THEY INTEND TO INHABIT	SHIPS/DATES OF ARRIVAL	
BOYLE (cont'd)							
P.	20		Farmer	Ireland	United States	Courier	16 May 1825
Patrick	17 6/12	M	Labourer	Ireland	U. States	Virginia	20 Jun 1825
Peter	26	M	Farmer	Ireland	United States	Dublin Packet	23 May 1828
Peter	29	M	Labourer	Great Britain	United States	Colossus	5 Jun 1827
Richard	30	M	Mariner	Ireland	Great Britian	Florida	13 Feb 1826
Richd.	40	M	Farmer	Ireland	U. States	William & John	10 Jul 1824
Robert	23	M	...	Great Britain	United States	Friends	13 Jun 1825
Rosua	25	F	None	Great Britain	United States	Colossus	5 Jun 1827
Susan	22	F	wife of E. Boyle	Ireland	United States	Asia	29 Jul 1829
Timothy	19	M		Great Britain	United States	Aspasia	16 Jul 1828
William	20		Tailor	Ireland	United States	Antioch	3 Dec 1827
William	26	M	Dyer	Scotland	United States	Mary & Susan	5 Aug 1828
BOYLEN, H...	15 6/12	M	...	England	America, U.S.	Illinois	3 Jun 1822
BOYNERT, Maur	10	F		Gaudaloup	Gaudaloup	Orono	5 Jun 1823
BOYNEST, —, Mr.	40	M	Planter	Gaudaloup	Gaudaloup	Orono	5 Jun 1823
Eduard	12	M		Gaudaloup	Gaudaloup	Orono	5 Jun 1823
Jeann	8	F		Gaudaloup	Gaudaloup	Orono	5 Jun 1823
BOYNSON, Alice	10	F		Great Britain	United States	Diana	20 Nov 1828
John	38	M	Farmer	Great Britain	United States	Diana	20 Nov 1828
Mary	37	F		Great Britain	United States	Diana	20 Nov 1828
BOYNTON, Amos	54	M	Merchant	United States	United States	Camberwell	2 Oct 1828
Jane	48	F		United States	United States	Camberwell	2 Oct 1828
BOYOT, Joseph	66	M	Farmer	France	United States	Montano	5 May 1828
Marguerite	8	F		France	United States	Montano	5 May 1828
Marguerite	55	F		France	United States	Montano	5 May 1828
Pierre	3	M		France	United States	Montano	5 May 1828
Suzanne	30	F		France	United States	Montano	5 May 1828
BOYRIE, Eugene	22	M	Gentleman	Spain	United States	Helen	5 Sep 1828
BOYS, E.	2	F	Labourer	Ireland	U. States	New Packet	16 Apr 1828
James	13 5/12	M	Lapederrry	Great Britain	U. States	Robert Fulton	3 Dec 1827
Sarah	20	F	Labourer	Ireland	U. States	New Packet	16 Apr 1828
BOYSE, John	20		Mason	Ireland	United States	Fabius	18 Mar 1829
BOYTAN, Andrew	30	M	Labourer	Drogheda	Drogheda	Howard Douglass	11 May 1827
BOZE, Louis R.	21 7/12	M	Farmer	France	U.S. America	Erie	19 Oct 1829
BR..., ...	...	M			U. States	South Carolina	2 Aug 1822
BR...E, Jane	22			Isle of Wight	G. Brit.	London	13 Dec 1822
BRACE, John	41	M	Tobacconist	U.S.	U.S.	Pactolus	19 Aug 1823
BRACEBRIDGE,							
Birkhead	30	M	Druggist	England	U. States	Acasta	21 Oct 1825
George	13	M	None	G.B.	U.S.A.	Silas Richard	30 Jun 1828
BRACEWELL, Ann	6	F		Great Brittain	United States	Nimrod	9 Jan 1827
B.	1	M		Great Brittain	United States	Nimrod	9 Jan 1827
C.	13	F		Great Brittain	United States	Nimrod	9 Jan 1827
E.	8	F		Great Brittain	United States	Nimrod	9 Jan 1827
Eliza	5	F		Great Brittain	United States	Nimrod	9 Jan 1827
H.	10	F		Great Brittain	United States	Nimrod	9 Jan 1827
John	20	M	Labourer	Great Brittain	United States	Nimrod	9 Jan 1827
Sarah	34	F		Great Brittain	United States	Nimrod	9 Jan 1827
BRACH, Judith	20	F	Spinster	Ireland	America	William	21 May 1825
Wm.	38	M	Mariner	U. States	U. States	General Jackson	5 Feb 1827
BRACHEER, A.	28	M	Dentist	France	U. States	Elizabeth Malvina	6 Dec 1827
BRACHER, Am	18	F	Servant	Ireland	America	Carolina Ann	7 Aug 1826
Jean	35	M	Taylor	Germany	United States	Origon	8 Jun 1824
Mary	19	F	Servant	Ireland	America	Carolina Ann	7 Aug 1826
Maryan	27	F		Germany	United States	Origon	8 Jun 1824
Maryann	1	F		Germany	United States	Origon	8 Jun 1824
Rosina	3	F		Germany	United States	Origon	8 Jun 1824
BRACHMIN, L.	35	M	Mechanic	France	U. States	Musidora	20 Feb 1823
BRACKENBRIDGE,							
John	25	M	Mason	Scotland	Washington	Curler	7 Jul 1827
Margaret	24	F		Scotland	Washington	Curler	7 Jul 1827
BRACKENRIDGE,							
James, Mr.	30		Army	Scotland	G.B.	Pacific	24 May 1824
BRACKER, Anne	18	F	Servant	Dublin	U. States	Hibernia	26 Oct 1826
Nicolas	34	M	Shoe Maker			Henri IV	17 May 1828
BRACKIN, John	25	M	Farmer	Great Britain	New York	Superior	5 Sep 1827

NAMES OF PASSENGERS	AGE	SEX	OCCUPATIONS	COUNTRY TO WHICH THEY BELONG	COUNTRY THEY INTEND TO INHABIT	SHIPS/DATES OF ARRIVAL	
BRACKLE, J.	30	M	Gent	Great Britan	W. Indies	Cadmus	28 May 1821
BRACKLER, Jas.	28			Ireland		Anacreon	7 Sep 1827
Margt.	4			Ireland		Anacreon	7 Sep 1827
Margt.	26			Ireland		Anacreon	7 Sep 1827
Thos.	3			Ireland		Anacreon	7 Sep 1827
BRACKLEY, James	10	M	Servant	Ireland	U. States	Nancy	25 Nov 1823
Janet	16	F	Servant	Ireland	U. States	Nancy	25 Nov 1823
Wm.	6	M	Shoemaker	Ireland	U. States	Nancy	25 Nov 1823
BRACO, J.	14	M	Student	Angustura	New York	United States	15 Jul 1824
BRADA, S.	40	M		Spain	U. States	Courier	31 Jul 1828
BRADBERRY, Samuel	26	M	Merchant	Great Britain	United States	Corinthian	2 Sep 1824
BRADBURY, Alice	2		Child, None	England	U.N. States	Corinthian	1 Sep 1823
Alice	45	F		Great Britain	United States	Ganges	8 Jul 1820
Andrew	14	M		Great Britain	United States	Ganges	8 Jul 1820
Ann	8	M		England	U.N. States	Helen	17 Dec 1827
Ann	9	F	None	Great Britain	United States	Roman	10 May 1828
Betsey	4	F	None	Great Britain	United States	Roman	10 May 1828
Betsey	21	F		England	America	Two Marys	24 Sep 1827
Betsey	38	F	None	Great Britain	United States	Roman	10 May 1828
Caroline A.	4	F		Great Britain	United States	Aspasia	16 Jul 1828
Elizabeth	26	F	None	Great Britain	United States	George Clinton	21 Oct 1826
Esther	27	F	Wife	England	U.N. States	Corinthian	1 Sep 1823
F. M.	26	M		Great Britain	United States	Aspasia	16 Jul 1828
George	16	M		Great Britain	United States	Ganges	8 Jul 1820
George	28	M	Stone Cutter	England	America	Two Marys	24 Sep 1827
George	50	M	Stone Cutter	England	America	Two Marys	24 Sep 1827
Hannah	9	F		Great Britain	United States	Aspasia	16 Jul 1828
Hannah	32	F	Spinster	England	U.N. States	Helen	17 Dec 1827
Hannah M.	2	M		England	U.N. States	Helen	17 Dec 1827
J. S.	0 3/12	M		Great Britain	United States	Aspasia	16 Jul 1828
James	10	M		England	U.N. States	Helen	17 Dec 1827
James	23	M	Mercht.	England	England	William Byrnes	14 Apr 1824
Jno.	21	M	Labourer	Great Britain	United States	Atlantic	28 May 1827
Jno.	33	M	Merchant	England	U.N. States	Corinthian	1 Sep 1823
Jno.	33	M	Merchant	Gt. Britain	United States	Corks	3 Aug 1824
John	12	M		England	U.N. States	Helen	17 Dec 1827
John	16	M	Farmer	England	U.N. States	William Byrnes	13 Aug 1829
John	21	M	None	Great Britain	United States	Roman	10 May 1828
John	29	M	Merchant	England	England	Meteor	22 Apr 1822
Mary	11	F		Great Britain	United States	Ganges	8 Jul 1820
Mathw.	26	M	Farmer	Stackport	United States	Aurelia	7 Jun 1826
Matthew	45	M		Great Britain	United States	Ganges	8 Jul 1820
Robt.	29	M	Farmer	Stackport	United States	Aurelia	7 Jun 1826
Saml.	6	M		England	U.N. States	Helen	17 Dec 1827
Sarah	6	F	None	Great Britain	United States	Roman	10 May 1828
T. F.	3	F		Great Britain	United States	Aspasia	16 Jul 1828
Thos.	28	M	Clothier	Great Britian	United States	George Clinton	21 Oct 1826
Thos., Mr.	42	M	Merchant	Gt. Britain	Gt. Britain	James Cropper	2 Aug 1827
Thos. E.	4	M		England	U.N. States	Helen	17 Dec 1827
William	1	M	None	Great Britain	United States	Roman	10 May 1828
Wm.	32	M	Carpenter	England	U. States	Lucy	25 Aug 1821
BRADDLY, Ann	59	F		G. Britain	U. States	Margaret Bogle	12 Jun 1828
Edmond	25	M	Farmer	G. Britain	U. States	Margaret Bogle	12 Jun 1828
Jean	29	F		G. Britain	U. States	Margaret Bogle	12 Jun 1828
John	28	M	Farmer	G. Britain	U. States	Margaret Bogle	12 Jun 1828
BRADE, Wm.	22	M	Merchant	England	England	Ann	3 Jul 1820
BRADEN, —, Mr.	30	M	Merchant	United States	United States	Mermaid	25 Oct 1822
A.	1		Farmer	Ireland	United States	Courier	16 May 1825
Geo.	20	M		U. States	United States	Crisis	6 Apr 1825
Jane	8	F	Child	Ireland	America	Josephine	8 Dec 1827
M.	20		Farmer	Ireland	United States	Courier	16 May 1825
Mary	27	F	Matron	Ireland	America	Josephine	8 Dec 1827
P.	28		Farmer	Ireland	United States	Courier	16 May 1825
BRADENCAMP, Conrad	31 5/12	M	Merchant	Germaney	Germaney	Edward Bonnaffe	13 Mar 1826
BRADENHOUSE, Eliza	3	F	None	Baltimore	U. States	Bayard	18 Jul 1823
BRADER, Joseph	18	M	Servant	Gt. Britain	U. States	New York	15 Jul 1825
BRADEY, Anney	18	F		Irland	U. States	Nancy	27 Jun 1823
Patrick	15	M		Irereland	America	Carolina Ann	20 Jun 1825

NAMES OF PASSENGERS	AGE	SEX	OCCUPATIONS	COUNTRY TO WHICH THEY BELONG	COUNTRY THEY INTEND TO INHABIT	SHIPS/DATES OF ARRIVAL	
BRADEY (cont'd)							
Patrick	25	M		Irereland	America	Carolina Ann	20 Jun 1825
BRADFERD, Saml. D.	25	M	Merch.	Boston	Boston	Wm. Thompson	13 Sep 1823
BRADFORD, —,							
daughter [of Sarah]	2	F		U. States	U. States	Jupiter	31 Mar 1826
B.	40	M	Mariner	New York	New York	Gertrude	6 May 1828
Charles	55	M	Mariner	U. States	U. States	Constitution	17 Mar 1823
Chas., Cap.	59	M	Sea Man	Alexandria, U.S.	Alexandria, U.S.	Panthea	22 Jul 1826
Josephine	36	F	Wife	England	United States should they approve of it	Robert Edwards	20 Jan 1829
L., Mr.			Lawyer	Philadelphia	United States	Henrietta	18 Aug 1829
Maria	19	F		Great Britain	United States	Thomas Dickason	14 Sep 1827
N.	21	M	Merchant	U. States	U. States	Hetta	11 Apr 1826
R.	21	M	Book Binder	Great Britain	United States	Thomas Dickason	14 Sep 1827
S. D.	28	M	Merchant	U. States	U. States	Columbia	20 Jul 1825
Sarah	20		Farmer	Ireland	United States	Courier	16 May 1825
Sarah	30	F		N. York	U. States	Jane	29 Aug 1822
Sarah, Miss	28	F	Servant	U. States	U. States	Jupiter	31 Mar 1826
Thos.	26		Farmer	Ireland	United States	Courier	16 May 1825
W.	20	M	Merchant	N. York	U. States	Pocahontas	18 May 1825
William	33	M	Joiner	England	United States should they approve of it	Robert Edwards	20 Jan 1829
Wm.	26	M		England		Anacreon	7 Sep 1827
Wm.	35	M	Distiller	Wales	America	Ulysses	1 May 1822
BRADICH, Wm.	37	M	Merchant	Ireland	U. States	Canada	4 Oct 1824
BRADIDER, John	23	M	Merchant	Holland	U. States	United States	7 Jul 1827
BRADIE, James	26	M	Farmer	Ireland	U. States	Camillus	27 Jul 1825
BRADISH, ...heaton	40	M	Merchant	...	New York	Britannia	3 Nov 1827
Harriot	25	F		U.S. America	Citizen	Leeds	7 Nov 1828
Luther	35 3/12	M	Counsellor at Law	United States	United States	Cadmus	9 Dec 1825
Whalen	40	M	Merchant	U.S. America	Citizen	Leeds	7 Nov 1828
Wheaton	34	M	Merchant	United States	United States	Thames	16 May 1821
Wheaton	38	M	Merchant	U. States	New York	James Cropper	21 Oct 1825
BRADIST, Jno.	35	M	Farmer	Ireland	America	Mary	29 May 1827
BRADLER, Me...			...			Amphion	31 May 1824
BRADLEY, Andrew	27	M	Labourer	Newton, Great Britain		Casanda	5 Sep 1827
Ann	40	F	Seamstress	G. Britain	U. States	Dalhouse Castle	12 Sep 1828
Barney	20	M	Plasterer	G. Britain	U. States	Camillus	8 Sep 1828
Catharine	23	F	Farmer	Scotland	U.S. States of Am.	Camillus	17 Sep 1823
Catherine	20	F	Spinster	Ireland	United States	Robert Fulton	24 Jul 1826
Davd.	21	M	Tailor	Ireland	United States	Henry Kneeland	7 Jun 1828
Dennis	25	M	Labourer	Ireland	United States	Robert Fulton	24 Jul 1826
Eliza	12	F		G. Britain	U. States	Dalhouse Castle	12 Sep 1828
Elizabeth	3	F	None			Importer	30 Oct 1820
Elizabeth	31	F	None			Importer	30 Oct 1820
George	7	M				Reuben & Eliza	21 Aug 1820
George H.	18	M	Shoe Maker	New Haven	U.S.	Lydia	7 Oct 1823
Helen	25	F	Farmer	Scotland	U.S. States of Am.	Camillus	17 Sep 1823
Helen	26	F	Spinster	Ireland	America	Camillus	12 Sep 1822
Isabella	27	F	Farmer	Scotland	U.S. States of Am.	Camillus	17 Sep 1823
James	20	M	Labourer	Irereland	America	Carolina Ann	20 Jun 1825
James	26	M	Labourer	Ireland	United States	Catharine	22 Jul 1825
Jane	7	F		G. Britain	U. States	Camillus	8 Sep 1828
Jas.	22	M	Tailor	Ireland	United States	Trident	16 May 1826
John	1 1/2			York County, G.B.	Ohio	Peru	30 May 1828
John	10	M				Reuben & Eliza	21 Aug 1820
John	26	M	Manufacturer	England	United States	Dalhouse Castle	6 Sep 1827
John	34		Cotton Maker	England	England	London	16 Aug 1824
Jos.		M	Mercht.	England	U.S. America	Huntress	6 Sep 1827
Jos.	26	M	...	England	U.S.	Chase	26 Jul 1824
Juliet	22	F	Spinster	Ireland	United States	Abigail	25 Jun 1822
Justus	52	M	Shoe Maker	New Haven	U.S.	Lydia	7 Oct 1823
Mar...	45	F	Matron	Ireland	U. States	Josephine	30 Aug 1828
Margaret	26			England	England	London	16 Aug 1824

| --- | --- | --- | --- | --- | --- | --- | --- |
BRADLEY (cont'd)							
Mary	4			York County, G.B.	Ohio	Peru	30 May 1828
Mary	20	F	Spinster	Ireland	America	Camillus	12 Sep 1822
Mary	21	F	Farmer	Scotland	U.S. States of Am.	Camillus	17 Sep 1823
Mary	27			York County, G.B.	Ohio	Peru	30 May 1828
Mathew	4	M		G. Britain	U. States	Dalhouse Castle	12 Sep 1828
Michael	28	M	Merchant	Ireland	United States	Sylvester Healy	17 Oct 1825
Michaels	28	M	Pedlar	Ireland	United States	Sylvester Healy	19 Aug 1825
Miles	26	M	Sadler	Ireland	United States	Clothier	22 Nov 1827
Nancy	1	F	None			Importer	30 Oct 1820
Nancy	10	F		G. Britain	U. States	Dalhouse Castle	12 Sep 1828
Patrick	23	M	Laborer	Ireland	America	Camillus	12 Sep 1822
Richard	3	M		G. Britain	U. States	Dalhouse Castle	12 Sep 1828
Sally	13	F		G. Britain	U. States	Dalhouse Castle	12 Sep 1828
Sarah	9	F		G. Britain	U. States	Camillus	8 Sep 1828
Sarah	14	F				Reuben & Eliza	21 Aug 1820
Sarah	2...		Laboring Class		United States	Atlantic	2 Apr 1827
Sarah	24	F	None	England	United States	Dalhouse Castle	6 Sep 1827
Sarah	35	F				Reuben & Eliza	21 Aug 1820
Susan	18	F	Spinster	Ireland	United States	Robert Fulton	24 Jul 1826
Susannah	12	F				Reuben & Eliza	21 Aug 1820
Thomas	38	M	Seaman	U. States	U. States	Golden Age	6 Jul 1821
Thos.	59	M	Weaver	England	United States	Dalhouse Castle	6 Sep 1827
Timothy	32		Miller	York County, G.B.	Ohio	Peru	30 May 1828
William	4		Child	England	England	London	16 Aug 1824
William	39	M	Farmer	England	United States of America	Jubilee	12 May 1828
Wm.	27	M	Mechanic	U.S.	U.S.	Clarissa	28 Apr 1824
BRADLY, Catharine	60	F	Farmer	Scotland	U.S. States of Am.	Camillus	17 Sep 1823
Daniel	25	M	Farmer	Ireland	United States	Belmont	30 Aug 1828
John		F		Ireland	America	Carolina Ann	7 Aug 1826
Noel	23	M	Labourer	Ireland	United States	Robert Fulton	24 Jul 1826
Rosanna	30	F	Farmer	Scotland	U.S. States of Am.	Camillus	17 Sep 1823
Thomas	15	M	Labourer	Ireland	America	Wilson	16 May 1825
William	60	M	Farmer	Scotland	U.S. States of Am.	Camillus	17 Sep 1823
Wm.	30	M	Farmer	Ireland	United States	Belmont	30 Aug 1828
BRADSHAW, George	2	M	None	england	U. St.	Manchester	7 Dec 1826
George	25	M	Farmer	Ireland	N. York	Josephine	10 Dec 1825
George	36	M	Grocer	England	U. St.	Manchester	7 Dec 1826
Maria	4	F	None	England	U. St.	Manchester	7 Dec 1826
Phebe	36	F	None	New York	U. St.	Manchester	7 Dec 1826
Thomas	21	M	Clerk	England	United States	Tom	2 Jul 1827
Willm. Iss.	23	M	Sadler	Ireland	U. States	Josephine	7 May 1827
BRADSLEY, George	42	M	Merchant	Great Britain	United States	Illinois	9 Oct 1820
George, Jur.	18	M	Farmer	Great Britain	United States	Illinois	9 Oct 1820
Mary	14	F	None	Great Britain	United States	Illinois	9 Oct 1820
BRADUCK, Thomas	31	M	Mariner	Great Britain	United States	Julia Ann	18 Sep 1826
BRADUM, Thomas	45	M	Merchant	U.S.	U.S.	Iris	3 Jul 1828
BRADUN, Thos.	38	M	Merchant	U.S.	U.S.	Richmond Packet	30 Oct 1827
BRADWELL, Elizabeth	20	F	Shoemaker	Great Britian	United States	Andes	19 Aug 1829
James	1	M	Shoemaker	Great Britian	United States	Andes	19 Aug 1829
Thomas	27	M	Shoemaker	Great Britian	United States	Andes	19 Aug 1829
BRADY, Alice	25	F	Servant	Ireland	New York	Atlantic	8 May 1828
Andw.	21	M	Farmer	England	U. States	Thomas Ritchie	2 Jul 1827
Ann	14	F	Spinster	Ireland	America	Josephine	8 Dec 1827
Ann	22	F	Spinster	Ireland	United States	Wilson	28 Nov 1828
Ann	28	F		Irland	United States	Nancy	28 Oct 1822
Ann	28	F		Ireland	United States	Aurora	9 Jul 1827
Ann	29	F		Ireland	U. States of America	Dale	14 Mar 1828
Be...	13	F	None	Ireland	United States	St. George	25 Aug 1829
Bessy	18 6/12	F	Servant	Ireland	New York	Atlantic	6 Oct 1828
Betsey	25	F	None	England	U. States	Roman	1 Dec 1828
Betty	13	F		Ireland	United States	St. George	25 Aug 1829
Biddy	30	F	Servant	Ireland	United States	Carolina Ann	14 May 1827
Bridget	14	F	Daughter	Ireland	New York	Atlantic	8 May 1828

NAMES OF PASSENGERS	AGE	SEX	OCCUPATIONS	COUNTRY TO WHICH THEY BELONG	COUNTRY THEY INTEND TO INHABIT	SHIPS/DATES OF ARRIVAL	
BRADY (cont'd)							
Bridget	16	F		Ireland	United States	Dalhouse Castle	8 May 1827
Bridget	20	F	Servant	Ireland	United States	Louisa	18 Apr 1827
Bridget	45	F	Matron	Ireland	America	Josephine	8 Dec 1827
Bryan	24	M	Farmers and Mechanics	Ireland	America	Constitution	1 Oct 1825
Catha.	12	F	Child	Ireland	America	Josephine	8 Dec 1827
Catharin	20	F		Ireland	U. States	Balaena	29 Apr 1825
Catharine	18/12	F				Governor Fenner	23 Jul 1829
Cathe.	22	F	Servant	G. Britain	U. States	Sarah G	5 Jun 1828
Catherine	20	F	Matron	Ireland	U. States	Josephine	23 Jan 1829
Cathrin	...	F		Great Britain	United States	Atlantic	28 May 1827
Champion	22	M	Merchant	England	U. States	Industry	20 Oct 1828
Champion, Esqr.	23	M	Gentleman	England	United States	Hudson	17 Mar 1828
Charles	23	M	Carpenter	U.S. America	U.S. America	Quill	5 Jun 1826
Cormick	23	M	Farmer	Ireland	New York	Governor Fenner	23 Jul 1829
Danl.	26		Weaver	Great Britain	U. States	Hamilton	28 Apr 1828
Edward	25	M	Farmer	Ireland	United States	Dublin Packet	29 Jun 1825
Edward	36	M	Shop Keeper	Great Britain	United States	Florida	10 Dec 1823
Edward	40	M	Labourer	Ireland	U.N. States	Jane	7 Oct 1826
Edwd.	18	M	Labourer	Ireland	United States	Louisa	18 Apr 1827
Eleanor	20	F				Governor Fenner	23 Jul 1829
Eliz.	22	F	None	Great Britain	United States	Aurora	10 Nov 1827
Eliza	26	F				Governor Fenner	23 Jul 1829
Eliza	33	F	Spinster	Ireland	United States	Dublin Packet	23 May 1828
Elizabeth	19	F	Spinster	Ireland	Und. Stts of America	Alexander Mansfield	18 Aug 1826
Elizabeth	20 1/12	F		Ireland	America	Carolina Ann	7 Apr 1826
Ellen	20	F		Ireland	U. States	Balaena	29 Apr 1825
Ellen	20	F		Ireland	America	Plutarch	18 Jul 1826
Ellen	24	F	None	Great Briton	United States	Mount Vernon	30 Dec 1828
Ellen	27	F	Spinster	Ireland	United States	Dublin Packet	24 Sep 1823
Ellen	50	F	Wife	Ireland	New York	Atlantic	8 May 1828
Florence	23	F	Labourer	Ireland	U. States	Two Marys	20 Apr 1825
Florence	60	F	Spinster	Ireland	Und. Stts of America	Alexander Mansfield	18 Aug 1826
Frances	23	F	Servant	Ireland	United States	St. Michaels	18 Jul 1826
Francis	27	M	Labourer	Ireland	America	Plutarch	18 Jul 1826
Hugh	20	M	Farmer	England	U. States	Thomas Ritchie	2 Jul 1827
Hugh	21	M	Labourer	Manchester	United States	Nile	17 May 1827
Hugh	22	M		Ireland	U. States	Balaena	29 Apr 1825
Hugh	27	M	Labourer	Ireland	America	Plutarch	18 Jul 1826
Hugh	30		Farmer	Ireland	U.S.	Hibernia	27 Jun 1821
Ja...	14	M	Weaver	Ireland	United States	St. George	25 Aug 1829
James	3 4/12	M	None	Great Briton	United States	Mount Vernon	30 Dec 1828
James	10	M	Farmer	Mertingar		Mount Vernon	7 Jun 1824
James	12	M	Labourer	Ireland	America	Wilson	27 Nov 1826
James	14	M	Weaver	Ireland	United States	St. George	25 Aug 1829
James	16	M		G. Britain	U. States	Great Britain	6 Sep 1828
James	22	M	Clerk	Ireland	U. States	Erin	5 Jul 1820
James	22	M	Labourer	Ireland	United States	Wilson	27 Jun 1826
James	24	M	Farmer	England		Marchioness	13 May 1828
James	25	M	Weaver	Ireland	U. States	Josephine	23 Jan 1829
James	58	M	Labourer	Ireland	New York	Atlantic	8 May 1828
Jane	22	F	Spinster	Ireland	Und. Stts of America	Alexander Mansfield	18 Aug 1826
John	9	M	Son	Ireland	New York	Atlantic	8 May 1828
John	18	M	Weaver	Ireland	New York	Louisa	18 Apr 1827
John	18 4/12	M		Ireland	U.S. of America	Douglass	6 Jul 1829
John	19	M	Labourer	Ireland	U. States	Courier	17 Mar 1828
John	19	M	Farmer	England		Marchioness	13 May 1828
John	20	M	Labourer	Great Britain	United States	Aurora	10 Nov 1827
John	23	M	Farmer	Ireland	United States	Dublin Packet	22 Oct 1827
John	23	M	Labourer	Ireland	United States	Jubilee	13 Jul 1829
John	24	M	Laborer	Scotland	United States	Camillus	28 Apr 1824
John	27	M	Farmer	Great Brit.	U.S.	Silvanus Jenkins	17 Mar 1828
John	32	M	Labourer	Great Britain	United States	Colossus	5 Jun 1827
John	33	M	Baker	Great Britain	United States	Orbit	23 Oct 1826
John	36	M	Farmer	Ireland	New York	Governor Fenner	23 Jul 1829

NAMES OF PASSENGERS	AGE	SEX	OCCUPATIONS	COUNTRY TO WHICH THEY BELONG	COUNTRY THEY INTEND TO INHABIT	SHIPS/DATES OF ARRIVAL	
BRADY (cont'd)							
John	50	M	Farmer	Ireland	United States	Dublin Packet	22 Apr 1822
Judith	20	F	Spinster	Ireland	America	Wilson	16 May 1825
Judith	20	F	Servant	Ireland	New York	Atlantic	8 May 1828
M.	19	M	Labourer	Ireland	United States	Josephine	30 Apr 1828
Marey	20	F		Irland	United States	Nancy	28 Oct 1822
Margeret	22	F	Spinster	Ireland	U. States	Josephine	23 Jan 1829
Mary	20	F	Servant	Ireland	America	Carolina Ann	7 Aug 1826
Mary	20	F	None	Great Britain		Moro Castle	6 Jul 1827
Mary	36	F		Ireland	America	Wilson	27 Nov 1826
Math.	19	M	Weaver	Ireland	New York	Louisa	18 Apr 1827
Mathew	22 7/12	M		Ireland	America	Carolina Ann	7 Apr 1826
Michael	16	M	Labourer	Ireland	America	Minerva	31 May 1824
Michael	30	M	Weaver	Ireland	United States	William	6 Oct 1828
Michl.	28	M	Clerk	Ireland	United States	Nile	17 May 1827
Nicholas	28	M	Labourer	Ireland	United States	Wilson	27 Jun 1826
Owen	28	M	Labourer	Ireland	U. States	Panthea	8 Apr 1826
Owen	33	M	Farmer	Ireland	United States	Dublin Packet	9 Jul 1827
P.	18	M	Labourer	Ireland	United States	Josephine	30 Apr 1828
Partrick	24	M	Labourer	Ireland	United States	Nile	17 May 1827
Pat	3 8/12	M		Ireland	U. States	Fabius	22 Sep 1828
Pat	20	M	Labourer	Ireland	United States	Essex	23 May 1828
Pat	20	M	Labourer	G. Britain	U. States	St. George	7 Jun 1828
Pat	20	M				Lady of the Lake	23 Aug 1828
*left ship							
Pat	22	M	Labourer	Ireland	United States	Dublin Packet	28 Apr 1824
Pat.	30	M	Gentleman	Ireland	U. States	Milton	20 Aug 1827
Patk.	23	M	Bricklayer	Ireland	United States	Wilson	27 Jun 1826
Patrick	21	M	Labourer	Ireland	U. States	Balaena	29 Apr 1825
Patrick	21 2/12		Weaver	Ireland	America	Carolina Ann	7 Apr 1826
Patrick	23	M	Labourer	Ireland	United States	Silas Richards	3 Apr 1826
Patrick	23	M	Labourer	Ireland	U. States	Josephine	7 May 1827
Patrick	25	M	Labourer	Ireland	U. States	Balaena	29 Apr 1825
Patrick	25	M	Laborer	Ireland	United States	Sarah G	19 Jun 1827
Patrick	28	M	Farmer	Ireland	United States	Aurora	9 Jul 1827
Patt	15	M	Labourer	Ireland	United States	Jubilee	13 Jul 1829
Philip	18	M	Labourer	Ireland	America	Josephine	8 Dec 1827
Philip	19	M	Distiller	G. Britain	U. States	St. George	7 Jun 1828
Philip	25	M	Weaver	St. Johns, N.B.	United States	Antioch	21 Sep 1827
Philip	26	M	Tailor	Ireland	U.N. States	Jane	7 Oct 1826
Philip	28 2/12	M		Ireland	America	Carolina Ann	7 Apr 1826
Rabby	9 6/12	F		Ireland	New York	Atlantic	6 Oct 1828
Rose	22	F	Wife	Ireland	New York	Louisa	18 Apr 1827
Rose	22	F		Great Britain	Philadelphia	Philetus	21 Jul 1827
Rose	23	F	Servant	Ireland	New York	Atlantic	8 May 1828
Sarah	20	F		G. Britain	U. States	St. George	7 Jun 1828
Tenniel	8	M	Farmer	Mertingar		Mount Vernon	7 Jun 1824
Terance	6/12	M	Child	Ireland	U. States	Josephine	23 Jan 1829
Terrance	15	M	Boy	Ireland	United States	Dublin Packet	29 Jun 1825
Terrence	27		Labourer	Ireland	America	Sarah	18 Aug 1829
Thomas	18	M	Farmer	Ireland	United States	Dublin Packet	22 Oct 1821
Thomas	19	M	Laborer	Ireland	United States	Indian Chief	16 Aug 1822
Thomas	20	M	Labourer	Ireland	U. States	Two Marys	20 Apr 1825
Thomas	22	M	Labourer	Ireland	United States	Dalhouse Castle	8 May 1827
Thomas	25	M	Labroer	Great Briton	United States	Mount Vernon	30 Dec 1828
Thos.	20	M	Farmer	Ireland	America	Mary	29 May 1827
Thos.	20	M	Mason	England	United States	Euphrates	18 Aug 1827
BRAE, John	21	M	Merchant	U. States	U. States	Betsey	31 Aug 1822
BRAELING, Ballen	60	F		Netherlands	New York	Louisa	6 Oct 1828
BRAGAN, Abby	14 6/12	F	Spinster	Ireland	U. States	Josephine	30 Aug 1828
Eliza	16 6/12	F	Spinster	Ireland	U. States	Josephine	30 Aug 1828
BRAGAR, Wm.	20 7/12	M	Gun Smith	America	America	Hiram	2 Apr 1828
BRAGAS, H.	25	M	Merchant	Spain	Spain	Prince Edward	25 Feb 1822
BRAGGAS, Antonia	42	M	Merchant			Eliza Ann	29 Sep 1820
BRAGLEN, Isabella	30	F	Servant	Great Britain	United States	Sylvester Healy	23 Nov 1825
BRAHR, Fredk.	50	M		Germany	U. States	Constitution	25 Jul 1823
BRAID, Christian	1	F	Child	Scotland	United States	Tom	2 Jul 1827
Janet	3	F	Child	Scotland	United States	Tom	2 Jul 1827

NAMES OF PASSENGERS	AGE	SEX	OCCUPATIONS	COUNTRY TO WHICH THEY BELONG	COUNTRY THEY INTEND TO INHABIT	SHIPS/DATES OF ARRIVAL	
BRAID (cont'd)							
Wm.	20		Farmer	Halifax	U. States	Edwin	26 Sep 1828
BRAIN, James	12	M	None	Ireland	U. States	Dalhouse	23 Mar 1829
John	10	M	None	Ireland	U. States	Dalhouse	23 Mar 1829
John H.	69	M	Merchant	N. York	N. York	Mark	1 Jun 1824
Mary	2			Ireland	United States	Geo. Canning	5 Jun 1828
Mary	14	F	None	Ireland	U. States	Dalhouse	23 Mar 1829
Nancy	38	F	None	Ireland	U. States	Dalhouse	23 Mar 1829
BRAINE, Hannah, Mrs.	64	F		Nova Scotia		Hopes Delight	31 May 1828
Janet, Miss	23	F		Nova Scotia		Hopes Delight	31 May 1828
Thomas	24	M	Labourer	G. Britain	U. States	Sarah G	5 Jun 1828
BRAINER, Christopher	38		Labourer	Scotland	United States	Camillus	3 May 1828
James	15	M				Acosta	28 Jul 1823
Joseph	17	M				Acosta	28 Jul 1823
Richard	7	M				Acosta	28 Jul 1823
Richard	30	M				Acosta	28 Jul 1823
Samuel	8	M				Acosta	28 Jul 1823
Sarah	12	F				Acosta	28 Jul 1823
Sarah	40	F				Acosta	28 Jul 1823
William	14	M				Acosta	28 Jul 1823
BRAITHWAIT, Anna	38	F	None	Great Britan	Great Britan	Columbia	11 Aug 1823
BRAITHWAITE, Anna, Mrs.	38	F	None	G. Bt.	G. Bt.	Canada	13 Oct 1825
Isaac	44	M	None	G. Bt.	G. Bt.	Canada	13 Oct 1825
Isaac	46	M	Merchant	Gt. Britain	Gt. Britain	Canada	5 Jun 1827
BRAITHWATER, Anna	39	F	Minister of the Gospel	Gt. Britain	Gt. Britain	Canada	5 Jun 1827
BRAKEFELD, —, Mrs.	51	F	Farmer	Great Britian	United States	Columbia	17 Apr 1827
Thos.	10	M	Farmer	Great Britian	United States	Columbia	17 Apr 1827
Thos.	50	M	Farmer	Great Britian	United States	Columbia	17 Apr 1827
Wm.	9	M	Farmer	Great Britian	United States	Columbia	17 Apr 1827
BRAKEFIELD, Charles	10			Kent, England		Cincinnatus	17 May 1823
Charles	33			Kent, England		Cincinnatus	17 May 1823
Elizabeth	6			Kent, England		Cincinnatus	17 May 1823
James	1			Kent, England		Cincinnatus	17 May 1823
John	4			Kent, England		Cincinnatus	17 May 1823
Mary	8			Kent, England		Cincinnatus	17 May 1823
Mary	31			Kent, England		Cincinnatus	17 May 1823
BRAKEN, Benj.	15	M	Labourer	G. Britain	U. States	St. George	7 Jun 1828
Thos.	25	M	Labourer	G. Britain	U. States	St. George	7 Jun 1828
BRAKLE, J. V.	35	M	Gentleman	St. Croix	U. States	Carlo	6 Oct 1827
John Rarr	35	M	Planter	St. Croix	U. States	South Carolina Packet	29 Aug 1826
Mary, Mrs.	60	F		St. Croix	U. States	South Carolina Packet	29 Aug 1826
BRALY, Henry	1	M	D. Maker	Ireland	N. York	Trusty	12 Sep 1828
John	3	M	D. Maker	Ireland	N. York	Trusty	12 Sep 1828
BRAMAGUE, John	26	M	Servant	France	U. States	Desdemona	21 Oct 1825
BRAMBLE, Louisa	28	F	Wife	England	New York	Lewis	29 Oct 1825
William	30	M	Painter	England	New York	Lewis	29 Oct 1825
BRAMER, S.	21	M	Merchant	Germany	U. States	Ann	19 Aug 1824
BRAMHARD, C. H.	22	M	Gentleman	Germany	United States	Origon	8 Jun 1824
BRAMLIN, ...	45	M	Merchant	Scotland	United States	Camillus	28 Apr 1824
BRAMMER, Mary S.	25	F	Professor of Music	Great Britain	Canada	Columbia	22 Sep 1828
BRAMNER, Susan	30	F		G. Britain	U. States	Camillus	8 Sep 1828
BRAN, Jas.	35	M	Labourer	England	England	Hudson	13 Jan 1827
BRANAGAN, Ellen	22	F		Ireland	United States	Princess Charlotte	26 Apr 1827
Mary	16	F	Spinster	Ireland	America	Josephine	8 Jan 1827
Mathew	23	M	Weaver	Ireland	United States	Princess Charlotte	26 Apr 1827
Patrick	20	M	Labourer	Ireland	United States	Princess Charlotte	26 Apr 1827
BRANAH, Arch.	32	M	Labourer	Ireland	United States	Meteor	26 Jun 1827
Jane	30	F	Labourer	Ireland	United States	Meteor	26 Jun 1827
Samuel	5	M	Labourer	Ireland	United States	Meteor	26 Jun 1827
Thomas	1	M	Labourer	Ireland	United States	Meteor	26 Jun 1827
William	8	M	Labourer	Ireland	United States	Meteor	26 Jun 1827
BRANAN, Ann	14/12	F	None	Great Brittan	United States	America	24 Jul 1827
Ann	21	F	None	Great Brittan	United States	America	24 Jul 1827

NAMES OF PASSENGERS	A G E	S E X	OCCUPATIONS	COUNTRY TO WHICH THEY BELONG	COUNTRY THEY INTEND TO INHABIT	SHIPS/DATES OF ARRIVAL	
BRANAN (cont'd)							
Bridget	17	M	Labourer			Evergreen	28 Jul 1820
Elizabeth	3	F		England	U.N. States	Helen	17 Dec 1827
Elizabeth	28	F		England	U.N. States	Helen	17 Dec 1827
James	5	M		England	U.N. States	Helen	17 Dec 1827
BRANAYAN, John	27	M	Weaver	U. States	U. States	St. Croix	13 Sep 1827
Lanta	30	M	Labourer	U. States	U. States	St. Croix	13 Sep 1827
Mary	26	F		U. States	U. States	St. Croix	13 Sep 1827
BRANCH, Gotlib	20	M	Hatter	Switzerland	U. States	Hewes	30 Oct 1829
J. H. L.	19	M	Merchant	U. States	U. States	Sarah Herrick	13 May 1826
BRAND, Abigail	23	F		G. Britain	New York	Brighton	26 Mar 1827
Alexander	25	M	Weaver	Ireland	United States	Romulus	24 Jun 1826
Anna Maria	7	F		France	United States	New England	29 Aug 1828
Anna Maria	17	F		France	United States	New England	29 Aug 1828
Anne	22	F		Ireland	United States	Romulus	24 Jun 1826
Baker	1	M		G. Britain	New York	Brighton	26 Mar 1827
Benjamin	2	M		G. Britain	New York	Brighton	26 Mar 1827
Benjamin	24	M	Butcher	G. Britain	New York	Brighton	26 Mar 1827
Catharine	5	F		France	United States	New England	29 Aug 1828
Charles	...	M		G. Britain	New York	Brighton	26 Mar 1827
Edward	24	M		G. Britain	New York	Brighton	26 Mar 1827
Heram	2	M		G. Britain	New York	Brighton	26 Mar 1827
Isabella	28	F		Scotland	United States	Camillus	27 Oct 1829
J.	3	F		France	United States	New England	29 Aug 1828
J.	31	M	Merchant	England	U. States	Ranger	2 Jul 1827
James	27	M	Joiner	Great Britain	United States	Colossus	5 Jun 1827
Janet	27	F	None	Great Britain	United States	Colossus	5 Jun 1827
John	3...	M	Farmer	G. Britain	New York	Brighton	26 Mar 1827
Joseph	15	M		France	United States	New England	29 Aug 1828
Joseph	50	M	Joiner	France	United States	New England	29 Aug 1828
Lucy	2	F	None	Great Britain	United States	Colossus	5 Jun 1827
Madelene	8	F		France	United States	New England	29 Aug 1828
Mary	26	F		G. Britain	New York	Brighton	26 Mar 1827
Thomas	13			England	England	Hudson	4 Sep 1823
Waller	3	M		G. Britain	New York	Brighton	26 Mar 1827
William	4	M	None	Great Britain	United States	Colossus	5 Jun 1827
BRANDEN, Hy.	22	M		Dublin	U. States	Hibernia	26 Oct 1826
J. S.	29	M	Merchant	Barbadoes	U. States	Elisa Pigott	24 Apr 1822
John	40	M	Carpenter	Germany	America	Orozimbo	1 Oct 1827
Joseph	22	M	Merchant	New York	New York	Athenian	9 Jan 1829
BRANDER, Wm.	30	M	Merchant	U.S.	U.S.	Agenoria	15 Jun 1822
BRANDIS, Lewis	25	M	Secretary to the Danish Legation	Denmark	United States	Baltic	1 Nov 1823
Louis	30	M	Secy. of the Danish Legation to the U. States	Denmark	U. States	Cincinnatus	22 Sep 1828
BRANDON, Abram R.	55	M	Merchant	Barbados	New York	Cannon	18 Aug 1821
John	23	M	Laborer	England	United States	London	21 May 1828
Joseph	19	M	Gentleman	Great Britain	United States	General Paez	28 Nov 1826
Joseph P.	26	M	Merchant	Curraco	Curraco	General Paez	30 Apr 1827
BRANDS, John	29 7/12	M	Student in Bardstown's College	Netherland	America	Henry	17 May 1828
BRANDT, Catherin	26	F	Sevant	Great Britan	United States	Columbia	11 Aug 1823
Frederick	28	M	Butcher	Germany	United States	Montano	5 May 1828
Fredk.		M	Merchant	Hamburg	Hamburgh	Swan	13 Nov 1821
T.	23	M	Sheperd	Germany	Uncertain	Jane	11 Jul 1828
BRANE, John	24	M	Mechanic	Germany	U. States	Hannibal	12 Oct 1829
BRANEN, Frances	1	F		Ireland	U. States	Convoy	10 Sep 1823
Isabella	4	F		Ireland	U. States	Convoy	10 Sep 1823
Margaret	3	F		Ireland	U. States	Convoy	10 Sep 1823
Mary	38	F		Ireland	U. States	Convoy	10 Sep 1823
BRANER, A.	24	M	Merchant	Bremen	Bremen	York	2 Dec 1828
BRANEY, Patrick	23	M	Labourer	Ireland	United States	Enterprize	23 Jul 1827
BRANIAR, Argate	3	F		Switzerland	U.S. America	Huntress	6 Sep 1827
Debor	5 4/12	F		Switzerland	U.S. America	Huntress	6 Sep 1827
J. P.	36	M	P...ter	Switzerland	U.S. America	Huntress	6 Sep 1827
M. W.	36	M	P...ter	Switzerland	U.S. America	Huntress	6 Sep 1827
Nichs.	10	M		Switzerland	U.S. America	Huntress	6 Sep 1827

NAMES OF PASSENGERS	AGE	SEX	OCCUPATIONS	COUNTRY TO WHICH THEY BELONG	COUNTRY THEY INTEND TO INHABIT	SHIPS/DATES OF ARRIVAL	
BRANIAR (cont'd)							
Sebastian	1	M		Switzerland	U.S. America	Huntress	6 Sep 1827
BRANIGAN, Charles	70	M	Farmer	Ireland	United States	Dublin Packet	22 Aug 1829
Jane	23	F	Spinster	Ireland	United States	Dublin Packet	22 Aug 1829
Thomas	30	M	Farmer	Ireland	United States	Dublin Packet	22 Aug 1829
BRANLEY, Ann	14	F	Spinster	Ireland	United States	Wilson	4 Oct 1827
BRANN, Huns	28	M	Cabinetmaker	Denmark	United States	Maria Elizabeth	6 Jan 1823
BRANNAIS, Edward	23	M	Weaver	Ireland	U. States	Josephine	30 Aug 1828
BRANNAN, Andw.	20	M	Labourer	England	U. States	Thomas Ritchie	2 Jul 1827
Ann	28	F		St. John	Gt. Britain	Isabella	18 Apr 1825
Dd.	45	M	Merchant	Ireland	U. States	Convoy	10 Sep 1823
Easter	37	F		Ireland	U. States	Virginia	20 Jun 1825
Elinor	15	F	...	Ireland	United States	Wilson	22 Jun 1824
James	24	M	Labourer	Ireland	United States	Robert Fulton	24 Jul 1826
M.	50	M	Mariner	U. States	U. States	Greek	8 Mar 1828
Michael	6	M	Farmer	Ireland	U. States	Hibernia	29 Nov 1821
Michael	20	M	Stonemason	Ireland	U. States	Virginia	20 Jun 1825
Sarah	50	F		St. John	Gt. Britain	Isabella	18 Apr 1825
Stephen	20	M	Labourer	England	U. States	Thomas Ritchie	2 Jul 1827
Thomas	42	M	Mechanic	Ireland	U. States	Convoy	10 Sep 1823
BRANNARD,							
Catherine	19 4/12	F	Domestic	Ireland	United States	London	6 Feb 1829
BRANNEN, Ea.	8	M		Ireland	U. States	Convoy	10 Sep 1823
Elizabeth	21	F		Ireland	U. States	Convoy	10 Sep 1823
Mary	5	F		Ireland	U. States	Convoy	10 Sep 1823
Thos.	23	M	Farmer	Ireland	U. States	Wilson	22 Apr 1822
BRANNER, —				G. Britain	U. States	Camillus	8 Sep 1828
F.	27	M	private	U. States	U. States	Enterprize	9 Aug 1825
BRANNIN, Eliza	18	F	None	Ireland	New York	Eliza Grant	29 Aug 1829
Eliza	18	F	None	Ireland		Eliza Grant	29 Aug 1829
William	15	M	None	Ireland	New York	Eliza Grant	29 Aug 1829
William	15	M	None	Ireland		Eliza Grant	29 Aug 1829
BRANNON, James	46	M	Weaver	Ireland	United States	Delta	24 Oct 1829
BRANSHAW, James	17	M	Chemist	England	New York	Louisa	10 Nov 1825
Lucy	36	F		England	New York	Louisa	10 Nov 1825
Wm.	43	M	Surgeon	England	New York	Louisa	10 Nov 1825
BRANSON, Josiah	34	F		G. Britain	U. States	St. George	16 Jan 1829
Thomas	42	M	Hosier	G. Britain	U. States	St. George	16 Jan 1829
BRANT, John	27	M	Gentleman	England	England	William	2 Sep 1822
Maria L.	11	F		America	Matanzas	Radius	12 Jul 1825
BRANTZ, Maria D.	8	F	Child	France	Havana	Robert Fulton	22 May 1824
BRAPHY, George	27	M	Clerk	Great Britain	United States	Orbit	23 Oct 1826
BRASH, James	30	M	Merchant	Scotland	U. States	Spartan	11 Mar 1823
BRASIER, Jno.	21	M	Cooper	Portland	Portland, N.Y.	Prize	10 Jun 1824
BRASILE, Daniel	24	M	Laborer	Ireland	America	Parrington	9 Jun 1827
BRASILL, Bridgett	20	F		...	United States	Combine	20 Nov 1824
Jno.	22	M	Laborer	...	United States	Combine	20 Nov 1824
BRASLEY, Mary	8	F		York, Great Britain		Casanda	5 Sep 1827
BRASLIN, John	20	M	Farmer	Ireland	United States	Trident	17 May 1825
BRATE, James	19	M		Great Britaian	United States	Margaret Ann	3 Apr 1822
BRATHWIT, Wm.	23	M	Weaver	Ireland	U. States	Atlantic	7 Aug 1823
BRATHWORTH, John	20	M	Grocer	Great Britain	United States	Marshal Wellington	3 May 1822
BRATT, George	40	M	Whitesmith	England	United States	Delta	24 Oct 1829
BRATY, John	35	M	Merchant	England	U. States	Crawford	4 Jan 1826
BRAU, Abigail	12	F	Farmer	England	Athens, N.Y.	Chelsea	16 May 1828
David	16	M	Farmer	England	Athens, N.Y.	Chelsea	16 May 1828
Louisa	8	F	Farmer	England	Athens, N.Y.	Chelsea	16 May 1828
Philadelphia	33 11/12	F	Farmer	England	Athens, N.Y.	Chelsea	16 May 1828
Richard	9	M	Farmer	England	Athens, N.Y.	Chelsea	16 May 1828
Susannah	1	F	Farmer	England	Athens, N.Y.	Chelsea	16 May 1828
Thomas	14	M	Farmer	England	Athens, N.Y.	Chelsea	16 May 1828
Thomas, & family	43 6/12	M	Farmer	England	Athens, N.Y.	Chelsea	16 May 1828
BRAUCK, Charles	20	M	...	G. Britain	G. Britain	General Marion	1 Sep 1824
BRAUN, Jane, Mrs.	23	F		Great Britain	England	Jay	18 Apr 1823
BRAVE, P.	30	M	Merchant	W. Indies	W. Indies	Hiram	8 Jul 1829

NAMES OF PASSENGERS	AGE	SEX	OCCUPATIONS	COUNTRY TO WHICH THEY BELONG	COUNTRY THEY INTEND TO INHABIT	SHIPS/DATES OF ARRIVAL	
BRAVO, —. (son)	6	M	Son of N. Bravo	Mexico		Joseph	20 Jul 1829
*died 8th July							
Nicholas		M	Vice President of				
			Mexico	Mexico		Joseph	20 Jul 1829
BRAWLEY, Edwd.	23		Farmer	Ireland	Great Britain	Robert Burns	14 Jun 1824
BRAWNOLEY, James	20	M	Carpenter	Scotland	Scotland	General Marion	17 Mar 1826
BRAY, B.	18	M	Mariner	U. States	U. States	Florida	25 Apr 1825
Betsey	17	F	None	Ireland	United States	Minerva	25 Aug 1823
C.	30		Hair Dresser	France		Edward	
						Bonnaffe	17 Mar 1828
D.	50	M	Mariner	U. States	U. States	Adeline	30 Apr 1821
David	50	M	Seaman	U. States	U. States	Boston	26 Sep 1820
Henry	25	M	Labourer	Germany	Newyork	Cortes	16 Jul 1827
Job	18	M	Painter	England	United States	Joseph	13 Oct 1823
Michae	19	M	Labourer	Ireland	United States	Minerva	25 Aug 1823
Thomas	40	M		Gt. Britain	U. States	Tantiva	7 Jul 1828
BRAYBORN, William	26		Musician	England	United States	Hudson	5 Apr 1826
BRAZ, Charles	33	M	Carpenter	Great Brittain	U. States	Florenzo	20 Mar 1827
Edwd.	4	M	None	Great Brittain	U. States	Florenzo	20 Mar 1827
BRAZAS, Frances	19	F		Portland	U. States	Robt. Y. Hayne	27 Jun 1825
BRAZIER, Jno.	21	M	Mechanic	U. States	U. States	Rebecca	27 May 1823
Thos.	28	M	Mechanic	United States	United States	Ann Maria	23 Oct 1820
BRAZIL, Edmund	24	M	Farmer	Great Britian	United States	Diamond	8 Nov 1824
BRE..., Philip	21	M		France	France	Edward Quesnel	3 Jul 1829
BREADBENT, Ben.	17	M	Merchant	England	United States	John Wells	22 May 1826
BREADY, Ann	60		Farmer	Belfast	Ireland	Carolina Ann	21 May 1823
Barney	25	M		Ireland	U. States	Nancy	16 Aug 1822
Biddy	3	F	Labourer	Ireland	U. States	Two Marys	20 Apr 1825
Bridget	20	F	Spinster	Ireland	U. States	Josephine	30 Aug 1828
John	19		Farmer	Belfast	Ireland	Carolina Ann	21 May 1823
Margaret	24	F	Spinster	New Brunswick	United States	Lady Hunter	27 Dec 1825
BREAL, John	25	M	Cotton Spinner	England	United States	Aurelia	7 Jun 1826
BREARD, Onnlis	31	M	Artist	France	United States	Bayard	15 Feb 1827
BREARLY, Isaac	47	M	Manufacturer	England	America	Britannia	22 Jul 1829
BREBIO, Antonis	30	M	Office of Spain	Spain	Spain	Hind	12 Jul 1820
BRECHNER, Christopher	23	M	Merchant	Germany	U. States	James M	15 Sep 1828
BRECINO, Ignaus	18	M	Nothing	Columbia	America	Britannia	5 Nov 1828
BRECK, Calvin	45	M	Farmer	America	United States	America	16 May 1827
BRECKDEN, Simon	29 4/12	M	Farmer	France	France	France	28 Mar 1829
BRECKENRIDGE,							
Danl.	33	M	Weaver	Great Britain	United States	Colossus	5 Jun 1827
James	21	M	Butcher	Glasgow	United States	Aurelia	7 Jun 1826
John	40	M	Farmer	Scotland	United States	Camillus	27 Oct 1829
BRECKER, John Ulerick	46	M	Farmer	Switzerland	United States	Elizabeth	27 Jul 1824
BRECKINRIDGE, Janet	32	F	Weaver	Great Britain	United States	Colossus	5 Jun 1827
BREDAN, P., Miss	25	F		United States		Howard	17 Oct 1822
BREELY, ...nda	...	F	...	England	New York	Wilson	10 Apr 1823
Catharine	36	F	...	England	New York	Wilson	10 Apr 1823
Maria	23	F	...	England	New York	Wilson	10 Apr 1823
Mary	1... 6/12	F	...	England	New York	Wilson	10 Apr 1823
Thos. F.	28	M	...	Ireland	New York	Wilson	10 Apr 1823
BREEN, J.	25	M	Mechanic	U. States	U. States	Mary	24 Feb 1823
Ls. A.	30	M	Merchant	Bordeaux	Jaqumel	President	21 Mar 1825
Michl.	30	M	Farmer	Anthrem	N. York	Nile	18 Aug 1829
Rick	25	M	Wife	Anthrem	N. York	Nile	18 Aug 1829
BREETEY, Elisb.	21	F				Henri IV	17 May 1828
Fredc.	26	M				Henri IV	17 May 1828
BREEZE, Allen	58	F		England	America	Plutarch	18 Jul 1826
Christopher	60	M	Gentleman	England	America	Plutarch	18 Jul 1826
Hanah	26	F		England	America	Plutarch	18 Jul 1826
Martha	21	F	Farmer	Ireland	United States	Justina	5 Aug 1823
Sarah Ellen	14	F		England	America	Plutarch	18 Jul 1826
William	22	M	Farmer	Ireland	United States	Justina	5 Aug 1823
BREFAN, Lewis	20	M	Weaver	France	United States	Bayard	23 Mar 1826
BREFAU, Catharine	12	F	Gardener	Canada	Quebec	Homer	28 Aug 1829
Franseau	43	M	Gardener	Canada	Quebec	Homer	28 Aug 1829
Genvave	47	F	Gardener	Canada	Quebec	Homer	28 Aug 1829
BREHM, E. G.	72	F	Farmer	Germany	America	Howard	27 Sep 1826
BREIDENBACH, Henry	26	M	painter	England	Newyork	Cortes	16 Jul 1827

127

NAMES OF PASSENGERS	AGE	SEX	OCCUPATIONS	COUNTRY TO WHICH THEY BELONG	COUNTRY THEY INTEND TO INHABIT	SHIPS/DATES OF ARRIVAL	
BREIS, Mary	23	F		England	United States	John Wells	16 May 1825
BREITEMBUCHER,							
Barbara	6	F		Switzerland	America, U.N.S.	Great Britain	3 Aug 1829
Elizabeth	17	F		Switzerland	America, U.N.S.	Great Britain	3 Aug 1829
Henri	13	M		Switzerland	America, U.N.S.	Great Britain	3 Aug 1829
Madelina	9	F		Switzerland	America, U.N.S.	Great Britain	3 Aug 1829
Margurita	40	F		Switzerland	America, U.N.S.	Great Britain	3 Aug 1829
Philip	43	M	Farmer	Switzerland	America, U.N.S.	Great Britain	3 Aug 1829
BREKER, John E.	22	M	Merchant	United States	United States	Tampico	21 Jan 1826
BRELAN, Willet	22	M	Laborer	Ireland	United States	St. Michaels	18 Jul 1826
BREMEN, Catherine	7	F	his family [Francios]	Germany	United States	Wm. Osborne	16 Sep 1828
Francios	5	M	his family [Francios]	Germany	United States	Wm. Osborne	16 Sep 1828
Francios	36	M	Painter	Germany	United States	Wm. Osborne	16 Sep 1828
James	24	M		G. Britain	U. States	Dalhouse Castle	12 Sep 1828
Maria	1	F	his family [Francios]	Germany	United States	Wm. Osborne	16 Sep 1828
Maria	36	F	his family [Francios]	Germany	United States	Wm. Osborne	16 Sep 1828
Phillip	13	M		Ireland	United States	Fabius	4 Jun 1828
BREMER, David	22	M	Shoemaker	Scotland	U.S. of America	Friends	10 May 1823
Detrick	26		Sugar Refiner	England	U. States	Corinthian	8 Oct 1828
John	20	M	Sugar Baker	Germany	New York	Constitution	20 Aug 1825
BREMNAR, Gordon	...		...	...	...	St. Michael	22 Sep 1824
BREMNER, Alex.	35	M	Merchant	N. York	N. York	Nancy	10 May 1825
B. E. 30 1/12 23/365 [?]		M	Merchant	United States	U. States	Panthea	5 Oct 1822
Benjn. E.	33	M	Gentleman	U. States	U. States	Quesnel	6 Sep 1824
Detrich	28	M	Sugar Refiner	England	U.S.	Acasta	11 May 1827
BREMON, James	21	M	Labourer	Ireland	America	Wilson	16 Nov 1824
BRENAN, Catherine	13	F	Child	Ireland	United States	Dublin Packet	9 Jul 1827
Eliza	12	F	Child	Ireland	United States	Dublin Packet	9 Jul 1827
James	19	M	Laborer	Ireland	United States	Dublin Packet	9 Jul 1827
Jno.	13	M	Laborer	Ireland	United States	Nancy Henrietta	3 Nov 1828
John	28	M	Farmer	Ireland	America	William	21 May 1825
Margaret	16	F	Spinster	...	United States	Erin	25 Dec 1820
Mary	25	F	Laborer or Spinster	Ireland	United States	Frances Miller	27 Jul 1827
Matthew	15	M	Laborer	Ireland	United States	Nancy Henrietta	3 Nov 1828
Wm.	33	M	Labourer	Ireland	Little York	Hope & Esther	21 Dec 1827
BRENDEL, Ferd.	32		Cordonnier [shoemaker]	Suisse		Deux Ernest	29 Dec 1827
*son épouse & 2 enfans [his wife and two children] Frederick, his Wife & two children *landed at Lewiston, Delw.			Shoemaker	Swisse	United States	Deux Ernest	29 Dec 1827
BRENDEN, T.	19	M	None	England	United States	Enterprize	19 Oct 1826
BRENDENBASH, Henry	4	M	Farmer	England	New York	Cortes	23 Nov 1827
Susanne, Mrs.	24	F	Farmer	England	New York	Cortes	23 Nov 1827
BRENEAU,							
Theophilus	21 1/12	M	Doctor	Cananda	Canada	Edward Bonnaffe	13 Mar 1826
BRENNAN, Betty	19	F		Ireland	U. States	Wilson	22 Apr 1822
Bidy	19	F	Spinster	Ireland	United States	Dublin Packet	13 Oct 1828
Catherine	4	F		Ireland	U. States	Wilson	22 Apr 1822
D.	3	M		With intention to become citizen		New York	18 Jul 1828
Dinah	40	F	Labourer	Ireland	United States	Essex	23 May 1828
Edmd.	17	M	Laborer	Gt. Britain		Dalhouse Castle	13 May 1828
Edmd.	25	M	Farmer	Ireland	New York	Commerce	24 Sep 1823
Eleanor	14	F	Servant	Ireland	United States	Wilson	27 Jun 1826
Eliza	14	F	Spinster	Ireland	America	Wilson	16 May 1825
Ellen	18	F	Spinster	Ireland	America	Wilson	16 May 1825
Ellenar	15	F	Spinster	Ireland	America	Wilson	16 May 1825
Jane	8	F		Ireland	U. States	Wilson	22 Apr 1822
John	14	M	None	Great Brittain	United States	Active	12 Sep 1828
Lawrance	6	M		Ireland	U. States	Wilson	22 Apr 1822

NAMES OF PASSENGERS	AGE	SEX	OCCUPATIONS	COUNTRY TO WHICH THEY BELONG	COUNTRY THEY INTEND TO INHABIT	SHIPS/DATES OF ARRIVAL	
BRENNAN (cont'd)							
Margt.	30	F		Ireland	U. States	Wilson	22 Apr 1822
Mary	1/2	F	Labourer	Ireland	United States	Essex	23 May 1828
Mary	22	F	Spinster	Ireland	U. States	Josephine	7 May 1827
Michl.	40	M	Labourer	Ireland	United States	Essex	23 May 1828
Neal	22	M	Labourer	Ireland	U. States	Josephine	7 May 1827
Patrick	13	M	Boy	Ireland	U. States	Josephine	7 May 1827
Peter	26	M	Labourer	Ireland	United States	Josephine	30 Apr 1828
Susan	9	F	Child	Ireland	U. States	Josephine	7 May 1827
William	16	M	Farmer	Ireland	United States	Dublin Packet	13 Oct 1828
Wm.	40	M	Mercht.	New York		Sarah Lee	29 May 1826
BRENNAND, Thos.	30	M		G. Brittain	U. States	Cincinnatus	2 Oct 1822
BRENNEN, Patrick	20	M	Labourer	Ireland	United States	Robert Fulton	10 Aug 1827
Patrick	24	M	Labourer	Ireland	U. States	Lady Hunter	9 Oct 1825
BRENNER, Margaret	18	F		Gt. Britain		Dalhouse Castle	13 May 1828
Mary	18	F		Gt. Britain		Dalhouse Castle	13 May 1828
BRENNON, Margaret	7	F	Child	Ireland	America	Wilson	16 Nov 1824
Mary	5	F	Child	Ireland	America	Wilson	16 May 1825
BRENT, Alfred, Mr.	24	M	Gent.	England	U.S.	Acasta	11 May 1827
Ann	40		Ladies and Gentlemen	England	United States	Corinthian	7 Jul 1829
Chas.	30	M	Labourer	England	United States	Essex	23 May 1828
Edgar Ellis	15		Ladies and Gentlemen	England	United States	Corinthian	7 Jul 1829
Edmund Vertue	17		Ladies and Gentlemen	England	United States	Corinthian	7 Jul 1829
Emma	14		Ladies and Gentlemen	England	United States	Corinthian	7 Jul 1829
Frances Isabella	9		Ladies and Gentlemen	England	United States	Corinthian	7 Jul 1829
Isabella	7		Ladies and Gentlemen	England	United States	Corinthian	7 Jul 1829
Julius	2		Ladies and Gentlemen	England	United States	Corinthian	7 Jul 1829
Samuel	41		Ladies and Gentlemen	England	United States	Corinthian	7 Jul 1829
BRENTNELL, Amos	17	M	Farmer			Importer	30 Oct 1820
Ann	7	F	None			Importer	30 Oct 1820
Catharine	39	F	None			Importer	30 Oct 1820
Eliza	2	F	None			Importer	30 Oct 1820
George	14	M	Farmer			Importer	30 Oct 1820
Harriet	5	F	None			Importer	30 Oct 1820
John	42	M	Farmer			Importer	30 Oct 1820
BRENTON, J.	28	M	Pilot	U. States	U. States	Don Quixote	15 Apr 1825
BRERETON, Hanh.	45	F	Wife	L...ts, Manchester, England	N. York	New Orleans	24 Aug 1827
John	7	M	Child	L...ts, Manchester, England	N. York	New Orleans	24 Aug 1827
John	34	M	Labourer	England	U. States	Comet	23 Aug 1828
Ralf	49	M	Weaver	Manchester, England	N. York	New Orleans	24 Aug 1827
BRESAC, Barie		M	Merchant	U. States		Frederick	18 Feb 1822
BRESLAW, Cornelius	24	M	Labourer	Ireland		William Tell	24 Oct 1829
BRESON, Wm.	20		Farmer	Ireland	United States	Robert Burns	18 Jun 1821
BRETIN, Georg	40	M		Ireland	United States	Nancy R. Crowell	21 Sep 1822
BRETON, Elizabeth	28	F		England	U.S.	Maria Caroline	12 Jul 1820
BRETT, Charles, Mr.	25	M	Gentleman	Ireland	United States	Dublin Packet	9 Jul 1827
John	30	M	Tailor	G. Britian	U. States	Neptune	24 Mar 1826
John H.	28	M	Brewer	Ireland	United States	Wilson	27 Jun 1826
Michael	26	M	Farmer	Ireland	United States	Dublin Packet	23 May 1828
BRETTELL, Edward	17	M	Locksmith	England	New York	Brighton	20 Aug 1825
BRETTON, Alexander	26	M	Labourer	Ireland	America	Minerva	31 May 1824
Archibald	25	M	Labourer	Ireland	America	Minerva	31 May 1824
BRETUNY, John	22	M	Labourer	Ireland	United States	Wilson	6 Jun 1828
BREW, Cathrine	1	F	None	Great Britain	United States	Penelope	11 Jun 1827
Jane	36	F	None	Great Britain	United States	Penelope	11 Jun 1827
John	4	M	None	Great Britain	United States	Penelope	11 Jun 1827

NAMES OF PASSENGERS	AGE	SEX	OCCUPATIONS	COUNTRY TO WHICH THEY BELONG	COUNTRY THEY INTEND TO INHABIT	SHIPS/DATES OF ARRIVAL	
BREW (cont'd)							
John	16	M	Boy	Ireland	U. States	Josephine	7 May 1827
Margret	6	F	None	Great Britain	United States	Penelope	11 Jun 1827
Robt.	8	M	None	Great Britain	United States	Penelope	11 Jun 1827
Robt.	32	M	Labourer	Great Britain	United States	Penelope	11 Jun 1827
BREWEN, James	45	M	Laborer	Great Brittan	Great Brittan	Tuscarora	26 Jan 1827
BREWER, Alfred,							
Master	14 1/12	M	None	New York	America	William & Mary	5 Jul 1826
Ann	47	F		U.S. America	U.S. America	Cincinnatus	31 Oct 1820
C...ia	23	F		Britain	U.S. America	Cincinnatus	31 Oct 1820
Caroline	21	F		Britain	U.S. America	Cincinnatus	31 Oct 1820
Catherine A.	27	F	None	United States	United States	John	6 Sep 1826
Charlotte, Miss	12 5/12	F	None	New York	America	William & Mary	5 Jul 1826
Chas. T.	17	M	Merchant	St. Croix	U. States	Gleaner	4 Oct 1828
Frances	6	F			U.S. America	Cincinnatus	31 Oct 1820
Francis	24	M	Cabinetmaker	England	United States	Delta	24 Oct 1829
H.	15	M	Farmer	Gt. Britain	United States	Robert Edwards	1 Jun 1826
Henry	34	M	...	England	United States	Danube	1 Nov 1827
James	29	M	Shoemaker	Maidstone, Kent		Colossus	27 Mar 1828
John	47	M	Merchant	U.S. America	U.S. America	Cincinnatus	31 Oct 1820
Louisa	3	F			U.S. America	Cincinnatus	31 Oct 1820
Rachal, Mrs.	32 6/12	F	None	Kingston, Jamaica	America	William & Mary	5 Jul 1826
S. W.	32	M	Merchant	U.S. America	U.S. America	James Cropper	29 Nov 1827
William	17	M	Labourer	England	America	Meteor	22 Apr 1822
William H.	8	M	None	Maidstone, Kent		Colossus	27 Mar 1828
Wm.	16	M	Farmer	Gt. Britain	United States	Robert Edwards	1 Jun 1826
Wm.	38	M	Farmer	Great Britain	Upper Canada	Zodiac	14 Jun 1822
BREWKIN, Eliza	22	F	Rabbit ...	Ireland	U. States	Atlantic	19 Aug 1825
BREWSTER, J. L.	38	M	Merchant	N. York	U. States	Hero	3 Sep 1823
Job	32	M	Farmer	England	U. States	Laburnum	10 Apr 1823
John	30	M	Farmer	Scotland	United States	Delta	24 Oct 1829
L. D.	44	M	Merchant	U. States	U. States	Frances	22 May 1827
Mary	30	F		England	U. States	Laburnum	10 Apr 1823
Mary	38 2/12	F		Ireland	U. States	Fabius	22 Sep 1828
Thos.	30	M	Farmer	Gt. Britain	United States	Crisis	13 Nov 1824
BRGNAL, Ann	30	F	Labourer	Gt. Britain	U. States	Panthea	21 Jul 1825
Richd.	4	M	Labourer	Gt. Britain	U. States	Panthea	21 Jul 1825
BRIAILY, Joseph	40	M	Card Maker	England		Fame	9 Dec 1826
BRIAN, Bridget	22	F	None	G. Britain	United States	Fairy	18 Feb 1825
Elizabeth		F	Chiefly farmers		United States	Factor	8 Jul 1829
James		M	Chiefly farmers		United States	Factor	8 Jul 1829
John		M	Chiefly farmers		United States	Factor	8 Jul 1829
John	21	M	Labourer	Ireland	U. States	Lady Hunter	9 Oct 1825
John	25	M	Farmer			Belle Savage	15 Aug 1820
John C.		M	Chiefly farmers		United States	Factor	8 Jul 1829
Mary		F	Chiefly farmers		United States	Factor	8 Jul 1829
Mary C.		F	Chiefly farmers		United States	Factor	8 Jul 1829
Patrick	19	M	Farmer	Gt. Britain	United States	Eliza Barker	11 Jan 1826
Thos.	29	M	Farmer	G. Britain	United States	Fairy	18 Feb 1825
Wm.	2	M	None	G. Britain	United States	Fairy	18 Feb 1825
BRIANT, Henry	28	M	Mechanic	Ireland	U. States	Bayard	11 Mar 1823
Nicholas	25	M	Farmer	Ireland	United States	Herald	7 Jun 1824
Sarah	22	F		London	U. States	Bayard	11 Mar 1823
BRIAR, Christopher	21	M		G. Britan	U. States	William Neilson	26 Jul 1828
Philip	40	M		G. Britan	U. States	William Neilson	26 Jul 1828
BRIARDY, Mary	3 2/12	F		Ireland	America	Carolina Ann	7 Apr 1826
Rose	30 1/12	F		Ireland	America	Carolina Ann	7 Apr 1826
BRIARLEY, Alice	40	F	...	G. Brittain	America	Robin Hood	20 Jul 1827
Ralph	43	M	...	G. Brittain	America	Robin Hood	20 Jul 1827
BRIBIO, —, Mr.	40	M	Merchant	Spain	U. States	Cadmus	12 Apr 1825
BRICE, Honora	30		Labourer	Ireland	United States	Geo. Canning	5 Jun 1828
Jame	20		Labourer	St. John	U. States	Lady Hunter	5 Jul 1823
Jane	26	F		Down, Ireland	New York	Anthusa	24 Aug 1825
Jas.	30	M	Weaver	Down, Ireland	New York	Anthusa	24 Aug 1825
John	1 6/12	M		Down, Ireland	New York	Anthusa	24 Aug 1825
John	28	M	Labourer	Ireland	U. States	Josephine	27 Jul 1825

NAMES OF PASSENGERS	AGE	SEX	OCCUPATIONS	COUNTRY TO WHICH THEY BELONG	COUNTRY THEY INTEND TO INHABIT	SHIPS/DATES OF ARRIVAL	
BRICE (cont'd)							
Mary	20		Labourer	Ireland	United States	Geo. Canning	5 Jun 1828
Thomas	2			Ireland	United States	Geo. Canning	5 Jun 1828
BRICEAU, —	27	M	Merchant	Switzerland		Edward Quesnel	13 Mar 1828
BRICENO, D., Dr.	42	M	Doctor	Colombia	U. States	Ocean	8 Jun 1826
BRICHOL, Ann M.	30	F	Farm	Ireland		Quatre Freres	29 Jul 1828
BRICK, Jno.	28	M	Labourer	Ireland	U.S. America	Traveller	10 Sep 1827
Jno.	30	M	Officer	U. States	U. States	Hannah	2 Feb 1822
BRICKETT, Edwin	24	M	Merchant	U. States	U. States	Hesper	16 Jun 1828
BRICKHEAD, —, Mr.	34	M	Merchant	U. States	U. States	Native	29 Apr 1825
BRICKLEY, John	23	M	Labourer	Ireland	United States	General Marion	6 Oct 1828
BRICKSON, James	30	M	Stone cutter	Great Britain	United States	Colossus	5 Jun 1827
BRIDGE, —, Mr.	28	M	Merchant	U. States	U. States	Columbia	7 Sep 1827
Elinor	1 6/12	F	Child	G. Brittan	U. States	Henry	24 Oct 1828
Harriet Shoe	22	F	Servant	G. Brittan	U. States	Henry	24 Oct 1828
J. B.	30	M	Gentleman	G. Britain		Diana	14 Sep 1820
John	23	M	Merchant	U. States	U. States	Echo	22 Apr 1823
John	25	M	Merchant	Germany	U. States	Columbia	22 Sep 1828
Stephen	20	M	Labourer	England	America	Two Marys	24 Sep 1827
BRIDGER, Emma	7	F	family of [Thomas]	U. Kingdom of Great Britain	United States	Cambria	7 May 1828
Harriet	3 4/12	F	family of [Thomas]	U. Kingdom of Great Britain	United States	Cambria	7 May 1828
Hester	1 6/12	F	family of [Thomas]	U. Kingdom of Great Britain	United States	Cambria	7 May 1828
James	13	M	family of [Thomas]	U. Kingdom of Great Britain	United States	Cambria	7 May 1828
James	20					Cincinnatus	29 Apr 1822
Mary	30 1/12	F	family of [Thomas]	U. Kingdom of Great Britain	United States	Cambria	7 May 1828
Mary Ann	5 6/12	F	family of [Thomas]	U. Kingdom of Great Britain	United States	Cambria	7 May 1828
Miriam	9	F	family of [Thomas]	U. Kingdom of Great Britain	United States	Cambria	7 May 1828
Philadelphia	11	F	family of [Thomas]	U. Kingdom of Great Britain	United States of Amer.	Cambria	7 May 1828
Thomas	34	M	Farmer	U. Kingdom of Great Britain	United States	Cambria	7 May 1828
BRIDGERS, Henry	21	M	Letter Cutter	Great Britain	U. States	Robert Fulton	3 Dec 1827
BRIDGES, Jas.	20	M	Farmer	Great Britian	United States	Columbia	17 Apr 1827
John	21	M	Joiner	England	America	Britannia	22 Jul 1829
Richard	15			New York	America	Rockingham	23 Aug 1822
Thomas	48		Painter	Milford	America	Rockingham	23 Aug 1822
BRIDGET, Henry	36	M	Tailor	England	America	Plutarch	18 Jul 1826
Thomas	22	M	Weaver	Ireland	United States	Borneo	2 Oct 1827
BRIDGEWOOD, Dan	55	M	Shoemaker			Lady of the Lake	23 Aug 1828
Dan, Jr.	20	M	Shoemaker			Lady of the Lake	23 Aug 1828
BRIDGLAND, James	12		None	England	England	Hudson	18 Jun 1825
William	18	M	Labourer	England	United States	Jubilee	12 May 1828
BRIDGMAN, Andrew H.	32		Mariner	London	England	London	13 Dec 1822
Susanna	24			New York	United States	London	13 Dec 1822
BRIDSON, Anne	17	F		L...n	United States	Java	9 Jul 1827
Caesar	6	M		L...n	United States	Java	9 Jul 1827
Jane	28	F	Farmer	L...n	United States	Java	9 Jul 1827
Thos.	39	M		L...n	United States	Java	9 Jul 1827
BRIEN, Catherine	25	F	Wife	Ireland	United States	Dublin Packet	23 May 1828
Denis	60	M	Labourer	Ireland	United States	Pallas	28 Oct 1828
Denis, Jr.	35	M	Labourer	Ireland	United States	Pallas	28 Oct 1828
James	30	M	Farmer	Ireland	United States	Dublin Packet	23 May 1828
Jane	25	F		Ireland	New York	Curler	7 Jul 1827
Johanna	20	F		Ireland	United States	Pallas	28 Oct 1828
John	25	M	Labourer	Ireland	New York	Curler	7 Jul 1827
BRIER, Eliza	5	F		Ireland	U. States	Cincinnatus	5 Oct 1824
M. F., Mrs.	25	F		Ireland	U. States	Cincinnatus	5 Oct 1824
Mary	21	F	None	Great Britain	United States	Aurora	5 Sep 1826
BRIERE, Marg.	16			Great Britain	U. States	Columbia	7 May 1828
BRIERLY, Ann	18	F	None	England	United States	Trident	18 Jul 1827

NAMES OF PASSENGERS	AGE	SEX	OCCUPATIONS	COUNTRY TO WHICH THEY BELONG	COUNTRY THEY INTEND TO INHABIT	SHIPS/DATES OF ARRIVAL	
BRIERLY (cont'd)							
John	22	M	Weaver	Rockdale, England	United States	Aurelia	7 Jun 1826
Joseph	21	M	Weaver	England	United States	Trident	18 Jul 1827
BRIERTZ, Alfred	8 2/12	M		Great Britain	United States	Samuel Wright	12 Oct 1829
Edward	12	M		Great Britain	United States	Samuel Wright	12 Oct 1829
Gideon	10	M		Great Britain	United States	Samuel Wright	12 Oct 1829
Jacob	24	F		Great Britain	United States	Samuel Wright	12 Oct 1829
Joseph	22	M	Cordmaker	Great Britain	United States	Samuel Wright	12 Oct 1829
Mary	8	F		Great Britain	United States	Samuel Wright	12 Oct 1829
BRIEVLEY, Benjamin	16	M		Great Britain	United States	Birmingham	15 Jun 1827
Esther	11	F		Great Britain	United States	Birmingham	15 Jun 1827
John	7	M		Great Britain	United States	Birmingham	15 Jun 1827
Lucy	14	F		Great Britain	United States	Birmingham	15 Jun 1827
BRIGG, George, Mr.	45	M	Farmer	England		Hercules	19 Jun 1821
John	8	M	Farmer	Great Brittan	U.S.	Emulous	29 Jun 1827
John	46					William	17 Aug 1820
Ths.	40	M	Farmer	Great Brittan	U.S.	Emulous	29 Jun 1827
George	20		Calico Printer	Kamsbottom	England	Great Britain	7 May 1827
BRIGGS, Ann	9	F		England	America	John Adams	2 Aug 1827
Anne	12	F	Child	Ireland	U.S. of America	Meteor	19 Mar 1828
Charles	5	M		England	America	John Adams	2 Aug 1827
Charles	28	M	Merchant	Gt. Britain	U. States	Panthia	13 Nov 1824
Chas.	30	M	Merchant	England	America	Silas Richard	24 Oct 1829
Chas.	40	M	Labourer	Yorkshire		Ocean	13 Jul 1827
Chs. [crossed out]	38	M	Merchant	England	U. States	New York	4 Nov 1824
Clement			Distressed Seaman			Boston	28 Aug 1821
E.	24	F				Hibernia	15 Aug 1820
Edward	72	M	Merchant	England	America	Silas Richard	24 Oct 1829
Eliza	9	F	Child	Ireland	U.S. of America	Meteor	19 Mar 1828
Fanny	78	F	Spinster	Ireland	U.S. of America	Meteor	19 Mar 1828
Francis	2	M		England	America	John Adams	2 Aug 1827
Francis	22	M	Getl.	England	U. States	Camillus	27 Jul 1825
H.	16	M	None	England	United States	Enterprize	19 Oct 1826
J.	22	M	None	England	United States	Enterprize	19 Oct 1826
Jas.	19	M	Butcher	England	America	John Adams	2 Aug 1827
Jessie	3	F		Ireland	United States	Louisa	7 Oct 1824
John	5	M	Child	Ireland	U.S. of America	Meteor	19 Mar 1828
John	10	M	None	Yorkshire		Ocean	13 Jul 1827
John	23	M	Weaver	Ireland	United States	Siroc	31 Oct 1829
Joseph	44	M	Joiner	England		Britannia	20 Jun 1827
Josiah	7	M	Child	Ireland	U.S. of America	Meteor	19 Mar 1828
Josiah	40	M	Farmer	Ireland	U.S. of America	Meteor	19 Mar 1828
Margaret	30	F		Ireland	United States	Louisa	7 Oct 1824
Mary	5	F	None	Yorkshire		Ocean	13 Jul 1827
Mary	7	F		England	America	John Adams	2 Aug 1827
Mary	33	F	Joiner	England		Britannia	20 Jun 1827
Mary	40	F	Wife	Ireland	U.S. of America	Meteor	19 Mar 1828
Robert	3	M	Child	Ireland	U.S. of America	Meteor	19 Mar 1828
Sally	45	F	None	Yorkshire		Ocean	13 Jul 1827
Sarah	16	F		England	America	John Adams	2 Aug 1827
Sarah	40	F		England	America	John Adams	2 Aug 1827
Thomas	9	M		Yorkshire	Pittsburg	Curler	7 Jul 1827
Thomas	23		Carver	England	United States	Thomas Dickason	5 Jun 1827
Thomas	31	M	Laborer	England	New York	Indian Chief	19 Jun 1823
W.	4	F				Hibernia	15 Aug 1820
William	10	M	Joiner	England		Britannia	20 Jun 1827
William	11	M		England	America	John Adams	2 Aug 1827
William	14	M		Ireland	U.S. of America	Meteor	19 Mar 1828
William	33	M	Farmer	Yorkshire	Pittsburg	Curler	7 Jul 1827
Wm.	30	M	Farmer	Ireland	United States	Siroc	31 Oct 1829
BRIGGY, Cathr.	20	F	Farmer	Ireland	U. States	Perserverance	21 Jul 1827
BRIGHAM, Robert W.	19	M	Farmer	England	Albany	Indian Chief	19 Jun 1823
Sabers	22	M	Druggist	Scotland	United States	Delta	24 Oct 1829
BRIGHT, Henry W.	19	M	Goldsmith	England	United States	Siroc	31 Oct 1829
BRILE..., Sarah	4	F		Great Britain	United States	John Jay	8 May 1828
BRILL, Ann	6	F	...	Ireland	United States	Wilson	22 Jun 1824
Margaret	4	F	...	Ireland	United States	Wilson	22 Jun 1824

NAMES OF PASSENGERS	AGE	SEX	OCCUPATIONS	COUNTRY TO WHICH THEY BELONG	COUNTRY THEY INTEND TO INHABIT	SHIPS/DATES OF ARRIVAL	
BRILL (cont'd)							
Sarah	1 6/12	F	...	Ireland	United States	Wilson	22 Jun 1824
BRIM, Alphonse	22	M	Gent	French	U. States	Charlemagne	19 Sep 1828
John	22	M	Labourer	Ireland	U. States	Combine	30 Nov 1825
BRIMLEY, Judy	28	F		Ireland	United States	Thompson	12 Sep 1827
Pat	40	M		Ireland	United States	Thompson	12 Sep 1827
BRIMNER, Betsey	40	F	Lady	Saint John, N.B.	Saint John, N.B.	Sarah G.	28 Nov 1827
Mary	17	F	Lady	Saint John, N.B.	Saint John, N.B.	Sarah G.	28 Nov 1827
BRIN, Edwd.	26	M	Labourer	England	United States	Margarett Scott	22 Aug 1827
BRINE, James	16	M			U. States	Greyhound	19 Aug 1820
BRINEN, Andrew	22	M	Farmer	Gt. Britan	America	Braganza	1 Dec 1824
Catherin	19	F	None	Gt. Britan	America	Braganza	1 Dec 1824
Mary	4/12	F	None	Gt. Britan	America	Braganza	1 Dec 1824
BRINER, —	17	F	None	Newfoundland	U. States	Mariner	11 Jul 1823
Margaret	26	F	Servant	France	U. States	Sully	15 Jul 1829
Mary	25	F	None	Newfoundland	U. States	Mariner	11 Jul 1823
Patrick	25	M	None	Newfoundland	U. States	Mariner	11 Jul 1823
BRINGEON,							
Emanuel	43 7/12	M	Merchant	France	Traveler	Cadmus	12 Dec 1823
BRINICK, Barbara	7	F		France	United States	Stephania	6 Dec 1827
Cath.	41	F		France	United States	Stephania	6 Dec 1827
Christian	10	M		France	United States	Stephania	6 Dec 1827
Henri	43	M	Cooper	France	United States	Stephania	6 Dec 1827
BRINKMAN, John	34	M	Farmer	Ireland	America	Wilson	16 May 1825
Margaret	28	F	Matron	Ireland	America	Wilson	16 May 1825
BRINLEY, Abby M.	22	F		America	America	Splendid	23 Mar 1829
Allcoffe	6/12	F		Columbia	America	Splendid	23 Mar 1829
Edward	6	M	Merchant	U. States	Laguira	Gertrude	16 May 1827
Francis A.	28	M	Merchant	America	America	Splendid	23 Mar 1829
Frs. W.	26	M	Merchant	New Jersey	U. States	Charleston	23 Oct 1825
Harriet	3	F		America	America	Splendid	23 Mar 1829
BRINLY, Janette	6	F	Servant	America	America	Splendid	23 Mar 1829
BRINNEFOUX, G. L.	37	M	Merchant	U. States	U. States	Edward Quesnel	16 Nov 1827
BRINNER, Andrew	26	M	Labourer	Ireland	U.S.	Lady Hunter	10 Jul 1826
BRINO, N. V. A.	17		Servant	Spain	Cuba	Draper	17 Dec 1823
R.	25	M	Mercht	Colombia	Colombia	Mary Jane	21 Dec 1825
BRINOBY, —, Mr.	31	M	Gentleman	Great Britain	U.S.	Robert Edwards	11 Nov 1822
BRINSDELL, John	22	M	Tailor	England	U.S. America	Ganges	15 Dec 1826
BRINTNALE, Charles	17			Denbey	England	Great Britain	7 May 1827
Paul	12			Denbey	England	Great Britain	7 May 1827
Sophia	22			Denbey	England	Great Britain	7 May 1827
BRINTNEL, Eliza	26			Denbey	England	Great Britain	7 May 1827
BRINTNELL, Amos	23		Farmer	Denbey	England	Great Britain	7 May 1827
Matilda	21			Denbey	England	Great Britain	7 May 1827
Paul	56		Farmer	Denbey	England	Great Britain	7 May 1827
Sarah	55			Denbey	England	Great Britain	7 May 1827
BRINTON, George	30	M	Labourer	Ireland	U. States	Lady Hunter	9 Oct 1825
BRION, Danl.	23			Ireland	United States	Geo. Canning	5 Jun 1828
BRIPTON, Thomas	21	M	Copper Smith	England	U.S.	Acasta	11 May 1827
BRISBANE, Abbot	23	M	Army U.S.A.	U.S.A.	U. States	Silas Richard	30 Jun 1828
Wm.	19	M	Gentleman	U.S.A.	U. States	Silas Richard	30 Jun 1828
BRISBOIS, Ansel	24	M	Farmer	Alsace in the Department of Upper and lower Rhine	Carolina	Augusta	16 May 1828
BRISE, Conly	25	M	Servant	Ireland	U. States	Henrietta	7 Jul 1825
BRISK, Pat	7	M		G. Britain	U. States	Dalhouse Castle	12 Sep 1828
BRISSELAU, T.	19	M	Merchant	Germany	United States	Plato	25 Aug 1829
BRISSOL, Anney	25		Seamstress	St. John	U. States	Lady Hunter	5 Jul 1823
BRISSON, Isabella	4/12	F	None	England	U.S.A.	Lima	6 Dec 1826
James	2	M	None	England	U.S.A.	Lima	6 Dec 1826
John	5	M	None	England	U.S.A.	Lima	6 Dec 1826
John	28	M	Farmer	England	U.S.A.	Lima	6 Dec 1826
Martha	27	F	None	England	U.S.A.	Lima	6 Dec 1826
Matilda	6	F	None	England	U.S.A.	Lima	6 Dec 1826
BRISTED, J.	43	M		Great Britain	United States	James Monroe	25 Apr 1822
BRISTEND, Ann	18	F	Labourer	Ireland	United States	Hope	12 Jun 1828
BRIT, James	25		Farmer	Ireland		Nancy	11 Sep 1820
P.	35	M	Merchant	U. States	U. States	Dover	17 Aug 1821

NAMES OF PASSENGERS	AGE	SEX	OCCUPATIONS	COUNTRY TO WHICH THEY BELONG	COUNTRY THEY INTEND TO INHABIT	SHIPS/DATES OF ARRIVAL	
BRITENBUCHER, Adam	28	M	Butcher	Native of Switzerland	United States	Canaris	30 Jun 1827
BRITON, James	27	M	Shoemaker	Manchester, England	Gt. Britain	Orozimbo	19 Oct 1822
BRITONNIERE, Auguste	17	M		France	United States	Montano	5 May 1828
Auguste	42	M	Baker	France	United States	Montano	5 May 1828
Elisa	3	F		United States	United States	Montano	5 May 1828
Jeanne	40	F		France	United States	Montano	5 May 1828
Josephine	15	F		France	United States	Montano	5 May 1828
BRITTAIN, Elizabeth	30	F		Ireland	U. States	Nancy	16 Aug 1822
BRITTEN, Elizabeth	39	F	Servant	Irereland	America	Carolina Ann	20 Jun 1825
BRITTIN, John	28	M	Cloth dresser	England	United States	Maria	12 May 1823
Sarah	26	F		England	United States	Maria	12 May 1823
BRITTLE, John	28	M	Pastry Cook	England	Albany	Stephania	13 Mar 1820
BRITTON, Andrew	34	M	Mercht.	Ireland	United States	Nestor	25 Jul 1823
Henry	15	M		England	United States	Aurora	9 Jul 1827
John	21	M	Carpenter	Ireland	United States	Atlantic	21 Jul 1827
John, Int.	17 6/12	M		Ireland	United States	Atlantic	21 Jul 1827
Joseph	52	M	Carpenter	England	United States	Aurora	9 Jul 1827
Margt.	25 6/12	F	Seamstress	Ireland	United States	Atlantic	21 Jul 1827
Martha	22 6/12	F	Matron	U. States	U. States	Josephine	23 Jan 1829
Martha G.	19	F	Farmer	Farmer	U. States	Wilson	2 Sep 1823
Mary	24	F	...	England	New York	Wilson	10 Apr 1823
Mary Ann	20 3/12	F		Ireland	United States	Atlantic	21 Jul 1827
N. M.	25	M	Merchant	America		Aspasia	19 Jul 1823
William	23	M	Farmer	England	United States	Acosta	28 Jul 1823
William	83	M	Merchant	Rhode Island	U. States	Augustus & John	10 Apr 1823
Wm.	27	M	Merchant	Gt. Britain	United States	Seeds	29 Sep 1824
Wm.	31	M	Officer	St. Johns	U. States	South Carolina	27 May 1823
BRIXTON, Charles C.	22	M	Merchant	United States	United States	Trident	31 Mar 1827
BRIZY, Philip	34 4/12	M	Gentleman	Perugia, Italy	Italy	Hazard	29 Jul 1829
BRO...WN, F...	23	...	...	Scotland	America	Nimrod	9 Jul 1827
BROAD, Jno.	19	M	Farmer	England	U.S. America	Cortes	19 May 1826
BROADBENT, Abraham	25	M	Merchant	U. States	Great Britain	Thompson	26 Apr 1828
Abraham	28	M	Weaver	England	U.N. States	Jane	7 Oct 1826
Abram	24	M	Merchant	England	United States	Cortes	10 Apr 1822
E.	32	M	Stone cutter	England	U.S. States	Splendid	14 Aug 1829
Edward	14	M	Woolen Manufacer.	England	America	Hannibal	28 May 1827
Elizabeth	30	F	None	Great Britain	United States	Colossus	1 Nov 1826
James	32	M	Merchant	Saddleworth, England	New York	New York	31 Jul 1829
James	42	M	Clothier	Great Britain	United States	Colossus	1 Nov 1826
Jas.	24	M	Merchant	Gt. Britain	U. States	Leeds	16 Apr 1825
John	22	M	Merchant	England	America	Hannibal	4 Oct 1822
John	23		Farmer	England	United States	Hugh Johnson	11 Jun 1828
John	48	M	Clothier	Great Britain	United States	Colossus	1 Nov 1826
Joseph	23	M	Woollen Manufacturer	Yorkshire	New York	New York	31 Jul 1829
Joseph	46	M	Clothier	Great Britain	United States	Colossus	1 Nov 1826
Mary	49	F	None	Great Britain	United States	Colossus	1 Nov 1826
Stephen	24	M	Gardner	Wakefield	United States	Dalhousie Castle	27 Jul 1826
Thomas	36	M	...	...	...	Meteor	16 Aug 1824
Timothy	28	M	Clothier	Great Britain	United States	Colossus	1 Nov 1826
William	30	M	Merchant	England	United States	Concordia	25 Aug 1827
BROADFIELD, Robt.	19	M	Tailor	England	United States	Acasta	14 Jun 1824
Willm.	45	M	Tailor	England	United States	Acasta	14 Jun 1824
Wm.	45	M	Tailor	England	U.S. America	Cortes	19 May 1826
BROADFOOT, William	44	M	Labourer	Scotland	United States	Samuel Robertson	9 May 1827
Willm.	44	M	Merchant	Great Britain	U.S. of America	Canada	1 Oct 1827
BROADFORT, —, Mr.	38	M	Merchant	United States	United States	Cortes	11 Dec 1822
BROADHEAD, Hannah	27	F	None	England	United States	Hamilton	13 Nov 1827
Jabez		M	None	England	United States	Hamilton	13 Nov 1827
John	28	M	Weaver	Great Britan	United States	Hamilton	19 Mar 1827
Mary	6	F	None	England	United States	Hamilton	13 Nov 1827
Mathew	25	F	Farier	Ireland	Ut. States	Courier	13 Jul 1826
Sarah	4	F	None	England	United States	Hamilton	13 Nov 1827

NAMES OF PASSENGERS	AGE	SEX	OCCUPATIONS	COUNTRY TO WHICH THEY BELONG	COUNTRY THEY INTEND TO INHABIT	SHIPS	DATES OF ARRIVAL
BROADHURST,							
John	28 2/12	M	Gentleman	England	England	Leeds	29 May 1824
William	23	M	Joiner	England	United States	Delta	24 Oct 1829
BROADLEY, P.	20		Farmer	Ireland	United States	Courier	16 May 1825
BROADSHAW, Jno.	...	M		...	...	Antioch	8 Oct 1827
BROADY, E.	26	F	Child	Ireland	N. York	Trusty	12 Sep 1828
BROANWY, Jean	6	M		Scotland	U. States	Superior	25 Sep 1828
BROAR, John	32	M		Great Britain	United States	Active	25 Mar 1828
BROAT, J.	34	M	Mariner	U. States	U. States	Defiance	18 May 1826
BROCK, John	34	M		Great Britain		Corinthian	27 Oct 1829
BROCKLERT, Ann	17	F	None	Great Britain	United States	Atlantic	28 May 1827
BROCKLESLY, Ann	5	F	None	Great Britain	United States	John	6 Oct 1820
Jno., Jr.	8	M	None	Great Britain	United States	John	6 Oct 1820
John	47	M	Farmer	Great Britain	United States	John	6 Oct 1820
Susan	12	F	None	Great Britain	United States	John	6 Oct 1820
BRODBENT, Joseph	26	M	Merchant	Great Britian	U. States	Orbit	29 Apr 1822
Joseph	38	M	Carpenter	Great Britan	United States	Clematis	8 May 1827
BRODBER, W.	23	F	Anything	Swiss	U. States	Edwd. Quesnel	30 Apr 1825
BRODEN, Thos.	24		Labourer	Ireland	United States	Geo. Canning	5 Jun 1828
BRODERICK, Cornelus	21	M	Farmer	Ireland	America	William	21 May 1825
BRODERMANN, Ann	45	F	Lady	Cuba	Cuba	New England	27 Jul 1829
Julius	8	M		Cuba	Cuba	New England	27 Jul 1829
BRODEY, Elizabeth	20	F	Servant	Great Britain	United States	Hanford	9 Oct 1829
BRODGE, B.	17	M	Merchant	U. States		Royal Oak	5 Aug 1820
E.	37	F	Spinster	U. States	U. States	Royal Oak	5 Aug 1820
Mary Ann	19	F	Spinster	Englang		Royal Oak	5 Aug 1820
BRODIE, Charlotte	17	F		Scotland	U. States	Camillus	29 Jan 1829
Elizab., Miss	28	F		Scotland	U.S. of America	Canada	1 Oct 1827
Elizabeth	20	F		Scotland	U. States	Camillus	29 Jan 1829
Francis	22	M	Merchant	Scotland	America	Mentor	21 Sep 1824
Helen	25	F		Britain	U. States	Florida	2 Jun 1828
James	24	M	Slater	Scotland	U. States	Camillus	27 Jun 1826
Janet	15	F		Scotland	U. States	Camillus	29 Jan 1829
BRODISH, John	25	M	Labourer			Andes	16 Sep 1820
BRODLE, Jno.		M		Scotland	U. States	Eliza	23 Dec 1822
BRODNANN, W.	19	M	Clerk	Hayti	Hayti	Robert Reade	13 Jul 1825
BRODRICK, Andw.	25		Victlar	Cork	New York	Schuylkill	22 Aug 1825
Ricd.	36	M	Labourer	Great Britain	United States	Penelope	11 Jun 1827
Thos.	40	M	Labourer	Great Britain	United States	Penelope	11 Jun 1827
BRODSKEN, Catharine	11	F		St. Johns	U. States	Wanderer	30 Oct 1828
BRODY, Hugh						Hero	19 May 1828
M.	25	M	Farmer	Scotland	United States	Indus	5 Sep 1827
BROFFY, Edmund	23	M	Farmer	Great Britain	United States	Eliza Barker	3 Jul 1826
BROGAN, Bridget	19	F	Spinster	Ireland	America	Wilson	16 May 1825
James	25	M	Pedler	U. States	U. States	United States	11 Sep 1828
John	22	M	Labourer	Ireland	America	Wilson	16 May 1825
Mary	27		Spinster	Ireland	United States	Courier	15 Oct 1827
Mathew	30	M	Labourer	Ireland	United States	Josephine	30 Apr 1828
BROGHAN, Patrick	23	M	Farmer	Ireland	United States	Lord Strangford	20 Jun 1826
BROHAM, Thomas	25	M	Blacksmith	G. Britain	U. States	Margaret Bogle	12 Jun 1828
BROIN, Ewd.	22	M	Labourer	Ireland		Robert Fulton	4 Jun 1828
Thos.	22	M	Mariner	U. States	U. States	Florida	25 Apr 1825
BROISER, —, Infant	2/12	F		Wertemburg	America, U.N.S.	Great Britain	3 Aug 1829
Cristiana	3	F		Wertemburg	America, U.N.S.	Great Britain	3 Aug 1829
Elisabeth	36	F		Wertemburg	America, U.N.S.	Great Britain	3 Aug 1829
Elizabeth	2	F		Wertemburg	America, U.N.S.	Great Britain	3 Aug 1829
Jaques	38	M	Carpenter	Wertemburg	America, U.N.S.	Great Britain	3 Aug 1829
Margarita	8 6/12	F		Wertemburg	America, U.N.S.	Great Britain	3 Aug 1829
BROLLY, James	35	M	Farmer	Scotland	United States	Curler	3 Mar 1828
BROMBERGEN, Johann	24		Tailor	Poland	New York	Europa	27 Dec 1827
BROMERICH, Isabella	12	F	None	England	United States	Mary & Harriet	9 Mar 1829
Lucy	3	F	None	England	United States	Mary & Harriet	9 Mar 1829
Lucy	57	F	None	England	United States	Mary & Harriet	9 Mar 1829
BROMKE, Honora	28	M	Laborer	Ireland	America	Parrington	9 Jun 1827
Margaret	26	F	Laborer	Ireland	America	Parrington	9 Jun 1827
Michael	30	M	Laborer	Ireland	America	Parrington	9 Jun 1827
BROMLEY, John	18	M	Blacksmith	Great Britain	United States	Thomas Dickason	31 Jul 1829
BROMONT, T.	30	M	Merchant	France	France	Medina	23 Apr 1828

135

NAMES OF PASSENGERS	AGE	SEX	OCCUPATIONS	COUNTRY TO WHICH THEY BELONG	COUNTRY THEY INTEND TO INHABIT	SHIPS/DATES OF ARRIVAL	
BRON, Catherine	62	F		France	France	Edward Quesnel	3 Jul 1829
Genevieve	23	F		France	France	Edward Quesnel	3 Jul 1829
John	30	M	Farmer	France	France	Edward Quesnel	3 Jul 1829
BRONAY, Rose Ann	21	M	Labourer	Ireland	United States	Hope	12 Jun 1828
BRONLY, W.	14	M	Servant	Denmark	America	Jupiter	8 Apr 1828
BRONNER, Barbara	4	F		France	United States	New England	29 Aug 1828
Christian	0 3/12	F		France	United States	New England	29 Aug 1828
Eliza	6	F		France	United States	New England	29 Aug 1828
Geo. Jacob	8	M		France	United States	New England	29 Aug 1828
Geo. Jacob	40	M	Weaver	France	United States	New England	29 Aug 1828
Jacob	65	M		France	United States	New England	29 Aug 1828
Jean	25	M	Servant	Guadeloupe	New York	Notre Dame	6 Oct 1827
Louiza	3	F		France	United States	New England	29 Aug 1828
Magdalena	14	F		France	United States	New England	29 Aug 1828
Maria Eliza	38	F		France	United States	New England	29 Aug 1828
Sophia	13	F		France	United States	New England	29 Aug 1828
T. J.	6	M		France	United States	New England	29 Aug 1828
BRONSON, Charles	32	M	Carpenter	United States		Mentor	23 May 1821
Reuben	24	M	Mason	United States	U. States	Planter	1 Mar 1822
BROODLY, Saml.	18	M	Clothier	Great Britain	United States	Samuel Wright	12 Oct 1829
William	16	M	Clothier	Great Britain	United States	Samuel Wright	12 Oct 1829
BROOK, Abel	24	M	Weaver	England	United States	Aurora	9 Jul 1827
Ann	47	F		England	New York	Corinthian	5 May 1827
Betsey	23	F		G. Britain	U.S.A.	Silas Richards	29 Oct 1827
Charles	17	M		G. Britain	U.S.A.	Silas Richards	29 Oct 1827
David	4	M				Hercules	25 Sep 1820
Elizabeth	32	F				Hercules	25 Sep 1820
George	11	M				Hercules	25 Sep 1820
Hannah	4	F		G. Britain	U.S.A.	Silas Richards	29 Oct 1827
Hannah	6	F				Hercules	25 Sep 1820
Jacob	26	M	Baker	Switzerland	U. States	Hewes	30 Oct 1829
James	11	M				Hercules	25 Sep 1820
James	23 5/12	M		Ireland	America	Carolina Ann	7 Apr 1826
James	38	M	Weaver			Hercules	25 Sep 1820
Jas.	41		Clothier	Great Britain	United States	Roman	10 Sep 1827
Jean	48	F		G. Britain	U.S.A.	Silas Richards	29 Oct 1827
John	3	M		England	United States	Aurora	9 Jul 1827
John	11	M				Hercules	25 Sep 1820
John	20	M	Clouthier	Ireland	Ut. States	Courier	13 Jul 1826
John	25	M	Paper Maker	Scotland	U. States	Czar	29 Aug 1829
John	50	M	Mechanic	G. Britain	U.S.A.	Silas Richards	29 Oct 1827
Joseph	1	M		England	United States	Aurora	9 Jul 1827
Joseph	13	M				Hercules	25 Sep 1820
Joseph	37	M	Weaver	England	United States	Siroc	31 Oct 1829
Joshua	18	M		G. Britain	U.S.A.	Silas Richards	29 Oct 1827
Martha	9	F				Hercules	25 Sep 1820
Mary	4/12	F				Hercules	25 Sep 1820
Mary	32	F				Hercules	25 Sep 1820
Matthew	12	M				Hercules	25 Sep 1820
Richard	2/12	M				Hercules	25 Sep 1820
Samuel	3	M				Hercules	25 Sep 1820
Samuel	10	M				Hercules	25 Sep 1820
Samuel	34	M	Weaver			Hercules	25 Sep 1820
Sarah	8	F				Hercules	25 Sep 1820
Sarah	22	F		England	United States	Aurora	9 Jul 1827
Teresa	20	F		G. Britain	U.S.A.	Silas Richards	29 Oct 1827
Thomas	40	M	Weaver	England	New York	Corinthian	5 May 1827
Walton	8	M				Hercules	25 Sep 1820
William	10	M				Hercules	25 Sep 1820
BROOKE, Charles J.	35	M	Merchant	U. States	Aux Caoyes	Venus	9 Sep 1820
Edmund	27	M	Merchant	Great Britain	U. States	Birmingham	12 Oct 1829
Thomas	27 11/12	M	Wheelright	Great Briton	United States	Mount Vernon	30 Dec 1828
BROOKES, Frances, Mrs.	28	F	Tailoress	England	U. States	Acasta	21 Oct 1825
John	30		Tailor	England	England	Hudson	4 Sep 1823
BROOKINS, Samuel	24	M	Blacksmith	Ireland	U. States	Lady Hunter	8 Aug 1826
BROOKMIN, Willm.	25	M	Printer	Ireland	America	Josephine	8 Dec 1827
BROOKS, —, Miss	10	F	None	England	U. States	Don Quixotte	27 Jun 1827

NAMES OF PASSENGERS	AGE	SEX	OCCUPATIONS	COUNTRY TO WHICH THEY BELONG	COUNTRY THEY INTEND TO INHABIT	SHIPS/DATES OF ARRIVAL	
BROOKS (cont'd)							
Alfred	21		Merchant	Midford	United States	William Thompson	13 May 1823
Alfred	21	M	Merchant	United States	United States	John Wells	22 May 1826
Alfred	26	M	Merchant	America	America	Britannia	5 Nov 1828
Ann	39	F		England		Anacreon	7 Sep 1827
Ann	43	F		England	New York	James Monroe	23 Aug 1822
Ann, Mrs.	38			Dedford/ Seddlescomb	Louis...	Venus	12 Apr 1821
Anna	9			Dedford/ Seddlescomb	Louis...	Venus	12 Apr 1821
Bess	4	F	Labourer	England	U. States	Ayrshire	12 May 1828
Bess	22	F	Labourer	Great Britain	U. States	Ayrshire	12 May 1828
Biddy	1	F	None	Great Brittan	U. States	Gem	26 Jul 1827
Cash	13	F	Labourer	England	U. States	Ayrshire	12 May 1828
Catherine	4			Dedford/ Seddlescomb	Louis...	Venus	12 Apr 1821
Charles	6			Dedford/ Seddlescomb	Louis...	Venus	12 Apr 1821
Charles J.	40	M	Merchant	United States	United States	Diana	1 May 1821
Chas., Mr.	37		Miller	Seddlescomb/ Seddlescomb	Louis...	Venus	12 Apr 1821
Daniel	27	M		England		Anacreon	7 Sep 1827
Ellen	16	F	Labourer	England	U. States	Ayrshire	12 May 1828
Frances Eliza	25			England	England	Hudson	4 Sep 1823
G.	30	M	Merchant	U. States	U. States	Bayard	25 Apr 1828
George	12	M	Labourer	England	U. States	Ayrshire	12 May 1828
Hannah	25	F		England	U. States	Amity	23 Sep 1823
Henry	2			Dedford/ Seddlescomb	Louis...	Venus	12 Apr 1821
Henry	22	M	Mercht.	U. States	U. States	William Thompson	19 Jan 1829
Horatio	20	M	Merchant	America	America	Soto	11 Nov 1828
James	6	M	Labourer	England	U. States	Ayrshire	12 May 1828
James	7		Farmer	Ireland	United States	Carolina Ann	12 Sep 1823
James	22	M	Machine Maker	Great Britain	United States	Roman	10 May 1828
Jane	30	F	Miliner	Great Britain	U. States	Fontine	4 Oct 1824
Jno.	30	M	Farmer	Great Brittan	U. States	Gem	26 Jul 1827
Jno., Mr.	35		Stationer	England	U.S. of America	Mary	21 Sep 1821
John	9		Farmer	Ireland	United States	Carolina Ann	12 Sep 1823
John	25	M	Labourer	England	U. States	Ayrshire	12 May 1828
John	37	M		England		Anacreon	7 Sep 1827
John	45	M	Merchant	London		New York	31 Jul 1829
Jonas	20	M		Ireland	U. States	Fame	15 Nov 1826
Joseph	45	M	Farmer	England	U.N. States	William Byrnes	13 Aug 1829
Lydia	25	F		England	U. States	Venus	4 Oct 1824
Marg.	46	F	Labourer	England	U. States	Ayrshire	12 May 1828
Mary	18	F	Labourer	England	U. States	Ayrshire	12 May 1828
Mary	26	F		England		Anacreon	7 Sep 1827
Mary	40		Farmer	Ireland	United States	Carolina Ann	12 Sep 1823
Oliver	27	M		U. States	U. States	Ambuscade	1 Jul 1820
Pat	17	M	Labourer	England	U. States	Ayrshire	12 May 1828
Peggy	5	F	None	Great Brittan	U. States	Gem	26 Jul 1827
Peggy	28	F	None	Great Brittan	U. States	Gem	26 Jul 1827
Peter	25	M	Labourer	Great Britain	U. States	Ayrshire	12 May 1828
Robert	4		Farmer	Ireland	United States	Carolina Ann	12 Sep 1823
Robert	10	M		England		Anacreon	7 Sep 1827
Robert	45		Farmer	Ireland	United States	Carolina Ann	12 Sep 1823
Robert S.	22 7/12	M	...	U.S. America	U.S. America	Edward	28 Oct 1825
Robt.	30	M	Military	England	England	Mary Hobin	29 May 1826
Saml.	27	M	Farmer	G. Britain	U. States	London	23 Sep 1828
Sophia	7			Dedford/ Seddlescomb	Louis...	Venus	12 Apr 1821
Thomas	19	M	Clerk	England	U. States	Louisa Matilda	9 Jun 1823
Thomas	30	M	Merchant	St. Iago de Cuba	Cuba	Eugenie	2 Oct 1829
William	3/12		Farmer	Ireland	United States	Carolina Ann	12 Sep 1823
Wm.	31			Great Britan	United States	Newry	11 Jul 1827
Wm. Walhook	12			Dedford/ Seddlescomb	Louis...	Venus	12 Apr 1821

NAMES OF PASSENGERS	A G E	S E X	OCCUPATIONS	COUNTRY TO WHICH THEY BELONG	COUNTRY THEY INTEND TO INHABIT	SHIPS/DATES OF ARRIVAL	
BROOKSBAUK, Robert	45	M	Farmer	Great Britain	United States	Florida	10 Dec 1823
BROOM, Alexander	2	M	None	Ireland	United States	Lord Wellington	28 May 1827
Benjn.	36	M	Black Smith	England	U.S.	Pacific	24 Oct 1828
Charles	26	M	Joiner	Great Britain	U. States	United States	8 Sep 1827
Elizabeth	42	F	...o...trade	Great Britain	United States	India	5 Sep 1827
James	58	M	Labourer	Glasgow, Barony, [Parish], Lanark [County]	New York	Hero	19 May 1828
*to look for Employment							
John	42	M	Labourer	Ireland	United States	Lord Wellington	28 May 1827
Mary	40	F	None	Ireland	United States	Lord Wellington	28 May 1827
Thos.	43	F		Great Britain	United States	India	5 Sep 1827
William	19	M	Farmer	England	Philadelphia	Indian Chief	19 Jun 1823
BROOMLE, James	45	M	Labourer	Bristol	U. States	Latona	7 Jul 1827
BROOZEY, Peter	23		Sugar Baker	Germany	U.S. of America	Mary	21 Sep 1821
BROPHEY, W.	45	M	Labourer	Ireland	U. States	Hope & Esther	27 Sep 1824
BROPHY, A.	19	M	Mechanic	Ireland	United States	Wm. Byrnes	30 Apr 1828
Catharine	38	F		Ireland	United States	Wm. Byrnes	30 Apr 1828
Catharine, Jr.	18	F		Ireland	United States	Wm. Byrnes	30 Apr 1828
Elisa.	1	F				Eliza Grant	6 Oct 1828
James	25	M				Eliza Grant	6 Oct 1828
John	1...	M	...	Ireland	United States	Wilson	22 Jun 1824
John	16	M	Mechanic	Ireland	United States	Wm. Byrnes	30 Apr 1828
Margaret	13	F		Ireland	United States	Wm. Byrnes	30 Apr 1828
Mary	8	F				Eliza Grant	6 Oct 1828
Mary	23	F		England		Eliza Grant	6 Oct 1828
Thomas	15	M	Mechanic	Ireland	United States	Wm. Byrnes	30 Apr 1828
BROSE, Fredk. Wm.	21	M	Engraver	Bremen	United States	Howard	6 Jul 1829
BROSS, S.	83	M	Farmer	Holland	U. States	Don Quixote	25 Oct 1828
BROSSARD, Augustin	27		Weaver	Switzerand	U. States	Parachute	14 May 1828
Francois	31		Baker	Switzerand	U. States	Parachute	14 May 1828
BROSSAT, Joseph	47	M	Distilor	Native of Vigil	New York	Superior	11 Oct 1828
Mary	42	F	Distilor	Native of Bourdoir	New York	Superior	11 Oct 1828
BROT, Jos. Y. D.	21	M	Marriner	Netherlands	Netherlands	Hippomenes	9 Jun 1821
BROTHER, T.	20	M	Clothier	Ireland	U. States	Wanderer	30 Sep 1828
BROTHWELL, Abraham	43	M	Farmer	England	New York	Governor Fenner	23 Jul 1829
Ann	51	F				Governor Fenner	23 Jul 1829
David	8	M				Governor Fenner	23 Jul 1829
BROUCARD, —, Miss	21	F	Lady	Aux Cayes	Aux Cayes	Curlew	3 Nov 1823
—, Mr.	65	M	Gentleman	France	Aux Cayes	Curlew	3 Nov 1823
BROUCE, Charles	18	M	Servant	Gt. Britian	United States	Nestor	16 Aug 1824
BROUDFOOT, William	29	M	Merchant	York, U. Canada	York, U. Canada	New York	14 Jul 1827
BROUDWAY, Cornelius	68	M	Farmer	England	U. States	Seine	10 Jun 1822
BROUGART, — Miss	25	F	None	Switzerland	Switzerland	Nestor	3 Nov 1820
BROUGHAN, Jno.	35	M	Weaver	England	U.S. America	Traveller	10 Sep 1827
BROUGHTON, Ann	40	F				Governor Fenner	23 Jul 1829
Ebenezer	18/12	M				Governor Fenner	23 Jul 1829
Job	4	M				Governor Fenner	23 Jul 1829
Job	37	M	Farmer	England	Ohio	Governor Fenner	23 Jul 1829
John	16	M				Governor Fenner	23 Jul 1829
John	21	M	Servant	London	G. Brittain	William Thompson	6 Sep 1822
Joshua	9	M				Governor Fenner	23 Jul 1829
Sarah	6	F				Governor Fenner	23 Jul 1829
William	14	M				Governor Fenner	23 Jul 1829
BROULLAND, G.	28	M	Mechanic	France	U. States	Bayard	25 Apr 1828
BROUTT, Chs.	47	M	Merchant	United States	United States	Weser	21 Oct 1823
BROW, Thomas	30			England	U. States	Corinthian	8 Oct 1828
BROWBEND, Laurence	30	M	Labourer	Great Britain	United States	Atlantic	28 May 1827
BROWER, Cuffy	46	M	Servant			Superior	27 Jun 1825
Jerm. W.	31	M	Mariner	U. States	U. States	Dart	5 Apr 1822
Jerome J.	21	M	Merchant	Robbnedon	United States	Champion	3 Nov 1827
Peter	25			England	U. States	Corinthian	8 Oct 1828
BROWING, Justus	26	M	Merchant	U. States	U. States	Elisa	1 May 1821
BROWLOW, John	21	M	Merchant	Bermuda	Bermuda	Samuel	23 Aug 1824
BROWN, —	58	M	Farmer	Ireland	U. States	Hazard	27 Aug 1821
—, Mr.			Merchant	England	England	Henrietta	18 Aug 1829

NAMES OF PASSENGERS	AGE	SEX	OCCUPATIONS	COUNTRY TO WHICH THEY BELONG	COUNTRY THEY INTEND TO INHABIT	SHIPS/DATES OF ARRIVAL	
BROWN (cont'd)							
—, Mr.	34	M	Mariner	Baltimore	U. States	Cornelia	16 Feb 1824
—, Mrs.		F		U. States	U. States	Indies	19 May 1823
—, Mrs.	20	F		Scotland	U.S.	Curler	19 Jul 1828
—, Mrs.	25	F		Nassau, N.P.	Nassau, N.P.	Superior	27 Jun 1825
—, Mrs.	30			U.S.	Philada.	Little William	14 Jun 1823
—, Mrs.	38	F	Wife	United States	United States	Bayard	13 Nov 1823
—, Mrs.	38	F		Scotland	New York	Joseph Hume	26 Oct 1829
...	12	F	Farmer			Manhattan	25 Dec 1820
... B.	25	M	Lawyer	N. York	U. States	Edward Quesnel	3 Sep 1826
...n	4	M		England	United States	Danube	22 Aug 1825
...y	13	M		England	United States	Danube	22 Aug 1825
Adaline	11	F		Nassau, N.P.	Nassau, N.P.	Superior	27 Jun 1825
Adelaide	21	F	None	England	New York	Brighton	16 Nov 1826
Adeline	9	F	Daughter	United States	United States	Bayard	13 Nov 1823
Adolphe	22	M	Bookseller	France	New York	Sully	4 Mar 1828
Adolphus	24	M	Farmer	United States	State of New York	Loire	3 Dec 1821
Adolphus	29	M	Labourer	America	U. States	Ice Plant	18 Dec 1820
Agnes	8	F		Scotland	New York	Joseph Hume	26 Oct 1829
Alex	48	M	Gentleman	Great Britain	United States	Mount Vernon	20 May 1822
Alexander	24	M	Tailor	Great Britain	United States	Rosina	28 May 1827
Alexr.	15	M	Servant	United States	United States	Thetis	28 Jun 1824
Alexr.	50	M	Farmer	Ireland	U. States	Alexander	28 Jul 1821
Amelia	12	F	Farmer			Helicon	3 Aug 1826
Andrew	11	M		Scotland	U.S.	Curler	19 Jul 1828
Andrew	28	M	Merchant	Great Britain	New York, U.S.	Florida	2 Oct 1828
Ann	1	F	None	Great Britain	United States	Atlantic	28 May 1827
Ann	1	F	Spinner	Great Britain	United States	Grecian	24 Sep 1828
Ann	2	F		Larse	United States	Carolina Ann	11 Jun 1824
Ann	4	F		Great Brittan	U.S.	Florida	17 May 1825
Ann	11	F		England	Albany	Cortes	16 Jul 1827
Ann	12	F	None	Gt. Brittian	Gt. Brittian	Manchester	21 Apr 1827
Ann	18	F		Gt. Britain	New York	Leeds	7 Nov 1828
Ann	20	F		Gt. Britain	United States	Silas Richards	20 Jun 1826
Ann	20	F	None	Ireland	U. States	Olive Branch	28 Aug 1828
Ann	21	F	None	Great Britain	United States	Atlantic	28 May 1827
Ann	24	F		Larse	United States	Carolina Ann	11 Jun 1824
Ann	25	F				Belfast	28 Sep 1820
Ann	28	F	Se[r]vant	United States	United States	Sylvester Healy	17 Oct 1825
Ann	32	F		Gt. Britain		Dalhouse Castle	13 May 1828
Ann	40	F		Gt. Britain	United States	Silas Richards	20 Jun 1826
Ann R.	28	F		Great Brittan	U.S.	Florida	17 May 1825
Annabella	6	F	Lady	England	United States	Cambria	8 Oct 1828
Archibald	6	M		Scotland	New York	Joseph Hume	26 Oct 1829
Arthur	5	M	Child	Ireland	U. States	Josephine	7 May 1827
Augusta	6	F	None	G. Britain	United States	Courier	23 Feb 1824
B.	15	F	Farmer	St. Johns	U. States	Isabella	28 Jun 1825
Barbara	6	F		Great Brittan	U.S.	Florida	17 May 1825
Benj.	13	M	U.S. Navy	U. States	U. States	Henry	27 Mar 1820
Benj.	14	M	...	England	U. States	York	10 Dec 1825
Benjn.	19	M	Farmer	Gt. Britain	United States	Silas Richards	20 Jun 1826
Betsey	8	F		Gt. Britain	United States	Columbia	7 Sep 1827
Bridget	28	F	Laborer	Ireland	U. States	Howard	25 Jul 1823
Briget	22	F	Spinster	England	United States	Sarah	31 Oct 1829
C...	11	M	Farmer			Manhattan	25 Dec 1820
Carol	45	F		England	United States	Danube	22 Aug 1825
Caroline	5	F	Daughter	United States	United States	Bayard	13 Nov 1823
Caroline	5	F		England	Albany	Cortes	16 Jul 1827
Caroline	7	M		England	United States	Danube	22 Aug 1825
Catharine	18	F		Ireland	U. States	William Barker	29 Aug 1827
Catharine	26	F		England	United States	Mount Vernon	9 Jun 1823
Catharine	29	F		Scotland	New York	Joseph Hume	26 Oct 1829
Catharine, (his wife) [Thomas]	26	F	Wife	Ireland	United States	Ann Maria	8 Jun 1824
Catherine	26	F	None	Great Britain	United States	Mary & Harriet	3 Jul 1829
Catherine	31	F	Matron	Ireland	U. States	Josephine	7 May 1827
Charles	3	M		United States	State of New York	Loire	3 Dec 1821
Charles	6	M		England	United States	Danube	22 Aug 1825
Charles	23	F	Musician	Gt. Britain	New York	Leeds	7 Nov 1828

139

NAMES OF PASSENGERS	AGE	SEX	OCCUPATIONS	COUNTRY TO WHICH THEY BELONG	COUNTRY THEY INTEND TO INHABIT	SHIPS/DATES OF ARRIVAL	
BROWN (cont'd)							
Charles	25	M	Foun...	Great Britain	United States	Orozimbo	7 Nov 1826
Charles, Mr.	26	M	Gentleman	England	America	Maine	16 Jul 1821
Charlotte	2	F		Great Brittan	U.S.	Florida	17 May 1825
Charlotte	8	F		Gt. Britain	United States	Silas Richards	20 Jun 1826
Chas.	26			England		Anacreon	7 Sep 1827
Chas.	40		Yeoman	England		Corinthian	11 Mar 1829
Chas. W.	30	M	Mariner	S. Buryrat [?]	U. States	Eliza Ann	17 Jul 1824
Chs.	10	M	None	Gt. Brittian	Gt. Brittian	Manchester	21 Apr 1827
Clementine	9/12	F	None	England	New York	Brighton	16 Nov 1826
D.	18	M	Merchant	U. States	U. States	Prudence	11 Jun 1825
D., Rvd.	49	M	Ecklesiastic	United States	United States	Maria Theresa	16 Nov 1820
Daniel	30	M	Farmer	Native of Switzerland	United States	Canaris	30 Jun 1827
Danl.	32	M	Merchant	New York	New York	Douglass	15 Oct 1824
David	2	M		Scotland	New York	Joseph Hume	26 Oct 1829
David	21	M	...	Great Britain	United States	Friends	13 Jun 1825
David	35	M	Mechanic	Great Brittan	U.S.	Florida	17 May 1825
David	40	M	Laborer	Ireland	United States	Mary	1 Jul 1829
David	53	M	Farmer	England	U.S.	Maria Caroline	12 Jul 1820
Dd. J. P.	26	M	Merchant	U. States	U. States	New York	8 Mar 1825
Donison	13	M	Farmer	Great Britain	United States	Ganges	8 Jul 1820
E., Miss	1		Merchant	Scotland		Zamoa	5 Nov 1828
Edmd.	25	M		Ireland		Lady Hunter	12 Apr 1823
Edward	14	M	Farmer			Helicon	3 Aug 1826
Edward	18	M	Laborer	Ireland	United States	St. Michael	21 Aug 1824
Edward	21	M	Student of Med.	Halifax	Philadelphia	Oliver Wolcott	3 Nov 1827
Edward	27	M	Yeoman	England	New York	Hudson	20 Nov 1828
Edward	30	M	Hatter	Manchester	United States	Nile	17 May 1827
Edwd.	24	M	Farmer	Ireland	America	Mary	29 May 1827
Edwd.	45	M	Merchant	Great Britain	United States	Ann Maria	23 Oct 1820
Elen	30	F				Lady of the Lake	23 Aug 1828
Elisabeth	28	F		England	United States	Cosmo	26 Aug 1829
Eliz.	2	F	Publican	England	U.S. States	Splendid	14 Aug 1829
Eliza	1	F	None	Scotland	United States	Orozimbo	11 Aug 1823
Eliza	11	F		Larse	United States	Carolina Ann	11 Jun 1824
Eliza	20	F	dress Maker	Ireland		Robert Fulton	4 Jun 1828
Eliza	24	F	Lady	New York	New York	Eagle	20 Nov 1820
Eliza	30			England		Anacreon	7 Sep 1827
Eliza Charlotte	3 1/2	F	None	England	America	Francis & Henrietta	11 Jul 1823
Elizabeth	2	F		England	Albany	Cortes	16 Jul 1827
Elizabeth	4	F		Native of Switzerland	United States	Canaris	30 Jun 1827
Elizabeth	7	F		England	United States	Danube	22 Aug 1825
Elizabeth	9	F	None	G. Britain	United States	Courier	23 Feb 1824
Elizabeth	23	F	Publican	England	U.S. States	Splendid	14 Aug 1829
Elizabeth	25	F		United States	State of New York	Loire	3 Dec 1821
Elizabeth	27	F	Lady	England	United States	Cambria	8 Oct 1828
Elizabeth	27	F		Scotland	New York	Joseph Hume	26 Oct 1829
Elizabeth	32	F		Native of Switzerland	United States	Canaris	30 Jun 1827
Elizabeth	36	F				Corinthian	11 Mar 1829
Elizabeth	37	F	None	Gt. Britain	United States	Union	9 Jan 1824
Elizabeth	39	F	Farmer	Great Britain	United States	Ganges	8 Jul 1820
Ellen	13	F	None	G. Britain	United States	Courier	23 Feb 1824
Ellen	15	F	Sailor's Child	America	America	Manhattan	12 May 1823
Emelly	14	M	Farmer	Gt. Britain	United States	Silas Richards	20 Jun 1826
Emily	2	F		Gt. Britain	United States	Silas Richards	20 Jun 1826
Emily Catherine	2	F	None	England	America	Francis & Henrietta	11 Jul 1823
Etha	45	F	Spinster	Ireland	United States	Decatur	5 Jul 1821
F.	22	M	Butcher	Gt. Britain	U. States	Camberwell	7 Apr 1828
Fanny	13	F		Larse	United States	Carolina Ann	11 Jun 1824
Francis	22	M	Seaman	New York	New York	Washington	19 Jun 1826
G.	22	M	Gentleman	France	U. States	Six Brothers	6 Jul 1824
Geo.	5	M		England	U. States	Charlotte	19 Feb 1822
Geo.	23	M	Merchant	U. States	U. States	New England	11 Sep 1828

NAMES OF PASSENGERS	AGE	SEX	OCCUPATIONS	COUNTRY TO WHICH THEY BELONG	COUNTRY THEY INTEND TO INHABIT	SHIPS/DATES OF ARRIVAL	
BROWN (cont'd)							
Geo.	29	M	Butcher	England	U. States	Marmion	29 Sep 1823
George	10	M	Farmer	Gt. Britain	United States	Silas Richards	20 Jun 1826
George	16	M	Mariner	U. States	U. States	La Grange	19 Apr 1826
George	20	M	Shoe Maker	Ireland	New York	Trusty	12 Sep 1828
George	23	M	Farmer	England	U. States	Rockingham	29 Nov 1821
George	25	M	School Master	England	Canada	Brighton	20 Aug 1825
George	26	M	Merchant	Scotland	United States	Union	6 May 1824
George	33	M	Spain	Scotland	U. States	York	4 Apr 1826
George	42	M	Farmer	England	United States	Albion	7 Feb 1820
George A., & Servant	27	M	Merchant	America	America	Galatea	20 Jul 1829
George K.	46	M	Farmer	Scotland	United States	James Cropper	26 Mar 1822
Grace	16	F	Servant	Ireland	United States	Eliza	29 Aug 1822
Grace	23	F	Farmer	Ireland	America	Superior	12 Jun 1824
H.	22	M	Merchant	U. States	U. States	Prudence	11 Jun 1825
Hamilton	28	M	Farmer	Great Britain	United States	Grecian	24 Sep 1828
Hannah	6	F	Farmer			Manhattan	25 Dec 1820
Hannah	30	F		U. States	U. States	Nassau	2 Nov 1825
Harriet	17	F	None	United States	United States	Hannibal	12 Oct 1829
Harrt.	3	F	None	England	New York	Brighton	16 Nov 1826
Harvey	31	M	Farmer	United States	United States	Concordia	25 Aug 1827
Henrietta C.	21	F		America	America	Britannia	22 Jul 1829
Henry	7	M		England	Albany	Cortes	16 Jul 1827
Henry	12	F	Farmer	..., ..., England	Philadelphia	New Orleans	24 Aug 1827
Henry	20	M	Farmer	England	United States	Justina	5 Aug 1823
Henry	21			Sussex England		Cincinnatus	17 May 1823
Henry	30	F	Publican	England	U.S. States	Splendid	14 Aug 1829
Henry	33	M	Saddler	England	United States	Delta	24 Oct 1829
Henry	abt. 35	M	Mariner	U.S.	U.S.	Courier	22 Aug 1829
Horice	28	M	Merchant	Port au Prince	United States	Artibonite	9 Sep 1826
Hugh	20	M	Laborer	Ireland	United States	Fabius	4 Jun 1828
Isaac	18		Laborer	Ireland	New York	Lady Hunter	19 Oct 1826
Isabella		F		Halifax	United States	Dodge Healy	14 Oct 1828
J.	29	M		England	America	Corinthian	1 Sep 1827
J.	30	F	Joiner	England	United States	India	8 Jun 1827
J.	41	M	Merchant	U. States	U. States	Dromo	24 Jul 1826
J. A., Col.	36	M	Merchant	G. Brittain	U. States	Canada	6 Jun 1825
J. L.	6	M	None	Brazil	U. States	Sarah	1 Aug 1827
Jacob	28		Seaman	Boston		Hudson	18 Jun 1825

*Officers, Seamen and Passengers belonging to the Ship Jane of Boston and taken from on board the Schooner Olive of St. Johns , N.B. on the 4th June 1825, Lat. 41.30, Long 53.19, which ship foundered on the 31st ultimo in Lat. 41.44 Long 52.

NAMES OF PASSENGERS	AGE	SEX	OCCUPATIONS	COUNTRY TO WHICH THEY BELONG	COUNTRY THEY INTEND TO INHABIT	SHIPS/DATES OF ARRIVAL	
James	3	M	None	Great Britain	United States	Mary & Harriet	3 Jul 1829
James	8	M	Sailor's Child	America	America	Manhattan	12 May 1823
James	11	M		Scotland	United States	Samuel Robertson	5 Oct 1827
James	14	M		U. States	U.S.	Bayard	10 Nov 1824
James	15	M	None	G. Britain	United States	Courier	23 Feb 1824
James	18	M	Farmer	Ireland	U. States	Nancy	14 Jan 1822
James	18	M	Shoe Maker	Ireland	New York	Trusty	12 Sep 1828
James	20	M	Cooper	U. States	U. States	Prize	19 Jun 1823
James	21	M	Carpenter	New Brunswick	United States	Lady Hunter	27 Dec 1825
James	23	M	Clerk	England	U.S.	Panthea	13 Nov 1823
James	24	M	Mason	Scotland	United States	Culloden	17 May 1828
James	24	M	Millwright	Scotland	United States	Mary & Susan	5 Aug 1828
James	25	M	Mariner	U. States	U. States	Leopard	31 Jul 1824
James	25	M	...	Great Britain	United States	Friends	13 Jun 1825
James	26	M	Labourer	Great Britain	United States	Mary & Harriet	3 Jul 1829
James	28	M	Weaver	Great Britain	United States	Colossus	5 Jun 1827
James	28	M	Labourer	Scotland	United States	Mary & Susan	5 Aug 1828
James	28		Yeoman	England	United States	Cambria	19 Oct 1829
James	29	M	Mechanic	England	United States	Concordia	25 Aug 1827
James	29	M	Merchant	Scotland	New York	Patriot	13 Aug 1828
James	30	M	Factor	England	United States	Hamlet	25 Aug 1825
James	30	M	Farmer	England	New York	Corinthian	5 May 1827
James	31		Merchant	Great Brittain	Great Brittain	Commerce	14 Mar 1823
James	34	M	Laborer	Ireland	U. States	Howard	25 Jul 1823
James	40	M	Merchant	England	United States	William Byrnes	6 Apr 1826
James	40	M	Farmer	U. States	U. States	General Jackson	15 Jan 1829
James	55	M	Farmer	England	United States	Justina	5 Aug 1823

NAMES OF PASSENGERS	AGE	SEX	OCCUPATIONS	COUNTRY TO WHICH THEY BELONG	COUNTRY THEY INTEND TO INHABIT	SHIPS/DATES OF ARRIVAL	
BROWN (cont'd)							
James, His Excellency			late Minister of the U.S. to the Court of France			Sully	26 Oct 1829
James, Mr.	15	M	Gentleman	Ireland	America	Birmingham	16 Oct 1826
James Garrett	33	M	Gentleman	Dalverton, Somerset	Canada	New York	31 Jul 1829
Jane	9/12	F	Child	Ireland	U. States	Josephine	7 May 1827
Jane	7	F		Larse	United States	Carolina Ann	11 Jun 1824
Jane	7	F	None	Westmoreland	U. States	Milton	21 May 1827
Jane	14	F	Spinster	Ireland	United States	Decatur	5 Jul 1821
Jane	18	F		Scotland	U. States	Superior	25 Sep 1828
Jane	20	F	Servant	Ireland	America	Carolina Ann	7 Aug 1826
Jane	20	F		Gt. Britain	United States	Columbia	7 Sep 1827
Jane	21	F	Spinster	Ireland	United States	Dublin Packet	3 Sep 1822
Jane	25	F		G. Britain	U. States	Camillus	8 Sep 1828
Jane	31 4/12	F	Lady	Denmark	Denmark	Jupiter	4 Aug 1829
Jas.	23	M	Merchant	Gt. Britain	Canada	Baltic	11 Apr 1825
Jas.	26	M	Domestic	St. Croix		Chase	5 Jul 1825
Jas.	47	F	Printer	England	United States	Danube	22 Aug 1825
Jean	14	F		Scotland	New York	Joseph Hume	26 Oct 1829
Jno.	24	M	Hatter	Gt. Britan	United States	Crisis	6 Apr 1825
Jno.	29	M	Gentleman	Gt. Britain	United States	Crisis	6 Apr 1825
Jno.	32	M	Merchant	England	U.S.	Leeds	7 Nov 1828
Jno.	38	M	Cooper	England	U. States	Charlotte	19 Feb 1822
Jno.	38	M	Mariner	England	U. States	Greek	17 May 1825
Jno.	40	M	Farmer	Gt. Britain	U. States	Superior	20 Aug 1825
Jno. C.	27	M	Merchant	England	U. States	New York	4 Nov 1824
John		M	Weaver	Halifax	United States	Dodge Healy	14 Oct 1828
John	2	M	Publican	England	U.S. States	Splendid	14 Aug 1829
John	4	M		Scotland	New York	Joseph Hume	26 Oct 1829
John	5	M		Larse	United States	Carolina Ann	11 Jun 1824
John	6	F		Gt. Britain		Dalhouse Castle	13 May 1828
John	9					Harmony	15 Jul 1820
John	14	M	None	G. Britain	United States	Courier	23 Feb 1824
John	19	M	...	United States	United States	Friends	21 Oct 1825
John	19	M	Printer	Great Britain	United States	Thomas Dickason	14 Sep 1827
John	19		Clerk	Ireland	United States	Courier	15 Oct 1827
John	20	M	Steward	U. States	U. States	Eunore Francis	18 Sep 1820
John	21	M	Stone Cutter	Ireland	United States	Fabius	31 Jul 1829
John	21	M	Joiner	England	United States	Paul Jones	14 Oct 1829
John	22	M	Mason	Parkhead, Barony [Parish], Lanark [County]	New York	Hero	19 May 1828
John	23	M	Merchant	Gt. Britain	U.S. America	Columbia	3 Apr 1826
John	23	M	Farmer	Scotland	U.S.	Curler	19 Jul 1828
John	24	M	Farmer	Ireland	United States	Princess Charlotte	6 Oct 1827
John	25	M	Printer	Great Brittan	United States	Hanford	3 Aug 1829
John	26	M	Labourer	G. Britain	U. States	George Clinton	10 Sep 1828
John	27	M	Merchant	England	United States	Euphrates	25 Jun 1824
John	27	M	Merchant	Scotland	Great Britian	Florida	13 Feb 1826
John	27	M	Mechanic	England	United States	Concordia	25 Aug 1827
John	28	M	Gentleman	England	United States	Hercules	21 Nov 1822
John	31	M	Gentleman	England	U. States	Morning Star	28 Apr 1824
John	31	M	Labourer	Great Britain	United States	William Dawson	18 Jun 1827
John	31	M	Farmer	..., ..., England	Philadelphia	New Orleans	24 Aug 1827
John	31		Mechanic	Scotland		Zamoa	5 Nov 1828
John	33	M	Labourer	G. Britain	U. States	Great Britain	6 Sep 1828
John	34	M	Baker	Great Britain	United States	Illinois	9 Oct 1820
John	34		Baker	New York	America	Rockingham	23 Aug 1822
John	35	M	Merchant	Port au Prince	Port au Prince	Artibonite	9 Sep 1826
John	35	M		Great Britain	United States	Active	25 Mar 1828
John	35	M	Merchant	Port au Prince	Port au Prince	Ann Eliza Jane	30 Jul 1828
John	36	M	Farmer	Ireland	America	Manhattan	20 Mar 1820
John	36		Shipmaster	U.S.	Philada.	Little William	14 Jun 1823
John	38	M	Farmer	Great Britain	United States	Ganges	8 Jul 1820

NAMES OF PASSENGERS	AGE	SEX	OCCUPATIONS	COUNTRY TO WHICH THEY BELONG	COUNTRY THEY INTEND TO INHABIT	SHIPS/DATES OF ARRIVAL	
BROWN (cont'd)							
John	38	M	Mecanick	England	America	William Thompson	18 Jan 1825
John	40		Labourer			Harmony	15 Jul 1820
John	40	M	Linen Draper	Larse	United States	Carolina Ann	11 Jun 1824
John	40	M	Merchant	United States of A.	United States	Florida	13 Feb 1826
John	40	M	Farmer	Great Britain	United States	William Dawson	18 Jun 1827
John	40	M	Weaver	Ireland	United States	Jubilee	13 Jul 1829
John	44	M	Teacher			Belfast	28 Sep 1820
John	46	M	Farmer			Manhattan	25 Dec 1820
John	48	M	Trader	England	U. States	Corinthian	2 May 1823
John	53	M	Merchant	England	England	James Cropper	16 Oct 1826
John	56	M	Farmer	Gt. Britain	United States	Silas Richards	20 Jun 1826
John	57	M	Merchant	Great Britain	United States	Orbit	31 Aug 1822
John	62	M	Seaman	N. York	N. York	St. Helena	18 Feb 1823
*Invalid from the U.S. Ship Cayenne, to be received in the Maine Hospital							
John, Junr.	5	M		Great Britain	United States	Ganges	8 Jul 1820
John, Mr.	24		...	England		Hercules	19 Jun 1821
John, Mr.	27	M	Sugar Refnr.	England	U. States	Acasta	3 Apr 1826
John, Mr.	27		Mercht.	England	United States	Acasta	16 Aug 1826
Jos.	22	M	...er	Great Britain	United States	Atlantic	28 May 1827
Joseph	9	M	Farmer			Manhattan	25 Dec 1820
Joseph	11	M				Reuben & Eliza	21 Aug 1820
Joseph	15	M	Printer	Great Britain	United States	Thomas Dickason	14 Sep 1827
Joseph	17	M	Farmer	Gt. Britain	United States	Silas Richards	20 Jun 1826
Joseph	22	M	Merchant	Ireland	America	Ann	11 Apr 1821
Joseph	23	M		England	Canada	Manhattan	12 May 1823
Joseph	27	M	Farner	Westmoreland	U. States	Milton	21 May 1827
Leonard	15	M	Farmer	England	England	Helicon	3 Aug 1826
Louisa	10	F	Farmer			Helicon	3 Aug 1826
M.	39	M	None	Halifax	England	Loire	7 Jun 1827
M.	44	F		U. States	United States	Florida	14 Sep 1827
Margaret	21	F		Scotland	New York	Joseph Hume	26 Oct 1829
Margaret	22	F		Ireland	U. States	William Barker	29 Aug 1823
Margaret	22	F	None	Ireland	United States	Princess Charlotte	6 Oct 1827
Margaret	32	F	Weaver	Great Britain	United States	Colossus	5 Jun 1827
Maria	1	F		England	U. States	Charlotte	19 Feb 1822
Maria	7	F	Farmer			Manhattan	25 Dec 1820
Martha	24	F		G. Britain	U. States	Camillus	8 Sep 1828
Mary	...	F	Spinster	Ireland	Unt. St. America	Wilson	21 May 1827
Mary	3	F		Great Britain	United States	Ganges	8 Jul 1820
Mary	8	F		Gt. Britain		Dalhouse Castle	13 May 1828
Mary	10	F	None	Westmoreland	U. States	Milton	21 May 1827
Mary	10	F		Scotland	New York	Joseph Hume	26 Oct 1829
Mary	12	F				Imperial	19 Jul 1820
Mary	12	F	None	G. Britain	United States	Courier	23 Feb 1824
Mary	14	F		England	United States	Danube	22 Aug 1825
Mary	15	M	None	Jamaica	Jamaica	Orion	12 Mar 1825
Mary	15	F		England	Albany	Cortes	16 Jul 1827
Mary	17	F	None	Westmoreland	U. States	Milton	21 May 1827
Mary	17	F	None	Great Britain	United States	Courier	26 Jun 1827
Mary	19	F		England		Britannia	20 Jun 1827
Mary	19 4/12	F	Spinster	Ireland	U. States	Josephine	30 Aug 1828
Mary	25	F	None	Scotland	United States	Orozimbo	11 Aug 1823
Mary	27	F	Spinster	Great Brittain		Corinthian	9 Jan 1827
Mary	30	F		England	United States	William Byrnes	6 Apr 1826
Mary	35	F	Sailor's Wife	America	America	Manhattan	12 May 1823
Mary	40	F		England	Albany	Cortes	16 Jul 1827
Mary	43	F		N. York	N. York	St. Helena	18 Feb 1823
Mary	46 7/12	F	None	G. Britain	United States	Courier	23 Feb 1824
Mary	49	F	Farmer			Manhattan	25 Dec 1820
Mary	50	F	None	Great Britain	United States	Martha	6 Feb 1822
Mary Ann	11	F	Sailor's Child	America	America	Manhattan	12 May 1823
Mary Ann	18	F	Spinster	Ireland	United States	Decatur	5 Jul 1821
Mary Ann	33	F	None	England	America	Francis & Henrietta	11 Jul 1823

NAMES OF PASSENGERS	AGE	SEX	OCCUPATIONS	COUNTRY TO WHICH THEY BELONG	COUNTRY THEY INTEND TO INHABIT	SHIPS/DATES OF ARRIVAL	
BROWN (cont'd)							
Mary Ann, Miss	26	F	None	U. States	U. States	Ribicon	13 Mar 1826
Matilda	9	F		Larse	United States	Carolina Ann	11 Jun 1824
Michael	33	M	Labourer	Ireland	Boston	Lima	5 Aug 1829
Michael	33	M	Labourer	Ireland	U. States	Lima	5 Aug 1829
Milte.	22	M	Farmer	Great Britain	United States	Atlantic	28 May 1827
Monica	4	F	None	G. Britain	United States	Courier	23 Feb 1824
Moses	34	M	Farmer	Gt. Britain	United States	Union	9 Jan 1824
Munrough G.	21 6/12	M	Hatter	United States	United States	Mount Vernon	30 Dec 1828
N., Mrs.			None	U.S.	U.S.	Sully	26 Oct 1829
Nancy	60	F	Semstress	Ballymony	United States	Minerva	30 Oct 1829
Nathaniel	28	M	Merchant	U. States	U. States	Caledonia	10 Sep 1828
Nathaniel	29	M	Merchant	U. States	U. States	Sarah	17 Mar 1829
Nelson	23	M	Merchant	U. States	U. States	Sea Nymph	7 Oct 1828
Owen	25	M	Labourer	Great Britain	United States	India	5 Sep 1827
P., Mrs.	20		Merchant	Scotland		Zamoa	5 Nov 1828
P. J., Mr.	22		Merchant	Scotland		Zamoa	5 Nov 1828
Pat	...	M	Labourer	Ireland	Unt. St. America	Wilson	21 May 1827
Pat	26	M	Labourer	Great Britian	United States	Princess Charlotte	6 Sep 1828
Pat	27	M	Labourer	Great Britian	United States	Princess Charlotte	6 Sep 1828
Pat	30	M	Black Smith			Hanford	17 Jul 1828
Patrick	50 1/12	M	Merchant	England	England	New York	7 Jul 1828
Patrick, Hon., Esqr.	45	M	Gentleman	Nassau, N.P.	Nassau, N.P.	Superior	27 Jun 1825
Paul	7	M	None	G. Britain	United States	Courier	23 Feb 1824
Peter	10	M	None	G. Britain	United States	Courier	23 Feb 1824
Peter	20	M	Printer	Great Brittan	United States	Cambria	11 Feb 1829
Peter	38	M	Groom	Ireland	U. States	Albion	11 May 1827
Peter	54	M	Gentleman	America	America	London Packet	25 Dec 1820
Phoebe	1 1/2	F		United States	State of New York	Loire	3 Dec 1821
Rachel	25	M		Scotland	U.S.	Curler	19 Jul 1828
Rebecca	9	F		Great Brittan	U.S.	Florida	17 May 1825
Rebecca	62	F	Farmer	Ireland	Pittsburg	Triton	12 Jul 1823
Richard	20	M	Merchant	Ireland	America	Hesperus	7 Jul 1820
Richard	30	M	Laborer	Ireland	America	Parrington	9 Jun 1827
Richard	34	M	Servant	Gt. Britain	United States	Crisis	13 Nov 1824
Richd.	48	M	Farmer	Westmoreland	U. States	Milton	21 May 1827
Robert	3	M		Gt. Britain		Dalhouse Castle	13 May 1828
Robert	15	M		Larse	United States	Carolina Ann	11 Jun 1824
Robert	20 2/12	M	Farmer	England	United States	London	6 Feb 1829
Robert	21	M	Labourer or Spinster	Ireland	United States	Champion	3 Nov 1827
Robert	22	M	Farmer	Ireland	America	Superior	12 Jun 1824
Robert	24	M	Farmer	Great Brittan	U. States	Gem	26 Jul 1827
Robert	25	M	Blacksmith	Scotland	U. States	Cygnet	23 Sep 1820
Robert Cuthburt	28	M	Gentleman	Great Britain	United States	Baltic	24 Dec 1824
Robt.	17	M	Servant	Nova Scotia	U. States	General Pulman	3 Jun 1828
Robt.	19	M	Farmer	England	United States	Silas Richards	27 Oct 1825
Robt.	25	M	Sadler	U. States	U. States	Olive Branch	28 Aug 1824
Robt.	35	M	Merchant	Great Britain	United States	Ann Maria	23 Oct 1820
Ruth	16	F		Gt. Britain	United States	Silas Richards	20 Jun 1826
S., Miss			None	U.S.	U.S.	Sully	26 Oct 1829
St. J. D.	27		U.S. Navy	United States		New Orleans	27 Feb 1829
Sally		F	Child	Halifax	United States	Dodge Healy	14 Oct 1828
Sally	16	F	Spinster	Ireland	United States	Decatur	5 Jul 1821
Saml.	6	M	None	England	New York	Brighton	16 Nov 1826
Saml.	16	M		Gt. Britain	United States	Columbia	7 Sep 1827
Saml.	30	M	Farmer	Serry	Ireland	Carolina Ann	11 Jun 1824
Saml.	50	M	Farmer	United States	United States	Silas Richards	27 Oct 1825
Samuel	3	M	None	Ireland	United States	Princess Charlotte	6 Oct 1827
Samuel	9	M		England	Albany	Cortes	16 Jul 1827
Samuel	23	M	Stone Cutter	Ireland	U. States	Hanford	29 Dec 1828
Samuel	48	M	Doctor	U. States	U.S.	Bayard	10 Nov 1824
Samuel	51	M	Carpenter	England	Albany	Cortes	16 Jul 1827
Samuel, M.D., Doctr.	39	M	Physician	U. States	U. States	Sully	24 Oct 1828
Sarah	3	F	None	Scotland	United States	Orozimbo	11 Aug 1823
Sarah	7	F	Child	Ireland	U. States	Josephine	7 May 1827

NAMES OF PASSENGERS	AGE	SEX	OCCUPATIONS	COUNTRY TO WHICH THEY BELONG	COUNTRY THEY INTEND TO INHABIT	SHIPS/DATES OF ARRIVAL	
BROWN (cont'd)							
Sarah	10	F		Gt. Britain	United States	Columbia	7 Sep 1827
Sarah	11	F		Great Britain	United States	Ganges	8 Jul 1820
Sarah	17	F	Farmer			Helicon	3 Aug 1826
Sarah	30		Farmer	Ireland	United States	Carolina Ann	12 Sep 1823
Sarah	35	F	Wife	U. States	U. States	Camille	1 Feb 1827
Sarah	40	F		England	U. States	York	12 Jul 1825
Sarah A.	8	F		England	U. States	York	12 Jul 1825
Sarah C.	6	F		Nassau, N.P.	Nassau, N.P.	Superior	27 Jun 1825
Stephen	22	M	Farmer	Ireland	United States	Diana	1 May 1826
Susan E.	3	F		Nassau, N.P.	Nassau, N.P.	Superior	27 Jun 1825
Susanna	18	F	Spinster	Ireland	United States	Asia	29 Jul 1829
T...	35	M	Gentleman	Great Britain	United States	Blakely	29 Sep 1826
Terry	26	M	Labourer	England	America	Josephine	24 Jul 1826
Thomas		M	Merchant	U. States	U. States	Elizabeth	7 Feb 1822
Thomas	11	M	None	G. Britain	United States	Courier	23 Feb 1824
Thomas	20	M		United States		Mentor	23 May 1821
Thomas	20	M	Farmer	Ireland	United States	L. M. Pelham	25 Jun 1822
Thomas	23	M	...	...	...	Camillus	18 Nov 1824
Thomas	24	M	Farmer		United States	Mount Vernon	9 Jun 1823
Thomas	26					Cincinnatus	17 May 1823
Thomas	32	M	Merchant	United States	United States	Nestor	3 Nov 1820
Thomas	32	M	Seaman	United States	United States	Ann Maria	8 Jun 1824
Thomas	45	M	Labourer	Great Britain	United States	Martha	6 Feb 1822
Thomas	45	M	Merchant	U. States	U. States	Patty & Sally	26 Aug 1822
Thomas	45	M	Manufacturer	England	West Indies	Adonis	29 Sep 1823
Thomas	47	M	Farmer	Great Britain	New York	Intrepid	8 Aug 1822
Thomas	47	M	Bookseller	Gt. Brittain	Gt. Brittian	Manchester	21 Apr 1827
Thomas	66	M	Merchant	U. States	U. States	Transit	28 Jun 1822
Thos.	12	M	None	Westmoreland	U. States	Milton	21 May 1827
Thos.	16	M	Farmer	England	U. States	Gem	28 Dec 1824
Thos.	19	M	Carpenter	St. Thomas	St. Thomas	Four Sons	8 Dec 1827
Thos.	24	M	Farmer	Westmoreland	U. States	Milton	21 May 1827
Thos.	30			England		Anacreon	7 Sep 1827
Thos.	41	M	Mariner	U. States	U. States	Brazillian	18 Oct 1824
Thos.	52	M	Merchant	U. States	United States	Florida	14 Sep 1827
Timothy	30	M	Captain	America	America	Nestor	13 Jul 1829
W.	21	M	Labourer	G. Britain	U. States	St. George	7 Jun 1828
W.	28	M	Taylor	Georgetown	Georgetown	Hope & Esther	19 Aug 1824
W.	28	M	Merchant	Ireland	U. States	Tampico	14 Jul 1825
W. C.	3/365					Corinthian	11 Mar 1829
*born on passage (died)							
Walter	42	M	Mariner	U. States	U. States	Magnet	18 Aug 1825
William	7/12	M	None	Great Britain	United States	Mary & Harriet	3 Jul 1829
William	9	M	Farmer	Great Britain	United States	Ganges	8 Jul 1820
William	15	M		England	United States	Danube	22 Aug 1825
William	18	M	Carpenter	England	Albany	Cortes	16 Jul 1827
William	20	M	Labourer	Scotland	United States	Friends	7 Jul 1827
William	21	M	Farmer	Great Briton	United States	Orion	18 Jun 1821
William	21	M	Farmer			Helicon	3 Aug 1826
William	23			England	England	London	16 Aug 1824
William	23	M	Merchant	England	England	William Thompson	19 Aug 1829
William	27	M	Farmer	England	New York	Corinthian	5 May 1827
William	27	M	Labourer	Scotland	United States	Mary & Susan	5 Aug 1828
William	47	M	Farmer			Helicon	3 Aug 1826
Willim.	9/12	M	None	England	New York	Brighton	16 Nov 1826
Willim.	26	M	Engineer	England	New York	Brighton	16 Nov 1826
Wm.	3	M			U. States	Rockingham	29 Nov 1821
Wm.	12	M	Farmer	Gt. Britain	United States	Silas Richards	20 Jun 1826
Wm.	19	M	Farner	Westmoreland	U. States	Milton	21 May 1827
Wm.	19	M		Scotland	U.S.	Curler	19 Jul 1828
Wm.	27	M		G. Britain	U. States	Margaret Bogle	12 Jun 1828
Wm.	30	F		England	U. States	Charlotte	19 Feb 1822
Wm.	30	M	Accountant	Great Britain	United States	Manhattan	18 Feb 1824
Wm.	30	M	Mason	Ireland	United States	Hopes Delight	29 Nov 1827
Wm.	35	M	Merchant	U. States	U. States	Nassau	2 Nov 1825
Wm.	37	M	Mariner	U. States	U. States	Hopes Delight	1 Sep 1827
Wm.	40	M	Merchant	Philadelphia	U. States	Nestor	9 Dec 1822

NAMES OF PASSENGERS	AGE	SEX	OCCUPATIONS	COUNTRY TO WHICH THEY BELONG	COUNTRY THEY INTEND TO INHABIT	SHIPS/DATES OF ARRIVAL	
BROWN (cont'd)							
Wm.	62	M	Farmer	Ireland	Pittsburg	Triton	12 Jul 1823
Wm.	64	M				Ann	17 May 1822
Wm., Mr.	25	M	Mercht.	Gt. Brittain	United States	Manchester	24 Aug 1827
Wm. J.	19	M	Merchant	New York	New York	Fly	12 Apr 1824
Wm. L.	21	M	Mariner	England	England	Athenian	3 Mar 1828
Wm. Linn	23	M	Gentleman	U.S.	U.S.	Corinthian	11 Mar 1829
BROWNE, Alexr.	21	M	Clerk	Ireland	United States	Carolina Ann	11 Dec 1826
Elizabeth	22	F	Mechanic	G.B.	U.S.A.	Silas Richard	30 Jun 1828
Francis	30	M	Grocer	Ireland	United States	James Cropper	26 Mar 1822
Francis	30	M	Labourer	Ireland	United States	Thomas	13 Dec 1827
Francis, Mrs.	25		Lady	Bath	United States	London	13 Dec 1822
Joseph	21	M	Surgeon	Ireland	United States	Carolina Ann	11 Dec 1826
Samuel J.	34		Gentleman	Bristol	United States	London	13 Dec 1822
Thomas	30	M	Farmer	England	Pensylvania	Lima	16 Mar 1829
BROWNEE, Ellen	2			Ireland	U.S.	Union	20 Aug 1827
Johanna	24			Ireland	U.S.	Union	20 Aug 1827
Patk.	28			Ireland	U.S.	Union	20 Aug 1827
BROWNELL, Silas	25	M	Carpenter	U. States	U. States	Magnet	1 Oct 1823
BROWNING, A.	26	M		Ireland	U. States	Fame	15 Nov 1826
Ann	31		going to her husband with family	Great Britain	United States	Camillus	12 Sep 1827
Isabella	4			Great Britain	United States	Camillus	12 Sep 1827
John	5			Great Britain	United States	Camillus	12 Sep 1827
John	8	M		Scotland	U. States	Superior	25 Sep 1828
John	10	M		Great Britain	United States	Exertion	17 Jul 1829
Maria	17	F	Dress Maker	Great Britain	United States	Exertion	17 Jul 1829
Wm.	48	M	Carpender	Great Britain	United States	Exertion	17 Jul 1829
BROWNLEE, E.	23		Farmer	Ireland	United States	Courier	16 May 1825
J.	1		Farmer	Ireland	United States	Courier	16 May 1825
J.	29		Farmer	Ireland	United States	Courier	16 May 1825
M.	4		Farmer	Ireland	United States	Courier	16 May 1825
BROWNLIE, James	25	M	Labourer	Scotland	United States	Friends	7 Jul 1827
BROWNLY, Henry	28	M	Weaver	Ireland	United States	Neury	27 Jan 1827
BROWNSON, Oliver	28	M	Phisician	G. Britton	U. States	Sully	25 Jun 1828
BROYER, Antoine	4	M	Farmer	Corgernon	U.S. America	Superior	18 Jun 1825
Margaret	29	F	Farmer	Corgernon	U.S. America	Superior	18 Jun 1825
BRUCE, —, Mrs.	25		Wife of George	Ireland	United States	Mexico	1 Jun 1821
A.	50	M	Merchant	Gt. Britian	United States	Nestor	16 Aug 1824
Alexr.	30	M	Grocer	U. States	U. States	Mary Howland	22 Sep 1828
Catharine	2			Scotland	United States	Camillus	3 May 1828
Charles	1...	M	None	Great Britain	Unknown	William Thompson	1 May 1827
Charles	21		Tailor	Scotland	United States	Isabella	5 Jul 1826
D.	36	M	Planter	Jamaica	Jamaica	Cadmus	14 Oct 1824
G. H. Henderson	28	M	Gentleman	Scotland	America	Pacific	13 Jan 1827
George	35		Stone Mason	Ireland	United States	Mexico	1 Jun 1821
Henry	25	M	Navy	U. States	U. States	Pacification	27 Apr 1824
James	23	M	Boot Maker	Scotland	United States	Cambria	8 Oct 1828
Janet	25	F		Scotland	United States	Camillus	27 Oct 1829
John	24	M	Labourer	Scotland	United States	Friends	7 Jul 1827
John	24		Farmer	Great Britain	United States	Camillus	12 Sep 1827
John	35	M	Merchant	U. States	U. States	Paquet des Cayes	25 Apr 1827
John	48	M	Merchant	U. States	U. States	Emily	12 Jan 1825
John, Mrs.	24		Spinster	Scotland	United States	Camillus	3 May 1828
Joshua	33		Farmer	England	America	Governor Griswold	6 Jun 1821
Maxwell	34	M	Carpenter	United States	United States	Mary Jane	7 Jan 1829
Phillip	23	M	Collier	Wales	U.S. States	Splendid	14 Aug 1829
R.	25	M	Servant	U. States	U. States	Medina	23 Apr 1828
Robert	25	M	Farmer	Scotland	United States	Friends	16 Aug 1824
Susan	9	F	Farmer	Scotland	United States	Friends	16 Aug 1824
Thomas	45	M	Merchant	Great Britain	Great Britain	General Marion	20 Jun 1826
William	2		Child [of George]	Ireland	United States	Mexico	1 Jun 1821
Wm. S.	23	M	Merchant	Boston	Boston	Lebago	30 Jun 1826
BRUCHLE, A.	28	M	Merchant	Havana	Havana	Crusader	23 Apr 1827
BRUDA, Agamemnon	37		Merchant	Italy	Italy	Silvanus Jenkins	30 Nov 1827

NAMES OF PASSENGERS	AGE	SEX	OCCUPATIONS	COUNTRY TO WHICH THEY BELONG	COUNTRY THEY INTEND TO INHABIT	SHIPS	DATES OF ARRIVAL
BRUE, Robt. ...	28	M	...	United States	New York	Albion	11 Jun 1821
BRUEN, G. W.	24	M		United States	U.S.	John Wills	21 May 1824
James	21	M	Pilot	Sligo	New York	Susquehana	27 Jun 1823
BRUENS, Frederica	29	F				Ceylon	14 Sep 1824
Thomas	46	M	Linnen Weaver	Konegreichs	State of N. York	Ceylon	14 Sep 1824
BRUGGER, Barbe	46	F	Farmer	Switzerland		Antioch	18 Aug 1829
Elizabeth	20	F	Farmer	Switzerland		Antioch	18 Aug 1829
Felix	17	M	Farmer	Switzerland		Antioch	18 Aug 1829
Jean	18	M	Farmer	Switzerland		Antioch	18 Aug 1829
Jno.	30	M	Gentleman	Sweden	U. States	Neptune	11 Jun 1822
Ubric	50	M	Farmer	Switzerland		Antioch	18 Aug 1829
BRUGIERE, Charles	52	M	Merchant	United States	United States	Henry	9 Jun 1826
Henry	29	M	Merchant	France	France	Greek	19 May 1826
BRUGMAN, W. R.	35	M	Merchant	Curacao	Curacao	General Paez	28 May 1828
BRUIN, E.	53	M	Planter	Spain	Spain	Frances	22 May 1827
BRUM, Cathrine	28	F	One Family [Start]	France	United States	Henri IV	2 Oct 1828
Charles	6	M	One Family [Start]	France	United States	Henri IV	2 Oct 1828
Elizabeth	7	F	One Family [Start]	France	United States	Henri IV	2 Oct 1828
Start	32	M	Butcher	France	United States	Henri IV	2 Oct 1828
BRUMAN, P.	20	M	Baker	West Indies	U.S.	Shepherdess	17 May
BRUMBERG, J.	18	M	Clerk	Hamburg	United States	Maria Elizabeth	2 Sep 1822
BRUMIN, Bridget	20	F	Spinster	Ireland	United States	Wilson	6 Jun 1828
BRUMLEY, Eliza V., Mrs.	33	F	Lady	U. States	U. States	Crisis	10 Nov 1823
BRUMMER, John	22	M	Black Smith	Hannover	U.N. States	Constitution	7 Dec 1827
BRUMMET, Abel	25	M	Weaver	Yorkshire	Pennsylvania	Curler	7 Jul 1827
BRUN, Edmund	26	M	Laborer	Great Britain	United States	Robert Fulton	1 Apr 1824
Ellen	18	F	None	U.S. America	U.S. America	Columbia	31 Jul 1826
Michel	30	M	Laborer	Great Britain	United States	Robert Fulton	1 Apr 1824
BRUNE, J. S.	47	M	Merchant	U. States	U. States	Sea Nymph	30 Apr 1828
Theophile	23	M	Farmer	France	U. States	France	14 Mar 1828
BRUNELL, E.	28	M	Merchant	France	U. States	Fair American	5 Apr 1822
BRUNET, Andrew	39	M		France	United States	Henri IV	2 Oct 1828
Francois	28	M	Gentleman	France	U.S.	Corinthian	11 Mar 1829
Lewis	45	M	Merchant	Spain	Spain	Transit	13 Nov 1823
Nicholas	13	M	School Boy	Spain	New York	Transit	17 Mar 1824
BRUNGEMAN, C.	40	M	Shepherd	Bremen	Bremen	Louise	30 Jun 1826
BRUNGER, James	19	M	Farmer	Great Britain	United States	Fame	26 May 1828
Joseph	19	M	Farmer	Great Britain	United States	Fame	26 May 1828
BRUNI, Barbara	6	F	Daughter	Swiss	United States	Elizabeth	4 Sep 1826
Catherina	3	F	Daughter	Swiss	United States	Elizabeth	4 Sep 1826
Christian	20	M	Son	Swiss	United States	Elizabeth	4 Sep 1826
David	10	M	Son	Swiss	United States	Elizabeth	4 Sep 1826
John	23	M	Son	Swiss	United States	Elizabeth	4 Sep 1826
Ma...ona	16	F	Daughter	Swiss	United States	Elizabeth	4 Sep 1826
Madelina	42	F	Wife	Swiss	United States	Elizabeth	4 Sep 1826
Peter	12	M	Son	Swiss	United States	Elizabeth	4 Sep 1826
Peter	45	M	Farmer	Swiss	United States	Elizabeth	4 Sep 1826
Samuel	1	M	Son	Swiss	United States	Elizabeth	4 Sep 1826
BRUNNER, Torn	27	M	Farmer	France	United States	Great Britain	18 Sep 1826
BRUNTEN, Amelia	1	F		England	New York	Louisa	10 Nov 1825
Amelia	22	F		England	New York	Louisa	10 Nov 1825
Philip	26	M	Plater	England	New York	Louisa	10 Nov 1825
BRUNTON, Bridget	20	F		Ireland	United States	Trio	13 Jun 1827
Henry	27	M	Student	Newburg	New York	Gratitude	25 Jun 1828
BRURICK, Edward	31	M	Cordwainer	Great Brittan	United States	Hanford	3 Aug 1829
Ellen	20	F	wife to [Edward]	Great Brittan	United States	Hanford	3 Aug 1829
BRURIE, John Henry	17	M		Great Britain		Corinthian	27 Oct 1829
BRUSE, Eliza	46	F	None	Ireland	Ut. States	Courier	13 Jul 1826
BRUSH, Ann	18	F	Spinster	Ireland	America	Josephine	8 Dec 1827
Elizabeth	16	F	Spinster	Ireland	America	Josephine	8 Dec 1827
Henry L.	18	M	Merchant	U. States	U. States	Clarice	1 Feb 1827
James	40 11/12	M		G. Brittian	United States	Louisa	14 Jun 1825
BRUSSO, Preteo	25	M	Physician	Italy	New York	Corinthian	27 Apr 1824
BRUTE, Simon	45	M	Devine	U. States	U.S.	Bayard	10 Nov 1824
BRUTSCHÉ, —	25	M		Swisse	United States	Deux Ernest	29 Dec 1827
*landed at Lewiston, Delw.							
BRUX, Augustus	32	M	Merchant	St. Domingue	U.S.	Bayard	30 Oct 1820
BRUY, Peter	22		Clerk	Paris	France	Ann	27 Nov 1820

NAMES OF PASSENGERS	AGE	SEX	OCCUPATIONS	COUNTRY TO WHICH THEY BELONG	COUNTRY THEY INTEND TO INHABIT	SHIPS/DATES OF ARRIVAL	
BRUYERES, Henry	24	M	Officer of Engineers	Great Britain	United States	Robert Fulton	27 Jun 1822
BRUZ, Francisca F.	25	F		Spain	U. States	Martha	25 Mar 1824
Jos. Asmezo	25	M	Merchant	Spain	U. States	Martha	25 Mar 1824
BRYAM, An...a	36	F	Servant	England	America	William	21 Sep 1821
Bel...	26	F	Spinster			Robert Burns	13 Jul 1820
Bridgett	18	F				Eliza Grant	6 Oct 1828
Catherine	12	F				Eliza Grant	6 Oct 1828
Chas.	28	M				Eliza Grant	6 Oct 1828
Dan.	32	M	Laborer	Ireland	U. States	Howard Douglass	29 Jan 1828
Denis	50	M	Farmer	Ireland	United States	Lord Strangford	20 Jun 1826
James	20	M	Farmer	Ireland	United States	Dublin Packet	3 May 1823
James	22	M	Labourer	U. States	U. States	United States	11 Sep 1828
James	32	M	Labourer	Great Britain	United States	Isaac Hicks	10 Jul 1827
Joh.	18	M				Eliza Grant	6 Oct 1828
John	20	M	Farmer	Ireland	United States	Wilson	22 Jun 1824
John	22	M	Labourer	Ireland	United States	Jubilee	13 Jul 1829
John	42	M	Carpenter	United States	United States	Nimrod	1 Jun 1821
Margaret	60	F	None	Great Britain	United States	Ganges	26 Oct 1826
Mary	2	F				Eliza Grant	6 Oct 1828
Mary	28	F	Labourer	England	U. States	Comet	23 Aug 1828
Mathew	20	M	Labourer	England	U. States	Comet	23 Aug 1828
Nicholas	23	M	Labourer	Great Britain	United States	Ganges	26 Oct 1826
Nicholas	24	M				Eliza Grant	6 Oct 1828
Patk.	27	M	Labourer	Ireland		Marchioness	13 May 1828
Patrick	13	M				Eliza Grant	6 Oct 1828
R.	28	M	Merchant	U. States	U. States	Alexander	31 Mar 1827
Robert	20	M	Farmer	Ireland	America	John Adams	2 Aug 1827
S.	36	M				Lady of the Lake	23 Aug 1828
Thomas	26	M	Farmer	Ireland	America	John Adams	2 Aug 1827
Timothy	18	M	Clerk	Ireland	United States	Jubilee	13 Jul 1829
Walter	29	M	Weaver	Gt. Britain	United States	Penelope	9 Sep 1828
William	28	M	Farmer	Ireland	America	William	21 May 1825
William	62	M	Merchant	London	United States	Hannibal	27 May 1822
Wm.	28	M	Merchant	American	U. States	Frederick	27 Jan 1823
BRYAND, Dan.	33	M	Farmer	England	U.S. America	Cortes	19 May 1826
BRYANT, —	35	M		Gt. Britain	U. States	Tantiva	7 Jul 1828
—, Mrs.	38	F		England	U. States	Milton	6 Dec 1825
C.	35	M		Gt. Britain	U. States	Tantiva	7 Jul 1828
F.	14	M		Gt. Britain	U. States	Tantiva	7 Jul 1828
Jerimiah	24	M	Merchant	Ireland	United States	Young Phoenix	26 Jul 1824
Joseph	32	M	Currier	England	United States should they approve of it	Robert Edwards	20 Jan 1829
Robt.	20	M	Labourer	Ireland	United S.	Hanford	19 Aug 1828
Timothy	34	M	...	America	United States	London Packet	25 Dec 1820
W.	40	M	Labourer	England	United States	Alicia	9 May 1827
BRYAR, Geo.	30	M	Merchant	U. States	U. States	Columbia	7 Sep 1827
BRYCE, Archd.	40	M	Mercht.	United States	United States	Nestor	13 Mar 1824
Archd., Mr.	37	M	Mercht.	Gt. Brittian	United States	Manchester	24 Aug 1827
BRYDEN, W.	38	M	Merchant	Jamaca	Jamaca	Active	25 Jun 1823
BRYDGES, Jane	26	F		Ireland	America	Wilson	27 Nov 1826
William	30	M	Labourer	Ireland	America	Wilson	27 Nov 1826
BRYDON, —, Mrs.	50	F		United States	United States	Don Quixote	18 Aug 1824
BRYEN, George	21	M	Farmer	England	New York	Robert Edwards	17 Mar 1828
John	25	M	Laborer	Ireland	United States	Trio	13 Jun 1827
Mary, his wife [George]	22	F		England	New York	Robert Edwards	17 Mar 1828
BRYER, Archd.	45	M	Merchant	Scotland	New York	York	8 Aug 1829
John	40	M	Farmer	Ireland	United States	Mary & Harriet	3 Jul 1829
Mary	39	F	None	Ireland	United States	Mary & Harriet	3 Jul 1829
Mary Anne	4	F	None	Ireland	United States	Mary & Harriet	3 Jul 1829
BRYERS, James	1	M		Ireland	United States	Romulus	24 Jun 1826
Jns.	21	M	Farmer	G. Britain		Ann Maria	3 Jul 1820
BRYINTON, B. A., Mr.	30		Merchant	U.S.	U.S.	Pacific	24 May 1824
BRYNE, Garret	50	M	Farmer	Ireland	U. States	Erin	5 Jul 1820
Judy	22	F	Farmer	Ireland	U. States	Erin	5 Jul 1820
BRYODEY, James	45	M	Labourer	Irereland	America	Carolina Ann	20 Jun 1825

NAMES OF PASSENGERS	AGE	SEX	OCCUPATIONS	COUNTRY TO WHICH THEY BELONG	COUNTRY THEY INTEND TO INHABIT	SHIPS/DATES OF ARRIVAL	
BRYON, John	25	M	Farmer	Ireland	New York	Phoenix	29 Apr 1826
BRYSON, John	22	M	Weaver	Ireland	United States	Meteor	27 Sep 1826
Margaret	20	F	Wife	Ireland	United States	Meteor	27 Sep 1826
Margaret	46		Servant	Ireland	United States	Robert Burns	18 Jun 1822
BUAH, Dennis	30	M		Ireland	U. States	Wanderer	1 Sep 1828
BUBLER, Caroline	25	F	Agriculture	Wirtemburg	United States	Henri IV	14 Oct 1829
Jas.	23	M	Agriculture	Wirtemburg	United States	Henri IV	14 Oct 1829
Philip	24	M	Hatmaker	Prussia		Constitution	20 Jun 1828
BUCA, Julia	21	F		Sweden	U. States	Hamilton	22 Sep 1828
BUCANNAN, John	20	M	Labourer	Ireland	U. States	Josephine	30 Aug 1828
Eliza Ann	16	F	Spinster	Ireland	United States	Fabius	31 Jul 1829
Mary	23	F	Spinster	Ireland	United States	Fabius	31 Jul 1829
BUCH, Anna Maria	3	F		France	U. States	Edward Bopnnaffe	30 Jul 1829
Barbara	37	F		France	U. States	Edward Bopnnaffe	30 Jul 1829
Christian	5	M		France	U. States	Edward Bopnnaffe	30 Jul 1829
Edward Brunoffi	1/12	M		France	U. States	Edward Bopnnaffe	30 Jul 1829
Johann [crossed out]	14	M	Farmer	France	U. States	Edward Bopnnaffe	30 Jul 1829
Madeisse	9 6/12	F		France	U. States	Edward Bopnnaffe	30 Jul 1829
Manuel	21	M	Servant	France	U. States	Lewis	6 Jul 1825
Marguerette	11	F		France	U. States	Edward	
Philip	8	M		France	U. States	Edward Bopnnaffe	30 Jul 1829
Philip J.	33	M	Hoabmaker [?]	France	U. States	Edward Bopnnaffe	30 Jul 1829
BUCHAN, James	32	M	Stationer	England	Gt. Britain	Electra	4 Sep 1827
Lucy	35	F		England	Gt. Britain	Electra	4 Sep 1827
Lucy Maria	8	F		England	Gt. Britain	Electra	4 Sep 1827
Robt.	24	M	Engineer	England	United States	Baltic	21 Apr 1827
BUCHANAN, —, Dr.	42	M	Physician	Scotland	U. States	Chase	6 Jun 1822
—, Mr.	30	F	None	England	U. States	Perseverance	18 Nov 1824
A. S.	25	M	Farmer	Ireland	United States	L. M. Pelham	25 Jun 1822
Adam	20	M	Smith	Switzerland	U. States	Hewes	30 Oct 1829
Alexander	15	M		Ireland	United States	Hannibal	6 Sep 1824
Alexander	23	M	Merchant	Canada		Amity	11 Sep 1820
And.	20	M	Merchant	Great Britain	United States	Cortes	18 Oct 1820
Archibald	31	M	Blacksmith	Scotland	America	Concord	4 Jun 1821
Christiann	20	F	...	England	United States	Milton	20 Oct 1827
Emelia	13	F	Servant	Island Jamaca	Island Jamaca	Agenora	19 Jun 1826
Geo.	41		Mercht.	England	U. States	New York	30 Oct 1827
George	45	M	Merchant	Great Britain	U.S.A.	Silas Richards	7 Mar 1825
Helen	19 2/12	F		G. Britain	United States	Dutchess of Portland	30 Oct 1826
James	19	M	None	United States	New York	Intrepid	8 Aug 1822
James	49	M	British Consul	Great Britain	Great Britain	Nestor	3 Nov 1820
Janet	45	F	None	Scotland	United States	Mary & Susan	5 Aug 1828
Jas.	20		Farmer	Great Britain	United States	Camillus	12 Sep 1827
Jas.	21	M	Laborer	Scotland	U. States	Czar	29 Aug 1829
Jas.	29	M	Farmer	Great Britain	America	Lady Gallatin	21 Jun 1820
Jas. C.	22	M	Gentleman	N. York	N. York	Canada	1 Nov 1823
John	23	M		Scotland	New York	Joseph Hume	26 Oct 1829
John	35 4/12	M	Gentleman	G. Britain	United States	Dutchess of Portland	30 Oct 1826
John L.	15	M	Mechanic	Germany	United States	Two Marys	12 Feb 1820
Mary	25	F	Servant	Ireland	U. States	Nancy	25 Nov 1823
Saml.	21	M	Farmer	Ireland	United States	Trident	16 May 1826
Thos.	20	M	Cordwainer	Great Britain	America	Lady Gallatin	21 Jun 1820
Wm.	23	M	Farmer	Ireland	United States	Trident	16 May 1826
BUCHANANNON, Robt.	21	M	B...	Ireland	United States	Gem	16 Jun 1824
BUCHANNAN, Ann	15	F		Ireland	U. States	Nancy	16 Aug 1822
George	26	M		Ireland	United States	William & George	14 May 1828
James	60	M	Dyer	Irereland	America	Carolina Ann	20 Jun 1825

NAMES OF PASSENGERS	AGE	SEX	OCCUPATIONS	COUNTRY TO WHICH THEY BELONG	COUNTRY THEY INTEND TO INHABIT	SHIPS/DATES OF ARRIVAL	
BUCHANNAN (cont'd)							
Mary	50	F	House Keeper	Irereland	America	Carolina Ann	20 Jun 1825
Rose	16	F		Ireland	U. States	Nancy	16 Aug 1822
BUCHANNIN, Eliza	20	F	Milliner	Irereland	America	Carolina Ann	20 Jun 1825
James	16	M	Dyer	Irereland	America	Carolina Ann	20 Jun 1825
BUCHANNON, Duncan	20	M		Ireland	United States	William & George	14 May 1828
John	22	M	Labourer	Ireland	United States	William & George	14 May 1828
BUCHANON, Andrew	37		Merchant	Scotland	Scotland	Triumph	23 Jul 1829
BUCHAR, Jno.	20	M	Laborer	Ireland	United States	Trio	13 Jun 1827
BUCHEN, Anne	6	F	his family [Pierce]	Germany	United States	Wm. Osborne	16 Sep 1828
Francios	1	M	his family [Pierce]	Germany	United States	Wm. Osborne	16 Sep 1828
Jean	8	M	his family [Pierce]	Germany	United States	Wm. Osborne	16 Sep 1828
Maria	7	F	his family [Pierce]	Germany	United States	Wm. Osborne	16 Sep 1828
Maria	20	F	his family [Pierce]	Germany	United States	Wm. Osborne	16 Sep 1828
Pierce	42	M	Farmer	Germany	United States	Wm. Osborne	16 Sep 1828
BUCHLAND, Henry	34	M	Merchant	England	U. States	William Thompson	17 Dec 1827
BUCHLER, Catharine	11	F	Farmer	Wortenberg	Lancaster	Louisa	6 Oct 1828
Elisabeth	8	F	Farmer	Wortenberg	Lancaster	Louisa	6 Oct 1828
George M.	38	M	Farmer	Wortenberg	Lancaster	Louisa	6 Oct 1828
Julaina Dorothea	45	F	Farmer	Wortenberg	Lancaster	Louisa	6 Oct 1828
BUCIERE, John T. L.	45		None	France		Bayard	10 Sep 1827
BUCK, Elizabeth	36	F	None			Manhattan	20 Sep 1821
Henery	29	M	Weelright	Warrington, Eng.	Pensylvania	Manhattan	20 Sep 1821
James	21	M	Labourer	Ireland	U. States	Loire	6 Dec 1827
Jane	9/12	F				Manhattan	20 Sep 1821
Michael	60	M	Glazier	G. Brittain	U. States	Cincinnatus	2 Oct 1822
Patrick	26	M	Labourer	Ireland	U. States	Combine	30 Nov 1825
Patrick	26	M	Labourer	Great Brittan	United States	America	24 Jul 1827
Robert	26	M	Farmer	United States	United States	John Dickinson	18 Feb 1822
Susan	54	F		G. Brittain	U. States	Cincinnatus	2 Oct 1822
Thomas	24	M				Manhattan	20 Sep 1821
BUCKAMAN, Mich	25	M	Farmer	Ireland	U. States	Dickinson	30 Jul 1825
BUCKAN, John	22	M		Great Britain	United States	Active	25 Mar 1828
BUCKANNON, J.	22	F		Ireland	Ireland	Alligator	15 Aug 1820
BUCKE, Richard	57 5/12	M	Officer ...	Philadelphia	U. States	Quito	9 Jul 1823
BUCKELMAN, Cat	24	M	Agriculture	Wirtemburg	United States	Henri IV	14 Oct 1829
BUCKET, A.	21	M	Merchant	France	U. States	Maria	19 Feb 1823
BUCKEY, —, Mrs.	30	M		England	United States	Manhattan	22 Sep 1823
John	30	M	Farmer	England	United States	Manhattan	22 Sep 1823
BUCKFORD, Jno.	22	M	Mariner	Salem	U. States	Galata	23 Jun 1823
BUCKHAM, John	18	M	Farmer	Scotland	United States	Commerce	17 Jul 1823
BUCKHANS, —, Miss	17	F		Saxony	United States	Constitution	6 Jul 1829
—, Mrs.	50	F		Saxony	United States	Constitution	6 Jul 1829
A.	17	F		Saxony	United States	Constitution	6 Jul 1829
E.	15	F		Saxony	United States	Constitution	6 Jul 1829
Oscar	15	M		Saxony	United States	Constitution	6 Jul 1829
BUCKHULZER, Ann	10	F		Switzerland	U. States	La Urania	3 Jul 1828
B.	7	M		Switzerland	U. States	La Urania	3 Jul 1828
Cathr.	19	F		Switzerland	U. States	La Urania	3 Jul 1828
Jean	8	M		Switzerland	U. States	La Urania	3 Jul 1828
Jean	41	M	Labourer	Switzerland	U. States	La Urania	3 Jul 1828
M. M.	40	F		Switzerland	U. States	La Urania	3 Jul 1828
Maria E.	17	F		Switzerland	U. States	La Urania	3 Jul 1828
BUCKINSHAW, Geo.	22	M	Laborer	England	U. States	Lady Hunter	14 Mar 1826
BUCKLAND, D., Mrs.	24	F	Lady	England	U.S.	Corinthian	11 Mar 1829
Edwd., Master	2					Corinthian	11 Mar 1829
Emily, Miss	4					Corinthian	11 Mar 1829
Frederick, Master	6	M				Corinthian	11 Mar 1829
BUCKLE, Gottl.	30	M	Farmer	Germany	United States	Martha	30 Jun 1823
BUCKLEAD, —, Mrs.	22	F		England	U. States	Hudson	23 Jul 1828
BUCKLER, A. C.	32	M	None	Prusia	U. States	Harriet	20 Oct 1824
Anna	20	F		Native of Switzerland	United States	Canaris	30 Jun 1827
Anna	46	F		Native of Switzerland	United States	Canaris	30 Jun 1827

150

NAMES OF PASSENGERS	AGE	SEX	OCCUPATIONS	COUNTRY TO WHICH THEY BELONG	COUNTRY THEY INTEND TO INHABIT	SHIPS/DATES OF ARRIVAL	
BUCKLER (cont'd)							
Chris	46	M	Farmer	Native of Switzerland	United States	Canaris	30 Jun 1827
Jeffy	23	M	Farmer	England	U. States	Hercules	6 Jul 1827
John	15	M		Native of Switzerland	United States	Canaris	30 Jun 1827
Maria	18	F		Native of Switzerland	United States	Canaris	30 Jun 1827
BUCKLES, Archy	18	M	Weaver	Ireland	United States	Robert Fulton	10 Aug 1827
BUCKLEY, —	24	M	Mariner (Capt.)	United States	United States	India	24 Mar 1826
—, (infant)	1			Ireland	United States	Geo. Canning	5 Jun 1828
—, Mr.	26	M	Merchant	G. Britain	New York	Corinthian	29 Apr 1826
Anne	40	F	None	Gt. Britain	U. States	Panthia	13 Nov 1824
C. J.	28	M	Gentleman	U.N. States	U. States	Washington	7 Jul 1824
Caroline	6	F		Great Britan	United States	Clematis	8 May 1827
Catherine	18	F	Labourer	Ireland	New York	Bowditch	27 Apr 1826
Charles	6	M	None	Gt. Britain	U. States	Panthia	13 Nov 1824
Cornelus	27	M	Farmer	Ireland	America	William	21 May 1825
Cornls.	22			Ireland	U.S.	Union	20 Aug 1827
Dennis	26	M	Clerk	Ireland	United States	Diana	1 May 1826
Eliza.	19	F		England	United States	Ganges	10 May 1828
Ellen	13	F	Servant	Ireland	United States	Trio	31 Oct 1827
Ellen	30	F	Spinster	Ireland	America	William	21 May 1825
G.	22	F	None	United States	U. States	Pacific	5 Sep 1827
H.	27	M	Merchant	Gt. Britain	United States	Seeds	29 Sep 1824
James	1	M		Great Britan	United States	Clematis	8 May 1827
James	18	M	Weaver	Gt. Britain	United States	Meteor	19 Aug 1829
James	19	M	Clothier	England	United States	John Wells	11 May 1827
James	20	M	Labourer	Meckelham County		Aurora	8 Jun 1827
James	22	M	Merchant	America	U. States	Wave	28 Dec 1821
James	36	M	Clothier	Great Britan	United States	Clematis	8 May 1827
James	36	M	brass founder	England	Newyork	Cortes	16 Jul 1827
Jane	34	F	Clothier	Great Britan	United States	Clematis	8 May 1827
Joana	25	F		England	United States	Ganges	10 May 1828
John	14					William	17 Aug 1820
John	18	M	None	Gt. Britain	U. States	Panthia	13 Nov 1824
John	18	M	Labourer	Ireland	United States	Aurelia	7 Jun 1826
John	22	M	Clothier	England	United States	John Wells	11 May 1827
John	23	M	Clothier	Great Britan	United States	Clematis	8 May 1827
John	40	M	Labourer	Great Britain	U. States	Ganges	21 Jun 1827
John	43	M	Iron Turner	Great Britan	United States	Hamilton	19 Mar 1827
John	48		Labourer	Ireland	United States	Geo. Canning	5 Jun 1828
Joseph	50	M	Weaver	England	America	Franklin	3 Dec 1827
Joshua	45	M	Merchant	England	United States	Manhattan	11 Oct 1824
Margaret	22					Trio	5 May 1828
Maria	7		Child	England	United States	Acasta	16 Aug 1826
Marianne	23	F	None	Gt. Britan	Gt. Britan	Canada	8 Jun 1826
Martha	3	F		Great Britain	United States	Clematis	8 May 1827
Mary	8	F		Great Britain	United States	Clematis	8 May 1827
Mary	12	F	None	Gt. Britain	U. States	Panthia	13 Nov 1824
Mary	26			Ireland	United States	Geo. Canning	5 Jun 1828
Mary	51	F	Spinster	..., ..., Ireland	N. York	New Orleans	24 Aug 1827
Mary Ann	29	F		England	Newyork	Cortes	16 Jul 1827
Mathew	23	M	None	Gt. Britan	Gt. Britan	Canada	8 Jun 1826
Matthew	55	M	Labourer	Ireland		Marchioness	13 May 1828
Micheal	62	M	Painter	United States	United States	Crisis	13 Nov 1824
Michl.	58		Painter			William	17 Aug 1820
Morris	50	M	Farmer	England	United States	Ganges	10 May 1828
Patrick	25	M	Labourer	Ireland	New York	Bowditch	27 Apr 1826
Peter	28	M	Weaver	England	United States	Bolivar	15 Jun 1826
Philip	10	M	None	Gt. Britain	U. States	Panthia	13 Nov 1824
Robt.	18	M	Labourer	England	U. States	Ayrshire	12 May 1828
Sally	56		Lady	England	United States	Acasta	16 Aug 1826
Sarah Ann	3 6/12	F	None	United States	U. States	Pacific	5 Sep 1827
Thos.	35	M	Labourer	Ireland		Marchioness	13 May 1828
William	8/12	M		England	Newyork	Cortes	16 Jul 1827
William	9	M		Great Britan	United States	Clematis	8 May 1827
Wm.	23	M	Labourer	Ireland	New York	Bowditch	27 Apr 1826

NAMES OF PASSENGERS	A G E	S E X	OCCUPATIONS	COUNTRY TO WHICH THEY BELONG	COUNTRY THEY INTEND TO INHABIT	SHIPS/DATES OF ARRIVAL	
BUCKLEY (cont'd)							
Wm.	27	M	Carpenter	U. States	U. States	Ann Maria	13 Dec 1824
Wm. R.	1 3/12	M		United States	U. States	Pacific	5 Sep 1827
BUCKLY, Danl.	30	M	Farmer	Great Britain	United States	Weser	9 May 1822
Jas.	18	M	Merchant	U. States		Charleston Packet	4 May 1821
Margaret	30	F	...	...	...	Braganza	8 Aug 1825
Matthew	30	M	...	...	...	Braganza	8 Aug 1825
BUCKMAN, H...	27	M	...	England	Ohio	Thames	6 Oct 1820
James	40	M	Pedlar	England	U. States	Robert Edwards	9 May 1827
Jane, & child	29	F	...	England	Ohio	Thames	6 Oct 1820
John	18	M	...	England	New York	Thames	6 Oct 1820
Michael	21	M	Farmer	France	France	Sully	15 Jul 1829
BUCKMANAN, Ann	7	F		Irland	United States	Nancy	28 Oct 1822
BUCKMASTER, E., Miss	18	F		Ireland	U. States	America	9 May 1822
BUCKNEY, Edward H.	26	M	Gentleman	North Carolina	U. States	Columbia	7 Jul 1824
BUCKRIGE, A.	28	F		G. Britain	U.S. America	Cincinnatus	31 Oct 1820
James	8	M		G. Britain	U.S. America	Cincinnatus	31 Oct 1820
John	4	M		G. Britain	U.S. America	Cincinnatus	31 Oct 1820
Mary	6	F		G. Britain	U.S. America	Cincinnatus	31 Oct 1820
BUCOMAN, Alexander	17	M	Taylor	Ireland	United States	Robert Fulton	10 Aug 1827
BUCT, Francoes	36 2/12	M	Tanner	France	America	Martha	2 Jul 1828
BUDAT, L.	40	M	Merchant	Spain	U. States	Native	15 Apr 1826
BUDD, G. K.	27	M	Gentn.	Pensylvania	Pensylvania	Florida	1 Jun 1827
George Knight	23	M	Mercht.	United States	U. States	Nimrod	24 Jan 1826
Thomas	34	M	Merchant	France	France	Lewis	10 Sep 1823
Thomas	40	M	Merchant	England	travelling	Desdemona	12 Jun 1826
BUDDEN, —, Mr.	31	M	Merchant	G. Britain	Canada	Corinthian	29 Apr 1826
BUDDENDORFF,							
Auguste Wilhelmine	4	F	family [of J. G.]	Prussia	Philadelphia	Maria Elizabeth	18 Jun 1827
Dorothea Elisabeth	42	F	family [of J. G.]	Prussia	Philadelphia	Maria Elizabeth	18 Jun 1827
J. G.	44	M	Storekeeper	Prussia	Philadelphia	Maria Elizabeth	18 Jun 1827
Louise Charlotte	11	F	family [of J. G.]	Prussia	Philadelphia	Maria Elizabeth	18 Jun 1827
Wilhelm Robert	6	M	family [of J. G.]	Prussia	Philadelphia	Maria Elizabeth	18 Jun 1827
BUDDY, Mary	23	F	Spinster			Commerce	22 Jun 1825
BUDGE, John	30	M	Tanner	Great Britain	Upper Canada	Horsley Hill	17 Jun 1823
John	31	M	Farmer	Great Britain	United States	Isaac Hicks	27 Sep 1826
Margaret	20	F	Wife	Great Britain	Upper Canada	Horsley Hill	17 Jun 1823
BUDGER, George	3	M	Farmer	England	U. States	Robert Edwards	9 May 1827
Henry	9	M	Farmer	England	U. States	Robert Edwards	9 May 1827
James	1	M	Farmer	England	U. States	Robert Edwards	9 May 1827
John	5	M	Farmer	England	U. States	Robert Edwards	9 May 1827
John	37	M	Farmer	England	U. States	Robert Edwards	9 May 1827
Lydia	32	F	Farmer	England	U. States	Robert Edwards	9 May 1827
William	7	M	Farmer	England	U. States	Robert Edwards	9 May 1827
BUDIMANN, Evalina G.	32	F		U. States	U. States	Montano	2 Sep 1828
James A.	38	M	Manufacturer	U. States	U. States	Montano	2 Sep 1828
James J.	10	M		U. States	U. States	Montano	2 Sep 1828
BUEL, Ahemez	34	M	Merchant	New York	St. Thomas	Genl. Pike	15 Jan 1827
BUELL, Ellis	24	M	Marinor	U. States	New York	London Packet	5 Jan 1829
BUELLER, John	55	M	Farmer	United States	United States	Aurora	5 Sep 1826
BUFFERVAUX,							
Rem Auguste	30	M	Lawyer	France	New Orleans	Brighton	16 Nov 1826
BUGAC, Math.	45	M	Merchant	U.S.	United States	Stephania	27 Nov 1826
BUGANO, Nicholas	29	M	Mechanic	Italy	United States	Cambridge	19 Sep 1828
BUGARD, E.	25	M	Mercht.	Swiss	U. States	Manchester Packet	23 May 1822
L.	30	M	Mercht.	Swiss	U. States	Manchester Packet	23 May 1822
BUGGY, Margaret	21	F	Labourer	Ireland	America	Otter	17 Mar 1828
Patrick	19	M	Labourer	Ireland	America	Otter	17 Mar 1828
Patrick	20	M	Farmer	Ireland	U. States	Perserverance	21 Jul 1827
BUGLEY, W.	18	M		G. Britain	U. States	St. George	7 Jun 1828
BUGOYNE, Isabella	18	F	Spinster	United States	United States	Pacific	24 Oct 1828
Wm.	49	M	Mercht.	United States	United States	Pacific	24 Oct 1828
BUHLMEN, Frederick	23	M	Belt Maker	Switzerland	United States	Elizabeth	27 Jul 1824
BUHRER, John			Missionary	Germany	Liberia	Sully	26 Oct 1829
BUIGAS, Pasqual, Dr.	24	M	Merchant	Spain	Cuba	Hesper	16 Jun 1828
BUILANGER, L.	29	M	Merchant	France	U. States	Quesnel	6 Sep 1824

152

NAMES OF PASSENGERS	AGE	SEX	OCCUPATIONS	COUNTRY TO WHICH THEY BELONG	COUNTRY THEY INTEND TO INHABIT	SHIPS	DATES OF ARRIVAL
BUILELER, Carl	14	M		Bardin	U. States	Bayard	5 Sep 1828
Carl	46	M		Bardin	U. States	Bayard	5 Sep 1828
Christian	28	M		Bardin	U. States	Bayard	5 Sep 1828
Christof	12	M		Bardin	U. States	Bayard	5 Sep 1828
G. J.	4	M		Bardin	U. States	Bayard	5 Sep 1828
J. A.	10	M		Bardin	U. States	Bayard	5 Sep 1828
J. Adm.	10	M		Bardin	U. States	Bayard	5 Sep 1828
Lousa	9	M		Bardin	U. States	Bayard	5 Sep 1828
Michal	39	M	Weaver	Bardin	U. States	Bayard	5 Sep 1828
BUIS, Gregonia	35	M	Merchant	Cuba	Cuba	Agenora	11 Jun 1824
BUKLEY, Rebecca	29	F		England	U. States	York	12 Jul 1825
Wm.	6	M		England	U. States	York	12 Jul 1825
Wm.	30	M	Watch maker	England	U. States	York	12 Jul 1825
BUKMAN, John	28	M	Seaman	Scotland	U. States	Camillus	17 Sep 1823
BULCOCK, John	26	M	Printer	England	United States	Aurelia	7 Jun 1826
BULDNER, Andrew	33	M	Black smith	Germany	United States	Virginia	31 May 1828
BULERN..., Carlos	26	M	Painter	Mexico	Germany	Conveyance	15 Jan 1827
BULES, Sarah	60	F		G. Britain	U. States	St. George	7 Jun 1828
BULGER, John	23	M	Male	Ireland	United States	Dublin Packet	3 Sep 1822
John	36	M		Great Britain	Canada	James Monroe	25 Apr 1822
M.	18	M	Farmer	Farmer	U. States	Wilson	2 Sep 1823
Patrick	21	M	Farmer	Ireland	United States	Dublin Packet	3 Sep 1822
BULKESLEY, Louiza	20	F		St. Croix	St. Croix	Caslo	8 Sep 1828
Wm. J.	41	M	Merchant	Connecticut	St. Croix	Caslo	8 Sep 1828
BULKLEY, C.	22	M	Mechanic	Connecticutt	U. States	Benjamin	1 Jun 1822
David	20		Farmer	England	England	Hudson	18 Jun 1825
H. D.	24 2/12	M	Merchant	U. States	U. States	Larch	6 Jul 1827
John	43		Cordwander	England		Hudson	23 Jul 1828
L.	30	M	Merchant	United States		Haitien	10 Jun 1822
Mary	20	F	None	England	United States	Hamilton	13 Nov 1827
Timothy	27	M	Farmer	Ireland	America	William	21 May 1825
BULL, George	27	M	Farmer	Ireland	United States	Wilson	22 Jun 1824
Jacob	35		Shipmaster	U.S.	N. York	Little William	14 Jun 1823
John	30	M	Harness maker	England	U. States	York	12 Jul 1825
John P.	41	M	Merchant	America	America	Britannia	5 Nov 1828
Lucius	32	M	Merchant	Connecticutt	U. States	Ganges	23 Jul 1824
Marcus	32	M	Merch.	America	America	William Thompson	18 Jan 1825
Margaret	26	F	Matron	Ireland	United States	Wilson	22 Jun 1824
Sarah	50	F	Seamstres	G. Brittain	America	Atlantic	11 Oct 1822
Thos.	42	M	Farmer	Gt. Britain	United States	John & Elizabeth	25 Sep 1827
BULLAND, Benjamin	12	M	Farmer	Great Britain	U. States America	Ann Maria	29 Nov 1821
Benjamin	48	M	Farmer	Great Britain	U. States America	Ann Maria	29 Nov 1821
Caroline	3	F	Farmer	Great Britain	U. States America	Ann Maria	29 Nov 1821
Elizabeth	17	F	Farmer	Great Britain	U. States America	Ann Maria	29 Nov 1821
Elizabeth	48	F	Farmer	Great Britain	U. States America	Ann Maria	29 Nov 1821
James	19	M	Farmer	Great Britain	U. States America	Ann Maria	29 Nov 1821
John	8	M	Farmer	Great Britain	U. States America	Ann Maria	29 Nov 1821
Jos.	6	M	Farmer	Great Britain	U. States America	Ann Maria	29 Nov 1821
Mary	10	F	Farmer	Great Britain	U. States America	Ann Maria	29 Nov 1821
Rebecca	15	F	Farmer	Great Britain	U. States America	Ann Maria	29 Nov 1821
BULLERS, John	10	M	Felemaker	Great Britan	United States	Silvanus Jenkins	10 Mar 1827
John	31	M	Miller	Scotland	U. States	Czar	29 Aug 1829
Thomas	12	M	Felemaker	Great Britan	United States	Silvanus Jenkins	10 Mar 1827
Wm.	45	M	Felemaker	Great Britan	United States	Silvanus Jenkins	10 Mar 1827
Wm., Junr.	17	M	Felemaker	Great Britan	United States	Silvanus Jenkins	10 Mar 1827
BULLETT, A. C.	30	M	Merchant	U. States	U. States	Carlo	19 Jun 1828
Mary	21	F		U. States	U. States	Carlo	19 Jun 1828
BULLION, Ann Maria	6	F	Family [of John]	France	America	La Grange	7 Aug 1828
Ann Maria	26	F	Family [of John]	France	America	La Grange	7 Aug 1828
John	30	M	Farmer	France	America	La Grange	7 Aug 1828
Peter	3	M	Family [of John]	France	America	La Grange	7 Aug 1828
BULLOCK, David	30	M	...	...	United States	Camillus	10 Dec 1825
John	21	M	Farmer	Great Britain	United States	Ganges	8 Jul 1820
Jos.	21	M	Labourer	England	U. States	Thomas Ritchie	2 Jul 1827
Rhodia	19	F		Great Britain	United States	Ganges	8 Jul 1820
W.	24	M	Miner	G. Brittain	U. States	Pacific	23 Jan 1826
BULLON, Lucy	52	F		U. States	United States	Loire	12 Dec 1820

NAMES OF PASSENGERS	AGE	SEX	OCCUPATIONS	COUNTRY TO WHICH THEY BELONG	COUNTRY THEY INTEND TO INHABIT	SHIPS/DATES OF ARRIVAL	
BULLON (cont'd)							
Simeon, Capt.	31	M	Gent.	England	Canada	Cortes	23 Nov 1827
BULLWORTH, Robt.	30	M	Weaver	England	United States	Bolivar	15 Jun 1826
BULLY, Robson	50	M	Merchant	Great Britian	United States	Orbit	31 Dec 1821
BULOCK, Joseph	70		Drayman	England	United States	Mary	15 Jul 1822
BULOW, Caroline A.	24	F		South Carolina	South Carolina	Hector	30 Dec 1820
John J.	44	M	Merchant	South Carolina	South Carolina	Hector	30 Dec 1820
BULSIGER, Samuel				Suisse		Deux Ernest	29 Dec 1827
*son épouse & 5 enfans [his wife and five children]							
Samuel, his Wife & five children	...	M		Swisse	United States	Deux Ernest	29 Dec 1827
*landed at Lewiston, Delw.							
BULWORTH, Wm.	24	M	Weaver	England	U. States	Thomas Ritchie	2 Jul 1827
BUMFORTH, Ann	40	F	None	England	U. States	Thomas Ritchie	2 Jul 1827
Ricd.	47	M	Shoemaker	England	U. States	Thomas Ritchie	2 Jul 1827
BUMNIETT, Douglass	20	M	Merchant	Barbados	Supposition is he will return	Superb	7 Jul 1823
BUMOTH, William	39	M	Land Surveyor	England	Great Britian	Florida	13 Feb 1826
BUMSTED, Henry	15	M	None	England	Troy	Indian Chief	19 Jun 1823
Mary	18	F	None	England	Troy	Indian Chief	19 Jun 1823
Mary	47	F	None	England	Troy	Indian Chief	19 Jun 1823
Stephen	4	M	None	England	Troy	Indian Chief	19 Jun 1823
Thomas	49	M	Farmer	England	Troy	Indian Chief	19 Jun 1823
William	3	M	None	England	Troy	Indian Chief	19 Jun 1823
BUNBURY, Pat	21	M	Carpenter	Gt. Britain	United States	Penelope	9 Sep 1828
BUNCE, Eliza	57 6/12	F		England	America	Aurora	22 Sep 1828
Wm.	47	M	Mechanic	England	America	Aurora	22 Sep 1828
BUNCH, Francisque	10	M	Farmer	Germany	United States	Oxford	14 Aug 1828
Jean	8	M	Farmer	Germany	United States	Oxford	14 Aug 1828
Joseph	50	M	Farmer	Germany	United States	Oxford	14 Aug 1828
Madalaine	40	F	Farmer	Germany	United States	Oxford	14 Aug 1828
Rob. H.	35	M	Merchant	England	South America	Stranger	29 Jun 1824
Sarah	20	F	Servant	U.S.	U.S.	Athenian	14 Oct 1828
BUNDSEN, Thomas	27	M	Maltsler	England	U. States	William Thompson	25 Aug 1828
William	25	M	Farmer	England	U. States	William Thompson	25 Aug 1828
BUNELL, James A.	21	M		U. States	U. States	Howard	22 Sep 1828
BUNHARDT, —	29	M	Agriculture	France	United States	Henri IV	14 Oct 1829
BUNHOLD, Gelh.	9	M		Great Britain		Caravan	8 Sep 1828
John	19	M		Great Britain		Caravan	8 Sep 1828
M.	7	M		Great Britain		Caravan	8 Sep 1828
BUNKER, Absalom	30 5/12	M	Mariner	America	Nantucket	Young Phenix	17 Jan 1825
B.	26	M	Gentleman	U. States		Star	7 Jan 1827
Daniel, Capt.	40	M		United States	United States	Only Daughter	26 Apr 1826
David	24	M	Mariner	Nantucket	New York	Indian Chief	19 Jun 1823
Edw.	10	M	None	United States	United States	Cortes	19 Nov 1821
F. E.	32	F	Mercht.	N. York	South America	Tampico	7 Jan 1828
F. O.	26	M	Merchant	N. York	U. States	United States	10 Jan 1825
Fredk. E.	28	M	Mercht.	U. States	U. States	Sully	15 Jul 1829
Jno.	28	M		Ireland	U. States	Robert Fulton	9 Feb 1822
John	3	M		G. Britain	U. States	London	23 Sep 1828
R.	51	M	Harness Maker	Vera Cruz	U. States	Eliza	11 Apr 1826
BUNKS, Daniel	8 9/12	M		Ireland	America	Rising States	7 Jul 1828
BUNN, Thomas	22	M	Servant	Great Britain	Great Britain	Roman	10 May 1828
BUNNEL, Jacob	28 5/12	M	Farmer	Switzerland	U. States	France	26 Jun 1828
John	26 8/12	M	Farmer	Switzerland	U. States	France	26 Jun 1828
BUNNELL, M.	38			Nantucket		Ocean	28 Jul 1820
Z.	14	M	Mechanic	U.S.	U. States	Jane	15 Jun 1824
BUNSRARTH, Carian	50	F	Farmer	Germany	United States	Oxford	14 Aug 1828
Catherine	16	F	Farmer	Germany	United States	Oxford	14 Aug 1828
Georges	14	M	Farmer	Germany	United States	Oxford	14 Aug 1828
Georges	50	M	Farmer	Germany	United States	Oxford	14 Aug 1828
Jaques	21	M	Farmer	Germany	United States	Oxford	14 Aug 1828
Jean	24	M	Farmer	Germany	United States	Oxford	14 Aug 1828
Mariane	9	F	Farmer	Germany	United States	Oxford	14 Aug 1828
Marion	19	F	Farmer	Germany	United States	Oxford	14 Aug 1828

NAMES OF PASSENGERS	AGE	SEX	OCCUPATIONS	COUNTRY TO WHICH THEY BELONG	COUNTRY THEY INTEND TO INHABIT	SHIPS/DATES OF ARRIVAL	
BUNSUM, Margt.	35	F	Lady	New York		Ann Maria	7 Sep 1827
BUNSWARTH, Mariane	45	F	Farmer	Germany	United States	Oxford	14 Aug 1828
BUNTIN, Alace	18	F	Farmer	Ireland	United States	L. M. Pelham	25 Jun 1822
Jno. W.	17	M	Gentleman	St. Barthole-mews	U. States	Thomas & Eliza	29 Jul 1823
BUNTING, Madalane	49	F	Servant	St. Croix	America	South Carolina Packet	2 Aug 1825
Thomas	19	M	Farmer	Ireland	U. States	Dickinson	30 Jul 1825
BUNTON, Margaret	25	F		United States	U. States	Hazard	17 Jul 1822
BURARY,							
Pier Francis	30 5/12	M	Gentleman	Switzerland	U.S. America	Edward	28 Oct 1825
BURAS, Benjamin	43	M	Labourer	Great Britain	United States	Robert	15 Jul 1822
BURCH, Ann	6	F	Tailor	Great Britain	United States	Thomas Dickason	31 Jul 1829
Cathe.	25	F		Columbia	Columbia	William Bayard	6 Aug 1825
Elinor	30	F	Brewer	Great Britan	United States	Clematis	8 May 1827
Eliza	23	F	Spinster	Ireland	U. States	Josephine	30 Aug 1828
Elizabeth	12	F	Brewer	Great Britan	United States	Clematis	8 May 1827
Esebella	0 4/12	F	Child	Ireland	U. States	Josephine	30 Aug 1828
Glorie	49 6/12	M	Farmer	Ireland	U. States	Josephine	30 Aug 1828
Jane	6	F	Brewer	Great Britan	United States	Clematis	8 May 1827
John	44	M	Brewer	Great Britan	United States	Clematis	8 May 1827
Mary	8	F	Brewer	Great Britan	United States	Clematis	8 May 1827
Rachel	43	F	Matron	Ireland	U. States	Josephine	30 Aug 1828
Robt.	3	M		Columbia	Columbia	William Bayard	6 Aug 1825
Robt. H.	32	M		Columbia	Columbia	William Bayard	6 Aug 1825
Sarah	18	F	Tailor	Great Britain	United States	Thomas Dickason	31 Jul 1829
Thomas	45	M	Tailor	Great Britain	United States	Thomas Dickason	31 Jul 1829
BURCHEN, Samuel	44	M	Black Smith	England	United States	Cambria	3 Jul 1829
BURCHENS, S. A.	35	F	Servant	Hamburg	United States	Maria Elizabeth	2 Sep 1822
BURCHER, George	13	M	None	England	America	Ann	2 Nov 1820
Wm.	56	M	Farmer	England	America	Ann	2 Nov 1820
BURCK, James	28	M	Joiner	Argyle (Tedland) Scotland	United States	Jean Hastie	27 Jul 1829
William	27	M	Farmer	Ireland	New York	Concordia	12 Oct 1826
BURCKE, Phillip	20	M	Gentleme	Great Briton	United States	Mount Vernon	30 Dec 1828
BURCKLE, Emanuel	29	M	Merchant	U. States	New York	Lewis	16 Mar 1826
P. J.	30	M	Merchant	U. States	U. States	Courier	9 Feb 1829
BURCKLEY, Wm.	26	M	Merchant	U. States	U. States	Eastern Star	15 Aug 1827
BURD, Eliza	39	F		G. Britain		Caravan	8 Sep 1828
Martin	39	M	Shepherd	G. Britain		Caravan	8 Sep 1828
BURDEN, Henry	36	M	Merchant	Scotland	United States	York	31 Mar 1828
Margaret	11	F		Ireland	United States	Leonidas	3 Aug 1825
BURDER, —, Mrs.	32	F	None	Scotland	United States	Camillus	28 Apr 1824
James	7	M	None	Scotland	United States	Camillus	28 Apr 1824
John	11	M	None	Scotland	United States	Camillus	28 Apr 1824
William	9	M	None	Scotland	United States	Camillus	28 Apr 1824
BURDET, Saml.	30	M	Gentleman	Uns. States	United States	Helen	5 Sep 1828
BURDETT, Charles	26	M	Rule Maker	G.B.	New York	Eliza Grant	29 Aug 1829
BURDING, Betsey		F	Spinster		United States	William	5 Oct 1822
BURDITT, Anne	6	F	None	Great Britain	United States	Mary & Harriet	3 Jul 1829
Charles	27	M	Farmer	Great Britain	United States	Mary & Harriet	3 Jul 1829
Mary	29	F	None	Great Britain	United States	Mary & Harriet	3 Jul 1829
Sarah	1	F	None	Great Britain	United States	Mary & Harriet	3 Jul 1829
BURDON, H.	18	M	Gentleman	England		Hudson	23 Jul 1828
BURDS, Edw.	21	M	Painter	Great Brittan	United States	Lewis	13 Jan 1827
BUREL, A.	31	M	Merchant	England	U. States	Flight	2 Nov 1825
BURELL, T. S.	22	M	Merchant	North America	Different	Tampico	11 Jul 1826
BURFITT, Ann M.	1	F		England	United States	Brighton	20 Aug 1825
Martha	6	F		England	United States	Brighton	20 Aug 1825
Martha	28	F		England	United States	Brighton	20 Aug 1825
Thomas	4	M		England	United States	Brighton	20 Aug 1825
Thomas	54	M	Farmer	England	United States	Brighton	20 Aug 1825
BURFORD, John	25	M	Artist	Great Britain	U. States	Columbia	22 Sep 1828
BURGAN, Curtis	40	M	Farmer	Great Britain	United States	Richmond	18 Feb 1820
BURGARD, Abel	6	M		Germany	U. States	Isabella	10 Aug 1829
Antoinnette	2	F		Germany	U. States	Isabella	10 Aug 1829

NAMES OF PASSENGERS	AGE	SEX	OCCUPATIONS	COUNTRY TO WHICH THEY BELONG	COUNTRY THEY INTEND TO INHABIT	SHIPS/DATES OF ARRIVAL	
BURGARD (cont'd)							
Elizabeth	19	F		Germany	U. States	Isabella	10 Aug 1829
Elizabeth	46	F		Germany	U. States	Isabella	10 Aug 1829
Frederick	13	M		Germany	U. States	Isabella	10 Aug 1829
Jacob	4	M		Germany	U. States	Isabella	10 Aug 1829
Johannes	17	F		Germany	U. States	Isabella	10 Aug 1829
Johannes	50	M	Farmer	Germany	U. States	Isabella	10 Aug 1829
Maria	9	F		Germany	U. States	Isabella	10 Aug 1829
BURGER, Catharina	18	F	...	Wirtemburg	United States	Wade	29 Aug 1825
Catharine	40	F		France	U. States	Danube	21 Nov 1826
John	38	M		France	U. States	Danube	21 Nov 1826
Magdalina	25	F	...	Wirtemburg	United States	Wade	29 Aug 1825
Margareth	3	F		France	U. States	Danube	21 Nov 1826
Richard	56	M	Watchmaker	United States	U. States	William Prince	13 Dec 1827
BURGES, James	22	M	None	England	United States	Montgomery	6 Mar 1829
BURGESS, Ane	20	F		Great Britain		Manhattan	7 Nov 1827
Ann	4	F	Child	England	United States	Cambria	3 Jul 1829
Edmond	3	M	Child	England	United States	Cambria	3 Jul 1829
Edmond	25	M	Farmer	England	United States	Cambria	3 Jul 1829
Edward	35	M	Farmer	G. Britain	Canada	Nancy	12 Aug 1820
Eliza	5	F	Farmer	Windsor	Canada	Pilgrim	1 Sep 1828
Elizabeth	21	F		Great Britain		Manhattan	7 Nov 1827
Elizabeth	43	F		Great Britain		Manhattan	7 Nov 1827
Elizabeth	44	F	Farmer	Windsor	Canada	Pilgrim	1 Sep 1828
Francis	13	F	Farmer	Windsor	Canada	Pilgrim	1 Sep 1828
Geo.	7	M	Farmer	Windsor	Canada	Pilgrim	1 Sep 1828
Hannah	15	F	Farmer	Windsor	Canada	Pilgrim	1 Sep 1828
Harriet	16	F		Great Britain		Manhattan	7 Nov 1827
James	14	M		Great Britain		Manhattan	7 Nov 1827
James	19	M	Farmer	Windsor	Canada	Pilgrim	1 Sep 1828
John	8/12	M	Child	England	United States	Cambria	3 Jul 1829
John	12	M	Farmer	Great Britian	United States	Columbia	21 Jan 1828
John	17	M	Farmer	Windsor	Canada	Pilgrim	1 Sep 1828
John	41	M	Merchant	Great Britain		Manhattan	7 Nov 1827
Mary	10	F	Farmer	Windsor	Canada	Pilgrim	1 Sep 1828
Racheal	32	F	Farmer	G. Britain	Canada	Nancy	12 Aug 1820
Sarah	25	F	Wife	England	United States	Cambria	3 Jul 1829
Wm.	22	F	Farmer	Windsor	Canada	Pilgrim	1 Sep 1828
Wm.	40	M	Farmer	Great Britian	United States	Columbia	21 Jan 1828
BURGETT, Charles	26	M	Bookbinder	Ireland		Eliza Grant	29 Aug 1829
BURGI, Benedict	2	M	Mason	Less	U.S. America	Superior	18 Jun 1825
Benedict	28	M	Mason	Less	U.S. America	Superior	18 Jun 1825
Elizabeth	5	M	Mason	Less	U.S. America	Superior	18 Jun 1825
John	2	M	Mason	Less	U.S. America	Superior	18 Jun 1825
Madelaine	30	F	Mason	Less	U.S. America	Superior	18 Jun 1825
BURGLE, Michael	25	M	Carpenter	Germany	United States	Origon	8 Jun 1824
BURGLEY, Allen, Capt.	26	M	Marener	U.N. States		Orient	9 Dec 1826
*sent Home by the Marican Counsell							
BURGMAN, Jno. Chr.	24	M	Sugar Baker	Germany	U.S.	Robert Edwards	11 Nov 1822
BURGOYNE, E.	14	F		United States	U. States	Panthea	5 Oct 1822
H.	16	F		United States	U. States	Panthea	5 Oct 1822
Wm.	42	M	Merchant	United States	U. States	Panthea	5 Oct 1822
BURGY, Eugenia, Mrs.			None	France	U.S.	Sully	26 Oct 1829
Henry	4		Merchant	France	U.S.	Sully	26 Oct 1829
Henry	34	M	...	U. States	U. States	Queen Mab	26 Jul 1824
BURIA, Antonia	25	M	Merchant	Spain	Havana	Packet	26 Dec 1823
Antonio	26	M	Merch.	United States	United States	Rapid	24 Oct 1823
BURINGKER, —, Mrs.	30	M		Switzerland	U. States	Martha	26 Dec 1823
P.	30	M	Carpenter	Switzerland	U. States	Martha	26 Dec 1823
BURK, Andrew	16	M	Clerk	Ireland	America	William	21 May 1825
Biddy	30	F	Wife	Ireland	U. States	Hanford	29 Dec 1828
David	23	M	Cooper	Ireland	Virginia	Susquehanna	9 Jan 1824
Elista	32	M		Ireland	America	Carolina Ann	14 Feb 1825
Elizabeth	1	F	Child	England	Pennsylvania	General Stark	12 Jun 1826
Fanny	28	F	Lady	Great Briton	United States	Erin	26 May 1821
James	1	M	Labourer	Great Britain	United States	Thomas Dickason	31 Jul 1829
James	23	M	Saddlier	Ireland	United States	Ann Maria	1 Apr 1826
Jas.	14	M		Ireland	U. States	William Byrnes	17 Jul 1825

NAMES OF PASSENGERS	AGE	SEX	OCCUPATIONS	COUNTRY TO WHICH THEY BELONG	COUNTRY THEY INTEND TO INHABIT	SHIPS/DATES OF ARRIVAL	
BURK (cont'd)							
Jno.	8	M		Ireland	U. States	William Byrnes	17 Jul 1825
John	16	M		Ireland	America	Carolina Ann	14 Feb 1825
John	28	M	Farmer	England	United States	Ganges	10 May 1828
Judah	42	M	Manufacturer	Ireland	U. States	William Byrnes	17 Jul 1825
Julia	5	F	Child	Ireland	U. States	Hanford	29 Dec 1828
Lawrence	30	M	Carpenter	England	Pennsylvania	General Stark	12 Jun 1826
Margaret	20	F	Spinster	Ireland	America	Wilson	16 Nov 1824
Margaret	25	F	Wife	England	Pennsylvania	General Stark	12 Jun 1826
Margt.	10	F		Ireland	U. States	William Byrnes	17 Jul 1825
Mary	18/12	F		Ireland	U. States	William Byrnes	17 Jul 1825
Mary	22	F		Gt. Britain	United States	John & Elizabeth	25 Sep 1827
Mary	30	F	Labourer	Great Britain	United States	Thomas Dickason	31 Jul 1829
Mathew	31	M	Farmer	Ireland	United States	Lord Strangford	20 Jun 1826
Michael	26	...	...	Ireland	United States	Lord Strangford	20 Jun 1826
Nelly	6/12	F	Child	Ireland	U. States	Hanford	29 Dec 1828
Owen	25	M	Laborer	Gt. Britain		Dalhouse Castle	13 May 1828
Pat	27	M		St. Johns	U. States	Wanderer	30 Oct 1828
Patrick	25	M	Farmer	Ireland	America	Josephine	24 Jul 1826
Peter	3	M	Labourer	Great Britain	United States	Thomas Dickason	31 Jul 1829
Peter	30	M	Labourer	Great Britain	United States	Thomas Dickason	31 Jul 1829
Richard	28	M	Butcher	Great Britain	United States	Richmond	18 Feb 1820
Rose	26	F	Spinster	Ireland	United States	Lord Strangford	20 Jun 1826
T.	21	M	Blacksmith	America	U. States	Ambuscade	11 Jul 1821
Thomas	34 3/12	M	Clerk	Great Briton	United States	Erin	26 May 1821
BURKARD, Antony	8/12	M	his family [Sebastian]	Germany	Philadelphia	Isabella	15 Sep 1828
Christina	25	F	his family [Sebastian]	Germany	Philadelphia	Isabella	15 Sep 1828
Sebastian	28	M	Farmer	Germany	Philadelphia	Isabella	15 Sep 1828
BURKE, An	35	F		Ireland	United States	Fabius	4 Jun 1828
Ann	41	F		England	United States	Copernicus	3 Aug 1829
Anne	7	F		Ireland	Cincinita	Lima	5 Aug 1829
Anne	7	F		England	U. States	Lima	5 Aug 1829
Anthony	21	M	Carpenter	Ireland	United States	Jubilee	13 Sep 1827
Briget	21	F		Great Britain	United States	India	5 Sep 1827
Cath.	7		No buseniss	England	America	Sarah	18 Aug 1829
Catharin	9	F		England	U. States	Lima	5 Aug 1829
Catharin	38	F		England	U. States	Lima	5 Aug 1829
Catherine	...	F		Ireland	Cincinita	Lima	5 Aug 1829
Catherine	38	F		Ireland	Cincinita	Lima	5 Aug 1829
Cathr.	17		No buseniss	England	America	Sarah	18 Aug 1829
Eleanor	16	F	None	Ireland	United States	Mary & Harriet	3 Jul 1829
Helen	8		No buseniss	England	America	Sarah	18 Aug 1829
Honor	17	F		Ireland	Cincinita	Lima	5 Aug 1829
Honor	17	F		England	U. States	Lima	5 Aug 1829 y
James	18	M	Laborer	Gt. Britain		Dalhouse Castle	13 May 1828
Jas.	35	M	None	Ireland	U. States	Dalhouse	23 Mar 1829
Jeremiah	18	M		Ireland	Cincinita	Lima	5 Aug 1829
Jeremiah	18	M		England	U. States	Lima	5 Aug 1829
Jno.	50	M	Manufacturer	Ireland	U. States	William Byrnes	17 Jul 1825
John	7	M		England	United States	Copernicus	3 Aug 1829
Jona.	17	M	Weaver	Great Britain	United States	India	5 Sep 1827
Joseph	40	M	Cooper	New Orleans	New Orleans	Brighton	20 Aug 1825
Leonard	9	M		England	United States	Copernicus	3 Aug 1829
Marten	42	M	Musician	England	United States	Copernicus	3 Aug 1829
Martha	6	F		Ireland	United States	Fabius	4 Jun 1828
Mary	17	F		Ireland	Cincinita	Lima	5 Aug 1829
Mary	17	F		England	U. States	Lima	5 Aug 1829
May	26	F		Gt. Britain	United States	Penelope	9 Sep 1828
Mich.	7	M		Ireland	United States	Fabius	4 Jun 1828
Michael	8	M		Ireland	Cincinita	Lima	5 Aug 1829
Michael	8	M		England	U. States	Lima	5 Aug 1829
Michl.	26	M	Laborer	Ireland	United States	Trio	13 Jun 1827
Pat	25	M	Farmer	Ireland	United States	Trio	13 Jun 1827

NAMES OF PASSENGERS	AGE	SEX	OCCUPATIONS	COUNTRY TO WHICH THEY BELONG	COUNTRY THEY INTEND TO INHABIT	SHIPS/DATES OF ARRIVAL	
BURKE (cont'd)							
Pat	44	M		Gt. Britain	United States	Penelope	9 Sep 1828
Richd.	6	M		Ireland	U. States	William Byrnes	17 Jul 1825
Thomas	2	M	Infant	Ireland	United States	Wilson	4 Oct 1827
Thomas	30	M	Yeoman	Ireland	United States	Dublin Packet	28 Apr 1824
Thomas	32	M	Farmer	Ireland	United States	Silas Richards	3 Apr 1826
William	4	M		England	United States	Copernicus	3 Aug 1829
BURKET, Daniel	21	M	Farmer	England	United States	Aurora	9 Jul 1827
Thomas	22	M	Drugist	England	England	Criterion	29 May 1822
BURKETT, George	38	M	Shoe Maker	England	Canada	Mentor	20 Oct 1825
John	24		Farmer	Ireland	United States	John Dickinson	28 Jun 1822
BURKHART, Jean, Capt.	38	M	Ship Master	United States	United States	Dromo	9 Oct 1828
BURKINGHAM,							
Joseph H.	21	M	Printer	U. States	U. States	York	13 Aug 1827
BURKLEY, Mary A.	18	F	None	Great Brittain	U. States	Florenzo	20 Mar 1827
BURLACK, Margaret							
E., Miss	12			St. Croix	New York	South Carolina Packet	19 Jun 1826
BURLEY, Jno.	20	M	Clerk	England	U. States	Wilson	2 Sep 1823
Nathaniel E., Capt.	32	M	Ship Master	United States	United States	Dromo	9 Oct 1828
Robert	31	M	Farmer	England	U.N. States	Jane	7 Oct 1826
BURLING, B. S.	40	M	Merchant	U. States	United States	Asaph	25 Dec 1827
Charles	19		Farmer	England	S. New York	Xenophon	25 Jul 1826
BURLINGHAM,							
Joseph, Mr.	38	M	Merchant	England	England	Manchester	8 Dec 1827
BURLOCK, —, Mrs.	22	F	Lady	America	U. States	Catharine	3 Sep 1821
D.	36	M	Merchant	America	U. States	Catharine	3 Sep 1821
David	20	M	Merchant	U. States	U. States	South Carolina Packet	4 Sep 1822
David L.	27	M	Merchant	America	America	Loire	7 Apr 1821
M. E., Miss	8	F		St. Croix	U. States	South Carolina Packet	4 Sep 1822
Mary R.	2	F	Child	America	U. States	Catharine	3 Sep 1821
BURMINGHAM, Mary	30	F		Limerick	N. York	Thomas & William	25 May 1827
BURMISTER, —, Mr.	18			Germany	United States	Henri IV	14 Sep 1827
BURN, Benjamin	22		Sadder	America	America	Commerce	14 Mar 1823
Biddy	19	F		Ireland	United States	Commerce	13 Jun 1828
James	25	M	Labourer	Ireland	United States	Lord Wellington	28 May 1827
John	21	M	Gentleman	England	United States	Hudson	17 Mar 1828
Mary	20	F	None	Ireland	United States	Lord Wellington	28 May 1827
Mary	20	F		England	United States	Hudson	17 Mar 1828
Michael	35	M	Labourer	Ireland	America	Ulysses	1 May 1822
Susan	20	F				Catherine	19 Aug 1825
Thos.	20	M	Labourer	G... S...	United States	Baltic	21 Apr 1827
Thos.	24	M	Farmer	Gt. Britain	United States	Penelope	9 Sep 1828
BURNAHY, Amelia	19	F	None	England	Canada	Brighton	11 Mar 1825
Richard	31	M	Gentleman	England	Canada	Brighton	11 Mar 1825
BURNAM, W.	25	M	Carpenter	Massachusetts	Boston	General Warren	8 Jul 1829
BURNANE, John	45	M	Farmer	Ireland	United States	Trio	31 Oct 1827
BURNARD, F. P.	28	M	Merchant	N. Orleans	U. States	Fabius	7 Dec 1825
BURNE, M.	2...	...	Marchent	St. Croix	West Indies	William & Frederick	16 Jun 1827
BURNELL, Margt.	24	F	Labourer	Great Britian	United States	Princess Charlotte	6 Sep 1828
Samuel	19	M		England	United States	Amelia	20 Aug 1829
BURNES, —, Mrs.	30	F		New Brunswick	New Brunswick	Abigale	9 Aug 1821
Alfred	1 6/12	M		England	United States	Hercules	25 Jan 1820
Ann	16	F	Spinster	Ireland	United States	Robert Fulton	24 Jul 1826
Ann Maria	4	F		England	United States	Hercules	25 Jan 1820
Bridget	23	F	None	Great Briton	United States	Mount Vernon	30 Dec 1828
Cathrine	4 1/12	F	None	Great Briton	United States	Mount Vernon	30 Dec 1828
Deborah	9	F		England	United States	Hercules	25 Jan 1820
Hannah	33	F		England	United States	Hercules	25 Jan 1820
James	26			Ireland	New York	General Marion	21 Nov 1828
James	34	M	Store Keeper	England	United States	Hercules	25 Jan 1820
James	50	M	Labourer	Great Britain	United States	Thomas Dickason	31 Jul 1829
Joseph	6	M		England	United States	Hercules	25 Jan 1820

NAMES OF PASSENGERS	AGE	SEX	OCCUPATIONS	COUNTRY TO WHICH THEY BELONG	COUNTRY THEY INTEND TO INHABIT	SHIPS/DATES OF ARRIVAL	
BURNES (cont'd)							
Judy	20	F	Spinster	Grt. Britain	United States	Robert Fulton	8 Oct 1828
Lewis	28	M	Merchant	England	England	Loire	7 Apr 1821
Ls.	25	M	Farmer	Ireland	U. States	Margaret	19 Mar 1825
Robt.	24	M	Butcher	England	U. States	Electra	7 Jul 1828
S.	30	M	Merchant	New Brunswick	New Brunswick	Abigale	9 Aug 1821
Samuel	16	M	Y. Man	Ireland	New York	Trusty	12 Sep 1828
Thomas	11	M		England	United States	Hercules	25 Jan 1820
BURNET, B.	39					Copernicus	3 Aug 1829
BURNETT, James	6	M	None	Great Britian	G. Britain	Enterprize	3 Jul 1826
Jona.	26	M	Farmer	England	U. States	Margarett Scott	22 Aug 1827
Peter, Mr.	27	M	Merchant	Scotland	Canada	Hector	11 May 1821
Wm.	21	M	Gentleman	Great Britian	U. States	Pallas	17 Aug 1824
BURNEY, James	21	M	Farmer	G. Brittian	United States	Louisa	14 Jun 1825
Sarah	19	F	Wife [of Thomas]	G. Brittian	United States	Louisa	14 Jun 1825
Thomas	30 9/12	M	Farmer	G. Brittian	United States	Louisa	14 Jun 1825
BURNFATHER, Ann	22	F		Great Britain	United States	Diana	6 Jul 1829
Thos.	1 6/12	M		Great Britain	United States	Diana	6 Jul 1829
Wm.	2	M		Great Britain	United States	Diana	6 Jul 1829
BURNGAN, Larrence	25	M	Labourer	Ireland	U. States	Combine	30 Nov 1825
BURNHAM, Catherine	3	F	None	England	Alexandria, U.S.	Roman	17 Oct 1826
Goerge	5	M	None	England	Alexandria, U.S.	Roman	17 Oct 1826
J.	36	M	Capt.	U. States	U. States	La Ville de Cayes	5 Dec 1826
James	35	M	Merchant	New York	New York	Emma	25 Oct 1825
Joseph	1	M	None	England	Alexandria, U.S.	Roman	17 Oct 1826
Joseph	28	M	Farmer	England	Alexandria, U.S.	Roman	17 Oct 1826
Mark	21	M				Helen	4 Aug 1829
Rebecca	29	F	None	England	Alexandria, U.S.	Roman	17 Oct 1826
W.	30	M	Merchant	American	U. States	Romulus	31 Jul 1823
BURNHARD,							
John George	28	M	Confectioner	Germany	United States	Elizabeth	4 Sep 1826
BURNIL, William	32	M	Merchant	Scotland	United States	Cortes	23 Mar 1824
BURNS, —	6			England	United States	Hugh Johnson	11 Jun 1828
—	36			England	United States	Hugh Johnson	11 Jun 1828
—	40		Labourer	England	United States	Hugh Johnson	11 Jun 1828
—, Mrs.	20		Wife, Going to her Husband	Scotland	United States	Camillus	3 May 1828
—, Mrs.	38	F	Iron Founder	Great Britain	United States	Olympia	20 Aug 1829
...	23	M	Clerk	Ireland	U. States	Wilson	2 Sep 1823
Agnes	11	F		Scotland	United States	Camillus	9 May 1827
Agnes	46	F		Scotland	United States	Camillus	9 May 1827
Alex.	30	M	Joiner	Scotland	United States	Essex	23 May 1828
Alex.	30	F		Ireland	United States	Commerce	13 Jun 1828
Alex., Jr.	8	M	Joiner	Scotland	United States	Essex	23 May 1828
Ann	8	F		Gt. Britain		Dalhouse Castle	13 May 1828
Ann	19	F	Labourer	Ireland	United States	Hope & Esther	17 Oct 1827
Ann	25	F		Ireland	U. States	Hope & Esther	27 Sep 1824
Anne	17	F	Iron Founder	Great Britain	United States	Olympia	20 Aug 1829
Archibald	19	M		Scotland	United States	Camillus	9 May 1827
Archibald	30	M		Scotland	United States	Camillus	9 May 1827
Arthur	40	M	Farmer	England		Marchioness	13 May 1828
Biddy	2	F		Gt. Britain		Dalhouse Castle	13 May 1828
Catharine	25 2/12	F	Wife	Ireland	America	Farmer	3 May 1824
Catherine	...	F		Ireland	United States	Sarah G.	20 Jul 1827
Catherine	23	F		Scotland	United States	Camillus	9 May 1827
D.	30	M	Confectioner	Halifax	U. States	Hope & Esther	12 May 1826
Dennis	24	M	Labourer	England	United States	Aurelia	7 Jun 1826
Edward	12	M	Spinster	England	U. States	Electra	7 Jul 1828
Eleanor	22		Servant	Ireland	United States	Robert Burns	30 May 1823
Elizabeth	1 1/2	F		Scotland	United States	Camillus	9 May 1827
Elizabeth	28	F	Spinster	Ireland	U. States	Panthea	8 Apr 1826
Ellen	14	F	Iron Founder	Great Britain	United States	Olympia	20 Aug 1829
Ellen	20	F	Spinster	Ireland	United States	Fabius	4 Jun 1828
Ellen	25	F		England	America	Two Marys	24 Sep 1827
Frederick	25	M	Farmer	U. States	U. States	Nancy	19 Oct 1821
Geo.	28			England	United States	India	8 Jun 1827
Georgiana	14	F	None	Scotland	United States	Dalhouse Castle	6 Sep 1827
Hannah	35	F		G. Britain	Canada	Nancy	12 Aug 1820

159

NAMES OF PASSENGERS	AGE	SEX	OCCUPATIONS	COUNTRY TO WHICH THEY BELONG	COUNTRY THEY INTEND TO INHABIT	SHIPS/DATES OF ARRIVAL	
BURNS (cont'd)							
Helen	12	F		Scotland	United States	Camillus	9 May 1827
Helen	25	F	Servant	England	U. States	Trident	1 Dec 1824
Henry	38 1/12	M	Chandler	Ireland	America	Farmer	3 May 1824
Isaac	30	M	Farmer	Great Britain	United States	William Dawson	18 Jun 1827
J.	32		Farmer	Ireland	United States	Courier	16 May 1825
James	3/12			Scotland	United States	Camillus	3 May 1828
James	21	M	Labourer	Ireland		Marchioness	13 May 1828
James	26	M	Farmer	Ireland	U. States	William & John	10 Jul 1824
James	27	M	Baker	G. Britain	U. States	Camillus	8 Sep 1828
James	32	M	Farmer	Great Britain	United States	Aurora	5 Sep 1826
Jane	14	F	Spinster	England	U. States	Electra	7 Jul 1828
Jane	52	F	None	Scotland	United States	Dalhouse Castle	6 Sep 1827
Janet	7	F		Scotland	United States	Camillus	9 May 1827
Jas.	18	M	Farmer	Ireland	New York	Phoenix	29 Apr 1826
Jas.	28	M	Labourer	Ireland	U. States	Hope & Esther	27 Sep 1824
Jesse		F	Carpenter	England	U. States	Electra	7 Jul 1828
Jno.	28	M	Plasterer	Ireland	United States	Dalhouse Castle	6 Sep 1827
Jno.	42	M	Farmer	England	U.S. America	Cortes	19 May 1826
Joh.	20	M	Labourer	Dublin	Dublin	Howard Douglass	11 May 1827
John	25	M	Farmer	Ireland	America	Superior	12 Jun 1824
John	25	M	Weaver	Ireland	America	Plutarch	18 Jul 1826
John	25	M	Weaver	Ireland	United States	Henry Kneeland	7 Jun 1828
John	28	M	Mechanic	G.B.	U.S.A.	Silas Richard	30 Jun 1828
John	34	F	Joiner	England	United States	India	8 Jun 1827
Joseph	23 5/12	M	...	England	America, U.S.	Illinois	3 Jun 1822
Joseph	25	M	Mechanic	Columbia	Columbia	Hesper	21 Sep 1827
Joseph	26	M	Carpenter	Ireland	America	Plutarch	18 Jul 1826
Joseph	48		Labourer	Manchester		Mount Vernon	18 Oct 1822
Lewis	40	M	Merchant	St. John, N.B.	St. John, N.B.	St. Michaels	11 May 1826
Lidia	18	M	Spinster	England	U. States	Electra	7 Jul 1828
M.	32	M		Ireland	United States	Commerce	13 Jun 1828
Margaret	3	F		Halifax	U. States	Hope & Esther	12 May 1826
Margaret	6	F	Spinster	England	U. States	Electra	7 Jul 1828
Margaret	10	F		Gt. Britain		Dalhouse Castle	13 May 1828
Margaret	13	F		Scotland	United States	Camillus	9 May 1827
Martha	3	F	Stone Mason	England	U. States	Electra	7 Jul 1828
Martha	9	F	Spinster	England	U. States	Electra	7 Jul 1828
Martin	18	M	Sugar Baker	Germany	U. States	Constitution	21 Jun 1824
Martock	28	M	Labourer	Ireland	U. States	Panthea	8 Apr 1826
Mary	16	F	Servant	Ireland	United States	Henry Kneeland	7 Jun 1828
Mary	18	F		Scotland	United States	Camillus	9 May 1827
Mary	22		Servant	Ireland	United States	Robert Burns	30 May 1823
Mary	24	F		Halifax	U. States	Hope & Esther	12 May 1826
Mary	26	F		Gt. Britain		Dalhouse Castle	13 May 1828
Mary	28	F	None	Ireland	U. States	Henry Kneeland	27 Jul 1825
Mathew	27	M	Labourer	England	America	Two Marys	24 Sep 1827
Michael	24	M	Farmer	Ireland	United States	Colossus	26 Aug 1828
Moses	39	M	Iron Founder	Great Britain	United States	Olympia	20 Aug 1829
Nace	30	M	Labourer	Dublin	Dublin	Howard Douglass	11 May 1827
Nancy	24	F	Servant	Ireland	United States	Henry Kneeland	7 Jun 1828
Nancy	25 6/12	F	Servant	Irereland	America	Carolina Ann	20 Jun 1825
Nicholas	20	M	Labourer	Ireland	United States	Trident	31 Mar 1827
Owen	25	M	Labourer	Ireland	United States	Hope & Esther	17 Oct 1827
Patrick	22	...	...	Ireland	United States	Carolina Ann	24 Oct 1825
Patrick	24	M	Farmer	Ireland	U. States	Nancy	29 Nov 1821
Patrick	27 0/12	M	Labourer	England	United States	John Wells	22 May 1826
Patrick	28	M	Labourer	Ireland	United States	Edwin	27 Oct 1828
Patt	20	M	Labourer	Great Britain	United States	India	5 Sep 1827
Peter	19	F	Labourer	Ireland	United States	Essex	23 May 1828
Phebe	21	F	Spinster	England	U. States	Electra	7 Jul 1828
Robert	23	M	Farmer	Great Britian	United States	Andes	19 Aug 1829
Sally	22	F		Ireland	United States	Enterprize	23 Jul 1827
Sandy	22	M	Weaver	Ireland	New York	Xenophon	3 Oct 1829
Sarah	4	F	Spinster	England	U. States	Electra	7 Jul 1828
Thomas	4	M		Scotland	United States	Camillus	9 May 1827
Thomas	20	M	Labourer	Ireland	Pensylvania	Lima	5 Aug 1829

NAMES OF PASSENGERS	AGE	SEX	OCCUPATIONS	COUNTRY TO WHICH THEY BELONG	COUNTRY THEY INTEND TO INHABIT	SHIPS/DATES OF ARRIVAL	
BURNS (cont'd)							
Thomas	20	M	Labourer	Ireland	U. States	Lima	5 Aug 1829
Thomas	23	M	Laborer	Ireland	United States	Sylvester Healy	17 Oct 1825
Thos.	8	M	Spinster	England	U. States	Electra	7 Jul 1828
Wm.	18	M	Spinster	England	U. States	Electra	7 Jul 1828
BURNSIDE, David	36	M	Merchant	Scotland	United States	Friends	13 Mar 1824
James	20	M	Sadler	Ireland	United States	Robert Fulton	10 Aug 1827
Jane	18	F	Spinster	Ireland	United States	Robert Fulton	10 Aug 1827
Jane	21	F	Matron	Ireland	United States	Robert Fulton	10 Aug 1827
Thomas	75			U.S.	U.S.	Silvanus Jenkins	30 Nov 1827
William	0 6/12	M	Child	Ireland	United States	Robert Fulton	10 Aug 1827
William	16	M	Sadler	Ireland	United States	Robert Fulton	10 Aug 1827
BURNSTED, Josiah F.	28	M	...	U. States	U. States	William Thompson	10 May 1825
BUROPP, Ann	22	F	Lady	Great Brittain	St. John	Nancy	18 Jul 1821
BURR, Hy.	23	M	Blacksmith	U. States	U. States	Boston Packet	5 Jul 1825
James	20	M	Laborer or Spinster	Ireland	United States	Sarah G.	15 Aug 1827
John	1 1/2		Child	Scotland	United States	Hope	5 Dec 1827
John	24	M	Farmer	England	U. States	Hercules	6 Jul 1827
John	27	M	Baker	Scotland	United States	Hope	5 Dec 1827
Mary	24	F		Scotland	United States	Hope	5 Dec 1827
Matthew	31	M	Labourer	Scotland	New York	Ariel	22 Feb 1823
R.	33	M	Mechanic	Philada.	U. States	Pocahontas	1 Feb 1825
Robert	23	M	Labourer	Scotland	New York	Ariel	22 Feb 1823
Yetty	25	F	Lady	U. States	U. States	Nancy	19 Oct 1821
BURRAS, Ann	22	F	wife	U. States	U. States	Pleiades	5 Nov 1828
D. B.	23	M	Merchant	New York	U. States	Angenora	16 Jan 1827
Mary Ann	18/12	F	Child	U. States	U. States	Pleiades	5 Nov 1828
Samuel	32	M	Seaman	U. States	U. States	Pleiades	5 Nov 1828
Samuel, Captain	30	M	Shipmaster	United States	United States	Trident	18 Jul 1827
BURRAWES, Thomas	22	M	Farmer, Labourer or Spinster	Ireland	U. States	Meteor	4 Oct 1827
BURRBROS, John	71	M	Farmer	Chadwell, Leeds, England	Gt. Britain	Orozimbo	19 Oct 1822
BURREL, Geo. Thompson	28	M	Mariner	United States	United States	General Warren	5 May 1828
*Distressd. Seaman from Schnr. Indus							
John	20	M	on a visit Returning home	Pensylvany	Inhabitant Pensylvany	Nile	18 Aug 1829
BURRELL, Charles	25	M	Farmer	Ireland	United States	Asia	29 Jul 1829
Dorothy	15	F	None			Evergreen	28 Jul 1820
Dorothy	50	F	None			Evergreen	28 Jul 1820
Eliza	14	F	Spinster	Ireland	United States	Asia	29 Jul 1829
Elizabeth	8	F	Spinster			Evergreen	28 Jul 1820
Ewd.	12	M	Farmer			Evergreen	28 Jul 1820
Ewd.	21	M	Farmer			Evergreen	28 Jul 1820
Geo.	35	M	Gentleman	U. States	U. States	Adeline	30 Apr 1821
George	25	M	Labourer			Evergreen	28 Jul 1820
Jane	50	F	his wife [John]	Ireland	United States	Asia	29 Jul 1829
John	20	M	Farmer	Ireland	United States	Asia	29 Jul 1829
John	24	M	Military	France	Martinique	General Pike	2 Oct 1826
John	28	M	Shoe Maker	G. Britain	U. States	Camillus	8 Sep 1828
John	60	M	Farmer	Ireland	United States	Asia	29 Jul 1829
Luthr.	18	M	Farmer			Evergreen	28 Jul 1820
Margaret	17	F	None			Evergreen	28 Jul 1820
Margery	10	F	Spinster			Evergreen	28 Jul 1820
Unity	18	M		G. Britain	U. States	Camillus	8 Sep 1828
BURRET, Poule	36	M	Capt. vessel	French Britain	U. States	Polly & Eliza	23 Mar 1826
BURRIADGE, Ann, Mrs.	40	F	Setler	England	New York	Maine	16 Jul 1821
BURRICH, D., Mr.	23	M	Merchant	G. Britain	Canada	Corinthian	29 Apr 1826
BURRIDGE, Elizabeth	24	F		England	England	Gulnard	24 Mar 1825
Jno.	30	M	Gardner	England	England	Gulnard	24 Mar 1825
William	36	M	Merchant	England	United States	Abigail	23 Nov 1820
BURRILL, Catharine	20	F	Servant	Ireland	United States	Lord Strangford	20 Jun 1826
James A.	19 10/12	M	Merchant	United States	United States	Clarice	27 Aug 1827
John	22	M	Cooper	Switzerland	U. States	Hewes	30 Oct 1829
Thomas	21	M	Labourer	England	America	Manhattan	20 Mar 1820
BURRIN, Lucien	19	M	Gentleman	France	United States	Aurora	11 Dec 1824
BURRIS, Robert	26	M	Manufactorer	England	United States	Orozimbo	1 Dec 1823

NAMES OF PASSENGERS	AGE	SEX	OCCUPATIONS	COUNTRY TO WHICH THEY BELONG	COUNTRY THEY INTEND TO INHABIT	SHIPS/DATES OF ARRIVAL	
BURROUGH, M., Dr.	28	M	Doctor	United States	U. States	Polly & Eliza	23 Mar 1826
BURROUGHS, George C.	32	M	Gentleman	Great Britain	U. States	York	7 Aug 1828
John S.	25	M	Gentleman	England	United States	Marion	25 Nov 1825
BURROW, Bartholomew	25	M	Yeoman	Ireland	United States	Borneo	9 Jul 1827
BURROWES, Isaac B.	47	M	Merchant	England	U. States	Pacific	5 Sep 1827
John	28	F				Splendid	14 Aug 1829
BURROWS, Eliza	25	F	Farmer	Gt. Brittian	United States	Manchester	16 Dec 1828
J. W.	30	M	Merchant	N. York	New York	Octavian	15 May 1824
Saml.	23	M	None	England	United States	Mary & Harriet	9 Mar 1829
Sarah	14	F	Cabin Servant	England	New York	Robert Edwards	17 Mar 1828
Silas E.		M	Merchant	Connecticutt	U. States	Post Captain	12 Dec 1822
Silas E.	32	M	Merchant	U. States	U. States	Medina	23 Apr 1828
William	22	M	Labourer	England	U. States	Comet	23 Aug 1828
Wm.	35	M	Farmer	Gt. Brittian	United States	Manchester	16 Dec 1828
BURSLEY, Maurice	26	M	Labourer	Ireland	United States	Sarah Ann	11 Jan 1827
BURST, John	30	M	Merchant	U. States	U. States	Tobasco	14 Apr 1828
Robert	23	M	Gardener	England	United States	Comet	6 Mar 1823
BURT, Arthur	46	M	Weaver	Ireland	Philadelphia	Carolina Ann	15 Oct 1824
Hannah	63		Shipwright	England	United States	Corinthian	30 May 1828
James	32	M	Supercargo	Connecticut	U. States	Ocean	23 Oct 1820
Mary	35	F	Wife	England	Canada	General Stark	12 Jun 1826
Peter	64		Shipwright	England	United States	Corinthian	30 May 1828
Sarah Ann	23	F		U. States	U. States	Native	29 Apr 1825
Thos. W.	31	M	Carpenter	U. States	U. States	Trent	23 Jan 1829
William	40	M	Minster	England	Canada	General Stark	12 Jun 1826
BURTAN, Betty	52	F	Farmer	Ireland	U. States	Dickinson	30 Jul 1825
John	21	M	Farmer	Ireland	U. States	Dickinson	30 Jul 1825
BURTE, Alice	10 2/12	F	Daughter	Ireland	United States	Louisa	27 Nov 1826
John	3 4/12	M	Son	Ireland	United States	Louisa	27 Nov 1826
Mary	14 3/12	F	Daughter	Ireland	United States	Louisa	27 Nov 1826
Mary Ann	34 2/12	F	Wife	Ireland	United States	Louisa	27 Nov 1826
Nathaniel	12	M	Son	Ireland	United States	Louisa	27 Nov 1826
Samuel	6 3/12	M	Son	Ireland	United States	Louisa	27 Nov 1826
William	17	M	Labourer	Ireland	United States	Louisa	27 Nov 1826
BURTING, F. L.	17	F		France	U. States	Diana	12 Apr 1825
BURTINSHAW, Hugh	35	M	Butcher	England	U.S.A.	Hudson	21 Aug 1829
BURTIS, Sarah	44	F	Lady	England	England	Nancy	16 Aug 1824
William	6	M	boy	England	England	Nancy	16 Aug 1824
Wm.	63	M	Gentleman	England	England	Nancy	16 Aug 1824
BURTLEY, W. B.	26	M		Great Britain	United States	Active	25 Mar 1828
BURTON, Alex.	35	M	Merchant	New York	U. States	Alexander	18 Mar 1822
Alexr.	36	M	Merchant	U. States	U. States	Boston	26 Sep 1820
Alfred G.	22	M	Merchant	New York	U. States	Mary & Eliza	2 Jul 1829
Ann	13					William	17 Aug 1820
Ann	41	F		Great Britain	U. States	Great Britain	18 Mar 1828
Benjamin	12	M		Great Britain	U. States	Great Britain	18 Mar 1828
Benjn.	34	M	Gentleman	gt. Britain	Great Britain	Manchester	12 Aug 1829
Catherine	22	F	None	U. States	U. States	Leader	2 Aug 1826
D.	28	M	Mariner	U. States	U. States	Rice Plant	20 Sep 1827
Daniel	40		Farmer	England	U. States	William	17 Aug 1820
Daniel, Junr.	15					William	17 Aug 1820
Daniel V.	22	M	Doctor	Great Britain	Great Britan	Nancy	13 Dec 1822
Eliza	25	F		England	New Jersey	Lima	5 Aug 1829
Eliza	25	F		England	New Jersey	Lima	5 Aug 1829
Elizabeth	14	F		Great Britain	U. States	Great Britain	18 Mar 1828
Elizabeth	17					William	17 Aug 1820
Hannah	1					William	17 Aug 1820
Isabella	16	F		England	U.S.A.	Robin Hood	6 May 1828
J.	36	M	Farmer	Great Britton	U. State	Earl of Liverpool	16 Aug 1826
James	9	M		Great Britain	U. States	Great Britain	18 Mar 1828
James	27	M	Labourer	Scotland	Pittsburgh	Orozimbo	8 Jun 1822
Jno.	28	M	Butcher	England	United States	Aurora	27 Apr 1825
Job	28	M	White Smith	England	New Jersey	Lima	5 Aug 1829
Job	28	M	Whitesmith	England	New Jersey	Lima	5 Aug 1829
John	18					William	17 Aug 1820
John	24	M		Great Brit.	Ohio	Gov. Griswald	3 Jul 1820
John	28	M	Hardward Man	England	United States	Copernicus	3 Aug 1829
John	30 2/12	M	...	England	America, U.S.	Illinois	3 Jun 1822
John, Dr.	22	M	Doctor	America	U. States	Florida	16 May 1827

162

NAMES OF PASSENGERS	A G E	S E X	OCCUPATIONS	COUNTRY TO WHICH THEY BELONG	COUNTRY THEY INTEND TO INHABIT	SHIPS/DATES OF ARRIVAL	
BURTON (cont'd)							
Jonathan	5	M		Great Britain	U. States	Great Britain	18 Mar 1828
Joseph	7	M		Great Britain	U. States	Great Britain	18 Mar 1828
Joshua	7	M		Great Britain	U. States	Ann Marria	6 Aug 1823
Joshua	55	M		Dranher Haff.	U. States	Manhattan	21 May 1821
Martha	3					William	17 Aug 1820
Mary	1	F		Great Britain	U. States	Ann Marria	6 Aug 1823
Mary	5					William	17 Aug 1820
Mary	38					William	17 Aug 1820
Richard	4/12	M		Great Britain	U. States	Great Britain	18 Mar 1828
Robert	10	M		Great Britain	U. States	Great Britain	18 Mar 1828
Robert	41	M	Miner	Great Britain	U. States	Great Britain	18 Mar 1828
Roda	5	F		Great Britain	U. States	Ann Marria	6 Aug 1823
Saml. J.	27	M	Military	G. Brittain	Canada	Hercules	24 Oct 1821
Samuel	7					William	17 Aug 1820
Sarah	27	F		Great Britain	U. States	Ann Marria	6 Aug 1823
Thom.	27	M		Great Britain	U. States	Ann Marria	6 Aug 1823
Thomas	2	M		Great Britain	U. States	Great Britain	18 Mar 1828
Thomas	37	M				Lady of the Lake	23 Aug 1828
*left ship							
Thos.	22	M	Blacksmith	Manchester	United States	Java	9 Jul 1827
Thos.	26	M	Farmer	England	United States	Aurora	27 Apr 1825
William	5	M		England	New Jersey	Lima	5 Aug 1829
William	5	M		England	New Jersey	Lima	5 Aug 1829
Wm.	14	M	Mariner	England	England or Jamaica	Packet	11 Oct 1823
BURTSURT, James	9	M		Gt. Britain	Gt. Britain	Silvanus Jenkins	24 Jul 1828
BURUS, Betsy	16	F	Spinster	Ireland	America	Wilson	16 Nov 1824
Catherine	12	F	Child	Ireland	America	Wilson	16 Nov 1824
BURWELL,							
Charlotte	28	F		Great Britain	United States	James Cropper	26 Mar 1822
Thomas	26 3/12	M	Farmer	Great Britain	United States	James Cropper	26 Mar 1822
BURY, James	21	M	Farmer	Gt. Britain	United States	Pacific	22 May 1826
BURZER, Eliza	18	F	Spinster	Ireland	United States	Fabius	4 Jun 1828
BUSAY, M.	46	M	Merchant	France	U. States	Le Pacquet des Cayes	6 Nov 1826
BUSBY, Bernard	30 9/12	M	Clerk	Ireland	U. States	Fabius	22 Sep 1828
James	22	...	...	Ireland	United States	Carolina Ann	24 Oct 1825
Thomas		M		Ireland	America	Carolina Ann	7 Aug 1826
BUSCAGLIA, M.	40	F	Merchant	Mexico	Mexico	Washington	29 Apr 1826
BUSCATO, Rolla	18	M	Merchant	Spain	Havana	Rolla	10 Feb 1824
BUSCH, George H.	27	M	Merchant	Germany	U. St.	Manchester	7 Dec 1826
George Henry	25	M	Merchant	Hamburg	Hamburg	James Cropper	7 Oct 1823
BUSCHMAN, Edward	23	M	Gentleman	Germany	Hambro [?]	Virginia	8 Mar 1828
BUSH, Arthur	3			Ireland	United States	Alexander Mansfield	9 Nov 1822
Ellen	2			Ireland	United States	Alexander Mansfield	9 Nov 1822
Eve, Mrs.	56		Servant	United States	United States	Acasta	16 Aug 1826
Mary	26			Ireland	United States	Alexander Mansfield	9 Nov 1822
BUSHBY, —, Mrs.	26	F		St. Croix	St. Croix	South Carolina Packet	16 Sep 1823
Jos.	44	M	Merchant	England	Boston	Jane	31 Jan 1827
Thomas	36	M	Merchant	England	U.S.	Chase	26 Jul 1824
W.	36	M	Merchant	St. Croix	St. Croix	South Carolina Packet	16 Sep 1823
BUSHE, George	30	M	Proffessor of Anatomy	Great Britain		Birmingham	11 Oct 1828
BUSHEY, Peter E.	29	M	Merchant	U. States	U. States	Burdett	11 Oct 1827
BUSKER, Catharine	50	F	None	...ford	...	Frances Henrietta	30 Jun 1827
James	25	M	...	...ford	...	Frances Henrietta	30 Jun 1827
Nicholas	9	M	None	...ford	...	Frances Henrietta	30 Jun 1827
Patrick	12	M	None	...ford	...	Frances Henrietta	30 Jun 1827

NAMES OF PASSENGERS	AGE	SEX	OCCUPATIONS	COUNTRY TO WHICH THEY BELONG	COUNTRY THEY INTEND TO INHABIT	SHIPS/DATES OF ARRIVAL	
BUSKER (cont'd)							
Richard	6	M	None	...ford	...	Frances Henrietta	30 Jun 1827
Thomas	20	M	...	...ford	...	Frances Henrietta	30 Jun 1827
BUSLARD, Wm.	20	M	Labourer	Ireland	United States	Trident	16 May 1826
BUSOHGENS, —	27	M	Brewer	Germany	U. States	Joseph	3 Oct 1820
BUSS, Edward	17					Xenophon	25 Jul 1826
George	5					Xenophon	25 Jul 1826
John	14					Xenophon	25 Jul 1826
Mary	9					Xenophon	25 Jul 1826
Richard	7					Xenophon	25 Jul 1826
Richard	49		Farmer	England	S. New York	Xenophon	25 Jul 1826
Sarah	48					Xenophon	25 Jul 1826
William	22					Xenophon	25 Jul 1826
BUSSELL, Alfred	6			Great Britain	United States	John	6 Oct 1820
Charles	2			Great Britain	United States	John	6 Oct 1820
Elizabeth	33	F		Great Britain	United States	John	6 Oct 1820
Geo., Jr.	7			Great Britain	United States	John	6 Oct 1820
George	33	M	Carpenter	Great Britain	United States	John	6 Oct 1820
Hannah	42	F	Wife to [John]	Scotland	United States	Samuel Robertson	9 May 1827
John	55	M	Labourer	Scotland	United States	Samuel Robertson	9 May 1827
Richd.	4			Great Britain	United States	John	6 Oct 1820
William	40	M	...	G. Britain	U. States	New England	28 Sep 1824
BUSSER, Cast. Ferd.	27	M	landed at	Oldenburg	U.N. States of America	Constitution	7 Dec 1827
BUST, Elizabeth	4			England	United States	Hudson	5 Apr 1826
Mary	23			England	United States	Hudson	5 Apr 1826
Sarah	1			England	United States	Hudson	5 Apr 1826
BUSTAMANTE, Jose	40	M	Gent.	Spain	Cuba	Fabius	24 Oct 1825
BUSTIO, Pablo	22	M	Mercht.	Spain	United States	Fox	9 Mar 1829
BUSTO, Lorenazo	28	M	Merchant	U.S. America	U.S. America	Claudio	22 Mar 1828
BUTCHER, Amos	4	M	None	England	United States	Jubilee	12 May 1828
Ann	6	F	Farmer	England	United States	New Packet	7 Aug 1826
Danl.	25	M	Merchant	Gt. Britain	U. States	Margaret	26 Jul 1828
David	1	M	None	England	United States	Jubilee	12 May 1828
Edward	9	M	None	England	United States	Jubilee	12 May 1828
Elisha	31	M	Farmer	Great Britain	United States	Fame	26 May 1828
Hannah	4	F	Farmer	England	United States	New Packet	7 Aug 1826
James	6	M	None	England	United States	Jubilee	12 May 1828
John	26 1/12	M	Tailor	England	Albany, N.Y.	Chelsea	16 May 1828
John	28	M	Farmer	England	United States	America	25 Dec 1827
John	39	M	Labourer	England	United States	Jubilee	12 May 1828
John, Lawyer	20 1/12	M	Lawyer	England	United States	Leeds	4 Jun 1827
Lydia	34	F	None	England	United States	Jubilee	12 May 1828
Lydia, Jr.	13	F	None	England	United States	Jubilee	12 May 1828
Maria	23	F		England	Albany, N.Y.	Chelsea	16 May 1828
Martha	21	F		England	United States	America	25 Dec 1827
Richard	9	M	Farmer	England	United States	New Packet	7 Aug 1826
Saml.	26	M	Merchant	England	U. States	Pacific	5 Sep 1827
Saml.	27	M	Merchant	Gt. Britain	U. States	Cortes	6 Apr 1825
Samuel	27	M	Merchant	Gt. Brittain	United States	Cortex	7 Mar 1823
Sarah	1	F	Farmer	England	United States	New Packet	7 Aug 1826
Susanna	28	F	Farmer	England	United States	New Packet	7 Aug 1826
Thomas	39	M				Acosta	28 Jul 1823
Thos.	8	M	Farmer	England	United States	New Packet	7 Aug 1826
William	14	M	None	England	United States	Jubilee	12 May 1828
William, child	2	M		England	United States	America	25 Dec 1827
Winifred	17	F	None	England	United States	Jubilee	12 May 1828
Wm.	23	M	Baker	Rye, England	United States	William	21 May 1828
Wm.	38	M	Farmer	England	United States	New Packet	7 Aug 1826
BUTEL, —	24	M	Carpenter	Brattain		L'Esperance	6 Sep 1828
BUTELOT, Stephen			Servant	France	U.S.	Sully	26 Oct 1829
BUTINER, Adolphs.	4	M			U. States	Hippomenes	9 Jun 1821
M.	30	F			U. States	Hippomenes	9 Jun 1821
S.	7	F			U. States	Hippomenes	9 Jun 1821
Sally	5	F			U. States	Hippomenes	9 Jun 1821

NAMES OF PASSENGERS	AGE	SEX	OCCUPATIONS	COUNTRY TO WHICH THEY BELONG	COUNTRY THEY INTEND TO INHABIT	SHIPS/DATES OF ARRIVAL	
BUTLER, —	1/12		born on the passage	Scotland	United States	Statird	26 Aug 1823
—	1/12		born on the passage	Scotland	United States	Statird	26 Aug 1823
A., Mrs.	27	F	Spinster	Ireland	United States	Dublin Packet	28 Apr 1824
Abigail	19	M	Labourer	Ireland	U. States	Wanderer	1 Sep 1828
Abigail	33	F	None	Great Britain	United States	Aurora	10 Nov 1827
Andrew	27	M	Mason	Ireland	U. States	Lady Hunter	8 Aug 1826
Ann	13					Agricola	1 Jul 1820
Ann	14	F		England	U.N. States	Helen	17 Dec 1827
Ann	18	F		U. States	Great Britain	Thompson	26 Apr 1828
Ann	34					Agricola	1 Jul 1820
Ann	36	F		England	U.N. States	Helen	17 Dec 1827
Betty	2	F	Child	United States	United States	Trident	16 May 1826
Bridget	30	F		Ireland	New York	Curler	7 Jul 1827
Catherine	8	F	Child	Ireland	United States	Dublin Packet	28 Apr 1824
Catherine	30	F	Servant	France	United States	American	27 Aug 1827
Cathrine	19	F	Labourer	Ireland	U. States	Virginia	20 Jun 1825
Charles	6	M	None	Scotland	United States	Statird	26 Aug 1823
Charles	6	M	Son	England	United States	Cambria	8 Oct 1828
David	8		Farmer	England	United States	Corinthian	30 May 1828
David	22 2/12	M	Laborer	England	United States	Rising States	16 Jan 1829
Edward	34	M	Farmer	Ireland	United States	Dublin Packet	28 Apr 1824
Eliza	3	F		Ireland	U. States	William	27 Jul 1824
Elizabeth	10	F	Daughter	England	United States	Cambria	8 Oct 1828
Ellen	23	F	Spinster	Ireland	United States	Dublin Packet	23 May 1828
F.	9	M	Farmer	U. States	U. States	Marmion	7 Jun 1824
Fanny	7	F	Child	United States	United States	Trident	16 May 1826
Francis Spilsbury	21 4/12	M	Merchant	England	United States	London	6 Feb 1829
Fredk.	19	M	None	England and Ireland	United States	Jubilee	12 May 1828
Geo.	5	M	Farmer	Great Britain	U. States	Yamacraw	4 Sep 1822
Grace	30	F	Wife	Ireland	United States	Trident	16 May 1826
Harriet	6					Cosmo	17 Mar 1828
Harriet [crossed out] *Died Augt. 26	2	F	Daughter	England	United States	Cambria	8 Oct 1828
Henry	13	M	Son	England	United States	Cambria	8 Oct 1828
J. L.	28	M	Military	Ireland	United States	York	31 Mar 1828
James	9	M	None	Great Britain	United States	Aurora	10 Nov 1827
James	17		Farmer	England	United States	Corinthian	30 May 1828
James *put on Board by the Consul	20	M	Mariner	America	America	Morning Star	16 Feb 1824
James	30	M	Farmer	Great Britian	United States	Andes	19 Aug 1829
James	33	M	Baker	England	United States	Trident	30 Sep 1826
James P.	27	M	Merchant	England	U. States	Dalhouse	23 Mar 1829
Janet	8	F	None	Scotland	United States	Statird	26 Aug 1823
Janet	32	F	Wife	Scotland	United States	Statird	26 Aug 1823
John	5	M		Ireland	U. States	William	27 Jul 1824
John	30	M	Farmer	Great Britain	United States	Mary & Harriet	3 Jul 1829
John	38	M	Farmer	England	U.N. States	Helen	17 Dec 1827
John	40	M	Farmer	Ireland	U. States	Perserverance	21 Jul 1827
John	54	M	Seaman	Norfolk	Norfolk	Olivebranch	15 Mar 1820
Jonathan	10					Agricola	1 Jul 1820
Jos., Jr.	3	M	None	Scotland	United States	Statird	26 Aug 1823
Joseph	22		Weaver	Bolton	England	Great Britain	7 May 1827
Joseph	46	M	Farmer	Scotland	United States	Statird	26 Aug 1823
Luke	26	M	Labourer	Ireland	America	Weser	26 Jun 1821
Margt.	20	F	None	England	U. States	Dalhouse	23 Mar 1829
Martin	25	M	Carpenter	Ireland	United States	Lady Hunter	27 Dec 1825
Mary	7	F	Child	Ireland	United States	Trident	16 May 1826
Mary	9	F	Child	United States	United States	Trident	16 May 1826
Mary	11	F	Daughter	England	United States	Cambria	8 Oct 1828
May	1 9/12	F				Robert Fulton	8 Mar 1823
May	22	F				Robert Fulton	8 Mar 1823
Michael	28	M	Labourer	Ireland	New York	Curler	7 Jul 1827
Philip	1					Cosmo	17 Mar 1828
Philippia	30			England	America	Cosmo	17 Mar 1828
Richard	11	M	None	Great Britain	United States	Aurora	10 Nov 1827
Richd.	32	M	Ship Master	British	S. America	Cleanthes	9 May 1825
Robert	4	M	Child	United States	United States	Trident	16 May 1826
Robert	35	M	Labourer	Ireland	United States	Trident	16 May 1826

NAMES OF PASSENGERS	AGE	SEX	OCCUPATIONS	COUNTRY TO WHICH THEY BELONG	COUNTRY THEY INTEND TO INHABIT	SHIPS/DATES OF ARRIVAL	
BUTLER (cont'd)							
Robr.	34	M	Farmer	Great Britain	U. States	Dominica	4 Jan 1823
Robt.	32	M	Labourer	Ireland	U. States	William	27 Jul 1824
Rosanna	3	F	Child	Ireland	United States	Dublin Packet	28 Apr 1824
Sally	1	F	Child	United States	United States	Trident	16 May 1826
Sarah	8	F	Daughter	England	United States	Cambria	8 Oct 1828
Sarah	41	F	Wife	England	United States	Cambria	8 Oct 1828
Stephen	19	M	Farmer	England	United States	Cincinnatus	21 Nov 1821
T.	45	M	Farmer	U. States	U. States	Marmion	7 Jun 1824
Thomas	10	M	Child	Ireland	United States	Dublin Packet	28 Apr 1824
Thomas	21	M	Son	England	United States	Cambria	8 Oct 1828
Thomas	36	M	Carpenter	England	United States	Cambria	3 Jul 1829
Thomas	42	M	Bricklayer	England	United States	Cambria	8 Oct 1828
Thos.	8	M		Ireland	U. States	William	27 Jul 1824
Thos.	34					Agricola	1 Jul 1820
Triphana [crossed out] *Died Augt. 26	3/12	F	Daughter	England	United States	Cambria	8 Oct 1828
W. H.	21	M	Merchant	America	U. States	William Byrnes	17 Jul 1825
William	4	M	Son	England	United States	Cambria	8 Oct 1828
William	30	M	Labourer	Ireland	United States	Wanderer	31 Aug 1829
Wm.	20	M	Farmer	Scotland	United States	Statird	26 Aug 1823
BUTONER, Saml.	23	M	Merchant	England	U.S.	Panthea	13 Nov 1823
BUTT, John	44	M	Gentm.	U. States	U. States	Lady Hunter	12 Apr 1823
William	19	M	Grocer	Great Britain	United States	Purrington	8 Dec 1827
BUTTELLE, ...vis F.	11	M	None	St. Croix	U.S.A.	Rampart	31 Aug 1826
Dashrood	4	M	None	St. Croix	U.S.A.	Rampart	31 Aug 1826
BUTTENS, Nathan	42	M	Gentleman	St. John	Gt. Britain	Isabella	18 Apr 1825
BUTTER, Ann	9	F		United States	United States	Robert Fulton	27 Jun 1822
Edward	28	M	Seaman	Massachusetts	U. States	Velocipede	24 May 1824
Francis	7	M		United States	United States	Robert Fulton	27 Jun 1822
J.	22	M	Pastry Cook	England	Albany	Stephania	13 Mar 1820
Joseph	26	M	Painter	Great Britain	United States	Ganges	26 Oct 1826
Margaret	20	F	None	Great Britain	United States	Ganges	26 Oct 1826
Miner	51	M	Gentleman	United States		Only Daughter	20 Feb 1826
Thomas	44	M	Planter	United States	United States	Robert Fulton	27 Jun 1822
BUTTERALL, Wm.	22	M	Farmer	England	United States	Curler	3 Mar 1828
BUTTERFIELD, Samuel	34	M	...	Halifax	New York	Frances Henrietta	30 Jun 1827
Samuel, Jr.	10	M	None	Halifax	New York	Frances Henrietta	30 Jun 1827
Thos.	40	M	Mariner	Bermuda	Bermuda	Eclipse	14 Feb 1820
William	12	M	None	Halifax	New York	Frances Henrietta	30 Jun 1827
BUTTERS, Joseph	17	M	House Carpenter	Great Britain	United States	Diana	30 Oct 1827
BUTTERSWORTH, Thomas	21	M	Weaver	England	America U. States	La Grange	27 Sep 1826
BUTTERVILLE, Geo.	30	M	Seaman	Canada	Canada	Radius	22 Aug 1820
BUTTERWORTH, Archd.	R.24	M	Accountant	Great Britain	United States	Minerva	28 Jul 1823
James	47	M	Woolen Manufr.	England	England	William Thompson	19 Aug 1829
John	30	M	Stone Mason	Great Britian	United States	George Clinton	21 Oct 1826
John	41	M	Labourer	G. Britain	U. States	Nimrod	31 Jul 1828
BUTTLER, Margaret	23	F		Ireland	U. States	William	27 Jul 1824
BUTTON, Charlotte	30			England	England	London	16 Aug 1824
Edward	6		Child	England	England	London	16 Aug 1824
Eveling	3		Child	England	England	London	16 Aug 1824
Harry	9		Child	England	England	London	16 Aug 1824
Lissey	8		Child	England	England	London	16 Aug 1824
Stephen	10		Child	England	England	London	16 Aug 1824
BUUCHONER, Theopolus	30	M	Farmer	Ireland		Quatre Freres	29 Jul 1828
BUVET, Thresa	40	F		Philadelphia	U. States	Marmion	8 Sep 1828
BUXHEDA, C.	31	M	Merchant	Catalonian	Catalonia	Charleston Packet	3 Jul 1823
BUXIA, Antonio, Don	38	M	Merchant	Spain	Spain	Eliza Jane	11 Jul 1822
BUXTON, An	5	F	Farmer	England	U. States	Franklin	7 Jul 1828
Charles	2 6/12		Farmer	England	U. States	Franklin	7 Jul 1828
Eliz.	49	F	Farmer	England	U. States	Franklin	7 Jul 1828

NAMES OF PASSENGERS	AGE	SEX	OCCUPATIONS	COUNTRY TO WHICH THEY BELONG	COUNTRY THEY INTEND TO INHABIT	SHIPS/DATES OF ARRIVAL	
BUXTON (cont'd)							
Geo.	4	M		England	United States	Acasta	25 Sep 1827
George	9	M	Farmer	England	U. States	Franklin	7 Jul 1828
George	25	M	Mate	Boston	U. States	Pioneer	6 May 1828
Henry	52	M	Farmer	England	U. States	Franklin	7 Jul 1828
Jno. P.	32	M	Mariner	Baltimore	U. States	Frances	6 Jan 1824
Jone	15	F	Farmer	England	U. States	Franklin	7 Jul 1828
Mary	1 9/12	F		England	United States	Acasta	25 Sep 1827
Mary	24	F		England	United States	Acasta	25 Sep 1827
Richard	23	M	Farmer	England	U. States	Franklin	7 Jul 1828
Robt.	19	M	Farmer	England	U. States	Franklin	7 Jul 1828
Sarah	6	F	Farmer	England	U. States	Franklin	7 Jul 1828
Thomas	13	M	Farmer	England	U. States	Franklin	7 Jul 1828
Thos.	2	M		England	United States	Acasta	25 Sep 1827
Wm.	24	M	Labourer	England	U. States	Comet	23 Aug 1828
BUYADA, Emily	3	F	Child	Spain	Spain	Virginia	26 May 1828
John	39	M	Merchant	Spain	Spain	Virginia	26 May 1828
Mary	28	F	Wife	Spain	Spain	Virginia	26 May 1828
BUYNES, John	9	M	Farmer	Great Britain	U. States	Eliza Barker	13 May 1824
John	30	M	Farmer	Great Britain	U. States	Eliza Barker	13 May 1824
Mary	29	F	Farmer	Great Britain	U. States	Eliza Barker	13 May 1824
Richard	12	M	Farmer	Great Britain	U. States	Eliza Barker	13 May 1824
Wm.	7	M	Farmer	Great Britain	U. States	Eliza Barker	13 May 1824
BYAN, Cornelius	40		Shoemaker	England	United States	Mary	15 Jul 1822
Margret	18	F	None	England	U. States	Thomas Ritchie	2 Jul 1827
Pat	30	M	Clerk	England	U. States	Thomas Ritchie	2 Jul 1827
Stephen	23	M	Servant	Ireland	U. States	Bayard	11 Mar 1823
BYANS, Peter	2	M	Child	Ireland	United States	Josephine	30 Apr 1828
BYARS, John	20	M	Labourer	G. Britain	U. States	Sarah G	5 Jun 1828
BYAS, Bartholomew	25	M	Merchant	Baltimore	Baltimore	Martha	3 Aug 1824
BYEN, Wm.	22	M	Labourer	Ireland	U. States	Liverpool	25 Mar 1828
BYERALIE, Catharine	24	F		England	England	Amity	31 May 1822
BYERS, Amelia	16	F		Ireland	America	Carolina Ann	7 Aug 1826
Charles	2...	M	...	...	...	Antioch	8 Oct 1827
Elisha	...	M	...	...	...	Antioch	8 Oct 1827
Eliza	18	F		Ireland	America	Carolina Ann	7 Aug 1826
Hugh	17	M	Labourer	Ireland		William Tell	24 Oct 1829
John	25	M	Weaver	Ireland	United States	Romulus	24 Jun 1826
Robert	11	M		England	New York	James Cropper	16 Oct 1826
BYFIELD, Francis	9	M		Great Britain	Canada	Marmion	13 Jun 1823
Richd.	26	M	Farmer	Great Brittan	United States	Cambria	11 Feb 1829
BYLIN, Peter	40	M		Great Britain		London	29 Apr 1824
BYRAM, Elizabeth	24	F		Antigua	United States	Betsey	18 Aug 1823
Jno.	40	M	Merchant	Gt. Brittain	United States	Cortes	5 Aug 1822
M.	39	M	Planter	Antigua	United States	Betsey	18 Aug 1823
BYRAN, Edward	25			England	U. States	Corinthian	8 Oct 1828
John	40	M	Merchant	Great Brittain	U. States	William Byrnes	23 Jul 1824
Wm.	30		Shoemaker	England	United States	Mary	15 Jul 1822
BYREN, John	20	M	Weaver	Ireland	New York	Trusty	12 Sep 1828
BYRES, Elizabeth, Mrs.	25 9/12	F		Scotland	United States	Mobile	21 Aug 1827
John	1 6/12	M		Scotland	United States	Mobile	21 Aug 1827
BYRIE, George	29	M	Printer	Great Britain		Moro Castle	6 Jul 1827
BYRN, Dennis	26	M	Labourer	Ireland	United States	Hope	12 Jun 1828
BYRNE, Andrew	22	M	Gentleman	New York	U. States	Only Son	14 Jun 1827
Bridget	20		Spinster	Ireland	United States	Courier	15 Oct 1827
Bridget	52	F	Spinster	Great Britain	United States	Wanderer	11 Jul 1826
Cath.	8	F	Child	Ireland	United States	Dublin Packet	29 Jun 1825
Catherine, his wife [Patrick]	24	F	Spinster	United States	United States	Andes	2 Oct 1828
E.	30	M	Tailor	Great Britain	United States	Saml. Wight	6 Sep 1827
Edward	34	M	Labourer	Ireland	United States	Lord Wellington	28 May 1827
Garret	60	M	Farmer	Ireland	United States	Dublin Packet	23 May 1828
Gregory	16	M	Farmer	Ireland	America	Farmer	15 Nov 1823
Henry	46	M	Labourer	Ireland	New York	Louisa	20 Jul 1826
Hugh	21	M	Labourer	Co. Cavan	Co. Cavan	Howard Douglass	11 May 1827
Jane	28	F	Spinster	Ireland	United States	Dublin Packet	29 Jun 1825
Jno.	27	M	Labourer	Ireland	United States	Thomas	13 Dec 1827

NAMES OF PASSENGERS	AGE	SEX	OCCUPATIONS	COUNTRY TO WHICH THEY BELONG	COUNTRY THEY INTEND TO INHABIT	SHIPS/DATES OF ARRIVAL	
BYRNE (cont'd)							
John	69	M	Clergyman	Great Britian	United States	London	24 Jun 1823
Judith	38	F	Widow	Ireland	United States	Dublin Packet	29 Jun 1825
Lawrence	30	M	Labourer	Ireland		Fame	9 Dec 1826
M.	22	M	Farmer	Great Britain	United States	Isaac Hicks	6 Dec 1827
Mary	3	F	None	Great Britain		Moro Castle	6 Jul 1827
Mary	16	F	None	Ba...y	Oxford, Gt. Britain	Howard Douglass	11 May 1827
Mary	19		Spinster	Ireland	United States	Courier	15 Oct 1827
Mary	21		Spinster	Ireland	United States	Courier	15 Oct 1827
Mary	22	F	None	Ba...y	Oxford, Gt. Britain	Howard Douglass	11 May 1827
Mary	22	F	None	Ireland	United States	Lord Wellington	28 May 1827
Mary	25	F	Servant	Ireland	Canada	James Monroe	18 Apr 1821
Mary	26	F	Spinster	Ireland	United States	Dublin Packet	23 May 1828
Mary	30	F	None	Great Britain		Moro Castle	6 Jul 1827
Mary	38	F	None	Ba...y	Oxford, Gt. Britain	Howard Douglass	11 May 1827
Mary Ann	16	F	Spinster	Ireland	United States	Dublin Packet	29 Jun 1825
Michal	30	M	Farmer	Ireland	United States	Andes	2 Oct 1828
Patrick	19	M	None	Gt. Brittain	United States	Balaena	21 Aug 1824
Patrick	25	M	Joiner	Ireland	United States	Andes	2 Oct 1828
Patt	38	M	Farmer	Ba...y	Oxford, Gt. Britain	Howard Douglass	11 May 1827
Robert	28	M	None	Ireland	N. York	Eliza Grant	29 Aug 1829
Sarah	40		Spinster	Ireland	United States	Courier	15 Oct 1827
Thomas	25	M	Labourer	Great Britain		Moro Castle	6 Jul 1827
William	20	M	Bleacher	G. Brittain	U. States	Cincinnatus	2 Oct 1822
Wm.	32	M	Servant	Gt. Britain	Canada	New York	15 Jul 1825
BYRNES, Ann	27	F	None	Great Brittan	U. States	Gem	26 Jul 1827
Catherine	19	F		Ireland	United States	Princess Charlotte	26 Apr 1827
James	25	M	Labourer	Ireland	United States	Trident	31 Mar 1827
John	19	M	Weaver	Ireland	United States	Princess Charlotte	26 Apr 1827
John	24	M	Shoe Maker	Ireland	United States	Princess Charlotte	26 Apr 1827
Mary Ann	1	F		United States	United States	Manhattan	24 Oct 1825
Mary Ann	23	F		United States	United States	Manhattan	24 Oct 1825
Patrick	18	M	Labourer	England	America	William	21 Sep 1821
R.	19	M	Clockmaker	Great Britain	United States	Isaac Hicks	6 Dec 1827
Robert	28	M	None	Ireland		Eliza Grant	29 Aug 1829
Rosanna	19	F		Great Britain		Robert Fulton	8 Mar 1823
Thomas	44	M	Merchant	United States	United States	Manhattan	24 Oct 1825
*Died on the 8th October 1825							
William	18	M	Labourer	Ireland	United States	Princess Charlotte	26 Apr 1827
BYRNS, W.	32	M	Handy Craft	Ireland	U. States	Alex Mansfield	1 Jun 1822
BYROM, Esther	3	F		Great Britain	United States	Birmingham	15 Jun 1827
John	5	M		Great Britain	United States	Birmingham	15 Jun 1827
Margaret	33	F		Great Britain	United States	Birmingham	15 Jun 1827
Robert	6/12	M		Great Britain	United States	Birmingham	15 Jun 1827
Sarah	8	F		Great Britain	United States	Birmingham	15 Jun 1827
BYRONS, Catherine	6	F	None	...	U. States	St. Michael	21 Jul 1824
Gormack	4	F	None	...	U. States	St. Michael	21 Jul 1824
Hannah	2	F	None	...	U. States	St. Michael	21 Jul 1824
Mary	30	F	None	...	U. States	St. Michael	21 Jul 1824
Patrick	8	M	None	...	U. States	St. Michael	21 Jul 1824
Thos.	28	M	Tailor	...	U. States	St. Michael	21 Jul 1824
BYSEN, Bennit	52	M		Switzerland	Ohio	Eugenie	20 Aug 1827
Eliz.	18	F		Switzerland	Ohio	Eugenie	20 Aug 1827
Elizabeth	50	F		Switzerland	Ohio	Eugenie	20 Aug 1827
BYSTAT, A.	31	M	Merchant	France	U. States	Edward Bonaffe	11 Dec 1827
BYUNS, Aley	20	F	Servant	Ireland	United States	Josephine	30 Apr 1828
C..., —	3	F	None	England	New York	Thames	6 Oct 1820
—	5	F	None	England	New York	Thames	6 Oct 1820

NAMES OF PASSENGERS	AGE	SEX	OCCUPATIONS	COUNTRY TO WHICH THEY BELONG	COUNTRY THEY INTEND TO INHABIT	SHIPS/DATES OF ARRIVAL	
C... (cont'd)							
—	6	F	None	England	New York	Thames	6 Oct 1820
...	34	M		England		Elias Burger	26 Jul 1821
A...	4	F	None	...	United States	Martha	22 Jul 1820
Abm.	27	M	Servant	Denmark	Denmark	Gleaner	31 Jul 1821
Elizabeth, Mrs.	28	F	None	England	New York	Thames	6 Oct 1820
Jane	2	F	None	...	United States	Martha	22 Jul 1820
Mark	...	...	...	...	...	William Thompson	30 Sep 1824
Mary...	...	F	Spinster	Ireland	Unt. St. America	Wilson	21 May 1827
C...AN, John Henry	...	M		Scotland	Great Britain	Rufus King	27 Jun 1821
C...B...D..., J., Mr.	44	M	Mercht.	Jamaica	Jamaica	Wallace	12 Apr 1824
C...GHAN, Catherine	...	F	Spinster	Ireland	Unt. St. America	Wilson	21 May 1827
C...ING, ...	...	F	...	Great Britain	New York	Dublin	21 Dec 1824
...	16	M	...	Great Britain	New York	Dublin	21 Dec 1824
C...L..., Mary	2...	...	...	...	...	St. Michael	22 Sep 1824
C...MAN, John G.	22		Wheelwright	England	England	Thames	25 Oct 1821
C...SON, Samuel	22	M	Assistant	England	England	Stephania	13 Sep 1821
C...TELL, Catherine	23	F		Limerick	N. York	Thomas & William	25 May 1827
Edmond	25	M	Labourer	Limerick	N. York	Thomas & William	25 May 1827
Honorah	1	F		Limerick	N. York	Thomas & William	25 May 1827
C...TOT, —, Mde.	26	F	Lady	France	France	Imperial	10 Dec 1821
CA..., Bridget	31	F	...	Scotland	America	Nimrod	9 Jul 1823
J...	33	M	None	West Indies	Canada	Martha	22 Jul 1820
CA...N, James	30	M	Farmer	Ireland	United States	Aurelia	7 Jun 1826
CA...ON, John	20	M	Labourer	New Brunswick [?]	U. States	St. Michael	5 May 1827
CA...SS, Patrick	16	M	Labourer	Sligo	New York	Susquehana	27 Jun 1823
CAALE, W.	18	M	Clerk	U. States	U. States	Tryon	25 Apr 1825
CAANAN, Owan	25	M	Farmer	England	United States	India	8 Jun 1827
Paterick	30	M	Weaver	England	United States	India	8 Jun 1827
CAARLO, John H.	49	M	Merchant	America	America	Pacific	13 Jan 1827
CABAHALL, C.	25	M	Merchant	Matanzas	U. States	Mary & Emily	23 Mar 1825
CABAL, A., Mr.	29	M	Merchant	France	France	Rebecca	2 May 1825
Robt. H.	25	M	Genn.	United States	United States	Henri IV	14 Oct 1829
Sal...a	22	F		United States	United States	Henri IV	14 Oct 1829
Sule W.	5	F		United States	United States	Henri IV	14 Oct 1829
CABANEL, F.	36	M	Merchant	France	France	Eliza	28 Apr 1827
CABANELL, Francis	36	M	Merchant	Spain	Vera Cruz	Droma	25 Mar 1826
CABANET, F.	34	M	Merchant	France	U. States	Neptunes Barge	1 Oct 1822
CABBY, Fleming	25	M		Great Britain	U. States	Ann Marria	6 Aug 1823
CABELLO, P.	28	M	Merchant	Havana	United States	James Monroe	3 Jul 1824
CABILLE, —, Mrs.	25	F		U. States	U.S.	Henri IV	14 Sep 1827
Jno.	3	F		U. States	U.S.	Henri IV	14 Sep 1827
CABIN, A.	17	M	Merchant	France	U. States	Waldo	19 Aug 1826
N.	7	M	Merchant	France	U. States	Waldo	19 Aug 1826
CABLES, James	29	M	Carpenter	Connecticutt	U. States	General Brooks	21 May 1824
CABOT, Edward	35	M	Merchant	America	America	Reliance	17 Jun 1828
Jno. H.	40	M	Merchant	Salem	U. States	Canton	6 May 1824
John H.	46 4/12	M	Merchant	America	America	France	28 Mar 1829
Stephen	36	M	Gentleman	G. Britian	U. States	Chase	17 Jan 1825
CACEY, Thos.	30	M	Cooper	Newfoundland	Newfoundland	Mariner	11 Jul 1823
CACUINEY, Robace	45	M	Butcher	Martinique	France	Alpha	27 Jul 1827
CADDELL, Peter	19	M	Laborer	Gt. Britain		Dalhouse Castle	13 May 1828
CADDIN, Cathine	45	F	Widdow	England	United States	Hanford	3 Jul 1829
Ellen	10	F	Child	England	United States	Hanford	3 Jul 1829
CADDOCK, Samuel	29	M	Engineer	England	England	Sully	15 Jul 1829
CADE, Thomas	38	M	Farmer	U. States	U. States	Cadmus	26 Oct 1821
CADET (see Bremon)							
CADLEY, Alexr.	1	M	Mechanic	Great Britain	United States	Thomas Dickason	31 Jul 1829
Ann	11	F	Mechanic	Great Britain	United States	Thomas Dickason	31 Jul 1829
Ellena	26	F	Mechanic	Great Britain	United States	Thomas Dickason	31 Jul 1829

NAMES OF PASSENGERS	AGE	SEX	OCCUPATIONS	COUNTRY TO WHICH THEY BELONG	COUNTRY THEY INTEND TO INHABIT	SHIPS/DATES OF ARRIVAL	
CADLEY (cont'd)							
Henry	1	M	Mechanic	Great Britain	United States	Thomas Dickason	31 Jul 1829
Thomas	3 6/12	M	Mechanic	Great Britain	United States	Thomas Dickason	31 Jul 1829
CADMORE, Daniel	12	M	None	Ireland	United States	Nestor	20 Nov 1821
Henry	23	M	Shoemaker	Ireland	United States	Nestor	20 Nov 1821
CADON, Cathr.	18	F		Ireland	U. States	Sarah G	7 May 1827
CADOT, J. B.	25	M	Cabinet Maker	France	United States	Howard	19 May 1826
CADWALLADER, Elizh.	26	F		Great Britain	United States	Isaac Hicks	10 Jul 1827
Job Owens	7	M		Great Britain	United States	Isaac Hicks	10 Jul 1827
Thos.	30	M	Farmer	Great Britain	United States	Isaac Hicks	10 Jul 1827
CADWELL, Nichs.	27	M	Labourer	Ireland		Marchioness	13 May 1828
CADY, Jesse	23	M	Merchant	U.S. America	U.S. America	Hiram	14 Aug 1829
CAEHO, L.	28	M		Mexico	U. States	Laveria	23 Jul 1828
CAELHO, Francesco	36	M	Merchant	Brazil	Brazil	Zepher	20 Oct 1827
CAEUS, Conway	30	M	Hatter	Ireland	New York	Trusty	12 Sep 1828
CAFFARA, Catharine	27			Liverpool		Mount Vernon	18 Oct 1822
CAFFARTY, Ant.	48	M	Labourer	Ireland	U. States	Panthea	8 Apr 1826
CAFFER, James	23	M	...	...	U. States	Louisiana	31 Oct 1827
CAFFERCADETTE, P.	45	M	Merchant	France	France	Day	24 Apr 1828
CAFFERY, Cathr.	30	F	Spinster	Lpool.	Lpool.	Howard Douglass	11 May 1827
CAFFIN, Charles M.	43	M	Sea Captain	America	New York	Hercules	10 Apr 1823
CAFFRAY, Jane	22	F	Milliner	Ireland	United States	Andes	2 Oct 1828
CAFREY, Ann	4	F		England	United States	Concordia	25 Aug 1827
Chatharine	35	F		England	United States	Concordia	25 Aug 1827
CAGGER, Mary	21	F	Spinster	Ireland	United States	Trident	16 May 1826
CAGIGA, Manuel, Don	28	M	Merchant	Spain	Spain	Lovinia	20 Nov 1828
CAGIYERO, Pedro C.	25	M	Gentleman	Havana	U. States	Hero	21 Jan 1825
CAGROUGH, John B.	22	M	Cabinet Maker	Great Britain	U. States	Robert Fulton	3 Dec 1827
CAHADO, Fernando	30	M	Merchant	Mexico	Mexico	Fancy	28 Apr 1825
CAHAINES, Thomas	4	M	Laborer	Ireland	United States	St. Michaels	25 May 1825
CAHALLE, Ann	19	F		Ireland	United States	William Byrnes	6 Apr 1826
CAHEL, Honor	20	F		Gt. Britain		Dalhouse Castle	13 May 1828
CAHER, Eliza	19	F	None	England	U. States	Montgomery	18 Oct 1828
James	30	M	Farmer	England	U. States	Montgomery	18 Oct 1828
CAHILL (see Colrill)							
Ann	1 6/12	F	Child	Ireland	United States	Dublin Packet	22 Aug 1829
Ann	24	F	Spinster	Ireland	United States	Wilson	22 Jun 1824
Ann	27	F	Wife	Ireland	United States	Dublin Packet	22 Aug 1829
Bridget	26	F	Spinster	Ireland	United States	Wilson	22 Jun 1824
Bryan	21	M	Laboror	Ireland	United States	Wilson	27 Jun 1826
Cathr.	20	F	None	England	United States	Aurelia	7 Jun 1826
Daniel	38	M	Farmer	Ireland	America	William	21 May 1825
Edward	36	M		U. States	U. States	Virginia	16 Apr 1822
Geo.	22	M	Shop Keeper	England	United States	Aurelia	7 Jun 1826
Honora	5	F	None	Ireland	United States	Jubilee	12 May 1828
John	33	M	Farmer	Great Brittain	U. States	Hibernia	8 Jul 1823
Margaret	7	F	None	Ireland	United States	Jubilee	12 May 1828
Michael	48	M	Labourer	Ireland	United States	Jubilee	12 May 1828
Michel	20	M	Labourer	Ireland	U. States	Josephine	7 May 1827
Pat	24	M	Labourer	Great Britain	United States	Ann Maria	12 Jul 1821
Peggy	30	F	None	Ireland	United States	Jubilee	12 May 1828
Susan	4	F	None	Ireland	United States	Jubilee	12 May 1828
Thos.	25	M	Labourer	Ireland		Marchioness	13 May 1828
CAHILLE, James	20	M	Labourer	Ireland	U. States	Josephine	27 Jul 1825
CAHINES, Berched	28	F	Servant	Ireland	United States	St. Michaels	25 May 1825
Mary	2	F	Child	Ireland	United States	St. Michaels	25 May 1825
CAHITLY, David	24	M	Merchant	Ireland	Ireland	Malibar	18 Nov 1823
CAHN, Cerf, Mr.	23	M	Mercht.	France	New York	Cadmus	27 Aug 1822
CAHOL, Edwd.	18	M	Gentleman	Ireland	U. States	Wilson	2 Sep 1823
CAHOON, James	20	M	Preacher	Lisbrew	United States	Carolina Ann	11 Jun 1824
William	22	M	Farmer	Ireland	United States	Dublin Packet	23 May 1828
CAHOR, Phillip	20	M	Tailor	France		Pallas	14 Jun 1828
CAIL, Bessy	21	F	Servant	Ireland	United States	Carolina Ann	11 Dec 1826
CAILLAS, Alfred	22	M	Merchant	United States	United States	Savannah	10 Jan 1828
CAIN, Abel	2	M		England	United States	Hannibal	25 Sep 1827
Ann	5	F	Labourer	England	U. States	Comet	23 Aug 1828

170

NAMES OF PASSENGERS	AGE	SEX	OCCUPATIONS	COUNTRY TO WHICH THEY BELONG	COUNTRY THEY INTEND TO INHABIT	SHIPS/DATES OF ARRIVAL	
CAIN (cont'd)							
Ann	6	F	None	England		Marchioness	13 May 1828
Catharine	1	F	Labourer	England	U. States	Comet	23 Aug 1828
Charles	22	M	Joiner	Isle of Man	United States	Nile	17 May 1827
Christian	40	F		England	United States	Hannibal	25 Sep 1827
Eliza	11	F		England	United States	Hannibal	25 Sep 1827
George	25	M	Labourer	Great Britan	United States	Bolivar	21 May 1827
James	7	M	Labourer	England	U. States	Comet	23 Aug 1828
James	22	M	Laborer	Ireland	United States	Fabius	4 Jun 1828
James	33	M	Labourer	Ireland	U. States	Frances Henrietta	25 Oct 1824
John	13	M	None	England		Marchioness	13 May 1828
John	14	M	Labourer	England	U. States	Comet	23 Aug 1828
John	24	M	Farmer	Ireland	U. States	Criterion	23 May 1826
John	27		Pedlar	Ireland	G. Britain	Robert Burns	14 Jun 1824
John	30	M	Artizan	England	United States	Jubilee	1 Oct 1828
John	38	M	Millwright	Scotland	New York	Commerce	24 Sep 1823
Judiah	37	F	Labourer	England	U. States	Comet	23 Aug 1828
Margaret	26	F	None	England		Marchioness	13 May 1828
Margret	25	F		G. Britain	U. States	Mary & Harriot	8 Sep 1828
Mary	27	F		G. Britain	U. States	Mary & Harriot	8 Sep 1828
Matthew	30	M	Mason	England		Marchioness	13 May 1828
Peter	27	M	Spinner	Scotland	United States	Orion	15 Jan 1827
Philip	4	M		England	United States	Hannibal	25 Sep 1827
Philip	4	M	None	England		Marchioness	13 May 1828
Sebastre	28	M	Labourer	G. Britain	U. States	Mary & Harriot	8 Sep 1828
Thomas	1	M	None	England		Marchioness	13 May 1828
Thomas	11	M	Labourer	England	U. States	Comet	23 Aug 1828
William	28	M	Labourer	G. Britain	U. States	Mary & Harriot	8 Sep 1828
Willm.	21	M	Clerk	Isle of Man	United States	Nile	17 May 1827
Wm.	9	M	Labourer	England	U. States	Comet	23 Aug 1828
Wm.	22	M	Mason	England	United States	Jubilee	12 May 1828
Wm.	40	M	Labourer	England	U. States	Comet	23 Aug 1828
CAINE, John	34	M	Engineer	Great Brittain	United States	United States	16 Feb 1827
William	22 6/12		Mill Wright	Great Britain	United States	Thomas Dickason	29 Aug 1828
CAINES, Christopher	27	M	Farmer	U. States	U. States	Cincinnatus	2 Oct 1822
CAINEY, Mary	50			Ireland	New York	Lady Hunter	19 Oct 1826
CAINS, J.	40	M	Mariner	Bermuda	U. States	Agnes	1 Jul 1825
CAIR, John	17	M	F...	Ireland	West Indies	Courier	17 Mar 1827
CAIRD, James	36	M	Farmer	Scotland	United States	Mary & Susan	5 Aug 1828
CAIRE, M.	30	M	Labourer	America	U. States	Olive Branch	30 Oct 1823
CAIREY, Jams.		M	Merchant	Port au Prince	U. States	Atlanta	5 Jul 1821
CAIRNES, John	23	M	Planter	Ireland	Ireland	Jupiter	4 Aug 1829
Lawrence	27	M	Laborer	Great Britain	United States	Corinthian	5 Jan 1824
CAIRNS, John	70	M	Baker	Scotland	U. States	Cowper	8 Jan 1827
Nancy	21	F	Mantumaker	Irereland	America	Carolina Ann	20 Jun 1825
Rob.	36	M	Merchant	Getchholm	England	Yamacraw	10 May 1821
Wm.	15 4/12	M	Clerk	Ireland	U. States	Fabius	22 Sep 1828
CAIRO, R.	30	M		Spain		Apollo	11 Jun 1828
CAIRON, R., Made.	67	F		U.S.		Henri IV	17 May 1828
CAIT, Jno.	44	M	Merchant	America	America	James Cropper	14 Oct 1822
CAITTE, Mary	28	F				Helen	4 Aug 1829
Samuel	4	M				Helen	4 Aug 1829
Samuel	32	M	Cabt. Maker			Helen	4 Aug 1829
CAJIGA, —, Mr.	27		Merchant	Mexico	Mexico	Brown	11 Jun 1827
CAKERY, Alexander	21	M	Wool Stapler	England	America	Comet	26 Jun 1822
CAKILL, Michl.	21	M	Labourer	Ireland		Marchioness	13 May 1828
CALAGHAN, John	21	M	...		Gall...	Catherine	19 Aug 1825
CALALA, Mare	21	M	Pastry Cook	France	New York	Harriot	1 May 1822
CALAMAN, Jno.		M	Carpenter	N. York	U. States	Cabbasso Conta	23 Aug 1824
CALAME, Fredk.	19	M	Farmer	Switzerland		Henri IV	17 May 1828
CALB, James	21	M	Laborer	Ireland	United States	Belleville	13 Oct 1827
CALBERT, Jas.	28	M	Mechanic	Ireland	U. States	Susan & Sarah	25 Apr 1825
CALBES, Gregory	31	M	Servant	Spain	Spain	Britannia	5 Nov 1828
CALBISON, H.	26	M	Mariner	American		Sarah Ann	5 Aug 1820
CALD...LL, John	24	M	Farmer	Scotland	U. States	Camillus	29 Jan 1829
CALDER, George	24	M	Labourer	Scotland	U. States	Superior	25 Sep 1828
James	22	M	Clark	Scotland	United States	Camillus	6 Apr 1821

NAMES OF PASSENGERS	AGE	SEX	OCCUPATIONS	COUNTRY TO WHICH THEY BELONG	COUNTRY THEY INTEND TO INHABIT	SHIPS/DATES OF ARRIVAL	
CALDER (cont'd)							
Joseph	45	M	Farmer	Great Britain	United States	Ganges	8 Jul 1820
Maria	26	F	Seamtress	U. States	U. States	Reaper	31 May 1824
William	40	M	Merchant	Great Britain	America	Samuel Robertson	26 Nov 1825
Wm.	40	M	Merchant	U. States	U. States	Caledonia	20 Jan 1829
CALDEREN, Joseph	18	M	F...t...	Havana	Havana	Stephania	29 Nov 1825
CALDO, Elizabeth	34	F	Servant	Great Britain		Canada	1 Oct 1827
CALDONS, Elizabeth	30	F	None	England	New York	Concordia	12 Oct 1826
CALDWALL, Wm.	25	M	Merchant	Scotland	U. States	Pedler	20 Aug 1827
CALDWELL, —, Mrs.	34	F	None	Scotland	U. States	Czar	29 Aug 1829
Abm.	26	M	Labourer	U. States	U. States	Robt. Reade	12 Apr 1825
Adam	20	M	Farmer, Labourer or Spinster	Ireland	U. States	Meteor	4 Oct 1827
Agns	26	F	Farmer	Scotland	U. States	Roger Stewart	9 Jun 1828
Alex	28	M	Farmer	Ireland	United States	Trident	16 May 1826
Anna	12	F	Farmer, Labourer or Spinster	Ireland	U. States	Meteor	4 Oct 1827
Brice	22	M	Farmer	Ireland	U. States	Dickinson	30 Jul 1825
Christian	6	F	Child	Scotland	United States	Tom	2 Jul 1827
Christian	32	F	Spinster	Scotland	United States	Tom	2 Jul 1827
David	33	M	Laborer	Scotland	United States	Tom	2 Jul 1827
Elisabeth	50	F	Spinster	Ireland	United States	Catharine	22 Jul 1825
Eliza	5	F		Great Britain	U. States	United States	8 Sep 1827
Elizabeth	16	F	Farmer, Labourer or Spinster	Ireland	U. States	Meteor	4 Oct 1827
Ellen	26	F	Wife	England	U.S.	Pacific	24 Oct 1828
Geo.	27	M	Manufacturer	Great Britain	United States	United States	8 Sep 1827
George	21	M	Manufacture	Scotland	U. States	York	4 Apr 1826
Helen	1	F	Child	Scotland	United States	Tom	2 Jul 1827
Helen	28	F	Wife	Scotland	United States	Tom	2 Jul 1827
Henry	19	M	Lawyer	Great Britain	United States	Henrietta	19 Oct 1825
James	5	M		Scotland	America	Eyder	7 Aug 1826
James	6	M	None	Scotland	U. States	Czar	29 Aug 1829
Jane	2	F	Child	England	U.S.	Pacific	24 Oct 1828
Janet	5	F	Child	Scotland	United States	Tom	2 Jul 1827
Janet	34	F	Spinster	Scotland	United States	Tom	2 Jul 1827
Janet	74	F	Wife	Scotland	United States	Tom	2 Jul 1827
Jas.	28	M	Tanner	Ireland	N. York	Salem	15 Mar 1828
Jean	16	F	Farmer	Scotland	U. States	Roger Stewart	9 Jun 1828
John	1	M		Great Britain	U. States	United States	8 Sep 1827
John	2	M	None	Scotland	U. States	Czar	29 Aug 1829
John	4	M	Farmer, Labourer or Spinster	Ireland	U. States	Meteor	4 Oct 1827
John	12	M		Scotland	America	Eyder	7 Aug 1826
John	19 5/12	M	Printer	Ireland	United States	Louisa	16 Mar 1826
John	28	M	Labourer	Ireland	United States	Catharine	22 Jul 1825
John	31	M	Joiner	Scotland	U. States	Czar	29 Aug 1829
John	35	M	...a...le	Scotland	United States	Tom	2 Jul 1827
John	44	M	Merchant	Scotland	United States	Corinthian	10 Jan 1826
Joseph	3	M		Great Britain	U. States	United States	8 Sep 1827
Joseph	2...	M		Ireland	United States	General Putnam	20 Jun 1825
Joseph	57	M	Minister	America	U. States	Cincinnatus	21 Feb 1825
Margaret	2	F	Child	Scotland	United States	Tom	2 Jul 1827
Margaret	15	F		Scotland	America	Eyder	7 Aug 1826
Margret	22	F	Farmer, Labourer or Spinster	Ireland	U. States	Meteor	4 Oct 1827
Martha	7	F		Scotland	America	Eyder	7 Aug 1826
Martha	50	F	Farmer, Labourer or Spinster	Ireland	U. States	Meteor	4 Oct 1827
Mary	7	F	Farmer, Labourer or Spinster	Ireland	U. States	Meteor	4 Oct 1827
Mary	60	F	Seamstress	Great Britain	United States	Henrietta	19 Oct 1825
Matilda	18	F	Farmer, Labourer or Spinster	Ireland	U. States	Meteor	4 Oct 1827
Richd.	6/12	M	Child	England	U.S.	Pacific	24 Oct 1828
Robert	4	M	Child	Scotland	United States	Tom	2 Jul 1827
Robt.	10	M		Scotland	America	Eyder	7 Aug 1826
Robt.	34	M	Labourer	Gt. Britain	U.S. America	James Cropper	2 Aug 1827

NAMES OF PASSENGERS	AGE	SEX	OCCUPATIONS	COUNTRY TO WHICH THEY BELONG	COUNTRY THEY INTEND TO INHABIT	SHIPS/DATES OF ARRIVAL	
CALDWELL (cont'd)							
Robt.	50	M	Farmer	Scotland	U. States	Roger Stewart	9 Jun 1828
Robt.	64	M	Laborer	Scotland	United States	Tom	2 Jul 1827
Sally	18	F	Farmer	Scotland	U. States	Roger Stewart	9 Jun 1828
Saml.	28	M	Smith	Great Britian	U. States	St. Michael	3 Jan 1825
Sarah	27	M		Great Britain	U. States	United States	8 Sep 1827
Susannah	45	F		Scotland	America	Eyder	7 Aug 1826
Thos.	45	M	Mariner	Philad.	U. States	John Adams	27 Sep 1827
William	10	M	Farmer, Labourer or Spinster	Ireland	U. States	Meteor	4 Oct 1827
Wm.	50	M	Farmer, Labourer or Spinster	Ireland	U. States	Meteor	4 Oct 1827
CALE, Anne	3			Great Britan	United States	Newry	11 Jul 1827
Jas.	45			Great Britan	United States	Newry	11 Jul 1827
Mary	15			Great Britan	United States	Newry	11 Jul 1827
Mary	40			Great Britan	United States	Newry	11 Jul 1827
Robert	40	M	Gentleman	England	England	Cincinnatus	19 Oct 1826
Sarah	1			Great Britan	United States	Newry	11 Jul 1827
CALEHOUN, John	36	M	servant	Boston	U. States	Zephyr	18 May 1825
Mary	30	F	Servant	Boston	U. States	Zephyr	18 May 1825
CALEMNARD, C.	28	M	Merchant	New York	N. York	Talma	23 Sep 1828
CALEN, E. T.	37	M	Merchant	England	England	Angenora	12 May 1826
CALENOR, F. M.	20	M		Spain	Mexico	Sarah	23 Sep 1826
CALENT, Caroline	4 5/12	F	Child	England	United States	Nimrod	28 Apr 1824
Elizabeth	5 7/12	F	Child	England	United States	Nimrod	28 Apr 1824
Elizabeth	26 11/12	F	Lady	England	United States	Nimrod	28 Apr 1824
John	26 5/12	M	Cabinet Maker	England	United States	Nimrod	28 Apr 1824
CALER, Michael	21	M	Seaman	N. Shorey [?]		Orient	10 Mar 1828
CALEY, Francis	33	M	Carpenter	County Long..., ..., Ireland	Boston	New Orleans	24 Aug 1827
Saml.	19	M	Farmer	Gt. Britain	United States	Robert Edwards	1 Jun 1826
CALHIL, John	22	M	Labourer	Ireland	United States	Edwin	27 Oct 1828
CALHOUN, J. E.	22	M	mariner	U. States	U. States	Actress	18 Feb 1825
Meredith	26	M	Merchant	Philadelphia	New York, U.S.	New York	14 Mar 1828
CALICE, Adam	8/12	M		France	United States	Charles Carroll	16 Jan 1829
Catharine	5 9/12	F		France	United States	Charles Carroll	16 Jan 1829
Eva	9 8/12	F		France	United States	Charles Carroll	16 Jan 1829
Eva	33 2/12	F		France	United States	Charles Carroll	16 Jan 1829
Francis	13 4/12	M		France	United States	Charles Carroll	16 Jan 1829
John	7 5/12	M		France	United States	Charles Carroll	16 Jan 1829
Margaret	3 1/12	F		France	United States	Charles Carroll	16 Jan 1829
Nicholas	33 6/12	M	Carpenter	France	United States	Charles Carroll	16 Jan 1829
CALIGAN, David	40	M	Labourer	Ireland	U. States	New Packet	16 Apr 1828
CALIN, Hugh	24	M	Ash Merchant	Irereland	America	Carolina Ann	20 Jun 1825
M.	20	F	Labourer	Ireland	United States	Combine	4 Jun 1825
CALINANN, —, Mr.	40	M	Carpenter	U. States	U. States	Cadmus	12 Apr 1825
CALISTER, Thomas, Jur.	18	M	Farmer	England	United States	Jubilee	1 Oct 1828
CALL, Barbery	2	F	Farmer	France	United States	Crescent	12 Jul 1827
Bernard	12			Great Britan	United States	Newry	11 Jul 1827
Catherine	11	F	Farmer	France	United States	Crescent	12 Jul 1827
Daniel	7			Great Britan	United States	Newry	11 Jul 1827
Edward, Mr.	42		Royal Navy	Philadelphia/ Sussex, Eng.	England	Venus	12 Apr 1821
George	45	M	Farmer	France	United States	Crescent	12 Jul 1827
Hans	5	M	Farmer	France	United States	Crescent	12 Jul 1827
James	19	M	Weaver	Ireland	United States	Commerce	13 Jun 1828
John	25	M	Labourer	England	United States	Jubilee	12 May 1828
John Gerge	9	M	Farmer	France	United States	Crescent	12 Jul 1827
José	26	M	Merchant	Spain	Spain	Claudio	22 Mar 1828
Margaret	18	F	Farmer	France	United States	Crescent	12 Jul 1827
Margaret	43	F	Farmer	France	United States	Crescent	12 Jul 1827
Phillip	10			Great Britan	United States	Newry	11 Jul 1827
Sampson	9/12	M	None	England	United States	Jubilee	12 May 1828
Sampson	18	M	Labourer	England	United States	Jubilee	12 May 1828
Sarah	24	F	None	England	United States	Jubilee	12 May 1828
Stephen	29	M	Labourer	England	United States	Jubilee	12 May 1828
CALLAGAN, Hellen	32	F	Labourer	Argyle (Tedland) Scotland	United States	Jean Hastie	27 Jul 1829
Humphrey	36	M	Labourer	Great Britain	United States	Aspasia	16 Jul 1828

NAMES OF PASSENGERS	AGE	SEX	OCCUPATIONS	COUNTRY TO WHICH THEY BELONG	COUNTRY THEY INTEND TO INHABIT	SHIPS/DATES OF ARRIVAL	
CALLAGAN (cont'd)							
Janet	34	F	Labourer	Argyle (Tedland) Scotland	United States	Jean Hastie	27 Jul 1829
Margaret	36	F	Labourer	Argyle (Tedland) Scotland	United States	Jean Hastie	27 Jul 1829
CALLAGER, —, Mrs.	34	F		U. States	U. States	Emma	15 Apr 1822
Ann	24	F	Labourer	England	U. States	Ayrshire	12 May 1828
Barnard	22	M	Labourer	England	U. States	Ayrshire	12 May 1828
Mary	13	F	Labourer	England	U. States	Ayrshire	12 May 1828
Mary	20	F	Labourer	England	U. States	Ayrshire	12 May 1828
Peter	19	M	Labourer	England	U. States	Ayrshire	12 May 1828
Thomas	21	M	Labourer	England	U. States	Ayrshire	12 May 1828
CALLAGHAN, Catha.	18	F	Wife	Ireland	United States	Trident	16 May 1826
Catharine	12					Trio	5 May 1828
Catherine	24	F		Ireland	United States	Trio	2 Oct 1828
Denis	50					Trio	5 May 1828
Denis, Jr.	14					Trio	5 May 1828
Honora	35	F		Ireland	United States	Pallas	28 Oct 1828
Jas.	26		Weaver	G. Britain	U. States	Hamilton	28 Apr 1828
Jeremiah	30	M	Labourer	Ireland	United States	Trio	2 Oct 1828
John	25	M	Servant	Scotland	United States	Tom	2 Jul 1827
Lawrance	38	M	Surgeon	Scotland	United States	Tom	2 Jul 1827
Lawrence	20	M	Labourer		Baltimore	Robert Fulton	8 Mar 1823
M.	23	M	Supercargo	Gt. Britan	U. States	Eliza	14 Mar 1825
Margaret	50					Trio	5 May 1828
Michal	27	M	Currier	Ireland	U. States	Josephine	23 Jan 1829
Neil	21	M	Labourer	Ireland	United States	Trident	16 May 1826
Patrick	18	M	Farmer	Ireland	United States	Romulus	24 Jun 1826
Patrick	26	M	Labourer	Gt. Britn.	United States	Union	9 Jan 1824
Patrick	26	M	Gentleman	Ireland	United States	Dublin Packet	13 Oct 1828
Rose	20	F		Ireland	Baltimore	Lima	5 Aug 1829
Rose	20	F		Ireland	U. States	Lima	5 Aug 1829
CALLAHAN, Mary	24	M	Farmer	Ireland	U. States	Edward	15 Jul 1825
Michael	22	M	Carpenter	Ireland	America	William	11 Nov 1825
P.	27	M	Farmer	Ireland	U. States	Edward	15 Jul 1825
Philip	25	M	Farmer	Ireland	U. States	Alexander	28 Jul 1821
CALLAN, Catherine	12	F	None	Ireland	United States	Lord Wellington	28 May 1827
Elizabeth	5	F	None	Ireland	United States	Lord Wellington	28 May 1827
Hugh	5/12	M	None	Ireland	United States	Lord Wellington	28 May 1827
Hugh	36	M	Labourer	Ireland	United States	Lord Wellington	28 May 1827
Mary	32	F	None	Ireland	United States	Lord Wellington	28 May 1827
Thomas	18	M	Clerk	Great Briton	United States	Erin	26 May 1821
Thomas	28	M	Labourer	Ireland	New York	Rambler	31 Aug 1829
William	30	M	Labourer	Ireland	United States	Lord Wellington	28 May 1827
CALLANAN, Cornelius	19	M	Farmer	Great Britain	United States	Aurora	5 Sep 1826
James	22	M	Farmer	Great Britain	United States	Aurora	5 Sep 1826
CALLANO, J. B.	29	M	Merchant	Columbia		Athenian	3 Sep 1827
CALLASTER, Thos.	18			Ireland		Anacreon	7 Sep 1827
CALLAY, Elizabeth	...	...	...	Ireland	United States	Carolina Ann	24 Oct 1825
CALLEHIN, Wm.	30	M		Great Britain	United States	Mary	11 Jul 1820
CALLEN, Eliza	70	F	None	Great Britain	United States	William Dawson	18 Jun 1827
James	30	M	Labourer	Ireland	United States	Lord Wellington	28 May 1827
CALLER, Eliza	47			England		Anacreon	7 Sep 1827
CALLERY, Abby	25	F		Ireland	United States	Lord Wellington	14 Nov 1827
James	28	M	Farmer	Ireland	United States	Lord Wellington	14 Nov 1827
CALLESTER, Thomas	50	M	Farmer	England	United States	Jubilee	1 Oct 1828
CALLEY, Patrick	30	M	Laborer	Great Britain	United States	Hanford	9 Oct 1829
CALLHON, Ann	28	F	Lady	Ireland	United States	Belleville	13 Oct 1827
John	26	M	Laborer	Ireland	United States	Belleville	13 Oct 1827
John, Jr.	2	M	Child	Ireland	United States	Belleville	13 Oct 1827
CALLIGHAN, Michl.	20	M	Wheelwright	Ireland	United States	Diana	1 May 1826
CALLIHAN, Mathew	32	M	Farmer	England	New York	Cincinnatus	16 Apr 1824
CALLIN, James	30			Great Britan	United States	Newry	11 Jul 1827
CALLINAN, Joseph	12	M	Labourer	Ireland	United States	Wilson	4 Oct 1827
CALLINANE, Thos.	35	M	Farmer	Ireland	U. States	Howard	25 Jul 1823
CALLISTER, Elisa	36	F		Great Britain	United States	Meridian	2 Jul 1827
Isabella	12	F		England		Anacreon	7 Sep 1827
Jane	9	F		Great Britain	United States	Meridian	2 Jul 1827
Jane	36	F		Great Britain	United States	Meridian	2 Jul 1827

NAMES OF PASSENGERS	AGE	SEX	OCCUPATIONS	COUNTRY TO WHICH THEY BELONG	COUNTRY THEY INTEND TO INHABIT	SHIPS/DATES OF ARRIVAL	
CALLISTER (cont'd)							
Jas.	1	F		Great Britain	United States	Meridian	2 Jul 1827
John	5	M		Great Britain	United States	Meridian	2 Jul 1827
John	13	M	Farmer	Great Britain	United States	Meridian	2 Jul 1827
John	34	M	Farmer	Great Britain	United States	Meridian	2 Jul 1827
Mary	6	F		Great Britain	United States	Meridian	2 Jul 1827
Thomas	40	M	Farmer	Great Britain	United States	Meridian	2 Jul 1827
Thos.	4	F		Great Britain	United States	Meridian	2 Jul 1827
Thos.	18	M	Farmer	Great Britain	United States	Meridian	2 Jul 1827
Wm.	10	M	Farmer	Great Britain	United States	Meridian	2 Jul 1827
CALLIVAN, Canner	23	M	Labourer	Ireland	U. States	Courier	17 Mar 1828
CALLOLY, James	24 7/12	M		Ireland	U.S. of America	Douglass	6 Jul 1829
John	22 3/12	M		Ireland	U.S. of America	Douglass	6 Jul 1829
CALLON, ...ace	7	F	child of J. Callon	Ireland	United States	Asia	29 Jul 1829
Ales	15	F	Spinster	Ireland	United States	Asia	29 Jul 1829
Anne	10	F		Ireland	U. States	Sarah G	30 Jun 1828
Bryan	9	M	child of J. Callon	Ireland	United States	Asia	29 Jul 1829
Hugh	40	M	Labourer	Ireland	U. States	Sarah G	30 Jun 1828
John	8	M		Ireland	U. States	Sarah G	30 Jun 1828
John	13	M	child of J. Callon	Ireland	United States	Asia	29 Jul 1829
John	50	M	Labourer	Ireland	United States	Asia	29 Jul 1829
Margaret	2/12	F	Sent for by her Father	Ireland	United States	Asia	29 Jul 1829
Mary	17	F	Spinster	Ireland	United States	Asia	29 Jul 1829
Mary	50	F	wife of J. Callon	Ireland	United States	Asia	29 Jul 1829
Peggy	38	F		Ireland	U. States	Sarah G	30 Jun 1828
Robert	6	M		Ireland	U. States	Sarah G	30 Jun 1828
Thomas	3	M		Ireland	U. States	Sarah G	30 Jun 1828
William	19	M	Labourer	Ireland	United States	Asia	29 Jul 1829
CALLOW, Ann	5	F	None	Isle of Man		Ocean	13 Jul 1827
Eliz.	1			England	United States	Hugh Johnson	11 Jun 1828
Ellen	1	F	None	Isle of Man		Ocean	13 Jul 1827
Isabella	34	F	None	Isle of Man		Ocean	13 Jul 1827
John	6	M	None	Isle of Man		Ocean	13 Jul 1827
John	23		Labourer	England	United States	Hugh Johnson	11 Jun 1828
Margret	20			England	United States	Hugh Johnson	11 Jun 1828
Mary	65	F		Great Britain	United States	William Dawson	18 Jun 1827
Thos.	3	M	None	Isle of Man		Ocean	13 Jul 1827
Thos.	28			England	United States	Hugh Johnson	11 Jun 1828
Thos.	32	M	Joiner	Isle of Man		Ocean	13 Jul 1827
CALLY, Ann	30	F	Merchant	Ireland	United States	Magnet	22 Aug 1822
Catherine	4	F	Child	Great Britain	United States	Hanford	9 Oct 1829
Jane	06	F	Child	Great Britain	United States	Hanford	9 Oct 1829
Janes	2	M	Child	Great Britain	United States	Hanford	9 Oct 1829
Nancy	28	F	Wife	Great Britain	United States	Hanford	9 Oct 1829
CALOGLY, Bridget	20	F	None	Ireland	America	Braganza	8 Aug 1825
CALOMEL, —, Infant				G. Britain	U. States	Robt. Edwards	4 Sep 1828
Charlotte	3	F		G. Britain	U. States	Robt. Edwards	4 Sep 1828
Charlotte	29	F		G. Britain	U. States	Robt. Edwards	4 Sep 1828
Eliza	18	F		G. Britain	U. States	Robt. Edwards	4 Sep 1828
Mary	2	F		G. Britain	U. States	Robt. Edwards	4 Sep 1828
Susan	56	F		G. Britain	U. States	Robt. Edwards	4 Sep 1828
Wm.	33	M	Wool draper	G. Britain	U. States	Robt. Edwards	4 Sep 1828
CALON, Monras	27	M	Labourer	Ireland	United States	Nancy Henrietta	3 Nov 1828
CALORRIS, Chris	20	M	Servant	Spain	United States	Alfred	3 Jun 1826
CALRISAS, Pablo	56	M	Merchant	Spain	Havana	Herald	21 Sep 1824
CALT, Elizabeth	3	F		Ireland	U. States	Nancy	29 Nov 1821
CALTEN, Walter	42	M	Merchant	New York	New York	American	18 Oct 1824
CALTER, Anna Maria	10	F	Family [of Anthony]	France	America	La Grange	7 Aug 1828
Anthony	12	M	Family [of Anthony]	France	America	La Grange	7 Aug 1828
Anthony	45	M	Farmer	France	America	La Grange	7 Aug 1828
Barbara	16	F	Family [of Anthony]	France	America	La Grange	7 Aug 1828
*Died on the Voyage							
Barbara	40	F	Family [of Anthony]	France	America	La Grange	7 Aug 1828

NAMES OF PASSENGERS	AGE	SEX	OCCUPATIONS	COUNTRY TO WHICH THEY BELONG	COUNTRY THEY INTEND TO INHABIT	SHIPS/DATES OF ARRIVAL
CALTER (cont'd)						
John	3...	M	Family			La Grange	7 Aug 1828
			[of Anthony]	France	America	La Grange	7 Aug 1828
CALTON, Adalster	52 4/12	F	Farmer	Switzerland	U. States	France	26 Jun 1828
Gorue	48 3/12	M	Farmer	Switzerland	U. States	France	26 Jun 1828
Josephine	14 2/12	F	Farmer	Switzerland	U. States	France	26 Jun 1828
Maria	18 3/12	F	Farmer	Switzerland	U. States	France	26 Jun 1828
CALUNT, Joseph	25	M	Mechanic	England	United States	Wm. Byrnes	30 Apr 1828
CALVAN, Nicholas	35	M	Merchant	Havana	U. States	Empress	7 Jul 1827
CALVART, H. N.	25	M	...	...	U.S. America	Columbia	26 Nov 1825
Margret	21	F	Servant	England	United States	Maria	12 May 1823
CALVELL, John, Esqr.	45	M	R. General w/army	Canada	Canada	Manhattan	21 May 1821
CALVEROS, Ns.	38	M	Merchant	Spain	United States	Alfred	3 Jun 1826
CALVERT, Is.	16	M	Baker	Great Britain	United States	Marshal Wellington	3 May 1822
John	19	M	Soldier	England	England	Hudson	21 Aug 1829
Will	54		Sh...	...	U. States	South Carolina Packet	17 May 1827
CALVERTON, Amos	30	M	Bookbinder	France	America	Saluda	16 Oct 1824
CALVIERE, Francis	32	M	Watchmaker	France		Edward Quesnel	17 Nov 1828
CALVILLE, T.	23	M	Mason	United States	United States	Indus	5 Sep 1827
CALVIN, Ann	50	F	Wife	Ireland	United States	Dublin Packet	13 Oct 1828
Joseph	30	M	Farmer	Ireland	United States	Dublin Packet	13 Oct 1828
William	21		Farmer	England	United States	Hudson	5 Apr 1826
William	33	M	Tailor	Isle of Man	United States	Lunar	5 May 1828
CALYAN, Thos	19	M	Farm	Ireland	U. States	Meteor	19 Jul 1828
CALZADIKA, Pablo	35	M	Servant	Tenerief	Spain	Orozimbo	16 Apr 1821
CAM, Henry	21	M	Officer	England	U. States	Hiram	17 Jun 1826
CAM..., Thomas	24 3/12	M	...	England	America, U.S.	Illinois	3 Jun 1822
CAMACHO, John							
Gomez	20	M	Joiner	Portugeese	United States	Mary Elizabeth	15 Oct 1829
CAMANE, John W.	14	M		U. States	U. States	Geo. Canning	2 Sep 1828
CAMANT, Mark	27	M	Blacksmith	England	U. States	Alert	22 Sep 1821
CAMAREN, Mary	21	F		Ireland	U. States	John Jay	17 Sep 1828
CAMBAULT, Peter	50	M	Merchant	Ireland	U. States	Jane	24 May 1822
CAMBAUTT, P. C.				France	U. States	General Ward	22 Jun 1821
CAMBEL, James	26	M	Cole burner	Emerica	Merican	Enterprize	14 Oct 1828
CAMBELE, Peter	26	M	Farmer	England	U. States	Electra	7 Jul 1828
CAMBELL, Bermand	20	M	Carpenter	Ireland	United States	Fabius	4 Jun 1828
Bridgett	16	F				Catherine	19 Aug 1825
Catherine	14	F				Catherine	19 Aug 1825
Catherine	20	F		Ireland	America	Wilson	27 Nov 1826
Charles	19	M				Betsey	17 Aug 1820
Eleanor	55	F		Ireland	United States	Fabius	4 Jun 1828
Francis	65	M	Carpenter	Ireland	United States	Fabius	4 Jun 1828
H.	50		Farmer	Ireland	United States	Courier	16 May 1825
Jane	13	F		Ireland	United States	Fabius	4 Jun 1828
John	8	M				Catherine	19 Aug 1825
John	21	M	Carpenter	Ireland	United States	Fabius	4 Jun 1828
John	22	M	...	Ireland	New York	Catherine	19 Aug 1825
John	41	M	Labourer			Catherine	19 Aug 1825
Margaret	28	F				Catherine	19 Aug 1825
Mary	18	F				Catherine	19 Aug 1825
Mary	45	F				Catherine	19 Aug 1825
Satira	32	F				Catherine	19 Aug 1825
Susanah	16	F		Ireland	United States	Fabius	4 Jun 1828
William	22	M	Miller	England	Newyork	Cortes	16 Jul 1827
William, Sir	71	M	...ad...	Great Brittan	Canada	Cambria	3 Jul 1829
CAMBLE, Bryan	27		Laborer	Ireland	Great Britain	Robert Burns	14 Jun 1824
Neill	15	M	Labourer	Grt. Britain	United States	Robert Fulton	8 Oct 1828
CAMBRELING, C. C.	38	M	Merchant	U. States	N. York	James Cropper	21 Oct 1825
CAMDEN, Bridget	18	F		England	United States	Danube	22 Aug 1825
John	29	M	Labourer	Great Brittain	United States	Sarah Ralston	27 Jan 1827
CAMDON, C.	25	M	Labourer	Great Brittain	United States	Sarah Ralston	27 Jan 1827
E.	18	F		Great Brittain	United States	Sarah Ralston	27 Jan 1827
CAMEL, Hugh	29	M	Mason	Halifax	U. States	Hope Return	20 Mar 1824
John	25	M	Farmer	Ireland	U. States	Nancy	12 Aug 1820
Mary	20	F		Ireland	U. States	Nancy	12 Aug 1820
CAMEN, N.	23	M	Farmer	Scotland	United States	Indus	5 Sep 1827

NAMES OF PASSENGERS	AGE	SEX	OCCUPATIONS	COUNTRY TO WHICH THEY BELONG	COUNTRY THEY INTEND TO INHABIT	SHIPS/DATES OF ARRIVAL	
CAMERA, P.	23	M	Clerk	Yucatan	Yucatan	Imperial	12 Aug 1825
CAMERFORD, Ally	26	F		Ireland	United States	Wilson	27 Jun 1826
Biddy	23	F	Servant	Ireland	United States	Wilson	27 Jun 1826
Elizabeth	11	F	Servant	Ireland	United States	Wilson	27 Jun 1826
John	30	M	Bricklayer	Ireland	United States	Wilson	27 Jun 1826
Mary	9	F	Servant	Ireland	United States	Wilson	27 Jun 1826
CAMERON, —, Mrs.	38	F	None	Great Britain	United States	Kate	2 Oct 1821
A.	40	M	Merchant	U. States	U. States	Prudence	11 Jun 1825
Alexander	19 4/12	M	Accountant	Great Britain	United States	Amity	1 Dec 1826
Alexr.	11	M	Farmer	Scotland	United States	Belmont	30 Aug 1828
Allan	9/12	M	Son	Scotland	United States	Cambria	8 Oct 1828
Allin	29	M	Farmer	England	England	New York Packet	8 May 1823
Amelia	45	F		Scotland	United States	Shakespeare	24 Jul 1828
Angus	20	M	Gardener	Scotland	U. States	Atlantic	27 Aug 1827
Angus	24	M	Farmer	Scotland	United States	Belmont	30 Aug 1828
Ann	24	F	None	Scotland	U. States	Czar	29 Aug 1829
Ann	30	F	Farmer	Argyle (Tedland) Scotland	United States	Jean Hastie	27 Jul 1829
Daniel	29	M	Coton Spiner	Great Britain	United States	Courier	26 Jun 1827
Danl.	21	M	Clerk	Great Britain	U.S. America	Prince Madoc	24 Sep 1821
Dunkin	30	M	Engineer	Scotland	Brooklin, S.S.	Essex	24 Aug 1829
E.	15	F		Scotland	United States	Shakespeare	24 Jul 1828
Eleser.	18	M	Labourer	Glasgow, Scotland	Gt. Britain	Orozimbo	19 Oct 1822
Elizabeth	3	F	Daughter	Scotland	United States	Cambria	8 Oct 1828
G.	18		Merchant		N. Brunswick	Charlotte Corday	15 Jul 1820
James	18	F	Labourer	Great Britain	United States	Kate	2 Oct 1821
James	23	M	Baker	Scotland	U. States	Atlantic	27 Aug 1827
James	41	M	Surveyor	Great Britain	United States	Kate	2 Oct 1821
James	46	M	Merchant	Scotland	United States	Herald	7 Jun 1824
Jean	16	F		Scotland	United States	Shakespeare	24 Jul 1828
Jno.	25	M	Mercht.	America	U. States	Ambuscade	5 Jul 1822
John	6	M	Son	Scotland	United States	Cambria	8 Oct 1828
John	23	M	Drugist	United States	United States	Charleston Packet	25 Jul 1821
John	25	M	Baker	Scotland	U. States	Czar	29 Aug 1829
John	38	M	Gardener	Scotland	United States	Cambria	8 Oct 1828
John	45	M	Merchant	Great Britian	U. States	Henry Kneedland	7 Aug 1826
John G.	14	M		Scotland	United States	Shakespeare	24 Jul 1828
Margaret	44	F	Wife	Scotland	United States	Cambria	8 Oct 1828
Mary	23	F	Spinster	Scotland	United States	Broke	16 Jul 1829
Peter	25	M	Painter	Edenborough	Edenborough	Howard Douglass	11 May 1827
Rob. A.	25	M	Tinman	U. States	U. States	Ann Maria	5 Aug 1824
CAMES, James	22	M	Mariner	Massachusetts	U. States	Falcon	19 Sep 1823
CAMFELD, Richd.	18	M	Labourer	G. Britain	U. States	St. George	7 Jun 1828
CAMIN, Fancis	20	M	Farmer	U. States	U. States	Nancy	19 Oct 1821
CAMMANN, O. ... S.	21	M	Mercht.	New York	New York	Columbia	5 Oct 1824
CAMMEL, James	21	M	Linnen weaver	Ireland	America	Franklin	13 Aug 1827
CAMMIEN, Frederick	18	M	Seaman	U. States	U. States	Boston	26 Sep 1820
CAMMINS,							
Anthony	24 2/12	M	...	...	United States	Lima	19 Jun 1824
Jane	12 7/12	F	...	Ireland	United States	Lima	19 Jun 1824
CAMMON, John	22		Slater	Scotland	United States	Camillus	3 May 1828
CAMON, John	25	M	Merchant	France	France	Altamira	24 Jun 1828
CAMONDSON, Jno.	57	M	Dealer	England	United States	Dalhouse Castle	8 May 1827
CAMP, J. W.	21	M	Mariner	U. States	U. States	Eliza	26 Jul 1825
John	20	M	Mechanic	Halifax	U. States	Penobscott Packet	1 Jul 1823
CAMPAGNE, —	33	M	Merchant			Sarah Ann	5 Aug 1820
CAMPAL, Danl.	26		Farmer			Charlotte Corday	15 Jul 1820
CAMPANN, M.	30	M	Soldier	Spain	Spain	Prince Edward	22 Jul 1824
CAMPBALL, John	30	M	Cooper	Aberdeen	U. States	Gowan	28 Aug 1822
CAMPBEL, Isabella,							
Mrs., his wife [Neil]	27	F		Scotland		Hercules	19 Jun 1821
Neil, Mr.	30	M	Labourer	Scotland		Hercules	19 Jun 1821
CAMPBELL, —	37	F	Spinster	Ireland	United States	Thomas	13 Dec 1827

NAMES OF PASSENGERS	AGE	SEX	OCCUPATIONS	COUNTRY TO WHICH THEY BELONG	COUNTRY THEY INTEND TO INHABIT	SHIPS/DATES OF ARRIVAL	
CAMPBELL (cont'd)							
—, Mrs.	23	F		Scotland	New York	Joseph Hume	26 Oct 1829
...	4	M				Lady of the Lake	23 Aug 1828
A.	45	M	Weaver			Lady of the Lake	23 Aug 1828
Adam G.	12	M	Boy	Ireland	U. States	Josephine	23 Jan 1829
Agnes	4	F	Gentleman	Scotland	United States	Camillus	9 May 1827
Alex	6	M	Gentleman	Scotland	United States	Camillus	9 May 1827
Alexander	8	M				Servant	30 Aug 1820
Alexander	34 3/12	M	Mason	England	America	John Dickinson	15 Oct 1826
Alexr.	25	M	Farmer	New Brunswick	Canada	Susan Morton	17 Jun 1823
Alexr.	26	M	Farmer	Killean, Gla..., Scotland	N. York	New Orleans	24 Aug 1827
Alexr.	28	M	Gentleman	Scotland	United States	Camillus	9 May 1827
Alexr.	30	M	Farmer	New Brunswick	Canada	Susan Morton	17 Jun 1823
Allan	30	M	Blacksmith	Scotland	United States	McDonough	3 Nov 1823
Amy	50	F		St. Johns	U. States	Nancy	10 Jul 1822
Andrew	40	M	Cartman	Ireland	United States	Neury	27 Jan 1827
Ann	1	F	None	Scotland	United States	Mary & Susan	5 Aug 1828
Ann	25	F		Scotland	St. Johns, N.B.	Isabella	10 Mar 1825
Ann	25	F		Gt. Britain		Dalhouse Castle	13 May 1828
Ann	30	F	Lady	Nova Scotia	Upper Canada	Hanford	10 Nov 1827
Archd.	2	M		Scotland	United States	Trent	10 Jul 1827
Archd.	2	M		Scotland	New York	Joseph Hume	26 Oct 1829
Archd.	30	M	Weaver	Scotland	United States	Trent	10 Jul 1827
Archibald	4/12	M	Child	Ireland	U. States	Josephine	23 Jan 1829
B.	22	M	Mariner	American	U. States	Sarah Ann	5 Aug 1820
Barney	21	M	Labourer	Ireland	U. States	Marcus	7 Apr 1825
Betsey	18	F	Spinstress	England	U. States	Ann	29 Jan 1820
Bridget	21	F	Farmer, Labourer or Spinster	Ireland	U. States	Meteor	4 Oct 1827
Caroline	6	F	Farmer	New Brunswick	Canada	Susan Morton	17 Jun 1823
Catharin	14/12	F	None	Great Brittan	U. States	Electra	28 Apr 1827
Catharine	19	F	Spinster	Ireland	United States	Lord Strangford	20 Jun 1826
Catharine	22	F	Spinster	Ireland	United States	Catharine	22 Jul 1825
Catharine	30	F		Great Brittian	United States	Carolina Augusta	2 Dec 1828
Catherine	7/12	F				Servant	30 Aug 1820
Catherine	5	F	Child	Ireland	U. States	Josephine	23 Jan 1829
Catherine	13		Spinster			Rufus King	7 Aug 1820
Catherine	23	F		Gt. Britain		Dalhouse Castle	13 May 1828
Catherine	26	F				Imperial	19 Jul 1820
Catherine	30	F	Farmeress			Servant	30 Aug 1820
Catherine	64	F		Mayo	America	Margaret	31 Jul 1824
Charles H.	3	M	None	New York	New York	Brighton	21 Jan 1826
Charlotte A.	31	F	None	New York	New York	Brighton	21 Jan 1826
Chas.	26	M	Farmer	Ireland	United States	Leonidas	3 Aug 1825
Chas. S.	22	M	Bookbinder	Great Britain	United States	Purrington	8 Dec 1827
Christian	28	F	Gentleman	Scotland	United States	Camillus	9 May 1827
Colin	35	M	Farmer	Scotland	U. States	Servant	30 Aug 1820
Colin	45	M	Gentleman	England	G. Brittain or her Collonies	Etheldred	17 Oct 1822
D. D.	24	M		America	America	Britannia	22 Jul 1829
Daniel	20	M	Labourer	Great Britian	U. States	Pallas	17 Aug 1824
Daniel	25	M	Labourer	Ireland	United States	Catharine	22 Jul 1825
Daniel	29	M	Blacksmith	Great Britain	United States	Fame	26 May 1828
Daniel	40 8/12	M	Labourer	G. Brittian	United States	Louisa	14 Jun 1825
Danl.	9		A Boy	Ireland	United States	Fabius	18 Mar 1829
David	40	M	Farmer	Mayo	America	Margaret	31 Jul 1824
Donald	30	M	Farmer	Great Britain	America	Samuel Robertson	26 Nov 1825
E.	35	M	Carpenter	Scotland	St. Johns, N.B.	Isabella	10 Mar 1825
Edward	30	M	Labour	Great Britain	United States	Samuel Wright	12 Oct 1829
Edwd.	47	M	...	Great Brittain	N. York	Albion	11 Jun 1821
Eleanor	4	F	Child	Ireland	U. States	Courier	17 Mar 1828
Eliza	5	F	Farmer	New Brunswick	Canada	Susan Morton	17 Jun 1823
Eliza	10	F	Child	Ireland	U. States	Josephine	23 Jan 1829
Eliza	28	F				Imperial	19 Jul 1820

CAMPBELL (cont'd)

NAMES OF PASSENGERS	AGE	SEX	OCCUPATIONS	COUNTRY TO WHICH THEY BELONG	COUNTRY THEY INTEND TO INHABIT	SHIPS/DATES OF ARRIVAL	
Elizabeth	13	F				Lady of the Lake	23 Aug 1828
Elizabeth	23	F	None	Great Britain	United States	Purrington	8 Dec 1827
Elizabeth	30	F	None	Ayrshire	United States	Dalhousie Castle	27 Jul 1826
Elizabeth	50	F				Imperial	19 Jul 1820
Ellen	30	F	None	Great Brittan	U. States	Electra	28 Apr 1827
Felix	25	M	Y. Man	Ireland	New York	Trusty	12 Sep 1828
Finlay	70	M	Gentleman	England	United States	Hamlet	25 Aug 1825
Flora	50	F	Spinster	Scotland	America	Concord	4 Jun 1821
Frans.	32	M	Auctioner	Great Britian	United States	London	24 Jun 1823
Fredk.	22	M	Gentleman			Helen	4 Aug 1829
G.	5	F		Scotland	United States	McDonough	3 Nov 1823
G. W., Lady & Two Children		M	Ambassador from the U.S. to the Court of St. Petersburg etc., etc.			Bayard	30 Oct 1820
George	3	M		Ireland	U. States	Josephine	27 Jul 1825
George	12	M	Farmer	Tyrone	United States	Carolina Ann	11 Jun 1824
George	29	M	Carpenter	Ireland	U. States	Courier	17 Mar 1828
Grace	21	F		Scotland	United States	McDonough	3 Nov 1823
H. W.	33	M	Merchant	Hayti	Hayti	Robert Reade	13 Jul 1825
Hannah	70	F				Imperial	19 Jul 1820
Helen	29	F		Scotland	United States	Trent	10 Jul 1827
Henry	22	M	Farmer	Ireland	United States	Asia	29 Jul 1829
Hugh	25	M				Lady of the Lake	23 Aug 1828
Isabella	20	F	Spinster	Ireland	U. States	William & John	10 Jul 1824
Isabella	22	F		Great Britian	U. States	Hector	17 Aug 1825
J.	12		Labourer	Ireland	United States	Thomas	13 Dec 1827
J.	23	M	Cooper	U. States	U. States	Columbus	23 Oct 1828
James	1	M	Gentleman	Scotland	United States	Camillus	9 May 1827
James	6	M				Servant	30 Aug 1820
James	21	M	Joiner	Scotland	United States	Shakespeare	24 Jul 1828
James	23	M	Farmer	Ireland	United States	Lord Strangford	20 Jun 1826
James	23	M	Labourer	Ireland	United States	Fabius	31 Jul 1829
James	24	M	Labour	Great Britain	United States	Samuel Wright	12 Oct 1829
James	25		Farmer	Ireland	America	Rufus King	7 Aug 1820
James	26	M	Farmer	Great Britain	United States	Colossus	5 Jun 1827
James	28	M	Servant	Ireland	United States	Nancy Henrietta	3 Nov 1828
James	28	M	Shoemaker	Scotland	U.S.A.	Dalhouse Castle	21 Aug 1829
James	28	M	Shoemaker	Scotland	United States	Dalhouse Castle	21 Aug 1829
James	32	M	Merchant	Scotland	United States	Plato	25 Aug 1829
James	40		Labourer	Ireland	United States	Fabius	18 Mar 1829
James M.	29	M	Merchant	New York	New York	Brighton	21 Jan 1826
James S. Mr.	25		Mechanic	U.S. America	America	Hesper	9 Jun 1827
Jane	1	F	Child	Ireland	U. States	William & John	10 Jul 1824
Jane	2	F		Ireland	United States	Neury	27 Jan 1827
Jane	4	F	None	Scotland	United States	Mary & Susan	5 Aug 1828
Jane	8	F	Gentleman	Scotland	United States	Camillus	9 May 1827
Jas.	3	M		Scotland	United States	McDonough	3 Nov 1823
Jas.	16	M	...	Ireland	U. States	Atlantic	19 Aug 1825
Jas.	20	M	Weaver	Ireland	United States	Trident	16 May 1826
Jas.	22	M	Merchant	U. States		Charleston Packet	4 May 1821
Jas.	30	M	Merchant	Scotland	England	Dart	24 Oct 1825
Jas. S.	25	M	Mechanic	U. States	U. States	Hannah & Rebecca	12 Jun 1824
Jno.	25	M	Weaver	England	U. States	Olive Branch	30 Oct 1823
John				Great Britain	United States	Colossus	5 Jun 1827
John	1 1/2	M		Ireland	New York	Rambler	31 Aug 1829
John	4	M		Scotland	United States	Trent	10 Jul 1827
John	6	M		Scotland	United States	McDonough	3 Nov 1823
John	8 6/12	M	Child	Ireland	U. States	Josephine	23 Jan 1829
John	16	M	Labourer	Ireland	United States	Catharine	22 Jul 1825
John	20	M	Labourer	Ireland	United States	Jubilee	12 May 1828
John	22	M	Farmer	New Brunswick	Canada	Susan Morton	17 Jun 1823
John	22	M	Gentleman	Scotland	Scotland	Morning Star	26 May 1824

NAMES OF PASSENGERS	A G E	S E X	OCCUPATIONS	COUNTRY TO WHICH THEY BELONG	COUNTRY THEY INTEND TO INHABIT	SHIPS/DATES OF ARRIVAL	
CAMPBELL (cont'd)							
John	22	M	Labourer	Ireland	U. States	William & John	10 Jul 1824
John	24	M	Labourer	England	United States	Nimrod	31 Jul 1828
John	28	M	Mercht.	Great Britian	U. States	Hector	17 Aug 1825
John	30	M	Farmer	Ireland	United States	Dublin Packet	13 Oct 1828
John	32 10/12	M	Weaver	Ireland	United States	Mobile	21 Aug 1827
John	36	M	...	Ireland	United States	Carolina Ann	24 Oct 1825
John	36	M	Labourer	Ireland	United States	Josephine	30 Apr 1828
Joseph	22	M		Ireland	United States	William & George	14 May 1828
M.	30	M	Gentleman	American	U. States	Romulus	31 Jul 1823
Margaret	18	F		Gt. Britain		Dalhouse Castle	13 May 1828
Margaret	25	F		Ireland	United States	Neury	27 Jan 1827
Margeret	7	F	Child	Ireland	U. States	Josephine	23 Jan 1829
Margery	30	F		Ireland	United States	Neury	27 Jan 1827
Margt.	17		Spinster			Rufus King	7 Aug 1820
Maria	3	F	Child	Ireland	U. States	Courier	17 Mar 1828
Maria	24	F	Matron	Ireland	U. States	Courier	17 Mar 1828
Marian	28	F	None	Scotland	United States	Mary & Susan	5 Aug 1828
Mary	1	F		Scotland	United States	McDonough	3 Nov 1823
Mary	1	F		Great Brittian	United States	Carolina Augusta	2 Dec 1828
Mary	3	F	Child	Ireland	U. States	Josephine	23 Jan 1829
Mary	5	F				Servant	30 Aug 1820
Mary	15		Spinster			Rufus King	7 Aug 1820
Mary	20			Ireland	United States	Robert Burns	30 May 1823
Mary	20	F		Great Britian	U. States	Pallas	17 Aug 1824
Mary	20	M	None	Ireland	United States	Leonidas	3 Aug 1825
Mary	20	F	Spinster	Ireland	United States	Lord Strangford	20 Jun 1826
Mary	22	F	Wife	England	United States	Hamlet	25 Aug 1825
Mary	22	F	None	Great Britain	United States	Penelope	11 Jun 1827
Mary	22	F		Ireland	New York	Rambler	31 Aug 1829
Mary	22 3/12	F	Spinner	G. Britain	United States	Dutchess of Portland	30 Oct 1826
Mary	25	F		Scotland	United States	Margaret Bogle	11 Jun 1824
Mary	25	F	Spinster	Ireland	United States	Catharine	22 Jul 1825
Mary	26	F		Scotland	United States	McDonough	3 Nov 1823
Mary	34	F				Imperial	19 Jul 1820
Mary	42	F		Mayo	America	Margaret	31 Jul 1824
Mary Ann	16	F		Tyrone	United States	Carolina Ann	11 Jun 1824
Mary Anne	19	F	Wife	Ireland	America	Dublin Packet	9 Oct 1820
May	31	F		Great Britain	U. States	Lady Hunter	28 May 1823
Michael	40	M	Labourer	Ireland	United States	Lord Wellington	28 May 1827
Michl.	19	M	Labourer	Great Britain	United States	Penelope	11 Jun 1827
Nancy	18	...	Servant	Irland	America	Belleville	7 Dec 1827
Nathl.	50	M	Farmer	New Brunswick	Canada	Susan Morton	17 Jun 1823
Neil	27	M	Mason	Scotland	U.S.A.	Calliope	15 Aug 1827
Oliver	24		Farmer			Rufus King	7 Aug 1820
P. A.	20	F	...	Ireland	U.S. America	Columbia	26 Nov 1825
P. F. A.	47	M	Gentleman	England	U. States	John Wells	16 May 1825
Patrick	5	M		Great Brittian	United States	Carolina Augusta	2 Dec 1828
Patrick	10	M	Boy	Ireland	United States	Lord Strangford	20 Jun 1826
Patrick	19	M	Plaisterer	Ireland	United States	Henry Kneeland	7 Jun 1828
Patrick	21	M	Labourer	Ireland	United States	Andes	2 Oct 1828
Patrick	30	M		Great Brittian	United States	Carolina Augusta	2 Dec 1828
Patrick	31	M	Labourer	Ireland	U. States	Marcus	7 Apr 1825
Peter	20 5/12	M	Printcutter	Scotland	United States	Mobile	21 Aug 1827
Peter	26	M	Planter	Scotland	U. States	Huntress	15 Oct 1823
Peter	27	M	Farmer, Labourer or Spinster	Ireland	U. States	Meteor	4 Oct 1827
Peter	30	M	Labourer	Ireland	New York	Rambler	31 Aug 1829
Peter	32	M	Merchant	Great Brittan	U. States	Electra	28 Apr 1827
Quentin	33	M	Farmer	Ayrshire	United States	Dalhousie Castle	27 Jul 1826
R.	25	M	Merchant	U. States	U. States	Rachel	14 Mar 1825
Rachel	28	F		Mayo	America	Margaret	31 Jul 1824
Rebecca	17	F	Wife	Great Britain	United States	Fame	26 May 1828
Richard	...4	...	...	Ireland	United States	Carolina Ann	24 Oct 1825
Robert	22	M	Shoemaker	Scotland	U.S.A.	Dalhouse Castle	21 Aug 1829
Robert	28	M	Labourer	Scotland	United States	Mary & Susan	5 Aug 1828

NAMES OF PASSENGERS	AGE	SEX	OCCUPATIONS	COUNTRY TO WHICH THEY BELONG	COUNTRY THEY INTEND TO INHABIT	SHIPS/DATES OF ARRIVAL
CAMPBELL (cont'd)						
Robt.	22	M	Shoemaker	Scotland	United States	Dalhouse Castle 21 Aug 1829
Robt.	35	M	Laborer	Scotland	United States	Trent 10 Jul 1827
Robt. E.	14	M	Boy	Ireland	U. States	Josephine 23 Jan 1829
Rose	3	F		Great Brittian	United States	Carolina Augusta 2 Dec 1828
Sandy	18	M	Farmer	New Brunswick	Canada	Susan Morton 17 Jun 1823
Sarah	6	F	Child	Ireland	U. States	Courier 17 Mar 1828
Sarah	8	F	Farmer	New Brunswick	Canada	Susan Morton 17 Jun 1823
Sarah	19	F	Servant	Ireland	N. York	Trusty 12 Sep 1828
Sarah	40		Housewife			Rufus King 7 Aug 1820
Seohn	25	M	Weaver	Scotland	United States	Trent 10 Jul 1827
Sophia	5/12	F	None	New York	New York	Brighton 21 Jan 1826
T.	38	M	Labourer	Ireland	United States	Thomas 13 Dec 1827
Thomas	29	M	Farmer	Mayo	America	Margaret 31 Jul 1824
Thos.	20	M	Labourer	Ireland	U. States	Balaena 29 Apr 1825
W.	42	M	Merchant	Scotland	America	James Cropper 10 Feb 1823
William	1	M	Child	Ireland	U. States	Courier 17 Mar 1828
William	2	M		Mayo	America	Margaret 31 Jul 1824
William	20	M	Shoemaker	Great Britain	United States	Fenwick 16 Aug 1826
William	45	M	Merchant	England	N. York	James Cropper 13 Mar 1826
William M.	14 5/12	M		Ireland	United States	Josephine 30 Apr 1828
Willm.	21	M	Laboror	Ireland	United States	Wilson 27 Jun 1826
Wm.	4	M	Child	Nova Scotia	Upper Canada	Hanford 10 Nov 1827
Wm.	19	M	Weaver			Lady of the Lake 23 Aug 1828
Wm.	23 6/12	M	Weaver	G. Britain	United States	Dutchess of Portland 30 Oct 1826
Wm.	24	M	Weaver	Ireland	New York	Atlantic 8 May 1828
Wm.	24	M	Weaver	Scotland	New York	Joseph Hume 26 Oct 1829
Wm.	25	M	Merchant	Great Brittan	U. States	John & Elizabeth 11 Dec 1826
Wm.	44	M	Mason	Scotland		Aurora 12 Mar 1827
Wm. B.	30			England		Anacreon 7 Sep 1827
CAMPBLE, James	29	M		Ireland	U. States	Concordia 11 Jun 1823
Jas.	20	M	Weaver	Ireland	United States	Alex. Mansfield 17 May 1823
CAMPELL, Elizabeth	34	F	Matron	Ireland	U. States	Josephine 23 Jan 1829
Ellen	32	F		Ireland	America	Carolina Ann 7 Aug 1826
Hugh	32	M	Weaver	Ireland	America	Carolina Ann 7 Aug 1826
Robert	43	M	Minister	Ireland	U. States	Josephine 23 Jan 1829
CAMPERO, Elias	28	M	Merchant	Mexico	U. States	Emma 15 Dec 1824
CAMPHSON, Ambrose	33	M	Merchant	G. Briton	United States	James Monroe 14 Dec 1820
CAMPION, Jas.	27	M	Labourer	Ireland	United States	Thomas 13 Dec 1827
John	20	M	Shopman	Ireland	New York	Hope & Esther 21 Dec 1827
CAMPOS, Pedro, Don	48	M	Merchant	Spain	Spain	Lovinia 20 Nov 1828
CAMPS, Maria	103	F		Spain	U.S.	Fabius 25 Aug 1829
CAMPTON, Wm.	21	M	Labourer	Great Brittan	U. States	John & Elizabeth 11 Dec 1826
CAMRON, Combs.			Boy	Ireland		Westmoreland 1 Aug 1826
Dennis	34		Farmer	Ireland		Westmoreland 1 Aug 1826
Edward	6		Child	Ireland		Westmoreland 1 Aug 1826
Eleanor	1		Child	Ireland		Westmoreland 1 Aug 1826
George	5	M		Germany	United States	Samuel Robertson 8 Aug 1828
Maria	32	F		Germany	United States	Samuel Robertson 8 Aug 1828
Michael	40	M	Gent		New York	Betsy 4 Sep 1820
Sally	10		Girl	Ireland		Westmoreland 1 Aug 1826
Stephon	31	M	Joiner	Germany	United States	Samuel Robertson 8 Aug 1828
Suisan	3		Child	Ireland		Westmoreland 1 Aug 1826
Susan	30		Wife	Ireland		Westmoreland 1 Aug 1826
CAMUN, Duncan	60	M	Weaver	England	U. States	Pacific 17 Jun 1828
CAMVER, Francis	25	M	Hatter	France	France	Cadmus 26 Apr 1824
CAMVIN, John	46	M	Yoman	Newbrunswick	Lower Canaday	America 1 Aug 1829
CAN..., Jn.	21	M	Jeweller	Great Britian	United States	London 24 Jan 1823
CANADA, John	25	M	None	England	U. States	Criterion 20 Nov 1823
Sarah	20	M	None	England	U. States	Criterion 20 Nov 1823
CANADAY, Barnard	27	M	Farmer	G. Brittian	United States	Louisa 14 Jun 1825
CANAHAN, Chas.	21	M	Plaisterer	Ireland	United States	Henry Kneeland 7 Jun 1828
CANAL, John	25	M	Farmer	Ireland	U. States	Henry Kneeland 27 Jul 1825
CANANLY, Frederick	27	M	Sugar Baker	Germany		Boyer 9 May 1825

NAMES OF PASSENGERS	AGE	SEX	OCCUPATIONS	COUNTRY TO WHICH THEY BELONG	COUNTRY THEY INTEND TO INHABIT	SHIPS/DATES OF ARRIVAL	
CANARAN, Thomas	26	M	Labourer	England	U. States	Comet	23 Aug 1828
CANARDAY, Andru	35	M	Labourer	Halifax, N.S.	Lansburg	Citizen	1 Nov 1828
Marget	30	F		Halifax, N.S.	Lansburg	Citizen	1 Nov 1828
Timothey	9/52	M		Halifax, N.S.	Lansburg	Citizen	1 Nov 1828
CANASEAN, Mary	3	F		G. Britain	U. States	Mary & Harriot	8 Sep 1828
CANAVILLE, R.	30	M	Merchant	Mexico	Mexico	Bogota	17 Jul 1828
CANAWAY, Bertty	28	F				Ocean	17 Aug 1820
CANBERY, Thos.	30	M	Labourer	Ireland	New York	Trusty	12 Sep 1828
CANCER, Barbara, his daughter [Jacob]	11/12	F		France	United States	William	31 Jul 1826
Barbara, his wife [Jacob]	38	F		France	United States	William	31 Jul 1826
Elizabeth, his daughter [Jacob]	7	F		France	United States	William	31 Jul 1826
Jacob	42 8/12	M	Farmer	France	United States	William	31 Jul 1826
John, his son [Jacob]	4	M		France	United States	William	31 Jul 1826
Margarita, his daughter [Jacob]	10	F		France	United States	William	31 Jul 1826
Thiebould, his son [Jacob]	3	M		France	United States	William	31 Jul 1826
CANDA, —, Madam	25	F		France	United States	Elbe	2 Aug 1822
Florimand	28	M	Architect	France	United States	Elbe	2 Aug 1822
CANDALA, Barnard	22	M	Mariner	Porto Rico	U. States	Martha	7 Jul 1826
CANDAN, Margaret	24	F	Spinster	Ireland	United States	Sarah Ann	18 Nov 1826
CANDAY, John	25	M	Carpenter	Ireland	United States	Ann Maria	4 Oct 1824
CANDELE, John	52	M	Farmer			Euphrates	8 Aug 1820
CANDLER, E., Mrs.	35			Marblehead	Great Brit.	London	13 Dec 1822
Eleanor	33	F		United States	United States	Venus	8 Sep 1820
Ellen, Miss	18			Marblehead	United States	London	13 Dec 1822
Isaac	20	M	Merchant	England		Howard	17 Oct 1822
Isaac	32	M	Merchant	Great Britain	United States	Mount Vernon	17 Jun 1825
CANDY, Abraham	27	M	Artist	England	New York	Brighton	29 Aug 1828
Ann	22	F	Farmer	Bristol, Engl.	England	Warrior	19 May 1828
John	21	M	Farmer	Bristol, Engl.	England	Warrior	19 May 1828
CANE, Edwd.	18	M	Labourer	Ireland	U. States	St. Michaels	25 Apr 1825
Eliza	34		Spinster			Charlotte Corday	11 Sep 1820
Elizabeth	28	F		Ireland	U. States	Nancy	10 Jul 1822
Hellen	34	F		England	New York	York	2 Dec 1828
J.	26		Farmer	Kerry	Philadelphia	Schuylkill	22 Aug 1825
James	25	M	Baker	Halafax, N.S.	New York	Citizen	1 Nov 1828
Justin	21	M	Farmer	Ireland		Cuba	24 Jun 1822
Margret	16	F		Ireland	United States	Nancy R. Crowell	21 Sep 1822
Michael	42	M	Farmer	Ireland		Cuba	24 Jun 1822
Morris	32	M	Merchant	Ireland	U. States	Hope	4 Jun 1821
Thos.	30	M	Labourer	Gt. Britain	U. States	Panthea	21 Jul 1825
CANEDO, Cipriano	18	M	Colegian	Mexico	U. States	Hiram	17 Jun 1826
Vincente	16	M	Colegian	Mexico	U. States	Hiram	17 Jun 1826
CANEN, J.	31	M	Merchant	Ireland	United States	Tontine	9 Jun 1827
CANER, Curtis	19	M	None	Great Britain	United States	Ganges	26 Oct 1826
CANES, —, Madam	26	F		U. States	U. States	Ambuscade	6 Oct 1821
—, Miss	6/12	F				Radius	21 Jul 1824
—, Miss	24	F		U. States	U. States	Ambuscade	6 Oct 1821
—, Miss	24	F		U.S.	U.S.	Radius	21 Jul 1824
—, Mrs.	30	F		U.S.	U.S.	Radius	21 Jul 1824
F.	26	M	Mercht.	U.S.	U.S.	Radius	21 Jul 1824
Fransisco	2	M	None	N. York	U. States	Ambuscade	6 Oct 1821
Joaquin A.	16	M	Merchant	Spain	United States	Hope	19 Jan 1820
CANEWEY, Catherine	29	F	Spinster			Catherine	19 Aug 1825
CANFIELD, —, Mr.	32	M	Merchant	St. Johns, N.B.	U. States	Maria	4 Sep 1823
—, Mrs.	20	F		St. Johns, N.B.	U. States	Maria	4 Sep 1823
Ann	26	F		Gt. Britain		Dalhouse Castle	13 May 1828
Martin	20	M	Labourer	Ireland	New York	Hope & Esther	21 Dec 1827
Mary	9	F	Child	Ireland	America	Wilson	16 May 1825
Richard	12	M	Boy	Ireland	America	Wilson	16 May 1825
CANGEVIN, Charles	34	M	Merchant	Great Britain	Quebec	Corinthian	27 Apr 1824
CANING, Matthew	18	M	Labourer	G. Britain	U. States	London	23 Sep 1828
CANIOT, Eliza	36	F	Merchant	France	U. States	Dawn	8 Jun 1827

NAMES OF PASSENGERS	AGE	SEX	OCCUPATIONS	COUNTRY TO WHICH THEY BELONG	COUNTRY THEY INTEND TO INHABIT	SHIPS/DATES OF ARRIVAL	
CANIOT (cont'd)							
Jacob	48	M	Merchant	France	U. States	Dawn	8 Jun 1827
CANLAN, —, Mrs.	19	F	Wife	Great Britain	United States	Corinthian	29 Apr 1826
Catherin	29	F	Spinster	Ireland	U. States	Josephine	30 Aug 1828
CANLAND, Joseph	22	M	Mariner	U.S.	U.S.	Cadmus	9 Dec 1826
CANLEY, Bridget	20	F	Spinster	Ireland	United States	Wilson	4 Oct 1827
CANLIN, Jams	3	M	Child	Ireland	United States	Robert Fulton	10 Aug 1827
Mary	5	F	Child	Ireland	United States	Robert Fulton	10 Aug 1827
Mary	24	F	Matron	Ireland	United States	Robert Fulton	10 Aug 1827
Patrick	32	M	Millar	Ireland	United States	Robert Fulton	10 Aug 1827
Rose	2	F	Child	Ireland	United States	Robert Fulton	10 Aug 1827
CANMYNE, Felecia							
Caroline	20	F		...	America	Columbia	6 Oct 1825
CANN, Jane	25	F	Farmer	Ireland	U. States	Dickinson	30 Jul 1825
Mary	60	F	Farmer	Ireland	U. States	Dickinson	30 Jul 1825
Robert	30	M	Farmer	Ireland	U. States	Dickinson	30 Jul 1825
CANNACH, B.	52	M	Colonel	G. Britain	U. States	Canada	19 Sep 1828
CANNALE, Eleanor	13	F		Great Britain	United States	Meridian	2 Jul 1827
James	11	M		Great Britain	United States	Meridian	2 Jul 1827
James	20	M	Farmer	Great Britain	United States	Meridian	2 Jul 1827
John	4	M		Great Britain	United States	Meridian	2 Jul 1827
Margt.	5	F		Great Britain	United States	Meridian	2 Jul 1827
Margt.	45	F		Great Britain	United States	Meridian	2 Jul 1827
Philip	6	M		Great Britain	United States	Meridian	2 Jul 1827
Philip	45	M	Farmer	Great Britain	United States	Meridian	2 Jul 1827
William	1	M		Great Britain	United States	Meridian	2 Jul 1827
CANNALL, Thomas	21			Isle of Man	N. York	Peru	30 May 1828
CANNAN, Alexr.	22	M	Printer	Scotland	New York	Joseph Hume	26 Oct 1829
CANNEDO, John	36	M	Atorney at Law	Mexico	Mexico	Maria	3 Oct 1822
CANNELL, Ann	6	F	Shoemaker	Great Britain	U.S. America	Chili	7 Jul 1827
Eleanor	25	F	Shoemaker	Great Britain	U.S. America	Chili	7 Jul 1827
James	11	M	Joiner	Great Britain	U.S. America	Chili	7 Jul 1827
Jane	17	F	Joiner	Great Britain	U.S. America	Chili	7 Jul 1827
Jane	20	F	Servant	G. Britain	U. States	Nimrod	31 Jul 1828
Jane	27	F	Farmer	Great Britain	U.S. America	Chili	7 Jul 1827
John	4	M	Farmer	Great Britain	U.S. America	Chili	7 Jul 1827
John	14	M	Joiner	Great Britain	U.S. America	Chili	7 Jul 1827
John	25		Labourer	Isle of Man	N. York	Peru	30 May 1828
John	27	M	Farmer	Great Britain	U.S. America	Chili	7 Jul 1827
Margaret	29	F	Farmer	Great Britain	U.S. America	Chili	7 Jul 1827
Margery	56	F	Joiner	Great Britain	U.S. America	Chili	7 Jul 1827
Mary	10	F	Joiner	Great Britain	U.S. America	Chili	7 Jul 1827
Patrick	72	M	Farmer	Great Britain	U.S. America	Chili	7 Jul 1827
Thomas	1	M	Farmer	Great Britain	U.S. America	Chili	7 Jul 1827
Thomas	1	M		G. Britain	U. States	Nimrod	31 Jul 1828
Thomas	2	M	Shoemaker	Great Britain	U.S. America	Chili	7 Jul 1827
Thos.	21	M	Farmer	Great Britain	U.S. America	Chili	7 Jul 1827
Thos.	30	M	Shoemaker	Great Britain	U.S. America	Chili	7 Jul 1827
Wm.	1	M	Farmer	Great Britain	U.S. America	Chili	7 Jul 1827
Wm.	20	M	Joiner	Great Britain	U.S. America	Chili	7 Jul 1827
Wm.	58	M	Joiner	Great Britain	U.S. America	Chili	7 Jul 1827
CANNES, Jno. L.	23	M		France	U. States	London	13 Sep 1824
CANNING, Anne	20			G. Britain	U. States	Great Britain	6 Sep 1828
Brien	24	M		Scotland	U.S.	Curler	19 Jul 1828
E. W.	24	M		U. States	Gt. Britain	Caledonia	10 Sep 1828
Ed.	50	M	Merchant	L'pool	N. York	James Cropper	4 Feb 1824
Edwd.	22	M	Merchant	England	U. States	James Cropper	17 Jun 1825
Ellen	8	F		Great Britain	United States	Sarah Ralston	27 Jan 1827
John	27	M	Labourer	Great Brittain	United States	Sarah Ralston	27 Jan 1827
Joseph	28		Farmer	Ireland	United States	John Dickinson	28 Jun 1822
Mary	28	F		Great Brittain	United States	Sarah Ralston	27 Jan 1827
Ns.	24	M	Farmer	Great Brittain	U. States	Dominica	4 Jan 1823
William	22	M		Ireland	United States	William & George	14 May 1828
Wm.	18		Clerk	Ireland	United States	Robert Burns	30 May 1823
CANNION, Jane	26	F		Great Brittain	United States	Active	12 Sep 1828
CANNON, Catharine	5	F		Ireland	U. States	St. Michael	27 Mar 1827
Cordelia, Miss	13	F		England	United States	Maria	29 Sep 1823
Cordelia, Mrs.	30	F		England	United States	Maria	29 Sep 1823

NAMES OF PASSENGERS	AGE	SEX	OCCUPATIONS	COUNTRY TO WHICH THEY BELONG	COUNTRY THEY INTEND TO INHABIT	SHIPS/DATES OF ARRIVAL	
CANNON (cont'd)							
Danl.	40		Weaver	Great Britain	United States	Camillus	12 Sep 1827
Elizabeth	8	F	Child	England	United States	Maria	29 Sep 1823
Ellenor	32	F		Ireland	U. States	St. Michael	27 Mar 1827
George	11	M		England	United States	Maria	29 Sep 1823
George	16	M		Ireland	United States	Nancy R. Crowell	21 Sep 1822
Henry P.	28	F		New York	New York	Eliza Jane	14 Jun 1828
Hugh	7	M		Ireland	U. States	St. Michael	27 Mar 1827
James	14		None	Ireland	New York	Albion	11 Oct 1821
James	30	M		Ireland	U. States	St. Michael	27 Mar 1827
Jane	6 4/12	F	Daughter	G. Brittan	U. States	Henry	24 Oct 1828
Jno.	19	M	Farmer	Ireland	U. States	Alex Mansfield	1 Jun 1822
Jno.	25	M	Merchant		Campeachy	Patriot	13 Nov 1823
John	25	M	Labourer	Ireland	United States	Catharine	22 Jul 1825
John	32	M	Labourer	Ireland	United States	Andes	2 Oct 1828
M.	28	F		Great Brittain	United States	Sarah Ralston	27 Jan 1827
Martin	29	M	Merchant	G. Brittan	U. States	Henry	24 Oct 1828
Mary	5	F	Child	England	United States	Maria	29 Sep 1823
Mary	28	F	Wife	G. Brittan	U. States	Henry	24 Oct 1828
Mary, his wife [John]	28	F	Housekeeper	Ireland	United States	Andes	2 Oct 1828
Matthew, their child [John & Mary]	4	M	Child	Ireland	United States	Andes	2 Oct 1828
Nathl. R.	45	M	Mariner	U.S. America	U.S. America	Franklin	2 Feb 1824
Pat	19	M	Labourer	Ireland		Robert Fulton	4 Jun 1828
Patrick	25	M	Labourer	Ireland	United States	William & George	14 May 1828
Peter	27		Farmer	Ireland		Westmoreland	1 Aug 1826
R.	28		Labourer	Halifax	U. States	Edwin	26 Sep 1828
Richard	2	M	Child	England	United States	Maria	29 Sep 1823
Wm.	19	M	Gentleman	Great Brittain	U. States	Hibernia	8 Jul 1823
CANNOP, John	32	M	Grate Maker	Great Brittain	America	Pacific	13 Jan 1827
CANON, Catherine	8	F		Halifax, N.S.	New York	Citizen	1 Nov 1828
James	6	M		Halifax, N.S.	New York	Citizen	1 Nov 1828
Mary	12	F	Coatleman	Halifax, N.S.	New York	Citizen	1 Nov 1828
Mary	24	F	Spinster	Ireland	United States	Trident	16 May 1826
Mary	31	F		Halifax, N.S.	New York	Citizen	1 Nov 1828
Partick	1	M		Halifax, N.S.	New York	Citizen	1 Nov 1828
Rose	40	F		U. States	U. States	Ductile	11 Feb 1822
Siney	2/52	M		Halifax, N.S.	New York	Citizen	1 Nov 1828
Tomas	32	M		Halifax, N.S.	New York	Citizen	1 Nov 1828
CANOVAN, James	26	M	Carpenter	Ireland	U. States	Josephine	30 Aug 1828
CANPBELL, Ann	36	F				Hanford	17 Jul 1828
CANPELL, John	20	M	Laboreer	Ireland	United States	Fabius	4 Jun 1828
CANRAY, Jno.	40	M	Merchant	England	U. States	Hiram	25 Jul 1828
CANT, James	26	M	Schoolmaster	Scotland, Great Britain	America	Superb	11 Oct 1821
William	21 3/12	M	Farmer	Scotland	U. States	Hopes Delight	21 Apr 1828
CANTALO, James	57	M	gun smith	Prince Edward Island	N. York	Resolution	6 Jun 1822
CANTELO, E.	20	M	Gun smith	G. Brittain	U. States	Hope & Esther	26 Nov 1822
James	58	M	Gun smith	G. Brittain	U. States	Hope & Esther	26 Nov 1822
Mary	54	F		G. Brittain	U. States	Hope & Esther	26 Nov 1822
Mary S.	36	F		G. Brittain	U. States	Hope & Esther	26 Nov 1822
CANTERBURY, —, Mrs.	30	F	None	United States	United States	Loire	18 Oct 1820
Edmund	2	M		United States	United States	Loire	18 Oct 1820
Mary	5	F		United States	United States	Loire	18 Oct 1820
Thos.	3	M		United States	United States	Loire	18 Oct 1820
Wm.	7	M		United States	United States	Loire	18 Oct 1820
CANTHS, Henry	35	M	Gentleman	England	U. States	Bayard	8 Mar 1825
CANTIN, Lewis	21	M	Merchant	France	France	Bayard	27 Jun 1821
CANTINE, James	19	M	Mariner	U. States	U. States	Florida	25 Apr 1825
CANTTREYS, Nancy	20		Spinster			Rufus King	7 Aug 1820
CANTWELL, Thomas	22	M	Baker	Ireland	United States	Marion	25 Nov 1825
CANUT, Chas.	22	M	Merchant	France	United States	India	4 Aug 1826
CAPAN, Peirre	27	M	Baker	France	U. States	Hyperion	7 Aug 1826
CAPANONA, S.	28	M	Gentleman	Spain	Porto Rico	Edward Quesnel	15 May 1826
CAPARILLA, J. Reyna	40	M		Spain	Spain	Fabius	3 Jun 1825
CAPE, —, Mrs.	22	F		England	England	Andreas	20 Aug 1821

NAMES OF PASSENGERS	AGE	SEX	OCCUPATIONS	COUNTRY TO WHICH THEY BELONG	COUNTRY THEY INTEND TO INHABIT	SHIPS/DATES OF ARRIVAL	
CAPE (cont'd)							
John	29	M	Carpenter	United States		Mentor	23 May 1821
Thomas	32	M	Merchant	England	England	Andreas	20 Aug 1821
CAPER, John	22	F	Foiler	England		Aurora	12 Mar 1827
CAPERTER, Sophie	22	F	Domestic	France		François I	19 Nov 1828
CAPEWELL, Ann	40	F	None	Great Brittain	United States	Robert Fulton	13 Mar 1827
Geo.	43	M	Bricklayer	Great Brittain	United States	Robert Fulton	13 Mar 1827
George	17	M	Bricklayer	Great Brittain	United States	Robert Fulton	13 Mar 1827
John	12	M		Great Brittain	United States	Robert Fulton	13 Mar 1827
Mary Ann	10	F		Great Brittain	United States	Robert Fulton	13 Mar 1827
Susannah	2	F		Great Brittain	United States	Robert Fulton	13 Mar 1827
Thomas	13	M	None	Great Brittain	United States	Robert Fulton	13 Mar 1827
CAPMEIR, Christiana	25	M	Wife	Germany	Germany	Virginia	8 Mar 1828
Henry	24	M	Locksmith	Germany	Germany	Virginia	8 Mar 1828
CAPPE, T.	25	M	Merchant	St. Thomas	St. Martin	Leonora	25 May 1826
CAPPER, E. P.	25	M	Merchant	Birmingham	United States	Hector	29 Nov 1823
F. B.		M	Officer	Portugal	Portugal	Diana	7 Jun 1823
W. S.	24	M	Merchant	Britain	United States	Hannibal	27 May 1822
William S.	23	M	Merchant	Great Britain	United States	Meteor	15 Apr 1823
William S.	24	M	Merchant	England	United States	William Byrnes	1 Dec 1824
William S.	25 4/12	M	Merchant	United States	United States	Leontine	13 Mar 1826
Wm. S.	23	M	Merchant	Birmingham	United States	Hector	29 Nov 1823
CAPPINGER, Anne	19	F	...	Ireland	U. States	Union	3 Jun 1822
Walter	10	M	...	Ireland	U. States	Union	3 Jun 1822
CAPPITO, Ignetius	1/12	M	None	Dublin	Dublin	Howard Douglass	11 May 1827
Ignetius	28	M	None	Dublin	Dublin	Howard Douglass	11 May 1827
Ignetius	50	M	Farmer	Dublin	Dublin	Howard Douglass	11 May 1827
Jas.	32	M	Farmer	Dublin	Dublin	Howard Douglass	11 May 1827
Lucy	26	F	None	Dublin	Dublin	Howard Douglass	11 May 1827
Mary	2	F	None	Dublin	Dublin	Howard Douglass	11 May 1827
CAPRON, Augustus	30	M	Merchant	United States	United States	Montano	31 May 1824
Augustus	30	M	Merchant	U. States	U. States	Bayard	8 Mar 1825
Augustus	30	M	Mercht.	America	America	Henry	11 Oct 1825
CAPSTICK, Elizabeth	26	F	Weaver	Ireland	U.S.A.	Dalhouse Castle	21 Aug 1829
Elizth.	26	F	Weaver	Ireland	United States	Dalhouse Castle	21 Aug 1829
Jonathan	4	M	None	Ireland	U.S.A.	Dalhouse Castle	21 Aug 1829
Jonn.	4	M	None	Ireland	United States	Dalhouse Castle	21 Aug 1829
Joseph	2	M	None	Ireland	U.S.A.	Dalhouse Castle	21 Aug 1829
Josh.	2	M	None	Ireland	United States	Dalhouse Castle	21 Aug 1829
CAR, John	18	M	Farmer	England	U. States	Lewis	1 Jul 1820
Samuel	34	M	Shoe Maker	Great Britain	United States	Illinois	9 Oct 1820
CAR..., John	32		Farmer	Lancaster	Utica	Peru	30 May 1828
CARABIN, Augustin	21	M	One Family [Joseph]	France	United States	Henri IV	2 Oct 1828
Caroline	6	M	One Family [Joseph]	France	United States	Henri IV	2 Oct 1828
Cathrine	45	F	One Family [Joseph]	France	United States	Henri IV	2 Oct 1828
Elizabeth	19	F	One Family [Joseph]	France	United States	Henri IV	2 Oct 1828
Francois	4	M	One Family [Joseph]	France	United States	Henri IV	2 Oct 1828
Isedor	14	F	One Family [Joseph]	France	United States	Henri IV	2 Oct 1828
Joseph	9	M	One Family [Joseph]	France	United States	Henri IV	2 Oct 1828
Joseph	51		Farmer	France	United States	Henri IV	2 Oct 1828
Lewis	7	M	One Family [Joseph]	France	United States	Henri IV	2 Oct 1828
Peter	23	M	One Family [Joseph]	France	United States	Henri IV	2 Oct 1828
CARADEN, William	16	M	Labourer	Ireland	U. States	Josephine	7 May 1827
CARAGAN, Margrate	18		Mantumaker	Ireland	New York	Marcella	18 May 1827

NAMES OF PASSENGERS	AGE	SEX	OCCUPATIONS	COUNTRY TO WHICH THEY BELONG	COUNTRY THEY INTEND TO INHABIT	SHIPS/DATES OF ARRIVAL	
CARAGE, Henry	23	M	Merchant	Grenada	Grenada	Criterion	24 May 1825
CARAGON, Cathr.	22	F	Servant	Ireland	U. States	Sarah G	30 Jun 1828
CARANDAZO, P.	48	M	Merchant	Spain	U. States	Native	15 Apr 1826
CARAPLER, Peter	21	M	Weaver	Ireland	United States	Louisa	18 Apr 1827
CARAVAN, Rebecca	24	F	Spinster	Ireland	U. States	Josephine	30 Aug 1828
CARAVASA, Calesto G.	22	M	Merchant	Spain	U. States	Bee	18 Dec 1821
CARBALLS, Jon	23	M	Gentleman	Havannah	Havannah	Rising State	15 Dec 1820
CARBERRY, Ann	5	F	None	Ireland	United States	Dalhouse Castle	6 Sep 1827
Kelly	9	F	None	Ireland	United States	Dalhouse Castle	6 Sep 1827
Mary	7	F	None	Ireland	United States	Dalhouse Castle	6 Sep 1827
CARBERY, Honer	...	F	None	Ireland	United States	Dalhouse Castle	6 Sep 1827
Margaret	15	F	None	Ireland	United States	Dalhouse Castle	6 Sep 1827
Patrick	13	M	None	Ireland	United States	Dalhouse Castle	6 Sep 1827
CARBEY, James	21	M	Gentn.	Ireland	United States	Dublin Packet	22 Oct 1821
John	26	M	Labourer	Great Brittain	United States	Active	12 Sep 1828
CARBLEY, Ann	3	F		Great B.	U. States	William Neilson	26 Jul 1828
Emma	6/12	F		Great B.	U. States	William Neilson	26 Jul 1828
John	56	M		Great B.	U. States	William Neilson	26 Jul 1828
Mary	26	F		Great B.	U. States	William Neilson	26 Jul 1828
Samuel	60	M		Great B.	U. States	William Neilson	26 Jul 1828
CARBOJAL, Rafael Gnz.	25	M	Merchant	Spain	U. States	Wicker	19 Jun 1826
CARBONDE, Rayd.							
Simon, Don	31	M	Merchant	Spain	Spain	Jas. Monroe	9 Jun 1826
CARBRIM, Michal	28	M	Gent	French	U. States	Charlemagne	19 Sep 1828
CARBY, Stephen	24	M	Farmer	Ireland	New York	Phoenix	29 Apr 1826
CARCOILE, Jas.	35	M		Switzerland	United States	Columbia	16 Jan 1829
CARD, Abigail	1	F	Child	Nova Scotia	Upper Canada	Hanford	10 Nov 1827
Abigail	52	F	Wilfe	Nova Scotia	Upper Canada	Hanford	10 Nov 1827
Catherine	9	F	Weaver	France	U.S.	Helen	3 May 1828
Catherine	43	F	Weaver	France	U.S.	Helen	3 May 1828
Christiana	1 7/12	F	Weaver	France	U.S.	Helen	3 May 1828
Daniel	14	M	Child	Nova Scotia	Upper Canada	Hanford	10 Nov 1827
Eliza	12	F	Child	Nova Scotia	Upper Canada	Hanford	10 Nov 1827
Enoch	2	M	Child	Nova Scotia	Upper Canada	Hanford	10 Nov 1827
Eunice	6	F	Child	Nova Scotia	Upper Canada	Hanford	10 Nov 1827
Henry	21	M	Musician	Great Brittan	United States	Cambria	11 Feb 1829
Jacque	7 3/12	M	Weaver	France	U.S.	Helen	3 May 1828
Jacque Jean	31	M	Weaver	France	U.S.	Helen	3 May 1828
John	54	M	Farmer	Nova Scotia	Upper Canada	Hanford	10 Nov 1827
Lockhart	16	M	Child	Nova Scotia	Upper Canada	Hanford	10 Nov 1827
Madelaine	3 4/12	F	Weaver	France	U.S.	Helen	3 May 1828
Margaret	5 6/12	F	Weaver	France	U.S.	Helen	3 May 1828
Margaret	28	F	Child	Nova Scotia	Upper Canada	Hanford	10 Nov 1827
Mary	19	F	Child	Nova Scotia	Upper Canada	Hanford	10 Nov 1827
Mercy	20	F	Child	Nova Scotia	Upper Canada	Hanford	10 Nov 1827
Perry	30	M	Child	Nova Scotia	Upper Canada	Hanford	10 Nov 1827
Stabra	8	F	Child	Nova Scotia	Upper Canada	Hanford	10 Nov 1827
Woodbury	25	M	Child	Nova Scotia	Upper Canada	Hanford	10 Nov 1827
CARDAZO, Dominciano							
Ernesto Dias		M	Officer	Portugal	Portugal	Diana	7 Jun 1823
CARDDUCH, Richard	36	M	Farmer	Great Britan	United States	Hamilton	19 Mar 1827
CARDEN, H., Mr.	40	F		S. Croix	S. Croix	Jupiter	29 Jun 1825
Russel, Mrs.	30 6/12	F	Lady	Denmark	Denmark	Jupiter	4 Aug 1829
CARDENA, John	11	M	None	Spain (Cuba)	Island of Cuba (Spain)	James Barron	26 Jun 1823
CARDENESON, J.	25	M	Span. Army	Havana	U. States	Silas Richards	29 Oct 1828
CARDER, Ed.	24	M	Merchant	Vera Cruz	U. States	Eliza	11 Apr 1826
Jane R., Miss	6 3/12	F	Lady	Denmark	Denmark	Jupiter	4 Aug 1829
CARDET, A.	22			Paris	France	Brown	11 Jun 1827
*Died on the passage							
CARDHAN,							
Abraham	58 4/12	M	Farmer	Switzerland	U. States	France	26 Jun 1828
Christy	4 2/12	F	Farmer	Switzerland	U. States	France	26 Jun 1828
Jonah	7 5/12	F	Farmer	Switzerland	U. States	France	26 Jun 1828
Rosonah	2 4/12	F	Farmer	Switzerland	U. States	France	26 Jun 1828
CARDIN, Thomas	22	M	Weaver	Ireland	New York	Louisa	20 Jul 1826
CARDNESS, J.	37	M	Merchant	Havana	U. States	Silas Richards	29 Oct 1828
CARDOT, Auguste	5	M		France	U. States	Leonarde	29 Aug 1828
Francoise	9	M		France	U. States	Leonarde	29 Aug 1828

NAMES OF PASSENGERS	AGE	SEX	OCCUPATIONS	COUNTRY TO WHICH THEY BELONG	COUNTRY THEY INTEND TO INHABIT	SHIPS/DATES OF ARRIVAL	
CARDOT (cont'd)							
Iredin	15	F		France	U. States	Leonarde	29 Aug 1828
Jaques	8	M		France	U. States	Leonarde	29 Aug 1828
Jean	16	M		France	U. States	Leonarde	29 Aug 1828
Jean B.	42	M	Farmer	France	U. States	Leonarde	29 Aug 1828
Jean B. P.	40	F		France	U. States	Leonarde	29 Aug 1828
Joseph	12	M		France	U. States	Leonarde	29 Aug 1828
Marie Rose				France	U. States	Leonarde	29 Aug 1828
*died on the passage							
CARDWELL, Henry B.	27	M	Merchant	England	Philidelphia	Florida	22 May 1826
Henry Booth	17	M	Merchant	England	United States	Florida	11 May 1822
John	24	M	Farmer	Ireland	U. States	Concordia	11 Jun 1823
John	37	M	Merchant	Great Britain	United States	Martha	3 May 1821
CAREDAY, John	25	M	Servant	Great Britian	U. States	St. Michael	3 Jan 1825
CAREERA, Jno.	28	M	Merchant	Spain	Spain	Nile	24 Aug 1821
CAREL, Charls	25	M	Laber	Irland	U. States	Nancy	27 Jun 1823
CARENET, Charles	24	M		Great B.	U. States	William Neilson	26 Jul 1828
CARERA, Antonio	50	M	Merchant	France	U. States	Victoria	9 Sep 1828
CARET, Afred	38	M	Merchant	France	France	Mary Livingston	14 May 1827
CAREW, Henry	28	M	Brick Maker	England	New York	Hudson	20 Nov 1828
Wm.	30	M	Merchant	England	U. States	William & Frederick	16 Feb 1824
CAREY, Ann Elizabeth	26	F	Lady	Nova Scotia	United States	Hanford	19 Aug 1828
Catherine	23	F		Ireland	United States	America	25 Dec 1827
Denis	26	M	Gardiner	Ireland	United States	America	25 Dec 1827
Denis	33	M	Mason	Ireland	United States	Trio	13 Jun 1827
Francis	30	M	Carpenter	United States	United States	Huntress	5 Apr 1826
Frank	30	M	Farmer	Ireland		Cuba	24 Jun 1822
Henry C., Mr.	32	M	Bookseller	U. States	U. States	Hudson	10 Nov 1825
James	23	M	Labourer	Ireland	U. States	Borneo	15 Apr 1828
Jas.	22	M	Shoemaker	Ireland	U. States	Ohio	21 Mar 1825
John	20	M	Labourer	Great Britain	United States	Ganges	26 Oct 1826
Julia Ann	5	F	Lady	Nova Scotia	United States	Hanford	19 Aug 1828
M.	32	M	Laborer	Ireland	United States	Trio	13 Jun 1827
Maria, Miss	27	F		U. States	U. States	Hudson	10 Nov 1825
Mary	25	F	Farmer	Ireland		Cuba	24 Jun 1822
Mary	28	F	Farmer	Ireland	U.S.A.	Dalhouse Castle	21 Aug 1829
Mary	28	F		Ireland	United States	Dalhouse Castle	21 Aug 1829
Mat	28	M	Farmer	Ireland	U.S.A.	Dalhouse Castle	21 Aug 1829
Mat	28	M		Ireland	United States	Dalhouse Castle	21 Aug 1829
Patty, Mrs.	28	F		U. States	U. States	Hudson	10 Nov 1825
Richd.	45	M	Merchant	Ireland	United States	St. John	5 Oct 1829
Thos.	32	M	Farmer	Ireland	United States	Nancy	15 Nov 1824
William	42 6/12	M	Jamaica Planter	England	Great Britain	Robert Cochran	29 Aug 1825
CARFRY, Mary	20	F		Ireland	United States	Kleber	23 Jul 1827
CARGA, —	1	F	Carpenter	Switzerland	U. States	Seine	30 Aug 1824
—, Mrs.	23	F	Carpenter	Switzerland	U. States	Seine	30 Aug 1824
Johannes	34	M	Carpenter	Switzerland	U. States	Seine	30 Aug 1824
CARGAN, Thomas	34	M	Labourer	Ireland	United States	Dublin Packet	22 Aug 1829
CARGROVE, Frank	32		Farmer	England	United States	Mary	15 Jul 1822
Peter	40		Farmer	England	United States	Mary	15 Jul 1822
CARIGAN, Andrew	14	M	Labourer			Evergreen	28 Jul 1820
Ann	18		Spinster	Co. Fermarah	Ireland	Carolina Ann	21 May 1823
Mary	16		Farmer	Co. Fermarah	Ireland	Carolina Ann	21 May 1823
Sally	18			Ireland	United States	Robert Burns	30 May 1823
CARINGTON, Chas.	28	M	Smith	Great Britain	United States	Meridian	2 Jul 1827
CARIVAN, Richard	21	M	Painter	Halifax	U. States	Adoro	14 Apr 1828
CARKILLO, Mary	18	F	Servant	Ireland	United States	Hannibal	25 Sep 1827
CARLAND, Ann	37	F		Ireland	U.S.	Lady Hunter	10 Jul 1826
Bernard	22	M	Farmer	Ireland	United States	Asia	29 Jul 1829
John	21	M	Planter	Scotland	U. States	Superior	25 Sep 1828
CARLAW, Margaret	19	F		Scotland	United States	Mazzinghi	3 Jan 1826
Wm. B.	27		Ship Master	Citizen of New York	U. States	Camille	31 Jul 1826
CARLE, E.	22	M	Farmer	Farmer	U. States	Wilson	2 Sep 1823
Edward	42	M	Labourer	Ireland	America	John Adams	2 Aug 1827
Henry	7	M		Ireland	U. States	Lady Hunter	8 Aug 1826
Kitty	18	F	Laborer or Spinster	Ireland	United States	Sarah G.	15 Aug 1827
CARLEON, B.	23	F				Hanford	17 Jul 1828

NAMES OF PASSENGERS	AGE	SEX	OCCUPATIONS	COUNTRY TO WHICH THEY BELONG	COUNTRY THEY INTEND TO INHABIT	SHIPS/DATES OF ARRIVAL	
CARLESS, Jim	28	M	...	U. States	U. States	Radius	21 Jul 1824
CARLET, Ann	30	F	None	Great Britain	United States	William Dawson	18 Jun 1827
Daniel	24	M	Weaver	Great Britain	United States	William Dawson	18 Jun 1827
James	3	M	None	Great Britain	United States	William Dawson	18 Jun 1827
Jane	21	F	None	Great Britain	United States	William Dawson	18 Jun 1827
Jane	30	F	None	Great Britain	United States	William Dawson	18 Jun 1827
Margt.	17	F	None	Great Britain	United States	William Dawson	18 Jun 1827
Phil	26	M	Shoemaker	Great Britain	United States	William Dawson	18 Jun 1827
Thos.	31	M	Labourer	Great Britain	United States	William Dawson	18 Jun 1827
Wm.	30	M	Tailor	Great Britain	United States	William Dawson	18 Jun 1827
CARLEY, J.	25	F	None	Gt. Brittain	United States	Balaena	24 Aug 1825
James	28	M	Labourer	Ireland	United States	Baltic	21 Apr 1827
Patrick	28	M	Baker	Gt. Brittain	United States	Balaena	24 Aug 1825
CARLIE, Edwd.	27	M	Merchant	G. Brittain	U. States	Canada	6 Jun 1825
George E.	24	M	Merchant	United States	United States	Benjamin Franklin	10 Apr 1827
CARLIFF, Mary	1 4/12	F		Great Britain	United States	Saml. Wight	6 Sep 1827
Sarah	22	F		Great Britain	United States	Saml. Wight	6 Sep 1827
CARLILE, Thos.	26	M	Surveyor	Scotland	Scotland	Abigail	10 May 1821
CARLIN, Alexander	23	M	Labourer	Ireland	United States	Robert Fulton	24 Jul 1826
James	29	M	Labourer	Ireland	United States	Robert Fulton	10 Aug 1827
John	21	M	Labourer	Ireland	United States	Edwin	27 Oct 1828
John	28	M	Butcher	England	U.S. States	Splendid	14 Aug 1829
Laurence	12	M		Great Britain	United States	Isaac Hicks	10 Jul 1827
Mary	26	F	Butcher	England	U.S. States	Splendid	14 Aug 1829
Phillis	20	F	Labourer	Ireland	United States	Edwin	29 Nov 1828
CARLING, Mary	19	F	None	England	United States	Jubilee	13 Jul 1829
CARLISLE, Ann	10	F	Child	England	United States	Trident	30 Sep 1826
Ann	45	F	Spinster	Scotland	United States	Friends	7 Jul 1827
Benjamin	46	M	Joiner	England	United States	Trident	30 Sep 1826
Daniel	11 5/12	M	Family [of Daniel]	G. Brittian	United States	Louisa	14 Jun 1825
Daniel	58	M	Miller	G. Brittian	United States	Louisa	14 Jun 1825
Elisabeth	38	F	Wife	England	United States	Trident	30 Sep 1826
Eliza	13	F	Family [of Daniel]	G. Brittian	United States	Louisa	14 Jun 1825
Elizabeth	16	F	Spinster	Scotland	United States	Friends	7 Jul 1827
Hannah	5	F	Child	England	United States	Trident	30 Sep 1826
Isabella	24 7/12	F	Family [of Daniel]	G. Brittian	United States	Louisa	14 Jun 1825
John	5	M	Farmer	Scotland	U. States	Roger Stewart	9 Jun 1828
John	16 3/12	M	Family [of Daniel]	G. Brittian	United States	Louisa	14 Jun 1825
John	25	M	Weaver	Great Britain	United States	Luella	15 Jun 1825
Maria	2	F	Child	England	United States	Trident	30 Sep 1826
Mary	9	F	Child	England	United States	Trident	30 Sep 1826
Mary	26	F		Ireland	United States	Princess Charlotte	26 Apr 1827
N. D.	21	M	Merchant	Providence	U. States	Eliza & Mary	14 Jan 1824
Ruth	7	M	Child	England	United States	Trident	30 Sep 1826
Sarah	18	F	Family [of Daniel]	G. Brittian	United States	Louisa	14 Jun 1825
Thos.	30	M	Merchant	G. Britain	U. States	Hanford	18 Sep 1828
CARLLO, Ramon	26	M	Merchant	Mexico	United States	Eliza	29 Dec 1827
CARLOHAM, John	35	M	Farmer	England	U. States	Emulous	22 Aug 1828
CARLON, John	18	M	Merchant	Ireland	New York	Wilson	28 Aug 1822
Peggy	25	F	Spinster	Ireland	United States	Sarah Ann	6 Mar 1827
Thos.	25	M	Mariner	America	U. States	Leo	30 Apr 1825
CARLOS, F. H.	28	M	Merchant	Spain	Spain	Virginia	26 May 1828
Jean	65	M	Mechanic	Marseilles	U. States	Plato	18 Apr 1826
Louisa	17	F	Wife	Spain	Spain	Virginia	26 May 1828
Mary Ann	23	F	Spinster	U. States	U. States	Frederick	5 May 1826
CARLOW, James	30	M	Labourer	Ireland	United States	Lord Wellington	28 May 1827
Sarah	...4	F	Wife	U. States	U. States	Camille	1 Feb 1827
Wm.	29	M	Mariner	U.S.	U.S.	Mordicae	24 Nov 1828
CARLTON, Ann	22	F		Ireland	U. States	Justina	7 Mar 1823
Ann	32	F	Servant	Great Britian	U. States	St. Michael	3 Jan 1825
CARLY, Patrick	19	M	Taylor	Ireland	U. States	Josephine	7 May 1827
CARMAGEN, Paul	24	M	Mercht.	U.S.	U.S.	Edward Quesnel	17 Jan 1825
CARMAN, Augustes	5	M		U. State	U. States	Trident	18 Aug 1820
John	25	M	Merchant	France	U. States	Sea Nymph	7 Jul 1827
John	48	M	Merchant	U. State	U. States	Trident	18 Aug 1820
S. M.	35	F	None	U. State	U. States	Trident	18 Aug 1820
CARMEN, Johan	35	M	Cabinet Maker	Prusia	U.S. America	Sereno	31 Jul 1826

NAMES OF PASSENGERS	AGE	SEX	OCCUPATIONS	COUNTRY TO WHICH THEY BELONG	COUNTRY THEY INTEND TO INHABIT	SHIPS/DATES OF ARRIVAL	
CARMICHAEL, Daniel	55		Merchant	United States	United States	John Dickinson	28 Jun 1822
David	24	M	Teacher	Ireland	United States	Friends	21 Oct 1825
John	15 2/12	M	Farmer	Ireland	America	Farmer	3 May 1824
John, Mr.	61		Merchant	Carlisle, Eng./ Carlisle, Eng.	New York	Venus	12 Apr 1821
M.	28	M	None	Great Britain	United States	James Monroe	25 Apr 1822
Samuel	24	M	Labourer	Ireland	United States	William & George	14 May 1828
CARMON, Bridget	20	F		Ireland	United States	Loore	9 Sep 1822
Cathr.	1	F		Great Britain	United States	Grecian	24 Sep 1828
Cathr.	50	F	Spinner	Great Britain	United States	Grecian	24 Sep 1828
Mary	18	F	None	Ireland	U.S.A.	Dalhouse Castle	21 Aug 1829
Mary	18	F	None	Ireland	United States	Dalhouse Castle	21 Aug 1829
P. B.	32	M	Mariner	U. States	U. States	Packet Margaret	19 Sep 1823
CARNAR, Ann Maria	11	F				Golden Grove	6 Sep 1820
Catherine	27	F				Golden Grove	6 Sep 1820
George Jacob	38	M				Golden Grove	6 Sep 1820
John Jacob	8	M				Golden Grove	6 Sep 1820
Margaret	1	F				Golden Grove	6 Sep 1820
CARNEGHIN, George	13/12	M		Irereland	America	Carolina Ann	20 Jun 1825
CARNEL, John	24	M	Servant	Ireland	United States	Sylvester Healy	19 Aug 1825
CARNES, —, Miss	3	F		U.S.		Radius	21 Jul 1824
Betty	3	F		Great Britain	United States	Atlantic	28 May 1827
Daniel	1	F		Great Britain	United States	Atlantic	28 May 1827
Ellen	2	F		Great Britain	United States	Atlantic	28 May 1827
Fras.	25	F	Gardner	Ireland	U. States	Margarett Scott	22 Aug 1827
James	26	M	Engineer	Great Britain	United States	Courier	26 Jun 1827
Jane	40	F		Great Britain	United States	Atlantic	28 May 1827
John	28	M	Farmer	Scotland	United States	John Dickinson	12 Aug 1824
John A.	5	M	Farmer	Ireland	Canada	Champion	26 Jul 1827
Jos.	57	M	Tailor	Great Britain	United States	Atlantic	28 May 1827
M.	31	M	Farmer	Ireland	Canada	Champion	26 Jul 1827
Margaret	3	F	None	Scotland	United States	John Dickinson	12 Aug 1824
Margery	24	F	None	Great Britain	United States	Courier	26 Jun 1827
Margret	6	F		Great Britain	United States	Atlantic	28 May 1827
Mary	1	F	None	Scotland	United States	John Dickinson	12 Aug 1824
Mary	27	F	None	Scotland	United States	John Dickinson	12 Aug 1824
Patrick	21	M	Labourer	St. Johns	Great Britain	St. Michael	5 Jan 1826
Wm.	24	M	Gardner	Ireland	U. States	Margarett Scott	22 Aug 1827
CARNESOLTAS, F.	48	M	Mercht.	Spain	Spain	Richmond Packet	10 Dec 1828
Manuel	14	M		Spain	Spain	Richmond Packet	13 Jun 1825
CARNEY, Ann	18	F	Labourer	Great Britain	United States	Thomas Dickason	31 Jul 1829
Ann	23	F	None	Ireland		Marchioness	13 May 1828
Ann	30	F	None			Eliza Jane	12 Sep 1820
Bridget	19	F	None	Great Britain	United States	Juno	5 Oct 1822
Catherine	7	F	None	Great Britain	United States	Juno	5 Oct 1822
Daniel, Jr.	29 1/12	M	Merchant	United States		Sabbattus	3 Mar 1828
Dennis	26	M	Labourer	Ireland	New York	America	1 Aug 1828
Ellen	4	F				Eliza Jane	12 Sep 1820
Ellen	26	F		Great Britain	Philadelphia	Philetus	21 Jul 1827
Geo.	20	M	Laborer			Commerce	22 Jun 1825
Hugh	29	M	Cooper	Great Britain	United States	Juno	5 Oct 1822
John	24	M	Labourer	England	America	Two Marys	24 Sep 1827
John M	17	M	Labourer	Ireland	U. States	Josephine	7 May 1827
Lauce.	21	M		Great Britain	Philadelphia	Philetus	21 Jul 1827
Mary	5	F	None	Great Britain	United States	Juno	5 Oct 1822
Mary	12	F	Servant	Ireland	United States	Josephine	30 Apr 1828
Mary	26	F	None	Great Britain	United States	Juno	5 Oct 1822
Michael	35	M	Farmer	Ireland	United States	William & George	14 May 1828
Michl.	7	M				Eliza Jane	12 Sep 1820
Michl.	30	M	Labourer	Ireland	U. States	William & John	10 Jul 1824
Nancy	22	F	Servant	Ireland	U. States	Edwin	1 Jul 1829
Owen M.	48	M	Bricklayer	Ireland	U. States	Josephine	7 May 1827
Pat	9	M				Eliza Jane	12 Sep 1820

NAMES OF PASSENGERS	AGE	SEX	OCCUPATIONS	COUNTRY TO WHICH THEY BELONG	COUNTRY THEY INTEND TO INHABIT	SHIPS/DATES OF ARRIVAL	
CARNEY, (cont'd)							
Patrick	24	M	Labourer	Ireland	United States	Catharine	22 Jul 1825
CARNIE, Agnes	3	F	None	Great Britain	United States	Colossus	5 Jun 1827
David	1	M	None	Great Britain	United States	Colossus	5 Jun 1827
Janet	5	F	None	Great Britain	United States	Colossus	5 Jun 1827
Jean	1	F	None	Great Britain	United States	Colossus	5 Jun 1827
John	10	M	None	Great Britain	United States	Colossus	5 Jun 1827
Margaret	8	M	None	Great Britain	United States	Colossus	5 Jun 1827
Mirian	12	F	None	Great Britain	United States	Colossus	5 Jun 1827
Mirian	30	F	None	Great Britain	United States	Colossus	5 Jun 1827
Wm.	6	M	None	Great Britain	United States	Colossus	5 Jun 1827
Wm.	31	M	Clerk	Great Britain	United States	Colossus	5 Jun 1827
CARNITER, John D.	18 4/12	M	Farmer	Switzerland	U. States	France	26 Jun 1828
CARNLEY, Robert	28	M	Ship Carpenter	United States	United States	Silvanus Jenkins	16 Aug 1826
CARNMEICHEL,							
Joseph	25	M	Farmer	Ireland	America	Carolina Ann	14 Feb 1825
CARNNER, Thomas	37	M	Farmer	France	United States	Virginia	31 May 1828
CARNOLY, Wm.	45	M	Shoemaker	Blackburn	Blackburn	Howard Douglass	11 May 1827
CARNS, John	30	M	Cooper	St. Johns	U. States	Champion	26 Jul 1827
Mary Ann	6	F	Farmer	Ireland	Canada	Champion	26 Jul 1827
CARNY, Biddey	19	F		Ireland	United States	Commerce	13 Jun 1828
Catherine	...	F	Spinster	Ireland	Unt. St. America	Wilson	21 May 1827
Cathrine	19			Ireland	New York	Marcella	18 May 1827
CAROL, Margaret	19	F	Servant	Ireland	United States	Wanderer	1 Aug 1828
CAROLEN, Richard	30	M				Splendid	14 Aug 1829
CAROLES, Ira	38	M	Merchant	America	America	David	4 May 1825
CAROLINE, Ann	20	F		Scotland	United States	Camillus	27 Oct 1828
CAROLL, Byran	27	M	Farmer	Ireland	U.S. States	Solon	25 Nov 1824
Margt.	26	F	Spinster	Ireland	United States	Dublin Packet	22 Oct 1821
CAROLTON, Augustes	15		Boy	America	America	William	5 Nov 1828
Cathren, Miss	19		Lady	America	America	William	5 Nov 1828
Hannah, Mrs.	49		Lady	America	America	William	5 Nov 1828
John	16		Boy	America	America	William	5 Nov 1828
William	11		Boy	America	America	William	5 Nov 1828
CARON, Rose	22	F	Servt.	Ireland	United States	St. Michaels	23 Dec 1826
CAROW, Isaac	49		Mercht.	United States	U. States	New York	30 Oct 1827
CAROY, Thos.	26	M	Labourer	Ireland	United States	William	20 Jul 1829
CARPENTER, —, Mr.	27	M		England	U. States	Perseverance	18 Nov 1824
Alex	35	M	Weaver	Scotland	Ama.	Expedition	19 May 1828
Allen	28	M	Clothier	England	United States	Warrior	6 Oct 1828
Arns	8	M		England	United States	Warrior	6 Oct 1828
Becky, his wife [William]	30	F		United States	United States	Only Daughter	29 Apr 1825
D.	30	M		England	U. States	Mary	24 Jun 1824
Eliza	1	F	Child	United States	United States	Only Daughter	29 Apr 1825
J.	14	M	None	U. States	U. States	Frances	22 May 1827
James	31	M	Laborer			Plato	31 Oct 1829
Lewis	26	M	Merchant	United States	United States	Ann Maria	7 Nov 1826
M.	35	M	Seaman	U. States	U. States	Mazinghi	15 Jan 1827
Mary	6	F	Child	United States	United States	Only Daughter	29 Apr 1825
Nelson	21	M	Tailor	England	United States	Warrior	6 Oct 1828
Walter	30	M	Mariner	N. York	U. States	Albatross	25 Jul 1821
William	34	F	Farmer	United States	United States	Only Daughter	29 Apr 1825
Wm.	37	M	Merchant	State of Ohio	State of Ohio	Hesper	25 Jul 1826
CARPENTIER, —	50	M	Mercht.	France	United States	Bayard	13 Nov 1823
CARR, ...ah	25			Ireland	U.S.	Hibernia	27 Jun 1821
...in	6/12	F		Ireland	United States	Kleber	23 Jul 1827
Ann	22	M		G. Britan	U. States	Dalmarnock	11 Dec 1828
Arthur	30	M	None	England	U.S.A.	Lima	6 Dec 1826
Benjn.	4	M		Great Britain	United States	Atlantic	28 May 1827
Betsey	8			Ireland	U.S.	Hibernia	27 Jun 1821
Bridget	35	F	None	Gt. Britain	U. States	Panthia	13 Nov 1824
Catharine	9	F	None	Gt. Britain	U. States	Panthia	13 Nov 1824
Catharine D.	30	F	Spinster	Glasgow	U.S. America	Camillus	10 Sep 1821
Catherine	3	F		Ireland	United States	Kleber	23 Jul 1827
Catherine	25	M	Yeoman	Ireland	United States	Borneo	9 Jul 1827
Edward	32	M	Labourer	Ireland		William Tell	24 Oct 1829
Eleanor	6/12	F		Ireland	United States	Kleber	23 Jul 1827

NAMES OF PASSENGERS	AGE	SEX	OCCUPATIONS	COUNTRY TO WHICH THEY BELONG	COUNTRY THEY INTEND TO INHABIT	SHIPS/DATES OF ARRIVAL	
CARR (cont'd)							
Elisa	16	F		Ireland	U. States	Nancy	2 May 1823
Ellen	2	F	Labourer	Ireland	United States	Borneo	2 Oct 1827
Geo.	28	M	Seaman	G. Britan	U. States	Dalmarnock	11 Dec 1828
Giles	8	F		Ireland	United States	Kleber	23 Jul 1827
Hannah	23	F		Great Britain	United States	Atlantic	28 May 1827
Isabella	46	F	Widow	Ireland	U. States	William & John	10 Jul 1824
J.	30	M	private	U. States	U. States	Enterprize	9 Aug 1825
James	10	M		Ireland	United States	Kleber	23 Jul 1827
James	12	M	Labourer	Ireland	United States	Kleber	23 Jul 1827
Jane	8	F		Ireland	U. States	Nancy	2 May 1823
Jane	18	F	Spinster	Ireland	U. States	William & John	10 Jul 1824
Jno.	28	M	Mechanic	England	U. States	Charlotte	19 Feb 1822
Jno.	36	M	Labourer	Great Britain	United States	Atlantic	28 May 1827
John	4	M	None	Gt. Britain	U. States	Panthia	13 Nov 1824
John	18	M	Labourer	Ireland	America	Weser	26 Jun 1821
John	30	M	Farmer	Ireland	U.S.A.	Dalhouse Castle	21 Aug 1829
John	30	M	None	Ireland	United States	Dalhouse Castle	21 Aug 1829
John	33	M	Weaver	Ireland	United States	Kleber	23 Jul 1827
Mary	19	F	Tailor	G. Britain	U. States	Perseverance	9 Jun 1827
Mary B.	25	F		Ireland	United States	Kleber	23 Jul 1827
Michael	19	M	Labourer	Ireland	United States	Kleber	23 Jul 1827
Michall	28	M	Labourer	Younghall, Great Britain	United States	Union	24 Sep 1823
Obed S.	26	M	Mariner	United States	United States	Mary Ann	7 Jan 1829
Owen	44	M	Farmer	Ireland	New York	Louisa	18 Apr 1827
Pat	24	M	Labourer	Ireland	United States	Commerce	13 Jun 1828
Pat	34	M	Labourer	England	U. States	Comet	23 Aug 1828
Robt.	45	M	Merchant	G. Britain		Emerald	9 Sep 1820
Sarah	22	F	Dressmaker	Ireland		William Tell	24 Oct 1829
Thomas	22	M	Gardener	England	New York	Governor Fenner	23 Jul 1829
Wm. B.	62	M	Mechanic	Great Britain	United States	Washington	3 Sep 1827
CARRAGAN, James	32	M	Merchant	Louisiana	Louisiana	Science	23 Sep 1824
CARRAGHAN, Mary	12		girl	Ireland	United States	Abigail	25 Jun 1822
CARRAL, J. P.	14	M	Merchant	Columbia	U. States	Canton	7 Feb 1826
Margret	28	F		Ireland	N. Jersey	Potomac	7 Aug 1827
Mary An.	5		Girl	Ireland	N. Jersey	Potomac	7 Aug 1827
Samuel	2		Boy	Ireland	N. Jersey	Potomac	7 Aug 1827
William	30	M	Weaver	Ireland	N. Jersey	Potomac	7 Aug 1827
CARRE, —	24	M	Mercht.	France	France	Don Quixote	3 Jan 1826
Bridget	23	F	Labourer	Ireland	United States	Borneo	2 Oct 1827
CARREA, Rachel	17	F		England	England	Tontin	13 Jun 1825
Sarah	55	F		England	England	Tontin	13 Jun 1825
CARRENS, Edwd.	23	M	Labourer	Great Britain	United States	William Dawson	18 Jun 1827
Eve	30	F	None	Great Britain	United States	William Dawson	18 Jun 1827
CARRERA, John	30	M	Mariner	Spain	U.S.	Anita	5 May 1821
CARRESS, —, Mrs.	35	F	Widow	France	United States	Bayard	13 Nov 1823
CARRET, Joseph	32	M	Merchant	Spain	U. States	Pomona	4 Apr 1823
CARRETT, A.	7	F		Great Britain	United States	Isaac Hicks	6 Dec 1827
B.	5	F		Great Britain	United States	Isaac Hicks	6 Dec 1827
E.	28	F		Great Britain	United States	Isaac Hicks	6 Dec 1827
H.	8	F		Great Britain	United States	Isaac Hicks	6 Dec 1827
J.	1	M		Great Britain	United States	Isaac Hicks	6 Dec 1827
James	36	M	Gentleman	U. States	U. States	William Thompson	27 May 1824
W.	36	M	Weaver	Great Britain	United States	Isaac Hicks	6 Dec 1827
CARREY, Betty	28	F	Servant	Ireland	United States	St. Michaels	18 Jul 1826
CARRICK, Alex	30	M	Merchant	Scotland	U. States	William Thompson	27 May 1824
Alexander	39	M	Merchant	Great Britain	Great Britain	Martha	25 Nov 1820
R.	36	M	Merchant	Gt. Britain	New York	Manchester	15 Apr 1828
Robert	26	M	Merchant	Scotland	America	Meteor	22 Apr 1822
CARRIE, David G.	26	M	Merchant	Glasgow	United States	Henry Clay	25 Apr 1822
Lewis E.	35	M	Merchant	France	N. Orleans	Queen Mab	20 Nov 1826
S. T.	24	M	Merchant	L'pool	N. York	James Cropper	4 Feb 1824
Thomas	28	M	Merchant	Glasgow	United States	Henry Clay	25 Apr 1822
CARRIERDA, J. F.	24	M	Organ Maker	Chile	Chile	Atlas	24 Jun 1828
CARRIGAN, Catherine	21	F	Spinster	Ireland	United States	Lady Hunter	29 Apr 1826
Matt.	20	M	Laborer	Gt. Britain		Dalhouse Castle	13 May 1828

NAMES OF PASSENGERS	AGE	SEX	OCCUPATIONS	COUNTRY TO WHICH THEY BELONG	COUNTRY THEY INTEND TO INHABIT	SHIPS/DATES OF ARRIVAL	
CARRINGTON, A. B.	28	M	Merchant	Connecticutt	U. States	Mary	10 Sep 1823
Mable	22	F	Lady	U. States	U. States	Chase	17 Jan 1825
CARRION, Antonia	50	F	Merchant	Spain	U. States	Commodore Chauncy	28 Nov 1825
Francisca	22	F	Merchant	Spain	U. States	Commodore Chauncy	28 Nov 1825
Juan	18	M	Merchant	Spain	U. States	Commodore Chauncy	28 Nov 1825
CARRIRRE, Joseph	38	M	Clergiman	France		Charlemagne	20 Aug 1829
CARRO, Antonio Jose	28	M	Gentleman	Columbia	Columbia	William Bayard	6 Aug 1825
CARROK, Cathe.	25	F	...	Co. Wicklow	United States	Java	9 Jul 1827
Christr.	25	M	...	Co. Wicklow	United States	Java	9 Jul 1827
Eliza	6/12	F	...	Co. Wicklow	United States	Java	9 Jul 1827
Jas.	4	M	...	Co. Wicklow	United States	Java	9 Jul 1827
Margt.	4	F	...	Co. Wicklow	United States	Java	9 Jul 1827
CARROL, Ann	25	F	Spinster	Ireland	United States	William & George	14 May 1828
Catharine	36	F	Labourer	England	U. States	Comet	23 Aug 1828
Elijah	28		Schoolmaster	Great Britain		John Dickinson	5 Apr 1821
Henry	19	M	Son [of Susan]	Ireland	New York	Atlantic	8 May 1828
Hugh	21	M	Farmer	Ireland	United States	William & George	14 May 1828
James	40	M	Farmer	Ireland	United States	William & George	14 May 1828
John	24 9/12	M	Farmer	Ireland	U. States	Virginia	20 Jun 1825
John	26 1/12	M	Farmer	England	U.S. of America	Illinois	16 Jun 1821
Maria	28			United States	United States	Planter	26 Jul 1822
Mary	10	F	Daughter [of Susan]	Ireland	New York	Atlantic	8 May 1828
Michael	40	M	Farmer	Ireland	United States	William & George	14 May 1828
Pat	...4 4/12	M	Labourer	Ireland	Unt. St. America	Wilson	21 May 1827
Patrick	70	M	Gentleman	U. States	U. States	St. Michaels	25 Apr 1825
Robert	15	M	Son [of Susan]	Ireland	New York	Atlantic	8 May 1828
Susan	40	F	Mother	Ireland	New York	Atlantic	8 May 1828
Thos.	40	M	Farmer	Ireland	United States	Meteor	27 Sep 1826
CARROLE, James	28	M	Labourer	Ireland	United States	Wilson	27 Jun 1826
CARROLL, Ann	4	F		England		Anacreon	7 Sep 1827
Ann	25	F		England		Anacreon	7 Sep 1827
B.	6		Farmer	Ireland	United States	Courier	16 May 1825
Biddy	25	F	Wife	South	Boston	Nile	18 Aug 1829
Bridget	16	F		Ireland	United States	Wm. Byrnes	30 Apr 1828
Bridget	25		None	Great Britain	United States	Roman	10 Sep 1827
Charles	19	M	Merchant	Baltimore	U.S.	Bayard	30 Oct 1820
Daniel	49	M	Farmer	Great Britain		Robert Fulton	8 Mar 1823
Edwerd	17	M	Gentleman	Great Britain	U. States	Lady Hunter	28 May 1823
Elizth.	18		Spinster	Ireland	United States	Courier	15 Oct 1827
Harry G.	34	M	Farmer	U. States	U. States	York	13 Aug 1827
Henry	18			Ireland	U. States	Lima	5 Aug 1829
James	9	M	None	Ireland	United States	Aurelia	7 Jun 1826
James	28	M	Clerk	Ireland	United States	Pallas	28 Oct 1828
Jane	28	F	Wife	Queens County, Leeds, Ireland	N. York	New Orleans	24 Aug 1827
John	6	M		England		Anacreon	7 Sep 1827
John	21	M	Farmer	Ireland	United States	Meteor	19 Aug 1829
John	30	M	Stone Mason	Ireland	United States	Princess Charlotte	26 Apr 1827
John	30	M		England		Anacreon	7 Sep 1827
John	33	M	Bookkeeper	Queens County, Leeds, Ireland	N. York	New Orleans	24 Aug 1827
M.	28	M	Farmer	Ireland	America	Mary	29 May 1827
M.	42		Farmer	Ireland	United States	Courier	16 May 1825
M. O.	30	M	Merchant	U. States	U. States	Eliza	20 Nov 1828
Margaret	19	F		Ireland	New York	Lima	5 Aug 1829
Margurita	19	F		Ireland	U. States	Lima	5 Aug 1829
Mary	6	F	None	Ireland	United States	Aurelia	7 Jun 1826
Mary	18	F	Spinster	Ireland	U. States	Josephine	30 Aug 1828
Mary	30	F	None	Ireland	United States	Aurelia	7 Jun 1826
Mary Ann	22	F	None	Great Britain		Moro Castle	6 Jul 1827
Maryann	25	F		Ireland	America	John Adams	2 Aug 1827

NAMES OF PASSENGERS	AGE	SEX	OCCUPATIONS	COUNTRY TO WHICH THEY BELONG	COUNTRY THEY INTEND TO INHABIT	SHIPS/DATES OF ARRIVAL	
CARROLL (cont'd)							
Michael	41	M	Labourer	England	U. States	Comet	23 Aug 1828
Micharl	20	M	Farmer	G. Brittian	United States	Louisa	14 Jun 1825
Michl.	19	M	Labourer	Great Britain		Moro Castle	6 Jul 1827
Michl.	20	M	Labourer	Ireland	United States	Wilson	6 Jun 1828
Miles	30	M	Labourer	Great Britain		Moro Castle	6 Jul 1827
Ml.	34	M	M...	Ireland	United States	Trio	13 Jun 1827
Morgan	34	F	Labourer	Great Britian	United States	Princess Charlotte	6 Sep 1828
Nancy	57	F		Great Britain	U. States	Lady Hunter	28 May 1823
Nichl.	22	M	Mechanic	Ireland	United States	Wm. Byrnes	30 Apr 1828
Patk.	60	M	None	Ireland	United States	Aurelia	7 Jun 1826
Patrick	20	M	Farmer	Ireland	United States	Meteor	19 Aug 1829
Patrick	28	M	Farmer	Ireland	United States	Abigail	25 Jun 1822
Patt	29	M	Labourer	South	Boston	Nile	18 Aug 1829
Peter	37	M	Labourer	Great Britian	United States	Princess Charlotte	6 Sep 1828
Roseann	20	F	Spinster	Ireland	U. States	Josephine	30 Aug 1828
T.	48		Farmer	Ireland	United States	Courier	16 May 1825
Thos.	1	M		England		Anacreon	7 Sep 1827
Thos.	30		Farmer	Great Britain	United States	Roman	10 Sep 1827
Wenny	18	F		Ireland	New York	Lima	5 Aug 1829
William	23	M	Laborer	Ireland	United States	Sarah G	19 Jun 1827
Wm.	2	M		England		Anacreon	7 Sep 1827
Wm.	15	M		Great Britain	U. States	Lady Hunter	28 May 1823
Wm.	19	M	Butcher	Gt. Britain	United States	Penelope	9 Sep 1828
CARRON, Briget	19	F	wife	Great Britain	United States	Hanford	3 Aug 1829
Hugh	24	M	Turner	Great Brittan	United States	Hanford	3 Aug 1829
Jno.	33	M		England		Anacreon	7 Sep 1827
John	23	M	Stone Cutter	Ireland	U. States	Hanford	29 Dec 1828
Nichs.	28	M	Weaver	France	United States	Stephania	24 Mar 1828
CARROT, M.	29	M	Labourer	England	America	Two Marys	24 Sep 1827
CARROTTE, —, Mr.	28	M	Merchant	Italy	Italy	Buck	24 Jul 1821
CARROW, Dominick	22	M	Labourer	Ireland	United States	Catharine	22 Jul 1825
CARRSON, Cathr.	30	F		Co. La...	United States	Java	9 Jul 1827
Margt.	6	F		Co. La...	United States	Java	9 Jul 1827
Owen	30	M	Labourer	Co. La...	United States	Java	9 Jul 1827
Patk.	1	M		Co. La...	United States	Java	9 Jul 1827
CARRUT, Jos.	28	M	Clothier	Great Britain	United States	Atlantic	28 May 1827
CARRUTHERS, Robert	30	M	Farmer	Scotland	Uncertain	Hannibal	28 May 1827
CARRY, Margaret	25	F	Spinster	Ireland	United States	Dublin Packet	23 May 1828
William	22	M	Carpenter	United States	United States	Bolivar	21 May 1827
CARRYE, Wm.	20	M	Spinster	Great Brittian	United States	Corinthian	9 Jan 1827
CARSE, John	28	M		Great Britain	United States	Active	25 Mar 1828
CARSEN, Maryann	21 2/12	F	Labourer	Ireland	America	Enterprize	29 Jun 1827
CARSIAN, Wm.	33	M	Merchant	England	U. States	Ranger	2 Jul 1827
CARSILO, Mary	6	F	Linnen weaver	Ireland	America	Franklin	13 Aug 1827
CARSON, Alex.	34		Farmer	United States		John Dickinson	5 Apr 1821
Ellis	28	F	Wife	Ireland	United States	St. Michaels	18 Jul 1826
John	8	M	Child	Ireland	United States	St. Michaels	18 Jul 1826
Johnston	16	M	Weaver	Ireland	United States	Robert Fulton	10 Aug 1827
Mary	2	F	Child	Ireland	United States	St. Michaels	18 Jul 1826
Nancy	24	F	None	Ireland	United States	Lord Wellington	28 May 1827
Peter	40	M	U.S. Navy	U. States	U. States	Ann	4 Mar 1826
Robt.	26	M	Tailor	U. States	U. States	Topaz	5 Jul 1825
Sarah	21	F	Dressmaker	Ireland	America	Carolina Ann	7 Aug 1826
Sarah	21	F	Gran Daughter	Armar	Baltimore	Nile	18 Aug 1829
Sydney	18	F	Spinster	Ireland	United States	Robert Fulton	10 Aug 1827
Thomas	22	M	Labourer	Ireland	United States	Lord Wellington	28 May 1827
William	6	M	Child	Ireland	United States	St. Michaels	18 Jul 1826
CARSSENS, H. N.	26	M	Merchant	United States	United States	Howard	27 Sep 1826
CARSTACK, Maria, Mrs.	34			United States	U. States	South Carolina Packet	30 May 1825
CARSTENS, D.		M	Mercht.	U. States	U. States	Atlantic	13 Aug 1824
CARSWELL, Joseph	26	M	Merchant	United States	United States	Hannibal	25 Sep 1827
Samuel K.	28	M	Gentleman	Germany	U. States	Rook	25 Jul 1827
CART, Catharine	18	F	Lady	Great Brittain	U. States	Nancy	18 Jul 1821
CARTAN, Patrick	34	M	Farmer	Ireland	United States	Dublin Packet	9 Jul 1827
*died July 3d 1827							

193

NAMES OF PASSENGERS	A G E	S E X	OCCUPATIONS	COUNTRY TO WHICH THEY BELONG	COUNTRY THEY INTEND TO INHABIT	SHIPS/DATES OF ARRIVAL	
CARTAN (cont'd)							
William	22	M		Ireland	United States	William & George	14 May 1828
CARTANIE, M.	30	M	Mariner	Genoa	Central America	Mary Levengston,	17 Jun 1826
CARTAR,	22	M	Shoemaker	Ireland	New York	Louisa	18 Apr 1827
CARTCELLANO, Andres	16	M		Spain	U. States	Independence	2 Sep 1824
CARTELS, Michael	...	M	...	Ireland	United States	Carolina Ann	24 Oct 1825
CARTEN, Elizabeth	30	F	Spinster	Ireland	United States	Robert Fulton	24 Jul 1826
CARTENCE, Ellen	29	F	Wife	Ireland	United States	St. Michaels	23 Dec 1826
Patrick	27	M	Carpenter	Ireland	United States	St. Michaels	23 Dec 1826
CARTENEY, Richd.	27	M	Servant	Ireland	U. States	Henrietta	7 Jul 1825
Walker	23	M	Segar Maker	Island of Cuba	United States	Betsey	28 Oct 1825
CARTER, ... H.	37	M	Merchant	United States	United States	Pacific	7 May 1827
Abraham	2		None	Ribchester, England	Great Britain	Franklin	22 Jun 1827
Abraham	41		Wood Turner	Ribchester, England	Great Britain	Franklin	22 Jun 1827
Agnes	28	F			U. States	Rockingham	29 Nov 1821
Ann	4		None	Henfield, England	Great Britain	Frances Henrietta	31 May 1824
Ann	22	F				Hector	11 Sep 1820
C.	15	F		United States	United States	Robert Edwards	1 Jun 1826
Charles	22	M	None	England	America	Silvanus Jenkins	17 Nov 1828
Chas.	22	M	Gentn.	United States	United States	Robert Edwards	1 Jun 1826
Edward	25	M	Merchant	England	England	William Thompson	27 May 1824
Edward	30	M	Merchant	England	England	Britannia	14 Mar 1828
Elizabeth	1 1/2		None	Henfield, England	Great Britain	Frances Henrietta	31 May 1824
Elizabeth	13	F	None	England	United States	Hamilton	13 Nov 1827
Elizabeth	37	F	None	England	United States	Hamilton	13 Nov 1827
Ewd.	11	M	Farmer	..., Dublin, Ireland	U. States	New Orleans	24 Aug 1827
Francis	8	M	None	England	United States	St. George	25 Aug 1829
Francis	8	M		England	United States	St. George	25 Aug 1829
G. D.	27		Merchant	U.S. America	Boston	Frederick	26 Apr 1824
Geo.	35	M	Servant	Antiqua	U. States	South Carolina	2 Aug 1822
Geo. D.	25	M	Merchant	United States	United States	Gertrude	19 May 1826
George	21	M	Cabinet Maker	Great Britain	United States	Diana	30 Oct 1827
Hannah	17	F	None	England	United States	Hamilton	13 Nov 1827
Harriet	5 7/12	F		England	America, U.S.	Illinois	3 Jun 1822
Hetta	1	M	None	England	United States	Hamilton	13 Nov 1827
J., Miss	19	F		United States	United States	Robert Edwards	1 Jun 1826
James	11 3/12	M		England	America, U.S.	Illinois	3 Jun 1822
James	45 3/12	M	Shoemaker	England	America, U.S.	Illinois	3 Jun 1822
Jane	3	F	Child	G. Brittan	U. States	Henry	24 Oct 1828
Jane	28	F		Ireland	U. States	Alexander	28 Jul 1821
John	9	M	None	England	United States	Hamilton	13 Nov 1827
John	16	M	Farmer	..., Dublin, Ireland	U. States	New Orleans	24 Aug 1827
John	16	M	Farmer	G. Britain	U. States	London	23 Sep 1828
John	18	M	Farmer	Ireland	United States	Dublin Packet	29 Jun 1825
John	22	M	Laborer	Ireland	United States	St. Michaels	18 Jul 1826
John	23	M	Farmer	U. Kingdom of Great Britain	United States	Cambria	7 May 1828
Joseph	3	M		Ireland	U. States	Alexander	28 Jul 1821
Joseph	20	M	Merchant	Havana	Havana	Robert Reade	9 Feb 1822
Judith	2	F		Ireland	U. States	Alexander	28 Jul 1821
Julian	19			Ireland	U.S.	Hibernia	27 Jun 1821
M.	16	F		United States	United States	Robert Edwards	1 Jun 1826
M. M.	18	F		United States	United States	Robert Edwards	1 Jun 1826
Marey	29	F	None	England	United States	St. George	25 Aug 1829
Margaret	21	F		G. Britain	U. States	London	23 Sep 1828
Maria	2	F	None	England	United States	St. George	25 Aug 1829
Maria	2	F		England	United States	St. George	25 Aug 1829
Maria	4	F	None	England	United States	Hamilton	13 Nov 1827
Martha	28		None	Ribchester, England	Great Britain	Franklin	22 Jun 1827

NAMES OF PASSENGERS	AGE	SEX	OCCUPATIONS	COUNTRY TO WHICH THEY BELONG	COUNTRY THEY INTEND TO INHABIT	SHIPS/DATES OF ARRIVAL	
CARTER (cont'd)							
Mary	11	F	None	England	United States	Hamilton	13 Nov 1827
Mary	28	F	None	Ireland	U. States	Erin	5 Jul 1820
Mary	29	F	None	England	United States	St. George	25 Aug 1829
Maryan	5	F	Child	G. Brittan	U. States	Henry	24 Oct 1828
N. H.	44	M	Gentleman	U. States	U. States	Perseverance	28 Apr 1828
Philadelphia	52		None	Henfield, England	Great Britain	Frances Henrietta	31 May 1824
Polly	27		None	Henfield, England	Great Britain	Frances Henrietta	31 May 1824
Pricilla	7	F	None	England	United States	Hamilton	13 Nov 1827
Rd.	22			Ireland	U.S.	Hibernia	27 Jun 1821
Richard	9	M	None	England	United States	St. George	25 Aug 1829
Richard	9	M		England	United States	St. George	25 Aug 1829
Richard	26	M	Servant	England	N. York	Lyon	6 Feb 1826
Robert, Mr.	26	M	Merchant	England	England	Lafayette	3 Dec 1827
Robt.	17	M	Farmer	Ireland	United States	Dublin Packet	29 Jun 1825
Robt.	35	M	Slater	G. Britain	U. States	Margaret Bogle	12 Jun 1828
Sarah	9 9/12	F		England	America, U.S.	Illinois	3 Jun 1822
Sarah	12	F	Child	G. Brittan	U. States	Henry	24 Oct 1828
Sarah	36	F	wife	G. Brittan	U. States	Henry	24 Oct 1828
Susannah	37 6/12	F		England	America, U.S.	Illinois	3 Jun 1822
Thomas		M	Merchant	U. States	U. States	Adonis	16 Jun 1825
Thomas	9	M	Farmer	..., Dublin, Ireland	U. States	New Orleans	24 Aug 1827
Thomas	20	M	Farmer	Ireland	United States	Dublin Packet	23 May 1828
Thomas	25 9/12	M	Shoemaker	England	America	Cincinnatus	22 May 1826
Thomas	58	M	Farmer	..., Dublin, Ireland	U. States	New Orleans	24 Aug 1827
Thomas, Esqr.	42	M	Merchant	America	America	Cincinnatus	22 May 1826
Thos.	33	M	Engine	G. Brittan	U. States	Henry	24 Oct 1828
Timothy	27	M		America	Boston	Cortes	23 Nov 1827
Walter	25	M	Farmer	Gt. Britain	U.S. of America	Friends	25 Sep 1823
William	25		Farmer	England	S. New York	Xenophon	25 Jul 1826
William	27	M	Gardener	Ireland	New York	Atlantic	8 May 1828
William	30	M	Carpenter	New York	United States	St. Michaels	12 Apr 1826
William	32	M	Farmer	Ireland	U. States	Alexander	28 Jul 1821
William	32		Labourer	...arsfield, England	Great Britain	Frances Henrietta	31 May 1824
Wm.	40	M	U.S. Navy	U. States	U. States	Hamlet	31 Jan 1825
CARTHELAZ, Ns.	26	M	Merchant	United States		Montano	3 Jan 1823
CARTHY, Elinor	18	F		Ireland	America	Wilson	27 Nov 1826
CARTIGAN, Bridget	45	M	Labourer	U. States	U. States	Wm. Penn	18 Sep 1827
Danl.	11	M	Labourer	U. States	U. States	Wm. Penn	18 Sep 1827
Eliza	20	M	Labourer	U. States	U. States	Wm. Penn	18 Sep 1827
James	17	M	Labourer	U. States	U. States	Wm. Penn	18 Sep 1827
Mary	15	M	Labourer	U. States	U. States	Wm. Penn	18 Sep 1827
CARTILLI, Lewis A.	21	M	Physician	United States	United States	Laurel	20 Apr 1826
CARTIN, Patrick	30	M	Labourer	Ireland	United States	Hope	12 Jun 1828
CARTIO, Vincente	28	M	Priest	Central America	Central America	Robert Y. Haynes	2 Oct 1829
CARTO, D.	36	M	Merchant	Spain	U. States	Mary Jane	29 Mar 1828
CARTRIGHT, Eliza	20	F	Servant	Irereland	America	Carolina Ann	20 Jun 1825
John	22	M	Weaver	Irereland	America	Carolina Ann	20 Jun 1825
CARTRO, —, Mr.	35	M	Merchant	Havana	Havana	Milo	15 May 1824
CARTSELANO, Augustin	13	M		Spain	U. States	Independence	2 Sep 1824
CARTWELL, James	32	M	Mariner	England	Canada	Bolina	16 Mar 1826
CARTWORTH, Joseph	35	M				Eliza Grant	6 Oct 1828
CARTWRIGHT, —, child [Sophia]		F		Canada	England	Bayard	30 Oct 1820
—, Mr.	40	M	Gentn.	Gt. Britain	United States	Robert Edwards	1 Jun 1826
Elizth.	30	F	...	Great Brittain	Montreal	Albion	11 Jun 1821
James	34	M	Machinist	Great Britian	United States	Andes	19 Aug 1829
John	42	M	Draper	England	America	Panthea	18 Jul 1823
Jonas	40	M	Farmer	Great Britain	United States	Aurora	5 Sep 1826
Sophia, Mrs.	22	F		Canada	England	Bayard	30 Oct 1820
CARTY, Ann	18	F	Spinster	Great Britain	United States	Wilson	26 Feb 1824
Anty	18	F	Spinster	Ireland	United States	Dublin Packet	6 Dec 1827
Catherine	2	F		Gt. Britain		Dalhouse Castle	13 May 1828

NAMES OF PASSENGERS	AGE	SEX	OCCUPATIONS	COUNTRY TO WHICH THEY BELONG	COUNTRY THEY INTEND TO INHABIT	SHIPS/DATES OF ARRIVAL	
CARTY (cont'd)							
John	24	M	Farmer	Ireland	United States	Dublin Packet	6 Dec 1827
John	37 2/12	M	Labourer	Ireland	America	Minerva	15 Jun 1825
Mail	27	M	Laborer	Scotland	United States	Trent	10 Jul 1827
Martin	34	M	Pilot	Sligo	New York	Susquehana	27 Jun 1823
Michael	40	M	Laborer	Ireland	New York	Munroe	27 May 1825
Patrick	27 6/12	M	Labourer	Ireland	America	Minerva	15 Jun 1825
Wm.	30	M	Stone Mason	England	United States	Essex	23 May 1828
CARUN, Wm.	23	M	Blacksmith	America	America	Splendid	23 Mar 1829
CARUS, Margt.	16	F	Servant	Ireland	United States	Henry Kneeland	7 Jun 1828
CARUTHERS, Mary	25	F	Servant	Ireland	New York	Louisa	20 Jul 1826
CARVAGAL, C. G.	25	M	Merchant	Spain	Spain	Prince Edward	25 Feb 1822
CARVAGH, Edward	18	M	Labourer	Ireland	United States	Curler	7 Jul 1827
CARVELL, Mary	2	F	None		United States	Mount Vernon	29 Aug 1828
CARVELLIRY, Isabella,							
Miss	11	F	Child	Spain		Orlando	8 May 1824
M., Mr.	19	M	Gentleman	Spain		Orlando	8 May 1824
CARVER, Charles	58	M	Farmer	Holland	U. States	Edward Bonaffe	23 Jul 1828
Francis	1	M		Holland	U. States	Edward Bonaffe	23 Jul 1828
Harietta, Miss	18	F	Lady	United States	United States	Florida	22 May 1826
Jacob	13	M		Holland	U. States	Edward Bonaffe	23 Jul 1828
John	30	M	Ship master	St. John, N.B.	St. John, N.B.	St. Michaels	24 Mar 1825
Margaret	18	F		Holland	U. States	Edward Bonaffe	23 Jul 1828
Marian	22	F	Farmer	Holland	U. States	Edward Bonaffe	23 Jul 1828
Mary	40	F		Holland	U. States	Edward Bonaffe	23 Jul 1828
Niclon	4	F		Holland	U. States	Edward Bonaffe	23 Jul 1828
Nicolus	7	M		Holland	U. States	Edward Bonaffe	23 Jul 1828
Saml. R.	23		Mercht.	England	U. States	New York	30 Oct 1827
W. H.	21	M	Nothing	United States	United States	Britannia	29 Oct 1829
CARVILL, Julia	22	F		England	United States	Florida	14 Sep 1827
CARVILLE, Charles	23	M	Merchant	England	U. States	Florida	16 May 1827
CARVIN, James	25 6/12	M		Ireland	U.S. of America	Douglass	6 Jul 1829
CARWAY, Bartly	30	M	Merchant	Sligo	New York	Susquehana	27 Jun 1823
Pat	21 8/12	M		Ireland	U.S. of America	Douglass	6 Jul 1829
CARWORTH, Nancy	...	...		...	...	St. Michael	22 Sep 1824
CARY, Edwd.	28	M	Labourer	Ireland	United States	Thomas	13 Dec 1827
Francis	30	M	cabinet Maker	American	United States	Conclusion	4 Feb 1829
Isabbella	29	F		England	U. States	Pacific	11 Sep 1824
James		M	Chiefly farmers		United States	Factor	8 Jul 1829
James	3	F		England	U. States	Pacific	11 Sep 1824
James	19	M				Lady of the Lake	23 Aug 1828
*left ship							
James, Mr.	19	M	Gentleman	Ireland	United States	Dublin Packet	9 Jul 1827
John	1	M		Ireland	America	John Adams	2 Aug 1827
John	18	M		Ireland	U. States	Nancy	10 Jul 1822
Mary	23	F		Ireland	America	John Adams	2 Aug 1827
Thomas	22	M	Farmer	Ireland	America	William	21 May 1825
Thomas	30	M	Tanner	Ireland	America	John Adams	2 Aug 1827
Thomas, Jr.	3	M		Ireland	America	John Adams	2 Aug 1827
Wm.	28	M	Mason	Ireland	United States	Francis	11 Apr 1825
CAS...NOUGH, Mary	18	F	Spinster	..., ..., Ireland	U. States	New Orleans	24 Aug 1827
CASADY, Michael	25	M	Farmer	Ireland		Cuba	24 Jun 1822
CASAGENES, R.	25	M	Merchant	Barcelona	U. States	New Priscilla	22 Aug 1823
CASALANAN, J.	28	M	Merchant	Vera Cruz	U. States	Eliza	11 Apr 1826
CASANEA, Lewis Page	25	M	Merchant	Spain	Spain	Napoleon	26 May 1828
CASANOVA, Domingo	27	M	Artist	Italy	U. States	Aerial	10 Nov 1825
CASAQUE, C.	14	M	Gentleman	U. States	U. States	Imperial	10 Dec 1821
H.	17	M	Gentleman	U. States	U. States	Imperial	10 Dec 1821
CASARUS, Frs.	14	M	Merchant	Mexico	U. States	Desdemona	15 Jun 1827
CASARY, Pedro	13	M	Merchant	Mexico	U. States	Desdemona	15 Jun 1827
CASASIMO, John	70	M	Priest	Spain	U. States	Mount Vernon	18 Dec 1824
CASAT, Jaques	20	M	Gentleman	France	U. States	Superb	9 Jul 1821
CASBEIN, Magdeline	22	F	Farmer	Switzerland	U.S.	C. Amelia	30 Jun 1828
CASBURY, A.	30	M	Maunfacturer	Ireland	U. States	John Wells	8 Sep 1897
Abram	62	M	Manufacturer	Ireland	U. States	John Wells	8 Sep 1897
Amelia	20	F	Manufacturer	Ireland	U. States	John Wells	8 Sep 1897
Ann	60	F	Maunfacturer	Ireland	U. States	John Wells	8 Sep 1897
Jane	18	F	Maunfacturer	Ireland	U. States	John Wells	8 Sep 1897

NAMES OF PASSENGERS	AGE	SEX	OCCUPATIONS	COUNTRY TO WHICH THEY BELONG	COUNTRY THEY INTEND TO INHABIT	SHIPS/DATES OF ARRIVAL	
CASBUSH, Thomas	20		Farmer	England	S. New York	Xenophon	25 Jul 1826
CASE, Henry	21	M	Groome	England	U.S.	Pacific	24 Oct 1828
Levi	32	M	Mariner	United States	United States	Langdon Cheeves	19 Mar 1827
Marget	16	F	Servant	Irereland	America	Carolina Ann	20 Jun 1825
CASEDAY, Samuel	31 2/12	M	Merchant	U.S.A.	U.S.A.	Silas Richards	27 Oct 1826
CASELEY, Jacob	30	M	Farmer	United States	United States	Globe	30 Aug 1828
Merebella	22	M	Farmer	United States	United States	Globe	30 Aug 1828
CASEMAN, Ann	6	F		G. Britain	U. States	Nimrod	31 Jul 1828
Ann	30	F		G. Britain	U. States	Nimrod	31 Jul 1828
Cath.	5	F		G. Britain	U. States	Nimrod	31 Jul 1828
Ewd.	31	M	Labourer	G. Britain	U. States	Nimrod	31 Jul 1828
Isabella	16	F		G. Britain	U. States	Nimrod	31 Jul 1828
Jane	11	M		G. Britain	U. States	Nimrod	31 Jul 1828
Robt.	1	M		G. Britain	U. States	Nimrod	31 Jul 1828
CASEY, —	2	M	Farmer	Ireland		Cuba	24 Jun 1822
—, Mr.	21	M	Merchant	France	U. States	Fair Play	29 Apr 1822
Andrew	5	M		Ireland	U. States	Fame	15 Nov 1826
Andrew	34	M		Ireland	U. States	Fame	15 Nov 1826
Ann	19	F	Wife of [Patk.]	Great Britain	United States	Aurora	5 Sep 1826
Ann	26		Labourer	England	United States	Hugh Johnson	11 Jun 1828
Betsey	14	F		England	America	Ann	3 Jul 1820
Catharine	1 6/12	F		Ireland	U. States	Fame	15 Nov 1826
Catharine	36	F		Ireland	U. States	Fame	15 Nov 1826
Cathr.	22	F		Gt. Britain	United States	Penelope	9 Sep 1828
Charles	8	M	None	U. States	U. States	Jannette Josephine	22 Aug 1820
Charles	29	M		London	London	Swift	7 Apr 1827
Daniel	6	M		Ireland	U. States	Fame	15 Nov 1826
Danl.	6	M		Ireland	U. States	Fame	15 Nov 1826
Ellen	3	F		Ireland	U. States	Fame	15 Nov 1826
Ellen	30	F		Ireland	U. States	Fame	15 Nov 1826
Francis	2/12	M		Ireland	U. States	Fame	15 Nov 1826
Frederick	33	M	Gentleman	G. Britian	U. States	Chase	17 Jan 1825
Frederick	34	M	Planter	Great Britain	Great Britain	Jane	7 Aug 1825
George	40	M		Ireland	U. States	Fame	15 Nov 1826
James	10	M	None	U. States	U. States	Jannette Josephine	22 Aug 1820
Jane	23		Spinster	Ireland	Ireland	Dewitt Clinton	26 Aug 1825
Jno.	18	M	Carpenter	Ireland	U. States	Edward	15 Jul 1825
Jno.	23		Labourer	Ireland	Ireland	Dewitt Clinton	26 Aug 1825
John	9	M		Ireland	U. States	Fame	15 Nov 1826
John	11	M		Ireland	U. States	Fame	15 Nov 1826
John	19	M	La	Glenneth & Cork	Co. Cork	Aldebaron	21 Jan 1826
John	20	M	None	Ireland	Und. Stts of Amer	Alexander Mansfield	18 Aug 1826
John	28		Labourer	England	United States	Hugh Johnson	11 Jun 1828
Joseph P.				Ireland		Hiram	14 Aug 1829
*Died Aug 1 of the Dissentary							
Lawrence	1 6/12	M		Ireland	U. States	Fame	15 Nov 1826
M.	15	M	Carpenter	Ireland	U. States	Edward	15 Jul 1825
Martin	28	M	Farmer	Ireland	U. States	Edward	15 Jul 1825
Mary	5	F		Ireland	U. States	Fame	15 Nov 1826
Mary	10	F		Ireland	United States	Trio	13 Jun 1827
Mary	29	F		Ireland	U. States	Fame	15 Nov 1826
Michl.	19	M	Labourer	Co. Lford	Co. Lford	Howard Douglass	11 May 1827
Neal	18	M	Turner	Great Britain	United States	Isaac Hicks	10 Jul 1827
Patk.	20	M	Labourer	Great Britain	United States	Aurora	5 Sep 1826
Patrick	14	M	Turner	Great Britain	United States	Isaac Hicks	10 Jul 1827
Patrick	24	M	...	Ireland	United States	Colossus	30 May 1825
Patrick	25	M	Mason	Ireland	United States	Fabius	4 Jun 1828
Sarah	3	F		England	America	Ann	3 Jul 1820
Thomas	6/12	M		Ireland	U. States	Fame	15 Nov 1826
Thos.	22		Labourer	England	United States	Hugh Johnson	11 Jun 1828
Thos.	33	M	Baker	England	U. States	Rising States	20 Sep 1828
William	14	M	None	U. States	U. States	Jannette Josephine	22 Aug 1820
CASH, Alexander	6	M		Ireland	United States	Meteor	27 Sep 1826

NAMES OF PASSENGERS	AGE	SEX	OCCUPATIONS	COUNTRY TO WHICH THEY BELONG	COUNTRY THEY INTEND TO INHABIT	SHIPS/DATES OF ARRIVAL	
CASH (cont'd)							
Ann	8	F		Ireland	United States	Meteor	27 Sep 1826
Ann	46	F	Wife	Ireland	United States	Meteor	27 Sep 1826
Hugh	14	M	Weaver	Ireland	United States	Meteor	27 Sep 1826
John	23	M	Goldsmith	England	U.S.A.	Brighton	21 Jan 1826
John	45	M	Weaver	Ireland	United States	Meteor	27 Sep 1826
John, Jr.	12	M	Weaver	Ireland	United States	Meteor	27 Sep 1826
Josh.	20	M	Dresser	England	U. States	Dalhouse	23 Mar 1829
Robert	10	M	Weaver	Ireland	United States	Meteor	27 Sep 1826
William	22	M	Weaver	Ireland	United States	Meteor	27 Sep 1826
CASHAN, Betty	40	F	None	England	U. States	Thomas Ritchie	2 Jul 1827
Dianna	5	F	None	England	U. States	Thomas Ritchie	2 Jul 1827
Jas.	6	M	None	England	U. States	Thomas Ritchie	2 Jul 1827
Jno.	15	M	None	England	U. States	Thomas Ritchie	2 Jul 1827
John	21	M	None	Great Brittan	U. States	John & Elizabeth	11 Dec 1826
Liddia	11	F	None	England	U. States	Thomas Ritchie	2 Jul 1827
Sally	13	F	None	England	U. States	Thomas Ritchie	2 Jul 1827
CASHEN, Wm., Jr.	25	M	Carver & Guilder	Liverpool	New York	Cadmus	22 Mar 1822
CASHIN, Catharine	26	F	None	Ireland		Eliza Grant	29 Aug 1829
Catherine	26	F		Ireland	New York	Eliza Grant	29 Aug 1829
Henry	24	M	Carpenter	Ireland	New York	Eliza Grant	29 Aug 1829
Henry	24	M	Carpenter	Ireland		Eliza Grant	29 Aug 1829
Henry	27	M	Carpenter	Ireland	New York	Eliza Grant	29 Aug 1829
Henry	27	M	Carpenter	Ireland		Eliza Grant	29 Aug 1829
James	2/12	M		Ireland	New York	Eliza Grant	29 Aug 1829
James	2/12	M		Ireland		Eliza Grant	29 Aug 1829
Joannah	27	F		Ireland	New York	Eliza Grant	29 Aug 1829
Joannah	27	F		Ireland		Eliza Grant	29 Aug 1829
Mary	2	F		Ireland	New York	Eliza Grant	29 Aug 1829
Mary	2	F		Ireland		Eliza Grant	29 Aug 1829
CASHMAN, —, Mrs.	35	F		U. States	U. States	Shamrock	17 Jun 1822
D. E.	55	M	Merchant		U. States	Silas Richards	29 Oct 1828
M.	40	M	Labourer	Ireland	U. States	Albion	11 May 1827
Mary	25	F	Servant	Ireland	America	Liverpool	31 Aug 1827
Mary	33	F	Spinster	Ireland	America	William	21 May 1825
Patrick	35	M	Coachman	Ireland	America	Liverpool	31 Aug 1827
CASIDY, B.	18	M		Gt. Britain	U. States	St. George	20 Sep 1828
B.	65	M	Turner	Gt. Britain	U. States	St. George	20 Sep 1828
Eliza	20	F		Gt. Britain	U. States	St. George	20 Sep 1828
Mary	62	F		Gt. Britain	U. States	St. George	20 Sep 1828
Peter	30	M		St. Johns	U. States	Wanderer	30 Oct 1828
CASIO, Sebastin D.	23	M	Merchant	South Americ	South America	Margaret	13 Mar 1826
CASKE, Janes	28	M	Baker	Ireland	United States	Fabius	4 Jun 1828
Mary	40	F		Ireland	United States	Fabius	4 Jun 1828
CASKETT, Jno.	31	M	Farmer	United States	United States	Nestor in Liverpool	29 Jul 1822
CASLETT, Michael	24	M	Weaver	England	United States	India	8 Jun 1827
CASLIN, Jno.	22	M	Mechanic	Ireland	United States	Vermont	10 Jan 1827
CASLON, Catharine	25	F		Irland	United States	Nancy	28 Oct 1822
CASMO, Wm.	35	M	Planter	Jamaica		Rebecca	25 Aug 1824
CASNOLL, Margeret	42	F	Spinstress	Great Briton	United States	Erin	26 May 1821
CASPAR, Jas.	33	M	Mechanic	Switzerland	U.S.	Howard	4 May 1827
CASPER,							
Ann Maria	36 9/12	F		France	United States	Catharine	10 Sep 1827
Asa B.	30	M	Seaman	U.S. America	U.S. America	Gibraltar	12 Oct 1829
Atelia	4 6/12	M		France	United States	Catharine	10 Sep 1827
Berinice M.	35	F	his Wife [Asa B.]	France	U.S. America	Gibraltar	12 Oct 1829
Caroline F.	9/12	F	Girl	France	U.S. America	Gibraltar	12 Oct 1829
E.	8 2/12	F		France	United States	Catharine	10 Sep 1827
Geo.	6 7/12	M		France	United States	Catharine	10 Sep 1827
George P.	4	M	Boy	France	U.S. America	Gibraltar	12 Oct 1829
Graner	40 6/12	M	Carpenter	France	United States	Catharine	10 Sep 1827
Isabella B.	2	F	Girl	France	U.S. America	Gibraltar	12 Oct 1829
Peter	10 10/12	M		France	United States	Catharine	10 Sep 1827
Phillip	28	M	Merchant	England	America	Cincinnatus	19 Oct 1826
CASS, Daniel	4	M		G. Britain	U. States	John Jay	17 Sep 1828
James	1	M		G. Britain	U. States	John Jay	17 Sep 1828
James	21	M	Feltmonger	England	America	Adams	21 Jun 1824

198

NAMES OF PASSENGERS	AGE	SEX	OCCUPATIONS	COUNTRY TO WHICH THEY BELONG	COUNTRY THEY INTEND TO INHABIT	SHIPS/DATES OF ARRIVAL	
CASS (cont'd)							
Jane	36	F		G. Britain	U. States	John Jay	17 Sep 1828
Jane, 2d.	12	F		G. Britain	U. States	John Jay	17 Sep 1828
John	10	M		G. Britain	U. States	John Jay	17 Sep 1828
John	23	M	Clerk	G. Britain	U. States	Margaret Bogle	12 Jun 1828
Thos.	14	M		G. Britain	U. States	John Jay	17 Sep 1828
CASSA, Ferdinand	38	M	Farmer or Mechanic	France	U.S.	Edward Quesnel	31 Jul 1827
CASSADY, Dominick	28	M	Labourer	Ireland	United States	William & Henry	19 Jul 1822
Elizth.	24	F		Great Britain	U. States	Hector	11 Oct 1824
John	5/...	M		Great Britain	U. States	Hector	11 Oct 1824
Michl.	...1	M	...	Great Britain	U. States	Hector	11 Oct 1824
Michl.	23	M	...	Great Britain	U. States	Hector	11 Oct 1824
Owen	22	M	Labourer	Gt. Britain	U. States	Frances Henrietta	18 Apr 1825
Patrick	3...	...	...	Ireland	United States	Carolina Ann	24 Oct 1825
Patrick	30	M	Sevt.	England	England	Manhattan	21 Sep 1822
CASSAGEMUS, Rafael	25	M	Merchant	Spain	Unknown	Mercury	2 Feb 1825
CASSAN, James	21	M	Servant	U. States	U. States	Douglass	14 Jul 1828
CASSANDY, Michael	21	M	Farmer	Ireland	New York	William	27 Aug 1827
CASSANT, Mary	30	F		Gt. Britain	U. States	Lima	22 Sep 1828
Peter	32	M	Mason	Gt. Britain	U. States	Lima	22 Sep 1828
Peter, Jr.	6	M		Gt. Britain	U. States	Lima	22 Sep 1828
CASSEDY, John	12	M	Labourer	Great Britain	United States	Atlantic	8 Dec 1827
William	23	M	Taylor	Ireland	United States	Meteor	19 Aug 1829
CASSEL, James	18		Mariner	Great Brittain	Great Brittain	Commerce	14 Mar 1823
CASSELLS, James M.	40	M	Farmer	Great Britain	United States	Colossus	5 Jun 1827
John	25	M	Farmer	Great Britain	United States	Colossus	5 Jun 1827
CASSELS, Elizabeth	28	F	Matron	England	America	Josephine	8 Jan 1827
Henry	1	M		England	America	Josephine	8 Jan 1827
Henry	33	M	Shoe Maker	England	America	Josephine	8 Jan 1827
Jane	3	F		England	America	Josephine	8 Jan 1827
CASSEN, Wm.	22	M	Gentleman	Belfast	Damerara	John & Edward	6 Jul 1824
CASSENS, Joh. Hein.	26	M	Sugar Baker	Germany	U. States	Constitution	21 Jun 1824
CASSERNA, Thos.	48	M	Labourer	G. Britain	U. States	St. George	7 Jun 1828
CASSERTY, Bernard	3	M		Gt. Britain	U. States	St. George	20 Sep 1828
Eugene	9	M		Gt. Britain	U. States	St. George	20 Sep 1828
Geo.	5	M		Gt. Britain	U. States	St. George	20 Sep 1828
James	1 1/2	M		Gt. Britain	U. States	St. George	20 Sep 1828
Joseph	7	M		Gt. Britain	U. States	St. George	20 Sep 1828
Margt.	28	F		Gt. Britain	U. States	St. George	20 Sep 1828
Pat	34	M	Farmer	Gt. Britain	U. States	St. George	20 Sep 1828
CASSEY, Peggy	40	F	None	Ireland	U.S. of America	Hamilton	18 Jul 1827
CASSICK, Mary	35	F	Servant	Ireland	U. States	St. Michaels	25 Apr 1825
CASSIDAY, Bridget	32	F	Spinster	Ireland	United States	Thomas	13 Dec 1827
Margt.	20	F	Spinster	Ireland	United States	Thomas	13 Dec 1827
Robt.	35	M	Labourer	Ireland	United States	Thomas	13 Dec 1827
CASSIDEY, Daniel	23	M	Stone Cutter	Ireland	U. States	Hanford	29 Dec 1828
T.	17	M	Labourer	Ireland	U. States	Two Marys	20 Apr 1825
CASSIDY, Barthol	30	M	Labourer	Ireland	United States	Mary & Harriet	3 Jul 1829
Biddy	16 3/12	F		Ireland	America	Carolina Ann	7 Apr 1826
Bridget	22	F	None	Ireland	United States	Wilson	27 Jun 1826
Cathe., Jr.	10	F	Child	Ireland	United States	Dublin Packet	22 Apr 1822
Catherine	...	F	Spinster	Ireland	United States	Wilson	6 Jun 1828
Catherine	38	F	Spinster	Ireland	United States	Wilson	6 Jun 1828
Catherine	40	F	Woman	Ireland	United States	Dublin Packet	22 Apr 1822
Cathn.	18 0/12	F		Ireland	America	Carolina Ann	7 Apr 1826
Ellen	20 11/12	F		Ireland	America	Carolina Ann	7 Apr 1826
Jane	30	F	None	Ireland	United States	Mary & Harriet	3 Jul 1829
John	3	M	None	Ireland	United States	Mary & Harriet	3 Jul 1829
John	14	M	Farmer			Commerce	22 Jun 1825
John	20	M	Servant	Ireland	United States	Josephine	30 Apr 1828
John	22	M		Belfast	New York	Anthusa	24 Aug 1825
John	22	M	Pa...	Ireland	United States	Trident	16 May 1826
Judith	22	F	Spinster	Ireland	U. States	Panthea	8 Apr 1826
Margret	26	F	Servant	Ireland	United States	Carolina Ann	14 May 1827
Mary	1/52	F	Died June 24	Ireland	United States	Mary & Harriet	3 Jul 1829
Mary	25	F	Spinster	Ireland	America	Mary	29 May 1827
Peter	22	M	Labourer	Ireland	United States	Josephine	30 Apr 1828

NAMES OF PASSENGERS	AGE	SEX	OCCUPATIONS	COUNTRY TO WHICH THEY BELONG	COUNTRY THEY INTEND TO INHABIT	SHIPS/DATES OF ARRIVAL	
CASSIDY (cont'd)							
Pierce	14	F	Servant	Ireland	United States	Carolina Ann	14 May 1827
Sally	22		Laboring Class		United States	Atlantic	2 Apr 1827
Sarah	30	F	Wife			Commerce	22 Jun 1825
CASSILS, Wm.	30	M	Merchant	Scotland	U. States	Hector	18 Apr 1825
CASSIN, Agnes	7	F	None	Gt. Britain	United States	Eliza Barker	11 Jan 1826
Betsey	15	F	None	Gt. Britain	United States	Eliza Barker	11 Jan 1826
John	16	M	Blacksmith	Gt. Britain	United States	Eliza Barker	11 Jan 1826
Margaret	48	F		Gt. Britain	United States	Eliza Barker	11 Jan 1826
Martha	14	F	None	Gt. Britain	United States	Eliza Barker	11 Jan 1826
Robert	10	M	None	Gt. Britain	United States	Eliza Barker	11 Jan 1826
Roger	45	M	Blacksmith	Gt. Britain	United States	Eliza Barker	11 Jan 1826
Wm.	19	M	Blacksmith	Gt. Britain	United States	Eliza Barker	11 Jan 1826
CASSITY, Ellen	22	M	Yeoman	Ireland	United States	Borneo	9 Jul 1827
CASSON, —	24	M	Seaman	France	France	Artibonite	9 Sep 1826
—, Mde.	28	F	Lady	France	France	Imperial	10 Dec 1821
Jane	6	F	Child	Ireland	United States	Trident	16 May 1826
Mary	19	F	Spinster	..., ..., Ireland	N. York	New Orleans	24 Aug 1827
Mary	30	F	Wife	Ireland	United States	Trident	16 May 1826
Robert	8	M	Child	Ireland	United States	Trident	16 May 1826
Robert	60	M	Farmer	Ireland	United States	Trident	16 May 1826
CASSWELL, Jno.	39	M	Merchant	Gt. Britain	Gt. Britain	St. Michael	28 Feb 1826
John	40	M	Merchant	Gt. Brittain	United States	Balaena	24 Aug 1825
CASTA, Peter M. S.	24	M	Weaver	Scotland	U. States	Atlantic	7 Aug 1823
CASTANEDA, Francisco	38	M	Merchant	Spain	Spain	Sciot	12 Mar 1828
Maria Antonia	18	F		Mexico	Spain	Sciot	12 Mar 1828
CASTAX, John R.	17	M	Gentleman	America	U. States	Sarah Herrick	11 Jun 1825
CASTELA, Bernard	25	M	Merchant	Havana	Spain	Fair American	24 Dec 1821
CASTELASO, Lewis	23	M	Merchant	Mexico	Lpool [Liverpool]	Niagara	4 Sep 1824
CASTELL, Cathr.	20	F		Ireland	United States	Potomac	28 Sep 1827
Francis	38	M	Planter	France	France	James Monroe	24 Feb 1826
Michael	47	M	Farmer	Germany	United States	Stephania	16 Aug 1827
CASTELLANO, P.	12	M		Spain	Havana	Bellona	3 May 1826
CASTELLIAR, John	21	M	Mercht.	Columbia	Columbia	Atlantic	31 Jan 1828
CASTELLO, Eliza	8	F		G. Britain		Corinthian	27 Oct 1829
John G.	31	M	Merchant	Spain	Spain	Charlotte Corday	16 Aug 1821
L.	19	M		Mexico	U. States	Laveria	23 Jul 1828
Manuel	25	M	Merchant	Spain	U. States	Abigail	16 Nov 1824
Manuel	35	M	Merchant	Spain	U. States	Susannah	20 Mar 1824
Maria	27	F		G. Britain		Corinthian	27 Oct 1829
Mary	26	F	Servant	Great Britain	United States	Sylvester Healy	23 Nov 1825
Michael	28	M	Labourer	Great Britain	United States	Sylvester Healy	23 Nov 1825
Patt	19	M	Farmer	Ireland	United States	Concordia	25 Aug 1827
R.	25	M	Mercht.	Spain	U. States	Abeona	5 Jul 1822
Salvador	30	M	Merchant	Mexaco	Mexaco	Frances	19 Jun 1826
CASTILLO, Charles	24	M	Mercht.	Havana	Boston, Mass.	Rubicon	22 May 1826
Fredk.	10	M			Spain	Emma	24 Jun 1822
Jose	7	M		Spain	United States	Georgetown Packet	15 Nov 1823
Justo	19	M	Servant	Mexico	Mexico	Virginia	8 Mar 1828
Manuel	38	M	Merchant	Mexico	U. States	Desdemona	15 Jun 1827
R.	18	M	Merchant	Spain	Spain	Victory	8 Oct 1821
Raymond	20	M	Mercht.	Havanna	Spain	Orozimbo	16 Apr 1821
S.	28	M	Merchant	U.S.	U. States	Toison	15 Dec 1828
CASTILO, R.	21	M	Merchant	Spain	U. States	Orion	15 Apr 1822
CASTIN, Kate	2	F	None	Ireland	U. States	Josephine	27 Jul 1825
Mary	30	F	None	Ireland	U. States	Josephine	27 Jul 1825
William	26	M	Farmer	Ireland	U. States	Josephine	27 Jul 1825
CASTINEYRA, Leno	9	M	School Boy	Spain	New York	Transit	17 Mar 1824
Mariano	25	M	Merchant	Spain	New York	Transit	17 Mar 1824
CASTININOS, J. M.	24	M	Merchant	Cuba	Spain	Jane	29 Jul 1823
CASTIO, Henry	40	M	Merchant	France	U. States	Canada	5 Feb 1827
CASTLE, Bridgit	26	M	Labourer	Ireland	United States	Wilson	6 Jun 1828
Jno. W.	60	M	Notary	France	U. States	Little John	20 Aug 1822
Joseph	30	M	Seaman	New York	New York	Mary & Elizabeth	7 Sep 1824
CASTLES, James	22	M	Merchant	U. States	U. States	Weymouth	16 Feb 1825
Patrick	22	M	Weaver	Ireland	U. States	Courier	17 Mar 1828
Wearey	20	F	Spinster	Ireland	United States	Wilson	6 Jun 1828

NAMES OF PASSENGERS	AGE	SEX	OCCUPATIONS	COUNTRY TO WHICH THEY BELONG	COUNTRY THEY INTEND TO INHABIT	SHIPS/DATES OF ARRIVAL	
CASTO, Hosto	30	M	Gentleman	Cuba		Alpha	7 Dec 1827
Jno. Baptist	19	M	Carpenter	Italy	Italy	Atlanta	20 May 1822
Manuel	36	M	Carpenter			Atlanta	20 May 1822
CASTOLEY, Thos. W.		M	Gentleman	Great Britain	United States	Elias Burger	25 Feb 1820
CASTOTAI, Lucile	21	M	Gentleman	Spain	U.S.	Edward Quesnel	21 Apr 1827
CASTREL, Saml.	30	M	Mechanic	New York	United States	St. Michaels	12 Jun 1826
CASTRO, C.	30	M	Planter	Spain	U.S.	Radius	29 Jul 1823
C.	30	M	Merchant	Spain		Radius	21 Jul 1824
Henry	41	M	Merchant	United States	U. States	York	7 Aug 1828
Manuel	6	M		Spain	United States	Georgetown Packet	15 Nov 1823
Matias	40	M	Merchant	Spain	United States	Georgetown Packet	15 Nov 1823
CASTRY, Henry	16	M	Shoemaker	Ireland	United States	Nancy	15 Dec 1824
Richard	48	M	Shoemaker	Ireland	United States	Nancy	15 Dec 1824
CASTWELL, William	48	M	Black Smith	England	U.S. America	New Hampshire	28 Sep 1826
CASWELL, H.	18	M		G. Britain	U. States	Canada	19 Sep 1828
Samuel	19	M	Gent.	U. States	U. States	Cadmus	28 May 1821
CASWORTH, John	1	M	None	England	United States	Trident	18 Jul 1827
Mary	24	F	None	England	United States	Trident	18 Jul 1827
CASWORTH, Thomas	2	M	None	England	United States	Trident	18 Jul 1827
CATCHEN, W. H.	40	M	Merchant	Philada.	U. States	Diana	1 Jun 1822
CATCHER, Catharine	14	F	Labourer	England	U. States	Comet	23 Aug 1828
Isabella	7	F	Labourer	England	U. States	Comet	23 Aug 1828
Margaret	11	F	Labourer	England	U. States	Comet	23 Aug 1828
Margaret	35	F	Labourer	England	U. States	Comet	23 Aug 1828
Thomas	4	M	Labourer	England	U. States	Comet	23 Aug 1828
Thomas	37	M	Labourer	England	U. States	Comet	23 Aug 1828
William	3	M	Labourer	England	U. States	Comet	23 Aug 1828
CATEMORE, George	29	M	Watch Maker	England	Canada	Brighton	14 Oct 1824
CATHALL, Betsey	14	F	Servant			Hercules	25 Sep 1820
Wm.	13	M	Servant			Hercules	25 Sep 1820
CATHART, Effey	18		Spinster	Ireland		Westmoreland	1 Aug 1826
CATHBERDSON, Barthw.	30	M	Spinner	Scotland	United States	Washington	2 Oct 1828
CATHBERT, Chr. Wm.	22	M		U. States	U. States	Cambria	3 Jul 1829
CATHCART, Effey	50		Wife	Ireland		Westmoreland	1 Aug 1826
George	18		Farmer	Ireland		Westmoreland	1 Aug 1826
Jas.	20		Farmer	Ireland		Westmoreland	1 Aug 1826
Magt.	16		Spinster	Ireland		Westmoreland	1 Aug 1826
Mary	1		Child	Ireland		Westmoreland	1 Aug 1826
Matthew	20		Labourer	Ireland	United States	Fabius	18 Mar 1829
Rebecca	20		Spinster	Ireland		Westmoreland	1 Aug 1826
Wm.	60		...	Ireland		Westmoreland	1 Aug 1826
CATHEL, Clementine	18	F	None	U. States	U. States	Arthenian	28 Apr 1827
Elmirra	10	F	None	U. States	U. States	Arthenian	28 Apr 1827
Matilda	40	F	None	U. States	U. States	Arthenian	28 Apr 1827
CATHELL, Clemente	47	M	Mariner	U. States	United States	Tampico	13 May 1828
CATHER, Andw.	27	M	Labourer	Ireland	U. States	Margarett Scott	22 Aug 1827
Biddy	26	F	Labourer	Ireland	U. States	Margarett Scott	22 Aug 1827
James	26	M	Labourer	Ireland	U. States	Margarett Scott	22 Aug 1827
Jane	50			St. John	U. States	Lady Hunter	5 Jul 1823
CATHERS, Amy	12		Laborer	St. John	U. States	Lady Hunter	5 Jul 1823
Francis	16		Seamstress	St. John	U. States	Lady Hunter	5 Jul 1823
John	22	M	Laborer	Ireland	United States	Mary	1 Jul 1829
Maria	19	F		Ireland	United States	Mary	1 Jul 1829
Maye	7		Serv...	St. John	U. States	Lady Hunter	5 Jul 1823
CATHERTON, Eliza	11	F	Child	Ireland	U. States	Sarah Ann	11 Jan 1827
CATHERY, Thomas	24	M	Merchant	Great Britain	England	Jay	18 Apr 1823
CATHLIERTS, James	33	M	Sevt.	England		Hudson	23 Jul 1828
CATHWICK, Henry	23	M	Machinist	England	Rhode Island	Governor Fenner	23 Jul 1829
CATLIN, —	12	M		Gt. Britain	U. States	Tantiva	7 Jul 1828
E.	13	M		Gt. Britain	U. States	Tantiva	7 Jul 1828
E.	30	M		Gt. Britain	U. States	Tantiva	7 Jul 1828
CATON, Isaac	20	M		Ireland	United States	William & George	14 May 1828
CATORA, A.	20	M	Merchant	Spain	France & Spain	Native	24 Aug 1825
CATT, Geo.	30	M	Clergyman	United States	United States	Columbia	16 Jan 1829
Isaac	22	M	Farmer	Rye, England	United States	William	21 May 1828
Joseph	24	M	Farmer	Rye, England	United States	William	21 May 1828

NAMES OF PASSENGERS	AGE	SEX	OCCUPATIONS	COUNTRY TO WHICH THEY BELONG	COUNTRY THEY INTEND TO INHABIT	SHIPS/DATES OF ARRIVAL	
CATT (cont'd)							
Martha	25	F	Clergyman	United States	United States	Columbia	16 Jan 1829
Samuel	20		Farmer	England	S. New York	Xenophon	25 Jul 1826
CATTERALL, C.	25	M	Mariner	U. States	U. States	Georgetown Packet	24 Feb 1823
CATTILLO, Joseph							
Ignacio	9	M		Spain	United States	Georgetown Packet	15 Nov 1823
CATTING, Robert	31	F	Farmer	England	United States	Acosta	28 Jul 1823
Thomas	24	F	Farmer	England	United States	Acosta	28 Jul 1823
CATTON, Elizth.	4	F	None	Great Britain	United States	Ann Maria	12 Jul 1821
Elizth.	27	F	None	Great Britain	United States	Ann Maria	12 Jul 1821
James	6	M	None	Great Britain	United States	Ann Maria	12 Jul 1821
Thomas	2	M	None	Great Britain	United States	Ann Maria	12 Jul 1821
CATTOR, Jno.	29	M		Great Britain	America	Lady Gallatin	21 Jun 1820
CATTS, Agustus	28	M	U.S. Navy	Portsmouth	Portsmouth	Florida	1 Jun 1827
CAUBEN, James	25	M	Servant	Ireland	U. States	Henrietta	7 Jul 1825
CAUFFON, Y.	38	M	Merchant	Hayti	Hayti	Robert Reade	13 Jul 1825
CAUGHAN, Peter	21	M	Weaver	Ireland	U. States	Edward	15 Jul 1825
CAUGHEY, Jane	30	F	Farmer	Ireland	U. States	Dickinson	30 Jul 1825
CAUGHY, Eliza		F		Ireland	America	Carolina Ann	7 Aug 1826
Jane	18	M		Ireland	America	Carolina Ann	7 Aug 1826
Robert	20	F		Ireland	America	Carolina Ann	7 Aug 1826
CAUKINS, Edward	19		Gentleman	Wales	United States	Cambria	19 Oct 1829
CAUL, Sarah	25	F		Ireland	United States	Princess Charlotte	26 Apr 1827
CAULAY, James	27	M	Labourer	Ireland	United States	Enterprize	23 Jul 1827
CAULDFIELD, James	30	M	Clerk	Ireland	New York	America	1 Aug 1828
Lucy	2	F	None	Ireland	New York	America	1 Aug 1828
Mary	26	F	None	Ireland	New York	America	1 Aug 1828
CAULDWELL, Jas.	...8	M	Labourer	Great Brittan	U. States	John & Elizabeth	11 Dec 1826
Thomas	27	M	Farmer	Great Britain	United States	Roman	10 May 1828
CAULEY, Eliza	25	F		Ireland	America	Plutarch	18 Jul 1826
Mary	2	F		Ireland	America	Plutarch	18 Jul 1826
Michael	35	M	Labourer	Ireland	United States	Montgomery	6 Mar 1829
Tim	28	M	Labourer	Ireland	America	Plutarch	18 Jul 1826
Wm.	23	M	Farmer	England	United States	Euphrates	18 Aug 1827
CAULFIELD, Catherine	20	F	.	Ireland	United States	Princess Charlotte	26 Apr 1827
D.	50		Farmer	Ireland	United States	Courier	16 May 1825
M.	3		Farmer	Ireland	United States	Courier	16 May 1825
M.	6		Farmer	Ireland	United States	Courier	16 May 1825
M.	45		Farmer	Ireland	United States	Courier	16 May 1825
Rose	22	F		Ireland	United States	Princess Charlotte	26 Apr 1827
S.	5		Farmer	Ireland	United States	Courier	16 May 1825
CAULTER, William	19	M	Labourer	Ireland	U. States	Josephine	30 Aug 1828
CAUMONT, St. Croix	40	M	Merchant	France	U. States	Edward Quesnel	15 May 1826
St. Croix	44	M	Merchant	France	United States	Stephania	22 Apr 1822
CAURASS, Jose	22	M	Merchant	Spain	America	Port Captain	6 Dec 1825
CAUTHELS, Mary	45	F	Servant	Waterford	U. States	Margaret Bogle	11 Sep 1827
CAUTULE, Isaac	35	M	Miller	England	U. States	Thomas Ritchie	2 Jul 1827
CAVALERA, John	50	M	Priest	Spain	U. States	Horatio	21 Jan 1829
CAVALERY, Peter	17	M	Merchant	Porto Rico	U. States	Ann Eliza Jane	6 Sep 1822
CAVALLIERY, Peter	22	M	Planter	Porto Rico	Porto Rico	Francis Jarvis	30 Aug 1826
CAVAN, Philip	60	M	Farmer	Great Britain	United States	Meridian	2 Jul 1827
CAVANAAN, Ann	17	F	...	Ireland	United States	Carolina Ann	24 Oct 1825
CAVANAGH, Ann	20	F	Spinster	Ireland	United States	Dublin Packet	29 Jun 1825
James	23	M	Farmer	Ireland	United States	Dublin Packet	29 Jun 1825
Thos.	24	M	Farmer	Ireland	America	Farmer	4 Aug 1825
CAVANAH, ...d.	27	F		Ireland	U.S.	Hibernia	27 Jun 1821
Ann	18	F	Spinster	Ireland	Und. Stts of America	Alexander Mansfield	18 Aug 1826
Maria	10	F		Ireland	U.S.	Hibernia	27 Jun 1821
CAVANHUGH, Patrick	23	M	Labourer	Ireland	New York	Trusty	12 Sep 1828
CAVANNAH, Ann	20	F	Spinster	Ireland	U. States	Josephine	7 May 1827
Anne	13	F	Spinster	Ireland	America	Mary	29 May 1827
Mary	21	F	Spinster	Ireland	U. States	Josephine	7 May 1827

NAMES OF PASSENGERS	AGE	SEX	OCCUPATIONS	COUNTRY TO WHICH THEY BELONG	COUNTRY THEY INTEND TO INHABIT	SHIPS/DATES OF ARRIVAL	
CAVANNAH (cont'd)							
Morris	40			Ireland		Anacreon	7 Sep 1827
CAVANOUGH, Chas.	23	M				Ocean	17 Aug 1820
CAVE, Elizabeth	16			London	England	Rockingham	23 Aug 1822
James	41		Carpenter	Isle of Wight	England	London	13 Dec 1822
William	56			Sutton	England	Rockingham	23 Aug 1822
CAVEL, Charles	18	M	Carpenter	England	America	Mary Lord	26 Oct 1829
CAVENAGH, Arthur	21	M	Labourer	Ireland	U. States	Marcus	7 Apr 1825
P.	26	M	Labourer	Ireland	United States	Princess Charlotte	6 Oct 1827
CAVENAUGH, Bernard	22	M	Student	Great Britain	United States	Juno	5 Oct 1822
Margaret	29	F				Reuben & Eliza	21 Aug 1820
Thomas	23	M				Reuben & Eliza	21 Aug 1820
CAVENDER, Kitty	20	F		G. Britain	U. States	Dalhouse Castle	12 Sep 1828
CAVENDISH, Charlotte	12	F				Eliza Grant	6 Oct 1828
John	30	M				Eliza Grant	6 Oct 1828
CAVERHILL, Agnes	22	F		Scotland	United States	Samuel Robertson	5 Oct 1827
Thomas	27	M	Farmer	Great Britain	United States	Rebecca	20 Mar 1824
William	24	M	Labourer	Scotland	United States	Samuel Robertson	5 Oct 1827
CAVERNE, F.	26	M	School Master	Switzerland	U. States	Marmion	18 Oct 1824
CAVERNNAH, Bryan	23	M	Farmer	England		Exchange	11 Jul 1823
CAVERON, Francis	18	M	Merchant	Spain	U. States	Alfred	22 May 1824
Jos.	45	M	Merchant	Spain	U. States	Alfred	22 May 1824
CAVILLO, J. M.	35	M	Planter	Cuba	Neuvitas	Income	29 May 1824
CAVINDISH, James	29	M	Artizan	England	United States	Jubilee	1 Oct 1828
CAW, John	28	M				Eliza Grant	6 Oct 1828
R.	27	M	Farmer	England	U.S. States	Splendid	14 Aug 1829
CAWAJAL, Calisto	21	M	Merchant	Spain	Matanzes	Mechanic	16 Apr 1824
CAWEY, Thos.	18			Ireland	Philidelphia	General Marion	21 Nov 1828
CAWFORD, ...	...	...	...	Scotland	America	Nimrod	9 Jul 1827
CAWLEY, James	20	M	Hatter	Ireland	Pensylvania	Eliza Grant	29 Aug 1829
James	20	M	Hatter	Ireland	U. States	Eliza Grant	29 Aug 1829
John	28	M	Cooper	Ireland	New York	Trusty	12 Sep 1828
CAWLING, Patty	19	F		Great Britain	Canada	Orozimbo	2 Oct 1824
CAWS, H. B.	27	M	Physician		U. States	Packet Margaret	20 Sep 1824
CAWSON, Anne	15	F	None	G.B.	U.S.A.	Silas Richard	30 Jun 1828
CAY, Isaac	24	M	Weaver	Ireland	State of New York	Louisa	18 Apr 1827
CAYAN, Mary	26	F		England	United States	William	4 Oct 1822
Michael	30	M	Painter	England	United States	William	4 Oct 1822
CAYLOR, James	20	M	Shoemaker	Manchester		Colossus	27 Mar 1828
CAZALES, M.	30	M	Merchant	Spain	U. States	William Bayard	25 Apr 1826
CAZALY, Fredk.	13	M	None	England	United States	Manhattan	11 Oct 1824
CAZEAU, J. M.	23			France	Interior	Desdemona	12 Jun 1826
CAZEAUX, Gerard, Mr.	48	M	Merchant	France	France	Stephania	28 Jul 1823
CAZENAMU, —, Madam	57	F		France	U. States	Lewis	25 Jun 1824
CAZENOVE, Chs. J.	25	M	Merchant	United States	United States	Nestor	16 Aug 1824
Louis	19	M	Gentn.	Virginia	Virginia	Cadmus	16 Aug 1826
CE...E, Mary	23	F	Servant	Ireland	United States	Carolina Ann	14 May 1827
CEA, Juan S.	21	M	Gentleman	Chile	Chile	Mapocho	9 Jan 1824
CEARNE, Wm.	40	M	Farmer	Great Britan	United States	Silvanus Jenkins	10 Mar 1827
CEARNS, William	33	M	Merchant	New York	New York	Hector	11 Oct 1822
CEARUS, Jacob	2	M	Boy	Ireland	America	Josephine	8 Dec 1827
Jacob	35	M	Weaver	Ireland	America	Josephine	8 Dec 1827
John	8	M	Boy	Ireland	America	Josephine	8 Dec 1827
Mary	34	F	Matron	Ireland	America	Josephine	8 Dec 1827
CEASY, John	24		Farmer	Cork	New York	Schuylkill	22 Aug 1825
CEBALLOS, Manuel	17	M	Mechanic	Havana	U. States	Courier	9 Feb 1829
CECIL, Joseph, Jr.	27	M	Merchant	Great Britain	Great Britain	Canada	20 Jun 1823
CEILY, Albert	12	M		England	United States	Cosmo	26 Aug 1829
Edward	5	M		England	United States	Cosmo	26 Aug 1829
Elisa	35	F		England	United States	Cosmo	26 Aug 1829
Emma	6	F		England	United States	Cosmo	26 Aug 1829
John	10			England	United States	Cosmo	26 Aug 1829
John	66	M	Writer	England	United States	Cosmo	26 Aug 1829
Matilda	3	F		England	United States	Cosmo	26 Aug 1829
Robert	2	M		England	United States	Cosmo	26 Aug 1829
Thomas	9			England	United States	Cosmo	26 Aug 1829

NAMES OF PASSENGERS	AGE	SEX	OCCUPATIONS	COUNTRY TO WHICH THEY BELONG	COUNTRY THEY INTEND TO INHABIT	SHIPS/DATES OF ARRIVAL	
CELES, A.	12	M	Student	Columbia	U. States	Sarah	5 Aug 1825
CELESTIN, B.	30	M	Gentleman	U. States	U. States	Native	31 Jan 1825
CELESTON, B.	35	M	Merchant	America	America	Paragon	22 Sep 1827
CELIS, Juan	28	M	Merchant	St. Domingo	New York	Curlew	1 Mar 1824
CELISS, C.	33	M	Merchant	Spain	U. States	Mary Livingston	26 Jul 1824
CELLAR, J.	25	M	Merchant	Spain	United States	Burdett	30 Apr 1828
CELLERS, Mary Ann	26	F	None	Lancashire	America	Hannibal	4 Apr 1823
CELNAR, John	28	M	Labourer	Ireland	U. States	Belville	5 Jul 1827
CELTERON, M.	30	F		Gaudaloup	U. States	Orono	5 Jun 1823
CENNAH, Thomas	23	M	Miner	Great Britain	United States	Thomas Dickason	31 Jul 1829
CENNY, Lawrence	16	M	Farmer	Great Britain	United States	Rosina	12 Aug 1823
CENROY, Ewd.	4	M		G. Britain	U. States	St. George	7 Jun 1828
James	20	M		G. Britain	U. States	St. George	7 Jun 1828
John	12	M		G. Britain	U. States	St. George	7 Jun 1828
Margt.	7	F		G. Britain	U. States	St. George	7 Jun 1828
Margt.	34	F		G. Britain	U. States	St. George	7 Jun 1828
Mary	9	F		G. Britain	U. States	St. George	7 Jun 1828
Pat	11	M		G. Britain	U. States	St. George	7 Jun 1828
Pat	35	M	Farmer	G. Britain	U. States	St. George	7 Jun 1828
CENTER, A.	12	M		Hudson		Nimrod	21 Sep 1820
Robert E.	21	M	Merchant	U. States	United States	Governor Griswold	4 Feb 1822
CERCEL, Wm., Jr.	29	M	Merchant	Great Brittain	America	Pacific	13 Jan 1827
CERMARTHY, Mary	30	F	None	England	United States	India	8 Jun 1827
CERON, —	30	M	Merchant	France	France	Asparia	1 Sep 1824
H.	22	M	Merchant	France	U. States	Pacification	6 Oct 1823
CERRALL, Mary	26	F	None		United States	Mount Vernon	29 Aug 1828
CERTINU, J.	32	M	Merchant	Spain	U. States	Mary Livingston	26 Jul 1824
CERVA, Thomas	30	M	Labourer	Great Britain	U. States	Balance	19 Jun 1824
CESAR, Lewis	26	M	Farmer	Bavaria	United States	American	27 Aug 1827
CESPEDES, Ramon	25	M	Lawyer	Island Cuba		Claudio	21 Aug 1827
CESSE, Catherine	40	F	Nurse	France	San Domingo	Victory	29 May 1821
CESSIER, N.	24	M	Merchant	France	U. States	Waldo	19 Aug 1826
CESSON, Wm.	18	M		Gt. Britain	Gt. Britain	Silvanus Jenkins	24 Jul 1828
CETCHAN, Isach	25	M	Merchant	United States	United States	Nancy	8 Mar 1822
CETTLE, Jaques	27	M	Labourer	France	America, U.N.S.	Great Britain	3 Aug 1829
CETZMAN, Y. F.	24	M	Merchant	Germany	Hambro [?]	Virginia	8 Mar 1828
CH..., John	29 5/12	M	Merchant	Ireland	New York	Globe	3 Dec 1821
CH...ILL, Arthur	42	M	Joiner	Great Brittan	U. States	Gem	26 Jul 1827
CH...TIAN, Cathe.	23	F		G. Britain	U. States	St. George	7 Jun 1828
CHABEND, J. A.	23	M	...	Great Britain	Nova Scotia	Loire	18 Oct 1820
CHABRAT, G. J., Revd.	34		Clergyman	Kentucky	Bardstown, N.C.	Manchester	30 May 1821
CHABROL, Peter	28	M	Silk printer	France		Corinthian	27 Oct 1829
CHACHT, Carl	34	M	Military	Prusia	Prusia	William	2 May 1821
CHADERTON, Thomas		M	Merchant	Barbados	unknown	Superb	23 Apr 1823
CHADET, A.	22	M	Merchant	France	France	Liberty	26 Mar 1827
CHADHAM, C.	30	M	Merchant	U. States	U. States	Topaz	7 Apr 1828
CHADOIR, P.	24	M	Merchant	Neather Lands	U. States	La Voltiquer	23 Jul 1822
CHADWICK, —, Mrs.	22	F		U. States	U. States	Maria	19 Feb 1823
Agnus	11	F	Child	England	Canada	Phoenix	29 Apr 1826
Ann	5	F	None	Great Britian	Canada	Galaxy	9 Sep 1826
Ann	25	F	None	Great Britian	Canada	Galaxy	9 Sep 1826
Ann	58	F	None	Great Britian	United States	Hamilton	21 Nov 1826
Benj.	27	M	Nail Maker	Yorkshire	United States	Dalhousie Castle	27 Jul 1826
Benjamin	29	M	Merchant	Great Britian	Canada	Galaxy	9 Sep 1826
Charles	7	M	Child	England	Canada	Phoenix	29 Apr 1826
Diannah	3/12	F	None	Great Britian	United States	Hamilton	21 Nov 1826
Eli	36	M	Reverand	England	Canada	Phoenix	29 Apr 1826
James	15	M	None	Great Britian	United States	Hamilton	21 Nov 1826
James	23 5/12	M	Spinner	England	Massachusetts	Concordia	12 Oct 1826
James	68	M	Calico Printer	Great Britian	United States	Hamilton	21 Nov 1826
Jane	3	F	None	Great Britian	Canada	Galaxy	9 Sep 1826
Jane	7	F	None	Great Britian	United States	Hamilton	21 Nov 1826
Jane	27	F	None	Great Britian	Canada	Galaxy	9 Sep 1826
Jn. W. ... J. W.	3	M	Child	England	Canada	Phoenix	29 Apr 1826
John	25	M	Merchant	Great Britian	United States	James Cropper	14 Oct 1824
John	29	M	Shoe Maker	Great Briton	New York	Brighton	12 Jun 1826
John	41	M	Calico Printer	Great Britian	United States	Hamilton	21 Nov 1826

NAMES OF PASSENGERS	AGE	SEX	OCCUPATIONS	COUNTRY TO WHICH THEY BELONG	COUNTRY THEY INTEND TO INHABIT	SHIPS/DATES OF ARRIVAL	
CHADWICK (cont'd)							
Josiah	3	M	None	Great Britain	United States	Hamilton	21 Nov 1826
Margaret	2	F	Child	England	Canada	Phoenix	29 Apr 1826
Margaret	36	F	Reverand	England	Canada	Phoenix	29 Apr 1826
Mary	2	F	None	Great Britain	Canada	Galaxy	9 Sep 1826
Mary	9	F	Child	England	Canada	Phoenix	29 Apr 1826
Mary	11	F	None	Great Britain	United States	Hamilton	21 Nov 1826
Mary	20	F		G. Britain	U. States	Mary Howland	22 Sep 1828
Saml.	22	M	Manufacturer	G. Britain	U. States	Mary Howland	22 Sep 1828
Samuel	26	M	Taylor	Great Britan	United States	Silvanus Jenkins	10 Mar 1827
Sarah	4	F	None	Great Britain	United States	Hamilton	21 Nov 1826
Susannah	34	F	None	Great Britain	United States	Hamilton	21 Nov 1826
W. N.	25	M	Merchant	U.S.	U.S.	Radius	27 Apr 1824
William	...	M	Merchant	England	New York	Amity	13 Sep 1821
CHAFFENER, Bab	34	F		Native of Switzerland	United States	Canaris	30 Jun 1827
Frets	1	M		Native of Switzerland	United States	Canaris	30 Jun 1827
Philip	13	M		Native of Switzerland	United States	Canaris	30 Jun 1827
CHAFFENERE, George H.	36	M	Weaver	Native of Switzerland	United States	Canaris	30 Jun 1827
CHAFFIE, H. B.	36	M	Merchant	Connecticutt	U. States	Hero	17 May 1825
CHAFFIELD, Charles	28	M	M...	Great Britain	U. States	Panthea	24 Mar 1825
CHAFMAR, H. S.	25	M	Merchant	London	U. States	Pacific	16 Apr 1825
CHAGEE, Isabella	24	F				John Dickinson	14 Sep 1820
Thos.	1	M				John Dickinson	14 Sep 1820
CHAGET, Adele	18	F		France	America	Saluda	16 Oct 1824
Theo.	23	M		France	America	Saluda	16 Oct 1824
CHAGOT, —	30	M	Mercht.	France	France	Don Quixote	3 Jan 1826
CHAIG, Anon	17	M	Farmer	Scotland	U. States	Roger Stewart	9 Jun 1828
Robt.	21	M	Farmer	Scotland	U. States	Roger Stewart	9 Jun 1828
CHAIN, A.	23	M		Great Britain	United States	Saml. Wight	6 Sep 1827
Eliza	3	F		Great Britain	United States	Saml. Wight	6 Sep 1827
Sarah	2	F		Great Britain	United States	Saml. Wight	6 Sep 1827
*Died 11th August							
Wm.	5	M		Great Britain	United States	Saml. Wight	6 Sep 1827
CHAISEL, D. B.	24	F		Porto Rico	N. York	Hanna	3 Jun 1828
D. R.	32	M	Planter	Porto Rico	N. York	Hanna	3 Jun 1828
F.	6	M		Porto Rico	N. York	Hanna	3 Jun 1828
M.	3	M		Porto Rico	N. York	Hanna	3 Jun 1828
CHALABRE, John	26	M	Student	America	United States	Margaret Bogle	11 Jun 1824
CHALAND, J. A.	24	M	Merchant	Cape of Good Hope	Cape of Good Hope	Abigail	10 May 1821
CHALDEN, —, Mr.	45	F	Lady	Guadaloupe	U. States	Turner	8 Jun 1824
CHALDREN, Henry	32	M	Wool ...ter	England	Uncertain	John Wells	22 Sep 1824
CHALLAC, Lewis	30	M	Hairdresser	France	U. States	Ariadne	15 Apr 1822
CHALLAR, Alexander	24	M	Carpenter	England	United States	Trident	31 Mar 1827
CHALLEMBERG, Bab	1	F		Native of Switzerland	United States	Canaris	30 Jun 1827
Bab	28	F		Native of Switzerland	United States	Canaris	30 Jun 1827
Catharine	8	F		Native of Switzerland	United States	Canaris	30 Jun 1827
Elizabeth	10	F		Native of Switzerland	United States	Canaris	30 Jun 1827
John	6	M		Native of Switzerland	United States	Canaris	30 Jun 1827
John	33	M	Farmer	Native of Switzerland	United States	Canaris	30 Jun 1827
CHALLET, Jean Henry	23	M	Planter	Switzerland	U. States	Little William	16 Jun 1821
CHALMER, John	33	M	Mechanic	U. States	U. States	Only Daughter	24 Oct 1827
CHALMERS, David	57	M	Clerk	Scotland	U. States	Psyche	16 May 1821
Isabella	33	F	Farmer	N. York	U. States	Loire	28 Aug 1824
Jas.	37	M	Joiner	G. Britain	U. States	Eliza	31 Jul 1828
John	24	M	Distiller	G. Britan	U. States	Dalmarnock	11 Dec 1828
Thomas	31	M	Grocer	New York	New York	Chief	14 Nov 1823
Wm.	43	M	Weaver	Scotland	America	Camillus	12 Sep 1822
CHALMON, Js.	26	M	Merchant	France	United States	Howard	19 May 1826

NAMES OF PASSENGERS	AGE	SEX	OCCUPATIONS	COUNTRY TO WHICH THEY BELONG	COUNTRY THEY INTEND TO INHABIT	SHIPS/DATES OF ARRIVAL
CHALON, —, Mr.	35	M	Merchant	France	United States	Neptunes Barge 23 Apr 1821
CHALRET, Hipolite	30	M	Merchant	France	U. States	Four Sons 30 Jul 1829
CHAMBAIN, Saml.	6/12	M	None	U. States	U. States	Georgiana 12 Nov 1822
CHAMBERLAIN, —, Mrs.		F	None	U. States	U. States	Georgiana 12 Nov 1822
Ann	23	F	Spinster	Great Britain	United States	Superior 31 Mar 1828
Edwd.	10	M	None	U. States	U. States	Georgiana 12 Nov 1822
J. G.	39	M	Mercht.	U. States	U. States	Alciope 6 Jul 1822
James	23	M	Merchant	England	U. States	Susannah 19 Apr 1823
John	20	M	Miller	Great Britain	United States	Freake 25 Aug 1829
John, her Son [Sarah]	10					Hercules 19 Jun 1821
Mark	23	M	Tailer	England	America	Sarah 18 Aug 1829
Mary, Daughter [Sarah]	3					Hercules 19 Jun 1821
Robt.	36		Farmer	England	America	Governor Griswold 6 Jun 1821
Sarah, Mrs.	34	F				Hercules 19 Jun 1821
Thomas	37	M		Great Brittian	United States	Carolina Augusta 2 Dec 1828
Thos.	29 1/12	M	Shoemaker	Great Britain	America	Magnet 13 Nov 1821
Wm.	27	M	Merchant	U. States	U. States	Hook 10 Feb 1827
Wm.	32	M	Merchant	U. States	U. States	Pacific 11 Sep 1824
Wm. F. R.	27	M	Mariner	U. States	U. States	General Brooks 3 Nov 1825
CHAMBERLANE, Maria	22	F	Lady	France	U. States	Pacific 11 Sep 1824
CHAMBERLEN, E.	52	M	Merchant	U. States	U. States	William Tell 3 Dec 1827
Henry	22	M	Supercargo	U. States	U. States	Deborah 11 Jun 1824
CHAMBERLIN, A. B., Miss	18	F		England	United States	Cincinnatus 21 Nov 1821
Jos.	38		Farmer	England	United States	Mary 15 Jul 1822
Joseph	35	M	Farmer	England	United States	Concordia 25 Aug 1827
Mary	21		Farmer	England	United States	Mary 15 Jul 1822
Mathew	22	F	Lady	America	America	Loire 7 Apr 1821
S., Mrs.	59	F		England	United States	Cincinnatus 21 Nov 1821
William	26	M	Mechanic	America	America	Loire 7 Apr 1821
CHAMBERS, Alec	32	M	Blacksmith	Scotland	U.S. States	Splendid 14 Aug 1829
Alexr.	42	M	Cooper			John Dickinson 14 Sep 1820
Barney	25	M		Irland	U. States	Nancy 27 Jun 1823
D.	3	M	Blacksmith	Scotland	U.S. States	Splendid 14 Aug 1829
E.	30	F	Blacksmith	Scotland	U.S. States	Splendid 14 Aug 1829
Edward	17	M	Printer	England and Ireland	United States	Jubilee 12 May 1828
Edward	21	M	Labourer	Ireland	United States	Ann Maria 2 Nov 1827
Edward	31	M	Farmer	England	America	Dewitt Clinton 27 Jul 1824
Edward	38	M	Plater	Great Britain	United States	Ganges 26 Oct 1826
Elizabeth	5	F		England	America	Dewitt Clinton 27 Jul 1824
Elizabeth	31	F		England	America	Dewitt Clinton 27 Jul 1824
Ellen	6	F				John Dickinson 14 Sep 1820
Francis	19	F		Scotland	United States	Commerce 17 Jul 1823
Frederick	3	M		England	America	Dewitt Clinton 27 Jul 1824
Henry	40	M	Farmer			John Dickinson 14 Sep 1820
Hugh	20	M	Sadler	Ireland	U. States	Courier 17 Mar 1828
Hugh	29 5/12	M	Supercargo	United States	United States	America 18 Jan 1820
Isabella	58	F				John Dickinson 14 Sep 1820
J., Mr.	30	M	Mercht.	Gt. Brittian	United States	Manchester 15 Aug 1826
James	19	M				John Dickinson 14 Sep 1820
Jane	35	F				John Dickinson 14 Sep 1820
John	9	M		England	America	Dewitt Clinton 27 Jul 1824
John	25	M				John Dickinson 14 Sep 1820
John	50	M	Farmer	England	United States	Enterprize 19 Oct 1826
Lydia H.	25	F	None	Jamaica	Jamaica	General Marion 17 Mar 1826
M. McN.	24	M	Farmer	Scotland	Scotland	Yamacraw 10 May 1821
Margaret	24	F		Ireland	U. States	Alexander 28 Jul 1821
Margret	22	F		Irland	U. States	Nancy 27 Jun 1823
Margret	42	F	Spinster	Ireland	United States	Henry Kneeland 7 Jun 1828
Maria	40	F	...	Ireland	United States	Carolina Ann 24 Oct 1825
Mary	1	F		England	America	Dewitt Clinton 27 Jul 1824
R.	14/12	M	Blacksmith	Scotland	U.S. States	Splendid 14 Aug 1829
Richard	22	M	Farmer	England	America	Dewitt Clinton 27 Jul 1824

NAMES OF PASSENGERS	AGE	SEX	OCCUPATIONS	COUNTRY TO WHICH THEY BELONG	COUNTRY THEY INTEND TO INHABIT	SHIPS/DATES OF ARRIVAL
CHAMBERS (cont'd)						
Robrt.	22	M				John Dickinson 14 Sep 1820
Sarah	7	F		England	America	Dewitt Clinton 27 Jul 1824
Thomas	1	M				John Dickinson 14 Sep 1820
Thomas	33	M	Merchant	Great Britian	U. States	Silas Richards 29 Oct 1828
Thomas	50	M	Merchant	United States	United States	Silas Richards 27 Oct 1825
Thomas	50	M	Merchant	G.B.		Silas Richards 29 Oct 1827
Ths.	50	M	Merchant	Great Brittain		Corinthian 9 Jan 1827
William	2	M				John Dickinson 14 Sep 1820
William	21 8/12	M	Farmer	England	U.S. of America	Illinois 16 Jun 1821
William	22	M	Farmer	Scotland	United States	Commerce 17 Jul 1823
Wm.	33		Spinner	Great Britain	United States	Camillus 12 Sep 1827
Z. E.	40	M	Mason	Jamaica	Jamaica	General Marion 17 Mar 1826
CHAMBIGE,						
Francis	20 5/12	M	Student	France	America	Henry 17 May 1828
CHAMBINWIE,						
Bernard	29	M	Gentleman	France	U.S.	Helen 3 May 1828
CHAMER, —	6/12	F	None	France	U. States	Luna 25 Jul 1825
—	3	F	None	France	U. States	Luna 25 Jul 1825
—, Madam	27	F	None	France	U. States	Luna 25 Jul 1825
CHAMPHY, P. F.	40	M	Physician	United States		Edward Quesnel 17 Nov 1828
CHAMPLER, A., Mrs.	21	F		United States	United States	Cincinnatus 21 Nov 1821
CHAMPLEY, Jane	19	F	Child	G. Britain	U. States	George Porter 23 Sep 1826
Mary	60	F	Wife	G. Britain	U. States	George Porter 23 Sep 1826
Priscilla	27	F	Child	G. Britain	U. States	George Porter 23 Sep 1826
Robt.	66	M	Carpenter	G. Britain	U. States	George Porter 23 Sep 1826
CHAMPONIER, T. C.	27			Clermont (France)	Bardstown, N.C.	Manchester 30 May 1821
CHAMPOUNNIER, W.	31	M		France	U. States	Desdemona 15 Feb 1826
CHAMPY, Antonete	9	F		Point Petre, Guadaloupe	United States	General Macombe 17 Jul 1827
Caroline	11	F		Point Petre, Guadaloupe	United States	General Macombe 17 Jul 1827
Clarissa	13	F		Point Petre, Guadaloupe	United States	General Macombe 17 Jul 1827
Emeline	14	F	Lady	Point Petre, Guadaloupe	United States	General Macombe 17 Jul 1827
F.	36	M	Physician	Point Petre, Guadaloupe	United States	General Macombe 17 Jul 1827
Fanny	38	F	Lady	Point Petre, Guadaloupe	United States	General Macombe 17 Jul 1827
Felix	7	M		Point Petre, Guadaloupe	United States	General Macombe 17 Jul 1827
Louis Jane	3	M		Point Petre, Guadaloupe	United States	General Macombe 17 Jul 1827
Sarah	33	F	Lady	Point Petre, Guadaloupe	United States	General Macombe 17 Jul 1827
CHANAER, George	10	M	Weaver	Ireland		Quatre Freres 29 Jul 1828
Jac	34	M	Weaver	Ireland		Quatre Freres 29 Jul 1828
Jack	7	M	Weaver	Ireland		Quatre Freres 29 Jul 1828
Margaret	33	F	Weaver	Ireland		Quatre Freres 29 Jul 1828
Thebared	4	M	Weaver	Ireland		Quatre Freres 29 Jul 1828
CHANCE, Geo.	33	M	Merchant	England		London 29 Apr 1824
CHANCELLOR, Henry	24	M	Merchant	U. States	U. States	Caledonia 10 Sep 1828
CHANCEY, Betsy	21	F	Cook	New Jersey	New Jersey	Annah 17 Dec 1823
CHANCLIFF, Simon	46	M	Labourer	England	U. States	Comet 23 Aug 1828
CHANDER, ...n	28	M	Farmer	Switzerland	United States	Elbe 2 Aug 1822
CHANDHIS, —	32	M	Mariner	Spain	U. States	Maria Ann 29 Sep 1823
*landed at Balize [Biloxi?], Missippi						
CHANDLER, ...	55	F				Belfast 28 Sep 1820
Benjamin	45	M	Merchant	United States	United States	Nancy 8 Mar 1822
Daniel	20	M	Farmer	England	New York	Thames 6 Oct 1820
Isaac	30		Mariner	Salem, Mass.	U. States	Lucy 16 Apr 1821
Jane	38	F		Canada	Canada	Thames 16 May 1821
John	26	M	Wheelwright	Great Britain	Pennsylvania	Venus 8 Sep 1820
Keneland	45	M	Gentleman	Canada	Canada	Thames 16 May 1821
Wm.	55	M	Grocer	U. States	U. States	Mary Howland 22 Sep 1828
CHANDLESS, Henry	22	M	M...	Great Britain	U. States	Panthea 24 Mar 1825
Henry	25	M		England		Britannia 20 Jun 1827

NAMES OF PASSENGERS	AGE	SEX	OCCUPATIONS	COUNTRY TO WHICH THEY BELONG	COUNTRY THEY INTEND TO INHABIT	SHIPS/DATES OF ARRIVAL	
CHANET, —, Miss	15	F	Spinster	Charleton	U. States	Othello	31 Aug 1824
CHANNERY, Nathaniel	39	M	Gentleman	United States	New Haven, U.S.	Florida	2 Oct 1828
CHANON, A.	22	M	Merchant	U. States	U. States	Waldo	19 Aug 1826
Edward	19	M	Artist	France	United States	Elbe	2 Aug 1822
M.	17	F		U. States	U. States	Waldo	19 Aug 1826
CHAPEL, S., Mr.	35	M	Merchant	N. York	U. States	Milo	23 Dec 1824
CHAPELL, S.	35	M	Mercht.	U.S. America		Brown	12 Oct 1824
CHAPEN, Abel	20	M	...	...	U.S. America	Columbia	26 Nov 1825
CHAPIN, Alexander	8	M		France	United States	Le Voltaire	19 Jul 1828
Cath. S.	2	F		France	United States	Le Voltaire	19 Jul 1828
M. Cath.	9/12	F		France	United States	Le Voltaire	19 Jul 1828
Maria M.	42	F		France	United States	Le Voltaire	19 Jul 1828
Rosina	7	F		France	United States	Le Voltaire	19 Jul 1828
Thiebaud	50	M	Farmer	France	United States	Le Voltaire	19 Jul 1828
CHAPLIN, Walter	50	M				Eliza Grant	6 Oct 1828
CHAPMAN, Ane	26	F		Scotland	United States	Camillus	27 Oct 1829
Ann	10		Family [of Wm.]	Great Britain	United States	Camillus	12 Sep 1827
Ann	18	F	Spinster	Ireland	United States	Dublin Packet	22 Aug 1829
Benj.	23	M		Great Britain	United States	James Monroe	25 Apr 1822
C., Miss	12	F	Comedian	England	U. States	Talma	23 Sep 1828
Catharine	6		Family [of Wm.]	Great Britain	United States	Camillus	12 Sep 1827
Catherine	60		Family [of Wm.]	Great Britain	United States	Camillus	12 Sep 1827
Charles	24		Merchant	Ireland	England	Hudson	4 Sep 1823
Charles	29	M	Merchant	Ireland	United States	Aurora	9 Jul 1827
Christian	6		Family [of Wm.]	Great Britain	United States	Camillus	12 Sep 1827
Christian	32		Wife [of Wm.]	Great Britain	United States	Camillus	12 Sep 1827
Elenor	6/12	F	None	Great Britain	United States	Eliza Barker	3 Jul 1826
Eles	1			York County	Ohio	Peru	30 May 1828
Elizabeth	26			York County	Ohio	Peru	30 May 1828
Elizabeth	28	F		Ireland	United States	Aurora	9 Jul 1827
Francis	30	M	Farmer	Great Britain	United States	Dapper	21 Aug 1828
Francis	30	M	Miner	England	U. States	Emulous	22 Aug 1828
Geo.	20	M	Labourer	Ireland	United States	Lord Wellington	28 May 1827
Geo.	22		Labourer	England	England	Hudson	14 Jun 1827
Geo.	37	M	Farmer	Great Britain	United States	William Dawson	18 Jun 1827
George	2	M	None	Great Britain	United States	Eliza Barker	3 Jul 1826
George	4	M		Ireland	United States	Aurora	9 Jul 1827
George	18 2/12	M	Hatclean	Great Briton	United States	Mount Vernon	30 Dec 1828
George	28			York County	Ohio	Peru	30 May 1828
George	28	M	Clerk	Ireland	United States	Pallas	28 Oct 1828
Henry	20	M	Merchant	Ireland	United States	Aurora	9 Jul 1827
Henry G.	20	M		...	U. States	Corinthian	2 Sep 1824
J.	40	M	Mariner	U. States	U. States	Swiftsure	14 Apr 1828
James	27	M	Laborer	Scotland	America	Camillus	12 Sep 1822
James	28	M	None	Great Britain	United States	Eliza Barker	3 Jul 1826
Jane	8		Family [of Wm.]	Great Britain	United States	Camillus	12 Sep 1827
Jane	18	F	None	Ireland	United States	Lord Wellington	28 May 1827
Jane	55	F		Ireland	United States	Aurora	9 Jul 1827
John	19	M	Labourer	Ireland	United States	Lord Wellington	28 May 1827
John	25		Upholster	United States	Philadelphia	Swift	9 Jan 1826
John J., Capt.	25	M	Armey	England	England	Manhattan	21 Sep 1822
Margaret	22	F	None	Great Britton	U. States	Factor	27 Mar 1827
Margt.	2		Family [of Wm.]	Great Britain	United States	Camillus	12 Sep 1827
Mary	6	F		Ireland	United States	Aurora	9 Jul 1827
Mary	27	F	None	Great Britain	United States	Eliza Barker	3 Jul 1826
S., Miss	19	F	Comedian	England	U. States	Talma	23 Sep 1828
Saml.	45	M	Comedian	England	U. States	Talma	23 Sep 1828
Samuel	29	M	Mercht.	U.S.	U.S.	Torch	21 Nov 1825
Sarah	40	F	Comedian	England	U. States	Talma	23 Sep 1828
T., Miss	5	F	Comedian	England	U. States	Talma	23 Sep 1828
William	20	M	...	England	America, U.S.	Illinois	3 Jun 1822
William	31	M	Seaman	Great Britton	U. States	Factor	27 Mar 1827
Willm.	44	M	Coper	Engd.	United States	Cosmo	21 Aug 1828
Wm.	4		Family [of Wm.]	Great Britain	United States	Camillus	12 Sep 1827
Wm.	6			York County	Ohio	Peru	30 May 1828
Wm.	34		Weaver	Great Britain	United States	Camillus	12 Sep 1827
Wm.	35	M	Merchant	G. Britain	Canada	Columbia	7 Sep 1827
CHAPPEL, S.	40	M	Merch.		U. States	William Bayard	2 Mar 1824
CHAPPELL, —, Mr.	35	M	Merchant	New York	New York	Native	30 Jun 1826

NAMES OF PASSENGERS	AGE	SEX	OCCUPATIONS	COUNTRY TO WHICH THEY BELONG	COUNTRY THEY INTEND TO INHABIT	SHIPS/DATES OF ARRIVAL	
CHAPPELL (cont'd)							
E.	30	M	Merchant	Greenock	U. States	Favorite	12 May 1823
Hannah	35					Xenophon	25 Jul 1826
Jacob	36	M	Mariner	U. States	U. States	James Monroe	24 Jan 1829
John	45		Blackine Mercht.	England	S. New York	Xenophon	25 Jul 1826
S.	32	M	Merchant	U. States	U. States	Swan	23 Jun 1823
CHAPPELLE, M.	41	M	Merchant	France	United States	St. Martin	10 Feb 1820
CHAPPELLS, Salvadore	35	M	Merchant	N. York	U. States	Betsey	4 Apr 1823
CHAPPER, Sarah	14	F		New York	U. States	Cambria	3 Jul 1829
CHAPPIN, Richard	17 10/12	M	Butcher	Great Britain	Philadelphia	Thames	16 May 1821
CHAPPLE, J.	45	M	Merchant	U. States	U. States	Superion	30 Apr 1825
S.	35	M		U. States	U. States	Native	16 Nov 1825
S.	40	M	Merchant	Spain	U. States	Native	15 Apr 1826
Salvador	35	M	Merchant	Spain	New York	Abeona	20 Dec 1823
Salvador	40	M	Merchant	New York	New York	Nile	18 Oct 1828
CHAPRON, —, Miss	12	F				Henri IV	14 Sep 1827
—, Mrs.	27	F				Henri IV	14 Sep 1827
A.	30	M	Merchant	U. States	U. States	Adze	24 Jul 1820
J., Mr.	40	M	Merchant	United States	U. States	Henri IV	14 Sep 1827
CHARAMON, F. J.	36	M	Waiter	France	U. States	America	22 Sep 1826
CHARART, Augustus	25		None	France		Bayard	10 Sep 1827
CHARBACH, Andries, Zyn Broeder (his brother [Joseph])	9	M		Bleicheim	United States	Juffraw Johanna	16 Oct 1821
Joseph	21	M	Boer	Bleicheim	United States	Juffraw Johanna	16 Oct 1821
CHARBACK, Cathrina	5 6/12	F	Daughter	Germany	United States	Elizabeth	4 Sep 1826
Christian	22	M	Son	Germany	United States	Elizabeth	4 Sep 1826
Felix	40	M	Farmer	Germany	United States	Elizabeth	4 Sep 1826
Joseph	9	M	Son	Germany	United States	Elizabeth	4 Sep 1826
Maria	6 6/12	F	Daughter	Germany	United States	Elizabeth	4 Sep 1826
Rosina	48	F	Wife	Germany	United States	Elizabeth	4 Sep 1826
CHARBONNET, Amable	38	M	Merchant	U. States	U. States	Sully	24 Oct 1828
CHARCHILLET, Brody	23	M	Gent.	France	West Indies	Adonis	29 Sep 1823
CHARD, Amelia	19	F			U. States America	Cambria	2 Jul 1821
Ann	40	F			U. States America	Cambria	2 Jul 1821
John	17	M			U. States America	Cambria	2 Jul 1821
William	21	M			U. States America	Cambria	2 Jul 1821
William	45	M	Farmer	England	U. States America	Cambria	2 Jul 1821
CHARDON, Edwd.	21	M	Merchant	France	United States	Bayard	13 Nov 1823
Francois	18	M	Merchant	France	America	Don Quixotte	2 Jun 1828
CHARESWORTH, John	23	M				Euphrates	8 Aug 1820
CHARICE, Adrien	3 6/12	F		Havre	N. York	Stephania	29 Nov 1825
Peter	7	M		Havre	N. York	Stephania	29 Nov 1825
CHARIER, Lewis	12	M		France	U. States of America	Brandt	21 May 1821
CHARITRY, Edward	27	M	Merchant	Gt. Britain	United States	Seeds	29 Sep 1824
CHARLE, Conaite	36	M	Baker	Germany	United States	Quito	16 Jun 1826
CHARLEDIN, W.	23		Farmer	Ireland	United States	Courier	16 May 1825
CHARLES, Alexander	23	M	Merchant	England	United States	Orbit	22 Apr 1824
Alexr.	20	M	Clerk	Ireland	U. States of America	Courier	17 Mar 1827
Geo.	26	M	Carpenter	France	America	Saluda	18 Jun 1825
John, Mr.	45	M	Hudson Bay Co.	Gt. Brittian	North Brittian		6 Apr 1826
Lewis		M	Servant	France	U. States	Desdemona	21 Oct 1825
Phebi	28	F		Great B.	U. States	William Neilson	26 Jul 1828
R.	50	M		Great B.	U. States	William Neilson	26 Jul 1828
Sarah	25	F		Great B.	U. States	William Neilson	26 Jul 1828
CHARLESTON, Catherine	57	F		Philadelphia	United States	Loire	12 Dec 1820
CHARLESWORTH, Maria	21	F		England	United States	Maria	3 Oct 1822
Reuben	25	M	Farmer	Great Brittain	U. States	Atticus	25 Apr 1822
William	26	M	Farmer	Great Britain	U. States America	Ann Maria	29 Nov 1821
CHARLETON, F.	19	M	Cabinet Maker	England	United States	Brilliant	24 Sep 1827
CHARLOT, Honorine, Nurse [with Irma Pochon]	28	F	Servant	France	United States	Montano	5 May 1828
CHARLOTTE, Francis	6	M		Gt. Britain	U. States	St. George	20 Sep 1828
Laurence	3	M		Gt. Britain	U. States	St. George	20 Sep 1828

NAMES OF PASSENGERS	AGE	SEX	OCCUPATIONS	COUNTRY TO WHICH THEY BELONG	COUNTRY THEY INTEND TO INHABIT	SHIPS/DATES OF ARRIVAL	
CHARLOTTE (cont'd)							
William	Infant	M		Gt. Britain	U. States	St. George	20 Sep 1828
CHARLTON, Dorothy	17	F	Farmer	Scotland	U. States	Mentor	5 Jul 1825
Ellen	27	F	None	Scotland	U. States	Mentor	5 Jul 1825
Jane	11	F	Farmer	Scotland	U. States	Mentor	5 Jul 1825
John	14	M	child of Charlton, Cabinet Maker, N. York	England	New York	Robert Edwards	17 Mar 1828
John	30	M	Weaver	Ireland	United States	Independence	10 Oct 1821
John F., Mr.	45	M	Musician	England	U. States	Emily	25 Aug 1827
Margt.	12	F	Farmer	Scotland	U. States	Mentor	5 Jul 1825
Michael	22	M	Farmer	Scotland	U. States	Mentor	5 Jul 1825
Penelope	43	F	Wife of Charlton, Cabinet Maker, N. York	England	New York	Robert Edwards	17 Mar 1828
Penelope, Junr.	17	F	child of Charlton, Cabinet Maker, N. York	England	New York	Robert Edwards	17 Mar 1828
Thos.	46	M	Grocer	Scotland	U. States	Mentor	5 Jul 1825
CHARLY, Fany	19	F	Servant	England	U.N. States	Earl of Liverpool	20 Aug 1825
CHARNALES,							
Chas. Francis, Don	23	M	Merchant	France		Seine	16 Jan 1827
CHARNLEY, Joseph	25	M	Calico Printer	England	America	Hercules	2 Nov 1825
Thos.	24	M	Tobacconist	England	England	William Byrnes	14 Apr 1824
CHARNOCH, Robert	20	F	Weaver	England		Aurora	12 Mar 1827
CHARNOCK, John	25	M	Merchant	Great Britain	United States	James Monroe	27 Jul 1821
CHARP, Frederick	11	M	None	England	U. States	Comet	28 Jul 1825
Frederick	40	M	Clock Maker	Swiss	U. States	Comet	28 Jul 1825
Harriet	36	F	None	England	U. States	Comet	28 Jul 1825
Manuel	6	M	None	Swiss	U. States	Comet	28 Jul 1825
CHARPEA, Amelia	22	F		Switzerland	U. States	Criterion	16 May 1825
C. H.	27	M	Mechanic	Switzerland	U. States	Criterion	16 May 1825
C. M.	26	M	Mechanic	Switzerland	U. States	Criterion	16 May 1825
CHARPENTIER, D. B.	41	M	Merchant	U. States	U. States	Edward Bonnaffe	4 May 1827
CHARPER, Mary	24	F	Servant	Wittenburg	U. States	Comet	28 Jul 1825
CHARRIER, —, Madam	23	F		France	U. States	Stephania	8 Mar 1823
Jno. Lewis	26	M	Plume Manufactorer	France	U. States	Stephania	8 Mar 1823
CHARROPPIN,							
Lafond, Mr.	30	M	Planter	Guadaloupe	France	Elizabeth	17 Jul 1823
Maria Augustine, Madam	20	F		Guadaloupe	France	Elizabeth	17 Jul 1823
CHARSELOT, H.	32	M	Merchant	France	United States	Edward Bonnaffe	24 Aug 1827
CHARTERS, ...	24	M	Merchant	Great Briton	U. States	Leontine	10 Jul 1826
Alexr.	27	M	Merchant	Ireland	United States	Florida	14 Sep 1827
Ellen	20	F		Ireland	United States	Florida	14 Sep 1827
John	26	M	Merchant	Ireland	America	Hannibal	4 Oct 1822
Joseph	22			Kilpatric	N. York	Peru	30 May 1828
Marg.	18		Labourer	Downpersmith	U. States	Carolina Ann	14 Feb 1824
Mary	25	F	None	Ireland	America	Hannibal	4 Oct 1822
CHARTON, Eleanor	11	F	Farmer	Scotland	U. States	Mentor	5 Jul 1825
CHARTRAM,							
Charlotte Adelaide	33	F		France	United States	Thetis	5 Jul 1821
CHARTRES, Alexander	26	M	Gentleman	United States	United States	William Bayard	17 May 1825
CHASADA, John	28	M	Weaver	Great Britain	U. States	St. Croix	13 Sep 1827
CHASAWINES, F.	32	M	Merchant	U. States	New York	Howard	11 Jan 1827
CHASE, Benj.	32	M	Mariner	U. States	U. States	La Grange	19 Apr 1826
Charles	21	M	Seaman	New York	New York	Mary & Elizabeth	7 Sep 1824
Damira	7	M				Perseverance	9 Jun 1827
Francis	37	F	Lady	United States	United States	Nimrod	30 Aug 1824
John	37	M	Mariner	U.S.A.	U.S.A.	Noble	5 Nov 1828
Philander, Revd.	50	M	Clergyman	United States	United States	Orbit	30 Aug 1824
Stephen	53	M	Farmer	Great Britan	Cannada	Columbia	11 Aug 1823
CHASHETON,							
Nicholas	32 3/12	M	Merchant	U.S. America	U.S. America	Erie	19 Oct 1829

NAMES OF PASSENGERS	AGE	SEX	OCCUPATIONS	COUNTRY TO WHICH THEY BELONG	COUNTRY THEY INTEND TO INHABIT	SHIPS/DATES OF ARRIVAL	
CHASLYN, Charles	15	M	...	England	America, U.S.	Illinois	3 Jun 1822
Robert	19 3/12	M	...	England	America, U.S.	Illinois	3 Jun 1822
CHASMER, Jane	25	F	None	England	United States	London	21 May 1828
Robert	1	M	None	England	United States	London	21 May 1828
Robert	25	M	Laborer	England	United States	London	21 May 1828
William	4	M	None	England	United States	London	21 May 1828
CHASTANT, Lewis	38	M	Merchant	U. States	U. States	America	7 Apr 1828
CHATARD, Ferdinand E.	23	M	Doctor	U. States	U. States	Sully	15 Jul 1829
J. H.	28	M	Merchant	France	France	William Bayard	25 Apr 1826
P. H.	22	M		France	France	Ambuscade	1 Jul 1820
CHATER, Sarah	5	F	None	England	United States	Martha	17 Sep 1821
CHATFIELD, Alfred	5			England	United States	Caspian	12 Jul 1821
Edward	10			England	United States	Caspian	12 Jul 1821
George	1			England	United States	Caspian	12 Jul 1821
Henry	16			England	United States	Caspian	12 Jul 1821
John	17			England	United States	Caspian	12 Jul 1821
Mary	20			England	United States	Caspian	12 Jul 1821
Richard	13			England	United States	Caspian	12 Jul 1821
Sarah	44			England	United States	Caspian	12 Jul 1821
William	23			England	United States	Caspian	12 Jul 1821
Wm.	49		Coach Trimmer	England	United States	Caspian	12 Jul 1821
CHATHAM, A.	38	F		Great Britain	United States	Isaac Hicks	6 Dec 1827
CHATILLON, —, Infant	8/12	M		Spain	U. States	Cadmus	28 May 1821
—, Madam	24	F		Spain	U. States	Cadmus	28 May 1821
CHATTERNEY, H.	42	M	Merct.	France	U.S.	Stephania	15 Aug 1825
CHATTERSON, John	51	M	Labourer	Great Britain	Great Britain	Nestor	3 Nov 1820
CHATTERTON, David	18 4/12	M	Farmer	England	U.S. of America	Illinois	16 Jun 1821
George	20 9/12	M	Farmer	England	U.S. of America	Illinois	16 Jun 1821
John	11 10/12	M		England	U.S. of America	Illinois	16 Jun 1821
John	30	M	Merchant	England	U. States	Brighton	14 Apr 1828
Jonathan	22 3/12	M	Farmer	England	U.S. of America	Illinois	16 Jun 1821
Lydia	8 4/12	F		England	U.S. of America	Illinois	16 Jun 1821
Martha	6 9/12	F		England	U.S. of America	Illinois	16 Jun 1821
Rebecka	4 4/12	F		England	U.S. of America	Illinois	16 Jun 1821
Sarah	38 8/12	F		England	U.S. of America	Illinois	16 Jun 1821
CHATTIN, Francois	21	M	Spoonmaker	Holland	U. States	Xenophon	15 Sep 1820
CHATTO, Lewis	22	M	Mariner	America	United States	Two Marys	12 Feb 1820
CHATTON, Jos.	33	M	Merchant	U.S.	U.S.	Radius	27 Apr 1824
CHATZ, Thos. J.	29	M	Gentleman	Barbadoes	Barbadoes	Falcon	4 Jun 1825
CHAUNCEY, H.	31	M	Merchant	U. States	U. States	Carlow	20 Apr 1826
John S.	22	M	Lt. U.S. Navy	U. States	U. States	Jasper	17 Jul 1826
Wm.	30	M	Merchant	United States		Hannibal	4 Apr 1823
Wm.	37	M	Merchant	U. States	U. States	Silas Richards	29 Oct 1828
CHAURDIN, —, Madame	32	F		France	U.S.	Edward Quesnel	19 Dec 1826
CHAUREY, Jean	36	F		Gt. Brittan		L'Esperance	6 Sep 1828
John	43	M	Cooper	Gt. Brittan		L'Esperance	6 Sep 1828
Peter	22	M		Gt. Brittan		L'Esperance	6 Sep 1828
CHAUVELOT,							
Caroline	2 6/12	F		France	U. States	Don Quixote	9 Oct 1827
E.	25	F		France	U. States	Don Quixote	9 Oct 1827
CHAVES, Alexr.	12		Scholar			Corsair	2 Oct 1820
Jose	14		Scholar	Havana		Corsair	2 Oct 1820
CHAYTER, William	23	M		Great Britain	United States	Ganges	8 Jul 1820
CHAYTOR, James	50	M	Merchant	U. States	U. States	General Paez	18 Aug 1828
Mary	25	F		Great Britain	United States	Ganges	8 Jul 1820
CHAZOURNES, F.	26	M	Merchant	France	United States	Nestor	6 Jul 1821
CHAZOUSUE, —, Mr.	32	M	Merchant	U. States	U.S.	Henri IV	14 Sep 1827
CHE...E, Thomas	27	...	...	...	United States	Criterion	27 Jun 1827
CHEATHAM, Margaret	20	F		England	United States	William Byrnes	15 Aug 1826
CHEATHEM, Jane	23	F	None	G.B.	U.S.A.	Silas Richard	30 Jun 1828
Mary	3	F	None	G.B.	U.S.A.	Silas Richard	30 Jun 1828
CHEAVEROTE, Chs.	22	M	Clergyman	Germany	U. States	America	22 Sep 1826
CHEBSEY, Charles	52	M	Glass Blower	Ireland	America	Evelina	10 Nov 1825
Esther	22	F	Lady	Ireland	America	Evelina	10 Nov 1825
CHEDEHOUX, Edmound	26	M	Officer in Army	France	England	Canada	4 Oct 1824
CHEDL, Benjamin, Junr.	9	M	None	Merrionthshire	U. States	Manhattan	21 May 1821
Benjn.	47	M	Farmer	Merrionthshire	U. States	Manhattan	21 May 1821
Elizabeth	19	M	None	Merrionthshire	U. States	Manhattan	21 May 1821
Marry	45	M	None	Merrionthshire	U. States	Manhattan	21 May 1821

NAMES OF PASSENGERS	A G E	S E X	OCCUPATIONS	COUNTRY TO WHICH THEY BELONG	COUNTRY THEY INTEND TO INHABIT	SHIPS/DATES OF ARRIVAL	
CHEDWICK, Samuel	21	M	Weaver	England	United States	Aurora	9 Jul 1827
CHEEKS, —, Mrs.	28	F	Farmer	Barbadoes	U. States	Azores	2 Jun 1824
Henrietta	4/12	F	Farmer	Barbadoes	U. States	Azores	2 Jun 1824
John	32	M	Merchant	Gt. Britain	Barbadoes	Crisis	13 Nov 1824
John R.	32	M	Merchant	Barbadoes	U. States	Rambler	8 Jul 1823
Wm.	12	M	Farmer	Barbadoes	U. States	Azores	2 Jun 1824
CHEERMON, B.	13	M	Boy	Barbadoes	Barbadoes	Azores	2 Jun 1824
Robt.	8	M	Boy	Barbadoes	Barbadoes	Azores	2 Jun 1824
Thos.	10	M	Boy	Barbadoes	Barbadoes	Azores	2 Jun 1824
CHEESBROUGH, Henry	45	M	Merchant	U. States	U. States	Pizarro	21 Oct 1825
CHEESEMAN, Ann	2					Corinthian	11 Mar 1829
Anna	11	F	daughter [of John C.]	New York	New York, U.S.	New York	14 Mar 1828
Hannah	36					Corinthian	11 Mar 1829
John C.	40	M	Doctor of Medn.	New York	New York, U.S.	New York	14 Mar 1828
Martha	30	F	Wife [of John C.]	New York	New York, U.S.	New York	14 Mar 1828
Mary	4					Corinthian	11 Mar 1829
Mathew	15					Corinthian	11 Mar 1829
Thimothy M.	3	M	Son [of John C.]	New York	New York, U.S.	New York	14 Mar 1828
CHEESMAN, Ann	26			Great Britain	U. States	Nile	30 Apr 1827
Farrer	3			Great Britain	U. States	Nile	30 Apr 1827
Maria	5			Great Britain	U. States	Nile	30 Apr 1827
Thomas	1			Great Britain	U. States	Nile	30 Apr 1827
Thomas	28			Great Britain	U. States	Nile	30 Apr 1827
William	51	M	Farmer	England	U.S. America	New Hampshire	28 Sep 1826
CHEETCH, Mary	26 2/12	F	None	Great Britain	America	Magnet	13 Nov 1821
CHEETERS, James	32	M	Spinner	England	U. States	Panthea	8 Apr 1826
CHEETHAM, Aaron	66	M	Farmer	Great Britain		Casanda	5 Sep 1827
John	22	M	Weaver	Great Britain	United States	Eliza Barker	3 Jul 1826
CHEEVER, —	28	M	Labourer	Baden	United States	Cavalier	25 Jul 1828
—, Wife	24	F		Baden	United States	Cavalier	25 Jul 1828
CHEGARAZ, F.	47	M	Merchant	United States	United States	Potomac	8 Dec 1826
CHEGUER, Catharan	10			England		Hudson	23 Jul 1828
Chanels	12					Hudson	23 Jul 1828
Martha	41		Boot Maker	England		Hudson	23 Jul 1828
Moran	20					Hudson	23 Jul 1828
Wm.	46		Boot Maker	England		Hudson	23 Jul 1828
CHELL, Mary	28	F	None	Great Britain	United States	Roman	19 Dec 1825
Robert	28	M	Shoe Maker	Great Britain	United States	Roman	19 Dec 1825
CHELTOON, Sarah	31	F	None	Great Briton	United States	Mount Vernon	30 Dec 1828
CHEMIN, Henry	30	M	Clerk	France	U. States	Dublin Packet	8 Feb 1825
CHEMOT, Jeacque	23	M	Weaver	France	U. States	C. Amelia	30 Jun 1828
Jean	31	F	Weaver	France	U. States	C. Amelia	30 Jun 1828
Marguarite	20	F	Wash	France	U. States	C. Amelia	30 Jun 1828
CHENANE, Ellen	25	F	Spinster	Ireland	America	William	21 May 1825
CHENARD, Anthy.	40	M	Merchant	France	United States	Stephania	27 Nov 1826
F.	38	M		France	U. States	Rampart	28 Nov 1823
CHENE, Jno.	50	M	Mechanic	U. States	U. States	Seine	16 Jun 1826
CHENELETTE, Anuel	50	M	Merchant	America	America	Exchange	25 Feb 1822
CHENNEBURG, Cath.	22	F		France	United States	Le Voltaire	19 Jul 1828
Francoise	8	F		France	United States	Le Voltaire	19 Jul 1828
Francoise	13	M		France	United States	Le Voltaire	19 Jul 1828
Jean	18	F		France	United States	Le Voltaire	19 Jul 1828
Joseph	15	M		France	United States	Le Voltaire	19 Jul 1828
Joseph	44	M	Farmer	France	United States	Le Voltaire	19 Jul 1828
Margt.	11	F		France	United States	Le Voltaire	19 Jul 1828
Marie	17	F		France	United States	Le Voltaire	19 Jul 1828
Marie	47	F		France	United States	Le Voltaire	19 Jul 1828
CHENNIS, ...am	26	M	Labourer	Great Brittain	United States	Sarah Ralston	27 Jan 1827
CHEQUER, Wm.	20	M	Servant			Helen	4 Aug 1829
CHERIOT, Henry	60	M	Merchant	France	U. States	Sea Serpent	21 Apr 1821
CHERONNET, Leon	24 6/12	M	Architect	French	French	Howard	4 May 1827
CHERRIAN, —, Miss	22	F		St. Domingo	United States	Paquet des Cayes	26 May 1828
CHERRIAUD, —, Madr.	42	F	None	Aux Cayes	Aux Cayes	Paquet des Cayes	10 Mar 1828
CHERRY, William	33	M	Weaver	Scotland	United States	Camillus	27 Oct 1829
CHERRYTREE, Trueman	26	M	Merchant	United States	United States	Wanderer	31 Aug 1829
CHESEMAN, Ann	3	F	Wife	G. Brittan	U. States	Henry	24 Oct 1828

NAMES OF PASSENGERS	AGE	SEX	OCCUPATIONS	COUNTRY TO WHICH THEY BELONG	COUNTRY THEY INTEND TO INHABIT	SHIPS/DATES OF ARRIVAL	
CHESEMAN (cont'd)							
Ann	35	F	Wife		U. States	Henry	24 Oct 1828
Ann	46	F	Wife	G. Brittan	U. States	Henry	24 Oct 1828
G.	7/12	M		G. Brittan	U. States	Henry	24 Oct 1828
J.	6	M			U. States	Henry	24 Oct 1828
Jacob	36	M	Carpenter	G. Brittan	U. States	Henry	24 Oct 1828
Mary	8	F	Wife	G. Brittan	U. States	Henry	24 Oct 1828
R.	11	F			U. States	Henry	24 Oct 1828
CHESHIRE, Emma	3					Hudson	5 Apr 1826
Geo.	24		Baker	England	United States	Hudson	5 Apr 1826
John	25	M	Lawler	Great Britain	U. States	Columbia	22 Sep 1828
Mary	26					Hudson	5 Apr 1826
CHESHOLM, —, Mrs.	63	F		Scotland	U. States	Hunter	19 Nov 1821
Donald	30	M	Blacksmith	Scotland	U. States	Hunter	19 Nov 1821
Jane	28	F		Scotland	U. States	Hunter	19 Nov 1821
Nancy	32	F		Scotland	U. States	Hunter	19 Nov 1821
Wm.	34	M	Blacksmith	Scotland	U. States	Hunter	19 Nov 1821
CHESLEY, Maria	25	F	Spinster	Ireland	United States	Dublin Packet	9 Jul 1827
CHESLIEN, George	17	M	Farmer	England		Marchioness	13 May 1828
William	16	M	Farmer	England		Marchioness	13 May 1828
CHESMOR, —, Mrs., & five children	40	F		Gt. Britain	U.S.	Robert Edwards	11 Nov 1822
CHESNUT, Sally	27		Servant	Ireland	Great Britain	Robert Burns	14 Jun 1824
CHESTER, —, Mrs.	24		None	New York	United States	William Thompson	13 May 1823
Elizabeth	30	F	Domestic	Great Britain	United States	India	5 Sep 1827
Johanna G.	21	M	Taylor	Wertemberg	Wertemberg	Edward Quesnel	3 Jul 1829
Nicholas	41 4/12	M	Merchant	England	England	Calais Packet	6 Nov 1828
Thomas	34	M	Shoemaker	Great Britain	United States	Spartan	25 Jul 1821
W., Mr.	35		Merchant	Connecticut	United States	William Thompson	13 May 1823
CHESTERMAN, Ame	25	F		Great Britain	U. States	Corinthian	2 Sep 1824
CHESTFIELD, Geo.	19	M	Farmer	Rye, England	United States	William	21 May 1828
Mary	25	F		Rye, England	United States	William	21 May 1828
Samuel	6	M	Farmer	Rye, England	United States	William	21 May 1828
CHESTON, William	24	M	Carpenter	U. States	U. States	Sall & Hope	12 Jul 1820
CHEVARD, Desire	20	M	Merchant	U. States	U. States	Marmion	29 Sep 1823
CHEVARSSE, F. X., Mr.	24		Merchant	France	New York	Romulus	15 May 1828
CHEVAT, Maria Threse	30	F		France	United States	New England	29 Aug 1828
CHEVER, Jas. W.	36	M	Mariner	Salem	U. States	Cygnet	17 Jan 1824
Thomas H.	24	M	Merchant	America	America	Minerva	8 Oct 1824
CHEVERIN, J.	41	M	Farmer	Germany	U. States	Isabella	10 Aug 1829
Johannes	8	M		Germany	U. States	Isabella	10 Aug 1829
Margareta	6 6/12	F		Germany	U. States	Isabella	10 Aug 1829
Margareta	38	F	Farmer	Germany	U. States	Isabella	10 Aug 1829
CHEVFILLS, G.	40	M	Mariner	Quebec	Quebec	Vermont	10 Jan 1827
CHEVROLAT, Hyppolite	28 3/12	M	Merchant	France	New York	Cadmus	19 Aug 1823
CHEW, Hannah	30	F	Wife	Great Brittain	United States	Corinthian	9 Jan 1827
Richard	35	M	Spinster	Great Brittain	United States	Corinthian	9 Jan 1827
S. C.	19	M	Gentleman	Connecticut	U. States	Seine	30 Aug 1824
CHEYNE, Wm., Mr.	21	M	Surgeon	Edenburgh	U. States	United States	29 Nov 1823
CHIA, John	27	M	Labourer	Ireland	Boston	General Marion	12 Jan 1829
CHICKAOS, Carolin	22	F		Germany	Unsurton	Orient	25 Nov 1825
Peter	35	M	Mechanic	Germany	Unsurton	Orient	25 Nov 1825
CHIDLY, Ann	20	F	Spinster	Ireland		Robert Fulton	4 Jun 1828
CHIFFMAN, —, Mrs.	25	F	Farmer	Switzerland	U. States	Seine	30 Aug 1824
D.	3	M	Farmer	Switzerland	U. States	Seine	30 Aug 1824
John	27	M	Farmer	Switzerland	U. States	Seine	30 Aug 1824
CHIGNE, Elizabeth	28	F		Germany	U. States	Isabella	10 Aug 1829
Johannes	28	M	Farmer	Germany	U. States	Isabella	10 Aug 1829
CHILCOT, John	38	M	Secretary	Great Britan	Great Britan	Columbia	11 Aug 1823
CHILD, Betsey M., Mrs.						Gratitude	3 Oct 1829
Charlotte	2	F		Great Britain	New York	Hesperus	13 Oct 1825
Daniel	45	M	Farmer	England	United States	Warrior	6 Oct 1828
Edward V.	25	M	Gent	U.S.	Boston	Silvanus Jenkins	27 Jul 1829
Elizabeth	10	F	None	England	United States	London	21 May 1828
Jasmana L.	10	F		Great Britain	New York	Hesperus	13 Oct 1825

NAMES OF PASSENGERS	AGE	SEX	OCCUPATIONS	COUNTRY TO WHICH THEY BELONG	COUNTRY THEY INTEND TO INHABIT	SHIPS/DATES OF ARRIVAL	
CHILD (cont'd)							
John	3/12	M		Great Britain	New York	Hesperus	13 Oct 1825
*Died							
John	3	M	None	England	United States	London	21 May 1828
John	23			Ireland	Philidelphia	General Marion	21 Nov 1828
Joseph	8	M		Great Britain	New York	Hesperus	13 Oct 1825
Joseph S.	36	M	...	Great Britain	New York	Hesperus	13 Oct 1825
Mary	11	F		Great Britair	New York	Hesperus	13 Oct 1825
Mary	12	F	None	Eng˙	United States	London	21 May 1828
Penelope	30	F		Great Bı...ain	New York	Hesperus	13 Oct 1825
Sarah	34	F	None	England	United States	London	21 May 1828
Sarah Jane	5	F	None	England	United States	London	21 May 1828
William	8	M	None	England	United States	London	21 May 1828
William	38	M	Laborer	England	United States	London	21 May 1828
CHILDS, C. B.	34	M	Navy	U. States	U. States	Eliza	13 Nov 1824
Fras.	17	M		England	United States	Ann Maria	27 Aug 1822
Lewis	9	M				Helen	4 Aug 1829
CHILLET, Francoise	7	F		France	United States	Le Voltaire	19 Jul 1828
Joseph	40	M	Weaver	France	United States	Le Voltaire	19 Jul 1828
Josh.	5	M		France	United States	Le Voltaire	19 Jul 1828
Margt. M.	30	F		France	United States	Le Voltaire	19 Jul 1828
Marie	9	F		France	United States	Le Voltaire	19 Jul 1828
Victorie	2	M		France	United States	Le Voltaire	19 Jul 1828
CHILLUS, David	2	M	...	England	United States	Milton	20 Oct 1827
Elinor	1...	F	...	England	United States	Milton	20 Oct 1827
Isabella	40	F	...	England	United States	Milton	20 Oct 1827
Louiser	11	F	...	England	United States	Milton	20 Oct 1827
CHILOES, Arthur	1	M	None	England	United States	Trident	18 Jul 1827
Margaret	20	F	None	England	United States	Trident	18 Jul 1827
CHILTON, Charles	19	M	Gentleman	Virginia	Virginia	Jupiter	27 May 1826
Thos.	29	M	Blacksmith	Ireland	United States	St. George	25 Aug 1829
CHIN, Caroline	3	F	None	Gt. Britain	United States	Crisis	13 Nov 1824
Ellen	39	F	None	Gt. Britain	United States	Crisis	13 Nov 1824
Frederick	20	M	Butcher	England	United States	Cosmo	26 Aug 1829
Geo.	3	M	None	Gt. Britain	United States	Crisis	13 Nov 1824
Geo.	10	M	None	Gt. Britain	United States	Crisis	13 Nov 1824
Michael	27	M	Labourer	Ireland	U. States	St. Michaels	25 Apr 1825
Samuel	5	M	None	Gt. Britain	United States	Crisis	13 Nov 1824
Wm.	8	M	None	Gt. Britain	United States	Crisis	13 Nov 1824
CHINA, A.		M	Merchant	U. States	U. States	Maria	2 Apr 1827
CHINAR, —	21	M	Cabinet Maker	France	United States	Stephania	24 Mar 1828
CHINCH, Benjamin	23	M	Merchant	New York	St. Andrews	Champion	27 Dec 1827
CHINDLER, Caroline	23	F		Bardin	U. States	Bayard	5 Sep 1828
Ch.	45	M	Talor	Bardin	U. States	Bayard	5 Sep 1828
Christian	3	F		Bardin	U. States	Bayard	5 Sep 1828
Dorthea	49	M		Bardin	U. States	Bayard	5 Sep 1828
Eliz.	27	F		Bardin	U. States	Bayard	5 Sep 1828
G. A.	28	M		Bardin	U. States	Bayard	5 Sep 1828
J. H.	17	M	Farmer	Bardin	U. States	Bayard	5 Sep 1828
Jacob	2	M		Bardin	U. States	Bayard	5 Sep 1828
Jacob	32	M		Bardin	U. States	Bayard	5 Sep 1828
CHINNS, Hny.	40	M	Farmer	Scotland	U. States	Roger Stewart	9 Jun 1828
Margaret	40	F	Farmer	Scotland	U. States	Roger Stewart	9 Jun 1828
CHINNY, Ann	30	F	None	Great Britian	United States	George Clinton	21 Oct 1826
Eliza	6/12	F	None	Great Britian	United States	George Clinton	21 Oct 1826
James	4	M	None	Great Britian	United States	George Clinton	21 Oct 1826
Susannah	6	F	None	Great Britian	United States	George Clinton	21 Oct 1826
CHINY, James	32	M	Stone Cutter	Great Britian	United States	George Clinton	21 Oct 1826
CHIO, A.	43	M	Merchant	France	U. States	Annawan	3 Apr 1826
CHIPMAN, —, Lady	26	F		Province of New Brunswick	to return to New Brunswick	Loire	23 May 1821
...	35	M	Gentleman	Great Britian	United States	London	24 Jun 1823
...	35	F		Great Britian	United States	London	24 Jun 1823
Edward	36	M	Merchant	Virginia	New York	Ann Howard	30 Dec 1828
Joseph	20	M	Doctor	Newbrunsick	Newbrunsick	Nancy	23 Oct 1823
Ward, Junr. Esqr.	30	M	His B. M. Agent under the fifth Article of the Treaty of Ghent	Province of New Brunswick	to return to New Brunswick	Loire	23 May 1821

NAMES OF PASSENGERS	AGE	SEX	OCCUPATIONS	COUNTRY TO WHICH THEY BELONG	COUNTRY THEY INTEND TO INHABIT	SHIPS/DATES OF ARRIVAL	
CHIPMAN (cont'd)							
Ward, The Honble	50	M	His B. M. Agent under the fifth Article of the Treaty of Ghent	Province of New Brunswick	to return to New Brunswick	Loire	23 May 1821
CHIRM, Robert	28 3/12	M	Farmer	Ireland	America	St. Michaels	25 Nov 1825
CHIS, Leonarde	62	F	Merchant	France	France	Henry	16 May 1827
CHISAN, Eliza	30	F		G. Britain	U. States	Wanderer	23 Jun 1828
Hugh	8	M		G. Britain	U. States	Wanderer	23 Jun 1828
CHISCHAM, Edwd.	18	M	Merchant	U. States	U. States	Hopes Delight	6 Aug 1823
CHISHOLM, Amelia	1 1/12	F		Scotland	United States	Mobile	21 Aug 1827
Donald A.	30	M	Merchant	U. States	United States	Tampico	13 May 1828
Elizabeth	17 4/12	F		Scotland	United States	Mobile	21 Aug 1827
Isabella, Mrs.	21 4/12	F		Scotland	United States	Mobile	21 Aug 1827
Robert	30	M	Dyer	Great Britain	United States	Courier	26 Jun 1827
CHISHOLME, Jane	60	F	Mother	G. Britain	U. States	Hynd	12 Jul 1820
CHISMEN, Henry	35	M	Merchant	Great Britain	Canada	Martha	3 May 1821
CHISNEAU, C.	41	M	Mariner	Spain	U. States	Maria Ann	29 Sep 1823
*landed at Balize [Biloxi?], Missippi							
CHISOLM, Jno. H.	25	M	Merchant	A.M.	U. States	Edgar	23 Nov 1824
CHITTENDEN, Eliz.	60	F		Switzerland	U.States	C. Amelia	30 Jun 1828
Stephen	20 4/12	M	Farmer	England	United States	Young Phoenix	26 Jul 1824
William	38		Carpenter	England	S. New York	Xenophon	25 Jul 1826
William Francis	13		Carpenter	England	S. New York	Xenophon	25 Jul 1826
CHITTEY, Willm.	26	M	Servant	Great Britain	U. States	Ann Marria	6 Aug 1823
CHIUCH, Philip	30	M	Brewer	United States	United States	Globe	30 Aug 1828
CHIVANTEAU, Ferdinand	21	M	Merchant	France	France	Isaac Hicks	22 Aug 1829
CHOATE, Florence	2 6/12	F		United States	United States	Samuel Robertson	5 Oct 1827
Jos.	27	M	Mechanic	Connecticutt	U. States	Benjamin	1 Jun 1822
Susan, Mrs.	21	F		United States	United States	Samuel Robertson	5 Oct 1827
Susan M.	1 6/12	F		United States	United States	Samuel Robertson	5 Oct 1827
CHOL, Francis	24	M		France	France	Montano	15 Jan 1829
Nancy	20	F		France	France	Montano	15 Jan 1829
CHOLLER, Lewis	18	M	Farmer	U. States	U. States	Combine	12 Nov 1821
CHORLEY, Charles	24	M	Merchant	G. Briton	United States	James Monroe	14 Dec 1820
CHOTTIN, F.	27	M	Merchant	France	U. States	L'Egide	8 Jun 1824
CHOW, James	14	M		England		Edward Quesnel	17 Nov 1828
CHRANLEY, Ml.	18	M		Ireland	U. States	Alex Mansfield	1 Jun 1822
CHRET..., Catharin	8	F		Switzerland		Pallas	14 Jun 1828
Catharin L.	3	F		Switzerland		Pallas	14 Jun 1828
Easter F.	13	M		Switzerland		Pallas	14 Jun 1828
George F.	10	M		Switzerland		Pallas	14 Jun 1828
Jaque C.	6	F	Farmer	Switzerland		Pallas	14 Jun 1828
Julie	6	F		Switzerland		Pallas	14 Jun 1828
Pe... F.	...	M		Switzerland		Pallas	14 Jun 1828
Perre F.	1	M		Switzerland		Pallas	14 Jun 1828
Susannah C.	...	F		Switzerland		Pallas	14 Jun 1828
CHRISFIELD, William	20	M		G. Britain	New York	Brighton	26 Mar 1827
CHRISHOLIN, James	25	M	Farmer	England	U. States	Emulous	22 Aug 1828
Mary	3/12	F		England	U. States	Emulous	22 Aug 1828
Mary	20	F		England	U. States	Emulous	22 Aug 1828
CHRISHOLM, Thomas	18	M	None	Great Britain	Canada	Roman	19 Dec 1825
CHRISHOLME, Isabella	40	F	Daughter	G. Britain	U. States	Hynd	12 Jul 1820
CHRISIAN, José	34	M	Servant	Mexico	Mexico	Virginia	9 Feb 1829
CHRIST..., A...m	59	M	Planter	Great Britain	Great Britain	Ann Maria	17 Apr 1827
CHRISTAL, Timothy	18	M	Labourer	Ireland	U. States	Wanderer	1 Sep 1828
CHRISTANIO, S.	30	M	Painter	Portugal	Portugal	Dart	8 Oct 1821
CHRISTEN, J. C.	32	M	Farmer	Great Britain	United States	Isaac Hicks	6 Dec 1827
CHRISTENER, Barbi	12		Turner	France	U. States	Elizabeth	9 Jul 1825
Christ.	10		Turner	France	U. States	Elizabeth	9 Jul 1825
John	41		Turner	France	U. States	Elizabeth	9 Jul 1825
Maria	41		Turner	France	U. States	Elizabeth	9 Jul 1825
Peter	6		Turner	France	U. States	Elizabeth	9 Jul 1825
Trene	4		Turner	France	U. States	Elizabeth	9 Jul 1825
CHRISTERLAM, Julia	24	F	Gent	France	U. States	Charlemagne	19 Sep 1828
CHRISTEY, Alias	40	M	Farmer	Great Brittain	United States	Active	12 Sep 1828

NAMES OF PASSENGERS	AGE	SEX	OCCUPATIONS	COUNTRY TO WHICH THEY BELONG	COUNTRY THEY INTEND TO INHABIT	SHIPS/DATES OF ARRIVAL	
CHRISTEY (cont'd)							
Eliza	2	F		Great Brittain	United States	Active	12 Sep 1828
John	6	M		Great Brittain	United States	Active	12 Sep 1828
Margret	8	F		Great Brittain	United States	Active	12 Sep 1828
Mary	40	F		Great Brittain	United States	Active	12 Sep 1828
William	4	M		Great Brittain	United States	Active	12 Sep 1828
CHRISTHOLM, Alexr.	28	M	Merchant	U. States	U. States	General Marion	12 Jul 1823
CHRISTIAL, Michael	25	M	Weaver	Ireland	U. States	Wanderer	1 Sep 1828
CHRISTIAN, Catharin	5			England	United States	Thomas Dickason	5 Jun 1827
Catharine	4	F		Switzerland	United States	Howard	27 Sep 1824
Catharine	22	F		Switzerland	United States	Howard	27 Sep 1824
Cathr.	20	F		England	United States	Nimrod	31 Jul 1828
Daniel	7	M		England	U. States	Pacific	17 Jun 1828
Daniel	10			England	United States	Thomas Dickason	5 Jun 1827
Elizabeth	15			England	United States	Thomas Dickason	5 Jun 1827
Enean	43		Mill Right	England	United States	Thomas Dickason	5 Jun 1827
Jane	3	F		England	U. States	Pacific	17 Jun 1828
Jane	7			England	United States	Thomas Dickason	5 Jun 1827
Jane	40			England	United States	Thomas Dickason	5 Jun 1827
Jas.	32	M	Farmer	England	U. States	Pacific	17 Jun 1828
Jno.	60	M	Farmer	England	United States	Essex	23 May 1828
John	22	M				Eliza Grant	6 Oct 1828
Margaret	3			England	United States	Thomas Dickason	5 Jun 1827
Margt.	42	F		England	U. States	Pacific	17 Jun 1828
Mary Ann	5	F		England	U. States	Pacific	17 Jun 1828
May	30	F		England	U. States	Pacific	17 Jun 1828
Peter	35 7/12	M	Merchant	America	America	Elias Burger	19 Dec 1820
Pether	28	M	Harness Maker	Switzerland	United States	Howard	27 Sep 1824
Sarah	23	F	None	England	United States	St. George	25 Aug 1829
Sarah	23	M		England	United States	St. George	25 Aug 1829
William	13			England	United States	Thomas Dickason	5 Jun 1827
Wm.	19		Labourer	England	United States	Hugh Johnson	11 Jun 1828
Wm.	20	M	Labourer	England	United States	Nimrod	31 Jul 1828
Wm.	38	M	Weaver	England	U. States	Pacific	17 Jun 1828
CHRISTIANSON,							
Rasmus	7	M	Farmer	Norway	United States	Salem	31 Aug 1829
CHRISTIE, —, Miss	19	F		Scotland	Jamaica	Little Cherub	11 Aug 1825
—, Mr.	35	M	Military	Mexico	Mexico	Pulaski	19 Oct 1825
Andrew	5			Great Britain	United States	Camillus	12 Sep 1827
Andrew	50	M		Scotland	United States	Camillus	9 May 1827
Catherin, Miss	12	F	None	Great Britan	U. States	Columbia	10 Mar 1824
Daniel	40	M	Labourer	Paisley, Abby [Parish], Renfrew [County]	New York	Hero	19 May 1828
*to look for Employment							
David	25	M	Merchant	Scotland	United States	Cato	8 Aug 1825
Helen	24	F		Abernethy, Abernethy [Parish], Perth [County]	New York	Hero	19 May 1828
*going to her friends							
Isabella	27		going to her friends	Great Britain	United States	Camillus	12 Sep 1827
James	19	M	Mariner	Scotland	U.S. America	Columbia	31 Jul 1826
Jane	3			Great Britain	United States	Camillus	12 Sep 1827
Jas. M.	58	M	Merchant	United States	New York	Elizabeth	9 Aug 1821
John	7			Great Britain	United States	Camillus	12 Sep 1827
Lawrence	35 11/12	M	Nail Maker	America	America	Peacock	26 Jul 1820
Mary, Miss	20	F	None	Great Britan	U. States	Columbia	10 Mar 1824
Richard	25	M	Merchant	Great Britain	United States	Pacific	7 May 1827

NAMES OF PASSENGERS	AGE	SEX	OCCUPATIONS	COUNTRY TO WHICH THEY BELONG	COUNTRY THEY INTEND TO INHABIT	SHIPS/DATES OF ARRIVAL	
CHRISTIN, Coplin	62	M	Farmer	France	United States	Belmont	30 Aug 1828
Enos	21	M	Farmer	England	U. States	Emulous	22 Aug 1828
CHRISTINA, Louis	55	M	Farmer	England	U.S.	Maria Caroline	12 Jul 1820
CHRISTMAN, Cathr.	24	F	Domestic	France	United States	Cavalier	25 Jul 1828
CHRISTMAS, —	48	M	Servant	St. Thomas	St. Thomas, U. States	Signal	11 Jul 1826
Elizabeth	1	F				Betsey	17 Aug 1820
Harriot	2	F				Betsey	17 Aug 1820
Harriot, Mrs.	27	F				Betsey	17 Aug 1820
John	27	M				Washington	16 Sep 1820
CHRISTOPHE, —, his Wife	45	F		France	United States	Cavalier	25 Jul 1828
R.	21	M	Labourer	France	United States	Cavalier	25 Jul 1828
CHRISTOPHER, Frans.	20	M	Merchant	Spain	Matanzas	William	14 Oct 1824
Henry	25	M	Labourer	Ireland	United States	Edwin	29 Nov 1828
Lod. Jacques	50	M	Carrier	France	United States	Elizabeth	4 Sep 1826
Patrick	23	M	Weaver	Ireland	Ireland	Sarah G.	28 Nov 1827
CHRISTOPHERSON, Christopher	10	M	Farmer	Norway	United States	Salem	31 Aug 1829
CHRISTY, A.	22	M	Farmer	Ireland	United States	Princess Charlotte	6 Oct 1827
A.	24	M	Labourer	Ireland	United States	Princess Charlotte	6 Oct 1827
B.	23	F	None	Ireland	United States	Princess Charlotte	6 Oct 1827
C.	20	M	Farmer	Ireland	United States	Princess Charlotte	6 Oct 1827
Charles	2	M	None	Ireland	United States	Princess Charlotte	6 Oct 1827
Elizabeth	12	F	None	Ireland	United States	Princess Charlotte	6 Oct 1827
Margaret	16	F	None	Ireland	United States	Princess Charlotte	6 Oct 1827
Mary	16 9/12	F	Spinster	Ireland	U. States	Josephine	30 Aug 1828
Mary	30	F	Wife	Ireland	United States	Nancy	16 Aug 1824
May Ann	18	F	None	Ireland	United States	Princess Charlotte	6 Oct 1827
Neal	4	M	Child	Ireland	United States	Nancy	16 Aug 1824
Peggy	5	F	Child	Ireland	United States	Nancy	16 Aug 1824
CHRITIN, Andrew	60 6/12	M	Farmer	Great Britain	United States	Robert Fulton	18 May 1825
Harriett	24	F	None	Great Britain	United States	Robert Fulton	18 May 1825
Jannett	62	F	None	Great Britain	United States	Robert Fulton	18 May 1825
Thomas	1 4/12	M	None	Great Britain	United States	Robert Fulton	18 May 1825
Thomas	23 6/12	M	Farmer	Great Britain	United States	Robert Fulton	18 May 1825
CHUB, Mary	45			England	England	Corinthian	8 Oct 1828
CHUBB, Emma	1	F	None	G. Britain	U. States	Rosalie	22 Aug 1820
Jeremiah	30	M	Mechanick	England	U.S.	Maria Caroline	12 Jul 1820
Lydia	8	F	None	G. Britain	U. States	Rosalie	22 Aug 1820
Lydia	30	F	None	G. Britain	U. States	Rosalie	22 Aug 1820
Wm.	4	M	None	G. Britain	U. States	Rosalie	22 Aug 1820
Wm.	30	M	Brushmaker	G. Britain	U. States	Rosalie	22 Aug 1820
CHUCRE, Elizabeth	20	F		Germany	U. States	Isabella	10 Aug 1829
Elizabeth	56	F		Germany	U. States	Isabella	10 Aug 1829
Jacob	60	M	Shoemaker	Germany	U. States	Isabella	10 Aug 1829
Johannes	19	M		Germany	U. States	Isabella	10 Aug 1829
CHULLE, Bernard	28	M	Tailor	Atherton, England	Gt. Britain	Orozimbo	19 Oct 1822
Eliza	12	F	Tailor	Atherton, England	Gt. Britain	Orozimbo	19 Oct 1822
Mary	27	M	Tailor	Atherton, England	Gt. Britain	Orozimbo	19 Oct 1822
CHULLON, Louisa	40	F	Merchant	U. States	U. States	Purrington	14 May 1827
CHUPPLE, J.	46	M	Merchant	Island Cuba	U. States	Havana Packet	27 Jul 1827
CHUR, Frederick	27	M	Black Smith	Germany	United States	Helen	5 Sep 1828
CHURCH, ...	...	M		England	U. States	Elizabeth	17 May 1822
...at	11	M		England	U. States	Elizabeth	17 May 1822
Edmond	18	M	None	U. States	U. States	Belville	5 Jul 1827
John	6	M		England	U. States	Elizabeth	17 May 1822

NAMES OF PASSENGERS	AGE	SEX	OCCUPATIONS	COUNTRY TO WHICH THEY BELONG	COUNTRY THEY INTEND TO INHABIT	SHIPS/DATES OF ARRIVAL	
CHURCH (cont'd)							
Samuel	40	M	Cooper	United States		Silk Worm	6 Mar 1820
*died 6 Feb							
Sarah	30	F		England	U. States	Elizabeth	17 May 1822
Sarah, Jr.	...	F		England	U. States	Elizabeth	17 May 1822
CHURCHHILL, Mary	24	F	Wife	New York	New York, U.S.	New York	14 Mar 1828
William	26	M	Merchant	New York	New York, U.S.	New York	14 Mar 1828
CHURCHILL, Henry	36	M	Farmer	England	America	Francis & Henrietta	11 Jul 1823
Stephen	40	M	Shipmaster	U. States	U. States	Tabasco	5 Aug 1826
CHURCHMAN, Charles	33	M	Merchant	G. Britain	G. Britain	Jane	18 Feb 1825
CHURCHOFER, Philip	27		Miller	France	U. States	Parachute	14 May 1828
CHUTE, Ellen	55	F		Ireland	America	Liverpool	31 Aug 1827
CID, Emanuel	35	M	Merct.	Havana	U. States	Greek	3 Aug 1825
Maria	21	F		Havana	U. States	Greek	3 Aug 1825
CIELAND, —, Miss	35	F		W. Indies	U. States	Jane	22 Mar 1824
CILDWELL, Fanny	20	F	Spinster	Great Britain	U. States	Morning Star	9 Nov 1824
Jane	13	F	Spinster	Great Britain	U. States	Morning Star	9 Nov 1824
CILLEN, Dennis	28	M		Ireland	U. States	Howard	25 Jul 1823
CILLER, D. J. M.	28		Merchant		U. States	Charlotte Corday	15 Jul 1820
CILLON, P. N.	34	M	Gentleman	France	U.S.A.	Noble	2 Nov 1826
CILPLES, Lewis	45 2/12	M	Merchant	U.S.A.	U. States	Silas Richards	27 Oct 1826
CINGAR, Anthony	7	M	Servant	Cuba	United States	Saluda	14 May 1827
CINNINGHE, Catharn	36	F		G. Britan	U. States	William Neilson	26 Jul 1828
CINTNEY, John	56	M	Tailor	Gt. Britain	U. States	Henry Kneeland	25 Sep 1827
CINTREE, Sibbilla	24	F		Pennsylvania		London	29 Apr 1824
CINUEL, John	25	M	Laborer	Ireland	United States	Lord Wellington	14 Nov 1827
CIPRIANA, —	14	M	Servant	France	U. States	Grampus	14 Apr 1823
CIRDMORE, Wm.	19	M	Shoemaker	Ireland	America	Parrington	9 Jun 1827
CIRSOVINS, Helen, Mrs.	24	F		Denmark	U.S. of America	Canada	1 Oct 1827
CISNERO, M.	30	M	Merchant	Spain	Spain	Richmond Packet	30 Oct 1827
CIVILAND, Bridget	30	F	Labourer			Lady Hunter	10 Jul 1826
Ellen	3	F	Girl	Ireland	U.S.	Lady Hunter	10 Jul 1826
John	1 6/12	M	Boy	Ireland	U.S.	Lady Hunter	10 Jul 1826
Mat	6	M	Boy	Ireland	U.S.	Lady Hunter	10 Jul 1826
Pat	28	M	Labourer	Ireland	U.S.	Lady Hunter	10 Jul 1826
CL..., ...	...	...	...	...	...	William Thompson	30 Sep 1824
CL...BERT, Ellen	20	F	...	...	...	Braganza	8 Aug 1825
CL...CHETT, William	27	M	Merchant	United States	United States	John Wells	18 Sep 1826
CL...S, —, Mr.	...	...	...	...	...	William Thompson	30 Sep 1824
CLACK, John	21	M	Tin Smith	Scotland	U. States	Rosina	27 Feb 1824
CLACKSON, Allan	24	M	Farmer	Ireland	Philadelphia	Angelica	18 Aug 1823
CLAFARTY, Anna	22	F				Catherine	19 Aug 1825
John	19	M	Weaver			Catherine	19 Aug 1825
CLAFFATON, Thos.	30	M	Draper	Great Britain		Moro Castle	6 Jul 1827
CLAGG, Henry	27	M	Mason	England	Boston	Curler	7 Jul 1827
John	25	M	Weaver	England	Boston	Curler	7 Jul 1827
CLAGGETT, H. B.	21	M	Merchant	America	United States	Maria Theresa	28 Aug 1821
CLAHILL, Joseph	25	M	Turner	Great Britain		Moro Castle	6 Jul 1827
CLAIR, Louis	14	M	Student	Point Peter	France	Pacific	14 May 1827
CLAISTON, Sarah	...			L...	England	Great Britain	7 May 1827
CLAN, Francis Y. N.	21	M	Merchant	Spain	U. States	Dromo	4 May 1827
CLANCEY, Honora	18	F	Spinster	Ireland	United States	Diana	1 May 1826
CLANCY, Ann	24	F	Lady	Ireland	United States	South Carolina Packet	25 Mar 1820
Elenor	24	F	Farmer, Labourer or Spinster	Ireland	U. States	Meteor	4 Oct 1827
Eliza	2 3/12	F	Child	Ireland	United States	South Carolina Packet	25 Mar 1820
George	30	M	Gentleman	Ireland	United States	South Carolina Packet	25 Mar 1820
Issabella	45	F	None	Great Britain	United States	Friends	13 Jun 1825
James	21	M	Labourer	U. States	U. States	United States	11 Sep 1828
Mary	18	F	Servt.	Sligo	New York	Susquehana	27 Jun 1823
Mary	27			Cormick	Gt. Britain	Enterprize	19 Feb 1822
William	35	M	Labourer	Ireland	U.S. America	Traveller	10 Sep 1827

NAMES OF PASSENGERS	AGE	SEX	OCCUPATIONS	COUNTRY TO WHICH THEY BELONG	COUNTRY THEY INTEND TO INHABIT	SHIPS/DATES OF ARRIVAL	
CLANEY, M.	20	M	Labourer	England	U. States	Comet	23 Aug 1828
CLANNON, Bridget	60	F	Spinster	Ireland	United States	Dublin Packet	9 Jul 1827
Catherine	20	F	Spinster	Ireland	United States	Dublin Packet	9 Jul 1827
Eleanor	21	F	Spinster	Ireland	New York	Wilson	28 Aug 1822
Robert	15	M	Labourer	Ireland	New York	Wilson	28 Aug 1822
CLAPHAM, —	28	M	Farmer	American	America	Mary Lord	26 Oct 1829
Martha	20	F		Gt. Britain	United States	Meteor	19 Aug 1829
William	24	M	Weaver	Gt. Britain	United States	Meteor	19 Aug 1829
CLAPLIN, Eliza, Miss	17	F	Yeoman	England	U. States	Acasta	11 Dec 1826
George, Master	15	M	Yeoman	England	U. States	Acasta	11 Dec 1826
CLAPP, Ambrose	3	M			U. States America	Cambria	2 Jul 1821
Benjamin	26	M	Gentleman	United States	United States	Elias Burger	25 Feb 1820
George	12	M			U. States America	Cambria	2 Jul 1821
George	48	M	Farmer	England	U. States America	Cambria	2 Jul 1821
Hannah	9	F			U. States America	Cambria	2 Jul 1821
John	16	M			U. States America	Cambria	2 Jul 1821
Richard	10	M			U. States America	Cambria	2 Jul 1821
Sarah	40	F			U. States America	Cambria	2 Jul 1821
CLAPSON, William	17	M	Farmer	England	New York	Chelsea	16 May 1828
CLARCK, James	21	M	Weaver	Ireland	United States	Fabius	4 Jun 1828
Wm.	23	M	Mechanic	England	United States	John Wells	15 Jan 1827
CLARDANEY, David	40	M	Farmer	U. States	G. Britain	Nancy	10 Jul 1820
CLARE, H.	35	M	Mechanic	U. States	U. States	Betsey	23 Jul 1824
CLAREDGE, P. J.	54	M	Merchant	United States	United States	Robert Edwards	3 Oct 1829
CLARENCE, Jack	23	M	Laborer	Ireland	United States	St. Michaels	23 Dec 1826
CLAREY, Anne	1					Trio	5 May 1828
Cathe., Jr.	14					Trio	5 May 1828
Catherine	36					Trio	5 May 1828
Edward	6					Trio	5 May 1828
J. C.	24	M	Taylor	Bermuda	Bermuda	Mary & Elizabeth	1 Apr 1824
James	9					Trio	5 May 1828
John	12					Trio	5 May 1828
Mary	18	F	Servant	Ireland	United States	St. Michaels	18 Jul 1826
Thos.	40					Trio	5 May 1828
CLARIE, Michael, Capn.	43	M	Sea Captain	Philadelph.	Philadelphia	Hannibal	28 Apr 1824
CLARINGBURN, Joseph	45	M		Great Britain	United States	Ganges	8 Jul 1820
CLARK, —	20	M	Greener		U.S. America	Camillus	10 Sep 1821
—, Mr.	25	M		England	U. States	Perseverance	18 Nov 1824
—, Mr.	35	M	Gent.	England	United States	Warrior	6 Oct 1828
—, Mrs.				Dublin	U. States	Hibernia	26 Oct 1826
—, Mrs.	32	F	None	U. States	U. States	Surprize	1 Aug 1825
...	25	M	Farmer			Robert Burns	13 Jul 1820
A.	40	M	Merchant	America	America	James Cropper	14 Oct 1822
Abraham	30 10/12	M	Blacksmith	England	U.S. of America	Hamilton	18 Jul 1827
Agness	19	F		G. Britain	U. States	Camillus	8 Sep 1828
Agness	27	F		Scotland	U.S. of America	Friends	10 May 1823
Alexr.	28	M	Mercht.	G.B.	Canada	George Canning	2 May 1828
Amy, Miss	6		Child	England	United States	Acasta	16 Aug 1826
Andrew	29	M	Laborer or Spinster	Ireland	United States	Frances Miller	27 Jul 1827
Andw.	24	M	Farmer	Ireland	United States	Orozimbo	5 Mar 1827
Ann	25	F	Laborer or Spinster	Ireland	United States	Frances Miller	27 Jul 1827
Ann	28	F		England	United States	Nimrod	31 Jul 1828
Ann	34	F	None	Great Britain	United States	Illinois	9 Oct 1820
Ann	36	F	None	America	U. States	St. Michaels	30 Sep 1823
Anne	71 1/12	F	None	England	U.S. of America	Hamilton	18 Jul 1827
Archd.	0 6/12	M		G. Britain	U. States	Camillus	8 Sep 1828
Arn	1	F	Child			Seine	10 Jun 1822
B. C.	28	M	Merchant	U. States	U. States	Elias Burger	21 Jun 1823
Benjamin	35	M	Mariner	U. States	U. States	Martha	7 Nov 1825
Biddy	21	F	Servant	Ireland	United States	Carolina Ann	11 Dec 1826
Bonnet	24	M	Gentleman	G. Britain	Canada	Content	28 Aug 1820
Bridget	26	F	None	Ireland	New York	Commerce	24 Sep 1823
C.	3	M		Switzerland	U. States	Romulus	24 Sep 1828
C.	23	M	Merchant	Boston	U. States	Eliza & Mary	14 Jan 1824
C.	25	M		Switzerland	U. States	Romulus	24 Sep 1828
C. H.	28	M	Citizen	New York	New York	Florida	1 Jun 1827
Caroline	7	F	None	America	U. States	St. Michaels	30 Sep 1823
Catharine	02	F	Child	Ireland	Ireland	Sarah G.	28 Nov 1827

NAMES OF PASSENGERS	AGE	SEX	OCCUPATIONS	COUNTRY TO WHICH THEY BELONG	COUNTRY THEY INTEND TO INHABIT	SHIPS/DATES OF ARRIVAL	
CLARK (cont'd)							
Cathe.	30		Servant	Great Britain	United States	Camillus	12 Sep 1827
Cathn.	30		Labourer	Great Britan	United States	Newry	11 Jul 1827
Chansey	30	M	Merchant	United States	U. States	Potosi	30 Nov 1826
Charles	18/12	M	No trade	Great Britain	United States	Courier	13 Mar 1820
Charlotte	5	F	Child			Seine	10 Jun 1822
Christen	4	F	None	Scotland	United States	Statird	26 Aug 1823
Danl.	17	M	Labourer	Ireland		Marchioness	13 May 1828
David	18 9/12	M	Weaver	Ireland	United States	Atlantic	21 Jul 1827
Debly	4	F		Ireland	U. States	Wanderer	1 Sep 1828
Ducan	27	M	Cooper	Great Britan	U. States	Hudson	12 Mar 1824
E., Mr.	25	M	Merchant	U.S.A.		François I	19 Nov 1828
E. H.	29	M	Merchant	England	U. States	Columbia	20 Jul 1825
Edward	25	M		Great Britain	United States	Origon	8 Jun 1824
Edward	26	M	Labourer	Ireland	New York	Trusty	12 Sep 1828
Edward	50	M	Mariner	U. States	U. States	Riendeer	5 Sep 1820
Edwin	25	M	Merchant	U. States	United States	Florida	14 Sep 1827
Edwin	25	M	Merchant	U. States	U. States	Edwin	1 Jul 1829
Eleanor	28	F	Spinster	Ireland	U. States	Josephine	7 May 1827
Eliza	3	F		G. Britain	U. States	Camillus	8 Sep 1828
Eliza	7			Great Britan	United States	Newry	11 Jul 1827
Eliza	7			Great Britan	United States	Newry	11 Jul 1827
Eliza	20	F		Ireland	United States	Marmion	17 Jun 1825
Eliza	26	F		Scotland	U. States	Dalmarnock	23 May 1823
Eliza	30	F	Spinster	Ireland	United States	Orozimbo	5 Mar 1827
Elizabeth	4 6/12	F		New York	U. States	Cambria	3 Jul 1829
Elizabeth	8	F	None	Scotland	United States	Statird	26 Aug 1823
Elizabeth	14		Farmer	England	England	Hudson	18 Jun 1825
Elizabeth	15	F	None	Great Britain	United States	Illinois	9 Oct 1820
Elizabeth	40	F	Wife	Scotland	United States	Statird	26 Aug 1823
Elizabeth	42	F		New York	U. States	Cambria	3 Jul 1829
Emily	17	F		Great Britain	United States	Origon	8 Jun 1824
Erastus	34	M	Merchant	St. Thomas		New York	26 Dec 1828
Erastus, Mr.	33		Merchant	United States	U. States	South Carolina Packet	30 May 1825
F.	24	M	Merchant	Charleston	U. States	Valiant	21 Oct 1822
F., Mrs.	35		Lady	England	United States	Acasta	16 Aug 1826
Frances	3	F	Child			Seine	10 Jun 1822
Frances	27	F	Lady			Seine	10 Jun 1822
Francis	37	M	Weaver	Ireland	United States	Borneo	28 Aug 1828
Frank	11	M	boy	Ireland	United States	Dublin Packet	24 Sep 1823
Frdk.	23	M	Merchant	U. States	U. States	Southern Trader	23 Apr 1823
Fredk.	36	M	Merchant	St. Domingo	U. States	Valiant	30 Jan 1823
Frs.	17	M	None	Jamaica	U. States	Hal	7 Jun 1824
Gelina	10		Farmer	England	England	Hudson	18 Jun 1825
Geo.	49	M	Farmer	New York	U. States	Cambria	3 Jul 1829
Geo. A.	40	M	Merchant	N. York	U. States	Morgiana	24 May 1821
George A.	40	M	Merchant	America		Wicker	1 Aug 1820
Grace	49			England	America	Robert Burns	8 Dec 1821
Hannah	36	F	None	England	America	Manhattan	21 Sep 1822
Helen	6	F		Scotland	United States	Samuel Robertson	5 Oct 1827
Henrey	23	M	Weaver	Ireland	America	Reindeer	18 Oct 1828
Henry	13	M	None	America	U. States	St. Michaels	30 Sep 1823
Henry Richard	6		Farmer	England	England	Hudson	18 Jun 1825
Hugh	19		Family [of Wm.]	Great Britain	United States	Camillus	12 Sep 1827
Isaac	10		Family [of Wm.]	Great Britain	United States	Camillus	12 Sep 1827
Isaac	45	M	Farmer	Connecticutt	U. States	Income	29 May 1824
Isabella	2	F		Scotland	U.S. of America	Friends	10 May 1823
J.	6/12	M	Merchant	N. York	U. States	Superior	25 Sep 1828
J., Mrs.	32	F	Lady	England	U. States	Acasta	11 Dec 1826
J. H.	37	M	Merchant	Boston	U. States	Nestor	7 Jan 1825
J. W.	11	M	None	U. States	U. States	Surprize	1 Aug 1825
James	1 6/12	M	None	Scotland	United States	Samuel Robertson	9 May 1827
James	7	M		New York	U. States	Cambria	3 Jul 1829
James	11	M	Labourer	Argyle (Tedland) Scotland	United States	Jean Hastie	27 Jul 1829
James	18	M	Merchant	Scotland	America	Orbit	1 Sep 1823

220

NAMES OF PASSENGERS	AGE	SEX	OCCUPATIONS	COUNTRY TO WHICH THEY BELONG	COUNTRY THEY INTEND TO INHABIT	SHIPS/DATES OF ARRIVAL	
CLARK (cont'd)							
James	23	M		Great Britain	United States	Ganges	8 Jul 1820
James	23	M	Labourer		U. States	Helen	4 Aug 1829
James	23 6/12		Gardiner	Ireland	New York	Marcella	18 May 1827
James	24	M	Labourer	Ireland	U. States	Meteor	19 Jul 1828
James	25	M				Cassack	25 Jul 1820
James	25	M	Labourer	Ireland	U. States	Belville	5 Jul 1827
James	27	M	Farmer			Seine	10 Jun 1822
James	29	M	Merchant	England	England	Hiram	31 Oct 1828
James	32	M	Merchant	Denmark	U. States	Elias Burger	21 Jun 1823
James	35		Merchant	U. States	U. States	Nancy	11 Sep 1820
James	35	M	Timber Sawer	England	United States	Margaret	5 Sep 1827
James	39	M	Merchant	Nova Scotia	U. States	Tantamount	25 Apr 1822
Jane	3		Labourer	Great Britan	United States	Newry	11 Jul 1827
Jane	11	F		G. Britain	U. States	London	23 Sep 1828
Jane	25	F	Joiner	Great Britain	U.S. America	Chili	7 Jul 1827
Jane	26	F	Spinster	G. Britain	U. States	Canada	19 Sep 1828
Jane	28	F	Seamstress	Ireland	New Jersey	Carolina Ann	15 Oct 1824
Jane	35	F		G. Britain	U. States	London	23 Sep 1828
Janet	30	F		G. Britain	U. States	Camillus	8 Sep 1828
Janet	36	F	Wife	Scotland	United States	Samuel Robertson	9 May 1827
Jannet	6	F		Scotland	U. States	Dalmarnock	23 May 1823
Jas.	30	M	Plater	U. States	Great Britain	Thompson	26 Apr 1828
Jean	4/12	F	None	Ireland	United States	Friends	21 Oct 1825
Jean	1	F		Scotland	U. States	Dalmarnock	23 May 1823
Jean	2	F	None	Scotland	United States	Statird	26 Aug 1823
Jeffrey	21	M	Farmer	England		Manhattan	22 May 1827
Jno.	25	M		Ireland		Ann	17 May 1822
Jno.	26	M	Merchant	Dublin	U. States	Hibernia	26 Oct 1826
Jno.	66	M	Farmer	Cookstown	Philad.	Favourite	8 Oct 1823
John	17	M	Farmer	England	U. States	Cincinnatus	24 May 1821
John	19	M	Paper Maker	England	United States	Hamlet	25 Aug 1825
John	20	M	Farmer	...ford, Ireland		Mount Vernon	7 Jun 1824
John	20	M	Labourer	Ireland	United States	Thompson	12 Sep 1827
John	20 6/12	M	Labourer	Ireland	U. States	Courier	17 Mar 1828
John	21	M	Labourer	Gt. Britain	U. States	Frances Henrietta	18 Apr 1825
John	21	M	Farmer	Ireland	U. States	Criterion	23 May 1826
John	22	M	St...t	U. States	U. States	William	27 Jul 1824
John	22	M	Weaver	York, Great Britain		Casanda	5 Sep 1827
John	22	M	Farmer	England	America	Silas Richard	24 Oct 1829
John	24	M	Farmer	Scotland	U.S. of America	Friends	10 May 1823
John	24	M	Farmer	Scotland	United States	Statird	26 Aug 1823
John	25	M	Joiner	England	United States	Oscar	21 Oct 1822
John	25		Shoemaker			Cincinnatus	16 Apr 1824
*distress'd American to whom passage was given							
John	25	M	Labourer	Ireland	U. States	Sarah G	30 Jun 1828
John	27	M				Hibernia	15 Aug 1820
John	27	M	Taylor	Ireland	United States	Wilson	28 Nov 1828
John	29	M	Farmer	England	United States	Silas Richards	3 Apr 1826
John	30	M	Seaman	Boston	America	Mary	2 Oct 1820
John	30		Farmer	Great Britan	United States	Newry	11 Jul 1827
John	30	M				Lady of the Lake	23 Aug 1828
*left ship							
John	30	M	Con...di...	United States	United States	Cambria	8 Oct 1828
John	32	M	Watch Maker	G. Britain	U. States	London	23 Sep 1828
John	32	M	Labourer	England	United States	Montgomery	6 Mar 1829
John	33	M	Clothier	Switzerland	U. States	Romulus	24 Sep 1828
John	35	M	Mechanic	France		Charlemagne	16 Jan 1829
John	50	M	Gent.	Great Britain	United States	Mary Howland	19 Jul 1827
John	52	M	Druggist	England	United States	Nimrod	31 Jul 1828
John	56	M	Manufactor	England	U. States	John Wells	16 May 1825
John W.	30	M	Musician	Great Britain	United States	Courier	13 Mar 1820
Jos. W.	24	M	Merchant	Albany	Albany	Jupiter	27 May 1826
Joseph	7	M	Merchant	Scotland	United States	Justina	5 Aug 1823
Joseph	9	M		G. Britain	U. States	London	23 Sep 1828

NAMES OF PASSENGERS	AGE	SEX	OCCUPATIONS	COUNTRY TO WHICH THEY BELONG	COUNTRY THEY INTEND TO INHABIT	SHIPS/DATES OF ARRIVAL	
CLARK (cont'd)							
Joseph	21	M	Laborer	Great Britain	United States	Freake	25 Jun 1827
Joseph	28	M	Merchant	Scotland	United States	Justina	5 Aug 1823
Joseph	41	M	Linen draper	England	America	Manhattan	21 Sep 1822
Joseph	42	M	Merchant	U. States	U. States	Dromo	4 May 1827
Julia	7	F	Child	Ireland	New York	Atlantic	8 May 1828
Julia	9	F		England	U. States	John Wells	16 May 1825
Julia	23	F	Servant	Ireland	Ireland	Sarah G.	28 Nov 1827
L.	32	M	Instrument Maker	England	America	Two Marys	24 Sep 1827
Laurence	7		Family [of Wm.]	Great Britain	United States	Camillus	12 Sep 1827
Luke	36	M	Tanner	Ireland	New York	Thames	6 Oct 1820
M.	21	F	Merchant	N. York	U. States	Superior	25 Sep 1828
M.	34	M	Merchant	Philada.	U. States	General Brown	10 Dec 1823
Malcolm	36	M	Bricklayer	Scotland	United States	Samuel Robertson	9 May 1827
Malcolm, Junr.	12	M	None	Scotland	United States	Samuel Robertson	9 May 1827
Margaret	5	F		Gt. Britain		Dalhouse Castle	13 May 1828
Margaret	6	F	None	Scotland	United States	Statird	26 Aug 1823
Margaret	10	F	Labourer	Argyle (Tedland) Scotland	United States	Jean Hastie	27 Jul 1829
Margaret	11		Farmer	England	England	Hudson	18 Jun 1825
Margt.	14		Family [of Wm.]	Great Britain	United States	Camillus	12 Sep 1827
Maria	18	F	None	Jamaica	U. States	Hal	7 Jun 1824
Mariann	7	F		U.S.	U.S.	Florida	30 Jun 1826
Martha	46	F	House Keeper	Irereland	America	Carolina Ann	20 Jun 1825
Martha Jane	5/12	F	Merchant	Scotland	United States	Justina	5 Aug 1823
Mary	9	F	Child	Ireland	New York	Atlantic	8 May 1828
Mary	10	F	None	Scotland	United States	Statird	26 Aug 1823
Mary	18	F	None	Ireland	United States	Friends	21 Oct 1825
Mary	20	F		Great Britain	United States	Origon	8 Jun 1824
Mary	20	F	Spinster	Ireland	U. States	Josephine	7 May 1827
Mary	22	F				Helen	4 Aug 1829
Mary	22	F	dress Maker	Great Britain	United States	Unity	20 Oct 1829
Mary	24	F		U.S.A.	U.S.A.	Hope	6 Jun 1823
Mary	24		Family [of Wm.]	Great Britain	United States	Camillus	12 Sep 1827
Mary	27	F		G. Britain	U. States	London	23 Sep 1828
Mary	30		Labourer	Great Britan	United States	Newry	11 Jul 1827
Mary	40			Ireland	U. States	Robert Burns	18 Jun 1822
Mary	40	F	Labourer	Argyle (Tedland) Scotland	United States	Jean Hastie	27 Jul 1829
Mary	53	F		Great Britain	United States	Origon	8 Jun 1824
Mary	53	F		England	U. States	John Wells	16 May 1825
Mary, Miss	9		Child	England	United States	Acasta	16 Aug 1826
Mary Ann	18	F		Great Britain	United States	Freake	25 Jun 1827
Mary Ann	28	F	Merchant	Scotland	United States	Justina	5 Aug 1823
Mary Ann	35	F		England	United States	Margaret	5 Sep 1827
Mary Ann	78	F	Merchant	Scotland	United States	Justina	5 Aug 1823
Mary Ann, Jr.	3	F	Merchant	Scotland	United States	Justina	5 Aug 1823
Mary L.	22	F	None	United States		General Paez	21 Jun 1826
Mary S.	15	F		New York	U. States	Marmion	8 Sep 1828
May	21		Family [of Wm.]	Great Britain	United States	Camillus	12 Sep 1827
May	47		Family [of Wm.]	Great Britain	United States	Camillus	12 Sep 1827
Michael	23	M	Labourer	Ireland	New York	Atlantic	8 May 1828
Michael	30	M	Labourer	Ireland	New York	America	1 Aug 1828
Michael	45 3/12	M	Labourer	G. Britain	United States	Dutchess of Portland	30 Oct 1826
Michal	2 6/12			Ireland	New York	Marcella	18 May 1827
Michl.	21	M	Labourer	Ireland		Marchioness	13 May 1828
Miles	25	M	Coachman	England	United States	Essex	23 May 1828
Molly	25	F	Spintress	Great Britain	United States	Courier	13 Mar 1820
— Mr.	40	M	Servant	Dublin	U. States	Hibernia	26 Oct 1826
Nancy	22	F				Hibernia	15 Aug 1820
Noel	21	M	Gentleman	U. States		Star	7 Jan 1827
Pat.	20	M	Labourer	Ireland	U. States	Alex Mansfield	1 Jun 1822
Patrick	20		Weaver	Ireland	America	Sarah	18 Aug 1829
Patrick	26	M	Labourer	Scotland	United States	Princess Charlotte	26 Apr 1827
Peter	17		Family [of Wm.]	Great Britain	United States	Camillus	12 Sep 1827

NAMES OF PASSENGERS	AGE	SEX	OCCUPATIONS	COUNTRY TO WHICH THEY BELONG	COUNTRY THEY INTEND TO INHABIT	SHIPS/DATES OF ARRIVAL	
CLARK (cont'd)							
Peter	20	M	Labourer	Great Britain	United States	William Dawson	18 Jun 1827
Peter	21	M	...	Ireland	United States	Carolina Ann	24 Oct 1825
Peter	30		Blacksmith	Dundalk	Ireland	Hudson	18 Jun 1825
*Officers, Seamen and Passengers belonging to the Ship Jane of Boston and taken from on board the Schooner Olive of St. Johns , N.B. on the 4th June 1825, Lat. 41.30, Long 53.19, which ship foundered on the 31st ultimo in Lat. 41.44 Long 52.							
Peter D.	51	M	Mariner	U. States	Jereme	Culloden	21 Oct 1823
Philip	13		Farmer	England	England	Hudson	18 Jun 1825
Phillip	39	M	Labourer	U. States	U. States	Hudson	8 Oct 1827
Poul				Ireland	U. States	Fabius	22 Sep 1828
Richard	10	M	None	Great Britain	United States	Illinois	9 Oct 1820
Richard	61	M	...	Great Britain	United States	Origon	8 Jun 1824
Robert	5			Ireland	U. States	Robert Burns	18 Jun 1822
Robert	12	F	None	America	U. States	St. Michaels	30 Sep 1823
Robert	19	M	Labourer	G. Britain	U. States	St. George	16 Jan 1829
Robert	26	M	Clerk	Scotland	U. States	Phocion	8 May 1824
Robert	30	M	Black Smith	Belfast	...	Frances Henrietta	30 Jun 1827
Robert	50	M	Labourer	Irereland	America	Carolina Ann	20 Jun 1825
Robt.	35		Carpenter	Great Britan	United States	Newry	11 Jul 1827
Robt., Mr.	15	M	Gent.	England	United States	Warrior	6 Oct 1828
Rose	23	F	Spinster	Ireland	United States	Wilson	28 Nov 1828
Sally	28			Ireland	New York	Marcella	18 May 1827
Sampson	25	M	Merchant	Ireland	St. John	Four Sons	4 Jun 1827
Samuel	5	M	None	Scotland	United States	Samuel Robertson	9 May 1827
Samuel	47	M	Supercargo or Ship Master	United States	United States	William	2 Feb 1820
Sarah, Miss	21	F	None	England	New York	Thames	6 Oct 1820
Sarah, Mrs.	30	F	Servnat	Ireland	United States	Dublin Packet	9 Jul 1827
Thomas	2	M		Ireland	U. States	Wanderer	1 Sep 1828
Thomas	4	M	None	Great Britain	United States	Illinois	9 Oct 1820
Thomas	18 2/12	M	Miller	Ireland	America	Carolina Ann	7 Apr 1826
Thomas	25	M	Labourer	Ireland	Ireland	Sarah G.	28 Nov 1827
Thomas	30	M	Miller	England	United States	Danube	13 Jul 1827
Thoms.	40	M	Weaver	Ireland	U.S. States	Splendid	14 Aug 1829
Thos.	1		Labourer	Great Britan	United States	Newry	11 Jul 1827
Thos.	17	M	Merchant	U. States	U. States	William & Henry	9 Sep 1826
Thos.	25	M		Great B.	U. States	William Neilson	26 Jul 1828
Thos.	27	M	Weaver	Ireland	United States	Orozimbo	5 Mar 1827
Thos.	28	M	Sawyer	Great Brittain	United States	Nimrod	9 Jan 1827
Thos.	35	M	Merchant	Great Britain	United States	James Cropper	27 Sep 1821
Thos. A.	21	M	Merchant	New York	U. States	Natchez	7 Feb 1825
W.	4	M		Scotland	U. States	Dalmarnock	23 May 1823
W.	5	M		G. Britain	U. States	London	23 Sep 1828
W.	30	M	Merchant	Scotland	U. States	Dalmarnock	23 May 1823
William	3	M	No trade	Great Britain	United States	Courier	13 Mar 1820
William	5	M				Helen	4 Aug 1829
William	7	M		G. Britain	U. States	London	23 Sep 1828
William	7	M		New York	U. States	Cambria	3 Jul 1829
William	17	M	...	...	...	Camillus	18 Nov 1824
William	20	M	Weaver	Ireland	United States	Princess Charlotte	26 Apr 1827
William	21	M		Irereland	America	Carolina Ann	20 Jun 1825
William	23	M	Carpenter	England	U.S. America	New Hampshire	28 Sep 1826
William	34	M	Mechanic	Ireland	U. States	Reuben & Eliza	21 Aug 1820
William	37	M	Shoemaker	Great Britain	United States	Unity	20 Oct 1829
William	49		Tallow Cahndler	England	America	Robert Burns	8 Dec 1821
William	50	M	Labourer	Scotland	United States	Samuel Robertson	5 Oct 1827
William, Junr.	19			England	America	Robert Burns	8 Dec 1821
William H.	34	M	Gentleman	Ireland	Western Country	British Hibernia	13 Mar 1820
Wm.	6			Ireland	U. States	Robert Burns	18 Jun 1822
Wm.	21	M	Farmer	Scotland	United States	Minerva	29 Oct 1822
Wm.	21	M	Baker	Gt. Britain	United States	Baltic	11 Apr 1825
Wm.	21	M	Merchant	Great Britain	United States	Meridian	2 Jul 1827
Wm.	21	M	Gentleman	...	...	Antioch	8 Oct 1827
Wm.	25	M	Farmer	Scotland	U. States	Roger Stewart	9 Jun 1828

NAMES OF PASSENGERS	A G E	S E X	OCCUPATIONS	COUNTRY TO WHICH THEY BELONG	COUNTRY THEY INTEND TO INHABIT	SHIPS/DATES OF ARRIVAL	
CLARK (cont'd)							
Wm.	45	M	Farmer	Scotland	United States	Statird	26 Aug 1823
Wm.	53		Farmer	Great Britain	United States	Camillus	12 Sep 1827
Wm.	55	M	Watch Maker	G. Britain	U. States	London	23 Sep 1828
Wm., Jr.	16	M	Farmer	Scotland	United States	Statird	26 Aug 1823
Wm. S.	32	M	Shipmaster	U. States Amer	U. States Amer	Juno	5 Oct 1822
CLARKE, —, Mrs.	40	F	Lady	U. States		Congress	21 Nov 1823
—, Mrs.	40	F	None	United States	United States	Hannibal	12 Oct 1829
A.	27	M	Merchant	Scotland	Philada.	Eclipse	3 Aug 1824
Abraham	6	M	None	England		Marchioness	13 May 1828
Abraham	41	M	Labourer	England		Marchioness	13 May 1828
Ann	20	F	Servant	Ireland	United States	Josephine	30 Apr 1828
Ann	21	F	Matron	Great Britain	United States	Wilson	26 Feb 1824
Austin C.	37	M	Farmer	Brittian	U. States	Acasta	28 Jan 1823
Catherine	28	F	Lady	Ireland	U. States	Meteor	4 Oct 1827
Catherine	64	F		England	United States	William Byrnes	1 Dec 1824
Chas.	6 6/12	M	Labourer	Co. Wicklow	United States	Java	9 Jul 1827
Daniel	20	M	Weaver	G. Brittian	United States	Louisa	14 Jun 1825
E.	25		Farmer	Ireland	United States	Courier	16 May 1825
Edward	31	M	Merchant	United States	United States	Cortes	10 Apr 1822
Edwd.	23	M	...	Co. Wicklow	United States	Java	9 Jul 1827
Edwd.	70	M	Labourer	Co. Wicklow	United States	Java	9 Jul 1827
El...	1	F	None	England		Marchioness	13 May 1828
Elizabeth	8	F	None	England		Marchioness	13 May 1828
Elizabeth B.	18	F		New York	U. States	Hudson	21 Aug 1829
Ellen	20	F	Servant	Ireland	United States	Carolina Ann	14 May 1827
Ellen	22	F	...	Ireland	United States	Carolina Ann	24 Oct 1825
Fanny	2			England	England	Hudson	4 Sep 1823
Fredk.	23	M	Merchant	Aquin	U. States	Sarah Ann	25 Jun 1822
G. W.	28	M	Mariner	U. States	U. States	Helecon	3 Dec 1821
Geo.	23	M	Weaver	Ireland	America	Mary	29 May 1827
Geo.	30	M	Mechanic	England	U. States	Hanover	12 Oct 1822
George H.	28	M	Gentleman	U. States		Colossus	27 Mar 1828
Hanah	10	F	None	England		Marchioness	13 May 1828
Hannah	26	F		England	United States	William Byrnes	1 Dec 1824
Harriot	25	F	Seamstress			John & Edward	25 Aug 1820
Henrietta	33	F	None	England		Marchioness	13 May 1828
J.	20		Farmer	Ireland	United States	Courier	16 May 1825
J. H.	38	M	Merchant	U. States	United States	James Barron	26 Jun 1823
James	5	M	None	England		Marchioness	13 May 1828
James	12	M	Weaver	Ireland	U.S. of America	Meteor	19 Mar 1828
James	20	M	Labourer	Ireland	United States	Concordia	25 Aug 1827
Jane	22	F	Labourer	Co. Wicklow	United States	Java	9 Jul 1827
Jane	30	F	Labourer	Co. Wicklow	United States	Java	9 Jul 1827
John	19	M	Labourer	Ireland	Canada	Pilgrim	1 Sep 1828
John	22	M	Mariner	Ireland	United States	Louisa	18 Apr 1827
John	24	M		Great Britain	United States	Wilson	26 Feb 1824
John	25	M	Farmer			John & Edward	25 Aug 1820
John	26	M	Farmer	Great Britain	United States	Mary Howland	19 Jul 1827
John	42	M	Farmer	Gt. Britain	United States	Importer	21 May 1821
John Y.	31	M	Merchant	U. States	U. States	Caledonia	10 Sep 1828
Joseph	20	M	Labourer	Ireland		Marchioness	13 May 1828
Joseph	60	M	None	England	United States	William Byrnes	1 Dec 1824
L. H.	46	M	Counsellor	New York	U. States	Hudson	21 Aug 1829
Mary	1	F		England	United States	William Byrnes	1 Dec 1824
Mary	2	F	Labourer	Co. Wicklow	United States	Java	9 Jul 1827
Mary	4	F	None	England		Marchioness	13 May 1828
Mary	22	F				Reuben & Eliza	21 Aug 1820
Mary Ann	24			England	England	Hudson	4 Sep 1823
Michael	30	M	Labourer	Ireland	United States	Ann Maria	8 Jun 1824
N., Jr.	26	M	Merct.	Massatt.	U. States	Imperial	12 Aug 1825
Peter	25	M	Weaver	Ireland	America	Mary	29 May 1827
Philip	25	M	Farmer	Ireland	United States	Dublin Packet	29 Jun 1825
Rebecca	19	F	Wife	Ireland	U.S. of America	Meteor	19 Mar 1828
Richard	50	M		Great Britain	United States	Ganges	8 Jul 1820
Robert	32	M	Farmer, Labourer or Spinster	Ireland	U. States	Meteor	4 Oct 1827
Robt.	23 4/12	M	Farmer	Ireland	Beaver Town	Triton	12 Jul 1823
Rose	1			England	England	Hudson	4 Sep 1823

NAMES OF PASSENGERS	AGE	SEX	OCCUPATIONS	COUNTRY TO WHICH THEY BELONG	COUNTRY THEY INTEND TO INHABIT	SHIPS/DATES OF ARRIVAL	
CLARKE (cont'd)							
Sarah	2/12	F	Labourer	Co. Wicklow	United States	Java	9 Jul 1827
Sarah Ann	2	F		England	United States	William Byrnes	1 Dec 1824
Thomas	3	M	None	England		Marchioness	13 May 1828
Thomas	35	M	...	Ireland	United States	Carolina Ann	24 Oct 1825
Thomas	38	M	Grocer	England	United States	William Byrnes	1 Dec 1824
Thos.	35	M	Labourer	Co. Wicklow	United States	Java	9 Jul 1827
Thos. W.	23	M	Barrister	Philadelphia	U. States	Howard	25 Jul 1823
William	28	M	Gentleman	Great Britain	U. States	Panthea	24 Mar 1825
Wm.	27	M	Farmer	Ireland	United States	Louisa	18 Apr 1827
CLARKSON, Agness	54	F	None	Scotland	U. States	Camillus	27 Jul 1825
Ann	18	F		England	United States	Nancy Henrietta	3 Nov 1828
Ann	19	F		England	U.N. States	William Byrnes	23 Jul 1824
George	12	M	None	Ireland	U. States	Josephine	27 Jul 1825
James	12	M		England	U.N. States	William Byrnes	23 Jul 1824
Jane	...0	F		England	U.N. States	William Byrnes	23 Jul 1824
Jno.	2/12	M		England	United States	Nancy Henrietta	3 Nov 1828
John	22	M	Weaver	Great Britain	United States	Aurora	5 Sep 1826
John	55	M	Taylor	Scotland	U. States	Camillus	27 Jul 1825
M.	22	F		Great Britain	United States	Isaac Hicks	6 Dec 1827
Robert	18	M	tin smith	Ireland	U. States	Josephine	27 Jul 1825
CLARRO, —, Mr.	25	M	Merchant	Havana	Havana	Milo	15 May 1824
CLARRY, Edwd. M.	20	M	Merchant	U. States	U. States	Bordeaux	21 Sep 1822
CLARY, Catharine	22	F		Ireland		Fame	9 Dec 1826
Francies	55	F		New York	New York	General Marion	21 Nov 1828
James	20	M	Laborer	Ireland	U. States	Edwin	1 Jul 1829
John	24	M	Farmer	England	United States	William Howland	5 Jul 1821
John	24	M	Lawyer	Ireland	N. York	Trusty	12 Sep 1828
John	28	M	Farmer	Ireland		Fame	9 Dec 1826
Thomas	16	M	Merchant	New York	New York	General Marion	21 Nov 1828
Timothy	25	M	Farmer	Great Briton	New York	Brighton	12 Jun 1826
CLASERY, Ann	20	F	Spinster	Ireland	United States	Wilson	6 Jun 1828
CLASKY, H. M.	20	M	Farmer	Ireland	U. States	Isabella	28 Jun 1825
CLASON, Augustus W.	28		Merchant	United States	United States	William Byrnes	25 Aug 1828
CLAUDE, August	5	M	Book Binder	France	United States	American	27 Aug 1827
Bolt	23	M	Farmer	France	United States	Virginia	31 May 1828
C. J.	47	M	Farmer	France	United States	Le Voltaire	19 Jul 1828
Eleanor	6	F	Book Binder	France	United States	American	27 Aug 1827
Eugene	3	M	Book Binder	France	United States	American	27 Aug 1827
Francis	1	M	Book Binder	France	United States	American	27 Aug 1827
John, Don	41	M	Book Binder	France	United States	American	27 Aug 1827
Maria	38	F	Book Binder	France	United States	American	27 Aug 1827
Rosina	7	F	Book Binder	France	United States	American	27 Aug 1827
Victore	13	F	Book Binder	France	United States	American	27 Aug 1827
CLAUSS, Jaques	36	M	Farmer	Germany	United States	Oxford	14 Aug 1828
CLAVES, Juan N.	28	M	Merchant	Spain	U. States	Seneca	14 May 1821
CLAVILL, Ruman	31	M	Merchant	Spain	United States	Dromo	22 Feb 1827
CLAVITT, John	30	M	Gentleman	Nassau	U.States	Venus	28 Jun 1825
CLAW, Thomas	24	M	Carpenter	Great Brittain	United States	United States	16 Feb 1827
William	15	M	Clerk	Great Britain	United States	Natchez	17 Aug 1822
CLAWSON, Ann	25	F	None	England	U. States	Radius	16 Mar 1822
CLAXTON, Ann	20	F	Spinster	Ireland	United States	Dublin Packet	29 Jun 1825
John	8	M	Boy	Ireland	United States	Dublin Packet	29 Jun 1825
Thomas	16	M	Boy	Ireland	United States	Dublin Packet	29 Jun 1825
CLAY, John	24	M	D...s...	G. Britain	U. States	Armadello	22 Jun 1827
Robert	22		Gentleman	Scotland	Scotland	Hudson	14 Jun 1827
S. H.	25	M	Merchant	Hanover	U. States	Minerva	13 Sep 1827
T.	24	M	Lawyer	U. States	U. States	Ranger	2 Jul 1827
William	40	M	Labourer	G. Britain	U. States	St. George	7 Jun 1828
CLAYHORN, J.	25	M	Merchant	Spain	U. States	Native	15 Apr 1826
CLAYSON, Nancy	24	F	None	England	U. States	Montgomery	18 Oct 1828
CLAYTON, —				G. Britain	U. States	Camillus	8 Sep 1828
Anne	43	F	Spinster	Great Britain	United States	Robert Fulton	1 Apr 1824
Eliza	2	F		G. Britain	U. States	Camillus	8 Sep 1828
Eliza	25	F		Co. L...	United States	Java	9 Jul 1827
Geo.	25	M	Tinplater	England	United States	Essex	23 May 1828
J. B.	24	M	Portrait Painter	England	New York	James Cropper	16 Oct 1826
J. B.	25	M	Clerk	Great Britain	United States	Cambria	26 Dec 1827

NAMES OF PASSENGERS	AGE	SEX	OCCUPATIONS	COUNTRY TO WHICH THEY BELONG	COUNTRY THEY INTEND TO INHABIT	SHIPS/DATES OF ARRIVAL	
CLAYTON (cont'd)							
John	19	M	Farmer	Roscommon		Mount Vernon	7 Jun 1824
John	22	M	Farmer	Ireland	U. States	Francis	6 Sep 1827
John	38		Mariner	U. States	U. States	Eliza Pigott	25 Sep 1820
Joshua	22	M		U. States	U. States	Brazillian	15 Mar 1824
M.	23	M	Mechanic	England	Newyork	Cortes	16 Jul 1827
Mary	21	F		G. Britain	U. States	Camillus	8 Sep 1828
Robert	32	M	...	Co. L...	United States	Java	9 Jul 1827
CLE...Y, John	20	M	Painter	England	America	Plutarch	18 Jul 1826
CLEADON, Charlotte	32		None	Boston	United States	Elizabeth	8 Dec 1821
Eliza	15		None	Boston	United States	Elizabeth	8 Dec 1821
James	10		None	Boston	United States	Elizabeth	8 Dec 1821
CLEAGAN, Eliza	40 5/12	F	Spinstress	Ireland	U. States	Fabius	22 Sep 1828
James	14 3/12	M		Ireland	U. States	Fabius	22 Sep 1828
John	2 7/12	M		Ireland	U. States	Fabius	22 Sep 1828
John	49 6/12	M	Labourer	Ireland	U. States	Fabius	22 Sep 1828
Mary Ann	17 9/12	F	Spinstress	Ireland	U. States	Fabius	22 Sep 1828
CLEAGWE, Catharine	48	F	Labourer	England	U. States	Comet	23 Aug 1828
Daniel	13	M	Labourer	England	U. States	Comet	23 Aug 1828
Esther	19	F	Labourer	England	U. States	Comet	23 Aug 1828
Hugh	6	M	Labourer	England	U. States	Comet	23 Aug 1828
Robt.	8	M	Labourer	England	U. States	Comet	23 Aug 1828
CLEAMAN, Frederick	43	M	Merchant	Russia	Virginia	Sarah	17 Aug 1825
CLEANDER, Frederick	28	M	Watch Maker	Germany	U. States	Rook	25 Jul 1827
CLEAR, George	23	M	Farmer	Switzerland	United States	Andes	5 May 1828
CLEARY, Catharine	50	F	None	Great Britain	United States	Comet	9 Aug 1822
Jno.	24		Laborer	Great Britain	United States	Comet	9 Aug 1822
John	23	M	Lawyer	Ireland	America	Parrington	9 Jun 1827
John	30	M	None	Gt. Britain	Gt. Britain	Adno	29 Apr 1825
Martin	25	M	Labourer	Great Britain	U. States	Robert Fulton	3 Dec 1827
Pat	24	M	Labourer	Great Britain		Moro Castle	6 Jul 1827
CLEASE, Tim	21	M	Farmer	Ireland	United States	Dublin Packet	29 Jun 1825
CLEAVES, Thomas	32	M	Merchant	Ireland	Great Britton	William	11 Dec 1820
CLEGG, Betsey	14	F		U. States	U. States	United States	11 Sep 1828
Edward	35 6/12	M	Merchant	Great Britain	Great Britain	James Monroe	27 Jul 1821
Ellis	35	M	Weaver	Ireland	U. States	Severn	12 Oct 1826
Emma	10	F		U. States	U. States	United States	11 Sep 1828
Fanny	45	F		U. States	U. States	United States	11 Sep 1828
Geo.	24	M	Weaver	Great Britain	United States	Washington	3 Sep 1827
John	17	M	Joiner	England	U. States	Emulous	22 Aug 1828
John	20	M	Labourer	England	U. States	Emulous	22 Aug 1828
John	25	M	Weaver	England	United States	Delta	24 Oct 1829
John	27			Isle of Man	N. York	Peru	30 May 1828
Sarah	12	F		U. States	U. States	United States	11 Sep 1828
Sarah	32	F		U. States	U. States	United States	11 Sep 1828
CLEGGERTT, Anna	4	F		England	U.N. States	Helen	17 Dec 1827
Eliza	7/12	F		England	U.N. States	Helen	17 Dec 1827
Frances	28	F		England	U.N. States	Helen	17 Dec 1827
Harriet	8	F		England	U.N. States	Helen	17 Dec 1827
Olive	12	F		England	U.N. States	Helen	17 Dec 1827
Richd.	35	M	Farmer	England	U.N. States	Helen	17 Dec 1827
Stephen	6	F		England	U.N. States	Helen	17 Dec 1827
CLEGGS, Agniss	22	F	Hatter	Great Britian	United States	George Clinton	13 Apr 1826
Harrietta	11	F	None	Great Britian	United States	George Clinton	13 Apr 1826
James	50	M	Hatter	Great Britian	United States	George Clinton	13 Apr 1826
CLEGHORN, Adam	13	M	None	Ireland	New York	America	1 Aug 1828
Christian	9	M	None	Ireland	New York	America	1 Aug 1828
Elizabeth	48	F	None	Ireland	New York	America	1 Aug 1828
James	1/12	M	None	Ireland	New York	America	1 Aug 1828
James	52	M	Labourer	Ireland	New York	America	1 Aug 1828
John	27	M	Labourer	Ireland	New York	America	1 Aug 1828
Margaret	3	F	None	Ireland	New York	America	1 Aug 1828
Maria	3	M	None	Ireland	New York	America	1 Aug 1828
Mary	11	F	None	Ireland	New York	America	1 Aug 1828
Mary	28	F	None	Ireland	New York	America	1 Aug 1828
Robert	5	M	None	Ireland	New York	America	1 Aug 1828
Thomas	22	M	Labourer	Ireland	New York	America	1 Aug 1828
Watson	7	M	None	Ireland	New York	America	1 Aug 1828
William	16	M	Labourer	Ireland	New York	America	1 Aug 1828

NAMES OF PASSENGERS	AGE	SEX	OCCUPATIONS	COUNTRY TO WHICH THEY BELONG	COUNTRY THEY INTEND TO INHABIT	SHIPS/DATES OF ARRIVAL	
CLELAND, Jas.	24		Farmer	Ireland	United States	John Dickinson	28 Jun 1822
Jas.	24		Farmer	Ireland	United States	John Dickinson	28 Jun 1822
Saml.	26	M	Merchant	Down, Ireland	New York	Anthusa	24 Aug 1825
CLELLAND, Saml.	30	M	Clerk	Scotland	United States	Camillus	27 Oct 1829
CLEMAN, John	23	M	Carpenter	Ireland	U. States	Vermont	19 Jun 1827
CLEMENS, Henry	8	M		Boston	U. States	South Carolina	2 Aug 1822
CLEMENT, —	30	M	Sea Capt.	France	France	Saluda	15 Jul 1826
Agnes	30	F		G. Britain	U. States	Camillus	8 Sep 1828
Ann	32	F		England	U. States	Criterion at London	10 May 1821
David	1	M		England	U. States	Criterion at London	10 May 1821
Elizabeth	45	F		U. States		Abigail	26 Sep 1820
Jane	2	F		America	U. States	Criterion at London	10 May 1821
Mary Ann	11	F		England	U. States	Criterion at London	10 May 1821
Richd.	40	M	Hatter	England	U. States	Criterion at London	10 May 1821
Samuel	14	M		England	U. States	Criterion at London	10 May 1821
William	4	M		America	U. States	Criterion at London	10 May 1821
William	34	M	Farmer	Scotland	United States	Camillus	27 Oct 1829
CLEMENTE-BOLAVER (see Bolaver)							
CLEMENTS, Elenor	20	F	Labourer	Grt. Britain	United States	Robert Fulton	8 Oct 1828
Henry	22	M	Labourer	Grt. Britain	United States	Robert Fulton	8 Oct 1828
James	22	M	Mechanic	Philada.	U. States	Sarah Herrick	7 Oct 1826
James	27 11/12	M	Labourer	Ireland	United States	Atlantic	21 Jul 1827
Mary	18	F	Labourer	Grt. Britain	United States	Robert Fulton	8 Oct 1828
Mary Ann	30 7/12	F	Wife	Ireland	United States	Atlantic	21 Jul 1827
Wm. W.	25	M	Farmer	Great Britain	United States	Grecian	24 Sep 1828
CLEMINSON, Jno.	27	M	Farmer	England	U. States	New York	11 Jul 1823
CLEMM, Joseph E.	32	M	Merchant	United States	United States	William Thompson	16 Jan 1826
CLEMONS, Easter	35	F	Labourer or Spinster	Ireland	United States	Champion	3 Nov 1827
John	28	M	Labourer or Spinster	Ireland	United States	Champion	3 Nov 1827
CLEMONT, Frederick	35	M	Captain	St. Johns	U. States	Nancy	10 Jul 1822
CLENDENNING, Willm.	37	M	Gentn.	England	U.S.A.	Lima	6 Dec 1826
CLENEY, J...s	24	M	Carpenter	Ireland	United States	Abigale	17 Jul 1822
CLENGUE, Charles	48	M	Labourer	England	U. States	Comet	23 Aug 1828
CLEONDLING, Andrew	6	M	Child	Ireland	U. States	Meteor	19 Jul 1828
Andrew	40	M	Farmer	Ireland	U. States	Meteor	19 Jul 1828
Eliz.	3	F	Child	Ireland	U. States	Meteor	19 Jul 1828
Eliz.	36	F	Wife	Ireland	U. States	Meteor	19 Jul 1828
Jane	1 6/12	F	Child	Ireland	U. States	Meteor	19 Jul 1828
Mary An	12	F	Child	Ireland	U. States	Meteor	19 Jul 1828
W.	8	M	Child	Ireland	U. States	Meteor	19 Jul 1828
CLEPHERE, George	48	M	Wallen Clt. [Wollen Cloth?]	England		Fame	9 Dec 1826
CLERER, Coenraad	36	M	Carpenter	Germany	Vermont	Orient	25 Nov 1825
CLERK, John	26	M	Labourer	Ireland	United States	Commerce	13 Jun 1828
Mary	15	F	Spinster	Ireland	United States	Dublin Packet	22 Oct 1821
CLERKON, Thos.	25			Great Britan	United States	Newry	11 Jul 1827
CLERMENIL, James	26	M	Merchant	France	United States	Don Quixote	7 May 1824
CLERMENT, P.	29	M	Labourer	England	America	Two Marys	24 Sep 1827
CLESSEY, Remond, Mr.	60		Mercht.	U.S.	U.S.	Brandt	7 Feb 1822
CLEVAN, Patt	26	M	Farmer	Co. ...th	United States	Java	9 Jul 1827
CLEVELAND, R. S.	51	M	Merchant	U. States	U. States	Edwd. Quesnel	30 Apr 1825
Richard J.	50	M	Merchant	United States	United States	Columbia	1 Dec 1823
CLEVEN, John	30	M	ropemaker	England	U.S. States	Splendid	14 Aug 1829
CLEVERIDA, Agata	5	F	Farmer	Switzerland	U. States	India	8 Dec 1826
Antonni	50	M	Farmer	Switzerland	U. States	India	8 Dec 1826
Antony	3	M	Farmer	Switzerland	U. States	India	8 Dec 1826
Chatarina	14	F	Farmer	Switzerland	U. States	India	8 Dec 1826
Francis	1	M	Farmer	Switzerland	U. States	India	8 Dec 1826

NAMES OF PASSENGERS	AGE	SEX	OCCUPATIONS	COUNTRY TO WHICH THEY BELONG	COUNTRY THEY INTEND TO INHABIT	SHIPS/DATES OF ARRIVAL	
CLEVERIDA (cont'd)							
Joseph	8	M	Farmer	Switzerland	U. States	India	8 Dec 1826
Maria	10	F	Farmer	Switzerland	U. States	India	8 Dec 1826
Martin	18	M	Farmer	Switzerland	U. States	India	8 Dec 1826
Theresa	17	F	Farmer	Switzerland	U. States	India	8 Dec 1826
Thofney	50	M	Farmer	Switzerland	U. States	India	8 Dec 1826
CLEWCAS, Margt.	24	F	None	Isle of Man		Ocean	13 Jul 1827
Wm.	2	M	None	Isle of Man		Ocean	13 Jul 1827
Wm.	27	M	Weaver	Isle of Man		Ocean	13 Jul 1827
CLIBBORN, J.	50	M	Merchant	United States	United States	John Jay	8 May 1828
CLICTEUR, John B.	23 4/12	M	Student in Bardstown's College	Nederland	America	Henry	17 May 1828
CLIFDEN, Arthur	23	M	Labourer	Ireland	United States	Lord Wellington	28 May 1827
CLIFF, Daniel	6	M		England	United States	Joseph	13 Oct 1823
Hannah	12	F		England	United States	Joseph	13 Oct 1823
Mary	11	F		England	United States	Joseph	13 Oct 1823
Samuel	8	M		England	United States	Joseph	13 Oct 1823
Sarah	4	F		England	United States	Joseph	13 Oct 1823
Sarah	36	F		England	United States	Joseph	13 Oct 1823
CLIFFE, Allice	26	F		Great Britain	United States	Isaac Hicks	10 Jul 1827
Elizabeth	6	F		Great Britain	United States	Isaac Hicks	10 Jul 1827
John H.	30	M	Surgeon	Great Britain	United States	Isaac Hicks	10 Jul 1827
Thomas	4	M		Great Britain	United States	Isaac Hicks	10 Jul 1827
CLIFFORD, Ann	22	F	Labourer	England	U. States	Ayrshire	12 May 1828
Ann	35	F		Great Britain	United States	Camberwell	2 Oct 1828
Bridget	26	F	Labourer	Ireland	New York	Bowditch	27 Apr 1826
C.	24	F	Servant	Ireland	U. States	Wanderer	30 Sep 1828
Cathr.	2	F	Labourer	Ireland	New York	Bowditch	27 Apr 1826
Cathr.	45	F	Linen Draper	Ireland	New York	Bowditch	27 Apr 1826
Dennis	22	M	Labourer	Ireland	United States	General Marion	6 Oct 1828
Geo.	2	M		Ireland	U. States	Wanderer	30 Sep 1828
James	5	M		Great Britain	United States	Camberwell	2 Oct 1828
James	8	M	Labourer	Ireland	New York	Bowditch	27 Apr 1826
James	26	M	Labourer	New York	New York	Bowditch	27 Apr 1826
James	35	M	Farmer	Ireland	U. States	Sabina	29 Apr 1825
James	56	M	Hat feller	Great Britain	United States	Birmingham	15 Jun 1827
John	4	M		Great Britain	United States	Camberwell	2 Oct 1828
John	20	M	Labourer	Ireland	New York	Bowditch	27 Apr 1826
Martin	30	M	Labourer	Ireland	New York	Bowditch	27 Apr 1826
Mary	3	F	Labourer	Ireland	New York	Bowditch	27 Apr 1826
Mary	17	F	Servant	Ireland	U. States	Wanderer	30 Sep 1828
Michl.	25	M		Ireland	United States	Essex	23 May 1828
Pat	35	M	Farmer	Ireland	U. States	Wanderer	30 Sep 1828
Peggy	8	F		Ireland	U. States	Wanderer	30 Sep 1828
Rebecca	40	F	None	Ireland	U. States	Franklin	7 Jul 1828
Robert	1	M		Great Britain	United States	Camberwell	2 Oct 1828
Thomas	35	M	Farmer	Great Britain	United States	Camberwell	2 Oct 1828
Timothy	15	M	Labourer	Ireland	U. States	Wanderer	30 Sep 1828
Wm.	6	M	Labourer	Ireland	New York	Bowditch	27 Apr 1826
CLIFORD, —, Miss	22	F	Lady	U. States	U. States	Milo	15 May 1824
CLIFTON, Ann	21	F	Lady	Great Britian	United States	Silvanus Jenkins	6 Apr 1826
Charles	21	M	Gentleman	Great Britian	United States	Silvanus Jenkins	6 Apr 1826
George	28	M	Farmer	Younghall, Great Britain	United States	Union	24 Sep 1823
Thomas	36	M	Baker	Great Britain	United States	George Clinton	27 Aug 1827
CLIGG, Wm.	1	M		L...n	United States	Java	9 Jul 1827
CLIGGE, Jas.	24	M	Shoemaker	L...n	United States	Java	9 Jul 1827
Mary	27	F		L...n	United States	Java	9 Jul 1827
CLINCY, Ann	18	F	Laborer	Ireland	U. States	Albion	9 Aug 1826
Bartholomew	40	M	Laborer	Ireland	U. States	Albion	9 Aug 1826
Bridget	12	F	Laborer	Ireland	U. States	Albion	9 Aug 1826
Bryan	14	M	Laborer	Ireland	U. States	Albion	9 Aug 1826
Catherine	40	F	Wife	Ireland	U. States	Albion	9 Aug 1826
May	16	F	Wife	Ireland	U. States	Albion	9 Aug 1826
Wm.	20	F	Laborer	Ireland	U. States	Albion	9 Aug 1826
CLINDEN, Henry	23	M	Lock Smith	Germany	America	Orozimbo	1 Oct 1827
CLINE, —, his Wife	40	F		France	United States	Cavalier	25 Jul 1828
Andrew	30		Gentn.	Great Britian	U. States	Columbia	7 May 1828

NAMES OF PASSENGERS	AGE	SEX	OCCUPATIONS	COUNTRY TO WHICH THEY BELONG	COUNTRY THEY INTEND TO INHABIT	SHIPS/DATES OF ARRIVAL	
CLINE (cont'd)							
Barbara	18	F		France	United States	Cavalier	25 Jul 1828
C.	38	M	Servant	Germany	Germany	Benjamin	10 Aug 1821
Christian	22		Weaver	France	U. States	Parachute	14 May 1828
Ignale	2	F		France	United States	Cavalier	25 Jul 1828
Jacob	22	M	Taylor	Germany	U. States	Isabella	10 Aug 1829
Jean	16	F		France	United States	Cavalier	25 Jul 1828
Jean	54	F	Wheelright	France	United States	Cavalier	25 Jul 1828
John	23		Gentn.	Great Britan	U. States	Columbia	7 May 1828
Joseph	21	M		France	United States	Cavalier	25 Jul 1828
M.	9	F		France	United States	Cavalier	25 Jul 1828
Peter	25		Tailor	France	U. States	Parachute	14 May 1828
Thre.	7	F		France	United States	Cavalier	25 Jul 1828
CLING, Alex	7	M	D. Maker	Ireland	N. York	Trusty	12 Sep 1828
Mary M.	10	F	Servant	Ireland	N. York	Trusty	12 Sep 1828
Sarah	30	F	Servant	Ireland	N. York	Trusty	12 Sep 1828
CLINKLEY, William F.	29	M	Gardiner			Nimrod	21 Sep 1820
CLINMOK, Francis	22	M	Baker	England	United States	Siroc	31 Oct 1829
CLINTON, Alice	35	F		Ireland	U.S. of America	Douglass	6 Jul 1829
Allan	25	M	Barrister	Scotland	U.S. States of Am.	Camillus	17 Sep 1823
Arthur Glynn	22	M	Barrister	Scotland	U.S. States of Am.	Camillus	17 Sep 1823
Bartholomew	37	M	Merchant	Ireland	U. States	Ganges	21 Jun 1827
Henry	20	M	Gentleman	England	United States	Marion	25 Nov 1825
Joseph	1 9/12	M		Ireland	U.S. of America	Douglass	6 Jul 1829
CLIOLOT, Adolphe	20	M	Merchant	France	Spain	Circassian	13 Jun 1825
CLIPERD, Allen	28	M		Ireland	United States	Sarah G.	20 Jul 1827
CLIRKIN, Peter	20	M	Baker	Ireland	U. States	Franklin	7 Jul 1828
CLISSOLD, Thomas	25	M	Laborer	England	United States	Danube	13 Jul 1827
CLOCK, C.	28	M	Shephard	Saxony	U. States	Minerva	23 May 1825
CLOGSTON, Agnes	24	F		Ireland	United States	John Dickinson	18 Feb 1822
Robert	22	M		Ireland	United States	John Dickinson	18 Feb 1822
CLOR, Adam	17	M		France	America, U.N.S.	Great Britain	3 Aug 1829
Adam	50	M	Farmer	France	America, U.N.S.	Great Britain	3 Aug 1829
Catharina	2	F		France	America, U.N.S.	Great Britain	3 Aug 1829
Effa	6	F		France	America, U.N.S.	Great Britain	3 Aug 1829
Elizabeth	12	F		France	America, U.N.S.	Great Britain	3 Aug 1829
Magdalina	4	F		France	America, U.N.S.	Great Britain	3 Aug 1829
Marguerita	16	F		France	America, U.N.S.	Great Britain	3 Aug 1829
Marguerita	40	F		France	America, U.N.S.	Great Britain	3 Aug 1829
Michel	14	M		France	America, U.N.S.	Great Britain	3 Aug 1829
Salime	3/12	F		France	America, U.N.S.	Great Britain	3 Aug 1829
CLOSE, Laurent	34	M	Professor at the American Asylum at Hartford, Connecticut			Brandt	21 May 1821
Mathew	23	M	Labourer	Ireland	United States	Wilson	22 Jun 1824
CLOSS, Margaret	20	F	Spinster	Ireland	United States	Erin	25 Dec 1820
Saml.	40	M	Servant	New York	U. States	William Thompson	6 Sep 1822
CLOTHIER, Edward	22	M	Farmer	England	America	Adams	21 Jun 1824
Edward	29					Copernicus	3 Aug 1829
James	29					Copernicus	3 Aug 1829
CLOUD, Ma.	26	M	Servent		St. Croix	Admittance	8 Mar 1826
CLOUGH, Amy	17 3/12	F	Spinster	Great Britain	United States	Corinthian	5 Jan 1824
James	19	M	Spinster	Great Brittain	United States	Corinthian	9 Jan 1827
Joseph	8	M		Great Britain	United States	Mary	11 Jul 1820
Joseph	40	M	Mechanic	Great Britain	United States	Corinthian	5 Jan 1824
Mary	6	F		Great Britain	United States	Mary	11 Jul 1820
Mary	37	F		Great Britain	United States	Mary	11 Jul 1820
Sarah	2	F		Great Britain	United States	Mary	11 Jul 1820
CLOUGHN, Alexander	6	M				Boston	28 Aug 1821
Eliza	24	F				Boston	28 Aug 1821
Thos.	33	M	Farmer	U. States	U. States	Boston	28 Aug 1821
CLOUREY, Eliz.	28	F	None	Ireland	U. States	Franklin	7 Jul 1828
CLOUSE, Anna	52	F		Germany	United States	Samuel Robertson	8 Aug 1828
Clouse	10	M		Germany	United States	Samuel Robertson	8 Aug 1828

NAMES OF PASSENGERS	AGE	SEX	OCCUPATIONS	COUNTRY TO WHICH THEY BELONG	COUNTRY THEY INTEND TO INHABIT	SHIPS/DATES OF ARRIVAL	
CLOUSE (cont'd)							
Joanas	18	F		Germany	United States	Samuel Robertson	8 Aug 1828
Joseph	22	M		Germany	United States	Samuel Robertson	8 Aug 1828
Maria	23	F		Germany	United States	Samuel Robertson	8 Aug 1828
Nicholas	55	M	Farmer	Germany	United States	Samuel Robertson	8 Aug 1828
CLOVER, Ann	10			England	U.S. America	Constitution	18 Jun 1827
Betsy	21	F		Great Britain	United States	Atlantic	28 May 1827
Catherine	9/12			England	U.S. America	Constitution	18 Jun 1827
Edward	30		Carpenter	England	U.S. America	Constitution	18 Jun 1827
Edward, Jr.	6			England	U.S. America	Constitution	18 Jun 1827
Eliza	3			England	U.S. America	Constitution	18 Jun 1827
Elizabeth	2			England	U.S. America	Constitution	18 Jun 1827
Frederick	5			England	U.S. America	Constitution	18 Jun 1827
George	1			England	U.S. America	Constitution	18 Jun 1827
Jane	7			England	U.S. America	Constitution	18 Jun 1827
Jane	32			England	U.S. America	Constitution	18 Jun 1827
Mary	8			England	U.S. America	Constitution	18 Jun 1827
Mary	28			England	U.S. America	Constitution	18 Jun 1827
Mary Ann	3			England	U.S. America	Constitution	18 Jun 1827
Wm.	24	M	...	Great Britain	United States	Atlantic	28 May 1827
CLOWES, John	34	M	Farmer	Great Britain	New York	Orozimbo	2 Oct 1824
Rachel	13	F		Great Britain	Canada	Orozimbo	2 Oct 1824
CLOWGAN, Peter	20	M		Great B.	U. States	William Neilson	26 Jul 1828
CLOWS, Thedoras	34	M	Merchant	United States	St. John	Nancy R. Crowell	21 Sep 1822
CLOYNE, Betty	1	F		Great Britain	United States	Atlantic	28 May 1827
Ellen	5	F		Great Britain	United States	Atlantic	28 May 1827
Micheal	25	M	Servant	Great Brittain	U. States	William Byrnes	23 Jul 1824
CLUCK, James	22	M	Merch.	U.S.	U.S.	Silvanus Jenkins	17 Mar 1828
CLUCKETT, Ann	18	F	Spinster	England	U. States	Electra	7 Jul 1828
James	19	M	Spinster	England	U. States	Electra	7 Jul 1828
CLUFF, Ann	20	F	Cabinet Maker	Gt. Britain	U.S.A.	Dalhouse Castle	21 Aug 1829
Ann	20	F		Great Britain	United States	Dalhouse Castle	21 Aug 1829
Eliza	4	F	Cabinet Maker	Gt. Britain	U.S.A.	Dalhouse Castle	21 Aug 1829
Eliza	4	F		Great Britain	United States	Dalhouse Castle	21 Aug 1829
Emily	2	F	Cabinet Maker	Gt. Britain	U.S.A.	Dalhouse Castle	21 Aug 1829
Emily	2	F		Great Britain	United States	Dalhouse Castle	21 Aug 1829
Joseph	29	M	Cabinet Maker	Gt. Britain	U.S.A.	Dalhouse Castle	21 Aug 1829
Joseph	29	M	Cabinet Maker	Great Britain	United States	Dalhouse Castle	21 Aug 1829
Susan Jane	3	F	Cabinet Maker	Gt. Britain	U.S.A.	Dalhouse Castle	21 Aug 1829
Susan Jane	3	F		Great Britain	United States	Dalhouse Castle	21 Aug 1829
CLUNN, Charles	35	M	Mariner	United States	U. States	Robert Reade	9 Feb 1822
CLUSKEY, Patrick	25	M	Farmer	Ireland	America	Minerva	31 May 1824
CLYBURN, Richard	55	M	Gentleman	Ireland	New York	Brighton	24 Aug 1827
CLYDE, John	31	M	Carpenter	New Brunswick	Canada	Belleville	29 Aug 1827
CO..., —	30	F		Switzerland	United States	Elbe	2 Aug 1822
Christian	38	M	Farmer	Switzerland	United States	Elbe	2 Aug 1822
Danl.	18	M	Farmer	Switzerland	United States	Elbe	2 Aug 1822
CO...CK, James	29	M	Labourer	Ireland		Marchioness	13 May 1828
CO...DY, Ja...	18		...			Amphion	31 May 1824
CO...MON, Luke	25	M	Labourer	Ireland	United States	Essex	23 May 1828
COAKLAY, Hy.	42	M	Mcht.	U. States	U. States	Nassau	24 Nov 1824
Daniel	27	M	Silk Weaver	England	U.S. American	Criterion	7 Jul 1824
COALES, John	...	...	...	Ireland	U. States of America	Courier	17 Mar 1827
COALTHURST, Anna	8	F				Splendid	14 Aug 1829
Elizabeth	35	F				Splendid	14 Aug 1829
Jacob	12	M				Splendid	14 Aug 1829
John	19	M				Splendid	14 Aug 1829
John	26	M	Farmer			Splendid	14 Aug 1829
Joseph	3	M				Splendid	14 Aug 1829
Margaret	10	F				Splendid	14 Aug 1829
Mary	17	F				Splendid	14 Aug 1829
Nerston	13	F				Splendid	14 Aug 1829
Robert	20	M	Farmer			Splendid	14 Aug 1829
Tanier	18	F				Splendid	14 Aug 1829

NAMES OF PASSENGERS	AGE	SEX	OCCUPATIONS	COUNTRY TO WHICH THEY BELONG	COUNTRY THEY INTEND TO INHABIT	SHIPS/DATES OF ARRIVAL	
COALTHURST (cont'd)							
Thomas	6	M				Splendid	14 Aug 1829
Thomas	48	M	Miner			Splendid	14 Aug 1829
COAN, Ann Maria	40			Ireland	United States	Jno. Dickinson	21 Sep 1821
Mathew	45		Mariner	United States	United States	Jno. Dickinson	21 Sep 1821
COANE, Wm.	35	M	Labourer	Ireland	America	Weser	26 Jun 1821
COAP, Margaret	75	F		Ireland	United States	Magnet	16 May 1823
Mary	18	F		Ireland	United States	Magnet	16 May 1823
COATES, Alice	6	M	None	Lancaster	Lancaster	Howard Douglass	11 May 1827
Ann	1	F	None	Lancaster	Lancaster	Howard Douglass	11 May 1827
Ann	14	F		England	United States	Amelia	20 Aug 1829
Ann	30	F	None	Lancaster	Lancaster	Howard Douglass	11 May 1827
Christr.	27	M	Farmer	Lancaster	Lancaster	Howard Douglass	11 May 1827
Francis	30	M	Labourer	Lancaster	Lancaster	Howard Douglass	11 May 1827
Helen	43	F		England	United States	Amelia	20 Aug 1829
James	3	M		England	United States	Amelia	20 Aug 1829
Janet	10	F	None	Lancaster	Lancaster	Howard Douglass	11 May 1827
John	2	M	None	Lancaster	Lancaster	Howard Douglass	11 May 1827
John	16	M		England	United States	Amelia	20 Aug 1829
John	48	M	Farmer	England	United States	Amelia	20 Aug 1829
Mary	11	F		England	United States	Amelia	20 Aug 1829
Richd.	7	M	None	Lancaster	Lancaster	Howard Douglass	11 May 1827
S. W.	30	M	Merchant	U.S. America	U.S. America	Cincinnatus	31 Oct 1820
Saml.	9	M	None	Lancaster	Lancaster	Howard Douglass	11 May 1827
Samuel	30	M	P...ter	Belfast	United States	Minerva	30 Oct 1829
Sarah	8	F		England	United States	Amelia	20 Aug 1829
Thomas	4	M	None	Lancaster	Lancaster	Howard Douglass	11 May 1827
Thomas	19	M		England	United States	Amelia	20 Aug 1829
Victor	15	M	...	Ireland	U.S. America	Columbia	26 Nov 1825
COATS, Agnes	40	F	None	Scotland	United States	Mary & Susan	5 Aug 1828
Ann	35	F	None	Great Britain	United States	Martha	6 Feb 1822
James	8	M	None	Scotland	United States	Mary & Susan	5 Aug 1828
Jane	12	F	None	Scotland	United States	Mary & Susan	5 Aug 1828
John	12	M	None	Great Britain	United States	Courier	26 Jun 1827
Johnn	40	M	Shop Keeper	Great Britain	United States	Martha	6 Feb 1822
William	50	M	Tailor	Great Britain	United States	Courier	26 Jun 1827
Wm., Jur.	17	M	Tailor	Great Britain	United States	Courier	26 Jun 1827
COBA, Euphrona, Miss	20			Spain	U. States	Greek	1 Oct 1825
Marcus	20/12	M		Spain	U. States	Greek	1 Oct 1825
COBB, Alexr.	29	M	Sailmaker	U. States	U. States	Sarah	4 Aug 1825
N., Mrs.	30			America		Meteor	25 Aug 1823
COBERN, Jane	19 1/12	F		Ireland	America	Carolina Ann	7 Apr 1826
COBERT, Jacob	40	M	Merchant	U. States	U. States	Beaver	2 Feb 1822
COBET, George	40	M	Miner	England	England	Eliza	31 Jul 1826
COBEZA, Francis	30	M	Gent.	Spain	Spain	Fabius	19 Mar 1825
COBIN, L.	42	M	Merchant	France	U. States	Waldo	19 Aug 1826
COBURGH, Abraham	14	M	Boyo	England	U.S.	Robert Edwards	11 Nov 1822
COBURN, D.	25		Farmer	Ireland	United States	Courier	16 May 1825
J.	50		Farmer	Ireland	United States	Courier	16 May 1825
R.	56		Farmer	Ireland	United States	Courier	16 May 1825
William	25	M	Farmer	Ireland	New York	Louisa	20 Jul 1826
COBY, Henry	33	M	...	Gt. Britain	United States	Crisis	13 Nov 1824
COCHERAN, William	22	M	Labourer	...	United States	Baltic	21 Apr 1827
COCHETEL, E., Mr.	12	M	None	U. States	U. States	Bayard	9 Jul 1824
G., Mrs.	32	F	None	U. States	U. States	Bayard	9 Jul 1824
COCHIN, —	38	M	Mariner	Spain	U. States	Maria Ann	29 Sep 1823
*landed at Balize [Biloxi?], Missippi							
COCHIS, E.	22	M	Merchant	Jemmny	U. States	Mary Livingston	26 Jul 1824
COCHLAN, L.	40	M	Farmer	Ireland	America	Mary	29 May 1827

NAMES OF PASSENGERS	AGE	SEX	OCCUPATIONS	COUNTRY TO WHICH THEY BELONG	COUNTRY THEY INTEND TO INHABIT	SHIPS/DATES OF ARRIVAL	
COCHLAN (cont'd)							
Timothy	26	M	Labourer	Great Britain	United States	Henrietta	19 Oct 1825
COCHRAN, —	40	M	Servant	Ireland	Ireland	Argus	12 Dec 1826
Alexander	1 6/12	M		Ballymopoly	...	Gleaner	24 May 1823
Alexr.	56	M	Chandler	Great Britain	U. States	United States	8 Sep 1827
Ann	6	F	Spinster	Ballymopoly	...	Gleaner	24 May 1823
Ann	24	F	Farmer	Longford		Mount Vernon	7 Jun 1824
Ann	35	F	Spinster	Ballymopoly	...	Gleaner	24 May 1823
Catharine	15	F		Ireland	United States	William & George	14 May 1828
Elenor	20	F		Ireland	United States	William & George	14 May 1828
Eliza	30	F		Great Britain	U. States	Lord Wellington	17 Mar 1823
Elizabeth	20		Milliner	Ireland	Great Britain	Robert Burns	14 Jun 1824
H.	35		Farmer	Ireland	United States	Courier	16 May 1825
Hugh	7	M		Great Britain	U. States	Lord Wellington	17 Mar 1823
Hugh	23	M	Coopper	Ireland	Ireland	Trident	17 May 1825
Isabella	27		Wife [of James]	Great Britain	United States	Camillus	12 Sep 1827
James	2	M		Ireland		Louisa	7 Oct 1824
James	4	M		Ballymopoly	...	Gleaner	24 May 1823
James	29	M	Clergyman	Ireland	United States	Louisa	7 Oct 1824
James	37		Weaver	Great Britain	United States	Camillus	12 Sep 1827
Jane	8	F		Ireland	United States	Louisa	7 Oct 1824
Jane	22	F		Ireland	United States	Romulus	24 Jun 1826
Jane	26	F		Ireland	United States	Louisa	7 Oct 1824
Janes	34	M	Midshipman	U. States	U. States	Factor	9 Mar 1829
Jas.	5		Family [of Margaret]	Great Britain	United States	Camillus	12 Sep 1827
Jno.	9		Family [of Margaret]	Great Britain	United States	Camillus	12 Sep 1827
John	4	M		Ireland	United States	Louisa	7 Oct 1824
John	20	M	Mill wright	Great Britain	U. States	United States	8 Sep 1827
John	25	M	Weaver	Ireland	United States	Romulus	24 Jun 1826
John	40		Farmer	Great Britain	United States	Camillus	12 Sep 1827
M.	27		Farmer	Ireland	United States	Courier	16 May 1825
Margaret	6/12	F		Ireland	United States	Romulus	24 Jun 1826
Margaret	9	F		Great Britain	U. States	Lord Wellington	17 Mar 1823
Margaret	27		Spinster and family going to her husband	Great Britain	United States	Camillus	12 Sep 1827
Margaret	46		Child [of James]	Great Britain	United States	Camillus	12 Sep 1827
Mary	7		Family [of Margaret]	Great Britain	United States	Camillus	12 Sep 1827
Michael	33	M	Labourer	Ireland	America	Dewitt Clinton	27 Jul 1824
Rebecca	52	F		Ireland	United States	William & George	14 May 1828
Robert	34	M	Merchant	Great Britain	U. States	Lord Wellington	17 Mar 1823
Robt.	50	M		Ireland	United States	William & George	14 May 1828
S.	37		Farmer	Ireland	United States	Courier	16 May 1825
Thomas	40	M	Merchant	Ireland	United States	Abigail	25 Jun 1822
William	32	M	Merchant	G. Britain	U. States	James Monroe	18 Apr 1821
Wm.	19		Labourer	St. John	U. States	Lady Hunter	5 Jul 1823
Wm.	27	M	Farmer	Ballymopoly	...	Gleaner	24 May 1823
COCHRANE, Ann	16	F		Ireland		Ocean	17 Aug 1820
David	15	M	None	Ireland	Und. Stts of Amer	Alexander Mansfield	18 Aug 1826
Ellen	5	F	None	England	U.S.A.	Lima	6 Dec 1826
H.	2	F		Scotland	U. States	Superior	25 Sep 1828
James	1	M	None	England	U.S.A.	Lima	6 Dec 1826
John	24	M	Shoe Maker	Scotland	New York	Joseph Hume	26 Oct 1829
John	30	M	Farmer	Ireland	United States	Samuel Robertson	9 Apr 1828
Mary	27	F	None	England	U.S.A.	Lima	6 Dec 1826
Moses	27	M	Farmer	Ireland	United States	Samuel Robertson	9 Apr 1828
Paterson	11	F	Farmer	Scotland	America	Mentor	21 Sep 1824
S.	22	F		Scotland	U. States	Superior	25 Sep 1828
Saml	60	M	Farmer			Ocean	17 Aug 1820

NAMES OF PASSENGERS	AGE	SEX	OCCUPATIONS	COUNTRY TO WHICH THEY BELONG	COUNTRY THEY INTEND TO INHABIT	SHIPS/DATES OF ARRIVAL	
COCHRANE (cont'd)							
Sarah	3	F	None	England	U.S.A.	Lima	6 Dec 1826
Sarah	50	F				Ocean	17 Aug 1820
Thomas	23	M	Labourer	Ireland	New York	America	1 Aug 1828
William	25	M	Labourer		New York	Prince Madore	28 Aug 1820
COCHREN, Ann	1/2		Child	Great Britain	United States	Camillus	12 Sep 1827
John	2 1/2		Child	Great Britain	United States	Camillus	12 Sep 1827
Mathew	1		Child	Great Britain	United States	Camillus	12 Sep 1827
COCK, —, Mr.	20	M		England	U. States	Milton	6 Dec 1825
—, Mr.	24	M		England	U. States	Milton	6 Dec 1825
H. H.	28	M	U.S. Navy	U. States	U. States	Pharos	10 Jun 1824
J.	45	M	Merchant	St. Johns	Great Britain	St. Michael	5 Jan 1826
Jno.	16	M	Farmer	Ireland	U. States	Edward	15 Jul 1825
John	27	M	Mechanic	England	United States	John Wells	22 May 1826
Thos.	36	M	Merchant	Scotland	United States	Orozimbo	5 Mar 1827
COCKAYNE, Joseph	28	M	Mercht.	Boston	U.S.	Esther	9 May 1825
COCKBURN, Barha	23	F	Spinster	Ireland		Robert Fulton	4 Jun 1828
Edward	30	M	Merchant	Scotland	United States	Commerce	17 Jul 1823
J.	42	M	Merchant	New York	America	Hannibal	4 Oct 1822
James	23	M		Scotland	New York	Cincinnatus	5 Dec 1825
Jane	35	F		Scotland	United States	Commerce	17 Jul 1823
John, Lieut	27	M	British Army	England	U. States	William Thompson	25 Aug 1828
Louisa, Mrs.	21	F		England	U. States	William Thompson	25 Aug 1828
COCKELL, David	23	M		Great Britian	United States	Andes	19 Aug 1829
Hugh	15	F		Great Britian	United States	Andes	19 Aug 1829
Margaret	20	F		Great Britian	United States	Andes	19 Aug 1829
Michael	40	M	Farmer	Great Britian	United States	Andes	19 Aug 1829
COCKER, Abrem	25	M	Laber	Irland	U. States	Nancy	27 Jun 1823
Benjamin	28	M	Farmer	Great Britain	United States	Eliza Barker	3 Jul 1826
Eliza	26	F	None	Great Britain	United States	Eliza Barker	3 Jul 1826
Elizabeth	4	F	None	Great Britain	United States	Eliza Barker	3 Jul 1826
Samuel	26	M	Mould	Scotland	United States	Camillus	27 Oct 1829
COCKEREN, John	25	M	Laborer	Ireland	United States	Nancey	8 Jun 1822
COCKERIN, Bridjet	37	F		Great Britain	New York	Philetus	21 Jul 1827
Thomas	25	M	Carpenter	England	United States	St. George	25 Aug 1829
Thos.	25	M	Carpenter	England	United States	St. George	25 Aug 1829
COCKEROFT, Elizabeth	25	F	None	Canada	Canada	Mentor	20 Oct 1825
Landale	38	M	Physician	Canada	Canada	Mentor	20 Oct 1825
COCKEY, John	30	M		Ireland	United States	William Byrnes	11 Dec 1827
COCKIN, Hannah	6	F	Weaver	Great Britain	U.S. America	Chili	7 Jul 1827
Harriet	4	F	Weaver	Great Britain	U.S. America	Chili	7 Jul 1827
John	13	M	Weaver	Great Britain	U.S. America	Chili	7 Jul 1827
John	41	M	Labourer	Great Britain		Casanda	5 Sep 1827
Joseph	8	M	Weaver	Great Britain	U.S. America	Chili	7 Jul 1827
Lenord	36	M	Weaver	Great Britain	U.S. America	Chili	7 Jul 1827
Martha	4/12	F	Weaver	Great Britain	U.S. America	Chili	7 Jul 1827
Mary	36	F	Weaver	Great Britain	U.S. America	Chili	7 Jul 1827
Matilda	11	F	Weaver	Great Britain	U.S. America	Chili	7 Jul 1827
Mellen	16	M	Weaver	Great Britain	U.S. America	Chili	7 Jul 1827
Sarah	45	F	None	Great Britain		Casanda	5 Sep 1827
Walter	2	M	Weaver	Great Britain	U.S. America	Chili	7 Jul 1827
COCKLETT, Sarah	21	F		England	U.N. States	Helen	17 Dec 1827
Thos.	24	M	Farmer	England	U.N. States	Helen	17 Dec 1827
COCKLIN, Nicholas	37	M	Tanner	Ireland	New York	Thames	6 Oct 1820
COCKMAN, Jane	25	F	Servant	Ireland	United States	Sarah G.	15 May 1828
COCKRAM, Thomas	27	M	Merchant	Great Britain	New York	Intrepid	8 Aug 1822
COCKRAN, Ann	40	F		St. Johns	St. Johns	St. Michael	26 Oct 1824
Ellen	30	F	Wife	Ireland	United States	Dublin Packet	13 Oct 1828
Fergus	23	M	Merchant	Great Britian	United States	George Clinton	13 Apr 1826
John	38	M	Weaver	Great Britain	United States	Colossus	5 Jun 1827
Patrick	28	M	Cooper	Ireland	U. States	Prize	10 Jun 1824
Saml.	18	M	Clerk	England	England	William Byrnes	14 Apr 1824
Thomas	2	M	Child	Ireland	United States	Dublin Packet	13 Oct 1828
William	16	M	Farmer	St. John, N.B.	St. John, N.B.	St. Michaels	24 Mar 1825
COCKRANE, James	26	M	Weaver	Great Britain	United States	Courier	26 Jun 1827
John	29	M	Labourer	Ireland	United States	Matvina	19 Oct 1826
COCKREN, Marey	21	F		Ireland	United States	Nancey	8 Jun 1822

NAMES OF PASSENGERS	AGE	SEX	OCCUPATIONS	COUNTRY TO WHICH THEY BELONG	COUNTRY THEY INTEND TO INHABIT	SHIPS/DATES OF ARRIVAL	
COCKRUN, James	31	M	Labourer	England	United States	Milton	20 Oct 1827
John	20	M	Labourer	England	United States	Milton	20 Oct 1827
COCKSAN, Mathew	27	M	Weaver	Ireland	United States	Meteor	27 Sep 1826
COCKSHOTT, W. R.	21	M	Merchant	Great Britan	Great Britan	Columbia	10 Mar 1824
COCKSON, Duncan	27	M	Marriner	Scotland	United States	Liverpool Trader	24 Oct 1825
COCODIVE, Eliz.	4	F				Hudson	23 Jul 1828
Hannah	2	F				Hudson	23 Jul 1828
May	26	F				Hudson	23 Jul 1828
COCOSAN, Philip	25	M	Joiner	England		Fame	9 Dec 1826
Thomas	21	M	Joiner	England		Fame	9 Dec 1826
COCRAN, M.	18	M	Merchant	United States	United States	Joseph	11 Jul 1821
CODAZZI, Augustine	31	M	Gentleman	Italy	South America	Louisiana	9 Aug 1826
CODD, Hannah	28	F		Ireland	U. States	Wilson	2 Sep 1823
John	29	M	Servant	St. John, N.B.	United States	Henrietta	3 Jun 1825
M. E.	31	F		Ireland	U. States	Wilson	2 Sep 1823
Maria	25	F		Ireland	U. States	Wilson	2 Sep 1823
Mathew	55	M	Merchant	Ireland	United States	Euphrates	12 May 1823
Patrick	24		Carpenter	Ireland	America	Sarah	18 Aug 1829
Phillis	37	F	Widow	Ireland	United States	Dublin Packet	9 Jul 1827
Robt.	30	M		Ireland	U. States	Fame	15 Nov 1826
Susannah	76	F	Widow	Ireland	United States	Dublin Packet	9 Jul 1827
CODDEN, Rosa	46	F	Seamstress	Great Britain	United States	Henrietta	19 Oct 1825
CODDIN, Bridget	8	F		Great Britain	United States	Henrietta	19 Oct 1825
CODDING, Pat.	10	M	Laborer	Ireland	U. States	Lady Hunter	14 Mar 1826
CODE, Eve	8	F		United States	United States	Globe	30 Aug 1828
Jacob	42	M	Farmer	United States	United States	Globe	30 Aug 1828
Regina	32	F		United States	United States	Globe	30 Aug 1828
CODERA..., William	24	M	Calico Printer	Great Britain	United States	Hamilton	21 Nov 1826
CODFIRSE, E. H.	32	F		Denmark	America	Jupiter	8 Apr 1828
CODMAN, George	27 9/12	M	Gentleman	United States	United States	Hector	8 Jan 1820
Richard	26	M	Merchant	United States	United States	Montano	31 May 1824
Sarah	40	F				Lady of the Lake	23 Aug 1828
CODRERDY, James	27		Laborer	Ireland	America	Parrington	9 Jun 1827
CODWIN, Edward	24		Accountant	United States	U. States	South Carolina Packet	4 Mar 1822
James	55	M	Farmer	U. States	United States	Eagle	26 Jul 1828
CODWISE, Geo. W.		M	Merchant	N. York	U. States	Boston	7 Nov 1823
George M.	32	M		U. States	U. States	Franklin	23 Jul 1827
James, Mrs.	50	F		St. Croix	St. Croix	Jupiter	19 Oct 1826
John	9	M	Schollar	St. Croix	New York	Jupiter	19 Oct 1826
CODY, Ann	20	F	Wife	Ireland	United States	Dublin Packet	22 Aug 1829
Ann	28			Ireland		Henrietta	26 Nov 1825
Catharine	8			Ireland		Henrietta	26 Nov 1825
Catharine	60			Ireland	Great Britain	Henrietta	26 Nov 1825
Edward	26		Labourer	Ireland	Great Britain	Henrietta	26 Nov 1825
James	5			Ireland		Henrietta	26 Nov 1825
John	30		Lawyer	Ireland	Great Britain	Henrietta	26 Nov 1825
John	65			Ireland	Great Britain	Henrietta	26 Nov 1825
Patrick	3			Ireland		Henrietta	26 Nov 1825
Patrick	35		Labourer	Ireland	Great Britain	Henrietta	26 Nov 1825
William	25		Labourer	Ireland	Great Britain	Henrietta	26 Nov 1825
COE, John	20	M	Farmer	England	United States	Caspian	12 Jul 1821
Jonathan	25	M	Miner	Mexico	England	Brown	23 Dec 1826
Thomas	55	M	Farmer	England	United States	Caspian	12 Jul 1821
COELER, Ann	25	F	Wife	Swiss	U. States	Comet	28 Jul 1825
John	34	M	Carpenter	Swiss	U. States	Comet	28 Jul 1825
John	infant	M	son	Swiss	U. States	Comet	28 Jul 1825
Margaret	infant	F	Daughter	Swiss	U. States	Comet	28 Jul 1825
COESTE, Timothy	...	...	...	...	...	St. Michael	22 Sep 1824
COFFARTT, Eliza	20	F	Lady	England	United States	Cambria	8 Oct 1828
COFFEE, Bernard	30	M	Butcher	Ireland	United States	Andes	2 Oct 1828
James	28	M	Medical Student	Ireland		Birmingham	11 Oct 1828
Susannah	32		Carpenter	England	United States	Corinthian	7 Jul 1829
Thomas	33		Carpenter	England	United States	Corinthian	7 Jul 1829
Wilham	23	M	Mason	Ireland	U.S.	Lady Hunter	10 Jul 1826
COFFER, D.	25	M	Taylor	Great Brit.	U. States	George	31 Jul 1820
Nicholas	22	M	Farmer	Ireland	Ut. States	Courier	13 Jul 1826
Timothy	28	M	Laborer or Spinster	Ireland	United States	Sarah G.	15 Aug 1827

NAMES OF PASSENGERS	AGE	SEX	OCCUPATIONS	COUNTRY TO WHICH THEY BELONG	COUNTRY THEY INTEND TO INHABIT	SHIPS/DATES OF ARRIVAL	
COFFEY, Betty	25	F	Servant	Ireland	United States	Josephine	30 Apr 1828
Mary	30	F		Great Britain	United States	Samuel Wright	12 Oct 1829
COFFIM, Mary	23	F	None	U. States	U. States	Asaph	23 Mar 1827
COFFIN, —, Capt.	40	M	Mariner	United States	United States	Great Britain	18 Sep 1826
—, Mr.	44	M	Painter	Marthas Vineyard	U. States	Alligator	15 Aug 1820
... [crossed out]	35	M	Mariner	United States	United States	Porcia	6 Apr 1826
B.	28	M	Mariner [crossed out]	U. States	United States	Porcia	6 Apr 1826
Caroline	36	F		U. States	U. States	Mattrawan	4 Jan 1826
D.	32	M	Merchant	U. States	U. States	Ladies Delight	7 Jul 1821
Daniel	31	M	Super Cargo			Ladies Delight	18 Sep 1820
Daniel	32	M	Mariner	U. States	U. States	Lady's Delight	21 Dec 1820
Danl.	33	M	Merchant	U. States	U. States	Ladies Delight	15 Oct 1821
Danl.	33	M	Merchant	U. States	U. States	Matteawan	6 Apr 1822
E., Mrs.	30	F	None	Great Britan	Canada	Canada	2 Jun 1824
Elia	27	M	Merchant	U. States	U. States	Lapwing	12 Jul 1828
Ellen	22	F		G. Britain	U. States	Sarah G	5 Jun 1828
Fethio	37	M	Mariner	Nantucket	Nantucket	Nimrod	21 Sep 1820
Francis C.	28	M	Mariner	U. States	U. States	Loire	17 Aug 1827
Frederick, Capt.	45 3/12	M	Mariner	America	America	Minerva	15 Jun 1825
Frederick M.	11	M	None	America	America	Minerva	15 Jun 1825
G. C., Major	40	M	Army Officer	Great Britan	Canada	Canada	2 Jun 1824
H., Capt.	50		Mariner	G. Britain	America	Magnet	24 Sep 1824
H., Captain	41	M	Ship Master	United States	United States	Meteor	17 Jan 1825
Hector	40	M	Merchant	America	America	Napoleon	26 May 1828
Isaac, Admiral Sir	66	M	Navy	Gt. Britan	Gt. Britan	Canada	8 Jun 1826
Isaac, Sir	50	M	Navy	Great Britain	Great Britain	Columbia	9 Aug 1822
J. J.	50	M	Merchant	U. States	U. States	Columbia	7 Sep 1827
Mary Jane	9 5/12	F	None	America	America	Minerva	15 Jun 1825
Sarah	42 4/12	F	None	America	America	Minerva	15 Jun 1825
Wm. H.	40		Merchant, white	England	England	Martha	10 Mar 1829
COFFON, William	30 6/12	M	Gentleman	Gt. Britain	U. States	Maria	22 May 1822
COFFRETT, William	28		Sadler	England	United States	Caspian	12 Jul 1821
COFFREY, Daniel	30	M	Laborer	Ireland	United States	St. Michaels	12 Jun 1826
COFFRUN, Jacob	36	M	Mercht.	U. States	U. States	Venus	10 Aug 1824
Nichs.	16	M	Mercht.	U. States	U. States	Venus	10 Aug 1824
COFFRY, Thomas	24	M	Labourer	Great Brittan	United States	America	24 Jul 1827
COFFY, Robt.	24	M	Labourer	England	U. States	Thomas Ritchie	2 Jul 1827
COFSTETES, Pierre	30	M	Weaver	Switzerland	United States	Thetis	5 Jul 1821
COG..., Mary ...	10	F		New Brunswick [?]	U. States	St. Michael	5 May 1827
COGAN, David A.	31		Merchant	England	England	London	16 Aug 1824
Hannah	22	F	Labourer	...	U. States	St. Michael	21 Jul 1824
John	19	M	Gardener	Ireland	New York	Munroe	27 May 1825
Joseph	8	M	Boy	Ireland	United States	Dublin Packet	23 May 1828
Micheal	27	M	Labourer	...	U. States	St. Michael	21 Jul 1824
Nancy	16	F	Labourer	...	U. States	St. Michael	21 Jul 1824
COGGALL, Geo.	45	M	Merchant	America	America	Corinthian	1 Sep 1827
COGGER, John	20	M	Labourer	Great Britian	United States	Mount Vernon	19 May 1823
COGGILL, Ann	39	F	Wife	America	America	Corinthian	1 Sep 1827
C. J.	13	M		America	America	Corinthian	1 Sep 1827
F. W.	4	M		America	America	Corinthian	1 Sep 1827
Geo.	16	M		America	America	Corinthian	1 Sep 1827
Heny.	17	M		America	America	Corinthian	1 Sep 1827
Julia	2	F		America	America	Corinthian	1 Sep 1827
Louisa	11	F		America	America	Corinthian	1 Sep 1827
Margaret Ann	19	F		America	America	Corinthian	1 Sep 1827
COGGINS, Bartholomew	21	M	Mason	Ireland	United States	Enterprize	23 Jul 1827
Fanny	18	F		Ireland	United States	Enterprize	23 Jul 1827
Pat	20	M	Labourer	Ireland	Unt. St. America	Wilson	21 May 1827
COGGSHALL, Freegift	34	M	Mainer	N. York	U. States	Herald	6 Feb 1824
Fregift	30	M	Mariner	America	U. States	New Priscilla	22 Aug 1823
George	50	M	Merchant	U. States	U. States	Gov. Clinton	1 Feb 1827
COGHILL, T.	27	M	Doctor	U.S.	U.S.	Toison	6 May 1828
COGHLAN, Anne	22	F		England	Canada	Leeds	7 Nov 1828
Anne Eliza	1 1/12	F		England	Canada	Leeds	7 Nov 1828
Bridget	11 4/12	F	Labourer	Ireland	America	Enterprize	29 Jun 1827
Elizabeth	20	F		Great Brittian	United States	Carolina Augusta	2 Dec 1828

NAMES OF PASSENGERS	AGE	SEX	OCCUPATIONS	COUNTRY TO WHICH THEY BELONG	COUNTRY THEY INTEND TO INHABIT	SHIPS/DATES OF ARRIVAL	
COGHLAN (cont'd)							
James	23	M	Laboror	Ireland	United States	Wilson	27 Jun 1826
James, Revd.	30	M	Clergyman	England	Canada	Leeds	7 Nov 1828
Jerh.	20	M	Laborer	Ireland	United States	Trio	13 Jun 1827
John	28	M		Great Brittian	United States	Carolina	
						Augusta	2 Dec 1828
COGHLIN, Elizabeth	27	F		Ireland	U. States	Grand Turk	3 Dec 1821
Mary	2	F		Ireland	U. States	Grand Turk	3 Dec 1821
COGIN, Jane	10	F		Great Britain	United States	Roanoak	19 Sep 1827
COGLAN, Bess	20	F		U. States	U. States	United States	11 Sep 1828
Danl.	22 6/12	M	Labourer	Ireland	America	Enterprize	29 Jun 1827
Garnot	47 5/12	M	Labourer	Ireland	America	Enterprize	29 Jun 1827
John	6	M		U. States	U. States	United States	11 Sep 1828
COGLER, Catherine	4	F		Germany	Missouri	Isabella	15 Sep 1828
Freda	36	F		Germany	Missouri	Isabella	15 Sep 1828
Johannes	40	M	Farmer	Germany	Missouri	Isabella	15 Sep 1828
Josephina	8	F		Germany	Missouri	Isabella	15 Sep 1828
Martin	2	F		Germany	Missouri	Isabella	15 Sep 1828
COGSWELL, Mary	38	F		Canary		Quill	11 May 1825
Nathl.	47	M	Merchant	Canary		Quill	11 May 1825
COHAN, Anna	20	F	None	England	New York	Brighton	19 Aug 1829
Anna	20	F	None	England		Brighton	19 Aug 1829
Esther	10	F	None	England	New York	Brighton	19 Aug 1829
Esther	10	F	None	England		Brighton	19 Aug 1829
Evelina	7	F	None	England	New York	Brighton	19 Aug 1829
Evelina	7	F	None	England		Brighton	19 Aug 1829
Henrietta	40	F	None	England	New York	Brighton	19 Aug 1829
Henrietta	40	F	None	England	New York	Brighton	19 Aug 1829
Julia	16	F	None	England	New York	Brighton	19 Aug 1829
Julia	16	F	None	England	New York	Brighton	19 Aug 1829
Michael	12	M	None	England	New York	Brighton	19 Aug 1829
Michael	12	M	None	England		Brighton	19 Aug 1829
COHEN, A.	8	M		Gt. Britain	United States	Robert Edwards	1 Jun 1826
A.	12	M		Gt. Britain	United States	Robert Edwards	1 Jun 1826
Abm.	3	M	Watchmaker	England	U. States	Cincinnatus	9 Jul 1825
C.	6	F		Gt. Britain	United States	Robert Edwards	1 Jun 1826
David	32	M	Watchmaker	England	U. States	Cincinnatus	9 Jul 1825
Elizabeth	5	F	Watchmaker	England	U. States	Cincinnatus	9 Jul 1825
Esdaire	28	M	Merchant	U. States	U. States	Caledonia	10 Sep 1828
Ester	58	F	Matron	Great Brittan	United States	Cambria	11 Feb 1829
Esther	8	F	Watchmaker	England	U. States	Cincinnatus	9 Jul 1825
Henry	16	M	Gentleman	G. Brittain	England	Abigail	25 Feb 1826
Isabella	20	F	None	Great Britain	United States	Hannibal	12 Oct 1829
James	22	M	None	Great Britain	United States	Hannibal	12 Oct 1829
John	2	M		Switzerland	Ohio	Eugenie	20 Aug 1827
John	25	M		Switzerland	Ohio	Eugenie	20 Aug 1827
Louis J.	25		Merchant	U.N.S.		Hudson	5 Apr 1826
M.	7/12	M		Gt. Britain	United States	Robert Edwards	1 Jun 1826
M.	40	M	Quill Maker	Gt. Britain	United States	Robert Edwards	1 Jun 1826
M. G.	2	M		Gt. Britain	United States	Robert Edwards	1 Jun 1826
Marie	28	F		Switzerland	Ohio	Eugenie	20 Aug 1827
Marie Ann	3	F		Switzerland	Ohio	Eugenie	20 Aug 1827
Phoebe	25	F	Watchmaker	England	U. States	Cincinnatus	9 Jul 1825
R.	32	F		Gt. Britain	United States	Robert Edwards	1 Jun 1826
Saj.	1	M	Watchmaker	England	U. States	Cincinnatus	9 Jul 1825
Samuel	27	M	Cabinet Maker	England	New York	Hudson	20 Nov 1828
Sarah	22	F		Great Brittan	United States	Cambria	11 Feb 1829
COHIN, Eleanor	27		his Wife			Cambria	19 Oct 1829
Ellen	11	F		Great Britain	U. States	Columbia	22 Sep 1828
Jane	2		his Daughter			Cambria	19 Oct 1829
Joseph S.	28		Cabinet Maker	England	United States	Cambria	19 Oct 1829
Maria	3		his Daughter			Cambria	19 Oct 1829
COHNOR, Ann	18	F	Scotland	Ireland	N. York	Lima	5 Aug 1829
COHOHA, Antonio	42	M	Priest	Spain	U. States	Horatio	21 Jan 1829
COIL, Edward	22	M		Ireland	United States	William Byrnes	15 Aug 1826
Eliza	25	F	Servant	St. Johns	U. States	Wanderer	30 Oct 1828
James	20	M	Labourer	Ireland	United States	Robert Fulton	24 Jul 1826
John	27	M	Labourer	Ireland	United States	Hope & Esther	17 Oct 1827
Margt.	23	F	Servant	Ireland	United States	Carolina Ann	11 Dec 1826

NAMES OF PASSENGERS	AGE	SEX	OCCUPATIONS	COUNTRY TO WHICH THEY BELONG	COUNTRY THEY INTEND TO INHABIT	SHIPS/DATES OF ARRIVAL	
COIL (cont'd)							
Pat	25	M	Labourer	St. Johns	U. States	Wanderer	30 Oct 1828
Thomas	28		Labourer	Scotland	United States	Camillus	3 May 1828
Thos.	4	M		St. Johns	U. States	Wanderer	30 Oct 1828
COILE, James	21	M	Laborer	Ireland	United States	Mary	1 Jul 1829
John	25		Labourer	County Carvan	N. York	Peru	30 May 1828
Mary	19	F		Ireland	United States	Mary	1 Jul 1829
Mary	30	F	None	Ireland	United States	Aurelia	7 Jun 1826
Patrick	29	M	Laborer	Ireland	United States	Mary	1 Jul 1829
COINEAU, J. G. P.	11	F		G. Britain	U. States	Hanford	18 Sep 1828
COIRHAN, Ann	30	F	None	Ireland	U. States	Henry Kneeland	27 Jul 1825
COISTRANE,							
Bridget	45 9/12	F		Ireland	U.S. of America	Douglass	6 Jul 1829
COIT, Elias L.	37	M	Merchant	New London	U. States	Rising Sun	19 Sep 1826
H.	22	M	Merchant	America, U.S.A.	United States	Belle	3 Aug 1822
H. A.	24	M	Merchant	N. York	U. States	Swan	24 Mar 1823
Henry	22	M	Merchant	U. States	U. States	Edgar	19 Aug 1820
Peter L.	27	M	Mariner	U.S.	U.S.	Abigail	21 Mar 1825
COITER, Philip	30		Baker	Germany	Germany	London	16 Aug 1824
COL...S, Richard F.	42	M	Tailor	England	Baltimore	Thames	6 Oct 1820
COLAN, Wm.	40	M	Merchant	Great Britain	United States	Cortes	19 Nov 1821
COLANAN, Isabela	17	F	Nurse	Ireland	U.S. America	New Hampshire	28 Sep 1826
Mary	19	F	Nurse	Ireland	U.S. America	New Hampshire	28 Sep 1826
Richard	49	M	Farmer	Ireland	U.S. America	New Hampshire	28 Sep 1826
COLAR, Barbara	16	F	Family [of John]	France	America	La Grange	7 Aug 1828
Catharine	8	F	Family [of John]	France	America	La Grange	7 Aug 1828
Elisabeth	12	F	Family [of John]	France	America	La Grange	7 Aug 1828
George	6	M	Family [of John]	France	America	La Grange	7 Aug 1828
John	14	M	Family [of John]	France	America	La Grange	7 Aug 1828
John	48	M	Farmer	France	America	La Grange	7 Aug 1828
Joseph	4	M	Family [of John]	France	America	La Grange	7 Aug 1828
Magdalene	4	F	Family [of John]	France	America	La Grange	7 Aug 1828
Magdalene	44	F	Family [of John]	France	America	La Grange	7 Aug 1828
COLARD, Cathan	56	F	Weaver	France		Pallas	14 Jun 1828
Catharn M.	25	F		France		Pallas	14 Jun 1828
George	39	M		France		Pallas	14 Jun 1828
COLASSO, Antho.	33	M	Mercht.	Spain	U. States	Fair American	16 Oct 1822
R.	25	M	Mercht.	Spain	U. States	Fair American	16 Oct 1822
COLBARNE, Elisabeth,							
Lady	38	F	Lady	England	U. Canada	Corinthian	8 Oct 1828
Jame, Miss	3	F	Gentln.	England	U. Canada	Corinthian	8 Oct 1828
John, Sir	48	M	Gentln.	England	U. Canada	Corinthian	8 Oct 1828
John S..., Mast.	2	M	Gentln.	England	U. Canada	Corinthian	8 Oct 1828
COLBERT, James	51	M	Labourer	Ireland	America	Franklin	13 Aug 1827
COLBORNE, Cordelia							
Ann Leathrony, Miss	4	F	Gentln.	England	U. Canada	Corinthian	8 Oct 1828
Edmund, Mast.	6	M	Gentln.	England	U. Canada	Corinthian	8 Oct 1828
Elizabeth, Miss	8	F	Gentln.	England	U. Canada	Corinthian	8 Oct 1828
Francis, Master	10	M	Gentln.	England	U. Canada	Corinthian	8 Oct 1828
Graham M., Mast.	5	M	Gentln.	England	U. Canada	Corinthian	8 Oct 1828
James, Master	12	M	Gentln.	England	U. Canada	Corinthian	8 Oct 1828
COLBRAN, John	44	M	Farmer	England	U. States	Commerce	2 Oct 1823
COLBRIDGE, Ann	27	F	Wife [of William]	Great Briton	United States	Orion	18 Jun 1821
William	36	M	Labourer	Great Briton	United States	Orion	18 Jun 1821
COLBURN, Zorah	20	M	Gentleman	America	United States	Euphrates	25 Jun 1824
COLCROFT, Hannah	26	F		Great Britain	United States	Samuel Wright	12 Oct 1829
Harriot	1	F		Great Britain	United States	Samuel Wright	12 Oct 1829
Jno.	5	M	Farmer	England	United States	Euphrates	18 Aug 1827
Mary	36	F	Farmer	England	United States	Euphrates	18 Aug 1827
Rob.	1	M	Farmer	England	United States	Euphrates	18 Aug 1827
Thomas	27	M	Carpet Weaver	Great Britain	United States	Samuel Wright	12 Oct 1829
COLD, Wm. T.	26	M	None	U. States	U. States	Birmingham	12 Oct 1829
COLDBECK, Wm.	42	M	Merchant	G. Britain	U. States	St. George	7 Jun 1828
COLDEN, —, Mrs.	60			G. Britain	America	Magnet	24 Sep 1824
David	27	M	None	New York	U. States	New York	15 Nov 1823
Francis	27	F	None	New York	U. States	New York	15 Nov 1823
COLDWELL, Alexr.	31 6/12	M	Captain	Gt. Britain	Gt. Britain	Betsey	18 Apr 1822
COLE, Ann	20	F	Dress Maker	Great Britain	United States	Exertion	17 Jul 1829
Cath.	20		Spinster	Ireland		Westmoreland	1 Aug 1826

NAMES OF PASSENGERS	A G E	S E X	OCCUPATIONS	COUNTRY TO WHICH THEY BELONG	COUNTRY THEY INTEND TO INHABIT	SHIPS/DATES OF ARRIVAL	
COLE (cont'd)							
Catherine	1	F		England	America	John Wells	11 Jun 1823
Charles	13		boy	Ireland	United States	Robert Burns	18 Jun 1821
Charles	25	M	Merchant	England	U. States	Ann Celia	29 Aug 1826
Domk.	25		Farmer	Ireland		Westmoreland	1 Aug 1826
E.	24	M	Clerk	G. Britain	U. States	Margaret Bogle	12 Jun 1828
Frances	6	F		United States	United States	Robert Edwards	1 Jun 1826
Frances	28	F		United States	United States	Robert Edwards	1 Jun 1826
Henry	20	M	Clerk of [John Cole]	U. Kingdom Great Britain	United States	Cambria	7 May 1828
Henry	22	M	Carpenter	New Brunswick	United States	Lady Hunter	27 Dec 1825
J.	28		Farmer	Ireland	United States	Courier	16 May 1825
Jane	27	F	Wife of [John]	U. Kingdom Great Britain	United States	Cambria	7 May 1828
Jane R.	27	F		England	America	John Wells	11 Jun 1823
Jno. D.	23	M	Servant	W. Indies	U. States	Matilda	27 Apr 1822
John	27	M	Surgeon	U. Kingdom Great Britain	United States	Cambria	7 May 1828
M.	25	M		Ireland	U. States	Balaena	29 Apr 1825
Mary	24	F		Ireland	U. States	Balaena	29 Apr 1825
Mineous	20	M	Labourer	Ireland	United States	Edwin	29 Nov 1828
Sanday	2		Child	Ireland		Westmoreland	1 Aug 1826
Sarah	16		Spinster	Ireland	United States	Robert Burns	18 Jun 1821
Thomas	2	M		England	America	John Wells	11 Jun 1823
Thomas	28	M	Farmer	England	America	John Wells	11 Jun 1823
Thos.	24		Laborer	Great Britain	United States	Comet	9 Aug 1822
W. J.	23	M	Merchant	U. States	U. States	Eliza	26 Jul 1825
William	...	...		...	...	St. Michael	22 Sep 1824
William	22 4/12	M	Blacksmith	Great Britain	U. States	Robert Fulton	3 Dec 1827
COLEAND, D. A.	30	M	Servant	Curracoa	U. States	Charleston	10 May 1825
Isabella	18	F	Servant	Curracoa	U. States	Charleston	10 May 1825
COLEBROOK, Ellen	5/12	F	None	England	United States	London	21 May 1828
Harriet	18	F	None	England	United States	London	21 May 1828
Richard	25	M	Laborer	England	United States	London	21 May 1828
COLEBURN, Elizabeth	30	F	None	England	Pennsylva.	Commerce	24 Sep 1823
Mary	6	F	None	England	Pennsylva.	Commerce	24 Sep 1823
Wm.	33	M	Coal Miner	England	Pennsylva.	Commerce	24 Sep 1823
COLEIN, Edwd.	52	M	Mechanic	England	U. States	Otter	30 Oct 1826
COLEMAN, —	25	M	Mechanic	Hamburger	U. States	Lady Tompkins	9 Feb 1825
Allice	18	F	None	Ireland	U.S.A.	Dalhouse Castle	21 Aug 1829
Allice	18	F	None	Ireland	United States	Dalhouse Castle	21 Aug 1829
Charlotte	3	F		U. States	U. States	Caledonia	10 Sep 1828
Charlotte	23	F		U. States	U. States	Caledonia	10 Sep 1828
Edward	13	M	Farmer	England	America	Sarah	18 Aug 1829
Fredc.	30	M	Agricultur	France	United States	Stephania	24 Mar 1828
Honora	21	F	Labourer	Ireland	United States	Trio	5 May 1828
James	23	M	Farmer	England	America	Sarah	18 Aug 1829
James	26	M	Farmer	Ireland	America	Minerva	31 May 1824
James	27					Trio	5 May 1828
Jane	18	F	Lady	St. Johns, N.B.	St. Johns, N.B.	Sarah G	11 Sep 1827
Jas.	2	M		Great Britain	United States	William Dawson	18 Jun 1827
Jas.	4	M	Labourer	Ireland	United States	Trio	5 May 1828
Lucy	55	F	Farmer	England	America	Sarah	18 Aug 1829
M.	25	F	...	...	U. States	Governor Tompkins	26 Jul 1824
Mary	22	F		Ireland	United States	Trio	2 Oct 1828
— Mrs.	30		Wife of Wm.	Ireland	United States	Mexico	1 Jun 1821
Patrick	20	M	Stonemason	Ireland	U. States	Virginia	20 Jun 1825
Richard	40		Cooper	Ireland	United States	Mexico	1 Jun 1821
Saria	47		Mariner	Nantucket	America	Rockingham	23 Aug 1822
William	15	M	Printer	England	U. States	Roman	1 Dec 1828
William	26	M	Farmer	Ireland	America	William	21 May 1825
Willm. H.	28		Counseller	...	U. States	South Carolina Packet	17 May 1827
Wm.	25	M	Mariner	New York	U. States	Baltimore	6 Dec 1823
Wm.	45	M	Farmer	England	America	Sarah	18 Aug 1829
COLEMARD, Charles	23	M	Merchant	France	United States	Henry	9 Jun 1826
COLEMBEL, Pierre	18	M	None	France	U. States	Bayard	9 Jul 1824
COLENDER, Charles, Jr.	21	M		Great Britain	U. States	Corinthian	2 Sep 1824

NAMES OF PASSENGERS	AGE	SEX	OCCUPATIONS	COUNTRY TO WHICH THEY BELONG	COUNTRY THEY INTEND TO INHABIT	SHIPS/DATES OF ARRIVAL	
COLERAIN, Thomas	19		Farmer			Rufus King	7 Aug 1820
COLERAKE, Patrick	20	M	Labourer	Ireland	America	Wilson	16 May 1825
COLES, Charles	23	M	Merchant	Great Britain	Great Britain	Mentor	26 Dec 1826
Francis	28	F		England	America	Criterion	27 Oct 1821
Wm.	9/12	M		America	America	Criterion	27 Oct 1821
Wm.	28	M	Grocer	England	America	Criterion	27 Oct 1821
COLESHOW, Talyor	20	M	Farmer	England	America	Silas Richard	24 Oct 1829
COLETT, John	1	M		Native of Switzerland	United States	Canaris	30 Jun 1827
COLEY, Esther	3	F	None	England	United States	London	21 May 1828
George	29	M	None	England	United States	London	21 May 1828
Jane	25	F	None	England	United States	London	21 May 1828
Thomas	27	M	Laborer	England	United States	London	21 May 1828
COLFAX, Schuyler	29	M	Accountant	New Jersey	U. States	Catharine	15 May 1822
COLGAN, Ann	6	F	...	Ireland	United States	General Putnam	20 Jun 1825
Laurance	30 6/12	M	Labourer	Ireland	America	Enterprize	29 Jun 1827
Mary	35 5/12	F	Servant	Ireland	United States	Atlantic	21 Jul 1827
Mary, Jur.	20 2/12	F	Servant	Ireland	United States	Atlantic	21 Jul 1827
Mich.	30	M	Farmer	Ireland	United States	General Putnam	20 Jun 1825
COLGEN, Elizabeth	25 1/12	F		Ireland	U.S. of America	Douglass	6 Jul 1829
Mary	50	F	Spinster	Ireland	United States	Ann Maria	8 Jun 1824
P.	25		Farmer	Ireland	United States	Courier	16 May 1825
COLGIN, John	30	M	Merchant	G. Britain	Canada	Nancy	12 Aug 1820
COLHOON, Robert	19	M	Labourer	Ireland	United States	Robert Fulton	10 Aug 1827
Francis	23	M	Gentleman	Ireland	United States	Trident	16 May 1826
Robert	10	M	Boy	Ireland	United States	Trident	16 May 1826
COLIER, Anna	25	F	None	...	Philadelphia	Frances Henrietta	30 Jun 1827
John	1 6/12	M	None	...	Philadelphia	Frances Henrietta	30 Jun 1827
Robert	29	M	...	...	Philadelphia	Frances Henrietta	30 Jun 1827
COLIGAN, Edwd.	21	M	Heckler	Ireland	United States	Louisa	18 Apr 1827
Ewd.	25	M	Carpenter	Ireland	United States	Jubilee	13 Sep 1827
COLIN, A.	6	F	Farmer	Switzerland	U. States	Alfred	8 Jul 1828
Anne	3	F	Farmer	Switzerland	U. States	Alfred	8 Jul 1828
J. B.	30	M	Farmer	Switzerland	U. States	Alfred	8 Jul 1828
M.	20	F	Farmer	Switzerland	U. States	Alfred	8 Jul 1828
P. S.	23	M	Farmer	Switzerland	U. States	Alfred	8 Jul 1828
COLINAUGH, Isabella	37	F	...			York	10 Dec 1825
Jos.	37	M	...	G. Brittain	U. States	York	10 Dec 1825
COLINBOURO, Ann	52	F	None	Great Britain	Great Britain	Bolivar	21 May 1827
COLINS, James	54	M	Merchant	Scotland	U. States	Aurora	18 Sep 1821
COLL, Hugh	20	M	Labourer	Ireland	United States	Hope	12 Jun 1828
COLLAFAX, R.	18	M	Mechanic	Ireland	United States	Vermont	10 Jan 1827
COLLAGHAN, Danl.	10		Labourer	Ireland	United States	Geo. Canning	5 Jun 1828
Danl.	52		Farmer	Ireland	United States	Geo. Canning	5 Jun 1828
Ellen	17			Ireland	United States	Geo. Canning	5 Jun 1828
James	23		Farmer	Ireland	United States	Geo. Canning	5 Jun 1828
Joanna	4			Ireland	United States	Geo. Canning	5 Jun 1828
John	23		Farmer	Ireland	United States	Geo. Canning	5 Jun 1828
Joseph	25		Farmer	Ireland	United States	Geo. Canning	5 Jun 1828
Margret	40			Ireland	United States	Geo. Canning	5 Jun 1828
COLLAN, John	19	M	Artisen	Ireland	United States	Jubilee	13 Jul 1829
Mary	16	F	None	Ireland	United States	Jubilee	13 Jul 1829
COLLAND, Daniel Fox	21		Gentleman	England	England	Hudson	18 Jun 1825
Frances	30	F		England	America	Criterion	27 Oct 1821
Wm.	26	M	Farmer	England	America	Criterion	27 Oct 1821
COLLAS, John	26	M	Gent.	England	United States	Cosmo	26 Aug 1829
COLLE, —, Mrs.	23	F		Spain	Spain	Sabina	5 May 1826
Jos.	45	M	Gentleman	Spain	Spain	Sabina	5 May 1826
Jos., Jr.	4	M		Spain	Spain	Sabina	5 May 1826
Louisa	1	F		Spain	Spain	Sabina	5 May 1826
COLLEGHAN, Pat	29	M	Labourer	Ireland	U. States	York	7 Aug 1828
COLLERBOURNE, Wm.	25	M	Comedian	England	U. States	Pacific	20 Aug 1825
COLLET, Aglac	5	F		France	U. States	Montano	2 Sep 1828
Alexander	8	M	her Son [Juliana]	France	United States	Helen	5 Sep 1828
Alexander	30		fireman	France		Bayard	10 Sep 1827
Clemantine	9	F		France	U. States	Montano	2 Sep 1828

NAMES OF PASSENGERS	AGE	SEX	OCCUPATIONS	COUNTRY TO WHICH THEY BELONG	COUNTRY THEY INTEND TO INHABIT	SHIPS/DATES OF ARRIVAL	
COLLET (cont'd)							
Eliza	50	F		G. Britain	U. States	St. George	7 Jun 1828
Helena	1	F		France	U. States	Montano	2 Sep 1828
Juliana	30	F	Seamstress	France	United States	Helen	5 Sep 1828
Leon	4	M		France	U. States	Montano	2 Sep 1828
Pat	42	M	Boat Builder	G. Britain	U. States	St. George	7 Jun 1828
Thomas	40	M	Farmer	England	United States	Delta	24 Oct 1829
Timothy	53	M	Gentleman	G. Britain	G. Britain	Brittania	17 Jul 1828
Virginia	33	F		France	U. States	Montano	2 Sep 1828
COLLETT, Augest	4	M		Native of Switzerland	United States	Canaris	30 Jun 1827
Eliza	3	F		England	America	Silas Richard	24 Oct 1829
Elizabeth	26	F		England	America	Silas Richard	24 Oct 1829
Frank	6	M		Native of Switzerland	United States	Canaris	30 Jun 1827
Jane	20	F		G. Britain	U. States	St. George	7 Jun 1828
Jno.	14	M	Comedian	England	U. States	Pacific	20 Aug 1825
John	8	M		Native of Switzerland	United States	Canaris	30 Jun 1827
John	23	M	Labourer	G. Britain	U. States	St. George	7 Jun 1828
Mary	18	F		Native of Switzerland	United States	Canaris	30 Jun 1827
Peter	20	F	Farmer	Native of Switzerland	United States	Canaris	30 Jun 1827
Richard	5	M		England	America	Silas Richard	24 Oct 1829
Victor	38	M		Native of Switzerland	United States	Canaris	30 Jun 1827
COLLETTE, Lanbert	37	M	Goldsmith	Belgiggne	United States	Montano	5 May 1828
COLLEY, Abigail	18	F	None	England	United States	London	21 May 1828
Edward	8	M		Great B.	U. States	William Neilson	26 Jul 1828
George	12	M	None	England	United States	London	21 May 1828
George	53	M	Mechanic	Great Britain	England	John Wells	29 Jan 1825
George, Junr.	23	M	Mechanic	Great Britain	England	John Wells	29 Jan 1825
James	10	M	None	England	United States	London	21 May 1828
John	14	M	None	England	United States	London	21 May 1828
Joseph	4	M	None	England	United States	London	21 May 1828
Joseph	25	M		Great B.	U. States	William Neilson	26 Jul 1828
Mary	6	F		U. States	U. States	John Wells	29 Jan 1825
Mary	30	F		Great B.	U. States	William Neilson	26 Jul 1828
Mary	50	F	None	England	United States	London	21 May 1828
Sarah	6	F	None	England	United States	London	21 May 1828
Sarah	20	F		Great B.	U. States	William Neilson	26 Jul 1828
COLLIE, Ann	21	F		Scotland	Unt. States	Robert Fulton	14 Mar 1829
Robt.	25	M	Taylor	Scotland	Unt. States	Robert Fulton	14 Mar 1829
COLLIER, ...	30	M	Clothier	G. Braitan	U. States	Cosmo	29 Jun 1826
Cath.	21	F		Ireland	United States	Curler	3 Mar 1828
James	18	M	Tin plate Worker	G. Britain	U. States	London	23 Sep 1828
Jas.	18	M	Postillion	France	U.S. America	Huntress	6 Sep 1827
John	19	M	Tin plate Worker	G. Britain	U. States	London	23 Sep 1828
John	28	M	Farmer	Ireland	United States	Curler	3 Mar 1828
Judah	3	F		Ireland	United States	Curler	3 Mar 1828
May	17	F		G. Britain	U. States	London	23 Sep 1828
Ralph	21	M	Tin plate Worker	G. Britain	U. States	London	23 Sep 1828
Sarah	45	F		G. Britain	U. States	London	23 Sep 1828
Thos.	32	M	Gardner	England	New York	Brighton	16 Nov 1826
William	43	M	Wire Drawer	Great Britain	New York	Superior	5 Sep 1827
Wm.	5	M		G. Britain	U. States	London	23 Sep 1828
COLLIGAN, Bernard	22	M	Labourer	Ireland	United States	Josephine	30 Apr 1828
Mary	20	F		Ireland	United States	Josephine	30 Apr 1828
Ml.	24	M	Farmer	Great Britain	U. States	Dominica	4 Jan 1823
Willian	24	M	Weaver	Ireland	United States	Josephine	30 Apr 1828
COLLILANE, Jas.	21					Trio	5 May 1828
COLLIN, Catherine	34	F	Spinster	Ireland	United States	Wilson	4 Oct 1827
John	26	M	Labourer	Great Britain	United States	Mary & Harriet	3 Jul 1829
Mary	20	F	None	Great Britain	United States	Mary & Harriet	3 Jul 1829
Michael	11	M		G. Britain	U. States	London	23 Sep 1828
Michael	22	M	Carpenter	Ireland	United States	Clothier	22 Nov 1827
Philipa	36		None	Gt. Britan	United States	James Monroe	11 Dec 1821

NAMES OF PASSENGERS	AGE	SEX	OCCUPATIONS	COUNTRY TO WHICH THEY BELONG	COUNTRY THEY INTEND TO INHABIT	SHIPS/DATES OF ARRIVAL	
COLLIN (cont'd)							
Robert	21	M	...	...	...	Frances	
						Henrietta	30 Jun 1827
COLLINDRIDGE, —	38 7/12	F		England	U.S. American	Criterion	7 Jul 1824
Hannah	16 7/12	F		England	U.S. American	Criterion	7 Jul 1824
Joseph	14 2/12	M	...	England	U.S. American	Criterion	7 Jul 1824
Rebecca	10 8/12	F		England	U.S. American	Criterion	7 Jul 1824
Sopha	13 1/12	F		England	U.S. American	Criterion	7 Jul 1824
William	40 11/12	M	...	England	U.S. American	Criterion	7 Jul 1824
COLLINGS, —, Mrs.	30	F		U.S.	U.S.	Radius	9 May 1823
COLLINGWOOD, Rich.	36	M	Carpenter	England	New York	Brighton	19 Aug 1829
Richard	36	M	Carpenter			Brighton	19 Aug 1829
COLLINS, —,							
3 children	12, etc.		(males and				
			female) None	England	New York	Thames	6 Oct 1820
Abigail	13	F	Lady	England	America	Criterion	27 Oct 1821
Alex	34	M	Farmer	Ireland	U. States	Howard	
						Douglass	29 Jan 1828
Amelia	14	F		U. States	U. States	Silvia	10 Sep 1827
Ann	21	F	Servant	G. Britain	U. States	Wanderer	23 Jun 1828
Ann	25		Seamster	Scotland	United States	Camillus	3 May 1828
Anna	6	F		U. States	U. States	Silvia	10 Sep 1827
Anne	23	F	...	...	...	Laurel	16 Nov 1824
Benoni	20	M	Tailor	England	U.S. America	Cortes	19 May 1826
Betsey	9	F		Ireland	United States	John & Adam	21 Sep 1822
Betsey	15	F	...	Ireland	United States	General Putnam	20 Jun 1825
Betsey	18	F	None	United States	United States	Abigale	9 Aug 1822
Betsy	14	F		Great Brittan	United States	Cambria	11 Feb 1829
Bridget	18	F		Great Brittan	United States	Cambria	11 Feb 1829
C. W.	23	M	Merchant	Philada.	U. States	Hero	17 May 1825
Caroline	0 6/12	F		England	United States	Nimrod	31 Jul 1828
Cath.	20	F		St. Johns	U. States	Wanderer	30 Oct 1828
Cath.	28	F		England	United States	Nimrod	31 Jul 1828
Catherine	6	F	Child	Ireland	United States	St. Michaels	23 Dec 1826
Cathr.	10	F		Ireland	U. States	Albion	11 May 1827
Charles	18	M		U. States	U. States	Silvia	10 Sep 1827
Charles	25	M	weaver	Ireland	United States	Josephine	30 Apr 1828
Charles	41	M	Ground work man	England	United States	Robert Edwards	3 Oct 1829
Charles	56	M	Liet. Gov. of				
			R. Island	U. States	U. States	Perseverance	28 Apr 1828
Danl.	18	M	Laborer or Spinster	Ireland	United States	Sarah G	11 Sep 1827
David	25	M	Painter	Ireland	Und. Stts of Amer	Alexander	
						Mansfield	18 Aug 1826
Dennis	16	M		Ireland	U. States	Albion	11 May 1827
Dennis	24	M	Farmer	Ireland	America	William	21 May 1825
Edd.	24	M	Clerk	Ireland	United States	Trident	16 May 1826
Edw. K.	21	M	Merchant	U. States	U. States	Bee	12 Apr 1823
Edwd.	6	M	None	England	United States	Orozimbo	11 Aug 1823
Edwd. Phillip, Lieut.	25	M	Royal Navy	England	Canada	Brighton	24 Aug 1827
Elenor	23	F	Spinster	Ireland	Und. Stts of Amer	Alexander	
						Mansfield	18 Aug 1826
Elizabeth	17	F	Servant	Ireland	New York	Atlantic	8 May 1828
Elizabeth	40	F	Wife	Great Brittan	United States	Cambria	11 Feb 1829
Ellen	6	F		St. Johns	U. States	Wanderer	30 Oct 1828
Fanny	...	...	...	...	United States	Minerva	30 Oct 1827
Francis	33	M	...	...	...	Laurel	16 Nov 1824
Fred. V.	19	M	Clerk	America		Peruvian	28 Jul 1824
George	40	M	Tailor	Scotland	U. States	Superior	25 Sep 1828
H.	4	M		Ireland	U. States	Albion	11 May 1827
Hale	30	M	Mariner	United States	United S.	Ariel	1 Mar 1828
Henretta	25 4/12	F		France	America	France	28 Mar 1829
Henry	27	M	Mariner	Great Britain	Great Britain	Cuba	25 Feb 1822
J.	2	F		Scotland	U. States	Superior	25 Sep 1828
J.	4	M		Scotland	U. States	Superior	25 Sep 1828
J.	37	F		U. States	U. States	Silvia	10 Sep 1827
J.	72	F		Scotland	U. States	Superior	25 Sep 1828
J. P.	35	M	Merchant	U. States	U. States	Leontine	19 May 1825
James	16	M	Gardner	Great Brittan	United States	Cambria	11 Feb 1829
James	21	M	Labourer	England	U.S. America	New Hampshire	28 Sep 1826

NAMES OF PASSENGERS	AGE	SEX	OCCUPATIONS	COUNTRY TO WHICH THEY BELONG	COUNTRY THEY INTEND TO INHABIT	SHIPS/DATES OF ARRIVAL	
COLLINS (cont'd)							
James	25	M	Blacksmith	England	America	Thames	27 May 1822
James	28	M	Mariner	United States	U.S.	Jane	18 Oct 1828
James	44	M	Labourer	G. Britain	United States	Edward	21 Apr 1821
Jane	20	F	None	United States	United States	Abigale	9 Aug 1822
Jane	25	F	Labourer	Gt. Britain	U. States	Panthea	21 Jul 1825
Jane	33	F	None	England	United States	Orozimbo	11 Aug 1823
Jas.	25		Butcher	England		Corinthian	11 Mar 1829
Jeremiah	10	M	Boy	Great Brittan	United States	Cambria	11 Feb 1829
Jno.	40	M	Merchant	Great Britain	United States	Minerva	28 Jul 1823
John	5	M	Child	Ireland	United States	St. Michaels	23 Dec 1826
John	19	M	Farmer	England	United States	William Howland	5 Jul 1821
John	22	M				Washington	16 Sep 1820
John	22	M	Corder	England	U.S. America	New Hampshire	28 Sep 1826
John	22	M		St. Johns	U. States	Wanderer	30 Oct 1828
John	27	M	Labourer	Ireland	United States	Sarah G.	15 May 1828
John	28	M	Tradesman	Ireland	America	Samuel Robertson	26 Nov 1825
John	28	M	weaver	Ireland	New York	Atlantic	8 May 1828
John	28	M	Mariner	U. States	U. States	Henry	3 Jun 1828
John	29	M	Marriner	U. States	U. States	Farmer	11 Feb 1826
John	35	M	Coachmaker	Ireland	New York	Brighton	24 Aug 1827
John	35	M	Labourer	Ireland	United States	Pallas	28 Oct 1828
John	40	M	Agriculturist	United States	United States	Columbia	16 Jan 1829
John	44	M	Farmer	St. Johns	U. States	Wanderer	30 Oct 1828
John, (Son [of John])	11	M	Coachmaker	Ireland	New York	Brighton	24 Aug 1827
John H.	2	M	Child	Great Brittan	United States	Cambria	11 Feb 1829
Joseph	8	M		U. States	U. States	Silvia	10 Sep 1827
Lewis	18	M	Servent	Cannada	N. York	Manhattan	21 May 1821
M.	23		Farmer	Cork	New York	Schuylkill	22 Aug 1825
M. J.	26	M	Military Officer	England	England	Almira	8 Aug 1822
Margaret	28	F		Ireland	United States	John & Adam	21 Sep 1822
Margaret	35	F	None	England	New York	Thames	6 Oct 1820
Mary	8	F	Child	Ireland	United States	St. Michaels	23 Dec 1826
Mary	16	F		Ireland	U. States	Albion	11 May 1827
Mary	20	F		England	America	Thames	27 May 1822
Mary	20	F		England	U. States	Emulous	22 Aug 1828
Mary	23		Farmer & Labourer	Great Britain & Ireland	United States	Trio	8 Feb 1827
Mary	31	F	Wife	Ireland	United States	St. Michaels	23 Dec 1826
Mary	40	F		Ireland	U. States	Albion	11 May 1827
Michael	2	M	Labourer	Gt. Britain	U. States	Panthea	21 Jul 1825
Michael	23	M	Servant	Ireland	United States	Sylvester Healy	19 Aug 1825
Michael	24	M	Farmer	St. Johns	U. States	Wanderer	30 Oct 1828
Michal	30	M	Labourer	Ireland	Ireland	Sarah G.	28 Nov 1827
Nancy	2			Scotland	United States	Camillus	3 May 1828
Nancy	18	F		St. Johns	U. States	Wanderer	30 Oct 1828
Own	38	M		Scotland	U. States	Superior	25 Sep 1828
Pat	21	M	Grocer	England	United States	Nimrod	31 Jul 1828
Pat	35	M	Laborer	Ireland	United States	Trio	13 Jun 1827
Pat.	17	M	Farmer	Ireland	United States	General Putnam	20 Jun 1825
Patrick	25	M	Servant	Ireland	United States	Sylvester Healy	19 Aug 1825
Patrick	25	M	Shoemaker	Ireland	United States	Edwin	29 Nov 1828
Patrick	28		Labourer	Scotland	United States	Camillus	3 May 1828
Peter	30	M	Labourer	Gt. Britain	U. States	Panthea	21 Jul 1825
Rebecca	25	F		England	England	Almira	8 Aug 1822
Robt.	2/12	M	D. Maker	Ireland	N. York	Trusty	12 Sep 1828
Samuel	22	M	Laborer	Ireland	United States	Sarah Ann	18 Nov 1826
Sarah	7	F	Girl	Great Brittan	United States	Cambria	11 Feb 1829
Sarah	29	F	Servant	Ireland	N. York	Trusty	12 Sep 1828
Stephen	35	M	Mariner	Boston	U. States	Jones	13 Mar 1822
Susan	2	F	Child	Ireland	United States	St. Michaels	23 Dec 1826
Susan	5	F	Child	Great Brittan	United States	Cambria	11 Feb 1829
Thomas	7	M		Ireland	U. States	Albion	11 May 1827
Thomas	24	M	Hatter	England	U.S. America	New Hampshire	28 Sep 1826
Thomas	45	M	Gardner	Great Brittan	United States	Cambria	11 Feb 1829
Thomas	59	M	Farmer	Ireland	U. States	Albion	11 May 1827
Thomas	60	M	Shoemaker	England	United States	Orozimbo	11 Aug 1823

NAMES OF PASSENGERS	AGE	SEX	OCCUPATIONS	COUNTRY TO WHICH THEY BELONG	COUNTRY THEY INTEND TO INHABIT	SHIPS/DATES OF ARRIVAL	
COLLINS (cont'd)							
Thomas, a black	30	M	Servant	U. States	U. States	Charlotte	19 Feb 1822
Thomas, Junr.	22		Gardener	Great Brittan	United States	Cambria	11 Feb 1829
Thomas P.	28	M	Gent.	Alabama	America	Wilson	27 Nov 1826
Thos.	37		Distiller	Ireland		Hudson	23 Jul 1828
W. H.	17/12	M		England	England	Almira	8 Aug 1822
William	...	...	...	...	United States	Minerva	30 Oct 1827
William	22	M	Gardner	Great Brittan	United States	Cambria	11 Feb 1829
Wm.	3	M	D. Maker	Ireland	N. York	Trusty	12 Sep 1828
Wm.	12	M		U. States	U. States	Silvia	10 Sep 1827
Wm.	14	F	None	Great Britain	New York	Superior	5 Sep 1827
Wm.	20	M	Laborer	Ireland	United States	Trio	13 Jun 1827
Wm.	20 4/12	M	Clerk	Ireland	U. States	Fabius	22 Sep 1828
Wm.	26		5 ft. 5 in., Owner	England	U. States	Rangers	2 Oct 1826
Wm.	54	M	Farmer	U. States	U. States	Silvia	10 Sep 1827
COLLIS, Frances	20	F		England	U. States	Camillus	29 Jan 1829
William	27	M	Chapman	England	U. States	Camillus	29 Jan 1829
COLLISTER, John	23	M	Labourer	...aeland	United States	Baltic	21 Apr 1827
COLLOMB, Felix	25	M	Accountant	Switzerland	United States	Bayard	13 Nov 1823
COLLOMORE, Jane	22	F	White Smith	England	U. States	Little William	16 Jun 1821
Thos.	22	M	White Smith	England	U. States	Little William	16 Jun 1821
COLLON, Bridgt.	30	F	Farmers and Mechanics	Ireland	America	Constitution	1 Oct 1825
Tim.	33	M	Farmers and Mechanics	Ireland	America	Constitution	1 Oct 1825
COLLONS, Giles	25	M	Labourer	Ireland	United States	Hope	12 Jun 1828
Mary	22	F	Labourer	Ireland	United States	Hope	12 Jun 1828
Wm.	18	M	Labourer	Ireland	United States	Hope	12 Jun 1828
COLLONY, Patrick	24	M	Labourer	Ireland	Great Brittain	St. Michael's	10 Feb 1827
COLLOSTER, Mary	15	F	None	...	...	Frances Henrietta	30 Jun 1827
COLLS, Peter	23	M	Taylor	Bavaria	Bavaria	Edward Quesnel	3 Jul 1829
COLLUM, Bridget	15	F	Spinster	Ireland	U. States	Courier	17 Mar 1828
John	18	M	Labourer	Ireland	U. States	Courier	17 Mar 1828
COLLWELL, James	25	M	Carpenter	Ireland	United States	Catharine	22 Jul 1825
COLLYER, —, Mr.	38	M	Merchant	England	U. States	Ann Maria	13 Mar 1823
Amy	Infant	F		England	U. States	Cincinnatus	24 May 1821
*Died on the passage							
Elizabeth	26	F		Scotland	United States	Orion	15 Jan 1827
John	2	M		England	U. States	Cincinnatus	24 May 1821
John	36	M	Farmer	England	U. States	Cincinnatus	24 May 1821
Margaret	1	F		Scotland	United States	Orion	15 Jan 1827
Mary	59	F		England	U. States	Cincinnatus	24 May 1821
Sarah	4	F		Scotland	United States	Orion	15 Jan 1827
William	23	M	Farmer	England	U. States	Cincinnatus	24 May 1821
COLMAN, Fanny	28			...	...	Hudson	14 Jun 1827
James	2	M	Child	Ireland	United States	Sarah G.	20 Jul 1827
James	28	M		Ireland	United States	Sarah G.	20 Jul 1827
Mary	25	F		Ireland	United States	Sarah G.	20 Jul 1827
COLMER...RES, V.	30	M		Spain	U. States	Montano	3 Jan 1825
COLNA, Fransisco	3	M	None	N. York	U. States	Ambuscade	6 Oct 1821
COLNARD, —, Mrs.	22	F		U. States	U. States	Ambuscade	6 Oct 1821
COLOMAN, —, Miss	4	F		France	U. States	Sabina	18 Oct 1824
B.	45	M	Gentleman	France	U. States	Sabina	18 Oct 1824
COLOMANS, —, Mrs.	28	F		France	U. States	Sabina	18 Oct 1824
COLOMB, Felix	32 5/12	M	Merchant	France	America	Erie	19 Oct 1829
COLOMBEL, Peter	25	M	Barber	France	U. States	Edward Quesnel	17 Mar 1829
COLOSIA, S.	30	M	Merchant	Spain	U. States	Mary Livingston	26 Jul 1824
COLOUGH, Francis	25	M	Clerk	New Castle	United States	Nile	17 May 1827
COLRAIN, —, Mrs.	40		None	England	New Jersey	Albion	11 Oct 1821
COLRAN, Nancy	27	F	Lady	Bermuda	U. States	Mary & Elizabeth	10 Jul 1824
COLRAT, Jacob	35	M	Farmer	Switzerland	United States	Elbe	2 Aug 1822
COLRIDGE, T. P. T.	28	M	Physician	United States	United States	Cincinnatus	21 Nov 1821
COLRIEN, John	26 4/12	M	Baker	Ireland	United States	Lunar	5 May 1828
COLRILL, Eliza	14	F	None			Frances	17 Aug 1820
George	16	M	None			Frances	17 Aug 1820
Jane	50	F	None			Frances	17 Aug 1820
Walter	17	M	Farmer			Frances	17 Aug 1820

NAMES OF PASSENGERS	AGE	SEX	OCCUPATIONS	COUNTRY TO WHICH THEY BELONG	COUNTRY THEY INTEND TO INHABIT	SHIPS/DATES OF ARRIVAL	
COLRILL (cont'd)							
William	56	M	Farmer			Frances	17 Aug 1820
COLRY, Domingoh	26	M	Merchant	France	Spain	William Henry	12 Sep 1820
COLSIN, William	30 .../12	M	Labourer	Ireland	America	Enterprize	29 Jun 1827
COLSON, Ann	30	F	Farmer	Ireland	United States	Justina	5 Aug 1823
Jane	6	F	Farmer	Ireland	United States	Justina	5 Aug 1823
Margaret		F	Farmer	Ireland	United States	Justina	5 Aug 1823
Mary Ann	2	F	Farmer	Ireland	United States	Justina	5 Aug 1823
Wm.	34	M	Farmer	Ireland	United States	Justina	5 Aug 1823
COLSTON, —, Mr.	26	M		France	U. States	Desdemona	21 Oct 1825
Michael	15	M		England	United States	Earl of Liverpool	29 Sep 1823
Raligh, Mr.	29	M	Gentleman	...a	U. States	Desdemona	21 Oct 1825
COLTEN, Waller	40	M	Supercargo	New York	U. States	Conveyance	27 Dec 1825
COLTERMOLE, Henry	25	M	Farmer	G. Britain	U.S.A.	Silas Richards	29 Oct 1827
William	14	M	Farmer	G. Britain	U.S.A.	Silas Richards	29 Oct 1827
COLTON, J.	32	M	Printer	U. States	U. States	Richard	26 Jun 1823
Walter	38	M	Merchant	U. States	U. States	Rampart	4 Jun 1822
Walter	41	M	Merchant	New York	New York	American	4 Aug 1823
COLUMBEL, Anthime	22 2/12	M	Merchant	France	Traveler	Cadmus	12 Dec 1823
COLUMBIANNIATO, St. Maria	35	M	G.	Mexico	U. States	Laveria	23 Jul 1828
COLVILL, Hosea	22	M	Confectioner	Great Britain	U. States	Hannibal	12 Oct 1829
COLVILLE, James	26		Gardiner	Great Britain	U. States	Nile	30 Apr 1827
COLVIN, John	10/12	M		England	America	Cincinnatus	22 May 1826
Josep	11	M		England	New York	Cincinnatus	5 Dec 1825
Mary	5	F		England	America	Cincinnatus	22 May 1826
Mary	30 9/12	F		England	America	Cincinnatus	22 May 1826
Susan	10	F		England	America	Cincinnatus	22 May 1826
Thomas	6	M		England	America	Cincinnatus	22 May 1826
Thomas	35	M	Shoemaker	England	New York	Cincinnatus	5 Dec 1825
William	3	M		England	America	Cincinnatus	22 May 1826
COLVY, Eliza	10	F		U. States	U. States	United States	11 Sep 1828
John	7	M		U. States	U. States	United States	11 Sep 1828
Piere	8	M		U. States	U. States	United States	11 Sep 1828
Robt.	14	M		U. States	U. States	United States	11 Sep 1828
COLWELL, Charles	25	M	Laborer	Ireland	United States	Ann Maria	18 Dec 1827
Isabella	23	F	Spinster	Ireland	United States	Catharine	22 Jul 1825
John	23	M	Labourer	Ireland	United States	Catharine	22 Jul 1825
COLYAN, John	20	M	Labourer	G. Britain	U. States	St. George	7 Jun 1828
COMACHA, J. A.	28	M	Merchant	Columbia	Columbia	Douglass	9 May 1825
COMACK, Wm.	18	M	Labourer	Great Britain	New York	Dublin	21 Dec 1824
COMAS, Joseph	16	M	Son of Narciso Comas	Spain	Porto Rico	Ann	26 May 1824
Narciso	40	M	Merchant	Spain	Porto Rico	Ann	26 May 1824
COMB, William	35	M	Merchant	Edinburgh	United States	Nancy Henrietta	3 Nov 1828
COMBE, —, Col.	36	M	Gentleman	France	U. States	Howard	14 Apr 1823
Mathew Heney	34	M	Mariner	England	England	Enterprize	14 Oct 1828
COMBERS, John	25	M	Clerk			Robert Edwards	8 Nov 1825
COMBIA, Cipriany	22		Mercht.	France	United States	Cadmus	24 Oct 1827
COMBS, —, Miss	13	F	Lady	U.S.	U.S.	Cadmus	26 Apr 1824
—, Mrs.	30	F	Lady	U.S.	U.S.	Cadmus	26 Apr 1824
Alonzo	26	M	Sadlier	G. Braitan	U. States	Cosmo	29 Jun 1826
Charlotte	7	M		England	America	Comet	26 Jun 1822
Elizabeth	1	F		England	America	Comet	26 Jun 1822
Elizabeth	32	F		England	America	Comet	26 Jun 1822
Elizabeth	34	F		Great Britain	United States	Fidelity	16 Oct 1820
H.	38	M	Mechanic	N. Orleans	U. States	Columbia	24 Mar 1823
Hannah	10	M		England	America	Comet	26 Jun 1822
Isabella	31	F		G. Braitan	U. States	Cosmo	29 Jun 1826
James	3	M		Great Britain	United States	Fidelity	16 Oct 1820
John	9	M		Great Britain	United States	Fidelity	16 Oct 1820
Lorenzo	10	F		G. Braitan	U. States	Cosmo	29 Jun 1826
Mary	5	M		England	America	Comet	26 Jun 1822
Moses	1	M		Great Britain	United States	Fidelity	16 Oct 1820
Richard	3	M		England	America	Comet	26 Jun 1822
Richard	40	M	Farmer	England	America	Comet	26 Jun 1822
Sarah	7	F		Great Britain	United States	Fidelity	16 Oct 1820

NAMES OF PASSENGERS	AGE	SEX	OCCUPATIONS	COUNTRY TO WHICH THEY BELONG	COUNTRY THEY INTEND TO INHABIT	SHIPS/DATES OF ARRIVAL	
COMBS (cont'd)							
Sarah	13	F		England	America	Comet	26 Jun 1822
Thomas	11	M		Great Britain	United States	Fidelity	16 Oct 1820
Thomas	35	M	Labourer	Great Britain	United States	Fidelity	16 Oct 1820
COMEBANTH, P.	50	M	Merchant	United States	U. States	Jane	18 Apr 1823
COMEGGE, J. B.	31	M	Merchant	United States	United States	William Henry	24 Mar 1828
COMEN..., Ann	7	F	None	Great Britain	United States	William Dawson	18 Jun 1827
Eliza	10	F	None	Great Britain	United States	William Dawson	18 Jun 1827
Henry	1	M	None	Great Britain	United States	William Dawson	18 Jun 1827
Isaac	45	M	Labourer	Great Britain	United States	William Dawson	18 Jun 1827
Maria	5	F	None	Great Britain	United States	William Dawson	18 Jun 1827
Mary	9	F	None	Great Britain	United States	William Dawson	18 Jun 1827
Millicent	2	F	None	Great Britain	United States	William Dawson	18 Jun 1827
Susan	33	F	None	Great Britain	United States	William Dawson	18 Jun 1827
William	8	M	None	Great Britain	United States	William Dawson	18 Jun 1827
COMENEY, Alex	30	M	Farmer	Scotland	United States	Camillus	27 Oct 1829
COMER, T.	38	M		Ireland	America	Corinthian	1 Sep 1827
COMERADE, Barbara	33	F				Henri IV	17 May 1828
Barbara	58	F				Henri IV	17 May 1828
Hannah	18	F				Henri IV	17 May 1828
Jacob	21	M				Henri IV	17 May 1828
Margarette	20	F				Henri IV	17 May 1828
Piere	68	M				Henri IV	17 May 1828
COMERFORD, James	20					Trio	5 May 1828
COMERSKY, Bridget	18	F	Spinster	Ireland	U. States	Courier	17 Mar 1828
COMES, Peter A.	40	M	Merchant	Baltimore	U. States	Laura Ann	8 Dec 1823
COMESKY, Owen	20	M	Laborer	Gt. Britain		Dalhouse Castle	13 May 1828
Patrick	12	M	Laborer	Gt. Britain		Dalhouse Castle	13 May 1828
COMESSES, Motimer	26	M	Doctor	U. States	U. States	Marmion	7 May 1827
COMET, Biddy	30	F		Ireland	U. States	Sarah G	30 Jun 1828
COMFORD, Wm.	21	M	Ropemaker	Ireland	New York	Washington	3 Mar 1828
COMMEL, Felix	29	M	Shoemaker	U. States	U. States	Cobbosse Conte	18 Apr 1823
COMMERSE, Francis	13	M	None	St. Domingo	United States	Protection	23 Nov 1824
COMMORS, Ellen	16	F	Spinster	Ireland	United States	Wilson	6 Jun 1828
COMOLANTA, M.	30	F	None	France	France	Arthenian	28 Apr 1827
COMOLANTE, John	7	M	None	France	France	Arthenian	28 Apr 1827
Peter	2	M	None	France	France	Arthenian	28 Apr 1827
COMON, Hance	25	M	Carpenter	France	France	Edward Quesnel	3 Jul 1829
COMPARD, Francis	30 2/12	M	Servant	Spaniard	New York	Leonidas	22 Jan 1829
COMPS, James	48	M	Merchant	France	United States	Maria Theresa	13 Apr 1822
COMPTON, James	26	M	...	...	...	Antioch	8 Oct 1827
COMSTICK, Charles	23	M	Farmer	United States	United States	Minerva	25 Aug 1823
COMY, Bridget	25	F	Servt.	Sligo	New York	Susquehana	27 Jun 1823
Catherine	14	F		Sligo	New York	Susquehana	27 Jun 1823
Catherine	25	F	Servt.	Sligo	New York	Susquehana	27 Jun 1823
CON, Murae	24	M	Talor	Holland	U. States	Edward Bonaffe	23 Jul 1828
CON..., Geo.	20	M	Surgeon	England	England	Elizabeth	17 May 1822
CON...EAVE, Biddy	29	F	Spinster	Ireland	United States	Sarah G	19 Jun 1827
CONANT, Samuel	44	M	Merchant	United States	United States	Alto	8 Jun 1827
CONANTS, Levi	24	M	Merchant	U. States	United States	Adams	17 Feb 1827
CONATY, John	24	M	Labourer	Ireland	America	Plutarch	18 Jul 1826
CONAVAN, D. H.	28	M	Merchant	Tortola	U. States	Andromacke	31 Aug 1821
CONBY, J.	27	M	Divinity	England	United States	Seine	7 Dec 1821
CONCANNON, John	25	M	Labourer	Ireland	United States	Jubilee	13 Sep 1827
Wm.	30	M	Shoe Maker	Ireland	United States	Jubilee	13 Sep 1827
CONCEL, Jas.	25		Farmer	Ireland	U. States	Schuylkill	22 Aug 1825
CONCIYCO, Maria	25	F	Spinster	Portugeese	United States	Mary Elizabeth	15 Oct 1829
CONCKLIN, —,							
Captain	30 to 40	M	Mariner	New York		Isabella	24 Oct 1829
CONCORAN, Thos.	32	M	Farmer	Ireland	U. States	Globe	14 Jul 1821
CONDER, Wm.	28	M	Gentleman	France	U. States	Mirope	8 Mar 1824
CONDON, Baptiste	17	M	Gardener	Italy	U. States	Sarah Lee	21 Jul 1821
Edward	35	M	Tailor	England	United States	Cambria	8 Oct 1828
Ellen	36	F	Wife	England	United States	Cambria	8 Oct 1828
James	8	M		Ireland	America	Liverpool	31 Aug 1827
Johana	2	F		Ireland	America	Liverpool	31 Aug 1827
Mary	16					Trio	5 May 1828
Nelly	29	F		Ireland	America	Liverpool	31 Aug 1827
Pat	32	M	Farmer	Ireland	America	Liverpool	31 Aug 1827

NAMES OF PASSENGERS	AGE	SEX	OCCUPATIONS	COUNTRY TO WHICH THEY BELONG	COUNTRY THEY INTEND TO INHABIT	SHIPS/DATES OF ARRIVAL	
CONDON (cont'd)							
Richd.	24	M	Labourer	Ireland	United States	Matvina	19 Oct 1826
CONDRY, D.	28	M	Mariner	U. States	U. States	Elias Burger	21 Jun 1823
CONEALLY, Phenic	24	M	Mason	Ireland	U. States	Adno	5 Jul 1828
CONEGAN, Patt	40	M	Farmer	County of Meath, Dublin, Ireland	N. York	New Orleans	24 Aug 1827
CONELL, Philip	20	M	Schoolmaster	Ireland	New York	America	1 Aug 1828
CONELLY, Ann	22		Farmer	France	U. States	Parachute	14 May 1828
CONELY, Bridget	22	F		Scotland	United States	Indus	5 Sep 1827
CONER, Charles	25	M	Labourer	Ireland	United States	Edwin	27 Oct 1828
James	26	M	Labourer	Ireland	United States	Hope	12 Jun 1828
N.	24	M	Mechanic	U. States	U. States	Edward Quesnel	15 May 1826
CONEY, Ellen	55	F		Ireland	United S.	Hanford	19 Aug 1828
CONFECT, T.	54	F	Nurse	Holland	U. States	Edward Bonaffe	23 Jul 1828
CONFLONG, —,							
the Servant	45		Servant	St. Martins		Mary Ann	10 Oct 1820
CONFORD, ...	25 2/12	M	Farmer	Switzerland	U. States	France	26 Jun 1828
CONGAN, Catherine	25	F		Gt. Britain		Dalhouse Castle	13 May 1828
Mary	3	F		Gt. Britain		Dalhouse Castle	13 May 1828
CONGAR, Anthony Joseph		M	Gentleman	Lisbon	Spain	Cabbasso Conta	23 Aug 1824
CONGER, Gilbert	32	M	Mechanic	France		Charlemagne	16 Jan 1829
J.	23	M	Carver	U. States	U. States	Rising States	23 Nov 1825
CONGLAN, Bridget	25	F	Spinster	Ireland	United States	Herald	29 Oct 1825
Nicholas	12	M	Child	Ireland	United States	Herald	29 Oct 1825
Patrick	28	M	Woolen factor	Ireland	United States	Herald	29 Oct 1825
CONGREVE, Chas.	39	M	...	Great Brittain	N. York	Albion	11 Jun 1821
CONIC, Tho.	21	M	Farmer	Ireland	U. States	Meteor	19 Jul 1828
CONIGAN, Margt.	22	F	Farmer	Ireland	U. States	Dickinson	30 Jul 1825
CONILL, Ann	9/12	F		Ireland		Fame	9 Dec 1826
James	16	M		Ireland		Fame	9 Dec 1826
John	3	M		Ireland		Fame	9 Dec 1826
Lawrence	14	M		Ireland		Fame	9 Dec 1826
Mary	36	F		Ireland		Fame	9 Dec 1826
Patrick	5	M		Ireland		Fame	9 Dec 1826
Sera	8	F		Ireland		Fame	9 Dec 1826
CONIN, Barney	30	M	Weaver	Ireland	United States	Carolina Ann	11 Dec 1826
Elizabeth	22	F	Spinster	Great Brittan	United States	Hanford	3 Aug 1829
John	10	M		Ireland	United States	Carolina Ann	11 Dec 1826
Mary	12	F		Ireland	United States	Carolina Ann	11 Dec 1826
CONING, Charles	45	M	Seaman	U.S.	U.S.	Radius	22 Aug 1820
Thos.	35	M	Sawyer	Scotland	United States	Commerce	17 Jul 1823
CONINGHAM, Jane	22	F		Ireland	United States	General Putnam	20 Jun 1825
Thos.	24	M	...	Ireland	United States	General Putnam	20 Jun 1825
CONIZARAS, Juan	27	M	Planter	Island of Cuba	Cuba	James Monroe	21 May 1825
CONKLIN, B.	23	M	Mariner	N. York	U. States	Sancho Panza	2 Jun 1824
Ben. T.	21	M	Gentleman	U. States	U. States	Vigilant	25 Nov 1822
Betsey	35	F		Ireland	U. States	Nancy	29 Nov 1821
John	8	M		Ireland	U. States	Nancy	29 Nov 1821
Jos.	6	M		Ireland	U. States	Nancy	29 Nov 1821
Lidey	32	F		U. States		Abigail	26 Sep 1820
CONKLING, —, Mrs.	26	F		United States	United States	Langdon Cheeves	19 Mar 1827
J. F.	28	M	Marriner	United States	United States	Langdon Cheeves	19 Mar 1827
CONKLYN, Hugh	23	M	Labourer	G. Britain	U. States	Mary & Harriot	8 Sep 1828
James	25	M	Labourer	G. Britain	U. States	Mary & Harriot	8 Sep 1828
Rose	6	F		G. Britain	U. States	Mary & Harriot	8 Sep 1828
CONLAN, Anthony	32	M	Sawyer	Ireland	United States	Atlantic	21 Jul 1827
John	21	M	Farmer	G. Brittian	United States	Louisa	14 Jun 1825
Patrick	26	M	Shoemaker	Ireland	America	Josephine	8 Dec 1827
CONLAR, Mary	30	F	Labourer	Ireland	United States	Thomas	13 Dec 1827
Wm.	30	M	Labourer	Ireland	United States	Thomas	13 Dec 1827
CONLEY, B.	30	F		Ireland	U. States	Wanderer	1 Sep 1828
Betty	22	F	Servant	Ireland	St. John, N.B.	Ann Maria	7 Aug 1826
Boddy	30	F		Ireland	New York	Four Sisters	25 Sep 1823
Edward	36	M	Mechanic	Ireland	New York	Four Sisters	25 Sep 1823
Florin	26 7/12	F	Joiner	France	U. States	France	26 Jun 1828
James	27	M	Labourer	Ireland	St. John, N.B.	Ann Maria	7 Aug 1826

NAMES OF PASSENGERS	AGE	SEX	OCCUPATIONS	COUNTRY TO WHICH THEY BELONG	COUNTRY THEY INTEND TO INHABIT	SHIPS/DATES OF ARRIVAL	
CONLEY (cont'd)							
John	5			Ireland	New York	Lady Hunter	19 Oct 1826
John	21	M	...	..., ..., Ireland	U. States	New Orleans	24 Aug 1827
Mary	23			Ireland	New York	Lady Hunter	19 Oct 1826
Pat.	28		Tanner	Ireland	New York	Lady Hunter	19 Oct 1826
Thomas		M		Ireland	America	Carolina Ann	7 Aug 1826
Thos.	3			Ireland	New York	Lady Hunter	19 Oct 1826
CONLEYS, Barney	23	M	Servant	Ireland	U. States	Hanford	29 Dec 1828
CONLIFF, John	27	M	Cotton Printer	Great Britain	United States	India	5 Sep 1827
CONLIN, Ann	36	F	Farmers and Mechanics	Ireland	America	Constitution	1 Oct 1825
Chas.	36	M	Farmers and Mechanics	Ireland	America	Constitution	1 Oct 1825
Michael	20		Labourer	Ireland	United States	Fabius	18 Mar 1829
Wm.	18		Labourer	Ireland	United States	Courier	15 Oct 1827
CONLIND, Bridget	24	F	Labourer	Great Britain	United States	Mount Vernon	17 Jun 1825
Eliza	1	F	Child	Great Britain	United States	Mount Vernon	17 Jun 1825
Patrick	31	M	Labourer	Great Britain	United States	Mount Vernon	17 Jun 1825
CONLON, Catherine	1 3/12	F	Agriculturist	France	U.S.	Helen	3 May 1828
Frederick	7	M	Agriculturist	France	U.S.	Helen	3 May 1828
George	32	M	Agriculturist	France	U.S.	Helen	3 May 1828
Rose	42	F	Agriculturist	France	U.S.	Helen	3 May 1828
CONLY, Boaday	3	M		Ireland	U. States	St. Michael's	10 Feb 1827
Catharine	40	F	Wife	Ireland	U. States	St. Michael's	10 Feb 1827
Ellen	25	F		Ireland	United States	Jubilee	13 Sep 1827
John	2	M		Ireland	U. States	St. Michael's	10 Feb 1827
M.	28	M	Labourer	Ireland	United States	Jubilee	13 Sep 1827
M.	32	M	Labourer	Ireland	U. States	Wanderer	1 Sep 1828
Mary	3/12	F		Ireland	U. States	St. Michael's	10 Feb 1827
Patrick	24	M	Mason	England	United States	Dalhouse Castle	8 May 1827
Paul	22	M	Labourer	Ireland	United States	Jubilee	13 Sep 1827
CONN, Robert	24	F		Ireland	America	Carolina Ann	7 Aug 1826
Robert, Jr.	24	M	Merchant	Ireland	United States	Florida	7 Feb 1825
CONNAH, John	23	M	Merchant	England	United States	Cortex	4 Dec 1824
CONNAHAN, James	20	M	Farmer	Ireland	Ireland	Trident	17 May 1825
CONNAL, Ann	26	F		Gt. Britain		Dalhouse Castle	13 May 1828
Thomas	40	M	Merchant	Chester	United States	Dalhousie Castle	27 Jul 1826
CONNALL, Archd.	35	M	Clergyman	Gt. Britain	United States	Neptune	23 Jan 1826
Bridget	10	F		Gt. Britain		Dalhouse Castle	13 May 1828
Hugh	27	M	Weaver	Isle of Man	Ohio	Curler	7 Jul 1827
Jane	25	F		Isle of Man	Ohio	Curler	7 Jul 1827
John	1	M		Isle of Man	Ohio	Curler	7 Jul 1827
Marg.	21	F		Isle of Man	Ohio	Curler	7 Jul 1827
Robert	24	M	Tailor	Isle of Man	Ohio	Curler	7 Jul 1827
William	1	M		Isle of Man	Ohio	Curler	7 Jul 1827
CONNALLY, Thomas	22	M	Cooper	Ireland	United States	Andes	2 Oct 1828
CONNAN, Anthony	9	M	Farmer	Ireland	United States	Dublin Packet	24 Sep 1823
James	24	M	Farmer	Ireland	United States	Dublin Packet	24 Sep 1823
John	22	M	Farmer	Ireland	United States	Dublin Packet	24 Sep 1823
Nancy	27	F	Spinster	Ireland	United States	Dublin Packet	24 Sep 1823
CONNANT, Mary	35			United States	United States	Hudson	18 Jun 1825
CONNEGAN, Jas.	32	M	Labourer	...	U. States	St. Michael	21 Jul 1824
CONNEL, Patrick	17	M	None	Great Britain	United States	Eliza Barker	3 Jul 1826
Richard	11	M	None	Great Britain	United States	Ocean	27 Jul 1825
CONNELL, Allicia	18	F	None	Ireland	United States	Exchange	5 Oct 1829
Ann	13	F		Ireland	United States	Curler	3 Mar 1828
Ann	18	F		Gt. Britain		Dalhouse Castle	13 May 1828
Ann	49	F	None	Ireland	United States	Exchange	5 Oct 1829
Betsey	19	M				Eliza Jane	12 Sep 1820
Biddy	17	F		Ireland	U. States	Olive Branch	30 Oct 1823
Ch.	13	M	Farmer	Ireland	United States	Curler	3 Mar 1828
Daniel	19	M	Labourer	Ireland	United States	Trio	2 Oct 1828
Dorothy	30	F	Farmer, Labourer or Spinster	Ireland	U. States	Meteor	4 Oct 1827
Frances	20	F		Gt. Britain		Dalhouse Castle	13 May 1828
Henry	4	M	Farmer, Labourer or Spinster	Ireland	U. States	Meteor	4 Oct 1827
Hugh	22	M	Laborer	Gt. Britain		Dalhouse Castle	13 May 1828
James	10		Boy	Ireland	United States	Dublin Packet	22 Aug 1829

NAMES OF PASSENGERS	AGE	SEX	OCCUPATIONS	COUNTRY TO WHICH THEY BELONG	COUNTRY THEY INTEND TO INHABIT	SHIPS/DATES OF ARRIVAL	
CONNELL (cont'd)							
James	22	M	Carpenter	Ireland	United States	Catharine	22 Jul 1825
James	26	M	Coachman	England		Marchioness	13 May 1828
James	28	M	Farmer	West Island		Mount Vernon	7 Jun 1824
James	30	M	Farmer	Scotland	United States	Curler	3 Mar 1828
James	40	M	Farmer	Ireland	U. States	Howard	25 Jul 1823
James	45	M	Merchant	St. John	St. John	St. Michael	27 Mar 1827
James	49	M	Slater	Ireland	United States	Exchange	5 Oct 1829
Jas.	23	M	Labourer	Scotland	U. States	Czar	29 Aug 1829
John	8	M				Eliza Jane	12 Sep 1820
John	25	M	Farmer	France	U. States	Great Britain	6 Sep 1828
John	37	M	Merchant	United States	United States	Cortes	5 Aug 1822
John	40	M	Merchant	America	United States	Marmion	13 Jun 1823
John	40	M	Merchant	United States	United States	William Thompson	16 Jan 1826
John, Mr.	44	M		U.S.		Henri IV	17 May 1828
Judy	18 3/12	F		Ireland	America	Carolina Ann	7 Apr 1826
Lawce.	15	M	Farmer	Ireland	United States	Curler	3 Mar 1828
Margeret	22	F	None	Ireland	New York	America	1 Aug 1828
Margt.	25	F	Servant	Ireland	United States	Wilson	27 Jun 1826
Mary	1	F	None	England		Marchioness	13 May 1828
Mary	18	F		Ireland	United States	Trio	2 Oct 1828
Mary	24	F	None	England		Marchioness	13 May 1828
Mary	39	F	None			Eliza Jane	12 Sep 1820
Mathew	23	M	Tobacconist	Ireland	United States	Romulus	24 Jun 1826
Nicholas	75	M	Farmer			Eliza Jane	12 Sep 1820
Patrick						Mary Howland	19 Jul 1827
Patrick	17	M	Farmer, Labourer or Spinster	Ireland	U. States	Meteor	4 Oct 1827
Patrick	27	M	Labourer	Ireland	United States	Fabius	31 Jul 1829
Patrick	40	M	Labourer	Ireland	United States	Nancy Henrietta	3 Nov 1828
Phillip	8	M				Eliza Jane	12 Sep 1820
Rachael	26	F		America	United States	Marmion	13 Jun 1823
Robert	6	M				Eliza Jane	12 Sep 1820
Robt.	24	M				Eliza Jane	12 Sep 1820
Rose	28	F	Labourer	Ireland	United States	Meteor	26 Jun 1827
Simon	28	M	Farmer	Ireland	United States	Dublin Packet	23 May 1828
Wm.	66	M	Marchant	N. York	U. States	Commodore Perry	9 Apr 1821
CONNELLEY, Garnet	36	M	Labourer	Ireland		Robert Fulton	4 Jun 1828
CONNELLY, Anne	64	F	Spinster	Ireland		Dublin Packet	30 Apr 1821
B.	20	F		Ireland	United States	Indus	5 Sep 1827
Bridget	14	F	Spinster	Ireland		Robert Fulton	4 Jun 1828
Daniel	22	M	Farmer	Ireland	United States	Trident	17 May 1825
Edwd.	9	M		Ireland		Robert Fulton	4 Jun 1828
Edwd.	55	M	Mason	G. Britain	U. States	Eliza	9 May 1827
Elith.	2	F		Ireland		Robert Fulton	4 Jun 1828
Hugh	18	M	Labourer	Ireland	U. States	Josephine	7 May 1827
John	10	M		Ireland		Robert Fulton	4 Jun 1828
John	25	M	Labourer	Ireland	America	Wilson	27 Nov 1826
John	30	M	Labourer	G. Britain	U. States	Mary & Harriot	8 Sep 1828
John	35	M	Farmer	Ireland	New York	Munroe	27 May 1825
Margaret	20	F	Spinster	Ireland	U. States	Josephine	7 May 1827
Mary	19	F	Spinster	Ireland	United States	Trident	17 May 1825
Mary	20	F		Ireland	U. States	Nancy	16 Aug 1822
Mary	27	F		Great Britain		London	29 Apr 1824
Mary Ann	15	F	Spinster	Ireland		Robert Fulton	4 Jun 1828
Michael	26	M	Taylor	Great Brittain	U. States	Hibernia	8 Jul 1823
P.	20	M	Labourer	Ireland	United States	Sarah G.	15 May 1828
Patk.	2/12	M		Ireland		Robert Fulton	4 Jun 1828
Susan	33	F	Spinster	Ireland		Robert Fulton	4 Jun 1828
Thos.	6	M		Ireland		Robert Fulton	4 Jun 1828
CONNELY, Catherine	15	F	None	Tullymore	Tullymore	Aldebaron	21 Jan 1826
Mary	62	F	Matron	Ireland	United States	Robert Fulton	24 Jul 1826
Pat	30	M	Farmer	Ireland	U. States	North Carolina	22 Oct 1827
Rose	19 6/12	F	Spinster	Ireland	United States	Robert Fulton	24 Jul 1826
CONNER, Clevebelt	19	M	Labourer	Ireland	United States	Hope	12 Jun 1828
Eliza	20	F	Farmer	Ireland	U. States	Francis	6 Sep 1827
Eliza	27	F	Labourer	Ireland	United States	Meteor	26 Jun 1827

NAMES OF PASSENGERS	AGE	SEX	OCCUPATIONS	COUNTRY TO WHICH THEY BELONG	COUNTRY THEY INTEND TO INHABIT	SHIPS/DATES OF ARRIVAL	
CONNER (cont'd)							
Jno.	18	M	Bookkeeper	England	U. States	Thomas Ritchie	2 Jul 1827
John	22	M	Labourer	Ireland	United States	Meteor	26 Jun 1827
John	30	M	Labourer			Lady of the Lake	23 Aug 1828
John	30	M	Labourer	Ireland	United States	General Marion	6 Oct 1828
M...ae	21	M	Labourer	Great Britain	United States	Atlantic	28 May 1827
Mary		F	None	Great Britain	United States	William Dawson	18 Jun 1827
Mary	20	F		England	United States	Siroc	31 Oct 1829
Mary	24		Labourer	Halifax	U. States	Edwin	26 Sep 1828
Mary [crossed out]	30	F	None	Great Britain	United States	William Dawson	18 Jun 1827
Michael	17	M	Labourer	Ireland	New York	America	1 Aug 1828
Michael	26	M	Labourer	Ireland	U. States	Pleiades	9 Oct 1829
Michl.	30	M	Labourer	Great Britain	United States	William Dawson	18 Jun 1827
Nolah	18	M	Labourer	Ireland	United States	Hope	12 Jun 1828
Patrick	30	M	Labourer	England	United States	John Wells	22 May 1826
Peter	22	M	Laborer	Ireland	U. States	Lady Hunter	8 Aug 1826
T. C.	25	M	Merchant	North America	Different	Tampico	11 Jul 1826
Thos. H.	38	M	Farmer	Ireland		Cuba	24 Jun 1822
Timy.	28			Ireland	U.S.	Union	20 Aug 1827
CONNERS, Hellen	3		Farmer & Labourer	Great Britain & Ireland	United States	Trio	8 Feb 1827
Jas.	5		Farmer & Labourer	Great Britain & Ireland	United States	Trio	8 Feb 1827
Mary D.	19	F		England	U. States	Rising States	20 Sep 1828
Pat	24	M	Cooper	England	U. States	Rising States	20 Sep 1828
Thos.	25	M	Farmer	Ireland	New York	Phoenix	29 Apr 1826
CONNERTON, Colr.	20	F	Labourer	Ireland	United States	Essex	23 May 1828
CONNERY, Edward	23		Farmer	Cork	New York	Schuylkill	22 Aug 1825
Thomas	28	M	Farmer	Ireland	America	William	21 May 1825
CONNESS, Richard	45	M	Gentleman	Great Briton	United States	Brighton	12 Jun 1826
CONNET, Jean	26	F	Manufacturer	France		Nimrod	21 Sep 1820
CONNEY, Daniel	25	M	Labourer	Ireland	U.S.	Lady Hunter	10 Jul 1826
John	30	M	Labourer	England	U.S. America	New Hampshire	28 Sep 1826
CONNIN, Josepha	16	M	Servant	France	France	Arthenian	28 Apr 1827
CONNING, Thomas	21	M	Labourer	Ireland	United States	Hope	12 Jun 1828
CONNLY, John	52	M	Labourer	Ireland	United States	Meteor	26 Jun 1827
Mary	19	F	Labourer	Ireland	United States	Meteor	26 Jun 1827
Mary	52	F	Labourer	Ireland	United States	Meteor	26 Jun 1827
Rose	12	F	Labourer	Ireland	United States	Meteor	26 Jun 1827
Thomas	16	M	Labourer	Ireland	United States	Meteor	26 Jun 1827
William	19	M	Labourer	Ireland	United States	Meteor	26 Jun 1827
CONNOLLY, Ann	13	F	going to the Father	G. Brittian	United States	Louisa	14 Jun 1825
B.	28	M		G. Britain	U. States	Camillus	8 Sep 1828
Betty	50	F	None	Scotland	U. States	Czar	29 Aug 1829
Catherine	1 11/12	F	None	Great Britain	United States	Blakely	29 Sep 1826
Catherine	30	F				Superb	18 Jul 1820
Danl.	30	M		Ireland	United States	John & Adam	21 Sep 1822
Eleanor	26	F	None	Great Britain	United States	Blakely	29 Sep 1826
Ellen	10	F	going to the Father	G. Brittian	United States	Louisa	14 Jun 1825
James	14					Superb	18 Jul 1820
James	25		Labourer	Ireland	United States	Geo. Canning	5 Jun 1828
Jane	23	F	Wife	Ireland	United States	Dublin Packet	6 Dec 1827
John	20	M		Gt. Britain	United States	Penelope	9 Sep 1828
John	23	M		Ireland	United States	John & Adam	21 Sep 1822
John	28	M	Farmer	Ireland	United States	Dublin Packet	6 Dec 1827
John	40	M	Carpenter	Ireland	U. States	Albion	9 Aug 1826
John	46	M	Stone Mason	Great Britain	United States	Blakely	29 Sep 1826
L.	18	F	Spinster	Ireland	United States	Thomas	13 Dec 1827
Margaret	56	F				Superb	18 Jul 1820
Mary	5	F	None	Great Britain	United States	Blakely	29 Sep 1826
Mary	12 3/12	F	going to the Father	G. Brittian	United States	Louisa	14 Jun 1825
Mary	20	F		Ireland	U. States	Virginia	20 Jun 1825
Mary	21	F		Ireland	America	Plutarch	18 Jul 1826
Mary	25	F	Spinster	Ireland	United States	Dublin Packet	9 Jul 1827
Michael	4	M	None	Great Britain	United States	Blakely	29 Sep 1826
Michl.	60	M	Shoemaker	Ireland	U. States	Superb	18 Jul 1820
Michl., Junr.	20	M				Superb	18 Jul 1820
Nelly	18					Superb	18 Jul 1820

NAMES OF PASSENGERS	AGE	SEX	OCCUPATIONS	COUNTRY TO WHICH THEY BELONG	COUNTRY THEY INTEND TO INHABIT	SHIPS/DATES OF ARRIVAL	
CONNOLLY (cont'd)							
Patrick	5	M		Ireland	U. States	Albion	9 Aug 1826
Sarah	40 7/12	F	going to the Husband	G. Brittian	United States	Louisa	14 Jun 1825
Susannah	22	F				Superb	18 Jul 1820
Thomas	20	M	Carpenter	Ireland	U. States	Albion	9 Aug 1826
William	19 2/12	M	going to the Father	G. Brittian	United States	Louisa	14 Jun 1825
CONNOLY, Allan	27	M	Labourer	Ireland	United States	Sarah G.	15 May 1828
John	23	M	Labourer	Ireland	United States	Sarah G.	15 May 1828
Mary	6	F		Ireland	United States	Sarah G.	15 May 1828
CONNON, Judith	24	F	Spinster	Ireland	U. States	Columbia	20 Jul 1825
CONNOR, —	49	F	Spinster	Ireland	United States	Thomas	13 Dec 1827
—, Count		M	Gentleman	France	France	Meteor	11 Apr 1825
Ann	18	F		Ireland	New York	Lima	5 Aug 1829
Bridget	20	F		G. Britain	U. States	Wanderer	23 Jun 1828
Catherine	22	F	Spinster	Ireland	United States	Dublin Packet	23 May 1828
Catherine	25	F		Gt. Britain		Dalhousie Castle	13 May 1828
David, Mr.	34	M	Gardner	England	U. States	Acasta	11 Dec 1826
Eliza	13	F	Farmer	U. States	U. States	Robt. Reade	12 Apr 1825
Francis	20	M	Laborer	England	United States	London	21 May 1828
Hetty	32	F		U. States	U. States	Robt. Reade	12 Apr 1825
Jas.	35	M	Farmer	U. States	U. States	Robt. Reade	12 Apr 1825
Johanna	23	F	Servant	Ireland	United States	Trio	31 Oct 1827
John	28	M	Tailor	Gt. Britain	U. States	Henry Kneeland	25 Sep 1827
John	70	M	Farmer	U. States	U. States	Robt. Reade	12 Apr 1825
Margaret	25	F		Ireland	United States	Concordia	25 Aug 1827
Margt.	19	F	Spinster	Ireland	U. States	Hibernia	3 Dec 1823
Mary	19	F	Spinster	Ireland	United States	Diana	1 May 1826
Mary	26		Farmer & Labourer	Great Britain & Ireland	United States	Trio	8 Feb 1827
Michael	28	M	Bootmaker	Gt. Britain		Corinthian	27 Oct 1829
Michael	30	M	Farmer	Ireland	United States	Concordia	25 Aug 1827
Nicholas	24	M	Labourer	Ireland		Marchioness	13 May 1828
Patrick	24	M	Weaver	Ireland	United States	Trio	2 Oct 1828
Peter	24	M	Farmer	Great Britan	United States	Clematis	8 May 1827
Peter	34	M	Labourer	Co. L...th	United States	Java	9 Jul 1827
Sarah, Mrs.	30	F	Gardner	England	U. States	Acasta	11 Dec 1826
Thos.	22		Farmer & Labourer	Great Britain & Ireland	United States	Trio	8 Feb 1827
William	26	M	Clerk	Great Britain	United States	Erin	26 May 1821
Wm.	41	M	Farmer	Ireland	New York	Robert Edwards	17 Mar 1828
CONNORS, Andrew	22	M	Labourer	Ireland	America	Plutarch	18 Jul 1826
Bridget	40	F		Ireland	America	Plutarch	18 Jul 1826
CONNOWAY, John	30	M	Spinner	Ireland	United States	Trident	31 Mar 1827
Judith	23	F	Farmer	England	U. States	Mentor	5 Jul 1825
Wm.	22	M	Farmer	Ireland	U. States	Mentor	5 Jul 1825
CONNOY, Ellen	25	F		Ireland	U. States	Albion	11 May 1827
John	4	M		Ireland	U. States	Albion	11 May 1827
Pat	32	M	Labourer	Ireland	U. States	Albion	11 May 1827
CONNYNGHAM, Michl.	20	M	Farmer, Labourer or Spinster	Ireland	U. States	Meteor	4 Oct 1827
CONOLEY, Anne	6	F	Child	C..., ..., ...land	U. States	New Orleans	24 Aug 1827
Michael	2	F	Child	C..., ..., ...land	U. States	New Orleans	24 Aug 1827
Nancy	30	F	Spinster	C..., ..., ...land	U. States	New Orleans	24 Aug 1827
CONOLLY, Alexander	23	M	Laborer	Cueshaugh	...	Gleaner	24 May 1823
John	28	M	Weaver	Ireland	United States	Meteor	19 Aug 1829
Margarett	10	F	Spiner	...aven	United States	Minerva	30 Oct 1829
Mary	26	F	Spiner	...aven	United States	Minerva	30 Oct 1829
Nathaniel	23	M	Laborer	Anaharham	...	Gleaner	24 May 1823
Richard	18	M	Clerk	Ireland	United States	Trio	2 Oct 1828
Thos.	18	M	Clerk	Ireland	U.S. America	Traveller	10 Sep 1827
CONOLY, Elanor	10	F	Servt.	Sligo	New York	Susquehana	27 Jun 1823
John	50	M	Labourer	Ireland	U. States	Meteor	19 Jul 1828
Mary	13	F	Servt.	Sligo	New York	Susquehana	27 Jun 1823
Peter	15	M	Labourer	Ireland	United States	Trident	31 Mar 1827
CONOR, Jane	20	F		England	America	Two Marys	24 Sep 1827
CONORAN, Ann	80	F	Servant	Ireland	United States	Josephine	30 Apr 1828
CONOROLLY, Bridget	21	F		G. Britain	U. States	Dalhouse Castle	12 Sep 1828

NAMES OF PASSENGERS	AGE	SEX	OCCUPATIONS	COUNTRY TO WHICH THEY BELONG	COUNTRY THEY INTEND TO INHABIT	SHIPS/DATES OF ARRIVAL	
CONOWAY, ...	...	F	...	Great Britain	United States	Aurora	10 Nov 1827
...y	...	F	...	Great Britain	United States	Aurora	10 Nov 1827
Richard	...	M	None	Great Britain	United States	Aurora	10 Nov 1827
CONRAD, C.	13	M		France	United States	La Flora	30 Jun 1828
Caroline	8	F		France	United States	La Flora	30 Jun 1828
F. F.	36	F		France	United States	La Flora	30 Jun 1828
J. N.	38	M	Joiner	France	United States	La Flora	30 Jun 1828
John P.	30	M	Farmer	Switzerland		Charlemagne	20 Aug 1829
Louis	10	M		France	United States	La Flora	30 Jun 1828
Philip	1 6/12	M		France	United States	La Flora	30 Jun 1828
T.	4	F		France	United States	La Flora	30 Jun 1828
CONRADE, W. D.	26	M	Carpenter	Philadelphia	U. States	Genl. Brooks	17 Jul 1825
CONRADT, Caroline, & child	30	F		Wertemburg	U.S. America	Sereno	31 Jul 1826
Charles A.	28	M	Founder	Wertemburg	U.S. America	Sereno	31 Jul 1826
CONRAY, C. H.	23	M	Farmer	England	U. States	Leeds	24 Sep 1827
CONRED, A.	4	M		France	U. States	Orleans	14 Dec 1821
J.	6	M		France	U. States	Orleans	14 Dec 1821
J. T.	34	M	Cabinet Maker	Prussia	U. States	Orleans	14 Dec 1821
L.	34	F		France	U. States	Orleans	14 Dec 1821
R.	2	F		France	U. States	Orleans	14 Dec 1821
CONREY, Michael	28	M	Labourer	Great Britian	United States	Mount Vernon	19 May 1823
CONRI, Ellen	20	F		England	United States	Ganges	10 May 1828
Thos.	22	M	Farmer	England	United States	Ganges	10 May 1828
CONROE, Patrick	20	M	Labourer	Ireland		Robert Fulton	4 Jun 1828
CONROGHAY, Jane	5	F	Weaver	Ireland	U. States	Ann Maria	5 Aug 1824
W. M.	32	M	Weaver	Ireland	U. States	Ann Maria	5 Aug 1824
Wm.	4	M	Weaver	Ireland	U. States	Ann Maria	5 Aug 1824
CONROY, Ann	50	F		Ireland	U. States	Lady Hunter	8 Aug 1826
Betty	27	F		Ireland	U.S. America	Traveller	10 Sep 1827
Daniel	35	M	Weaver	Ireland	United States	Lord Wellington	14 Nov 1827
Francis	10	M	Labourer	Ireland	U.S.A.	Dalhouse Castle	21 Aug 1829
Fras.	10	M	Labourer	Ireland	United States	Dalhouse Castle	21 Aug 1829
Harriot, Miss	22	F	None	Ireland	United States	Nestor	25 Jul 1823
Honora	24	F	Spinster	Ireland	Unt. St. America	Wilson	21 May 1827
Hugh	7	F	None	Ireland	New York	America	1 Aug 1828
James	28	M	Labourer	Ireland	U.S.A.	Dalhouse Castle	21 Aug 1829
James	28	M	Labourer	Ireland	United States	Dalhouse Castle	21 Aug 1829
Johanna	4	F		Ireland	U.S. America	Traveller	10 Sep 1827
John	23	M	Student	Great Britain	United States	Juno	5 Oct 1822
Margt.	24	F	Servant	Ireland	United States	Wilson	27 Jun 1826
Mary	2	F		Ireland	U.S. America	Traveller	10 Sep 1827
Terence	21	M	Labourer	Ireland	New York	America	1 Aug 1828
CONRY, James	34	M	Weaver	Great Britain	United States	Thomas Dickason	31 Jul 1829
CONSEIL, Ada., Made.	20	F		France		Henri IV	17 May 1828
Antoine	32	M	Merchant	France	United States	Montano	5 May 1828
CONSFINE, Edward	41	M				Eliza Grant	6 Oct 1828
CONSTABLE, Daniel	47	M	Pedestrian	England	New York & ...	Thames	6 Oct 1820
CONSTANCE, Maria R.	16	F	Servant	Honduras	Great Britain	Penobscot Packet	4 May 1826
CONSTANT, F.	30	M	Mechanic	France	U. States	Bayard	25 Apr 1828
CONSTANTIA, —, Mrs.	45	F		from Portugal	U. States	Phocion	19 Sep 1822
M.	38	M	Minister plenipotentiary	from Portugal	U. States	Phocion	19 Sep 1822
CONSTANTINE, John	34	M	Gunsmith	Manchester	United States	Nile	17 May 1827
CONTESSE, Celestine	21	F				Henri IV	17 May 1828
John B.	50	M	Machanic			Henri IV	17 May 1828
CONTHARD, James	22	M	Labourer	Great Britain	United States	Sylvester Healy	23 Nov 1825
CONTHERS, Ann	5	F	None	Scotland	U. States	Franklin	7 Jul 1828
Ann	40	F	None	Scotland	U. States	Franklin	7 Jul 1828
Ester	12	F	None	Scotland	U. States	Franklin	7 Jul 1828
Jerry	14	F	None	Scotland	U. States	Franklin	7 Jul 1828
John	2	M	Spinner	Scotland	U. States	Franklin	7 Jul 1828
Johnathan	22	M	Spinner	Scotland	U. States	Franklin	7 Jul 1828
Margaret	9	F	None	Scotland	U. States	Franklin	7 Jul 1828
Robbin	7	M	Spinner	Scotland	U. States	Franklin	7 Jul 1828
Wm.	16	M	Spinner	Scotland	U. States	Franklin	7 Jul 1828
CONTI, Augustus	38	M	Mariner	United States	United States	Genl. Brown	3 Dec 1821

NAMES OF PASSENGERS	AGE	SEX	OCCUPATIONS	COUNTRY TO WHICH THEY BELONG	COUNTRY THEY INTEND TO INHABIT	SHIPS/DATES OF ARRIVAL	
CONTIAN, Jno. B.	20	M	Merchant	United States	United States	Weser	21 Oct 1823
CONTOIS, S. B.	45	M	Merchant	France	Cape Haytien	Inspector	26 May 1828
CONTON, J.	35	M	Printer	Massachusetts	U. States	Abigail	17 Sep 1822
CONTY, Mary	40	F	Lady	Great Britain	United States	Sylvester Healy	23 Nov 1825
CONVOY, Humphry	37	M	Baker	Great Britain	U. States	Princess	
						Charlotte	6 Sep 1828
CONWAY, —, Mr.	25		Actor	G. Britain	America	Magnet	24 Sep 1824
—, Mrs.	27		Actor	G. Britain	America	Magnet	24 Sep 1824
Alice	26	F		Gt. Britain		Dalhouse Castle	13 May 1828
Ann, Mrs.	27	F	Carpenter	England	U.S.	Acasta	11 May 1827
Bridget	18	F	Laborer	Ireland	U. States	Albion	9 Aug 1826
Charles	20		Labourer	Desmore	Gt. Britain	Enterprize	19 Feb 1822
Charles	26	M	Labourer	Ireland	United States	Catharine	22 Jul 1825
Charles	36	M	Farmer	Ireland	United States	William &	
						Henry	19 Jul 1822
Elizabeth	16	F		Gt. Britain		Dalhouse Castle	13 May 1828
John	3	M	None	Ireland	U.S.A.	Dalhouse Castle	21 Aug 1829
John	3	M	None	Ireland	United States	Dalhouse Castle	21 Aug 1829
Luke	27	M	Surgeon	Great Britain	U. States	Lord Wellington	17 Mar 1823
Martha	34	F		Ireland	United States	William &	
						Henry	19 Jul 1822
Mary	15 2/12	F		Ireland	U.S. of America	Douglass	6 Jul 1829
Mary	28	F	None	Ireland	U.S.A.	Dalhouse Castle	21 Aug 1829
Mary	28	F	None	Ireland	United States	Dalhouse Castle	21 Aug 1829
Michael	21	M	Labourer	Ireland	U. States	Wanderer	1 Sep 1828
Molly	25	M	Servant	Ireland	United States	Neury	27 Jan 1827
Patt	15	M		Galway	U. States	Eliza Ann	30 Jul 1823
Peter	25	M	Labourer	Great Britan	United States	Clematis	8 May 1827
Phillip	25	M	Yeoman	Ireland	United States	Borneo	9 Jul 1827
W. A.	34	M	Comedian	Great Britain	Great Britain	Columbia	1 Dec 1823
Wm., Mr.	28	M	Carpenter	England	U.S.	Acasta	11 May 1827
CONWELL, Mary	19	F		Ireland	United States	Gem	16 Jun 1824
CONY, John	23	M	Miller	England	United States	Criterion	27 Oct 1820
CONYNGHAM, Edward	18 3/12		Labourer	Ireland	United States	Helen	5 Jul 1820
William	20		Farmer	Ireland	United States	Robert Burns	30 May 1823
COOBET, John	24	M	Tailor	Scotland	U. States	General Graham	9 May 1827
COOD, George	27	M	Farmer	Great Britain	United States	Dapper	21 Aug 1828
COOES, Henry, Servant			Servant to				
to Edward Steward	23	M	Mr. E. Steward	England	United States	Caspian	12 Jul 1821
COOGAN, James	24 2/12	M	Labourer	Ireland	United States	Atlantic	21 Jul 1827
Joseph	18	M	Labourer	Ireland	America	Wilson	16 May 1825
COOK, —, Mrs.	22	F	None	United States	United States	Loire	18 Oct 1820
Ann	17		Servant	England	U. States	Venus	4 Oct 1821
Ann	36	F	None	Great Britain	N. York	Josephine	10 Dec 1825
Ann, of Baltimore	19	F		England	America	Mary Lord	26 Oct 1829
Anna	37 5/12	F		England	U.S. of America	Illinois	16 Jun 1821
B.	2	F		Great Britain	United States	Isaac Hicks	6 Dec 1827
Betsey	7/12	F		United States	United States	Loire	18 Oct 1820
C. E.	29	M	Merchant	U. States	United States	Howard	20 Aug 1827
D. S.	32	M	Mariner	U. States	U. States	Louisa Matilda	4 Dec 1821
Daniel	21	M	Laborer	Ireland	Baltimore	Munroe	27 May 1825
David	23		Shoe Maker	England	America	Sarah	18 Aug 1829
Diana	3 6/12	F		England	U.S. of America	Illinois	16 Jun 1821
Elias	9		Tailor	England	U. States	Venus	4 Oct 1821
Eliza, Wife							
[of Robert]	25	F		England	New York	Brighton	24 Aug 1827
Elizabeth	13	F	Weaver	Great Britain	U.S.A.	Dalhouse Castle	21 Aug 1829
Elizabeth	17	F	Spinster	Great Britain	United States	Ann	24 Sep 1822
Elizabeth	30	F	Sevant	Great Britan	Great Britan	Columbia	11 Aug 1823
Elizabeth,							
of Baltimore	21	F		England	America	Mary Lord	26 Oct 1829
Elizth.	13	F		Great Britain	United States	Dalhouse Castle	21 Aug 1829
Emma	12		Blacksmith	England	U. States	Venus	4 Oct 1821
Geo.	17	M	Carpenter	Bristol	New York	Cosmo	25 Sep 1827
George	9 2/12	M		England	U.S. of America	Illinois	16 Jun 1821
George	24 2/12	M	...	England	America, U.S.	Illinois	3 Jun 1822
H.	27	F		Great Britain	United States	Isaac Hicks	6 Dec 1827
Hannah	6 8/12	F		England	U.S. of America	Illinois	16 Jun 1821
Hannah	30	F		England	U. States America	Columbus	23 Mar 1829

NAMES OF PASSENGERS	AGE	SEX	OCCUPATIONS	COUNTRY TO WHICH THEY BELONG	COUNTRY THEY INTEND TO INHABIT	SHIPS/DATES OF ARRIVAL	
COOK (cont'd)							
Harriet	11	F		Great Britian	United States	Robert Quayle	29 Jul 1822
Harriet, of Baltimore	8	F		England	America	Mary Lord	26 Oct 1829
Horatio	30	M	Laborer	England	America	Silas Richard	24 Oct 1829
Hy.	33	M	Servant	Baltimore	U. States	New York	15 Nov 1823
J.	13	M	Carpenter	Bristol	New York	Cosmo	25 Sep 1827
James	23	M		Ireland	United States	William Byrnes	15 Aug 1826
James, of Baltimore	16	M	Gentleman	England	America	Mary Lord	26 Oct 1829
Jane	50	F	Weaver	Great Britain	U.S.A.	Dalhouse Castle	21 Aug 1829
Jane	50	F		Great Britian	United States	Dalhouse Castle	21 Aug 1829
Jane, of Baltimore	11	F		England	America	Mary Lord	26 Oct 1829
Jas.	28	M	Farmer	Great Britain		Casanda	5 Sep 1827
Jno.	22	M	Labourer	Great Britain	United States	Juno	5 Oct 1822
John	11/12	M		Great Britian	United States	Columbia	21 Jan 1828
John	7	M		Great Britian	United States	Robert Quayle	29 Jul 1822
John	8	M	None	Great Britan	United States	Hamilton	19 Mar 1827
John	22	M	Labourer	Ireland	United States	William	20 Jul 1829
John	27	M	Farmer	Ireland	U. States	Mentor	5 Jul 1825
John	31	M	Cotton Spinner	Eyesson, Lancashire	Eyesson	Colossus	27 Mar 1828
John	35	M	Merchant	England	U. States America	Columbus	23 Mar 1829
Joseph	9	F		Great Britian	United States	Robert Quayle	29 Jul 1822
Joseph	51	M	Farmer	Great Britian	United States	Robert Quayle	29 Jul 1822
Joshua	22	M	Farmer	Great Briton	United States	Orion	18 Jun 1821
Lydia	4	F	Lady	G. Brittain		Mary & Elizabeth	17 May 1824
Lydia	26	F	Lady	G. Brittain		Mary & Elizabeth	17 May 1824
Margaretta	1	F		England	U. States America	Columbus	23 Mar 1829
Martha	4	F		Great Britian	United States	Robert Quayle	29 Jul 1822
Mary	2	F	None	Great Britian	U.S.A.	Dalhouse Castle	21 Aug 1829
Mary	3		Tailor	England	U. States	Venus	4 Oct 1821
Mary	19	F	Spinster	Great Britain	United States	Ann	24 Sep 1822
Mary	20	F		Great Britain	United States	Dalhouse Castle	21 Aug 1829
Mary	27	F	None	Great Britain		Casanda	5 Sep 1827
Mary, of Baltimore	18	F		England	America	Mary Lord	26 Oct 1829
Moses	22		Farmer	Ireland	United States	Robert Burns	18 Jun 1821
R. A.	25	M	Merchant	N. York	U. States	Paulina Julia	22 Feb 1823
Richard	29	M	Farmer	England	United States	Roman	12 Jun 1826
Robert	5		Tailor	England	U. States	Venus	4 Oct 1821
Robert	23	M	Weaver	Great Britain	U.S.A.	Dalhouse Castle	21 Aug 1829
Robert	30	M	Butcher	England	New York	Brighton	24 Aug 1827
Robt.	23	M	Farmer	Great Britain	United States	Dalhouse Castle	21 Aug 1829
Robt.	24	M	Weaver	Ireland	N. York	Trusty	12 Sep 1828
Saml.	55	M	Gent.	Engd.	United States	Cosmo	21 Aug 1828
Sarah	3/12	F	None	Great Britain		Casanda	5 Sep 1827
Sarah	13	F		Great Britian	United States	Robert Quayle	29 Jul 1822
Sarah	13 5/12	F		England	U.S. of America	Illinois	16 Jun 1821
Sarah	15		Servant	England	U. States	Venus	4 Oct 1821
Sarah	19	F	Servant	G. Brittain		Mary & Elizabeth	17 May 1824
Sarah	22	F		Great Britian	United States	Columbia	21 Jan 1828
Sarah	41		Servant	England	U. States	Venus	4 Oct 1821
Sarah	44	F		Great Britian	United States	Robert Quayle	29 Jul 1822
Sarah, & family of Baltimore	49	F	Lady	England	America	Mary Lord	26 Oct 1829
Sarah, of Baltimore	22	F		England	America	Mary Lord	26 Oct 1829
Sarah Ann	19	F		U. States	Great Britain	Thompson	26 Apr 1828
Sophia	1			U. States	United States	Canton	13 Oct 1824
Sophia	3	F		England	U. States America	Columbus	23 Mar 1829
Sophia	24		Lady	U. States	United States	Canton	13 Oct 1824
Susan	66	F	Gent.	Engd.	United States	Cosmo	21 Aug 1828
Susannah, of Baltimore	14	F		England	America	Mary Lord	26 Oct 1829
Thomas	38	M	Merchant	Great Brittain	U. States	Atticus	25 Apr 1822
William	2			U. States	United States	Canton	13 Oct 1824
William	2	M	None	Great Britain	U.S.A.	Dalhouse Castle	21 Aug 1829
William	6	M	Farmer	Great Britain	U.S.A.	Dalhouse Castle	21 Aug 1829
William	11		Tailor	England	U. States	Venus	4 Oct 1821

NAMES OF PASSENGERS	AGE	SEX	OCCUPATIONS	COUNTRY TO WHICH THEY BELONG	COUNTRY THEY INTEND TO INHABIT	SHIPS/DATES OF ARRIVAL	
COOK (cont'd)							
William	44	M	Farmer	England	U.S. of America	Illinois	16 Jun 1821
William	56	M	Weaver	Great Britain	U.S.A.	Dalhouse Castle	21 Aug 1829
Wm.	2	M		Great Britain	United States	Dalhouse Castle	21 Aug 1829
Wm.	6	M		Great Britain	United States	Dalhouse Castle	21 Aug 1829
Wm.	24	M		U. States	Great Britain	Thompson	26 Apr 1828
Wm.	30	M	Comb Maker	Great Britian	United States	Columbia	21 Jan 1828
Wm.	48	M	Carpenter	Bristol	New York	Cosmo	25 Sep 1827
Wm.	56	M	Weaver	Great Britain	United States	Dalhouse Castle	21 Aug 1829
Wm. A.	24	M	Watch maker	Great Britan	United States	Hamilton	19 Mar 1827
Wm. Henry	7	M		England	U. States America	Columbus	23 Mar 1829
Wm. S.	10/12	M		U. States	Great Britain	Thompson	26 Apr 1828
COOKE, —, Mrs.	20	F	None	United States	U. States	John Wells	16 May 1825
Ann	1	F		England	United States	William Byrnes	1 Dec 1824
Catharine	25	F	Servant	Ireland	New York	Atlantic	8 May 1828
Edwd.	17	M	None	U. States	U. States	Abeona	20 Aug 1827
Eliza	8	F	Spinster	Ireland	United States	Dublin Packet	3 Sep 1822
Elizabeth	18	F	...	Ireland	United States	Carolina Ann	24 Oct 1825
Ellen	9	F	Spinster	Ireland	United States	Dublin Packet	3 Sep 1822
John	6	M		England	United States	William Byrnes	1 Dec 1824
Joseph	31	M	...	England	United States	William Byrnes	1 Dec 1824
Martha	29	F		England	United States	William Byrnes	1 Dec 1824
Mary	20	F	...	Ireland	United States	Carolina Ann	24 Oct 1825
Mary	23	F	Lady	England	United States	Cambria	8 Oct 1828
Mary	26	F	Servant	Ireland	United States	Josephine	30 Apr 1828
Robert	31	M	Butcher	England	United States	Cambria	8 Oct 1828
Thomas	27 3/12	M	Tailor	England	United States	Acasta	25 Sep 1827
COOKMAN, George G.	21	M	Gentleman	Great Britain	Great Britain	Ann	24 Sep 1822
COOKS, Thos.	25	M	Joiner	Great Britain	United States	William Dawson	18 Jun 1827
COOKWORTHEY, Alice	3	F		Great Britain		Ulysses	29 Oct 1822
Anna	12	F		Great Britain		Ulysses	29 Oct 1822
Eliza	5	F		Great Britain		Ulysses	29 Oct 1822
Jane	14	F		Great Britain		Ulysses	29 Oct 1822
Jane	32	F		Great Britain		Ulysses	29 Oct 1822
John	30	M	Farmer	Great Britain	U.N. States	Ulysses	29 Oct 1822
Mary	7	F		Great Britain		Ulysses	29 Oct 1822
Samuel	9	M		Great Britain		Ulysses	29 Oct 1822
William	16	M		Great Britain		Ulysses	29 Oct 1822
COOL...Y, J. H.	25	M	Merchant	U. States	U. States	Leontine	10 Jul 1826
COOLEY, Mary	11	F	Labourer	Ireland	U. States	Virginia	20 Jun 1825
COOLIDGE, Chas. Henry	19	M	Gentleman	Boston	Boston	New York	14 Nov 1826
COOLIER, Elizabeth	45	M				Washington	16 Sep 1820
COONEY, Alice	22	F	Wife	Ireland	New York	Louisa	20 Jul 1826
Ann	6	F	None	Ireland	United States	Lord Wellington	28 May 1827
Anne	21	M	None	Great Brittan	U. States	John & Elizabeth	11 Dec 1826
Catherine	38	F	None	Ireland	United States	Lord Wellington	28 May 1827
Charles	42	M	Labourer	Ireland	United States	Lord Wellington	28 May 1827
Christopher	4	M	None	Ireland	United States	Lord Wellington	28 May 1827
James	21	M	Farmer	Great Brittan	U. States	John & Elizabeth	11 Dec 1826
John	20	M	Labourer	Ireland	United States	Thompson	12 Sep 1827
John	22	M	Farmer	Ireland	America	William	21 May 1825
John	30	M	Servant	Younghall, Great Britain	United States	Union	24 Sep 1823
Judith	8	F	None	Ireland	United States	Lord Wellington	28 May 1827
Lawrence	6/12	M	None	Ireland	United States	Lord Wellington	28 May 1827
Mary	10	F	None	Ireland	United States	Lord Wellington	28 May 1827
Michal	24	M	Weaver	Ireland	New York	Louisa	20 Jul 1826
Patrick	12	M	None	Ireland	United States	Lord Wellington	28 May 1827
COOP, Joshua	25	M	Weaver	England	U. States	Severn	12 Oct 1826
COOPER, —, Mrs.	33	F		England	U. States	Amos Palmer	17 Aug 1826
...uel	39	M	Farmer	Gt. Britain	U. States	Maria	22 May 1822
Ambrose	20	M	Mechanic	England	United States	New Packet	7 Aug 1826
Amia	45	F	None	England	New Jersey	Concordia	12 Oct 1826
Ann	6	F		England	U. States	Amos Palmer	17 Aug 1826
Ann	11	F	None	England	New Jersey	Concordia	12 Oct 1826
Ann	36		Farmer	England	United States	Corinthian	30 May 1828
Anne	3	F				Eliza Grant	6 Oct 1828

NAMES OF PASSENGERS	AGE	SEX	OCCUPATIONS	COUNTRY TO WHICH THEY BELONG	COUNTRY THEY INTEND TO INHABIT	SHIPS/DATES OF ARRIVAL	
COOPER (cont'd)							
Charles	4		Farmer	England	United States	Corinthian	30 May 1828
Charles	26		Merchant	U. States		Fenelon	15 Dec 1823
Chas.	23	M	Labourer	Great Britain	United States	Frances Henrietta	17 Sep 1827
E. O.	26	M	Mariner	U. States	U. States	William	31 Jan 1826
Edward	32		Farmer	England	United States	Corinthian	30 May 1828
Elizabeth	17		Farmer	England	U. States	Venus	4 Oct 1821
Ellen	25	F	Farmer	Great Britain	U. States	Princess Charlotte	6 Sep 1828
Emeline	3		Farmer	England	United States	Corinthian	30 May 1828
Emma	2	F		England	U. States	Amos Palmer	17 Aug 1826
Grenville C.	28	M	Purser U.S.N.	U. States	U. States	Edward Quesnel	4 Aug 1828
Hannah	2	F	None	England		Manhattan	22 May 1827
Henry	25		Clerk	Ireland	United States	Courier	15 Oct 1827
Henry	26	M	Merchant	England	Central America	Tampico	29 Apr 1826
Henry	29	M	Weaver	England		Manhattan	22 May 1827
J.	28	M	Merchant	U. States	U. States	United States	7 Dec 1827
James	4	M		England	U. States	Amos Palmer	17 Aug 1826
James	5		Farmer	England	United States	Corinthian	30 May 1828
James	24	M	Baker	Great Britain	U. States	Robert Fulton	3 Dec 1827
James	26	M	Gentleman	Ireland	United States	Marion	25 Nov 1825
James	37	M	Clerk	England	United States	Jubilee	13 Jul 1829
James	38 5/12	M	Merchant	Scotland	England	Leeds	29 May 1824
Jane	25	M	Labourer	Ireland	United States	Jubilee	13 Jul 1829
Jesse	1		Farmer	England	United States	Corinthian	30 May 1828
John	1	M	Farmer	Great Britain	U. States	Princess Charlotte	6 Sep 1828
John	15	M	None	England	New Jersey	Concordia	12 Oct 1826
John	21	M	None	Great Britain	United States	Hannibal	12 Oct 1829
John	22	M	Tailor	Great Britain	United States	Diana	6 Jul 1829
John	23	M	Ironworker	G. Britian	U. States	Howard	27 Jan 1825
John	45		Servant	St. Croix	United States	South Carolina Packet	22 Jun 1822
Jonothan	29	M				Eliza Grant	6 Oct 1828
Joseph	27	M	Merchant	England	U.N. States	Corinthian	1 Sep 1823
Joseph	30	M	Manufacture	England	U. States	York	4 Apr 1826
Joseph	30		Wool Comber	Great Britain	United States	Roman	10 Sep 1827
Joseph, Mr.	26	M	Merchant	England	England	Hector	20 Sep 1821
Julian	28	M	Servant	St. Croix	United States	Carlo	28 Jun 1826
Margaret	5		Farmer	England	United States	Corinthian	30 May 1828
Maria	20	F	None	England	United States	New Packet	7 Aug 1826
Maria	24		Farmer	England	United States	Corinthian	30 May 1828
Martha	3	F		England	U. States	Amos Palmer	17 Aug 1826
Mary	32	F	None	England		Manhattan	22 May 1827
Moses	28	M	Farmer	Great Britain	U. States	Princess Charlotte	6 Sep 1828
Rob.	36	M	Weaver	England	U. States	Amos Palmer	17 Aug 1826
Robert	23	M	Farmer	Suffolk, Engl.	U. States	Atlantic	13 Jul 1824
Robert	23	M	Farmer	England	United States	Jubilee	1 Oct 1828
Robert, Jur.	40	M	Farmer	England	United States	Jubilee	1 Oct 1828
Samuel	25	M	Servant	U. States	U. States	Jasper	17 Jul 1826
Samuel	32 6/12	M	pudler		uncertain	Mount Vernon	29 Aug 1828
Sarah	1		Farmer	England	United States	Corinthian	30 May 1828
Sarah, Mrs.	64	F		England	U. States	Emily	25 Aug 1827
Soloman	5	M				Eliza Grant	6 Oct 1828
Stephen	29		Farmer	England	United States	Corinthian	30 May 1828
Susan	26	F				Eliza Grant	6 Oct 1828
Thomas	6	M	Farmer	Great Britain	U. States	Princess Charlotte	6 Sep 1828
Thomas	19	M	None	Great Britain	United States	Hannibal	12 Oct 1829
Thomas	28	M	Mechanic	N. York	U. States	Betsey	4 Apr 1823
Thomas	47	M	Weaver	Great Britain		Olive Branch	9 Oct 1829
Thomas, Mr.	68	M	Farmer	England	U. States	Emily	25 Aug 1827
Thos.	22	M	Hater	Ireland	United States	William	20 Jul 1829
Thos.	27	M	Clerk	Great Britain	United States	Diana	6 Jul 1829
Thos.	28	M	Mechanic	U. States	U. States	Trimmer	30 Apr 1825
W. S.	40	M	Merchant	U. States	U. States	Bengal	30 Jun 1823
William	7		Farmer	England	United States	Corinthian	30 May 1828

NAMES OF PASSENGERS	AGE	SEX	OCCUPATIONS	COUNTRY TO WHICH THEY BELONG	COUNTRY THEY INTEND TO INHABIT	SHIPS/DATES OF ARRIVAL	
COOPER (cont'd)							
William	28	M	...	Great Britian	United States	Robert Quayle	29 Jul 1822
William	35	M	Merchant	Gt. Britian	United States	Nestor	16 Aug 1824
William	41	M	Mason	England	New Jersey	Concordia	12 Oct 1826
William S.	48	M	...	U.S. America	U. States	Victory	21 Jun 1824
Wm.	4	M	Farmer	Great Britain	U. States	Princess Charlotte	6 Sep 1828
Wm.	25	M	None	New York	U. States	New York	15 Nov 1823
Wm.	27	M	Engineer	London	U. States	Plato	18 Apr 1826
Wm. D.	24		None	Sussex	England	Elizabeth	8 Dec 1821
COORENGEL, Charles G.	20	M	Merchant	Holland	Holland	Essex	20 Oct 1820
COOS, Thomas	26	M	Shoemaker	County of Cork, Ireland	New York City	Thorny Close	3 May 1826
COPE, J.	29	M	Carpenter	Philadela.	U. States	Planter	28 Apr 1823
Philip	25	M	Cooper	U. States	U. States	Sall & Hope	12 Jul 1820
Sarah	28	F	None	England	United States	Great Britain	5 Sep 1827
COPEL, John	25	M	Baker	Genoa	America	Exchange	25 Feb 1822
COPELAND, Charlotte	9/12	F		Great Britain		Robert Fulton	8 Mar 1823
J.	38	M	Ship master	U.S. America	U.S. America	Claudio	22 Mar 1828
James	13		Boy	Ireland	United States	Courier	15 Oct 1827
Jas., Capt.	40	M	Captain	U. States	U. States	Brutus	3 Feb 1827
Mary	22	F		Great Britain		Robert Fulton	8 Mar 1823
Robert	11		Boy	Ireland	United States	Courier	15 Oct 1827
William Thomas	35	M	Merchant	Great Britain	Great Britain	Frances Miller	24 May 1827
Wm.	16	M	Merchant	U.S.	U.S.	Agenoria	15 Jun 1822
COPEMAN, Alfred	9	M		Gt. Britain		Corinthian	27 Oct 1829
Amelia	7	F		Gt. Britain		Corinthian	27 Oct 1829
Arthur	17	M		Gt. Britain		Corinthian	27 Oct 1829
Charles	42	M	Farmer	Gt. Britain		Corinthian	27 Oct 1829
Emma	5	F		Gt. Britain		Corinthian	27 Oct 1829
Lucretia	11	F		Gt. Britain		Corinthian	27 Oct 1829
Maria	47	F		Gt. Britain		Corinthian	27 Oct 1829
Matilda	19	F		Gt. Britain		Corinthian	27 Oct 1829
Minerva	13	F		Gt. Britain		Corinthian	27 Oct 1829
COPES, James	26		Labourer	England	United States	Hudson	5 Apr 1826
COPISCH, A.	30		Merchant	Hanover	England	Brown	11 Jun 1827
COPLAND, Alexd.	12	M		Scotland	U.S. of America	Friends	10 May 1823
Mary	28	F		U. States	U. States	Ariodne	17 Nov 1821
Saml.	20	M	Merchant	Philada.	U. States	Jane	9 Dec 1822
COPNNARTY, Sally	19			County of Carvan	Ohio	Peru	30 May 1828
COPP, —	50	M				Ben & James	15 Aug 1820
COPPENGER, —, Col.	33	M	Lawer	Spain	Spain	Saluda	15 Jul 1826
—, Genl.	54	M	Army	Spain	Spain	Saluda	15 Jul 1826
Charles C.	32	M	Merchant	U. States	U. States	Agness	19 Mar 1827
COPPER, Francis	27	M	Merchant	England	United States	Euphrates	25 Jun 1824
W. S.	24	M	Merchant	St. Britain	United States	Prince Edward	1 Apr 1825
COPPINS, James	21	M	Turner	England	America	Mary Lord	26 Oct 1829
COPPUCH, Peter V.	22	M	Watch Maker	U. States	U. States	Emigrant	10 Feb 1827
COPS, James	26	M	Game Keeper	United States	United States	Robert Edwards	3 Oct 1829
Susannah	26	F	Wife	United States	United States	Robert Edwards	3 Oct 1829
COPSALL, Geo.	25	M	Mechanic	G. Britain	G. Britain	Brittania	17 Jul 1828
COQUELLAT, Manuel	37	M	Merchant	Havannah	U. States	Eliza	20 Aug 1827
COQUENARD, Joseph	24	M	Farmer	Germany	U. States	Isabella	10 Aug 1829
CORAGA, John	48		Mariner	Portugal	United States	Othello	6 Nov 1823
CORAL, Catharine	10	F		Ireland	United States	Wm. Byrnes	30 Apr 1828
CORAN, Ann	22	F	Spinster	Ireland	America	Josephine	8 Dec 1827
Sarah	46	F	Widdow	Ireland	America	Josephine	8 Dec 1827
CORBAIL, Frs.	30	M	Merchant	France	S. America	Mentor	8 Sep 1821
CORBEL, —, Mrs.	25	F		G. Britain	U. States	Camillus	8 Sep 1828
CORBET, Danl.	24	M	Farmer	Ireland	America	Farmer	4 Aug 1825
Edward	28	M	Merchant	Great Britian	U. States	Cortes	13 Aug 1825
J. B.	42	M	Merchant	France	United States	La Coralie	18 Oct 1824
Joseph	10	M				John Dickinson	14 Sep 1820
Margaret	9	F				John Dickinson	14 Sep 1820
Mathias	20	M	Farmer	Ireland		Cuba	24 Jun 1822
Rebecca	3	F		G. Britain	U. States	Camillus	8 Sep 1828
CORBETT, Corns.	40	M	Weaver	Ireland	United States	Trio	13 Jun 1827
Eliza	8	F	Farmer	Ireland	U. States	Dickinson	30 Jul 1825

NAMES OF PASSENGERS	AGE	SEX	OCCUPATIONS	COUNTRY TO WHICH THEY BELONG	COUNTRY THEY INTEND TO INHABIT	SHIPS/DATES OF ARRIVAL	
CORBETT (cont'd)							
John	17	M	None	Isle of Man		Ocean	13 Jul 1827
John	34	M	Farmer	Ireland	U. States	Dickinson	30 Jul 1825
CORBIN, Joseph	24	M		England	U. States	Acosta	28 Jul 1823
CORBINE, Elisabeth	32	F		Scotland	United States	Camillus	9 May 1827
Thomas	30	M		Scotland	United States	Camillus	9 May 1827
CORBIT, Thos.	25	M	Farmer	Ireland	U. States	Edward	15 Jul 1825
CORBITT, John				America	America	Medina	4 Sep 1828
*Distressed Seaman							
CORBUTT, Thomas	31	M	Farier	Scotland	Ut. States	Courier	13 Jul 1826
CORCORAN, Bridget	20	F	Servant	Ireland	United States	Eliza	29 Aug 1822
Jno.	22	M	Labourer	Ireland	United States	Essex	23 May 1828
John	35	M	Labourer	Ireland		Marchioness	13 May 1828
Margaret	38	F		Ireland	United States	Princess Charlotte	26 Apr 1827
Mary	22	F	Servant	Ireland	America	Plutarch	18 Jul 1826
Michael	15	M	...	Ireland	U. States	William	27 Jul 1824
Michael	28	M	Farmer	Ireland	United States	Eliza	29 Aug 1822
Patrick	38	M	Labourer	Ireland	United States	Princess Charlotte	26 Apr 1827
Peter	28	M	Laborer	Ireland	United States	Carolina Ann	11 Dec 1826
Thomas	22	M	Farmer	Ireland	United States	Eliza	29 Aug 1822
Thomas	40	M	Farmer	Ireland	United States	Wilson	22 Jun 1824
William	26	M	Gentleman	Ireland, G.B.	U. States	Ann	29 Jan 1820
CORCORANE, Jas.	40	M	Planter	St. Croix	St. Croix	Telegraph	5 Aug 1824
CORDERO, Diego	16	M	School Boy	Spain	Spain	Emulation	22 Jun 1825
CORDES, Christian	27	M	Mechanic	Germany	U. States	Constitution	2 Mar 1826
J. J.	24	M	None	United States	United States	New York	12 Nov 1822
CORDIAL, Ellen	30	F	None	Ireland	United States	Elizabeth	8 Jun 1827
Honnor	21	F	None	Ireland	U.S.A.	Dalhouse Castle	21 Aug 1829
Honnor	21	F	None	Ireland	United States	Dalhouse Castle	21 Aug 1829
CORDMORE, William	46	M	Farmer	Great Britan	United States	Clematis	8 May 1827
CORDOVER, J. R. D.	40	M	Gentleman	G. Britain		Diana	14 Sep 1820
CORDREI, Samuel	28	M	...	...	United States	Wade	29 Aug 1825
COREG, Jos. D.	27	M	Merchant	New York	U. States	Ambuscade	12 Jan 1822
CORELLOEZ, Andrew	25	M	Segar Maker	Island of Cuba	United States	Betsey	28 Oct 1825
CORET, Jacob	40	M	Farmer	Switzerland	United States	Elbe	2 Aug 1822
CORETT, Christ	8	M		Switzerland	United States	Elbe	2 Aug 1822
Christian	4	M		Switzerland	United States	Elbe	2 Aug 1822
Danl.	7	M		Switzerland	United States	Elbe	2 Aug 1822
Jacob	9	M		Switzerland	United States	Elbe	2 Aug 1822
Jacob	11	M		Switzerland	United States	Elbe	2 Aug 1822
Joseph	1	M		Switzerland	United States	Elbe	2 Aug 1822
Mathew	6	M		Switzerland	United States	Elbe	2 Aug 1822
Pier	10	M		Switzerland	United States	Elbe	2 Aug 1822
COREY, J. D.	28	M	Merchant	America	United States	Sisters	24 Jan 1820
Michael	29	M	Labourer	Ireland	U. States	Vermont	19 Jun 1827
S. D.	25	M	Merchant	U. States		General Brown	17 Oct 1820
Thomas	77	M	Farmer	New York	U. States	Champion	26 Jul 1827
CORFIELD, Charles	17	M	Clerk	U. Kingdom Great Britain	United States	Cambria	7 May 1828
Richard	30	M	...	Great Britain	New York	Panthea	24 Mar 1825
CORGET, Jenny	8	F	Gentleman	France	U. States	Bayard	11 Jul 1825
S.	30	M	Gentleman	France	U. States	Bayard	11 Jul 1825
CORGIAN, Jno. N.	42	M	Mariner	United States	United States	Weser	21 Oct 1823
CORHAM, Wm. S.	21	M	Gent	U. States	U. States	Charlemagne	19 Sep 1828
CORIGAN, Ann	20	F	Spinster	Ireland	U. States	Josephine	7 May 1827
William	35	M	Labourer	Ireland		Dublin Packet	30 Apr 1821
CORISH, Peter	21	M	Mechanic	Ireland	United States	Wm. Byrnes	30 Apr 1828
CORK, Janes	9	M	Wever	Ireland	United States	Fabius	4 Jun 1828
Joseph	5	M	Wever	Ireland	United States	Fabius	4 Jun 1828
Joshua	23	M	Brewer	Great Britain	United States	Ann	24 Sep 1822
Patrick	22	M	Wever	Ireland	United States	Fabius	4 Jun 1828
Patt	45	M	Wever	Ireland	United States	Fabius	4 Jun 1828
Wm.		M	None	United States	United States	United States	18 Sep 1826
CORKAN, —	4	F		Ireland	New York	Amanda	23 May 1827
Jno.	22	M	Labourer	Ireland	New York	Amanda	23 May 1827
M.	26	F		Ireland	New York	Amanda	23 May 1827
Mary	7	F		Ireland	New York	Amanda	23 May 1827

NAMES OF PASSENGERS	AGE	SEX	OCCUPATIONS	COUNTRY TO WHICH THEY BELONG	COUNTRY THEY INTEND TO INHABIT	SHIPS/DATES OF ARRIVAL	
CORKAN (cont'd)							
Patt	32	M	Labourer	Ireland	New York	Amanda	23 May 1827
CORKELL, Harry	27			Isle of Man	N. York	Peru	30 May 1828
Margaret	25			Isle of Man	N. York	Peru	30 May 1828
CORKER, James	21	M	Farmer	Ireland	U. States	Hibernia	29 Nov 1821
CORLATT, Elinor	16			Great Britain	United States	Thomas Dickason	29 Aug 1828
Jane	28			Great Britain	United States	Thomas Dickason	29 Aug 1828
Mary	19			Great Britain	United States	Thomas Dickason	29 Aug 1828
Phillip	13 6/12			Great Britain	United States	Thomas Dickason	29 Aug 1828
CORLE, Patt M.	30	M	Labourer	Ireland	In Country	Potomac	7 Aug 1827
CORLETT, Charles	6	M	Farmer	Great Britain	U.S. America	Chili	7 Jul 1827
Eleanor	2	F	Farmer	Great Britain	U.S. America	Chili	7 Jul 1827
Eleanor	37	F	Farmer	Great Britain	U.S. America	Chili	7 Jul 1827
Jane	4	F	Farmer	Great Britain	U.S. America	Chili	7 Jul 1827
John	11	M	Farmer	Great Britain	U.S. America	Chili	7 Jul 1827
Mary	15	F	Farmer	Great Britain	U.S. America	Chili	7 Jul 1827
Thos.	9	M	Farmer	Great Britain	U.S. America	Chili	7 Jul 1827
Wm.	17	M	Farmer	Great Britain	U.S. America	Chili	7 Jul 1827
Wm.	23	M	Ropemaker	England	United States	Jubilee	12 May 1828
Wm.	39	M	Farmer	Great Britain	U.S. America	Chili	7 Jul 1827
CORLEY, Cathe.	24 4/12	F	Servant	Ireland	United States	Atlantic	21 Jul 1827
CORM, Aguste	25	M	Sausage Maker	France	U. States	Montano	2 Sep 1828
CORMAN, John H.	35	M	Doctor	U. States	U. States	Pedlar	17 Sep 1824
CORMELLY, Jery.	21	M	Yeoman	Ireland	United States	Borneo	9 Jul 1827
CORMELY, Dennis	27	M	Yeoman	Ireland	United States	Borneo	9 Jul 1827
Eleanor	27	F	Lady	Ireland	United States	Borneo	9 Jul 1827
CORMEN, Carroll	7	M	Child	..., ..., Ireland	N. York	New Orleans	24 Aug 1827
Eliza	5	F	Child	..., ..., Ireland	N. York	New Orleans	24 Aug 1827
John	11	M	Child	..., ..., Ireland	N. York	New Orleans	24 Aug 1827
John	44	M	Shoe ...	..., ..., Ireland	N. York	New Orleans	24 Aug 1827
Julia	9	F	Child	..., ..., Ireland	N. York	New Orleans	24 Aug 1827
Mary	3	F	Child	..., ..., Ireland	N. York	New Orleans	24 Aug 1827
Timothy	13	M	Child	..., ..., Ireland	N. York	New Orleans	24 Aug 1827
CORMICHAEL,							
Jane	24 3/12	F	Wife	Ireland	United States	Atlantic	21 Jul 1827
Jessy	1 1/12	F	Child	Ireland	United States	Atlantic	21 Jul 1827
Wm.	30	M	Farmer	Ireland	United States	Atlantic	21 Jul 1827
CORMICK, Dennis	23	M	Farmer	Citazen	U.S. States	Splendid	14 Aug 1829
Fredk.	23	M	Farmer	Ireland	America	Mary	29 May 1827
H.	24	M	Labourer	Ireland	U. States	Albion	11 May 1827
Honer	22	F	Spinster	Ireland	America	Mary	29 May 1827
Jas.	25	M	Labourer	Great Britain	United States	Penelope	11 Jun 1827
Mary	21	F	Farmer	Citazen	U.S. States	Splendid	14 Aug 1829
Michl.	18	M	Labourer	Great Britain	United States	William Dawson	18 Jun 1827
Wm.	25	M	Labourer	Ireland	U. States	Albion	11 May 1827
CORMICKS, Samuel	26	M	Merchant	England	U. States	Alexander Mansfield	9 Jul 1827
CORMIER,							
Maria Theresa	24	F	Labourer	France	New York	Sully	30 Oct 1827
CORMOCK, Daniel	49					Trio	5 May 1828
CORMONT, Alexander	26	M	Clerk	Ireland		Camillus	29 Jan 1829
CORNA, Fernd.	22	M		Galway	U. States	Eliza Ann	30 Jul 1823
CORNALDI, Jacob	9	M	Lad	Jamaica	U. States	America	17 Sep 1827
CORNAU, Adolphe	23	M	White Smith	France	United States	Montano	5 May 1828
CORNBOUER, Daniel	18	M	Kleermaker	Limbach	United States	Juffraw Johanna	16 Oct 1821
CORNE, Wm.	26	M	Merchant	England	United States	Cincinnatus	21 Nov 1821
CORNEAL, Christopher	40	M	Labourer	Ireland	United States	Thomas	13 Dec 1827
CORNELIOUS,							
Theodore	35	M	Merchant	France	France	Lovinia	20 Nov 1828
CORNELL, Bridget	9	F		Ireland	U. States	William	27 Jul 1824
Catharine	1	F		Great Britian	United States	Andes	19 Aug 1829
Isabella	30	F		Great Britian	United States	Andes	19 Aug 1829
Janett	3	F		Great Britian	United States	Andes	19 Aug 1829
Judith	24	F	...	Ireland	U. States	William	27 Jul 1824
Patrick	26	M	...	Ireland	U. States	William	27 Jul 1824

NAMES OF PASSENGERS	AGE	SEX	OCCUPATIONS	COUNTRY TO WHICH THEY BELONG	COUNTRY THEY INTEND TO INHABIT	SHIPS/DATES OF ARRIVAL	
CORNELL (cont'd)							
Patt	30	M	Labourer	Great Britain	United States	Blakely	29 Sep 1826
Robert	5	M		Great Britian	United States	Andes	19 Aug 1829
Robert	31	M	Farmer	Great Britian	United States	Andes	19 Aug 1829
T.	30	M	None	Ireland	U. States	Criterion	23 May 1826
W.	23	M	Mariner	N. York	U. States	Adams	27 Jun 1825
Whitehead	26	M	Mariner	United States	United States	Tampico	29 Apr 1826
Whitehead	28	M	Merchant	America	U. States	Governor Lincoln	10 Jul 1827
CORNER, July	6	F		England	America	Mary Lord	26 Oct 1829
Margaret	28	F		England	America	Mary Lord	26 Oct 1829
Mary	1	F		England	America	Mary Lord	26 Oct 1829
Patrick	29	M	Pollisher	England	America	Mary Lord	26 Oct 1829
CORNETTE, Catherine	28	F	Agriculturist	France	U.S.	Helen	3 May 1828
Charles	4	M	Agriculturist	France	U.S.	Helen	3 May 1828
Edmund, Mr.	20	M	Planter	Gaudaloupe	Morristown, N.J.	Horace	31 May 1822
Maryann	2	F	Agriculturist	France	U.S.	Helen	3 May 1828
*killed on board							
Peter	26	M	Agriculturist	France	U.S.	Helen	3 May 1828
CORNEVAEL, Jno.	30	M	Merct.	France	U.S.	Stephania	15 Aug 1825
CORNFORTH, Jno.	28	M	Glazer	Great Brittain	U. States	Laburnum	24 Aug 1822
CORNING, John	65	M	Gentleman	Great Britain	United States	Jupiter	14 Sep 1827
Leonard	31	M	Merchant	United States	United States	Isabella	1 Aug 1829
CORNISH, Ann	13	F	None	Great Britain	United States	William Dawson	18 Jun 1827
Chas.	55	M	Farmer	Great Britain	United States	William Dawson	18 Jun 1827
E.	24	F		England	U. States	Laveria	23 Jul 1828
J.	1	M		England	U. States	Laveria	23 Jul 1828
J.	22	M	Miner	England	U. States	Laveria	23 Jul 1828
Jane	16	F	None	Great Britain	United States	William Dawson	18 Jun 1827
Jane	55	F	None	Great Britain	United States	William Dawson	18 Jun 1827
Margt.	22	F	None	Great Britain	United States	William Dawson	18 Jun 1827
Martha	22	F		Great Britain	U. States	Ganges	21 Jun 1827
Mary	21	F	None	Great Britain	United States	William Dawson	18 Jun 1827
Thomas	1	M		Great Britain	U. States	Ganges	21 Jun 1827
Will	19	M	None	Great Britain	United States	William Dawson	18 Jun 1827
William	23	M	Farmer	Great Britain	U. States	Ganges	21 Jun 1827
William E.	49		Weaver	Great Britain	United States	Thomas Dickason	29 Aug 1828
CORNNECHER, Alexr.	28	M		G. Britain	U. States	Leavitts	25 Aug 1828
CORNT, Jno.	17	M	Labourer	England	United States	Essex	23 May 1828
CORNWALL, C., Mrs.	25	F	Md. Woman	England	Halifax	Stephania	28 Jul 1823
Charlotte	34		Farmer	England	United States	Corinthian	7 Jul 1829
George	2		Farmer	England	United States	Corinthian	7 Jul 1829
Herbert	30	M	Lt. in B. Army	England	Halifax	Stephania	28 Jul 1823
John	4		Farmer	England	United States	Corinthian	7 Jul 1829
John	25	M	Seaman	Great Britain	United States	Ann Maria	9 Mar 1820
John	28	M	Merchant	United States	United States	Montano	31 May 1824
Spencer	1		Farmer	England	United States	Corinthian	7 Jul 1829
Thomas	31		Farmer	England	United States	Corinthian	7 Jul 1829
CORNWELL, Francis	26	M	Sawyer	Ireland	United States	New Packet	15 Nov 1828
John	18	M	Labourer	Ireland	U.S. of America	Meteor	19 Mar 1828
John	30	M	Merchant	U. States	U. States	Bayard	8 Mar 1825
CORNY, Jane	13	F				Hudson	23 Jul 1828
Josey	11	F				Hudson	23 Jul 1828
Mary	14	F				Hudson	23 Jul 1828
Polly	12	F				Hudson	23 Jul 1828
CORNZILLE, Stephen	46	M	Merchant	St. Domingo	France	Orozimbo	21 May 1821
COROLEY, Ann	19	F		England	United States	Essex	23 May 1828
Hny.	23	M	Fisherman	England	United States	Essex	23 May 1828
Jno.	16	M	Fisherman	England	United States	Essex	23 May 1828
CORONADO, Peter	35	M	Officer in the Army	Mexico		Pagasus	21 Mar 1829
CORP, B.	70	M	Farmer	Bristol	New York	Cosmo	25 Sep 1827
CORR, Jerusha	30					Borneo	28 Aug 1828
Sarrah	19	F	Spinster	Ireland	United States	Fabius	4 Jun 1828
CORRALL, Lewis	18	M	Planter	U.S.	U.S.	Minerva	3 Dec 1821
CORRAN, Adam	40	M				Imperial	19 Jul 1820
CORREGAN, James	39	M	Labourer	England	U. States	Ayrshire	12 May 1828
CORREO, Jos.	45	M	Servant	Spain	U. States	Lucy Ann	4 Sep 1822
CORRER, J.	28	M	Merchant	England	U.S.	York	1 Dec 1827
Saml.	21	M	Farmer	G. Brittain	U. States	Huldah & Judah	21 Jun 1822

NAMES OF PASSENGERS	AGE	SEX	OCCUPATIONS	COUNTRY TO WHICH THEY BELONG	COUNTRY THEY INTEND TO INHABIT	SHIPS/DATES OF ARRIVAL	
CORREVACHER, Samuel	24	M	Mason	Scotland	U. States	General Graham	9 May 1827
CORREY, Joseph D.	26		Merchant	New York		Iris	26 Jun 1821
CORRIE, George, Mast.	10	M	Publican	England	U.S.	Acasta	11 May 1827
Thomas, Mr.	50	M	Publican	England	U.S.	Acasta	11 May 1827
CORRIGAN, Ann	25	F		Ireland	U.S. of America	Douglass	6 Jul 1829
Bridget	18	F		Ireland	U.S. of America	Douglass	6 Jul 1829
James	19	M	Labourer	Ireland	United States	Wilson	6 Jun 1828
James	27	M	Labourer	G. Britain	U. States	Hanford	18 Sep 1828
John	21	M	Cottonspinner	Ireland	New York	Louisa	20 Jul 1826
John	26	M	Laborer	Ireland	New York	Munroe	27 May 1825
Luke	24	M	Labourer	Ireland	United States	Lord Wellington	28 May 1827
Mary	22			Ireland	United States	Fabius	18 Mar 1829
Patrick	24	M	Laborer	Ireland	New York	Munroe	27 May 1825
Richard	20		Currier	Ireland	United States	Fabius	18 Mar 1829
CORRIN, B.	30	M	Mercht.	Switzerland	U. States	Manchester Packet	23 May 1822
CORRY, David	6	M	None	Ireland	United States	Lord Wellington	28 May 1827
James	32	M	Labourer	Ireland	United States	Lord Wellington	28 May 1827
John	3	M	None	Ireland	United States	Lord Wellington	28 May 1827
John	31	M	Planter	...land	United States	South Carolina Packet	3 Jan 1825
Jos. D.	25	M	Merchant	U. States	U. States	Irene	14 Apr 1821
Mary	28	F	None	Ireland	United States	Lord Wellington	28 May 1827
Nancy	24	F	None	Ireland	United States	Lord Wellington	28 May 1827
Thomas	25	M	Labourer	Ireland	United States	Lord Wellington	28 May 1827
William	2	M	None	Ireland	United States	Lord Wellington	28 May 1827
CORSAN, Thom	18	M	Labourer	Ireland	America	Wilson	16 May 1825
CORSCADEN, Isabella	22	F	Spinster	Ireland	United States	Trident	17 May 1825
CORSID, Augustin	19	M		Spain	U. States	Independence	2 Sep 1824
CORSON, James	30	M	Farmer	Scotland	Uncertain	John Wells	22 Sep 1824
William	26	M	Carpenter	United States	United States	Lady Hunter	27 Dec 1825
CORT, Daniel W.	38	M	Merchant	U. States	U. States	Danube	2 Sep 1828
CORTAYS, Jno. E.	28	M	Labourer	England	U. States	James Monroe	14 Jan 1823
CORTENGAN, Christiane	7	F		U. States	U. States	Edward Quesnel	16 Nov 1827
Felix D.	12	M		U. States	U. States	Edward Quesnel	16 Nov 1827
Henriette	15	F		U. States	U. States	Edward Quesnel	16 Nov 1827
Jean Marie	52	M	Merchant	U. States	U. States	Edward Quesnel	16 Nov 1827
CORTES, Jno.	20	M	Cooper	Nova Scotia	U. States	Morning Star	9 Nov 1824
CORTEX, Jno.	19	M	Gentleman	Havana	U. States	New Packet	5 May 1823
CORTILLE, L. A.	21	M	Doctor	N. York	N. York	Robert Cochran	14 Mar 1825
CORTWRIGHT, R.	24	M	...	U. States	U. States	Pacific	11 Sep 1824
Wm.	7	M		St. Croix	St. Croix	Commerce	13 Nov 1823
CORTY, Beley	26	F		Ireland		Fame	9 Dec 1826
John	26	M	Labourer	Ireland		Fame	9 Dec 1826
Mary	1	F		Ireland		Fame	9 Dec 1826
Thomas	22	M	Servant	Ireland		Fame	9 Dec 1826
CORVELL, Nora	22	F		Ireland	U. States	Phocion	19 Sep 1822
CORWAN, David	24		Spinner			Zamoa	5 Nov 1828
Joseph	27	M	Farmer	England	U.S.A.	Brighton	21 Jan 1826
CORWELL, Nicholas	17	M	Labourer	Great Britain	U. States	Great Britain	18 Mar 1828
CORWEN, H.	18	M	Super Cargo	U. States	U. States	Nancy & Maria	11 Jun 1825
CORWIN, Joshua	28	M	Carpenter	New York	United States	St. Michaels	12 Apr 1826
CORY, J. D.	25	M	Merchant	U. States	U. States	Adze	24 Jul 1820
Patrick	32	M	Carpenter	Ireland	New York	Patriot	13 Aug 1828
COSBROOK, Ann	25	F		England	U. States	Hudson	8 Oct 1827
COSES, Joseph	40	M	Keeper of beasts	England	United States should they approve of it	Robert Edwards	20 Jan 1829
COSGRAVE, James	25	M	Farmer, Labourer or Spinster	Ireland	U. States	Meteor	4 Oct 1827
COSGRED, Peter	24	M	Laborer	Ireland	New York	Indian Chief	19 Jun 1823
COSGREVE, Bridget	25	F				Lady of the Lake	23 Aug 1828
*left ship James	30	M				Lady of the Lake	23 Aug 1828
*left ship COSGRIEF, Rose	23	F	None	Ireland	United States	Jubilee	13 Jul 1829
COSGROVE, Catharine	15	F	None	Great Britain	United States	Roman	10 May 1828
Denny	32	M	Merchant			John & Edward	25 Aug 1820

NAMES OF PASSENGERS	AGE	SEX	OCCUPATIONS	COUNTRY TO WHICH THEY BELONG	COUNTRY THEY INTEND TO INHABIT	SHIPS/DATES OF ARRIVAL	
COSGROVE (cont'd)							
Eliza	9	F	None	Great Britain	United States	Roman	10 May 1828
John	18	M	None	Great Britain	United States	Roman	10 May 1828
Margaret	20	F	None	Great Britain	United States	Roman	10 May 1828
Margaret	45	F	None	Great Britain	United States	Roman	10 May 1828
Mary	9	F	None	Great Britain	United States	Roman	10 May 1828
Michel	8/12	M		Irereland	America	Carolina Ann	20 Jun 1825
Patrick	16	M	None	Ireland	United States	Exchange	5 Oct 1829
Richard	11	M	None	Great Britain	United States	Roman	10 May 1828
Rose	30	F		Irereland	America	Carolina Ann	20 Jun 1825
Thos.	30	M	Laborer	Ireland	United States	Sarah G.	11 Jan 1828
COSHEL, Betsey	6	F		Ireland	United States	Potomac	28 Sep 1827
Cathy	32	F		Ireland	United States	Potomac	28 Sep 1827
COSIMER, Elisabeth	6	F	Family [of Roland]	France	America	La Grange	7 Aug 1828
Elisabeth	36	F	Family [of Roland]	France	America	La Grange	7 Aug 1828
Josephine	3	F	Family [of Roland]	France	America	La Grange	7 Aug 1828
*Died on the Voyage							
Maria	10	F	Family [of Roland]	France	America	La Grange	7 Aug 1828
Roland	45	M	Farmer	France	America	La Grange	7 Aug 1828
COSKEY, Elanor	20	F	None	Ireland	United States	Leonidas	3 Aug 1825
Patrick	30	M	Farmer	Ireland	United States	Leonidas	3 Aug 1825
COSLER, John H.	22	M	Gentleman	America	U. States	James Cropper	10 Jun 1823
COSLIN, Betsey	17	F		Germany	United States	Rent	13 May
COSLINE, Ann	28	F	House Keeper	Irereland	America	Carolina Ann	20 Jun 1825
Eliza	25	F	Carpenter	Irereland	America	Carolina Ann	20 Jun 1825
COSMAN, Mary	44	F		Prusia	U.S. America	Sereno	31 Jul 1826
COSREA, W. F.	22	M	Gentleman	Spain	U. States	Native	16 Nov 1825
COSSINGHAM, George	2/12					Xenophon	25 Jul 1826
Leah	23	F		England	S. New York	Xenophon	25 Jul 1826
COSSINGTON, Jonathan	54		Shipwright	England	United States	Corinthian	30 May 1828
COSTA, John, Master	1	M	Farmer	England	U. States	Acasta	21 Oct 1825
COSTAR, Elizabeth	20	F	Farmer	England	U. States	Acasta	21 Oct 1825
John	20	M	Farmer	England	U. States	Acasta	21 Oct 1825
COSTATES, Mariano	22	M	Mercht.	Guatemela	Central America	Savannah	22 May 1827
COSTELLA,							
Catharine, Mrs.	37	F	None	U. States	U. States	Sully	25 Jun 1828
Elizabeth, Mrs.	16	F	None	U. States	U. States	Sully	25 Jun 1828
COSTELLO, Alice	30	F	Servant	Ireland	America	Weser	26 Jun 1821
Anne	26	F	Servant	Ireland	America	Weser	26 Jun 1821
Bartly	56 6/12	M		Ireland	U.S. of America	Douglass	6 Jul 1829
Catherine	20	F	Servant	Ireland	America	Weser	26 Jun 1821
Mary	45 8/12	F		Ireland	U.S. of America	Douglass	6 Jul 1829
Michl.	30	M	Labourer	Ireland	America	Weser	26 Jun 1821
Thomas	19	M	Farmer	Ireland	United States	Lima	19 Jun 1824
COSTEN, Andres	26	M	Merchant	Columbia	Columbia	Tampico	20 Apr 1825
COSTER, Elizabeth	27		...	...	...	Hudson	14 Jun 1827
Thomas	12		...	...	...	Hudson	14 Jun 1827
Thomas	33		...	...	...	Hudson	14 Jun 1827
COSTERISAN, August	18	M	Merchant	France		Charlemagne	20 Aug 1829
COSTILO, Wall	17	M	Labourer	Ireland	United States	Wilson	6 Jun 1828
COSTLOW, Ann	18	F	Merchant	Ireland	United States	Carolina Ann	24 Oct 1825
Michael	39	M	...	Ireland	United States	Carolina Ann	24 Oct 1825
COSTOLA, Margaret	22	F	Servant	Ireland	United States	Eliza	29 Aug 1822
COSTON, William H.	25	M	Merchant	Holland	U. States	United States	7 Jul 1827
COTE, Samuel W.	23	M	Carpenter	America, Connecticut	America	William	16 Apr 1823
COTERSON, John	25			Great Britan	United States	Newry	11 Jul 1827
COTHER, William	38	M	Planter	Denmark	Denmark	Elias Burger	3 Dec 1821
Wm.		M	Mercht.	S. Carolina	U. States	South Carolina	22 Dec 1824
Wm.	13	M	Merchant	England	U. States	Gleaner	4 Oct 1828
COTLEY, Thos.	22	M	Saddler	England	U. States	Unity	5 Sep 1828
COTOLY, David	5	M	Child	Ireland	U. States	Meteor	19 Jul 1828
David	32	M	Labourer	Ireland	U. States	Meteor	19 Jul 1828
Jane	1	F	Child	Ireland	U. States	Meteor	19 Jul 1828
Mary	1	F	Child	Ireland	U. States	Meteor	19 Jul 1828
Robt.	7	M	Child	Ireland	U. States	Meteor	19 Jul 1828
Sarah	30	F	Spinster	Ireland	U. States	Meteor	19 Jul 1828
COTS, John	33	M	Merchant	England	United States	St. Michaels	23 Dec 1826
COTTAIN, Catherine	53	F	Farmer	England	America	Thames	27 May 1822

NAMES OF PASSENGERS	AGE	SEX	OCCUPATIONS	COUNTRY TO WHICH THEY BELONG	COUNTRY THEY INTEND TO INHABIT	SHIPS/DATES OF ARRIVAL	
COTTAIN (cont'd)							
John	18	F	Farmer	England	America	Thames	27 May 1822
Mary	8	F	Farmer	England	America	Thames	27 May 1822
Reebecca	12	F	Farmer	England	America	Thames	27 May 1822
Vincent	48	M	Farmer	England	America	Thames	27 May 1822
William	16	M	Farmer	England	America	Thames	27 May 1822
COTTAN, John	29	M	Smith	Ireland	New York	Indian Chief	19 Jun 1823
COTTEN, G. B.		M	Merchant	U. States		Levantine	7 Nov 1825
COTTER, Edward	12	M		England	United States	Manhattan	22 Sep 1823
Elizth.	8	F		England	United States	Manhattan	22 Sep 1823
Elizth.	35	F		England	United States	Manhattan	22 Sep 1823
Ellen	10	F		England	United States	Manhattan	22 Sep 1823
Hugh C.	1 6/12	M		St. Johns, N.B.	United States	Henrietta	17 Aug 1825
James W.	3 6/12	M		St. Johns, N.B.	United States	Henrietta	17 Aug 1825
Jeremiah	32	M	Weaver	Ireland	America	William	21 May 1825
John	7			Ireland	Great Britain	Henrietta	26 Nov 1825
John	25	M	Farmer	St. Johns, N.B.	United States	Henrietta	17 Aug 1825
Mary	6	F		England	United States	Manhattan	22 Sep 1823
Mary	19			Ireland	Great Britain	Henrietta	26 Nov 1825
Mary	23	F		St. Johns, N.B.	United States	Henrietta	17 Aug 1825
Mary	35			Ireland	Great Britain	Henrietta	26 Nov 1825
Michael	17			Ireland	Great Britain	Henrietta	26 Nov 1825
Patrick	9			Ireland	Great Britain	Henrietta	26 Nov 1825
COTTEREAU, Luce	54	F	Lady	U. States	U. States	Lewis	10 Sep 1823
COTTEREL, Michael	19	M	Labourer	Ireland	United States	Combine	4 Jun 1825
COTTERMOLE, H. H.	23	M	Butcher	Gt. Britan	United States	Crisis	6 Apr 1825
COTTET, Maria	1		Farmer	France	U. States	Elizabeth	9 Jul 1825
Maria	23		Farmer	France	U. States	Elizabeth	9 Jul 1825
COTTIER, William	20	M	Tailor	Isle of Man	United States	Aurora	9 Jul 1827
COTTLE, A.	4	F	Farmer	St. Johns	U. States	Isabella	28 Jun 1825
J.	28	F	Farmer	St. Johns	U. States	Isabella	28 Jun 1825
J.	35	M	Farmer	St. Johns	U. States	Isabella	28 Jun 1825
M. J.	3	M	Farmer	St. Johns	U. States	Isabella	28 Jun 1825
S.	6	F	Farmer	St. Johns	U. States	Isabella	28 Jun 1825
COTTMAN, William	24	M	Carpenter	U.S. America	U. States	Messenger	10 Jul 1829
COTTON, ...ia	24	F	None	England	U. States America	Ann Maria	29 Nov 1821
Benjn.	7	M		Great Britian	United States	Columbia	21 Jan 1828
Benjn.	31	M	Farmer	Manchester	United States	Nile	17 May 1827
Elizabeth	20	F		Liston	Ireland	Carolina Ann	11 Jun 1824
George, an infant		M		Liston	Ireland	Carolina Ann	11 Jun 1824
Hannah	4	F		Great Britian	United States	Columbia	21 Jan 1828
Hannah	28	F		Great Britian	United States	Columbia	21 Jan 1828
Jane	18	F	Gran Daughter	Armar	Baltimore	Nile	18 Aug 1829
Jas.	51	M	Clerk	England	U. States	James Cropper	10 Jun 1823
Jas., Jr.	13	M		England	U. States	James Cropper	10 Jun 1823
John	6	M		Great Britian	United States	Columbia	21 Jan 1828
John	26	M	Weaver	Liston	Ireland	Carolina Ann	11 Jun 1824
Josep	45	M	Labourer	Great Britain	United States	Cambria	26 Dec 1827
Joseph, Junr.	3	M	None	Great Britain	United States	Cambria	26 Dec 1827
M. R.	23	M	Merchant	Connecticutt	U. States	Charity	18 Nov 1823
Martha	1	F		Great Britian	United States	Columbia	21 Jan 1828
Martha	40	F	None	Great Britian	United States	Cambria	26 Dec 1827
Mary	8	F		Great Britian	United States	Columbia	21 Jan 1828
Mary	21	F	Gran Daughter	Armar	Baltimore	Nile	18 Aug 1829
N.	20	F	Spinster	Ireland		Robert Fulton	4 Jun 1828
Sarah	11	F		Great Britian	United States	Columbia	21 Jan 1828
Thos.	23	M	Labourer	England	United States	Nancy	15 Mar 1820
Thos.	33	M	Pedlar	Great Britian	U. States	Pallas	17 Aug 1824
Wm.	10	M		Great Britian	United States	Columbia	21 Jan 1828
Wm. R.	30	M	Merchant	Connecticutt	U. States	Concord	10 Nov 1824
COTTREAU, Henry W.	42	M	Mariner	Baltimore	Baltimore	Levant	18 Nov 1824
COTTRELL, —, Mr.	20	M	Gentleman	England	G. Brittain or her Collonies	Etheldred	17 Oct 1822
COTTRILL, Jessee	23		Mechanic	U.S.	U.S.	Abeona	24 May 1822
COUBAN, Michl.	28	M	Labourer	Great Britain	United States	Penelope	11 Jun 1827
COUBER, Ann	24	F	Servant	Ireland	U. States	Henrietta	7 Jul 1825
COUCHMAN, James	45	M	Farmer	U. Kingdom of Great Britain	United States	Cambria	7 May 1828
COUD, Jean	1	M	Farmer	England	United States	Oxford	14 Aug 1828

NAMES OF PASSENGERS	AGE	SEX	OCCUPATIONS	COUNTRY TO WHICH THEY BELONG	COUNTRY THEY INTEND TO INHABIT	SHIPS/DATES OF ARRIVAL	
COUD (cont'd)							
Jeanne	37	F	Farmer	England	United States	Oxford	14 Aug 1828
John	40	M	Farmer	England	United States	Oxford	14 Aug 1828
Louis	18	M	Farmer	England	United States	Oxford	14 Aug 1828
Mazerina	7	F	Farmer	England	United States	Oxford	14 Aug 1828
Presillia	9	F	Farmer	England	United States	Oxford	14 Aug 1828
Robert	11	M	Farmer	England	United States	Oxford	14 Aug 1828
William	13	M	Farmer	England	United States	Oxford	14 Aug 1828
COUET, Amand	26	M	Farmer	France	U. States	Bayard	25 Apr 1828
COUFFIN, Thomas	20	M	Farmer	Ireland	United States	Asia	29 Jul 1829
COUGDON, Stephen	23	M	Mechanic	Rhode Island	U. States	Columbia	24 Mar 1823
COUGHAY, Eliza	2	F		Ireland	U. States	Ann Maria	5 Aug 1824
COUGHIN, Pat	24	M	Labourer	England	United States	Aurelia	7 Jun 1826
COUGHLAN, James	26	M	Labourer	Ireland	United States	Trio	31 Oct 1827
Mary	23	F		Ireland	United States	Trio	31 Oct 1827
COUGHLAND, Julia	13	F		England	U.S. America	Cortes	19 May 1826
COUGHLIN, Ellen	24	F		England	United States	Ganges	10 May 1828
John	27	M	Farmer	England	United States	Ganges	10 May 1828
Wm.	25	M	Farmer	England	United States	Ganges	10 May 1828
COUGHY, Margeret	45	F	Matron	Ireland	U. States	Josephine	30 Aug 1828
COUGLIN, Patrk.	24	M	Farmer	Great Britain	United States	Ann Maria	12 Jul 1821
COULILE, Sarah	74	F	Farmer	England	U. States	Franklin	7 Jul 1828
COULLARD, —, Mr.	23	M	Merchant	France	U.S.	Francois I	8 Aug 1829
COULTER, Andrew	23		Carpenter	Ireland	Great Britain	Robert Burns	14 Jun 1824
Charles	20	M	Labourer	Ireland	United States	Princess Charlotte	26 Apr 1827
Christopher	25	M	Labourer	Ireland	U.States	Nancy	31 May 1823
Geo.	14			Ireland	United States	Jno. Dickinson	21 Sep 1821
Henry	20	M	Labourer	Ireland	Unt. St. America	Wilson	21 May 1827
James	22	M	Labourer	Ireland	U. States	Josephine	7 May 1827
Jno.	23	M	Merchant	Great Britain	United States	Cortes	18 Oct 1820
John	19		Farmer	Ireland	Great Britain	Robert Burns	14 Jun 1824
Mary	8			Ireland	United States	Jno. Dickinson	21 Sep 1821
William	15	M	Labourer	Ireland	United States	Robert Fulton	24 Jul 1826
William	22	M	Labourer	Ireland	U.States	Nancy	31 May 1823
COULTHUS, Thomas	30	M	Mason	England	New York	Lima	5 Aug 1829
Thomas	30	M	Maison	England	U. States	Lima	5 Aug 1829
COULTON, Chas.	21		Farmer	Ireland		Westmoreland	1 Aug 1826
John	1		Boy	Ireland		Westmoreland	1 Aug 1826
Pat	1		Boy	Ireland		Westmoreland	1 Aug 1826
COUMBRA, C.	24	M	Merchant	France	France	Altamira	24 Jun 1828
COUN..., Bridget	20	F		Great Britain	United States	Orozimbo	7 Nov 1826
COUNEND, F.	45	M	Gentleman	Havana	U. States	Queen Mab	22 Jul 1825
COUNIE, B., Mrs.	31	F	Servant	England	U. States	Florida	16 May 1827
COUNT, John	27 6/12	M	Taylor	France	U.S.A.	Hesper	7 Dec 1827
COUNTS, Edward	37	M	Bookkeeper	Younghall, Great Britain	United States	Union	24 Sep 1823
COUPE, Thomas	32	M	Spinner	Great Britain	United States	Isaac Hicks	10 Jul 1827
COUPEL, Lewis A.	24	M	Book Binder	France	United States	American	27 Aug 1827
Paulina D.	24	F	Book Binder	France	United States	American	27 Aug 1827
COUPLAND, Ann	15	F	None	England	Pittsburgh	Orozimbo	8 Jun 1822
Caroline, her daughter [Caroline]	8	F		...	United States	Dawn	15 Oct 1827
Caroline, Mrs.	30	F		...	United States	Dawn	15 Oct 1827
Charles	16	M	Farmer	England	Pittsburgh	Orozimbo	8 Jun 1822
Eliza	10	F	None	England	Pittsburgh	Orozimbo	8 Jun 1822
George	4	M	None	England	Pittsburgh	Orozimbo	8 Jun 1822
George	18	M	Farmer	England	Pittsburgh	Orozimbo	8 Jun 1822
Henry	1	M	None	England	Pittsburgh	Orozimbo	8 Jun 1822
Henry	22	M	Farmer	England	Pittsburgh	Orozimbo	8 Jun 1822
John	30	M	Farmer	England	Pittsburgh	Orozimbo	8 Jun 1822
Mary, her daughter [Caroline]		F		...	United States	Dawn	15 Oct 1827
Rebecca	50	F	None	England	Pittsburgh	Orozimbo	8 Jun 1822
Sarah	30	F	None	England	Pittsburgh	Orozimbo	8 Jun 1822
William, her son [Caroline]	6	M		...	United States	Dawn	15 Oct 1827
COURIE, Ellen	23	F	Wife	Ireland	U. States	Hanford	29 Dec 1828
COURIER, John, Mr.	24	M	Merchant	United States	United States	Manchester	8 Dec 1827

NAMES OF PASSENGERS	AGE	SEX	OCCUPATIONS	COUNTRY TO WHICH THEY BELONG	COUNTRY THEY INTEND TO INHABIT	SHIPS/DATES OF ARRIVAL	
COURLAND, Michal	28	M	Carpenter	Ireland	U. States	Franklin	7 Jul 1828
COURLET, Louisa	5	F	Servant	U. States	U. States	Imperial	10 Dec 1821
COURLETT, John	26	M	Farmer	Isle of Man	United States	Curler	3 Mar 1828
COUROAGH, Martin, Mr.		M	Planter	London		Genl. A. Jackson	15 Jul 1820
COURSEN, E.	12	M	Merchant	France	United States	Burdett	30 Apr 1828
COURT, Samue	25	M		Great B.	U. States	William Neilson	26 Jul 1828
COURTE, Gabriel	22	M	C...try ...a...	Havre	N. York	Stephania	29 Nov 1825
COURTNEY, Daniel	6	M	Laborer	Ireland	United States	Sarah G	19 Jun 1827
Ellen	30	F	Wife	Ireland	United States	Sarah G	19 Jun 1827
James	35	M	Laborer	Ireland	United States	Sarah G	19 Jun 1827
John	8	M	Laborer	Ireland	United States	Sarah G	19 Jun 1827
John	32	M	Farmer	Canada	Canada	Bowditch	27 Apr 1826
Margt.	27	F	Joiner	England	New York	Bowditch	27 Apr 1826
Mary	3	F	Laborer	Ireland	United States	Sarah G	19 Jun 1827
Wm.	37	M	Joiner	England	New York	Bowditch	27 Apr 1826
COURTSLAND, Hinriotte	22	F		Bremen	America	Franklin	14 Jan 1828
COURVOISIR, David L.	71	M	Farmer	Neufehatel	U.S. America	Superior	18 Jun 1825
Francois	17	M	Taylor	Neufehatel	U.S. America	Superior	18 Jun 1825
Louis A.	32	M	Shoemaker	Neufehatel	U.S. America	Superior	18 Jun 1825
Louis H.	39	M	Farmer	Neufehatel	U.S. America	Superior	18 Jun 1825
COUSHMAN, Charles	6/12	M	Farmer	England	In the Country	Chelsea	16 May 1828
*Died May 11th							
Charlotte	2	F	Farmer	England	In the Country	Chelsea	16 May 1828
*Died May 11th							
George, & family	28	M	Farmer	England	In the Country	Chelsea	16 May 1828
Sarah	23	F	Farmer	England	In the Country	Chelsea	16 May 1828
COUSSADO, Louis	21	M	Merchant	Bordeaux	U. States	Elizabeth	23 Oct 1828
COUSTADT, Bolongne	33	M	Merchant	Maragalante	U. States	Mary	29 Dec 1823
COUTON, M.	39	M	Merchant	Holland	U.S. America	Columbia	31 Jul 1826
COUTSHUFF, John	25	M	Calico Printer	England	America	Hercules	2 Nov 1825
COUTY, J., Mrs.	35	F		S. Carolina	United States	Cato	8 Aug 1825
James	30	M		Scotland	United States	Cato	8 Aug 1825
John	29	M	Civil Engineer	U. States	U. States	Frances Henrietta	25 Oct 1824
John	45	M	Land Surveyor	S. Carolina	United States	Cato	8 Aug 1825
COVEN, John M.	6/12	M	Child	Ireland	U. States	Meteor	19 Jul 1828
COVENTRY, Fanny	22			England	Canada	Venus	4 Oct 1821
James	27		Servant	England	U. States	Venus	4 Oct 1821
James	35	M	Laborer	Scotland	United States	Camillus	28 Apr 1824
Wm.	30	M	M.D.	U.S.	U. States	John Jay	17 Sep 1824
COVER, Elisabeth	13	F	Daughter	Swiss	U. States	Comet	28 Jul 1825
Elisabeth	37	F	Wife	Swiss	U. States	Comet	28 Jul 1825
Manuel	66	M	Farmer	Swiss	U. States	Comet	28 Jul 1825
COVERCLAT, John	22	M	Musician	Spain	U. States	Leader	20 Apr 1827
COVERDALE, David	12	M		England	Utica	Indian Chief	19 Jun 1823
Jonathan	10	M		England	Utica	Indian Chief	19 Jun 1823
Joseph	54	M	Farmer	Great Britain	United States	Magnet	28 Jun 1821
Kitturah	13	F	None	England	Utica	Indian Chief	19 Jun 1823
Thomas	54	M	Farmer	England	Utica	Indian Chief	19 Jun 1823
William	21	M	Wheelright	England	Utica	Indian Chief	19 Jun 1823
COVERELL, A.	40	M	Merchant	France	France	Medina	17 Dec 1828
COVERLY, N. T.	17	M	Boy	U. States	U. States	Worromontogus	23 Jun 1823
Thomas	38	M	Gardener	Inverlecthing, Inverlecthing [Parish], Roxburgh [County]	New York	Hero	19 May 1828
*to follow his occupation							
COVERN..., Edward	20	M	Weaver	England	United States	India	8 Jun 1827
COVERT, Jacob	43	M	Merchant	U. States	U. States	Maria	2 Apr 1827
COVEY, Mary Jane	19		Spinster	Ireland	United States	Courier	15 Oct 1827
Nancy	30 6/12	F	None	Ireland	United States	Atlantic	21 Jul 1827
Wm. J.	29		Cooper	Ireland	United States	Courier	15 Oct 1827
COVILL, Wm.	40	M	Farmer	Lincoln		Aurora	8 Jun 1827
COVIN, William	25	M	Laborer	Ireland	United States	Nancey	8 Jun 1822
COVINGTON, John R.	40	M	U.S. Navy	United States	U. States	Nimrod	24 Jan 1826
COW, Ann	23	F	Servant	Ireland	U. States	Edwin	1 Jul 1829
Tim	30	M	Merchant	...moy	China	Ajax	15 May 1822
COWACE, Wm.	22	M	Lawer	Spain	Spain	Saluda	15 Jul 1826

NAMES OF PASSENGERS	AGE	SEX	OCCUPATIONS	COUNTRY TO WHICH THEY BELONG	COUNTRY THEY INTEND TO INHABIT	SHIPS/DATES OF ARRIVAL	
COWAN, Charlotte	6	F		Britain	U. States	Florida	2 Jun 1828
David	37 8/12	M	Printcutter	Scotland	United States	Mobile	21 Aug 1827
Duncan	56	M	Merchant	Britain	U. States	Florida	2 Jun 1828
Ed.	20	M	Merchant	G. Brittain	G. Brittain	Franklin	28 Feb 1825
Edwd.	21	M	Labourer	Ireland	New York	Louisa	18 Apr 1827
Helen	11	M		Britain	U. States	Florida	2 Jun 1828
Janet	17	F		Britain	U. States	Florida	2 Jun 1828
Jno.	32	M	Farmer	Great Britain	United States	Atlantic	28 May 1827
John	30			Great Britan	United States	Newry	11 Jul 1827
Josh.	28	M	Pencil Mr.	England	U. States	Dalhouse	23 Mar 1829
M.	19	M		Britain	U. States	Florida	2 Jun 1828
Michael	27	M	Labourer	Ireland	United States	Nancy	16 Aug 1824
Michael	30	M	Labourer	Ireland	United States	St. Michaels	24 Mar 1825
Patrick	3	M		Ireland	United States	Princess Charlotte	26 Apr 1827
*Died on the Voyage							
Thomas	24	M	Wheelright	Ireland	U. States	Josephine	7 May 1827
W.	31	M	Merchant	United States	United States	Claudio	16 Oct 1827
William	13		Hatter	Ireland	G. Britain	Robert Burns	14 Jun 1824
Wm.	30	M	Taylor	Ireland	U. States	Hunter	30 May 1827
COWANS, G.	2	M		Scotland	U. States	Superior	25 Sep 1828
G.	3	M		Scotland	U. States	Superior	25 Sep 1828
S.	26	F		Scotland	U. States	Superior	25 Sep 1828
S.	38	F		Scotland	U. States	Superior	25 Sep 1828
Wm.	32	M	Merchant	Scotland	U. States	Superior	25 Sep 1828
COWBURN, George	18	M	Dyer	Great Britain	United States	Freak	14 oct 1828
COWDEN, Ann	28	F				Lady of the Lake	23 Aug 1828
Jo	39	M	Labourer			Lady of the Lake	23 Aug 1828
COWELL, Betty	2	F	Labourer	England	U. States	Comet	23 Aug 1828
Esther	33	F	Labourer	England	U. States	Comet	23 Aug 1828
Frances	19			England	England	Thames	25 Oct 1821
John	10	M	Labourer	England	U. States	Comet	23 Aug 1828
John	25	M	Farmer	England	New York	Eliza	8 Mar 1827
Joseph	4	M	Labourer	England	U. States	Comet	23 Aug 1828
Mary	32	F	Farmer	England	New York	Eliza	8 Mar 1827
Thomas	7	M	Labourer	England	U. States	Comet	23 Aug 1828
Thomas	20	M	Labourer	Great Brittain	United States	Active	12 Sep 1828
Thomas	34	M	Labourer	England	U. States	Comet	23 Aug 1828
William	1	M	Labourer	England	U. States	Comet	23 Aug 1828
COWEN, Alice	1	F		Ireland	United States	Princess Charlotte	26 Apr 1827
Arthur	19	M	Labourer	Ireland	America	Wilson	27 Nov 1826
Catherine	4	F		Ireland	United States	Princess Charlotte	26 Apr 1827
Catherine	30	F		Ireland	United States	Princess Charlotte	26 Apr 1827
Eliza	2	F		Ireland	United States	Princess Charlotte	26 Apr 1827
Janny	16	F		Ireland	America	Wilson	27 Nov 1826
John	30	M	Stone Mason	Ireland	United States	Princess Charlotte	26 Apr 1827
Joseph	23 1/12	M	Taylor	Ireland	United States	London	6 Feb 1829
Mary	6	F		Ireland	United States	Princess Charlotte	26 Apr 1827
Patt	25	M	Farmer	Ireland	United States	Dublin Packet	29 Jun 1825
COWERSIAN, Judah	26	F		G. Britain	U. States	Mary & Harriot	8 Sep 1828
COWHAN, Dennis	25	M	Labourer	Ireland	U. States	Sarah G	30 Jun 1828
Joseph	50		Merchant	Jamaica	Great Britain	Henrietta	26 Nov 1825
COWHLAN, John	40	M	Stone Cutter	Ireland	United States	Enterprize	23 Jul 1827
COWING, Andrew, a son [of William]	9	M		Scotland	N. York State	Resolution	6 Jun 1822
Cristiaen, daughter [of William]	24	F		Scotland	N. York State	Resolution	6 Jun 1822
Jane, daughter [of William]	14	F		Scotland	N. York State	Resolution	6 Jun 1822
S. L.	35	M	Merchant	United States	United States	William Byrnes	1 Dec 1824

NAMES OF PASSENGERS	AGE	SEX	OCCUPATIONS	COUNTRY TO WHICH THEY BELONG	COUNTRY THEY INTEND TO INHABIT	SHIPS/DATES OF ARRIVAL	
COWING (cont'd)							
Thomas, son							
[of William]	22	M	farmer & merchant	Scotland	N. York State	Resolution	6 Jun 1822
William	53	M	farmer & merchant	Scotland	N. York State	Resolution	6 Jun 1822
COWL, Ann	5	F		England	United States	Ann Maria	27 Aug 1822
John	7	M		England	United States	Ann Maria	27 Aug 1822
Sarah	3	F		England	United States	Ann Maria	27 Aug 1822
W.	9	M		England	United States	Ann Maria	27 Aug 1822
COWLBY, Adam	37	M	Farmer	United States	New York	Rambler	31 Aug 1829
COWLE, Ann	50	F	None	Isle of Man		Ocean	13 Jul 1827
Anne	12	F	None	Great Britain	United States	Mary & Harriet	3 Jul 1829
Catherine	6	F	None	Great Britain	United States	Mary & Harriet	3 Jul 1829
Chas.	32	M	Labourer	Great Britain	United States	Mary & Harriet	3 Jul 1829
Elizh.	30	F	None	Isle of Man		Ocean	13 Jul 1827
Esther	32	F	None	Great Britain	United States	Mary & Harriet	3 Jul 1829
Jane	6	F	None	Isle of Man		Ocean	13 Jul 1827
John	35	M	Farmer	Isle of Man		Ocean	13 Jul 1827
Wm.	40	M	Labourer	Isle of Man		Ocean	13 Jul 1827
Wm. John	9	M	None	Isle of Man		Ocean	13 Jul 1827
COWLEN, Betsey	1...	F	...	England	United States	Milton	20 Oct 1827
COWLER, John	20	M	Labourer	Isle of Man		Ocean	13 Jul 1827
COWLES, Ira, &							
apprentice		M	Trader	Connecticut		Antelope	21 Aug 1820
COWLEY, Charles	26 1/12	M	Miner	Ireland	United States	London	6 Feb 1829
Ellen	20	F		Ireland	New York	William	26 Apr 1823
Harriet	20	F	Ladies Maid	England	America	Criterion	27 Oct 1821
James	23	M	Weaver	Ireland	New York	Lima	5 Aug 1829
James	23	M	Weaver	Ireland	New York	Lima	5 Aug 1829
John	40	M	Labourer	G. Britain	U. States	London	23 Sep 1828
Loarami	18 2/12	F	daughter of				
			Richd. Cowley	New York	New York	Thames	16 May 1821
Mary	22	F		Scotland	United States	Indus	5 Sep 1827
Mary	27	F		G. Britain	U. States	London	23 Sep 1828
Pat	27	M	Labourer	Ireland	United States	Wilson	6 Jun 1828
Patrick	15	M	Labourer	Ireland	New York	William	26 Apr 1823
Richd.	20	M	Labourer	Isle of Man		Ocean	13 Jul 1827
Saml.	47	M	Labourer	Great Britain	United States	Atlantic	28 May 1827
Sarah	20	F		G. Britain	U. States	London	23 Sep 1828
T.	24	M	Farmer	Scotland	United States	Indus	5 Sep 1827
Thomas	3	M		G. Britain	U. States	London	23 Sep 1828
Thos.	1 3/12	M		Scotland	United States	Indus	5 Sep 1827
Wm.	19	M	Mechanic	England	U. States	Birmingham	16 Jun 1828
Wm.	20	M	Labourer	G. Britain	U. States	Nimrod	31 Jul 1828
COWLING, Richard	25	M	Grocer	Great Britain	Pensylvania	Orozimbo	2 Oct 1824
COWLISHAW, George	36	M	Butcher	England	New York	Brighton	19 Aug 1829
George	36	M	Butcher			Brighton	19 Aug 1829
John	4	M	None	England	New York	Brighton	19 Aug 1829
John	4	M	None			Brighton	19 Aug 1829
Martha	33	F	None	England	New York	Brighton	19 Aug 1829
Martha	33	F	None			Brighton	19 Aug 1829
William	3	M	None			Brighton	19 Aug 1829
Willm.	3	M	None	England	New York	Brighton	19 Aug 1829
COWLOY, Catherine	23	F	Spinster	Ireland	United States	St. Michaels	23 Dec 1826
COWLY, Ann	4	F	None	Isle of Man		Ocean	13 Jul 1827
John	2	M	None	Isle of Man		Ocean	13 Jul 1827
Mary	27	F	None	Isle of Man		Ocean	13 Jul 1827
Wm.	2	M	None	Isle of Man		Ocean	13 Jul 1827
Wm.	30	M	Farmer	Isle of Man		Ocean	13 Jul 1827
COWNEY, John	20	M	Labourer	Ireland	United States	Wilson	6 Jun 1828
COWNIS, —, Mrs.	42	F	Lady	G. Britain	G. Britain	Wallace	12 Apr 1824
COWPER, Geo.	27	M	Gentn.	Gt. Brittain	United States	Robert Edwards	1 Jun 1826
Josiah	50	M	Mariner	United States	United States	Genl. Brown	3 Dec 1821
COWPTOW, Margret	11	F	Girl	Ireland	United States	Henry Kneeland	7 Jun 1828
COWS, Lucy	3/12	F	None	New York	New York	Elizabeth	6 Oct 1827
Phillis	40	F	None	New York	New York	Elizabeth	6 Oct 1827
Rachel	11	F	None	New York	New York	Elizabeth	6 Oct 1827
COWSICZ, Mary	35	F	...	Great Britian	U. States	St. Michael	3 Jan 1825
COWTHORP, Elizabeth	24	F		Great Britain	United States	Freake	25 Jun 1827
Joseph	3	M		Great Britain	United States	Freake	25 Jun 1827

NAMES OF PASSENGERS	AGE	SEX	OCCUPATIONS	COUNTRY TO WHICH THEY BELONG	COUNTRY THEY INTEND TO INHABIT	SHIPS/DATES OF ARRIVAL	
COWTHORP (cont'd)							
Joseph	32	M	Farmer	Great Britain	United States	Freake	25 Jun 1827
Mary	1	F		Great Britain	United States	Freake	25 Jun 1827
Thomas	5	M		Great Britain	United States	Freake	25 Jun 1827
COX, —, Mrs.	30	F		Pennsylvania	U. States	United States	29 Nov 1823
A., Mr.	40	M	Merchant	Pennsylvania	U. States	United States	29 Nov 1823
Abigail	3 6/12	F		England		Ann Maria	26 Apr 1822
Andrew	28	M	Mason	Ireland	United States	Belleville	13 Oct 1827
Ann	2					Xenophon	25 Jul 1826
Betsey	27			England	Maryland	Caroline	10 Mar 1828
C. L.	8	F		United States	United States	Trio	2 Oct 1828
Charlotte B.	28	F		United States	United States	Trio	2 Oct 1828
Clara, Mrs.	19	F	None	U. States	U. States	Canada	13 Oct 1825
Cornich	63	M	Labourer	Ireland	U. States	Josephine	30 Aug 1828
E.	1 6/12	F		England		Ann Maria	26 Apr 1822
E.	21	M	Farmer	England	United States	Earl of Liverpool	28 Apr 1824
E. B.	22	M		Great Brittan	U.S.	Florida	17 May 1825
E. H., Mrs.	40	F	Spinster	United States	U. States	William Thompson	29 Jan 1823
Edward	6	M		Ireland	United States	Eliza	29 Aug 1822
Elen	24	F		Ireland	U. States	Lady Hunter	8 Aug 1826
Eliza	5	F		Great Britain	United States	Isaac Hicks	10 Jul 1827
Elizabeth	1 2/12	F		England	United States	Eliza Grant	7 Jun 1827
Elizabeth	9	F		Ireland	United States	Eliza	29 Aug 1822
Elizabeth	32	F		England	U. States	Ann Maria	26 Apr 1822
Elizabeth	38	F		Great Britain	United States	Isaac Hicks	10 Jul 1827
Ellen	2	F		United States	United States	Trio	2 Oct 1828
Enoch	26	M	Tiler	England	United States	Cosmo	21 Aug 1828
Fanny	20	F	Miller's wife	England	England	Stephania	13 Sep 1821
Francis	29 2/12	M	Painter	Gt. Britain	New York	Betsey	18 Apr 1822
Geo.	1		Child	Ireland	United States	Eliza	29 Aug 1822
Geo.	34	M	Farmer	Ireland	United States	Eliza	29 Aug 1822
George	27		Surgeon	Scotland	England	London	16 Aug 1824
George	32	M	Smith	England	U. States	Ann Maria	26 Apr 1822
Henry	5	M	None	United States	U. States	William Thompson	29 Jan 1823
Henry	20	M		Ireland	United States	John & Adam	21 Sep 1822
James	...		Weaver		United States	Atlantic	2 Apr 1827
James	21	M	Laborer	Ireland	United States	Belleville	13 Oct 1827
James	23	M	None	England	England	Leeds	24 Sep 1827
James	28	M	Labourer	Ireland	New York	America	1 Aug 1828
James	29	M	Miller	England	England	Stephania	13 Sep 1821
James	32		Farmer	England	S. New York	Xenophon	25 Jul 1826
James, Mr.	20	M	None	G. Britian	U. States	Corinthian	4 Jan 1825
Jane	4	F		Ireland	United States	Eliza	29 Aug 1822
Jane	20	F	None	St. Johns	U. States	Sarah G	7 May 1827
Jane	25	F	Wife	Ireland	Canada	Ann Maria	7 Aug 1826
John	2	F		Great Britain	United States	Isaac Hicks	10 Jul 1827
John	3	M		England	United States	Eliza Grant	7 Jun 1827
John	21	M	Shoemaker	Ireland	New York	America	1 Aug 1828
John	26	M	Merchant	G. Brittain	United States	Hercules	24 Oct 1821
John	27	M	Farmer	Ireland	Canada	Ann Maria	7 Aug 1826
John	28	M	Merchant	Gt. Britain	United States	Seeds	29 Sep 1824
John	30	M		U. States	U. States	United States	11 Sep 1828
John	39	M	Engineer	Great Britain	United States	Isaac Hicks	10 Jul 1827
John	39	M	Farmer	America	America	Britannia	5 Nov 1828
Jos.	28	M	Merchant	Great Brit.	Great Britain	Martha	4 Oct 1822
Joseph	23	M	Druggist	Great Britain	U. States America	Maria	22 May 1822
Joseph	29	M	Tanner	America	America	Britannia	5 Nov 1828
Joseph	30	M	None	U. States	U. States	Canada	13 Oct 1825
Joseph	33	M	Merchant	U. States	United States	Florida	14 Sep 1827
Lawrence	21	M	Farmer	Ireland	United States	Helen	27 Jun 1821
Margaret	16	F		Great Brittan	U.S.	Florida	17 May 1825
Mary	4					Xenophon	25 Jul 1826
Mary	5	F		England	United States	Eliza Grant	7 Jun 1827
Mary	11	F		Great Britain	United States	Isaac Hicks	10 Jul 1827
Mary	17	F	Farmer	England	U. States	Lewis	1 Jul 1820
Mary, Mrs.	24 6/12	F		England	United States	Eliza Grant	7 Jun 1827

NAMES OF PASSENGERS	AGE	SEX	OCCUPATIONS	COUNTRY TO WHICH THEY BELONG	COUNTRY THEY INTEND TO INHABIT	SHIPS/DATES OF ARRIVAL	
COX (cont'd)							
Mary Ann	3	F		U. States	U. States	United States	11 Sep 1828
Michael	25	M	Labourer	Ireland	New York	America	1 Aug 1828
Michael	27	M	Labourer	Ireland		Marchioness	13 May 1828
Owen	16	M	Laborer	Ireland	United States	Fabius	4 Jun 1828
Patrick	15	M	Shoemaker	Ireland	New York	America	1 Aug 1828
Patt	20	M		Ireland	United States	William Byrnes	6 Apr 1826
Rachel	34	F	Spinster	Ireland	United States	Eliza	29 Aug 1822
Rebecca	6					Xenophon	25 Jul 1826
Rebecca	29					Xenophon	25 Jul 1826
Richard	8					Xenophon	25 Jul 1826
Robert	24	M	Farmer	England	United States	Manhattan	11 Oct 1824
Rosana	19	F	Spinster	Ireland	U. States	Josephine	30 Aug 1828
Rosanna	22	F	Spinster	Ireland	America	Josephine	8 Dec 1827
S. H.	24	M	Gentleman	Ireland	United States	John & Adam	21 Sep 1822
S. H.	32	M	Gent.	United States	United States	Trio	2 Oct 1828
Saml.	23	M	Spinster	Great Brittan	United States	Corinthian	9 Jan 1827
Sarah	9	F		Great Britain	United States	Isaac Hicks	10 Jul 1827
Susan	7	F		Great Britain	United States	Isaac Hicks	10 Jul 1827
Susanah	63	F	Matron	Ireland	U. States	Josephine	30 Aug 1828
Thomas	21 9/12	M	Stone Mason	England	United States	Eliza Grant	7 Jun 1827
Thomas	38		Farmer	England	Maryland	Caroline	10 Mar 1828
Thos.	15	M	Farmer	England	America	Britannia	5 Nov 1828
W.	60	M	Merchant	Antigua	Antigua	Collector	7 Aug 1826
W. J.	21	M	Gent.	United States	United States	Trio	2 Oct 1828
William	27	M	tailor	England	Newyork	Cortes	16 Jul 1827
William	50	M	Publican	American	Amemerica	Arcadia	5 May 1828
William B.	22	M	Merchant	St. Johns	U. States	Nancy	27 Jun 1823
Wm.	22	M	Farmer	St. Johns	St. John, N.B.	Brothers	17 Oct 1823
Wm.	27	M		Great Brittan	U.S.	Florida	17 May 1825
Wm.	37	M	Doctor	G. Britain	London	Agness	20 Jan 1829
COXAT, Ernst	35	F		U. States	U. States	Columbia	22 Sep 1828
COXHEAD, Frereck	2	M		Germany	U. States	Columbia	22 Sep 1828
COY, Jose S.	27	M	Merchant	Spain	Spain	Circassian	13 Jun 1825
COYLE, And.	1	M		Ireland	America	Mary	29 May 1827
Ann	20	F	None	Ireland	United States	Jubilee	13 Jul 1829
Ann	23	F		Gt. Britain		Dalhouse Castle	13 May 1828
Bridget	26	F		Ireland	United States	Aurora	9 Jul 1827
Cat.	1/2	F	None	England	United States	India	8 Jun 1827
Cathn.	28	F		Ireland	United States	Aurora	9 Jul 1827
Charles	24	M	Weaver	Ireland	U. States	Josephine	30 Aug 1828
Danl.	35	M	Labourer	Ireland		Robert Fulton	4 Jun 1828
Elenr.	17	F		Ireland	United States	Aurora	9 Jul 1827
Hugh	28	M	Farmer	Ireland	United States	Aurora	9 Jul 1827
James	18			County Carvan	N. York	Peru	30 May 1828
James	36	M	...	...	...	Meteor	16 Aug 1824
John	3	M	Child	Ireland	United States	Dublin Packet	9 Jul 1827
Jos.	27	M	Farmer	Ireland	America	Mary	29 May 1827
Judy	20	F	Servant	Ireland	United States	Josephine	30 Apr 1828
Margaret	24	F	Wife	Ireland	United States	Dublin Packet	9 Jul 1827
Margt.	21	F	Servant	Ireland	United States	Carolina Ann	14 May 1827
Mary	20	F	Servant	Ireland	New York	Atlantic	8 May 1828
Mary	20			County Carvan	N. York	Peru	30 May 1828
Mary	22	F	Spinster	Ireland	America	Mary	29 May 1827
Mary	23	F	None	England	United States	India	8 Jun 1827
Mary	24	F	Spinster	Ireland	United States	Robert Fulton	24 Jul 1826
Michael	18	M	Labourer	Great Britain	United States	Isaac Hicks	22 Aug 1828
Michal	20	M	Weaver	Great Briton	uncertain	Mount Vernon	29 Aug 1828
Patrick	17	M		Ireland	U. States	Virginia	20 Jun 1825
Peter	20	M	Servant	Ireland	United States	Josephine	30 Apr 1828
Peter	21	M	Farmer	England	United States	India	8 Jun 1827
Philip	23	M	Farmer	Ireland	United States	Dublin Packet	28 Apr 1824
Rose	20 8/12	F	Seamstress	Ireland	United States	Atlantic	21 Jul 1827
Sarah	22	F	Spinster	Ireland	United States	Trident	17 May 1825
COYLEY, Ann	23	F	None	Ireland	U. States	Dalhouse	23 Mar 1829
COYNE, George	26	M	Baker	Ireland	Und. Stts of Amer	Alexander Mansfield	18 Aug 1826
COZER, M.	23	M	Merchant	France	U. States	Waldo	19 Aug 1826
COZIA, Andrew	20	M	Farmer	Great Britian	United States	Diamond	8 Nov 1824

NAMES OF PASSENGERS	AGE	SEX	OCCUPATIONS	COUNTRY TO WHICH THEY BELONG	COUNTRY THEY INTEND TO INHABIT	SHIPS/DATES OF ARRIVAL	
COZINS, Wm.	27	M	Clerk	Gt. Britain	United States	Seeds	29 Sep 1824
COZZENS, Sarah	55	F	Servant	England	U.S.A.	Hudson	21 Aug 1829
COZZINS, Elizabeth	36	M	Farmer	Great Britain	United States	Frances Henrietta	17 Sep 1827
CR..., Eliza	18	F		Ireland	United States	Nancey	8 Jun 1822
H...	32	F	None	St. Thomas	United States	Martha	22 Jul 1820
CRAB, J.	19	M	Mercht.	U.S.	U.S.	Toison	6 May 1828
John	12	M		France	France	Lincoln	12 Jun 1824
CRABB, Charles J.	20	M	Merchant	U.S.	U.S.	New England	27 Jul 1829
Jno. N.	48	M	Planter	Spain	U.S.	Emma	24 Jun 1825
Thos., Sr.	41	M	U.S. Navy	U.S.A.	U.S.A.	Potomac	25 Jul 1829
CRABTREE, Edward	54	M	Farmer	Yorkshire	U. States	Atlantic	13 Jul 1824
James	55	M	Shoe Maker	England	America	Josephine	8 Jan 1827
CRACELINI, Lud.	28	M	Merchant	Carleruke in Netherlands	New York	Louisa	6 Oct 1828
CRACHARTE, Fred	44	M	Weaver	France	U. States	C. Amelia	30 Jun 1828
CRADDOCK, —, Infant Child	9/12	F		England	New York	Lima	16 Mar 1829
Anne	24	F		England	New York	Lima	16 Mar 1829
John	27	M	Joiner	England	U. States	Josephine	23 Jan 1829
CRADOCK, Wm.	31	M	Miller	Great Britain	United States	Diana	6 Jul 1829
CRAFIELD, Edward	25	M	Laborer	Ireland	United States	Sarah G.	20 Jul 1827
Marey	1	F	Child	Ireland	United States	Sarah G.	20 Jul 1827
Margaret	23	F		Ireland	United States	Sarah G.	20 Jul 1827
CRAFT, Charles	9	M		England	United States	Euphrates	2 Sep 1823
Geo.	35	M	Farmer	Germany	United States	Lydia	18 Jun 1828
Harriott	7	F		England	United States	Euphrates	2 Sep 1823
John	21	M	Shoemaker	England	America	Franklin	19 Nov 1828
John	34	M	Farmer	England	United States	Euphrates	2 Sep 1823
Lewis F.	17	M	Farmer or Mechanic	France	U.S.	Edward Quesnel	31 Jul 1827
Margaret	49	F		England	United States	Euphrates	2 Sep 1823
Mary Ann	11	F		England	United States	Euphrates	2 Sep 1823
Wm. C.	18	M	Farmer	Gt. Britain	United States	Robert Edwards	1 Jun 1826
CRAFTS, R. A.	29	M	Merchant	U. States	U. States	Napolean	26 Sep 1828
CRAGG, John	25	M	Carpenter	With intention to become citizen		New York	18 Jul 1828
CRAGGS, Charles	8	M	None	Gt. Britain	U.S.A.	Dalhouse Castle	21 Aug 1829
Chs.	8	M	None	Great Britain	United States	Dalhouse Castle	21 Aug 1829
Elizabeth	2	F	None	Gt. Britain	U.S.A.	Dalhouse Castle	21 Aug 1829
Elizth.	2	F	None	Great Britain	United States	Dalhouse Castle	21 Aug 1829
Francis	23	M	Smith	England	New York	Cortes	23 Nov 1827
Henry	2	M	None	Gt. Britain	U.S.A.	Dalhouse Castle	21 Aug 1829
Henry	2	M	None	Great Britain	United States	Dalhouse Castle	21 Aug 1829
Isabella	34	F	None	Gt. Britain	U.S.A.	Dalhouse Castle	21 Aug 1829
Isabella	34	F	None	Great Britain	United States	Dalhouse Castle	21 Aug 1829
Jane	23	F	None	Gt. Britain	U.S.A.	Dalhouse Castle	21 Aug 1829
Jane	23	F	None	Great Britain	United States	Dalhouse Castle	21 Aug 1829
Jessey	1	F	None	Great Britain	United States	Dalhouse Castle	21 Aug 1829
Jessy	1	F	None	Gt. Britain	U.S.A.	Dalhouse Castle	21 Aug 1829
Saml.	10	M	None	Great Britain	United States	Dalhouse Castle	21 Aug 1829
Samuel	10	M	None	Gt. Britain	U.S.A.	Dalhouse Castle	21 Aug 1829
Sarah	4	F	None	Gt. Britain	U.S.A.	Dalhouse Castle	21 Aug 1829
Sarah	4	F	None	Great Britain	United States	Dalhouse Castle	21 Aug 1829
William	6	M	None	Gt. Britain	U.S.A.	Dalhouse Castle	21 Aug 1829
Wm.	6	M	None	Great Britain	United States	Dalhouse Castle	21 Aug 1829
CRAIG, Agnes	25	F	Spinster	Ireland	America	Superior	12 Jun 1824
Alexr.	27	M	Slater	Ireland	United States	Carolina Ann	11 Dec 1826
Amelia	4	F	None	Great Britain	America	Remittance	24 Aug 1825
Andrew	20	M	Weaver	Ireland	United States	Commerce	13 Jun 1828
Andrew	25	M	Merchant	Ireland	United States	Carolina Ann	11 Dec 1826
Anne	15	F	Spinster	Ireland	America	Superior	12 Jun 1824
C. L.	22	M	Accountant	Great Britain	U. States	Great Britain	18 Mar 1828
Chrisn.	40	M	None	Great Britain	America	Remittance	24 Aug 1825
David	15 6/12	M	distressed seaman	Philadelphia	United States	Florida	27 Aug 1825
David S.	25	M	Gentleman	N. York	U. States	Quito	15 Mar 1824
Dd. S.	25	M	Merchant	N. York	U. States	Flight	12 Dec 1825
Eliza	18	F	Spinster	Ireland	America	Superior	12 Jun 1824
Ellen	20	F	Servant	Great Britain	United States	Leeds	29 Sep 1823
Hester	7			Ireland	United States	Courier	15 Oct 1827

269

NAMES OF PASSENGERS	AGE	SEX	OCCUPATIONS	COUNTRY TO WHICH THEY BELONG	COUNTRY THEY INTEND TO INHABIT	SHIPS/DATES OF ARRIVAL	
CRAIG (cont'd)							
Hester	30		Spinster	Ireland	United States	Courier	15 Oct 1827
J. Mayar	40	M	C.A.	U.S.	U. States	Athenian	18 Oct 1826
James	13	M	Farmer	Ireland	America	Superior	12 Jun 1824
James	22	M	Merchant	Scotland	New York	Xenophon	3 Oct 1829
James	25	F		Swinetrees, Lochwinnoch [Parish], Renfrew [County]	New York	Hero	19 May 1828
*going with their friends							
James	60	M	Farmer	Ireland	America	Superior	12 Jun 1824
Jane	4	F	None	Great Britain	United States	Courier	26 Jun 1827
Jane	5			Ireland	United States	Courier	15 Oct 1827
Jane	11	F	Farmer	Ireland	America	Superior	12 Jun 1824
Jane	24		Seamstress	Scotland	City New York	Rufus King	3 Sep 1822
Jane	27	F	None	Great Britain	United States	Courier	26 Jun 1827
Jane	27	F	None	Scotland	U.S. of America	Hamilton	18 Jul 1827
Jane	45	F	Farmer	Ireland	America	Superior	12 Jun 1824
Jno.	19	M	None	Great Britain	America	Remittance	24 Aug 1825
John	3	M	Farmer	Ireland	America	Superior	12 Jun 1824
John	20	M	None	Scotland	U. States	Czar	29 Aug 1829
John	27	M	Taylor	Scotland	U.S. of America	Hamilton	18 Jul 1827
John	42	M	None	Abberdinstine	Berpoterk	Aldebaron	21 Jan 1826
Kitty	35	F	Servant	England	America	Britannia	5 Nov 1828
Mary	6	F	None	Great Britain	United States	Courier	26 Jun 1827
Mary	22	F	Spinster	Ireland	America	Superior	12 Jun 1824
Mary	35	F	None	Great Britain	America	Remittance	24 Aug 1825
Robert	2			Ireland	United States	Courier	15 Oct 1827
Samuel B.	30	M	Merchant	N. York	Philadelphia	Independence	25 Oct 1828
Sarah	2/12	F	None	Great Britain	United States	Courier	26 Jun 1827
Sarah	9			Ireland	United States	Courier	15 Oct 1827
William	8	M	Farmer	Ireland	America	Superior	12 Jun 1824
Wm.	21	M	None	Great Britain	United States	Meridian	2 Jul 1827
Wm.	25	M	Blacksmith	Scotland	United States	Belmont	30 Aug 1828
Wm.	28	M	Farmer	Swinetrees, Lochwinnoch [Parish], Renfrew [County]	New York	Hero	19 May 1828
*Farmer to follow his occupation							
Wm.	32	M	Bookkeeper	Gt. Britain	United States	Eliza Barker	11 Jan 1826
Wm.	34	M	Weaver	Ireland	United States	Essex	23 May 1828
CRAIGAN, James	20	M	Farmer	Ireland	United States	Baltic	21 Apr 1827
CRAIGE, Hugh	22	M	Labourer	Ireland	U. States	Two Marys	20 Apr 1825
Jas.	18	M	Labourer	Ireland	U. States	Two Marys	20 Apr 1825
CRAIGEN, John	1 6/12	M	Child	Ireland	United States	Champion	3 Nov 1828
CRAIGO, William	33	M	Labourer	Ireland	United States	Wilson	28 Nov 1828
CRAIN, Thomas	22	M	Labourer	Ireland	U. States	Sarah G	30 Jun 1828
CRAINE, John	6			Great Britain	United States	Thomas Dickason	29 Aug 1828
John	21		Joiner	Great Britain	United States	Thomas Dickason	29 Aug 1828
Mary	36			Great Britain	United States	Thomas Dickason	29 Aug 1828
Thomas	33		Joiner	Great Britain	United States	Thomas Dickason	29 Aug 1828
CRAMER, William	29	M	Gentleman	Holland	United States	Jason	3 Nov 1828
CRAMIL, Felix	17		Boy	Ireland	United States	Courier	15 Oct 1827
CRAMP, Ann	5	F	family of [Samuel]	U. Kingdom of Great Britain	United States	Cambria	7 May 1828
David	2 6/12	M	family of [Samuel]	U. Kingdom of Great Britain	United States	Cambria	7 May 1828
Priscilla	30	F	family of [Samuel]	U. Kingdom of Great Britain	United States.	Cambria	7 May 1828
Samuel	8 6/12	M	family of [Samuel]	U. Kingdom of Great Britain	United States.	Cambria	7 May 1828
Samuel	32	M	Mason	U. Kingdom of Great Britain	United States	Cambria	7 May 1828
CRAMPTON, Ann Jane	23	F	Mantuamaker	Ireland	New York	Atlantic	6 Oct 1828
Elizabeth	3	M	Daughter	Ireland	New York	Atlantic	6 Oct 1828

NAMES OF PASSENGERS	AGE	SEX	OCCUPATIONS	COUNTRY TO WHICH THEY BELONG	COUNTRY THEY INTEND TO INHABIT	SHIPS/DATES OF ARRIVAL	
CRAMSBY, John	35	M	Labourer	Ireland	United States	Robert Fulton	10 Aug 1827
CRAMSEY, Mary	20	F	Servant	Ireland	United States	William & George	14 May 1828
CRANCH, Charles	15	M	Carpenter	England	Albany	Chelsea	16 May 1828
Elizabeth	9	F	Carpenter	England	Albany	Chelsea	16 May 1828
Frederick	12	M	Carpenter	England	Albany	Chelsea	16 May 1828
George	17	M	Carpenter	England	Albany	Chelsea	16 May 1828
Hannah	5	F	Carpenter	England	Albany	Chelsea	16 May 1828
Levi, & family	44	M	Carpenter	England	Albany	Chelsea	16 May 1828
Samuel	7	M	Carpenter	England	Albany	Chelsea	16 May 1828
Sarah *Died May 11th	2	F	Carpenter	England	Albany	Chelsea	16 May 1828
Sarah	43	F	Carpenter	England	Albany	Chelsea	16 May 1828
CRANE, Ann	25	F		Wales	United States	Lord Wellington	14 Nov 1827
Cathe.	29	F	Wife	..., ..., England	Pittsburg	New Orleans	24 Aug 1827
Elisa	30	F		Ireland	United States	Nancy Henrietta	3 Nov 1828
J.	34	M	Architect	United States		Howard	17 Oct 1822
Jane	12	M	Child	..., ..., England	Pittsburg	New Orleans	24 Aug 1827
Jane	22	F	None	G.B.	U.S.A.	Silas Richard	30 Jun 1828
John	1	F	Child	..., ..., England	Pittsburg	New Orleans	24 Aug 1827
John	26	M	Painter	..., ..., England	Pittsburg	New Orleans	24 Aug 1827
Philip	21	M	Labourer	England	United States	Nimrod	31 Jul 1828
Robert	30	M	None	G.B.	U.S.A.	Silas Richard	30 Jun 1828
Sam.	28	M	Shoemaker	Ireland	U. States	Palestine	1 May 1821
Thos.	25	M	Gentleman	Ireland	United States	Jubilee	13 Sep 1827
William	27	M	Rifle Maker	Wales	United States	Lord Wellington	14 Nov 1827
CRANFIELD, Nathaniel G.	22		Cooper	England	U.S. of America	Mary	21 Sep 1821
CRANGAN, Thos.	21	M	...	England	Canada	William Thompson	10 May 1825
CRANIN, Francis	28	M	Tanner	Ireland	United States	Maria	12 May 1823
CRANSTON, Wm.	20	M	Labourer	Argyle (Tedland) Scotland	United States	Jean Hastie	27 Jul 1829
CRANWALL, James	19	M	La	Glenneth & Cork	Co. Cork	Aldebaron	21 Jan 1826
CRANWELL, Joseph	20	M	La	Glenneth & Cork	Co. Cork	Aldebaron	21 Jan 1826
CRAREY, Charels	26	M	Labourer	Ireland	U. States	Meteor	19 Jul 1828
Petre	20	M	Labourer	Irereland	America	Carolina Ann	20 Jun 1825
CRARY, Edward C.	22	M	Mercht.	U.S.	N. York	George Canning	2 May 1828
John	35	M	Labourer	Ireland	United States	Hope	12 Jun 1828
John S.	39		Merchant	Connecticut	New York	James Cropper	12 Jul 1822
Patrick	27	M	Labourer	Ireland	United States	Hope	12 Jun 1828
CRATHERS, Robt.	30	M	Weaver	G. Britain	U. States	Camillus	8 Sep 1828
CRATON, John	21	M	Painter	Ireland	United States	Washington	2 Oct 1828
CRATT, A.	30	M	Shoemaker	Great Britain	United States	Isaac Hicks	6 Dec 1827
CRAULEY, Jerry	25	M	Laborer	Ireland	United States	Sarah G.	11 Jan 1828
Johanna	25	F		Ireland	United States	Pallas	28 Oct 1828
Michl.	25	M	Labourer	Ireland	United States	Pallas	28 Oct 1828
Will	25			Great Britan	United States	Newry	11 Jul 1827
CRAVEN, George	20 6/12	M	Sawyer	Great Britain	America	Hannibal	12 Oct 1826
Robert	23	M	Farmer	England	United States	Panthia	7 Feb 1822
CRAVENS, Will	21	M	Farmer			Hector	11 Sep 1820
CRAVIS, Elizabeth	39	F	None	Great Britain	U. States	Balance	19 Jun 1824
CRAWDER, Joseph	30	M	Manufacr.	Great Britain		Dalmannock	24 Ocg 1826
CRAWFAID, John, Mr.	24	M	Merchant	Gt. Britain	Gt. Britain	Pacific	22 May 1826
CRAWFORD, Agnes	14	F				Harmony	15 Jul 1820
Alexr.	27	M		Scotland	New York	Joseph Hume	26 Oct 1829
Alexr.	40	M	Mercht.	England	U.S.A.	Lima	6 Dec 1826
And.	40	M	Farmer	Ireland	U. States	Nancy	29 Nov 1821
Andrew	23	M	Labourer	Ireland	United States	William & George	14 May 1828
Ann	27		Wife, going to her husband	Scotland	United States	Camillus	3 May 1828
Catherine	26	F				Frances	17 Aug 1820
Charles	14	M	Weaver	Ireland	N. Jersey	Potomac	7 Aug 1827
Conyngham	28 3/12	M	Doctor of Medicine	Gt. Britain	United States	St. Michael	28 Feb 1826
David	19	M	Labourer	Ireland	United States	William & George	14 May 1828
David	22	M	Farmer	Scotland	United States	Commerce	17 Jul 1823

NAMES OF PASSENGERS	AGE	SEX	OCCUPATIONS	COUNTRY TO WHICH THEY BELONG	COUNTRY THEY INTEND TO INHABIT	SHIPS/DATES OF ARRIVAL	
CRAWFORD (cont'd)							
Dd.	8	M	Farmer	Ireland	U. States	Nancy	29 Nov 1821
Donald	33	M	Farmer			Frances	17 Aug 1820
Eliza	18	F	Shoemaker	G. Britain	U. States	Perseverance	9 Jun 1827
Ellen	30	F	Farmer, Labourer or Spinster	Ireland	U. States	Meteor	4 Oct 1827
Frederick	24	M	Shoemaker	Ireland	U. States	Nancy	25 Nov 1823
Gangee	6	M				Harmony	15 Jul 1820
George	46	M	Merchant			Harmony	15 Jul 1820
Gilbert	30	M	Teacher			Frances	17 Aug 1820
Isabella	3/12	F		Glasgow	New York	Anthusa	24 Aug 1825
James	5	M		Glasgow	New York	Anthusa	24 Aug 1825
James	28	M	Weaver	Ireland	U. States of America	Courier	17 Mar 1827
James	35	M	Baker	Glasgow	New York	Anthusa	24 Aug 1825
Jane	6	F	Farmer, Labourer or Spinster	Ireland	U. States	Meteor	4 Oct 1827
Jane	32	F		Glasgow	New York	Anthusa	24 Aug 1825
Janet	3/12			Scotland	United States	Camillus	3 May 1828
Janet	11	F				Harmony	15 Jul 1820
Janet	12	F	Gentleman	Scotland	United States	Camillus	9 May 1827
Janet	19		Spinster	Glasgow, Scotland	Great Britain	Iris	15 Jun 1822
Jno.	18	M				Harmony	15 Jul 1820
John	10	M	Farmer	Ireland	U. States	Nancy	29 Nov 1821
John	20	M	...	Ireland	United States	General Putnam	20 Jun 1825
John	21	M	Farmer	Ireland	America	Carolina Ann	14 Feb 1825
John	22	M	Weaver	Ireland	United States	Enterprize	23 Jul 1827
John	23		Merchant	Quebec	Great Britain	William Thompson	13 May 1823
John	23	M	Baker	G. Britain	United States	Ariel	21 May 1827
John	24	M	Shoemaker	G. Britain	U. States	Perseverance	9 Jun 1827
John	31	M	Labourer	Ireland	America	Splendid	23 Mar 1829
John	45	M	Merchant	United States	United States	Agnes	12 Apr 1821
John H.	2	M		Glasgow	New York	Anthusa	24 Aug 1825
John L.	28	M	Merchant	England	England	Birmingham	16 Jun 1828
John L., Mr.	21		Merchant	Quebec	G.B.	Pacific	24 May 1824
Margaret	40	F				Harmony	15 Jul 1820
Margret	20	F				Harmony	15 Jul 1820
Margt.	2			Scotland	United States	Camillus	3 May 1828
Maria	19	F				Harmony	15 Jul 1820
Mary	36		...	Ireland	United States	Robert Burns	18 Jun 1822
Matthew	20	M	Founder	G. Britain	United States	Ariel	21 May 1827
Peter	28	M	Farmer			Frances	17 Aug 1820
Peter	60	M	Farmer	Great Britain	U.S. America	Prince Madoc	24 Sep 1821
Rachel	29	F	None	Glasgow	Glasgow	New York	14 Nov 1826
Robert	11		...	Ireland	United States	Robert Burns	18 Jun 1822
Robert, & Servant	36		Merchant	Ireland	United States	Bogota	25 Oct 1827
Saml.	25	M	Farmer	G. Britan	U. States	Corinthian	4 Jan 1825
Samuel	3	M	Farmer, Labourer or Spinster	Ireland	U. States	Meteor	4 Oct 1827
Sarah	17	F	Spinster	Great Britain	U.S. America	Prince Madoc	24 Sep 1821
Sarah	24	F				Frances	17 Aug 1820
Sarah	38	F		Ireland	U. States	Nancy	29 Nov 1821
Sarah	58	F	Spinster	Great Britain	U.S. America	Prince Madoc	24 Sep 1821
T. L.	24	M	Merchant	England	Canada	Corinthian	20 Apr 1825
Thomas	38	M	Consul	Scotland	America	Concord	4 Jun 1821
Thos.	33	M	Labourer	Ireland	America	Splendid	23 Mar 1829
William	1	M	Farmer, Labourer or Spinster	Ireland	U. States	Meteor	4 Oct 1827
William	14		Clerk	Ireland	U. States	Xenophon	28 May 1822
William	24	M	Merchant	Antrin	United States	Carolina Ann	11 Jun 1824
William	40	M	Farmer	Scotland	United States	Princess Charlotte	26 Apr 1827
Wm.	8		...	Ireland	United States	Robert Burns	18 Jun 1822
Wm.	32	M	Merchant	England	U. States	Florida	16 May 1827
CRAWLEY, James	21		Farmer	Cork	New York	Schuylkill	22 Aug 1825
Mary	25	F		Great Britain	United States	Meridian	2 Jul 1827
Pat	23	M	Labourer	Great Britain	United States	Meridian	2 Jul 1827
CRAWSHA, Joseph	40	M	Farmer	England	United States	Panthia	7 Feb 1822

NAMES OF PASSENGERS	AGE	SEX	OCCUPATIONS	COUNTRY TO WHICH THEY BELONG	COUNTRY THEY INTEND TO INHABIT	SHIPS/DATES OF ARRIVAL	
CRAWSHAW, James	23	M	Joiner	Great Britain	United States	Freake	25 Aug 1829
Sarah	27	F		Great Britain	United States	Freake	25 Aug 1829
CRAWTHER, Robt.	40	M	Cotton Spinner	Great Britain	New York	Superior	5 Sep 1827
CRAY, —, Mr.	22	M	Merchant	St. Martins	U. States	Matilda	11 Oct 1824
William	20	M	Labourer	Isle of Man	Ohio	Curler	7 Jul 1827
William	31	M	Butcher	Great Britain	United States	Courier	26 Jun 1827
Wm.	21	M	Merchant	Ireland	New York	Carolina Ann	15 Oct 1824
CRAYLING, Radcliff	20	M	Labourer	Isle of Man		Ocean	13 Jul 1827
CRAYTON, David	28	M	Farmer	Scotland	U.S. American	Criterion	7 Jul 1824
CRAZER, Thomas	22	M	Merchant	Ireland	United States	Edwin	27 Oct 1828
CREA, John	24	M	Labourer	Scotland	United States	Mary & Susan	5 Aug 1828
CREAG, Agnes	28	F		Scotland	United States	Orion	15 Jan 1827
Thomas	28	M	Merchant	Scotland	United States	Orion	15 Jan 1827
CREAGH, A.	14	F		Ireland	United States	John & Adam	21 Sep 1822
E.	19	F		Ireland	United States	John & Adam	21 Sep 1822
F.	39	F		Ireland	United States	John & Adam	21 Sep 1822
James	26	M	Carpenter	Ireland	United States	Trio	2 Oct 1828
M.	16	F		Ireland	United States	John & Adam	21 Sep 1822
Wm.	9	M		Ireland	United States	John & Adam	21 Sep 1822
CREAN, Patk.	32 9/12	M	Clerk	Ireland	New York	Atlantic	6 Oct 1828
CREARY, William	34	M	Carpenter	England	America	Franklin	13 Aug 1827
CREASE, John H.	35	M	Merchant	U. States	U. States	Horatio	25 Jun 1828
CREATE, Fredk., Mr.	30	M	Sugar Refnr.	England	U. States	Acasta	3 Apr 1826
CREAUGH, Sebastian	25	M	Merchant	Spain	Mexico	Sarah	23 Sep 1826
CREDEN, Daniel	24	M	Farmer	Ireland	America	William	21 May 1825
CREDRAN, H.	28		Farmer	Ireland	United States	Courier	16 May 1825
CREED, Johnson	22	M				Cassack	25 Jul 1820
Penelope	52	F				Cassack	25 Jul 1820
CREEFOASSE, J.	22	M	Merchant	France	U. States	Waldo	19 Aug 1826
CREELMAN, Mathew	20	M	Weaver	Gt. Britain	U. States	Frances Henrietta	18 Apr 1825
CREER, Charlotte	1	F	Child	..., ..., England	N. York	New Orleans	24 Aug 1827
Eliza	60	F	Spinster	..., ..., England	N. York	New Orleans	24 Aug 1827
Hannah	36	F	Spinster	..., ..., England	N. York	New Orleans	24 Aug 1827
James	4	M	Child	..., ..., England	N. York	New Orleans	24 Aug 1827
Martha	6	F	Child	..., ..., England	N. York	New Orleans	24 Aug 1827
Wm.	8	M	Child	..., ..., England	N. York	New Orleans	24 Aug 1827
CREES, Fredk. Coxe	25	M	Printer	England	Philidelphia	Brighton	16 Nov 1826
CREESE, Harriette	19	F		England	Newyork	Cortes	16 Jul 1827
CREFOT, Louisa C.	28	F	None	France	U. States	Bayard	18 Jul 1823
CREGG, Andrew	14	M	Fer.	Wales	U. States	Franklin	7 Jul 1828
Ann	12	F	Fer.	Wales	U. States	Franklin	7 Jul 1828
Josph.	2	M	Fer.	Wales	U. States	Franklin	7 Jul 1828
Margaret	40	F	Fer.	Wales	U. States	Franklin	7 Jul 1828
Mary	6	F	Fer.	Wales	U. States	Franklin	7 Jul 1828
Robt.	16	M	Fer.	Wales	U. States	Franklin	7 Jul 1828
CREGGY, Catharn	16	F	Spinster	Ireland	U. States	Meteor	19 Jul 1828
CREHRAN, F.	25		Farmer	Ireland	United States	Courier	16 May 1825
CREIG, James	27	M	Weaver	Great Britain	United States	Colossus	5 Jun 1827
Robert	23	M	Spiner	Great Britain	United States	Colossus	5 Jun 1827
CREIGH, Biddy	25	F	Labourer	Ireland	U. States	Marcus	7 Apr 1825
Jas.	28	M	Labourer	Ireland	U. States	Marcus	7 Apr 1825
CREIGHTON, Agnas	4	F	his family [James]	Scotland	U.N. States	Jane	7 Oct 1826
Agnes	30	F		Scotland	U. States	Hind	28 Jan 1822
Ar.	32	M	Dyer	Scotland	U. States	Hind	28 Jan 1822
Cecelia	2	F		Scotland	U. States	Hind	28 Jan 1822
Charles	24	M	Merchant	U. States	England	York	7 Aug 1828
Georgina	2 6/12	F	his family [James]	Scotland	U.N. States	Jane	7 Oct 1826
Isabella	6	F	his family [James]	Scotland	U.N. States	Jane	7 Oct 1826
Isabella	39	F	his family [James]	Scotland	U.N. States	Jane	7 Oct 1826
James	10	M	his family [James]	Scotland	U.N. States	Jane	7 Oct 1826
James	38	M	Merchant	Scotland	U.N. States	Jane	7 Oct 1826
James	51	M	Mechanic	G.B.	G.B.	George Canning	26 Aug 1829
John	35	M	Labourer	U. States	U. States	Robt. Reade	12 Apr 1825
Mary	25	F	Servant	Ireland	United States	Sarah G.	15 May 1828
Ogden	31	M	Army	Great Britain		Birmingham	11 Oct 1828
Peter	1 5/12			Scotland	U. States	Hind	28 Jan 1822
Ruger	1 6/12	M	his family [James]	Scotland	U.N. States	Jane	7 Oct 1826
William	13	M	his family [James]	Scotland	U.N. States	Jane	7 Oct 1826

NAMES OF PASSENGERS	AGE	SEX	OCCUPATIONS	COUNTRY TO WHICH THEY BELONG	COUNTRY THEY INTEND TO INHABIT	SHIPS/DATES OF ARRIVAL	
CRELE, Abraham	19	M	None	...	United States	Wade	29 Aug 1825
CRELIN, Esther	24	M	Shoemaker	England	U. States	Emulous	22 Aug 1828
John	24	M	Farmer	England	U. States	Emulous	22 Aug 1828
Thos.	26	M	Farmer	England	U. States	Emulous	22 Aug 1828
CRELLIN, Cath.	24	F		Ireland	United States	Nimrod	31 Jul 1828
Esther	4	F		Ireland	United States	Nimrod	31 Jul 1828
John	4	M		Ireland	United States	Nimrod	31 Jul 1828
John	26	M	Taylor	Ireland	United States	Nimrod	31 Jul 1828
Thomas	1	M		Ireland	United States	Nimrod	31 Jul 1828
CREMARTY, David	35	M	Farmer	Scotland	United States	Belmont	30 Aug 1828
CREMIN, Danl.	37	M	Carpenter	Ireland	United States	Trio	13 Jun 1827
CRENAN, Margaret	6	F		Ireland	U. States	Wilson	2 Sep 1823
CRENER, Jacob	27	M	Farmer	France	U. States	Edward Bonaffe	23 Jul 1828
CRENNAN, Elizabeth	22	F	Spinster	Ireland	United States	Dublin Packet	23 May 1828
William	30	M	Farmer	Ireland	United States	Dublin Packet	23 May 1828
CRENNER,							
Francis W. Stein	40	M	Merchant	New York	N. York	Charlemagne	20 Aug 1829
CRENNY, Martin	21	M	Labourer	England	U.N. States	Reindeer	20 Aug 1828
CRENSHAW, John	33	M	Gardiner	Great Britain	United States	Aurora	5 Sep 1826
CRESHO, Augustin	24	M	Merchant	Colombia	Tenerrif	Port Captain	6 Dec 1825
CRESLEY, Peter	32	M	U.S. Navy	U. States	U. States	Ardelle	27 Nov 1826
CRESMASS, —	80	F	None	U. States	U. States	Rice Plant	22 May 1827
CRESPIN, Danl.	4	M	Spinster	England	U. States	Electra	7 Jul 1828
Eliz.	6	M	Spinster	England	U. States	Electra	7 Jul 1828
Elizabeth	30	F	Spinster	England	U. States	Electra	7 Jul 1828
Margaret	40	F	Spinster	England	U. States	Electra	7 Jul 1828
Wm.	11	M	Spinster	England	U. States	Electra	7 Jul 1828
CRESPO, Agostine	30	M	Merchant	Spain	Spain	Hesperus	13 Mar 1826
Agostine, Mr.	25	M	Trader	Spain	Spain	Hesper	2 May 1826
CRESSIL, Amelia	9	F	None	Great Britain	U. States	Hannibal	12 Oct 1829
Charles	4	M	None	Great Britain	U. States	Hannibal	12 Oct 1829
Francis	13	M	None	Great Britain	U. States	Hannibal	12 Oct 1829
George	7	M	None	Great Britain	U. States	Hannibal	12 Oct 1829
Mary Ann	16	F	None	Great Britain	U. States	Hannibal	12 Oct 1829
Mary Ann	41	F	None	Great Britain	U. States	Hannibal	12 Oct 1829
Walter	11	M	None	Great Britain	U. States	Hannibal	12 Oct 1829
William	15	M	None	Great Britain	U. States	Hannibal	12 Oct 1829
William	42	M	Carpenter	Great Britain	U. States	Hannibal	12 Oct 1829
CRESSOT, Emily Em	2	F	None	Baltimore	U. States	Bayard	18 Jul 1823
CRESSWELL, Robert	52	M	Farmer	Ireland	New York	Carolina Ann	15 Oct 1824
Robert, Jun.	36	M	Farmer	Ireland	New York	Carolina Ann	15 Oct 1824
CRESWALL, Mary	10			Ireland	New York	Marcella	18 May 1827
Maryan	6			Ireland	New York	Marcella	18 May 1827
Sabina	36			Ireland	New York	Marcella	18 May 1827
CRESWELL, Elizh.	17	F	Spinster	Ireland	United States	Trident	16 May 1826
CREUGH,							
Bartholomew	19 8/12	M	...	Ireland	U. States	Union	3 Jun 1822
John	3 3/12	M	...	Ireland	U. States	Union	3 Jun 1822
Robert	11 11/12	M	...	Ireland	U. States	Union	3 Jun 1822
CREVALIN, —, Mrs.	20	F		France	U. States	Pocahontas	28 Jun 1824
H.	30	M		France	U. States	Pocahontas	28 Jun 1824
CREVICH, Jane	2	F	None	Great Britain	United States	Atlantic	28 May 1827
Jane	33	F	None	Great Britain	United States	Atlantic	28 May 1827
Ricd.	65	F	None	Great Britain	United States	Atlantic	28 May 1827
*dead							
Wm.	32	M	Farmer	Great Britain	United States	Atlantic	28 May 1827
CREW, Mathew	30	M	Weaver	England	United States	Lord Wellington	14 Nov 1827
CREWLAN, Thomas	29	M		Great B.	U. States	William Neilson	26 Jul 1828
CREYLING, Cathe.	12	F	None	Isle of Man		Ocean	13 Jul 1827
Roseanna	24	F	None	Isle of Man		Ocean	13 Jul 1827
Thos.	2/12	M	None	Isle of Man		Ocean	13 Jul 1827
Thos.	26	M	Labourer	Isle of Man		Ocean	13 Jul 1827
Wm.	2	M	None	Isle of Man		Ocean	13 Jul 1827
Wm.	38	M	Taylor	Isle of Man		Ocean	13 Jul 1827
CRIAG, Janet	1	F		Swinetrees, Lochwinnoch [Parish], Renfrew [County]	New York	Hero	19 May 1828

*going with their friends

NAMES OF PASSENGERS	AGE	SEX	OCCUPATIONS	COUNTRY TO WHICH THEY BELONG	COUNTRY THEY INTEND TO INHABIT	SHIPS/DATES OF ARRIVAL
CRIAG (cont'd)						
William	4	M		Swinetrees, Lochwinnoch [Parish], Renfrew [County]	New York	Hero	19 May 1828
*going with their friends						
CRIBENER, Stephen	24	M	Carpenter	New York	United States	Abigail	23 Nov 1820
CRICHTON, James	39	M	Stone Cutter	United States	U. States	Albion	7 Feb 1820
John	51	M	Planter	U. States	U. States	Pacific	11 Sep 1824
Margt.	61	F	None	Great Britain	United States	Kate	2 Oct 1821
CRICK, George	28	F	Merchant	England	U. States	Florida	16 May 1827
Mary Ann	4	F	None	England	U. States	Florida	16 May 1827
CRICO, Antonio	35	M	Merchant	Spain	Spain	Virginia	8 Mar 1828
CRIELEY, John	24	M	Turner	Ireland	Und. Stts of America	Alexander Mansfield	18 Aug 1826
CRIER, James	32	M		Great Britain	United States	Active	25 Mar 1828
Matthias	27	M	... Smith	...	...	Frances Henrietta	30 Jun 1827
CRIETCHFIELD, Onan M.	28	M	Merchant	United States		Edward Quesnel	17 Nov 1828
CRIFFIS, George	22	M	Merchant	England	England	Brittannia	28 Feb 1827
CRIGHTON, Daniel	20	M	Spinster	Great Brittain	United States	Corinthian	9 Jan 1827
Eliza	30	F		Scotland	U.S.	Curler	19 Jul 1828
Esther	27	F	Farmer	England	United States	Essex	23 May 1828
James	28	M	...b...	Scotland	United States	Camillus	27 Oct 1829
Jane	16	F		Scotland	U.S.	Curler	19 Jul 1828
Mary	12	F		Scotland	U.S.	Curler	19 Jul 1828
Robt.	14	M		Scotland	U.S.	Curler	19 Jul 1828
Thos.	50	M	Seaman	England	United States	Essex	23 May 1828
W.	40	M		Scotland	U.S.	Curler	19 Jul 1828
Wm.	28	M	Farmer	England	United States	Essex	23 May 1828
CRINGAN, Thos.	30	M	Merchant	Great Britain	Canada	Pacific	7 May 1827
CRINGE, Rose	17	F	Spinster	Ireland	United States	Dublin Packet	22 Oct 1821
CRIPIN, Catherine	24	F	Milener	England	America	Lygonia	12 Oct 1829
John	25	M	Mason	England	America	Lygonia	12 Oct 1829
CRIPPIN, Elizabeth	17	F		London	New York	Hudson	20 Nov 1828
Elizabeth	35	F	Sempstress	London	New York	Hudson	20 Nov 1828
Henry	10	M		London	New York	Hudson	20 Nov 1828
Mary	8	F		London	New York	Hudson	20 Nov 1828
CRIPPS, George	30	M	Merchant	England	United States	Robert Edwards	3 Oct 1829
Mary	58	F		Great Britain	United States	Spartan	25 Jul 1821
Sophia	22	F		Great Britain	United States	Spartan	25 Jul 1821
Wm.	24	M	Merchant	England	England	John Wells	14 Oct 1823
CRIPT, Yarly	45	F	None	England	United States	Nancy	28 Oct 1822
CRISFIELD, Edward	17	M	Butcher	England	America	Cincinnatus	22 May 1826
Jane	20		None	London	England	Elizabeth	8 Dec 1821
John	1		None	London	England	Elizabeth	8 Dec 1821
John	24		Merchant	London	England	Elizabeth	8 Dec 1821
CRISP, —, Lady					U. States	Montgomery	18 Oct 1828
Alclyde	2	M		Gt. Britain	Philadelphia	Leeds	7 Nov 1828
Charlotte	20			Great Britain	U. States	Columbia	7 May 1828
John, Mr.					U. States	Montgomery	18 Oct 1828
Mary	30	F		Gt. Britain	Philadelphia	Leeds	7 Nov 1828
Perseues Orpheus	3	M		Gt. Britain	Philadelphia	Leeds	7 Nov 1828
Wm.	30		Joiner	Great Britain	U. States	Columbia	7 May 1828
CRISPAN, Richard	28			England	England	Corinthian	8 Oct 1828
CRISPE, Thomas	33	M	Acct.	England	U. States	Douglass	14 Oct 1828
CRISPER, J.	28	M	Merchant	Spain	U. States	Native	15 Apr 1826
CRISPO, Lorenzo	19	M	Merchant	Spain	Spain	Virginia	8 Mar 1828
CRISTANGER, Fredk.	3		Boy	Swtserland	America	Saluda	18 Jun 1825
Joan	13	F		Swtserland	America	Saluda	18 Jun 1825
Mary	11	F		Swtserland	America	Saluda	18 Jun 1825
Rodolph	6		Boy	Swtserland	America	Saluda	18 Jun 1825
CRISTY, Wm. S.	40	M	Mariner	Maryland	Maryland	Cannon	6 Nov 1824
CRITCHER, William	39	M	Baker	Great Britain	United States	George Clinton	27 Aug 1827
CRITCHLEY, Ellen	26	F	None	Great Britain	United States	Magnet	28 Jun 1821
CRITON, Edward	47	M	Labourer	Scotland	United States	Friends	7 Jul 1827
CRITTENDEN, Elizabeth	39	F	None	England	United States	London	21 May 1828
Harriet	3	F	None	England	United States	London	21 May 1828
James	7	M	None	England	United States	London	21 May 1828

NAMES OF PASSENGERS	AGE	SEX	OCCUPATIONS	COUNTRY TO WHICH THEY BELONG	COUNTRY THEY INTEND TO INHABIT	SHIPS/DATES OF ARRIVAL	
CRITTENDEN (cont'd)							
Mary	14	F	None	England	United States	London	21 May 1828
Timothy	17	M		Georgetown, D.C.		Gleaner	6 Dec 1827
William	18	M	Laborer	England	United States	London	21 May 1828
William	38	M	Labourer	England	United States	London	21 May 1828
CRO..., James	...	...	...	...	...	William Thompson	30 Sep 1824
CROAK, R.	25	M		Gt. Britain	U. States	Tantiva	7 Jul 1828
Thos.	30	M		Gt. Britain	U. States	Tantiva	7 Jul 1828
CROCE, Annette M.	21 1/12	F	Confectioner	France	United States	Catharine	10 Sep 1827
Joseph	16 19/12	M	Confectioner	France	United States	Catharine	10 Sep 1827
CROCHRANE, Alexdr.	9		one family [William Reid]	Ireland	Und. Stts of Amer	Alexander Mansfield	18 Aug 1826
James	12		one family [William Reid]	Ireland	Und. Stts of Amer	Alexander Mansfield	18 Aug 1826
CROCKER, B.	47	F		Great Britain	United States	Isaac Hicks	6 Dec 1827
Chas.	23	M	Printer	U. States	U. States	Loire	8 Sep 1820
M.	18	F		Great Britain	United States	Isaac Hicks	6 Dec 1827
Richd.	21	M	Weaver	Ireland	United States	Louisa	18 Apr 1827
S.	12	F		Great Britain	United States	Isaac Hicks	6 Dec 1827
Thos.	27	M	Merchant	Boston	Massachusetts	Alto	8 Jun 1827
CROCKET, Betsey	26		Spinster	Ireland	United States	Robert Burns	18 Jun 1821
David	20		Merchant	New York	United States	Robert Burns	18 Jun 1821
Eliza	56		Widow	Ireland	United States	Robert Burns	18 Jun 1821
Jane	24		Spinster	Ireland	United States	Robert Burns	18 Jun 1821
Mary	28		Spinster	Ireland	United States	Robert Burns	18 Jun 1821
Ths.	16		Farmer	Ireland	United States	Robert Burns	18 Jun 1821
CROCKETT, J. W. S.	18	M	Gentleman	Gt. Britain	U. States	Panthia	13 Nov 1824
CRODDOCK, Jno.	23	M	Grocer	Great Britain	U. States	Dominica	4 Jan 1823
CROES, Sam	32	M	Merchant	U. States	U. States	Georgetown Packet	6 Nov 1822
Saml.	30	M	Merchant	New York	U. States	Ranger	16 May 1822
Thomas	24	M	Farmer	England	United States	Cambria	3 Jul 1829
CROFER, Charles	13	M	Cabinet Maker	Great Britain	United States	Exertion	17 Jul 1829
James H.	56	M	Yeoman	Great Britain	United States	Exertion	17 Jul 1829
Richard	23	M	Cabinet Maker	Great Britain	United States	Exertion	17 Jul 1829
Sarah	54	F	Yeoman	Great Britain	United States	Exertion	17 Jul 1829
CROFERD, David	25	M	Laborer	Ireland	United States	Ann Maria	18 Dec 1827
CROFF, ...	48	M	Button Maker	Great Britain	United States	Superior	31 Mar 1828
CROFFER, Sarah	10	M	Cabinet Maker	Great Britain	United States	Exertion	17 Jul 1829
CROFFET, Benjamin	48	M	Tanner	Great Briton	United States	Brighton	12 Jun 1826
CROFFORD, Andrews	23	M	Farmer	St. Johns, N.B.	New York	Loire	9 Aug 1821
CROFORD, James	19	M	Labourer	Ireland	U. States	Josephine	30 Aug 1828
CROFT, George	66	M	Farmer	England	England	Nancy	16 Jul 1824
James	49	M	Merchant	England	United States	Persia	19 Sep 1823
Thos.	39	M	Farmer	Great Brittan	U. States	Gem	26 Jul 1827
CROFTO, Moses	22	M	Labourer	England	U. States	Ayrshire	12 May 1828
CROFTS, R. A.	27	M	Merchant	U. States	U. States	Leeds	24 Sep 1827
CROGAN, Thomas	27	M	Weaver	Ireland	United States	Carolina Ann	14 May 1827
CROGGAN, Dennis	50	M	Labourer	Great Britain	United States	Samuel Wright	12 Oct 1829
Ellen	22	F		Great Britain	United States	Samuel Wright	12 Oct 1829
Mary	25	F		Great Britain	United States	Samuel Wright	12 Oct 1829
CROGIN, Eliza	12	F		Great Britain	United States	Roanoak	19 Sep 1827
Eliza	28	F		Great Britain	United States	Roanoak	19 Sep 1827
John	55	M	Weaver	Great Britain	United States	Roanoak	19 Sep 1827
John, Jr.	14	M	Weaver	Great Britain	United States	Roanoak	19 Sep 1827
M.	8	F		Great Britain	United States	Roanoak	19 Sep 1827
Nancy	16	F	Spinstress	Great Britain	United States	Roanoak	19 Sep 1827
Wm.	5	M		Great Britain	United States	Roanoak	19 Sep 1827
CROILE, Barney	18	M	Laborer	Gt. Britain		Dalhouse Castle	13 May 1828
CROIPANT, Susanah E.	10	F	Weaver	France	U. States	C. Amelia	30 Jun 1828
CROIPANTE, Cath.	50	F	Farmer	France	U. States	C. Amelia	30 Jun 1828
Jane	50	M	Farmer	France	U. States	C. Amelia	30 Jun 1828
CROKER, John	27	M	Student			Evergreen	28 Jul 1820
CROM...OO., John	24	M	Joiner	Great Britain	United States	Mary Howland	19 Jul 1827
CROMBIE, William	28	M		Dundee	Noagards	Robert	28 Aug 1829
CROMELIN, R.	24	M	Merchant	G. Brittain	U. States	Pacific	23 Jan 1826
CROMMIE, Catherine	45	F	None	Great Britan	U. States	Ann Marria	6 Aug 1823

NAMES OF PASSENGERS	AGE	SEX	OCCUPATIONS	COUNTRY TO WHICH THEY BELONG	COUNTRY THEY INTEND TO INHABIT	SHIPS/DATES OF ARRIVAL	
CROMMIE (cont'd)							
Henery	9	M	None	Great Britan	U. States	Ann Marria	6 Aug 1823
Jane	10	F	None	Great Britan	U. States	Ann Marria	6 Aug 1823
Patrick	18	M	Labourrer	Great Britan	U. States	Ann Marria	6 Aug 1823
CROMMOND, Wm.	40	M	Merchant	England	U. States	Neptunes Barge	1 Oct 1822
CROMONEY, J. S.	30	M	Planter	W. Indies	U. States	Matilda	27 Apr 1822
CROMPT, John	29	M		England	United States	Hannibal	25 Sep 1827
CROMPTON, Ann	23	F		Great Britain	U.S. of America	Gratitude	3 Oct 1829
Jno.	25	M	Farmer	Great Britain	U.S. of America	Gratitude	3 Oct 1829
Richard	24	M	Labourer	England		Britannia	20 Jun 1827
Wm.	22	M	Weaver	England	U. States	Thomas Ritchie	2 Jul 1827
CROMWELL, Arlene	14	F	None	U. States	U. States	Sully	25 Jun 1828
James T.	23	M	Physician	U.S.	U. States	Edward Quesnel	16 Nov 1827
James T.	24	M	Phisician	U. States	U. States	Sully	25 Jun 1828
Jno.	26					Stephania	6 Dec 1827
*an American passage Fal...							
John	30	M	Mason	England	New York	Brighton	14 Oct 1824
CRON, Thos.	35	M	Labourer	...	U. States	St. Michael	21 Jul 1824
CRONAN, Catharine	28	F	Seamstress	Ireland	New York	Concordia	12 Oct 1826
Daniel	50	M	Labourer	Ireland	New York	General Marion	12 Jan 1829
Francis	20	M	Labourer	Ireland	U.S. of America	Meteor	19 Mar 1828
James	20	M	Labourer	G. Britain	U. States	Convivial	10 Nov 1826
Thomas	22	M	Labourer	G. Britain	U. States	Convivial	10 Nov 1826
CRONATCH, Mary	30	F		Halifax	U.S.	Oliver Wolcott	3 Nov 1827
CRONELEY, Sarah	28	F		Ireland	U. States	Nancy	16 Aug 1822
Wm.	30	M	...	Ireland	U. States	Nancy	16 Aug 1822
CRONEN, John	25	M	Farmer	England	United States	Ganges	10 May 1828
CRONIERE, Peter	40	M	Merchant	England	U. States	Mary	18 Jul 1822
CRONIN, John	28	M	Shoemaker	Ireland	United States	Essex	23 May 1828
CRONING, Mary	45	F	Servant	England	U. States	Pacific	5 Sep 1827
CRONLY, Mary	16	F	Spinster	Ireland	United States	Dublin Packet	6 Dec 1827
William		M		Ireland	U. States	St. Michael's	10 Feb 1827
CRONNAN, Elizabeth	28	F	Labourer	England	U. States	Comet	23 Aug 1828
Ellen	5	F	Labourer	England	U. States	Comet	23 Aug 1828
CRONON, Mary	18	F	None	Ireland	United States	Jubilee	13 Jul 1829
CROOK, Harnah	56	F		England	United States	Cosmo	21 Aug 1828
John	14	M		New York	New York	Independence	25 Apr 1828
Martha	22	F		England	United States	Cosmo	21 Aug 1828
Mary	45	F		England	United States	Cosmo	21 Aug 1828
Perpetual	9	M		England	United States	Cosmo	21 Aug 1828
Rosanna	20	F		England	United States	Cosmo	21 Aug 1828
Zaban	17	M		England	United States	Cosmo	21 Aug 1828
CROOKES, Samuel	25 6/12	M	Stationer	Great Britain	Great Britain	Euphrates	3 Apr 1822
CROOKS, Ramsay	33	M	Mercht.	United States	United States	Importer	21 May 1821
CROOKSHANK, Danl.	29	M	Merchant	Denmark		Frederick	25 Jan 1820
Grace			Lady	England	United States	Corinthian	30 May 1828
William	27	M	Merchant	Canada	Great Britain	St. Michaels	12 Apr 1826
CROOP, James	21	M	Joiner	America	United States	Ann	22 Dec 1821
CROP, George	22	M	Joiner	England	United States	Trident	30 Sep 1826
CROPPER, Mary	42	F	None	Wanington	America, New York	Washington	3 Mar 1828
Thomas	48	M	Cooper	Great Britain	America, New York	Washington	3 Mar 1828
Vincent	44	M	Joiner	United States	United States	James Cropper	26 Mar 1822
CROPSAY, Caroline	20	F	Lady	U. States	U. States	Belle	10 Sep 1824
CROSBIE, Ann	20	F	Servant	Ireland	United States	Wilson	27 Jun 1826
Catherine	1	F		York, Great Britain		Casanda	5 Sep 1827
John	23	M	Farmer	York, Great Britain		Casanda	5 Sep 1827
Margaret	30	F		England	United States	Danube	13 Jul 1827
Mary	15	F	Spinster	Ireland	U. States	Josephine	7 May 1827
William	30	M	Joiner	England	United States	Danube	13 Jul 1827
Wineford	19	F	None	York, Great Britain		Casanda	5 Sep 1827
CROSBY, Anw.	28	M	Mariner	Philada.	Philada.	Emma	14 Oct 1825
Asa	36	M	Saddler	New Hampshire	New York	Curlew	3 Nov 1823
Hugh	30	M	Joiner	G. Britain	U. States	St. George	7 Jun 1828
John	29	M	Butcher	Scotland		Zamoa	5 Nov 1828
P. P.	34	M	Silk Weaver	England	Gt. Britain	Electra	4 Sep 1827
Peter	25	M	Mariner	Boston	Boston	Carlo	16 Oct 1825

NAMES OF PASSENGERS	AGE	SEX	OCCUPATIONS	COUNTRY TO WHICH THEY BELONG	COUNTRY THEY INTEND TO INHABIT	SHIPS/DATES OF ARRIVAL	
CROSBY (cont'd)							
Thomas	30	M	Farmer	Ireland	United States	Elizabeth	8 Jun 1827
CROSCH, Antoine	36	M	Farmer	Switzerland	U. States	Alfred	8 Jul 1828
F.	2	F	Farmer	Switzerland	U. States	Alfred	8 Jul 1828
M.	7	F	Farmer	Switzerland	U. States	Alfred	8 Jul 1828
M.	8	F	Farmer	Switzerland	U. States	Alfred	8 Jul 1828
Maria	40	F	Farmer	Switzerland	U. States	Alfred	8 Jul 1828
N.	6	F	Farmer	Switzerland	U. States	Alfred	8 Jul 1828
CROSCHILD, Edward	24	M	Merchant	England	United States	Dalhouse Castle	6 Sep 1827
CROSCO, Nicholas, Don	24	M	Lawyer	Pernania	S. America	Superior	17 Jan 1825
CROSDALE, —, Mrs.	49	F	None	Ireland	United States	John Wells	22 Sep 1824
CROSE, S. B.		M	Ship Master	Lundon	Lundon	Warren	10 Sep 1824
CROSHAN, Alice	32	F	Servant	G.B.	G.B.	George Canning	26 Aug 1829
CROSHING, Joseph	28	M	Farmer	France	America	La Grange	7 Aug 1828
CROSLAND, John	40	M	Farmer	Great Brittan	U. States	John & Elizabeth	11 Dec 1826
CROSLEY, Betty	2	F		Great Britain	United States	Atlantic	28 May 1827
Jane	1	F		Great Britain	United States	Atlantic	28 May 1827
Jno.	27	M	Clothier	Great Britain	United States	Atlantic	28 May 1827
Patrick	15	M	Boy	Ireland	United States	Dublin Packet	3 Sep 1822
Sarah	27	F		Great Britain	United States	Atlantic	28 May 1827
CROSLY, John	22	M	Farmer	Ireland	United States	Fabius	4 Jun 1828
CROSMAN, Antony	28	M	Farmer	Ireland	United States	Lima	19 Jun 1824
CROSNER, Thos.	22	M	Merchant	Switzerland	U. States	La Urania	3 Jul 1828
CROSS, Abraham	4	M	Miner	Great Britain	United States	Unity	20 Oct 1829
Agness	2	F		Great Britain	United States	Robert Fulton	22 Oct 1821
Ann	27	F	Miner	Great Britain	United States	Unity	20 Oct 1829
Anne	22	F	Wife	Dublin, Dublin, Ireland	Philadelphia	New Orleans	24 Aug 1827
Anthony	14	M	Family [of Joseph]	France	America	La Grange	7 Aug 1828
Barbara	8	F	Family [of Joseph]	France	America	La Grange	7 Aug 1828
Barbara	38	F	Wife [of Joseph]	France	America	La Grange	7 Aug 1828
Catharin	18	M	Servant	Ireland	United States	Fabius	4 Jun 1828
Christopher, Mr.	27	M	Baker	England	U. States	Acasta	11 Dec 1826
Daniel	15	M	Farmer	England	New York	Thames	6 Oct 1820
David	38	M	Grocer	Scotland	United States	Samuel Robertson	9 May 1827
Ellen	10	F		Ireland	U. States	Nancy	16 Aug 1822
Frederick	6	M	None	Great Britton	U. States	Factor	27 Mar 1827
George	26	M	Shoemaker	Great Britain	United States	Robert Fulton	22 Oct 1821
George	40	M	Mechanic	England	Pensylvania	William	2 Sep 1822
George, Junr.	12	M		England	Pensylvania	William	2 Sep 1822
Isaac	6	M		Ireland	U. States	Nancy	16 Aug 1822
Isabell	1/12		her Child [Isabella]	Ireland	United States	Rufus King	4 Sep 1823
Isabella	26		To her Brother	Ireland	United States	Rufus King	4 Sep 1823
J. O.	27	M	Merchant	England	America	New York Packet	8 May 1823
James	8	M		Ireland	U. States	Nancy	16 Aug 1822
James	10	M	None	Scotland	United States	Samuel Robertson	9 May 1827
Jas.	39	M	Cabinet Maker	Great Britain	United States	William Dawson	18 Jun 1827
Jno.	21	M	Labourer	Scotland	United States	Morning Star	25 Jun 1822
John	22	M	Farmer	England	U. States	Margarett Scott	22 Aug 1827
John	25	M	Auctionear	Cty. of Longford, Dublin, Ireland	Philadelphia	New Orleans	24 Aug 1827
John	29	M	Watchmaker	England	United States	Nancy	15 Mar 1820
John	30	M		Ireland	U. States	Nancy	16 Aug 1822
John	34	M	Farmer	Great Britton	U. States	Factor	27 Mar 1827
John	63	M	Farmer	England	U. States	Acasta	21 Oct 1825
Jos.	36	M	Officer of the U.S. Navy	U. States	U. States	Chinchille	14 Apr 1825
Joseph	28	M	Miner	Great Britain	United States	Unity	20 Oct 1829
Joseph	42	M	Farmer	France	America	La Grange	7 Aug 1828
Julia	10/12	F		England	United States	Nancy	15 Mar 1820
Lydia	27	F	None	Great Britton	U. States	Factor	27 Mar 1827
Lydia	40	F	None	Great Britton	U. States	Factor	27 Mar 1827
Mary	8	F		England	New York	York	2 Dec 1828
Mary	16	F		Ireland	U. States	Nancy	16 Aug 1822

NAMES OF PASSENGERS	AGE	SEX	OCCUPATIONS	COUNTRY TO WHICH THEY BELONG	COUNTRY THEY INTEND TO INHABIT	SHIPS/DATES OF ARRIVAL	
CROSS (cont'd)							
Mary	29	F		Great Britain	United States	Robert Fulton	22 Oct 1821
Paulina	6	F	Family [of Joseph]	France	America	La Grange	7 Aug 1828
Rachel	20	F	Spintress	England	United States	Nancy	15 Mar 1820
Richard	4	M		Ireland	U. States	Nancy	16 Aug 1822
Robt. W.	36	M	Stinter	Scotland	U. States	Dalhouse	23 Mar 1829
Rosina	4	F	Family [of Joseph]	France	America	La Grange	7 Aug 1828
Ruth	1	F	Miner	Great Britain	United States	Unity	20 Oct 1829
Saml.	48		Servant	United States	New York	Albion	11 Oct 1821
Sarah	28	F		Ireland	U. States	Nancy	16 Aug 1822
Vincent	1	M		Great Britain	United States	Robert Fulton	22 Oct 1821
William	4	M	None	Great Britton	U. States	Factor	27 Mar 1827
William	21	M	Mariner	U. States	U. States	Atlas	24 Jun 1828
Wm.	35	M	Farmer	England	New York	York	2 Dec 1828
CROSSCAN, Ann	45	F	...	Ireland	United States	Carolina Ann	24 Oct 1825
James	40	M	...	Ireland	United States	Carolina Ann	24 Oct 1825
CROSSE, Thos.	25	M	Merchant	England	United States	Brilliant	24 Sep 1827
CROSSEN, James	13 9/12	M		Ireland	U. States	Fabius	22 Sep 1828
John	14 6/12	M		Ireland	U. States	Fabius	22 Sep 1828
CROSSIN, Ellis	26	F	Spinster	N. York	N. York	Wm. Thompson	13 Sep 1823
Patrick	20	M	Laborer	Ireland	United States	Mary	1 Jul 1829
CROSSINGHAM, George	26	M	Baker	Great Briton	New York	Brighton	12 Jun 1826
CROSSLEY, Abbey	18		Servant	Ireland	United States	Courier	15 Oct 1827
David	26		Farmer	Ireland	United States	John Dickinson	28 Jun 1822
E.	24	M	Printer	Great Britain	United States	Isaac Hicks	6 Dec 1827
E. G.	22	F	Spinster	Ireland	U. States	Concordia	11 Jun 1823
Henry	17	M	Farmer	Aahar Honn	...	Gleaner	24 May 1823
James	25	M	Weaver	Ireland	U. States	Josephine	30 Aug 1828
James	26	M				Lady of the Lake	23 Aug 1828
*left ship							
Jas.	28	M	Merchant	Gt. B.	Gt. B.	Caledonia	20 Jan 1829
Thomas	65	M	Weaver	Ireland	U. States	Josephine	30 Aug 1828
Wm.	17	M	Weaver	Ireland	U. States	Concordia	11 Jun 1823
CROSSLY, George	5	M	Farmer	Ireland	United States	Fabius	4 Jun 1828
James	31	M	Weaver	Great Britain	U.S. America	Chili	7 Jul 1827
Nancy	60	F	Spinster	Ireland	United States	Fabius	4 Jun 1828
CROSSON, Ann	17	F		Ireland	America	Carolina Ann	7 Aug 1826
Sarah	30	F		Ireland	America	Carolina Ann	7 Aug 1826
William	4	M		Ireland	America	Carolina Ann	7 Aug 1826
CROSSTLY, Jas.	25	M	Merchant	England	U. States	New York	8 Mar 1825
CROSTHWAITE, Edward	25	M	Merchant	Ireland	United States	Manhattan	24 Oct 1825
Harriet	22	F		Ireland	United States	Manhattan	24 Oct 1825
James P.	27	M	Merchant	Ireland	United States	Manhattan	24 Oct 1825
James P.	30		Merchant	Ireland	Ireland	William Byrnes	25 Aug 1828
James S.	26	M	Merchant	England	United States	Manhattan	11 Oct 1824
Martha	22	M	None	England	United States	Manhattan	11 Oct 1824
Rachael	19	F		Ireland	United States	Manhattan	24 Oct 1825
CROSWAITH, Edwa.	24	F	Spinster	Ireland	Western Country	British Hibernia	13 Mar 1820
James	22	M	Clerk	Ireland	Western Country	British Hibernia	13 Mar 1820
CROSWIEN, Joseph	43	M	Merchant	Great Britain	United States	Cortes	19 Nov 1821
CROTTEY, Patrick	27	M	Farmer	Ireland	America	William	21 May 1825
CROTTY, Jer.	25		Labourer	Ireland	United States	Geo. Canning	5 Jun 1828
CROUCH, Catharine	23	F		Gt. Britain	U. States	Maria	22 May 1822
Frances [with John]	34	F	Farmer	England	Troy, N.Y.	Chelsea	16 May 1828
George [with John]	5	M	Farmer	England	Troy, N.Y.	Chelsea	16 May 1828
James [with John]	14	M	Farmer	England	Troy, N.Y.	Chelsea	16 May 1828
John, and family	35	M	Farmer	England	Troy, N.Y.	Chelsea	16 May 1828
John F.	2 6/12	M		Gt. Britain	U. States	Maria	22 May 1822
Martha [with John]	10	F	Farmer	England	Troy, N.Y.	Chelsea	16 May 1828
Mary	25			England	England	Thames	25 Oct 1821
Mary [with John]	8	F	Farmer	England	Troy, N.Y.	Chelsea	16 May 1828
Sarah [with John]	3	F	Farmer	England	Troy, N.Y.	Chelsea	16 May 1828
Sophia [with John]	1	F	Farmer	England	Troy, N.Y.	Chelsea	16 May 1828
Thomas	8/12	M		Gt. Britain	U. States	Maria	22 May 1822
Thomas	25			England	England	Thames	25 Oct 1821
William	23	M	Farmer	Gt. Britain	U. States	Maria	22 May 1822
William [with John]	12	M	Farmer	England	Troy, N.Y.	Chelsea	16 May 1828

NAMES OF PASSENGERS	AGE	SEX	OCCUPATIONS	COUNTRY TO WHICH THEY BELONG	COUNTRY THEY INTEND TO INHABIT	SHIPS/DATES OF ARRIVAL	
CROULY, Florence	26	M	Weaver	County of Cork, Ireland	New York City	Thorny Close	3 May 1826
Margaret	26	F		County of Cork, Ireland	New York City	Thorny Close	3 May 1826
CROUMILLER, John	30	M	Carpenter	U. States	U. States	Horatio	10 Feb 1827
CROUSE, Frs.	14 5/12	M	Farmer	Switzerland	U. States	France	26 Jun 1828
George	16 5/12	M	Farmer	Switzerland	U. States	France	26 Jun 1828
John	6 7/12	M	Farmer	Switzerland	U. States	France	26 Jun 1828
John	60 9/12	M	Farmer	Switzerland	U. States	France	26 Jun 1828
Joseph	6 7/12	M	Farmer	Switzerland	U. States	France	26 Jun 1828
Madalin	9 4/12	F	Farmer	Switzerland	U. States	France	26 Jun 1828
Madalin	41 6/12	F	Farmer	Switzerland	U. States	France	26 Jun 1828
Margaret	10 5/12	F	Farmer	Switzerland	U. States	France	26 Jun 1828
Mariah	19 4/12	F	Farmer	Switzerland	U. States	France	26 Jun 1828
CROUTHER, John	35 9/12	M	Labourer	Scotland	United States	London	6 Feb 1829
CROW, Charles	22		Labourer	Ireland	Great Britain	Robert Burns	14 Jun 1824
Eliza	31	F		Ireland	U. States	Wanderer	30 Sep 1828
John	7	M		Ireland	U. States	Wanderer	30 Sep 1828
John	30	M	Labourer	Ireland	U. States	Wanderer	1 Sep 1828
Pat	2	M		New York	U. States	Wanderer	30 Sep 1828
Pat	26	M	Labourer	Ireland	U. States	Wanderer	30 Sep 1828
Rachal ...	28	F		New York	New York	Nancy	16 Aug 1822
Wm.	4	M		Ireland	U. States	Wanderer	30 Sep 1828
CROWE, Elen	4			Isle of Man	Rochester	Peru	30 May 1828
Ellen	21					Trio	5 May 1828
Isabelle	6			Isle of Man	Rochester	Peru	30 May 1828
Jane	10			Isle of Man	Rochester	Peru	30 May 1828
Jane	38			Isle of Man	Rochester	Peru	30 May 1828
John	5					Trio	5 May 1828
John	36		Bacon Drier	England	S. New York	Xenophon	25 Jul 1826
Mary	26					Trio	5 May 1828
Mary, Jr.	3					Trio	5 May 1828
Mathias	41		Stone Mason	Isle of Man	Rochester	Peru	30 May 1828
Sarah	8			Isle of Man	Rochester	Peru	30 May 1828
Thos.	20	M	None	G.B.	United States	Corinthian	29 Apr 1826
Wm.	40	M	Labourer	Isle of Man		Ocean	13 Jul 1827
CROWEL, Elisa Ann	21	F		Ireland	United States	Borneo	28 Aug 1828
CROWELL, Henry	40	M	Calico Printer	Ireland	U. States of America	Courier	17 Mar 1827
Joseph	29		Artist	England	England	Thames	25 Oct 1821
Thomas	24	M	Chairmaker	New York	U. States	Dolphin	15 Apr 1822
CROWERT, John Frederick	15	M	...	Switzerland	United States, the State of Ohio	Florian	28 Sep 1824
John William	50	M	...	Switzerland	United States, the State of Ohio	Florian	28 Sep 1824
CROWES, James	22	M	Farmer	Ireland	New York, U.S.	Angelica	18 Aug 1823
CROWFORD, William	25	M	Farmer	G. Britain	U. States	Nancy	12 Aug 1820
CROWLAY, Michal	15	M	boy	Ireland	Pennsylvania	Susquehanna	9 Jan 1824
CROWLEY, Cornelus	26	M	Farmer	Ireland	America	William	21 May 1825
Danl.	23	M	Farmer	England	United States	Ganges	10 May 1828
Margaret	21	F		Ireland	United States	Trio	2 Oct 1828
Nelley	21	F	Spinster	Great Brittan	United States	Hanford	3 Aug 1829
Nelly	52	F		Ireland	United States	Trio	2 Oct 1828
CROWLY, Catherine	19	F		England	America	Silas Richard	24 Oct 1829
CROWN, Anthony	1	M	Boy	Ireland	United States	Trident	17 May 1825
Anthony	30	M	Mason	Ireland	United States	Trident	17 May 1825
Ellenor	30	F	Spinster	Ireland	United States	Trident	17 May 1825
Mary	6	F	Girl	Ireland	United States	Trident	17 May 1825
CROWNAN, Dennis	20	M	Farmer	Ireland	New York	General Marion	12 Jan 1829
CROWNINSHIELD, Jacob	27	M	Gentleman	Uns. States	United States	Helen	5 Sep 1828
CROWRY, —	29	M	Merchant	St. Martins	St. Martins	Matilda	10 Sep 1821
CROWTHER, Elizabeth	7	F	None	Great Britain	United States	Ann Maria	12 Jul 1821
Elizabeth	21	F	None	Ireland	United States	Jubilee	13 Jul 1829
George	20	M	Col... Maker	England	Kentuckey	Debby & Eliza	20 Nov 1820
James	31	M	Merchant	Great Britain	United States	Ann Maria	12 Jul 1821
John	44	M	Col... Maker	England	Kentuckey	Debby & Eliza	20 Nov 1820
Margt.	1	F	None	Great Britain	United States	Ann Maria	12 Jul 1821
Mary	12	F		England	Kentuckey	Debby & Eliza	20 Nov 1820

NAMES OF PASSENGERS	AGE	SEX	OCCUPATIONS	COUNTRY TO WHICH THEY BELONG	COUNTRY THEY INTEND TO INHABIT	SHIPS/DATES OF ARRIVAL	
CROWTHER (cont'd)							
Mary	31	F	None	Great Britain	United States	Ann Maria	12 Jul 1821
Mary Ann	9	F	None	Great Britain	United States	Ann Maria	12 Jul 1821
Sarah E.	4	F	None	Great Britain	United States	Ann Maria	12 Jul 1821
Thos.	22	M	Stone Cutter	England	U. States	Emulous	22 Aug 1828
William	22	M	Servant	Great Britain	United States	Ganges	26 Oct 1826
CROZER, Catharine	24	F	Spinster	Ireland	U. States	Lady Hunter	9 Oct 1825
Elizabeth	24	F	Spinster	Ireland	U. States	Lady Hunter	9 Oct 1825
John	34	M	Labourer	Ireland	U. States	Lady Hunter	9 Oct 1825
CROZET, Adolphi	22		Merchant	France	U. States	Nymph	5 Jul 1820
Alexandrine	35	F		France	United States	Montano	27 Aug 1827
Eliza	8	F		France	United States	Montano	27 Aug 1827
CROZIER, Christ.	25		Farmer	Ireland		Westmoreland	1 Aug 1826
Fhibe	24 1/12		Spinster	Scotland	U.S. of America	Helen	8 Feb 1822
James	22	M	Farmer	Ireland	United States	Trident	30 Sep 1826
Jane	13	F	Spinster	Ireland	U. States	Josephine	7 May 1827
John	26 2/12		Farmer	Scotland	U.S. of America	Helen	8 Feb 1822
William	19	M	Labourer	Ireland	U. States	Josephine	7 May 1827
William	21		Farmer	Ireland		Westmoreland	1 Aug 1826
CROZIOR, Elizabeth	35 2/12	F	Seamstress	G. Britain	United States	Louisa	14 Jun 1825
CRUDON, John	30		Labourer	Ireland	United States	Geo. Canning	5 Jun 1828
CRUGAN, John	24	M	Labourer	Ireland	United States	General Marion	20 Aug 1828
CRUGER, B. P.	48	M	Gentleman	United States	United States	Montano	4 Nov 1823
B. P.	50	M	Merchant	America		Chase	11 Sep 1820
B. P.	50	M		U. States	U. States	Dispatch	7 Dec 1825
B. P.	52	M	Merchant	U. States	U. States	Mattewan	20 Oct 1827
B. V.	48	M	Gentleman	U. States	U. States	Fame	3 Sep 1824
Bertram	45	M	Merchant	United States	United States	Virginia	24 Jul 1821
C.	25	M			U. States	Edward Quesnel	3 Sep 1826
P.	45	M	Planter	W. Indies	U. States	Elias Burger	12 Sep 1822
CRUICKSHANK, Rich.	25	M	Laborer	New Air	New York	James Margaret	17 May 1827
CRUISE, Francis	40	M	Farmer	Germany	United States	Stephania	16 Aug 1827
Patrick	25	M	None	England	New York	Brighton	29 Aug 1828
Robert	2	M	None	England	New York	Brighton	29 Aug 1828
Theresa	23	F	None	England	New York	Brighton	29 Aug 1828
CRUMBY, Wm.	27	M	Mechanic	Great Britain	Great Britain	Hercules	6 Oct 1828
CRUMLEY, John	14	M	Farmer	Ireland	United States	Asia	29 Jul 1829
CRUMMEY, Catherine	48	F	None	Gt. Brittain	United States	Balaena	21 Aug 1824
Edward	20	M	Butcher	Great Britain	United States	Favorite	10 Dec 1822
CRUMNOR, Adam	6	M		Holland	U. States	Edward Bonaffe	23 Jul 1828
Carvile	12	M		Holland	U. States	Edward Bonaffe	23 Jul 1828
Charlot	10	F	Farmer	Holland	U. States	Edward Bonaffe	23 Jul 1828
Jacob	13	M		Holland	U. States	Edward Bonaffe	23 Jul 1828
Jacob	36	M	Farmer	Holland	U. States	Edward Bonaffe	23 Jul 1828
Margaret	35	F		Holland	U. States	Edward Bonaffe	23 Jul 1828
Mary	3/12	F	Farmer	Holland	U. States	Edward Bonaffe	23 Jul 1828
CRUMPTON, Ann	48	F		Great Britain	United States	John Jay	8 May 1828
Nancy	9	F		Great Britain	United States	John Jay	8 May 1828
Robt.	24	M	Mechanic	Great Britain	United States	John Jay	8 May 1828
CRUNDETT, Aaron	21	M	Carpenter	England	Gt. Britain	Electra	4 Sep 1827
Joseph	25	M	Carpenter	England	Gt. Britain	Electra	4 Sep 1827
Stephen	15	M		England	Gt. Britain	Electra	4 Sep 1827
CRUSE, Maria	17	F	Spinster	Great Britain	United States	Wilson	26 Feb 1824
CRUX, James	6/12		his Son			Cambria	19 Oct 1829
Jane	28		his Wife			Cambria	19 Oct 1829
Thomas	2		his Son			Cambria	19 Oct 1829
Thomas	30		Miller	England	United States	Cambria	19 Oct 1829
CRUZ, J.	18	M	Merchant	Spain	U. States	Ranger	2 Jul 1827
Jose M.	8	M	Scholar	Philadelphia	Phila.	Alto	8 Jun 1827
CRYAN, Betty	28	F		Ireland	U.S. of America	Douglass	6 Jul 1829
Catherine	15	F	Spinster	Ireland	America	William	21 May 1825
James	24 6/12	M		Ireland	U.S. of America	Douglass	6 Jul 1829
Michael	40	M	Farmer	Ireland	America	William	21 May 1825
Nancy	36	F	Spinster	Ireland	America	William	21 May 1825
CRYDER, John	28	M	Merchant	Philada.	U. States	Cato	2 Jan 1824
John	32		Merchant	U.S.	Philada.	Little William	14 Jun 1823
CRYSTAL, John	41	M	Labourer	Ireland	America	Weser	26 Jun 1821
CRYSTALL, Bess	6	F		Ireland	New York	Vigilant	6 May 1822
Mary	20	F		Ireland	U.S. of America	Douglass	6 Jul 1829

NAMES OF PASSENGERS	AGE	SEX	OCCUPATIONS	COUNTRY TO WHICH THEY BELONG	COUNTRY THEY INTEND TO INHABIT	SHIPS/DATES OF ARRIVAL	
CRYSTALL (cont'd)							
Michael	3	M	Labourer	Ireland	New York	Vigilant	6 May 1822
Nancy	18 4/12	F		Ireland	U.S. of America	Douglass	6 Jul 1829
Wm.	19	M		Ireland	New York	Vigilant	6 May 1822
CRYTCH, J.	49	M	Physician	Denmark		Fanny	31 Mar 1825
CUBBOUR, John	22	M	Joiner	U. States	U. States	United States	11 Sep 1828
Wm.	24	M	Black Smith	U. States	U. States	United States	11 Sep 1828
CUBERT, Jos.	23	M	Labourer	Great Britain	United States	Atlantic	28 May 1827
CUCHEVAL, James	42	M	Merchant	Sweden	U. States	Pacific	5 Sep 1827
CUDDEN, Henry	30	M	Labourer	Ireland	New York	Orozimbo	2 Oct 1824
Pat	26	M	Farmer	Gt. Britain	United States	Penelope	9 Sep 1828
CUDDY, Patt	21	M	Labourer	Ireland	United States	Concordia	25 Aug 1827
Thos.	20 2/12	M	Clerk	Ireland		Cririe	18 Sep 1820
CUDER, Moses	20	M	Mariner	Philada.	U. States	Iris	8 Jan 1824
CUDIFF, Elizebeth, Miss	18	F	Gentn.	England	U. States	Acasta	3 Apr 1826
CUDLAND, Eliza, & Son	30 4/12	F	Lady	United States	Philadelphia	Gleaner	30 Apr 1821
CUDLIF, Charles	18		Barber	Port...a, E.	England	Packet	27 Aug 1822
CUDMORE, Wm.	19	M	Shoemaker	Wales	U. States	Richard Mead	26 Jun 1821
CUE, David	7	M	Labourer	Argyle (Tedland) Scotland	United States	Jean Hastie	27 Jul 1829
Euphereme	11	F	Labourer	Argyle (Tedland) Scotland	United States	Jean Hastie	27 Jul 1829
Janett	36	F	Labourer	Argyle (Tedland) Scotland	United States	Jean Hastie	27 Jul 1829
Jno.	3	M	Labourer	Argyle (Tedland) Scotland	United States	Jean Hastie	27 Jul 1829
Robert	5	M	Labourer	Argyle (Tedland) Scotland	United States	Jean Hastie	27 Jul 1829
Simpson	22	F	Labourer	Argyle (Tedland) Scotland	United States	Jean Hastie	27 Jul 1829
William	9	M	Labourer	Argyle (Tedland) Scotland	United States	Jean Hastie	27 Jul 1829
Wm.	33	M	Labourer	Argyle (Tedland) Scotland	United States	Jean Hastie	27 Jul 1829
CUET, F.	35	M	Mechanic	France	U. States	Bayard	25 Apr 1828
CUFF, John	25	M	Labourer	Bristol	U. States	Latona	7 Jul 1827
CUGGY, Jeremiah	20	M	Labourer	Ireland	United States	Andes	2 Oct 1828
CUGIGAL, Jose M.	23	M	Mercht.	Spain	U. States	Brown	7 Jul 1826
CUGUY, John	29	M	Farmer	Switzerland	United States	Howard	11 Jun 1824
CUHEL, Jean Batiste	18	M	Farmer	France	U. States	C. Amelia	30 Jun 1828
CUISHING, Edward	21	M	Whealwright	England	United States	Jubilee	4 Mar 1829
CUIT, James	7	M		G. Britain	U. States	George Clinton	10 Sep 1828
Jane	20	F		G. Britain	U. States	George Clinton	10 Sep 1828
CUIT, Thos.	24	M	Baker	G. Britain	U. States	George Clinton	10 Sep 1828
CULBERT, Ml.	30	M	Farmer	Ireland	United States	Trio	13 Jun 1827
CULBERTSON, John	23	M	Farmer	Great Britain	United States	Natchez	17 Aug 1822
Robert	30	M	Farmer	Great Britain	United States	Natchez	17 Aug 1822
CULERANE, William	30	M	Farmer	Ireland	America	William	21 May 1825
CULL, Margaret	30			Great Britan	United States	Newry	11 Jul 1827
CULLAGHAN, Jno.	30	M	Laborer	Ireland	United States	Trio	13 Jun 1827
CULLAM, Ann	20	F	None	Ireland	U.S. of America	Hamilton	18 Jul 1827
Peter	39	M	Stone Cutter	Great Brittan	U. States	John & Elizabeth	11 Dec 1826
CULLAN, Jas.	22	M	Labourer	Great Britain	United States	Penelope	11 Jun 1827
Patrick	40	M	Distiller	Ireland	United States	Spartan	25 Jul 1821
Stephen	30	M	Cabinet Maker	Ireland	New York	Concordia	12 Oct 1826
CULLEN, A.	40	F		England	United States	Dalhouse Castle	8 May 1827
Andrew	28	M		Ireland	U.S. of America	Douglass	6 Jul 1829
Hannah	25	F	None	U. States	U. States	Martha	20 Jun 1825
Jas.	24	M	Farmer	U. States	U. States	Martha	20 Jun 1825
John	22 8/12	M	Labourer	Ireland	United States	Atlantic	21 Jul 1827
John	25	M	Servant	Ireland	United States	Dublin Packet	29 Jun 1825
John	28	M	Shoe Maker	England	U. States	Acasta	21 Oct 1825
John	36	M	Laborer	Ireland	United States	Danube	13 Jul 1827
M.	34	M	Grocer	With intention to become citizen		New York	18 Jul 1828
Patrick	9/12	M	None	U. States	U. States	Martha	20 Jun 1825

NAMES OF PASSENGERS	AGE	SEX	OCCUPATIONS	COUNTRY TO WHICH THEY BELONG	COUNTRY THEY INTEND TO INHABIT	SHIPS/DATES OF ARRIVAL	
CULLEN (cont'd)							
Thomas	25	M	Farmer	Ireland	United States	Dublin Packet	29 Jun 1825
CULLER, Elizabeth	20	F	Taylor	Ireland	U. States	Virginia	20 Jun 1825
John	9	F	None	Gt. Britain	U.S. of America	Friends	25 Sep 1823
Margaret	18	F	None	Gt. Britain	U.S. of America	Friends	25 Sep 1823
Rosira	50	F	None	Gt. Britain	U.S. of America	Friends	25 Sep 1823
CULLEY, Biddy	22	F	Labourer	Ireland	U. States	Marcus	7 Apr 1825
John	40	M	Farmer	England	U. States	Trident	1 Dec 1824
CULLIE, Bernard	34	M	Carpenter	Ireland	United States	Fabius	4 Jun 1828
CULLILLI, Augustus	57	M	Doctor	Matanzas	Cuba	Magnet	18 Aug 1825
CULLIN, Simon	19	M	Merchant	Scotland	U. States	Atlantic	13 Jul 1824
Thos.	40		Labourer	Great Britan	United States	Newry	11 Jul 1827
CULLINANE, James	18	M	Labourer	Ireland	United States	Trio	5 May 1828
CULLING, Allen	30	M	Cooper	New York	U. States	Prize	10 Jun 1824
CULLINS, Adam	30	M	Farmer	England	U.N. States	Jane	7 Oct 1826
CULLIVEN, Peter	22	M	Labourer	Ireland	U. States	Courier	17 Mar 1828
CULLUM, Eliza	3	F	None	England	America	Manhattan	20 Mar 1820
Eliza	28	F	None	England	America	Manhattan	20 Mar 1820
George	1	M	None	England	America	Manhattan	20 Mar 1820
Robert	28	M	Farmer	England	America	Manhattan	20 Mar 1820
CULLY, Nancy	20	F	Labourer	Ireland	U. States	Meteor	19 Jul 1828
CULMAN, Honora	13			Ireland	America	Liverpool	31 Aug 1827
CULMERT, Jas.	27	M	Mason	G. Britain	U. States	Eliza	31 Jul 1828
Sarah	27	F		G. Britain	U. States	Eliza	31 Jul 1828
CULPEPPER, Frs.	7	M		England, Born in Barbadoes	U. States	Cannon	15 Jul 1822

*all the children have come under the care of Mrs. Fenwick for their education

NAMES OF PASSENGERS	AGE	SEX	OCCUPATIONS	COUNTRY TO WHICH THEY BELONG	COUNTRY THEY INTEND TO INHABIT	SHIPS/DATES OF ARRIVAL	
CULVERT, John	27		Merchant	Cumberland	England	Great Britain	7 May 1827
CUMANE, Michl.	19 4/12	M		Ireland	U.S. of America	Douglass	6 Jul 1829
CUMARD, Thos.	20	M	Brazer	England	U. States	Franklin	7 Jul 1828
CUMBLE, Owen	24	M	Labourer	Gt. Britain	U. States	Frances Henrietta	18 Apr 1825
CUMEL, Eliza	18		Farmer	Ireland	U. States	Schuylkill	22 Aug 1825
CUMERSLEY, Mary	21	F	...	Ireland	United States	Wilson	22 Jun 1824
CUMESKEY, Patrick	20	M	Labourer	Gt. Britain	U. States	Frances Henrietta	18 Apr 1825
CUMINGHAM, Helen	32	F		Great Britian	United States	Brok	29 Aug 1823
Robert	30	M	Taylor	Great Britian	United States	Brok	29 Aug 1823
CUMINGTON, Catherine	3	F	Farmer	England	America	Hercules	10 Apr 1823
Margrate	28	F	Farmer	England	America	Hercules	10 Apr 1823
CUMINS, Mary	21	F	Spinster	Ireland	U. States	Josephine	30 Aug 1828
CUMMIN, S.	45	M	Merchant	United States	U. States	Baltic	29 Jul 1829
CUMMING, —	45	F	Spinster	Scotland	United States	Friends	7 Jul 1827
Archd.	18			Scotland	United States	Camillus	3 May 1828
C.	42	M	Merchant	Great Britain		Robert Fulton	9 Jul 1823
Chs.	30	M	Merchant	Great Britian	United States	Robert Quayle	29 Jul 1822
Edward	7	M	None	Scotland	United States	Friends	7 Jul 1827
Fran...	24	F		Great Britian	United States	Robert Quayle	29 Jul 1822
George	22	M	Merchant	Ireland	United States	Dublin Packet	29 Jun 1825
George B.	28	M	Merchant	U. States	U. States	Canada	4 Oct 1824
George Miers	20	F	None	Scotland	United States	Friends	7 Jul 1827
Janet	17		Spinster	Scotland	United States	Camillus	3 May 1828
John	25	M	Labourer	Ireland	United States	Aurelia	7 Jun 1826
John	28	M	Labourer	Ireland	America	Dewitt Clinton	27 Jul 1824
John	45	M	Planter	Ireland	U. States	Elias Burger	12 Sep 1822
Matilda	10			Scotland	United States	Camillus	3 May 1828
Nancy	17	F		Ireland	America	Carolina Ann	7 Apr 1826
Pat	32	M	Labourer	Ireland	United States	Wilson	6 Jun 1828
Rebecca	12			Scotland	United States	Camillus	3 May 1828
Robert	16		Weaver	Scotland	United States	Camillus	3 May 1828
Wm.	45	M	Merchant	Great Britain	United States	Martha	25 Nov 1820
CUMMINGS, Alexander	24	M	Labourer	Scotland	United States	Mary & Susan	5 Aug 1828
Bridget	5/12	F		Ireland	United States	Aurora	9 Jul 1827
Bridget	21	F		Ireland	United States	Aurora	9 Jul 1827
Bryan	30	M	Labourer	Ireland	Unt. St. America	Wilson	21 May 1827
C.	10	M		Scotland	U. States	Superior	25 Sep 1828
Catharine	38	F	Spinster	Philadelphia	U. States	Virginia	3 Dec 1827
Daniel	20	M	Farmer	Great Brittan	U. States	Gem	26 Jul 1827

NAMES OF PASSENGERS	AGE	SEX	OCCUPATIONS	COUNTRY TO WHICH THEY BELONG	COUNTRY THEY INTEND TO INHABIT	SHIPS/DATES OF ARRIVAL	
CUMMINGS (cont'd)							
Daniel	24	M	Farmer	Ireland	United States	William & Henry	19 Jul 1822
H.	6	F		Scotland	U. States	Superior	25 Sep 1828
Henry	28		Seaman			Cincinnatus	16 Apr 1824
*distress'd American to whom passage was given							
James	14	M		Scotland	U. States	Superior	25 Sep 1828
James	21	M	BrickLayer	England	America	Ann	11 Apr 1821
James	27	M	Tailor	Ireland	United States	Aurora	9 Jul 1827
Jas.	35	M	Farmer	Great Brittan	U. States	Gem	26 Jul 1827
Josiah	30	M	Joiner	U. States	U. States	Virginia	8 Mar 1828
Michiel S.	24	M	Woolen Draper	Great Britain		Olive Branch	9 Oct 1829
Patk.	28	M	Laboror	Ireland	United States	Wilson	27 Jun 1826
Robert	25	M	Merchant	Ireland	United States	Indian Chief	16 Aug 1822
S.	4	F		Scotland	U. States	Superior	25 Sep 1828
Sally	18	F	Spinster	Ireland	United States	Dublin Packet	29 Jun 1825
Sarah	25	F	None	Great Brittan	U. States	Gem	26 Jul 1827
Susan	2	F	None	Great Brittan	U. States	Gem	26 Jul 1827
CUMMINS, Bridget	17 5/12	F		Ireland	U.S. of America	Douglass	6 Jul 1829
Catharine	10/12	F		Ireland	U.S. America	Traveller	10 Sep 1827
Ellen	25	F	Servt.	Ireland	U.S. America	Traveller	10 Sep 1827
Francis	28	M	Servt.	Ireland	U.S. America	Traveller	10 Sep 1827
James	38	M	Laborer	Ireland	New York	Munroe	27 May 1825
John	24	...	...	...	...	Pioneer	21 Jun 1825
Mary	1...	F	Spinster	Ireland	Unt. St. America	Wilson	21 May 1827
Mary J., Mrs.		F	Lady	Barbados	unknown	Superb	23 Apr 1823
Nancy	34	F	None	Ireland	New York	Munroe	27 May 1825
Peggy	20	F	Sevnt.	Ireland	United States	Lima	19 Jun 1824
Thomas	35	M	Mercht.	England	U.S.A.	Lima	6 Dec 1826
CUMMISKY, James	20	M		Ireland	United States	William Byrnes	15 Aug 1826
CUMMOCK, John	20	M	Wright	Scotland	U.S.A.	Calliope	15 Aug 1827
CUMPERLAND, Thomas	20		Labourer	England	United States	Hugh Johnson	11 Jun 1828
CUMRIE, Wm.	1	F		G. Britain	U. States	Hanford	18 Sep 1828
CUMSKY, Christopher	25	M	Labourer	U. States	U. States	United States	11 Sep 1828
CUNCANNON, Rick	25	M	Laborer	Ireland	New York	Amanda	23 May 1827
CUNDLE, William	22	M	Tin Man	England	United States	Cambria	16 Aug 1827
CUNDLIFFE, John	31	M	Engineer	England	U.S. America	Columbia	31 Jul 1826
CUNERRA, M.	55	M	Mercht.	United States	U. States	Hiram	4 Sep 1824
CUNIN, Denis	32	M	Farmer	Ireland	America	Farmer	4 Aug 1825
Elenor	20	F	Farmer	Ireland	America	Farmer	4 Aug 1825
CUNINGHAM, A.	28		Farmer	Ireland	United States	Courier	16 May 1825
J.	28		Farmer	Ireland	United States	Courier	16 May 1825
John	17	M	Labourer	Ireland	United States	Trident	16 May 1826
John	40	M	Labourer	Kilmaronock	U.S. America	Camillus	10 Sep 1821
Peter	18	M	Tailor	Ireland	United States	Trident	16 May 1826
R.	25		Farmer	Ireland	United States	Courier	16 May 1825
Robt.	18		Farmer	Ireland	United States	Robert Burns	30 May 1823
Thomas	27	M	Joiner	Scotland	United States	Mary & Susan	5 Aug 1828
CUNNAGAN, Mary	5	F	Child	Ireland	United States	St. Michaels	25 May 1825
CUNNEEN, Frances	32	F	None	Ireland	United States	Roman	12 Jun 1826
John	36	M	Cordwainer	Ireland	United States	Roman	12 Jun 1826
Michael	9	M	None	Ireland	United States	Roman	12 Jun 1826
CUNNEY, James	20	M	Farmer	Ireland	United States	Trident	17 May 1825
CUNNIF, Jeremiah	23		Weaver	Cork	Philadelphia	Schuylkill	22 Aug 1825
CUNNIGAN, Hannah	30	F	Servant	Ireland	United States	St. Michaels	25 May 1825
CUNNIN, Martin	50	M	Labourer	Ireland	United States	Catharine	22 Jul 1825
Mary	5	F	None	Ireland	United States	Catharine	22 Jul 1825
Sarah	26	F	Spinster	Ireland	United States	Catharine	22 Jul 1825
CUNNING, Thomas	30	M	Labourer	Great Britain	United States	Meridian	2 Jul 1827
CUNNINGHAM, Ann	5	F	None	Great Britain	United States	Roman	10 May 1828
Ann	19	F	Spinster	Ireland	United States	Robert Fulton	24 Jul 1826
Ann	24	M	Farmer	Ireland	U. States	Napolean	26 Sep 1828
Bernard	20	M	Shoemaker	Ireland	United States	Romulus	24 Jun 1826
Bernd.	45		Farmer	Great Britan	United States	Newry	11 Jul 1827
Betsey	19	F		Ireland	United States	Trio	2 Oct 1828
Betty	20 6/12	F	None	Ireland	United States	Atlantic	21 Jul 1827
Bidy	16	F	Labourer	Ireland	United States	Hope	12 Jun 1828
Charles	7	M	Her Child [Jane]	Scotland	U.S. of America	Camillus	16 Apr 1822
Charles	24	M	Merchant	Honduras	Honduras	Favourite	25 Mar 1824

NAMES OF PASSENGERS	AGE	SEX	OCCUPATIONS	COUNTRY TO WHICH THEY BELONG	COUNTRY THEY INTEND TO INHABIT	SHIPS/DATES OF ARRIVAL	
CUNNINGHAM (cont'd)							
Charles	29	M	Merchant	U. States	U. States	Boston	26 Sep 1820
Charles	30	M	Labourer	Ireland	United States	Princess Charlotte	26 Apr 1827
Chas.	45	M		Scotland	New York	Joseph Hume	26 Oct 1829
Christopher	22	M	Labourer	Great Britain	United States	Penelope	11 Jun 1827
Condy	30	M	Farmer			Robert Burns	13 Jul 1820
Eliza	19	F		U. States	United States	Wade	29 Aug 1825
Francis	22	M	Laborer	Ireland	United States	Dublin Packet	9 Jul 1827
Grace	75	F		N. York	U. States	Weaver	26 Nov 1822
Henry	34	M	Labourer	Ireland	United States	Lord Wellington	28 May 1827
Horace	26	M	Merchant	United States	United States	Canada	20 Jun 1823
Hy.	18	M	Gentleman	England	U. States	Acasta	21 Jan 1825
J.	22	M		Dublin	U. States	Hibernia	26 Oct 1826
J.	40		Farmer	Ireland	United States	Courier	16 May 1825
J. A.	25	M	M.D.	America	America	Britannia	5 Nov 1828
J. A.	39	M	Merchant	U.S. America	U.S. America	Canada	30 Jan 1829
J. C.	26	M	Mariner	United States	United States	Frances	19 Feb 1829
James	21	M	Mercht.			Ocean	17 Aug 1820
James	21	M	Laborer	Gt. Britain	U.S. of America	Friends	25 Sep 1823
James	23	M	Servant	Island Jamaca	Island Jamaca	Agenora	19 Jun 1826
James	25	M	Merchant	United States	U.S.	William Byrnes	11 Dec 1827
James	26	M	Farmer	Ireland	U. States	Napolean	26 Sep 1828
James	27	M	...			Catherine	19 Aug 1825
James	28	M	Baker	Dublin	New York	New York	31 Jul 1829
James	30	M	Farmer	England		Exchange	11 Jul 1823
Jane	18	F	Seamstress	Great Britain	United States	Grecian	24 Sep 1828
Jane	33	F	to Her Husband	Scotland	U.S. of America	Camillus	16 Apr 1822
Jas.	25	M	Labourer	Ireland	U. States	Albion	11 May 1827
Jas.	33	M	Merchant	Boston	Boston	Carib	11 Apr 1825
Jno.	16	M	None	U. States	New York	Missouri	10 Apr 1821
John	6/12	M		Ireland	United States	Romulus	24 Jun 1826
John	12	M	Her Child [Jane]	Scotland	U.S. of America	Camillus	16 Apr 1822
John	20	M	Farmer	Ireland	United States	Dublin Packet	23 May 1828
John	20	M	Mechanic	Great Britain	United States	Grecian	24 Sep 1828
John	21	M		Irereland	America	Carolina Ann	20 Jun 1825
John	22	M	Cooper	Ireland	U. States	Lady Hunter	14 Mar 1826
John	26	M	Merchant	Ireland	United States	Magnet	22 Aug 1822
John	28	M	Labourer	Ireland	United States	Robert Fulton	10 Aug 1827
John	32 2/12	M	Merchant	U. States	U. States	Nestor	15 Dec 1828
Joseph	29	M	Merchant	Ireland	U. States	Erin	5 Jul 1820
Joseph	54	M	Artist	England	U. States	Acasta	21 Jan 1825
Luke	22	M	Weaver	England	United States	Ganges	10 May 1828
Magnus	28	M	Labourer	Scotland	United States	Orion	15 Jan 1827
Margaret	19	F		Ireland	United States	Romulus	24 Jun 1826
Margaret	23	F	Labourer	England	U. States	Comet	23 Aug 1828
Margaret	24	F	Labourer	England	U. States	Comet	23 Aug 1828
Margaret	34	F	None	Ireland	United States	Lord Wellington	28 May 1827
Margt.	9	F	Her Child [Jane]	Scotland	U.S. of America	Camillus	16 Apr 1822
Margt.	20	F	...	Ireland	U. States	William	27 Jul 1824
Mary	19	F	Spinster	Ireland	United States	Wilson	6 Jun 1828
Mary	20	F	Spinster	United States	United States	Hannah Eliza	23 Sep 1826
Mary	22 4/12	F	Seamstress	Ireland	United States	Atlantic	21 Jul 1827
Mary	28	F	Spinster	Ireland	United States	Trident	17 May 1825
Maurice	21	M	Carpenter	Ireland	United States	Trio	2 Oct 1828
Mcaty	23	M	Spinster	Ireland		Robert Fulton	4 Jun 1828
Miles	20	M	Labourer	Ireland	United States	Maria	19 Oct 1829
Patk.	20	M	Farmer	Ireland	America	Mary	29 May 1827
Patrick	16	M	Youth	Ireland	United States	Romulus	24 Jun 1826
Patrick	19	M	Labourer	Ireland	United States	Maria	19 Oct 1829
Patrick	26	M	Farmer	Ireland	United States	Abigail	25 Jun 1822
Rhoda	7	F	Child	Ireland	United States	St. Michaels	25 May 1825
Richd.	23	M	Merchant	United States	United States	New York	12 Nov 1822
Rose	18	F	None	Ireland	America	Braganza	8 Aug 1825
Rose	20	F		Ireland	United States	Aurora	9 Jul 1827
Saml. W.	38	M	Traveller	England	West Indies	Conestoga	23 Nov 1825
Samuel	24	M	Farmer	Ireland	U. States	William & John	10 Jul 1824
Sarah	50 6/12	F		Ireland	U.S. of America	Douglass	6 Jul 1829
Thomas	19	M	Labourer	Ireland	United States	Sarah Ann	11 Jan 1827

NAMES OF PASSENGERS	AGE	SEX	OCCUPATIONS	COUNTRY TO WHICH THEY BELONG	COUNTRY THEY INTEND TO INHABIT	SHIPS/DATES OF ARRIVAL	
CUNNINGHAM (cont'd)							
Thomas	28	M	Labourer	Ireland	St. John, N.B.	Ann Maria	7 Aug 1826
Thomas	30	M	Labourer	England	...	Braganza	8 Aug 1825
Thos.	30	M	Farmer	Ireland	U.S. America	Traveller	10 Sep 1827
Wm.	18	M	Cook	Ireland	United States	Hannah Eliza	23 Sep 1826
CUNNION, James	20	M	Taylor	Ireland	U. States	Virginia	20 Jun 1825
CUNTEE, David C.	30	M	Merchant	U. States	U.S. America	York	4 Aug 1826
CUPED, John	27	M	Mason	St. Croix	St. Croix	Chase	22 May 1827
CUPPS, Wm.	22	M	Merchant	England	America	Governor Griswold	6 Jun 1821
CURBITT, John	30	M	Labourer	England		Marchioness	13 May 1828
CURBRAIN, R.	50	M	Merchant	U. States	U. States	Purrington	14 May 1827
CUREY, Thomas	28	M	Labourer	G. Britain	United States	Louisa	14 Jun 1825
CURHBERTSON,							
Wm. Davd.	27	M	Merchant	England	New York	Robert Edwards	17 Mar 1828
CURLES, Anne Jane	1 6/12	F	None	England	United States	London	21 May 1828
Arabella	5	F	None	England	United States	London	21 May 1828
Charlotte	37	F	None	England	America	London	21 May 1828
Charlotte, Jr.	18	F	None	England	America	London	21 May 1828
Harriet	8	F	None	England	United States	London	21 May 1828
Letitia	3	F	None	England	United States	London	21 May 1828
William	38	M	Labourer	England	America	London	21 May 1828
CURLETT, Ann	1	F		Great Britain	United States	Meridian	2 Jul 1827
Ann	3	F		Isle of Man	Ohio	Curler	7 Jul 1827
Eliza	24	F		Isle of Man	Ohio	Curler	7 Jul 1827
Jane	5	F		Great Britain	United States	Meridian	2 Jul 1827
Jane	20	F		Great Britain	United States	Meridian	2 Jul 1827
Jane	24	F		England	United States	Nimrod	31 Jul 1828
Jane	28	F		England	United States	Nimrod	31 Jul 1828
Jas.	11	M		Great Britain	United States	Meridian	2 Jul 1827
Jno.	6	M		Great Britain	United States	Meridian	2 Jul 1827
Jno.	40	M	Farmer	Great Britain	United States	Meridian	2 Jul 1827
John	1	M		Isle of Man	Ohio	Curler	7 Jul 1827
John	19	M	Labourer	Isle of Man	Ohio	Curler	7 Jul 1827
John	20	M		Great Britain	United States	Meridian	2 Jul 1827
Leta.	36	F		Great Britain	United States	Meridian	2 Jul 1827
Robt.	3	M		Great Britain	United States	Meridian	2 Jul 1827
Thomas	3	M		England	United States	Nimrod	31 Jul 1828
Thomas	5	M		Isle of Man	Ohio	Curler	7 Jul 1827
Thomas	28	M	Farmer	Isle of Man	Ohio	Curler	7 Jul 1827
Thos.	13	M		Great Britain	United States	Meridian	2 Jul 1827
Wm.	8	M		England	United States	Nimrod	31 Jul 1828
Wm.	25	M	Labourer	England	United States	Nimrod	31 Jul 1828
Wm.	30	M	Labourer	England	United States	Nimrod	31 Jul 1828
CURLEY, Cornelius	1	M	Child	Ireland	Ireland	Sarah G.	28 Nov 1827
Eliza	50	F		Ireland	United States	Princess Charlotte	26 Apr 1827
Ellen	25	F	Servant	Ireland	Ireland	Sarah G.	28 Nov 1827
Ennis	16	M	Labourer	Gt. Britain	U. States	Sarah G.	14 Apr 1828
James	24	M	Labourer	Ireland	United States	Fabius	31 Jul 1829
CURLFORD, Edward	25	M	Labourer	Gt. Britain	U. States	Sarah G.	14 Apr 1828
CURLOW, —, Mrs.	50	F			U. States	Cygnet	22 Jun 1821
Marg.	12	F			U. States	Cygnet	22 Jun 1821
Rob.	10	M			U. States	Cygnet	22 Jun 1821
Thos.	52	M	Mechanic	Scotland	U. States	Cygnet	22 Jun 1821
CURLY, Cathr.	23	F		G. Britain	U. States	St. George	7 Jun 1828
James	21	M	Labourer	G. Britain	U. States	St. George	7 Jun 1828
James	22	M	Labourer	Ireland	United States	Hope	12 Jun 1828
CURMAN, Augustua T.	24	M	Gentleman	New York	U. States	Bayard	7 Mar 1825
CURMNEY, John	28	M	Butcher	Great Britain	New York	Hesperus	13 Oct 1825
CURNIER, Mary	20	F	Labourer	Ireland	United States	Essex	23 May 1828
CURR, John	10	M		G. Britain	U. States	Dalhouse Castle	12 Sep 1828
CURRAN, Edward	20		Servant			Amphion	31 May 1824
James	14		Farmer			Amphion	31 May 1824
Margt.	26	F		Ireland	United States	William Byrnes	6 Apr 1826
Mary	2	F		Ireland	United States	William Byrnes	6 Apr 1826
Mary	16	F	Spinster	Ireland	America	Josephine	8 Dec 1827
Mary	20	F	None	Ireland	United States	Jubilee	12 May 1828
Mary	21	F		Ireland	America	Alexander	28 Jul 1821

NAMES OF PASSENGERS	AGE	SEX	OCCUPATIONS	COUNTRY TO WHICH THEY BELONG	COUNTRY THEY INTEND TO INHABIT	SHIPS/DATES OF ARRIVAL	
CURRANT, Anne	1 2/12	F	Child	Ireland	Pensilva	Louisa	18 Apr 1827
Anne	22	F	Wife	Ireland	Pensilva	Louisa	18 Apr 1827
Thos.	24	M	Weaver	Ireland	Pensilva	Louisa	18 Apr 1827
CURREN, Elizabeth	20	F		Ireland	U. States	Hope & Esther	12 May 1826
Jane	22	F	Spinster	Ireland	America	Superior	12 Jun 1824
Thomas	25	M		Ireland	America	Superior	12 Jun 1824
Thomas	25	M	Labourer	Ireland	U. States	Hope & Esther	12 May 1826
CURRER, Francus	23	M	Weaver	France		Pallas	14 Jun 1828
Georg	1	M		France		Pallas	14 Jun 1828
George	22	M	Labourer	France		Pallas	14 Jun 1828
Perree	17	M		France		Pallas	14 Jun 1828
CURRIE, Cath.	60	F		G. Britain	U. States	Camillus	8 Sep 1828
Frs.	19	M	Musician	Gent.	U. States	Lewis	20 Feb 1824
George	22	M	Labourer	Kilmarnock	U.S. America	Camillus	10 Sep 1821
Jas.	18	M	Laborer			Commerce	22 Jun 1825
Lucy	17	F	Spinster			Commerce	22 Jun 1825
Mary	22	F	Spinster			Commerce	22 Jun 1825
Mary	58	F	Spinster			Commerce	22 Jun 1825
Philip	20	M	Farmer	Ireland	U. States	Camillus	27 Jul 1825
Rolf	24	M	Laborer			Commerce	22 Jun 1825
Wm.	58	M	Seaman	G. Britain	U. States	Camillus	8 Sep 1828
CURRIN, Jos., Dr.	38		Physician	Ireland	United States	John Dickinson	28 Jun 1822
Judith	17	F	Spinster	Ireland	United States	Wilson	4 Oct 1827
CURRY, Archibald	...	M	None	Great Brittan	Great Brittan	Tuscarora	26 Jan 1827
David	3	M		France		Pallas	14 Jun 1828
David	9	M	Son	Ireland	United States	Cambria	8 Oct 1828
David	29	M	Merchant	United States	United States	Orion	1 Feb 1820
David	37	M	Boot Maker	Ireland	United States	Cambria	8 Oct 1828
Geo.	27	M	Farmer	Ireland	America	Mary	29 May 1827
John	7	M	Son	Ireland	United States	Cambria	8 Oct 1828
John	38	M	Weaver	Ireland	Und. Stts of Amer	Alexander Mansfield	18 Aug 1826
Joseph	21		Labourer	Ireland	Great Britain	Robert Burns	14 Jun 1824
Mary	18	F	Black Smith	Ireland	U. States	Virginia	20 Jun 1825
Mary	26	F	Spinster	Ireland	America	Mary	29 May 1827
Mungo	33	M	Merchant	Scotland	U. States	Hector	18 Apr 1825
Sarah	37	F	Wife	Ireland	United States	Cambria	8 Oct 1828
Surac	4	M	Labourer	France		Pallas	14 Jun 1828
William R.	30	M	Merchant	Pensilvania	Philadelphia	John London	8 Dec 1823
CURSON, Saml.	45	M	Merchant	U. States	U. States	Sea Nymph	7 Jul 1827
CURTAIN, Betty	31	F		Ireland	United States	Trio	2 Oct 1828
Bridget	20			Dilmore	Gt. Britain	Enterprize	19 Feb 1822
Honora	11	F		Ireland	United States	Trio	2 Oct 1828
Joanna	9	F		Ireland	United States	Trio	2 Oct 1828
Mary	6	F		Ireland	United States	Trio	2 Oct 1828
Pat	22	M	Labourer	Ireland	United States	Trio	2 Oct 1828
CURTEMUS, Fredk. W.	19	M	Merchant	New York	New York	Canton	13 Dec 1824
CURTENS, Jas.	27	M	Mariner	Baltimore	U. States	Swift	31 Mar 1825
CURTHBERT, James	27	M	Weaver	Scotland	United States	Nimrod	1 Jun 1821
CURTION, Anthaid	23	M	Cutler	France	U.S. America	Gibraltar	12 Oct 1829
CURTIS, Abraham M.	35	M	Ship master	United States	United States	Rising States	8 Aug 1825
Ambrose S.	27	M	Merchant	United States	United States	William Thompson	16 Jan 1826
Ann	40		Farmer	Ireland	United States	Carolina Ann	12 Sep 1823
Benjn.	35	M	Merchant	U. States	U. States	Sully	24 Oct 1828
Benjn., Mr.	34	M	Mercht.	New York	N. York	Cadmus	16 Aug 1826
Betsey	16	F	Daghter	New York	United States	St. Michaels	18 Jul 1826
Betsey	50	F	Lady	New York	United States	St. Michaels	18 Jul 1826
Chas.	21	M	Merchant	U. States	U. States	Escort	30 Jun 1828
Chs.	24	M	Gentleman	U. States	U. States	Isabella	18 Apr 1825
D. B.	40	M	Mechanic	Rhode Island	U. States	Columbia	24 Mar 1823
Ellen	14	F	Child	New York	United States	St. Michaels	18 Jul 1826
Franklin	6	M	Child	New York	United States	St. Michaels	18 Jul 1826
Hannah	35	F	Servant	U.S.	U.S.	Emma	24 Jun 1825
Jacob	50	M	Mariner	U. States	U. States	Exchange	29 Apr 1822
James F.	26	M	Navy	Boston	Boston	Trimmer	12 Apr 1824
John	1		Farmer	Ireland	United States	Carolina Ann	12 Sep 1823
Joseph	18	M	Sailor	New York	United States	St. Michaels	18 Jul 1826
Martha	22			England	U. States	Corinthian	8 Oct 1828

NAMES OF PASSENGERS	AGE	SEX	OCCUPATIONS	COUNTRY TO WHICH THEY BELONG	COUNTRY THEY INTEND TO INHABIT	SHIPS/DATES OF ARRIVAL	
CURTIS (cont'd)							
Mary	10	F	Child	New York	United States	St. Michaels	18 Jul 1826
Mary	30	F		Ireland	United States	Concordia	25 Aug 1827
Samuel	40	M	Mariner	N. York	U. States	Dart	24 Oct 1825
T.	19	M	Servant	U. States	U. States	Cobbosse Conte	18 Apr 1823
Thomas	9	M		Ireland	United States	Concordia	25 Aug 1827
CURTZ, Mary	25	F	Labourer	Ireland	United States	Essex	23 May 1828
Robt.	8	M	Labourer	Ireland	United States	Essex	23 May 1828
CURWEN, Joseph	47	M	Merchant	U.S.	U.S.	George Canning	20 Jan 1829
CUSACK, Edward	50	M	Merchant	England	England	Pacific	17 Jun 1828
Nicholas	21	M	Laboror	Ireland	United States	Wilson	27 Jun 1826
CUSCHEROPP,							
Christian	23	M	Tailor	Prusia	U. States	Franklin	3 Jul 1820
CUSHAR, Patrick	25	M	Labourer	Ireland	United States	Carolina Ann	14 May 1827
CUSHMAN, Arch.	29	M		Mallon	U. States	Manhattan	21 May 1821
Bat	27	M	Labourer	Ireland	Ireland	Sarah G.	28 Nov 1827
Mary	25	F	Servant	Ireland	Ireland	Sarah G.	28 Nov 1827
CUSHNER, Thomas	18	M	Accountant	Mayo	America	Margaret	31 Jul 1824
CUSIE, Bridget	1	F		Ireland	U. States	Josephine	27 Jul 1825
Bridget	25	F		Ireland	U. States	Josephine	27 Jul 1825
Thomas	25	M	Weaver	Ireland	U. States	Josephine	27 Jul 1825
CUSSASA, Jose	17	M	Merchant	Havana	U. States	Emblem	14 May 1827
CUSSING, Patrick	30		Labourer	Ireland	United States	Geo. Canning	5 Jun 1828
CUSTIS, Deborah	13	F	Servant	Denmark	U. States	Catherine	3 Jul 1820
CUSTLE, Bryan	36	M	Labourer	Ireland	United States	Wilson	6 Jun 1828
CUSUCH, J.	28	M	Labourer	Ireland	United States	Combine	4 Jun 1825
CUSUELE, —, Mr.	28	M	Printer	U. States	U. States	Cadmus	12 Apr 1825
CUTH, John	30	M	Gentleman	England	England	Jubilee	1 Dec 1827
CUTHAL, Ann	30	F	Spinster			Servant	30 Aug 1820
CUTHBERT,							
Barbra, Mrs.	27 3/12	F		Scotland	United States	Mobile	21 Aug 1827
James	7 2/12	M		Scotland	United States	Mobile	21 Aug 1827
James	22		None	Philadelphia	England	Elizabeth	8 Dec 1821
James	39		Servant	England		Hudson	5 Apr 1826
Jane	18		None	Bath	England	Elizabeth	8 Dec 1821
Janet Fife	1/12	F		Scotland	United States	Mobile	21 Aug 1827
John	34 10/12	M	...	Scotland	United States	Mobile	21 Aug 1827
Mary	22	F		Scotland	United States	Nimrod	1 Jun 1821
Ross	50	M				Acasta	14 Jun 1824
William	24	M	Shoemaker	Ireland	United States	Catharine	22 Jul 1825
CUTHWAIT, A. W.	32	M	Mariner	U. States	U. States	Mary Palmer	28 Aug 1821
CUTLER, Alice	26	F	None	England	United States	Dalhouse Castle	6 Sep 1827
Ann	3	F	None	England	United States	Dalhouse Castle	6 Sep 1827
C...y	24			Bl...	England	Great Britain	7 May 1827
Elizh.	3			Bl...	England	Great Britain	7 May 1827
Jane	4	F	None	England	United States	Dalhouse Castle	6 Sep 1827
Jane	29			Bl...	England	Great Britain	7 May 1827
Jno.	1	M	None	England	United States	Dalhouse Castle	6 Sep 1827
John	1/2			Bl...	England	Great Britain	7 May 1827
John	50		Farmer	Bl...	England	Great Britain	7 May 1827
Nancy	5			Bl...	England	Great Britain	7 May 1827
Thos.	6	M	None	England	United States	Dalhouse Castle	6 Sep 1827
CUTTEER, A.	35	M	Mechanic	U. States	U. States	Mary	19 May 1823
CUTTEN, Elizabeth	21	F	Spinster	England	United States	Trident	31 Mar 1827
CUTTER, James	17	M	Tailor	N. York	N. York	Albion	17 Jan 1825
CUTTING, —	36	M	Gentleman	America	U. States	Leo	30 Apr 1825
Alfred	3	M		England	United States	Acasta	12 Dec 1823
Amelia	18	F		England	United States	Acasta	12 Dec 1823
Anna Maria	40	F		England	United States	Acasta	12 Dec 1823
Augusta	12	F		England	United States	Acasta	12 Dec 1823
Charles	11	M		England	United States	Acasta	12 Dec 1823
Elizabeth	17	F		England	United States	Acasta	12 Dec 1823
Ema	5	F		England	United States	Acasta	12 Dec 1823
F. B., Mr.	22	M	Atty.	United States	United States	Manchester	15 Aug 1826
Fulton	14	M		U.S.	U.S.	Francois I	8 Aug 1829
Henry	14	M	Farmer	France	France	Augusta	8 Dec 1821
*Deceased 27 Sep 1821							
Henry	20	M		England	United States	Acasta	12 Dec 1823
John	26	M	Merchant	England	United States	Acasta	14 Jun 1824

NAMES OF PASSENGERS	AGE	SEX	OCCUPATIONS	COUNTRY TO WHICH THEY BELONG	COUNTRY THEY INTEND TO INHABIT	SHIPS/DATES OF ARRIVAL	
CUTTING (cont'd)							
Louisa	13	F		England	United States	Acasta	12 Dec 1823
Robt.	16	M		U.S.	U.S.	Francois I	8 Aug 1829
Sarah	25		Ladies and Gentlemen	England	United States	Corinthian	7 Jul 1829
CUVELLIN, Austin	45	M	Merchant	Gt. Britain	Canada	Caledonia	10 Sep 1828
CUYSHLY, Cathrine	8			County of Carvan	Boston	Peru	30 May 1828
James	30		Croper	County of Carvan	N. York	Peru	30 May 1828
Margret	30			County of Carvan	Boston	Peru	30 May 1828
Rdmond	2/12			County of Carvan	Boston	Peru	30 May 1828
CUZACK, John	32	M	Labourer	Ireland	United States	Combine	4 Jun 1825
CYNE, Phillip	13		Clerk	England	Upper Canada	Xenophon	25 Jul 1826
D..., Abraham	30	M	Merchant	United States	United States	Pacific	7 May 1827
Ann	...	...	...	...	...	St. Michael	22 Sep 1824
Bettey Ann	22	F		Dunnmore	Ireland	Carolina Ann	11 Jun 1824
George	55	M	Mariner	U. States	U. States	Boston	28 Aug 1821
James	20		Farmer			Amphion	31 May 1824
Jan...	...	...	...	...	...	St. Michael	22 Sep 1824
John	...	...	...	...	...	William Thompson	30 Sep 1824
John	12	M	Gentleman	Ireland	United States	Dublin Packet	9 Jul 1827
Patrick	19		...			Amphion	31 May 1824
Thomas	...	...	...	...	...	St. Michael	22 Sep 1824
Thos.	21	M		Great Britain	Baltimore	Philetus	21 Jul 1827
William	34	M	Farmer	Antrim	Ireland	Carolina Ann	11 Jun 1824
D...A...ALLY, Andrew	23	M	Labourer	Ireland	United States	Carolina Ann	14 May 1827
D...A...H..., William	22	M	Carpenter	Ireland	United States	Carolina Ann	14 May 1827
D...ONE, Elizabeth	42 3/12	F	Lady	Philadelphia	Philadelphia	Quito	9 Jul 1823
D...P..., Elizabeth	29	F	...	Scotland	America	Nimrod	9 Jul 1827
John	30	M	...	Scotland	America	Nimrod	9 Jul 1827
D...TY, ...	4	M				Robert Burns	13 Jul 1820
...	6	F				Robert Burns	13 Jul 1820
...	24	M	Carpenter			Robert Burns	13 Jul 1820
...	24	M	Labourer			Robert Burns	13 Jul 1820
...	24	F	Spinster			Robert Burns	13 Jul 1820
D...VOY, Charles	35	M	Fisherman	Ireland		William Tell	24 Oct 1829
D. COSTER, W. S.	10	M		St. Croix	U. States	Carlo	6 Oct 1827
D'ARANGE, M., Miss	17	F		Madeira	Madeira	Industrioza	12 Nov 1827
R.	29	M	Merchant	Madeira	Madeira	Industrioza	12 Nov 1827
D'ARMAN, Alexander	15					Henrietta	26 Nov 1825
Alexander	52		Farmer	Nova Scotia	G. Britain	Henrietta	26 Nov 1825
Charles	8					Henrietta	26 Nov 1825
David	10					Henrietta	26 Nov 1825
Elizabeth	19					Henrietta	26 Nov 1825
Jane	17					Henrietta	26 Nov 1825
Mary	51					Henrietta	26 Nov 1825
Robert	12					Henrietta	26 Nov 1825
Susan	14					Henrietta	26 Nov 1825
Thomas	22					Henrietta	26 Nov 1825
D'AVELLAR, J. S.	12	M	Gentleman	Portugal		New Packet	29 Aug 1822
D'ISLER, Augustin	26	M	Merchant	France	New York	Lewis	16 Mar 1826
D'OTRANTE,							
Armand, Count			None	France	U.S.	Sully	26 Oct 1829
Athanase			None	France	U.S.	Sully	26 Oct 1829
D'SILVIA, Jos.	30	M	Merchant	Portugal	Portugal	Quill	31 Oct 1825
D'WOLF, —	6/12	M		U. States	U. States	Alabama	21 May 1823
—, Mrs.	20	F		U. States	U. States	Alabama	21 May 1823
C.	20	M	Merchant	U. States	U. States	Leontine	19 May 1825
Geo., Mr.	19	M	Student	United States	Rhode Island	Stephania	28 Jul 1823
M. A.	22	M	Gentleman	U. States	U. States	Alabama	21 May 1823
D'WOLFE, Charles H.	21	M	Gentleman	U. States	U. States	Perseverance	26 May 1827
DA..., Mary	22	F	Servant	Ireland	United States	Carolina Ann	14 May 1827
DA...E, ...	31	M			U. States	Edward Quesnel	3 Sep 1826
M.	20	M	Farmer	Ireland	Canada	Pilgrim	1 Sep 1828

NAMES OF PASSENGERS	AGE	SEX	OCCUPATIONS	COUNTRY TO WHICH THEY BELONG	COUNTRY THEY INTEND TO INHABIT	SHIPS/DATES OF ARRIVAL	
DABNEY, John S.	22	M				Patty & Sally	30 Aug 1820
DABUHOFF, —, Mr.	25	M	Cabinet Maker	Copenhagen, Denmark	going to reside in Clearfield, Pennsylvania	Friketon	7 Nov 1823
DACEY, Denis	28	M	Labourer	Ireland	United States	Trio	2 Oct 1828
DA COSTA, E. C. M.	28	M	Merchant	St. Thomas	St. Thomas	Velocipede	24 May 1824
DACY, Margaret	1	F		Ireland	United States	Delta	24 Oct 1829
Mary	30	F		Ireland	United States	Delta	24 Oct 1829
DADAGEN, Wm.	28	M	Labourer	Ireland	United States	Hope	12 Jun 1828
DADE, Charles	27	M		Great Britain		Corinthian	27 Oct 1829
DAEGNET, Camille	27	M	Merchant	France	U. States	Edward Quesnel	16 Nov 1827
DAELLINBACK, Jacob	42	M	Farmer	Germany	United States	Origon	8 Jun 1824
DAETON, Margt.	25	F		G. Britain	U. States	Dalhouse Castle	12 Sep 1828
DAEZ, Michl.	21	M	Farmer	Ireland	America	Liverpool	31 Aug 1827
DAFF, Michael	4	M		G. Britain	U. States	Mary & Harriot	8 Sep 1828
DAFFIELD, John	13	M	Merchant	England	America	Silas Richard	24 Oct 1829
DAFFIN, Benjamin	25	M	Shopkeeper	England		Manhattan	22 May 1827
Mary	28	F	None	England		Manhattan	22 May 1827
DAGGETT, H.	27	M	Merchant	United States	United States	Tontine	9 Jun 1827
Horace	26	M	Merchant	U. States	U. States	Colossus	21 Apr 1827
DAGITEL, —	40	M	Sea Captain	France	France	Maria Ann	11 Aug 1820
DAGNELL, Mary	22	F	Labourer	England	U. States	Ayrshire	12 May 1828
DAGUET, Nicolas Barthelmy	40	M	Gardener	France	New York	Cadmus	19 Aug 1823
DAHERTY, Wm.	20		Farmer	Ireland	United States	Robert Burns	18 Jun 1827
DAHN, Henrick	24	M	Sugar Baker	Germany		Boyer	9 May 1825
DAIGHTON, Joseph	30	M	Military	Great Britain	Great Britain	Fontine	4 Oct 1824
DAIL, Andw.	21	M	Farmer	Great Britain	United States	Atlantic	28 May 1827
DAILEY, —, Mr.	20	M		Dublin	U. States	Hibernia	26 Oct 1826
Bernard	7	M	Child	Great Britain	United States	Wilson	26 Feb 1824
Bridet	2	F	Child	...	United States	Hanford	17 Oct 1828
Briget	24	F	...	...	United States	Hanford	17 Oct 1828
Catherin	50	F	widdow	Great Brittan	United States	Hanford	3 Aug 1829
Hugh	24	M	Merchant	England	England	William Byrnes	24 Apr 1827
James	30	M	Farmer	Ireland	United States	Eliza	29 Aug 1822
John	14	M	Child	Great Britain	United States	Wilson	26 Feb 1824
M.	28	M	Farmer	Ireland	U. States	Beaver	27 Oct 1828
Michael	12	M	Child	Great Britain	United States	Wilson	26 Feb 1824
Patrick	30	M	Labourer	...	United States	Hanford	17 Oct 1828
DAILTON, Martin	28	M	Farmer	Great Britain	U.N. States	Reindeer	10 Dec 1827
DAILY, Ann	2	F	None	Ireland	Alexandria, U.S.	Roman	17 Oct 1826
Briget	6	F	None	Ireland	Alexandria, U.S.	Roman	17 Oct 1826
David	14	M	None	Ireland	Alexandria, U.S.	Roman	17 Oct 1826
Hugh	33	M	Gent.	Ireland	U. States	Meteor	19 Jul 1828
James	30	M	Merchant	England	United States	Loire	6 Jul 1821
John	7	M	Labourer	Ireland	United States	Carolina Ann	24 Oct 1825
Kitty	20	F		Ireland	United States	Neury	27 Jan 1827
Margaret	20	F	None	Ireland	Alexandria, U.S.	Roman	17 Oct 1826
Mary	1	F	...	Ireland	United States	Carolina Ann	24 Oct 1825
Mary	23	F	None	Ireland	Alexandria, U.S.	Roman	17 Oct 1826
Mary	50				Alexandria, U.S.	Roman	17 Oct 1826
Mathew	49	M	Farmer	Ireland	Alexandria, U.S.	Roman	17 Oct 1826
Michael	22	M		Ireland	Alexandria, U.S.	Roman	17 Oct 1826
Sarah	8	F		Ireland	U. States	Wilson	22 Apr 1822
Thomas	25	M	Weaver	Ireland	United States	Fabius	4 Jun 1828
Timothy	10	M	None	Ireland	Alexandria, U.S.	Roman	17 Oct 1826
DAIS, Joh. Gorge	26	M	Farmer	Germany	America	Falcon	28 Aug 1828
DAIX, Aglat	19	F	None	France	U. States	Marmion	7 Jun 1824
Marria	25	F	None	France	U. States	Marmion	7 Jun 1824
DAJANI, Carl, Miss	17	F	None	France	France	Canada	27 Sep 1826
DAKE, Catharine	26	F		Ireland	United States	William Byrnes	15 Aug 1826
DAKIN, Aboot	18	M	Baker	U.S.		Venus	11 Aug 1820
Gustavis G., Mr.	23	M	Merchant	Gt. Britain	Gt. Britain	Pacific	22 May 1826
DAKY, Justine	24	F		France	France	Edward Quesnel	3 Jul 1829
DALAGAN, Catharn	9	F	Child	Ireland	U. States	Meteor	19 Jul 1828
Ed	7	M	Child	Ireland	U. States	Meteor	19 Jul 1828
John	34	M	Farmer	Ireland	U. States	Meteor	19 Jul 1828
May	5	F	Child	Ireland	U. States	Meteor	19 Jul 1828

NAMES OF PASSENGERS	AGE	SEX	OCCUPATIONS	COUNTRY TO WHICH THEY BELONG	COUNTRY THEY INTEND TO INHABIT	SHIPS/DATES OF ARRIVAL	
DALBY, Dominick	24	M	Gentleman	Gt. Britian	United States	Cortes	11 Dec 1822
Margaret	24	F		Great Britain		London	29 Apr 1824
DALDRICH, John	24	M	Gardner	Scotland	United States	Commerce	17 Jul 1823
Mary	27	F		Scotland	United States	Commerce	17 Jul 1823
DALE, —, Mrs.	35	F				Day	11 Jun 1823
Alice, Mrs.	55	F	Wife	England	U.N. States	Corinthian	1 Sep 1823
Banj.	25	M	Tailor	England		Marchioness	13 May 1828
Benj.	13	M	None	England	U.N. States	Corinthian	1 Sep 1823
Charles A.	37	M	Gentleman	U. States	U. States	Day	11 Jun 1823
George	24	M	Farmer	Manchester	United States	Nile	17 May 1827
Hannah	19	F	Wife	Manchester	United States	Nile	17 May 1827
Hugh	28	M	Merchant	G. Britain	U. States	Hercules	24 Oct 1821
James	18	M	Farmer	Ireland	U. States	Francis	6 Sep 1827
Jno.	25	M	Navy	U. States	U. States	Columbia	12 Apr 1826
Johanna	46					Mount Vernon	26 Aug 1820
John	23	M	Labourer	Ireland	U.S. of America	Hamilton	18 Jul 1827
John	67		Farmer			Mount Vernon	26 Aug 1820
John, Junr.	10					Mount Vernon	26 Aug 1820
Josh.	26	M	Weaver	England	U.N. States	Corinthian	1 Sep 1823
Judah	7	F	Spinster	Ireland	U. States	Meteor	19 Jul 1828
Margt.	27	F		Great Britain	United States	Washington	3 Sep 1827
Martha	21	F	Wife	England	U.N. States	Corinthian	1 Sep 1823
Mary Ann	20	F	Spinster	England	U.N. States	Corinthian	1 Sep 1823
Rachel	2					Mount Vernon	26 Aug 1820
Richd.	23	M	Farmer	Manchester	United States	Nile	17 May 1827
Samuel	24	M	Labourer	England and Ireland	United States	Jubilee	12 May 1828
Thos.	23	M	Hatter	Great Britain	New York	Superior	5 Sep 1827
Ths.	17	M	Labourer	Ireland	U. States	Meteor	19 Jul 1828
William	20	M	Labourer	England and Ireland	United States	Jubilee	12 May 1828
DALER, Thos.	50	M	Reed Maker	England	United States	Dalhouse Castle	6 Sep 1827
DALEY, Betty	1	F	Child	Ireland	United States	Leonidas	3 Aug 1825
Elizabeth	16	F		Ireland	United States	Trio	2 Oct 1828
John	22	M		Ireland	New York	Lady Hunter	5 Jun 1826
John	23		Labourer	Halifax	U. States	Edwin	26 Sep 1828
Julian	13	F		Ireland	America	Liverpool	31 Aug 1827
Margt.	23	F	Servant	Ireland	United States	Wilson	27 Jun 1826
Nony, ...	30	F		Ireland	United States	Trio	2 Oct 1828
T.	27	M	Gentleman	Ireland	Western Country	British Hibernia	13 Mar 1820
Thomas	24 5/12	M	Jeweler	England	America	Peacock	26 Jul 1820
DALHBECK, John	48	M	Hatter	Hamburg	United States	Howard	28 Aug 1828
DALL, Alexander	30	M	Farmer	Scotland	United States	Natchez	22 Apr 1822
Helen	25	F		Scotland	United States	Natchez	22 Apr 1822
DALLAS, Chas. C.	16	M		Barbadoes	U. States	Hiram	10 Dec 1825
DALLETT, John	15	M	Gentleman	United States	United States	Georgetown Packet	15 Nov 1823
DALLEY, James	40	M	Stone Mason	Irereland	America	Carolina Ann	20 Jun 1825
DALLMAN,							
Amelia, Miss	20	F	Yeoman	England	U. States	Acasta	11 Dec 1826
Carline, Miss	6	F	Yeoman	England	U. States	Acasta	11 Dec 1826
Drusilla, Miss	3	F	Yeoman	England	U. States	Acasta	11 Dec 1826
Henry, Master	8	M	Yeoman	England	U. States	Acasta	11 Dec 1826
Laury, Miss	10	F	Yeoman	England	U. States	Acasta	11 Dec 1826
Maria, Miss	21	F	Yeoman	England	U. States	Acasta	11 Dec 1826
Maria, Mrs.	45	F	Yeoman	England	U. States	Acasta	11 Dec 1826
Thomas, Master	12	M	Yeoman	England	U. States	Acasta	11 Dec 1826
William	21		Farmer	England	United States	Corinthian	30 May 1828
William, Mr.	45	M	Yeoman	England	U. States	Acasta	11 Dec 1826
DALLO, John	40	M	Pudder	G. Britain	U. States	Great Britain	6 Sep 1828
DALLY, Am	9		Farmer & Labourer	Great Britain & Ireland	United States	Trio	8 Feb 1827
Elias M.	23	M	Chair Maker	U. States	U. States	Dromo	28 Feb 1829
John	30	M	Miner	Great Britain	Mexico	Corinthian	27 Apr 1824
John	40	M	Labourer	Gt. Britain	U. States	Frances Henrietta	18 Apr 1825
Lewis	47		Farmer & Labourer	Great Britain & Ireland	United States	Trio	8 Feb 1827

NAMES OF PASSENGERS	A G E	S E X	OCCUPATIONS	COUNTRY TO WHICH THEY BELONG	COUNTRY THEY INTEND TO INHABIT	SHIPS/DATES OF ARRIVAL	
DALLY (cont'd)							
Margt.	10		Farmer & Labourer	Great Britain & Ireland	United States	Trio	8 Feb 1827
DALLYWIMPLE, G. H.	22	M	Mariner	England	Barbadoes	Celia	15 Oct 1825
DALMAN, H. G.	52	M	Gentleman	Stockholm	U. States	Crisis	10 Nov 1823
DALMAR, Thos.	30	M	Merchant	Spain	Havana	James Monroe	21 Apr 1824
DALMOUR, H. P.	28	M	Merchant	England	U. States	Ysdva	11 Sep 1828
DALRIGG, O.		M	Merchant	N. Orleans	N. Orleans	Julia	9 Aug 1827
DALRIMPLE, R.	25		...	Ireland	United States	Alexander Mansfield	23 Nov 1824
DALRYMPLE, Ann	35	F	None	G. Britain	United States	New York	12 Nov 1822
Davison	22	M	Carpenter	Scotland		Marchioness	13 May 1828
Dora	10	F	None	G. Britain	United States	New York	12 Nov 1822
DALT, John	27	M	Joiner	Scotland	U. States	Czar	29 Aug 1829
DALTON, Ann	40	F	Wife	Ireland	United States	Dublin Packet	23 May 1828
Augusta	8	F	Dress Maker	England	New York	Brighton	16 Nov 1826
Edwin	20	M	Artist	Great Britain	U. St.	Manchester	7 Dec 1826
Elizabeth	40	F	Dress Maker	England	New York	Brighton	16 Nov 1826
Henry	32					Splendid	14 Aug 1829
James	26	M		Great Brittain	United States	Active	12 Sep 1828
*Died on the Passage							
John	6	M	Boy	Ireland	United States	Dublin Packet	23 May 1828
John	19	M	Farmer	England	U.N. States	William Byrnes	13 Aug 1829
John	35	M	Clerk	Ireland	United States	Euphrates	12 Mar 1824
John	50	M	Farmer	Great Britian	United States	George Clinton	13 Apr 1826
Julia	6	F	None	England	New York	Brighton	16 Nov 1826
Louisa	19	F	Dress Maker	England	New York	Brighton	16 Nov 1826
Margaret	32	F		Ireland	U. States	Josephine	27 Jul 1825
Marice	27					Trio	5 May 1828
Mary	4	F	Child	Ireland	United States	Dublin Packet	23 May 1828
Mary	13	F		Gt. Britain		Dalhouse Castle	13 May 1828
Michael	21	M	Framer	Ireland	U. States	Globe	14 Jul 1821
Michael	23	M	Labourer	Great Brittain	United States	Active	12 Sep 1828
Pat	30	M	Labourer	England	U. States	Ayrshire	12 May 1828
Patrick	25	M	Labourer	Ireland		Marchioness	13 May 1828
Patrick	28	M	Farmer	Great Britain	United States	Eliza Barker	3 Jul 1826
Richd.	2	M	None	England	New York	Brighton	16 Nov 1826
Richd.	45	M	Mercht.	England	New York	Brighton	16 Nov 1826
Rose	20		Maid Servant	Ireland	America	Sarah	18 Aug 1829
Samuel	23	M	Artist	Great Britain	U. St.	Manchester	7 Dec 1826
Sarah	18	F	Dress Maker	England	New York	Brighton	16 Nov 1826
Ths.	13	M	None	Great Brittan	U. States	John & Elizabeth	11 Dec 1826
Walter	40	M	Farmer	Ireland	United States	Dublin Packet	23 May 1828
DALY, Ann	40	F		Ireland	U. States	Albion	11 May 1827
Anne	28	F	Spinster	Ireland	United States	Thomas	13 Dec 1827
Bartholomew	30	M	Teacher	Great Britain		Panthea	15 Jun 1822
Catharine	28	F	Spinster	Ireland	United States	Dublin Packet	22 Oct 1821
Catherine	9	F		Ireland	America	Liverpool	31 Aug 1827
D.	29	M	Gentleman	Ireland	Canada	York	31 Mar 1828
Daniel	20 3/12	M	Weaver	Ireland	United States	Atlantic	21 Jul 1827
Danl.	27	M	Labourer	Ireland	U. States	Albion	11 May 1827
E.	19	M	Merchant	Baltimore	U. States	Cato	4 Apr 1823
Edward	30	M	Mariner	Great Britian	United States	Columbia	21 Jan 1828
Elizabeth	30	F	Lady	Ireland	United States	Sarah Ann	11 Jan 1827
Felix	28	M	Labourer	Ireland	United States	Thomas	13 Dec 1827
Fiobert	24	M	Shoemaker	Ireland	U. States	Union	3 Jun 1822
H.	7	M		Ireland	U. States	Albion	11 May 1827
James	25	F	Farmer	Great Britain	United States	William Dawson	18 Jun 1827
James	26	M	Labourer	England	United States	Dalhouse Castle	8 May 1827
Jane	25	F		Great Britian	United States	Columbia	21 Jan 1828
John	6/12	M		Great Britian	United States	Columbia	21 Jan 1828
John	10	M	Child	Ireland	New York	Wilson	28 Aug 1822
John	20	M	Laborer	Ireland	United States	Carolina Ann	11 Dec 1826
John	21	M	Labourer	Great Britain		Olive Branch	9 Oct 1829
John	24	M	Mechanic	New York	U. States	St. Michaels	21 Apr 1824
John	25	M	Farmer	Great Britain		Panthea	15 Jun 1822
Joshua	17	M		Ireland	U. States	Albion	11 May 1827
Lawrence	24	M	Blacksmith	Ireland	United States	Thomas	13 Dec 1827

NAMES OF PASSENGERS	AGE	SEX	OCCUPATIONS	COUNTRY TO WHICH THEY BELONG	COUNTRY THEY INTEND TO INHABIT	SHIPS/DATES OF ARRIVAL	
DALY (cont'd)							
Margaret	10 2/12	F	Servant	Ireland	United States	Atlantic	21 Jul 1827
Margaret	18	M	Spins.	Ireland	United States	Dublin Packet	3 Sep 1822
Margaret	26	F	Farmer	Ireland	America	Superior	12 Jun 1824
Margt.	16	F	Servant	Ireland	United States	William	20 Jul 1829
Margt.	20		Spinster	Ireland	United States	Courier	15 Oct 1827
Margt.	27	F		Ireland	U. States	Albion	11 May 1827
Mary	1	F		Ireland	United States	Thomas	13 Dec 1827
Mary	9	F		Ireland	United States	William	20 Jul 1829
Mary	18	F	None	Great Britain	United States	Aurora	10 Nov 1827
Mary	19	F		Ireland	U. States	Albion	11 May 1827
Mary	26	F		Ireland	United States	William Byrnes	15 Aug 1826
Mathew	1	M	Labourer	Ireland	U. States	Albion	11 May 1827
Mathew	4	M		Ireland	U. States	Albion	11 May 1827
Michael	2 1/2	M		Ireland	United States	William Byrnes	15 Aug 1826
Michael	21	M	Farmer	Ireland	United States	Dublin Packet	22 Oct 1821
Pat.	20	M	Labourer	Ireland	United States	Wilson	6 Jun 1828
Rose	28	F	Servant	Ireland	U. States	Sarah G	30 Jun 1828
Sarah	15	F		Ireland	United States	Thomas	13 Dec 1827
Simon	11	M		Ireland	America	Liverpool	31 Aug 1827
Thomas	21	M	Labourer	Great Britain	United States	Aurora	10 Nov 1827
Thomas	30	M	Tailor	Great Britain		Panthea	15 Jun 1822
William	27	M	Farmer	Ireland	America	Superior	12 Jun 1824
DALY...ILL, John	38	...	...	Scotland	America	Nimrod	9 Jul 1827
Walter	23	...	...	Scotland	America	Nimrod	9 Jul 1827
DALZELE, Jean	8	F	Farmer	Scotland	U. States	Roger Stewart	9 Jun 1828
Margaret	22	F	Farmer	Scotland	U. States	Roger Stewart	9 Jun 1828
Mary	18	F	Farmer	Scotland	U. States	Roger Stewart	9 Jun 1828
Rena	10	F	Farmer	Scotland	U. States	Roger Stewart	9 Jun 1828
DALZELL, —, Mrs.	45	F	Ireland	Ireland	U. States	Hiram	25 Jul 1828
Joseph	38	M	Ireland	Ireland	U. States	Hiram	25 Jul 1828
Willm.	38	M	Farmer	America	America	Carolina Ann	7 Apr 1826
DAMAIRE, Juan	22	M	Merchant	Spain	U. States	Fabius	7 Dec 1825
DAMARA, C., Don	32	M	Merchant	Spain	Mexico	Nancy	1 Oct 1824
DAMERON, Phebe	45	F	Wife	U.S.	U.S.	Pacific	24 Oct 1828
Wm.	58	M	Mercht.	U.S.	U.S.	Pacific	24 Oct 1828
DAMET, F. A.	23	M	Gentleman	France	U. States	Amos Palmer	29 Sep 1827
DAMEY, H. Josep	36	M	Mariner	Neather Lands	U. States	La Voltiquer	23 Jul 1822
Henry	28	M	Mariner	Neather Lands	U. States	La Voltiquer	23 Jul 1822
DAMIELS, Rosa	23	F	Servant	England	U.S. America	Cortes	19 May 1826
DAMON, John W.	35	M	Merchant	U. States	U.S.	Burdett	7 Dec 1827
DAMOR, Richd.							
Francois	18	M	Basket Maker	France	United States	Acasta	15 Jul 1822
DAMPSEY, Wm.	29	M	Gent.	Ireland	United States	Siroc	31 Oct 1829
DAN, Edward	27	M	Farmer	Gt. Britain	United States	Robert Edwards	1 Jun 1826
DAN..., Wm.	38	M	Farmer	Ireland	New York	Margaret	18 May 1825
DANA, Francis	19	M	Miner	U.S.A.		George	10 Jul 1826
Frs., Jr.	18	M	Merchant	U. States	U. States	Minerva	23 May 1825
Richd.	41	M	Mariner	Boston	U. States	Amphion	14 Mar 1823
DANAGH, Henry	15	M	Farmer	Ireland	U. States	Dickinson	30 Jul 1825
DANAHOE, Daniel	19	M	Labourer	Ireland	United States	Jubilee	13 Jul 1829
Mary	20	F	None	Ireland	U.S. of America	Hamilton	18 Jul 1827
DANAHY, James	5	M	Child	Ireland	U. States	Josephine	30 Aug 1828
John	44 6/12	M	Weaver	Ireland	U. States	Josephine	30 Aug 1828
Mary	7	F	Child	Ireland	U. States	Josephine	30 Aug 1828
DANAKY, John	24	M	Weaver	Ireland	United States	Robert Fulton	10 Aug 1827
William	25	M	Weaver	Ireland	United States	Robert Fulton	10 Aug 1827
DANALASAN, William	20	M	Farmer	Ireland	U. States	Dickinson	30 Jul 1825
DANALDBOR, Elizabeth	22	F		Ireland	America	John Adams	2 Aug 1827
Terenier	32	M	Cooper	Ireland	America	John Adams	2 Aug 1827
DANBAR, Robert T.	25	M	Planter	America	America	Britannia	5 Nov 1828
DANBERT, Chs. L.	23	M	Clergyman	Germany	U. States	America	22 Sep 1826
DANBREVILLE, —	25	M	Mechanicien	France		François I	19 Nov 1828
DANCALF, Richard	23	M	Miner	England	England	Ranger	15 Jan 1827
DANCANGAT, V.	18	M	Mechanic	France	U. States	Harriet	3 Sep 1823
DANCE, Thomas	36	M	Merchant	England	America	James Cropper	14 Oct 1822
DANDICOLLE, Pierre	26	M	Mariner	France	France	Traveller	11 Dec 1824
DANDO, E.	17	M	Gentleman	England	U. States	Milton	6 Dec 1825
DANE, E.	30	M		Scotland	U. States	Superior	25 Sep 1828

NAMES OF PASSENGERS	AGE	SEX	OCCUPATIONS	COUNTRY TO WHICH THEY BELONG	COUNTRY THEY INTEND TO INHABIT	SHIPS/DATES OF ARRIVAL	
DANEGGERE, Magdelen	29	F	None	France	N. York	Charlemagne	20 Aug 1829
DANELL,							
Thos. A., Jr.	22 2/12	M	Merchant Bmda.	Bermuda	Bermuda	Florida	27 Aug 1825
DANEY, James	27	M	Labourer	Gt. Britain	U. States	Panthea	21 Jul 1825
DANFORTH,							
George, Esqr.	31		Carpenter	United States	United States	South Carolina Packet	22 Jun 1822
DANGERFD., Saarah A.	20	F		England	U.S.A.	Robin Hood	6 May 1828
DANGERFIELD, Edwd.	24	M	Merchant	United States	United States	Britannia	29 Oct 1829
Will	55	M	Engineer	England	U.S.A.	Robin Hood	6 May 1828
DANGLY, Oowen	40	F	Servant	Ireland	N. York	Trusty	12 Sep 1828
S.	5	F	Servant	Ireland	N. York	Trusty	12 Sep 1828
DANIE, George	47	M	Shipmaster	U. States	U. States	Mary Livingston	6 Dec 1827
DANIEL, Betty	6	F	None	Great Britain	United States	Mary & Harriet	3 Jul 1829
George	27	M	Mechanic	England	New York	Curler	7 Jul 1827
Hannah	7	F	None	Great Britain	United States	Mary & Harriet	3 Jul 1829
Hen.	30	M	Labourer	Great Britain	United States	Mary & Harriet	3 Jul 1829
Isaac	19	M	Smith	G. Britain	America	Spring	12 Oct 1821
James	1	M	None	Great Britain	United States	Mary & Harriet	3 Jul 1829
James	22	M	Mechanic	England	New York	Curler	7 Jul 1827
Jno.	38	M	Farmer	Great Britain	U.S.	Nestor	6 Jul 1821
John	3	M	None	Great Britain	United States	Mary & Harriet	3 Jul 1829
Mary	27	F	None	Great Britain	United States	Mary & Harriet	3 Jul 1829
Miller	25	M	Servant	Garmine	Garmine	Douglass	9 Nov 1827
Thos.	16	M	Joiner	Great Brittan	U. States	Gem	26 Jul 1827
DANIELS, Eliza	28	F	None	England	United States	Great Britain	5 Sep 1827
Eliza Ann	4	F	None	England	United States	Great Britain	5 Sep 1827
George	2	M	None	Great Britain	U. States	Gem	26 Jul 1827
George	27	M	Merchant	England	United States	John Wells	22 May 1826
Henry	27	M	Gentleman	United States	New York	Astrea	21 Oct 1823
James	23	M	Servant	United States	United States	Corinthian	2 Sep 1824
Josiah	30	M	Merchant	U.S.	U.S.	Frances	21 Jul 1827
Martha	60	M	Farmer	Great Britain	United States	John	6 Oct 1820
Mary	4	F	None	Great Britain	U. States	Gem	26 Jul 1827
Sarah	20	F	None	Great Britain	U. States	Gem	26 Jul 1827
Thos.	17	M	Farmer	Great Britain	U. States	Gem	26 Jul 1827
DANIELSON, Henry	7	M	None	St. Croix	St. Croix	Matteawan	30 Nov 1826
John	5/12	M	None	St. Croix	St. Croix	Matteawan	30 Nov 1826
Mary	30	F	None	St. Croix	St. Croix	Matteawan	30 Nov 1826
DANIGAN, James	20		Tailor			Zamoa	5 Nov 1828
DANISH, Susan	36	F	Spinster	Germany	Missouri	Isabella	15 Sep 1828
DANKES, Ann	24	F	None	England	Pennsylva.	Commerce	24 Sep 1823
John	32	M	Coal Miner	England	Pennsylva.	Commerce	24 Sep 1823
Lidia	2	F	None	England	Pennsylva.	Commerce	24 Sep 1823
Peter	4	M	None	England	Pennsylva.	Commerce	24 Sep 1823
DANLAN, Mary	20	F	None	Ireland	New York	America	1 Aug 1828
Patrick	24	M	Labourer	Ireland	New York	America	1 Aug 1828
DANLEY, Sarah	55	F	Spinner	Great Britain	United States	Atlantic	8 Dec 1827
DANLY, John	17	M	Labourer	Ireland	U. States	Wanderer	1 Sep 1828
Michael	20	M	Labourer	Ireland	U. States	Wanderer	1 Sep 1828
DANNENBERG, Nathan	20	M	Joiner	Hesse	United States	Constitution	2 Aug 1826
DANNOTT, Peter	21		Labourer	Ireland	United States	Courier	15 Oct 1827
DANOAFEDELE, C.	25	M	Merchant	France	Matanzas	Radius	12 Jul 1825
DANOLSON, Eugene	22 4/12	M	...	...	U.S. America	Edward	28 Oct 1825
DANONAN, Edwd.	22		Blacksmith	Ireland	United States	Geo. Canning	5 Jun 1828
DANPSON, Mary	24		Laborer	Ireland	New York	Lady Hunter	19 Oct 1826
DANS, Barbara	37	F		Brattain		L'Esperance	6 Sep 1828
Catherine	7	F		Gt. Brittan		L'Esperance	6 Sep 1828
Ignan	38		Shoemaker	Brattain		L'Esperance	6 Sep 1828
John	40	M	Printer	Gr. Britain		Moro Castle	6 Jul 1827
DANSCOTH, James	22	M	Farmer			Orion	21 Aug 1820
DANSON, Edmund	29	M	Merchant	Great Britain	Great Britain	Hannibal	12 Oct 1829
DANTARY, Wm.	21	M	Printer			John Dickinson	14 Sep 1820
DANTILLAE, Victor	23 2/12	M	Hair Dresser	France	New York	Harriot	1 May 1822
DANTZMANN, David	13	M		France	America, U.N.S.	Great Britain	3 Aug 1829
David	40	M	Farmer	France	America, U.N.S.	Great Britain	3 Aug 1829
Effa	20	F		France	America, U.N.S.	Great Britain	3 Aug 1829
Henri	12	M		France	America, U.N.S.	Great Britain	3 Aug 1829
Jacob	16	M		France	America, U.N.S.	Great Britain	3 Aug 1829

NAMES OF PASSENGERS	AGE	SEX	OCCUPATIONS	COUNTRY TO WHICH THEY BELONG	COUNTRY THEY INTEND TO INHABIT	SHIPS/DATES OF ARRIVAL	
DANTZMANN (cont'd)							
Madeline	18	F		France	America, U.N.S.	Great Britain	3 Aug 1829
Mader	40	F		France	America, U.N.S.	Great Britain	3 Aug 1829
Michel	1 6/12	M		France	America, U.N.S.	Great Britain	3 Aug 1829
DANVERS, James	26	M	Labourer	Great Briton	uncertain	Mount Vernon	29 Aug 1828
William	28	M	Blacksmith	Great Briton	uncertain	Mount Vernon	29 Aug 1828
DANWORTH, E.	30	F		England	U. States	Howard Douglass	29 Jan 1828
Francis	11	M		England	U. States	Howard Douglass	29 Jan 1828
Geo.	36	M	Brick Maker	England	U. States	Thomas Ritchie	2 Jul 1827
DANZERSEN,							
Anna Maria	3	F	Daughter	Germany	United States	Elizabeth	4 Sep 1826
Barbara	6	F	Daughter	Germany	United States	Elizabeth	4 Sep 1826
Barbara	25	F	Wife	Germany	United States	Elizabeth	4 Sep 1826
Christien	5	M	Son	Germany	United States	Elizabeth	4 Sep 1826
Jacob	21	M	Son	Germany	United States	Elizabeth	4 Sep 1826
Madelina	17	F	Daughter	Germany	United States	Elizabeth	4 Sep 1826
Mathias	43	M	Waggoner	Germany	United States	Elizabeth	4 Sep 1826
DANZERSIN, Zalabeha	12	F	Daughter	Germany	United States	Elizabeth	4 Sep 1826
DANZIESEN, Catharine	28	F	None	Germany	U. States	Sully	24 Oct 1828
Catharine, Jr.	4	F	None	Germany	U. States	Sully	24 Oct 1828
Charles F.	0 9/12	M	None	Germany	U. States	Sully	24 Oct 1828
Elizabeth	2	F	None	Germany	U. States	Sully	24 Oct 1828
Jacob	32	M	Farmer	Germany	U. States	Sully	24 Oct 1828
Jacob, Jr.	6	M	None	Germany	U. States	Sully	24 Oct 1828
Sophia	8	F	None	Germany	U. States	Sully	24 Oct 1828
DAOLY, John	22	M	Labourer	Ireland		Robert Fulton	4 Jun 1828
DAOTT, Bid	56	F	Spinster	Ireland		Robert Fulton	4 Jun 1828
Bridget	16	F	Spinster	Ireland		Robert Fulton	4 Jun 1828
DAPONCHAL, Edward	21	M	Mechanic	France	U.S.	Montano	24 Jun 1823
DAPY, Peeared	10	M	Shoe Maker	Germany	United States	Virginia	31 May 1828
DARAN, Allen	20	M	Labourer	U. States	U. States	Nancy	19 Oct 1821
DARBA, Ann	38	F		G. Britain	U. States	London	23 Sep 1828
Ann	40	F		G. Britain	U. States	London	23 Sep 1828
Diana	14	F		G. Britain	U. States	London	23 Sep 1828
Eliza	3	F		G. Britain	U. States	London	23 Sep 1828
William	12	M		G. Britain	U. States	London	23 Sep 1828
Wm.	45	M	Shoe Maker	G. Britain	U. States	London	23 Sep 1828
DARBY, G. J.	26	M	Farmer	Gt. Britain	United States	Columbia	7 Sep 1827
Joseph	27	M	Merchant	London	Boston	George	6 Aug 1823
Maria	28	F		Gt. Britain	United States	Columbia	7 Sep 1827
Robt.	24	M		Great Brittain	U. States	Atticus	25 Apr 1822
DARCEY, Ann	2	F		York, Great Britain		Casanda	5 Sep 1827
Cathe.	13	F		York, Great Britain		Casanda	5 Sep 1827
Dennis	10	M		York, Great Britain		Casanda	5 Sep 1827
James	15	M	Labourer	Ireland	United States	Wilson	4 Oct 1827
John	6	M		York, Great Britain		Casanda	5 Sep 1827
John	22	M	Labourer	G. Britain	U. States	St. George	7 Jun 1828
John	45	M		York, Great Britain		Casanda	5 Sep 1827
Mary	15	F		York, Great Britain		Casanda	5 Sep 1827
Patt	4	M		York, Great Britain		Casanda	5 Sep 1827
Rose	20	F	Spinster	Ireland	United States	Wilson	4 Oct 1827
Thos.	18	M		York, Great Britain		Casanda	5 Sep 1827
DARCIEY, William	21	M	Farmer	Ireland	United States	Dublin Packet	13 Oct 1828
DARCY, Julia	40	F		York, Great Britain		Casanda	5 Sep 1827
DARDEN, John	17		Stone Mason	England	United States	Corinthian	7 Jul 1829
DARE, Charles	21	M	Shoe Maker	England		Manhattan	22 May 1827
Simon	30	M	Mason	England	United States	Hannibal	25 May 1827
DAREAN, J. M.	40	M	Clergiman	U. States	U. States	Silas Richards	29 Oct 1828

NAMES OF PASSENGERS	AGE	SEX	OCCUPATIONS	COUNTRY TO WHICH THEY BELONG	COUNTRY THEY INTEND TO INHABIT	SHIPS/DATES OF ARRIVAL	
DARETY, Harey	28	F		Irland	U. States	Nancy	27 Jun 1823
DARIELL, James	19	M	Farmer	Ireland	U. States	William Penn	20 Oct 1825
DARIER, J.	26	M	Merchant	Sweden	U. States	Cadmus	28 May 1821
DARIES, A.	70	F		Scotland	U.S.	Curler	19 Jul 1828
Cath.	65	F		Scotland	U.S.	Curler	19 Jul 1828
Mary	3	F		Scotland	U.S.	Curler	19 Jul 1828
Mary	34	F		Scotland	U.S.	Curler	19 Jul 1828
May	27	F		Scotland	U.S.	Curler	19 Jul 1828
Robt.	38	M		Scotland	U.S.	Curler	19 Jul 1828
Wm.	3/4	M		Scotland	U.S.	Curler	19 Jul 1828
DARION, Bobington	4		Boy	Ireland	N. Jersey	Potomac	7 Aug 1827
DARKER, John	25 7/12	M	Labourer	England	United States	London	6 Feb 1829
DARKES, James	18	M	Weaver	Ireland	United States	Ann Maria	4 Oct 1824
John	16	M	Weaver	Ireland	United States	Ann Maria	4 Oct 1824
DARKEY, Bridget	19	F	Spinster	Ireland	United States	Fabius	31 Jul 1829
DARKS, Jos.	24	M	Printer	England	U. States	Ann Maria	13 Mar 1823
DARLEY, Caroline	7	F	Child	G. Brittan	U. States	Henry	24 Oct 1828
Edward	2	M	Child	G. Brittan	U. States	Henry	24 Oct 1828
Harriet H.	11	F	Child	G. Brittan	U. States	Henry	24 Oct 1828
Lousia	6	F	Child	G. Brittan	U. States	Henry	24 Oct 1828
Thos.	4	M	Child	G. Brittan	U. States	Henry	24 Oct 1828
DARLING, Andrew	6	M	Dyer	Scotland	U. States	Orozimbo	7 Jul 1825
Ann	18	F	None	Great Britan	Great Britan	United States	21 May 1827
Christ.	13	M	Dyer	Scotland	U. States	Orozimbo	7 Jul 1825
David	16	M	Dyer	Scotland	U. States	Orozimbo	7 Jul 1825
Eliza	45	F	Dyer	Scotland	U. States	Orozimbo	7 Jul 1825
Hannah	31		Servt.	England	U. States	New York	30 Oct 1827
James	23		Labourer	Scotland	United States	Camillus	3 May 1828
Jas.	13	M	Dyer	Scotland	U. States	Orozimbo	7 Jul 1825
John	7	M	Dyer	Scotland	U. States	Orozimbo	7 Jul 1825
M.	18	M	Dyer	Scotland	U. States	Orozimbo	7 Jul 1825
Mary	12	F	Dyer	Scotland	U. States	Orozimbo	7 Jul 1825
Wm.	23	M	Carpenter	U. States	U. States	Rodman	28 May 1825
DARLY, James	27	M	Cloth Cutter	England	U.N. States	Jane	7 Oct 1826
Peter	22	M	Tailor	Great Britain	United States	Penelope	11 Jun 1827
DARMOTY, Michl.	18	M	Labourer	England	United States	John Wells	22 May 1826
DARNEHARD, C.	25	M	Soldier	France	France	Rebecca	1 Aug 1825
DARNEL, Rachel	18	F	Servant	Great Britain	U. States of America	Junius	5 Jul 1820
DARNING, Pat	...	M		Ireland	United States	General Putnam	20 Jun 1825
DARNLEY, John	25	M	M...ter	Hudd...sfield	...	Frances Henrietta	30 Jun 1827
DAROUGH, Martha	0 6/12	F	Child	Ireland	United States	Robert Fulton	24 Jul 1826
DARRACH, Alexander	14	M	Farmer	Ireland	Pittsburg	Triton	12 Jul 1823
Ann	23			Great Britain		John Dickinson	5 Apr 1821
Matilda	2			Great Britain		John Dickinson	5 Apr 1821
Willm.	24		Physician	Philadelphia	Philadelphia	Albion	5 Feb 1822
DARRAGH, Christn.	70	F		Ireland	Redstone	Triton	12 Jul 1823
Geo.	23	M	Weaver	Ireland	U. States	Hunter	30 May 1827
DARRELL, R. G. B.	18	M	Merchant	Bermuda	Bermuda	Leander	30 Oct 1826
Wm. H.	19	M	Merchant	Bermuda	Bermuda	Leander	30 Oct 1826
DARRIE, Farnes	28	M	...	G. Britain	U. States	New England	28 Sep 1824
DARROCH, Andrew	4	M		G. Britain	U. States	Camillus	8 Sep 1828
Geo.	8	M		G. Britain	U. States	Camillus	8 Sep 1828
Helen	23	F		G. Britain	U. States	Camillus	8 Sep 1828
Margt.	2	F		G. Britain	U. States	Camillus	8 Sep 1828
Wm.	8	M		G. Britain	U. States	Camillus	8 Sep 1828
DARROTT, Jane	29			Birmingham	N. York	Peru	30 May 1828
Joseph	35		Goldsmith	Birmingham	N. York	Peru	30 May 1828
Wm.	8			Birmingham	N. York	Peru	30 May 1828
DARROUGH, Mary	21	F	Spinster	Ireland	United States	Robert Fulton	24 Jul 1826
DARSTON, Charlotte	28	F	None	England	New York	Brighton	16 Nov 1826
Montagew	25	M	Carpenter	England	New York	Brighton	16 Nov 1826
DARTEY, Lisa	4	F		Irland	U. States	Nancy	27 Jun 1823
Pat	2	M		Irland	U. States	Nancy	27 Jun 1823
Robert	8	F		Irland	U. States	Nancy	27 Jun 1823
DARVALE, ...	25	F		Great Britian	United States	London	24 Jun 1823
...	28	M		Great Britian	United States	London	24 Jun 1823
DARVILLE, Timy.	28	M	Farmer	Ireland	New York	Robert Edwards	17 Mar 1828
DARVIN, Elizabeth	45	F	Lady	St. Domingo	United States	Bayard	13 Nov 1823

NAMES OF PASSENGERS	AGE	SEX	OCCUPATIONS	COUNTRY TO WHICH THEY BELONG	COUNTRY THEY INTEND TO INHABIT	SHIPS/DATES OF ARRIVAL	
DARY, Archd.	31	M	Farmer	Scotland	United States	Samuel Robertson	5 Oct 1827
James	21	M	Servant	Ireland	U. States	Wanderer	1 Sep 1828
DASBEFEALLE, C.	22	M	Merchant	France	N. York	Margaret	7 Dec 1825
DASCHARMES, —,							
Mrs.	30	F		France	United States	Alexander	20 Aug 1828
Edward Olympe	30	M	Merchant	France	United States	Alexander	20 Aug 1828
Felix Pasot	35	M	Merchant	France	United States	Alexander	20 Aug 1828
DASH, A. Z., Mrs.	26	F	None	U. States	U. States	Canada	13 Oct 1825
Daniel B.	1	M	None	U. States	U. States	Canada	13 Oct 1825
Daniel B.	33	M	None	U. States	U. States	Canada	13 Oct 1825
Margaret B.	3	F	None	U. States	U. States	Canada	13 Oct 1825
DASHER, H.	23	M	Sugar Baker	Ireland	U. States	Frederick	2 Apr 1828
DASHIEL, Geo.			Distressed Seaman	Virginia	U. States	Mary & Eliza	2 Jul 1829
DASHWOOD, Ann	26	F	Lady	St. John, N.B.	United States	St. Michaels	11 May 1826
John	20	M	Compositor	England	United States	Cambria	8 Oct 1828
Mary	12	F	None	England	America	Manhattan	20 Mar 1820
Mary	64	F	Lady	United States	United States	St. Michaels	11 May 1826
Robert	5	M	None	England	America	Manhattan	20 Mar 1820
Sophia	2	F	None	England	America	Manhattan	20 Mar 1820
Sophia	42	F	None	England	America	Manhattan	20 Mar 1820
Thomas	10	M	None	England	America	Manhattan	20 Mar 1820
Thos.	8	M	None	England	America	Manhattan	20 Mar 1820
DASHY, Michl.	34	M	Farmer	Ireland	America	Liverpool	31 Aug 1827
Norry	30	F	servt.	Ireland	America	Liverpool	31 Aug 1827
DA SILVA, Vicente Julio		M		Portugal	U. States	Sarah Louisa	10 Oct 1822
DASKER, Claus	23	M	Carpenter	Germany	Newyork	Cortes	16 Jul 1827
DASKEY, John	22	M	Servant	Ireland	U. States	Henrietta	7 Jul 1825
DASON, Anderson	25	M	Labourer	Ireland	United States	Hope	12 Jun 1828
DASQUE, J.	17	M	Comm... Marchand	France	Phyladelphia	Charles Miller	31 May 1825
DASTRE, P.	40	M	Merchant	Cuba	U. States	Ladies Delight	9 Aug 1823
DATER, John, Capt.		M	Mariner	United States	United States	India	24 Mar 1826
DATSON, James	20 5/12	M	Farmer	England	United States	Young Phoenix	26 Jul 1824
DAUB, Joh. Fr.	26	M	Servant	Germany	New York	Maria Elizabeth	16 Mar 1829
DAUDSON, Andrew	29	M	Farmer	Scotland	Unt. States	Robert Fulton	14 Mar 1829
DAUGHERTY, Bridget	24	F	Spinster	Ireland	Unt. St. America	Wilson	21 May 1827
Catharine	1	F	...		America	Ann	11 Apr 1821
Charles	28	M	Labourer	Ireland	United States	Robert Fulton	10 Aug 1827
Ellen	9	F	None	Great Britian	U. States	Pallas	17 Aug 1824
Ellen	19	F		Ireland	America	Ann	11 Apr 1821
James	28	M	Farmer	Ireland	America	Ann	11 Apr 1821
Jane	12	F	None	Great Britian	U. States	Pallas	17 Aug 1824
Mary	20	F	Matron	Ireland	United States	Robert Fulton	10 Aug 1827
Mary	25	F			America	Ann	11 Apr 1821
Mary	27	F		Ireland	U. States	Wilson	22 Apr 1822
Michael	23	M	Farmer	Ireland	America	Ann	11 Apr 1821
Morgan	22	M	Farmer	Ireland	U. States	Wilson	22 Apr 1822
Rebecca	41	F	None	Great Britian	U. States	Pallas	17 Aug 1824
Thos.	1	M		Ireland	America	Ann	11 Apr 1821
DAULBY, Wm., Mr.	28	M	Merchant	England	England	Manhattan	21 Sep 1822
DAULEY, Robt.	27	M	Lawyer	U. States	U. States	United States	11 Sep 1828
DAUMENGE, Aglac	7	F		Toulon	New York	Pedler	14 May 1828
Clair	44	F		Toulon	New York	Pedler	14 May 1828
Fortunie	21	F		Toulon	New York	Pedler	14 May 1828
Joseph	17	M	Sailmaker	Toulon	New York	Pedler	14 May 1828
DAUSEN, Candy	21	M		Ireland	U. States	Nancy	16 Aug 1822
DAV..., Jas. [crossed out]		M	Ship Master	United States	United States	Cortes	5 Aug 1822
DAVAING, Alley	20	F		Ireland	United States	Sarah G.	20 Jul 1827
DAVALLAN, John,							
her Son [Sarah]	9/12					Hercules	19 Jun 1821
Sarah, Mrs.	23	F				Hercules	19 Jun 1821
DAVARE, Edmund	19	M	Farmer	England	U. States	New York	11 Jul 1823
DAVEN, George Wm.	3	M	Boy	England	United States	Cambria	8 Oct 1828
DAVENPERT, John	26	M	Calico Printer	Great Britain	United States	Aurora	5 Sep 1826
DAVENPORT, Ann	6	F	None	Great Britain	United States	William Dawson	18 Jun 1827
Augusta	17	F		New York	New York	Triton	11 Jul 1826
Eliza	27	F	None	Great Britain	United States	William Dawson	18 Jun 1827
Elizabeth	25	F	None	England	United States	Trident	18 Jul 1827
Ellen	4	F	None	England	United States	Trident	18 Jul 1827

NAMES OF PASSENGERS	AGE	SEX	OCCUPATIONS	COUNTRY TO WHICH THEY BELONG	COUNTRY THEY INTEND TO INHABIT	SHIPS/DATES OF ARRIVAL	
DAVENPORT (cont'd)							
Fennus	22	M	Merchant	R. Island	N. York	Albion	17 Jan 1825
George	44	M	Merchant	U. States	U. States	Canada	12 May 1828
J.	25	M	Merchant	Great Britan	U. States	Aspasia	23 Nov 1825
Jabez	25	M	Baker	Great Britain	U. States	Great Britain	18 Mar 1828
Maria	1	F	Mantusmith	Ireland	United States	Marmion	17 Jun 1825
Mary	1	F	None	England	United States	Trident	18 Jul 1827
Mary Ann	4	F	None	Great Britain	United States	William Dawson	18 Jun 1827
Murray	2	M	None	England	United States	Trident	18 Jul 1827
Peter	36	M	Shoemaker	Great Britain	United States	William Dawson	18 Jun 1827
Robert	15	M	None	Gt. Britain	United States	Neptune	24 May 1824
Robert F.	15 6/12	M	Accountant	New York	New York	Triton	11 Jul 1826
Saml.	19	M	Gentleman	United States	United States	Emma	12 May 1826
Saml. O.	21	M	Merchant	U. States		Charlotte Corday	15 Aug 1820
Thos.	18		Gentleman	Ireland		Westmoreland	1 Aug 1826
William	17		Writer			Rufus King	7 Aug 1820
William	20	M	Merchant	Bermuda	Bermuda	Angenora	5 May 1826
DAVES, E.	28	F	Farmer	Gt. Britain	U. States	Columbia	7 Sep 1827
DAVEY, Eliza	31	F	Lady	England	United States	Cambria	8 Oct 1828
Elizabeth Anne	8	F	Girl	England	United States	Cambria	8 Oct 1828
Henry	2	M	Boy	England	United States	Cambria	8 Oct 1828
Nicholas	28	M	Farmer	Ireland	Philadelphia	General Marion	12 Jan 1829
Richard	27	M	Merchant	England	New York	Florida	22 May 1826
William	40	M	Farmer	Great Britain	United States	Cambria	26 Dec 1827
DAVID, —, Mrs.	26	F	Seamstress	Paris	Philadelphia	Cadmus	27 Aug 1822
B. L.	21	M	Merchant	Germany	U. States	Xenophon	15 Sep 1820
David	50	M	...	England	Canada	Venus	4 Oct 1824
Felix	18	M				Reuben & Eliza	21 Aug 1820
J.	53	M	Officer	France	U. States	Edwd. Quesnel	30 Apr 1825
James	23	M	Clerk	Ireland	United States	Corinthian	10 Jan 1826
Jno. T.	30	M	Merchant	Philada.	U. States	Cato	9 Aug 1823
John	34	M	Farmer	Scotland	U. States	Brilliant	19 Mar 1828
John	60	M	Merchant	United States	Philadelphia	Cadmus	27 Aug 1822
John Batich	54	M	Merchant	France		Leader	9 Nov 1825
Mary	60	F	Servant	Island Jamaica	Island Jamaca	Agenora	19 Jun 1826
Victor	33	M	Merchant	U. States	U. States	Birmingham	12 Oct 1829
DAVIDS, Andrew	43	M	Mariner	U. States	U. States	Constitution	17 Mar 1823
David	21	M	Labourer	G. Britain	U. States	Aisthorpe	22 May 1827
DAVIDSON, —, Mr.	55	M	Labourer	Dundee, Scotland	U. States	Hector	16 May 1821
Abm.	38	M	None	Scotland	United States	Euphrates	8 Nov 1821
Agnes	8	F	family of Merchant [William]	England	United States	Comet	6 Mar 1823
Agnes	26	F		Great Britain		Dalmannock	24 Ocg 1826
Alexander	22	M	...	Great Britain	United States	Ann	24 Sep 1822
Andrew	33	M	Merchant	Scotland	United States	Friends	13 Mar 1824
Ann	18	F		Dundee, Scotland	U. States	Hector	16 May 1821
Ann	40	F	family of Merchant [William]	England	United States	Comet	6 Mar 1823
Charles	3	M	family of Merchant [William]	England	United States	Comet	6 Mar 1823
D.	40	M	Traveler	England	Surinam	Bolivar Liberator	8 Dec 1826
Donald A.	20	M		Jamaica	England	Pleiades	13 Nov 1826
Edward	4	M	family of Merchant [William]	England	United States	Comet	6 Mar 1823
Eliza	2	F		Scotland	U.S.	Curler	19 Jul 1828
Elizabeth	13	F		Dundee, Scotland	U. States	Hector	16 May 1821
Ellen	27	F		Scotland	U.S.	Curler	19 Jul 1828
Fanny	30	F	Lady	Great Britain	United States	Cambria	26 Dec 1827
Geo.	20	M	Mechanic	England	U. States	Cygnet	22 Jun 1821
George	28	M	Printer	G.B.	Rhode Island	Eliza Grant	29 Aug 1829
George	28	M	Printer	Great Britain		Eliza Grant	29 Aug 1829
Isabella	28	F		Dundee, Scotland	U. States	Hector	16 May 1821
Isabella	55	F		Dundee, Scotland	U. States	Hector	16 May 1821

NAMES OF PASSENGERS	AGE	SEX	OCCUPATIONS	COUNTRY TO WHICH THEY BELONG	COUNTRY THEY INTEND TO INHABIT	SHIPS/DATES OF ARRIVAL	
DAVIDSON (cont'd)							
James	16	M	family of Merchant [William]	England	United States	Comet	6 Mar 1823
Jane	4	F		Scotland	U.S.	Curler	19 Jul 1828
John	25	M	Teacher	Great Britain		Dalmannock	24 Ocg 1826
John	33	M	Mason	Scotland	U.S.	Curler	19 Jul 1828
John	37	M	Merchant	Quebec	U. States	New York	15 Nov 1823
John	45	M		Great Brittain		Corinthian	9 Jan 1827
Joseph	7			Ireland	United States	Jno. Dickinson	21 Sep 1821
Louellan	33	M	Farmer	Great Britain	United States	Favorite	10 Dec 1822
Margt.	42	F				Cassack	25 Jul 1820
Mary	10	F		Dundee, Scotland	U. States	Hector	16 May 1821
Mary	11			Ireland	United States	Jno. Dickinson	21 Sep 1821
Mary	18	F	Labourer	Alvey Invonsshire, Scotland	Gt. Britain	Orozimbo	19 Oct 1822
Mary Jane	9	F	family of Merchant [William]	England	United States	Comet	6 Mar 1823
Philip	...	M	...	...	...	Frances Henrietta	30 Jun 1827
Richard	1	M	family of Merchant [William]	England	United States	Comet	6 Mar 1823
Sarah	25			Ireland	United States	Jno. Dickinson	21 Sep 1821
Thomas	29	M	Planter	America	U. States	Brutus	21 May 1824
Thomas	30	M	Merchant	Boston	Boston	Herald	23 Jun 1827
Thomas	40	M	Gentleman	London	America	Evelina	10 Nov 1825
Thos.	20	M	Labourer			Hanford	17 Jul 1828
Thos.	32	M	Merchant	Connecticut	U. States	Mentor	26 Jul 1825
Thos.	40	M	Merchant	Scotland	New York	Hector	11 Oct 1822
Virginia	6	F	family of Merchant [William]	England	United States	Comet	6 Mar 1823
W., Jr.	25	M	Merchant	Gt. Britian	United States	Cortes	11 Dec 1822
William	25	M	Farmer	Great Britain	United States	Mary & Harriet	3 Jul 1829
William	26	M	Merchant	England	World	James Cropper	3 Mar 1825
William	28	M	Merchant	Scotland	England	New York	3 Apr 1826
William	50	M	Merchant	England	United States	Comet	6 Mar 1823
William	52 4/12	M	Merchant	Great Britain	U.S.A.	Silas Richards	27 Oct 1826
Wm.	20	M	Merchant	British ...	American States	Loyalty	9 Sep 1822
Wm.	21	M	Merchant	Great Britain	United States	Cortes	18 Oct 1820
Wm. A.	22	M	Merchant	Charleston	United States	Hogarth	12 Oct 1829
DAVIE, Albert	29		C...	United States	U. States	New York	30 Oct 1827
Allison	25	M	Shipmaster	Great Britiann	United States	Nestor	13 Mar 1824
Catharine	24			Great Britain	United States	Gomer	21 May 1828
David	1			Great Britain	United States	Gomer	21 May 1828
Robert	27		Farmer	Great Britain	United States	Gomer	21 May 1828
DAVIES, Ann	3	F		Ireland	U. States	William	27 Jul 1824
Ann	10	F	None	Wales		Marchioness	13 May 1828
Ann	27	F	Farmer	Britain	U. States	Fame	3 Jun 1828
Ann	43	F	None	Wales	Utica, U.S.	Angelica	18 Aug 1823
Benj.	29	M	Shoemaker	G. Braitan	U. States	Cosmo	29 Jun 1826
C. F.	24	M	Merchant	U. States	United States	Burdett	30 Apr 1828
Catharine	38	F		Ireland	U. States	William	27 Jul 1824
Daniel	34	M	Spinner	England	United States	Trident	30 Sep 1826
David	1	M	None	Wales		Marchioness	13 May 1828
David	5	M		Ireland	U. States	William	27 Jul 1824
David	25	M	Farmer	England	United States	Jubilee	1 Oct 1828
David	27	M	Merchant	New Orleans	New Orleans	Tabasco	6 Apr 1826
David	36	M	Labourer	Wales		Marchioness	13 May 1828
Edward	33		Joiner	Cardigan		Mount Vernon	18 Oct 1822
Edwd.	25	M	Farmer	G. Britain	United States	Fairy	18 Feb 1825
Edwin	43	M	None	Great Brittan	United States	America	24 Jul 1827
Elisabeth	47	F	None	Great Brittan	United States	America	24 Jul 1827
Elizabeth	2	F		Ireland	U. States	William	27 Jul 1824
Ellen	6	F	None	Wales	Utica, U.S.	Angelica	18 Aug 1823
Ellen	22	F	None	England	United States	Jubilee	1 Oct 1828
Enoch	25		Chair Maker	U. States	U. States	Wave	21 May 1821
Evan	23	M	Farmer	Great Britain	United States	Mary & Harriet	3 Jul 1829
Ewan	42	M	Weaver	Wales	Utica, U.S.	Angelica	18 Aug 1823

NAMES OF PASSENGERS	AGE	SEX	OCCUPATIONS	COUNTRY TO WHICH THEY BELONG	COUNTRY THEY INTEND TO INHABIT	SHIPS/DATES OF ARRIVAL	
DAVIES (cont'd)							
Geo.	24	M	Farmer	G. Braitan	U. States	Cosmo	29 Jun 1826
Hannah	3	F	None	Wales		Marchioness	13 May 1828
Hy.	16	M		England	United States	Exchange	18 Nov 1822
Jacob D.	23 10/12	M	Merchant	America	America	Elias Burger	19 Dec 1820
Jane	7			Cardigan		Mount Vernon	18 Oct 1822
John	1			Cardigan		Mount Vernon	18 Oct 1822
John	6	M	None	Wales		Marchioness	13 May 1828
John	24	M	Farmer	England	United States	Cosmo	21 Aug 1828
John	33	M	Farmer	Ireland	U. States	William	27 Jul 1824
John Lloyd	26		Gentn.	England	United States	Corinthian	30 May 1828
Judith	37	F	None	Wales		Marchioness	13 May 1828
Margaret	2	F		Ireland	U. States	William	27 Jul 1824
Margaret	9	F	None	Wales	Utica, U.S.	Angelica	18 Aug 1823
Mary	1	F		Ireland	U. States	William	27 Jul 1824
Mary	6	F	None	Scotland	United States	Washington	2 Oct 1828
Mary	26	F		Ireland	U. States	William	27 Jul 1824
Naome	34			Cardigan		Mount Vernon	18 Oct 1822
Richard	3	M		Ireland	U. States	William	27 Jul 1824
Richd.	24	M	Farmer	Britain	U. States	Fame	3 Jun 1828
Robert	3	M	None	Wales	Utica, U.S.	Angelica	18 Aug 1823
Thomas	5	M	None	Wales		Marchioness	13 May 1828
Thomas	22	M	Labourer	Ireland	United States	Trident	18 Jul 1827
Thomas	28	M	Labourer	Wales	United States	Orozimbo	11 Aug 1823
William	45	M	Farmer	Great Brittan	United States	America	24 Jul 1827
William	52	M	Farmer	U. States	U. States	Corinthian	4 Jan 1825
Wm.	46	M	Cradleman	England	United States	Exchange	18 Nov 1822
DAVILA, Vecente	34	M	Merchant	Spain	United States	Juliana	25 Jan 1820
DAVILLAUX, John	29	M	Merchant	New York	America	Don Quixotte	2 Jun 1828
DAVIN, Lighton	24	M	Labourer	Ireland	U. States	Nancy	1 Sep 1823
DAVIS, —, Capt.	40	M	Capt. Brig	England	U. States	Bayard	5 Sep 1828
—, Lawrence wife	35	F	L	America	U. States	Rebecca	17 Aug 1824
—, Mr.	38	M	Merchant	England	England	Tontine	1 Jun 1826
—, Mrs.	25	F	None	England	England	Manchester	8 Dec 1827
...	32	F		Great Britian	United States	London	24 Jun 1823
Albert	21	M		England	England	Amity	31 May 1822
Andrew	23	M	Labourer	Ireland	New York	America	1 Aug 1828
Ann	9	F	None	Great Britain	United States	Milton	21 Mar 1828
Ann	20	F	Seamstress	England	United States	Ganges	10 May 1828
Ann	22	F	Blacksmith	Great Britain	United States	Thomas Dickason	31 Jul 1829
Ann	28	F		Jamaica	U. States	Milo	24 Jun 1824
Ann	35	F	None	Great Britain	United States	Milton	21 Mar 1828
Ann, Miss	11	F	None	Grate Britain	...	Courier	14 Jun 1825
Ann Jane	22	F	Milliner	Irereland	America	Carolina Ann	20 Jun 1825
Archd.	34	M	Tailor	Scotland	United States	Samuel Robertson	5 Oct 1827
B.	22	M	Merchant	U. States	U. States	Betsey	6 May 1826
Ben...	...			Stonebridge	England	Great Britain	7 May 1827
Benjamin	11	M		Great Britian	United States	London	24 Jun 1823
Benjamin	26 7/12	M	pudler		uncertain	Mount Vernon	29 Aug 1828
Benjm.	8	M				Rebecca	17 Aug 1824
Benjn.	21	M	Shoemaker	England	United States	Euphrates	12 May 1823
Benjn.	38	M	Merchant	England	United States	Great Britain	5 Sep 1827
Benn.	23		Labourer	Stonebridge	England	Great Britain	7 May 1827
C. A.	25	M	Merchant	New York	U. States	New Priscilla	22 Aug 1823
Caroline	2	F	None	Great Britain	United States	Milton	21 Mar 1828
Caroline	3	F	Farmer	England	Troy, N.Y.	Chelsea	16 May 1828
Catharine	26	F	Labourer	Ireland	United States	General Marion	6 Oct 1828
Catherine, Miss	21	F	None	Grate Britain	...	Courier	14 Jun 1825
Charles	35	M	Labourer	England	England	Sir James Kempt	10 Dec 1827
Chas.	30	M	Merchant	U. States	U. States	Hiram	17 Feb 1827
Clarah	22	F	Labourer	Ireland	United States	General Marion	6 Oct 1828
Clement	26	M	...ter	Great Britian	United States	Columbia	17 Apr 1827
Daniel	2	M	None	Grate Britain	...	Courier	14 Jun 1825
Daniel	23	M	Gentleman	United States		Elias Burger	28 May 1821
Daniel	40	M	Gentn.	England	England	William Byrnes	13 Aug 1829
Danl., Jr.	25	M	Labourer	Ireland	U. States	William & John	10 Jul 1824
David	9	M		Great Britian	United States	London	24 Jun 1823

NAMES OF PASSENGERS	AGE	SEX	OCCUPATIONS	COUNTRY TO WHICH THEY BELONG	COUNTRY THEY INTEND TO INHABIT	SHIPS/DATES OF ARRIVAL	
DAVIS (cont'd)							
David	12	M		Great Britain	United States	Mary	11 Jul 1820
David	22	M	Merchant	Wales	U. States	Constitution	16 Sep 1823
David	25	M	Carpenter	U. States	United States	Trident	22 Jan 1822
David	35		Weaver	England	United States	Hudson	5 Apr 1826
David	50	M		Great Britain	United States	Mary	11 Jul 1820
David, Mr.	15	M	None	Grate Britain	...	Courier	14 Jun 1825
Delia	1	F	Child	Ireland	United States	Sarah G.	20 Jul 1827
E. A.	26 3/12	M	Mariner	U. States	U. States	Gleaner	6 Jun 1828
Edward	23	M	Miner	Great Britain	United States	Thomas Dickason	31 Jul 1829
Edward	32	M		Gt. Britain	Gt. Britain	Silvanus Jenkins	24 Jul 1828
Edwd.	19	M	Doctor	Great Britten	England	Cortes	6 Mar 1827
Eleanor, Wife [of John]	39	F	Farmer	Wales		Gomer	22 May 1827
Elie	28	M	Barber	France	United States	Paris	10 Sep 1823
Eliza	12	F	None	Great Britain	United States	Milton	21 Mar 1828
Eliza, Miss	18	F	Spinster	U. States	U. States	Arringdon	8 May 1826
Eliza Jane	20			Great Britain	United States	Thomas Dickason	29 Aug 1828
Elizabeth	26 11/12	F		Great Britain	United States	Courier	23 Feb 1824
Elizabeth	38	F		South Wales	U. States	Hudson	10 Nov 1825
Elizabeth	50	F	Seamstress			Hudson	23 Jul 1828
Elizabeth, Miss	17	F	None	Grate Britain	...	Courier	14 Jun 1825
Ellenor	20	F		Irereland	America	Carolina Ann	20 Jun 1825
Emelia	16	F		England	U. States	Criterion	12 Jun 1823
F. A.	27	M	Gentleman	England	U. States	Milton	6 Dec 1825
Francis J.	25	M	Merchant	St. Johns	United States	Nancey	13 May 1822
G. Y.	35	M	Merchant	England	U. States	New York	4 Nov 1824
Geo.	4	M		England	U. States	Columbia	7 Jul 1824
George	1	M	None	Great Britain	United States	Milton	21 Mar 1828
George	6	M	Child	Ireland	United States	Sarah G.	20 Jul 1827
George	24	M	Merchant	U. States	U. States	Margaret Mercer	3 May 1826
George	35	M	Gentleman	Ireland	United States	Sarah G.	20 Jul 1827
Golder	7	M		Great Britian	United States	London	24 Jun 1823
Griffith	21	M	Labourer	Wales		Gomer	22 May 1827
Hannah	21	F		England	U. States	John Wells	16 May 1825
Hannah	31	F		Gloucestershire	New York	New York	31 Jul 1829
Harriet	3	F	Farmer	England	In the Country	Chelsea	16 May 1828
Henry	15	M	Farmer	England	In the Country	Chelsea	16 May 1828
Henry	17	M	Farmer	G. Britain	United States	New York	12 Nov 1822
Henry	42	M	Mechanic	England	U. States	Criterion	12 Jun 1823
Henry	45	M	Mercht.	G. Britain	G. Britain	Wallace	12 Apr 1824
*Died							
Hugh	24		Servant	England	England	Hudson	18 Jun 1825
Hugh	39		Planter	Great Britain	unknown	South Carolina Packet	7 Jul 1821
Hugh	51	M	Confectioner	England	U. States	Cincinnatus	9 Jul 1825
Humphrey	8	M		Great Britian	United States	London	24 Jun 1823
J.	28	M	Mercht.	London	Engld.	Criterion	9 Aug 1826
J.	41	M	Merchant	England	Canada	James Monroe	29 Apr 1823
J. C.	26	M	Farmer	England	America	Farmer	15 Nov 1823
J. F.	29	M	Ma...	New York	New York	Elizabeth	6 Oct 1827
J. M.	27	M	Merchant	U. States	U. States	General Paez	30 Apr 1827
Jacob	29	M	Merchant	America	United States	Euphrates	12 May 1823
Jacob	34	M	Leather Merchant	G. Britain	G. Britain	Brittania	17 Jul 1828
James	18	M	Farmer	England	In the Country	Chelsea	16 May 1828
James	26	M	...	Ireland	U. States	William & John	10 Jul 1824
James	41	M	Merchant	England	U. States	Columbia	7 Jul 1824
James R.	22	M	Mariner	Boston	U. States	Trident	13 Aug 1823
Jane	17	F				Acosta	28 Jul 1823
Jane	25	F		England	America	Two Marys	24 Sep 1827
Jane	32	F	Farmer	England	Albany, N.Y.	Chelsea	16 May 1828
Jno.	20		Seaman	North Yarmouth		Hudson	16 Jun 1825

*Officers, Seamen and Passengers belonging to the Ship Jane of Boston and taken from on board the Schooner Olive of St. Johns , N.B. on the 4th June 1825, Lat. 41.30, Long 53.19, which ship foundered on the 31st ultimo in Lat. 41.44 Long 52.

Jno.	20	M	Farmer	Great Britain	United States	John Jay	8 May 1828
Jno.	24	M	Farmer	Great Britain	America	Lady Gallatin	21 Jun 1820
Jno.	24	M	Curier	England	U. States	William	17 Jun 1823

NAMES OF PASSENGERS	AGE	SEX	OCCUPATIONS	COUNTRY TO WHICH THEY BELONG	COUNTRY THEY INTEND TO INHABIT	SHIPS/DATES OF ARRIVAL	
DAVIS (cont'd)							
Jno. H.	32	M	Mariner	Salem	U. States	Cygnet	17 Jan 1824
John	1	M		England	U. States	John Wells	16 May 1825
John	8	M	Farmer	England	Albany, N.Y.	Chelsea	16 May 1828
John	10	M		Great Britian	United States	London	24 Jun 1823
John	18	M	Manuir	England	United States	Dalhouse Castle	6 Sep 1827
John	22	M	...	G. Britain	U. States	New England	28 Sep 1824
John	24	M	Farmer	Ireland	United States	Princess Charlotte	6 Oct 1827
John	24	M	Farmer	England	Troy, N.Y.	Chelsea	16 May 1828
John	24	M	Labourer	G. Britain	U. States	St. George	7 Jun 1828
John	29	M	Shoemaker	G. Britain	U. States	Armadello	22 Jun 1827
John	29	M	Goldsmith	Germany	United States	Henry Kneeland	5 Nov 1828
John	32	M		England	England	Amity	31 May 1822
John	32	M	Farmer	Machias	U. States	Borneo	4 Dec 1824
John	32	M	Master Mariner	United States	United States	Eliza	12 May 1828
John	32	M	Cotton Spinner	Great Britain	U.S. of America	Gratitude	3 Oct 1829
John	34 6/12	M	Merchant	Spain	Spain	Henry	29 May 1828
John	36 9/12	M	Gentleman	Great Britain	United States	Courier	23 Feb 1824
John	38	M	Merchant	England	New York	Brighton	9 Dec 1828
John	40	M	Farmer	Wales		Gomer	22 May 1827
John	40	M	Labourer	England	New Jersey	Lima	5 Aug 1829
John	40	M		Ireland	U. States	Lima	5 Aug 1829
John	50 3/12	M	Ship Master	U. States	U. States	Jupiter	4 Aug 1829
John, & family	36 1/12	M	Farmer	England	Albany, N.Y.	Chelsea	16 May 1828
John, & family	50	M	Farmer	England	In the Country	Chelsea	16 May 1828
John, child [of John]	16	M	Farmer	Wales		Gomer	22 May 1827
Jonathan	22	M	Farmer	West Island		Mount Vernon	7 Jun 1824
Jonathan	24	M	Merchant	England	United States	Great Britain	5 Sep 1827
Jos.	19	M		G. Britain	U. States	Canada	19 Sep 1828
Joseph	5	M	Confectioner	England	U. States	Cincinnatus	9 Jul 1825
Joseph	24	M	Miner	England	U.S. States	Splendid	14 Aug 1829
Joseph L.	35	M	Servant	England	America	William	21 Sep 1821
Josephine	35	F		New York	New York	John London	8 May 1823
Joshua	2	M		England	U. States	Columbia	7 Jul 1824
Joshua	25	M	Carpenter	England	U. States	Washington	7 Jul 1824
Joshua	40	M	Planter	England	U. States	Zion	7 Oct 1823
Joshua	48	M	Nailmaker	Great Briton	United States	Mount Vernon	30 Dec 1828
Kildedale	26	M	Brewer	Great Brittan	U.S.	Emulous	29 Jun 1827
Kitty	33	F	Wife	Ireland	United States	Sarah G.	20 Jul 1827
Latitia	48			Great Britain	United States	Thomas Dickason	29 Aug 1828
Lawrence	10	M		America	U. States	Rebecca	17 Aug 1824
Lawrence A.	40	M	Gentleman	America	U. States	Rebecca	17 Aug 1824
Lucretier	39			England	U. States	Corinthian	8 Oct 1828
Lydia	15	F		New York	New York	John London	8 May 1823
Lydia	42	F		Gt. Brittain	United States	Herald	24 May 1826
Margaret	59			Great Britain	United States	Mary	11 Jul 1820
Margaret A.	22			Great Britain	United States	Thomas Dickason	29 Aug 1828
Marry	32 6/12	F	...	Great Britain	United States	Hopes Delight	26 Aug 1829
Mary	1 1/2	F		South Wales	U. States	Hudson	10 Nov 1825
Mary	2	F	Blacksmith	Great Britain	United States	Thomas Dickason	31 Jul 1829
Mary	10	F		Great Britain	United States	Mary	11 Jul 1820
Mary	16	M		Great Britain	United States	Mary	11 Jul 1820
Mary	18	F		Great Brittan	U. States	Prince Leopold	2 Jul 1821
Mary	25	F	None	America	United States	Euphrates	12 May 1823
Mary	26	F		England	England	Amity	31 May 1822
Mary	30	F	Servant	Great Britain	U. States	Columbia	22 Sep 1828
Mary	34	F		England	Canada	Acasta	14 Jun 1824
Mary	35	F	None	Great Britain		Casanda	5 Sep 1827
Mary	40	F	None	United States	New York	Cincinnatus	16 Apr 1824
Mary, child [of John]	18	F	Farmer	Wales		Gomer	22 May 1827
Mary, Miss	13	F	None	Grate Britain	...	Courier	14 Jun 1825
Mary, Miss	18	F		England	Havana	Eliza Pigott	23 Mar 1824
Mary, Mrs.	40	F	None	Grate Britain	...	Courier	14 Jun 1825
Mary Ann	4	F	None	America	United States	Euphrates	12 May 1823
Mary Ann	28	F	None	Halifax	U. States	Loire	7 Jul 1827

NAMES OF PASSENGERS	AGE	SEX	OCCUPATIONS	COUNTRY TO WHICH THEY BELONG	COUNTRY THEY INTEND TO INHABIT	SHIPS/DATES OF ARRIVAL	
DAVIS (cont'd)							
Mathew	26	M	Mechanic	England	U. States	John Wells	16 May 1825
Matilda	5	F	None	Great Britain	United States	Milton	21 Mar 1828
Matilda	18	F		U. States	U. States	Pedler	2 Jul 1823
Mose	61		Merchant	Germany	United States	Hudson	18 Jun 1825
Neal	26	M	Brewer	Great Brittan	U.S.	Emulous	29 Jun 1827
O.	50	M	Farmer	Great Britain	United States	Saml. Wight	6 Sep 1827
Oscar	26	M	Navy Officer	Philadelphia	Philadelphia	Independence	25 Oct 1828
Pedre	20	M	Servant	United States	United States	Frances	19 Feb 1829
Rebecca	2	F		Bristol, Engl.	...	Warrior	19 May 1828
Rebecca	28	F		Bristol, Engl.	...	Warrior	19 May 1828
Rebecca	38	F	Confectioner	England	U. States	Cincinnatus	9 Jul 1825
Richard	59	M	Hair Dresser	England	New York	Indian Chief	19 Jun 1823
Richard, Mr.	9	M	None	Grate Britain	...	Courier	14 Jun 1825
Richd.	9	M	Confectioner	England	U. States	Cincinnatus	9 Jul 1825
Richd.	23	M	Labourer	Great Britain		Moro Castle	6 Jul 1827
Robt.	19	M	...	G. Britain	U. States	New England	28 Sep 1824
Roger	18		None	Ireland	New York	Albion	11 Oct 1821
S., Miss	25	F		England	Havana	Eliza Pigott	23 Mar 1824
Saml.	28	M	Sadler	U. States	U. States	Prince Edward	5 Jul 1825
Saml. J.	3	M	Confectioner	England	U. States	Cincinnatus	9 Jul 1825
Samuel	1	M	Farmer	England	Albany, N.Y.	Chelsea	16 May 1828
Sarah	40	M	Merchant	England	U. States	Columbia	7 Jul 1824
Sarry	24					Amphion	31 May 1824
Shadrick, Mast.	6	M	None	Grate Britain	...	Courier	14 Jun 1825
Shadrick, Revd.	45	M	Minister of Gos.	Grate Britain	...	Courier	14 Jun 1825
Stephen	31	M	Mechanic	N. York	U. States	Elizabeth	24 Feb 1823
Stephen S.	35	M	Merchant	United States	United States	Orient	17 Feb 1829
T.	23	M	Shoe Maker	G. Brittain	U. States	Elias Burger	30 Nov 1822
Thomas	3	M	Child	Ireland	United States	Sarah G.	20 Jul 1827
Thomas	8	M	None	Great Britain	United States	Milton	21 Mar 1828
Thomas	10	M	Farmer	England	Albany, N.Y.	Chelsea	16 May 1828
Thomas	17	M	Brewer	G. Britain	G. Britain	Brittania	17 Jul 1828
Thomas	22	M	Weaver	Ireland	U. States	Josephine	7 May 1827
Thomas	22	M	Moulder	England		Britannia	20 Jun 1827
Thomas	22	M	Blacksmith	Great Britain	United States	Thomas Dickason	31 Jul 1829
Thomas	25	M	Laborer			Plato	31 Oct 1829
Thomas	26	M	Curier	England	U. States	William	17 Jun 1823
Thomas	27	M	Engineer	England	United States	Corinthian	10 Jan 1826
Thomas	28	M	Carpenter	Bristol, Engl.	...	Warrior	19 May 1828
Thomas	30	M	Weaver	Scotland	United States	Washington	2 Oct 1828
Thomas	35		Carpenter	United States	United States	Iris	26 Jun 1821
Thomas	40	M	Mariner	U. States	U. States	Tuscaloosa	31 Oct 1825
Thomas	42	M	Merchant	United States	United States	Robert Read	19 Oct 1825
Thoms.	22	M	Miner	England	U.S. States	Splendid	14 Aug 1829
Thos.	27	M	...	U. States	U. States	York	10 Dec 1825
Thos.	33 8/12	M	Carpenter	New York	New York	Harriot	1 May 1822
Tobias	24 1/12	M	Seaman	Salem	United States	Eagle	20 Mar 1824
Virginia	4	F		Jamaica	U. States	Milo	24 Jun 1824
W.	35	M	Grass Cutter	Great Britian	United States	London	24 Jun 1823
W.	40	M	Farmer	G. Britain	U. States	St. George	7 Jun 1828
Walther	70	M	Farmer	Gt. Britain	United States	Robert Edwards	1 Jun 1826
William	12	M	Farmer	England	Albany, N.Y.	Chelsea	16 May 1828
William	14			Great Britain	United States	Thomas Dickason	29 Aug 1828
William	21	M	Farmer	England	In the Country	Chelsea	16 May 1828
William	21	M	Grocer			Plato	31 Oct 1829
William	28	M	Sailor	United States	United States	Jeune Antoinette	31 Oct 1829
William	30	M	Labourer	England	America	William	21 Sep 1821
William	32	M	Farmer	Scotland	U.S. of America	Friends	10 May 1823
William	35	M	Gent.	England	United States	Cosmo	26 Aug 1829
William	35	M	Tailor	G.B.	New York	Eliza Grant	29 Aug 1829
William	35	M	Tailor	Great Britain		Eliza Grant	29 Aug 1829
William	48	M	Cabinet Maker	South Wales	U. States	Hudson	10 Nov 1825
William	52		Architect	Great Britain	United States	Thomas Dickason	29 Aug 1828
Wm.	4	M	None	Scotland	United States	Washington	2 Oct 1828
Wm.	4	M	None	Scotland	United States	Washington	2 Oct 1828

NAMES OF PASSENGERS	AGE	SEX	OCCUPATIONS	COUNTRY TO WHICH THEY BELONG	COUNTRY THEY INTEND TO INHABIT	SHIPS/DATES OF ARRIVAL	
DAVIS (cont'd)							
Wm.	7	M	Confectioner	England	U. States	Cincinnatus	9 Jul 1825
Wm.	19	M	Clerk	Younghall, Great Britain	United States	Union	24 Sep 1823
Wm.	45	M	Farmer	G. Britain	United States	New York	12 Nov 1822
Wm.	45	M	Farmer	United States	United States	Corinthian	29 Apr 1826
Wm. Lane	30	M	Gentl.	Willington, Lalap	London	Aldebaron	21 Jan 1826
DAVISE, Benj.	18	M	Fruit Seller	England	United States	Acasta	25 Sep 1827
David	60	M	Clothier	England	United States	Acasta	25 Sep 1827
Eltha	52	F		England	United States	Acasta	25 Sep 1827
Fanny	11 2/12	F		England	United States	Acasta	25 Sep 1827
Henry	20 1/12	M	Fruit Seller	England	United States	Acasta	25 Sep 1827
Maria	26	F		England	United States	Acasta	25 Sep 1827
Mark	22 4/12	M	Fruit Seller	England	United States	Acasta	25 Sep 1827
Rachel	24	F		England	United States	Acasta	25 Sep 1827
Solomon	9	M	Fruit Seller	England	United States	Acasta	25 Sep 1827
DAVISON, Alex	20	M	Tailor	Gt. Britain	U. States	Eldon	21 Aug 1827
Christie	12	F	Labourer	Ireland	United States	Meteor	26 Jun 1827
George	40	M	Weaver	Ireland	N. Jersey	Potomac	7 Aug 1827
Hannah	25	F		Gt. Britain	Canada	Diana	28 Apr 1828
James	4/12		Boy	Ireland	N. Jersey	Potomac	7 Aug 1827
John	6/12	M		Gt. Britain	Canada	Diana	28 Apr 1828
John	34	M	Farmer	Gt. Britain	Canada	Diana	28 Apr 1828
John E.						Venus	12 Apr 1821
Margaret	20	F	Servant	St. John, N.B.	St. John, N.B.	Loire	3 Dec 1821
Mary	5	F	Labourer	Ireland	United States	Meteor	26 Jun 1827
Mary	28	F		Ireland	N. Jersey	Potomac	7 Aug 1827
Robert	2	M		Gt. Britain	Canada	Diana	28 Apr 1828
Robert	4	M	Labourer	Ireland	United States	Meteor	26 Jun 1827
Sarah	9	F	Labourer	Ireland	United States	Meteor	26 Jun 1827
Sarah	32	F	Labourer	Ireland	United States	Meteor	26 Jun 1827
Thomas	5	M		Gt. Britain	Canada	Diana	28 Apr 1828
Thos.	24	M	Labourer	Ireland	U.S.	Oliver Wolcott	3 Nov 1827
DAVISS, Elizabeth	28	F	None	Scotland	United States	Washington	2 Oct 1828
Mary	28	F	Servant	Ireland	United States	Sylvester Healy	19 Aug 1825
DAVISSON, Benjamin	21	M	Baker	Great Britain	U. States	Hannibal	12 Oct 1829
DAVIT, Nancey	28	F		Ireland	United States	Nancy R. Crowell	21 Sep 1822
DAVITT, Mary	18	F	Servant	Ireland	America	Carolina Ann	7 Aug 1826
DAVOL, George	10	M	Student	U.N. States	U.N. States	Ariel	5 Dec 1828
DAVY, H. C.	45	M	Mariner	U. States	U. States	Mary Olivia	10 Jul 1824
Thomas	16	M	Labourer	England and Ireland	United States	Jubilee	12 May 1828
DAW, Edmund	18		Carpenter	England	S. New York	Xenophon	25 Jul 1826
DAWN, Ellen	20	F		England	United States	Ann Maria	27 Aug 1822
DAWNS, Helen	2		Child	Glasgow, Scotland	Great Britain	Iris	15 Jun 1822
Mary	30		Widow	Glasgow, Scotland	Great Britain	Iris	15 Jun 1822
DAWS, Augustus	1/12	M	Child	Great Brittan	United States	Cambria	11 Feb 1829
Sarah	30	F	Wife	Great Brittan	United States	Cambria	11 Feb 1829
Sophia	1 4/12	F	Child	Great Brittan	United States	Cambria	11 Feb 1829
William	27	M	Farmer	Great Brittan	United States	Cambria	11 Feb 1829
William	56	M	Husbandry	Great Britain	United States	Bolivar	21 May 1827
William, Jr.	2 6/12	M	Child	Great Brittan	United States	Cambria	11 Feb 1829
DAWSON, Allen	8	M		G. Britain	U. States	Freak	9 Jun 1828
Allice	28	F	None	Blackburn	Blackburn	Howard Douglass	11 May 1827
Andrew	30	M	Labourer	Great Brittain	United States	Active	12 Sep 1828
Ann	6	F	None	Blackburn	Blackburn	Howard Douglass	11 May 1827
Ann	35	F		G. Britain	U. States	Freak	9 Jun 1828
Arthur	35	M	Merchant	England	U. States	Pomona	4 Apr 1823
Catherine	2	F	Child of T. Dawson	St. John, N.B.	United States	St. Michaels	12 Jun 1826
Charles	35	M	Labourer	Great Britain		Moro Castle	6 Jul 1827
Christina	27	...	...	Great Britain	United States	Colossus	5 Jun 1827
David	25	M	Accoantant	Scotland	America	Franklin	19 Nov 1828
Edward	45	M	Stone Mason	Great Britian	United States	George Clinton	21 Oct 1826

NAMES OF PASSENGERS	AGE	SEX	OCCUPATIONS	COUNTRY TO WHICH THEY BELONG	COUNTRY THEY INTEND TO INHABIT	SHIPS/DATES OF ARRIVAL	
DAWSON (cont'd)							
Elisabeth	27	F	Labourer	Ireland	United States	Meteor	26 Jun 1827
Elizabeth	7 3/12	F	Domestic	Ireland	United States	London	6 Feb 1829
Elizabeth	20	F		England	America	John Adams	2 Aug 1827
F.	23	M	Merchant	England	U. States	Columbia	20 Jul 1825
Geo.	16	M	Labourer	Ireland	United States	Thomas	13 Dec 1827
George	4	M	Child of T. Dawson	St. John, N.B.	United States	St. Michaels	12 Jun 1826
George	26 9/12	M	Taylor	Ireland	United States	London	6 Feb 1829
Hannah	9 6/12	F	Domestic	Ireland	United States	London	6 Feb 1829
Hannah	29	F	None	Great Britain	United States	Cortes	18 Oct 1820
Henry	4	M	None	Blackburn	Blackburn	Howard Douglass	11 May 1827
Henry	6	M	Child of T. Dawson	St. John, N.B.	United States	St. Michaels	12 Jun 1826
James	27	M	Weaver	Great Britain	United States	Colossus	5 Jun 1827
Jane	29	F		England	U. States	Grand Turk	19 Aug 1823
Jno. Wm.	20	M	Planter	Jamaica		Rebecca	25 Aug 1824
John	2	M	None	Great Britain	United States	Colossus	5 Jun 1827
John	4 5/12	M	Domestic	Ireland	United States	London	6 Feb 1829
John	20	M	Farmer	Ireland	U. States	Dickinson	30 Jul 1825
John	22	M	Farmer	Ireland	United States	Lord Strangford	20 Jun 1826
John	23	M	Fuller	England	U. States	Thomas Ritchie	2 Jul 1827
John	28	M	Farmer	Great Britain	United States	Cortes	18 Oct 1820
John	42	M	Weaver	Blackburn	Blackburn	Howard Douglass	11 May 1827
John, Jr.	1	M	None	Great Britain	United States	Cortes	18 Oct 1820
John P.	50	M	Traveller	Ireland	United States	Delta	24 Oct 1829
Joseph	26 3/12	M	Painter	England	New York or Boston	Concordia	12 Oct 1826
Lucy	18	F		St. Johns	United States	Nancey	13 May 1822
M. S.	14	M		U. States	U. States	Atlanta	5 Jul 1821
Margaret	9/12	F	None	Great Britain	United States	Colossus	5 Jun 1827
Margaret	18	F	Child of T. Dawson	St. John, N.B.	United States	St. Michaels	12 Jun 1826
Margaret	30 2/12	F	Domestic	Ireland	United States	London	6 Feb 1829
Patk.	25	M	Labourer	United States	United States	Trident	16 May 1826
Rachel	14	F	Child of T. Dawson	St. John, N.B.	United States	St. Michaels	12 Jun 1826
Rachel	58	F	Wife of T. Dawson	St. John, N.B.	United States	St. Michaels	12 Jun 1826
Richard	30	M	Farmer, Labourer or Spinster	Ireland	U. States	Meteor	4 Oct 1827
Robert	20	M	Labourer	Scotland	United States	Mary & Susan	5 Aug 1828
Robert	50	M	Blacksmith	G. Britain	U. States	Freak	9 Jun 1828
Robt.	25		Mason	Great Britain	United States	Camillus	12 Sep 1827
Saml.	32	M	Labourer	England	U. States	Frances Henrietta	9 Dec 1823
Stephen	18	M	Merchant	U. States	U. States	Montano	2 Sep 1828
Susan	20	F	Farmer	Ireland	United States	L. M. Pelham	25 Jun 1822
Thomas	12	M	Child of T. Dawson	St. John, N.B.	United States	St. Michaels	12 Jun 1826
Thomas	19	M	...	...	...	Laurel	16 Nov 1824
Thomas	26	M	Carpenter	England	U. States	Grand Turk	19 Aug 1823
Thomas	60	M	Farmer	St. John, N.B.	United States	St. Michaels	12 Jun 1826
Thos.	24	M	Measurer	St. Johns	United States	Antioch	21 Sep 1827
Thos.	40	M	Farmer	G. Britain	Canada	Nancy	12 Aug 1820
William	8	M	Child of T. Dawson	St. John, N.B.	United States	St. Michaels	12 Jun 1826
William	48	M	Merchant	United States	United States	Ariadne	25 Jul 1822
Wm.	37	M	Sadler	Philada.	U. States	Frances Jarvis	11 May 1822
Wm. A.	18	M	Merchant	Port Au Prince	United States	Mazzinghi	27 Feb 1824
DAY, Abel	20	M	Mason	Great Britain	United States	Atlantic	28 May 1827
Ann	16	F	Servant	Great Briton	United States	Erin	26 May 1821
Ann	18	F		Ireland	United States	Thompson	12 Sep 1827
B...	...	F	None	France	U. States	Sully	25 Jun 1828
George O.	2	M		America	America	Silas Richard	24 Oct 1829
J.	30	M	Merchant	England		New York	14 Jul 1827
James	28	M	Husbandry	Great Britan	United States	Bolivar	21 May 1827
James	40	M	Shipmaster	U. States Amer	U. States Amer	Juno	5 Oct 1822
Jane	25	F	None	Great Britain	United States	Bolivar	21 May 1827
Jane	32	F	Spinster	Great Britain	United States	Magnet	28 Jun 1821
Jno.	27	M	Joiner			Belfast	28 Sep 1820
Jno.	48	M	Merchant	England	U. States	New York	4 Nov 1824
John	20	M	Merchant	St. Johns	U. States	Nancy	10 Jul 1822
John	23	M	Tailor	England	United States	Cosmo	26 Aug 1829
John	45 9/12	M	Marinor	U. States	Salem	London Packet	5 Jan 1829

NAMES OF PASSENGERS	AGE	SEX	OCCUPATIONS	COUNTRY TO WHICH THEY BELONG	COUNTRY THEY INTEND TO INHABIT	SHIPS/DATES OF ARRIVAL	
DAY (cont'd)							
John	53	M	Merchant	America	America	Silas Richard	24 Oct 1829
John James	20	M		England	England	Lady Gallatin	26 Sep 1823
Joseph	48	M	Weaver	France	U. States	Sully	25 Jun 1828
L...	...	M	None	France	U. States	Sully	25 Jun 1828
Margaret	11	F	Neice [of Elizabeth Harple]	England	Pennsylvania	General Stark	12 Jun 1826
Margaret	33	F	Spinster	Great Britain	United States	Magnet	28 Jun 1821
Margaret	35	F		America	America	Silas Richard	24 Oct 1829
Mary	42	F	None	France	U. States	Sully	25 Jun 1828
Mary Jane	26	F		Britain	Great Britain	Thompson	26 Apr 1828
S.	21	M	U.S. Army	U. States	U. States	Amos Palmer	29 Sep 1827
Sherman	22 7/12	M		America	America	France	28 Mar 1829
Susan	30	F	None	Port au Prince	United States	Director	6 Sep 1826
William	38	M	Mariner	United States	United States	Eliza	10 Jul 1827
William	73	M	Farmer	Great Britain	United States	Magnet	28 Jun 1821
DAYLE, James	20	M	Hatter	Ireland	U. States	Eliza Grant	29 Aug 1829
DAYLEY, James	29 4/12	M	Mechanic	England	United States	John Wells	22 May 1826
Jas.	19	M	Labourer	Ireland	United States	Essex	23 May 1828
Jas.	22	M	Shoemaker	England	United States	Essex	23 May 1828
DAYTON, Benjamin	29	M	Shipmaster	U. States	U. States	Euphrates	8 Aug 1820
Charles W.	28		Merchant	U.N.S.		Hudson	5 Apr 1826
G.	23	M	Mariner	U. States	U. States	Laura Ann	25 May 1822
Geo. S.	21	M	Clerk	U. States		Mattrawan	7 Jul 1824
Michiel	25 3/12	M	Farmer	Ireland	U.S. America	Illinois	16 Oct 1822
DAZ, Emile	24	F		France	U. States	Danube	21 Nov 1826
DE ...LLO, Frans.	20	M	Mercht.	Spain	U. States	Fair American	16 Oct 1822
DEA...LORE, William	34	M	Farmer	Great Britian	United States	Silvanus Jenkins	6 Apr 1826
DEACON, Ann	24		Farmer	England	U.S. of America	Mary	21 Sep 1821
Ann	25	F	Girl	Ireland	United States	Dublin Packet	22 Apr 1822
Ann	26	F		Great Britain	United States	Spartan	25 Jul 1821
James	27		Carpenter	England	U.S. of America	Mary	21 Sep 1821
John	3	M		Great Britain	United States	Spartan	25 Jul 1821
John	23	M	Cotton Printer	England	America	Hercules	2 Nov 1825
John	57	M	Accountant	United States	United States	Bolivar	21 May 1827
Saml.	26	M	Butcher	England	United States	Siroc	31 Oct 1829
W.	52	M	Merchant	Ireland	U. States	Clarissa	14 Jul 1821
DEAGAN, James M.	24	M	Merchant	United States	United States	Dandy	15 Apr 1824
DEAGO, F.	19	M	Merchant	Spain	U. States	Dromo	22 May 1826
Jos.	30	M	Servant	Spain	Spain	Governor Von Schollen	7 Nov 1827
DEAGON, Milly	12	F		G. Britain	U. States	Dalhouse Castle	12 Sep 1828
DE AGRITTEZ,							
Jerrenino	55	M	Merchant	Portugal	U. States	Minos	24 Oct 1828
DE AIANGO FORISTA,							
Maria Ameria	13	F		Brazil	Brazil	America	16 May 1827
Maria Constantia	12	F		Brazil	Brazil	America	16 May 1827
DEAIR, John	33	M	None	Great Britian	Canada	Silvanus Jenkins	6 Apr 1826
DEAKES, Thomas	20	M	Labourer	Ireland	United States	Atlantic	21 Jul 1827
DEAL, P. Berry	30	M	Merchant	France	U. States	Montano	3 Jan 1825
Wm.	20	M	Labourer	Great Britain		Moro Castle	6 Jul 1827
DEALAFIELD, John	34	M	Merchant	G. Britain		Cassack	25 Jul 1820
DEALEY, Rose	24 2/12	F		Ireland	America	Nancy	28 Jan 1820
DE ALVARA, Manuel	25	M	Gentleman	Spain	U. States	Vigilant	14 Apr 1823
DEALY, Dennis	30		Farmer	Cork	Baltimore	Schuylkill	22 Aug 1825
Jane	35	F	Family	Ireland	United States	Loire	26 May 1828
Jane Eliza	6	F	Family	Ireland	United States	Loire	26 May 1828
John	4	M	Family	Ireland	United States	Loire	26 May 1828
Mary Ann	2	F	Family	Ireland	United States	Loire	26 May 1828
DE ALZOLA, Y.	27	M	Merchant	Spain	Columbia	Don Quixote	15 Apr 1825
DEAMOND, Andrew	36	M	Merchant	England	England	Tontine	1 Jun 1826
DEAN, Alice	3	F		England	United States	Siroc	31 Oct 1829
Alice	32	F		England	United States	Siroc	31 Oct 1829
Ann Jane	15	F	None	Ireland	United States	Princess Charlotte	6 Oct 1827
Benjamin	25	M	Black Maker	England	United States	Siroc	31 Oct 1829
Benjn., Jr.	5	M		England	United States	Siroc	31 Oct 1829
Charles	22	M	Merchant	England	U. States	Calais Packet	3 Sep 1827
Chas.	30	M	Mercht.	Gt. Brittian	United States	Nestor	14 Nov 1823

NAMES OF PASSENGERS	AGE	SEX	OCCUPATIONS	COUNTRY TO WHICH THEY BELONG	COUNTRY THEY INTEND TO INHABIT	SHIPS/DATES OF ARRIVAL	
DEAN (cont'd)							
Chas. A.	18	M	Army	Great Brittain	Canada	Canada	5 Feb 1827
Daniel	43	M	Labourer	Ireland	America	Cincinnatus	22 May 1826
Edward	31	M	Whitener	Ireland	U. States	Hudson	10 Nov 1825
Fanny	18	F	Servant	Ireland	United States	Sylvester Healy	17 Oct 1825
Fradk.	25 5/12	M	...	America	America	Cincinnatus	22 May 1826
Frederick	21	M	Butcher	Brittian	U. States	Acasta	28 Jan 1823
Frederick	27	M	Farmer	U. States	U. States	Hudson	8 Oct 1827
Hannah	40	F		Ireland	America	Liverpool	31 Aug 1827
Henry	50	M	Glass Blower	Ireland	America	Liverpool	31 Aug 1827
Hugh	11	M		Ireland	New York	Atlantic	6 Oct 1828
James	10	M		England	United States	Siroc	31 Oct 1829
James	14	M		Ireland	New York	Atlantic	6 Oct 1828
James	30	M	Merchant	Bolton le Moors	New York	New York	31 Jul 1829
Jas. E.	32	M	Gentleman	Nova Scotia	United States	McDonough	3 Nov 1823
Jean	8	M		England	United States	Siroc	31 Oct 1829
John	3/12	M		Ireland	U. States	Hudson	10 Nov 1825
John	6	M		England	United States	Siroc	31 Oct 1829
John	14	M		Ireland	New York	Atlantic	6 Oct 1828
John B.	32	M	Planter	Barbados, U.S.	West Indies	Spartan	24 Jul 1826
Margaret	12	F		England	United States	Siroc	31 Oct 1829
Margaret	20	F		Great Britain	United States	Lady Hunter	26 Nov 1823
Mariah	27	F	Lady	Nova Scotia	United States	Wanderer	31 Aug 1829
Mary	17	F	None	Ireland	United States	Princess Charlotte	6 Oct 1827
Mary	26	F		Ireland	U. States	Hudson	10 Nov 1825
May	12	F	None	Ireland	United States	Princess Charlotte	6 Oct 1827
Mery	22			St. John	U. States	Lady Hunter	5 Jul 1823
Peter	1	M		England	United States	Siroc	31 Oct 1829
Robert	14	M	None	Ireland	United States	Princess Charlotte	6 Oct 1827
Robert	27	M	Labourer	Ireland	United States	Princess Charlotte	6 Oct 1827
S. H.	20	M	Merchant	U. States	U. States	Rodman	22 Mar 1825
Samuel	18	M	Mechanic	U. States	U. States	Rodney	19 Jun 1827
*Passenger from the Wreck of Schooner Gen. Marion from Charleston to N.Y.							
Sarah	9	F	None	Ireland	United States	Princess Charlotte	6 Oct 1827
Solomon	50	M	Farmer	America	United States	Hesperus	14 Feb 1820
Thomas	23	M	Merchant	England	U.S.	Panthea	13 Nov 1823
Thomas	27	M	Mercht.	United States	United States	Manchester	17 Aug 1825
Thomas	33	M	Stone Mason	Great Britian	United States	George Clinton	21 Oct 1826
W.	31	M	Merchant	U. States	U. States	Enterprize	28 May 1821
*died							
W...	24			St. John	U. States	Lady Hunter	5 Jul 1823
William	30	M		England	New York	Cincinnatus	16 Apr 1824
DE ANDRE, Adolph	8	M	Son of Consul of France	France	United States	Bayard	13 Nov 1823
Alexandrine Durant	13	F	Daughter of Consul of France	France	United States	Bayard	13 Nov 1823
Charlotte	12	F	Daughter of Consul of France	France	United States	Bayard	13 Nov 1823
Durant	46	M	Consul of France	France	United States	Bayard	13 Nov 1823
Durant, Mrs.	31	F	Wife of Consul of France	France	United States	Bayard	13 Nov 1823
Maurice	9/12	M	Son of Consul of France	France	United States	Bayard	13 Nov 1823
Sophie	6	F	Daughter of Consul of France	France	United States	Bayard	13 Nov 1823
DEANE, Ann	55	F		Halifax	New York	Loire	11 Jun 1824
James	30	M	Merchant	Great Brittain	Great Brittain	James Cropper	23 Mar 1827
Maria	14	F		Halifax	New York	Loire	11 Jun 1824
Peter	24	M	Printer	Ireland	United States	Aurelia	7 Jun 1826
DEANS, Elizabeth	20	F	Spinster	Ireland	United States	Robert Fulton	24 Jul 1826
Jane	14	F	Spinster	Ireland	Unitd pStates	Robert Fulton	24 Jul 1826
Mary	54	F	Matron	Ireland	United States	Robert Fulton	24 Jul 1826
DE APBEL, Dom.	42	M	Merchant	United States		General Warren	8 Jul 1829

NAMES OF PASSENGERS	AGE	SEX	OCCUPATIONS	COUNTRY TO WHICH THEY BELONG	COUNTRY THEY INTEND TO INHABIT	SHIPS/DATES OF ARRIVAL	
DEAR, E. Horry, Mr.	24 11/12		Physician	America (U.S.)	South Carolina	Romulus	15 May 1828
John	29	M		England	United States	Hercules	25 Jan 1820
Richard	22	M		England	United States	Hercules	25 Jan 1820
DE ARA, Felix	24	M	Mercht.	Havama	United States	Brown	26 Apr 1826
DE ARAMBUNE, C., Don	31	M	Merchant	Spain	Mexico	Nancy	1 Oct 1824
DEARAND, Alexis	35	M	Miner	England	England	Eliza	31 Jul 1826
DEARDON, James	2...	M	Lab.	Haslender	Haslender	Howard Douglass	11 May 1827
DEAREN, Cathe.	21	F	None	Great Brittan	U. States	Gem	26 Jul 1827
Dennis	24	M	Farmer	Great Brittan	U. States	Gem	26 Jul 1827
Pat	1	M	None	Great Brittan	U. States	Gem	26 Jul 1827
DE ARJARDIN, V.	18	M	Merchant	Cape Hayti	U. States	Topaz	7 Apr 1828
DE ARO, Bar...ola	24	F		Mexico	Spain	Sciot	12 Mar 1828
Maria	7	F		Mexico	Spain	Sciot	12 Mar 1828
DE ARTECHEA, A. J.	21	M	Merchant	Spain	U. States	Jesse	14 Aug 1826
DEARTH, Golden	38	M	Mariner	United States	U. States	Jane	18 Apr 1823
DEAS, Marcos	11	M	None	Cuba	Cuba	Agenora	11 Jun 1824
William	24	M	Laborer	St. John, N.B.	United States	St. Michaels	11 May 1826
DEASEY, Margaret	27					Trio	5 May 1828
DEASY, Mary	23	F	Labourer	Ireland	United States	William & George	14 May 1828
DEATER, L.	33	M	Merchant	U. States	U. States	Napolean	26 Sep 1828
DEATH, Alfred	5	M	None	England	Philadelphia	Orozimbo	8 Jun 1822
Caroline	3	F	None	England	Philadelphia	Orozimbo	8 Jun 1822
Charlotte	23	F	None	England	Philadelphia	Orozimbo	8 Jun 1822
Elizabeth	40	F	None	England	Philadelphia	Orozimbo	8 Jun 1822
Emma	4	F	None	England	Philadelphia	Orozimbo	8 Jun 1822
Francis	8	M	None	England	Philadelphia	Orozimbo	8 Jun 1822
George	6	M	None	England	Philadelphia	Orozimbo	8 Jun 1822
Isaac	1 6/12	M	None	England	Philadelphia	Orozimbo	8 Jun 1822
Jereh.	14	M	None	England	Philadelphia	Orozimbo	8 Jun 1822
John	49	M	Baker	England	Philadelphia	Orozimbo	8 Jun 1822
Mary	22	F	None	England	Philadelphia	Orozimbo	8 Jun 1822
Rebecca	1 6/12	F	None	England	Philadelphia	Orozimbo	8 Jun 1822
Sophia	7	F	None	England	Philadelphia	Orozimbo	8 Jun 1822
DEATON, —, Mr.	46	M	Gentleman	St. Croix	St. Croix	Carlo	19 Apr 1828
DE AUGELES, Gideon	22	M	Gentleman	France	U. States	Vigilant	14 Apr 1823
DEAVIS, Thomas	25					Trio	5 May 1828
DE AYERRAN, Joaquin	36		Gentleman	Mexico	Mexico	Othello	6 Nov 1823
DE AYERRARAN, Antonio Carlos	3		Child of J. De A [Joaquin De Ayerran]	Spain	Mexico	Othello	6 Nov 1823
Dolores	6		Child of J. De A [Joaquin De Ayerran]	Spain	Mexico	Othello	6 Nov 1823
Gaudalup	1		Child of J. De A [Joaquin De Ayerran]	Spain	Mexico	Othello	6 Nov 1823
Joaquin	4		Child of J. De A [Joaquin De Ayerran]	Spain	Mexico	Othello	6 Nov 1823
Luisa	0		Child of J. De A [Joaquin De Ayerran]	Spain	Mexico	Othello	6 Nov 1823
Magdalena	7		Child of J. De A [Joaquin De A yerran]	Spain	Mexico	Othello	6 Nov 1823
R., Mrs.	27		Lady	Spain	Mexico	Othello	6 Nov 1823
DEAYSIN, —, Mrs.	48					Pomona	28 May 1822
DEAZE, Janet	37	F		Scotland	U. States	Superior	25 Sep 1828
DE BASABE, Benanco	40	M	Merchant	Columbia	U. States	Tampico	19 Oct 1826
DEBASQUE, Lewis	35	M	Merchant	U. States	U. States	Andrew Jackson	16 Jun 1821
DEBASTRO, H.	40	M	Merchant	G. Britain		Hope & Polly	17 Aug 1827
DEBAUFAIS, Lewis Athenise	25	M	Farmer	France	United States	Elizabeth	13 Nov 1824
DE BEAR, Adeline	17	F		Charleston	U. States	Rover	28 Oct 1825
Charles A.	9	M		Charleston	U. States	Rover	28 Oct 1825

NAMES OF PASSENGERS	AGE	SEX	OCCUPATIONS	COUNTRY TO WHICH THEY BELONG	COUNTRY THEY INTEND TO INHABIT	SHIPS/DATES OF ARRIVAL	
DE BEAR (cont'd)							
Mary F.	57	F		Charleston	U. States	Rover	28 Oct 1825
DE BEARYSON, Cather.	56	F		Canada	Canada	Cambria	3 Jul 1829
Cather. Char.	20	F		Canada	Canada	Cambria	3 Jul 1829
Geo. R.	19	M	Law	Canada	Canada	Cambria	3 Jul 1829
Terense	58	M	Proprietor	Canada	Canada	Cambria	3 Jul 1829
DE BEHL, De Behl	2	M		Germany	United States	Samuel Robertson	8 Aug 1828
Elizabeth	27	F		Germany	United States	Samuel Robertson	8 Aug 1828
Hance	36	M	Farmer	Germany	United States	Samuel Robertson	8 Aug 1828
DEBELLE, Dan. F.	40	M	Merchant	Isld. Cuba	I. Cuba	Blue Ey'd Mary	26 Jun 1823
Renole	7	M	a boy	Isld. Cuba	I. Cuba	Blue Ey'd Mary	26 Jun 1823
DE BENNE, Jno.	24	M	Brewer	France	United States	Stephania	24 Mar 1828
DEBLACK, Barrish	24	M	Jeweller	Raden	U. States	Comet	28 Jul 1825
DEBOIS, Josephine	20	F	Servant	Nassau, N.P.	Nassau, N.P.	Superior	27 Jun 1825
DE BORJA MONTOTO,							
Francis, Mr.	25	M	Gentleman	Spain	Spain	Florida	26 Sep 1826
DEBOST, C.	40		Merchant	France	U. States	Brown	11 Jun 1827
DE BOUSTON, Ann	23	F		Charleston	U. States	Rover	28 Oct 1825
DE BOYMAKER, Vincent	26	M	Clergyman	Flanders	Kentucky	Abigail	9 Aug 1821
DE BREE, William	28	M	Merchant	United States	United States	Cambria	7 May 1828
DE BRESSEN, Charels	30	M		France	France	Caledonia	10 Sep 1828
DEBRIE, —, Mr.	22	M	Chair Maker	U.S.	U.S.	Robert Edwards	11 Nov 1822
DE BROGUE, Eliza	51	M	Lady	United States	France	Stephania	13 Sep 1821
DEBROUX, M.	30	M	Merchant	France	U. States	Plato	5 Feb 1822
DEBROWE, Ls.	25	M	Merchant	Spain	Spain	Sarah Ann	8 May 1822
DE BUSSON, Chas.	25	M	Sec... Legation	France	France	Montano	3 Jan 1823
DE CAIX, E.	22	M	Gentn.	France	United States	Howard	20 Aug 1827
H.	17	F		U. States	United States	Howard	20 Aug 1827
DE CALA, —, Mrs.	22	F		Mexico	U. States	Desdemona	15 Jun 1827
Manuel	38	M	Merchant	Mexico	U. States	Desdemona	15 Jun 1827
DE CALEUZ DOMINGUES,							
Juan	17	M	A...	Colombia	Colombia	Bunker Hill	10 Dec 1825
DE CAMP, V.	40	M	Comedian	London	U. States	New York	15 Nov 1823
DE CAMPOS, A.	21	M		Portugal	Mexico	York	8 Aug 1829
DECAN, John	20	M	Labourer	Ireland	United States	Dublin Packet	30 Apr 1821
DECARY, Eugene	21	M	Merchant	Nancy	N. York	Stephania	29 Nov 1825
DECASSE, Peter	38	M	Merchant	New Orleans	France	Wilson	25 Sep 1820
DE CASTA, A. Terro.	48	M	Belonging to the Portuguese Legation	Portugal	belonging to the Portuguese Legation	Alexander	18 Mar 1822
Chas.	18	M	Belonging to the Portuguese Legation	Portugal	belonging to the Portuguese Legation	Alexander	18 Mar 1822
DE CASTANEDA,							
M. Josefa	1	F		Mexico	Spain	Sciot	12 Mar 1828
DE CASTELBAGDE, R.	25	M	Courier	France	U.S.	Edward Quesnel	21 Apr 1827
DE CASTRO, Josefa,							
Miss	30			Spain	Mexico	Othello	6 Nov 1823
DE CAUMAN, José							
Jorivio	20	M	Merchant	Spain	U. States	Fabius	9 Jul 1824
DE CAVALLÉE,							
Armand	40	M	Mercht.	France	U. States	Sully	15 Jul 1829
DE CAVES, Joseph	22	M		Spain	Spain	Bayard	16 May 1827
DECEREE, P.	42	M	B...	France	America	La Grange	7 Aug 1828
DE CHAMENT, C. V.	27		Merchant	Hamburg		Constitution	5 Jan 1829
DE CHAMPS, Jos.	35	M	Mechanic	France	U. States	Emblem	15 Apr 1826
DE CHAPPOTIN,							
François	20	M	Merchant	Havana	Spain	Bayard	30 Oct 1820
DE CHATTERTON,							
Henry	42	M	Officer in the Army	France	U. States	Huntress	29 May 1822
DE CHEVET,							
Augustus A.	28	M	Officer	France	France	Cadmus	26 Apr 1824
DE CHRISTO, A.	65	M	Mercht.	Venice, Italy		Aldebaron	21 Jan 1826
DECK, Antoinne	50	M	Farmer	Switzerland	U. States	Henri IV	7 May 1827
Mary	52	F		Switzerland	U. States	Henri IV	7 May 1827

NAMES OF PASSENGERS	AGE	SEX	OCCUPATIONS	COUNTRY TO WHICH THEY BELONG	COUNTRY THEY INTEND TO INHABIT	SHIPS/DATES OF ARRIVAL	
DECKER, Ebenezer K.	45	M	Mechanick	U.S.	U. States	Venus	11 Aug 1820
Jno.	16	M		England		New York Packet	20 Mar 1824
DECKIN, Mary	60	F	Servant	Ireland	United States	Wilson	27 Jun 1826
DECKNER, N. W.	29	M	Grocer	Scotland	United States	Euphrates	8 Nov 1821
DE COMKIR, Abraham	20	M	Farmer	New York		Olive Branch	9 Oct 1829
DECONDER, A.	55	M	Gentleman	France	France	Jupiter	8 Apr 1828
DECONICK, James D.	30	M	Mechanic	Antwerp	Antwerp	Otter	30 Oct 1826
DE CORDOVA, E.	21			Great Britian	Halifax	America	28 Jul 1826
J. R.	28		Merchant	Great Britian	Halifax	America	28 Jul 1826
R.	19/12			Great Britian	Halifax	America	28 Jul 1826
DE COREÉ, d'Agerone	40	M	Farmer	France	U. States	Edward Quesnel	4 Aug 1828
DE COST, Betsy	39	F		U. States	U. States	Cortes	13 Aug 1825
C.	40	M	Merchant	U. States	U. States	Lucy Ann	6 Sep 1826
DE COSTA, James	21	M	Gentleman	Spain	New York	Cordelia	23 Apr 1821
John L.	21	M	Merchant	United States	U.S. of America	Hannibal	17 Dec 1823
Peregrine	38	M	Merchant	England	U. States	Napolean	8 Sep 1828
DECOSTA, O. M.	27	M	Merchant	England	U. States	Hippomenes	30 Aug 1821
DE COSTER, Julia	12	F		St. Croix	U. States	Carlo	6 Oct 1827
DE COUDEY, L.	26	M	Merchant	Havana	Spain	William	1 Apr 1822
DE COUDRY HOLSTIEN, H. L. W.	68	M	Military	Germany	U. States	Mattrawan	5 Apr 1824
DE COURDRAY, L.	27	M	Gentleman	France	U. States	Artibonite	31 Jan 1827
DECOURSEY, Mathew	20	M	Labourer	Ireland	United States	Fabius	31 Jul 1829
DECOUSTE, —, Mrs.	30	F	Lady	France	U. States	Queen Mab	16 Jun 1827
DECREA, M.	24	M	Gentleman	France	U. States	Six Brothers	6 Jul 1824
DE CYAO Y MATAS, Joseph	21	M	Merchant	Spain	Mexico	Leader	19 Aug 1825
DEDE, F.	25	M	Merchant	Germany	Charleston	Maria Elizabeth	16 Feb 1826
DE DENSERD, Wm.	26	M	bearer of dispatches & saild to England		U. States	Hiram	17 Jun 1826
DEDERICK, F.	32	M	Farmer	Holland	U. States	Criterion	12 Jun 1823
DEDRICKEN, N. J.	20	M	Mechanic	Denmark	U. States	Chase	5 Oct 1824
DEE, Mary	28	F	None	Russia	United States	Baltic	17 Aug 1824
Mary	30	F	Lady	England	U. States	Robert Edwards	9 May 1827
DE EASRO GUIMARAINS, Bento, Jr.	13 6/12	M	Gent.	Brazil	New York	American	4 Aug 1823
DEEHEEN, James	22	M	Labourer	Ireland	United States	Trident	16 May 1826
DEEN, J.	20	M	Servant	England	St. Johns	Silvanus Jenkins	24 Jul 1828
DEENY, Fanny	1	F		Ireland	United States	Enterprize	23 Jul 1827
James	35	M	Shoe Maker	Ireland	United States	Enterprize	23 Jul 1827
John	6	M		Ireland	United States	Enterprize	23 Jul 1827
Margaret	30	F		Ireland	United States	Enterprize	23 Jul 1827
Patrick	2	M		Ireland	United States	Enterprize	23 Jul 1827
Thomas	4	M		Ireland	United States	Enterprize	23 Jul 1827
DEEPONTE, Chas.	21	M	Merchant	U. States	U. States	White Oak	24 Apr 1826
DEER, —	...	M	...	Great Britain	United States	Aurora	10 Nov 1827
DE ERNEST, F.		M	Officer	Portugal	Portugal	Diana	7 Jun 1823
DEERY, Mary	20	F	Spinster	Ireland	United States	Robert Fulton	24 Jul 1826
DE ESTRADA, J. M. Gutierrer	26	M	Diplomatic agent	Mexico	Mexico	York	2 Dec 1828
DE ESTRADO, F. G.	21	M	Gentleman	Mexico	South America	York	7 Aug 1828
DEETZ, Fredk.	21	M	Cabt. Maker	France	U. States	Sully	24 Oct 1828
Marguerite	21	F	Merchant	United States		Cincinnatus	29 Apr 1822
DE FABARIN, Jos.	30	M	Merchant	Columbian Republic	Columbian Republic	Meta	5 Jun 1824
DE FERAR CAVALLO, Chicos	33		Planter			Corsair	2 Oct 1820
DE FERNAX, Jean	30	M	Dr. in theology	Geneva	United States	Henry	9 Jun 1826
DEFERRIER, Angel	57 7/12	M	Merchant	U.S. America	U.S. America	Edward Bonnaffe	20 Jun 1826
DE FIGANER, John	13	M	None	Portugal	United States	Emulous	7 Oct 1822
Selina, Madam	20	F		Portugal	United States	Emulous	7 Oct 1822
DE FIGANERO Y MOSEN, H., Chevr.	24	M	Consul of Portugal	Portugal	United States	Emulous	7 Oct 1822
DE FONTERMAN, C.	31	M	Merchant	Netherlands	United States	Union	9 Jan 1824

NAMES OF PASSENGERS	AGE	SEX	OCCUPATIONS	COUNTRY TO WHICH THEY BELONG	COUNTRY THEY INTEND TO INHABIT	SHIPS/DATES OF ARRIVAL	
DE FOREST, A.	36	M	Merchant	New York	United States	Excel	26 Apr 1827
Benjn.	24	M	Merchant	U. States	U. States	South Carolina Packet	28 Apr 1823
L.	40	M	Merchant	Connecticutt	U. States	Parthian	10 May 1824
Lemuel	30	M	Merchant	U. States	U. States	Laura Ann	2 Feb 1820
Lemuel	35	M	Merchant	U. States	U. States	Jason	25 May 1822
S.	29	M	Mercht.	U. States	U. States	Patriot	23 May 1821
DEFOREST, Sidney	38	M	Merchant	Connecticutt	U. States	Susannah	13 Jul 1824
DEFOUST, Alfred	34	M	Merchant	U. States	U. States	South Carolina	30 Jun 1824
DEFREES, Elizabeth, Mrs.	27	F		Massa.	Nantucket	South America	29 Aug 1826
Henry T., Capt.	35	M	Mariner	Massa.	Nantucket	South America	29 Aug 1826
DE FRETERS, M. R.	22	M	Merchant	U. States		Emerald	27 Mar 1822
DE FUGA, Manuel	41	M	Merchant	U. States	U. States	Frances	22 May 1827
DE GANEZ, M.	35	M	Gentleman	Columbia	Columbia	William Bayard	6 Aug 1825
DEGARD, Elizh.	10	F		England	U. States	Auritz	20 May 1823
George	1	M		England	U. States	Auritz	20 May 1823
James	8	M		England	U. States	Auritz	20 May 1823
John	5	M		England	U. States	Auritz	20 May 1823
Joseph	29	M	Store Keeper	England	U. States	Auritz	20 May 1823
Martha	25	F		England	U. States	Auritz	20 May 1823
Mary	3	F		England	U. States	Auritz	20 May 1823
DEGENETAIS, Anne	11 6/12	F		France	United States	Montano	29 Apr 1826
Sophia	38	F		France	United States	Montano	29 Apr 1826
DEGNAN, Ellen	16	F	Servant	Ireland	New York	Atlantic	8 May 1828
DE GRISARRI, Antonio Jose	40	M	Gentleman	Guatemala	South America	York	4 Aug 1826
DEGROAT, Wm. E.	19	M	Merchant	U. States	U. States	McDonough	31 Jul 1821
DE GROEN, Antonious	40	M	Horlogiemaker	Ouden-bosche	United States	Juffraw Johanna	16 Oct 1821
DE GROOT, Jno.	28	M	Merchant	United States	United States	York	31 Mar 1828
John	30	M	Merchant	United States	United States	John Wells	18 Sep 1826
DE GUERRO, M.	50	M	Gentleman	Spain	Spain	Catharine Rogers	6 Oct 1823
DE GYTER, Angimur	23	M	Teacher	England	U.S. America	Cortes	19 May 1826
DEHAMA, John R.	27	M	Merchant	France	U. States	Rodman	19 Dec 1825
DE HANNA, Isah Victor	27	M	Grocer	Great Britian	U. States	Hudson	12 Mar 1824
DEHANNE, Jas.	23	M	Marchant	N. York	U. States	Commodore Perry	9 Apr 1821
DE HART, J. M.	25	M		Holland	Surinam	Factor	10 May 1821
DE HETIAGE, Juan	33	M	Merchant	Spain	U. States	Farmer	16 Feb 1825
DEHIE, Francis	17	M		France	U. States	Damon	18 Nov 1826
DE HIL, Rosalia	26	F		Mexico	Spain	Sciot	12 Mar 1828
*died the 11th March at 7 P.M.							
DEHN, Barbe	30	F	his family [George]	Germany	United States	Wm. Osborne	16 Sep 1828
Catherine	4	F	his family [George]	Germany	United States	Wm. Osborne	16 Sep 1828
Charles	6/12	M	his family [George]	Germany	United States	Wm. Osborne	16 Sep 1828
George	6	M	his family [George]	Germany	United States	Wm. Osborne	16 Sep 1828
George	40	M	Farmer	Germany	United States	Wm. Osborne	16 Sep 1828
Jacob	7	M	his family [George]	Germany	United States	Wm. Osborne	16 Sep 1828
Jean	2	M	his family [George]	Germany	United States	Wm. Osborne	16 Sep 1828
DEHRING, C.	29	M	Tanner	Germany	Germany	Minerva	17 May 1828
DEIDERIDE, Robt.	18	M		New York	U. States	London	13 Sep 1824
DEIGET, Francis	21	M	Merchant	Spain	U. States	Virginia	3 Dec 1827
DEIGHTON, George	20	M	Farmer	Great Britain	United States	Cambria	26 Dec 1827
George	21	M	Mechanic	Great Brittan	United States	Cambria	11 Feb 1829
DE INSER, Jose	34	M	Merchant	Spain	U. States	Albany Packet	23 Mar 1827
DEITZ, Andrew	25	M	Merchant	U. States	U. States	Paquet des Cayes	25 Apr 1827
DEIZ, Charles W.	7	M	her Son [Elizabeth Weissinger]	Germany	United States	Helen	5 Sep 1828
DEJARDIN, J.	26	M	Merchant	Cape Hayti	U. States	Topaz	7 Apr 1828
J. L.	26	M	Mercht.	France	U. States	Edward Bonnaffe	12 Oct 1826
DE JARDIN, G.	14	M		France	United States	India	4 Aug 1826
John	39	M	Farmer	France	United States	Thetis	5 Jul 1821
L.	8	F		France	United States	India	4 Aug 1826
DEJEAN, —, Revd.	26	M	Revd.	France	U. States	Othello	31 Aug 1824
DE JOEZA, Jose	30	M	Merchant	Pernambuca	Pernambuca	Venus	4 Mar 1825
DEJONG, Stvn. K.	35	M	Mechanic	Great Britain	England	John Wells	29 Jan 1825
DE JURA SOLER, Thos.	28	M	Mercht.	Cuba	U. States	Brown	8 Aug 1825

NAMES OF PASSENGERS	AGE	SEX	OCCUPATIONS	COUNTRY TO WHICH THEY BELONG	COUNTRY THEY INTEND TO INHABIT	SHIPS/DATES OF ARRIVAL	
DE KAY, Geo. C.	29	M	Mariner	United States	United States	Frances	19 Feb 1829
DEKAY, B. E.	36	M	Gentn.	New York	New York	Florida	1 Jun 1827
Geo. C.	28	M	Mariner	United States	U. States	Saml. Smith	24 Jul 1826
DE KNELL, F. A. G.	25	M	Merchant	France	U. States	Franklin	6 May 1828
DE KOVEN, H. L.	43	M	Merchant	United States	United States	Splendid	27 Mar 1828
DEKUM, Mary	33	F	None	St. John, N.B.	United States	Edwin	29 Nov 1828
DE LA BARUTE,							
Francisco A.	40	M	Merchant	Braziles	Braziles	Tampico	19 Oct 1826
DE LABORIE, Roux	18	M	Beaver ...	France	United States	Martha	17 Sep 1821
DE LA CASTA, M. C.	33	M	Merchant	Bragils	Petergal	Calypso	1 Jun 1821
Mary	25	F				Calypso	1 Jun 1821
DE LA CERNA, F.	42 5/12	M	Merchant	Spain	Spain	Brillante	24 May 1822
DELACOUR		M	Merchant	U. States	U. States	Fredrick	18 Feb 1822
DE LA COVA, —	2/12	M		U. States	Caracao	Radius	12 Jul 1825
D.	17	F		U. States	Caracao	Radius	12 Jul 1825
L.	3	M		U. States	Caracao	Radius	12 Jul 1825
N.		M		U. States	Caracao	Radius	12 Jul 1825
DELACRETAZ, —, Mr.	41	M	Chemist	France		François I	19 Nov 1828
—, Mrs.	32	F		France		François I	19 Nov 1828
Caroline	3	F		France		François I	19 Nov 1828
Ernest	6	M		France		François I	19 Nov 1828
Ida	1 3/12	F		France		François I	19 Nov 1828
DELA CROIX, Chas.	46	M	Clergyman	U. States		Antioch	18 Aug 1829
DE LA CUESTA, J. L., Mr.	21	M	...	Havanna	Spain	Cadmus	11 Jul 1827
DELADE, Parqoi	20	M	Notary	France	N. York	France	29 Nov 1827
DELAFIELD, A. E.	25	F				Cassack	25 Jul 1820
Chas.	5	M				Cassack	25 Jul 1820
Emma	4	F				Cassack	25 Jul 1820
John	7	M				Cassack	25 Jul 1820
Mary A.	6	F				Cassack	25 Jul 1820
DELAFOLIE, Ann	26	F		U. States	U. States	Bayard	16 May 1827
Caroline	6	F		U. States	U. States	Bayard	16 May 1827
Clarisa	5/12	F		U. States	U. States	Bayard	16 May 1827
DELAFOLN, Francis	32	M	Merchant	France	N. York	France	29 Nov 1827
DE LA FORA, Manuel		M		Spain	U. States	Madison	22 May 1822
DE LA FOREST, —, Master	6	M		France	France	Six Brothers	4 Jun 1822
—, Miss	2	F		France	France	Six Brothers	4 Jun 1822
—, Miss	4	F		France	France	Six Brothers	4 Jun 1822
—, Mrs.	33	F		France	France	Six Brothers	4 Jun 1822
DELAFOREST, ...	42	M	Consul	France	France	Imperial	10 Dec 1821
DELAGADO, Felipe	13	M	Mercht.	Spain	Spain	Juliana	2 Sep 1826
DE LA GUITANA, Pedro	26	M	Merchant	Spainard		Spark	17 Sep 1821
DELA HOUSSAYE, —,							
Mrs.	28		Lady	England	England	Monroe	29 Nov 1823
J. C.	30		Major	England	England	Monroe	29 Nov 1823
DELAHUNTY, John	29	M	Cloth dresser	Ireland	America	Josephine	24 Jul 1826
Mary	18	F	Matron	Ireland	America	Josephine	24 Jul 1826
DELAHURST, James	30	M	Labourer	Ireland	New York	Curler	7 Jul 1827
DE LAISEL, Allustine	28	F		France		Roanoke	21 May 1828
DELA KOVA, L.	29	M	Merchant	Carraccas	Carracas	Robert Fulton	2 Aug 1824
DELALANDO, —	22	M	Painter	France	U. States	Belle	28 Dec 1824
DELA LASTRA, Fernan	35	M	Merchant	Spain	Campicho	Charles	5 Mar 1824
DELAM, Phebe	42	F	Shopkeeper	England	U. States	Alonzo	16 Jul 1821
DELAMAR, Catherine	32	F	None	Ireland	New York	Colossus	2 Oct 1827
Margaret	9	F	None	Ireland	New York	Colossus	2 Oct 1827
Patrick	36	M	Machinist	Ireland	New York	Colossus	2 Oct 1827
DELAMARE, J. A.	23	M	Baker	France	U. States	Edward Bonaffe	11 Dec 1827
DE LA MATA, Pedro	22	M	Merchant	Spain	U. States	Fabius	9 Jul 1824
DE LA MOTH,							
Jean Baptiste	63	M	Writing Master	France	U. States	Elizabeth	29 Sep 1823
DELANCY, Jas.	28	M	Merchant	Gt. Britain	Great Britain	Martha	4 Oct 1822
Mary	28	F	None	Gt. Britain	Great Britain	Martha	4 Oct 1822
DELANE, Timothy	27	M	Gardner	Ireland	United States	Trio	2 Oct 1828
DELANENVILLE,							
Louis Auguste,							
Mr.	29 6/12	M	Merchant	France	New York & Paris	Cadmus	27 Aug 1822
DELANEY, —, Mrs.	35	F		London	U. States	Zephyr	2 Oct 1826
Ann	35	F	None	Gt. Brittain	United States	Balaena	21 Aug 1824
Anthony	29	M	Engineer	Ireland	United States	Herald	7 Jun 1824

NAMES OF PASSENGERS	AGE	SEX	OCCUPATIONS	COUNTRY TO WHICH THEY BELONG	COUNTRY THEY INTEND TO INHABIT	SHIPS/DATES OF ARRIVAL	
DELANEY (cont'd)							
Ellen	5	F	None	Ireland		Marchioness	13 May 1828
Ellen	24	F	None	Ireland		Marchioness	13 May 1828
J. Dw.	18	M	Merchant	America	America	David	4 May 1825
James	21	M	Labourer	England	U. States	Comet	23 Aug 1828
Kervan	3	M	None	Ireland		Marchioness	13 May 1828
Margret	18			Ireland	U.S.	Union	20 Aug 1827
Wm.	40	M	Shoemaker	Ireland		Marchioness	13 May 1828
DELANO, A.	20	M	Merchant	U. States	U. States	Frederick	5 May 1826
J. C.	26	M	Captain	U.S.	U.S.	Porcia	4 Jan 1828
DELANTY, Danial	40	M	Labourer	Great Britain	U. States	Robert Fulton	3 Dec 1827
Johannah	6 6/12	F	Child	Great Britain	U. States	Robert Fulton	3 Dec 1827
John	36	M	Labourer	Ireland		Ocean	13 Jul 1827
Margaret	30 6/12	F	Matron	Great Britain	U. States	Robert Fulton	3 Dec 1827
Mary	8 6/12	F	Child	Great Britain	U. States	Robert Fulton	3 Dec 1827
Michal	5	M	Child	Great Britain	U. States	Robert Fulton	3 Dec 1827
Michl.	26	M	Labourer	Ireland		Ocean	13 Jul 1827
Ross	35	M	Labourer	Ireland		Ocean	13 Jul 1827
DELANUE, M.	21	M	Merchant	France	United States	St. Martin	10 Feb 1820
DELANY, A.	25	F	None	Ireland	U. States	Criterion	23 May 1826
Catharine	21	F	Wife	Ireland	United States	Dublin Packet	13 Oct 1828
Michael	25	M	Tailor	Ireland	New York	America	1 Aug 1828
Patrick	20	M	Farmer	Ireland	United States	Dublin Packet	13 Oct 1828
Patrick	23	M	Farmer	Ireland	U. States	Criterion	23 May 1826
Patrick	27	M	Farmer	Ireland	U. States	Criterion	23 May 1826
William	28	M	Labourer	Ireland	United States	Jubilee	13 Jul 1829
DELAP, H. L.	40	M	Mercht.	Great Britain	U. States	Java	20 Jun 1825
Mary	30	F		England	Great Britain	Robert Cochran	29 Aug 1825
Patt	22	M	Weaver	Ireland	New York	Amanda	23 May 1827
DE LA PENA, Joseph	35	M	Merchant	Cadiz		Nimrod	21 Aug 1827
DELAPLAINE, E.	35	M	...	U. States	U.S.	Queen Mab	26 Nov 1825
P. P.	33	M	Merchant	U. States	U. States	Chase	24 Jul 1823
DE LA PORT, John	21	M	Merchant	Italy	U. States	Sally	8 Aug 1820
DELA PORTELLO,							
Bruno Gonzalez, Don	45	M	Merchant	Spain	Spain	Frances	21 Mar 1827
DE LARA, Joaquin	10	M		Island of Cuba	Cuba	James Monroe	21 May 1825
Jose Mariano	9	M		Island of Cuba	Cuba	James Monroe	21 May 1825
Lino	11	M		Island of Cuba	Cuba	James Monroe	21 May 1825
Pio	42	M	Planter	Island of Cuba	Cuba	James Monroe	21 May 1825
DELA REED, F.	21	M	Merchant	Spain	Spain	Hesperus	13 Mar 1826
J.	17	M	Merchant	Spain	Spain	Hesperus	13 Mar 1826
Mary	33	F		New York	America	Rebecca	31 Oct 1825
Maxima	30	M	Merchant	Spain	America	Rebecca	31 Oct 1825
DELARUA, Gerald	21	M	Gentleman	Ireland	Ireland	Dublin Packet	28 Apr 1824
DELARUE, —, Madam	45	F	Lady	France	America	Lima	11 Dec 1823
Alfred	20	M	Gentleman	France	America	Lima	11 Dec 1823
DELARY, Danl.	32	M	Shoe Maker	America	U. States	Robt. Edwards	4 Sep 1828
DE LASA, Barner	20	M	Merchant	Spain	Havanna	Ann Maria	23 Oct 1820
Jos. M.	28	M	Merchant	Spain	Havanna	Ann Maria	23 Oct 1820
DE LA SENNA, Ramona	26	M	Merchant	Spain		Alfred	20 Dec 1821
DE LA SERRIA, Ramon	28	M	Merchant	Spain	Spain	Radius	14 Feb 1826
DE LAS L'CAMORAS, R.	22	M	Mercht.	Havana	U. States	Evelina	31 May 1825
DELA TERREGO, H.	16		Merchant	Spain	U. States	Alfred	24 Jul 1828
DELATONE, W.	30	F	Spinster	France	America	Alexander	28 Jul 1821
DE LA TORRES, J. L.	25	M		Spain	Spain	Fabius	3 Jun 1825
DE LAUNAY, Victor	22	M	Merchant	France	U. States	Sully	24 Oct 1828
DELAUNAY, A.	15	M	Farmer	France	Canada	Quesnel	6 Sep 1824
DE LAVACQUE,						Nestor in	
Stanislaus	30	M	Merchant	France	United States	Liverpool	29 Jul 1822
DELAVAN, Ed. C.	31	M	Merchant	U. States	U. States	Canada	14 Feb 1824
Hy. W.	33	M	Merchant	America	America	Albion	4 Oct 1820
DELAVILLE, E.	25	M	Mechanic	Switzerland	U. States	Don Quixote	14 Aug 1826
DELAVY, ...	32		Farmer	Ireland	U.S.	Hibernia	27 Jun 1821
DELAWAN, Enoch S.	35		Mechanic	U. States	U. States	Venus	4 Oct 1821
DEL BARRIO, R. J.	25	M	Merchant	Guatemala	Guatemala	Stephania	26 Apr 1824
DEL BOIS, J.	20	M	Merchant	Spain	Spain	Sarah Ann	8 May 1822
DELBOS, —	20	M	Merchant	France	U. States	Othello	3 Jun 1823
Charles	21 2/12	M	Merchant	France	New York, U.S.	Europa	6 Oct 1828
DEL BRESTER, L.	26	M	Merchant	Spain	Spain	Brown	15 Nov 1825

NAMES OF PASSENGERS	A G E	S E X	OCCUPATIONS	COUNTRY TO WHICH THEY BELONG	COUNTRY THEY INTEND TO INHABIT	SHIPS/DATES OF ARRIVAL	
DEL BRUTO, A.	30	M	Merchant	Havana	Havana	Crusader	23 Apr 1827
DELBURTO, L.	28	M	Merchant	Havana	Havana	Crusader	23 Apr 1827
DEL CARMEN DE COUDRY							
HOLSTIEN, Maria	24	F		Spain	U. States	Mattrawan	5 Apr 1824
DEL CASTELLA,							
Vincent	35	M	Merchant	Havana	U. States	Hesper	28 Dec 1825
DEL CASTILLO,				Trinidad in			
Manuel Jose	25	M	Merchant	Cuba	U. States	Fortune	23 Nov 1821
DELECANT,							
Marie Francoise	24	F	Servant	Netherlands	United States	Montano	31 May 1824
DELECROIX, Andre	30	M	Merchant	France	France	Meteor	17 Jan 1825
DELEMAN, Wm.	18		Seaman	Boston		Hudson	18 Jun 1825
*Officers, Seamen and Passengers belonging to the Ship Jane of Boston and taken from on board the Schooner Olive of St. Johns , N.B. on the 4th June 1825, Lat. 41.30, Long 53.19, which ship foundered on the 31st ultimo in Lat. 41.44 Long 52.							
DELEMONG, Catherine	7	F	Farmer	France	United States	Crescent	12 Jul 1827
Dellemoney	18	M	Farmer	France	United States	Crescent	12 Jul 1827
Francess	38	F	Farmer	France	United States	Crescent	12 Jul 1827
Jack	4	M	Farmer	France	United States	Crescent	12 Jul 1827
Joseph	12	M	Farmer	France	United States	Crescent	12 Jul 1827
Thiebot	22	M	Farmer	France	United States	Crescent	12 Jul 1827
Xavier	49	M	Farmer	France	United States	Crescent	12 Jul 1827
DELENAO, James	19	M	Farmer	Great Britain	New York	Superior	5 Sep 1827
DELENBACK, Andrias	1	M	Farmer	Switzerland	U. States	India	8 Dec 1826
Charatina	31	F	Farmer	Switzerland	U. States	India	8 Dec 1826
Christian	5	M	Farmer	Switzerland	U. States	India	8 Dec 1826
Fred'k	4	M	Farmer	Switzerland	U. States	India	8 Dec 1826
Galfrina	8	F	Farmer	Switzerland	U. States	India	8 Dec 1826
Gattile	2	M	Farmer	Switzerland	U. States	India	8 Dec 1826
Hons.	6	M	Farmer	Switzerland	U. States	India	8 Dec 1826
John	30	M	Farmer	Switzerland	U. States	India	8 Dec 1826
Ann	47	F	Farmer	Switzerland	U. States	India	8 Dec 1826
Anna	15	F	Farmer	Switzerland	U. States	India	8 Dec 1826
Christian	53	M	Farmer	Switzerland	U. States	India	8 Dec 1826
Elizabeth	11	F	Farmer	Switzerland	U. States	India	8 Dec 1826
Fre'd	22	M	Farmer	Switzerland	U. States	India	8 Dec 1826
Geresia	7	F	Farmer	Switzerland	U. States	India	8 Dec 1826
Han. C.	23	F	Farmer	Switzerland	U. States	India	8 Dec 1826
John	16	M	Farmer	Switzerland	U. States	India	8 Dec 1826
Maria	9	F	Farmer	Switzerland	U. States	India	8 Dec 1826
DE LE NORAL, Cipivane	28	M	Merchant	Spain	unknown	Juanita	13 Oct 1829
DE LEON, Ponce	25	M	Merchant	Spain	U. States	William Thompson	24 Aug 1827
DELERAA, James, Mr.	17	M	Gentln.	England	U. States	Corinthian	8 Oct 1828
DELERNER, Ricr.	20	M	Farmer	Great Britain	United States	Atlantic	28 May 1827
DELESCAR, John	34	M	Merchant	England	U. States	Brighton	9 Dec 1828
DELESDENIER, J., Mrs.	20	F		U. States	U. States	Tipporah	22 Dec 1828
DELESDERMIER, —, Mrs.	19	M		U. States	U. States	Zipporah	13 Jun 1828
DELFEN, Mono	26 4/12	F	Confectioner	France	United States	Catharine	10 Sep 1827
DELFOSSA, Larencee	45	M	Merchant	U. States	U. States	Ariosto	4 Jun 1823
DELFOSSE, Casimir	40	M	Merchan	Switzerland	U. States	Ariosto	4 May 1821
Cassimer	50	M	Merchant	United States	U. States	Falcon	11 Oct 1824
DEL GADA, B.	28	M	Merchant	U. States	U. States	Hippomenes	9 Jun 1821
DELGADO, Joseph,							
Servant	33	M	Servant	Spain	Cuba	James Cropper	2 Aug 1827
R.	14	M	School Boy	Columbia	U. States	Exchange	26 Jul 1824
DELGARDO, W. B.	30	M	Merchant	Spain	U. States	Hippomenes	22 Dec 1821
DEL HOIJO, Carlos	22	M	Gentleman	Mexico	U. States	Emilia	30 Jul 1827
DELHONY, Philip	36		Pavor	Ireland		Hudson	23 Jul 1828
DELHUMEN, —, Mr.	36	M	Merchant	France	U.S.	Francois I	8 Aug 1829
DELIAS, Hy.	20	M	Merchant	Bremen	U. States	New York	15 Nov 1823
DE LIDERER, —, Baron	50	M	Austrian Consul General	Austria	U. States	Don Quixote	9 Oct 1827
A., Miss	18	F	Daughter	Austria	U. States	Don Quixote	9 Oct 1827
DE LILLERS, —, Count	25	M	Gentleman	France	France	Bayard	16 May 1827
DE LIMA, Antonio Alfonzo	21	M	Merchant	Oporto	Oporto	Annabal	15 Nov 1824
DELINS, Geo.	34	M	Merchant	Germany	United States	Cortes	10 Apr 1822
DELISLE DU FIEFFE, Jules	23	M	Gentleman	France	United States	Montano	5 May 1828
DELITANT, Augustus	55	M	Supercargo	France	France	Chatham	8 Aug 1822

NAMES OF PASSENGERS	AGE	SEX	OCCUPATIONS	COUNTRY TO WHICH THEY BELONG	COUNTRY THEY INTEND TO INHABIT	SHIPS/DATES OF ARRIVAL	
DELITANT (cont'd)							
Augustus, Jr.	20	M	Gentleman	France	France	Chatham	8 Aug 1822
DELIUS, Henry	26	M		Germany	U. States	Florida	2 Jun 1828
DEL JEMER, Merced	17	F	Servant	Cuba (Cold. Servant)	U. States	Zephyr	18 May 1825
DELKIO, Agipito	20	M	Merchant	Cololumbia	Columbia	Ann	4 Mar 1826
Jose	18	M	Merchant	Cololumbia	Columbia	Ann	4 Mar 1826
DELL, Jane	36	F	Labourer	England	U. States	Ayrshire	12 May 1828
Pheoby	6	F	Labourer	England	U. States	Ayrshire	12 May 1828
Richard R.	36	M	Labourer	England	U. States	Ayrshire	12 May 1828
Wingat	5	F	Labourer	England	U. States	Ayrshire	12 May 1828
DELLAGER, —, Melle.	38		Couturière [seamstress]	Suisse		Deux Ernest	29 Dec 1827
DELLA TORRE, Joseph	41	M	Merchant	Citizen of U. States	U. States	Packet	20 Feb 1823
DELLATORRE, Antonio	21	M	Merchant	England	New York	Cortes	23 Nov 1827
DELLEN, Wm.	22	M	Mason	Ireland	New York	Cadmus	22 Mar 1822
DELLENIORE, Thomas	30	M	Labourer	England	U. States	Ayrshire	12 May 1828
DELLRIGER, —, Miss	38	F	Seamstress	Swisse	United States	Deux Ernest	29 Dec 1827
*landed at Lewiston, Delw.							
DELMER, Wilhelme	16	F			U. States	Maria Elizabeth	9 Jun 1826
DELMONICCO, John	29	M	Merchant	United States		Spartan	13 Apr 1826
DELMONIER, A.	18 6/12	F	Confectioner	France	United States	Catharine	10 Sep 1827
Anette	0 11/12	F	Confectioner	France	United States	Catharine	10 Sep 1827
Cathr.	3 6/12	F	Confectioner	France	United States	Catharine	10 Sep 1827
Cathr.	43 1/12	M	Confectioner	France	United States	Catharine	10 Sep 1827
Francis	24 6/12	M	Confectioner	France	United States	Catharine	10 Sep 1827
Honora	3 4/12	M	Confectioner	France	United States	Catharine	10 Sep 1827
John	40 4/12	M	Gentleman	France	United States	Catharine	10 Sep 1827
Josephine	11 11/12	F	Confectioner	France	United States	Catharine	10 Sep 1827
Peter A.	43 7/12	M	Confectioner	France	United States	Catharine	10 Sep 1827
Rosa	7 3/12	F	Confectioner	France	United States	Catharine	10 Sep 1827
Siro	19 7/12	M	Confectioner	France	United States	Catharine	10 Sep 1827
DELMONTE, D., Mr.	25	M		Spain		François I	19 Nov 1828
DELMOUR, T. W.	28	M	Grocer	England	United States	Manhattan	22 Sep 1823
DELOLINE, Jno. C.	38	M	Merchant	Geneva	U. States	Eagle	18 Jul 1822
DELOLME, Joseph	36	M	Doctor	Germany	U. States	Florida	16 May 1827
DELORM, Joseph P.	18	M	Student	France	U. States	Horace	23 Jun 1827
DELORME, Anthony	25		Merchant	Geneve	Switzerland	London	13 Dec 1822
DELOSREGES, Anthony	21	M	Servant	Spain	West Indies	Union Packet	9 Feb 1827
DELPECH, Dolorés, Mrs.	35	F	Lady	Colombia	Colombia	Sully	15 Jul 1829
Louis	20	M	Student	Colombia	Colombia	Sully	15 Jul 1829
DELPH, Geo.	34	M	Seaman	Germany	U. States	Criterion	15 Oct 1822
DELPHRICK, A.	23	M	Gentleman	Switzerland	U. States	Ohio	18 Jul 1821
DELPRICH, —, Mrs.	51	F	Wife	Switzerland	United States	Bayard	13 Nov 1823
Francis	50	M	Merchant	Switzerland	United States	Bayard	13 Nov 1823
DEL RIO, J. Garcia, Mr.	34 2/12		Proprietor	Colombia	Traveling	Romulus	15 May 1828
DELSUE, Wm.	30	M	Founder	France	W. Indies	Cadmus	28 May 1821
DELTON, —, Miss	15		Actor	G. Britain	America	Magnet	24 Sep 1824
DELTVEILER, Jean	18	M	Carpenter	Brattain		L'Esperance	6 Sep 1828
DE LUCE, —	9/12	M	None	Gt. Britain	United States	Iris	30 Aug 1824
—	1 9/12	F	None	United States	United States	Iris	30 Aug 1824
—	3	M	None	United States	United States	Iris	30 Aug 1824
—	5	M	None	United States	United States	Iris	30 Aug 1824
—	7	M	None	United States	United States	Iris	30 Aug 1824
Susan	32	F	None	United States	United States	Iris	30 Aug 1824
William	42	M	Musician	England	England	Criterion	29 May 1822
Wm.	36	M	Musician	Gt. Brittain	United States	Iris	30 Aug 1824
DE LUZE, Louis P.	26 5/12	M	Merchant	Neufchatel	United States	Hector	8 Jan 1820
DELUZE, —	29	M	Mercht.	Switzerland	U.S.	Cadmus	20 Dec 1824
DEL VALLE, Francisca	30	F		Island of Cuba	Cuba	James Monroe	21 May 1825
Raymond	25	M	Merchant	Spain	non Resident	Charleston Packet	25 Jul 1821
DELVALLE, J. A.	34	M	Merchant	Spain	Spain	Claudio	29 Dec 1827
DEL VECCHIO, John	23	M	Merchant	G. Brittain	U. States	York	10 Dec 1825
DEL VECHIO, John	20	M	Merchant	Ireland		Cincinnatus	29 Apr 1822
DEL VENOT, W.	12	M	Merchant	U. States	U. States	Prudence	11 Jun 1825
DELVERSNE, James	27	M	Gentleman	Italy	United States	New York	14 Jul 1827

NAMES OF PASSENGERS	A G E	S E X	OCCUPATIONS	COUNTRY TO WHICH THEY BELONG	COUNTRY THEY INTEND TO INHABIT	SHIPS/DATES OF ARRIVAL	
DEL VISTO, Lorenzo	23	M	Gentleman	Spain		Charleston Packet	4 May 1821
DELWAR, Joseph	17	M	Manuir	England	United States	Dalhouse Castle	6 Sep 1827
DE MAGNA, B.	31	M	Gentleman	France	France	Eliza	28 Apr 1827
DEMAIRE, Daniel	1			France	U. States	Parachute	14 May 1828
Fredk.	4			France	U. States	Parachute	14 May 1828
Fredk.	28		Mechanic	France	U. States	Parachute	14 May 1828
Madalin	25			France	U. States	Parachute	14 May 1828
Madeline	3			France	U. States	Parachute	14 May 1828
Philip	7			France	U. States	Parachute	14 May 1828
DE MANELLA, Galan	25	M	Tutor	Italy	U. States	Day	11 Jun 1823
DE MARI, Jose Fountis, Don	28	M	Merchant	Spain	Spain	Lovinia	20 Nov 1828
DE MARIA CORPOS, Antonio	20	M	Mercht.	Spain	Spain	Savannah	10 Jan 1828
DE MARTOIS, Eugene	38	M	Soldier	France	U.S.	Edward Quesnel	17 Jan 1825
DE MATTOS, M. L. F.		M	Officer	Portugal	Portugal	Diana	7 Jun 1823
DE MAYTER, —, Mrs.	35	F		Havana	So. America	Hesperion	28 Oct 1823
Frederick	3	M		Havana	So. America	Hesperion	28 Oct 1823
Jose, Jr.	19	M	Merchant	Havana	U. States	Hesperion	28 Oct 1823
Jose, Senr.	48	M	Merchant	Havana	So. America	Hesperion	28 Oct 1823
Mary Ann	7	F		Havana	So. America	Hesperion	28 Oct 1823
Rose	14	F		Havana	So. America	Hesperion	28 Oct 1823
Seroro	2/12	F		Havana	So. America	Hesperion	28 Oct 1823
Trinodat	16	M		Havana	So. America	Hesperion	28 Oct 1823
DE MAZAS, F.	28	M	Mercht.	United States	U. States	Sisters	7 Jul 1826
DEMENTH, Philip	27	M	Cultivator	Gt. Brittan		L'Esperance	6 Sep 1828
DEMERT, George	28	M	Farmer	Alsace in the Department of Upper and lower Rhine	United States	Carolina Augusta	16 May 1828
DE MEVGAS, France.	29	M	Merchant	Philadelphia	Phila.	Alto	8 Jun 1827
DE MEZA, Raphael	19	M	Merchant	Holland	Holland	General Paez	14 Apr 1826
DE MICHEL, John	37	M	Merchant	U. States	U. States	Sully	24 Oct 1828
DE MIER, Pablo	15	M	Merchant	Spain	Havana	Commodore Chauncy	28 Nov 1825
DE MINA, Jose Maria	35 6/12	M	Gentleman	Cuba	Mexico	Potosi	28 May 1825
DEMING, Frederic	28	M	Servant	France	U. States	Edward Bopnnaffe	30 Jul 1829
DEMINGO, Manl.	19	M	Merchant	Mexico	Mexico	Washington	29 Apr 1826
DE MIOT DE MILLITO, —, Count	52	M	Gentleman	France		Cadmus	9 Aug 1825
DEMITIN, F.	25	M	Merchant	France	Mexico	Washington	29 Apr 1826
DEMMISON, Auguste	36	M	Mechanic	France		Charlemagne	16 Jan 1829
DE MONKTON, —	14	M	Servant	Nassau, N.P.	Nassau, N.P.	Superior	27 Jun 1825
DEMONSARDIN, O.	48	F	Spinster	Holland	United States	Howard	19 May 1826
DEMONT, R.	22	M	Merchant	U. States	U. States	Betsey	6 May 1826
Victoire	50	F	Servt.	France	United States	Bayard	13 Nov 1823
DE MONTEBELLO, —, Duke	27	M		France	France	Caledonia	10 Sep 1828
DEMOREAU, Eliza	11	F	Spinster	United States	United States	Abaco	20 Oct 1829
DEMOT, —, Mr.	21	M	Butcher	New York	New York	Mary & Elizabeth	7 Sep 1824
DEMOTE, John	12	M		Great Britian	United States	Brok	29 Aug 1823
DEMOUTZEY, Antoine	36	M	Doctor	France	U. States	Edward Bopnnaffe	30 Jul 1829
Joseph	29	M	Doctor	France	U. States	Edward Bopnnaffe	30 Jul 1829
DEMPERLY, Nicholas	24	M	Farmer	Great Britain	United States	Roman	10 May 1828
DEMPREY, James	30	M	Labourer	Gt. Britain	U. States	Frances Henrietta	18 Apr 1825
DEMPSART, Gilbert	45	M	Merchant	Holland	Holland	Cadmus	9 Dec 1826
DEMPSEY, Bernard	25	M	Farmer	England	United States	Siroc	31 Oct 1829
Biddy	29	F	None	Ireland	United States	Jubilee	4 Mar 1829
Bridget	17	F		Gt. Britain		Dalhouse Castle	13 May 1828
Briget	24	F	None	Ireland	United States	Baltic	21 Apr 1827
Dennis	23	M	Farmer	Ireland	U.S.A.	Silas Richards	28 Jun 1825
Francis	1	M	None	Great Britain	United States	Eliza Barker	3 Jul 1826
Francis	19	F	None	Great Britain	United States	Eliza Barker	3 Jul 1826

NAMES OF PASSENGERS	AGE	SEX	OCCUPATIONS	COUNTRY TO WHICH THEY BELONG	COUNTRY THEY INTEND TO INHABIT	SHIPS/DATES OF ARRIVAL	
DEMPSEY (cont'd)							
James	1 7/12	M	None	Ireland	United States	Colossus	26 Aug 1828
James	22	M	Labourer	Ireland		Marchioness	13 May 1828
James	30	M	Labourer	Ireland	United States	Baltic	21 Apr 1827
John	24	M	Farmer	Ireland	United States	Dublin Packet	9 Jul 1827
John	60	M	Merchant	Ireland	U. States	Ariadne	12 Dec 1822
Margaret	20	F		Gt. Britain		Dalhouse Castle	13 May 1828
Margaret	20	F	None	Ireland		Marchioness	13 May 1828
Mary	25	F	Labourer	Ireland	United States	Essex	23 May 1828
Mary	25	F	None	Ireland	United States	Colossus	26 Aug 1828
Mary	36			Yorkshire	...	Hudson	14 Jun 1827
Michael	32	M	Soap Boiler	Ireland	United States	Roman	12 Jun 1826
Murty	17	M	Labourer	Ireland	United States	Baltic	21 Apr 1827
Patk.	25	M	Tobacconist	Ireland	United States	William	20 Jul 1829
Richard	26	M	Labourer	Ireland	U. States	Josephine	7 May 1827
Sampson	1 9/12	M		Ireland	U. States	Fabius	22 Sep 1828
Susan	36 5/12	F	Spinstress	Ireland	U. States	Fabius	22 Sep 1828
Thomas	21	M	Laborer, Spinster or Child	Ireland	United States	Ann Maria	4 Aug 1827
Thos.	25	M	Labourer	Ireland	United States	Essex	23 May 1828
William	25	M	None	Great Britain	United States	Eliza Barker	3 Jul 1826
DEMPSTER, Agnes	3	...	...	Scotland	America	Nimrod	9 Jul 1827
Gilbert	30	M	Farmer	Ireland	America	Hesperus	7 Jul 1820
James	38	M		Great Britain	United States	Active	25 Mar 1828
Jane	26	F	Housekeeper	Scotland	United States	Andes	2 Oct 1828
William	22	M	Taylor	Scotland	United States	Andes	2 Oct 1828
DEMPSY, Ann	10	F	Child	Ireland	United States	Dublin Packet	9 Jul 1827
Joseph	28	M	Farmer	Ireland	U.S.A.	Dalhouse Castle	21 Aug 1829
Josh.	28	M	Farmer	Ireland	United States	Dalhouse Castle	21 Aug 1829
Margaret	27	F	None	Ireland	U. States	Union	3 Jun 1822
Mary	16	F	Child	Ireland	United States	Dublin Packet	9 Jul 1827
Rodger	25	M	Farmer, Labourer or Spinster	Ireland	U. States	Meteor	4 Oct 1827
DEMSEE, James	35	M				Hanford	17 Jul 1828
DEMSEY, Peter	25	M	Labourer	Ireland	U. States	Two Marys	20 Apr 1825
DE MULDER, C., Mr.	49	M	Mercht.	Holland	Holland	Manchester	21 Apr 1827
DEMULT, Benjamin	41		Merchant	United States	United States	James Monroe	11 Dec 1821
DEMUTER, Jean	37	M	Merchant	Netherlands	United States	James Monroe	14 Dec 1820
DENA, Mark	24	M	Labourer	Ireland	U. States	Combine	30 Nov 1825
Martin	26	M	Labourer	Ireland	U. States	Combine	30 Nov 1825
DENAKEE, Lawrence	23	M	Farmer	England	United States	India	8 Jun 1827
DENAM, Barnard	31	M	Labourer	Ireland	United States	Borneo	14 Aug 1827
DENAUX, Edmd.	21	M	Mason	France	U. States	India	8 Dec 1826
DENBY, Patrick	19	M	Farmer	Ireland	United States	Lima	19 Jun 1824
DENCHLER, Catherine	35	F				Golden Grove	6 Sep 1820
Mac	5					Golden Grove	6 Sep 1820
Max	37	M	Farmer	Bonden	Pennsylvania	Golden Grove	6 Sep 1820
Phillip	1 6/12					Golden Grove	6 Sep 1820
DENCK, Henry	34	M	Mechanic	New York	U. States	Sea Bird	8 Feb 1827
DENE, Alphenso	25	M	Mariner	France	France	Traveller	11 Dec 1824
DE NECKER, Leo	29	M	Clergyman	America, U.N.S.	America, U.N.S.	Great Britain	3 Aug 1829
DENEFORD, —, Mrs.	25	F		England	U. States	Six Brothers	4 Jun 1822
Wm.	22	M	Mercht.	England	U. States	Six Brothers	4 Jun 1822
DENEGO, John	30		Farmer	Ireland	Philidelphia	General Marion	21 Nov 1828
DENEMAN, —, Mrs.	45	F		Nantucket	U. States	Baltimore	6 Dec 1823
DENEVEN, J.	25	F		Gt. Britain	U. States	Sarah G.	14 Apr 1828
Margaret	22	F		Gt. Britain	U. States	Sarah G.	14 Apr 1828
DENGHOLAYAN, Patrick	28	M	Farmer	Ireland	U. States	Mentor	5 Jul 1825
DENHAM, Eliza	20	F	Lady	Scotland	United States	Friends	7 Jul 1827
Josiah	7 10/12	M	Son	England	United States	Robert Edwards	3 Oct 1829
Josiah	35 6/12	M	Baptist Minister	England	United States	Robert Edwards	3 Oct 1829
DENICK, —, Mr.	25	M	Sugar Baker	G. Britain	U.S.	Robert Edwards	11 Nov 1822
DENIER, Therese	50	F		France	U. States	Edward Bopnnaffe	30 Jul 1829
DENIERE, Charles	17	M		France	U. States	Edward Bopnnaffe	30 Jul 1829
Jean	54	M	Doctor	France	U. States	Edward Bopnnaffe	30 Jul 1829

NAMES OF PASSENGERS	AGE	SEX	OCCUPATIONS	COUNTRY TO WHICH THEY BELONG	COUNTRY THEY INTEND TO INHABIT	SHIPS/DATES OF ARRIVAL	
DENIERE, (cont'd)							
Julie	15	F		France	U. States	Edward Bopnnaffe	30 Jul 1829
Marie	19	F		France	U. States	Edward Bopnnaffe	30 Jul 1829
DENIFF, Patrick	25	M	Labourer	Ireland	U. States	Combine	30 Nov 1825
DE NIGO, H.	29	M	Merchant	Mexico	Mexico	Bogota	17 Jul 1828
DENING, Am	31	M	Gent	French	Switzerland	Charlemagne	19 Sep 1828
B.	13	M	Gent	French	Switzerland	Charlemagne	19 Sep 1828
C.	13	M	Gent	French	Switzerland	Charlemagne	19 Sep 1828
F.	39	M	Gent	French	Switzerland	Charlemagne	19 Sep 1828
DENIORD, Martha	31	F	None	England	New York	Brighton	19 Aug 1829
Martha	31	F	None			Brighton	19 Aug 1829
Richard	32	M	Engineer	England	New York	Brighton	19 Aug 1829
Richard	32	M	Engineer			Brighton	19 Aug 1829
DENIS, Caroline	25	F				Columbia	16 Jan 1829
Harriet	12/12	F				Columbia	16 Jan 1829
Hugh	11			Ireland	United States	Jno. Dickinson	21 Sep 1821
Jane	17	F	Farmer	Ireland	U. States	Dickinson	30 Jul 1825
John A.	25	M	Merchant	France	U. States	Queen Mab	31 Jul 1826
John Charles	30	M	Merchant	Holland	United States	Columbia	16 Jan 1829
P.	29	M	Servant	Vera Cruz	U. States	Eliza	11 Apr 1826
DENISON, J.	40	M	Mariner	U. States	U. States	Henry	3 Jun 1828
John	64	M	Farmer	Canada	Canada	Ann	29 Jan 1820
DENISTON, Samuel B.	32	M	Merchant	United States		France	6 Feb 1829
DENLY, Joseph	25	M		Ireland	U. States	Nancy	16 Aug 1822
DENMAN, Charles	3	M		Scotland	United States	Margaret Bogle	11 Jun 1824
Fredrick	2	M		Scotland	United States	Margaret Bogle	11 Jun 1824
James	20	M	Merchant	England	U. States	Howard	27 Feb 1824
Mary, & Child	28	F		Scotland	United States	Margaret Bogle	11 Jun 1824
William	30 2/12	M	Merchant	England	United States	Nimrod	28 Apr 1824
Wm.	31	M	Merchant	England	U. States	Cincinnatus	21 Feb 1825
DENMORE, Chrs.	40	M	Merchant	England	U. States	Charles Hamilton Aberdeen	2 Nov 1824
Frs.	40	F		England	U. States	Charles Hamilton Aberdeen	2 Nov 1824
DENNAHY, Jane	27	F		Ireland	United States	Trio	31 Oct 1827
DENNAN, Andw.	27		Farmer	Great Britan	United States	Newry	11 Jul 1827
Ann	23			Great Britan	United States	Newry	11 Jul 1827
Eliza	2			Great Britan	United States	Newry	11 Jul 1827
Esther	3			Great Britan	United States	Newry	11 Jul 1827
DENNANT, Elisabeth	22	F		Great Britain	United States	Meteor	15 Apr 1823
Saml. Calvin	23	M	Merchant	Great Britain	United States	Meteor	15 Apr 1823
DENNASON, John	24	M	Gentleman	England	Great Britain	New York	22 Jul 1824
DENNE, Bridt.	28	F	None	Great Britain	United States	William Dawson	18 Jun 1827
John	30	M	Labourer	Great Britain	United States	William Dawson	18 Jun 1827
DENNEGAN, Michael	40	M	Farmer	Great Britain	New York	Superior	5 Sep 1827
DENNEN, Patrick	32	M	Merchant	Ireland	U. States	Commerce	11 Dec 1824
DENNERY, John	18	M	Labourer	England and Ireland	United States	Jubilee	12 May 1828
DENNETT, Moses	40	M	Farmer	England	In the country	Chelsea	16 May 1828
DENNEY, B.	0 4/12	F		Great Britain	United States	Washington	3 Sep 1827
E.	24	F		Great Britain	United States	Washington	3 Sep 1827
Pat	22	M	Farmer	Great Britain	United States	Washington	3 Sep 1827
Thomas	29	M	Weaver	Ireland	New Jersey	Curler	7 Jul 1827
DENNIN, Thomas	28	M	Labourer	Ireland	United States	Jubilee	12 May 1828
DENNING, Esabella	37	F	Spinster	Ireland		Robert Fulton	4 Jun 1828
Sarah	15	F	Spinster	Ireland		Robert Fulton	4 Jun 1828
Wm.	68	M	Labourer	Ireland		Robert Fulton	4 Jun 1828
DENNIS, Charles	27	M	Farmer	England	U. States	Elizabeth	20 Sep 1822
Etienne	22	M	Gentleman	France	U.S.	Edward Quesnel	19 Oct 1829
John	25	M	Super Cargo	New Londn.	United States	Windham	7 Mar 1823
John	50	M	Mariner	N. York	U. States	Hope	17 Apr 1824
Sarah	25	F	Dressmaker	England	U.S. America	Josephine	24 Jul 1826
DENNISON, Charles	16	M	Farmer	G. Britain	U. States	Freak	9 Jun 1828
Mary	10	F	Merchant	America	U. States	Nancy	13 Dec 1822
Mary Ann	30	F	Merchant	America	U. States	Nancy	13 Dec 1822
Thomas	8	M	Child	America	U. States	Nancy	13 Dec 1822
Wm.	25	M	Foyal Engineer	England	U. States	Florida	16 May 1827

NAMES OF PASSENGERS	AGE	SEX	OCCUPATIONS	COUNTRY TO WHICH THEY BELONG	COUNTRY THEY INTEND TO INHABIT	SHIPS/DATES OF ARRIVAL	
DENNISTON, Henry	22	M	Labourer	Ireland	U.S.	Lady Hunter	10 Jul 1826
DENNISTOWN, John	24	M	Merchant	Great Britain, Ireland	New York	Britannia	3 Nov 1827
DENNIT, Fras.	35	M	Weaver	Scotland	Ama.	Expedition	19 May 1828
DENNS, Thomas	24	M	Sadler	England	New York	Corinthian	5 May 1827
DENNY, Elly	36			Ireland	Great Britain	Robert Burns	14 Jun 1824
James	20	M		Scotland		Factor	10 May 1821
*died 4 May							
James	22	M	Merchant	G. Britain	United States	Robert Burns	13 Jul 1820
Margaret	25			Ireland	Great Britain	Robert Burns	14 Jun 1824
Patrick	2			Ireland	Great Britain	Robert Burns	14 Jun 1824
Rebecca	23			Ireland	Great Britain	Robert Burns	14 Jun 1824
Wm.	11			Ireland	Great Britain	Robert Burns	14 Jun 1824
DENONETTE, V.	34	M	Merchant	France	France	Favourite	18 Aug 1823
DENRY, Frd.	36 5/12	M	Farmer	Switzerland	U. States	France	26 Jun 1828
DENSILLIER, Augustus	60	M	Artist	France	U. States	Jane Blossom	28 Aug 1826
DENSNAUP, Joh	50	M	Farmer	England	America	Erin	7 Nov 1821
DENT, Ann	30	F	None	England		Manhattan	22 May 1827
Elizabeth	18	F	None	England		Manhattan	22 May 1827
Jane	14	F	None	England		Manhattan	22 May 1827
John D.	22	M	Merchant	England	U. States	William & Frederick	16 Feb 1824
Margaret	19	F		G.B.	G.B.	George Canning	26 Aug 1829
Mary	20	F	None	England		Manhattan	22 May 1827
Thos.	30	M	Chemist	G. Britain	U. States	Canada	19 Sep 1828
DENTON, Ann	48	F		Ireland	New York	Lima	5 Aug 1829
Ann	48	F		Ireland	New York	Lima	5 Aug 1829
DENTZLINGER, Joe	28	M	Weaver	Germany	United States	Helen	5 Sep 1828
DE NULLY, John	32	M	Merchant	Denmark	U. States	Chase	30 Dec 1822
DE NUNES, Juliana	36	F		Mexico	Spain	Sciot	12 Mar 1828
DENY, B.	28	M	Merchant	France	United States	Joseph	11 Jul 1821
John	22	M	Weaver	Ireland	United States	Henry Kneeland	7 Jun 1828
Michael	20	M	Labourer	Ireland	United States	Wanderer	1 Aug 1828
Nathanil	20	M	Gentleman	U. States Amer		Charlotte Corday	7 Mar 1820
DE OEA, Jose M.	22	M	Mercht.	Spain	Spain	Magnet	18 Aug 1825
DE ORLIGA, J. G.	28	M	Consul	Cuba	Columbia	Tampico	14 Jul 1825
DEOSON, Thos.	21		Painter	Ma...shton	England	Great Britain	7 May 1827
DEOT, C.	30	F		Holland	U. States	Talma	23 Sep 1828
DE OTERO, Jose	19	M	Labourer	Spain	U. States	Mercid	10 Jul 1826
DEOVNUX, Martin	22	M	Brazer	New York	New York or Boston	Concordia	12 Oct 1826
DEPAU, Frans., Jr.	28	M	Merchant	U. States	U. States	Ann	4 Mar 1826
Fras., Jr.	28	M	Merchant	U. States	New York	Sully	11 Mar 1829
DE PENNIE,							
Antonio, Don	32	M	Merchant	Portugal	Portugal	Bee	2 Oct 1820
DE PERNOY, S. E., Mrs.	36	F	None	So. America	U. States	Eclipse	10 Jun 1823
DE PEYSTER, F., Jr.	25	M	Merchant	U. States	U. States	Elias Burger	11 Jul 1822
F. A.	32	M	Ship Master	France	France	Augusta	8 Dec 1821
Rob. G. L.	26	M	Merchant	U. States	U. States	Elias Burger	11 Jul 1822
DEPEYSTER, F. A.	38	M	Captain	U. States	U. States	Signal	3 Jan 1827
DE PINARD, J.	21	M	Merchant	U.S.		Cadmus	9 Aug 1825
DE PINTO, J. F.	35	M	Captain	Portugal	U. States	St. George	20 Sep 1828
DEPLIDGE, Thos.	50		Farmer	G. Britain		Casanda	5 Sep 1827
DE POORTER,							
Benedictine, Miss	33	F	Teacher	Nederland	America	Henry	17 May 1828
DE POUVILLION, Josef.	J.25		Merchant	France	United States	Othello	6 Nov 1823
DEPRATT, Lewis	35	M	Merchant	France	U. States	Eliza Ann	16 Apr 1824
Lewis	38	M	Merchant	France	New York	Enterprize	3 Nov 1824
DE PUGE, Manuel	40	M	Merchant	U. States	United States	Dromo	22 Feb 1827
DE PUGO, Manuel	42	M	Merchant	U.S. America	U.S. America	Claudio	22 Mar 1828
DE PYRMONT, August	45	M	Merchant	France	France	Isaac Hicks	22 Aug 1829
DE QUARTEL, H. W.	48	M	Capt. Netherlands Navy	Netherlands	Netherlands	General Paez	22 Nov 1828
J. S.	6	M		Netherlands	Netherlands	General Paez	22 Nov 1828
P. F.	10	M		Netherlands	Netherlands	General Paez	22 Nov 1828
DEQUEYLA, Jean	26	M	Merchant	Gaudaloupe	Gaudaloupe	Jane	13 Aug 1827
DE QUFE, Morris	32	M	Merchant	Germany	U. States	Edward Quesnel	4 Aug 1828
DERAISMES, Jean	24	M	Merchant	French	French	Howard	4 May 1827

NAMES OF PASSENGERS	AGE	SEX	OCCUPATIONS	COUNTRY TO WHICH THEY BELONG	COUNTRY THEY INTEND TO INHABIT	SHIPS/DATES OF ARRIVAL	
DERAISMUS,							
John T.	26 4/12	M	Merchant	France	France	France	28 Mar 1829
Napolean H.	12 5/12	M		France	France	France	28 Mar 1829
DERAUX, John	4 6/12	M		France	France	Edward Quesnel	3 Jul 1829
John Francis	27	M	Farmer	France	France	Edward Quesnel	3 Jul 1829
Maria Theresa	27	F		France	France	Edward Quesnel	3 Jul 1829
Peter	1 6/12	M		France	France	Edward Quesnel	3 Jul 1829
DERAY, Theodore	27 4/12	M		France	U.S. America	Edward Bonnaffe	20 Jun 1826
DE RAYS, P.	23	M	Merchant	Portugal	U. States	Stephania	8 Mar 1823
DERBY, Richard	60	M	Gentleman	Cuba	United States	Ariel	30 Jun 1828
DERBYSHIRE, John	23	M	Mason	Great Britain	United States	Isaac Hicks	10 Jul 1827
DERDEN, Hannah	9	F		Great Britain	United States	India	5 Sep 1827
Mary	48	F		Great Britain	United States	India	5 Sep 1827
Richd.	47	M	Yarn Dresser	Great Britain	United States	India	5 Sep 1827
DERDRICK, Joseph	38	M	Mechanic	Hamburg	U. States	Minerva	13 Sep 1827
DERGAN, Betty	16	F	None	Ireland		Marchioness	13 May 1828
DERGER, James	13	M	Servant	Ireland	America	Carolina Ann	7 Aug 1826
DERHAM, Wm.	22	M	Labourer	Ireland	U. States	Sarah G	30 Jun 1828
DE RIGO CORENBA,							
Joze Comez	32	M	Milatary	Perambuco	Brazil	Jane	17 Jan 1825
DE RIGULES, José	26	M	Merchant	Spain	New York	Abeona	20 Dec 1823
DE RIVAFINOLE,							
Le Cher.	30	M	Merchant	Italy	U. States	Nestor	9 Dec 1822
DE RIVAFINOLI,							
Vincent	37	M	Mine Inspector	Italy	Mexico	Corinthian	27 Apr 1824
DERLIN, John	35	M	Weaver	Ireland	America	Carolina Ann	7 Aug 1826
Sally	22	F	Servant	Ireland	America	Carolina Ann	7 Aug 1826
DERMAN, John	23	M		G. Britan	U. States	William Neilson	26 Jul 1828
DERMODY, Francis	18	M	Weaver	Gt. Britain		Dalhouse Castle	13 May 1828
Henry	20	M	Labourer	Ireland	United States	Josephine	30 Apr 1828
DERMOT, Charles	...	...	...	Ireland	United States	General Putnam	20 Jun 1825
Edward	...	...	...	Ireland	United States	General Putnam	20 Jun 1825
John	19 5/12	M		Ireland	U.S. of America	Douglass	6 Jul 1829
Laurence	20	M	Labourer	Ireland	New York	Louisa	20 Jul 1826
DERMOTT, John	23	M	Labourer	Ireland	United States	Wilson	6 Jun 1828
Ryan	22	F	Coachman	Ireland	United States	Essex	23 May 1828
DERMSAY, Bridget	24	F		England	United States	India	8 Jun 1827
Elza	24	F	None	England	United States	India	8 Jun 1827
Margt.	21	F	None	England	United States	India	8 Jun 1827
DE ROA, Frs.	18	M	School Boy	Spain	Spain	Emulation	22 Jun 1825
DEROCHE, David L.	25	M	Farmer	Grandval	U.S. America	Superior	18 Jun 1825
Samuel	1	M	Farmer	Grandval	U.S. America	Superior	18 Jun 1825
Solomon	3	M	Farmer	Grandval	U.S. America	Superior	18 Jun 1825
Susan	30	F	Farmer	Grandval	U.S. America	Superior	18 Jun 1825
DE ROCHEBLANC, Pierre	55	M	Gentleman	Canada	Canada	Corinthian	5 May 1827
DEROIGNE, Chs. L.	36		Farmer	France	U. States	Elizabeth	9 Jul 1825
DEROIGNER, C. E.	5		Farmer	France	U. States	Elizabeth	9 Jul 1825
Chs. L.	6		Farmer	France	U. States	Elizabeth	9 Jul 1825
DERREN, Aaron	24	M		U. States	United States	Loire	12 Dec 1820
William	26	M	Paper Maker	Great Brittain	United States	Loire	12 Dec 1820
DER RHEINE, M.	37	M	Merchant	U.S.	Havanna	Auritz	20 May 1823
DERRIN, John	24	M	Labourer	Ireland	United States	Hope	12 Jun 1828
DERRING, F. S.	30	M	Merchant	U. States	U. States	Belvidera	28 Dec 1825
J. G.	26	M	Merchant	Germany	U. States	Sancho Panza	2 Jun 1824
DERRY, Chas.	20	M	Labourer	Ireland	United States	Henry Kneeland	7 Jun 1828
DERTMER, G.	11	M		Germany	U. States	Minerva	9 Jan 1827
DE RUGER, W.	35	M	Merchant	Citizen U. States	U. States	Leontine	10 Jul 1826
DE RUSSY, R. A.	29	M	Merchant	U. States	New York	Howard	11 Jan 1827
DE RUYTER, Benoit	32	M	Merchant	Holland	Holland	Paris	10 Sep 1823
DERVAL, Henry	30	M	Merchant	France	France	Ariel	1 Mar 1828
DERVAND, T.	42		Sqr.	Limoges (France)	New York	Manchester	30 May 1821
DERVELAND, Michal	19	M	Commisur	Bardin	U. States	Bayard	5 Sep 1828
DERWIN, Patrick	28	M		Ireland	U. States	Nancy	10 Jul 1822
DERZEL, John	52	M	Carpenter	Ireland	U. States	Concordia	11 Jun 1823
DE SACH, —, Count	55	M	Traveller	Berlin, Ga.	Different	Tampico	11 Jul 1826
DE ST. AGNAN, P. H. P.	28	M	Merchant	France	U. States	Robert Y. Haynes	22 Mar 1827

NAMES OF PASSENGERS	AGE	SEX	OCCUPATIONS	COUNTRY TO WHICH THEY BELONG	COUNTRY THEY INTEND TO INHABIT	SHIPS/DATES OF ARRIVAL	
DE ST. CROIX, B.	18	M	Doctor	Anapolis	U. States	Molly	30 Oct 1823
Euphemia	56	F	Lady	State New York	United States	St. Michaels	7 Jun 1827
P. Louis	20	M	Medicine	Nova Scotia	United States	McDonough	3 Nov 1823
DE ST. GEORGE, —,							
Baron	33	M	Gentleman	France	United States	Brighton	11 Dec 1827
DE SALAZAR, Luciano	23	M	Diplomatic	Spain	Philadelphia	Maria Elizabeth	16 Mar 1829
DE SALVEIRA, Helen B.	2	F	None	Brazil	U. States	Sarah	1 Aug 1827
Helen B.	29	F	None	Portugal	U. States	Sarah	1 Aug 1827
Joqueen N.	5	M	None	Brazil	U. States	Sarah	1 Aug 1827
Josse N.	6	M	None	Portugal	U. States	Sarah	1 Aug 1827
DESANNET, Vangull	25	M	Farmer	Switzerland		Nimrod	21 Sep 1820
DESAQUE, Francis	25	M	Mariner	U. States	U. States	Mary Livingston	14 May 1827
DESAULLES, Sarah	44	F	Lady	United States	United States	Harriet Smith	18 Oct 1821
DESBA...ES, J. L.	30	M	Gentleman	Great Britain	United States	Hamilton	21 Nov 1826
DESBAYET, E.	28	M	Watchmaker	Switzerland	U. States	Romulus	24 Sep 1828
DESBRAZA, Albert	23	M	Clergyman	St. John, N.B.	St. John, N.B.	St. Michaels	11 May 1826
DESBREST, A.	20	M	Merchant	France	U. States	Seine	16 Jun 1826
DESBROW, N.	65	M	Merchant	U. States	United States	Sarah G.	15 May 1828
DESBY, John	23	M	Merchant	U. States	Newyork	Sally Ann	28 Mar 1820
DESCHAMPE, Amie	12	F		United States	United States	Montano	27 Aug 1827
Coupard	30	F		United States	United States	Montano	27 Aug 1827
Edmond	34	M	Dyer	United States	United States	Montano	27 Aug 1827
Edward	9	M		United States	United States	Montano	27 Aug 1827
Francis	5	M		United States	United States	Montano	27 Aug 1827
Gustave	1 3/12	M		United States	United States	Montano	27 Aug 1827
DE SCHAUMBURG, H.	35	M	Merchant		United States	Brighton	29 Aug 1828
DES CHEMIS, S. Bois	10	F		Spain	U.S.	Radius	27 Apr 1824
DES CONDER, Lewis P.	45	M	Planter	U.S.	U.S.	Minerva	3 Dec 1821
DESDIERS, Henry	28	M	Merchant	Havana	U. States	Senica	17 Mar 1824
DESEAM, Rebecca	25	F	None	N. York	U. States	St. Michael	21 Jul 1824
DE SECHENDORFF, —,							
Mr.	46	M	Prof. of Phil.	Germany	Kentuckey	Elizabeth	5 Jul 1821
DE SEERE, A.	...	M	Merchant	W. Indis	W. Indis	Hiram	8 Jul 1828
A.	32	M	Merchant	W. Indies	W. Indies	Hiram	8 Jul 1829
DESEILLE, Nathalie	29	F	Nurse	Holland	U. States	America	22 Sep 1826
DE SELDERNY, Charles	30	M	Merchant	U. States	U. States	Manchester Packet	5 Dec 1826
DE SERIENE, A. L. P.	40	M	Merchant	Holland	U. States	Thule	29 Apr 1825
DESERMAUX, Anthony F.	44	M	Merchant	St. Martins	France	Brandt	11 Oct 1824
DES FONTAINE, Maria	27	F		United States	United States	Don Quixote	18 Aug 1824
DES FRALS, L. Jouquin	16	M		Madeira	U. States	Orion	19 Jun 1826
DESHEYS, —, Mr.	28	M	Merchant	United States	United States	Don Quixote	18 Aug 1824
DESHILOS, Ab.	25	M	Mearchnt.	United States	United States	Planter	26 Jul 1822
DE SIDANNE, M.	50	M	Gentleman	Spain	U. States	Mechanic	14 Dec 1822
DE SILVA, Francisco	46	M	Merchant	Spain	Havana	Draper	18 Nov 1822
Manuel	12	M	Merchant	Spain	Havana	Draper	18 Nov 1822
Manuel Henrique	28	M	Gentm.	Madeira	U. States	General Warren	19 Jan 1829
S. J.	19	M	Merchant	Brazil	U. States	Angenora	12 May 1826
DE SILVEIRA,							
Jaquin N., Mr.	36	M	Gentleman	U.S. Am.	U.S. Am.	Henry IV	5 Feb 1827
DE SILVIA LISBON,							
André	28	M	Secretary of Legation	Brazils	U. States	Bolivar	9 Dec 1826
Juan C.	7	M	Secretary of Legation	Brazils	U. States	Bolivar	9 Dec 1826
DESIRE D'EGREMONT,							
Prosper	22	M		France	France	Topaz	27 May 1828
DESJARDIN, Jules	27	M	Merchant	France		Edward Quesnel	17 Nov 1828
DESJARDINS, —	40	M	Farmer	France	United States	Marmion	13 Jun 1823
Cecilia	8	F		France	United States	Marmion	13 Jun 1823
Eliza	7	F		France	United States	Marmion	13 Jun 1823
DESLINER, ...	...	...	...	...	...	Seine	29 Jun 1827
DESMOLD, Christian	16	M	Gentleman	Germany	United States	Brandt	26 Jun 1826
DESMOLELINES, P.	27	M	Merchant	France	Jacmel	Arinthia Bell	31 Mar 1824
DESMONTIUS, Camille	30	M	Merchant	France	France	Hope Return	6 Jun 1823
DESMOULIUS, H. C.	30	M	Merchant	France	France	Fair American	25 Jul 1822
DESOBY, L.	20	M	Merchant	U. States	U. States	Waldo	19 Aug 1826
P.	17	M	Merchant	U. States	U. States	Waldo	19 Aug 1826

NAMES OF PASSENGERS	AGE	SEX	OCCUPATIONS	COUNTRY TO WHICH THEY BELONG	COUNTRY THEY INTEND TO INHABIT	SHIPS/DATES OF ARRIVAL	
DE SOLA, H.	26	M	None	Curraco	U. States	Ann Elizabeth	13 Jul 1826
DE SONTAG, Foturned.	28	M	Sect. To the Lagate Paris	France	America	Silvanus Jenkins	17 Nov 1828
DE SORIA, Pablo	48	M	Merchant	Spain	Spain	Martha	15 Jan 1822
DESOUCHES, Victory	24	F	Servant	France	U. States	Sully	25 Jun 1828
DESP...ACES, O. Tho...ier	55	M	Merct.	France	U.S.	Stephania	15 Aug 1825
DESPARD, Francis	11	M	Boy	Great Briton	United States	Erin	26 May 1821
Henrietta	11	F	Spinster	Ireland	United States	Dublin Packet	28 Apr 1824
Richard	12	M	Boy	Great Briton	United States	Erin	26 May 1821
DESPLACES, A.	59		Merchant	France		Edward	
Thoisnice						Bonnaffe	17 Mar 1828
DESREA, T.	45	M	Merchant	Spanish America	U. States	Endymion	22 May 1822
DES REVIERS, Francis W.	29	M	Advocate	Montreal	U. States	New York	15 Nov 1823
DES RUELLES, Gerrit	35	M	Koopman	Amsterdam	United States	Juffraw Johanna	16 Oct 1821
DESS, Antonio	9	M		France	France	Edward Quesnel	3 Jul 1829
Antonio	51	M	Farmer	France	France	Edward Quesnel	3 Jul 1829
Catherine	34	F		France	France	Edward Quesnel	3 Jul 1829
DESSANE, Bernard Demort	42	M	Dyer	England	U. States	Elizabeth	20 Sep 1822
DE SYLON, —, Baron	19	M	Gentleman	United States	United States	Don Quixote	18 Aug 1824
DE TICA, Manuel	30	M	Gentleman	Spain	United States	Orris	12 Mar 1825
DETMER, Geo. H.	43	M	Comissioner	Hamburg		Caesar	24 Aug 1829
George	41	M	Comissioner	Germany	U. States	Minerva	9 Jan 1827
DETTNER, F.	40	M	Saddler	Swiss	U. States	Montano	2 Sep 1828
DEUBLER, Andrew	32	M	Agriculture	Wirtemburg	United States	Henri IV	14 Oct 1829
DEUHURST, George	36	M	Reed Maker	England	United States	Dalhouse Castle	6 Sep 1827
DEUJNLOP, Agness	21	F	None	Scotland	United States	Washington	2 Oct 1828
DEULON, Rob.	17	M	Merchant	France	U. States	Magnet	1 Oct 1823
DE URRIA, P.	30	M	Planter	Cuba	U.S.	Edward Quesnel	31 Jul 1827
DEUTCH, ... [crossed out]	4	F	None	Germany	U. States	Sully	24 Oct 1828
Jacob	18	M	Weaver	Germany	U. States	Sully	24 Oct 1828
Joseph	4	M	Germany	France	U. States	Sully	24 Oct 1828
Maria	10	F	None	Germany	U. States	Sully	24 Oct 1828
Michael	21	M	Farmer	France	France	Sully	15 Jul 1829
Rosina	38	F	None	Germany	U. States	Sully	24 Oct 1828
DEVAL, Albin	30	M	Farmer	France	France	Edward Quesnel	3 Jul 1829
Ann R.	28	F		France	France	Edward Quesnel	3 Jul 1829
DEVAN, Ann	21	F	Spinster	Ireland	U. States	Josephine	30 Aug 1828
William	23	M	Weaver	Ireland	United States	Borneo	2 Oct 1827
DE VANCE, C...	26	M	Joiner	France	U.S.	Cadmus	9 Dec 1826
DEVANCY, Thos.	25	M	Farmer	Ireland	New York	Phoenix	29 Apr 1826
DEVANPORT, Geo. F.	21	M	Merchant	England	U. States	Falcon	12 Oct 1822
John	27	M	Merchant	U. States	U. States	President	3 Apr 1826
W.	18	M	Merchant	Bermuda	Bermuda	William	11 Nov 1823
Wm. A.	22	M	Merchant	Bermuda	Bermuda	Clio	6 Nov 1826
DEVANS, Sam	47	M	Merchant	U. States	U. States	William Bayard	25 Apr 1826
DEVANTRAY, L.	37	M	Farmer	Sweden	U. States	Cadmus	28 May 1821
DEVANY, Bridgit	20	F	Spinster	Ireland	United States	Wilson	6 Jun 1828
Cathrine	20	F	Taylor	Ireland	U. States	Virginia	20 Jun 1825
DEVARENY, Jane	20 10/12	F		Ireland	U.S. of America	Douglass	6 Jul 1829
DEVELIN, James	20	M	Labourer	Ireland	U. States	Josephine	30 Aug 1828
John	18	M	Weaver	Ireland	U. States	Josephine	30 Aug 1828
Nancy	21	F	Spinster	Ireland	United States	Leonidas	3 Aug 1825
DEVEN, Ann	20	F		Ireland	United States	Thompson	12 Sep 1827
DEVENPORT, H.	24	M	Gentleman	Boston	United States	Howard	14 May 1825
DEVENY, Anna	30	F	Hosier	Ireland		William Tell	24 Oct 1829
Rebecca	20		Spinster	Ireland	United States	Robert Burns	18 Jun 1821
DEVER, Edward	29	M	Labourer			Catherine	19 Aug 1825
James	29	M	Labourer	G. Britain	U. States	Hanford	18 Sep 1828
Margaret	27	F				Catherine	19 Aug 1825
Mary	6	F				Catherine	19 Aug 1825
Sarah	27	F		G. Britain	U. States	Hanford	18 Sep 1828
DEVERAUX, John	7	M	None	Great Brittan	U. States	John &	

NAMES OF PASSENGERS	AGE	SEX	OCCUPATIONS	COUNTRY TO WHICH THEY BELONG	COUNTRY THEY INTEND TO INHABIT	SHIPS/DATES OF ARRIVAL	
DEVERAUX (cont'd)							
John	49	M	Merchant	Great Brittan	U. States	John &	
						Elizabeth	11 Dec 1826
DEVERELL, Margaret	10	F		England	U. States	Trident	1 Dec 1824
W. R.	20	M	Gentleman	England	U. States	Trident	1 Dec 1824
DEVEREUX, George P.	30	M	Planter	U. States	United States	John & Edward	7 Nov 1825
M. N.	20		Farmer	Cork	Baltimore	Schuylkill	22 Aug 1825
R.	31	M	Carpenter	U. States	U. States	Swift	28 Jan 1828
DEVERIN, Chales	32	M	Gent	France	U. States	Charlemagne	19 Sep 1828
DEVERISE, John	30	M	Clerk	Ireland	America	Dublin Packet	9 Oct 1820
DEVETER, Margret	23	F		Ireland	United States	Nancey	8 Jun 1822
DEVETT, Felix	27	M		England	United States	Essex	23 May 1828
DEVHURST, Richard	20	M	Farmer	G.B.	U.S.A.	Silas Richard	30 Jun 1828
DEVIEME, Patt	40			England	United States	Hugh Johnson	11 Jun 1828
DEVIES, John	31	M	Farmer	G. Braitan	U. States	Cosmo	29 Jun 1826
DEVILIN, John		M	Chiefly farmers		United States	Factor	8 Jul 1829
DEVILLALAUR, Piere	43	M	Gold Smith	France	United States	Bayard	15 Feb 1827
DE VILLEBACH,							
Renaud	35	M	...	France	U.S.	Queen Mab	26 Nov 1825
DE VILLENEUEX,							
Alexr. Guyot	19	M	Student	France	New York	Lewis	29 Oct 1825
DE VILLERS,							
F. D. Petit, Mr.	68	M	Merchant	U. States	U. States	Sully	24 Oct 1828
DEVILLEZE, Peirre	25	M	Merchant	France	U. States	Admittance	10 Nov 1825
DEVIN, James	24	M	Farmer	Ireland	United States	Dublin Packet	29 Jun 1825
John	22	F	Labourer	Ireland	United States	Hope	12 Jun 1828
DEVINA, Ann	30	F	Farmer	Ireland	U. States	Edward	15 Jul 1825
Ann	70	F	Farmer	Ireland	U. States	Edward	15 Jul 1825
Catharine	35	F	Farmer	Ireland	U. States	Edward	15 Jul 1825
Hugh	31	M	Farmer	Ireland	U. States	Edward	15 Jul 1825
Hugh	70	M	Farmer	Ireland	U. States	Edward	15 Jul 1825
Mich.	22	M	Farmer	Ireland	U. States	Edward	15 Jul 1825
DEVINE, Eliza	21	F		Ireland	U. States	Olive Branch	30 Oct 1823
Ellen	23	F	None	Ireland	United States	Colossus	26 Aug 1828
Hugh	21	M	Labourer	Great Brittan	U. States	Pallas	17 Aug 1824
James	21	M	None	Ireland	U. States	Criterion	23 May 1826
John	20	M	Carpenter	U. States	U. States	Commodore	
						Perry	9 Apr 1821
John	28	M	Labourer	Ireland	United States	Fabius	31 Jul 1829
Mary	19	F	None	Ireland	United States	Colossus	26 Aug 1828
Mary	55	F	None	Ireland	United States	Colossus	26 Aug 1828
Partrick	12	M	None	Ireland	United States	Colossus	26 Aug 1828
Samuel	21		Laborer	Ireland	United States	Robert Burns	18 Jun 1821
Thomas	20	M	Labourer	Ireland	United States	Jubilee	12 May 1828
W.		M	Carpenter	U. States	U. States	David	19 Apr 1824
DEVING, Bridget	30	F				Catherine	19 Aug 1825
James	35	M				Catherine	19 Aug 1825
John	8	M				Catherine	19 Aug 1825
Mary	11	F				Catherine	19 Aug 1825
Patrick	4	M				Catherine	19 Aug 1825
Sarah	14	F				Catherine	19 Aug 1825
Sarah	20	F	Spinster			Catherine	19 Aug 1825
DEVINGREW,							
Anna, Miss	63					Alfred	8 Jul 1822
DEVIR, James	24	M	Labourer	Ireland	United States	Catharine	22 Jul 1825
DEVISON, L.	25	M	Merchant	England	U. States	Diana	12 Apr 1825
DEVITT, Thomas	25	M	Labourer	Ireland	United States	Meteor	26 Jun 1827
DEVLIN, Arthur	20		Farmer	Ireland		Westmoreland	1 Aug 1826
Pat.	...	...	...	Ireland	United States	General Putnam	20 Jun 1825
Patrick	26	M	Weaver	Monymore	N. York	Favourite	8 Oct 1823
DEVOE, John	25	M	Farmer	Great Brittain	U. States	Nancy	18 Jul 1821
DEVOIGNER, Marianna	30		Farmer	France	U. States	Elizabeth	9 Jul 1825
DEVOL, Charles	20	M	Labourer	Germany	United States	Samuel	
						Robertson	8 Aug 1828
DEVOLIN, Daniel	9	M		G. Britain	U. States	Camillus	8 Sep 1828
DEVON, A. C. F.	56	M	Merchant	France	U. States	Canning	18 Jul 1828
DEVONSHIRE, Jane	70	F		America	United States	Loire	12 Dec 1820
DEVONY, Patrick	28	M	Farmer	Great Britain	United States	Ocean	27 Jul 1825
DEVOTION, Josephine	20	F	Lady	U. States	U. States	Abeona	1 Oct 1823

NAMES OF PASSENGERS	AGE	SEX	OCCUPATIONS	COUNTRY TO WHICH THEY BELONG	COUNTRY THEY INTEND TO INHABIT	SHIPS/DATES OF ARRIVAL	
DEVOY, Dennis	50	M	Farmer	Great Britain	United States	Ocean	27 Jul 1825
Dennis, Jr.	25	M	Farmer	Great Britain	United States	Ocean	27 Jul 1825
DEVOY, Nicholas	27	M	Farmer	Great Britain	United States	Ocean	27 Jul 1825
DEVREX, John	38 4/12	M	Sencral	Iland	U. States	France	26 Jun 1828
DE VRGUEFO, Dionisis	33	M	Merchant	Spain	New York	Abeona	20 Dec 1823
DEVRICK, George	20	M	Harness Maker	G. Britain	U.S. America	Cincinnatus	31 Oct 1820
DEVRY, Rose	20	F		Gt. Britain		Dalhouse Castle	13 May 1828
DE VUSTAMANTU, Pedro, Don	52	M	Merchant	Spain	Spain	Centurion	22 Dec 1828
DEWAR, John	19	M	Merchant	Scotland	U. States	Spartan	11 Mar 1823
Rt.	30	M	Grocer	Glasgow, Barony [Parish], Lanark [County]	New York	Hero	19 May 1828
*to follow his occupation							
DEWBLER, Christina	2	F	there child [Martin & Dorothy]	Germany	United States	Helen	5 Sep 1828
Dorothy	27	F	his wife [Martin]	Germany	United States	Helen	5 Sep 1828
Elizabeth	1	F	there child [Martin & Dorothy]	Germany	United States	Helen	5 Sep 1828
Frederick	8	M	there child [Martin & Dorothy]	Germany	United States	Helen	5 Sep 1828
George	7	M	there child [Martin & Dorothy]	Germany	United States	Helen	5 Sep 1828
Joan	4	F	there child [Martin & Dorothy]	Germany	United States	Helen	5 Sep 1828
Martin	38	M	Farmer	Germany	United States	Helen	5 Sep 1828
DEWENT, J. G.	25	M	Tailor	U. States	U. States	Cannon	10 Dec 1821
DEWER, Wm.	25	M	Laborer or Spinster	Ireland	United States	Sarah G	11 Sep 1827
DEWHIRST, Ann	33	F		Great Britain	United States	Thomas Dickason	14 Sep 1827
John	36	M	White Smith	Great Britain	United States	Thomas Dickason	14 Sep 1827
Newton	7	F		Great Britain	United States	Thomas Dickason	14 Sep 1827
Peter	48	M	Stone Mason	Great Britan	United States	Clematis	8 May 1827
Sarah	2 9/12	F		Great Britain	United States	Thomas Dickason	14 Sep 1827
DEWHUNT, Margaret	20	M	Weaver	England	U. States	York	4 Apr 1826
DEWHURST, Ann	17	M	Reed Maker	England	United States	Dalhouse Castle	6 Sep 1827
John Johnson	32	M	House Joiner	Great Britain	America	Lady Gallatin	21 Jun 1820
Paul	24	M	Sawyer	Great Britain	United States	Penelope	11 Jun 1827
DE WINT, Isaac	23	M	Taylor	America	United States	Andrew Jackson	9 Jul 1822
DEWITT, S.	22	M	Merchant	Alaenburg		Constitution	20 Jun 1828
DEWNVIN, James	20	M		Ireland	America	Carolina Ann	7 Aug 1826
DE WOLF, G.	20	M	Merchant	U. States	U. States	Leontine	19 May 1825
Jacob	22	M	Carpenter	Connecticut	Connecticut	Governor Griswold	15 Jul 1826
M. A.	25	M	Merchant	U. States	U. States	Lincoln	12 Jun 1824
DEWOLF, N. H.	18	M		Norfolk	U. States	John Dickinson	13 May 1823
Wm. Henry	31	M	Gentleman	Rhode Island	U. States	Romulus	26 Apr 1822
DE WOLFE, M. A.	25	M	Merchant	U. States	U. States	Eagle	2 Jul 1825
DEWZEY, Jos.	35	M	Ship Master	Columbus	Columbus	Prudence	19 Apr 1826
DEXTER, George	30	M	Merchant	England	St. Domingo	Euphrates	8 Aug 1820
George M.	22	M	Merchant	U. States	U. States	York	10 Dec 1825
Katharine	55	F		United States	United States	Robert Fulton	27 Jun 1822
DEY, Caroline	28	F		U. States	U. States	Silas Richards	27 Jun 1827
Mary	50	F		England	U.N. States	Earl of Liverpool	20 Aug 1825
DEYER, William	23	M	Merchant	U. States	U. States	Queen Mab	16 Mar 1825
DE YNZA, Frans.	38	M	Merchant	Spain	U. States	Albany Pkt.	2 Jun 1828
Jose	42	M	Mercht.	Spain	Spain	Albany Packet	14 Nov 1826
DE YOLAS, Jose	25	M	Barrister	Spain	U. States	Rubicon	8 Jun 1827
DE YONG, Alex	24	F	Wife	G. Brittan	U. States	Henry	24 Oct 1828
Elizabeth	65	F	infant	G. Brittan	U. States	Henry	24 Oct 1828
Isaack S.	32	M	Merchant	G. Brittan	U. States	Henry	24 Oct 1828
Manna	2	F	infant	G. Brittan	U. States	Henry	24 Oct 1828
Mary	27	M	Merchant	G. Brittan	U. States	Henry	24 Oct 1828
Saml. Jacob	19	M	Merchant	England	United States	Acasta	14 Jun 1824
DEZPLACES, Chris W.	60	M	Merch.	France	United States	Henri IV	14 Oct 1829

NAMES OF PASSENGERS	AGE	SEX	OCCUPATIONS	COUNTRY TO WHICH THEY BELONG	COUNTRY THEY INTEND TO INHABIT	SHIPS/DATES OF ARRIVAL	
DEZPLACES, Chris W.	60	M	Merch.	France	United States	Henri IV	14 Oct 1829
DHARA, Pedro	39	M	Merchant	American born	U. States	Leontine	18 Mar 1825
DHITTENDEN, Asabel	24	M	...	England	United States	Exchange	18 Nov 1822
DIAMON, Joseph	27	M	Taylor	England	United States	William & Henry	19 Jul 1822
DIAMOND, Catharine	4	F	Farmer	Ireland	U. States	Dickinson	30 Jul 1825
Cathrine	27	F		Ireland	New York	Carolina Ann	15 Oct 1824
George	21	M	Shoemaker	U. States	U. States	Swift	28 Jan 1828
Hugh	25		Marble ...			Amphion	31 May 1824
Mary	9	F		Ireland	New York	Carolina Ann	15 Oct 1824
Mary	62	F	Widdow	Ireland	U. States	Josephine	7 May 1827
Nancy	6	F	Farmer	Ireland	U. States	Dickinson	30 Jul 1825
Richard	30	M	Shoemaker	Ireland	U. States	Josephine	7 May 1827
Sarah Jane *Dead				Ireland	New York	Carolina Ann	15 Oct 1824
Susan	30	F	Servant	Great Brittian	Jamaica	Four Sons	31 May 1828
DIAMONT, Julia	25		Laboring Class		United States	Atlantic	2 Apr 1827
DIANE, Thos.	28	M				Hibernia	15 Aug 1820
DIANEL, Ann	15		Spinster	Ireland	United States	Courier	15 Oct 1827
DIAR, Fernando	14	M	Merchant	Columbian Republic	Columbian Republic	Meta	5 Jun 1824
Manuel Ma.	32	M	Merchant	Columbian Republic	Columbian Republic	Meta	5 Jun 1824
DIAS, A. L.	32	M	Mercht.	U.S.	U.S.	Edward Quesnel	21 Apr 1827
Alexis L.	30	M	Merchant	United States		France	6 Feb 1829
Alfred Wm.	6	M	Child	England	United States	Cambria	3 Jul 1829
Eliza	4	F	Child	England	United States	Cambria	3 Jul 1829
John	35	M	Merchant	United States	United States	Patty & Sally	8 Dec 1821
John	38	M	Hatter	U. States	U. States	Francis Jarvis	17 Oct 1822
John	40	M	Hatter	U. States	U. States	Nassau	2 Nov 1825
Robert	35	M	Lighterman	England	United States	Cambria	3 Jul 1829
Sarah	31	F	Wife	England	United States	Cambria	3 Jul 1829
Sarah Ann	7	F	Child	England	United States	Cambria	3 Jul 1829
Sydney Smith	8/12	M	Child	England	United States	Cambria	3 Jul 1829
DIAZ, Joaquin	25	M	Gentleman	Costafirme	Mexico	Noble	2 Nov 1826
Manuel	40	M	Merchant	Spain	U. States	Dromo	4 May 1827
DIBBIN, Ann	20 4/12	F	None	Ireland	America	Minerva	31 May 1824
Mary	1 9/12	F	None	Ireland	America	Minerva	31 May 1824
Thomas	27 6/12	M	Labourer	Ireland	America	Minerva	31 May 1824
DIBBLE, Jonathan	35	M	Merchant	U. States	U. States	Sarah Herrick	13 May 1826
DICK, Ben	40	M	Carpenter	Switzerland	United States	Howard	27 Sep 1824
Benjamin, Child	9	M	...	Switzerland	United States, the State of Ohio	Florian	28 Sep 1824
Bennoit	32	F	Miller	Switzerland	U. States	Lewis	11 Nov 1824
David	25	M	Mechanic	Scotland	United States	Trent	10 Jul 1827
Elizabeth	12	F	...	Switzerland	United States, the State of Ohio	Florian	28 Sep 1824
Elizabeth	20	F	Farmer	Switzerland	U. States	Sully	15 Jul 1829
George	23	M	Farmer	Scotland	U. States	Camillus	27 Jun 1826
Hannah	11/12	F	...	Switzerland	United States, the State of Ohio	Florian	28 Sep 1824
Hannah	9	F	...	Switzerland	United States, the State of Ohio	Florian	28 Sep 1824
Henry	17	M	Farmer	Britain	America	Camillus	9 Oct 1820
Hugh	30	M	Merchant	England	England	Splendid	31 Aug 1827
Isabella	35	F		Switzerland	United States	Howard	27 Sep 1824
J.	21	M	Miller	Switzerland	U. States	Marmion	18 Oct 1824
Jane	5	F		Scotland	United States	Camillus	27 Oct 1829
John	38	M	...	Switzerland	United States, the State of Ohio	Florian	28 Sep 1824
John, child	12	M	...	Switzerland	United States, the State of Ohio	Florian	28 Sep 1824
Jonah	8	M	...	Switzerland	United States, the State of Ohio	Florian	28 Sep 1824
Margaret	3	F	...	Switzerland	United States, the State of Ohio	Florian	28 Sep 1824
Margt.	29	F		Scotland	United States	Camillus	27 Oct 1829
Mary Ann	10	F	...	Switzerland	United States, the State of Ohio	Florian	28 Sep 1824

NAMES OF PASSENGERS	AGE	SEX	OCCUPATIONS	COUNTRY TO WHICH THEY BELONG	COUNTRY THEY INTEND TO INHABIT	SHIPS/DATES OF ARRIVAL	
DICK (cont'd)							
Materlane	8	F	...	Switzerland	United States, the State of Ohio	Florian	28 Sep 1824
Nannah	6	F	...	Switzerland	United States, the State of Ohio	Florian	28 Sep 1824
Nicholas	4	M	...	Switzerland	United States, the State of Ohio	Florian	28 Sep 1824
Nicholas	13	M	...	Switzerland	United States, the State of Ohio	Florian	28 Sep 1824
Nicholas	23	M	Farmer	Switzerland	U. States	Sully	15 Jul 1829
Nicholas	33	M	...	Switzerland	United States, the State of Ohio	Florian	28 Sep 1824
Richard	35	M	Merchant	England	U. States	William Thompson	17 Dec 1827
Ruenon, his wife [Nicholas]	34	F	...	Switzerland	United States, the State of Ohio	Florian	28 Sep 1824
Sarah	38	F	...	Switzerland	United States, the State of Ohio	Florian	28 Sep 1824
Wm.	22	M	Labourer	British ...	American States	Loyalty	9 Sep 1822
DICKERS, John	40	M	Farmer	England	New York	Brighton	11 Dec 1827
DICKERSON, Thomas	43	M	Sail Maker	United States	United States	Only Daughter	29 Apr 1825
DICKES, James	13	M		Gt. Brittain	U. States	Courier	30 Dec 1824
John	25	M	Farmer	England	England	Gulnard	24 Mar 1825
Joseph	49	M	Farmer	Gt. Brittain	U. States	Courier	30 Dec 1824
Thomas	11	M		Gt. Brittain	U. States	Courier	30 Dec 1824
Wm.	14	M		Gt. Brittain	U. States	Courier	30 Dec 1824
DICKEY, ...s	3...	...	...	Scotland	America	Nimrod	9 Jul 1827
E., Revnd.	48	M	Clergyman	United States	United States	Nestor	3 Nov 1820
Elizabeth	...	...	...	Scotland	America	Nimrod	9 Jul 1827
Ezekiel	28	M	Farmer	Ireland	United States	Gem	16 Jun 1824
George	19	M	Gentleman	U. States	U. States	Carlo	30 Jul 1827
Henry	...	...	...	Scotland	America	Nimrod	9 Jul 1827
Ja...	...	...	...	Scotland	America	Nimrod	9 Jul 1827
Jane	...3	F	Spinster	Ireland	United States	Gem	16 Jun 1824
John	...	M	...	Scotland	America	Nimrod	9 Jul 1827
William	...	M	...	Scotland	America	Nimrod	9 Jul 1827
DICKIE, John	34	M	Weaver	Great Britain		Dalmannock	24 Ocg 1826
DICKINS, George	54	M	Plastere	G.B.	New York	Eliza Grant	29 Aug 1829
George	54	M	Plasterer	Great Britain		Eliza Grant	29 Aug 1829
DICKINSON, Alice	37	F	None			Manhattan	8 Aug 1820
Charles	7	M	None	England	America	Ann	2 Nov 1820
Eliza	8	F	None	England	America	Ann	2 Nov 1820
Elizabeth	42	F		England	United States	Amelia	20 Aug 1829
F. H.	1		None	United States	United States	Roman	10 Sep 1827
Geo.	45	M	Merchant	United States	United States	Manhattan	22 Sep 1823
George	41	M	Clerk	Great Britain	United States	Manhattan	8 Aug 1820
Henry	9	M	None	England	America	Ann	2 Nov 1820
Isabella	22		None	United States	United States	Roman	10 Sep 1827
Jas.	25	M	Mill Wright	Scotland	U. States	Henri IV	3 Feb 1829
John	14	M		England	United States	Amelia	20 Aug 1829
John	30	M	Woolsater	Ireland	U. States	Lima	5 Aug 1829
John	47	M	Farmer	England	United States	Amelia	20 Aug 1829
John K.	26		Farmer	Germany	United States	Corinthian	30 May 1828
Mary	21		None	Charl..., Canada	America	Frances Henrietta	31 May 1824
P.	29	M	Mariner	U. States	U. States	Sentiment	30 Jul 1827
Sarah	26	F	None	England	America	Ann	2 Nov 1820
T.	45	M	Planter	Matanzas	U. States	New England	23 Apr 1827
Taylon	38	M	Farmer	England	America	Ann	2 Nov 1820
Wm.	23	M		England		Anacreon	7 Sep 1827
DICKISON, W. A.	31	M	Merchant	England	U. States	York	12 Jul 1825
DICKMON, Wm. Smith	29	M	Merchant	G. Bt.	G. Bt.	Canada	13 Oct 1825
DICKS, Johahn	7	M		Gt. Brittain	U. States	Courier	30 Dec 1824
Mary	4	F		Gt. Brittain	U. States	Courier	30 Dec 1824
Mary	49	F		Gt. Brittain	U. States	Courier	30 Dec 1824
DICKSON, Ann	32	F	Farmer	England	United States	Justina	5 Aug 1823
Augh	25	M		Ireland	America	Superior	12 Jun 1824
Biddy	27	F		Ireland	America	Carolina Ann	7 Apr 1826
Daniel	25		Farmer			Rufus King	7 Aug 1820

NAMES OF PASSENGERS	AGE	SEX	OCCUPATIONS	COUNTRY TO WHICH THEY BELONG	COUNTRY THEY INTEND TO INHABIT	SHIPS/DATES OF ARRIVAL	
DICKSON (cont'd)							
Elizabeth	2/12	F	Farmer	England	United States	Justina	5 Aug 1823
James	9	M	Shoemaker	U. States	U. States	Robt. Reade	12 Apr 1825
John	10	M	Farmer	U. States	U. States	Robt. Reade	12 Apr 1825
John	30	M	Woolsorter	England	New York	Lima	5 Aug 1829
John H.	30	M	Merchant	Philada.	U. States	James Murdock	2 Jan 1822
Joseph	32	M	Cabinet Maker	Great Britain	United States	Wilson	26 Feb 1824
Julia	30	F	Farmer	U. States	U. States	Robt. Reade	12 Apr 1825
Mary	2	F	Farmer	England	United States	Justina	5 Aug 1823
Patrick	30		Farmer			Rufus King	7 Aug 1820
Richard	20	M	...man	United States	United States	Silas Richards	27 Oct 1825
Richard	25	M	Merchant	Scotland	United States	Camillus	9 May 1827
Samuel	19	M	Weaver	Ireland	United States	Romulus	24 Jun 1826
Thomas	32	M	Farmer	England	United States	Justina	5 Aug 1823
William	25	M	Merchant	United States	United States	Actress	17 Mar 1820
William	25	M	Carpenter	England	United States	Jubilee	1 Oct 1828
Wm.	14	M	Farmer	U. States	U. States	Robt. Reade	12 Apr 1825
Wm.	30	M	Cord weaver	England	U. States	Electra	7 Jul 1828
DICKY, Jno.	18	M	Farmer	Ireland	United States	Marmion	17 Jun 1825
DICONSON,							
E... [crossed out]						Franklin	7 Jul 1828
*Died on the voyage, 23 Jun 1828							
Eliz.	30	F	En.	England	U. States	Franklin	7 Jul 1828
Hannah	10/12	F	En.	England	U. States	Franklin	7 Jul 1828
DIDEN, Jefferson F.	21	M	Merchant	France	U. States	Bayard	9 Nov 1825
DIDIER, Alphonse	17	M	Merchant	France	France	Washington	7 Dec 1827
J. F.	23	M	Merchant	Baltimore	U. States	Altamira	5 Aug 1826
Peter	18	M	Barber	Italy	United States	Montano	13 Jan 1826
DIECONE, Pire	30	M	Laborer	Switzerland	U.States	C. Amelia	30 Jun 1828
DIEHR, Clement	52	M	Farmer	Swizerland		Antioch	18 Aug 1829
Marguerite	32	M	Farmer	Swizerland		Antioch	18 Aug 1829
DIEL, Caspar	30	M	Joiner	Baden	Baden	Sully	15 Jul 1829
DIELLY, Connor	34	M	Labourer	Gt. Britain	U. States	Frances Henrietta	18 Apr 1825
DIEMAN'S, M.	32	M	Cooper	Hessian	U. States	Howard	13 Feb 1829
DIEMARTRAY, Alferri	30	M	Merchant	France	Central America	Ned	1 Oct 1829
DIEPEN, J. J. A.	23	M	Merchant	Holland	U. States	Columbia	24 Dec 1822
DIETORICH, Mary M.	26	F		America	U. States	Charlemagne	19 Sep 1828
Saturne	34	M	Gent.	America	U. States	Charlemagne	19 Sep 1828
Wm. H.	31	M		America	U. States	Charlemagne	19 Sep 1828
DIETRIEK, Clements	22	M	Baker	France	U. States	Edward Quesnel	4 Aug 1828
DIETSCHY, Rodolph			Missionary	Germany	Liberia	Sully	26 Oct 1829
DIEUDONNÉ,							
Louis Henri	25 9/12	M	Merchant	St. Thomas	St. Thomas	Wanderer	4 Aug 1829
DIEUX, L.	25	M	None	France	United States	Marmione	20 Nov 1821
DIEZ, Wilhelmina	17	F		Germany	Ohio	James Noble	27 Aug 1827
DIGEL, Barbara	40	F	Baker	France	United States	Globe	30 Aug 1828
John	42	M	Baker	France	United States	Globe	30 Aug 1828
DIGGIN, Timothy	35	M	Tailor	Great Britain	United States	Mary Howland	19 Jul 1827
DIGGLE, Abraham	16	M	Weaver	England		Britannia	20 Jun 1827
James	28	M	Weaver	Ireland	United States	Lord Wellington	14 Nov 1827
DIGGLES, Nathaniel	17	M	Dyer	England	Red Island	Curler	7 Jul 1827
Wm.	24	M	Spinner	Great Britain	United States	Penelope	11 Jun 1827
DIGGS, David	31	M	Farmer	U. States	U. States	Robt. Reade	12 Apr 1825
Ephram	10	M	Farmer	U. States	U. States	Robt. Reade	12 Apr 1825
Nancy	4	F	Farmer	U. States	U. States	Robt. Reade	12 Apr 1825
Rachel	28	F	Farmer	U. States	U. States	Robt. Reade	12 Apr 1825
DIGHT, John	32	M	Clergyman	England	U. States	Manhattan	12 Jun 1824
DIGIN, Peter	24	M		Native of Switzerland	United States	Canaris	30 Jun 1827
DIGMAN, Jno.	33	M	Weaver	Great Britain	United States	Penelope	11 Jun 1827
Rose	21	F	None	Great Britain	United States	Penelope	11 Jun 1827
DIGNAN, Eleanor	21	F	Spinster	Ireland	United States	Dublin Packet	9 Jul 1827
DIGNEN, Thos.	25	M	Weaver			Hanford	17 Jul 1828
DIJOUX, Pictor	24	M	Cooper	France	United States	Olympia	20 Aug 1829
DIKE, John	1	M	Spinster	Great Britain	United States	Asia	14 Jul 1829
Lucy	23	F	Spinster	Great Britain	United States	Asia	14 Jul 1829
DILCHARD, Samul, Mr.	26	M	Carpenter	England	U.S.	Acasta	11 May 1827
DILES, Raymond	28	M	Merchant	Spain	Spain	Douglass	25 Nov 1825

NAMES OF PASSENGERS	AGE	SEX	OCCUPATIONS	COUNTRY TO WHICH THEY BELONG	COUNTRY THEY INTEND TO INHABIT	SHIPS/DATES OF ARRIVAL	
DILL, David	25	M				Imperial	19 Jul 1820
David	50	M	Farmer			Imperial	19 Jul 1820
Hannah	20	F				Imperial	19 Jul 1820
Margaret	45	F				Imperial	19 Jul 1820
Moile	23	F				Imperial	19 Jul 1820
Nancy	25	F				Imperial	19 Jul 1820
Nathan J.	36	M	Merchant	Bermuda	Great Britian	Two Brothers	6 Sep 1823
Nathl.	38	M	Mariner	Bermuda	U. States	Anna	12 May 1823
Saml.	28	M	Farmer			Imperial	19 Jul 1820
DILLAN, Francis	3	M	Child	Ireland	U. States	Josephine	30 Aug 1828
DILLEN, Ann	30	F	Matron	Ireland	U. States	Josephine	30 Aug 1828
Francis	22	M	Labourer	Ireland	United States	Edwin	29 Nov 1828
James	5	M	Child	Ireland	U. States	Josephine	30 Aug 1828
DILLENBACK, Christian	51	M	Farmer	Switzerland	United States	Don Quixote	7 May 1824
Samuel	17	M	Farmer	Switzerland	United States	Don Quixote	7 May 1824
DILLETT, John	28	M	Gentleman	St. Domingo	U. States	John London	26 Jun 1822
DILLIGAN, Phillip	20	M	Shoemaker			Commerce	22 Jun 1825
DILLION, Ellen	22	F	Wife	Ireland	United States	Ann Maria	2 Nov 1827
William	23	M	None	Ireland	United States	Ann Maria	2 Nov 1827
DILLIS, Mary	7	F	Spinster	Ireland	United States	Wilson	6 Jun 1828
DILLON, Akira	30		Lady	Ireland		Hibernia	15 Aug 1820
Bartholls.	30	M	Farmer	Ireland	United States	Lord Strangford	20 Jun 1826
Bridget	8	F	Child	Ireland	United States	Dublin Packet	28 Apr 1824
Catharine	7		Lady			Hibernia	15 Aug 1820
Christopher	31	M	Farmer	Gt. Britain	United States	Elbe	8 Jun 1824
Danl.	57	M	Farmer	Great Britain	U.S. of America	Gratitude	3 Oct 1829
Henry	16	M	Gentleman	Ireland	U. States	York	7 Aug 1828
J.	29	M	Smith	Great Britain	United States	Isaac Hicks	6 Dec 1827
John	20	M	Farmer	Ireland	America	Farmer	4 Aug 1825
Jos.	13	M	Labourer	Ireland	United States	Essex	23 May 1828
Joseph	26 10/12		Labourer	Ireland	Savanna	Marcella	18 May 1827
Julia	5	F	Child	Ireland	United States	Dublin Packet	28 Apr 1824
Mary	30	F	Spinster	Ireland	United States	Dublin Packet	28 Apr 1824
Michael	40	M	Clerk	Ireland	United States	Thompson	12 Sep 1827
Patrick	10	M	Child	Ireland	United States	Dublin Packet	28 Apr 1824
Patrick	28	M	Farmer	Ireland	United States	Abigail	25 Jun 1822
Patrick	33	M	Farmer	Ireland	United States	Dublin Packet	28 Apr 1824
Thomas	10	M	Labourer	Ireland	U. States	William & John	10 Jul 1824
Thos.	24	M	Labourer	Ireland		Marchioness	13 May 1828
William	32	M	Merchant	U. States	U. States	Nassau	2 Nov 1825
DILMORE, Christ.	32	M	Farmer	England	U. States	Auritz	20 May 1823
DILY, Margt.	24	F		Ireland	U. States	Sarah G	30 Jun 1828
DIMANN, Anthony	27	M	Paper Hanger	England	New York	Thames	6 Oct 1820
DIMDERDALE,							
Cleaveland	8	M	None	Leeds	New York	New York	14 Nov 1826
Forbes	10	M	None	Leeds	New York	New York	14 Nov 1826
John	19	M	None	Leeds	New York	New York	14 Nov 1826
Joseph	13	M	None	Leeds	New York	New York	14 Nov 1826
Maria	15	F	None	Leeds	New York	New York	14 Nov 1826
Maria S.	38	F	None	Leeds	New York	New York	14 Nov 1826
Mary	12	F	None	Leeds	New York	New York	14 Nov 1826
Sarah	17	F	None	Leeds	New York	New York	14 Nov 1826
Susannah	6	F	None	Leeds	New York	New York	14 Nov 1826
DIMOCH, Charles	25	M	Officer	U. States	U.S.	Bayard	10 Nov 1824
DIMON, H.	22	M	Mechanic	Gt. Britain	U. States	Swift	25 Apr 1828
DIMOND, Rachal	20	F		Ireland	America	Carolina Ann	7 Aug 1826
DIMS, David	40	M	Merchant	United States	United States	Nancy	28 Oct 1822
DINAN, Patrick	30		Laborer	Great Britan	U. States	Columbia	7 May 1828
DINATCH, Agness	19	F		Gt. Britain	U. States	Lima	22 Sep 1828
DINGWELL, Roderick	39	M	Planter	Scotland	U.S.A.	Orator	1 Oct 1829
DINING, Hannah	24	F		New York	United States	Mount Vernon	9 Jun 1823
DINKLINGER, Barbara	28	F	his wife [Christian]	Germany	United States	Helen	5 Sep 1828
Christian	32	M	Farmer	Germany	United States	Helen	5 Sep 1828
Francis X.	4	M	there child [Christian & Barbara]	Germany	United States	Helen	5 Sep 1828
Mary	3	F	there child [Christian & Barbara]	Germany	United States	Helen	5 Sep 1828

NAMES OF PASSENGERS	A G E	S E X	OCCUPATIONS	COUNTRY TO WHICH THEY BELONG	COUNTRY THEY INTEND TO INHABIT	SHIPS/DATES OF ARRIVAL	
DINN, Edward	7	M		Philadelphia	U. States	Howard	25 Jul 1823
Edward	41	M		Ireland	U. States	Howard	25 Jul 1823
DINNAN, Sarah	45	F		England	United States	Lord Wellington	14 Nov 1827
William	26	M	Canal Cutter	England	United States	Lord Wellington	14 Nov 1827
DINNEY, Richard	26	M	Laborer	Ireland	United States	St. Michaels	12 Jun 1826
DINNUN, John	20	M	Labourer	Ireland	U. States	Combine	30 Nov 1825
DINNY, Nelly	19	F	Spinster	Ireland	United States	Trident	16 May 1826
DINSMORE, Elizabeth	21		Spinster			Rufus King	7 Aug 1820
DINTON, Jas.	20	M	Hatter	England	United States	Loire	26 May 1828
Thomas	25	M	Farmer	Ireland	United States	Lord Wellington	14 Nov 1827
DIOS, John	38		Merchant	Citizen of New York	U. States	Camille	31 Jul 1826
DIRKWORTH, A.	10	F		Great Britain	United States	Isaac Hicks	6 Dec 1827
DIRLUZ, Edmund	22		Merchant	America		Margarett	2 Mar 1820
DIRWAN, Patrick	50	M	...	Ireland	United States	Wilson	22 Jun 1824
DISAGUS, Lewis	25	M	Merchant	U. States	U. States	Henrietta	13 Nov 1822
DISBROW, Noah	52	M	Merchant	G. Brittain, St. Johns	St. Johns, N.B.	Constitution	14 May 1822
Noah	68	M	Merchant	St. Johns	U. States	Abigail	26 Sep 1820
Noah, Jr.	12	M		G. Brittain, St. Johns	St. Johns, N.B.	Constitution	14 May 1822
Phoebe Ann	28	M		St. Johns, N.B.	St. Johns, N.B.	Isabella	21 May 1825
DISCOLE, John	40		Labourer	Ireland	United States	Geo. Canning	5 Jun 1828
DISH, Catherine	40	F	Wife to [Dominic]	Austria	America	Bayard	15 Dec 1828
Christian	9	M	None	Austria	America	Bayard	15 Dec 1828
Daniel	1	M	None	Austria	America	Bayard	15 Dec 1828
Dominic	13	M	None	Austria	America	Bayard	15 Dec 1828
Dominic	50	M	Farmer	Austria	America	Bayard	15 Dec 1828
Jacob	19	M	Weaver	Austria	America	Bayard	15 Dec 1828
Laurence	7	M	None	Austria	America	Bayard	15 Dec 1828
Maria	14	F	None	Austria	America	Bayard	15 Dec 1828
Martin	23	M	Weaver	Austria	America	Bayard	15 Dec 1828
DISHER, Diana	31	F	Wife	Scotland	United States	Tom	2 Jul 1827
James	1	M	Child	Scotland	United States	Tom	2 Jul 1827
Margaret	6	F	Child	Scotland	United States	Tom	2 Jul 1827
William	3	M	Child	Scotland	United States	Tom	2 Jul 1827
Wm.	30	M	Joiner	Scotland	United States	Tom	2 Jul 1827
DISMON, Saml.	28	M		U. States	U. States	Charlemagne	19 Sep 1828
DISOLE, Lewis F.	38	M	Planter	Porto Rico	Porto Rico	Ann Maria	7 Nov 1826
DIT ANGE, Engel	36	M	Gentleman	Switzerland	United States	Aurora	11 Dec 1824
DITMAR, Frederic	38	M	Sadder	Switzerland	America	Bolivar	2 Oct 1826
DITS, Anne Marie	26	F		France	U. States	Edward Quesnel	16 Nov 1827
Jos., Junr.	26	M	Lamp Maker	France	U.S.	Edward Quesnel	21 Apr 1827
DITTE, Frans.	27	M	Goldsmith	France	U. States	Edward Bopnnaffe	30 Jul 1829
DITTON, Alfred	7			Great Brit.	U. States	Columbia	7 May 1828
Catherine	40			Great Brit.	U. States	Columbia	7 May 1828
Charlotte	6/12			Great Brit.	U. States	Columbia	7 May 1828
Colin	20			Great Brit.	U. States	Columbia	7 May 1828
Daniel	2			Great Brit.	U. States	Columbia	7 May 1828
Mary	23	F		Ireland	U. States	Cincinnatus	5 Oct 1824
Mary	27	F	None	England		Marchioness	13 May 1828
Richard	4			Great Brit.	U. States	Columbia	7 May 1828
Robert	1			Great Brit.	U. States	Columbia	7 May 1828
Robert	27	M	Labourer	England		Marchioness	13 May 1828
Robert	40		Farmer	Great Brit.	U. States	Columbia	7 May 1828
Sarah	6			Great Brit.	U. States	Columbia	7 May 1828
Thos.	9			Great Brit.	U. States	Columbia	7 May 1828
Wm.	3			Great Brit.	U. States	Columbia	7 May 1828
DITTOR, —, Mrs., & Infant	41	F		England	United States	Richmond	4 Aug 1826
Charles	11	M		England	United States	Richmond	4 Aug 1826
George	17	M		England	United States	Richmond	4 Aug 1826
Harriet	5	F		England	United States	Richmond	4 Aug 1826
Henry	19	M		England	United States	Richmond	4 Aug 1826
James	13	M		England	United States	Richmond	4 Aug 1826
John	41	M	Farmer	England	United States	Richmond	4 Aug 1826
Mary	7	F		England	United States	Richmond	4 Aug 1826
Oved	15	M		England	United States	Richmond	4 Aug 1826

NAMES OF PASSENGERS	AGE	SEX	OCCUPATIONS	COUNTRY TO WHICH THEY BELONG	COUNTRY THEY INTEND TO INHABIT	SHIPS/DATES OF ARRIVAL	
DITTOR (cont'd)							
Sally	3	F		England	United States	Richmond	4 Aug 1826
William	9	M		England	United States	Richmond	4 Aug 1826
DITZ, Andrew	12	M	...	...tin	Pennsylvania	Frances Henrietta	25 Aug 1825
Caroline	7	F	...	...tin	Pennsylvania	Frances Henrietta	25 Aug 1825
Ferdinand	15	M	...	...tin	Pennsylvania	Frances Henrietta	25 Aug 1825
Jacob	9	M	...	...tin	Pennsylvania	Frances Henrietta	25 Aug 1825
John	39	M	...	...tin	Pennsylvania	Frances Henrietta	25 Aug 1825
Magadline	2	F	...	...tin	Pennsylvania	Frances Henrietta	25 Aug 1825
Magdaline	38	F	...	...tin	Pennsylvania	Frances Henrietta	25 Aug 1825
Matthew	5	M	...	...tin	Pennsylvania	Frances Henrietta	25 Aug 1825
DIVAN, Edward	25	M	Teacher	Scotland	United States	Samuel Robertson	9 May 1827
John	24	M	Laborer	Ireland	New York	Indian Chief	19 Jun 1823
Marie	22	F	Servant	Curacoa	Jacqumel	Orion	30 Mar 1825
DIVE, M.	12	M		G. Britain	U. States	Freak	9 Jun 1828
DIVEN, Edward	18	M	Laborer or Spinster	Ireland	United States	Sarah G	11 Sep 1827
DIVER, Hannah	23	F	Spinster	Ireland	United States	Robert Fulton	24 Jul 1826
James	21	M	Clerk	Ireland	New York	Louisa	18 Apr 1827
James	24	M	Farmer	Ireland	United States	Asia	29 Jul 1829
John	22	M	Miller	Ireland	United States	Robert Fulton	24 Jul 1826
Margaret	20	F	Spinster	Ireland	United States	Asia	29 Jul 1829
W.	25	M	Mariner	England	U. States	Edward D. Douglass	6 Jun 1823
DIVERETT, William	20	M	Smith	England	United States	Cosmo	26 Aug 1829
DIVIN, Francis	21	M	Labourer	Ireland	United States	General Putnam	20 Jun 1825
DIVINE, Catherine	17	F	Spinster	Ireland	United States	Trident	17 May 1825
Charles	48	M	Shoemaker	United States	United States	Robert Burns	13 Jul 1820
Dennis	23	M	Farmer	Great Briton	Virginia	Brighton	12 Jun 1826
Jas.	21	M	Labourer	Ireland	U. States	William & John	10 Jul 1824
John	33	M	Labourer	Ireland	U. States	Borneo	15 Apr 1828
Manus	24	M	Weaver	Ireland	U. States	Virginia	20 Jun 1825
Nicholas	23	M	Farmer	Great Britain	United States	Robert Fulton	1 Apr 1824
Patrick	21	M	Farmer	Great Britain	United States	Robert Fulton	1 Apr 1824
DIVON, Thos.	19	M	Farmer	Great Britain	United States	Grecian	24 Sep 1828
DIX, C. M.	18	F		U.S.A.	U. States	Edward Bonnaffe	12 Oct 1826
Jno. A.	28	M	Officer U.S.A.	U.S.A.	U. States	Edward Bonnaffe	12 Oct 1826
Timy. H.	30	M	Mariner	Connecticutt	U. States	Planter	16 Mar 1824
DIXBY, Lambert	23	M	Merchant	United States	United States	John Wells	18 Sep 1826
DIXEY, John	22	M	Farmer	England	United States	Roman	12 Jun 1826
DIXIE, Richard	40	M	Bootmaker	G. Britain	U. States	London	23 Sep 1828
DIXINS, William	20	M	Laborer	Ireland	United States	Nancey	8 Jun 1822
DIXON, Abraham	12	M	Merchant	England	U. States	Florida	16 May 1827
Alexander	18	M	Gentleman	England	America	Josephine	8 Jan 1827
Ann	3	F	Joiner	England	United States	Paul Jones	14 Oct 1829
Ann	21	F	Joiner	England	United States	Paul Jones	14 Oct 1829
Ann	24					Amphion	31 May 1824
Anthony	16 3/12	M	Gentleman	Guadaloupe	Guadaloupe	General Hand	27 Aug 1827
Danl.	20	M	Labourer	Ireland	U. States	Marcus	7 Apr 1825
E.	31	F		Great Britain	United States	Aspasia	16 Jul 1828
Eliza	1	F	Weaver	Gt. Britain	U.S.A.	Dalhouse Castle	21 Aug 1829
Eliza	1	F		Great Britain	United States	Dalhouse Castle	21 Aug 1829
Eliza	20	F	Spinster	Great Britain	U. States	Robert Fulton	3 Dec 1827
Elizabeth	4	F	Farmer	England	United States	Resign	7 Oct 1822
Francis, Rev.	28	M		Scotland	Isle Bermuda	Hesperus	2 Nov 1820
George	4	M	Joiner	England	United States	Paul Jones	14 Oct 1829
George	10	M	None			Evergreen	28 Jul 1820
George	24	M	Laborer	Great Britain	United States	Samuel Wright	12 Oct 1829
George	26	M	Die Tinker	Great Britain	United States	Corinthian	2 Sep 1824

NAMES OF PASSENGERS	AGE	SEX	OCCUPATIONS	COUNTRY TO WHICH THEY BELONG	COUNTRY THEY INTEND TO INHABIT	SHIPS/DATES OF ARRIVAL	
DIXON (cont'd)							
George	34	M	Merchant	Great Brittain	Great Brittain	James Cropper	23 Mar 1827
George	43	M	Clerk			Evergreen	28 Jul 1820
H.	1	M		Great Britain	United States	Aspasia	16 Jul 1828
Henry	25	M	Merchant	Ireland	United States	Silas Richards	27 Oct 1825
Henry	27	M	Merchant	England	England	Britannia	14 Mar 1828
James	42	M	Weaver	Gt. Britain	U.S.A.	Dalhouse Castle	21 Aug 1829
James	42	M	Weaver	Great Britain	United States	Dalhouse Castle	21 Aug 1829
Jane	1	F	Farmer	England	United States	Resign	7 Oct 1822
Jane	6	F	Weaver	Gt. Britain	U.S.A.	Dalhouse Castle	21 Aug 1829
Jane	6	F		Great Britain	United States	Dalhouse Castle	21 Aug 1829
Jane	40	F	Weaver	Gt. Britain	U.S.A.	Dalhouse Castle	21 Aug 1829
Jane	40	F		Great Britain	United States	Dalhouse Castle	21 Aug 1829
Jas.	26	M	Labourer	Scotland	New York	Joseph Hume	26 Oct 1829
John	19	M	Tailor	Ireland	United States	Carolina Ann	11 Dec 1826
John	20	M	Saddler	England	America	Two Marys	24 Sep 1827
John	24	M	Laborer	Scotland	U. States	Howard Douglass	29 Jan 1828
John	24	M	Joiner	England	United States	Paul Jones	14 Oct 1829
John	25 6/12	M	Painter	England	America	John Dickinson	15 Oct 1826
John	27	M	...	England	U. States	Margarett Scott	22 Aug 1827
John	29	M	Seaman	U. States	U. States	Boston	26 Sep 1820
John	37	M	Farmer	England	United States	Resign	7 Oct 1822
John, Jr.	24	M	Merchant	England	United States	Aurora	27 Apr 1825
John E.	24	M	Mill wright	Gt. Britain	U. States	St. George	20 Sep 1828
Joseph	16	M	Merchant	England	U. States	Florida	16 May 1827
Joseph	33	M	Merchant	England	United States	New York	14 Jul 1827
Joseph, Junr.	19	M	Merchant	G. Britain	U. States	Panthia	23 Apr 1824
Joseph, Mr.	21	M	Merchant	England		Douglass	8 May 1826
Madyer	10	F	Child	Ireland	U. States	Courier	17 Mar 1828
Margaret	34	F	None			Evergreen	28 Jul 1820
Margaret	45	F	Matron	Ireland	United States	Wilson	22 Jun 1824
Mary	24	F	Farmer	England	United States	Resign	7 Oct 1822
May	5	M		Ireland	United States	Carolina Ann	11 Dec 1826
Patrick	24	M	Farmer	Droghan		Mount Vernon	7 Jun 1824
Rott.	21	M		Great Britain	United States	Ganges	8 Jul 1820
Sarah	15	F	Weaver	Gt. Britain	U.S.A.	Dalhouse Castle	21 Aug 1829
Sarah	15	F		Great Britain	United States	Dalhouse Castle	21 Aug 1829
Susan	8	F	Weaver	Gt. Britain	U.S.A.	Dalhouse Castle	21 Aug 1829
Susan	8	F		Great Britain	United States	Dalhouse Castle	21 Aug 1829
Thomas	20	M	Farmer	England	United States	Resign	7 Oct 1822
Thomas	28	M	Merchant	Great Britain	United States	Martha	3 May 1821
Thomas	30	M	Merchant	England	United States	Orbit	22 Apr 1824
Thomas	35	M	Farmer	G. Britain	U. States	Freak	9 Jun 1828
Thomas	50	M	Labourer	Bristol	U. States	Latona	7 Jul 1827
Thos.	20	M	Labourer	Ireland		Marchioness	13 May 1828
Thos.	29	M	Merchant	Great Britain	U. States	Columbia	24 Dec 1822
Thos.	32	M	Merchant	England	U. States	Florida	16 May 1827
William	12	M	Weaver	Gt. Britain	U.S.A.	Dalhouse Castle	21 Aug 1829
William	20	M		Ireland	America	Carolina Ann	7 Aug 1826
Wm.	12	M	Weaver	Great Britain	United States	Dalhouse Castle	21 Aug 1829
DIXSON, Edward	21	M	Merchant	Ireland	America	Carolina Ann	14 Feb 1825
DIZE, Barbe	17 8/12	F	Farmer	Switzerland	America	Henry	17 May 1828
Catherine	18 5/12	F	Farmer	Switzerland	America	Henry	17 May 1828
Emily	8 1/12	F	Farmer	Switzerland	America	Henry	17 May 1828
George	11 4/12	M	Farmer	Switzerland	America	Henry	17 May 1828
George	47 5/12	M	Farmer	Switzerland	America	Henry	17 May 1828
Jacob	5 9/12	M	Farmer	Switzerland	America	Henry	17 May 1828
Madeline	4	F	Farmer	Switzerland	America	Henry	17 May 1828
Margaret	50	F	Farmer	Switzerland	America	Henry	17 May 1828
Margot	20 8/12	F	Farmer	Switzerland	America	Henry	17 May 1828
Micheal	2 7/12	M	Farmer	Switzerland	America	Henry	17 May 1828
DO..., ...	40	F	Farmer	England	U. States	Electra	7 Jul 1828
...	46	M	Cord weaver	England	U. States	Electra	7 Jul 1828
Ann	8	M	Farmer	England	U. States	Electra	7 Jul 1828
Anthon	12	M	Farmer	England	U. States	Electra	7 Jul 1828
Edmond	20	F	Farmer	England	U. States	Electra	7 Jul 1828
John	15	M	Farmer	England	U. States	Electra	7 Jul 1828
Phillip	6	M	Farmer	England	U. States	Electra	7 Jul 1828

NAMES OF PASSENGERS	AGE	SEX	OCCUPATIONS	COUNTRY TO WHICH THEY BELONG	COUNTRY THEY INTEND TO INHABIT	SHIPS/DATES OF ARRIVAL	
DO... (cont'd)							
Samuel	10	M	Farmer	England	U. States	Electra	7 Jul 1828
Sophia	5	M	Farmer	England	U. States	Electra	7 Jul 1828
Zacariah	18	F	Farmer	England	U. States	Electra	7 Jul 1828
DO...RTY, James	23	M	Machinst	Great Britain	United States	Colossus	5 Jun 1827
DOAK, Cathr.	16	F	Spinster			Commerce	22 Jun 1825
Mary	42	F		U. States	United States	Wade	29 Aug 1825
DOAN, J. P.	25	M	Mcht.	U. States	U. States	Nassau	24 Nov 1824
DOANE, Norman	22		Mariner	United States		New Orleans	27 Feb 1829
Randall	23	M	Mariner	U. States	U. States	Florida	25 Apr 1825
DOAR, Michael	23	M	Farmer	Switzerland	United States	Andes	5 May 1828
DOAT, George	8	M	Farmer	England	United States	Young Phoenix	26 Jul 1824
Jannet	6 2/12	F	Farmer	England	United States	Young Phoenix	26 Jul 1824
Mary	4	F	Farmer	England	United States	Young Phoenix	26 Jul 1824
Mary	34 4/12	F	Farmer	England	United States	Young Phoenix	26 Jul 1824
Thomas	2 3/12	M	Farmer	England	United States	Young Phoenix	26 Jul 1824
DOATE, George	30	M	Farmer	England	United States	Young Phoenix	26 Jul 1824
DOBBER, Peter	23	M	Sugar Baker	Holland	U. States	United States	7 Jul 1827
DOBBIE, John	20	M	Bookbinder	Scotland	United States	Camillus	27 Oct 1829
DOBBIN, David	46	M	Farmer	Ireland	United States	Herald	29 Oct 1825
John	40	M	Mechanic	U. States	U. States	Mary Olivia	10 Jul 1824
Nancy	26	F	Spinster	Ireland	United States	Herald	29 Oct 1825
DOBBMAN, Gotfred	21	M	Merchant	Prusia	U. States	Harmony	6 Jan 1823
DOBBS, Jane	5	F		England	United States	Yobah	26 Sep 1827
Job	9	M		England	United States	Yobah	26 Sep 1827
John	9	M		England	United States	Yobah	26 Sep 1827
Mary	3	F		England	United States	Yobah	26 Sep 1827
Sophia	39	F		England	United States	Yobah	26 Sep 1827
Thomas	13	M		England	United States	Yobah	26 Sep 1827
William	24	M	Wheelwright	England	America	Thames	27 May 1822
Wm.	2	M		England	United States	Yobah	26 Sep 1827
Wm.	29	M		England	United States	Yobah	26 Sep 1827
DOBILL, Ann	21	F		Great Britain	United States	Fame	26 May 1828
Samuel	22	M	Farmer	Great Britain	United States	Fame	26 May 1828
DOBIN, Mary	26	F	Labourer	Ireland	United States	Jubilee	13 Jul 1829
DOBLER, Carolina	9	F		Germany	America	Falcon	28 Aug 1828
Christian	55	M	Farmer	Germany	America	Falcon	28 Aug 1828
Christin	1	M		Germany	America	Falcon	28 Aug 1828
Cristina R.	14	F		Germany	America	Falcon	28 Aug 1828
George Fredk.	17	M		Germany	America	Falcon	28 Aug 1828
Johann Jacob	6	M		Germany	America	Falcon	28 Aug 1828
Louisa D. F.	44	F		Germany	America	Falcon	28 Aug 1828
DOBSON, Eliza	23	F		Scotland	United States	Indus	5 Sep 1827
John	...		Paper Maker	...ll...	England	Great Britain	7 May 1827
Thos.	26	M	Labourer	Scotland	United States	Indus	5 Sep 1827
DOBY, Jno.	24	M	Coachman	Great Britain	United States	Comet	9 Aug 1822
DOBZELL, James	36	M		Scotland	U. States	Roger Stewart	9 Jun 1828
Mary	27	F	Weaver	Scotland	U. States	Roger Stewart	9 Jun 1828
DOCETY, Nancey	22	F		Ireland	United States	Nancy R. Crowell	21 Sep 1822
DOCHERTY, Agnes	25	F	his wife [George]	Great Britain	United States	Rosina	28 May 1827
George	37	M	Mason	Great Britain	United States	Rosina	28 May 1827
James	34	M	Labourer	Ireland	U.S.A.	Lima	6 Dec 1826
DOCHRELL, Jarves	26	M	Labourer	England	U. States	Comet	23 Aug 1828
DOCKERTY, Geo.	40		Farmer	Halifax	U. States	Edwin	26 Sep 1828
J.	25		Labourer	Halifax	U. States	Edwin	26 Sep 1828
John	26	M	Glass Cutter	G. Britain	U. States	Mary & Harriot	8 Sep 1828
Patrick	25	M	Servant	Ireland	U. States	Henrietta	7 Jul 1825
Richard	22	M	Glass Cutter	G. Britain	U. States	Mary & Harriot	8 Sep 1828
Thos.	44	M	Labourer	Isle of Man		Ocean	13 Jul 1827
DOCKHERT, Francis	18	M	Labourer	...	U. States	St. Michael	21 Jul 1824
DOCTON, Franceois	24		Farmer	France	U. States	Elizabeth	9 Jul 1825
Joseph	29		Farmer	France	U. States	Elizabeth	9 Jul 1825
Lousa	25		Farmer	France	U. States	Elizabeth	9 Jul 1825
DOCULA, Jas.	14	M		St. Lucia	U. States	Lady of the Lake	11 Apr 1825
DODD, A.	27	F		America	U. States	Calais Packet	7 Jul 1828
Abijah	28	M	Paper Maker	America	U. States	Calais Packet	7 Jul 1828
Ann	36	F	Calico Printer	England	United States	Amelia	20 Aug 1829
Danl.	22		Labourer	Ireland	Ireland	Dewitt Clinton	26 Aug 1825

NAMES OF PASSENGERS	AGE	SEX	OCCUPATIONS	COUNTRY TO WHICH THEY BELONG	COUNTRY THEY INTEND TO INHABIT	SHIPS/DATES OF ARRIVAL	
DODD (cont'd)							
Ellen	20	F		Great Britain	United States	John Wells	18 Sep 1826
Henry	41	M	Farmer	England	America, U.S.	Illinois	3 Jun 1822
John	1/12	M		England	America, U.S.	Illinois	3 Jun 1822
John	21	M	Farmer	Great Britain	United States	John Wells	18 Sep 1826
John	26		Tailor	Ireland	N. York at present	Marcella	18 May 1827
John	30			York County	Ohio	Peru	30 May 1828
Joseph	14 4/12	M		England	America, U.S.	Illinois	3 Jun 1822
Margaret	35 4/12	F		England	America, U.S.	Illinois	3 Jun 1822
Mary	38			York County	Ohio	Peru	30 May 1828
Mary	42	F	None	England	America	Francis & Henrietta	11 Jul 1823
Patrick	30	M	Gentleman	Ireland	United States	Dublin Packet	13 Oct 1828
Richd.	26		Labourer	Ireland	Ireland	Dewitt Clinton	26 Aug 1825
Richd.	42	M	Farmer	England	America	Francis & Henrietta	11 Jul 1823
Timothy	49	M	Merchant	United States	United States	Hannibal	12 Oct 1829
DODDS, James	35 8/12	M	Farmer	Great Britain	Great Britain	Amity	1 Dec 1826
DODER, Morris	27		Servant	Halifax	U. States	Almira	15 Jul 1822
DODGE, Ed.	24	M	Mariner	Boston	U. States	Amos Palmer	17 Aug 1826
Gideon	30	M	Mechanic	Vermont	U. States	Reporter	27 Sep 1823
Joseph	30		Consul at Verseilles	Massachusetts	Boston	James Cropper	12 Jul 1822
Joshua	34	M	Consul at Marseilles	Salem		Desdemona	12 Jun 1826
P.	20	M	Merchant	U. States	U. States	Quesnel	6 Sep 1824
DODGEY, Samuel	32	M	Glass Cutter	Ireland	America	Evelina	10 Nov 1825
DODGSON, Isaac	53	M	Merchant	G. Britain	U. States	America	17 Oct 1825
DODIEZ, Henri	21	M	Farmer	France		Henri IV	17 May 1828
Henriette	23	F				Henri IV	17 May 1828
DODLING, Wm.	16			England	United States	Hugh Johnson	11 Jun 1828
DODNING, Charles	22	M	Clerk	Ireland	United States	Nile	17 May 1827
DODS, Agnes	8	F		Scotland	United States	Broke	16 Jul 1829
Elen	42	F	Farmer	Scotland	United States	Broke	16 Jul 1829
Margaret	17	F		Scotland	United States	Broke	16 Jul 1829
Mary	10	F		Scotland	United States	Broke	16 Jul 1829
Robert	5	M		Scotland	United States	Broke	16 Jul 1829
Robert	45	M	Farmer	Scotland	United States	Broke	16 Jul 1829
DODSON, Jos.		M	Seaman	United States	United States	Agenoria	27 Jun 1823
DODSWORTH, Charles	4	M	None	Great Britain	United States	Mary & Harriet	3 Jul 1829
Elizth.	35	F	None	Great Britain	United States	Mary & Harriet	3 Jul 1829
Harvey	6	M	None	Great Britain	United States	Mary & Harriet	3 Jul 1829
Ida	9	F	None	Great Britain	United States	Mary & Harriet	3 Jul 1829
James	1	M	None	Great Britain	United States	Mary & Harriet	3 Jul 1829
DODWORTH, Allen	9	M		G. Britain	U. States	St. George	7 Jun 1828
Thos.	27	M		G. Britain	U. States	St. George	7 Jun 1828
DOE, Agnes	20	F	Farmer, Labourer or Spinster	Ireland	U. States	Meteor	4 Oct 1827
DOEBLY, John	29	M	Tailor	Switzerland	United States	Thetis	5 Jul 1821
DOEN, Mary	20			Ireland	New York	Lady Hunter	19 Oct 1826
DOERES, John	17	M	Laborer	Gt. Britain		Dalhouse Castle	13 May 1828
DOERING, F. G.	31	M	Merch.	U. States		Hebe	14 Jun 1825
Frederick	22	M	Gentleman	Germany	U. States	Acasta	28 Jan 1823
DOEY, Bridget	30	F	Wife	Ireland	United States	Trident	16 May 1826
John	2	M	Child	Ireland	United States	Trident	16 May 1826
John	24	M	Labourer	Ireland	United States	Trident	16 May 1826
Wm.	26	M	Labourer	Ireland	United States	Trident	16 May 1826
DOFFATT, James	27	M	Labourer	Whipsey		Aurora	8 Jun 1827
DOFFEE, Denis	25	M		Ireland	United States	Nancy R. Crowell	21 Sep 1822
Mancey	20	F		Ireland	United States	Nancy R. Crowell	21 Sep 1822
DOGAN, Rose	...	...	...	Ireland	United States	Carolina Ann	24 Oct 1825
DOGGET, Ebenezer	25	M	Carpenter	America, Mas [Massachusetts]	America	William	16 Apr 1823
DOGGETT, Henry	27	M	Merchant	Gt. Britain	New York	Stephania	2 Jan 1824
DOGHERTY, Andrew	21		Servant	Ireland	United States	Robert Burns	18 Jun 1821
Ann	36	F		Ireland	New York	Lima	5 Aug 1829

NAMES OF PASSENGERS	AGE	SEX	OCCUPATIONS	COUNTRY TO WHICH THEY BELONG	COUNTRY THEY INTEND TO INHABIT	SHIPS/DATES OF ARRIVAL	
DOGHERTY (cont'd)							
Betty	30	F	Farmer	Ireland	U. States	Dickinson	30 Jul 1825
Elizth.	17			Ireland	United States	Robert Burns	30 May 1823
Ewd.	22	M	Weaver	Great Britain	United States	Frances Henrietta	17 Sep 1827
John	3	M		Ireland	New York	Lima	5 Aug 1829
John	25	M	Mechanic	Scotland	United States	Orion	15 Jan 1827
Mary	26		Servant	Ireland	United States	Robert Burns	18 Jun 1821
Robert	25	M	Labourer	Ireland	United States	Jubilee	12 May 1828
Rose	22		Servant	Ireland	United States	Robert Burns	18 Jun 1821
Thomas	33	M	Mason	Ireland	New York	Lima	5 Aug 1829
Wm.	16	M	Labourer	Ireland	U.S. of America	Meteor	19 Mar 1828
Wm. H.	24	M	Revenue Officer of N.P.	England	Antigua	Crawford	4 Jan 1826
DOGLE, Mary	16	F	None	Ireland	New York	America	1 Aug 1828
DOHA, Ann	21	F	Servant	Great Britain	United States	Ann Maria	17 Apr 1827
James	...	M	Labourer	Great Britain	United States	Ann Maria	17 Apr 1827
Sarah	...	F	Wife	Great Britain	United States	Ann Maria	17 Apr 1827
DOHARTY, Ellen	18	F	...	Ireland	United States	General Putnam	20 Jun 1825
John	...	M	...	Ireland	United States	General Putnam	20 Jun 1825
Pat	22	M	Labourer	Ireland	United States	General Putnam	20 Jun 1825
DOHENTY, Andrew	30	M	Laborer	Ireland	U. States	Edwin	1 Jul 1829
DOHERDAY, Neil	21	M	Labourer	Ireland	U. States	Lady Hunter	18 Jul 1825
DOHERTY, Ann	20	M	Labourer	Ireland	United States	Hope	12 Jun 1828
Ann	22	F	Spinner	Great Britain	United States	Atlantic	8 Dec 1827
Anne	21	F	Spinster	Ireland	United States	Trident	16 May 1826
Biddy	3	F	Spinster	Ireland	United States	Marmion	17 Jun 1825
Bridget	14	F	Child			Commerce	22 Jun 1825
Bridget	28	F	Spinster	Ireland	United States	Trident	16 May 1826
Charles	4	M		Ireland	United States	Gem	16 Jun 1824
Charles	20	M	Labourer	Ireland	United States	Catharine	22 Jul 1825
Daniel	6	M	Labourer	Ireland	United States	Hope	12 Jun 1828
Daniel	18	F	Labourer	Ireland	United States	Hope	12 Jun 1828
Dennis	30	M	Labourer	Ireland	United States	Trident	16 May 1826
Edward	6/12	M	None	Ireland	United States	Catharine	22 Jul 1825
Edward	20	M	Labourer	Ireland	United States	Hope	12 Jun 1828
Edward	22	M	Merchant	Ireland	United States	Sylvester Healy	17 Oct 1825
Eleanor	14	F	Spinster	Ireland	U. States	William & John	10 Jul 1824
Esebeler	6	F	Laborer	Ireland	U. States	Edwin	1 Jul 1829
Esebeler	30	F	Laborer	Ireland	U. States	Edwin	1 Jul 1829
George	10	M	Child	Ireland	U. States	William & John	10 Jul 1824
George	19	M	Shoemaker	New Brunswick	United States	New Packet	15 Nov 1828
George	20	M	Farmer	Ireland	United States	Gem	16 Jun 1824
George	50	M	Farmer	Ireland	U. States	William & John	10 Jul 1824
Grace	25	F	Spinster	Ireland	United States	Gem	16 Jun 1824
James	9	M	Child	Ireland	U. States	William & John	10 Jul 1824
Jas.	20	M	Labourer	Ireland	U. States	Lady Hunter	18 Jul 1825
Jas.	20	M	Labourer	Ireland	United States	Trident	16 May 1826
John	4	M	Child	Ireland	U. States	Edwin	1 Jul 1829
John	18	M	Labourer	Ireland	United States	Trident	16 May 1826
John	20	M	Shoemaker	Ireland	United States	Trident	16 May 1826
John	20	M	Farmer	Ireland	United States	Asia	29 Jul 1829
John	22	M	Labourer	Ireland	United States	Trident	16 May 1826
John	25	M	Labourer	Ireland	United S.	Hanford	19 Aug 1828
John	25	M	Merchant	Great Britain	United States	Hanford	9 Oct 1829
John	29	M	Carman	Ireland	United States	Trident	16 May 1826
Margaret	...	...	...	...	...	St. Michael	22 Sep 1824
Margaret	10	F	Child			Commerce	22 Jun 1825
Margt.	27	F	Wife	Ireland	United States	Trident	16 May 1826
Mary	26	F	Spinster	Ireland	United States	Asia	29 Jul 1829
Mary Ann	1	F	Child	Ireland	U. States	Edwin	1 Jul 1829
Michael	22	M	Smith	G. Britain	New York	Brighton	26 Mar 1827
Patk.	26	M	Labourer	Ireland	United States	Trident	16 May 1826
Patrick	21	M	Laborer	Ireland	United States	Mary	1 Jul 1829
Rose	28	F	Spinster	Ireland	United States	Catharine	22 Jul 1825
Sally	12	F	Child	Ireland	U. States	William & John	10 Jul 1824
Sally	50	F	wife to [George]	Ireland	U. States	William & John	10 Jul 1824
Susan	17	M	Labourer	Ireland	United States	Hope	12 Jun 1828
Willm.	19	M	Labourer	Ireland	United States	Trident	16 May 1826

NAMES OF PASSENGERS	AGE	SEX	OCCUPATIONS	COUNTRY TO WHICH THEY BELONG	COUNTRY THEY INTEND TO INHABIT	SHIPS/DATES OF ARRIVAL	
DOHERTY (cont'd)							
Wm.	21	M	Farmer	Ireland		L. M. Pelham	12 May 1823
DOIG, John	28	M	Merchant	Scotland	United States	Cato	8 Aug 1825
Paul	33	M		Scotland	United States	Camillus	9 May 1827
DOIL, Margaret	29	F	Lady	Ireland	United States	Borneo	2 Oct 1827
Patrick	29	M	Labourer	Ireland	United States	Borneo	2 Oct 1827
DOLAGHAN, Martha	32	F	Wife	Ireland	United States	Meteor	27 Sep 1826
DOLAM, John	23	M	Labourer	Ireland	United States	Wilson	6 Jun 1828
DOLAN, Catherine	16	F	Spinster	Ireland	United States	Wilson	6 Jun 1828
Catherine	24	M	None	Ireland	U. States	William Byrnes	24 Apr 1827
J.	20	F		Great Britain	United States	Isaac Hicks	6 Dec 1827
James	15 6/12	M		Ireland	U.S. of America	Douglass	6 Jul 1829
James	26	M	Labourer	Ireland	United States	Trident	30 Sep 1826
James	33	M		Gt. Britain	United States	Penelope	9 Sep 1828
Jas.	17	M		Ireland	U. States	William Byrnes	17 Jul 1825
John	13	M		Great Britain	United States	Mary Howland	19 Jul 1827
John	20	M	Labourer	Ireland	United States	John Wells	11 May 1827
John	44	M	Labourer	Ireland	U. States	Courier	17 Mar 1828
Lawrence	23	M	Labourer	Ireland	America	Wilson	27 Nov 1826
Margaret	15	F		Great Britain	United States	Mary Howland	19 Jul 1827
Margareth	27	F	Wife	Ireland	United States	Trident	30 Sep 1826
Mary	18	F	Labourer	Ireland	U.S.A.	Dalhouse Castle	21 Aug 1829
Mary	18	F	None	Ireland	United States	Dalhouse Castle	21 Aug 1829
Michl.	45	M	Labourer	Ireland	United States	Thomas	13 Dec 1827
Pat	8	M	None	Great Britain	United States	Aurora	10 Nov 1827
Patk.	17	M	Labourer	Ireland	United States	Wilson	6 Jun 1828
Thomas	26	M	Weaver	Ireland	United States	Enterprize	23 Jul 1827
Thomas	28	M	Labourer	Ireland	United States	New Packet	15 Nov 1828
Thos.	45	M		Baltimore	U. States	Eliza Ann	30 Jul 1823
DOLBERG, Jacob	29	M	Shoemaker	Sweden	U. States	Oscar	4 Sep 1823
DOLBIES, Jonathan A.	27	M	Carpenter	U. States	U. States	Prince Edward	29 Jul 1823
DOLBY, Danl.	72		Labourer	Northamp- tonshire	England	Great Britain	7 May 1827
John	45	M	Mercht.	England	U. States	Perseverance	18 Nov 1824
Sarah	64			Northamp- tonshire	England	Great Britain	7 May 1827
DOLE, Daniel	24	M	Merchant	United States	United States	Hanford	3 Aug 1829
DOLESON, George	30	M	Labourer	Ireland	America	Plutarch	18 Jul 1826
DOLEY, Mary	26	F	Spinster	Ireland	United States	Robert Fulton	24 Jul 1826
Michal	26	M	Labourer	Ireland	United States	Robert Fulton	24 Jul 1826
DOLIER, Ann	29	F	Servant	St. Croix	U. States	Elias Burger	18 Apr 1823
DOLLAN, Mary	20	F	None	Ireland	United States	Jubilee	13 Jul 1829
DOLLAR, D.	6	M		G. Britain	U. States	London	23 Sep 1828
DOLLAS, G.	32	M		Scotland	U.S.	Curler	19 Jul 1828
DOLLON, Ann	30	F	Servant	Ireland	United States	Eliza	29 Aug 1822
Charles	40	M	Farmer	Ireland	United States	Eliza	29 Aug 1822
Francis	19	M	Farmer	Ireland	United States	Eliza	29 Aug 1822
DOLLY, Charles	28	M	Merchant	France	United States	Brighton	9 Dec 1828
James	28	M	Servant	United States	United States	Cortes	19 Nov 1821
DOLY, William	26	M	Labourer	Great Britain	U. States	Superb	28 May 1821
DOME, P. F.	53	M	Carpenter	France	United States	New England	29 Aug 1828
DOMEC, —, Mrs.	36	F	Lady	Spain		Orlando	8 May 1824
Felix	5 5/12	M	Child	Spain		Orlando	8 May 1824
DOMERAGE, Therese	20	F	Spinster	Marseilles	U. States	Conveyance	9 Feb 1825
DOMEZA, Abigail, Miss	9	F	...	Curacao	Curacao	Hippomenes	4 Nov 1820
Abigail, Mrs.	47	F	...	Curacao	Curacao	Hippomenes	4 Nov 1820
DOMICK, Otis	32	M	Mercht.	U. States		Betsey	15 Jun 1827
DOMINGO, Trevjo	20	M	Gentleman	Spain	Spain	Ariel	9 Mar 1829
DOMINGUEZ, Manl.	25	M	Merchant	Spain	New York	Abeona	20 Dec 1823
DOMINICI, Fernando	46	M	Gentn.	Spain	Spain	Fabius	2 Oct 1826
DOMINICK, Eliza	20	F	Lady	St. John, N.B.	St. John, N.B.	St. Michaels	25 May 1825
F. W.	35	M	Mariner	U. States	U. States	Julia	18 Apr 1828
Frs. W.	35	M	Mariner	U. States	U. States	Rampart	4 Jun 1822
James	18	M	Clerk	St. John, N.B.	St. John, N.B.	St. Michaels	25 May 1825
DOMINIGER, Daniel	24	M	Shoemaker	Switzerland	U.S.	Francois I	8 Aug 1829
DOMIRA, Vincente	...	M	Gentn.	Spain	Spain	Fabius	2 Oct 1826
DOMMANGE, Achille	27	M	Farmer	France	U. States	Elizabeth	20 Mar 1824
Auguste	2	M	None	France	U. States	Elizabeth	20 Mar 1824
Maxance	25	F	Spinster	France	U. States	Elizabeth	20 Mar 1824

335

NAMES OF PASSENGERS	AGE	SEX	OCCUPATIONS	COUNTRY TO WHICH THEY BELONG	COUNTRY THEY INTEND TO INHABIT	SHIPS/DATES OF ARRIVAL	
DOMNICK, John	28	M	Shoe Maker	Ireland	U. States	Sarah G	30 Jun 1828
DOMODY, Margt.	28	F	Labourer	Ireland	U. States	Marcus	7 Apr 1825
DOMONICKS, Frances W.	35	M	Mariner	U. States	U. States	Falcon	1 Jun 1827
DOMSLA, George	31	M	Merchant	Portugal		Abigail	2 Oct 1820
DON, Catharine	17	F		England	U. States	Rising Sun	1 May 1823
DON...LLY, Bridget	23	F	...	England	United States	Milton	20 Oct 1827
DONACHO, Joseph	24		Planter	Ireland	Ireland	Agnes	27 Mar 1828
DONADAN, Ann	20	F				Lady of the Lake	23 Aug 1828
DONAFORT, Barbe	55	F	Farmer	Switzerland	America	Henry	17 May 1828
Edam	59 5/12	M	Farmer	Switzerland	America	Henry	17 May 1828
DONAGEE, William	24	M	Wever	Ireland	United States	Fabius	4 Jun 1828
DONAGH, James	22	M	Carpenter	Drummore	United States	Carolina Ann	11 Jun 1824
DONAGHOE, Catherine	24	F	Matron	Ireland	U. States	Courier	17 Mar 1828
James	26 6/12	M	Labourer	Ireland	U. States	Courier	17 Mar 1828
Patt	20	M	Labourer	Ireland	United States	Jubilee	13 Jul 1829
DONAGHOR, Patrick	19	M	Preacher	Ireland	United States	Trio	31 Oct 1827
DONAGHTY, Edward	31	M	Farmer	Ireland	United States	Meteor	27 Sep 1826
DONAGHUE, Jno.	24	M	Farmer	Great Britain	America	Remittance	24 Aug 1825
Margt.	24	F		Ireland	United States	William Byrnes	6 Apr 1826
Mary	1	F	None	Great Britain	America	Remittance	24 Aug 1825
Mary	25	F	None	Great Britain	America	Remittance	24 Aug 1825
Michl.	30	M	Farmer	Great Britain	America	Remittance	24 Aug 1825
Morgan	9	M		Ireland	United States	William Byrnes	6 Apr 1826
Patrick	2	M		Ireland	United States	William Byrnes	6 Apr 1826
DONAGHY, Biddy	25	F	Spinster	Ireland	United States	William & George	14 May 1828
J.	26	M	Clergyman	Scotland	United States	Spartan	21 Aug 1824
DONAHO, Mary	20	F	Spinster	Ireland	United States	Asia	29 Jul 1829
DONAHOE, Bridget	18	F	None	Ireland	United States	Jubilee	13 Jul 1829
Eliztth	20	F	None			India	8 Jun 1827
J.	32	M	Mason	Ireland	U. States	Frederick	2 Apr 1828
James	17	M	Labourer	Ireland	United States	Jubilee	13 Jul 1829
John	21	M	Labourer	Ireland	United States	Jubilee	13 Jul 1829
John	22	M	Labourer	Gt. Britain	U. States	Isaac Hicks	18 Apr 1825
Mary	20	F		Ireland	U. States	Frederick	2 Apr 1828
Rose	18	F	Servant	Ireland	United States	Josephine	30 Apr 1828
DONAHOO, Edward	18	M	Labourer	Ireland	U. States	Josephine	27 Jul 1825
Mary	20	F	Servant	Ireland	America	Carolina Ann	7 Aug 1826
DONAHOV, Micheal	22 1/12	M		Ireland	America	Carolina Ann	7 Apr 1826
DONAHU, Danl.	47	M	Mechanic	Ireland	U. States	Liberty	7 Jun 1826
DONAHUE, Bridget	16	F	Farmer	Ireland	U. States	Sabina	29 Apr 1825
Davis	13	M	Farmer	Ireland	U. States	Sabina	29 Apr 1825
Hugh	20	M	Farmer	Ireland	U. States	Sabina	29 Apr 1825
James	24	M	Farmer	Ireland	U. States	Sabina	29 Apr 1825
Michael	26	M	Farmer	Ireland	U. States	Sabina	29 Apr 1825
DONAHUGH, Hugh	50	M	Labourer	Ireland	New York	Trusty	12 Sep 1828
DONAL, William	21	M	Labourer	Ireland		Robert Fulton	4 Jun 1828
DONALD, Andrew	26	M	Labourrer	Great Britan	U. States	Ann Marria	6 Aug 1823
Ann	25	F	Lady	Greece	U. States	Edward Bonnaffe	4 May 1827
Benjamin	24		None	United States	United States	James Monroe	11 Dec 1821
Berther	35	F		Aberdeen		James Margaret	17 May 1827
Hugh	40	M	Mechanic	Ireland	United States	Concordia	25 Aug 1827
James	22	M	Mercht.	U.S.A.	U. States	Edward Bonnaffe	12 Oct 1826
James	40	M	Laborer	Aberdeen	New York	James Margaret	17 May 1827
John	25	M	Mercht.	U.S.A.	U. States	Edward Bonnaffe	12 Oct 1826
Rober	32	M	Shipmaster	Great Britain	United States	Orozimbo	5 Mar 1827
Robert	20	M	Labourer	Ireland	United States	Catharine	22 Jul 1825
Thos.	20	M	Weaver	Scotland	Ama.	Expedition	19 May 1828
Walter	28	M	Blacksmith	Scotland	United States	Ann Maria	9 Jun 1824
DONALDSON, —, Miss	50	F	Lady	Jamaica	Jamaica	Wallace	12 Apr 1824
Alexander	14 5/12	M	Cotton spinner	Scotland	United States	Mobile	21 Aug 1827
Andrew	18 1/12	M	Cotton spinner	Scotland	United States	Mobile	21 Aug 1827
Andrew	43 4/12	M	Cotton spinner	Scotland	United States	Mobile	21 Aug 1827
Ann	2	F		G. Britain	U. States	Eliza	9 May 1827

NAMES OF PASSENGERS	AGE	SEX	OCCUPATIONS	COUNTRY TO WHICH THEY BELONG	COUNTRY THEY INTEND TO INHABIT	SHIPS/DATES OF ARRIVAL	
DONALDSON (cont'd)							
Ann	11 7/12	F		Scotland	United States	Mobile	21 Aug 1827
Ann	19	F		G. Britain	U. States	Eliza	9 May 1827
Ann	28	F		G. Britain	U. States	Eliza	9 May 1827
Betty	9	F		G. Britain	U. States	Eliza	9 May 1827
Betty	31	F		G. Britain	U. States	Eliza	9 May 1827
Betty	65	F		G. Britain	U. States	Eliza	9 May 1827
Catherine	3 2/12	F		Scotland	United States	Mobile	21 Aug 1827
Catherine, Mrs.	42 2/12	F		Scotland	United States	Mobile	21 Aug 1827
David	23	M	Joiner	G. Britain	U. States	Eliza	9 May 1827
Duncan	28		Farmer	Great Britain	United States	Camillus	12 Sep 1827
Elizabeth	8 2/12	F		Scotland	United States	Mobile	21 Aug 1827
Ellen	22	F	Servant	Montreal, Canada	Great Britain	James Cropper	7 Oct 1823
Geo.	12	M	Child			Commerce	22 Jun 1825
James	21	M	Gentleman	United States	United States	Columbia	1 Dec 1823
James	21	M	Cabinet Maker	Glasgow, St. Johns [Parish], Lanark [County]	New York	Hero	19 May 1828
*to follow his occupation							
James	30	M	Mason	Great Britain	United States	Roanoak	19 Sep 1827
Jane	26	F		New Brunswick	United States	Edwin	27 Oct 1828
Jane	38	F	Spinster			Commerce	22 Jun 1825
Jas.	33	M	Mason	G. Britain	U. States	Eliza	9 May 1827
Jesse	6	F		G. Britain	U. States	Eliza	9 May 1827
John	5 7/12	M		Scotland	United States	Mobile	21 Aug 1827
John	24	M	Farmer	Ireland	United States	Asia	29 Jul 1829
John	28	M	Clerk	Great Briton	United States	Erin	26 May 1821
John	34	M	Brewer	Scotland	United States	Broke	16 Jul 1829
John	40	M	Miller	Ireland	United States	Marmion	17 Jun 1825
Joseph	...	M	...	Ireland	United States	General Putnam	20 Jun 1825
Katherine	2	F	None	Great Britain	United States	Colossus	5 Jun 1827
Mary	14	F	Child			Commerce	22 Jun 1825
Mary	21	F	None	Great Britain	United States	Colossus	5 Jun 1827
Mary	30	F		Ireland	New York	Carolina Ann	15 Oct 1824
Robert	22		None	United States	United States	James Monroe	11 Dec 1821
Robert	24	M	Gentleman	United States	United States	Cortex	4 Dec 1824
Sarah	21	F		Ireland	United States	Romulus	24 Jun 1826
Sarh.	...	...	...	Ireland	United States	General Putnam	20 Jun 1825
William	16 3/12	M	Baker	Scotland	United States	Mobile	21 Aug 1827
William	43	M	...	G. Britain	U. States	Belle Savage	15 Aug 1820
Wm.	1	M		G. Britain	U. States	Eliza	9 May 1827
Wm.	1	M	None	Great Britain	United States	Colossus	5 Jun 1827
Wm.	27	M	Dyer	Great Britain	United States	Colossus	5 Jun 1827
Wm.	29	M	Mason	Scotland	United States	Camillus	27 Oct 1829
Wm.	65	M	Shoe Maker	G. Britain	U. States	Eliza	9 May 1827
Wm. P.	21	M	Merchant	United States	U. States	Angenora	22 Dec 1826
DONALLY, Biddy	25	F	Spinster	Ireland	United S.	Hanford	19 Aug 1828
Catherine	25		Laboring Class		United States	Atlantic	2 Apr 1827
Elanur	24	F	D. Maker	Ireland	N. York	Trusty	12 Sep 1828
Mary, Mrs.	28	F	Milliner	Ireland	United States	Astrea	21 Oct 1823
Nancy	30	F		Ireland	U.S. of America	Douglass	6 Jul 1829
DONALSON, Mary	33	F	None	England	United States	Montgomery	6 Mar 1829
Peter	24	M	Cotton Spinner	England	United States	Montgomery	6 Mar 1829
DONALTY, Mary	20	F	None	England	United States	India	8 Jun 1827
DONALY, Neal	21	M	Labourer	Ireland	U. States	Meteor	19 Jul 1828
DONASON, John	36	M	Apothecary	Ireland	United States	Euphrates	12 Mar 1824
DONATHON, John	23	M	Labourer	Ireland	United States	Edwin	29 Nov 1828
DONATTI, Dominic	40	M	Misionary	Italy	Kentucky	Abigail	9 Aug 1821
DONAVAN, Timothy	25	M	Labourer	Ireland	United States	Jubilee	13 Jul 1829
DONAWIN, Dai...	6	M	Child	Ireland	United States	St. Michaels	27 Nov 1824
Jane	35	F	Wife	Ireland	United States	St. Michaels	27 Nov 1824
John	2	M	Child	Ireland	United States	St. Michaels	27 Nov 1824
Patty	8	F	Child	Ireland	United States	St. Michaels	27 Nov 1824
DONBY, Charles	20	M	W. Maker	Ireland	New York	Trusty	12 Sep 1828
DONCE, —, Mrs.	34	F		Copenhagen	St. Croix	Sarah	25 Oct 1825
DONCOURT, Elizabeth	22	F		France	U. States	Stephania	26 Apr 1824
J. H.	27	M	Merchant	France	U. States	Stephania	26 Apr 1824

NAMES OF PASSENGERS	AGE	SEX	OCCUPATIONS	COUNTRY TO WHICH THEY BELONG	COUNTRY THEY INTEND TO INHABIT	SHIPS/DATES OF ARRIVAL	
DONDAKIN, Margaret	17 6/12	F		Ireland	U.S. of America	Douglass	6 Jul 1829
Sibby	20	F		Ireland	U.S. of America	Douglass	6 Jul 1829
DONE, Chs.	25	M	Farmer	Ireland	U. States	Edward	15 Jul 1825
Wm.	27	M	Carpenter	France	U. States	David	5 Oct 1824
DONEGAIN, Francis	26	M	Merchant	Italy	U. States	Edward Bonaffe	11 Dec 1827
DONEGAN, Jno.	26	M	Gentleman	Canada	Canada	New York	13 Mar 1824
DONEGANE, B.	22	M	Merchant	Canada	U. States	Edward Bonaffe	11 Dec 1827
DONEHOE, Rose	25	F		Ireland	United States	Nancy R. Crowell	21 Sep 1822
DONEL, John	30	M	Taylor	Ireland	United States	Edwin	27 Oct 1828
Matin	24	M	Farmer	Ireland		Cuba	24 Jun 1822
DONELLON, Biddy	11	F		Ireland		L. M. Pelham	12 May 1823
John	2	M		Ireland		L. M. Pelham	12 May 1823
Mary	10	F		Ireland		L. M. Pelham	12 May 1823
DONELLY, Betsey	17	F	going to her Father	G. Brittian	United States	Louisa	14 Jun 1825
Catharine	45 7/12	F	going to her Husband	G. Brittian	United States	Louisa	14 Jun 1825
Edwd.	34	M	Moulder	Gt. Britain	New York	Columbia	3 Apr 1826
Margaret	12	F	going to her Father	G. Brittian	United States	Louisa	14 Jun 1825
Mary	1	F	None	United States	United States say Philadelphia	Union	19 Apr 1826
Mary	21	F	going to her Father	G. Brittian	United States	Louisa	14 Jun 1825
Nancy	5	F	going to her Father	G. Brittian	United States	Louisa	14 Jun 1825
Patrick	10	M	going to [his] Father	G. Brittian	United States	Louisa	14 Jun 1825
Sarah	15	F	going to her Father	G. Brittian	United States	Louisa	14 Jun 1825
Walter	30		Labourer	Warford	N. York	Peru	30 May 1828
*died on the passage							
Wm.	30	M	Labourer	Ireland	U. States	William & John	10 Jul 1824
DONEY, James	22	M	Labourer	Gt. Britain	U. States	Sarah G.	14 Apr 1828
DONGEY, M.	20	F	Servant	Ireland	N. York	Trusty	12 Sep 1828
DONGHEY, Barnard	20	M	Tailor	Ireland	New York	Trusty	12 Sep 1828
DONGLEY, Rosey	20	M	D. Maker	Ireland	N. York	Trusty	12 Sep 1828
Sarah	16	M	D. Maker	Ireland	N. York	Trusty	12 Sep 1828
DONGLY, Edw.	9	M	D. Maker	Ireland	N. York	Trusty	12 Sep 1828
DONHAM, Thomas L.	21	M	Clerk	United States	United States	William	11 Dec 1820
DONHASEN, Henry	19	M	Gentleman	Great Britain	England	John Wells	29 Jan 1825
Stephen	19	M	Gentleman	Great Britain	England	John Wells	29 Jan 1825
DONHOLEY, Abraham	25	M	Manufacturer	Great Britain	United States	Illinois	9 Oct 1820
DONICKS, Richard	25	M	Plaister	Great Britain	United States	Blakely	29 Sep 1826
DONIGAN, John	26	M	Cooper	Ireland	United States	William	20 Jul 1829
Mary	13	F	Spinster	Ireland	America	Mary	29 May 1827
Mary	22	F	Servant	Ireland	United States	William	20 Jul 1829
DONIGH, Ellen	18	F		Gt. Britain		Dalhouse Castle	13 May 1828
DONIHOO, Betsy	20	F	Spinster	Ireland	United States	Dublin Packet	3 May 1823
Mary	6/12	F	Child	Ireland	United States	Dublin Packet	3 May 1823
DONILLY, John	20		Labourer	Ireland	New York	Marcella	18 May 1827
DONILON, Austin	4	F		Ireland	Pensylvania	Marcella	18 May 1827
Bridget	10	F		Ireland	Pensylvania	Marcella	18 May 1827
Carthrine	20	F		Ireland	Pensylvania	Marcella	18 May 1827
Margrate	6	F		Ireland	Pensylvania	Marcella	18 May 1827
Mary	8	F		Ireland	Pensylvania	Marcella	18 May 1827
Mary	35	F		Ireland	Pensylvania	Marcella	18 May 1827
Michal	2	M		Ireland	Pensylvania	Marcella	18 May 1827
Pat	11 6/12	M	Laberor	Ireland	Pensylvania	Marcella	18 May 1827
Sally	45	F		Ireland	New York	Marcella	18 May 1827
DONIS, Ant., Don	22	M	Leiutenant in ...	Spain	Spain	James Monroe	5 Apr 1820
DONIVERT, Catherine	2	F	Farmer	France	United States	Crescent	12 Jul 1827
Catherine	28	F	Farmer	France	United States	Crescent	12 Jul 1827
Jacob	28	M	Farmer	France	United States	Crescent	12 Jul 1827
Michal	3	F	Farmer	France	United States	Crescent	12 Jul 1827
DONLAN, Ann	21	F	None	England	United States	London	21 May 1828
DONLERS, J.	22		Farmer	Ireland	United States	Courier	16 May 1825
DONLEY, Andrew	20	M		G. Britan	U. States	William Neilson	26 Jul 1828
B.	1			Great Britain	United States	Isaac Hicks	6 Dec 1827
B.	30	F		Great Britain	United States	Isaac Hicks	6 Dec 1827
James	20	M	Laborer	Ireland	United States	Sarah Ann	18 Nov 1826
Joseph	16	M	Farmer	Ireland	United States	Lima	19 Jun 1824
Mary Ane	...	F	...	...	United States	Hanford	17 Oct 1828

NAMES OF PASSENGERS	AGE	SEX	OCCUPATIONS	COUNTRY TO WHICH THEY BELONG	COUNTRY THEY INTEND TO INHABIT	SHIPS/DATES OF ARRIVAL	
DONLEY (cont'd)							
T.	21	M	Farmer	Great Britain	United States	Isaac Hicks	6 Dec 1827
DONLIN, John	27	M	Farmer	Ireland	United States	Dublin Packet	29 Jun 1825
DONLY, Dl.	26	M	Shoemaker	U. States	U. States	Laura Ann	2 Feb 1820
R.	20	F	Servant	Ireland	U. States	Sarah G	7 May 1827
Stephen	25	M	Labourer	Great Briton	uncertain	Mount Vernon	29 Aug 1828
DONN, William	36	M	Labourer	United States	United States	Robert Fulton	13 Mar 1827
DONNA..., Danl.	24	M	Farmer	England	U. States	Gem	28 Dec 1824
DONNAGHY, Sarah	25	F	None	Ireland	Pittsburgh	Indian Chief	16 Aug 1822
DONNAHOE, John	25	M	Farmer	Great Brittain	U. States	Hibernia	8 Jul 1823
DONNAHOO, Bridget	22	F		Irereland	America	Carolina Ann	20 Jun 1825
DONNALD, Andrew							
[crossed out]	26	M	Labourer	G. Britan	U. States	Ann Marria	6 Aug 1823
Jane	20	F	Spinster	Ireland		Robert Fulton	4 Jun 1828
Nathaniel, Mr.	28		Cotton Spinner	Glasgow		Hercules	19 Jun 1821
DONNALDSON, Jane	30	F	Lady	St. John, N.B.	United States	Sarah G.	11 Jan 1828
Lochlan	39	M	Merchant	St. John, N.B.	St. John, N.B.	Ann Maria	1 Apr 1826
Sarah	14	F	Lady	St. John, N.B.	St. John, N.B.	Ann Maria	1 Apr 1826
DONNALLAN, John	25	M	Farmer	Ireland	New York	Munroe	27 May 1825
Peter	20	M	Farmer	Ireland	New York	Munroe	27 May 1825
DONNALLY, Ann	28	F	None	Ireland	United States	Elizabeth	8 Jun 1827
Biddy	24	F		Gt. Britain		Dalhouse Castle	13 May 1828
W., Revd.	26	M	Clergiman	Ireland	United States	Essex	23 May 1828
DONNALSON, Andw.	19	M	Farmer	Ireland	United States	Trident	17 May 1825
DONNALY, Edward	23	M	Labourer	Ireland		Marchioness	13 May 1828
DONNAN, Wm.	26	M	Schoolmaster	Scotland	New York	Commerce	24 Sep 1823
DONNEGAN, Margrett	20	F	...	...	United States	Hanford	17 Oct 1828
DONNEL, Mary	20	F	Wife	Ireland	United States	Meteor	27 Sep 1826
DONNELL, John	18	M	Farmer	Great Britain	United States	Grecian	24 Sep 1828
John	28	M	Farmer	Great Britain	United States	Grecian	24 Sep 1828
Mary	21	F	Labourer	England	U. States	Comet	23 Aug 1828
Pat	28	M	Farmer	Ireland	America	Mary	29 May 1827
Thomas	17	M	None	Great Britain	United States	George Clinton	27 Aug 1827
Wm.	45		Farmer			Rufus King	7 Aug 1820
DONNELLON, Honer	30	F		Ireland		L. M. Pelham	12 May 1823
Patr.	30	M	Farmer	Ireland		L. M. Pelham	12 May 1823
Thomas	3	M		Ireland		L. M. Pelham	12 May 1823
DONNELLY, Ann	8 7/12	F	None	Ireland	United States	Atlantic	21 Jul 1827
Ann	25	F	None	United States	United States say Philadelphia	Union	19 Apr 1826
Bernard	2	M		Ireland	America	Plutarch	18 Jul 1826
Biddy	2	F		Ireland	United States	Dalhouse Castle	8 May 1827
Biddy	20	F		Ireland	United States	Alex. Mansfield	17 May 1823
Donnock	21	M	Labourer	Ireland		Marchioness	13 May 1828
Eliza	3	F		Ireland	America	Plutarch	18 Jul 1826
Ellen	19	F	None	Ireland	United States	Baltic	21 Apr 1827
Henry	25	M	Labourer	Ireland	United States	Sarah Ann	11 Jan 1827
Hugh	20	M	Labourer	Great Britain	United States	Meridian	2 Jul 1827
James	21	M	Farmer	Ireland	United States	Lord Strangford	20 Jun 1826
James	30	M	Laborer	Gt. Britain		Dalhouse Castle	13 May 1828
James	34	M	Farmer	Ireland	U.S.A.	Silas Richards	28 Jun 1825
Jas.	11	M	Weaver	Great Britain	United States	Atlantic	8 Dec 1827
John	0 6/12	M		Great Britain	United States	Atlantic	8 Dec 1827
John	4	M		Ireland	United States	Dalhouse Castle	8 May 1827
John	11	M	Flax dresser	Great Britain	United States	Atlantic	8 Dec 1827
John	26	M	Farmer	Ireland	U.S.A.	Silas Richards	28 Jun 1825
John	32	M	Labourer	Ireland	America	Plutarch	18 Jul 1826
Judith	25	F		England	United States	Dalhouse Castle	8 May 1827
Margaret	18	F	None	G.B.	U.S.A.	Silas Richard	30 Jun 1828
Margt.	30	F	Spinner	Great Britain	United States	Atlantic	8 Dec 1827
Margt.	40	F	Farmer	Ireland	U. States	Dickinson	30 Jul 1825
Mary	20	F	Farmer	Ireland	U. States	Dickinson	30 Jul 1825
Mary	26	F		Ireland	America	Plutarch	18 Jul 1826
Molly	18	F		Ireland	United States	Alex. Mansfield	17 May 1823
P.	25	M		Ireland	United States	William Byrnes	6 Apr 1826
Patrick	22 8/12	M	Labourer	Ireland	United States	Atlantic	21 Jul 1827
Peter	30	M	Accountant	United States	United States say Philadelphia	Union	19 Apr 1826
Rossanna	28		Sempstress	Ireland	Great Britain	Henrietta	26 Nov 1825

NAMES OF PASSENGERS	AGE	SEX	OCCUPATIONS	COUNTRY TO WHICH THEY BELONG	COUNTRY THEY INTEND TO INHABIT	SHIPS/DATES OF ARRIVAL	
DONNELLY (cont'd)							
William	19	M	Laborer	Ireland	United States	Carolina Ann	11 Dec 1826
Wm.	25	M	Weaver	Ireland	America	Mary	29 May 1827
DONNELSON, David	28		Baker	England		Hudson	23 Jul 1828
DONNELY, Eliza	22	F	Spinster	Ireland	United States	Trident	16 May 1826
Peter	28	F	Servant	Ireland	United States	Louisa	18 Apr 1827
Wm.	20	M	Wailie	Ireland	United States	Trident	16 May 1826
DONNER, Denis	4	M		Ireland	U. States	St. Michael	26 Oct 1824
Timothy	27	M		Ireland	U. States	St. Michael	26 Oct 1824
DONNEY, Sarah	20	F		Great Britain	U. States	Lady Hunter	28 May 1823
DONNIGAN, Michael	66	M	Farmer	Great Brittain	United States	Active	12 Sep 1828
DONNISS, John	38	M	Merchant	England	England	Tontine	1 Jun 1826
DONNOHOW, Catherine	18	F		G. Britain	U. States	Mary & Harriot	8 Sep 1828
Elizabeth	14	F		G. Britain	U. States	Mary & Harriot	8 Sep 1828
DONNOLLY, Ann, Jr.	2	F	None	Ireland	United States	Elizabeth	8 Jun 1827
Jane	17	F		G. Britain	U. States	Hamilton	28 Apr 1828
John	75	M		G. Britain	U. States	Hamilton	28 Apr 1828
Mary	9	F		G. Britain	U. States	Hamilton	28 Apr 1828
Mary	33	F		G. Britain	U. States	Hamilton	28 Apr 1828
Mary A.	12	F		G. Britain	U. States	Hamilton	28 Apr 1828
R.	45	M	Labourer	G. Britain	U. States	Hamilton	28 Apr 1828
W.	30			G. Britain	U. States	Hamilton	28 Apr 1828
DONNOLY, Eliza	18	F	Servant	Ireland	N. York	Trusty	12 Sep 1828
DONNONS, John	28	M	Merchant	United States	St. John	Nancy R. Crowell	21 Sep 1822
DONNWULTH, Jean	24	F	Brewer	Switzerland	Swizland	Le Voltaire	19 Jul 1828
DONOCHO, James	24	M	Planter	G. Britton	Ireland	Eliza Davidson	12 Feb 1829
Owen	40	M	Planter	Ireland	Ireland	Eliza Davidson	1 Dec 1828
DONOGHOE, Betsey	18	M		England	United States	Essex	23 May 1828
Bridget	30	F	Servant	Ireland	New York	Atlantic	8 May 1828
Daniel	40	M	Carpenter	New York	New York	Harriot	1 May 1822
Dl.	46	M	Carpenter	Ireland	U. States	Antelope	23 Mar 1824
Pat	25	M	Labourer	Ireland	New York	Atlantic	8 May 1828
Thomas	42	M	Carpenter	Ireland	U. States	Antelope	23 Mar 1824
DONOGHUE, Rose	21	F		Great Britain	Philadelphia	Philetus	21 Jul 1827
DONOHAN, Catherine	19	F		Ireland		Lady Hunter	12 Apr 1823
DONOHO, Biddy	56	F		Ireland	U. States	Alfred	7 Jun 1824
H.	14	M	Farmer	Ireland	U. States	Alfred	7 Jun 1824
James	18	M	Farmer	Ireland	U. States	Alfred	7 Jun 1824
James	23		Labourer	Carvan	N. York	Peru	30 May 1828
Patrick	21	M	Farmer	Ireland	U. States	Alfred	7 Jun 1824
DONOHOE, —	2	F		Dublin	U. States	Hibernia	26 Oct 1826
—	7	F		Dublin	U. States	Hibernia	26 Oct 1826
—	9	F		Dublin	U. States	Hibernia	26 Oct 1826
—	14	M		Dublin	U. States	Hibernia	26 Oct 1826
—	16	M		Dublin	U. States	Hibernia	26 Oct 1826
—, Mr.	34	M		Dublin	U. States	Hibernia	26 Oct 1826
—, Mr.	50	M		Dublin	U. States	Hibernia	26 Oct 1826
—, Mrs.	34	F		Dublin	U. States	Hibernia	26 Oct 1826
Catharin	18	F		Gt. Britain	U. States	Isaac Hicks	18 Apr 1825
Daniel	45	M	Engineer	U.S.	U.S.	Frances	21 Jul 1827
Evestaine	50	F	Matron	Ireland	America	Wilson	16 May 1825
John	26	M	Servant	Ireland	United States	Abigail	25 Jun 1822
Patrick	24	M	Clerk	Ireland	America	Wilson	16 May 1825
DONOHOO, Mary	19	F	Spinster	Ireland	United States	Dublin Packet	22 Apr 1822
DONOHOUGH, Ann	24	F	Labourer	Great Britain	U. States	Ganges	21 Jun 1827
Joseph	25	M	Labourer	Great Britain	U. States	Ganges	21 Jun 1827
DONOHUA, Mary	26	F		Ireland	United States	William Byrnes	15 Aug 1826
DONOHUE, James	13	M	Boy	Ireland	United States	Dublin Packet	3 Sep 1822
Winifred	14	F	Spinster	Ireland	United States	Dublin Packet	3 Sep 1822
Wm.	26	M	Farmer	Ireland	United States	Dublin Packet	3 Sep 1822
DONOLDSON, Sarah	5	F	Child	Scotland	America	Concord	4 Jun 1821
DONOLLEY, Thos.	25	M	Labourer	Ireland	United States	Edwin	29 Nov 1828
DONOLLON, Michl.	40	M	Farmer	Ireland		L. M. Pelham	12 May 1823
Pat	50	M	Farmer	Ireland		L. M. Pelham	12 May 1823
DONOR, Margaret	16	F	Labourer	Ireland	United States	Hope	12 Jun 1828
DONOUGHEW, Wm.	28	M	Farmer	C..., ..., Ireland	U. States	New Orleans	24 Aug 1827
DONOUGHOO, C.	4/12	F	None	Ireland	United States	Aurelia	7 Jun 1826
*died on passage							

NAMES OF PASSENGERS	AGE	SEX	OCCUPATIONS	COUNTRY TO WHICH THEY BELONG	COUNTRY THEY INTEND TO INHABIT	SHIPS/DATES OF ARRIVAL	
DONOUGHOO (comt'd)							
Denis	26	M	None	Ireland	United States	Aurelia	7 Jun 1826
James	3	M	None	Ireland	United States	Aurelia	7 Jun 1826
John	26	M	Tailor	Manchester	United States	Aurelia	7 Jun 1826
Mary	20	F	None	Ireland	United States	Aurelia	7 Jun 1826
Mary	21	F	None	Ireland	United States	Aurelia	7 Jun 1826
Thomas	40	M	Farmer	Great Britain	United States	India	5 Sep 1827
DONOUGHY, John	26 5/12	M		England	U.S. of America	Illinois	30 Apr 1823
DONOVAN, Ann	45			England	West Indies	Robert Burns	8 Dec 1821
Charlotte	20		Laborer	Great Britan	U. States	Columbia	7 May 1828
D. D.	5			England	West Indies	Robert Burns	8 Dec 1821
Honora	19	F	None	Ireland	New York	America	1 Aug 1828
James	22	M	Farmer	Ireland	United States	Andes	2 Oct 1828
Johanna	22			England	West Indies	Robert Burns	8 Dec 1821
John	35	M	Labourer	Ireland	United States	Trio	13 Jun 1827
Margt.	50	F	Labourer	Ireland	United States	Trio	5 May 1828
Mary	26	F	Lady	Ireland	United States	Ann Maria	1 Apr 1826
Michael	30		Laborer	Great Britan	U. States	Columbia	7 May 1828
Patrick	18	M	None	Ireland	New York	America	1 Aug 1828
Ths. B.	...0		Planter	England	West Indies	Robert Burns	8 Dec 1821
DONOVEN, Timothy	28	M	Laborer or Spinster	Ireland	United States	Sarah G	11 Sep 1827
DONOVIN, Michael	21	M	Labourer	Ireland	United States	Robert Edwards	3 Oct 1829
DONTISS, Francis	23	M	Farmer	France	United States	American	27 Aug 1827
DONYTHAN, Michael		M	Miner	America		Iris	7 Dec 1827
DOOBIN, Patt	24	M	Farmer	Ireland	United States	Dublin Packet	29 Jun 1825
DOOGAN, John	19	M	Labourer	Ireland		Marchioness	13 May 1828
DOOLAN, Timothy	25	M	Farmer	Ireland	United States	Trident	31 Mar 1827
DOOLEN, Thomas	23	M		Ireland	Ireland	Britannia	22 Jul 1829
DOOLEY, Martin	35	M	Farmer	Ireland	Cannada	Hesperus	2 Nov 1820
Winfield	23	M	Taylor	U. States	U. States	Climax	24 Sep 1827
DOOLIN, Peter	26	M	Farmer	Great Britain	United States	Robert Fulton	1 Apr 1824
DOOLING, May	15	F		Ireland	United States	Thomas	13 Dec 1827
Mgt.	40	F		Ireland	United States	Thomas	13 Dec 1827
Pat	10	M		Ireland	United States	Thomas	13 Dec 1827
DOOLITTLE, Anze	32	M	Teacher	U.S.		Venus	11 Aug 1820
J.	32	M	Gent.	U. States	U. States	Cadmus	28 May 1821
DOOLY, Ann	40	F		England	United States	Nimrod	31 Jul 1828
M.	50	M	Farmer	England	United States	Nimrod	31 Jul 1828
Sally	22	F	Spinster	Ireland	United States	Dublin Packet	9 Jul 1827
Tim	26	M				Lady of the Lake	23 Aug 1828
*left ship							
DOON, John	18	M	Merchant	U.S.A.	U.S.A.	Gallego	13 Mar 1829
DOONAGAN, E.	27	F		Great Brittain	United States	Sarah Ralston	27 Jan 1827
DOONERZAN, M.	30	M	Labourer	Great Brittain	United States	Sarah Ralston	27 Jan 1827
DOONEY, Hugh	22	M	Labourer	Ireland	New York	Curler	7 Jul 1827
DOORIS, James	19	M	Smith	Ireland	United States	Carolina Ann	11 Dec 1826
John	22	M	Laborer	Ireland	United States	Carolina Ann	11 Dec 1826
DOORLING, Joseph, Mr.	25		Stenographer	England	returns to England	Mary	21 Sep 1821
DOOTEY, Haner	22	F				Nancey	25 Jan 1823
Thomis	6	M				Nancey	25 Jan 1823
DOR..., Jo...	...3	...	...	...	...	Pioneer	21 Jun 1825
DORA, James	50		Gentleman	Halifax, N.S.	United States	Mexico	1 Jun 1821
John	22		Gentleman	Halifax, N.S.	United States	Mexico	1 Jun 1821
DORAM, Bridget	30	F	Spinster	Ireland	United States	Wilson	6 Jun 1828
Mary	2	F	Spinster	Ireland	United States	Wilson	6 Jun 1828
Thos.	32	M	Labourer	Ireland	United States	Wilson	6 Jun 1828
DORAN, Alice	16	F		Ireland	United States	Romulus	24 Jun 1826
Alice	21	F		Ireland	U. States	Alexander	28 Jul 1821
Allicia	6/12	F	Servant	Ireland	United States	Wilson	27 Jun 1826
Ann	19	F		Ireland	U. States	Alexander	28 Jul 1821
Ann	25	F		Great Britain	U.S.A.	Silas Richards	28 Jun 1825
Arthur	34	M	Labourer	Scotland	United States	Friends	7 Jul 1827
Bridget	8 6/12	F	Servant	Ireland	United States	Wilson	27 Jun 1826
Catharine	14	F	Spinster	Ireland	United States	Dublin Packet	22 Oct 1821
Catharine	22	F	Spinster	Ireland	United States	Abigail	25 Jun 1822
Catharine	24 8/12	F	Spinstress	Ireland	U. States	Fabius	22 Sep 1828
Dennis	30	M	Gardner	Ireland		Ocean	13 Jul 1827
Edward	28	M	Farmer	Ireland	United States	Abigail	25 Jun 1822

NAMES OF PASSENGERS	AGE	SEX	OCCUPATIONS	COUNTRY TO WHICH THEY BELONG	COUNTRY THEY INTEND TO INHABIT	SHIPS/DATES OF ARRIVAL
DORAN (cont'd)						
Edward	28	M	Labourer	Ireland	United States	Lord Wellington 28 May 1827
Francis	24	M	Servant	Ireland	United States	Josephine 30 Apr 1828
Honer	15	F	Farmer	Ireland		Cuba 24 Jun 1822
Hugh	21	M	Farmer	Ireland	U. States	Alexander 28 Jul 1821
Hugh	21	M	Labourer	Ireland	United States	Josephine 30 Apr 1828
James	10	M	Child	Ireland	United States	Dublin Packet 9 Jul 1827
James	16		Laboring Class		United States	Atlantic 2 Apr 1827
James	20	M	Labourer	Borstro...	United States	Carolina Ann 11 Jun 1824
James	21 1/12		Labourer	Ireland	United States	Helen 5 Jul 1820
James	22	M	Waiter	Great Britain		London 29 Apr 1824
James	23	M	Calico Printer	Great Britain	U.S.A.	Silas Richards 28 Jun 1825
James	23	M	Labourer	U. States	U. States	United States 11 Sep 1828
James	32	M	Farmer	Ireland	United States	Abigail 25 Jun 1822
James	57 3/12		Merchant	Ireland	United States	Helen 5 Jul 1820
John	1 6/12	M	Servant	Ireland	United States	Wilson 27 Jun 1826
John	21	M	Farmer	Ireland	U. States	Alexander 28 Jul 1821
John	23	M	Labourer	Great Britain	United States	William Dawson 18 Jun 1827
John	30	M	Labourer	Ireland	United States	Lord Wellington 28 May 1827
John	45	M	Farmer	Ireland	United States	Dublin Packet 22 Aug 1829
John	50	M	Farmer	Ireland		Cuba 24 Jun 1822
Kitty	14	F	Farmer	Ireland		Cuba 24 Jun 1822
Margt.	20	F	Servant	Ireland	United States	Wilson 27 Jun 1826
Mary	17	F	Servant	Ireland	United States	Wilson 27 Jun 1826
Mary	18	F	None	Great Britain	United States	Frances Henrietta 17 Sep 1827
Mary	19	F	Servant	Ireland	United States	Josephine 30 Apr 1828
Mary	20	F	Servant	Ireland	United States	Wilson 27 Jun 1826
Mary	30	F	Servant	Ireland	United States	Wilson 27 Jun 1826
Mary	50	F	Farmer	Ireland		Cuba 24 Jun 1822
Mary, Senr.	27	F	Servant	Ireland	United States	Josephine 30 Apr 1828
Michael	22	M	Yeoman	Ireland	United States	Borneo 9 Jul 1827
Pat	24	M	Cooper	Gt. Britain	U. States	St. George 20 Sep 1828
Patk.	30	M	Farmer	Ireland	United States	Wilson 27 Jun 1826
Patrick	25 6/12	M	Labourer	England	United States	John Wells 22 May 1826
Patt	12	M	Farmer	Ireland		Cuba 24 Jun 1822
Peter	24	M		England	United States	Yobah 26 Sep 1827
Saly	16	F	Spinster	Ireland	United States	Fabius 31 Jul 1829
Thos.	26	M		England	United States	Yobah 26 Sep 1827
Wm.	26	M	Millwright	Brunswick	U.S. America	Commodore Preble 17 Dec 1825
DORANTES, Mariano	22	M	Mercht.	Guatemela	Central America	Savannah 22 May 1827
Ramon	17	M	Mercht.	Guatemela	Central America	Savannah 22 May 1827
DORATHY, Abigail	30	F	Servant	Ireland	United States	Wanderer 1 Aug 1828
DORDELLY, Peter	25	M	Merchant	New York	New York	Hope Mary Ann 19 Jan 1825
DORDILLY, P.	25	M	Merchant	Italy	U. States	Ann Elizabeth 28 Feb 1824
Peter	28	M	Merchant	France	S. America	Mentor 8 Sep 1821
DOREGH, John	25	M	Laborer	Ireland	United States	St. Michael 21 Aug 1824
DOREH, Edward	25	M	Gent.	Ireland	U. States	Meteor 19 Jul 1828
DORELL, Jabish	45	M	Merchant	United States	U. States	Romulus 26 Dec 1825
Simon	30	M	Carpenter	Ireland	United States	Tampico 29 Apr 1826
DOREN, John	20	M	Labourer	Ireland	United States	Meteor 26 Jun 1827
Susan	20	F	Labourer	Ireland	United States	Meteor 26 Jun 1827
DORETH, Louisa	27	F	Farmer	Switzerland		Pallas 14 Jun 1828
DOREWERT, Catherine	8	F	Farmer	France	United States	Crescent 12 Jul 1827
George	41	M	Farmer	France	United States	Crescent 12 Jul 1827
Magdalen	5	F	Farmer	France	United States	Crescent 12 Jul 1827
Magdalen	43	F	Farmer	France	United States	Crescent 12 Jul 1827
Margaret	12		Farmer	France	United States	Crescent 12 Jul 1827
Margaret	22	F	Farmer	France	United States	Crescent 12 Jul 1827
Yerneg	17	M	Farmer	France	United States	Crescent 12 Jul 1827
DORGAN, Michael	30	M	boiler Maker	England	United States	Nancy Henrietta 3 Nov 1828
DORGERTY, Philip	19	M	Labourer	Ireland	America	Franklin 13 Aug 1827
DORIGHEN, James	22 7/12	M	Servant	United States	United States	Criterion 27 Oct 1820
DORIN, John	26	M	Taylor	Ireland	U. States	Amity 23 Sep 1823
Philip	30	M	Laborer	Canada	Canada	Active 29 Nov 1820
Rose	30	F	Spinner	Great Britain	United States	Atlantic 8 Dec 1827
DORINGER, Caspar	41	M	Chemist	Prussia	United States	Pioneer 28 Jun 1827
Rupperta	31	F		Prussia	United States	Pioneer 28 Jun 1827

NAMES OF PASSENGERS	AGE	SEX	OCCUPATIONS	COUNTRY TO WHICH THEY BELONG	COUNTRY THEY INTEND TO INHABIT	SHIPS/DATES OF ARRIVAL	
DORIS, Washington	19	M		U. States	U. States	Doris	2 Jun 1828
DORITY, James	20	M	Weaver	Ireland	United States	Kleber	23 Jul 1827
DORIVAL, —, Mrs.	31	F	Priestess	France	U.S.	Edward Quesnel	31 Jul 1827
DORLAN, John	30	M		England	United States	Yobah	26 Sep 1827
M.	24	M		England	United States	Yobah	26 Sep 1827
DORLY, E.	38	F	Child	G. Brittan	U. States	Henry	24 Oct 1828
T.	16	M	Child	G. Brittan	U. States	Henry	24 Oct 1828
W.	13	M	Child	G. Brittan	U. States	Henry	24 Oct 1828
DORMAN, Andrew	25	M	Weaver	Ireland	United States	Trident	18 Jul 1827
DORMER, —, Mrs.	24	F	Milliner	Ireland	U. States	Telegraph	14 Feb 1820
John M.	27	M	Trader	Ireland	U. States	Telegraph	14 Feb 1820
DORMON, John M.	40	M	Merchant	U. States	U. States	Echo	22 Apr 1823
DORMOND, John	28		Sugar Baker	Hanovurine	United States	Hudson	5 Apr 1826
DORMOODY, Phillip	23	M	Gardener	Ireland	New York	Munroe	27 May 1825
DORMOY, G.	28	M	Planter	St. Martins	U. States	Matilda	23 May 1826
DORNAN, James	60	M	Farmer	U.S.A.	U.S.	Fame	26 Jul 1822
DORNCOT, Eliza	20	F	Servant	Ireland, Great Britain	U.S. of America	Dublin	21 Feb 1826
DORNE, Catharine	34	F		Nova Scotia	United States	McDonough	3 Nov 1823
DORNEN, Catharine	23	F	Servant	U. States	U. States	Cincinnatus	24 May 1821
DORNICK, P. E.	50	M	Physician	Great Britain	United States	Isaac Hicks	6 Dec 1827
DORNY, James	23	M	Labourer	Ireland	United States	Princess Charlotte	6 Oct 1827
DORODOYER, Peter	27	M	Baker	France	U. States	Sully	25 Jun 1828
DOROLAN, Katr.	17	F	Servant	Ireland	United States	Carolina Ann	11 Dec 1826
DOROLARO, Sebastian	12			Columbia	Columbia	Pettrell	15 Sep 1826
DOROTY, Pattey	20	M	Labourer	Ireland	U. States	Nancy	1 Sep 1823
Peggy	70	F		Ireland	U. States	Nancy	1 Sep 1823
Sally	22	F		Ireland	U. States	Nancy	1 Sep 1823
DORR, Edward	21	M	Merchant	U. States	U. States	Robert Edwards	25 Apr 1821
Frederick H.	23	M	Merchant	U. States	U. States	Leader	7 Aug 1829
J.	58	M	Merchant	U.S.	U.S.	Edward Quesnel	31 Jul 1827
Job	22	M	Merchant	U.S. America	U.S. America	Columbia	31 Jul 1826
John, Junr.	24	M	Merchant	U.S. America	U.S. America	Columbia	31 Jul 1826
S.	52	M	Merchant	U.S.	U.S.	Edward Quesnel	31 Jul 1827
Samuel F.	19	M	Merchant	United States		William Byrnes	6 Apr 1826
DORRAH, John	29	M	Carpenter	Ireland	United States	Lady Hunter	27 Dec 1825
DORRAN, Jane	14 1/12	F		Ireland	U.S. of America	Douglass	6 Jul 1829
John	57	M		Ireland	U.S. of America	Douglass	6 Jul 1829
Mary	50 7/12	F		Ireland	U.S. of America	Douglass	6 Jul 1829
DORRELL, —, Mr.	23	M	Merchant	Bermuda	Bermuda	Improvement	6 Jun 1826
DORSEY, Felix	33 9/12	M	Labourer	Ireland	United States	Atlantic	21 Jul 1827
James	17	M	Gentleman	U.S., N. York		Congress	21 Nov 1823
Mary	22	F	Seamstress	Ireland	United States	Eliza	29 Aug 1822
DORSOMEVILLE, Ls.	26	M	Merchant	Louisiana	U. States	Altamira	31 Jan 1826
DORSON, Richd.	21	M	Farmer	G. Britain	U. States	Wanderer	23 Jun 1828
William	25	M	Labourer	England	United States	Maria	12 May 1823
DORSONVELL, Lewis	28	M	Merchant	Louisiana	U. States	Mary & Eliza	13 Dec 1828
DORTY, M.	20	M	Labourer	G. Britain	U. States	Hanford	18 Sep 1828
DOS SANTOS, F. Joaquim	32	M	Milatary	Perambuco	Brazil	Jane	17 Jan 1825
Francisco	25	M	Mechanic	Madeira	U. States	Howard	3 Mar 1828
DOUBLET, Edward	24	M	Merchant	France	America	Don Quixotte	2 Jun 1828
DOUCET, Francis O.	36	M	Phisician	Switzerland	U. States	Sully	25 Jun 1828
DOUCHER, Jaques	40	M	Servt.			Henri IV	17 May 1828
DOUDE, Anne	14	F	Farmer	England	America	Thames	27 May 1822
Elizabeth	8	F	Farmer	England	America	Thames	27 May 1822
James	4	M	Farmer	England	America	Thames	27 May 1822
Joseph	infant	M	Farmer	England	America	Thames	27 May 1822
Lucy	6	F	Farmer	England	America	Thames	27 May 1822
Martha	5	F	Farmer	England	America	Thames	27 May 1822
Mary	12	F	Farmer	England	America	Thames	27 May 1822
Mary	40	F	Farmer	England	America	Thames	27 May 1822
Molly	13	F	Farmer	England	America	Thames	27 May 1822
Richard	10	M	Farmer	England	America	Thames	27 May 1822
Vincent	40	M	Farmer	England	America	Thames	27 May 1822
DOUDIKIN, Catherin	21	F	Spinster	Great Brittan	United States	Hanford	3 Aug 1829
Wm.	25	M	Labourer	Great Brittan	United States	Hanford	3 Aug 1829
DOUGALE, John	45	M	Farmer	Great Britain	United States	Rosina	12 Aug 1823
DOUGALL, Jno.	22	M	Merchant	Gt. Britain	Canada	Baltic	11 Apr 1825

NAMES OF PASSENGERS	AGE	SEX	OCCUPATIONS	COUNTRY TO WHICH THEY BELONG	COUNTRY THEY INTEND TO INHABIT	SHIPS/DATES OF ARRIVAL	
DOUGALL (cont'd)							
Wm.	22	M	Farmer	Ireland	United States	Trident	17 May 1825
DOUGAN, M.	20	M	Farmer	Ireland	U. States	Napolean	26 Sep 1828
DOUGGERTY, Michl.	22	M	Labourer	Ireland		Robert Fulton	4 Jun 1828
DOUGHARTY, Charles	20	M	Labourer	Ireland	United States	Nancy	16 Jul 1824
DOUGHERTY,							
Alexander	26 11/12	M	Weaver	Ireland	United States	Louisa	27 Nov 1826
Ann	...	F	...	Ireland	United States	General Putnam	20 Jun 1825
Ann	12	F		England	U. States	Manhattan	20 Jun 1825
Ann	17	F	None	Ireland	U. States	Belville	5 Jul 1827
Ann	36	F		England	U. States	Lima	5 Aug 1829
Bette [crossed out]	30	F		Ireland	United States	Asia	29 Jul 1829
Bridget	20	F	S...	Ireland	United States	Henry Kneeland	7 Jun 1828
Bridget	67	F		England	United States	John Wells	22 May 1826
C., Mrs.	19	F	Revenue Officer of N.P.	England	Antigua	Crawford	4 Jan 1826
Catherin	33	F	Spinster	Ireland	United States	Robert Fulton	10 Aug 1827
Catherine	18	F	Spinster	Ireland	United States	Robert Fulton	24 Jul 1826
Charles	23	M	Labourer	Ireland	United States	Robert Fulton	10 Aug 1827
Charles	32	M	Farmer	St. Johns, N.B.	United States	Henrietta	17 Aug 1825
Chas.	...	M	...	Ireland	United States	General Putnam	20 Jun 1825
Chas.	20 5/12	M	Labourer	England	United States	John Wells	22 May 1826
Chas.	28	M	Baker	Ireland	United States	Henry Kneeland	7 Jun 1828
Con	13	F	Boy	Ireland	United States	Henry Kneeland	7 Jun 1828
Con.	21	M	Farmer	Ireland	United States	Henry Kneeland	7 Jun 1828
Corns.	21	M		Ireland	United States	William & George	14 May 1828
Danl.	40	M	Fisherman	Ireland	United States	Henry Kneeland	7 Jun 1828
Edward	19	M	Merchant	Ireland	United States	Sylvester Healy	11 May 1825
Edward	20	M	Labourer	Ireland	United States	Robert Fulton	24 Jul 1826
Elinor	20	F	Spinster	Ireland	United States	Robert Fulton	10 Aug 1827
George	16	M	Miller	Ireland	United States	Trident	17 May 1825
Henry	38	M	...	Ireland	U. States	Ann Maria	6 Jul 1824
Hn.	20		Farmer	Ireland		Westmoreland	1 Aug 1826
Hugh	21	F	Servant	Ireland	United States	Henry Kneeland	7 Jun 1828
Hugh	22	M	Shoemaker	Ireland	United States	Henry Kneeland	7 Jun 1828
Hugh	43		Farmer	Ireland	Great Britain	Robert Burns	14 Jun 1824
Hy.	30		Farmer	Ireland		Westmoreland	1 Aug 1826
James	2/12	M	Child	Ireland	New York	Atlantic	6 Oct 1828
James	18	M	Labourer	Ireland	United States	Henry Kneeland	7 Jun 1828
James	25	M	Labourer	Ireland	United States	Henry Kneeland	7 Jun 1828
James	28	M	Mason	United States		Mentor	23 May 1821
James	30	M	Farmer	Ireland	United States	General Putnam	20 Jun 1825
Jane	16	F	Spinner	Scotland	United States	Orion	15 Jan 1827
Jane	24	F	Servant	Ireland	United States	Atlantic	21 Jul 1827
John	...	M	...	Ireland	United States	General Putnam	20 Jun 1825
John	3	M		England	U. States	Lima	5 Aug 1829
John	5	M	None	Great Britian	U. States	Pallas	17 Aug 1824
John	17	M	Labourer	Ireland	United States	Robert Fulton	10 Aug 1827
John	20	M	Labourer	Ireland	United States	Robert Fulton	24 Jul 1826
John	22		Labourer	Ireland	G. Britain	Robert Burns	14 Jun 1824
John	24	M	shoe Maker	Ireland	United States	Josephine	30 Apr 1828
John	30	M	Mechanic	England	Great Britain	Manchester Packet	30 Nov 1822
Joseph	30	M	Labourer	Ireland	United States	Hope	12 Jun 1828
Leal	25	M	Labourer	Ireland	United States	Henry Kneeland	7 Jun 1828
M.	19	F	Labourer	Ireland	United States	Hope	12 Jun 1828
Margaret	68	F	Mother	Ireland	New York	Atlantic	8 May 1828
Mariah	21	F	Wife	Ireland	United States	Henry Kneeland	7 Jun 1828
Mary	9	F	Wife	Ireland	New York	Atlantic	6 Oct 1828
Mary	20	F	Spinster	Ireland	United States	Robert Fulton	24 Jul 1826
Mary	21	F	Wife	Ireland	United States	Henry Kneeland	7 Jun 1828
Mary	21	F	Servant	Ireland	United States	Henry Kneeland	7 Jun 1828
Mary	22	F		England	U. States	Manhattan	20 Jun 1825
Mary	27	F	Spinster	Ireland	U. States	Meteor	19 Jul 1828
Michal	5	M	Child	Ireland	U. States	Meteor	19 Jul 1828
Michal	23	M	Labourer	Ireland	United States	Robert Fulton	24 Jul 1826
Michal	29	M	Labourer	Ireland	United States	Hope	12 Jun 1828
Nancy	26	F		Ireland	United States	General Putnam	20 Jun 1825

NAMES OF PASSENGERS	AGE	SEX	OCCUPATIONS	COUNTRY TO WHICH THEY BELONG	COUNTRY THEY INTEND TO INHABIT	SHIPS/DATES OF ARRIVAL	
DOUGHERTY (cont'd)							
Nancy	50	F		Ireland	United States	General Putnam	20 Jun 1825
Neil	21		Labourer	Ireland	Great Britain	Robert Burns	14 Jun 1824
Neil	23	M	Farmer	Ireland	United States	Henry Kneeland	7 Jun 1828
Noat	33	F	Labourer	Ireland	United States	Hope	12 Jun 1828
Pat	27	M		Gt. Britain	United States	Penelope	9 Sep 1828
Patrick	22	M	Farmer	Ireland	United States	Trident	17 May 1825
Patrick	25	M	Labourer	Ireland	United States	Robert Fulton	10 Aug 1827
Peggy	38	F	Wife	Ireland	United States	Henry Kneeland	7 Jun 1828
Peter	3	M	Child	Ireland	U. States	Meteor	19 Jul 1828
Peter	22	M	Labourer	Ireland	United States	Henry Kneeland	7 Jun 1828
Philip	30	M	Weaver	Scotland	United States	Delta	24 Oct 1829
Rebecca	3	F	None	Great Britian	U. States	Pallas	17 Aug 1824
Robt.	54	M	Farmer	England	U. States	Manhattan	20 Jun 1825
Robt., Jr.	26	M	Weaver	England	U. States	Manhattan	20 Jun 1825
Sarah	27	F	Labourer	Ireland	United States	Hope	12 Jun 1828
Stewart	21		Weaver	Ireland	United States	Robert Burns	30 May 1823
Susan	60			Ireland	Great Britain	Robert Burns	14 Jun 1824
Thomas	20	M	Spinner	Scotland	United States	Orion	15 Jan 1827
Thomas	25	M	Carpenter	Ireland	United States	Clothier	22 Nov 1827
Thomas	33	M	Maison	England	U. States	Lima	5 Aug 1829
William	19	M	Labourer	Ireland	United States	Silas Richards	3 Apr 1826
Wm.	...	M	...	Ireland	United States	General Putnam	20 Jun 1825
Wm.	2/12	M	Child	Ireland	New York	Atlantic	6 Oct 1828
Wm.	19	M	Spinner	Scotland	United States	Orion	15 Jan 1827
Wm.	24 9/12	M	Labourer	England	United States	John Wells	22 May 1826
DOUGHLASS, —	11	M				Hibernia	15 Aug 1820
DOUGHT...Y, ...	12	M				Robert Burns	13 Jul 1820
DOUGHTERLY, Ann	18	F	Labourer	Ireland	United States	Hope	12 Jun 1828
Patrick	26	M	Labourer	Ireland	United States	Hope	12 Jun 1828
Wm.	28	M	Labourer	Manchester	United States	Aurelia	7 Jun 1826
DOUGHTERY, Jas.	8	M				Robert Burns	13 Jul 1820
Wm.	13	M				Robert Burns	13 Jul 1820
DOUGHTRY, Rose	38	F	Spinster			Robert Burns	13 Jul 1820
DOUGHTY, Geo.	26	M	Labourer	Sligo	U. States	Panthea	8 Apr 1826
Mary	18	F	Spinster	Ireland		Robert Fulton	4 Jun 1828
Michael	27	M	Labourer	New York, Roscommon	United States	Solon	21 Jun 1824
Wm.	21	M	Labourer	New York, Roscommon	United States	Solon	21 Jun 1824
DOUGIN, Auther	7	M		Ireland	United States	Borneo	28 Aug 1828
Daniel	5	M		Ireland	United States	Borneo	28 Aug 1828
John	3	M		Ireland	United States	Borneo	28 Aug 1828
Mary	30	F		Ireland	United States	Borneo	28 Aug 1828
William	0 2/12	M		Ireland	United States	Borneo	28 Aug 1828
William	30	M	Farmer	Ireland	United States	Borneo	28 Aug 1828
DOUGLAS, Isabella	40	F		Ireland	New York	Carolina Ann	15 Oct 1824
John	40	M	Brewer	Ireland	New York	Carolina Ann	15 Oct 1824
Margaret, Child	13	F		Ireland	New York	Carolina Ann	15 Oct 1824
William	26	M	Merchant	Canada	Canada	Monroe	18 May 1827
William	26 2/12	M	Merchant	Great Brittian	Canada	Four Sons	31 May 1828
Willm.	28	M	Cooper	Ireland	United States	Aurelia	7 Jun 1826
Wm.	22 6/12	M	Merchant	Scotland	Canada	Globe	3 Dec 1821
DOUGLASS, —, Capt.	30	M	Seaman	U.S.	U.S.	Radius	22 Aug 1820
—, Mr.	21	M	Clerk	England	U. States	Ann Maria	13 Mar 1823
...	74	F	...	Scotland	America	Nimrod	9 Jul 1827
...ret	35	F	Child	Scotland	America	Nimrod	9 Jul 1827
Andrew	5	M	Farmer	Argyle (Tedland) Scotland	United States	Jean Hastie	27 Jul 1829
Andrew	36	M	Farmer	Argyle (Tedland) Scotland	United States	Jean Hastie	27 Jul 1829
Ann	21			England	America	Governor Griswold	6 Jun 1821
Charles	27	M	Mercht.	..., ..., Scotland	U. States	New Orleans	24 Aug 1827
Chas.	36	M	Mercht.	United States	U. States	Betsey	7 Sep 1822
Christian	33	F	Farmer	Argyle (Tedland) Scotland	United States	Jean Hastie	27 Jul 1829
Christopher	3	M	Farmer	Argyle (Tedland) Scotland	United States	Jean Hastie	27 Jul 1829

NAMES OF PASSENGERS	AGE	SEX	OCCUPATIONS	COUNTRY TO WHICH THEY BELONG	COUNTRY THEY INTEND TO INHABIT	SHIPS/DATES OF ARRIVAL	
DOUGLASS (cont'd)							
D.	18	F		Great Britain	United States	Isaac Hicks	6 Dec 1827
David	24	M	Gentleman	Great Britan	U. States	Ann Marria	6 Aug 1823
Elizabeth	18			England	America	Governor Griswold	6 Jun 1821
Elizabeth	18	F	None	Scotland	U.S. America	Columbia	31 Jul 1826
Elizabeth	55			England	America	Governor Griswold	6 Jun 1821
Isabella	30	F	None	Scotland	U.S.A.	Dalhouse Castle	21 Aug 1829
Isabella	30	F	None	Scotland	United States	Dalhouse Castle	21 Aug 1829
J.	32	M	Merchant	United States	U. States	Prince Edward	26 Mar 1827
James				England	America	Sarah	18 Aug 1829
James	17	M	Farmer	G. Britain	U. States	St. George	16 Jan 1829
James	30	M	Merchant	Scotland	New Brunswick	Hector	30 Dec 1820
James	50	M	Merchant	England	America	Governor Griswold	6 Jun 1821
Jane	9	F	Child	Great Britian	United States	Emulation	21 Sep 1821
Jas.	26	M	None	York, Great Britain		Casanda	5 Sep 1827
John				England	America	Sarah	18 Aug 1829
John	2	M	None	Scotland	U.S.A.	Dalhouse Castle	21 Aug 1829
John	2	M	None	Scotland	United States	Dalhouse Castle	21 Aug 1829
John	9	M	Farmer	Argyle (Tedland) Scotland	United States	Jean Hastie	27 Jul 1829
John	15			England	America	Governor Griswold	6 Jun 1821
John	35	M	Gentleman	Great Britain	United States	Andes	19 Aug 1829
John	36	M	Farmer	United States	United States	Emily Cook	29 Aug 1825
Margaret	26	F	Lady	Great Britain	Great Britain	Sylvester Healy	23 Nov 1825
Margaret	50	F		Great Britain	Jersey	Zodiac	14 Jun 1822
Margarett	1	M		England	America	Sarah	18 Aug 1829
Margarett	26	M	Shepherd	England	America	Sarah	18 Aug 1829
Maria	23	F	Wife of Mercht. [Chas.]	United States	U. States	Betsey	7 Sep 1822
Mary	18	F	Spinster			Emily Cook	29 Aug 1825
Mary	36	F		Great Britian	United States	Andes	19 Aug 1829
Mathew	1	M	Farmer	Argyle (Tedland) Scotland	United States	Jean Hastie	27 Jul 1829
Rachael	80			Ireland	United States	Jno. Dickinson	21 Sep 1821
Robert	35	M	Trader	England	United States	Jubilee	13 Jul 1829
Sarah	6	F	Daughter of Mercht. [Chas.]	United States	U. States	Betsey	7 Sep 1822
Sidney	21	M	Merchant	United States	United States	Amelia	20 Aug 1829
Thomas	13			England	America	Governor Griswold	6 Jun 1821
William	7	M	Farmer	Argyle (Tedland) Scotland	United States	Jean Hastie	27 Jul 1829
William	25	M	Teacher	Scotland	U. States	Sceptre	24 Jul 1822
William	25	M	Merchant	Scotland	United States	Herald	29 Oct 1825
William	34	M	Gentleman	Scotland	America	Nimrod	9 Jul 1827
William	34	M	Shepherd	England	America	Sarah	18 Aug 1829
William	34	M	Miller	Scotland	U.S.A.	Dalhouse Castle	21 Aug 1829
William, Jr.	30	M	Child	Scotland	America	Nimrod	9 Jul 1827
Wm.	22	M	Cordwainer	Great Britain	America	Lady Gallatin	21 Jun 1820
Wm.	32	M	Merchant		U. States	Chase	6 Jun 1822
Wm.	34	M	Miller	Scotland	United States	Dalhouse Castle	21 Aug 1829
DOUGSON, J.	28	M	Farmer	England	Pennsylvania	York	8 Aug 1829
DOUN, Ann	20			Kilkenny	Ireland	Hudson	18 Jun 1825

*Officers, Seamen and Passengers belonging to the Ship Jane of Boston and taken from on board the Schooner Olive of St. Johns , N.B. on the 4th June 1825, Lat. 41.30, Long 53.19, which ship foundered on the 31st ultimo in Lat. 41.44 Long 52.

NAMES OF PASSENGERS	AGE	SEX	OCCUPATIONS	COUNTRY TO WHICH THEY BELONG	COUNTRY THEY INTEND TO INHABIT	SHIPS/DATES OF ARRIVAL	
DOUNE, J. S.	49	M	Merchant	France	U. States	Eliza	28 Apr 1827
DOUNER, Ann	22	F		Scotland	United States	Samuel Robertson	5 Oct 1827
William	25	M	Labourer	Scotland	United States	Samuel Robertson	5 Oct 1827
DOUNES, Mary	15	F	Spinster	Ireland	U. States	William & John	10 Jul 1824
DOUNNOZ, Thomas	30	M	Stone Cutter	Ireland	U. States	Bellville	14 May 1827
DOURGAUX, M. A.	31	M	Merchant	United States		Edward Quesnel	17 Nov 1828
DOUROSOY, Perr	42	M	Baker	France		Pallas	14 Jun 1828

NAMES OF PASSENGERS	AGE	SEX	OCCUPATIONS	COUNTRY TO WHICH THEY BELONG	COUNTRY THEY INTEND TO INHABIT	SHIPS/DATES OF ARRIVAL	
DOURSAY, Maryaritta	32	F		France		Pallas	14 Jun 1828
DOURTY, William	35	M	Labourer	Ireland	United States	Meteor	26 Jun 1827
DOUTRELINNGNER,							
Peter Jos.	33	M	Student in Bardstown's College	Netherland	America	Henry	17 May 1828
DOVE, James	30	M	Merchant	N. York	New York	Wickes	27 Feb 1826
Jno.	22	M	Merchant	America	U. States	Caroline	9 May 1822
DOVENICK, Margaret	19	F	Lady	U. States	U. States	Marcellus	2 Sep 1820
DOVER, James	30	M	Watchmaker	Scotland	United States	Nancy Henrietta	3 Nov 1828
John	23	M	Farmer	England	America	Hercules	10 Apr 1823
Mary	13	F		Scotland	United States	Nancy Henrietta	3 Nov 1828
Rebecca	28	F		Scotland	United States	Nancy Henrietta	3 Nov 1828
William	5	M		Scotland	United States	Nancy Henrietta	3 Nov 1828
DOW, —, Mrs.	30	F		U. States	U. States	Lark	11 Jun 1828
Ann	18	F		Gt. Britain	U. States	St. George	20 Sep 1828
Catherine	24	F	None	England	Alexandria, U.S.	Roman	17 Oct 1826
Edward	23	M	Mason	Great Britain	United States	Fame	26 May 1828
Elisabeth	26			G. Britain	U. States	Hamilton	28 Apr 1828
James	17			G. Britain	U. States	Hamilton	28 Apr 1828
James	26	F	Merchant	England	United States	Great Britain	5 Sep 1827
John	24		Grocer	G. Britain	U. States	Hamilton	28 Apr 1828
Margaret	11			G. Britain	U. States	Hamilton	28 Apr 1828
Margaret Agnew, Miss	19	F	Lady	England	United States	Florida	26 Sep 1826
Mary	20			G. Britain	U. States	Hamilton	28 Apr 1828
Mary, Mrs.	50	F	Lady	England	United States	Florida	26 Sep 1826
Richd.	9	M	Servant	Spain	U. States	Abeona	11 Sep 1828
Robert	26		Surveyor	G. Britain	U. States	Hamilton	28 Apr 1828
DOW...S, Mary	30	F	Spinster	Ireland	U. States	Josephine	7 May 1827
DOWALL, Robt.	22	M		Scotland	United States	McDonough	3 Nov 1823
DOWAN, Patt	30	M	Labourer	England	U. States	Ayrshire	12 May 1828
DOWD, Ann	16	F	None	Great Britain	United States	Meteor	17 Jan 1825
Ann	20	F	None	England	U. States	Thomas Ritchie	2 Jul 1827
Catharine	7	F	None	United States	United States	Meteor	17 Jan 1825
Cecilia	18	F	None	Great Britain	United States	Meteor	17 Jan 1825
Eliza	38	F	None	United States	United States	Meteor	17 Jan 1825
George	46	M	Tallow Chandler	United States	United States	Meteor	17 Jan 1825
George W.	13	M	None	United States	United States	Meteor	17 Jan 1825
James	9	M	None	United States	United States	Meteor	17 Jan 1825
Margaret	25	F		Ireland	United States	Enterprize	23 Jul 1827
Mary	3	F		Ireland	United States	Enterprize	23 Jul 1827
Mary	27	F	None	Great Britain	United States	Penelope	11 Jun 1827
Michl.	22	M	Labourer	England	U. States	Thomas Ritchie	2 Jul 1827
Miles	25	M	Labourer	England	U. States	Thomas Ritchie	2 Jul 1827
Owen	5	M	None	Great Britain	United States	Meteor	17 Jan 1825
Pat	1	M	None	Great Britain	United States	Penelope	11 Jun 1827
Patrick	27	M	Weaver	Ireland	United States	Enterprize	23 Jul 1827
Peter	30	M	Labourer	Great Britain	United States	Penelope	11 Jun 1827
Phillip	11	M	None	United States	United States	Meteor	17 Jan 1825
Thomas	22	M	Labourer	Ireland	United States	Enterprize	23 Jul 1827
Thomas	24	M	Weaver	Ireland	United States	Wilson	27 Jun 1826
DOWDALE, Andrew	24		Labourer	Ireland	America	Sarah	18 Aug 1829
DOWDALL, Alice	13	F		Ireland	America	Alexander	28 Jul 1821
Christr.	40 2/12		Labourer	Ireland	United States	Helen	5 Jul 1820
Daniel	13 10/12	M		Ireland	America	Alexander	28 Jul 1821
Mary	45	F		Ireland	America	Alexander	28 Jul 1821
DOWDEGAN, Edward	22	M	Labourer	Ireland	America	Plutarch	18 Jul 1826
DOWDIGAN, Bridgit	9	M	Boy	Ireland	United States	Wilson	6 Jun 1828
DOWDILL, Dan	25	M	Labourer			Lady of the Lake	23 Aug 1828
DOWELL, Saml.	16	M	Labourer	Ireland	New York	Trusty	12 Sep 1828
DOWEN, James	28	M	Labourer	Gt. Britain	U. States	Sarah G.	14 Apr 1828
Sally	27	F	Servant	Gt. Britain	U. States	Sarah G.	14 Apr 1828
DOWER, John	26	M		Ireland	U. States	St. Michael	26 Oct 1824
DOWERTY, John	30	M	Weaver	Scotland	Ut. States	Courier	13 Jul 1826
DOWEY, T.	39	M	Engineer	New York	N. York	James Cropper	4 Feb 1824
DOWING, —, Mr.	44	M	Sugar Baker	U.K. Gt. Britain	U.S. America	James Cropper	29 Nov 1827
—, Mrs., & Infant	24	F	None	U.K. Gt. Britain	U.S. America	James Cropper	29 Nov 1827
DOWLAN, Patrick	23	M	Labourer	Ireland		Marchioness	13 May 1828

NAMES OF PASSENGERS	AGE	SEX	OCCUPATIONS	COUNTRY TO WHICH THEY BELONG	COUNTRY THEY INTEND TO INHABIT	SHIPS/DATES OF ARRIVAL	
DOWLAND, Mary	27	F	None	Great Britain	United States	Mount Vernon	17 Jun 1825
DOWLER, Thomas	21	M	Brass founder	Great Britain	United States	Ganges	26 Oct 1826
DOWLEY, Joseph	24	F	Bricklayer	England	United States	Danube	22 Aug 1825
DOWLING, —, Mr.	47	M	Farmer	England	U. States	Milton	6 Dec 1825
Ann	4	F		Ireland	United States	Thomas	13 Dec 1827
Catherine	5	F	Child	Ireland	America	Josephine	24 Jul 1826
Chs.	2	M		Ireland	United States	Thomas	13 Dec 1827
Edward	11	M	Weaver	Ireland	America	Josephine	24 Jul 1826
Edward	28	M	Labourer	Great Brittain	United States	Sarah Ralston	27 Jan 1827
Henry	24	M	Carpenter	Great Britain	U.S. of America	Gratitude	3 Oct 1829
James	28	M	Labourer	Ireland	America	Reindeer	18 Oct 1828
James	35	M	Weaver	Ireland	America	Josephine	24 Jul 1826
Johanna	11	F		Great Brittain	United States	Sarah Ralston	27 Jan 1827
John	13	M	Weaver	Ireland	America	Josephine	24 Jul 1826
Judith	35	F	Matron	Ireland	America	Josephine	24 Jul 1826
Kyran	7	M	Child	Ireland	America	Josephine	24 Jul 1826
M.	17	M	Farmer	Ireland	Beaver Town	Triton	12 Jul 1823
Mgt.	7	F		Ireland	United States	Thomas	13 Dec 1827
Michael	3	M	Child	Ireland	America	Josephine	24 Jul 1826
Pat	30	M	Labourer	Great Brittain	United States	Sarah Ralston	27 Jan 1827
Patrick	9	M	Weaver	Ireland	America	Josephine	24 Jul 1826
Richd.	27	M	Farmer	England	U.N. States	Helen	17 Dec 1827
Robt.	14	M	Farmer	Ireland	Beaver Town	Triton	12 Jul 1823
William	2	M	Child	Ireland	America	Josephine	24 Jul 1826
DOWLY, Ml.	27	M				Lady of the Lake	23 Aug 1828
*left ship							
DOWN, Ann	10			England	U.S. America	Constitution	18 Jun 1827
Ann	20			England	U.S. America	Constitution	18 Jun 1827
Charlotte	4			England	U.S. America	Constitution	18 Jun 1827
Edward	56		Farmer	England	U.S. America	Constitution	18 Jun 1827
Edward, Jr.	23		Farmer	England	U.S. America	Constitution	18 Jun 1827
Edward, 3d.	1			England	U.S. America	Constitution	18 Jun 1827
Edwd.	19					Schuylkill	22 Aug 1825
George	19			England	U.S. America	Constitution	18 Jun 1827
H. P.	24	M	Merchant	New York	U. States	Abeona	23 May 1823
Isaac	16			England	U.S. America	Constitution	18 Jun 1827
James	2			England	U.S. America	Constitution	18 Jun 1827
*James Down died at Sea May 13th of a falling in the Canal							
Nancy	26	F	Spinster	Ireland	Unt. St. America	Wilson	21 May 1827
Robert	12			England	U.S. America	Constitution	18 Jun 1827
Sarah	8			England	U.S. America	Constitution	18 Jun 1827
Sarah	23			England	U.S. America	Constitution	18 Jun 1827
Stephen	6/12			England	U.S. America	Constitution	18 Jun 1827
William	13			England	U.S. America	Constitution	18 Jun 1827
DOWNER, John	18	M	Merchant	Scotland	United States	Commerce	17 Jul 1823
DOWNES, H. P.	25	M	Merchant	Great Britain	U.S. of Ama.	Robert Fulton	16 Aug 1824
Hugh	24	M	Farmer	Ireland	U. States	William & John	10 Jul 1824
DOWNEY, Elizth.	27	F	wife	St. John, N.B.	United States	Henrietta	3 Jun 1825
Hugh	50	M	Mechanic	St. John, N.B.	United States	Henrietta	3 Jun 1825
James	28	M	Taylor	Ireland	U. States	Nancy	1 Sep 1823
John	4	M	None	England	U. States	Thomas Ritchie	2 Jul 1827
Margret	27	F	None	England	U. States	Thomas Ritchie	2 Jul 1827
Michael	21	M	Laborer	Ireland	New York	Amanda	23 May 1827
Robt.	26	M	Labourer	Ireland	United States	Phocian	5 Aug 1826
Robt.	50	M	Mechanic	St. John, N.B.	United States	Henrietta	3 Jun 1825
Thomas	29	M	Merchant	W. Indies	U. States	Matilda	27 Apr 1822
Walter	28	M	Cotton ...	G. Brittain	America	Robin Hood	20 Jul 1827
DOWNIE, Alexr.	14	M		Gt. Britain		Atlantic	7 Nov 1828
Ann	9	F				Atlantic	7 Nov 1828
James	13	M				Atlantic	7 Nov 1828
Jane	5	F				Atlantic	7 Nov 1828
John	31	M	Merchant	U. States	Great Britain	Thompson	26 Apr 1828
Jos.	32	M	Merchant	Ireland	U. States	Marshall	12 Jun 1824
Margaret	34	F	Lady	Gt. Britain	U. States	Atlantic	7 Nov 1828
Margaret	56		Spinster	Great Britain	United States	Camillus	12 Sep 1827
Preston	11	F				Atlantic	7 Nov 1828
Robt.	38		Farmer	Great Britain	United States	Camillus	12 Sep 1827
DOWNIG, William	23	M	Labourer	Ireland	United States	Mary & Harriet	3 Jul 1829

NAMES OF PASSENGERS	AGE	SEX	OCCUPATIONS	COUNTRY TO WHICH THEY BELONG	COUNTRY THEY INTEND TO INHABIT	SHIPS/DATES OF ARRIVAL	
DOWNING, Betsey	18	F	Wife	Ireland	United States	Ann Maria	5 May 1824
Biddy	29	F		Ireland	United States	Dalhouse Castle	26 Dec 1827
John	26	M		Ireland	United States	John & Adam	21 Sep 1822
Matha	60	F		England	England	James Cropper	16 Oct 1826
S. W.	30	M	Lieutenant, U.S. Navy	United States	United States	Louisiana	9 Aug 1826
Thos.	22		Labourer	Ireland	United States	Geo. Canning	5 Jun 1828
William	30	M	Carpenter	Ireland	United States	Ann Maria	5 May 1824
DOWNIST, Biddy	16	F	Spinster	Stewarttown	N. York	Favourite	8 Oct 1823
DOWNS, Andrew	14	M	Clerk	U. States	U. States	Hope & Esther	12 Nov 1825
Ann	31	F				Hudson	23 Jul 1828
Catharine	1 6/12	F	None	U.S.A.		Olive Branch	9 Oct 1829
Hugh	18	M	Farmer	Great Brittian		Merchant	22 Apr 1822
James	26	M	Labourer	Great Brittian		Merchant	22 Apr 1822
James	40	M	Mariner	U. States	U. States	James & Caroline	3 May 1826
John	22	M	Musician	Great Britain		Olive Branch	9 Oct 1829
John	30	M	Labourer			Lady of the Lake	23 Aug 1828
John	40	M	Hatter	Lancaster Shire	England	Helicon	3 Aug 1826
Margaret	28	F	None	Great Britain	United States	Milton	21 Mar 1828
Mary	22	F	None	Great Britain		Olive Branch	9 Oct 1829
Mary	26	F		Lancaster Shire	England	Helicon	3 Aug 1826
DOWNY, Judith	18	F	Servant	Great Britian	U. States	St. Michael	3 Jan 1825
Mary	28	F	Servant	Ireland	Ireland	Sarah G.	28 Nov 1827
Thomas	30	M	Farmer	Great Britain	United States	Ann Maria	12 Jul 1821
Thos.	30	M	Mason	Great Britian	U. States	St. Michael	3 Jan 1825
Timothy	26	M	Farmer	Great Britain	U. States	St. Croix	13 Sep 1827
William	21		Writer			Rufus King	7 Aug 1820
Wm.	29	M	Shoe Maker	England	U. States	Thomas Ritchie	2 Jul 1827
DOWRAN, Patrick	32			Ireland	Philidelphia	General Marion	21 Nov 1828
DOWRIS, Catharine	16	F	Servant	Ireland	New York	Atlantic	8 May 1828
Denis	12	M	Child	Ireland	New York	Atlantic	8 May 1828
Patrick	33	M	Black Smith	Ireland	New York	Atlantic	8 May 1828
DOWRY, Charlotte	4	F		Gt. Britain	United States	Robert Edwards	1 Jun 1826
Hannah	24	F		Gt. Britain	United States	Robert Edwards	1 Jun 1826
S. J.	2	F		Gt. Britain	United States	Robert Edwards	1 Jun 1826
Saml.	27	M	Farmer	Gt. Britain	United States	Robert Edwards	1 Jun 1826
DOWSEE, Christian	9 3/12	M		America	America	Nancy	28 Jan 1820
George	12 1/12	M		America	America	Nancy	28 Jan 1820
DOWSON, Ann E.	6			England	England	Hudson	4 Sep 1823
Charles	32	M	Knife Grinder	Great Britain	U.S. of America	Gratitude	3 Oct 1829
Elizabeth Jane	28			New Providence	England	Hudson	4 Sep 1823
Sarah	4			England	England	Hudson	4 Sep 1823
William	36		Clergyman	England	England	Hudson	4 Sep 1823
William F.	7			W. Indies	England	Hudson	4 Sep 1823
DOWSTAN, Charles	12	M	Taylor	England	United States	Concordia	25 Aug 1827
John	34	M	Taylor	England	United States	Concordia	25 Aug 1827
DOWTON, James	26	M	Rope Maker	England	United States	Cambria	16 Aug 1827
Sarah	60	F		England	United States	Cambria	16 Aug 1827
DOXSHOO, Pat	25	M	Farmer	U. States	U. States	Erin	5 Jul 1820
DOYLE, Ann	3	F		Gt. Britain		Dalhouse Castle	13 May 1828
Ann	7	F	Child	Ireland	America	Wilson	16 May 1825
Ann	23	F		Great Britain	New York	Dublin	21 Dec 1824
Ann	27	M	Labourer	England	America	Two Marys	24 Sep 1827
Barry	48	M	Farmer	Ireland	United States	Belmont	30 Aug 1828
Bridget	18	F	Spinster	Ireland	America	Wilson	16 May 1825
Bridget	20	F	Spinster	Ireland		Robert Fulton	4 Jun 1828
Bridget	21	F	Spinster	Ireland	United States	Dublin Packet	29 Jun 1825
Bryan	6	M		Gt. Britain		Dalhouse Castle	13 May 1828
Catharine	20	M	Servant	Ireland	U. States	Hanford	29 Dec 1828
Catherine	23	F	None	England		Exchange	11 Jul 1823
Charles	26	M	Weaver	Ireland	America	Carolina Ann	7 Apr 1826
Charles	35	M	Labourer	Ireland	United States	Dublin Packet	22 Aug 1829
Daniel	21	M	Y. Man	Ireland	New York	Trusty	12 Sep 1828
Denis	26	M	Farmer	Ireland	U. States	Globe	14 Jul 1821
Elenor	20	F		Gt. Britain	U. States	Panthea	21 Jul 1825
Henry	23	M	Labourer	Gt. Britain	U. States	St. George	20 Sep 1828
Henry, Rev.	30			Great Britain		John Dickinson	5 Apr 1821

NAMES OF PASSENGERS	AGE	SEX	OCCUPATIONS	COUNTRY TO WHICH THEY BELONG	COUNTRY THEY INTEND TO INHABIT	SHIPS/DATES OF ARRIVAL	
DOYLE (cont'd0							
J...	20	M	Hatter	Ireland	Pensylvania	Eliza Grant	29 Aug 1829
James	25	M	Farmer	Great Brittain	U. States	Nancy	18 Jul 1821
James	25	M	Labourer	Ireland	U. States	Combine	30 Nov 1825
James	29	M	None	Great Britain	United States	Eliza Barker	3 Jul 1826
John	19		Farmer	Ireland	U. States	Schuylkill	22 Aug 1825
John	25	M	Farmer	G. Britain	U. States	Margaret Bogle	12 Jun 1828
John	34	M	Farmer	Ireland	United States	Meteor	19 Aug 1829
John	36	M	Laborer	Ireland	United States	Dublin Packet	22 Oct 1821
M.	28	F		England	America	Two Marys	24 Sep 1827
Mary	18		Servant	Ireland	United States	Rufus King	4 Sep 1823
Mary	21	F	Labourer	Gt. Britain	U. States	Panthea	21 Jul 1825
Mary Ann	18	M	Servant	Ireland	U. States	Hanford	29 Dec 1828
Michael	33	M	Labourer	Great Britian	United States	Princess Charlotte	6 Sep 1828
N. H.	25	M	Grocer	Ireland	America	Francis & Henrietta	11 Jul 1823
Pat	31	M	Laborer	Ireland	U. States	Howard Douglass	29 Jan 1828
Pat, Junr.	26	M	Laborer	Ireland	U. States	Howard Douglass	29 Jan 1828
Patr.	33	M	Taylor	Ireland	New York or Boston	Concordia	12 Oct 1826
Patr.	50	M	Merchant	Ireland	America	Dublin Packet	9 Oct 1820
Patrick	...	M	...	...	...	Frances Henrietta	30 Jun 1827
Patrick	20	M	Labourer	Ireland	United States	Dalhouse Castle	8 May 1827
Pattk.	36	M	Grocer	Ireland	America	Plutarch	18 Jul 1826
Simon	38		Farmer	Gt. Britan	United States	James Monroe	11 Dec 1821
Thomas	22		Farmer	Gt. Britan	United States	James Monroe	11 Dec 1821
Thomas	30	M	Labourer	England	United States	Enterprize	19 Oct 1826
Thos.	26	M	...	Ireland	U. States	William	27 Jul 1824
Wm.	23	M	Acountant	G. Brittan	U. States	Henry	24 Oct 1828
DRABBLE, James	38	M	Merchant	England	England	Nestor	20 Nov 1821
Wm.	30	M	Miner	England	England	Ranger	15 Jan 1827
DRACKINE, Ignacio	40	M	Mercht.	Spain	United States	Georgetown Packet	15 Nov 1823
DRAFAGE, John	19	M	Servant	Russia	U. States	Balance	28 Sep 1822
DRAGNER, Ko...	21	...	F	England	America, U.S.	Illinois	3 Jun 1822
William	35 4/12	M	...	England	America, U.S.	Illinois	3 Jun 1822
DRAKE, Ann	7	F	Spinster	Spain (Cuba)	Island of Cuba (Spain)	James Barron	26 Jun 1823
Ann	34	F		G. Britain	U. States	Mary & Harriot	8 Sep 1828
Ann	50	F		Great Britain	U. States	United States	8 Sep 1827
Benj.	22	M	Gentleman	United States	U. States	York	7 Aug 1828
Catherine	9	F		G. Britain	U. States	Mary & Harriot	8 Sep 1828
Catherine	45	F	Lady		St. Johns	Charlotte Corday	15 Aug 1820
Charles	24	M	Mercht.	Havana	Boston, Mass.	Rubicon	22 May 1826
Charlotte	15	F	Spinster	Spain (Cuba)	Island of Cuba		
Charlotte	39	F	Spinster	Spain (Cuba)	Island of Cuba (Spain)	James Barron	26 Jun 1823
Chas.	10	M		G. Britain	U. States	Mary & Harriot	8 Sep 1828
D., Mrs.	27	F		Gt. Britain	U. States	Charles	21 Jul 1825
David	6/12	M		Gt. Britain	U. States	Charles	21 Jul 1825
David	29	M	Merchant	Gt. Britain	U. States	Charles	21 Jul 1825
E., Master	2	M		U.S.	U.S.	Henri IV	17 May 1828
Emilia	19	F	Spinster	Spain (Cuba)	Island of Cuba (Spain)	James Barron	26 Jun 1823
Fr.	14	M			Spain	Emma	24 Jun 1822
Francis	5	M		G. Britain	U. States	Mary & Harriot	8 Sep 1828
Francis	32	M	Weaver	G. Britain	U. States	Mary & Harriot	8 Sep 1828
Geo.	2	M		Gt. Britain	U. States	Charles	21 Jul 1825
Geo.	10	M			Spain	Emma	24 Jun 1822
Gilbert M.	23	M	Merchant	St. John, N.B.	St. John, N.B.	Nancy	2 May 1823
Henry	7	M		G. Britain	U. States	Mary & Harriot	8 Sep 1828
J., Master	4	M		U.S.	U.S.	Henri IV	17 May 1828
James	18	M	Merchant	N. York	U. States	Nestor	7 Jan 1825
James	57	M	Merchant	Spain (Cuba)	Island of Cuba (Spain)	James Barron	26 Jun 1823
James, Jr.	25	M	Mercht.	U. States	U. States	Rubicon	8 Jun 1827

NAMES OF PASSENGERS	AGE	SEX	OCCUPATIONS	COUNTRY TO WHICH THEY BELONG	COUNTRY THEY INTEND TO INHABIT	SHIPS/DATES OF ARRIVAL	
DRAKE (cont'd)							
James., Junr.	25 11/12	M	Merchant	America	America	Henry	18 Oct 1826
Jno.	26	M	Artist	England	U. States	Liberty	20 Jun 1821
John	1	M		G. Britain	U. States	Mary & Harriot	8 Sep 1828
John	18		...	Ireland	United States	Alexander Mansfield	23 Nov 1824
John	46	M	Farmer	Great Britain	U. States	United States	8 Sep 1827
Jonat. W.	26 10/12	M	Gentleman	America	America	Henry	18 Oct 1826
L. R., Mrs.	20	F		America	America	Henry	18 Oct 1826
Luis	10	M	None	Spain (Cuba)	Island of Cuba (Spain)	James Barron	26 Jun 1823
Maria A.	8	F	Spinster	Spain (Cuba)	Island of Cuba (Spain)	James Barron	26 Jun 1823
Samuel	59		Merchant	St. John, N.B.		Catherine	28 Dec 1820
Susan	25	F		England	U. States	Liberty	20 Jun 1821
Thomas	28	M	Surgeon			Robert Edwards	8 Nov 1825
William	21	M	Merchant	New Brunswick	New Brunswick	Wanderer	31 Aug 1829
William F.	20 6/12	M	Merchant	N. Brunswick	N. Brunswick	Josephine	23 Jan 1829
DRAKESFORD, Jane	18/12	F				Governor Fenner	23 Jul 1829
Mary Ann	33	F				Governor Fenner	23 Jul 1829
Thomas	7	M				Governor Fenner	23 Jul 1829
William	3	M				Governor Fenner	23 Jul 1829
William	32	M	Farmer	England	Ohio	Governor Fenner	23 Jul 1829
DRANSFIELD, John A.	75	M	Farmer	Ireland	United States	L. M. Pelham	25 Jun 1822
DRAPER, George	42	M	Weaver	Great Britain	United States	Thomas Dickason	31 Jul 1829
Major	45	M	Mechanick	U. States	U. States	Union	22 Jul 1820
Simeon, Jr.	23	M	Merchant	Boston	New York	Sully	11 Mar 1829
William B.	23	M	Merchant	U. States	Boston	Sully	30 Oct 1827
DRASEY, Joana	25					Trio	5 May 1828
DRAY, Andreas	12	M	Merchant	Havana	U. States	Emblem	14 May 1827
DRAYASHE, Joseph	32	M	Miner	England	U. States	Vermont	19 Jun 1827
DRAYER, Agness	16	F	Lady	Ireland	U. States	Howard	25 Jul 1823
DRAYHN, John	22	M	Mechanic	U. States	U. States	Betsey	23 Jul 1824
DRAYTON, John	22	M	Merchant	United States	United States	Robert Read	19 Oct 1825
Patrick	18	M	Framer	Ireland	U. States	Globe	14 Jul 1821
DREAMONT, Jas.	24	M	Merchant	France	U. States	Topaz	23 Feb 1827
DREBS, Charlotte	8	F		Germany	Charlston	Cotton Plant	15 Nov 1823
DRECHLER, Sebastian	23	M	Farmer	Germany	America	Orozimbo	1 Oct 1827
DREESKE, Mitchel	18	M	Farmer	Germany	United States	Virginia	31 May 1828
DREFENDACH, Ansel	15	F		Germany	U. States	Isabella	10 Aug 1829
Augustus	11	M		Germany	U. States	Isabella	10 Aug 1829
Christin	45	F		Germany	U. States	Isabella	10 Aug 1829
Christine	20	F		Germany	U. States	Isabella	10 Aug 1829
Jacob	17	M		Germany	U. States	Isabella	10 Aug 1829
Jean	4	M		Germany	U. States	Isabella	10 Aug 1829
Maria	8	F		Germany	U. States	Isabella	10 Aug 1829
Michael	46	M	Farmer	Germany	U. States	Isabella	10 Aug 1829
DREGAL, Ann Maria	9	F		Switzerland	U.S.	Francois I	8 Aug 1829
Barbara	11	F		Switzerland	U.S.	Francois I	8 Aug 1829
Dorothea	6	F		Switzerland	U.S.	Francois I	8 Aug 1829
Jacob	46	M	Taylor	Switzerland	U.S.	Francois I	8 Aug 1829
Johannes	15	M		Switzerland	U.S.	Francois I	8 Aug 1829
Renegana	4	F		Switzerland	U.S.	Francois I	8 Aug 1829
Renegana	38	F		Switzerland	U.S.	Francois I	8 Aug 1829
DREGGS, Asa S.	21	M	Doctor	U. States	U. States	Toison	20 Apr 1827
Benjamin	20	M	Merchant	U.S.	U.S.	Bruce	6 Aug 1828
DREGHORN, Allen	24	M	Gentleman	Scotland	United States	Liverpool Trader	24 Oct 1825
Hannah	10	F		Scotland, Great Britain	America	Superb	11 Oct 1821
Jane	12	F		Scotland, Great Britain	America	Superb	11 Oct 1821
John	4	M		Scotland, Great Britain	America	Superb	11 Oct 1821
Margret	7	F		Scotland, Great Britain	America	Superb	11 Oct 1821
Mary	19	F		Scotland, Great Britain	America	Superb	11 Oct 1821

NAMES OF PASSENGERS	AGE	SEX	OCCUPATIONS	COUNTRY TO WHICH THEY BELONG	COUNTRY THEY INTEND TO INHABIT	SHIPS/DATES OF ARRIVAL	
DREGHORN (cont'd)							
William	46	M	Farmer	Scotland, Great Britain	America	Superb	11 Oct 1821
DREHER, John	22	M	Farmer	Great Britain	United States	William Dawson	18 Jun 1827
DREOBI, Anestine	16 6/12	F		Holland	United States	Jason	3 Nov 1828
DRERR, Geo.	8/12	M	None	U. States	United States	Seine	7 Dec 1821
DRESDEL, Anna	28	F	Servant	C...	U. States	Agness	23 Jun 1827
DRESS, —, Mrs.	24	F	Spinster	U. States	United States	Seine	7 Dec 1821
DREUX, Louis			Hair dresser	France	U.S.	Sully	26 Oct 1829
Louisa			None	France	U.S.	Sully	26 Oct 1829
DREW, B.				Ireland	United States	Potomac	28 Sep 1827
Betty	20	F		Ireland	U. States	Nancy	13 Dec 1822
Ellen	18		None	G. Britain	United States	Roman	10 Sep 1827
Freeman	35	M	Merchant	France	U. States	Eliza Ann	16 Apr 1824
John	0 3/12	F		Ireland	United States	Potomac	28 Sep 1827
Leonard Perfect	27	M	Perfumer	France	United States	Elizabeth	13 Nov 1824
Mary	9	F		Ireland	United States	Potomac	28 Sep 1827
Mary	22	F	None			Evergreen	28 Jul 1820
Mary	30	F		Ireland	United States	Potomac	28 Sep 1827
Mathew	15	M	Joiner	Scotland	United States	Samuel Robertson	5 Oct 1827
Thos.	20	M		Gt. Britain	United States	Penelope	9 Sep 1828
Wm.	7	M		Ireland	United States	Potomac	28 Sep 1827
DREWGAN, Owen	23	M	Farmer	Ireland	United States	Fabius	4 Jun 1828
DREYER,							
Frederick Adol.	17	M		Bremen	U. States	Massachusetts	30 Oct 1829
Gustavus Wm.	22	M	Chemist	Bremen	U. States	Massachusetts	30 Oct 1829
H.	26	M	Merchant	Vera Cruz	U. States	Eliza	11 Apr 1826
John Henry, Jun.	15	M		Bremen	U. States	Massachusetts	30 Oct 1829
John Henry, Revd.	52	M		Bremen	U. States	Massachusetts	30 Oct 1829
Peter Henry	21		Merchant	Bremen	New York	Franklin	18 Aug 1827
DREYFAUS, D.	36	M	Pedler	France	U. States	Edward Quesnel	15 May 1826
DREYFOUS, Jos.	35	M	Mercht.	U.S.	U.S.	Edward Quesnel	21 Apr 1827
DRIAN, —, Mrs.	30	F	Lady	France	New York	Cadmus	16 Aug 1826
DRICHOT, Marie	40	M	Cultivator	Gt. Brittan		L'Esperance	6 Sep 1828
DRIGGS, B.	38	M	Mariner	U. States	U. States	Rebecca & Sally	16 Oct 1822
Eliza	17	F	Druggist	United States	U. States	Fair Trader	25 Jul 1820
Joseph	11/12	M	infant	United States	U. States	Fair Trader	25 Jul 1820
Joseph	8	M		U.S.	U.S.	Florida	30 Jun 1826
Lloyd	28	M	Merchant	U.S.	U.S.	Florida	30 Oct 1826
S.	32	M	Doctor	U. States	U. States	Hannah	19 Jul 1822
Sam.	35	M	Planter	Connecticutt	U. States	Abigail	16 Nov 1824
Saml.	6	M		U. States	U. States	Abigail	16 Jul 1824
Saml.	42	M	Merchant	U.S.	U.S.	Florida	30 Jun 1826
Seth	27	M	Druggist	United States	U. States	Fair Trader	25 Jul 1820
Seth	32	M	Merchant	Trinerdard		George	10 Jul 1826
DRINKER, J. R., Jr.	29	M	Merchant	United States	United States	Langdon Cheeves	19 Mar 1827
Jos. D., Jr.	26	M	Merchant	American	U. States	Plough Boy	16 Oct 1823
DRINKWATER, Charles	28	M	British Navy	England	England	Canton Packet	13 Oct 1829
Mack	70	M	Gentleman	New York	U. States	Tidal	28 Oct 1824
DRIRNTZY, —, Mr.	25	M	None	Great Britain	Great Britain	Cornelia	12 Mar 1825
DRISCO, Danniel	30	M	Labourer	England	U.N. States	Reindeer	20 Aug 1828
DRISCOLL, Catharine	28	F		Ireland	United S.	Hanford	19 Aug 1828
Catherine	4	F		Ireland	United S.	Hanford	19 Aug 1828
Cornelus	17	M	Farmer	Ireland	America	William	21 May 1825
Daniel	16			Ireland	U.S.	Union	20 Aug 1827
Danl.	24	M	Farmer	Gt. Britain	United States	Silas Richards	20 Jun 1826
Frances	22	F		Ireland	New York	Lima	5 Aug 1829
Francis	22	F		Ireland	U. States	Lima	5 Aug 1829
Jerimia	14			Ireland	U.S.	Union	20 Aug 1827
Mary Ann	40			Ireland	U.S.	Union	20 Aug 1827
Timothy	38	M	Carpenter	Ireland	United States	Hannah Eliza	23 Sep 1826
William	31	M	Labourer	Ireland	New York	Lima	5 Aug 1829
William	31	M	Labourer	Ireland	U. States	Lima	5 Aug 1829
DRISCOW, Miry	40		Dress Maker	Ireland	England	London	16 Aug 1824
DRISDALE, Jno.	27	M	Black Smith	Scotland	United States	Essex	23 May 1828
DRISKEL, Timothy	21	M	Carder	Ireland		Eliza Grant	29 Aug 1829
DRISKELL, Timothy	21	M	Carder	G.B.	New York	Eliza Grant	29 Aug 1829

NAMES OF PASSENGERS	AGE	SEX	OCCUPATIONS	COUNTRY TO WHICH THEY BELONG	COUNTRY THEY INTEND TO INHABIT	SHIPS/DATES OF ARRIVAL	
DRISNEAU, Elizabeth	45	F		U. States	U. States	Edward Quesnel	16 Nov 1827
Eugenie	1...	F		U. States	U. States	Edward Quesnel	16 Nov 1827
DRISON, Sandy	26	M	Laborer, Spinster or Child	Ireland	United States	Ann Maria	4 Aug 1827
DRISWOLD, Florine	26		Painter	Ireland	United States	Geo. Canning	5 Jun 1828
DRITON, Thos.	30 4/12	M	Shoemaker			Cririe	18 Sep 1820
DRITTON, Chst.	27	M	Bricklayer	Great Britain	U. States America	Maria	22 May 1822
DRIVAL, —, Mrs.	55	F		France	U. States	Centurion	20 Oct 1828
DRIVER, Eliz.	40	F		England	U. States	Howard Douglass	29 Jan 1828
John	40	M	Gent.	England	U. States	Howard Douglass	29 Jan 1828
John	40		Mariner	United States		New Orleans	27 Feb 1829
John, Jr.	20	M	Gent.	England	U. States	Howard Douglass	29 Jan 1828
DRODELET, Nicholas	36	M	Brewer	Germany	United States	Wm. Osborne	16 Sep 1828
DROGHARTY, Ann	2	F	None			Importer	30 Oct 1820
Ann	32	F	None			Importer	30 Oct 1820
Elizabeth	7	F	None			Importer	30 Oct 1820
Henry	3	M	None			Importer	30 Oct 1820
Lucy	1	F	None			Importer	30 Oct 1820
Peter	33	M	Farmer			Importer	30 Oct 1820
Thomas	5	M	None			Importer	30 Oct 1820
DROIX, —, Mr.	51			Switzerland	United States	Henri IV	14 Sep 1827
DROLLET, Francis	25	M	Doctor	Canada	Canada	Hudson	13 Jan 1827
DROMGOALE, Henry	41		Labourer	Great Britan	United States	Newry	11 Jul 1827
DRONEY, Michael	30	M	Merchant	Great Britian	U. States	Orbit	29 Apr 1822
DROUT, L.	30	M	Tanner	Saxony	United States	Constitution	6 Jul 1829
DROZ, Chas. Emanuel	24	M	Mechanic	Switzerland	U. States	Little William	16 Jun 1821
DRUE, John	24	M	Manufacturer	England	U. States	York	12 Jul 1825
DRULOUX, Reese S.	33	M	Carpenter	Belfoit	U.S. America	Superior	18 Jun 1825
DRUM, Ann	16	F	...	Ireland	United States	Carolina Ann	24 Oct 1825
Ann	21	F	Spinster	Ireland	U. States	Wilson	22 Apr 1822
Bridget	16	F	Servant	Ireland	New York	Atlantic	6 Oct 1828
James	19 6/12	M	Stonemason	Ireland	U. States	Virginia	20 Jun 1825
James	60	M	Farmer	Ireland	U. States	Virginia	20 Jun 1825
John	20	M	...	Ireland	United States	Carolina Ann	24 Oct 1825
Mary Ann	10	F	None	Scotland	United States	Mary & Susan	5 Aug 1828
Patrick	24	M	Laborer	Ireland	United States	Indian Chief	16 Aug 1822
DRUMAN, David	23	M		Scotland	U.S.	Curler	19 Jul 1828
DRUMLING, F.	58	M	Accountant	U.S.	U.S.	Edward Quesnel	31 Jul 1827
DRUMMAN, John	25	M		Jamaica	England	Pleiades	13 Nov 1826
DRUMMENSHLAGER, Anthony	26	M	Clothier	...	Ohio	Frances Henrietta	25 Aug 1825
DRUMMER, Antony	4	M		Germany	United States	Samuel Robertson	8 Aug 1828
Christian	40	F		Germany	United States	Samuel Robertson	8 Aug 1828
Egnancy	9	M		Germany	United States	Samuel Robertson	8 Aug 1828
John	6	M		Germany	United States	Samuel Robertson	8 Aug 1828
Joseph	11	M		Germany	United States	Samuel Robertson	8 Aug 1828
Kover	38	F		Germany	United States	Samuel Robertson	8 Aug 1828
Peter	39	M	Joiner	Germany	United States	Samuel Robertson	8 Aug 1828
DRUMMOND, —		F	infant	Scotland	United States	Belmont	30 Aug 1828
—, Mrs.	25	F		Philadelphia	U. States	Abeona	25 Apr 1828
—, Mrs.	32	F		Scotland	United States	Belmont	30 Aug 1828
A. C.	24	M	Painter	U. States	U. States	Lady Hunter	9 Oct 1825
Alexr.	10	M		Scotland	United States	Belmont	30 Aug 1828
Andrew	23	M	Smith	Scotland	New York	Frances Henrietta	3 Apr 1826
Daniel	28	M	Labourer	Scotland	United States	Mary & Susan	5 Aug 1828
Elizabeth	5	F		Philadelphia	U. States	Abeona	25 Apr 1828
Hannah	3	F		Philadelphia	U. States	Abeona	25 Apr 1828

NAMES OF PASSENGERS	AGE	SEX	OCCUPATIONS	COUNTRY TO WHICH THEY BELONG	COUNTRY THEY INTEND TO INHABIT	SHIPS/DATES OF ARRIVAL	
DRUMMOND (cont'd)							
James	26	M	Labourer	Scotland	United States	Mary & Susan	5 Aug 1828
Janet	3	F		Scotland	United States	Belmont	30 Aug 1828
John	4	M		Scotland	United States	Belmont	30 Aug 1828
Margt.	8	F		Scotland	United States	Belmont	30 Aug 1828
Mary	7	F		Philadelphia	U. States	Abeona	25 Apr 1828
William	29	M	Merchant	Connecticut	D...	Loire	11 Jun 1824
DRUMOND, Jno.	47	M	Merchant	Great Britan	Great Britan	Robert Read	25 Aug 1824
DRUMTED, Joseph	27	M	Shoemaker	Germany	Missouri	Isabella	15 Sep 1828
DRUNMOND, William	21	M	Mariner	United States	United States	Richmond	2 May 1828
DRURY, Jno.	21	M	Weaver	Ireland	United States	Orozimbo	5 Mar 1827
DRYDAN, Lambt.	34	M	Merchant	U. States	U. States	Canada	6 Jun 1825
DRYFOUS, Joseph	28	M	Merchant	U.S.	United States	Stephania	13 Sep 1821
Joseph	32	M	Merchant	U.S.	U.S.	Montano	24 Jun 1823
DRYSDALE, Alex.	23	M	Mill Wright	Scotland	United States	Louisiana	3 Nov 1827
Isobella	22	F	Black Smith	Scotland	United States	Essex	23 May 1828
Jas.	27	M	Carpenter	Scotland	U. States	Alert	22 Sep 1821
DU...S, George	30	M	C...	Scotland	U.S. of America	Friends	10 May 1823
DUAMS, Wm.	30	M	Gardiner	Ireland	United States	Trio	13 Jun 1827
DUAND,							
William, Col. 63 2/12		M	Gentleman	Philadelphia	Philadelphia	Quito	9 Jul 1823
DUANE, Jno.	26	M	Butcher	Ireland	United States	Essex	23 May 1828
Thomas	30			Ireland	U.S.	Union	20 Aug 1827
DUBA, Minett	54	F	Mulatto	Martinico	United States	Falcon	1 May 1824
DUBAN, S. J. A.	25	M	Merchant	St. Domingo	U. States	Superior Hope	15 Feb 1825
DUBAR, Morice	20	M	Mechanic	France	U. States	Native	29 May 1824
DUBBS, Wm. J.	27	M	Mercht	U. States	U. States	Mary Jane	21 Dec 1825
DUBELA, John P.	23	M	Farmer or Mechanic	Surry	U.S.	Edward Quesnel	31 Jul 1827
DU BERCEAU, D.							
Laviotte, Mrs.	49	F		Gaudaloupe	Morristown, N.J.	Horace	31 May 1822
Laviotte, Mr.	29	M	Planter	Gaudaloupe	Morristown, N.J.	Horace	31 May 1822
Laviotte, Mrs.	28	F		Gaudaloupe	Morristown, N.J.	Horace	31 May 1822
Matilda, Mrs.	25	F		Gaudaloupe	Morristown, N.J.	Horace	31 May 1822
DUBEREAW, Lavolle	32	M	Mercht.	France	France	Clio	7 Aug 1826
DU BOIS, L.	29	M	Planter	France	gone to France	Diana	9 Aug 1823
DUBOIS, —, Mr.	40	M	Merchant	France	U.S.	Francois I	8 Aug 1829
—, Mrs.	22	F	Lady	U. States	U. States	Milo	15 May 1824
—, Mrs.	26	F		France	U. States	Topaz	27 May 1828
Charles Ignace	17	M	Domestic	Switzerland	United States	Thetis	5 Jul 1821
Jone	32	M	Wagon maker	Bardin	U. States	Bayard	5 Sep 1828
Jules	15	M	Watchmaker	Switzerland	United States	Don Quixote	7 May 1824
L.	9	F	None	Swiss	U. States	Edwd. Quesnel	30 Apr 1825
Lucien	19	M	Watchmaker	Switzerland	United States	Don Quixote	7 May 1824
S.	45	F	Child Maker	Swiss	U. States	Edwd. Quesnel	30 Apr 1825
Salley	2	F	Child	U. States	U. States	Leader	2 Aug 1826
Salley	22	F	None	U. States	U. States	Leader	2 Aug 1826
DUBOISSON, P.	56	M	Dentist	France	U. States	Elizabeth Malvina	6 Dec 1827
DUBOLA, Jacob	25	M	Lock Smith	Germany	U. States	Sully	25 Jun 1828
DUBOLD, Cathern	24	F	None	France	U. States	Sully	25 Jun 1828
DUBORDEUR, J.	27	M	Cooper	France	U. States	Brunswick	14 Feb 1829
DUBOST, C.	40	M	Merchant	U. States	U. States	Trimmer	30 Apr 1825
DUBROCA, Valentine	20	M	Merchant	Louisiana	Baton Rouge	Packet	11 Nov 1824
DU CANARCEY, Lewis	21	M	Merchant	Port au Prince	Spain	Harmony	16 Oct 1821
DUCASS, —, Mrs.	35	F		Bordeaux	U. States	Smyrna	30 Apr 1825
John	60	M	Merchant	Bordeaux	U. States	Smyrna	30 Apr 1825
DUCAT, A.	22	F		France	U. States	Edward Bonaffe	11 Dec 1827
Ewd.	37	M	Refiner	France	U. States	Edward Bonaffe	11 Dec 1827
Fanny	17	F		France	U. States	Edward Bonaffe	11 Dec 1827
DUCATEL, E., Mr.	17	M	Student	Baltimore	U. States	Stephania	11 Apr 1825
Julius	24	M	Merchant	Baltimore	U.S.	Bayard	30 Oct 1820
DU CHABONET,							
Hugoureau, Mr. Dr.	22	M	D...	France	France	Cadmus	11 Jul 1827
DUCHAMP, Jno. B.	54	M	Mercht.	U.S.	U.S.	New York	29 Jun 1827
John B.	54	M	Mercht.	America	America	Exertion	26 Jul 1824
DUCHANCE, Peter 24 5/12		M	...	France	United States	Criterion	13 Oct 1825
DUCHEND, —, Mrs.	40	F		France	U. States	Manchester Packet	23 May 1822
DUCHESE, Genereux	20	M	Clerk	France	United States	Elbe	2 Aug 1822

NAMES OF PASSENGERS	AGE	SEX	OCCUPATIONS	COUNTRY TO WHICH THEY BELONG	COUNTRY THEY INTEND TO INHABIT	SHIPS/DATES OF ARRIVAL	
DUCK, Thomas	30	M		G. Britain	U. States	London	23 Sep 1828
DUCKINFEILD,							
Charles	6/12					Agricola	1 Jul 1820
Ellen	31					Agricola	1 Jul 1820
Geo.	27		Taylor			Agricola	1 Jul 1820
DUCKLOTT, George	27	M	Butcher	Germany	United States	Howard	15 Jun 1825
DUCKWORTH, Abram	5			England	America	Florida	14 Oct 1829
Eliza	14		Calico Printer	England	America	Florida	14 Oct 1829
Emma	3			England	America	Florida	14 Oct 1829
Geo.	28	M	Farmer	England	U. States	Severn	12 Oct 1826
George	11		Calico Printer	England	America	Florida	14 Oct 1829
James	30	M	Carpenter	Liverpool	United States	Nile	17 May 1827
James	30	M	Labourer	Great Britain	United States	William Dawson	18 Jun 1827
James	44	M	Farmer	Great Britain	United States	William Dawson	18 Jun 1827
Jas.	23	M	Mercht.	England	Philadea.	Canada	1 Nov 1823
Mary A.	13		Calico Printer	England	America	Florida	14 Oct 1829
Sarah	34		Calico Printer	England	America	Florida	14 Oct 1829
T.	33	M		England	America	Corinthian	1 Sep 1827
DUCLAS, P.	5	M	Servant	France	U. States	Bayard	11 Jul 1825
V.	7	M	Servant	France	U. States	Bayard	11 Jul 1825
DUCLEREAS, M.	35	M	Merchant	Cape Hayten	U. States	Deaux Amis	29 Oct 1828
DUCOMMANE, Gustave	22	M	Planters	Switzerland	U. States	Little William	16 Jun 1821
DUCONDEY, Mary R.	25	F	Lady	Cuba	Cuba	New England	27 Jul 1829
DUCRET, Hortence	19	F	Lady	France	United States	Helen	5 Sep 1828
John F.	26	M	Merchant	France	United States	Helen	5 Sep 1828
DUCY, Mary	27	F	None	Ireland	United States	Jubilee	13 Jul 1829
Patt	30	M	Labourer	Ireland	United States	Jubilee	13 Jul 1829
Patt, Jr.	1	M	None	Ireland	United States	Jubilee	13 Jul 1829
DUDGINS, William	23	M	Farmer	Ireland	America	Fairy	8 Aug 1821
DUDLEY, —, Mrs.	26	F		With intention to become citizen		New York	18 Jul 1828
A.	2	M		With intention to become citizen		New York	18 Jul 1828
Ann	34	F	Labourer	England	New York	Brighton	19 Aug 1829
Ann	34	F	Labourer			Brighton	19 Aug 1829
Frederick	12	M	Labourer			Brighton	19 Aug 1829
Fredk.	12	M	Labourer	England	New York	Brighton	19 Aug 1829
Harriett	11	F	Labourer	England	New York	Brighton	19 Aug 1829
Harriett	11	F	Labourer			Brighton	19 Aug 1829
James	21	M	Farmer	Ireland	U. States	Sabina	29 Apr 1825
John	34 4/12	M	Ship Master	N. Carolina	New York	American	4 Aug 1823
Timothy	29	M	Pocket Book Maker	With intention to become citizen		New York	18 Jul 1828
William	34	M	Labourer	England	New York	Brighton	19 Aug 1829
William	34	M	Labourer			Brighton	19 Aug 1829
William	40 1/12	M	...	England	America, U.S.	Illinois	3 Jun 1822
Wm.	8	M		With intention to become citizen		New York	18 Jul 1828
DUDRICKS, Emerline	23	F	Servant	Germany	United States	Maria Elizabeth	6 Jan 1823
DUERCUT, J. F.	23	M	Manufacturer	France	United States	Howard	19 May 1826
DUETER, Jacque	24	M	Agriculturist	France	U.S.	Helen	3 May 1828
DUETT, J.	23	M	Farmer	St. Johns	U. States	Isabella	28 Jun 1825
DUFAIR, J. B.	45	M	Merchant	France	U. States	Neptunes Barge	1 Oct 1822
DUFARR, J. B.	39	M	Merchant	U. States	U. States	New Packet	5 May 1823
DUFAU, Catherine	23	F	Merchant	France	France	Henry	16 May 1827
Jean Baptiste	11	M	Merchant	France	France	Henry	16 May 1827
DUFAUX, Dorotha	33	F		France	U. States	Don Quixote	25 Oct 1828
John David	40	M	Chemist	United States	United States	Columbia	16 Jan 1829
DUFF, Anastatia	30	F	None	...	...	Frances Henrietta	30 Jun 1827
Catharine	18	F	None	G. Britain	U. States	Courier	16 Aug 1824
Deniss	10	M		Ireland	U. States	Lady Hunter	18 Jul 1825
Edward	1	M	None	...	...	Frances Henrietta	30 Jun 1827
Elenor	8	F		Ireland	U. States	Lady Hunter	18 Jul 1825
George	30	M	Merchant	Ireland	U. States	Frederick	5 May 1826
George	32	M		England	United States	Lewis	30 May 1823
Harriet	1 6/12	F	None	...	...	Frances Henrietta	30 Jun 1827

NAMES OF PASSENGERS	AGE	SEX	OCCUPATIONS	COUNTRY TO WHICH THEY BELONG	COUNTRY THEY INTEND TO INHABIT	SHIPS/DATES OF ARRIVAL	
DUFF (cont'd)							
Henry	16	M	None	G. Britain	U. States	Courier	16 Aug 1824
Isabella	34	F	None	...	...	Frances	
						Henrietta	30 Jun 1827
J.	20	M				Hibernia	15 Aug 1820
James	5	M	None	G. Britain	U. States	Courier	16 Aug 1824
James	21	M		Scotland	U.S.	Curler	19 Jul 1828
Jane	12	F	None	G. Britain	U. States	Courier	16 Aug 1824
Jane	35	F	None	G. Britain	U. States	Courier	16 Aug 1824
Jno.	31	M	Shoemaker	Ireland	U. States	Lady Hunter	18 Jul 1825
John	40	M	...il...	...	...	Frances	
						Henrietta	30 Jun 1827
Marther	1	F	None	G. Britain	U. States	Courier	16 Aug 1824
Martin	23	M		Ireland	United States	William Byrnes	11 Dec 1827
Mary	3	F	None	...	...	Frances	
						Henrietta	30 Jun 1827
Mary	25		Lady			Hibernia	15 Aug 1820
Mary	32	F		Ireland	U. States	Lady Hunter	18 Jul 1825
Mary	47	F	Spinster	Ireland	United States	Dublin Packet	3 Sep 1822
Mary Ann	3	F	None	...	...	Frances	
						Henrietta	30 Jun 1827
Mathw.	30 2/12	M	Clerk			Cririe	18 Sep 1820
Pat	7/12		Child			Hibernia	15 Aug 1820
Pat	24		Surgeon	Great Britain		Moro Castle	6 Jul 1827
Philip	25	M	Servant	Havana	U. States	Patriot	13 Nov 1823
Timothy	6	M		Ireland	U. States	Lady Hunter	18 Jul 1825
William	30	M	...il...	...	...	Frances	
						Henrietta	30 Jun 1827
Wm.	7	M	None	G. Britain	U. States	Courier	16 Aug 1824
DUFFAN, John	24	M	Labourer	Ireland	United States	Commerce	13 Jun 1828
DUFFAY, Thomas	28	M	Cropper	Gt. Brittan	America	Reindeer	3 Aug 1827
DUFFE, Barnard	23	M	Labourer	Great Britian	United States	Mount Vernon	19 May 1823
Bridgit	21	F	Spinster	Ireland	United States	Wilson	6 Jun 1828
John, Mr.	35	M	Merchant	Scotland	New York	Hannibal	28 Apr 1824
Mary	22	F		Great Britian	United States	Mount Vernon	19 May 1823
DUFFEE, Betty	18	F	Servant	Ireland	United States	Henry Kneeland	7 Jun 1828
Denis	24	M		Irland	U. States	Nancy	27 Jun 1823
James	22	M	Farmer	Ireland	United States	Lord Strangford	20 Jun 1826
James	42	M	Servant	U. States	U. States	Francis Jarvis	16 Feb 1822
Margaret	18	F	Spinster	Ireland	United States	Lord Strangford	20 Jun 1826
Mary	22	F	Servant	Ireland	United States	Henry Kneeland	7 Jun 1828
Mary Ann	6/12	F				Hercules	25 Sep 1820
DUFFEY, Edward	25	M	Farmer	Ireland	U. States	William & John	10 Jul 1824
Eliza	3	F		Ireland	United States	Curler	7 Jul 1827
Eliza	36	F		Ireland	United States	Curler	7 Jul 1827
Hugh	18		Farmer	Ireland	United States	John Dickinson	28 Jun 1822
Hugh	20	M	Labourer	Grt. Britain	United States	Robert Fulton	8 Oct 1828
John	21	M	Turner	Ireland	New York	Governor Fenner	23 Jul 1829
John	25	M	Labourer	Grt. Britain	United States	Robert Fulton	8 Oct 1828
Margt.	24	F	None	Liverpool	Liverpool	Howard	
						Douglass	11 May 1827
Mary	3	F	Labourer	Liverpool	Liverpool	Howard	
						Douglass	11 May 1827
Mary	19	F	Servant	Ireland	America	Carolina Ann	7 Aug 1826
Mary	20	M	Baker	...	...	Laurel	16 Nov 1824
Mary Ann	1	F	Labourer	Liverpool	Liverpool	Howard	
						Douglass	11 May 1827
Mathew	35	M	Farmer	Great Britain	United States	Ganges	8 Jul 1820
Patrick	55	M	Weaver	Ireland	United States	Curler	7 Jul 1827
Patt.	22	M	Baker	...	...	Laurel	16 Nov 1824
Peter	27	M	Labourer	Liverpool	Liverpool	Howard	
						Douglass	11 May 1827
Sarah	18	F	Spinster			Commerce	22 Jun 1825
Terence	23 6/12	M	Labourer	Ireland	New York	Louisa	20 Jul 1826
Thos.	24	M	Labourer	Ireland	U. States	Marcus	7 Apr 1825
Turrenes	26	F	...	Great Britain	U. States	Hamilton	28 Apr 1828
Wm.	20	M	Labourer	England	U. States	Ayrshire	12 May 1828
DUFFICER, A.	12	M	Student	France	U.S.	Cadmus	20 Dec 1824
DUFFIE, Hugh	22	M	Labourer	Ireland		Robert Fulton	4 Jun 1828

NAMES OF PASSENGERS	AGE	SEX	OCCUPATIONS	COUNTRY TO WHICH THEY BELONG	COUNTRY THEY INTEND TO INHABIT	SHIPS/DATES OF ARRIVAL	
DUFFIE (cont'd)							
Jane	3	F		Ireland	U. States	Concordia	11 Jun 1823
John	23		Labourer	Ireland	Great Britain	Henrietta	26 Nov 1825
Mary	8	F		Ireland	U. States	Concordia	11 Jun 1823
Mary	30	F	Servant	Ireland	U. States	Concordia	11 Jun 1823
DUFFIES, James	23	M	Blacksmith			Hercules	25 Sep 1820
Mary	21	F				Hercules	25 Sep 1820
DUFFIN, Wm.	20	M	Gentn.	England	U. States	Trident	8 Mar 1824
DUFFY, Ann	16	F	Spinster	Ireland	America	Josephine	8 Dec 1827
Ann	20	F		Great Britain	United States	Grecian	24 Sep 1828
Ann	29	F	Servant	Ireland	U. States	James Cropper	17 Jun 1825
Anna	10	F		Great Britain		Robert Fulton	8 Mar 1823
Anthony	20	M		Ireland	United States	William & George	14 May 1828
B.	19	F	Servant	Ireland	United States	Josephine	30 Apr 1828
B.	23	M	Labourer	Great Brittain	United States	Sarah Ralston	27 Jan 1827
B.	27	M	Labourer	Great Britain	U. States	Hamilton	28 Apr 1828
Bridjet	20	F		Great Britain	New York	Philetus	21 Jul 1827
Cath.	12 10/12	F		Ireland	U. States	Fabius	22 Sep 1828
Catherine	57	F	Spinster	Ireland		Robert Fulton	4 Jun 1828
Cathr.	27	F		Ireland	United States	Commerce	13 Jun 1828
Chas.	53	M	...	Ireland	United States	General Putnam	20 Jun 1825
Danl.	26	M	Labourer	Ireland	United States	Hope	12 Jun 1828
David	21	M	Labourer	Great Brittain	United States	Sarah Ralston	27 Jan 1827
Elizabeth	40	F	None	Ireland	United States	Jubilee	13 Jul 1829
Ewd.	30	M	Labourer	Ireland	United States	Commerce	13 Jun 1828
Harriet	24	F		Gt. Britain	United States	Penelope	9 Sep 1828
Hugh	18	M	Labourer	Ireland		Robert Fulton	4 Jun 1828
James	4	M		Great Britain	United States	Grecian	24 Sep 1828
James	10	M	Boy	Ireland	U. States	Josephine	30 Aug 1828
James	20	M	Tailor	England	United States	Peru	23 May 1827
James	24	M	Labourer	Great Brittain	United States	Sarah Ralston	27 Jan 1827
James	28	M	Labourer	Ireland	America	Plutarch	18 Jul 1826
James, Mr.	29	M	Farmer	Ireland		Hercules	19 Jun 1821
John	11/12	M	Laborer	Ireland	United States	Weser	29 Jul 1823
John	1	M		Gt. Britain	United States	Penelope	9 Sep 1828
John	17	M	Farmer, Labourer or Spinster	Ireland	U. States	Meteor	4 Oct 1827
John	18	M		Great Britain	New York	Philetus	21 Jul 1827
John	21	M	Labourer	Ireland	United States	Wilson	28 Nov 1828
John	22	M	Labourer	Great Brittain	United States	Sarah Ralston	27 Jan 1827
John	24	M	...	Ireland	United States	General Putnam	20 Jun 1825
John	24	M	Farmer	Ireland	U. States	Henry Kneeland	27 Jul 1825
John	25	M	Labourer	Ireland, Great Britain	U.S. of America	Dublin	21 Feb 1826
Kate	33	F	Laborer	Ireland	United States	Weser	29 Jul 1823
Margt.	20	F	None	England	U. States	Thomas Ritchie	2 Jul 1827
Mary	5	F	...	Ireland	United States	General Putnam	20 Jun 1825
Mary	13	F	None	England	U. States	Thomas Ritchie	2 Jul 1827
Mary	16 5/12	F		Ireland	U.S. of America	Douglass	6 Jul 1829
Mary	19	F		Great Brittain	United States	Active	12 Sep 1828
Mary	24	F	Spinster	Ireland	America	Josephine	8 Dec 1827
Mary	27	F		England	United States	Peru	23 May 1827
Michael	14	M		Great Britain	United States	Grecian	24 Sep 1828
Michal	27	M	Currier	Ireland	America	Ann	2 Nov 1820
Michl.	10	M	...	Ireland	United States	General Putnam	20 Jun 1825
Michl.	22	M	Labourer	England	U. States	Thomas Ritchie	2 Jul 1827
Nichl.	23	M	Labourer	Great Brittain	United States	Active	12 Sep 1828
Owen	10	M	None	Ireland		Marchioness	13 May 1828
Pat	14	M	...	Ireland	United States	General Putnam	20 Jun 1825
Pat	23	M	Labourer	Great Brittain	United States	Sarah Ralston	27 Jan 1827
Pat	24	M		Gt. Britain	United States	Penelope	9 Sep 1828
Pat	25	M	Labourer	Great Brittain	United States	Sarah Ralston	27 Jan 1827
Patk.	26	M	Laborer	Ireland	United States	Weser	29 Jul 1823
Patrick	24	M	Blacksmith	Great Britain	United States	Ocean	27 Jul 1825
Patrick	25	M	Labourer	Ireland	U. States	Hanford	29 Dec 1828
Patrick	33	M	Farmer	Ireland	U. States	Henry Kneeland	27 Jul 1825
Patt	17	M		Ireland	United States	William Byrnes	6 Apr 1826
Patt	19	M		Ireland	United States	William Byrnes	6 Apr 1826

NAMES OF PASSENGERS	AGE	SEX	OCCUPATIONS	COUNTRY TO WHICH THEY BELONG	COUNTRY THEY INTEND TO INHABIT	SHIPS/DATES OF ARRIVAL	
DUFFY (cont'd)							
Peggy	50	F	None	England	U. States	Thomas Ritchie	2 Jul 1827
Philip	26	M	Labourer	Great Britain	U. States	Princess Charlotte	6 Sep 1828
Rose, Miss, his Sister [James]	27	F		Ireland		Hercules	19 Jun 1821
Sarah	17	F		Great Britain	United States	Grecian	24 Sep 1828
T.	24	M	Labourer	Great Brittain	United States	Sarah Ralston	27 Jan 1827
Thos.	5	M	Farmer	Ireland	United States	General Putnam	20 Jun 1825
Ths.	25		Merchant	Ireland	United States	Robert Burns	18 Jun 1821
Wm.	1	M	None	England	U. States	Thomas Ritchie	2 Jul 1827
Wm.	25	M	Farmer	Ireland	United States	Curler	3 Mar 1828
DUFORSON, Paul	24	M	Merchant	France	United States	Stephania	22 Apr 1822
DUFOUGERAIS, F. B.	21	M	None	Paris	France	Natches	13 Sep 1823
DUFOUR, —	26	M	Merchant	France	U. States	Maria Ann	29 Sep 1823
*landed at Balize [Biloxi?], Missippi							
DUFURE, J. B.	28	M	Merchant	France	U. States	Rapid	24 Jun 1822
DUG...KIN, Thomas	21		... Maker	London	Great Britain	Frances Henrietta	31 May 1824
DUGAN, Bryan	20	M	Labourer	Ireland	United States	Mary & Harriet	3 Jul 1829
Chas.	20	M	...	Ireland	United States	General Putnam	20 Jun 1825
Cornelius	29	M	Labourer	Ireland	United S.	Hanford	19 Aug 1828
Edward	26	M		Ireland	New York	Lady Hunter	5 Jun 1826
Ellen	20	F		Ireland	United S.	Hanford	19 Aug 1828
Hugh	27	M	Laborer	Ireland	United States	Mary	1 Jul 1829
James	...		Labourer	...horn...	England	Great Britain	7 May 1827
Patrick	20	M	Smith	Ireland	United States	Josephine	30 Apr 1828
Patrick	30	M	Labourer	Ireland	United States	Mary & Harriet	3 Jul 1829
Peter	21	M	None	Ireland	United States	Lord Wellington	28 May 1827
DUGARY, Enrigo, Don	25	M	Merchant	Spain	Mexico	Rubicon	19 Dec 1827
DUGAS, Louis	46	M	Planter	U. States	U. States	Edward Quesnel	16 Nov 1827
Victor, Revd.	35	M	Theology	France	United States	Lexington	14 Aug 1828
DUGDALE, Ann	1	F	None	England	U. States	Montgomery	18 Oct 1828
Betty	19	F	None	England	U. States	Montgomery	18 Oct 1828
DUGEDON, James	22	M	Farmer	Ireland	United States	Trident	31 Mar 1827
DUGEN, Henry	20	M	Weaver	Ireland	United States	St. Michaels	18 Jul 1826
DUGGAN, Archibald	29	M	Taylor	Ireland	New York	Lima	5 Aug 1829
Archibald	29	M	Taylor	Ireland	U. States	Lima	5 Aug 1829
Honorra	47	F		Ireland	United States	Trio	13 Jun 1827
John, Mr.	21	M	Gentn.	England	American	Acasta	3 Apr 1826
M.	30		Farmer	Ireland	U. States	Schuylkill	22 Aug 1825
DUGGIN, Anne	16	F		Ireland	U. States	Union	3 Jun 1822
John	9	M		Gt. Britain		Dalhouse Castle	13 May 1828
Sarah	17		Laboring Class		United States	Atlantic	2 Apr 1827
Sarah	20	F	Servant	Scotland	United States	Mary & Susan	5 Aug 1828
William	18		Laboring Class		United States	Atlantic	2 Apr 1827
DUGHTY, Fras.	23	M	Farmer	Ireland	Neward	Triton	12 Jul 1823
DUGLAS, Thomas	22	M	Y. Man	Ireland	New York	Trusty	12 Sep 1828
DUGLASS, David	25	M	Weaver	England		Fame	9 Dec 1826
DUGLISH, G.	30	F		Great Britain	Great Britain	William	1 Jul 1828
P.	10/12	M		Great Britain	Great Britain	William	1 Jul 1828
P.	35	M	Gardener	Great Britain	Great Britain	William	1 Jul 1828
DUGMAN, C.	4 6/12	F		England	United States	Acasta	25 Sep 1827
Elysha	30	F		England	United States	Acasta	25 Sep 1827
Geo.	34	M	Cork warner	England	United States	Acasta	25 Sep 1827
DUGUEL, John	26	M		G. Britan	U. States	William Neilson	26 Jul 1828
DUGUEYT, C.	34	M	Merchant	France	U. States	Quesnel	6 Sep 1824
Clara	32	F	Wife	France	U. States	Quesnel	6 Sep 1824
DUHAMEL, —	48	M	Merchant	U. States	U. States	Imperial	10 Dec 1821
Robert L.	50	M	Merchant	U. States	U.S.	Bayard	10 Nov 1824
DUHURST, Henry	22	M	Gentleman	St. Croix	England	South Carolina Packet	16 Sep 1820
DUIE, Amy	16		Farmer & Grazier	England	United States	Corinthian	7 Jul 1829
Caroline	17		Farmer & Grazier	England	United States	Corinthian	7 Jul 1829
Charles	7		Farmer & Grazier	England	United States	Corinthian	7 Jul 1829
Edward	4		Farmer & Grazier	England	United States	Corinthian	7 Jul 1829
George	20		Farmer & Grazier	England	United States	Corinthian	7 Jul 1829
Harriette	15		Farmer & Grazier	England	United States	Corinthian	7 Jul 1829
John	9		Farmer & Grazier	England	United States	Corinthian	7 Jul 1829

NAMES OF PASSENGERS	AGE	SEX	OCCUPATIONS	COUNTRY TO WHICH THEY BELONG	COUNTRY THEY INTEND TO INHABIT	SHIPS/DATES OF ARRIVAL	
DUIE (cont'd)							
Margaret	14		Farmer & Grazier	England	United States	Corinthian	7 Jul 1829
Mary Ann	1		Farmer & Grazier	England	United States	Corinthian	7 Jul 1829
Sarah	44		Farmer & Grazier	England	United States	Corinthian	7 Jul 1829
Thomas	51		Farmer & Grazier	England	United States	Corinthian	7 Jul 1829
DUIN, Anne	52	F		England	United States	Siroc	31 Oct 1829
Daniel	17	M		England	United States	Siroc	31 Oct 1829
James	18	M		England	United States	Siroc	31 Oct 1829
Lydia	13	F		England	United States	Siroc	31 Oct 1829
Rebecca	20	F		England	United States	Siroc	31 Oct 1829
Samuel	19	M		England	United States	Siroc	31 Oct 1829
Thomas	51	M	Shoemaker	England	United States	Siroc	31 Oct 1829
DUKE, B.	30	M	Farmer	Scotland	United States	Indus	5 Sep 1827
James	22	M	Shoemaker	England	U. States	Frances Henrietta	9 Dec 1823
John	22		Farmer	England	America	Sarah	18 Aug 1829
John	30	M	Farmer	United States	United States	Atlantic	3 Dec 1821
Johnathan	22	M	Mason	Great Britain		Eliza Grant	29 Aug 1829
Jonathan	22	M	Brick Mason	G.B.	New York	Eliza Grant	29 Aug 1829
Mary	23	F		G.B.	New York	Eliza Grant	29 Aug 1829
Mary	23	F		Great Britain		Eliza Grant	29 Aug 1829
Samuel	56		Farmer	England	America	Sarah	18 Aug 1829
DUKES, Sarah	20	F		England	United States	Amelia	20 Aug 1829
DULANY, Hy.	24	M	Citizen	U. States	U. States	New York	15 Jul 1825
Ruth	20	F	Spinster	Ireland	Unt. St. America	Wilson	21 May 1827
DULEAW, M.		M		Port au Prince	Port au Prince	Nature	17 Aug 1824
DULECHAUF, Austin	29	M	Farmer or Mechanic	France	U.S.	Edward Quesnel	31 Jul 1827
DULION, A. S. J.	24	M	Merchant	St. Domingo	U. States	Industry	5 Jan 1824
J. J. A.	26	M	Merchant	New York	New York	Industry	5 Apr 1824
DULITH, Alexander	30	F		United States	United States	Montano	27 Aug 1827
DULLEMON, A.	25	M	Merchant	Spain	Havana	Bellona	3 May 1826
DULLEN, —	40	M		St. Croix	St. Croix	Carlo	19 Apr 1828
DULLON, B.	18	M	Servant	Ireland	U. States	Sarah G	30 Jun 1828
DUMAN, Alexander	17	M	Gentleman	Scotland	New York, U.S.	Amity	31 Jan 1822
DUMATT, George	35	M		England	England	Pleiades	13 Nov 1826
DUMAULET, Jane	32		Lady	United States	United States	Corinthian	30 May 1828
DUMAZEAU, E.	23	M	Merchant	France	America	Don Quixotte	2 Jun 1828
DUMFRES, ...	64	M	Farmer		New York	Governor Clinton	3 Jul 1827
DUMIS, Addele	6	F		France	U. States	Charlemagne	19 Sep 1828
Loies F.	40	M	Gent	France	U. States	Charlemagne	19 Sep 1828
Mary	32	F		France	U. States	Charlemagne	19 Sep 1828
DUMNORD, Geo.	13	M	Servant	U. States	U. States	Napolean	26 Sep 1828
DU MONDRA, Louis		M	None	United States	United States	United States	18 Sep 1826
DUMONSIE, —,							
Madam	12 6/12	F	Lady	France	Nuyork	Louisa	17 Jul 1826
Clara, Madam	14 6/12	F	Lady	France	Nuyork	Louisa	17 Jul 1826
Veure, Madam	38	F	Lady	France	Nuyork	Louisa	17 Jul 1826
DUMOT, P. M.	25	M	Farmer	America	America	Nancy	18 Aug 1821
DUMPSTER, Mary	...	...	...	Scotland	America	Nimrod	9 Jul 1827
DUMWOOL, George	39	M	Cooper	Germany	United States	Samuel Robertson	8 Aug 1828
DUN, Edward	20	M	Labourer	Ireland	America	Josephine	8 Jan 1827
James	13	M	None	England	America	Lygonia	13 Aug 1829
John	48	M	Weaver	England	America	Lygonia	13 Aug 1829
Katharina	10	F	...	Baden	United States	Wade	29 Aug 1825
R.	23	M	Labourer	England	America	Two Marys	24 Sep 1827
Tobias	40	M	...	Baden	United States	Wade	29 Aug 1825
DUNA, John Antonio Cryoso	28	M	Merchant	Spain	U. States	Virginia	3 Dec 1827
DUNAFTEN, Constant	23	M	Farmer	Geneva	U.S. America	New Hampshire	28 Sep 1826
DUNAN, Adolpus	24	M	Doctor	United States	United States	Elbe	2 Aug 1822
DUNAVEN, Cath.	20	F		England	United States	Ganges	10 May 1828
Corns.	22	M	Farmer	England	United States	Ganges	10 May 1828
Ellen	2	F		England	United States	Ganges	10 May 1828
John	21	M	Farmer	England	United States	Ganges	10 May 1828
Kate	22	F		England	United States	Ganges	10 May 1828
Mary	3	F		England	United States	Ganges	10 May 1828
Mary	3	F		England	United States	Ganges	10 May 1828

NAMES OF PASSENGERS	AGE	SEX	OCCUPATIONS	COUNTRY TO WHICH THEY BELONG	COUNTRY THEY INTEND TO INHABIT	SHIPS/DATES OF ARRIVAL	
DUNAVEN (cont'd)							
Mary	24	F		England	United States	Ganges	10 May 1828
Richd.	24	M	Farmer	England	United States	Ganges	10 May 1828
Wm.	20	M	Farmer	England	United States	Ganges	10 May 1828
DUNBAIN, Mary	16	F	Lady	Ireland	United States	Belleville	13 Oct 1827
DUNBAR, Mary	22	F		Great Brittain	U. States	Atticus	25 Apr 1822
Mary	26			S... ...h	England	Great Britain	7 May 1827
William	26	M	Baker	Gt. Brittan	America	Reindeer	3 Aug 1827
DUNBIE, George	19		Servant	United States	United States	William Byrnes	25 Aug 1828
DUNCAN, —, Mr.	21	M	Printer	England	U. States	Spartan	21 Apr 1826
—, Mr.	30	M	Gent.	England	U.S.	Stephania	15 Aug 1825
—, Mrs.	28	F	Lady	England	U.S.	Stephania	15 Aug 1825
—, Mrs.	35	F	Labourer	Scotland	U. States	New Packet	16 Apr 1828
...	26	F	Spinster	Ireland	U. States	Josephine	7 May 1827
Abm.	8	M		Great Brittain	United States	Active	12 Sep 1828
Alex., Jr.	22	M	Servant	Great Britain	U.S. of America	Canada	1 Oct 1827
Ann	3	F		Great Britain	U. States	Lady Hunter	28 May 1823
Ann	8	F	Child	Halifax	New York	Hope & Esther	9 Jun 1827
Archd.	23	M	Joiner	Scotland	United States	Samuel Robertson	5 Oct 1827
Bejm.	23	M		Galway	U. States	Eliza Ann	30 Jul 1823
Chs.	24	M	Labourer	Great Britain	New York	Dublin	21 Dec 1824
David	22	M	Merchant	Great Britain	U. States	Indiana	11 Sep 1827
Eliz.	14	F	Child	Halifax	New York	Hope & Esther	9 Jun 1827
Eliza	9/12		None	Great Britain	United States	Roman	10 Sep 1827
F. A.	22	F		U. States	U. States	Caledonia	10 Sep 1828
Fleming	30	M		Great Britain	United States	Roman	10 May 1828
Flemming	34		Watch Maker	Great Britain	United States	Roman	10 Sep 1827
G. C.	28	M	Merchant	Gt. Britain	U. States	Caledonia	10 Sep 1828
G. Currie	23	M	Merchant	England	United States	Hercules	21 Nov 1822
George	40	M	Farmer	Great Britian	United States	Brok	29 Aug 1823
H.	21	M				Lady of the Lake	23 Aug 1828
J. R.	40			Great Britian	Halifax	America	28 Jul 1826
James	16	M	Mariner	Great Britain	Great Britain	Cuba	25 Feb 1822
James	21	M	Joiner	Scotland	United States	Samuel Robertson	5 Oct 1827
James A.	1/2	M	Child	N. York	New York	Hope & Esther	9 Jun 1827
Jane	5	F	Child	Halifax	New York	Hope & Esther	9 Jun 1827
Jane	21	F	Spinster	Ireland	United States	Asia	29 Jul 1829
Jas.	25	M	Joiner	Scotland	United States	Essex	23 May 1828
John	27	M	Weaver	Ireland	U. States	Josephine	7 May 1827
John	32	M	Mason	Great Britain	U. States	Lady Hunter	28 May 1823
John	40	M	Labourer	Scotland	U. States	New Packet	16 Apr 1828
John	54	M	Joiner	Scotland	United States	Samuel Robertson	5 Oct 1827
Margaret	50	F		Scotland	United States	Samuel Robertson	5 Oct 1827
Mary	28		None	Great Britain	United States	Roman	10 Sep 1827
Mary	35	F		Great Britain	U. States	Lady Hunter	28 May 1823
Mary	38	F	Lady	New York	New York	Hope & Esther	9 Jun 1827
Mary Ann	11	F	Maunfacturer	Ireland	U. States	John Wells	8 Sep 1897
Peter	25	M	Laborer	Ireland	United States	Ann Maria	18 Dec 1827
Robert	15	M	Clerk	Scotland	United States	Samuel Robertson	5 Oct 1827
Robt.	26	M	Labourer	G. Britain	U. States	St. George	7 Jun 1828
Robt.	28	M		Great Britain	United States	Washington	3 Sep 1827
Thos.	20	M		Gt. Britain	United States	John & Elizabeth	25 Sep 1827
William	32	M	Labourer	Great Britain	U. States	Princess Charlotte	6 Sep 1828
Wm.	28	M	Merchant	Great Britain		Andromache	7 Feb 1820
Wm., Mr.	23		Gentleman	England	United States	Acasta	16 Aug 1826
DUNCANSON, John	21	M	Joiner	Great Britain	United States	Courier	26 Jun 1827
DUNCK, —, & Wife	28	M	Merchant	England	U. States	Sarah Ann	5 Aug 1820
DUNCOM, —, Mr.	12	M	Merchant	G. Britain	G. Britain	Endeavor	4 Jun 1823
Robt.	44	M	Merchant	G. Britain	G. Britain	Endeavor	4 Jun 1823
DUNCOME, Alfred	11	M	Son	G. Britain	U. States	Endeavour	1 May 1826
C.	20	M	Gent.	Nassau, N.P.	Great Brittan	Ranger	9 Jan 1824

NAMES OF PASSENGERS	AGE	SEX	OCCUPATIONS	COUNTRY TO WHICH THEY BELONG	COUNTRY THEY INTEND TO INHABIT	SHIPS/DATES OF ARRIVAL	
DUNCOME (cont'd)							
Edward	2	M	Son	G. Britain	U. States	Endeavour	1 May 1826
Eliza	30	F	Lady	G. Britain	U. States	Endeavour	1 May 1826
Frederic	8	M	Son	G. Britain	U. States	Endeavour	1 May 1826
Mary	6	F	Daughter	G. Britain	U. States	Endeavour	1 May 1826
Robert	40	M	Merchant	G. Britain	U. States	Endeavour	1 May 1826
Robert, Esqr.	40		Gentleman			Superior	27 Jun 1825
Thos.	28	M	Merchant	G. Britain	U. States	Endeavour	1 May 1826
William	14	M	Servant			Superior	27 Jun 1825
DUNCON, Judeth	19	F	None	Ireland	New York	Eliza Grant	29 Aug 1829
Judeth	19	F	None	Ireland		Eliza Grant	29 Aug 1829
DUNDAS, Jno.	53	M	Mechanic	Ireland	New York	Phoenix	29 Apr 1826
Wm.	25	M	Mechanic	Ireland	New York	Phoenix	29 Apr 1826
DUNDEN, Maria	28					Trio	5 May 1828
Mary	24					Trio	5 May 1828
DUNDERDALE, Mary	28	F		England	U. States	Criterion at London	10 May 1821
Mary	39	F	Mason	England	U. States	Acasta	21 Oct 1825
Thos.	25	M	Farmer	England	U. States	Criterion at London	10 May 1821
DUNE, John	38	M	...	...	Canada	Hanford	17 Oct 1828
Mary	16	F	Spinster	England	United States	Euphrates	18 Aug 1827
DU NEESON, Louis S.	27	M	Merchant	Swiss	U. States	Montano	2 Sep 1828
DUNET, Jos.	40	M	Merchant	U. States	U. States	Prince Edward	25 Feb 1822
DUNEVAN, Jernimiah	31	M	Labourer	...	United States	Hanford	17 Oct 1828
DUNFORD, Elizabeth	50	F	Lady	G. Brittain		Mary & Elizabeth	17 May 1824
James	29	M	Merchant	G. Brittain		Mary & Elizabeth	17 May 1824
Jas.	28	M	Mercht.	Bermuda	Bermuda	Mary & Elizabeth	1 Apr 1824
John	23	M	Farmer	Ireland	U. States	Perserverance	21 Jul 1827
John	27	M	Gentleman	U. States	U. States	Diana	14 Sep 1820
DUNGAN, Biddy	20	F	None	England	U. States	Thomas Ritchie	2 Jul 1827
DUNGIN, James	22	M	Farmer	U. States	U. States	Nancy	19 Oct 1821
Mary	25	F	Wife [of James]	U. States	U. States	Nancy	19 Oct 1821
DUNHAM, Catherine	12	F	Spinster	New Brunswick	Upper Canada	Lady Hunter	22 Aug 1825
Catherine	22	F	Spinster	New Brunswick	Upper Canada	Lady Hunter	22 Aug 1825
Catherine	60	F	Widow	New Brunswick	Upper Canada	Lady Hunter	22 Aug 1825
Clara	2	F	Child	New Brunswick	Upper Canada	Lady Hunter	22 Aug 1825
Daniel	48	M	Farmer	New Brunswick	Upper Canada	Lady Hunter	22 Aug 1825
David	26	M	Farmer	New Brunswick	Upper Canada	Lady Hunter	22 Aug 1825
Grace	20	F	Spinster	New Brunswick	Upper Canada	Lady Hunter	22 Aug 1825
Henry	6	M	Child	New Brunswick	Upper Canada	Lady Hunter	22 Aug 1825
James	22	F	Spinster	New Brunswick	Upper Canada	Lady Hunter	22 Aug 1825
John	28	M	Farmer	New Brunswick	Upper Canada	Lady Hunter	22 Aug 1825
DUNING, Frederick	20	M	Farmer	Germany	Germany	Cadmus	9 Dec 1826
DUNIVEN, Eliza	20	F	None	Great Britain	America	Remittance	24 Aug 1825
John	25	M	Tailor	Great Britain	America	Remittance	24 Aug 1825
DUNK, Betsey	25	F	Servant	Gt. Britain	U.S.	Fabius	25 Aug 1829
Charles	22	M	...	Scotland	unknown	Robert Edwards	4 Jun 1824
David	21	M	Miller	Great Britain	United States	Fame	26 May 1828
Henry	30	M	...	Scotland	unknown	Robert Edwards	4 Jun 1824
Jane	29	F	Wheelwright	Rye, England	United States	William	21 May 1828
Jenne	7	F	Wheelwright	Rye, England	United States	William	21 May 1828
John	30	M	Wheelwright	Rye, England	United States	William	21 May 1828
Robert	30	M	Labourer	Great Britain	United States	Juno	5 Oct 1822
Sarah	5	F	Wheelwright	Rye, England	United States	William	21 May 1828
DUNKEE, Joseph D., (Super Cargo)	28	M	Merchant	United States	United States	Quill	31 Oct 1825
DUNKELL, Erastus A.	25 7/12	M	Doctor	America	America	Peacock	26 Jul 1820
DUNKIN, Henry	29	M	Farmer	England	U. States	Cincinnatus	24 May 1821
Henry	49	M	Farmer	Great Britain	United States	George Clinton	27 Aug 1827
John	14	M	Farmer	Great Britain	United States	George Clinton	27 Aug 1827
Martha	32 3/12	F		Great Britain	United States	Thames	16 May 1821
Matilda	6 2/12	F		Great Britain	United States	Thames	16 May 1821
Rebecca	39	F	Servant	Jamaica	Jamaica	Ambuscade	12 Nov 1823
Summeshays	41 10/12	M	Gentleman	Great Britain	United States	Thames	16 May 1821

NAMES OF PASSENGERS	AGE	SEX	OCCUPATIONS	COUNTRY TO WHICH THEY BELONG	COUNTRY THEY INTEND TO INHABIT	SHIPS/DATES OF ARRIVAL	
DUNKUN, Betty	18	F	Spinster	England	United States	Euphrates	18 Aug 1827
DUNLAP, David	18	M	Farmer	Scotland	United States	Minerva	29 Oct 1822
David	28	M	...	United States	United States	Ann	24 Sep 1822
David	30	M	Merchant	United States	United States	Alexander Mansfield	16 Sep 1823
Durham H.	15	M	Boy	Ireland	America	Josephine	8 Dec 1827
F.	18	M		Philada.	U. States	Indian Queen	12 May 1823
George	22	M	Weaver	Ireland	United States	Fabius	4 Jun 1828
James	25	M	Merchant	Great Britain	United States	John Jay	8 May 1828
John	46	M	Mariner	U. States	U. States	William & Henry	17 Sep 1822
Maria	20	F	Farmer	Great Britain	United States	John Jay	8 May 1828
Martha	28	F	Farmer	Scotland	United States	Minerva	29 Oct 1822
Wm.	34	M	Carpenter	Scotland	America	Franklin	19 Nov 1828
Wm.	72	M	Farmer	Ireland	United States	Henry Kneeland	7 Jun 1828
DUNLARY, James	12	M	Farmer	Ireland	U.S.A.	Dalhouse Castle	21 Aug 1829
Jas.	12	M	Farmer	Ireland	United States	Dalhouse Castle	21 Aug 1829
DUNLEAR, Joseph	35	M	Farmer	Ireland		Quatre Freres	29 Jul 1828
Mary	26	F	Farmer	Ireland		Quatre Freres	29 Jul 1828
DUNLER, Ann	13	F	Farmer	Ireland		Quatre Freres	29 Jul 1828
Ann M.	9	F	Farmer	Ireland		Quatre Freres	29 Jul 1828
John	25	M	Farmer	Ireland		Quatre Freres	29 Jul 1828
DUNLEVY, Chas.	17	M	Gentleman	Ireland	America	Liverpool	31 Aug 1827
DUNLOP, —, Mrs.	48	F	None	Great Britain	United States	James Monroe	5 Apr 1820
Alexander	33	M	Advocate	Scotland	Scotland	New York	5 Jul 1826
Andrew	24	M	Hatter	Ireland	U. States	Josephine	7 May 1827
Campbele	38	M	Gentleman	Scotland	U. States	Robert Edwards	9 May 1827
Cathr.	25	F	Servant	Ireland	United States	Josephine	30 Apr 1828
Elizabeth	14 5/12	F		Ireland	America	Carolina Ann	7 Apr 1826
James	22	M	Gentleman	United States	New York	Britannia	3 Nov 1827
James	23	M	Farmer	Great Britain	United States	Friends	13 Jun 1825
James	58	M	Merchant	Scotland	Sctoland	Nestor	20 Nov 1821
Jane	12 10/12	F		Ireland	America	Carolina Ann	7 Apr 1826
Janet	12	F	None	Great Britain	United States	James Monroe	5 Apr 1820
John	10	M		Ireland	America	Carolina Ann	7 Apr 1826
John	30	M	Merchant	England	U. States	Pacific	5 Sep 1827
John B.	35	M	Merchant	St. Croix	St. Croix	Ludwig	10 Aug 1825
John B.	37	M	Merchant	U. States	U. States	Carlo	10 Nov 1826
Letitia	20 4/12	F		Ireland	America	Carolina Ann	7 Apr 1826
Margaret	26	F	None	Scotland	Scotland	New York	5 Jul 1826
Margt.	24 4/12	F		Ireland	America	Carolina Ann	7 Apr 1826
Mary	16 4/12	F		Ireland	America	Carolina Ann	7 Apr 1826
Mary	17	F	Spinster	Ireland	U. States	Josephine	7 May 1827
Mary	23	F	Matron	Ireland	U. States	Josephine	7 May 1827
Mary	41	F		Ireland	America	Carolina Ann	7 Apr 1826
Matthew	14	M	None	Great Britain	United States	James Monroe	5 Apr 1820
Robert	5	M	None	Scotland	Scotland	New York	5 Jul 1826
Robert	17	M	Farmer	Great Britain	United States	Friends	13 Jun 1825
Robert	24	M	Merchant	Great Britain	Great Britain	Nestor	3 Nov 1820
Robt.						Carolina Ann	7 Apr 1826
Robt.	30			Great Britan	United States	Newry	11 Jul 1827
William	15 4/12	M		Great Britain		Silas Richards	27 Oct 1826
DUNLOPS, Andreca	22		Farmer	Ireland	United States	Carolina Ann	12 Sep 1823
DUNN, —, Capt.	38	M	Officer	England	U. States	Corinthian	20 Apr 1825
..., Capt.	35	M	British Officer	Cannada	Canada	Manhattan	21 May 1821
A. S. A.	14	M	Merchant	Boston	Boston	William Bayard	24 Jan 1825
Ann	1	F	None	Ireland	United States	Jubilee	1 Oct 1828
Ann	32	F	None	England	United States	Hamilton	13 Nov 1827
Ann	33	F	None	Ireland	Canada	Mentor	20 Oct 1825
Arthur	24	M	Labourer	G. Britain	U. States	London	23 Sep 1828
Cath.	28	F	Servant	Ireland	U. States	Marcus	7 Apr 1825
Catharine	30	F		Ireland	U. States	Nancy	10 Jul 1822
Catherine	22	F	None	Ireland	United States	Jubilee	1 Oct 1828
Charles	40	M	Baker	Ireland	Canada	Mentor	20 Oct 1825
Cristopher	27	M	Farmer	Ireland	United States	Lord Strangford	20 Jun 1826
Denis	29	M	Labourer	Ireland	U. States	Combine	30 Nov 1825
Dennis	21	M	Labourer	Ireland	United States	Baltic	21 Apr 1827
E.	26	F		G. Britain	U. States	Albion	19 Jun 1828
Edward	22	M	Shepherd	England	America	Sarah	18 Aug 1829

NAMES OF PASSENGERS	AGE	SEX	OCCUPATIONS	COUNTRY TO WHICH THEY BELONG	COUNTRY THEY INTEND TO INHABIT	SHIPS/DATES OF ARRIVAL	
DUNN (cont'd)							
Edwd.	30	M	Laborer	Ireland	United States	Trio	13 Jun 1827
Eliza	10	F		England	United States	John &	
						Elizabeth	25 Sep 1827
Elizabeth	4	F		Scotland	United States	Ann	11 Sep 1827
Emily	28	F		England	U. States	Cato	9 Aug 1823
Finten	30	M	Shoe Maker	Ireland	United States	Lord Wellington	14 Nov 1827
Francis	20	M	Labourer	Ireland	New York	Governor Fenner	23 Jul 1829
Geo.	29	F	Mechanic	England	United States	John &	
						Elizabeth	25 Sep 1827
George	22					Amphion	31 May 1824
George	43 9/12	M	Labourer			Cririe	18 Sep 1820
Henry	27	M	Clergyman	G. Britain	U. States	Albion	19 Jun 1828
Isabella	6	F		Ireland	United States	Mary	1 Jul 1829
James	3	M	Laborer	Ireland	United States	Mary	1 Jul 1829
James	9	M	None	Ireland	Canada	Mentor	20 Oct 1825
James	21	M	Gentleman	Ireland	United States	Dublin Packet	13 Oct 1828
James	22	M	Laborer	Ireland	New York	Eliza Grant	29 Aug 1829
James	22	M	Labourer	Great Britain		Eliza Grant	29 Aug 1829
James	23	M	Joiner	Ireland		Ocean	13 Jul 1827
James	24	M		Ireland	U. States	Balaena	29 Apr 1825
James	25	M	Labourer	Ireland	United States	Mary	1 Jul 1829
James	27	M	Farmer	Ireland	United States	Samuel	
						Robertson	9 Apr 1828
Jane	21	M	Labourer	Great Britian	United States	Sarah	11 Jul 1829
Jane	28	F	None	Ireland	United States	Jubilee	1 Oct 1828
Jere	24	M	Yeoman	Ireland	United States	Borneo	9 Jul 1827
John	2	M		England	United States	John &	
						Elizabeth	25 Sep 1827
John	18	M	Boy	Ireland	United States	Dublin Packet	29 Jun 1825
John	20	M		Ireland	U. States	Balaena	29 Apr 1825
John	24					Amphion	31 May 1824
John	24	M	Laborer	Ireland	United States	Trio	13 Jun 1827
John	24	M	Labourer	Ireland	United States	Jubilee	1 Oct 1828
John	30	M	Labourer	England	U. States	Montgomery	18 Oct 1828
John	30	M	Farmer	Ireland	Philadelphia	General Marion	12 Jan 1829
John	32	M	Labourer	Great Britain	United States	Isaac Hicks	10 Jul 1827
John	40	M	Farmer	Great Britain	United States	Diana	6 Jul 1829
Louisa	24	F		Great Britain	United States	Isaac Hicks	10 Jul 1827
Margaret	2	F		Philadelphia	U. States	Howard	25 Jul 1823
Margaret	10	F		Scotland	United States	Ann	11 Sep 1827
Margaret	28	F		Scotland	United States	Ann	11 Sep 1827
Martin	1	M	None	Ireland	United States	Jubilee	1 Oct 1828
Mary	7	F	None	Ireland	Canada	Mentor	20 Oct 1825
Mary	18	F	None	Great Briton	uncertain	Mount Vernon	29 Aug 1828
Mary	20	F		England	U. States	Alert	22 Sep 1821
Mary	26	F		Great Britain	United States	Isaac Hicks	10 Jul 1827
Mary	30	F		Ireland	United States	Mary	1 Jul 1829
Mary	35	F	Lady	Ireland	U. States	Nancy	25 Nov 1823
Mary Ann	5	F	None	Ireland	Canada	Mentor	20 Oct 1825
Michael	24	M	Farmer	England	United States	Aurelia	7 Jun 1826
Nancy	4	F		Ireland	United States	Mary	1 Jul 1829
Oliver	30	M	Gentleman	U. States	U. States	Robert Edwards	9 May 1827
P.	28	M	private	U. States	U. States	Enterprize	9 Aug 1825
Pat	22	M	Weaver	Gt. Britain	United States	Penelope	9 Sep 1828
Peggy	54	F		Ireland	U. States	Howard	25 Jul 1823
Peter	11	M	None	Ireland	Canada	Mentor	20 Oct 1825
Peter	27	M	Farmer	Ireland	United States	Orozimbo	11 Aug 1823
Peter	40	M	Weaver	Great Britan	Great Britan	United States	21 May 1827
R. S.	35	M	Merchant	United States	America	Pacific	13 Jan 1827
Robert	1	M	Laborer	Ireland	United States	Mary	1 Jul 1829
Robt.	6	M		England	United States	John &	
						Elizabeth	25 Sep 1827
Robt.	24	M	Labourer	Ireland	U. States	Atlantic	19 Aug 1825
Robt.	45	M	...	...	...	Diamond	27 Jul 1824
Samuel	18	M	Labourer	England	America	Constitution	1 Oct 1825
Samuel	18	M	Farmer	Ireland	U. States	Lady Hunter	9 Oct 1825
Thomas	10	M	Boy	Ireland	United States	Dublin Packet	29 Jun 1825
Thomas	23	M		Irereland	America	Carolina Ann	20 Jun 1825

NAMES OF PASSENGERS	A G E	S E X	OCCUPATIONS	COUNTRY TO WHICH THEY BELONG	COUNTRY THEY INTEND TO INHABIT	SHIPS/DATES OF ARRIVAL	
DUNN (cont'd)							
Thomas	24	M	Labourer	Scotland	N. York	Resolution	6 Jun 1822
Thomas	30	M	Farmer	Ireland	United States	Jubilee	1 Oct 1828
Thos.	7	M		England	United States	John & Elizabeth	25 Sep 1827
Thos.	38	M	Merchant	England	United States	John & Elizabeth	25 Sep 1827
William	4/12	M		Scotland	United States	Ann	11 Sep 1827
William	27	M	Farmer	Ireland	United States	Dublin Packet	29 Jun 1825
William	30	M	Distiller	British ...	Upper Canada	Loyalty	9 Sep 1822
William	32	M	Labourer	Great Britain	United States	Isaac Hicks	10 Jul 1827
William	33	M	Weaver	Scotland	United States	Ann	11 Sep 1827
William	35	M	Laborer	Ireland	United States	Mary	1 Jul 1829
William, Mr.	40	M	Military	Gt. Britain	Gt. Britain	James Cropper	14 Mar 1828
Willm.	23	M	Labourer	Ireland	United States	Wilson	27 Jun 1826
Wm.	20	M	Labourer	Great Brittain	United States	Nimrod	9 Jan 1827
Wm.	22	M	Shoemaker	England	U. States	Howard Douglass	29 Jan 1828
Wm.	23	M	Bucher	England	United States	Hamilton	13 Nov 1827
Wm.	25	M	Farmer	England	U. States	Thomas Ritchie	2 Jul 1827
Wm.	26	M	Laborer	Great Britian	United States	Columbia	17 Apr 1827
DUNNE, Andrew	30		Weaver	Kellahy	Ireland	Carolina Ann	21 May 1823
DUNNEGAN, Jane	1	F		Ireland	Pensylvania	Lima	5 Aug 1829
Jane	1	F		England	U. States	Lima	5 Aug 1829
Margaret	24	F		Ireland	Pensylvania	Lima	5 Aug 1829
Margaret	24	F		England	U. States	Lima	5 Aug 1829
Owen	30	M	Weaver	Ireland	Pensylvania	Lima	5 Aug 1829
Owen	30	M		England	U. States	Lima	5 Aug 1829
DUNNEY, Catherine	25	F		Ireland	United States	Enterprize	23 Jul 1827
DUNNIN, Judath	38	F		Gt. Brittan	America	Reindeer	3 Aug 1827
DUNNING, C. S.	30	M	Mariner	U. States	U. States	Beaver	2 Apr 1828
DUNO, Anthony	50	M	Farmer	Native of Switzerland	United States	Canaris	30 Jun 1827
Francis	10	M		Native of Switzerland	United States	Canaris	30 Jun 1827
Margaret	50	F		Native of Switzerland	United States	Canaris	30 Jun 1827
Peter	12	M		Native of Switzerland	United States	Canaris	30 Jun 1827
DUNOHO, A. N. V.	2	F	None	Great Britain	U. States	Balance	19 Jun 1824
Judish	15	F	None	Great Britain	U. States	Balance	19 Jun 1824
Wm.	18	M	Farmer	Great Britain	U. States	Balance	19 Jun 1824
DUNOHOE, John	10	M	None	Great Britain	U. States	Balance	19 Jun 1824
John	40	M	Shoemaker	Great Britain	U. States	Balance	19 Jun 1824
Michael	12	M	None	Great Britain	U. States	Balance	19 Jun 1824
Nancy	40	F	None	Great Britain	U. States	Balance	19 Jun 1824
Wm.	11	M	None	Great Britain	U. States	Balance	19 Jun 1824
DUNOTHO..., Mary	...	...	Servant	Ireland	United States	Edwin	29 Nov 1828
DUNPSTER, Henry		M		Jamaica		Antelope	22 Aug 1820
John		M	Mason	Jamaica		Antelope	22 Aug 1820
— Mrs.		F		Jamaica		Antelope	22 Aug 1820
DUNRAH, M.	60	F		Gaudaloup	U. States	Orono	5 Jun 1823
DUNRIE, Cath.	30	F		G. Britain	U. States	Hanford	18 Sep 1828
DUNRODIE, Charles	28	M		England	U. States	Birmingham	16 Jun 1828
Mary	20	F		England	U. States	Birmingham	16 Jun 1828
DUNSCOMB, —, Mr.	21	M	Merchant	Bermuda	Bermuda	Improvement	6 Jun 1826
Caroline	14	F			U. States	Greyhound	19 Aug 1820
Eliza	17	F			U. States	Greyhound	19 Aug 1820
J. W.	16	M	Student	Bermuda, W.I.		Norval	12 Jun 1826
John, Esqr.	41	M	Merchant	NewfdLand	U. States	Greyhound	19 Aug 1820
Thos. T.	45	M	Merchant	G. Britain	U. States	Hope Success	16 Jul 1828
DUNSCOMBE, Edward	17	M	Student	United States	U. States	Combine	9 Sep 1824
DUNSHAW, Cathrine	45	F	Lady	Ireland	United States	Belleville	13 Oct 1827
DUNSON, Elisabeth	24 9/12	F		Bristol, Engl.	...	Warrior	19 May 1828
Samuel	28	M	Farmer	Bristol, Engl.	...	Warrior	19 May 1828
DUNSTERVILLE, Elizabeth	27	F		...	United States	Dawn	15 Oct 1827
DUNT, Martha	66	F		England	U.S.A.	Hudson	21 Aug 1829
DUNTE, J. C.	29	M	Merchant	Bremen	New York	Louisa	9 Jul 1828

NAMES OF PASSENGERS	AGE	SEX	OCCUPATIONS	COUNTRY TO WHICH THEY BELONG	COUNTRY THEY INTEND TO INHABIT	SHIPS/DATES OF ARRIVAL	
DUNTHART, Thos.	26	M	Weaver	Ireland	United States	Alex. Mansfield	17 May 1823
DUNTON, John L.	10	M			U. States of America	Junius	5 Jul 1820
Robert	18	M	Merchant	England	United States	John Wells	11 May 1827
William	15	M	None	England	United States	John Wells	11 May 1827
DUNVILLE, Benj.	20	M	Butcher	England		Marchioness	13 May 1828
DUNWIDDIE, ...	11	M		Scotland		Ann	17 May 1822
DUPANT, Charles	30	M	Goldsmith	Marseiles	New York	Pedler	14 May 1828
DUPARET, Eugene	1	F		France	New York	Isabella	15 Sep 1828
Eugene	3	F		France	New York	Isabella	15 Sep 1828
J.	33	M	Hatter	Germany	Philadelphia	Isabella	15 Sep 1828
Ufrus	2/12	F		France	New York	Isabella	15 Sep 1828
Ufrus	28	F		France	New York	Isabella	15 Sep 1828
DUPART, Ferdinand	38	M	Merchant	France	France	Don Quixote	12 Feb 1829
DUPASQUES, J.	33	M	Merct.	France	U.S.	Stephania	15 Aug 1825
DUPHER, Loris	44	M	Merchant	U. States	U. States	Montano	2 Sep 1828
DUPIERRIS, Martial	26	M	Merchant	France	U. States	Ann Eliza Jane	6 Sep 1822
DUPIN, Frs.	19	M	Merchant	Curacoa	United States	Rebecca & Sally	18 Jul 1823
DUPINE, E.		F		Holland	U. States	Talma	23 Sep 1828
DUPL...IS, F. L.	35	M	Actor	Switzerland	New York	Stephania	28 Jul 1823
DUPLIN, Amanda	25	F	Farm	France		Pallas	14 Jun 1828
Mariah C.	61	F	Carpenter	France		Pallas	14 Jun 1828
Mariah M.	28	F	Farm	France		Pallas	14 Jun 1828
Perre	58	M	Labour	France		Pallas	14 Jun 1828
DUPON, Pall	52	M	Merchant	United States	U. States	Alpha	27 Jul 1827
DU PONT, Jenny	20		Servant	France	U. States	Brandt	14 Aug 1823
DUPONT, —	36	M	Mechanic	New York	U. States	Diana	1 Jun 1822
J.	28	M	Merchant	U.S.	U. States	Toison	15 Dec 1828
DUPONY, André	32	M	Merchant	France	travelling	Desdemona	12 Jun 1826
DUPORT, John M.	26	M	Baker	France	U. States	Hyperion	7 Aug 1826
Pierre	31	M	Merchant	France	France	Alto	8 Jun 1827
DUPRAT, Pierre	32	M	Mechanic	France	U. States	Desdemona	6 Oct 1824
DUPRE, Maurice	26		Farmer	France	U. States	Elizabeth	9 Jul 1825
T.	26	M	Merchant	France	U. States	Talma	23 Sep 1828
DUPRÉE, Joseph	28	M	Merchant	France	New York & Paris	Cadmus	27 Aug 1822
DUPREY, Francis	12	M	Child	Spain		Orlando	8 May 1824
Peter	14	M	Child	Spain		Orlando	8 May 1824
DUPRIR, John	29	M	Merchant	France	U. States	Columbia	10 Mar 1824
DUPRIS, Maurice	44	M	Gardner	France	United States	American	27 Aug 1827
DUPRUY, J. A.	32	M	Merchant	France	U. States	Grampus	14 Apr 1823
DUPRY, Francis	36 5/12	F	Farmer	Switzerland	U. States	France	26 Jun 1828
Madaline	39 2/12	M	Farmer	Switzerland	U. States	France	26 Jun 1828
DUPUCK, —, Madam	30	F	Lady	U. States	U. States	Maria Ann	21 Oct 1826
John	14	M		U. States	U. States	Maria Ann	21 Oct 1826
DUPUIS, Charles	47	M	Hat maker	France	United States	Montano	5 May 1828
DUPUY, Jno.	47	M	Merchant	France	United States	Polly & Sophia	13 Sep 1821
John	40	M	Gentleman	France	U. States	Wave	7 Mar 1822
DUQUERST, Camille	38	M	Merchant	France	N. York	Charlemagne	20 Aug 1829
DURAN, Lou	55	M	Merchant	Switzerland	U.S.	C. Amelia	30 Jun 1828
M.	42	M	Merchant	U. States	U. States	John	18 Sep 1824
Maneual	30	M	Merchant	New York	The United States	Sally	11 Oct 1820
Maniel	36	M	Mariner	Portugal	U. States	Union	21 Nov 1822
Marie	40	F		Switzerland	U.S.	C. Amelia	30 Jun 1828
DURANCE, John	27	M	Merchant	U. States	U. States	Quesnel	6 Sep 1824
DURAND, B.	40	M	Merchant	Brooklin	Brooklin	Hero	5 Jul 1828
Benjamin	34	M	Merchant	United States		Bucksport	8 Dec 1827
Cecilia	9	F	Spinster	United States	United States	Paris	10 Sep 1823
E.	31	M	Merchant	France	U. States	Edwd. Quesnel	30 Apr 1825
Frances	16 6/12	F	Spinster	Ireland	U. States	Josephine	30 Aug 1828
James, Mrs.	40	F		United States	United States	Paris	10 Sep 1823
James B.	45	M	Merchant	United States	United States	Paris	10 Sep 1823
John	22		Farmer			Caroline	10 Mar 1828
John	45	M	Merchant	France	France	Lovinia	20 Nov 1828
Joseph	12	M	None	France	U. States	Alabama	21 May 1823
Joseph	20	M	Merchant	United States	United States	William	31 Mar 1828
Joseph	28	M	Merchant	U. States	U. States	John	15 Sep 1827
Louisa	15	F	None	U. States	U. States	Lewis	25 Jun 1824
Mary	16	F	None	U. States	U. States	Lewis	25 Jun 1824
Theodore	23	M	Merchant	France	U. States	Confiance	26 Apr 1828

NAMES OF PASSENGERS	AGE	SEX	OCCUPATIONS	COUNTRY TO WHICH THEY BELONG	COUNTRY THEY INTEND TO INHABIT	SHIPS/DATES OF ARRIVAL	
DURANT, —, Miss	20	F		Norfolk	Norfolk	South Carolina Packet	16 Sep 1823
—, Mr.	25	M	Merchant	France	U. States	Eugenie	29 Jan 1827
—, Mrs.	28	F		St. Croix	St. Croix	South Carolina Packet	16 Sep 1823
—, Mrs.	57	F		France		François I	19 Nov 1828
J...	...	F		Irland	United States	Nancy	28 Oct 1822
Lewis	18	M	Printer	Saint John	Saint John	Sarah G.	28 Nov 1827
Thomas	...	M		Irland	United States	Nancy	28 Oct 1822
DURATO, Jno.	31	M	Planter	St. Martins	U. States	Matilda	16 Aug 1822
DURCHOLD, Louisa A.	60 5/12	F	None	Prussia	America	John Dickinson	9 Oct 1828
DURDEN, Richd.	27	M	C. Printer	Great Britain	United States	Amelia	20 Aug 1829
DUREMENT, Augusta	11	F		France	United States	Le Voltaire	19 Jul 1828
Cath. M.	32	F		France	United States	Le Voltaire	19 Jul 1828
Eugene	2	F		France	United States	Le Voltaire	19 Jul 1828
Julie	7	F		France	United States	Le Voltaire	19 Jul 1828
Pierre C.	41	M	Farmer	France	United States	Le Voltaire	19 Jul 1828
Sophie	9	F		France	United States	Le Voltaire	19 Jul 1828
DURESSEL, Louis	23 5/12	M	Joiner	France	U. States	France	26 Jun 1828
DURET, John	45	M	Shoe Maker	Ireland		Quatre Freres	29 Jul 1828
Maryan	26	F	Shoe Maker	Ireland		Quatre Freres	29 Jul 1828
DURGAN, Bridget	6	F	Child	Ireland	America	Wilson	16 May 1825
Bridget	19	F	Spinster	Ireland	America	Wilson	16 May 1825
DURHAM, David R.	32	M	Merchant	U.S.A.	U. States	Edward Quesnel	17 Mar 1829
DURHURST, Thomas	26	M	Labourer	Ireland	United States	Jubilee	13 Jul 1829
DURIER, Paul Joseph	29	M	Jeweller	France	United States	Marseilles	14 Jan 1826
DURINGBURG, Barbara	3	F	Child	Switzerland	United States	Andes	5 May 1828
Catherine	22	F	Spinster	Switzerland	United States	Andes	5 May 1828
Catherine	48	F	Spinster	Switzerland	United States	Andes	5 May 1828
George	10	M	Farmer	Switzerland	United States	Andes	5 May 1828
Michel	17	M	Farmer	Switzerland	United States	Andes	5 May 1828
Michel	48	M	Farmer	Switzerland	United States	Andes	5 May 1828
DURKEE, Justus	40	M	Mariner	United States	United States	Genl. Brown	3 Dec 1821
DURKER, Samuel	31 2/12	M	Farmer	United States	United States	Nimrod	28 Apr 1824
DURLY, Charles	30		Hatter	Great Brit.	U. States	Columbia	7 May 1828
DURM, Charles, his Wife & three Children *landed at Lewiston, Delw.	37	M	Weaver	Rothalban	United States	Deux Ernest	29 Dec 1827
DURNAKIN, Andrew	21	M	Farmer	Great Britain	United States	John Jay	8 May 1828
DURNELL, Grace	...	...	...	Ireland	United States	General Putnam	20 Jun 1825
DURNEY, Simon	40	M	Manufact.	United States	United States	St. John	5 Oct 1829
DURNS, Alexander	24	M	Farmer			Hector	11 Sep 1820
DURNY, John	14		Tailor	Ireland	New York	Marcella	18 May 1827
DURON, Charles *son épouse & 3 enfans [his wife and three children]	37		Cisseraux [?]	Rothalbon		Deux Ernest	29 Dec 1827
DURR, James J.	29	M	Merchant	U. States	U. States	Edward Bonnaffe	4 May 1827
DURRER, Patrick	30	M	...	G. Britain	U. States	New England	28 Sep 1824
DURRICH, Pat	20	M	Ploughman	Ireland	United States	Josephine	30 Apr 1828
DURRNOT, Elizabeth	25	F	Spinster	County Longford, ..., England	U. States	New Orleans	24 Aug 1827
DURRONE, Susanah	63	F	Lady	Connecticut	United States	St. Michaels	12 Jun 1826
DURROUGH, Andrew	24	M	Weaver	Scotland	United States	Princess Charlotte	26 Apr 1827
Robert	27	M	Carpenter	Scotland	United States	Princess Charlotte	26 Apr 1827
DURRY, Joseph	22	M	Farmer	Switzerland	United States	Andes	5 May 1828
DURSHURE, Stephen	14	M	...	Ireland	U. States	Union	3 Jun 1822
DURYIA, Rich.	26	M	Merchant	France	U. States	Edgar	1 Oct 1822
DURYOK, William	22	M	Laborer	Ireland	United States	Fabius	4 Jun 1828
DU ST. GEORGES, —, Madam	55	F		St. Domingo	St. Domingo	Cadmus	11 Jul 1827
DUSTER, Francis	30	M	Mechanic	France	France	Splendid	31 Aug 1827
DUSTON, M.	25	M	Carpenter	England	United States	Brilliant	24 Sep 1827
DUSTY, Berard, Doct.	30	M	Surgeon	France	France	Athenian	1 Dec 1827
DUTCH, Alfred P.	17	M	Sailor	New York	U. States	Virginia	3 Dec 1827
DUTHER, A.	23	M	Merchant	St. Petersburg	America	Wm. Tell	9 Jan 1827

NAMES OF PASSENGERS	AGE	SEX	OCCUPATIONS	COUNTRY TO WHICH THEY BELONG	COUNTRY THEY INTEND TO INHABIT	SHIPS/DATES OF ARRIVAL	
DU TOUR, —, Mrs.	39	F	Priestess	France	U.S.	Edward Quesnel	31 Jul 1827
DUTTENHOFFER, A.	31	M	Engineer	Germany	Germany	Frances Miller	1 May 1826
DUTTON, Abm.	44	M	Farmer	United States	United States	Trident	30 Sep 1826
DUVAEL, Etenll	28	F		Brattain		L'Esperance	6 Sep 1828
Jh.	38	M	Saddler	Brattain		L'Esperance	6 Sep 1828
DUVAL, Eugene	27	M	Merchant	France	Porto Rico	Concordia	8 Nov 1822
Jno. Chs.	30	M	Mercht.	France	U.S.	Cadmus	20 Dec 1824
L.	27	M	Gilder	France	U. States	Alexander Le Grand	9 Sep 1823
Peter Eugene	30	M	Merchant	France	U. States	Buck	7 Aug 1822
DUVALL, H.	34	M	Confectioner	France	United States	Robert Fulton	2 Aug 1824
Stephen	56	M	Mariner	U. States	U. States	Sarah Sheaf	13 Jun 1825
*Captain of the Ship Orion							
DUVAR, Margaret	22	F	None	Scotland	United States	Camillus	28 Apr 1824
DUVELIN, Cathr.	53	F	Weaver	Gt. Britan	U. States	Sarah Skeafe	10 Sep 1827
Joseph	14	M	Weaver	Gt. Britan	U. States	Sarah Skeafe	10 Sep 1827
Mary	13	F	Weaver	Gt. Britan	U. States	Sarah Skeafe	10 Sep 1827
DUVIGNY, H.	30	M	Traveller	France		Howard	4 Feb 1826
DUVOISAN, Lewis	25	M	Mercht.	Switzerland	U.S.	Edward Quesnel	17 Jan 1825
DUXBURY, Wm.	39	M	Weaver	Gt. Howard	U. States	Milton	21 May 1827
DWELIN, James	17	M	Weaver	Ireland	United States	Commerce	13 Jun 1828
DWELLING, James	30	M	Farmer	Ireland	United States	Jubilee	13 Jul 1829
Jane	3	F	None	Ireland	United States	Jubilee	13 Jul 1829
John	1	M	None	Ireland	United States	Jubilee	13 Jul 1829
Martha	30	F	None	Ireland	United States	Jubilee	13 Jul 1829
DWENAN, Henry	19	M	Labourer	Ireland	United States	Aurelia	7 Jun 1826
*died on passage							
DWIGHT, Alex.	...	...	...	...	...	Diamond	27 Jul 1824
G. A., Mr.	23	M	Merchant	U.S.	U.S.	Frances	21 Mar 1827
Henry E., Mr.	30	M	Gentn.	U.S.	U.S.	Cadmus	11 Jul 1827
John	23	M	Merchant	U. States	U. States	Pacific	11 Sep 1824
Theodore, Jr.	24	M	Gentn.	United States	United States	Magnet	28 Jun 1821
Timo.	21	M	Merch.	U. States	U. States	Eagle	16 Aug 1823
DWOLF, John	40	M	Mariner	United States	United States	Balance	12 Oct 1821
DWYER, —, Miss	19	F		Great Britain	United States	Isaac Hicks	6 Dec 1827
Alexander	36	M	Merchant	Great Britain	United States	Corinthian	2 Sep 1824
Barney	19	M	Labourer	Great Britain	U. States	Hope & Esther	13 Oct 1829
Bridget	30	F	Servant	Great Britain	U. States	Hope & Esther	13 Oct 1829
C., Mrs.	16	M		Great Britain	United States	Isaac Hicks	6 Dec 1827
Catharine	30	F	Breeder	Ireland	New York	Phoenix	29 Apr 1826
Cathr.	20	F		U. States	U. States	United States	11 Sep 1828
Charles	3	M		Great Britain	United States	Isaac Hicks	6 Dec 1827
Daniel	10	M		Great Britain	United States	Isaac Hicks	6 Dec 1827
E., Miss	19	F		Great Britain	United States	Isaac Hicks	6 Dec 1827
Edward	19	M	Merchant	Great Britain	United States	Isaac Hicks	6 Dec 1827
Edward	20	M	Farmer	England	United States	Mary & Harriet	9 Mar 1829
Henry	23	M	Farmer	Ireland	United States	Justina	5 Aug 1823
Jn.	32	M	Farmer	Ireland	New York	Phoenix	29 Apr 1826
John	12	M		Gt. Britain	U. States	Panthea	21 Jul 1825
John	24	M	Merchant	Great Britain	United States	Isaac Hicks	6 Dec 1827
Joseph	19	M	Merchant	Great Britain	United States	Isaac Hicks	6 Dec 1827
Judith	6	F	Child	Ireland	New York	Phoenix	29 Apr 1826
Martha	45	F		Gt. Britain	U. States	Panthea	21 Jul 1825
Mary Ann	15	F		Gt. Britain	U. States	Panthea	21 Jul 1825
Michael	4	M	Child	Ireland	New York	Phoenix	29 Apr 1826
Patrick	19	M	Papermaker	Ireland	United States	Meteor	19 Aug 1829
Patrick	27	M	Farmer	Ireland	United States	Abigail	25 Jun 1822
Robt.	14	M		Gt. Britain	U. States	Panthea	21 Jul 1825
Robt.	45	M	Merchant	Gt. Britain	U. States	Panthea	21 Jul 1825
S., Miss	14	F		Great Britain	United States	Isaac Hicks	6 Dec 1827
Susana	50	F		U. States	U. States	United States	11 Sep 1828
Timothy	1	M	Child	Ireland	New York	Phoenix	29 Apr 1826
W.	51	M	Merchant	Great Britain	United States	Isaac Hicks	6 Dec 1827
Wm., Junr.	17	M		Great Britain	United States	Isaac Hicks	6 Dec 1827
Wrs.[Mrs.?]	45	F		Great Britain	United States	Isaac Hicks	6 Dec 1827
DWYNE, Mag.	18	F				Lady of the Lake	23 Aug 1828

*left ship

NAMES OF PASSENGERS	A G E	S E X	OCCUPATIONS	COUNTRY TO WHICH THEY BELONG	COUNTRY THEY INTEND TO INHABIT	SHIPS/DATES OF ARRIVAL	
DWYNE (cont'd)							
Mary	26	F				Lady of the Lake	23 Aug 1828
*left ship							
T.	27	M				Lady of the Lake	23 Aug 1828
*left ship							
DWYRE, James	22	M	Labourer	Ireland	Philadelphia	Curler	7 Jul 1827
Peggy	34	F	None	Ireland	United States	Aurelia	7 Jun 1826
DYCKE, Sam. D.	16	M		N. York	U. States	Indian Queen	18 Feb 1825
DYDAL, John	24	M	Weaver	Ireland	Und. Stts of Amer	Alexander Mansfield	18 Aug 1826
DYELL, Maxwell	29	F	Servant	Scotland		Amity	31 Jan 1822
DYER, David	23		Carpenter	Cam...inshire, South Wales/ London	Susquehannah P	Venus	12 Apr 1821
Dinah	43	F	None	England	United States	London	21 May 1828
Eliza	20	F	None	England	United States	London	21 May 1828
H.	22	M	Mechanic	France	U. States	Harriet	3 Sep 1823
John	33	M	Mercht.	England	U.S. America	Cortes	19 May 1826
Mary Ann	10	F	None	England	United States	London	21 May 1828
DYETT, M.	28	M	Merchant	W. Indies	U. States	Elias Burger	12 Sep 1822
DYKE, John	25	M	Carpenter	Bristol	New York	Cosmo	25 Sep 1827
DYKEMAN, George	14	M	Family	United States	Lower Canada	New Packet	15 Nov 1828
Jacob	11	M	Family	United States	Lower Canada	New Packet	15 Nov 1828
Rebecca	17	F	Family	United States	Lower Canada	New Packet	15 Nov 1828
Sarah	6	F	Family	United States	Lower Canada	New Packet	15 Nov 1828
Statira	42	F	Wife	United States	Lower Canada	New Packet	15 Nov 1828
William	8	M	Family	United States	Lower Canada	New Packet	15 Nov 1828
DYKER, M.	65	M	Merchant	U. States	U. States	Planter	17 Jul 1826
DYKES, Alexander	5	M	None	Great Britain	United States	Hamilton	21 Nov 1826
Alfred	2	M	None	Great Britain	United States	Hamilton	21 Nov 1826
Ann	11	F	None	Great Britain	United States	Hamilton	21 Nov 1826
Diannah	45	F	None	Great Britain	United States	Hamilton	21 Nov 1826
Isabella	40	F	None	Great Britain	United States	Courier	26 Jun 1827
John	19	M	Manufacturer	Great Britain	United States	Hamilton	21 Nov 1826
John	30 6/12	M	Weaver	G. Britain	United States	Dutchess of Portland	30 Oct 1826
Joseph	9	M	None	Great Britain	United States	Hamilton	21 Nov 1826
Joseph	41	M	Manufacturer	Great Britain	United States	Hamilton	21 Nov 1826
Mary Ann	13	F	None	Great Britain	United States	Hamilton	21 Nov 1826
Robert	24	M	Weaver	Scotland	United States	Camillus	9 May 1827
Samuel	16	M	Manufacturer	Great Britain	United States	Hamilton	21 Nov 1826
Thomas	17	M		Holland	United States	Ocean	10 Sep 1823
DYLON, Allen	1	M	None	Great Britain	United States	William Dawson	18 Jun 1827
Ann	24	F	None	Great Britain	United States	William Dawson	18 Jun 1827
John	27	M	...	Great Britain	United States	William Dawson	18 Jun 1827
DYMAK, Saml.	30 4/12	M	Joiner	Gt. Britain	New York	Betsey	18 Apr 1822
DYNEAN, William	31	M	Farmer	Ireland	America	William	21 May 1825
DYNES, Willm.	30	M	Laborer	Ireland	United States	Trio	13 Jun 1827
DYOIS, Thos.	20	M	Laborer	Ireland	America	Parrington	9 Jun 1827
DYRE, Katura	26	F		England	U.S.	Maria Caroline	12 Jul 1820
Levi	24	M	Mechanick	England	U.S.	Maria Caroline	12 Jul 1820
DYSAN, Geo.	22	M	Clothier	Huddlespits	Huddlespits	Howard Douglass	11 May 1827
DYSON, Ann	6	F	None	Great Britain	United States	William Dawson	18 Jun 1827
Ann	40	F	None	Great Britain	United States	William Dawson	18 Jun 1827
Chls.	6	M		G. Brittain	U. States	York	10 Dec 1825
D. S.	26	M	Merchant	U. States	U. States	Birmingham	11 Oct 1828
Dunbar	18	M	Merchant	Scotland	United States	Ann	22 Dec 1821
George	17	M	Clothier	Great Britain	United States	William Dawson	18 Jun 1827
George	26	M		America	America	Braganza	1 Dec 1824
James	21	M	Machinist	Great Britain	U.S. of America	Gratitude	3 Oct 1829
Jane	13	F	None	Great Britain	United States	William Dawson	18 Jun 1827
Jno.	9/12	M		Great Britain	United States	William Dawson	18 Jun 1827
John	8	M	None	Great Britain	United States	William Dawson	18 Jun 1827
John	29	M	Farmer	Great Britain	United States	Fame	26 May 1828
John	50	M	Cloth dresser	England	United States	Andes	2 Oct 1828
Joseph	22	M	Weaver	England	America U. States	La Grange	27 Sep 1826

NAMES OF PASSENGERS	AGE	SEX	OCCUPATIONS	COUNTRY TO WHICH THEY BELONG	COUNTRY THEY INTEND TO INHABIT	SHIPS/DATES OF ARRIVAL	
DYSON (cont'd)							
May F.	2	F		England	U. States	Hudson	8 Oct 1827
Ruth	15	F	None	Great Britain	United States	William Dawson	18 Jun 1827
Sarah	1	F	None	Great Britain	United States	William Dawson	18 Jun 1827
Sarah	29	F		England	U. States	Hudson	8 Oct 1827
Thomas	20	M	Laborer	Great Britain	United States	Samuel Wright	12 Oct 1829
Thomas	22	M	Steam Engineer	England	United States	Lunar	5 May 1828
Thos.	27	M	Joiner	Great Britain	U.S. America	Chili	7 Jul 1827
William	25	M	Weaver	Ireland	United States	Amelia	20 Aug 1829
Wm.	45	M	Mercht.	Rathsham, Sheffield, England	N. York	New Orleans	24 Aug 1827
E..., —, Mrs.	...	...	...	...	...	William Thompson	30 Sep 1824
EACOIT, R.	25	M	Labourer	England	United States	Alicia	9 May 1827
EADIE, John	19	M	Labourer	Scotland	U. States	Camillus	27 Jul 1825
John	45	M	Cordwainer	G. Britain	U. States	Panthia	23 Apr 1824
Robt.	15	M	Cordwainer	G. Britain	U. States	Panthia	23 Apr 1824
EAGAN, —, Mr.	55	F		Ireland	G. Britain	Venus	27 Jun 1821
Alice	22	F	Servant	Ireland	United States	Lord Wellington	14 Nov 1827
Edward	27	M	...	Ireland	United States	Wilson	22 Jun 1824
J. *died	60	M				Venus	27 Jun 1821
Jno.	11	M	boy Student	Denmark	U. States	Chase	24 Jul 1823
EAGER, B.	40		Farmer	Ireland	United States	Courier	16 May 1825
Bridget	24	F		Ireland	United States	Princess Charlotte	26 Apr 1827
Joel	22	M	Mechanic	N. York	U. States	St. Michaels	21 Apr 1824
M.	3		Farmer	Ireland	United States	Courier	16 May 1825
M.	20		Farmer	Ireland	United States	Courier	16 May 1825
M.	20		Farmer	Ireland	United States	Courier	16 May 1825
M.	20		Farmer	Ireland	United States	Courier	16 May 1825
Timothy	24	M	Stone Mason	Ireland	United States	Princess Charlotte	26 Apr 1827
EAGIN, Honor	22	F		Ireland	America	Plutarch	18 Jul 1826
John	18	M	Shoemaker	Ireland	America	Plutarch	18 Jul 1826
Patt	26	M	Shoemaker	Ireland	America	Plutarch	18 Jul 1826
EAGLE, Henry	23	M	Officer	U.S. America		Phoebe Ann	27 Dec 1825
EAGLES, Nelson	22	M	Farmer	G. Britain	Upper Canada	Perseverance	9 Jun 1827
EAGLESFIELD, William	44	M	Farmer	Great Britain	U. States	Ann Maria	26 Apr 1822
EAJOR, John	25	M	...	England	U.N. States	William Byrnes	23 Jul 1824
EAL, Eliza	64		Merchant	Halifax	U. States	Edwin	26 Sep 1828
EALER, A. G.	22	M	Doctor	U. States	England	Brown	23 Dec 1826
EALING, John	26	M	Farmer	Great Britain	U. States	Ann Maria	26 Apr 1822
EALY, Fris.	13	M	Boy	Ireland	N. York	Trusty	12 Sep 1828
EAMES, Cutter	27	M	Merchant	U. States	U. States	Jane	13 Sep 1828
John	21	M	Farmer	Great Britain	United States	Zodiac	29 Oct 1822
EAR...MANN, John	31	M	Servant	Switzerland	United States	Howard	11 Jun 1824
EARDEN, Francis	20	M	Sadler	Switzerland	United States	American	27 Aug 1827
EARKIN, E.	20	F	D. Maker	Ireland	N. York	Trusty	12 Sep 1828
EARL, Elizabeth	25	F	his daughter [J.]	St. John, N.B.	Canada	Henrietta	3 Jun 1825
Francis	24	F		Great Britain		Robert Fulton	9 Jul 1823
J.	50	M	Merchant	St. John, N.B.	Canada	Henrietta	3 Jun 1825
John	30	M	Labourer	Ireland	New York	America	1 Aug 1828
John	34	M	Merchant	Great Britain		Robert Fulton	9 Jul 1823
Polly	30	F	his daughter [J.]	St. John, N.B.	Canada	Henrietta	3 Jun 1825
Sally	23	F	his daughter [J.]	St. John, N.B.	Canada	Henrietta	3 Jun 1825
William	29		Merchant	England	United States	Florida	11 Mar 1829
EARLE, Dl.	25	M	Merchant	United States	United States	Argus	3 Oct 1825
Morgan P.	22	M	Merchant	United States	United States	Roman	17 Oct 1826
William	26	M	Blacksmith	England	England	Hazard	17 Jul 1822
EARLEY, Bridget	22	F	None	Great Britan	U. States	Ann Marria	6 Aug 1823
Devin	30	M	Labourer	Great Britan	U. States	Ann Marria	6 Aug 1823
Pat	22	M	Labourer	Ireland	N. York	Trusty	12 Sep 1828
Phillip	26	M	Labourer	Ireland	U.S. of America	Hamilton	18 Jul 1827
EARLY, Bridget	18	F		Gt. Britain		Dalhouse Castle	13 May 1828
Cath.	13	F		Ireland	America	Mary	29 May 1827
Catharine	20	F	...	Ireland	U. States	William	27 Jul 1824
Charles	20	M	Weaver	Great Britain	United States	Isaac Hicks	22 Aug 1828

NAMES OF PASSENGERS	AGE	SEX	OCCUPATIONS	COUNTRY TO WHICH THEY BELONG	COUNTRY THEY INTEND TO INHABIT	SHIPS/DATES OF ARRIVAL	
EARLY (cont'd)							
Patrick	19	M	Blacksmith	Gt. Britain		Dalhouse Castle	13 May 1828
Patrick	60	M	Farmer	Ireland	United States	Dublin Packet	13 Oct 1828
Rose	18	F		Gt. Britain		Dalhouse Castle	13 May 1828
William	19	M	Wever	Ireland	United States	Fabius	4 Jun 1828
EARNSHAW, Johnathan	26	M	Mechanic	England	Great Briton	Lafayette	3 Dec 1827
EARSHAW, George	23	M	S. Mason	G.B.	Philad.	Eliza Grant	29 Aug 1829
George	23	M	Stone Mason	Ireland		Eliza Grant	29 Aug 1829
EASLEY, Mary	22	F		England	United States	John Wells	22 May 1826
EASSON, —, Mr.	28	M	Planter	Jamaica	Jamaica	Huntress	15 Oct 1823
—, Mrs.	28	F		Jamaica	Jamaica	Huntress	15 Oct 1823
Alexr.	47	M	Labourer	G. Britain	U. States	Hynd	12 Jul 1820
EASTAFF, F.	21	M	Sailor	America	U. States	Hiram	17 Jun 1826
EASTARD, John	31	M	Labourer	G. Britain	U. States	Mary & Harriot	8 Sep 1828
EASTBROOK, —, Mrs.	34	F		American	U. States	Shallet	21 Apr 1821
D.	2	M		England	U. States	Shallet	21 Apr 1821
J.	34	M	Naval Officer	England	U. States	Shallet	21 Apr 1821
EASTBURN,						South Carolina	
Charlotte, Mrs.	40	F	Lady	United States	United States	Packet	15 Jan 1820
Hollis	48	M	Merchant	England	United States	Cincinnatus	21 Nov 1821
James	53	M	Mercht.	United States	United States	Manchester	17 Aug 1825
James	54	M	Merchant	United States	New York	Britannia	3 Nov 1827
Menton, Mr.	19	M	Gentleman	United States	United States	South Carolina	
						Packet	15 Jan 1820
EASTBURNE, James, Mr.	53	M	Merchant	United States	U.S.	Pacific	22 May 1826
Wallace	49	M		G. Brittain	U. States	Cincinnatus	2 Oct 1822
EASTMAN, Hester	7	F		England	U.S.A.	Hudson	21 Aug 1829
Hester	34	F		England	U.S.A.	Hudson	21 Aug 1829
Louisa	10	F		England	U.S.A.	Hudson	21 Aug 1829
Lucina	2	F		England	U.S.A.	Hudson	21 Aug 1829
Mary	12	F		England	U.S.A.	Hudson	21 Aug 1829
EASTMOND, John P.	26	M	Farmer	Great Brittan	United States	Cambria	11 Feb 1829
EASTON, An	15	F	None	Ireland	United States	Catharine	22 Jul 1825
An	45	F	Spinster	Ireland	United States	Catharine	22 Jul 1825
C.	23	M	Merchant	America	United States	South Carolina	14 Aug 1823
C.	25	M	Gentleman	N. York	U. States	Chase	5 Jul 1825
Catharine	25	F	Spinster	Ireland	United States	Catharine	22 Jul 1825
Collin	1 6/12	M		St. Croix	U. States	Chase	5 Jul 1825
E.	33	F		Nantucket	U. States	Favorite	13 Jun 1821
Hamilton	13	M	None	Ireland	United States	Catharine	22 Jul 1825
James	35	M	Farmer	Ireland	United States	Catharine	22 Jul 1825
James	50		Weaver	Huddersfield, England	Great Britain	Franklin	22 Jun 1827
John	2	M	None	Ireland	United States	Catharine	22 Jul 1825
John	45	M	Farmer	Ireland	United States	Catharine	22 Jul 1825
John, Jr.	25	M	cabinet maker	Ireland	United States	Catharine	22 Jul 1825
Joseph	60	M		Great Brittain	United States	Sarah Ralston	27 Jan 1827
Julia	19	F	Lady	St. Croix	U. States	Chase	5 Jul 1825
Margaret	4	F	None	Ireland	United States	Catharine	22 Jul 1825
Margaret	18	F	Spinster	Ireland	United States	Catharine	22 Jul 1825
Maria	24	F	Servant	Great Britian	United States	Diamond	8 Nov 1824
Rebecca	17	F	None	Ireland	United States	Catharine	22 Jul 1825
Robert	23	M	Farmer	Ireland	United States	Catharine	22 Jul 1825
Sally	4	F		St. Croix	U. States	Chase	5 Jul 1825
EASTWOOD, John	22	M	Mechanic	England	Great Briton	Lafayette	3 Dec 1827
EATEN, F.	25	M	Labourer	Ireland	United States	Combine	4 Jun 1825
EATING, Ann	25	F	Farmer	Great Britain	United States	Zodiac	29 Oct 1822
John	3	M	Farmer	Great Britain	United States	Zodiac	29 Oct 1822
EATON, Charles J. M.	20	M	Merchant	U. States	U. States	France	14 Mar 1828
Chs. T. M.	18	M	Mercht.	United States	United States	Manchester	17 Aug 1825
George	7 7/12	F		England	America	Britannia	22 Jul 1829
J. S. L.	26	M	Merchant	England	America	Atlantic	8 May 1828
James B.	44 2/12	M	Silversmith	United States	United States	London	6 Feb 1829
Louisa	3	F		England	America	Britannia	22 Jul 1829
*Dead							
Mary	29	F		England	America	Britannia	22 Jul 1829
Mary Ann	5	F		England	America	Britannia	22 Jul 1829
*Dead							
Moses	33		Gentleman	United States	United States	Maria Ann	18 May 1825

370

NAMES OF PASSENGERS	AGE	SEX	OCCUPATIONS	COUNTRY TO WHICH THEY BELONG	COUNTRY THEY INTEND TO INHABIT	SHIPS/DATES OF ARRIVAL	
EATON (cont'd)							
Ol...	40	M	Mechanic	Great Britian	United States	Andes	19 Aug 1829
Peter	27	M	Laborer	England	United States	Danube	13 Jul 1827
Sarah	5/12	F		England	America	Britannia	22 Jul 1829
William	34	M	Farmer	England	America	Britannia	22 Jul 1829
EAVES, Jno.	20	M	Labourer	England	United States	Essex	23 May 1828
EAVLY, Thomas	30	M	Blacksmith	Ireland	New York	Potomac	7 Aug 1827
EAYRS, Willm.		M	Merchant	U.S.A.	U.S.A.	Hope	6 Jun 1823
EBARLER, Georg	4	M		Switzerland	United States	Elizabeth	27 Jul 1824
Georg	35	M	Shoemaker	Switzerland	United States	Elizabeth	27 Jul 1824
Gottbed	2	M		Switzerland	United States	Elizabeth	27 Jul 1824
Jacob	5	M		Switzerland	United States	Elizabeth	27 Jul 1824
Magdalina	31	F		Switzerland	United States	Elizabeth	27 Jul 1824
EBBEANEY, John	30	M	Labourer	Ireland	United States	William & George	14 May 1828
EBBIT, Humphry	36	M	Shoe Maker	Irereland	America	Carolina Ann	20 Jun 1825
EBELE, George	35	M	Merchant	England	United States	Ann Maria	23 Oct 1820
EBERHAD, Anna	21	F	Weaver	Berne	U.S. America	Superior	18 Jun 1825
Jacob	5	M	Weaver	Berne	U.S. America	Superior	18 Jun 1825
Madeline	7	F	Weaver	Berne	U.S. America	Superior	18 Jun 1825
Madeline	47	F	Weaver	Berne	U.S. America	Superior	18 Jun 1825
Maria	18	F	Weaver	Berne	U.S. America	Superior	18 Jun 1825
Nicolas	17	M	Weaver	Berne	U.S. America	Superior	18 Jun 1825
Nicolas	45	M	Weaver	Berne	U.S. America	Superior	18 Jun 1825
EBERHAIKIN, William D.	26	M				Reuben & Eliza	21 Aug 1820
EBERHARD, Jeane	13	F	Weaver	Berne	U.S. America	Superior	18 Jun 1825
EBERHART, Charles	3	M		Native of Switzerland	United States	Canaris	30 Jun 1827
Elizabeth	31	F		Native of Switzerland	United States	Canaris	30 Jun 1827
Frank C.	28	M	Farmer	Native of Switzerland	United States	Canaris	30 Jun 1827
EBERHE, Charles S.	42	M	Merchant	U. States	U. States	Splendid	8 Jan 1829
EBERLE, Christian	24	M	Butcher	Switzerland	U. States	Hewes	30 Oct 1829
G.	18	M	Tailor	Germany	America	Falcon	28 Aug 1828
J.	18	M	Shoemaker	Germany	America	Falcon	28 Aug 1828
Rosina	23	F	Wife	Switzerland	U. States	Hewes	30 Oct 1829
EBERSOLD, Anna	4	F	Framer	Switserland	Ohio	Danube	20 Jul 1826
Christian	2	M	Framer	Switserland	Ohio	Danube	20 Jul 1826
Magdelena	22	F	Framer	Switserland	Ohio	Danube	20 Jul 1826
St. John	30	M	Framer	Switserland	Ohio	Danube	20 Jul 1826
EBITT, George	22	M	Clerk	Great Britain	United States	Florida	10 Dec 1823
EBRENTZ, Louis			Taylor	France	U.S.	Sully	26 Oct 1829
EBRIENT, —	4	F		U. States	U. States	Peter Remsen	30 Jun 1828
D.	12	F		U. States	U. States	Peter Remsen	30 Jun 1828
EBY, Edwin A.	22	M	Doctor	U. States	U. States	Edwin	10 Feb 1829
EBZRA, Wm., Mr.	21	M	Farmer	England	U. States	Acasta	12 May 1825
ECCLES, Ann Maria	20		Ladies and Gentlemen	United States	United States	Corinthian	7 Jul 1829
James	50		Ladies and Gentlemen	United States	United States	Corinthian	7 Jul 1829
John	7	M		England	United States	Dalhouse Castle	26 Dec 1827
Mary	32	F		England	United States	Dalhouse Castle	26 Dec 1827
Robert	5	M		England	United States	Dalhouse Castle	26 Dec 1827
Samuel	22 2/12	M	Farmer	England	United States	Young Phoenix	26 Jul 1824
Thomas	4	M		England	United States	Dalhouse Castle	26 Dec 1827
ECELESTON, —, Abbé	26	M	Priest	U.S.	U.S.	Edward Quesnel	31 Jul 1827
Edwd.	33	M	Merchant	Great Britain	United States	Pacific	11 Mar 1829
ECFORD, Walter	27	M	Spiner	Great Britain	United States	Courier	26 Jun 1827
ECH...IRE, Hoza Antonio, Mr.	39	M	Officer Army	Mexico	New York	Leonidas	22 Jan 1829
ECHEGURIA, J. N.	26	M	Merchant	Baltimore	U. States	Eclipse	10 Jun 1823
ECHELMIN, Juan	13	M	Seaman	Carracas	U. States	Velocipede	24 May 1824
ECHENEGIE, Jose	37	M	Merchant	S. America	Spain	Galatea	20 Jul 1829
ECHENSCHVILLER, Joseph	48	M	...	...	Ohio	Frances Henrietta	25 Aug 1825
ECHESUNA, M.	39	F		So. America	U. States	Eclipse	10 Jun 1823
ECKART, Isaac Roberts	21	M	Gentn.	Gt. Brittain	Canada	York	6 Dec 1826

NAMES OF PASSENGERS	AGE	SEX	OCCUPATIONS	COUNTRY TO WHICH THEY BELONG	COUNTRY THEY INTEND TO INHABIT	SHIPS/DATES OF ARRIVAL	
ECKENSTEIN, J. R.	44	M	Merchant	Switzerland	U. States	Little William	16 Jun 1821
ECKFARD, John H.	22	M	Merchant	United States	United States	Pacific	7 May 1827
ECKLER, Margret	38	F		Germany	Cincinatti	Isabella	15 Sep 1828
Marian	1	F		Germany	Cincinatti	Isabella	15 Sep 1828
Philip	6	M		Germany	Cincinatti	Isabella	15 Sep 1828
Sebastian	5	M		Germany	Cincinatti	Isabella	15 Sep 1828
Silvestre	33	M	Farmer	Germany	Cincinatti	Isabella	15 Sep 1828
Simon	3	M		Germany	Cincinatti	Isabella	15 Sep 1828
ECKLES, G. E.	24	M	Weaver	Great Britain	United States	Isaac Hicks	6 Dec 1827
ECKSTEIN, John F. J.	35	M	Farmer	Coburg	Ohio	Caesar	24 Aug 1829
John Jacob	9	M	Farmer	Coburg	Ohio	Caesar	24 Aug 1829
Maria Barbara	40	F	Farmer	Coburg	Ohio	Caesar	24 Aug 1829
ED...ARDS, Geo.	29	M	Coach Maker	G. Britain	U. States	St. George	7 Jun 1828
EDANGHUE, John		M	Merchant	Ireland	United States	Oxford	14 Aug 1828
EDDERSHAW, Eliz.	47	M	Planter	England	U. States	Electra	7 Jul 1828
Thos.	61	M		England	U. States	Electra	7 Jul 1828
Wellington	17	M	Labourer	England	U. States	Electra	7 Jul 1828
EDDES, James	28	M	Paper Maker	England	United States	Brighton	11 Mar 1825
EDDY, B.	48	M	Merchant	U.S.	U.S.	Jacob	23 Mar 1826
Henry	25	M	Labourer	England	U. States	Emulous	22 Aug 1828
Jennett	8	F		G. Britain	U. States	Eliza	9 May 1827
Jennett	34	F		G. Britain	U. States	Eliza	9 May 1827
Joseph	30	M	Merchant	England	England	Virginia	26 May 1828
Margeret	9/12	F		G. Britain	U. States	Eliza	9 May 1827
Minigo	45	M	Carpenter	G. Britain	U. States	Eliza	9 May 1827
Minigo, Jr.	3	M		G. Britain	U. States	Eliza	9 May 1827
Patrick	27	M	Stone Cutter	Ireland	United States	Trio	31 Oct 1827
Robert	24	M	Collier	Scotland	United States	Camillus	27 Oct 1829
Saml.	21	M	Mechanic	England	United States	Concordia	25 Aug 1827
EDELINS, J. B.	25	M	Merchant	France	U. States	Huntress	30 Jun 1824
EDEN, Edward	7	M	Labourer	Ireland	United States	Meteor	26 Jun 1827
EDES, B., Mrs.	38 7/12	F		United States	United States	Henry	10 Feb 1825
Catharine	19	F		America	U. States	Mogul	20 Jul 1825
H., Miss	10 8/12	F		United States	United States	Henry	10 Feb 1825
S. B.	60	M	Mariner	U. States	U. States	Don Quixote	15 Apr 1825
Saml., Capt.	40	M		U.S.		Henri IV	17 May 1828
EDEY, Frere	40	M	Merchant	Barbados	Supposition is he will return	Superb	7 Jul 1823
EDGAN, John J.	27	M	Musician	G. Britain	U. States	John Jay	17 Sep 1828
EDGAR, A.	32	M	Labourer	Great Brittan	U. States	British King	4 Apr 1827
Eliza	44	F				Lady of the Lake	23 Aug 1828
F...	34	M	Nerchant	New Jersey	United States	Martha	22 Jul 1820
H. M.	22	F	None	New Jersey	United States	Martha	22 Jul 1820
Jas.	50	M				Lady of the Lake	23 Aug 1828
Jo	20	M				Lady of the Lake	23 Aug 1828
*left ship							
Robert	26	M	Farmer	Ireland	America	Superior	12 Jun 1824
Thomas	21	M				Lady of the Lake	23 Aug 1828
EDGE, Ann	5	F		England	Pittsburg	Curler	7 Jul 1827
James	2	M		England	Pittsburg	Curler	7 Jul 1827
John	3	M		England	Pittsburg	Curler	7 Jul 1827
Martha	26	F		England	Pittsburg	Curler	7 Jul 1827
Richard	22	M	Weaver	England	United States	Siroc	31 Oct 1829
Thomas	26	M	Engineer	England	Pittsburg	Curler	7 Jul 1827
EDGECOMBE, Charlotte	24	F	Servant	England	Halifax	Stephania	28 Jul 1823
EDGECUMBE, Caroline	27	F	None	England	New York	Brighton	20 Aug 1825
Henry	1	M	None	England	New York	Brighton	20 Aug 1825
Henry	25	M	Carpenter	England	New York	Brighton	20 Aug 1825
EDGELAND, John	26	M	Book Binder	Great Britain	United States	Milton	21 Mar 1828
EDGERLY, John	54 4/12	M	Tavernkeeper	United States	New York	Venus	8 Sep 1820
Thomas	16	M	Grocer	G. Britain	U. States	James Monroe	18 Apr 1821
EDGERTON, Hy.	40	M	Carpenter	U. States	U. States	Lady Hunter	18 Jul 1825
EDGEWORTH, Lloyd E., Mr.	26	M	None	...	...	Hector	11 May 1821

NAMES OF PASSENGERS	AGE	SEX	OCCUPATIONS	COUNTRY TO WHICH THEY BELONG	COUNTRY THEY INTEND TO INHABIT	SHIPS/DATES OF ARRIVAL	
EDME, Durand	34	M	Doctor	France	France	Charlotte Corday	8 Nov 1823
EDMENSTEN, Jane	23		Spinster	Ireland	United States	Fabius	18 Mar 1829
EDMESTON, Robt.	25		Gentn.	England	U. States	New York	30 Oct 1827
EDMINSTON, Edward	36	M	Mason	Gt. Britain	United States	Meteor	19 Aug 1829
Margaret	6	F		Gt. Britain	United States	Meteor	19 Aug 1829
Mary	25	F	Labourer	Ireland	United States	Meteor	26 Jun 1827
Mary	38	F		Gt. Britain	United States	Meteor	19 Aug 1829
Robert	12	M		Gt. Britain	United States	Meteor	19 Aug 1829
Robert	25	M	Labourer	Ireland	United States	Meteor	26 Jun 1827
Samuel	21	M	Mason	Gt. Britain	United States	Meteor	19 Aug 1829
William	9	M		Gt. Britain	United States	Meteor	19 Aug 1829
EDMISTON, John	1	M	Farmer, Labourer or Spinster	Ireland	U. States	Meteor	4 Oct 1827
Margret	28	F	Farmer, Labourer or Spinster	Ireland	U. States	Meteor	4 Oct 1827
William	4	M	Farmer, Labourer or Spinster	Ireland	U. States	Meteor	4 Oct 1827
EDMISTONE, Robt.	23	M	Gent.	Gt. Britain	U.S. America	Columbia	3 Apr 1826
EDMITON, James	26	M	Labourer	Ireland	United States	Hope	12 Jun 1828
John	20	M	Labourer	Ireland	United States	Hope	12 Jun 1828
EDMOND, James	26	M	Farmer	Scotland	U.S.	Curler	19 Jul 1828
EDMONDS, Arthur	1					Xenophon	25 Jul 1826
Harriet	22					Xenophon	25 Jul 1826
Robert	51	M	Builder	Ireland	New York	Louisa	20 Jul 1826
Thomas	23		Farmer	England	S. New York	Xenophon	25 Jul 1826
William	25	M	Clerk	England	United States	Cosmo	26 Aug 1829
EDMONDSON, Alice	27	F	None	Great Britain	U. States	Balance	19 Jun 1824
Ann	3	F	None	Great Britain	U. States	Balance	19 Jun 1824
John	5	M	None	Great Britain	U. States	Balance	19 Jun 1824
John	31	M	Farmer	Great Britain	U. States	Balance	19 Jun 1824
Wm.	1	M	None	Great Britain	U. States	Balance	19 Jun 1824
EDMONSTON, A.	41	M	Gentleman	U.N. States	U. States	Washington	7 Jul 1824
EDMONSTONE, William	25	M		Canada	Canada	Britannia	22 Jul 1829
EDMSTON, Robt.	35		Laboring Class		United States	Atlantic	2 Apr 1827
EDMUND, Chas.	32	M	Lieut. B. Navy	Great Brittain	Great Brittain	Tontine	25 Jan 1827
H.	25	M	Merchant	U. States	U. States	Rubicon	16 Feb 1827
Wm.	18	M	Farmer	England	U. States	Hercules	6 Jul 1827
EDMUNDS, C.	23	M	Merchant	England	United States	Brilliant	24 Sep 1827
Eliza	19	F		United States	United States	Mazzinghi	31 Mar 1826
Jas., Mr.	15	M	boot Maker	England	New York	Cortes	23 Nov 1827
John	23	M	Farmer	Great Britain	U.S. America	Prince Madoc	24 Sep 1821
Lydia	14	F		United States	United States	Mazzinghi	31 Mar 1826
Margaret, Mrs.	25	F	Farmer	England	New York	Cortes	23 Nov 1827
EDMUNDSON, Mary	20	F	Wife [of Robert]	England	America	Ann	23 Jul 1821
Robert	20	M	Child [of Robert]	England	America	Ann	23 Jul 1821
Robert	24	M	Farmer	England	America	Ann	23 Jul 1821
EDMUNSTON, E.	22	M	Labourer	G. Britain	U. States	London	23 Sep 1828
Robt., Mr.	35	M	Mercht.	England	United States	Manchester	16 Dec 1828
EDNEY, Ann	27	F		England	U. States	Hudson	8 Oct 1827
Jno.	18	M		England	U. States	Hudson	8 Oct 1827
Wm.	50	M	Carpenter	England	U. States	Hudson	8 Oct 1827
EDRIDGE, Elizh., Miss	17			London	England	London	13 Dec 1822
EDSON, Wm. P. *Dead	22	M	Merchant	U. States	U. States	Leontine	10 Jul 1826
EDWARD, Anderew	35	M	Labourer	Ireland	N. York	Trusty	12 Sep 1828
David	23	M	Farmer	Britain	U. States	Fame	3 Jun 1828
Edward	23	M	Farmer	Great Britain	United States	John Jay	8 May 1828
Eliza	30	F		Great Britain	United States	Aspasia	16 Jul 1828
James	19	M	Labourer	Ireland	U. States	Loire	6 Dec 1827
John H. C.	25	M	Planter	Gt. Britain	United States	Eagle	26 Jul 1828
W.	22	M	Mechanic	U. States	U. States	Hannah & Rebecca	12 Jun 1824
EDWARDS, —, Mr.	35	M	Waiter	England	U.S.A.	Bayard	25 Aug 1829
—, Mrs.	36	F	Lady	England	U.S.A.	Bayard	25 Aug 1829
...	... 3/12	M		England	America, U.S.	Illinois	3 Jun 1822
...	19	M	Farmer			Manhattan	25 Dec 1820
...	21	F	Farmer			Manhattan	25 Dec 1820
...	22	M	Farmer			Manhattan	25 Dec 1820

NAMES OF PASSENGERS	A G E	S E X	OCCUPATIONS	COUNTRY TO WHICH THEY BELONG	COUNTRY THEY INTEND TO INHABIT	SHIPS/DATES OF ARRIVAL	
EDWARDS (cont'd)							
...	75	F	Farmer			Manhattan	25 Dec 1820
Ageness	16	F		England	America	Mary Lord	26 Oct 1829
Alfred P.	42	M	Merchant	New York	U. States	Sultana	20 Sep 1824
Ann	12	F		England	America	Plato	31 Oct 1829
Ann	18	F	Farmer	Great Britian	U. States	Hudson	12 Mar 1824
Anne Jane	7	F		Great Britain	United States	Aspasia	16 Jul 1828
C.	4	F				Lady of the Lake	23 Aug 1828
*left ship							
C. W.	27	M	Merchant	Hamburgh	England	Rebecca	2 May 1825
Carlina	13	F	Farmer	Great Britian	U. States	Hudson	12 Mar 1824
Catharine	1 6/12		Child	England	United States	Delta	24 Oct 1829
Catharine	28	F	his Wife [Francis]	England	United States	Delta	24 Oct 1829
Charles	2	M		Great Britain	United States	Aspasia	16 Jul 1828
Charles	13	M		England	America	Plato	31 Oct 1829
Charles	25	M	Forgeman	Great Britain	United States	Isaac Hicks	10 Jul 1827
Crispin	26	M	Shoemaker	Camling township		Colossus	27 Mar 1828
David	5		Farmer	Wales	Great Britain	Oglethorpe	25 Aug 1825
David	42		Labourer	G. Britian	G. Britian	Dewitt Clinton	26 Aug 1825
Edward	24	M	None	United States	U. States	Hudson	10 Nov 1825
Edwards	6/12	M		England	America	Plato	31 Oct 1829
Eliza	5	F		England	America	Plato	31 Oct 1829
Elizabeth	35		Farmer	Wales	Great Britain	Oglethorpe	25 Aug 1825
Elizabeth	47	F	Farmer	Great Britian	U. States	Hudson	12 Mar 1824
Ellen	8	F	Farmer	Great Britian	U. States	Hudson	12 Mar 1824
Ewd.	21	M		England	United States	Acasta	25 Sep 1827
Francis	45	F	Manufacturer	England	United States	Delta	24 Oct 1829
Frederick	30	M	Merchant	Great Britain	United States	Mary & Harriet	3 Jul 1829
Frederick, Mr.	22	M	Merchant	England	United States	Dublin Packet	23 May 1828
G.	25	M				Lady of the Lake	23 Aug 1828
*left ship							
Geo.	4	M		G. Britain	U. States	St. George	7 Jun 1828
George	19	M	Bricklayer	England	America	Mary Lord	26 Oct 1829
H.	29		Merchant	U.S.A.		Edward Bonnaffe	17 Mar 1828
Henry	8	M		England	America	Plato	31 Oct 1829
Henry	12	M	Bricklayer	England	America	Mary Lord	26 Oct 1829
Hy.	25	M	Carpenter	G. Britain	U. States	Cosmo	15 May 1827
James	10	M	Farmer	Great Britian	U. States	Hudson	12 Mar 1824
James	10	M		England	America	Plato	31 Oct 1829
James	22	M	Cloth Dresser	England	United States	Siroc	31 Oct 1829
James	24	M	Shoemaker	Great Britain	U.S. America	Mentor	22 Jul 1823
James	45	M	Farmer	Great Britian	U. States	Hudson	12 Mar 1824
James, Mr.	32	M	Gentn.	England	American	Acasta	3 Apr 1826
Jane	...6 7/12	F		England	America, U.S.	Illinois	3 Jun 1822
Jane	3		Farmer	Wales	Great Britain	Oglethorpe	25 Aug 1825
Jane	24	F				Lady of the Lake	23 Aug 1828
*left ship							
Jas.	40		Farmer	England	England	Gulnard	24 Mar 1825
Jno. George	26	M	Gentleman	Great Britain	England	York	7 Aug 1828
Jno. L.	2/365	M	None	Gt. Britan	U. States	Earl of Liverpool	12 Apr 1825
John	... 8/12	M	Farmer	England	America, U.S.	Illinois	3 Jun 1822
John	1 4/12	M	Fringe Maker	Great Briton	Boston	Brighton	12 Jun 1826
John	7	M		Great Britain	United States	Saml. Wight	6 Sep 1827
John	9	M		England	America	Mary Lord	26 Oct 1829
John	18	M	Farmer	Great Britain	United States	Mary Howland	19 Jul 1827
John	24	M	Servant	United States	United States	Planter	26 Jul 1822
John	24	M	Farmer	England	United States	Jubilee	13 Jul 1829
John	25	M	Shoe Maker	Wales	New York	Angelica	18 Aug 1823
John	26	M	Mechanic	G.B.	G.B.	George Canning	20 Jan 1829
John	30		Cloth Weaver	Somerset	...	Hudson	14 Jun 1827
John	37	M	Bricklayer	England	America	Mary Lord	26 Oct 1829
John	38	M	Tailor	England	America	Plato	31 Oct 1829
John, Dr.	35	M	Surgeon	England	United States	Trident	18 Jul 1827

NAMES OF PASSENGERS	AGE	SEX	OCCUPATIONS	COUNTRY TO WHICH THEY BELONG	COUNTRY THEY INTEND TO INHABIT	SHIPS/DATES OF ARRIVAL	
EDWARDS (cont'd)							
John, Mr.	34	M	Surgeon	England	England	Florida	26 Sep 1826
Jos.	27	M	Carpenter	G. Britain	U. States	Cosmo	15 May 1827
Joseph	... 4/12	M		England	America, U.S.	Illinois	3 Jun 1822
Joseph	23	M	Cotton Spinner	England	United States	Mary & Harriet	9 Mar 1829
M., Mrs.	33	F	None	Gt. Britan	U. States	Earl of Liverpool	12 Apr 1825
Martha	5	F	Farmer	Great Britian	U. States	Hudson	12 Mar 1824
Martin	40	M	Labourer	G. Britain	U. States	Mary & Harriot	8 Sep 1828
Mary	... 4/12	F		England	America, U.S.	Illinois	3 Jun 1822
Mary	7		Farmer	Wales	Great Britain	Oglethorpe	25 Aug 1825
Mary	25	F	Fringe Maker	Great Briton	Boston	Brighton	12 Jun 1826
Mary	33	F		England	America	Plato	31 Oct 1829
Mary	45	F		Great Britain	United States	Saml. Wight	6 Sep 1827
Mary	47 6/12	F		England	America, U.S.	Illinois	3 Jun 1822
Mary, Miss	20	F	Lady	England	American	Acasta	3 Apr 1826
Mary Ann	3	F		England	America	Plato	31 Oct 1829
N.	40	M	Mariner	U. States	U. States	Atlas	24 Jun 1828
Nathan	35	M	Cooper	America, Connecticut	America	William	16 Apr 1823
Phobe, (Lady's Maid)	26	F		England	Canada	Cortes	23 Nov 1827
R.	25	M	Ship Master	U. States	U. States	Dromo	28 Feb 1829
R. D.	32	M	Farmer	Scotland	U. States	Rampart	16 Apr 1825
Rees	25	M	Linnen draper	Wales	New York	Curler	7 Jul 1827
Richd.	46	M	Farmer			Manhattan	25 Dec 1820
S.	2	F				Lady of the Lake	23 Aug 1828
*left ship							
Samuel	36	M	Milk Man	England	United States	Siroc	31 Oct 1829
Sarah	40	F		England	America	Mary Lord	26 Oct 1829
Stephen, Mr.	28	M	Gentn.	England	American	Acasta	3 Apr 1826
Thomas	14	M	Bricklayer	England	America	Mary Lord	26 Oct 1829
Thomas	25	M	Whever	England	America	Mary Lord	26 Oct 1829
Thomas	30	M	Merchant	England	U. States	William Thompson	17 Dec 1827
Thomas	36 7/12	M	Farmer	England	America, U.S.	Illinois	3 Jun 1822
Thomas	39	M	Tailor	England	England	William Thompson	19 Aug 1829
Thomas	55	M	Minister	England	United States	Bolivar	15 Jun 1826
Thomas	57 6/12	M	Farmer	England	America, U.S.	Illinois	3 Jun 1822
Thos.	25	M	Servant	England	U. States	Sarah Thornton	13 Sep 1828
Thos.	30	M	Butcher	England	United States	St. John	5 Oct 1829
Thos., Jr.	20	M	Surgeon	England	United States	Bolivar	15 Jun 1826
W.	5	M		Great Britain	United States	Saml. Wight	6 Sep 1827
W.	9		Farmer	Wales	Great Britain	Oglethorpe	25 Aug 1825
William	... 6/12	M		England	America, U.S.	Illinois	3 Jun 1822
William	3 6/12	M	Fringe Maker	Great Briton	Boston	Brighton	12 Jun 1826
William	6	M		England	America	Mary Lord	26 Oct 1829
William	24	M	Shoemaker	G. Britain	New York	Brighton	26 Mar 1827
William	27	M	Fringe Maker	Great Briton	Boston	Brighton	12 Jun 1826
William	40	M	Farmer	Britain	U. States	Fame	3 Jun 1828
Wm.	24 6/12	M	Merchant	America	United States	Hiram	31 Oct 1828
Wm.	34	M	Jeweller	G.B.	U.S.	London	19 Dec 1823
EDWIN, John	28	M	Musician	England	America	Leeds	2 Aug 1828
Mary	25	F	None	England	New York	Brighton	29 Aug 1828
EENGE, John	29	M	Farmer	Switzerland	United States	Elbe	2 Aug 1822
EERS, Patrick	19	M	None	Ireland	U. States	Rice Plant	22 May 1827
EFTI, Catherine	30	F		Switzerland	U.S.	Francois I	8 Aug 1829
EGAGNETH, F. P.	9	M	Boy	Carracas	U. States	Morning Star	28 Apr 1824
EGAN, Andw.	32	M	Labourer	Ireland	United States	Wilson	27 Jun 1826
Ann	23	F		Ireland	United States	Dublin Packet	30 Apr 1821
Anne	4	F	Child	L... Cty., Dundalk, Ireland	U. States	New Orleans	24 Aug 1827
Arabella	27	F	None	England	United States	London	21 May 1828
Bridget	20	F	Spinster	Ireland	United States	Dublin Packet	23 May 1828
Catherine	6	F	None	England	United States	London	21 May 1828
Daniel	23			Longford	N. York	Peru	30 May 1828
Danl.	27	M	Servant	Ireland	U. States	Albion	11 May 1827

NAMES OF PASSENGERS	AGE	SEX	OCCUPATIONS	COUNTRY TO WHICH THEY BELONG	COUNTRY THEY INTEND TO INHABIT	SHIPS/DATES OF ARRIVAL	
EGAN (cont'd)							
Dennis	1	M	Child	L... Cty., Dundalk, Ireland	U. States	New Orleans	24 Aug 1827
George	7	M	None	England	United States	London	21 May 1828
James	20	M	Laboror	Ireland	United States	Wilson	27 Jun 1826
John	3 6/12	M	Child	Ireland	U. States	Albion	11 May 1827
John	18	M	Labourer	Ireland	United States	Concordia	25 Aug 1827
John	26	M	Labourer	G. Britain	U. States	Mary & Harriot	8 Sep 1828
John	30		Labourer			Euphrates	8 Aug 1820
John, Junr.	7		Merchant			Euphrates	8 Aug 1820
M.	23	M	Weaver	Ireland	America	Mary	29 May 1827
Margaret	20	F	None	Ireland	U.S.A.	Dalhouse Castle	21 Aug 1829
Margt.	20	F	None	Ireland	United States	Dalhouse Castle	21 Aug 1829
Martha	25	F	None	England	United States	London	21 May 1828
Mary	10	F		G. Britain	U. States	Mary & Harriot	8 Sep 1828
Mary	26	F	Wife	Ireland	U. States	Albion	11 May 1827
Mary	30	F	Wife	L... Cty., Dundalk, Ireland	U. States	New Orleans	24 Aug 1827
Mary Ann	16	F	None	England	United States	London	21 May 1828
Patrick	20	M	Labourer	Ireland	United States	Jubilee	13 Sep 1827
Patrick	24	M	Laborer	Ireland	Philadelphia	Indian Chief	19 Jun 1823
Patrick	28	M	Bookkeeper	Ireland	United States	Robert Fulton	22 Oct 1821
Robert	4	M	None	England	United States	London	21 May 1828
Sarah	10	F	None	England	United States	London	21 May 1828
Thomas	7	M		G. Britain	U. States	Mary & Harriot	8 Sep 1828
Thomas	22	M	Laborer	Ireland	New York	Amanda	23 May 1827
Thomas	30	M	Stone Mason	L... Cty., Dundalk, Ireland	U. States	New Orleans	24 Aug 1827
Thomas	30	M	Labourer	Ireland	United States	Jubilee	12 May 1828
William	23	M	Farmer	Ireland	United States	Dublin Packet	29 Jun 1825
Wm.	25	M	Labourer	Ireland	United States	Jubilee	13 Sep 1827
EGAR, Bridget	18	F	Servant	Ireland	U. States of America	Courier	17 Mar 1827
Danl.	28	M	Labourer	Ireland	United States	Essex	23 May 1828
Jacques	30	M	Farmer	Switzerland		Antioch	18 Aug 1829
Mary	10	F		Ireland	United States	Romulus	24 Jun 1826
EGATER, David	3	M		Germany	United States	Samuel Robertson	8 Aug 1828
Doffet	34	M	Farmer	Germany	United States	Samuel Robertson	8 Aug 1828
Frederick	25	M	Farmer	Germany	United States	Samuel Robertson	8 Aug 1828
Margaret	33	F		Germany	United States	Samuel Robertson	8 Aug 1828
Maria	6	F		Germany	United States	Samuel Robertson	8 Aug 1828
EGEN, Frederick	26	M	Farmer	Germany	United States	Helen	5 Sep 1828
EGENTON, Mary	50	F	None	Ireland	United States	John Wells	11 May 1827
William	38	M	Merchant	France	U. States	Danube	21 Nov 1826
Wm.	35	M	Mechanic	U. States	U. States	Aolus	1 Aug 1823
EGERTON, E...d	25	M	Labourer	Ireland	America	Plutarch	18 Jul 1826
William	23	M	Labourer	Ireland	America	Plutarch	18 Jul 1826
EGGERT, Michael	24	M	Farmer	France	U. States	France	14 Mar 1828
EGGERTON, Cath.	20	F	Labourer	Ireland	U. States	Marcus	7 Apr 1825
John	16	M	Labourer	Ireland	U. States	Marcus	7 Apr 1825
EGGLERS, Catherine	40	F	Lady	Ireland	United States	Dublin Packet	3 Sep 1822
EGGLESTON, Robt.	28	M	Tallow Chandler	United States	New York	Albion	11 Jun 1821
EGGON, John	29	M	Farmer	Great Britain	U.N. States	Reindeer	10 Dec 1827
Margart	27	F		Great Britain	U.N. States	Reindeer	10 Dec 1827
EGLAND, James	28	M	Merchant	England	America	Manhattan	22 Sep 1823
EGLESHAW, Richard	29	M	Labourer	England	Pennsylvania	Governor Fenner	23 Jul 1829
EGLY, Jacob	44	M	Farmer	United States	United States	Globe	30 Aug 1828
EHERMAN, M. E.	15	F		France	U.S.A.	Bayard	25 Aug 1829
P. F.	38	M		France	U.S.A.	Bayard	25 Aug 1829
S. S.	40	F		France	U.S.A.	Bayard	25 Aug 1829
EHNINGER, Geo.	26	M	Merchant	U. States	U. States	Seneca	15 Mar 1820
EIBELLE, S.	27	M	Cabinet Maker	Switzerland	U. States	La Urania	3 Jul 1828

NAMES OF PASSENGERS	AGE	SEX	OCCUPATIONS	COUNTRY TO WHICH THEY BELONG	COUNTRY THEY INTEND TO INHABIT	SHIPS/DATES OF ARRIVAL	
EIDAN, John	30	M	foile cutter	Great Briton	United States	Mount Vernon	30 Dec 1828
EIDESTON, Edward	24	M	Gentleman	Ireland	United States	Dublin Packet	24 Sep 1823
EIFFE, W.	39	M	Artist	Germany	U. States	Mount Parnassas	2 Sep 1828
EISBRALGO, —, Master	9	M	None	Havana	U. States	Milo	15 May 1824
EISELE, Anna Cath.	37	F		Germany	America	Falcon	28 Aug 1828
Jacob	43	M		Germany	America	Falcon	28 Aug 1828
EISENBARTH, Catharina	20	F		Germany	America	Falcon	28 Aug 1828
Joh. Jacob	26	M		Germany	America	Falcon	28 Aug 1828
EISENMINGER, Ludwig	55	M	None	Switzerland	U. States	Manhattan	20 Jun 1825
EISLEZ, Barbara	42	F	Servant	Switzerland	U.S.	Henri IV	17 May 1828
EIVERS, James	54	M	Merchant	New York	New York	John Adams	17 Jul 1827
Owen	46	M	Merchant	New York	New York	John Adams	17 Jul 1827
EKELAND, C. G.	23	M	Mariner	Sweden	U. States	Anna Christina	24 Dec 1821
EKER, Sarah B.	43	F	Dress Maker	Great Britain	United States	Fame	26 May 1828
EKLARD, Jacques	26	M	Taylor	Gt. Brittan		L'Esperance	6 Sep 1828
ELAER, Joseph	26	M	Weaver	France	U. States	Edward Bonaffe	23 Jul 1828
ELAMB, Catherine	34	F		France	U. States	C. Amelia	30 Jun 1828
ELBE, Francis	7	M		Switzerland	U. States	Romulus	24 Sep 1828
Joseph	11	M		Switzerland	U. States	Romulus	24 Sep 1828
M.	6	F		Switzerland	U. States	Romulus	24 Sep 1828
M.	16	F		Switzerland	U. States	Romulus	24 Sep 1828
M.	41	F		Switzerland	U. States	Romulus	24 Sep 1828
M.	44	M	Weaver	Switzerland	U. States	Romulus	24 Sep 1828
ELDE, Henry	40	M	Merchant	U. States	United States	Eagle	26 Jul 1828
ELDER, —, Mr.	33	M	Schoolmaster	Scotland	U. States	Packet	2 Aug 1824
—, Mrs.	66	F		Glasgow	U. States	Florozen	29 Jun 1826
Christian	49	F	Wife	Scotland	United States	Tom	2 Jul 1827
David	11	M	Child	Scotland	United States	Tom	2 Jul 1827
George	27	M	Cooper	Great Brittan	U. States	Electra	28 Apr 1827
James	8	M	Child	Scotland	United States	Tom	2 Jul 1827
James	30	M		Scotland	America	Nimrod	9 Jul 1827
Jane	30	F	Upolsterer	U. States		Hudson	23 Jul 1828
John	19	M	Laborer	Scotland	United States	Tom	2 Jul 1827
John	25	M	Machinist	Great Britain	United States	Colossus	5 Jun 1827
John	66	M	Weaver	Glasgow	U. States	Florenzo	29 Jun 1826
Robert	13	M	Child	Scotland	United States	Tom	2 Jul 1827
Wm.	4	M		Glasgow	U. States	Florenzo	29 Jun 1826
Wm.	58	M	Laborer	Scotland	United States	Tom	2 Jul 1827
Wm., Jr.	15	M	Child	Scotland	United States	Tom	2 Jul 1827
ELDERBERRY, Nicholas	34	M	Merchant	Russia	U. States	Minerva	13 Sep 1827
ELDRIDGE, A. H.	25	M	Mariner	United States	U. States	Robert Reade	9 Feb 1822
Edward	1	M		America	United States	America	16 May 1827
Edward	30	M	Merchant	America	United States	America	16 May 1827
Hannah	27	F		America	United States	America	16 May 1827
Lucinda	18	F	Lady	U. States	U. States	Nancy	19 Oct 1821
Mary Ann	4	F		America	United States	America	16 May 1827
Ruben	27	M	Mariner	America	America	Peruvian	11 Mar 1822
Thos.	28	M	Merchant	N. York	U. States	Franklin	27 Aug 1822
Vindel	22 2/12	M	Farmer	America	America	Hiram	2 Apr 1828
William	25	M	Farmer	England	Albany, N.Y.	Chelsea	16 May 1828
ELDRIGE, E.	26	M	Seaman	America	America	Paragon	22 Sep 1827
Sophy	16	F	Servant	England	U. States	Cincinnatus	24 May 1821
ELE..., Jos.	...	...	...	...	...	William Thompson	30 Sep 1824
ELENTON, James	35	M	Merchant	Great Britain		Robert Fulton	8 Mar 1823
ELEXANDER, Catherine	10	F	None	Wales South	U. States	Oglethorpe	8 Jul 1824
Eleanor	12	F	None	Wales South	U. States	Oglethorpe	8 Jul 1824
Jeremiah	26	M	Joiner	America	America	Hope	15 Oct 1821
Mariah	23	F	None	Wales South	U. States	Oglethorpe	8 Jul 1824
Robert	1 6/12	M	None	Wales South	U. States	Oglethorpe	8 Jul 1824
Thos.	8	M	None	Wales South	U. States	Oglethorpe	8 Jul 1824
Thos.	37	M	Farmer	Wales South	U. States	Oglethorpe	8 Jul 1824
Wm.	7	M	None	Wales South	U. States	Oglethorpe	8 Jul 1824
ELGALSBY, James	21	M	Tailor	Ireland	New Jersey	Atlantic	6 Oct 1828
ELGAN, James	40	M	Farmer	England		Hudson	23 Jul 1828
ELGER, L.	15	M	Painter	Jacmel	New Orleans	Hero	5 Jul 1828
ELHINNEY, Mary	55	F		Ireland	United States	William & George	14 May 1828
ELINOR, John	30 2/12	M	Farmer	France	United States	Catharine	10 Sep 1827

NAMES OF PASSENGERS	AGE	SEX	OCCUPATIONS	COUNTRY TO WHICH THEY BELONG	COUNTRY THEY INTEND TO INHABIT	SHIPS/DATES OF ARRIVAL	
ELIOT, Mary, Miss	20	F		England	U. States	Panthea	22 Nov 1826
ELIOTT, Richard	42	M	...	Great Brittain	Philadelphia	Albion	11 Jun 1821
ELIS, George	50	M		Great Britain	U. States	Ann Marria	6 Aug 1823
ELISAICAIR, —, Mr.	28	M	Merchant	Spain	U. States	Lucy Ann	4 Sep 1822
—, Mrs.	25	F	Merchant	Spain	U. States	Lucy Ann	4 Sep 1822
ELISER, H.	28	M	Merchant	Vera Cruz	U. States	Eliza	11 Apr 1826
ELISHAR, James	10	M	None	Havama	United States	Brown	26 Apr 1826
ELIZAB, Catharun	41	M		Bardin	U. States	Bayard	5 Sep 1828
ELIZAENDO, Marter	25	M	Grocer	Hayti		Ranger	29 Jul 1828
ELKINDORF, M.	35	M	Doctor	France	U. States	Lima	13 Nov 1822
ELLAM, E.	5	F		England	U. States of America	Dale	14 Mar 1828
James	30	M	Farmer	England	U. States of America	Dale	14 Mar 1828
Mary	26	F		England	U. States of America	Dale	14 Mar 1828
O.	3	M	Farmer	England	U. States of America	Dale	14 Mar 1828
P.	6	M	Farmer	England	U. States of America	Dale	14 Mar 1828
ELLARD, George	35	M	Carpenter	Ireland	America	Liverpool	31 Aug 1827
ELLAS, Dennis	11	M		Switzerland	U. States	Robert Edward	2 Nov 1827
Jas.	3	M		Switzerland	U. States	Robert Edward	2 Nov 1827
Martha	9	F		Switzerland	U. States	Robert Edward	2 Nov 1827
Thos.	1	M		Switzerland	U. States	Robert Edward	2 Nov 1827
ELLEIS, William	18 6/12	M	Labourer	Ireland	U. States	Josephine	30 Aug 1828
ELLEN, Hannah	43	F	Weaver	G. Britain	U. States	London	23 Sep 1828
Henry	16	M		G. Britain	U. States	London	23 Sep 1828
James	18	M		G. Britain	U. States	London	23 Sep 1828
Mark	31	M	Carpenter	England	America	Josephine	8 Jan 1827
Sarah	13	F		G. Britain	U. States	London	23 Sep 1828
Sarah	19	F		G. Britain	U. States	London	23 Sep 1828
Sidney	23	M	Knife Forger	Great Britain	U.S. of America	Gratitude	3 Oct 1829
Thomas	9	M		G. Britain	U. States	London	23 Sep 1828
ELLERBY, Edward	27	M	Miller	Great Britain	United States	Marshal Wellington	3 May 1822
ELLERHORST, Eberhart	26	M	Baker	Bremen		Caesar	24 Aug 1829
ELLERY, Alfred	24	M	Mason	England	U. States	Montgomery	18 Oct 1828
Henry	27	M	Laborer	England	United States	London	21 May 1828
John S.	45	M	Merchant	United States	United States	Maria	12 May 1823
ELLES, Betsy	8	F		Switzerland	U. States	Robert Edward	2 Nov 1827
ELLIN, James	47	M		England	United States	Yobah	26 Sep 1827
ELLING, Flew	40	M	Wheelwright	Canada	Canada	Ann Maria	7 Sep 1827
ELLINGHAM, Ann	33	F		G. Brittain	U. States	Cincinnatus	2 Oct 1822
Jane	8	F		G. Brittain	U. States	Cincinnatus	2 Oct 1822
John	10	M		G. Brittain	U. States	Cincinnatus	2 Oct 1822
Maria	6	F		G. Brittain	U. States	Cincinnatus	2 Oct 1822
Robert	27		Farmer			Mount Vernon	26 Aug 1820
Sarah		F		G. Brittain	U. States	Cincinnatus	2 Oct 1822
ELLINGSWORTH, Lewis	20	M	Labourer	Ireland	United States	Jubilee	13 Jul 1829
ELLIOT, —, Mrs.	38	F		United States	United States	Robert Edwards	21 Sep 1821
Ann	2	F	Farmer	England	In the Country	Chelsea	16 May 1828
C.	28	M	Mechanic	New York	U. States	Star	4 Oct 1826
Charles	23		Weaver	Ireland	G. Britain	Robert Burns	14 Jun 1824
Geo.	30	M		Scotland	U.S.	Curler	19 Jul 1828
George	34	M	Gentleman	U. States	U. States	Robert Edwards	9 May 1827
Harriet	7 6/12	F	Farmer	England	In the Country	Chelsea	16 May 1828
Heny.	21	M	Lace Maker	Great Britain	United States	Penelope	11 Jun 1827
James	12	M	Farmer	England	In the Country	Chelsea	16 May 1828
James	25	M	Taylor	Ireland	United States	Roman	12 Jun 1826
James	28			Great Britan	United States	Newry	11 Jul 1827
James	36	M	Shoemaker	Ireland	America	Josephine	8 Dec 1827
Janet	24	F		Scotland	United States	Camillus	9 May 1827
Jno.	25	M	Merchant	N. York	U. States	Brutus	1 Feb 1825
John	15 9/12	M	Merchant	Irereland	America	Carolina Ann	20 Jun 1825
John	26	M		Scotland	United States	Camillus	9 May 1827
John	27	M	Cooper	Ireland	United States	Roman	12 Jun 1826
John, & family	33	M	Farmer	England	In the Country	Chelsea	16 May 1828
Joseph	5	M	None	England	U. States	Courier	25 Aug 1825
Lucy	31	F	Farmer	England	In the Country	Chelsea	16 May 1828
Luke	21	M	Smith	England	America	Two Marys	24 Sep 1827
Mary	3	F	None	England	U. States	Courier	25 Aug 1825
Mary	18	F		Nova Scotia	U. States	General Pulman	3 Jun 1828

NAMES OF PASSENGERS	A G E	S E X	OCCUPATIONS	COUNTRY TO WHICH THEY BELONG	COUNTRY THEY INTEND TO INHABIT	SHIPS/DATES OF ARRIVAL	
ELLIOT (cont'd)							
Mary	26	F	None	England	U. States	Courier	25 Aug 1825
Rebecca	50	F	Servant	Antigua	United States	Betsey	18 Aug 1823
Sarah	9	F	Farmer	England	In the Country	Chelsea	16 May 1828
Thomas	28	M	Farmer	England	U. States	Courier	25 Aug 1825
Thomas	43	M	Gardner	Great Britain	United States	Roman	10 May 1828
William	30	M	Merchant	Elizabeth, N.C.	U. States	Jones & Samuel	22 Sep 1826
Wm.	27	M		Scotland	U.S.	Curler	19 Jul 1828
ELLIOTT, —, Mrs.	26	M	Military	U. States	U. States	Doris	2 Jun 1828
Bridget	30	F	Farmer	England	U. States	Mentor	5 Jul 1825
Charlotte	20	F	Spinster	Ireland	United States	Asia	29 Jul 1829
Eliza	8 4/12	F		U.S.A.	U.S.A.	Silas Richards	27 Oct 1826
Elliott	18	M	Spinster	Ireland	United States	Asia	29 Jul 1829
Francis	24	M	Labourer	Ireland	United States	Catharine	22 Jul 1825
Francis	24	M	Cottonspinner	Ireland	New York	Louisa	20 Jul 1826
George A.	30	M	Merchant	England	U. Canada	Lama	7 Nov 1825
Henry	...		...	...	...	St. Michael	22 Sep 1824
Henry	25	M	Furrier	England	U. States	Brutus	2 Dec 1823
Hugh	26	M	Merchant	Great Britain	United States	Isaac Hicks	6 Dec 1827
John	32	M	Farmer	England	U. States	Mentor	5 Jul 1825
John	36	M	Merchant	Great Britain	United States	Mary & Harriet	3 Jul 1829
John	41	M	Labourer	Ireland	America	Weser	26 Jun 1821
Maria	29 5/12	F		U.S.A.	U.S.A.	Silas Richards	27 Oct 1826
Mary	9 3/12	F		U.S.A.	U.S.A.	Silas Richards	27 Oct 1826
Mary	58	F	None	England	America	Meteor	19 Aug 1825
Nelson J.	22	M	Merchant	United States	United States	Pacific	11 Mar 1829
Susannah	23	F	Spinster	Ireland	United States	Asia	29 Jul 1829
Wm. P.	22	M	None	U. States	U. States	Sully	15 Jul 1829
ELLIS, Amer	6	F				Xenophon	25 Jul 1826
Ann	6/12		their Child [James and Henrietta]	England	United States	Rufus King	4 Sep 1823
Ann	6	F		Great Britain	United States	Gomer	21 May 1828
Ann	10	F		Great B.	U. States	William Neilson	26 Jul 1828
Ann	40		his Wife [James]	England	United States	Rufus King	4 Sep 1823
Ann, Child [of Griffith]	4	F	Farmer	Wales		Gomer	22 May 1827
C.	55	M	Merchant	America	America	Corinthian	1 Sep 1827
Catherine, Wife [of Griffith]	28	F	Farmer	Wales		Gomer	22 May 1827
Christopher	28	M	Attorney	Great Britian	United States	Isaac Hicks	13 Jan 1826
Danl.	24	M	Merchant	England	United States	Dalhouse Castle	6 Sep 1827
Eleanor, Child [of Griffith]	5	F	Farmer	Wales		Gomer	22 May 1827
Elias	4	M		Great Britain	United States	Gomer	21 May 1828
Eliza, Mrs.	30	F	Lady	Ireland	United States	Dublin Packet	13 Oct 1828
Elizabeth	33	F		Great Britain	United States	Diana	6 Jul 1829
Elizabeth	54	F	None	England	United States	New Packet	7 Aug 1826
F.	48	M	Mariner	U. States	U. States	Villard de Cayes	10 Apr 1827
Felix N.	28	M	Merchant	France	U. States	Bayard	9 Nov 1825
Francis	2/12	M		Great Britain	United States	Diana	6 Jul 1829
Frederick	2		their Child [James and Henrietta]	England	United States	Rufus King	4 Sep 1823
George	...	M	...	Ireland	United States	General Putnam	20 Jun 1825
George	10	M		Great Britain	United States	Diana	6 Jul 1829
George	18	M	Weaver	England	United States	Siroc	31 Oct 1829
Griffith	29	M	Farmer	Wales		Gomer	22 May 1827
Henrietta	13		their Child [James and Henrietta]	England	United States	Rufus King	4 Sep 1823
Izzabella	20	F	Wife	Ireland	United States	St. Michaels	7 Jun 1827
James	...	M		Ireland	United States	General Putnam	20 Jun 1825
James	9		their Child [James and Henrietta]	England	United States	Rufus King	4 Sep 1823
James	23	M	Merchant	Scotland	Halifax, N.S.	Hunter	2 Aug 1822
James	40		Farmer	England	United States	Rufus King	4 Sep 1823
Jane	...	F		Ireland	United States	General Putnam	20 Jun 1825
Jane	3	F	Spinster	Ireland		Robert Fulton	4 Jun 1828
Jane	11					Xenophon	25 Jul 1826
Jas.	50	M		United States	United States	Essex	23 May 1828
John	...	...	...	Ireland	United States	General Putnam	20 Jun 1825
John	8					Xenophon	25 Jul 1826

NAMES OF PASSENGERS	AGE	SEX	OCCUPATIONS	COUNTRY TO WHICH THEY BELONG	COUNTRY THEY INTEND TO INHABIT	SHIPS/DATES OF ARRIVAL	
ELLIS (cont'd)							
John	8	M		Great Britain	United States	Diana	6 Jul 1829
John	10	F		Great B.	U. States	William Neilson	26 Jul 1828
John	36		Farmer	England	Albany	Xenophon	25 Jul 1826
John	39	M	Plumber	Great Britan	United States	Bolivar	21 May 1827
Josep	55	M	Farmer	Great Britain	United States	Gomer	21 May 1828
Lowry	53	F		Great Britain	United States	Gomer	21 May 1828
M. M.	25	M	Merchant	U.S. America	U.S. America	Claudio	22 Mar 1828
Margaret	30	F	Servant	U. States	U. States	Cadmus	28 May 1821
Margaret	38	F		U. States	U.S.	Edward Quesnel	19 Dec 1826
Margt.	...	...	...	Ireland	United States	General Putnam	20 Jun 1825
Mark	27	M	Stone Mason	Great Britain	United States	Cortes	18 Oct 1820
Mary	2	F		Great Britain	United States	Diana	6 Jul 1829
Pat	24	M	Labourer	England	United States	Aurelia	7 Jun 1826
Richard	34	M	Carpenter	Great Britain	United States	Diana	6 Jul 1829
Richard H.	23	M	Mariner	U. States	U. States	Lion	5 Sep 1828
Riuth	2	F		Great Britain	United States	Gomer	21 May 1828
Robert	9					Xenophon	25 Jul 1826
Robt.	43	M	Labourer	England	United States	Bolivar	15 Jun 1826
Sarah	35					Xenophon	25 Jul 1826
Thomas	5					Xenophon	25 Jul 1826
Thomas	11	M		Great Britain	United States	Gomer	21 May 1828
Thos.	5	M		Great Britain	United States	Diana	6 Jul 1829
William	11		their Child [James and Henrietta]	England	United States	Rufus King	4 Sep 1823
William	13					Xenophon	25 Jul 1826
William	17	M	Labourer	Wales		Gomer	22 May 1827
William	19	M	Clothier	England	U. St.	Manchester	7 Dec 1826
William	20		Labourer	England	United States	Corinthian	7 Jul 1829
Wm.	6	M		Great Britain	United States	Diana	6 Jul 1829
ELLISON, Barthw.	13	M	Farmer	Great Britain	America	Remittance	24 Aug 1825
Christopher	22	M	Merchant	England	U.N. States	Corinthian	1 Sep 1823
Henry	10 5/12		Farmer	Scotland	U.S. of America	Helen	8 Feb 1822
John	24	M	Weaver	England	United States	Peru	23 May 1827
Jos.	19	M	Farmer	G. Brittain	U. States	Rockingham	17 May 1821
Joseph	25	M	Farmer	Great Britain	America	Remittance	24 Aug 1825
Mary	22	F		England	United States	Peru	23 May 1827
Mary	30	F		Gt. Britan	U. States	Magnet	9 Apr 1825
Richd.	17	M	Farmer	Great Britain	America	Remittance	24 Aug 1825
Thos.	34	M	None	Gt. Britan	U. States	Magnet	9 Apr 1825
ELLOT, James	34	M	Labourer	Gt. Britain	U. States	Frances Henrietta	18 Apr 1825
Margaret	22	F	Spinster	Gt. Britain	U. States	Frances Henrietta	18 Apr 1825
Mary	33	F	Spinster	Gt. Britain	U. States	Frances Henrietta	18 Apr 1825
Thomas	17	M	Labourer	Gt. Britain	U. States	Frances Henrietta	18 Apr 1825
ELLSWORTH, Ewd.	22	M	Labourer	England	United States	Nimrod	31 Jul 1828
Henry	33 6/12	M	Counsellor	U.S.A.	U. States	Silas Richards	27 Oct 1826
Moses	50	M	Labourer	England	United States	Nimrod	31 Jul 1828
Pat	18	M	Servant	Ireland	U. States	Sarah G	30 Jun 1828
V. D.	29	M	Merchant	United States	United States	Corinthian	10 Jan 1826
ELLWOOD, Ann	26	F	None	Great Britain	United States	Comet	9 Aug 1822
James	30	M				Eliza Grant	6 Oct 1828
ELMASH, Phillip J.	42	M	Farmer	England	America	John Wells	11 Jun 1823
ELMHIRST,							
Phillip James	45	M	Farmer	England	Canada	Roman	12 Jun 1826
ELMWOOD, H.	19	M	Merchant	U. States	U. States	Beaver	18 Feb 1823
ELPHENSTONE, W. H.	20	M	Gentn.	England	America	Leeds	2 Aug 1828
ELPHIE, Charlotte	10	F	Miller	England	United States	Euphrates	18 Aug 1827
Hanah	12	F	Miller	England	United States	Euphrates	18 Aug 1827
Hanah	44	F	Miller	England	United States	Euphrates	18 Aug 1827
Jn...	18	M	Miller	England	United States	Euphrates	18 Aug 1827
Jno.	47	M	Miller	England	United States	Euphrates	18 Aug 1827
Mary Ann	16	F	Miller	England	United States	Euphrates	18 Aug 1827
Sarah	8	F	Miller	England	United States	Euphrates	18 Aug 1827
ELRENTZ, —, Mrs.	28	F		Philadelphia	U. States	Peter Remsen	30 Jun 1828
ELTON, John	20	M	Labourer	England		Britannia	20 Jun 1827

NAMES OF PASSENGERS	AGE	SEX	OCCUPATIONS	COUNTRY TO WHICH THEY BELONG	COUNTRY THEY INTEND TO INHABIT	SHIPS/DATES OF ARRIVAL	
ELTON (cont'd)							
Romeo	36	M	Professor	United States		Britannia	20 Jun 1827
Sarah	17	F		England		Britannia	20 Jun 1827
ELVEMAS, Octavius	50	M	Gentleman	France	France	Stephania	13 Sep 1821
ELVIN, Wm.	27	M	Taylor	Great Brittan	U. States	Electra	28 Apr 1827
ELWEIN, Johannes	21	M	Farmer	Wirtemburg	United States	Wade	29 Aug 1825
ELWELL, Hannah	35	F		England	America	Hudson	20 Nov 1828
Henry	26	M	Teacher	England	America	Hudson	20 Nov 1828
ELWOOD, Thomas	64	M	Farmer	Great Britain	United States	Comet	9 Aug 1822
ELWYN, John, Mr.	21		Merchant	England	U.S.	Pacific	24 May 1824
ELY, D. D.	20	M	Merchant	United States		Howard	17 Oct 1822
J. T.	21	M	Mercht.	N. York	New York	Howard	26 Aug 1823
Jonathan	18	M		Connecticut	U.S.	Bayard	30 Oct 1820
EMAND, Joseph	44	M	Farmer	France	U.S.	C. Amelia	30 Jun 1828
EMANUEL, Jonathan	26	M	Merchant	Gt. Britain	U. States	Canada	4 Oct 1824
Michael	43	M	Merchant	United States	United States	William	6 Oct 1828
EMARD, Peter	35					Prometheus	30 Aug 1828
EMBDEN, A.	30	M	Merchant	Hamburgh	U. States	Enterprize	14 Jul 1823
H.	34	M	Mercht.	U. States	U. States	Howard	13 Feb 1820
EMBRY, John	21	M	Watch Maker	Germany	U. States	Rook	25 Jul 1827
EMBURG, Peter	27 7/12		Merchant	New York	New York	Agnes	27 Mar 1828
EMERSON, Ann	7	F	None	Great Brittain	U. States	Louisa	11 Jun 1824
Elizabeth	32	F	None	Great Brittain	U. States	Louisa	11 Jun 1824
Hannah	18	F	None	Cuba	United States	Ariel	30 Jun 1828
James	26	M	Labourer	Ireland	United States	Jubilee	13 Jul 1829
Jane	24	F	None	New York		Olive Branch	9 Oct 1829
John	17	M	Farmer, Labourer or Spinster	Ireland	U. States	Meteor	4 Oct 1827
John	25	M	Carpenter	New York		Olive Branch	9 Oct 1829
Joseph	29	M	Blacksmith	New York		Olive Branch	9 Oct 1829
Mary	1 6/12	F	None	New York		Olive Branch	9 Oct 1829
Ralph	22	M	Mercht.	U. States	U. States	Malaga	10 Jul 1828
Thos.	18	M	Gentleman	U.S.	U.S	Radius	18 Feb 1823
Thos.	32	M	Merchant	Great Britain	U. States	Columbia	22 Sep 1828
Wm.	5					Splendid	14 Aug 1829
EMERY, Jno.	25	M	Labourer			Robert Edwards	8 Nov 1825
John	30	M	Minister	America	America	Albion	4 Oct 1820
William	28	M	Dyer	Great Britain	United States	Isaac Hicks	27 Sep 1826
EMES, John	22	M		Ireland	America	Carolina Ann	7 Aug 1826
EMICK, Jno.	27	M	Labourer	Ireland	U. States	Lady Hunter	18 Jul 1825
EMLENSEN, Eleanor	22		Spinster	Ireland	United States	Fabius	18 Mar 1829
EMMERING, Aron	19	M	Clerk	Holland	New York	Falcon	21 Oct 1826
EMMERSON, Elizabeth	5	F		Great Britain	United States	Freak	14 oct 1828
George	2	M		Great Britain	United States	Freak	14 oct 1828
Hannah	21					Mount Vernon	26 Aug 1820
Harriet	3	F		Great Britain	United States	Freak	14 oct 1828
John	9	M		Great Britain	United States	Freak	14 oct 1828
John	28		Farmer	United States		John Dickinson	5 Apr 1821
Mary	7	M		Great Britain	United States	Freak	14 oct 1828
Rebecca	42	F		Great Britain	United States	Freak	14 oct 1828
Robert	10	M		Great Britain	United States	Freak	14 oct 1828
Robt.	4	M	Farmer	Great Britain	United States	Freak	14 oct 1828
Thomas	13	M		Great Britain	United States	Freak	14 oct 1828
William	12	M		Great Britain	United States	Freak	14 oct 1828
William	30		Farmer			Mount Vernon	26 Aug 1820
EMMES, Margaret	35	F	Lady			Helen	4 Aug 1829
William	50	M	Gentleman	England		Helen	4 Aug 1829
EMMET, John	26	M	Loom Maker	Great Britain	U.S. of America	Gratitude	3 Oct 1829
EMMETT, David	30	M	Farmer	Great Britain	United States	John Jay	8 May 1828
EMMONS, Woodh.	30	M	Merchant	United States	U.S.	Maria Ann	7 Apr 1823
EMMUEL, Jacob	25	M	Smith	Great Britian	U. States	Pallas	17 Aug 1824
EMNET, George	39	M	Butcher			Splendid	14 Aug 1829
EMORY, Isiah	25	M	Barber	America	America	Leeds	2 Aug 1828
EMPEREAN, Chs.	27	M	Merchant	England	England	Bunker Hill	20 Sep 1827
END, Charles	4	M	Farmer	Germany	United States	Oxford	14 Aug 1828
Eloise	31	F	Farmer	Germany	United States	Oxford	14 Aug 1828
Mariane	30	F	Farmer	Germany	United States	Oxford	14 Aug 1828

NAMES OF PASSENGERS	AGE	SEX	OCCUPATIONS	COUNTRY TO WHICH THEY BELONG	COUNTRY THEY INTEND TO INHABIT	SHIPS/DATES OF ARRIVAL	
ENDAL, Francis	32	M	Farmer	Alsace in the Department of Upper and lower Rhine	United States	Carolina Augusta	16 May 1828
ENDERSON, Robert	25	M		Ireland	United States	Nancy R. Crowell	21 Sep 1822
ENERES, A.	24	F	Labourer	England	U. States	Hope & Esther	10 Jul 1827
ENGATHURST, E.	36	F	Farmer	Switzerland	U. States	Alfred	8 Jul 1828
Eliza	7	F	Farmer	Switzerland	U. States	Alfred	8 Jul 1828
F.	6	F	Farmer	Switzerland	U. States	Alfred	8 Jul 1828
J.	1	F	Farmer	Switzerland	U. States	Alfred	8 Jul 1828
Jos.	44	M	Farmer	Switzerland	U. States	Alfred	8 Jul 1828
M.	4	F	Farmer	Switzerland	U. States	Alfred	8 Jul 1828
W.	3	F	Farmer	Switzerland	U. States	Alfred	8 Jul 1828
ENGEL, C.	37	M	Brush Maker	Switzerland	U. States	Romulus	24 Sep 1828
Faver	4	F		Switzerland	U. States	Romulus	24 Sep 1828
Mary	40	F		Switzerland	U. States	Romulus	24 Sep 1828
Rosina	17	F		Switzerland	U. States	Romulus	24 Sep 1828
ENGELKER, Domi	24	M	Labourer	Prussia		Constitution	20 Jun 1828
ENGEMAN, A.	24	M		Germany	United States	Robert Edwards	1 Jun 1826
ENGLAND, E.	23	M	Hatter	England	U.S.	York	1 Dec 1827
James	25	M	Merchant	England	U. States	Manhattan	26 Feb 1825
Mary	26					Xenophon	25 Jul 1826
Michl.	24	M	Farmer	England		Marchioness	13 May 1828
Robert	37		Farmer	England	S. New York	Xenophon	25 Jul 1826
Saml.	33	M	Painter	England	United States	Hudson	17 Mar 1828
ENGLANDHAND, Elias	32		Painter			Caledonian	16 Aug 1820
ENGLE, Barthol, Zyn Lusters Kinder [Daniel Haffner's sister's child]	7	M		Zweybruck	United States	Juffraw Johanna	16 Oct 1821
Christine				Switzerland	U. States	Romulus	24 Sep 1828
Emanuel	30	M	Cooper	Wertemburg	America, U.N.S.	Great Britain	3 Aug 1829
Frederik, Zyn Lusters Kinder [Daniel Haffner's sister's child]	13	M		Zweybruck	United States	Juffraw Johanna	16 Oct 1821
Isaac E.	28	M	Mercher	U.S.	U.S.	Charleston Allen	15 Nov 1826
Maria, Zyn Susters Kinder [Daniel Haffner's sister's child]	13	F		Zweybruck	United States	Juffraw Johanna	16 Oct 1821
ENGLEE, Bernhard	24	M	Farmer	Hamburg	U. States	Martha	4 Sep 1828
Eben.	25	M	Mechanic	New York	U. States	St. Michaels	21 Apr 1824
Parsons	25	M	Mechanic	New York	U. States	St. Michaels	21 Apr 1824
ENGLEMAY, Victor L.	26	M	Merchant	France	U. States	Cincinnatus	24 May 1821
ENGLES, Fredk.	24	M	Merchant	Prusia	U. States	Horizon	23 Aug 1822
ENGLISH, —, Mr.	30	M	Gentleman	U.S.	U.S.	Robert Edwards	11 Nov 1822
B.	38	M	Merchant	Connecticett	U. States	Spartan	20 Feb 1826
Elisha N.	38	M	Merchant	U. States	U. States	Moro	26 Aug 1824
Wm., Revd.	30	M		Ireland	United States	Potomac	28 Sep 1827
ENICK, Willm.	32	M	Farmer	England	U.S.A.	Lima	6 Dec 1826
ENIS, Badget	22	F		Great Brittain	United States	Sarah Ralston	27 Jan 1827
ENMAN, William	22	M	Mariner	New York	New York	Baltic	20 Aug 1821
ENNIS, —	22	M	Weaver	Gt. Britain	United States	Penelope	9 Sep 1828
Ann	20	F	Spinster	Gt. Britain	U. States	Frances Henrietta	18 Apr 1825
Bridget	9	F	Labourer	Ireland	U. States	Two Marys	20 Apr 1825
Catharine	5	F	Labourer	Ireland	U. States	Two Marys	20 Apr 1825
Eliza	50	F		Ireland	U. States	Two Marys	20 Apr 1825
John	18	M	Labourer	Ireland	U. States	Two Marys	20 Apr 1825
John	38	M	Gentleman	United States	United States	Wyton	12 May 1821
M.	13	M	Labourer	Ireland	U. States	Two Marys	20 Apr 1825
M.	24		Coachman	Great Britain	United States	Comet	9 Aug 1822
Michael	6	M		United States	United States	Wyton	12 May 1821
Patrick	24	M	Labourer	Ireland	U. States	Two Marys	20 Apr 1825
Thomas	34	M	Mason	United States	U. States	Great Britain	18 Mar 1828
ENO, Richard	29	M	Gentleman	Citazen	U.S. States	Splendid	14 Aug 1829

NAMES OF PASSENGERS	AGE	SEX	OCCUPATIONS	COUNTRY TO WHICH THEY BELONG	COUNTRY THEY INTEND TO INHABIT	SHIPS/DATES OF ARRIVAL	
ENO (cont'd)							
Richard	68	M	Gentleman	England	U.S. States	Splendid	14 Aug 1829
William	20	M	Joiner	Great Britain	United States	Isaac Hicks	27 Sep 1826
ENOVER, Joseph	21	M	Carpenter	England	New York	Brighton	29 Aug 1828
ENRICO, John	28	M	Engineer	Italy	Mexico	Corinthian	27 Apr 1824
ENSALAN, Estein	36	M	Painter	Mexico	Germany	Conveyance	15 Jan 1827
ENTROPE, —	30	M	Merchant	France	U. States	Magnet	1 Oct 1823
ENTWERLE, Ann	1	F	None	England	United States	Enterprize	19 Oct 1826
L.	27	F	None	England	United States	Enterprize	19 Oct 1826
M.	5	F	None	England	United States	Enterprize	19 Oct 1826
T.	3	M	None	England	United States	Enterprize	19 Oct 1826
ENTWISE, James	33	M	Shoemaker	England	United States	Enterprize	19 Oct 1826
ENTWISLE, Edward	10	M	None	Bolton		Aurora	8 Jun 1827
Edward	41	M	Merchant	Bolton		Aurora	8 Jun 1827
Henry	10	M	None	Bolton		Aurora	8 Jun 1827
James	16	M	None	Bolton		Aurora	8 Jun 1827
Mary	32	F	None	England	New York	Cincinnatus	16 Apr 1824
Mary	38	F	None	Bolton		Aurora	8 Jun 1827
ENTWISTE, Mary Anne	36	F	Farmer	England	England	Criterion	29 May 1822
ENTWISTLE, Wm.	25	M	Farmer	England	United States	John Wells	15 Jan 1827
ENTZ, Abr. Frederic	30 7/12	M	Merchant	Switzer	Philadelphia, U.S.	Europa	6 Oct 1828
ENWARD, William	50	M	Merchant	St. John	St. John	St. Michael	24 Jun 1824
ENWOOD, Sarah	28	F	Farmer	Great Britain	United States	Wanderer	14 May 1828
EPENOZA DE CAMARA PERESTRELLO, Frns. Cicento, Esqr, etc. etc.		M	Consul Genl.	Portugal	U. States	Sarah Louisa	10 Oct 1822
EPERY, Hy.	20	M	Book Binder	England	U. States	Acasta	21 Jan 1825
EPLOTTENICE, F. L.	33		Merchant	Switzerland		Edward Bonnaffe	17 Mar 1828
EPPS, John	21	M	Farmer	Gt. Britain	Clyde, N.Y.	Leeds	7 Nov 1828
Wm.	28	M	Farmer	Gt. Britain	Clyde, N.Y.	Leeds	7 Nov 1828
EQUICE, J. B.	23	M	Gentleman	Belboa	South America	Columbus	2 May 1826
EQUIN, Patrick	27	M	Laborer	Ireland	United States	Belleville	13 Oct 1827
EQUIRA, Joaquim J.	60	M	Merchant	Portugal	U. States	Haxall	21 Oct 1826
ERANS, Sarah	28	F	Servant	Great Britain	U. States	Columbia	22 Sep 1828
ERCHBORN, Philip	20	M	Merchant	Prussia	Prussia	Columbia	10 Mar 1824
ERCHIN, —	28	M	Labourer	France	United States	Cavalier	25 Jul 1828
—, his Wife	28	F		France	United States	Cavalier	25 Jul 1828
Pierre	1 6/12	F		France	United States	Cavalier	25 Jul 1828
ERDMAND, H.	28	M	Merchant	Germany	Germany	Lady Washington	31 Dec 1827
ERDMANN, H.	28	M	Merchand	Germany		Amos Palmer	9 Jan 1829
ERECARVANA, G. A.	22	M	Merchant	Spain	U. States	Canning	18 Jul 1828
ERICKSON, Christian	40	M	Master	Philadelphia	United States	Richmond	18 Feb 1820
ERLEMS, Antonio	30	M	Merchant	Brazil	Brazil	Zepher	20 Oct 1827
ERLER, Carl Gottleib	26	M	Tailor	Saxony		François I	19 Nov 1828
ERLES, Elizabeth	35	F	None	Great Britain	United States	John	6 Oct 1820
Job	4	M	None	Great Britain	United States	John	6 Oct 1820
Wm.	40	M	Manufacturer	Great Britain	United States	John	6 Oct 1820
Wm., Jr.	7	M	None	Great Britain	United States	John	6 Oct 1820
ERMATINGER, Bernard	34	M	Merchant	Lu...terland	N. York	Stephania	29 Nov 1825
ERMETENGER, B.	32	M	Merchant	Spain	U. States	Anne	20 Jun 1828
ERNENPUSCH, T. C.	28	M	Merchant	Germany	United States	Florida	14 Sep 1827
ERNIT, Bernard	55	M		Germany	U. States	Falcon	11 Jun 1827
ERNNEST, Sarah	18	M		Great Britain	United States	Isaac Hicks	22 May 1826
Wm.	22	M	Gentleman	Great Britian	United States	Isaac Hicks	22 May 1826
ERNSHAN, Geo.	25	M	Weaver	Alloa	U. States	Sprightly	14 Jun 1822
ERNSHAW, ...ham	1 6/12	M	None	Halifax	...	Frances Henrietta	30 Jun 1827
Elizabeth	24	F	None	Halifax	...	Frances Henrietta	30 Jun 1827
John	30	M	...	Halifax	...	Frances Henrietta	30 Jun 1827
ERNST, Bernard	20	M	Locksmith	Germany	U. States	Falcon	11 Jun 1827
Charles	24	M	Cooper	Germany	U. States	Falcon	11 Jun 1827
Elizabeth	16	F		Germany	U. States	Falcon	11 Jun 1827
L.	8	M		Germany	U. States	Falcon	11 Jun 1827
Rosina	26	F		Germany	U. States	Falcon	11 Jun 1827

NAMES OF PASSENGERS	AGE	SEX	OCCUPATIONS	COUNTRY TO WHICH THEY BELONG	COUNTRY THEY INTEND TO INHABIT	SHIPS/DATES OF ARRIVAL	
ERNST (cont'd)							
Stifft. Christian	47	M	Miner	Garmine	Garmine	Douglass	9 Nov 1827
ERNST JORDAN, —,							
Mrs.	30	F		Saxony	New York	Constitution	29 Aug 1821
Carl G. E.	52	M	Chemist	Saxony	New York	Constitution	29 Aug 1821
ERPEL, C. S. H.	42	M	Planter	Germany	Bermuda	Industry	26 Jul 1825
ERSKINE, William	30	M		Scotland	United States	Camillus	9 May 1827
Willm.	22	M	Farmer	Ireland	U. States	Dickinson	30 Jul 1825
ERSON, Francis	36	M	Farmer	England	U.S. States	Splendid	14 Aug 1829
ERTHINGTON,							
James	25 4/12	M	Farmer	England	U.S. of America	Illinois	16 Jun 1821
ERVENS, Owen	41	M	Merchant	Ireland	U. States	Alfred	17 Sep 1822
ERVIN, Pierre	51		Farmer	France	U. States	Parachute	14 May 1828
ERVINE, Gillis	21	M	Labourer	Ireland	United States	Hope	12 Jun 1828
ERVING, Alexander	18	M	Labourer	Ireland	United States	Hope	12 Jun 1828
James	45	M	Farmer	Scotland	U. States	Roger Stewart	9 Jun 1828
ERVITRE, A.	16	M	Son	Hessee	U. States	Henry	24 Oct 1828
A.	48	M		Hessee	U. States	Henry	24 Oct 1828
Caselia	13	F	Dauter	Hessee	U. States	Henry	24 Oct 1828
Elizabeth	26	F	Lady	Hessee	U. States	Henry	24 Oct 1828
Sarah	38	F	Lady	Hessee	U. States	Henry	24 Oct 1828
ERWIN, John	10	M	child	U. States	U. States	Nancy	19 Oct 1821
Robert	45	M	Labourer	Ireland	U. States	Josephine	30 Aug 1828
Thomas	35	M	Labourer	U. States	U. States	Nancy	19 Oct 1821
ESA, Hosa	3...	M	Meriner	Spain	Spain	Florida	30 Jun 1826
ESCAVAN, Jean	43	M		Spain		Apollo	11 Jun 1828
ESCHENBURG, Eliza	24	F		United States	United States	Romulus	13 Aug 1829
Ellen	3	F		Buenos Ayres	United States	Romulus	13 Aug 1829
Emily	4	F		Buenos Ayres	United States	Romulus	13 Aug 1829
Isabella	6/12	F		Buenos Ayres	United States	Romulus	13 Aug 1829
John Rodney	2	M		Buenos Ayres	United States	Romulus	13 Aug 1829
ESCHER, George	18	M	Baker			Nancy	1 Sep 1823
ESCHERALDER, F.	44	M	Farmer	France	U. States	Lewis	6 Jul 1825
ESCONDON, —	21	M	Merchant	Havana	Spain	Fair American	24 Dec 1821
ESCOVEGALA, Barnardo	14	M	School Boy	Spain	Spain	Emulation	22 Jun 1825
ESDRA, Moses	28	M	Watchmaker	France	New York	Homer	28 Aug 1829
ESENLABEN, Joel F.	23	M	Farmer	Holland	America	Gamacraw	28 Sep 1820
ESERT, Ge.	16	M		Switzerland	U.States	C. Amelia	30 Jun 1828
Jean	50	M		Switzerland	U.States	C. Amelia	30 Jun 1828
May	6	F	Tailor	Switzerland	U.States	C. Amelia	30 Jun 1828
ESH, Parbsour	21	F	None	Switzerland	United States	Ospray	2 Sep 1824
ESIMETE, Bernard	25	M	Mercht.	Campeachy	Campeachy	Margaret Wright	20 May 1825
ESK, Christia	3	F	None	Switzerland	United States	Ospray	2 Sep 1824
Sophronia	2	F	None	Switzerland	United States	Ospray	2 Sep 1824
ESMARALDO, Angelina	36	F	Lady	Madeira	Madeira	Uniao	19 Aug 1829
Francisco	32	M	Merchant	Madeira	Madeira	Uniao	19 Aug 1829
Louisa	30	F	Lady	Madeira	Madeira	Uniao	19 Aug 1829
Mary	6	F	Child	Madeira	Madeira	Uniao	19 Aug 1829
ESNARD, —, Mrs.	30					Prometheus	30 Aug 1828
Elisa	10					Prometheus	30 Aug 1828
ESPADERO, Carman	3	F		Spain		Boyer	9 May 1825
Dolores	26	F		Spain		Boyer	9 May 1825
Manuel	35	M		Spain		Boyer	9 May 1825
ESPALAZO, Juan	36	M		Holland		Apollo	11 Jun 1828
ESPARDERO, Rajla		F		Spain		Boyer	9 May 1825
ESPARDO, J. M.	28	M	Commercial agent for Campeachy to the U. States	U. States	U. States	Favourite	18 Aug 1823
ESPENVILLE, D.	18	M	Secretary	France	France	Imperial	10 Dec 1821
ESPIE, George	19	M	Youth	Ireland	United States	Romulus	24 Jun 1826
Isabella	33		Spinster	Great Britain	United States	Camillus	12 Sep 1827
Jane	56		Spinster	Great Britain	United States	Camillus	12 Sep 1827
ESPINOSA, Jose	30	M	Mercht.	Teneriffe		Marcella	15 Mar 1827
Raphael	30	M	Military	Mexico	Mexico	Virginia	9 Feb 1829
Teresa	18	F	Wife	Spain	Mexico	Virginia	9 Feb 1829
ESPREO, J.	40	M	Merchant	Spain	U. States	Aspasia	23 Nov 1825
ESPUE, Jas.	20		Farmer	Great Britain	United States	Camillus	12 Sep 1827
ESQUIVEL, M.	31	M	Gentleman	Central America	U. States	Mary Levengston,	17 Jun 1826

NAMES OF PASSENGERS	AGE	SEX	OCCUPATIONS	COUNTRY TO WHICH THEY BELONG	COUNTRY THEY INTEND TO INHABIT	SHIPS/DATES OF ARRIVAL	
ESRAGOLA, L.	39	M		Spain	U. States	Courier	31 Jul 1828
ESSEX, John	45		Merchant	Worcester	England	London	13 Dec 1822
ESTANO, G.	28	M	Merchant	Spain	Spain	Victory	8 Oct 1821
ESTE, Olivia, Miss	24	F		France	United States	Alexander	20 Aug 1828
ESTEPH, Geo. S.	61	M		Germany	United States	Lydia	18 Jun 1828
ESTERA, Gabriel	23	M	Gentleman	Spain	United States	Liberty	7 Aug 1821
ESTEVES, Joaquin	35	M	Servant	Island of Cuba	Cuba	James Monroe	21 May 1825
Ramon	25	M	Merchant	Cuba	Cuba	New England	27 Jul 1829
ESTHER, George	20	M	Baker	Germany	United States	St. Michaels	12 Apr 1826
ESTOFAL, Christobal	35	M	Merchant	France	France	Albert	17 Jan 1828
ESTRANDO, Joaquim G.	22	M	Merchant	Mexico	U. States	Desdemona	15 Jun 1827
ESTRANGE, Lawrence	24	M	Farmer	Ireland	United States	Dublin Packet	23 May 1828
ETESTE, A.	35	M	Merchant	France	St. Domingo	Elionor	5 Aug 1828
ETIENNE, D. G.	42	M	Professor of Music	France	N. York	Talma	23 Sep 1828
Francois	6/12	M				Henri IV	17 May 1828
Joseph	28	M	Tailer			Henri IV	17 May 1828
Mary Ann	28	F				Henri IV	17 May 1828
Nicolas	2	M				Henri IV	17 May 1828
ETNEILLE, Samuel, Rev.	32	M	Minister of Gospel	Grate Britain	...	Courier	14 Jun 1825
ETRER, Maddan	42	F		St. Domingo	Baltimore	Proxy	20 Jul 1826
ETTAR, Marten	26		Baker	Germany	Philadelphia	Xenophon	25 Jul 1826
ETTERSHANKS, John H.	14	M	...	England	United States	Cincinnatus	21 Nov 1821
ETTWAS, ...m. Fra...	5	M		Great Britian	United States	London	24 Jun 1823
EUHRISTE, James	26	M	Merchant			Hercules	25 Sep 1820
EUNVIN, Robert	18	M	Mariner	Scotland	U. States	Douglass	7 Aug 1827
EUSTIS, J., Mr., Jr.	34	M	Merchant	U.S.A.		François I	19 Nov 1828
EVAN, Martin	20	M	Labourer	Great Brittain	United States	Active	12 Sep 1828
EVANGALZ, Christopher	12	M	Merchant	Greece	U. States	Harriet	3 Mar 1828
EVANS, ...	50		Shipbuilder	England	U.S. of America	Mary	21 Sep 1821
Abraham	28	M	Farmer	Ireland	United States	Justina	5 Aug 1823
Alan	8	F	None	Great Britan	U. States	Ann Marria	6 Aug 1823
Alice	22	F	Spinster	Wales		Gomer	22 May 1827
Andrew	32	M	Grocer	Wales	America	Francis & Henrietta	11 Jul 1823
Andw.	24	M	Sawyer	Cl...	Wales	Howard Douglass	11 May 1827
Ann	36		Farmer	England	United States	Corinthian	30 May 1828
Ann	50	F	None			James Monroe	8 Aug 1820
Benj.	28	M	Mercht.	U. States	U. States	Eugene	15 Dec 1828
Benjamin	12	M		Ireland	Bermuda	Triton	24 Oct 1826
Benjamin	24	M	Merchant	Philada.	U. States	Dewitt Clinton	16 Dec 1825
Bessey	23	F	Spinster	Ireland	United States	Dublin Packet	28 Apr 1824
Betsey	19		his family	England	U.S. of America	Mary	21 Sep 1821
Caroline	11		his family	England	U.S. of America	Mary	21 Sep 1821
Catharine	18	F	Farmer	G. Britian	U. States	Messouri	17 Jun 1824
Charlotte	5	F	Farmer	Great Britain	U. States	Columbia	22 Sep 1828
David	18		Black Smith	Cardigan		Mount Vernon	18 Oct 1822
David	22	M	Merchant	England	New York	Cincinnatus	16 Apr 1824
David	24	M				Splendid	14 Aug 1829
David	29	M	Farmer	England	U.S. of America	Illinois	16 Jun 1821
Ed.	32	M	Farmer	Ireland	U. States	Margaret	19 Mar 1825
Edward	26	M	Woolster	Wales	Wales	Helicon	3 Aug 1826
Edward	38		Farmer	England	United States	Corinthian	30 May 1828
Elanor	55	F		England	America U. States	La Grange	27 Sep 1826
Eleanor	10	F	Farmer	Wales		Gomer	22 May 1827
Eleanor	23	F		G. Britain	U. States	William Thompson	30 Apr 1822
Elias	25	M	Labourer	England	United States	Orozimbo	11 Aug 1823
Eliza	6	F	None	Great Britan	U. States	Ann Marria	6 Aug 1823
Emma	20	F	None	England	New York	Cincinnatus	16 Apr 1824
Evan	4	M	Labourer	Wales	U. States	Franklin	28 Jun 1825
Evan	14		Black Smith	Cardigan		Mount Vernon	18 Oct 1822
Evan	32	M	Farmer	Great Brittain	U. States	Louisa	11 Jun 1824
Evan	45		Black Smith	Cardigan		Mount Vernon	18 Oct 1822
Eyre	28	M	Farmer	Great Brit.	U. States	George	31 Jul 1820
Francis, Mr.	9	M	Gentn.	England	Canada	Acasta	21 Oct 1825
Frs.	14	M	Clerk	Ireland	U. States	Alex Mansfield	1 Jun 1822
Grace	32	F	Labourer	Wales	U. States	Franklin	28 Jun 1825
Griffith	30	M	Farmer	Wales	United States	Orozimbo	11 Aug 1823

NAMES OF PASSENGERS	AGE	SEX	OCCUPATIONS	COUNTRY TO WHICH THEY BELONG	COUNTRY THEY INTEND TO INHABIT	SHIPS/DATES OF ARRIVAL	
EVANS (cont'd)							
Griffith	31	M	Farmer	Ireland	United States	Aurelia	7 Jun 1826
Griffith	36	M	Farmer	Wales		Gomer	22 May 1827
Gwan	27	F	None	Great Brittain	U. States	Louisa	11 Jun 1824
Gwen	1	F	Labourer	Wales	U. States	Franklin	28 Jun 1825
Hannah	2	F	None	Wales	United States	Orozimbo	11 Aug 1823
J.	14	M	Farmer	Ireland	America	Liverpool	31 Aug 1827
J.	30	M	Printer	U. States	U. States	Columbia	7 Sep 1827
Jacob	28 1/12	M	Butcher	New York	New York	Florida	27 Aug 1825
James	22	M	None	England	New York	Brighton	16 Nov 1826
James F.	36	M	Blacksmith	Wales	United States	Lord Wellington	14 Nov 1827
Jane	6			Cardigan		Mount Vernon	18 Oct 1822
Jane	6	F	None	Great Brittain	U. States	Louisa	11 Jun 1824
Jane	43			Cardigan		Mount Vernon	18 Oct 1822
Jane	60	F		Ireland	America	Carolina Ann	7 Apr 1826
Jane, Daughter [of Griffith]	13	F	Farmer	Wales		Gomer	22 May 1827
Janes	25	F	None	Wales	United States	Orozimbo	11 Aug 1823
Jas.	20	M	Mechanic	England	U. States	Acasta	21 Jan 1825
Jno.	26	M	Farmer	G. Brittain	U. States	Favorite	13 Jun 1821
John	10	M	None	Great Britan	U. States	Ann Marria	6 Aug 1823
John	11		Black Smith	Cardigan		Mount Vernon	18 Oct 1822
John	13		his family	England	U.S. of America	Mary	21 Sep 1821
John	21	M	Merchant	England	America	Plato	31 Oct 1829
John	30		Farmer	Ireland	United States	Abigail	25 Jun 1822
John	35	M	Farmer	Great Britain	U. States	Columbia	22 Sep 1828
John	45	M	Farmer			James Monroe	8 Aug 1820
John, Child [of Griffith]	1	M	Farmer	Wales		Gomer	22 May 1827
Josh.	38	M	Mariner	England	Quebec	New England	12 Apr 1825
Lewis	31	M	Labourrer	Great Britan	U. States	Ann Marria	6 Aug 1823
Magn.	23	F		Gt. Britain		Dalhouse Castle	13 May 1828
Margaret	7	F	Labourer	Wales	U. States	Franklin	28 Jun 1825
Margaret	23	F		Great Britain	United States	John Jay	8 May 1828
Maria Sophia, Mrs.	21	F	Lady	England	Canada	Acasta	21 Oct 1825
Marry	31	F	None	Great Britan	U. States	Ann Marria	6 Aug 1823
Mary	6	F	Farmer	Wales		Gomer	22 May 1827
Mary	27	F		England	England	Tontin	13 Jun 1825
Mary, Wife [of Robert]	21	F	Labourer	Wales		Gomer	22 May 1827
Mary, Wife [of Griffith]	36	F	Farmer	Wales		Gomer	22 May 1827
Mary Ann	3	F	Farmer	Great Britain	U. States	Columbia	22 Sep 1828
Nancy	21		his family	England	U.S. of America	Mary	21 Sep 1821
Nancy	43		his family	England	U.S. of America	Mary	21 Sep 1821
Owen	32	M	...later	G. Britain	U. States	Convivial	10 Nov 1826
Rabecca	6/12	F	Farmer	Great Britain	U. States	Columbia	22 Sep 1828
Rebecca	25	F	None	Wales	United States	Orozimbo	11 Aug 1823
Richard	20		Black Smith	Cardigan		Mount Vernon	18 Oct 1822
Richd.	12	M	Mechanic	England	U. States	Acasta	21 Jan 1825
Richd.	14	M	None	England	New York	Brighton	16 Nov 1826
Richd.	44	M	Artist	England	England	General Warren	6 Mar 1829
Robert	23	M	Labourer	Wales		Gomer	22 May 1827
Robt.	9	M	None	Great Brittain	U. States	Louisa	11 Jun 1824
Sarah	18		his family	England	U.S. of America	Mary	21 Sep 1821
Sarah	28	F	Farmer	Great Britain	U. States	Columbia	22 Sep 1828
Sarah	38	F				Acasta	28 Jul 1823
Thomas	4			Cardigan		Mount Vernon	18 Oct 1822
Thomas	5	M				Acasta	28 Jul 1823
Thomas	35		Farmer	England	America	Governor Griswold	6 Jun 1821
Thos.	42		Shop Keeper	Great Britain	United States	Comet	9 Aug 1822
Thos.	48	M	Gentn.	England	Canada	Brighton	16 Nov 1826
W.	22	M	Merchant	England	U. States	Pacific	16 Apr 1825
W. S.	27	M	Merchant	Great Britain	Baltimore	Corinthian	27 Apr 1824
William	22		his family	England	U.S. of America	Mary	21 Sep 1821
William	22	M	Carpenter	Bristol, Engl.	...	Warrior	19 May 1828
Winniford	3	M	None	Great Britan	U. States	Ann Marria	6 Aug 1823
Wm.	29	M	Labourer	Wales	U. States	Franklin	28 Jun 1825

NAMES OF PASSENGERS	AGE	SEX	OCCUPATIONS	COUNTRY TO WHICH THEY BELONG	COUNTRY THEY INTEND TO INHABIT	SHIPS/DATES OF ARRIVAL	
EVANS (cont'd)							
Wm.	33		Farmer	England	U. States	Charlotte	26 Aug 1825
Wm.	38	M	Mariner	Bermuda	Bermuda	Rover	17 Apr 1827
Wm.	40	M	Merchant	Ireland	Bermuda	Triton	24 Oct 1826
Wm. Hy.	34	M	Gentleman	Charleston, S.C.	Charleston, S.C.	New York	31 Jul 1829
EVARS, E.	18			Ireland	United States	Geo. Canning	5 Jun 1828
Mary	54			Ireland	United States	Geo. Canning	5 Jun 1828
EVE, Cordelia	15/12	F	None	Great Britain	United States	Orlando	8 Nov 1826
Dorcas T.	27	F	None	Great Britain	United States	Orlando	8 Nov 1826
EVELEIGH, N. W.	32	M	Mariner	U. States	U. States	Queen Mab	16 Jun 1827
EVENE, C.	30	M	Tanner	Switzerland	U. States	Romulus	24 Sep 1828
EVENS, —, Mr.	30	M	Merchant	England	U. States	Baltimore	6 Dec 1823
David	11	M	Farmer	Britain	U. States	Fame	3 Jun 1828
Even	24 2/12	M	Preacher of the Gospel	North Wales	United States	Missouri	21 May 1827
G.	18	M	White Smith	U. States	U. States	John & Robert	4 Sep 1827
Mary	26	F		North Wales	United States	Missouri	21 May 1827
Rufus	23	M	Merchant	N. Hampshire	U. States	Weymouth	13 Aug 1822
Thomas	24	M	Laborer	Scotland	New York	Indian Chief	19 Jun 1823
EVERAERTS, John	40	M	Consul	Hayti		Ranger	29 Jul 1828
EVERARD, Jno.	21	M	Harness Maker	Great Britain	United States	Penelope	11 Jun 1827
John	30	M	Stone Cutter	G. Britain	U. States	St. George	16 Jan 1829
Thomas	70	M	Preacher	Great Britain	United States	Robert Fulton	22 Oct 1821
Thomas	70	M	Clergyman	United States	United States	Silas Richards	27 Oct 1825
EVERDEN, Jane	12	F				Acosta	28 Jul 1823
John	15	M				Acosta	28 Jul 1823
Thomas	55	M	Gardner			Acosta	28 Jul 1823
EVERETT, Alex. H.	40 2/12	M	Gentleman	U.S. America	U.S. America	Erie	19 Oct 1829
Benjamin C.	12	M	Boy	England	United States	Cambria	3 Jul 1829
Charles	40	M		U. States	U. States	Florida	2 Jun 1828
Charles, Jr.	17	M	Merchant	Britain	U. States	Florida	2 Jun 1828
Christopher	28	M		Ireland	United States	Essex	23 May 1828
Eliza	37	F		U. States	U. States	Florida	2 Jun 1828
Elizabeth	5	F	None	Denbagh	U. States	New York	11 Jul 1823
Elizabeth	27	F	None	Denbagh	U. States	New York	11 Jul 1823
Jno.	40	M		English	England	Prudence	19 Apr 1826
Jno. R.	3	M	None	Denbagh	U. States	New York	11 Jul 1823
Louisa	16 5/12	F	Lady	U.S. America	U.S. America	Erie	19 Oct 1829
Lucretia	36 4/12	F	Lady	U.S. America	U.S. America	Erie	19 Oct 1829
Mary	3	F	None	England	U. States	New York	11 Jul 1823
Mary	20	F		Ireland	United States	Essex	23 May 1828
Mary	30	F	None	England	U. States	New York	11 Jul 1823
Mary	50	F	Weaver	Ireland	United States	Essex	23 May 1828
Newman	36	M	Miller	England	United States	Cambria	3 Jul 1829
Robt.	10/12	M	None		U. States	New York	11 Jul 1823
Robt.	5	M	None	England	U. States	New York	11 Jul 1823
Robt.	33	M	Minister	Denbagh	U. States	New York	11 Jul 1823
Thomas	34	M	Merchant	U.S.		Pacific	29 Dec 1824
Thos.	27	M	Book Keeper	Manchester	U. States	New York	11 Jul 1823
EVERHART, Wm.	36	M	Merchant	United States	United States	Columbia	9 Aug 1822
EVERING, George W.	29 8/12	M	Gentlman.	America	America	France	28 Mar 1829
EVERS, Ann	17	F	Servant	Ireland	New York	Atlantic	8 May 1828
Jno.	25	M		Ireland	United States	Essex	23 May 1828
Owen	26	M	Clerk	Ireland	U. States	Henry Kneeland	27 Jul 1825
EVERSLEY, John	5/12	M		Bardos	United States	McFingal	9 Dec 1826
Leonore	24	F	None	Bardos	United States	McFingal	9 Dec 1826
EVERSOM, Roberson	22	M	Laborer	Ireland	United States	Fabius	4 Jun 1828
EVES, —, Mr.	34	M	Merchant	Dublin	U. States	Hibernia	26 Oct 1826
EVETT, Alley	20			Ireland	United States	John Dickinson	28 Jun 1822
Humphrey	13			Ireland	United States	John Dickinson	28 Jun 1822
John	13			Ireland	United States	John Dickinson	28 Jun 1822
EVINS, Hugh	65	M	Surgeon	Wales	United States	Euphrates	23 Jun 1826
EVIO, Banardo	19	M	Gent.	Spain	Cuba	Fabius	24 Oct 1825
EWART, David	18	M	Weaver	Liston	Ireland	Carolina Ann	11 Jun 1824
James	20 9/12	M	Farmer	G. Britain	United States	Louisa	14 Jun 1825
James	27	M	Merchant	England	Canada	William Byrnes	11 Dec 1827
Mary	66	F	Wife	Armar	Baltimore	Nile	18 Aug 1829
William	30	M	Son	Armar	Baltimore	Nile	18 Aug 1829

NAMES OF PASSENGERS	AGE	SEX	OCCUPATIONS	COUNTRY TO WHICH THEY BELONG	COUNTRY THEY INTEND TO INHABIT	SHIPS/DATES OF ARRIVAL	
EWART (cont'd)							
William	66	M	Farmer	Armar	Baltimore	Nile	18 Aug 1829
EWBANK, Mary	26	F		United States	New York	Venus	8 Sep 1820
Thos. Harrison	2	M		United States	New York	Venus	8 Sep 1820
EWEN, Edward	30	M	Mariner	U.S.	U.S.	Athenian	14 Oct 1828
EWERBANK, James	32	M	Carver	Gt. Britain	U. States	St. George	20 Sep 1828
T. M.	42	F		Gt. Britain	U. States	St. George	20 Sep 1828
EWERLAGE, Frans, Mr.	43	M	Seaman	Oldenburg	New York	Europa	12 Oct 1829
Mathilda, Miss	9 10/12	F		Hamburg	New York	Europa	12 Oct 1829
Mathilda, Mrs.	44 5/12	F		Hamburg	New York	Europa	12 Oct 1829
EWIN, Isabella	29	F	Housekeeper	Scotland	United States	Liverpool Trader	24 Oct 1825
Peter	29	M	Print Cotton	Great Britain	United States	Robert Fulton	18 May 1825
EWINE, Rob.	25	M	Merchant	U. States		Charleston Packet	4 May 1821
Saml.	26	M	Joiner	Wol..., H..., Scotland	U. States	New Orleans	24 Aug 1827
EWING, A.	35	M	Merchant	Londonderry	United States	Hector	29 Nov 1823
Amelia	18	F	None	London	United States	Dalhousie Castle	27 Jul 1826
Eliza	18	F	Servant	Ireland	America	Carolina Ann	7 Aug 1826
Gabrial	30	M	Weaver	Ireland	United States	Marmion	17 Jun 1825
Geo. W.	50	M	Gentleman	U. States	U. States	Six Brothers	4 Jun 1822
George	7			Ireland	United States	John Dickinson	28 Jun 1822
James	17	M	Labourer	Ireland	U. States	William & John	10 Jul 1824
James	18	M	G. Blower	Scotland	U. States	Spartan	21 Apr 1826
James	23	M	Servant	Ireland	America	Carolina Ann	7 Aug 1826
James	26 1/12	M		Ireland	U.S. of America	Douglass	6 Jul 1829
James	30	M	Merchant	Great Britain	St. Johns, N.B.	Columbia	9 Aug 1822
James	50	M	Farmer	Ireland	U. States	Hanford	29 Dec 1828
John	26	M	Laborer	Carrah Cayr, Derry	...	Gleaner	24 May 1823
Judith	5			Ireland	United States	John Dickinson	28 Jun 1822
Judith	26			Ireland	United States	John Dickinson	28 Jun 1822
Mary	20	M		Great Britain	U. States	Lady Hunter	26 Nov 1823
Robert	8			Ireland	United States	John Dickinson	28 Jun 1822
William	1 6/12	M	Servant	Ireland	America	Carolina Ann	7 Aug 1826
William	24		Farmer			Rufus King	7 Aug 1820
Wm.	3			Ireland	United States	John Dickinson	28 Jun 1822
EWINGTON, Henry	61	M	Schoolmaster	London	United States	Dalhousie Castle	27 Jul 1826
Mary	6...	F	None	London	United States	Dalhousie Castle	27 Jul 1826
Sophia	24	F	None	London	United States	Dalhousie Castle	27 Jul 1826
EWINS, John, Mr.	23		Farmer	England		Hercules	19 Jun 1821
EWRING, James	50	M	Merchant	England	United States	Great Britain	5 Sep 1827
EWRY, John	7	M	Labourer	England	U. States	Emulous	22 Aug 1828
Richard	5	M	Labourer	England	U. States	Emulous	22 Aug 1828
EXCHENBAUB,							
Catherine	1 6/12	F	there child [James & Magdelene]	France	United States	Helen	5 Sep 1828
George	15	M	there child [James & Magdelene]	France	United States	Helen	5 Sep 1828
James	48	M	Farmer	France	United States	Helen	5 Sep 1828
Magdelene	3	F	there child [James & Magdelene]	France	United States	Helen	5 Sep 1828
Magdelene	37	F	his wife [James]	France	United States	Helen	5 Sep 1828
EXLEY, Anne	18	F	None	England	United States	Jubilee	12 May 1828
John	56	M	Weaver	England	United States	Jubilee	12 May 1828
Mary	53	F	None	England	United States	Jubilee	12 May 1828
Mary, Jr.	12	F	None	England	United States	Jubilee	12 May 1828
EXLY, E...	40	M	Clothier	Great Britain	United States	Atlantic	28 May 1827
EXMANDER, E. M.	12	M	boy	Cuba	U. States	James Monroe	8 Sep 1824
Joseph F.	8	M	boy	Cuba	U. States	James Monroe	8 Sep 1824
Joseph M.	10	M	boy	Cuba	U. States	James Monroe	8 Sep 1824
EXTON, Ed.	24		Farmer	England	United States	Hugh Johnson	11 Jun 1828
Eliz.	22			England	United States	Hugh Johnson	11 Jun 1828
Joseph	34		Farmer	England	United States	Hugh Johnson	11 Jun 1828
Thos.	26		Farmer	England	United States	Hugh Johnson	11 Jun 1828

NAMES OF PASSENGERS	AGE	SEX	OCCUPATIONS	COUNTRY TO WHICH THEY BELONG	COUNTRY THEY INTEND TO INHABIT	SHIPS/DATES OF ARRIVAL	
EYBACHER, I							
George Frema	50	M	Farmer	Wortenberg	Lancaster	Louisa	6 Oct 1828
Margaretha	11	F	Farmer	Wortenberg	Lancaster	Louisa	6 Oct 1828
EYMAR, ...nd	30	M	Mercht.	France	U. States	Charles	11 Jul 1823
Antonio	35	M	Merchant	Spain	Spain	Plough Boy	16 Oct 1823
EYQUEN, Marie	18	F	Merchant	France	France	Henry	16 May 1827
EYR, Thomas	20	M	Labourer	England	U. States	Emulous	22 Aug 1828
EYRE, —, Mr.	32	M	Mariner	U. States	U. States	Cicero	24 Oct 1823
Catherine	12	F	None	England	United States	Hogarth	12 Oct 1829
Eliza	13	F	None	England	United States	Hogarth	12 Oct 1829
James	9	M	None	England	United States	Hogarth	12 Oct 1829
James	38	M	Mechanic	England	United States	Hogarth	12 Oct 1829
Jane	37	F	None	England	United States	Hogarth	12 Oct 1829
Joshua	2	M	None	United States	United States	Hogarth	12 Oct 1829
Mary Ann	10	F	None	England	United States	Hogarth	12 Oct 1829
EYRNTEN, Wm.	20	M	None	U. States	U. States	Bayard	9 Jul 1824
EYTINGE, —, Mrs.	34	F		Amsterdam	U. States	Heroine	19 Jun 1828
Eliza	9	F		Amsterdam	U. States	Heroine	19 Jun 1828
Hannah	4	F		Amsterdam	U. States	Heroine	19 Jun 1828
J.	52	M	Merchant	Amsterdam	U. States	Heroine	19 Jun 1828
Jane	11	F		Amsterdam	U. States	Heroine	19 Jun 1828
Louis D.	66	M		Holland	N. York	Salem	15 Mar 1828
Margt.	2	F		Amsterdam	U. States	Heroine	19 Jun 1828
May	7	F		Amsterdam	U. States	Heroine	19 Jun 1828
Simon	38	M	Merchant	Amsterdam	U. States	Heroine	19 Jun 1828
EZEKIEL, Esther	17 5/12	F	None	Great Brittian	United States	Four Sons	31 May 1828
Leah	40 6/12	F	None	Great Brittian	United States	Four Sons	31 May 1828
EZPELETA, Francisco	10/12	M		Mexico	Spain	Virginia	9 Feb 1829
Francisco, Mr.	30	M	Merchant	Spain	Spain	Virginia	9 Feb 1829
Maria, Mrs.	19	F	Wife	Mexico	Spain	Virginia	9 Feb 1829
F..., Edwd.	86	M	...	Switzerland	U. States	Robert Edward	2 Nov 1827
F...A...LLES, —, Mrs.	28	F		Great Britian	United States	London	24 Jun 1823
F...CO, Wm. H.	35 11/12	M	Merchant	America	America	Josephine	8 Jan 1827
F...DGE, Michal	24	M		Great B.	U. States	William Neilson	26 Jul 1828
F...DLINGTON, ...	30 3/12	M	...	England	America, U.S.	Illinois	3 Jun 1822
F...L, Mary	26	F	Servant Maid	Ireland	America	Plutarch	18 Jul 1826
F...NN..., George	...		Labourer	...on	England	Great Britain	7 May 1827
FABB, Abraham	27	M	Weaver	Germany	United States	Origon	8 Jun 1824
Balary	22	F		Germany	United States	Origon	8 Jun 1824
FABBY, Michael	27	M	Labourer	Great Britain	United States	Henrietta	19 Oct 1825
FABER, Adamine, Miss	24	F		...mark		Howard	6 Jul 1829
Esthe	45	F		U. States	U. States	Hamilton	22 Sep 1828
J.	47	M	Merchant	United States	United States	Robert Fulton	2 Aug 1824
John R.	32	M	Mariner	United States	United States	John Wells	16 Feb 1824
L.	13	M	Merchant	New York	U. States	Confiance	26 Apr 1828
FABIE, Jno. A.	22	M	Merchant	Mexico	Mexico	Washington	29 Apr 1826
FABINE, C.	35	M	Merchant	Germany	U. States	Neptune	19 Nov 1828
FABOR, C. W.	27	M	...	...	U.S. America	Columbia	26 Nov 1825
FABRICK, Jno.	27	M	Ma[r]iner	France	U. States	Vigilant	14 Apr 1823
FABRICO, C.	21	M	Merchant	Panama	Panama	Morhey	3 Mar 1825
FABRIN, J.						Dromo	14 Aug 1829
FACEY, Mary	40	F	Gent.	Jamaica	U. States	Brown	11 Jan 1825
FACKINTER, James	0 6/12	M	Laborer or Spinster	Ireland	United States	Sarah G	11 Sep 1827
Margaret	23	F	Laborer or Spinster	Ireland	United States	Sarah G	11 Sep 1827
FACON, —, Mdme.	47	F		Spain	Spain	Cadmus	11 Jul 1827
—, Miss	18	F		Spain	Spain	Cadmus	11 Jul 1827
—, Miss	22	F		Spain	Spain	Cadmus	11 Jul 1827
—, Mr.	21	M		Spain	Spain	Cadmus	11 Jul 1827
—, Mr.	47	...	...for	Spain	Spain	Cadmus	11 Jul 1827
—, Mr., Jr.	20	M		Spain	Spain	Cadmus	11 Jul 1827
FADDOMS, Jno.	22	M	Mechanic	U.S.	U.S.	Mordicae	24 Nov 1828
FADER, —	69	F		New Brunswick	United States	Edwin	27 Oct 1828
FADERELLE, Jas.	25	M	Merchant	France	Honduras or South America	Alabama	3 Dec 1823
FADINO, Louis	32	M	Merchant	Italy	West Indies	Sally	15 Sep 1820
FAERBER, E. F.	36	M	Merchant	Prussia	Prussia	Columbia	10 Mar 1824
FAERICH, Wm.	30	M	Currier	Gt. Britain	New York	Betsey	18 Apr 1822
FAG, Ann	22	F	Servant	Ireland	U. States	Henrietta	7 Jul 1825

NAMES OF PASSENGERS	AGE	SEX	OCCUPATIONS	COUNTRY TO WHICH THEY BELONG	COUNTRY THEY INTEND TO INHABIT	SHIPS/DATES OF ARRIVAL	
FAG (cont'd)							
Edwd	25	M	Servant	Ireland	U. States	Henrietta	7 Jul 1825
FAGAIN, Ellen	32	F	Servant	Ireland	America	Carolina Ann	7 Aug 1826
FAGAN, Catherine	24	F	Spinster	Ireland	United States	Dublin Packet	9 Jul 1827
Christopher	20	M	Victualler	Ireland	U. States	Albion	11 May 1827
Daniel	26	M	Merchant			Hercules	25 Sep 1820
Eliza	12	F	Servant	Ireland	United States	Carolina Ann	14 May 1827
Farel	28			b. Weaver of Land, last of Longford	Newyork	Peru	30 May 1828
James	19		Gentleman	Ireland	America	Florida	14 Oct 1829
James	22	M	Farmer	Ireland	United States	Dublin Packet	29 Jun 1825
John	23	M	Cordwainer	Ireland	U.S.A.	Robin Hood	6 May 1828
Mary	20	M	Servant	England	United States	Nimrod	31 Jul 1828
Mary	25	F	Servant	Ireland	United States	Carolina Ann	14 May 1827
Mathew	26	M		Gt. Britain	United States	Penelope	9 Sep 1828
Patt	25	M	Farmer	Ireland	United States	Dublin Packet	29 Jun 1825
Peter	23	M	Carpenter	Ireland	U. States	Josephine	7 May 1827
Peter	25	M	Farmer	Ireland	America	Mary	29 May 1827
Thomas	28	M	Planter	Demerara	Island of Cuba	Adrianna	7 Apr 1823
FAGEN, Pat	21	M		Great Britain	United States	Atlantic	28 May 1827
FAGERTY, Jacob	29	M	Farmer	Alsace in the Department of Upper and lower Rhine	United States	Carolina Augusta	16 May 1828
FAGG, Elizabeth	17	M	Labourer	England	America	Sarah	18 Aug 1829
George	5	M	Labourer	England	America	Sarah	18 Aug 1829
Henry	3/12	M	Labourer	England	America	Sarah	18 Aug 1829
James	13	M	Labourer	England	America	Sarah	18 Aug 1829
John	19	M	Labourer	England	America	Sarah	18 Aug 1829
John	42	M	Labourer	England	America	Sarah	18 Aug 1829
Joseph	3	M	Labourer	England	America	Sarah	18 Aug 1829
Mary	43	F	Labourer	England	America	Sarah	18 Aug 1829
Samuel	11	M	Labourer	England	America	Sarah	18 Aug 1829
Stephen	7	M	Labourer	England	America	Sarah	18 Aug 1829
William	15	M	Labourer	England	America	Sarah	18 Aug 1829
FAGGAN, Jno.	22	M		Ireland	U. States	Alex Mansfield	1 Jun 1822
FAHR, Joseph	30	M	Carpenter	France	U. States	Cowper	8 Jan 1827
FAHTMAN, Detrich	24	M	Sugar Refiner	England	U.S.	Acasta	11 May 1827
FAHY, Bridget	22	F		Ireland	United States	Meteor	19 Aug 1829
H., Miss	12	F		England		Hudson	23 Jul 1828
James	22	M		Galway	U. States	Eliza Ann	30 Jul 1823
Patrick	1	M		Ireland	United States	Meteor	19 Aug 1829
William	25	M	Taylor	Ireland	United States	Meteor	19 Aug 1829
FAILE, Patrick	28	M	Labourer	Ireland	U. States	Marcus	7 Apr 1825
FAILES, B., Mr.						Dromo	14 Aug 1829
FAILEY, Joshua	25	M	Labourer	Great Britain	U. States	Hamilton	28 Apr 1828
FAINNEN, Thos.	30	M	Mariner	U. States	U. States	John Wells	14 Oct 1823
FAINOT, George	25	M	Agriculturist	France	U.S.	Helen	3 May 1828
John	31	M	Agriculturist	France	U.S.	Helen	3 May 1828
FAINY, Mary	26	F	Spinster	Ireland	United States	St. Michaels	23 Dec 1826
FAIR, John	45	M	Officer	England	U. States	Hiram	17 Jun 1826
Thomas	48	M		Ireland	United States	Fabius	4 Jun 1828
FAIRBANK, Allen	8		None	Great Britain	United States	Roman	10 Sep 1827
Ann	2		None	Great Britain	United States	Roman	10 Sep 1827
Fanny	15		None	Great Britain	United States	Roman	10 Sep 1827
Francis	48	M	Cloth Manufacturer	England	United States	Montano	27 Aug 1827
Harriet	17		None	Great Britain	United States	Roman	10 Sep 1827
Jane	44		None	Great Britain	United States	Roman	10 Sep 1827
Jas.	13		None	Great Britain	United States	Roman	10 Sep 1827
Jno.	21		Weaver	Great Britain	United States	Roman	10 Sep 1827
Nancy	10		None	Great Britain	United States	Roman	10 Sep 1827
Stepn.	37	M	Mercht.	Boston	Boston	Canada	1 Nov 1823
FAIRBANKS, Elizabeth	35	F		Nova Scotia	Brazil	America	16 May 1827
George E.	30	M	Physician	Nova Scotia	Brazil	America	16 May 1827
FAIRBROTHER, Eliza	25	F	None	Great Britton	U. States	Factor	27 Mar 1827
Wm.	28	M	Book Binder	Great Britton	U. States	Factor	27 Mar 1827
FAIRBURN, Archd.	20	M	Butcher	Scotland	U.S. of America	Friends	12 May 1826
FAIRCLOUGH, John	9	M	None	Great Britan	United States	Silvanus Jenkins	10 Mar 1827

NAMES OF PASSENGERS	AGE	SEX	OCCUPATIONS	COUNTRY TO WHICH THEY BELONG	COUNTRY THEY INTEND TO INHABIT	SHIPS/DATES OF ARRIVAL
FAIRCLOUGH (cont'd)						
John	30	M	Forgeman	Great Britan	United States	Silvanus Jenkins 10 Mar 1827
Joseph	2	M	None	Great Britan	United States	Silvanus Jenkins 10 Mar 1827
Mary	7	F	None	Great Britan	United States	Silvanus Jenkins 10 Mar 1827
Mary	29	F	None	Great Britan	United States	Silvanus Jenkins 10 Mar 1827
FAIREN, James	23	M	Weaver	Ireland	Ireland	Trident 17 May 1825
FAIRFIELD, Anistatia,						
Miss	20	F	Lady	Ireland	United States	Dublin Packet 23 May 1828
Anistatia, Mrs.	50	F	Lady	Ireland	United States	Dublin Packet 23 May 1828
Francis	1	F		England	U. States	Unity 5 Sep 1828
Harriet	6	F		England	U. States	Unity 5 Sep 1828
Hugh	48	M	Glass Blower	England	United States	Justina 5 Aug 1823
L.	40	F	Lady	France & Switzerland	U. States	Bayard 14 Jul 1826
Martha	26	F		England	U. States	Unity 5 Sep 1828
S. L.	23	M	Gentleman	France & Switzerland	U. States	Bayard 14 Jul 1826
Samuel	21	M	Farmer	England	U. States	Unity 5 Sep 1828
Sophia	3	F		England	U. States	Unity 5 Sep 1828
FAIRHURST, Edward	6	M	None	England	United States	Trident 18 Jul 1827
Ellis	2	M	None	England	United States	Trident 18 Jul 1827
Joseph	4	M	None	England	United States	Trident 18 Jul 1827
Mary	35	F	None	England	United States	Trident 18 Jul 1827
Mary Anne	7	F	None	England	United States	Trident 18 Jul 1827
Thomas	9	M	None	England	United States	Trident 18 Jul 1827
FAIRIER, Ed.	22	M	Mechanic	Rhode Island	U. States	Columbia 24 Mar 1823
FAIRINGTON, Elijah	28	M	Gentleman	New York	U. States	Dolphin 15 Apr 1822
FAIRLIN, Peter	18	M		Ireland	U. States	Howard 25 Jul 1823
FAIRLOUGH, H.	15	M	None	Great Brittain	U. States	Florenzo 20 Mar 1827
FAIRLY, Jno.	24	M	Farmer	Ireland	U. States	Edward 15 Jul 1825
FAIRO, P.	38	M	Merchant	England	Britain	Savannah 24 Apr 1828
FAIRWEATHER, S.	22	M	Farmer	New Brunswick	United States	Edwin 27 Oct 1828
FAISLEY, Biddy	28	F	Servant	Ireland	United States	John Wells 22 Sep 1824
FAITH, Francois	30	M	Carpenter	Switzerland	U.S.	C. Amelia 30 Jun 1828
FAITHFUL, Hannah	50	F	Servant	Great Britain	United States	Fidelity 16 Oct 1820
Rebecca	10	F	None	Great Britain	United States	Fidelity 16 Oct 1820
FALARDE, Jose	30	M	Merchant	Spain	Spain	Galatea 20 Jul 1829
FALCONE, Charles	80	M	Oculist	United States	New York	Gleaner 30 Apr 1821
Malvina	16	F		United States	New York	Gleaner 30 Apr 1821
Nancy	32	F		United States	New York	Gleaner 30 Apr 1821
FALCONER, Agnes	60	F		Scotland	United States	Camillus 9 May 1827
Alexr.	16	M		Scotland	United States	Camillus 9 May 1827
Jas.	45	M	Merchant	New York	New York	Leeds 26 Sep 1826
Margaret	17	F		Scotland	United States	Camillus 9 May 1827
FALENTINE, James	56	M	Fa...	United States	United States	Cambria 8 Oct 1828
FALES, Samuel C.	28	M	Merchant	U. States	United States	Neptune 5 Jul 1820
Wm.	21	M	None	U.S.	U.S.	Fame 22 Mar 1826
FALHAM, Ann, Jr.	15	F		Great Britain	U. States	Dominica 4 Jan 1823
FALHAN, Ann	52	F		Great Britain	U. States	Dominica 4 Jan 1823
FALKER, John	22	M	Weaver	Ireland	New York	Trusty 12 Sep 1828
FALKNER, Richard, Mr.	31 11/12		Banker	England	travelling	Romulus 15 May 1828
FALKNIER, James	4	M		England	Gt. Britain	Electra 4 Sep 1827
Wm.	6	M		England	Gt. Britain	Electra 4 Sep 1827
FALL, John	23	M	Laborer	Ireland	United States	St. Michaels 23 Dec 1826
FALLAGAR, Ann	12	F	Farmer	England	U. States	Robert Edwards 9 May 1827
Elizebeth	16	F	Farmer	England	U. States	Robert Edwards 9 May 1827
Elizebeth	41	F	Farmer	England	U. States	Robert Edwards 9 May 1827
Ellinnneh	21	F	Farmer	England	U. States	Robert Edwards 9 May 1827
George	10	M	Farmer	England	U. States	Robert Edwards 9 May 1827
John	18	M	Farmer	England	U. States	Robert Edwards 9 May 1827
Richard	14	M	Farmer	England	U. States	Robert Edwards 9 May 1827
Richard	44	M	Farmer	England	U. States	Robert Edwards 9 May 1827
FALLAN, Jane	4	F		Ireland	United States	Curler 3 Mar 1828
Jane	45	F		Ireland	United States	Curler 3 Mar 1828
Marcellis	27	M	Farmer	Ireland	United States	Curler 3 Mar 1828
Thomas	2	M		Ireland	United States	Curler 3 Mar 1828
Wm.	26	M	Farmer	Ireland	United States	Curler 3 Mar 1828
FALLE, Issack	30	M	Weelright	Switzerland	U. States	Sully 25 Jun 1828

NAMES OF PASSENGERS	AGE	SEX	OCCUPATIONS	COUNTRY TO WHICH THEY BELONG	COUNTRY THEY INTEND TO INHABIT	SHIPS/DATES OF ARRIVAL	
FALLER, Anton	20	M	Agriculturist	France	U.S.	Helen	3 May 1828
FALLIGARB, Lewis	49	M	Mercht.	U. States	U. States	Rachel Ann	11 Mar 1826
FALLON, Bridget	5/6	F		Ireland	America	Plutarch	18 Jul 1826
Eleanor	13	F		Ireland	New York	Vigilant	6 May 1822
M.	7	F		Ireland	New York	Vigilant	6 May 1822
Margret	25	M		Ireland	America	Plutarch	18 Jul 1826
Mary	10	F		Ireland	New York	Vigilant	6 May 1822
Mary	30	F		Ireland	New York	Vigilant	6 May 1822
Nelly	20	F	Farmer	Great Britian	United States	Andes	19 Aug 1829
Pat	20	M	Farmer	Great Britian	United States	Andes	19 Aug 1829
Patt	30	M	Weaver	Ireland	America	Plutarch	18 Jul 1826
FALLOW, Edwd.	28	M	Merchant	Younghall, Great Britain	United States	Union	24 Sep 1823
FALLOWS, John	35		Farmer	England	United States	Corinthian	30 May 1828
FALLS, Jas.	25	M	Merchant	Great Britain	United States	Ann Maria	23 Oct 1820
Wm.	17	M	Joiner	Great Britain	United States	Colossus	5 Jun 1827
FALVEY, Dennis	6	M	Child	Ireland	United States	Nancy	15 Dec 1824
Edward, Mr.	31	M	Brush Maker	England	U.S.	Acasta	11 May 1827
Ellin	30	F	Brush Maker	England	U.S.	Acasta	11 May 1827
John	3	M	Child	Ireland	United States	Nancy	15 Dec 1824
Mary	24	F	Wife	Ireland	United States	Nancy	15 Dec 1824
Thomas	30	M	Mason	Ireland	United States	Nancy	15 Dec 1824
FALYERE, C.	15	M	Student	France	U.S.	Cadmus	20 Dec 1824
FAMIN, Juls Raymond	36	M	Merchant	Point Peter	France	Pacific	14 May 1827
FAMLEY, Valentine	45	M	Merchant	England	U. States	Nymph	5 Jul 1820
FANAGHAN, John	26	M	Labourer	Ireland		Marchioness	13 May 1828
FANE, John R.	3	M	Merchant	United States	United States	Prince Edward	22 Jul 1824
FANLANER, Johannes	28	M	Labourer	Prussia		Constitution	20 Jun 1828
FANMAN, John	24	M	Merchant	Bremen	U. States	Louise	30 Jun 1826
FANN, Ann	27	F	None	Gt. Britain	United States	Crisis	13 Nov 1824
Charles	10	M	None	Gt. Britain	United States	Crisis	13 Nov 1824
Edward	4	M	None	Gt. Britain	United States	Crisis	13 Nov 1824
Emma	8/12	F	None	Gt. Britain	United States	Crisis	13 Nov 1824
Henry	7	M	None	Gt. Britain	United States	Crisis	13 Nov 1824
John	8	M	None	Gt. Britain	United States	Crisis	13 Nov 1824
John	34	M	Farmer	Gt. Britain	United States	Crisis	13 Nov 1824
Mary	2	F	None	Gt. Britain	United States	Crisis	13 Nov 1824
Sarah	4	F	None	Gt. Britain	United States	Crisis	13 Nov 1824
FANNAER, Laurence	30	M	Founder	Ireland	U. States	Meteor	19 Jul 1828
FANNAN, Bathw.	24	M	Labourer	England	U. States	Comet	23 Aug 1828
Luke	23 2/12	M	Shoe Maker	Ireland	United States	London	6 Feb 1829
FANNARD, Philip	22	M	Farmer	Ireland	America	Farmer	4 Aug 1825
FANNER, Edwd. P.	36	M	Miller	Brattain		L'Esperance	6 Sep 1828
FANNIN, Patrick	24 2/12	M		England	U.S. of America	Illinois	30 Apr 1823
FANNING, Betty	13	F	None	Ireland	United States	Lord Wellington	28 May 1827
Catherine	40	F	None	Ireland	United States	Lord Wellington	28 May 1827
James	23	M	Labourer	Ireland	United States	Lord Wellington	28 May 1827
Judith	24	F	None	Ireland	United States	Colossus	26 Aug 1828
Michael	11	M	None	Ireland	United States	Lord Wellington	28 May 1827
Michael	30	M	Boat Builder	Maine	Pennsyvania	Champion	27 Dec 1827
Nancy	16	F	None	Ireland	United States	Lord Wellington	28 May 1827
Peggy	6	F	None	Ireland	United States	Lord Wellington	28 May 1827
Rose	9	F	None	Ireland	United States	Lord Wellington	28 May 1827
Thomas	29 1/12	M	Mariner	United States	United States	Atlantic	16 Dec 1825
Wm.	23	M	Merchant	Gt. Britain	U. States	St. George	20 Sep 1828
FANNO, Francis	20	M	Labourer	Ireland	United States	Ann Maria	8 Jun 1824
FANNY, Mary	20	F	Spinster	Ireland	U. States	Meteor	19 Jul 1828
FANSHAW, Edward, Lt. Col.	45	M	Royal Engineer	Great Britain	Great Britain	Roman	10 May 1828
FANTON, John	28	M	Stone Cutter	Scotland	U. States	Loire	18 Jul 1828
FANTORE, Gabriel	35	M	Cook	France	U. States	Brunswick	14 Feb 1829
FANVIL, G., Fils [son]	35	M	Gentleman	France	U. States	Ohio	18 Jul 1821
FANWICK, Jos.		M	Merchant	U. States	U. States	Governor Griswold	18 Jun 1821
FAOLIN, Mary	17	F	None	Great Brittan	United States	America	24 Jul 1827
FARADAY, Mary	23	F	None	Ireland	New York	America	1 Aug 1828
FARALL, Eleanor	30	F	...	...	U. States	Governor Tompkins	26 Jul 1824
Jas.	40	M	...	...	U. States	Governor Tompkins	26 Jul 1824

NAMES OF PASSENGERS	AGE	SEX	OCCUPATIONS	COUNTRY TO WHICH THEY BELONG	COUNTRY THEY INTEND TO INHABIT	SHIPS/DATES OF ARRIVAL	
FARALL (cont'd)							
Thomas	7	M	...	...	U. States	Governor Tompkins	26 Jul 1824
FARAN, Rosanna	19	F		Ireland	United States	Borneo	28 Aug 1828
FARANGE, Wm.	60	M	Farmer	...	America	Laurel	16 Nov 1824
FAREL, Ann	25			b. County of Westmouth, last of Kilpatric	N. York	Peru	30 May 1828
Katey	20			Longford	Boston	Peru	30 May 1828
FARELET, C.	25	F		France		Pallas	14 Jun 1828
C. M.	2	F		France		Pallas	14 Jun 1828
Catherin	11	F		France		Pallas	14 Jun 1828
Fransis	25	M		France		Pallas	14 Jun 1828
Jams	45	M		France		Pallas	14 Jun 1828
Jaqus	1	M		France		Pallas	14 Jun 1828
Jaqus	20	F		France		Pallas	14 Jun 1828
Jean R.	50	F	Wm. Drou [?]	France		Pallas	14 Jun 1828
Mari	2	F		France		Pallas	14 Jun 1828
Mary	20	F	Wm. Drou [?]	France		Pallas	14 Jun 1828
Perre	12	M	Shoe Maker	France		Pallas	14 Jun 1828
FAREQUE, Ching	30	M	Merchant	P. A. Prince	P. A. Prince	Fancy	28 Apr 1824
FARGUES, C.	32	M	Jeweller	Spain	Spain	General Brown	10 Dec 1823
FARICH, M.	28	F		Gt. Britain	New York	Betsey	18 Apr 1822
FARINGTON, M.				Cork	New York	Schuylkill	22 Aug 1825
FARLADOUX, J. F., Mr.	23	M		France		Henri IV	17 May 1828
L., Made.	20	F		France		Henri IV	17 May 1828
FARLAND, Isaac	30	M	Laborer	Ireland	U. States	Lady Hunter	14 Mar 1826
James	20	M	Labourer	Ireland	Philadelphia	Lady Hunter	5 Jun 1826
FARLEY, Ann	28 7/12	F		Ireland	America	Carolina Ann	7 Apr 1826
Catharine	18	F	Servant	Ireland	United States	Josephine	30 Apr 1828
Geo. G.	29	M	Mariner	U. States	U. States	Tampico	20 Apr 1825
Geo. W.	24	M	Shipmaster	U. States	U. States	Ladies Delight	18 Sep 1820
John	20	M	Merchant	Great Britain	United States	Atlantic	8 Dec 1827
Michael	31		Seaman	Boston		Hudson	18 Jun 1825

*Officers, Seamen and Passengers belonging to the Ship Jane of Boston and taken from on board the Schooner Olive of St. Johns , N.B. on the 4th June 1825, Lat. 41.30, Long 53.19, which ship foundered on the 31st ultimo in Lat. 41.44 Long 52.

NAMES OF PASSENGERS	AGE	SEX	OCCUPATIONS	COUNTRY TO WHICH THEY BELONG	COUNTRY THEY INTEND TO INHABIT	SHIPS/DATES OF ARRIVAL	
Michl.	25	M	Labourer	Co. Cavan	Co. Cavan	Howard Douglass	11 May 1827
Patrick	24	M	Labourer	Irereland	America	Carolina Ann	20 Jun 1825
Rose	14	F	Servant	Ireland	United States	Josephine	30 Apr 1828
Thomas	25	M	Gentleman	England	England	William	2 Sep 1824
FARLIX, M.	15	M	Merchant	Columbia	Columbia	Franklin	27 May 1825
FARLOW, Julia	57	F	Widow	Gt. Britain	U. States	St. George	20 Sep 1828
FARMAN, Joseph	24	M	Clerk	Meatah	Meath	Aldebaron	21 Jan 1826
FARMER, —, Miss	2	F	Farmer	Barbadoes	U. States	Azores	2 Jun 1824
—, Mrs.	21	F	Farmer	Barbadoes	U. States	Azores	2 Jun 1824
Emma	7 6/12	F		Bristol, Engl.	England	Warrior	19 May 1828
Euphemia	2	F		G. Britain	U. States	Eliza	9 May 1827
Felix	20	M	Sawyer	Ireland	United States	Romulus	24 Jun 1826
George	2 6/12	M		Bristol, Engl.	England	Warrior	19 May 1828
Jas.	7	M		Switzerland	U. States	Robert Edward	2 Nov 1827
John	20	M	Labourer	England	New York	America	1 Aug 1828
John	30	M	Farmer	England	U. States	Electra	7 Jul 1828
Judith	2	F		Switzerland	U. States	Robert Edward	2 Nov 1827
Louisa	5	F		Bristol, Engl.	England	Warrior	19 May 1828
Margaret	4	F		G. Britain	U. States	Eliza	9 May 1827
Margaret, Mrs.	27	F		G. Britain	U. States	Eliza	9 May 1827
Martha	32	...	...	Switzerland	U. States	Robert Edward	2 Nov 1827
Mary	11	F		Bristol, Engl.	England	Warrior	19 May 1828
Mary	34	F		Bristol, Engl.	England	Warrior	19 May 1828
Patrick	14	M	Joiner	Ireland	United States	Romulus	24 Jun 1826
R. H.	22	M	Farmer	Barbadoes	U. States	Azores	2 Jun 1824
Sarah	9	F		Bristol, Engl.	England	Warrior	19 May 1828
Stephen	5	M		Switzerland	U. States	Robert Edward	2 Nov 1827
Stephen	37	...	...	Switzerland	U. States	Robert Edward	2 Nov 1827
Thomas						Hesperus	29 Sep 1827

*Died on the Voyage

Thomas	21	M	Joiner	Ireland	United States	Romulus	24 Jun 1826

NAMES OF PASSENGERS	AGE	SEX	OCCUPATIONS	COUNTRY TO WHICH THEY BELONG	COUNTRY THEY INTEND TO INHABIT	SHIPS/DATES OF ARRIVAL	
FARMER (cont'd)							
William	4	M		Bristol, Engl.	England	Warrior	19 May 1828
William A.	31	M	Merchant	Great Britian	United States	George Clinton	21 Oct 1826
FARMLEE, Eleazer	26	M	Gentleman	America	U. States	Hudson	26 Jan 1825
FARNER, John	19	M	Labourer	England	U. States	Ayrshire	12 May 1828
FARNES, Joseph	11	M	None	Cuba	Cuba	Agenora	11 Jun 1824
FARNIER, Thomas	39	M	Labourer	England	U. States	Ayrshire	12 May 1828
FARNIGAN, James	29	M	Laborer, Spinster or Child	Ireland	United States	Ann Maria	4 Aug 1827
FARNIVAL, Saml.	5	M	None	Great Brittain	New York	Albion	11 Jun 1821
FARNSWORTH, J.	36	M	Merchant	U. States	U. States	Birmingham	12 Oct 1827
James	37	M	Merchant	U. States	United States	Wm. Byrnes	30 Apr 1828
Thos.	28	M	Captain or Mariner	U. States	U. States	Forest	15 Dec 1827
FARON, Thomas	17	M	Merchant	England	New York	Brighton	20 Aug 1825
FARQUHAUER, Jos. C.	19	M	Merchant	Scotland	U. States	Fair American	26 Jul 1825
FARR, Edd.	...	...	...	Ireland	U. States of America	Courier	17 Mar 1827
F.	50	M	Mariner	France	France	Swiftsure	14 Apr 1828
FARRAL, Ann	41	F	Labourer	Ireland	America	Otter	17 Mar 1828
Christopher	9	M	Labourer	Ireland	America	Otter	17 Mar 1828
John	20	M	Labourer	Great Britain		Olive Branch	9 Oct 1829
Paterick	40	M	Labourer	Ireland	America	Otter	17 Mar 1828
FARRALL, Allace	32	F		Denmark	St. Croix	Jupiter	8 Apr 1828
Ann	25	F	Labourer	Ireland	U.S. of America	Hamilton	18 Jul 1827
Mary	26	F	None	Ireland	U.S. of America	Hamilton	18 Jul 1827
FARRALLY, Tarrance	28	M	Whitesmith	Ireland	New York	Governor Fenner	23 Jul 1829
FARRAN, John Smith	31	M	Captain, Officers & crew of the Brig George of New York (wrecked at Fayal)	U.S. America	U.S.A.	Gallego	13 Mar 1829
Neal	11	M	Boy	Ireland	United States	Trident	17 May 1825
FARRAR, Henry	21		Traveller	England	England	Hudson	18 Jun 1825
James	26	M	...	England	Canada	William Thompson	10 May 1825
James	29	M	Taylor	England	United States	Marion	25 Nov 1825
FARREL, Andrew	24	M	Labourer	Ireland	America	Plutarch	18 Jul 1826
Ann	20	F		Ireland	America	Plutarch	18 Jul 1826
Catherin	16	F		Ireland	America	Wilson	27 Nov 1826
Catherine	3	F	None	England	New York	America	1 Aug 1828
Daubney	25	M	Planter	America	Kentucky	Stephania	13 Mar 1820
Elizabeth	18	F		Ireland	America	Wilson	27 Nov 1826
Ellen	14	F	Labourer	England	United States	John Wells	22 May 1826
Isabella	1	F	Labourer	Ireland	United States	Meteor	26 Jun 1827
James	12	M	Labourer	Ireland	United States	Meteor	26 Jun 1827
James	13	M	Labourer	England	United States	John Wells	22 May 1826
James	31	M	Farmer	Ireland	America	William	21 May 1825
Jane	21	F	Labourer	Ireland	United States	Meteor	26 Jun 1827
John	25	M	Labourer	Ireland	United States	Meteor	26 Jun 1827
Margret	20	F	Servantmaid	Ireland	America	Plutarch	18 Jul 1826
Mary	9	F	None	England	New York	America	1 Aug 1828
Mary	17	F	Spinster	Ireland	United States	Wilson	6 Jun 1828
Michael	27	M	Merchant	Ireland	United States	Nancy Henrietta	3 Nov 1828
Patrick	1	M	None	England	New York	America	1 Aug 1828
Robert	40	M	Labourer	England	United States	John Wells	22 May 1826
Sarah	20 1/12	F		Ireland	America	Carolina Ann	7 Apr 1826
Thomas	31	M	Labourer	Ireland	America	Plutarch	18 Jul 1826
William	4	M		Ireland	America	Plutarch	18 Jul 1826
William	15	M	Labourer	Ireland	United States	Meteor	26 Jun 1827
FARRELL, Ann	12	F		Great Britain	United States	Mary Howland	19 Jul 1827
Ann	16	F	None	Ireland	United States	Washington	2 Oct 1828
Ann	40	F		Great Britain	United States	Mary Howland	19 Jul 1827
Ann	40	F	Spinster	Ireland	United States	Wilson	6 Jun 1828
Ann	40	F	None	Ireland	United States	Washington	2 Oct 1828
Brian	30	M	Laborer	G. Bt.	U. States	Canada	12 May 1828
Bridget	2	F		Gt. Britain	United States	John & Elizabeth	25 Sep 1827
Bridget	18	F		Gt. Britain		Dalhouse Castle	13 May 1828
Catharine	25	F	Spinster	Ireland	Unt. St. America	Wilson	21 May 1827

NAMES OF PASSENGERS	AGE	SEX	OCCUPATIONS	COUNTRY TO WHICH THEY BELONG	COUNTRY THEY INTEND TO INHABIT	SHIPS/DATES OF ARRIVAL	
FARRELL (cont'd)							
Catharine	40	F		Great Brittian	United States	Carolina	
						Augusta	2 Dec 1828
Catherine	19	F	Servant	Ireland	United States	Lord Wellington	14 Nov 1827
Catherine	32	F	None	Ireland	New York	America	1 Aug 1828
Catherine	35	F	None	England	New York	America	1 Aug 1828
Cathr.	27	F	Milliner	Ireland	United States	Aurelia	7 Jun 1826
Charles L.	26	F				Washington	15 Sep 1821
Corns.	48	M		France	U. States	Ohio	18 Jul 1821
Daniel	1	M		Gt. Britain	United States	John &	
						Elizabeth	25 Sep 1827
Dennis	16	M	Labourer	Ireland	New York	Lima	5 Aug 1829
Dennis	16	M	Labourer	Ireland	N. York	Lima	5 Aug 1829
Edward	20	M	Farmer	Gt. Brittian	United States	Balaena	8 Jan 1825
Edward	23	M		Ireland	United States	Thompson	12 Sep 1827
Edwd.	21	M	Labourer	Ireland		Marchioness	13 May 1828
Eliza	18	F		Gt. Britain	U. States	St. George	20 Sep 1828
Elizabeth	22	F	Servant	Ireland	U. States	Sarah G	7 May 1827
Elizath.	4	F	Child	Great Britain	United States	Wilson	26 Feb 1824
Hamilton	19	M	Labourer	Ireland	United States	Fabius	31 Jul 1829
Hugh	21	M	Labourer	Ireland	U. States	Loire	6 Dec 1827
Isabella	52	F	Spinster	Ireland	United States	Fabius	31 Jul 1829
James	5	M	None	Ireland	New York	America	1 Aug 1828
James	17	M	Y. Man	Ireland	New York	Trusty	12 Sep 1828
James	25	M		Ireland	United States	Thompson	12 Sep 1827
James	30	M	School Master	Ireland	New York	Commerce	24 Sep 1823
James	60	M	Labourer	Ireland	U. States	Jefferson	7 Aug 1820
Jane	2	F				Washington	15 Sep 1821
Jno.	25	M	Labourer	Ireland	United States	Essex	23 May 1828
John	11	M	None	Ireland	United States	Washington	2 Oct 1828
John	18	M		Ireland	U. States	Balaena	29 Apr 1825
John	18	M	Labourer	Ireland	United States	William	20 Jul 1829
John	20			Ireland	U.S.	Union	20 Aug 1827
John	20	M	Laborer	Gt. Britain		Dalhouse Castle	13 May 1828
John	28	M	Labourer	...th...ck	United States	Solon	21 Jun 1824
John	30	M	Calico Printer	Great Britain	Taunton, Mass.	Hesperus	13 Oct 1825
John	30	M	Farmer	Ireland	New York	Lima	16 Mar 1829
John	34	M	Labourer	Ireland	New York	Wilson	28 Aug 1822
John	50	M	Merchant	Ireland	United States	Washington	2 Oct 1828
Jos.	20	M	Laborer	Ireland	United States	Carolina Ann	11 Dec 1826
Laurence	25	M	Labourer	Ireland	United States	Josephine	30 Apr 1828
Malki	24			Ireland	U.S.	Union	20 Aug 1827
Margeret	9	F	None	Ireland	New York	America	1 Aug 1828
Margt.	30	F		Denmark	St. Croix	Jupiter	8 Apr 1828
Maria	30	F		Gt. Britain	United States	Columbia	7 Sep 1827
Mary	...	F	Labourer	England	U. States	Comet	23 Aug 1828
Mary	10	F		Great Britain	United States	Mary Howland	19 Jul 1827
Mary	18	F	None	Ireland	United States	Washington	2 Oct 1828
Mary	19	F		Ireland	U. States	Ganges	21 Jun 1827
Mary	23	F		Gt. Britain	United States	John & Elizabeth	25 Sep 1827
Mary	27	F	Spinster	Ireland	United States	Dublin Packet	24 Sep 1823
Mary	30	F		Great Britain	United States	Mary Howland	19 Jul 1827
Mary	34	F	Matron	Great Britain	United States	Wilson	26 Feb 1824
Matthew	26	M	Masson	Ireland	U. States	Jefferson	7 Aug 1820
Michael	1	M		Great Britain	United States	Mary Howland	19 Jul 1827
Michael	21 1/12	M	Labourer	Ireland	United States	Atlantic	21 Jul 1827
Michael	25	M	Labourer	Great Britain	United States	Washington	9 Apr 1821
Michol	28	M	Stone Cutter	Ireland	U. States	Courier	17 Mar 1828
Patrick	20	M		Gt. Britain	United States	John & Elizabeth	25 Sep 1827
Patrick	34	M	Labourer	Great Britain	United States	Frances	
						Henrietta	17 Sep 1827
Patt	21	M	Carpenter	Ireland	New York	Lima	5 Aug 1829
Patt	21	M	Carpenter	Ireland	N. York	Lima	5 Aug 1829
Patt	22	M	Labourer	Great Britain	U. States	Great Britain	18 Mar 1828
Peggy	35	F	Seamstress	Ireland	United States	Essex	23 May 1828
Richard	7	M	Child	Great Britain	United States	Wilson	26 Feb 1824
Richd.	30	M	Merchant	Ireland	U. States	Jubilee	1 Jul 1823
Robt.	23	M	Labourer	Ireland	United States	Aurelia	7 Jun 1826
Roger	40	M		Great Britain	United States	Mary Howland	19 Jul 1827

NAMES OF PASSENGERS	AGE	SEX	OCCUPATIONS	COUNTRY TO WHICH THEY BELONG	COUNTRY THEY INTEND TO INHABIT	SHIPS/DATES OF ARRIVAL	
FARRELL (cont'd)							
Rose	22	F	None	Great Britain		Moro Castle	6 Jul 1827
T.	23	M	Labourer	England	U. States	Hope & Esther	10 Jul 1827
Thomas	7	M	None	Ireland	New York	America	1 Aug 1828
Thos.	20	M	Labourer	...th...ck	United States	Solon	21 Jun 1824
Walter	20 3/12	M	Shoemaker	Ireland	United States	Atlantic	21 Jul 1827
Wm.	13	M	None	Ireland	United States	Washington	2 Oct 1828
Wm.	22	M	Labourer	Co. La...gford	La...gford	Howard Douglass	11 May 1827
FARREN, Anne	18	M		G. Britain	U. States	Great Britain	6 Sep 1828
Dennis	20	M	Farmer	G. Britain	U. States	St. George	7 Jun 1828
Dennis	22	M		Ireland	British Amera.	William & George	14 May 1828
Mary	19	F	Servant	Ireland	United States	Henry Kneeland	7 Jun 1828
Mary	20	F	None	England	United States	India	8 Jun 1827
FARRENDER, Isaac	25	M	Shoemaker	Ireland	United States	Essex	23 May 1828
FARRER, Thos.	20	M	Labourer	Ireland	United States	Trident	16 May 1826
FARRERO, Charles J.	20	M		U. States	U. States	Pacific	17 Jun 1828
Jane Ann	45	F		U. States	U. States	Pacific	17 Jun 1828
FARRES, P.	14	M		Spain	U. States	Emeline	12 Sep 1823
FARRET, Andrew	20	M	Labourrer	Great Britan	U. States	Ann Marria	6 Aug 1823
FARRETT, Joseph, Junr.	29	M	Merchant	G. Britan	G. Britan	Canada	27 Sep 1826
FARRIENT, C.	13	M		Spain	U. States	Rodman	28 May 1825
FARRIER, Jno. M.	40	M	Merchant	France	U. States	Herald	21 May 1824
Rob.	36	M	Labourer	Ireland	United States	Essex	23 May 1828
FARRIL, Ann	20	F	None	Great Britain	United States	Isaac Hicks	22 Aug 1828
FARRILL, Ann	1 1/2	F		Great Brittian	United States	Carolina Augusta	2 Dec 1828
Catharine	5	F		Great Brittian	United States	Carolina Augusta	2 Dec 1828
Eliza	18	F	Spinster	Ireland	United States	Dublin Packet	22 Apr 1822
Fergus	22	M	Farmer	Ireland	United States	Lord Strangford	20 Jun 1826
Mary	3	F		Great Brittian	United States	Carolina Augusta	2 Dec 1828
Thomas	14	M		Great Brittian	United States	Carolina Augusta	2 Dec 1828
FARRILLY, Patrick	19	M	Labourer	Ireland	America	Wilson	16 May 1825
FARRIN, Mary	20	F	Spinster	Ireland	United States	Robert Fulton	10 Aug 1827
FARRINGTON, Elijah	27	M	Chairmaker	American	New York	Boon	26 Feb 1820
Eliza	17	F		Gt. Britain	U. States	St. George	20 Sep 1828
James	24	M	Merchant	United States	United States	Ardelle	18 Jan 1828
Jane Ann	20	F		England	Canada	Silas Richards	27 Oct 1825
John	22		Farmer	Cork	New York	Schuylkill	22 Aug 1825
Joseph	28	M	Merchant	England	Canada	Silas Richards	27 Oct 1825
Maria	43	F		England	Canada	Silas Richards	27 Oct 1825
Mary	10			Cork	New York	Schuylkill	22 Aug 1825
P.	25	M	M...	U. States	U.S.	Ann	31 Mar 1825
FARRIS, David	50	M	Merchant	East Port	East Port	General Marion	20 Jul 1829
Elizabeth	46	F	Matron	Ireland	America	Wilson	16 May 1825
FARROE, Thomas	20	M	Carpenter	Great Britain	United States	Ocean	27 Jul 1825
FARROL, Mary	22	F	Servant	Great Britian	U. States	Henry Kneedland	7 Aug 1826
FARROLL, Mic.	30	M	Farmer	Gt. Britain	United States	Penelope	9 Sep 1828
Wm.	24	M	Farmer	Gt. Britain	United States	Penelope	9 Sep 1828
FARRON, Grace	20	F	Lady		New York	Betsy	4 Sep 1820
Mary	20	F		Ireland	United States	Loore	9 Sep 1822
Michael	20	M	Labourer	Ireland	United States	Loore	9 Sep 1822
FARRONLY, James	25	M	Miner	U. States	U. States	Frances	23 Mar 1827
FARROTT, John	25	M	Mariner	U. States	U. States	Atlas	24 Jun 1828
FARROW, Allice	27	F		England	U. States	Severn	12 Oct 1826
Ebenezer	24	M	U.S. Navy	United States	U. States	Frances	6 Feb 1829
John	30	M	Labourer	England	United States	India	8 Jun 1827
Peter	15	M	Labourer	England	United States	India	8 Jun 1827
Robt.	27	M	Weaver	England	U. States	Severn	12 Oct 1826
FARSON, Henry	32 3/12	M	distressed seaman, mate	Philadelphia	United States	Florida	27 Aug 1825
FARUST, Ann	25	F	Servant	Ireland	U. States	Sarah G	30 Jun 1828
Bill	30	M	Labourer	Ireland	U. States	Sarah G	30 Jun 1828
Mary	20	F		Ireland	U. States	Sarah G	30 Jun 1828

NAMES OF PASSENGERS	AGE	SEX	OCCUPATIONS	COUNTRY TO WHICH THEY BELONG	COUNTRY THEY INTEND TO INHABIT	SHIPS/DATES OF ARRIVAL	
FARUST (cont'd)							
Mary	20	F	Servant	Ireland	U. States	Sarah G	30 Jun 1828
Robt.	35	M	Labourer	Ireland	U. States	Sarah G	30 Jun 1828
FARVEY, R.	18	F		Ireland	United States	Commerce	13 Jun 1828
FARWAY, M.	22	F	Spinster	G. Britain	U. States	Hanford	10 Jun 1828
FARY, Elenor	20	F	Lady	Ireland	United States	Ann Maria	1 Apr 1826
FAS, Samuel	46	M	Merchant	Great Britain	New York	Zodiac	14 Jun 1822
FASENMEYER, Andreas	10	M	Son	Germany	United States	Elizabeth	4 Sep 1826
Felix	13	M	Son	Germany	United States	Elizabeth	4 Sep 1826
Felix	43	M	Carpenter	Germany	United States	Elizabeth	4 Sep 1826
Maria	35	F	Wife	Germany	United States	Elizabeth	4 Sep 1826
FASENMYER,							
Celestinas	3/12	M	Son	Germany	United States	Elizabeth	4 Sep 1826
Johanna	4	F	Daughter	Germany	United States	Elizabeth	4 Sep 1826
FASS, A.	28	M	Servant	Curacoa	Curacoa	Dover	17 Aug 1821
Ben	26	M	Farmer	Germany	United States	Samuel Robertson	8 Aug 1828
Isaac A.	17	M	Merchant	Great Britain	United States	Mount Vernon	17 Jun 1825
FASSNERY, John A.	25	M	Gentleman	Great Brittan	United States	Napoleon	28 Jan 1829
FAST, J. A.	21	M	Farmer	Bardin	U. States	Bayard	5 Sep 1828
FASTUA, J. M.	25	M	Stone Cutter	Germany	U. States	Falcon	11 Jun 1827
FASY, John H.	30	M	Merchant	Demerara	U. States	Ariadne	12 Dec 1822
FATHAN, Rob.	60	M		Great Britain	U. States	Dominica	4 Jan 1823
FATTAN, Fredk. Lewis	60	M	Gentleman	Switzerland	U. States	Robert Edward	2 Nov 1827
Louise	38	F		Switzerland	U. States	Robert Edward	2 Nov 1827
Sophia	13	F		Switzerland	U. States	Robert Edward	2 Nov 1827
FATTERSAL, Lawrence	46	M	Farmer	England	U. States	Trident	8 Mar 1824
FATTRICK, M., Miss	17	M	None	United States	United States	Atlantic	3 Dec 1821
M., Mrs.	50	M	None	United States	United States	Atlantic	3 Dec 1821
Peter	60	M	Merchant	United States	United States	Atlantic	3 Dec 1821
FAU, Jennet	20	F		Scotland	Canada	Braganza	16 Apr 1825
FAUL, Henry	28	M	One Family [Michael Zeigler]	France	United States	Henri IV	2 Oct 1828
FAULDER, William	30	M	Farmer	England	United States	Aurelia	7 Jun 1826
FAULDS, Hugh	24	M				Czar	29 Aug 1829
FAULKNER, Bridget	25	F	Matron	Ireland	United States	Robert Fulton	24 Jul 1826
Francis	46	M	Weaver	England	Ut. States	Courier	13 Jul 1826
James	28	M		Ireland	United States	Sarah G.	20 Jul 1827
John	25	M	Labourer	Ireland	United States	Robert Fulton	24 Jul 1826
John, Mr.	22	M	Manufacturer	Scotland	New York	Broughty Castle	18 Dec 1826
Margeret	30	F	Matron	Ireland	United States	Robert Fulton	24 Jul 1826
Neil	21	M	Labourer	Ireland	U. States	Lady Hunter	18 Jul 1825
Rose	60	F	Matron	Ireland	United States	Robert Fulton	24 Jul 1826
William	28	M		England	New York	Cincinnatus	5 Dec 1825
FAULKNIER, Harriet	1	F		England	Gt. Britain	Electra	4 Sep 1827
FAULKS, William	34	M	Farmer	England	New York	Brighton	9 Dec 1828
Wm.	3...	M	...		U. States	Ann Maria	6 Jul 1824
FAULS, Andw.	24	M	Shoemaker	Scotland	United States	Essex	23 May 1828
Marg.	22	F		Scotland	United States	Essex	23 May 1828
FAUQUETT, Jean L.	34	M	Store Keeper	Switzerland		Edward Quesnel	17 Nov 1828
FAURBURN, Wm.	18	M	Labourer	Great Brittan	U. States	John & Elizabeth	11 Dec 1826
FAURBURNE, Jaine	25	F	Spinster	Great Brittan	U. States	John & Elizabeth	11 Dec 1826
FAURE, Jno. R.	11	M		U. States	U. States	Native	16 Nov 1825
Margaret	30	F		New York	U. States	Native	16 Nov 1825
FAURES, Francis	27		Merchant	...		Little John	4 Nov 1820
FAUREST, Ellin	23 9/12	F	Servant	Ireland	New York	Atlantic	6 Oct 1828
FAVEAU, A., Mr.	30	M	Planter	France		François I	19 Nov 1828
FAVER, F. W.	28	M	Merchant	Holland	New York	Louisa	10 May 1828
FAVEREAU, Francis	40	M	Merchant	United States	New York	Cadmus	19 Aug 1823
Francis, Jr.	12	M		United States	New York	Cadmus	19 Aug 1823
FAVIER, Charles	12	M	Servant	France	America	Britannia	5 Nov 1828
FAVIGNON, M. D.	32	F		France	U. States	Circassian	26 Jun 1823
FAVIRE, Celentine	16	F		France	United States	Le Voltaire	19 Jul 1828
Constance	7	M		France	United States	Le Voltaire	19 Jul 1828
Francoise C.	12	F		France	United States	Le Voltaire	19 Jul 1828
Joseph	49	M	Farmer	France	United States	Le Voltaire	19 Jul 1828
Laurent	18	F		France	United States	Le Voltaire	19 Jul 1828

NAMES OF PASSENGERS	AGE	SEX	OCCUPATIONS	COUNTRY TO WHICH THEY BELONG	COUNTRY THEY INTEND TO INHABIT	SHIPS/DATES OF ARRIVAL	
FAVIRE (cont'd)							
Marie	49	M		France	United States	Le Voltaire	19 Jul 1828
FAVOANE, Apoline	12	F	Daughter	France	U. States	Comet	28 Jul 1825
Constant	1	M	Son	France	U. States	Comet	28 Jul 1825
Joseph	8	M	Son	France	U. States	Comet	28 Jul 1825
Josette	3	F	Daughter	France	U. States	Comet	28 Jul 1825
La Joseph	39	M	Farmer	France	U. States	Comet	28 Jul 1825
Rosse	35	F	Wife	France	U. States	Comet	28 Jul 1825
FAVOURET, F. M.	44	M	Gentleman	France	N. York	Stephania	7 Aug 1824
FAVRE, Augustis	27	M	Gentleman	Switzerland	U. States	Edward Quesnel	16 Nov 1827
Henry	22	M	Watchmaker	Suisse	United States	Montano	5 May 1828
James	20	M	Watchmaker	Prussia	U.S.	Edward Quesnel	19 Oct 1829
L., Capt.	45	M	Ship Master	France	France	Claudio	16 Oct 1827
FAVY, Mary	17			Longford	Boston	Peru	30 May 1828
FAWCETT, John	28	M	Merchant	Great Britan	Great Britan	Columbia	10 Mar 1824
FAX, M. C.	12	F		Denmark	Denmark	Agness	23 Jun 1828
FAY, Claude	31 1/12	M	Priest	France	Canada	Cadmus	12 Dec 1823
H.	1	M		Switzerland	U. States	La Urania	3 Jul 1828
James	21	M	Labourer	Irereland	America	Carolina Ann	20 Jun 1825
Jane	18	F	Spinster	Ireland	United States	Dublin Packet	22 Oct 1821
John	44		Varnish maker	French	America	Romulus	15 May 1828
M.	31	F		Switzerland	U. States	La Urania	3 Jul 1828
Nicholas	14	M	Boy	Ireland	United States	Dublin Packet	9 Jul 1827
O.	24	M	Black Smith	Switzerland	U. States	La Urania	3 Jul 1828
Peter	24	M	...	Ireland	U. States	William	27 Jul 1824
Rose	28	F	None	Ireland	United States	Trident	18 Jul 1827
Saml. Howard	24	M	Merchant	United States	Savannah, U.S.	Florida	2 Oct 1828
FAYE, Ann	20 6/12	F		Ireland	America	Carolina Ann	7 Apr 1826
FAYLE, John	23	M	Baker	Great Britain	United States	William Dawson	18 Jun 1827
John	25					Trio	5 May 1828
Jos.	35	M	Merchant	G. Brittain	U. States	Pacific	23 Jan 1826
FAYLEN, —, Mrs.	27	F		Ireland	U. States	Lukey	12 Jun 1822
Wm.	28	M	Mechanic	Ireland	U. States	Lukey	12 Jun 1822
FAYLOR, Jas.	30	M	...	G. Britain	United States	Fairy	18 Feb 1825
FAYOLLE, —, Mrs.	43	F		United States		Howard	17 Oct 1822
A., Miss	15	F		United States		Howard	17 Oct 1822
E. B.	34	M	Merchant	United States	United States	Romulus	3 Dec 1827
FAYOUGA, Jose T.	27	M	Gentleman	Mexico	England	Brown	23 Dec 1826
FAYRE, Elizy.	24	F	Washer	France	U. States	C. Amelia	30 Jun 1828
FEAGAN, Rose	17	F	None	Ireland	United States	Jubilee	13 Jul 1829
FEALD, Andrew, Mr.	22	M	Farmer	England	U. States	Acasta	3 Apr 1826
FEALY, Pat	23	M	Farmer	Ireland	United States	Leonidas	3 Aug 1825
Peter	23	M	Farmer	Ireland	United States	Leonidas	3 Aug 1825
FEAN, M.	20	M	Servant	Ireland	U. States	Courier	31 Jul 1828
FEANCY, John	23	M	Labourer	England	U. States	Montgomery	18 Oct 1828
FEARENPACK,							
Andrews	2 6/12	M	Son	Germany	United States	Elizabeth	4 Sep 1826
Angnes	24	F	Wife	Germany	United States	Elizabeth	4 Sep 1826
Johanna	2/12	F	Daughter	Germany	United States	Elizabeth	4 Sep 1826
Mathias	27	M	Farmer	Germany	United States	Elizabeth	4 Sep 1826
FEARN, Edwd.	24	M	Labourer	Ireland	United States	William	20 Jul 1829
FEARNLY, Mary Ann	13	F	...	Ireland	United States	Colossus	30 May 1825
FEARON, Ann	3/12	F	None	Great Britain	United States	Eliza Barker	3 Jul 1826
Edward	20	M	Printer	Great Britain	United States	Eliza Barker	3 Jul 1826
Mary Ann	23	F	None	Great Britain	United States	Eliza Barker	3 Jul 1826
FEASON, Robert	19	M	Meason	Tyrone	Ireland	Carolina Ann	11 Jun 1824
FEATHERSTON, Esther	40	F	None	England	United States	Bolivar	15 Jun 1826
Wm.	46	M	Farmer	England	United States	Bolivar	15 Jun 1826
FEATHERSTONE, Thomas	34		Mechanic	...	...	James Cropper	28 Jun 1824
FEATHERSTONHAUGH,							
—, Mrs.	47			U. States	U. States	Napoleon	10 Jan 1828
G. W.	47			U. States	U. States	Napoleon	10 Jan 1828
G. W., Jr.	16			U. States	U. States	Napoleon	10 Jan 1828
J. D.	12			U. States	U. States	Napoleon	10 Jan 1828
FEBHER, Antiocha	2/52	F				Antioch	18 Aug 1829
*Born on Voyage							
Barbara	29	F	Farmer	Switzerland		Antioch	18 Aug 1829
Christian	39	M	Farmer	Switzerland		Antioch	18 Aug 1829
Elizabeth	4	F	Farmer	Switzerland		Antioch	18 Aug 1829

NAMES OF PASSENGERS	AGE	SEX	OCCUPATIONS	COUNTRY TO WHICH THEY BELONG	COUNTRY THEY INTEND TO INHABIT	SHIPS/DATES OF ARRIVAL	
FEBHER (cont'd)							
Elizabeth	5	F	Farmer	Switzerland		Antioch	18 Aug 1829
Elizabeth	32	F	Farmer	Switzerland		Antioch	18 Aug 1829
Frederic	29	M	Farmer	Switzerland		Antioch	18 Aug 1829
Maria	2	F	Farmer	Switzerland		Antioch	18 Aug 1829
Marie	3	F	Farmer	Switzerland		Antioch	18 Aug 1829
FECKWORTH, John	29	M	Sawyer	Gt. Britain	U. States	Diana	28 Apr 1828
FECTALY, ...	11	F		United States	United States	Seine	21 Oct 1822
Bautista	7	F		United States	United States	Seine	21 Oct 1822
E.	52	M	Farmer	United States	United States	Seine	21 Oct 1822
Elizabeth	15	F		United States	United States	Seine	21 Oct 1822
H.	53	M	Farmer	United States	United States	Seine	21 Oct 1822
Johannes	20	M	Farmer	United States	United States	Seine	21 Oct 1822
John	57	M	Farmer	United States	United States	Seine	21 Oct 1822
Maria	24	F	Farmer	United States	United States	Seine	21 Oct 1822
W.	24	M	Farmer	United States	United States	Seine	21 Oct 1822
FEE, Ann	22	F	Labourer	Great Britain	U. States	Princess Charlotte	6 Sep 1828
Jane	3	F	Labourer	Great Britain	U. States	Princess Charlotte	6 Sep 1828
Mary	23	F	Laborer or Spinster	Ireland	United States	Sarah G	11 Sep 1827
Robt.	22	M	Labourer	Great Britain	U. States	Princess Charlotte	6 Sep 1828
Sally	1	F	Laborer or Spinster	Ireland	United States	Sarah G	11 Sep 1827
William	24	M	Laborer or Spinster	Ireland	United States	Sarah G	11 Sep 1827
Wm.	26	M	Labourer	Great Britain	U. States	Princess Charlotte	6 Sep 1828
FEEALY, Nancy	8	F	Sevt.	Sligo	New York	Susquehana	27 Jun 1823
Patrick	14	M	Sevt.	Sligo	New York	Susquehana	27 Jun 1823
FEEHILY, Mary	18	F	Servt.	Sligo	New York	Susquehana	27 Jun 1823
FEELER, D.	21	M		Germany	United States	Lydia	18 Jun 1828
FEENAGHTY, Thomas	23	M	Farmer	Great Britain	United States	Mount Vernon	17 Jun 1825
FEENARTY, Thomas	20	M	Farmer	Ireland	United States	Lima	19 Jun 1824
FEENER, John	38	M	Mason	Scotland	Ama.	Expedition	19 May 1828
FEENEY, Pat	28	M	Labourer	Ireland	America	Weser	26 Jun 1821
FEENIGAN, Mary	20	F	Servt. made	Sligo	Kentucky	Susquehana	27 Jun 1823
FEGAN, Catharine	50	F	Spinster	Ireland	United States	Eliza	29 Aug 1822
Thomas	20	M	Mathematical Teacher	Ireland	United States	Eliza	29 Aug 1822
FEHR, —, Coll.	54	M	Militaire	Switzerland	U.S.	Francois I	8 Aug 1829
Edmond	16	M	Merchant	Switzerland	U. States	Queen Mab	16 Mar 1825
FEILEY, Catherine	26	F	Spinster	Ireland	United States	Fabius	31 Jul 1829
Catherine, Jr.	3	F	Child	Ireland	United States	Fabius	31 Jul 1829
FEILLET, —, Capt.	34	M	France	France	France	Anna Elizabeth	14 Jun 1824
FEINON, Francis	20	F		Ireland	United States	Mary	1 Jul 1829
FEINQUARD, William	21		Mechanic	London	England	Rockingham	23 Aug 1822
FEINS, William	32	M	Servant	New York	United States	St. Michaels	15 Feb 1825
FELARITY, Biddy	23	F	None	Ireland		Eliza Grant	29 Aug 1829
FELCON, A.	26	M	Servant	Italy	Italy	Governor Von Schollen	7 Nov 1827
FELICEANA, Antonio	25	M	Merchant	Catalona	Gibara	Abigail	18 Mar 1824
FELIMAE, Joseph	55	M	M...	...	New York	Curlew	28 Jun 1824
FELIX, George	25	M	Physician	Germany		George	10 Mar 1823
Louisa	25	F		France	U. States	North Star	27 Oct 1828
M. C.	39	M	Baker	France	U. States	North Star	27 Oct 1828
S.	4...	M	Merchant	Pourtigese	W. Sammea	Sloop Packet	5 Oct 1821
S.	40	M	Merchant	U. States		General Brown	17 Oct 1820
S.	42	M	Merchant	Spain	U.States	Sally	16 Apr 1821
Salvadore	38	M	Mariner	U. States	U. States	Ambuscade	1 Jul 1820
FELL, Ann	13	F		Isle of Man	Ohio	Curler	7 Jul 1827
James	41	M	...	England	U.S. American	Criterion	7 Jul 1824
Richard	22	M	Labourer	England	United States	Roman	12 Jun 1826
FELLER, Regina	62	F		France	France	Edward Quesnel	3 Jul 1829
FELLEW, Felix	32	M	Merchant	France	France	Annah	21 Jun 1826
FELLMAN, John	29	M	Farmer	France	United States	American	27 Aug 1827
FELLOW, Jams	18	M	Labourer	Ireland	United States	Hope	12 Jun 1828
FELLOWS, S.	26	M	Merchant	Great Britian		Radius	21 Jul 1824
William	29	M	Merchant	U. States	U. States	Dromo	28 Feb 1829
FELTER, Henry	23		Carpenter	New York	New York	Leonora	9 May 1828

NAMES OF PASSENGERS	AGE	SEX	OCCUPATIONS	COUNTRY TO WHICH THEY BELONG	COUNTRY THEY INTEND TO INHABIT	SHIPS/DATES OF ARRIVAL	
FELTMAN, Agust	28 4/12	M	Joiner	France	U. States	France	26 Jun 1828
FELTON, A. M., Mrs.	30	F	Lady	England	Canada	Acasta	11 Dec 1826
B.	45	M	Clothier			Lady of the Lake	23 Aug 1828
Edward, Master	1	M	Boy	England	Canada	Acasta	11 Dec 1826
Eli	7	M	...	...	...	Diamond	27 Jul 1824
George	5	M	...	...	...	Diamond	27 Jul 1824
S.	40		Labourer	Halifax	U. States	Edwin	26 Sep 1828
Sarah	25	F	...	...	...	Diamond	27 Jul 1824
William, Esq.	40	M	Gent.	England	Canada	Acasta	11 Dec 1826
FELTONE, John Henry	40	M	Musician	Prussia		Constitution	20 Jun 1828
FELWAY, Chas.	12	M	Boy	Ireland	United States	Trident	16 May 1826
FENCOHR, Dethery	25		Sugar Baker	Germany		Pomona	28 May 1822
FENELY, B.	25	F	Wife	Great Britain	United States	Washington	3 Sep 1827
Cathr.	5	F	Child	Great Britain	United States	Washington	3 Sep 1827
FENERTY, Edward	30	M	Labourer	Ireland	United States	Enterprize	23 Jul 1827
FENERY, George		M	Farmer	Alsace in the Department of Upper and lower Rhine	United States	Carolina Augusta	16 May 1828
George	32	M	Farmer	Alsace in the Department of Upper and lower Rhine	United States	Carolina Augusta	16 May 1828
Jacob		M	Farmer	Alsace in the Department of Upper and lower Rhine	United States	Carolina Augusta	16 May 1828
Maria		F	Farmer	Alsace in the Department of Upper and lower Rhine	United States	Carolina Augusta	16 May 1828
Maria	31	F	Farmer	Alsace in the Department of Upper and lower Rhine	United States	Carolina Augusta	16 May 1828
FENION, Francis	25	M	Weaver	Ireland	United States	Clothier	22 Nov 1827
FENNARY, David	27	M	Farmer			Robert Fulton	8 Mar 1823
FENNEL, Micheal	27		Shoemaker	England	United States	Mary	15 Jul 1822
FENNELL, Elliss	45	M	Labour	Great Britain	United States	Samuel Wright	12 Oct 1829
Mary	21	F	Farmer	Citazen	U.S. States	Splendid	14 Aug 1829
William, Junr.	38	M	Merchant	U. States	U. States	Queen Mab	16 Mar 1825
Wm., Jr.		M	Merchant	U. States	U. States	Atlanta	5 Jul 1821
Wm. [crossed out]	22	M	Mariner	United States	...	Mechanic	11 Apr 1826
FENNER, W., Revd.	40	M	Church	Switzerland	U. States	Manchester Packet	23 May 1822
FENNET, Joseph	23	M		France	United States	Bayard	13 Nov 1823
FENNING, Rose	23	F	Servant	Ireland	United States	Edwin	27 Oct 1828
FENNO, Ellinora	7	F		Denmark	St. Croix	Jupiter	8 Apr 1828
Jas.	39	M	Merchant	U. States	U. States	Chase	19 Sep 1823
FENOKIA, Jno.	27	M	Merchant	England	U. States	Bee	18 Dec 1821
FENRY, Margaretta		F	Farmer	Alsace in the Department of Upper and lower Rhine	United States	Carolina Augusta	16 May 1828
Martin	37	M	Labourer	Ireland	United States	Enterprize	23 Jul 1827
FENTIN, James	22	M	Farmer	Ireland	U. States	Combine	30 Nov 1825
FENTON, Ann	37	F	None	England	Canada	Hercules	24 Oct 1821
Benj.	27	M	Whitesmith	Ireland	United States	Trident	17 May 1825
J.	26	M	Carpenter	U. States	U. States	Signal	3 Jan 1826
James	3	M	None	England	Camada	Hercules	24 Oct 1821
Robt.	26	M	Farmer	Scotland		Domestic	31 Aug 1820
FENWICH, Edward	55	M		America	America	Braganza	1 Dec 1824
FENWICK, Edward	26	M	Merchant	Switzerland	America, U.N.S.	Great Britain	3 Aug 1829
Elizabeth	52	F	Teacheress	England	U. States	Cannon	15 Jul 1822
Mathew	25	M	Farmer	Great Brit.	Ohio	Gov. Griswald	3 Jul 1820
P.	18	F	Servant	Barbadoes	U. States	Cannon	15 Jul 1822
Thomas	30	M	Farmer	Great Brit.	Ohio	Gov. Griswald	3 Jul 1820
FEORILLI, Barthelmi	40	M	Merchant	U. States	U. States	Queen Mab	16 Mar 1825

NAMES OF PASSENGERS	AGE	SEX	OCCUPATIONS	COUNTRY TO WHICH THEY BELONG	COUNTRY THEY INTEND TO INHABIT	SHIPS/DATES OF ARRIVAL	
FEORNSIXO, Jose	2					Apollo	11 Jun 1828
FER, Jacob	20	M	Labourer	Wittenburg	U. States	Comet	28 Jul 1825
FERALLY, Cath.	13	F	Spinster	Ireland	America	Mary	29 May 1827
FERANDA, Jno. S.	30	M	Grocer	Cape Hatien	U. States	Eugene	12 Jul 1822
FERANDE, Thomas	4	M		U. States	U. States	Imperial	10 Dec 1821
FERARD, Francis		M	Lock Smith	France		Frederick	18 Feb 1822
FERAT, Chs.	35		Confectioner	American	America	Romulus	15 May 1828
FERBER, Jacob	25		Tailor	France	U. States	Parachute	14 May 1828
FERBES, Alexr.	22	M	Merchant	U. States	U. States	Isaac McKim	23 May 1826
FERBNER, Caroline	1			France	U. States	Parachute	14 May 1828
Catherine	3			France	U. States	Parachute	14 May 1828
Margaret	26			France	U. States	Parachute	14 May 1828
FERDENUMD, ...ocher	21	M		France	State of N. York	Danube	20 Jul 1826
FERDIN, Jose	62	M	Mercht.	Spain	Spain	Juliana	2 Sep 1826
FEREIRA, Antonio	22	M	Mariner	Portuges	United States	Fox	9 Mar 1829
FEREMAN, Ann	16	F		Great Britain	New York	Radius	7 Jul 1821
FEREN, Anna	39 7/12	F	Farmer	Switzerland	America	Henry	17 May 1828
Catherine	5 3/12	F	Farmer	Switzerland	America	Henry	17 May 1828
George	3 9/12	M	Farmer	Switzerland	America	Henry	17 May 1828
Margaret	1 11/12	F	Farmer	Switzerland	America	Henry	17 May 1828
Peter	48 3/12	M	Farmer	Switzerland	America	Henry	17 May 1828
FERER, —, Mr.	33	M	Merchant	Spain	U. States	Cadmus	12 Apr 1825
FERGASON, Edward	18 10/12	M		Ireland	U.S. of America	Douglass	6 Jul 1829
Joseph	26	M	Weaver	Ireland	New York	Colossus	2 Oct 1827
FERGEMAN, H.		M	Merchant	Hamburgh	U. States	Nancy	23 Aug 1823
FERGERSON, Peter	35			Great Britain	U. States	Columbia	7 May 1828
FERGURSON, David	22	M	Farmer	Gt. Britain	United States	Eliza Barker	11 Jan 1826
FERGUS, David	60	M	Preacher	Great Britain	United States	Natchez	17 Aug 1822
Janet	60	F		Great Britain	United States	Natchez	17 Aug 1822
Mary	26	F		Great Britain	United States	Natchez	17 Aug 1822
FERGUSON, —, Mr.	25	M	Merchant	England	U. States	Robert Edwards	11 Mar 1822
—, Mrs.	45	F	Spinster	Scotland	U.S. States of Am.	Camillus	17 Sep 1823
Alexr.	35	M	France	G. Britain	United States	Siroc	13 Sep 1828
Andrew	10	M	Child	Scotland	United States	Samuel Robertson	5 Oct 1827
Ann	0 9/12	F		Great Britain	U. States	United States	8 Sep 1827
Ann	24	F		Ireland	United States	Commerce	13 Jun 1828
Ann	29	F		Great Britain	U. States	United States	8 Sep 1827
Ann	34	F		Scotland	United States	Samuel Robertson	5 Oct 1827
Donald	26	M	Farmer	Scotland	U. States	Czar	29 Aug 1829
Duncan	22	M	Millwright	Scotland	U.S.A.	Calliope	15 Aug 1827
Elisabeth	6/52			Ireland	United States	Antioch	3 Dec 1827
Elisabeth	20			Ireland	United States	Antioch	3 Dec 1827
Eliz.	2	F		England	U. States	Howard Douglass	29 Jan 1828
Eliza	19	F		America	America	Silas Richard	24 Oct 1829
Elizth.	28	F	None	Scotland		Marchioness	13 May 1828
George	33	M	Merchant	Scotland	U. States	Rapid	25 Feb 1822
George, Sr.	22		Mercht.	United States	United States	Emily	11 Mar 1826
Georgiana	16	F		America	America	Silas Richard	24 Oct 1829
Henry	20		Weaver	Ireland	United States	Antioch	3 Dec 1827
Henry	22	M	Carpenter	Scotland	United States	Broke	16 Jul 1829
Isabella	7	F		England	U. States	Howard Douglass	29 Jan 1828
Isabella	44	F		England	U. States	Howard Douglass	29 Jan 1828
James	2	M		Great Britain	U. States	United States	8 Sep 1827
James	6	M		England	U. States	Howard Douglass	29 Jan 1828
James	8	M	Child	Scotland	United States	Samuel Robertson	5 Oct 1827
James	22		Marble ...			Amphion	31 May 1824
James	27		Labourer	Ireland	G. Britain	Robert Burns	14 Jun 1824
James	27	M	Carpenter	Ireland	U. States	Lady Hunter	9 Oct 1825
James	28		Printer	Scotland	United States	Camillus	3 May 1828
James	29	M	Weaver	Great Britain	U. States	United States	8 Sep 1827
James	30	M	Laborer	Ireland	United States	Mary	1 Jul 1829
James	35	M	Merchant	United States	United States	Atlantic	3 Dec 1821

NAMES OF PASSENGERS	AGE	SEX	OCCUPATIONS	COUNTRY TO WHICH THEY BELONG	COUNTRY THEY INTEND TO INHABIT	SHIPS/DATES OF ARRIVAL	
FERGUSON (cont'd)							
James	36	M	Labourer	Scotland	United States	Samuel Robertson	5 Oct 1827
James	57	M	Farmer	G. Briton	United States	James Monroe	14 Dec 1820
Jane Ellen	3	F		Ireland	United States	Princess Charlotte	26 Apr 1827
Jas.	24	M	Farmer	Scotland	U. States	Czar	29 Aug 1829
Jno.	21	M	Merchant	England	U. States	New York	4 Nov 1824
Jno.	21	M	Blacksmith	England	United States	Essex	23 May 1828
John	20	M	Weaver	Scotland	U.S. States of Am.	Camillus	17 Sep 1823
John	22	M	Farmer	Great Britain	United States	Dapper	14 Mar 1828
John	23	M	Merchant	New York	New York	New York	14 Nov 1826
John	23	M	Laborer, Spinster or Child	Ireland	United States	Ann Maria	4 Aug 1827
John	28	M	Labourer	Scotland		Marchioness	13 May 1828
John	38	M	Merchant	U.S. America	U.S. America	Columbia	3 Apr 1826
John	41	M	Mercht.	U.S.	U.S.	George Canning	2 May 1828
John	65	M	Carpenter	Ireland	U. States	Lady Hunter	9 Oct 1825
Mar.	6	F		England	U. States	Howard Douglass	29 Jan 1828
Mar.	36	F		England	U. States	Howard Douglass	29 Jan 1828
Margaret	1	F	None	Scotland		Marchioness	13 May 1828
Margaret	22		Spinster	Ireland	United States	Robert Burns	18 Jun 1821
Margaret	38	F		Ireland	United States	Princess Charlotte	26 Apr 1827
Mariancoe	16	F		England	U. States	Howard Douglass	29 Jan 1828
Mary	16			Ireland	G. Britain	Robert Burns	14 Jun 1824
Mary	32	F		Scotland	Jamaica	Little Cherub	11 Aug 1825
Rob.	30	M	Mercht.	Glasgow	U. States	Ossian	18 Feb 1822
S.	27	M		Ireland	America	Corinthian	1 Sep 1827
Saml.	24	M	Mercht.	Ireland	United States	St. John	5 Oct 1829
Sarah	20	F		America	America	Silas Richard	24 Oct 1829
Thomas	23	M	Merchant	St. Johns	Great Britain	St. Michael	5 Jan 1826
Thos.	25	M	Farmer	Gt. Britain	United States	Penelope	9 Sep 1828
William	4	M		England	U. States	Howard Douglass	29 Jan 1828
Wm.	11	M		England	U. States	Howard Douglass	29 Jan 1828
FERICOT, Eliz.	29	F	Farmer	France		Pallas	14 Jun 1828
Geo. H.	3	M		France		Pallas	14 Jun 1828
Jean G.	27	F		France		Pallas	14 Jun 1828
Perre	6	M	Farmer	France		Pallas	14 Jun 1828
FERKIN, Joseph	34	M	Labourer	...fferty, Staplton, England	U. States	New Orleans	24 Aug 1827
FERLAT, Stephen	41 3/12	M	...	...	U.S. America	Edward	28 Oct 1825
FERMAN, A.	41	M		Great Brittan	U.S.	Florida	17 May 1825
Danl.	13	M		Great Brittan	U.S.	Florida	17 May 1825
FERMER, Ann	18		Spinster	Ireland	United States	Robert Burns	18 Jun 1821
James	23		Farmer	Pennsylvania	United States	Robert Burns	18 Jun 1821
FERN, Elizabeth	9					William	17 Aug 1820
Emund	45	M	Farmer	Derbeyshire, Bradbern	U. States	Manhattan	21 May 1821
James	10	M	None	Derbeyshire, Bradbern	U. States	Manhattan	21 May 1821
James	13					William	17 Aug 1820
James	40		Farmer			William	17 Aug 1820
John	18	M	None	Derbeyshire, Bradbern	U. States	Manhattan	21 May 1821
Joseph	18					William	17 Aug 1820
Lawrence	4					William	17 Aug 1820
Marry	44	F	None	Derbeyshire, Bradbern	U. States	Manhattan	21 May 1821
Samuel	12	M	None	Derbeyshire, Bradbern	U. States	Manhattan	21 May 1821
Sarah	10					William	17 Aug 1820
Sarah	44					William	17 Aug 1820
Wm.	15					William	17 Aug 1820

NAMES OF PASSENGERS	AGE	SEX	OCCUPATIONS	COUNTRY TO WHICH THEY BELONG	COUNTRY THEY INTEND TO INHABIT	SHIPS/DATES OF ARRIVAL	
FERN (cont'd)							
Wm.	15	M	None	Derbeyshire, Bradbern	U. States	Manhattan	21 May 1821
FERNAIN, Elanor	2	F	Labourer	Sligo	New York	Susquehana	27 Jun 1823
Marg.	4	F	Labourer	Sligo	New York	Susquehana	27 Jun 1823
Margaret	27	F	Labourer	Sligo	New York	Susquehana	27 Jun 1823
FERNALD, Mark	33	M	Mariner	U. States	U. States	Combine	22 May 1824
FERNAN, Ann	24	F	None	England	U. States	Montgomery	18 Oct 1828
Hugh	25	M	Labourer	Ireland	United States	Wilson	4 Oct 1827
John	30	M	Labourer	England	U. States	Montgomery	18 Oct 1828
FERNANDER, Ferua	8	F	Merchant	Spain	Havana	Commodore Chauncy	28 Nov 1825
Francesca	13	M	Merchant	Spain	Havana	Commodore Chauncy	28 Nov 1825
Francisco	11	M	Merchant	Spain	Havana	Commodore Chauncy	28 Nov 1825
Getrades	17	F	Merchant	Spain	Havana	Commodore Chauncy	28 Nov 1825
Isabel	6	F	Merchant	Spain	Havana	Commodore Chauncy	28 Nov 1825
Manuel	16	M	Merchant	Spain	Havana	Commodore Chauncy	28 Nov 1825
Ramon	4	M	Merchant	Spain	Havana	Commodore Chauncy	28 Nov 1825
Rosaria, Da.	23	F	Merchant	Spain	Havana	Commodore Chauncy	28 Nov 1825
Solodad	18	F	Merchant	Spain	Havana	Commodore Chauncy	28 Nov 1825
FERNANDES, Antonio	28	M	Merchant	Spain	U. States	Ariadne	15 Apr 1822
FERNANDEZ, A.	25	M	Gentleman	American	U. States	Harmony	12 Jul 1821
Andrez	27	M	Merchant	Spain	Spain	Claudio	22 Mar 1828
Anthony	26	M	...	...	United States	Abeona	26 Jun 1824
Antonio	34	M	Merchant	Havana	Havana	Crusader	23 Apr 1827
Benith	20	M	Merchant	Havana	Havana	Boon	26 Feb 1820
Carlos	34	M	Merchant	Mexico	Mexico	Splendid	31 Aug 1827
Carlos	38	M	Merchant	Spain	U. States	Pomona	4 Apr 1823
D.		M	Merchant	Spain		Levantine	7 Nov 1825
E.	27	M	Merchant			Eliza Ann	29 Sep 1820
F.	20	M	Servant	Spain	U. States	Quesnel	6 Sep 1824
Hypolite, Mr.	35	M	Merchant	Porto Rico	Porto Rico	Jupiter	6 Aug 1826
J. M.	41	M	Merchant	Spain	U. States	Ysdva	11 Sep 1828
Jno.		M	Gentleman	Spaniard		Happy Return	23 Jul 1821
Jose	35	M	Marchant	Spain	Spain	Atrevida	26 Jul 1820
Joseph	22	M	Merchant	France	France	Swiftsure	27 Feb 1826
Juan Antonio	57	M	Merchant	Spain	Havana	Commodore Chauncy	28 Nov 1825
Miguel	30	M	Military	Mexico	Mexico	Virginia	9 Feb 1829
Saml.	28	M	Mariner	U. States	U. States	Ambuscade	1 Jul 1820
FERNANDOZ, H., Don	30	M	Merchant	Spain	Mexico	Nancy	1 Oct 1824
FERNEOUGH, Thomas	20	M	Farmer	England	United States	Jubilee	13 Jul 1829
FERNESS, John	28			Westmoreland	Ohio	Peru	30 May 1828
Joseph	22			Westmoreland	Ohio	Peru	30 May 1828
FERNON, Marcibio	30	M	Merchant	Spain	U. States	William Thompson	24 Aug 1827
FERNS, Thomas	16	M	Merchant	England	America	Silas Richard	24 Oct 1829
Thomas	30	M	Merchant	England	United States	Bogota	16 Dec 1826
Thos.	30	M		G. Britain	U. States	Canada	19 Sep 1828
Thos.	31	M	Merchant	Gt. Brittain	United States	Cortes	5 Aug 1822
Thos.	32	M	Merchant	Great Britain	United States	Leeds	29 Sep 1823
William W.	40	M	Mechanic	Ireland	U.S.	George Canning	26 Aug 1829
FERNSIDE, ...	21	F	Farmer	Torres..., Scotland	Gt. Britain	Orozimbo	19 Oct 1822
...	28	F	Farmer	Torres..., Scotland	Gt. Britain	Orozimbo	19 Oct 1822
Jas.	6/12	M	Farmer	Torres..., Scotland	Gt. Britain	Orozimbo	19 Oct 1822
Martha	3	F	Farmer	Torres..., Scotland	Gt. Britain	Orozimbo	19 Oct 1822

NAMES OF PASSENGERS	AGE	SEX	OCCUPATIONS	COUNTRY TO WHICH THEY BELONG	COUNTRY THEY INTEND TO INHABIT	SHIPS/DATES OF ARRIVAL	
FERNSIDE (cont'd)							
Thomas	21	M	Farmer	Torres..., Scotland	Gt. Britain	Orozimbo	19 Oct 1822
Thos.	5	M	Farmer	Torres..., Scotland	Gt. Britain	Orozimbo	19 Oct 1822
FERON, Augustus	3 4/12	M		Great Britain	U. States	New York	19 Nov 1828
Elizabeth	29	F		Great Britain	U. States	New York	19 Nov 1828
Letitia	45	F		Great Britain	U. States	New York	19 Nov 1828
FERRABY, Edward	21	M	Famer	Gt. Britain	U. States	Maria	22 May 1822
FERRALL, Sidney	25	M	Merchant	Ireland	United States	Alexander Mansfield	9 Jul 1829
FERRAN, Hugh	25	M	Labourer	Great Britain	United States	Penelope	11 Jun 1827
Rich.	30	M	Labourer	Great Britain	United States	Penelope	11 Jun 1827
FERRAND, P. F.	32	M	Mercht.	France	N. York	Howard	26 Aug 1823
V.	23	M	Merchant	Charleston	U. States	Manchester Packet	21 Aug 1823
FERRARA, John	26	M	Boot Maker	England		Exchange	11 Jul 1823
FERRELL, Ann	5	F	None			Importer	30 Oct 1820
Ann	30	F	None			Importer	30 Oct 1820
C.	35	F		U. States	U. States	Penobscott Packet	1 Jul 1823
Cathrine	7	F	Child	Ireland	United States	Dublin Packet	24 Sep 1823
Edward	7	M	None			Importer	30 Oct 1820
Edward	26	M	Weaver			Washington	15 Sep 1821
James	33	M	Farmer			Importer	30 Oct 1820
Michael	22	M	Farmer	Ireland	United States	Dublin Packet	22 Apr 1822
FERREN, Edwd.	28	M	Labourer	Ireland	United States	Essex	23 May 1828
Mary	26	F	Labourer	Ireland	United States	Essex	23 May 1828
FERREORA, Loreta	21	F		Mexico	Mexico	Virginia	9 Feb 1829
Soledad	23	F		Mexico	Mexico	Virginia	9 Feb 1829
FERRI, Isabella	30	F	...	Ireland	United States	Carolina Ann	24 Oct 1825
FERRIGAN, Amy	20	F	...	Ireland	United States	Carolina Ann	24 Oct 1825
John	25	M	...	Ireland	United States	Carolina Ann	24 Oct 1825
FERRILL, —, Miss		F		St. Croix	St. Croix	Ludwig	10 Aug 1825
Jno.	23	M	Farmer	Ireland	America	Mary	29 May 1827
Thos.	20	M	Cooper	...	United States	Combine	20 Nov 1824
FERRIN, Francis	22	M	Labourer	Ireland	United States	Edwin	29 Nov 1828
FERRINGTON, Benjm.	28	M	Mechanic	U. States	U. States	Abeona	11 Mar 1823
Elija	35	M	Mechanic	U. States	U. States	Abeona	11 Mar 1823
Henry	29		Planter	Great Britain	St. Croix	South Carolina Packet	7 Jul 1821
FERRIRA, Antonio	19	M	Mechanic	Madeira	U. States	Howard	3 Mar 1828
FERRIS, Eliza	35	F		U. States	U. States	Penobscott Packet	1 Jul 1823
Eliza M., Miss	12	F	Lady	Ireland	United States	Dublin Packet	24 Sep 1823
Henry	52	M	Farmer	...	United States	Erin	25 Dec 1820
Thomas	31	M	Shoemaker	Ireland	United States	Edwin	27 Oct 1828
Thomas E., Doctor	25	M	Doctor	United States	United States	Dublin Packet	24 Sep 1823
FERRIT, Ann	18	F	Spinster	Ireland	United States	Lord Strangford	20 Jun 1826
FERRNAICE, —	41	M	Labourer	France	United States	Cavalier	25 Jul 1828
—, Wife	31	F		France	United States	Cavalier	25 Jul 1828
Agatha	3	F		France	United States	Cavalier	25 Jul 1828
Caspur	2	M		France	United States	Cavalier	25 Jul 1828
Cath.	6	F		France	United States	Cavalier	25 Jul 1828
Selie	9	F		France	United States	Cavalier	25 Jul 1828
FERRO, John	28	M	Merchant	Spain	Spain	Liberty	27 Mar 1826
Peter	32 5/12	M	Merchant	Gibraltar	Vera Cruz	Clarice	27 Aug 1827
FERROLL, Mary	20	F	None	Philadelphia	Philadelphia	Washington	3 Mar 1828
FERROW, Rose	16	M	Labourer	Ireland	United States	Hope	12 Jun 1828
FERRUGAN, Andrew	20	M	Labourer	Ireland	United States	Mary & Harriet	3 Jul 1829
FERRUS, W.	30	M	Servant	England	U. States	Rising Sun	1 May 1823
FERRY, Alice	19	F		Ireland	United States	Clothier	22 Nov 1827
Andrew	22	...	...	Ireland	United States	Carolina Ann	24 Oct 1825
Anne	...	...		Ireland	United States	Carolina Ann	24 Oct 1825
Charles	45	M	Priest	Ireland	U. States	Nancy	14 Jan 1822
James	24	...	...	Ireland	United States	Carolina Ann	24 Oct 1825
John	18	M	Merchant	U. States	U. States	Prince Edward	25 Feb 1822
John	20	M	Merchant	U.S.	America	Wave	15 Aug 1821
Michael	21	M	Labourer	Ireland	America	Plutarch	18 Jul 1826

NAMES OF PASSENGERS	A G E	S E X	OCCUPATIONS	COUNTRY TO WHICH THEY BELONG	COUNTRY THEY INTEND TO INHABIT	SHIPS/DATES OF ARRIVAL	
FERRY (cont'd)							
Neal O.	21	M	Labourer	Ireland	United States	Hope	12 Jun 1828
Patrick	10	...	...	Ireland	United States	Carolina Ann	24 Oct 1825
Sarah	...	...	...	Ireland	United States	Carolina Ann	24 Oct 1825
Winny	...	...	...	Ireland	United States	Carolina Ann	24 Oct 1825
FERTH, John	24	M	Farmer	England	United States	Aurelia	7 Jun 1826
FERTUSON, Jas.	27	M	Weaver	Scotland	New York	Joseph Hume	26 Oct 1829
FERUGAN, John	18	M	Labourer	Sligo	New York	Susquehana	27 Jun 1823
FESEHART, Fredrick	30	M	Farmer	France	United States	Virginia	31 May 1828
FESEMAN, Joseph	22	M	Weaver	Switzerland	U. States	Romulus	24 Sep 1828
Joseph	22	M	Joiner	Switzerland	U. States	Romulus	24 Sep 1828
FESENMEIER, Joseph	31	M	Agriculturist	France	U.S.	Helen	3 May 1828
FESSART, —	36	M	Merchant	U. States	U. States	Imperial	10 Dec 1821
A.	36	M	Merchant	France	U. States	William Thompson	29 Jan 1823
FETCHIS, Mary	7	F	Child	New York	New York	Atlantic	8 May 1828
FETE, Spencer	40	M	Servant	United States	United States	William Bayard	17 May 1825
FETHERSHIELD, John	17	M	Laborer	United States	United States	Globe	30 Aug 1828
FETHERSTON, John	27	M	Clerk	Ireland	Great Britan	Columbia	11 Aug 1823
FETHERSTONE, Ann	4	F	None	Great Britain	United States	Cambria	26 Dec 1827
Ann	33	F	None	Great Britain	United States	Cambria	26 Dec 1827
Eliza	12	F	None	Great Britain	United States	Cambria	26 Dec 1827
Thomas	33	M	Blacksmith	Great Britain	United States	Cambria	26 Dec 1827
FETNAN, Christopher	7	M		Philadelphia	U. States	Howard	25 Jul 1823
FETTER, John	40	M	Gardner	Switzerland	United States	Eliza Grant	18 Aug 1826
FEVER, Hannah	53 6/12	F		England	America	Cincinnatus	22 May 1826
John	48 3/12	M	Shoemaker	England	America	Cincinnatus	22 May 1826
FEVRE, Christr.	9	F		France	United States	Le Voltaire	19 Jul 1828
Eliz. G.	38	F		France	United States	Le Voltaire	19 Jul 1828
Ja...ue	20	F		France	United States	Le Voltaire	19 Jul 1828
Jean	13	F		France	United States	Le Voltaire	19 Jul 1828
Jean	42	F	Weaver	France	United States	Le Voltaire	19 Jul 1828
Pievre	17	F		France	United States	Le Voltaire	19 Jul 1828
FEW, Anna M.	16	F	his family [Joseph]	Germany	Pensylvania	Isabella	15 Sep 1828
C.	26	F	Servant	Ireland	U. States	St. Michaels	25 Apr 1825
Christian	10	M	his family [Joseph]	Germany	Pensylvania	Isabella	15 Sep 1828
Christina	30	F	his family [Joseph]	Germany	Pensylvania	Isabella	15 Sep 1828
Edward	3	M		England	United States	Delta	24 Oct 1829
Elizabeth	5	F		England	United States	Delta	24 Oct 1829
Fredereck	8	M	his family [Joseph]	Germany	Pensylvania	Isabella	15 Sep 1828
George	6	M	his family [Joseph]	Germany	Pensylvania	Isabella	15 Sep 1828
Jacob	5	M	his family [Joseph]	Germany	Pensylvania	Isabella	15 Sep 1828
John	2	M		England	United States	Delta	24 Oct 1829
John	24	M	Carpenter	England	United States	Delta	24 Oct 1829
Joseph	40	M	Carpenter	Germany	Pensylvania	Isabella	15 Sep 1828
Mary	18	F		N. York	U. States	Brandt	20 Sep 1822
Rebecca *Died	6/12	F		England	United States	Delta	24 Oct 1829
Rebecca	22	F	his wife	England	United States	Delta	24 Oct 1829
Rosina	1 6/12	F	his family [Joseph]	Germany	Pensylvania	Isabella	15 Sep 1828
FEXELI, Vincenzo	39	M		Roma	Philadelphia	Falcon	10 Sep 1823
FEYAN, Jas.	30	M	Calico Printer	Great Britain	United States	Aurora	5 Sep 1826
FEZAN, Catherine	29	F	his family [Henry]	Germany	United States	Wm. Osborne	16 Sep 1828
Jean	3	M	his family [Henry]	Germany	United States	Wm. Osborne	16 Sep 1828
Jean	29	M	his family [Henry]	Germany	United States	Wm. Osborne	16 Sep 1828
FHISTER, Alex P.	45	M	Merchant	U. States	U. States	Marmion	7 May 1827
FIBBS, John	38	M	pudler		uncertain	Mount Vernon	29 Aug 1828
FICHE, H.	26	F		France	United States	La Flora	30 Jun 1828
FICHETY, Wm.	21	M	Farmer	Ireland	United States	Diana	1 May 1826
FICHITY, Micheal	32	M	Farmer	Ireland	United States	Diana	1 May 1826
FICKS, John Lewis, Dr.	35	M	Art...	Germany	Germany	Acasta	12 May 1825
FICTEW, Anthony	4	M	Family [of Hans]	France	America	La Grange	7 Aug 1828
Catharine	8	F	Family [of Hans]	France	America	La Grange	7 Aug 1828
Gertrude	14	F	Family [of Hans]	France	America	La Grange	7 Aug 1828
Gertrude	40	F	Family [of Hans]	France	America	La Grange	7 Aug 1828
Hans	45	M	Farmer	France	America	La Grange	7 Aug 1828
Joseph	10	M	Family [of Hans]	France	America	La Grange	7 Aug 1828
FIDDLER, Thos.	20	M	Stone Cutter	Great Britain	United States	William Dawson	18 Jun 1827
FIDEA, Paul	35	M	Merchant	France	Baracoa	Paulina Julia	15 Apr 1824

NAMES OF PASSENGERS	AGE	SEX	OCCUPATIONS	COUNTRY TO WHICH THEY BELONG	COUNTRY THEY INTEND TO INHABIT	SHIPS/DATES OF ARRIVAL	
FIDEON, Thos.	38	M	Mercht.	Gt. Britain	Mexico	William Thompson	19 Jan 1829
Thos.	55	M	Mercht.	Gt. Britain	Mexico	William Thompson	19 Jan 1829
FIEDING, Maria M.	45	F		Germany	U. States	Falcon	11 Jun 1827
FIELD, Ann	6/12	F	None	Great Britain	United States	Cambria	26 Dec 1827
Ann	32	F	None	Great Britain	United States	Cambria	26 Dec 1827
George	26		Miller	Kent	...	Hudson	14 Jun 1827
Henry	3	M	Child	U. States	U. States	Edwin	1 Jul 1829
Isaac	38	M	Merchant	U. States	U. States	Leader	31 Dec 1827
James	31	M	Cordwainer	G. Britain	U. States	Panthia	23 Apr 1824
James	45	M	Merchant	New York	United States	Abigail	23 Nov 1820
Jas. O.	33		Shoemaker	England		Corinthian	11 Mar 1829
John	6	M	Child	U. States	U. States	Edwin	1 Jul 1829
John	27	M	Merchant	United States	United States	Cortes	18 Oct 1820
Martha	32	F	None	U. States	U. States	Edwin	1 Jul 1829
Mary	20	F	Lady	United States	United States	Hopes Delight	22 Jul 1829
Michael	19	M			Great Britain	U. States	Great Britain	18 Mar 1828
Michael	23	M	Farmer	Ireland	United States	Lord Strangford	20 Jun 1826
Thomas	17	M		Great Britain	U. States	Great Britain	18 Mar 1828
Thomas	26			Kent	...	Hudson	14 Jun 1827
Thos.	27	M		Ireland	United States	Thompson	12 Sep 1827
William	32	M	Carpenter	Great Britain	United States	Cambria	26 Dec 1827
Wm.	17	M	Manuir	England	United States	Dalhouse Castle	6 Sep 1827
FIELDCHER, Wm.	46	M				Eliza Grant	6 Oct 1828
Wm., Jr.	18	M				Eliza Grant	6 Oct 1828
FIELDEN, Caroline	20	F	Servant	Great Britain	U. States	Hope & Esther	13 Oct 1829
William	25	M	Servant	Great Britain	U. States	Hope & Esther	13 Oct 1829
FIELDING, Andrew	36		Weaver	Great Britain	United States	Camillus	12 Sep 1827
Ann	30	F		Ireland	U. States	Fame	15 Nov 1826
Charles	6	M		Ireland	America	Carolina Ann	7 Apr 1826
George	8	M		Ireland	America	Carolina Ann	7 Apr 1826
James	72	M	Machine Maker	England	Patterson	Curler	7 Jul 1827
Jane						Carolina Ann	7 Apr 1826
Johanah	11	F		Ireland	America	Liverpool	31 Aug 1827
John	5	M		Ireland	U. States	Fame	15 Nov 1826
John	23	M	Student	England	United States	Jubilee	4 Mar 1829
John	28	M	Servant	Great Britian	United States	Columbia	21 Jan 1828
Joseph	20	M	Mariner	U.S. America	U.S. America	Ganges	15 Dec 1826
*Destitute Seaman put on board by the American Consul in London							
Mary	18	F	Servant	Ireland	United States	Edwin	29 Nov 1828
Mary	31 2/12	F		Ireland	America	Carolina Ann	7 Apr 1826
Robt.	30	M	Labourer	Gt. Britain	U. States	Frances Henrietta	18 Apr 1825
Robt.	35	M	Wheelwright	Ireland	U. States	Fame	15 Nov 1826
Thos.	25	M		Ireland	U. States	Robert Fulton	9 Feb 1822
William	10 3/12	M		Ireland	America	Carolina Ann	7 Apr 1826
FIELDS, Isaac, Mr.			Merchant	U.S.	U.S.	Sully	26 Oct 1829
Thomas	17	M	Carpenter	Ireland	U. States	Josephine	7 May 1827
FIENGO, Mary, Mrs.	30	F	Lady	United States	United States	Maria	29 Sep 1823
Nicholas	4	M	Child	United States	United States	Maria	29 Sep 1823
Sarah	5	F	Child	United States	United States	Maria	29 Sep 1823
FIERNAN, A.	25	M	Labourer	Co. L...th	United States	Java	9 Jul 1827
Peter	22	M	Labourer	Co. L...th	United States	Java	9 Jul 1827
FIERNY, James	22	M	Tailor	Ireland	America	Wilson	16 May 1825
FIFE, —, Mrs.	52	F		G. Britain	U. States	Camillus	8 Sep 1828
Agnes	35	F		Scotland	United States	Commerce	17 Jul 1823
Christian	11	F		Scotland	United States	Commerce	17 Jul 1823
Jams	40	M	Reed Maker	Scotland	United States	Commerce	17 Jul 1823
Janet	18 3/12	F		Scotland	United States	Mobile	21 Aug 1827
John	66 7/12	M	Weaver	Scotland	United States	Mobile	21 Aug 1827
John, ...	15	M	Mechanic	Scotland	United States	Commerce	17 Jul 1823
Maria	20 6/12	F		Scotland	United States	Mobile	21 Aug 1827
May	20	F		Scotland	United States	Commerce	17 Jul 1823
Wm.	20		Farmer	Ireland	United States	Robert Burns	18 Jun 1821
FIFER, Barbara	17	F		Germany	United States	Samuel Robertson	8 Aug 1828
Barnard	5	M		Germany	United States	Samuel Robertson	8 Aug 1828

406

NAMES OF PASSENGERS	AGE	SEX	OCCUPATIONS	COUNTRY TO WHICH THEY BELONG	COUNTRY THEY INTEND TO INHABIT	SHIPS/DATES OF ARRIVAL	
FIFER (cont'd)							
Dorathy	9	F		Germany	United States	Samuel Robertson	8 Aug 1828
George	3	M		Germany	United States	Samuel Robertson	8 Aug 1828
George	41	M	Taylor	Germany	United States	Samuel Robertson	8 Aug 1828
Matalana	19	F		Germany	United States	Samuel Robertson	8 Aug 1828
Matalana	49	F		Germany	United States	Samuel Robertson	8 Aug 1828
Salana	7	F		Germany	United States	Samuel Robertson	8 Aug 1828
FIGARA, J. Theodore	14	M	Trader	U. States	U. States	Rodney	19 Jun 1827
FIGEN, Paulo Joaqn.	28	M	Merchant	Portugal	U. States	Minos	24 Oct 1828
FIGG, William	63	M	Sawyer	England	U.S.A.	Hudson	21 Aug 1829
FIGUESROA VASCOS, Antonio Pedro, Eqr.		M	Secretary to Consul Genl.	Portugal	U. States	Sarah Louisa	10 Oct 1822
FILAN, John	23	M	None	Ireland	U. States	Criterion	23 May 1826
FILER, James	22	M	Labourer	G. Britain	U. States	Sarah G	5 Jun 1828
FILES, Flamhest	25	M	Merchant	Jacqumel	Rebublic of Hayti	Renuniero	3 Jan 1822
FILEY, John	21	M	Farmer	Ireland	New York	Margaret	18 May 1825
FILIPPI, Giovanni D.	26	M	Merchant	Piedmont	United States	Pedler	29 May 1826
FILL, Alfred	6	M		England	United States	Eliza Grant	7 Jun 1827
Charlotte, Miss	9	F		England	United States	Eliza Grant	7 Jun 1827
Emma, Miss	11	F		England	United States	Eliza Grant	7 Jun 1827
George	5	M		England	United States	Eliza Grant	7 Jun 1827
H. A.	22	M	Merchant	Barbadoes	Barbadoes	Sudan	6 Aug 1823
Harry	3	M		England	United States	Eliza Grant	7 Jun 1827
Marg., Miss	20	F		England	United States	Eliza Grant	7 Jun 1827
Molly, Mrs.	39	F		England	United States	Eliza Grant	7 Jun 1827
FILLMAN, H.	42	M	Shp. Carpenter	G. Brittan	U. States	Henry	24 Oct 1828
FILLY, Mary	24	F		Ireland		Lady Hunter	12 Apr 1823
FILMER, Charles	23	M	Farmer	England	U. States	Cincinnatus	24 May 1821
FILMONT, James D.	33	M	None	France	U. States	Sully	25 Jun 1828
FILS, Larchhelle	30	M	Merchant		U. States	Diana	1 Jun 1822
FIMBLE, James	22		Weaver	Ireland	United States	Courier	15 Oct 1827
FIMINGHAM, Hannah	40	F		Bermuda	Bermuda	Wormontogus	17 May 1822
FIN, John	25	M	Labourer	Ireland	United States	Antioch	21 Sep 1827
Pat	25	M	Labourer	Ireland	United States	Antioch	21 Sep 1827
FINALEY, Benjamin	27	M				Splendid	14 Aug 1829
FINAN, Bridget	19	F	Spinster	Ireland	United States	Dublin Packet	22 Apr 1822
FINBY, Eleanor	17	F		Ireland	United States	Wm. Byrnes	30 Apr 1828
Jas.	13	M	Mechanic	Ireland	United States	Wm. Byrnes	30 Apr 1828
Mary	11	F		Ireland	United States	Wm. Byrnes	30 Apr 1828
FINCENT, Vincent	22	M	Paper Maker	England	U. States	Rising States	20 Sep 1828
FINCH, Ann	12	F		Ireland	U. States	Nancy	16 Aug 1822
Caroline	22	F	Labourer	G. Britain	U. States	London	23 Sep 1828
David	25	M	Merchant	U. States	U. States	Pacific	28 Mar 1822
John	30	M	Labourer	England	U. States	Emulous	22 Aug 1828
Ralph K.	20	M	Gentleman	United States	United States	Spartan	16 Nov 1827
William	37	M	Joiner	England	United States	London	21 May 1828
FINCHEN, —	12	F	None	England		Marchioness	13 May 1828
—	29	F	None	England		Marchioness	13 May 1828
Elisha	34	M	Labourer	England		Marchioness	13 May 1828
FINCHEY, Hannah	20	F	...	Wirtemburg	United States	Wade	29 Aug 1825
Regina	24	F	...	Wirtemburg	United States	Wade	29 Aug 1825
FINDLAY, M.	22	M	Farmer	U. States	U. States	Infant	10 Jul 1821
FINDLEY, Janet	18	F	None	Scotland	U.S. of America	Friends	12 May 1826
Nicholas	25	M	Labourer	Ireland	United States	Alexander Mansfield	16 Sep 1823
Sarah	30	F	Servant	G. Britain	U. States	Endeavour	1 May 1826
FINDON, John	17	M	Nob n By [?]	Ireland	U. States	Electra	7 Jul 1828
FINEGAN, Authur	12	M	Gentleman	Ireland	United States	Dublin Packet	13 Oct 1828
Ellen	21	F	Spinster	Ireland	U. States	Josephine	30 Aug 1828
John	18		Painter	Dros...da, Ireland	Great Britain	Franklin	22 Jun 1827
John	30		Chandler	Dros...da, Ireland	Great Britain	Franklin	22 Jun 1827
Patrick	20	M	Labourer	Ireland	United States	Elizabeth	8 Jun 1827

NAMES OF PASSENGERS	AGE	SEX	OCCUPATIONS	COUNTRY TO WHICH THEY BELONG	COUNTRY THEY INTEND TO INHABIT	SHIPS/DATES OF ARRIVAL	
FINEGAN (cont'd)							
Patrick	30	M	Weaver	Ireland	United States	Romulus	24 Jun 1826
FINEGUR, Catharine	18	F		Irereland	America	Carolina Ann	20 Jun 1825
FINEL, Marie, (Widow)	55	F		France	United States	Montano	5 May 1828
FINERTY, Catherine	19	F	Spinster	Ireland	America	Wilson	16 May 1825
FINGAN, James	28	M	Weaver	U. States	U. States	United States	11 Sep 1828
Mary	24	F		U. States	U. States	United States	11 Sep 1828
FINIGAN, Barney	15	M	Farmer	Ireland	United States	Silas Richards	3 Apr 1826
Cormick	45	M	Farmer	Ireland	United States	Silas Richards	3 Apr 1826
Jas.	35	M	Taylor	Ireland	United States	Neury	27 Jan 1827
Mary	15	F		Ireland	United States	Neury	27 Jan 1827
Patrick	18	M	Farmer	Ireland	United States	Silas Richards	3 Apr 1826
Philip	22	M	Labourer	Ireland	United States	Lord Wellington	28 May 1827
FINIQUE, Chery	43	M	Mariner	West Indies	U. States	Nassau	2 Nov 1825
FINK, Abraham	36	M	Farmer	Switzerland	United States	Andes	5 May 1828
Alexr.	25	M	Butcher	U.S.	U.S.	Superb	27 Sep 1820
Catharan	17	F		Bardin	U. States	Bayard	5 Sep 1828
Johname	24	F	Farmer	Germany	U. States	United States	3 Sep 1828
FINKERTON, Ann	21	M		Ireland	United States	Fabius	4 Jun 1828
Janes	21	M		Ireland	United States	Fabius	4 Jun 1828
FINKIN, E.	31	F	Lady	U. States	U. States	Diana	18 Jul 1820
FINLAY, James	34	M	Merchant	St. Croix	St. Croix	St. Helena	18 Feb 1823
John	23	M	Merchant	Gt. Britain	Canada	Friends	25 Sep 1823
John	30	M	Gentleman	St. Croix	St. Croix	Jupiter	31 Mar 1826
Reubin	21		Baker	Ireland	United States	Fabius	18 Mar 1829
Robert	20	M	Joiner	England	New York	America	1 Aug 1828
Wm.	25	M	Gentleman	Ireland	U. States	Erin	5 Jul 1820
Wm., Mr.	38			Scotland	G.B.	Pacific	24 May 1824
FINLAYSON, Finlay	26	M	Labourer	Scotland	Cape Britan	Mary & Susan	5 Aug 1828
FINLEY, Ann	30	F		Scotland	U.S.A.	Calliope	15 Aug 1827
Cathr.	22	F	None	Ireland	United States	Aurelia	7 Jun 1826
James	1	M	None	Scotland	U.S.A.	Calliope	15 Aug 1827
James	27	M		Argyle (Tedland) Scotland	United States	Jean Hastie	27 Jul 1829
Jas.	25	M	Taylor	Great Britain	United States	Science	16 Sep 1826
Jean	5	F		Scotland	U.S.A.	Calliope	15 Aug 1827
Jennet	7	F		Scotland	U.S.A.	Calliope	15 Aug 1827
John	3	M		Scotland	U.S.A.	Calliope	15 Aug 1827
John	23	M	Shoe Maker	Ireland	United States	Aurelia	7 Jun 1826
John	27		Merchant	...	...	James Cropper	28 Jun 1824
Margeret	10	F		Scotland	U.S.A.	Calliope	15 Aug 1827
Michael	20	M	Labourer	Ireland	America	Plutarch	18 Jul 1826
Mon	8	M		Scotland	U.S.A.	Calliope	15 Aug 1827
Robt.	42	M	Weaver	Scotland	U.S.A.	Calliope	15 Aug 1827
Susan	21	F		G. Britain	U. States	Dalhouse Castle	12 Sep 1828
Thomas	20		Merchant	...	...	James Cropper	28 Jun 1824
William	24	M	Labourer	Ireland	United States	Hopes Delight	29 Nov 1827
FINLEYSON, David	24	M	Cooper	Scotland	New York	Monroe	20 Jan 1825
FINLY, William	32	M	Baker	Ireland	United States	Nancey	25 Jan 1823
FINN, Ann	32	F	None	Ireland	U.S.A.	Dalhouse Castle	21 Aug 1829
Ann	32	F	None	Ireland	United States	Dalhouse Castle	21 Aug 1829
Catherine	13	F		England	U. States	Hudson	8 Oct 1827
Edmond	18					Trio	5 May 1828
Eliza, Mrs.	55	F	Teacher	England	America	Maine	16 Jul 1821
H. J.	34	M	Gentleman	Great Britain	United States	Juno	5 Oct 1822
John	20	M		Ireland	United States	John & Adam	21 Sep 1822
Joseph	23	M	Farmer	Germany	Missouri	Isabella	15 Sep 1828
Lawrence	41	M	Merchant	England	U. States	Hudson	8 Oct 1827
Patrick	32	M	Laborer	Ireland	United States	St. Michaels	12 Jun 1826
Sarah	13	F		England	U.S.A.	Hudson	21 Aug 1829
Sebastian	21	M	Farmer	Germany	Missouri	Isabella	15 Sep 1828
Thomas	35	M	Cloth Dresser	Ireland	U.S.A.	Dalhouse Castle	21 Aug 1829
Thos.	35	M	Cloth Dresser	Ireland	United States	Dalhouse Castle	21 Aug 1829
Timothy	12	M	None	Ireland	U.S.A.	Dalhouse Castle	21 Aug 1829
Timy.	12	M	None	Ireland	United States	Dalhouse Castle	21 Aug 1829
FINNAGHTY, Edward	3/12	M	Child	England	United States	Hanford	3 Jul 1829
Elsa	26	F	Wife	England	United States	Hanford	3 Jul 1829
Mary Ann	10	F	Child	England	United States	Hanford	3 Jul 1829
FINNAN, Mary	19	F	None	Ireland	United States	Silas Richards	3 Apr 1826

NAMES OF PASSENGERS	AGE	SEX	OCCUPATIONS	COUNTRY TO WHICH THEY BELONG	COUNTRY THEY INTEND TO INHABIT	SHIPS/DATES OF ARRIVAL	
FINNAN (cont'd)							
Pegg	28	F		S...off...ton	United States	Java	9 Jul 1827
FINNEGAN, Elizabeth	24	F	Matron	Ireland	U. States	Courier	17 Mar 1828
John	25	M	Labourer	Ireland	U. States	Courier	17 Mar 1828
FINNERY, Abraham	2	M	Labourer	England	U. States	Ayrshire	12 May 1828
Bridget	56	F	Labourer	England	U. States	Ayrshire	12 May 1828
Catharine	18	F	Labourer	England	U. States	Ayrshire	12 May 1828
Harriet	4	F	Labourer	England	U. States	Ayrshire	12 May 1828
Thomas	22	M	Labourer	England	U. States	Ayrshire	12 May 1828
Thomas	56	M	Labourer	England	U. States	Ayrshire	12 May 1828
FINNEY, John	26	M	Farmer	United States	United States	Trident	30 Sep 1826
Martin	24	M	Labourer	Ireland	U. States	Hanford	29 Dec 1828
FINNIE, Alexander	8	M	Child	Salkirk	U.S. America	Camillus	10 Sep 1821
George	10	M	Child	Salkirk	U.S. America	Camillus	10 Sep 1821
Mary	40	F	Wife	Salkirk	U.S. America	Camillus	10 Sep 1821
Melser	5	M	Child	Salkirk	U.S. America	Camillus	10 Sep 1821
Thomas	11	M	Child	Salkirk	U.S. America	Camillus	10 Sep 1821
FINNIGAN, Ann	16		Maid Servant	Ireland	America	Sarah	18 Aug 1829
Catherine	25	F	None	Ireland	United States	Mary & Harriet	3 Jul 1829
James	23	M	Farmer	England	America	Panthia	17 Sep 1821
James	26	M	Labourer	Ireland	United States	Mary & Harriet	3 Jul 1829
T.	24	M	Weaver	Great Britain	United States	Amelia	20 Aug 1829
FINNIGHAN, Barnard	30	M	Labourer	Ireland	U.S. of America	Meteor	19 Mar 1828
FINNY, Ann	30	F	Spinster	Ireland	United States	Trident	17 May 1825
Betty	5	F	Girl	Ireland	United States	Trident	17 May 1825
Charles	2	M	Child	Ireland	United States	Trident	17 May 1825
Ellenor	1	F	Child	Ireland	United States	Trident	17 May 1825
Mary	6	F	Girl	Ireland	United States	Trident	17 May 1825
FINTON, John	21	M	Farmer	England	America	Francis & Henrietta	11 Jul 1823
FIONTATRA, Juan F.	20	M	Merchant	Spain	France	Fly	17 Jan 1824
FIRMAN, Biddy	18	F	None	Great Britain	United States	Atlantic	28 May 1827
FIRNANDS, Joseph M.	33	M	Merchant	Cuba	U. States	James Monroe	8 Sep 1824
FIRTH, Eli	21	F	None	Gr. Britain		Moro Castle	6 Jul 1827
Eliza	50	F	Seamstress	G. Brittain	America	Atlantic	11 Oct 1822
Ellen	3	F		England	United States	Ann Maria	27 Aug 1822
Jane	4	F		G. Brittain	America	Atlantic	11 Oct 1822
John	8	M		G. Brittain	America	Atlantic	11 Oct 1822
John	20	M	Labourer	Gr. Britain		Moro Castle	6 Jul 1827
M.	25	F		England	United States	Ann Maria	27 Aug 1822
M.	27	M	Shoemaker	England	United States	Ann Maria	27 Aug 1822
Mery Ann	1	F		England	United States	Ann Maria	27 Aug 1822
Sarah	62	F	None	England	United States	John Wells	11 May 1827
FIS..., John	4...		Weaver	...defort	England	Great Britain	7 May 1827
FISCHER, Adam	30	M	Farmer	Germany	United States	Helen	5 Sep 1828
Catherine	5	F	there child [Adam & Catherine]	Germany	United States	Helen	5 Sep 1828
Catherine	28	F	his wife [Adam]	Germany	United States	Helen	5 Sep 1828
Elizabeth	8	F	there child [Adam & Catherine]	Germany	United States	Helen	5 Sep 1828
Frederick	19	M	Weaver	Brunswick	United States	Howard	6 Jul 1829
George	17	M	there child [Adam & Catherine]	Germany	United States	Helen	5 Sep 1828
FISCKE, John	...	...	...	...	...	...	26 Mar 1823
FISH, —, Mrs., & infant	35	F		England	United States	Richmond	4 Aug 1826
A.	39	M	Merchant	United States	U. States	Seneca	23 Oct 1826
Ambrose	18	M	Mariner	Connecticut, U.S.	Connecticut, U.S.	Tryon	20 Jun 1826
Charles	6	M		England	United States	Richmond	4 Aug 1826
Emma	16	F		England	United States	Richmond	4 Aug 1826
Giles	3	M		England	United States	Richmond	4 Aug 1826
Hannah	8	F		England	United States	Richmond	4 Aug 1826
Mary	55	F		U. States	U. States	Silas Richards	29 Oct 1828
Preserved	60	M	Gent.	U. States	U. States	Silas Richards	29 Oct 1828
Ralph	25	M	Weaver	Blakleer	Blakleer	Howard Douglass	11 May 1827
Robert	21	M	Weaver	England	Ut. States	Courier	13 Jul 1826
Rodger	36	M	Weaver	England	Ut. States	Courier	13 Jul 1826

NAMES OF PASSENGERS	AGE	SEX	OCCUPATIONS	COUNTRY TO WHICH THEY BELONG	COUNTRY THEY INTEND TO INHABIT	SHIPS/DATES OF ARRIVAL	
FISH (cont'd)							
Saml.	10	M		England	United States	Richmond	4 Aug 1826
Saml.	42	M	Labourer	England	United States	Richmond	4 Aug 1826
Wm.	25	M	Weaver	Darvin	Darvin	Howard Douglass	11 May 1827
Wm.	25	M	Weaver	Darnien	Darnien	Howard Douglass	11 May 1827
Wm. M.	17	M		U. States	U. States	Silas Richards	29 Oct 1828
FISHBURN, Wm.	24	M	Engraver	England	U. States	Florida	13 Jan 1827
FISHBURS, Henry	26	M	Bookkeeper	Ireland	Ut. States	Courier	13 Jul 1826
FISHER, —, Mr.	40	M				Henri IV	14 Sep 1827
—, Mrs.	43	F		Scotland	Upper Canada	Lima	5 Aug 1829
—, Mrs.	43	F	Scotland	Upper Canada	N. York	Lima	5 Aug 1829
...	3	F		Scotland	Upper Canada	Lima	5 Aug 1829
Alexander	25	M	Merchant	United States	United States	Chili	9 Jan 1829
Alice	21	F	Spinster	Ireland	United States	Lord Strangford	20 Jun 1826
Amelia	17	F	None	England	United States	Great Britain	5 Sep 1827
Ann	18	F	Lady		N. York	Betsy	4 Sep 1820
Ann	24	F		Great Britian	United States	Brok	29 Aug 1823
Anna	27	F	None	England	Albany	Indian Chief	19 Jun 1823
C.	38	M	Merchant	Germany	U. States	Napolean	2 Sep 1828
Caroline	19	F	None	England	United States	Great Britain	5 Sep 1827
Catharine	10	F	Girl	Ireland	United States	Lord Strangford	20 Jun 1826
Catharine	28	F		France	Canada	Abby Jones	12 Jul 1827
Charles	10	M		United States	United States	Frances	19 Feb 1829
Charles	30	M	Merchant	U. States	U. States	Comet	28 Jul 1825
Christian	42 ...	M	Farmer	Switzerland	United States	Criterion	13 Oct 1825
Clara	16	F	None	England	United States	Great Britain	5 Sep 1827
Corina	8	F		United States	United States	Frances	19 Feb 1829
Cristian	24	M	Tailor	Wirtemberg	America, U.N.S.	Great Britain	3 Aug 1829
Daniel	16	M	Labourer	Scotland	United States	Friends	7 Jul 1827
Daniel	22	M	Blacksmith	Great Britain	United States	Elizabeth & Mary	20 Mar 1828
Daniel	34	M	...	Great Brittain	Montreal	Albion	11 Jun 1821
David	39	M	Labourer	Great Britain		Moro Castle	6 Jul 1827
Eleanor	17	F		Scotland	Upper Canada	Lima	5 Aug 1829
Eleanor	17	F	Scotland	Upper Canada	N. York	Lima	5 Aug 1829
Elenor	5/12	F	Child		U. States	Acasta	28 Jan 1823
Elenor J.	25	F	Wife	Brittian	U. States	Acasta	28 Jan 1823
Eliz.	30	M	None	England	U. States	Electra	7 Jul 1828
Elizabeth	28			England	Nantucket	Xenophon	25 Jul 1826
Elizabeth A.	2 4/12	F	Child	Brittian	U. States	Acasta	28 Jan 1823
Elizth.	10	F	...	Great Brittain	Montreal	Albion	11 Jun 1821
Ellen	24	F	None	Russia	U. States	Bayard	9 Nov 1825
F. A.	23	M	Butcher	Germany	U. States	Minerva	23 Aug 1824
Francis W.	38	M	Carrier	Germany	New York	Lewis	29 Oct 1825
Fras. W.	22	M	Merchant	England	U.S.	Panthea	13 Nov 1823
Frederick	25	M	Bainter	Germany	United States	Rent	13 May
Frederick	33	M	Merchant	England		Ann Maria	3 Jul 1827
G.	22	M	Brass founder	England	United States	India	8 Jun 1827
Galen	3	M		United States	United States	Frances	19 Feb 1829
George	11/12	F		Scotland	Upper Canada	Lima	5 Aug 1829
George	11/12	M	Scotland	Upper Canada	N. York	Lima	5 Aug 1829
Hannah D.	29	F		United States	United States	Frances	19 Feb 1829
Henry	24	M	Merchant	New York	New York, U.S.	New York	14 Mar 1828
Henry	40	M	Merchant	England	America	Hannibal	4 Oct 1822
Isabela	20	F		Scotland	Upper Canada	Lima	5 Aug 1829
Isabela	20	F	Scotland	Upper Canada	N. York	Lima	5 Aug 1829
J., Mr.	44	M	Gent	United States	U.S.	Henri IV	14 Sep 1827
James	19	M	Weaver	Ireland	New York	Trusty	12 Sep 1828
James	25	M	Farmer	Great Britain	United States	Ganges	8 Jul 1820
James	30	M	Merchant	England	U. States	Florida	16 May 1827
James	56	M	Labourer	Scotland	United States	Friends	7 Jul 1827
James	62	M		Great Britian	United States	Brok	29 Aug 1823
James M.	21	M	Saddler	Nova Scotia	United States	Nancy	16 Aug 1824
Jams	12	M	None	England	U. States	Electra	7 Jul 1828
Jane	3	F		Scotland	Upper Canada	Lima	5 Aug 1829
Jane	3	F	Scotland	Upper Canada	N. York	Lima	5 Aug 1829
Jane	6	F	None	England	Albany	Indian Chief	19 Jun 1823

NAMES OF PASSENGERS	AGE	SEX	OCCUPATIONS	COUNTRY TO WHICH THEY BELONG	COUNTRY THEY INTEND TO INHABIT	SHIPS/DATES OF ARRIVAL	
FISHER (cont'd)							
Jane	24	F	None	England	United States	Great Britain	5 Sep 1827
Jane	30	F	None	England	United States	Great Britain	5 Sep 1827
Jane	56	F	None	England	United States	Great Britain	5 Sep 1827
Jane, child	2	F	None	England	United States	Great Britain	5 Sep 1827
Janet	12	F		Great Britian	United States	Brok	29 Aug 1823
Jean	49	M		France	United States	La Flora	30 Jun 1828
Jean	50	F	Spinster	Scotland	United States	Friends	7 Jul 1827
Jno.	16	M	Labourer			Harmony	15 Jul 1820
Jno., Mr.	35	M	Merchant	Canada	Canada	Napoleon	26 May 1828
John	2	M	None	England	Albany	Indian Chief	19 Jun 1823
John	8	M	Boy	Ireland	United States	Lord Strangford	20 Jun 1826
John	10	M	None	England	U. States	Electra	7 Jul 1828
John	18	M		England	America	Ann	3 Jul 1820
John	19	M	Clerk	Great Britian	United States	Brok	29 Aug 1823
John	25	M	Merchant	Bermuda	U. States	Alpha	28 May 1823
John	25	M	Cooper	Scotland	United States	Broke	16 Jul 1829
John	26	M	Potter	Wertemberg	Wertemberg	Edward Quesnel	3 Jul 1829
John	30	M		England	America	Ann	3 Jul 1820
John	33		Merchant	Montreal	Great Britain	William Thompson	13 May 1823
John	33	M	Farmer	England	Albany	Indian Chief	19 Jun 1823
John	40	M	Merchant	G. Britain		Sarahs Delight	13 May 1823
John	44 3/12	M	Merchant	Ireland	United States	Leeds	6 Feb 1826
John A.	27	M	None	England	United States	Great Britain	5 Sep 1827
John Michael	35	M	Smith	Wirtemburg, Germany	New York	Frances Henrietta	25 Aug 1825
Joseph	10	M	Servant Boy	Ireland	United States	William	20 Jul 1829
Julia	12	F	Girl	Ireland	United States	Lord Strangford	20 Jun 1826
Lawerence	24	M	None	Ireland	U. States	Henry Kneeland	27 Jul 1825
Margaret, Mrs.	25	F	Merchant	Canada	Canada	Napoleon	26 May 1828
Margarett *Deceased	16	F	Semstress	Belfast		Minerva	30 Oct 1829
Mary	33	F		England	America	Cincinnatus	22 May 1826
Mary Ann	16	F	Spinster	Ireland	United States	Lord Strangford	20 Jun 1826
Mary W.	40	F		Great Britian	United States	London	24 Jun 1823
Michael	5	M	Boy	Ireland	United States	Lord Strangford	20 Jun 1826
Mirzal	27	M	...	...	...	Josephine	10 Dec 1825
Nelva	26	F		Scotland, Great Britain	America	Superb	11 Oct 1821
Peter	45	M	Farmer	Scotland, Great Britain	America	Superb	11 Oct 1821
Peter	46	M	Gentleman	England	England	Hercules	21 Nov 1822
Richd.	18	M	Merchant	Bermuda	Bermuda	Alpha	7 Oct 1823
S. R.	32	M	Merchant	New York	New York	Julia	8 Feb 1827
S. R.	35	M	Merchant	U. States	United States	Asaph	25 Dec 1827
Sam	35	M	Tanner	Ireland	U. States	Electra	7 Jul 1828
Sarah	3	F	None	England	Albany	Indian Chief	19 Jun 1823
Seth	3	M				Xenophon	25 Jul 1826
Susan	22	F		Great Britian	United States	Brok	29 Aug 1823
Thomas	21	M	Weaver	Ireland	New York	Trusty	12 Sep 1828
Thomas	30	M	Labourer	Great Britian	United States	Brok	29 Aug 1823
Thomas	37	M	...	England	America	Cincinnatus	22 May 1826
Thos.	8	M	None	Ilan...	U. States	Electra	7 Jul 1828
Thos.	28	M	Labourer	Ireland	United States	Thomas	13 Dec 1827
W.	27	M	Weaver	Great Brittain	United States	Robert Fulton	13 Mar 1827
Walter	25	M	Tailor	United States	United States	Deborah	3 Jul 1824
William	5	M	Scotland	Upper Canada	N. York	Lima	5 Aug 1829
William	24	M	Whitesmith	England	Louisville	Thames	6 Oct 1820
William	25	M	Blacksmith	Scotland	America	Sarah	18 Aug 1829
Wm.	2			Ilan...	U. States	Electra	7 Jul 1828
Wm.	55	M	Labourer			Harmony	15 Jul 1820
FISHERS, James	28	M	Mason	Great Britain	United States	Roanoak	19 Sep 1827
FISK, Anna	11			England	United States	Caspian	12 Jul 1821
Anthony	7		None	Great Brittain	Great Brittain	Commerce	14 Mar 1823
Anthony	44		Farmer	Great Brittain	Great Brittain	Commerce	14 Mar 1823
Edward	10			England	United States	Caspian	12 Jul 1821
Francis	26		Merchant	London	Great Britain	William Thompson	13 May 1823

411

NAMES OF PASSENGERS	A G E	S E X	OCCUPATIONS	COUNTRY TO WHICH THEY BELONG	COUNTRY THEY INTEND TO INHABIT	SHIPS/DATES OF ARRIVAL	
FISK (cont'd)							
Geo. B.	28 1/12	M	Merchant	America	America	Magnet	13 Nov 1821
George	5			England	United States	Caspian	12 Jul 1821
Henry	13			England	United States	Caspian	12 Jul 1821
James	4			England	United States	Caspian	12 Jul 1821
Jemina	30		None	Great Brittain	Great Brittain	Commerce	14 Mar 1823
Mahala	38	F		England	United States	Caspian	12 Jul 1821
Mary	8		None	Great Brittain	Great Brittain	Commerce	14 Mar 1823
Richard	40	M	Grocer	England	United States	Caspian	12 Jul 1821
Susan	8			England	United States	Caspian	12 Jul 1821
William	5		None	Great Brittain	Great Brittain	Commerce	14 Mar 1823
William	15			England	United States	Caspian	12 Jul 1821
FISKE, Isaac	33	M	Mercht.	U. States	U. States	Savannah	22 May 1827
FISTER, Alexr. N. P.	35	M	Merchant	New York	U. States	Marmion	8 Sep 1828
John R.	13	M	Merchant	New York	U. States	Marmion	8 Sep 1828
FITCH, Beriah		M	Mariner	U. States		Horatio	19 Jul 1823
Douglas W.	23	M	Merchant	Boston	U. States	Acasta	27 Aug 1821
James, Mr.	26		Planter	Ireland	United States	South Carolina Packet	22 Jun 1822
FITCH.GERALD, Edwd.	22	M	Farmer	Ireland	New York	Robert Edwards	17 Mar 1828
FITE, Elisabeth	22	F	Spinster	Switzerland	United States	Andes	5 May 1828
FITMAN, Anne	56		Farmer	Ireland	U. States	Schuylkill	22 Aug 1825
Mary	26		Farmer	Ireland	U. States	Schuylkill	22 Aug 1825
FITNAM, Bridget	25	F		Ireland	U. States	Ganges	21 Jun 1827
Christopher	1	M		Ireland	U. States	Ganges	21 Jun 1827
Thomas	24	M	Labourer	Ireland	U. States	Ganges	21 Jun 1827
FITRANCE, Ann	27	F	None	France		Brighton	19 Aug 1829
FITRANE, Gravt.	27	M	Carpenter	France		Brighton	19 Aug 1829
FITSGERALL, James	23		None	Cork	come out to his friends	Pomona	28 May 1822
FITSGIBBINS, Patrick	28	M	Labourer	Ireland	United States	Hopes Delight	29 Nov 1827
FITSIMONS, Mary	12	F	None	West Island		Mount Vernon	7 Jun 1824
FITSMENS, Andrew	10	F	Farmer	Gt. Britain	U. States	Champion	19 Apr 1828
Mary	18	F	Farmer	Gt. Britain	U. States	Champion	19 Apr 1828
Mary	30	F	Farmer	Gt. Britain	U. States	Champion	19 Apr 1828
Wm.	55	M	Farmer	Gt. Britain	U. States	Champion	19 Apr 1828
FITSPATERCK, Andrew	25	M	Weaver	Ireland	N. Jersey	Potomac	7 Aug 1827
FITSPATICK, Sarah	20	F	Servant	Ireland	N. Jersey	Potomac	7 Aug 1827
FITSPATRIC, John	1			County of Carvan	Ohio	Peru	30 May 1828
Margret	20			County of Carvan	Ohio	Peru	30 May 1828
Patric	26			County of Carvan	Ohio	Peru	30 May 1828
FITSPATRICK, Thos.	21	M	Servant	Ireland	United States	William	20 Jul 1829
FITS SIMMONS, M.	25	M	Farmer	Ireland	United States	Justina	5 Aug 1823
FITSUMMONS, Ann	6	F	None	Great Britain	United States	Roman	10 May 1828
James	32	M	Weaver	Great Britain	United States	Roman	10 May 1828
FITT, H. A.	23	M	Merant.	Barbadoes	Halifax, N.S.	Salumith	17 Nov 1826
FITZ..., Geo.		M	...	...	United States	Minerva	30 Oct 1827
FITZANCE, Ann	27	F	None	France	New York	Brighton	19 Aug 1829
FITZANE, Grant	27	M	Carpenter	France	New York	Brighton	19 Aug 1829
FITZESIMONS, Mary	20	F	Spinster	Ireland	United States	Fabius	4 Jun 1828
FITZ GEARL, James	25	M	Laborer or Spinster	Ireland	United States	Sarah G	11 Sep 1827
FZ. GERALD, George	28	M	Labourer	Limerick	N. York	Thomas & William	25 May 1827
FITZ GERALD, Eliza	22	F		Ireland	U. States	Howard	25 Jul 1823
Garet	23	M		Ireland	U. States	Howard	25 Jul 1823
John	22	M		Ireland	U. States	Howard	25 Jul 1823
John	34	M		St. Johns	U. States	Wanderer	30 Oct 1828
John	36	M	Farmer	Ireland	U. States	Howard	25 Jul 1823
Lucinda	18	F	None	Great Britain		Casanda	5 Sep 1827
Maria	28	F	None	Great Britain		Casanda	5 Sep 1827
Mary Ann	16	F	None	Great Britain		Casanda	5 Sep 1827
Michl.	27	M	Labourer	Great Britain		Casanda	5 Sep 1827
Morris	20		Farmer	England	United States	Corinthian	30 May 1828
Nicholas	30	M	Weaver	Ireland	United States	Clothier	22 Nov 1827
Richard	35	M	Blacksmith	England	United States	Nimrod	30 Aug 1824
Thomas	52	M	Gentleman	Great Britan	United States	Hamilton	19 Mar 1827

NAMES OF PASSENGERS	AGE	SEX	OCCUPATIONS	COUNTRY TO WHICH THEY BELONG	COUNTRY THEY INTEND TO INHABIT	SHIPS/DATES OF ARRIVAL	
FITZGERALD, —, Mrs.	51			New York		Ocean	28 Jul 1820
Ann	13	F	Child	Ireland	America	Parrington	9 Jun 1827
Catherine	15	F		Ireland	America	Liverpool	31 Aug 1827
Catherine	24	F	Married Woman	Ireland	United States	Robert Edwards	3 Oct 1829
Cathn.	23	F	Wife	Roscommon	Baltimore	Nile	18 Aug 1829
Daniel	22	M	Farmer	Ireland	United States	Mary & Harriet	9 Mar 1829
Edward	27	M	Mason	Ireland	America	William	21 May 1825
Eliza	9	F	Child	Ireland	America	Parrington	9 Jun 1827
Elizabeth *deceased	30	F		Ireland	America	Parrington	9 Jun 1827
Ellen	2	F		Ireland	America	Liverpool	31 Aug 1827
Ellen	6 6/12	F	Child	Ireland	America	Parrington	9 Jun 1827
Ewd.	25	M	Distiller	Roscommon	Baltimore	Nile	18 Aug 1829
Jas.	13	M				Trio	5 May 1828
Jas.	19	M	Farmer	Ireland	America	Liverpool	31 Aug 1827
Jas.	40	M	Labourer	England	U. States	Thomas Ritchie	2 Jul 1827
Johannah	54	F	Spinster	Ireland	America	William	21 May 1825
John	11	M		Ireland	America	Liverpool	31 Aug 1827
John	23	M	Farmer	Great Britain	United States	Minerva	28 Jul 1823
John	26	M	Labourer	Ireland	United States	Combine	4 Jun 1825
John	27	M	Labourer	Ireland	United S.	Hanford	19 Aug 1828
John	42	M	Farmer	Ireland	United States	Huron	26 Dec 1827
Julian	4	F		Ireland	America	Liverpool	31 Aug 1827
Julian	35	F		Ireland	America	Liverpool	31 Aug 1827
Lettia	8	F		Ireland	America	Liverpool	31 Aug 1827
Mary	3 6/12	F	Daughter	Ireland	United States	Robert Edwards	3 Oct 1829
Mary	5	F	Child	Ireland	America	Parrington	9 Jun 1827
Mary	13	F		Ireland	America	Liverpool	31 Aug 1827
Mary	26	F	Brewer	Gt. Britain	U. States	Panthea	21 Jul 1825
Mary	50	F	Matron	Ireland	United States	Ganges	20 Aug 1825
Mary	50	F	Spinster	Ireland	United States	Lord Strangford	20 Jun 1826
Michael	1 9/12	M	Child	Ireland	America	Parrington	9 Jun 1827
Michael	20	M	Mason	Ireland	America	William	21 May 1825
Nathaniel	30	M	Seaman	New York	New York	Mary & Elizabeth	7 Sep 1824
Patrick	6	M		Ireland	America	Liverpool	31 Aug 1827
Patrick	11	M	Child	Ireland	America	Parrington	9 Jun 1827
Patrick	27		Laborer	Ireland	America	Parrington	9 Jun 1827
Patt	25	M	Gardiner	Ireland	United States	Delta	24 Oct 1829
Robert	21	M	Mason	Ireland	America	William	21 May 1825
Roberto	40	M	Merchant	Ireland	U. States	Jane	24 May 1822
Thomas	22	M	Mason	Ireland	America	William	21 May 1825
Thomas	34	M	Farmer	Ireland	America	Parrington	9 Jun 1827
Thos.	32	M	Brewer	Gt. Britain	U. States	Panthea	21 Jul 1825
Thos.	50	M	Gentleman	Ireland	America	Liverpool	31 Aug 1827
Wm.	3	M	Brewer	Gt. Britain	U. States	Panthea	21 Jul 1825
FITZGERRALD, Wm.	22	M	Labourer	Co. La...gford	La...gford	Howard Douglass	11 May 1827
F GERRELD, John	29		Labourer	Ireland	Pensylvania	Marcella	18 May 1827
FITZGIBBEN, John	19					Trio	5 May 1828
FITZ GIBBON,							
Dorothy, Mrs.	40	F		England	Niagara	Cadmus	27 Aug 1822
Eleanor, Miss	12	F		England	Niagara	Cadmus	27 Aug 1822
Eliza	4 10/12	F		England	Niagara	Cadmus	27 Aug 1822
Maria Louisa	6	F		England	U. States	Cincinnatus	24 May 1821
Mary L. B.	3 1/12	F		England	Niagara	Cadmus	27 Aug 1822
McMamara, Mr.	10	M		England	Niagara	Cadmus	27 Aug 1822
Sophia, Miss	14	F		England	Niagara	Cadmus	27 Aug 1822
Thos., Mr.	49 8/12	M	Mercht.	England	Niagara	Cadmus	27 Aug 1822
Thos. Henry, Mr.	19	M		England	Niagara	Cadmus	27 Aug 1822
FITZGIBBONS, Jno.	20	M	Labourer	Ireland	United States	Thomas	13 Dec 1827
FITZHENRY, B.	28	F		Scotland	U.S.	Curler	19 Jul 1828
Honora	27					Trio	5 May 1828
John	29	M		Scotland	U.S.	Curler	19 Jul 1828
Kitty	22					Trio	5 May 1828
Patt	26					Trio	5 May 1828
Sarah	33					Trio	5 May 1828
FITZHUGH, John K.	31	M	Gentlen.	U.S.	U.S.	Bayard	18 Oct 1826
FITZIMINS, Henry	26	M	Farmer	Scotland	United States	Broke	16 Jul 1829

NAMES OF PASSENGERS	AGE	SEX	OCCUPATIONS	COUNTRY TO WHICH THEY BELONG	COUNTRY THEY INTEND TO INHABIT	SHIPS/DATES OF ARRIVAL	
FITZIMINS (cont'd)							
Margaret	24	F		Scotland	United States	Broke	16 Jul 1829
FITZIMMONS, B.	24	M		G. Britain	U. States	Great Britain	6 Sep 1828
Charles	36	M		Ireland	United States	Thomas	13 Dec 1827
E.	15	M		G. Britain	U. States	Great Britain	6 Sep 1828
E.	32	M		G. Britain	U. States	Great Britain	6 Sep 1828
Michael	22	M	Shoemaker	Ireland	U. States	Henry Kneeland	27 Jul 1825
FITZIMONS, Patrick	30	M	House Carpenter	Irereland	America	Carolina Ann	20 Jun 1825
FITZMON, Cath.	18	F	Servant	Ireland	U. States	Marcus	7 Apr 1825
Margt.	19	F	Labourer	Ireland	U. States	Marcus	7 Apr 1825
FITZMONS, Biddy	20	F	Servant	Ireland	N. York	Trusty	12 Sep 1828
FITZ MORRIS, C. J.	30	M	Army	Ireland	U. States	Exchange	19 Aug 1822
FITZMORRIS, C. J.	28	M	Mariner	U.S.	U.S.	Aginoria	16 Apr 1821
Elen	30	F				Lady of the Lake	23 Aug 1828
FITZPATRIC, Biddy	29			Carvan	N. York	Peru	30 May 1828
FITZ PATRICK, Barney	26	M	Farmer	Ireland	U. States	Sabina	29 Apr 1825
Daniel	31	M	Labourer	Great Britan	United States	Silvanus Jenkins	10 Mar 1827
Ellen	20	F	Seamstress	Ireland	U.S. States	Splendid	14 Aug 1829
Hannah	20	F		Ireland	United States	Thompson	12 Sep 1827
John	20 3/12		Farmer	Scotland	U.S. of America	Helen	8 Feb 1822
Mary	14			Ireland	Philidelphia	General Marion	21 Nov 1828
Mary	30	F	None	...	United States	Minerva	30 Oct 1827
Mary	30			Ireland	Philidelphia	General Marion	21 Nov 1828
Michael	27	M		Ireland	United States	Thompson	12 Sep 1827
Owen	22	M	Farmer	Ireland	U. States	Sabina	29 Apr 1825
Patrick	...	M	...	England	United States	Milton	20 Oct 1827
Peter	1			Ireland	Philidelphia	General Marion	21 Nov 1828
Peter	40			Ireland	Philidelphia	General Marion	21 Nov 1828
Rose	10			Ireland	Philidelphia	General Marion	21 Nov 1828
Thos.	22	M	Labourer	...	United States	Minerva	30 Oct 1827
Wm.	41	M	Farmer	England	United States	Ganges	10 May 1828
FITZPATRICK, Charles	27	M	Labourer	C. Anthrem	Baltimore	Nile	18 Aug 1829
Dennis	25	M	Clerk	Ireland	America	William	21 May 1825
Dennis	25	M	Clerk	Ireland	United States	Diana	1 May 1826
Edward	30	M	Tailor	U. States	U. States	Nancy	11 Apr 1822
Gregory	28	M	Labourer	Ireland	United States	Matvina	19 Oct 1826
Helenora	8	F		England	United States	Danube	22 Aug 1825
Hugh	3	M	None	Gt. Britain	U. States	Frances Henrietta	18 Apr 1825
James	23	M	Labourer	England	U. States	Rising States	20 Sep 1828
Jane	3	F		England	United States	Danube	22 Aug 1825
John	30	M	Labourer	Ireland	United States	William	20 Jul 1829
Judy	20	F		Ireland	United States	Trio	2 Oct 1828
Julia	28	F		Ireland	United States	Sarah G.	20 Jul 1827
Margt.	19	F	Spinster	Ireland	U. States	William	27 Jul 1824
Martin	30	M	Farmer	Ireland	United States	Dublin Packet	29 Jun 1825
Mary	28	F		England	United States	Danube	22 Aug 1825
Mary	32	F	Labourer	Ireland	United States	Essex	23 May 1828
Michael	24	M	Farmer	Ireland	United States	Dublin Packet	13 Oct 1828
Pat	32	M	Labourer	Ireland	United States	Essex	23 May 1828
Patk.	30	M	Farmer	England	United States	Danube	22 Aug 1825
Patrick	30	M	Weaver	Ireland	United States	Enterprize	23 Jul 1827
Patrick	30	M	Labourer	Ireland	United States	Princess Charlotte	6 Oct 1827
Peter	2	...	...	Ireland	United States	Carolina Ann	24 Oct 1825
Peter	18 4/12	M		Ireland	U. States	Fabius	22 Sep 1828
Phillip	22	M	Labourer	Ireland	U. States	Two Marys	20 Apr 1825
Rose Ann	30	F	Spinster	Gt. Britain	U. States	Frances Henrietta	18 Apr 1825
Samuel B.	23	M	Merchant	United States	Georgia	Lark	28 Jun 1824
Terance	32	M	Planter	Ireland	United States	Jupiter	12 May 1827
Terrence	32	M	Mechanic	Ireland	U. States	Agness	9 Oct 1828
Thomas	17	M	...	Ireland	United States	Carolina Ann	24 Oct 1825
Thos.	18	M	Lab.	Rathangar	K. Co.	Howard Douglass	11 May 1827
Thos.	28	M	Labourer	Ireland	U. States	Hercules	4 Oct 1824
W. C.	25	M	Mercht.	Cuba	Cuba	Criterion	9 Aug 1826

NAMES OF PASSENGERS	AGE	SEX	OCCUPATIONS	COUNTRY TO WHICH THEY BELONG	COUNTRY THEY INTEND TO INHABIT	SHIPS/DATES OF ARRIVAL	
FITZPATRIK, Martin	22	M	Weaver	England	New York	America	1 Aug 1828
FITZSIMANY, Pat	20	M	Y. Man	Ireland	New York	Trusty	12 Sep 1828
Thomas	20	M	Y. Man	Ireland	New York	Trusty	12 Sep 1828
FITZ SIMMONS, B...y	3	M	None	England	United States	India	8 Jun 1827
Catharine	24	F	Spinster	Ireland		Dublin Packet	30 Apr 1821
Ellen	22	F		Ireland	United States	Siroc	31 Oct 1829
John	18	M	Labourer	Ireland		Dublin Packet	30 Apr 1821
John	35	M				Splendid	14 Aug 1829
Lucy	20	F	Spinster	Ireland		Dublin Packet	30 Apr 1821
Margaret	22	F	Spinster	Ireland		Dublin Packet	30 Apr 1821
Mary	19	F	None	England	United States	India	8 Jun 1827
Mary	22	F	None	England	United States	India	8 Jun 1827
Pat	24	M	Labourer	England	United States	India	8 Jun 1827
Pat	33	F	None	England	United States	India	8 Jun 1827
Richd.	24	M	Farmer	Great Brittain	U. States	Hibernia	8 Jul 1823
Wm.	20	M	Farmer	Ireland	United States	Siroc	31 Oct 1829
FITZSIMMONS, Ann	10	F		Gt. Britain		Dalhouse Castle	13 May 1828
Ann	60	F		Gt. Britain		Dalhouse Castle	13 May 1828
Bridget	35	F		Gt. Britain		Dalhouse Castle	13 May 1828
Edward	16		Taylor	Ireland	United States	Robert Burns	18 Jun 1822
Esther	17		Laboring Class		United States	Atlantic	2 Apr 1827
Francis	27	M	Labourer	England	U. States	Thomas Ritchie	2 Jul 1827
Garret	23		Laboring Class		United States	Atlantic	2 Apr 1827
John	24	M	Labourer	Ireland	America	Plutarch	18 Jul 1826
Margaret	8	F		Gt. Britain		Dalhouse Castle	13 May 1828
Margaret	18	F	None	Ireland		Marchioness	13 May 1828
Mary	40	F	Matron	Ireland	America	Wilson	16 May 1825
Patrick	6	M		Gt. Britain		Dalhouse Castle	13 May 1828
Patrick	26	M	Farmer	Ireland	Pennsylvania	Curler	7 Jul 1827
Sarah	18	M	None	Ireland	U. States	William Byrnes	24 Apr 1827
Simon	40	M	Labourer	Ireland	United States	John Wells	11 May 1827
FITZ SIMONS, Hugh	16	M	Labourer	Ireland		Dublin Packet	30 Apr 1821
FITZSIMONS, John	24	M	Carpenter	Ireland	America	Wilson	16 May 1825
John	34	M	Labourer	Ireland	Ireland	Helicon	3 Aug 1826
Nancy	14	F	None	West Island		Mount Vernon	7 Jun 1824
FITZSUMONS, Mch.	21	M	Y. Man	Ireland	New York	Trusty	12 Sep 1828
FITZWILLIAM, Henry	35	M	Merchant	Great Britian	United States	Diamond	12 Mar 1824
Maria	24	F		U. States	U. States	Yamacraw	9 Mar 1822
FIVENCH, John W.	32	M	Ship Master	America		Amos Palmer	9 Jan 1829
FIZGARLD, James	28	M	Labourer	Ireland	U. States	Combine	30 Nov 1825
FL..., B...y	19	F	None	Ireland	United States	Dalhouse Castle	21 Aug 1829
FLACH, Mitchel						Olympia	12 Aug 1828

*After having been at Sea a Number of Days was ascertaining the quantity of Baggage to report found the under mentioned persons had secreted themselves away notwithstanding our searach with the Gendearmes at the of leaving the port

FLACK, Mary Ann	20	F	Merchant	Ireland	England	Eliza	22 Dec 1826
FLAGET, Benedict	18 7/12	M	Student	France	America	Henry	17 May 1828
E., Miss	23		None	Clermont	Bardslow, N.C.	Manchester	30 May 1821
FLAGG, Robt.	46	M		Gt. Britain	U. States	St. George	20 Sep 1828
FLAGHERTY, Winney	20	F	Spinster			Commerce	22 Jun 1825
FLAGLER, Letetia	37	F	Lady	United States	St. John, N.B.	Ann Maria	21 May 1827
FLAHERTY, James	14	M	Labourer	Great Britain	United States	Washington	3 Sep 1827
FLAKE, Jos.	28	M	Silver Smith	Switzerland	United States	Ospray	2 Sep 1824
FLANAGAN, Allice	18	F	Labourer	Ireland	U. States	Two Marys	20 Apr 1825
Ann	22	F	Spinster	Ireland	United States	Wilson	4 Oct 1827
Ann	30	F	None	Ireland	New York	Concordia	12 Oct 1826
Bryan	23	M	Taylor	Ireland	United States	William	5 Oct 1822
Cathrine	17	F	Spinster	Ireland	United States	Wilson	4 Oct 1827
E...th.	1 8/12	F	None	Ireland	New York	Concordia	12 Oct 1826
Frans.	26	M	Labourer	Ireland	United States	Essex	23 May 1828
John	30	M	Farmer	Ireland	United States	Dublin Packet	13 Oct 1828
Joseph	20	M	Taylor	Ireland	New York	Concordia	12 Oct 1826
Patt	36	M	...er	Ireland	America	Farmer	4 Aug 1825
Peter	22			Longford	N. York	Peru	30 May 1828
FLANAGIN, Wm.		M	Planter	Ireland	G. Brittain	Catharine	23 Jun 1821
FLANDERS, Benjn.	23	M	Sail Maker	Massachusetts	U. States	Borneo	4 Dec 1824
FLANEGAN, Catharine	26	F	Spinster	Ireland	United States	Dublin Packet	22 Oct 1821
FLANER, Richd.	61	M	Merchant	England	U. States	New York	4 Nov 1824
FLANERY, Henry	25			Great Britan	United States	Newry	11 Jul 1827
FLANGAN, Michael	35	M	Labourer	Ireland	United States	Jubilee	13 Sep 1827

415

NAMES OF PASSENGERS	AGE	SEX	OCCUPATIONS	COUNTRY TO WHICH THEY BELONG	COUNTRY THEY INTEND TO INHABIT	SHIPS/DATES OF ARRIVAL	
FLANIGAN, Ann	26	F	None	Ireland	United States	Lord Wellington	28 May 1827
Catharine	26	F	Servant	Ireland	New York	Atlantic	6 Oct 1828
Eliza	22	F		Ireland	United States	Princess Charlotte	26 Apr 1827
Felix	26	M	Labourer	Ireland	United States	Lord Wellington	28 May 1827
John	16 9/12	M	Tailor	Ireland	New York	Atlantic	6 Oct 1828
John	17	M	Carpenter	Ireland	United States	Princess Charlotte	26 Apr 1827
Patrick	15	M		Ireland	United States	Princess Charlotte	26 Apr 1827
FLANLY, Ann	27	F	Spinster	Ireland	United States	Wilson	6 Jun 1828
FLANNAGAN, Catharine	11	F		Ireland	New York	Curler	7 Jul 1827
Geo. P.	18	M	Gentleman	Great Brittain	U. States	Hibernia	8 Jul 1823
John	9	M		Ireland	New York	Curler	7 Jul 1827
John	40	M	Weaver	Ireland	New York	Curler	7 Jul 1827
Margaret	6	F		Ireland	New York	Curler	7 Jul 1827
Mary	13	F		Ireland	New York	Curler	7 Jul 1827
Mary	25	F		Ireland	New York	Curler	7 Jul 1827
Patrick	5	M		Ireland	New York	Curler	7 Jul 1827
Richard	1	M		Ireland	New York	Curler	7 Jul 1827
Thomas	3	M		Ireland	New York	Curler	7 Jul 1827
FLANNAGIN, James	19	M	Shoe Maker	Ireland	New York	William	27 Aug 1827
FLANNERY, Patrick	22		Labourer	Dunganin	Gt. Britain	Enterprize	19 Feb 1822
FLANNIGAN, Ellen	18		Shoemaker	England	United States	Mary	15 Jul 1822
FLARHETY, Hugh, Eqr.	38	M	Merchant	England	England	Charlotte Corday	24 Jan 1820
FLARTY, Patrick	26			Ireland	U.S.	Union	20 Aug 1827
FLASH, Edward	3/12	M		England	England	Tontine	1 Jun 1826
Judiah	3/12	F		England	England	Tontine	1 Jun 1826
Rachael	19	F		England	England	Tontine	1 Jun 1826
FLATT, Thos.	35	M	Farmer	Ireland	U. States	Orozimbo	7 Jul 1825
FLATTERY, Cathe.	24	F				Trio	5 May 1828
Edmund	34	M				Trio	5 May 1828
Ellen	4	F				Trio	5 May 1828
Mary	30	F				Trio	5 May 1828
Patrick	4	M				Trio	5 May 1828
Wm.	31	M				Trio	5 May 1828
FLEAR, John	25		Wheelwright	England	America	Sarah	18 Aug 1829
FLEET, Jno. M.	28	M	Merchant	U. States	U. States	James	4 Jun 1825
FLEIG, Fredk., Mr.	39	M	Farmer	Switzerland	United States	Henri IV	14 Sep 1827
FLEIGHT, Charles Soln.	4	M	Child	England	United States	Cambria	3 Jul 1829
Emely	2	F	Child	England	United States	Cambria	3 Jul 1829
Mary	30	F		England	United States	Cambria	3 Jul 1829
Mary S.	7	F	Child	England	United States	Cambria	3 Jul 1829
Samuel T.	6	M	Child	England	United States	Cambria	3 Jul 1829
FLEIND, Bengam	34	M	Child	G. Brittan	U. States	Henry	24 Oct 1828
FLEMEN, Briget	23	F	None	Ireland	U. States	Vermont	19 Jun 1827
John	1	M		Ireland	U. States	Vermont	19 Jun 1827
FLEMING, Agnes	7	F		Great Britian	United States	Brok	29 Aug 1823
Ann	9	F		Great Britian	United States	Brok	29 Aug 1823
Charles	4	M		Great Britian	United States	Brok	29 Aug 1823
Daniel	30	M	Drysalter	England	New York	Robert Edwards	17 Mar 1828
David	19	M	Farmer	Ireland	United States	Trident	16 May 1826
Eliza, his wife [Daniel]	28	F		England	New York	Robert Edwards	17 Mar 1828
Elizabeth	34	F		England	America	Cincinnatus	22 May 1826
Francis	8	M		Bermuda	U. States	Agnes	1 Jul 1825
Helen, child of D & E Fleming	4	F		England	New York	Robert Edwards	17 Mar 1828
James	29	M	Planter	United States	United States	Ductile	30 Nov 1822
Janet, child of D & E Fleming	1	F		England	New York	Robert Edwards	17 Mar 1828
Jas.	30	M	Merchant	Scotland	U. States	Alert	22 Sep 1821
John	19	M		Great Britain	United States	Kate	2 Oct 1821
John	20	M	France	G. Britain	United States	Siroc	13 Sep 1828
John	29	M	Laborer	Aberdeen	New York	James Margaret	17 May 1827
Joseph	17		Weaver	Ireland	United States	Robert Burns	30 May 1823
Joseph	22	M	Baker	England	America	Cincinnatus	22 May 1826
Peter	35	M	Land surveyor	Great Britian	United States	Brok	29 Aug 1823

NAMES OF PASSENGERS	AGE	SEX	OCCUPATIONS	COUNTRY TO WHICH THEY BELONG	COUNTRY THEY INTEND TO INHABIT	SHIPS/DATES OF ARRIVAL	
FLEMING (cont'd)							
Peter, Jr.	13	M		Great Britian	United States	Brok	29 Aug 1823
Peter, Mr.	45	M	Mercht.	Gt. Brittian	New York	Manchester	21 Apr 1827
Saml., child of D & E Fleming	6	M		England	New York	Robert Edwards	17 Mar 1828
William	17	M	Clerk	Great Britian	United States	Brok	29 Aug 1823
William	43	M	Mechanic	Great Britain	U. States	Hannibal	12 Oct 1829
William, Esqr.	28		Carpenter	United States	United States	South Carolina Packet	22 Jun 1822
FLEMMING, Ann	25	F	Spinster	Ireland	United States	Robert Fulton	24 Jul 1826
Jas.	23	M	...	G. Britain	U. States	Cosmo	15 May 1827
John	15	M	Labourer	Ireland	United States	Robert Fulton	10 Aug 1827
John	25	M	None	Ireland	U. States	Criterion	23 May 1826
Joseph	30	M	Merchant	Great Britain	U. States	Hector	11 Oct 1824
Mack	32	M	Weaver	Great Britain	United States	Colossus	5 Jun 1827
Mary	19	F	Spinster	Ireland	United States	Robert Fulton	10 Aug 1827
Mary	24	F	Gent.	U. States	U. States	Hunter	27 Oct 1824
N. G.	21	M	Merchant	France		Pallas	14 Jun 1828
Nathaniel	23	M	Gentleman	U. States	U. States	Hunter	27 Oct 1824
FLEMMINS, —, Miss	17	F		St. Andrews	U. States	Mary Louisa	6 Mar 1827
—, Miss	19	F		St. Andrews	U. States	Mary Louisa	6 Mar 1827
FLENEGAN, Eliza	20	F	Farmer	Ireland	United States	Helen	27 Jun 1821
FLETCHER, Ann	27	F		England	America	Two Marys	24 Sep 1827
Cath.	38	F		Germany	United States	Lydia	18 Jun 1828
Catharine	28	F	...	Ireland	United States	Colossus	30 May 1825
Elizabeth	...	F	...	Ireland	United States	Colossus	30 May 1825
Elizabeth	35		Lock Smith	England	United States	Mary	15 Jul 1822
Geo.	1	M		England	America	Two Marys	24 Sep 1827
Geo.	24	M	Farmer	Great Britain	United States	Washington	3 Sep 1827
Geo.	34	M	Brewer	England	America	Two Marys	24 Sep 1827
Geo.	38	M		Germany	United States	Lydia	18 Jun 1828
George	8	M	Farmer	Scotland	United States	Commerce	17 Jul 1823
George	9		Lock Smith	England	United States	Mary	15 Jul 1822
Hannah	... 1/12	F	...	Ireland	United States	Colossus	30 May 1825
J.	40		Lock Smith	England	United States	Mary	15 Jul 1822
James	25	M	Farmer	Scotland	United States	Commerce	17 Jul 1823
Janet	45	F		Scotland	United States	Commerce	17 Jul 1823
John	10	M		Germany	United States	Lydia	18 Jun 1828
John, Junr.	20	M	Merchant	G. Bt.	G. Bt.	Canada	13 Oct 1825
Joseph	2		Lock Smith	England	United States	Mary	15 Jul 1822
Joseph	29	M	Taylor	Ireland		Ocean	13 Jul 1827
Joseph	53	M	Clothier	England	United States	Aurora	9 Jul 1827
Margret	26	F		England	United States	Aurora	9 Jul 1827
Margt.	12	F		Scotland	United States	Commerce	17 Jul 1823
Mary	18	F		Scotland	United States	Commerce	17 Jul 1823
Mary	23	F	Miliner	Ireland		Cuba	24 Jun 1822
Mary Ann	3	F		England	America	Two Marys	24 Sep 1827
Nelly	9	F		Scotland	United States	Commerce	17 Jul 1823
Pat.	8	M	...	...	U. States	Governor Tompkins	26 Jul 1824
Patrick	27	M	Farmer	Ireland	United States	Cuba	24 Jun 1822
Richard	33	M	...	Ireland	United States	Colossus	30 May 1825
Robert	28	M	Farmer	Great Britain	United States	Elizabeth & Mary	20 Mar 1828
Robert	50	M	Farmer	Scotland	United States	Commerce	17 Jul 1823
Robt.	24	M		Ireland	U. States	Fame	15 Nov 1826
Sabra	50	F		England	United States	Aurora	9 Jul 1827
Samuel	25	M	Farmer	England	United States	Panthia	7 Feb 1822
Sarah	5	F		England	United States	Aurora	9 Jul 1827
Thomas	22	M	Farmer	England	United States	Panthia	7 Feb 1822
Thomas	32	M	Farmer	Ireland	America	Farmer	15 Nov 1823
William	26	M	Merchant	England	United States	Martha	21 Mar 1820
Wm.	34	M	Merchant	France	France	Abigail	6 May 1822
FLETERT, Jos. Panlin	32	M	Planter	United States	United States	Euphrates	15 Jul 1822
FLEURIAN, Cathrine	18	F	One Family [Joseph]	France	United States	Henri IV	2 Oct 1828
George	13	M	One Family [Joseph]	France	United States	Henri IV	2 Oct 1828
Joseph	52	M		France	United States	Henri IV	2 Oct 1828

NAMES OF PASSENGERS	AGE	SEX	OCCUPATIONS	COUNTRY TO WHICH THEY BELONG	COUNTRY THEY INTEND TO INHABIT	SHIPS/DATES OF ARRIVAL	
FLEURIAN (cont'd)							
Juliana	17	F	One Family [Joseph]	France	United States	Henri IV	2 Oct 1828
Magdalain	16	F	One Family [Joseph]	France	United States	Henri IV	2 Oct 1828
Mary	52	F	One Family [Joseph]	France	United States	Henri IV	2 Oct 1828
FLEURY, Elizabeth	48	F	his wife [Francis]	Switzerland	United States	Helen	5 Sep 1828
Francis	2	M	there child [Francis & Elizabeth]	Switzerland	United States	Helen	5 Sep 1828
Francis	45	M	Weaver	Switzerland	United States	Helen	5 Sep 1828
Xavier	11	M	there child [Francis & Elizabeth]	Switzerland	United States	Helen	5 Sep 1828
FLEWELLING, Benjamin	13	M	Child	St. John, N.B.	Canada	Sarah Ann	18 Nov 1826
David	7	M	Child	St. John, N.B.	Canada	Sarah Ann	18 Nov 1826
Elijah	19	M	Child	St. John, N.B.	Canada	Sarah Ann	18 Nov 1826
Fanny	16	F	Child	St. John, N.B.	Canada	Sarah Ann	18 Nov 1826
Jacob	50	M	Farmer	St. John, N.B.	Canada	Sarah Ann	18 Nov 1826
Joseph	9	M	Child	St. John, N.B.	Canada	Sarah Ann	18 Nov 1826
Olivet	17	F	Child	St. John, N.B.	Canada	Sarah Ann	18 Nov 1826
Sarah Ann	11	F	Child	St. John, N.B.	Canada	Sarah Ann	18 Nov 1826
Susannah	5	F	Child	St. John, N.B.	Canada	Sarah Ann	18 Nov 1826
FLEWERY, —, Mr.	32	M	Doctor	France	U. States	Pedler	28 Feb 1825
FLEWILLING, Sarah	45	F	Wife	St. John, N.B.	Canada	Sarah Ann	18 Nov 1826
FLI..., Betty	23	F	Servant	Ireland	United States	Carolina Ann	14 May 1827
FLICK, Joseph	24	M		Switzerland	U.S.	Francois I	8 Aug 1829
FLIGHT, Joseph	5	M	Boy	England	United States	Cambria	3 Jul 1829
FLIN, Biddy	19	F	None	Ireland	U.S.A.	Dalhouse Castle	21 Aug 1829
FLING, Barney	32	M	Dyer	Great Britain	United States	Colossus	5 Jun 1827
FLINN, Ann	9	F	None	Great Brittain	U. States	Louisa	11 Jun 1824
B.	5	F		Great Brittain	United States	Sarah Ralston	27 Jan 1827
Betsey	20	F	...	England	United States	Milton	20 Oct 1827
Bridget	24	F				Trio	5 May 1828
Catharine	22	F		Ireland	U. States	Lima	5 Aug 1829
Catharine	23	F	Labourer	Great Brittain	United States	Sarah Ralston	27 Jan 1827
Catherine	6	F	his family [Ferdinand]	Germany	United States	Wm. Osborne	16 Sep 1828
Catherine	22	F		Ireland	New York	Lima	5 Aug 1829
Cathr.	23	F		England	America	Two Marys	24 Sep 1827
Daniel	25	M	Labourer	Ireland	U.S.	Lady Hunter	10 Jul 1826
E.	6	M		Great Brittain	United States	Sarah Ralston	27 Jan 1827
Edd.	25	M	Laborer	Ireland	U. States	Howard Douglass	29 Jan 1828
Eleonar	20	F	Spinster	Ireland	United States	Wilson	6 Jun 1828
Elisabeth	11	F	None	Great Brittain	U. States	Louisa	11 Jun 1824
Elisabeth	38	F	None	Great Brittain	U. States	Louisa	11 Jun 1824
Elza	20	F				Trio	5 May 1828
Ferdinand	2	M	his family [Ferdinand]	Germany	United States	Wm. Osborne	16 Sep 1828
Ferdinand	25	M	Shoemaker	Germany	United States	Wm. Osborne	16 Sep 1828
George	7	M	his family [Ferdinand]	Germany	United States	Wm. Osborne	16 Sep 1828
Gerfried	20	F	his family [Ferdinand]	Germany	United States	Wm. Osborne	16 Sep 1828
Hannah	26	F		America	United States	John & Elizabeth	25 Sep 1827
Helen	42	F	None	Gt. Brittain	United States	Balaena	21 Aug 1824
James		M	Farmer	Ireland	America	Farmer	4 Aug 1825
James	21	M	Labourer	Ireland	United States	Baltic	21 Apr 1827
Jno.	6	M	None	Great Brittain	U. States	Louisa	11 Jun 1824
Jno.	40	M	Labourer	Great Brittain	U. States	Louisa	11 Jun 1824
John	20	M	Farmer	Ireland	U. States	Nancy	29 Nov 1821
John	23	M	Weaver	England	United States	Bolivar	15 Jun 1826
John	30	M	Weaver	Ireland	United States	Baltic	21 Apr 1827
John	34	M	Pilot	America	United States	John & Elizabeth	25 Sep 1827
Joseph	4	M	his family [Ferdinand]	Germany	United States	Wm. Osborne	16 Sep 1828
Js.	30	M	Shoemaker	Great Brittan	U. States	John & Elizabeth	11 Dec 1826

NAMES OF PASSENGERS	AGE	SEX	OCCUPATIONS	COUNTRY TO WHICH THEY BELONG	COUNTRY THEY INTEND TO INHABIT	SHIPS/DATES OF ARRIVAL	
FLINN (cont'd)							
Laurence	24	M	Labourer	Ireland	New York	Lima	5 Aug 1829
Laurence	24	M	Labourer	Ireland	U. States	Lima	5 Aug 1829
Margaret	2/12	F	...	England	United States	Milton	20 Oct 1827
Margt.	28	F		Great Britain	United States	Britannia	29 Oct 1829
Mary	12	F	None	Gt. Brittain	United States	Balaena	21 Aug 1824
Mary	17	F	Spinster	Ireland	United States	Dublin Packet	29 Jun 1825
Mary	30	F		Great Brittain	United States	Sarah Ralston	27 Jan 1827
Nancy	23		Farmer & Labourer	Great Britain & Ireland	United States	Trio	8 Feb 1827
Nickolas	7	M	None	Gt. Brittain	United States	Balaena	21 Aug 1824
Patk.	17	M	None	Gt. Brittain	United States	Balaena	21 Aug 1824
Patrick	40	M	Labourer	Ireland	United States	Carolina Ann	14 May 1827
Philip	8	M	his family [Ferdinand]	Germany	United States	Wm. Osborne	16 Sep 1828
Robert	2	M		Great Brittain	United States	Sarah Ralston	27 Jan 1827
Thomas	20	M	Farmer	Ireland	United States	Silas Richards	3 Apr 1826
Thomas	30	M	Labourer	Great Brittain	United States	Sarah Ralston	27 Jan 1827
Thos.	24	M	Labourer	Dublin	Dublin	Howard Douglass	11 May 1827
FLINNAGAN, Catherine	3			Killany	Ireland	Hudson	18 Jun 1825

*Officers, Seamen and Passengers belonging to the Ship Jane of Boston and taken from on board the Schooner Olive of St. Johns , N.B. on the 4th June 1825, Lat. 41.30, Long 53.19, which ship foundered on the 31st ultimo in Lat. 41.44 Long 52.

James	28			Killany	Ireland	Hudson	18 Jun 1825

*Officers, Seamen and Passengers belonging to the Ship Jane of Boston and taken from on board the Schooner Olive of St. Johns , N.B. on the 4th June 1825, Lat. 41.30, Long 53.19, which ship foundered on the 31st ultimo in Lat. 41.44 Long 52.

Mary	30			Killany	Ireland	Hudson	18 Jun 1825

*Officers, Seamen and Passengers belonging to the Ship Jane of Boston and taken from on board the Schooner Olive of St. Johns , N.B. on the 4th June 1825, Lat. 41.30, Long 53.19, which ship foundered on the 31st ultimo in Lat. 41.44 Long 52.

Patrick	5			Killany	Ireland	Hudson	18 Jun 1825

*Officers, Seamen and Passengers belonging to the Ship Jane of Boston and taken from on board the Schooner Olive of St. Johns , N.B. on the 4th June 1825, Lat. 41.30, Long 53.19, which ship foundered on the 31st ultimo in Lat. 41.44 Long 52.

FLINT, Alexander	49	M	Merchant	W. Brittain	U.S.	Bliss	28 Jul 1821
James	40	M	Gent.	England	U. States	William Thompson	25 Aug 1828
Jno.	35	M	None	Columbia	U. States	Theresa	10 Dec 1825
John	23	M	Joiner	Great Britain	United States	Elizabeth & Mary	20 Mar 1828
Thos.	30	M		Great B.	U. States	William Neilson	26 Jul 1828
William	22	M	Merchant	Gt. Britian	United States	Nestor	16 Aug 1824
FLINTER, Steward	20	M	Farmer	Ireland	United States	Dublin Packet	23 May 1828
FLINTOFF, Ann	9	F	Farmer	England	United States	Meteor	16 Aug 1824
Ellen	5	F	Farmer	England	United States	Meteor	16 Aug 1824
Geoge	50	M	Farmer	St. John	U. States	Lady Hunter	5 Jul 1823
George	13	M	Farmer	England	United States	Meteor	16 Aug 1824
James	7	M	Farmer	England	United States	Meteor	16 Aug 1824
James	53	M	Farmer	St. John	U. States	Lady Hunter	5 Jul 1823
John	14	M	Farmer	England	United States	Meteor	16 Aug 1824
Mary	37	F	Farmer	England	United States	Meteor	16 Aug 1824
Robert	4	M	Farmer	England	United States	Meteor	16 Aug 1824
Sarah	6/12	F	Farmer	England	United States	Meteor	16 Aug 1824
Thomas	16	M	Farmer	England	United States	Meteor	16 Aug 1824
FLIX, Ann Maria	43	F		Germany	United States	Samuel Robertson	8 Aug 1828
Catherine	16	F		Germany	United States	Samuel Robertson	8 Aug 1828
George	48	M	Mason	Germany	United States	Samuel Robertson	8 Aug 1828
Joseph	20	M	Mason	Germany	United States	Samuel Robertson	8 Aug 1828
Madaline	4	F		Germany	United States	Samuel Robertson	8 Aug 1828
Peter	8	M		Germany	United States	Samuel Robertson	8 Aug 1828
FLOKER, John	40	M	Gentleman	St. Cruz	U. States	Manchester Packet	29 Jan 1825
FLOOD, Ann	3	F		Great Brittan	U.S.	Florida	17 May 1825
Ann	4 3/12	F		Ireland	United States	Atlantic	21 Jul 1827
Ann	13	F	None	Ireland	U.S.A.	Dalhouse Castle	21 Aug 1829

NAMES OF PASSENGERS	AGE	SEX	OCCUPATIONS	COUNTRY TO WHICH THEY BELONG	COUNTRY THEY INTEND TO INHABIT	SHIPS/DATES OF ARRIVAL	
FLOOD (cont'd)							
Ann	13	F	None	Ireland	United States	Dalhouse Castle	21 Aug 1829
Ann	24	F		Great Brittan	U.S.	Florida	17 May 1825
Ann	25 9/12	F	Servant	Ireland	United States	Atlantic	21 Jul 1827
Arthur	26	M	Labourer	G. Brittain	U.S. America	York	4 Aug 1826
B.	16	F	Farmer	Ireland	United States	Josephine	30 Apr 1828
Barney	25	M	Labourer	Ireland	U. States	Marcus	7 Apr 1825
Biddy	25	F	Labourer	Ireland	U. States	Marcus	7 Apr 1825
Cathe.	24	F	Wife	..., ..., England	Boston	New Orleans	24 Aug 1827
Cather.	40	F		Ireland	United States	William Byrnes	6 Apr 1826
Cornelius	25	M	Labourer			Evergreen	28 Jul 1820
Elizabeth	2	F		Great Britian	United States	Isaac Hicks	13 Jan 1826
Ellen	14	F	Farmer	Ireland	United States	Josephine	30 Apr 1828
Ellen	22	F	None	Ireland	U.S.A.	Dalhouse Castle	21 Aug 1829
Ellen	22	F	None	Ireland	United States	Dalhouse Castle	21 Aug 1829
Ewd.	28	M				Hibernia	15 Aug 1820
Fanny	5	F		Great Britian	United States	Isaac Hicks	13 Jan 1826
J. S.	5	M		Great Brittan	U.S.	Florida	17 May 1825
John	18	M	Labourer	Ireland	United States	Lady Hunter	29 Apr 1826
John	20 3/12	M	Weaver	Ireland	United States	Atlantic	21 Jul 1827
John	62	M	Farmer	Ireland	United States	Josephine	30 Apr 1828
Judy	31	F	Servant	Ireland	United States	Carolina Ann	14 May 1827
Mary	26	F	Spinster	Ireland	U. States	Josephine	7 May 1827
Mary	29	F	None	Ireland		Marchioness	13 May 1828
Michl.	19	M	Laborer	Ireland	United States	Trio	13 Jun 1827
Owen	28	M	Labourer	Ireland	U. States	Marcus	7 Apr 1825
Pat	20	M	Black smith	Ireland	United States	Josephine	30 Apr 1828
Pat	25	M				Hibernia	15 Aug 1820
Patrick	2 7/12	M		Ireland	United States	Atlantic	21 Jul 1827
Patrick	4	M	Farmer	Ireland	U.S.A.	Dalhouse Castle	21 Aug 1829
Patrick	4	M	None	Ireland	United States	Dalhouse Castle	21 Aug 1829
Peter	20	M	Labor	England		Exchange	11 Jul 1823
Peter	30	M	Shoe Maker	..., ..., England	Boston	New Orleans	24 Aug 1827
Philip	21	M	Farmer	Ireland	United States	Aurora	9 Jul 1827
Rose	20	F	None	Ireland	United States	Colossus	26 Aug 1828
Rose	22	F	Spinster	Ireland	U. States	Josephine	7 May 1827
Sarah	25	F		Great Britian	United States	Isaac Hicks	13 Jan 1826
Stephen	1	M		Great Britian	United States	Isaac Hicks	13 Jan 1826
Thomas	24	M	Farmer	Ireland	United States	Aurora	9 Jul 1827
Thos.	20	M				Hibernia	15 Aug 1820
FLORA, Jno. N.	35	M	Merchant	Mexico	U. States	Prince Edward	5 Jul 1825
FLORENCE, Lewis	23	M	Merchant	U. States	U. States	Mary Olivia	10 Jul 1824
FLORES, Antonio	33	M	Mercht.	Spain	Spain	Richmond Packet	28 Oct 1825
FLOREZ, Terrasa	45	F		Spain	Spain	Dromo	5 Oct 1829
FLORITY, Biddy	23	F		Ireland	Phila.	Eliza Grant	29 Aug 1829
FLORRAND, Clara	21 1/12	F	Joiner	France	U. States	France	26 Jun 1828
FLOWER, Joseph	16	M	Merchant	Great Britain	United States	Isaac Hicks	6 Dec 1827
FLOWERS, ...	15	M	Farmer	England	U. States	Acasta	12 May 1825
Hannah, Miss	4	F	Carpenter	England	U.S.	Acasta	11 May 1827
John, Mast.	6	M	Carpenter	England	U.S.	Acasta	11 May 1827
Maria, Mrs.	32	F	Carpenter	England	U.S.	Acasta	11 May 1827
Mercy, Miss	10	F	Carpenter	England	U.S.	Acasta	11 May 1827
Sarah	20	F	None	England	United States	Jubilee	13 Jul 1829
Wm., Mast.	2	M	Carpenter	England	U.S.	Acasta	11 May 1827
FLOWES, —	22	F		St. Croix	St. Croix	Carlo	19 Apr 1828
FLOYD, Charles B.	23	M	Lieu. U.S. Marines	United States	Boston	Cortes	7 Jul 1821
Culliss	30	M	Baker	Great Brittain	U. States	Florenzo	20 Mar 1827
Esther	30	F	Spinster	Great Britain	U. States	Boston	28 Aug 1821
Isaac	45		Gardner	London, England	Great Britain	Franklin	22 Jun 1827
James	20	M	Weaver	Ireland	United States	Nancy	15 Dec 1824
John	3	M	Child	Great Britain	U. States	Boston	28 Aug 1821
Margaret	5	F	Child	Great Britain	U. States	Boston	28 Aug 1821
Mary	30	F	Lady	United States	United States	Sylvester Healy	17 Oct 1825
Patrick	7	M	Child	Great Britain	U. States	Boston	28 Aug 1821
Saml.	27	M				Imperial	19 Jul 1820
Thomas	20	M	Farmer	Ireland	United States	Trident	17 May 1825
FLUERY, Wm.	20	M	Labourer	G. Britain	U. States	Mary & Harriot	8 Sep 1828

NAMES OF PASSENGERS	AGE	SEX	OCCUPATIONS	COUNTRY TO WHICH THEY BELONG	COUNTRY THEY INTEND TO INHABIT	SHIPS/DATES OF ARRIVAL	
FLUNNER, Mary			Born Sea	Great B.	U. States	William Neilson	26 Jul 1828
FLUON, H.	30	M	Merchant	France		Sarah Ann	5 Aug 1820
FLURRY, Henry	21	M	Farm	Ireland		Quatre Freres	29 Jul 1828
FLUTLY, Sara	24	F	Merchant	England	England	Venus	15 Apr 1822
FLUWEY, John	22	M		Gt. Britain	United States	John & Elizabeth	25 Sep 1827
FLYER, Ann	21	F		G. Britan	U. States	William Neilson	26 Jul 1828
FLYN, Briget	6			Ireland	U.S.	Union	20 Aug 1827
Catharine	27		Farmer	Ireland	U. States	Schuylkill	22 Aug 1825
Catherine	4			Ireland	U.S.	Union	20 Aug 1827
Daniel	1 1/2			Ireland	U.S.	Union	20 Aug 1827
Daniel	21	M	Labourer	Ireland	U.S.	Lady Hunter	10 Jul 1826
Daniel	45			Ireland	U.S.	Union	20 Aug 1827
John	20			Ireland	U.S.	Union	20 Aug 1827
Julia	16			Ireland	U.S.	Union	20 Aug 1827
Margret	10			Ireland	U.S.	Union	20 Aug 1827
Mary	45			Ireland	U.S.	Union	20 Aug 1827
Simon	8			Ireland	U.S.	Union	20 Aug 1827
Thomas	18			Ireland	U.S.	Union	20 Aug 1827
FLYNER, Margaret	26	M		G. Britan	U. States	William Neilson	26 Jul 1828
FLYNN, Andrew	19	M	Labourer	Ireland	U. States	Josephine	7 May 1827
Bernard	16	M	Servant	Ireland	America	Plutarch	18 Jul 1826
Bridget	9	F		Ireland	United States	Pallas	28 Oct 1828
Bridget	30	M	Merchant	Ireland		Athenian	3 Sep 1827
Dennis	20	M	Farmer	England	United States	Ganges	10 May 1828
Ellen	11	F		Ireland	United States	Pallas	28 Oct 1828
Ellen	35	F		Ireland	United States	Pallas	28 Oct 1828
Ellen	55	F		Ireland	United States	Pallas	28 Oct 1828
James	1	M		Ireland	United States	Pallas	28 Oct 1828
James	24	M	Labourer	Sligo	New York	Susquehana	27 Jun 1823
John	8	M		Ireland	United States	Pallas	28 Oct 1828
John	21	M	Labourer	Ireland	United States	Jubilee	12 May 1828
Michael	28	M	Labourer	Ireland	U.S. America	Traveller	10 Sep 1827
Patrick	22	M	Whitener	Ireland	U. States	Hudson	10 Nov 1825
Thomas	3	M		Ireland	United States	Pallas	28 Oct 1828
William	19 3/12	M	Labourer	Ireland	America	Enterprize	29 Jun 1827
FOADOAZ, Henry	44	M	Plaisterer	Guadaloupe	Guadaloupe	Genl. Irdelle	13 Sep 1828
FOALA, Christian	22	M	Mechanic	Switzerland	U. States	Queen Mab	7 Apr 1826
FOANTEZ, F.	25	M	Merchant	Havana	U. States	Greek	17 May 1825
FOBERT, William	33	M	Miller	Ireland	United States	Lunar	5 May 1828
FOE, Daniel	40	M	Farmer			Splendid	14 Aug 1829
FOGARTHEY, John	27	M	Farmer	Gt. Britain	United States	Penelope	9 Sep 1828
FOGARTY, Mary	25	F		Ireland	United States	Danube	13 Jul 1827
Mary, Mrs.	36	F		St. Croix	U. States	South Carolina Packet	4 Sep 1822
Patrick	30	M	Farmer	Ireland	United States	Meteor	19 Aug 1829
FOGER, Fredk.	35	M	Merchant	U. States	U. States	Exchange	25 Sep 1826
FOGERTY, Mary, Mrs.	34			St. Croix	New York	South Carolina Packet	19 Jun 1826
Michael	30	M	Bricklayer	Ireland	United States	Danube	13 Jul 1827
Patrick	22	M	Labourer	Ireland	United States	Jubilee	13 Jul 1829
FOGG, J. P.	37	M	Merchant	U. States	U. States	Cobbosse Conte	18 Apr 1823
J. V.	35	M	Merchant	United States	United States	Agenora	11 Jun 1824
John	16	M	Manuir	England	United States	Dalhouse Castle	6 Sep 1827
John	35	M	House Joiner		U. States	Clio	8 Apr 1828
FOIL, Gil	20	M	Labour	Great Britain	United States	William Dawson	18 Jun 1827
Jno.	21	M	Labour	Great Britain	United States	William Dawson	18 Jun 1827
FOIS, Jean	25	M	Merchant	Spain	Spain	Iris	3 Jul 1828
FOISDYK, Francois	59		Dyer	France	U. States	Parachute	14 May 1828
Louis	31		Dyer	France	U. States	Parachute	14 May 1828
FOLAGN, M. L.	50	M	Farmer	U. States	U. States	General Coffin	9 Mar 1827
FOLDS, Elenor	40	F		Great Brittain	United States	Active	12 Sep 1828
Hannah	2	F		Great Brittain	United States	Active	12 Sep 1828
Henrietta	36	F		Great Brittain	United States	Active	12 Sep 1828
John	26	M		Great Brittain	United States	Active	12 Sep 1828
Wm.	1	M		Great Brittain	United States	Active	12 Sep 1828
Wm.	28	M		Great Brittain	United States	Active	12 Sep 1828
*Died on the Passage							
FOLEY, Allen	24	F	Spinster	Ireland	United States	Mary & Harriet	9 Mar 1829

NAMES OF PASSENGERS	AGE	SEX	OCCUPATIONS	COUNTRY TO WHICH THEY BELONG	COUNTRY THEY INTEND TO INHABIT	SHIPS/DATES OF ARRIVAL	
FOLEY (cont'd)							
Ann	18	F	None	Great Britain	United States	Roman	10 May 1828
Biddy	30	F		Ireland	United States	Trio	2 Oct 1828
Burasset	5	F	...	G. Britain	U. States	New England	28 Sep 1824
Cath.	12	F	Farmer	G. Britain	Canada	Cosmo	25 Nov 1826
Catharine	42	F	Farmer	Great Britain	U. States	Columbia	22 Sep 1828
Catherine	20	F	Spinster	Ireland	America	William	21 May 1825
Charles	...	...	...	Ireland	United States	Carolina Ann	24 Oct 1825
Charles	25	M	...	G. Britain	U. States	New England	28 Sep 1824
David	24	M	Labourer	Ireland	U. States	Packet	23 Sep 1820
Edmd.	2	M	Farmer	G. Britain	Canada	Cosmo	25 Nov 1826
Edward	16	M	...	G. Britain	U. States	New England	28 Sep 1824
Edward	53	M	...	G. Britain	U. States	New England	28 Sep 1824
Edwd.	48	M	Farmer	Great Britain	U. States	Columbia	22 Sep 1828
Elizabeth	...	...	...	Ireland	United States	Carolina Ann	24 Oct 1825
Ellen	7	F	Farmer	G. Britain	Canada	Cosmo	25 Nov 1826
Ellinor	40	F	Farmer	G. Britain	Canada	Cosmo	25 Nov 1826
Giles	22	F	Spinster	Ireland	United States	Wilson	6 Jun 1828
Hugh	30	M	...	G. Britain	U. States	New England	28 Sep 1824
James	17	M	...	G. Britain	U. States	New England	28 Sep 1824
James	35	M	Cloth Maker	Ireland	New York	Thames	6 Oct 1820
Jas.	18	M	Farmer	G. Britain	Canada	Cosmo	25 Nov 1826
Jas.	43	M	Gentleman	G. Britain	Canada	Cosmo	25 Nov 1826
John	7/12	M	Boy	Ireland	U.S.	Panthea	22 Jul 1826
John	3	M		Great Britain	U. States	Columbia	22 Sep 1828
John	9	M	Farmer	G. Britain	Canada	Cosmo	25 Nov 1826
John	41	M	Farmer	G. Britain	Canada	Cosmo	25 Nov 1826
John	45		Labourer	Ireland	United States	Geo. Canning	5 Jun 1828
Margaret	23	F		Ireland	U. States	Packet	23 Sep 1820
Mary	15	F	...	G. Britain	U. States	New England	28 Sep 1824
Mary	21	F	Lady	Ireland	U.S.	Panthea	22 Jul 1826
Michael	28	M	Labourer	Ireland	U. States	William Byrnes	17 Jul 1825
Michael	30	M	Labourer	Limerick	N. York	Thomas & William	25 May 1827
Micheal	27	M	Farmer	Ireland	America	William	21 May 1825
Pat	12	M	Farmer	G. Britain	Canada	Cosmo	25 Nov 1826
Patrick	21	M	...	G. Britain	U. States	New England	28 Sep 1824
Sarah	9	F	Farmer	Great Britain	U. States	Columbia	22 Sep 1828
Sarah	21 6/12	F	Spinster	Ireland	United States	Wilson	6 Jun 1828
Thos.	5	M	Farmer	G. Britain	Canada	Cosmo	25 Nov 1826
Wm.	7	M	Farmer	G. Britain	Canada	Cosmo	25 Nov 1826
Wm.	21	M	Mechanic	Ireland	United States	Vermont	10 Jan 1827
FOLGE, F. S.	27	M	Merchant	U. States	U. States	Eliza Allen	30 May 1827
FOLGER, B. H.	23	M	Merchant	United States	U. States	Pacific	5 Sep 1827
F. L.	28	M	Merchant	N. York	U. States	Rising States	23 Apr 1825
F. L.	29	M	Merchant	U. States	New York	Hope Mary Ann	21 Aug 1824
F. L.	35	M	Merchant	United States	United States	William	6 Oct 1828
Fredk.	35	M	Merchant	Hudson	U. States	Mattrawan	16 Dec 1823
Fredk. L.	28	M	Merchant	N. York	N. York	Exchange	1 May 1824
Fredk. L.	31	M	Merchant	U. States	U. States	Mattrawan	15 Sep 1823
Fredr. L.	51	M	Merchant	U. States	U. States	Mattrawan	31 Jan 1823
R. W.	32	M	Merchant	U. States	U. States	Mattrawan	1 Oct 1822
FOLIEN, Peter	36	M	Merchant	England	United States	Jubilee	1 Oct 1828
FOLIET, A.	30	M	Carpenter	England	United States	Lewis	30 May 1823
FOLIN, Bartty	9	M	Farmer	Ireland		Cuba	24 Jun 1822
Bidy	16	F	Farmer	Ireland		Cuba	24 Jun 1822
Pat.	13	M	Farmer	Ireland		Cuba	24 Jun 1822
Thady	40	M	Farmer	Ireland		Cuba	24 Jun 1822
Thos.	10	M	Farmer	Ireland		Cuba	24 Jun 1822
FOLK, E. C.	40	M	Lock Smith	Germany		Ariel	24 Sep 1827
Mathew	25	M	Taylor	England	United States	Eliza Grant	7 Jun 1827
FOLKES, Ann	27	F		England	America	Two Marys	24 Sep 1827
Francis	32	M	Carpenter	England	United States	Warrior	6 Oct 1828
Ralph	34	M	Weaver	England	America	Two Marys	24 Sep 1827
FOLKS, Thomas	7	M	Collier	England	United States	Amelia	20 Aug 1829
FOLL...MON, Conner	21	M	Labourer	England	...	Braganza	8 Aug 1825
FOLLEY, Patrick	3	M	None	Great Britain	United States	Orbit	23 Oct 1826
Richard	30	M	Shoemaker	Great Britain	United States	Orbit	23 Oct 1826
FOLLINS, Chas.	31		Merchant	Charleston	Charleston	Matilda	31 Jan 1826

NAMES OF PASSENGERS	AGE	SEX	OCCUPATIONS	COUNTRY TO WHICH THEY BELONG	COUNTRY THEY INTEND TO INHABIT	SHIPS/DATES OF ARRIVAL	
FOLLY, Catharine	30	F	None	Great Britain	United States	Orbit	23 Oct 1826
Ellen	23	F		Ireland	United States	Trio	13 Jun 1827
John	2	M	None	Great Britain	United States	Orbit	23 Oct 1826
FOLMER, —, Infant	2/365	M		Wertemburg	America, U.N.S.	Great Britain	3 Aug 1829
Andre	35	M	Farmer	Wertemburg	America, U.N.S.	Great Britain	3 Aug 1829
Baptist	58		Farmer	German	America	Romulus	15 May 1828
Charlote	10		Farmer	German	America	Romulus	15 May 1828
Frederica	34	F		Wertemburg	America, U.N.S.	Great Britain	3 Aug 1829
George	18		Farmer	German	America	Romulus	15 May 1828
Indie	2	M		Wertemburg	America, U.N.S.	Great Britain	3 Aug 1829
Jacob	5		Farmer	German	America	Romulus	15 May 1828
Magdalin	47		Farmer	German	America	Romulus	15 May 1828
FOLOGER, Ann	28	F		England	Albany	Cortes	16 Jul 1827
Caroline	8/12	F		England	Albany	Cortes	16 Jul 1827
Mary	2 6/12	F		England	Albany	Cortes	16 Jul 1827
Samuel	28	M	Farmer	England	Albany	Cortes	16 Jul 1827
FOLSOM, Geo. W.	11	M	Mariner	Newburyport	U. States	Essex	8 Oct 1823
Lewis	40	M	Mariner	Newburyport	U. States	Essex	8 Oct 1823
FOLY, Rebecca	34	F		Ireland	New York	Vigilant	6 May 1822
Timothy	38	M	Servant	Gt. Britain	United States	John & Elizabeth	25 Sep 1827
FOMARD, Chas.		M	Mariner	France	U. States	Nonparel	11 Jun 1824
FONAN, Julia	30	M	Lady	Ireland	United States	William	20 Jul 1829
FONE, Robt.	23	M	Saddler	Great Britain	United States	William Dawson	18 Jun 1827
FONTAIN, —	43	M	Merchant	France	America	Saluda	16 Oct 1824
Augustine	32	M	Soldier	France	Uncertain	Belfast	21 Mar 1820
P.	31	M		France	U. States	London	13 Sep 1824
FONTAINE, Eloph	42		None	France		Bayard	10 Sep 1827
So.	45	M	Marchant	N. York	U. States	Commodore Perry	9 Apr 1821
FONTANAL, Marino	22	M	Gentleman	Havana	Spain	William	1 Apr 1822
FONTE, Susan	26	F	Servant	Switzerland	U.S.	Henri IV	17 May 1828
FOOLEY, Thomas	27	M	Weaver	Ireland	United States	Enterprize	23 Jul 1827
FOORD, Jane	30	F		Great Britain	United States	Diana	6 Jul 1829
Thomas	2 6/12	M		Great Britain	United States	Diana	6 Jul 1829
W.	29	M	Farmer	Great Britain	United States	Diana	6 Jul 1829
FOOT, Benjm.	36	M	Mechanic	Connecticutt	U. States	Henry	11 Apr 1823
George	17	M	Servant	England	Upper Canada	Hudson	21 Aug 1829
Isabella	40	F		G. Brittain	U. States	Cincinnatus	2 Oct 1822
John F.	42	M		G. Brittain	U. States	Cincinnatus	2 Oct 1822
FOOTE, Andrew	1	M		Scotland	United States	Culloden	17 May 1828
James L.	33	M	Mariner	Massachusetts	U. States	Abigail	25 Mar 1822
John	28	M	Carpenter	America	America	Splendid	23 Mar 1829
John	40	M	Joiner	Scotland	United States	Culloden	17 May 1828
Mary	36	F		Scotland	United States	Culloden	17 May 1828
Saml. E.	38	M	Merchant	U. States	U. States	Splendid	11 Apr 1826
Thos.	23	M	Mason	U. States	U. States	Richard	26 Jun 1823
FOOTENAN, Eleanor	40	F	None	Ireland	United States	Jubilee	13 Jul 1829
Ellen	13	F	None	Ireland	United States	Jubilee	13 Jul 1829
James	20	M	Farmer	Ireland	United States	Jubilee	13 Jul 1829
Laurence	9	M	None	Ireland	United States	Jubilee	13 Jul 1829
Laurence	40	M	Farmer	Ireland	United States	Jubilee	13 Jul 1829
Mary	11	F	None	Ireland	United States	Jubilee	13 Jul 1829
Patt	14	M	Farmer	Ireland	United States	Jubilee	13 Jul 1829
FOR...TH, James	...1		Labourer	...ton	England	Great Britain	7 May 1827
FORBES, —, Miss	22	F		Boston, U.S.		Robert Edwards	8 Nov 1825
...as	58	M	Weaver	Gt. Britain	U. States	Maria	22 May 1822
A.	21	M	Merchant	U. States	U. States	Colossus	21 Apr 1827
Alexr.	30	M	Mason	Demshult, Auchlemuchly [Parish], Fife [County]	New York	Hero	19 May 1828
*to follow his occupation							
Andw.	25	M		Ireland	U. States	Nancy	10 Jul 1822
Betsey	19	F		G. Britain	U. States	Eliza	31 Jul 1828
Charles J.	43 7/12	M	Military	Great Britain		Silas Richards	27 Oct 1826
Duncan	22	M	Farmer	Scotland	United States	Commerce	17 Jul 1823
Duncan	24	M	Weaver	Gt. Britain	U. States	St. George	20 Sep 1828
Edgar	5	M		Great Brittian	United States	Carolina Augusta	2 Dec 1828
Elizabeth	10	F		Great Brittian	United States	Carolina Augusta	2 Dec 1828

NAMES OF PASSENGERS	AGE	SEX	OCCUPATIONS	COUNTRY TO WHICH THEY BELONG	COUNTRY THEY INTEND TO INHABIT	SHIPS/DATES OF ARRIVAL
FORBES (cont'd)						
Elizabeth	35	F		Great Brittian	United States	Carolina Augusta 2 Dec 1828
Hannah	7 3/12	F		England	England	Venus 15 Apr 1822
Hannah, Mrs.	35	F	Lady	England	United States	Maria 29 Sep 1823
Henry	8	M		Gt. Britain	U. States	Maria 22 May 1822
J.	26	M	None	Ireland	U. States	Criterion 23 May 1826
James	1 6/12	F	Merchant	England	England	Venus 15 Apr 1822
James	22	M	Labourer	Ireland	United States	Carolina Ann 24 Oct 1825
James	40	M	Painter	Great Brittian	United States	Carolina Augusta 2 Dec 1828
Janet	58	F		G. Britain	U. States	Eliza 31 Jul 1828
Jean	27	F		Demshult, Auchlemuchly [Parish], Fife [County]	New York	Hero 19 May 1828
*going with her husband						
John	24	M	Labourer	Scotland	U. States	Superior 25 Sep 1828
Jos.	60	M	Currier	G. Britain	U. States	Eliza 31 Jul 1828
Mary	15	F		Gt. Britain	U. States	Maria 22 May 1822
Mary	26 7/12	F		England	England	Venus 15 Apr 1822
Mary	49	F		Gt. Britain	U. States	Maria 22 May 1822
Mary, Junr.	9	F		England	England	Venus 15 Apr 1822
P. S.	21	M	Merchant	U. States	U. States	Emma 26 May 1827
Robert	18	M	Labourer	Ireland	United States	Catharine 22 Jul 1825
Sarah	12	F		Gt. Britain	U. States	Maria 22 May 1822
Thomas	18	M	Weaver	Gt. Britain	U. States	Maria 22 May 1822
Thomas T.	23 9/12	M	Merchant	U.S. America	U.S. America	Leeds 5 Feb 1827
Ths.	35	F	Merchant	England	England	Venus 15 Apr 1822
Ths., Junr.	4	F	Merchant	England	England	Venus 15 Apr 1822
William	7	M		Great Brittian	United States	Carolina Augusta 2 Dec 1828
Wm.	36	M	Labourer	Glasgow, Barony [Parish], Lanark [County]	New York	Hero 19 May 1828
*to look for employment						
Wm., Mr.	23	M	British Army	Great Britain		Florida 3 Jun 1824
FORCARD, Charles, Mr.	29	M	Merchant	Switzerland	Switzerland	Cadmus 11 Jul 1827
FORCE, Philip	26	M	Merchant	St. John, N.B.	St. John, N.B.	Ann Maria 2 Nov 1827
FORCHER, George	42	M	Shoemaker	France	United States	Helen 5 Sep 1828
FORD, Alfred	2	M	Farmer	England	U. States	Robert Edwards 9 May 1827
An	30	F	Child	Ireland	N. York	Trusty 12 Sep 1828
Ann	9/12	F		G. Brittian	U. States	Cincinnatus 2 Oct 1822
Augustus	38	M	U. States	U. States	U. States	Columbia 1 Dec 1824
B.	28	M	Labourer	Ireland	U. States	Sarah G 30 Jun 1828
Bridget	60	F	Servant	Ireland	United States	Josephine 30 Apr 1828
Caleb	44	M	Blacksmith	Great Britain	U.S. America	Chili 7 Jul 1827
Charity	22	F	Merchant	England	U. States	Calais Packet 3 Sep 1827
Chas.	19	M	Smith	England	United States	Cosmo 21 Aug 1828
Danie	33	M	Farmer	England	U. States	Robert Edwards 9 May 1827
Daniel	1	M		England	United States	Cosmo 21 Aug 1828
Daniel	10	M	Farmer	England	U. States	Robert Edwards 9 May 1827
Edward	4	M	Farmer	England	U. States	Robert Edwards 9 May 1827
Edward	40	M	Bootmaker	Gt. Britain		Corinthian 27 Oct 1829
Elizabeth	21	F	Servant	Ireland	United States	Josephine 30 Apr 1828
Elizebeth	6	F	Farmer	England	U. States	Robert Edwards 9 May 1827
Elizebeth	28	F	Farmer	England	U. States	Robert Edwards 9 May 1827
F. J.	26		Merchant	Baltimore	U. States	Brown 11 Jun 1827
Francis	22	M	Chandler	Great Britain	U. States	Ganges 21 Jun 1827
G.	23		Farmer	Ireland	United States	Courier 16 May 1825
George	8	M	Farmer	England	U. States	Robert Edwards 9 May 1827
George	30	M	Servant	England	Barbadoes	Jupiter 27 Jun 1828
H.	30	M	Labourer	Ireland	U. States	Sarah G 30 Jun 1828
Hester	4	F		England	United States	Cosmo 21 Aug 1828
Ja.	2	M	D. Maker	Ireland	N. York	Trusty 12 Sep 1828
James	50	M	Teacher	United States	United States	Robert Edwards 3 Oct 1829
Jane	8	F	Laborer	Great Britian	U. States	Henry Kneedland 7 Aug 1826
Jno.	21	M	Farmer	Great Britain	America	Remittance 24 Aug 1825
John	20	M	Lawyer	Ireland	N. York	Trusty 12 Sep 1828
John	60	M	Laborer	Great Britian	U. States	Henry Kneedland 7 Aug 1826

NAMES OF PASSENGERS	AGE	SEX	OCCUPATIONS	COUNTRY TO WHICH THEY BELONG	COUNTRY THEY INTEND TO INHABIT	SHIPS/DATES OF ARRIVAL	
FORD (cont'd)							
Jon	8	M		England	United States	Cosmo	21 Aug 1828
Mary	6	F		Gt. Britain		Corinthian	27 Oct 1829
Mary	32	F		England	United States	Cosmo	21 Aug 1828
Nathan	64	M	Agriculturist	United States	United States	Four Sons	31 May 1828
Patrick	10	M		Ireland	U. States	Wilson	2 Sep 1823
Sarah	6	M		England	United States	Cosmo	21 Aug 1828
Sophia	24	F		G. Brittain	U. States	Cincinnatus	2 Oct 1822
Stephen	25	M		G. Brittain	U. States	Cincinnatus	2 Oct 1822
Susan	10	F		England	United States	Cosmo	21 Aug 1828
Thomas	1	M	Child	Ireland	United States	Josephine	30 Apr 1828
Thomas	26	M	Laborer	Ireland	America	Parrington	9 Jun 1827
Thos. R.	32	M	Planter	New York	U. States	Catharine	12 Nov 1821
William	12	M	Farmer	England	U. States	Robert Edwards	9 May 1827
William	27	M	Labourer	Ireland	N. York	Trusty	12 Sep 1828
FORDE, A.	35	M	Doctor	Spain	U. States	Thankfull Winslow	23 Aug 1826
FORDGE, Juna	32	F	None	Great Britain	United States	James Monroe	5 Apr 1820
Sampson	25	M	Collier	Great Britain	United States	James Monroe	5 Apr 1820
Solomon	27	M	Collier	Great Britain	United States	James Monroe	5 Apr 1820
FORDHAM, Elizabeth	24	F		England	United States	Cincinnatus	21 Nov 1821
Joseph	22	M	Miller	England	United States	Cincinnatus	21 Nov 1821
FORE, John	30	M	Miner	England	England	Eliza	31 Jul 1826
FOREHALL, Catharine	40	F	None	Gt. Britain	U. States	Panthia	13 Nov 1824
FORENAN, Etiene	43	M	Gent.	France	United States	Henri IV	14 Oct 1829
FOREST, —, child of							
Mrs. Forest [Forrest]	4	F		Guadaloupe	U. States	Turner	8 Jun 1824
Alfred D., Mr.	34		Merchant	United States	U. States	South Carolina Packet	30 May 1825
F.	38	M	U.S. Navy	U. States	U. States	Brown	29 Apr 1825
Fanny	14	F		American	U. States	John London	1 Sep 1823
G.	60	M	Labourer	American	U. States	John London	1 Sep 1823
James	50	M	Gentleman	U. States	U. States	Superb	9 Jul 1821
John	26	M	Laborer	Ireland	United States	St. Michaels	23 Dec 1826
FORESTEN, Janet	70	F		Great Britain	New York	Intrepid	8 Aug 1822
William	30	M	Labourer	Great Britain	New York	Intrepid	8 Aug 1822
FORESTT, Edmond	25	M	Labourer	Ireland	U. States	Combine	30 Nov 1825
FORESYTH, Thomas	20	M	Plasterer		New York	Governor Clinton	3 Jul 1827
FORGARTY, Richard	23	M	Labourer	Ireland	America	Plutarch	18 Jul 1826
FORGATY, John	23	M	Labourer	Ireland	U. States	Combine	30 Nov 1825
FORGE, A.	35	M	B...	France	America	La Grange	7 Aug 1828
FORGERSON, Elisebeth	38	F		Irland	United States	Nancy	28 Oct 1822
James	8	M	Labor	Irland	United States	Nancy	28 Oct 1822
Karther	40	M	Laborer	Irland	United States	Nancy	28 Oct 1822
Letis	10	F		Irland	United States	Nancy	28 Oct 1822
Martha	60	F	Servant	Ireland	America	Carolina Ann	7 Aug 1826
Richard	35	M	White Smith	Ireland	America	Carolina Ann	7 Aug 1826
FORGESON, John	15	M	Laborer, Spinster or Child	Ireland	United States	Ann Maria	4 Aug 1827
FORGO, Christiaan	37	M	Boer	Hechgen	United States	Juffraw Johanna	16 Oct 1821
FORGUSON, Isabella	22	F	Spinster	Scotland	America	Camillus	12 Sep 1822
FORIANO, Joaquim	30	M	...	Spain	Spain	Queen Mab	26 Nov 1825
FORIOSO, Janett	30	F	Theatrical Performer or Play Actor	France	U.S. America	Sicily	7 Oct 1829
Marie	26	F	Theatrical Performer or Play Actor	France	U.S. America	Sicily	7 Oct 1829
Rosalie	18	F	Theatrical Performer or Play Actor	France	U.S. America	Sicily	7 Oct 1829
FORITUNE, Michael	24	M	Artist	Italy	U. States	Eliza	24 Aug 1825
FORLEY, Catharine	3	F	Agriculturist	France	U.S.	Helen	3 May 1828
Catharine	31	F	Agriculturist	France	U.S.	Helen	3 May 1828
Jean	27	M	Agriculturist	France	U.S.	Helen	3 May 1828
Margaret	3/12	F	Agriculturist	France	U.S.	Helen	3 May 1828
FORMAN, Abijah	28	F		U. States	U. States	Robt. Reade	4 Apr 1825
Jane	24	F		United States	U. States	General Pulman	3 Jun 1828
John	21	M	Farmer	Great Britain	United States	Washington	9 Apr 1821
FORME, Alever	21	M	Watch Maker	Germany	U. States	Rook	25 Jul 1827
FORMOSIA, Peter	24	M	None	Great Britain		Casanda	5 Sep 1827

NAMES OF PASSENGERS	AGE	SEX	OCCUPATIONS	COUNTRY TO WHICH THEY BELONG	COUNTRY THEY INTEND TO INHABIT	SHIPS/DATES OF ARRIVAL	
FORMULA, Sarah	21	F		England	United States	Cosmo	26 Aug 1829
FORNADE, —, Md.	32	F	Shop Keeper	U. States	U. States	Imperial	10 Dec 1821
FORO, Frs., Dn.	35	M	Merchant	Mexico	for London	Alexander	6 May 1824
FORRACT, James	19	M	Glass Cutter	Scotland	U. States	Camillus	17 Sep 1823
FORRER, Francis S.	2	M		France		Pallas	14 Jun 1828
Jean C.	30	F	Baker	France		Pallas	14 Jun 1828
Rose S.	27	F		France		Pallas	14 Jun 1828
FORREST, —, Mrs.	35	F	Lady	Guadaloupe	U. States	Turner	8 Jun 1824
Betty	22	M	None	Cork	Cork	Howard Douglass	11 May 1827
Bridget	22	F	Farmer	Gt. Britain	U. States	Superior	20 Aug 1825
Catha.	1	F	Farmer	Gt. Britain	U. States	Superior	20 Aug 1825
James	20	M	Labourer	Cork	Cork	Howard Douglass	11 May 1827
James	47	M	Labourer	Cork	Cork	Howard Douglass	11 May 1827
Jas.	25	M	Farmer	Gt. Britain	U. States	Superior	20 Aug 1825
L.	25	M	unknown	U. States	U. States	Mary	7 Nov 1822
R., Revd.	29			United States	U. States	New York	30 Oct 1827
Thos.	30	M	Preacher	G. Britain	N. York	Aurora	21 Dec 1820
Thos. F.	20	M	Merchant	Gt. Brittain	United States	York	6 Dec 1826
FORRESTAL,							
Richard	26 3/12	M	Labourer	Ireland	New York, U. States	Combine	1 Aug 1825
Walter	22	M	Labourer	Ireland	U. States	Combine	30 Nov 1825
FORRESTER, Caroline	1	F			United States	William	5 Oct 1822
Elenor	4	F			United States	William	5 Oct 1822
Hamah	31	F	Spinster	Ireland	United States	William	5 Oct 1822
Jas.	26	M	Merchant	Scotland	U. States	Flight	9 Jul 1825
John	25	M	Labourer	Scotland	United States	Samuel Robertson	9 May 1827
John	27	M		Great Britain	United States	Active	25 Mar 1828
Lucy	6	F			United States	William	5 Oct 1822
Robt.	20	M	Labourer	Scotland	United States	Tom	2 Jul 1827
Sally	14	F			United States	William	5 Oct 1822
Susan	7	F			United States	William	5 Oct 1822
Willm. R.	31		Tobacconist	England	United States	Rufus King	4 Sep 1823
FORRINGTON, James	47	M	Merchant	U. States	U. States	Virginia	3 Dec 1827
FORRISON, Margaret	39	M	Merchant	Wales	England	Germania	15 Jun 1825
Wm.	45	M	Merchant	Wales	England	Germania	15 Jun 1825
FORRISTER, Augustus	34	M	Merchant	France	U. States	Columbia	9 Aug 1822
Peter	74	M	Physician	U. States	U. States	Marmion	7 Jun 1824
FORRODE, John	10	M	Farmer	Germany	U. States	Bayard	16 May 1827
FORS, Juan	22	M	Merchant	Spain	Cuba	Isis	17 Nov 1828
Juan	27	M	Mercht.	Spain	Spain	Angelina	28 May 1827
FORSE, Ann	21	F	Farmer	Canada	Canada	Edwin	1 Jul 1829
Catherina	18	F	Farmer	Canada	Canada	Edwin	1 Jul 1829
George	10	M	Farmer	Canada	Canada	Edwin	1 Jul 1829
Hannah	16	F	Farmer	Canada	Canada	Edwin	1 Jul 1829
John	14	M	Farmer	Canada	Canada	Edwin	1 Jul 1829
Peter	68	M	Farmer	Canada	Canada	Edwin	1 Jul 1829
Rohdy	64	F	Farmer	Canada	Canada	Edwin	1 Jul 1829
FORSETT, Thomas	23		Gentleman	England	England	Hudson	14 Jun 1827
FORSTAL, Felix S.	27	M	Merch.	U. States	United States	Henri IV	14 Oct 1829
FORSTALE, Edmund J.	26	M	Merchant	U. States	New Orleans	James Monroe	23 Aug 1822
FORSTER, George	30	M	Sadler	England	New York	Robert Edwards	17 Mar 1828
Joseph	30	M	Mercht.	Switzerland	United States	Columbia	16 Jan 1829
Josiah	34	M	Gentn.	England	St. Croix	Stephania	16 Aug 1827
Robert, Mr.	40	M	Gentn.	England	England	Acasta	21 Oct 1825
FORSTICK, Mary Ann	30			England	United States	Hudson	14 Jun 1827
FORSTING, Andris H.	6 3/12	M		Holland	America	Martha	16 Mar 1829
Derick H.	9/12	M		Holland	America	Martha	16 Mar 1829
Johan H.	4 6/12	M		Holland	America	Martha	16 Mar 1829
Johan Hendrik	33 10/12	M	Tanner	Holland	America	Martha	16 Mar 1829
Johana	28	F	Servant	Netherlands	U. States	Edward Quesnel	17 Mar 1829
FORSYTH, Catharine	15	F		Ireland	U. States	Nancy	16 Aug 1822
Clara	12	F		U. States	U. States	Othello	3 Jun 1823
Ebenezer	30	M	Farmer	U.S.	America	Pacific	13 Jan 1827
H. G.	23		Merchant	Aberdeen	Great Britain	William Thompson	13 May 1823

NAMES OF PASSENGERS	AGE	SEX	OCCUPATIONS	COUNTRY TO WHICH THEY BELONG	COUNTRY THEY INTEND TO INHABIT	SHIPS/DATES OF ARRIVAL	
FORSYTH (cont'd)							
Henry	16	M		Ireland	U. States	Nancy	16 Aug 1822
Henry K.	26	M	Merchant	Great Britain	United States	Grecian	24 Sep 1828
J. B.	23	M	Merchant	Great Britain	Great Britain	John Jay	8 May 1828
James	20	M		Ireland	U. States	Nancy	10 Jul 1822
James	20	M		Ireland	U. States	Nancy	16 Aug 1822
James	22	M		England	England	Amity	31 May 1822
John	4	M		U. States	U. States	Othello	3 Jun 1823
John	17	M		England	England	Amity	31 May 1822
John	22	M		Ireland	U. States	Nancy	10 Jul 1822
John	45	M	Merchant	Ireland	U. States	Nancy	10 Jul 1822
John	46	M	Envoy from U.S. to Spain	U. States	U. States	Othello	3 Jun 1823
John	55	M		England	England	Amity	31 May 1822
Julia	16	F		U. States	U. States	Othello	3 Jun 1823
Martha	12	F		Ireland	U. States	Nancy	16 Aug 1822
Mary	14	F		U. States	U. States	Othello	3 Jun 1823
Mary	18	F		Ireland	U. States	Nancy	16 Aug 1822
Mary	35	F		U. States	U. States	Othello	3 Jun 1823
Rachael	43	F		Ireland	U. States	Nancy	10 Jul 1822
Robert [crossed out]	23	M	Seaman	United States	United States	Leonidas	3 Aug 1825
Robt.	34	M	Carpenter	Amer.	Ama.	Expedition	19 May 1828
Samuel	47	M	Carver & Gilder	Great Britain	United States	Robert Fulton	27 Jun 1822
Virginia	7	F		U. States	U. States	Othello	3 Jun 1823
Wm.	15	M		England	England	Amity	31 May 1822
FORSYTHE, Elizth.	25		Spinster	Ireland	United States	Courier	15 Oct 1827
Robert	28		Weaver	Ireland	United States	Courier	15 Oct 1827
FORT, Harriet	20	F	his Wife	England	United States	Delta	24 Oct 1829
Henry	6/12	M		England	United States	Delta	24 Oct 1829
William	22	M	Joiner	England	United States	Delta	24 Oct 1829
FORTEN, John	28	M	Clerk	England	America	Leeds	2 Aug 1828
FORTER, —	30	F	None	Newcastle	United States	James & Margaret	30 May 1825
J.	30	M	Bookbinder	Newcastle	United States	James & Margaret	30 May 1825
Jane	5	F				James & Margaret	30 May 1825
Robert	2	M				James & Margaret	30 May 1825
FORTH, Ann M., Mrs. & Child	23	F		Bermuda		Lancatter	5 Jul 1820
Hezekiah	55	M	Merchant	Bermuda		Lancatter	5 Jul 1820
Hezekiah, Junr.	28	M	Merchant	Bermuda		Lancatter	5 Jul 1820
John	4	M		Great Britain	United States	Freake	25 Aug 1829
John	32	M	Farmer	Great Britain	United States	Freake	25 Aug 1829
Joseph	6	M		Great Britain	United States	Freake	25 Aug 1829
Mary	37	F		Great Britain	United States	Freake	25 Aug 1829
Richard	9/12	M		Great Britain	United States	Freake	25 Aug 1829
Sarah	11	F		Great Britain	United States	Freake	25 Aug 1829
FORTIN, John F.	25	M	Gentleman	U. States	U. States	Vigilant	25 Nov 1822
Wm.	20	M	Gentleman	U. States	U. States	Vigilant	25 Nov 1822
FORTSON, Joseph	45	M	France	France	U. States	Edward Bonaffe	23 Jul 1828
Maryan	44	F	France	France	U. States	Edward Bonaffe	23 Jul 1828
FORTUNATAS, Angelo, dos.	24	M	Merchant	Portugeese	United States	Mary Elizabeth	15 Oct 1829
FORTUNATE, Amelia, his wife	30 4/12	F	Bonet maker	Braband	New York	Dawn	12 Jun 1826
Joseph	36 2/12	M	Merchant	Holland	New York	Dawn	12 Jun 1826
FORTUNE, James	28	M	Farmer	Ireland	United States	Aurelia	7 Jun 1826
FORTURE, James	10	M	Servant to Mr. Hearny	Ireland	United States	Rufus King	27 Jun 1821
FORY, Thos.	23	M	Farmer	England	United States	Danube	22 Aug 1825
FOSETT, Ann	22	F	None	Ireland	United States	Jubilee	13 Jul 1829
FOSLAY, Chals. Augs.	46	M	Mecanick	Germany	America	William Thompson	18 Jan 1825
FOSONE, Joseph A.	26	M	Mechanic	Italy	United States	Eliza Jane	14 Sep 1826
FOSS, Elizabeth	1 6/12	F	None	Great Britain	United States	Richmond	18 Feb 1820
Ellen	4	F	None	Great Britain	United States	Richmond	18 Feb 1820
John	7	M	None	Great Britain	United States	Richmond	18 Feb 1820

NAMES OF PASSENGERS	AGE	SEX	OCCUPATIONS	COUNTRY TO WHICH THEY BELONG	COUNTRY THEY INTEND TO INHABIT	SHIPS/DATES OF ARRIVAL	
FOSS (cont'd)							
Lydia	34	F	None	Great Britain	United States	Richmond	18 Feb 1820
Robert	34	M	Butcher	Great Britain	United States	Richmond	18 Feb 1820
Sarah	3	F	None	Great Britain	United States	Richmond	18 Feb 1820
FOSSET, William	24	M	Mechanic	Great Britain	United States	Hannibal	12 Oct 1829
FOSSETT, James	21	M	Perfumer	England	New York	Hudson	20 Nov 1828
John	19	M	Perfumer	England	New York	Hudson	20 Nov 1828
FOSTER, —, Miss	7	F	None	United States	United States	Stephania	3 Oct 1822
—, Miss	20	F	None	United States	United States	Stephania	3 Oct 1822
—, Mr.	16	M	Merchant	England	U. States	Robert Edwards	11 Mar 1822
—, Mr.	24	M	Merchant	U. States	Havana	Robert Fulton	22 May 1824
—, Mrs.	45	F	None	United States	United States	Stephania	3 Oct 1822
A., Jr.	22	M	Merchant	N. York	U. States	Frances	16 Aug 1822
Andrew	52	M	Merchant	United States	United States	Corinthian	10 Jan 1826
Andrew, Jr.	27	M	Merchant	United States	New York	Britannia	3 Nov 1827
Andrew, Junr.	24	M	Merchant	U. States	U. States	Canada	4 Oct 1824
Andw., Jr.	28	M	Merchant	United States	United States	Britannia	29 Oct 1829
Ann N...n...	15	F		Great Britian	United States	London	24 Jun 1823
Arthur	6	M	Farmer	Great Britian	United States	Andes	19 Aug 1829
Benjamin	24	M	Tailor	St. Johns	St. Johns	Ann Maria	7 Sep 1827
Benjamin	30	M		Great Britain	New York	Philetus	21 Jul 1827
C.	19	M	Clerk	Ireland	U. States	Alex Mansfield	1 Jun 1822
C.	28	M	Shoe Maker	America	America	Hiram	2 Apr 1828
C. C.	39	M	Merchant	U. States	U. States	Canada	2 Jun 1824
Charles	10	M	Farmer	Great Britian	United States	Andes	19 Aug 1829
Charles	12	M	Boy	...	United States	Erin	25 Dec 1820
Claudine	26	M	Gent.	England	U.S. America	Columbia	31 Jul 1826
E.	35	M	Cabinet Maker	U. States	U. States	Rising States	23 Nov 1825
Eliza	18	F	Spinster	...	United States	Erin	25 Dec 1820
Eliza	25	F	None	America	United States	Exchange	5 Oct 1829
Elizabeth	23		Female			Mount Vernon	26 Aug 1820
Elizabeth	50	F	Farmer	Great Britian	United States	Andes	19 Aug 1829
G. B.	23		...	...	...	Alert	12 Oct 1824
George	13	M	Labourer	Ireland	America	Wilson	16 May 1825
George	24	M	Doctor	U. States	U. States	Betsey	6 May 1826
George	25		Honble. Company & Service	England	England	Hudson	4 Sep 1823
H. A.	19	M	None	Lincolnshire		Hannibal	28 Jul 1823
Henry	16/365					Mount Vernon	26 Aug 1820
Hugh	1	M		Ireland	United States	Meteor	27 Sep 1826
Isabella	18	F	Spinster	Ireland	America	Wilson	16 May 1825
J.	36	M	Shipmaster	U. States	U. States	Olive Branch	20 Mar 1824
Jacob	35		Mercht.	U. States		Columbia	7 May 1828
James	14	M	Farmer	Great Britian	United States	Andes	19 Aug 1829
James	36	M	School Master	Ireland	United States	Meteor	27 Sep 1826
Jas.	38		Taylor	Sh...ham/ She...ham	New York	Venus	12 Apr 1821
Jno. F.	31 1/12	M	Merchant	Virginia, Richmond	Virginia, Richmond	Florida	13 Jan 1827
Johanna	48	F		Saxony	United States	Wade	29 Aug 1825
John	9	M		Ireland	United States	Meteor	27 Sep 1826
John	20	M	Farmer	Great Britain	America	Lady Gallatin	21 Jun 1820
John	20	M	Black Smith	Ireland	United States	Josephine	30 Apr 1828
John	22	M	...			Importer	30 Oct 1820
John	26	M	Farmer	England	United States	Panthia	7 Feb 1822
John	29	M	Mariner	United States	United States	Mary Ann	7 Jan 1829
John	36		Butcher			Mount Vernon	26 Aug 1820
Joseph	23	M	Cloth Dresser	Great Britain	United States	Dapper	21 Aug 1828
Joseph	26	M	Gentleman	London		South Carolina Packet	16 Sep 1820
Joseph	50	M	Farmer	Great Britian	United States	Andes	19 Aug 1829
Josiah	34		Planter	St. Croix	St. Croix	Emelia	26 Jun 1828
Margaret	22	F	Lady	St. John, N.B.	St. John, N.B.	St. Michaels	18 Jul 1824
Mary	7	F		Ireland	United States	Meteor	27 Sep 1826
Mary	8	F	Farmer	Great Britian	United States	Andes	19 Aug 1829
Mary	39	F	Labourer	Ireland	U.S.A.	Dalhouse Castle	21 Aug 1829
Mary	39	F	Labourer	Ireland	United States	Dalhouse Castle	21 Aug 1829
N.	40	M	Painter	U. States	U. States	Rising States	12 May 1827
Paul	3	M		Ireland	United States	Meteor	27 Sep 1826

NAMES OF PASSENGERS	AGE	SEX	OCCUPATIONS	COUNTRY TO WHICH THEY BELONG	COUNTRY THEY INTEND TO INHABIT	SHIPS/DATES OF ARRIVAL	
FOSTER (cont'd)							
Rachael	34	F	Wife	Ireland	United States	Meteor	27 Sep 1826
Sarah	24	F		U. States	U. States	Betsey	6 May 1826
Selden	28	M	Mariner	America	U. States	Harmony	6 Jan 1823
Thomas	16	M	Farmer	Great Britian	United States	Andes	19 Aug 1829
Thomas	25		Farmer	England	America	Sarah	18 Aug 1829
Thomas	28	M	Iron Roller	Gt. Britain	U.S. America	James Cropper	14 Mar 1828
Thos.	32	M	Accountant	Great Britain	United States	Nimrod	5 Apr 1821
Thos.	37	M	Merchant	St. Croix	U. States	Carlo	6 Oct 1827
William	6	M		Ireland	United States	Meteor	27 Sep 1826
William	20	M	Farmer, Labourer or Spinster	Ireland	U. States	Meteor	4 Oct 1827
William	26 2/12	M	pudler		uncertain	Mount Vernon	29 Aug 1828
Wm.	28	M	Mercht.	Great Britian	United States	Columbia	21 Jan 1828
FOTHERGALLE, Robt.	24	M		England	U. States	Birmingham	16 Jun 1828
FOTHERINGHAM,							
Elizabeth	19	F	wife & family of James Fotheringham	Great Britain		Panthea	15 Jun 1822
James	17	M	wife & family of James Fotheringham	Great Britain		Panthea	15 Jun 1822
James	46	M	Mason	Great Britain		Panthea	15 Jun 1822
Jannett	40	F	wife & family of James Fotheringham	Great Britain		Panthea	15 Jun 1822
Margaret	12	F	wife & family of James Fotheringham	Great Britain		Panthea	15 Jun 1822
Robert	10	M	wife & family of James Fotheringham	Great Britain		Panthea	15 Jun 1822
FOTHERSTON, Aen	10	F	Labourer	Ireland	United States	Essex	23 May 1828
FOTTERALL, L. G.	29	M	Mercht.	U.S.	N. York	George Canning	2 May 1828
Stephen G.	28	M	Merchant	U. States	U. States	New York	13 Mar 1824
FOUAR, A.	20	M	Merchant	France	France	Howard	27 Sep 1826
FOUCARD, John A.	4...	M	Merchant	U. States	U. States	Edward Quesnel	16 Nov 1827
FOUCHER, —, Madam	45	F		Louisiana	Louisania	Cadmus	16 Aug 1826
Louis, Mr.	60	M	Gentn.	Louisiana	Louisania	Cadmus	16 Aug 1826
FOUGERES, Louis	28 8/12	M	Merchant	France	America	Otho	2 Jan 1822
FOULE, Adam	...	M	...	...	...	George	23 Sep 1824
Ann Maria	9	F	...	...	...	George	23 Sep 1824
Elizabeth	19	F	...	...	...	George	23 Sep 1824
Margaret	1	F	...	...	...	George	23 Sep 1824
Margaret, (Wife)	40	F	...	...	...	George	23 Sep 1824
Ottelia	5	F	...	...	...	George	23 Sep 1824
Philip	...	M	...	...	...	George	23 Sep 1824
FOULER, Wm.	26	M		U. States	United States	Exchange	18 Nov 1824
FOULIS, Als.	24	M	Laborer	Ireland	United States	Belleville	13 Oct 1827
FOULK, Gebhard	40	M	...	...	...	George	23 Sep 1824
FOULKE, —, Mrs.	30	F		U. States	U. States	Douglass	27 Apr 1824
Charlote	40	F	None	United States	United States	General Paez	28 May 1828
Jno. B.	21	M	Merchant	America	U. States	Abeona	17 May 1825
Jos.	45	M	Merchant	U. States	U. States	Douglass	27 Apr 1824
Joseph	48	M	Merchant	United States	United States	General Paez	28 May 1828
FOULKNER, Eliza	12			Dublin		Mount Vernon	18 Oct 1822
Jane	9			Dublin		Mount Vernon	18 Oct 1822
John	6			Dublin		Mount Vernon	18 Oct 1822
Sarah	42			Dublin		Mount Vernon	18 Oct 1822
FOUNTAIN, Betsey	24	F	None	Halifax	U. States	Hunter	2 Jul 1824
Peter	33	M	Confectioner		Pittsburge	Hunter	25 May 1824
FOUNTOWN, Elizabeth	30	F	Lady	New Haven	New Haven	Hope & Esther	9 Jun 1827
FOURCHET, John	26	M	Servt.	France	U. States	Henri IV	7 May 1827
FOURE, L. D., Madam						Dromo	14 Aug 1829
FOURNEL, G.	31		Merchant	France		Edward Bonnaffe	17 Mar 1828
FOURNIER, Fred.	29	M	Weaver	France	United States	Montano	5 May 1828
FOWERK, Jennett	24	F	Servant	Great Britain	U. States	Columbia	22 Sep 1828
FOWHEY, Catherine	26	F	Spinster	Ireland	America	William	21 May 1825

NAMES OF PASSENGERS	AGE	SEX	OCCUPATIONS	COUNTRY TO WHICH THEY BELONG	COUNTRY THEY INTEND TO INHABIT	SHIPS/DATES OF ARRIVAL	
FOWHEY (cont'd)							
Ellen	1 9/12	F		Ireland	America	William	21 May 1825
James	24	M	Farmer	Ireland	America	William	21 May 1825
Margret	18	F	Spinster	Ireland	America	William	21 May 1825
FOWKS, Abraham	13	M		Great Britain	United States	Mary Howland	19 Jul 1827
Elisabeth	2	F		Great Britain	United States	Mary Howland	19 Jul 1827
Francis	28	F		Great Britain	United States	Mary Howland	19 Jul 1827
Lasarus	1	M		Great Britain	United States	Mary Howland	19 Jul 1827
Philip	4	M		Great Britain	United States	Mary Howland	19 Jul 1827
Rachel	6	F		Great Britain	United States	Mary Howland	19 Jul 1827
Thomas	9	M		Great Britain	United States	Mary Howland	19 Jul 1827
Thomas	20	M	Farmer	Great Britain	United States	Mary Howland	19 Jul 1827
FOWL, Ed.	23	M	S... C...	Italy	U. States	Edward Bonnaffe	12 Oct 1826
FOWLDS, Henry	31		Merchant	Scotland	England	Elizabeth	8 Dec 1821
James	3		None	Scotland	England	Elizabeth	8 Dec 1821
Jane	30		None	Scotland	England	Elizabeth	8 Dec 1821
FOWLE, H.	27	M	Merchant	New York	New York	Gertrude	6 Mar 1827
John	25	M	Mercht.	Bermuda	Bermuda	Andromache	29 May 1821
John	25	M	Merchant	U. States	U. States	Arthenian	28 Apr 1827
John	35	M	Officer U.S.	U.S.	U.S.	Edward Quesnel	17 Jan 1825
Robt.	22	M	Joiner	England	U. States	Alexander Mansfield	9 Jul 1827
Theophilus	46	M	Labourer	England	United States	Jubilee	12 May 1828
FOWLER, ...	23	M	Gentleman	U. States	U. States	Liberty	23 Feb 1820
Benjamin	43	M	Merchant	U. States	U. States	Betsey	1 Apr 1824
Benjn.	24	M	Merchant	England	U. States	Milton	16 Jun 1823
David	32	M	Labourer	Ireland	U. States	St. Michaels	25 Apr 1825
Elizabeth	21 4/12	F	Farmer	England	United States	Young Phoenix	26 Jul 1824
G. W.	34	M	Shoemaker	New York	New York	New Packet	15 Nov 1828
George	8		None			Emulous	19 Feb 1822
Gilbert	40 2/12	M	Master	United States	United States	Hector	8 Jan 1820
H. W.	35	M	Gentleman	United States	United States	Enterprize	9 Aug 1825
Henry	11		None			Emulous	19 Feb 1822
Henry	14		None			Emulous	19 Feb 1822
Isabella	30	F	None	Scotland	United States	Mary & Susan	5 Aug 1828
J.	28	M	Merchant	American	U. States	Peter Francisco	7 Jun 1822
J. D.	22	M	Gent.	U.S.	U.S.	Trimmer	28 Nov 1826
J. S.	35	M	Merchant	America	U. States	Gen. A. Jackson	10 Sep 1821
Jacob D.	20	M	Merchant	U. States	U. States	Zephyr	2 Oct 1826
James	24	M	Farmer, Labourer or Spinster	Ireland	U. States	Meteor	4 Oct 1827
James	35	M	Officer	England	U. States	Hiram	17 Jun 1826
Jane	18	F	Lady	New York	United States	St. Michael	24 Jan 1824
Jane	36	F		Ireland	U. States	Xenophon	13 Jun 1823
John	6		None			Emulous	19 Feb 1822
John	20	M	Labourer	England	U. States	Hope & Esther	10 Jul 1827
John	30	M	Schoolmaster	United States	United States	St. Michaels	23 Dec 1826
John, Consul's Man			Seaman			Athenian	1 Dec 1827
Joseph	24	M	Merchant	England	U. States	Atlantic	26 Aug 1820
Lydia	4		None			Emulous	19 Feb 1822
Maria	15	F	None	England	America	Hannibal	4 Oct 1822
Mary	14		None			Emulous	19 Feb 1822
Mary	35		None			Emulous	19 Feb 1822
Patrick	27	M	Weaver	Ireland	Ireland	Sarah G.	28 Nov 1827
Simon	38	M	Farmer			Emulous	19 Feb 1822
Thomas	27	M	Farmer	England	America	Comet	26 Jun 1822
Thomas F.	38	M	Gent.	Great Britten	United States	Cortes	6 Mar 1827
William	9		None			Emulous	19 Feb 1822
Wm.	27 3/12	M	Farmer	England	United States	Young Phoenix	26 Jul 1824
Wm.	43	M	Farmer	Great Brittan	U. States	John & Elizabeth	11 Dec 1826
Wm. W.	27	M	Merchant	U.States	U. States	Willmot	21 Jul 1820
Z.	22	M	Gentm.	St. Johns, N.B.	U. States	Lady Hunter	12 Apr 1823
FOWRER, John	28	M	Farmer	Switzerland	U. States	Sully	15 Jul 1829
FOX, ...	16	F	Manufacturer			Manhattan	25 Dec 1828
Anna	8	F	his family [Joseph]	Germany	Cincanatti	Isabella	15 Sep 1828
Anna	41	F	his family [Joseph]	Germany	Cincanatti	Isabella	15 Sep 1828
Barbe	7	F	his family [Joseph]	Germany	Cincanatti	Isabella	15 Sep 1828
Biddy	13	F		Ireland	America	Mary	29 May 1827

NAMES OF PASSENGERS	AGE	SEX	OCCUPATIONS	COUNTRY TO WHICH THEY BELONG	COUNTRY THEY INTEND TO INHABIT	SHIPS/DATES OF ARRIVAL	
FOX (cont'd)							
Brian	26	M	Farmer	Ireland	United States	Lord Strangford	20 Jun 1826
Catherine	14	F	his family [Joseph]	Germany	Cincanatti	Isabella	15 Sep 1828
Charles	25	M	Comb Maker		U. States	Cowper	8 Jan 1827
Daniel	30	M	Farmer	Ireland	U.S.A.	Dalhouse Castle	21 Aug 1829
Daniel	30	M	Farmer	Ireland	United States	Dalhouse Castle	21 Aug 1829
Daniel	36	M	Labourer	Great Brittain	New York	Albion	11 Jun 1821
Edward	35	M	Labourer	Antrim, Ireland	Pennsylvania	Anthusa	24 Aug 1825
Elizabeth, Mrs.	25	F	Lady	United States	United States	Florida	22 May 1826
Geo. S.	26		Merchant	New York	United States	William Thompson	13 May 1823
George	35	M	Comb Maker	England	U. States	Cowper	8 Jan 1827
Gorick	2	M	his family [Joseph]	Germany	Cincanatti	Isabella	15 Sep 1828
Henry	34	M	Mechanic	Scotland	United States	Concordia	25 Aug 1827
Highram	26	M	Cooper	United States	U.S. States	Thrasher	4 Dec 1822
Ignatius	4	M	his family [Joseph]	Germany	Cincanatti	Isabella	15 Sep 1828
J.	39	M	Farmer	U. States	U. States	Great Britain	6 Sep 1828
James	25	M	Merchant	England	United States	Martha	17 Sep 1821
James	26	M	Farmer	Ireland	Pennsylvania	Curler	7 Jul 1827
James	32	M	Merchant	England	England	Pacific	17 Jun 1828
James, Mr.	29	M	Merchant	England	United States	Florida	22 May 1826
Jas.	25	M	Merchant		United States	Columbia	11 Apr 1822
John	22		Labourer	Great Britan	United States	Newry	11 Jul 1827
John	30	M	Weaver	Ireland	United States	Baltic	21 Apr 1827
John	41	M	Weaver	England	United States	Robert Edwards	3 Oct 1829
Joseph	11	M	his family [Joseph]	Germany	Cincanatti	Isabella	15 Sep 1828
Joseph C.	43	M	Shoemaker	Germany	Cincanatti	Isabella	15 Sep 1828
Joseph Gott.	22	M	Joiner	Yorkshire		Ocean	13 Jul 1827
Louisa	19	F	his family [Joseph]	Germany	Cincanatti	Isabella	15 Sep 1828
Lucretia	22	F	None	United States	U. States	Planter	1 Mar 1822
Mannard	9	M	his family [Joseph]	Germany	Cincanatti	Isabella	15 Sep 1828
Mary	17	F	Spinster	Ireland	United States	Wilson	6 Jun 1828
Mary	25	F	None	Great Britain	United States	Magnet	19 Aug 1822
Mary	29	F		England	Canada	Acasta	14 Jun 1824
Rebecca	18	F	None	Great Britain	United States	Magnet	19 Aug 1822
Richard	36	M	Clerk	Ireland	United States	Dublin Packet	6 Dec 1827
Sam	35	M	Merchant	U. States	U. States	Exchange	29 Apr 1822
Saml.	40	M	Labourer	England	United States	Nestor	25 Jul 1823
Solomon	26	M	Cooper	United States	U.S. States	Thrasher	4 Dec 1822
Thomas	21	M	Mason	England	Upper Canada	Lima	5 Aug 1829
Thomas	21	M		England	Upper Canada	Lima	5 Aug 1829
Thomas	25	M	Servant	Ireland	America	Plutarch	18 Jul 1826
Thomas	26	F	Carpenter	Ireland	U. States	Adno	5 Jul 1828
Walter	3	M	None	Great Britain	United States	Magnet	19 Aug 1822
Warren	25		Mariner	United States		Midas	16 Jun 1827
William	40	M	Labourer	England	U.N. States	Reindeer	20 Aug 1828
Wm.	25		Blacksmith	Great Britan	United States	Newry	11 Jul 1827
Wm.	59	M	Carpenter	Great Britain	United States	Diana	6 Jul 1829
FOXHALL, James	28	M	Shoemaker	Ireland	U. States	Josephine	27 Jul 1825
FOXY, Margt.	14 9/12	F	Spinstress	Ireland	U. States	Fabius	22 Sep 1828
Sarah	13 5/12	F		Ireland	U. States	Fabius	22 Sep 1828
FOY, Anthony	25	M	Servant	Ireland	United States	Sylvester Healy	19 Aug 1825
Betsey	25	F		Ireland	U. States	Nancy	29 Nov 1821
Bridget	30	F	Farmer	Ireland	U. States	Sabina	29 Apr 1825
James	27		Farmer	Ireland		Westmoreland	1 Aug 1826
Jera.	8	F		Ireland	U. States	Nancy	29 Nov 1821
John	22	M	Labourer	Ireland	United States	Nile	17 May 1827
John	28	M	Mechanic	English	United States	Ann	11 Sep 1827
Mary	9	F	Farmer	Ireland	U. States	Sabina	29 Apr 1825
Michol	28	M	Stone Cutter	Ireland	U. States	Courier	17 Mar 1828
Patrick	33	M	Farmer	Ireland	U. States	Sabina	29 Apr 1825
Peter	7	M	Farmer	Ireland	U. States	Sabina	29 Apr 1825
Thos.	11/12	M	Farmer	Ireland	U. States	Sabina	29 Apr 1825
FOYE, Moses	27	M	Mariner	U. States	U. States	Florida	25 Apr 1825
FOYLE, Ann	30	F		Ireland	U. States	Howard Douglass	29 Jan 1828
John	30	M	Weaver	Ireland	U. States	Howard Douglass	29 Jan 1828
Joshua	25		Merchant	Belfast	Ireland	Carolina Ann	21 May 1823

NAMES OF PASSENGERS	A G E	S E X	OCCUPATIONS	COUNTRY TO WHICH THEY BELONG	COUNTRY THEY INTEND TO INHABIT	SHIPS/DATES OF ARRIVAL	
FOYLES, John	20	M	Farmer	Ireland	U. States	Howard Douglass	29 Jan 1828
Louisa	23	F		Ireland	U. States	Howard Douglass	29 Jan 1828
Sam.	27	M	Farmer	Ireland	U. States	Howard Douglass	29 Jan 1828
Thomas	2	M		Ireland	U. States	Howard Douglass	29 Jan 1828
FR...ARIC, Joaquin	21	M	Mercht.	Spain	U. States	Brown	7 Jul 1826
FRAAS, Hanicke	18 10/12	M	Sugar baker	Hanover	New York	Thames	16 May 1821
FRADGLEY, Ann, Mrs.	60		Lady	England	United States	Acasta	16 Aug 1826
FRAECHER, Johanna	28	F	Agriculturist	France	U.S.	Helen	3 May 1828
FRAEND, C.	35	M	Royal Navy	England	Different	Tampico	11 Jul 1826
FRAGEN, Matthew	28	M	Labourer	Ireland	United States	Nancy Henrietta	3 Nov 1824
FRAGMAN, Thos.	21	M		Galway	U. States	Eliza Ann	30 Jul 1823
FRAICE, Jane	25	F	None	Great Britain	United States	Colossus	1 Nov 1826
FRAISER, Jno. A.	20	M	Accountant	France	U. States	Brandt	8 Nov 1828
FRAIZARE, Nalbraugh	25	M	...	United States	U. States	Seine	20 Dec 1821
FRALY, Patrick	25	M	Labourer	Ireland	U. States	Combine	30 Nov 1825
FRAM, Elizabeth	9	F	Lady	Berlin	Berlin	Wanderer	4 Aug 1829
Matilda	7	F	Lady	Berlin	Berlin	Wanderer	4 Aug 1829
Mona	46	F	Lady	Berlin	Berlin	Wanderer	4 Aug 1829
FRAME, John	25	M	Baker	Great Britain	United States	Rebecca	20 Mar 1824
Thos.	60	M	Servant	Ireland	United States	Henry Kneeland	7 Jun 1828
FRAMPTON, Maria	2	F		England	U. States	Unity	5 Sep 1828
Sarah	21	F		England	U. States	Unity	5 Sep 1828
William	23	M	None	England	United States	Seine	7 Dec 1821
Wm.	21	M	Brick Layer	England	U. States	Unity	5 Sep 1828
FRAN, Hugh	6	M		Scotland	Gt. Britain	Friends	29 Apr 1822
Margaret	19	F		Scotland	Gt. Britain	Friends	29 Apr 1822
Robert	15	M		Scotland	Gt. Britain	Friends	29 Apr 1822
FRANATTI, John	22	M	Seaman	Greece	U. States	Factor	9 Mar 1829
FRANBÉ, Charlotte	18	F	None	Nassau, N.P.	U. States	Brown	8 Aug 1825
FRANCE, Geo.	30	M	...	Great Brittain	New York	Albion	11 Jun 1821
George	26	M	Farmer	Switzerland	United States	Andes	5 May 1828
James	30	M	Rope Maker	G. Britain	G. Britain	Brittania	17 Jul 1828
FRANCELON, C.	24	M	Merchant	Switzerland	U. States	Mary Jane	29 Dec 1821
FRANCER, —	26	M	Servant	Africa		Calypso	1 Jun 1821
FRANCES, —, Mrs.	19	F	Lady	England	England	Electra	17 Nov 1828
R.	43	M	Merchant	France	U. States	Flight	2 Nov 1825
FRANCHY, Carlos	28	M	Merchant	Spain	U. States	Amphion	24 Aug 1821
FRANCIA, John L.	22	M	Merchant	Gibralter	U. States	Mary Jane	8 Dec 1826
John L.	26	M	Merchant	G. Britain	U. States	La Plata	6 Jun 1828
FRANCINE, J. L.	39	M	Merchant	Spain	U. States	Hippomenes	1 Mar 1823
James L.	36	M	Merchant	France	United States	Don Quixote	7 May 1824
FRANCIS, Ann	6	F		Great Britain	America	Lady Gallatin	21 Jun 1820
Benjamin	21	M	Labourer	Ireland	America	Minerva	31 May 1824
C.	35	M	Mariner	France	Honduras or South America	Alabama	3 Dec 1823
Catherine	30	F		Limerick	N. York	Thomas & William	25 May 1827
Charles	5	M	None	England	U. States	Birmingham	12 Oct 1827
Cherry	29	M	Baker	France	Ohio	Eugenie	20 Aug 1827
Dorothy	4	F		Great Britain	America	Lady Gallatin	21 Jun 1820
Elisha	48	M	Farmer	Ireland	U. States	Orbit	10 mar 1823
Emily	33	F	None	England	U. States	Birmingham	12 Oct 1827
Fos.	2	M		France	Ohio	Eugenie	20 Aug 1827
George	3	M	None	England	U. States	Birmingham	12 Oct 1827
Henry	21	M	Weaver	St. Johns, N.B.	New York	Nancy	26 Nov 1822
Henry	37	M	Tinplate	G.B.	U.S.	Silvanus Jenkins	27 Jul 1829
Isaac	12	M	Boy	Ireland	U. States	Courier	17 Mar 1828
James	3	M		Limerick	N. York	Thomas & William	25 May 1827
James	24		Farmer	England	S. New York	Xenophon	25 Jul 1826
James	30	M	Ship Master	America	America	Commodore Chauncy	19 Jan 1826
Jane	24					Xenophon	25 Jul 1826
Jeremiah	9/12					Xenophon	25 Jul 1826
Jno.	49	M	Merchant	N. York	U. States	Panther	9 Jul 1825

NAMES OF PASSENGERS	AGE	SEX	OCCUPATIONS	COUNTRY TO WHICH THEY BELONG	COUNTRY THEY INTEND TO INHABIT	SHIPS/DATES OF ARRIVAL	
FRANCIS (cont'd)							
John	5					Xenophon	25 Jul 1826
John	21	M	Physician	U. States America	Philadelphia	Ann Maria	29 Nov 1821
John	24	M	Labourer	Ireland	United States	Jubilee	13 Sep 1827
John	25	M	Captain, Officers & crew of the Brig George of New York (wrecked at Fayal)	U.S. America	U.S.A.	Gallego	13 Mar 1829
John	30	M	Laborer	Scotland	United States	Tom	2 Jul 1827
John	54	M	Farmer	Great Britain	America	Lady Gallatin	21 Jun 1820
John, Jr.	13	M		Great Britain	America	Lady Gallatin	21 Jun 1820
Lewis	19	M	Labourer	U. States	U. States	Only Daughter	24 Oct 1827
Mary	9	F		Great Britain	America	Lady Gallatin	21 Jun 1820
Mary	23	F		St. John	Great Britain	General Coffin	9 Mar 1827
Mary	23	F	Tinplate	G.B.	U.S.	Silvanus Jenkins	27 Jul 1829
Mary	25	F		England	U. States	Pacific	5 Sep 1827
Mary	41	F		Great Britain	America	Lady Gallatin	21 Jun 1820
Philip	33	M	Gentleman	England	U. States	Birmingham	12 Oct 1827
Richd.	2	M	None	England	U. States	Birmingham	12 Oct 1827
Rose	25	F		France	Ohio	Eugenie	20 Aug 1827
Susannah	4					Xenophon	25 Jul 1826
Tero	4	M		France	Ohio	Eugenie	20 Aug 1827
Thomas	34	M	Farmer	Great Britain	United States	Elizabeth	10 Apr 1826
Thomas, Mrs.	33	M	Setler	England	New York	Maine	16 Jul 1821
Victor	4	M		France	Ohio	Eugenie	20 Aug 1827
William	22	M	Shoemaker	G. Britain	U. States	Armadello	22 Jun 1827
William	26	M	Labourer	England	U. States	Emulous	22 Aug 1828
FRANCISCO, —	20	M	Servant	Spain	Spain	Sabina	5 May 1826
—	22	M	Farmer	Madeira	U. States	John Laird	16 Jun 1827
—	30	M	Servant	Spain	Spain	Sabina	5 May 1826
—, Don	40	M	Seaman	Malaga	Malaga	Pleiades	5 Nov 1828
John	18	M	B. N. Service	England	West Indies	Soto	11 Nov 1828
FRANCOER, Mertin	35	M	Doctor	France	U. States	Herald	4 Oct 1824
FRANCOIS, Allen	1	M		France	Louisiana	Abby Jones	12 Jul 1827
Allen	36	M	Farmer	France	Louisiana	Abby Jones	12 Jul 1827
Balthasar	35	M	Mechanic	France		France	6 Feb 1829
Catharine	7	F		France	Louisiana	Abby Jones	12 Jul 1827
Joseph	...	M	Servant	Isle of France	Lower Canada	Amity	13 Sep 1821
Mary	13	F		France	Louisiana	Abby Jones	12 Jul 1827
Mary	35	F		France	Louisiana	Abby Jones	12 Jul 1827
Mary Ann	9	F		France	Louisiana	Abby Jones	12 Jul 1827
Mary Jane	5	F		France	Louisiana	Abby Jones	12 Jul 1827
Philisty	3	F		France	Louisiana	Abby Jones	12 Jul 1827
R.	22	M	Merchant	Spain	Spain	Richmond Packet	30 Oct 1827
Sebastian	11	M		France	Louisiana	Abby Jones	12 Jul 1827
FRANER, Antony	2	M	Child	Ireland	St. John, N.B.	Ann Maria	7 Aug 1826
Charles	1	M	Child	Ireland	St. John, N.B.	Ann Maria	7 Aug 1826
Hannah	4	F	Child	Ireland	St. John, N.B.	Ann Maria	7 Aug 1826
Mary	27	F	Servant	Ireland	St. John, N.B.	Ann Maria	7 Aug 1826
Mary Ann	3	F	Child	Ireland	St. John, N.B.	Ann Maria	7 Aug 1826
FRANK, J.	30	M	Farmer	France	U. States	Bayard	25 Apr 1828
Peter	7	M		Sweden	U. States	Hamilton	22 Sep 1828
FRANKAUSER, Jean	23	M	Cultivator	Brattain		L'Esperance	6 Sep 1828
FRANKLAND,							
Benjamin	27 3/12	M	Hatter	Great Britain	New York	Thames	16 May 1821
Benjm.	29	M	Clerk	Gt. Britain	United States	Union	9 Jan 1824
Ellen	26	F	None	England	United States	London	21 May 1828
Henry	3	M	None	England	United States	London	21 May 1828
James	1	M	None	England	United States	London	21 May 1828
James	40	M	Mason	England	United States	Dalhouse Castle	8 May 1827
Joseph	25	M	Miller	England	United States	Herald	29 Oct 1825
Robert	20	M	Farmer	Great Britain	United States	Diana	6 Jul 1829
William	40	M	Draper	Lancashire, England	United States	Aurelia	7 Jun 1826
Wm.	24	M	Farmer	Great Britain	United States	Diana	6 Jul 1829
FRANKLIN, Abm.	20	M	Gentleman	N. York	U. States	Jane	29 Apr 1822

NAMES OF PASSENGERS	AGE	SEX	OCCUPATIONS	COUNTRY TO WHICH THEY BELONG	COUNTRY THEY INTEND TO INHABIT	SHIPS/DATES OF ARRIVAL	
FRANKLIN (cont'd)							
Alis	6	F	None	Great Britan	Great Britan	United States	21 May 1827
Ann	2	F	None	Great Britan	Great Britan	United States	21 May 1827
Ann	26	F	None	Great Britan	Great Britan	United States	21 May 1827
B.	5	F	None	England	America	Corinthian	1 Sep 1827
Benj.	20	M	Mill wright	Great Britain	U. States	United States	8 Sep 1827
Charles	32	M	Stone Cutter	Great Britan	Great Britan	United States	21 May 1827
Elizabeth	13	F		Barbadoes	United States	Only Daughter	26 Apr 1826
Ellen	26	F	Wife	England	America	Corinthian	1 Sep 1827
George	26	M	...	Ireland	America	Farmer	4 Aug 1825
Henry	12	M				Washington	16 Sep 1820
James	21	M	Labourer	England	America	Corinthian	1 Sep 1827
Jane	36	F	None	Great Britan	Great Britan	United States	21 May 1827
Joseph	1	M	None	Great Britan	Great Britan	United States	21 May 1827
Joseph	10	M	None	Great Britan	Great Britan	United States	21 May 1827
Margaret	5	F	None	Great Britan	Great Britan	United States	21 May 1827
Margaret	13	F	None	Great Britan	Great Britan	United States	21 May 1827
Ralph	6	M	None	Great Britan	Great Britan	United States	21 May 1827
Thomas	28	M	Farmer	England	New York	Brighton	20 Aug 1825
Thomas D.	24	M		England	U. States	Acosta	28 Jul 1823
Thos.	36	M	Stone Cutter	Great Britan	Great Britan	United States	21 May 1827
William	5	M	None	Great Britan	Great Britan	United States	21 May 1827
William	46		Spinner	Great Britain	United States	Thomas Dickason	29 Aug 1828
FRANKPELT, Mary	38	F	Servant	England	New York	Brighton	16 Nov 1826
FRANKPILL, Febe	55	F	Seamstress	England	New York	Brighton	20 Aug 1825
FRANKPITT, James	50	M	Mariner	England	United States	Hudson	17 Mar 1828
Mary	36	F	None	Great Briton	New York	Brighton	12 Jun 1826
FRANKS, Charles	26	M		Great Britten	U. States	Magnet	29 Sep 1823
Frances	26	F	None	England	U. States	Columbia	7 Jul 1824
Harriet	9	F		Great Britian	United States	London	24 Jun 1823
John	40	M	Merchant	United States	United States	Maria	12 May 1823
Louisa	7	F		Great Britian	United States	London	24 Jun 1823
Thomas	30	M	Merchant	England	U. States	Columbia	7 Jul 1824
FRANNECIS, A.	19	M	Farmer	France	U.S.	Stephania	15 Aug 1825
FRANQUENCE, L.	28	M	Servant	Switzerland	U. States	Six Brothers	21 Nov 1822
FRANTZ, Margaret	18	F	Spinster	Belfoit	U.S. America	Superior	18 Jun 1825
Marie T.	20	F	Spinster	Belfoit	U.S. America	Superior	18 Jun 1825
FRANY, Arabella	29	F	Labourer	England	U. States	Comet	23 Aug 1828
John	29	M	Labourer	England	U. States	Comet	23 Aug 1828
FRANZ, Dominick	23	M	Blacksmith	Ireland	United States	Borneo	14 Aug 1827
FRAQUIN, J.	25	M	Gentleman	Belgian	U. States	Harmony	12 Jul 1821
J.	29	M	Gentleman	Belgian	U. States	Harmony	12 Jul 1821
M.	27	M	Gentleman	Belgian	U. States	Harmony	12 Jul 1821
FRARARD, Fredrick	23	M	Farmer	France	United States	Virginia	31 May 1828
FRASER, Alex	35	M	Mason	Great Britian	United States	Brok	29 Aug 1823
Alex., Revd.	35	M		New York	New York	Napoleon	26 May 1828
Archibald	30	M	Mason	G. Britain	United States	Ariel	21 May 1827
James	17	M	Gentleman	Great Britain	United States	George Clinton	10 Oct 1825
John	19	M		Scotland	United States	Broke	16 Jul 1829
John	23	M	Merchant	G. Brittain	U. States	Rengal	9 Oct 1822
John	26	M	Royal Navy	England	U. States	Florida	16 May 1827
John	35	M	Gentleman	Edenburgh	England	Orbit	31 Aug 1822
P. W.	24	M	Merchant	United St.	United States	Nancy	23 Oct 1823
FRASH, Bernard	24	M	Instrument Maker	Switzerland	U. States	Hewes	30 Oct 1829
FRASHER, Jas.	23	M	Doctor	Denmark	U. States	Jane	28 Jul 1826
FRASIER, Alexd.	43	M	Laborer	Scotland	U.S. of America	Friends	10 May 1823
Alexr.	37	M	Labourer	Great Britain	United States	Baltic	24 Dec 1824
Catharine	32	F		Scotland	U.S. of America	Friends	10 May 1823
Christian	12	F		Scotland	U.S. of America	Friends	10 May 1823
Christian	45	F		Scotland	U.S. of America	Friends	10 May 1823
Elisabeth	6	F		Scotland	U.S. of America	Friends	10 May 1823
Elizabeth	1	F		Scotland	U.S. of America	Friends	10 May 1823
James	18	M	Spinner	Scotland	U.S. of America	Friends	10 May 1823
Margaret	15	F		Scotland	U.S. of America	Friends	10 May 1823
William	45	M	Labor	Scotland	U.S. of America	Friends	10 May 1823
FRASSER, James	66	M	None	Scotland	U. States	Camillus	27 Jun 1826
FRAVES, Abraham	27		Weaver	Bolton	England	Great Britain	7 May 1827
Joseph	2...		Weaver	Bolton	England	Great Britain	7 May 1827

NAMES OF PASSENGERS	AGE	SEX	OCCUPATIONS	COUNTRY TO WHICH THEY BELONG	COUNTRY THEY INTEND TO INHABIT	SHIPS/DATES OF ARRIVAL	
FRAVES (cont'd)							
Mary	23			Bolton	England	Great Britain	7 May 1827
FRAWL, Bridget	24	F	Labourer	Ireland	United States	Hope & Esther	17 Oct 1827
FRAY, Frederick	25	M	Gardiner	Swiss	U. States	Comet	28 Jul 1825
Jack	27	M	Farmer	France	United States	Crescent	12 Jul 1827
Jean	63	M	Farmer	Germany	United States	Origon	8 Jun 1824
FRAYLE, John	28	M	Merchant	Ireland	U. States	Amity	21 Feb 1823
FRAYNOR, Catherine	27	F	his Wife presented by U.S. seaman	Ireland	United States	Asia	29 Jul 1829
FRAZER, —, Mrs.	47	F		Halifax, N.S.	New York	Citizen	1 Nov 1828
A.	22	M	Seaman	U. States	U. States	Atlantic	15 Oct 1821
Addum	13	M		Halifax, N.S.	New York	Citizen	1 Nov 1828
Ann	2	F	child	England	U. States	Trident	8 Mar 1824
Ann	28	F	wife	England	U. States	Trident	8 Mar 1824
Barbra, Mrs.	24 4/12	F		Scotland	United States	Mobile	21 Aug 1827
Christin	26			France	U. States	Parachute	14 May 1828
Christin	56			France	U. States	Parachute	14 May 1828
David	9	M		Halifax, N.S.	New York	Citizen	1 Nov 1828
Duncan	18	M	Labourer	Scotland	United States	Friends	7 Jul 1827
J.	40	M	Mariner	U. States	U. States	Loire	18 Jul 1828
James	21	M	James Frazer Jur.	Halifax, N.S.	New York	Citizen	1 Nov 1828
James	23	M	Merchant	St. Croix	St. Croix	Edward D. Douglass	11 Aug 1824
James	35	M	Butcher	England	U. States	Trident	8 Mar 1824
John	20	M	Labourer	Gt. Britain	America	Ariel	20 Jul 1822
John	34 11/12	M	Weaver	Scotland	United States	Mobile	21 Aug 1827
John	36	M		Gt. Britain	U. States	Napolean	26 Sep 1828
Joseph	13			France	U. States	Parachute	14 May 1828
Joseph	20	M	Doctor	Ireland	United States	Nancy	16 Jul 1824
Madaline	26			France	U. States	Parachute	14 May 1828
Manuel	56		Mason	France	U. States	Parachute	14 May 1828
Margaret	1 2/12	F		Scotland	United States	Mobile	21 Aug 1827
Marget	16	F		Halifax, N.S.	New York	Citizen	1 Nov 1828
Maria	1	F	child	England	U. States	Trident	8 Mar 1824
Mary	9/12	F		Pennsylvania	U. States	Yamacraw	28 Jul 1823
Mary	3	F		Halifax, N.S.	New York	Citizen	1 Nov 1828
Maryan	10	F		Halifax, N.S.	New York	Citizen	1 Nov 1828
Oswald	21	M	Clark	Scotland	United States	Camillus	6 Apr 1821
Sophia	18			France	U. States	Parachute	14 May 1828
William	45	M	Merchant	United States	United States	Eliza Pigott	27 Mar 1820
FRAZIER, —, Master	14	M		U.S.	U.S.	Robert Edwards	11 Nov 1822
—, Mr.	47	M	Merchant	U.S.	U.S.	Robert Edwards	11 Nov 1822
—, Mrs.	23	F		Pennsylvania	U. States	Yamacraw	28 Jul 1823
Ann	14		Merchant	Halifax	U. States	Edwin	26 Sep 1828
Charles	20		Merchant	Halifax	U. States	Edwin	26 Sep 1828
Harris	6		Merchant	Halifax	U. States	Edwin	26 Sep 1828
James	23	M	Accountant	Scotland	U. States	Edward D. Douglass	16 Jun 1824
Jane	16		Merchant	Halifax	U. States	Edwin	26 Sep 1828
Jane	54		Merchant	Halifax	U. States	Edwin	26 Sep 1828
Jas.	60		Merchant	Halifax	U. States	Edwin	26 Sep 1828
Jno.	29	M	Farmer	Pennsylvania	U. States	Yamacraw	28 Jul 1823
John	8		Merchant	Halifax	U. States	Edwin	26 Sep 1828
Malbro	23	M	Merchant	Philada.	U. States	Dick	4 Sep 1823
Mary	12		Merchant	Halifax	U. States	Edwin	26 Sep 1828
Robert	10		Merchant	Halifax	U. States	Edwin	26 Sep 1828
Wm.	42	M	Planter	America	America	Samuel Robertson	26 Nov 1825
FRE..., Mary L.	41	M	Lady	United States	France	Stephania	13 Sep 1821
FREAM, Wm.	37	M	Merchant	U. States	U. States	Isaac McKim	25 Nov 1824
FREAN, Wm.	35	M	Merchant	United States	United States	Ductile	30 Nov 1822
Wm.	40	M	Merchant	United States	U. States	Midas	6 Oct 1823
FREARY, Meltune	32	M	Labourer	Great Brittan	United States	Hanford	3 Aug 1829
FREASY, Edward	40	M	Labourer	Ireland	United States	Fabius	31 Jul 1829
Hugh	21	M	Labourer	Ireland	United States	Fabius	31 Jul 1829
FRECHANTIZ, Abraham	9	M	Farmer	Switzerland	Ohio	Frances Henrietta	25 Aug 1825
Alexander	2	M	Farmer	Switzerland	Ohio	Frances Henrietta	25 Aug 1825

NAMES OF PASSENGERS	AGE	SEX	OCCUPATIONS	COUNTRY TO WHICH THEY BELONG	COUNTRY THEY INTEND TO INHABIT	SHIPS/DATES OF ARRIVAL	
FRECHANTIZ (cont'd)							
Catharine	38	F	Farmer	Switzerland	Ohio	Frances Henrietta	25 Aug 1825
Eliza	6/12	F	Farmer	Switzerland	Ohio	Frances Henrietta	25 Aug 1825
Jacob	32	M	Farmer	Switzerland	Ohio	Frances Henrietta	25 Aug 1825
John	7	M	Farmer	Switzerland	Ohio	Frances Henrietta	25 Aug 1825
Rosalie	4	F	Farmer	Switzerland	Ohio	Frances Henrietta	25 Aug 1825
FREDERIC, John						Olympia	12 Aug 1828

*After having been at Sea a Number of Days was ascertaining the quantity of Baggage to report found the under mentioned persons had secreted themselves away notwithstanding our search with the Gendearmes at the of leaving the port

NAMES OF PASSENGERS	AGE	SEX	OCCUPATIONS	COUNTRY TO WHICH THEY BELONG	COUNTRY THEY INTEND TO INHABIT	SHIPS/DATES OF ARRIVAL	
FREDERICK, Benjn.	13	M	Boy	Matanzas	N. York	New England	7 Jul 1826
Catharine	30	F	Labourer	France	Louisiana	Sully	30 Oct 1827
Daniel	23	M	Merchant	France	United States	Stephania	3 Oct 1822
Geo.	58	M	Farmer	Holland	U. States	Martha	13 Sep 1827
James	21	M	Merchant	England	U. States	Brighton	14 Apr 1828
Joseph	21	M	Mechanic	France	United States	Stephania	3 Oct 1822
L.	30	M	Butcher	U. States	United States	Autumn	1 Aug 1828
Louis	19		Farmer	France	U. States	Parachute	14 May 1828
Louis	40	M	Goldsmith	Guadaloupe	Guadaloupe	Martha	23 Jun 1825
Martin	35	M	Labourer	U. States	Louisiana	Sully	30 Oct 1827
FREDRICH, Andreas	10	M	Farmer	Wortenberg	Lancaster	Louisa	6 Oct 1828
Christian	3	M	Farmer	Wortenberg	Lancaster	Louisa	6 Oct 1828
Eberfend	27	M	Farmer	Wortenberg	Lancaster	Louisa	6 Oct 1828
Eva	9	F	Farmer	Wortenberg	Lancaster	Louisa	6 Oct 1828
Johann	4 6/12	M	Farmer	Wortenberg	Lancaster	Louisa	6 Oct 1828
Johannes	8	M	Farmer	Wortenberg	Lancaster	Louisa	6 Oct 1828
FREDRICK, Jen...	44 5/12	F	Farmer	Switzerland	U. States	France	26 Jun 1828
John	12 4/12	M	Farmer	Switzerland	U. States	France	26 Jun 1828
John	12 4/12	M	Farmer	Switzerland	U. States	France	26 Jun 1828
FREDY, John	11	M	Labourer	Great Britain	United States	William Dawson	18 Jun 1827
Thos.	34	M	Labourer	Great Britain	United States	William Dawson	18 Jun 1827
FREE, Rubin	22	M	Farmer	England	U. States	Hercules	6 Jul 1827
FREED, Caroline	4	F		England	United States	Richmond	4 Aug 1826
Edmund	8	M		England	United States	Richmond	4 Aug 1826
Edward	12	M		England	United States	Richmond	4 Aug 1826
George	14	M		England	United States	Richmond	4 Aug 1826
Henry	6	M		England	United States	Richmond	4 Aug 1826
James	1...		Bricklayer	Gil...	England	Great Britain	7 May 1827
Joseph	45	M	Farmer	England	United States	Richmond	4 Aug 1826
Mary	18	F		England	United States	Richmond	4 Aug 1826
Richard	10	M		England	United States	Richmond	4 Aug 1826
Sarah	64			Gil...	England	Great Britain	7 May 1827
William	56		Labourer	Gil...	England	Great Britain	7 May 1827
Wm., & Infant	35	F		England	United States	Richmond	4 Aug 1826
FREEL, Denis	20	M	Laborer	Ireland	United States	Mary	1 Jul 1827
James	22	M	Labourer	Ireland	United States	General Putnam	20 Jun 1825
FREELAN, Maria	18	F	None	Ireland		Aurora	12 Mar 1827
FREELAND, —, Mrs.	40	F	Merchant	N. York	U. States	Four Sons	31 May 1823
A.	25	M	Merchant	Louisiana	U. States	Altamira	31 Jan 1826
John	13	M		Ireland	United States	Commerce	13 Jun 1828
John, Esqr.	33	M	...t	...	New York	Curlew	28 Jun 1824
Sarah	40	F		Ireland	United States	Commerce	13 Jun 1828
Wm.	15	M		Ireland	United States	Commerce	13 Jun 1828
FREELY, Peter	27	M	Merchant	G. Britain	U. States	Freak	9 Jun 1828
FREEMAN, Ann	18	F		Ireland	United States	Essex	23 May 1828
Ann	24	F	his wife [John]	Ireland	United States	Asia	29 Jul 1829
Catharine	59	F		Ireland	United States	Trio	2 Oct 1828
Charity	18	F		American	United States	William	28 Feb 1826
Elizabeth	24	F	Seamstress	Penrith	St. Johns	James	31 Oct 1822
F.	46	M	Shoe Maker	England	America	Two Marys	24 Sep 1827
John	8	M	Shoe Maker	England	America	Two Marys	24 Sep 1827
John	18	M	Labourer	Ireland	United States	Euphrates	12 Mar 1824
John	20	M	Land Surveyor	Ireland	United States	Asia	29 Jul 1829
John	28 6/12	M	Weaver	Scotland	U. States	Hopes Delight	21 Apr 1828
John	38	M	Farmer	England	United States	Ann Maria	26 Apr 1822

NAMES OF PASSENGERS	AGE	SEX	OCCUPATIONS	COUNTRY TO WHICH THEY BELONG	COUNTRY THEY INTEND TO INHABIT	SHIPS/DATES OF ARRIVAL	
FREEMAN (cont'd)							
Jona.	20	M	Merchant	Jersey	U. States	Mary Ann	12 Jul 1824
Maria	29	F	None	England	United States	Bolivar	15 Jun 1826
Mary	_/12	F	their child				
			[John & Ann]	Ireland	United States	Asia	29 Jul 1829
N.	37	M	Merchant	United States	United States	Maria	25 Mar 1829
Pat	20	M	Labourer	Ireland	United States	Essex	23 May 1828
Rebecca	20	F		American	United States	William	28 Feb 1826
Seth	50	M	Marriner	United States	United States	Cicero	26 Sep 1826
Thomas	22		Brick layer	England	United States	Hudson	5 Apr 1826
Thomas	28	M	Labourer	England	United States	Bolivar	15 Jun 1826
William, Capt.	38	M	Master	U. States	U. States	Cygnet	23 Sep 1820
Wm.	26	M	Servant	Gt. Britain	United States	Crisis	13 Nov 1824
FREEMANY, James	27 6/12	M	Gentleman	Great Briton		Mount Vernon	29 Aug 1828
FREEMENT, Hippolite	3	M		France		Acosta	28 Jul 1823
FREEMONT,							
Adile Martele	32	F		France	United States	Acosta	28 Jul 1823
Selena	4	F		France		Acosta	28 Jul 1823
Victorine	5	F		France		Acosta	28 Jul 1823
FREENAN, Grace	33	F	Wife	Ireland	United States	Meteor	27 Sep 1826
FREENSWAR, —	18	M	Servant	Curraco	Curraco	General Paez	30 Apr 1827
FREER, Wm.	26	M	Merchant	G. Britain	Canada	Congress	23 Mar 1824
FREESON, Edmond	30	M	Farmer	Great Brittain	U. States	William Byrnes	23 Jul 1824
FREEZE, Eve	48	F		United States	United States	Globe	30 Aug 1828
Jacob	50	M	Farmer	United States	United States	Globe	30 Aug 1828
Jacob, Jr.	28	M		United States	United States	Globe	30 Aug 1828
Louisa	14	F		United States	United States	Globe	30 Aug 1828
Peter	24	M		United States	United States	Globe	30 Aug 1828
Peter, Jr.	4	M		United States	United States	Globe	30 Aug 1828
FREITAS, Joseph	26	M	Meriner	Un. States	Philadelphy	Rebecca Groves	31 Jul 1829
FRELOLET, Frs.	36	M	Gent	French	U. States	Charlemagne	19 Sep 1828
FREMONT, Bertroud	20	F		France	United States	Montano	27 Aug 1827
Henry	45	M	Mercht.	France	America	Lima	11 Dec 1823
Louis	23	M	Shoe Maker	France	United States	Montano	27 Aug 1827
FREMONT DE LORRIERE,							
Auguste	19	M	Merchant	United States	United States	Montano	5 May 1828
Charles	59	M	Merchant	United States	United States	Montano	5 May 1828
FRENCH, ...	2	F		Great Britian	United States	London	24 Jun 1823
...	22	F		Great Britian	United States	London	24 Jun 1823
Anne	1/12	F	Farmer	Ireland	U. States	Atlantic	19 Aug 1825
B.	11	M	Farmer	England	U.S. States	Splendid	14 Aug 1829
C.	22	M	Merchant	U. States	U. States	Prudence	11 Jun 1825
Charlotte	3	F	Farmer	England	U.S. States	Splendid	14 Aug 1829
D. A.	32	M	Teacher	U. States	U. States	Euphrates	9 Apr 1825
Elizabeth Ann	2	F	Child	England	United States	Cambria	3 Jul 1829
Ezth.	3	F	None	Connecticut	U. States	Ann Maria	1 Jun 1824
Francis	7	F	Child	England	United States	Cambria	3 Jul 1829
George	24	M	Yeoman	England	America	Cincinnatus	22 May 1826
Hannah	30	F	Seamstress	England	New York	Brighton	20 Aug 1825
Hannah	30	M	Farmer	England	U.S. States	Splendid	14 Aug 1829
Henry	1			b. Kent County, last of Rye	N.York	Peru	30 May 1828
Henry	24		Shipwright	b. Kent County, last of Rye	N.York	Peru	30 May 1828
J.	9	M	Farmer	England	U.S. States	Splendid	14 Aug 1829
J.	15	M	Farmer	England	U.S. States	Splendid	14 Aug 1829
James	12	M	Child	England	United States	Cambria	3 Jul 1829
James	23	M	Farmer	England	United States	William Howland	5 Jul 1821
John	29	M	Farmer	Ireland	U. States	Atlantic	19 Aug 1825
Joseph	25	M	Baker	England	United States	Criterion	27 Oct 1820
Mary	7	F	Farmer	England	U.S. States	Splendid	14 Aug 1829
Mary	30	F		Ireland	United States	Alex. Mansfield	17 May 1823
Mary Ane	5	F	Farmer	England	U.S. States	Splendid	14 Aug 1829
Matilda	29	F	Farmer	Ireland	U. States	Atlantic	19 Aug 1825
Naomi	20			b. Kent County, last of Rye	N.York	Peru	30 May 1828
Rachel	14	F	None	England	United States	Nestor	20 Nov 1821

NAMES OF PASSENGERS	AGE	SEX	OCCUPATIONS	COUNTRY TO WHICH THEY BELONG	COUNTRY THEY INTEND TO INHABIT	SHIPS/DATES OF ARRIVAL	
FRENCH (cont'd)							
Sarah	17	F		Barbados	United States	Cannon	18 Aug 1821
Sarah	38	F		England	United States	Cambria	3 Jul 1829
Sarah	53	F	None	England	United States	Mentor	28 Apr 1824
Sarah Ann	14	F		England	United States	Cambria	3 Jul 1829
Sheppard	13	F	None	England	United States	Mentor	28 Apr 1824
Stephen	10	M	Child	England	United States	Cambria	3 Jul 1829
T.	13	M	Farmer	England	U.S. States	Splendid	14 Aug 1829
Thomas	29	M	Weaver	England	U. States	Pleiades	9 Oct 1829
Thoms.	46	M	Farmer	England	U.S. States	Splendid	14 Aug 1829
William	17	M	Farmer	England	U.S. States	Splendid	14 Aug 1829
Wm.	25	M	Miller	Great Britian	United States	London	24 Jun 1823
FRENSUCHEIN, Wm.	25	M	Shoe Maker	Ireland	America	Meteor	26 Dec 1825
FRENTE, G.	30	M	Merchant	Cuba	U. States	Brown	29 Apr 1825
FRESE, Francis	24	M	Cooper	Germany	United States	Constitution	2 Aug 1826
FRESHAM, Henry	22	M	Merchant	England	England	Pacific	17 Jun 1828
FRESSIE, Thomas	28	M	Engineer	England	U. States	Messenger	10 Jul 1829
William	37	M	Engineer	England	U. States	Messenger	10 Jul 1829
FRETAGEST, A.	11	M	Student	France	U.S.	Cadmus	20 Dec 1824
FREW, James	20	M	Farmer	Scotland	United States	Margaret Bogle	11 Jun 1824
FREY, —		F	None	Ship Sully	U. States	Sully	24 Oct 1828
Ann Maria	38	F	None	Germany	U. States	Sully	24 Oct 1828
C.	33	M	Merchant	Bremen	to return	Louisa	16 May 1826
Christian	10	M	None	Germany	U. States	Sully	24 Oct 1828
Eliza	32	F	Merchant	Switzerland	United States	Factor	1 Sep 1823
Eliza Caroline	9	F	Merchant	Switzerland	United States	Factor	1 Sep 1823
Frederich	18	M	None	Germany	U. States	Sully	24 Oct 1828
Fredrick	12	M	Merchant	Switzerland	United States	Factor	1 Sep 1823
George	42	M	Weaver	Germany	U. States	Sully	24 Oct 1828
Gustavus	6	M	Merchant	Switzerland	United States	Factor	1 Sep 1823
Jean	22	M	Farmer	Germany	U. States	Isabella	10 Aug 1829
John G.	6 6/12	M	None	Germany	U. States	Sully	24 Oct 1828
Julia	4	F	Merchant	Switzerland	United States	Factor	1 Sep 1823
Lewis	7	M	Merchant	Switzerland	United States	Factor	1 Sep 1823
Madelina	2	F	None	Germany	U. States	Sully	24 Oct 1828
Mary C.	5 6/12	F	None	Germany	U. States	Sully	24 Oct 1828
Mary M.	15	F	None	Germany	U. States	Sully	24 Oct 1828
Philip	23	M	Potter	France	United States	New England	29 Aug 1828
Rosina	8	F	None	Germany	U. States	Sully	24 Oct 1828
Sophia	2	F	Merchant	Switzerland	United States	Factor	1 Sep 1823
Theolopeus	45	M	Merchant	Switzerland	United States	Factor	1 Sep 1823
Theolopheus	13	M	Merchant	Switzerland	United States	Factor	1 Sep 1823
FREYBOURGERS, Aperlo	20	M	Weaver	Germany	Canada	Virginia	31 May 1828
Frances	24	F	Weaver	Germany	Canada	Virginia	31 May 1828
Jane	69	F	Weaver	Germany	Canada	Virginia	31 May 1828
John	71	M	Weaver	Germany	Canada	Virginia	31 May 1828
Marier	36	F	Weaver	Germany	Canada	Virginia	31 May 1828
Materlane	21	F	Weaver	Germany	Canada	Virginia	31 May 1828
FREYMAN, —, Mrs.	37	F		Germany	U. States	Minerva	18 Oct 1828
Cath.	2 1/12	F		Germany	U. States	Minerva	18 Oct 1828
Cathr.	4	F		Germany	U. States	Minerva	18 Oct 1828
D.	6	M		Germany	U. States	Minerva	18 Oct 1828
M.	13	M		Germany	U. States	Minerva	18 Oct 1828
M.	57	M	Farmer	Germany	U. States	Minerva	18 Oct 1828
N.	9	M		Germany	U. States	Minerva	18 Oct 1828
FREYRE, Antonio	24		Merchant	Cuba	Cuba	Sarah	26 Dec 1827
Antonio M.	24	M	Merchant	Cuba	Cuba	Sarah	24 Mar 1828
FRIAR, L.	0 6/12	M		Great Britain		Caravan	8 Sep 1828
L.	10	M		Great Britain		Caravan	8 Sep 1828
L.	12	M		Great Britain		Caravan	8 Sep 1828
L.	38	M	Black Smith	Great Britain		Caravan	8 Sep 1828
M	36	M		Great Britain		Caravan	8 Sep 1828
FRIBURGHHAUSEN, Anna	25	F	Wife of [Bennoist]	Switzerland	United States	Aurora	21 Jun 1824
Bennoist	5	M	Child of [Bennoist]	Switzerland	United States	Aurora	21 Jun 1824
Bennoist	28	M	Farmer	Switzerland	United States	Aurora	21 Jun 1824
Christian	1	M	Child of [Bennoist]	Switzerland	United States	Aurora	21 Jun 1824
John	4	M	Child of [Bennoist]	Switzerland	United States	Aurora	21 Jun 1824
FRIDAY, Catherine	23	F		Germany	United States	Samuel Robertson	8 Aug 1828

NAMES OF PASSENGERS	AGE	SEX	OCCUPATIONS	COUNTRY TO WHICH THEY BELONG	COUNTRY THEY INTEND TO INHABIT	SHIPS/DATES OF ARRIVAL	
FRIDAY (cont'd)							
Catherine	48	F		Germany	United States	Samuel Robertson	8 Aug 1828
Clostres	55	F		Germany	United States	Samuel Robertson	8 Aug 1828
George	8	M		Germany	United States	Samuel Robertson	8 Aug 1828
Margaret	10	F		Germany	United States	Samuel Robertson	8 Aug 1828
Michael	47	M	Farmer	Germany	United States	Samuel Robertson	8 Aug 1828
FRIDELANCE, J. B.	53		Carpenter	France	U. States	Elizabeth	9 Jul 1825
FRIEDRIK, Johan	7	M	Farmer	Wortenberg	Lancaster	Louisa	6 Oct 1828
FRIEL, Bryan	23	M		Ireland	United States	William & George	14 May 1828
Hugh	23	M		Ireland	United States	William & George	14 May 1828
FRIELL, James	22	M	Laborer	Ireland	United States	Ann Maria	21 May 1827
Mary	30	F	Spinster	Ireland	United States	Ann Maria	21 May 1827
FRIEND, Chs.	30	M	Merchant	England	England	Medina	23 Apr 1828
FRIER, Jean	27	M	Farmer	Switzerland	U. States	Alfred	8 Jul 1828
FRIGOS, Manuel M.	35	M	Gentleman	Columbia	Columbia	William Bayard	6 Aug 1825
FRILD, James	22	M	Labourer	Ireland	United States	Henry Kneeland	7 Jun 1828
FRILL, Bridget	25	F		Ireland	U. States	St. Michael	27 Mar 1827
Hugh	3	M		Ireland	U. States	St. Michael	27 Mar 1827
Patrick	28	M	Labourer	Ireland	U. States	St. Michael	27 Mar 1827
Rose	6	F		Ireland	U. States	St. Michael	27 Mar 1827
FRIO, Domingo	18	M		Mexico	New York	Prince Edward	8 Aug 1829
FRISBY, Adolphus	26	M	Labourer	Gt. Britain	U. States	Maria	22 May 1822
William	25	M	Tailor	England	New Eng.	Thames	6 Oct 1820
FRISHER, Catharine	38	F	Wife	Switzerland	U. States	Hewes	30 Oct 1829
Christian	14	M	her children [Catharine]	Switzerland	U. States	Hewes	30 Oct 1829
Christina	7	F	her children [Catharine]	Switzerland	U. States	Hewes	30 Oct 1829
Frederick	5	M	her children [Catharine]	Switzerland	U. States	Hewes	30 Oct 1829
FRISK, Mary	39 6/12	F		England	United States	John Wells	22 May 1826
FRISLE, Christin	23		Tailor	France	U. States	Parachute	14 May 1828
FRISLER, Ann Maria	1	F	Book Binder	Bavaria	United States	American	27 Aug 1827
Barbara	7	F	Book Binder	Bavaria	United States	American	27 Aug 1827
Catherine	13	F	Book Binder	Bavaria	United States	American	27 Aug 1827
Elisa	9	F	Book Binder	Bavaria	United States	American	27 Aug 1827
Jacob	4	F	Book Binder	Bavaria	United States	American	27 Aug 1827
Louisa	5	F	Book Binder	Bavaria	United States	American	27 Aug 1827
Louisa	41	F	Book Binder	Bavaria	United States	American	27 Aug 1827
Margret	18	F	Book Binder	Bavaria	United States	American	27 Aug 1827
Michael	15	F	Book Binder	Bavaria	United States	American	27 Aug 1827
Michael	48	M	Book Binder	Bavaria	United States	American	27 Aug 1827
Peter	2 6/12	F	Book Binder	Bavaria	United States	American	27 Aug 1827
FRISNEDO, D.	18	M	Merchant	Spain	U. States	Joseph S. Lewis	6 Dec 1822
FRITAS, M... R. D.	22	M	Mercht.	Oporto	Portugal	Eliza	16 Oct 1821
FRITH, —, Miss	11	F	Merchant	Bermuda	Bermuda	Improvement	6 Jun 1826
Eliza	1	F	None	England	U. States	Thomas Ritchie	2 Jul 1827
Geo.	23	M	Mason	England	U. States	Thomas Ritchie	2 Jul 1827
H.	35	M	Merchant	Bermuda	Bermuda	Improvement	6 Jun 1826
Hannh.	35	F	None	England	U. States	Thomas Ritchie	2 Jul 1827
Hezekiah, Mr., Jun.	17	M		Bermuda	visiting New York	Camden	14 May 1825
Hezekiah, Mr., Sr.	60	M		Bermuda	visiting New York	Camden	14 May 1825
Jas.	35	M	Mason	England	U. States	Thomas Ritchie	2 Jul 1827
Jno.	3	M	None	England	U. States	Thomas Ritchie	2 Jul 1827
John	40	M	Miller	Ireland	U.S.A.	Dalhouse Castle	21 Aug 1829
John	40	M	Miller	Ireland	United States	Dalhouse Castle	21 Aug 1829
Mary	6	F	None	England	U. States	Thomas Ritchie	2 Jul 1827
Mary	32	F	None	England	U. States	Thomas Ritchie	2 Jul 1827
Saml.	32	M	Mason	England	U. States	Thomas Ritchie	2 Jul 1827
W., Master	8	M		Bermuda	visiting New York	Camden	14 May 1825
Wm.	6	M	None	England	U. States	Thomas Ritchie	2 Jul 1827

NAMES OF PASSENGERS	AGE	SEX	OCCUPATIONS	COUNTRY TO WHICH THEY BELONG	COUNTRY THEY INTEND TO INHABIT	SHIPS/DATES OF ARRIVAL	
FRITZ, P.	32	M	Farmer	Holland	U. States	Don Quixote	25 Oct 1828
FRIZZI, D.	37	M	Gentleman	Spain	Mexico	Pharos	10 Jun 1824
Rafala	26	F	Lady	Spain	Mexico	Pharos	10 Jun 1824
FROCOICE, R.	30	M	Merchant	Spain	Spain	Iris	3 Jul 1828
FRODING, Elizabeth	1 2/12			United States	United States	Hudson	18 Jun 1825
Mary	22			United States	United States	Hudson	18 Jun 1825
FROGENT, Anoine	11			Switzerland	U. States	Parachute	14 May 1828
Fancis	16			Switzerland	U. States	Parachute	14 May 1828
J. Pierre	8			Switzerland	U. States	Parachute	14 May 1828
Marie	46			Switzerland	U. States	Parachute	14 May 1828
Mary Ann	6			Switzerland	U. States	Parachute	14 May 1828
Mary J.	18			Switzerland	U. States	Parachute	14 May 1828
FROGGAT, David	32	M		England	United States	Essex	23 May 1828
FROGGET, Hannah	1	F		England	United States	Essex	23 May 1828
Susan	30	F		England	United States	Essex	23 May 1828
Wm.	5	M		England	United States	Essex	23 May 1828
FROIDERAUX, Genevieve	30	F		France	France	Edward Quesnel	3 Jul 1829
FROIGENT, J. P.	51		Mechanic	Switzerland	U. States	Parachute	14 May 1828
FROIS, Mordecai	26	M	Merchant	Holland	Holland	Rebecca Ann	5 Dec 1821
FROM, Barbis	25	M	Mechantile	Germany	U. States	Alexander	1 May 1826
Jno.	25	M	Farmer	England	U. States	New York	11 Jul 1823
FROMAGERT, —, Miss	13	F		U. States	United States	Henri IV	14 Sep 1827
FROMONT, Nichs. A.	42	M	Officer	France	N. Carolina	Stephania	13 Mar 1820
FRONCAYET, —, Mrs.	36	F			United States	Henri IV	14 Sep 1827
FRONTE, G.	40	M	Merchant	America	U. States	Mary Jane	2 Jul 1828
FROST, A.	70	M	...	United States	United States	Loire	18 Oct 1820
Ca.	30	F		G. Britain	U. States	Cosmo	15 May 1827
Elizabeth	6	F	None	Great Britain	United States	Penelope	11 Jun 1827
Elizabeth	30	F	None	Great Britain	United States	Penelope	11 Jun 1827
Gideon	25	M	Merchant	Boston	U. States	Margaret	16 May 1825
Jas.	12	M	None	Great Britain	United States	Penelope	11 Jun 1827
Jno.	31	M	Chandler	Ireland	United States	Essex	23 May 1828
Jno.	39	M	Merchant	U. States	U. States	Circassian	13 Jun 1825
John	3	M	None	Great Britain	United States	Penelope	11 Jun 1827
John	34	M	Mariner	United States	United States	Edward	21 Apr 1821
John	40	M	Labourer	Great Britain	United States	Penelope	11 Jun 1827
Mary		F	Mechanic	American		Happy Return	23 Jul 1821
Rebecca	5	F	None	Great Britain	United States	Penelope	11 Jun 1827
S. A.	10	F		G. Britain	U. States	Cosmo	15 May 1827
S. J.	21	M	Grocer	U. States	U. States	Oglethorpe	9 Nov 1824
Thomas	30	M	...b...	...shire	U. States	Panthea	24 Mar 1825
William	18	M	Laborer	Ireland	United States	St. Michaels	18 Jul 1826
Wm.	8	M		G. Britain	U. States	Cosmo	15 May 1827
Wm.	38	M	fuller	G. Britain	U. States	Cosmo	15 May 1827
FROSTE, Joseph	23 3/12	M	Merchant	England	Canada	Leeds	4 Jun 1827
Maria	28	F		Great Britain	United States	Robert Fulton	27 Jun 1822
Robt.	36	M	Merchant	Great Britain	United States	Robert Fulton	27 Jun 1822
T.	30	M	Merchant	England	Canada	Birmingham	12 Oct 1827
FROTH, Peter	30	M	Tailor	Holland	U. States	Edward Bonaffe	23 Jul 1828
FROTHINGHAM, N. L., Revd. Mr.	35	M	Divine	United States	United States	Manchester	24 Aug 1827
FROY, Philip	23	M	Baker	Ireland	United States	Trio	2 Oct 1828
FRUCAUFF, Eugene A.	21	M	Merchant	U. States	U.S.	William Byrnes	11 Dec 1827
FRUCHEBAS, Francois	18			Savannah	travellers	Desdemona	12 Jun 1826
FRUEL, Joseph	35	M	Farmer	England	U. States	Washington	7 Jul 1824
FRUIT, Josph.	30	M		France	United States	Le Voltaire	19 Jul 1828
Marie	22	F		France	United States	Le Voltaire	19 Jul 1828
Pierre	1 /12	M		France	United States	Le Voltaire	19 Jul 1828
*Born at Sea							
FRURER, John	7	M	None	Ireland	U. States	Franklin	7 Jul 1828
Mary	28	F	None	Ireland	U. States	Franklin	7 Jul 1828
Orsila	9	F	None	Ireland	U. States	Franklin	7 Jul 1828
FRUSCO, L. Baronder	39	M	Gentleman	France	England	Ranger	15 Jan 1827
FRY, Antoney	30	M	Laberer	Irland	U. States	Nancy	27 Jun 1823
Charles	1	M	Gent		United States	Cosmo	21 Aug 1828
Geo. N.	32	M	unknown	U. States	U. States	Mary	7 Nov 1822
Helury	6	F		Irland	U. States	Nancy	27 Jun 1823
Henry	22	M	Merchant	England	U. States	Trident	1 Dec 1824

NAMES OF PASSENGERS	AGE	SEX	OCCUPATIONS	COUNTRY TO WHICH THEY BELONG	COUNTRY THEY INTEND TO INHABIT	SHIPS/DATES OF ARRIVAL	
FRY (cont'd)							
Marey	28	F		Irland	U. States	Nancy	27 Jun 1823
Mathew	20		Clock Maker	Germany	United States	Hudson	5 Apr 1826
Wm.	37	M	...			Manhattan	8 Aug 1820
FRYE, Francis J.	21	M	Watch Maker	Germany	U. States	Rook	25 Jul 1827
FRYER, Martha	34		Farmer	England	United States	Corinthian	30 May 1828
Samuel	30		Farmer	England	United States	Corinthian	30 May 1828
FRYERS, Owen	27 2/12	M	Labourer	Ireland	New York	Louisa	20 Jul 1826
FRYNISS, Dion	31	M	Merchant	Balboa	Havana	Mary	1 Nov 1824
FUCHEZ, Thom, Capt.	29	M	Marinor	U. States	Baltimore	London Packet	5 Jan 1829
FUDD, Joseph	30	M	Farmer	Great Britian	United States	Andes	19 Aug 1829
FUDGE, Hy.	30	M	Farmer	Ireland	U. States	Mentor	5 Jul 1825
Mary	22	F	Farmer	Ireland	U. States	Mentor	5 Jul 1825
FUENTES, Ferdinand	17	M	Merchant	...	America	Columbia	6 Oct 1825
Gabriel	19	M	Merchant	...	America	Columbia	6 Oct 1825
Ralph, Junr.	21	M	Merchant	...	America	Columbia	6 Oct 1825
Ralph, Senr.	49	M	Merchant	...	America	Columbia	6 Oct 1825
FUESTARDO, J. B.	49	M	Merchant	Great Britain	Great Britain	Dromo	28 Feb 1829
FUGASON, Mary Ann	18	F		Ireland	America	Enterprize	29 Jun 1827
FUGLE, Charles	20	M	Merchant	England	England	Eugenie	2 Oct 1829
FUILLET, —	32	M	Merchant	France	France	Imperial	10 Dec 1821
FULELOT, A.	40	M	Merchant	France	U. States	Othello	3 Jun 1823
FULEY, Honor	32	F	Servant	Ireland	America	Weser	26 Jun 1821
James	1 6/12	M	Child	Ireland	America	Weser	26 Jun 1821
FULFAIR, Dorbina	30	M	Carpenter	Switzerland	U. States	Bayard	9 Jul 1824
FULFORD, —, Mrs.	33	F		G. Bridain		Trio	27 Jun 1823
Catherine	9	F		G. Bridain		Trio	27 Jun 1823
William	15	M		G. Bridain		Trio	27 Jun 1823
FULHERRIN, —	72	F		Germany	U. States	Falcon	11 Jun 1827
FULKNIER, Danl.	30	M	Farmer	England	Gt. Britain	Electra	4 Sep 1827
Mary	28	F		England	Gt. Britain	Electra	4 Sep 1827
FULLAGAR, Sarah	20	F		Gt. Britain	U. States	Maria	22 May 1822
William	27	M	Carpenter	Gt. Britain	U. States	Maria	22 May 1822
FULLAM, Mary	17	F	None	Ireland		Marchioness	13 May 1828
Patrick	19 3/12	M	Weaver	Ireland	America	Carolina Ann	7 Apr 1826
FULLAN, Michael	19	F		Ireland	America	Carolina Ann	7 Aug 1826
FULLATRE, James	35	M	Callico printer	France	United States	Helen	5 Sep 1828
FULLER, Ann	8			Sussex, England		Cincinnatus	17 May 1823
Anthony	30			Sussex, England		Cincinnatus	17 May 1823
Edward	8	M		Great Britain		Robert Fulton	8 Mar 1823
Eliza	2			Sussex, England		Cincinnatus	17 May 1823
Ester	9			Sussex, England		Cincinnatus	17 May 1823
Ester	26			Sussex, England		Cincinnatus	17 May 1823
George	5			Sussex, England		Cincinnatus	17 May 1823
Godfrey	3			Sussex, England		Cincinnatus	17 May 1823
Han.	1			Sussex, England		Cincinnatus	17 May 1823
*died							
Hannah	34	F	Wife	Ireland	U. States	Meteor	19 Jul 1828
Harreott	19	F		Great Brittan	United States	Cambria	11 Feb 1829
Henry	5			Sussex, England		Cincinnatus	17 May 1823
Henry	29	M	England	England	United States	Aurora	21 Jun 1824
Henry	33	M	Apothecary	England	America	Bayard	15 Dec 1828
Jno.	30	M	Block Maker	Baden	Carlisle, Pensa.	Leeds	7 Nov 1828
Karl	28	M	Professor	Germany		Cadmus	20 Dec 1824
Mary	4			Sussex, England		Cincinnatus	17 May 1823
Mary	6	F		England	America	Brittannia	28 Feb 1827
Mary	26			Sussex, England		Cincinnatus	17 May 1823
Richd.	6			Sussex, England		Cincinnatus	17 May 1823
Richd.	32			Sussex, England		Cincinnatus	17 May 1823
Robert	1			Sussex, England		Cincinnatus	17 May 1823
Samuel	26	M	Mechanic	Great Britain	U.S. Am.	Eliza	12 May 1828
Thos.	15	M	Labourer	Ireland	U. States	Meteor	19 Jul 1828
W. B.	45	M	Gentleman	England	America	Brittannia	28 Feb 1827
Willm.	36	M	Gentn.	England	New York	Brighton	16 Nov 1826
FULLERSTON, D.	21		Farmer	Ireland	United States	Courier	16 May 1825
FULLERTON, Geo.	30	M	Engineer	England	U. States	Clio	8 Apr 1828
James	36	M	Merchant	U. States	U. States	Tobasco	14 Apr 1828
Jane	50	F	Seamstress	Great Britain	United States	Grecian	24 Sep 1828
Wm.	37	M	Labourer	Ireland	United States	Meteor	26 Jun 1827

NAMES OF PASSENGERS	AGE	SEX	OCCUPATIONS	COUNTRY TO WHICH THEY BELONG	COUNTRY THEY INTEND TO INHABIT	SHIPS/DATES OF ARRIVAL	
FULLIAMS, William	26		Farmer	... Eng./G...th, Eng.	New York	Venus	12 Apr 1821
FULLSON, Hugh	16	M	Servant	Ireland	United States	Carolina Ann	11 Dec 1826
FULMER, John	28	M	Shoemaker	Germany	U. States	Sully	24 Oct 1828
FULSEN, Nathl., Captn.	27	M	Shipmaster	Portsmouth, N.H.	United States	Zodiac	14 Jun 1822
FULSTON, Robert	21	M	Tradesman	Great Britain	United States	Diana	20 Nov 1828
FULTAN, Benjaman	18	M	Weaver	Ireland	United States	Robert Fulton	10 Aug 1827
FULTON, Cordelia	11	F				Day	11 Jun 1823
Eleanor	3		Child	Ireland	United States	Courier	15 Oct 1827
Elizabeth	22 4/12		Spinster	Scotland	U.S. of America	Helen	8 Feb 1822
George	45	M	Merchant	America	America	Panthia	17 Sep 1821
Henry	20 1/12		Farmer	Scotland	U.S. of America	Helen	8 Feb 1822
Hugh	24		Carpenter	Scotland	United States	Camillus	3 May 1828
*died on the passage							
Isabella	3		Spinster	Great Britain	United States	Camillus	12 Sep 1827
James	26	M	Labourer	Ireland		William Tell	24 Oct 1829
John	10	M	Boy	Ireland	United States	Courier	15 Oct 1827
Joseph	31		Farmer			Rufus King	7 Aug 1820
Js.	35	M	Labourer	Great Brittan	U. States	John & Elizabeth	11 Dec 1826
Julia	13	F				Day	11 Jun 1823
Mary	9	F				Day	11 Jun 1823
Matilda	2		Child	Ireland	United States	Courier	15 Oct 1827
Robert	15	M				Day	11 Jun 1823
Thos.	1/4		Child	Ireland	United States	Courier	15 Oct 1827
FULTZ, James	20	M	unknown	U. States	U. States	Mary	7 Nov 1822
FUMAER, Wm., Jr.	26	M	...	...	...	Antioch	8 Oct 1827
FUNCEH, Cherry	40	M	Merchant	U. States	Jereme	Culloden	21 Oct 1823
FUNCK, C.	21	M	Sugar refiner	Gt. Britain	United States	Europa	20 Apr 1825
James	32 5/12	M	Mariner	America	America	Braganza	7 Oct 1823
James P.	23	M	Clergyman	United States	United States	Illinois	9 Oct 1820
Jos. A.	35 2/12	M	Clerk	America	U. States	France	26 Jun 1828
FUNDARA, Fransisco	41	M	Planter	Spain	U. States	Ambuscade	6 Oct 1821
FUNK, Carl F.	35	M	Joiner	France	United States	New England	29 Aug 1828
David	27	M	Sail Maker		America	Loire	7 Apr 1821
FUNROD, Ann	33	F	None	Ireland	United States	Jubilee	13 Jul 1829
FURDON, Henry	47	M	Plate in Steel	Gt. Britain	New York	Leeds	7 Nov 1828
Henry, Junr.	10	M		Gt. Britain	New York	Leeds	7 Nov 1828
FURGASON, —,							
Childe	3/12	F		Ireland	America	Enterprize	29 Jun 1827
An	8	F	None	Great Britain	United States	Courier	26 Jun 1827
Elenor	9	F		Ireland	America	Enterprize	29 Jun 1827
Elenor	44	F		Ireland	America	Enterprize	29 Jun 1827
Elizabeth	3	F		Ireland	America	Enterprize	29 Jun 1827
Elizabeth	25	F	None	Great Britain	United States	Courier	26 Jun 1827
John	4	M	None	Great Britain	United States	Courier	26 Jun 1827
John	5	M		Ireland	America	Enterprize	29 Jun 1827
William	6	M	None	Great Britain	United States	Courier	26 Jun 1827
Wm.	55	M	Spinner	England	U. States	Panthea	22 Nov 1826
FURGERSON, Goerge	20	M	Labourer	Ireland	United States	Nancy	16 Jul 1824
FURGESON, Elizabeth	23	F	None	G.B.	U.S.	Silvanus Jenkins	27 Jul 1829
John	66	M	Farmer	America	United States	Belmont	30 Aug 1828
William	2 6/12	M	None	G.B.	U.S.	Silvanus Jenkins	27 Jul 1829
FURGSON, Bridget	7	F		Ireland	America	Enterprize	29 Jun 1827
Charles	15	M		Ireland	America	Enterprize	29 Jun 1827
FURGUSON, Christian	28	F		Scotland	U.S. of America	Friends	10 May 1823
Edward	22	M	Merchant	United States	United States	York	31 Mar 1828
James	3	M		Scotland	U.S. of America	Friends	10 May 1823
Robert	13	M	None	Ireland	America	Hesperus	7 Jul 1820
FURIE, Cherry	26	M	Trader	U. States	U. States	Robt. Reade	12 Apr 1825
FURIGAN, Margaret	20	F		Ireland	United States	Princess Charlotte	26 Apr 1827
FURLONG, Balthazar	50	M	Merchant	Mexico	N. York	Charlemagne	20 Aug 1829
Jno.	25	M	Merchant	Alexandria	Alexandria	Robert Cochran	6 Nov 1824
John	23	M	Laboror	Ireland	United States	Wilson	27 Jun 1826
Seaquim	48	M	Merchant	Mexico	N. York	Charlemagne	20 Aug 1829
Thos.	27	M	Labourer	Great Britain	United States	Penelope	11 Jun 1827
Walter	30	M	Mechanic	Ireland	United States	Wm. Byrnes	30 Apr 1828

NAMES OF PASSENGERS	AGE	SEX	OCCUPATIONS	COUNTRY TO WHICH THEY BELONG	COUNTRY THEY INTEND TO INHABIT	SHIPS/DATES OF ARRIVAL	
FURMAN, Wm. N.	19	M	Merchant	United States	U.S.	Maria Ann	7 Apr 1823
FURN, Elen	22	F	None	Derbeyshire, Bradbern	U. States	Manhattan	21 May 1821
Emund, Junr.	21	M	None	Derbeyshire, Bradbern	U. States	Manhattan	21 May 1821
FURNACE, Allen	19	F		G. Britan	U. States	William Neilson	26 Jul 1828
Charles	4	M	None	Great Britain	New York	Superior	5 Sep 1827
Jno.	6	M	None	Great Britain	New York	Superior	5 Sep 1827
Maria	8	F	None	Great Britain	New York	Superior	5 Sep 1827
Mary Ann	10	F	None	Great Britain	New York	Superior	5 Sep 1827
Wm.	2	M	None	Great Britain	New York	Superior	5 Sep 1827
FURNESS, Connaut	40	M	Moulder	England	U. States	Florida	16 May 1827
Joseph	12	M	Moulder	England	U. States	Florida	16 May 1827
FURNHARD, Eliza	1			England	America	Governor Griswold	6 Jun 1821
FURNHEAD, James	38		Mechanic	England	America	Governor Griswold	6 Jun 1821
Mary	10			England	America	Governor Griswold	6 Jun 1821
Mary	38			England	America	Governor Griswold	6 Jun 1821
Wm.	12			England	America	Governor Griswold	6 Jun 1821
FURNISS, Sophia	2	F		St. Croix	U. States	Chase	9 Aug 1827
Sophia	38	F		St. Croix	U. States	Chase	9 Aug 1827
Wm.	6	M		St. Croix	U. States	Chase	9 Aug 1827
Wm.	40	M	Merchant	St. Croix	U. States	Chase	9 Aug 1827
FURNIVAL, Ann	32	F	None	Great Brittain	New York	Albion	11 Jun 1821
Jane	12	F	None	Great Brittain	New York	Albion	11 Jun 1821
Mary A.	9	F	None	Great Brittain	New York	Albion	11 Jun 1821
W. Jos.	7	M	None	Great Brittain	New York	Albion	11 Jun 1821
FURRIER, J. S.	24	M	Merchant	G. Brittain	U. States	Pacific	23 Jan 1826
FURSE, Robert	40	M	Gardner	Great Britain	U. States	Hannibal	12 Oct 1829
FURST, A.	22	M	Capmaker	Prussia	U. States	Brutus	2 Dec 1823
FURY, Ann	3	F	Child	Ireland	United States	Dublin Packet	24 Sep 1823
Mary	5	F	Child	Ireland	United States	Dublin Packet	24 Sep 1823
Sarah	30	F	Wife	Ireland	United States	Dublin Packet	24 Sep 1823
FUSSEL, James	22	M	Collier	Scotland	United States	Camillus	27 Oct 1829
FUTCHER, Joseph	20	M	Merchant	England	U. States	Cincinnatus	24 May 1821
FYACK, William	37	M	Merchant	U. States	U. States	Calliope	20 Mar 1824
FYFE, —, child	8/12			U. States	U. States	Morgiana	18 Sep 1821
John	35	M	Merchant	Scotland	United States	Camillus	9 May 1827
Martha	30	F		U. States	U. States	Morgiana	18 Sep 1821
FYNE, James	30	M	Labourer	England	U. States	Comet	23 Aug 1828
FYRLE, Patrick	24	M	Baker	Ireland	United States	Borneo	9 Jul 1827
G..., James	...	M	Silver Plater	England	America	Josephine	8 Jan 1827
G...D, John	...2	M	Farmer	...	United States	Minerva	30 Oct 1827
G...E...Y, Margaret	17	F	Dress Maker	Ireland	United States	Carolina Ann	14 May 1827
G...EPEAR, Victor...	35	M	Merchant	France	France	Cadmus	9 Dec 1826
G...EVER, Henry	24	M	Teacher	Switzerland	United States	Elbe	2 Aug 1822
G...ING, James	24	M	Labourer	Great Britain	United States	Frances Henrietta	17 Sep 1827
Robert	27	M		England	America	Ann	11 Apr 1821
G...LAND, Michael	21	M	Labourer	Limerick	Baltimore	Thomas & William	25 May 1827
G...LL..., Robert	28 1/12	M	Weaver	Great Briton	United States	Mount Vernon	30 Dec 1828
GA..., Jacob	30	M	Weaver	Switzerland	United States	Elbe	2 Aug 1822
GA...ACA, Anne	22	F		Switzerland	United States	Elbe	2 Aug 1822
Barbara	44	F		Switzerland	United States	Elbe	2 Aug 1822
Catherina	20	F		Switzerland	United States	Elbe	2 Aug 1822
GA...Y, J.	36		Farmer	Ireland	United States	Courier	16 May 1825
GABA, Rebecca	45	F	None	Jamaica	U. States	Essex	20 May 1823
GABART, John	30	M	Merchant	France	France	Hannah Elizabeth	14 Sep 1827
GABBORY, Francis	20	M	Labourer	Ireland	United States	Belleville	13 Oct 1827
GABBY, William	22	M	Labourrer	Great Britan	U. States	Ann Marria	6 Aug 1823
GABENS, N.	48	F		France	United States	New England	29 Aug 1828
GABERAILLI, John	24	M	Silversmith	Boston	U. States	Congress	9 Mar 1829

NAMES OF PASSENGERS	AGE	SEX	OCCUPATIONS	COUNTRY TO WHICH THEY BELONG	COUNTRY THEY INTEND TO INHABIT	SHIPS/DATES OF ARRIVAL	
GABERT, Jacob	35	M	Mechanic	Bordeaux	U. States	Curlew	1 Mar 1823
GABESH, John C.	20	M	Merchant	Russia	United States	Robert Edwards	1 Jun 1826
GABIL, Caroline	20	F		Denmark	United States	Pioneer	28 Jun 1827
GABORY, Albert	22	M	Gentleman	France	U.S.	Edward Quesnel	21 Apr 1827
GABRELLA, Vincent	46	M	Store Keeper	Philadelphia	Philadelphia	London	19 Dec 1823
GABRIEL, John	22	M	Sugar Baker	Germany	United States	Robert Edwards	1 Jun 1826
GACK, Maria	40	F		France	America, U.N.S.	Great Britain	3 Aug 1829
Martin	50	M	Farmer	France	America, U.N.S.	Great Britain	3 Aug 1829
GADD, George	35	M	Lace Weaver	England	United States	Euphrates	18 Aug 1827
GADDIS, Gann	17	M		Killinchey	United States	Carolina Ann	11 Jun 1824
William	19	M	Farmer	Killinchey	United States	Carolina Ann	11 Jun 1824
GADEN, M.	28	M	Gent.	England	U. States	James Cropper	17 Jun 1825
GADERSELLER, L.	36	M	C...	Germany	Prussia	Florida	17 May 1825
GADONA, —, Madan	26	F	None			Howard	21 May 1827
Janny	4	F	None			Howard	21 May 1827
GADSBY, Edward	30	M	Farmer	Ireland	United States	Colossus	30 May 1825
Elizabeth	25	F	...	Ireland	United States	Colossus	30 May 1825
James	29	M	Farmer	...lson	United States	Solon	21 Jun 1824
Thos.	32	M	Farmer	...lson	United States	Solon	21 Jun 1824
GAEBER, John	18	M	Joiner	Switzerland	United States	Elbe	2 Aug 1822
Ulrich	15	M		Switzerland	United States	Elbe	2 Aug 1822
GAEL..., John	42	M	Weaver	Switzerland	United States	Elbe	2 Aug 1822
GAELAN, Francis	22	M	Accountant	United States	United States	Altimira	21 Feb 1827
GAFF, Catherine	49 8/12	F	Farmer	Switzerland	America	Henry	17 May 1828
George	17 5/12	M	Farmer	Switzerland	America	Henry	17 May 1828
Jacob	21 7/12	M	Farmer	Switzerland	America	Henry	17 May 1828
John	54 3/12	M	Farmer	Switzerland	America	Henry	17 May 1828
GAFFAY, Michl.	30	M		Ireland	United States	William Byrnes	6 Apr 1826
GAFFENEY, Charles	34	M	Labourer	Ireland	America	Plutarch	18 Jul 1826
Hugh	4	M		Ireland	America	Plutarch	18 Jul 1826
Margret	6	F		Ireland	America	Plutarch	18 Jul 1826
Mary	8	F		Ireland	America	Plutarch	18 Jul 1826
Owen	30	M	Brick setter	Ireland	America	Plutarch	18 Jul 1826
Winny	34	F		Ireland	America	Plutarch	18 Jul 1826
GAFFNEY, Bridget	24	F	Spinster	Ireland	United States	Dublin Packet	3 Sep 1822
Charles	22	M	Labourer	Great Britain	United States	Thomas Dickason	14 Sep 1827
John	28	M	Mercht.	Ireland		Fame	9 Dec 1826
M.	15 6/12	M	Labourer	Great Britain	United States	Thomas Dickason	14 Sep 1827
Mary	19	F	Servant	Irereland	America	Carolina Ann	20 Jun 1825
Patrick	26	M	Labourer	Ireland	U.S. of America	Hamilton	18 Jul 1827
Rose	10 7/12	F		Ireland	America	Carolina Ann	7 Apr 1828
Thomas	20	M	Farmer	Ireland	United States	Dublin Packet	3 Sep 1822
GAFFNY, Cath.	5	F	None	Ireland	United States	Dalhouse Castle	21 Aug 1829
Catharine	5	F	None	Ireland	U.S.A.	Dalhouse Castle	21 Aug 1829
GAFFREY, Ann	8	F	None	England	United States	India	8 Jun 1827
Bridget	18			Ireland		Anacreon	7 Sep 1827
Cathe.	15			Ireland		Anacreon	7 Sep 1827
Elisabeth	30	F	Spinster	Ireland	United States	Ann Maria	8 Jun 1824
Ellen	15	F	None	England	United States	India	8 Jun 1827
Jas.	12	M	None	England	United States	India	8 Jun 1827
John	36			Ireland		Anacreon	7 Sep 1827
John, (her Child) [Elisabeth]	9	M	Boy	Ireland	United States	Ann Maria	8 Jun 1824
William	10	M	None	England	United States	India	8 Jun 1827
GAFFRY, Maria	5	F		Ireland	America	Josephine	8 Jan 1827
Mary	25	F	Matron	Ireland	America	Josephine	8 Jan 1827
Michael	4	M		Ireland	America	Josephine	8 Jan 1827
Thomas	30	M	Clerk	Ireland	America	Josephine	8 Jan 1827
GAFFY, Owen	46	M	Labourer	Ireland	United States	Hope	12 Jun 1828
GAFNEY, Ann	35	F		England	United States	Danube	22 Aug 1825
Bridget	7	M		England	United States	Danube	22 Aug 1825
Ellenor	13	F		England	United States	Danube	22 Aug 1825
Margaret	Infant	F		England	United States	Danube	22 Aug 1825
Mary	15	F		England	United States	Danube	22 Aug 1825
Michael	4	M		England	United States	Danube	22 Aug 1825
Michael	40	M	Farmer	England	United States	Danube	22 Aug 1825
Patrick	9	M		England	United States	Danube	22 Aug 1825

NAMES OF PASSENGERS	AGE	SEX	OCCUPATIONS	COUNTRY TO WHICH THEY BELONG	COUNTRY THEY INTEND TO INHABIT	SHIPS/DATES OF ARRIVAL	
GAFNEY (cont'd)							
Peter	11	M		England	United States	Danube	22 Aug 1825
Philip	17	M	Labourer	Ireland	United States	Josephine	30 Apr 1828
GAFREY, Edward	27	M	Labourer	Ireland	America	Wilson	16 Nov 1824
Mary	24	F	Matron	Ireland	America	Wilson	16 Nov 1824
GAFT, Catharin	54	F		France		Pallas	14 Jun 1828
Henry	55	M	Farm	France		Pallas	14 Jun 1828
Jean P.	12	F		France		Pallas	14 Jun 1828
Joseph	19	F	Farm	France		Pallas	14 Jun 1828
Margaretta	22	F		France		Pallas	14 Jun 1828
Perre	18	F		France		Pallas	14 Jun 1828
GAGAR, Julius	21	M	Merchant	Denmark	U. States	Martha	5 Sep 1827
GAGE, Arnold	17	M	Clerk	Ireland	U. States	Dawn	15 Jul 1828
E. W.	30	M	Planter	Boston	U. States	Circassian	3 Jun 1826
Henry	25	M	Gentleman	U. States	U. States	Genl. A. Jackson	6 Sep 1820
John T.	20	M	Clerk	London	London	Cato	2 Jan 1824
W.	32	M	Farmer	Germany	United States	Lydia	18 Jun 1828
GAGGAIN, A. H.	26	M	Merchant	U. States	U. States	St. George	20 Sep 1828
GAGOX, Ana Maria	5	F		Switzerland	United States	Elizabeth	27 Jul 1824
Elizabeth	4	F		Switzerland	United States	Elizabeth	27 Jul 1824
Maria Ana	1	F		Switzerland		Elizabeth	27 Jul 1824
*died on the passage							
Samuel	3	M		Switzerland	United States	Elizabeth	27 Jul 1824
Samuel	30	M	Weaver	Switzerland	United States	Elizabeth	27 Jul 1824
Verena	34	F		Switzerland	United States	Elizabeth	27 Jul 1824
GAGUE, James	15	M	Merch.	Great Brit.	U.S.	Silvanus Jenkins	17 Mar 1828
GAHAGAN, Owen	26	M	Labourer	Ireland	United States	William	20 Jul 1829
GAIL, Edward	24	M	Farmer	England	United States	Siroc	31 Oct 1829
Ellen	4	F		England	United States	Siroc	31 Oct 1829
Mary	22	F	Farmer	England	United States	Siroc	31 Oct 1829
William	2	M		England	United States	Siroc	31 Oct 1829
GAILEY, John	20	M	Labourer	Ireland	United States	William & George	14 May 1828
GAILLARD, John	35	M	Merchant	France	U.S.	Bayard	10 Nov 1824
GAILLUME, Abraham	13	M		Germany	United States	Origon	8 Jun 1824
Abrm.	1	M		Germany	United States	Origon	8 Jun 1824
Christ	25	M	Farmer	Germany	United States	Origon	8 Jun 1824
Elizabeth	25	F		Germany	United States	Origon	8 Jun 1824
GAILROIS, Jean	28	M	Potter Baker	France	U. States	Leonarde	29 Aug 1828
GAIMAUND, Joseph	9	M	None	Cuba	Spain	Ariel	30 Jun 1828
GAIN, Mary	6	F		Irland	U. States	Nancy	27 Jun 1823
Pat	4	M		Irland	U. States	Nancy	27 Jun 1823
GAINER, James	25	M		Ireland	United States	William Byrnes	6 Apr 1826
GAINES, Pory	32	F		Ireland	U. States	Howard Douglass	29 Jan 1828
GAINING, Pat	20	M	Labourer	Ireland	U. States	Loire	6 Dec 1827
GAINOR, Peter	21	M	Labourer	Ireland	U.N. States	Jane	7 Oct 1826
GAINS, Edward	20		Laboring Class		United States	Atlantic	2 Apr 1827
James	20		Laboring Class		United States	Atlantic	2 Apr 1827
GAIR, Samuel	30	M	Merchant	United States	United States	Nestor	3 Nov 1820
GAIT, J. W.	21	M	Merchant	U. States		Star	7 Jan 1827
GAITLAND, Nicholas	40	M	Farmer	Ireland	United States	Trident	18 Jul 1827
GALAGAN, Magrat	3	F	None	Ireland	U.S.	Pacific	24 Oct 1828
Mary	35	F	Wife	Ireland	U.S.	Pacific	24 Oct 1828
Tho.	34	M	Farmer	Ireland	U. States	Meteor	19 Jul 1828
GALAGAR, Sarah	21	F	Labourer	Ireland	United States	Hope	12 Jun 1828
GALAGELER, Agurtha	7	F	Swiss	Ireland		Quatre Freres	29 Jul 1828
Catharen	0 1/12	F	Swiss	Ireland		Quatre Freres	29 Jul 1828
*Born on the Passage							
Francis	2	M	Swiss	Ireland		Quatre Freres	29 Jul 1828
Jane	24	F	Carpenter	Ireland		Quatre Freres	29 Jul 1828
Joseph	36	M	Carpenter	Ireland		Quatre Freres	29 Jul 1828
Perre	4	M	Swiss	Ireland		Quatre Freres	29 Jul 1828
GALAGER, Mary	18	F	Labourer	Ireland	United States	Hope	12 Jun 1828
GALAGHAN, Patrick	28	M	Labourer	Ireland	United States	New Packet	15 Nov 1828
GALAGHER, Hugh	20	M	Labourer	Ireland	United States	William & George	14 May 1828

NAMES OF PASSENGERS	AGE	SEX	OCCUPATIONS	COUNTRY TO WHICH THEY BELONG	COUNTRY THEY INTEND TO INHABIT	SHIPS/DATES OF ARRIVAL	
GALAGHER (cont'd)							
John	25	M	Labourer	Ireland	United States	William & George	14 May 1828
Neal	21	M		Ireland	United States	William & George	14 May 1828
Patrick	22	M		Ireland	United States	William & George	14 May 1828
GALAHAR, Owen	26	M	Labourer	Ireland	United States	Hope	12 Jun 1828
GALAHER, Patk.	13	M		Limerick	Kentucky	Thomas & William	25 May 1827
Sarah	24	F	Spinster	Ireland		Robert Fulton	4 Jun 1828
GALAN, Nicholas	30	M	Labourer	Great Britain	U. States	Great Britain	18 Mar 1828
GALAUGHER,							
Bridget	15 6/12	F	Spinster	Ireland	United States	Robert Fulton	24 Jul 1826
Danial	24	M	Labourer	Ireland	United States	Robert Fulton	24 Jul 1826
Hugh	23	M	Baker	Ireland	United States	Robert Fulton	24 Jul 1826
GALAVAN, Ellen	14	F		Ireland	United States	Trio	2 Oct 1828
Margaret	16	F		Ireland	United States	Trio	2 Oct 1828
Margaret	46	F		Ireland	United States	Trio	2 Oct 1828
GALAWAY, Ann	24	F	Lady	Ireland	United States	Belleville	13 Oct 1827
John	30	M	Laborer	Ireland	United States	Belleville	13 Oct 1827
Mary	3/12	F	Child	Ireland	United States	Belleville	13 Oct 1827
GALBODEA, Joseph	24	M	Artizen	Iterly	United States	Jubilee	13 Jul 1829
GALBRAITH, Hugh	30	M	Labourer	Ireland, Great Britain	U.S. of America	Dublin	21 Feb 1826
James	25	M	Labourer	Scotland	United States	Friends	7 Jul 1827
Margt.	14	F		Ireland	New York	Triton	12 Jul 1823
Mary	12		Spinster	Ireland	United States	Robert Burns	18 Jun 1821
Wm.	21	M	Labourer	Great Britain	United States	Atlantic	8 Dec 1827
GALBREATH, Samuel	39		Farmer	U. States	United States	Robert Burns	18 Jun 1821
GALBRETH, A.	22	M	Farmer	Scotland	U. States	Superior	25 Sep 1828
GALBRIETH, Thomas	42	M	Shoemaker	Ireland	America	Farmer	4 Aug 1825
GALBROUTH, Hugh	1 6/12	M		Scotland	United States	St. John	5 Oct 1829
Isabella	13	F		Scotland	United States	St. John	5 Oct 1829
Margaret	30	F		Scotland	United States	St. John	5 Oct 1829
Robert	33	M	Manufacturer	Scotland	United States	St. John	5 Oct 1829
GALBURG, John M.	42	M	Mariner	U. States	U. States	London Packet	8 Mar 1825
GALBURTH, M.	8	F	...	...	U. States	Governor Tompkins	26 Jul 1824
GALDEN, Samuel	35	M	Farmer	Scotland	U. States	General Graham	9 May 1827
GALDESHEAD, William	32	M	Labourer	Scotland	United States	Samuel Robertson	5 Oct 1827
GALE, Catharine	3 6/12			England	United States	Thomas Dickason	5 Jun 1827
Easter	26			England	United States	Thomas Dickason	5 Jun 1827
Emma, Miss	2	F	Lady	England	U. States	Acasta	21 Oct 1825
Harriet	12	F		St. John	U.States	Nancy	31 May 1823
Henrietta	15	F	None	New York, U. States	United States	James Cropper	7 Oct 1823
John	45		Weaver	England	United States	Thomas Dickason	5 Jun 1827
John, Jr.	15			England	United States	Thomas Dickason	5 Jun 1827
L. H.	31	M	Merchant	U. States	U. States	Dromo	24 Jul 1826
Sophia, Mrs.	28	F	Lady	England	U. States	Acasta	21 Oct 1825
Thos.	10 3/12		Servt. to Mr. Wright	Great Britain	Pennsylvania	Venus	8 Sep 1820
GALEMON, Benjn.	15	M	Labourer	England	United States	John Dickinson	30 Sep 1823
GALESPIE, James	15	M	Clerk	Scotland	United States	Friends	16 Aug 1824
GALHOUN, Mathew	20	M	Labourer	Ireland		Robert Fulton	4 Jun 1828
GALIANO, Thomas	37	M	Gentleman	Spain	U. States	Brunswick	14 Feb 1829
GALIGAN, Alice	27	F	Spinster	Ireland	United States	Dublin Packet	6 Dec 1827
GALIGER, Margaret	20	F		Ireland		Lady Hunter	12 Apr 1823
GALIHER, David, Mast.	4	M	Carpenter	England	U.S.	Acasta	11 May 1827
Edward, Mast.	6	M	Carpenter	England	U.S.	Acasta	11 May 1827
Jane, Mrs.	30	F	Carpenter	England	U.S.	Acasta	11 May 1827
John	32	M	Carpenter	England	U.S.	Acasta	11 May 1827
John, Mast.	2	M	Carpenter	England	U.S.	Acasta	11 May 1827
GALINDO, Antonio		M	Gentleman	Spaniard		Happy Return	23 Jul 1821

NAMES OF PASSENGERS	AGE	SEX	OCCUPATIONS	COUNTRY TO WHICH THEY BELONG	COUNTRY THEY INTEND TO INHABIT	SHIPS/DATES OF ARRIVAL	
GALIVAN, Thomas	19	M	Sadler	Ireland	United States	Clothier	22 Nov 1827
GALLAGAR, Mary	18	F	Child	Ireland	N. York	Trusty	12 Sep 1828
—, Dr.	48	M	Doctor	U. States	U. States	Emma	15 Apr 1822
Edward	17	M	Taylor	Ireland	U. States	Courier	17 Mar 1828
Elizabeth	18	F	Spinster	Ireland	U. States	Courier	17 Mar 1828
Mary Ann	13 6/12	F	Spinster	Ireland	U. States	Courier	17 Mar 1828
GALLAGHAN, Bridget	27	F				Governor Fenner	23 Jul 1829
Farral	27	M	Labourer	Ireland	Pennsylvania	Governor Fenner	23 Jul 1829
John	9/12	M				Governor Fenner	23 Jul 1829
Thos.	47	M	Weaver	Ireland	United States	Henry Kneeland	7 Jun 1828
GALLAGHAR, Ann	21	F	None	Great Britain	United States	Eliza Barker	3 Jul 1826
Antig	32	F	Wife	Ireland	United States	St. Michaels	23 Dec 1826
Bernard	21	M	Tanner	Ireland	United States	Louisa	18 Apr 1827
George	38	M	Merchant	U. States	U. States	York	10 Dec 1825
GALLAGHER, —,							
an infant	6/12	M		Ireland	United States	Trio	31 Oct 1827
—, Mrs.	60	F		U. States	U. States	Queen Mab	7 Apr 1826
Amelia	23	F		U. States	U. States	Queen Mab	7 Apr 1826
Andrew	20	M	Farmer	Ireland	United States	Asia	29 Jul 1829
Ann	5	F		Ireland	United States	Trio	31 Oct 1827
Ann	22	F		Ireland	United States	Trio	31 Oct 1827
Anne	16	F	Spinster	Ireland	United States	Asia	29 Jul 1829
Arthur	21	M	Labourer	Ireland		William Tell	24 Oct 1829
Bridget	...		Laboring Class		United States	Atlantic	2 Apr 1827
Bridget	6	F	None	Great Britain	United States	Columbia	9 Aug 1822
Bridget	19	F		Ireland	U. States	Virginia	20 Jun 1825
Catherine	5	F	Child	Ireland	United States	St. Michaels	23 Dec 1826
Catherine	22	F	Spinster	England	United States	Trident	31 Mar 1827
Charlotte	18	F	Farmer, Labourer or Spinster	Ireland	U. States	Meteor	4 Oct 1827
Chris	30	M		Great Britain	United States	Aurora	5 Sep 1826
E.	14	M		Ireland	United States	Antioch	21 Sep 1827
Edward	20	M	Farmer	Ireland	United States	Dublin Packet	9 Jul 1827
Ellen	33	F	Child	Ireland	United States	Henry Kneeland	7 Jun 1828
Fanny	20	F	Farmer, Labourer or Spinster	Ireland	U. States	Meteor	4 Oct 1827
Francis	4	M	None	Great Britain	United States	Columbia	9 Aug 1822
George	5	M	Child	Ireland	United States	Henry Kneeland	7 Jun 1828
George	18	M		Ireland	New York	Potomac	7 Aug 1827
George	22	M	Merchant	United States	United States	Isaac Hicks	22 May 1826
Hugh	22	M	Farmer	Gt. Britain	United States	Penelope	9 Sep 1828
Isabella	20	F	Spinster	Ireland	United States	Asia	29 Jul 1829
James	9	M	Child	Ireland	United States	Henry Kneeland	7 Jun 1828
James	24	M	Labourer	Ireland	U. States	Hanford	29 Dec 1828
James	25	M	Labourer	Ireland	U. States	Sarah G	7 May 1827
James	35	M	Child	Ireland	United States	Henry Kneeland	7 Jun 1828
James	40	M	Merchant	Ireland	United States	Antioch	21 Sep 1827
James, Jr.	7	M		Ireland	United States	Antioch	21 Sep 1827
Jann	34	F	None	Great Britain	United States	Columbia	9 Aug 1822
Jno.	24	M	Merchant	Ireland	United States	Trident	17 May 1825
John	1	M	Child	Ireland	United States	St. Michaels	23 Dec 1826
John	1	M	Child	Ireland	United States	Henry Kneeland	7 Jun 1828
John	1 1/12	M	None	England	United States	Trident	31 Mar 1827
John	19	M	Labourer	Ireland		Robert Fulton	4 Jun 1828
John	30	M	Labourer	Ireland	U. States	Nancy	1 Sep 1823
Louisa	19	F		U. States	U. States	Queen Mab	7 Apr 1826
Margaret	9		Laboring Class		United States	Atlantic	2 Apr 1827
Margret	12	F	Child	Ireland	United States	Henry Kneeland	7 Jun 1828
Martha	6	F		Ireland	United States	Antioch	21 Sep 1827
Mary	3	F	Child	Ireland	United States	St. Michaels	23 Dec 1826
Mary	20	F	Spinster	Ireland	United States	Fabius	4 Jun 1828
Mary	23	F	Servant	Ireland	U. States	Sarah G	7 May 1827
Mary	28	F	Labourer	Ireland	U. States	Nancy	1 Sep 1823
Mary	32	F		Ireland	U. States	Virginia	20 Jun 1825
Mary	60	F	Farmer, Labourer or Spinster	Ireland	U. States	Meteor	4 Oct 1827
Owen	30	M	Labourer	Ireland	United States	Trio	31 Oct 1827
Patrick	3	M		Ireland	United States	Trio	31 Oct 1827
Patrick	3	M	Child	Ireland	United States	Henry Kneeland	7 Jun 1828

NAMES OF PASSENGERS	AGE	SEX	OCCUPATIONS	COUNTRY TO WHICH THEY BELONG	COUNTRY THEY INTEND TO INHABIT	SHIPS/DATES OF ARRIVAL	
GALLAGHER (cont'd)							
Patt	20	M	Mason	Ireland	New York	Lima	5 Aug 1829
Patt	20	M	Mason	Ireland	New York	Lima	5 Aug 1829
Sally	14	F	Child	Ireland	United States	Henry Kneeland	7 Jun 1828
Sally	19	F	Spinster	Ireland		Robert Fulton	4 Jun 1828
William	7	M	Child	Ireland	United States	Henry Kneeland	7 Jun 1828
GALLAGINER, Jas.	10	M	None	Great Britain	United States	Columbia	9 Aug 1822
GALLAGUR, Mary	8	F	None	Great Britain	United States	Columbia	9 Aug 1822
GALLAHER, Allis	48	F		Ireland	New York	Potomac	7 Aug 1827
Catharine	20	F	Spinster	Ireland	United States	Catharine	22 Jul 1825
GALLANGER, Rose	22	F	Spinster	Ireland	United States	Robert Fulton	24 Jul 1826
GALLATIN, —, Miss	18	F		U. States	U. States	Silvanus Jenkins	30 Nov 1827
—, Mrs.	58	F		U. States	U. States	Silvanus Jenkins	30 Nov 1827
Albert	21	M	Gent.	U. States	U. States	Cadmus	28 May 1821
Albert	66	M	Merchant	U. States	U. States	Silvanus Jenkins	30 Nov 1827
Francis	18	F		United States	U.S.	Montano	24 Jun 1823
Gallancy Albert, Sir Esqr.	60	M	Ambassader	United States	U.S.	Montano	24 Jun 1823
James	26	M	Ambassader	United States	U.S.	Montano	24 Jun 1823
Mary	50	F		United States	U.S.	Montano	24 Jun 1823
GALLATION, Giles	20	M	Merchant	U. States	Laguira	Gertrude	16 May 1827
GALLAUGHAR, John	1...	M	Labourer	Ireland	Unt. St. America	Wilson	21 May 1827
GALLAUGHER, Dennis	10		Boy	Ireland		Westmoreland	1 Aug 1826
Domk.	12		Boy	Ireland		Westmoreland	1 Aug 1826
James	30		Labourer			Rufus King	7 Aug 1820
John	20	M	Cord Wainer	Ireland	United States	Asia	29 Jul 1829
John	40		Labourer			Rufus King	7 Aug 1820
Mary	15	F	Spinster	Ireland	Unt. St. America	Wilson	21 May 1827
Patrick	45	M	Labourer	Ireland	United States	Robert Fulton	24 Jul 1826
GALLAYNON, Owen	...	M	Cooper	Ireland	U. States	Henry Kneeland	27 Jul 1825
GALLE, Florance	24	M	Mariner	Italy	Italy	Eliza	22 Dec 1826
GALLEGAR, Hugh	22	M	Hacklemakerer	Ireland	America	Franklin	13 Aug 1827
GALLEGHER, James	23	M	Labourer	Ireland	America	Plutarch	18 Jul 1826
GALLERY, James	33	M	Musician	France		Fame	9 Dec 1826
GALLET, Pierre A.	29	M	Fancy Dealer	France	U. States	Montano	2 Sep 1828
Virginia	25	M	Fancy Dealer	France	U. States	Montano	2 Sep 1828
GALLFORD, Catherine	4	F	his family [Paul]	Germany	United States	Wm. Osborne	16 Sep 1828
Elizabeth	6	F	his family [Paul]	Germany	United States	Wm. Osborne	16 Sep 1828
Henry	8	M	his family [Paul]	Germany	United States	Wm. Osborne	16 Sep 1828
Margret	1	F	his family [Paul]	Germany	United States	Wm. Osborne	16 Sep 1828
Paul	38	M	Blacksmith	Germany	United States	Wm. Osborne	16 Sep 1828
Salme	38	F	his family [Paul]	Germany	United States	Wm. Osborne	16 Sep 1828
Susanne	2	F	his family [Paul]	Germany	United States	Wm. Osborne	16 Sep 1828
GALLGER, George	18	M	Labourer	Ireland		Robert Fulton	4 Jun 1828
GALLIGAN, Ann	24	F	Matron	Ireland	U. States	Josephine	30 Aug 1828
Eliza	20	F	None	Ireland	United States	Trident	18 Jul 1827
Jas.	25	M	Labourer	England	U. States	Thomas Ritchie	2 Jul 1827
Peter		M	Farmer	Ireland	U. States	Dickinson	30 Jul 1825
Wm.	12	M	Labourer	Ireland	United States	Louisa	18 Apr 1827
GALLIHER, Francis	24		Seaman	United States		Cynosure	4 Mar 1828

*Consul's man, put on bord by the american Consil at St. Michal's Belonging to the brig Emeline of Portland Was Rackt on the 25 of Dec 1827 in the Harber of St. Michals

NAMES OF PASSENGERS	AGE	SEX	OCCUPATIONS	COUNTRY TO WHICH THEY BELONG	COUNTRY THEY INTEND TO INHABIT	SHIPS/DATES OF ARRIVAL	
GALLINGHER, Manasses	...	M	Labourer	Ireland	Unt. St. America	Wilson	21 May 1827
GALLISKI, Maria	25	F	Spinster	England	United States	Sarah	31 Oct 1829
GALLIVAN, Danl.	29	M	Farmer	Ireland	U. States	Gem	28 Dec 1824
Denis	27	M	Labourer	Ireland	U. States	Combine	30 Nov 1825
Mary	21	F		Ireland	U. States	Gem	28 Dec 1824
Nelley	9/12	F		Ireland	U. States	Gem	28 Dec 1824
GALLONY, C.	22	M	Merchat	United States	United States	Indus	5 Sep 1827
GALLOP, Thomas	28			England	United States	Hugh Johnson	11 Jun 1828
GALLOS, Anny	44	F		France	U. States	Lewis	6 Jul 1825
Caspar	17	M	Carpenter	France	U. States	Lewis	6 Jul 1825
Catharine	12	F		France	U. States	Lewis	6 Jul 1825
John	19	M		France	U. States	Lewis	6 Jul 1825
GALLOWAY, Ann	17	F	Child [of John]	Great Briton	United States	Orion	18 Jun 1821
Elizabeth	11	F	Child [of John]	Great Briton	United States	Orion	18 Jun 1821
Elizabeth	44	F	Wife [of John]	Great Briton	United States	Orion	18 Jun 1821
Isabella	6	F	Child [of John]	Great Briton	United States	Orion	18 Jun 1821
Jane, Jr.	12	F	Child [of John]	Great Briton	United States	Orion	18 Jun 1821

NAMES OF PASSENGERS	AGE	SEX	OCCUPATIONS	COUNTRY TO WHICH THEY BELONG	COUNTRY THEY INTEND TO INHABIT	SHIPS/DATES OF ARRIVAL	
GALLOWAY (cont'd)							
John	22	M	Plumber	Scotland	U. States	Atlantic	27 Aug 1827
John	44	M	Dealer	Great Briton	United States	Orion	18 Jun 1821
John, Jr.	15	M	Child [of John]	Great Briton	United States	Orion	18 Jun 1821
Mary	18	F	Child [of John]	Great Briton	United States	Orion	18 Jun 1821
Micheal	28	M	Farmer	Scotland	United States	Commerce	17 Jul 1823
Thomas	4	M	Child [of John]	Great Briton	United States	Orion	18 Jun 1821
GALLOWNEY, John	28	M	Cooper	Spain	Havana	Commodore Chauncy	28 Nov 1825
GALLY, Daniel	35	M	Farmer	England	United States	Cambria	3 Jul 1829
Deborah	34	F	Wife	England	United States	Cambria	3 Jul 1829
Ellen	10	F	Child	England	United States	Cambria	3 Jul 1829
GALMICH, F. C.	42	M		France	United States	Le Voltaire	19 Jul 1828
F. V.	16	M		France	United States	Le Voltaire	19 Jul 1828
Favier	9	M		France	United States	Le Voltaire	19 Jul 1828
Jean C.	4	F		France	United States	Le Voltaire	19 Jul 1828
Joseph F.	6	M		France	United States	Le Voltaire	19 Jul 1828
Margret	19	M		France	United States	Le Voltaire	19 Jul 1828
Nicholas	43	M	Farmer	France	United States	Le Voltaire	19 Jul 1828
GALOUGHER,							
Bridget	39 6/12	F	Matron	Ireland	United States	Robert Fulton	24 Jul 1826
James	52	M	Labourer	Ireland	United States	Fabius	31 Jul 1829
John	27 6/12	M	Labourer	Ireland	United States	Wilson	28 Nov 1828
GALPIN, J. F.	20	M	Gentleman	United States	United States	Charles Amburger	16 Aug 1826
GALPINE, Francis J.	38	M	Merchant	Great Britain	U. States	Superior	5 Jun 1826
GALSORAN, Nicholas	24	M	Merchant	Spain	Spain	Commodore Preble	17 Dec 1825
GALT, Alexr.	11	M		England	Canada	Brighton	14 Apr 1828
Eliza	40	F		England	Canada	Brighton	14 Apr 1828
John	13	M		England	Canada	Brighton	14 Apr 1828
John	42	M	Gentn.	England	Canada	Brighton	16 Nov 1826
Margt.	19	F	None	Whitehaven	Canada	Aldebaron	21 Jan 1826
Thomas	12	M		England	Canada	Brighton	14 Apr 1828
GALTON, William	36	M	Mariner			Robert Edwards	8 Nov 1825
GALTREATH, Cathe.	28		going to her friends	Great Britain	United States	Camillus	12 Sep 1827
Jas.	5			Great Britain	United States	Camillus	12 Sep 1827
Jno.	3			Great Britain	United States	Camillus	12 Sep 1827
GALTRES, Wm.	30	M	Farmer	England		Marchioness	13 May 1828
GALVAN, John	28		Labourer	Longford	Virginia	Peru	30 May 1828
GALVIN, Bridget	26			Longford	Virginia	Peru	30 May 1828
John	26	M	Laborer	Ireland	United States	Trio	13 Jun 1827
Martin	24	M	Labourer	Ireland	Baltimore	Lima	5 Aug 1829
Martin	24	M	Labourer	Ireland	Baltimore	Lima	5 Aug 1829
Mary	32			Longford	Virginia	Peru	30 May 1828
GALWAY, John	18		Servant	Ireland	Great Britain	Robert Burns	14 Jun 1824
Mary	15			Ireland	Great Britain	Robert Burns	14 Jun 1824
Mary	50			Ireland	Great Britain	Robert Burns	14 Jun 1824
William	21 3/12	M	Farmer	Ireland	United States	Wilson	22 Jun 1824
GALWERK, Mary	1 1/2		Child	Great Britain	United States	Camillus	12 Sep 1827
GAMBELL, Lenard	20	M	Flax Dresser	Ireland	In Country	Potomac	7 Aug 1827
GAMBINO, Leus	29	M	Engineer	Italy	Mexico	Corinthian	27 Apr 1824
GAMBLE, Aarther	20	M	Labourer	Ireland	U. States	Courier	17 Mar 1828
Andrew	6			Ireland	United States	Robert Burns	30 May 1823
Ann	1...	F	Labourer	England	U. States	Comet	23 Aug 1828
Edward	32	M	Labourer	England	U. States	Comet	23 Aug 1828
Ellen	18	F	None	England	United States	Jubilee	1 Oct 1828
Esther	27	F	Farmer	Lundarry	United States	Minerva	30 Oct 1829
James	6	M	Child	Kilmarnock	U.S. America	Camillus	10 Sep 1821
James	32		Farmer	Ireland	United States	Robert Burns	30 May 1823
Jane	3	F	Farmer	Lundarry	United States	Minerva	30 Oct 1829
Jane	30			Ireland	United States	Robert Burns	30 May 1823
Jane	36	F	Wife	Kilmarnock	U.S. America	Camillus	10 Sep 1821
Janet	3	F	Child	Kilmarnock	U.S. America	Camillus	10 Sep 1821
John	9	M	Farmer	Lundarry	United States	Minerva	30 Oct 1829
John	21	M	Tailor	England	America	Two Marys	24 Sep 1827
John W.	22	M	Merchant	Canada	Canada	Brighton	20 Aug 1825
Margaret	6/52			Ireland	United States	Robert Burns	30 May 1823
Margarett	5	F	Farmer	Lundarry	United States	Minerva	30 Oct 1829

NAMES OF PASSENGERS	AGE	SEX	OCCUPATIONS	COUNTRY TO WHICH THEY BELONG	COUNTRY THEY INTEND TO INHABIT	SHIPS/DATES OF ARRIVAL	
GAMBLE (cont'd)							
Mary	7	F	Farmer	Lundarry	United States	Minerva	30 Oct 1829
Nancy	2	F	Farmer	Lundarry	United States	Minerva	30 Oct 1829
Nathl.	23	M	Gentleman	Ireland	United States	Trident	16 May 1826
Robert	1	M	Child	Kilmarnock	U.S. America	Camillus	10 Sep 1821
Robert	38	M	Carpenter	England	United States	Jubilee	1 Oct 1828
Robt.	50	M	Farmer	Lundarry	United States	Minerva	30 Oct 1829
Sarah	30	F	None	England	United States	Jubilee	1 Oct 1828
Sarah	34	F	Labourer	England	U. States	Comet	23 Aug 1828
William	15	M	Farmer	Lundarry	United States	Minerva	30 Oct 1829
William	20	M	Farmer	Ireland	United States	Princess Charlotte	26 Apr 1827
Wm.	8	M	Child	Kilmarnock	U.S. America	Camillus	10 Sep 1821
GAMELL, Richard	22	M	Land Surveyor	Great Britain	United States	Birmingham	15 Jun 1827
GAMERO, M.	35	M	Merchant	Spain	U. States	Mary Jane	2 Jul 1828
GAMERON, H.	25	F		Scotland	U. States	Superior	25 Sep 1828
M.	13	F		Scotland	U. States	Superior	25 Sep 1828
M.	14	F		Scotland	U. States	Superior	25 Sep 1828
W.	41	M	Plasterer	Scotland	U. States	Superior	25 Sep 1828
GAMFELL, Jas.	44	M	Farmer	Gt. Britain	U. States	New York Packet	6 Aug 1824
GAMIEL, Alexr.	22					Charlotte Corday	15 Jul 1820
GAMIRE, Thomas	24	M	Labourer	Irereland	America	Carolina Ann	20 Jun 1825
GAMMEL, Anne	2					James Monroe	8 Aug 1820
Garrett	3	F				James Monroe	8 Aug 1820
Jane	20	F		Scotland		James Monroe	8 Aug 1820
GAMMELL, James	32	M				Ocean	17 Aug 1820
GAMMIS, Peter	29	M	Planter	Scotland	Jamaica	Rolla	16 Nov 1824
GAMSBY, Robt.	21	M	Mariner	Ireland	U. States	Champion	26 Jul 1827
GAMY, Patrick	23	M	Farmer	Ireland	U. States	Sabina	29 Apr 1825
GANAHL, Charles	2	M		America	Newyork	Cortes	16 Jul 1827
Charlotte	26	F		America	Newyork	Cortes	16 Jul 1827
Henry	6	M		America	Newyork	Cortes	16 Jul 1827
Joseph	30	M	Merchant	America	Newyork	Cortes	16 Jul 1827
GANCHETT, John	42	M	Merchant	N. York	United States	Huntress	25 Mar 1822
GANDARD, Jno. Francis	29	M	Merchant	France	U. States	Stephania	8 Mar 1823
GANDER, Mathias	56	M	Farmer	Germany	United States	Elizabeth	4 Sep 1826
GANDERWICH, Thomas	21	M	...	...	...	Sublime	6 Dec 1824
Willm.	32	M	...	...	...	Sublime	6 Dec 1824
GANDOLPH, Antonio	44	M	Gardener	Italy	U. States	Sarah Lee	21 Jul 1821
GANES, Richd.	60	M	Naval Officer	England	United States	Aurora	11 Dec 1824
GANEY, Peter	33	M	Stone Cutter	Great Brittan	U. States	John & Elizabeth	11 Dec 1826
GANGES, Hannah	22	F		United States	United States	Oscar	21 Oct 1822
GANGET, Frederick	22		Gentm.	Prussia	United States	Cadmus	24 Oct 1827
GANGON, Victor	23	M	Mechanic	France	U.S.	Montano	24 Jun 1823
GANIOR, Ewd.	18	M	Labourer	Great Britain	United States	Penelope	11 Jun 1827
GANLEY, John	32	M	Carpenter	G. Britain		Perseverance	9 Jun 1827
GANNET, Betsey	17	F	Seamstress	England		Hudson	23 Jul 1828
GANNETTY, James	26	M	Weaver	England	U. States	Montgomery	18 Oct 1828
Robert	18	M	Weaver	England	U. States	Montgomery	18 Oct 1828
Robert	56	M	Weaver	England	U. States	Montgomery	18 Oct 1828
GANNING, Robt.	24	F		Ireland	U. States	Wanderer	1 Sep 1828
Thomas	26	M	Labourer	Ireland	U. States	Wanderer	1 Sep 1828
GANNON, Mary	21	F	Wife	Ireland	United States	Dublin Packet	9 Jul 1827
Peter	25	M	Printer	England	United States	Silas Richards	3 Apr 1826
GANOLL, Francis	20	M	Clerk	Germany	Germany	Stephania	13 Sep 1821
GANS, James	21		Labourer	England	United States	Corinthian	7 Jul 1829
GANSLOS, F. P.	11	M	Merchant	Spain	Havana	James Monroe	21 Apr 1824
GANT, John	2	M		Scotland	United States	Concordia	25 Aug 1827
Mary	27	F		Scotland	United States	Concordia	25 Aug 1827
GANTON, Robert	28	M	Labourer	Scotland	United States	Mary & Susan	5 Aug 1828
GANTRO, Thomas	25	M	...	England	U. States	Chase	26 Jul 1824
GANTY, James	25	M	Farmer	Ireland	United States	Dublin Packet	29 Jun 1825
GANTZ, B. M.	19	M	Farmer	Ireland	U. States	New England	12 Apr 1825
GAPPER, —, Miss	26	F	Gent.	England	United States	Warrior	6 Oct 1828
—, Mr.	25	M	Gent.	England	United States	Warrior	6 Oct 1828
—, Mrs.	27	F	Gent.	England	United States	Warrior	6 Oct 1828
—, Mrs.	58	M	Gent.	England	United States	Warrior	6 Oct 1828

NAMES OF PASSENGERS	AGE	SEX	OCCUPATIONS	COUNTRY TO WHICH THEY BELONG	COUNTRY THEY INTEND TO INHABIT	SHIPS/DATES OF ARRIVAL	
GARAN, Joseph	43	M	Merchant	France		Stephania	24 Jul 1820
GARATY, Margaret	30 5/12	F		Ireland	U.S. of America	Douglass	6 Jul 1829
Mary	10 1/12	F		Ireland	U.S. of America	Douglass	6 Jul 1829
GARAY, Anthony	22	M	Merchant	Mexico	Mexico	Saltana	18 Apr 1825
GARBA, A.	42	M	Mason	Great Britain		Caravan	8 Sep 1828
An	44	M	Mason	Great Britain		Caravan	8 Sep 1828
Catiania	5	M	Joiner	Great Britain		Caravan	8 Sep 1828
G.	3	M		Great Britain		Caravan	8 Sep 1828
L.	1	M		Great Britain		Caravan	8 Sep 1828
Louis	14	M	Joiner	Great Britain		Caravan	8 Sep 1828
P.	9	M	Mason	Great Britain		Caravan	8 Sep 1828
U.	9	M	Joiner	Great Britain		Caravan	8 Sep 1828
GARBALDY, Antonio	24	M		G. Britain	United States	Siroc	13 Sep 1828
John	24	M		G. Britain	United States	Siroc	13 Sep 1828
GARBELE, G.	36	M		Italy	United States	Siroc	13 Sep 1828
GARBER, Michael	...	M	Clog Maker	Switzerland	United States	Elbe	2 Aug 1822
GARBET, Jno.	43	M	Farmer	U. States	U. States	Isaac Hicks	18 Apr 1825
GARBIDAR, Gab.	14	M	Merchan	Spain	Maracaibo	William	14 Dec 1826
Juan	42	M	Merchan	Spain	Maracaibo	William	14 Dec 1826
GARBIOS, John B.	10 5/12	M	Boy	Collumbia	Collumbia	Dolphin	31 May 1824
GARBRECHT,							
Henry Ludewic	16	M	Mason	Germany	United States	Constitution	2 Aug 1826
Margeret	18	F		Hanover	United States	Constitution	6 Jul 1829
Theodore	18	M	Mechanic	Germany	U. States	Constitution	2 Mar 1826
GARBURN, Paul	80			France	U. States	Parachute	14 May 1828
GARBY, John	25	M	Cooper	United States	United States	Seine	21 Oct 1822
GARCEN, Rosalie, Miss	20	F	Governess	Brussels	Brussels	Lewis	29 Oct 1825
GARCIA, Anna	18	F	Wife	Mexico	Columbia	Virginia	26 May 1828
Antonio	42	M	Merchant	Spain	Spain	Virginia	26 May 1828
Augustine	1	F	None	Spain	U. States	Frances	22 May 1827
Augustine	22	F	None	Spain	U. States	Frances	22 May 1827
Clamato	4	M	None	Spain	U. States	Frances	22 May 1827
Consatia	2	F	None	Spain	U. States	Frances	22 May 1827
Eligeo	30	F	Wife	Mexico	Mexico	Virginia	9 Feb 1829
J. P.	21	M	Merchant	Spain	U. States	Native	15 Apr 1826
J. P.	26	M	Merchant	Spain	U. States	Frances	22 May 1827
J. R.	25	M	Gentn.	Spain	Spain	Fabius	2 Oct 1826
Jno. P.	28	M	Merchant	Spain	Havana	James Monroe	21 Apr 1824
Joseph	28	M	Merchant	Guatemala	Guatemala	Helen Mar	29 Jun 1827
L.	28	M	Merchant	Spain	Spain	Richmond Packet	30 Oct 1827
M.	20	M	Merchant	Spain	U. States	Leontine	10 Jul 1826
Manuel	16	M	Gentleman	Vara Cruz	U. States	New Packet	5 May 1823
Manuel	25	M	Merchant	Spain	U. States	Virginia	8 Mar 1828
Manuel, Don	40	M	Gent.	Spain	Cuba	Fabius	24 Oct 1825
Michael	30	M	Merchant	Spain	U. States	St. Croix	31 Jul 1827
Michael	30	M	Merchant	Columbia	Columbia	Virginia	26 May 1828
Migual, Don	35	M	Attached to the Columbian Legation	Columbia	United States	Mercid	21 Oct 1824
Paricheta	35	F		Columbia	America	Splendid	23 Mar 1829
Victer	12	M	Boy	Colombia	United States	Bogota	28 Mar 1827
GARCIA DE TOLSA,							
Concepcion	28	F		Spain	Mexico	Virginia	9 Feb 1829
GARCIDE, Robert	18	M	Clothier	Great Brittain	United States	Nimrod	9 Jan 1827
GARCIN, Andrew	11	M	Cook	France	New York	Pacific	5 Jul 1820
James	54	M	Cook	France	New York	Pacific	5 Jul 1820
Jno.	10	M	Cook	France	New York	Pacific	5 Jul 1820
R.	13	F	Cook	France	New York	Pacific	5 Jul 1820
GARDADE, Joseph	21	M	Farmer	England	U.S. America	Cortes	19 May 1826
GARDEN, Bernard	28 8/12	M	Carpenter	Ireland	United States	Atlantic	21 Jul 1827
Edward	28	M	Merchant	France	U.S.	Edward Quesnel	19 Dec 1826
George	45	M	Merchant	Gt. Britian	United States	Nestor	16 Aug 1824
Jas.	28	M	Mercht.	Bristol	Jamaica	Canada	1 Nov 1823
GARDER, John	38	M	Officer	Great Brittan	Gr. Brittain	Nancy	13 Dec 1822
Mary	35	F	Lady	Great Brittan	Gr. Brittain	Nancy	13 Dec 1822
GARDERA, Francis Benjn.	26	M	Gent.	France	United States	Elizabeth	13 Nov 1824
GARDERE, F. V.	25	M	Merchant	U. States	U. States	Fly	22 Oct 1823
GARDIAN, Joseph	40	M	Merchant	France	France	Nile	13 Aug 1828

NAMES OF PASSENGERS	AGE	SEX	OCCUPATIONS	COUNTRY TO WHICH THEY BELONG	COUNTRY THEY INTEND TO INHABIT	SHIPS/DATES OF ARRIVAL	
GARDICH, Alfred	7	M		U.S.	U.S.	New England	27 Jul 1829
GARDIEN, Edmund	2	M	Child	France	United States	Galaxy	31 Jan 1828
Maria	21	F		United States	United States	Galaxy	31 Jan 1828
GARDIN, Doming	20	M	Merchant	Matanzas	U. States	Orono	21 May 1827
Nath	35	M	Gentleman	...	United States	Antioch	8 Oct 1827
GARDINER, —, Capt.	59	M	Mariner	United States	United States	Great Britain	18 Sep 1826
...ndr...	30	M	Weaver	Great Britain	United States	Colossus	5 Jun 1827
A. E.	21	F	Lady	United States	United States	Sylvester Healy	14 Jun 1825
A. W.	35	M	Merchant	United States	United States	Iris	21 Sep 1821
Alexr.	45		Mason	Great Britain	United States	Camillus	12 Sep 1827
Archd.	3	M	None	Great Britain	United States	Colossus	5 Jun 1827
Archibald	26	M	Labourer	Perth	Noagards	Robert	28 Aug 1829
Edward	28	M	Drovener	U.S. American	U.S. American	Criterion	7 Jul 1824
Ellen	30	F	None	United States	United States	Sally	26 Jun 1822
James	25		Fom...	Great Britain	United States	Camillus	12 Sep 1827
Janet	24	F	None	Great Britain	United States	Colossus	5 Jun 1827
Jas.	29		Steward	Wooster		Hudson	18 Jun 1825
*Officers, Seamen and Passengers belonging to the Ship Jane of Boston and taken from on board the Schooner Olive of St. Johns , N.B. on the 4th June 1825, Lat. 41.30, Long 53.19, which ship foundered on the 31st ultimo in Lat. 41.44 Long 52.							
John	20		Farmer	England	England	Hudson	4 Sep 1823
John D.	25	M	Mariner, Ship Master	United States		Orozimbo	8 Mar 1826
Lewis	33	M	Farmer	Swtserland	America	Saluda	18 Jun 1825
Stephen H.	25	M	Mariner	U. States	United States	Pionier	4 Mar 1828
Wm.	8/12	M	None	Great Britain	United States	Colossus	5 Jun 1827
*Died							
Wm.	32	M	Joiner	Scotland	United States	Leda	30 Aug 1828
GARDMAN, Louisa	73	F	Spinster	Germany	Missouri	Isabella	15 Sep 1828
GARDNER, Alexander	4	M		Scotland	U. States	Superior	25 Sep 1828
Antonia	33	M	House Carpenter	Germany	United States	Virginia	31 May 1828
Antonio	8	M	House Carpenter	Germany	United States	Virginia	31 May 1828
B.	32	M	Distiller	France	France	Cadmus	9 Apr 1825
C., Mrs.	55	F	None	U. States	U. States	Canada	2 Jun 1824
D.	28	M	Clothier	Bristol	New York	Cosmo	25 Sep 1827
David	29	M	Labourer	Scotland	U. States	Superior	25 Sep 1828
Detherick	16	M	Farmer	England	In the country	Chelsea	16 May 1828
Edward	34	M	Tailor	England	America	Plato	31 Oct 1829
Elisa	8	F		England	United States	Cosmo	21 Aug 1828
Elizabeth	6	F		Scotland	U. States	Superior	25 Sep 1828
Elizabeth	10	F		England	United States	Cosmo	21 Aug 1828
Geo.	36	M	Gentleman	U. States	U. States	Henry	21 Dec 1822
George	19	M	Joiner	Great Britain	United States	Courier	26 Jun 1827
George	24		Mariner	United States		New Orleans	27 Feb 1829
George G.	37	M	Mariner	U. States	U. States	Charles Amburger	22 Apr 1822
H., Miss	14	F	None	U. States	U. States	Canada	2 Jun 1824
Hanah	6	F		England	United States	Cosmo	21 Aug 1828
Henry	1	M		England	United States	Cosmo	21 Aug 1828
Henry	7	M		England	America	Plato	31 Oct 1829
Henry, Jr.	42	M	Miner			Plato	31 Oct 1829
Isaac	10	M		England	United States	Warrior	6 Oct 1829
J. L.	29	M	Merchant	Boston	Boston	Stephania	2 Jan 1824
James	17	M		England	United States	Cosmo	21 Aug 1828
Jane	3	F		England	America	Plato	31 Oct 1829
Janet	29	F		Scotland	U. States	Superior	25 Sep 1828
John	3/12	M		Scotland	U. States	Superior	25 Sep 1828
John	16	M	Servant	N. York	U. States	Parthian	10 May 1824
John	21	M	Sadler	Ireland	United States	Henry Kneeland	7 Jun 1828
John	22	M	Labourer	Great Britain		Olive Branch	9 Oct 1829
John	29	F	Farmer	Scotland	United States	Friends	16 Aug 1824
John	38	M	Miner			Plato	31 Oct 1829
John, Jr.	28	M	Supercargo	United States	United States	Ceres	20 Nov 1824
John, Jr.	29	M	Merchant	U. States	U.S.	Ceres	16 Jan 1826
Joseph, Doctr.	24	M	Physician	U. States	U. States	Sully	24 Oct 1828
Louisa	5	F		England	America	Plato	31 Oct 1829
Lucy	4	F	House Carpenter	Germany	United States	Virginia	31 May 1828
Margret	1/2	F	House Carpenter	Germany	United States	Virginia	31 May 1828
Mary	16	F		England	United States	Cosmo	21 Aug 1828
Mary	28	F		Irland	United States	Nancy	2 Jan 1824

NAMES OF PASSENGERS	AGE	SEX	OCCUPATIONS	COUNTRY TO WHICH THEY BELONG	COUNTRY THEY INTEND TO INHABIT	SHIPS/DATES OF ARRIVAL	
GARDNER (cont'd)							
Mary	33	F		England	America	Plato	31 Oct 1829
Mary Ann	11	F		England	America	Plato	31 Oct 1829
Materlane	6	F	House Carpenter	Germany	United States	Virginia	31 May 1828
Materlane	30	F	House Carpenter	Germany	United States	Virginia	31 May 1828
Matilda	9	F		England	America	Plato	31 Oct 1829
Mitchell	2	M	House Carpenter	Germany	United States	Virginia	31 May 1828
Robert	25	M	Farmer, Labourer or Spinster	Ireland	U. States	Meteor	4 Oct 1827
Samuel	4	M		England	United States	Cosmo	21 Aug 1828
Sarah	28	F		England	United States	Warrior	6 Oct 1828
Sarah	43	F		England	United States	Cosmo	21 Aug 1828
William	20	M	Merchant	Scotland, Great Britain	America	Superb	11 Oct 1821
Wm.	8	M		Scotland	U. States	Superior	25 Sep 1828
Wm.	38	M	Merchant	America	Hayti	Paragon	22 Sep 1827
GARDNIN, Henry	22	M	Merchant	United States	United States	James Monroe	14 Dec 1820
GARDOCK, W.	35	M	Merchant	Prussia	U. States	Minerva	23 May 1825
GARDY, Jno. Fras.	15	M	Servant	Guadaloupe	Guadaloupe	Baltic	20 Aug 1821
GARECK, Rob.	36	M	Mariner	St. Johns, N.B.	St. Johns, N.B.	Maine	24 Jun 1824
GARESCHE, —, Mrs.	34	F		France		François I	19 Nov 1828
Edwd.	4	M		U.S.A.		François I	19 Nov 1828
Paul, Mr.	53	M	Merchant	France		François I	19 Nov 1828
GARETSON, James	42	M	Hatter	New York	U.S.	Lydia	7 Oct 1823
GARETT, Jane	30	F	None	Great Brittan	U.S.	Emulous	29 Jun 1827
Joseph	25	M	Gentn.	Ireland	United States	Dublin Packet	22 Oct 1821
GARETTY, Margaret	25	F	Spinster	Ireland	United States	Lord Strangford	20 Jun 1826
GARETY, Ann	2	F		Ireland	U. States	St. Michael	27 Mar 1827
Biddy	8 7/12	F		Ireland	U.S. of America	Douglass	6 Jul 1829
Catherine	22	F	Spinstres	Ireland	New York	Xenophon	3 Oct 1829
Daniel	30	M	Labourer	Ireland	United States	Hannah Eliza	23 Sep 1826
Danl.	27	M	Labourer	Ireland	U. States	St. Michael	27 Mar 1827
Ellin	3	F	Child	Ireland	New York	Xenophon	3 Oct 1829
Etty	6	F		Ireland	U. States	St. Michael	27 Mar 1827
James	4	M		Ireland	U. States	St. Michael	27 Mar 1827
John	1 6/12	M		Ireland	New York	Xenophon	3 Oct 1829
Martin	1	M		Ireland	U. States	St. Michael	27 Mar 1827
Matt	27	M	Labourer	Great Brittan	United States	America	24 Jul 1827
Thomas	26	M	Weaver	Ireland	New York	Xenophon	3 Oct 1829
GAREY, Peter	19	M	Farmer	Ireland	United States	Lord Strangford	20 Jun 1826
Timothy	27	M	Labourer	Ireland	Ireland	Sarah G.	28 Nov 1827
GARFORTH, John	29	M	Farmer	Great Britain	United States	Mary & Harriet	3 Jul 1829
Margt.	24	F	Farmer	Great Britain	United States	Mary & Harriet	3 Jul 1829
GARG, Peter	12	M	None	France	New York	Billow	1 Jun 1826
Shan	13	M	None	France	New York	Billow	1 Jun 1826
GARGIN, Patrick	22	M	Farmer	Gt. Brittian	Gt. Brittian	Manchester	21 Apr 1827
GARIA, F. S. F.	38	M	Mariner	Spain	U. States	Ospray	11 Apr 1825
GARIDARD,							
Ferdinand	32 7/12	M	Merchant	France	United States	France	6 Oct 1828
GARLAM, Burk	23	M	Clerk	Ireland	United States	Trio	2 Oct 1828
GARLAND, Benj.	32		Labourer	England	America	Sarah	18 Aug 1829
GARLICK, Benjn.	28	M	Spinner	Oldham	Oldham	Howard Douglass	11 May 1827
Hannah	6	F	None	Great Britain		Casanda	5 Sep 1827
Hugh	37	M	Labourer	Great Britain		Casanda	5 Sep 1827
Joseph	13	M	None	Great Britain		Casanda	5 Sep 1827
Mary	35	F	None	Great Britain		Casanda	5 Sep 1827
Mary Ann	5	F	None	Great Britain		Casanda	5 Sep 1827
Rbt.	40	M	Weaver	England	America	Two Marys	24 Sep 1827
Susan	3	F	None	Great Britain		Casanda	5 Sep 1827
Wm.	15	M	None	Great Britain		Casanda	5 Sep 1827
Wm.	32		Mason	England		Corinthian	11 Mar 1829
GARLINE, Mary	16	F	Sevant			Royal Oak	5 Aug 1820
GARLON, Wm.	20	M	Farmer	Great Brittian		Merchant	22 Apr 1822
GARNER, Patt	25	M	Labourer	Ireland	N. Jersey	Potomac	7 Aug 1827
Thomas	21	M	Craper	England		Fame	9 Dec 1826
GARNET, Christopher	9	M	Farmer			Evergreen	28 Jul 1820
John	58	M	Farmer			Importer	30 Oct 1820
Joseph	22	M	Tanner	France	United States	Spartan	21 Aug 1824

NAMES OF PASSENGERS	AGE	SEX	OCCUPATIONS	COUNTRY TO WHICH THEY BELONG	COUNTRY THEY INTEND TO INHABIT	SHIPS/DATES OF ARRIVAL	
GARNETT, Alice	64	F	None	Great Britain	United States	James Monroe	27 Jul 1821
J. Stewart	21	M	Merchant	England	U. States	William Thompson	17 Dec 1827
Margt.	30	F	None	Lancaster	Lancaster	Howard Douglass	11 May 1827
Thos.	29	M	Labourer	Lancaster	Lancaster	Howard Douglass	11 May 1827
Wm.	3/12					Howard Douglass	11 May 1827
GARNEY, Rose	20	F	None	Gt. Brittain	United States	Balaena	21 Aug 1824
GARNIER, J., Jr.	25	M	Mariner	Havre	United States	Superior	14 Apr 1825
Jno.	38	M	Mechanic	France	U. States	Herald	21 May 1824
Labon	40	M	Merchant	U. States Amer	U.S. America	George	17 Jul 1823
GARNISS, John	48		Farmer			Agricola	1 Jul 1820
Susannah	40					Agricola	1 Jul 1820
GARON, Ann	13	F		Great Brittian	United States	Carolina Augusta	2 Dec 1828
Ann	17	F		Great Brittian	United States	Carolina Augusta	2 Dec 1828
Patrick	6	M		Great Brittian	United States	Carolina Augusta	2 Dec 1828
GAROTY, Patrick	40 1/12	M	Shoe Maker	Ireland	America	Minerva	15 Jun 1825
GARR, Andrew	19	M	Clerk	United States	United States	Laurel	20 Apr 1826
Andrew	20	M	Merchant	U. States	U. States	Colossus	21 Apr 1827
Catherine	7	F		Switzerland	U.S.	Francois I	8 Aug 1829
Catherine	32	F		Switzerland	U.S.	Francois I	8 Aug 1829
Chas.	35		Gardiner	England		Corinthian	11 Mar 1829
Dorothea	10	F		Switzerland	U.S.	Francois I	8 Aug 1829
Elizabeth	2	F		Switzerland	U.S.	Francois I	8 Aug 1829
Jacob	4	M		Switzerland	U.S.	Francois I	8 Aug 1829
GARRACK, Robert	46	M	Ship Master	England	United States	Edwin	27 Oct 1828
GARRANNS, M.	27	F		France	U. States	Harriet	3 Sep 1823
GARRATIA, Joseph	28	M	Merchant	Spain		Eliza Ann	29 Sep 1820
GARRATT, Ann J.	5	F	None	Great Britain		Casanda	5 Sep 1827
Betsey Ann	2	F	None	Great Britain		Casanda	5 Sep 1827
Margt.	25	F	None	Great Britain		Casanda	5 Sep 1827
Sophia	4	F	None	Great Britain		Casanda	5 Sep 1827
Wm.	29	M	Tanner	Great Britain		Casanda	5 Sep 1827
Wm. Hy.	4	M	None	Great Britain		Casanda	5 Sep 1827
GARRATTY, Bridget	16	F	None	Ireland	New York	America	1 Aug 1828
Thomas	40	M	Labourer	Ireland	New York	America	1 Aug 1828
GARRCIO, Jose	47	M	Merchant	Havana	U. States	Dromo	13 Nov 1827
GARRENE, Jacob	20	M	Mechanic	France	U. States	Harriet	3 Sep 1823
GARRET, A.	22	M	Taylor	U. States	U. States	Isabella	10 Mar 1825
Geo.	35	M	Joiner	Scotland	United States	Delta	24 Oct 1829
James	18	M	Joiner	Great Britain	U. States	Hamilton	28 Apr 1828
Joseph	17	M	Labor	Great Britten	U. States	Magnet	29 Sep 1823
Robt.	23	M	Shoemaker	Isle of Man		Ocean	13 Jul 1827
Thos.	1	M	None	Great Britain	United States	William Dawson	18 Jun 1827
GARRETT, Ann	16			England		Anacreon	7 Sep 1827
Ann	47	F		England		Anacreon	7 Sep 1827
Ellen	8			England		Anacreon	7 Sep 1827
Esther	5			England		Anacreon	7 Sep 1827
Frederick	19	M	Gentn.	Ireland	United States	Dublin Packet	22 Oct 1821
Geo.	30	M	Farmer	Gt. Brittain	United States	Balaena	8 Jan 1825
James	24	M		Ireland	U. States	Adno	5 Jul 1828
Jane	11			England		Anacreon	7 Sep 1827
John	4	M	None	Great Brittan	U.S.	Emulous	29 Jun 1827
John	25	M	Currier	U. States	U. States	United States	11 Sep 1828
John	28	M	Farmer	Great Brittan	U.S.	Emulous	29 Jun 1827
John	30	M	Cooper	Sligo, ..., Ireland	N. York	New Orleans	24 Aug 1827
Mary	31	F	Wife	Sligo, ..., Ireland	N. York	New Orleans	24 Aug 1827
Philip	13			England		Anacreon	7 Sep 1827
Phillip	55	M		England		Anacreon	7 Sep 1827
Susan	18	F		Gt. Britain		Corinthian	27 Oct 1829
Thos.	27	M	Shoemaker	Isle of Man	Isle of Man	Howard Douglass	11 May 1827
Thos.	30	M	Carpenter	England	U. States	Cincinnatus	24 May 1821
Ths.	8/52	M	None	Great Brittan	U.S.	Emulous	29 Jun 1827

NAMES OF PASSENGERS	AGE	SEX	OCCUPATIONS	COUNTRY TO WHICH THEY BELONG	COUNTRY THEY INTEND TO INHABIT	SHIPS/DATES OF ARRIVAL	
GARRETT (cont'd)							
William	30	M	Farmer	Gt. Britain		Corinthian	27 Oct 1829
Wm.	19			England		Anacreon	7 Sep 1827
Wm.	25		Labourer	England	United States	Hugh Johnson	11 Jun 1828
Wm., Junr.	23	M	Mechanic	United States	America	John Wells	11 Jun 1823
GARRETY, Jane	23		Laboring Class		United States	Atlantic	2 Apr 1827
GARRIAN, John	25	M	Labourer	G. Britain	U. States	St. George	7 Jun 1828
GARRICK, Eliza	33	F		England	United States	Edwin	27 Oct 1828
John	5	M				Splendid	14 Aug 1829
Mary	26	M				Splendid	14 Aug 1829
Thomas	2	M				Splendid	14 Aug 1829
GARRIEL, F.	25	M	Merchant	France	U. States	Cannon	10 Dec 1821
GARRIER, F.	39	M		Spain		Apollo	11 Jun 1828
GARRIGAN, John	24	M	Labourer	Ireland	U.S.	Lady Hunter	10 Jul 1826
GARRINE, Matilda	20	F	Spinster	Ireland	U. States	William & John	10 Jul 1824
Saml.	20	M	Farmer	Ireland	U. States	William & John	10 Jul 1824
GARRISON, Wm.	23	M	...	Ireland	U. States	Atlantic	19 Aug 1825
GARRITY, B.	16	F				Hanford	17 Jul 1828
GARROIN, Adel S.	9	F	Farmer	Ma...f...	U.S. America	Superior	18 Jun 1825
Ferdinand	2	M	Farmer	Ma...f...	U.S. America	Superior	18 Jun 1825
Isaac	41	M	Farmer	Ma...f...	U.S. America	Superior	18 Jun 1825
Lydia	35	F	Farmer	Ma...f...	U.S. America	Superior	18 Jun 1825
Marian	4	F	Farmer	Ma...f...	U.S. America	Superior	18 Jun 1825
Rosalie	4	F	Farmer	M...	U.S. America	Superior	18 Jun 1825
Ules	13	F	Farmer	Ma...f...	U.S. America	Superior	18 Jun 1825
GARRY, —, Mrs.	25	F				Neptunes Barge	23 Apr 1821
Henry	36	M	Labor	Rhode Island	United States	Jane	17 Jul 1821
James	22	M	Labourer	England	United States	Trident	31 Mar 1827
Nicholas	39	M	Merchant	London	Great Brittan	Amity	11 May 1821
Patrick	15	M	Labourer	Ireland	Amarica	United States	22 Mar 1824
GARSCHE, Alexr.	40	M	Merchant	Wilmington	U. States	Circassian	3 Jun 1826
Frederick	3	M	Child	Wilmington	U. States	Circassian	3 Jun 1826
L., Mrs.	32	F	Lady	Wilmington	U. States	Circassian	3 Jun 1826
Vital	10/12	M	Child	Philadelphia	U. States	Circassian	3 Jun 1826
GARSE, Betty	42	F		England	Patterson	Curler	7 Jul 1827
Elizabeth	4	F		England	Patterson	Curler	7 Jul 1827
John	2	M		England	Patterson	Curler	7 Jul 1827
John	46	M	Carpenter	England	Patterson	Curler	7 Jul 1827
Margaret	6	F		England	Patterson	Curler	7 Jul 1827
GARSELL, E. A.	19	F		N. Orleans	U. States	Hope Return	20 Mar 1824
GARSIDE, Jas.	50	M	Clothier	Great Brittain	United States	Nimrod	9 Jan 1827
John	15	M	Clothier	Great Brittain	United States	Nimrod	9 Jan 1827
John	31	M	...	England	United States	Milton	20 Oct 1827
Joshua	22	M	Clothier	Great Brittain	United States	Nimrod	9 Jan 1827
Robt.	22	M	Manufacturer	England	U. States	Amity	25 Sep 1822
Samuel	17	M	Clothier	Great Brittain	United States	Nimrod	9 Jan 1827
GARSIDES, Abraham	27	M	Labourer	Great Britain	United States	Penelope	11 Jun 1827
Esther	25	F	None	Great Britain	United States	Penelope	11 Jun 1827
Nancy	1	F	None	Great Britain	United States	Penelope	11 Jun 1827
GARSIER, Frs.	14	M		Spain	N. Haven	Herald	14 Mar 1825
GARSON, Mary	35	F	Spinster	England	U.S.	Pacific	24 Oct 1828
GARSTON, Alexr.	25	M	Farmer	Antrin	United States	Carolina Ann	11 Jun 1824
GARTH, George	25	M	None	England	United States	Enterprize	19 Oct 1826
Sarah	27	F		England	United States	Dalhouse Castle	8 May 1827
GARTNER, Jacob	27	M	Farmer	Hessian-Germany	Canada	Caesar	8 Sep 1828
GARTON, Benjm.	35	M	Merchant	Galacia	U. States	Hero	3 Sep 1823
GARTY, Jane, his wife [Terrance]	26	F	Housekeeper	Ireland	United States	Andes	2 Oct 1828
Terrance	30	M	Labourer	Ireland	United States	Andes	2 Oct 1828
GARUSCHA, Duponceau T.	18	M	Student	U.S.	U.S.	Edward Quesnel	3 Jul 1829
GARVAN, Mary	34					Trio	5 May 1828
Robert	30					Trio	5 May 1828
GARVARD, Mae P.	24	F		Switzerland	Havana	Helen Mar	29 Jun 1827
GARVER, Bridget	10	F	Lady	Ireland	United States	Borneo	2 Oct 1827
Catharine	5	F	Lady	Ireland	United States	Borneo	2 Oct 1827
Catherine	44	F	Lady	Ireland	United States	Borneo	2 Oct 1827
Dennis	7	M	Child	Ireland	United States	Borneo	2 Oct 1827

NAMES OF PASSENGERS	AGE	SEX	OCCUPATIONS	COUNTRY TO WHICH THEY BELONG	COUNTRY THEY INTEND TO INHABIT	SHIPS/DATES OF ARRIVAL	
GARVER (cont'd)							
Jeremiah	50	M	Gentleman	Ireland	United States	Borneo	2 Oct 1827
John	20	M	Labourer	England	U. States	Comet	23 Aug 1828
Margaret	19	F	Lady	Ireland	United States	Borneo	2 Oct 1827
Mary	13	F	Labourer	England	U. States	Comet	23 Aug 1828
Mary	46	F	Labourer	England	U. States	Comet	23 Aug 1828
Mathew	9	M	Labourer	England	U. States	Comet	23 Aug 1828
Patrick	9	M	Boy	Ireland	United States	Borneo	2 Oct 1827
Sarah	19	F	Labourer	England	U. States	Comet	23 Aug 1828
Thomas	14	M	Labourer	England	U. States	Comet	23 Aug 1828
Wm.	24	M	Labourer	England	U. States	Comet	23 Aug 1828
Wm.	48	M	Labourer	England	U. States	Comet	23 Aug 1828
GARVEY, John	21	M	Clerk	Ireland	United States	Princess Charlotte	26 Apr 1827
Thomas	32	M	Laborer	Ireland	New York	Thames	6 Oct 1820
GARVIN, Hugh	30	M		Ireland	U. States	Nancy	10 Jul 1822
John	22	M	Weaver	Ireland	United States	Louisa	18 Apr 1827
GARVON, Bryan	17	M		Great Brittian	United States	Carolina Augusta	2 Dec 1828
James	4	M		Great Brittian	United States	Carolina Augusta	2 Dec 1828
James	30	M		Great Brittian	United States	Carolina Augusta	2 Dec 1828
John	15	M		Great Brittian	United States	Carolina Augusta	2 Dec 1828
Mary	11	F		Great Brittian	United States	Carolina Augusta	2 Dec 1828
Matthew	3	M		Great Brittian	United States	Carolina Augusta	2 Dec 1828
May	30	F		Great Brittian	United States	Carolina Augusta	2 Dec 1828
GARVY, Ann	1	F	Carpenter	Great Briton	New York	Brighton	12 Jun 1826
Bridget	35	F	Carpenter	Great Briton	New York	Brighton	12 Jun 1826
Elenor	7	F	Carpenter	Great Briton	New York	Brighton	12 Jun 1826
John	2	M	Carpenter	Great Briton	New York	Brighton	12 Jun 1826
John	35	M	Carpenter	Great Briton	New York	Brighton	12 Jun 1826
Mary	10 6/12	F	Carpenter	Great Briton	New York	Brighton	12 Jun 1826
Michael	5 4/12	M	Carpenter	Great Briton	New York	Brighton	12 Jun 1826
GARWOOD, Robt.	28	M	Comb Maker	Great Britian	United States	Columbia	21 Jan 1828
GARY, Cath.	29	M	Laborer	Switzerland	U.S.	C. Amelia	30 Jun 1828
F.	26	M	Merchant	Spain	France & Spain	Native	24 Aug 1825
Geo. C.	25	M	Mariner	Virginia	U. States	Favourite	27 Jun 1823
George C.	25	M	Mariner	U. States	United States	Pionier	4 Mar 1828
James	25	M	Labourer	Ireland	U.S.	Oliver Wolcott	3 Nov 1827
GASCELET, J.	33	M	Merchant	France		Soldado Espanol	8 Jul 1822
*Died							
GASCOIGNE, Ann	40	F	None	United States	United States	Pacific	24 Oct 1828
James B.	40	M	Mercht.	United States	United States	Pacific	24 Oct 1828
James W.	7	M	None	United States	United States	Pacific	24 Oct 1828
John	3	M	None	United States	United States	Pacific	24 Oct 1828
Phebe B.	5	F	None	United States	United States	Pacific	24 Oct 1828
GASCON, Raymon	44 5/12	M	Pastry Cook	France	New York	Harriot	1 May 1822
GASCONE, Wm.	21	M	Labourer	Glasgow, Barony [Parish], Lanark [County]	New York	Hero	19 May 1828
*to look for employment							
GASHAM, Mary	8	F		G. Britain	U. States	Mary & Harriot	8 Sep 1828
GASKELL, Mary	27	F	None	U. States	U. States	Birmingham	12 Oct 1829
Thos. Penn	29	M	None	U. States	U. States	Canada	13 Oct 1825
Thos. Penn	33	M	None	U. States	U. States	Birmingham	12 Oct 1829
GASNER, Geo.				Switzerland	U.S.	C. Amelia	30 Jun 1828
GASPER, Bernard	2	M	Farmer	Alsace in the Department of Upper and lower Rhine	United States	Carolina Augusta	16 May 1828
Francis	24	M	Shoe Maker	Ireland		Quatre Freres	29 Jul 1828

456

NAMES OF PASSENGERS	AGE	SEX	OCCUPATIONS	COUNTRY TO WHICH THEY BELONG	COUNTRY THEY INTEND TO INHABIT	SHIPS/DATES OF ARRIVAL	
GASPER (cont'd)							
George	6	M	Farmer	Alsace in the Department of Upper and lower Rhine	United States	Carolina Augusta	16 May 1828
Henry	11	M	Farmer	Alsace in the Department of Upper and lower Rhine	United States	Carolina Augusta	16 May 1828
Jacob	19	M	Farmer	Alsace in the Department of Upper and lower Rhine	United States	Carolina Augusta	16 May 1828
John	45	M	Farmer	Alsace in the Department of Upper and lower Rhine	United States	Carolina Augusta	16 May 1828
Margaretta	18	F	Farmer	Alsace in the Department of Upper and lower Rhine	United States	Carolina Augusta	16 May 1828
Margaretta	43	F	Farmer	Alsace in the Department of Upper and lower Rhine	United States	Carolina Augusta	16 May 1828
Philip	15	M	Farmer	Alsace in the Department of Upper and lower Rhine	United States	Carolina Augusta	16 May 1828
GASQUET, —, Mr.	24	M	Valet	France	U.S.	Robert Edwards	11 Nov 1822
Joseph	28		Servant	France		Cincinnatus	29 Apr 1822
GASQUIT, Elizabeth	28	F		England	U. States	Hudson	8 Oct 1827
GASS, Ann	6/12	F		Germany	United States	Samuel Robertson	8 Aug 1828
Catherine	9	F		Germany	United States	Samuel Robertson	8 Aug 1828
George	40	M	Shoemaker	Germany	United States	Samuel Robertson	8 Aug 1828
Magdalana	18	F		Germany	United States	Samuel Robertson	8 Aug 1828
Magdalana	38	F		Germany	United States	Samuel Robertson	8 Aug 1828
Margaret	6	F		Germany	United States	Samuel Robertson	8 Aug 1828
Marion	4	F		Germany	United States	Samuel Robertson	8 Aug 1828
Michael	2	M		Germany	United States	Samuel Robertson	8 Aug 1828
Porrie	22	F	Farmer	Switzerland	U.S.	C. Amelia	30 Jun 1828
Rodolphe	40	M	Merchant	Switzerland	New York	Sully	4 Mar 1828
GASSE, Frank	24	M	Blacksmith	Native of Switzerland	United States	Canaris	30 Jun 1827
GASSELMANN, Ann	17 6/12	F	Servant			Weser	24 Jul 1820
GASSER, Heller	26			England	U. States	Corinthian	8 Oct 1828
GASSETT, H.	15					Olympia	12 Aug 1828
GASSEY, Isaac	17	M	Farmer	Irereland	America	Carolina Ann	20 Jun 1825
William	21	M	Labourer	Irereland	America	Carolina Ann	20 Jun 1825
GASSGITT, Joseph	32	M	Servant	France	U. States	Danube	11 Apr 1826
GASSIRA, A.	29	M	Soldier	Spain	Spain	Prince Edward	22 Jul 1824
GASSMEUX, J. T.	60	M	Weaver	Gt. Britain	United States	Penelope	9 Sep 1828
GASTON, —	2	M		Havana	U. States	Senica	17 Mar 1824
—	4	M		Havana	U. States	Senica	17 Mar 1824
—	6	M		Havana	U. States	Senica	17 Mar 1824
Augustes, Dr.	30	M	Merchant	Havana	U. States	Senica	17 Mar 1824
Bernardo	32	M	Mercht.	Campeache	Campeache	Emma	14 Oct 1825
H.	55	M	Planter	Porto Rico	N. York	Hanna	3 Jun 1828
J.	26	M	Merchant	Spain	Havana	John and Edward	6 Jan 1824

NAMES OF PASSENGERS	AGE	SEX	OCCUPATIONS	COUNTRY TO WHICH THEY BELONG	COUNTRY THEY INTEND TO INHABIT	SHIPS/DATES OF ARRIVAL	
GASTON (cont'd)							
Jane	23	F	Spinster	Gt. Britain	U. States	Frances Henrietta	18 Apr 1825
Mary	19	F		Porto Rico	N. York	Hanna	3 Jun 1828
Wm.	35		Merchant	United States	Savannah	Albion	11 Oct 1821
Wm.	36	M	Merchant	U. States	U. States	Amity	23 Sep 1823
Wm.	39	M	Merchant	U. States	United States	Florida	14 Sep 1827
GATEAU, Louis	29	M	Farmer	France	U. States	Sully	15 Jul 1829
GATEHOUSE, John	40	M	Stone Cutter	England	U. States	Emulous	22 Aug 1828
Margt.	35	F	Stone Cutter	England	U. States	Emulous	22 Aug 1828
GATES, Chas.	35	M	Gun Smith	Great Britain	Green turtle Key	Cicero	21 Aug 1823
Ed.	28	M	Labourer	Great Britain	United States	Mary & Harriet	3 Jul 1829
Eliza	24	F	None	Great Britain	United States	Mary & Harriet	3 Jul 1829
Samuel	32	M	Farmer	Great Britain	United States	John Jay	8 May 1828
Thomas	2	M	None	Great Britain	United States	Mary & Harriet	3 Jul 1829
Thomas	40	M	Merchant	England	U. States	William Thompson	17 Dec 1827
GATHEN, Jno.	2... 3/12	M	Merchant	Philadelphia	U. States	Quito	9 Jul 1823
GATHMEY, Ann	20	F		Gt. Britain		Dalhouse Castle	13 May 1828
GATIERRE, Philip	25	M	Grocer	Hayti		Ranger	29 Jul 1828
GATJEN, Jacob	23	M	Blacksmith	Germany	U. States	Constitution	21 Jun 1824
GATMAN, Christian	8	F	Gent	French	Switzerland	Charlemagne	19 Sep 1828
Eliz.	30	F	Gent	French	Switzerland	Charlemagne	19 Sep 1828
Fredrick	10	M	Gent	French	Switzerland	Charlemagne	19 Sep 1828
Jacob	35	M	Gent	French	Switzerland	Charlemagne	19 Sep 1828
GATREAUD, Peter	19	M	None	France	United States	Seine	7 Dec 1821
GATS, Christopher	20	M	Silver Smith	Switzerland	United States	Ospray	2 Sep 1824
GATTE, Antonio Lionel Jorte	17	M	Gent.	Lisbon	U. States	L. M. Pelham	17 Aug 1820
GATTERSON, F. M.	35	M	Planter	Germany	U. States	Dromo	24 Sep 1827
GATTES, Jean B.	20	M	Tailor	Switzerland	U.S.	C. Amelia	30 Jun 1828
GATTIKE, —	32	M	Distiller	Holland	United States	Wilmot	14 Mar 1820
GATTITLEY, Christiane	27 6/12	F	Wife of Gattitley [James]	Scotland	Canada	Globe	3 Dec 1821
James	27 6/12	M	Farmer	Scotland	Canada	Globe	3 Dec 1821
Joseph	1 8/12	M	Child [of James]	Scotland	Canada	Globe	3 Dec 1821
GATTLAND, John	32	M	Labourer	Ireland	United States	Lord Wellington	28 May 1827
GATTSBERGER, Francis	42		Servant			Weser	24 Jul 1820
GATWOLD, Henry	26	M		Pennsylvania	U. States	William	30 Jul 1824
GATZ, C. F.	50	M	Merchant	Germany	United States	Comet	24 Dec 1821
GAUBADAN, John	42	M	Gentleman	U. States	U. States	Elizabeth	20 Sep 1822
GAUDARD, Francis	33	M	Merchant	France	United States	Howard	27 Sep 1824
Francis	40	M	Merchant	Hayti	Hayti	Artibonite	3 Jul 1826
GAUGHAN, Edeward	23	M	Labourer	Ireland	America	Dewitt Clinton	27 Jul 1824
GAUGHLEN, Margaret	16	F	Servant	Mayo	America	Margaret	31 Jul 1824
GAUGHREN, Jno.	27	M	Labourer	England	U. States	Thomas Ritchie	2 Jul 1827
GAUL, —, child	4/12			Nova Scotia	United States	William	9 Aug 1821
—, Mrs.	25	F		Nova Scotia	United States	William	9 Aug 1821
Hugh	28	M	Sailor	N. Scotia	Upper Canada	Infant	21 Nov 1820
John	32	M	Blaise Dr...	Great Britain	Wilmington, Del.	Zodiac	14 Jun 1822
GAULDING, Jas.	23	M	None	Great Britian	U. States	Henry Kneedland	7 Aug 1826
Margaret	20	F	None	Great Britian	U. States	Henry Kneedland	7 Aug 1826
Robt.	25	M	None	Great Britian	U. States	Henry Kneedland	7 Aug 1826
GAULHIAC, Desirée Roy	26	F	None	France	America	Bayard	15 Dec 1828
Jean	30	M	Hair Dresser	France	America	Bayard	15 Dec 1828
GAULT, Margaret, Mrs.	50	F	Lady	Ireland	United States	Dublin Packet	9 Jul 1827
GAUMER, Catherine	7	F	Farmer	Switzerland	United States	Olympia	12 Aug 1828
Catherine	23	F	Farmer	Switzerland	United States	Olympia	12 Aug 1828
Ferdinand	5	M	Farmer	Switzerland	United States	Olympia	12 Aug 1828
Jacob	10	M	Farmer	Switzerland	United States	Olympia	12 Aug 1828
Michel	36	M	Farmer	Switzerland	United States	Olympia	12 Aug 1828
Philipine	35	F	Farmer	Switzerland	United States	Olympia	12 Aug 1828
GAUNT, Amey	20	F		Great Britain	U. States	Ann Marria	6 Aug 1823
Ann	14	F		Great Britain	U. States	Ann Marria	6 Aug 1823
Ann	48	F		Great Britain	U. States	Ann Marria	6 Aug 1823
Bridget	10	F		Great Britain	U. States	Ann Marria	6 Aug 1823

NAMES OF PASSENGERS	AGE	SEX	OCCUPATIONS	COUNTRY TO WHICH THEY BELONG	COUNTRY THEY INTEND TO INHABIT	SHIPS/DATES OF ARRIVAL	
GAUNT (cont'd)							
Jessey	13	F		Great Britain	U. States	Ann Marria	6 Aug 1823
John	16	M		Great Britain	U. States	Ann Marria	6 Aug 1823
John	54	M		Great Britain	U. States	Ann Marria	6 Aug 1823
Marry	9	F		Great Britain	U. States	Ann Marria	6 Aug 1823
Wm.	21	M		Great Britain	U. States	Ann Marria	6 Aug 1823
GAURAN, Michael	42	M	Merchant	United States		Edward Quesnel	17 Nov 1828
GAURT, W.	20		Carpenter	Great Britain	U. States	Hamilton	28 Apr 1828
GAUSMAN, Earl C.	19 9/12	M	Baker	Holland	America	Martha	2 Jul 1828
GAUTHIER, Jos.	32	M	Merchant	New York	United States	Ann Maria	5 Nov 1821
GAUTIER, Alexis	28	M	Professor of Languages	France	America	Bayard	15 Dec 1828
Caroline	23	F	Servt.	France	United States	Bayard	13 Nov 1823
GAUTZ, A. *died 12th April		M	Mechanic	U. States	U. States	Radius	18 Apr 1825
GAUVANER, Saml., Jr.	57	M	Merchant	U. States	U. States	Montano	2 Sep 1828
GAUVIN, Charles	30	M	Labourer			Evergreen	28 Jul 1820
GAVARD, Peter	23	M	Merchant	Switzerland	Havana	Helen Mar	29 Jun 1827
GAVARONE, Nicholas	27	M	Merchant	Italian	America	Port Captain	6 Dec 1825
GAVEY, Jno.	18	M		Ireland	U. States	Alex Mansfield	1 Jun 1822
Ml.	33	M	Merchant	Ireland	U. States	Alex Mansfield	1 Jun 1822
GAVIL, Jno.	28	M	Mariner	U. States	U. States	Hippomenes	22 Dec 1821
GAVIN, Francis	28	M	Labourer	Great Britain	United States	Ann Maria	12 Jul 1821
Susan	25		Laboring Class		United States	Atlantic	2 Apr 1827
GAVON, James	24		Blacksmith	Ireland	New York	Marcella	18 May 1827
GAVOOL, N.	42	M	Mercht.	Havana	U. States	Greek	17 May 1825
GAWEN, John	32	M	...	Ireland	United States	Borneo	2 Oct 1827
GAWN, Ann	30	F	None	Isle of Man	United States	Aurelia	7 Jun 1826
Daniel	4	M	None	Isle of Man	United States	Aurelia	7 Jun 1826
Eliza	7	F	None	Isle of Man	United States	Aurelia	7 Jun 1826
Ellem	1		Labourer	England	United States	Hugh Johnson	11 Jun 1828
Ellem	26			England	United States	Hugh Johnson	11 Jun 1828
John	9	M	None	Isle of Man	United States	Aurelia	7 Jun 1826
John	34	M	Fisherman	Isle of Man	United States	Aurelia	7 Jun 1826
Thos.	28		Labourer	England	United States	Hugh Johnson	11 Jun 1828
GAWNE, John	22		Baker	Great Britain	United States	Thomas Dickason	29 Aug 1828
William	21		Tailor	Great Britain	United States	Thomas Dickason	29 Aug 1828
GAY, Christian	45	F	None	Great Britain	United States	Roman	19 Dec 1825
David	19	M	Shoe Maker	Ireland	United States	Borneo	9 Jul 1827
Hy.	10	M		G. Britain	U. States	Cosmo	15 May 1827
Thomas	27	M	Farmer	Ireland	America	Farmer	15 Nov 1823
William	30	M	Merchant	Scotland	England	New York	3 Apr 1826
GAYAROLA, J.		M	Merchant	Spain	Spain	Packet	13 Jun 1821
GAYLER, C. J.	30	M	Mercht.	England	New York	Brighton	16 Nov 1826
Eliza	11		Shipwright	England	United States	Corinthian	30 May 1828
Louisa	7		Shipwright	England	United States	Corinthian	30 May 1828
GAYLOR, Helen	21	F	None	Scotland		Marchioness	13 May 1828
Henry	23	M	Labourer	Germany	U.S.A.	Hudson	21 Aug 1829
GAYMAINE, F. J.	22	M	Carpenter	Germany	United States	Origon	8 Jun 1824
GAYNOR, John	50	M	Grocer	American		Dublin Packet	30 Apr 1821
GAYOT, L.	28	M	Merchant	France	United States	La Coralie	18 Oct 1824
GAYTON, Elizt.	19	F	Carpenter	G. Britain	Canada	Cosmo	25 Nov 1826
Jack	3			England	United States	Warrior	6 Oct 1828
James	12			England	United States	Warrior	6 Oct 1828
James	46	M	Cloth worker	England	United States	Warrior	6 Oct 1828
Jas.	17	M	Carpenter	G. Britain	Canada	Cosmo	25 Nov 1826
Mary	13			England	United States	Warrior	6 Oct 1828
Rosa	16			England	United States	Warrior	6 Oct 1828
Rosa	47	F		England	United States	Warrior	6 Oct 1828
Susan	7			England	United States	Warrior	6 Oct 1828
GAZOUR, C.	39	M	Ship master	France	France	Favourite	18 Aug 1823
GÉ, Cornelius Lewis	3/12	M		France	U.S.	Edward Quesnel	31 Jul 1827
Eliza	20	F		U.S.	U.S.	Edward Quesnel	31 Jul 1827
GE..., Ulrich	...	M	Farmer	Switzerland	United States	Elbe	2 Aug 1822
GEAR, James	36	M	Labourer	England	United States	India	8 Jun 1827
May	19	M	Weaver	England	United States	India	8 Jun 1827
GEARDSON, James J.	26	M	Mercht.	Boston	Boston	Andromache	29 May 1821

NAMES OF PASSENGERS	AGE	SEX	OCCUPATIONS	COUNTRY TO WHICH THEY BELONG	COUNTRY THEY INTEND TO INHABIT	SHIPS/DATES OF ARRIVAL	
GEARY, Daniel	11			Cove	Gt. Britain	Enterprize	19 Feb 1822
Margt.	22	F		Ireland	U.S.	Oliver Wolcott	3 Nov 1827
Mary	30			Cove	Gt. Britain	Enterprize	19 Feb 1822
Thomas	3			Cove	Gt. Britain	Enterprize	19 Feb 1822
Thomas	22	M	Farmer	England	United States	Ganges	10 May 1828
GEBBONE, Austin	20	M	Merchant	Mayo	America	Margaret	31 Jul 1824
GEBEIRY, Michael	41	M	Colonel	Mexico	Mexico	Frances	17 Dec 1825
GEBETMER, Francois	21	M		France	United States	Henri IV	2 Oct 1828
GEBHARD, James	30	M	Merchant	France	New York	Curlew	1 Mar 1824
John	22	M	Farmer	Switzerland	U. States	Romulus	24 Sep 1828
GEBNER, Michael	9	M	None	Ireland	United States	Jubilee	4 Mar 1829
Thomas	19	M	Labourer	Ireland	United States	Jubilee	4 Mar 1829
GECCI, S. S.	36		Merchant	U. States	U.S.	Silvanus Jenkins	30 Nov 1827
GED, D.	29	M	Musician	G. Britain	U. States	Nimrod	31 Jul 1828
GEDGE, Eliza	5/12	F	Lady	Great Britain	United States	Cambria	26 Dec 1827
John	23 6/12	M	Merchant	Great Britain	United States	Cambria	26 Dec 1827
Rebecca	22 9/12	F	Lady	Great Britain	United States	Cambria	26 Dec 1827
GEDNEY, Catherine	20	F	Wife	Ireland	United States	St. Michaels	18 Jul 1826
Isaac	30	M	Farmer	Ireland	United States	St. Michaels	18 Jul 1826
Joseph	2	M	Child	Ireland	United States	St. Michaels	18 Jul 1826
Mary Ann	6/12	F	Child	Ireland	United States	St. Michaels	18 Jul 1826
GEE, Antonio	27	M	Artizen	Iterly	United States	Jubilee	13 Jul 1829
Henry	33	M	Mechanic	England	United States	Richmond	4 Aug 1826
John	40	M	Joiner	Ireland	U.S.A.	Dalhouse Castle	21 Aug 1829
John	40	M	Joiner	Ireland	United States	Dalhouse Castle	21 Aug 1829
GEEHAN, Edwd. M.	25	M	Labourer	Ireland	U. States	William & John	10 Jul 1824
GEER, John	21	M		Scotland	U.S.	Curler	19 Jul 1828
GEERE, Alexander	44	M	Glassblower	England	United States	Maria	29 Sep 1823
James	1	M	Child	England	United States	Maria	29 Sep 1823
GEFFRES, Winifred	18	M		Ireland	America	Carolina Ann	7 Aug 1826
GEGAR, Christopher	41	M	Mason	Italy	U. States	Sarah Lee	21 Jul 1821
GEGORY, Thomas	12	M	Labourer	Ireland	U. States	Meteor	19 Jul 1828
GEIBBI..., John	20	M	Labourer	Ireland	United States	Princess Charlotte	26 Apr 1827
GEIGEL, Hipolito	15	M	for Schooling	Spain	Porto Rico	Ann	26 May 1824
GEIT, D.	26	M	Tanner	Germany	United States	Howard	15 Jun 1825
GELARD, Denis	21 5/12	M	...	France	United States	Criterion	13 Oct 1825
GELCHIN, Jane	18	F	Servant	Ireland	United States	Wilson	27 Jun 1826
Mary	20	F	Servant	Ireland	United States	Wilson	27 Jun 1826
GELDEN, Sarah	21	F		Halifax	Great Britton	William	11 May 1821
GELDENER, R.	26	M	Merchant	Sweden	Sweden	Elias Burger	11 Jul 1822
GELHOOLY, Peter	20	M	Baker	Ireland	United States	Nancy Henrietta	3 Nov 1828
GELHORN, Andrew	40	M		France	United States	Henri IV	2 Oct 1828
GELLARD, James	30	M	Brass Founder	Great Britian	United States	Mount Vernon	19 May 1823
GELLEN, Kitty	8 3/12	F		Ireland	U.S. of America	Douglass	6 Jul 1829
Patrick	22	M	Servant	Ireland	U. States	Henrietta	7 Jul 1825
GELLER, Joseph	49	M	Sailor	England	U. States	Hiram	17 Jun 1826
GELLGIER, S.	25	M	Merchant	England	England	Ductile	12 May 1826
GELLING, Cathe.	9	F	None	Isle of Man		Ocean	13 Jul 1827
Cathe.	28	F	None	Isle of Man		Ocean	13 Jul 1827
Ellen	7	F	None	Isle of Man		Ocean	13 Jul 1827
John	1	M	None	Isle of Man		Ocean	13 Jul 1827
Mary	5	F	None	Isle of Man		Ocean	13 Jul 1827
Paul	3	M	None	Isle of Man		Ocean	13 Jul 1827
Paul	30	M	Farmer	Isle of Man		Ocean	13 Jul 1827
GELMACH, Edward	21	M	Labourer	Ireland	U. States	Lady Hunter	18 Jul 1825
GELMARTIN, William	18	M	Labourer	Ireland		Robert Fulton	4 Jun 1828
GELMER, F. W.	6	M	...	United States	United States	Crisis	13 Nov 1824
GELPAY, Thos.	25	M	Farmer	Ireland	U. States	Sabina	29 Apr 1825
GELSTON, John	26	M	Weaver	Scotland	United States	Princess Charlotte	26 Apr 1827
GEMIL, Thos.	39	M		Great Britain	United States	Mary	11 Jul 1820
GEMMILL, Alexr.	40	M	Joiner	Scotland	New York	Joseph Hume	26 Oct 1829
GENDER, Joseph	20	M	Ribbonweaver	Switzerland	U. States	Hewes	30 Oct 1829
GENENIGER, John	33	M	Carpenter	Netherlands	Philadelphia	Louisa	6 Oct 1828
GENER, Benja.	5	M		Cuba	U. States	Zephyr	18 May 1825
Francesco	22	M	Merchant	Spain	Spain	Commodore Chauncy	19 Jan 1826

NAMES OF PASSENGERS	AGE	SEX	OCCUPATIONS	COUNTRY TO WHICH THEY BELONG	COUNTRY THEY INTEND TO INHABIT	SHIPS/DATES OF ARRIVAL	
GENER (cont'd)							
Guadeloupe	19	M		Cuba	U. States	Zephyr	18 May 1825
Jos.	16	M	Merchant	Cuba	U. States	Zephyr	18 May 1825
Jose	40	M	Merchant	Matanzas	U. States	Orono	21 May 1827
GENERY, Jos.	50	M	Merchant	N. York	U. States	Caravan	1 May 1824
GENJALN, P.	26	M	Merchant	Mexico	America	Tampico	14 Jul 1825
GENT, Abm.	44	M	Merchant	England	U. States	Packet	23 Sep 1820
C.	19	F	Actress	France	America	Don Quixotte	2 Jun 1828
Henry	28	M	Doctor	England	U. States	Eliza Pigott	15 Oct 1821
Jno.	26		Labourer	G. Britain	United States	Roman	10 Sep 1827
Maria	47	F	Actress	France	America	Don Quixotte	2 Jun 1828
Ralph	44		Laborer	United States	United States	Robert Burns	14 Jun 1824
Ralph G.	18		Weaver	Ireland	G. Britain	Robert Burns	14 Jun 1824
GENTHALLER, Joshua	20	M		Ireland	United States	Essex	23 May 1828
GENTIL, Jacob P.	32	M	Farmer	France	United States	American	27 Aug 1827
Susanah	31	F	Farmer	France	United States	American	27 Aug 1827
GENTLE, James	30	M	Gentleman	Scotland	Scotland	Morning Star	26 May 1824
Peter	36	M	Carpenter	Great Brittain	U.S.	Trafalgar	22 Jun 1821
GENTZ, Catherine	36	F		Gt. Britain		Dalhouse Castle	13 May 1828
John	40	M	Shoemaker	Gt. Britain		Dalhouse Castle	13 May 1828
GEO, Elizabeth	21	F	Gent		United States	Cosmo	21 Aug 1828
GEOCK, John	16	M	Farmer	Switzerland	U. States	Seine	30 Aug 1824
GEOFFER, John	25	M	Servant	Ireland	U. States	Henrietta	7 Jul 1825
GEOMY, George	40	M	Farmer	France	United States	Crescent	12 Jul 1827
Julie	8	F	Farmer	France	United States	Crescent	12 Jul 1827
Margaret	4	F	Farmer	France	United States	Crescent	12 Jul 1827
Thereze	36	F	Farmer	France	United States	Crescent	12 Jul 1827
GEORDING, John	50	M	Farmer	Switzerland		Charlemagne	20 Aug 1829
Joseph	14	M	Farmer	Switzerland		Charlemagne	20 Aug 1829
Margaret	6/12	F	Farmer	Switzerland		Charlemagne	20 Aug 1829
Margaret	40	F	Farmer	Switzerland		Charlemagne	20 Aug 1829
Robert	10	M	Farmer	Switzerland		Charlemagne	20 Aug 1829
Sam	6	M	Farmer	Switzerland		Charlemagne	20 Aug 1829
Wm.	16	M	Farmer	Switzerland		Charlemagne	20 Aug 1829
GEORGE, Alm	14	F		Scotland	U.S.	Curler	19 Jul 1828
Amelia	21	F	None	England	United States	Hamilton	13 Nov 1827
Andrew	21		Baker	England	United States	Acasta	16 Aug 1826
Ann	16	M		England	America	Sarah	18 Aug 1829
Ann	28	F	Servant	G. Britain	U. States	Wanderer	23 Jun 1828
Augustus	27	M	Merchant	Canada	Canada	James Monroe	18 Apr 1821
Charlotte	14	M		England	America	Sarah	18 Aug 1829
Charlotte	22	F	Servant	G. Britain	U. States	Wanderer	23 Jun 1828
Christien	8	F		Scotland	U.S.	Curler	19 Jul 1828
David	16	M		Scotland	U.S.	Curler	19 Jul 1828
E., Jr.	27	M	Merchant	Philada.	U. States	Margaret	11 Mar 1823
Elenor	1 6/12	F		Ireland	America	Wilson	27 Nov 1826
Elizabeth	4	M		England	America	Sarah	18 Aug 1829
Elizabeth	11	F		Scotland	U.S.	Curler	19 Jul 1828
Elizabeth	42	F		Scotland	U.S.	Curler	19 Jul 1828
Francis	6	M		England	America	Sarah	18 Aug 1829
Geo. S.	13	M	pupil	G. Brittain	U. States	Frances Henrietta	19 Feb 1823
George	37	M	Farmer	England	America	Sarah	18 Aug 1829
Harman	26		Farmer	Switzerland	United States	Henri IV	14 Sep 1827
Harriett	17	M		England	America	Sarah	18 Aug 1829
Henry	25	M	Merchant	U. States	U. States	St. George	20 Sep 1828
J.	43	M	Merchant	America	U. States	Queen Mab	22 Jul 1825
James	7/12	M		England	America	Sarah	18 Aug 1829
James	19 5/12	M	Farmer	Great Britain	Upper Canada	Amity	1 Dec 1826
Jane	12	M		England	America	Sarah	18 Aug 1829
Janes	50	M		Scotland	U.S.	Curler	19 Jul 1828
John	27 7/12	M	Farmer	England	America	Nimrod	1 Dec 1827
John	28	M	Agriculture	Wirtemburg	United States	Henri IV	14 Oct 1829
John G.	30	M	Merchant	United States	United States	Otter	25 Feb 1822
John R.	25	M	Merchant	England	U. States	Virginia	3 Dec 1827
Margaret	3 6/12	F		Ireland	America	Wilson	27 Nov 1826
Margaret	30	F		Ireland	America	Wilson	27 Nov 1826
Martha	38	M		England	America	Sarah	18 Aug 1829
Peter	19	M		Scotland	U.S.	Curler	19 Jul 1828

NAMES OF PASSENGERS	AGE	SEX	OCCUPATIONS	COUNTRY TO WHICH THEY BELONG	COUNTRY THEY INTEND TO INHABIT	SHIPS/DATES OF ARRIVAL	
GEORGE (cont'd)							
Philip	23	M	Merchant	U. States	U. States	St. George	20 Sep 1828
Richard P.	23	M	Merchant	England	U. States	Virginia	3 Dec 1827
Richard P.	24	M	Merchant	Gt. Brittain	United States	York	6 Dec 1826
Rupert D., Sir	27	M	Gentleman	England	England	William Thompson	29 Jan 1824
Sarah	26	F	Semstress	New York	United States	Minerva	30 Oct 1829
Thomas	10	M		England	America	Sarah	18 Aug 1829
Wm.	18	M		Scotland	U.S.	Curler	19 Jul 1828
GEORGEN, John	22	...	...	Ireland	United States	Carolina Ann	24 Oct 1825
GEOSIA, David	19 6/12	M	...	...	United States	Wade	29 Aug 1825
GERAEU, M. M.	30	M	Merchant	United States	United States	Tontine	9 Jun 1827
GERALDE, Peter	32	M	Merchant	France	U. States	Union	21 Jul 1825
GERAND, John Joseph	55	M	Merchant	France	U.S. America	Triton	10 May 1828
GERARD, —, Master	2	M		United States		Howard	17 Oct 1822
A.	20	M	Watch Maker	Swiss	U. States	Edwd. Quesnel	30 Apr 1825
Ann	28	F	Milner	England	U. States	Florida	13 Jan 1827
Chr.	36	M	Farmer	Brattain		L'Esperance	6 Sep 1828
David L.	46	M	Farmer or Mechanic	Switzerland	U.S.	Edward Quesnel	31 Jul 1827
F.	30	M	Watch Maker	St. ...	U.S.	Stephania	15 Aug 1825
J.	35	M	Merchant	France	United States	Neptunes Barge	23 Apr 1821
Jean P.	4	M		France	U. States	Leonarde	29 Aug 1828
John	35	M	Merchant	England	England	Bunker Hill	20 Sep 1827
Madelaine	1	F		France	U. States	Leonarde	29 Aug 1828
Marianne	12	F		France	U. States	Leonarde	29 Aug 1828
Marianne P.	38	F		France	U. States	Leonarde	29 Aug 1828
Marie	14	F		France	U. States	Leonarde	29 Aug 1828
Martin	7/12			Hamburg		Ann Maria	28 Mar 1822
Mary	14	F		England	England	Amity	31 May 1822
Michel	7	M		France	U. States	Leonarde	29 Aug 1828
Paul	38	M	Farmer	France	U. States	Leonarde	29 Aug 1828
Peter	40 1/12	M	Cabinet Maker	Paris	New York	Harriot	1 May 1822
S.	26	M	Merchant	France	U. States	Laveria	23 Jul 1828
Samuel	52	M		Canada	Canada	Britannia	22 Jul 1829
GERATH,							
Chas. Augt.	30 4/12	M	Doctor	Germany	U. States	Kanhawa	6 May 1828
GERAU, Patric	32	M	Farmer	Ireland	U.S. America	Josephine	24 Jul 1826
GERAUD, Daniel	38	M	Merchant	U. States	U. States	Emeline	5 Jul 1823
Francis	18	M	None	France	New York	Sully	11 Mar 1829
John	40	M	None	France	United States	Hannibal	12 Oct 1829
GERBER, Antoine	16	M		Switzerland	U. States	La Urania	3 Jul 1828
Maria N.	53	F		Switzerland	U. States	La Urania	3 Jul 1828
Piere	53	M	Labourer	Switzerland	U. States	La Urania	3 Jul 1828
GERBERLE, George	19	M	there child [George & Margret]	Germany	United States	Helen	5 Sep 1828
George	55	M	Farmer	Germany	United States	Helen	5 Sep 1828
John	16	M	there child [George & Margret]	Germany	United States	Helen	5 Sep 1828
Margret	21	F	there child [George & Margret]	Germany	United States	Helen	5 Sep 1828
Margret	53	F	his wife [George]	Germany	United States	Helen	5 Sep 1828
GERCKEN, Henrich	28	M	Mechanic	Germany	U. States	Constitution	2 Mar 1826
GERDING, Teo. Fredk.	22	M	Mechanic	Germany	U. States	Constitution	2 Mar 1826
GERDON, Alice	26	F	Spinster	England	United States	Euphrates	18 Aug 1827
GERE, J.	27	M	Dyer		Canada	Edward Quesnel	3 Sep 1826
GEREKLOPT, C. T.	27	M	Merchant	Germany	U. States	Dido	26 Apr 1825
GERGONUS, Aadam	3	M	Shoe Maker	Ireland		Quatre Freres	29 Jul 1828
Cassener	1/12	M	Shoe Maker	Ireland		Quatre Freres	29 Jul 1828
*Born on the Passage							
Margaret	5	M	Shoe Maker	Ireland		Quatre Freres	29 Jul 1828
Margaret	30	F	Shoe Maker	Ireland		Quatre Freres	29 Jul 1828
Peter	11	M	Shoe Maker	Ireland		Quatre Freres	29 Jul 1828
Sebastien	40	M	Shoe Maker	Ireland		Quatre Freres	29 Jul 1828
Soloman	8	M	Shoe Maker	Ireland		Quatre Freres	29 Jul 1828
GERGUSON, John	18	M	Farmer	Scotland	United States	Commerce	17 Jul 1823
GERKE, Julius Henry	19	M	Ropemaker	Brunswick	United States	Howard	6 Jul 1829
GERLING, Augustus	40	M	Shoemaker	Germany	United States	Wm. Osborne	16 Sep 1828
Catherine	40	F		Germany	United States	Wm. Osborne	16 Sep 1828
GERMAIN, Abrm.	37	M	Carpenter	France	United States	Le Voltaire	19 Jul 1828

NAMES OF PASSENGERS	AGE	SEX	OCCUPATIONS	COUNTRY TO WHICH THEY BELONG	COUNTRY THEY INTEND TO INHABIT	SHIPS/DATES OF ARRIVAL	
GERMAIN (cont'd)							
Augustin	56	M	Merchant	Canada	Canada	Henry	9 Jun 1826
Cath.	7	F		France	United States	Le Voltaire	19 Jul 1828
Chas.	1/12	M		France	United States	Le Voltaire	19 Jul 1828
*Born at Sea							
Chas. C.	1/12	M		France	United States	Le Voltaire	19 Jul 1828
*Born at Sea							
Chas. C.	9	M		France	United States	Le Voltaire	19 Jul 1828
Cristopher	30	M	Carpenter	France	United States	Le Voltaire	19 Jul 1828
Geo.	26	M	Carpenter	France	United States	Le Voltaire	19 Jul 1828
Jean F.	32	F		France	United States	Le Voltaire	19 Jul 1828
Lewis	12	M		France	United States	Le Voltaire	19 Jul 1828
Margret C.	36	F		France	United States	Le Voltaire	19 Jul 1828
Pierre F.	3	M		France	United States	Le Voltaire	19 Jul 1828
Sophia	1 3/12	F		France	United States	Le Voltaire	19 Jul 1828
Susanah C.	6	M		France	United States	Le Voltaire	19 Jul 1828
Susanah C.	22	M		France	United States	Le Voltaire	19 Jul 1828
Susanah C.	34	M		France	United States	Le Voltaire	19 Jul 1828
GERMAN, Cathe.	27			Ireland		Anacreon	7 Sep 1827
Elizabeth	43	F		Down, Ireland	Rhode Island	Anthusa	24 Aug 1825
GERMS, Henry	28	M	Sadler	England	U. States	Otter	30 Oct 1826
GERNESEUS, Jerome	37	F	None	Switzerland	U. States	Sully	25 Jun 1828
GERNLY, Ann	16	F	Spinster	Ireland	United States	Fabius	4 Jun 1828
Bridget	18	F	Spinster	Ireland	United States	Fabius	4 Jun 1828
Eliza	21	F	Spinster	Ireland	United States	Fabius	4 Jun 1828
Hermard	14	M		Ireland	United States	Fabius	4 Jun 1828
James	12	M		Ireland	United States	Fabius	4 Jun 1828
Mary	15	F	Spinster	Ireland	United States	Fabius	4 Jun 1828
Sarah	10	F	Spinster	Ireland	United States	Fabius	4 Jun 1828
GEROME, Charles	38	M	Merchant	America	U. States	Dawn	8 Jun 1827
Maria	36	F		America	U. States	Dawn	8 Jun 1827
Philip	19	M		America	U. States	Dawn	8 Jun 1827
GEROMPH, G. J.	28	M	Merchant	Germany	U. States	Lewis	6 Jul 1825
GERRA, Ruffus	27	M	Merchant	Spain	Spain	Weymouth	13 Aug 1822
GERRAN, Joseph	26	M	Merchant	Gt. Brittain	United States	Cortes	7 Dec 1825
GERRAND, Danl.	38	M	Merchant	U. States	U. States	Othello	11 Jul 1825
GERRARD, Jno.	24	M	Merchant	Great Brittan	Great Brittain	Florida	17 May 1825
John	33	M	Gentleman	England	Great Britain	New York	22 Jul 1824
Jos.	22	M	Merchant	England	United States	Cortes	10 Apr 1822
Richard	26	M	Gentleman	Canada	Canada	Silas Richards	27 Jun 1827
Richd.	26	M	Merchant	Great Brittan	Great Brittain	Florida	17 May 1825
GERRARDT, J. P.	22	M	Doctor	W. Indies	U. States	Elias Burger	12 Sep 1822
GERRAT, J. B.	42		Sevant	France	America	Courier	24 Jul 1820
GERREST, Ann	48	F		England	United States	Marion	25 Nov 1825
Stephen	50	M	Shopkeeper	England	United States	Marion	25 Nov 1825
GERRIN, Elias	22	M	Merchant	...	America	Columbia	6 Oct 1825
GERRINGLY, Ja...s.	27	M	Tailor	England	United States	India	8 Jun 1827
GERRITY, Owen	21	M	Farmer	Ireland	United States	Dublin Packet	9 Jul 1827
GERROIS, Charles	34	M	Merchant	U. States	U. States	Sully	24 Oct 1828
GERRON, Patrick	42	M	Silk Mercer	Ireland	Great Britain	Florida	26 Sep 1826
GERRY, C.	25	M	Farmer	Ireland	N. York	Elizabeth	20 Jun 1828
GERT, Celestin	28	M	Agriculture	France	United States	Henri IV	14 Oct 1829
Frs.	29	M	Merchant	France	U. States	William Bayard	25 Apr 1826
GERUX, Peter	28	M	Mercht.	France	United States	Rapid	24 Oct 1823
GERVAIS, George	35	M	Farmer	Ireland	United States	Asia	29 Jul 1829
GESFORD, John	14	M		Great Britton	U. State	Earl of Liverpool	16 Aug 1826
Mary	6	F		Great Britton	U. State	Earl of Liverpool	16 Aug 1826
Richard	10	F		Great Britton	U. State	Earl of Liverpool	16 Aug 1826
Robt.	12	M		Great Britton	U. State	Earl of Liverpool	16 Aug 1826
Sarah	8	F		Great Britton	U. State	Earl of Liverpool	16 Aug 1826
Susan	33	F		Great Britton	U. State	Earl of Liverpool	16 Aug 1826
GESINGS, Christopher	23	M	Merchant	England	U. States	Chase	28 Sep 1826
GESNON, J.	43	M	Merchant	Gaudaloupe	U. States	La Marie Adele	8 Jan 1827
GESSER, Catherin	35	F	Farmer	Germany	United States	Oxford	14 Aug 1828
Catherine	7	F	Farmer	Germany	United States	Oxford	14 Aug 1828
Jean	1	M	Farmer	Germany	United States	Oxford	14 Aug 1828
Jean	35	M	Farmer	Germany	United States	Oxford	14 Aug 1828
Marie	5	F	Farmer	Germany	United States	Oxford	14 Aug 1828
Rosine	3	F	Farmer	Germany	United States	Oxford	14 Aug 1828

NAMES OF PASSENGERS	AGE	SEX	OCCUPATIONS	COUNTRY TO WHICH THEY BELONG	COUNTRY THEY INTEND TO INHABIT	SHIPS/DATES OF ARRIVAL	
GESTAVO, F. A.	35	M	Merchant	G. Brittain	England	Abigail	25 Feb 1826
GESTLING, George	20	M	Joiner	Germany	Philadelphia	Falcon	21 Oct 1826
GESTUN, Christopher	27		Sugar boiler	Germany	Germany	Hudson	18 Jun 1825
GETHERSON, James	4	M	child	Ireland	United States	Andes	2 Oct 1828
GETTY, Eliza	20	F	Spinster	Ireland	U. States	William & John	10 Jul 1824
Ellen	7	F	Child	Ireland	U. States	William & John	10 Jul 1824
Jane	13	F	Child	Ireland	U. States	William & John	10 Jul 1824
Matilda	9	F	Child	Ireland	U. States	William & John	10 Jul 1824
Robt.	11	M	Child	Ireland	U. States	William & John	10 Jul 1824
Saml.	54	M	Farmer	Ireland	U. States	William & John	10 Jul 1824
Samuel	6	M	Child	Ireland	U. States	William & John	10 Jul 1824
GHERCI, —	27	M	Seaman	France	France	Artibonite	9 Sep 1826
GHIERHOF, E. J.	19	F	Spinster	Germany	New York	Constitution	20 Aug 1825
GHILIONE, R.	30	M	Merchant	Italy	U. States	Logan	22 May 1823
GHILOME, J.	25	M	Merchant	France	France	Morning Star	6 Oct 1823
GHIO, Catharine	29	M		Fishkill	U. States	Phoebe Ann	23 Nov 1824
GIBB, Alexander	40	M	Farmer	Scotland	United States	Samuel Robertson	5 Oct 1827
Benjamin	28	M	Merchant	Gt. Britan	Gt. Britan	Canada	8 Jun 1826
Charles	10	M		Scotland	United States	Samuel Robertson	5 Oct 1827
Helen	2	F		Scotland	United States	Samuel Robertson	5 Oct 1827
Helen	38	F		Scotland	United States	Samuel Robertson	5 Oct 1827
James	1	M		Scotland	United States	Samuel Robertson	5 Oct 1827
John	6	M		Scotland	United States	Samuel Robertson	5 Oct 1827
Margaret	11	F		Scotland	United States	Samuel Robertson	5 Oct 1827
Nancy	5	F		Scotland	United States	Samuel Robertson	5 Oct 1827
GIBBER, Ann	28	F	Seamstress	St. Johns, N.B.	United States	Henrietta	17 Aug 1825
GIBBES, Thomas	40	M	Gentleman	St. Bartholomew	U. States	Bunker Hill	12 Aug 1828
GIBBINS, Charles	22	M	Merchant	Ireland	Ireland	Reindeer	15 Aug 1820
Margaret	26	F		Ireland	U. States	Nancy	10 Jul 1822
William	32	M	Merchant	Ireland	Ireland	Reindeer	15 Aug 1820
GIBBON, F. S.	31	M	Officer of the U.S. Navy	U. States	U. States	Chinchille	14 Apr 1825
M.	50	M	Farmer	Great Britain	New York	Dublin	21 Dec 1824
Samues	16	M	Farmer	Darry	Pitsburg	Nile	18 Aug 1829
W.	25	M	Bookbinder	Ireland		Eliza Jane	12 Sep 1820
GIBBONEY, Thomas	22	M	Labourer	Ireland	Philadelphia	Curler	7 Jul 1827
GIBBONS, Chas.	26	M	Printer	Great Britain	U. States	Columbia	22 Sep 1828
Hannah	22		Wife	Ireland	G. Britain	Robert Burns	14 Jun 1824
James	22	M	Farmer	Ireland	America	William	21 May 1825
Jane	20	F	Servant	Ireland	United States	St. Michaels	15 Feb 1825
John	23		Weaver	Ireland	G. Britain	Robert Burns	14 Jun 1824
Sarah, Miss	21	F	Servant	Bermuda		Friends Delight	5 Dec 1825
Wm.	30	M	Gentleman	G. Braitan	U. States	Cosmo	29 Jun 1826
GIBBS, Agnes	31	F	None	England	United States	Brighton	11 Mar 1825
C. G.	30	M	Mariner	America	U. States	Ambuscade	5 Jul 1822
Cathr.	25	F		G. Britain	U. States	Margaret Bogle	12 Jun 1828
Danl.	26	M	Merchant	U. States	U. States	George Henry	24 Mar 1823
David	32	M	Merchant	England	United States	Brighton	11 Mar 1825
Elijah	6	M	None	Great Britian	United States	Diamond	8 Nov 1824
Eliza	8	F	None	Great Britian	United States	Diamond	8 Nov 1824
Emma	7	F		England	U. States	Cincinnatus	21 Feb 1825
G.		M	Marriner	Great Britain		Oregon	15 Nov 1824
George	17	M	Gentleman	Turks Island	U. States	Eliza Jane	29 Oct 1821
George E.	48	M	Locksmith	U. States	U. States	Jefferson	29 Nov 1828
Helen	26	F		G. Britain	U. States	Robt. Edwards	4 Sep 1828
Henertta	9	F		England	U. States	Cincinnatus	21 Feb 1825
Jane	11	F	None	Great Britian	United States	Diamond	8 Nov 1824
Jno.	38	M	Gentleman	England	G. Brittain	Chase	24 Aug 1822
John	2	M	None	Great Britian	United States	Diamond	8 Nov 1824
John	24	M	Butcher	Scotland	New York	Joseph Hume	26 Oct 1829
John	29	M	Dyer	England	United States	Maria	12 May 1823

NAMES OF PASSENGERS	A G E	S E X	OCCUPATIONS	COUNTRY TO WHICH THEY BELONG	COUNTRY THEY INTEND TO INHABIT	SHIPS/DATES OF ARRIVAL	
GIBBS (cont'd)							
Laura	9	F	None	England	United States	Brighton	11 Mar 1825
Mary	3	F	None	England	United States	Brighton	11 Mar 1825
Mary	27	F	None	Great Britian	United States	Diamond	8 Nov 1824
Mary Ann	32	F		England	U. States	Cincinnatus	21 Feb 1825
Richd.	25	F		G. Britain	U. States	Margaret Bogle	12 Jun 1828
Richd.	29	M	Farmer	Great Britian	United States	Diamond	8 Nov 1824
Sarah	19	F		G. Britain	U. States	Camillus	8 Sep 1828
Susannah	35	F	None	Great Britian	United States	Diamond	8 Nov 1824
Thomas	13	M	None	England	United States	Brighton	11 Mar 1825
William	4	M	None	Great Britian	United States	Diamond	8 Nov 1824
GIBNEY, Michael	23	M	Currier	Ireland	America	John Adams	2 Aug 1827
Owen	27	M	Labourer	Halifax	U. States	Loire	7 Jul 1827
GIBS, Charles	28	M	None	United States	United States	Orozimbo	1 Dec 1823
GIBSON, —, Mr.	27	M	...nt	England	U. States	Robert Edwards	11 Mar 1822
A. P.	31	M	Gentleman	United States	U.S.	Panthea	13 Mar 1823
Agnes	36	F		Scotland		Samuel Robertson	5 Oct 1827
*Dead							
Andw.	30	M	Labourer	Ireland	U. States	Two Marys	20 Apr 1825
Ann	24	F	Matron	Ireland	U. States	Josephine	7 May 1827
Benj.	2/12	M	Farmer	England	United States	Justina	5 Aug 1823
Benj.	29		Grocer	Huddersfield, England	Great Britain	Franklin	22 Jun 1827
Benjn.	26	M	Farmer	Ireland	United States	Eliza	29 Aug 1822
Charles	7		child	Ireland	U. States	Xenophon	28 May 1822
Charles	13	M	Farmer	England	United States	Justina	5 Aug 1823
Charles	45	M	Farmer	England	United States	Justina	5 Aug 1823
Clarissa	12	F		New York	New York	New Packet	9 May 1827
David	14	M	Farmer	England	United States	Justina	5 Aug 1823
David	23	M	Baker	Scotland	U. States	Dalhouse	23 Mar 1829
Edward	...7	M	...	...	Mississippa	Josephine	10 Dec 1825
Edward	35	M	Merchant	England		Reuben & Eliza	21 Aug 1820
Effy	30	F	Lady	Bermuda	U. States	Mary & Elizabeth	10 Jul 1824
Elizabeth	18		Spinster	Great Britain	United States	Camillus	12 Sep 1827
G.	21	M	Gentleman	American	U. States	Abeona	1 Apr 1824
George	...	...	...	Scotland	America	Nimrod	9 Jul 1827
George	22	M	Servant	Bermuda	U. States	Susan	2 Aug 1822
Hannah	19	F	Farmer	England	United States	Justina	5 Aug 1823
Hannah	38	F	Farmer	England	United States	Justina	5 Aug 1823
Harriett	27	F	Lady	County Renagh, Ireland	England	Hanford	15 May
Henry	60	M	Farmer	England	U. States	Commerce	2 Oct 1823
Isaac	21	M	Merchant	Great Britian	U. States	Dalhouse Castle	28 Feb 1826
J.	21	M	Merchant	England	England	John Wills	21 May 1824
J.	21	M	Brass Founder	G. Britain	U. States	St. George	7 Jun 1828
James	11	M	Tailor	Great Britain	U.S.A.	Dalhouse Castle	21 Aug 1829
James	11	M	Tailor	Great Britain	United States	Dalhouse Castle	21 Aug 1829
James	36	M	Merchant	Scotland	United States	Commerce	17 Jul 1823
James	36	M	Farmer	Scotland	United States	Samuel Robertson	5 Oct 1827
Jane	3/12	F	Farmer	England	U. States	Commerce	2 Oct 1823
Jane	60	F	Farmer	England	United States	Justina	5 Aug 1823
Janet	4	F		Scotland	United States	Samuel Robertson	5 Oct 1827
Jno. William	9					Cannon	18 Aug 1821
John	15/12	M	...	...	Mississippa	Josephine	10 Dec 1825
John	18	M	Farmer	G. Britain	U. States	Freak	9 Jun 1828
John	22	M	Farmer	Scotland	United States	Camillus	27 Oct 1829
John	30	M	Labourer	G. Britain	U. States	George Clinton	10 Sep 1828
John	30	M	Tailor	Great Britain	U.S.A.	Dalhouse Castle	21 Aug 1829
John	30	M	Tailor	Great Britain	United States	Dalhouse Castle	21 Aug 1829
John	34	M	Farmer	Great Britain	United States	Minerva	28 Jul 1823
Joseph	11	M	Farmer	England	United States	Justina	5 Aug 1823
Joseph	22	M		Ireland	United States	William & George	14 May 1828
Margaret	20	F	Farmer	England	U. States	Commerce	2 Oct 1823

465

NAMES OF PASSENGERS	AGE	SEX	OCCUPATIONS	COUNTRY TO WHICH THEY BELONG	COUNTRY THEY INTEND TO INHABIT	SHIPS/DATES OF ARRIVAL	
GIBSON (cont'd)							
Margaret	20	F	Seamstress	Scotland	U. States	Camillus	27 Jun 1826
Margaret	24	F	Farmer	England	U. States	Commerce	2 Oct 1823
Margaret, & Infant	27	F		England	New York	James Monroe	23 Aug 1822
Mary	2	F	child	Great Britain	United States	Minerva	28 Jul 1823
Mary	4		child	Ireland	U. States	Xenophon	28 May 1822
Mary	15	F	None	Scotland	U. States	Camillus	27 Jun 1826
Mary	25	F	his wife [Thos.]	St. John, N.B.	United States	Henrietta	3 Jun 1825
Mary	32	F	his Wife [John]	Great Britain	United States	Minerva	28 Jul 1823
Peter	32	M	Weaver	Scotland	Massachusetts	Governor Fenner	23 Jul 1829
Phebe	25	F	Spinster	Ireland	United States	Dublin Packet	29 Jun 1825
Phillis	50	F	House wife	New York	New York	New Packet	9 May 1827
Richard	25	M	Dyer	Great Britain	United States	Birmingham	15 Jun 1827
Robert	16	M	Farmer	Great Britain	United States	Florida	10 Dec 1823
Robert	17	M	Farmer	England	United States	Justina	5 Aug 1823
Robert	17	M		G. Britain	U. States	Camillus	8 Sep 1828
Robert	34	M	Gentleman	England	U. States	John Marshall	1 Aug 1825
Robert	43	M	Cooper	Great Britain	United States	Birmingham	15 Jun 1827
Rowland Thos.	13	M	None	Barbados		Cannon	18 Aug 1821
Samuel S.	10	M				Cannon	18 Aug 1821
Sarah	21	F	Spinster	Great Britain	United States	Washington	3 Sep 1827
Sarah	34	F	Wife	Scotland	America	Concord	4 Jun 1821
Sarah	36		Spinster	Ireland	U. States	Xenophon	28 May 1822
Sarah E.	33	F		England, Born in Barbadoes	U. States	Cannon	15 Jul 1822
Serah	18	F	Spinster	Ireland	U. States	Josephine	23 Jan 1829
Susan	18	F		England, Born in Barbados	U. States	Cannon	15 Jul 1822
*all the children have come under the care of Mrs. Fenwick for their education							
T. G.	30	M	Merchant	Massachusetts	United States	Tontine	9 Jun 1827
Thomas	21	M	Bru...b...	Scotland	United States	Camillus	27 Oct 1829
Thomas	23	M	Baker	Great Britain	New York	Superior	5 Sep 1827
Thomas	26	M	Schoolmaster	England	United States	John Dickinson	30 Sep 1823
Thomas	28		Haberdasher	England	S. New York	Xenophon	25 Jul 1826
Thomas	37		White Gentleman	Barbadoes	U. States	Cannon	12 Sep 1820
Thomas	38	M	Farmer	Barbados	United States	Cannon	18 Aug 1821
Thos.	20	M	Servant	Engd.	Engd.	Napoleon	26 May 1828
Thos.	25	M	Mechanic	St. John, N.B.	United States	Henrietta	3 Jun 1825
W.	31	M	Gentleman	U. States	U. States	Patriot	23 May 1821
William	19	M	Farmer	Ireland	United States	Princess Charlotte	6 Oct 1827
William	40	M	Merchant	Great Britain	U. States	Hopes Return	5 Aug 1825
William	59	M	Merchant	America	America	Britannia	5 Nov 1828
Wm.	23	M	Farmer	Gt. Britain	U. States	Diana	28 Apr 1828
Wm.	50	M	Merchant	Great Britain	Great Britain	Martha	25 Nov 1820
Wm., Mr.	30	M	Mercht.	Gt. Brittian	Gt. Brittian	Manchester	21 Apr 1827
Wood, Mr.	24	M	Merchant	England	America	Hector	20 Sep 1821
GIBVILLE, Sophie	25	F	Servant	England	Halifax	Stephania	28 Jul 1823
GICHTE, Henry	24	M	Cooper	France	U. States	Lewis	6 Jul 1825
GIDDES, Joseph	28		...	Ireland	United States	Alexander Mansfield	23 Nov 1824
GIDDINGS, B.	50	M		U. States	U. States	Napolean	2 Sep 1828
GIDDONES, Muse	40	M	Merchant	Swis	United States	Iris	21 Sep 1821
GIDION, —	45	F	Lady	France	U. States	Sally	14 May 1821
Maria	5	F	Child	France	U. States	Sally	14 May 1821
GIDNEY, Aggus	19	F		Halifax	U. States	Rufus King	11 Mar 1822
Catherine	23	F	Servant	Great Britain	U.S. of America	Gratitude	3 Oct 1829
Eleazer	29	M	Dentist	United States	United States	Bolivar	21 May 1827
GIENIER, Jean	35	M	Merchant	France	N. Orleans	Frances Augusta	19 Aug 1825
GIEQUEL, Chs.	2	M		France	United States	Howard	20 Aug 1827
GIGAS, J.	50	M		Spain		Apollo	11 Jun 1828
GIGGIE, James	40		Mechanic	Scotland	American	Agnes	27 Mar 1828
GIGGINS, Anthony	18	M	Shoe Maker	Ireland	United States	Enterprize	23 Jul 1827
GIGLY, Nancy	19	F	Servant	Ireland	United States	Ann Maria	4 Oct 1824
GIGNAEZO, Anthy.	28	M	Merchant	Italy	U. States	Neptune	25 Jan 1823
GIJON, Claudius F.	27	M	Professor	France	United States	Maria Theresa	13 Apr 1822
GILBERT, —, Miss	29	F	None	New York	New York	Industry	11 Jun 1821
—, Mrs.	20	F	Merchant	Bermuda	Great Britian	Two Brothers	6 Sep 1823
—, Mrs.	35	F		Bermuda	Bermuda	Industry	26 Jul 1825

NAMES OF PASSENGERS	AGE	SEX	OCCUPATIONS	COUNTRY TO WHICH THEY BELONG	COUNTRY THEY INTEND TO INHABIT	SHIPS/DATES OF ARRIVAL	
GILBERT (cont'd)							
Abram	10	M		G. Britain	U. States	Mary & Harriot	8 Sep 1828
Alexander	4	M	...	Ireland	United States	Carolina Ann	24 Oct 1825
Alphonsa	17		Hair dresser	France		Bayard	10 Sep 1827
Elias	28					Cincinnatus	29 Apr 1822
Elias	56					Cincinnatus	29 Apr 1822
Elis	18	M	Cloth Dresser	England	United States	Siroc	31 Oct 1829
Elizabeth	18					Cincinnatus	29 Apr 1822
Elizabeth	50					Cincinnatus	29 Apr 1822
Emma	13					Cincinnatus	29 Apr 1822
Frederck	9					Cincinnatus	29 Apr 1822
George	22		Merchant	St. Johns	N. Brunswick	Charlotte Corday	15 Jul 1820
Goleth	30	F	Servant	Point Petre	New Jersey	Proxy	20 Jul 1826
Gorge	18	M		G. Britain	U. States	Mary & Harriot	8 Sep 1828
Henry	3					Cincinnatus	29 Apr 1822
Henry	19	M	None	Great Britain	Great Britain	Nestor	3 Nov 1820
Henry R.	31	M	Merch.	U. States	United States	Henri IV	14 Oct 1829
J. H.	35	M	Merchant	Bermuda	Bermuda	Industry	26 Jul 1825
James	5	M		England	America	Ulysses	1 May 1822
James	12					Cincinnatus	29 Apr 1822
James C.	30	M	Merchant	U. States	U. States	Lady Tompkins	13 Apr 1824
Jno.	37	M	Farmer	England	America	Ulysses	1 May 1822
John	20	M	Farmer	Gt. Britain	United States	Penelope	9 Sep 1828
John, Jr.	12	M		England	America	Ulysses	1 May 1822
John H.	25	M	Merchant	Bermuda	Great Britian	Two Brothers	6 Sep 1823
Joseph	43	M	Shop Keeper	England	U.S. of America	Hannibal	17 Dec 1823
Louis	53		Hair dresser	France		Bayard	10 Sep 1827
Louise L.	52	M	Hair Dresser	France	U. States	America	22 Sep 1826
Lucea	8	F		G. Britain	U. States	Mary & Harriot	8 Sep 1828
Martin	13	M		G. Britain	U. States	Mary & Harriot	8 Sep 1828
Mary	13	F		England	America	Ulysses	1 May 1822
Mary	33	F		England	America	Ulysses	1 May 1822
P.	35	M	Merchant	U. States	U. States	Fancy	1 Apr 1824
Richd.	27	M	Merchant	U. States	U. States	Montano	2 Sep 1828
Robt.	45	M	Labourer	G. Britain	U. States	Mary & Harriot	8 Sep 1828
Sarah	16					Cincinnatus	29 Apr 1822
Sarah	40	F	Labourer	G. Britain	U. States	Mary & Harriot	8 Sep 1828
Stepun	20					Cincinnatus	29 Apr 1822
Susan	3	F	...	Ireland	United States	Carolina Ann	24 Oct 1825
Susan	17	F	...	Ireland	United States	Carolina Ann	24 Oct 1825
Thomas	8	M		England	America	Ulysses	1 May 1822
Thos. Jno.	20	M	Merchant	Bermuda	U. States	Wormontagus	11 Apr 1823
William	30	M	Farman	St. John, N.B.	St. John, N.B.	Nancy	18 Oct 1824
William	30	M	Merchant	St. John, N.B.	St. John, N.B.	Sarah G	19 Jun 1827
Wm.	22	M	...	...	U.S. America	Columbia	26 Nov 1825
Wm.	26	M	Farmer	G. Britain	United States	Fairy	18 Feb 1825
GILBORNE, Wm. S.	28	M	Seaman	Canada	U. States	Ductile	4 Oct 1825
GILBRAOTH, Elizabeth	79	F	Spinster	Ireland	United States	Robert Fulton	10 Aug 1827
GILBREBRECHT, Adam	26	M	Boer	Mausbach	United States	Juffraw Johanna	16 Oct 1821
Christiaan, Kinder (his child [Adam])	1 6/12	F		Alt bornback	United States	Juffraw Johanna	16 Oct 1821
Daniel, Kinder (his child [Adam])	3	M		Alt bornback	United States	Juffraw Johanna	16 Oct 1821
Dorothea, Zyn Vrouw (his wife [Adam])	26	F		Alt bornback	United States	Juffraw Johanna	16 Oct 1821
Maria, Kinder (his child [Adam])		F		Alt bornback	United States	Juffraw Johanna	16 Oct 1821
Susana, Kinder (his child [Adam])	4 6/12	F		Alt bornback	United States	Juffraw Johanna	16 Oct 1821
GILBURN, J. J.	25	M	Merchant	Boston	U. States	Ice Plant	5 Jun 1823
GILCHRIST, Alexa.	23	M	Dyer	Scotland	U.S.A.	Calliope	15 Aug 1827
Ann	6			Scotland	United States	Camillus	3 May 1828
Ann	26	F		Great Britain	New York	Philetus	21 Jul 1827
Catherine	24	F	Wife	Great Britain	United States	Hanford	9 Oct 1829
Cathne.	34		his Wife [Michl.]	Ireland	United States	Rufus King	4 Sep 1823
Hugh	21	M	Weaver	Scotland	United States	Andes	2 Oct 1828
James	9	F	None	...ford, Ireland		Mount Vernon	7 Jun 1824
James	30	M	Farmer	Scotland	United States	Belmont	30 Aug 1828

NAMES OF PASSENGERS	AGE	SEX	OCCUPATIONS	COUNTRY TO WHICH THEY BELONG	COUNTRY THEY INTEND TO INHABIT	SHIPS/DATES OF ARRIVAL	
GILCHRIST (cont'd)							
James	52	M	Farmer	Scotland	United States	Broke	16 Jul 1829
Jane	3/12	F		Great Britain	New York	Philetus	21 Jul 1827
Jane	25	F		Gt. Britain		Dalhouse Castle	13 May 1828
Jas.	38	M	Seaman	England	United States	Orozimbo	5 Mar 1827
John	0 2/12	M	Child	Great Britain	United States	Hanford	9 Oct 1829
John	2			Scotland	United States	Camillus	3 May 1828
John	35	M	Dyer	England	New York	Joseph Hume	26 Oct 1829
Margaret	2	F		Gt. Britain		Dalhouse Castle	13 May 1828
Margt.	8			Scotland	United States	Camillus	3 May 1828
Mary	10			Scotland	United States	Camillus	3 May 1828
Mary	12	F	None	...ford, Ireland		Mount Vernon	7 Jun 1824
Mary	17	F	house maid	Ireland	United States	William	20 Jul 1829
Mary	40	F	None	...ford, Ireland		Mount Vernon	7 Jun 1824
Michl.	45		Farmer	Ireland	United States	Rufus King	4 Sep 1823
Nancy	14	F	None	...ford, Ireland		Mount Vernon	7 Jun 1824
Peggy	20	F	None	...ford, Ireland		Mount Vernon	7 Jun 1824
Thos.	2	M		Great Britain	New York	Philetus	21 Jul 1827
William	32 3/12	M	Spinner	Great Britain	United States	Amity	1 Dec 1826
Wm.	3...	M		Great Britain	New York	Philetus	21 Jul 1827
Wm., Mrs.	28		Wife, Going to her Husband	Scotland	United States	Camillus	3 May 1828
GILDEMEISTER,							
Adrian H.	6/12	M		Netherlands	U. States	Edward Quesnel	17 Mar 1829
Catharine A.	30	F		Netherlands	U. States	Edward Quesnel	17 Mar 1829
Hugo C.	33	M	Merchant	Netherlands	U. States	Edward Quesnel	17 Mar 1829
Peter S.	7	M		Netherlands	U. States	Edward Quesnel	17 Mar 1829
GILDEN, Wm. C.	26	M	Mariner	Baltimore	U. States	Cannon	29 Dec 1825
GILE, Catharan	20	F		Great B.	U. States	William Neilson	12 Jun 1828
Elisabeth	24	F	Farmer	Ireland	U. States	Dickinson	30 Jul 1825
John	23	M	Farmer	Ireland	U. States	Dickinson	30 Jul 1825
Thomas	24	M		Great B.	U. States	William Neilson	26 Jul 1828
GILES, Ann	10	F		Jamaica	Great Britain	Kingston	1 Jul 1829
Ann	11	F		England	U. States	Elizabeth	17 May 1822
Ann	39	F	Farmer	Great Britton	U. State	Earl of Liverpool	16 Aug 1826
B.	3	F	Farmer	Great Britton	U. State	Earl of Liverpool	16 Aug 1826
Elizabeth	1	F		England	U. States	Elizabeth	17 May 1822
J.	10	M	Farmer	Great Britton	U. State	Earl of Liverpool	16 Aug 1826
James	29	M	Farmer	Rye, England	United States	William	21 May 1828
Jane	8	F		England	U. States	Elizabeth	17 May 1822
John	13	M		England	U. States	Elizabeth	17 May 1822
John	22	M	Joiner	Ireland	United States	Neury	27 Jan 1827
John	40	M	Servant	England	U.S. America	Columbia	31 Jul 1826
Joshua	4	M		England	U. States	Elizabeth	17 May 1822
L.	28	M	Taylor	France	U. States	John London	1 Sep 1823
S.	12	F	Farmer	Great Britton	U. State	Earl of Liverpool	16 Aug 1826
Sarah	34	F		England	U. States	Elizabeth	17 May 1822
T.	8	M	Farmer	Great Britton	U. State	Earl of Liverpool	16 Aug 1826
T.	35	M	Farmer	Great Britton	U. State	Earl of Liverpool	16 Aug 1826
Thos.	6	M		England	U. States	Elizabeth	17 May 1822
Thos.	34	M	Labourer	England	England	Elizabeth	17 May 1822
William	27	M	Farmer	Rye, England	United States	William	21 May 1828
Wm.	6	M	Farmer	Great Britton	U. State	Earl of Liverpool	16 Aug 1826
GILESPIE, Robert	17	M	Merchant	United States	U. States	Manhattan	25 Dec 1820
GILFALLAN, William	20		Weaver	Ireland	United States	Robert Burns	30 May 1823
GILFILBIN, Stuart	25	F		Great Britian	United States	London	24 Jun 1823
GILFILLAN, Alexander	21	M	Labourer	Ireland	United States	Robert Fulton	24 Jul 1826
GILFILLIN, George	20	M	Farmer	Ireland	United States	General Putnam	20 Jun 1825
GILFORD, John	30	M	Labourer	Ireland	New York	Bowditch	27 Apr 1826
GILGID, Carla	20	M		Germany	United States	Lydia	18 Jun 1828
John	27	F	Shoe Maker	Germany	United States	Lydia	18 Jun 1828
Sophia	23	F		Germany	United States	Lydia	18 Jun 1828

NAMES OF PASSENGERS	AGE	SEX	OCCUPATIONS	COUNTRY TO WHICH THEY BELONG	COUNTRY THEY INTEND TO INHABIT	SHIPS/DATES OF ARRIVAL	
GILHALY, Michael	34	M		Great Britain	United States	Roman	10 May 1828
GILHAM, Jonathan	22	M	Physician	United States	U.S.	Fanny	31 Mar 1825
GILHOOLEY, Bridget	28	F	Spinster	Ireland	United States	Wilson	4 Oct 1827
GILHOP, Mary	13	F	...	Ireland	United States	Wilson	22 Jun 1824
GILHULLY, Barnard	2	M		Ireland	U. States	William Byrnes	17 Jul 1825
Bridget	16	F		Ireland	U. States	William Byrnes	17 Jul 1825
Bridget	25	F		Ireland	U. States	William Byrnes	17 Jul 1825
Catharine	20	F		Ireland	U. States	William Byrnes	17 Jul 1825
Charles	22	M	Mason	Ireland	U. States	Champion	26 Jul 1827
Francis	26	M		Ireland	U. States	William Byrnes	17 Jul 1825
Pat	1	M		Ireland	U. States	William Byrnes	17 Jul 1825
GILHURY, Thady	26	M	Labourer	Ireland	America	Weser	26 Jun 1821
GILIGIN, Barnibus	25	M	...	...	...	Dawn	19 Aug 1825
GILISPIE, Jabez	28	M	Ship master	United States	U. States	Potosi	30 Nov 1826
GILIVET, Gilbert	15	M		France	U. States	Niger	29 Jan 1827
GILKISON, Archbald	18		Gentleman	Canada	America	Florida	14 Oct 1829
Cornish	13		Gentleman	Scotland	America	Florida	14 Oct 1829
Jasper	15		Gentleman	Canada	America	Florida	14 Oct 1829
William	50		Gentleman	Scotland	America	Florida	14 Oct 1829
GILKS, Thomas	30	M		Gt. Britain	U. States	Tantiva	7 Jul 1828
GILL, —, Mr.	20	M	Merchant	Balt.U. States	U.S.	Love	12 Oct 1827
...	7	F	Manufacturer			Manhattan	25 Dec 1820
...	8	F	Manufacturer			Manhattan	25 Dec 1820
...	11	F	Manufacturer			Manhattan	25 Dec 1820
...	40	F	Manufacturer			Manhattan	25 Dec 1820
...	42	M	Manufacturer			Manhattan	25 Dec 1820
A. R., Miss	14		Lady	America	America	Birmingham	16 Oct 1826
Allen	6 6/12	M		England	United States of A.	New York	3 Apr 1826
B.	30	M	Merchant	Cuba	U. States	Ductile	12 May 1826
B., Mr.	41	M	Merchant	America	America	Birmingham	16 Oct 1826
Bennington	40	M	Merchant	United States	United States of A.	New York	3 Apr 1826
Betty	15	F	None	Great Britain	United States	William Dawson	18 Jun 1827
Bregit	27					Agricola	1 Jul 1820
Bridget	25	F		Great Brittain	United States	Sarah Ralston	27 Jan 1827
Catharine	40	F	Spinster	...	U. States	New Orleans	24 Aug 1827
Charlotte	15				U. States	Nymph	5 Jul 1820
Christian	30	F	Spintres	U. States	U. States	Servant	30 Aug 1820
E. P., Miss	15		Lady	America	America	Birmingham	16 Oct 1826
E. S.	46	M	Merchant	England	England	Pacific	17 Jun 1828
Elizabeth	16 9/12	F	None	Great Briton	United States	Mount Vernon	30 Dec 1828
Ellen	1	F	None	Great Britain	United States	William Dawson	18 Jun 1827
Ellen	24	F	None	England	United States	Hamilton	13 Nov 1827
Eustachio	35	M	Minister	Spain	America	Rebecca	31 Oct 1825
F.	38	M	Labourer	G. Britain	U. States	Hanford	18 Sep 1828
Frances	40	F		England	England	Pacific	17 Jun 1828
Geo.	53	M	Labourer	Great Britain	United States	Kate	2 Oct 1821
Grace	20	F	None	Great Britain	United States	William Dawson	18 Jun 1827
Hugh	6	M	Labourer	Ireland	New York	Vigilant	6 May 1822
Hugh	16	M	Labourer	Sligo	America	Ocean	17 Aug 1820
James	4	M				Governor Fenner	23 Jul 1829
James	9	M	Labourer	Ireland	New York	Vigilant	6 May 1822
James	21	M	Weaver			Hanford	17 Jul 1828
James	25	M	Merchant	U. States	United States	Cortes	18 Oct 1820
Jas.	21	F			U. States	Nymph	5 Jul 1820
Jno.	35	M	Mechanic	Ireland	U. States	Chase	9 May 1823
John	17	M	Labourer	England	United States	Jubilee	12 May 1828
John	23	M	Brass Founder	England	U.S.A.	Lima	6 Dec 1826
John	26	M	Labourer	Scotland	United States	Coquet	6 Jun 1827
John	27	M	Clothier	Great Britain	United States	William Dawson	18 Jun 1827
John	63	M	Gentleman	Barbadoes	Barbadoes	Falcon	4 Jun 1825
Joseph	21	M	Farmer	Ireland	United States	Lord Strangford	20 Jun 1826
M.	20	F		Great Britain	United States	Isaac Hicks	6 Dec 1827
M.	30	M	Brick Layer	Great Britain	United States	Aspasia	16 Jul 1828
M. H., Miss	12		Lady	America	America	Birmingham	16 Oct 1826
Margaret	21	F	None	Great Britain	United States	Kate	2 Oct 1821
Maria	19					Agricola	1 Jul 1820
Mary	1	F		Great Brittain	United States	Sarah Ralston	27 Jan 1827
Mary	3	F		Ireland	New York	Vigilant	6 May 1822
Mary	15	F	Spinster	...	U. States	New Orleans	24 Aug 1827

469

NAMES OF PASSENGERS	AGE	SEX	OCCUPATIONS	COUNTRY TO WHICH THEY BELONG	COUNTRY THEY INTEND TO INHABIT	SHIPS/DATES OF ARRIVAL	
GILL (cont'd)							
Mary	35	F				Governor Fenner	23 Jul 1829
Mary	39	F	None	Great Briton	United States	Mount Vernon	30 Dec 1828
Nancy	16	F	Spinster			Ocean	17 Aug 1820
Nancy	22	F	Spinster	Ireland		Robert Fulton	4 Jun 1828
Owen	22	M	Labourer			Ocean	17 Aug 1820
Pat	70	M		Great Brittain	United States	Sarah Ralston	27 Jan 1827
Patrick	23	M	Labourer	Ireland	U. States	Marcus	7 Apr 1825
Patrick	28	M	Laborer	Ireland	United States	Sarah G	19 Jun 1827
Peter	2	M		Great Brittain	United States	Sarah Ralston	27 Jan 1827
Peter M.	32	M	Merchant	Great Britain	Canada	Canada	20 Jun 1823
R.	34	M	Weaver	Great Britain	United States	Isaac Hicks	6 Dec 1827
Richard	22	M	Shoemaker	Great Britain	U. States	Ganges	21 Jun 1827
Richard	29	M	Maltster	England	Pennsylvania	Curler	7 Jul 1827
Robert	48	M	Farmer	England	U. States	Nymph	5 Jul 1820
S., Miss	8		Lady	America	America	Birmingham	16 Oct 1826
S. A., Miss	10		Lady	America	America	Birmingham	16 Oct 1826
S. P., Mrs.	35		Lady	America	America	Birmingham	16 Oct 1826
Theodore Paul	2	M		America	America	Birmingham	16 Oct 1826
Thomas	4	M		Great Brittain	United States	Sarah Ralston	27 Jan 1827
Thomas	40	M	Farmer	Great Briton	United States	Mount Vernon	30 Dec 1828
Thomas, Jun.	11 4/12	M	None	Great Briton	United States	Mount Vernon	30 Dec 1828
Unner	30	F		Ireland	New York	Vigilant	6 May 1822
Will	3	M		Great Britain	United States	William Dawson	18 Jun 1827
Will K.	34	M	Braizer	England	U.S.A.	Robin Hood	6 May 1828
William	15	M	None	Great Briton	United States	Mount Vernon	30 Dec 1828
William	30		Cloth ...	England		Agricola	1 Jul 1820
William	34	M	Labourer	England	New York	Governor Fenner	23 Jul 1829
Wm.	29	M	Painter	Great Britain	United States	Minerva	28 Jul 1823
GILLA...TT, H. C.	21	M	Merchant	U. States	U. States	Hector	11 Oct 1824
William	25	M	Merchant	Great Britain	U. States	Hector	11 Oct 1824
GILLAHEE, Patk.	24	M	Boat Carpenter	Ireland	United States	Trident	16 May 1826
GILLAN, George	20	M	Farmer	Great Britain	U. States	Great Britain	18 Mar 1828
Hugh	12 1/12	M	Labourer	Ireland	New York	Louisa	20 Jul 1826
Hugh	60	M	Carpenter	England	U.S.	Panthea	13 Nov 1823
Jane	60	F		England	U.S.	Panthea	13 Nov 1823
John	18 1/12	M	Labourer	Ireland	New York	Louisa	20 Jul 1826
Luke	19	M	Black Smith	Ireland	U. States	Virginia	20 Jun 1825
Mary	10 4/12	F	Labourer	Ireland	New York	Louisa	20 Jul 1826
Mary	50	F	Mother of [Thomas]	Ireland	New York	Louisa	20 Jul 1826
Thomas	21 3/12	M	Labourer	Ireland	New York	Louisa	20 Jul 1826
GILLARD, Elizabeth	30	F	None	England	New Jersey	Commerce	24 Sep 1823
James	3	M	None	England	New Jersey	Commerce	24 Sep 1823
John	7	M	None	England	New Jersey	Commerce	24 Sep 1823
Joseph	50	M	Merchant	France	U. States	Bayard	9 Nov 1825
Sarah	5	F	None	England	New Jersey	Commerce	24 Sep 1823
Wm.	1	M	None	England	New Jersey	Commerce	24 Sep 1823
GILLASPIA, Henry	26 4/12		Farmer	Scotland	U.S. of America	Helen	8 Feb 1822
GILLDAIR, David	20	M	Weaver	Belfast	United States	Minerva	30 Oct 1829
GILLEN, Barnard	15	M	Farmer	Ireland	United States	Trident	17 May 1825
Charles	19	M	Farmer	Ireland	United States	Trident	17 May 1825
Edward	12	M	Farmer	Ireland	United States	Trident	17 May 1825
Ellen	40	F	Spinster	Ireland	United States	Trident	17 May 1825
Fanny	8	F	Girl	Ireland	United States	Trident	17 May 1825
Henry		M	Chiefly farmers		United States	Factor	8 Jul 1829
Margt.	16	F	Spinster	Ireland	United States	Trident	17 May 1825
Mary		F	Chiefly farmers		United States	Factor	8 Jul 1829
Michl.	28	M	Labourer	Great Brittain	United States	Active	12 Sep 1828
Phillip	9	M	Boy	Ireland	United States	Trident	17 May 1825
GILLENDER,							
Mary Anne, Mrs.	21	F	None	Liverpool	Liverpool	Hector	11 May 1821
Theos.	8	M	None	New York	United States	Hector	29 Nov 1823
Wm. C.	22	M	Mercht.	U. States	U. States	America	17 Oct 1825
Wm. O.	23	M	Mercht.	New York	New York	Panthea	22 Jul 1826
GILLENEAU, Peter	33	M	Officer	Columbia	U. States	Govr. Von Scholten	23 Apr 1825
GILLERN, Victor	22	M	Doctor	United States	United States	General La Fayette	1 Aug 1829
GILLES, Annes	7	F	Facterist	Scotland	Canada	Swift	16 Jul 1827

NAMES OF PASSENGERS	AGE	SEX	OCCUPATIONS	COUNTRY TO WHICH THEY BELONG	COUNTRY THEY INTEND TO INHABIT	SHIPS/DATES OF ARRIVAL	
GILLES (cont'd)							
Daniel	16	M	Facterist	Scotland	Canada	Swift	16 Jul 1827
Daniel	48	M	Farmer	Scotland	Canada	Swift	16 Jul 1827
Dunkin	14	M	Facterist	Scotland	Canada	Swift	16 Jul 1827
Jane	42	F	Farmer	Scotland	Canada	Swift	16 Jul 1827
John	21	M	Facterist	Scotland	Canada	Swift	16 Jul 1827
John	26	M	Mason	Scotland	U. States	Camillus	27 Jun 1826
Margeret	10	F	Facterist	Scotland	Canada	Swift	16 Jul 1827
GILLESPE, Isabella	23	F	Spinster	Ireland	United States	Robert Fulton	24 Jul 1826
GILLESPIE, —, Mrs.	32	F		England	New York	Lima	5 Aug 1829
—, Mrs.	32	F		England	U. States	Lima	5 Aug 1829
Alex.	16	M	Mechanic	Great Brittan	Great Brittain	Florida	17 May 1825
Anna	14	F	Mechanic	England	United States	Hercules	24 Oct 1821
Anthony	8	M		England	New York	Lima	5 Aug 1829
Anthony	8	M		England	U. States	Lima	5 Aug 1829
Biddy	15	F	Spinster	Ireland	United States	Trident	16 May 1826
Catherine	12	F	Spinster	Ireland	United States	Trident	16 May 1826
Cecilia	47	F	Wife	Ireland	United States	Trident	16 May 1826
Collin	54	M	Merchant	England	U. States	William Thompson	17 Dec 1827
Daniel	26	M	Labourer	Ireland	St. John, N.B.	Ann Maria	7 Aug 1826
Dennis	19	M	Servant	Ireland	United States	Trident	16 May 1826
Edward	50	M	Labourer	Ireland	United States	Trident	16 May 1826
Edwd.	10	M	Boy	Ireland	United States	Trident	16 May 1826
Henry	23	M	Mechanic	England	United States	Hercules	24 Oct 1821
Hugh [crossed out]	19	M	Farmer	Ireland	United States	Leonidas	3 Aug 1825
Jame	30		Labourer	Great Britan	United States	Newry	11 Jul 1827
James	2	M		Glasgow, Barony [Parish], Lanark [County]	New York	Hero	19 May 1828
*going to her friends							
James [crossed out]	20	M	Farmer	Ireland	United States	Leonidas	3 Aug 1825
Janet	27	F		Glasgow, Barony [Parish], Lanark [County]	New York	Hero	19 May 1828
*going to her friends							
Jno. F.	32	M	Merchant	U. States		Charleston Packet	4 May 1821
John	18	M	Farmer	Ireland	United States	Trident	16 May 1826
John	20	M	Cutler	Scotland	U. States	Czar	29 Aug 1829
John	30		Labourer	Great Britan	United States	Newry	11 Jul 1827
John [crossed out]	25	M	Farmer	Ireland	United States	Leonidas	3 Aug 1825
Marcus	16	M	Labourer	Ireland	United States	Trident	16 May 1826
Martha	38	F	None	Great Britain	United States	Orozimbo	7 Nov 1826
Martha	56	F	Mechanic	England	United States	Hercules	24 Oct 1821
Mary	11	F	Mechanic	England	United States	Hercules	24 Oct 1821
Mary Ann	2			Great Britan	United States	Newry	11 Jul 1827
Michael	4	M		England	New York	Lima	5 Aug 1829
Michael	4	M		England	U. States	Lima	5 Aug 1829
Michael	25	M	Farmer	Scotland	United States	Tom	2 Jul 1827
Nancy	18	F	Spinster	Ireland	United States	Trident	16 May 1826
Peter	20	...	...	Scotland	America	Nimrod	9 Jul 1827
R.	47	M	Merchant	U. States	Great Britain	Thompson	26 Apr 1828
Robert	27	M	Mercht.	G.B.	Canada	George Canning	2 May 1828
Robert	38	M	Merchant	G. Briton	United States	James Monroe	14 Dec 1820
Robert	40	M	Merchant	Scotland	Gt. Britain	Columbia	31 Jul 1826
Robert	64	M	Farmer	Scotland	U. States	Hope	21 Oct 1823
Robt.	48	M	Merchant	Scotland	U.S.	Florida	17 May 1825
Sarah	15	F	Spinster	Ireland	United States	Trident	17 May 1825
Susannah	24	F	Spinster	Ireland	United States	Asia	29 Jul 1829
Thomas	40	M	Weaver	Ireland	United States	Atlantic	21 Jul 1827
William	...	M	...	Great Britain	United States	Orozimbo	7 Nov 1826
William	48	M	Dyer	Great Britain	United States	Orozimbo	7 Nov 1826
Wm.	18	M	Farmer	Ireland	United States	General Putnam	20 Jun 1825
GILLET, Augustus W.	31	M	Merchant	U.S.	U. States	Canada	5 Feb 1827
Augustus W.	33	M	Merchant	U. States	U. States	Birmingham	23 Feb 1829
Daniel	23	M	Labourer	Gt. Britain	U. States	Sarah G.	14 Apr 1828
Jno.	28	M	...	Canada	N.Y.	Julia	28 Jul 1824

NAMES OF PASSENGERS	AGE	SEX	OCCUPATIONS	COUNTRY TO WHICH THEY BELONG	COUNTRY THEY INTEND TO INHABIT	SHIPS/DATES OF ARRIVAL	
GILLET (cont'd)							
Philader		M	Merchant	U. States	U. States	Hannah & Elizabeth	13 Jun 1825
Thos.	17 7/12	M	distressed seaman	Philadelphia	United States	Florida	27 Aug 1825
GILLEW, Mathew	2/12	M	Child	Ireland	United States	Wilson	6 Jun 1828
Michl.	17	M	Labourer	Ireland	United States	Wilson	6 Jun 1828
GILLEY, Terrence	16	M	Labourer	Ireland	New York	Lima	5 Aug 1829
Terrence	16	M	Labourer	Ireland	U. States	Lima	5 Aug 1829
GILLIAN, Jane	24	F	Seamstress	Ireland	New York	Louisa	18 Apr 1827
Mary	22 6/12	F	Seamstress	Ireland	New York	Louisa	18 Apr 1827
GILLIARD, Ed.	10	M	Merchant	Philada.	U. States	Dewitt Clinton	16 Dec 1825
GILLIAT, Sophia	28	F		England	America	Courier	24 Jul 1820
William	29	M	Merchant	England	America	Courier	24 Jul 1820
GILLIE, George	22	M	Husband	Ireland	United States	Louisa	18 Apr 1827
GILLIES, J. R.	33	M	Millwright	Scotland	United States	Orozimbo	11 Aug 1823
William	33 1/12	M	Farmer	Great Britain	United States	Amity	1 Dec 1826
GILLIGAN, Mary	4	F		Ireland	United States	Thompson	12 Sep 1827
Patrick	19	M	Farmer			Commerce	22 Jun 1825
Patt	6	M		Ireland	United States	Thompson	12 Sep 1827
Peter	20	M	Mechanic	Ireland	United States	Wm. Byrnes	30 Apr 1828
GILLIGHAN, John	20	M	Labourer	Ireland		Robert Fulton	4 Jun 1828
GILLILAND, H.	37	M	Mechanic	Ireland	England	Franklin	31 Jan 1825
GILLIMAND, R.	24	M	Bleacher	Ireland	United States	Josephine	30 Apr 1828
GILLIN, Ann	23	F	None	Great Britain	America	Remittance	24 Aug 1825
Brien	19	M	Farmer	Ireland	United States	Lima	19 Jun 1824
Patk.	27	M	Farmer	Great Britain	America	Remittance	24 Aug 1825
GILLING, Wolfgang	19	M	Baker	Germany	Philadelphia	Falcon	21 Oct 1826
GILLIPA, Conelious	22	M	Labourer	Ireland	N. Jersey	Potomac	7 Aug 1827
GILLIS, A. W.	22	M	Merchant	St. Johns	U. States	Nancy	10 Jul 1823
Agns	35	F	Weaver	Scotland	U. States	Roger Stewart	9 Jun 1828
Charles	1	M		Ireland	United States	Borneo	28 Aug 1828
Harriet	23	F	Matron	Ireland	America	Josephine	8 Dec 1827
John	28	M	Weaver	Scotland	U. States	Roger Stewart	9 Jun 1828
Margaret	2	F	Weaver	Scotland	U. States	Roger Stewart	9 Jun 1828
Martha	25	F	Weaver	Scotland	U. States	Roger Stewart	9 Jun 1828
Mary	6/12	F	Weaver	Scotland	U. States	Roger Stewart	9 Jun 1828
Owen	20	M	Labourer	Ireland	America	Franklin	13 Aug 1827
Susanna	22	F		Ireland	United States	Borneo	28 Aug 1828
Wm.	26	M	Weaver	Stland	U. States	Roger Stewart	9 Jun 1828
Wm.	28	M		Great B.	U. States	William Neilson	26 Jul 1828
GILLISPIE, Alice	5 11/12	F		England	America, U.S.	Illinois	3 Jun 1822
Billy	18	F				Superb	18 Jul 1820
Francis	26	M	Laborer	Scotland	America	Friends	28 Sep 1822
George	46 3/12	M	...	England	America, U.S.	Illinois	3 Jun 1822
Thos.	30		Couchman	Ireland	England	London	16 Aug 1824
Wm.	25	M	Tailor	Scotland	America	Friends	28 Sep 1822
GILLISSON, Thomas	21	...	...	...	United States	Criterion	27 Jun 1827
GILLMAN, R. K.	21	M	Merchant	U. States	U. States	Pizarro	21 Oct 1825
Wm.	23	M	Mercht.	England	Buenos Ayres	Perserverance	2 Mar 1822
GILLMARTIN, Mary	12	F		Sligo	New York	Susquehana	27 Jun 1823
Mary	35	F	Sevt.	Sligo	New York	Susquehana	27 Jun 1823
GILLMORE, ... [Ann?]	60	F	Spinster			Robert Burns	13 Jul 1820
GILLMOUR, John	5 3/12	M	Gentleme	Great Briton	incerter [uncertain]	Mount Vernon	30 Dec 1828
GILLNOUR, Thomas	32	M	Gentleme	Great Briton	uncertan	Mount Vernon	30 Dec 1828
GILLON, Barry	20	M	Labourer	Ireland	United States	Henry Kneeland	7 Jun 1828
Cath.	12	F	Spinster	Ireland	United States	Thomas	13 Dec 1827
George	26	M	Labourer			Ocean	17 Aug 1820
Hugh	24	M	Labourer			Superb	18 Jul 1820
Sarah	20	F	Spinster	Ireland	United States	Thomas	13 Dec 1827
GILLOON, Ow[e]n	40	M	Trader			Superb	18 Jul 1820
GILLOW, Brdgit	15	F	Spinster	Ireland	United States	Wilson	6 Jun 1828
Catherine	21	F	Spinster	Ireland	United States	Wilson	6 Jun 1828
Margret	14	F	Spinster	Ireland	United States	Wilson	6 Jun 1828
GILLS, Ely	30	F	Spinster	Ireland	U. States	Meteor	19 Jul 1828
George	28	M	Tailor			Lady of the Lake	23 Aug 1828
James	25		Wool Courer	Ireland	United States	Geo. Canning	5 Jun 1828
James	38	M	Cloth finisher	England	United States	Andes	2 Oct 1828
GILMAN, James	30	M	Labourer	G. Britain	U. States	Mary & Harriot	8 Sep 1828

NAMES OF PASSENGERS	AGE	SEX	OCCUPATIONS	COUNTRY TO WHICH THEY BELONG	COUNTRY THEY INTEND TO INHABIT	SHIPS/DATES OF ARRIVAL	
GILMAN (cont'd)							
R. H.	30	M	Merchant	U. States	U. States	Robert Read	30 Jan 1826
Rufus K.	20 3/12	M	G...	United States	United States	Ann Maria	8 Jun 1824
Thomas	26	M	Laborer	Ireland	U. States	Lady Hunter	8 Aug 1826
Wm.	18	M		G. Britain	U. States	Mary & Harriot	8 Sep 1828
GILMARTIN, Alica	2	F		New York	U. States	Virginia	20 Jun 1825
Ann	22	F	Black Smith	Ireland	U. States	Virginia	20 Jun 1825
Bridget	30	F	Spinster	Ireland		Robert Fulton	4 Jun 1828
Catharine	14	F	Spinster	Ireland		Robert Fulton	4 Jun 1828
Daniel	6	M	Labourer	Ireland		Robert Fulton	4 Jun 1828
Edward	2	M		New York	U. States	Virginia	20 Jun 1825
Margret	15	F	Spinster	Ireland		Robert Fulton	4 Jun 1828
Mary	5	F	Spinster	Ireland		Robert Fulton	4 Jun 1828
Mary	20	F	Spinster	Ireland	United States	Wilson	4 Oct 1827
Mary	24	F	Spinster	Ireland	United States	Lima	19 Jun 1824
Patrick	30	M	Farmer	New York	U. States	Virginia	20 Jun 1825
Rose	32	F		New York	U. States	Virginia	20 Jun 1825
William	3	M	Labourer	Ireland		Robert Fulton	4 Jun 1828
Winniford	6	F		New York	U. States	Virginia	20 Jun 1825
GILMER, James A.	12	M	...	United States	United States	Prudence	31 Oct 1827
GILMOINE, Chrs.	30	M	Farmer	England	U. States	Thomas Ritchie	2 Jul 1827
GILMOR, John	27 9/12	M	Merchant	Ireland	United States	Louisa	27 Nov 1826
GILMORE, Abm.	60	M	Farmer			Robert Burns	13 Jul 1820
Abm., Junr.	20	M				Robert Burns	13 Jul 1820
Agnes	22	F	None	England	U. States	Montgomery	18 Oct 1828
Elizh.	11/12	F		Ireland	U. States	Marcus	7 Apr 1825
Francis	23	M	Carpenter	Ireland	U. States	Marcus	7 Apr 1825
Jane	21	F	None	England	U. States	Montgomery	18 Oct 1828
Jannett	26	F	None	England	U. States	Montgomery	18 Oct 1828
John	19	M	Merchant	Virginia	U. States	United States	1 Apr 1828
John	23	M	Black Smith	United States	U.S. States	Thrasher	4 Dec 1822
Margarett	60	F	None	England	U. States	Montgomery	18 Oct 1828
Mary	35	F	Servant	Ireland	U. States	Marcus	7 Apr 1825
Mary T.	24	F		Ireland	U. States	Marcus	7 Apr 1825
Patrick	24	M	Gentleman	Mexico	England	Brown	23 Dec 1826
Patrick	25	M	Weaver	Ireland	United States	Enterprize	23 Jul 1827
Peggy	18	F	Spinster			Robert Burns	13 Jul 1820
Thomas	60	M	Farmer	England	U. States	Montgomery	18 Oct 1828
GILMOUR, David	25	M		Scotland	United States	Camillus	9 May 1827
Hugh	29	M		Scotland	United States	Camillus	9 May 1827
Martha	27	F	Spinster	Ireland	United States	Trident	16 May 1826
Patrick	27	M	Merchant	Ireland	United States	Herald	7 Jun 1824
GILNER, Elizabeth	12	F		G. Britain	U. States	Mary & Harriot	8 Sep 1828
Henry	50	M	Farmer	G. Britain	U. States	Mary & Harriot	8 Sep 1828
Margret	10	F		G. Britain	U. States	Mary & Harriot	8 Sep 1828
Sally	18	F		G. Britain	U. States	Mary & Harriot	8 Sep 1828
Sarah	50	F		G. Britain	U. States	Mary & Harriot	8 Sep 1828
GILONE, John	48	M	Farmer	Great Britian	United States	Isaac Hicks	22 May 1826
GILPATRICK, Asa	31	M	Mariner	American	United States	Exchange	16 Feb 1822
GILPIN, Richd.	16	M	Mercht.	U.S.	U.S.	Pacific	24 Oct 1828
Wm.	25	M	None	Ireland	America	Hesperus	7 Jul 1820
GILRANY, Hugh	20	M	Weaver	Ireland	U. States	Virginia	20 Jun 1825
GILROW, Pat.	20	F	Spinster	Ireland	United States	Wilson	6 Jun 1828
GILROY, Ann	40	F	Spinster	Ireland	United States	Wilson	4 Oct 1827
Cathrine	6	F	Spinster	Ireland	United States	Wilson	4 Oct 1827
Hugh	10	M	Labourer	Ireland	United States	Wilson	4 Oct 1827
James	8	M	Labourer	Ireland	United States	Wilson	4 Oct 1827
Michal	12	M	Labourer	Ireland	United States	Wilson	4 Oct 1827
Patt	14	M	Labourer	Ireland	United States	Wilson	4 Oct 1827
Thomas	40	M	Weaver	Scotland	United States	Confidence	5 Sep 1828
GILSHAM, Christopher	30	M	Labourer	Ireland	United States	Andes	2 Oct 1828
Mary, his wife [Christopher]	25	F	Housekeeper	Ireland	United States	Andes	2 Oct 1828
GILSON, Anthony	25	M	Farmer	H...ll	United States	Solon	21 Jun 1824
Chas.			Prisoner taken by the U.S. Ship Cyane and sent by the Consul at St. Iago			Maria	20 Jul 1820
James	20	M	Labourer	Ireland	United States	Hope	12 Jun 1828
W.	30	M	Sailor	England	U. States	Hiram	17 Jun 1826
GILSTON, Bridget	40	F	Lady	Ireland	United States	Dublin Packet	3 Sep 1822

NAMES OF PASSENGERS	AGE	SEX	OCCUPATIONS	COUNTRY TO WHICH THEY BELONG	COUNTRY THEY INTEND TO INHABIT	SHIPS/DATES OF ARRIVAL	
GILSTON (cont'd)							
Saml.		M	Merchant	U. States	U. States	General Ward	22 Jun 1821
GILVAREY, John	28	M	Labourer	Ireland	United States	Robert Fulton	24 Jul 1826
GIMMEL, C.	16	F	Gent	French	Switzerland	Charlemagne	19 Sep 1828
C.	35	F	Gent	French	Switzerland	Charlemagne	19 Sep 1828
Gerance	39	F	Gent	French	Switzerland	Charlemagne	19 Sep 1828
L.	10	M	Gent	French	Switzerland	Charlemagne	19 Sep 1828
M.	6	F	Gent	French	Switzerland	Charlemagne	19 Sep 1828
M.	18	F	Gent	French	Switzerland	Charlemagne	19 Sep 1828
S.	14	F	Gent	French	Switzerland	Charlemagne	19 Sep 1828
T.	12	F	Gent	French	Switzerland	Charlemagne	19 Sep 1828
GINDELL, Antonio	29	M	Merchant	Italy	United States	Dolphin	7 May 1822
GINDER, Lorenzo	30	M	Miller	...	New York	Frances Henrietta	25 Aug 1825
GINNESSER, Joseph	70	M	Merchant	U. States	U. States	Virginia	26 May 1828
GINO, T., Don	48		Gentleman	Spain	Cuba	Draper	17 Dec 1823
GINOL, Henry	26	M	Clergiman	Bevarian	U.N.S.	Robert Edwards	20 Jan 1829
GIO, Francis	35	M	Weaver	France	United States	Globe	30 Aug 1828
*landed at this Port, Custom House, Portland, Aug 19, 1828							
Maria	30	F	Weaver	France	United States	Globe	30 Aug 1828
*landed at this Port, Custom House, Portland, Aug 19, 1828							
GIRADLEY, Robt.	26	M	Labourer	Scotland	United States	Margaret Bogle	11 Jun 1824
GIRAND, Daniel	40	M	Merchant	United States	United States	Emeline	21 Nov 1823
Jno. P.	23	M	Merchant	U. States	U. States	Chase	27 Feb 1824
Marin	26	M	Merchant	N. York	U. States	Governor Tompkins	7 Apr 1823
GIRARD, —	24	M	Merchant	U. States	U. States	Quesnel	6 Sep 1824
—, Mr.	25	M	Merchant	France	France	Desdemonia	9 Jun 1825
Arseni	25			Germany	Interior	Desdemona	12 Jun 1826
Emile	16	M	Engineer			Henri IV	17 May 1828
Jacob P.	42	M	Merchant	United States	United States	White Oak	30 Oct 1820
James	29	M	Farmer or Mechanic	France	U.S.	Edward Quesnel	31 Jul 1827
John D.	26	M	Weaver	Wertemberg	Wertemberg	Edward Quesnel	3 Jul 1829
Joseph	30	M	Surgeon	Tuscany	Italy	Eliza	20 Mar 1824
GIRARDIN, Jonakeal	35	M	Militaire	France		Charles Carroll	16 Jan 1829
GIRARDO, Catharan	4 5/12	F	Farmer	Switzerland	U. States	France	26 Jun 1828
Coneverrena	2 4/12	F	Farmer	Switzerland	U. States	France	26 Jun 1828
Mary	65 5/12	F	Farmer	Switzerland	U. States	France	26 Jun 1828
GIRARRD, Danl.	45	M	Merchant	U. States	U. States	Tuscaloosa	19 Mar 1827
GIRAUD, Danl.	42	M	Merchant	New York	U. States	Tuscaloosa	8 May 1826
GIRAUDIN, F.	19	M	Machine Maker	France	United States	Le Voltaire	19 Jul 1828
GIRDINAGO, L.	37	M	Mariner	U. States	U. States	Tampico	20 Apr 1825
GIRGENBUHLER, Anna	28	F	Farmer	France	U. States	Lewis	6 Jul 1825
John	18	M	Farmer	France	U. States	Lewis	6 Jul 1825
GIRRE, Francis	30		Servent	Mexico	Mexico	Cicero	18 Aug 1829
GIRREY, Thomas	20	M	Stone Cutter	Ireland	United States	Sarah Ann	18 Nov 1826
GIRVAN, Margaret	30		Farmer	Ireland	United States	Carolina Ann	12 Sep 1823
GISE, Catherine	4	F	Farmer	Swizerland		Antioch	18 Aug 1829
Christine	28	F	Farmer	Swizerland		Antioch	18 Aug 1829
Joseph	28	M	Farmer	Swizerland		Antioch	18 Aug 1829
GISM, Jean	36	M	Labourer	Brattain		L'Esperance	6 Sep 1828
GISNER, David H.	25	M	Merchant	St. John, N.B.	St. John, N.B.	St. Michaels	27 Nov 1824
GITNAY, Peter	22	M	Servant	Great Britain	United States	Ganges	26 Oct 1826
GITTENS, Rose	25	F	None	Great Britain	United States	Mary & Harriet	3 Jul 1829
GIVAN, Robert	35	M	Merchant	Great Britain	United States	Martha	3 May 1821
GIVANS, John	6	M		Ireland	U. States	Nancy	29 Nov 1821
Margt.	20	F		Ireland	U. States	Nancy	29 Nov 1821
Wm.	4	M		Ireland	U. States	Nancy	29 Nov 1821
Wm.	22	M		Ireland	U. States	Nancy	29 Nov 1821
GIVEN, Jno. M.	29	M	Carpenter	U. States	U. States	Georgiana	25 Jun 1824
Robert	8	M	Child	Nova Scotia	United States	Sarah Ann	18 Nov 1826
GL...N, James	30	M		G. Britain	U. States	Camillus	8 Sep 1828
GLACE, Isaac	30	M	Merchant	United States	United States	Gertrude	19 May 1826
GLADHILL, Matthew	40	M	Manufacturer	Great Britain	United States	Ganges	26 Oct 1826
GLADWICK, A.	8	F		Gt. Britain	United States	Robert Edwards	1 Jun 1826
H.	42	M	Miller	Gt. Britain	United States	Robert Edwards	1 Jun 1826
H., Jr.	10	M		Gt. Britain	United States	Robert Edwards	1 Jun 1826
M.	48	F		Gt. Britain	United States	Robert Edwards	1 Jun 1826

NAMES OF PASSENGERS	AGE	SEX	OCCUPATIONS	COUNTRY TO WHICH THEY BELONG	COUNTRY THEY INTEND TO INHABIT	SHIPS/DATES OF ARRIVAL	
GLANCEY, Michel	21	M	Labourer	Ireland	United States	Wilson	4 Oct 1827
Oriney	28	F		Ireland	U.S. of America	Douglass	6 Jul 1829
GLANCY, Catharine	18	F		Ireland	U. States	Nancy	1 Sep 1823
GLANEY, Bidey	16	F	Merchant	Ireland	United States	Magnet	22 Aug 1822
GLANTZEN, C. F.	30	M	Watchmaker	Germany	U. States	George	9 Jul 1825
GLARDON, Ann C.	35	F		France	France	Edward Quesnel 3 Jul 1829	
Catherine	6	F		France	France	Edward Quesnel 3 Jul 1829	
Catherine	62	F		France	France	Edward Quesnel 3 Jul 1829	
Frederick	10	M		France	France	Edward Quesnel 3 Jul 1829	
George	1 5/12	M		France	France	Edward Quesnel 3 Jul 1829	
Jaquet Christopher	35	M		France	France	Edward Quesnel 3 Jul 1829	
Perre D.	65	M		France	France	Edward Quesnel 3 Jul 1829	
Perre Louis	4 6/12	M		France	France	Edward Quesnel 3 Jul 1829	
GLARE, James	24	M	Labourer	Scotland	America	Minerva	8 Oct 1824
GLASEA, Emanul	28	F		Spain	U. States	Ambuscade	6 Oct 1821
GLASER, Catharine	21	F				Caesar	24 Aug 1829
GLASGON, John	21	M	Turner	Ireland	America	John Adams	2 Aug 1827
GLASGOW, James	25	M	Machanic	U. States	U. States	Packet Frances	30 Jun 1828
Jas.	34	M	Mercht.	England	U. States	Perseverance	18 Nov 1824
GLASHAN, Chas. M.	45	M	Mariner	Scotland	G. Britain	Nassau	20 Dec 1823
GLASON, James	21	M	...	Ireland	United States	Colossus	30 May 1825
Sophia	31	F	Farmer	France	France	Sully	15 Jul 1829
GLASS, A.	27	M	Merchant	U. States	U. States	Eliza	26 Jul 1825
An	15	F	None	Great Britain	United States	Courier	26 Jun 1827
Barbaretta	27	F	Spinster	Switzerland	United States	Andes	5 May 1828
E. B.	50	F		N. York	America	Jupiter	8 Apr 1828
Eleanor	20		Servant	Ireland	Great Britain	Robert Burns	14 Jun 1824
Eliza	...	F	...	Ireland	United States	General Putnam 20 Jun 1825	
John	21	M	...	Ireland	United States	General Putnam 20 Jun 1825	
John	24	M		Ireland	U. States	Nancy	16 Aug 1822
John	41	M	Merchant	Great Britain	United States	Courier	26 Jun 1827
Michael	23	M	Farmer	Switzerland	United States	Andes	5 May 1828
William	23		Shoe Maker	Ireland	G. Britain	Henrietta	26 Nov 1825
GLASSAN, Jas.	25	M	Farmer	Ireland	U. States	Abeona	16 Mar 1820
GLASSE, F.	43 5/12		Merchant	England	England	Jackin	15 May 1828
GLASSER, Andr.	3	M		Switzerland	U.States	C. Amelia	30 Jun 1828
Cath.	5	F		Switzerland	U.States	C. Amelia	30 Jun 1828
Hy.	37	M		Switzerland	U.States	C. Amelia	30 Jun 1828
Jean	7	F		Switzerland	U.States	C. Amelia	30 Jun 1828
Maria	1 9/12	F		Switzerland	U.S.	C. Amelia	30 Jun 1828
GLASSEY, Betty	18	F	Servant	Ireland	United States	Carolina Ann	11 Dec 1826
Isaac	64	M	Farmer	Ireland	United States	Carolina Ann	11 Dec 1826
Martha	17	F	Servant	Irereland	America	Carolina Ann	20 Jun 1825
Rachel	20	F	Spinster	Ireland	United States	Fabius	31 Jul 1829
Robt.	2 1/12	M		Ireland	America	Carolina Ann	7 Apr 1826
Susan	23 5/12	F	Mantuamaker	Ireland	America	Carolina Ann	7 Apr 1826
William	20	M	Laborer	Ireland	United States	Carolina Ann	11 Dec 1826
GLASSON, John	30	M	Blacksmith	Great Britain	Mexico	Corinthian	27 Apr 1824
Saml.	23	M	Mariner	St. Johns, N.B.	England	Peruvian	7 Oct 1825
GLATTZARD, Ann	33	F		Switzerland	Switzerland	Edward Quesnel 3 Jul 1829	
Catherine	4	F		Switzerland	Switzerland	Edward Quesnel 3 Jul 1829	
Catherine	27	F		Switzerland	Switzerland	Edward Quesnel 3 Jul 1829	
Christian	4 6/12	M		Switzerland	Switzerland	Edward Quesnel 3 Jul 1829	
Christian	31	M	Mason	Switzerland	Switzerland	Edward Quesnel 3 Jul 1829	
Cristian	56	M	Cooper	Switzerland	Switzerland	Edward Quesnel 3 Jul 1829	
Elizabeth	15	F		Switzerland	Switzerland	Edward Quesnel 3 Jul 1829	
Frederick	1 6/12	M		Switzerland	Switzerland	Edward Quesnel 3 Jul 1829	
John	1	M		Switzerland	Switzerland	Edward Quesnel 3 Jul 1829	
John	27	M	Cooper	Switzerland	Switzerland	Edward Quesnel 3 Jul 1829	
Margaret	24	F		Switzerland	Switzerland	Edward Quesnel 3 Jul 1829	
Margaret	55	F		Switzerland	Switzerland	Edward Quesnel 3 Jul 1829	
Margareta	3	F		Switzerland	Switzerland	Edward Quesnel 3 Jul 1829	
Peter	24	M	Mason	Switzerland	Switzerland	Edward Quesnel 3 Jul 1829	
Roadolphe	4	M		Switzerland	Switzerland	Edward Quesnel 3 Jul 1829	
Susanna	24	F		Switzerland	Switzerland	Edward Quesnel 3 Jul 1829	
GLAUZE, Julein	24	M	Merchant	France	United States	Maria	3 Oct 1822
GLAVIN, Philip	34	M	Farmer	Ireland	U. States	Criterion	23 May 1826
GLAWSON, Elizabeth	19	F	Servant	Ireland	United States	Wanderer	31 Aug 1829
James	21	M	Servant	Ireland	United States	Wanderer	31 Aug 1829

NAMES OF PASSENGERS	AGE	SEX	OCCUPATIONS	COUNTRY TO WHICH THEY BELONG	COUNTRY THEY INTEND TO INHABIT	SHIPS/DATES OF ARRIVAL	
GLAWSON (cont'd)							
Sophia	23	F	Mantuamaker	Ireland	United States	Wanderer	31 Aug 1829
GLAZER, Ferdinand	14	M	Farmer	Switzerland	U. States	Hewes	30 Oct 1829
Joseph	24	M	Cooper	Switzerland	U. States	Hewes	30 Oct 1829
GLEAN, F. R.	13	M	Planter	U.S.	U.S.	New England	11 Jul 1827
James E.	42	M	Merchant	U. States	U. States	Diligence	29 Jul 1823
GLEASANCE, Patrick	25	M	Laborer	Ireland	United States	St. Michaels	23 Dec 1826
GLEASEN, Margaret	21 5/12	F	None	Great Briton	United States	Mount Vernon	30 Dec 1828
GLEASON, John	55	M	Wever	Switserland	Ohio	Danube	20 Jul 1826
GLEDSKILL, Jos.	34	M	Labourer	Great Britain	United States	Cortes	18 Oct 1820
GLEENWOOD, Mary	40			b. Westmoreland, last of Ohio	Ohio	Peru	30 May 1828
GLEESON, David	44	M	Labourer	Ireland	U. States	Perserverance	21 Jul 1827
Edwd.	36	M	Farmer	Ireland	U. States	Sabina	29 Apr 1825
Ridy	25	M	Labourer	Ireland	New York	Bowditch	27 Apr 1826
Timothy	22	M	...	...	America	Farmer	11 Sep 1824
GLEESSEY, Thomas	22	M	Farmer	Ireland	United States	Lord Strangford	20 Jun 1826
GLEN, —, Mrs.	26	F		Scotland	U.S.	Curler	19 Jul 1828
Alexr.	18	M	Joiner	Scotland	U. States	Brilliant	19 Mar 1828
Alexr.	29		Merchant	Great Britain	United States	Camillus	12 Sep 1827
Ann	11	F		Scotland	United States	Commerce	17 Jul 1823
Ann	50	F		Scotland	United States	Commerce	17 Jul 1823
Christan		F		Scotland	U.S.	Curler	19 Jul 1828
David	21	M	Farmer	Scotland	United States	Commerce	17 Jul 1823
David	60	M	Farmer	Scotland	United States	Commerce	17 Jul 1823
George	40	M	Law	U. States	United States	New York	12 Nov 1822
Jams	14	M	Farmer	Scotland	United States	Commerce	17 Jul 1823
Janet	22	F		Scotland	United States	Commerce	17 Jul 1823
John	10	M		Scotland	United States	Commerce	17 Jul 1823
John	37	M	Merchant	Columbia	Columbia	Athenian	14 Oct 1828
William	16	M	Farmer	Scotland	United States	Commerce	17 Jul 1823
GLENEY, Geo. G.	30	M	Taylor	St. Domingo	St. Domingo	Robert Y. Haynes	13 Mar 1826
GLENN, Dan.	24	M	Merchant	Hamburg	U. States	Hope	18 Jun 1824
Eduard G., & Servant	20		Merchant	Canada	Canada	Bogota	25 Oct 1827
Robert	28	M	Weaver	Great Britain	United States	Colossus	5 Jun 1827
Wm.	30	M	Mariner	U. States	U. States	Cannon	15 Jul 1822
GLENNA, Rodger	30	M	Labourer	Ireland	U. States	Josephine	30 Aug 1828
GLENNAN, Edward	21	M	Farmer	Ireland	United States	Andes	2 Oct 1828
John	6	M	Child	Ireland	United States	Dublin Packet	9 Jul 1827
Judith	9	F	Child	Ireland	United States	Dublin Packet	9 Jul 1827
Margaret	16	F	Child	Ireland	United States	Dublin Packet	9 Jul 1827
Mary	12	F	Child	Ireland	United States	Dublin Packet	9 Jul 1827
GLENNIN, John	19		Labourer	Ireland	America	Sarah	18 Aug 1829
GLENROSE, Margaret	28	F	Farmer	Scotland	United States	Friends	16 Aug 1824
GLENSON, —, Mr.	30	M		Dublin	U. States	Hibernia	26 Oct 1826
—, Mrs.	24	F		Dublin	U. States	Hibernia	26 Oct 1826
—, Mrs.	30	F		Dublin	U. States	Hibernia	26 Oct 1826
GLENTWORTH, James B.	20	M	Officer U.S.N.	Pennsylvania	Pennsylvania	Potosi	28 May 1825
GLENTWORTH, Wm.	19	M	Gentleman	U. States	U. States	Abeona	1 Oct 1823
GLERNEY, Barney	42	M	Weaver	Great Britain	United States	Magnet	19 Aug 1822
GLIDE, Catharine	9	F		Native of Switzerland	United States	Canaris	30 Jun 1827
Catharine	34	F		Native of Switzerland	United States	Canaris	30 Jun 1827
George	36	M	Carpenter	Native of Switzerland	United States	Canaris	30 Jun 1827
Joseph	11	M		Native of Switzerland	United States	Canaris	30 Jun 1827
GLIDHILL, Henry	20	M	Shoemaker	Great Britain		Moro Castle	6 Jul 1827
GLINCUR, Ferdinand	24	M	Merchant	Welsh	U. States	Dawn	8 Jun 1827
GLINZ, D.	27	M	Merchant	Germany	Germany	Don Quixote	12 Feb 1829
GLODEN, A.	30	M	Merchant	Martinique	U. States	Rover	11 Jun 1823
GLOON, Elias	43	M	Cooper	G. Britain	U. States	St. George	16 Jan 1829
GLORDON, Elizabeth	31	F		France		Pallas	14 Jun 1828
Jaques	25	M	Farm	France		Pallas	14 Jun 1828
Jerinry J.	2	F		France		Pallas	14 Jun 1828
GLOTHING, Hugh	24	M	Labourer	Ireland	United States	Ann Maria	4 Oct 1824
GLOUDON, Andr.	24	M	Merchant	U. States	U. States	Diana	4 Dec 1821

NAMES OF PASSENGERS	AGE	SEX	OCCUPATIONS	COUNTRY TO WHICH THEY BELONG	COUNTRY THEY INTEND TO INHABIT	SHIPS/DATES OF ARRIVAL	
GLOVER, Amelia	8/12		None	U.S.	U.S.	Sully	26 Oct 1829
Benjamin	45	M	Mechanic	Great Britain	United States	Thomas Dickason	31 Jul 1829
Catherine	57	F		Switzerland	U.S.	Francois I	8 Aug 1829
Daniel			None	U.S.	U.S.	Sully	26 Oct 1829
Elias	45	M	Filer	Great Britian	United States	Baltic	5 Apr 1826
Eliza	6	F		G.B.	New Jersey	Eliza Grant	29 Aug 1829
Eliza	6	F	None	Ireland		Eliza Grant	29 Aug 1829
Harriet	25	F	Mechanic	Great Britain	United States	Thomas Dickason	31 Jul 1829
James	28		Miner	Scotland	United States	Camillus	3 May 1828
Joseph	21	M	Mechanic	Great Britain	United States	Thomas Dickason	31 Jul 1829
Joseph	24	M	Farmer	Great Britain	United States	William Dawson	18 Jun 1827
Maria	17	F		Great Britian	United States	Baltic	5 Apr 1826
Mary	25	F	None	G.B.	New Jersey	Eliza Grant	29 Aug 1829
Mary	25	F	None	Ireland		Eliza Grant	29 Aug 1829
Mary, Mrs.			None	U.S.	U.S.	Sully	26 Oct 1829
Peter	20	M	Filer	Great Britian	United States	Baltic	5 Apr 1826
Susannah	46	F		Great Britian	United States	Baltic	5 Apr 1826
Wm.	29	M		Ireland	U. States	Fame	15 Nov 1826
GLYNN, Edward	39	M	Mechanic	England	U. States	Alpha	7 Oct 1823
Elizabeth	20	F		Gt. Britain		Dalhouse Castle	13 May 1828
John	25 3/12	M	White Smith	England	United States	Eliza Grant	7 Jun 1827
GNECH, Charles D.	45	M	Watch Maker	Poland	United States	William Thompson	19 Aug 1829
Charles T.	7	M	None	United States	United States	William Thompson	19 Aug 1829
GOALD, Richd.	24	M	Draper		U. States	Robt. Edwards	4 Sep 1828
GOB, William	21	M	Seaman	U. States	U. States	Boston	26 Sep 1820
GOBLE, Ann	36	F	Agriculturist	France	U.S.	Helen	3 May 1828
Catherine	10	F	Agriculturist	France	U.S.	Helen	3 May 1828
Elizabeth	5 6/12	F	Agriculturist	France	U.S.	Helen	3 May 1828
George	13	M	Agriculturist	France	U.S.	Helen	3 May 1828
George	33	M	Agriculturist	France	U.S.	Helen	3 May 1828
Louisa	2 4/12	F	Agriculturist	France	U.S.	Helen	3 May 1828
Peter	7	M	Agriculturist	France	U.S.	Helen	3 May 1828
GOBRY, George	29	M	Mason	Great Britain	United States	Exertion	17 Jul 1829
GOBVILLE, Jaques	25	M	Servant	England	Halifax	Stephania	28 Jul 1823
GOCHLE, Anthony	28	M	Sugar Baker	Germany	United States	Cambria	16 Aug 1827
Henry	20	M	Sugar Baker	Germany	United States	Cambria	16 Aug 1827
GODALE, William	30	M	Laborer	Ireland	United States	St. Michaels	12 Jun 1826
GODBEHER, William	53		Farmer	Great Britain	United States	Comet	9 Aug 1822
GODDARD, Ann E.	5	F		U. States	U. States	Silas Richards	27 Jun 1827
Harriet	0 4/12	F		U. States	U. States	Silas Richards	27 Jun 1827
Lina	22	M	Farmer	England	U.S.A.	Brighton	21 Jan 1826
Louisa	7	F		U. States	U. States	Silas Richards	27 Jun 1827
Lucretia	3 4/12	F		U. States	U. States	Silas Richards	27 Jun 1827
Mehetabel	30	F		U. States	U. States	Silas Richards	27 Jun 1827
S. A.	30	M	Merchant	Birmingham	England	Silas Richards	9 Mar 1829
Samuel	39	M	Merchant	U. States	U. States	Silas Richards	27 Jun 1827
GODDEN, George	5	M	Labourer	England	America	Sarah	18 Aug 1829
Stephen	3	M	Labourer	England	America	Sarah	18 Aug 1829
Susan	28	F	Labourer	England	America	Sarah	18 Aug 1829
Thomas	26	M	Machine Maker	England	U.S. America	New Hampshire	28 Sep 1826
Thomas	30	M	Labourer	England	America	Sarah	18 Aug 1829
GODDING, Chas.	18	M	Mechanic	England	America	Britannia	5 Nov 1828
Elias	42	M				Hudson	23 Jul 1828
Mark	30	M	Gardener	U. Kingdom of Great Britain	United States	Cambria	7 May 1828
Mary	50	F				Hudson	23 Jul 1828
GODEFMAN, Amst.	33	M	Farmer	Germany	United States	Wm. Osborne	16 Sep 1828
Anne	6	F	his family [Amst.]	Germany	United States	Wm. Osborne	16 Sep 1828
Barbe	30	F	his family [Amst.]	Germany	United States	Wm. Osborne	16 Sep 1828
Catherine	4	F	his family [Amst.]	Germany	United States	Wm. Osborne	16 Sep 1828
Daniel	2	M	his family [Amst.]	Germany	United States	Wm. Osborne	16 Sep 1828
Jaques	7	M	his family [Amst.]	Germany	United States	Wm. Osborne	16 Sep 1828
Walmhen	8	M	his family [Amst.]	Germany	United States	Wm. Osborne	16 Sep 1828
GODEMAT, N.	22	M	Blacksmith	France	U. States	Queen Mab	22 Jul 1825

NAMES OF PASSENGERS	AGE	SEX	OCCUPATIONS	COUNTRY TO WHICH THEY BELONG	COUNTRY THEY INTEND TO INHABIT	SHIPS/DATES OF ARRIVAL	
GODEWIN, E.	19	M	Hair Dresser	France	U. States	Montano	2 Sep 1828
GODFREY, Betsey	22	F		N. York	U. States	Eliza Jane	29 Oct 1821
H.	32	M	Mariner	Massachusetts	U. States	Eliza Jane	29 Oct 1821
Kemp	21		Painter	England	United States	Caspian	12 Jul 1821
GODIER, Aaron	54	M	Farmer	United States		Casanda	5 Sep 1827
Thos.	34	M	Farmer	United States		Casanda	5 Sep 1827
GODING, Joseph	22	M	Carpenter	U. Kingdom Great Britain	United States	Cambria	7 May 1828
W. P.	24	M	Merchant	Barbadoes	Intend to return	Chasseur	17 Aug 1824
GODKELER, Godfried	25	M	Farmer	Germany	America	Falcon	28 Aug 1828
GODQUIN, E. F.	24	M	Hair Dresser	France	U. States	America	22 Sep 1826
Francis	18		Hair dresser	France		Bayard	10 Sep 1827
Polly	3		Hair dresser	France		Bayard	10 Sep 1827
Victor	28		Hair dresser	France		Bayard	10 Sep 1827
GODSON, D.	21	M	Labourer	G. Britain	U. States	St. George	7 Jun 1828
GODWIN, Mithle, Mr.	36	M	Sculpturer	England	United States	Montano	18 Dec 1827
GOERSON, Peter	45	M	Blacksmith	U. States	U. States	John London	21 Mar 1825
GOETHE, G. J. D.	26	M	Farmer	United States	United States	Hebe	30 Apr 1821
GOETS, T.	30	F	Mechanic	Swiss	U. States	Don Quixote	15 Apr 1825
GOETZ, J. J.	32	M	Mechanic	Swiss	U. States	Don Quixote	15 Apr 1825
GOFELMEN, Augustus	30	M		Denmark	Denmark	Pleiades	13 Nov 1826
GOFF, James	40	M	Mechanic	U. States	U. States	Mary	19 May 1823
Jno.	25	M	Mechanic	Great Brittan	Great Brittain	Florida	17 May 1825
John	45	M	Laboror	U.States	U. States	Patty & Sally	25 Apr 1821
Maria	1					Agricola	1 Jul 1820
Susannah	21					Agricola	1 Jul 1820
Thos.	26					Agricola	1 Jul 1820
William	18 4/12	M	Farmer	England	U.S. of America	Illinois	16 Jun 1821
GOFFE, Ann	25	F				Robert Edwards	8 Nov 1825
Daniel	30	M	Baker	England		Robert Edwards	8 Nov 1825
With.	1 6/12	M				Robert Edwards	8 Nov 1825
GOFFRENT, John C.	2		Farmer	France	U. States	Elizabeth	9 Jul 1825
GOFFREY, Mary	30	F	Spinster	Ireland	United States	Dublin Packet	22 Oct 1821
Michl.	22	M	Labourer			Evergreen	28 Jul 1820
GOFT, C.	30	F		Germany	United States	Lydia	18 Jun 1828
Geo.	4	M		Germany	United States	Lydia	18 Jun 1828
M.	2	M		Germany	United States	Lydia	18 Jun 1828
M.	33	M		Germany	United States	Lydia	18 Jun 1828
T.	6	F		Germany	United States	Lydia	18 Jun 1828
GOGGIN, Wm.	18		Labourer	Ireland	N. York at present	Marcella	18 May 1827
GOGULA, C.	25	M	Merchant	France	France & Spain	Native	24 Aug 1825
GOKELIN, Bernard	18	M	Labourer	Prussia		Constitution	20 Jun 1828
GOL..., Phyllip	...		Labourer	Pe....	England	Great Britain	7 May 1827
GOLA, Jas. M.	27	M	Mariner	U. States	U. States	Tampico	20 Apr 1825
GOLATHAN, Nancy	25	F		Irland	United States	Nancy	28 Oct 1822
GOLD, Alexander	26	M	Joiner	Scotland	United States	Shakespeare	24 Jul 1828
Charlot	23	F	Farmer	America	United States	Julia Ann	24 Jul 1820
John	38	M	Farmer	America	United States	Julia Ann	24 Jul 1820
GOLDEN, Andrew	18	M	Labourer	Ireland	United States	Fabius	31 Jul 1829
Bridget	20	F	Spinster	Ireland	America	Josephine	8 Dec 1827
Catherine	60	F	Widow	Ireland	America	Josephine	8 Dec 1827
Caty	3	F	Farmer	Ireland	Canada	Champion	26 Jul 1827
Daniel	60	M	Labourer	Ireland	United States	Fabius	31 Jul 1829
Daniel, Jr.	20	M	Labourer	Ireland	United States	Fabius	31 Jul 1829
Edwd.	20	M	Shoemaker	Ireland	United States	Trident	17 May 1825
Margarett	60	F	Spinster	Ireland	United States	Fabius	31 Jul 1829
Margarett, Jr.	13	F	Spinster	Ireland	United States	Fabius	31 Jul 1829
Margt.	16	F	...	...	United States	Minerva	30 Oct 1827
Mary	22	F	Matron	Ireland	America	Josephine	8 Dec 1827
Patrick	30	M	Carpenter	Ireland	U. States	Hope & Esther	4 Oct 1825
Peter	22	M	Mason	Great Britain	United States	Mount Vernon	17 Jun 1825
Thomas	6	M	Child	Ireland	America	Josephine	8 Dec 1827
GOLDIN, Andrew	...4	M	Carpenter	Ireland	America	Corinthian	1 Sep 1827
John	23	M		Ireland	America	Corinthian	1 Sep 1827
Maria	18	F		Ireland	America	Corinthian	1 Sep 1827
GOLDING, John	34 3/12	M	Gentleman	United States	United States	Brighton	12 Jun 1826
Mary	...		Servant			Amphion	31 May 1824
Patrick M.	27	M	Farmer	Ireland	Canada	Champion	26 Jul 1827
Saml., Mr.	28	M	Merchant	England	U. States	Hudson	10 Nov 1825

478

NAMES OF PASSENGERS	AGE	SEX	OCCUPATIONS	COUNTRY TO WHICH THEY BELONG	COUNTRY THEY INTEND TO INHABIT	SHIPS/DATES OF ARRIVAL	
GOLDING (cont'd)							
Sophia	25	F	Lady	United States	United States	Alfred	8 Jul 1822
Thomas R.	4	M	Farmer	Ireland	U. States	Champion	26 Jul 1827
GOLDSBOROUGH,							
Nicholas	26	M	Mariner	U.S.	U.S.	Athenian	14 Oct 1828
Sarah, Mrs.	30	F	Lady	United States	United States	Maria	29 Sep 1823
GOLDSCHMID, Catherine	4	F	there child				
			[Fredk. & Jaquet] Germany		United States	Helen	5 Sep 1828
Christian	6/12	M	there child				
			[Fredk. & Jaquet] Germany		United States	Helen	5 Sep 1828
Fredk.	30	M	Farmer	Germany	United States	Helen	5 Sep 1828
Jaquet	27	F	his wife [Fredk.]	Germany	United States	Helen	5 Sep 1828
GOLDSCHMIDT,							
Adolphus	27 3/12	M	Merchant	Great Britain	England	John Wells	29 Jan 1825
GOLDSMITH, Daniel	35	M	Labourer	New York	New York	Hesperus	2 Nov 1820
George	5	M	Farmer	England	U. States	Robert Edwards	9 May 1827
Isaac	45	M	Farmer	England	U. States	Robert Edwards	9 May 1827
John	45	M	Furrier	U.S.	New York	Brighton	12 Jun 1826
Lydia	37	F	Farmer	England	U. States	Robert Edwards	9 May 1827
Mary	1	F	Farmer	England	U. States	Robert Edwards	9 May 1827
Silas	43	M	Mariner	U. States	U. States	Florida	25 Apr 1825
GOLDTHWAIT, Anne	49	F	Lady	United States	United States	Cambria	8 Oct 1828
GOLFORT, Edward	9	M	None	Scotland	United States	Mary & Susan	5 Aug 1828
Margaret	26	F	None	Scotland	United States	Mary & Susan	5 Aug 1828
GOLFS, Henry	21	M	Sugar Baker	Bremen	U. States	Huntress	29 May 1822
GOLGAVE, Biddy	28	F	Spinster	Ireland	United States	Sarah G	19 Jun 1827
Patrick	1	M	Child	Ireland	United States	Sarah G	19 Jun 1827
GOLIKER, Nany	18	F	Servant	Ireland	U. States	Wanderer	1 Sep 1828
GOLLAGHER, James	30	M	F...	Ireland	New York	Wilson	10 Apr 1823
GOLLER, M.	23	M	Butcher	Germany		Ariel	24 Sep 1827
GOLLETT, Henry	24	M	Farmer	England	United States	Hudson	17 Mar 1828
GOLLIEZ, Louisa			Servant	France	U.S.	Sully	26 Oct 1829
GOLLIGER, Martin	25	M	Labourer	Ireland	United States	Wilson	6 Jun 1828
Michael	30	M	Labourer	Ireland	United States	Wilson	6 Jun 1828
GOLLIGHER, Nidd [?]	28	M		Ireland	U. States	St. Michael	27 Mar 1827
GOLOGER, Cate.	16	F	Farmer	England	United States	India	8 Jun 1827
GOLONGER, Mary	24	F	Spinster	Ireland	United States	Robert Fulton	24 Jul 1826
GOLOZER, Peter	26	M	Farmer	Ireland	United States	Trident	30 Sep 1826
GOLWELL, Oppier	25	M	Farmer	Switzerland	United States	Olympia	12 Aug 1828
GOMAN, Hannah	20	F		Ireland	U. States	Virginia	20 Jun 1825
GOMAR, Jose	50	M	Merchant	Spanyard	U. States	Romulus	31 Jul 1823
GOMAZ, Jose	30	M	Mercht.	Spain	Spain	Sally	11 Oct 1820
GOMBARETT, Augustus	36		Merchant	France	U. States	Nymph	5 Jul 1820
GOME, M.	30	F		America	America	Paragon	22 Sep 1827
GOMERSY, Pat	16	M	Labourer			Hanford	17 Jul 1828
GOMEZ, —	7/12	F		Mexico	Caracas	Herald	21 Sep 1824
—	9/12	M		Mexico	Caracas	Herald	21 Sep 1824
—, Miss	20	F	Lady	United States	Curacao	Anna Elizabeth	14 Jun 1824
—, Mr.	45	M	Merchant	New York		Genl. A. Jackson	15 Jul 1820
—, Mrs.	26	F		Spain	Havana	Lady Tompkins	10 Nov 1823
—, Mrs.	36	F		Spain	U. States	Emma	25 Oct 1825
Adeline	1 6/12	F		Spain	U. States	Emma	25 Oct 1825
Charles	4	M		Spain	Havana	Lady Tompkins	10 Nov 1823
George	31	M	Merchant	Spain		Star	7 Jan 1827
Gregorio	26	M	Merchant	Spain	United States	Montano	4 Nov 1823
Joaquin, Don	10	M	Student	U. States	U. States	Greek	1 Oct 1825
John	2	M		Spain	U. States	Emma	25 Oct 1825
Jose	25	M	Merchant	Spain	U. States	Sally	8 Aug 1820
Juan Maria	29	M		Columbia	U. States	Julia	18 Apr 1828
Lorenza	9	F		Spain	Havana	Lady Tompkins	10 Nov 1823
M.	19	M	Merchant	United States	United States	General Jackson	12 Aug 1824
M.	32	M	Merchant	Baltimore	U. States	Nestor	7 Jan 1825
Maria	44	F	None	U. States	U. States	Hal	7 Jun 1824
Rosalia	22	F		Mexico	Caracas	Herald	21 Sep 1824
S.	20	F		Columbia	U. States	Julia	18 Apr 1828
Stephen	40	M	Segar Maker	Spain	N. York	Emma	25 Oct 1825
GOMINE, Ann	26	F	Spinster	Ireland		Robert Fulton	4 Jun 1828
GOMLEY, Owen	25	M	Labourer	Ireland	U. States	Nancy	1 Sep 1823
GOMM, Thomas	21	M	Carpenter	England	Utica	Cortes	16 Jul 1827

NAMES OF PASSENGERS	AGE	SEX	OCCUPATIONS	COUNTRY TO WHICH THEY BELONG	COUNTRY THEY INTEND TO INHABIT	SHIPS/DATES OF ARRIVAL	
GONDOLF, Jose	27		Merchant	Campeachy	U. States	Alfred	24 Jul 1828
GONE, Francis	35	M	Plaisterer	England		Marchioness	13 May 1828
GONELLY, Sally	21	F	Labourer	Ireland	U. States	Two Marys	20 Apr 1825
GONER, Kady	26	M	Farmer	Ireland	America	Superior	12 Jun 1824
GONFIEVILLE, B.	41	M	Dyer	France	U.S.	Francois I	8 Aug 1829
C.	29	M	Dyer	France	U.S.	Francois I	8 Aug 1829
GONGORA, Carromla	28	F	Merchant	Spain	Havana	Commodore Chauncy	28 Nov 1825
GONIGAL, Nancy	16	F	Spinster	Ireland	United States	Lima	19 Jun 1824
GONNELL, John	20	M	Farmer	Ireland	United States	Dublin Packet	29 Jun 1825
GONNELLY, Hugh	21	M	Labourer	Ireland	U. States	Two Marys	20 Apr 1825
GONREL, James	25	M	Labourer	Ireland	America	Plutarch	18 Jul 1826
GONSALEZ, —, son of [A.J.]	10	M	Merchant	Spain	United States	Burdett	30 Apr 1828
A. J.	40	M	Merchant	Spain	United States	Burdett	30 Apr 1828
Agostine	15	M	Boy, Mariner	U.S.	U.S.	Hesper	2 May 1826
GONSATER, V.	32	M	Cooper	Spain	Havana	United States	13 Dec 1824
GONSREAUME, Francis	20	M	Merchant	France	U. States	Edward Bonaffe	11 Dec 1827
GONTZENBACH, Augt.	23		Mercht.	Switzerland	U. States	New York	30 Oct 1827
GONVALES, Thos.	40	M	Merchant	Spain	Matanzas	Betsey	10 Nov 1826
GONVERNER, Laman	40	M	Labourer	Ireland	U.S. America	New Hampshire	28 Sep 1826
GONZALAS, F.	13	M	None	Spain	U. States	Frances	22 May 1827
F.	14	F	None	Spain	U. States	Frances	22 May 1827
P.	13	M	Mercht.	Spain	Spain	Richmond Packet	11 Jul 1827
GONZALES, Calisto	25	M	Mercht.	Spain	U. States	Ambuscade	6 Oct 1821
F.	36	M	Merchant	France	U. States	Manchester Packet	21 Aug 1823
Frs., Don	31	M	Merchant	Havana	U. States & Spain	Seneca	21 May 1825
GONZALET, Jose	58	M	Priest	Spain	Spain	Virginia	8 Mar 1828
GONZALEZ, Manuel	67	M	Gentn.	Spain	Spain	Fabius	2 Oct 1826
N.	23	M	Gentleman	Spain	U. States	Vigilant	14 Apr 1823
N.	33	M	Merchant	Havana	Havana	Crusader	23 Apr 1827
Ygnacio	33	M	Merchant	St. Johns, Puerto Rico	St. Johns, Puerto Rico	George	6 Aug 1823
GONZALLES, R.	22	M	Mercht.	Spain	U. States	Caroline	21 Jun 1823
GONZALS, T.	24	M	Gentleman	Porto Rico	U. States	Tidal	28 Oct 1824
GONZALVEZ, Juan		M	Prisoner charged with Piracy			Oswego	12 Apr 1824
GONZOLES, J. G.	34	M	Merchant	Spain	Spain	Virginia	8 Mar 1828
GONZOLOZ, Jose	25	M	Merchant	Spain	Spain	Claudio	22 Mar 1828
GOOD, George	20 2/12	M	...	England	America, U.S.	Illinois	3 Jun 1822
Jane, Miss	19	F		England	U. States	Tipporah	22 Dec 1828
W. W.	27	M	Gentleman	New York	U. States	Craven	9 Jul 1823
William	23	M	Cabinet Maker	Bristol, Engl.	...	Warrior	19 May 1828
GOODACRE, Wm.	25	M	Artist	England	U. States	Don Quixote	25 Oct 1828
GOODALE, Lyman	28	M	Gentleman	U.S.	U.S	Radius	18 Feb 1823
GOODALL, Benjm.	8	M		England	U. States	York	12 Jul 1825
James	24	M	Mate	America	U. States	Mt. Vernon	1 Apr 1824
Prudence	49	F		England	U. States	York	12 Jul 1825
Richard	25	M	Doctor	England	U.N.S.	Helen	16 Mar 1829
Thomas	12	M		England	U. States	York	12 Jul 1825
Thomas	21	M	Labourer	Ireland	United States	Jubilee	13 Jul 1829
Wm.	50	M	Labourer	England	U. States	York	12 Jul 1825
GOODAPLE, Catherine	31	F		Germany	United States	Samuel Robertson	8 Aug 1828
George	7	M		Germany	United States	Samuel Robertson	8 Aug 1828
Maria	2	F		Germany	United States	Samuel Robertson	8 Aug 1828
Michael	13	M		Germany	United States	Samuel Robertson	8 Aug 1828
Michael	33	M	Weaver	Germany	United States	Samuel Robertson	8 Aug 1828
GOODAU, James	26	M	Merchant	Madeira	U. States	Factor	28 Sep 1822
GOODCHILD, Henry	23	M	Organist	England	U. States	Frances Henrietta	9 Dec 1823
GOODELL, Asa	34	M	Mechanic	Massachusetts	U. States	Stranger	13 Jun 1823
GOODFELLOW, David	20	M	Farmer	Ireland	United States	Trident	30 Sep 1826

NAMES OF PASSENGERS	AGE	SEX	OCCUPATIONS	COUNTRY TO WHICH THEY BELONG	COUNTRY THEY INTEND TO INHABIT	SHIPS/DATES OF ARRIVAL
GOODFELLOW, (cont'd)						
Healey	23	M	Labourer	Great Britain	United States	Mary & Harriet 3 Jul 1829
Margret	19	F	Labourer	Great Britian	United States	Princess
						Charlotte 6 Sep 1828
Robert	30	M	Painter	England	United States	Delta 24 Oct 1829
GOODHALL, Ann	17	F				Eliza Grant 6 Oct 1828
Elizabeth	55	F		England	United States	Eliza Grant 6 Oct 1828
John	20	M				Eliza Grant 6 Oct 1828
John Newton	28	M	Gardner	Great Britain	United States	Superior 31 Mar 1828
Maria	18	F	Spinster	Great Britain	United States	Superior 31 Mar 1828
Richard	28	M				Eliza Grant 6 Oct 1828
Thomas	20	M				Eliza Grant 6 Oct 1828
GOODILES, Benito	25	M	Mercht.	Spain	United States	Georgetown
						Packet 15 Nov 1823
GOODIN, Ebenezer	25	M	Blacksmith	England	U. States	Emulous 22 Aug 1828
GOODING, Albert	45	M	Merchant	United States	United States	Enterprize 11 May 1827
George	21	M	Grocer	Great Britain	United States	Robert Fulton 27 Jun 1822
Jonald	19	M	Farmer	Great Britain	United States	Robert Fulton 27 Jun 1822
William	24	M	Farmer	Great Britain	United States	Robert Fulton 27 Jun 1822
GOODKIN, Foster	27	M	Gentleman	America	America	Wilson 16 May 1825
GOODLAKE, James	29	M	Merchant	England	U. States	Indiana 11 Sep 1827
GOODMAN, Elizabeth	28	F		England	U. States	Pleiades 9 Oct 1829
George	6/12	M	None	England		Marchioness 13 May 1828
George	26	M	Plumber	England		Marchioness 13 May 1828
J.	68	M	...	England	U.S.	Chase 26 Jul 1824
James	5	M		England	U. States	Pleiades 9 Oct 1829
Jane	21	F	None	England		Marchioness 13 May 1828
John	34	M	Labourer	England	U. States	Pleiades 9 Oct 1829
Louisa	8	F		England	U. States	Pleiades 9 Oct 1829
Marcus	35	M	Merchant	Spain	United States	Saluda 14 May 1827
Mary Ann	6	F		England	U. States	Pleiades 9 Oct 1829
S.	60	M	Merchant	U. States	U. States	Prudence 11 Jun 1825
GOODRICH, Chauncy M.	35	M	Professor—			
			Yale Colledge	United States	United States	Roman 17 Oct 1826
J.	28	M	Mechanic	Connecticut	U. States	Clarissa 14 Jul 1821
James	52	M	Mariner	U. States	U. States	Merope 6 Dec 1825
O.	27	M	Mechanic	N. Jersey	U. States	Andromache 30 Jul 1823
Samuel G.	30	M	Merchant	United States	United States	John Wells 22 Sep 1824
GOODSELL, —, Mr.	36		Merchant	U.S.	U.S.	Pacific 24 May 1824
—, Mrs.	26			U.S.	U.S.	Pacific 24 May 1824
John	22	M	Wheelwright	England	New York	America 1 Aug 1828
GOODSON, Joseph	19		Farmer	England	United States	Corinthian 30 May 1828
GOODWIN, ...ll...	50	F	None	England	New York	Thames 6 Oct 1820
Ann	3	F		G. Britain	U. States	St. George 7 Jun 1828
Eliza	28	F	None	Ireland	America	Manhattan 20 Mar 1820
Eliza, Miss	20	F	None	England	New York	Thames 6 Oct 1820
F. H.	25	M	Merchant	America		Aspasia 19 Jul 1823
G. H.	26	M	Merchant	Boston	U. States	Cato 9 Aug 1823
Geo.	7	M		G. Britain	U. States	St. George 7 Jun 1828
Geo.	40	M		Gt. Britain	U. States	Tantiva 7 Jul 1828
Geo. W.	27	M	Merchant	Boston	U. States	Cato 2 Jan 1824
Geo. W.	27	M	Merchant	U. States	U. States	Fancy 28 Apr 1825
George W.	27	M	Merchant	United States	United States	Howard 11 Jun 1824
Harriet	4	M		G. Britain	U. States	St. George 7 Jun 1828
Hugh	30	M	Labourer	Ireland	America	Manhattan 20 Mar 1820
Hy.	24	M	Farmer	Gt. Britain	United States	Robert Edwards 1 Jun 1826
Isabella	24	F		Great Britain	United States	Frances
						Henrietta 17 Sep 1827
James	42	M		England		Ann 17 May 1822
John	25	M	Mariner	U. States	U. States	Panthia 23 Apr 1824
Jos.	35	M	Merchant	U. States	U. States	Lady Tompkins 13 Apr 1824
M. H.	36	F		G. Britain	U. States	St. George 7 Jun 1828
Oliver	23	M	Labourer	G. Brittian	United States	Louisa 14 Jun 1825
Ozias, Jr.	26	M	Merchant	U. States	U. States	Maria 7 Feb 1820
Patrick	24	M	Farmer	Great Britain	United States	Frances
						Henrietta 17 Sep 1827
R.	35	M	Labourer	G. Britain	U. States	St. George 7 Jun 1828
Richd.	9	M		G. Britain	U. States	St. George 7 Jun 1828
Saml.	35	M	Farmer	Gt. Britain	United States	Robert Edwards 1 Jun 1826

NAMES OF PASSENGERS	A G E	S E X	OCCUPATIONS	COUNTRY TO WHICH THEY BELONG	COUNTRY THEY INTEND TO INHABIT	SHIPS/DATES OF ARRIVAL	
GOODWIN (cont'd)							
Thomas, Mr.	25	M	Musician	England	U. States	Emily	25 Aug 1827
Thos.	21	M	Mercht.	Great Britain	United States	Nestor	6 Jul 1821
Thos.	41	M	Gentleman	England	U. States	Corinthian	20 Apr 1825
William	23	M	Baker	G. Britain	New York	Brighton	26 Mar 1827
Willm.	25	M	Servant	England	New York	Brighton	16 Nov 1826
Wm.	5	M		G. Britain	U. States	St. George	7 Jun 1828
GOOLDING, James	29 4/12	M	Labourer	England	United States	London	6 Feb 1829
GOOLRICK, J. C.	29	M	Merchant	U. States	U. States	Canton	7 Feb 1826
GOOUVERNIEAR, S., Mr.	28	M	Merchant	United States	Curacao	Anna Elizabeth	14 Jun 1824
GORACK, Thos.	22	M	Carpenter			Hudson	23 Jul 1828
GORALDI, J. Jose	44	M	Servant	Spain	Spain	Savannah	24 Apr 1828
GORAM, Magt.	27	F	None	England	United States	India	8 Jun 1827
Peter	23	M	Student of Divinity	England	United States	India	8 Jun 1827
GORATE, Jose	25	M	Merchant	U. States	U.S.	Ambuscade	14 Mar 1820
GORBETT, Joseph	23	M	Laborer	Great Britain	United States	India	5 Sep 1827
GORBITT, Magart	1	F	Nurse	England	U.S. America	New Hampshire	28 Sep 1826
Margaret	23	F	Nurse	England	U.S. America	New Hampshire	28 Sep 1826
Mary Ann	3	F	Nurse	England	U.S. America	New Hampshire	28 Sep 1826
Robt.	23	M	Carver & Gilder	England	U.S. America	New Hampshire	28 Sep 1826
GORCIA, Monuel	23	M	Gentleman	Spain	Spain	Governor Von Schollen	7 Nov 1827
GORDAN, James	31	M	Smith	Scotland	United States	Louisiana	3 Nov 1827
John	3	M		Scotland	United States	Louisiana	3 Nov 1827
John	25		Clerk	Scotland	United States	Rufus King	4 Sep 1823
M.	7	F		Scotland	United States	Louisiana	3 Nov 1827
M.	30	F	Milliner	Scotland	United States	Louisiana	3 Nov 1827
Mary Ann	15	F	Spinster	Ireland	United States	Dublin Packet	13 Oct 1828
GORDEN, M.	21	M		Gt. Britain	United States	John & Elizabeth	25 Sep 1827
Margret	23	F	Servant	Ireland	United States	Henry Kneeland	7 Jun 1828
GORDERMANN, Carl M.	17	M	Goldsmith	France	U. States	Edward Bopnnaffe	30 Jul 1829
John	43	M	Goldsmith	France	U. States	Edward Bopnnaffe	30 Jul 1829
GORDON, —, Mrs.	21	F		Scotland	U. States	Majestic	27 Jul 1829
—, Mrs.	28	F		N. York	U. States	Robt. Y. Hayne	27 Jun 1825
—, Ms.	23	F		Massachusetts	U. States	Swift	11 May 1824
A.	24	M	Merchant	Scotland	N. Orleans	Queen Mab	20 Nov 1826
A.	28	M	Clerk	G. Britain	U. States	George Clinton	10 Sep 1828
Agness	48	F		Ireland	United States	Commerce	13 Jun 1828
Alexr.	3	M	Child	Scotland	America	Camillus	12 Sep 1822
Alexr.	32	M	Gardner	Great Britain	Great Britain	Moro	19 Dec 1827
Alexr.	42	M	Merchant	Netherlands	N. York	Adonis	17 Aug 1824
Andrew	14	M	Servant	St. Croix	America	South Carolina Packet	2 Aug 1825
Ann	9	F	Child	Scotland	America	Camillus	12 Sep 1822
Ann	20	F	None	Scotland	United States	Mary & Susan	5 Aug 1828
Ann	22	F	Servant	Ireland	N. York	Trusty	12 Sep 1828
Archibald	20	M	Merchant	Great Britain	United States	Columbia	9 Aug 1822
Archibald	27	M	Merchant	Great Britian		France	6 Feb 1829
Barbara	10	F	None	Scotland	United States	Mary & Susan	5 Aug 1828
Benj.	18	M		Ireland	United States	Commerce	13 Jun 1828
Benjamin	22		Watch Maker	Islington	England	London	13 Dec 1822
Bridget	20	F	Farmer	Ireland		Cuba	24 Jun 1822
C. H.	26	M	Merchant	U. States	U. States	Huntress	6 May 1823
Daniel	17	M	...	England	United States	Robert Edwards	4 Jun 1824
Duncan	7/12	M		Scotland	U. States	Majestic	27 Jul 1829
Duncan	11	M	Child	Scotland	America	Camillus	12 Sep 1822
Eliza	7	F	Child	Scotland	America	Camillus	12 Sep 1822
G.	20	M	Carpenter	England	U.S. States	Splendid	14 Aug 1829
Gabriel	65	M	Gentleman	Great Britain	Great Britain	Manchester	12 Aug 1829
Geo.	3	M		N. York	U. States	Robt. Y. Hayne	27 Jun 1825
Geo.	30	M	Army	England	England	Elias Burger	11 Jul 1822
George	31	M	Gentleman	St. Croix	Great Britain	Chase	4 Sep 1821
George B.	12	M	Artist	G. Britian	U. States	William Byrnes	23 Aug 1827
James	22	M	Farmer	Ireland	United States	John Dickinson	18 Feb 1822
James	28	M	Laborer	Ireland	Pittsburgh	Indian Chief	16 Aug 1822

482

NAMES OF PASSENGERS	AGE	SEX	OCCUPATIONS	COUNTRY TO WHICH THEY BELONG	COUNTRY THEY INTEND TO INHABIT	SHIPS/DATES OF ARRIVAL	
GORDON (cont'd)							
James	28	M	Sailor	England	U. States	Hiram	17 Jun 1826
James, Mr.	39	M	Surgeon	England	England	Helen	17 Dec 1827
Jane	15	F	None	Scotland	United States	Mary & Susan	5 Aug 1828
Janet	39	F		Scotland	America	Camillus	12 Sep 1822
Jesse	7	F	None	Scotland	United States	Mary & Susan	5 Aug 1828
John	16	M	None	England	New York	Brighton	29 Aug 1828
John	20	F		Ireland	United States	Commerce	13 Jun 1828
John	22	M	Farmer	Ireland	United States	William & George	14 May 1828
John	25	M	Labourer	Meldmaghn, Scotland	Gt. Britain	Orozimbo	19 Oct 1822
John	26	M	Sugar Baker	Germany	U.S. America	Cincinnatus	31 Oct 1820
Joseph	20	M	Farmer	England	England	William Byrnes	14 Apr 1824
Lewis	20	M	Farmer	G. Brittan	U. States	Trafalgar	4 Jun 1822
M.	33	M	Merchan	Spain	U. States	Dromo	22 May 1826
Margt.	21	F		Ireland	United States	Commerce	13 Jun 1828
Martha	14	F		Ireland	United States	Commerce	13 Jun 1828
Mary	40	F	None	Scotland	United States	Mary & Susan	5 Aug 1828
Mary Ann	17	F	None	Scotland	United States	Mary & Susan	5 Aug 1828
Oliver	30	M	Farmer	Great Britian	United States	Andes	19 Aug 1829
Patrick	30	M	Labourer	Ireland	United States	Wilson	4 Oct 1827
Phillip	29	M	on Bussiness	Germany	United States	Martha	30 Jun 1823
Robt.	12	M		Ireland	United States	Commerce	13 Jun 1828
Saml.	50	M	Labourer	Ireland	United States	Commerce	13 Jun 1828
Samuel	18	M	Merchant		United States	Columbia	11 Apr 1822
Sarah	23	F		United States		France	6 Feb 1829
Thos.	18			Ireland	United States	Jno. Dickinson	21 Sep 1821
W.	22	M	Merchant		United States	Columbia	11 Apr 1822
W.	26	M	Merchant	Massachusetts	U. States	Swift	11 May 1824
W.	28	M	Merchant	N. York	U. States	Robt. Y. Hayne	27 Jun 1825
W.	30	M	Mercht.	U.S. America	U. States	Mount Parnasse	17 Jul 1829
William	25	M	Artist	G. Britian	U. States	William Byrnes	23 Aug 1827
William	34	M	Merchant	Maine	Portland	Curlew	3 Nov 1823
William	35	M	Merchant	U.S. America	U.S. America	Vermont	7 Oct 1828
William	45	M	Farmer	Scotland	America	Camillus	12 Sep 1822
William, Esqr.	36	M	Gentn.	U.S. America	U. States	St. Thomas	24 May 1824
William, Mr.	23	M	Farmer	Scotland	U. States	Majestic	27 Jul 1829
GORDOVA, Manuel	32	M	Gentleman	Mexico	England	Brown	23 Dec 1826
GORE, Ann	30	F	Servant	Canada	Canada	New York	5 Jul 1826
George	30	M	Merchant	U. State	U. States	Trident	18 Aug 1820
Henry	23	M	Planter	England	America	Comet	26 Jun 1822
John	38	M	Glass Blower	Great Britain	United States	Lord Gambier	4 Feb 1829
Patrick	22	M		Ireland	United States	William & George	14 May 1828
Patrick	30	M		Great B.	U. States	William Neilson	26 Jul 1828
Richard	32	M	Merchant	Great Britain	United States	Hamilton	21 Nov 1826
Thos.	31	M	Seaman	Cape Cod	United States	Venus	8 Sep 1820
GORENICH, Joaquin	22		Merchant	Porto Rico		Telegraph	24 Mar 1828
GORER, Phillip G.	47	M	Merchant	Maryland	U. States	Columbia	7 Jul 1824
GOREVERNEUR, Saml., Junr.	36	M	Merchant	U. States	U. States	Edward Quesnel	16 Nov 1827
GORGE, Andrew	30	M	Laborer	England	United States	Jubilee	1 Oct 1828
GORGET, August	7	M	Merchant	France	U. States	Dawn	8 Jun 1827
J.	33	F	Merchant	France	U. States	Dawn	8 Jun 1827
GORGLIN, Mary	26	F		Great B.	U. States	William Neilson	26 Jul 1828
GORHAM, Ann	8	F		G. Britain	U. States	Mary Howland	22 Sep 1828
E.	20	F			U. States	Mary Howland	22 Sep 1828
Eliza	35	F		G. Britain	U. States	Mary Howland	22 Sep 1828
Hannah	4	F		G. Britain	U. States	Mary Howland	22 Sep 1828
Harrot	22	F		G. Britain	U. States	Mary Howland	22 Sep 1828
James	12	M		G. Britain	U. States	Mary Howland	22 Sep 1828
Jno.	18	M	Gentleman	U. States	United States	Alfred	3 Jun 1826
John	49	M	Farmer	G. Britain	U. States	Mary Howland	22 Sep 1828
Sarah	18	F		G. Britain	U. States	Mary Howland	22 Sep 1828
Wm.	6	M		G. Britain	U. States	Mary Howland	22 Sep 1828
GORINAM, Cathrine	28	F	None	Ireland	New York	Eliza Grant	29 Aug 1829
GORINLEY, Owen	30	M	Labourer	Ireland	United States	Pallas	28 Oct 1828

NAMES OF PASSENGERS	AGE	SEX	OCCUPATIONS	COUNTRY TO WHICH THEY BELONG	COUNTRY THEY INTEND TO INHABIT	SHIPS/DATES OF ARRIVAL	
GORLY, James	18	M	Farmer	Parish of Norhill, Parish of ..., Ireland	N. York	New Orleans	24 Aug 1827
GORMAN, Ann	12	F		Ireland	U. States	Virginia	20 Jun 1825
Ann	21	F	Labourer	England	U. States	Hope & Esther	10 Jul 1827
Arn	16	F	Child			Commerce	22 Jun 1825
Bridget	18	F	Spinster	Ireland	United States	Wilson	6 Jun 1828
Catharine	25	F		Ireland	U. States	Josephine	27 Jul 1825
Catherine	27	F	Servant	Ireland	United States	Henry Kneeland	7 Jan 1827
Dennis	25	M	Blacksmith	Great Britain	U.N. States	Reindeer	10 Dec 1827
Ellen	22	F	Spinster	Ireland	U. States	Hibernia	29 Nov 1821
Francis	26	M	Labourer	Ireland	United States	New Packet	15 Nov 1828
Geo.	21		None	G. Britain	United States	Roman	10 Sep 1827
George	20	M	Laborer	Ireland	United States	Fabius	4 Jun 1828
J., 19	19	M				Hibernia	15 Aug 1820
James	19	M	Labourer	Ireland	U. States	Josephine	7 May 1827
James	21	M	Labourer	Ireland	United States	Sarah Ann	11 Jan 1827
John	26	M	Merchant	U	U	Charlotte Corday	24 Jan 1820
John	29 8/12	M	Shoe Maker	Ireland	U. States	Fabius	22 Sep 1828
Mary	5	F	Child	Ireland	United States	Ann Maria	8 Jun 1824
Mary	20	F	Spinster			Commerce	22 Jun 1825
Mary	50	F	Spnster.	Ireland	United States	Ann Maria	8 Jun 1824
Mathew	35		Farmer & Labourer	Great Britain & Ireland	United States	Trio	8 Feb 1827
Michael	24	M	Gentlemen	Ireland	United States	South Carolina Packet	25 Mar 1820
Michael	28	M	Carpenter	Ireland	U. States	Josephine	27 Jul 1825
Michl.	30	M	Farmer	Ireland	United States	Wilson	27 Jun 1826
Nancy	19	F	Spinster	Ireland	United States	Lima	19 Jun 1824
Patrick	25	M	Labourer	Ireland	Ireland	Sarah G.	28 Nov 1827
Patt	24	M	Farmer	Ireland	United States	Dublin Packet	29 Jun 1825
Rebecca	28 6/12	F		Ireland	U. States	Fabius	22 Sep 1828
Robert	22		Servant	Ireland	G. Britain	Robert Burns	14 Jun 1824
Rosy	21	F	Wife	Ireland	United States	Sarah Ann	11 Jan 1827
T.	23	M	Bookbinder	Ireland		Eliza Jane	12 Sep 1820
GORMBY, Cormk.	29	M	Labourer	Great Britain	United States	William Dawson	18 Jun 1827
Edwd.	21	M	Labourer	Great Britain	United States	William Dawson	18 Jun 1827
Mary	2	F	None	Great Britain	United States	William Dawson	18 Jun 1827
Mary	28	F	None	Great Britain	United States	William Dawson	18 Jun 1827
GORMDEN, John	33	M	Farmer	Ireland	U. States	Napolean	26 Sep 1828
Mary	26	M	Farmer	Ireland	U. States	Napolean	26 Sep 1828
GORMLEY, An	17	F	Spinster	Ireland	United States	Catharine	22 Jul 1825
An	46	F	Spinster	Ireland	United States	Catharine	22 Jul 1825
Barnard	20	M	Labourer	Ireland	United States	Catharine	22 Jul 1825
Eleanor	16	F	Spinster	Ireland	United States	Catharine	22 Jul 1825
Francis	50	M	Mechanic	Ireland	United States	Concordia	25 Aug 1827
James	12	M	Labourer	Ireland	United States	Catharine	22 Jul 1825
Mary	22	F	Spinster	Ireland	United States	Catharine	22 Jul 1825
Mary	50	F		Ireland	United States	Concordia	25 Aug 1827
Patrick	19		Laborer	Ireland	Great Britain	Robert Burns	14 Jun 1824
GORNICK, John	8	M	Child	Ireland	U. States	Meteor	19 Jul 1828
John	28	M		G. Britan	U. States	William Neilson	26 Jul 1828
Thos.	21	M		G. Britan	U. States	William Neilson	26 Jul 1828
GORNLY, Patrick	24	M	Labourer	Ireland	America	John Adams	2 Aug 1827
GORNSLEY, Biddy	1	F	None	Great Britain	United States	William Dawson	18 Jun 1827
Frances	38	F	None	Great Britain	United States	William Dawson	18 Jun 1827
Francis	2	F	None	Great Britain	United States	William Dawson	18 Jun 1827
Mary	6	F	None	Great Britain	United States	William Dawson	18 Jun 1827
Rose	38	F	None	Great Britain	United States	William Dawson	18 Jun 1827
GORNSLY, Bridget	17	F	Farmer	Ireland	U. States	Champion	26 Jul 1827
GORREON, —, Mr.	50	M	Merchant	Havana	Havana	Milo	15 May 1824
GORSUCH, Henry	...	...	...	...	...	Diamond	27 Jul 1824
GORTNEY, Ann	3/12	F	Servant	Ireland	United States	Wilson	27 Jun 1826
Ann	18	F	Servant	Ireland	United States	Wilson	27 Jun 1826
Mary	6/12	F	Child	Ireland	United States	Wilson	27 Jun 1826
Patk.	30	M	Laboror	Ireland	United States	Wilson	27 Jun 1826
Rose	25	F	Servant	Ireland	United States	Wilson	27 Jun 1826
GORTON, Thomas	1	M	Child	Scotland	America	Camillus	12 Sep 1822
GOS..., G., Mrs.	27	F		United States	U.S.	Gleaner	31 Jul 1821

NAMES OF PASSENGERS	AGE	SEX	OCCUPATIONS	COUNTRY TO WHICH THEY BELONG	COUNTRY THEY INTEND TO INHABIT	SHIPS/DATES OF ARRIVAL	
GOSHEN, William	19	M	Farmer	England	America	Plutarch	18 Jul 1826
GOSLET, Thos. B.	23	M	Merchant	U. States	U. States	Carolina Ann	5 Jul 1822
GOSLIN, A.	24	F	lady	Denmark	Denmark	Superb	18 Oct 1821
GOSLING, Georgte	30	M	Planter	St. Croix	St. Croix	South Carolina Packet	16 Sep 1820
Sarah	32	F	Sempstress	Bristol, Engl.	...	Warrior	19 May 1828
GOSMAN, Catharine	28	F	None	Ireland		Eliza Grant	29 Aug 1829
GOSQUET, Elizabeth	25	F		G. Brittain	U. States	Cincinnatus	2 Oct 1822
GOSS, Ann	22	F		Ireland	U. States	St. Michael	27 Mar 1827
Barbe	26	F	Farmer	Switzerland	U.S.	C. Amelia	30 Jun 1828
Catherine	22	F	Spinster	Switzerland	United States	Andes	5 May 1828
George	62	M	Farmer	Switzerland	U.S.	C. Amelia	30 Jun 1828
John	3	M		Ireland	U. States	St. Michael	27 Mar 1827
Joseph	26	M		Germany	Missouri	Isabella	15 Sep 1828
M. A.	26	F	Weaver	Switzerland	U.States	C. Amelia	30 Jun 1828
Marthy	50	F				John Dickinson	14 Sep 1820
GOSSAGE, —, Mrs.	27	F		U.S.	U.S.	Radius	9 May 1823
GOSSALER, P.	32	M	Merchant	France	U. States	Georgiana	25 Jun 1824
GOSSAMER, C.	22	F	Coachman	Germany	U. States	Exchange	28 Aug 1828
J.	24	M	Baker	Germany	U. States	Exchange	28 Aug 1828
GOSSELIN, Victor	19	M	Clerk	France	U.S.	Cadmus	20 Dec 1824
GOSSIN, Marian	26	F	Servant	France	U. States	Bayard	16 May 1827
GOSSLEE, Henry John, Mr.	21	M	Merchant	Hamburgh	America	Birmingham	16 Oct 1826
GOSSLER, Henry	25 2/12	M	Merchant	U. States	U. States	Columbia	30 Jun 1828
Julia, Miss	20	F	Lady	England	United States	New York	14 Jul 1827
GOSTER, Jno.	36	M	Farmer	Germany	United States	Stephania	16 Aug 1827
GOTIER, Lewis	22	M	Mechanic	N. York	U. States	Hope Return	13 Jan 1826
GOTLEP, A. Hatfield	25	M	Merchant	Engld.	Engld.	Napoleon	26 May 1828
GOTOBEA, William	21	M	Accountant	Great Britain	United States	Washington	22 Mar 1820
GOTT, Joseph	23	M		England	U.N. States	Ariel	9 Mar 1829
Mary	29	F	None	England	America	Ann	23 Jul 1821
GOTTER, Constan	29	M	Mariner		France	Packet Margaret	20 Sep 1824
GOTTLICH, Cath.	26	F	Asst. Cordwinder	Swiss	U. States	Edwd. Quesnel	30 Apr 1825
J. W.	30	M	Cordwinder	Swiss	U. States	Edwd. Quesnel	30 Apr 1825
GOTTNESS, David	9	M		Scotland	United States	Camillus	9 May 1827
GOTZ, Jacob	29	M	Sadelmaker	Baden	New York	Louisa	6 Oct 1828
GOUBOULT, G. N.	28	M	Saddler	French	U. States	Topaz	23 Jul 1828
GOUCH, Jacob	32	M	Farmer	Germany	U. States	United States	3 Sep 1828
GOUFF, Adah	6	F	None	Great Britan	United States	Silvanus Jenkins	10 Mar 1827
Benjamin	29	M	Moulder	Great Britan	United States	Silvanus Jenkins	10 Mar 1827
Emma	2 6/12	F	None	Great Britan	United States	Silvanus Jenkins	10 Mar 1827
John	11/12	M	None	Great Britan	United States	Silvanus Jenkins	10 Mar 1827
Mary	26	F	None	Great Britan	United States	Silvanus Jenkins	10 Mar 1827
Thomas	10	M	None	Great Britan	United States	Silvanus Jenkins	10 Mar 1827
GOUFFAIN, Domin.	29	M	Merchant	St. Thomas		Reliance	17 Jun 1828
Wm.	34	M	Servant	St. Thomas		Reliance	17 Jun 1828
GOUGERARD, Aug.	40	M	Merchant	Spain		Aspasia	19 Jul 1823
GOUGH, Anne	32	F		England		Fame	9 Dec 1826
John	5	M		England		Fame	9 Dec 1826
John	13	M				Helen	4 Aug 1829
John	48	M	Weaver	England		Fame	9 Dec 1826
Michael	40	M	Weaver	England		Fame	9 Dec 1826
Nancy	40	F		England		Fame	9 Dec 1826
Thomas, Mr.	22	M	Gentleman	England	United States	Maria	29 Sep 1823
GOUIGON, V.	32	M	Merchant	France	U. States	Julia	16 Nov 1824
GOULD, Charles	21	M	Merchant	Albany	Albany	Jupiter	27 May 1826
E.	11	M	Farmer	Great Britton	U. State	Earl of Liverpool	16 Aug 1826
George	25	M	Farmer	Ireland	Great Britton	William	11 Dec 1820
John	30	M	Carpenter	England		Marchioness	13 May 1828
Juan Bautisto	27	M	Merchant	Italy	U. States	Robert Y. Haynes	22 Mar 1827
Nathl.	40	M	Merchant	England	England	Birmingham	16 Jun 1828
Warren	26	M	Merchant	Beverly	U. States	Bramin	30 Mar 1825
William	40	M	Shipmaster	U. States	U. States	Boston	26 Sep 1820
GOULDCAP, Isaac	20	M	Merchant	England	U. States America	Columbus	23 Mar 1829
GOULDING, Anna	35	F		G. Britain	U. States	Hanford	10 Jun 1828
Catherine	1 1/12	F	None	Ireland	United States	Trident	31 Mar 1827

NAMES OF PASSENGERS	AGE	SEX	OCCUPATIONS	COUNTRY TO WHICH THEY BELONG	COUNTRY THEY INTEND TO INHABIT	SHIPS/DATES OF ARRIVAL	
GOULDING (cont'd)							
Charlotte	6	F		G. Britain	U. States	Hanford	10 Jun 1828
Hiram	3	M		G. Britain	U. States	Hanford	10 Jun 1828
John	24	M	Farmer	Ireland	United States	Trident	31 Mar 1827
John	27	M	Labourer	Ireland	United States	Trident	18 Jul 1827
Mary	23	F	None	Ireland	United States	Trident	31 Mar 1827
GOULET, John N.	37		Confectioner	French	America	Romulus	15 May 1828
GOULEY, Ann	32 10/12	F	Dress Maker	G. Brittian	United States	Louisa	14 Jun 1825
GOULON, Clementine1 6/12		F	there child [Peter J. & Francis]	France	United States	Helen	5 Sep 1828
Francis	34	F	his wife [Peter J.]	France	United States	Helen	5 Sep 1828
Peter E.	6	M	there child [Peter J. & Francis]	France	United States	Helen	5 Sep 1828
Peter J.	40	M	Taven Keeper	France	United States	Helen	5 Sep 1828
Stans. A.	3	M	there child [Peter J. & Francis]	France	United States	Helen	5 Sep 1828
GOULY, James	8	M	going to [his] Father	G. Brittian	United States	Louisa	14 Jun 1825
Jane	5	F	going to [her] Father	G. Brittian	United States	Louisa	14 Jun 1825
Nivilla	9	F	going to [her] Father	G. Brittian	United States	Louisa	14 Jun 1825
GOUNIER, A.	31	M	Physician	France	U. States	Edwd. Quesnel	30 Apr 1825
GOUNIN, Agustus	24	M	Tanner	France	United States	Elizabeth	4 Sep 1826
GOUNLIER, Philip	18	M	None	France	United States	Montano	4 Nov 1823
GOURAUD, F.	38 6/12	M	Doctor	Washington	America	Henry	15 Feb 1826
GOURDIN, Julia L., Miss	23	F	Lady	France	America	Lima	11 Dec 1823
GOURDON, Henry	19	M	Merchant	America	America	Silas Richard	24 Oct 1829
GOURE, Augustus	25	M	Merchant	Spain	U. States	Pocahontas	9 Jun 1823
GOURJON, Victor	55	M	Manufacturer	France	U. States	Marmion	7 Jun 1824
GOURLAY, Alexr.	23	M		Ireland	United States	William & George	14 May 1828
GOURLAY, John	50		Millwright	Scotland	United States	Cambria	19 Oct 1829
GOURNARSE, Antoine	37	M	Agriculturist	France	U.S.	Helen	3 May 1828
GOURUZAX, S. T.	38	M	Merchant	France	U. States	Bayard	9 Nov 1825
GOUSEELEUS, A. M.			Prisoner taken by the U.S. Ship Cyane and sent by the Consul at St. Iago			Maria	20 Jul 1820
GOUSSET, Georges	31	M	Farmer	Germany	United States	Oxford	14 Aug 1828
GOUSTES, —, Madam	54	F		Havre	N. York	Stephania	29 Nov 1825
GOUTER, Joseph	22	M	Farm	Ireland		Quatre Freres	29 Jul 1828
GOUTZ, George	25	M	Merchant	U. States	U. States	Cyno	21 Jul 1824
GOUVERNEUR, Samuel	36	M	Merchant	United States	United States	General Paez	14 Apr 1826
GOUVOLT, —, Marchioness of Gouvolt	32	F	None	France	U. States	Sully	25 Jun 1828
GOVASLEY, Waker	22	M	Merchant	Spain	U. States	Union	21 Jul 1825
GOVERNER, Murdin	22	M	Segar Maker	Island of Cuba	United States	Betsey	28 Oct 1825
GOVERTS, P. D.	45	M	Mercht.	Germany	U. States	Sarah Ralston	20 Feb 1826
P. D.	51	M	Merchant	U. States	U. States	Henrietta	27 Mar 1824
GOVES, Cath.	35	F		Switzerland	U. States	Romulus	24 Sep 1828
Charles	7	M		Switzerland	U. States	Romulus	24 Sep 1828
Gaite	7	M		Switzerland	U. States	Romulus	24 Sep 1828
Geo.	1	M		Switzerland	U. States	Romulus	24 Sep 1828
Hennis	12	F		Switzerland	U. States	Romulus	24 Sep 1828
Henry	37	M	Farmer	Switzerland	U. States	Romulus	24 Sep 1828
James	45	M	Farmer	G. Britain	U. States	Robt. Edwards	4 Sep 1828
Maria	4	F		Switzerland	U. States	Romulus	24 Sep 1828
Mary	18	F		Switzerland	U. States	Romulus	24 Sep 1828
Nicholas	10	M		Switzerland	U. States	Romulus	24 Sep 1828
GOVISS, D. P.	50	M	Merchant	America	Baltimore	Prince Edward	8 Aug 1829
GOW, Charles	24	M	Joiner	Great Britain	United States	Courier	26 Jun 1827
David Lith	22	M	Smith	Argyle (Tedland) Scotland	United States	Jean Hastie	27 Jul 1829
James, Mast.	10	M	Carpenter	England	U.S.	Acasta	11 May 1827
Mary, Mrs.	33	F	Carpenter	England	U.S.	Acasta	11 May 1827
GOWAN, Bridget	21	F	Spinster	Ireland	U. States	Josephine	7 May 1827
James	3	M	None	Isle of Man		Ocean	13 Jul 1827

NAMES OF PASSENGERS	AGE	SEX	OCCUPATIONS	COUNTRY TO WHICH THEY BELONG	COUNTRY THEY INTEND TO INHABIT	SHIPS/DATES OF ARRIVAL	
GOWAN (cont'd)							
James	23	M	Taylor	England	United States	Cincinnatus	21 Nov 1821
Jane	8	F	None	Isle of Man		Ocean	13 Jul 1827
John		M		Scotland	U.S.	Curler	19 Jul 1828
John	30	M	Labourer	Isle of Man		Ocean	13 Jul 1827
Ml.	50	M	Musician	U. States	U. States	Hannah & Rebecca	12 Jun 1824
Ml., Mr.	13	M		U. States	U. States	Hannah & Rebecca	12 Jun 1824
Ml., Mr.	28	M		U. States	U. States	Hannah & Rebecca	12 Jun 1824
Rosanna	27	F	None	Isle of Man		Ocean	13 Jul 1827
Wm.	20	M	Farmer	Great Britian	United States	Columbia	17 Apr 1827
GOWEL, Daniel	18	M	Labourer	Ireland	United States	Trio	5 May 1828
GOWEN, Daniel	19	M	Merchant	Gt. Britain	Gt. Britain	Clarice	1 Feb 1827
Graseck	40	F		Irland	United States	Nancy	28 Oct 1822
Lara	8	F		Irland	United States	Nancy	28 Oct 1822
Mical	6	M		Irland	United States	Nancy	28 Oct 1822
N. C.	45	M	Planter	Spain	U.S.	Emma	24 Jun 1825
R.	32		Farmer	England	England	Hudson	4 Sep 1823
Richd.	46	M		Great Brittan	U.S.	Florida	17 May 1825
GOWER, Adeliza *died	8/12	F	Child	England	United States	Herald	29 Oct 1825
Elizabeth	6	F	Child	England	United States	Herald	29 Oct 1825
Elizabeth	28	F	Spinster	England	United States	Herald	29 Oct 1825
Esther	16	F	None	Gt. Britain	U.S. America	James Cropper	2 Aug 1827
James *died	8/12	M	Child	England	United States	Herald	29 Oct 1825
John	4	M	Child	England	United States	Herald	29 Oct 1825
Juan W.	27	M	Sec. Col. Leg. [Secretary Columbian Legation?]	Columbia	U. States	Pacific	20 Aug 1825
Rachl.	12	F	None	Gt. Britain	U.S. America	James Cropper	2 Aug 1827
Richard	3	M	Child	England	United States	Herald	29 Oct 1825
GOWERY, Michael	19	M	Weaver	Ireland	United States	Clothier	22 Nov 1827
GOWRIE, Joseph	28	M	Merchant	England	United States	Hamlet	25 Aug 1825
GOWSPON, William	23	M	Labourer	Ireland	United States	Hope	12 Jun 1828
GOYLE, David	45	M	Farmer	Scotland	United States	Commerce	17 Jul 1823
GOZEN, Nicholas	23	M	Labourer	Switzerland	U. States	La Urania	3 Jul 1828
GRA...ER, —	29	F		Switzerland	United States	Elbe	2 Aug 1822
GRABANT, Ws.	22	M	Carpenter	New Jersey	U. States	Prize	10 Jun 1824
GRABOLD, Augustine	36	M	Artizen	Iterly	United States	Jubilee	13 Jul 1829
GRABOUR, John	26	M	Farmer	Switzerland	U. States	Criterion	16 May 1825
GRACE, Catherine	1 1/12	F	Child	Switzerland	United States	Andes	5 May 1828
Christina	22	F	Spinster	Switzerland	United States	Andes	5 May 1828
Christina	47	F	Spinster	Switzerland	United States	Andes	5 May 1828
Frs.	25	F	Lady	New York	New York	Native	30 Jun 1826
Henery J.	30	M	Merchant	Great Britan	Great Britan	George	25 May 1825
J. A. *Landed at Cape May	25	M	Planter	Cuba	Cuba	Dover	17 Aug 1821
Jacob	42	M	Baker	Germany	U. States	Ann	19 Aug 1824
Jno. A.	35	M	Merchant	England	England	John Wells	14 Oct 1823
John	19	M	Labourer	Ireland	U.S.	Oliver Wolcott	3 Nov 1827
Philip	20	M	Farmer	Switzerland	United States	Andes	5 May 1828
Philip	46	M	Farmer	Switzerland	United States	Andes	5 May 1828
Samuel	21	M	Gentleman	U. States	U. States	Bramin	13 Jun 1828
Sophy	5	F	Child	Switzerland	United States	Andes	5 May 1828
GRACEY, Rebecca	19	F	Nothing	Ireland	New York	Louisa	20 Jul 1826
GRACHE, Charles	30	M	Mercht.	Port au Prince	America	Fox	21 Dec 1821
GRACIA, Jose M.	42			Spain		Victory	12 Jul 1820
GRACIE, Archd., Jr.	30	M	Mercht.	United States	United States	Manchester	6 Dec 1825
Archibald, Jr.	25		Merchant	New York	New York	Braganza	9 Oct 1820
Archibald, Junr.	30	M	Mercht.	U.S.	U.S.	Edward Quesnel	21 Apr 1827
Joseph Maria	33	M	Mercht.	Havanna	Spain	Orozimbo	16 Apr 1821
Wm.	35	M	Merchant	New York	United States	Lewis	30 May 1823
Wm. R.	24	M	Merchant	N. York	U. States	Plato	18 Apr 1826
GRACO, Sam	14	M		England	U. States	Prize	23 Mar 1824
GRACY, John	27	M		G. Britain	U. States	St. George	7 Jun 1828

NAMES OF PASSENGERS	AGE	SEX	OCCUPATIONS	COUNTRY TO WHICH THEY BELONG	COUNTRY THEY INTEND TO INHABIT	SHIPS/DATES OF ARRIVAL	
GRADHAM, Thomas	38	M	Farmer	England	United States	Jubilee	1 Dec 1827
GRADY, Catherine	2/12	F	...	Ireland	United States	Wilson	22 Jun 1824
Catherine	4	F	...	Ireland	United States	Wilson	22 Jun 1824
Edwin	30	M	...	Ireland	United States	Wilson	22 Jun 1824
John C.	26	M	Mariner	United States	U. States	Leopard	30 Aug 1826
Margret	21	F		Ireland		L. M. Pelham	12 May 1823
GRAEAGR, Sarey	48	F		St. Johns	U. States	Nancy	27 Jun 1823
GRAER, Patrick	24	M	Farmer	Ireland	United States	Dublin Packet	3 Sep 1822
GRAF, G.	35	M	Tanner	Germany	Germany	Minerva	17 May 1828
GRAFE, J. F.	26	M	Gentleman	France	France	Superb	18 Oct 1821
GRAFF, W.	38	M	Tanner	U. States	U. States	Minerva	23 May 1825
GRAFFEN, Ann	19	F		Irereland	America	Carolina Ann	20 Jun 1825
John	33	M	Labourer	Great Britain	U. States	Hope & Esther	13 Oct 1829
Morris	30	M	Labourer	Great Britain	U. States	Hope & Esther	13 Oct 1829
GRAFFIN, Jane	20	F	Mantua Maker	Great Britain	United States	Atlantic	8 Dec 1827
GRAFFTY, Ellen	12	F		Great B.	U. States	William Neilson	26 Jul 1828
GRAFT, George	19 7/12	M	Taylor	Germany	U.S. American	Criterion	7 Jul 1824
GRAFTON, D. C.	27	M	Merchant	Great Brittan	U. States	Cadmus	5 Apr 1826
Nathaniel	26	M	Merchant	England	New York	Brighton	19 Aug 1829
Nathaniel	26	M	Merchant	England		Brighton	19 Aug 1829
GRAHAM, ...	1	M	None	Great Brittain	New York	Albion	11 Jun 1821
A. M.	3/12	F		Philada.	U. States	Fancy	1 Oct 1825
Agness	7	F	Labourer	Great Britain	U. States	Princess Charlotte	6 Sep 1828
Alex	30	M	Labourer	Scotland	U. States	Czar	29 Aug 1829
Alexander	17	M	Labourer	G. Britain	United States	Louisa	14 Jun 1825
Alexander	26 6/12	M	Merchant	Scotland	United States	New York	3 Apr 1826
Alexdr.	20	M	Weaver	Ireland	United States	Trident	17 May 1825
Amabella	6	F	None	Scotland	U. States	Czar	29 Aug 1829
And., Jr.	33	M	Joiner	Scotland	U. States	Czar	29 Aug 1829
And., Sr.	53	M	Merchant	Scotland	U. States	Czar	29 Aug 1829
Andrew	4 1/2	M		Scotland	United States	Camillus	27 Oct 1829
Andrew	21	M	Weaver	Ireland	New York	Trusty	12 Sep 1828
Ann	20	F	None	Great Britain	United States	Orbit	23 Oct 1826
Ann	23	F	None	Ireland	Pittsburgh	Indian Chief	19 Jun 1823
Ann Maria	5	F		Great Brittain	United States	Sarah Ralston	27 Jan 1827
Anne	6 3/12	F	Daughter	Ireland	New York	Louisa	20 Jul 1826
Augustus	44	M	Merchant	Scotland	United States	Nestor	3 Nov 1820
Bridget	20	F	Spinster	Ireland	United States	Fabius	4 Jun 1828
Catherine	55	F		Sligo	Kentucky	Susquehana	27 Jun 1823
Cathrin	25	F		Scotland	United States	Camillus	27 Oct 1829
Charine	28		Spinster	Ireland		Westmoreland	1 Aug 1826
Charlotte		F	None	Ireland	U. States	Josephine	27 Jul 1825
Chas.	30	M	Joiner	Scotland	United States	Dalhouse Castle	6 Sep 1827
Christian	33	F		Scotland	United States	Camillus	27 Oct 1829
Danl.	20	M	Farmer	Ireland	U. States	Orozimbo	7 Jul 1825
Dary	3	M	Labourer	Great Britain	U. States	Princess Charlotte	6 Sep 1828
David	18	M	Son	Ireland	New York	Louisa	20 Jul 1826
David	21	M	Weaver	Ireland	U. States	Courier	17 Mar 1828
David	55	M	Farmer	Ireland	New York	Louisa	20 Jul 1826
E., Miss	18		Merchant	Scotland		Zamoa	5 Nov 1828
Elisa	8	F	Daughter	Ireland	New York	Louisa	20 Jul 1826
Elisa	49	F	Wife	Ireland	New York	Louisa	20 Jul 1826
Eliza	6	F		Great Brittain	United States	Sarah Ralston	27 Jan 1827
Elizabeth, Miss	30	F	None	Scotland	New York	Hector	11 May 1821
Elizabeth, Mrs.	36	F		Scotland	United States	Samuel Robertson	5 Oct 1827
Ellen	7	F	Farmer	N. Brunswick	New Brunswick	Abigale	9 Aug 1821
Ellen	26	F	None			Manhattan	25 Dec 1820
Ellen	28	F		Scotland	United States	Camillus	27 Oct 1829
Ellen	30	F	None	Scotland	U. States	Czar	29 Aug 1829
Esther	21		Spinster	Ireland		Westmoreland	1 Aug 1826
Esther	29	F	Labourer	Great Britain	U. States	Princess Charlotte	6 Sep 1828
Fanny	6			Cork	Gt. Britain	Enterprize	19 Feb 1822
Francis	23	M	Labourer	England	England	William Byrnes	14 Apr 1824
G. B.	37	M	Merchant	G. Britain	United States	New York	12 Nov 1822
George	6	M		Ireland	U. States	Nancy	1 Sep 1823

NAMES OF PASSENGERS	AGE	SEX	OCCUPATIONS	COUNTRY TO WHICH THEY BELONG	COUNTRY THEY INTEND TO INHABIT	SHIPS/DATES OF ARRIVAL	
GRAHAM (cont'd)							
George	40	M	Farmer	Ireland	New York	Carolina Ann	15 Oct 1824
Grace	4/12	F		Scotland	United States	Camillus	27 Oct 1829
Hannah	16			Cork	Gt. Britain	Enterprize	19 Feb 1822
Henry	24	M	Weaver	Gt. Britain	U. States	Frances Henrietta	18 Apr 1825
Henry	50	M	Grocer	Sligo	Kentucky	Susquehana	27 Jun 1823
Hugh	12 3/12	M	Son	Ireland	New York	Louisa	20 Jul 1826
Isaac	6	M		Great Brittain	United States	Sarah Ralston	27 Jan 1827
Isabella	1		Girl	Ireland		Westmoreland	1 Aug 1826
Isabella	9	F	None	Scotland	U. States	Czar	29 Aug 1829
Isabella	14 3/12	F	Daughter	Ireland	New York	Louisa	20 Jul 1826
Isabella	30	F	Seamstress	Scotland	U. States	Reaper	31 May 1824
Isabella	50		Wife	Ireland		Westmoreland	1 Aug 1826
J.	30	M	Merchant	U. States	U. States	Henry	17 Sep 1827
J.	50	F	None	United States	United States	Euphrates	15 Nov 1824
J., Mrs.	40		Merchant	Scotland		Zamoa	5 Nov 1828
J. S.	16	M		G. Brittain	U. States	Canada	6 Jun 1825
James		M	Chiefly farmers		United States	Factor	8 Jul 1829
James	3	M		Scotland	United States	Camillus	27 Oct 1829
James	18	M	Weaver	Ireland	United States	Trident	17 May 1825
James	21	M	Weaver	Scotland	U.S.A.	Calliope	15 Aug 1827
James	22	M	Labourer	Great Britain	United States	Orbit	23 Oct 1826
James	23	M	Reedmaker	Ireland	Pittsburgh	Indian Chief	19 Jun 1823
James	26	M	Bricklayer	England		Marchioness	13 May 1828
James	30	M	Farmer, Labourer or Spinster	Ireland	U. States	Meteor	4 Oct 1827
James, her Son [Sarah]	12	M				Criterion	27 Oct 1820
Jams	2 1/2	M		Scotland	United States	Camillus	27 Oct 1829
Jams	28	M	Blacksmith	Scotland	United States	Camillus	27 Oct 1829
Jane	1		Girl	Ireland		Westmoreland	1 Aug 1826
Jane	5	F	Trader	Ireland	U. States	Telegraph	14 Feb 1820
Jane	20 3/12	F	Daughter	Ireland	New York	Louisa	20 Jul 1826
Jane	22	F	Spinster	Ireland	United States	Catharine	22 Jul 1825
Jane	25	F	Spinster	Ireland	United States	Fabius	31 Jul 1829
Jane, Miss	13	F	Spinster	Ireland	United States	Dublin Packet	13 Oct 1828
Janet	1	F	None	Scotland	U. States	Czar	29 Aug 1829
Jas.	30		Farmer	Ireland		Westmoreland	1 Aug 1826
Jasper	46	M	Gentleman	Scotland	U. States	Huntress	15 Oct 1823
Jno.	25	M	Labourer			Harmony	15 Jul 1820
John	1	M	Labourer	Great Britain	U. States	Princess Charlotte	6 Sep 1828
John	4	M	None	Great Brittain	New York	Albion	11 Jun 1821
John	6 1/2	M		Scotland	United States	Camillus	27 Oct 1829
John	16	M	None	Scotland	U. States	Czar	29 Aug 1829
John	22	M	Laborer	Ireland	United States	Robert Burns	18 Jun 1821
John	22	M	Merchant	England	Jamaica	Favorite	9 Oct 1823
John	22	M	Servant	Ireland	America	Carolina Ann	7 Aug 1826
John	23	M	Farmer	Ireland	America	Superior	12 Jun 1824
John	23	M	Labourer	Ireland	United States	Fabius	31 Jul 1829
John	25		Farmer	Ireland	G. Britain	Robert Burns	14 Jun 1824
John	27	M	Bricklayer	England		Marchioness	13 May 1828
John	28 5/12	M	Doctor	Ireland	United States	Josephine	30 Apr 1828
John	30	M	Labourer	Ireland	U. States	Nancy	1 Sep 1823
John	31	M	Cloth Dresser	England	Massachusetts	Indian Chief	19 Jun 1823
John	33	M	Farmer	Ireland	America	Superior	12 Jun 1824
John	35	M	None	Great Britain	U. States America	Ann Maria	29 Nov 1821
John	35	M	Labourer	Great Britain		Moro Castle	6 Jul 1827
John	40	M	Seaman	Ireland	United States	Friends	21 Oct 1825
John	40	M	Farmer	Great Brittain	United States	United States	16 Feb 1827
John	54		Merchant	Scotland		Zamoa	5 Nov 1828
John, boy	14	M		Ireland	New York	Carolina Ann	15 Oct 1824
Jonas	25		Farmer	England	United States	Mary	15 Jul 1822
Kitty	25	F		Tyrone, Ireland	Pennsylvania	Anthusa	24 Aug 1825
Louiza	7	M		G. Britain	U. States	Great Britain	6 Sep 1828
M.	21	F	None	Great Brittain	New York	Albion	11 Jun 1821
M. E.	23	F		Philada.	U. States	Fancy	1 Oct 1825
Magt.	6	F		Scotland	United States	Camillus	27 Oct 1829

NAMES OF PASSENGERS	A G E	S E X	OCCUPATIONS	COUNTRY TO WHICH THEY BELONG	COUNTRY THEY INTEND TO INHABIT	SHIPS/DATES OF ARRIVAL	
GRAHAM (cont'd)							
Margaret	4	F	None	Ireland	U. States	Josephine	27 Jul 1825
Margaret	12			Cork	Gt. Britain	Enterprize	19 Feb 1822
Margaret	26	F	None	Ireland	U. States	Telegraph	14 Feb 1820
Margaret	26	F				Harmony	15 Jul 1820
Margaret	34	F	None	Ireland	U. States	Josephine	27 Jul 1825
Margaret	40			Cork	Gt. Britain	Enterprize	19 Feb 1822
Margaret	45	F	None	Ireland	U. States	Franklin	7 Jul 1828
Margret	16		Spinster	Ireland		Westmoreland	1 Aug 1826
Margret	60	F		Ireland	United States	Fabius	4 Jun 1828
Margt.	6	F	None	Scotland	U. States	Czar	29 Aug 1829
Margt.	19	F	None	Ireland	New York	America	1 Aug 1828
Margt.	60	F	None	Ireland	New York	America	1 Aug 1828
Margt.	68	F	None	Scotland	U. States	Czar	29 Aug 1829
Maria	6/12		Spinster	Ireland		Westmoreland	1 Aug 1826
Martha	2	F		Ireland	America	Superior	12 Jun 1824
Martha	10 3/12	F	Daughter	Ireland	New York	Louisa	20 Jul 1826
Martha	18		Spinster	Ireland		Westmoreland	1 Aug 1826
Martha	24	F	Farmer	Ireland	America	Superior	12 Jun 1824
Mary	2	F		Ireland	America	Superior	12 Jun 1824
Mary	18	F	None	Scotland	U. States	Czar	29 Aug 1829
Mary	22	F	Spinster	Ireland	United States	Trident	17 May 1825
Mary	23	F		Tyrone, Ireland	Pennsylvania	Anthusa	24 Aug 1825
Mary	46	F	None	Scotland	U. States	Czar	29 Aug 1829
Mary	50	F	Labourer	Ireland	United States	Hope	12 Jun 1828
Mathew	28	M	Labourer	Ireland	U. States	Nancy	1 Sep 1823
Mathew	38	M	Labourer	Great Britain	United States	Thomas Dickason	31 Jul 1829
Michael	20		Laboring Class		United States	Atlantic	2 Apr 1827
Nancy	1		Spinster	Ireland		Westmoreland	1 Aug 1826
Owen M.	38	M	Servant	Ireland	United States	Henry Kneeland	7 Jun 1828
Patrick	1 3/12	M	None	Ireland	Pittsburgh	Indian Chief	19 Jun 1823
Peter	24	M	Merchant	Ireland	America	Weser	26 Jun 1821
Peter	26	M	Labourer	Ireland	United States	Hope	12 Jun 1828
Petre	48	M	Weaver	Scotland	U.S.A.	Calliope	15 Aug 1827
Pridget	19	F	Servant	Ireland	America	Carolina Ann	7 Aug 1826
Ralph	25	M		Great Brittain	United States	Sarah Ralston	27 Jan 1827
Rebecca	6/12		Spinster	Ireland		Westmoreland	1 Aug 1826
Richard	55	M	Labourer	Ireland	United States	Hope	12 Jun 1828
Robert	13	M	None	Scotland	United States	Samuel Robertson	9 May 1827
Robert	55		Farmer	Ireland		Westmoreland	1 Aug 1826
Robt.	17	M	Labourer			Harmony	15 Jul 1820
Robt.	27	M	Weaver	Scotland	U.S.A.	Calliope	15 Aug 1827
Robt.	28	M	Farmer	Scotland	United States	Dalhouse Castle	6 Sep 1827
Rosa	21		Laboring Class		United States	Atlantic	2 Apr 1827
Samuel	19	M	None	Great Britian	U. States	Pallas	17 Aug 1824
Sarah	21	F	Weaver	Ireland	United States	Wanderer	31 Aug 1829
Sarah	33	F		England	United States	Criterion	27 Oct 1820
Sarah	35	F	None	Great Britain		Moro Castle	6 Jul 1827
Simson	21	M	Cabinetmaker	Great Britain	United States	Thomas Dickason	31 Jul 1829
Susan	2	F	None	Scotland	U. States	Czar	29 Aug 1829
T.	52	M	Baker	United States	United States	Euphrates	15 Nov 1824
Thomas	5	M				Harmony	15 Jul 1820
Thomas	6	M		Great Brittain	United States	Sarah Ralston	27 Jan 1827
Thomas C.	24	M	Merchant	New York	United States	New York	14 Jul 1827
Thos.	29	M	Farmer	N. Brunswick	New Brunswick	Abigale	9 Aug 1821
W. C.	36	M	Mercht.	U.S. America	U. States	Mount Parnasse	17 Jul 1829
Walter	25		Farmer	England	United States	Mary	15 Jul 1822
William	1 4/12	M	Child	Ireland	United States	Fabius	31 Jul 1829
William	3 7/12	M	Son	Ireland	New York	Louisa	20 Jul 1826
William	18	M	Labourer			Imperial	19 Jul 1820
William	30	M	Farmer	Ireland	U. States	Josephine	27 Jul 1825
Wm.	...6	M	Labourer	Ireland	United States	Hope	12 Jun 1828
Wm.	3	M		Great Brittain	United States	Sarah Ralston	27 Jan 1827
Wm.	16	M	Laborer			Commerce	22 Jun 1825
Wm.	20	M	Gent.	scotland	U. States of Amer	Dale	14 Mar 1828
Wm.	24		Cooper	England	United States	Mary	15 Jul 1822

NAMES OF PASSENGERS	AGE	SEX	OCCUPATIONS	COUNTRY TO WHICH THEY BELONG	COUNTRY THEY INTEND TO INHABIT	SHIPS/DATES OF ARRIVAL	
GRAHAM (cont'd)							
Wm.	30	M	Labourer	Great Britain	U. States	Princess Charlotte	6 Sep 1828
Wm.	35 3/12	M	Mariner	United States	U. States	Panthea	5 Oct 1822
Wm.	48	M	Merchant	Scotland	U. States	Columbia	7 Jul 1824
Wm. C.	26	M	Merchant	Philada.	U. States	Fancy	1 Oct 1825
GRAHAME, Elizabeth	21	F	Dress maker	Scotland	United States	Tom	2 Jul 1827
GRAHAMS, Molly	24	F	Spinster	Ireland	U.S. of America	Meteor	19 Mar 1828
GRAHAN, A.	26	M	Weaver			Hanford	17 Jul 1828
Maurice	24	M	...	Ireland	United States	Carolina Ann	24 Oct 1825
GRAHANN, John	20	M	Labourer	Great Brittan	United States	Hanford	3 Aug 1829
GRAIN, Eugenie	22	F	Lady	France	United States	Stephania	22 Apr 1822
GRAINGER, Andrew	8	M		England	United States	Acasta	14 Jun 1824
Chas.	13	M		England	United States	Acasta	14 Jun 1824
Elizh.	35	F		England	United States	Acasta	14 Jun 1824
Francis	10	M		England	United States	Acasta	14 Jun 1824
Jane	5	F		England	United States	Acasta	14 Jun 1824
Willm.	16	M		England	United States	Acasta	14 Jun 1824
GRAM, O. P.	47	M	Merchant	Denmark	U. States	Carlo	28 Mar 1827
Otto	24	M	Sugar Baker	Germany		Boyer	9 May 1825
GRAMEN, Catharine	28	F		United States	United States	Globe	30 Aug 1828
John	36	M	Farmer	United States	United States	Globe	30 Aug 1828
Louis	4	M		United States	United States	Globe	30 Aug 1828
GRAN, Christain	8	F		Bardin	U. States	Bayard	5 Sep 1828
Elizabeth	10	F		Bardin	U. States	Bayard	5 Sep 1828
Jacob	1/4	M		Bardin	U. States	Bayard	5 Sep 1828
Jacob	34	M		Bardin	U. States	Bayard	5 Sep 1828
Lousia	3	F		Bardin	U. States	Bayard	5 Sep 1828
Lousia	32	F		Bardin	U. States	Bayard	5 Sep 1828
GRANADOS, J. G.	23	M	Merchant	Guatemala	Guatemala	Stephania	26 Apr 1824
GRANAGHAN, Elizabeth	18	F	Farmer, Labourer or Spinster	Ireland	U. States	Meteor	4 Oct 1827
GRANAHAN, Edward	25	M	Labourer	Ireland	United States	Robert Fulton	24 Jul 1826
GRANBY, Bridget	29	F	Servant	Ireland	New York	Louisa	18 Apr 1827
Martha	9/12	F	Child	Ireland	New York	Louisa	18 Apr 1827
GRAND, Jean C.	20	M	Weaver	France	U. States	C. Amelia	30 Jun 1828
GRANDA, —	25	M	Painter	France	America	Saluda	18 Jun 1825
GRANDEN, Helene C.	12	F	Servant	Sweden	United States	William Howland	10 Nov 1825
GRANDER, J., Jr.	18	M	Farmer	Piedemont	U. States	Ohio	18 Jul 1821
James	60	M	Farmer	England	U. States	Ohio	18 Jul 1821
GRANDISTON, Arch.	46	M	Taylor	Scotland	U. States	Czar	29 Aug 1829
Isabella	16	F	None	Scotland	U. States	Czar	29 Aug 1829
Isabella	40	F	None	Scotland	U. States	Czar	29 Aug 1829
Margt.	20	F	None	Scotland	U. States	Czar	29 Aug 1829
GRANDLEINARD, Abm.	28		Wheelwright	France	U. States	Elizabeth	9 Jul 1825
Maria	24		Wheelwright	France	U. States	Elizabeth	9 Jul 1825
GRANDPIK, Rhapel	25	M	Mechanic	France	U.S.	Helen	3 May 1828
GRANER, Edwd.	29	M	Labourer	Brattain		L'Esperance	6 Sep 1828
Henry			Missionary	Germany	Liberia	Sully	26 Oct 1829
Martin	21	M	Weaver, Nephew to Vilman	Austria	America	Bayard	15 Dec 1828
GRANGE, Benjn.	42	M		U. States	U. States	Radius	12 Jul 1825
GRANGER, B.	45	M	Merchant	U.S.	U.S.	New England	27 Jul 1829
B.	47	M	Planter	U.S.	U.S.	New England	11 Jul 1827
John	13	M				Acosta	28 Jul 1823
Joshua	38	M				Acosta	28 Jul 1823
Peater	14	M		Ireland	United States	Nancy R. Crowell	21 Sep 1822
Peter	22	M	Miner	England	U. States	Laveria	23 Jul 1828
GRANIE, George W.	21	M	Gentleman	New York	not known	Greyhound	20 Mar 1820
GRANJAR, John	40	M	Merchant	Mexico	Mexico	Eliza	31 Jul 1826
GRANNEY, Margt.	20		Spinster	Ireland	United States	Courier	15 Oct 1827
GRANSBURY, George	7	M		England	United States	Copernicus	3 Aug 1829
John	11	M		England	United States	Copernicus	3 Aug 1829
Mary	32	F		England	United States	Copernicus	3 Aug 1829
Oliver	9	M		England	United States	Copernicus	3 Aug 1829
Phila.	4	F		England	United States	Copernicus	3 Aug 1829
Steplin	32	M	Labourer	England	United States	Copernicus	3 Aug 1829

NAMES OF PASSENGERS	AGE	SEX	OCCUPATIONS	COUNTRY TO WHICH THEY BELONG	COUNTRY THEY INTEND TO INHABIT	SHIPS/DATES OF ARRIVAL	
GRANSBURY (cont'd)							
William	8	M		England	United States	Copernicus	3 Aug 1829
GRANSMORE, John	45	M	Mariner	Great Britain	Great Britain	Protection	6 Nov 1826
GRANT, —, Mrs.	22	F		St. Croix	United States	Carlo	28 Jun 1826
...lliam	40		unknown	Favore, E.	England	Packet	27 Aug 1822
A.	30		Farmer	Ireland	United States	Courier	16 May 1825
A. A.	33	M	Planter	United States	United States	New Packet	19 Oct 1826
Alex	14	M	Child	Scotland	United States	Tom	2 Jul 1827
Alex.	27	M	Farmer	Scotland	United States	Commerce	17 Jul 1823
Alexr.	44	M	Merchant	U. States	U. States	Isaac Hicks	18 Apr 1825
Amelia	28	F		Bermuda	England	Florida	28 Jun 1825
Ann	38		unknown	Chichester, E.	England	Packet	27 Aug 1822
Archd.	29	M	Farmer	Scotland	United States	Commerce	17 Jul 1823
B.	12	F		Scotland	United States	Indus	5 Sep 1827
Barbara	22	F	Spinster	Scotland	United States	Tom	2 Jul 1827
Bernard	18	M	Labourer	Ireland	U. States	Atlantic	19 Aug 1825
Bernd.	30		Carpenter	Great Britan	United States	Newry	11 Jul 1827
C.	25	M	Merchant	Canada	Canada	James Monroe	29 Apr 1823
Caroline	30	F	...	Great Brittain	Montreal	Albion	11 Jun 1821
Charlotte	4	F	...	Great Brittain	Montreal	Albion	11 Jun 1821
Charlotte	10	F	Farrier	Great Brittain	United States	Dapper	21 Aug 1828
Chas. D.	6	M	...	Great Brittain	Montreal	Albion	11 Jun 1821
Dorothe	22	F	Gentlewoman	British	Brittain	Govenor Lincoln	15 Feb 1827
Eliza	2	F		Scotland	United States	Indus	5 Sep 1827
Eliza	3	F	Farrier	Great Britain	United States	Dapper	21 Aug 1828
Eliza	30		Carpenter	Great Britan	United States	Newry	11 Jul 1827
Elizabeth Ann Waite	34	F	Lady	England	America	Panthea	18 Jul 1823
Elizazabeth	25	F	Servant	Ireland	United States	St. Michaels	18 Jul 1826
Esther	14		unknown	Cork, E.	England	Packet	27 Aug 1822
George	5	M	Farrier	Great Britain	United States	Dapper	21 Aug 1828
George	27	M	Wallhauseman	England	United States	Orozimbo	11 Aug 1823
Hannah	3	F		Bermuda	England	Florida	28 Jun 1825
Harriet, of Baltimore	46	F	Lady	England	America	Mary Lord	26 Oct 1829
Henry	26	M	Weaver	Ireland	United States	Princess Charlotte	26 Apr 1827
James	6	M		Scotland	United States	Indus	5 Sep 1827
James	20	M	Clerk	G. Britain	U. States	Camillus	8 Sep 1828
James	21	M	Farmer	Scotland	U. States	Camillus	17 Sep 1823
James	27	M	Mechanic	Ireland	United States	Concordia	25 Aug 1827
Jas. Chas.	35	M	Advocate	Canada	Canada	New York	19 Nov 1828
Jean	49	F	Wife	Scotland	United States	Tom	2 Jul 1827
Jess	18	F		Scotland	United States	Belmont	30 Aug 1828
Jno. D.	8/12	M		Great Britain	United States	Brutus	6 May 1828
John	28	M	Labourer	Ireland	United States	Wilson	22 Jun 1824
John Henry	26	M	Solicitor	British	Brittain	Govenor Lincoln	15 Feb 1827
Juan Jose	35	M	Gentn.	Spain	Spain	Fabius	2 Oct 1826
L. S.	40	M	None	England	United States	Manhattan	24 Oct 1825
Magt.	28 1/12	F	Servant	Ireland	United States	Wilson	27 Jun 1826
Margaret	7	F	Child	Scotland	United States	Tom	2 Jul 1827
Margaret	20	F		Great Britain	United States	Brutus	6 May 1828
Maria	2/12	F	Farrier	Great Britain	United States	Dapper	21 Aug 1828
Maria	32	F	Farrier	Great Britain	United States	Dapper	21 Aug 1828
Mary	4	F		Scotland	United States	Indus	5 Sep 1827
Mary	13			Great Britan	United States	Newry	11 Jul 1827
Mary	28	F	None	England	New York	Brighton	19 Aug 1829
Mary	28	F	None	England		Brighton	19 Aug 1829
Mary	30	F		Scotland	United States	Indus	5 Sep 1827
Mary	70	F		Bermuda	N. York	Magnet	10 Jul 1820
Peter	12	M	Child	Scotland	United States	Tom	2 Jul 1827
Petre	43	M	Musision	Irereland	America	Carolina Ann	20 Jun 1825
R. J.	30	M	Merchant	St. Croix	United States	Carlo	28 Jun 1826
Robert	50	M	Gardner	England	United States	Hamlet	25 Aug 1825
Saml.	21	M	Clark	Scotland	Canada	Honduras Packet	30 Jun 1823
Sidney	22	M	Carpenter	United States	U.S. States	Thrasher	4 Dec 1822
Thomas	31	M	Farrier	Great Britain	United States	Dapper	21 Aug 1828
Thomas	35	M	Merchant	England	Ut. States	Courier	13 Jul 1826

NAMES OF PASSENGERS	AGE	SEX	OCCUPATIONS	COUNTRY TO WHICH THEY BELONG	COUNTRY THEY INTEND TO INHABIT	SHIPS/DATES OF ARRIVAL	
GRANT (cont'd)							
Thomas	37	M	Agent to the Royal Naval Institute at Baltimore	England	England	Florida	28 Jun 1825
William	7	M	Farrier	Great Britain	United States	Dapper	21 Aug 1828
William	25	M	Mason	Scotland	United States	Commerce	17 Jul 1823
William	28	M	Labourer	Scotland	United States	Mary & Susan	5 Aug 1828
William, of Baltimore	23	M	Gentleman	England	America	Mary Lord	26 Oct 1829
William, of Baltimore	50	M	Gentleman	England	America	Mary Lord	26 Oct 1829
Wm.	10	M		Scotland	United States	Indus	5 Sep 1827
Wm.	35	M		Scotland	United States	Indus	5 Sep 1827
Wm. D.	44			England	U. States	Brown	11 Jun 1827
GRANVILLE, Bevill L.	28	M	Mechanic	U.S.	U.S.	Panthea	22 Jul 1826
GRAOS, William	24	M	Farmer	England	America	Francis & Henrietta	11 Jul 1823
GRAPE, Thos. R.	20	M		Great Britain	U. States Ame	Maria	22 May 1822
GRASETT, Henry	48	M	Surgeon to H. B. Forbes	England	Cannada	Acasta	28 Jan 1823
GRASON, Robert		M	Joiner	Scotland		Eliza Grant	29 Aug 1829
*3 August Jumped over board insane							
GRASS, Carl	22	M	Agriculture	France	United States	Henri IV	14 Oct 1829
GRATE, Joseph	25	M	Mercht.	Havanna	Spain	Orozimbo	16 Apr 1821
GRATER, Francois	32			Germany	Interior	Desdemona	12 Jun 1826
GRATICOA, Roman	25	M	...	Columbia	U. States	Victory	21 Jun 1824
GRATTAN, Edward	17	M	Gentn.	Ireland	United States	Dublin Packet	22 Oct 1821
GRATTEN, Thomas	20	M	Shoe Maker	Ireland	United States	Enterprize	23 Jul 1827
GRATTIN, Wm.	21	M	Lab.	Rathangar	K. Co.	Howard Douglass	11 May 1827
GRATTON, B.	14	M				Pleiades	13 Nov 1826
George	40	F	Spinster	England	United States	Mary & Harriet	9 Mar 1829
John	21	M	Merchant	Ireland	America	Erin	14 Feb 1820
Susan	30	F	None			Pleiades	13 Nov 1826
GRATZNELL, Wm.	27	M	Farm	France		Pallas	14 Jun 1828
GRAVANO, P.	34	M		Spain	Spain	Fabius	3 Jun 1825
GRAVE, Henry J.	23	M	Farmer	England	England	Criterion	29 May 1822
GRAVEA, Manuel	22		Gentleman	Spain	Spain	Florida	1 Dec 1828
GRAVELEY, John, Mr.	27	M	Merchant	England	England	Florida	26 Sep 1826
John	24	M	Merchant	Great Britain	United States	James Cropper	27 Sep 1821
GRAVELY, John	23	M	Merchant	Gt. Britain	U. States	Napolean	26 Sep 1828
John	26	M	Merchant	Great Britain	United States	Thomas Dickason	14 Sep 1827
GRAVES, A.	19	M	Merchant	American	New York	Bolivar	10 Aug 1827
A.	50	M	Merchant	U. States	U. States	Adze	24 Jul 1820
A., Supercargo	54	M	Mariner	Spain	U. States	Sally	7 Nov 1821
Ann	1			G. Britain	U. States	Hamilton	28 Apr 1828
Ann	4	F		Ireland	United States	Sarah G.	15 May 1828
Anthy.	67 2/12	M	Mariner	New York	New York	Victor	3 Jul 1829
Antonia	46	M	Mariner	Portugal	U. States	Union	21 Nov 1822
Antonio	55	M	Mariner	U. States	U. States	Eliza Davidson	28 Jul 1828
David	31	M	Farmer	England	England	Venus	15 Apr 1822
Edwd.	43	M	Merchant	England	U. States	James Cropper	17 Jun 1825
Ellen	6	F		Ireland	United States	Sarah G.	15 May 1828
Frances	26	F		England	United States	Ariadne	7 May 1821
George	23	M	Rope Maker	Great Britain	United States	Dapper	14 Mar 1828
George R.	23		Weaver	Great Britain	United States	Thomas Dickason	29 Aug 1828
Hannah	27			G. Britain	U. States	Hamilton	28 Apr 1828
Jane	20	F	Servant	England	America	Ann	3 Jul 1820
Jane R.	32			Great Britain	United States	Thomas Dickason	29 Aug 1828
John	40	M	Weaver	England	United States	Delta	24 Oct 1829
Joseph	2	M		Ireland	United States	Sarah G.	15 May 1828
Joseph	12			G. Britain	U. States	Hamilton	28 Apr 1828
Mary	6			G. Britain	U. States	Hamilton	28 Apr 1828
Mary	25			G. Britain	U. States	Hamilton	28 Apr 1828
Mary	38	F		America	U. States	Amity	21 Feb 1823
Mary	42	F		Ireland	United States	Sarah G.	15 May 1828

NAMES OF PASSENGERS	A G E	S E X	OCCUPATIONS	COUNTRY TO WHICH THEY BELONG	COUNTRY THEY INTEND TO INHABIT	SHIPS/DATES OF ARRIVAL	
GRAVES (cont'd)							
Richard, Admiral	63	M	Admrl.	England	America	Liverpool Packet	23 Mar 1822
Saml. Collolan, Eqr.	34	M	Gentleman	England	England	Manhattan	21 Sep 1822
Samuel R.	31		Weaver	Great Britain	United States	Thomas Dickason	29 Aug 1828
Seth	26	M	Jeweller	U. States	United States	Neptune	5 Jul 1820
Sophia	1	F		Ireland	United States	Sarah G.	15 May 1828
Stephen	8	M		Ireland	United States	Sarah G.	15 May 1828
Thos.	40	M	Seaman	U. States	U. States	Boston	26 Sep 1820
William L.	27		None	United States	United States	Bayard	17 Dec 1827
Wm.	23	M	Merchant	New York	New York	Douglass	3 Nov 1823
Wm.	27		Farmer	G. Britain	U. States	Hamilton	28 Apr 1828
Wm.	35	M	Merchant	America	U. States	Amity	21 Feb 1823
Wm.	39	M	Weaver	Scotland	United States	Orozimbo	5 Mar 1827
GRAVIER, J.	23		Merchant	New Orleans	U. States	Brown	11 Jun 1827
GRAVILLON,							
Augustin	23 11/12	M	Merchant	France	New York	Dawn	12 Jun 1826
GRAVIN, Ruth	20	F		Great Britain	United States	Ganges	8 Jul 1820
GRAVIS, Anthony	53	M	Merchant	U.S. of Amer	U.S. of Amer	Harmony	20 Nov 1820
GRAY, —,							
Child & Sevant	25			Bermuda		Ocean	28 Jul 1820
—, Mr.	18	M	Merchant	Boston	U. States	Nestor	10 Jan 1823
—, Mrs.	49	F		Scotland	U. States	James & Margaret	15 Jul 1822
—, Wife	24	F		Bermuda		Ocean	28 Jul 1820
...	22			Ireland	U.S.	Hibernia	27 Jun 1821
...	26 5/12	M	Merchant	Denmark	Denmark	Elias Burger	18 Sep 1821
Alexr.	36	M	Shoemaker	Great Britain	United States	William Dawson	18 Jun 1827
Andrew	14	M	None	Ireland	United States	Lord Wellington	28 May 1827
Andrew	24	M	Merchant	Great Britain	United States	Florida	2 Sep 1822
Andrew	25	M	Merchant	Gt. Britain	United States	Seeds	29 Sep 1824
Arthur	30	M	Weaver	Great Britain	United States	Colossus	5 Jun 1827
Biddy	7	F	Labourer	Great Britian	United States	Princess Charlotte	6 Sep 1828
Biddy	20	F	Servant	Ireland	United States	Josephine	30 Apr 1828
Biddy	22	F	Labourer	Ireland	U. States	Two Marys	20 Apr 1825
Biddy	27	F	Labourer	Great Britain	United States	Princess Charlotte	6 Sep 1828
Bridget	22	F		Ireland	America	Plutarch	18 Jul 1826
Cathrine	13	F	One Family [Peter]	France	United States	Henri IV	2 Oct 1828
Daniel	25	M	Merchant	United States	United States	Climax	24 Oct 1829
David	6	M		St. Thomas	St. Croix	Chase	2 Oct 1823
David	12	M	None	Ireland	United States	Lord Wellington	28 May 1827
David	25	M	Farmer	Scotland	United States	Margaret Bogle	11 Jun 1824
David, Mr.	35	M	Merchant	Gt. Britain	Gt. Britain	James Cropper	2 Aug 1827
Edward	20	M	Chymist	Great Britain	United States	Ann	24 Sep 1822
Eleanor	45	F	Spinster	Ireland	United States	Thomas	13 Dec 1827
Eliza	18	F	None	Ireland	United States	Lord Wellington	28 May 1827
Elizabeth	13	F	Spinster	Great Britain	United States	Ann	24 Sep 1822
Elizabeth	26	F	None	Gt. Britain	United States	Neptune	23 Jan 1826
Elizabeth	27 1/12	F		Great Briton	Canada	Brighton	12 Jun 1826
Felicite	15	F	One Family [Peter]	France	United States	Henri IV	2 Oct 1828
Francis	13 3/12	M		Great Briton	Canada	Brighton	12 Jun 1826
Hester, Mr.	23	F		Ireland	St. Croix	Chase	2 Oct 1823
Hugh	21	M	Weaver	Ireland	United States	John Dickinson	18 Feb 1822
Isabella	23	F		England	U. States	Union	10 Mar 1823
Isabella	37	F	None	Scotland	U. States	Camillus	27 Jun 1826
James	6	M		Irereland	America	Carolina Ann	20 Jun 1825
James	7			Scotland	U. States	James & Margaret	15 Jul 1822
James	17	M	Blacksmith	Scotland	U. States	Rosina	27 Feb 1824
James	22	M	Clerk	Ireland	United States	William & Henry	19 Jul 1822
James	25		Clerk	Ireland	Great Britain	Robert Burns	14 Jun 1824
James	26	M	Labourer	Great Britain	United States	India	5 Sep 1827
James	26	M	Labourer	Ireland	America	Josephine	8 Dec 1827
James	27	M	Farmer	Gt. Britain	United States	Neptune	23 Jan 1826
James	30 2/12	M	Gentleman	Great Briton	Canada	Brighton	12 Jun 1826

NAMES OF PASSENGERS	AGE	SEX	OCCUPATIONS	COUNTRY TO WHICH THEY BELONG	COUNTRY THEY INTEND TO INHABIT	SHIPS/DATES OF ARRIVAL	
GRAY (cont'd)							
James	40	M	Farmer	Great Britian	United States	Andes	19 Aug 1829
James	42	M	Farmer	Scotland	U. States	James & Margaret	15 Jul 1822
James	60	M	Labourer	Ireland	United States	Lord Wellington	28 May 1827
Jane	22	F	Spinster	Great Britain	United States	Ann	24 Sep 1822
Jane	33	F		Irereland	America	Carolina Ann	20 Jun 1825
Jas.	27	M	Mechanic	U. States	U. States	Beluga	26 Apr 1825
Jno.	10			Scotland	U. States	James & Margaret	15 Jul 1822
John	2	M		England	U. States	Union	10 Mar 1823
John	23	M	Farmer	Ireland	United States	Fabius	4 Jun 1828
John	24	M	Iron Founder	Great Britain	United States	Courier	26 Jun 1827
John	28	M	Labourer			Lady of the Lake	23 Aug 1828
John H.	23	M	Merchant	Boston		Desdemona	12 Jun 1826
Laurence	25	M	Mason	Great Britain	England	Jay	18 Apr 1823
Margaret	12		Farmer	Ireland	United States	Carolina Ann	12 Sep 1823
Martha	22	F	Servant	Ireland	United States	William & George	14 May 1828
Mary	8			Scotland	U. States	James & Margaret	15 Jul 1822
Mary	32	F	One Family [Peter]	France	United States	Henri IV	2 Oct 1828
Mary	60	F	...	Ireland	United States	General Putnam	20 Jun 1825
Mary	75	F		Ireland	United States	Fabius	4 Jun 1828
Mary Ann	16	F	Spinster	Great Britain	United States	Ann	24 Sep 1822
Michael	43	M	Taylor	Great Britian	United States	Princess Charlotte	6 Sep 1828
Pat	42	M	Labourer	Great Britian	United States	Princess Charlotte	6 Sep 1828
Patrick	21	M		Ireland	New York	Lady Hunter	5 Jun 1826
Peter	40	M	Taylor	France	United States	Henri IV	2 Oct 1828
Rew	12			Scotland	U. States	James & Margaret	15 Jul 1822
Robert	20	M	Labourer	Ireland	United States	Lord Wellington	28 May 1827
Robert	31 6/12		Shoe Maker	Ireland	America	Farmer	3 May 1824
Robert	36	M	Farmer	Ireland	United States	Fabius	4 Jun 1828
Robt.	16	M	Labourer	Ireland	U. States	Atlantic	19 Aug 1825
Robt.	85	M	Farmer	Ireland	United States	Fabius	4 Jun 1828
S.	23	M	Merchant	U. States	U. States	John Wells	14 Oct 1823
Saml.	31	M	Merchant	U. States	U. States	Prize	10 Jun 1824
Thomas	31	M				Lady of the Lake	23 Aug 1828
*left ship							
Thomas	32	M	Merchant	St. Thomas	St. Croix	Chase	2 Oct 1823
Thos.	19	M	Merchant			Hanford	17 Jul 1828
Thos.	23	M	Labourer	Ireland	United States	Trident	16 May 1826
Thos.	30	M	Mercht.	Bermuda		Ocean	28 Jul 1820
Thos., Mr., Jr.	24	M	Docter	U.S.A.		François I	19 Nov 1828
V.	8	M	Merchant	Havana	U. States	Hero	3 Sep 1823
W.	9			Scotland	U. States	James & Margaret	15 Jul 1822
W.	18	M	Merchant	U. States	U. States	John Wells	14 Oct 1823
W.	30	M	Sailor	England	U. States	Hiram	17 Jun 1826
Walter	48	M	Clerk	Gt. Britain	United States	Neptune	23 Jan 1826
William	20	M	Labourer	Ireland	U. States	Josephine	7 May 1827
William	23	M	Hater	Ireland	America	Plutarch	18 Jul 1826
William	23	M	Labourer	Ireland	United States	William & George	14 May 1828
William	23	M	Weaver	Ireland	New York	Trusty	12 Sep 1828
William	28	M	Farmer	Bristol, Engl.	...	Warrior	19 May 1828
William	45	M	Mariner	U. States	U. States	Leopard	31 Jul 1824
William	49	M	Glass blower	Great Britain	United States	Ann	24 Sep 1822
Winthrop	22 4/12	M	Gent.	America	America	Napoleon	26 May 1828
Wm.	18	M	Laborer	Ireland	U. States	Howard Douglass	29 Jan 1828
Wm.	28		Merchant	Pennsylvania	United States	Robert Burns	18 Jun 1821
Wm.	42	M	Seamen	U. States	U. States	Wm. Tell	22 Jul 1828
GRAYCOX, Wm.	30	M	Farmer	America	America	Nancy	18 Aug 1821

NAMES OF PASSENGERS	AGE	SEX	OCCUPATIONS	COUNTRY TO WHICH THEY BELONG	COUNTRY THEY INTEND TO INHABIT	SHIPS/DATES OF ARRIVAL	
GRAYSON, Ellen	35	F	None	Ireland	United States	John Wells	11 May 1827
John	22	M	Joiner	Great Britain	U.S. of America	Gratitude	3 Oct 1829
John	40	M	Farmer	Ireland	United States	Mary & Harriet	9 Mar 1829
Mary	54	M	Clerk	Great Britain	New York	Superior	5 Sep 1827
William	40	M	Doctor of Medicine	United States	United States	Robert Edwards	3 Oct 1829
Wm.	37	M	Joiner	Great Britain	New York	Superior	5 Sep 1827
GRAZALEZ, M.	40	M	Merchant	Spain	Spain	Richmond Packet	30 Oct 1827
GRE..., Lewis	40	M	Merchant	France	America	Saluda	18 Jun 1825
GREADY, Madalin	31	F	Waserwoman	Ireland		Quatre Freres	29 Jul 1828
GREAINGLE, Catherine	24	F	Agriculturist	France	U.S.	Helen	3 May 1828
GREAN, William	38	M	Merchant	United States	United States	Bogota	28 Mar 1827
GREASLEY, Ann	21	F		Great Britain	U. States	Great Britain	18 Mar 1828
Henry	34	M	Farmer	Great Britain	U. States	Great Britain	18 Mar 1828
Martha	1	F		Great Britain	U. States	Great Britain	18 Mar 1828
GREASTON, George	13	M	Basketmaker	England	United States	Andes	2 Oct 1828
GREATREM, J.	35	M	Labourer	G. Britann		Manchester	29 Aug 1828
GREAVATT, Geo.	37	M	Farmer	England	United States	New Packet	7 Aug 1826
Sarah	31	F	None	England	United States	New Packet	7 Aug 1826
GREAVE, Robt.	77	M	Farmer	England	New York	Joseph Hume	26 Oct 1829
GREAVES, Alexdr.	46	M	Gentleman	England	U.S.	Leeds	7 Nov 1828
Betsey	47	F	None	Great Britain	United States	Richmond	18 Feb 1820
Chas.	26	M	Mason	Great Britain	United States	Penelope	11 Jun 1827
Dorothy	19 6/12	F	None	Great Britain	America	Hannibal	12 Oct 1826
Edward	44	M	Merchant	Great Britain	United States	Leeds	29 Sep 1823
Henry	23		Farmer	England	United States	Corinthian	30 May 1828
John	4		None	Great Britain	United States	Richmond	18 Feb 1820
John, Mr.	34	M	Gentleman	England	England	Florida	26 Sep 1826
Joseph	43	M	Farmer	Great Britain	United States	Richmond	18 Feb 1820
Martha	9	F	None	Great Britain	United States	Richmond	18 Feb 1820
Warren Philip	37	M		Great Britain	U. States	Great Britain	18 Mar 1828
GREAVS, Matthew	36	M	Weaver	Lancaster Shire	England	Helicon	3 Aug 1826
GREBAN, Wm.	30	M	Laborer			Emulous	19 Feb 1822
GREE, Albert G.	20	M	Merchant	U. States	U. States	Sarah	17 Mar 1829
GREEEN, Isaac	45	M	Farmer	United States	United States	Prize	23 Sep 1822
GREEGG, Michael	25	M		Ireland	United States	Thompson	12 Sep 1827
GREEK, Jane	41	F	Spinster	Ireland	United States	Fabius	4 Jun 1828
GREELEY, Martin	22	M		Ireland	U. States	Howard	25 Jul 1823
GREEN, —, Mr.	28	F		England	U.S.	Henri IV	14 Sep 1827
—, Mrs.	24	F		U. States	U. States	Mary	24 Feb 1823
—, Mrs.	25	F		England		Robert Edwards	8 Nov 1825
—, Mrs. Green baby	3/12	F		England		Robert Edwards	8 Nov 1825
Alexr.	22 6/12	M	Merchant	Ireland	United States	Atlantic	21 Jul 1827
Alice	30	F	None	England	United States	Mary & Harriet	9 Mar 1829
Ann	3	F		Great Britain	United States	Isaac Hicks	10 Jul 1827
Ann	6 6/12	F	her Daughter [Rebecca]	Great Britain	Utica Onida	Venus	8 Sep 1820
Ann	17	M	Spinster	England	England	Venus	15 Apr 1822
Ann	24	F		Ireland	United States	Nancey	8 Jun 1822
Ann	26			England	U. States	Corinthian	8 Oct 1828
Anthony	12	M	None	England	U. States	Montgomery	18 Oct 1828
Anthony	26		Weaver	Ireland	United States	Robert Burns	30 May 1823
Arch	13	F		Great Britain	United States	Freake	25 Aug 1829
Barney	20	M	Laborer	Ireland	United States	Sylvester Healy	14 Jun 1825
Biddy	15	F		Limerick	N. York	Thomas & William	25 May 1827
Bridget	18	F	Spinster	Ireland	United States	Wilson	4 Oct 1827
Briget	40	F	None	Ireland	New York	Concordia	12 Oct 1826
Catharan	11	F	None	Ireland	U. States	Franklin	7 Jul 1828
Cathrine	18	F	...	Ireland	United States	General Putnam	20 Jun 1825
Caty.	7	F		G. Britain	U. States	Cosmo	15 May 1827
Charles	17	M	B. N. Service	England	West Indies	Soto	11 Nov 1828
Charles	21	M	Weaver	England	America U. States	La Grange	27 Sep 1826
Charles	40	M	Merchant	United States	United States	John Jay	8 May 1828
Christian Fredrich	33	M	Grocer	American	U.S.A.	Robert Wilson	2 Dec 1828
Cornelia	30	F		U. States	U. States	Silas Richards	29 Oct 1828
Cs.	6	M		G. Britain	U. States	Cosmo	15 May 1827
Daniel	17	M	...	Ireland	United States	General Putnam	20 Jun 1825
Daniel	19	M	Labourer	England	U. States	Montgomery	18 Oct 1828

NAMES OF PASSENGERS	AGE	SEX	OCCUPATIONS	COUNTRY TO WHICH THEY BELONG	COUNTRY THEY INTEND TO INHABIT	SHIPS/DATES OF ARRIVAL	
GREEN (cont'd)							
David	22	M	Farmer	England	U.S. States	Splendid	14 Aug 1829
E.	25	F	Servant	New York	United States	Astrea	16 Nov 1825
Edward	55	M	Farmer	Pensylvania	Pensylvania	Anthusa	24 Aug 1825
Eliz	16	F	...	Ireland	United States	General Putnam	20 Jun 1825
Eliza	12	F		G. Britain	U. States	Cosmo	15 May 1827
Eliza	22	F		Ireland	United States	Nancey	8 Jun 1822
Elizabeth	14	M	Spinster	England	England	Venus	15 Apr 1822
Elizabeth	18	F		U. States	United States	Loire	12 Dec 1820
Elizabeth	27	F		Great Britain	United States	Samuel Wright	12 Oct 1829
Elizabeth	30	F	Servent	United States		Britannia	20 Jun 1827
Elizabeth	33	F	None	Bristoll		Aurora	8 Jun 1827
Elizabeth R.	2	F	Child	Ireland	United States	Sarah G.	11 Jan 1828
Esther	11	F		G. Britain	U. States	Cosmo	15 May 1827
F.	4	F	Farmer	Germany	United States	Lydia	18 Jun 1828
Fisher	30	M	Cooper	United States	United States	Sarah	24 Mar 1828
Frances	10	M	None	Ireland	New York	Concordia	12 Oct 1826
Frances	45	M	Cabinet Maker	Ireland	New York	Concordia	12 Oct 1826
Francis	7			Hampshire/ Sutton	New York	Venus	12 Apr 1821
Fs.	...	M		G. Britain	U. States	Cosmo	15 May 1827
Fy.	14	F		G. Britain	U. States	Cosmo	15 May 1827
Geo.	31	M	Mariner	U. States		Cumberland	5 May 1828
George	4 1/12	M		England	U.S. of America	Illinois	16 Jun 1821
George	28	M	Labourer	Ireland	United States	William & George	14 May 1828
George	58	M	Farmer	Great Britain	United States	Freake	25 Aug 1829
Harriet	38	F		G. Britain	U. States	Cosmo	15 May 1827
Henrietta	30			Hampshire/ Sutton	New York	Venus	12 Apr 1821
Henry	8	M	Mariner	United States	United States	Prince Edward	13 Apr 1824
Henry	27	M	Labourer	England	America	John Adams	2 Aug 1827
Henry, Master	9	M	Farmer	England	U. States	Acasta	11 Dec 1826
Herman A.	26	M	Merchant	U. States	U. States	Sarah	17 Mar 1829
Hy.	1	M		G. Britain	U. States	Cosmo	15 May 1827
J. D.	46	M	Mariner	U. States	U. States	Jane	13 Dec 1824
J. F.	28	M	Merchant	U. States	U. States	Seneca	7 Nov 1825
Jacob	36	M	Farmer	Germany	United States	Lydia	18 Jun 1828
Jacob, Profr.	37	M	Professor	U. States	U. States	Sully	24 Oct 1828
James	17 1/12	M	Gentleman	England	United States	Young Phoenix	26 Jul 1824
James	19	M		Limerick	N. York	Thomas & William	25 May 1827
James	19	M	Joiner	Gt. Britain	United States	Meteor	19 Aug 1829
James	20	M	Labourer	Ireland	Baltimore	Lima	5 Aug 1829
James	22	M	Merchant	Ireland	St. John, N.B.	Ann Maria	7 Aug 1826
James	24	M	Farmer	England		Manhattan	22 May 1827
James	25 10/12		Farmer	Scotland	U.S. of America	Helen	8 Feb 1822
James	27	M	Farmer	England	United States	Andes	2 Oct 1828
James	34	M	Hatter	Great Britain	United States	Roman	10 May 1828
James	38	M	Ship Master	America	America	Friends	28 Sep 1822
James	50	M	Farmer	England	United States	Silas Richards	27 Oct 1825
Jane	20	F	...	Ireland	United States	General Putnam	20 Jun 1825
Jane	43 10/12	F		England	U.S. of America	Illinois	16 Jun 1821
Jane McH.	36 2/12	F	Wife	England	United States	Robert Edwards	3 Oct 1829
Jas.	33	M	Merchant	England	U. States	Lycurgus	3 Dec 1821
Jesse	28	M	Mechanic	G. Britain	America	Quill	19 Jun 1828
Jnn.	50	M	Mariner	United States	United States	Prince Edward	13 Apr 1824
Jno.	21	M	None	Columbia	U. States	Theresa	10 Dec 1825
Jno.	27	M	Professor Musick	England		Robert Edwards	8 Nov 1825
Johanna	38	F	None	U. States	U. States	Duplicate	22 May 1827
John	1 1/2	M		Gt. Britain	United States	Meteor	19 Aug 1829
John	5		Farmer	England	United States	Hugh Johnson	11 Jun 1828
John	5			England	U. States	Corinthian	8 Oct 1828
John	14	M	...	Ireland	United States	General Putnam	20 Jun 1825
John	17	M		America	America	Friends	28 Sep 1822
John	19	M	Tailor	G. Britain	U. States	Camillus	8 Sep 1828
John	25	M	Dye Sinker	Great Britain	U. States	Great Britain	18 Mar 1828
John	26	M	Labourer	Limerick	N. York	Thomas & William	25 May 1827

497

NAMES OF PASSENGERS	AGE	SEX	OCCUPATIONS	COUNTRY TO WHICH THEY BELONG	COUNTRY THEY INTEND TO INHABIT	SHIPS/DATES OF ARRIVAL	
GREEN (cont'd)							
John	29	M	Merchant	Gt. Britain	New York	Stephania	2 Jan 1824
John	30	M	Farmer	Ireland		Cuba	24 Jun 1822
John	31	M	Mariner	American	America	Britania	27 Mar 1820
John	31	M	Cooper			Hanford	17 Jul 1828
John	34	M	Farmer	England	United States	Mary & Harriet	9 Mar 1829
John	39		Millwright	Sutton/Sutton	New York	Venus	12 Apr 1821
John	48	M	Farmer	England	U.S. of America	Illinois	16 Jun 1821
John C.	28	M	Merchant	U. States	U. States	Panama	9 Apr 1828
Jos. H.	30		Mechanic	United States	U.N. States	James	27 May 1824
Joseph	8/12	M		England	U.S. of America	Illinois	16 Jun 1821
Joseph	20	M	Clerk	Great Britan	United States	Silvanus Jenkins	10 Mar 1827
M.	2	F	Farmer	Germany	United States	Lydia	18 Jun 1828
Maria	1	F	None	England	United States	Mary & Harriet	9 Mar 1829
Martha	26	F		Gt. Britain	United States	Meteor	19 Aug 1829
Martha	35	F	None	England	United States	Mary & Harriet	9 Mar 1829
Martin	40	M	Labourer	England	U. States	Comet	23 Aug 1828
Mary	1 1/2	F	None	Bristoll		Aurora	8 Jun 1827
Mary	19	F	Spinster	Ireland	United States	Fabius	4 Jun 1828
Mary	21	F	Farmer, Labourer or Spinster	Ireland	U. States	Meteor	4 Oct 1827
Mary	21	F		Great Britain	United States	Freake	25 Aug 1829
Mary	21 3/12	M	Spinster	England	England	Venus	15 Apr 1822
Mary	22	F	Servant	Ireland	United States	Sarah G.	11 Jan 1828
Mary	23	F	Servant	Ireland	United States	William & George	14 May 1828
Mary	25	F		American	America	Britania	27 Mar 1820
Mary	25	F		Great Britain	United States	Isaac Hicks	10 Jul 1827
Mary	60	F		Gt. Britain		Corinthian	27 Oct 1829
Mary Ann	6			England	U. States	Corinthian	8 Oct 1828
Mary Jane	2 2/12		Spinster	Scotland	U.S. of America	Helen	8 Feb 1822
Mathew, Mr.	50	M	Farmer	England	U. States	Acasta	11 Dec 1826
Matthew	26	M	Machinist	Great Britain	United States	Colossus	5 Jun 1827
Michl.	22	M	Labourer	Ireland		Marchioness	13 May 1828
Naby	22	F	Spinster	Ireland	United States	Wilson	28 Nov 1828
Nancy	19	F	Spinster	Ireland	United States	Dublin Packet	13 Oct 1828
Nancy	21	F	None	Ireland	U. States	Franklin	7 Jul 1828
Nancy	22 3/12		Spinster	Scotland	U.S. of America	Helen	8 Feb 1822
Oliver	21	M	Gentleman	Co...	U. States	Henry	13 Oct 1827
Oliver, twin	10/12			England	U. States	Corinthian	8 Oct 1828
P. C.	32	M	Merchant	U. States	U. States	Union	21 Jul 1825
Patk.	12	M		Limerick	N. York	Thomas & William	25 May 1827
Patrick	22	M	Labourer	Ireland	United States	Trio	31 Oct 1827
Peter C.	23		Mechanic	United States	U.N. States	James	27 May 1824
Ralph	37		Farmer	England	New York	Rufus King	3 Sep 1822
Rebecca	18	F		Great Britain	United States	Freake	25 Aug 1829
Rebecca	54	F		Great Britain	United States	Freake	25 Aug 1829
Richard	36 6/12	M	Cagemaker	England	United States	Robert Edwards	3 Oct 1829
Richard	40	M	Merchant	Great Britain	United States	Florida	2 Oct 1828
Richd.	42	M	Merchant	G. Brittian	U. States	Pacific	19 Oct 1829
Richd., Major	40	M	Major in the ... Rgmt.	England	England	William Thompson	29 Jan 1824
Robert	20	M	Mechanic	England	United States	Concordia	25 Aug 1827
Robert	25	M	Seaman	Ireland	United States	Aurora	27 Apr 1825
Robert	33	M	Seaman	U. States	U. States	Golden Age	6 Jul 1821
Robert	36	M	Labourer			John & Edward	25 Aug 1820
Robert	40	M	Joiner	Great Britain	United States	Samuel Wright	12 Oct 1829
Rose	9	F	...	Ireland	United States	General Putnam	20 Jun 1825
Rose	50	F	...	Ireland	United States	General Putnam	20 Jun 1825
Rose, Miss	6	F	Farmer	England	U. States	Acasta	11 Dec 1826
Samuel	1	M		U. States	United States	Loire	12 Dec 1820
Samuel	23	M	Farmer	Great Briton	New York	Brighton	12 Jun 1826
Samuel	25		Merchant	U. States	U. States	Swan	29 May 1821
Samuel	33	M	Wool Comber	Great Britain		Olive Branch	9 Oct 1829
Sarah	23	F	Lady	England	United States	Cambria	8 Oct 1828
Sarah	23	F	Wife	Great Brittan	United States	Cambria	11 Feb 1829
Sarah	40			London/London	New York	Venus	12 Apr 1821
Sarah	40			England	United States	Hugh Johnson	11 Jun 1828

NAMES OF PASSENGERS	AGE	SEX	OCCUPATIONS	COUNTRY TO WHICH THEY BELONG	COUNTRY THEY INTEND TO INHABIT	SHIPS/DATES OF ARRIVAL	
GREEN (cont'd)							
Sofer	26 1/12	F		England	U.S. of America	Illinois	16 Jun 1821
Sophia	34	F	Farmer	Germany	United States	Lydia	18 Jun 1828
Susan, twin	10/12			England	U. States	Corinthian	8 Oct 1828
Thomas	26			England	U. States	Corinthian	8 Oct 1828
Thomas	27	M	Labourer	Lancaster	Lancaster	Howard Douglass	11 May 1827
Thomas	32	M	Manufacturer	Great Britain	United States	Illinois	9 Oct 1820
Thomas	39	M	Labourer	Bristoll		Aurora	8 Jun 1827
Thos.	19	M	Farmer	Great Britain	United States	Freake	25 Aug 1829
Thos.	24	M	None	Great Britain	United States	Eliza Barker	3 Jul 1826
Thos.	37		Labourer	England	United States	Hugh Johnson	11 Jun 1828
Tim	27	M	Farmer	England	U. States	Thomas Ritchie	2 Jul 1827
W.	6	F	Farmer	Germany	United States	Lydia	18 Jun 1828
W. W.	38	M	Merchant	America		Jane	18 Feb 1825
William	2 6/12	M		England	U.S. of America	Illinois	16 Jun 1821
William	26	M	Joiner	Gt. Britain	United States	Meteor	19 Aug 1829
William	27	M	Labourer	Great Britain	United States	Isaac Hicks	10 Jul 1827
William	34	M	Watchmaker	England	U.S.A.	Hudson	21 Aug 1829
William A.	19	M	Gentleman	New York	American	Midas	9 May 1827
Willm. J.	7 6/12	M	Son	England	United States	Robert Edwards	3 Oct 1829
Wm.		M	Servant, Negro		U.S.	Emma	24 Jun 1825
Wm.	26	M		Great Britain	America	Lady Gallatin	21 Jun 1820
Wm.	35	M	Merchant	U. States	U. States	Silas Richards	29 Oct 1828
Wm.	36		Labourer	England	United States	Hugh Johnson	11 Jun 1828
Wm.	39	M	Farmer	G. Britain	U. States	Cosmo	15 May 1827
GREENAN, Rose	9/12	F		Ireland	United States	Meteor	27 Sep 1826
GREENATT, Abm.	26	M		England	England	John Wills	21 May 1824
GREENE, Abby	3	F	Child	Ireland	United States	Dublin Packet	23 May 1828
Ann	25	F		Great Britian	United States	Andes	19 Aug 1829
John C.	22		Merchant	United States	United States	James Monroe	11 Dec 1821
John H.	30	M	Merchant	Boston	Boston	Hector	30 Dec 1820
Margaret	28	F	Wife	Ireland	United States	Dublin Packet	23 May 1828
William	28	M	Farmer	Ireland	United States	Dublin Packet	23 May 1828
GREENFIELD,							
Alexander	27	M	Farmer	Ireland	United States	Carolina Ann	14 May 1827
Ann	1 6/12	F		Great Britain	United States	Diana	6 Jul 1829
Edwin	9	M		Great Britain	United States	Diana	6 Jul 1829
Emma	3	F		Great Britain	United States	Diana	6 Jul 1829
Enoch	8	M		Great Britain	United States	Diana	6 Jul 1829
George	22		Weaver	Kellahy	Ireland	Carolina Ann	21 May 1823
Jane	30	F	Housekeeper	Ireland	United States	Carolina Ann	14 May 1827
John	30	M	Weaver	Irereland	America	Carolina Ann	20 Jun 1825
John V.	23	M	Merchant	United States	United States	Seeds	29 Sep 1824
M.	35	F		Great Britain	United States	Diana	6 Jul 1829
Martha	11	F		Great Britain	United States	Diana	6 Jul 1829
Mary	6	F		Great Britain	United States	Diana	6 Jul 1829
Michael	67	M	Labourer	Ireland	United States	Carolina Ann	14 May 1827
Nancy	67	F	Housekeeper	Ireland	United States	Carolina Ann	14 May 1827
Robert	20	M	Shoe Maker	Irereland	America	Carolina Ann	20 Jun 1825
Saml.	35	M	Farmer	Ireland	U. States	Ohio	21 Mar 1825
Samuel	18	M	Labourer	Ireland	United States	Carolina Ann	14 May 1827
Thomas	55	M	Farmer	Ireland	United States	Carolina Ann	14 May 1827
William	24	M	Miller & Baker	England	United States	Andes	2 Oct 1828
GREENH...LCH, John	2...		Painter	Bolton	England	Great Britain	7 May 1827
GREENHA...GH, Edwd.	27	M	Farmer	Great Britain	United States	Blakely	29 Sep 1826
GREENHALGH,							
Allicis	1 6/12	F		England	U. States	Severn	12 Oct 1826
John	27	M	Weaver	England	U. States	Severn	12 Oct 1826
Margt.	6/12	F		England	U. States	Severn	12 Oct 1826
Nelly	25	F		England	U. States	Severn	12 Oct 1826
GREENHOFF, Thos.	23	M		England	U. States	Favourite	2 Sep 1822
GREENHOUR, James G.	32	M	Merchant	Great Britain	United States	Milton	20 Oct 1827
GREENHOW, Rob.	23	M	M.D.	U. States	U. States	Marmion	29 Sep 1823
GREENLAND, —,							
Child born on board	5/52		Tailor	England	U. States	Venus	4 Oct 1821
John	18/12		Blacksmith	England	U. States	Venus	4 Oct 1821
Sarah	22		Tailor	England	U. States	Venus	4 Oct 1821
William	27		Tailor	England	U. States	Venus	4 Oct 1821

NAMES OF PASSENGERS	AGE	SEX	OCCUPATIONS	COUNTRY TO WHICH THEY BELONG	COUNTRY THEY INTEND TO INHABIT	SHIPS/DATES OF ARRIVAL	
GREENLAW, John	44	M	Mariner	Howick	Howick	Maine	2 Nov 1827
GREENLEAF, Samuel	23	M	Seaman	Boston	U. States	Pioneer	6 May 1828
GREENLEY, Isabella	1	F		Great Britain	United States	Diana	6 Jul 1829
Margaret	4	F		Great Britain	United States	Diana	6 Jul 1829
Sarah	28	F		Great Britain	United States	Diana	6 Jul 1829
Wm.	28	M	Farmer	Great Britain	United States	Diana	6 Jul 1829
GREENMAN, —, Miss	1	F		Providence	U. States	New York	3 Oct 1826
—, Miss	2	F		Providence	U. States	New York	3 Oct 1826
—, Mrs.	28	F		Providence	U. States	New York	3 Oct 1826
Wm.	35	M	Merchant	Providence	U. States	New York	3 Oct 1826
GREENSHIELD, Jno.	40	M	Merchant	England	U. States	Edwin	10 Feb 1829
GREENUP, George	23	M		Gt. Britain	Gt. Britain	Canada	4 Oct 1824
Wm. M.	25	M	Merchant	Great Britain	United States	Leeds	29 Sep 1823
Wm. M.	26	M		Gt. Britain	Gt. Britain	Canada	4 Oct 1824
GREENWALL, Polly Ann	16	F		United States	United States	Fair American	24 Jul 1821
GREENWAY, Edwd. M.	27	M	Mercht.	U. States	U. States	Columbia	1 Dec 1824
Francis	...	...	...		United States	London Packet	25 Dec 1820
Thomas	27	M	Wheelwright	Great Britain	United States	Unity	20 Oct 1829
Thomas G.	...	...	...		United States	London Packet	25 Dec 1820
GREENWOOD, Abm.	28			England	United States	Hugh Johnson	11 Jun 1828
C.	20	F		Amsterdam	Westindies	Bolivar Liberator	8 Dec 1826
Daniel	22	M	Weaver	Ireland	America	Plutarch	18 Jul 1826
Eliza	22	F		England	Great Britain	New York	22 Jul 1824
Elizabeth	30	F	None	England	United States	Baltic	21 Apr 1827
Hannah	5	F	None	Great Britain	United States	Penelope	11 Jun 1827
James	45	M	Weaver	England	U. States	Howard Douglass	29 Jan 1828
Jno.	32	M	Miller	Great Britain	United States	Penelope	11 Jun 1827
John	19	M	Laborer	Great Britain	United States	Cortes	18 Oct 1820
John	22	M	Farmer	England	United States	Aurora	9 Jul 1827
John	30	M				Splendid	14 Aug 1829
John	36	M	Tullir	England	United States	Siroc	31 Oct 1829
John	40	M	Weaver	England	U. States	Howard Douglass	29 Jan 1828
L.	25	M	Merchant	St. Croix	St. Croix	South Carolina Packet	16 Sep 1823
M.	30	M	Gentleman	St. Croix	U. States	Carlo	30 Jul 1827
Sam.	18	M	Weaver	England	U. States	Howard Douglass	29 Jan 1828
Sam.	34	M	Weaver	England	U. States	Howard Douglass	29 Jan 1828
Sophia	16	F	None	England	United States	Dalhouse Castle	6 Sep 1827
Susan	32	F	None	Great Britain	United States	Penelope	11 Jun 1827
Tabathy	26			England	United States	Hugh Johnson	11 Jun 1828
Thos.	22	M	Laborer	Great Britain	United States	Cortes	18 Oct 1820
Thos.	24	M	Weaver	G. Britain	U. States	St. George	16 Jan 1829
William	22	M	Weaver	England	Great Britain	Florida	26 Sep 1826
Wm.	20	M	Merchant	New York	New York	Lady Hunter	22 Aug 1825
GREER, Barnard	18	M	Stonecutter	Scotland	New York	America	1 Aug 1828
Catherine	16	F	Spinster	Ireland	United States	Robert Fulton	10 Aug 1827
David	14	M	Boy	Ireland	United States	Robert Fulton	10 Aug 1827
Eliza	30	F	Matron	Ireland	United States	Robert Fulton	10 Aug 1827
J.	40		Farmer	Ireland	United States	Courier	16 May 1825
James	3	M	Child	Ireland	United States	Robert Fulton	10 Aug 1827
James	40	M	Weaver	Ireland	United States	Robert Fulton	10 Aug 1827
M.	23		Farmer	Ireland	United States	Courier	16 May 1825
M.	29		Farmer	Ireland	United States	Courier	16 May 1825
Margaret	18	M		Scotland	U. States	William	18 Mar 1822
Margaret	21	F	None	Great Britain	United States	Courier	26 Jun 1827
Mary	30		None	G. Britain	United States	Roman	10 Sep 1827
Mary Ann	8		None	G. Britain	United States	Roman	10 Sep 1827
Mathey	10		None	G. Britain	United States	Roman	10 Sep 1827
Patrick	4		None	G. Britain	United States	Roman	10 Sep 1827
Rebecca	11	F	Child	Ireland	United States	Robert Fulton	10 Aug 1827
GREERSON, Jas.	36	M	Captain	Scotland	Canada	Indian Queen	5 Dec 1825
GREEVES, A.	54	M	Mariner	New York	U. States	Abeona	23 May 1823
A.	65	M	Mariner	U. States	U. States	Franklin	14 Jul 1827
Anthony	52	M	Mercht.	N. York	N. York	Orozimbo	16 Apr 1821

NAMES OF PASSENGERS	AGE	SEX	OCCUPATIONS	COUNTRY TO WHICH THEY BELONG	COUNTRY THEY INTEND TO INHABIT	SHIPS/DATES OF ARRIVAL	
GREEVES (cont'd)							
Peter	2...	M	Weaver	Great Britian	United States	George Clinton	21 Oct 1826
GREFFINGER, James	27	M	Butcher	Germany	United States	Helen	5 Sep 1828
GREG, Margaret	...0		Servant	Ireland	Great Britain	Robert Burns	14 Jun 1824
GREGER, Rodolph C.	24	M	Shipmaster	U.S.	U.S.	Emma	7 Jul 1824
GREGG, Alexander P.	45	M	Merchant	Scotland	United States	Natchez	22 Apr 1822
Ann	8	F		United States	United States	Natchez	22 Apr 1822
David	5	M		United States	United States	Natchez	22 Apr 1822
Margaret	45	F		Scotland	United States	Natchez	22 Apr 1822
Thomas	14	M	no trade	Ireland	United States	Carolina Ann	11 Dec 1826
GREGIL, Francis	30	M	Carpenter	France	U. States	Brandt	8 Nov 1828
GREGORY, —, Mr.	29	M		England	U. States	Milton	6 Dec 1825
Alexander	17	M	Clark	Scotland, Great Britain	America	Superb	11 Oct 1821
Alfred	9			Somerset	...	Hudson	14 Jun 1827
Ann	...	F	...	...	United States	Minerva	30 Oct 1827
Ann	14			Somerset	...	Hudson	14 Jun 1827
Ann	37			Somerset	...	Hudson	14 Jun 1827
Anna	2 2/12	F	Domestic	England	United States	London	6 Feb 1829
Ben	30	M	Farmer	Ireland	America	Mary	29 May 1827
Bridget	40 9/12	F		Ireland	America	Carolina Ann	7 Apr 1826
Briorn	48	M	Sawyer	England	United States	Nancy Henrietta	3 Nov 1828
Con	25			Great Britan	United States	Newry	11 Jul 1827
Daniel	7			Somerset	...	Hudson	14 Jun 1827
Edward	35	M	...	Naples	U. States	Columbia	7 Jul 1824
Eliza	30	F	Spinster	Ireland	America	Mary	29 May 1827
Elizabeth	5			Somerset	...	Hudson	14 Jun 1827
Emma	3			Somerset	...	Hudson	14 Jun 1827
Francis	14	M	Labourer	Ireland	United States	Dalhouse Castle	8 May 1827
G., Mr.	26	M	Merchant	U.S.A.		François I	19 Nov 1828
George	8			Somerset	...	Hudson	14 Jun 1827
James	17	M		Ireland	America	Carolina Ann	7 Apr 1826
James	3...	M	Labourer	Ireland	United States	Princess Charlotte	26 Apr 1827
James	32	M	Labourer	Ireland	United States	Princess Charlotte	26 Apr 1827
Jno.	6...	M	...	...	United States	Minerva	30 Oct 1827
John		M	...	...	United States	Minerva	30 Oct 1827
John	13 2/12	M		Ireland	America	Carolina Ann	7 Apr 1826
John	28	M		Ireland	America	Carolina Ann	7 Apr 1826
Joseph	11			Somerset	...	Hudson	14 Jun 1827
Lucretia	16			Somerset	...	Hudson	14 Jun 1827
Lydia	31	F		Gt. Britain	U. States	St. George	20 Sep 1828
Margaret	40	F	None	Ireland	United States	Dalhouse Castle	8 May 1827
Martha	44 5/12	F	Domestic	England	United States	London	6 Feb 1829
Mary	...	F	...	...	United States	Minerva	30 Oct 1827
Mary	4 6/12	F	Domestic	England	United States	London	6 Feb 1829
Mary	20	F		Ireland	United States	Dalhouse Castle	8 May 1827
Mathew	15 7/12	M		Ireland	America	Carolina Ann	7 Apr 1826
Matilda	12			Somerset	...	Hudson	14 Jun 1827
Michael	16	M	Labourer	Ireland	United States	Dalhouse Castle	8 May 1827
Michael	26	M	Labourer	Ireland	United States	Princess Charlotte	26 Apr 1827
Micheal	11 5/12	M		Ireland	America	Carolina Ann	7 Apr 1826
Patrick	9 0/12	M		Ireland	America	Carolina Ann	7 Apr 1826
Patrick	12	M	Labourer	Ireland	United States	Dalhouse Castle	8 May 1827
Peter	7 1/12	M		Ireland	America	Carolina Ann	7 Apr 1826
Peter	20 3/12	...		Ireland	America	Carolina Ann	7 Apr 1826
Peter	24	M	Labourer	Ireland	United States	Dalhouse Castle	8 May 1827
Phillip	30	M	Weaver	Ireland	United States	Princess Charlotte	26 Apr 1827
Richard	60			Somerset	...	Hudson	14 Jun 1827
Robert	33		Merchant	England	U. States	Jackin	15 May 1828
Saml.	29	M	Calico Printer	Gt. Britain	U. States	St. George	20 Sep 1828
Samuel	35	M	Gentleman	Great Britain	United States	Juno	5 Oct 1822
Samuel	42	M	Brick Layer	Great Britten	America	Cortes	6 Mar 1827
Sarah	24 2/12	F	Domestic	England	United States	London	6 Feb 1829
Sarah	37	M	Brick Layer	Great Britten	America	Cortes	6 Mar 1827

NAMES OF PASSENGERS	AGE	SEX	OCCUPATIONS	COUNTRY TO WHICH THEY BELONG	COUNTRY THEY INTEND TO INHABIT	SHIPS/DATES OF ARRIVAL	
GREGORY (cont'd)							
Thomas	21	M	Labourer	Ireland	United States	Princess Charlotte	26 Apr 1827
Thomas	45 2/12	M	Bricklayer	England	United States	London	6 Feb 1829
Thos.	40	M	Merchant	U. States	U. States	William & John	21 Aug 1822
William	17			Somerset	...	Hudson	14 Jun 1827
William	26	M	Stonemason	England	New York	America	1 Aug 1828
Wm.	24	M	Labourer	..., ..., England	Sommersworth (N.Y)	New Orleans	24 Aug 1827
GREGSON, Betty	9/12	F	None	England and Ireland	United States	Jubilee	12 May 1828
Esther	2	F	None	England and Ireland	United States	Jubilee	12 May 1828
Rebecca	30	F	None	England and Ireland	United States	Jubilee	12 May 1828
Richard	52	M	None	England	New York	America	1 Aug 1828
William	52	M	Farmer	England	United States	Concordia	25 Aug 1827
GREIG, Clarissa	36	F	None	Scotland	United States	New York	5 Jul 1826
David	15	M	None	Scotland	United States	New York	5 Jul 1826
John	30	M				Czar	29 Aug 1829
John	46	M	None	Scotland	United States	New York	5 Jul 1826
John W.	13	M	None	Scotland	United States	New York	5 Jul 1826
Sara	20	F		Java	Java	Eunore Francis	18 Sep 1820
GREIL, Henrich	17	M	Agriculture	Wirtemburg	United States	Henri IV	14 Oct 1829
Jacob	20	M	Agriculture	Wirtemburg	United States	Henri IV	14 Oct 1829
Jane	53	F	Agriculture	Wirtemburg	United States	Henri IV	14 Oct 1829
Jeant.	54	M	Agriculture	Wirtemburg	United States	Henri IV	14 Oct 1829
GREISHAM, Ellen	22	M	Surgeon	Ireland	United States	Dublin Packet	6 Dec 1827
GREIT, B.	30	M	Mercht.	England		Antioch	18 Aug 1829
R.	25	F		England		Antioch	18 Aug 1829
GREIVES, Willm.	30	M	Mechanic	St. John, N.B.	United States	Henrietta	3 Jun 1825
GREIZLE, Beata	7	F		Switzerland	U. States	Hewes	30 Oct 1829
Calina	2	F		Switzerland	U. States	Hewes	30 Oct 1829
Christina	31	F	his Wife [Gotlib]	Switzerland	U. States	Hewes	30 Oct 1829
Gotlib	5 6/12	M		Switzerland	U. States	Hewes	30 Oct 1829
Gotlib	32	M	Tailor	Switzerland	U. States	Hewes	30 Oct 1829
Maria	4 6/12	F		Switzerland	U. States	Hewes	30 Oct 1829
GRELAND, John	36	M	Merchant	U.S. America	U.S. America	Columbia	15 Nov 1826
GRELOS, John	33	M	Farmer	France	France	Edward Quesnel	3 Jul 1829
GREN, James	20	M		Ireland	U. States	Lima	5 Aug 1829
GRENADER, Bernard	1	F		Gt. Britain	United States	Penelope	9 Sep 1828
James	26	M	Farmer	Gt. Britain	United States	Penelope	9 Sep 1828
Mary	23	F		Gt. Britain	United States	Penelope	9 Sep 1828
GRENADO, Giassen	20	M	Lawyer	Republic Guatemalla	Gutamilta	Robert Fulton	22 May 1824
GRENAN, Inan	27		Gentleman	Spain	Spain	Florida	1 Dec 1828
GRENARD, John	19	M	Labourer	Ireland	United States	John Wells	11 May 1827
GRENELY, Philip	20	M	Farmer	England	United States	India	8 Jun 1827
GRENET, Christian	46	M	Farmer	Switzerland	United States	Andes	5 May 1828
Christina	17	F	Spinster	Switzerland	United States	Andes	5 May 1828
Henry	15	M	Farmer	Switzerland	United States	Andes	5 May 1828
Madalena	2	F	Child	Switzerland	United States	Andes	5 May 1828
Margaretta	46	F	Spinster	Switzerland	United States	Andes	5 May 1828
GRENICKER, William	23	M	Seaman	U. States	U. States	Golden Age	6 Jul 1821
GRENIER, Francisco	65	M	Military	Spain	Columbian Government	William Bayard	24 Jan 1825
GRENNEL, Dennis	28	M	Merchant	Ireland	United States	Trident	30 Sep 1826
GRENOT, John B.	29	M	Confectioner	France	U.S. America	Sicily	7 Oct 1829
GRENUP, George	24	M	Mercht.	G. Britian	U. States	America	17 Oct 1825
GRENVILLE, Ann	10			Suffolk	England	Hudson	14 Jun 1827
Benjamin	37		Brick Maker	Middlesex	England	Hudson	14 Jun 1827
Emeline	2			Middlesex	England	Hudson	14 Jun 1827
Geo.	12			Suffolk	England	Hudson	14 Jun 1827
Jane	4/12			Middlesex	England	Hudson	14 Jun 1827
Mary	26			Middlesex	England	Hudson	14 Jun 1827
GREOÁ, Parqual	17	M	Servant	Spain	United States	Georgetown Packet	15 Nov 1823
GRERE, John	28 2/12	M	Merchant	United States	United States	Rising States	16 Jan 1829
GRESELAERDT, Joseph	25	M	Weaver	Scotland	Canada	Ann	11 Sep 1827
GRESMER, Jacque	22	M	Agriculturist	France	U.S.	Helen	3 May 1828

NAMES OF PASSENGERS	AGE	SEX	OCCUPATIONS	COUNTRY TO WHICH THEY BELONG	COUNTRY THEY INTEND TO INHABIT	SHIPS/DATES OF ARRIVAL	
GRESSART, Catharine	3	F	Farmer	France	France	Sully	15 Jul 1829
John	23	M	Farmer	France	France	Sully	15 Jul 1829
Merritte	26	F	Farmer	France	France	Sully	15 Jul 1829
Susanne	2	F	Farmer	France	France	Sully	15 Jul 1829
GRESSEMEYER,							
...therine	7	F		France	U. States	Edward Quesnel	4 Aug 1828
Caroline	3	F		France	U. States	Edward Quesnel	4 Aug 1828
Catherine	30	F		France	U. States	Edward Quesnel	4 Aug 1828
Madalina	5	F		France	U. States	Edward Quesnel	4 Aug 1828
Margaretta	1	F		France	U. States	Edward Quesnel	4 Aug 1828
Nicholas	32	M	Baker	France	U. States	Edward Quesnel	4 Aug 1828
GREVES, Eliza	15	F				Lady of the Lake	23 Aug 1828
J. B.	50	M	Weaver			Lady of the Lake	23 Aug 1828
John	1	M	None	Great Britain	United States	Richmond	18 Feb 1820
John	16	M				Lady of the Lake	23 Aug 1828
John	20	M	Labourer	England		Marchioness	13 May 1828
Mary	4	F	None	Great Britain	United States	Richmond	18 Feb 1820
Mary	36	F				Lady of the Lake	23 Aug 1828
Samuel	29	M	Farmer	Great Britain	United States	Richmond	18 Feb 1820
Sarah	25	F	None	Great Britain	United States	Richmond	18 Feb 1820
Sarah	40	F				Lady of the Lake	23 Aug 1828
GREW, —, Mr.	30	M	Merchant	America	St. Domingo	Eliza Ann	17 Jul 1824
Eliza	20	F		United States		Corinthian	27 Oct 1829
Henry	47	M		United States		Corinthian	27 Oct 1829
GREY, Arther	36	M	Labourer	United States	United States	Only Daughter	29 Apr 1825
Bird	11	F		Gt. Britain	New York	Leeds	7 Nov 1828
Cath.	33	F		Gt. Britain	New York	Leeds	7 Nov 1828
Cornelius B., Master	4	M	Child	St. Croix	Ireland	Jupiter	21 Nov 1825
Elizth.	9		Farmer	Ireland	United States	Carolina Ann	12 Sep 1823
James	7	M		Gt. Britain	New York	Leeds	7 Nov 1828
Mark	9	M		Gt. Britain	New York	Leeds	7 Nov 1828
Mary	2	F		Gt. Britain	New York	Leeds	7 Nov 1828
Mary, Miss	6	F	Child	St. Croix	Ireland	Jupiter	21 Nov 1825
Patric	25	M	Labourer	Ireland	America	Wilson	16 May 1825
Peotras	19	M	Laborer	Ireland	United States	Sylvester Healy	17 Oct 1825
Sally	32	F		United States	United States	Only Daughter	29 Apr 1825
Wm.	7	M	None	U. States	U. States	Hibernia	24 Aug 1820
GREYSON, John	44	M	Merchant	Ireland	America	Josephine	8 Dec 1827
GRIBBEN, Peter	30 5/12		Labourer	Ireland	United States	Helen	5 Jul 1820
GRIBBIN, Andw.	27			Great Britan	United States	Newry	11 Jul 1827
Danl.	30		Farmer	Great Britan	United States	Newry	11 Jul 1827
John [crossed out]	45			Great Britan	United States	Newry	11 Jul 1827
GRIBBON, Charles	25	M	Manufacturer	Arnagallan	United States	Minerva	30 Oct 1829
Mary	20	F	Semstress	Arnagallan	United States	Minerva	30 Oct 1829
GRIBI, Jean	30	M	Weaver	Beeren	U.S. America	Superior	18 Jun 1825
Jean S.	27	M	Taylor	Beeren	U.S. America	Superior	18 Jun 1825
GRIDLEA, James	29	M	Gent. Servant	Gt. Britain	United States	Meteor	19 Aug 1829
GRIDWELL, Jenney	25	F	Colored Servant	America		Elias Burger	28 May 1821
GRIEM, Alexr.	26					Charlotte Corday	15 Jul 1820
GRIENDER, Georges	38	M	Farmer	Switzerland	United States	Olympia	12 Aug 1828
Joseph	27	M	Farmer	Switzerland	United States	Olympia	12 Aug 1828
GRIEOR, David	20	M	Paper Maker	Scotland	United States	Camillus	9 May 1827
GRIER, Ann	1	F		Great Britain	United States	Active	25 Mar 1828
James	30	M		Great Britain	United States	Active	25 Mar 1828
P. C.	23	M	Labourer	France	U. States	Edward Bonaffe	11 Dec 1827
Sarah	28	F		Great Britain	United States	Active	25 Mar 1828
GRIERNE, George H.	18	M	Professor			Henri IV	17 May 1828
GRIERSON, Robert	28	M	Jeweller	Great Britain	United States	Purrington	8 Dec 1827
Thomas	28	M	Commedian	England		Britannia	20 Jun 1827
GRIESHAM, James	22	M	Surgeon	Ireland	United States	Dublin Packet	6 Dec 1827
GRIEVE, J. H.	18		Mechanic	Scotland		Zamoa	5 Nov 1828
GRIEVES, Anne	27	F	Spinster	England	United States	Herald	29 Oct 1825
James	7	M	Child	England	United States	Herald	29 Oct 1825

NAMES OF PASSENGERS	AGE	SEX	OCCUPATIONS	COUNTRY TO WHICH THEY BELONG	COUNTRY THEY INTEND TO INHABIT	SHIPS/DATES OF ARRIVAL	
GRIEVES (cont'd)							
Janet	27	F	Farmer	Scotland	United States	Friends	16 Aug 1824
John	32	M	Clothier	England	United States	Herald	29 Oct 1825
Maria	40	F	Farmer	Scotland	United States	Friends	16 Aug 1824
Samuel	2	M	Child	England	United States	Herald	29 Oct 1825
GRIFFEN, Daniel	20		Farmer & Labourer	Great Britain & Ireland	United States	Trio	8 Feb 1827
Daniel	25	M	Labourer	Ireland	New York	General Marion	12 Jan 1829
Dennis	22		Farmer & Labourer	Great Britain & Ireland	United States	Trio	8 Feb 1827
James	3		Farmer & Labourer	Great Britain & Ireland	United States	Trio	8 Feb 1827
Judy	22		Shoe Maker	Great Britain & Ireland	United States	Trio	8 Feb 1827
Mary	2		Farmer & Labourer	Great Britain & Ireland	United States	Trio	8 Feb 1827
Mary	28	F	Labourer	Ireland	Boston	General Marion	12 Jan 1829
Maurice	22		Farmer & Labourer	Great Britain & Ireland	United States	Trio	8 Feb 1827
Peggy	22		Farmer & Labourer	Great Britain & Ireland	United States	Trio	8 Feb 1827
Thomas	25		Shoe Maker	Great Britain & Ireland	United States	Trio	8 Feb 1827
GRIFFET, Joseph	26	M	stationer	France	U. States	Leonarde	29 Aug 1828
GRIFFETH, Arthur	11	M	None	England	United States	John Dickinson	30 Sep 1823
GRIFFIN, A.	23	M	Labourer	U. States	U. States	St. Croix	13 Sep 1827
Danl.	10		Farmer	Limerick	Silver Lake	Schuylkill	22 Aug 1825
Ellen	22	F		Ireland	United States	Sarah G.	20 Jul 1827
H.	1	M		Ireland	United States	Sarah G.	15 May 1828
J.	28	F	Spinster	Ireland	United States	Sarah G.	15 May 1828
James	19		Farmer	Limerick	Silver Lake	Schuylkill	22 Aug 1825
James	26	M	Labourer	Ireland	United States	William & George	14 May 1828
James	30	M		Ireland	United States	Sarah G.	20 Jul 1827
James	35	M	Labourer	Ireland	U. States	Liverpool	25 Mar 1828
Jno.	23			Ireland		Anacreon	7 Sep 1827
John	...	M	Servt.	Ireland	Washington	Amity	13 Sep 1821
John	1	M		G. Britain	U. States	Sarah G	5 Jun 1828
John	2	M	Child	France	United States	Chatham	8 Aug 1822
John	21	M	Labourer	England	U.N. States	Reindeer	20 Aug 1828
John	27	M	Shoe ...	..., ..., Ireland	N. York	New Orleans	24 Aug 1827
John	28	M	Farmer	France	U. States	Bayard	16 May 1827
John	28	M	Farmer	England	United States	Ganges	10 May 1828
John	35	M	Confectioner	France	United States	Chatham	8 Aug 1822
Margt.	7	F		G. Britain	U. States	Sarah G	5 Jun 1828
Martha	27	M	Farmer	Ireland	U. States	Erin	5 Jul 1820
Mary	22	F	Farmer	France	U. States	Bayard	16 May 1827
Mary	35	F	Servant	G. Britain	U. States	Sarah G	5 Jun 1828
Morris	30	M	Labourer	Ireland	United States	Sarah G.	15 May 1828
Richd.	27	M	Farmer	England	U.S.A.	Lima	6 Dec 1826
Robert	20	M	Farmer	New Brunswick	United States	Henrietta	19 Oct 1825
Sarah	20	F	Lady	Philadelphia	Great Britain	Sylvester Healy	23 Nov 1825
GRIFFING, Jas.	22	M	Mariner	U. States	U. States	Cicero	24 Oct 1823
Jno.	22	M	Farmer	U. States	U. States	Martha	20 Jun 1825
Timothy	25		Farmer	Limerick	Silver Lake	Schuylkill	22 Aug 1825
GRIFFIS, John	9/12	M		Wales	America	Ulysses	1 May 1822
John	32	M		Wales	America	Ulysses	1 May 1822
Margaret	21	F	None	England	United States	Orozimbo	1 Dec 1823
Sarah	30	F		Wales	America	Ulysses	1 May 1822
Wm.	22	M	Labourer	Wales	America	Ulysses	1 May 1822
GRIFFITH, A. E.	4 1/12	F		G. Britain	U. States	Wanderer	23 Jun 1828
Ann	1			Great Britain	United States	Gomer	21 May 1828
Ann	18	F	Servant	Great Britan	U. States	Canada	2 Jun 1824
Ann	29	F	None	England	U. St.	Manchester	7 Dec 1826
Ann	40		Servant	Great Britain	United States	Gomer	21 May 1828
Catherine	16	F		Great Britain	United States	Robert	15 Jul 1822
Cathrine	1	F		Great Britain	United States	Gomer	21 May 1828
Charles	30	M	Labourer	Great Britain	United States	Robert	15 Jul 1822
Charlotte	3	F		Albany	United S.	Hanford	19 Aug 1828

NAMES OF PASSENGERS	AGE	SEX	OCCUPATIONS	COUNTRY TO WHICH THEY BELONG	COUNTRY THEY INTEND TO INHABIT	SHIPS/DATES OF ARRIVAL	
GRIFFITH (cont'd)							
David	24	M	Farmer	Wales	United States	Mount Vernon	9 Jun 1823
David	24	M	...	...	America	Farmer	4 Aug 1825
David	25	M	...	...	...	Diamond	27 Jul 1824
David	30	M	Hatter	Gt. Britain	U. States	Panthea	21 Jul 1825
David	34		Farmer	Great Britain	United States	Gomer	21 May 1828
Dorothy	17	F		Fyncoes	United States	Marquis of Anglesea	8 Jun 1827
Edward	5	M		Great Britain	United States	Robert	15 Jul 1822
Edward	7	M	None	England	U. St.	Manchester	7 Dec 1826
Edward	29	M	Jeweller	England	U. St.	Manchester	7 Dec 1826
Edward	44	M	Mariner	America	U. States	Cincinnatus	9 Jul 1825
Eleanor	28	F	Spinster	Wales		Gomer	22 May 1827
Elinor	5			Great Britain	United States	Gomer	21 May 1828
Elinor	40			Great Britain	United States	Gomer	21 May 1828
Eliza	7	F	Child	Ireland	America	Dublin Packet	9 Oct 1820
Eliza	9	F	None	England	United States	John Dickinson	30 Sep 1823
Ellen	3	F		Great Britain	United States	Gomer	21 May 1828
Ellen	40	F		Cardiga	United S.	Hanford	19 Aug 1828
Ellin	28	F		Aberdaron	United States	Marquis of Anglesea	8 Jun 1827
George	5	M	Child	Ireland	America	Dublin Packet	9 Oct 1820
George	20	M	Merchant	Great Britain	U. States	Ganges	21 Jun 1827
George	40 3/12	M	Warehouseman	America	America	Braganza	7 Oct 1823
Griffeth	4			Great Britain	United States	Gomer	21 May 1828
Griffith Humphrey	28	M	Tanner	U.S.A.	U.S.A.	Silas Richards	28 Jun 1825
Hannah	35	F		G. Britain	U. States	Wanderer	23 Jun 1828
Henry	9	M	Child	Ireland	America	Dublin Packet	9 Oct 1820
Hugh	26		Farmer	Great Britain	United States	Gomer	21 May 1828
Hugh	35	M	Missionry	Ireland	United States	Panthea	11 Nov 1825
James	18	M	...	...	...	Diamond	27 Jul 1824
James	21	M	Glassmaker	Great Britain	United States	Isaac Hicks	27 Sep 1826
James	28	M	Clerk	Ireland	U.S.	Hibernia	27 Jun 1821
Jane	2			Great Britain	United States	Gomer	21 May 1828
Jane	13	F		Fyncoes	United States	Marquis of Anglesea	8 Jun 1827
Jane	14	F		Aberdaron	United States	Marquis of Anglesea	8 Jun 1827
Jane	25	F	Farmer	Ireland	United States	Justina	5 Aug 1823
Jane	29			Great Britain	United States	Gomer	21 May 1828
Jane	35	F		Fyncoes	United States	Marquis of Anglesea	8 Jun 1827
Jas.	2	F	None	Great Britain	America	Remittance	24 Aug 1825
Jas.	5			Ireland	U.S.	Hibernia	27 Jun 1821
John	1/12	M		G. Britain	U. States	Wanderer	23 Jun 1828
John	8	M		England	America	William	21 Sep 1821
John	22	M	Farmer	Ireland	United States	Justina	5 Aug 1823
John	27	M	Labourer	Wales	U. States	Sabina	29 Apr 1825
John	35	M	Labourer	Cardiga	United S.	Hanford	19 Aug 1828
John	70	M	Farmer	Wales		Gomer	22 May 1827
Joseph	34	M	Farmer	G. Britain	U. States	Wanderer	23 Jun 1828
Margaret	3/12	F		Fredericton (N.B.)	United S.	Hanford	19 Aug 1828
Margaret	27	F		Wales	U. States	Sabina	29 Apr 1825
Margrt.	28	F		Great Britain	United States	Gomer	21 May 1828
Margt.	7 4/12	F		G. Britain	U. States	Wanderer	23 Jun 1828
Mary	1	F		Aberdaron	United States	Marquis of Anglesea	8 Jun 1827
Mary	18	F		Aberdaron	United States	Marquis of Anglesea	8 Jun 1827
Mary	25	F		Ireland	U.S.	Hibernia	27 Jun 1821
Mary	26	F	None	Great Britain	America	Remittance	24 Aug 1825
Mary	28	F		U.S.A.	U.S.A.	Silas Richards	28 Jun 1825
Mary	38	F		Great Britain	United States	Robert	15 Jul 1822
Mary Ann	5	F		Albany	United S.	Hanford	19 Aug 1828
Matilda	2	F	None	England	U. St.	Manchester	7 Dec 1826
May	34	F		England	America	William	21 Sep 1821
Morris	14	M	None	Great Britian	United States	Isaac Hicks	23 Aug 1825
Patt	28	M	Land Surveyor	Great Britain	United States	India	5 Sep 1827

505

NAMES OF PASSENGERS	AGE	SEX	OCCUPATIONS	COUNTRY TO WHICH THEY BELONG	COUNTRY THEY INTEND TO INHABIT	SHIPS/DATES OF ARRIVAL	
GRIFFITH (cont'd)							
R.	24	M	Sergeon	United States	United States	Atlantic	3 Dec 1821
Rees	32	M	Farmer	England	United States	William Byrnes	1 Dec 1824
Richard	27	M	Merchant	G.B.	U.S.A.	Silas Richards	29 Oct 1827
Robert	5	M	None	England	United States	John Dickinson	30 Sep 1823
Robert	30	M	Farmer	Great Britain	United States	Gomer	21 May 1828
Robt.	18	M	Shoe Maker	North Wales	United States	Magnet	16 May 1823
Rus. H.	7/12	M		U.S.A.	U.S.A.	Silas Richards	28 Jun 1825
S. M., Dr.	28	M	Army	America	America	Medina	4 Sep 1828
Saml. M., Dr.	30	M	Physician	England	England	Athenian	17 Jul 1829
Samuel, Dr.	28	M	Surgeon	England	England	Athenian	1 Dec 1827
Susannah, Mrs.	40	F	Wife	Ireland	America	Dublin Packet	9 Oct 1820
Thomas	25	M	Merchant	England	America	William	21 Sep 1821
Thomas	43	M	Labourer	Great Britain	United States	Robert	15 Jul 1822
Thos.	...	...	...	...	...	Diamond	27 Jul 1824
William	3 7/12	M		G. Britain	U. States	Wanderer	23 Jun 1828
William	12	M		Aberdaron	United States	Marquis of Anglesea	8 Jun 1827
Wm.	1	M		Fyncoes	United States	Marquis of Anglesea	8 Jun 1827
Wm.	18	M	Labourer	England	U. States	Ayrshire	12 May 1828
Wm.	27	M		England	U. States	Mary	24 Jun 1824
GRIFFITHS, Ann	40	F	Farmer	Britain	U. States	Fame	3 Jun 1828
David	28	M	Joiner	G. Britain	U. States	Aisthorpe	22 May 1827
Eben	28	M	Professional			Plato	31 Oct 1829
Edward	25	M		Ireland	New York	Lady Hunter	5 Jun 1826
Edward	35	M	Farmer	Wales	United States	Mount Vernon	9 Jun 1823
Eleanor	35	F		Gt. Brittain	United States	Herald	24 May 1826
Eliza	6	F	None	Wales	United States	Orozimbo	11 Aug 1823
Eliza	39	F	None	Wales	United States	Orozimbo	11 Aug 1823
Evan	12	M	None	Wales	United States	Orozimbo	11 Aug 1823
Griffith	1	M	None	Wales	United States	Orozimbo	11 Aug 1823
Griffith	8	M	Labourer	Wales	United States	Orozimbo	11 Aug 1823
Griffith	26	M	Farmer	Gt. Britain	United States	Euphrates	10 Apr 1827
Helen	23	F	Servant	Great Britain	United States	James Monroe	5 Apr 1820
James	34	M	Farmer	Wales	United States	Orozimbo	11 Aug 1823
Jane	3	F	None	Wales	United States	Orozimbo	11 Aug 1823
Jane	32	F	None	Wales	United States	Orozimbo	11 Aug 1823
Jno. R.	45	M		G. Britain	U. States	William Thompson	30 Apr 1822
John	2	M		Gt. Brittain	United States	Herald	24 May 1826
John	24	M	Farmer	Wales	United States	Orozimbo	11 Aug 1823
Joseph	27	M		Great Britain	United States	Mary Howland	19 Jul 1827
Margaret	5	F	None	Wales	United States	Orozimbo	11 Aug 1823
Margaret	21	F	None	Wales	United States	Orozimbo	11 Aug 1823
Mary	7	F		Gt. Brittain	United States	Herald	24 May 1826
Mary	49	F	None	England	United States	Roman	12 Jun 1826
Owen	10	M		Gt. Brittain	United States	Herald	24 May 1826
Owen	22	M				Splendid	14 Aug 1829
Richd.	24	M	Farmer	Wales	United States	Orozimbo	11 Aug 1823
Rowland	42	M	Labourer	Gt. Brittain	United States	Herald	24 May 1826
Thomas	1	M	None	Wales	United States	Orozimbo	11 Aug 1823
Thomas	4	M		New York	U.S.A.	Silas Richards	29 Oct 1827
William	27	M	Farmer	England	United States	Mount Vernon	9 Jun 1823
Wm.	10	M	None	Wales	United States	Orozimbo	11 Aug 1823
Wm.	39	M	Labourer	Wales	United States	Orozimbo	11 Aug 1823
GRIFFUN, George	13	M		Ireland	United States	Trio	2 Oct 1828
GRIFFY, Thomas	42	M	Servant	put on board by the American Consul		Cincinnatus	24 May 1821
GRIGARTY, M.	28	M	Labourer	Ireland	United States	Princess Charlotte	6 Oct 1827
GRIGG, Andrew	36	M		Gt. Britain	United States	John & Elizabeth	25 Sep 1827
Ann	30	F	...	Great Brittain	Quebec	Albion	11 Jun 1821
Eliza	60	F	...	Ireland	United States	Carolina Ann	24 Oct 1825
Francis	6	M	...	Great Brittain	Quebec	Albion	11 Jun 1821
Frederick	43	M	...	Great Brittain	Quebec	Albion	11 Jun 1821
Frederick, Jr.	9	M	...	Great Brittain	Quebec	Albion	11 Jun 1821

NAMES OF PASSENGERS	AGE	SEX	OCCUPATIONS	COUNTRY TO WHICH THEY BELONG	COUNTRY THEY INTEND TO INHABIT	SHIPS/DATES OF ARRIVAL	
GRIGG (cont'd)							
Lucinda	66	F		Ireland	United States	Clothier	22 Nov 1827
Mary	17	F	...	Ireland	United States	Carolina Ann	24 Oct 1825
Mary	20	F		Ireland	United States	General Putnam	20 Jun 1825
Robert	24	M	Farmer	Ireland	United States	General Putnam	20 Jun 1825
GRIGGS, Stephn.	27	M	Merchant	U. States	U. States	Elias Burger	21 Jun 1823
GRILON, Itr.	18	M	Merchant	France	France	Hiram	8 Jul 1828
GRIM, George	33	M	Shoemaker	England	United States	Jubilee	1 Dec 1827
GRIMARUE, Jacques	50	M	Mariner	France	France	Traveller	11 Dec 1824
GRIME, John	29	M	Blacksmith	Gt. Britain	United States	Silas Richards	20 Jun 1826
Joseph	39	M	Gunsmith	Gt. Britain	United States	Silas Richards	20 Jun 1826
GRIMES, Ann	26	F	None	Great Britain	United States	William Dawson	18 Jun 1827
Catherine	23	F				Hesperus	2 Nov 1820
Cathn.	15 2/12	F		Ireland	America	Carolina Ann	7 Apr 1826
Henry	1/12	M	None	Great Britain	United States	William Dawson	18 Jun 1827
James	27	M	Labourer	Great Britain	United States	William Dawson	18 Jun 1827
Jas.	34	M	Labourer	Ireland	United States	Margarett Scott	22 Aug 1827
John	1	M				Hesperus	2 Nov 1820
John	36	M	Taylor	England	New York	Concordia	12 Oct 1826
Nancy	19	F	Spinster	Ireland		Robert Fulton	4 Jun 1828
Patrick	20	M	Labourer	Ireland	New York	Atlantic	8 May 1828
Robert	30	M			Indianna	Hesperus	2 Nov 1820
Wm.	25	M	Labourer	Ireland		Robert Fulton	4 Jun 1828
GRIMLEY, Hannah	20	F		Ireland	United States	Princess Charlotte	26 Apr 1827
GRIMM, Elizabeth	30 1/12	F	Servant	Gt. Britain	U. States	Maria	22 May 1822
Jean	20	M	Paper Maker	Swisse	United States	Deux Ernest	29 Dec 1827
*landed at Lewiston, Delw.							
Jean	20		Md. de papier	Suisse		Deux Ernest	29 Dec 1827
John	18	M	Labourer	Germany	United States	Constitution	2 Aug 1826
GRIMS, Elizabeth	36	F	Spinner	England	U. States	Panthea	22 Nov 1826
Esther	14	F	Spinner	England	U. States	Panthea	22 Nov 1826
Henry	5	M		England	U. States	Panthea	22 Nov 1826
James	2	M		England	U. States	Panthea	22 Nov 1826
John	13	M	Spinner	England	U. States	Panthea	22 Nov 1826
Sally	13	F	Spinner	England	U. States	Panthea	22 Nov 1826
GRIMSHANT, Jas.	25	M	Merchant	G. Brittain	U. States	Pacific	23 Jan 1826
GRIMSHAW, Betsey	2	F	Child			Helen	4 Aug 1829
James	26	M	Merchant	Great Brittain	America	Pacific	13 Jan 1827
Jas., Mr.	30	M	Merchant	England	England	Manchester	8 Dec 1827
John	20	M	Merchant	Great Britain	Great Britain	Nestor	3 Nov 1820
Mary	23	F				Helen	4 Aug 1829
Thos.	25		Currier			Helen	4 Aug 1829
Wm.	21	M	Farmer	Great Britain	United States	Meridian	2 Jul 1827
GRIMSTON, Robert	34	M	Merchant	England	America	Orozimbo	1 Oct 1827
GRIMWOOD, Abraham	2	M		Suffolk, Engl.	U. States	Atlantic	13 Jul 1824
Ann	1	F		Suffolk, Engl.	U. States	Atlantic	13 Jul 1824
Eliza	9	F		Suffolk, Engl.	U. States	Atlantic	13 Jul 1824
Hannah	11	F		Suffolk, Engl.	U. States	Atlantic	13 Jul 1824
Isaac	12	M		Suffolk, Engl.	U. States	Atlantic	13 Jul 1824
Isaac	45	M	Farmer	Suffolk, Engl.	U. States	Atlantic	13 Jul 1824
Jacob	3	M		Suffolk, Engl.	U. States	Atlantic	13 Jul 1824
Joseph	6	M		Suffolk, Engl.	U. States	Atlantic	13 Jul 1824
Mary Ann	15	F		Suffolk, Engl.	U. States	Atlantic	13 Jul 1824
Sarah	13	F		Suffolk, Engl.	U. States	Atlantic	13 Jul 1824
Sophia	19	F		Suffolk, Engl.	U. States	Atlantic	13 Jul 1824
Susan	17	F		Suffolk, Engl.	U. States	Atlantic	13 Jul 1824
Susan	46	F		Suffolk, Engl.	U. States	Atlantic	13 Jul 1824
William	7	M		Suffolk, Engl.	U. States	Atlantic	13 Jul 1824
GRINDAD, Rachel	10	F	None	Great Brittan	U. States	John & Elizabeth	11 Dec 1826
Wm.	50	M	None	Great Brittan	U. States	John & Elizabeth	11 Dec 1826
Wm., Jur.	33	M	None	Great Brittan	U. States	John & Elizabeth	11 Dec 1826
GRINDID, Rachel	50	F	Spinster	Great Brittan	U. States	John & Elizabeth	11 Dec 1826
GRINDLAY, James	26	M	Lawyer	G. Britain	U. States	Camillus	8 Sep 1828

NAMES OF PASSENGERS	AGE	SEX	OCCUPATIONS	COUNTRY TO WHICH THEY BELONG	COUNTRY THEY INTEND TO INHABIT	SHIPS/DATES OF ARRIVAL	
GRINDLEY, James	12	M	...	...	United States	Camillus	10 Dec 1825
Margaret	18	F	...	...	United States	Camillus	10 Dec 1825
GRINDRED, Math.	24		Weaver	Rochdale, England	Great Britain	Franklin	22 Jun 1827
GRINMORY, Patrick	26	M	Mechanic	U.S.	U.S.	Emma	7 Jul 1824
GRINNELL, Henry	43	M	Merchant	America	America	Silas Richard	24 Oct 1829
Moses H.	22	M		...	U. States	Corinthian	2 Sep 1824
GRINSE, W. F.	42	M	Merchant	U. States	U. States	Tabasco	5 Aug 1826
GRINSHAW, Thos.	35	M	Farmer	Great Britain	United States	William Dawson	18 Jun 1827
GRIS, Henry Jeanneret	54	M	Watch Maker	Switzerland	United States	Thetis	5 Jul 1821
GRISSARD, Cathena	36	F	Farmer	Alsace in the Department of Upper and lower Rhine	United States	Carolina Augusta	16 May 1828
Catherine	5	F	Farmer	Alsace in the Department of Upper and lower Rhine	United States	Carolina Augusta	16 May 1828
Charles	2	M	Farmer	Alsace in the Department of Upper and lower Rhine	United States	Carolina Augusta	16 May 1828
Louise	4	F	Farmer	Alsace in the Department of Upper and lower Rhine	United States	Carolina Augusta	16 May 1828
Peter F.	40	M	Farmer	Alsace in the Department of Upper and lower Rhine	United States	Carolina Augusta	16 May 1828
GRIST, Geo.	30	M	Millwright	G. Britain	U. States	Cosmo	15 May 1827
Wm. B.	21	M	Merchant	United States	United States	Combine	9 Aug 1825
GRISWOLD, Ann	25	F		N. York	U. States	Perseverance	25 Oct 1821
E. C.	4...	M	Merchant	United States	United States	Cambria	8 Oct 1828
Elizabeth	25	F		U.S. America	U.S. America	Cincinnatus	31 Oct 1820
Elizh.	26	F		United States	United States	Acasta	14 Jun 1824
George	22	M	Student	United States	United States	Rolla	8 May 1823
Jacob	45	M	Carpenter	New York	United States	Ann Maria	4 Oct 1824
Josiah	35	M	m...	...	U. States	Julia	20 Dec 1825
Mary	2	F		United States	United States	Acasta	14 Jun 1824
Mary	14	F	Daughter	New York	United States	Ann Maria	4 Oct 1824
Nancy	33	F	Wife	New York	United States	Ann Maria	4 Oct 1824
GRISWOOD, John	33	M	Farmer	Great Briton	United States	Mount Vernon	30 Dec 1828
GROAGER, Benj.	42	M	Mariner	U. States	U. States	Telegraph	14 Jun 1828
GROENING, F.	45	M	Distiller	Denmark	U. States	Cincinnatus	3 Sep 1827
GROETA, Ettaien	21	M	Joiner	France	United States	Stephania	4 Aug 1826
GROGAN, James	20	M	Merchant	Ireland	U. States	Phocion	19 Sep 1822
Mic.	40	F		Great Britain	United States	Samuel Wright	12 Oct 1829
Wm.	45	M	Labourer	Great Britain	United States	Zodiac	29 Oct 1822
GROGGET, Thomas	24	M	Labourer	Argyle (Tedland) Scotland	United States	Jean Hastie	27 Jul 1829
GROGONY, Joseph	43	M	Labourer	Scotland	United States	Indus	5 Sep 1827
GROHAM, Henry	24	M	Miller	England	U. States	Unity	5 Sep 1828
GROING, Catherine	19	F		Gt. Britain		Dalhouse Castle	13 May 1828
GROJON, Alexander Jonas	20	M	Labourer	Swiss	U. States	Comet	28 Jul 1825
GROKEN, Edward	45	M	Farmer	Great Britain	U. States	Columbia	22 Sep 1828
Eliza	40	F	Farmer	Great Britain	U. States	Columbia	22 Sep 1828
Elizabeth	2 6/12	F	Farmer	Great Britain	U. States	Columbia	22 Sep 1828
James	6/12	M	Farmer	Great Britain	U. States	Columbia	22 Sep 1828
Susan	3	F	Farmer	Great Britain	U. States	Columbia	22 Sep 1828
GROLER, Abraham	21 7/12	M	Farmer	Switzerland	U. States	France	26 Jun 1828
Colin	6 4/12	M	Farmer	Switzerland	U. States	France	26 Jun 1828
Elizabeth	1 3/12	F	Farmer	Switzerland	U. States	France	26 Jun 1828
John	3 5/12	M	Farmer	Switzerland	U. States	France	26 Jun 1828
Madolin	29 4/12	F	Farmer	Switzerland	U. States	France	26 Jun 1828
Saml.	8 5/12	M	Farmer	Switzerland	U. States	France	26 Jun 1828
Samul	22 5/12	M	Farmer	Switzerland	U. States	France	26 Jun 1828
GROLON, Jh.	28	M	Merchant	France	France	Hiram	8 Jul 1829

NAMES OF PASSENGERS	AGE	SEX	OCCUPATIONS	COUNTRY TO WHICH THEY BELONG	COUNTRY THEY INTEND TO INHABIT	SHIPS/DATES OF ARRIVAL	
GROMLY, John	30	M	Labourer	Ireland	United States	Princess Charlotte	26 Apr 1827
GROOM, Ann	26	F	...	England	America	Ann	11 Apr 1821
Eliza	5	F		Gt. Britain	Gt. Britain	Silvanus Jenkins	24 Jul 1828
Emily	3	F		Gt. Britain	Gt. Britain	Silvanus Jenkins	24 Jul 1828
John	7	M		Gt. Britain	Gt. Britain	Silvanus Jenkins	24 Jul 1828
John	32	M	Farmer	Gt. Britain	Gt. Britain	Silvanus Jenkins	24 Jul 1828
Richard	0 3/12	M		Gt. Britain	Gt. Britain	Silvanus Jenkins	24 Jul 1828
Robert	36	M	Shoemaker	G. Britain	America	Spring	12 Oct 1821
Sarah	9	F		Gt. Britain	Gt. Britain	Silvanus Jenkins	24 Jul 1828
Sarah	34	F		Gt. Britain	Gt. Britain	Silvanus Jenkins	24 Jul 1828
Thomas	10	M	Child	Gt. Britain	Gt. Britain	Silvanus Jenkins	24 Jul 1828
GROONEY, Henry	19	M	Bricklayer	Ireland	U. States	Josephine	30 Aug 1828
GROOS, John	30	M	Mechanic	G. Britain	U. States	Mary Howland	22 Sep 1828
GROS, —, Infant	2	F	Farmer	Switzerland	U. States	Bayard	9 Nov 1825
George F.	12	M	Farmer	Switzerland	U. States	Bayard	9 Nov 1825
John G.	42	M	Farmer	Switzerland	U. States	Bayard	9 Nov 1825
M. N.	30	F	Farmer	Switzerland	U. States	Bayard	9 Nov 1825
GROSBY, John	27	M	Labourer	Whipsey		Aurora	8 Jun 1827
GROSCLAUDE, —				Germany	Unsurton	Orient	25 Nov 1825
*bierth 4 November							
Catarin	3	F		Germany	Unsurton	Orient	25 Nov 1825
Hanryett	7	F		Germany	Unsurton	Orient	25 Nov 1825
James	9	M		Germany	Unsurton	Orient	25 Nov 1825
Louis	35	M	Mechanic	Germany	Unsurton	Orient	25 Nov 1825
Louise	32	F		Germany	Unsurton	Orient	25 Nov 1825
GROSELIN, N. W.	19	M		Ireland	U. States	Geo. Canning	2 Sep 1828
GROSENBACKER, Samuel	20	M	Farmer	Switzerland	U.S.	Francois I	8 Aug 1829
GROSMAN, Christian	26	M		Wertemberg	Wertemberg	Edward Quesnel	3 Jul 1829
Christopher	18	M		Wertemberg	Wertemberg	Edward Quesnel	3 Jul 1829
Elizabeth B.	50	F		Wertemberg	Wertemberg	Edward Quesnel	3 Jul 1829
Frederick	24	M	Ropemaker	Wertemberg	Wertemberg	Edward Quesnel	3 Jul 1829
GROSON, John	30	M	Farmer	Great Brittan	U.S.	Emulous	29 Jun 1827
GROSS, Andrew	19	M	Baker	France	U. States	Edward Quesnel	4 Aug 1828
Catherine	4	F		Switzerland	U. States	Henri IV	7 May 1827
Charles	4	M		Switzerland	U. States	Henri IV	7 May 1827
Elizabeth	2	F		Switzerland	U. States	Henri IV	7 May 1827
Elizabeth	33	F		Switzerland	U. States	Henri IV	7 May 1827
Elizh.	32	F		Switzerland	U. States	Henri IV	7 May 1827
Jaques	5	M		Switzerland	U. States	Henri IV	7 May 1827
Jaques	9	M		Switzerland	U. States	Henri IV	7 May 1827
Jaques	34	M	...	Switzerland	U. States	Henri IV	7 May 1827
John M.	40 1/12	M	Blacksmith	France	United States	William	31 Jul 1826
Mark	10	M		Switzerland	U. States	Henri IV	7 May 1827
Mark	23	M		Switzerland	U. States	Henri IV	7 May 1827
Nicholas	...	M		Switzerland	U. States	Henri IV	7 May 1827
Nicholas	32	M		Switzerland	U. States	Henri IV	7 May 1827
Philip	2	M		Switzerland	U. States	Henri IV	7 May 1827
Philip	12	M		Switzerland	U. States	Henri IV	7 May 1827
Sophia	7	F		Switzerland	U. States	Henri IV	7 May 1827
GROSSIMER, Lewis	31	M	...man	United States	United States	Silas Richards	27 Oct 1825
GROSSMAN, Barbara	6	F	Farmer	Holland	U. States	Don Quixote	25 Oct 1828
Catharine	6	F	Farmer	Holland	U. States	Don Quixote	25 Oct 1828
Cathr.	40	F	Farmer	Holland	U. States	Don Quixote	25 Oct 1828
Christiana	10	F	Farmer	Holland	U. States	Don Quixote	25 Oct 1828
Elizabeth	21	F	Farmer	Holland	U. States	Don Quixote	25 Oct 1828
G.	17	M	Farmer	Holland	U. States	Don Quixote	25 Oct 1828
Jacob	19	M	Farmer	Holland	U. States	Don Quixote	25 Oct 1828
Jacob	51	M	Farmer	Holland	U. States	Don Quixote	25 Oct 1828
Johannes	9	F	Farmer	Holland	U. States	Don Quixote	25 Oct 1828
Ludwic	4	M	Farmer	Holland	U. States	Don Quixote	25 Oct 1828
Philip	20	M	Farmer	Holland	U. States	Don Quixote	25 Oct 1828
Rosina	24	F	Farmer	Holland	U. States	Don Quixote	25 Oct 1828
GROSVENOR, J.	28	M	Merchant	United States	United States	James Monroe	25 Apr 1822
S. W.	30	M	Merchant	U. States	U. States	Mary	22 May 1822
Seth	38	M	Merchant	U. States	U. States	Silas Richards	29 Oct 1828
Willm.	19	M	Merchant	St. John, N.B.	St. John, N.B.	St. Michael	28 Feb 1826
GROTT, S. Elizbh.	30	F		Bermuda	Bermuda	Magnet	10 Jul 1820

NAMES OF PASSENGERS	AGE	SEX	OCCUPATIONS	COUNTRY TO WHICH THEY BELONG	COUNTRY THEY INTEND TO INHABIT	SHIPS/DATES OF ARRIVAL	
GROTZ, Fredrick	22	M	None	France	U. States	Sully	25 Jun 1828
GROUCH, Charlotte	4	F	Farmer	England	U. States	Electra	7 Jul 1828
Emma	8	F	Farmer	England	U. States	Electra	7 Jul 1828
James	11	M	Farmer	England	U. States	Electra	7 Jul 1828
Jesse	13	M	Farmer	England	U. States	Electra	7 Jul 1828
John	41	M	Farmer	England	U. States	Electra	7 Jul 1828
Levi	6	M	Farmer	England	U. States	Electra	7 Jul 1828
Sarah	1	M	Spinster	England	U. States	Electra	7 Jul 1828
Sarah	38	M	Farmer	England	U. States	Electra	7 Jul 1828
GROUCHÉ, Eugene	30	M	Gentleman	France	United States	Bayard	23 Mar 1826
GROULIER, Maurice	52	M	Farmer	France	America	Bayard	15 Dec 1828
GROUP, Robt.	26	M	Seaman	Wilmington	United States	Venus	8 Sep 1820
GROUT, Nicholas	30	M	Farmer	Ireland	United States	Dublin Packet	13 Oct 1828
GROVE, Anne	10	F		G. Britain	United States	United States	11 Sep 1828
Cath.	10	F		G. Britain	United States	United States	11 Sep 1828
Ewd.	12	M		G. Britain	United States	United States	11 Sep 1828
Geo., Mr.	29	M	Merchant	England	Philadelphia	Hannibal	28 Apr 1824
H. D.	23	M	Farmer	not to Remain in the U. States	U. States	Maria Elizabeth	9 Jun 1826
H. D.	28		Merchant	Germany	United States	Albion	27 Jun 1827
Jno.	37	M	Farmer	England	U. States	Hudson	8 Oct 1827
John	34	M	Farmer	Great Britain	United States	James Monroe	27 Jul 1821
Sarah	77	F		G. Britain	United States	United States	11 Sep 1828
GROVER, Alexander	26		Merchant	England	U. States	Hudson	4 Sep 1823
Chs.	30	M	Mariner	U. States	U. States	Worromontogus	23 Jun 1823
Hannah S.	5	F		G. Britain	U.S. America	Cincinnatus	31 Oct 1820
John	42	M	Farmer	G. Britain	U.S. America	Cincinnatus	31 Oct 1820
Kitty	39	F		G. Britain	U.S. America	Cincinnatus	31 Oct 1820
Kitty, Junr.	17	F		G. Britain	U.S. America	Cincinnatus	31 Oct 1820
P.	30	F	None	Mexico	U. States	Cincinnatus	9 Jul 1825
GROVES, Ann	60	F	None	England		Marchioness	13 May 1828
John	20		Laborer	Ireland	United States	Robert Burns	18 Jun 1822
Richard	52	M	Farmer	England	United States	Roman	12 Jun 1826
Sam	30	M	Seaman	U. States	U. States	Income	12 Mar 1822
Thomas	41	M	Shipmaster	U. States Amer	United States	Lark	10 Mar 1823
GROVNEY, James	25	M	Labourer	Ireland	New York	Eliza	8 Mar 1827
GROWNCY, Michl.	23	M	Bricklayer	Ireland	America	Wilson	16 May 1825
GROYER, Polandon	30	M	Servant	U. States	U. States	Seine	10 Jun 1822
GROZIER, Rosalie	17	F	None	Germany	America	Orozimbo	1 Oct 1827
GRUATULLS, Wm.	20	M	Labourer	Great Britain		Moro Castle	6 Jul 1827
GRUBB, Thomas	27	M	Farmer	Great Britain	U. States	Ganges	21 Jun 1827
GRUBBE, J. H.	24	M	Gentleman	Gt. Britain	Canada	Corks	3 Aug 1824
GRUDGE, Isabella	23	F	Servant	Ireland	United States	Sylvester Healy	17 Oct 1825
Wm.	26	M	Laborer	Ireland	United States	Sylvester Healy	17 Oct 1825
GRULLER, G.	3...	M		Jamaica	England	Pleiades	13 Nov 1826
GRUMBOT, Nicholas	23	M	Farmer	Alsace in the Department of Upper and lower Rhine	United States	Carolina Augusta	16 May 1828
GRUNDER, Barb.	16	F	Farmer	Piedemont	U. States	Ohio	18 Jul 1821
Catharine	20	F	Farmer	Piedemont	U. States	Ohio	18 Jul 1821
GRUNDERTON, Archabold	22	M	Labourer	England	U. States	Ayrshire	12 May 1828
GRUNDY, Elias	...			A...	England	Great Britain	7 May 1827
John	36		Bleacher	A...	England	Great Britain	7 May 1827
Margaret	40			A...	England	Great Britain	7 May 1827
Mary	13			A...	England	Great Britain	7 May 1827
Samuel	2			A...	England	Great Britain	7 May 1827
Samuel	45	M	Merchant			Courier	13 Mar 1820
GRUNENTHAL, Abr., Mr.	17 4/12	M	Clerk	Dusseldorf	Boston	Cadmus	27 Aug 1822
GRUNHALGH, Saml.	2	M		Great Britain	U. States	United States	8 Sep 1827
Sarah	20	F		Great Britain	U. States	United States	8 Sep 1827
GRUNNON, James	35	M	Farmer	Ireland	United States	Justina	5 Aug 1823
GRUNUP, Wm. M., Mr.	25	M	Merchant	Gt. Britain	Gt. Britain	Pacific	22 May 1826
GRUTZ, Benjamin	35	M	Merchant	United States	United States	William	7 Jan 1828
GRUVERNEUR, Saml.	35	M	...	U. States	U.S.	Queen Mab	26 Nov 1825
GSCHWEILLER, Christopher	33	M	Tailor	France	United States	Thetis	5 Jul 1821

NAMES OF PASSENGERS	AGE	SEX	OCCUPATIONS	COUNTRY TO WHICH THEY BELONG	COUNTRY THEY INTEND TO INHABIT	SHIPS/DATES OF ARRIVAL	
GSCHWIND,							
Charles Henry	30	M	Merchant	Switzerland	United States	Henry	9 Jun 1826
Joseph	42	M	Tailor	Switzerland	United States	Thetis	5 Jul 1821
GUARKUT, Cristine	8	F	Farmer	Switzerland	United States	Olympia	12 Aug 1828
Cristine	38	F	Farmer	Switzerland	United States	Olympia	12 Aug 1828
Frederick	40	M	Farmer	Switzerland	United States	Olympia	12 Aug 1828
Jacob	6	M	Farmer	Switzerland	United States	Olympia	12 Aug 1828
Margaret	7	F	Farmer	Switzerland	United States	Olympia	12 Aug 1828
GUCED, John	28	M	Sawyer	G. Britain	Upper Canada	Perseverance	9 Jun 1827
GUDMUNDSDOTER,							
Anned	3 6/12	F	Farmer	Norway	United States	Salem	31 Aug 1829
Berta	8 6/12	F	Farmer	Norway	United States	Salem	31 Aug 1829
Tarbot	1 6/12	F	Farmer	Norway	United States	Salem	31 Aug 1829
GUEDRON, J. G.	30	M	Merchant	U. States	U. States	Rodman	9 Mar 1826
GUELLEN, A.	30		Merchant	France	U. States	Alfred	24 Jul 1828
C.	9		Merchant	France	U. States	Alfred	24 Jul 1828
Eliza	5		Merchant	France	U. States	Alfred	24 Jul 1828
Fran	36		Doctor	France	U. States	Alfred	24 Jul 1828
Frans	28		Merchant	Campeachy	U. States	Alfred	24 Jul 1828
M.	1		Merchant	France	U. States	Alfred	24 Jul 1828
GUENA, Francis Salber	23	M	Shu Maker	Medaira	New York	Rebecca Groves	31 Jul 1829
GUENIN, Francois	29	M		France	United States	Henri IV	2 Oct 1828
GUERADE, Frs.	20	M	Merchant	Aquin	Aquin, St. Domingo	Emily	2 Jun 1824
GUERBER, Augustus	19	M	Merchant	Switzerland	United States	Montano	31 May 1824
GUEREY, Jno.	27	M				Trio	5 May 1828
GUERIN, Francis	11	M	Boy	Nantz, France	United States	Nestor	8 Mar 1827
Francis	35	M	Merchant	New York	New York	Cannon	19 Dec 1820
GUERNSEY, Peter B.	25	M	Physician	New York	U. States	Crisis	26 May 1824
GUERORET, Isaac Abm.	25	M	Engraver	France	U.S.	Edward Quesnel	19 Oct 1829
GUERRIER, Henry	22	M	Taylor	France	United States	Montano	5 May 1828
GUERVA, A. Maria	25	F		Cuba	Neuvitas	Income	29 May 1824
GUEST, James	20 11/12	M	Printer	New Brunswick	United States	Hanford	19 Aug 1828
John	28	M	Shoemaker	Gt. Brittan		L'Esperance	6 Sep 1828
Mary	33	F		England	United States	Delta	24 Oct 1829
Thomas	25	M	Carpenter	Ireland	United States	Ann Maria	4 Oct 1824
GUFFER, —	7	F		Gt. Britain	U. States	Tantiva	7 Jul 1828
—	8	F		Gt. Britain	U. States	Tantiva	7 Jul 1828
Edmond	36	M		Gt. Britain	U. States	Tantiva	7 Jul 1828
N.	29	F		Gt. Britain	U. States	Tantiva	7 Jul 1828
GUGGER, Joan	30	M	Cooper	Switzerland	United States	Howard	27 Sep 1824
GUGGI, Lewis	44	M	Merchant	Spain	U. States	Anne	20 Jun 1828
GUI...UND, Thos.	27	M	Labourer	Great Britain	United States	William Dawson	18 Jun 1827
GUIBART, James	31	M		France	United States	Ariadne	25 Jul 1822
GUIBERT, —, Mdm.	30	F		Philada.	U. States	Little John	20 Aug 1822
GUIDAHCOROS, A.	45	M	Minister of the Gospel	Turkey	U. States	Douglass	4 Aug 1823
GUIGA, Anna	27	F		Germany	United States	Origon	8 Jun 1824
GUIGON, Augustine	7	M	None	France	U. States	Howard	21 Aug 1826
Josephine	3	F	None	France	U. States	Howard	21 Aug 1826
Thirese	34	F	None	France	U. States	Howard	21 Aug 1826
GUIL, Thomas	24	M	Joiner	Great Britain	United States	Courier	26 Jun 1827
GUILBER, Peter	11	M		Guersey	New York	Comet	19 Oct 1826
GUILBERT, Thomas	18	M	Taylor	Guersey	New York	Comet	19 Oct 1826
GUILBOT, P.	32	M	Mercht.	U.S.		Antioch	18 Aug 1829
GUILD, Jane	20		Daughter [of Wm.]	Great Britain	United States	Camillus	12 Sep 1827
Margt.	19		Wife [of Wm.]	Great Britain	United States	Camillus	12 Sep 1827
William	24	M		G. Britain	U. States	Florida	2 Jun 1828
Wm.	25		Weaver	Great Britain	United States	Camillus	12 Sep 1827
GUILE, Barbary	37	F	Agriculturist	Germany	U.S.	Helen	3 May 1828
George	4	M	Agriculturist	Germany	U.S.	Helen	3 May 1828
Henry	21	M	Candle Manfr.	Great Britain		Dalmannock	24 Ocg 1826
Jacque	36	M	Agriculturist	Germany	U.S.	Helen	3 May 1828
Peter	8	M	Agriculturist	Germany	U.S.	Helen	3 May 1828
Solomon	2	M	Agriculturist	Germany	U.S.	Helen	3 May 1828
GUILL, Ann	25	F	Milliner	Gt. Brittan	America	Reindeer	3 Aug 1827
Edward	30	M	Mason	G. Britain	U. States	Eliza	9 May 1827
GUILLAMOD, J. H. D.	15	F		Prussia	United States	Origon	8 Jun 1824
R.	13	F		Prussia	United States	Origon	8 Jun 1824
V. F.	11	M		Prussia	United States	Origon	8 Jun 1824

NAMES OF PASSENGERS	AGE	SEX	OCCUPATIONS	COUNTRY TO WHICH THEY BELONG	COUNTRY THEY INTEND TO INHABIT	SHIPS/DATES OF ARRIVAL	
GUILLARD, Adele	28	F		U.S.	N. York	France	29 Nov 1827
John	37	M	Merchant	U.S.	N. York	France	29 Nov 1827
GUILLARS, S.	27	M	Miller	Great Britton	U. State	Earl of Liverpool	16 Aug 1826
GUILLE, Catherine	8	F		Scotland	United States	Camillus	9 May 1827
Gavin	3	M		Scotland	United States	Camillus	9 May 1827
Gavin	32	M		Scotland	United States	Camillus	9 May 1827
Jane	30	F		Scotland	United States	Camillus	9 May 1827
John	6	M		Scotland	United States	Camillus	9 May 1827
Robert	4	M		Scotland	United States	Camillus	9 May 1827
William	1	M		Scotland	United States	Camillus	9 May 1827
GUILLET, —, Mr.	26	M	Merchant	France	U.S.A.	Bayard	25 Aug 1829
—, Mrs.	22	F	Lady	U.S.A.	U.S.A.	Bayard	25 Aug 1829
Inderi	22	M	Merchant	Switzerland	U. States	Queen Mab	16 Mar 1825
Isedore	24	M	Merchant	France	United States	Montano	27 Aug 1827
L. J.	50	M	Litterati	France	France	Edward Quesnel	21 Apr 1827
Peter	30	M	Planter	U. States	U. States	Diana	18 Jul 1820
GUILLING, C. G.	20	M		France	U. States	Talma	23 Sep 1828
GUILLMAN, A.	22	M	Merchant	Spain	U. States	Dromo	22 May 1826
GUILLOUNE, A.	21	M	Merchant	France	United States	Elizabeth	22 May 1822
GUIN, Ann	21	F		Great Britain	United States	Isaac Hicks	10 Jul 1827
GUINLER, Adam	23	M	Cabinet Maker	France	United States	New England	29 Aug 1828
GUINSHAW, Ame	11	F	None	England	United States	Dalhouse Castle	6 Sep 1827
Betty	6	F	None	England	United States	Dalhouse Castle	6 Sep 1827
George	9	M	None	England	United States	Dalhouse Castle	6 Sep 1827
Hannah	3	F	None	England	United States	Dalhouse Castle	6 Sep 1827
Mary	56	F	None	England	United States	Dalhouse Castle	6 Sep 1827
Thos.	13	M	None	England	United States	Dalhouse Castle	6 Sep 1827
GUIRCAUZ, J. D.	19	M	Farmer	Switzerland	America	Don Quixotte	2 Jun 1828
GUIRET, Franscois	30	F		Cooper	United States	Spartan	21 Aug 1824
GUISHORE, Peter S.	29	M	Merchant	U. States	U. States	Pedlar	17 Sep 1824
GUISNARD, Louis	45 2/12	M	Lawyer	France	France	Erie	19 Oct 1829
GUIVEINA, Chas. F.	32	M	Watchmaker	Prussia	U.S.	Edward Quesnel	19 Oct 1829
GUJALVA, Peter, Jr.	24	M	Merchant	Teneriffe	Teneriffe	Merury	14 Dec 1824
GULE, Hugh	26	M	Labourer	Ireland	United States	Hope	12 Jun 1828
GULION, L.	41	M	Merchant	Italy	New York	Income	12 Feb 1824
GULIVAN, Henry	30	M	Farmer	Ireland	United States	Antioch	21 Sep 1827
Mary	21	F	Spinster	Ireland	United States	Antioch	21 Sep 1827
GULLAT, Francis	36	M	F. Tutor	Ireland		Quatre Freres	29 Jul 1828
GULLEN, John	29	M	Joiner	Scotland	U. States	Roger Stewart	9 Jun 1828
Mary	19	F	Farmer	Scotland	U. States	Roger Stewart	9 Jun 1828
GULLERHAN, Bridget	20	F		Ireland	United States	Kleber	23 Jul 1827
Mary	19	F		Ireland	United States	Kleber	23 Jul 1827
Thomas	24	M	Labourer	Ireland	United States	Kleber	23 Jul 1827
GULLET, Fredrick	30	M	Wheel Right	Ireland		Quatre Freres	29 Jul 1828
Stephen	47	M	None	U. States	U. States	James Monroe	8 Aug 1820
GULLEY, Chatherine	6	F	None	England	United States	Hamilton	13 Nov 1827
Dora	8	M	None	England	United States	Hamilton	13 Nov 1827
Henry	30	M	Carpenter	England	United States	Hamilton	13 Nov 1827
Margret	4	F	None	England	United States	Hamilton	13 Nov 1827
Mary	40	F	None	England	United States	Hamilton	13 Nov 1827
Morris	2	M	None	England	United States	Hamilton	13 Nov 1827
Sarah Amelia	1/12	F	None	None	United States	Hamilton	13 Nov 1827
GULLIVAN, D.	9		Farmer	Ireland	U. States	Schuylkill	22 Aug 1825
GUMBALE, John B.	26	M	Merchant	U.S. America	U.S. America	Columbia	15 Nov 1826
GUMBER, Louisa	1	F		Gt. Britain	New York	Leeds	7 Nov 1828
Louisa	23	F		Gt. Britain	New York	Leeds	7 Nov 1828
Stephen	24	M	Engeneer	Gt. Britain	New York	Leeds	7 Nov 1828
Stephen, Jur.	3	M		Gt. Britain	New York	Leeds	7 Nov 1828
GUNAN, Bernard	30	M	Plasterer	G. Britain	U. States	Camillus	8 Sep 1828
GUNBIRT, J.	36	M	Merchant		U. States	John London	1 Sep 1823
GUNCHINA, Margt.	18	F	None	Great Britain	United States	William Dawson	18 Jun 1827
Owen	25	M	Smith	Great Britain	United States	William Dawson	18 Jun 1827
GUNDL, G. H.	23	M	Merchant	U. States	U. States	Minerva	9 Jan 1827
Maria	20	F	Wife	Germany	U. States	Minerva	9 Jan 1827
GUNN, Chas.	10	M		Ireland	U. States	Olive Branch	30 Oct 1823
John	31 10/12	M	Farmer	England	Gallaway, N.Y.	Chelsea	16 May 1828
Mary	20	F		Ireland	N. Jersey	Potomac	7 Aug 1827
Sarah	2	F	Farmer	England	Gallaway, N.Y.	Chelsea	16 May 1828

NAMES OF PASSENGERS	AGE	SEX	OCCUPATIONS	COUNTRY TO WHICH THEY BELONG	COUNTRY THEY INTEND TO INHABIT	SHIPS/DATES OF ARRIVAL	
GUNN (cont'd)							
Sarah	25	F	Farmer	England	Gallaway, N.Y.	Chelsea	16 May 1828
GUNNELL, Betsey	10	F	Artist	England	U. States	Cincinnatus	9 Jul 1825
Betsey	37	F	Artist	England	U. States	Cincinnatus	9 Jul 1825
Ellen	7	F	Artist	England	U. States	Cincinnatus	9 Jul 1825
Emma	3	F	Artist	England	U. States	Cincinnatus	9 Jul 1825
Jessy	1	F	Artist	England	U. States	Cincinnatus	9 Jul 1825
John	35	M	Artist	England	U. States	Cincinnatus	9 Jul 1825
William T.	30	M	Manufacturer	U. States	U.S.	Bayard	10 Nov 1824
GUNNING, Ed.	29	M	Merchant	England	U. States	Little John	20 Aug 1822
Edward	2					Little John	20 Aug 1822
Henry	1/12					Little John	20 Aug 1822
Henry	30	M	Farmer	U. States	U. States	Josephine	30 Aug 1828
S. E.	23	F		England	U. States	Little John	20 Aug 1822
GUNNMAN, Alfred	60	M	Engineer	England	U. States	Messenger	10 Jul 1829
GUNNOCCIA,							
Dominicco	41	M	Gardner	Italy	United States	Cambridge	19 Sep 1828
GUNRICH, Luaver	28	M	Shoe maker	Germany	United States	Virginia	31 May 1828
GUNSENBAER,							
Ferdinand D.	22	M	None	Switzerland	U. States	Manhattan	20 Jun 1825
GUNSHALD, Bridget	18	F	Labourer	Ireland	United States	Essex	23 May 1828
GUNSON, Thomas	24	M	...	Ireland	United States	Colossus	30 May 1825
GUNT, Richard	81		Cloth ...			Agricola	1 Jul 1820
GUNTERS, Saml.	23	M	Labourer			Evergreen	28 Jul 1820
GUNTHER, Anne Maria	50	F	Farmer	Switzerland		Antioch	18 Aug 1829
Catherine	6	F		Switzerland	U.S.	Francois I	8 Aug 1829
Catherine	35	F		Switzerland	U.S.	Francois I	8 Aug 1829
Elizabeth	10	F		Switzerland	U.S.	Francois I	8 Aug 1829
Jean	20	M	Farmer	Switzerland		Antioch	18 Aug 1829
Jean	56	M	Farmer	Switzerland		Antioch	18 Aug 1829
Magdalen	3	F		Switzerland	U.S.	Francois I	8 Aug 1829
Maria	6/12	F		Switzerland	U.S.	Francois I	8 Aug 1829
Marie	18	F	Farmer	Switzerland		Antioch	18 Aug 1829
Nicholas	12	M		Switzerland	U.S.	Francois I	8 Aug 1829
Peter	15	M		Switzerland	U.S.	Francois I	8 Aug 1829
Peter	30	M	Farmer	Switzerland	U.S.	Francois I	8 Aug 1829
Weinhold	6	M	Farmer	Switzerland		Antioch	18 Aug 1829
GUNTON, Isabella	50	F		England	United States	Ann Maria	27 Aug 1822
GURARD, S.	19	M	Merchant	St. Domingo	U. States	Rover	11 Jun 1823
GURDETTE, Jno. B.	21	M	Mercht.	U.S.	U.S.	Toison	6 May 1828
GURDON, E.	28			Ireland	New York	General Marion	21 Nov 1828
GURENET, Z.	34	M	Merchant	Sweden	U. States	Cadmus	28 May 1821
GURES, A.	40	M	Merchant	Portugal	U. States	Sally	4 Aug 1821
GURGLEY, Charles	30	M	None	Canada	U. States	William & Nancy	31 Jan 1823
GURLING, Sa... R.	7			England	England	Thames	25 Oct 1821
Susan	28			England	England	Thames	25 Oct 1821
GURMAN,							
Catharine	12 9/12	F		Switzerland	United States	Criterion	13 Oct 1825
Elizabeth	14 11/12	F		Switzerland	United States	Criterion	13 Oct 1825
Elizabeth	40 ...	F		Switzerland	United States	Criterion	13 Oct 1825
John B.	5 .../12	M		Switzerland	United States	Criterion	13 Oct 1825
Joseph A.	7 .../12	M		Switzerland	United States	Criterion	13 Oct 1825
Joseph A.	43 ...	M	Gentleman	Switzerland	United States	Criterion	13 Oct 1825
Maria	15 ...	F		Switzerland	United States	Criterion	13 Oct 1825
Mary B.	4 6/12	F		Switzerland	United States	Criterion	13 Oct 1825
GURNEY, Chas.	33	M	Farmer	England	U. States	Pleiades	9 Oct 1829
Jane	13	F		England	U. States	Pleiades	9 Oct 1829
Martha	1	F		England	U. States	Pleiades	9 Oct 1829
Mary Ann	23	F		England	U. States	Pleiades	9 Oct 1829
Thos.	30	M	Labourer	...	U. States	St. Michael	21 Jul 1824
GURRETT, Richard	24	M	Carpenter	Gt. Britain		Corinthian	27 Oct 1829
GURRIK, John	20	M	Labourer	Ireland		Robert Fulton	4 Jun 1828
GURRY, Eliza	5	F				Neptunes Barge	23 Apr 1821
John	50	M	Merchant	France	America	Martha Pond	7 Sep 1820
GURSDON, Augustus	25	M	Merchant	France		Charlemagne	20 Aug 1829
GURSELL, Isaac	30	M		England	England	Pleiades	13 Nov 1826
GURWOOD, John	38 3/12	M	Line Col. of the Army	Great Brittion	Great Grittian	Four Sons	31 May 1828
GUSSER, Gaspard	39		Farmer	France	U. States	Elizabeth	9 Jul 1825

513

NAMES OF PASSENGERS	AGE	SEX	OCCUPATIONS	COUNTRY TO WHICH THEY BELONG	COUNTRY THEY INTEND TO INHABIT	SHIPS/DATES OF ARRIVAL	
GUTBROD, David	24 6/12	M	Tailor	Germany	Pensylvania	James Noble	27 Aug 1827
GUTHER, G.	20	M	Farmer	Great Britain	United States	Isaac Hicks	6 Dec 1827
GUTHERIE, Ann	51	F	None	America	America	Hesperus	7 Jul 1820
GUTHERY, Bridget	38	F		St. Johns	U. States	Nancy	10 Jul 1822
GUTHMEN, An	22	F	Farm	France		Pallas	14 Jun 1828
Ann	45	F	Baker	France		Pallas	14 Jun 1828
Catheran	16	F	Farm	France		Pallas	14 Jun 1828
Joseffe	59	M		France		Pallas	14 Jun 1828
Mariah	18	F		France		Pallas	14 Jun 1828
Mary	20	F	Weaver	France		Pallas	14 Jun 1828
GUTHRE, Jane	32	F		U. States	U. States	Buck	21 Nov 1822
Jno.	1	M		U. States	U. States	Buck	21 Nov 1822
GUTHREE, Eliza	1 6/12	F	None	Scotland	United States	William	19 Jan 1820
H.	8/12	F	None	Scotland	United States	William	19 Jan 1820
H. F.	32	M	Currier	United States	United States	William	19 Jan 1820
Lucy	26	F	None	United States	United States	William	19 Jan 1820
GUTIERRIS, J. M.	23	M	Merchant	Mexico	Mexico	Stephania	26 Apr 1824
GUTIORES, Jose	40	M	Gentleman	Mexico	Mexico	Lady Washington	31 Dec 1827
GUTPERMEN, Ann	20	F	Agriculture	Wirtemburg	United States	Henri IV	14 Oct 1829
GUTTENB..., Philippe Gerard	27	M	...t	Germany	United States	Montano	8 May 1827
GUTTERY, Jane	22	F	Servant	Ireland	United States	Ann Maria	5 May 1824
GUTUMES DE ESTRADA, J. M.	27	M	Gentleman	Mexico	Mexico	Virginia	8 Mar 1828
GUVEN, Alexr.	26	M		St. Johns	U. States	Wanderer	30 Oct 1828
GUY, A. G.	35	M	Merchant	U. States	U. States	William Thompson	24 Aug 1827
Allice	20	F	Labourer	Ireland	U. States	Two Marys	20 Apr 1825
Anna	24	F	Farmer's wife	Ireland	America	Farmer	15 Nov 1823
Caroline	21	F		England	Canada	Hudson	20 Nov 1828
Esther	...0	F	Labourer	Ireland	U. States	Two Marys	20 Apr 1825
Henry	22	M	Farmer	England	New York	Chelsea	16 May 1828
John	9	M	Labourer	Ireland	U. States	Two Marys	20 Apr 1825
Jonathan	18	M	Farmer	England	New York	Chelsea	16 May 1828
Margaret	20	F	Spinster	Ireland	U. States	William & John	10 Jul 1824
Robert	20	M	Labourer	Ireland	U. States	William & John	10 Jul 1824
Robt.	16	M	Labourer	Ireland	U. States	Two Marys	20 Apr 1825
Wm.	4	M	Labourer	Ireland	U. States	Two Marys	20 Apr 1825
Wm.	9	M		G. Britain	U. States	Cosmo	15 May 1827
GUYAHOA, Peter	25	M	Merchant	Canary Islands	Canary Islands	Virginia	8 Mar 1828
GUYLE, Jno. Deman	66	M	Merchant	Dane	Para	Director	20 Sep 1824
GUYNN, Eliza	12	F	Child	England	United States	Hanford	3 Jul 1829
George	50	M	Trader	England	United States	Hanford	3 Jul 1829
Hannah Mariah	7	F	Child	England	United States	Hanford	3 Jul 1829
Mary Ann	14	F	Child	England	United States	Hanford	3 Jul 1829
Rose Ann	12	F	Child	England	United States	Hanford	3 Jul 1829
Rose Ann	46	F	Wife to [George]	England	United States	Hanford	3 Jul 1829
Stewart	9	F	Child	England	United States	Hanford	3 Jul 1829
GUYTER, J.	3...	M	Labourer	England	United States	Alicia	9 May 1827
GUZMAN, Cipriano	25	M	Servant	Guatemala	United States	Favorite	9 Oct 1823
M.	45	M	Merct.	Yucatan	Yucatan	Imperial	12 Aug 1825
Ml.	12	M	Boy	Yucatan	Yucatan	Imperial	12 Aug 1825
P.	45	M	Merct.	Yucatan	Yucatan	Imperial	12 Aug 1825
GWENDALE, Thomas	21	M	Labourer	Ireland	U. States	Loire	6 Dec 1827
GWIRNER, Fred	29	M	Brewer	France	United States	New England	29 Aug 1828
GWYN, Mergart	20	F	Spinster	Ireland	United States	Marmion	17 Jun 1825
GYBBS, Stephen	28	M	Mariner	U. States	U. States	Amazon	29 Aug 1825
GYLIN, Elizabeth	60	F	Farmer	Switzerland		Antioch	18 Aug 1829
Jean	32	M	Farmer	Switzerland		Antioch	18 Aug 1829
GYLLENGRANT, —, Madame	33	F	Lady	Sweeden	Sweeden	Tapperheten	12 Jun 1826
GYNOUR, —, Madam	25	F		Bordeaux	U. States	Hero	3 Sep 1823
B.	33	M	Merchant	Bordeaux	U. States	Hero	3 Sep 1823
GYPSIN, Richd.	27	M	Farmer	England	New York	Commerce	24 Sep 1823
GYSON, George	25	M	Servant	United States	United States	Only Daughter	29 Apr 1825
H..., Antono	...	M	Farmer	Switzerland	United States	Elbe	2 Aug 1822
Christianna	Infant					Packet	27 Aug 1822

NAMES OF PASSENGERS	AGE	SEX	OCCUPATIONS	COUNTRY TO WHICH THEY BELONG	COUNTRY THEY INTEND TO INHABIT	SHIPS/DATES OF ARRIVAL	
H... (cont'd)							
David	30	M	Farmer	Great Britian	United States	Robert Quayle	29 Jul 1822
H...ARD, George	32	M	Weaver	England	United States	Trident	30 Sep 1826
H...CHILD, Henrick	22	M	Servant	Hamburg	United States	Maria Elizabeth	2 Sep 1822
H...D, Jno.	...	...	...	...	United States	Minerva	30 Oct 1827
H...ICH, Christian	3	F		Switzerland	United States	Elbe	2 Aug 1822
H...K, Andrew ..., Revd.	35	M	Clergyman	England	New York	Thames	6 Oct 1820
H...SS, Dolly	21	F	None	Great Britain	United States	Atlantic	28 May 1827
H...T, Ann	21	F		Gt. Britain		Dalhouse Castle	13 May 1828
H...THER, Robert	30	M	Miner	Great Britain	United States	Colossus	5 Jun 1827
H...VILLE, James	21	M	Labourer	Ireland	United States	Meteor	26 Jun 1827
HA..., Benjamin	25	M	Clothier	Great Britain	United States	Frances Henrietta	17 Sep 1827
HA...DON, Elenor	11	F		Ireland	U. States	Virginia	20 Jun 1825
HA...TY, James	45	M	Merchant	Great Britain	U. States	Hector	11 Oct 1824
HAAGA, Ann Maria	14	F		Wertemberg	Wertemberg	Edward Quesnel	3 Jul 1829
Catherine	49	F		Wertemberg	Wertemberg	Edward Quesnel	3 Jul 1829
Christopher F.	16	M		Wertemberg	Wertemberg	Edward Quesnel	3 Jul 1829
Gottleib	7	M		Wertemberg	Wertemberg	Edward Quesnel	3 Jul 1829
Gottleib	45	M	Farmer	Wertemberg	Wertemberg	Edward Quesnel	3 Jul 1829
John	9	M		Wertemberg	Wertemberg	Edward Quesnel	3 Jul 1829
Maria Agnes	18	F		Wertemberg	Wertemberg	Edward Quesnel	3 Jul 1829
HAAKE, Geo.	24	M	Printer	Germany	U. States	Constitution	25 Jul 1823
HAAS, —, a child born on board	3/12	F		Germany	U. States	Three Brothers	21 Mar 1825
—, his Child [Jacob Joseph]	3	F		Germany	U. States	Three Brothers	21 Mar 1825
—, Mrs., his Wife [Jacob Joseph]	25	F		Germany	U. States	Three Brothers	21 Mar 1825
Eberhard	40	M	Farmer	Germany	Pensylvania	James Noble	27 Aug 1827
Elizabeth	4	F		France	America, U.N.S.	Great Britain	3 Aug 1829
Elizabeth	5	F		France	America, U.N.S.	Great Britain	3 Aug 1829
Elizabeth	34	F		France	America, U.N.S.	Great Britain	3 Aug 1829
Henri	6	M		France	America, U.N.S.	Great Britain	3 Aug 1829
Jacob Joseph	28	M	Farmer	Germany	U. States	Three Brothers	21 Mar 1825
Jean	34	M	Mason	France	America, U.N.S.	Great Britain	3 Aug 1829
John	6/12	M		France	America, U.N.S.	Great Britain	3 Aug 1829
Marguerita	7 6/12	F		France	America, U.N.S.	Great Britain	3 Aug 1829
Martin	8	M		France	America, U.N.S.	Great Britain	3 Aug 1829
Philip	37	M	Farmer	France	America, U.N.S.	Great Britain	3 Aug 1829
Rosina	25	F	Servant	Wirtemberg	America, U.N.S.	Great Britain	3 Aug 1829
HABACKER, Christian	41	M	Farmer	Switserland	Ohio	Danube	20 Jul 1826
Magtalino	36	F	Framer	Switserland	Ohio	Danube	20 Jul 1826
HABART, John	20	M	Clerk	Great Britian	U. States	Henry Kneedland	7 Aug 1826
HABBIN, Francis	20	M	Cord weaver	England	U. States	Electra	7 Jul 1828
John	22	M	Cord weaver	England	U. States	Electra	7 Jul 1828
HABERT, J. B.	25	M	Merchant	France	France	L. Emilie Marie	12 Jul 1820
HABLITZ, F.	18	M	Weaver	Switzerland	U. States	La Urania	3 Jul 1828
HABUTTEE, Louis	26	M	Merchant	U. States	U. States	Pizarro	21 Oct 1825
HACK, Anne	26	F	Farmer	France	France	Sully	15 Jul 1829
Christiana	37	F				Golden Grove	6 Sep 1820
Christopher	1	M				Golden Grove	6 Sep 1820
D.	40	M	Docter	American	U. States	Robert Edwards	11 Mar 1822
Eliza	23	F	Domestic	France	United States	Cavalier	25 Jul 1828
Jacob	30	M	Farmer	France	France	Sully	15 Jul 1829
Phillip	38	M				Golden Grove	6 Sep 1820
HACKEL, Jane	40	F	Labourer	Ireland	United States	Meteor	26 Jun 1827
Mary	25	F	Labourer	Ireland	United States	Meteor	26 Jun 1827
Patrick	21	M	Labourer	Ireland	United States	Meteor	26 Jun 1827
HACKENDORN,							
Sarah	30 4/12	F	Milliner	Switzerland	United States	France	6 Oct 1828
Verine	21 2/12	F	Milliner	Switzerland	United States	France	6 Oct 1828
HACKENRATH,							
Leon, Mr.	27	M	Merchant	Holland	U. States	Hudson	10 Nov 1825
HACKERSON, C.	25	M	Carpenter	U. States	U. States	Palestine	1 May 1821
HACKET, Catherine	20	F	Wife	Ireland	United States	Matvina	19 Oct 1826
James	3	M	Child	Ireland	United States	Matvina	19 Oct 1826
Lawrence	30	M	Labourer	Ireland	United States	Matvina	19 Oct 1826

NAMES OF PASSENGERS	AGE	SEX	OCCUPATIONS	COUNTRY TO WHICH THEY BELONG	COUNTRY THEY INTEND TO INHABIT	SHIPS/DATES OF ARRIVAL	
HACKET (cont'd)							
Michal	33	M	Farmer	Ireland	U. States	Combine	30 Nov 1825
Thomas	18	M	Bookkeeper	England	United States	Enterprize	19 Oct 1826
Wm.	25	M	Sawyer	G. Britain	Upper Canada	Perseverance	9 Jun 1827
HACKETT, Allen	22	M	Laborer	Ireland	United States	Sarah G	19 Jun 1827
Cordin	2	M		England	America	William	21 Sep 1821
Dennis	21	M	Weaver	Ireland	New York	Louisa	20 Jul 1826
Eliza	4	F		England	America	William	21 Sep 1821
Eliza	23	F		England	America	William	21 Sep 1821
Eliza	30	F	None	Great Brittan	U. States	Gem	26 Jul 1827
James	23	M	Laborer or Spinster	Ireland	United States	Sarah G	11 Sep 1827
James	33	M	Merchant	U.S.	New York	Brighton	24 Aug 1827
Jane	22	F	Spinster	Ireland	New York	Louisa	20 Jul 1826
Jno.	21					Trio	5 May 1828
Mary	25	F	Spinster	Ireland	United States	Asia	29 Jul 1829
Maurice	25		Cooper	Ireland	United States	Rufus King	4 Sep 1823
Michael	20	M	Mechanic	U. States	U. States	Birmingham	16 Jun 1828
Michael M.	21	M	None	England	England	Britannia	23 Mar 1829
Pat	47	M	Labourer	Ireland	United States	Essex	23 May 1828
Patty	26	F		Great Britain	United States	Meridian	2 Jul 1827
William	30	M	Farmer	England	America	William	21 Sep 1821
HACKING, Joseph	42	M	Clothier	Great Britain	United States	William Dawson	18 Jun 1827
HACKLEE, William	22	M	Labourer	England	United States	Concordia	25 Aug 1827
HACKMAN, A.	18	F	Gent	French	Switzerland	Charlemagne	19 Sep 1828
Christian	46	M	Gent	French	Switzerland	Charlemagne	19 Sep 1828
Eliz.	42	F	Gent	French	Switzerland	Charlemagne	19 Sep 1828
James	24	M	Labourer		New York	Prince Madore	28 Aug 1820
Jane	13	F	Spinster		New York	Prince Madore	28 Aug 1820
Margt.	10	F	Spinster		New York	Prince Madore	28 Aug 1820
Mary	25	F	Spinster		New York	Prince Madore	28 Aug 1820
HACKNES, Nancy	28	F	Spinster	Ireland	U.S. of America	Meteor	19 Mar 1828
HACKSTAFF, Charles L.	22	M	None	United States	United States	Manhattan	24 Oct 1825
William G.	26	M	Mariner	U.S.	U.S.	George Canning	20 Jan 1829
HADAKA, Frederick	28	M	Catler	Germany	U. States	Jane	11 Jul 1828
HADCROFT, James	64	M	Farmer	England	America	Silas Richard	24 Oct 1829
HADDEN, Adam	5	M		England	New York	James Monroe	23 Aug 1822
David	53	M	Merchant	U. States	United States	Florida	14 Sep 1827
Eliz.	22			England	United States	Hugh Johnson	11 Jun 1828
Emma	2	F		England	New York	James Monroe	23 Aug 1822
Isabella	17	F		U. States	United States	Florida	14 Sep 1827
Jane	7	F		England	New York	James Monroe	23 Aug 1822
Janey	31	F		England	New York	James Monroe	23 Aug 1822
Mary	21	F		Ireland	New York	Amanda	23 May 1827
Saml.	24	M	Farmer	Great Britain	U. States America	Maria	22 May 1822
HADDER, Wm.	24	M	Shoemaker	Ireland	U. States of America	Courier	17 Mar 1827
HADDIN, John	23	M	Farmer	Goland Tyrom	...	Gleaner	24 May 1823
HADDLE, Henry	56		Farmer	England	United States	Hugh Johnson	11 Jun 1828
HADDOCH, H.	23	M	Merchant	St. Bartholmas	St. Martin	Leonora	25 May 1826
HADDOCK, Addam	5...	M	Gent	French	Switzerland	Charlemagne	19 Sep 1828
E.	22	F	Gent	French	Switzerland	Charlemagne	19 Sep 1828
Edward	39	M	None	Great Britain	United States	Ann Maria	9 Mar 1820
F.	18	M	Gent	French	Switzerland	Charlemagne	19 Sep 1828
H.	26	F	Gent	French	Switzerland	Charlemagne	19 Sep 1828
H.	45	F	Gent	French	Switzerland	Charlemagne	19 Sep 1828
Isaac	40	F	Spinster	Great Britain	U. States	Boston	28 Aug 1821
J.	22	M	Gent	French	Switzerland	Charlemagne	19 Sep 1828
Jacob	54	M	Gent	French	Switzerland	Charlemagne	19 Sep 1828
James	37	M	Weaver	Ireland	United States	L. M. Pelham	25 Jun 1822
Jane	12			Cork	Philadelphia	Schuylkill	22 Aug 1825
M.	48	F	Gent	French	Switzerland	Charlemagne	19 Sep 1828
Marion	24	M	Farmer	Great Britain	U. States	Boston	28 Aug 1821
Marsden	61	M	None	Great Britain	United States	Ann Maria	9 Mar 1820
Martha	64	F	Spinster	Great Britain	U. States	Boston	28 Aug 1821
R.	24	F	Gent	French	Switzerland	Charlemagne	19 Sep 1828
Wm.	24	M	Farmer	Ireland	United States	L. M. Pelham	25 Jun 1822
HADDON, —, Miss	3	F		St. Croix	America, U.S.	Jupiter	6 Aug 1826
—, Miss	7	F		St. Croix	America, U.S.	Jupiter	6 Aug 1826
—, Mrs.	35	F		St. Croix	America, U.S.	Jupiter	6 Aug 1826
Lewis	40	M	Planter	St. Croix	America, U.S.	Jupiter	6 Aug 1826

NAMES OF PASSENGERS	AGE	SEX	OCCUPATIONS	COUNTRY TO WHICH THEY BELONG	COUNTRY THEY INTEND TO INHABIT	SHIPS/DATES OF ARRIVAL	
HADEN, Henery	25	M	Cordwainer	England	United States	Cambria	16 Aug 1827
Michael	26	M	Labourrer	Great Britan	U. States	Ann Marria	6 Aug 1823
HADESS, B.	22	M	Merchant	U. States	U. States	Colossus	21 Apr 1827
HADFIELD, —, Mrs.	26	F		G. Britain	Canada	Columbia	7 Sep 1827
John	1	M		Gt. Britain	United States	Columbia	7 Sep 1827
Wm.	28	M	Farmer	G. Britain	Canada	Columbia	7 Sep 1827
HADIN, Thomas D.	20	M	Plater	U. States		Hudson	23 Jul 1828
HADKINS, Henry	23	M	Jeweller	London	New York	New York	31 Jul 1829
John	40	M	Farmer	England	United States	Jubilee	13 Jul 1829
Walter	16	M	Farmer	England	United States	Jubilee	13 Jul 1829
HADLEY, Anne M., Mrs.	55	F		England	U. States	Hudson	10 Nov 1825
Hasten	38	M	Farmer	Great Britain	Great Britain	Columbia	1 Dec 1823
Ritter	23	M	Carpenter	New York	Boston, Mass.	Rubicon	22 May 1826
Wm.	23	M	Shoemaker	Leicester	Leicester	Aldebaron	21 Jan 1826
HADLOCK, —, Madam	22	F		Prussia	United States	Henry	9 Jun 1826
—, Miss	3/12	F		France	United States	Henry	9 Jun 1826
Samuel	34 2/12	M	Merchant	United States	United States	Henry	9 Jun 1826
HADLOW, Henry	47 9/12	M	Gardner	Great Briton	uncertain	Mount Vernon	29 Aug 1828
HADSON, L.	27	M	Merchant	U. States	U. States	St. Croix	13 Sep 1827
HADSWELL, Jas.	36	M	Hatter	England	United States	India	8 Jun 1827
HAEGLER, Elizabeth	45	F	...ian	England	New York	Frances Henrietta	25 Aug 1825
Jacob	40	M	...ian	England	New York	Frances Henrietta	25 Aug 1825
HAEKSLEY, Mary Ann	30	F	Seamstress	England	United States	Essex	23 May 1828
HAENSJENS, Chas.	32	M	Merchant	Germany	United States	Cortex	4 Dec 1824
HAENTJENS, C.	32	M	Merchant	Holland	Port au Prince	Fancy	28 Apr 1824
HAENZLAER, Johan Gotliep	28	M	Boer & Finikerbaker	Sleesinger	United States	Juffraw Johanna	16 Oct 1821
HAERTTER, Jacob	43	M	Smith	Wirtemburg, Germany	New York	Frances Henrietta	25 Aug 1825
Mary	46	F	Smith	Wirtemburg, Germany	New York	Frances Henrietta	25 Aug 1825
HAFF, Jno. F.	25	M	Mechanic	Germany	U. States	Condstitution	21 Mar 1825
John		M	Gentleman	United States		Mary	16 Mar 1820
John	30	M	Farmer	United States	United States	Sarah G	11 Sep 1827
L.	27	M	Merchant	U.S.	U.S.	Radius	10 Aug 1822
HAFFAM, Wm.	24	M	Taylor	England	United States	William	4 Oct 1822
HAFFENER, Charlotte, Kinder (his child [Jacob])				Homburg	United States	Juffraw Johanna	16 Oct 1821
Charlotte, Zyn Vrouw (his wife [Peter])	24	F		Zwartsenacker	United States	Juffraw Johanna	16 Oct 1821
Chatarina, Kinder (his child [Peter])	13	F		Inwilder	United States	Juffraw Johanna	16 Oct 1821
Elizabeth, Kinder (his child [Peter])	11	F		Inwilder	United States	Juffraw Johanna	16 Oct 1821
Elizabeth, Zyn Vrouw (his wife [Jacob])	29	F		Homburg	United States	Juffraw Johanna	16 Oct 1821
Frederik, Kinder (his child [Peter])	18	M		Inwilder	United States	Juffraw Johanna	16 Oct 1821
Hendrick, Kinder (his child [Peter])	7	M		Inwilder	United States	Juffraw Johanna	16 Oct 1821
Jacob	27	M	Boer	Einert	United States	Juffraw Johanna	16 Oct 1821
Jacob, Kinder (his child [Jacob])	3	M		Homburg	United States	Juffraw Johanna	16 Oct 1821
Maria, Kinder (his child [Peter])	3	F		Inwilder	United States	Juffraw Johanna	16 Oct 1821
Marigs, Kinder (his child [Peter])		F		Inwilder	United States	Juffraw Johanna	16 Oct 1821
Peter	36	M	Boer	Zwenbrugge	United States	Juffraw Johanna	16 Oct 1821
HAFFEY, Catharine	20		Dress Maker			Amphion	31 May 1824
Mary	17		Dress Maker			Amphion	31 May 1824
HAFFLIGER, Ann Maria	23	F		Swiss	United States	Iris	21 Sep 1821
Ann Maria	53	F		Swiss	United States	Iris	21 Sep 1821
Anna	19	F		Swis	United States	Iris	21 Sep 1821
Bernard	21	M	Farmer	United States		Iris	21 Sep 1821
Daniel	8	M		Swis	United States	Iris	21 Sep 1821
Frena	11	F		Swis	United States	Iris	21 Sep 1821

NAMES OF PASSENGERS	A G E	S E X	OCCUPATIONS	COUNTRY TO WHICH THEY BELONG	COUNTRY THEY INTEND TO INHABIT	SHIPS/DATES OF ARRIVAL	
HAFFLIGER (cont'd)							
John	9	M		Swis	United States	Iris	21 Sep 1821
Rudolph	23	M	Farmer	Swiss	United States	Iris	21 Sep 1821
HAFFNER, Daniel	26	M	Boer en Smit	Zweybruck	United States	Juffraw Johanna	16 Oct 1821
HAFFY, Ellen	16	F	...	Ireland	United States	Carolina Ann	24 Oct 1825
HAFLIN, John	6	M	Laborer or Spinster	Ireland	United States	Sarah G	11 Sep 1827
Paddy	30	M	Laborer or Spinster	Ireland	United States	Sarah G	11 Sep 1827
Rosa	29	F	Laborer or Spinster	Ireland	United States	Sarah G	11 Sep 1827
Thos.	3	M	Laborer or Spinster	Ireland	United States	Sarah G	11 Sep 1827
HAFONNE, Martha	21	F	Labourer	Ireland	United States	Hope	12 Jun 1828
HAGAMIN, —, Madam	35	F		Switzerland	U.S. America	Elbe	21 Sep 1821
...	3	F		Switzerland	U.S. America	Elbe	21 Sep 1821
...	5	F		Switzerland	U.S. America	Elbe	21 Sep 1821
E...	7	F		Switzerland	U.S. America	Elbe	21 Sep 1821
HAGAN, Ann	26	F		Great Britain	U. States	Hamilton	28 Apr 1828
Ann	40 3/12	F	Cook	Ireland	United States	Atlantic	21 Jul 1827
Catherine	45	F	Servant	Ireland	United States	Dublin Packet	9 Jul 1827
Charles	19	M	Weaver	Ireland	United States	Sarah Ann	11 Jan 1827
Claus	36	M	farmer	Germany	Newyork	Cortes	16 Jul 1827
Edw.	27			Great Britain	U. States	Hamilton	28 Apr 1828
Francis	13	M	Boy	Ireland	U. States	Josephine	7 May 1827
James	...	M	Farmer	Ireland	U. States	Dickinson	30 Jul 1825
James	7	M		M...felt	United States	Carolina Ann	11 Jun 1824
James	35	M	Labourer	Ireland	U.S. America	Columbia	31 Jul 1826
James	40	M	Farmer	M...felt	United States	Carolina Ann	11 Jun 1824
Jane	32	F		M...felt	United States	Carolina Ann	11 Jun 1824
John	11	M		M...felt	United States	Carolina Ann	11 Jun 1824
John	16		Boy	Ireland	United States	Courier	15 Oct 1827
John	21	M	Labourer	Great Britain	United States	Atlantic	28 May 1827
Michael	19	M	Farmer	Ireland	U. States	Dickinson	30 Jul 1825
Michal	22	M	Labourer		New York	Governor Clinton	3 Jul 1827
Nancy	18	F	Spinster	Ireland	U. States	Josephine	7 May 1827
Patrick	27		Labourer	Great Britain	U. States	Hamilton	28 Apr 1828
Paul	18 8/12	M	Weaver	Ireland	America	Carolina Ann	7 Apr 1826
Richard	9	M		M...felt	United States	Carolina Ann	11 Jun 1824
Robert, an infant		M		M...felt	United States	Carolina Ann	11 Jun 1824
Sally	13	F		M...felt	United States	Carolina Ann	11 Jun 1824
T.	45	M	private	U. States	U. States	Enterprize	9 Aug 1825
Terence	21 1/12	M		Ireland	America	Carolina Ann	7 Apr 1826
Thomas	5	M		M...felt	United States	Carolina Ann	11 Jun 1824
William	2	M		M...felt	United States	Carolina Ann	11 Jun 1824
Wm.	4...	...	...	Ireland	U. States of Amer	Courier	17 Mar 1827
HAGANGAS, Harman	22	M	Merchant	St. Thomas & Denmark	U.S.	Bliss	28 Jul 1821
HAGAR, Benjamin	43		Mariner	Montreal		Buffalo	27 Mar 1820
Charles	28	M	Labourer	Ireland	U. States	St. Michaels	25 Apr 1825
HAGARTY, James	25	M	Merchant	United States	U. States	New York	19 Nov 1828
James	38	M	...	Virginia	U. States	Columbia	7 Jul 1824
James	39	M	Merchant	Virginia	New York, U.S.	New York	14 Mar 1828
John	18	M	Labourer	Ireland	U.States	Nancy	31 May 1823
John	25	M	Labourer	Ireland		Marchioness	13 May 1828
Sarah	21	F		United States	U. States	New York	19 Nov 1828
HAGEA, Peggy	20 1/12	F		Ireland	America	Nancy	28 Jan 1820
HAGEAONE, G.	17	M	Merchant	Germany	U. States	Dido	26 Apr 1825
HAGEL, Got.	58	M	Farmer	Bardin	U. States	Bayard	5 Sep 1828
Johnthan	50	M		Bardin	U. States	Bayard	5 Sep 1828
HAGELBERGER, Magdalina	20	F	Servant	Switzerland	America, U.N.S.	Great Britain	3 Aug 1829
HAGEN, Wm.	15	M	Student	N. York	N. York	London	19 Dec 1823
HAGERTY, Charles	2	M	Child	Ireland	United States	Nancy	18 Oct 1824
Danl.	23	M	Labourer	Ireland	United States	Trident	16 May 1826
Eliza	26	F	Sister [of William]	G. Brittian	United States	Louisa	14 Jun 1825
Jas.	23	M	Servant	Ireland	U. States	Henrietta	7 Jul 1825
Jas.	25	M	Carpenter	Ireland	New York	Triton	12 Jul 1823
Margry	15	F	Spinster	Ireland	United States	Trident	17 May 1825
Mary	1	F	Child	Ireland	United States	Nancy	18 Oct 1824
Mary	3	F		Ireland	United States	Sarah G.	20 Jul 1827
Mary	25	F		Ireland	United States	Sarah G.	20 Jul 1827

NAMES OF PASSENGERS	AGE	SEX	OCCUPATIONS	COUNTRY TO WHICH THEY BELONG	COUNTRY THEY INTEND TO INHABIT	SHIPS/DATES OF ARRIVAL	
HAGERTY (cont'd)							
Mary	34	F	Servant	Ireland	United States	Nancy	18 Oct 1824
Nancy	4	F	Child	Ireland	United States	Nancy	18 Oct 1824
Nancy	23	F	Spinster	Ireland	United States	Trident	16 May 1826
Peter	23	M	Laborer or Spinster	Ireland	United States	Frances Miller	27 Jul 1827
William	30 4/12	M	Labourer	G. Brittian	United States	Louisa	14 Jun 1825
HAGERY, Bridgt.	22	F	None	Great Britain		Moro Castle	6 Jul 1827
HAGETY, James	25	M	Laborer, Spinster or Child	Ireland	United States	Ann Maria	4 Aug 1827
HAGG, James	22	M	Merchant	G. Brittian	U. States	Pacific	19 Oct 1829
HAGGAN, Joseph	28	M	Labourer	Ireland	United States	Fabius	31 Jul 1829
HAGGARTY, J. A.	21	M	Merchant	U. States	U. States	Carlow	20 Apr 1826
James	21	M		Ireland	New York	Lady Hunter	5 Jun 1826
HAGGELBERGER,							
Balthazar	45	M	Farmer	France	America, U.N.S.	Great Britain	3 Aug 1829
Caspar	6 1/12	M		France	America, U.N.S.	Great Britain	3 Aug 1829
Madeline	16	F		France	America, U.N.S.	Great Britain	3 Aug 1829
Madeline	40	F		France	America, U.N.S.	Great Britain	3 Aug 1829
Michel	19	M		France	America, U.N.S.	Great Britain	3 Aug 1829
Pulser	10	M		France	America, U.N.S.	Great Britain	3 Aug 1829
HAGGERSON, Edgar	24	M	Merchant	England	U. States	South Carolina	27 May 1823
HAGGERTY, C.	32	M	Spinner	England	America	Two Marys	24 Sep 1827
James	7	M	None	Scotland	United States	Mary & Susan	5 Aug 1828
M... [crossed out]	10	F	None	Scotland	United States	Mary & Susan	5 Aug 1828
Nancy	48	F	None	Scotland	United States	Mary & Susan	5 Aug 1828
Nancy, Jr.	14	F	None	Scotland	United States	Mary & Susan	5 Aug 1828
Patrick	28	M	Teacher	Great Brittian		Merchant	22 Apr 1822
Rosina	11	F	None	Scotland	United States	Mary & Susan	5 Aug 1828
Wm.	23	M	Servant	United States	United States	Hogarth	12 Oct 1829
HAGGETT, Ann	19	F	None	England and Ireland	United States	Jubilee	12 May 1828
Charles	3	M	Labourer	England and Ireland	United States	Jubilee	12 May 1828
Edward	21	M	Labourer	England and Ireland	United States	Jubilee	12 May 1828
Ellen	24	F	None	England and Ireland	United States	Jubilee	12 May 1828
Harriet	14	F	None	England and Ireland	United States	Jubilee	12 May 1828
Mary	50	F	None	England and Ireland	United States	Jubilee	12 May 1828
Richard	22	M	Labourer	England and Ireland	United States	Jubilee	12 May 1828
Richard, Jr.	27	M	Labourer	England and Ireland	United States	Jubilee	12 May 1828
Robert	1	M	Labourer	England and Ireland	United States	Jubilee	12 May 1828
HAGGIN, Thomas	28	M	Farmer	G. Britain	U. States	Margaret Bogle	12 Jun 1828
HAGHERTY, Jeremiah	34	M	Labourer	Ireland	United States	Trio	2 Oct 1828
Mary	67	F		Ireland	United States	Trio	2 Oct 1828
HAGIN, —,							
Infant on breast				Ireland	United States	Trio	13 Jun 1827
Ellen	28	F		Ireland	United States	Trio	13 Jun 1827
John	30	M	Laborer	Ireland	United States	Trio	13 Jun 1827
John, Jnr.	4	M		Ireland	United States	Trio	13 Jun 1827
Pat	2 3/12	M		Ireland	United States	Trio	13 Jun 1827
HAGLIN, Cathrine	25	F		Ireland	Und. Stts of Amer	Alexander Mansfield	18 Aug 1826
John	28	M	Tapper Maker	Ireland	Und. Stts of Amer	Alexander Mansfield	18 Aug 1826
HAGON, Robert	23	M	...ar...	Ireland	New York	Wilson	10 Apr 1823
HAGOR, Ann	30	F	Tailor	Great Britten	America	Cortes	6 Mar 1827
Henry	2	M	Tailor	Great Britten	America	Cortes	6 Mar 1827
John	27	M	Tailor	Great Britten	America	Cortes	6 Mar 1827
HAGS, James	20	M	Labourer	Ireland	U. States	Lady Hunter	9 Oct 1825
HAGTER, Henry	25	M	Officer	Great Britain	G.B.	Greyhound	27 Nov 1820
HAGUE, Benjn.	31	M	Labourer	Great Britain	United States	William Dawson	18 Jun 1827
Charles	32	M	Spinner	Great Britain	United States	Freake	25 Jun 1827
Henry	26			Ireland		Anacreon	7 Sep 1827

NAMES OF PASSENGERS	AGE	SEX	OCCUPATIONS	COUNTRY TO WHICH THEY BELONG	COUNTRY THEY INTEND TO INHABIT	SHIPS/DATES OF ARRIVAL	
HAGUE (cont'd)							
James	48	M	Mariner	U.S.	U.S.	London	19 Dec 1823
Margaret	61	F		Great Britain	United States	Isaac Hicks	10 Jul 1827
Peggy	19	F		Great Britain	United States	Isaac Hicks	10 Jul 1827
Robert	38	M	Merchant	Phila.	U. States	Aletta	12 May 1823
Stephen	60	M	Farmer	Great Britain	United States	Isaac Hicks	10 Jul 1827
Thomas	22	M	Carpenter	Scotland	New York	Hudson	20 Nov 1828
HAHN, Andrew	1	M		Gt. Brittan		L'Esperance	6 Sep 1828
Antone	40	M	Labourer	Gt. Brittan		L'Esperance	6 Sep 1828
Barbara	4	M		Gt. Brittan		L'Esperance	6 Sep 1828
Carolina	7	F	Farmer	Wortenberg	Lancaster	Louisa	6 Oct 1828
Catharina	8	F	Farmer	Wortenberg	Lancaster	Louisa	6 Oct 1828
Catherine	9	F		Gt. Brittan		L'Esperance	6 Sep 1828
Christian Fredrica	5	F	Farmer	Wortenberg	Lancaster	Louisa	6 Oct 1828
Elizabeth	34	F		Gt. Brittan		L'Esperance	6 Sep 1828
Eva	1 3/12	F	Farmer	Wortenberg	Lancaster	Louisa	6 Oct 1828
Fredrica	35	F	Farmer	Wortenberg	Lancaster	Louisa	6 Oct 1828
J. F.	22	M	Baker	Germany	U. States	Jane	11 Jul 1828
Johan Adam	36	M	Farmer	Wortenberg	Lancaster	Louisa	6 Oct 1828
Johann Adam	11	F	Farmer	Wortenberg	Lancaster	Louisa	6 Oct 1828
John	3	M		Ireland		L. M. Pelham	12 May 1823
Louza	12	F	Farmer	Wortenberg	Lancaster	Louisa	6 Oct 1828
Mary	30	F		Ireland		L. M. Pelham	12 May 1823
Mary Ann	8	F		Ireland		L. M. Pelham	12 May 1823
Xavier	7	M		Gt. Brittan		L'Esperance	6 Sep 1828
HAIGERTY, ...t	16	M		Ireland	United States	John & Adam	21 Sep 1822
Ellen	55	F		Ireland	United States	John & Adam	21 Sep 1822
Hannah	21	F		Ireland	United States	John & Adam	21 Sep 1822
Janet	7	M		Ireland	United States	John & Adam	21 Sep 1822
Michael	19	F		Ireland	United States	John & Adam	21 Sep 1822
HAIGH, Richard	13	M	None	Great Britain	United States	Ganges	26 Oct 1826
Ruth	50	F	None	Great Britain	United States	Ganges	26 Oct 1826
HAIGHT, Charles T.	30	M	Merchant	Great Britain	United States	James Cropper	14 Oct 1824
D. H.	20	M	Merchant	United States	United States	Britannia	29 Oct 1829
Hannah	25	F	None	Great Britain	United States	James Cropper	14 Oct 1824
John	4	M	None	Great Britain	United States	James Cropper	14 Oct 1824
John G.	21	M	Merchant	New York	U. States	Zephyr	18 May 1825
R. K.	23	M	Merchant	United States	United States	Cortes	5 Aug 1822
Richd. W.	25	M	Merchant	United States	New York	Florida	22 May 1826
Thomas	29	M	Mason	G.B.	G.B.	Cadmus	26 Apr 1824
Wm.	2	M		Great Britain	United States	James Cropper	14 Oct 1824
HAIGT, Patrick	60	M	Mariner	U. States	U. States	Virginia	26 May 1828
HAIL, Charles	22	M	Cloth Washer	G.B.	U.S.	Silvanus Jenkins	27 Jul 1829
Easter	28	F	None	G.B.	U.S.	Silvanus Jenkins	27 Jul 1829
Elizabeth	2 6/12	F	None	G.B.	U.S.	Silvanus Jenkins	27 Jul 1829
Hannah	1 6/12	F	None	G.B.	U.S.	Silvanus Jenkins	27 Jul 1829
Hannah	30	F	None	G.B.	U.S.	Silvanus Jenkins	27 Jul 1829
Lawrance	25	M	None	G.B.	U.S.	Silvanus Jenkins	27 Jul 1829
Samul	24	M	Cloth Washer	G.B.	U.S.	Silvanus Jenkins	27 Jul 1829
HAILER, Jacob	28	M	Farmer	Germany	Pensylvania	James Noble	27 Aug 1827
HAILES, Harris	27	M	Gentleman	Europe	Europe	Champion	1 Sep 1820
Isabella	50	F		St. John, N.B.	St. John, N.B.	Loire	3 Dec 1821
M. C.	24	M	Gentn.	Great Britain	Great Britain	Magnet	28 Jun 1821
Michael C.	25	M	Attorney at Law	St. John, N.B.	St. John, N.B.	Loire	3 Dec 1821
Micheal	30	M	Gentleman	Europe	Europe	Champion	1 Sep 1820
HAILEY, Andw.	28	M	Founder	Scotland	New York	Joseph Hume	26 Oct 1829
Ann	27	F	None	England		Marchioness	13 May 1828
James	24	M	Founder	Scotland	New York	Joseph Hume	26 Oct 1829
Thos.	27	M	Wheelwright	England		Marchioness	13 May 1828
HAILS, Elizabth	38		Maid	London		Pomona	28 May 1822
Sarah	22		Maid	London		Pomona	28 May 1822
HAIMAN, Martin	8	M		Gt. Britan	U. States	Magnet	9 Apr 1825
R.	44	M	Millwright	Gt. Britan	U. States	Magnet	9 Apr 1825
HAIN, Napolin	22 2/12	M	Merchant	France	United States	Montano	12 Jan 1827
HAINE, Ann	24	F	Dress Maker	Great Britain		Olive Branch	9 Oct 1829
Saml. B.	20	M	Tailor	United States	United States	Gertrude	19 May 1826
HAINES, Benjamin	27	M	Mechanic	U. States	U. States	Packet Frances	30 Jun 1828
John	20	M	Weaver	England	United States	Ganges	10 May 1828
HAINS, Robert	25		Baker	Scotland	United States	Camillus	3 May 1828

NAMES OF PASSENGERS	AGE	SEX	OCCUPATIONS	COUNTRY TO WHICH THEY BELONG	COUNTRY THEY INTEND TO INHABIT	SHIPS/DATES OF ARRIVAL	
HAINVILLE, Geo.	13	M	Farmer	Ireland	U. States	Atlantic	19 Aug 1825
HAIR, James	50	M			U. States	Robt. Edwards	4 Sep 1828
Maurice	42	M	Merch.	Ireland	America	William Thompson	18 Jan 1825
HAIRET, A.	25	M	Merchant	U. States	U. States	Eliza	3 Jan 1826
HAISTINGS, Jos. S.	35	M	Merchant	U. States	U. States	Martha	18 Oct 1824
HAITLEY, Alice	21	F	None	England	United States	Dalhouse Castle	6 Sep 1827
Christopher	8	M	None	England	United States	Dalhouse Castle	6 Sep 1827
Hannah	24	F	None	England	United States	Dalhouse Castle	6 Sep 1827
Robert	13	M	None	England	United States	Dalhouse Castle	6 Sep 1827
Robt.	13	M	None	England	United States	Dalhouse Castle	6 Sep 1827
Roger	59	M	Stone cutter	England	United States	Dalhouse Castle	6 Sep 1827
HAITY, Thos.	28	M	Laborer or Spinster	Ireland	United States	Sarah G	11 Sep 1827
HALAGGER, Jean	40	M	Farmer	Truo	U.S. America	Superior	18 Jun 1825
HALBACH, G.	27 2/12	M	Merchant	Germany	United States	Cadmus	9 Dec 1825
HALBERSTADT, Elias G.	42	M	Merchant	Germany		France	6 Feb 1829
HALBERSTEAD, John	28	M	Merchant	U. States	U. States	Virginia	30 May 1827
HALBERT, J...	1/12	F		Scotland	U.S.	Curler	19 Jul 1828
John	25	M	Slater	England	United States	Peru	23 May 1827
Louis, Mr.	15	M	Student	New Orleans	New York	Stephania	28 Jul 1823
Marrice	5	F		Scotland	U.S.	Curler	19 Jul 1828
Mary	6	F		Scotland	U.S.	Curler	19 Jul 1828
Robert	2	M		Scotland	U.S.	Curler	19 Jul 1828
Robert	4	M		Scotland	U.S.	Curler	19 Jul 1828
Wm.	8	M		Scotland	U.S.	Curler	19 Jul 1828
HALBROUN, Isador	30	M	Mercht.	Germany	United States	Nestor	14 Nov 1823
HALBURTON, J.	26	M	Mercht.	U. States	U. States	Patriot	23 May 1821
HALCOMB, D.	20	M	Mechanic	Connecticutt	U. States	Benjamin	1 Jun 1822
HALDEN, Robt.	13	M				James Monroe	8 Aug 1820
Thomas	40	M	Weaver	Great Britain	United States	Courier	26 Jun 1827
HALE, C.	27	M	Merchant		Canada	York	8 Aug 1829
Charlotte	6	F				Hercules	25 Sep 1820
Ed...	18	M		Great Britian	United States	Robert Quayle	29 Jul 1822
Geo. C.	24	M	Merchant	U. States	U. States	Sarah	17 Mar 1829
H. H.	21	M	Merchant	America	America	Catherine & Jane	4 Nov 1820
Henry	11	M				Hercules	25 Sep 1820
Henry	50	M	Weaver			Hercules	25 Sep 1820
Jane	8	F				Hercules	25 Sep 1820
John	22	M				Hercules	25 Sep 1820
John	36	M	Merchant	Great Britain	U.S. of Ama.	Robert Fulton	16 Aug 1824
John	39	M	Merchant	England	Central America	Tampico	29 Apr 1826
John	39	M	Merchant	England	South America	James Cropper	16 Oct 1826
John	40	M	Merchant	U. States	U. States	Robt. Reade	12 Apr 1825
John	45	M	Merchant	England	England	Robert Y. Haynes	2 Oct 1829
Mara	13	F				Hercules	25 Sep 1820
Martin	28	M	Mercht.	Ireland	U. States	Abeona	5 Jul 1822
Mary	19	F				Hercules	25 Sep 1820
Mary	42	F				Hercules	25 Sep 1820
Matilda	4	F				Hercules	25 Sep 1820
S.	50	M	Servant	Baltimore	U. States	New York	15 Nov 1823
William	2	M				Hercules	25 Sep 1820
William	13	M	Boy	Ireland	United States	Trident	17 May 1825
HALEDAY, Thos.	25	M	Engraver	G. Brittan	U. States	Henry	24 Oct 1828
HALEGAN, Mary	17	F	Spinster	Ireland	U. States	Josephine	30 Aug 1828
HALEM, Hannah	30	F		Great Brit.	Ohio	Gov. Griswald	3 Jul 1820
HALERIN, Martin	24	M	Farmer	Wirtermberg	United States	Olympia	20 Aug 1829
HALERINE, Catherine	60	F	Farmer	Switzerland	United States	Olympia	20 Aug 1829
HALES, Elisa	8	F		Irland	United States	Nancy	28 Oct 1822
Frs.	3	F		Irland	United States	Nancy	28 Oct 1822
Mary	35	F		Irland	United States	Nancy	28 Oct 1822
HALEY, —, Mrs.	35	F	Lady	W. Indies	U. States	Congress	21 Nov 1823
Catherine	20	M	None	Ireland	U. States	William Byrnes	24 Apr 1827
Ed. B.	23	M	Merchant	Barbadoes	Intend to return	Chasseur	17 Aug 1824
Hunislaag	5	M				Congress	21 Nov 1823
Isabella	42 4/12	F		France	France	France	28 Mar 1829

NAMES OF PASSENGERS	AGE	SEX	OCCUPATIONS	COUNTRY TO WHICH THEY BELONG	COUNTRY THEY INTEND TO INHABIT	SHIPS/DATES OF ARRIVAL	
HALEY (cont'd)							
James	11	M				Congress	21 Nov 1823
John	22	M	Carpenter	Ireland	America	Wilson	16 May 1825
M.	30	M		Gt. Britain	U. States	Tantiva	7 Jul 1828
Robert	8	M				Congress	21 Nov 1823
S.	20	M	Black Smith	Ireland	U. States	Wanderer	1 Sep 1828
HALFFERING, Mary	24	F	None	Gr. Britain		Moro Castle	6 Jul 1827
HALFIN, Patrick	22	M	Laborer	Ireland	U. States	Lady Hunter	8 Aug 1826
HALFORD, Ann, Miss	10	F	None	Grate Britain	...	Courier	14 Jun 1825
James, Mas.	4	M	None	Grate Britain	...	Courier	14 Jun 1825
John, Mr.	40	M	Farmer	Grate Britain	...	Courier	14 Jun 1825
Mary, Miss	6	F	None	Grate Britain	...	Courier	14 Jun 1825
Mary, Mrs.	36	F	None	Grate Britain	...	Courier	14 Jun 1825
Mary, Mrs.	50	F	None	Grate Britain	...	Courier	14 Jun 1825
Silbrham, Mr.	8	M	None	Grate Britain	...	Courier	14 Jun 1825
HALFWORTH, M.	25	F	Mariner	Virginia	U. States	Favourite	27 Jun 1823
HALGHAN, Samuel	25	M	Farmer	G. Britain	U. States	Mary & Harriot	8 Sep 1828
HALIDAY, David	19	M	Weaver	Ireland	U. States	Josephine	7 May 1827
HALKET, J.	50	M	Gentleman	Scotland	Washington	Amity	13 Sep 1821
HALKGARD, Jno. W.	30	M	Merchant	England	England	Agricola	19 Jul 1824
HALL, —	30		Cordonnier [shoemaker]	Suisse		Deux Ernest	29 Dec 1827
*son épouse & 2 enfans [his wife and two children]							
—, Miss	23	F		England	America	Birmingham	16 Oct 1826
Abraham	35	M	Farmer	Gt. Britain	United States	Meteor	19 Aug 1829
Ainsley, Mr.	37	M	Gentleman	England	New York	Thames	6 Oct 1820
Alexd.	33	M	Merchant	Ireland	West Indies	Spartan	24 Jul 1826
Alexr. H.	24	M	Merchant	Philad.	U. States	Velocipede	16 Dec 1824
Amelia	34	F	None	England	U. States	Birmingham	12 Oct 1827
And.	24	M	Mason	Argyle (Tedland) Scotland	United States	Jean Hastie	27 Jul 1829
Andr. T.	21	M	Merchant	America	U. States	Orazimbo	7 Jan 1821
Andrew	12	M		Sligo	New York	Susquehana	27 Jun 1823
Ann	1			G. Britain		Casanda	5 Sep 1827
Ann	18	F		G. Britain	U. States	George Clinton	10 Sep 1828
Ann	23	F	None	Great Britan	United States	Bolivar	21 May 1827
Ann	24	F			U. States	Margaret	3 Jun 1822
Ann	33	F	wife Wm. Hale of New York		New York	Thames	16 May 1821
Ann	38	F	None	Great Britain		Casanda	5 Sep 1827
Ann	40	F		G. Britain	U. States	George Clinton	10 Sep 1828
Ann L. M.	24	F	None		United States	London Packet	25 Dec 1820
B., Capt.	38	M	Royal Navy	England	U. States	Florida	16 May 1827
B., Mrs.	27	F	Lady	England	U. States	Florida	16 May 1827
Betty	10	F	None	England	U. States	Birmingham	12 Oct 1827
C. J.	25	M	Merchant	Massachusetts	U. States	Franklin	20 Apr 1826
Caroline	6 1/12	F	child Wm. Hall of New York		New York	Thames	16 May 1821
Caroline	26	F	None	Boston	Boston	New York	14 Nov 1826
Charles	3	M	None	Great Britain	United States	Colossus	5 Jun 1827
Daniel Hire	24	M	Baker	France	U.S.	Montano	24 Jun 1823
David	33	M	Calico Printer	England	United States	Siroc	31 Oct 1829
Edward	2	M	Farmer	Gt. Brittian	United States	Manchester	16 Dec 1828
Edward	22	M	Painter	United States	United States	Gertrude	19 May 1826
Edward	34	M		G. Britain		Casanda	5 Sep 1827
Edwd.	32	M	Cordwainer	Great Brittan	U. States	Gem	26 Jul 1827
Eleanor	27	F	Linnen weaver	Ireland	America	Franklin	13 Aug 1827
Elen	20	F		U. States	U. States	Charlemagne	19 Sep 1828
Eliakim	50	M	Butcher	Connecticut	U. States	Hippomenes	5 Jul 1820
Eliza	6	F		Ireland	America	Carolina Ann	7 Aug 1826
Eliza	28	F		Ireland	America	Carolina Ann	7 Aug 1826
Eliza Jane, Miss	14/12	F	Lady	England	U. States	Florida	16 May 1827
Elizabeth	5	F	None	Boston	Boston	New York	14 Nov 1826
Elizabeth	14	F	None	Great Britain	United States	Fidelity	16 Oct 1820
Emma	9 1/12	F	child Wm. Hall of New York		New York	Thames	16 May 1821
Esther	22 6/12	F		Great Britain	United States	James Cropper	26 Mar 1822
Esther	43			C...tla...	England	Great Britain	7 May 1827
Frances	30	F	None	Great Brittan	U. States	Gem	26 Jul 1827

NAMES OF PASSENGERS	AGE	SEX	OCCUPATIONS	COUNTRY TO WHICH THEY BELONG	COUNTRY THEY INTEND TO INHABIT	SHIPS/DATES OF ARRIVAL	
HALL (cont'd)							
Frederick	2	M	child Wm. Hall of New York		New York	Thames	16 May 1821
George	27 5/12	M	Waggoner	Scotland	United States	London	6 Feb 1829
George	38	M	Farmer	England	United States	Siroc	31 Oct 1829
George	58	M	Minor	England	United States	Siroc	31 Oct 1829
H.	25	M	Sailor	England	U. States	Hiram	17 Jun 1826
Hanna	25	F		Gt. Britain	United States	Meteor	19 Aug 1829
Hannah	46	F	None	Great Britain	United States	Fidelity	16 Oct 1820
Helen	23	F			U. States	Margaret	3 Jun 1822
J. C.	29 4/12	M	Marine Corps of U.S.	U. States		Maria	24 Oct 1829
Jacob	5	M	None	Great Britain	United States	Fidelity	16 Oct 1820
James	7	M		United States	United States	General Marion	20 Aug 1828
James	18	M	Tabacconist	Ireland	United States	Delta	24 Oct 1829
James	26	M	Pattern Maker	Great Britain	United States	Colossus	5 Jun 1827
James	27 8/12	M	Joiner	England	United States	Lunar	5 May 1828
James	30	M	Plasterer	England	Alexandria, U.S.	Roman	17 Oct 1826
James	48	M	Merchant	England	England	Hannibal	28 May 1827
James, Junr.	47	M			U. States	Margaret	3 Jun 1822
James, Senr.	72	M	Merchant		U. States	Margaret	3 Jun 1822
Jane	5	F		United States	United States	General Marion	20 Aug 1828
Jane	6	F	None		United States	London Packet	25 Dec 1820
Jane	8	F		G. Britain		Casanda	5 Sep 1827
Jane	26	F			U. States	Margaret	3 Jun 1822
Jane	36	F		G. Britain		Casanda	5 Sep 1827
Jas.	18			Ireland	U.S.	Hibernia	27 Jun 1821
Jas.	29	M		Argyle (Tedland) Scotland	United States	Jean Hastie	27 Jul 1829
Jean	1/2	F	None	Great Britain	United States	Colossus	5 Jun 1827
Jno. James	25	M	Merchant	England	Cuba	Abigail	29 May 1822
Jno. R.	34	M				Cassack	25 Jul 1820
Joh...	30	M	Mason	England	America	Two Marys	24 Sep 1827
John	3	M		United States	United States	General Marion	20 Aug 1828
John	21	M			U. States	Margaret	3 Jun 1822
John	30	M	Merchant	Barbados	Supposition is he will return	Superb	7 Jul 1823
John	32	M	Merchant	U.S.	New York	Auritz	20 May 1823
John	36	M	Merchant	Gt. Britain	New York	Stephania	2 Jan 1824
John	38	M	Merchant	England	England	Cadmus	9 Dec 1825
John	40	M	Butcher	Great Brittain	United States	Nimrod	9 Jan 1827
John, Child [of Jane]	1	M	None		United States	London Packet	25 Dec 1820
John, Junr.	31	M	Merchant	Boston	Boston	New York	14 Nov 1826
Jos.	3	M	None	England	U. States	Birmingham	12 Oct 1827
Joseph	6			C...tla...	England	Great Britain	7 May 1827
Joseph	32	M	Farmer	Ireland	America	Carolina Ann	7 Aug 1826
Joseph	35	M	Merchant	U. States	U. States	Queen Mab	16 Mar 1825
Josh.	31	M	Labourer	Great Britain		Moro Castle	6 Jul 1827
Louisa, Child [of Jane]	...	F	None		United States	London Packet	25 Dec 1820
Lucy	26	F	None	England	United States	Enterprize	19 Oct 1826
M.	30	F	Spinster	U. States	U. States	Don Quixote	15 Apr 1825
M. J.	22	M	Mercht.	U. States	U. States	Caroline	21 Jun 1823
Marfret	33	F		United States	United States	General Marion	20 Aug 1828
Margard	4	F		Ireland	America	Carolina Ann	7 Aug 1826
Margaret	5	F	None	Great Britain	United States	Colossus	5 Jun 1827
Margaret	23	F	None	Great Britain	United States	Colossus	5 Jun 1827
Mary	9	F		United States	United States	General Marion	20 Aug 1828
Mary	10	F	None	Great Britain	United States	Fidelity	16 Oct 1820
Mary	12	F		G. Britain		Casanda	5 Sep 1827
Mary	18	F			U. States	Margaret	3 Jun 1822
Mary	47	F	None	England	United States	Hamilton	13 Nov 1827
Mary	48	F		St. Croix	U. States	Ann	29 Apr 1825
Mary	58	F	Minor	England	United States	Siroc	31 Oct 1829
Mary Ann	8	F	None	Great Britain	United States	Fidelity	16 Oct 1820
Mary C., Mrs.	23 10/12	F		United States		Leonidas	22 Jan 1829
Matthew	3	M	None	Great Britain	United States	Fidelity	16 Oct 1820
Nathaniel, Child [of Jane]	4	M	None		United States	London Packet	25 Dec 1820
Ralph	40	M	Farmer	Great Britain		Casanda	5 Sep 1827

NAMES OF PASSENGERS	AGE	SEX	OCCUPATIONS	COUNTRY TO WHICH THEY BELONG	COUNTRY THEY INTEND TO INHABIT	SHIPS/DATES OF ARRIVAL	
HALL (cont'd)							
Richard	25 6/12		Merchant	Liverpool, England		Pegassus	7 Aug 1829
Robert	18 3/12	M	Carpenter	England	United States	Rising States	16 Jan 1829
Saml.	3...		Weaver	C...tla...	England	Great Britain	7 May 1827
Saml.	40	M	Farmer	England	United States	Siroc	31 Oct 1829
Samuel	6	M		Ireland	America	Carolina Ann	7 Aug 1826
Samuel	6	M	Farmer	Gt. Brittian	United States	Manchester	16 Dec 1828
Samuel	29	M	Schoolmaster	Great Britain	United States	James Cropper	26 Mar 1822
Samuel	30	M	Traveller	United States	United States	Henry	9 Jun 1826
Samuel C.	30	M	Shipmaster	United States	United States	William	12 Oct 1827
Sarah	3			G. Britain		Casanda	5 Sep 1827
Sarah	6	F	None	England	United States	Enterprize	19 Oct 1826
Sarah	35	F	Farmer	Gt. Brittian	United States	Manchester	16 Dec 1828
Sarah, Mrs.	29	F		England	New York	Thames	6 Oct 1820
Thomas	7 3/12	M	child Wm. Hall of New York		New York	Thames	16 May 1821
Thomas	36 5/12	M	Carpenter	United States	United States	General Marion	20 Aug 1828
Thomas	45	M	Labourer	England	America	Two Marys	24 Sep 1827
Thomas	50	M	None	Great Britan	United States	Bolivar	21 May 1827
Thos.	32	M	None	Ireland	United States	Weser	29 Jul 1823
Thos.	36	M	Carpenter	United States		General Marion	6 Oct 1828
W.	3	M	None	England	United States	Enterprize	19 Oct 1826
W., Jr.	21		Gentn.	United States	United States	Othello	6 Nov 1823
W. C.	34	M	M...ld	U. States	U. States	Pacific	20 Aug 1825
Washington, Child [of Jane]	10	M	None		United States	London Packet	25 Dec 1820
William	4 1/12	M	child Wm. Hall of New York		New York	Thames	16 May 1821
William	23	M	Labourer	Great Britan	United States	Bolivar	21 May 1827
William	31	M	Carpenter	U. States	New York	William	31 Aug 1820
William	42	M	Farmer	Great Britain	United States	Fidelity	16 Oct 1820
William	44	M	Merchant	England	America	Friends	28 Sep 1822
William, Mr.	52	M	Farmer	Gt. Brittian	United States	Manchester	16 Dec 1828
William C.	37		Merchant	United States	United States	London	16 Aug 1824
Wm.	8	M		England	U. States	Packet	23 Sep 1820
Wm.	22	M	Mariner	Norfolk	United States	Levant	15 Aug 1823
Wm.	23	M	Seaman	U. States Amer	U. States Amer	Honor & Amey	15 Mar 1823
Wm.	34	M	Merchant	Boston	U. States	New York	11 Jul 1823
Wm.	35	M	Mechanic	England	U. States	Packet	23 Sep 1820
Wm. B.	22	M	Merchant	U. States	United States	Burdett	30 Apr 1828
HALLAGAN, Jno.	40		Labourer	Great Britain	United States	Roman	10 Sep 1827
HALLAGHAN, James	6	M		Ireland	America	Corinthian	1 Sep 1827
John	4	M		Ireland	America	Corinthian	1 Sep 1827
John	50	M	Stationer	Ireland	America	Corinthian	1 Sep 1827
Margt.	24	F	Wife	Ireland	America	Corinthian	1 Sep 1827
Richd.	14	M		Ireland	America	Corinthian	1 Sep 1827
HALLAHAN, Agnes	25		Laboring Class		United States	Atlantic	2 Apr 1827
Ann	60	F	Spinster	Ireland	United States	Catharine	22 Jul 1825
David	25	M	Farmer	Ireland	America	William	21 May 1825
Hannah	18	F	Spinster	Ireland	United States	Catharine	22 Jul 1825
John	30	M	Farmer	Ireland	America	William	21 May 1825
William, Jr.	18	M	Labourer	Ireland	United States	Catharine	22 Jul 1825
HALLAIRD, Thomas	24		Labourer	Ireland	United States	Robert Burns	30 May 1823
HALLAM, Fanny	24	F	Commedian	England		Britannia	20 Jun 1827
G. W.	22	M	Gentleman	England	U. States	Bayard	11 Jul 1825
John	19	M	Merchant	England	U. States	Shaw	23 May 1827
John	36	M	Commedian	England		Britannia	20 Jun 1827
Thos.	26	M	Cotton Spinner	Great Britain	United States	Aurora	5 Sep 1826
HALLAN, Amelia	28			England		Anacreon	7 Sep 1827
Edward	31			England		Anacreon	7 Sep 1827
Eliza	9			England		Anacreon	7 Sep 1827
George	3			England		Anacreon	7 Sep 1827
Rebecca	5			England		Anacreon	7 Sep 1827
Wm.	6			England		Anacreon	7 Sep 1827
HALLARHAN, Thomas	20			Ireland	U.S.	Union	20 Aug 1827
HALLAWAY, Ailica	1	F	None	England	U. States	Thomas Ritchie	2 Jul 1827
Esther	26	F	None	England	U. States	Thomas Ritchie	2 Jul 1827
HALLCOCK, John	21	M	Plasterer	Great Brittain	America	Pacific	13 Jan 1827

NAMES OF PASSENGERS	AGE	SEX	OCCUPATIONS	COUNTRY TO WHICH THEY BELONG	COUNTRY THEY INTEND TO INHABIT	SHIPS/DATES OF ARRIVAL	
HALLE, Joanna	33	M	Turner	Germany	America	Saluda	18 Jun 1825
HALLEN, Benjn.	32	M	Farmer	Great Britain	United States	Ann Maria	12 Jul 1821
HALLER, Conrad	20	M	...	Wirtemburg	United States	Wade	29 Aug 1825
Danniel	2 6/12	M	Farmer	Wortenberg	Lancaster	Louisa	6 Oct 1828
Eva	6	F	Farmer	Wortenberg	Lancaster	Louisa	6 Oct 1828
Eve Cathrine	30	F	Farmer	Wortenberg	Lancaster	Louisa	6 Oct 1828
Frederika	11	F	Farmer	Wortenberg	Lancaster	Louisa	6 Oct 1828
Gottfried	5	M	Farmer	Wortenberg	Lancaster	Louisa	6 Oct 1828
Gottlob	0 4/12	M	Farmer	Wortenberg	Lancaster	Louisa	6 Oct 1828
Jacob	15	M	Farmer	Wortenberg	Lancaster	Louisa	6 Oct 1828
Johann F.	47	M	Farmer	Wortenberg	Lancaster	Louisa	6 Oct 1828
Johannes	14	M	Farmer	Wortenberg	Lancaster	Louisa	6 Oct 1828
Rosina	18	F	Farmer	Wortenberg	Lancaster	Louisa	6 Oct 1828
Thelona	17	F	Farmer	Wortenberg	Lancaster	Louisa	6 Oct 1828
HALLERIN, David	32	M	Farmer	Wirtermberg	United States	Olympia	20 Aug 1829
HALLET, James	24	M	Labourer	Ireland	U. States	Nancy	2 May 1823
Margaret	25	F		New York	U. States	Almira	3 Sep 1822
Mary	22	F		Ireland	U. States	Nancy	2 May 1823
Peggy	20	F		New York	U. States	Almira	3 Sep 1822
Sarah	38	F		New York	U. States	Almira	3 Sep 1822
Wm.	16	M	Farmer	England	U. States	Acasta	12 May 1825
HALLETS, Benjamin	36	M	Carpenter	England	New York	Cortes	23 Nov 1827
Joseph	12	M		England	New York	Cortes	23 Nov 1827
HALLETT, David	3/12	M		England	United States	New York Packet	14 Oct 1823
Eliza	34	F		England	United States	New York Packet	14 Oct 1823
Elizabeth	2	F		England	United States	New York Packet	14 Oct 1823
George	5	M		England	United States	New York Packet	14 Oct 1823
Jas.	11	M		England	United States	New York Packet	14 Oct 1823
John	7	M		England	United States	New York Packet	14 Oct 1823
John	37	M	Farmer	England	United States	New York Packet	14 Oct 1823
Mary	14	F		England	United States	New York Packet	14 Oct 1823
Saml.	12	M		England	United States	New York Packet	14 Oct 1823
Sarah	9	F		England	United States	New York Packet	14 Oct 1823
HALLEY, Gerard	23	M	Mechanic	Ireland	United States	Wm. Byrnes	30 Apr 1828
Wm.	21	M	Mechanic	England	United States	Wm. Byrnes	30 Apr 1828
HALLICK, Elizabeth	28	F	Spinster	Ireland	United States	Sarah G	19 Jun 1827
Henry	30	M	Laborer	Ireland	United States	Sarah G	19 Jun 1827
John	5	M	Child	Ireland	United States	Sarah G	19 Jun 1827
HALLIDAY, Ann	32	F		Gt. Britain	U. States	Diana	28 Apr 1828
John	26		Labourer	Ireland	United States	Fabius	18 Mar 1829
Mary	7	F		Gt. Britain	U. States	Diana	28 Apr 1828
Robert	48	M	Merchant	G. Briton	United States	James Monroe	14 Dec 1820
Thomas	30	M	Brick Layer	Gt. Britain	U. States	Diana	28 Apr 1828
HALLIGAN, —, Mr.	34	M	Distiller	Dublin	U. States	Hibernia	26 Oct 1826
—, Mrs.	30	F	Distiller	Dublin	U. States	Hibernia	26 Oct 1826
Ann	14	F	None	Ireland	United States	Jubilee	12 May 1828
Christopher	8	M	Distiller	Dublin	U. States	Hibernia	26 Oct 1826
James	3	M	Distiller	Dublin	U. States	Hibernia	26 Oct 1826
James	26	M	Labourer	Ireland	United States	Jubilee	12 May 1828
Jas.	9	M				Hibernia	15 Aug 1820
Joseph	10	M	Distiller	Dublin	U. States	Hibernia	26 Oct 1826
Margt.	11	F				Hibernia	15 Aug 1820
Mary	17	F	None	Ireland	United States	Jubilee	12 May 1828
Simon	12	M	Distiller	Dublin	U. States	Hibernia	26 Oct 1826
William	19	M	Labourer	Ireland	United States	Jubilee	12 May 1828
HALLINGHAM, Jas.	20	M	Weaver	England	U. States	Mentor	5 Jul 1825
HALLINGTON, Saml.	21	M	Farmer	England	America	Francis & Henrietta	11 Jul 1823

NAMES OF PASSENGERS	AGE	SEX	OCCUPATIONS	COUNTRY TO WHICH THEY BELONG	COUNTRY THEY INTEND TO INHABIT	SHIPS/DATES OF ARRIVAL	
HALLINGWORTH,							
Fredk.	24	M	P. gentleman	Ireland	United States	William	20 Jul 1829
HALLISON, John	26	M	Labourer	England	Pittsburgh	Orozimbo	8 Jun 1822
HALLIWELL, Daniel	6	M	None	Hyde, near Stockpost	Hyde	Colossus	27 Mar 1828
Dorothy	8	F	None	Hyde, near Stockpost	Hyde	Colossus	27 Mar 1828
Margaret	15	F	None	Hyde, near Stockpost	Hyde	Colossus	27 Mar 1828
Mary	11	F	None	Hyde, near Stockpost	Hyde	Colossus	27 Mar 1828
Noah	13	M	None	Hyde, near Stockpost	Hyde	Colossus	27 Mar 1828
Simeon	17	M	None	Hyde, near Stockpost	Hyde	Colossus	27 Mar 1828
HALLOW, John	25	M	Labourer	Gt. Britain	U. States	Panthea	21 Jul 1825
HALLOWAY, John	25	M				Cassack	25 Jul 1820
John	40	M	Manufacturer	England	New York	Frances Henrietta	3 Apr 1826
Russel	31	M				Cassack	25 Jul 1820
HALLOWELL, Jas.	25	M	Lawer	United States	Jamaica	Active	25 Jun 1823
HALLSTOCK, George	8	M	None	England	United States	London	21 May 1828
Harriet	10	F	None	England	United States	London	21 May 1828
Sarah	33	F	None	England	United States	London	21 May 1828
Sarah Ann	5/12	F	None	England	United States	London	21 May 1828
William	35	M	Laborer	England	United States	London	21 May 1828
HALLSTON, James	38	M	Mariner	U. States	U. States	Nassau	30 Mar 1824
HALLUS, Jno. B.	34	M	Captain	England	England	Florida	17 May 1825
HALLY,							
Abraham Heyman	38		Merchant	Germany	Boston on the Brig ...o...brad	Manhattan	20 Jun 1826
HALME, —, Mr.	48	M	Merchant	England	England	Desdemonia	9 Jun 1825
HALMON, Edwd.	13	M	None	England	United States	Peru	23 May 1827
HALPEN, Paget	29	M	Shugar Planter	New Orleans	New Orleans	Hope Mary Ann	3 May 1824
HALPIN, Ann, Mrs.	30	F	Carpenter	England	U.S.	Acasta	11 May 1827
Charles	20	M	...	Ireland	United States	Trident	18 Jul 1827
John	28		Laborer	Ireland	New York	Lady Hunter	19 Oct 1826
Mary	20	F	Spinster	Ireland	United States	Diana	1 May 1826
Robert	33	M	Carpenter	England	U.S.	Acasta	11 May 1827
Robert, Mast.	1	M	Carpenter	England	U.S.	Acasta	11 May 1827
Wm., Mast.	4	M	Carpenter	England	U.S.	Acasta	11 May 1827
HALPON, Thos.	50	M	Farmer	Limerick	N. York	Thomas & William	25 May 1827
HALRAGE, Wm.	37 5/12	M	Merchant	England	England	Julius Seesar	29 Jul 1820
HALSBERGER,							
Bernard	20	M	Farmer	Holland	U. States	Don Quixote	25 Oct 1828
HALSENBECK, C.	27	M	Merchant	Hamburgh	U. States	Robert Burns	1 Dec 1823
HALSER, Antoine C.	47		Farmer	France	United States	Parachute	14 May 1828
Catharine	48			France	United States	Parachute	14 May 1828
Marian	6			France	United States	Parachute	14 May 1828
HALSEY, Abm. A.	29		Merchant	New York		Hudson	5 Apr 1826
C.		M	Merchant	N. York	U. States	Maine	19 Sep 1823
C.	39	M	Merchant	N. York	U. States	Sally Ann	29 Mar 1824
C.	45	M	Merchant	New York	U. States	Sarah Herrick	7 Oct 1826
Cephas	30	M	Merchant	U. States	U. States	Maine	25 Jan 1823
Cephas	38	M	Mercht.	America	U. States	Sarah Herrick	11 Jun 1825
Cephas	40	M	Mercht.	United States	United States	Sarah Herrick	24 Oct 1825
Ciphar	40	M	Mercht.	America	America	Exertion	26 Jul 1824
D. T.	30	M	Gent.	U.S. America	U.S. America	Exchange	10 Aug 1826
J. M.	36	M	Purser U.S. Navy	U. States	U. States	Jasper	17 Jul 1826
Thomas	27	M	Mechanic	England	U. States	Trimmer	3 Jan 1826
HALSO, Ellis	13	M	Mechanic	England	United States	Manchester	15 Aug 1826
Moses	33	M	Mechanic	England	United States	Manchester	15 Aug 1826
HALT, Mary	22	F		Great Britten	U. States	Magnet	29 Sep 1823
HALTER, Christine	22	F	Mantuamaker	Gt. Brittan		L'Esperance	6 Sep 1828
David	2	M		Brattain		L'Esperance	6 Sep 1828
Maria	23	F		Brattain		L'Esperance	6 Sep 1828
Sebastian	32	M	Labourer	Brattain		L'Esperance	6 Sep 1828
HALTON, Ann	20	F	Spinster	Ireland	United States	Dublin Packet	13 Oct 1828

NAMES OF PASSENGERS	AGE	SEX	OCCUPATIONS	COUNTRY TO WHICH THEY BELONG	COUNTRY THEY INTEND TO INHABIT	SHIPS/DATES OF ARRIVAL	
HALTON (cont'd)							
Rebecca	19	F		G.B.	America	Pacific	13 Jan 1827
Wm. H.	24	M	Labourer	G.B.	America	Pacific	13 Jan 1827
HALY, —, Miss	18	F	None	England	U. States	Criterion	20 Nov 1823
—, Mrs.	42	F	None	England	U. States	Criterion	20 Nov 1823
Hugh	22	M	Labourer	Ireland	U. States	Sarah G	30 Jun 1828
Margaret	24	F		Ireland	United States	Trio	31 Oct 1827
HALYIARD, Ann	4	F	Child	England	United States	Cambria	3 Jul 1829
Charity	23	F	Wife	England	United States	Cambria	3 Jul 1829
Henry	2	M	Child	England	United States	Cambria	3 Jul 1829
Michiel	28	M	Farmer	England	United States	Cambria	3 Jul 1829
HALZER, Charlotte	25	F		France	U. States	Acasta	21 Jan 1825
Edwd.	30	M	Gentleman	Germany	U. States	Acasta	21 Jan 1825
Eugene	2 1/2	F		France	U. States	Acasta	21 Jan 1825
Julia	1/2	F		France	U. States	Acasta	21 Jan 1825
HAM, Mary	21	F		Ireland	New York	Lady Hunter	5 Jun 1826
Thomas	24	M	Labourer	Ireland	U. States	Combine	30 Nov 1825
HAMAGH, Wm.	23	M	Spinster	Great Brittain	United States	Corinthian	9 Jan 1827
HAMAR, James	37	M	Calicoe Printer	Great Britain	U.S. of America	Gratitude	3 Oct 1829
William	33	M	Merchant	England		Amity	11 Sep 1820
HAMAY, Richd.	24	M	Farmer	Ireland	U. States	Orozimbo	7 Jul 1825
HAMBER, Edmund	32	M	Printer	England	United States	Comet	6 Mar 1823
HAMBLA, Thomas	24	M	Miner	England	U. States	Laveria	23 Jul 1828
HAMBLETON, —	3	F		Gt. Britain	U. States	Tantiva	7 Jul 1828
—	7	F		Gt. Britain	U. States	Tantiva	7 Jul 1828
—	8	F		Gt. Britain	U. States	Tantiva	7 Jul 1828
—	10	F		Gt. Britain	U. States	Tantiva	7 Jul 1828
Ann	28	F		Gt. Britain	U. States	Tantiva	7 Jul 1828
Elizabeth	20		Spinster			Rufus King	7 Aug 1820
John	30	M	Mason	Gt. Britain	U. States	Tantiva	7 Jul 1828
HAMBLIN, Elizabeth	25	F		U. Kingdom, G. Britain & Ireland	New York	James Cropper	21 Oct 1825
Thomas	25	M	Gentleman	U. Kingdom, G. Britain & Ireland	New York	James Cropper	21 Oct 1825
HAMBLY, John	31	M	Miner	Great Britain	United States	Thomas Dickason	14 Sep 1827
HAME, John	40	M		England	England	Amity	31 May 1822
HAMEE, Charles	22	M	Farmer	Switzerland	America	Don Quixote	2 Jun 1828
HAMEROG, M.	33	M	Pedler	Ireland	U. States	Montano	2 Sep 1828
HAMILTON, —, Mr.	24	M	Merchant	G. Britain	Canada	Corinthian	29 Apr 1826
—, Mr.	27	M	Gent.	England	United States	Warrior	6 Oct 1828
—, Mrs.	32	F		Gt. Britain	U. States	Columbia	7 Sep 1827
A.	40	M	Surgeon	Great Britain	United States	Isaac Hicks	6 Dec 1827
Agnes	25	F		Scotland	U.S.	Curler	19 Jul 1828
Alexander	35	M	Mercht.	U. States		Hector	17 Aug 1825
Alice	1	M		Gt. Britain	United States	Columbia	7 Sep 1827
Allexander	23	M	Labourer	Ireland	New York	Trusty	12 Sep 1828
Alston	1	F	None	Scotland	United States	Manhattan	11 Oct 1824
And.	24	M	Mercht.	Glasgow	U. States	Ossian	18 Feb 1822
Andrew	15	M		Ireland	U. States	Nancy	10 Jul 1822
Andrew	21	M	Gentleman	Ireland	United States	General Putnam	20 Jun 1825
Andrew	23	M	Grocer	Great Britain	United States	Isaac Hicks	10 Jul 1827
Andrew	23	M	Carpenter	Ireland	United States	Fabius	31 Jul 1829
Ann	19	F	Child	Ireland	N. York	Trusty	12 Sep 1828
Ann	27	F	Merchant	North Shields, Scotland	Gt. Britain	Orozimbo	19 Oct 1822
Charles	6	M	Farmer	Germany	U. States	Bayard	16 May 1827
Chas.	16	M	Servant	Ireland	United States	Trident	16 May 1826
Crosier	12		Farmer	Ireland	United States	Carolina Ann	12 Sep 1823
David	18	M	Labourer	Ireland	N. York	Trusty	12 Sep 1828
E., Mrs.	30	F	Lady	England	U.S. America	Leeds	6 Jun 1826
Edward	2	M	Farmer	Ireland	United States	Neury	27 Jan 1827
Edward	40	M	Farmer	Ireland	United States	Neury	27 Jan 1827
Eliza	1			Scotland	United States	Camillus	3 May 1828
Eliza	20	F	Spinster	Ireland	United States	Thomas	13 Dec 1827
Elizabeth	13	F	None	Scotland	United States	Manhattan	11 Oct 1824
Elizh. Thompson	40	F	None	Scotland	United States	Manhattan	11 Oct 1824

NAMES OF PASSENGERS	AGE	SEX	OCCUPATIONS	COUNTRY TO WHICH THEY BELONG	COUNTRY THEY INTEND TO INHABIT	SHIPS/DATES OF ARRIVAL	
HAMILTON (cont'd)							
Ellen		F	Housemaid	Halifax	United States	Dodge Healy	14 Oct 1828
Ellenor	18	F		Ireland	U. States	Nancy	10 Jul 1822
Euphemia	16	F	None	Scotland	United States	Manhattan	11 Oct 1824
Francis	5	M	Farmer	Ireland	United States	Neury	27 Jan 1827
George	40	M		Ireland	U. States	Nancy	10 Jul 1822
Giles	25	M	Farmer	New York	New York	Gertrude	24 Jul 1820
Hannah	40	F	Lady	St. Croix	Ireland	Jupiter	6 Aug 1826
Hans	1 3/12	M	Son	Ireland	New York	Atlantic	6 Oct 1828
Henry	44		Farmer	Ireland	United States	Carolina Ann	12 Sep 1823
Isabella	8	F	None	Scotland	United States	Manhattan	11 Oct 1824
James	...	M			New York	Hero	19 May 1828
James	6	M	Farmer	Ireland	United States	Neury	27 Jan 1827
James	8	M	None	Scotland	U.S. of America	Friends	12 May 1826
James	10	M	None	Scotland	United States	Manhattan	11 Oct 1824
James	16	M		Scotland	United States	Camillus	9 May 1827
James	20	M		Ireland	U. States	Nancy	10 Jul 1822
James	20	M	Accountant	America	America	Trafalgar	18 Jan 1828
James	20	M	Farmer	Ireland	United States	Asia	29 Jul 1829
James	21	M	Colour Maker	Scotland	U.S.A.	Calliope	15 Aug 1827
James	30	M	Mercht.	Glasgow	U. States	Ossian	18 Feb 1822
James	44	M	Labourer	Ireland	N. York	Trusty	12 Sep 1828
James	58	M	Gentleman	Great Britain	United States	James Cropper	27 Sep 1821
Jane	2 6/12	F	Daughter	Ireland	New York	Atlantic	6 Oct 1828
Jane	11	F	None	Scotland	United States	Manhattan	11 Oct 1824
Jane	14		Farmer	Ireland	United States	Carolina Ann	12 Sep 1823
Jas.	22	M	Merchant	England	Canada	Corinthian	20 Apr 1825
Jeanett	16	F	None	Scotland	United States	Manhattan	11 Oct 1824
Jennet	15	M	None	Scotland	United States	Manhattan	11 Oct 1824
Jessia	12		Niece [of John Lirtch]	Great Britain	United States	Camillus	12 Sep 1827
Jno.	23	M	Planter	United States	United States	Agenora	3 Oct 1826
John	5	M	Son	Ireland	New York	Atlantic	6 Oct 1828
John	16	M	Servant	Scotland	U.S. of America	Camillus	16 Apr 1822
John	18	M	Gentleman	Great Britain	...	Hector	18 Jul 1822
John	20	M	Gentleman	Ireland	United States	Romulus	24 Jun 1826
John	21	M	Farmer	England	U.S. of America	Illinois	16 Jun 1821
John	23	M	Boot Maker	Antrim, Ireland	New York	Anthusa	24 Aug 1825
John	24	M	Farmer	Gt. Britain	U. States	Columbia	7 Sep 1827
John	24	M	Baker	Scotland	United States	Hope	5 Dec 1827
John	25	M		Gt. Britain	U. States	Napolean	26 Sep 1828
John	55	M	...	Scotland	United States	Manhattan	11 Oct 1824
Joseph	27	M	Surgeon	Canada	America	Minerva	8 Oct 1824
Joseph	32	M		Gt. Britain	U. States	Napolean	26 Sep 1828
Magret A.	32	F	Spinster	Ireland	United States	Robert Fulton	10 Aug 1827
Margaret	9		Farmer	Ireland	United States	Carolina Ann	12 Sep 1823
Margaret	35			Great Britan	United States	Newry	11 Jul 1827
Margaret	60	F	Lady	Great Britain	United States	James Cropper	27 Sep 1821
Mary	2	F	Spinster	Ireland	United States	Thomas	13 Dec 1827
Mary	6	F	None	Scotland	United States	Manhattan	11 Oct 1824
Mary	10	F				John Dickinson	14 Sep 1820
Mary	10	F	Child	Ireland	United States	Robert Fulton	10 Aug 1827
Mary	20	F		Ireland	United States	Trio	2 Oct 1828
Mary	23	F	Spinster	Ireland	United States	Hesperus	14 Feb 1820
Mary	24	F	Spinster	Gt. Britain	U. States	Frances Henrietta	18 Apr 1825
Mary	24	F	Wife	Ireland	New York	Atlantic	6 Oct 1828
Mary	30		Seamster	Scotland	United States	Camillus	3 May 1828
Mary Ann	40		Farmer	Ireland	United States	Carolina Ann	12 Sep 1823
Mary Ann	45	F	Spinster	Grt. Britain	United States	Robert Fulton	8 Oct 1828
Mary Ann L.	19	F	Lady	United States	United States	Tampico	13 Oct 1825
P.	27	M	Supercargo	America	U. States	Queen Mab	22 Jul 1825
Partrick	22	M	Weaver	Great Britain	United States	Courier	26 Jun 1827
R. M., Capt.	39	M	Mariner	U.S.	U.S.	Frances	21 Mar 1827
Rachel	6		Farmer	Ireland	United States	Carolina Ann	12 Sep 1823
Rachel	22	F		America	America	Brittannia	28 Feb 1827
Robert	2		Farmer	Ireland	United States	Carolina Ann	12 Sep 1823
Robert	4	M	Farmer	Ireland	United States	Neury	27 Jan 1827
Robert M.	45	M	Mercht.	U.S.	U.S.	Wm. Henry	11 Mar 1826

NAMES OF PASSENGERS	AGE	SEX	OCCUPATIONS	COUNTRY TO WHICH THEY BELONG	COUNTRY THEY INTEND TO INHABIT	SHIPS/DATES OF ARRIVAL	
HAMILTON (cont'd)							
Robt.		M	Sailor			Favorite	9 Oct 1823
Robt.	28	M	Merchant	Scotland	U. States	Servant	30 Aug 1820
Rose	35	M	Farmer	Ireland	United States	Neury	27 Jan 1827
S., Mr.	45	M	Merchant	England	England	Acasta	12 May 1825
Saml.	30	M	Merchant	Ireland	N. York	Trusty	12 Sep 1828
Samuel	28	M	Weaver	Irereland	America	Carolina Ann	20 Jun 1825
Sarah	40	F	Widow	Ireland	United States	Trident	16 May 1826
Susan	18	F		Ireland	United States	William & George	14 May 1828
Thompson	4	F	None	Scotland	United States	Manhattan	11 Oct 1824
W.	28	M	Farmer	Ireland	United States	L. M. Pelham	25 Jun 1822
W. B.	43	M	Gentleman	Great Britain	U. States	Lord Wellington	17 Mar 1823
William	25	M	Clerk	Grt. Britain	United States	Henry Kneeland	5 Nov 1828
William	28		Weaver	Ireland	United States	Mexico	1 Jun 1821
Willm.	28	M	Farmer	Ireland	America	Josephine	8 Dec 1827
Wm.	0 6/12	M		Gt. Britain	United States	Columbia	7 Sep 1827
Wm.	20			Great Britan	United States	Newry	11 Jul 1827
Wm.	21		...	Ireland		Westmoreland	1 Aug 1826
Wm.	22	M	Gardner	Scotland	United States	Margaret Bogle	11 Jun 1824
Wm.	30	M	Weaver	Ireland	New York	Atlantic	6 Oct 1828
Wm.	40	M	...	...	U. States	Mount Parnassus	13 Nov 1827
Wm. R.	40	M	Writer	Gt. Britain	U. States	Frances Henrietta	18 Apr 1825
HAMIN, Wm.	26	M	Weaver	Great Britain	United States	Atlantic	28 May 1827
HAMINGSON,							
James	24 4/12	M	Yeoman			Cririe	18 Sep 1820
HAMION, —	14	M	Gentleman	U. States	U. States	Imperial	10 Dec 1821
HAMLEN, G. T.	39	M	Clerk	United States	United States	Agricola	19 Jul 1824
HAMLIN, Robt.	45	M	None	England	America	Silvanus Jenkins	17 Nov 1828
HAMLINTON, William	25	M	Weaver	C. Armannar [Armagh or Farmanagh?]	N. York	Nile	18 Aug 1829
HAMLON, James	20	M	Labourer	England	U. States	Ayrshire	12 May 1828
HAMMAND, H.	27	M	Merchant	U. States	U. States	Orion	19 Jun 1826
HAMMEL, A. C.	43	F	Farmer	Germany	America	Howard	27 Sep 1826
Adolph	30	M	Mercht.	France	France	Savannah	10 Jan 1828
Jacob	22	M	...	...	...	George	23 Sep 1824
HAMMELL, Elizabeth	27	F	Servant	Ireland	New York	Atlantic	8 May 1828
James	28	M	Block Maker	Ireland	U. States	St. Michael's	10 Feb 1827
John	26	M	Servant	Ireland	New York	Atlantic	8 May 1828
Margaret	26	F	Wife	Ireland	U. States	St. Michael's	10 Feb 1827
HAMMEN, Catharine	40	F		United States	United States	Globe	30 Aug 1828
Dorothy	14	F		United States	United States	Globe	30 Aug 1828
Nicholas	46	M	Farmer	United States	United States	Globe	30 Aug 1828
Sophia	21	F		United States	United States	Globe	30 Aug 1828
HAMMER, Isaac	57	M	Farmer	U.S.	U. States	Canada	5 Feb 1827
John	25	M	Farmer	England	U.S. States	Splendid	14 Aug 1829
HAMMERSMITH,							
Barbara	6	F		United States	United States	Globe	30 Aug 1828
Bernhard	49	M	Farmer	United States	United States	Globe	30 Aug 1828
Catharine	8	F		United States	United States	Globe	30 Aug 1828
Catharine	40	F		United States	United States	Globe	30 Aug 1828
Magdalene	1	F		United States	United States	Globe	30 Aug 1828
HAMMINGSTON,							
Samuel G.	20	M	Farmer	Great Brittain	U. States	Nancy	18 Jul 1821
HAMMOCK, Charles	21	M	Cutter	G. Brittain	U. States	Cincinnatus	2 Oct 1822
HAMMON, Edward	31	M	Merchant	United States		Robert Fulton	8 Mar 1823
HAMMOND, Alexander	60	M	Farmer	Ireland	United States	Asia	29 Jul 1829
C. H.	23	M	Farmer	G. Britain	U. States	St. George	7 Jun 1828
Cy.	30	M		U. States	U. States	Robt. Reade	12 Apr 1825
Edwd.	31	M	Weaver	Ireland	U. States	Pleiades	9 Oct 1829
Eleanor	22	F	his wife [Robert]	Ireland	United States	Asia	29 Jul 1829
Furnothy	22	M	Farmer	Ireland	United States	Asia	29 Jul 1829
Geo.	26	M	Merchant	U. States	U. States	Adeline	30 Apr 1821
H.	22	M	Merchant	Jamaica	U. States	Carlo	6 Oct 1827
J.	50	M	Merchant	Jamaica	U. States	Carlo	6 Oct 1827
James	25		Gentleman	Great Britain	United States	Thomas Dickason	29 Aug 1828

NAMES OF PASSENGERS	AGE	SEX	OCCUPATIONS	COUNTRY TO WHICH THEY BELONG	COUNTRY THEY INTEND TO INHABIT	SHIPS/DATES OF ARRIVAL	
HAMMOND (cont'd)							
John	13		Farmer	England	United States	Corinthian	7 Jul 1829
John	50	M	Mariner	United States	United States	Phoebe	7 Jun 1824
Margaret	55	F	his Wife				
			[Alexander]	Ireland	United States	Asia	29 Jul 1829
Mary	15	F	Lady	St. John	U. States	Ann Maria	6 Jul 1824
Ogden	27	M	Merchant	United States	United States	Cortes	7 Dec 1825
Phebee, Miss	11	F		England	United States	Hercules	25 Jan 1820
Richard	26	M	Farmer	Ireland	United States	Asia	29 Jul 1829
Robert	26	M	Farmer	Ireland	United States	Asia	29 Jul 1829
Sarah	13	F	Lady	St. John	U. States	Ann Maria	6 Jul 1824
Sarah	40	F	Lady	St. John	U. States	Ann Maria	6 Jul 1824
William	25	M	Labourer	Ireland	U. States	Hanford	29 Dec 1828
Wm.	7	M	Merchant	Jamaica	U. States	Carlo	6 Oct 1827
HAMOR, —, Mrs.	30	F	None	U. States	U. States	John	10 Aug 1825
L., Miss	21	F	None	U. States	U. States	John	10 Aug 1825
HAMPHILL, James	19	M	Officer	U.S. America		Phoebe Ann	27 Dec 1825
HAMPSEN, Henry	32	M	Joiner	England	U. States	Thomas Ritchie	2 Jul 1827
Jas.	30	M	Joiner	England	U. States	Thomas Ritchie	2 Jul 1827
HAMPSON, Edward	1	M	Hatter	England	New York	Bowditch	27 Apr 1826
Geo.	23	M	Hatter	Great Britain	New York	Superior	5 Sep 1827
Geo.	25	M	Hatter	England	New York	Bowditch	27 Apr 1826
George	4	M	None	Great Britain	New York	Superior	5 Sep 1827
Hannah	3	F	Hatter	England	New York	Bowditch	27 Apr 1826
James	56	M	Hatter	England	United States	Peru	23 May 1827
Jane	25	F		England	United States	Peru	23 May 1827
John	16	M	Weaver	England	United States	Trident	18 Jul 1827
Maria	22	F	Hatter	England	New York	Bowditch	27 Apr 1826
Saml.	32	M	Gardner	England	United States	Peru	23 May 1827
HAMPTON, —, Mrs.	35	F	None	Great Britton	U. States	Factor	27 Mar 1827
Bridget	3 8/12	F	family [of Valintine]	Ireland	United States	Atlantic	21 Jul 1827
E.	18	F		Gt. Britain	United States	Robert Edwards	1 Jun 1826
John	32	M	Carpenter	Great Britton	U. States	Factor	27 Mar 1827
Margaret	...	...	...	Ireland	United States	Carolina Ann	24 Oct 1825
Mary	25	F	None	Great Britton	U. States	Factor	27 Mar 1827
May	28 6/12	F	family				
			[of Valintine]	Ireland	United States	Atlantic	21 Jul 1827
Sarah	28	F	Lady	U. States Amer		Charlotte Corday	7 Mar 1820
Stephen	30	M	Servant	N. York	N. York	Rebecca	1 May 1824
Thomas	9/12	M	family				
			[of Valintine]	Ireland	United States	Atlantic	21 Jul 1827
Thomas	30	M	Millman		uncertain	Mount Vernon	29 Aug 1828
Valintine	25 5/12	M	Farmer	Ireland	United States	Atlantic	21 Jul 1827
William	10	M	...	Ireland	United States	Carolina Ann	24 Oct 1825
HAMSON, James, Mr.	25	M	Carpenter	England	U.S.	Acasta	11 May 1827
Justus	38	M	Merchant	America	America	Shepherdess	9 May 1822
HANACKE, Augt.	22		None	America	America	Courier	24 Jul 1820
HANAGAN, James	22	M	Labourer	Ireland	United States	Jubilee	13 Jul 1829
Thos.	19 6/12	M	Labourer	Ireland	United States	Wilson	6 Jun 1828
HANAH, Hannah	3	F	None	England	United States	Dalhouse Castle	6 Sep 1827
John	1	M	None	England	United States	Dalhouse Castle	6 Sep 1827
M.	25	M	Merchant	France	U. States	Waldo	19 Aug 1826
HANAHAN, J. C.	23	M	Gentleman	U. States	U. States	Birmingham	12 Oct 1827
HANANG, A.	40	M	Planter	France	Spain	Ann Maria	11 Jun 1828
HANARY, Thomas	23	M	Labourer	Ireland	U. States	Combine	30 Nov 1825
HANBY, Cecil	21	M	Farmer	Great Brittan	U. States	Gem	26 Jul 1827
HANCE, J. F.	36	M	Professor	England	United States	Elizabeth	22 May 1822
Jno.	21	M	Carpenter	U. States	U. States	Eliza	14 Mar 1825
Jno.	23	M	Carpenter	U. States	U. States	Vigilant	25 Nov 1822
HANCHEN, F. H.	28	M	Dyer	Germany	U. States	Franklin	8 Jun 1827
HANCKAMP, Johannis	25	M	Smit	Oldenburg	United States	Juffraw Johanna	16 Oct 1821
HANCKSERE, Hugh	41	M	Butcher	Germany	U. States	Frances	27 Dec 1826
HANCOCK, Adam	11	M		Great Britain	United States	Asia	14 Jul 1829
Ainne	4					Xenophon	25 Jul 1826
Alice	60	M	Labourer	Ireland	United States	Meteor	26 Jun 1827
Crawford C.	27		Tanner	United States	United States	London	16 Aug 1824
Elizabeth	33					Xenophon	25 Jul 1826
Elizabeth	38	F		England	United States	Hercules	21 Nov 1822
Enfield	1					Xenophon	25 Jul 1826

NAMES OF PASSENGERS	AGE	SEX	OCCUPATIONS	COUNTRY TO WHICH THEY BELONG	COUNTRY THEY INTEND TO INHABIT	SHIPS/DATES OF ARRIVAL	
HANCOCK (cont'd)							
George	16	M	Merchant	Great Britain	United States	Asia	14 Jul 1829
Hannah	18	F	None	Great Britain	U. States	Hannibal	12 Oct 1829
Henry	23			Ireland	United States	Geo. Canning	5 Jun 1828
John	8	M		England	United States	Hercules	21 Nov 1822
John	27		Farmer	England	S. New York	Xenophon	25 Jul 1826
Mary	22	F		Ireland	United States	Geo. Canning	5 Jun 1828
Mary Anna	1 6/12	F		England	United States	Hercules	21 Nov 1822
Mirea	20	F		Ireland	America	Carolina Ann	7 Aug 1826
P.	40	M	Merchant	United States	United States	Isaac Hicks	6 Dec 1827
Peter	2					Xenophon	25 Jul 1826
W.	26	M	Merchant	U.S.	U.S.	Mary Ann	1 Jun 1822
William	10					Xenophon	25 Jul 1826
HANCOX, Benjn.	27	M	Servant	England	Canada	Brighton	16 Nov 1826
Brooke	30	M	Merchant	Great Britan	Canada	Canada	2 Jun 1824
HANCROFT, Joseph	21	M	Labourer	Great Britan	U. States	Canada	2 Jun 1824
HAND, Bridget	40	F		Ireland	America	John Adams	2 Aug 1827
Catharine	5	F		Ireland	America	John Adams	2 Aug 1827
Charles	22	M		England	United States	Siroc	31 Oct 1829
Christopher	44	M	Farmer	Ireland	America	John Adams	2 Aug 1827
Christopher, Jr.	6	M		Ireland	America	John Adams	2 Aug 1827
Elizabeth	9	F		Switzerland	U. States	Robert Edward	2 Nov 1827
Ellen	10	F	None	England	U. States	Thomas Ritchie	2 Jul 1827
Emma	1	F		Switzerland	U. States	Robert Edward	2 Nov 1827
Geo.	13	M		Switzerland	U. States	Robert Edward	2 Nov 1827
Hannah	17	F		Switzerland	U. States	Robert Edward	2 Nov 1827
Jno.	3	M	None	England	U. States	Thomas Ritchie	2 Jul 1827
John	4	M		Ireland	America	John Adams	2 Aug 1827
John	29 2/12	M	Planter	England	England	St. Michaels	25 Nov 1825
John	30	M	Plasterer	England	U. States	Thomas Ritchie	2 Jul 1827
Jonathan	7	M		Switzerland	U. States	Robert Edward	2 Nov 1827
Lucy	5	F		Switzerland	U. States	Robert Edward	2 Nov 1827
Margret	1	F	None	England	U. States	Thomas Ritchie	2 Jul 1827
Margret	28	F	None	England	U. States	Thomas Ritchie	2 Jul 1827
Mary	32	F		Switzerland	U. States	Robert Edward	2 Nov 1827
Mary Ann	11	F		Switzerland	U. States	Robert Edward	2 Nov 1827
N.	43	M		N. Jersey	U. States	William	30 Jul 1824
Thomas	1	M		Ireland	America	John Adams	2 Aug 1827
Wm.	16	M	Weaver	Ireland	U. States	Edward	15 Jul 1825
HAND COCK, Georg	30	M	Brass Maker			Hudson	23 Jul 1828
HANDCOCK, Ledia	24	F	Spinster	Ireland	United States	Asia	29 Jul 1829
HANDEROAGH, Jacobus	32	M	Merchant	Germany	Philadelphia	Cumberland	25 Feb 1826
HANDERSIDE, A.	20	M	Mechanic	England	U. States	London Packet	5 Jul 1823
HANDERSON, Isaac	35	M	Laborer	Ireland	U. States	Lady Hunter	8 Aug 1826
William	30 5/12	M	Labourer	England	America	St. Michaels	25 Nov 1825
HANDET, —, Miss	17	F	None	Madeira	Madeira	Howard	18 Sep 1828
HANDEY, Bester	39	M	Cole burner	Emerica	Merican	Enterprize	14 Oct 1828
HANDLY, Helen	17	F	Spinster	Ireland	United States	Wilson	6 Jun 1828
Thos.	28	M	Labourer	Ireland	United States	Wilson	6 Jun 1828
HANDRIDE, A.	31	M	Merchant	England	U. States	Pacific	11 Sep 1824
HANDS, Elizabeth	1 3/12	F		Great Britain	U. States	Silas Richards	27 Jun 1827
Elizabeth	20	F		Great Britain	U. States	Silas Richards	27 Jun 1827
Frederick	23	M	Laborer	Gt. Britain	United States	Silas Richards	20 Jun 1826
Hy.	3	M		Gt. Britain	United States	Silas Richards	20 Jun 1826
Patrick	21	M	Labourer	Ireland	U. States	Two Marys	20 Apr 1825
HANDSOME, Robt.	26	M	Farmer	Great Britain	United States	Diana	6 Jul 1829
HANDY, L.	22	M	Mechanic	Connecticutt	U. States	Benjamin	1 Jun 1822
Samuel	20	M	Merchant	Scotland	U. States	Atlantic	13 Jul 1824
Thomas	12	M	Boy	Ireland	United States	Dublin Packet	3 Sep 1822
HANDYSIDE, Robert	32	M	Merchant	Great Britain		Panthea	15 Jun 1822
HANE, Johanns	22	M	Silver Smith	Switzerland	United States	Ospray	2 Sep 1824
HANEY, Bess	18	F	on a visit	C. Armannar [Armagh or Farmanagh?]	Boston	Nile	18 Aug 1829
Biddy	20	F		Ireland	United States	Thompson	12 Sep 1827
Bridget	14	F	None	Ireland	United States	Jubilee	4 Mar 1829
James	30	M		Ireland	United States	Thompson	12 Sep 1827
Michael	38	M	Mason	Ireland	United States	Jubilee	4 Mar 1829
Robert	22	M	Weaver	Ireland	United States	Jubilee	4 Mar 1829

NAMES OF PASSENGERS	AGE	SEX	OCCUPATIONS	COUNTRY TO WHICH THEY BELONG	COUNTRY THEY INTEND TO INHABIT	SHIPS/DATES OF ARRIVAL	
HANEY (cont'd)							
Thomas	35	M	Laborer	Ireland	United States	Ann Maria	3 Jul 1827
HAÑEZ, Manuel	27	M	Merchant	Spain	United States	Enterprize	9 Aug 1825
HANFORD, Amelia	26					Charlotte Corday	11 Sep 1820
Ann	65	F	Lady	St. John	St. John	Ann Maria	5 May 1824
Thomas	21	M	Merchant	St. John	St. John	Nancy	19 Oct 1821
Thos.	22	M	Merchant	St. John	St. John	St. Michael	27 Mar 1827
HANG, Amaria	48	F		Switzerland	U. States	Hewes	30 Oct 1829
Catell	19	F		Switzerland	U. States	Hewes	30 Oct 1829
Christina	24	F		Switzerland	U. States	Hewes	30 Oct 1829
George	17	M		Switzerland	U. States	Hewes	30 Oct 1829
Gotfrid	11 6/12	M		Switzerland	U. States	Hewes	30 Oct 1829
Gotfrid	51	M	Tailor	Switzerland	U. States	Hewes	30 Oct 1829
Magdalina	10	F		Switzerland	U. States	Hewes	30 Oct 1829
HANGLY, Wm.	28	M	Labourer	Ireland	United States	Hope	12 Jun 1828
HÀNHLE, Christian	12	M		Germany	Pensylvania	James Noble	27 Aug 1827
Jacob	24	M	Hatter	Germany	Pensylvania	James Noble	27 Aug 1827
HANIFEN, Thos. S.	25	M	Mariner	America	U. States	Brown	8 Aug 1825
HANIGAN, Hugh	20	M	Labourer	Ireland	United States	Robert Fulton	10 Aug 1827
HANING, Elizabeth	22	F	Spinster	Ireland	America	Josephine	8 Dec 1827
HANK, Geo.	21	M	Labourer	Germany	Newyork	Cortes	16 Jul 1827
HANKLEY, Thos.	19	M	Farmer	New York		Olive Branch	9 Oct 1829
HANKS, Wotten Wright	14	M	None	Gt. Britain	Canada	New York	5 Jul 1826
HANKSLEY, Wm.	35	M	Chandler	England	United States	Essex	23 May 1828
HANLAN, Jas.	23	M	Farmer	Ireland	New York	Concordia	12 Oct 1826
John			Servant	Ireland	England	General Starke	17 Jul 1827
HANLEN, Michael	21	M	Gentleman	England	Great Britain	New York	22 Jul 1824
HANLEY, Ann	1	F	None	Great Britain	United States	William Dawson	18 Jun 1827
Catherine	18	F	Spinster	Ireland	United States	Wilson	6 Jun 1828
Chas.	20	M	Taylor	England	U. States	William	28 Nov 1823
Daniel	24	M	Weaver	Great Britian	United States	Andes	19 Aug 1829
Dennis	20	M	Weaver	Great Britian	United States	Andes	19 Aug 1829
Edward	19	M	...	Ireland	United States	Wilson	22 Jun 1824
John	27	M	Labourer	Ireland	U. States	Combine	30 Nov 1825
Mary	20	F	None	Great Britain	United States	William Dawson	18 Jun 1827
William	22	M	...	Ireland	United States	Wilson	22 Jun 1824
Wm.	26	M	Labourer	Great Britain	United States	William Dawson	18 Jun 1827
HANLIN, John	24	M	Farmer	Great Brittain	U. States	Hibernia	8 Jul 1823
Thos.	18	M	Farmer	County of ..., Dublin, Ireland	N. York	New Orleans	24 Aug 1827
HANLON, Barney	23	M	Weaver	Gt. Britain		Dalhouse Castle	13 May 1828
Eliza, Mrs.	36	F	Lady	Ireland	United States	Dublin Packet	9 Jul 1827
Ellen, Miss	18	F	Lady	Ireland	United States	Dublin Packet	9 Jul 1827
Esther	20	F	Spinster	Ireland	United States	Dublin Packet	28 Apr 1824
James	21	M	Farmer	Ireland	United States	Dublin Packet	28 Apr 1824
James	26	M	Weaver	Ireland	U. States	Courier	17 Mar 1828
Margaret	22		Dress Maker	Great Britain	United States	Thomas Dickason	29 Aug 1828
Mary Ann	23	F	Dress Maker	Great Britain	United States	Atlantic	8 Dec 1827
T.	21		Farmer	Ireland	United States	Courier	16 May 1825
HANMER, Simon	25	M	Carpenter	Boston	Boston	Governor Griswold	15 Jul 1826
HANN, James	30	M	Farmer	Ireland		L. M. Pelham	12 May 1823
HANNA, Athony., Revd.	26	M	Gentleman	Ireland	United States	Erin	25 Dec 1820
James	32	M	Labourer	Ireland	New York	Atlantic	6 Oct 1828
John	24	M	Labourer	Ireland	United States	Josephine	30 Apr 1828
Maria	17	F		Ireland	United States	Romulus	24 Jun 1826
HANNABURY, Jas.	23	M	Sailor	Novascotia	U. States	Prince Edward	5 Dec 1821
HANNAGAN, Patrick	27	M	Laborer	England	United States	Peru	23 May 1827
William	20	M	Tailor	England	United States	Peru	23 May 1827
HANNAH, Ann	27	F		West Indies	U. States	Hudson	8 Oct 1827
Ann	30	F		Ireland	United States	Sarah G.	20 Jul 1827
B.	24	M	Merchant	U. States	U. States	Emma	15 Apr 1822
Catherine	13 6/12	F	Child	Scotland	United States	Samuel Robertson	9 May 1827
Elizabeth	19	F		Irereland	America	Carolina Ann	20 Jun 1825
Hannah	2	F		Ireland	United States	Sarah G.	20 Jul 1827

NAMES OF PASSENGERS	AGE	SEX	OCCUPATIONS	COUNTRY TO WHICH THEY BELONG	COUNTRY THEY INTEND TO INHABIT	SHIPS/DATES OF ARRIVAL	
HANNAH (cont'd)							
Heborah	3	F	None	England	United States	Dalhouse Castle	6 Sep 1827
J. L.	27	M	Doctor	N. York	U. States	Hunter	1 Jul 1828
James	27	M	Farmer	G. Britain	U. States	George Clinton	10 Sep 1828
Jas. L.	36	M	M.D.	West Indies	U. States	Hudson	8 Oct 1827
Jas. Washington	10/12	M		West Indies	U. States	Hudson	8 Oct 1827
John	28	M	Laborer	Scotland	U. States	Ice Plant	18 Dec 1820
John, The Revd.	36	M	Minister of the Gospel	Great Britan	Great Britan	Columbia	10 Mar 1824
Kenny	20	M	Farmer	Ireland	U. States	Champion	26 Jul 1827
Marey Ann	1	F		Ireland	United States	Sarah G.	20 Jul 1827
Robert	27 5/12	M	Farmer	Wales	America	Minerva	15 Jun 1825
Sarah	22	F	Spinster	America	U. States	Ice Plant	18 Dec 1820
Sarah	23	F		G. Britain	U. States	George Clinton	10 Sep 1828
William	4	M		Ireland	United States	Sarah G.	20 Jul 1827
HANNAN, Ellen	21	F	None	Great Britain	United States	Cortes	11 Dec 1822
Ellen, Jr.	39	F	None	Great Britain	United States	Cortes	11 Dec 1822
James	23		Shomaker	Ireland	United States	Geo. Canning	5 Jun 1828
Peter	2_ 6/12	M	Child	Ireland	America	Weser	26 Jun 1821
HANNAR, Margaret	22	F	Spinster	Ireland	U. States	Meteor	19 Jul 1828
HANNATY, Elizth.	16	F	Spinster	Ireland	America	Josephine	8 Dec 1827
Margt.	17	F	Spinster	Ireland	America	Josephine	8 Dec 1827
Owen	20	M	Baker	Ireland	America	Josephine	8 Dec 1827
HANNAY, Anstice	16	F		Gt. Britain		Dalhouse Castle	13 May 1828
HANNEN, John	25	M	Smith	Germany	America	Orozimbo	1 Oct 1827
HANNENMON, Fred, Doct.	41 6/12	M	Physician	Germany	U. States	Enterprize	2 Jun 1828
HANNESSY, Ann	32	F	None	Ireland	Alexandria, U.S.	Roman	17 Oct 1826
George	21	M	Iron Monger	Ireland	Alexandria, U.S.	Roman	17 Oct 1826
HANNEY, Charles	11					Cincinnatus	29 Apr 1822
D.	20	M		France & Switzerland	U. States	Bayard	14 Jul 1826
Eliza	17					Cincinnatus	29 Apr 1822
Emma	16					Cincinnatus	29 Apr 1822
James	8					Cincinnatus	29 Apr 1822
Jane	10					Cincinnatus	29 Apr 1822
Jean	20	M		Great Brittain	United States	Active	12 Sep 1828
Jennett	51					Cincinnatus	29 Apr 1822
Matilda	15					Cincinnatus	29 Apr 1822
Michael	22	M	Laborer	Gt. Britain		Dalhouse Castle	13 May 1828
N.	18	F		France & Switzerland	U. States	Bayard	14 Jul 1826
Thomas	13					Cincinnatus	29 Apr 1822
William	53		Farmer	England		Cincinnatus	29 Apr 1822
HANNI, Elizabeth	15	F	Farmer	Switzerland	U. States	Sully	15 Jul 1829
John	25	M	Farmer	Switzerland	U. States	Sully	15 Jul 1829
HANNICK, Joseph	58	M	Merchant	United States	U. States	Saml. Smith	24 Jul 1826
HANNIE, Frederick	3	M		Switzerland	America, U.N.S.	Great Britain	3 Aug 1829
Jacob	6	M		Switzerland	America, U.N.S.	Great Britain	3 Aug 1829
Jean	35	M	Farmer	Switzerland	America, U.N.S.	Great Britain	3 Aug 1829
John	5	M		Switzerland	America, U.N.S.	Great Britain	3 Aug 1829
Maria	35	F		Switzerland	America, U.N.S.	Great Britain	3 Aug 1829
HANNIGAN, Catharine	30	F	Farmer	Ireland	U.S.A.	Dalhouse Castle	21 Aug 1829
Cathr.	30	F		Ireland	United States	Dalhouse Castle	21 Aug 1829
Pat	29	M	Farmer	Ireland	U.S.A.	Dalhouse Castle	21 Aug 1829
HANNIN, Wm.	22	M	Mariner	America	U. States	Ambuscade	11 Jul 1821
HANNINGTON, Henry	27	M	Musician	England	United States	Eliza Grant	7 Jun 1827
Robert	30	M	Musician	England	United States	Eliza Grant	7 Jun 1827
HANNION, Thomas	24	M	Labourer	Ireland	New York	Amanda	23 May 1827
HANNITY, Rose	40	F	Labourer	Great Britian	United States	Princess Charlotte	6 Sep 1828
HANNY, Sarah	20	F	Spinster	Ireland	Unt. St. America	Wilson	21 May 1827
HANO, Jose		M	Merchant	Spain	Spain	Packet	13 Jun 1821
HANORA, Isabella	20	F		Ireland	New York	Carolina Ann	15 Oct 1824
HANRAHAN, Daniel	36					Trio	5 May 1828
HANRALTY, Margaret	60	M	Spinster	Ireland	U. States	Globe	14 Jul 1821
HANRATTY, Bridget	25			Great Britan	United States	Newry	11 Jul 1827
HANRY, Eliza	26	F		Scotland	U.S.	Curler	19 Jul 1828
Jane	3	F		Scotland	U.S.	Curler	19 Jul 1828

NAMES OF PASSENGERS	AGE	SEX	OCCUPATIONS	COUNTRY TO WHICH THEY BELONG	COUNTRY THEY INTEND TO INHABIT	SHIPS/DATES OF ARRIVAL	
HANRY (cont'd)							
Peter	45	M		Scotland	U.S.	Curler	19 Jul 1828
HANSCKETT, T. J.	45	M	Merchant	Denmark	U. States	Elias Burger	12 Sep 1822
HANSEL, Christiania	24	F		Germany	America	Falcon	28 Aug 1828
HANSEN, Henry	20	M	Builder	England	U. States	Cincinnatus	24 May 1821
HANSET, A. J.	22	M	Mercht.	France	U. States	Edward Bonnaffe	12 Oct 1826
HANSICK, Edward	29	M	Merchant	U. States	U. States	Birmingham	12 Oct 1829
HANSIN, —, Mrs.	24	F		N. York	U. States	William Smith	9 May 1822
Peter	32	M	Merchant	N. York	U. States	William Smith	9 May 1822
HANSON, Abm.	11	M	None	England	U. States	Thomas Ritchie	2 Jul 1827
Charles	1	M	Labourer	Great Britain	U. States	Ganges	21 Jun 1827
Chrs.	45	M	Merchant	Denmark	Denmark	Algerine	27 Sep 1828
Edw.	6	F	None	England	U. States	Thomas Ritchie	2 Jul 1827
Edward	13	M	Labourer	Great Britain	U. States	Ganges	21 Jun 1827
Elisabeth	4	F	Labourer	Great Britain	U. States	Ganges	21 Jun 1827
Elisabeth	38	F	Labourer	Great Britain	U. States	Ganges	21 Jun 1827
Emma	3	F	Labourer	Great Britain	U. States	Ganges	21 Jun 1827
Fredk. F.	33	M	Lawyer	Denmark	U. States	Chase	2 Oct 1826
George	6	M	Labourer	Great Britain	U. States	Ganges	21 Jun 1827
Henry	9	M	None	England	U. States	Thomas Ritchie	2 Jul 1827
Janett	30	F		Scotland	Great Britain	Camillus	28 Apr 1823
Jno.	23	M	Manufacturer	England	U. States	Thomas Ritchie	2 Jul 1827
John	34	M	Sawyer	England	Newyork	Cortes	16 Jul 1827
Joseph	12	M	Labourer	Great Britain	U. States	Ganges	21 Jun 1827
Joseph	36	M	Labourer	Great Britain	U. States	Ganges	21 Jun 1827
Martha	45	F	None	England	U. States	Thomas Ritchie	2 Jul 1827
Richd.	24	M	Auctionear	Dublin, Dublin, Ireland	Philadelphia	New Orleans	24 Aug 1827
Robert	1	M		Scotland	Great Britain	Camillus	28 Apr 1823
Saml.	4	M	None	England	U. States	Thomas Ritchie	2 Jul 1827
Sarah	13	F	None	England	U. States	Thomas Ritchie	2 Jul 1827
Thos.	38	M	Merchant	U. States	U. States	Sanford William	28 Jan 1823
William	50	M	Machinemaker	Great Britain, Ireland	New York	Britannia	3 Nov 1827
HANSTON, B.	15	M		G. Britain	U. States	London	23 Sep 1828
E.	9	F		G. Britain	U. States	London	23 Sep 1828
Margt.	40	F		G. Britain	U. States	London	23 Sep 1828
Mary	2	F		G. Britain	U. States	London	23 Sep 1828
Wm.	13	M		G. Britain	U. States	London	23 Sep 1828
HANT, E. D.	30	M	Clergyman	France		Antioch	18 Aug 1829
HANTEMAN, Jacob	21	M	Hatmaker			Constitution	20 Jun 1828
HANTER, Wm.	36	M		Great Brittian	United States	Carolina Augusta	2 Dec 1828
HANTIN, Daniel	19	M	Labourer	Ireland	United States	Hope	12 Jun 1828
John	27	M	Labourer	Ireland	United States	Hope	12 Jun 1828
Richard	22	M	Labourer	Ireland	United States	Hope	12 Jun 1828
HANTON, Mary	18	F		Ireland	U. States	Virginia	20 Jun 1825
HANVEY, David	4	M		England	United States	Hannibal	25 Sep 1827
Geo.	2	M		England	United States	Hannibal	25 Sep 1827
Jane	0 4/12	F		England	United States	Hannibal	25 Sep 1827
Margt.	32	F		England	United States	Hannibal	25 Sep 1827
Wm.	7	M		England	United States	Hannibal	25 Sep 1827
Wm.	32	M	Painter	England	United States	Hannibal	25 Sep 1827
HANYAN, William	24	M	Labourer	Ireland	United States	Lord Wellington	28 May 1827
HANZELL, Jacob	26	M	Brewer	United States	United States	Globe	30 Aug 1828
HAPENNY, Richd.	26	M	Labourer	Ireland	U.S.	Oliver Wolcott	3 Nov 1827
HAPER, Robt.	2	M		Ireland		Triton	12 Jul 1823
HAPFOLDT, J. M.	20	M	Baker	Germany	United States	Maria Theresa	28 Aug 1821
HAPPEN, James	32	M	Laborer	Ireland	United States	St. Michaels	23 Dec 1826
Mary	30	F	Wife	Ireland	United States	St. Michaels	23 Dec 1826
HAPWORTH, Joseph	1 6/12	M	None	Great Briton	United States	Mount Vernon	29 Aug 1828
Susannah	26	F	None	Great Briton	United States	Mount Vernon	29 Aug 1828
HARA, Jos.	15		Labourer	G. Britian	G. Britian	Dewitt Clinton	26 Aug 1825
HARACEY, William	25	M	Merchant	Jamaica		Midas	9 May 1827
HARAGAN, Timothy	19	M	Baker	Ireland	United States	Borneo	14 Aug 1827
HARALD, Thos.	27	M	Miner	England	England	Eliza	31 Jul 1826
HARAM, Thos.	38	M	Tailor		U. States	Cowper	8 Jan 1827
HARAN, Jno.	32	M	Mechanic	Gt. Britain	United States	St. Michael	28 Feb 1826

NAMES OF PASSENGERS	AGE	SEX	OCCUPATIONS	COUNTRY TO WHICH THEY BELONG	COUNTRY THEY INTEND TO INHABIT	SHIPS/DATES OF ARRIVAL	
HARANDUS, A.	25	M	Merchant	Cuba	Spain	Transit	13 Nov 1823
HARBERT, Ha.	16	M	Cooper	Great Britain	U. States	Dominica	4 Jan 1823
John H.	18	M	Merchant	United States	U. States	Leopard	30 Aug 1826
HARBIE, J. W.	21	M	Merchant	U. States	U. States	Mary Ann	13 Jun 1821
HARBISON, Betsey	35		Farmer	England	United States	Mary	15 Jul 1822
Charles	5		Farmer	England	United States	Mary	15 Jul 1822
James	6		Farmer	England	United States	Mary	15 Jul 1822
Thomas	4		Farmer	England	United States	Mary	15 Jul 1822
Wm.	7		Farmer	England	United States	Mary	15 Jul 1822
HARBOTTLE, James	23	M	Labourer	England	Alexandria, U.S.	Roman	17 Oct 1826
Wm.	19	M	Carpenter	G. Britain	U. States	Cosmo	15 May 1827
HARBURGH, Wm.	24	M	Sugar Baker	Germany	U.S.	Robert Edwards	11 Nov 1822
HARCEY, John	24	M	Labourer	England	U. States	Comet	23 Aug 1828
HARD, Charles	13	M	Officer	England	U. States	Hiram	17 Jun 1826
John	44 5/12	M	Accountant	Barbadous	U.S. America	Illinois	16 Oct 1822
HARDCASTLE, William	20	M	Linen dresser	Great Britain	United States	Orozimbo	28 Jun 1827
HARDDEN, Jas.	36			Great Britain	U. States America	Maria	22 May 1822
Jas., Jr.	13			Great Britain	U. States America	Maria	22 May 1822
HARDEMAN, Benjamin	23	M	Farmer	Ireland	United States	Trident	31 Mar 1827
HARDEN, Betty	3	F		Ireland	United States	Sarah G.	20 Jul 1827
Bridget	26	F		Ireland	United States	Sarah G.	20 Jul 1827
George	23	M	Merchant	Ireland	America	Hannibal	4 Apr 1823
Sarah	16	F	Servant	Ireland		William Tell	24 Oct 1829
HARDENBERG, Allmina	20	F		England	New York	Brighton	24 Aug 1827
HARDENBROOK, Rebecca	31	F	None	U. States	U. States	Edwin	1 Jul 1829
HARDI, T.	18	M	Clerk	France	return in the vessel	Andreas	20 Aug 1821
HARDIE, —				G. Britain	U. States	Camillus	8 Sep 1828
—, Mrs.	28	F		G. Britain	U. States	Camillus	8 Sep 1828
D. C.	44	M	Merchant	United States	United States	Rose in Bloom	12 Apr 1821
Isabella	40	F		Scotland	United States	Camillus	9 May 1827
James	26	M	Farmer	Scotland	United States	Samuel Robertson	9 May 1827
HARDING, Ann	28	F	None	G. Britain	U. States	Rosalie	22 Aug 1820
Betty	24	F		Ireland	Pensylvania	Lima	5 Aug 1829
Betty	24	F		England	U. States	Lima	5 Aug 1829
Clara	1	F	None	G. Britain	U. States	Rosalie	22 Aug 1820
Dominick	24	M	Labourer	Ireland	U.S.	Lady Hunter	10 Jul 1826
Ebenr.	21	M	None	Nova Scotia	United States	Loire	18 Oct 1820
Frank	4	M	None	G. Britain	U. States	Rosalie	22 Aug 1820
Frs.	9	M		England, Born in Barbadoes	U. States	Cannon	15 Jul 1822

*all the children have come under the care of Mrs. Fenwick for their education

H.	24	M	Farmer	Great Britton	U. State	Earl of Liverpool	16 Aug 1826
James	6			England	United States	Warrior	6 Oct 1828
Jno.	7	M		England, Born in Barbadoes	U. States	Cannon	15 Jul 1822

*all the children have come under the care of Mrs. Fenwick for their education

John	4/12	M	None	England	United States	London	21 May 1828
John	23	M	Laborer	England	United States	London	21 May 1828
John	30	M	Steam Engineer	England	United States	Lunar	5 May 1828
Mary	20	F	Labourer	Ireland	U.S.	Lady Hunter	10 Jul 1826
Mary Ann	23	F	None	England	United States	London	21 May 1828
Phabe	2	F	None	England	United States	London	21 May 1828
Rachel	28	F		England	United States	Warrior	6 Oct 1828
Richd.	11	M		England, Born in Barbadoes	U. States	Cannon	15 Jul 1822

*all the children have come under the care of Mrs. Fenwick for their education

Robert	5			England	United States	Warrior	6 Oct 1828
Robert	30	M	Shoemaker	Ireland	United States	Trio	2 Oct 1828
S. K.	24	M	Merchant	U. States	U. States	Magnola	7 Mar 1827
Theresa	7	F	None	G. Britain	U. States	Rosalie	22 Aug 1820
Thomas	24	M	Farmer	Great Britian	United States	Andes	19 Aug 1829
Vallentin	63	M	Merchant	United	United States	Sarah	31 Oct 1829
Wm.	9	M		G. Britain	U. States	Rosalie	22 Aug 1820
HARDLEY, H.	18	M	Weaver	Great Britain	United States	Isaac Hicks	6 Dec 1827
HARDMAN, Curtis	20	M	Hatter	Ireland	United States	Jubilee	13 Sep 1827
Eliz.	20	F	None	Gt. Britain	U.S. America	James Cropper	2 Aug 1827

NAMES OF PASSENGERS	AGE	SEX	OCCUPATIONS	COUNTRY TO WHICH THEY BELONG	COUNTRY THEY INTEND TO INHABIT	SHIPS/DATES OF ARRIVAL	
HARDMAN (cont'd)							
George	18	M	None	Ireland	United States	St. George	25 Aug 1829
James	11	M	None	Great Britain	United States	Frances Henrietta	17 Sep 1827
John	21	M	Fisher	Gt. Britain	U.S. America	James Cropper	2 Aug 1827
John	30	F	Weaver	England	United States	Helen	17 Dec 1827
Mary	30	F	None	Great Britain	United States	Frances Henrietta	17 Sep 1827
Richd.	17	M	Machine Maker	Great Britain	United States	Frances Henrietta	17 Sep 1827
Samuel	6	M	None	Great Britain	United States	Frances Henrietta	17 Sep 1827
Thos. L.	45		Merchant	Massachusetts	N. Orleans	James Cropper	12 Jul 1822
Wm.	13	M	Machine Maker	Great Britain	United States	Frances Henrietta	17 Sep 1827
HARDON, Wm. H.	24		Cotton Spinner	Ireland	United States	Courier	15 Oct 1827
HARDREAU, James	25		Blacksmith	Ireland	United States	Courier	15 Oct 1827
HARDRY, H. A.	37	M	Merchant	U. States	U. States	Prince Edward	29 Jul 1823
HARDS, Ann	2		Shoe Maker	England	United States	Corinthian	7 Jul 1829
Ann	25		Shoe Maker	England	United States	Corinthian	7 Jul 1829
William	5		Shoe Maker	England	United States	Corinthian	7 Jul 1829
William	25		Shoe Maker	England	United States	Corinthian	7 Jul 1829
HARDY, Alex	27	M	Farmer	Scotland	United States	Curler	3 Mar 1828
Ann	8	F	None	Great Britain	United States	Illinois	9 Oct 1820
Ann	17	F	None	Great Britain	United States	William & Jane	22 Aug 1820
Anna	28	F	Wife [of William H.]	Great Briton	United States	Orion	18 Jun 1821
Anne	48	F	None	Great Britain	United States	Mary & Harriet	3 Jul 1829
Billy	25	F	None	Great Britain	United States	Illinois	9 Oct 1820
Edward	32	M	Merchant	New York	New York	Brighton	20 Aug 1825
Edwd.	40	M	Farmer			Splendid	14 Aug 1829
Eliz.	9	F				Splendid	14 Aug 1829
Elizabeth	1 6/12	F	Child [of William H.]	Great Briton	United States	Orion	18 Jun 1821
Elizth.	14	F	None	Great Britain	United States	Mary & Harriet	3 Jul 1829
Encord	34	M	Labourer	Ireland	United States	Hope	12 Jun 1828
Hannah	23	F	None	Great Britain	United States	William & Jane	22 Aug 1820
Henry	24		Merchant			Charlotte Corday	11 Sep 1820
J. L. C.			...	U. States	U. States	Day	14 Jun 1822
James	18	M	None	Great Britain	United States	Mary & Harriet	3 Jul 1829
Jane	6/12	F	None	Great Britain	United States	Illinois	9 Oct 1820
Jane	26					Charlotte Corday	11 Sep 1820
John	15	M	None	Great Britain	United States	Mary & Harriet	3 Jul 1829
John	23	M	Attached to his British Majesty's Consulate Maricaibo	England	U. States	Fame	9 Feb 1827
John	50	M	Farmer	Great Britain	United States	Mary & Harriet	3 Jul 1829
Joseph	5	M	None	Great Britain	United States	Illinois	9 Oct 1820
M.	25	M	Shoe Maker	Ireland	United States	Jubilee	13 Sep 1827
Manin	27	M	Labourer	Ireland	United States	Hope	12 Jun 1828
Martha	22	F	None	New York	New York	Brighton	20 Aug 1825
Martin	23	M	Laborer	England	America	Silas Richard	24 Oct 1829
Mary	10	F	None	Great Britain	United States	Illinois	9 Oct 1820
Mary	20	F		Ireland	United States	Jubilee	13 Sep 1827
Mary	55	F	None	Great Britain	United States	William & Jane	22 Aug 1820
Mary	60	F		Great Brittian	United States	Carolina Augusta	2 Dec 1828
R. K.	20	M		Ireland	U. States	Geo. Canning	2 Sep 1828
Richard	28	M	Farmer	England	United States	Nancy Henrietta	3 Nov 1828
Robert	8	M	None	Great Britain	United States	Mary & Harriet	3 Jul 1829
Thomas	3	M	infant	Great Britain	United States	William & Jane	22 Aug 1820
Thomas	40	M	Merchant	G.B.		Silas Richards	29 Oct 1827
Thomas	40	M	Merchant	England	America	Silas Richard	24 Oct 1829
Thos.	45	M	Schoolmaster	British ...	American States	Loyalty	9 Sep 1822
Thos.	45	M	Merchant	Great Britian	U. States	Silas Richards	29 Oct 1828
William H.	32	M	Merchant	Great Briton	United States	Orion	18 Jun 1821

NAMES OF PASSENGERS	AGE	SEX	OCCUPATIONS	COUNTRY TO WHICH THEY BELONG	COUNTRY THEY INTEND TO INHABIT	SHIPS/DATES OF ARRIVAL	
HARDYEAR, Stephen	20	M	Teacher	Derby	U. States	Matilda	1 Sep 1823
HAREKS, Isaac	16	M	Merchant	France	U. States	Victoria	9 Sep 1828
HAREN, Michl.	22	M	Labourer	Ireland	United States	Nile	17 May 1827
HARES, —, Miss	19	F		Bristol	New York	Cosmo	25 Sep 1827
HARFORD, ...enedict	62	M	...	...	Boston	Frances Henrietta	30 Jun 1827
Ann	47	F	None	...	Boston	Frances Henrietta	30 Jun 1827
Henry	37		Butcher	Leicester, England	Great Britain	Franklin	22 Jun 1827
HARGERTY, Biddy	5	F		Ireland	United States	Sarah G.	20 Jul 1827
HARGOOD, William, Mr.	32	M	Attorney	Great Britain	United States	Birmingham	15 Jun 1827
HARGRANS, Heny	29	M	Weaver	England	U. States	Severn	12 Oct 1826
HARGRAVE, Charles	21		Gentleman	England	England	London	16 Aug 1824
David	45	M	Cloth deeler	G. Britain	United States	Fairy	18 Feb 1825
Sanf.	30			England		Anacreon	7 Sep 1827
HARGRAVES, Ann	20	F	None	Great Britian	United States	George Clinton	21 Oct 1826
Hannah	2 6/12	F	None	Great Britian	United States	George Clinton	21 Oct 1826
James	24	M	Black Smith		New York	Governor Clinton	3 Jul 1827
John	25	M		Lancashire	U. States	Atlantic	13 Jul 1824
John	25	M	Bobinet Maker	Great Britian	United States	George Clinton	21 Oct 1826
Lawrence	38	M	Farmer	Great Britan	U. States	Ann Marria	6 Aug 1823
Mary	6	F	None	Great Britian	United States	George Clinton	21 Oct 1826
Raechal	22	F	None		New York	Governor Clinton	3 Jul 1827
William	6/12	M	None	Great Britian	United States	George Clinton	21 Oct 1826
HARGREAVES, James	18	M	Printer	England	United States	Aurelia	7 Jun 1826
James	27	M	Blacksmith	Rosedale	Rosedale	Howard Douglass	11 May 1827
James	27	M	Blacksmith	Rosedale	Rosedale	Howard Douglass	11 May 1827
James	40	M	Weaver	Great Britain	U.S. of America	Gratitude	3 Oct 1829
HARGRONIES, George	32	M	Weaver	England	United States	Baltic	21 Apr 1827
Wm.	27	M	Weaver	England	United States	Baltic	21 Apr 1827
HARHIDE, Patrick	30	M	Farmer	Ireland	United States	General Putnam	20 Jun 1825
HARIG, Maria	30	F	Govorness	Switzerland	United States	Howard	27 Sep 1824
HARIGAN, John	20	M	Farmer	Ireland	United States	Clothier	22 Nov 1827
HARINGTON, D.	30		Sailor	Halifax	U. States	Almira	15 Jul 1822
Mary	30		Sailor	Halifax	U. States	Almira	15 Jul 1822
HARISON, Andrew	10	M	Labourer	Ireland		Robert Fulton	4 Jun 1828
Jas.	22	M	Printer	England	New York	James Cropper	16 Oct 1826
Mary	3	F	Spinster	Ireland		Robert Fulton	4 Jun 1828
William	50	M	Turner	England	New York	James Cropper	16 Oct 1826
Wm., Jr.	28	M	Turner	England	New York	James Cropper	16 Oct 1826
HARKEN, James	30	M	Farmer	Derby	Derby	Howard Douglass	11 May 1827
HARKENS, Ann	22	F	Farmer	G. Britain	Upper Canada	Perseverance	9 Jun 1827
Danl.	23	M	Farmer	G. Britain	Upper Canada	Perseverance	9 Jun 1827
HARKERTY, Morgan	23	M	Laborer	Ireland	Baltimore	Munroe	27 May 1825
HARKIN, Chas.	28	M	Merchant	Ireland	U. States	Falcon	19 Sep 1823
Daniel	21	M	Farmer	Ireland	United States	Dublin Packet	28 Apr 1824
Edwd.	21	M	Shoemaker	Ireland	United States	Trident	16 May 1826
HHugh	22	M	Farmer	Ireland	United States	Trident	17 May 1825
John	19	M	Farmer	Ireland	United States	Silas Richards	3 Apr 1826
Mary	18	F	Spinster	Ireland	United States	Trident	17 May 1825
HARKINS, John	24	M	Cooper	Ireland	America	Franklin	13 Aug 1827
HARKNESS, Andrew	26	M	Weaver	Ireland	United States	Henry Kneeland	7 Jun 1828
Edwd.	21		None	England	...	James Cropper	28 Jun 1824
Jame	21	F	Servant	Ireland	United States	Henry Kneeland	7 Jun 1828
M...gt.	26	F	Wife	Ireland	United States	Henry Kneeland	7 Jun 1828
Saml.	22	M	Labourer	Ireland	United States	Henry Kneeland	7 Jun 1828
HARL..., John	...		Spinner	...der	England	Great Britain	7 May 1827
HARLAN, Ain, Wife	30	F	Labour	St. Croix	New York	Citizen	14 Jul 1829
Cathrine	2 1/2	F	Labour	St. Croix	New York	Citizen	14 Jul 1829
Drizels	1 1/12	M	Labour	St. Croix	New York	Citizen	14 Jul 1829
Jercy	30	M	Labour	St. Croix	New York	Citizen	14 Jul 1829
HARLAND, Jos.	25	M	Mariner	G. Brittain	England	Packet	26 Dec 1823
HARLEIGH, Biddy	18	F	Spinster	Ireland	United States	Trident	17 May 1825

NAMES OF PASSENGERS	AGE	SEX	OCCUPATIONS	COUNTRY TO WHICH THEY BELONG	COUNTRY THEY INTEND TO INHABIT	SHIPS/DATES OF ARRIVAL	
HARLEN, Ann	24	F	None	Great Britain	United States	Atlantic	28 May 1827
HARLERIN, Jane	18	M	Farmer	Wirtermberg	United States	Olympia	20 Aug 1829
HARLEY, Ann	20	F		County of Cork, Ireland	New York City	Thorny Close	3 May 1826
Catherine	24 6/12	F	Spinster	Ireland	U. States	Josephine	30 Aug 1828
John	24	M	Weaver	County of Cork, Ireland	New York City	Thorny Close	3 May 1826
John	31	M	Farmer	St. Johns, N.B.	United States	Henrietta	17 Aug 1825
Mary	8/12	F		County of Cork, Ireland	New York City	Thorny Close	3 May 1826
HARLING, Robt.	28	M	Missionary	Great Brittan	United States	Euphrates	12 Mar 1824
HARLOWE, Biddy	24	M	Spinster			Robert Burns	13 Jul 1820
Joseph	33	M	Tin plate worker	England	United States	Great Britain	5 Sep 1827
HARLY, John	1	M	Child	Ireland	Ireland	Sarah G.	28 Nov 1827
Mary	3	F	Child	Ireland	Ireland	Sarah G.	28 Nov 1827
Mary	35	F	Servant	Ireland	Ireland	Sarah G.	28 Nov 1827
Nelly	6	F	Servant	Ireland	Ireland	Sarah G.	28 Nov 1827
HARM, John	26	M				Lady of the Lake	23 Aug 1828
*left ship							
Joseph	33	M	Farmer	Gt. Britain	United States	John & Elizabeth	25 Sep 1827
HARMAN, Henry	46	M	Labourer	England	United States	Jubilee	12 May 1828
Jacob, Jr.	35	M	Mariner	Philada.	U. States	Cato	2 Jan 1824
Jacob, Junr.	34	M	Mariner	United States	U. States	Emma	25 Feb 1826
John	37	M	Potter	England	U. States	Pleiades	9 Oct 1829
Mary	21	F	Spinster	Ireland	United States	Dublin Packet	23 May 1828
N.	39	M	Weaver	France	United States	La Flora	30 Jun 1828
Patrick	18	M	Laborer	Ireland	U. States	Lady Hunter	14 Mar 1826
Wm.	19	M	Shoemaker	Wales	U. States	Richard Mead	26 Jun 1821
HARMANDA, Francis	38	M	Consul	Spain	Spain	Circassian	13 Jun 1825
HARMANDUS, J.	30	M	Merchant	Spain	U. States	St. Croix	31 Jul 1827
HARMAS, N.	20		Laborer	Hannover		Constitution	5 Jan 1829
HARMEN, John	51	M	Carpenter	U.S. America	U.S. America	Cincinnatus	31 Oct 1820
HARMER, —, Mrs.	26	F		St. Croix	St. Croix	Carlo	19 Apr 1828
HARMIT, E.	22		Farmer	Cork	Virginia	Schuylkill	22 Aug 1825
Richd.	17		Farmer	Cork	Virginia	Schuylkill	22 Aug 1825
HARMON, Wm.	25	M	Navay Officer	England	U. States	Dalmarnock	17 May 1822
HARMONY, Adam	22	M	Merchant	Germany	United States	Wm. Osborne	16 Sep 1828
Anne	22	F	his family [Adam]	Germany	United States	Wm. Osborne	16 Sep 1828
Jean	4	M	his family [Adam]	Germany	United States	Wm. Osborne	16 Sep 1828
Joachin, Mr.	20	M	Merchant	Spain	U. States	Halsey	16 Sep 1823
Manuel H.	12	M		Spain	U. States	Adams	13 Jan 1827
Maria	20	F	his family [Adam]	Germany	United States	Wm. Osborne	16 Sep 1828
HARMS, John	26	M	Cooper	England	United States	Robert Edwards	3 Oct 1829
Maria	26	F	Wife	England	United States	Robert Edwards	3 Oct 1829
HARN, James	25	M	Carpenter	Scotland	United States	Samuel Robertson	9 May 1827
HARNESS, Henry	20	M	Merchant	Prussia	U. States	Minerva	13 Sep 1827
Richard	30	M	Canal Cutter	England	United States	Lord Wellington	14 Nov 1827
HARNEY, James	24	M	Laborer or Spinster	Ireland	United States	Sarah G.	15 Aug 1827
HARNIS, Robt.	26	M	Labourer	Great Britain	United States	Penelope	11 Jun 1827
Sophia	24	F	None	Great Britain	United States	Penelope	11 Jun 1827
Wm.	40	M	Labourer	Great Britain	United States	Penelope	11 Jun 1827
HAROCK, Charles	27	M	Gentleman	...land	United States	Belle	3 Aug 1822
HAROLD, Andrew	28	M	Blacksmith	Ireland	New York	Angelica	18 Aug 1823
Daniel	28	M	Labourer	Ireland	United States	Robert Fulton	10 Aug 1827
HAROLY, John	20	M	Labourer	Ireland	United States	General Putnam	20 Jun 1825
HARPER, Abraham	23	M	Weaver	Ireland	U. States	Josephine	30 Aug 1828
Alex.	36	M		Scotland	U. States	Camillus	27 Jun 1826
Daniel	21	M	Smith	Antrim, Ireland	Pennsylvania	Anthusa	24 Aug 1825
Grace	22	F	Spinster	Ireland	United States	Fabius	4 Jun 1828
Hugh	...	...	...	Ireland	United States	Carolina Ann	24 Oct 1825
Hugh	26	M	Weaver	Ireland	United States	General Marion	20 Aug 1828
Isaac	21	M	None	England		Marchioness	13 May 1828
Isabella	2	F	None	Scotland	U. States	Camillus	27 Jun 1826
Isabella	28	F		Scotland	U. States	Camillus	27 Jun 1826
John	3	M	Farmer	Ireland	Pittsfield	Triton	12 Jul 1823
John	8	M	None	Scotland	U. States	Camillus	27 Jun 1826

NAMES OF PASSENGERS	AGE	SEX	OCCUPATIONS	COUNTRY TO WHICH THEY BELONG	COUNTRY THEY INTEND TO INHABIT	SHIPS/DATES OF ARRIVAL	
HARPER (cont'd)							
John	15	M	Far...	Ireland	United States	Henry Kneeland	7 Jun 1828
John	20	M	Labourer	Ireland	Ireland	Sarah G.	28 Nov 1827
John	21	M	Merchant	Great Brigain	United States	New Packet	19 Oct 1826
John	25	M	Carpenter	United States	United States	Elizabeth & Mary	23 Nov 1820
John	28	M	Jeweller	England	Gt. Britain	Electra	4 Sep 1827
John	45	M	Farmer	England	United States	Jubilee	1 Oct 1828
Mary	25	F	Farmer	Ireland	Pittsfield	Triton	12 Jul 1823
Matilda	17	F	Spinster	Ireland	United States	Henry Kneeland	7 Jun 1828
Nichs.	32	M	Engineer	United States	U. States	Angenora	22 Dec 1826
Richard P.	8	M		Balize	Spanish Main	Favorite	9 Oct 1823
Samuel B.	26	M	Merchant	Virginia	Virginia	Constitution	9 Dec 1824
Thos.	25	M	Merchant	U.S. of America	U.S. of America	Harmony	20 Nov 1820
Thos.	27	M	Farmer	England	U. States	Auritz	20 May 1823
William	6	M	None	Scotland	U. States	Camillus	27 Jun 1826
William	16	M	Gentleman	Ireland	United States	Dublin Packet	13 Oct 1828
William	25	M	Farmer	Ireland	Pittsfield	Triton	12 Jul 1823
Wm.	39	M	Mariner	N. York	N. York	Boston Packet	7 Jul 1825
HARPHAM, Joseph	38 3/12	M	Gent.	Great Britain	America	Magnet	13 Nov 1821
HARPLE, Ann	32	F	Lady	England	Pennsylvania	General Stark	12 Jun 1826
Elizabeth	1	M	Child	England	Pennsylvania	General Stark	12 Jun 1826
Elizabeth	40	F	Lady	England	Pennsylvania	General Stark	12 Jun 1826
Geo.	5	M	Child	England	Pennsylvania	General Stark	12 Jun 1826
John	7	M	Child	England	Pennsylvania	General Stark	12 Jun 1826
Mary	3	M	Child	England	Pennsylvania	General Stark	12 Jun 1826
Seth	9	M	Son	England	Pennsylvania	General Stark	12 Jun 1826
HARR, Jas.	6	M	Labourer	Ireland	United States	Margarett Scott	22 Aug 1827
John	19	M	Labourer	Ireland	United States	Margarett Scott	22 Aug 1827
Magt.	7	F	Labourer	Ireland	United States	Margarett Scott	22 Aug 1827
Mary	12	F	Labourer	Ireland	United States	Margarett Scott	22 Aug 1827
Mary	40	F	Labourer	Ireland	United States	Margarett Scott	22 Aug 1827
Peter	1	M	Labourer	Ireland	United States	Margarett Scott	22 Aug 1827
Tammy	17	F	Labourer	Ireland	United States	Margarett Scott	22 Aug 1827
Wm.	5	M	Labourer	Ireland	United States	Margarett Scott	22 Aug 1827
Wm.	60	M	Labourer	Ireland	United States	Margarett Scott	22 Aug 1827
HARR...ON..., ...	...	F		England	...	Lima	5 Aug 1829
HARRAGAN, Biddy	...	F		Ireland	America	Mary	29 May 1827
Chs.	6	M		Ireland	America	Mary	29 May 1827
Francis	1	M		Ireland	America	Mary	29 May 1827
Mary	30	F	Spinster	Ireland	America	Mary	29 May 1827
Owen	30	M	Farmer	Ireland	America	Mary	29 May 1827
HARRALD, T.	60	F	None	U. States	U. States	Fanny	17 Sep 1827
HARRAN, James	28	M		Ireland	New York	Lady Hunter	5 Jun 1826
William	13	M	None	Great Britan	United States	Bolivar	21 May 1827
HARRELL, Thomas	40	M	Labourer	England	U. States	Ayrshire	12 May 1828
HARREY, J. S.	18	M	Machine Maker	Europe	United States	Aspasia	5 Sep 1827
HARRIER, Joseph	30		Weaver	Liverpool	Great Britain	Oglethorpe	25 Aug 1825
Martin	19	M	Labourer	Ireland	United States	Wilson	6 Jun 1828
HARRIGAN, C.	30	F	Labourer	Scotland	U. States	New Packet	16 Apr 1828
Cathar	1	F	Labourer	Scotland	U. States	New Packet	16 Apr 1828
D.	33	M	Labourer	Scotland	U. States	New Packet	16 Apr 1828
David	7	M	Labourer	Scotland	U. States	New Packet	16 Apr 1828
John	6	M	Labourer	Scotland	U. States	New Packet	16 Apr 1828
HARRIGON, John	30	M	Labourer	Great Brittan	United States	Hanford	3 Aug 1829
Michael	22	M	House Carpenter	Great Brittan	United States	Hanford	3 Aug 1829
HARRIMAN, Eliza	38	F		United States	United States	Brighton	12 Jun 1826
HARRIMER, S.	24	M	Mechanic	Connecticutt	U. States	Benjamin	1 Jun 1822
HARRIMON, John	22	M	Spinster	Ireland	United States	Asia	29 Jul 1829
HARRIN, Caroline	5	F	None	Great Britan	United States	Bolivar	21 May 1827
John	11	M	None	Great Britan	United States	Bolivar	21 May 1827
Lamuel	40	M	Common Carter	Great Britan	United States	Bolivar	21 May 1827
Mary	16	F	None	Great Britan	United States	Bolivar	21 May 1827
Mary	38	F	None	Great Britan	United States	Bolivar	21 May 1827
Robert	9	M	None	Great Britan	United States	Bolivar	21 May 1827
HARRINGTON, Amelia	30	F		Ireland	United States	John & Adam	21 Sep 1822
Cathn.	18	F	Servant	Ireland	United States	William	20 Jul 1829
Jas.	24	M	Black Smith	Ireland	United States	New Packet	7 Aug 1826
John	26	M	Labourer	Ireland	United States	General Marion	20 Aug 1828
M.	27	M		G. Britain	U. States	Hanford	18 Sep 1828

NAMES OF PASSENGERS	AGE	SEX	OCCUPATIONS	COUNTRY TO WHICH THEY BELONG	COUNTRY THEY INTEND TO INHABIT	SHIPS/DATES OF ARRIVAL	
HARRINGTON (cont'd)							
Margt.	16	F		Ireland	U. States	Fame	15 Nov 1826
Mary, Senr.	27	F	None	Gt. Brittian	Gt. Brittian	Manchester	24 Aug 1827
Robert	28	M	Naturalist	England	America	Leeds	2 Aug 1828
Thos.	35	M	Labourer	Ireland	United States	Thomas	13 Dec 1827
W. B.	25	M	Merchant	America	United States	Andrew Jackson	9 Jul 1822
Wm.	25	M	Farmer	Ireland	U. States	Mentor	5 Jul 1825
Wm. J.	27	M	Merchant	England	America	Leeds	2 Aug 1828
HARRIOT, Cal	34	M				Cassack	25 Jul 1820
Geo. C.	26	M	Merchant	U. States	U. States	Fancy	1 Apr 1824
HARRIS, —, Mrs.	28	F		England	U. States	Edward Bonaffe	11 Dec 1827
Alfred	6	M		Germany	U. States	Columbia	22 Sep 1828
Ann	20	F		G. Britain	U. States	William Thompson	30 Apr 1822
Ann	29	F	Weaver	England	New York	Brighton	19 Aug 1829
Ann	30	F	Agriculturist	Great Britain	U. States	Columbia	22 Sep 1828
Benjamin	2	M	None	Great Britain		Olive Branch	9 Oct 1829
C.	34	M	Shipmaster	U. States	U. States	Caroline	21 Jun 1823
Catherine	20					William	17 Aug 1820
David	22	M	Farmer	Ohio, U.S.	United States	Cosmo	21 Aug 1828
Edward	3			England		Anacreon	7 Sep 1827
Edward	28	M	Gentleman	U. States	U. States	Birmingham	12 Oct 1827
Eliza	20	F		Ireland	United States	Fabius	4 Jun 1828
Elizabeth	55	F	None	England	America	Francis & Henrietta	11 Jul 1823
Enos	40	M	Ship Master	U. States	United States	Motion	15 Mar 1825
Francis	65	M	Gentleman	England	United States	Mount Vernon	9 Jun 1823
Francis, Junr.	27	M	Gentleman			Mount Vernon	9 Jun 1823
Frs.	14	M		Ireland	U. States	Magnet	6 Feb 1823
G.	32	M		N. York	United States	Abigale	9 Aug 1821
G.	45	M	Purser in U.S. Navy	U. States	U. States	Factor	9 Mar 1829
George	30	M	Weaver	Ireland	New York	Louisa	18 Apr 1827
George	35	M	Distiller	New York	U.S.	Nancy	1 Sep 1823
George	35	M	Farmer			Robert Edwards	8 Nov 1825
H.	16	M	Merchant	U. States	U. States	Betsey	6 May 1826
Hannah	14	F		England	United States	Dalhouse Castle	8 May 1827
Hannah	16	F	Seamstress	England	New York	Brighton	20 Aug 1825
Henry	4	M	None	Great Britain		Olive Branch	9 Oct 1829
Henry	20		Miller	England	United States	Cambria	19 Oct 1829
Huldah	32	F		New York	U.S.	Nancy	1 Sep 1823
J., Jr.	20	M	Merchant	U.S.	U.S.	Radius	1 May 1822
J., Jr.	23	M	Merchant	U. States	Cuba	Magnet	18 Aug 1825
J. H.	26		Merchant			Charlotte Corday	15 Jul 1820
Jacob	44	M	Merchant	U. States	U. States	Birmingham	23 Feb 1829
James	11	M	Farmer	England	America	Francis & Henrietta	11 Jul 1823
James	20	M	Labourer	U. States	U. States	Robt. Reade	12 Apr 1825
James	24		Shoemaker			William	17 Aug 1820
James	24	M	Merchant	England	United States	Dublin Packet	3 Sep 1822
James, Mr.	40	M	Mercht.	United States	United States	Manchester	16 Dec 1828
Jane	9/12	F	None	Great Britian	U. States	Henry Kneedland	7 Aug 1826
Jane	8	F	Farmer	Ireland	U. States	Orozimbo	7 Jul 1825
Jane	9	F	None	England	America	Francis & Henrietta	11 Jul 1823
Jane	30	F		Gt. Britain	U. States	Sarah G.	14 Apr 1828
Jane	55	F	Lady	New York	New York	New Packet	24 Jul 1827
Jas.	20 6/12	M	Taylor	Great Britian	U. States	Henry Kneedland	7 Aug 1826
Jas. H.	30	M	Clergyman	Uper Canada	Uper Canada	Britannia	29 Oct 1829
Jehaboa	11					Charlotte Corday	15 Jul 1820
Jno.	1	M	None	Great Britain	United States	Comet	9 Aug 1822
Jno.	17	M	Merchant	G. Britain	U. States	William Thompson	30 Apr 1822
Jno.	27	M	Farmer	England	America	Francis & Henrietta	11 Jul 1823
Jno.	35	M	Merchant	Gt. Britain	U. States	Cortes	6 Apr 1825
Jno.	35	M	Merchant	United States	United States	York	31 Mar 1828

NAMES OF PASSENGERS	AGE	SEX	OCCUPATIONS	COUNTRY TO WHICH THEY BELONG	COUNTRY THEY INTEND TO INHABIT	SHIPS/DATES OF ARRIVAL	
HARRIS (cont'd)							
John	1			England		Anacreon	7 Sep 1827
John	9	M	None	Great Britain		Olive Branch	9 Oct 1829
John	10	M	Farmer	Ireland	U. States	Orozimbo	7 Jul 1825
John	11	F	None	Great Britain		Olive Branch	9 Oct 1829
John	22		Labourer	England	U.S. America	Constitution	18 Jun 1827
John	25	M	Carpenter	United States	United States	Elizabeth & Mary	23 Nov 1820
John	30	M	Carpenter	Ireland	United States	Fabius	4 Jun 1828
John	30	M	Captain, Officers & crew of the Brig George of New York (wrecked at Fayal)	U.S. America	U.S.A.	Gallego	13 Mar 1829
John	40	M	Labourer	Great Britain		Moro Castle	6 Jul 1827
John	47	M	Farmer	Ireland	U. States	Orozimbo	7 Jul 1825
John A.	25	F		Uper Canada	Uper Canada	Britannia	29 Oct 1829
Joseph	27	M	Merchant	U. States	U. States	Silas Richards	27 Jun 1827
Joseph	30	M	Merchant	England	U. States	Panthea	22 Nov 1826
Joseph	30	M	Weaver	England	New York	Brighton	19 Aug 1829
Joseph	30	M	Farmer			Brighton	19 Aug 1829
Levell	13	M		United States	U. States	Corinthian	2 Sep 1824
Lindsay	21	M	Watch Maker	Ireland	New York	Trusty	12 Sep 1828
Lovett	45	M	Gentleman	United States	U.S.	Edward Quesnel	19 Oct 1829
M.	2	M	Farmer	Ireland	U. States	Orozimbo	7 Jul 1825
M. L.	22	F	None	U. States	U. States	Birmingham	12 Oct 1827
Marg.	22	F	Weaver	Ireland	U. States	Franklin	7 Jul 1828
Margaret	4	F	Child	New York	New York	New Packet	24 Jul 1827
Mary	...	M	Labourer	Ireland	Unt. St. America	Wilson	21 May 1827
Mary	3	F	None	Great Britain	United States	Comet	9 Aug 1822
Mary	17		None	Cheshire, England	Great Britain	Franklin	22 Jun 1827
Mary	18	F		England	U. States	Rising States	20 Sep 1828
Mary	19		Lady			Charlotte Corday	15 Jul 1820
Mary	20	F		Ireland	U. States	Wanderer	1 Sep 1828
Mary	24	F	None	Great Britian	U. States	Henry Kneedland	7 Aug 1826
Mary	26			England		Anacreon	7 Sep 1827
Mary	27	F	None	Great Britain	United States	Comet	9 Aug 1822
Mary	34	F	None	Great Britain		Olive Branch	9 Oct 1829
Mary	35	F				Robert Edwards	8 Nov 1825
Mary	39	F	Farmer	Ireland	U. States	Orozimbo	7 Jul 1825
Morris	23	M	Taylor	Great Britain	New York	Thames	16 May 1821
N. C.	24	M	Printer	Tenesse	U. States	Catharine & Jane	18 Feb 1823
Nancy	8	F		Ireland	U. States	Nancy	1 Sep 1823
Phillip	2	M	None	Great Britain	United States	Penelope	11 Jun 1827
R.	30	M	Iron Founder	England	U. States	Edward Bonaffe	11 Dec 1827
Reuben	25	M	Labour	U. States	U. States	Georgetown Packet	12 Mar 1825
Richard	25		Miller	England	United States	Cambria	19 Oct 1829
Richard	33	M	Laborer	Great Britain	United States	Comet	9 Aug 1822
Samuel	28	M	Merchant	Ireland	United States	Pallas	28 Oct 1828
Sarah	10	F	None	England	America	Francis & Henrietta	11 Jul 1823
Sarah Ann	32	F				Mount Vernon	9 Jun 1823
Solomon	19	M	Farmer	Great Britain	United States	Asia	14 Jul 1829
Spencer	35		Hat Manufacturer	England	United States	Corinthian	7 Jul 1829
Thomas	20	M	Labourer	Ireland	America	Wilson	27 Nov 1826
Thomas	28	M	Cabnet Maker	Ireland	United States	Ann Maria	28 Jan 1828
Thomas	57	M	Farmer	England	America	Francis & Henrietta	11 Jul 1823
Thomas	77	M	None	G. Brittian	U. States	Pacific	19 Oct 1829
Thos.	7	M		Germany	U. States	Columbia	22 Sep 1828
Thos.	22	M	Miner	England	England	Eliza	31 Jul 1826
Thos.	27			England		Anacreon	7 Sep 1827
Thos.	35	M	Agriculturist	Great Britain	U. States	Columbia	22 Sep 1828
Thos.	43	M	Mason	Great Britain	U. States	Ann Maria	26 Apr 1822

NAMES OF PASSENGERS	AGE	SEX	OCCUPATIONS	COUNTRY TO WHICH THEY BELONG	COUNTRY THEY INTEND TO INHABIT	SHIPS/DATES OF ARRIVAL	
HARRIS (cont'd)							
Thos., Jun.	18	M	Farmer	England	America	Francis & Henrietta	11 Jul 1823
William	2	M		Germany	U. States	Columbia	22 Sep 1828
William	7	M	None	Great Britain		Olive Branch	9 Oct 1829
William	25		Carpenter	Nova Scotia	Great Britain	Henrietta	26 Nov 1825
William	35	M	Labourer	Great Britain		Olive Branch	9 Oct 1829
William	40	M	Engineer	U. States	United States	Dispatch	16 Jul 1827
William	52	M	Dyer	England	U.N. States	Jane	7 Oct 1826
Wm.	3	M	None	Great Britain	United States	Penelope	11 Jun 1827
Wm.	18	M		Gt. Britain	United States	Columbia	7 Sep 1827
Wm.	25	M	Weaver	Ireland	U. States	Franklin	7 Jul 1828
Wm.	36	M	Farmer	England	United States	Acasta	15 Jul 1822
Wm. D.	25	M	Merchant	U. States	U. States	Jane	10 Jan 1824
HARRISON, —	22	F		England	United States	Ariadne	7 May 1821
—, Mr.	25	M	Inkeeper	New York	Ny...	Nancy	26 Nov 1822
—, Mr.	45	M	Merchant	England	U. States	William & Ezra	18 Oct 1824
—, Mrs.	12	F	Inkeeper	New York	Ny...	Nancy	26 Nov 1822
—, Mrs.	30	F			U. States	William & Ezra	18 Oct 1824
—, Mrs.	35	F		New York	United States	Vermont	10 Jan 1827
—, Mrs.	40	M		England	U. States	Robert Edwards	11 Mar 1822
Adam	13	M	Farmer	Great Britain	U. States	Princess Charlotte	6 Sep 1828
Ann	4	F	None	Isle of Man		Ocean	13 Jul 1827
Ann	8	F	Farmer	Great Britain	U. States	Princess Charlotte	6 Sep 1828
Ann	23	F		England	U. States	Lima	5 Aug 1829
Ann	29	F	None	Ireland	New Jersey	Commerce	24 Sep 1823
Ann	32	F		England	U. States	Birmingham	16 Jun 1828
Ann	36	F		England	America	John Adams	2 Aug 1827
Annette	0 4/12	F		England	U. States	Birmingham	16 Jun 1828
Arthur	35	M	Farmer	Ireland	United States	Leonidas	3 Aug 1825
Caroline	9	F		U. States	U. States	Industry	30 Jul 1822
Cathe.	6	F	None	Isle of Man		Ocean	13 Jul 1827
Cathe.	27	F	None	Isle of Man		Ocean	13 Jul 1827
David	25	M	Gentleman	G. Britain		Diana	14 Sep 1820
E.	4	F		England	America	Corinthian	1 Sep 1827
Edmund	3	M		England	America	John Adams	2 Aug 1827
Edward	1 3/12	M	None	Great Britain	United States	Isaac Hicks	27 Sep 1826
Eliza	7	F	Farmer	Great Britain	U. States	Princess Charlotte	6 Sep 1828
Eliza	8	F		England	United States	Dalhouse Castle	8 May 1827
Eliza	21	F		G. Britain	U. States	St. George	7 Jun 1828
Eliza	27	F	Farmer	Great Britain	U. States	Princess Charlotte	6 Sep 1828
Elizabeth	19	F		U. States	U. States	Colosso Conti	17 Apr 1822
Elizabeth	23	F	Spinster	Ireland	America	Josephine	8 Dec 1827
Elizabeth	24	F	Matron	Ireland	America	Josephine	8 Dec 1827
Emma	11	F	None	Great Britain	United States	Isaac Hicks	27 Sep 1826
Emma	25	M	Servant	England		Catharine	19 Jul 1822
Esther	24	F	None	Isle of Man		Ocean	13 Jul 1827
Felix	18	M	Baker	Ireland	America	Josephine	8 Dec 1827
G., Mr.	29	M	Merchant	America	America	Galatea	20 Jul 1829
Geo.	14	M	Inkeeper	New York	Ny...	Nancy	26 Nov 1822
Geo.	28	M	Farmer	Great Britain	U. States	Princess Charlotte	6 Sep 1828
George	20 3/12	M	Jamaica Planter	England	Great Britain	Robert Cochran	29 Aug 1825
George	27	M	Labourer	England	U. States	Ayrshire	12 May 1828
H. N., Mr.	21	M	Gent.	U. States	U. States	James Monroe	24 Jan 1829
Hannah	35	F		England	Philadelphia	Debby & Eliza	20 Nov 1820
Henry	13	M	Farmer	Ireland	United States	Leonidas	3 Aug 1825
Hugh	6	M	None	Ireland	United States	Leonidas	3 Aug 1825
Hugh	76	M	Gent.	Mayo	America	Margaret	31 Jul 1824
J...h.	32		Baker	Bl...	England	Great Britain	7 May 1827
James	7/12	M	Labourer	England	United States	Dalhouse Castle	8 May 1827
James	2		Mason	Bl...	England	Great Britain	7 May 1827
James	20	M	Farmer	Ireland	United States	Princess Charlotte	26 Apr 1827

NAMES OF PASSENGERS	AGE	SEX	OCCUPATIONS	COUNTRY TO WHICH THEY BELONG	COUNTRY THEY INTEND TO INHABIT	SHIPS/DATES OF ARRIVAL	
HARRISON (cont'd)							
James	20	M	Farmer	Great Britain	U. States	Princess Charlotte	6 Sep 1828
James	27	M	Servant	Great Britain	Mexico	Corinthian	27 Apr 1824
James	27	M	Labourer	Ireland	America	Josephine	8 Dec 1827
James	50	M	Farmer	Great Britain	U. States	Princess Charlotte	6 Sep 1828
Jane	...			Bl...	England	Great Britain	7 May 1827
Jane	1	F	None	Isle of Man		Ocean	13 Jul 1827
Jane	19	F		England	America	Corinthian	1 Sep 1827
Jas.	3	M	None	Great Britain	United States	Ann Maria	23 Oct 1820
Jeptha	29	M	Clergy Man	New Jersey	New Jersey	Charleston	1 Jun 1826
Jno.	25	M	Merchant	U. States	U. States	Douglass	30 Oct 1826
Jno. C.	28	M	Merchant	America	U. States	Abeona	17 May 1825
John	3 6/12	M	None	Great Britain	United States	Isaac Hicks	27 Sep 1826
John	8	M		England	Philadelphia	Debby & Eliza	20 Nov 1820
John	12	M		England	United States	Dalhouse Castle	8 May 1827
John	14	M		England	America	John Adams	2 Aug 1827
John	19	M	Farmer	Brittian	U. States	Acasta	28 Jan 1823
John	19	M	Farmer	Ireland	United States	Leonidas	3 Aug 1825
John	24	M	Gentn.	England	U. States	Trident	8 Mar 1824
John	29	M	Clerk	Ireland	New Jersey	Commerce	24 Sep 1823
John	30	M	Labourer	Sligo	U. States	Panthea	8 Apr 1826
John	32	M	Cabinet Maker	America	America	Paragon	22 Sep 1827
John	34	M	Farman	St. John, N.B.	United States	Nancy	18 Oct 1824
John	39	M	Joiner	England	Philadelphia	Debby & Eliza	20 Nov 1820
John	39	M	Mechanic	England	U. States	Birmingham	16 Jun 1828
John	40	M	Weaver	England	U.S.A.	Peru	2 Oct 1827
John	73	M	Labourer	England	United States	Dalhouse Castle	8 May 1827
John S.	30	M	Merchant	New York	United States	Vermont	10 Jan 1827
Jos.	34	M	Preacher	Great Britain	United States	Ann Maria	23 Oct 1820
Joseph	5	M	None	Great Britain	United States	Isaac Hicks	27 Sep 1826
Joseph	9			Bl...	England	Great Britain	7 May 1827
Joseph	15	M	Farmer	Ireland	United States	Leonidas	3 Aug 1825
Joseph	17	M	Weaver	Ireland	United States	Commerce	13 Jun 1828
Joseph	21	M	Farmer	Ireland	United States	Dublin Packet	13 Oct 1828
Joseph	24	M	Farmer	Great Britain	United States	John Wells	18 Sep 1826
Joseph	33	M	Glassmaker	Great Britain	United States	Isaac Hicks	27 Sep 1826
Joseph	52	M	Farmer	Great Britain	U. States	Princess Charlotte	6 Sep 1828
Justus	34	M	Merchant	U. States	U. States	Huron	30 Jan 1827
Justus, Supercargo	32	M	Merchant	N. Haven	U. States	Shepherdess	16 May 1821
Lewis	35	M	Mariner	N. York	U. States	Nancy	29 Nov 1821
Margaret	50	F	None	England	America	Minerva	31 May 1824
Margret	19	F	Farmer	Great Britain	U. States	Princess Charlotte	6 Sep 1828
Mark	7	M		England	America	John Adams	2 Aug 1827
Martha	2...		Shoemaker	Bl...	England	Great Britain	7 May 1827
Martha	23	F		England	America	John Adams	2 Aug 1827
Mary	9	F		England	Philadelphia	Debby & Eliza	20 Nov 1820
Mary	20	F	None	Ireland	United States	Jubilee	12 May 1828
Mary	28	F	None	Great Britain	United States	Isaac Hicks	27 Sep 1826
Mary	35	M		N. York	U. States	Nancy	29 Nov 1821
Mary	37	M	Labourer	England	United States	Dalhouse Castle	8 May 1827
Mary Ann	8	F			U. States	William & Ezra	18 Oct 1824
Mary Ann	8	F	None	Great Britain	United States	Isaac Hicks	27 Sep 1826
Mary Ann	17	F	None	England	United States	Brighton	11 Mar 1825
May	27			Great Britan	United States	Newry	11 Jul 1827
May	37	F	Wife	United States	United States	Hanford	3 Jul 1829
Michal	27	M	Labourer	England	U. States	Ayrshire	12 May 1828
Nancy	45	F		England	United States	Dalhouse Castle	8 May 1827
Nichs.	40 3/12	M	Farmer	Ireland	United States	Atlantic	21 Jul 1827
Parker	20	M	Farmer	Ireland	United States	Leonidas	3 Aug 1825
Patt	25	M	Labourer	Ireland		Marchioness	13 May 1828
Richard	26	M	Shoemaker	England	U. States	Lima	5 Aug 1829
Richard	50	M	Farmer	Great Britain	United States	Freake	11 Dec 1827
Richd.	4		Tailor	Bl...	England	Great Britain	7 May 1827
Robert	38	M	Labourer	England	United States	Dalhouse Castle	8 May 1827
Robert	40	M	Wheelwright	England	America	John Adams	2 Aug 1827

NAMES OF PASSENGERS	AGE	SEX	OCCUPATIONS	COUNTRY TO WHICH THEY BELONG	COUNTRY THEY INTEND TO INHABIT	SHIPS/DATES OF ARRIVAL	
HARRISON (cont'd)							
Robert	56	M	...	G. Britain	U. States	New England	28 Sep 1824
Robt.	25	M	Carpenter	England	United States	Ariadne	7 May 1821
Robt.	27	M	Smith	Isle of Man		Ocean	13 Jul 1827
S.	3	F		Gt. Britain	United States	Robert Edwards	1 Jun 1826
S.	31	F		Gt. Britain	United States	Robert Edwards	1 Jun 1826
Saml.	17	M	Farmer	Great Britain	U. States	Princess Charlotte	6 Sep 1828
Saml.	49	M	Farmer	Great Britain	U. States	Princess Charlotte	6 Sep 1828
Sarah	6	F		England	Philadelphia	Debby & Eliza	20 Nov 1820
Stephen	47	M	Seaman	U. States	U. States	Boston	26 Sep 1820
Swainstone	13	M		England	America	John Adams	2 Aug 1827
Thomas	2	M		England	America	John Adams	2 Aug 1827
Thomas	9	M		England	United States	Dalhouse Castle	8 May 1827
Thomas	21	M	Mechanic	England	United States	Concordia	25 Aug 1827
Thomas	25	M	Labourer	England	U. States	Ayrshire	12 May 1828
Thomas	32	M	Merchant	Philada.	U. States	New York	3 Oct 1826
Thos.	8	M	None	Isle of Man		Ocean	13 Jul 1827
Thos.	36	M	Labourer	Isle of Man		Ocean	13 Jul 1827
Thos. [inserted sideways]	25		So...	Engd.		Napoleon	26 May 1828
W.	5	M		Gt. Britain	United States	Robert Edwards	1 Jun 1826
W.	17	M		G. Britain	U. States	St. George	7 Jun 1828
Will	28			Great Britan	United States	Newry	11 Jul 1827
William	2	M		England	Philadelphia	Debby & Eliza	20 Nov 1820
William	3	M	Labourer	England	United States	Dalhouse Castle	8 May 1827
William	11	M		England	America	John Adams	2 Aug 1827
William	15	M	Farmer	Great Britain	U. States	Princess Charlotte	6 Sep 1828
William	18	M	Farmer	England	United States	Oscar	24 Jul 1823
William	21 ...	M	...	England	America, U.S.	Illinois	3 Jun 1822
William	22	M	Turner	Ireland	United States	Princess Charlotte	26 Apr 1827
William	31	M	Joiner	England	America	Britannia	22 Jul 1829
Wm.	27	M	Farmer	Ireland	United States	Leonidas	3 Aug 1825
Wm.	36	M	Labourer	England	U. States	Comet	23 Aug 1828
Wm. Henry	31	M	Barrister	United States	New York	Florida	22 May 1826
HARRISS, —		M	Servant	U. States	U. States	George	12 Jul 1821
HARRISSON, Alfred	20	M	Farmer	England	U.S. America	Criterion	27 Oct 1821
John	25	M	None	Ireland	Und. Stts of Amer	Alexander Mansfield	18 Aug 1826
John	28	M	Hatter	Great Britain	New York	Superior	5 Sep 1827
Peter	57	M	Weaver	G.B.	U.S.	Silvanus Jenkins	27 Jul 1829
HARROCKS, John	28	M	Spinner	England	United States	Trident	31 Mar 1827
Wm.	20	M	Spinner	England	United States	Trident	31 Mar 1827
HARRON, Bell	45			Ireland	United States	William & George	14 May 1828
John	19	M		Ireland	United States	William & George	14 May 1828
John	50	M	Merchant	Hayti		Nestor	20 Oct 1827
John	50	M		Ireland	United States	William & George	14 May 1828
Joseph	12/12	M		Ireland	United States	William & George	14 May 1828
Mary	8/12	F		Ireland	United States	William & George	14 May 1828
Robt.	17	M		Ireland	United States	William & George	14 May 1828
William	6/52	M		Ireland	United States	William & George	14 May 1828
HARROP, John	22	M	Tailer	England	America	Sarah	18 Aug 1829
Thos.	22	M	Farmer	England	United States	Aurelia	7 Jun 1826
HARROPP, John	24	M	None	York, Great Britain		Casanda	5 Sep 1827
HARROPS, Samuel	24	M	Gentleman	United States		Elias Burger	28 May 1821
HARROW, Bridget	20	F	Spinster	Ireland	United States	Catharine	22 Jul 1825
Charles	24	M	Weaver	Ireland	United States	Catharine	22 Jul 1825
HARROWER, Alexr.	45	M	Merchant	Montreal	U. States	Orlando	1 Aug 1826

NAMES OF PASSENGERS	AGE	SEX	OCCUPATIONS	COUNTRY TO WHICH THEY BELONG	COUNTRY THEY INTEND TO INHABIT	SHIPS/DATES OF ARRIVAL	
HARRSEL, James	10	M	Farmer	Germany	U. States	Bayard	16 May 1827
HARRUN, G.	18		Farmer	Ireland	United States	Courier	16 May 1825
HARRY, Anna	1	F		Scotland	United States	Shakespeare	24 Jul 1828
Mary O.	30	F		Scotland	United States	Shakespeare	24 Jul 1828
HARSEN, G.	35	M	Mariner	New York	N. York	Remittance	14 Oct 1824
HART, ...	24	M	Mechanic	Great Briton	U. States	Leontine	10 Jul 1826
Alexr., and Family constg.							
[consisting]	51 9/12	M	Gunsmith	England	New York	Chelsea	16 May 1828
Amelia	14 6/12	F		England	New York	Chelsea	16 May 1828
Anne	16	F	Spinster	Ireland	United States	Wilson	6 Jun 1828
Bathsheba	24	F		United States		Panthea	15 Jun 1822
Benjm.	45	M	Merchant	England	Canada	Corinthian	20 Apr 1825
Betsey	42	F	Woman	Ireland	America	Erin	14 Feb 1820
Biddy	36	F	Spinster	New York	United States	Antioch	21 Sep 1827
Bloomy	16 6/12	F		England	New York	Chelsea	16 May 1828
Bridget	27	F		Ireland	U. States	Virginia	20 Jun 1825
Bridgit	20	F	Spinster	Ireland	United States	Wilson	6 Jun 1828
Catharine	17 2/12	F		Ireland	U.S. of America	Douglass	6 Jul 1829
Cathr.	4	F		New York	United States	Antioch	21 Sep 1827
Cathrine	19	F	Taylor	Ireland	U. States	Virginia	20 Jun 1825
Charles	17	M	Farmer	Ireland	America	Farmer	15 Nov 1823
Charlotte	34	F	Farmer	Great Britain	United States	Roman	10 May 1828
Cornelius	35	M	Farmer	Ireland	United States	Dublin Packet	13 Oct 1828
Donnel	24	M	Laborer	Ireland	United States	Sarah Ann	18 Nov 1826
Elizabeth	23	F	Farmer	Great Britain	United States	Roman	10 May 1828
Elizabeth	51 6/12	F		England	New York	Chelsea	16 May 1828
Ellen	1	F	Farmer	Great Britain	United States	Roman	10 May 1828
Emanuel B.	19	M	Bookseller	New York	New York	Sully	4 Mar 1828
Geo. L.	27	M	Mariner	Connecticett	U. States	Spartan	20 Feb 1826
George	7	M	Farmer	Great Britain	United States	Roman	10 May 1828
George	18	M	Farmer	Ireland	New York	Phoenix	29 Apr 1826
George	18	M	Merchant	Great Britain	United States	Brutus	6 May 1828
Hannah	22 9/12	F		England	New York	Chelsea	16 May 1828
Henry	16	M	Merchant	United States	United States	Hanford	3 Aug 1829
Henry	19	M	Gunsmith	England	New York	Chelsea	16 May 1828
Henry	24	M	Labourer	Ireland, Great Britain	U.S. of America	Dublin	21 Feb 1826
Henry	27	M	Cooper	Ireland	U. States	Champion	26 Jul 1827
Henry	59	M	Mercht.	England	England	Britannia	5 Nov 1828
Isaac	12 6/12	M	Gunsmith	England	New York	Chelsea	16 May 1828
J. Horatia	18 6/12	F	None	United States	United States	Manchester	12 Aug 1829
Jacob	8 9/12	M	Gunsmith	England	New York	Chelsea	16 May 1828
James	11	M	Boy	Ireland	United States	Wilson	6 Jun 1828
James	18	M	Labourer	Ireland	U. States	Wanderer	1 Sep 1828
James	30	M	Farmer	Ireland	N. Jersey	Potomac	7 Aug 1827
James	31	M	Artist	England	United States	Hamilton	13 Nov 1827
James	31	M	Farmer	Great Britain	United States	Roman	10 May 1828
James	39	M	Farmer	England	United States	Trident	31 Mar 1827
Jas.	26	M	Labourer	Great Britain	United States	Penelope	11 Jun 1827
Joel	44 7/12	M	Physician	United States	United States	Manchester	12 Aug 1829
John	18	M	Merchant	St. John, N.B.	United States	Edwin	29 Nov 1828
John	20	M	Labourer	England	U. States	Ayrshire	12 May 1828
John	25	M	Lasler [?]	England	U. States	Howard Douglass	29 Jan 1828
John	28	M	Baker	Great Britain	U. States	Great Britain	18 Mar 1828
John	29	M	Planter	...on...	Antigua	Industry	15 Oct 1825
John	35	M	Wollen Manufacturer	Great Britain	United States	Roman	10 May 1828
John, Mr.	26	M	Gentn.	American	American	Acasta	3 Apr 1826
Julia	21 7/12	F		England	New York	Chelsea	16 May 1828
Lazarus	56	M	Hawker	Holland	United States	Robert Fulton	1 Apr 1824
Lydia	27	F	Spinster	Ireland	United States	Wilson	6 Jun 1828
Mair H.	30	M	Merchant	Great Britain	United States	New York	19 Nov 1828
Margaret	24	F	Lady	Ireland	United States	Borneo	9 Jul 1827
Maria	6	F	Farmer	Great Britain	United States	Roman	10 May 1828
Martha	30	F		Great Brittian	United States	Carolina Augusta	2 Dec 1828
Mary	6	F		New York	United States	Antioch	21 Sep 1827

NAMES OF PASSENGERS	AGE	SEX	OCCUPATIONS	COUNTRY TO WHICH THEY BELONG	COUNTRY THEY INTEND TO INHABIT	SHIPS/DATES OF ARRIVAL	
HART (cont'd)							
Mary	8	F		New York	United States	Antioch	21 Sep 1827
Mary	19	F	Servant	Ireland	New York	Atlantic	6 Oct 1828
Mary	22	F	Spinster	Ireland	United States	Wilson	4 Oct 1827
Mary	56	F		Ireland	United States	Nancy Henrietta	3 Nov 1828
Mary C.	20	F	Spinster	Ireland	America	Farmer	15 Nov 1823
Mathew	35	M	Labourer	Great Brittian	United States	Carolina Augusta	2 Dec 1828
Mazrath	10	F		Ireland	U. States	Virginia	20 Jun 1825
Michael	22	M	Labourer	Ireland	U. States	Wanderer	1 Sep 1828
Michel	24	M	Labourer	Ireland	United States	Wilson	4 Oct 1827
Morly	35	M	Merchant	Europe	United States	Braganza	30 Nov 1827
Owen	16 6/12	M		Ireland	U.S. of America	Douglass	6 Jul 1829
Owen	26	M	Yeoman	Ireland	United States	Borneo	9 Jul 1827
P.	20	M	Merchant	England	U.S. America	Cortes	19 May 1826
Patk.	25	M	Weaver	Ireland	United States	Wilson	27 Jun 1826
Patrick	20	M	Child	Ireland	United States	Dublin Packet	9 Jul 1827
Patrick	23	M	Farmer	Ireland	America	Farmer	15 Nov 1823
Philip	35	M	Coachman	New York	United States	Antioch	21 Sep 1827
Robert D., Mr.	18	M	Merchant	U. States	U. States	Hudson	10 Nov 1825
Silvy	16	F	Spinster	Ireland	Unt. St. America	Wilson	21 May 1827
Susan	18	F	Servant	Ireland	United States	Ann Maria	5 May 1824
Thomas	19	M	Clerk	Ireland	United States	Dublin Packet	13 Oct 1828
Thomas	24	M	Farmer	Great Britain	United States	Freake	25 Aug 1829
Thomas	32	M	Farmer			Euphrates	8 Aug 1820
Thos.	20	M	Farmer	Ireland	New York	Phoenix	29 Apr 1826
William	9	M	Farmer	Great Britain	United States	Roman	10 May 1828
William	21	M	Laborer	Ireland	United States	Sylvester Healy	17 Oct 1825
William	38	M	Farmer	Great Britain	United States	Roman	10 May 1828
Wm.	27	M	Farmer	Grate Brittan	New York	Susquehanna	9 Jan 1824
Wm. B.	24	M	Gentleman	United States		Panthea	15 Jun 1822
HARTE, John, Jr.	32		Mariner	United States		Cynosure	4 Mar 1828
HARTEJIN, John	33 6/12	M	Labourer	England	America	Minerva	15 Jun 1825
HARTEN, Bernard	33	M	Weaver	Ireland	U. States	Josephine	7 May 1827
HARTER, Catherine	4	F		France	U. States	Edward Quesnel	4 Aug 1828
Catherine	40	F		France	U. States	Edward Quesnel	4 Aug 1828
Clara	6	F		France	U. States	Edward Quesnel	4 Aug 1828
Francis	42	M	Carpenter	France	U. States	Edward Quesnel	4 Aug 1828
Magdalina	5/12	F		France	U. States	Edward Quesnel	4 Aug 1828
Maria	8	F		France	U. States	Edward Quesnel	4 Aug 1828
Nandeline	16	F		France	U. States	Edward Quesnel	4 Aug 1828
HARTFORD, Patrick	28	M	Labourer	Ireland	United States	Meteor	19 Aug 1829
HARTHORN, Jude	30	M	Seaman	U. States	U. States	Traveller	2 Jun 1822
HARTINE, E.	28	M	Merchant	Vera Cruz	U. States	Eliza	11 Apr 1826
HARTLAND, Ben	27	M	Labourer	England	U. States	Ayrshire	12 May 1828
HARTLEY, Christopher	35	M	...	G. Britain	U. States	New England	28 Sep 1824
George L., Mr.	28	M	Gentleman	Ireland	United States	Dublin Packet	22 Aug 1829
John	30	M	Stone Mason	England	United States	Dalhouse Castle	8 May 1827
Nevley	30	M	Farmer	Ireland	U. States	Champion	26 Jul 1827
Roger	27	M	Stone Mason	England	United States	Dalhouse Castle	8 May 1827
HARTLY, Barnard	21	M	Stone Mason	England	United States	Dalhouse Castle	8 May 1827
George	19	M	Farmer	England	U. States	Manhattan	12 Jun 1824
Henry	22	M	Br. Army	G.B.	G.B.	London	19 Dec 1823
Jane	20	F	None	England	U. States	Thomas Ritchie	2 Jul 1827
John	29	M	Tailor	England	U. States	Thomas Ritchie	2 Jul 1827
Theophilus	22	M	Farmer	Great Britian	United States	Andes	19 Aug 1829
William	14	M	Stone Mason	England	United States	Dalhouse Castle	8 May 1827
HARTMAN, —	24	M	Taylor	U. States	U. States	Alexander Le Grand	9 Sep 1823
Brill	26	F	Nurse	Holland	U. States	Edward Bonaffe	23 Jul 1828
C.	7	F		France	United States	La Flora	30 Jun 1828
Catherine	26	F		Germany	United States	Samuel Robertson	8 Aug 1828
Doris	4	F		Germany	United States	Samuel Robertson	8 Aug 1828
E.	11	F		France	United States	La Flora	30 Jun 1828
E.	46	F		France	United States	La Flora	30 Jun 1828
J.	44	M	Mason	France	United States	La Flora	30 Jun 1828
J. A. D.	25	M	Merchant	Denmark	U. States	Minerva	9 Jan 1827

NAMES OF PASSENGERS	AGE	SEX	OCCUPATIONS	COUNTRY TO WHICH THEY BELONG	COUNTRY THEY INTEND TO INHABIT	SHIPS/DATES OF ARRIVAL	
HARTMAN (cont'd)							
John	30	M	Farmer	Germany	United States	Samuel Robertson	8 Aug 1828
M.	4	F		France	United States	La Flora	30 Jun 1828
M.	18	F		France	United States	La Flora	30 Jun 1828
Mariana	2	F		Germany	United States	Samuel Robertson	8 Aug 1828
Stedman	30	M	Planter	St. Croix	U. States	South Carolina Packet	4 Sep 1822
HARTMANN, Barthw.	32	M	Merchant	Switzerland	United States	Helen	5 Sep 1828
E.	24		Merchant	Paris	France	Brown	11 Jun 1827
HARTNELL, Catherine	22	F		Ireland	U.S. America	Traveller	10 Sep 1827
Wm.	27	M	Shoe Maker	Ireland	U.S. America	Traveller	10 Sep 1827
HARTNESS, David	38	M	Labourer	Scotland	United States	Indus	5 Sep 1827
Elizabeth	17	M	Farmer	Ireland	United States	Fabius	4 Jun 1828
HARTNET, Jas.	50		Farmer & Labourer	Great Britain & Ireland	United States	Trio	8 Feb 1827
HARTNETT, Cathe.	2					Trio	5 May 1828
Ellen	6					Trio	5 May 1828
Margt.	27					Trio	5 May 1828
Mary	3					Trio	5 May 1828
HARTON, Richard	24	M	Farmer	Great Britian	United States	Andes	19 Aug 1829
HARTRIDGE, Charles	28	M	Merchant	United States	Savannah, U.S.	Florida	2 Oct 1828
HARTSHORN, Fanny	4 4/12	F		England	New York	Exertion	3 Dec 1828
Hannah	2 3/12	F		England	New York	Exertion	3 Dec 1828
James	30 3/12	M	Miner	England	New York	Exertion	3 Dec 1828
Mary	24 2/12	F		England	New York	Exertion	3 Dec 1828
HARTSHORNE, P. J.	38	M	Mercht.	U.S.	U. States	Hamlet	4 Aug 1823
Richard	22	M	Seaman	U. States	U. States	Natchez	18 Aug 1828
W.	56	M	Merchant	U. States	U. States	Marcellus	26 Feb 1824
HARTSON, James	34	M	Labourer	Ireland	New York	Mary	13 Dec 1821
HARTT, Geo.	25	M	Servant	England	U. States	Seine	10 Jun 1822
Mason	34	M	Farmer	Great Britain	U. St.	Manchester	7 Dec 1826
HARTWELL, Francis	26	F	Servant	U.S. Am.	U.S. Am.	Henry IV	5 Feb 1827
Jas.	20	M	Laborer	Ireland	United States	Trio	13 Jun 1827
John	24	M	Laborer	Ireland	United States	Trio	13 Jun 1827
Matt.	33	M	Laborer	Ireland	United States	Trio	13 Jun 1827
Thos.	25	M	Laborer	Ireland	United States	Trio	13 Jun 1827
HARVARD, Mary	27	F	None	United States	United States	William Thompson	16 Jan 1826
HARVAT, Peter C.	20	M	Farmer	Spain	U. States	General Jackson	15 Jan 1829
HARVE, John	20	M	Silver Smith	United States	United States	Hopes Delight	22 Jul 1828
HARVEY, Aaron	25	M	Engineer	England	United States	Eliza Grant	7 Jun 1827
Alicia	9	F		Ireland	United States	Thomas	13 Dec 1827
Amelia	28		Lady	England	United States	Corinthian	30 May 1828
Ann	3	F		Ireland	United States	Mary	1 Jul 1829
Ann	9	F		Ireland	United States	Concordia	25 Aug 1827
Benjamin	5	M		Ireland	United States	Concordia	25 Aug 1827
Briget	27	F		Ireland	United States	Concordia	25 Aug 1827
Catharine	3	F		Ireland	United States	Concordia	25 Aug 1827
Catharine	20	F		Ireland	United States	Mary	1 Jul 1829
Catherine	23	F	None	Scotland	United States	Trident	31 Mar 1827
Daniel	5	M		Ireland	United States	Thomas	13 Dec 1827
Eliza	6		Farmer	Ireland	U. States	Schuylkill	22 Aug 1825
Elizabeth	12	F		Ireland	United States	Thomas	13 Dec 1827
Elizabeth	20 10/12	F	Wife	Ireland	United States	Atlantic	21 Jul 1827
Francis Amelia	10		Lady	England	United States	Corinthian	30 May 1828
George	22	M	None	England	Canada	Thames	6 Oct 1820
H.	23	M	Mechanic	Connecticutt	U. States	Benjamin	1 Jun 1822
Harriet	1	F		Ireland	United States	Concordia	25 Aug 1827
Harriet	8		Lady	England	United States	Corinthian	30 May 1828
Henrietta	8	F		Ireland	United States	Thomas	13 Dec 1827
Henry	14	M	Laborer	Ireland	United States	Mary	1 Jul 1829
Henry	33		Gent.	England	United States	Corinthian	30 May 1828
Henry Chas.	24	M	Engraver	Gt. Britain		Corinthian	27 Oct 1829
Horatio	17	M	None	Great Britain	United States	Mary & Harriet	3 Jul 1829
James	1	M	None	Scotland	United States	Trident	31 Mar 1827
James	3	M	Child	Ireland	United States	Sylvester Healy	14 Jun 1825
James	20	M	Labourer	Ireland		Robert Fulton	4 Jun 1828

547

NAMES OF PASSENGERS	AGE	SEX	OCCUPATIONS	COUNTRY TO WHICH THEY BELONG	COUNTRY THEY INTEND TO INHABIT	SHIPS/DATES OF ARRIVAL	
HARVEY (cont'd)							
James	35	M	Laborer	Ireland	United States	Mary	1 Jul 1829
James	38	M	Mechanick	England	United States	Robert Edwards	3 Oct 1829
James	46	M	Carpenter			Helen	4 Aug 1829
Jno.	5		Farmer	Ireland	U. States	Schuylkill	22 Aug 1825
Jno.	22		Farmer	Ireland	U. States	Schuylkill	22 Aug 1825
Jno.	34	M	Gentleman	London	U. States	Criterion	15 Oct 1822
John	14	M	Servant	Ireland	America	Carolina Ann	7 Aug 1826
Joseph	25	M	Weaver	Scotland	United States	Trident	31 Mar 1827
Joseph	25	M	Labourer	Great Britain	United States	Mary & Harriet	3 Jul 1829
M.	28		Farmer	Ireland	U. States	Schuylkill	22 Aug 1825
Margaret	3	F	None	Scotland	United States	Trident	31 Mar 1827
Margret	27	F	Spinster	Ireland	U. States	Josephine	30 Aug 1828
Maria	26			Birmingham	England	London	13 Dec 1822
Mary	6	F		Ireland	United States	Concordia	25 Aug 1827
Mary	28	F	Wife	Ireland	United States	Sylvester Healy	14 Jun 1825
Mary	32	F	Spinster	Ireland	United States	Thomas	13 Dec 1827
Mary	35	F		Ireland	United States	Mary	1 Jul 1829
Patrick	16	M	Weaver	Ireland	America	Carolina Ann	7 Apr 1826
Patrick	30 2/12	M	Dealer	Ireland	United States	Atlantic	21 Jul 1827
Rebecca	40		Farmer	Ireland	U. States	Schuylkill	22 Aug 1825
Robert	25	M	Farmer	Ireland	United States	Sylvester Healy	14 Jun 1825
Rose Ann	20	F	Servant	Ireland	America	Carolina Ann	7 Aug 1826
Samuel	20	M	Labourer	Great Britain	United States	Mary & Harriet	3 Jul 1829
Thos.	54	M	Farmer	England	U. States	Panthea	8 Apr 1826
Virginia	25	F		Paris	U. States	Criterion	15 Oct 1822
William	3	M		Ireland	United States	Thomas	13 Dec 1827
William	14	M	Laborer	Ireland	United States	Mary	1 Jul 1829
William	28	M	Merchant	England	New York	Brighton	11 Dec 1827
William	50	M	Labourer	Great Britain	United States	Mary & Harriet	3 Jul 1829
HARVY, Lemuel	45	M	Mariner	United States	United States	Concordia	8 Sep 1823
HARWAGEN,							
Ellias Galtlieb	29	M	Gent.	Bavaria	United States	Orozimbo	28 Jun 1827
HARWALL, B. T.	29	F		France	United States	Le Voltaire	19 Jul 1828
Joseph A.	3	M		France	United States	Le Voltaire	19 Jul 1828
Nichoals	33	M	Hatter	France	United States	Le Voltaire	19 Jul 1828
HARWOOD, —, Miss	28	F		Gt. Britain	United States	Columbia	7 Sep 1827
J.	22	M	None	England	United States	Enterprize	19 Oct 1826
Joseph	26	M	Farmer	England	United States	Jubilee	1 Oct 1828
Robt. W.	27	M	...	England	Canada	William Thompson	10 May 1825
William	25	M	Farmer	England	United States	Jubilee	1 Oct 1828
Wm.	29	M	Merchant	Gt. Britain	Canada	Caledonia	10 Sep 1828
Wm., Junr.	28	M	Merchant	Great Britain	Canada	Canada	20 Jun 1823
HARY, John	20	M	Labourer	Ireland		Robert Fulton	4 Jun 1828
Joseph	40	M	L. Maker	France	U. States	Edward Bonaffe	23 Jul 1828
HARZEN, Fredk. F.	41	M	Merchant	Denmark	Denmark	Herald	21 Sep 1824
HARZER, Xavier	23	M	Weaver	Gt. Brittan		L'Esperance	6 Sep 1828
HASBURGH, John	53	M	Merchant	Great Britain	United States	Hamilton	21 Nov 1826
HASEL, Antonia	35	M	Planter	Germany	U. States	Lycurgus	3 Dec 1821
H.	30	F		Germany	U. States	Lycurgus	3 Dec 1821
HASELY, Ruth	21	F	Spinster	Ireland	America	Josephine	8 Dec 1827
HASEN, Charles	25	M	Merchant	St. Johns	United States	St. Michaels	7 Jun 1827
HASERAN, Wm.	30			Ireland	New York	General Marion	21 Nov 1828
HASETT, Joanna	21	F		Ireland	United States	Trio	2 Oct 1828
HASEY, Anne	15	F	None	Ireland	United States	Mary & Harriet	3 Jul 1829
Robert	20	M	Labourer	Ireland	United States	Meteor	26 Jun 1827
HASHING, Richard	23	M	Miner	England	England	Ranger	15 Jan 1827
HASKEL, Chas.	30	M	Meckanic	Prussia	United States	Maria Elizabeth	2 Sep 1822
N.	37	M	Farmer	Germany	United States	Lydia	18 Jun 1828
Wm.	16	M	Carpenter	Ireland	U. States	Concordia	11 Jun 1823
HASKELL, Sidney	40	M	Merchant	U. States	U. States	Canada	8 Jun 1826
HASKER, James	33	M	Miner	England	England	Virginia	8 Mar 1828
HASKET, Jeremiah	25	M	Labourer	Ireland	U. States	Nancy	2 May 1823
HASKILL, Wm. N.	26	M	Mechanic	U. States	U. States	William Tell	3 Dec 1825
HASLAM, James	23	M	Weaver	Barry	Barry	Howard Douglass	11 May 1827
HASLAN, James	24	M	Farmer	England	U.N. States	Jane	7 Oct 1826

NAMES OF PASSENGERS	A G E	S E X	OCCUPATIONS	COUNTRY TO WHICH THEY BELONG	COUNTRY THEY INTEND TO INHABIT	SHIPS/DATES OF ARRIVAL	
HASLEHURST,							
Catherine	38	F		Great Britain	United States	Birmingham	15 Jun 1827
Edwin	8	M		Great Britain	United States	Birmingham	15 Jun 1827
Elizabeth	50	F	Weaver	Great Britain	United States	Birmingham	15 Jun 1827
Emma	6	F		Great Britain	United States	Birmingham	15 Jun 1827
Fanny	21	F		Great Britain	United States	Birmingham	15 Jun 1827
George	4	M		Great Britain	United States	Birmingham	15 Jun 1827
James	2	M		Great Britain	United States	Birmingham	15 Jun 1827
James	17	M	Weaver	Great Britain	United States	Birmingham	15 Jun 1827
James	55	M	Weaver	Great Britain	United States	Birmingham	15 Jun 1827
Jane	2	F		Great Britain	United States	Birmingham	15 Jun 1827
John	34	M	Filer & Turner	Great Britain	United States	Birmingham	15 Jun 1827
Mary	10	F		Great Britain	United States	Birmingham	15 Jun 1827
Peter	10	M		Great Britain	United States	Birmingham	15 Jun 1827
HASLEM, John	36	M	Labourer	Great Brittain	United States	Robert Fulton	13 Mar 1827
HASLER, James	20	M	Weaver	Ireland	United States	St. George	25 Aug 1829
Janes	20	M	Weaver	Ireland	United States	St. George	25 Aug 1829
Mary	30	F		G. Britann		Manchester	29 Aug 1828
HASLEY, Ellis	24	M	Manufacture	Great Britain	United States	Blakely	29 Sep 1826
HASLVILL, George D.	22	M	Printer	G. Brittan	U. States	Henry	24 Oct 1828
W.	11	M	Child	G. Brittan	U. States	Henry	24 Oct 1828
HASON, Judah	22	M	Merchant	England	New Orleans	Brighton	9 Dec 1828
Sarah	22	F	None	England	New Orleans	Brighton	9 Dec 1828
HASPEL, G. L.	36	M	Merchant	Winterburg	U. States	Minerva	13 Sep 1827
HASSALL, Ann	26	F	None	Londonderry	United States	Hector	29 Nov 1823
John	26	M	Labourer	Isle of Man		Ocean	13 Jul 1827
Josiah	27	M	Merchant	Nantuck	United States	Hector	29 Nov 1823
HASSAM, Bridget	18	F		Ireland	U. States	Nancy	16 Aug 1822
HASSAN, Isaac	26	M		Gibraltar	Jamaica	Little Cherub	11 Aug 1825
Mary	15		Child	Ireland	England	Emulous	26 Jul 1821
Thomas	25	M	Labourer	G. Britain	U. States	Mary & Harriot	8 Sep 1828
HASSARD, Saml.	20	M	Student	New Haven	U. States	Ambuscade	12 Nov 1823
HASSEL, Ann	40	F		England	U. States	Washington	7 Jul 1824
Barbara	30	F		England	U. States	Washington	7 Jul 1824
Eliza	7	F		England	U. States	Washington	7 Jul 1824
Harriet	16	F		England	U. States	Washington	7 Jul 1824
Horrace	3	M		England	U. States	Washington	7 Jul 1824
Mary	13	F		England	U. States	Washington	7 Jul 1824
Reuben	10	M		England	U. States	Washington	7 Jul 1824
Richard	34	M		England	U. States	Washington	7 Jul 1824
Rob.	30	M		England	U. States	Washington	7 Jul 1824
Thos.	5	M		England	U. States	Washington	7 Jul 1824
W.	32	M		England	U. States	Washington	7 Jul 1824
HASSELL, Abr.	16	M	Domestic	St. Thomas	St. Croix	Chase	2 Oct 1823
Richd.	50	M	Farmer	England	U. States	Washington	7 Jul 1824
HASSEN, Arthur	50		Labourer	Ireland	England	Emulous	26 Jul 1821
David	32	M	Pedlar	England	U. States	Robert Edwards	9 May 1827
Edward	19		Labourer	Ireland	England	Emulous	26 Jul 1821
Michael	21		Labourer	Ireland	England	Emulous	26 Jul 1821
Sarah	17		Spinster	Ireland	England	Emulous	26 Jul 1821
HASSER, Geo.	10	M		Switzerland	U.S.	C. Amelia	30 Jun 1828
Jacob	40	F	Laborer	Switzerland	U.S.	C. Amelia	30 Jun 1828
Jean	7	M		Switzerland	U.S.	C. Amelia	30 Jun 1828
HASSETT, David	23	M	Labourer	Gt. Brittain	United States	Balaena	21 Aug 1824
Ellen	1	F	None	Ireland	America	Evelina	10 Nov 1825
Ellen	30	F	None	Ireland	America	Evelina	10 Nov 1825
Jermiah	36	M	Farmer	England	U. States	Oglethorpe	9 Nov 1824
Mary	6	F		England	U. States	Oglethorpe	9 Nov 1824
HASTADO, Pedro Maria	20	M		Spain	Spain	Wallace	18 May 1825
HASTER, Thos.	21			Kilpatric	N. York	Peru	30 May 1828
HASTHEY, ...ny	26	M	Watch Maker	Switzerland	United States	Elbe	2 Aug 1822
HASTING, John	20	M	Merchant	Ireland	U. States	Nancy	14 Jan 1822
John	24	M	Merchant	St. John, N.B.	St. John, N.B.	Nancy	2 May 1823
John	29	M	Doctor	Newbrunsick	Newbrunsick	Nancy	23 Oct 1823
HASTINGS, John	22	M		Ireland	U. States	St. Michael	26 Oct 1824
John	28	M	Merchant	St. John, N.B.	St. John, N.B.	St. Michaels	24 Mar 1825
John	31	M	Merchant	Great Britain	United States	Sylvester Healy	23 Nov 1825
HASTIS, John	17	M	Clerk	Great Britain	United States	Grecian	24 Sep 1828

NAMES OF PASSENGERS	AGE	SEX	OCCUPATIONS	COUNTRY TO WHICH THEY BELONG	COUNTRY THEY INTEND TO INHABIT	SHIPS/DATES OF ARRIVAL	
HASTMAN, Henry D.	26	M	Joiner	Native of Switzerland	United States	Canaris	30 Jun 1827
HASTNET, Cathrin	4	F		Irland	U. States	Nancy	27 Jun 1823
Jusca	23	M		Irland	U. States	Nancy	27 Jun 1823
Marey	25	F		Irland	U. States	Nancy	27 Jun 1823
HASTY, Betty	25	F		Ireland	New York	Phoenix	29 Apr 1826
George	21	M	Labourer	Ireland	United States	William & George	14 May 1828
Margaret	17	F		Ireland	United States	William & George	14 May 1828
Patrick	40	M	Laborer	Ireland	United States	Sarah Ann	18 Nov 1826
HASWELL, George	16	M	Servant	London		Hannibal	28 Jul 1823
HAT..., Thomas	35	M	Farmer	England	United States	William & Henry	19 Jul 1822
HATCH, —, Miss	21	F		Providence	U. States	New York	3 Oct 1826
Anselm	35	M	Mariner	U. States	U. States	Tuscaloosa	19 Mar 1827
Martyn	25	M	Merchant	U. States		Volant	19 Apr 1826
N. C.	30	M	Accountant	Ireland	America	Hannah	8 Nov 1821
Sarah	38 10/12	F		U. States	U. States	Clarice	19 Sep 1828
Thos.	27	M	Weaver	Ireland	United States	Robert Fulton	10 Aug 1827
Wm.	22	M	Farmer	Ireland	Pennsylvania	Susquehanna	9 Jan 1824
HATCHER, Charles	26	M	Laborer	England	United States	London	21 May 1828
Geo.	53	M	Farmer	Germany	United States	Lydia	18 Jun 1828
M.	16	M	Farmer	Germany	United States	Lydia	18 Jun 1828
M.	40	F		Germany	United States	Lydia	18 Jun 1828
Margt.	19	F		Germany	United States	Lydia	18 Jun 1828
R.	14	F		Germany	United States	Lydia	18 Jun 1828
Susannah	23	F	None	England	United States	London	21 May 1828
HATCHNIS, E.	26	M	Merchant	Vera Cruz	U. States	Eliza	11 Apr 1826
HATFELD, Gabriel	22	M	Clockmaker	United States	St. John, N.B.	Ann Maria	7 Aug 1826
HATFIELD, Ann	5	F		England	America	Thames	27 May 1822
Ann	32	F		England	America	Thames	27 May 1822
Betsy	1	F		England	America	Thames	27 May 1822
Edward	13	F		England	America	Thames	27 May 1822
Henry	33	M	Sadler	England	America	Thames	27 May 1822
John	4	M		England	America	Thames	27 May 1822
John	24	M	Laborer	Ireland	United States	Nancey	8 Jun 1822
Margaret	19	F		Halifax	U. States	Hope & Esther	12 May 1826
Peter	30	M	Esquire	Saint John	St. John	Nancy	11 Apr 1822
Sampson	24	M	Tailor	Halifax	U. States	Hope & Esther	12 May 1826
Sarah	9	F		England	America	Thames	27 May 1822
Sidney B.	21	M	Painter	England	United States	Acasta	12 Dec 1823
Thomas	7	M	Farmer	England	America	Thames	27 May 1822
HATHAM, Frs.	37	F		Great Brittain	U. States	Laburnum	24 Aug 1822
Geo.	9	M		Great Brittain	U. States	Laburnum	24 Aug 1822
Hannah	3	F		Great Brittain	U. States	Laburnum	24 Aug 1822
Jno.	11	M		Great Brittain	U. States	Laburnum	24 Aug 1822
Ra.	39	M	Farmer	Great Brittain	U. States	Laburnum	24 Aug 1822
Thomas	7	M		Great Brittain	U. States	Laburnum	24 Aug 1822
Wm.	5	M		Great Brittain	U. States	Laburnum	24 Aug 1822
HATHAN, —, Madam	40	F		France	U. States	Danube	21 Nov 1826
HATHAWAY, Enoch B.	23	M	Mariner	America	Dighton	Rachel Ann	13 Mar 1829
F. S.	20	M	Merchant	United States	United States	Florida	23 Aug 1825
George	25		Merchant			Mount Vernon	26 Aug 1820
James W.	18	M		United States	U. States	Edward Bopnnaffe	30 Jul 1829
Joseph [crossed out]	23	M	Merchant	United States	...	Mechanic	11 Apr 1826
Mary	13		None	London	England	Elizabeth	8 Dec 1821
William	40	M	Mariner	U.S. America	U.S. America	James Cropper	23 Mar 1827
Wm., Junr., Capt.	27		Mariner	U.S. of America	U.S. America	Mary	10 Mar 1826
Wm. G.	30	M	Servant	England	U. States	Pacific	5 Sep 1827
HATHWAY, Job						Venus	12 Apr 1821
John	23		Seaman	United States		Cynosure	4 Mar 1828

*Consul's man, put on bord by the american Consil at St. Michal's Belonging to the brig Emeline of Portland Was Rackt on the 25 of Dec 1827 in the Harber of St. Michals

HATLAN, Robt.	36	M	Labourer	Ireland	United States	Commerce	13 Jun 1828
HATRICK, Robt.	22	M	Labourer	Ireland	United States	Hope	12 Jun 1828
Wm.	28	M	Merchant	Ireland	United States	Samuel Robertson	5 Oct 1827

NAMES OF PASSENGERS	AGE	SEX	OCCUPATIONS	COUNTRY TO WHICH THEY BELONG	COUNTRY THEY INTEND TO INHABIT	SHIPS/DATES OF ARRIVAL	
HATSON, James	23	M	Gentleman	G. Britain	U. States	Kennebeck Trader	16 Jul 1822
HATTER, Caroline	8			Sussex, England		Cincinnatus	17 May 1823
Elizabeth	30			Sussex, England		Cincinnatus	17 May 1823
Hannah	6			Sussex, England		Cincinnatus	17 May 1823
James	2			Sussex, England		Cincinnatus	17 May 1823
*died							
James	34		Farmer	Sussex, England		Cincinnatus	17 May 1823
Martha	3			Sussex, England		Cincinnatus	17 May 1823
Patrick	24	M	Labourer	G. Britain	U. States	Mary & Harriot	8 Sep 1828
Richard	33	...	...	...	United States	Criterion	27 Jun 1827
HATTERSLEY, Thos.	17	M	Cutter	England	United States	Peru	23 May 1827
HATTON, Edward	18 7/12	M	Clerk			Cririe	18 Sep 1820
Edward	19	M	Forgeman	Great Britan	United States	Silvanus Jenkins	10 Mar 1827
Henry	10/12	M	None	Great Britan	United States	Silvanus Jenkins	10 Mar 1827
John	45	M	Forgeman	Great Britan	United States	Silvanus Jenkins	10 Mar 1827
John, Junr.	24	M	Forgeman	Great Britan	United States	Silvanus Jenkins	10 Mar 1827
Levina	2/12	F	None	Great Britan	United States	Silvanus Jenkins	10 Mar 1827
Margary	45	F	None	Great Britan	United States	Silvanus Jenkins	10 Mar 1827
Mary	17	F	None	Great Britan	United States	Silvanus Jenkins	10 Mar 1827
Mary A.	25	F	None	Great Britan	United States	Silvanus Jenkins	10 Mar 1827
R. W.	50	M	Mariner	Norfolk	U. States	Cordelia	16 Apr 1824
Rob.	35	M	Schoolmaster	England	United States	Essex	23 May 1828
Roland	12	M	None	Great Britan	United States	Silvanus Jenkins	10 Mar 1827
Sarah	19	F	None	England		Manhattan	22 May 1827
William	32	M	Laborer	Scotland	U. States	Camillus	17 Sep 1823
Wm.	21	M	Forgeman	Great Britan	United States	Silvanus Jenkins	10 Mar 1827
Wm.	33	M	Merchant	G. Brittain	U. States	General Jackson	15 Jan 1829
HATTONER, Antoni	35	M	Farmer	Ireland		Quatre Freres	29 Jul 1828
HATTRICK, Margt.	17		Seamster	Scotland	United States	Camillus	3 May 1828
Margt.	35		Seamster	Scotland	United States	Camillus	3 May 1828
HATTY, Eliza	27			United States	United States	Hudson	18 Jun 1825
HATWOTH, John	7	M		G. Britain	U. States	St. George	7 Jun 1828
HAUBBAND, David	22	M	Weaver	France	America, U.N.S.	Great Britain	3 Aug 1829
HAUBER, C.	18	F	Gent	French	Switzerland	Charlemagne	19 Sep 1828
C.	20	M	Gent	French	Switzerland	Charlemagne	19 Sep 1828
Didlin	40	F	Gent	French	Switzerland	Charlemagne	19 Sep 1828
Wm.	45	M	Gent	French	Switzerland	Charlemagne	19 Sep 1828
HAUCH, Oswald	23	M	Shoemaker	Switzerland	U. States	Hewes	30 Oct 1829
HAUEL, Eliza	12	F		County of Down, Ireland	U. States	Lady Washington	16 Oct 1821
James	55	M	Miller	County of Down, Ireland	U. States	Lady Washington	16 Oct 1821
Jane	5	F		County of Down, Ireland	U. States	Lady Washington	16 Oct 1821
Magret	51	F		County of Down, Ireland	U. States	Lady Washington	16 Oct 1821
Mary	16	F		County of Down, Ireland	U. States	Lady Washington	16 Oct 1821
HAUFER, Gottlenpina	33	M		Wertemberg	Wertemberg	Edward Quesnel	3 Jul 1829
John A.	27	M	Taylor	Wertemberg	Wertemberg	Edward Quesnel	3 Jul 1829
HAUG, Carol Frederick	6	M		Switzerland	United States	Elizabeth	27 Jul 1824
Caspar	53	M	Weaver	Switzerland	United States	Elizabeth	27 Jul 1824
Magdelina	53	F		Switzerland	United States	Elizabeth	27 Jul 1824
HAUGHEY, Hugh	21		Weaver	Ireland	G. Britain	Robert Burns	14 Jun 1824
HAUGHHEY, John	34	M	Merchant	Ireland	United States	Ann Maria	3 Jul 1827
HAUGHTON, Wm.	20		Merchant	Carlow	Ireland	Carolina Ann	21 May 1823
HAULY, Elizabeth	25	F	Sevant			James Monroe	8 Aug 1820
HAUNON, Jane	18	F	Miliner	Ireland	United States	Nile	17 May 1827
HAUPT, Jacob	49	M	Chirugyn	Altenburg in Sachse	United States	Juffraw Johanna	16 Oct 1821
HAURIET, James	52	M	...	...	...	Meteor	16 Aug 1824
Jula	22	F	...	...	...	Meteor	16 Aug 1824
HAUS, Edward	5	M		Wales South	U. States	Oglethorpe	8 Jul 1824
Elizabeth	23	F		Wales South	U. States	Oglethorpe	8 Jul 1824
Henry	1 6/12	M		Wales South	U. States	Oglethorpe	8 Jul 1824
Jas.	31	M	Farmer	Wales South	U. States	Oglethorpe	8 Jul 1824
Samuel	4	M		Wales South	U. States	Oglethorpe	8 Jul 1824
HAVARD, Anty.		M	Merchant	France		Frederick	18 Feb 1822

NAMES OF PASSENGERS	AGE	SEX	OCCUPATIONS	COUNTRY TO WHICH THEY BELONG	COUNTRY THEY INTEND TO INHABIT	SHIPS/DATES OF ARRIVAL	
HAVARTH, Eliza	19	F	None	England	United States	Jubilee	1 Oct 1828
George	52	M	Farmer		Perien [?]	Governor Clinton	3 Jul 1827
HAVEL, Germain, (Student)	14	M	Lad	France	New York	Sully	30 Oct 1827
HAVER, Catherine	9	F	Spinster	Switzerland	United States	Andes	5 May 1828
Johaves	36	M	Farmer	Switzerland	United States	Andes	5 May 1828
Margaret	3	F	Child	Switzerland	United States	Andes	5 May 1828
Maria	5	F	Child	Switzerland	United States	Andes	5 May 1828
Maria	33	F	Spinster	Switzerland	United States	Andes	5 May 1828
Sally	1 6/12	F	child	Switzerland	United States	Andes	5 May 1828
HAVERSTOCK, Danl.	34	M	Carpenter	Switzerland	United States	Factor	1 Sep 1823
Danl., Jr.	1	M	None	Switzerland	United States	Factor	1 Sep 1823
Mary	28	F		Switzerland	United States	Factor	1 Sep 1823
HAVERTY, John	22	M	Grocer	England	U. States	Mary Howland	22 Sep 1828
HAVEY, John	48	M	Labourer	Ireland	United States	Jubilee	12 May 1828
Michael	25	M	Labourer	Ireland	United States	Jubilee	12 May 1828
HAVICELM, Cathe.	19	M	Servant	Ireland	U. States	Ann Maria	13 Dec 1824
HAVIDING, John	25	M	Laborer or Spinster	Ireland	United States	Sarah G	11 Sep 1827
HAVILAND, John	32	M	Taylor	Great Britain	United States	Exertion	17 Jul 1829
Mary	18		Spinster	Ireland	United States	Robert Burns	18 Jun 1821
Patrick	23	M	Weaver	Ireland	United States	Trident	17 May 1825
HAVLIN, Bryan	17	M	Labourer	Ireland	United States	Henry Kneeland	7 Jun 1828
Margt.	25	F	Servant	Ireland	United States	Henry Kneeland	7 Jun 1828
HAVRE, Geo.	30	M	Labourer	Ireland	U. States	Atlantic	19 Aug 1825
HAVY, Girrard Lalor	18	M	British Army	U. States	U. States	Canada	27 Sep 1826
HAWARD, Gregoria	41	M	Merchant	Spain	Spain	Ambuscade	1 Jul 1820
James	22	M	Weaver	England	United States	Siroc	31 Oct 1829
Wm.	25	M		Great Britain	United States	India	5 Sep 1827
HAWE, Geo.	24	M	Merchant	Sweden	U. States	Pacific	5 Sep 1827
HAWERTH, Will	25	M	Farmer	England	U.S.A.	Robin Hood	6 May 1828
HAWETT, Thos.	30	M		England		Ann	17 May 1822
HAWKER, Henry	32	M	Mason	Great Britain	United States	Robert Fulton	22 Oct 1821
HAWKES, Ann L.	30	F	None	U. States	U. States	Columbia	24 Dec 1822
Helen	5	F	Mariner	Virginia	U. States	Favourite	27 Jun 1823
John	13	M	Mercht.	England	United States	Hannibal	6 Sep 1824
HAWKESWORTH, Jas.	31	M	Merchant	Barbados, U.S.	West Indies	Spartan	24 Jul 1826
HAWKEY, Thomas	29	M	Farmer	Ireland	U. States	Erin	5 Jul 1820
HAWKINS, A.	28	M	Carpenter	America	U. States	Ambuscade	5 Jul 1822
Ann Maria	1	F		United States		Edward Quesnel	17 Nov 1828
Caleb	30			G. Britain	U. States	Hamilton	28 Apr 1828
Charles E.	20	M	Merchant	U. States	U. States	Fanny	24 Oct 1822
E.	25	F		U. States	U. States	Edward Quesnel	3 Sep 1826
Eliza	26	F		United States		Edward Quesnel	17 Nov 1828
George	16	M	Carpenter	England	U. States	Electra	7 Jul 1828
George	26	M	Grocer	England	America	Leeds	2 Aug 1828
Hannah	22	F	Labrer	Ireland	U. States	Edwin	1 Jul 1829
James, Mr.	31	M	Farmer	England	New York	Cortes	23 Nov 1827
John	19	M	Carpenter	England	U. States	Electra	7 Jul 1828
John	25	M	Mariner	England	U. States	Criterion at London	10 May 1821
John	28	M	Labrer	Ireland	U. States	Edwin	1 Jul 1829
John	37	M	Farmer	Gt. Britain	United States	Crisis	13 Nov 1824
John, a distressed American Seaman put on board by W. J. Watchmon, American Consul						Andes	22 Oct 1821
Owen	19	M		Ireland	U.S. of America	Douglass	6 Jul 1829
Philip	24	M	Labourer	England	U. States	Emulous	22 Aug 1828
Richard	25	M	Shoe Maker	England	U. States	Franklin	7 Jul 1828
Robert	22	M				Lady of the Lake	23 Aug 1828
*left ship							
Sarah	40	F				Lady of the Lake	23 Aug 1828
*left ship							
Sophia, Miss	17	F		England	New York	Cortes	23 Nov 1827
Thomas	32	M	Carpenter	U.S. America	U.S. America	Quill	5 Jun 1826
Thos.	23	M	Mechanic	Gt. Britain	United States	John & Elizabeth	25 Sep 1827
William	12 6/12	M		Ireland	U.S. of America	Douglass	6 Jul 1829
William, Mastr.	18	M		England	New York	Cortes	23 Nov 1827

NAMES OF PASSENGERS	AGE	SEX	OCCUPATIONS	COUNTRY TO WHICH THEY BELONG	COUNTRY THEY INTEND TO INHABIT	SHIPS/DATES OF ARRIVAL	
HAWKLY, Samuel	15	M	Servant	England	Pensylvania	Lima	5 Aug 1829
Samuel	15	M	Servant	England	U. States	Lima	5 Aug 1829
Susannah	19	F		England	Pensylvania	Lima	5 Aug 1829
HAWKS, Henry	18	M	Carpenter	U. States	U. States	Jay	18 Apr 1823
HAWKYARD, James	24	M	Weaver	England	U.N. States	Jane	7 Oct 1826
HAWLEY, —, Mrs.	28	F	None	Great Britain	U. States America	Columbia	15 Nov 1826
Abr. M.	34	M	Merchant	Philada.	U. States	New York	3 Oct 1826
Betsey	8	F	None	Great Britain	U. States America	Columbia	15 Nov 1826
C.	22	M	Mechanic	Connecticut	U. States	Clarissa	14 Jul 1821
Charlotte	7	F	None	Great Britain	U. States America	Columbia	15 Nov 1826
H.	35	M	Rope Maker	England	U.S. America	Columbia	31 Jul 1826
Jonas	3	M	None	Great Britain	U. States America	Columbia	15 Nov 1826
M.	9	F	None	Great Britain	U. States America	Columbia	15 Nov 1826
Phoebe	2	F	None	Great Britain	U. States America	Columbia	15 Nov 1826
Thos.	5	M	None	Great Britain	U. States America	Columbia	15 Nov 1826
HAWORTH, Betty	30	F		England	U. States	Emulous	22 Aug 1828
Conad	4	M		England	U. States	Emulous	22 Aug 1828
Donnial	24	M	Wool ...mer		New York	Governor Clinton	3 Jul 1827
Elisabeth	6	F		England	U. States	Emulous	22 Aug 1828
Elizabeth	3	F	None	Great Britain	United States	Penelope	11 Jun 1827
Henry	1	M		England	U. States	Emulous	22 Aug 1828
James	3	M		England	U. States	Emulous	22 Aug 1828
James	25	M	Weaver	Great Britain	United States	Penelope	11 Jun 1827
John	1	M	None	Great Britain	United States	Penelope	11 Jun 1827
John	40	M	Merchant	Great Britain	U. States	Ganges	21 Jun 1827
Precilla	24	F	None	Great Britain	United States	Penelope	11 Jun 1827
HAWRIGHT, Mary	16	F				Eliza Grant	6 Oct 1828
HAWS, Jas.	7	M		Wales South	U. States	Oglethorpe	8 Jul 1824
HAWSON, Benjamin	19	F	Joiner	England		Aurora	12 Mar 1827
Francis	25	M	Labourer	Ireland	United States	Lord Wellington	28 May 1827
HAWSWELL, John	21	M	Farmer	Great Britain	United States	Zodiac	29 Oct 1822
John	40	M	Farmer	Great Britain	United States	Zodiac	29 Oct 1822
Mary	52	F	Farmer	Great Britain	United States	Zodiac	29 Oct 1822
Sarah		F	Farmer	Great Britain	United States	Zodiac	29 Oct 1822
HAWTHORN, Ann	30	F	Lady	England	Canada	Phoenix	29 Apr 1826
David	17		None	...	...	James Cropper	28 Jun 1824
Hugh	31		Machine maker	Scotland	United States	Camillus	3 May 1828
Jane	21 6/12	F		Ireland	U. States	Fabius	22 Sep 1828
John M.	24	M	Merchant	Philadelphia	America	Hannibal	4 Oct 1822
John M.	27	M	Merchant	United States	United States	Herald	29 Oct 1825
Nancy	34		Spinster	Scotland	United States	Camillus	3 May 1828
R.	16	M		G. Britain	U. States	William Thompson	30 Apr 1822
R. H.	22	M	Merchant	America	U. States	Meteor	4 Oct 1827
Robt.	13 7/12	M		Ireland	U. States	Fabius	22 Sep 1828
Robt.	33	M	Gentleman	England	Canada	Phoenix	29 Apr 1826
William	17	M	Farmer	Ireland	Ohio	Atlantic	8 May 1828
William W.	23	M	Physician	America	America	Wilson	16 May 1825
HAWYER, Anna M.	30	F		Switzerland	U. States	Romulus	24 Sep 1828
Charles	60	M	Shoe Maker	Switzerland	U. States	Romulus	24 Sep 1828
H. John	14/12	M		Switzerland	U. States	Romulus	24 Sep 1828
Margt.	3	F		Switzerland	U. States	Romulus	24 Sep 1828
Mary	6	F		Switzerland	U. States	Romulus	24 Sep 1828
S.	14/12	M		Switzerland	U. States	Romulus	24 Sep 1828
HAWYON, Bartholomew	57	M	Comedian	Ireland	United States	Belleville	13 Oct 1827
HAXTON, John	23	M	Horse Doctor	Scotland	United States	Culloden	17 May 1828
HAY, Adam	8	M		France	U. States	Edward Bonaffe	23 Jul 1828
Ain	50	F	Stranger	Scotland	U. States	Roger Stewart	9 Jun 1828
Alexander	21	M	Printer	Ireland	New York	Lima	5 Aug 1829
Alfred	11	M		France	U. States	Edward Bonaffe	23 Jul 1828
Ann	28	F	None	England	United States	Trident	18 Jul 1827
Ann	44	F		Great Britain	United States	Ann	24 Sep 1822
Charles	18	M	Farmer	G. Britain	U. States	George Clinton	10 Sep 1828
Christian	14	F	None	Scotland	United States	Camillus	28 Apr 1824
Christian	53	F	None	Scotland	United States	Camillus	28 Apr 1824
Folden	43	F	Water	France	U. States	Edward Bonaffe	23 Jul 1828
Henry	15	M	None	Scotland	United States	Camillus	28 Apr 1824
Hiram	26	M	Farmer	Great Britain	United States	William Dawson	18 Jun 1827

NAMES OF PASSENGERS	AGE	SEX	OCCUPATIONS	COUNTRY TO WHICH THEY BELONG	COUNTRY THEY INTEND TO INHABIT	SHIPS/DATES OF ARRIVAL	
HAY (cont'd)							
Isablla	11	F		Scotland	U. States	Roger Stewart	9 Jun 1828
James	8	M		U. States	U. States	Nancy	19 Oct 1821
James	8	M	Child	U. States	U. States	St. Michael	26 Oct 1824
James	44	M		Ireland	U. States	Fame	15 Nov 1826
James, Junr.	29 8/12	M	Merchant	N. York	U. States	Charlotte Corday	15 Aug 1820
Jane	14	F	None	Scotland	United States	Camillus	28 Apr 1824
John	24	M	Farmer	Great Britain	New York	Intrepid	8 Aug 1822
John	24	M	Farmer	Gt. Britain	U. States	Atlantic	17 May 1828
John	28	M	Mason	Great Britain	United States	Colossus	5 Jun 1827
Margaret	13	F		France	U. States	Edward Bonaffe	23 Jul 1828
Mary	18	F		France	U. States	Edward Bonaffe	23 Jul 1828
Mary	20	F	None	Great Britain	United States	William Dawson	18 Jun 1827
Mary	39	F		France	U. States	Edward Bonaffe	23 Jul 1828
Nancy	32	F	Wife	Ireland	New York	Louisa	20 Jul 1826
Pat.	24	M	Ropemaker	Great Britain	New York	Dublin	21 Dec 1824
Rebecca	26	F	Lady	U. States	U. States	Nancy	19 Oct 1821
Richard	24	M	Gentleman	Great Britain	Great Britain	Ann	24 Sep 1822
Richard	24 11/12	M	Gentleman	United St. Ama.	Utica, N.Y.	Chelsea	16 May 1828
Robert	25	M	Farmer	Scotland	United States	Minerva	29 Oct 1822
Robert	38	M	Labourer	Ireland	New York	Louisa	20 Jul 1826
Robt.	19	M	Baker	Scotland	U. States	Roger Stewart	9 Jun 1828
Saml.	23	M	Merchant	Great Britain	Great Britain	Columbia	15 Nov 1826
Samuel	30	M	Merchant	England		Athenian	3 Sep 1827
Thomas	17					William	17 Aug 1820
Thomas	27	M	Merchant	St. John, N.B.	St. John, N.B.	Ann Maria	1 Apr 1826
Thomas	60	M	Farmer	England	United States	Trident	18 Jul 1827
W.	39	M	Farmer	Gt. Britain	U. States	Superior	20 Aug 1825
William	25	M	Baker	St. John	U. States	Nancy	16 Aug 1822
Willian	20	M	Labourer	Ireland	N. York	Trusty	12 Sep 1818
Wm.	46	M		Scotland	U. States	Roger Stewart	9 Jun 1828
HAYARD, Eliza	20	F		G. Brittain	U. States	Hope & Esther	26 Nov 1822
HAYBURN, John	22	M	...	G. Britain	U. States	New England	28 Sep 1824
Mary	19	F	...	G. Britain	U. States	New England	28 Sep 1824
HAYCOCK, Hamilton	21	M	Laborer	Ireland	United States	Sylvester Healy	14 Jun 1825
HAYCOK, Henry	20	M		Great Britain	United States	James Monroe	25 Apr 1822
HAYDEN, —, Mrs.	30			U.S.	U.S.	Pacific	24 May 1824
Anson	40	M	Merchant	U. States	U. States	Canada	8 Jun 1826
Ar., Mr.	36		Merchant	U.S.	U.S.	Pacific	24 May 1824
Edwd.	17	M	Merchant	Ireland	United States	Pallas	28 Oct 1828
Eli	72	M	Merchant	U. States	U. States	Comet	10 Mar 1825
Henry	21	M	Farmer	England	U. States	Auritz	20 May 1823
J. C.	24	M	Docter	U.S.		Don Quixote	3 Jan 1826
James	28	M	Merchant	Greorgier	United States	Siroc	31 Oct 1829
Laurence	28	M	Labourer	Ireland	Boston	General Marion	12 Jan 1829
Lawce.	32	M	Merchant	Ireland	United States	Pallas	28 Oct 1828
Thoms	56	M	Toy Maker	England	U. States	Montgomery	18 Oct 1828
Wm. A.	23	M	Merchant	U. States	U. States	Marmion	30 Apr 1828
HAYDOCK, Henry	35 1/12	M	Weaver	Ireland	New York	Louisa	20 Jul 1826
Margaret	28	F	Wife	Ireland	New York	Louisa	20 Jul 1826
HAYEN, Robt.	23	M	Merchant	Ireland	U. States	Pacific	16 Apr 1825
HAYER, Jacob	26	M	Weaver	Germany	United States	Ohio	10 Jul 1820
HAYES, —, Infant						Trio	5 May 1828
—, Infant						Trio	5 May 1828
—, Mr.	35	M	Clerical	Ireland	U. States	Elias Burger	11 Jul 1822
And.	4	M	Family	Ireland	United States	Loire	26 May 1828
Ann	20	F	Labourer	Ireland	United States	Meteor	26 Jun 1827
B. M.	25	M	Physician	U. States	U. States	New Packet	20 Sep 1826
Bridget	17	F	Spinster	Ireland	America	William	21 May 1825
Charles	23	M	Merchant	England	Great Britain	James Barron	26 Jun 1823
David	1/2	M	Labourer	Ireland	United States	Meteor	26 Jun 1827
David	17	M	Shoe Maker	Ireland	United States	Josephine	30 Apr 1828
Denis	20					Trio	5 May 1828
Edmond	8	M	Family	Ireland	United States	Loire	26 May 1828

NAMES OF PASSENGERS	AGE	SEX	OCCUPATIONS	COUNTRY TO WHICH THEY BELONG	COUNTRY THEY INTEND TO INHABIT	SHIPS/DATES OF ARRIVAL	
HAYES (cont'd)							
Fredk.	20	F	Labourer	Ireland	United States	Meteor	26 Jun 1827
H. M.	35	M	Merchant	United States	United States	William Byrnes	6 Apr 1826
Hy.	12	M	Weaver	England	U. States	Panthea	8 Apr 1826
James	24	M	Stonemason	Ireland	New York	Louisa	20 Jul 1826
James	49	M	Merchant	England	America	Silas Richard	24 Oct 1829
Jas.	6	M	Family	Ireland	United States	Loire	26 May 1828
John	27	M	Sawyer	Ireland	United States	Diana	1 May 1826
John W.	26	M	Meriner	England	England	Samaritan	30 May 1828
Jonathan	27	M				Eliza Grant	6 Oct 1828
Margaret	35	F	Family	Ireland	United States	Loire	26 May 1828
Mary	18	F		G. Britain	U. States	London	23 Sep 1828
Norry	16	F		Ireland	America	Liverpool	31 Aug 1827
Patk.	24		Labourer	Ireland	United States	Geo. Canning	5 Jun 1828
Patrick	24	M	Labourer	Ireland	United States	Trio	2 Oct 1828
Patrick	28	M	Baker	Ireland	United States	Combine	4 Jun 1825
Patrick	45	M	Taylor	Ireland	United States	Jubilee	13 Sep 1827
Patrick	54	M	Mariner	Philada.	U. States	Fly	9 Apr 1823
Robt.	22	M	Farmer	Ireland	United States	Gem	16 Jun 1824
Thomas	23	M	Shoemaker	Ireland	New York	Louisa	20 Jul 1826
Thomas	23	M	Farmer	Great Britian	United States	Andes	19 Aug 1829
Thos.	12	M	Family	Ireland	United States	Loire	26 May 1828
Wm.	20	M	Millworker	Great Britain	United States	William Dawson	18 Jun 1827
HAYLAND, Fras.	22	M	Merchant	England	America	Albion	4 Oct 1820
Fras.	26	F		England	America	Albion	4 Oct 1820
HAYLEY, Patrick	25 6/12	M	Labourer	England	United States	John Wells	22 May 1826
HAYMAN, Heinr.	51	M	Agriculture	Bavaria	United States	Henri IV	14 Oct 1829
HAYNE, David	22	M	Black Smith	Ireland	Canada	Pilgrim	1 Sep 1828
HAYNES, Andrew	23	M	Stationer	Great Britian	U. States	Henry Kneedland	7 Aug 1826
Ann	14	F				Belfast	28 Sep 1820
Ann	38	F		England	U. States	Cincinnatus	24 May 1821
David	3	M		England	America	Britannia	22 Jul 1829
Edward	43	M	Mechanic	U. States	U. States	Robt. Reade	12 Apr 1825
Edwd.	22	M	...	...	...	Antioch	8 Oct 1827
Elizabeth	24	F		England	United States	America	25 Dec 1827
Elizabeth B.	47	F	None	England	U. States	New York	11 Jul 1823
Emma	7	F		England	America	Britannia	22 Jul 1829
Hohton	23	M	Painter	Great Britain	United States	Ganges	26 Oct 1826
John	5	M		England	America	Britannia	22 Jul 1829
John	31	M	Planter	Great Britain	Great Britain	Fontine	4 Oct 1824
John	36	M	Chymist	England	U. States	Cincinnatus	24 May 1821
John	41	M	Druggist	Gt. Britain		Corinthian	27 Oct 1829
Martha Q.	14	F	None	England	U. States	New York	11 Jul 1823
Mary	47	F		England	United States	Earl of Liverpool	29 Sep 1823
Penelope	32	F		England	America	Britannia	22 Jul 1829
Robt. J.	16	M	None	England	U. States	New York	11 Jul 1823
Robt. J.	54	M	Planter	England	U. States	New York	11 Jul 1823
Thomas	25	M	Candle Maker	England	United States	America	25 Dec 1827
Thos.	12	M	None	England	U. States	New York	11 Jul 1823
Thos.	29	M	Servant	England	U. States	New York	11 Jul 1823
HAYOCK, Wm.	26	M	Gent.	England	U.S. America	Columbia	31 Jul 1826
HAYS, Ann	19		Spinster	Ireland	United States	Mexico	1 Jun 1821
Anna Maria	27	F	None			James Monroe	8 Aug 1820
Charles	35	M	Merchant	Ireland	Ireland	James Monroe	8 Aug 1820
Geo.	55	M	Shoemaker	England	U. States	Panthea	8 Apr 1826
H.	14			Cork	Philadelphia	Schuylkill	22 Aug 1825
Henry	33	M	Weaver	Great Brittain		Corinthian	9 Jan 1827
James	22	M	Ropemaker	Ireland	United States	Nancy Henrietta	3 Nov 1828
Jane	20		Spinster	Ireland	United States	Mexico	1 Jun 1821
John	12			Cork	Philadelphia	Schuylkill	22 Aug 1825
John	23	M	Labourer	England	U. States	Ayrshire	12 May 1828
John	27	M	Farmer	Ireland		Cuba	24 Jun 1822
John	34	M	Carpenter	Gt. Britain	U. States	Lima	22 Sep 1828
Mary	35	F	Weaver	Great Brittain		Corinthian	9 Jan 1827
Patrick	20		Farmer	Cork	Philadelphia	Schuylkill	22 Aug 1825
Ricd.	25 6/12	M	Mechanic	England	United States	John Wells	22 May 1826

555

NAMES OF PASSENGERS	AGE	SEX	OCCUPATIONS	COUNTRY TO WHICH THEY BELONG	COUNTRY THEY INTEND TO INHABIT	SHIPS/DATES OF ARRIVAL	
HAYS (cont'd)							
Robert	23	M	Merchant	Great Britan	Great Britan	Columbia	10 Mar 1824
Wm.	25	M				Eliza Grant	6 Oct 1828
HAYSE, John	27	M	Labourer	Ireland	United States	Jubilee	13 Jul 1829
Margaret	30	F	None	Ireland	United States	Jubilee	13 Jul 1829
HAYTHESON, Jonas	36	...	...	...	United States	Criterion	27 Jun 1827
HAYTHORN, Elizabeth	41	...	...	...	United States	Criterion	27 Jun 1827
HAYTON, James	49	M	Rope Maker	U. States	U. States	Abigail	26 Sep 1820
HAYVOY, Bridget	4	F		Ireland	Ut. States	Courier	13 Jul 1826
Bridget	28	F	Farmer	Ireland	Ut. States	Courier	13 Jul 1826
James	35	M	Farmer	Ireland	Ut. States	Courier	13 Jul 1826
John	22	M		Ireland	Ut. States	Courier	13 Jul 1826
Margt.	6/12	F		Ireland	Ut. States	Courier	13 Jul 1826
Mary	3	F		Ireland	Ut. States	Courier	13 Jul 1826
HAYWARD, Anthony	13	M	None	Gt. Britain	United States	Neptune	24 May 1824
Charles	18	M	Labourer	England	U. States	Comet	23 Aug 1828
Charlotte	5	F	Labourer	England	U. States	Comet	23 Aug 1828
Elisabeth	32	F		Bristol, Engl.	...	Warrior	19 May 1828
Elizabeth	12	F	Labourer	England	U. States	Comet	23 Aug 1828
Joshua H.	26	M	Physician	Boston	U.S.	Cadmus	17 Aug 1824
Levi F.	30	M	Merchant	Massachusetts	Boston	Curlew	3 Nov 1823
Leweyan	18	M	Labourer	England	U. States	Comet	23 Aug 1828
Mark	7	M	Labourer	England	U. States	Comet	23 Aug 1828
Mary	69	F	Labourer	England	U. States	Comet	23 Aug 1828
Mary Ann	10	F		G. Braitan	U. States	Cosmo	29 Jun 1826
Sarah	31	F		G. Braitan	U. States	Cosmo	29 Jun 1826
Thomas	31	M	Farmer	Bristol, Engl.	...	Warrior	19 May 1828
Wm.	10	M	Labourer	England	U. States	Comet	23 Aug 1828
Wm.	29	M	Gentleman	G. Braitan	U. States	Cosmo	29 Jun 1826
Wm.	30	M	Schoolmaster	England	U. States	Amulet	9 Jan 1829
Wm.	49	M	Labourer	England	U. States	Comet	23 Aug 1828
HAYWOOD, A.	28	M	Gentleman	England	United States	Earl of Liverpool	28 Apr 1824
Buxom	23	M	Blacksmith	Great Britain	United States	Samuel Wright	12 Oct 1829
Eliz., Miss	20		Spinster	England	United States	Acasta	16 Aug 1826
J., Mr.	20	M		U. States	U.S.	Henri IV	14 Sep 1827
John	25	M		Great Britain	Canada	James Monroe	25 Apr 1822
Peter	58		Farmer	England	United States	Hugh Johnson	11 Jun 1828
Thos.	13			England	United States	Hugh Johnson	11 Jun 1828
Thos.	47		Baker	Great Britain	United States	Roman	10 Sep 1827
Wm.	27	M	Trader	Great Britain	U. States	Birmingham	12 Oct 1829
Mary	22	F		England	United States	Acasta	25 Sep 1827
HAZARD, D.	34	M	Mariner	U. States		Star	7 Jan 1827
Samuel	29 4/12	M	Merchant	United States	United States	Hector	8 Jan 1820
HAZELDEN, William	49	M	Shoemaker	England	United States	Delta	24 Oct 1829
HAZELLWOOD,							
William	24			England	United States	Thomas Dickason	5 Jun 1827
HAZELTON, Abraham	40	M	Tanner	Ireland	America	Hesperus	7 Jul 1820
John	4	M	None	Ireland	America	Hesperus	7 Jul 1820
Sarah	35	F	Spinner	Ireland	America	Hesperus	7 Jul 1820
Thomas	2	M	None	Ireland	America	Hesperus	7 Jul 1820
HAZER, Georges	22	M	Farmer	Germany	United States	Oxford	14 Aug 1828
HAZLET, Jas.	40	M	Button maker	Germany	U. States	Spartan	16 Feb 1825
HAZLETON, —	60		Widow	Ireland	United States	Robert Burns	18 Jun 1821
Abraham, Jn.	9	M	None	Ireland	America	Hesperus	7 Jul 1820
Edwd.	33	M	Weaver	Ireland	United States	Alex. Mansfield	17 May 1823
Richd.	10	M	None	Ireland	America	Hesperus	7 Jul 1820
Wm.	7	M	None	Ireland	America	Hesperus	7 Jul 1820
HAZLEY, William	56	M	Weaver	United States	Pensylvania	Rambler	31 Aug 1829
HEA...SEUR, Mary Ann	3	F		Great Britian	United States	Robert Quayle	29 Jul 1822
HEAD, Ann	9	F		Great Britan	United States	Clematis	8 May 1827
Elizabeth	1	F		Great Britian	United States	Robert Quayle	29 Jul 1822
George	2	M	Farmer	Great Britan	United States	Clematis	8 May 1827
George	35	M	Sk...	Great Britian	United States	Robert Quayle	29 Jul 1822
Jane	4	F		Great Britian	United States	Robert Quayle	29 Jul 1822
Mary	33	F	Farmer	Great Britan	United States	Clematis	8 May 1827
Ruth	5	F	Farmer	Great Britan	United States	Clematis	8 May 1827
Sarah	32	F		Great Britian	United States	Robert Quayle	29 Jul 1822

NAMES OF PASSENGERS	AGE	SEX	OCCUPATIONS	COUNTRY TO WHICH THEY BELONG	COUNTRY THEY INTEND TO INHABIT	SHIPS/DATES OF ARRIVAL	
HEADFIELD, Robt.	17 9/12		Accointtant	England	U. States	France	26 Jun 1828
HEADLEY, Charlotte	10	F	None	England	America	Cincinnatus	19 Oct 1826
Henry	2	M	None	England	America	Cincinnatus	19 Oct 1826
John	41	F	None	England	America	Cincinnatus	19 Oct 1826
HEAF, James	23	M	Weaver	England	U. States	Severn	12 Oct 1826
HEAGH, John	27	M	Joiner	Keeghley	Yorkshire	Howard Douglass	11 May 1827
Joseph	29	M	Joiner	Keeghley	Yorkshire	Howard Douglass	11 May 1827
HEALD, Jno.	20	M	Brick Maker	England	U. States	Thomas Ritchie	2 Jul 1827
HEALEY, Barthw.	...	M	Labourer	Ireland	Unt. St. America	Wilson	21 May 1827
Margaret	12	F	Child	Ireland	United States	Dublin Packet	23 May 1828
Mary	50	F	Wife	Ireland	United States	Dublin Packet	23 May 1828
Samuel	30	M	Weaver	England	United States	Trident	30 Sep 1826
HEALLEY, Ben.	17	M	Laborer	Ireland	U. States	Howard Douglass	29 Jan 1828
HEALLY, Edd.	25	M	Laborer	Ireland	U. States	Howard Douglass	29 Jan 1828
Pat	19	M	Labourer	Great Britain		Moro Castle	6 Jul 1827
HEALY, Alice	41	F		G. Britain		Caravan	8 Sep 1828
Anchen	17	F		G. Britain		Caravan	8 Sep 1828
Ann	...	F	Spinster	Ireland	Unt. St. America	Wilson	21 May 1827
Ann	26	F		Ireland	U. States	Virginia	20 Jun 1825
Anne	9	F		Sligo	New York	Susquehana	27 Jun 1823
Anne	2_ 6/12	F	Child	Ireland	America	Weser	26 Jun 1821
Ber...	26	F	Spinster	Ireland	Unt. St. America	Wilson	21 May 1827
Bridget	22	F	Farmer	Ireland	U. States	Virginia	20 Jun 1825
Catharine	44	F	Spinster	Ireland	United States	Helen	27 Jun 1821
Catherine	40	F	Gousekeeper	Sligo	New York	Susquehana	27 Jun 1823
Davett	20	F		G. Britain		Caravan	8 Sep 1828
David	40	M	Millwright	G. Britain		Caravan	8 Sep 1828
Edmund	23	M	Farmer	Great Britain	United States	Eliza Barker	3 Jul 1826
Edward	74	M	Boy	Ireland	United States	Dublin Packet	23 May 1828
Elinor	14	F	Spinster	Ireland	United States	Helen	27 Jun 1821
Harriet	9	F		G. Britain		Caravan	8 Sep 1828
Henry	11	M		G. Britain		Caravan	8 Sep 1828
James	4	M		Sligo	New York	Susquehana	27 Jun 1823
James	7	M	Spinster	Ireland	United States	Helen	27 Jun 1821
James	23		Farmer	Kerry	New York	Schuylkill	22 Aug 1825
John	12	M	Taylor	Ireland	U. States	Virginia	20 Jun 1825
John	50	M	Labourer	Ireland	U. States	Courier	17 Mar 1828
Joseph	7	F		G. Britain		Caravan	8 Sep 1828
Margert	14	F	Servant	Ireland	America	Weser	26 Jun 1821
Martin	25	M	Taylor	Ireland	U. States	Virginia	20 Jun 1825
Mary	6	F		Ireland	U. States	Virginia	20 Jun 1825
Mary	7	F		Sligo	New York	Susquehana	27 Jun 1823
Mary	13	M	Servant	Sligo	New York	Susquehana	27 Jun 1823
Mary	25	F		Ireland	U. States	Virginia	20 Jun 1825
Nicholas	36	M	Farmer	Ireland	America	Josephine	24 Jul 1826
Owen	15	M	Labourer	Sligo	New York	Susquehana	27 Jun 1823
Patrick	9	M		Ireland	U. States	Virginia	20 Jun 1825
Peter	25	M	Labourer	Ireland	Unt. St. America	Wilson	21 May 1827
Sarah	18	F		Ireland	America	Plutarch	18 Jul 1826
Thomas	22	M	Weaver	Ireland	U.S.	Lady Hunter	10 Jul 1826
HEAM, Sarah	53	F		England	America	Cincinnatus	22 May 1826
HEANEY, Pat	30			Great Britan	United States	Newry	11 Jul 1827
Patrick	27		Farmer	Great Britan	United States	Newry	11 Jul 1827
HEANNON, Betsey	18	F	Spinster	Ireland	United States	Fabius	31 Jul 1829
Bridget	24	F	Spinster	Ireland	United States	Fabius	31 Jul 1829
HEANSON, Jane	27	F		Irland	U. States	Nancy	27 Jun 1823
HEANY, Grace	30	F		Ireland	United States	Thomas	13 Dec 1827
Hugh	30	M	Labourer	Ireland	U. States	Josephine	30 Aug 1828
Pat	8	M	Labourer	Ireland	United States	Thomas	13 Dec 1827
Pat	30	M	Labourer	Ireland	United States	Thomas	13 Dec 1827
Patrick	25	M	Weaver	Great Britain	United States	Roman	10 May 1828
HEAP, Abraham	36	M	Cordwainer	Manchester	United States	Nile	17 May 1827
Alice	21	F		Great Britain	United States	Mary Howland	19 Jul 1827
Anne	12	F	None	England and Ireland	United States	Jubilee	12 May 1828

NAMES OF PASSENGERS	AGE	SEX	OCCUPATIONS	COUNTRY TO WHICH THEY BELONG	COUNTRY THEY INTEND TO INHABIT	SHIPS/DATES OF ARRIVAL	
HEAP (cont'd)							
Betsey	27	F	Joiner	England	United States	Amelia	20 Aug 1829
Betty	4	F	None	England and Ireland	United States	Jubilee	12 May 1828
Betty	30	F	None	England and Ireland	United States	Jubilee	12 May 1828
George	26	M	Joiner	England	United States	Amelia	20 Aug 1829
Henry	2	M	None	England and Ireland	United States	Jubilee	12 May 1828
James	6	M	None	England and Ireland	United States	Jubilee	12 May 1828
John	1	M		England	United States	Amelia	20 Aug 1829
John	3	M	None	England and Ireland	United States	Jubilee	12 May 1828
John	32	M	Fullinmille	Manchester	United States	Nile	17 May 1827
John	40	M	Builder	Great Britain	United States	Mary Howland	19 Jul 1827
John, Jun.	20	M		Great Britain	United States	Mary Howland	19 Jul 1827
Johnathan	32	M	...	...	...	Frances Henrietta	30 Jun 1827
Joseph	21	M	Shoe Maker	England	America	William Byrnes	22 Dec 1828
Joshua	12	M		U. States	U. States	United States	11 Sep 1828
Laurence	50	M	Weaver & Spinner	U. States	U. States	United States	11 Sep 1828
Mary	50	F		U. States	U. States	United States	11 Sep 1828
William	13	M		Great Britain	United States	Mary Howland	19 Jul 1827
Wm.	16	M		U. States	U. States	United States	11 Sep 1828
HEAPS, Charlotte	22	F				Governor Fenner	23 Jul 1829
John	23	M	Labourer	England	New York	Governor Fenner	23 Jul 1829
HEAR, Hannah	7	F		G. Britain	U. States	Dalhouse Castle	12 Sep 1828
HEARD, Edward	16	M	Clerk	United States	U. States	Baltic	29 Jul 1829
H., Mrs.	23	F	None	Gt. Britain	...	Corks	3 Aug 1824
Nich. T.	40	M	Merch.	N. York	N. York	Wm. Thompson	13 Sep 1823
Wm.	45	M	Merchant	United States	United States	Corks	3 Aug 1824
HEARNE,							
Dorothy H.	30 2/12	F		England	England	Gleaner	6 Jun 1828
John	33 8/12	M	Merchant	England	England	Gleaner	6 Jun 1828
HEARNEY, —, Mrs.	25			G. Britain	America	Magnet	24 Sep 1824
Jno. W.	45	M	Merchant	N. York	N. York	Chase	29 Apr 1824
HEARNS, Hugh	19	M	Farmer	Ireland	U. States	Dickinson	30 Jul 1825
John	12	M	Farmer	Ireland	U. States	Dickinson	30 Jul 1825
HEARNY, —, Mrs.	...	F		...	United States	Rufus King	27 Jun 1821
... M.	1	F		...	United States	Rufus King	27 Jun 1821
Ann	2	F		...	United States	Rufus King	27 Jun 1821
David	4	M		...	United States	Rufus King	27 Jun 1821
Hugh	30	M	Saddler	Ireland	United States	Fabius	4 Jun 1828
John	...	M		...	United States	Rufus King	27 Jun 1821
John	1	M		...	United States	Rufus King	27 Jun 1821
Michael	...	M		...	United States	Rufus King	27 Jun 1821
P. J.	19	M	Merchant	N. York	N. York	Chase	29 Apr 1824
HEARON, Jas.	20		Joiner	Great Britain	United States	Roman	10 Sep 1827
HEARSAY, Wm.	30	M	Mariner	Boston	U. States	Thomas	3 Sep 1822
HEARST, James	28 7/12	M	Mechanic	England	United States	John Wells	22 May 1826
HEART, George	18	M	Student	Gt. Britain	U. States	Sarah G.	14 Apr 1828
Jonas C.	35	M	Merchant	America	America	Britannia	5 Nov 1828
Nichs. T.	30	M	Merchant	U. States	U. States	New York	15 Jul 1825
HEARTLEY, —		M	Chiefly farmers		United States	Factor	8 Jul 1829
Charles	34	M	Farmer	Ireland	United States	Meteor	27 Sep 1826
Eliza		F	Chiefly farmers		United States	Factor	8 Jul 1829
Job		M	Chiefly farmers		United States	Factor	8 Jul 1829
John		M	Chiefly farmers		United States	Factor	8 Jul 1829
Mary		F	Chiefly farmers		United States	Factor	8 Jul 1829
Michae	23	M	Farmer	G. Britain	U.S. America	Cincinnatus	31 Oct 1820
HEATE, Charles	25	M	Weaver	G. Britain	U. States	London	23 Sep 1828
HEATH, —, Caitn.	60	M	Merchant	England	U. States	Venus	4 Oct 1824
—, Miss	20	F		England	U. States	Venus	4 Oct 1824
—, Miss	22	F		England	U. States	Venus	4 Oct 1824
—, Mr.	28	M	Merchant	G. Britain	Canada	Corinthian	29 Apr 1826

NAMES OF PASSENGERS	AGE	SEX	OCCUPATIONS	COUNTRY TO WHICH THEY BELONG	COUNTRY THEY INTEND TO INHABIT	SHIPS/DATES OF ARRIVAL	
HEATH (cont'd)							
John	20	M	Farmer	G.B.	U.S.A.	Silas Richard	30 Jun 1828
Saml. B.	23	M	Mechanic	New York	New York	Panthea	22 Jul 1826
HEATHCATL, John	31	M	Farmer	England	America	Panthia	17 Sep 1821
HEATHEN, Thomas	23	M	Farmer	Ireland	America	Superior	12 Jun 1824
HEATHOCK, Wm.	21	M	Farmer	England	United States	Aurelia	7 Jun 1826
HEATON, Robt.	26	M	Labourer	Great Britain		Moro Castle	6 Jul 1827
Wm.	26	M		England	Ut. States	Courier	13 Jul 1826
HEAVEN, Rcd.	18	M	None	G. Brittain	U. States	Canada	6 Jun 1825
HEAVEN, Thos., Mr.	25	M	Merchant	England	England	Helen	17 Dec 1827
HEBBLEWHITE, Wm.	23	M	Merchant	Gt. Brittain	United States	York	6 Dec 1826
HEBKIRK, J. B.	23	M	Merchant	Savannah	U. States	Hope Return	6 Oct 1824
HEBLER, John	18	M	Cultivator	Brattain		L'Esperance	6 Sep 1828
HECEVER, John	33	M	Mash. Manufectry	America	America	Mary Lord	26 Oct 1829
HECHT, —, Mrs.	30	F		England	America	Britannia	5 Nov 1828
HECKBISHER, Charles A.	22	M	Merchant	Germany	U. States	Florida	2 Jun 1828
HECKENDORF, Robert	26	M	Mercher	U.S.	U.S.	Charleston Allen	15 Nov 1826
HECKET, Mary	22	F	Seamtress	Ireland	United States	Louisa	18 Apr 1827
HECTOR, James	31 4/12	M	Farmer	Scotland	United States	Euphrates	25 Mar 1820
HEDDEN, David	37	M	... Maker	Halifax	New York	Hope & Esther	25 Aug 1827
HEDDERWICK, Alexr.	3	M			U. States	Margaret	3 Jun 1822
James	9	M			U. States	Margaret	3 Jun 1822
Jane	13	F			U. States	Margaret	3 Jun 1822
Jas.	40	M	...		U. States	Margaret	3 Jun 1822
Joanna	31	F			U. States	Margaret	3 Jun 1822
John	11	M			U. States	Margaret	3 Jun 1822
Margaret	6	F			U. States	Margaret	3 Jun 1822
Robt.	15	M			U. States	Margaret	3 Jun 1822
Wm.	1	M			U. States	Margaret	3 Jun 1822
HEDDING, Eli	70	M	Merchant	Boston	U. States	Protector	21 Apr 1823
HEDEIT, Jaques	30	M				Henri IV	17 May 1828
John P.	10	M				Henri IV	17 May 1828
Mary	58	F				Henri IV	17 May 1828
Mary B.	13	F				Henri IV	17 May 1828
Nicolas	20	F				Henri IV	17 May 1828
HEDELIUS, —, Mr.	29	M	Mariner	U. States	U. States	Hope Return	9 Mar 1827
HEDERTON, John	20	M	Labourer	Ireland	United States	Nile	17 May 1827
Patrick	22	M	Labourer	Ireland	United States	Nile	17 May 1827
HEDGE, F. H.	18	M	Merchant	Boston	U. States	Eagle	17 Feb 1823
John	37	M	Farmer	England	United States	William & Henry	19 Jul 1822
HEDGES, Eliza	20	F		Great Britain	U. States	Albert	1 Apr 1822
M., Mr.	45	M	Barber	U. States	U. States	William	25 Sep 1821
HEDGRLEY, Ann	18	F	None	England	New York	Concordia	12 Oct 1826
Mary	11	F	None	England	New York	Concordia	12 Oct 1826
Thomas	19	M	Smith	England	New York	Concordia	12 Oct 1826
Thomas	45	M	Smith	England	New York	Concordia	12 Oct 1826
HEDLAND, Lovysa	12	F	Servant	Sweden	United States	William Howland	10 Nov 1825
HEDLEY, Edwd.	3	M	None	Great Brittain	U. States	Louisa	11 Jun 1824
James	10	M	None	Great Brittain	U. States	Louisa	11 Jun 1824
Rebecca	44	F	None	Great Brittain	U. States	Louisa	11 Jun 1824
Wm.	6	M	None	Great Brittain	U. States	Louisa	11 Jun 1824
HEDLINGWORTH, Benjamin	21	M		Great Britain	United States	Ganges	8 Jul 1820
HEEDER, F. X.	30	M		France	America	Saluda	16 Oct 1824
HEEGER, Benj.	24	M	United States Army	United States	United States	Britannia	29 Oct 1829
HEEHAN, Elenor	18	F	Spinster	Ireland	United States	Wilson	4 Oct 1827
HEELY, Ann	34	F		England	United States	Aurora	9 Jul 1827
James	3	M		England	United States	Aurora	9 Jul 1827
Joseph	34	M	Clothier	England	United States	Aurora	9 Jul 1827
William	8	M		England	United States	Aurora	9 Jul 1827
HEENY, Catherine	15	F	Farmers and Mechanics	Ireland	America	Constitution	1 Oct 1825
Catherine	48	F	Farmers and Mechanics	Ireland	America	Constitution	1 Oct 1825
Ellen	13	F	Farmers and Mechanics	Ireland	America	Constitution	1 Oct 1825

NAMES OF PASSENGERS	AGE	SEX	OCCUPATIONS	COUNTRY TO WHICH THEY BELONG	COUNTRY THEY INTEND TO INHABIT	SHIPS/DATES OF ARRIVAL	
HEENY (cont'd)							
Jno.	10	M	Farmers and Mechanics	Ireland	America	Constitution	1 Oct 1825
Jno.	60	M	Farmers and Mechanics	Ireland	America	Constitution	1 Oct 1825
Patk.	3	M	Farmers and Mechanics	Ireland	America	Constitution	1 Oct 1825
Rose	7	F	Farmers and Mechanics	Ireland	America	Constitution	1 Oct 1825
HEERY, Lawe.	23	M	Farmer	England	U. States	Thomas Ritchie	2 Jul 1827
Mary	19	F	None	England	U. States	Thomas Ritchie	2 Jul 1827
HEESE, Henry	22	M	Labourer	Ireland	U. States	Calais Packet	7 Jul 1828
HEFF, Ann Catherine	20	F	Farmer	France	United States	Crescent	12 Jul 1827
Anthony	52	M	Farmer	France	United States	Crescent	12 Jul 1827
Antony	22	M	Farmer	France	United States	Crescent	12 Jul 1827
Barbery	48	F	Farmer	France	United States	Crescent	12 Jul 1827
Francis	23	M	Farmer	France	United States	Crescent	12 Jul 1827
John Peter	7	M	Farmer	France	United States	Crescent	12 Jul 1827
HEFFARNAN, Helen	27	F	None	England	New York	Brighton	29 Aug 1828
HEFFENSTIEN, Jno. C.	40	M	late in the Army	Great Britain	Canada	James Monroe	5 Apr 1820
HEFFERMAN, Wm.	39	M	Labourer	Ireland	U. States	Albion	11 May 1827
HEFFERN, Andrew	30	M		Ireland	United States	Thompson	12 Sep 1827
HEFFERNAN, Biddy	25	F		Limerick	N. York	Thomas & William	25 May 1827
Bridget	4	F		Ireland	U. States	Albion	11 May 1827
Catherine	9	F	his Child [John]	Ireland	U. States	Albion	9 Aug 1826
Corns.	37	M				Trio	5 May 1828
Frances	22	F		Ireland	U. States	Manhattan	20 Jun 1825
H.	10	F	Labourer	Ireland	U. States	Albion	11 May 1827
Helen, & Infant	26	F	his Wife [John]	Ireland	U. States	Albion	9 Aug 1826
J.	36	M	Labourer	Ireland	U. States	Albion	11 May 1827
Jno.	25	M	Labourer	Limerick	N. York	Thomas & William	25 May 1827
Johanna	6	F		Ireland	U. States	Albion	11 May 1827
John	16	M	Labourer	Ireland	U. States	Albion	11 May 1827
John	34	M	Laborer	Ireland	U. States	Albion	9 Aug 1826
John	50	M	Merchant	United States	United States	Georgetown Packet	6 May 1824
John	52	M	Mercht. & supercargo	U.S.	U.S.	Amazon	22 Jun 1827
M.	8	F	Labourer	Ireland	U. States	Albion	11 May 1827
Margt.	4	F	his Child [John]	Ireland	U. States	Albion	9 Aug 1826
Mary	1	F	None	England	New York	Brighton	29 Aug 1828
Mary	7	F	his Child [John]	Ireland	U. States	Albion	9 Aug 1826
Mary	13	F	Labourer	Ireland	U. States	Albion	11 May 1827
Mary T.	4	F		Ireland	U. States	Manhattan	20 Jun 1825
Michael	27	M	Labourer	Great Britain	United States	Henrietta	19 Oct 1825
Patrick	30	M	Farmer	Ireland	America	William	21 May 1825
William	30	M	Mason	England	New York	Brighton	29 Aug 1828
HEFTE, Mathew	14	M	Merchant	Swiss	U. States	Franklin	6 May 1828
HEFTY, C.	25	M	Tradesman	Switzerland	United States	Acosta	28 Jul 1823
Caspar	28	M	Merchant	Switzerland	United States	Montano	31 May 1824
F.	18	M	Tradesman	Switzerland	United States	Acosta	28 Jul 1823
HEGAN, John	21	M	Labourer	Ireland		Robert Fulton	4 Jun 1828
John	45	M	Scholar	Ireland	United States	Dalhouse Castle	21 Aug 1829
Mat	20	M	Farmer	Ireland	U.S.A.	Dalhouse Castle	21 Aug 1829
Susan	21	F	Farmer	Ireland	U.S.A.	Dalhouse Castle	21 Aug 1829
Thomas	25	M		Ireland	U. States	Nancy	16 Aug 1822
HEGARTY, Noble	14	F	Spinster	Ireland	United States	Trident	16 May 1826
Thos.	25	M	Laborer	Ireland	United States	Trio	13 Jun 1827
HEGEDY, John	20	M	Weaver	Switzerland	U. States	Sully	25 Jun 1828
HEGGIE, Robert	30	M	Weaver	Great Britain	United States	Colossus	5 Jun 1827
HEGUE, George	30	M	Labourer	England	U. States	Ayrshire	12 May 1828
HEHR, Julius	17	M	Merchant	Switzerland	United States	Helen Mar	29 Jun 1827
HEIBRIDGE, Ann	13	F	Farmer	Great Britian	United States	Andes	19 Aug 1829
Elizabeth	15	F	Farmer	Great Britian	United States	Andes	19 Aug 1829
James	45	M	Farmer	Great Britian	United States	Andes	19 Aug 1829
John	8	M	Farmer	Great Britian	United States	Andes	19 Aug 1829
Martha	47	F	Farmer	Great Britian	United States	Andes	19 Aug 1829

NAMES OF PASSENGERS	AGE	SEX	OCCUPATIONS	COUNTRY TO WHICH THEY BELONG	COUNTRY THEY INTEND TO INHABIT	SHIPS/DATES OF ARRIVAL
HEIBRIDGE (cont'd)						
Saml.	10	M	Farmer	Great Britian	United States	Andes 19 Aug 1829
William	19	M	Farmer	Great Britian	United States	Andes 19 Aug 1829
HEIGH, Thos.	35	M	Joiner	Great Britain	United States	William Dawson 18 Jun 1827
HEIGHLEHEY, Ann	50	F			United States	Greyhound 19 Aug 1820
HEIGHT, W.	25	M	Clergyman	England	U. States	Cincinnatus 5 Oct 1824
HEIGHTMAN, Henry	9	M		England	U. States	Josephine 27 Jul 1825
Henry	33	M	Blacksmith	England	U. States	Josephine 27 Jul 1825
Isaac	5	M		England	U. States	Josephine 27 Jul 1825
John	8	M		England	U. States	Josephine 27 Jul 1825
Joseph	7	M		England	U. States	Josephine 27 Jul 1825
Mary	6	F		England	U. States	Josephine 27 Jul 1825
Mary	35	F		England	U. States	Josephine 27 Jul 1825
HEIGUAND, —, Miss	35	F	Lady	St. Croix	on a Visit	Carlo 27 Aug 1829
HEILBANN, Adolphus	30	M	Gentleman	Germany	U. States	Hudson 26 Jan 1825
HEILBORN, A.	30	M	Merchant	Great Britain	Canada	Columbia 7 Sep 1827
HEILER, Charles	18	M	Merchant	U. States	U. States	Tally Ho 22 Mar 1825
Christian	3	F		Switzerland	U. States	Hewes 30 Oct 1829
Christine	26	F	Wife	Switzerland	U. States	Hewes 30 Oct 1829
Johan	32	M	Turner	Switzerland	U. States	Hewes 30 Oct 1829
HEILEY, Mary	...	F	...	...	United States	Hanford 17 Oct 1828
HEILL, Martin	35	M	Labourer	Ireland	America	Wilson 16 May 1825
HEILLER, Benjn.	24	M	Cotton Spinster	Great Britain	United States	Aurora 5 Sep 1826
HEILLNEN, J.	25	M	Merchant	Oldenburg	U. States	Indiana 20 Sep 1828
L.	16	M		Bavaria	U. States	Indiana 20 Sep 1828
L.	26	M	Mechanic	Prussia	U. States	Indiana 20 Sep 1828
HEILLY, Mary	20	F	Spinster	Ireland	United States	Thomas 13 Dec 1827
HEIMMISSEY, Timothy	45	M	Farmer	Great Britain	United States	Frances Henrietta 17 Sep 1827
HEINA, H.	17 6/12	M	Mercht.	Hanover	U. States	Howard 13 Feb 1829
HEINCK, Catherine	9	F	there child [George A. & Salome]	Germany	United States	Helen 5 Sep 1828
George	5	M	there child [George A. & Salome]	Germany	United States	Helen 5 Sep 1828
George A.	33	M	Shoemaker	Germany	United States	Helen 5 Sep 1828
Henry	7	M	there child [George A. & Salome]	Germany	United States	Helen 5 Sep 1828
Louisa	8	F	there child [George A. & Salome]	Germany	United States	Helen 5 Sep 1828
Salome	35	F	his wife [George A.]	Germany	United States	Helen 5 Sep 1828
William	6	M	there child [George A. & Salome]	Germany	United States	Helen 5 Sep 1828
HEINDS, Parvin	41	F		Switzerland	U.S.	C. Amelia 30 Jun 1828
HEINE, Elisa	26 4/12	F	Farmer	Switzerland	United States	France 6 Oct 1828
James	39	M	Farmer	England	United States	Cambria 3 Jul 1829
HEINHALT, Fred.	23	M	Carpenter	Germany	Newyork	Cortes 16 Jul 1827
HEINLAN, Alexander	18	M	Farmer	Ireland	United States	Asia 29 Jul 1829
HEINNAN, Munson	38	M	Mariner	United States	United States	Chili 9 Jan 1829
HEINOLD, A.	8	F		Switzerland	U. States	Romulus 24 Sep 1828
A. (Adam)	40	M	Gun Smith	Switzerland	U. States	Romulus 24 Sep 1828
C.	11	F		Switzerland	U. States	Romulus 24 Sep 1828
G.	8	F		Switzerland	U. States	Romulus 24 Sep 1828
J.	2	M	child of Adam Heinold			Romulus 24 Sep 1828
*Died on the Voyage						
J.	36	F		Switzerland	U. States	Romulus 24 Sep 1828
HEINREICH,						
Michael	20 3/12	M	None	Germany	America	John Dickinson 9 Oct 1828
HEINRICH, Wm.	20	M	...	Great Britain	United States	Atlantic 28 May 1827
HEINTJINSEN, Chas	25	M	Merchant	Germany	Germany	Vorwartz 21 Aug 1822
HEINTZER, Antoine	13	M	Weaver	Switzerland	U. States	La Urania 3 Jul 1828
Barbara	7	F		Switzerland	U. States	La Urania 3 Jul 1828
Cathls.	44	F		Switzerlànd	U. States	La Urania 3 Jul 1828

NAMES OF PASSENGERS	AGE	SEX	OCCUPATIONS	COUNTRY TO WHICH THEY BELONG	COUNTRY THEY INTEND TO INHABIT	SHIPS/DATES OF ARRIVAL	
HEINTZER (cont'd)							
Geo.	3	M		Switzerland	U. States	La Urania	3 Jul 1828
Jacque	10	M		Switzerland	U. States	La Urania	3 Jul 1828
Jean	17	M		Switzerland	U. States	La Urania	3 Jul 1828
Jean	44	M	Labourer	Switzerland	U. States	La Urania	3 Jul 1828
Joseph	8	M		Switzerland	U. States	La Urania	3 Jul 1828
Joseph	15	M	Weaver	Switzerland	U. States	La Urania	3 Jul 1828
M.	5	F		Switzerland	U. States	La Urania	3 Jul 1828
M.	6	F		Switzerland	U. States	La Urania	3 Jul 1828
M.	11	F		Switzerland	U. States	La Urania	3 Jul 1828
Maria	40	F		Switzerland	U. States	La Urania	3 Jul 1828
Martin	4	M		Switzerland	U. States	La Urania	3 Jul 1828
Michl.	9	M		Switzerland	U. States	La Urania	3 Jul 1828
P.	40	M		Switzerland	U. States	La Urania	3 Jul 1828
Piere	2	M		Switzerland	U. States	La Urania	3 Jul 1828
HEIRLDY, Edward	16	M	Labourer	Great Brittan	United States	Hanford	3 Aug 1829
HEISEZER, Andras	72	M		France	United States	New England	29 Aug 1828
HEISSER, Lorentz	27	M	Farmer	France	United States	New England	29 Aug 1828
HEITMAN, Cha...	22	M	Carpenter	Swisse	United States	Deux Ernest	29 Dec 1827
*landed at Lewiston, Delw.							
HEITMANN, Chs.	22 1/2		Charper. [carpenter]	Suisse		Deux Ernest	29 Dec 1827
HEITZ, Eva	45	F	Farmer	Prussia	Ohio	Caesar	24 Aug 1829
L. J.	47	M	Farmer	Prussia	Ohio	Caesar	24 Aug 1829
Peter	3	M	Farmer	Prussia	Ohio	Caesar	24 Aug 1829
Philip	9	M	Farmer	Prussia	Ohio	Caesar	24 Aug 1829
HELAN, J. S.	25	M	Merchant	N. York	U. States	Panther	9 Jul 1825
HELBERT, H.	30	M	Mercht.	England	England	Andreas	20 Aug 1821
HELBLING, Elizabeth	32	F	Farmer	...	Ohio	Frances Henrietta	25 Aug 1825
John	51	M	Farmer	...	Ohio	Frances Henrietta	25 Aug 1825
HELBOUR, Isidor	23	M	Merchant	Canada	U. States	William Thompson	27 May 1824
HELD, Cath.	25	F		Switzerland	U.S.	C. Amelia	30 Jun 1828
HELDEN, John	16	M	Carpenter	Ireland	United States	Aurora	9 Jul 1827
HELDITCH, Richard	57	M	Draper	Great Briton	United States	Orion	18 Jun 1821
HELDWIEN, John C.	25	M	Farmer	Germany	United States	Helen	5 Sep 1828
HELGROVE, Ann	24	F		G. Britain	U. States	London	23 Sep 1828
Ann	32	F		G. Britain	U. States	London	23 Sep 1828
Thomas	20	M		G. Britain	U. States	London	23 Sep 1828
Wm.	28	M	Labourer	G. Britain	U. States	London	23 Sep 1828
HELIE, J.	19	M	Merchant	Hayti	U. States	Jean Baptiste	2 Dec 1826
HELL, J.	23		Farmer	Kerry	Philadelphia	Schuylkill	22 Aug 1825
Mary	24	F	Servant	Ireland	United States	Edwin	27 Oct 1828
HELLASON, Thomas	27	M	Merchant	Great Brittan	U. States	John & Elizabeth	11 Dec 1826
HELLEN, Lewis	40	M	Mariner	U. States	U. States	Ranger	29 Jul 1824
HELLER, Agness	3			England	United States	Hugh Johnson	11 Jun 1828
Eliz.	2			England	United States	Hugh Johnson	11 Jun 1828
Geogianna	32			England	United States	Hugh Johnson	11 Jun 1828
Hugh	20			England	United States	Hugh Johnson	11 Jun 1828
William	3			England	United States	Hugh Johnson	11 Jun 1828
HELLIS, Mary Ann	25	F	Labourer	Great Britian	United States	Sarah	11 Jul 1829
Robert	20	M	Labourer	Great Britian	United States	Sarah	11 Jul 1829
HELLWIG, A.	30	M	Merchant	Germany	United States	Nestor	16 Aug 1824
HELMARTIN, Libby	19	F	Spinster	Ireland	United States	Helen	27 Jun 1821
HELMEN, Jern	49	M	Carpenter	Germany	United States	Virginia	31 May 1828
Mariah	46	F	Carpenter	Germany	United States	Virginia	31 May 1828
Materlean	15	F	Carpenter	Germany	United States	Virginia	31 May 1828
Mitchell	7	M	Carpenter	Germany	United States	Virginia	31 May 1828
HELMER, J.	8	M	Farmer	Switzerland	U. States	Alfred	8 Jul 1828
HELMOTH, Francis	21	M	School Master	England	Ut. States	Courier	13 Jul 1826
HELMSLEY, Mary	6/12	M		England		Edward Quesnel	17 Nov 1828
HELMUT, Lewis	25 7/12	M		England	U.S. America	Edward Bonnaffe	20 Jun 1826
HELRACY, William	32	M	U.S. Consul at Guayama	United States	United States	St. Anna	16 Aug 1828
HELTER, Barb...	14	F	None	Switzerland	U. States	Sully	25 Jun 1828
David	16	M	None	Switzerland	U. States	Sully	25 Jun 1828

NAMES OF PASSENGERS	AGE	SEX	OCCUPATIONS	COUNTRY TO WHICH THEY BELONG	COUNTRY THEY INTEND TO INHABIT	SHIPS/DATES OF ARRIVAL	
HELTER (cont'd)							
John	46	M	Farmer	Switzerland	U. States	Sully	25 Jun 1828
John, Jr.	11	M	None	Switzerland	U. States	Sully	25 Jun 1828
Mary	9	F	None	Switzerland	U. States	Sully	25 Jun 1828
Medelina	40	F	None	Switzerland	U. States	Sully	25 Jun 1828
Peter	7	M	None	Switzerland	U. States	Sully	25 Jun 1828
Vanesa	15	F	None	Switzerland	U. States	Sully	25 Jun 1828
HELVER, Cathr.	10 3/12	F	Farmer	France	United States	Catharine	10 Sep 1827
Jacob	6 3/12	M	Farmer	France	United States	Catharine	10 Sep 1827
Lewis	40 3/12	M	Farmer	France	United States	Catharine	10 Sep 1827
Mary	37 4/12	F	Farmer	France	United States	Catharine	10 Sep 1827
HELVESTON, Jno.	23	M	Carpenter	U. States	U. States	Gipsey	5 Sep 1823
HELVITIA, Francis	56	M	Merchant	U. States	U. States	Packet	11 Dec 1820
HELZ, Ann M.	19	F		Switzerland	United States	Aurora	21 Jun 1824
Rudolph	20	M	Saddler	Switzerland	United States	Aurora	21 Jun 1824
HELZEL, Frances	1	F		France	U. States	Edward Quesnel	4 Aug 1828
Fras. Josh.	5	F		France	U. States	Edward Quesnel	4 Aug 1828
Magdalina	7	F	Weaver	France	U. States	Edward Quesnel	4 Aug 1828
Mary Ann	3	F		France	U. States	Edward Quesnel	4 Aug 1828
HEMANDER, N.	21	M	Merchant	Island Cuba	U. States	Havana Packet	27 Jul 1827
HEMEZLING, Dominick	33	M		France	United States	New England	29 Aug 1828
HEMING, J.	24	M	Wheelwright	France	U. States	Great Britain	6 Sep 1828
William	34	M	Merchant	Canada	U. States	William & Nancy	31 Jan 1823
HEMINGWAY (see Way)							
John	45	M	C...thier	Great Britain	United States	Aurora	10 Nov 1827
Thomas	16	M	...	Great Britain	United States	Aurora	10 Nov 1827
HEMLIN, Mathias	33	M	Merchant	Spain	Spain	Swiftsure	6 Dec 1826
HEMMEZLING, Anna	7	F		France	United States	New England	29 Aug 1828
Anna Maria	1	F		France	United States	New England	29 Aug 1828
Catarina	16	F		France	United States	New England	29 Aug 1828
HEMOLTY, Anne	1	F	Child	...	N. York	New Orleans	24 Aug 1827
Bernard	30	M	Carpenter	...	N. York	New Orleans	24 Aug 1827
Cathe.	25	F	Wife	...	N. York	New Orleans	24 Aug 1827
Mary	...	F	Child	...	N. York	New Orleans	24 Aug 1827
Patt.	3	M	Child	...	N. York	New Orleans	24 Aug 1827
HEMPSTED, Benjamin	27	M	Merchant	U. States	U. States	York	13 Aug 1827
HEMSWORTH, James	8	M		Great Brittain	United States	Active	12 Sep 1828
Mary	10	F		Great Brittain	United States	Active	12 Sep 1828
Mary	50	F		Great Brittain	United States	Active	12 Sep 1828
Thomas	50	M	Labourer	Great Brittain	United States	Active	12 Sep 1828
William	12	M		Great Brittain	United States	Active	12 Sep 1828
HEN, Domonich	35			Ireland	Philidelphia	General Marion	21 Nov 1828
Mary	28			Ireland	Philidelphia	General Marion	21 Nov 1828
HENAN, George	22	M	Stone Cutter	Scotland	New York	Hope & Esther	21 Dec 1827
HENARY, Heny	30	F	Spinster	Ireland	U. States	Meteor	19 Jul 1828
HENBERGER, S.	22	M	Clergyman	France		Antioch	18 Aug 1829
HENCHAFT, Hannah	37	F	None		New York	Governor Clinton	3 Jul 1827
HENCHCLIFFE, Luke	38	M	Plaisterer	Great Britain	United States	Robert Fulton	27 Jun 1822
Mary	37	F		Great Britain	United States	Robert Fulton	27 Jun 1822
HENCHON, Jas.	25	M	Farmer	Gt. Brittain	United States	Balaena	21 Aug 1824
Jenny	3	F	None	Gt. Brittain	United States	Balaena	21 Aug 1824
Jenny	24	F	None	Gt. Brittain	United States	Balaena	21 Aug 1824
HENCKER, H.	21	M	Mechanic	Germany	U. States	Condstitution	21 Mar 1825
HENDAGY, Cristopher	22	M	Farmer	Germany	United States	Oxford	14 Aug 1828
HENDALE, James	24	M		England	England	Amity	31 May 1822
HENDARSON, William	53	M	gardner	United States	United States	Mount Vernon	30 Dec 1828
HENDER, Joseph	25		Farmer	France	U. States	Elizabeth	9 Jul 1825
HENDERNERS, Hugh	21	M	Servant	England	U. States	Virginia	3 Dec 1827
HENDERS, Thos.	41	M	Gentleman	St. Croix	United States	Chase	4 Sep 1821
HENDERSON, —, Mrs.	22	F	None	Great Britain	U. States America	Columbia	15 Nov 1826
Alexander	45	M		United States	United States	Samuel Robertson	5 Oct 1827
Alexander	48	M	Merchant	Scotland	U.S. of America	Camillus	16 Apr 1822
Alixr.	28	M	Labourer	Ireland	United States	Fabius	31 Jul 1829
Anabella	30	F	Spinster	Great Britain	United States	Colossus	5 Jun 1827
Ann	30	F		Scotland	United States	Leda	30 Aug 1828
Ann	55	F	Spinster	Ireland	United States	Fabius	31 Jul 1829

NAMES OF PASSENGERS	AGE	SEX	OCCUPATIONS	COUNTRY TO WHICH THEY BELONG	COUNTRY THEY INTEND TO INHABIT	SHIPS/DATES OF ARRIVAL	
HENDERSON (cont'd)							
Ann, Jr.	15	F	Spinster	Ireland	United States	Fabius	31 Jul 1829
Catharine	infant	F		Killiloage	United States	Carolina Ann	11 Jun 1824
Catherine	22	F	Spinster		U. States	Margaret	3 Jun 1822
Catherine	24	F	None	Ireland	United States	Diana	1 May 1826
Catherine	36	F			U. States	Margaret	3 Jun 1822
Christina	40	F		Scotland	United States	Isabella	5 Jul 1826
David	29	M	Mechanic	Great Britain, Ireland	Ohio	Britannia	3 Nov 1827
David	35	M	Farmer			John Dickinson	14 Sep 1820
Denny	14	F	Wife	Ireland	United States	Sylvester Healy	19 Aug 1825
Elisabeth	30	F	Spinster	Ireland	United States	Catharine	22 Jul 1825
Elizabeth	37	F		Scotland	United States	Isabella	5 Jul 1826
Ellen	3	F		Killiloage	United States	Carolina Ann	11 Jun 1824
Ellen	22	F	Lady	Ireland	United States	Sylvester Healy	19 Aug 1825
George	20	M	Labourer	Ireland	United States	Fabius	31 Jul 1829
George	21	M	Mason	Scotland	United States	Culloden	17 May 1828
George	25	M	Clerk	Gt. Britain	United States	Neptune	23 Jan 1826
George H.	24	M	Merchant	Scotland	Scotland	William Byrnes	24 Apr 1827
Hellen	25 8/12	F	Farmer	Scotland	United States	Euphrates	25 Mar 1820
Howd.	32		Mercht.	United States	U. States	New York	30 Oct 1827
Hugh	25	M	Farmer	Scotland	United States	Camillus	28 Apr 1824
Isaac	1	M	Farmer	Ireland	U. States	Champion	26 Jul 1827
Isabella	20	F	Spinster			Commerce	22 Jun 1825
James	2 2/12	M	Farmer	Scotland	United States	Euphrates	25 Mar 1820
James	20	M	Labourer	Ireland	United States	Sylvester Healy	19 Aug 1825
James	20	M	Merchant	England	U. States	William Thompson	17 Dec 1827
James	37	M	Draper	Great Britain	United States	Albion	18 Feb 1823
James	38	M	Labourer	Ireland	United States	Wilson	4 Oct 1827
Jane	22	F			U. States	Margaret	3 Jun 1822
Jane	25	F		Killiloage	United States	Carolina Ann	11 Jun 1824
Jane	25	F	Lady	Ireland	United States	Sylvester Healy	19 Aug 1825
Jane	35	F	Farmer	Ireland	U. States	Champion	26 Jul 1827
Jas.	12	M		Ireland	U. States	Alex Mansfield	1 Jun 1822
Jas.	22	M	Doctor, M.D.	Scotland	Scotland	Yamacraw	10 May 1821
Jeane	26		Seamster	Scotland	United States	Camillus	3 May 1828
John	11	M	Child	Ireland	United States	Marmion	17 Jun 1825
John	20	M	Laborer	St. John	United States	St. Michael	24 Jun 1824
John	27	M	Farmer	Killiloage	United States	Carolina Ann	11 Jun 1824
John	38	M	Merchant		U. States	Margaret	3 Jun 1822
Jonathan	17	M		Novascotia	Newyork	Exertion	9 Oct 1828
Margaret	16	F	Spinster	Ireland	United States	Catharine	22 Jul 1825
Martha	30			England	England	Thames	25 Oct 1821
Mary	9	F	Farmer	Ireland	U. States	Champion	26 Jul 1827
Mary	18	F	Spinster	Ireland	United States	Trident	17 May 1825
Mary	22	F	Spinster	Scotland	United States	Tom	2 Jul 1827
Mary Ann	45	F	Lady	Ireland	United States	Sylvester Healy	19 Aug 1825
Mgt.	14/12	F	Labourer	St. Halter, Scotland	Gt. Britain	Orozimbo	19 Oct 1822
Mgt.	22	F	Labourer	St. Halter, Scotland	Gt. Britain	Orozimbo	19 Oct 1822
Peter	71	M	Gentleman	Gt. Brittain	United States	Leeds	19 May 1823
Ralph	21	M	Servant	Ireland	United States	William & George	14 May 1828
Rebecca	11	F	Farmer	Ireland	U. States	Champion	26 Jul 1827
Richard	28	M	Merchant	Hayti	Hayti	Artibonite	3 Jul 1826
Richard	44	M	Labourer	England	U. States	Pleiades	9 Oct 1829
Robert	6/12	M	Farmer	Scotland	United States	Euphrates	25 Mar 1820
Robt.	18		Farmer	Great Britain	United States	Camillus	12 Sep 1827
Stephen	24	M	Farmer	Ireland	United States	Asia	29 Jul 1829
Thomas	13	M	Boy	Ireland	United States	Fabius	31 Jul 1829
Thomas	22	M	Labourer	Ireland	United States	Catharine	22 Jul 1825
Thomas	22	M	Accountant	Great Britain	United States	Bolivar	21 May 1827
Thomas	30	M	Taylor	Scotland	United States	Leda	30 Aug 1828
Thomas	30 8/12	M	Farmer	Scotland	United States	Euphrates	25 Mar 1820
William	21	M		Scotland	United States	Camillus	9 May 1827
William	50	M		Killiloage	United States	Carolina Ann	11 Jun 1824
William	51	M	Labourer	Ireland	United States	Fabius	31 Jul 1829

NAMES OF PASSENGERS	AGE	SEX	OCCUPATIONS	COUNTRY TO WHICH THEY BELONG	COUNTRY THEY INTEND TO INHABIT	SHIPS/DATES OF ARRIVAL	
HENDERSON (cont'd)							
William	70	M		Killiloage	United States	Carolina Ann	11 Jun 1824
Wm.	5	M	Lawyer	Scotland	U. States	Fortune	28 Jul 1825
Wm.	29	M		G. Britain	U. States	Robt. Edwards	4 Sep 1828
HENDLE, Christian	21	M	Baker	Switzerland	U. States	Hewes	30 Oct 1829
James	25	M	shoemaker	England	United States	Hudson	17 Mar 1828
HENDLING, Jack	62	M		France	United States	Henri IV	2 Oct 1828
Mary	68	F		France	United States	Henri IV	2 Oct 1828
HENDLY, Ralph	25	M				Lady of the Lake	23 Aug 1828
*left ship							
HENDREW, Joseph	29	M	Merchant	Havannah	U. States	Eliza	20 Aug 1827
HENDRICK, Benjamin	24	M	Labourer	Germany	Newyork	Cortes	16 Jul 1827
Christian	32	M	Farmer	Switzerland	United States	Elbe	2 Aug 1822
Dennis	30		Mason	Great Britain	United States	Birmingham	15 Jun 1827
Mary	18			Ireland	United States	Robert Burns	30 May 1823
Sarah	29	F		Great Britain	United States	Birmingham	15 Jun 1827
HENDRICKS, Barnard	41	M	Doctor	United States	United States	Seine	21 Oct 1822
H.	42	M	Gentleman	Gt. Britain	England	Paragon	22 Sep 1827
HENDRICKSMENDG, Rob.	50	M	None	Jamaica	U. States	Essex	20 May 1823
HENDRICKSON, Henry	21	M	Farmer	Georgia	United States	Silas Richards	3 Apr 1826
HENDRIKS, Harmon	38		Merchant	England	England	Hudson	14 Jun 1827
Michael	16			Jamaica	England	Hudson	14 Jun 1827
HENDSOM, Bridget	33	F	Spinster	Ireland		Robert Fulton	4 Jun 1828
HENEDEA, Jose	50	M	None	Cuba	Spain	Ariel	30 Jun 1828
HENEERY, John	21	M	Farmer	Ireland	United States	Dublin Packet	22 Aug 1829
HENEGAN, Cathe.	28	F		England	United States	Ganges	10 May 1828
HENEGE, Frederick	24	F	Farmer	Wirtermberg	United States	Olympia	20 Aug 1829
HENERY, Hannah	12	F		Ireland	America	Weser	26 Jun 1821
James	14	M		Ireland	America	Weser	26 Jun 1821
Jane	24	F	Servant	Ireland	America	Weser	26 Jun 1821
Jno.	40	M	Farmer	Ireland	America	Weser	26 Jun 1821
Margret	32	F		Ireland	America	Weser	26 Jun 1821
Robert	40	M	Mechanic	Philadelphia	Phila.	Lady Hunter	22 Aug 1825
HENESEY, Ellen	4	F		England	United States	Ganges	10 May 1828
Mary	6	F		England	United States	Ganges	10 May 1828
Mary	37	F		England	United States	Ganges	10 May 1828
HENESSEY, Wm.	30	M	Farmer	Ireland	New York	Hope & Esther	21 Dec 1827
HENESSY, Norry	18	F		Ireland	United States	Trio	2 Oct 1828
HENESTON, Wm.	39 7/12	M	Merchant	England	Trinidad	Bucksport	9 Jul 1828
HENESY, James	34	M	Clerk	Ireland	United States	Erin	25 Dec 1820
HENETT, Lydia	4	F	Farmer	Scotland	U. States	Orozimbo	7 Jul 1825
Mary	24	F	Farmer	Scotland	U. States	Orozimbo	7 Jul 1825
P.	28	M	Farmer	Scotland	U. States	Orozimbo	7 Jul 1825
HENEY, Catherine	5	F	Child	Switzerland	United States	Andes	5 May 1828
Elizabeth	27	F	Spinster	Switzerland	United States	Andes	5 May 1828
Frederick	3	M	child	Switzerland	United States	Andes	5 May 1828
Jacob	1	M	Child	Switzerland	United States	Andes	5 May 1828
John	35	M	Farmer	Switzerland	United States	Andes	5 May 1828
HENG, E.	26	M		G. Britain	U. States	Canada	19 Sep 1828
HENGIRY, Ann	35	F	Wife	Wittenburg	U. States	Comet	28 Jul 1825
Henry	32	M	None	Wittenburg	U. States	Comet	28 Jul 1825
Jacob	7	M	Son	Wittenburg	U. States	Comet	28 Jul 1825
Jacob	32	M	Farmer	Wittenburg	U. States	Comet	28 Jul 1825
T.	8	F	Daughter	Wittenburg	U. States	Comet	28 Jul 1825
HENIGAN, David	22	M	Sawyer	England	United States	Ganges	10 May 1828
Joana	3	F		England	United States	Ganges	10 May 1828
Joe	32	M	Black Smith	England	United States	Ganges	10 May 1828
Mary	15	F		England	United States	Ganges	10 May 1828
Michael	4	M		England	United States	Ganges	10 May 1828
HENISEE, Thos.	17	M		G. Britain	U. States	St. George	7 Jun 1828
HENISWORTH, John	24	M	Labourer	Great Brittain	United States	Active	12 Sep 1828
HENKER, Hanke	18	M	Black Smith	Germany	United States	Constitution	2 Aug 1826
HENKING, Charles	19	M	Merchant	Switzerland	United States	Henry	9 Jun 1826
HENLAND, Joseph, Jr.		M	None	United States	United States	United States	18 Sep 1826
HENLEY, D.	35	M	Merchant	U. States	U. States of A.	William	30 May 1826
Ellen	7			Ireland	United States	Geo. Canning	5 Jun 1828
Geo.	1			Ireland	United States	Geo. Canning	5 Jun 1828

NAMES OF PASSENGERS	AGE	SEX	OCCUPATIONS	COUNTRY TO WHICH THEY BELONG	COUNTRY THEY INTEND TO INHABIT	SHIPS/DATES OF ARRIVAL	
HENLEY (cont'd)							
James	4			Ireland	United States	Geo. Canning	5 Jun 1828
Joanna	35			Ireland	United States	Geo. Canning	5 Jun 1828
Michl.	9			Ireland	United States	Geo. Canning	5 Jun 1828
Wm. F.	24	M	Gentleman	U.S. America		Ospray	30 Jul 1827
HENLY, Bridget	22	F	Spinster	Ireland	United States	Dublin Packet	23 May 1828
HENMERLIN, Blancis	39	M		France	United States	New England	29 Aug 1828
Margaret	42	F		France	United States	New England	29 Aug 1828
HENMIGAN, James	28 6/12	M		Ireland	U.S. of America	Douglass	6 Jul 1829
HENNELL, Eliz.	31	F	None	Ireland	New York	America	1 Aug 1828
HENNES, Jacob	22	M	Smith	Switzerland	U. States	Hewes	30 Oct 1829
HENNESEY, Kate	8	F		England	United States	Ganges	10 May 1828
Pat	27	M	Weaver	England	United States	Ganges	10 May 1828
HENNESSY, James	30	M	Farmer	England	Alexandria, U.S.	Roman	17 Oct 1826
HENNEY, Peter	26	M	Laborer	Gt. Britain		Dalhouse Castle	13 May 1828
HENNI, Elizabeth	16/12	F	child of [Hieronymus]	Switzerland	United States	Aurora	21 Jun 1824
Fred	4	M	child of [Hieronymus]	Switzerland	United States	Aurora	21 Jun 1824
Hieronymus	43	M	Gunsmith	Switzerland	United States	Aurora	21 Jun 1824
John M.	22 8/12	M	Student in Bardstown's College	Switzerland	America	Henry	17 May 1828
Maria	32	F	Wife of [Hieronymus]	Switzerland	United States	Aurora	21 Jun 1824
HENNIGAN, Wm.	20 5/12	M		Ireland	U.S. of America	Douglass	6 Jul 1829
HENNIGE, David	33	M	Farmer	Switzerland	U. States	Hewes	30 Oct 1829
HENNING, Ezekial	20	F	Labourer	Ireland	U. States	Atlantic	19 Aug 1825
M. A., Miss	18		Spinster	England	U.S. of America	Mary	21 Sep 1821
Mary	53	F	Labourer	Ireland	U. States	Atlantic	19 Aug 1825
Wm.	28	M	Merchant	St. John	St. John	St. Michael	27 Mar 1827
HENNIS, Christopher	23	M	Cooper	Ireland	America	John Adams	2 Aug 1827
HENNISWEY, C.	7	F		Great Britain	United States	Aspasia	16 Jul 1828
Harriet	5	F		Great Britain	United States	Aspasia	16 Jul 1828
Jane	9	F		Great Britain	United States	Aspasia	16 Jul 1828
Jesse	11	F		Great Britain	United States	Aspasia	16 Jul 1828
M.	49	F		Great Britain	United States	Aspasia	16 Jul 1828
Sarah	13	F		Great Britain	United States	Aspasia	16 Jul 1828
HENNIVER, Aleci	38	M	Weaver	Switzerland	U. States	Hewes	30 Oct 1829
Alice	6	M		Switzerland	U. States	Hewes	30 Oct 1829
Caroline	7	F		Switzerland	U. States	Hewes	30 Oct 1829
Ignatze	2	M		Switzerland	U. States	Hewes	30 Oct 1829
Mary Ann	36	F	his Wife [Aleci]	Switzerland	U. States	Hewes	30 Oct 1829
HENNS, Jos. M.	20	M	Merchant	Mexico	U. States	Prince Edward	5 Jul 1825
HENNSON, Wm.	20	M	Baker	Scotland	America	Friends	24 Sep 1821
HENOEQ, C.	20		Merchant	France		Edward Bonnaffe	17 Mar 1828
HENOLL, Joseph	18	M		Scotland	United States	Indus	5 Sep 1827
HENRALTY, Patrick	36	M	Farmer	Ireland	U. States	Globe	14 Jul 1821
HENRI, Ewd.	13	M	Labourer	England	United States	Nimrod	31 Jul 1828
Louis	36	M	Farmer	France	France	Sully	15 Jul 1829
HENRICH, A.						Francois I	8 Aug 1829
A. F.	25	F	Farmer	Germany	America	Howard	27 Sep 1826
Angus	3 4/12			Hamburg		Ann Maria	28 Mar 1822
Johann	3 6/12	M	Farmer	Wortenberg	Lancaster	Louisa	6 Oct 1828
Maria	1 6/12	F	Farmer	Wortenberg	Lancaster	Louisa	6 Oct 1828
V. L.	27	M	Farmer	Germany	America	Howard	27 Sep 1826
HENRICHS, Maria	33	F		Copenhagen, Denmark	going to reside in Clearfield, Pennsylvania	Friketon	7 Nov 1823
HENRICK, Andres	26	M	Farmer	Switzerland	United States	Elizabeth	27 Jul 1824
HENRIETTA, Francis	39	F	Merchant	St. John	Canada	Henrietta	7 Jul 1825
HENRIQUES, Aaron	5	M		England	England	Tontin	13 Jun 1825
Aaron	10	M		England	England	Tontin	13 Jun 1825
Abigale	41	F		England	England	Tontin	13 Jun 1825
Alexander	3	M		England	England	Tontin	13 Jun 1825
David	42	M	Merchant	England	England	Tontin	13 Jun 1825
Esther	32	F		England	England	Tontin	13 Jun 1825
Eugenia	14/12	M		England	England	Tontin	13 Jun 1825

NAMES OF PASSENGERS	AGE	SEX	OCCUPATIONS	COUNTRY TO WHICH THEY BELONG	COUNTRY THEY INTEND TO INHABIT	SHIPS/DATES OF ARRIVAL	
HENRIQUES (cont'd)							
H. C.	24	M	Merchant	Curacoa	U. States	McDonough	31 Jul 1821
J.	49	M	Merchant	England	England	Tontin	13 Jun 1825
Leman	3	F		England	England	Tontin	13 Jun 1825
Luna	23	M		England	England	Tontin	13 Jun 1825
M.	15	M	Supercargo	Curraco	U. States	Ann Elizabeth	13 Jul 1826
Moses	9	M		England	England	Tontin	13 Jun 1825
Rebecca	5	F		England	England	Tontin	13 Jun 1825
HENRIQUEZ, Abigail	15	F		England	U.S. America	Cortes	19 May 1826
Moses	16	M	Gentleman	England	U.S. America	Cortes	19 May 1826
HENRITE, Dennis		M	Joiner	Halifax	United States	Dodge Healy	14 Oct 1828
John		M	Child	Halifax	United States	Dodge Healy	14 Oct 1828
Michael		M	Child	Halifax	United States	Dodge Healy	14 Oct 1828
Nancy		F		Halifax	United States	Dodge Healy	14 Oct 1828
HENRY, A., Miss	16	F		U. States	U. States	Hebe	27 Jan 1827
A., Mrs.	28	F		U. States	U. States	Hebe	27 Jan 1827
Alexander	25	M	Gentleman	Great Brittian	Great Brittian	Governor Von Schollen	7 Nov 1827
Alfred	30	M	Merchant	Great Britian	U. States	Silas Richards	29 Oct 1828
Ann	3/12	F				Governor Fenner	23 Jul 1829
B.	28	F		France & Switzerland	U. States	Bayard	14 Jul 1826
Bridget	25	F	Farmer, Labourer or Spinster	Ireland	U. States	Meteor	4 Oct 1827
Bridget	30	F	Wife to a farm	England	United States	Danube	22 Aug 1825
Catharan	18	F		G. Britan	U. States	William Neilson	26 Jul 1828
Charles	21	M	Labourer	England	U. States	Ayrshire	12 May 1828
Charles	24	M		G. Britan	U. States	William Neilson	26 Jul 1828
Denis	20	M	Weaver	Ireland	New York	Atlantic	6 Oct 1828
Eleanor	38	F				Governor Fenner	23 Jul 1829
Elisa	72	F	Servant	Ireland	United States	Josephine	30 Apr 1828
Eliza An	1	F		G. Britain	U. States	St. George	7 Jun 1828
Elizabeth	18	F	None	United States	United States	Isaac Hicks	22 Aug 1828
Elizabeth	48	F	None	United States	United States	Isaac Hicks	22 Aug 1828
Essy	26	F	Servant	Ireland	United States	Josephine	30 Apr 1828
F.	20	M	Farmer	France	U. States	Lewis	6 Jul 1825
Felix	2/12	F		Ireland	U. States	Charles	19 Dec 1822
Felix	24 5/12	M	Weaver	Ireland	U. States	Fabius	22 Sep 1828
Felix	38	M	Labourer	Great Britain	United States	Hector	8 Jan 1820
G.	35	M	Merchant	Aquin	U. States	Rover	11 Jan 1823
Geo. A.	14	M	Servent	G. Britain	U. States	Diligence	29 Jul 1823
Geo. H.	32	M	Merchant	U. States	U. States	Robt. Reade	12 Apr 1825
Helenor	18/12	F		Ireland	U. States	Charles	19 Dec 1822
Henry	40	M	Artist	England	England	Constitution	17 Mar 1823
J.	21	M	Labourer	England	U. States	Ayrshire	12 May 1828
J.	34	M		America	America	Paragon	22 Sep 1827
James	23	M	Weaver	Ireland	United States	Hannah Eliza	6 Jun 1826
James	48	M		Gt. Britain	United States	John & Elizabeth	25 Sep 1827
Jane	27	F	Milner	England	U. States	Florida	13 Jan 1827
Jas.	24	M	Farmer	Ireland	America	Mary	29 May 1827
John	6	M	Farmer, Labourer or Spinster	Ireland	U. States	Meteor	4 Oct 1827
John	18	M	Labourer	Ireland	U. States	Lady Hunter	9 Oct 1825
John	21	M	Tanner	Rhode Island	Rhode Island	Jean Baptiste	11 Aug 1828
John	27	M	Painter	Ireland	U.S.A.	Dalhouse Castle	21 Aug 1829
John	28	M	Labourer	G. Britain	United States	Louisa	14 Jun 1825
John	42	M	Chandler	Great Britain	United States	Washington	3 Sep 1827
John S.	24	M	Merchant	England	America	Courier	24 Jul 1820
John S.	25	M	Merchant	U. States	U. States	James Monroe	18 Apr 1821
Jos. A.	2	M		England	England	Tontin	13 Jun 1825
Josep	38	M	Labour	U. States	U. States	Georgetown Packet	12 Mar 1825
Josh.	18		Labourer	England	United States	Hugh Johnson	11 Jun 1828
L. V.	28	M		France & Switzerland	U. States	Bayard	14 Jul 1826
Margaret	28	F	Servant	Ireland	United States	Josephine	30 Apr 1828

NAMES OF PASSENGERS	AGE	SEX	OCCUPATIONS	COUNTRY TO WHICH THEY BELONG	COUNTRY THEY INTEND TO INHABIT	SHIPS/DATES OF ARRIVAL	
HENRY (cont'd)							
Margret	4	F	Farmer, Labourer or Spinster	Ireland	U. States	Meteor	4 Oct 1827
Mark	18	M	Weaver	Ireland	New York	Atlantic	6 Oct 1828
Mary	9	F				Governor Fenner	23 Jul 1829
Mary	20	F		Ireland	New York	Lady Hunter	5 Jun 1826
Mary	24	F		G. Britain	U. States	St. George	7 Jun 1828
Mary Ann	20	F	None	United States	United States	Isaac Hicks	22 Aug 1828
Nelly	30		Laborer	Ireland	New York	Lady Hunter	19 Oct 1826
Patrick	17	M				Governor Fenner	23 Jul 1829
Robert	28	M	Seaman	New York	New York	Charleston	1 Jun 1826
Robert	28 2/12	M	Farmer	Ireland	New York	Globe	3 Dec 1821
Robt.	25	M	Mercht.	England	England	Savannah	10 Jan 1828
Robt.	35	M	Mariner	U.S.	U.S.	Agenoria	7 Jan 1822
S.	37	F		Ireland	U. States	Charles	19 Dec 1822
Sally	36	F	Servant	G. Britain	U. States	Wanderer	23 Jun 1828
Saml.	29	M	Merchant	America	America	Brittania	17 Jul 1828
Saml.	29	M		England	England	Brittania	17 Jul 1828
Samuel	23	M	Merchant	England	England	William Thompson	19 Aug 1829
Sarah	1	F	Farmer, Labourer or Spinster	Ireland	U. States	Meteor	4 Oct 1827
Thomas	39	M	Farmer	Ireland	New York	Governor Fenner	23 Jul 1829
Walter	14	M				Governor Fenner	23 Jul 1829
William	49	M	Tailorman	England	New York	Brighton	29 Aug 1828
Wm.	17	M	Chandler	Great Britain	United States	Washington	3 Sep 1827
HENSEMEN, Frederich	33	M	Farmer	Switzerland	United States	Olympia	12 Aug 1828
Georges	4	M	Farmer	Switzerland	United States	Olympia	12 Aug 1828
Jean	18	M	Farmer	Switzerland	United States	Olympia	12 Aug 1828
Margaret	3	F	Farmer	Switzerland	United States	Olympia	12 Aug 1828
Margaret	33	F	Farmer	Switzerland	United States	Olympia	12 Aug 1828
HENSHAW, E.	25	F		G. Britain	G. Britain	Brittania	17 Jul 1828
James	37	M	Farmer	Nova Scotia		Aurora	12 Mar 1827
Robt.	21	M		Ireland	U. States	Fame	15 Nov 1826
Susan	40	F		New York	New York	Brighton	20 Aug 1825
Wm.	18	M	Shoemaker	England	United States	Delta	24 Oct 1829
HENSON, J. W.	23	M	Merchant	United States	United States	Eugenie	2 Oct 1829
HENSTON, John	1		Farmer	England	United States	Hugh Johnson	11 Jun 1828
HENTEN, Thomas	20	M	Weaver	Ireland	U. States	Josephine	30 Aug 1828
HENTHE, John	26	M	Labourer	Ireland	United States	Wilson	28 Nov 1828
HENTLENBECK,							
Catherine	29	F		Wertemberg	Wertemberg	Edward Quesnel	3 Jul 1829
Christian	10/12	M		Wertemberg	Wertemberg	Edward Quesnel	3 Jul 1829
Micheal	28	M	Stone cutter	Wertemberg	Wertemberg	Edward Quesnel	3 Jul 1829
HENTZ, André	10	M		France	U. States	Edward Quesnel	17 Mar 1829
Hy.	23	M	Weelwright	Switzerland	U.S.	C. Amelia	30 Jun 1828
HENVETY, Pat	12 11/12	M		Ireland	U.S. of America	Douglass	6 Jul 1829
HEPBURN, Geo.	44	M	Mariner	St. Johns, N.B.	St. Johns, N.B.	Maine	24 Jun 1824
James	25	M	Carpenter	Scotland	Ama.	Expedition	19 May 1828
HEPHUM, Thos.	25	M	Furier	Great Britain		Eliza Grant	29 Aug 1829
HEPINSTALL, Chas.	24	M	Farmer	England	Canada	Phoenix	29 Apr 1826
Richard	21	M	Currier	England	Albany	Indian Chief	19 Jun 1823
Sarah	29	F	Spinner	Great Britain	United States	Isaac Hicks	10 Jul 1827
HEPINSTATE, A...	9	F		Great Britain	Albany	Zodiac	14 Jun 1822
Christopher	57	M	Farmer	Great Britain	Albany	Zodiac	14 Jun 1822
George	11	M		Great Britain	Albany	Zodiac	14 Jun 1822
Hannah	13	F		Great Britain	Albany	Zodiac	14 Jun 1822
Sarah	18	F		Great Britain	Albany	Zodiac	14 Jun 1822
HEPPERNAN, Michel	21			Ireland	U.S.	Union	20 Aug 1827
HEPWORTH, Wm.	23	M	Farmer	Gt. Britain	United States	Pacific	22 May 1826
HERALD, Amy	17	F	Servant	Ireland	U. States	Wanderer	1 Sep 1828
C.	30		Farmer	Ireland	United States	Courier	16 May 1825
Cris	50	M	Shoe Maker	Ireland	U. States	Wanderer	1 Sep 1828
E.	9		Farmer	Ireland	United States	Courier	16 May 1825
L.	5		Farmer	Ireland	United States	Courier	16 May 1825

NAMES OF PASSENGERS	AGE	SEX	OCCUPATIONS	COUNTRY TO WHICH THEY BELONG	COUNTRY THEY INTEND TO INHABIT	SHIPS/DATES OF ARRIVAL	
HERALD (cont'd)							
L.	30		Farmer	Ireland	United States	Courier	16 May 1825
P.	6		Farmer	Ireland	United States	Courier	16 May 1825
R.	25		Farmer	Ireland	United States	Courier	16 May 1825
Stoner	27	M	Shoe Maker	Ireland	U. States	Wanderer	1 Sep 1828
HERARTY, Alice	22	F	Servant	Ireland	America	Weser	26 Jun 1821
HERBERT, Cathr.	20	F		Gt. Britan	U. States	Sarah Skeafe	10 Sep 1827
Frederick	23	M	Farmer	Bavarian	United States	American	27 Aug 1827
James	1 5/12	M		Gt. Britan	U. States	Sarah Skeafe	10 Sep 1827
John	22	M	Baker	Gt. Britan	U. States	Sarah Skeafe	10 Sep 1827
Patrick	30	M	Brick Layer	Europe	United States	Aspasia	5 Sep 1827
Phoebe	18	F		Ireland	U. States	William Byrnes	17 Jul 1825
HERBERTSON, R. H.	27	M	Merchant	Glasgow	U. States	Marshall	12 Jun 1824
HERBET, W.	21	M	Labourer	Ireland	U. States	William Byrnes	17 Jul 1825
HERBETTE, F. P. L.	48	M	Merct.	France	U.S.	Stephania	15 Aug 1825
HERCKENRATH,							
Leon J.	27 8/12	M	Merchant	U.S. America	U.S. America	Leeds	5 Feb 1827
HERDING, J. E.	24 1/12	M	Merchant	Germany	United States	Helen Mar	29 Jun 1827
HERDMAN, Ann	22	F	Weaver	Bally Cary	United States	Minerva	30 Oct 1829
James	1	M		Bally Cary	United States	Minerva	30 Oct 1829
Mary	16	F	Spinster	Ireland	United States	Dublin Packet	23 May 1828
Nancy	32		Lady	Ireland	U. States	Xenophon	28 May 1822
Ralph	50	M	Sailor		U.S.	Helen	4 Aug 1829
Thomas	18	M	Farmer	Ireland	United States	Dublin Packet	23 May 1828
Thos.	80	M	Mercht.	Belfast	Troy	Favourite	8 Oct 1823
HEREART, Louis	17	M		Italy	United States	Ariadne	25 Jul 1822
HERERA, Ignatio	21	M	Merchant	Spain	U. States	William Thompson	24 Aug 1827
HERERO, A.	23	M	Merchant	Spain	France & Spain	Native	24 Aug 1825
HERGAN, John	2	M	Child	Ireland	United States	St. Michaels	25 May 1825
John	26	M	Laborer	Ireland	United States	St. Michaels	25 May 1825
Mary	24	F	Wife	Ireland	United States	St. Michaels	25 May 1825
HERING, Robert S.	26	M	Merchant	England	United States	Cincinnatus	21 Nov 1821
HERIT, Jas.	27	M	Farmer	Great Britain	United States	Atlantic	28 May 1827
HERKER, Geo.	38	M	Shopkeeper	U. States	U. States	Ambuscade	1 Jul 1820
HERLHIE, John	23	M	Preacher	Ireland	United States	Trio	31 Oct 1827
HERLIHY, Danl.	26	M	Labourer	Ireland	U.S. America	Traveller	10 Sep 1827
Patrick	28	M	Seaman	Ireland	U.S. America	Traveller	10 Sep 1827
HERLILEY, John	19	M	Clerk	Ireland	United States	Pallas	28 Oct 1828
HERLY, Margaret	50	F	Senpstress	France	America	La Grange	7 Aug 1828
HERM, Jas.	38	M	Gentleman	England	U. States	Bayard	11 Jul 1825
Rachel	19	F				Apollo	11 Jun 1828
Richard	26	M	Taylor	Gt. Britain	U. States	Frances Henrietta	18 Apr 1825
HERMAN, Barbara	9	F		Wurtemburg	United States	Jason	3 Nov 1828
Barbary	14	F	Spinster	England	United States	Hanford	3 Jul 1829
Catherine	21	M	Farmer	Alsace in the Department of Upper and lower Rhine	United States	Carolina Augusta	16 May 1828
Cathrine	60			b. County of Sligo, last of London	N. York	Peru	30 May 1828
Christine	31	F		Wurtemburg	United States	Jason	3 Nov 1828
Constina	3	F		Wurtemburg	United States	Jason	3 Nov 1828
Fortine	25	M	Dyer	Brattain		L'Esperance	6 Sep 1828
Gotfred	9/12	M		Wurtemburg	United States	Jason	3 Nov 1828
Johannah	6	M		Wurtemburg	United States	Jason	3 Nov 1828
Joseph	9	M		Switzerland	United States	Elbe	2 Aug 1822
Joseph	28	M	Furrier	Russia	New York	Indian Chief	19 Jun 1823
Margarette	12	F		Wurtemburg	United States	Jason	3 Nov 1828
Otto	22		Farmer	Bremen	Germany	Hudson	14 Jun 1827
HERMANDES, A.	24	M	Merchant	Spanish Maine	U. States	Diana	31 Oct 1822
HERMANDEZ, Antonia M.	24	M	Merchant	Trinidad in Cuba	U. States	Fortune	23 Nov 1821
HERMANGE, Anthony	26	M	Physician	United States	United States	Purrington	8 Dec 1827
HERMANN, Carl	1/12	M		France	America, U.N.S.	Great Britain	3 Aug 1829
Francois	12	M		France	America, U.N.S.	Great Britain	3 Aug 1829
Francois J.	43	M	Farmer	France	America, U.N.S.	Great Britain	3 Aug 1829
George	10	M		France	America, U.N.S.	Great Britain	3 Aug 1829

NAMES OF PASSENGERS	AGE	SEX	OCCUPATIONS	COUNTRY TO WHICH THEY BELONG	COUNTRY THEY INTEND TO INHABIT	SHIPS/DATES OF ARRIVAL	
HERMANN (cont'd)							
Madalein	36	F		France	America, U.N.S.	Great Britain	3 Aug 1829
Madaleina	8	F		France	America, U.N.S.	Great Britain	3 Aug 1829
Marianne	4	F		France	America, U.N.S.	Great Britain	3 Aug 1829
Philippe	6 2/12	M		France	America, U.N.S.	Great Britain	3 Aug 1829
HERMANS, Jno. G.	62	M	Merchant	Germany	Germany	William Byrnes	6 Apr 1826
HERME, C.	39		Servant	U. States	U. States	Napoleon	10 Jan 1828
HERMEGE, John	4	M		Switzerland	U. States	Romulus	24 Sep 1828
John Joshua	33	M	Farmer	Switzerland	U. States	Romulus	24 Sep 1828
Jos.	9	M		Switzerland	U. States	Romulus	24 Sep 1828
M.	7	F		Switzerland	U. States	Romulus	24 Sep 1828
M.	29	F		Switzerland	U. States	Romulus	24 Sep 1828
HERMENETA, Jose	15	M	Gentleman	Chile	Chile	Mapocho	9 Jan 1824
HERNANDES, Antonio	26	M	Gentleman	Cuba	U. States	Mary & Eliza	8 Mar 1823
C.	3	M	Merchan	Spain	U. States	Dromo	22 May 1826
C.	21	M	Merchan	Spain	U. States	Dromo	22 May 1826
Francisco	1	M	Merchan	Spain	U. States	Dromo	22 May 1826
Francisco	50	M	Merchant	Spain	U. States	Fabius	7 Dec 1825
Parmes	10	M		Spain	United States	Georgetown Packet	15 Nov 1823
T.	26	M	Merchan	Spain	U. States	Dromo	22 May 1826
HERNANDEZ, —, Miss	6	F		Spain	U. States	Madison	22 May 1822
—, Miss	11	F		Spain	U. States	Madison	22 May 1822
—, Miss	13	F		Spain	U. States	Madison	22 May 1822
—, Mrs.	38	F		Spain	U. States	Madison	22 May 1822
Anthony	30	M	Merchant	Trinadad	Trinadad in Cuba	Topaz	23 Nov 1824
Antonio	27	M	Merchant	Spain	New York	Transit	17 Mar 1824
Carlos, Master	5	M		Spain	U. States	Madison	22 May 1822
D. Frs.	58	M	Gentleman	Spain	U. States	Madison	22 May 1822
Domingo	25	M	Merchant	Spain	Spain	Franklin	14 Jul 1827
Francisco	26	M	Columbian Navy	Columbia	Columbia	General Paez	17 Aug 1825
Francisco	28	M	Columbian Navy	Columbia	Columbia	General Paez	17 Aug 1825
Hipolito		M		Spain	U. States	Madison	22 May 1822
Juana	22	F		Island of Cuba	Cuba	James Monroe	21 May 1825
Modest	14	M	Columbian Navy	Columbia	Columbia	General Paez	17 Aug 1825
P.	28	M	Merchant	Spain	Cuba	Brown	30 Jan 1826
Raphaiel, Master	1 6/12	M		Spain	U. States	Madison	22 May 1822
Sebastian	36		Planter			Corsair	2 Oct 1820
W.	38	M	Merchant	Pensacola	U. States	Charleston	23 Oct 1825
HERNER, Charles	26	M	Merchant	U. States	United States	United States	16 Feb 1827
HERNESDEZ, Antonia	23	M	Planter	Spain	Spain	Louisa	10 May 1821
HERNIN, Owen	25	M	Laborer	Ireland	United States	Belleville	13 Oct 1827
HERNON, Eleanor	21	F	Spinster	Ireland	United States	Fabius	31 Jul 1829
HEROC, Henry	37	M	Artist	England	U. States	Venus	11 Aug 1820
HEROMMURES,							
Catharan	6/12	F	Brewer	Ireland		Quatre Freres	29 Jul 1828
George	5	M	Brewer	Ireland		Quatre Freres	29 Jul 1828
Isaack	62	M	Brewer	Ireland		Quatre Freres	29 Jul 1828
Margaret	1	F	Brewer	Ireland		Quatre Freres	29 Jul 1828
Margaret	25	F	Brewer	Ireland		Quatre Freres	29 Jul 1828
HERON, Christof	30	M	Farmer	Switzerland	U. States	Hewes	30 Oct 1829
James	30	M	Labourer	Scotland	United States	Friends	7 Jul 1827
Patt	24	M	Farmer	Ireland	United States	Dublin Packet	22 Aug 1829
William	32	M	Merchant	Scotland	United States	Friends	7 Jul 1827
HERPEY, Benj.	35	M	Mariner	U. States	U. States	Horatio	14 Mar 1829
HERR, Anton	34	M	Cooper & Brewer	Germany	U. States	Falcon	11 Jun 1827
C.	1 1/4	F		Germany	U. States	Falcon	11 Jun 1827
Dorothy L.	29	F		Germany	U. States	Falcon	11 Jun 1827
Henry	2	M		Germany	U. States	Falcon	11 Jun 1827
HERREMANS, Herbert	32	M	Gentleman	Holland	United States	Isaac Hicks	10 Jul 1827
HERRERO, A.	31	M	Merchant	Havan	U. States	Greek	3 Mar 1825
HERRICK, John	25	M	Farmer	Switzerland	U. States	Bayard	9 Nov 1825
Jona. K.	30	M	Merchant	United States	United States	Hannibal	12 Oct 1829
HERRICO, Dolores	22	F		Mexico	U. States	Virginia	3 Dec 1827
Manuel	47	M	Merchant	Spain	U. States	Virginia	3 Dec 1827
HERRIN, Chas.	26	M	Farmer	Great Britain	United States	Meridian	2 Jul 1827
Robert	31		...	Ireland	United States	Alexander Mansfield	23 Nov 1824
Thos.	26	M	Farmer	Great Britain	United States	Meridian	2 Jul 1827

NAMES OF PASSENGERS	AGE	SEX	OCCUPATIONS	COUNTRY TO WHICH THEY BELONG	COUNTRY THEY INTEND TO INHABIT	SHIPS/DATES OF ARRIVAL	
HERRING, Chas.	28	M	Merchant	London	U. States	Mary Jane	23 Mar 1829
Elizabeth	6	F	None	Derbeyshire	U. States	Manhattan	21 May 1821
Hannah	12	F	None	Derbeyshire	U. States	Manhattan	21 May 1821
Hannah	40	F	None		U. States	Manhattan	21 May 1821
James	8	M	None	Derbeyshire	U. States	Manhattan	21 May 1821
James	42	M			U. States	Manhattan	21 May 1821
Jane	15	F	None	Derbeyshire	U. States	Manhattan	21 May 1821
John	10	M	None	Derbeyshire	U. States	Manhattan	21 May 1821
John	20	M	Weaver	Ireland	United States	Asia	29 Jul 1829
Jonas	2	M	None	Derbeyshire	U. States	Manhattan	21 May 1821
Joseh	14	M	None	Derbeyshire	U. States	Manhattan	21 May 1821
Marry	2	F	None	Derbeyshire	U. States	Manhattan	21 May 1821
R. G.	30	M	Merchant	Gt. Britain	United States	Seeds	29 Sep 1824
Robert G.	27	M		U. States	U. States	Cincinnatus	2 Oct 1822
William	4	M	None	Derbeyshire	U. States	Manhattan	21 May 1821
HERRINGS, Ann	25	F		Ireland	New York	Lady Hunter	5 Jun 1826
Owen	27	M		Ireland	New York	Lady Hunter	5 Jun 1826
HERRINGTON, Betsey	1	F	...	England	United States	Milton	20 Oct 1827
Ellen	22	F	...	England	United States	Milton	20 Oct 1827
HERRIOT, Adelaide	4	F		France	U. States	Leonarde	29 Aug 1828
Jean M. M.	36	F		France	U. States	Leonarde	29 Aug 1828
Joseph	40	M	Farmer	France	U. States	Leonarde	29 Aug 1828
Julie	13	F		France	U. States	Leonarde	29 Aug 1828
Marie F.	1 9/12	F		France	U. States	Leonarde	29 Aug 1828
Simeon	11	M		France	U. States	Leonarde	29 Aug 1828
HERROD, Robert	38		Coff Smith	England	U. States	Corinthian	8 Oct 1828
HERSANT, M. E.	28	M	Secretary to French Ambassador	France	U. States	Amity	21 Feb 1823
HERSCHEL, Esau	18	M	Instrument Maker	Poland	New York	Indian Chief	19 Jun 1823
HERSENT, James S.	32	M	Merchant	France	New York	Sully	4 Mar 1828
HERSEY, Paul						Venus	12 Apr 1821
HERSH, B.	1	F		Switzerland	U. States	Romulus	24 Sep 1828
Charles	3	M		Switzerland	U. States	Romulus	24 Sep 1828
Charles	15	M		Switzerland	U. States	Romulus	24 Sep 1828
John	12	M		Switzerland	U. States	Romulus	24 Sep 1828
John	42	M	Farmer	Switzerland	U. States	Romulus	24 Sep 1828
M.	6	F		Switzerland	U. States	Romulus	24 Sep 1828
M.	10	F		Switzerland	U. States	Romulus	24 Sep 1828
M.	36	F		Switzerland	U. States	Romulus	24 Sep 1828
N.	8	M		Switzerland	U. States	Romulus	24 Sep 1828
HERSHELMAN, Jno. J.	51	M	Turner	Switzerland	United States	Aurora	21 Jun 1824
Rosann	23	F	Wife of [Jno. J.]	Switzerland	United States	Aurora	21 Jun 1824
HERSHON, Margritt	20	F	Spinster	County Renagh, Ireland	United States	Hanford	15 May
HERSNLICH, Ca.	18 9/12	M	Farmer	France	United States	Catharine	10 Sep 1827
Cathe.	47 3/12	F	Farmer	France	United States	Catharine	10 Sep 1827
Charles	4 1/12	M	Farmer	France	United States	Catharine	10 Sep 1827
D.	16 6/12	F	Farmer	France	United States	Catharine	10 Sep 1827
F.	7 6/12	M	Farmer	France	United States	Catharine	10 Sep 1827
Jacob	13 5/12	M	Farmer	France	United States	Catharine	10 Sep 1827
Philip J.	42 9/12	M	Farmer	France	United States	Catharine	10 Sep 1827
HERSTED, Susan, Miss	22	F	Lady	U. States	U. States	Buffaloe	14 Sep 1820
HERTENSTON, John	18	M	Farmer	Scotland	United States	Commerce	17 Jul 1823
HERTIG, P. G.	22	M	Gentleman	Swisserland	United States	Montano	13 Jan 1826
HERTON, James	22	M	Labourer	Ireland	United States	Meteor	26 Jun 1827
HERTZ, Maurice, Mr.	43	M	Merchant	Hamburg	Hamburg	Minerva	17 May 1828
HERTZICK, Alexander	1 2/12	M		Switzerland	America, U.N.S.	Great Britain	3 Aug 1829
Benedict	35	M	Shoemaker	Switzerland	America, U.N.S.	Great Britain	3 Aug 1829
Jonis	3 1/12	M		Switzerland	America, U.N.S.	Great Britain	3 Aug 1829
Suzanna	29	F		Switzerland	America, U.N.S.	Great Britain	3 Aug 1829
HERVAY, George	46	M	Gentleman	Scotchman	United States	London Packet	25 Dec 1820
HERVE, John	22	M	Printer	France	U.S.	Bayard	18 Oct 1826
HERVÉ, Chs., Mr.	24	M				Henri IV	17 May 1828
HERVEY, Edward M.	23 1/12	M	Mariner	U. States	U. States	Perry	21 Jun 1828
Jacob	25		Merchant	New York	Ireland	Carolina Ann	21 May 1823
Lydia	19	F	Spinster	Ireland	United States	Wilson	6 Jun 1828

NAMES OF PASSENGERS	AGE	SEX	OCCUPATIONS	COUNTRY TO WHICH THEY BELONG	COUNTRY THEY INTEND TO INHABIT	SHIPS/DATES OF ARRIVAL	
HERVEY (cont'd)							
Wm. J.	26	M	Merchant	London	London	Orlando	23 Mar 1826
HERVILLY, D., Mr.	22	M	Merchant	United States	United States	Don Quixote	18 Aug 1824
Felix D.	25		None	France	United States	Bayard	17 Dec 1827
HERVSTEN, Mary	23	F	Servant	Ireland	United States	Florida	14 Sep 1827
HERVY, Arthur	25	M	Shoe Maker	Ireland	United States	Clothier	22 Nov 1827
Charlot	1	F		Ireland	United States	Clothier	22 Nov 1827
Mary	12	F		Ireland	United States	Clothier	22 Nov 1827
HERY, Wm.	65	M	Labourer	Ireland		Robert Fulton	4 Jun 1828
HERZOG, C. C. G.	22	M	Mechanic	Saxony	U. States	Minerva	9 Jan 1827
Gregoire	22	M	Labourer	Switzerland	United States	Thetis	5 Jul 1821
Martha	40	F	Farmer	France	United States	Globe	30 Aug 1828
Phillip	51	M	Farmer	France	United States	Globe	30 Aug 1828
Victoire	23	F		Switzerland	United States	Thetis	5 Jul 1821
HESCOX, —, Mrs.	33	F		England	United States	Cosmo	26 Aug 1829
Benjn.	11	M		England	United States	Cosmo	26 Aug 1829
Ellen	3	F		England	United States	Cosmo	26 Aug 1829
Mary	5	F		England	United States	Cosmo	26 Aug 1829
Thos.	4	M		England	United States	Cosmo	26 Aug 1829
HESIGOYEN, Peter	41	M	Merchant	Philadelphia	America	Laurel	3 Jun 1828
HESKESTAD, John	31	M	Merchant	Norway	U.S.A.	Vigilance	26 Aug 1829
HESLIN, Biddy	19	F		Great Britain	New York	Philetus	21 Jul 1827
HESLY, John	20	M	Tailor	G. Britain	U. States	Mary Howland	22 Sep 1828
HESS, Adolph	33	M	Tailor	Switzerland	N. York	France	29 Nov 1827
Ann	35	M		Switzerland	N. York	France	29 Nov 1827
Fanny	1	F			United States	Spartan	21 Aug 1824
Harriett	49	F			United States	Spartan	21 Aug 1824
Jenny	22	F			United States	Spartan	21 Aug 1824
John	49	M		Shoemaker	United States	Spartan	21 Aug 1824
HESSELL, Christien	39	M		Bardin	U. States	Bayard	5 Sep 1828
Covle	42	M	Farmer	Bardin	U. States	Bayard	5 Sep 1828
J. C.	15	M		Bardin	U. States	Bayard	5 Sep 1828
J. T.	11	M		Bardin	U. States	Bayard	5 Sep 1828
HESSER, G. A.	38	M	Gardner	Germany	U. States	Falcon	11 Jun 1827
HESSNER, Joseph	52	F		France	United States	Deux Ernest	29 Dec 1827
*landed in New York							
HETCHER, Hannah	25	F				Imperial	19 Jul 1820
HETHERING, John	27	M	...	England	Canada	William Thompson	10 May 1825
Thos.	22	M	...	England	Canada	William Thompson	10 May 1825
HETHERINGTON,							
Ann Mary	25	F		Great Britain	Canada	Lord Gambier	4 Feb 1829
Eling	9	F				Governor Fenner	23 Jul 1829
Eliza	24	F	None	Yorkshire		Ocean	13 Jul 1827
Elizabeth	27	F				Governor Fenner	23 Jul 1829
Harriet	3	F				Governor Fenner	23 Jul 1829
James	6	M				Governor Fenner	23 Jul 1829
John P.	28	M	Missionary	Great Britain	Canada	Lord Gambier	4 Feb 1829
Joseph	11	M				Governor Fenner	23 Jul 1829
Joseph George	26	M	Painter	England	United States	Aurora	9 Jul 1827
Margaret	17	F		Ireland	New York	Carolina Ann	15 Oct 1824
Richd.	37	M	Shoemaker	Yorkshire		Ocean	13 Jul 1827
Saml.	19	M		Ireland	New York	Carolina Ann	15 Oct 1824
Thos.	24	M	Merchant	Gt. Britain	Gt. Britain	Canada	5 Jun 1827
William	34	M	Labourer	England	Canada	Governor Fenner	23 Jul 1829
HETHERTON, Catharine	3	F	None	Halifax	U. States	Loire	7 Jul 1827
Margaret	26	F	None	Halifax	U. States	Loire	7 Jul 1827
Mathew	30	M	Labourer	Halifax	U. States	Loire	7 Jul 1827
Patrick	4	M	None	Halifax	U. States	Loire	7 Jul 1827
Peter	1	M	None	Halifax	U. States	Loire	7 Jul 1827
HETTER, Ann M.	54	F	Farmer	Ireland		Quatre Freres	29 Jul 1828
Catharan	20	F	Farmer	Ireland		Quatre Freres	29 Jul 1828

NAMES OF PASSENGERS	AGE	SEX	OCCUPATIONS	COUNTRY TO WHICH THEY BELONG	COUNTRY THEY INTEND TO INHABIT	SHIPS/DATES OF ARRIVAL	
HETTER (cont'd)							
Magdaline	25	F	Farmer	Ireland		Quatre Freres	29 Jul 1828
HETTICK, Felix	28	M	Carpenter	Brattain		L'Esperance	6 Sep 1828
John	27	M	Labourer	Brattain		L'Esperance	6 Sep 1828
HETTY, Catharine	47	F	Farmer	France	U. States	Lewis	6 Jul 1825
HETZE, Augustus W.	38	M	Merchant	Great Britain	New York	Superior	5 Sep 1827
Wm. Henry	8	M	None	Great Britain	New York	Superior	5 Sep 1827
HEUCK, Eliza	25	F		England	United States	Yobah	26 Sep 1827
John	1	M		England	United States	Yobah	26 Sep 1827
Wm.	27	M		England	United States	Yobah	26 Sep 1827
HEUSTON, Benjm.	22	M	Doctor	America	U. States	Ice Plant	18 Dec 1820
HEVA, M.	22	M	Merchant	Spain	France & Spain	Native	24 Aug 1825
HEVENS, Thos.	21	M	Merchant	G. Brittain	U. States	Canada	6 Jun 1825
HEVODER, Michal	17	M		Bardin	U. States	Bayard	5 Sep 1828
HEVRON, Robt.	21	M	Labourer	Ireland	United States	Fabius	31 Jul 1829
HEVYER, G. J.	26	M	Merchant	Curacao	Curacao	General Paez	18 Aug 1828
HEW, Anna	21	F	None	Wales South	U. States	Oglethorpe	8 Jul 1824
HEWAS, John	6	M		Great Britain	America	Lady Gallatin	21 Jun 1820
HEWEL, Henry	8	M		County of Down, Ireland	U. States	Lady Washington	16 Oct 1821
HEWELL, Charles	23	M	Carpenter	Massachusetts	Boston	General Warren	8 Jul 1829
HEWES, Mathew	29	M	Baker	England	United States	Copernicus	3 Aug 1829
Richd.	28	M	Labourer	Great Britian	United States	Sarah	11 Jul 1829
Richd.	49	M	Farmer	Great Britain	America	Lady Gallatin	21 Jun 1820
Siday	34	M	Gentleman	England	United States	Magnet	16 May 1823
HEWET, Magrath	16	F	Stonemason	Ireland	U. States	Virginia	20 Jun 1825
HEWETT, John	26	M	Farmer	Great Britian	U. States	Hudson	12 Mar 1824
William	22	M	Silver Smith	G.B.	St. New York	Eliza Grant	29 Aug 1829
William	27	M	Farmer	Scotland	United States	Samuel Robertson	9 May 1827
HEWISEN, John	28	M	Smith	England	U. States	Patriot	31 Oct 1822
Mary Ann	9/12	F				Patriot	31 Oct 1822
Mary Ann	22	F				Patriot	31 Oct 1822
HEWIT, Elisabet	30 1/12	F	Weaver	Ireland	New York	Louisa	20 Jul 1826
Eliza	35		None	Manchester, England	Great Britain	Franklin	22 Jun 1827
Mary	10		None	Manchester, England	Great Britain	Franklin	22 Jun 1827
HEWITT, Adam	55	M	Labourer	Ireland	U. States	Atlantic	19 Aug 1825
Caroline	44	M	Shoe Maker	English	United States	Ann	11 Sep 1827
Charles	29	M	None	Great Britian	Great Britian	Thankful Winslow	9 Jun 1826
Jas.	18	M	Farmer	Ireland	U. States	Atlantic	19 Aug 1825
Jasper	38	M	Shoe Maker	English	United States	Ann	11 Sep 1827
S.	23	M	Labourer	Ireland	United States	Sarah G.	15 May 1828
HEWLET, John	54	M	Boot Maker	Great Britain	United States	Asia	14 Jul 1829
HEWLETT, —, Mrs.	60	F		England	America	Britannia	5 Nov 1828
Emma	7	F		England	America	Britannia	5 Nov 1828
F. A., Jr.	20	F		England	America	Britannia	5 Nov 1828
J. J. Adams	33	M	Farmer	England	America	Britannia	5 Nov 1828
Wm.	24	M	Merchant	U. States	U. States	Nile	11 Jul 1822
HEWLIN, Ann	24	F				Lady of the Lake	23 Aug 1828
*left ship							
James	24	M				Lady of the Lake	23 Aug 1828
*left ship							
Nancy	15	F	Servant	Ireland	United States	Josephine	30 Apr 1828
HEWLY, Daniel	40	M	Gentleman	Barbadoes	Barbadoes	Falcon	4 Jun 1825
HEWNER, Frederick	27	M	Sugar Baker	Ireland	U. States	Frederick	2 Apr 1828
HEWON, Jno.	4	M		Great Britain	United States	William Dawson	18 Jun 1827
HEWS, Barbara	12	F	Spinster	Switzerland	United States	Andes	5 May 1828
Grader	10	M	Spinster	Switzerland	United States	Andes	5 May 1828
Jacob	45	M	Farmer	Switzerland	United States	Andes	5 May 1828
Lena	9	F	Spinster	Switzerland	United States	Andes	5 May 1828
Maria	46	F	Spinster	Switzerland	United States	Andes	5 May 1828
Matthew	28	M	Mechanic	Great Brittan	United States	Cambria	11 Feb 1829
Philip	6	M	Child	Switzerland	United States	Andes	5 May 1828

NAMES OF PASSENGERS	AGE	SEX	OCCUPATIONS	COUNTRY TO WHICH THEY BELONG	COUNTRY THEY INTEND TO INHABIT	SHIPS/DATES OF ARRIVAL	
HEWSON, George	24	M	Farmer	Ireland	United States	Dublin Packet	29 Jun 1825
John	35	M	Farmer	England	U.N. States	William Byrnes	13 Aug 1829
Joseph	27	M	Farmer	England	U.N. States	William Byrnes	13 Aug 1829
HEWVAS, C.	22	M	Carpenter	Ireland	United States	Dalhouse Castle	8 May 1827
HEY, John	40	M		England	United States	William Byrnes	11 Dec 1827
HEYAC, Carola	5	F		France	America	George	6 Oct 1827
Charles	2/12	M		France	America	George	6 Oct 1827
Francis	36	M	Musician	France	America	George	6 Oct 1827
Rosina	28	F		France	America	George	6 Oct 1827
HEYAN, John	45	M	Scholar	Ireland	U.S.A.	Dalhouse Castle	21 Aug 1829
HEYCOCK, Henry	21	M	Merchant	Gt. Brittain	United States	Leeds	19 May 1823
Henry	22	M	Merchant	Great Britan	Great Britan	Columbia	10 Mar 1824
William	28		Merchant	England	United States	Florida	11 Mar 1829
Wm.	25	M	Mercht.	Gt. Brittian	United States	Nestor	14 Nov 1823
HEYDENRICK,							
Frederic	20 3/12	M	Tanner	France	United States	France	6 Oct 1828
HEYDER, Henry F.	19	M	Farmer	Hannover	U. States	Warren	7 Jul 1826
HEYER, Henry	35	M	Carver	America	America	Leeds	2 Aug 1828
HEYLAND, John	48	M	Labourer	Ireland	U. States	Two Marys	20 Apr 1825
M.	50	M	Labourer	Ireland	U. States	Two Marys	20 Apr 1825
Pely	12	F	Labourer	Ireland	U. States	Two Marys	20 Apr 1825
HEYLEGIER, Henry	36	M	Merchant	Connecticutt	U. States	Charity	18 Nov 1823
HEYLIGER, Sarah	65	M	Merchant	N. York	U. States	Chase	12 May 1826
HEYODRE, Babuch	11	F		Switzerland		Pallas	14 Jun 1828
Christof	...	M		Switzerland		Pallas	14 Jun 1828
Christof	...0	M	Weaver	Switzerland		Pallas	14 Jun 1828
F...	...	F		Switzerland		Pallas	14 Jun 1828
Moriah	...	F		Switzerland		Pallas	14 Jun 1828
Moriah	...7	F		Switzerland		Pallas	14 Jun 1828
HEYWOOD, Ellenor	27	F	None	Great Britain	United States	Illinois	9 Oct 1820
John	29	M	Farmer	Great Britain	United States	Illinois	9 Oct 1820
S.	9	M	Labourer	England	America	Sarah	18 Aug 1829
HIAMSON, Hiam	60	M	Merchant	England	New Orleans	Brighton	9 Dec 1828
HIBB, Louisa	25	F		England	England	Ranger	15 Jan 1827
Phillip	20	M	Miner	England	England	Ranger	15 Jan 1827
HIBBEL, Charles	14	M		Great Britain	United States	Comet	9 Aug 1822
Robert	29	M	Gardener	Great Britain	United States	Comet	9 Aug 1822
Susan	27	F	None	Great Britain	United States	Comet	9 Aug 1822
HIBBERD,							
Mary Elizabeth	22	F	Spinster	England	United States	Maria	12 May 1823
HIBBERT, ...	18	M	Gentl.	Great Britian	United States	London	24 Jun 1823
John	21	M	Printer	England	United States	Aurelia	7 Jun 1826
HIBBY, J.	38	M	Organ Builder	Great Britain	United States	Isaac Hicks	6 Dec 1827
HIBLER, Thos.	23	M	Labourer	England	United States	Nancy	15 Mar 1820
HICHY, John	35	M	None	England	America	Silvanus Jenkins	17 Nov 1828
HICK, Richd.	27	M	Farmer	England	United States	Florida	1 Sep 1823
Willet	52	M	Merchant	United States	United States	Atlantic	3 Dec 1821
William	20	M	Pedler	Ireland	United States	St. Michael	21 Aug 1824
HICKBAR, Dory	28	F	None	Halifax	U. States	Hunter	2 Jul 1824
Jane	6/12	F	None	Halifax	U. States	Hunter	2 Jul 1824
John	4	M	None	Halifax	U. States	Hunter	2 Jul 1824
HICKCOX, Samuel B.	33	M	Merchant	U. States	New York	James Cropper	21 Oct 1825
HICKE, John	30	M	Mason	Ireland	U. States	Albion	11 May 1827
HICKEY, Ann	10	F	None	Ireland	U.S.A.	Dalhouse Castle	21 Aug 1829
Ann	10	F	None	Ireland	United States	Dalhouse Castle	21 Aug 1829
Barney	15	M	Farmer	Ireland	United States	Dalhouse Castle	21 Aug 1829
James	14	M	Farmer	Ireland	United States	Dalhouse Castle	21 Aug 1829
James	20	M	Butcher	Ireland	America	William	11 Nov 1825
John	6	M	None	Ireland	U.S.A.	Dalhouse Castle	21 Aug 1829
Luke	45	M	Labourer	Ireland	America	Cincinnatus	22 May 1826
Mary	12	F	None	Ireland	U.S.A.	Dalhouse Castle	21 Aug 1829
Mary	12	F	None	Ireland	United States	Dalhouse Castle	21 Aug 1829
Mary	44	F		Ireland	United States	Dalhouse Castle	21 Aug 1829
Matt	26	M	Farmer	Ireland	United States	Dublin Packet	29 Jun 1825
Michael	8	M	None	Ireland	U.S.A.	Dalhouse Castle	21 Aug 1829
Michl.	8	M	None	Ireland	United States	Dalhouse Castle	21 Aug 1829
Peter	25	M	Butcher	Ireland	United States	William	20 Jul 1829
Richard	25	M	Cooper	G. Britain	U. States	America	17 Oct 1825
Robert	25	M	Farmer	Ireland	United States	Dublin Packet	9 Jul 1827

NAMES OF PASSENGERS	AGE	SEX	OCCUPATIONS	COUNTRY TO WHICH THEY BELONG	COUNTRY THEY INTEND TO INHABIT	SHIPS/DATES OF ARRIVAL	
HICKIE, Edmund	31	M	Labourer	Ireland	United States	Trio	31 Oct 1827
HICKINS, George	20	M	Labourer	Ireland	United States	Robert Fulton	10 Aug 1827
HICKLAN, William	24	M	Machine Maker	Ireland	United States	Fabius	31 Jul 1829
HICKMAN, J.	28	F		Gt. Britain	United States	Columbia	7 Sep 1827
Wm.	18		Carpenter	Essex	England	Elizabeth	8 Dec 1821
HICKMANN, Saml.	42		Mercht.	England	U. States	New York	30 Oct 1827
HICKS, Agness	2	F	None	Great Brittain	U. States	Louisa	11 Jun 1824
Ann	32	F		England	U.S.A.	Hudson	21 Aug 1829
Ann	36	F	None	Great Brittain	U. States	Louisa	11 Jun 1824
Bettey	4	F		Great Brittan	United States	Euphrates	12 Mar 1824
David	30	M	Gentleman	England	United States	Wade	29 Aug 1825
Edwd.	8	M		Stafford	United States	Java	9 Jul 1827
Eliza	16	F		Stafford	United States	Java	9 Jul 1827
Eliza	32	F		Stafford	United States	Java	9 Jul 1827
Eliza H.	20	F		U.S.	U.S.	George Canning	26 Aug 1829
Elizabeth	1	F		Great Brittan	United States	Euphrates	12 Mar 1824
Gilbert	26	M		U. States	U. States	Admittance	17 May 1826
Hannah	35	F		Maine	U. States	Five Brothers	9 Jul 1822
Henrietta	11	F		England	U.S.A.	Hudson	21 Aug 1829
Henry W.	25	M	Merchant	U.S.	U.S.	George Canning	26 Aug 1829
J. J.	40	M	Merchant	Germany	Germany	Jubilee	26 Jul 1828
Jno. H.	25		Merchant	U.S.	U.S.	Silvanus Jenkins	30 Nov 1827
John	20	M	Hatter	Great Brittan	United States	Euphrates	12 Mar 1824
John	30	M	Miner	England	England	Ranger	15 Jan 1827
John	45	M	Tinnor	Stafford	United States	Java	9 Jul 1827
Joseph	6	M	None	Great Brittain	U. States	Louisa	11 Jun 1824
Mary	...	...	...	...	...	St. Michael	22 Sep 1824
Mary	4	F		Stafford	United States	Java	9 Jul 1827
Mary	11	F	None	Great Brittain	U. States	Louisa	11 Jun 1824
Mary	30			Great Britain	U. States	Columbia	7 May 1828
Mary An	24	F		Great Brittan	United States	Euphrates	12 Mar 1824
Oliver	38	M	Mariner	America	U. States	Globe	14 Jul 1821
Philip C.	22	M	Seaman	U. States	U. States	Nassau	7 Jun 1826
R.	50	M	Gentleman	Rhode Island	U. States	Columbia	12 Sep 1827
Robert	65	M	Servant	Ireland	United States	Sylvester Healy	19 Aug 1825
Samuel	18	M		N. York	U. States	Criterion	12 Jun 1823
Sarah	6	F		Stafford	United States	Java	9 Jul 1827
Sarah H.	40	F		U.S.	U.S.	George Canning	26 Aug 1829
William	8	M		England	U.S.A.	Hudson	21 Aug 1829
William	40		Farmer	Great Britain	U. States	Columbia	7 May 1828
Wm.	9	M	None	Great Brittain	U. States	Louisa	11 Jun 1824
Wm.	41	M	Farmer	Great Brittain	U. States	Louisa	11 Jun 1824
HICKSON, James	1	M	None	England	United States	Trident	18 Jul 1827
Margaret	22	F	None	England	United States	Trident	18 Jul 1827
HICKY, Joana	18					Trio	5 May 1828
John	8					Trio	5 May 1828
HIDDEN, E.	32	M	Mechanic	U. States	U. States	General Marion	12 Jul 1823
HIDDLESTON, John	32	M	Merchant	England	America	Britannia	5 Nov 1828
HIDE, John	24	M	Farmer	England	United States	Ganges	10 May 1828
HIENER, A.	9 9/12	F		France	United States	Catharine	10 Sep 1827
Ann Maria	42 3/12	F	Farmer	France	United States	Catharine	10 Sep 1827
Eliza	3 3/12	F		France	United States	Catharine	10 Sep 1827
Joseph	8 7/12	M		France	United States	Catharine	10 Sep 1827
Joseph	43 3/12	M	Farmer	France	United States	Catharine	10 Sep 1827
Michl.	13 6/12	M	Farmer	France	United States	Catharine	10 Sep 1827
HIEST, Sarah	29	F	None	Great Britain	New York	Superior	5 Sep 1827
HIFFERNON, John	30	M	Laborer	Ireland	America	Parrington	9 Jun 1827
HIFFERTAN, James	36	M	Butcher	Great Britain	United States	John Jay	8 May 1828
HIGABOTHIM, Eliza	50	F	None	Great Brittan	U.S.	Emulous	29 Jun 1827
John	20	M	Farmer	Great Brittan	U.S.	Emulous	29 Jun 1827
John	50	M	Farmer	Great Brittan	U.S.	Emulous	29 Jun 1827
Ths.	18	M	Farmer	Great Brittan	U.S.	Emulous	29 Jun 1827
Wm.	73	M	Farmer	Great Brittan	U.S.	Emulous	29 Jun 1827
HIGDEN, George	21	M	Farmer	Great Britain	Uncertain	Roman	10 May 1828
HIGGANS, B.	23	M	Secy. Legation	Netherlands	Netherlands	Talma	23 Sep 1828
HIGGENS, Cathn.	26	F	Servant	Ireland	United States	Wilson	27 Jun 1826
HIGGET, John R. S.	23	M	Gentleman	New York	U.S. America	Superior	18 Jun 1825
HIGGIN, Edwd.	38	M	Joiner	Great Britain		Moro Castle	6 Jul 1827
John	1	M	None	Great Britain		Moro Castle	6 Jul 1827

NAMES OF PASSENGERS	AGE	SEX	OCCUPATIONS	COUNTRY TO WHICH THEY BELONG	COUNTRY THEY INTEND TO INHABIT	SHIPS/DATES OF ARRIVAL	
HIGGET, John R. S.	23	M	Gentleman	New York	U.S. America	Superior	18 Jun 1825
Mary	9	F	None	Great Britain		Moro Castle	6 Jul 1827
Mary	34	F	None	Great Britain		Moro Castle	6 Jul 1827
Robert	36	M	Merchant	Great Britain	United States	New York	19 Nov 1828
Rose	11	F	None	Great Britain		Moro Castle	6 Jul 1827
Thomas	6	M	None	Great Britain		Moro Castle	6 Jul 1827
HIGGINBOTTOM,							
Harriet	27	F	None	Great Britain	United States	Mary & Harriet	3 Jul 1829
HIGGINBOTTON, Jno.	32	M	Labourer	Great Britain	United States	Atlantic	28 May 1827
HIGGINS, —, Revd.	29			Ireland		Anacreon	7 Sep 1827
Ann	21			England		Anacreon	7 Sep 1827
Ann	30	F		Ireland	In Country	Potomac	7 Aug 1827
Anne	24	F	Spinster	Ireland	America	Mary	29 May 1827
Betty	21	F		Ireland	United States	Borneo	28 Aug 1828
C.	20	F	Servant	Ireland	United States	Josephine	30 Apr 1828
Cath.	20	M	Spinster	Ireland	U. States	Meteor	19 Jul 1828
Charles	20	M	Merchant	United	U. States	Sarah G	30 Jun 1828
D.	13	M	Labourer	Great Brittain	United States	Sarah Ralston	27 Jan 1827
Francis	3		Boy	Ireland	In Country	Potomac	7 Aug 1827
Francis	24	M	Farmer	Ireland	United States	Wanderer	31 Aug 1829
George	16	M	Laborer	Ireland	United States	St. Michael	24 Jun 1824
James	20	M	Weaver	Ireland	N. Jersey	Potomac	7 Aug 1827
James	24	M	Cabinet Maker	St. Johns, N.B.	United States	Antioch	21 Sep 1827
Jeremiah	25	M	Farmer			Robert Fulton	8 Mar 1823
Jno.	24	M	Mercht.	G. Britain	G. Britain	Wallace	12 Apr 1824
*Died							
John	1	M		St. Johns	U. States	Wanderer	30 Oct 1828
John	20	M	Labourer	Ireland	U. States	St. Michael's	10 Feb 1827
John	28	M	Farmer			Robert Fulton	8 Mar 1823
John	30	M	Farmer	Ireland	In Country	Potomac	7 Aug 1827
M.	21			Great Britan	United States	Newry	11 Jul 1827
M.	25	M	Labourer	Ireland	United States	Potomac	28 Sep 1827
Margaret	19	F	Spinster	Ireland	United States	Dublin Packet	9 Jul 1827
Margaret	26			Ireland	United States	Robert Burns	30 May 1823
Margret	29	F	Spinster	Ireland	United States	Wilson	6 Jun 1828
Maria	30	F	Mantua Maker	St. Johns	U. States	Wanderer	30 Oct 1828
Mary	1		Girl	Ireland	In Country	Potomac	7 Aug 1827
Mary	20	F	Spinster	Ireland	Unt. St. America	Wilson	21 May 1827
Mary	20	F	Lady	Ireland	United States	Belleville	13 Oct 1827
Mary	28	F	Servant	U. States	Great Britain	Thompson	26 Apr 1828
Michl.	32	M	Labourer	Ireland	U.S. America	Traveller	10 Sep 1827
Ns.	40	M	Farmer	Ireland	U. States	Margaret	19 Mar 1825
Pat	25 3/12	M		Ireland	U.S. of America	Douglass	6 Jul 1829
Patrick	27	M	Labourer	Great Britian	U. States	St. Michael	3 Jan 1825
Patrick	28	M	Labourer	Ireland	U.S. America	Traveller	10 Sep 1827
R.	32	M	Merchant	England	U. States	New York	15 Nov 1823
Rebecca	30	F		U. States	U. States	Pilgrim	16 Aug 1821
Richard	26	M	Mechanic	U.S.	U.S.	Richmond Packet	13 Jun 1825
Richard	32	M	Miner	England	England	Ranger	15 Jan 1827
Richd.	34	M	Mariner	U. States	U. States	Pilgrim	16 Aug 1821
Robert	34	M	Merchant	Ireland	United States	Silas Richards	27 Oct 1825
Roger	30	M	Farmer	Ireland	U.S. America	Traveller	10 Sep 1827
Rosana	23	M	Labourer	Ireland	U. States	Sarah G	30 Jun 1828
Sally	20	F	Captain's Wife	United States	United States	Beaver	29 Aug 1829
Thomas	6	M	Child	Ireland	United States	Dublin Packet	9 Jul 1827
Thomas	21	M	Labourer	Ireland	United States	Robert Fulton	24 Jul 1826
Thos.	26			England		Anacreon	7 Sep 1827
William	5	M	Child	Ireland	United States	Dublin Packet	9 Jul 1827
William	40	M	Labourer	England	New York	Lima	5 Aug 1829
William	40	M	Labourer	Ireland	U. States	Lima	5 Aug 1829
HIGGINSON, Edgar	22	M	Gentleman	England	England	Ann	11 Apr 1821
Edgar	24	M	Farmer	England	U. States	Elizabeth	20 Sep 1822
Edgar	29	M	Merchant	United States	United States	Emulation	17 Dec 1825
Eliza	27	F	None	Great Britain	New York	Superior	5 Sep 1827
George	71	M	None	England		Manhattan	22 May 1827
Phoebe	25	F	None	Great Britain	New York	Superior	5 Sep 1827
R.	27	M	Merchant	U. States	U. States	Tabasco	5 Aug 1826

NAMES OF PASSENGERS	AGE	SEX	OCCUPATIONS	COUNTRY TO WHICH THEY BELONG	COUNTRY THEY INTEND TO INHABIT	SHIPS/DATES OF ARRIVAL	
HIGGINSON (cont'd)							
Stephen	40	M	...	...field...	...	Frances Henrietta	30 Jun 1827
Thos.	67	M	Weaver	Great Britain	New York	Superior	5 Sep 1827
HIGGS, B., Mr.	40	M	Taylor	Bermuda	Missouri	Camden	14 May 1825
Benj.	35	M	Mercht. Tailer	Bermuda	U. States	Mary & Elizabeth	10 Jul 1824
Betsey	32	F	Lady	Bermuda	U. States	Mary & Elizabeth	10 Jul 1824
Patrick	22 3/12	M	Malster	Ireland	United States	London	6 Feb 1829
R. M.	30	M	Minister	Bermuda		Wave	29 Apr 1822
Robert, Mr.		M	Merchant		Philadelphia	Florida	3 Jun 1824
Thomas	23	M	Clerk	Ireland	America	Erin	14 Feb 1820
HIGHAM, Findlay J.	25	M	Merchant	United States	United States	Isaac Hicks	13 Jan 1826
Thomas	50	M	Gentleman	Charleston	United States	Brighton	11 Dec 1827
HIGHCET, Campbell D.	18	M	Baker	Scotland	United States	Camillus	27 Oct 1829
HIGHLAND, Ann	25	F		Great Briton	Ohio	Brighton	12 Jun 1826
Elizabeth	50	F		Great Briton	Ohio	Brighton	12 Jun 1826
Robert	54	M	Farmer	Great Briton	Ohio	Brighton	12 Jun 1826
HIGHMAN, Jacob	20	M	Pedler	Prussia	United States	William & Henry	19 Jul 1822
HIGHTOWER, ...	...	M	...	Great Britain	New York	Dublin	21 Dec 1824
...	30	M	...	Great Britain	New York	Dublin	21 Dec 1824
...m...	...	F	...	Great Britain	New York	Dublin	21 Dec 1824
Cather...	13	F	...	Great Britain	New York	Dublin	21 Dec 1824
Fredk.	...	M	...	Great Britain	New York	Dublin	21 Dec 1824
Jas.	9	M	...	Great Britain	New York	Dublin	21 Dec 1824
Jos.	14	M	...	Great Britain	New York	Dublin	21 Dec 1824
HIGHUM, Thos.	40	M	Merchant	U. States	U. States	Seine	10 Jun 1822
HIGINBOTHOM, Wm. R.	39	M	U.S. Commercial Agent	U. States	U. States	Superior Hope	27 Oct 1824
HIGUE, James	27	M	Shoe Maker	England	New York	Xenophon	3 Oct 1829
HIGUER, A.	16	M	Merchant	Spain	U. States	Fabius	30 Aug 1827
HIHGHAM, Thos.	23	M	Cooper	England	United States	Acasta	25 Sep 1827
HIL, Andres	35	M	Merchant	Spain	Spain	Sciot	12 Mar 1828
HILADOY, James	30	F	Mason	Scotland	U. States	Roger Stewart	9 Jun 1828
HILBERT, Johannes	48	M	Tailor	New York	New York	Maria Elizabeth	18 Jun 1827
HILD, Christian	33	M	...	Wirtemburg	United States	Wade	29 Aug 1825
Christina	1	F	...	Wirtemburg	United States	Wade	29 Aug 1825
Ferderick	9	M	...	Wirtemburg	United States	Wade	29 Aug 1825
Jacob	6	M	...	Wirtemburg	United States	Wade	29 Aug 1825
Jonen	3	F	...	Wirtemburg	United States	Wade	29 Aug 1825
HILDEBRAND, Z.	18	M	Laborer	Hannover	United States	Constitution	6 Jul 1829
HILDITCH, George	21	M	Farmer	Great Briton	United States	Orion	18 Jun 1821
Richard, Jr.	14	M	Boy	Great Briton	United States	Orion	18 Jun 1821
HILDT, John D. G.	24	M	Backer	Stackhard	New York	Maria Elizabeth	18 Jun 1827
HILFOIL, John	30	M	Labourer	Ireland	United States	William	20 Jul 1829
HILGER, L.	40	M	Mercht.	Philadelphia	United States	Howard	28 Aug 1828
HILKEN, John	27	M	Sugar Baker	England	New York	Cortes	23 Nov 1827
HILL, —	6/12					Neptunus	13 Nov 1820
—	1 6/12					Neptunus	13 Nov 1820
—	1 6/12					Neptunus	13 Nov 1820
—	2					Neptunus	13 Nov 1820
—	3					Neptunus	13 Nov 1820
—	4					Neptunus	13 Nov 1820
—	8					Neptunus	13 Nov 1820
—, Infant	0 2/12	F		Great Britain	United States	Jupiter	14 Sep 1827
—, Mrs.	35	F		Great Britain	United States	Jupiter	14 Sep 1827
A.	7	F		Great Britain	United States	Jupiter	14 Sep 1827
A. J.	21	M	Merchant	Great Britain	U. States of America	Junius	5 Jul 1820
A. J.	25	M	Merchant	England	U. States	Falcon	12 Oct 1822
Abraham	22	M	Millman		uncertain	Mount Vernon	29 Aug 1828
Agness	8	F		Great Britain	United States	Jupiter	14 Sep 1827
Ain	27	F	Farmer	England	U.S. States	Splendid	14 Aug 1829
Alexander	9	M		Scotland	U. States	Camillus	29 Jan 1829
Alexdr.	20	M	Farmer	England	U.N. States	Helen	17 Dec 1827
Ann	10	F		England	U.N. States	Helen	17 Dec 1827
Ann	17	F	None	Great Britain	United States	Hannibal	12 Oct 1829
Ann	19	F		U.S.	U.S.	New York	29 Jun 1827

NAMES OF PASSENGERS	AGE	SEX	OCCUPATIONS	COUNTRY TO WHICH THEY BELONG	COUNTRY THEY INTEND TO INHABIT	SHIPS/DATES OF ARRIVAL	
HILL (cont'd)							
Ann	32			England	United States	Neptunus	13 Nov 1820
Ann	33	F	None	England	U. States	Franklin	7 Jul 1828
Ann	46			England	United States	Thomas Dickason	5 Jun 1827
Ann Eliza	22	F	None	U. States	U. States	Canada	4 Oct 1824
Anthony J.	24	M	Merchant	G. Britan	G. Britan	Ariadne	4 Apr 1823
Austin, Rev.	42	M	Clergyman	England	Kentucky	Abigail	9 Aug 1821
Benjamin	1 10/12	M	None	Great Briton	United States	Mount Vernon	29 Aug 1828
Charles	9			England	United States	Thomas Dickason	5 Jun 1827
Charles	31	M	Weaver	England	United States	Peru	23 May 1827
Charles	65	M	Gentleman	Great Briton	Canada	Brighton	12 Jun 1826
Charlotte	25	F		England	U. States	Pleiades	9 Oct 1829
David	20	M	Labourer	Ireland	United States	Ann Maria	4 Oct 1824
David A.	49	M	Merchant	Ireland	U. States	Waterville	19 Dec 1825
Dianna	45	F		England	U.N. States	Helen	17 Dec 1827
Diner	3 6/12			England	United States	Thomas Dickason	5 Jun 1827
E.	4	F		Great Britain	United States	Isaac Hicks	6 Dec 1827
E.	26	M	Spinner	Great Britain	United States	Isaac Hicks	6 Dec 1827
Elen	24	F	Spinster	Ireland	United States	Robert Fulton	24 Jul 1826
Elisabeth	3	F		Great Britain	United States	Mary Howland	19 Jul 1827
Elisabeth	3					Splendid	14 Aug 1829
Elisabeth, Mrs.	26	F		England	U. States	Emily	25 Aug 1827
Elizabeth	6			England	United States	Thomas Dickason	5 Jun 1827
Elizabeth	8	M	Farmer	Philadelphia	Phila.	Sarah Herrick	10 Aug 1827
Elizabeth	25	F		Scotland	U. States	Camillus	29 Jan 1829
Elizabeth	32	F		Scotland	U. States	Camillus	29 Jan 1829
Elly	5	F	None	England	U. States	Franklin	7 Jul 1828
Emelia	10	F		Great Britain	United States	Jupiter	14 Sep 1827
Erlon	8	F	Farmer	England	U.S. States	Splendid	14 Aug 1829
G. R. G., Revd.	24	M	Clergeman	Jamaca	Jamaca	Peruvian	11 Mar 1822
George	11			England	United States	Thomas Dickason	5 Jun 1827
George	11					Cosmo	17 Mar 1828
George	18	M	Spinner	England	United States	Siroc	31 Oct 1829
George	22	M	Farmer	America	America	Evelina	10 Nov 1825
George	30	M	Shoemaker	Scotland	U.S. of America	Camillus	16 Apr 1822
George	43	M	Farmer	Great Britain	United States	Magnet	28 Jun 1821
George	44	M	Farmer	England	U.N. States	Helen	17 Dec 1827
Hannah	12 4/12			England	United States	Thomas Dickason	5 Jun 1827
Hariet	36			England	United States	Neptunus	13 Nov 1820
Harriot	10/12			England	United States	Thomas Dickason	5 Jun 1827
Henry						Bayard	15 Dec 1828
*November 24th Died, sent on board at Havre by the American Consul to be carried to the United States							
Henry	7	M	Farmer	England	U. States	Franklin	7 Jul 1828
Hugh	30	M	Mercht.	United States	United States	Manchester	6 Dec 1825
J. B.	28	M	Doctor	United States	U.S.	Stephania	13 Sep 1821
James	5	M		Great Britain	United States	Jupiter	14 Sep 1827
James	24	M	Farmer	G. Britain	U. States	Mary & Harriot	8 Sep 1824
James	25	M		Great Brittian	United States	Carolina Augusta	2 Dec 1828
James	28	M	Farmer	Scotland	U.S. of America	Camillus	16 Apr 1822
James	28	M	Mechanic	Great Britain	United States	Mary & Harriet	3 Jul 1829
James	29	M	Merchant	Greenock	U. States	Favorite	12 May 1823
James	32	M	...	...	...	Sublime	6 Dec 1824
Jane	26	F	Farmer			Splendid	14 Aug 1829
Janes	1					Splendid	14 Aug 1829
Jeremiah	4	M		U.S.	U.S.	New York	29 Jun 1827
John	18/12	M		England	U. States	Emily	25 Aug 1827
John	9	F		England	U.N. States	Helen	17 Dec 1827
John	13					Cosmo	17 Mar 1828
John	16			England	United States	Thomas Dickason	5 Jun 1827
John	20	M	teacher or Goldlace Maker	England	New York	Cortes	23 Nov 1827

578

NAMES OF PASSENGERS	AGE	SEX	OCCUPATIONS	COUNTRY TO WHICH THEY BELONG	COUNTRY THEY INTEND TO INHABIT	SHIPS/DATES OF ARRIVAL	
HILL (cont'd)							
John	24	M	Farmer	England	U. States	Electra	7 Jul 1828
John	25	M	Farmer	Ireland	United States	Aurora	9 Jul 1827
John	25	M	Clothier	Great Britain	United States	Samuel Wright	12 Oct 1829
John	3...	M	Mariner	G. Britain	Baltimore	Brighton	26 Mar 1827
John	30	M	Mariner	Ireland	New York	Brighton	24 Aug 1827
John	34	F	Farmer			Splendid	14 Aug 1829
John	36 1/12	M		England	U.S. of America	Illinois	30 Apr 1823
John	40	M	Barber	Halifax	U. States	William	28 Jul 1825
John Manuel	35	M	Merchant	Spain		Exploit	18 Jun 1827
Jos.	10					Neptunus	13 Nov 1820
Joseph	29 3/12	M	Joiner	Great Briton	United States	Mount Vernon	29 Aug 1828
Leonard, Mr.	38	M	Grocer	England	U. States	Emily	25 Aug 1827
M.	1	F		Great Britain	United States	Isaac Hicks	6 Dec 1827
Margaret	5					Splendid	14 Aug 1829
Margaret	14	M	Farmer	Philadelphia	Phila.	Sarah Herrick	10 Aug 1827
Mariah	22	F	Wife	Ireland	United States	Ann Maria	4 Oct 1824
Marth.	19	F	Spinster	Ireland		Robert Fulton	4 Jun 1828
Martha	4	F		Great Britain	United States	Mary Howland	19 Jul 1827
Martha	26			Ireland	United States	Fabius	31 Jul 1829
Mary	11	F		Great Britain	United States	Jupiter	14 Sep 1827
Mary	13	F		England	U.N. States	Helen	17 Dec 1827
Mary	13 6/12			England	United States	Thomas Dickason	5 Jun 1827
Mary	16	F		Bristol	New York	Cosmo	25 Sep 1827
Mary	17	F		Scotland	U. States	Camillus	29 Jan 1829
Mary	18	F	Farmer	Great Britain	United States	Magnet	28 Jun 1821
Mary	22	F	Spinster	Ireland		Robert Fulton	4 Jun 1828
Mary	24 9/12	F	None	Great Briton	United States	Mount Vernon	29 Aug 1828
Mary	40	M	Farmer	Philadelphia	Phila.	Sarah Herrick	10 Aug 1827
Mary	40					Cosmo	17 Mar 1828
Mary	40	F	Servant	U. States	U. States	Henry	24 Oct 1828
Michael	32	M	Farmer	Great Britain	United States	Mount Vernon	17 Jun 1825
Nancy	10			England	United States	Thomas Dickason	5 Jun 1827
Patrick	70	M	Labourer	Ireland	United States	Robert Fulton	24 Jul 1826
Richard	...	...	...	...	...	St. Michael	22 Sep 1824
Richd.	25	M	Labourer	Great Britain		Moro Castle	6 Jul 1827
Robard	10	M		England	U. States	Emily	25 Aug 1827
Robert	5	M		Co. Antrim	Co. Antrin	Aldebaron	21 Jan 1826
Robert	5	M		Scotland	U. States	Camillus	29 Jan 1829
Robert	25	M	Turner	England	U.S.A.	Hudson	21 Aug 1829
Robert	35	M	Farmer	Ireland	United States	Atlantic	16 Dec 1825
Robert	40	M	Oficer	England	U. States	Hiram	17 Jun 1826
Robet	26	M	Merchant	Grat Britan	Great Britan	Columbia	7 Apr 1823
S.	25	F		Great Britain	United States	Isaac Hicks	6 Dec 1827
Sally	5					Neptunus	13 Nov 1820
Saml.	11	M		Bristol	New York	Cosmo	25 Sep 1827
Saml.	23	M	Shoemaker	G. Britain	U. States	Congress	23 Mar 1824
Samuel	19	F	Farmer	Great Britain	United States	Magnet	28 Jun 1821
Samuel	25 4/12	M	weaver	Ireland	United States	Atlantic	21 Jul 1827
Samuel	30	M	Shoemaker	England	United States	William Howland	5 Jul 1821
Samuel	30	M	Cotton Spinner	Great Britain	United States	Samuel Wright	12 Oct 1829
Sarah	6/12	F		Great Britain	United States	Mary Howland	19 Jul 1827
Sarah	8			England	United States	Thomas Dickason	5 Jun 1827
Sarah	34	F		Great Britain	United States	Mary Howland	19 Jul 1827
Serah	30	F	Spinster	Ireland	United States	Robert Fulton	24 Jul 1826
T.	36	M	Seamen	America	U. States	Minerva	18 Oct 1828
Thomas	6	M		Great Britain	United States	Mary Howland	19 Jul 1827
Thomas	14 6/12			England	United States	Thomas Dickason	5 Jun 1827
Thomas	22		Labourer	England	United States	Hugh Johnson	11 Jun 1828
Thomas	27	M	Labourer	England	U. States	Ayrshire	12 May 1828
Thomas	34	M	Farmer	England	U. States	Franklin	7 Jul 1828
Thomas	46			England	United States	Thomas Dickason	5 Jun 1827
Thoms.	2	F	Farmer	England	U.S. States	Splendid	14 Aug 1829

NAMES OF PASSENGERS	AGE	SEX	OCCUPATIONS	COUNTRY TO WHICH THEY BELONG	COUNTRY THEY INTEND TO INHABIT	SHIPS/DATES OF ARRIVAL	
HILL (cont'd)							
Thoms.	4	F	Farmer	England	U.S. States	Splendid	14 Aug 1829
Thos.	1	M	Farmer	England	U. States	Franklin	7 Jul 1828
Thos.	3	M		Great Britain	United States	Jupiter	14 Sep 1827
Thos.	40	M	Merchant	Boston	U. States	New Priscilla	22 Aug 1823
Thos., Capt.	26	M	Seaman	Liverpool	Liverpool	Leo	31 Jul 1826
Thos. H.	38	M	Planter	Great Britain	United States	Jupiter	14 Sep 1827
William	7	M		Scotland	U. States	Camillus	29 Jan 1829
William	20		Merchant	Ireland		Nancy	11 Sep 1820
William	22	M	Merchant	United States	United States	Tampico	13 Oct 1825
William	34	M	Merchant	New Orleans	New Orleans	Hector	11 Oct 1822
William	40	F	Rope Maker	England	United States	Danube	22 Aug 1825
Willm.	11	F		England	U.N. States	Helen	17 Dec 1827
Willm.	44	M	Ship Master	U. States	U. States	Dromo	28 Feb 1829
Wm.	7					Neptunus	13 Nov 1820
Wm.	7	M		Co. Antrim	Co. Antrin	Aldebaron	21 Jan 1826
Wm.	36	M	Merchant	Gt. Britain	U. States	Canada	4 Oct 1824
Wm.	38	M	Farmer	England	U.S. States	Splendid	14 Aug 1829
Wm., Junr.	6	F	Farmer	England	U.S. States	Splendid	14 Aug 1829
Wm. Scott	8/12	M	None	U. States	U. States	Canada	4 Oct 1824
HILLAN, G.	37	M		Germany	United States	Robert Edwards	1 Jun 1826
HILLARD, Martha	22	F		Connecticut	U. States	Zephyr	18 May 1825
Moses	42	M	Mariner	Connecticutt	U. States	Edgar	23 Nov 1824
Rob.	40	M	Mariner	U. States	U. States	Morning Star	6 Oct 1823
HILLARGIN, Richard	30	M	Labourer	Ireland		Marchioness	13 May 1828
HILLER, Benj.			late Master			Vernon	17 Dec 1828
*Died on the Voyage							
Benjn.	32	M	Mariner	New York	N. York	Columbia	14 Apr 1824
T.	24	M	Mariner	U. States	U. States	Elias Burger	30 Nov 1822
HILLES, David	20	M	Labourer	Ireland	United States	Lord Wellington	28 May 1827
HILLEY, Edward	36	M	...	Ireland	U. States	Argus	26 Dec 1825
HILLIARD,							
William	35 1/12	M	Gentleman	England	United States	France	6 Oct 1828
Wm.	46	M	Bookseller	U. States	U. States	Canada	2 Jun 1824
HILLIKAR, R.	41	M	Clothier	G. Britain	Canada	Cosmo	25 Nov 1826
HILLINGWORTH,							
Ann	60	F	None	Great Briton	United States	Mount Vernon	30 Dec 1828
Bartley	11 5/12	M	None	Great Briton	United States	Mount Vernon	30 Dec 1828
HILLMAN, Ann	9	F		England	United States	Cosmo	21 Aug 1828
Ann	39	F		England	United States	Cosmo	21 Aug 1828
Caroline	4	F		England	United States	Cosmo	21 Aug 1828
Harry	8	M		England	United States	Cosmo	21 Aug 1828
Hester	20	F		England	United States	Cosmo	21 Aug 1828
John	40	M	Clothier	Bristol	New York	Cosmo	25 Sep 1827
Joseph	1	M		England	United States	Cosmo	21 Aug 1828
Peter	11	M		Bristol	New York	Cosmo	25 Sep 1827
HILLOCK, Andrew	19	M	Labourer	Ireland	N. York	Trusty	12 Sep 1828
Andrew	40	M	Labourer	Ireland	N. York	Trusty	12 Sep 1828
Bess	7	F	Servant	Ireland	N. York	Trusty	12 Sep 1828
Eliz.	12	F	Servant	Ireland	N. York	Trusty	12 Sep 1828
Eliz.	44	F	Servant	Ireland	N. York	Trusty	12 Sep 1828
Geo.	17	M	Labourer	Ireland	N. York	Trusty	12 Sep 1828
John	9	M	D. Maker	Ireland	N. York	Trusty	12 Sep 1828
Mary	14	F	Servant	Ireland	N. York	Trusty	12 Sep 1828
Rachel	24	F		Scotland	U. States	Sceptre	24 Jul 1822
Stephen	20	M	Labourer	Scotland	U. States	Sceptre	24 Jul 1822
HILLS, Alfred	3	M		England	U. States	Hudson	8 Oct 1827
Ann	9	F		England	U. States	Hudson	8 Oct 1827
Edwin	5	M		England	U. States	Hudson	8 Oct 1827
Elizabeth	29	F		United States	United States	Canada	20 Jun 1823
H. W.	36 1/12	M	Merchant	United States	U. States	Panthea	5 Oct 1822
John	30	M	Gentleman	U.S.	United States	Josephine	24 Jul 1826
Joseph	32	M	Farmer	England	United States	John Wells	15 Jan 1827
May	26	F		England	U. States	Hudson	8 Oct 1827
Robt.	7	M		England	U. States	Hudson	8 Oct 1827
Sarah	1	F		England	U. States	Hudson	8 Oct 1827
Stephen	22	M	Merchant	American	U. States	Nestor	9 Dec 1822
Stephen	51	M	Architect	United States	United States	Canada	20 Jun 1823
HILLSON, Mary	19	F	Spinster	America	America	Concord	4 Jun 1821

NAMES OF PASSENGERS	AGE	SEX	OCCUPATIONS	COUNTRY TO WHICH THEY BELONG	COUNTRY THEY INTEND TO INHABIT	SHIPS/DATES OF ARRIVAL	
HILLYER, Edward	36		Seaman	England	England	Hudson	4 Sep 1823
Hetty	34	F		U. States	U. States	Prospect	4 Apr 1822
Nathaniel	26 6/12	M	Merchant	United States	New York	Loire	9 Aug 1821
HILPERT, Peter	43	M	Smith			Constitution	20 Jun 1828
HILSTON, Charlotte	2	F		Great Britain		Dalmannock	24 Ocg 1826
Elizabeth	34	F		Great Britain		Dalmannock	24 Ocg 1826
Jessee	9	F		Great Britain		Dalmannock	24 Ocg 1826
Robert	12	M		Great Britain		Dalmannock	24 Ocg 1826
HILTON, James	34	M	Laborer	Gt. Britain	United States	Silas Richards	20 Jun 1826
Margt.	26	F		G. Britain	U. States	George Clinton	10 Sep 1828
Peter	28	M	Finisher Cloth	England	N. York	Salem	15 Mar 1828
Saul	...	M	...	...	U. States	Louisiana	31 Oct 1827
Susan	...	F	...	...	U. States	Louisiana	31 Oct 1827
William	...	M	...	...	U. States	Louisiana	31 Oct 1827
William	22	M	Grocer	Great Britain	U. States	Ann Maria	29 Nov 1821
HILTS, Barby	8	F		Sweden	Ohio	Abby Jones	12 Jul 1827
Catharine	2	F		Sweden	Ohio	Abby Jones	12 Jul 1827
Christian	4	M		Sweden	Ohio	Abby Jones	12 Jul 1827
Frany	36	F		Sweden	Ohio	Abby Jones	12 Jul 1827
John	9	M		Sweden	Ohio	Abby Jones	12 Jul 1827
Peter	6	M		Sweden	Ohio	Abby Jones	12 Jul 1827
Peter	36	M	Farmer	Sweden	Ohio	Abby Jones	12 Jul 1827
HILVETH, William	22	M	Silver Smith	Great Britain		Eliza Grant	29 Aug 1829
HILZEL, Catherine	17	F	Weaver	France	U. States	Edward Quesnel	4 Aug 1828
Elizabeth	9	F	Weaver	France	U. States	Edward Quesnel	4 Aug 1828
Joseph	42	M	Weaver	France	U. States	Edward Quesnel	4 Aug 1828
Magdalina	41	F	Weaver	France	U. States	Edward Quesnel	4 Aug 1828
HIMELY, A., Mrs.						Brandt	7 Feb 1822
Ann Eliza, Miss				U.S.	U.S.	Brandt	7 Feb 1822
Caroline, Miss				U.S.	U.S.	Brandt	7 Feb 1822
H. B., Mr.	22		Mercht.	U.S.	U.S.	Brandt	7 Feb 1822
J. J., Mr.	26		Mercht.	U.S.	U.S.	Brandt	7 Feb 1822
HIMEN, A. B.	23	M	Merchant	U. States	U. States	Juno	4 Sep 1824
HINBURY, Matthias	46	M	Carpenter	England	U. States	Don Quixote	25 Oct 1828
HINCAIN, George	30	M	Weaver	Gt. Brittain	United States	Balaena	8 Jan 1825
HINCKEN, Theodore S.	22		Merchant	U. States	U. States	Eliza Pigott	25 Sep 1820
HINCKLEY, Mary Ann	22	F		America	U. States	Calais Packet	7 Jul 1828
HINCKSON, Sussan	21			England	England	Corinthian	8 Oct 1828
HIND, Ann	30	F	None	Great Britain	U. States	Balance	19 Jun 1824
Bridget	18	F	Spinster	Ireland	America	Wilson	16 May 1825
Caroline	2	F	None	Great Britain	U. States	Balance	19 Jun 1824
Hy.	6/12	M	None	Great Britain	U. States	Balance	19 Jun 1824
John	3	M	None	Great Britain	U. States	Balance	19 Jun 1824
John	30	M	Labourer	Great Britain	U. States	Balance	19 Jun 1824
Martha	26	F	None	Great Britain	U. States	Balance	19 Jun 1824
Richd.	28	M	Labourer	Great Britain	U. States	Balance	19 Jun 1824
Sarah	3	F	None	Great Britain	U. States	Balance	19 Jun 1824
Thos.	6/12	M	None	Great Britain	U. States	Balance	19 Jun 1824
William	36	M	Planter	Jamaica	Jamaica	Leo	31 Jul 1826
Wm.	2/12	M	None	Great Britain	U. States	Balance	19 Jun 1824
HINDHOUGH, R. S.	56	M	Shoemaker	Great Britain	United States	Dapper	24 Aug 1827
HINDMAN, Elizabeth	18	F	Spinster	Scotland	United States	Friends	7 Jul 1827
Isabella	10	F	Spinster	Scotland	United States	Friends	7 Jul 1827
Leany	42	F	Spinster	Scotland	United States	Friends	7 Jul 1827
Margret	7	F	Spinster	Scotland	United States	Friends	7 Jul 1827
Mary	5	F	Spinster	Scotland	United States	Friends	7 Jul 1827
Robert	45	M	Labourer	Scotland	United States	Friends	7 Jul 1827
Robert	46	M	Miner	Scotland	United States	Orion	15 Jan 1827
HINDS, Elizabeth	54	F		England	America	Thames	27 May 1822
Ewd.	15	M	Gentleman	Ireland	United States	Jubilee	13 Sep 1827
George	6	M		England	America	Thames	27 May 1822
Hugh	19	M	Weaver	Ireland	U. States	Adno	5 Jul 1828
Hugh	26	M	Weaver	Ireland	U. States	Adno	5 Jul 1828
James	28	M	Farmer	Ireland	America	Josephine	8 Jan 1827
Jas.	27	M	Labourer	Ireland	United States	Thomas	13 Dec 1827
Johan	50	M	...	England	America	Thames	27 May 1822
John	4	M		Ireland	America	Josephine	8 Jan 1827
John, Jr.	15	M		England	America	Thames	27 May 1822
Joseph	16	M	Gentleman	Ireland	United States	Jubilee	13 Sep 1827

NAMES OF PASSENGERS	AGE	SEX	OCCUPATIONS	COUNTRY TO WHICH THEY BELONG	COUNTRY THEY INTEND TO INHABIT	SHIPS/DATES OF ARRIVAL	
HINDS (cont'd)							
M.	20	M		Ireland	U. States	Adno	5 Jul 1828
Mary	20	F		Ireland	U. States	Adno	5 Jul 1828
Patrick	20	M	Gentleman	Ireland	United States	Jubilee	13 Sep 1827
Richard	2	M		Ireland	America	Josephine	8 Jan 1827
Robert	29	M		England	America	Thames	27 May 1822
HINE, David	24		Carpenter	Guilford	England	Rockingham	23 Aug 1822
HINERACA, G.	44	M	Merchant	Spain	U. States	Native	15 Apr 1826
HINES, Bridget	1 6/12	F		U. States	U. States	Albion	23 Apr 1822
John	25	M	Glazier	United States	U. States	Sarah Ralston	20 Feb 1826
Sarah	2	F		U. States	U. States	Albion	23 Apr 1822
Sarah	25	F		U. States	U. States	Albion	23 Apr 1822
HINGEN, Mary	19	F		Gt. Britain	United States	John & Elizabeth	25 Sep 1827
HINGHAM, James	51	M	...	Halifax	New York	Frances Henrietta	30 Jun 1827
John	13	M	None	Halifax	New York	Frances Henrietta	30 Jun 1827
HINGHCLIFFE, Josuah	20	M	Weaver	Blakleer	Blakleer	Howard Douglass	11 May 1827
HINHOFER,							
Johann Martin	20	M	Weaver	Baden	United States	Jason	3 Nov 1828
Johannes	22	M	Weaver	Baden	United States	Jason	3 Nov 1828
Joseph	53	M	Weaver	Baden	United States	Jason	3 Nov 1828
HINILAY, Manus	28	M	Laborer	Ireland	United States	Ann Maria	18 Dec 1827
HINKELL, Abraham	21	M	Ship Carpenter	Halifax, N.S.	Halifax	St. Michael	28 Feb 1826
HINKEN, Louisa	2	F		United States	United States	Acasta	12 Dec 1823
Mary	39	F		United States	United States	Acasta	12 Dec 1823
HINKLEY, Saml.	30	M	Merchant	Massachusetts	U. States	Abigail	11 Apr 1823
HINLEY, John James	24	M	Merchant	United States	U. States	Active	23 Mar 1820
HINMAN, A.	17	M	Child	Switzerland	U. States	Romulus	24 Sep 1828
Antoine	45	M	Potter	Switzerland	U. States	Romulus	24 Sep 1828
Benjamin	24	M	Farmer	U.S.		Venus	11 Aug 1820
C.	18	F		Switzerland	U. States	Romulus	24 Sep 1828
F.	5	M		Switzerland	U. States	Romulus	24 Sep 1828
J.	16	M		Switzerland	U. States	Romulus	24 Sep 1828
M.	12	M		Switzerland	U. States	Romulus	24 Sep 1828
M.	13	M		Switzerland	U. States	Romulus	24 Sep 1828
M.	19	F		Switzerland	U. States	Romulus	24 Sep 1828
Munson	30	M	Mariner	U. States	U. States	Jane	16 Oct 1821
Munson	35	M	Merchant	Connecticut	U. States	Prince Edward	2 Sep 1822
Munson	35	M	Mariner	U. States	U. States	Enterprize	24 Mar 1823
T.	3	M		Switzerland	U. States	Romulus	24 Sep 1828
T.	40	F		Switzerland	U. States	Romulus	24 Sep 1828
HINS, Ann	20	F		Ireland	United States	Dalhouse Castle	8 May 1827
Claus	17	M	Labourer	Germany	United States	Constitution	2 Aug 1826
HINST, Joseph	34	M	Clothier	Great Britain	United States	John Wells	18 Sep 1826
HINTON, Ann	19	F		Great Britain	U. States	Great Britain	18 Mar 1828
HINTZ, Anthony	40	M	Ship Master	United States	Massachusetts	Monroe	12 Dec 1825
Jane H.	29	F	None	United States	Massachusetts	Monroe	12 Dec 1825
HINWET, Peter	36			Ireland	U.S.	Union	20 Aug 1827
HIPPE, W. H.	40	F		France	U. States	Sarah Ann	5 Aug 1820
HIPPOLITI, Jno.	20	M	Taylor	America	U. States	Ambuscade	11 Jul 1821
HIPSWELLING, Francis	28	M	F	France	Canada	Abby Jones	12 Jul 1827
HIPVARD, Catharine	41	F	None	Switzerland	U. States	Isaac Hicks	22 Aug 1829
Francis	65	M	Farmer	Switzerland	U. States	Isaac Hicks	22 Aug 1829
HIPWORTH, Hannah	32	F		Great Britain	U.S. of America	Gratitude	3 Oct 1829
Joshua	61	M	Courier	Great Britain	U.S. of America	Gratitude	3 Oct 1829
Louisa	1	F		Great Britain	U.S. of America	Gratitude	3 Oct 1829
HIRD, Maria	18	F	None	Canada	Canada	Nestor in Liverpool	29 Jul 1822
HIRON, —, Servant	16	M	Servant	France	France	Imperial	10 Dec 1821
HIRSCHOCKS, Henry	47	M	Mason	Winterborn	Bavaris	New York Packet	19 Aug 1820
Johannes	20	M	Mason	Winterborn	Bavaris	New York Packet	19 Aug 1820
Maria, his Wife	37	F		Winterborn	Bavaris	New York Packet	19 Aug 1820
HIRST, Hiram	23		Merchant	England	England	Hudson	4 Sep 1823

NAMES OF PASSENGERS	AGE	SEX	OCCUPATIONS	COUNTRY TO WHICH THEY BELONG	COUNTRY THEY INTEND TO INHABIT	SHIPS/DATES OF ARRIVAL	
HIRST (cont'd)							
Jonathan	40		Brick Layer	G. Britain		Casanda	5 Sep 1827
Lydia	34	F		G. Britain	U.S.A.	Silas Richards	29 Oct 1827
Mary	53	F	Servant	England	U.N. States	Corinthian	1 Sep 1823
Samuel	45	M	Farmer	G. Britain	U.S.A.	Silas Richards	29 Oct 1827
Sarah	19		None	Great Britain	United States	Roman	10 Sep 1827
Thos.	20	M	Merchant	Great Britain	United States	Martha	3 May 1821
William	26	M	Labourer	Great Britain	United States	Frances Henrietta	17 Sep 1827
Wm.	35	M	Linen man	Gt. Britain	United States	Robert Edwards	1 Jun 1826
HIRTH, John J.	24	M		Brattain		L'Esperance	6 Sep 1828
HIRTZ, Victor	38	M	Musician	France	U. States	Edward Quesnel	17 Mar 1829
HISCOCK, Arthur	23	M	Farmer	England	United States	William Howland	5 Jul 1821
HISKOCK, Wm.	37	M	Carpenter	Great Britain	United States	Asia	14 Jul 1829
HISSEY, Charles	40	M	Gentleman	England	New York	Brighton	24 Aug 1827
HITCH, Robert	25	M	Weaver	England	United States	Delta	24 Oct 1829
HITCHCOCK, Edward	20	M	Clerk	England	United States	Cosmo	26 Aug 1829
Electa	35	F	Merchant	N. York	U. States	Four Sons	31 May 1823
Elizabeth	35 8/12	F		England	U.S. of America	Illinois	16 Jun 1821
James	16 3/12	M		England	U.S. of America	Illinois	16 Jun 1821
Jno.	40	M	Merchant	N. York	U. States	Four Sons	31 May 1823
L. M.	45	M	Mariner	U. States	U. States	Douglass	30 Oct 1826
William	39 8/12	M	Carpenter	England	U.S. of America	Illinois	16 Jun 1821
HITCHCOX, J.	30	M	Merchant	United States	United States	Abigail	25 Jun 1822
HITCHELLS, John	29	M	Mechanic	Great Britain		Birmingham	11 Oct 1828
HITCHINGS, William	23	M	Engineer	England	U. States	Messenger	10 Jul 1829
HITCHINS, E.	30		Servant	Great Britan	U. States	Napoleon	10 Jan 1828
HITTER, Henie	24	M	Weaver	France	U. States	Edward Bopnnaffe	30 Jul 1829
HO..., John	25		Farmer	Edcom	England	Packet	27 Aug 1822
Sophia	24			Edcom	England	Packet	27 Aug 1822
HO...ARD, Thomas	27	M	Farmer	Ireland	United States	Trident	30 Sep 1826
HO...D, John	48		Farmer			Splendid	14 Aug 1829
HOAK, John	20	M	Labourer	Ireland	United States	Ann Maria	4 Oct 1824
HOAN, Eliza	35	F	Servant	Ireland	America	Carolina Ann	7 Aug 1826
HOAR, John	10	M	Child	England	United States	Maria	29 Sep 1823
Patrick	27 2/12	M	Labourer	England	United States	John Wells	22 May 1826
HOARAN, Kosanna	16	F	Spinster	Ireland	United States	General Marion	20 Aug 1828
HOARY, Catharar	14	F	Brewer	France		Pallas	14 Jun 1828
Grusa Jean	40	M	Labourer	France		Pallas	14 Jun 1828
HOATH, Charlotte	3	F		England	United States	Danube	13 Jul 1827
Henry	39	M	Mason	Manchester	United States	Nile	17 May 1827
James	1	M		England	United States	Danube	13 Jul 1827
James	25	M	Mason	Manchester	United States	Nile	17 May 1827
John	2	M		England	United States	Danube	13 Jul 1827
Mary	30	F		England	United States	Danube	13 Jul 1827
Thomas	27	M	Laborer	England	United States	Danube	13 Jul 1827
HOB, John	20	M	Watchmaker	Swiss	Switzerland	Stephania	13 Sep 1821
HOBBINS, Thos., (Sevt.)	14	M	Servant	Great Briton	United States	Orion	18 Jun 1821
HOBBS, Danl.	23	M	Butcher	England	U. States	Hudson	8 Oct 1827
Edward	24	M	Farmer	England	U. States	Acasta	12 May 1825
Esther	22	F		England	U. States	Hudson	8 Oct 1827
Mary Ann	35	F		England	United States	Cosmo	26 Aug 1829
HOBBY, Gust.	40	M	Merchant	Germany	U. States	Bayard	5 Sep 1828
HOBERT, —, The Right Revd. Bishop	49	M	Bishop	U. States	U. States	Canada	13 Oct 1825
HOBSON, Charles	19	M	Farmer	Great Britain	U. States	Yamacraw	4 Sep 1822
Elizabeth	42	F	Farmer	Great Britain	U. States	Yamacraw	4 Sep 1822
Francis	25	M	Merchant	England	England	William Thompson	19 Aug 1829
George	20		Clothier	Great Britain	United States	Roman	10 Sep 1827
George	29	M	Cloathier	..., ...ester, England	U. States	New Orleans	24 Aug 1827
James	8	M	Farmer	Great Britain	U. States	Yamacraw	4 Sep 1822
James	15	M	Farmer	Great Britain	U. States	Yamacraw	4 Sep 1822
James	24	M	Farmer	England	U. States	Roman	1 Dec 1828
James	55	M	Farmer	Great Britain	U. States	Yamacraw	4 Sep 1822
Jno.	13	M	Farmer	Great Britain	U. States	Yamacraw	4 Sep 1822

NAMES OF PASSENGERS	AGE	SEX	OCCUPATIONS	COUNTRY TO WHICH THEY BELONG	COUNTRY THEY INTEND TO INHABIT	SHIPS/DATES OF ARRIVAL	
HOBSON (cont'd)							
John C., Mr.	23	M	Merchant	Gt. Britain	Gt. Britain	Pacific	22 May 1826
Mary	11	F	Farmer	Great Britain	U. States	Yamacraw	4 Sep 1822
Peter	17	M	Farmer	Great Britain	U. States	Yamacraw	4 Sep 1822
Peter J.	16	M	Attorney			Amity	11 Sep 1820
Rob.	8	M	Farmer	Great Britain	U. States	Yamacraw	4 Sep 1822
Thomas	13	M	Farmer	Great Britain	U. States	Yamacraw	4 Sep 1822
Wm.	25			England		Anacreon	7 Sep 1827
HOCH, Christian	10	M	there child [John G. & Jaynet]	Germany	United States	Helen	5 Sep 1828
Christina	4	F	there child [John G. & Jaynet]	Germany	United States	Helen	5 Sep 1828
Jaquet	2	F	there child [John G. & Jaynet]	Germany	United States	Helen	5 Sep 1828
Jaynet	38	F	his wife [John G.]	Germany	United States	Helen	5 Sep 1828
John	2	M	there child [John G. & Jaynet]	Germany	United States	Helen	5 Sep 1828
John G.	40	M	Farmer	Germany	United States	Helen	5 Sep 1828
Philip	5	M	there child [John G. & Jaynet]	Germany	United States	Helen	5 Sep 1828
Theos.	8	M	there child [John G. & Jaynet]	Germany	United States	Helen	5 Sep 1828
HOCK, M.	20	M		Switzerland	U.S.	Francois I	8 Aug 1829
HOCKENCABB,							
George Michl.	27	M	Farmer	Germany	America	Falcon	28 Aug 1828
HOCKING, Saml.	16	M	Servant	Great Britain	Mexico	Corinthian	27 Apr 1824
HOCKINGS, Mary	46	F	Miner	Great Britain	United States	Thomas Dickason	31 Jul 1829
Oliver	50	M	Miner	Great Britain	United States	Thomas Dickason	31 Jul 1829
HOCKLEY, Thomas	23	M	Merchant	United States	United States	New Been	18 Jan 1820
Thos.	22	M	Merchant	U. States	U. States	Marcellus	26 Feb 1824
HOCKWALD, Adam	17	M	Tinner	Switzerland	U. States	Hewes	30 Oct 1829
HOCRANS, Lorenso	28	M	Merchant	Portugal	U. States	Minos	24 Oct 1828
HOCTOR, Ann	12			Ireland	Philidelphia	General Marion	21 Nov 1828
Jas.	34	M	Labourer	Great Britain		Moro Castle	6 Jul 1827
John	14			Ireland	Philidelphia	General Marion	21 Nov 1828
John	30			Ireland	Philidelphia	General Marion	21 Nov 1828
HODG, Helen	23	F	None	Scotland	U. States	Czar	29 Aug 1829
HODGE, Eliza	9	F	None	Ireland	United States	Lord Wellington	28 May 1827
Francis	40	M	Labourer	Ireland	United States	Lord Wellington	28 May 1827
Geo.	20	M	Apothecary	America	U. States	Cincinnatus	9 Jul 1825
H. A., Mr.	26	M	Merchant	U.S.A.		François I	19 Nov 1828
Jane	9	F	None	Ireland	United States	Lord Wellington	28 May 1827
John	7	M	None	Ireland	United States	Lord Wellington	28 May 1827
John	24	M	Taylor	Scotland	U. States	Czar	29 Aug 1829
John	27	M	Farmer	Scotland	America	Friends	24 Sep 1821
John L.	44	M	Merchant	Philadelphia	U. States	Montano	19 Feb 1824
M. F.	28	M	Merchant	U. States	U. States	Ann Elizabeth	24 Jun 1823
Margaret	16	F	None	Ireland	United States	Lord Wellington	28 May 1827
Mary	12	F	None	Ireland	United States	Lord Wellington	28 May 1827
Nancy	13	F	None	Ireland	United States	Lord Wellington	28 May 1827
Sally	6/12	F	None	Ireland	United States	Lord Wellington	28 May 1827
Susan	35	F	None	Ireland	United States	Lord Wellington	28 May 1827
Wm.	20	M	Servant	St. Croix	U. States	Carlo	30 Jul 1827
Wm. C.	30	M	Merchant	England	U.S.	Pacific	24 Oct 1828
HODGEKINS, John	21		Stone Cutter	G. Britain	America	Grand Turk	10 Jul 1820
HODGES, C.	30	M	Clergy Man	U. States	U. States	Caledonia	10 Sep 1828
Chas.	40	M	Military	Ireland	United States	Exchange	16 Feb 1822
Edward	35	M	Merchant	Phila.	U. States	Margaret	11 Mar 1823
Hannah	1	F	Child	Ireland	United States	Dublin Packet	9 Jul 1827
J. W.						Day	14 Jun 1822
Jno. H.	24	M	Merchant	U.S.	U.S.	Florida	17 May 1825

NAMES OF PASSENGERS	AGE	SEX	OCCUPATIONS	COUNTRY TO WHICH THEY BELONG	COUNTRY THEY INTEND TO INHABIT	SHIPS/DATES OF ARRIVAL	
HODGES (cont'd)							
John	24					Splendid	14 Aug 1829
John	32	M	Farmer	Ireland	United States	Dublin Packet	9 Jul 1827
John H.	26	M	Merchant	U. States	U. States	Canada	5 Jun 1827
Joseph	45	M	Seaman	United States	United States	Augusta	27 Aug 1829
Samuel, Junr.	31	M	U.S. Consul for the Cape de Verd Islands	United States	United States	Oswego	12 Apr 1824
Sophia	37	F	Wife	Ireland	United States	Dublin Packet	9 Jul 1827
HODGESS,							
William, Jr.	10 6/12	M	None	Great Britain	State of N. York	Robert Fulton	30 Dec 1824
William, Sr.	36	M	Musician	Great Britain	State of N. York	Robert Fulton	30 Dec 1824
HODGINS, Henry	20	M	Farmer	England	U. States	Commerce	2 Oct 1823
James	20	M	Steward	Ireland	New York	Bowditch	27 Apr 1826
James	22	M	Farmer	England	U. States	Commerce	2 Oct 1823
Margaret	27	F	Farmer	England	U. States	Commerce	2 Oct 1823
HODGKINTON, Wm. G.	28	M	Farmer	America	America	Napoleon	26 May 1828
HODGKISSON, Ann	40	F		G. Britain	U. States	Mary Howland	22 Sep 1828
John	45	M	Smith	G. Britain	U. States	Mary Howland	22 Sep 1828
HODGSHER, John	23	M				Eliza Grant	6 Oct 1828
HODGSON, A. L.	23	M	Merchant	United States	United States	Emma	12 May 1826
Betsey	5	F		Great Britain	United States	Ann	22 Dec 1821
Donald	12	M	None	Jamaica	U. States	Hal	7 Jun 1824
E.	40	F	None	U. States	U. States	Hal	7 Jun 1824
Elizabeth	26	F		Great Britain	United States	Ganges	8 Jul 1820
Feilden	26	M	Merchant	G. Bt.	G. Bt.	Canada	13 Feb 1826
Henry	36	M	Captain	England	U.S.	Lewis	29 Oct 1825
Henry, Capt.	33	M	Mariner	U.S.	U.S.	Cadmus	26 Apr 1824
Isabella		F	Infant	Great Britain	United States	Ganges	8 Jul 1820
James	23			Cumberland	Ohio	Peru	30 May 1828
Johana	21	F	None	Jamaica	U. States	Hal	7 Jun 1824
Margt.	9	F		Great Britain	United States	Ann	22 Dec 1821
Margt.	29	F		Great Britain	United States	Ann	22 Dec 1821
Mary	5	F		Great Britain	United States	Ganges	8 Jul 1820
Mary	10	F		Great Britain	United States	Ann	22 Dec 1821
Robert	22	M	Farmer	England	United States	Jubilee	1 Oct 1828
Saml.	7	F		Great Britain	United States	Ann	22 Dec 1821
Sarah	12	F		Great Britain	United States	Ann	22 Dec 1821
Thomas	11	M		Great Britain	United States	Ann	22 Dec 1821
William	29 2/12	M	Engineer	England	U. States	Mary Ann	2 Jan 1829
Wm.	3	M		Great Britain	United States	Ganges	8 Jul 1820
Wm.	25	M		Great Britain	United States	Ganges	8 Jul 1820
Wm.	28	M	Miller	Great Britain	United States	Ann	22 Dec 1821
HODKINS, John	35		Lock Smith	England	United States	Mary	15 Jul 1822
Sarah	30			England	United States	Mary	15 Jul 1822
Sarah	42	F	None	United States	United States	Mount Vernon	29 Aug 1828
HODSON, ...has.	21		Clerk	Ireland	U.S.	Hibernia	27 Jun 1821
Bridget	3	F	None	Jamaica	U. States	Hal	7 Jun 1824
Elizabeth	2	F	None	Jamaica	U. States	Hal	7 Jun 1824
John	23	M	Woolsorter	Great Britian	United States	George Clinton	21 Oct 1826
Thomas	20	M	Painter	England	United States	Siroc	31 Oct 1829
W. G.	40	M	Merchant	England	England	William Byrnes	14 Apr 1824
HOE, Ann M.	11					Agricola	1 Jul 1820
C. S.	4					Agricola	1 Jul 1820
Fred. M.	3					Agricola	1 Jul 1820
Luisa	1					Agricola	1 Jul 1820
Mary	30					Agricola	1 Jul 1820
Richard	40		Brick Layer			Agricola	1 Jul 1820
Robert R.	10					Agricola	1 Jul 1820
HOEFFER, Bernard	9	M	Farmer	France	France	Sully	15 Jul 1829
Dorothy	2/12	F	Farmer	France	France	Sully	15 Jul 1829
Henry	45	M	Farmer	France	France	Sully	15 Jul 1829
Jacob	6	M	Farmer	France	France	Sully	15 Jul 1829
Michael	2	M	Farmer	France	France	Sully	15 Jul 1829
Philip	11	M	Farmer	France	France	Sully	15 Jul 1829
Salomé	38	F	Farmer	France	France	Sully	15 Jul 1829
Salomé, Jr.	4	F	Farmer	France	France	Sully	15 Jul 1829

NAMES OF PASSENGERS	AGE	SEX	OCCUPATIONS	COUNTRY TO WHICH THEY BELONG	COUNTRY THEY INTEND TO INHABIT	SHIPS/DATES OF ARRIVAL
HOEFINGER, Barbara, Zyn Moeder (his mother [Frederik])	40	F			United States	Juffraw Johanna 16 Oct 1821
Chatrina, Zyn Suster (his sister [Frederik])	40	F			United States	Juffraw Johanna 16 Oct 1821
Frederik	40	M	Boer	Wurtenberg	United States	Juffraw Johanna 16 Oct 1821
HOELTZEL, Barbara	6	F	there child [John G. & Salome]	France	United States	Helen 5 Sep 1828
Caroline	13	F	there child [John G. & Salome]	France	United States	Helen 5 Sep 1828
Catherine	8	F	there child [John G. & Salome]	France	United States	Helen 5 Sep 1828
Chistina	3	F	there child [John G. & Salome]	France	United States	Helen 5 Sep 1828
Elizabeth	16	F	there child [John G. & Salome]	France	United States	Helen 5 Sep 1828
James	19	M	there child [John G. & Salome]	France	United States	Helen 5 Sep 1828
John G.	52	M	Farmer	France	United States	Helen 5 Sep 1828
Salome	45	F	his wife [John G.]	France	United States	Helen 5 Sep 1828
Solome	18	F	there child [John G. & Salome]	France	United States	Helen 5 Sep 1828
HOEROLDT, John	38	M	Butcher	Germany	United States	Plato 25 Aug 1829
HOF, John	19	M	Taylor	Switzerland	United States	Elizabeth 27 Jul 1824
HOFAS, John	24	M	Farmer	Great Britian	United States	Andes 19 Aug 1829
HOFER, Barbara	25	F		Baden	United States	Jason 3 Nov 1828
Jagnatch	33	M	Weaver	Baden	United States	Jason 3 Nov 1828
HOFF, Betty	26	F	None	Great Britain	United States	James Monroe 5 Apr 1820
John	4	M	None	Great Britain	United States	James Monroe 5 Apr 1820
Lydia	...	...	...	...	...	St. Michael 22 Sep 1824
HOFFANAR, John	23	M	...	Germany	New York	Constitution 20 Aug 1825
HOFFER, Rudolf	23	M	Framer	Switserland	Ohio	Danube 20 Jul 1826
HOFFIN, John	30	M	Labourer	Ireland	U.S. America	New Hampshire 28 Sep 1826
HOFFISTER, Nicolas	46	M	Mason	France	United States	New England 29 Aug 1828
HOFFMAN, ...n...y	...	...	...	...	...	St. Michael 22 Sep 1824
Andreas	32	M	Candidate	Rhyn Hessen	United States	Jason 3 Nov 1828
C.	35	M	Merchant	France		Athenian 3 Sep 1827
C. D.	25	M	Physician	U. States	U. States	Prince Edward 29 Jul 1823
Emily	13	F		U. States	U. States	York 12 Jul 1825
G.	21	M	Merchant	Germany	U. States	Pocahontas 28 Jun 1824
G.	45	M	Chair Maker	Holland	U. States	Harmony 6 Jan 1823
Geo.	11	M	Servant	Great Brittan	Great Brittain	Florida 17 May 1825
Jeremiah	40	M	Merchant	United States		Cincinnatus 29 Apr 1822
Jeremiah	41	M	Gentleman	U. States	U. States	York 12 Jul 1825
M. S. L.	24	M	Doctor	U. States	U. States	Georgetown Packet 24 Feb 1823
Margareth	17	F	Farmer	Coburg	Ohio	Caesar 24 Aug 1829
Willm.	35	M	Gentn.	United States	Baltimore	Brighton 16 Nov 1826
HOFFMANN, John G.	31	M	Wever	Switzerland	Ohio	Danube 20 Jul 1826
HOFFMIRE, Edwd.	21	M	Machenic	New York	U. States	Tartar 23 Jun 1824
HOFFNER, Antoine	40	M	Agriculturist	Germany	U.S.	Helen 3 May 1828
Elizabeth	29	F		U.S.A.	U.S.A.	Ceres 23 Sep 1826
Jacob	28	M	Baker	U.S.A.	U.S.A.	Ceres 23 Sep 1826
Jacque	1 3/12	M	Agriculturist	Germany	U.S.	Helen 3 May 1828
Joseph	3	M	Agriculturist	Germany	U.S.	Helen 3 May 1828
Margaret	32	F	Agriculturist	Germany	U.S.	Helen 3 May 1828
Michel	6	M	Agriculturist	Germany	U.S.	Helen 3 May 1828
HOFFORD, Elisabeth	30	F		Great Britian	United States	Andes 19 Aug 1829
William	30	M	Weaver	Great Britian	United States	Andes 19 Aug 1829

NAMES OF PASSENGERS	AGE	SEX	OCCUPATIONS	COUNTRY TO WHICH THEY BELONG	COUNTRY THEY INTEND TO INHABIT	SHIPS/DATES OF ARRIVAL	
HOFFSELLER, James	37	M	Merchant	U. States	U. States	Cowper	8 Jan 1827
HOFIES, John	40	M	Labourer			Hanford	17 Jul 1828
HOGAN, —	20		Cooper	Great Britan	United States	Newry	11 Jul 1827
Ann	20	F	Servant	Ireland	United States	Josephine	30 Apr 1828
Bernard	25	M	Clerk	Great Britain	United States	Corinthian	29 Apr 1826
Biddy	5	F		Ireland	America	Mary	29 May 1827
Catherine	20	F	Wife	Great Britain	United States	Corinthian	29 Apr 1826
Charlotte Mary	19	F	Lady	Nova Scotia	New York	Hope & Esther	21 Dec 1827
D. E.	28	M	Phisician	Havana	Havana	Nile	18 Oct 1828
David	30	M	Farmer	England		Marchioness	13 May 1828
Edward	13	M		G. Britain	U. States	New York	6 Mar 1827
Edward	25	M	Labourer	Ireland	U.S.A.	Dalhouse Castle	21 Aug 1829
Francis	21	M	Labourer	Ireland	United States	Josephine	30 Apr 1828
George	1	M	Child	Ireland	New York	Xenophon	3 Oct 1829
Jas.	6	M		Ireland	America	Mary	29 May 1827
John	1 6/12	M		Great Britain	United States	Corinthian	29 Apr 1826
John	20	M	Farmer	Ireland	U. States	Combine	30 Nov 1825
John	21	M	Labourer	Ireland	United States	Wilson	6 Jun 1828
John	36	M	Farmer	England	United States	Warrior	6 Oct 1828
Juda	26	F	Spinster	Ireland	America	Mary	29 May 1827
Julia	60	F	Spinster	Ireland	United States	Diana	1 May 1826
M.	30	M	Merchant	Ireland	Cuba	Abigail	25 Jun 1822
Margaret	35	F		England	United States	Warrior	6 Oct 1828
Mary	8	F		Ireland	America	Mary	29 May 1827
Mary	28	F	Spinster	Ireland	New York	Xenophon	3 Oct 1829
May	20	F		G. Britain	U. States	London	23 Sep 1828
Michael	18					Trio	5 May 1828
Michl.	21	M	Labourer	Halifax	U.S.	Oliver Wolcott	3 Nov 1827
Murthy	21	M	Laborer	Ireland	New York	Amanda	23 May 1827
Nelly	18	F		Ireland	New York	Amanda	23 May 1827
P. J.	17	M	Merchant	Ireland	Cuba	Abigail	25 Jun 1822
Pat	40	M	Labourer	Ireland	U. States	Albion	11 May 1827
Patk.	20					Trio	5 May 1828
S. Gardet	28	M	Merchant	France		Cadmus	9 Aug 1825
Thomas	26	M	Weaver	Ireland	New York	Xenophon	3 Oct 1829
Thos.	30	M	Farmer	Ireland	America	Mary	29 May 1827
W.	28	M	Merchant	Ireland	U. States	Sanford William	16 Feb 1822
Wm.	20	M	Labourer	G. Britain	U. States	London	23 Sep 1828
HOGANS, Mary	22	F		Great Britain	United States	Samuel Wright	12 Oct 1829
Thomas	1	M		Great Britain	United States	Samuel Wright	12 Oct 1829
Wm.	26	M		Tyrone, Ireland	New York	Anthusa	24 Aug 1825
HOGANT, May	7	F		G. Britain	U. States	London	23 Sep 1828
HOGART, Augustus S., Mr.	51	M	Merchant	United States	Philadelphia	Cadmus	27 Aug 1822
HOGARTH, George	25	M	Farmer	Baltimore	U. States	Paquet Des Cayes	11 Oct 1827
HOGARTY, Edward	23	M	Weaver	Ireland	United States	Wanderer	1 Aug 1828
HOGATH, John, Mas.	7/12	M	None	Grate Britain	...	Courier	14 Jun 1825
Joseph, Mr.	21	M	Black Smith	Grate Britain	...	Courier	14 Jun 1825
Mary, Mrs.	20	F	None	Grate Britain	...	Courier	14 Jun 1825
HOGAY, Nicholas	22	M		Great Britain	United States	Active	25 Mar 1828
HOGBEN, Richd.	35	F	Farmer	England	United States of Am.	Helen	17 Dec 1827
HOGDEN, Jno., child	2/12	M	None	England	United States	Great Britain	5 Sep 1827
Mary	23	F	None	England	United States	Great Britain	5 Sep 1827
HOGE, Elizabeth	26	F				Euphrates	8 Aug 1820
Hannah	4	F				Euphrates	8 Aug 1820
William	6 4/12	M	Farmer			Euphrates	8 Aug 1820
HOGES, John	25	M	Laborer	Ireland	America	Parrington	9 Jun 1827
Michael	23	M	Laborer	Ireland	America	Parrington	9 Jun 1827
HOGG, Ann	1	F	Labourer	Ireland	United States	Meteor	26 Jun 1827
Ann	25	F	Labourer	Ireland	United States	Meteor	26 Jun 1827
Dorothy	2	F	None	Great Britain	United States	Robert Fulton	18 May 1825
Elizabeth	8	F	None	Great Britain	United States	Robert Fulton	18 May 1825
Elizabeth	35	F	None	Great Britain	United States	Robert Fulton	18 May 1825
George	10	M	None	Great Britain	United States	Robert Fulton	18 May 1825
George, of Baltimore	24	M	Bookbinder	England	America	Mary Lord	26 Oct 1829
Hannah	13	F		Great Britain	United States	Diana	6 Jul 1829
Harriet, infant	2/12	F		England	America	Mary Lord	26 Oct 1829
Harriet, of Baltimore	24	F		England	America	Mary Lord	26 Oct 1829

NAMES OF PASSENGERS	AGE	SEX	OCCUPATIONS	COUNTRY TO WHICH THEY BELONG	COUNTRY THEY INTEND TO INHABIT	SHIPS/DATES OF ARRIVAL	
HOGG (cont'd)							
James	2	M	None	Great Britain	United States	Robert Fulton	18 May 1825
James	26	...	...	Scotland	America	Nimrod	9 Jul 1827
James	28	M	Clerk	Scotland	U. States	Camillus	27 Jun 1826
Jane	12	F		Great Britain	United States	Diana	6 Jul 1829
Jas.	7	M		England	U.S. America	Criterion	27 Oct 1821
Jean	22	...	...	Scotland	America	Nimrod	9 Jul 1827
John	24	...	...	Scotland	America	Nimrod	9 Jul 1827
John	42	M	Farmer	Great Britain	United States	Diana	6 Jul 1829
Mary	33	F		England	U.S. America	Criterion	27 Oct 1821
Mary	37	F		Great Britain	United States	Diana	6 Jul 1829
Moses	26	M	Farmer	Ireland	U. States	Dickinson	30 Jul 1825
Peter	5	M		England	U.S. America	Criterion	27 Oct 1821
Robert	24	...		Scotland	America	Nimrod	9 Jul 1827
Robert	35	M	Labourer	Ireland	United States	Meteor	26 Jun 1827
Robert Fulton	20/365	M	None	Great Britain	United States	Robert Fulton	18 May 1825
Sophia	14 6/12	F	None	Great Britain	United States	Robert Fulton	18 May 1825
Thomas	22	M	Merchant	United States	United States	Brighton	11 Mar 1825
Thos.	20/12	M		England	U.S. America	Criterion	27 Oct 1821
Thos.	43	M	Gardiner	England	U.S. America	Criterion	27 Oct 1821
William	32	M	Seaman	Great Brittan		Voltigeuse	4 Oct 1827
William	35	M	Farmer	Great Britain	United States	Robert Fulton	18 May 1825
William A.	6	M	None	Great Britain	United States	Robert Fulton	18 May 1825
HOGGARD, John	34	M	Planter	Antigua	U. States	Spartan	17 Dec 1823
HOGGE, Anne	22 2/12	F	None	Great Briton	United States	Mount Vernon	30 Dec 1828
Robert	40 10/12	M	Merchant	United States	United States	Mount Vernon	30 Dec 1828
HOGGINS, H. S.	2	F		United States	New York	Rambler	31 Aug 1829
Hannah	27	F		United States	New York	Rambler	31 Aug 1829
James	31	M	Shoe Maker	United States	New York	Rambler	31 Aug 1829
HOGINS, J. B.	30	M	Merchant	Spain	U. States	Mary Jane	29 Mar 1828
HOGSKIN, Ann	11	F	None	Great Britain		Olive Branch	9 Oct 1829
Elizabeth	35	F	None	Great Britain		Olive Branch	9 Oct 1829
Hannah	9	F	None	Great Britain		Olive Branch	9 Oct 1829
John	4	M	None	Great Britain		Olive Branch	9 Oct 1829
Joseph	49	M	Plush Weaver	Great Britain		Olive Branch	9 Oct 1829
Mary	14	F	None	Great Britain		Olive Branch	9 Oct 1829
William	7	M	None	Great Britain		Olive Branch	9 Oct 1829
HOGUE, John	35	M	Silversmith	Great Britain	United States	George Clinton	27 Aug 1827
John, Junr.	9	M		Great Britain	United States	George Clinton	27 Aug 1827
Michel	30	M	Confection	France	U. States	Sully	25 Jun 1828
HOGUET, A. F.	53	M	Merchant	U. States	U. States	Martha	18 Oct 1824
HOGUIN, F. E.	23	M	Advocate	France	U. States	Lewis	6 Jul 1825
HOHN, Frederic	22	M	Combmaker	Bavaria	United States of Am.	Constitution	6 Jul 1829
HOHNKE, Jno. C.	22	M	Jail Maker	Altona	U. States	Orion	3 Apr 1823
HOILE, Geo. C., K...	39	M	...	U.S.	England	Florida	17 May 1825
HOIST, John	35	M	Merchant	G. Brittain	United States	Hercules	24 Oct 1821
HOLBACK, —	18	M	Mariner	U. States	U. States	Mary	29 Feb 1820
HOLBERSTADT, Geo.	21	M	Merchant	Philadelphia	U. States	Prince Edward	3 Apr 1826
HOLBROOK (see Houlbroak)							
—	30	M	Seaman	United States	United States	Paquet des Cayes	26 May 1828
Edward	25		Physician	Charlston, S.C.	Massachusetts	Albion	5 Feb 1822
Geo.	40	M	Joiner	England	U. States	William	28 Nov 1823
Geo., Jr.	12	M		England	U. States	William	28 Nov 1823
Luke	50	M	Farmer	Great Britain	United States	Robert Fulton	18 May 1825
HOLBURG, Richd.	27	M	Shoe Maker	Sweden	U. States	Hamilton	22 Sep 1828
HOLDAN, Robert	22	F	Shue Right	England	United States	Danube	22 Aug 1825
HOLDAY, Betsy	...			England	U.S. America	Constitution	18 Jun 1827
Catharine	26	F	...ss Maker	Great Britain		Olive Branch	9 Oct 1829
Charlotte	14			England	U.S. America	Constitution	18 Jun 1827
Charlotte	41			England	U.S. America	Constitution	18 Jun 1827
Edward	41		Tailor	England	U.S. America	Constitution	18 Jun 1827
Hannah	6			England	U.S. America	Constitution	18 Jun 1827
William	10			England	U.S. America	Constitution	18 Jun 1827
HOLDEN, Abm.	9	M		England	U. States	Severn	12 Oct 1826
Abm.	40	M	Dyer	England	U. States	Severn	12 Oct 1826
Abrm.	31	M	Farmer	England	U.S.	Panthea	22 Jul 1826
Alexander	15	M	None	England	New York	Brighton	9 Dec 1828
Alice	18	F				James Monroe	8 Aug 1820

NAMES OF PASSENGERS	AGE	SEX	OCCUPATIONS	COUNTRY TO WHICH THEY BELONG	COUNTRY THEY INTEND TO INHABIT	SHIPS/DATES OF ARRIVAL	
HOLDEN (cont'd)							
Ann	39	F		Great Britain	United States	John Jay	8 May 1828
Ann M.	23	F		England	United States	Acasta	15 Jul 1822
Arthur	3	M	None	Great Britain	United States	Washington	9 Apr 1821
Charlotte	31	F	Farmer	England	U.S.	Panthea	22 Jul 1826
Edward	26	M	Merchant	Manchester, England	United States	Robert Fulton	22 Oct 1821
Edward H. S.	22	M	Apothecary	England	United States	Acasta	15 Jul 1822
Edwd.	28	M	Merchant	Great Britain	United States	Leeds	29 Sep 1823
Edwd.	35		Mercht.	England	U. States	New York	30 Oct 1827
Eliza	5	F				James Monroe	8 Aug 1820
Esther	8/12	F		Great Britain	United States	Corinthian	2 Sep 1824
Ewd.	25	M	Merchant			Hercules	25 Sep 1820
James	21	M	Mechanic	Great Britain	United States	John Jay	8 May 1828
James	24	M	Labourer	Halifax	U.S.	Oliver Wolcott	3 Nov 1827
James, Mr.	50		Gent.	England	U.S. of America	Mary	21 Sep 1821
Jno.	13	M		England	U. States	Severn	12 Oct 1826
John	11	M				James Monroe	8 Aug 1820
John	19	M	Miller	England	United States	Cincinnatus	21 Nov 1821
Margarett	11	F		Great Britain	United States	Corinthian	2 Sep 1824
Martha	30	F		Great Britain	United States	Corinthian	2 Sep 1824
Mary	4	F		Great Britain	United States	Corinthian	2 Sep 1824
Mary	20	F		Gt. Britain		Dalhouse Castle	13 May 1828
Mary, Mrs.	45			England	U.S. of America	Mary	21 Sep 1821
Mary Ann	54	F	Servant	England	U. States	New York	11 Jul 1823
Mary Ann, Miss	29			England	U.S. of America	Mary	21 Sep 1821
Richard	34	M	Mechanic	Great Britain	United States	John Jay	8 May 1828
Robert	27	M	...	Great Britain	United States	Corinthian	2 Sep 1824
Salina	18	F		England	U. States	Severn	12 Oct 1826
Sarah	4	F	Farmer	England	U.S.	Panthea	22 Jul 1826
Sarah, Miss	20			England	U.S. of America	Mary	21 Sep 1821
Thomas	19	M	Butcher	England	United States	Delta	24 Oct 1829
Thomas S.	20	M	Merchant	United States	United States	Pilot	27 Feb 1826
William	6	M		Great Britain	United States	Corinthian	2 Sep 1824
Wm. B.	2	M	Farmer	England	U.S.	Panthea	22 Jul 1826
HOLDERS, S.	30	M	Sargeant	U. States	U. States	Enterprize	9 Aug 1825
HOLDGATE, James	28		Farmer	Middlesex, Engd.		Cincinnatus	17 May 1823
HOLDING, Jesse	42	M	Calico Printer	Great Britain	United States	Aurora	5 Sep 1826
Mary	15	F		England	United States	Yobah	26 Sep 1827
Mary	38	F		England	United States	Yobah	26 Sep 1827
Wm.	38	M		England	United States	Yobah	26 Sep 1827
HOLDINGS, John	32	M	Merchant	U. States	U. States	Tampico	19 Oct 1826
HOLDMAN, Nicholas	22		Sugar boiler	Germany	Germany	Hudson	18 Jun 1825
HOLDREDGE, Sarah	30 5/12	F		America	America	France	28 Mar 1829
HOLDREGE, Eliza	28	F		United States	United States	Howard	27 Sep 1824
HOLDRIDGE, David	31 2/12	M	Merchant	U.S.A.	U.S.A.	Silas Richards	27 Oct 1826
George	25	M	Farmer	Great Briton	United States	Orion	18 Jun 1821
Mary	24	F	Wife [of George]	Great Briton	United States	Orion	18 Jun 1821
HOLDRIGE, —, Mrs.	27	F		N. York	New York	Howard	26 Aug 1823
Barbra C.	24	F		U. States	U. States	Silas Richards	27 Jun 1827
Henry	34	M	Mariner	New York	U. States	Crisis	26 May 1824
Lois	28	F	Lady	New York	U. States	Crisis	26 May 1824
HOLDRIT, Peter P.	23	M	Farmer	France	U. States	Edward Quesnel	4 Aug 1828
HOLDSTOCK, Elizabeth	10	F		England	Ohio	Brighton	14 Oct 1824
Enoch	7	M		England	Ohio	Brighton	14 Oct 1824
James	31	M	Farmer	England	Ohio	Brighton	14 Oct 1824
Margaret	27	F		England	Ohio	Brighton	14 Oct 1824
Mary	4	F		England	Ohio	Brighton	14 Oct 1824
HOLDSWORTH, Eliza	4	F	None	Great Britain	United States	Cortes	18 Oct 1820
Elizabeth	7	F	None	Great Britain	United States	Cortes	18 Oct 1820
F.	29	M	Merchant	England	U. States	Laveria	23 Jul 1828
Jacob	10	M	None	Great Britain	United States	Cortes	18 Oct 1820
Jas.	3	M	None	Great Britain	United States	Cortes	18 Oct 1820
John	40	M	Gardiner	Great Britain	United States	Cortes	18 Oct 1820
Jos.	15	M	None	Great Britain	United States	Cortes	18 Oct 1820
Mary	36	F	None	Great Britain	United States	Cortes	18 Oct 1820

NAMES OF PASSENGERS	AGE	SEX	OCCUPATIONS	COUNTRY TO WHICH THEY BELONG	COUNTRY THEY INTEND TO INHABIT	SHIPS/DATES OF ARRIVAL	
HOLDT, Ed	16	M	None	Great Britain	United States	James Monroe	25 Apr 1822
HOLDWORTH, M..., Mr.	24		Drugist	England		Hercules	19 Jun 1821
HOLEMAN, John F.	45	M	Watch Maker	Germany	New York	Eliza	8 Mar 1827
HOLENSHEAD, James	25	M	Merchant	England	U. States	Merchant	22 Oct 1821
HOLESBERRY, John	24		Farmer	Germany	United States	Corinthian	30 May 1828
HOLEST, C.	26	M	Merchant	Copenhage	U. States	Greek	3 Mar 1825
HOLESWORTH, Wm.	23	M	Merchant	Great Britain	United States	Cortes	19 Nov 1821
HOLEY, William H.	27	M	Mercht.	U. States	U. States	Nancy	13 Dec 1822
HOLGER, Herman	30		Mason	Germany	U. States	Columbia	7 May 1828
HOLIDAY, George	6	F	Farmer	Scotland	U. States	Roger Stewart	9 Jun 1828
HOLIKAN, Danl.	24	M	Labourer	England	U. States	Rising States	20 Sep 1828
John	24	M	Labourer	England	U. States	Rising States	20 Sep 1828
Philip	34	M	Labourer	England	U. States	Rising States	20 Sep 1828
HOLINGSHEAD, —, Mr.	30	M	Merchant	United States	United States	Mermaid	25 Oct 1822
HOLL, Dedrick	31	M	Merchant	Louisiana	U. States	Canada	13 Feb 1826
Mary	17	F		England	New York	Triton	11 Jul 1826
William	14	M		England	England	Triton	11 Jul 1826
HOLLADAY, Robt.	23	M	Seaman	New York	United States	Venus	8 Sep 1820
HOLLAND, —, Mr.	30	M	Merchant	Gt. Britain	U. States	Columbia	7 Sep 1827
—, Mrs.	25	F		Gt. Britain	U. States	Columbia	7 Sep 1827
Andrew	22		Farmer & Labourer	Great Britain & Ireland	United States	Trio	8 Feb 1827
Ann	22	F	Servant			Cassack	25 Jul 1820
Anthony H.	41	M	None	Halifax	England	Loire	7 Jun 1827
Danniel	25	F				Helen	4 Aug 1829
Edward	18	M	Labourer	England	United States	Jubilee	12 May 1828
Elizabeth	22	F	...	Ireland	United States	Carolina Ann	24 Oct 1825
Frances	30					Xenophon	25 Jul 1826
Francis	18	M	Farmer	Ireland	United States	Lady Hunter	27 Dec 1825
Hannah	22	F		England	United States	Hercules	25 Jan 1820
Isaac	48	M	Hatter	Great Britain	U. States	Edward Quesnel	17 Mar 1829
James	24	M	Bookkeeper	Ireland	New York	Margaret	18 May 1825
James	30	M	Shoemaker	Ireland	U. States	Nancy	25 Nov 1823
James	38	M		Irland	United States	Nancy	2 Jan 1824
James	40	M	Labourer	G. Britain	U. States	Sarah G	5 Jun 1828
John	20		Farmer & Labourer	Great Britain & Ireland	United States	Trio	8 Feb 1827
John	27	M	Blacksmith	Great Britain	U. States	Ganges	21 Jun 1827
John	30	M	Wheelwright	England	United States	Montgomery	6 Mar 1829
John	50	M	None	England	U. States	Sully	15 Jul 1829
Margaret	19	F	...	Ireland	United States	Carolina Ann	24 Oct 1825
Mary	40	F	Merchantress		England	Helen	4 Aug 1829
Mary A.	27	F		England	United States	Peru	23 May 1827
May	20	F	Seamstres	G. Brittain	America	Atlantic	11 Oct 1822
Stephen, Capt.	32		late of the Brig Chatham	Newburyport	United States	Hudson	18 Jun 1825

*Officers, Seamen and Passengers belonging to the Ship Jane of Boston and taken from on board the Schooner Olive of St. Johns , N.B. on the 4th June 1825, Lat. 41.30, Long 53.19, which ship foundered on the 31st ultimo in Lat. 41.44 Long 52., late

NAMES OF PASSENGERS	AGE	SEX	OCCUPATIONS	COUNTRY TO WHICH THEY BELONG	COUNTRY THEY INTEND TO INHABIT	SHIPS/DATES OF ARRIVAL	
Thomas	3	M		England	United States	Hercules	25 Jan 1820
William	24	M	Merchant	England	U.S. of America	Hannibal	17 Dec 1823
William	28		Farmer	England	S. New York	Xenophon	25 Jul 1826
HOLLARER, Richard	30	M	Gardener	England	U. States	Acasta	21 Oct 1825
HOLLARID, B.	6		Labourer	Halifax	U. States	Edwin	26 Sep 1828
B.	40		Labourer	Halifax	U. States	Edwin	26 Sep 1828
C.	3		Labourer	Halifax	U. States	Edwin	26 Sep 1828
HOLLEBREAD,							
Daniel	16 8/12	M	Bookbinder	England	United States	Robert Edwards	3 Oct 1829
HOLLER, Barbara	42	F		Wirtemburg	United States	Wade	29 Aug 1825
James	29	M	Stone Mason	Ireland		Eliza Grant	29 Aug 1829
HOLLERAN, Timothy	22	M	Farmer	Ireland	U. States	Criterion	23 May 1826
HOLLEVARA, Jno.	...	...	...	...	...	Ontario	25 Mar 1823
HOLLEY, James	29	M	Stone Mason	Ireland	New York	Eliza Grant	29 Aug 1829
HOLLHUYSEN, H.	14	F		U. States	U. States	Hippomenes	23 Jun 1823
HOLLIDAY, James	27 9/12	M	Print Cutter	Ireland	America	Farmer	3 May 1824
Robt.	40	M	Mercht.	Gt. Britian	U. States	Columbia	1 Dec 1824
HOLLIGNAN, Danl.	27	M		Ireland	U. States	Fame	15 Nov 1826
Mary	20	F		Ireland	U. States	Fame	15 Nov 1826
HOLLINGEN, J. H.	21	M	Merchant	France	U. States	Canada	6 Jun 1825

NAMES OF PASSENGERS	AGE	SEX	OCCUPATIONS	COUNTRY TO WHICH THEY BELONG	COUNTRY THEY INTEND TO INHABIT	SHIPS/DATES OF ARRIVAL	
HOLLINGS, John	13	M				Euphrates	8 Aug 1820
Mary	30	F				Euphrates	8 Aug 1820
Thomas	43	M	Farmer			Euphrates	8 Aug 1820
William	2	M				Euphrates	8 Aug 1820
HOLLINGSHEAD, Jas.	30	M	Drugist	England	United States	William	4 Oct 1822
Mary	25	F		England	United States	William	4 Oct 1822
HOLLINGSWORTH,							
—, Mrs.	25	F		U. States	U. States	Sarah Herrick	13 May 1826
B.	40	M	Manufacturer	Great Britain	United States	Isaac Hicks	6 Dec 1827
B.	46	F		Great Britain	United States	Isaac Hicks	6 Dec 1827
E.	10	F		Great Britain	United States	Isaac Hicks	6 Dec 1827
Emanuel	4	M		U. States	U. States	Sarah Herrick	13 May 1826
George	3	M		U. States	U. States	Sarah Herrick	13 May 1826
H.	1	F		Great Britain	United States	Isaac Hicks	6 Dec 1827
J.	16	F		Great Britain	United States	Isaac Hicks	6 Dec 1827
Jabes	22	M	Weaver	Great Britain	United States	Hamilton	21 Nov 1826
Joseph	25	M	Currier	G. Britain	U.S. America	Defence	13 Dec 1827
R.	4	F		Great Britain	United States	Isaac Hicks	6 Dec 1827
Wm.	30	M	Merchant	Baltimore	U. States	Cherub	1 Nov 1821
Wm.	45	M	Gentleman	America	U. States	Amity	21 Feb 1823
HOLLINGWORTH,							
George	46	M	Labourer	G. Britain	U.S.A.	Silas Richards	29 Oct 1827
Wm.	23	M	... Maker	Scotland	United States	Indus	5 Sep 1827
HOLLINSLEY, Edwd.	45	M	Farmer	Great Britain	United States	William Dawson	18 Jun 1827
Elizabeth	14	F	None	Great Britain	United States	William Dawson	18 Jun 1827
HOLLINSLEY, Sarah	35	F	None	Great Britain	United States	William Dawson	18 Jun 1827
HOLLINSWORTH,							
George	27	M	Mechanic	England	United States	Alexander Mansfield	9 Jul 1829
HOLLIS, Denzel	14	M	Farmer	England	U.S. of America	Illinois	16 Jun 1821
Elisabeth	8 4/12	F		England	U.S. of America	Illinois	16 Jun 1821
Elisabeth	40 1/12	F		England	U.S. of America	Illinois	16 Jun 1821
Elizabeth	43	F	None	Great Britain	U. States	Hannibal	12 Oct 1829
Emma	1 2/12	F		England	U.S. of America	Illinois	16 Jun 1821
George	6 7/12	M		England	U.S. of America	Illinois	16 Jun 1821
Henry	11	M	None	Gt. Britain	United States	Union	9 Jan 1824
Humphrey	74 2/12	M	Farmer	England	U.S. of America	Illinois	16 Jun 1821
Humphry	41 6/12	M	Farmer	England	U.S. of America	Illinois	16 Jun 1821
James	51	M	Merchant	Gt. Britain	United States	Union	9 Jan 1824
Jesse	17	M	Shoemaker	Great Britian	United States	Isaac Hicks	22 May 1826
John	16	M	None	Great Britain	U. States	Hannibal	12 Oct 1829
John	40	M	None	Great Britain	U. States	Hannibal	12 Oct 1829
Maria	9 5/12	F	.	England	U.S. of America	Illinois	16 Jun 1821
Salina	5	F	None	Great Britain	U. States	Hannibal	12 Oct 1829
Thomas	16 4/12	M	Farmer	England	U.S. of America	Illinois	16 Jun 1821
William	11 2/12	M		England	U.S. of America	Illinois	16 Jun 1821
HOLLOND, James	35	M	Pedler	Ireland	United States	St. Michael	21 Aug 1824
HOLLOWAY, Eliza		F				Cassack	25 Jul 1820
Eliza	25	F				Cassack	25 Jul 1820
Heny	22	M	Tailor	G. Britain	G. Britain	Brittania	17 Jul 1828
HOLLOWDAY, Ann	10	F	Farmer	Scotland	Canada	Swift	16 Jul 1827
Barbrey	5	F	Farmer	Scotland	Canada	Swift	16 Jul 1827
Charls	3	M	Farmer	Scotland	Canada	Swift	16 Jul 1827
Cillea	41	F	Farmer	Scotland	Canada	Swift	16 Jul 1827
James	41	M	Farmer	...ginia	Canada	Swift	16 Jul 1827
Margret	12	F	Farmer	Scotland	Canada	Swift	16 Jul 1827
William	7	M	Farmer	Scotland	Canada	Swift	16 Jul 1827
HOLLWAYS, Martin	26	M	Butcher	Germany	New York	Constitution	20 Aug 1825
HOLLY, John	23	M	Mason	England	America	Two Marys	24 Sep 1827
John	25	M	Laborer	Ireland	United States	Sylvester Healy	14 Jun 1825
Peter	20	M	Baker	England	America	Two Marys	24 Sep 1827
Sally	23	F	Wife	Ireland	United States	Sylvester Healy	14 Jun 1825
Saml.	24	M	Carpenter	England	America	Two Marys	24 Sep 1827
Steven	32	M	Farmer	U. States	U. States	Oglethorpe	9 Nov 1824
HOLLYER, W. T.	35	M	Merchant	England	United States	Cortex	4 Dec 1824
HOLMAN, Adam	2	M		Native of Switzerland	United States	Canaris	30 Jun 1827
Eliza	25	F		England	United States	Columbia	16 Jan 1829

NAMES OF PASSENGERS	AGE	SEX	OCCUPATIONS	COUNTRY TO WHICH THEY BELONG	COUNTRY THEY INTEND TO INHABIT	SHIPS/DATES OF ARRIVAL	
HOLMAN (cont'd)							
George	11	M		Native of Switzerland	United States	Canaris	30 Jun 1827
Harriet	7	F		Gt. Britain		Corinthian	27 Oct 1829
Harriet	26	F		Gt. Britain		Corinthian	27 Oct 1829
John	4	M		Gt. Britain		Corinthian	27 Oct 1829
John	8	M		Native of Switzerland	United States	Canaris	30 Jun 1827
John	30	M	Carpenter	Great Britan	United States	Bolivar	21 May 1827
John	31	M	Ship wright	Gt. Britain		Corinthian	27 Oct 1829
John	35	M	Brick Layer	Native of Switzerland	United States	Canaris	30 Jun 1827
Joseph S.	35 3/12	M	Merchant	England	U. States	France	26 Jun 1828
Margaret	5	F		Native of Switzerland	United States	Canaris	30 Jun 1827
Margaret	39	F		Native of Switzerland	United States	Canaris	30 Jun 1827
Mary	6	F		Gt. Britain		Corinthian	27 Oct 1829
Mary	20	F		Native of Switzerland	United States	Canaris	30 Jun 1827
Peter	2	M		Native of Switzerland	United States	Canaris	30 Jun 1827
Thomas	1	M		Gt. Britain		Corinthian	27 Oct 1829
HOLMDEN, Walter	22	M	Mechanic	England	United States	Columbia	16 Jan 1829
HOLME, J.	26	M	Merchant	Sweden	U. States	Gustava	9 Jul 1827
William	23	M	Joiner	Great Britain	United States	Isaac Hicks	10 Jul 1827
HOLMES, —, Mr.				England	U. States	Franklin	7 Jul 1828
—, Mrs.				England	U. States	Franklin	7 Jul 1828
Abram	30	M	Mariner	G. Bridain		Trio	27 Jun 1823
Albert	30	M	Servant	Great Britain	United States	Roman	19 Dec 1825
Alexander	23	M	Labourer	Ireland	United States	Robert Fulton	24 Jul 1826
Ann	8	F	None	England	United States	Jubilee	13 Jul 1829
Ann	24	F	Labourer	England	U. States	Comet	23 Aug 1828
Anthony	3	M	None	England	United States	Jubilee	13 Jul 1829
Betty	21	F	Labourer	England	U. States	Comet	23 Aug 1828
C.	37	M	Merchant	Connecticutt	U. States	Argo	5 Aug 1824
Francis	25	M	Mercht.	America	America	Kenhawa	20 Jan 1823
Henry	8	M	None	Scotland	U. States	Czar	29 Aug 1829
Isaac	30	M	Mechanic	U. States	U. States	Yamacraw	9 Mar 1822
James	23	M	None	United States	Philadelphia	Orozimbo	2 Oct 1824
James	25	M	Farmer	G. Britain	U. States	Mary & Harriot	8 Sep 1828
James	27	M	Labourer	England	U. States	Comet	23 Aug 1828
James	46	M	Weaver	Scotland	U. States	Roger Stewart	9 Jun 1828
Jane	60	F	Labourer	England	U. States	Comet	23 Aug 1828
Jno.	19	M	Merchant	Great Brittain	U. States	Atticus	25 Apr 1822
Jno.	45	M	Merchant	Warwickshire	G. Brittain	William Thompson	6 Sep 1822
John	11	M	Mason	Scotland	U. States	Roger Stewart	9 Jun 1828
John	30	M	Labourer	England	New York	Hercules	11 Feb 1822
John	44	M	Weaver	England	Philadelphia	Curler	7 Jul 1827
John	45	M	Farmer	Great Britian	U. States	Orbit	29 Apr 1822
Julia	22	F	Cloth Dresser	Great Britain	United States	Dapper	21 Aug 1828
Mary	12	F	Mason	Scotland	U. States	Roger Stewart	9 Jun 1828
Mary	35	F	Spinster	Ireland	America	Mary	29 May 1827
Mary	36	F	Mason	Scotland	U. States	Roger Stewart	9 Jun 1828
Peter	19	M	Captain, Officers & crew of the Brig George of New York (wrecked at Fayal)	U.S. America	U.S.A.	Gallego	13 Mar 1829
Robert	23	M	Cloth Dresser	Great Britain	United States	Dapper	21 Aug 1828
Robert	40	M	Laborer	Scotland	U. States	Czar	29 Aug 1829
Robt.	6	M	None	Scotland	U. States	Czar	29 Aug 1829
Saml.	60	M	Labourer	England	U. States	Comet	23 Aug 1828
Samuel	23	M	Marriner	Great Britian	United States	George Clinton	13 Apr 1826
Thomas	25	M	Super Cargo	N. York	N. York	Peruvian	8 Nov 1826
Thomas	25	M	Gun Maker	England		Fame	9 Dec 1826
Thomas	30	M	Merchant	England	United States	Indian Chief	16 Aug 1822
Thomas	54	M	Mariner	St. Johns, N.B.	England	Peruvian	7 Oct 1825

NAMES OF PASSENGERS	AGE	SEX	OCCUPATIONS	COUNTRY TO WHICH THEY BELONG	COUNTRY THEY INTEND TO INHABIT	SHIPS/DATES OF ARRIVAL	
HOLMES (cont'd)							
Thos.	17	M	Mechanic	England	Great Briton	Lafayette	3 Dec 1827
Thos.	25	M	Merchant	U. States	U. States	Ductile	11 Feb 1822
Valentine	20	M	Merchant	G. Britain	United States	Robert Burns	13 Jul 1820
Vincent	29		Mariner	U. States	U. States	Logan	14 Aug 1820
William	2	M				Hector	11 Sep 1820
William	9	M		Great Britain	U. States	United States	8 Sep 1827
William	24	M	Farmer	England	United States	Jubilee	1 Oct 1828
William	28	M		America	New York	Cincinnatus	5 Dec 1825
William	36	M	Manufacturer	Great Britain	U. States	United States	8 Sep 1827
Wm.	3	M	Mason	Scotland	U. States	Roger Stewart	9 Jun 1828
Wm.	20		Merchant	Ireland	United States	Robert Burns	18 Jun 1822
Wm.	27	M	Mechanic	G.B.	G.B.	George Canning	26 Aug 1829
HOLMS, J. H.	21	M	None	Gt. Brittain	United States	Cortes	5 Aug 1822
HOLMSE, Charles	40	M	Farmer	England	United States	Jubilee	13 Jul 1829
Sarah	40	F	None	England	United States	Jubilee	13 Jul 1829
HOLMUS, Alexander	23	M	Weaver	Ireland	United States	Robert Fulton	10 Aug 1827
HOLO, Jacob	30	M	Smith	G. Britain		Caravan	8 Sep 1828
HOLOHAN, Mary	20	F		Great Britain	New York	Philetus	21 Jul 1827
HOLRATH, Andreas	35	M	Tailor	Germany	United States	Elizabeth	4 Sep 1826
Felix	6 6/12	M	Son	Germany	United States	Elizabeth	4 Sep 1826
Madelena	2 6/12	F	Daughter	Germany	United States	Elizabeth	4 Sep 1826
Maria	33	F	Wife	Germany	United States	Elizabeth	4 Sep 1826
HOLRIN, M.	22	F	Labourer	Ireland	United States	Combine	4 Jun 1825
HOLROY, Thomas S.	21	F	Bricklayer	England		Aurora	12 Mar 1827
HOLROYD, Geo.	34	M	Servant	Great Britain	United States	Aurora	5 Sep 1826
Wm.	33	M	Paper dealer	St...land		Aurora	8 Jun 1827
HOLST, C. Aug.	25	M	Machanic	Germany	U. States	Lycurgus	3 Dec 1821
Hans	37	M	Merchant	Norway	...	Martha	24 Aug 1829
HOLSTEIN, Berenise	37		Farmer	France	U. States	Elizabeth	9 Jul 1825
L. D.	65	M	Gentleman	Germany	U. States	Elisa Pigott	24 Apr 1822
HOLSTEINE, Lewis	24		Farmer	France	U. States	Elizabeth	9 Jul 1825
HOLSTOCK, Margaret	17	F		Nova Scotia	United States	McDonough	3 Nov 1823
HOLT, Adam	15	M	Weaver	England	U. States	Thomas Ritchie	2 Jul 1827
Ann	17	F		Great Britain	United States	Mary Howland	19 Jul 1827
Betsey	5	F		Great Britain	United States	Mary Howland	19 Jul 1827
Betty	45	F	None	Great Britain	United States	Mary Howland	19 Jul 1827
Carl	13	M		Bardin	U. States	Bayard	5 Sep 1828
Catharan	19	M		Bardin	U. States	Bayard	5 Sep 1828
Christian	60	M	Farmer	Bardin	U. States	Bayard	5 Sep 1828
Cyrus	12	M		Great Britain	United States	Mary Howland	19 Jul 1827
Fanny	15	F		Great Britain	United States	Mary Howland	19 Jul 1827
Francis	27	M	Farmer	England	U.S. America	Cortes	19 May 1826
G. A.	10	M		Bardin	U. States	Bayard	5 Sep 1828
G. Ad.	17	M	Farmer	Bardin	U. States	Bayard	5 Sep 1828
James	22	M		Great Britain	United States	Mary Howland	19 Jul 1827
James, Mr.	30	M	Merchant	England	Canada	Birmingham	16 Oct 1826
Jno.	18	M	Weaver	England	U. States	Thomas Ritchie	2 Jul 1827
Jno.	41	M	Farmer	England	U. States	Severn	12 Oct 1826
John	11			Ireland	United States	Geo. Canning	5 Jun 1828
John	24	M	Calico Printer	Great Britain	United States	Aurora	5 Sep 1826
John	24	M	Cook	England	New York	Brighton	19 Aug 1829
Joseph	2	M		Great Britain	United States	Mary Howland	19 Jul 1827
Josh.	48	M	Weaver	England	U. States	Thomas Ritchie	2 Jul 1827
Louisa	1	F		London	U. States	Criterion	15 Oct 1822
Martha	2	F	None	England	America	Ann	2 Nov 1820
Mary	9	F		Great Britain	United States	Mary Howland	19 Jul 1827
Mary	22	F	None	England	America	Ann	2 Nov 1820
Mary	25	F		London	U. States	Criterion	15 Oct 1822
Mary	26	F	Lady	England	United States	Siroc	31 Oct 1829
Osterhall	24		Farmer	England	United States	Corinthian	30 May 1828
Rich	23	M	Mechanic	London	U. States	Criterion	15 Oct 1822
Thomas	23	M		Great Britain	United States	Mary Howland	19 Jul 1827
Wm.	16	M		Bardin	U. States	Bayard	5 Sep 1828
HOLTERMANN, Henry	22	M	Merchant	Hannover	United States of Am.	Constitution	6 Jul 1829
HOLTON, Eliza	26	F	Spinster	Ireland	United States	Dublin Packet	3 Sep 1822
John	24	M	Labourer	Germany	U. States	Hudson	26 Jan 1825
Patt	24	M	Farmer	Ireland	United States	Dublin Packet	29 Jun 1825
Sarah	27	F				Freake	25 Aug 1829

NAMES OF PASSENGERS	AGE	SEX	OCCUPATIONS	COUNTRY TO WHICH THEY BELONG	COUNTRY THEY INTEND TO INHABIT	SHIPS/DATES OF ARRIVAL	
HOLTON (cont'd)							
Wiliam	28	M		United States	United States	Freake	25 Aug 1829
William, Mr.	26	M	Watch Maker	Grate Britain	...	Courier	14 Jun 1825
HOLTZ, —	15	M	Cooper	Baltimore	Baltimore	Louisa	16 May 1826
—	30	M	Cooper	Baltimore	Baltimore	Louisa	16 May 1826
HOLWORTH, Thompson	42	M	Shoe maker	Halifax		Aurora	8 Jun 1827
HOLZ, Kitty	13	F		Ireland		L. M. Pelham	12 May 1823
HOME, Caroline	1	M	Farmer	England	U. States	Robert Edwards	9 May 1827
Daniel	9	M	Farmer	England	U. States	Robert Edwards	9 May 1827
Edward	5	M	Farmer	England	U. States	Robert Edwards	9 May 1827
Elizebeth	13	F	Farmer	England	U. States	Robert Edwards	9 May 1827
Elizebeth	33	F	Farmer	England	U. States	Robert Edwards	9 May 1827
John	11	M	Farmer	England	U. States	Robert Edwards	9 May 1827
John	35	M	Farmer	England	U. States	Robert Edwards	9 May 1827
Joseph	30	M	Tanner	Great Britain	United States	Orbit	23 Oct 1826
Mary	7	F	Farmer	England	U. States	Robert Edwards	9 May 1827
Sarah	3	M	Farmer	England	U. States	Robert Edwards	9 May 1827
HOMEL, Johnston	16 5/12	M	Farmer	Switzerland	U. States	France	26 Jun 1828
HOMER, Benjn.	40	M	None	Great Britian	U. States	Henry Kneedland	7 Aug 1826
Eliz.	42	F	Farmer	England	United States	Euphrates	18 Aug 1827
Henry	37	M	Merchant	U. States	U. States	Hesper	16 Jun 1828
Jacob	48	M	Mariner	U. States	U. States	Sally Ann	27 Oct 1825
P. J.	24	M	Merchant	United States	United States	York	31 Mar 1828
Peter T.	23	M	Merchant	United States	U. States	William Byrnes	24 Apr 1827
Robert	34		None	G. Britain		Casanda	5 Sep 1827
Sarah	29	F	None	G. Britain		Casanda	5 Sep 1827
Timothy	32	M	...b...	...shire	U. States	Panthea	24 Mar 1825
HOMES, Elisbath	18	F	Spinster	Ireland	United States	Fabius	31 Jul 1829
Jane	60	F		Ireland	United States	Marmion	17 Jun 1825
John	25	M	Farmer	Ireland	United States	Marmion	17 Jun 1825
Margaret	25	F		Ireland	United States	Marmion	17 Jun 1825
HOMEWOOD, Charles	5	M		Great Britain	United States	Fame	26 May 1828
Edward	29	M	Farmer	Great Britain	United States	Fame	26 May 1828
Elizabeth	1	F		Great Britain	United States	Fame	26 May 1828
Elizabeth	27	F		Great Britain	United States	Fame	26 May 1828
James	3	M		Great Britain	United States	Fame	26 May 1828
John	22		Farmer	England	S. New York	Xenophon	25 Jul 1826
Mary	24					Xenophon	25 Jul 1826
HOMMENSHAUS,							
William	44	M	Watch maker		United States	Constitution	2 Aug 1826
HONDS, Mary Ann	24	M	Sevt.			Hudson	23 Jul 1828
HONE, Eliza	26	F	Lady	United States	New York	Brighton	16 Nov 1826
George	21	M	Mechanic	Ireland	United States	Concordia	25 Aug 1827
Gerizel	30	F		Scotland	U. States	Superior	25 Sep 1828
Henry	20	M	Merchant	New York	U.S.	Bayard	30 Oct 1820
John	1	M	Child	Ireland	United States	Henry Kneeland	7 Jun 1828
John	25	M	Bleacher	Ireland	United States	Henry Kneeland	7 Jun 1828
John	25	M		Scotland	U. States	Superior	25 Sep 1828
Maria, Mrs.	26	F	Lady	U.S.	U.S.	Sully	15 Jul 1829
Sally	25	F	Wife	Ireland	United States	Henry Kneeland	7 Jun 1828
Thomas	21	M	Bleacher	Ireland	United States	Henry Kneeland	7 Jun 1828
HONEGAR, John	42	M	Merchant	St. John, N.B.	St. John, N.B.	Sylvester Healy	17 Oct 1825
HONER, Benj.	2	M	Farmer	England	United States	Euphrates	18 Aug 1827
Corn.	5	M	Farmer	England	United States	Euphrates	18 Aug 1827
Elizabeth	16	F	Farmer	England	United States	Euphrates	18 Aug 1827
Hy.	14	M	Farmer	England	United States	Euphrates	18 Aug 1827
Jno.	13	M	Farmer	England	United States	Euphrates	18 Aug 1827
Mary Ann	7	M	Farmer	England	United States	Euphrates	18 Aug 1827
W.	12	M	Farmer	England	United States	Euphrates	18 Aug 1827
HONESTALE, Patrick	25	M	Labourer	Ireland	Boston	General Marion	12 Jan 1829
HONESTER, Thos.	26	M	Mason	England	United States	Euphrates	18 Aug 1827
HONEY, —, Miss	38	F		Bermuda	Missouri	Camden	14 May 1825
HONEYMON, Michael	30	M	Artist			Servant	30 Aug 1820
HONEYSETT, Elizabeth	33	F	None	England	United States	Trident	31 Mar 1827
James	3	M	None	England	United States	Trident	31 Mar 1827
James	35	M	None	England	United States	Trident	31 Mar 1827
Mary	4 6/12	F	None	England	United States	Trident	31 Mar 1827
Rhoda	12	F	None	England	United States	Trident	31 Mar 1827

NAMES OF PASSENGERS	AGE	SEX	OCCUPATIONS	COUNTRY TO WHICH THEY BELONG	COUNTRY THEY INTEND TO INHABIT	SHIPS/DATES OF ARRIVAL	
HONEYSETT (cont'd)							
Thomas	6	M	None	England	United States	Trident	31 Mar 1827
Virtue	8	F	None	England	United States	Trident	31 Mar 1827
HONEYVILLE, Ann	18	F	Lady	United States	United States	Sylvester Healy	17 Oct 1825
HONEYWELL, Martha	28	F		N. York	U. States	Edward Bonaffe	11 Dec 1827
HONFLEURE, Ada	22	F		England	U. States	Brighton	14 Apr 1828
Juan	2	M		England	U. States	Brighton	14 Apr 1828
Juan	23	M		England	U. States	Brighton	14 Apr 1828
HONGLEY, James	23	M	Labourer	Ireland	New York	Trusty	12 Sep 1828
HONGLY, Patrick	21	M	Labourer	Ireland	United States	Hope	12 Jun 1828
HONIGE, Ami	30	M	Farmer	Wirtermberg	United States	Olympia	20 Aug 1829
HONOR, Francis	20	M	Farmer	Ireland	United States	Dublin Packet	23 May 1828
HONOT, M.	35	M	Merchant	Frenchman	Charleston	Maria Elizabeth	16 Feb 1826
HONOUGHLING, William	23	M	Farmer	England		Exchange	11 Jul 1823
HONOUR, John	28		Merchant	Jermany		Hudson	23 Jul 1828
HONRAY, Neal	23	F	Labourer	Ireland	United States	Hope	12 Jun 1828
HONSEM, Julia	23	F		England	England	Hudson	13 Jan 1827
HONSLOW, Henry	28	M	Gentn.	England	U. States	Dalhouse	23 Mar 1829
HONSON, Francis	24	M	Labourer	England	United States	Silas Richards	27 Oct 1825
John	32	M	Clothier	Ireland	U.S. America	New Hampshire	28 Sep 1826
HOOD, Agness	27	F	Spinster	Trobotton	U.S. America	Camillus	10 Sep 1821
Alexander	22	M	Joiner			Lady of the Lake	23 Aug 1828
Andrew	25	M	Baker	England	New York	Brighton	21 Jan 1826
Elizabeth	24	F	None	Gt. Britain	U.S. of America	Friends	25 Sep 1823
James	2	M		G. Britain	U. States	Armadello	22 Jun 1827
James	3	M	Merchant	Great Britain	United States	Martha	3 May 1821
James	34	M	Farmour	Trobotton	U.S. America	Camillus	10 Sep 1821
Jane	3	F		G. Britain	U. States	Armadello	22 Jun 1827
Jane	14	F	No Occupation but chance concerns	England	America	Meteor	22 Apr 1822
Jane	23	F	Family	Scotland	United States	Loire	26 May 1828
Jane	44	F	No Occupation but chance concerns	England	America	Meteor	22 Apr 1822
Janet	50	F	None	Gt. Britain	U.S. of America	Friends	25 Sep 1823
John	1	M	Family	Scotland	United States	Loire	26 May 1828
John	13	M	Boy	Glasgow	U.S. America	Camillus	10 Sep 1821
John	22	M	Merchant	Ireland	U. States	Concordia	11 Jun 1823
John	25	M	Gentleman	Ireland	United States	Romulus	24 Jun 1826
John	30	M	Laborer	Ireland	United States	St. Michaels	23 Dec 1826
Margaret	40	F	Spinster	Trobotton	U.S. America	Camillus	10 Sep 1821
Mary	30	F		G. Britain	U. States	Armadello	22 Jun 1827
Mary Ann	4	F		G. Britain	U. States	Armadello	22 Jun 1827
Matilda	14	F	Spinster	Ireland	United States	Robert Fulton	10 Aug 1827
Matthew	25	M	Mechanic	Great Britan	United States	Franklin	15 Apr 1826
Peter	28	M	Farmour	Trobotton	U.S. America	Camillus	10 Sep 1821
Rebecca	16	F	None	Gt. Britain	U.S. of America	Friends	25 Sep 1823
Thomas	29 4/12	M	Farmer	Scotland	U. States	Hopes Delight	21 Apr 1828
William	10	M	No Occupation but chance concerns	England	America	Meteor	22 Apr 1822
William	10	M	None	Gt. Britain	U.S. of America	Friends	25 Sep 1823
William	16	M	Farmer	G. Britain	U. States	Armadello	22 Jun 1827
William	35	M	Super Cargo	England	England	Severn	12 Oct 1826
Wm.	45	M	Merchant	Great Britain	West Indies	Columbia	24 Dec 1822
HOODLESS, W. R.	28	M	Captain	America	U. States	Mary Jane	29 Mar 1828
HOODS, Hugh	40			Great Britan	United States	Newry	11 Jul 1827
Margaret	7			Great Britan	United States	Newry	11 Jul 1827
Nancy	30			Great Britan	United States	Newry	11 Jul 1827
HOOK, Cecilia	5	F		England	U. States	York	12 Jul 1825
Cecilia	26	F		England	U. States	York	12 Jul 1825
Elijah	24	M	Merchant	United States	United States	Climax	24 Oct 1829
Jane	2	F		England	U. States	York	12 Jul 1825
Stephen, Jr.	15	M	Farmer	Rye, England	United States	William	21 May 1828
Thomas	58	M	Farmer	Rye, England	United States	William	21 May 1828
Thomas, Sr.	17	M	Farmer	Rye, England	United States	William	21 May 1828
Wm.	3	M		England	U. States	York	12 Jul 1825
Wm.	26	M		England	U. States	York	12 Jul 1825
HOOKER, J.	30	M	Farmer	Wirtemburg	United States	Wade	29 Aug 1825
HOOKS, James	25	M	Weaver	Ireland	United States	Romulus	24 Jun 1826
HOOL, John	24	M	Dyer	Ireland	United States	Josephine	30 Apr 1828

NAMES OF PASSENGERS	AGE	SEX	OCCUPATIONS	COUNTRY TO WHICH THEY BELONG	COUNTRY THEY INTEND TO INHABIT	SHIPS/DATES OF ARRIVAL	
HOOLE, ...	15	F		Gt. Britain	U. States	Maria	22 May 1822
Edmund	17	M		Gt. Britain	U. States	Maria	22 May 1822
Eliza	18	F		Gt. Britain	U. States	Maria	22 May 1822
Hannah	48	F		Gt. Britain	U. States	Maria	22 May 1822
Joseph	6	M		Gt. Britain	U. States	Maria	22 May 1822
Mary Ann	13	F		Gt. Britain	U. States	Maria	22 May 1822
Robert	11	M		Gt. Britain	U. States	Maria	22 May 1822
Samuel	53	M	Merchant	Great Britan	United States	Hamilton	19 Mar 1827
William	13	M		Gt. Britain	U. States	Maria	22 May 1822
HOONAM, George	7	M		Switzerland	United States	Elbe	2 Aug 1822
HOOPER, Alfred	27		Merchant	England	England	William Byrnes	25 Aug 1828
Ann	13	F		Great Britton	U. State	Earl of Liverpool	16 Aug 1826
Eliza	50	F		Great Britton	U. State	Earl of Liverpool	16 Aug 1826
Geo.	25	M	Farmer	Gt. Britan	U. States	Earl of Liverpool	12 Apr 1825
Jno.	12	M	Farmer	Gt. Britan	U. States	Earl of Liverpool	12 Apr 1825
Robt. C., Mr.	30	M	Mercht.	United States	United States	Manchester	16 Dec 1828
HOOPEY, R.	26	M	Servant	England	U. States	Sarah Thornton	13 Sep 1828
HOOTIN, Ann	20	F		England	America	Thames	27 May 1822
Benjamin	infant	M		England	America	Thames	27 May 1822
Elizabeth	14	F		England	America	Thames	27 May 1822
George	7	M		England	America	Thames	27 May 1822
John	47	M		England	America	Thames	27 May 1822
Joseph	9	M	Farmer	England	America	Thames	27 May 1822
Mary	46	F		England	America	Thames	27 May 1822
William	19	M	Farmer	England	America	Thames	27 May 1822
HOPE, A.	21	M	Merchant	England	U. States	Hero	17 May 1825
Agnes	30	F		England		Britannia	20 Jun 1827
Archd.	20	M	Merchant	England	U. States	Dart	3 Aug 1822
David	29	M	Canal Cutter	England	United States	Lord Wellington	14 Nov 1827
Horatio Nelson	24	M	Gentleman	Great Britain	U. States	Hope & Esther	12 Nov 1825
Thomas	25	M	...	Ireland	United States	Trident	18 Jul 1827
HOPKINS, Ann	37	F	Spinster	England	U.N. States	Helen	17 Dec 1827
C.	30	M	Labourer	G. Britain	U. States	Nimrod	31 Jul 1828
Catha.	5	F	Farmer	Gt. Britain	U. States	Superior	20 Aug 1825
Charles	6	F	Spinster	England	U.N. States	Helen	17 Dec 1827
D.	...			U. States	United States	Iris	24 Oct 1827
David	2/12	F		England	U.N. States	Helen	17 Dec 1827
David	41	M	Weaver	Ireland	America	Josephine	8 Dec 1827
Edward	28	M	Merchant	England	New York	Brighton	11 Dec 1827
Evan	6/12	M	Farmer	Gt. Britain	U. States	Superior	20 Aug 1825
James	4			England	U.N. States	Helen	17 Dec 1827
James D.	19	M	Miner	United States	U. States	Saml. Smith	24 Jul 1826
Jas.	8	M	Farmer	Gt. Britain	U. States	Superior	20 Aug 1825
Jas.	38	M	Farmer	Gt. Britain	U. States	Superior	20 Aug 1825
John	25	M	Coachman	England	United States	Jubilee	1 Oct 1828
John	35	M	Merchant	England	England	Alpheus	5 May 1828
Joseph	36	M	Labourer	Great Britain	U. States	Ganges	21 Jun 1827
Lewis	36	M	Farmer	England	America	New York Packet	8 May 1823
M.	27	M		G. Britain	U. States	Canada	19 Sep 1828
Margt.	35	F	Farmer	Gt. Britain	U. States	Superior	20 Aug 1825
Nicholas	30	M	Merchant	U. States	U. States	Thule	29 Apr 1825
Nicholas	39		Mariner	Providence	America	Rockingham	23 Aug 1822
Richard [crossed out]	36	M	Laborer			New York Packet	14 Oct 1823
*left in Bristol							
Robt.	1	M	Farmer	Gt. Britain	U. States	Superior	20 Aug 1825
Saml.	32	M	Mercht.	U.S.	U.S.	Floyd	31 May 1824
Susanna	10	F	Spinster	England	U.N. States	Helen	17 Dec 1827
Thos.	3	M	Farmer	Gt. Britain	U. States	Superior	20 Aug 1825
W.	6	M	Farmer	Gt. Britain	U. States	Superior	20 Aug 1825
Wm. J.	22	M	Gentn.	U.S.	U.S.	Cadmus	26 Apr 1824
HOPKINSON, Allen	49	M	Farmer	Great Britian	United States	Andes	19 Aug 1829
Charles	30	M	Coach builder	Great Britian	New York	Thames	16 May 1821
James	13	M	Farmer	Great Britian	United States	Andes	19 Aug 1829

NAMES OF PASSENGERS	AGE	SEX	OCCUPATIONS	COUNTRY TO WHICH THEY BELONG	COUNTRY THEY INTEND TO INHABIT	SHIPS/DATES OF ARRIVAL	
HOPKINSON (cont'd)							
John	19	M	Farmer	Great Britian	United States	Andes	19 Aug 1829
Martha	16	F	Farmer	Great Britian	United States	Andes	19 Aug 1829
Richard	49	M	Farmer	Great Britian	United States	Andes	19 Aug 1829
William	11	M	Farmer	Great Britian	United States	Andes	19 Aug 1829
HOPNER, C. C.	37	M	Officer	Germany	U. States	Ductile	12 Apr 1825
HOPPER, Barbara	12	F		Irereland	America	Carolina Ann	20 Jun 1825
Biddy	20 2/12	F		Ireland	U.S. of America	Douglass	6 Jul 1829
George	26	M	Farmer	Rye, England	United States	William	21 May 1828
Rebecca	17	F		Irereland	America	Carolina Ann	20 Jun 1825
Sarah	15	F		Irereland	America	Carolina Ann	20 Jun 1825
Thomas	35	M	Farmer	England	United States	Young Phoenix	26 Jul 1824
William	8	M		Irereland	America	Carolina Ann	20 Jun 1825
HOPPS, Joseph	22	M	Mercht.	England	England	Pacific	24 Oct 1828
HOPSON, Issac	29	M	Moulder	Great Britain	U. States America	Columbia	15 Nov 1826
HOPWOOD, Charles	28	M	Shoe Maker	England	United States	Lord Wellington	14 Nov 1827
Charles Henry	2	M	None	Great Britain	United States	Roman	10 May 1828
Elizabeth	11	F	None	Great Britain	United States	Roman	10 May 1828
Frank. Roman	0 1/12	M	None	Great Britain	United States	Roman	10 May 1828
John	25	M	Labourer	Great Britian	United States	George Clinton	21 Oct 1826
Martha	7	F	None	Great Britain	United States	Roman	10 May 1828
Mary	34	F	None	Great Britain	United States	Roman	10 May 1828
Mary Ann	9	F	None	Great Britain	United States	Roman	10 May 1828
Richard	5	M	None	Great Britain	United States	Roman	10 May 1828
HOR...I..., Ann	6	F	None	Great Britain	United States	Atlantic	28 May 1827
Elizh.	2	F	None	Great Britain	United States	Atlantic	28 May 1827
Ewd.	39	M	...er	Great Britain	United States	Atlantic	28 May 1827
Mary	13	F	None	Great Britain	United States	Atlantic	28 May 1827
Sarah	4	F	None	Great Britain	United States	Atlantic	28 May 1827
Sarah	36	F	None	Great Britain	United States	Atlantic	28 May 1827
HORAN, Michael	40	M	Labourer	Ireland	U.N. States	Jane	7 Oct 1826
Morris	32	M		Ireland	U. States	Fame	15 Nov 1826
HORARTY, Pat	20	M	Labourer	Ireland	America	Weser	26 Jun 1821
Thomas	20	M	Labourer	Ireland	America	Weser	26 Jun 1821
HORDE,							
Henriette, Mrs.	34 6/12	F		Hamburg	Charleston in North Carolina	Europa	12 Oct 1829
Jacob, a Child	2 1/12	M		Hamburg	Charleston in North Carolina	Europa	12 Oct 1829
Jacob, Mr.	37 4/12	M	Grocer	Norway	Charleston in North Carolina	Europa	12 Oct 1829
HORDMAN, Ann	19	F	None	Ireland	United States	Elizabeth	8 Jun 1827
Mary	40	F	None	Ireland	United States	Elizabeth	8 Jun 1827
HORE, Mary	32	F		G. Britann		Manchester	29 Aug 1828
HOREIS, B. M.	25	M	Laborer	Hanover	United States	Constitution	6 Jul 1829
HOREN, Elizabeth	17	F	None	Great Britain	United States	Purrington	8 Dec 1827
HOREY, ...	30	F	None	Great Britain	United States	Dalhouse Castle	21 Aug 1829
...	40	M		Great Britain	United States	Dalhouse Castle	21 Aug 1829
Ann	4	F	None	Great Britain	U.S.A.	Dalhouse Castle	21 Aug 1829
Cathr.	20	F		Ireland	U. States	Sarah G	7 May 1827
Eliza	1	F	None	Great Britain	United States	Dalhouse Castle	21 Aug 1829
Elizabeth	1	F	None	Great Britain	U.S.A.	Dalhouse Castle	21 Aug 1829
Elizabeth	6	F	None	Great Britain	U.S.A.	Dalhouse Castle	21 Aug 1829
Elizabeth	30	F	None	Great Britain	U.S.A.	Dalhouse Castle	21 Aug 1829
Elizth.	6	F	None	Great Britain	United States	Dalhouse Castle	21 Aug 1829
James	25	M	Shoemaker	Ireland	U. States	Sarah G	7 May 1827
John	8	M	None	Great Britain	U.S.A.	Dalhouse Castle	21 Aug 1829
John	40	M	Knitter	Great Britain	U.S.A.	Dalhouse Castle	21 Aug 1829
Nancy	17	F		Great Brittain	United States	Active	12 Sep 1828
Sarah	12	F	None	Great Britain	U.S.A.	Dalhouse Castle	21 Aug 1829
William	2	M	None	Great Britain	U.S.A.	Dalhouse Castle	21 Aug 1829
HORGAN, Daniel	28	M	Plaistere	Ireland	St. New York	Eliza Grant	29 Aug 1829
Elizabeth	26	F		Ireland	St. New York	Eliza Grant	29 Aug 1829
Micheal	9/12	M		Ireland	St. New York	Eliza Grant	29 Aug 1829
HORIGAN, Wm.	34	M	Labourer	Ireland	U. States	Albion	11 May 1827
HORIN, P.	32	M	Labourer	Ireland	U. States	Hope & Esther	27 Sep 1824
HORLAN, Arthur	4	M		Bristol	New York	Cosmo	25 Sep 1827
John	4	M		Bristol	New York	Cosmo	25 Sep 1827
HORLAR, Ann	29	F		Bristol	New York	Cosmo	25 Sep 1827

NAMES OF PASSENGERS	AGE	SEX	OCCUPATIONS	COUNTRY TO WHICH THEY BELONG	COUNTRY THEY INTEND TO INHABIT	SHIPS/DATES OF ARRIVAL	
HORLAR (cont'd)							
Mary Ann	12	F		Bristol	New York	Cosmo	25 Sep 1827
HORLOCK, Thomas	28	M	Farmer	England	America	Comet	26 Jun 1822
HORN, Albert	3	M		Spain	Spain	Circassian	13 Jun 1825
Charles E.	36	M	Composer	Great Britain	U.S. of America	Canada	1 Oct 1827
Charles J.	22	M	Farmer or Mechanic	Great Britan	U.S.	Edward Quesnel	31 Jul 1827
Francis	1	M		Spain	Spain	Circassian	13 Jun 1825
George	27	M	Farmer or Mechanic	Great Britan	U.S.	Edward Quesnel	31 Jul 1827
Jas.	31	M	Gardiner	G. Britain		Caravan	8 Sep 1828
John	32	M	Merchant	Ireland	England	Eliza	22 Dec 1826
Julia	5	F		Spain	Spain	Circassian	13 Jun 1825
Julia	27	F		England	England	Circassian	13 Jun 1825
Magdalena	60	M	Milliner	G. Britain		Caravan	8 Sep 1828
Thomas	24	M	Farmer	Ireland	America	William	21 May 1825
William	7	M		England	England	Circassian	13 Jun 1825
HORNBERGER, Catharine	6	F	Farmer	Switzerland	United States	Olympia	12 Aug 1828
Elizabeth	7	F	Farmer	Switzerland	United States	Olympia	12 Aug 1828
Jacob	4	M	Farmer	Switzerland	United States	Olympia	12 Aug 1828
Jaque	38	M	Farmer	Switzerland	United States	Olympia	12 Aug 1828
Magdeline	8	F	Farmer	Switzerland	United States	Olympia	12 Aug 1828
Magdeline	38	F	Farmer	Switzerland	United States	Olympia	12 Aug 1828
HORNBY, Alexander	12	M	Son of Mrs. Hornby	United States	Broom County	Venus	8 Sep 1820
Charlotte	2 4/12	F	Daughter of Mrs. Hornby	United States	Broom County	Venus	8 Sep 1820
Elizabeth	15	F	her Daughter [Mary Ann]	United States	Broom County	Venus	8 Sep 1820
Frederic	5	M	Son of Mrs. Hornby	United States	Broom County	Venus	8 Sep 1820
James	7 6/12	M	Son of Mrs. Hornby	United States	Broom County	Venus	8 Sep 1820
Jane	10 1/12	F	Daughter of Mrs. Hornby	United States	Broom County	Venus	8 Sep 1820
John	8	M	Son of Mrs. Hornby	United States	Broom County	Venus	8 Sep 1820
Mary Ann	10 6/12	F	her Daughter [Mary Ann]	United States	Broom County	Venus	8 Sep 1820
Mary Ann	39	F	Wife of Jno. Hornby	United States	Broom County	Venus	8 Sep 1820
HORNCASTLE, Amelia	6	F	None	England	U. States	Thomas Ritchie	2 Jul 1827
Eliza	32	F	None	England	U. States	Thomas Ritchie	2 Jul 1827
Henry	5	M	None	England	U. States	Thomas Ritchie	2 Jul 1827
Thos.	1	M	None	England	U. States	Thomas Ritchie	2 Jul 1827
Thos.	33	M	Labourer	England	U. States	Thomas Ritchie	2 Jul 1827
HORNE, Augustas	8	M	None	New York, U. States	United States	James Cropper	7 Oct 1823
Eliza	12	F	None	New York, U. States	United States	James Cropper	7 Oct 1823
Elizabeth	45	F	None	London, England	United States	James Cropper	7 Oct 1823
George Thos.	50	M	Physician	Richmond, York, Eng.	United States	James Cropper	7 Oct 1823
Jeffrey	50		Merchant	C..., England	Great Britain	Frances Henrietta	31 May 1824
Mary	54		None	London, England	Great Britain	Frances Henrietta	31 May 1824
Thomas	20	M	None	London, England	United States	James Cropper	7 Oct 1823
HORNEL, D.	18	M	Gentleman	Great Britain	United States	Isaac Hicks	6 Dec 1827
HORNELL, Chris	24	M	Farmer	U. States	U. States	United States	11 Sep 1828
HORNER, Dorrithey	24	F	None			Manhattan	20 Sep 1821
Francis	3	M				Manhattan	20 Sep 1821
George	27	M	Weaver	Antrim, Ireland	New York	Anthusa	24 Aug 1825
Hanah	6/12	F				Manhattan	20 Sep 1821
William	28	M	Sergeon	United States	United States	Atlantic	3 Dec 1821
HORNET, Celetta	28	M	Gardner	France	United States	American	27 Aug 1827
HORNSEY, Christopher	18	M	Farmer	Great Britain	United States	Florida	10 Dec 1823
HORNUNG, George	8 6/12	M		Amarica	Amarica	John Dickinson	19 Jun 1827
John	40 6/12	M	...rt	Amarica	Amarica	John Dickinson	19 Jun 1827

NAMES OF PASSENGERS	AGE	SEX	OCCUPATIONS	COUNTRY TO WHICH THEY BELONG	COUNTRY THEY INTEND TO INHABIT	SHIPS/DATES OF ARRIVAL	
HORRCOT, Richard	34	M	Merchant	G. Brittan	U. States	Henry	24 Oct 1828
HORRICK, Betty	25	F	None	Great Britain	New York	Superior	5 Sep 1827
John	24	M	Weaver	Barry	Barry	Howard	
						Douglass	11 May 1827
HORRIDEN, John	31	M	Labourer	Great Britain	United States	Aurora	5 Sep 1826
HORRING, Charles, Jr.	27	M	Merchant	G.B.		Silas Richards	29 Oct 1827
K. G.	30	M	Merchant	Great Britain	United States	Leeds	29 Sep 1823
HORRINGTON, Eugene	22	M	Surgeon	England	U. States	Electra	7 Jul 1828
HORSAFALL, Richard	30	M	Farmer	England	United States	Jubilee	13 Jul 1829
HORSE, Michael	26	M	Labourer	Ireland	United States	Mary & Harriet	3 Jul 1829
HORSELEY, John	26	M	...	G. Britain	U. States	New England	28 Sep 1824
HORSEMAN, Margaretta	21	F	Farmer	Alsace in the			
				Department of			
				Upper and lower			
				Rhine	United States	Carolina	
						Augusta	16 May 1828
HORSEY, Margt.	25	F		G. Britain	U. States	St. George	7 Jun 1828
Peter	16	M		G. Britain	U. States	St. George	7 Jun 1828
HORSFORD, James	36	M	Mariner	U. States	U. States	Atlas	24 Jun 1828
Jno. B.	32	M	Physician	U. States	U. States	Wm. Penn	6 Feb 1822
P.	34	M	Mariner	U. States	U. States	Atlas	24 Jun 1828
HORSIF...ER, Mary	22			Kamsbottom	England	Great Britain	7 May 1827
HORSINGTON, Richd.	26	M	Farmer	Bristol, Engl.	...	Warrior	19 May 1828
HORSLEY, Mary	22	F	Labourer	England	U. States	Comet	23 Aug 1828
Wm.	24	M	Labourer	England	U. States	Comet	23 Aug 1828
HORST, Henry	30	M	Shop Man	Great Britain	Great Britain	Nestor	3 Nov 1820
HORSTMAN, W. H.	38	M	Manufacturer	U. States	U. States	Marmion	7 Jun 1824
HORT, ..., Mr.	19	M	Gent.	France		Henri IV	7 May 1827
HORTH, —	39	M	Labourer	France	United States	Cavalier	25 Jul 1828
—, Wife	32	F		France	United States	Cavalier	25 Jul 1828
Antoine	1	M		France	United States	Cavalier	25 Jul 1828
Jacob	3	M		France	United States	Cavalier	25 Jul 1828
Joseph	13	M		France	United States	Cavalier	25 Jul 1828
Pierre	8	M		France	United States	Cavalier	25 Jul 1828
HORTON, David	22	M	Merchant	G. Brittain	U. States	Rockingham	17 May 1821
Edward H.	27	M	Merchant	United States	United States	Superb	27 Mar 1820
J.	30	M	Farmer	England	U. States	Orazimbo	7 Jan 1821
Mary	45	F	Lady	Island Jamaca	Island Jamaca	Agenora	19 Jun 1826
HORWOOD, Jno.	30 11/12	M	Merchant	England	United States	Hiram	31 Oct 1828
HORY, John	8	M	None	England	United States	Trident	18 Jul 1827
Peter	45	M	Black Smith	France		Pallas	14 Jun 1828
HOSACK, Alexr. E.	22	M	Doctor	N. York	New York	Lewis	29 Oct 1825
Hamilton	20	M	Merchant	New York	New York	Stephania	2 Jan 1824
Mary	30	F		G. Britain	U.S. America	Defence	13 Dec 1827
Nathl. P.	23	M		America	America	Britannia	22 Jul 1829
HOSCHAN, —	40	F		Switzerland	U.S.	Francois I	8 Aug 1829
Abel	5	F		Switzerland	U.S.	Francois I	8 Aug 1829
Catherine	12	F		Switzerland	U.S.	Francois I	8 Aug 1829
Margaret	7	F		Switzerland	U.S.	Francois I	8 Aug 1829
Maria	3	F		Switzerland	U.S.	Francois I	8 Aug 1829
Maria	8	F		Switzerland	U.S.	Francois I	8 Aug 1829
Mariaberg	16	F		Switzerland	U.S.	Francois I	8 Aug 1829
Nicholas	38	M	Carpenter	Switzerland	U.S.	Francois I	8 Aug 1829
Unice	10	F		Switzerland	U.S.	Francois I	8 Aug 1829
HOSEA, Jabez	28	M	Sailor	United States	United States	New Packet	20 Oct 1827
*distressed Seaman							
HOSER, John	21	M	Tailor	Gt. Brittan		L'Esperance	6 Sep 1828
HOSHAN, Dennis	30	M	Labourer	Ireland	United States	Jubilee	13 Jul 1829
Joannah	30	F	None	Ireland	United States	Jubilee	13 Jul 1829
HOSIER, Thos.	23	M	None	Ireland	U.S. America	Columbia	31 Jul 1826
Vintey	22	M	Teacher	Ireland	U.S. America	Columbia	31 Jul 1826
HOSKERNE, George H.	26	M	Sugar Refr.	England		Henri IV	17 May 1828
HOSKING, Charles	28		Mines	England	England	Triumph	23 Jul 1829
James	49		Mines	England	England	Triumph	23 Jul 1829
John	24		Miner	England	England	Triumph	23 Jul 1829
HOSKINS, C. N.	43	M	Merchant	England	New York	York	8 Aug 1829
HOSLEY, Hannah	22	F		Gt. Britain	United States	Crisis	6 Apr 1825
Wm.	27	M	Tailor	Gt. Britain	United States	Crisis	6 Apr 1825
HOSMER, A. P.	25	M	Merchant	U. States	U. States	Collasas	21 Oct 1826

NAMES OF PASSENGERS	AGE	SEX	OCCUPATIONS	COUNTRY TO WHICH THEY BELONG	COUNTRY THEY INTEND TO INHABIT	SHIPS/DATES OF ARRIVAL	
HOSNER, Elias	24	M	Grocer	Ley Bran		Manhattan	20 Sep 1821
HOSNINGHAUS,							
Justar A.	22	M	Student	Germany	New York	Lewis	29 Oct 1825
HOSS, Hans	35	M		Norway	America	Wm. Tell	22 Sep 1828
HOSSALL, Joseph	28	M	Merchant	G.B.	United States	Orozimbo	31 May 1824
HOSSAN, Bernard	18	M	Labourer	Ireland	United States	Robert Fulton	24 Jul 1826
Dennis	24	M	Labourer	Ireland	United States	Robert Fulton	24 Jul 1826
HOSSEY, Andrew	46	M	Seaman	America	America	Soto	1 Aug 1829
HOSSON, Jane	11	F		G. Britain	U. States	Mary & Harriot	8 Sep 1828
Mary	7	F		G. Britain	U. States	Mary & Harriot	8 Sep 1828
Samuel	9	M		G. Britain	U. States	Mary & Harriot	8 Sep 1828
Thomas	42	M		G. Britain	U. States	Mary & Harriot	8 Sep 1828
Wm.	19	M		G. Britain	U. States	Mary & Harriot	8 Sep 1828
HOT BLACK, John	27	M	Jeweller	England	U. States	Bayard	11 Mar 1823
Servina	21	F		England	U. States	Bayard	11 Mar 1823
HOTCHKISS, Daniel	24	M	Carpenter	United States		Mentor	23 May 1821
E.	45	M	Mercht.	U. States	U.S.	Shepherdess	17 May
Ezra	50	M	Merchant	N. Haven	U. States	Gleaner	4 Oct 1828
HOTHAM, Ann	23	F		Great Britain	United States	Mary	11 Jul 1820
Emme	2	F		Great Britain	United States	Mary	11 Jul 1820
HOTT, John	30	M	Weaver	England	Alexandria, U.S.	Roman	17 Oct 1826
HOTTIN, Lucy	infant	M		England	America	Thames	27 May 1822
HOTTON, Ann	19 6/12	F		Irereland	America	Carolina Ann	20 Jun 1825
HOUBLER, Catharine	7			France	U. States	Parachute	14 May 1828
Catharine	32			France	U. States	Parachute	14 May 1828
Christin	1			France	U. States	Parachute	14 May 1828
Greg	31		Farmer	France	U. States	Parachute	14 May 1828
Jean	4			France	U. States	Parachute	14 May 1828
HOUGH, Elizabeth	29	F	Farmer	Scotland	U. States	Hope	21 Oct 1823
Henry	26	M	Weaver	Great Brittain		Corinthian	9 Jan 1827
J. B.	53	M	Merchant	Philadelphia	U. States	Tuscaloosa	8 May 1826
Janet	60	F	Farmer	Scotland	U. States	Hope	21 Oct 1823
Margaret	45	F	Weaver	Great Brittain		Corinthian	9 Jan 1827
R. G.	23	M	Clerk	Alexander	U. States	Adams	27 Jun 1825
Willian	24	M	Gentlm.	England	Canada	James Cropper	13 Mar 1826
HOUGHTON, Catharine	28	F	None	Great Britain	United States	Mount Vernon	17 Jun 1825
Danl.	33	M	Mercht.	America, U.S.	Connt.	Orozimbo	16 Apr 1821
E.	24	M	Gentleman	England	U. States	Cyno	22 Jul 1826
James	28	M	Taylor	Great Britian	United States	Diamond	8 Nov 1824
Jno.	28	M				Cassack	25 Jul 1820
John	22	M	Gardner	Great Britain	United States	Mount Vernon	17 Jun 1825
Patrick	29	M	Gardner	Great Britain	United States	Mount Vernon	17 Jun 1825
Thomas W.	20	M	Merchant	United States	United States	Pedler	29 May 1826
Thomas W.	20	M	Mariner	U. States	U. States	Mary Jane	21 May 1827
HOULBROAK, Jesse	44	M	Supercargo	Bermuda		Lancatter	5 Jul 1820
HOULDING, James	28	M	Labourer	Great Britain	United States	Penelope	11 Jun 1827
HOULIHIN, Elenor	17	F	Spinster	Ireland	United States	General Marion	20 Aug 1828
HOUMAR, Honour	34	M	Clark	Ireland		Quatre Freres	29 Jul 1828
HOUNSFIELD, Geo.	27	M	Merchant	Gt. Britain	Grt. Britain	Britannia	29 Oct 1829
HOURIHAN, Mary	20	F	Spinster	Ireland	U. States	Josephine	7 May 1827
HOURTSHAM, John N.	24	M	Shipmaster	U. States	U. States	William Thompson	27 May 1824
HOUSE, Chas.	33	M	Sailor	Great Brittain	United States	Nimrod	9 Jan 1827
Francis	30 10/12	M	Attorny (at Law)	Englishman	America	Meteor	19 Aug 1825
HOUSEMAN, Hannah	15	F		Staten Island	U. States	South Carolina	2 Aug 1822
HOUSER, Susannah	53	F		England	United States	Acasta	15 Jul 1822
HOUSSY, Leod.	24	M	Carpenter	Switzerland	America	Henry	11 Oct 1825
HOUSTAN, Mary	40	F	Matron	Ireland	U. States	Josephine	30 Aug 1828
HOUSTEN, Alexander	7	M	Child	Ireland	U. States	Josephine	30 Aug 1828
Alexander	38	M	Millar	Ireland	U. States	Josephine	30 Aug 1828
George	12	M	Child	Ireland	U. States	Josephine	30 Aug 1828
Jane	10	F	Child	Ireland	U. States	Josephine	30 Aug 1828
John	14	M	Labourer	Ireland	U. States	Josephine	30 Aug 1828
HOUSTON, Henrietta	23	F	...	Scotland	America	Nimrod	9 Jul 1827
James	27	M	weaver	Great Britain	United States	Courier	26 Jun 1827
Jane	17	F	Spinster	Ireland	United States	Trident	16 May 1826
John	23	M	...	Scotland	America	Nimrod	9 Jul 1827
John	30	M	Weaver	Ireland	America	Carolina Ann	7 Apr 1826
Mary	...	F	...	Scotland	America	Nimrod	9 Jul 1827

NAMES OF PASSENGERS	AGE	SEX	OCCUPATIONS	COUNTRY TO WHICH THEY BELONG	COUNTRY THEY INTEND TO INHABIT	SHIPS/DATES OF ARRIVAL	
HOUSTON (cont'd)							
Mary	20 3/12	F		Ireland	America	Carolina Ann	7 Apr 1826
HOUTTON, Margert	18 6/12	F	Spinster	Ireland	U. States	Josephine	30 Aug 1828
HOVARES, Jonathan	50	M	Joiner	England	United States	Trident	18 Jul 1827
HOVE, Gideon, Mr.	33	M	Baker	England	U. States	Acasta	11 Dec 1826
HOW, Cathrine	16	F	Taylor	Ireland	U. States	Virginia	20 Jun 1825
Elizabeth	32	F	Farmer	Great Britain	U. States America	Ann Maria	29 Nov 1821
Frances	21	F		Great Britain	Pennsylvania	Thames	16 May 1821
Henry	23 3/12	M	Farmer	Great Britain	Pennsylvania	Thames	16 May 1821
James	20	M	Labourer	England	United States	India	8 Jun 1827
John	7	M	Farmer	Great Britain	U. States America	Ann Maria	29 Nov 1821
John W. S.	27	M	Merchant	England	United States	Cortex	4 Dec 1824
Jonathan	5	M	Farmer	Great Britain	U. States America	Ann Maria	29 Nov 1821
Maria	24	F		New York	U. States	Zephyr	18 May 1825
William	3	M	Farmer	Great Britain	U. States America	Ann Maria	29 Nov 1821
William	26 6/12	M	Farmer	Great Britain	Pennsylvania	Thames	16 May 1821
William	27		...	Ipswich, England	Great Britain	Frances Henrietta	31 May 1824
William, Jr.	1 8/12	M		Great Britain	Pennsylvania	Thames	16 May 1821
HOWALD, Ana	19	F	Farmer	Switzerland	United States	Elizabeth	27 Jul 1824
Christina	26	F	Farmer	Switzerland	U. States	Sully	15 Jul 1829
Henry	2	M	Farmer	Switzerland	U. States	Sully	15 Jul 1829
Jacob	28	M	Farmer	Switzerland	U. States	Sully	15 Jul 1829
John Ulerick	28	M	Farmer	Switzerland	United States	Elizabeth	27 Jul 1824
HOWARD, —, Miss	3	F		England	U. States	Edwin	10 Feb 1829
Alfred	4	M		England	New York	Hudson	20 Nov 1828
Alfred	6	M		England	U. States	Edwin	10 Feb 1829
Allen	...9	...	...	...	United States	John London	3 Aug 1824
Andw.	25	M	Labourer	England	U. States	Thomas Ritchie	2 Jul 1827
Ann	24 4/12	F	None	Great Britain	United States	James Monroe	27 Jul 1821
Betsy, Miss	7	F		England	U. States	Hudson	10 Nov 1825
Bridget	35	F		Ireland	U. States	Nancy	9 Jun 1821
Catherine	27	F	Lady	Ireland	United States	Borneo	9 Jul 1827
Charles	20	M	Gardener	England	New York	America	1 Aug 1828
Daniel	5	M	Farmer	Great Britain	U. States America	Ann Maria	29 Nov 1821
Daniel	35	M	Farmer	Ireland	U. States	Nancy	9 Jun 1821
David	21			Ireland	U.S.	Union	20 Aug 1827
Fanel	28	F		England	U. States	Edwin	10 Feb 1829
Favell	2	F		England	New York	Hudson	20 Nov 1828
Favell	30	F		England	New York	Hudson	20 Nov 1828
Frances Ann	20	F	Lady	St. Johns	United States	St. Michaels	7 Jun 1827
Frederick	32	M	Esq.	Ireland	Ireland	Thetis	17 Aug 1824
Henry	8	M		England	New York	Hudson	20 Nov 1828
Henry	25	M		England	Ut. States	Courier	13 Jul 1826
Henry	30	M	Gentleman	England	U. States	Acasta	28 Jan 1823
Henry	33	M	Merchant	England	New York	Hudson	20 Nov 1828
Henry	35	M	Merchant	England	U. States	Edwin	10 Feb 1829
Henry, Jr.	8	M		England	U. States	Edwin	10 Feb 1829
Hiram E.	26	M	Gentleman	United States	U. States	Saml. Smith	24 Jul 1826
James	7	M	Farmer	Great Britain	U. States America	Ann Maria	29 Nov 1821
James	26	M		Great Britain	United States	Ganges	8 Jul 1820
Jeane	25	M	Farmer	England	Alexandria, U.S.	Roman	17 Oct 1826
John	2/1/12	M	None	Great Britain	United States	James Monroe	27 Jul 1821
John	27	M	Shoe Maker	Ireland	United States	Borneo	9 Jul 1827
John	29	M	Farmer	Great Britain	U. States America	Ann Maria	29 Nov 1821
John	35	M		Ireland	U. States	Fame	15 Nov 1826
Jos. W.	29	M	Merchant	Massachusetts	U. States	Swift	11 May 1824
Joseph	26	M		America	America	Britannia	22 Jul 1829
Joseph, Master	2 1/2	M		England	U. States	Hudson	10 Nov 1825
Lewis	49	M	Merchant	United States	United States	Weser	21 Oct 1823
M.	28	M	Mining Agent	England	England	Medina	17 Dec 1828
Maria	10	F	Farmer	Ireland	U. States	Nancy	9 Jun 1821
Maria, Miss	4 1/2	F		England	U. States	Hudson	10 Nov 1825
Martha	27	F	Farmer	Great Britain	U. States America	Ann Maria	29 Nov 1821
Mary	34	F	Servant	Great Brittian	United States	Cortes	18 Oct 1820
Mary, Mrs.	26	F		England	U. States	Hudson	10 Nov 1825
Patience	51	F	Lady	State New York	United States	St. Michaels	7 Jun 1827
Patrick	12	M		Ireland	U. States	Nancy	9 Jun 1821
R.	17	M				Hanford	17 Jul 1828

NAMES OF PASSENGERS	AGE	SEX	OCCUPATIONS	COUNTRY TO WHICH THEY BELONG	COUNTRY THEY INTEND TO INHABIT	SHIPS/DATES OF ARRIVAL	
HOWARD (cont'd)							
Robert	27	M	Traveller	Great Britian	United States	Isaac Hicks	22 May 1826
Thomas	37	M	Labourer	Great Britain	United States	Washington	3 Sep 1827
Thos.	49 6/12	M	Ship Master	United States	New York	Manhattan	20 Feb 1826
William	29 10/12	M	Merchant	Great Britain	United States	Courier	23 Feb 1824
William, Master	4 1/2	M		England	U. States	Hudson	10 Nov 1825
HOWARTH, ...serd	30	M	Stone Mason		New York	Governor Clinton	3 Jul 1827
Allice	24	F	None	England	United States	Jubilee	13 Jul 1829
Ann	2			F...	England	Great Britain	7 May 1827
Ann	5	F	None		New York	Governor Clinton	3 Jul 1827
Ann	37	F	None		New York	Governor Clinton	3 Jul 1827
Anne	10	F		U. States	U. States	United States	11 Sep 1828
Catharine	11	M		England	England	Criterion	29 May 1822
Catharine	40	M		England	England	Criterion	29 May 1822
Charles	9	F		England	England	Criterion	29 May 1822
Charles	41	M	W. Manufatory	Great Britain	U. States America	Columbia	15 Nov 1826
Christiana	2	F	None	...	United States	Minerva	30 Oct 1827
Dennis	21	M	Farmer	Gt. Britain	U. States	Champion	19 Apr 1828
Edmund	5			F...	England	Great Britain	7 May 1827
Edward	4	M	None		New York	Governor Clinton	3 Jul 1827
Elizabeth	33	F	None	...	United States	Minerva	30 Oct 1827
Elizh.	29			F...	England	Great Britain	7 May 1827
Ellen	55	F	Farmer	Gt. Britain	U. States	Champion	19 Apr 1828
Emma	13	M		England	England	Criterion	29 May 1822
George	13	M	None	England	United States	Jubilee	13 Jul 1829
Gilbert	1	M	None		New York	Governor Clinton	3 Jul 1827
Gurtham	11	M		England	England	Criterion	29 May 1822
Hannah	33	F	None	Great Britain	United States	Eliza Barker	3 Jul 1826
Henry	7	M	None	...	United States	Minerva	30 Oct 1827
Henry	16	M	Blacksmith	England	United States	Jubilee	13 Jul 1829
Honey	1			F...	England	Great Britain	7 May 1827
Inmanul	23	M	Farmer	Switzerland	United States	Elizabeth	27 Jul 1824
James	19	M	Blacksmith	England	United States	Jubilee	13 Jul 1829
Jane	22	F		U. States	U. States	United States	11 Sep 1828
Jas.	17	M	None	...	United States	Minerva	30 Oct 1827
John	22	M	Blacksmith	England	United States	Jubilee	13 Jul 1829
John	30	M	None	Great Britain	United States	Eliza Barker	3 Jul 1826
Mary	8	F	None		New York	Governor Clinton	3 Jul 1827
Richard	...		Wheelright	F...	England	Great Britain	7 May 1827
Robert	21	M	Stone Mason		New York	Governor Clinton	3 Jul 1827
Sophia	16	F	Farmer	Gt. Britain	U. States	Champion	19 Apr 1828
HOWDEN, Allexander	19	M	...	...	United States	Hanford	17 Oct 1828
Archibald	17	M	...	...	United States	Hanford	17 Oct 1828
Christian	46	F	wife	...	United States	Hanford	17 Oct 1828
James	12	M	...	...	United States	Hanford	17 Oct 1828
Marion	15	M	...	...	United States	Hanford	17 Oct 1828
Peter	3	M	...	...	United States	Hanford	17 Oct 1828
William	43	M	Minister	Great Brittain	Great Brittain	St. Michael's	10 Feb 1827
William	50	M	Minister	St. John, N.B.	St. John, N.B.	St. Michaels	15 Feb 1825
Wm.	7	M	...	...	United States	Hanford	17 Oct 1828
Wm.	44	M	...	...	United States	Hanford	17 Oct 1828
HOWDLEY, Wm.	24	M	Merchant	G. Brittain	U. States	York	10 Dec 1825
HOWE, Anne	18	F		Mayo	America	Margaret	31 Jul 1824
G. G.	35	M	Merchant	Hayti	U. States	Curlew	16 Jun 1823
George	29	M	Supercargo	United States	United States	Neptune	29 Oct 1821
Isabella	25			England	England	Hudson	4 Sep 1823
James	27		Farmer	England	England	Hudson	4 Sep 1823
John	25	M	Weaver	Mayo	America	Margaret	31 Jul 1824
John	33	M	Farmer	Great Britain	U. States America	Ann Maria	29 Nov 1821
Joseph	40	M	Farmer	Great Britain	U. States America	Ann Maria	29 Nov 1821
Margaret	16	F		Mayo	America	Margaret	31 Jul 1824
Mary	52	F		Mayo	America	Margaret	31 Jul 1824

NAMES OF PASSENGERS	AGE	SEX	OCCUPATIONS	COUNTRY TO WHICH THEY BELONG	COUNTRY THEY INTEND TO INHABIT	SHIPS/DATES OF ARRIVAL	
HOWE (cont'd)							
Mary Ann	2	F		Great Britain	U. States America	Ann Maria	29 Nov 1821
Philip	41	M	Merchant	United States	New York, U.S.	Amity	31 Jan 1822
Robert	60	M	Mason	Mayo	America	Margaret	31 Jul 1824
Sarah	32	F		Great Britain	U. States America	Ann Maria	29 Nov 1821
Stephen B.	25	M	Merchant	United States	United States	Pilot	27 Feb 1826
HOWEL,							
Sophia, Miss	12 2/12	F		America	America	Henry	19 Jun 1825
Sophia, Mrs.	44	F		America	America	Henry	19 Jun 1825
HOWELL, —	32	M	Merchant			James Monroe	3 Jul 1824
Alexander	30	M	Merchant	U. States	U. States	Don Quixote	20 Mar 1827
C.	25	M	Merchant	France	U. States	New Packet	5 May 1823
Caroline	9	F	None	England	Upper Canada	Indian Chief	16 Aug 1822
Elizabeth	7	F	None	England	Upper Canada	Indian Chief	16 Aug 1822
Elizabeth	31	F	None	England	Upper Canada	Indian Chief	16 Aug 1822
Henry	29	M	Distiller	Englishman	America	Meteor	19 Aug 1825
John	45	M	Mechanic	England	U.S.	George Canning	26 Aug 1829
Mary	31	F	Seamstress	England	America	Meteor	19 Aug 1825
Peter	22	M	Svt.	Gt. Brittain	United States	Cortes	5 Aug 1822
Sarah	18	F		England	U.S.	George Canning	26 Aug 1829
Thomas	3	M	None	England	Upper Canada	Indian Chief	16 Aug 1822
HOWELLS, Thomas	32	M	Malster	England	United States	Warrior	6 Oct 1828
HOWER, —, child	4/12	M				Lingan	16 Jul 1822
—, Mrs.	20	F				Lingan	16 Jul 1822
Patrick	23	M	Farmer	Ireland	United states	Lingan	16 Jul 1822
Thos.	25		Laborer	Great Britan	U. States	Columbia	7 May 1828
HOWEY, Henry	26	M	Farmer	Stackport	United States	Aurelia	7 Jun 1826
HOWIE, Jas.	32	M		Scotland	New York	Joseph Hume	26 Oct 1829
HOWITH, Deny	52	M	Stone Mason	England	America	Belleville	7 Dec 1827
John	12	M	Stone Mason	England	America	Belleville	7 Dec 1827
HOWLAND, —, Mrs.		F		U. States	U. States	Monroe	23 Aug 1824
Caroline	13		Farmer	England	United States	Corinthian	7 Jul 1829
Celia	7		Farmer	England	United States	Corinthian	7 Jul 1829
Celia	30		Farmer	England	United States	Corinthian	7 Jul 1829
Geo. M.	20	M	Merchant	American	U.S.	Alexander	15 Oct 1827
Geo. M.	22	M	Merchant	U. States	U. States	Ospray	8 Mar 1828
Heneryett	23	F	...	...	...	Dawn	19 Aug 1825
Jane	9		Farmer	England	United States	Corinthian	7 Jul 1829
Jessy	5		Farmer	England	United States	Corinthian	7 Jul 1829
Joanna	30	F		United States	United States	Britannia	29 Oct 1829
Joseph	39	M	Merchant	U. States	U. States	Amity	11 Sep 1820
Lloyd	35	M	Master Mariner	United States	United States	New York	14 Jul 1827
Louisa	11		Farmer	England	United States	Corinthian	7 Jul 1829
Margaret	2		Farmer	England	United States	Corinthian	7 Jul 1829
Reuben	52	M	Mariner	U. States	U. States	John London	1 Oct 1822
Sam. S.	39	M	Merchant	United States	United States	Britannia	29 Oct 1829
Ths.	30	M	Labourer	Great Brittan	U. States	John & Elizabeth	11 Dec 1826
William	27		Joiner	England	U. States	Venus	4 Oct 1821
William	38		Farmer	England	United States	Corinthian	7 Jul 1829
William W.	24	M	Merchant	United States	United States	Louisa	6 Apr 1822
Wm. H.	17	M	Merchant	Massachusetts	U. States	Ganges	23 Jul 1824
HOWLEN, Mathew	28	M	Carpenter	United States	United States	Hannah Eliza	23 Sep 1826
HOWNY, Andrew	20	M	Baker	...aven	United States	Minerva	30 Oct 1829
HOWORTH, Abram	22		Calico Printer	England	America	Florida	14 Oct 1829
Samuel	44	M	Gentleman	England	U.S. America	Criterion	27 Oct 1821
HOWS, William	22	M	Machine Maker	England	U.S. America	New Hampshire	28 Sep 1826
HOWSON, —, Mrs.	25		None	England	Canada	Bolivar	25 Nov 1826
Agnes	3		None	England	Canada	Bolivar	25 Nov 1826
Alfred	15		None	England	Canada	Bolivar	25 Nov 1826
Fras.	27		Caver	England	Canada	Bolivar	25 Nov 1826
Wm.	9/12		None	England	Canada	Bolivar	25 Nov 1826
HOWSTON, Elizabeth	24	F	Spinster	England	United States	Trident	31 Mar 1827
HOXEY, Elizabeth	22	F	Servant	Ireland	America	Carolina Ann	7 Aug 1826
HOY, Alexr.	12	M		Ireland	New York	Atlantic	6 Oct 1828
Edward	50		Weaver	Ireland	United States	Mexico	1 Jun 1821
Jane	25	F		Great Britain	United States	Meridian	2 Jul 1827
John	23	M		Ireland	New York	Lady Hunter	5 Jun 1826
Owen	26	M	Labourer	Great Britain	United States	Meridian	2 Jul 1827

NAMES OF PASSENGERS	AGE	SEX	OCCUPATIONS	COUNTRY TO WHICH THEY BELONG	COUNTRY THEY INTEND TO INHABIT	SHIPS/DATES OF ARRIVAL	
HOYCE, Ann	25	F		U. States	U. States	United States	11 Sep 1828
Bess	28	F		U. States	U. States	United States	11 Sep 1828
John	30	M	Labourer	U. States	U. States	United States	11 Sep 1828
Mary	24	F		U. States	U. States	United States	11 Sep 1828
HOYL, John	20	M	Weaver	Gt. Britain		Dalhouse Castle	13 May 1828
HOYLE, Betsey	3	F	Weaver	Great Britain	U.S. America	Chili	7 Jul 1827
Chippendale	8	F		England	U. States	Packet	23 Sep 1820
Ellen	18	F	None	Great Britain	United States	Penelope	11 Jun 1827
Giles	22	M	Weaver	Great Britain	United States	Penelope	11 Jun 1827
Jane	19	F		England	U. States	Packet	23 Sep 1820
Jane	42	F		England	U. States	Packet	23 Sep 1820
John	1	M	Weaver	Great Britain	U.S. America	Chili	7 Jul 1827
John	30	M	Weaver	Great Britain	U.S. America	Chili	7 Jul 1827
John	35	M	Bookkeeper	Great Brittain	U. States	William Byrnes	23 Jul 1824
Joseph	41	M	Farmer	England	United States	Concordia	25 Aug 1827
Raphael	16	F		England	U. States	Packet	23 Sep 1820
Sarah	26	F	Weaver	Great Britain	U.S. America	Chili	7 Jul 1827
Stephen	3	M		England	U. States	Packet	23 Sep 1820
Thos.	17	M	Weaver	Great Britain	United States	Penelope	11 Jun 1827
William	46	M	Sailor			Belle Savage	15 Aug 1820
William, Junr.	17	M	Sailor			Belle Savage	15 Aug 1820
Zilpha	1	F		England	U. States	Packet	23 Sep 1820
HOYLES, Michael	32	M	Clergiman	England	U.S.	Acasta	11 May 1827
Williams	24	M	Farmer	England	Great Brittan	Venus	15 Apr 1822
HOYSTMAN, Louis	23	M	Farmer	Germany	United States	Virginia	31 May 1828
HOYT, Aneel	40	M	Doctor	U. States	U. States	Holly	8 Feb 1827
Charles W.	28	M	Seaman	U. States		Virginia	31 Dec 1827
J. C.	25	M	Mariner	U. States	U. States	Caseo	26 Apr 1828
Margaret	14	F	Lady	United States	United States	Ann Maria	21 May 1827
Moses	36	M	Farmer	St. Johns, N.B.	Novascotia	Lady Hunter	22 Mar 1824
Sarah	37	F	Lady	United States	United States	Ann Maria	21 May 1827
Shadrack	50	M	Mariner	Connecticut	Connecticut	Planter	7 Jan 1827
HOYTE, Jas.	37	M	Merchant	U. States	U. States	Canada	13 Feb 1826
HOZIER, James	20	M	Farmer	Ireland	United States	Dublin Packet	24 Sep 1823
Ventrey	18	M	Farmer	Ireland	United States	Dublin Packet	24 Sep 1823
HRYAS, Edmond	35	M	Labourer	Ireland	United States	Hope & Esther	17 Oct 1827
HU..., Francis	...		Weaver	Jo...	England	Great Britain	7 May 1827
HUARD, Charles	19	M	Merchant	France	Havanna	Desdemona	21 Oct 1825
HUART, N.	34	F		France	U. States	Asia	5 Jul 1823
HUBARD, James	15	M	Mercht.	England	United States	Hannibal	6 Sep 1824
Sarah	40	F		U. States	U. States	Penobscott Packet	1 Jul 1823
HUBBARD, Benjm.	30	M	Farmer	England	United States	Ariadne	7 May 1821
Caroline	25	F		Spain	Havana	Liberty	31 Jan 1826
Cellen	28	F		England	United States	Ariadne	7 May 1821
Charles	1	M		England	United States	Ariadne	7 May 1821
D.	54	M	Mariner	U. States	U. States	Centurion	2 Jan 1826
Daniel		M	Merchant	U.S.	U. States	Active	9 Feb 1827
David, Age Estimated at	20 6/12	M	Merchant	U. States	U. States	Port Captain	26 May 1824
Eunice	17	F		U.S.	U.S.	Abeona	24 May 1822
John	23	M	Marchant	N. York	U. States	Commodore Perry	9 Apr 1821
Wm.	4	M		England	United States	Ariadne	7 May 1821
Wm. W.	26	M	Seaman	America	U. States	Sarah	26 Jul 1824
HUBBELL, A.	25	M	Merchant	New York	New York	Samuel	14 Feb 1826
Charles	23	M	Mechanic	U. States	U. States	Rodney	19 Jun 1827
*Passenger from the Wreck of Schooner Gen. Marion from Charleston to N.Y.							
Geogg.	29		Merchant	United States	U. States	Cadet	11 Jan 1826
Henry W.	21	M	Merchant	U. States	U. States	Sabina	25 Apr 1828
HUBBLE, Catherine	10	F	Child	New Brunswick	Upper Canada	Lady Hunter	22 Aug 1825
Elizabeth	30	F	Wife	New Brunswick	Upper Canada	Lady Hunter	22 Aug 1825
H. W.	19	M	Gentleman	U. States	U. States	Sabina	5 May 1826
Jacob	4	M	Child	New Brunswick	Upper Canada	Lady Hunter	22 Aug 1825
Mary	9	F	Child	New Brunswick	Upper Canada	Lady Hunter	22 Aug 1825
Sofrina	7	F	Child	New Brunswick	Upper Canada	Lady Hunter	22 Aug 1825
Thomas	21	M	pudler		uncertain	Mount Vernon	29 Aug 1828
HUBBS, D. J.	40	M	Merchant	United States	United States	Splendid	27 Mar 1828

NAMES OF PASSENGERS	AGE	SEX	OCCUPATIONS	COUNTRY TO WHICH THEY BELONG	COUNTRY THEY INTEND TO INHABIT	SHIPS/DATES OF ARRIVAL	
HUBENSHALL, Henry	48	M		Hesler		Constitution	20 Jun 1828
John C.	28	M	Labourer	Hanover		Constitution	20 Jun 1828
HUBENTHAL, J. H.	46	M	Farmer	not to Remain in the U. States	U. States	Maria Elizabeth	9 Jun 1826
HUBER, Anthony	40	F	One Family [Henry]	France	United States	Henri IV	2 Oct 1828
Christian	15	M	One Family [Henry]	France	United States	Henri IV	2 Oct 1828
Frederica	7	F	One Family [Henry]	France	United States	Henri IV	2 Oct 1828
George	13/12	M	One Family [Henry]	France	United States	Henri IV	2 Oct 1828
Godfrey	20	M	One Family [Henry]	France	United States	Henri IV	2 Oct 1828
Gotliebe	6	F		Wirtemburg	United States	Wade	29 Aug 1825
Henry	17	M	One Family [Henry]	France	United States	Henri IV	2 Oct 1828
Henry	42	M	Agriculturalist	France	United States	Henri IV	2 Oct 1828
Joh. Fred.	3	M		Wirtemburg	United States	Wade	29 Aug 1825
John	9	M	One Family [Henry]	France	United States	Henri IV	2 Oct 1828
Louis	11	M	One Family [Henry]	France	United States	Henri IV	2 Oct 1828
Magdalina	20	F	...	Wirtemburg	United States	Wade	29 Aug 1825
Samuel	9/12	M		Wirtemburg	United States	Wade	29 Aug 1825
HÜBER, Godlob	18	M	Saddler	Wirtemburg	United States	Wade	29 Aug 1825
HUBERT, Dorothia	21	F	Maid to Mrs. Jukel	France	France	Bayard	30 Oct 1820
Jean	32	M	None	France	U. States	Ganges	21 Jun 1827
Josephine	25	F		France	United States	Henri IV	14 Oct 1829
Stephen	30 5/12	M	Mechanic	France	United States	Cadmus	9 Dec 1825
HUCHERSON, David	20	M	Shoe Maker	Ireland	United States	Borneo	28 Aug 1828
HUCHET, Heloise	16	F	Lady	Charleston, S.C.	U. States	Elba	21 May 1825
HUCKER, Saml.	23		Weaver	St. John	U. States	Lady Hunter	5 Jul 1823
HUCKET, Joseph	15	M	Merchant	U. States	U. States	Sully	24 Oct 1828
HUCKETT, Chas.	50	M	Merchant	France	U. States	John & Edward	18 Jul 1822
P.	15	F	Merchant	France	U. States	John & Edward	18 Jul 1822
HUCTCHINSON, Henry	12	M		Ireland	America	Carolina Ann	7 Apr 1826
HUDDESA, S.	34	M	Labourer	Europe	United States	Aspasia	5 Sep 1827
HUDDLESO, John	37	M	Farmer	Europe	United States	Aspasia	5 Sep 1827
HUDDLESON, James	26	M	Merchant	Gt. Britain	Gt. Britain	Thetis	28 Jun 1824
HUDDLESTON, J.	25	M	Merchant	Scotland	U. States	Ductile	12 May 1826
J.	26	M	Supercargo	Scotland	U. States	Genl. Scott	19 Apr 1825
James	25	M	Merchant	Scotland	U. States	Hope	5 Mar 1824
James	40	M	Labourer	Lancaster	Lancaster	Howard Douglass	11 May 1827
Robert	29	M	...	England	United States	Danube	1 Nov 1827
HUDDY, William	12	M		Scotland	United States	Hope	5 Dec 1827
HUDGISSON, R.	30	M	Grocer	England	U. States	Mary Howland	22 Sep 1828
HUDNAN, Wm.	24			Ireland	U.S.	Union	20 Aug 1827
HUDS, George	26	M	Blacksmith	Switzerland	U.S.	Francois I	8 Aug 1829
HUDSON, ...lliam	5	M				Hesperus	2 Nov 1820
Adam	7	M	...	United States	United States	John London	20 Dec 1825
Alice	40	F	None		...a...	Governor Clinton	3 Jul 1827
Amelia	20	F	...	United States	United States	John London	20 Dec 1825
Ann	1 1/2	F	None	England	U. States	Hercules	6 Jul 1827
Ann	10	F	None		...a...	Governor Clinton	3 Jul 1827
David	10	M	...	United States	United States	John London	20 Dec 1825
Dinah	18		Farmer	Great Britain	Upper Canada	Nestor	6 Jul 1821
Edwd.	10		Farmer	Great Britain	Upper Canada	Nestor	6 Jul 1821
Eli	36	M	Joiner		...a...	Governor Clinton	3 Jul 1827
Elisabeth	40	F	Wife			Splendid	14 Aug 1829
Eliza	4		Farmer	Great Britain	Upper Canada	Nestor	6 Jul 1821
Ellen	30	F		Great Britain	United States	Foster	23 Mar 1829
Ellen C.	24	F	None	U. States	U. States	Canada	13 Feb 1826
Geo.	13		Farmer	Great Britain	Upper Canada	Nestor	6 Jul 1821
Geofry	45	M	Farmers and Mechanics	Ireland	America	Constitution	1 Oct 1825
George	34	M	Shoemaker	Great Britain	U.S. of America	Gratitude	3 Oct 1829
George, Jr.	4	M		Great Britain	U.S. of America	Gratitude	3 Oct 1829
Hanah	6	F	Child			Splendid	14 Aug 1829
Hannah	41	F	...	United States	United States	John London	20 Dec 1825
Hannah, Jr.	18	F	...	United States	United States	John London	20 Dec 1825
Hans	23		Joiner	Otley, England	Great Britain	Franklin	22 Jun 1827
Henry	25	M	Surgeon	Ireland	United States	Lord Strangford	20 Jun 1826

NAMES OF PASSENGERS	AGE	SEX	OCCUPATIONS	COUNTRY TO WHICH THEY BELONG	COUNTRY THEY INTEND TO INHABIT	SHIPS/DATES OF ARRIVAL	
HUDSON (cont'd)							
Henry	32	M	Mariner	U. States	U. States	Lapwing	12 Jul 1828
Henry	34	M	Labourer	Ireland		Marchioness	13 May 1828
Jacob	46	M	Farmer	United States	United States	Robert Read	19 Oct 1825
James	11	M	None		...a...	Governor Clinton	3 Jul 1827
Jane	1	F				Splendid	14 Aug 1829
Jane	30	F	None	England	U. States	Hercules	6 Jul 1827
Jno.	19		Farmer	Great Britain	Upper Canada	Nestor	6 Jul 1821
John	10	M	None	England	U. States	Hercules	6 Jul 1827
John	20		Merchant	America	America	Meteor	25 Aug 1823
John	30	M	Weaver	England	United States	Roman	12 Jun 1826
John	30	M	Gent.	U.S. America	U. States	William Thompson	25 Aug 1828
John	32	M	...	England	America	William Thompson	10 May 1825
John	35	M	Farmer	England	U. States	Panthea	22 Nov 1826
John	7...	M	None		Ra...	Governor Clinton	3 Jul 1827
Josa.	2...	M	Merchant	New York	New York	Amity	13 Sep 1821
Joseph	15		Farmer	Great Britain	Upper Canada	Nestor	6 Jul 1821
Joseph	24	M	Miner	England	U.S. States	Splendid	14 Aug 1829
Joseph	30	M	Merchant	U. States	U. States	Canada	13 Feb 1826
Joseph, Rvd.	25	M	Chaplin	Gt. Britian	Canada	Pacific	22 May 1826
Joshua	30	M	Couh Maker	England	U. States	Franklin	7 Jul 1828
Julia	5	F	...	United States	United States	John London	20 Dec 1825
Mary	8		Farmer	Great Britain	Upper Canada	Nestor	6 Jul 1821
Mary	40	F	Farmers and Mechanics	Ireland	America	Constitution	1 Oct 1825
Mary	44		Farmer	Great Britain	Upper Canada	Nestor	6 Jul 1821
Michael	35	M	Mechanic	Great Britain	United States	Ann	24 Sep 1822
R.	38	M	Lawyer	U. States	U.S.	Panthea	13 Nov 1823
W. L.	30	M	Mariner	N. York	U. States	Adams	27 Jun 1825
W. W., Surgeon	28	M	Surgeon	Ireland	United States	Dublin Packet	9 Jul 1827
*Drowned May 18th 1827							
William	15	M	...	United States	United States	John London	20 Dec 1825
Wm.	8		Child			Splendid	14 Aug 1829
Wm.	34		Miner			Splendid	14 Aug 1829
HUES, John	34	M	Carpenter	U. States	U. States	John & Robert	4 Sep 1827
HUESMAN,							
Henry Fredric	22	M	Labourer	Germany	United States	Constitution	2 Aug 1826
HUFFEY, John	29		Farmer	Great Britan	United States	Newry	11 Jul 1827
HUFFMAN, Cathrine	27	F	Spinster	Great Brittan	U. States	John & Elizabeth	11 Dec 1826
Joanne	21	F	Spinster	Great Brittan	U. States	John & Elizabeth	11 Dec 1826
Julia	20	F	Spinster	Great Brittan	U. States	John & Elizabeth	11 Dec 1826
Mary	28	M	Refiner	Great Brittan	U. States	John & Elizabeth	11 Dec 1826
Michl.	27	M	Labourer	G. Britain	U. States	Sarah G	5 Jun 1828
HUFUR, Front	22	M	Deyer	Ireland		Quatre Freres	29 Jul 1828
HUGE, Wm. C.	25	M	M.D.	South Carolina	S. Carolina	York	8 Aug 1829
HUGES, Artuhur	15	M	Farmer	Ireland	U. States	Atlantic	19 Aug 1825
Eleanor	5	F	Farmer	Ireland	U. States	Atlantic	19 Aug 1825
Eliza	9	F		England	England	Criterion	29 May 1822
Esther	29	F		England	England	Criterion	29 May 1822
Fras.	6	F	Farmer	Ireland	U. States	Atlantic	19 Aug 1825
Henry	2	M		England	England	Criterion	29 May 1822
James	30	M		Great Brittain	United States	Active	12 Sep 1828
Jane	10	F	Farmer	Ireland	U. States	Atlantic	19 Aug 1825
Michl.	13	M	Farmer	Ireland	U. States	Atlantic	19 Aug 1825
HUGGENBURGER,							
Bernard	19	M	Weaver	Swis	United States	Iris	21 Sep 1821
HUGGERN, —	1 6/12	M	D. Maker	Ireland	N. York	Trusty	12 Sep 1828
HUGGETT, Ann	32	F	Farmer	England	United States	Euphrates	18 Aug 1827
Ann, Jr.	6	F	Farmer	England	United States	Euphrates	18 Aug 1827
Frances	4	F	Farmer	England	United States	Euphrates	18 Aug 1827
Jane	1	F	Farmer	England	United States	Euphrates	18 Aug 1827

NAMES OF PASSENGERS	AGE	SEX	OCCUPATIONS	COUNTRY TO WHICH THEY BELONG	COUNTRY THEY INTEND TO INHABIT	SHIPS/DATES OF ARRIVAL	
HUGGETT (cont'd)							
Thos.	38	M	Farmer	England	United States	Euphrates	18 Aug 1827
HUGGINS, Margaret	25	F	Married Woman	England	United States	Robert Edwards	3 Oct 1829
HUGH, Fritz, Mrs.	29	M	Merchant	England	England	Albion	4 Oct 1820
HUGHES, Alexr.	27	M	Farmer	Scotland	United States	Samuel Robertson	9 May 1827
Ann	1	F	None	Great Brittan	United States	America	24 Jul 1827
Ann	12	F		Great Britain	United States	Mary Howland	19 Jul 1827
Ann	34	F	None	Great Britain	United States	Cortes	18 Oct 1820
Ann	37	F	None	Great Brittan	United States	America	24 Jul 1827
Ann, Wife [of Richard]	45	F	Farmer	Wales		Gomer	22 May 1827
Anne, Child [of Richard]	6	F	Farmer	Wales		Gomer	22 May 1827
B. F.	27	M	Merchant	Hayti	Hayti	Camille	1 Nov 1826
Benjn. F.	24	M	Clergyman	England	United States	Corinthian	10 Jan 1826
Bernard	28	M		Great Brittain	United States	Active	12 Sep 1828
Bridget	15	F	Wever	Ireland	United States	Fabius	4 Jun 1828
Bridget	22	F	Farmer	Ireland	United States	Justina	5 Aug 1823
Bridget	22	F	Servant	Ireland	New York	Atlantic	8 May 1828
Cath.	19	F		Ireland	United States	Curler	3 Mar 1828
Catharine	21	F		Wales	America	John Adams	2 Aug 1827
Catharine	60	F	None	Great Britain	U. States America	Ann Maria	29 Nov 1821
Catharine	82	F	family [of John]	Ireland	United States	Atlantic	21 Jul 1827
Catharine, Child [of William]	3	F	Farmer	Wales		Gomer	22 May 1827
Catherine	15 3/12	F		Ireland	United States	Atlantic	21 Jul 1827
Cathr.	12	F		Ireland	United States	Commerce	13 Jun 1828
Cathr.	38	F		G. Britain	U. States	London	23 Sep 1828
Charles	20	M	Wever	Ireland	United States	Fabius	4 Jun 1828
Charles	30	M	Merchant	England	United States	Panthia	7 Feb 1822
Charles	38	M	Merchant	Baltimore	U.S.	Bayard	30 Oct 1820
Charles J., Mr.	7	M	Child	U. States	U.S.	Lewis	29 Oct 1825
Christopher	35	M	Ch...ff...	U. States	U.S.	Lewis	29 Oct 1825
David	35	M	Gentleman	Wales	England	Astrea	21 Oct 1823
E.	24	M	Labourer	England	United States	Enterprize	19 Oct 1826
Edward	2	M	None	Great Britain	U. St.	Manchester	7 Dec 1826
Edward	10	M		Great Britain	United States	Mary Howland	19 Jul 1827
Edward	11 4/12	M		Ireland	United States	Atlantic	21 Jul 1827
Edward [crossed out]						Enterprize	19 Oct 1826
Edwd.	1 1/2	M	Merchant	England	N. York	Salem	15 Mar 1828
Edwd.	26	M	Shop Keeper	Gt. Brittain	United States	Balaena	21 Aug 1824
Edwd.	32	M	Merchant	England	N. York	Salem	15 Mar 1828
Edwin	26	M	Farmer	Great Britain	United States	John Jay	8 May 1828
Eleanor	6	F	None	Great Brittan	United States	America	24 Jul 1827
Eleanor	19	F	Farmer	Wales, Gt. Bn.	United States	Orozimbo	31 May 1824
Elennor	18 1/12	F		Ireland	United States	Atlantic	21 Jul 1827
Elisabeth	8	F	None	Great Britain	U. St.	Manchester	7 Dec 1826
Eliza	3	F	Merchant	England	N. York	Salem	15 Mar 1828
Eliza	15	F	None	England	America	Manhattan	20 Mar 1820
Eliza Mary	21	F	Wife	England	U.N. States	Robert Edwards	20 Jan 1829
Elizabeth	16	F	Milliner	Ireland	United States	Wanderer	1 Aug 1828
Elizabeth	23	F	None	Aberdaron	United States	Marquis of Anglesea	8 Jun 1827
Elizabeth	25	F	Wife	Ireland	New York	Atlantic	8 May 1828
Elizabeth	26	F	None	England	United States	Hogarth	12 Oct 1829
Ellen	30	F		Aberdarorgen, Great Britain	United States	Marquis of Anglesea	8 Jun 1827
F. B.	27	M	Priest	U. States	Hayti	Robert Reade	13 Jul 1825
Fanny	4			Ireland	United States	Alexander Mansfield	23 Nov 1824
Fanny	5	F		G. Britain	U. States	Dalhouse Castle	12 Sep 1828
George	24	M		Ireland	United States	William & George	14 May 1828
Hannah	1	F	Child	Ireland	United States	Wanderer	1 Aug 1828
Harriett	25	F		Ireland	U. States	Manhattan	20 Jun 1825
Henry	13 3/12	M		Ireland	United States	Atlantic	21 Jul 1827
Henry, Child [of Richard]	3	M	Farmer	Wales		Gomer	22 May 1827

NAMES OF PASSENGERS	AGE	SEX	OCCUPATIONS	COUNTRY TO WHICH THEY BELONG	COUNTRY THEY INTEND TO INHABIT	SHIPS/DATES OF ARRIVAL	
HUGHES (cont'd)							
Hugh, Child							
[of William]	1 1/2	M	Farmer	Wales		Gomer	22 May 1827
Hugh, Child							
[of Richard]	11	M	Farmer	Wales		Gomer	22 May 1827
J.	23	M	Labourer	England	U.S.	York	1 Dec 1827
James	3/12	M	None	England	United States	Hogarth	12 Oct 1829
James	19 5/12	M		Ireland	America	Carolina Ann	7 Apr 1826
James	20	M	Baker	Ireland	New York	Trusty	12 Sep 1828
James	30	M	B. Smith	Great Britain	United States	Blakely	29 Sep 1826
James	57	M	Merchant	U. States	U. States	Abigail	26 Sep 1820
James	59	M	Merchant	Philadelphia	Philadelphia	Wilson	28 Aug 1822
Jane	13	F	None	England	America	Manhattan	20 Mar 1820
Jas.	24	M	Weaver	Antrim, Ireland	New York	Anthusa	24 Aug 1825
Jas.	25	M	stone Mason	Great Brittan	U.S.	Emulous	29 Jun 1827
John	2			Ireland	United States	Alexander Mansfield	23 Nov 1824
John	6	M		G. Britain	U. States	Dalhouse Castle	12 Sep 1828
John	17	M	Clerk	Great Britain	United States	Aurora	10 Nov 1827
John	19	M	Labourer	Ireland	United States	Commerce	13 Jun 1828
John	21	M		Great Brittain	United States	Mary Howland	19 Jul 1827
John	23	M	Merchant	Great Brittan	U. States	John & Elizabeth	11 Dec 1826
John	25	M	Labourer	G. Britain	U. States	London	23 Sep 1828
John	32	M	Farmer	England	United States	Cosmo	26 Aug 1829
John	45 3/12	M	Farmer	Ireland	United States	Atlantic	21 Jul 1827
Johnathan, Infant		M		Great Britain	United States	Mary Howland	19 Jul 1827
Joseph	20	M	Farmer	Saint John	St. John	Nancy	11 Apr 1822
Josh.	22	M		Ireland		Lady Hunter	12 Apr 1823
Judith	42 2/12	F	family [of John]	Ireland	United States	Atlantic	21 Jul 1827
Kitty	20	F	Spinster	Ireland	America	Josephine	8 Dec 1827
Laura, Mrs.	28	F	Wife	U. States	U.S.	Lewis	29 Oct 1825
Lawery	52	F	Farmer	Wales, Gt. Bn.	United States	Orozimbo	31 May 1824
Lewis, Child							
[of Richard]	4	M	Farmer	Wales		Gomer	22 May 1827
Margaret	6			Ireland	United States	Alexander Mansfield	23 Nov 1824
Margaret	8	F	Child	Ireland	New York	Atlantic	8 May 1828
Margaret	21	F	Spinster	Great Brittan	Canada	Florida	17 May 1825
Margaret, Child							
[of Richard]	13	F	Farmer	Wales		Gomer	22 May 1827
Margt.	37	F		G. Britain	U. States	London	23 Sep 1828
Margt.	45	F	None	England	America	Manhattan	20 Mar 1820
Mary	3	F	None	Great Brittan	United States	America	24 Jul 1827
Mary	6	F	None	England	America	Manhattan	20 Mar 1820
Mary	8			Ireland	United States	Alexander Mansfield	23 Nov 1824
Mary	8	F		Great Britain	United States	Mary Howland	19 Jul 1827
Mary	14	F	Servant	Ireland	New York	Atlantic	8 May 1828
Mary	15	F	None	Great Britain	United States	Aurora	10 Nov 1827
Mary	18		Spinster	Ireland	United States	Courier	15 Oct 1827
Mary	30	F	Merchant	England	N. York	Salem	15 Mar 1828
Mary	32			Ireland	United States	Alexander Mansfield	23 Nov 1824
Mary	35	F	Wife	Ireland	United States	Wanderer	1 Aug 1828
Mary	40	F		Wales	America	John Adams	2 Aug 1827
Mary	42	F		Great Britain	United States	Mary Howland	19 Jul 1827
Mary	45	F	Farmer	Ireland	U. States	Atlantic	19 Aug 1825
Mary, Child							
[of Richard]	16	F	Farmer	Wales		Gomer	22 May 1827
Mary, Wife							
[of William]	26	F	Farmer	Wales		Gomer	22 May 1827
Michael	6 5/12	M		Ireland	United States	Atlantic	21 Jul 1827
Michl.	35	M	Labour	Great Britain	United States	Cortes	18 Oct 1820
Neal	35 1/12	M	Smith	Ireland	United States	Atlantic	21 Jul 1827
Pat	16	M	Labourer	Ireland	United States	Commerce	13 Jun 1828
Pat	44	M		England	United States	Yobah	26 Sep 1827
Patarick	45	M	Farmer	Ireland	U. States	Atlantic	19 Aug 1825
Patr.	20	M	Laborer	Ireland	United States	Carolina Ann	11 Dec 1826

NAMES OF PASSENGERS	AGE	SEX	OCCUPATIONS	COUNTRY TO WHICH THEY BELONG	COUNTRY THEY INTEND TO INHABIT	SHIPS/DATES OF ARRIVAL	
HUGHES (cont'd)							
Patrick	1 2/12	M		Ireland	United States	Atlantic	21 Jul 1827
Patrick	31	M	Farmer, Labourer or Spinster	Ireland	U. States	Meteor	4 Oct 1827
Patrick	35	M	Farmer	Ireland	United States	Justina	5 Aug 1823
Peter	30	M	Weaver	Ireland	United States	Meteor	19 Aug 1829
Peter	32		Blacksmith	Ireland	United States	Alexander Mansfield	23 Nov 1824
Peter	40	M	Weaver	Great Britain	United States	Atlantic	8 Dec 1827
Rachel	23	F	Spinster	Great Brittan	Canada	Florida	17 May 1825
Rachel	50	F	Spinster	Great Brittan	Canada	Florida	17 May 1825
Richard	20	M	Labourer	Wales	America	John Adams	2 Aug 1827
Richard	55	M	Farmer	Wales		Gomer	22 May 1827
Richd.	52	M	Labourer	Scotland	United States	Indus	5 Sep 1827
Robert	23	M	Labourer	Aberdarorgen, Great Britain	United States	Marquis of Anglesea	8 Jun 1827
Robert	40	M	None	United States	United States	William Thompson	19 Aug 1829
Robt. B. M.	24	M	Sculptor	England	U.N. States	Robert Edwards	20 Jan 1829
Rose	2 7/12	F		Ireland	United States	Atlantic	21 Jul 1827
Rose	10			Ireland	United States	Alexander Mansfield	23 Nov 1824
Rose	60	F		Ireland	New York	Atlantic	8 May 1828
Sally	12			Ireland	United States	Alexander Mansfield	23 Nov 1824
Sarah	9	F	None	Great Brittan	United States	America	24 Jul 1827
Sarah	10	F	Labourer	Wales	America	John Adams	2 Aug 1827
Sarah	20	F		Great Britain	United States	Mary Howland	19 Jul 1827
Sarah	20		Spinster	Ireland	United States	Courier	15 Oct 1827
Sarah	35	F	None	Great Britain	U. St.	Manchester	7 Dec 1826
Simon	2	M		Great Britain	United States	Mary Howland	19 Jul 1827
Susan	21	F		Ireland	United States	Romulus	24 Jun 1826
Susannah	6	F		Great Britain	United States	Mary Howland	19 Jul 1827
Susannah	8	F	Merchant	England	N. York	Salem	15 Mar 1828
Thomas	2	M	Child	Ireland	United States	Wanderer	1 Aug 1828
Thomas	17	M		Great Britain	United States	Mary Howland	19 Jul 1827
Thomas	21	M	Weaver	Ireland	United States	Commerce	13 Jun 1828
Thomas	25	M		Ireland	America	Carolina Ann	7 Aug 1826
Thomas	60	M		Great Britain	United States	Mary Howland	19 Jul 1827
William	4 6/12	M		Ireland	United States	Atlantic	21 Jul 1827
William	9	M	None	England	America	Manhattan	20 Mar 1820
William	11	M	None	Great Brittan	United States	America	24 Jul 1827
William	15	M		Great Britain	United States	Mary Howland	19 Jul 1827
William	20	M	Labourer	Ireland	United States	Commerce	13 Jun 1828
William	27	M	Farmer	Wales		Gomer	22 May 1827
Willm.	22	M	Stone Cutter	England	England	William Byrnes	14 Apr 1824
Wm.	17	M		Great B.	U. States	William Neilson	26 Jul 1828
Wm.	31	M	Labourer	Aberdarorgen, Great Britain	United States	Marquis of Anglesea	8 Jun 1827
Wm.	33	M	Farmer	England	United States	John Dickinson	30 Sep 1823
Wm. M.	37	M	Merchant	England	U. States	Martha	1 Feb 1822
Wm. W.	25		Merchant	America		Robert Burns	8 Dec 1821
HUGHEY, Anderson	22	M	Joiner	Ireland	United States	Borneo	28 Aug 1828
HUGHIES, William	37	M	Farmer	Great Brittan	United States	America	24 Jul 1827
HUGHS, Ann	17	F	Spinster	U.S.	U.S.	Pacific	24 Oct 1828
Arthur	20	M	Labourer	Gt. Britain	U. States	Frances Henrietta	18 Apr 1825
Arthur	34	M	Mason	Great Britain	United States	Colossus	5 Jun 1827
Barrnard	23	M	Labourer	Ireland	U.S. of America	Meteor	19 Mar 1828
Biddy	22	F	Spinster	Gt. Britain	U. States	Frances Henrietta	18 Apr 1825
Christopher		M	Gentleman	America	U. States	James Cropper	10 Jun 1823
Dav...	24	M	Farmer	Great Britian	United States	London	24 Jun 1823
Edward	20	M	Labourer	England	U. States	Ayrshire	12 May 1828
Elias	22	M	Dr...	Gt. Britain	U. States	Frances Henrietta	18 Apr 1825
Elinor	28	F	Spinster	Ireland	U. States	Josephine	30 Aug 1828
Felix	30	M	Labourer	Ireland	U. States	William Byrnes	17 Jul 1825
Francis	26	M	Baker	Ireland	America States	Beaver	18 Aug 1827

NAMES OF PASSENGERS	A G E	S E X	OCCUPATIONS	COUNTRY TO WHICH THEY BELONG	COUNTRY THEY INTEND TO INHABIT	SHIPS/DATES OF ARRIVAL	
HUGHS (cont'd)							
H.	24	M	Brager	Ireland		Eliza Grant	29 Aug 1829
Harrett	24	M		G.B.	Philad.	Eliza Grant	29 Aug 1829
Henry	17	M	Labourer	Ireland	U.S. of America	Meteor	19 Mar 1828
Hugh	50	M	Weaver	Gt. Britain	U. States	Frances Henrietta	18 Apr 1825
Jas.	22		Farmer	Ireland	United States	Courier	16 May 1825
John	22	M	Tailor	U.S.	U.S.	Pacific	24 Oct 1828
Marey	23	F	Mantumaker	Ireland	America States	Beaver	18 Aug 1827
Margret	2	F	Child	Ireland	America States	Beaver	18 Aug 1827
Margt.	23	F		Ireland	U. States	William Byrnes	17 Jul 1825
Mary	9	F	None	U.S.	U.S.	Pacific	24 Oct 1828
Mary	17	F	Servant	Ireland	N. York	Trusty	12 Sep 1828
Mary	20	F	Spinster	Gt. Britain	U. States	Frances Henrietta	18 Apr 1825
Mary	20	F	Spinster	Gt. Britain	U. States	Frances Henrietta	18 Apr 1825
Mary	20	F	Labourer	England	U. States	Ayrshire	12 May 1828
Mary	25	F		Ireland	U.S.	George Canning	26 Aug 1829
Mary	34	F	None	Great Britain	United States	Colossus	5 Jun 1827
Maryan	8/12	F	Child	Ireland	America States	Beaver	18 Aug 1827
Nathaniel	31	M	Farmer		U. States	Charlotte Corday	15 Aug 1820
Patrick	23	M	Labourer	Ireland	United States	Wilson	28 Nov 1828
Patrick	27	M	Farmer	Ireland	United States	Trident	31 Mar 1827
Peter	22	M	Labourer	Gt. Britain	U. States	Frances Henrietta	18 Apr 1825
Robt.	14	M	None	U.S.	U.S.	Pacific	24 Oct 1828
T. A. M.				U. States	U. States	Frances Henrietta	18 Apr 1825
William	24	M	Braizer	G.B.	Philad.	Eliza Grant	29 Aug 1829
William	24	M	Brager	Ireland		Eliza Grant	29 Aug 1829
Wm.	13	M	None	U.S.	U.S.	Pacific	24 Oct 1828
HUGHSON, Elizabeth	38	F	Family [of Joseph]	Great Britain	United States	Hanford	9 Oct 1829
Harriet	26	F	Lady	St. Johns	St. Johns	Ann Maria	7 Sep 1827
James	1	M	Family [of Joseph]	Great Britain	United States	Hanford	9 Oct 1829
Jamima	2	F	Family [of Joseph]	Great Britain	United States	Hanford	9 Oct 1829
Jeremy	20	M	Merchant	St. John, N.B.	St. John, N.B.	Sylvester Healy	19 Aug 1825
Jerry	28	M	Merchant	New Brunswick	New Brunswick	Wanderer	31 Aug 1829
Jerry D.	22	M	Merchant	St. Johns	St. Johns	Ann Maria	7 Sep 1827
Joseph	40	M	Farmer	Great Britain	United States	Hanford	9 Oct 1829
Julia Ann	12	F	Family [of Joseph]	Great Britain	United States	Hanford	9 Oct 1829
Margaret	4	F	Family [of Joseph]	Great Britain	United States	Hanford	9 Oct 1829
Mary	6	F	Family [of Joseph]	Great Britain	United States	Hanford	9 Oct 1829
Wenworth	8	M	Family [of Joseph]	Great Britain	United States	Hanford	9 Oct 1829
William	10	M	Family [of Joseph]	Great Britain	United States	Hanford	9 Oct 1829
HUGIL, Ann	18 1/12	F				Cririe	18 Sep 1820
Eleanor	11 5/12	F				Cririe	18 Sep 1820
Eleanor	47 3/12	F				Cririe	18 Sep 1820
Elizabeth	7 2/12	F				Cririe	18 Sep 1820
Hannah	4 7/12	F				Cririe	18 Sep 1820
Jane	9 7/12	F				Cririe	18 Sep 1820
John	12 8/12	M				Cririe	18 Sep 1820
John	49 4/12	M	...	England	United States	Cririe	18 Sep 1820
Jonah	16 7/12	M				Cririe	18 Sep 1820
Jonathan	74 9/12	M				Cririe	18 Sep 1820
HUGILL, Betsey	6/12	F		England	America	John Adams	2 Aug 1827
Jane	26	F		England	America	John Adams	2 Aug 1827
Thomas	30	M	Farmer	England	America	John Adams	2 Aug 1827
Thos.	35	M	Labourer	G. Britain	U. States	London	23 Sep 1828
HUGLE, Augusta	28	F		Germany	U. States	Isabella	10 Aug 1829
Catherine	8	F		Germany	U. States	Isabella	10 Aug 1829
Catherine	38	F		Germany	U. States	Isabella	10 Aug 1829
Jacob	6	M		Germany	U. States	Isabella	10 Aug 1829
Jean	2	M		Germany	U. States	Isabella	10 Aug 1829
Johannes	30	M	Farmer	Germany	U. States	Isabella	10 Aug 1829
Margareta	9/12	F		Germany	U. States	Isabella	10 Aug 1829
Maria	5	F		Germany	U. States	Isabella	10 Aug 1829
Michael	40	M	Farmer	Germany	U. States	Isabella	10 Aug 1829

NAMES OF PASSENGERS	A G E	S E X	OCCUPATIONS	COUNTRY TO WHICH THEY BELONG	COUNTRY THEY INTEND TO INHABIT	SHIPS/DATES OF ARRIVAL	
HUGNE, Jos.	26			England		Anacreon	7 Sep 1827
HUGO, B. D.	29	M	Mechanic	Germany	United States	Two Marys	12 Feb 1820
HUGON, Bernard	44	M	Weaver	Ireland	United States	Josephine	30 Apr 1828
HUGREER, Jules	25		Farmer	Switzerland	United States	Henri IV	14 Sep 1827
HUGUENIN, Emelie	48	M		U.S.A.		François I	19 Nov 1828
HUINGUES, Louis B.	38		Merchant	France	U. States	Brandt	14 Aug 1823
HULBERT, Barnard	20	M	Weaver	France	United States	Virginia	31 May 1828
HULCHASSER, James	23	M	Farmer	New Jersey	United States	St. Michaels	18 Jul 1826
HULEN, Jose	24	M	Merchant	Switzerland	U. States	Alexander	18 Mar 1822
HULIN, —	17		Sailor	France	U. States	Almira	15 Jul 1822
Chrs.	20 6/12	F		France	U. States	Bonnaffe	27 Jan 1827
HULL, A.	23	M	Labourer	U. States	U. States	Robt. Reade	12 Apr 1825
Henry	20	M	Attorney	England	U.S.	Helen	3 May 1828
John	23	M	Suger Baker	Germany	United States	Hope	5 Dec 1827
Peter	21	M	Carpenter	G.B.	New Jersey	Eliza Grant	29 Aug 1829
Robt.	22	M	Labourer	England	U. States	Ayrshire	12 May 1828
William	38	M	Farmer	England	New York	Cincinnatus	16 Apr 1824
William C.	40	M	Merchant	U. States	U. States	Edward Quesnel	16 Nov 1827
HULLAND, Wallter	19	M	Farmer	England	U. States	Hercules	6 Jul 1827
HULLER, Charles	25	M	Farmer	Swisserland	United States	Montano	13 Jan 1826
HULLERAY, John	40	M	Merchant	England	U. States	Orozimbo	7 Jul 1825
HULLIGAN, Patrick	28	M	Labourer	England	United States	Dalhouse Castle	8 May 1827
HULLOCK, James	21	M	Labourer	England	United States	Nimrod	31 Jul 1828
HULLOP, Will	20		Hatter	Rochester, England	Great Britain	Franklin	22 Jun 1827
HULLY, John	47	M	Clothier	England	Alexandria, U.S.	Roman	17 Oct 1826
HULM, Joseph	28	M	Military	France	United States	Elizabeth	13 Nov 1824
HULME, Ann	22	F	None	France	U. States	Bayard	9 Nov 1825
Elizabeth	20	F	None	France	U. States	Bayard	9 Nov 1825
John	17	M	Merchant	France	U. States	Bayard	9 Nov 1825
Thomas	18	M	Merchant	France	U. States	Bayard	9 Nov 1825
HULOME, Thomas	30	M	Labourer	Great Britain	U. States America	Maria	22 May 1822
HULT, Anders M.	20	M	Clerk	Sweden	U.S. America	Freden	24 Oct 1820
HUMANA, Manuel, Don	20	M	Attached to the Mexican Legation	Mexico	United States	Mercid	21 Oct 1824
HUMBER, Pocahontas	18	F	Servant	United States	United States	Only Daughter	29 Apr 1825
HUMBERT, George	25	M	Farmer	France	France	Sully	15 Jul 1829
HUMBIRD, John	29	M	Farmer	New York		Olive Branch	9 Oct 1829
HUMBLE, Ewd.	49	M	Sailor	America	U. States	Robt. Edwards	4 Sep 1828
George	29	M	None	England	United States	Herald	7 Jun 1824
Mary	23	F	None	England	United States	Herald	7 Jun 1824
Thomas	16	M		Great Brittain	United States	Active	12 Sep 1828
HUMBRIGHT, M.	38	M	Farmer	Ireland	America	Mary	29 May 1827
HUME, Francis	20	M	Farmer	England	U.S.A.	Brighton	21 Jan 1826
James	25	M	Gentleman	Scotland	Upper Canada	Camillus	29 Jan 1829
Thomas	39	M	Merchant	United States	United States	Florida	13 Feb 1826
HUMER, David	23	M	Cutter	Swiss	U. States	Comet	28 Jul 1825
David	48	M	Farmer	Swiss	U. States	Comet	28 Jul 1825
Mary Ann	26	F	None	Swiss	U. States	Comet	28 Jul 1825
Susan	65	F	None	Swiss	U. States	Comet	28 Jul 1825
HUMES, Walter	35	M	Merchant	St. John, N.B.	United States	St. Michaels	25 May 1825
HUMFIELD, George	30	M	Weaver	England	America	John Adams	2 Aug 1827
HUMPACH, Barbara	13	F	Farmer	...t...ia	Pennsylvania	Frances Henrietta	25 Aug 1825
Vincent	8	M	Farmer	...t...ia	Pennsylvania	Frances Henrietta	25 Aug 1825
Vincent	43	M	Farmer	...t...ia	Pennsylvania	Frances Henrietta	25 Aug 1825
HUMPEY, Caspar	19	M	Baker	Norway	U. States	Hyperion	21 Mar 1827
HUMPHRES, Moss	21	M	Leather Dresser	Ireland	United States	Henry Kneeland	7 Jun 1828
HUMPHREY, Daniel	2	M	None	Great Britain	United States	Mary & Harriet	3 Jul 1829
Edwd.	49	M	Carpenter	Ireland	United States	Trio	13 Jun 1827
Mary Anne	24	F	None	Great Britain	United States	Mary & Harriet	3 Jul 1829
Owen	36	M	Fer.	Wales	U. States	Franklin	7 Jul 1828
Robt.	29	M	Fer.	Wales	U. States	Franklin	7 Jul 1828
Thomas	34	M	Baker	England	United States	Hudson	17 Mar 1828
William	26	M	Farmer	Great Britain	United States	Mary & Harriet	3 Jul 1829
Wm.	10	M		Ireland	United States	Trio	13 Jun 1827

NAMES OF PASSENGERS	AGE	SEX	OCCUPATIONS	COUNTRY TO WHICH THEY BELONG	COUNTRY THEY INTEND TO INHABIT	SHIPS/DATES OF ARRIVAL	
HUMPHREYS, Ann	52	F		Great Britain	United States	Thomas Dickason	14 Sep 1827
Despain	15		...	Ireland	United States	Alexander Mansfield	23 Nov 1824
Isabella	1	F		Great Britain	United States	Thomas Dickason	14 Sep 1827
Isabella	20	F		Great Britain	United States	Thomas Dickason	14 Sep 1827
James	50	M	Farmer	England	United States	Cambria	3 Jul 1829
Jno.	22	M	Merchant	U. States	U. States	Columbia	20 Jul 1825
John	15	M		Great Britain	United States	Thomas Dickason	14 Sep 1827
Mary	18	F	None	Great Britain	United States	William & Jane	22 Aug 1820
Mary	30	F	Lady	Ireland	United States	Nancy	20 Sep 1821
Mary	52	F	None	Wales	United States	Orozimbo	11 Aug 1823
Mary Ann	3	F		Great Britain	United States	Thomas Dickason	14 Sep 1827
Mary Ann	28	F		Great Britain	United States	Thomas Dickason	14 Sep 1827
Owen	51	M	Farmer	Wales	United States	Orozimbo	11 Aug 1823
Richard	64		Joiner	Kidderminster		Mount Vernon	18 Oct 1822
Richd.	7	M	Farmer	Wales, Gt. Bn.	United States	Orozimbo	31 May 1824
Sarah Ann	5	F		Great Britain	United States	Thomas Dickason	14 Sep 1827
Wm.	13	M	None	Great Britain	United States	William & Jane	22 Aug 1820
Wm.	50	M	Grocer	Great Britain	United States	William & Jane	22 Aug 1820
HUMPHRIES, Ann	25	F	Labourer	England	U. States	Ayrshire	12 May 1828
Ann	40			Ireland	United States	Alexander Mansfield	9 Nov 1822
David	22	M	Labourer	England	U. States	Ayrshire	12 May 1828
Jane	52	F	None	U. States	U. States	New York	11 Jul 1823
John	29		Gentleman	England	Boston	Xenophon	25 Jul 1826
John	55	M	Draper	U. States	U. States	New York	11 Jul 1823
Samuel	43	M	Mechanic	United States	United States	Acasta	15 Jul 1822
HUMPHRY, Edwd.	30	M	Collier	Wales	U.S. States	Splendid	14 Aug 1829
Elizabeth	13	F		U. States	U. States	William Thompson	24 Aug 1827
Jane	19	F		Aberdarorgen, Great Britain	United States	Marquis of Anglesea	8 Jun 1827
John	1	M	None	Aberdarorgen, Great Britain	United States	Marquis of Anglesea	8 Jun 1827
John	24	M	Merchant	U. States	U. States	William Thompson	24 Aug 1827
Wm.	22	M	Labourer	Aberdarorgen, Great Britain	United States	Marquis of Anglesea	8 Jun 1827
HUMPSON, Hy.	28	M	Farmer	England	U. States	Mary	24 Jun 1824
HUNARDY, Aug.	23	M	Merchant	Havana	U. States	Hero	3 Sep 1823
HUNARDY, Manuel	10	M	Merchant	Havana	U. States	Hero	3 Sep 1823
HUNCKETT, Isaac	28	M	Weaver	Ireland	United States	Trident	30 Sep 1826
HUNDECKER, E.	40	M	Merchant	Germany	United States	Nestor	16 Aug 1824
HUNDERSHELL, Geo.	26	M	Merchant	U. States	U. States	Flight	9 Jul 1825
HUNEKER, Catharine	3	F		Ireland	America	John Adams	2 Aug 1827
Eliza	7	F		Ireland	America	John Adams	2 Aug 1827
Mary	32	F		Ireland	America	John Adams	2 Aug 1827
Patrick	3/12	M		Ireland	America	John Adams	2 Aug 1827
Ron	3	F		Ireland	America	John Adams	2 Aug 1827
Walter	36	M	Carpenter	Ireland	America	John Adams	2 Aug 1827
HUNMAN, Chas.	25		Merchant	New York	New York	James Cropper	12 Jul 1822
HUNN, John	23	M	Farmer	Stockport	United States	Aurelia	7 Jun 1826
Sarah	50	F	Lady	United	United States	Sarah	31 Oct 1829
HUNNS, William	65		Mechanic	England	England	Hudson	4 Sep 1823
HUNNY, Thos.	45	M	Mechanic	England	United States	Wm. Byrnes	30 Apr 1828
HUNSFELD, James, Mr.	34		Merchant	England	G.B.	Pacific	24 May 1824
Jos., Mr.	45		Merchant	England	G.B.	Pacific	24 May 1824
HUNSWORTH, Robert	44	M	Weaver	Great Britain	United States	India	5 Sep 1827
HUNT, —, Mrs.	60	F	Spinster	Ireland	New York	British Hibernia	13 Mar 1820
A.	30	M	Servant	France	U. States	Desdemona	21 Oct 1825
Adelade	23	F		France	U. States	Desdemona	21 Oct 1825
Alexr.	5	M	None	Great Britan		Colossus	27 Mar 1828

NAMES OF PASSENGERS	AGE	SEX	OCCUPATIONS	COUNTRY TO WHICH THEY BELONG	COUNTRY THEY INTEND TO INHABIT	SHIPS/DATES OF ARRIVAL	
HUNT (cont'd)							
Alexr.	60	M	Merchant	England	United States	Nancy Henrietta	3 Nov 1828
Arthur	...	M	Gentleman	G. C. N. Carolina	G. C. N. Carolina	Amity	13 Sep 1821
Caroline	13	F		G. Britain	U. States	Armadello	22 Jun 1827
Charles	19	M		G. Britain	U. States	Armadello	22 Jun 1827
Charlotte	1	M				Cassack	25 Jul 1820
Clarissa	6	M				Cassack	25 Jul 1820
Eliza	28	F	Lady	St. John, N.B.	St. John, N.B.	St. Michaels	25 May 1825
Elizabeth	18	F	Servant	America	U. States	William Byrnes	17 Jul 1825
Elizabeth	19 1/12	F	Servant			Criterion	27 Oct 1820
F.	17	M	Carpenter	Bristol	New York	Cosmo	25 Sep 1827
Geo.	17	M				Cassack	25 Jul 1820
George	24	M	Labourer	Great Britain	United States	Colossus	5 Jun 1827
H. B.	35	M		G. Britain	U. States	John Jay	17 Sep 1828
Hannah	14	F		G. Britain	U. States	Armadello	22 Jun 1827
Harry	50	M	Merchant	U. States	U. States	Reunion	28 Sep 1821
Henry	13	M				Cassack	25 Jul 1820
James	8	M				Cassack	25 Jul 1820
Jer.	3	M				Cassack	25 Jul 1820
John	8	M				Cassack	25 Jul 1820
John	38	M	None	Gt. Brittain	United States	Balaena	21 Aug 1824
John	63	M	Sch...	G. Britain	U. States	Armadello	22 Jun 1827
Jonathan	30	M	Merchant	Liverpool		Colossus	27 Mar 1828
Joseph	17	M		G. Britain	U. States	Armadello	22 Jun 1827
Joseph	41	M	Currier	Great Britain	U. States	Lady Hunter	28 May 1823
Julien	4	M		France	U. States	Desdemona	21 Oct 1825
Lucy	38	M				Cassack	25 Jul 1820
Lydia	35	F		G. Britain	U. States	John Jay	17 Sep 1828
Maria	18	F	Maid	Brittian	U. States	Acasta	28 Jan 1823
Mary	16	F		G. Britain	U. States	Dalhouse Castle	12 Sep 1828
Moses, Junr.	25	M	Mariner	U. States	United States	Fox	9 Mar 1829
Philip	26	M	Farmer	France	U. States	Desdemona	21 Oct 1825
Rob.	20	M	Gentleman	Charleston	U. States	William Thompson	6 Sep 1822
S. B.	35	M	Merchant	England	England	Canada	14 Feb 1824
Saml.	32	M				Cassack	25 Jul 1820
Sarah	54	F		G. Britain	U. States	Armadello	22 Jun 1827
Tamar	54	F		Great Britain	Great Britain	Lady Hunter	28 May 1823
Thomas	21	M	Gentleman	England	United States	Acasta	12 Dec 1823
William	40	M	Doctor	Great Britain	Great Britan	Nancy	13 Dec 1822
HUNTER, —, Mrs.	24					London	19 Dec 1823
—, Mrs.	28	F		Scotland	U.S.	Curler	19 Jul 1828
...	4	M	Spinster	Glasgow	United States	Henry Clay	25 Apr 1822
Aaron	4	M	Boy	Ireland	Ireland	Trident	17 May 1825
Adam	28	M		Scotland	U.S.	Curler	19 Jul 1828
Alexander	36	M		...	U. States	Corinthian	2 Sep 1824
Alfred	1	M		England	United States	Siroc	31 Oct 1829
Alfred	25	M	Cutler	England	United States	Siroc	31 Oct 1829
An.	1	F		Scotland	U.S.	Curler	19 Jul 1828
Andw.	28	M	Farmer	Ireland	United States	Trident	17 May 1825
Ann	4	F	Child	Ireland	Ireland	Trident	17 May 1825
Catherine	1	F	Child	Ireland	Ireland	Trident	17 May 1825
Chas. G.	20	M	U.S. Navy	U.S.A.	U.S.A.	Potomac	25 Jul 1829
E.	26	M	Labourer	Ireland	U. States	Lady Hunter	9 Oct 1825
Eleanor	23	F		Ireland	U. States	Ohio	21 Mar 1825
Eliza	6	F	Girl	Ireland	Ireland	Trident	17 May 1825
Eliza	10	F	Girl	Ireland	Ireland	Trident	17 May 1825
Elizabeth	38	F	Spinster	Glasgow	United States	Henry Clay	25 Apr 1822
Frans.	35	M	Merchant	Nova Scotia	U. States	Tantamount	25 Apr 1822
Henry	31	M	Cutler	England	United States	Siroc	31 Oct 1829
James	21	M	Equestrian	England	United States	Maria	3 Oct 1822
James	26	M	Copper Smith	Ireland	United States	Asia	29 Jul 1829
Jane	23	F		Great Britian	United States	Brok	29 Aug 1823
Jane	25	F	Spinster	Ireland	United States	Trident	17 May 1825
Jane	27	F	Spinster	Ireland	United States	Trident	17 May 1825
Janet	6/12	F		Scotland	United States	Samuel Robertson	5 Oct 1827
Janny	41	F		Ireland	U. States	Emigrant	23 Jul 1822

HUNTER (cont'd)

NAMES OF PASSENGERS	AGE	SEX	OCCUPATIONS	COUNTRY TO WHICH THEY BELONG	COUNTRY THEY INTEND TO INHABIT	SHIPS/DATES OF ARRIVAL	
Jas. H.	19	M	Merchant	Belfast	Ireland	Carolina Ann	11 Jun 1824
Jeffrey	26	M	Servant	Gt. Britain	U. States	Maria	22 May 1822
Jno.	24	M	Farmer	Ireland	U. States	Ohio	21 Mar 1825
Jno.	33	M		Ireland	U. States	Emigrant	23 Jul 1822
John	4 2/12	M	Merchant	Great Britain	United States	Cambria	26 Dec 1827
John	5	M		Scotland	United States	Samuel Robertson	5 Oct 1827
John	9	M	Spinster	Glasgow	United States	Henry Clay	25 Apr 1822
John	18 6/12	M	Shoe Maker	Ireland	U. States	Fabius	22 Sep 1828
John	27	M	Printer	Great Britain	United States	William Dawson	18 Jun 1827
John	30	M		Ireland	United States	William & George	14 May 1828
John	31	M	Joiner	Scotland	United States	Belmont	30 Aug 1828
John	35	M	Mechanic	England	U. States	Trident	8 Mar 1824
John	35	M	Mechanic	Ireland	United States	Vermont	10 Jan 1827
John, Jr.	6	M	Boy	Ireland	Ireland	Trident	17 May 1825
John, Senr.	45	M	Farmer	Ireland	Ireland	Trident	17 May 1825
John D.	28	M	Gentleman	Virginia	U. States	Columbia	7 Jul 1824
John E.	28	M	Carpenter	New Brunswick	to return thither	Lady Hunter	14 Mar 1826
John E.	28	M	Merchant	St. John, N.B.	St. John, N.B.	St. Michaels	11 May 1826
John S.	29	M	Ship Master	United States	United States	General Macombe	17 Jul 1827
John W.	18	M	Midshipman in the U.S. Navy	United States	United States	Virginia	9 Apr 1821
Joseph	3	M	Boy	Ireland	United States	Trident	17 May 1825
Joseph	38	M	Merchant	England	Canada	Florida	11 May 1822
Lelenor	20	F	Lady	England	United States	Siroc	31 Oct 1829
Letitia	33	F		U. States	U. States	Birmingham	11 Oct 1828
Margaret	18	F	Spinster	Scotland	United States	Samuel Robertson	5 Oct 1827
Margaret	22	F		Prusia	U. States	Harmony	6 Jan 1823
Margaret	25	F	Servant	Ireland	Ireland	Sarah G.	28 Nov 1827
Margret	30	F		Scotland, Great Britain	America	Superb	11 Oct 1821
Martha	32	F	Spinster	Ireland	Ireland	Trident	17 May 1825
Mary		F	None	Ireland	United States	Catharine	22 Jul 1825
Mary	...	F	Spinster	Ireland	United States	Catharine	22 Jul 1825
Mary	8	F	Girl	Ireland	Ireland	Trident	17 May 1825
Mary	25	F		G. Britain	U. States	London	23 Sep 1828
Mary	35	F	Mechanic	Ireland	United States	Vermont	10 Jan 1827
Mary	60	F	Spinster	Ireland	United States	Trident	17 May 1825
Mary J.	1	F	Spinster	Glasgow	United States	Henry Clay	25 Apr 1822
Meriah	24	F	None	England	United States	Jubilee	13 Jul 1829
Nicholas	36	M	Labourer	Scotland	United States	Samuel Robertson	5 Oct 1827
Rachel	16	F		Ireland	U. States	Emigrant	23 Jul 1822
Rachel	29	F		Great Britain	U.S. of America	Gratitude	3 Oct 1829
Ri... R.	36		Am. Consul	U.S.	U.S.	London	19 Dec 1823
Richd.	53	M	Planter	Antigua	U. States	Laurel	26 Jul 1825
Robert	35	M				Reuben & Eliza	21 Aug 1820
Robert R.	40	M	Gentleman	U. States	U. States	Birmingham	11 Oct 1828
Robt.	6	M	Spinster	Glasgow	United States	Henry Clay	25 Apr 1822
Samuel	5	M	Boy	Ireland	United States	Trident	17 May 1825
Samuel	24	M	Farmer	Ireland	United States	Catharine	22 Jul 1825
Sarah	5	F		Great Britain	U.S. of America	Gratitude	3 Oct 1829
Sarah	29	F		England	United States	Dalhouse Castle	8 May 1827
Sarah	40	M		Scotland	U. States	Eliza	12 May 1823
Susan	27	F	Lady	England	United States	Siroc	31 Oct 1829
Thomas	31	M	Saddler	Great Britain	U.S. of America	Gratitude	3 Oct 1829
Thomas	45	M	Farmer	England	United States	London	21 May 1828
Thomas, Jr.	18	M	Farmer	England	United States	London	21 May 1828
Thos.	28	M	Printer	Ireland	United States	Carolina Ann	11 Dec 1826
W.	27	M	Weaver			Commerce	22 Jun 1825
W. G.	20	M	Gentleman	America	America	Romulus	27 Nov 1821
Wallace	26	M	Tanner	England	United States	Jubilee	13 Jul 1829
William	38 6/12	M	Merchant	Great Britain	United States	Cambria	26 Dec 1827
Wm.	16	M	Mechanic	Ireland	United States	Vermont	10 Jan 1827

NAMES OF PASSENGERS	AGE	SEX	OCCUPATIONS	COUNTRY TO WHICH THEY BELONG	COUNTRY THEY INTEND TO INHABIT	SHIPS/DATES OF ARRIVAL	
HUNTERMILLER, H. W.	29	M	Merchant	Bremen	Bremen	Francis	4 May 1826
HUNTIG, A. G. L.	40	M	Bricklayer	Germany	United States	Daphne	20 May 1823
HUNTINGDON, Thomas	40	M	Carpenter	England	United States	Siroc	31 Oct 1829
HUNTINGTON, —, Mrs.	25	F		U. States	United States	Nile	5 Oct 1827
E.	32	M	Merchant	U. States	U. States	Sarah	5 Aug 1825
E. W.	25	M	Merchant	U. States	U. States	Rodman	22 Mar 1825
E. W.	30	M	Merchant	United States	U. States	Midas	6 Oct 1823
Elisha	28	M	Merchant	United States	United States	Actress	17 Mar 1820
John	26	M				Lady of the Lake	23 Aug 1828
John	40	M	Mason	U. States	U. States	Cornelia	30 Jul 1827
Louisa	14	F		U. States	St. Domingo	Genl. Warren	10 Jul 1828
Mary	10	F		U. States	St. Domingo	Genl. Warren	10 Jul 1828
N.	35	F		U. States	St. Domingo	Genl. Warren	10 Jul 1828
R.	12	M		U. States	St. Domingo	Genl. Warren	10 Jul 1828
S.	45	M	Merchant	U. States	St. Domingo	Genl. Warren	10 Jul 1828
Saml.	2	M		U. States	St. Domingo	Genl. Warren	10 Jul 1828
HUNTLINGTON, H.	32	M	Merchant	America	America	Brittania	17 Jul 1828
L. M.	26 11/12	F		America	America	Brittania	17 Jul 1828
HUNTON, George	28	M	Merchant	England	United States	Corinthian	10 Jan 1826
HUNTZENBERG, Apponse O.	32	M	Merchant	France	Neworleans	Danube	20 Jul 1826
HUPEDEN, J., Mr.	29	M		Germany	U.S.	Henri IV	14 Sep 1827
HUPERTI, Justus	37	M	Merchant	England	England	Virginia	9 Feb 1829
HUQUENIN, J.	18	M	Mechanic	Switzerland	U. States	Don Quixote	14 Aug 1826
L.	19	M	Mechanic	Switzerland	U. States	Don Quixote	14 Aug 1826
HURBERT, Wm.	35	M	Planter	U. States	U. States	Emigrant	20 Sep 1823
HURD, Anne	2 6/12			Great Britain	United States	Thomas Dickason	29 Aug 1828
Cyrus	30	M	Mercht.	U. States	U. States	Mary Livingston	6 Dec 1827
John	4			Great Britain	United States	Thomas Dickason	29 Aug 1828
John	28		Joiner	Great Britain	United States	Thomas Dickason	29 Aug 1828
Mary	4			Great Britain	United States	Thomas Dickason	29 Aug 1828
Norman, Capt.	37	M	Mariner	United States	United States	Leader	19 Aug 1825
Rebecca	7/12			Great Britain	United States	Thomas Dickason	29 Aug 1828
Rebecca	26			Great Britain	United States	Thomas Dickason	29 Aug 1828
Thomas	45	M	Shoemaker	England		Marchioness	13 May 1828
HURDS, Wm.	29	M	Brazer	York, Great Britain		Casanda	5 Sep 1827
HURDY, Thomas	43	M	Farmer	Hull, England	United States	Aurelia	7 Jun 1826
HURE, F. F.	21	M	Planter	St. Martin	St. Martin	Leonora	25 May 1826
HUREL, F. F.	36	M	Engineer	France	France	Howard	27 Sep 1826
HURISAN, W.	19	M	Merchant	Scotland	U. States	Eliza	23 Dec 1822
HURLAN, Philip	18	M	White Smith	Ireland	U. States	Josephine	30 Aug 1828
HURLEY, Angel	22	F	Servant	Ireland	United States	Sylvester Healy	17 Oct 1825
Daniel	17	M	Farmer	Ireland	America	William	21 May 1825
Eliza	24	F	Spinster	Ireland	America	William	21 May 1825
Elizabeth	1 10/12	F		Ireland	America	William	21 May 1825
Elizabeth	30	F	Laborer or Spinster	Ireland	United States	Sarah G	11 Sep 1827
Ellen	6	F	Laborer or Spinster	Ireland	United States	Sarah G	11 Sep 1827
Ellen	25	F		Ireland	U. States	Nancy	16 Aug 1822
James	20	M		Great Britain	United States	Lady Hunter	26 Nov 1823
Jeremiah	28	M	Farmer	Ireland	America	William	21 May 1825
Jeremiah	42	M	Farmer	Ireland	America	William	21 May 1825
Jno.	8	M	Laborer or Spinster	Ireland	United States	Sarah G	11 Sep 1827
Jno.	35	M	Labourer	Ireland	United States	Sarah G	11 Sep 1827
John	24	M	Weaver	Ireland	U.S.	Oliver Wolcott	3 Nov 1827
John	28	M	Laborer	Ireland	United States	Sylvester Healy	17 Oct 1825
Margret	44	F	Spinster	Ireland	America	William	21 May 1825
Mary	3	F	Laborer or Spinster	Ireland	United States	Sarah G	11 Sep 1827
Mary	6	F		Ireland	U. States	Nancy	16 Aug 1822
May	40	F			New York	Robert Fulton	8 Mar 1823
Michael	10	M			New York	Robert Fulton	8 Mar 1823

NAMES OF PASSENGERS	AGE	SEX	OCCUPATIONS	COUNTRY TO WHICH THEY BELONG	COUNTRY THEY INTEND TO INHABIT	SHIPS/DATES OF ARRIVAL	
HURLEY (cont'd)							
Michl.	16	M	Farmer	Ireland	United States	Diana	1 May 1826
Patrick	26	M	Farmer	Ireland	United States	Diana	1 May 1826
Randall	25	M	...	Ireland	U. States	Nancy	16 Aug 1822
Randell	3	M	Child	Ireland	United States	Sylvester Healy	17 Oct 1825
Wm.	28	M		Ireland	U. States	Sarah G	30 Jun 1828
HURLY, Jno.	2	M	None	Gt. Brittain	United States	Horizon	8 Aug 1823
John	13	M		Ireland	America	William	21 May 1825
Mary	3	F	None	Gt. Brittain	United States	Horizon	8 Aug 1823
Nora	24	F	None	Gt. Brittain	United States	Horizon	8 Aug 1823
Eliza Ann	40 4/12	F		U.S. of America	U.S. of Amer	Illinois	30 Apr 1823
HURSELL, Robert	23	M	Tailer	England	America	Sarah	18 Aug 1829
HURST, Absolem	29	M	Weaver	England	U. States	Favourite	2 Sep 1822
Alphonso J.	16	M	Merchant	Bermuda	Bermuda	Leander	30 Oct 1826
Ann	25	F		U. States	U. States	Orbit	31 Dec 1821
Anna	35	F	None	England	U.N. States	William Byrnes	13 Aug 1829
Anna	70	F	None	England	U.N. States	William Byrnes	13 Aug 1829
Barney	1	M		Great Britain	United States	Mary Howland	19 Jul 1827
Biddy	28	F		Great Britain	United States	Mary Howland	19 Jul 1827
Edward	1	M		Great Britain	United States	Mary Howland	19 Jul 1827
Edwin	2	F	None			Importer	30 Oct 1820
Eliza	9	F	None	Great Britain	United States	Roman	10 May 1828
Elizabeth	4	F	None			Importer	30 Oct 1820
Elizabeth	25	F	None	Gt. Brittain	United States	Balaena	8 Jan 1825
Elizabeth	43	F	None			Importer	30 Oct 1820
George	13	M	Farmer			Importer	30 Oct 1820
Hannah	24	F		England	United States	Curler	3 Mar 1828
Jane	21	F	his wife [Thomas]	Ireland	United States	Asia	29 Jul 1829
Jeremiah	50	M	Merchant	Great Britain	U. States of Amer	Junius	5 Jul 1820
John	9	M	None			Importer	30 Oct 1820
John	12	M	None	Great Britain	United States	Roman	10 May 1828
John, Infant		M		Great Britain	United States	Mary Howland	19 Jul 1827
Mary	17	F	None			Importer	30 Oct 1820
Mary	30	F		Great Britain	United States	Mary Howland	19 Jul 1827
Mary	40	F		Great Britain	United States	Roman	10 May 1828
Michael	35	M	Farmer	Great Britain	United States	Mary Howland	19 Jul 1827
Peter	30	M		Great Britain	United States	Mary Howland	19 Jul 1827
Saml.	26	M	Farmer	England	United States	Curler	3 Mar 1828
Samuel	6	M	None			Importer	30 Oct 1820
Thomas	25	M	Farmer	Ireland	United States	Asia	29 Jul 1829
HURSTIN, T.	45	M	Mariner	U. States	U. States	Genl. Victoria	7 Apr 1828
HURSTON, Maria	24	F		Great Brittain	United States	Sarah Ralston	27 Jan 1827
HURTEL, Peter	49	M	Merchant	U. States	United States	Seine	7 Dec 1821
HURTZMAN, Fidell	21	M	Watch Maker	Germany	U. States	Rook	25 Jul 1827
HUSBAND, —, Mrs.	20	F	Merchant	Great Britain	Canada	Columbia	7 Sep 1827
George	19	M	Painter	England	U. States	Frances	26 May 1827
HUSE, Otto	26	M	Doctor	U. States	U. States	Hannah	2 Feb 1822
HUSHTON, John	42	M		Great Brit.	Ohio	Gov. Griswald	3 Jul 1820
Margaret	39	F		Great Brit.	Ohio	Gov. Griswald	3 Jul 1820
Thos.	12	M		Great Brit.	Ohio	Gov. Griswald	3 Jul 1820
HUSLESS, Samuel C.	35	M	Merchant	U. States	U. States	Abeona	20 Aug 1827
HUSLEY, Ann	22	F		England	Ut. States	Courier	13 Jul 1826
James	35	M	Merchant	England	Ut. States	Courier	13 Jul 1826
Mary	26			Cork	Philadelphia	Schuylkill	22 Aug 1825
Michael	30		Weaver	Cork	Philadelphia	Schuylkill	22 Aug 1825
HUSSAN, J.	23	M	Farmer	Ireland	U. States	Isabella	28 Jun 1825
HUSSEY, L. H.	42	M	Merchant	U. States	U. States	Annawan	3 Apr 1826
Patrick	20	M		Great B.	U. States	William Neilson	26 Jul 1828
Robert	45	M	Mariner	U. States	U. States	Doris	21 Jan 1826
Saml. W.	38	M	Merchant	U. States	U. States	American Hero	28 Jul 1824
Samuel W.	40	M	Merchant	U. States	U. States	Prince Edward	11 Oct 1825
HUSTACE, B. A.	22	M	Farmer	St. Johns	U. States	Isabella	28 Jun 1825
D. S.	32	M	Farmer	St. Johns	U. States	Isabella	28 Jun 1825
HUSTICE, Walter	24	M	Servant	Ireland	U. States	Bayard	11 Mar 1823
HUSTIS, Banjaman	63	M	Farmer	New York	New York	Reindeer	20 Aug 1828
HUSTON, Adam	27	M	Merchant	Scotland	United States	Friends	16 Aug 1824
David	26	M	Farmer	Ireland	United States	Catharine	22 Jul 1825
Elenor	10	F		Great Britan	United States	Delaware	20 Aug 1829
Elenor	34	F		Great Britan	United States	Delaware	20 Aug 1829

NAMES OF PASSENGERS	AGE	SEX	OCCUPATIONS	COUNTRY TO WHICH THEY BELONG	COUNTRY THEY INTEND TO INHABIT	SHIPS/DATES OF ARRIVAL	
HUSTON (cont'd)							
Filo	46	F	Spinster	Ireland	United States	Catharine	22 Jul 1825
Henry	20	M	Labourer	Ireland	United States	Robert Fulton	10 Aug 1827
Jacob, Mr.	28	M	Bricklayer	England	U. States	Acasta	3 Apr 1826
Jane	3/12	F	None	Ireland	United States	Catharine	22 Jul 1825
Jane	7	F		Great Britan	United States	Delaware	20 Aug 1829
John	5	M		Great Britan	United States	Delaware	20 Aug 1829
John	22	M	Merchant	U. States	U. States	Genl. Victoria	7 Apr 1828
Mary	67	F	Weaver	Great Britan	United States	Delaware	20 Aug 1829
Mary Ann	12	F		Great Britan	United States	Delaware	20 Aug 1829
Paul	19	M	Clerk	Ireland	United States	Trident	16 May 1826
Robert	2	M		Great Britan	United States	Delaware	20 Aug 1829
Sarah	21	F	Spinster	Ireland	United States	Catharine	22 Jul 1825
Stewart	30	M	Weaver	Ireland	United States	Alex. Mansfield	17 May 1823
HUTCHESON, Alex.	5	M		Killiloage	United States	Carolina Ann	11 Jun 1824
Andrew	2	M		Killiloage	United States	Carolina Ann	11 Jun 1824
Jane	7	F		Killiloage	United States	Carolina Ann	11 Jun 1824
John	30	M	Farmer	Killiloage	United States	Carolina Ann	11 Jun 1824
Mary	27	F		Killiloage	United States	Carolina Ann	11 Jun 1824
HUTCHETT, Eugene	6	M		France	U. States	John & Edward	18 Jul 1822
M.	50	F	Merchant	France	U. States	John & Edward	18 Jul 1822
HUTCHINGS, Harriet	22	F	Servant	Baltimore, U.S.	Baltimore, U.S.	Pagasus	21 Mar 1829
Henry	25	M	Planter	England	England	Tontine	1 Jun 1826
John	45	M	Farmer	England	Boston	Lima	5 Aug 1829
Philip	23	M	Tailor	Gt. Britain		Corinthian	27 Oct 1829
Thoms.	0 6/12	M		Gt. Britain		Corinthian	27 Oct 1829
William	34	M	Carpenter	England	Canada	Brighton	9 Dec 1828
HUTCHINGTON,							
Bridgit	21		Bonnet Maker or Milliner	Ireland	United States	Geo. Canning	5 Jun 1828
Thos.	37		Hater	Ireland	United States	Geo. Canning	5 Jun 1828
HUTCHINS, Eliza	28	F	Lady	Great Britain	United States	Cambria	26 Dec 1827
Geo. B.	31	M	Lieut. Royal Navy	Gt. Brittain	United States	Leeds	19 May 1823
Harriett	...	F	Married Woman	...land	United States	Robert Edwards	3 Oct 1829
John	30	M	...t...	G. Britain	U. States	Armadello	22 Jun 1827
Philip	2	M		Gt. Britain		Corinthian	27 Oct 1829
R. L.	46	M	Merchant	United States	United States	Cambria	8 Oct 1828
Sarah	47	F	family of [Margaret]	United States	United States	Cambria	7 May 1828
HUTCHINSON, —, Leut.	40	M	Lieut.	Great Britian	Great Britian	Vermont	17 Nov 1826
A.	40	M	Labourer	Ireland	United States	Princess Charlotte	6 Oct 1827
Agnes	18	F	None	Ireland	United States	Princess Charlotte	6 Oct 1827
Alex	40	M	Farmer		United States	William	5 Oct 1822
Andrew	22	M	Bookbinder	Scotland	United States	Camillus	27 Oct 1829
Betsey	9	F		N. York	U. States	Lewis	24 Oct 1821
Clemtia	9	F		Great Brittain	United States	Active	12 Sep 1828
E.	36	F	None	Ireland	United States	Princess Charlotte	6 Oct 1827
Eliza	3	F			United States	William	5 Oct 1822
Eliza	34	F	Spinster	Ireland	America	Mary	29 May 1827
Eunice	12	F		Great Brittain	United States	Active	12 Sep 1828
Fredric O.	20		None	...	...	James Cropper	28 Jun 1824
George	11	M			United States	William	5 Oct 1822
George	18	M	Farmer	Great Brittain	United States	Active	12 Sep 1828
Hannah	45	F		N. York	U. States	Lewis	24 Oct 1821
James	17	M			United States	William	5 Oct 1822
James	27	M	Boot Maker	Scotland	United States	Cambria	8 Oct 1828
James	57	M		Great Brittain	United States	Active	12 Sep 1828
*Died on the Passage							
Jane	...	F	...	Ireland	United States	General Putnam	20 Jun 1825
Jane	13	F			United States	William	5 Oct 1822
Jane	26	F		Great Brittain	United States	Active	12 Sep 1828
Jas.	37	M	Carpenter	Great Brittain	United States	Nimrod	9 Jan 1827
John	6	M		Great Brittain	United States	Active	12 Sep 1828
John	20	M	Labourer	Great Britian	United States	Mount Vernon	19 May 1823
John	23	M	Nail Maker	Yorkshire	United States	Dalhousie Castle	27 Jul 1826
John	23	M	Bookbinder	Scotland	United States	Camillus	27 Oct 1829

NAMES OF PASSENGERS	AGE	SEX	OCCUPATIONS	COUNTRY TO WHICH THEY BELONG	COUNTRY THEY INTEND TO INHABIT	SHIPS/DATES OF ARRIVAL	
HUTCHINSON (cont'd)							
Joseph	16	M	Farmer	Great Brittain	United States	Active	12 Sep 1828
Josh.	48	M	Farmer	Great Brittain	United States	Active	12 Sep 1828
Margaret	9	F			United States	William	5 Oct 1822
Margt.	34	F		America	America	Carolina Ann	7 Apr 1826
Martha	4	F		England	New York	Corinthian	5 May 1827
Martha	29	F		England	New York	Corinthian	5 May 1827
Mary	14	F	None	Ireland	United States	Princess Charlotte	6 Oct 1827
Mary	14	F		Great Brittain	United States	Active	12 Sep 1828
Mary	40	F			United States	William	5 Oct 1822
Mary	48	F	Farmer	Great Brittain	United States	Active	12 Sep 1828
Mary J.	1	F		Ireland	America	Mary	29 May 1827
Mary Jane	22	F		Gt. Britain		Corinthian	27 Oct 1829
Nancy	10	F		Great Brittain	United States	Active	12 Sep 1828
P.	15				United States	William	5 Oct 1822
Rebecca	5	F			United States	William	5 Oct 1822
Robert	32	M	Paisterer	Bury	Bury	Howard Douglass	11 May 1827
Tamor	2	F		Great Brittain	United States	Active	12 Sep 1828
Thomas	8	M		Great Brittain	United States	Active	12 Sep 1828
William	7	M			United States	William	5 Oct 1822
William	27	M	Merchant	Great Britain	U.S. of America	Canada	1 Oct 1827
William	30	M	Tanner	England	United States	Ann Maria	26 Apr 1822
William	37	M		England	New York	Corinthian	5 May 1827
Wm.	...	M		Ireland	United States	General Putnam	20 Jun 1825
Wm.	28	M	Farmer	Ireland	America	Mary	29 May 1827
HUTCHISON, Allen	20	M	Labourer	Ireland	U. States	Josephine	30 Aug 1828
Ann	24	F	Matron	Ireland	United States	Wilson	22 Jun 1824
Betsey	20	F		Ireland	N. Jersey	Potomac	7 Aug 1827
H.	40	M	Mariner	Scotland	United States	Louisiana	3 Nov 1827
James	17	M	Labourer	Ireland	U. States	Josephine	30 Aug 1828
Jane	11 6/12	F	Child	Ireland	U. States	Josephine	30 Aug 1828
John	17	M	Labourer	Ireland	United States	Trident	16 May 1826
Margaret	25	F		Scotland	U.S. States of Am.	Camillus	17 Sep 1823
Martha	3	F	...	Ireland	United States	Wilson	22 Jun 1824
Rebecca	44 6/12	F	Matron	Ireland	U. States	Josephine	30 Aug 1828
Samuel	26	M	Weaver	Ireland	N. Jersey	Potomac	7 Aug 1827
Thomas	...	M	...	Ireland	United States	Wilson	22 Jun 1824
Thos.	27	M	Cabinet Maker	Scotland	U.S. States of Am.	Camillus	17 Sep 1823
William	21 6/12	M	Hatter	Ireland	U. States	Josephine	30 Aug 1828
William	25	M	Merchant	England	United States	William Byrnes	1 Dec 1824
Wm.	40	M	Merchant	U. States	U. States	Birmingham	23 Feb 1829
HUTEN, Catherin	18	F		Irland	U. States	Nancy	27 Jun 1823
HUTER, Jacob	40	M	Merchant	United States	South Carolina	Arab	10 Nov 1826
HUTHERSON, Kitty	25	F	None	England	U. States	Franklin	7 Jul 1828
HUTHWORTH, Johannes	36	M	Farmer			New York Packet	19 Aug 1820
HUTSON, Cath.	17			England	United States	Hugh Johnson	11 Jun 1828
Geo.	32	M	Shepherd	G. Brittan	U. States	Trafalgar	4 Jun 1822
Helen	30	F	wife to Shepherd [Geo.]	G. Brittan	U. States	Trafalgar	4 Jun 1822
Henry	34	M	Carpenter	U. States	U.S.	Adrianna	8 Aug 1822
Louisa	28	F	None	Great Britan	Great Britan	United States	21 May 1827
Robt. D.	3	M	None	Great Britan	Great Britan	United States	21 May 1827
Thomas	33	M	Grocer	Great Britan	Great Britan	United States	21 May 1827
Thos. H.	1	M	None	Great Britan	Great Britan	United States	21 May 1827
HUTT, Margaretha	29	F	Farmer	Wortenberg	Lancaster	Louisa	6 Oct 1828
Matthew	35	M	Farmer	Wortenberg	Lancaster	Louisa	6 Oct 1828
HUTTEN, John	20	M	...	England	United States	Hamilton	13 Nov 1827
HUTTER, A.	20	F	Anything	Swiss	U. States	Edwd. Quesnel	30 Apr 1825
An M.	9	F	Washewoman	Ireland		Quatre Freres	29 Jul 1828
Bovler	21	F	Farm	Ireland		Quatre Freres	29 Jul 1828
Catharan	19	F	Washewoman	Ireland		Quatre Freres	29 Jul 1828
Jaques	78	M	Farmer	Ireland		Quatre Freres	29 Jul 1828
HUTTMAN, John	45	M	Carpenter			Betsey	17 Aug 1820
HUTTON, D. F.	31	M	Merchant	Scotland	U. States	Superior	25 Sep 1828
George	32	M	Merchant	England	U. States	Sully	24 Oct 1828
Robt.	30	M	Gentleman	U. States	U. States	La Fayette	7 Apr 1825

NAMES OF PASSENGERS	AGE	SEX	OCCUPATIONS	COUNTRY TO WHICH THEY BELONG	COUNTRY THEY INTEND TO INHABIT	SHIPS/DATES OF ARRIVAL	
HUTTON (cont'd)							
Thomas	23 6/12	M	Wheelright	Great Briton	United States	Mount Vernon	30 Dec 1828
Wm.	23	M	Surgeon	Great Britain	America	Lady Gallatin	21 Jun 1820
HUXLEY, Patrick	2	M		Ireland	America	William	21 May 1825
HUXLEY, Thos.	38	M	B. Armey	England	England	Corinthian	2 May 1823
HUYDEKEPER, Albert	18	M	Merchant	Holland		Louisa	12 Jun 1826
HYAMS, Rebecca	22	F		England	United States	Acasta	14 Jun 1824
HYANES, William	32	M	Joiner	England	America	Britannia	22 Jul 1829
HYDE, Abel	29	M		G. Britain		Casanda	5 Sep 1827
Betty	28	F		G. Britain		Casanda	5 Sep 1827
George	4	M	None		United States	Mount Vernon	29 Aug 1828
Hannah	12	F	None	Great Britian	United States	George Clinton	21 Oct 1826
Hannah	23	F	None		United States	Mount Vernon	29 Aug 1828
Henry	1	M	None	England	Virginia	Brighton	20 Aug 1825
James	1	M	None		United States	Mount Vernon	29 Aug 1828
James	25	M	Farmer	Ireland	America	William	21 May 1825
Jane	27	F	None	England	Virginia	Brighton	20 Aug 1825
John	24	M	Laborer	England	U. States	Howard Douglass	29 Jan 1828
John E.	47	M	Merchant	United States	New York, U.S.	Florida	2 Oct 1828
L.	27	M	Merchant	Vermont	U. States	Circassian	3 Jun 1826
Sarah	30	F	Servant	Great Brittain	Savannah	Albion	11 Jun 1821
Simeon	54	M	Merchant	U. States	U. States	Amity	23 Sep 1823
HYDEOLA, Benjm.	14	M	Watchmaker	England	U. States	Cincinnatus	9 Jul 1825
HYLAND, David	5/12	M		England	England	Venus	15 Apr 1822
Gans	16		Labourer	England	United States	Corinthian	7 Jul 1829
Geo.	16 11/12	M	Tanner	Great Britain	United States	Venus	8 Sep 1820
Hannah	22 6/12	F	his wife [Henry]	Great Britain	United States	Venus	8 Sep 1820
Helena	18		Servant	England	England	London	16 Aug 1824
Henry	39 6/12	M	Tanner	Great Britain	Albany	Venus	8 Sep 1820
Henry, Jr.	19 7/12	M	Tanner	Great Britain	United States	Venus	8 Sep 1820
John	23 2/12	F	Printer	England	England	Venus	15 Apr 1822
John	26	M	Joiner	Great Britain	United States	Fame	26 May 1828
Mary Ann	3	F		Great Britain	United States	Fame	26 May 1828
Mary Ann	25	F		Great Britain	United States	Fame	26 May 1828
Peter	28	M	Printer	Ireland	United States	Carolina Ann	11 Dec 1826
Rebecca	20	F	Printer	England	England	Venus	15 Apr 1822
Rossanna	30	F	Lady	Ireland	United States	Dublin Packet	13 Oct 1828
Ruth	1	F		Great Britain	United States	Fame	26 May 1828
William	14		Labourer	England	United States	Corinthian	7 Jul 1829
HYMAN, Abraham	24	M	Watch Maker	England	New York	Brighton	19 Aug 1829
Abraham	24	M	Watch Maker			Brighton	19 Aug 1829
Henry	21	M	Watch Maker	England	New York	Brighton	19 Aug 1829
HYNAMENI, John	28	M	Merchant	Italy	America	Hercules	5 Sep 1826
HYNDMAN, Jas.	29	M	Labourer	Ireland	United States	Trident	16 May 1826
HYNE, M.	19	F		Gt. Britain	U. States	Tantiva	7 Jul 1828
M.	19	F		Gt. Britain	U. States	Tantiva	7 Jul 1828
HYNER, Catherine	22	F	Servant	Ireland	United States	Ann Maria	5 May 1824
HYNES, Dorathy	27	F	Labourer	Ireland	United States	Lady Hunter	27 Dec 1825
Henry	6	M		England	United States	St. John	5 Oct 1829
James	22	M	Labourer	Ireland	U.S. of America	Hamilton	18 Jul 1827
Jno. Thos.	24	M	Clergyman	Ireland	Kentucky	Abigail	9 Aug 1821
John	40	M	Labourer	Ireland	America	John Adams	2 Aug 1827
Lowery	6	M		England	United States	St. John	5 Oct 1829
Mary A.	40	F		England	United States	St. John	5 Oct 1829
Michael	25	M	Laborer	Ireland	New York	Amanda	23 May 1827
Patt	22	M	Laborer	Ireland	New York	Amanda	23 May 1827
Thomas	10	M		England	United States	St. John	5 Oct 1829
HYPPOLET, H.	25	M	Merchant	France	United States	Edward Bonnaffe	24 Aug 1827
HYPPOLIH, D... Adolphe	22	M	Merchant	France	U. States	Dawn	8 Jun 1827
HYSLOP, Andw.	28	M	Gardner	England	America	Braganza	1 Dec 1824
Margt.	18	F		U. States	U. States	Montano	2 Sep 1828
Rob., Jr.	25	M	Merchant	U. States	U. States	Seneca	14 May 1821
Robert	24	M		America		Buffalo	7 Feb 1820
Saml. C.	35	M	Merchant	U. States	U. States	Abeona	11 Sep 1828
HYSUCH, Patrick	6			England	U. States	Corinthian	8 Oct 1828
HYTON, Robt.	27	M	Mason	England	United States	Trident	30 Sep 1826

NAMES OF PASSENGERS	AGE	SEX	OCCUPATIONS	COUNTRY TO WHICH THEY BELONG	COUNTRY THEY INTEND TO INHABIT	SHIPS/DATES OF ARRIVAL	
IBARD, Hugh	25	M	Farmer	Ireland	United States	Justina	5 Aug 1823
IBBOLETTER, Henry	31	M	Cutter	G. Britain	U. States	Canada	19 Sep 1828
ICARD, A.	23	M	None	Marseilles	Martinique	L'Amitus	2 Mar 1827
A.	35	M	Merchant	Mexico	U. States	Laveria	23 Jul 1828
ICK, Ann	24	F		England	U. States	Elias Burger	12 Sep 1822
Charles	2	M		England, Antigua	England	Fanny	8 May 1824
Emma	4	F		England, Antigua	England	Fanny	8 May 1824
Francis	25	F		England, Antigua	England	Fanny	8 May 1824
George	38	M		England, Antigua	England	Fanny	8 May 1824
M.	38	M	Merchant	England	U. States	Elias Burger	30 Nov 1822
William	8	M		England, Antigua	England	Fanny	8 May 1824
ICOBESKIE, Alburtz	20	M	Servant	Curacoa	Curacoa	William Prince	30 May 1825
IDALGOS, Ignacio	38	M	Priest	Mexico	Spain	Virginia	8 Mar 1828
IDARRA, John	29	M	Clothier	Great Britain	United States	Frances Henrietta	17 Sep 1827
Joseph	19	M	Clothier	Great Britain	United States	Frances Henrietta	17 Sep 1827
William	21	M	Labourer	Great Britain	United States	Frances Henrietta	17 Sep 1827
IDELMAN, Soloman	20	M	Merchant	Poland	U.S. America	Huntress	6 Sep 1827
IDLER, Charles	17	M	Merchant	U. States	U. States	Robert Y. Haynes	22 Mar 1827
Margaretha	20	F		Germany	America	Falcon	28 Aug 1828
IDOMS, Edward	40	M	Laborer	England	New York	Indian Chief	19 Jun 1823
ILLINGWORTH, William	55	M	Farmer	Yorkshire	United States	Dalhousie Castle	27 Jul 1826
William, Jr.	19	M	Farmer	Yorkshire	United States	Dalhousie Castle	27 Jul 1826
ILLMAN, Thomas	26		Cooper	England	United States	Corinthian	30 May 1828
ILSLEY, —, Mr.	18	M	Mercht.	Ireland	U. States	Brown	11 Jan 1825
David S.	25	M	Mercht.	U. States		Union	6 Nov 1826
ILVINE, Murtock	22	M	Farmer	Ireland	United States	Fabius	4 Jun 1828
ILWING, Edwd. A.	21	M	Merchant	New York	U.S.	Florida	17 May 1825
IMAN, John Thos.	28	M				Golden Grove	6 Sep 1820
IMHOFF, Durs	21	M	Weaver	Switzerland	United States	Thetis	5 Jul 1821
Jacob	21	M	Shoemaker	Switzerland	United States	Thetis	5 Jul 1821
IMLAH, Alexr.	40	M	Merchant	Scotland	U. States	Flight	9 Jul 1825
IMLAY, Jno.	12	M		St. Bartholo- mews	U. States	Fox	14 Sep 1822
Mary	10	F		St. Bartholo- mews	U. States	Fox	14 Sep 1822
IMMAN, John	16	M	Laborer	Hannover	U.N. States	Constitution	7 Dec 1827
INCH, Andrew	29	M	Labourer	Ireland	United States	Hope	12 Jun 1828
Spencer	23	M	Cabinet Maker	Ireland	New York	Carolina Ann	15 Oct 1824
INCLAIN, —	25	M	Merchant	Spain	Spain	Commodore Perry	24 Nov 1820
INCLIN, Stephen	21	M	Merchant	Spain		Agnes	30 Sep 1820
INELAND, Stephen	20	M		Spain	Spain	Ambuscade	1 Jul 1820
INEN, J.	7	M	Farmer	Switzerland	U. States	Alfred	8 Jul 1828
J.	10	M	Farmer	Switzerland	U. States	Alfred	8 Jul 1828
J.	45	M	Farmer	Switzerland	U. States	Alfred	8 Jul 1828
L.	5	M	Farmer	Switzerland	U. States	Alfred	8 Jul 1828
Maria	36	F	Farmer	Switzerland	U. States	Alfred	8 Jul 1828
S.	9	M	Farmer	Switzerland	U. States	Alfred	8 Jul 1828
INGALS, John	58	M		New York	United States	Juno	26 Nov 1821
INGER, Joseph	20	M	Servant	Great Britain	Great Britain	Roman	10 May 1828
INGERSOLL, John	33	M	Mariner	United States	United States	Mary Ann	7 Jan 1829
INGESLY, Pat	26	M	Labourer	U. States	U. States	United States	11 Sep 1828
INGHAM, Anthony	21	M	Weaver	England	United States	Trident	30 Sep 1826
Charles	4	M		United States	United States	Camberwell	2 Oct 1828
James	41	M	Merchant	England	United States	Florida	14 Sep 1827
Jane	28	F	Merchant	England	United States	Florida	14 Sep 1827
Jas.	23	M	Gentn.	Gt. Brittain	United States	York	6 Dec 1826
John	40	M	Labourer	England	United States	Amelia	20 Aug 1829
John	42	M	Merchant	United States	United States	Camberwell	2 Oct 1828

NAMES OF PASSENGERS	AGE	SEX	OCCUPATIONS	COUNTRY TO WHICH THEY BELONG	COUNTRY THEY INTEND TO INHABIT	SHIPS/DATES OF ARRIVAL	
INGHAM (cont'd)							
Katharine	6	F		United States	United States	Camberwell	2 Oct 1828
Sarah	...	...	...	...	...	St. Michael	22 Sep 1824
INGLAS, John	25	M	Lock Smith	Ireland	U.N. States	Jane	7 Oct 1826
INGLEE, Hiram	23	M	Merchant	U. States	U. States	Ardell	14 May 1828
INGLEMAN, B.	24	M	Baker	United States	United States	Seine	21 Oct 1822
INGLES, And.	6	M	None	Scotland	U. States	Czar	29 Aug 1829
Cath.	10	F	None	Scotland	U. States	Czar	29 Aug 1829
John	8	M	None	Scotland	U. States	Czar	29 Aug 1829
Julia	45	F	None	Scotland	United States	Mary & Susan	5 Aug 1828
William	40	M	Merchant	Scotland	United States	Camillus	6 Apr 1821
INGLIS, Catherine	2	F	None	Scotland	United States	Mary & Susan	5 Aug 1828
James	8	M	None	Scotland	United States	Mary & Susan	5 Aug 1828
Jane	16	F	Weaver	Scotland	United States	Mary & Susan	5 Aug 1828
Janet	19	F	Weaver	Scotland	United States	Mary & Susan	5 Aug 1828
Margaret	13	F	Weaver	Scotland	United States	Mary & Susan	5 Aug 1828
Mariann	10	F	Weaver	Scotland	United States	Mary & Susan	5 Aug 1828
Mary	24	F	Weaver	Scotland	United States	Mary & Susan	5 Aug 1828
Wm. B.	51	M	Merchant	U. States	U. States	Marcellus	2 Sep 1820
INGLISS, John	21	M		Scotland	United States	John Dickinson	12 Aug 1824
INGOLD, Andrew	5	M		Switzerland	United States	Elizabeth	27 Jul 1824
Doras	22	M	Weaver	Switzerland	United States	Elizabeth	27 Jul 1824
Fredr.	42	M	Weaver	Switzerland	United States	Elizabeth	27 Jul 1824
Jacob	4	M		Switzerland	United States	Elizabeth	27 Jul 1824
Johanes	12	M		Switzerland	United States	Elizabeth	27 Jul 1824
Johanes	48	M	Weaver	Switzerland	United States	Elizabeth	27 Jul 1824
Verena	48	F	Weaver	Switzerland	United States	Elizabeth	27 Jul 1824
INGOLDSBY, Felix	25	M	Merchant	Ireland	U.S.	Panthea	13 Nov 1823
INGOLSLY, Felix	30	M	Merchant	Great Britian	United States	Diamond	8 Nov 1824
INGRAHAM, —, Mastr.	8	M	None	U. States	U. States	Sea Nymph	7 Jul 1827
—, Mrs.	35	M	None	U. States	U. States	Sea Nymph	7 Jul 1827
Caroline	28 2/12	F		Gt. Britain	U. States	Maria	22 May 1822
N. G.	36	M	Merchant	N. York	U. States	Hero	3 Sep 1823
N. G., Mr.	34	M	Merchant	America	America	Manhatten	4 Feb 1822
Thomas	5	M		Gt. Britain	U. States	Maria	22 May 1822
INGRAM, Alice	7	F		Antrim	Ireland	Carolina Ann	11 Jun 1824
Alice	46	F		Antrim	Ireland	Carolina Ann	11 Jun 1824
Ann Jane	19	F		Antrim	Ireland	Carolina Ann	11 Jun 1824
Edwd.	5	M		Antrim	Ireland	Carolina Ann	11 Jun 1824
Eliza	2	F		Antrim	Ireland	Carolina Ann	11 Jun 1824
Hannah	17	F		Antrim	Ireland	Carolina Ann	11 Jun 1824
Henry	18	M		Antrim	Ireland	Carolina Ann	11 Jun 1824
James	9	M		Antrim	Ireland	Carolina Ann	11 Jun 1824
John	2	M		Antrim	Ireland	Carolina Ann	11 Jun 1824
Maria	40		Farmer	Ireland	United States	Carolina Ann	12 Sep 1823
Nathaniel	12	M		Antrim	Ireland	Carolina Ann	11 Jun 1824
Thos.	50	M		Antrim	Ireland	Carolina Ann	11 Jun 1824
Wm.	19		Farmer	Glars	Ireland	Carolina Ann	21 May 1823
INGRAN, Thomas	16		Farmer	Glars	Ireland	Carolina Ann	21 May 1823
INGWERSON, Jacob	31	M	Merchant	France	United States	Galaxy	17 Feb 1824
INHOF, Johanes	25	M	Weaver	Switzerland	United States	Elizabeth	27 Jul 1824
Peter	18	M	Weaver	Switzerland	United States	Elizabeth	27 Jul 1824
INLAT, Ann	15	F		United States	U. States	Nymph	5 Jul 1820
Jaqueline	36	F		United States	U. States	Nymph	5 Jul 1820
INMAN, Jane	28	F		N. York	U. States	Prize	20 Sep 1823
John	23	M	Law	U. States	U. States	Canada	5 Jun 1827
Robert	25	M	None	England	United States	Montgomery	6 Mar 1829
Saml.	21	M	Cotton Spinner	England	United States	Andes	2 Oct 1828
William	28	M	Farmer	Rye, England	United States	William	21 May 1828
INNES, Anne	40	F		England	U. States	Manhattan	20 Jun 1825
Chas.	21	M	Pr. Gentleman	Ireland	United States	William	20 Jul 1829
Elizabeth	17	F		England	U. States	Manhattan	20 Jun 1825
George	35	M	Labourer	Tyrone, Ireland	New York	Anthusa	24 Aug 1825
James	58	M	Merchant	U. States	U. States	Canada	8 Jun 1826
John	12	M	None	Gt. Britan	U. States	Canada	8 Jun 1826
John	51	M	Merchant	England	U. States	Manhattan	20 Jun 1825
Sarah	11	F		England	U. States	Manhattan	20 Jun 1825
William, Mr.	12	M		England	United States	Cosmo	26 Aug 1829

NAMES OF PASSENGERS	AGE	SEX	OCCUPATIONS	COUNTRY TO WHICH THEY BELONG	COUNTRY THEY INTEND TO INHABIT	SHIPS/DATES OF ARRIVAL	
INNESS, G.	23	M	Supercargo	U. States	U. States	Hope	2 Apr 1827
James	22	M	Silversmith	New York	New York	Reindeer	16 Mar 1820
James	22	M	Farmer	Scotland	United States	Andes	2 Oct 1828
James	23	M	Chair Maker	U. States		Ambuscade	30 Dec 1820
INNEY, John	22	M	Joiner	Denny, Denny [Parish], Stirling [County]	New York	Hero	19 May 1828
*to follow occupation							
INNIS, Daniel	38	M	Blacksmith	Scotland	Cuba	Frances	7 Aug 1826
Elizabeth	16	F		St. Johns, N.B.	United States	Henrietta	17 Aug 1825
George	1	M	Weaver	Great Britain	United States	Thomas Dickason	31 Jul 1829
James	20	M	Farmer			Nancy	12 Aug 1820
Jane	18	F	Farmer	Great Britain	United States	Wanderer	14 May 1828
John	4	M	Weaver	Great Britain	United States	Thomas Dickason	31 Jul 1829
John	54	M	...	St. Johns, N.B.	United States	Henrietta	17 Aug 1825
Margaret	20	F		G. Britain		Nancy	12 Aug 1820
Margaret	50	F		St. Johns, N.B.	United States	Henrietta	17 Aug 1825
Mary	18	F				Nancy	12 Aug 1820
Matilda	24	F	Weaver	Great Britain	United States	Thomas Dickason	31 Jul 1829
Moses	19	M		St. Johns, N.B.	United States	Henrietta	17 Aug 1825
Thomas	3	M		St. Johns, N.B.	United States	Henrietta	17 Aug 1825
William	2	M	Weaver	Great Britain	United States	Thomas Dickason	31 Jul 1829
William	13	M		St. Johns, N.B.	United States	Henrietta	17 Aug 1825
William	30	M	Weaver	Great Britain	United States	Thomas Dickason	31 Jul 1829
INSKEEP, —, wife	25	F	...	England	New York	Thames	6 Oct 1820
James, Mr.	33	M	...	England	New York	Thames	6 Oct 1820
INTINGER, J.	28	M	Merchant	Amsterdam	Antwert	Nestor	20 Nov 1821
IRAPENAN, Lewis	41	M	Merchant	U. States	U. States	York	2 Dec 1828
IRELAND, —, Mrs.	34	M	Farmer	Gt. Britain	U. States	Constitution	19 Jul 1825
Ann	19	F				Hanford	17 Jul 1828
James	21	M	Farmer	Scotland	U. States	Reaper	31 May 1824
Joana	21	F	Farmer	Scotland	U. States	Reaper	31 May 1824
Thomas	21	M	Labourer			Hanford	17 Jul 1828
William	39	M	Mariner	U. States	U. States	Jane	3 Apr 1823
Wm.	1 6/12	M				Hanford	17 Jul 1828
IREMOL, J.	22	M	Merchant	Tarugona	Tarrugona	Prize	10 Jun 1824
IREWIN, Johnson	22	M	Labourer	Ireland	U. States	Atlantic	19 Aug 1825
IRISH, —, Mrs.	34	F		England	U. States	Vermont	19 Mar 1827
Ann ...	18	M		Great Britian	United States	London	24 Jun 1823
Caroline	27	F	Lady	England	New York	Robert Edwards	17 Mar 1828
IRLAND, Rachal	54	F	going to her Son	Scotland	America	Camillus	12 Sep 1822
IRLETT, Charles	25	M	Merchant	Switzerland	U. States	Falcon	11 Oct 1824
IRMER, John	18	M	Farmer	England	United States	Cambria	3 Jul 1829
IRON, Dennis	23	M	Labourer	Ireland	United States	General Marion	6 Oct 1828
George	20	M	Farmer	England	United States	Euphrates	18 Aug 1827
Robt.	22		...			Amphion	31 May 1824
Thomas	23	M	Black Smith	Ireland	U. States	Wanderer	1 Sep 1828
IRONCOSA, R.	27	M	Mercht.	Spain	Spain	Richmond Packet	10 Dec 1828
IRROE, Dennis	20	M	Currier	Ireland	United States	Princess Charlotte	26 Apr 1827
IRSLER, Maria	35 2/12	F	Accointtant	France	U. States	France	26 Jun 1828
IRUDLAIRD, John	20	M	Farmer	Ireland	U. States	Mentor	5 Jul 1825
IRVIN, And.	Dead	M	Merchant	U. States	U. States	Mattewan	20 Oct 1827
*Dead							
Ann	6	M	Family/child [of Lowther]	G. Britain	United States	Louisa	14 Jun 1825
Ann	16	F	Child	Ireland	United States	Sarah G.	20 Jul 1827
Ann	41 5/12	F	Wife [of Lowther]	G. Britain	United States	Louisa	14 Jun 1825
Archibald	24	M	Labourer	Ireland	United States	Edwin	27 Oct 1828
Archibald	28	M	Labourer	Ireland	U. States	Josephine	7 May 1827
Charles	16	M	Boy	Ireland	U. States	Josephine	7 May 1827
David	13	M		G. Britain	United States	Louisa	14 Jun 1825
Edward	3	M	None	Great Britan	Great Britan	United States	21 May 1827

NAMES OF PASSENGERS	AGE	SEX	OCCUPATIONS	COUNTRY TO WHICH THEY BELONG	COUNTRY THEY INTEND TO INHABIT	SHIPS/DATES OF ARRIVAL	
IRVIN (cont'd)							
George	24	M	Mechanic	United States	United	Greyhound	27 Nov 1820
Grace	65	F		Ireland	U. States	Adno	5 Jul 1828
Henry	17	M	Labourer	Ireland	United States	Commerce	13 Jun 1828
James	10 3/12	M	Family/child [of Lowther]	G. Britain	United States	Louisa	14 Jun 1825
James	14	M	Boy	Ireland	U. States	Josephine	7 May 1827
James	22	M	Farmer	G. Britain	U. States	George Clinton	10 Sep 1828
Jane	13	M	Family/child [of Lowther]	G. Britain	United States	Louisa	14 Jun 1825
Jered	45	M	Painter	Ireland	America	Hannah	8 Nov 1821
John	5	M	Labourer	Ireland	United States	Edwin	27 Oct 1828
John	22	M	Taylor	Ireland	U. States	Nancy	1 Sep 1823
John	25	M	Farmer	Ireland	United States	Dublin Packet	28 Apr 1824
Louther	1 1/12	M	Family/child [of Lowther]	G. Britain	United States	Louisa	14 Jun 1825
Lowther	41 1/12	M	Bricklayer	G. Britain	United States	Louisa	14 Jun 1825
Mary	7	F		Ireland	U. States	Adno	5 Jul 1828
Mary	50	F	Widdow	Ireland	U. States	Josephine	7 May 1827
Richard	22	M	Merchant	Great Britain	U. States	Columbia	24 Dec 1822
Samuel	31	M	Merchant	U. States	U. States	Camillus	7 Mar 1825
Sarah	24	F		Ireland	U. States	Adno	5 Jul 1828
Steward	22	M	Labourer	Ireland		Robert Fulton	4 Jun 1828
Thos.	59	M	Merchant	Scotland	United States	Columbia	11 Aug 1823
William	5	M	None	Great Britan	Great Britan	United States	21 May 1827
Wm.	4	M		Ireland	U. States	Adno	5 Jul 1828
Wm.	34	M	Weaver	Ireland	Philadelphia	Carolina Ann	15 Oct 1824
IRVINE, James	20	M	Laborer	Ireland	United States	Mary	1 Jul 1829
James	24		Merchant	Ireland	United States	John Dickinson	28 Jun 1822
Jane	21	F	Matron	Ireland	U. States	Josephine	7 May 1827
IRVING, Eliza	28	F	Labourer	Ireland	U. States	Two Marys	20 Apr 1825
Ester	3	F	Labourer	Ireland	U. States	Two Marys	20 Apr 1825
Hy.	7	M	Labourer	Ireland	U. States	Two Marys	20 Apr 1825
James	7	M	Child	Ireland	United States	Edwin	27 Oct 1828
John	1	M	Labourer	Ireland	U. States	Two Marys	20 Apr 1825
John	25	M	Gentleman	Nassau	U.States	Venus	28 Jun 1825
John	35	M	Labourer	Ireland	U. States	Two Marys	20 Apr 1825
Margt.	9	F	Labourer	Ireland	U. States	Two Marys	20 Apr 1825
Mary	5	F	Labourer	Ireland	U. States	Two Marys	20 Apr 1825
Pierre	26		Attorney at Law	United States	United States	Hudson	14 Jun 1827
Thos.	24	M	Stone Cutter	Great Britain		Olive Branch	9 Oct 1829
IRVINS, Andw.	19		Farmer	Kerry	U. Canada	Schuylkill	22 Aug 1825
James	21		Farmer	Kerry	U. Canada	Schuylkill	22 Aug 1825
IRWIN, And.	22		Farmer	Ireland		Westmoreland	1 Aug 1826
Charles	21	M	Shoemaker	Ireland	United States	Clothier	22 Nov 1827
Edward	26	M	Farmer	England	United States	Delta	24 Oct 1829
Elizabeth	20		Spinster	Ireland	U. States	Xenophon	28 May 1822
Jerry	33	M	Farmer	Ireland	United States	Trident	30 Sep 1826
John	23	M	Weaver	Gt. Britan	America	Braganza	1 Dec 1824
John	23	M	Weaver	Ireland	United States	Romulus	24 Jun 1826
Joseph	23		Farmer	Ireland		Westmoreland	1 Aug 1826
Robt.	22 7/12	M	Baker	Ireland	America	Carolina Ann	7 Apr 1826
William	15 8/12	M	Labourer	Ireland	United States	Louisa	16 Mar 1826
IRWINE, Wm.	48 7/12	M	Weaver	Ireland	United States	Atlantic	21 Jul 1827
IRWINER, Patrick	28		Farmer			Rufus King	7 Aug 1820
ISAAC, Israel	21	M	Tailor	Rusia	United States	Elizabeth	8 Jun 1827
John	21	M	Servant	Gt. Britain	U. States	New York Packet	6 Aug 1824
Samuel	50	M	Traveller	Jeruselam	U. States	Hudson	12 Mar 1824
Tabatha	35	F	Servant	St. Croix	on a Visit	Carlo	27 Aug 1829
Thos.	48	M	Farmer	Gt. Britain	U. States	New York Packet	6 Aug 1824
Willm.	18	M	Servant	Gt. Britain	U. States	New York Packet	6 Aug 1824
ISAACKS, Moses	49	M	Merchant	England	Columbia	Chapman	21 Apr 1826
ISAACS, B. C.	55	M	Mercht.	Holland	New York	Panthea	22 Jul 1826
Eliza	25	F	Lady	G. Britain	U. States	Endeavour	1 May 1826
Henry	23	M	Gentleman	England	U. States	Bunker Hill	12 Aug 1828
R. B.	23	M	Clerk	U. States	U. States	Elbe	13 Jun 1827

NAMES OF PASSENGERS	AGE	SEX	OCCUPATIONS	COUNTRY TO WHICH THEY BELONG	COUNTRY THEY INTEND TO INHABIT	SHIPS/DATES OF ARRIVAL	
ISAACS (cont'd)							
R. B.	23	M	Merchant	American	U.S.	Alexander	15 Oct 1827
R. R.	24	M	Merchant	America	America	Nestor	13 Jul 1829
Tabitha	40	F	Servant	Denmark	Denmark	Mary Ann	5 May 1828
ISAACSON, Morris	22	M	...	Switzerland	U. States	Robert Edward	2 Nov 1827
ISAMBARDI, J. B.	28	M	Merchant	Switzerland	U. States	Leonidas	1 Aug 1822
ISBELL, Thomas	39	M	Coachman	United States	New York	Leonidas	22 Jan 1829
ISBILE,							
Constantin Gig Dupre	45	M	Planter	Guadaloupe	Guadaloupe	Baltic	20 Aug 1821
ISCH, Barbara	34	F	Farmer	Switzerland	U. States	Sully	15 Jul 1829
Barbara, Jr.	3	F	Farmer	Switzerland	U. States	Sully	15 Jul 1829
Benidict	1	M	Farmer	Switzerland	U. States	Sully	15 Jul 1829
Elizabeth	5	F	Farmer	Switzerland	U. States	Sully	15 Jul 1829
John	7	M	Farmer	Switzerland	U. States	Sully	15 Jul 1829
Maria	11	F	Farmer	Switzerland	U. States	Sully	15 Jul 1829
Nicholas	39	M	Farmer	Switzerland	U. States	Sully	15 Jul 1829
Nicholas, Jr.	9	M	Farmer	Switzerland	U. States	Sully	15 Jul 1829
ISELAND, William	22	M	Labourer	Ireland	United States	Meteor	26 Jun 1827
ISELIN, A., Master	9	M				Henri IV	17 May 1828
E., Miss	2	F				Henri IV	17 May 1828
Heln., Miss	16	F				Henri IV	17 May 1828
J., Mr.	44	M	Merchant	U. States	U.S.	Henri IV	17 May 1828
J., Mrs.	34	F				Henri IV	17 May 1828
W., Master	7	M				Henri IV	17 May 1828
ISHAIN, Benj.	43	M	Merchant	Philada.	Philada.	Neptune	11 Feb 1826
ISIDORE, Jacques	35	M	Wagoner	France	U. States	Edward Bopnnaffe	30 Jul 1829
Louis	7	M		France	U. States	Edward Bopnnaffe	30 Jul 1829
Marie	40	F	Wagoner	France	U. States	Edward Bopnnaffe	30 Jul 1829
ISLA, —, Mrs.	28	F	None	France	U. States	Luna	25 Jul 1825
J. R.	25	M	Merchant	America	U. States	Ladies Delight	9 Aug 1823
ISLAR, —, Mr.	29	M	None	France	U. States	Luna	25 Jul 1825
ISLE, Salamia	22	F	Sister-in-Law	Germany	United States	Elizabeth	4 Sep 1826
ISLER, Christian	22	M	Farmer	Germany	U. States	Isabella	10 Aug 1829
Christian	28	M	Farmer	Germany	U. States	Isabella	10 Aug 1829
ISLES, Christopher	28	M	Laborer	Ireland	United States	Mary	1 Jul 1829
ISLEY, —, Miss	15	F	lady	Ireland	U. States	Brown	11 Jan 1825
ISMON, Catherine	19	F		Germany	Pensylvania	Isabella	15 Sep 1828
Christian	10	M		Germany	Pensylvania	Isabella	15 Sep 1828
Jacob	2 6/12	M		Germany	Pensylvania	Isabella	15 Sep 1828
Joseph	8	M		Germany	Pensylvania	Isabella	15 Sep 1828
Joseph	42	M	Farmer	Germany	Pensylvania	Isabella	15 Sep 1828
Magdelene	18	F		Germany	Pensylvania	Isabella	15 Sep 1828
Teresa	40	F		Germany	Pensylvania	Isabella	15 Sep 1828
William	9	M		Germany	Pensylvania	Isabella	15 Sep 1828
ISRAEL, Moses S.	24	M	Mercht.	Great Britain		Governor Von Scholten	29 Jun 1827
S.	15	M	Merchant	England	U. States	Diana	12 Apr 1825
ISRAL, Sarah	30	M		Ressina	U. States	William Neilson	26 Jul 1828
ISRELLESUN, —, Miss	33					Weser	24 Jul 1820
ITHIER, John Babtist	30	M	Comb Maker	France	America	Hercules	5 Sep 1826
IVANS, David	21	M	Padler	Wales	America	Josephine	24 Jul 1826
Martin	34	M	Labourer	England	U. States	Comet	23 Aug 1828
Timothy	18	M	Farmer	Wales	America	Josephine	24 Jul 1826
IVER, Iloz	16	M	Bortour	France	U. States	Edward Bonaffe	23 Jul 1828
Joseph	13	M	Bortour	France	U. States	Edward Bonaffe	23 Jul 1828
IVERS, Howard	20	M	Merchant	U. States	U. States	James Cropper	17 Jun 1825
James	23	M	Labourer	Ireland	United States	Jubilee	12 May 1828
Michael	22	M	Labourer	Ireland	United States	Jubilee	13 Jul 1829
IVES, John	25	M	Merchant	U. States	U. States	Gertrude	12 Aug 1826
IVESON, Thomas	23	M	Sadler	Great Britian	United States	Isaac Hicks	22 May 1826
IVIES, B.	30	M	Farmer	Ireland	America	Mary	29 May 1827
H.	22	F		Ireland	America	Mary	29 May 1827
IVORY, Ann	1 6/12	F			Baltimore	Robert Fulton	8 Mar 1823
Christopher	58	M	Labourer		Baltimore	Robert Fulton	8 Mar 1823
Margaret	9/12	F			Baltimore	Robert Fulton	8 Mar 1823
Margaret	40	F			Baltimore	Robert Fulton	8 Mar 1823

NAMES OF PASSENGERS	AGE	SEX	OCCUPATIONS	COUNTRY TO WHICH THEY BELONG	COUNTRY THEY INTEND TO INHABIT	SHIPS/DATES OF ARRIVAL	
IVORY (cont'd)							
Mary	8	F			Baltimore	Robert Fulton	8 Mar 1823
Theresa	5 6/12	F			Baltimore	Robert Fulton	8 Mar 1823
IVY, Catherine	21	F	Servant	Ireland	United States	Henry Kneeland	7 Jun 1828
Danl.	20	M	Labourer	Ireland	United States	Henry Kneeland	7 Jun 1828
Patrick	23	M	Labourer	Ireland	United States	General Marion	6 Oct 1828
Sally	19	F	Servant	Ireland	United States	Henry Kneeland	7 Jun 1828
IWIN, Jno.	26	M	Blacksmith	Great Britain	United States	Comet	9 Aug 1822
IZDER, John	26	M	Laborer	England	United States	Earl of Liverpool	29 Sep 1823
IZOD, William H.	45		Baker	Great Brittan	United States	Cambria	11 Feb 1829
J..., Margaret	19	F		Ireland	America	Wilson	27 Nov 1826
J...T, Margaret	25	F	Servant	Ireland	New York	Atlantic	6 Oct 1828
J...ZÉ, Joseph	45	M	Merchant	Savannah, Geo.	United States	Henri IV	2 Oct 1828
JABBA, Frederick	18	M	Farmer	Ma...f...	U.S. America	Superior	18 Jun 1825
JABLEAU, Abby	2	F		Germany	U. States	Isabella	10 Aug 1829
Jean	8	M		Germany	U. States	Isabella	10 Aug 1829
Jean	36	M	Shoemaker	Germany	U. States	Isabella	10 Aug 1829
Matta	4	F		Germany	U. States	Isabella	10 Aug 1829
Matta	34	F		Germany	U. States	Isabella	10 Aug 1829
JACABUS, G.	22	M	Merchant	U. States	U. States	Prince Edward	25 Feb 1822
JACK, Agness	26	F		Great Britain	United States	Birmingham	15 Jun 1827
Andrew	21	M	Paper Maker	Britain	America	Camillus	9 Oct 1820
David	19		Spinner	Great Britain	United States	Camillus	12 Sep 1827
James	27	M	Weaver	Great Britain	United States	Birmingham	15 Jun 1827
John	19	M	Laborer	Scotland	America	Camillus	12 Sep 1822
John	20	M	Labourer	Scotland	United States	Mary & Susan	5 Aug 1828
Mary	9/12	F		Great Britain	United States	Birmingham	15 Jun 1827
Wm.	21	M	Shoemaker	Scotland	United States	Belmont	30 Aug 1828
JACKMAN, Jno.	26	M	Farmer	...	United States	Combine	20 Nov 1824
JACKS, Ann	40 6/12	F	None	America	America	Magnet	13 Nov 1821
James	55 3/12	M	Merchant	America	America	Magnet	13 Nov 1821
Lewis	28	M	Mercht.	U. States	U. States	Savannah	22 May 1827
JACKSON, —	25	M	Cook	U. States	U. States	Margaret Mercer	21 Dec 1825
—	25	M	Pedlar	St. John, N.B.	St. John, N.B.	St. Michaels	18 Jul 1826
—, Mr.	25	M	Merchant	G. Britain	Canada	Corinthian	29 Apr 1826
—, Mrs.	60	F		Scotland	New York	Joseph Hume	26 Oct 1829
...	1	F	Wife	...	Philadelphia	New Orleans	24 Aug 1827
A.	20		Servant	New Jersey	Halifax	America	28 Jul 1826
Abraham	20	M	Writer	Gt. Britain	U. States	Frances Henrietta	18 Apr 1825
Alexander	16	M	None	United States	United States	Pacific	24 Oct 1828
Alexr.	24	M	Mariner	U. States	U. States	Florida	25 Apr 1825
Ann	6			S... ...h	England	Great Britain	7 May 1827
Ann	6	F		Great Britain	United States	Freake	25 Jun 1827
Ann	8			England	United States	Hugh Johnson	11 Jun 1828
Ann	23	F	Servant	U. States	U. States	Canada	13 Oct 1825
Ann	25	F		Scotland		Ann	17 May 1822
Ann, Mrs.	52	F		Scotland		Ann	17 May 1822
Annabella	4	F	Child	Ireland	United States	Sarah Ann	6 Mar 1827
B.	28	M	Merchant	Leeds	G. Brittain	William Thompson	6 Sep 1822
Benjamin	26	M	Merchant	England	United States	Martha	17 Sep 1821
Benjn.	28	M	Merchant	England	U. States	Corinthian	20 Apr 1825
Bolton	40	M	Mercht.	U.S.	U.S.	George Canning	26 Aug 1829
C. H.				United States	U. States	Perseverance	25 Jun 1821
Charles	24	M	Cotton Spinner	England	United States	Montgomery	6 Mar 1829
Charles	30	M	Merchant	London	New York	Ann Maria	24 Feb 1824
Charles	44	M	Gentleman	Massachusetts	U. States	Columbia	7 Jul 1824
Charles	83	M	None	United States	United States	James Monroe	14 Dec 1820
Edmund P.	38	M	Merchant	Jamaica	Jamaica	Scio	24 Jul 1826
Edward	11	M		G. Britain	New York	Brighton	26 Mar 1827
Edward	17		Shipwright	England	United States	Corinthian	30 May 1828
Edward	22	M	Weaver	England	United States	Trident	31 Mar 1827
Edward	28	M	Farmer	Great Britain	United States	Leeds	29 Sep 1823
Edwin	21	M	None	United States	United States	James Monroe	14 Dec 1820
Eliz.	...2			England	United States	Hugh Johnson	11 Jun 1828
Eliz.	4			England	United States	Hugh Johnson	11 Jun 1828

NAMES OF PASSENGERS	AGE	SEX	OCCUPATIONS	COUNTRY TO WHICH THEY BELONG	COUNTRY THEY INTEND TO INHABIT	SHIPS/DATES OF ARRIVAL	
JACKSON (cont'd)							
Elizabeth	17	F	Spinster	United States	United States	James Monroe	12 Aug 1828
Elizabeth	26	F	None	Great Britian	United States	George Clinton	21 Oct 1826
Elizabeth	28	F	None	England	United States	Dalhouse Castle	6 Sep 1827
Frances	40	F	None	Massachusetts	U. States	Columbia	7 Jul 1824
Francis Gin	9	M	None	Great Britan	Great Britan	Columbia	11 Aug 1823
Fs.	22	M		Scotland		Ann	17 May 1822
Geo.	42		Farmer	England	United States	Hugh Johnson	11 Jun 1828
Geor.	50	M	...	Great Britain	United States	Cortes	18 Oct 1820
George	10			S... ...h	England	Great Britain	7 May 1827
George	37	M	British Commisioner	Great Britan	Great Britan	Columbia	11 Aug 1823
Georgiana	5	F	None	Great Britan	Great Britan	Columbia	11 Aug 1823
H.	28	M	Merchant	U. States	U. States	Atlantic	26 Aug 1820
Hamen	35	M	Merchant	Great Britain	United States	Milton	21 Mar 1828
Hannah	20	F	None	Great Britain	United States	Cortes	18 Oct 1820
Harriet	23	F				Lady of the Lake	23 Aug 1828
Harriet	41	M	Gentleman	Massachusetts	U. States	Columbia	7 Jul 1824
Henrietta Cordelia	8	F	None	Great Britan	Great Britan	Columbia	11 Aug 1823
Henry	22	M	Clark	Ireland	U. States	Combine	30 Nov 1825
Henry	36	M	Merchant	New York	New York	New York	14 Nov 1826
Isaac R.	24	M		America	America	Britannia	22 Jul 1829
J.	29	M	Mason	Great Britain	United States	Isaac Hicks	6 Dec 1827
J.	35	M	Teacher	England	United States	Hogarth	12 Oct 1829
James	...	M	None	Great Britain	U. States America	Columbia	15 Nov 1826
James	11	M	None	Great Britain	United States	Milton	21 Mar 1828
James	18 6/12	M	Tailor	Ireland	New York	Atlantic	6 Oct 1828
James	22	M	Shoemaker	Ireland	United States	Abigale	17 Jul 1822
James	22	M	Farmer	Great Britain	United States	Mary & Harriet	3 Jul 1829
James	23	M	House Carpenter	United States	United States	Charleston Packet	25 Jul 1821
James	30	M	Servant	Great Brittan	Great Brittain	Florida	17 May 1825
James	31		Clerk	England	England	General Starke	17 Jul 1827
James	35	M	Organ Maker	Great Britain	U. States America	Columbia	15 Nov 1826
James	36	M	Mechanic	England	U.S.	Panthea	22 Jul 1826
James	40	M	Taylor	Ireland	New York	Louisa	18 Apr 1827
James	53	M	Cabinet Maker	U. States	United States	Cambria	3 Jul 1829
Jane	17	F		U. States	U. States	Native	16 Nov 1825
Jane	25	F	Servant	Ireland	U. States	William & John	10 Jul 1824
Jane	30			S... ...h	England	Great Britain	7 May 1827
Jas.	30	M	Bookeeper	Gt. Britan	U. States	Magnet	9 Apr 1825
Jas.	30	M	Weaver	England	U. States	Thomas Ritchie	2 Jul 1827
Jas. T.	24	M	Merchant	U. States	U. States	Ductile	12 Apr 1825
Jeremy	18	M	Servant	New York		Milo	4 Jun 1827
Jno.	39	M	Farmer	England	U. States	Henry	13 Oct 1827
Joan	33	M	...	England	U. States	Chase	26 Jul 1824
John	3	M		Great Britain	United States	Freake	25 Jun 1827
John	4	M	None	Gt. Britain	U. States	Frances Henrietta	18 Apr 1825
John	23	M	Mechanic	Great Britain	United States	Mary & Harriet	3 Jul 1829
John	25	M	Farmer	Great Brit.	Ohio	Gov. Griswald	3 Jul 1820
John	25	M	Farmer	Ireland	United States	Abigale	17 Jul 1822
John	25	M	Farmer	England	United States	Jubilee	1 Oct 1828
John	25 6/12	M	Physicon	Great Briton	uncertain	Mount Vernon	29 Aug 1828
John	27	M	Painter			Lady of the Lake	23 Aug 1828
John	28	M	Clerk	Ireland	U. States	Margarett Scott	22 Aug 1827
John	30	M	Farmer	Ireland	United States	Nancy	16 Jul 1824
John	30	M	Gentleman	...	Philadelphia	New Orleans	24 Aug 1827
John	34	M		G. Britan	U. States	Geo. Canning	2 Sep 1828
John	35	M	Farmer	Great Britain	United States	Freake	25 Jun 1827
John	40 7/12	M	Merchant	Great Britain	Great Britain	Hector	8 Jan 1820
John	55	M	Farmer	Great Britain	N. York	Josephine	10 Dec 1825
John, Mr.	41	M	Glass Blower	United States	United States	Maria	29 Sep 1823
Joseph	27	M	Farmer	Great Britain	United States	Diana	6 Jul 1829
Joseph	54	M	Mariner	United States	United States	Florida	23 Aug 1825
Lucy	9	F		England	United States	Cosmo	21 Aug 1828
Lydia	26	F	Wife	...	Philadelphia	New Orleans	24 Aug 1827

JACKSON (cont'd)

NAMES OF PASSENGERS	AGE	SEX	OCCUPATIONS	COUNTRY TO WHICH THEY BELONG	COUNTRY THEY INTEND TO INHABIT	SHIPS/DATES OF ARRIVAL
M.	27	M				Hibernia 15 Aug 1820
Margaret	24	F		Ireland	United States	Nancy 16 Jul 1824
Mary	2			England	United States	Hugh Johnson 11 Jun 1828
Mary	20	F	Paper Maker	Ireland	U. States	Margarett Scott 22 Aug 1827
Mary	22	M	Machinist	England	United States	Montgomery 6 Mar 1829
Mary	24	F	None	Great Britain	United States	Mary & Harriet 3 Jul 1829
Mary	27	F	...	...	...	Meteor 16 Aug 1824
Mary	30	F	Spinster	Gt. Britain	U. States	Frances Henrietta 18 Apr 1825
Mary	30	F	None	Great Britian	United States	George Clinton 21 Oct 1826
Mary	45	F	None	Great Britain	United States	Cortes 18 Oct 1820
Mary, Mrs.	35	F	None	Great Britain	United States	Nestor 3 Nov 1820
Mary A.	1	F	None	Great Britain	United States	Cortes 18 Oct 1820
Mary Ann	15	F	None	Great Britain	United States	Cortes 18 Oct 1820
Mathew	34	M	Merchant	Great Britain	United States	Atlantic 3 Dec 1821
Matthew	26	M	Merchant	Great Britain	United States	Leeds 29 Sep 1823
May	20	F	Servant	Ireland	N. York	Trusty 12 Sep 1828
Peter	37	M	...	Great Britain	United States	Cortes 18 Oct 1820
R.	20	M	Land Surveyor	Ireland	United States	Asia 29 Jul 1829
R.	22	M	Merchant	Gt. Britain	Canada	Baltic 11 Apr 1825
Racheal	24	F	Lady	U. States	U. States	Atlantic 26 Aug 1820
Ralph	5	M		Great Britain	United States	Freake 25 Jun 1827
Rebecca	3	F	None	Great Britain	United States	Leeds 29 Sep 1823
Rebecca	23	F	None	Great Britain	United States	Leeds 29 Sep 1823
Richard	29	M	Farmer	England	U.N. States	Jane 7 Oct 1826
Riddle Alexand.	3	M	None	Great Britan	Great Britan	Columbia 11 Aug 1823
Robert	25	M	Shoemaker	Great Britain	United States	Roman 10 May 1828
Robert	26	M	Merchant	England		Reuben & Eliza 21 Aug 1820
Robert	29	M	Farmer	Great Britian	United States	George Clinton 21 Oct 1826
Robt.	37	M	Labourer	U. States	U. States	Robt. Reade 12 Apr 1825
Robt.	45	M	Farmer	Great Britain	United States	Albion 18 Feb 1823
S. H.	45	M	Merchant	Great Britain	United States	Orbit 31 Aug 1822
Samuel	21	M	Farmer	Great Britain	United States	Illinois 9 Oct 1820
Samuel	24	M	Nail Maker	Ashton Under Line	United States	Dalhousie Castle 27 Jul 1826
Samuel	38	M	Surgeon	U. States	U. States	Jasper 17 Jul 1826
Sarah	...	F	None	Great Britain	U. States America	Columbia 15 Nov 1826
Sarah	1/12	F	None	Great Britain	United States	Leeds 29 Sep 1823
Sarah	4	F	None	England	United States	Dalhouse Castle 6 Sep 1827
Sarah	18	F	None	Great Britain	United States	Cortes 18 Oct 1820
Sarah	19	M	Servant	England	United States	Cambria 3 Jul 1829
Sarah	21	F	None	Great Britain	United States	Leeds 29 Sep 1823
Sarah	22	F	None	Great Britain	America	Hannibal 12 Oct 1826
Sarah	27	F		Great Britain	United States	Freake 25 Jun 1827
Sarah	30	F		England	United States	Amelia 20 Aug 1829
Sarah	35	F	None	Great Britain	U. States America	Columbia 15 Nov 1826
Thomas	2	M		Great Britain	United States	Freake 25 Jun 1827
Thomas	5	M	Farmer	Ireland	United States	Nancy 16 Jul 1824
Thomas	21	M	T...	...	U. States	New Orleans 24 Aug 1827
Thomas	21	M	Farmer	England	United States	Jubilee 12 May 1828
Thomas	33	M	Silk Manufact.	England	United States	Amelia 20 Aug 1829
Thomas	48	M	Labourer	England	America	Sarah 18 Aug 1829
Thos.	25		Labourer	Rochester, England	Great Britain	Franklin 22 Jun 1827
Thos.	26	M	Farmer	Great Britain	United States	Mary & Harriet 3 Jul 1829
Thos. W.	30	M	Merchant	Gt. Britain	U. States	Frances Henrietta 18 Apr 1825
Timothy	53 7/12	M	Gentleman	Great Britain	Great Britain	Venus 8 Sep 1820
W.	21	M				Hibernia 15 Aug 1820
W.	42	M	Labourer	Scotland	United States	Morning Star 25 Jun 1822
William	2	M	None	Gt. Britain	U. States	Frances Henrietta 18 Apr 1825
William	30	M	Merchant	Ireland	Ireland	Helicon 3 Aug 1826
William	54	M	Merchant	U. States	U. States	Panthea 22 Nov 1826
William C.	28	M	Gentleman	England	England	Brittannia 28 Feb 1827
Willm.	39	M	Mechanic	Scotland	United States	Concordia 25 Aug 1827
Wm.	19	M	Labourer	Great Britain	U. States America	Maria 22 May 1822
Wm.	19	M	Labourer	England	United States	Essex 23 May 1828

NAMES OF PASSENGERS	AGE	SEX	OCCUPATIONS	COUNTRY TO WHICH THEY BELONG	COUNTRY THEY INTEND TO INHABIT	SHIPS/DATES OF ARRIVAL	
JACKSON (cont'd)							
Wm.	24	M	Wheelwright			Lady of the Lake	23 Aug 1828
Wm.	26	F	Currier	England	U.S. States	Splendid	14 Aug 1829
Wm.	31	M	Dyer	England	United States	Dalhouse Castle	6 Sep 1827
Wm.	45	M	Farmer	England	America	Manhattan	21 Sep 1822
Wm.	60	M	Merchant	New York	United States	Hogarth	12 Oct 1829
Wm., Mr.	27		Merchant	England	G.B.	Pacific	24 May 1824
JACKY, Cristien	21	M	Weaver	France	America, U.N.S.	Great Britain	3 Aug 1829
JACOB, Cathr.	20	F		France	United States	Cavalier	25 Jul 1828
Celestin	23	M	Watchmaker	Suisse	United States	Montano	5 May 1828
E. C. L.	27	M	Mercht.	France	U. States	London	13 Sep 1824
Erchin	71	M	Labourer	France	United States	Cavalier	25 Jul 1828
Ewa.	22	M	Labourer	Great Britain	United States	Penelope	11 Jun 1827
Francoise	9	F		France	United States	Cavalier	25 Jul 1828
Hy.	9		Farmer	Ireland	U. States	Schuylkill	22 Aug 1825
Hy.	12		Farmer	Ireland	U. States	Schuylkill	22 Aug 1825
Isaac	26	M	Labourer	Switzerland	United States	Eliza Grant	18 Aug 1826
Jacob	26	M	Tailor	England	New York	Hudson	20 Nov 1828
Jean	25	F		France	United States	Cavalier	25 Jul 1828
Joseph	22	M		France	United States	Cavalier	25 Jul 1828
Lewis	20	M	Gentleman	G. Britain	U. States	Loire	8 Sep 1820
Maria	14	F		France	United States	Cavalier	25 Jul 1828
Peter	40	M	Farmer	Switzerland	America	Bayard	15 Dec 1828
William S.	48	M	Physician	St. Croix	St. Croix	Ludwig	10 Aug 1825
Wm.	23	M	Merchant	U. States	U. States	Canada	13 Oct 1825
JACOBS, —, Madam	18	F		France	West Indies	Adonis	29 Sep 1823
C...h...	22 5/12	M	Farmer	Switzerland	U. States	France	26 Jun 1828
David	29	M	Tailor	England	New York	Chelsea	16 May 1828
Jerh.	32	M	Merchant	U. States	U. States	Nile	11 Jul 1822
Jno.	28	M	Merchant	England	Demerara	Jane	9 Mar 1824
John	30	M	Merchant	England		Cuba	3 Jan 1823
Louis	26	M	Lawyer	France	West Indies	Adonis	29 Sep 1823
Lyon	14	M		England	U.S.A.	Hudson	21 Aug 1829
Saml.	33	M	Mercht.	Camden	U.S.	Esther	9 May 1825
Simon G.	23	M	Merchant	St. Thomas	St. Thomas	Monroe	18 May 1827
Solomon	10		Gentleman	England	England	Hudson	18 Jun 1825
JACOBSON, Swen	53	M	Farmer	Norway	United States	Salem	31 Aug 1829
JACOBUS, Giles	27	M	Merchant	U. States	U. States	Nile	12 May 1823
JACOBY, A.	19	M	Merchant	Prussian	U. States	Minerva	18 Oct 1828
JACOT, Edw. H.	17	M	Gent.	America	America	Napoleon	26 May 1828
William	25	M	Merchant	U. States	U. States	Napolean	26 Sep 1828
JACOX, William	55	M	Farmer	State New York	United States	Sarah G.	15 Aug 1827
JACQU...MANT, Victor	25	M	Physician	France	France	Cadmus	9 Dec 1826
JACQUE, Josephine	29	F		Paris	Philadelphia	Falcon	10 Sep 1823
JACQUED, Keiper	32	M	Farmer	Germany	United States	Virginia	31 May 1828
Seebale	27	M	Farmer	Germany	United States	Virginia	31 May 1828
JACQUEMONT, F.	28	M	Merchant	Port au Prince	Port au Prince	Artibonite	9 Sep 1826
V.	20	M	Gentleman	Havana	U. States	Artibonite	2 Jul 1827
JACQUENET, Francis	30	M	Farmer	France	United States	American	27 Aug 1827
Hermoine	29	F	Farmer	France	United States	American	27 Aug 1827
JACQUES, M.	21	M	Merchant	Bristol	New York	Cosmo	25 Sep 1827
JACQUIMIN, Auguste	40	M	Servant to Mr. Harper	France	France	Bayard	30 Oct 1820
Prosper	18	M	Servant to Mr. Harper	France	France	Bayard	30 Oct 1820
JADD, John	19	M	Doctor			Superb	18 Jul 1820
JADWOOD, James	43	M	Seaman	N. York	N. York	St. Helena	18 Feb 1823
*Invalid from the U.S. Ship Cayenne, to be received in the Maine Hospital							
JAEGGE, —	26	M	Weaver	Brattain		L'Esperance	6 Sep 1828
JAFFRAY, James	29	M		G. Brittain	U. States	Cincinnatus	2 Oct 1822
James	40	M	Merchant	England	New York	Brighton	24 Aug 1827
John	35	M	Merchant	Great Britain	Great Britain	Martha	25 Nov 1820
JAFFREY, Alexr.	21	M	Tailor	Paisley, Renfrew [County]	New York	Hero	19 May 1828
*to follow his occupation							
JAGGER, Geo.	25	M		England		Ann	17 May 1822
Joseph	23	M	Mercht.	Yorkshire	N. York	Manhattan	21 May 1821

628

NAMES OF PASSENGERS	AGE	SEX	OCCUPATIONS	COUNTRY TO WHICH THEY BELONG	COUNTRY THEY INTEND TO INHABIT	SHIPS/DATES OF ARRIVAL	
JAGGERN, Chrs. ...	20	M	baker	Germany	New York	Constitution	20 Aug 1825
JAGGERS, Charles	35	M	Moulder	England	Pittsburg	Curler	7 Jul 1827
JAGGI, Elisabeth	38	F	Farmer	United States	United States	Montano	13 Jan 1826
JAGRENESS, Isaac	26	M	Tailor	Scotland	U. States	General Graham	9 May 1827
JAHNCKE, Fredricke	40	M	Merchant	Germany	U. States	Canada	8 Jun 1826
JAHNEST, Terietis	28	M	Farmer	Germany	United States	Oxford	14 Aug 1828
JAIGEN, John	28	M	Laborer	Gt. Britain		Dalhouse Castle	13 May 1828
JAINON, Peter	55	M	Merchant	French		Friendship	26 Feb 1820
JAIRSON, John	17	M	Farmer	G. Britain	U. States	St. George	7 Jun 1828
JAKES, C.	4 2/12	M		England	United States	Acasta	25 Sep 1827
John	6	M		England	United States	Acasta	25 Sep 1827
John	22	M	stocking Maker	Great Britain		Olive Branch	9 Oct 1829
John	30	M	Mechanic	Ireland		Venus	11 Aug 1820
John	31	M	Glass Manufacturer	England	United States	Acasta	25 Sep 1827
Joseph	24	M	Stocking weaver	Great Britain		Olive Branch	9 Oct 1829
Sarah	20	F	Dress Maker	Great Britain		Olive Branch	9 Oct 1829
JALAMAU, Francis	28	M	Marriner	America	America	Trafalgar	18 Jan 1828
JAMBOURH,							
Frederick	16 3/12	M	Farmer	Switzerland	America	Henry	17 May 1828
George	43 5/12	M	Farmer	Switzerland	America	Henry	17 May 1828
Madeline	5 8/12	F	Farmer	Switzerland	America	Henry	17 May 1828
Margaret	8 4/12	F	Farmer	Switzerland	America	Henry	17 May 1828
Margaret	44	F	Farmer	Switzerland	America	Henry	17 May 1828
JAMEISON, Jno.	30	M	Merchant	Great Britain	Great Britain	John Jay	8 May 1828
JAMERSON, Wm.		M	Merchant	Scotland	U. States	Martha	19 May 1823
JAMES, —, Miss	20	F		England	England	Desdemonia	9 Jun 1825
—, Mr.	25	M	Merchant	Dublin	U. States	Hibernia	26 Oct 1826
—, Mr.	60	M	Merchant	England	England	Desdemonia	9 Jun 1825
—, Mrs.	35	F		England	U. States	Diana	30 Apr 1824
Aaron	29	M	Merchant	Ireland	U. States	Concordia	11 Jun 1823
Ann	4	F		Wales	New York	Eliza Grant	29 Aug 1829
Ann	14	F				Reuben & Eliza	21 Aug 1820
Ann	22	M	None	U. States	U. States	Hope & Hannah	28 Mar 1827
Ann	31	F	None	Wales	United States	Mentor	28 Apr 1824
Benjamin	25	M	Farmer	Ireland	America	Dublin Packet	9 Oct 1820
Caroline	2	F	None	England	New York	America	1 Aug 1828
Cathr.	5	F	None	England	America	Meteor	21 Aug 1822
Charles	9/12	M	Son	England	United States	Cambria	8 Oct 1828
Charles	31	M	Merchant	United States	U. States	Pacific	5 Sep 1827
Chs. Needham	28	M	Surgeon	England	United States	Trident	30 Sep 1826
Columbus	23	M	Mariner	Baltimore	Baltimore	Rebecca & Sally	17 May 1825
David	9	M	None	Ireland	Uitica, U.S.	Angelica	18 Aug 1823
Ed. K.	22	M	None	G. Bt.	G. Bt.	Canada	13 Oct 1825
Edward	32	M		England	U. States	Cincinnatus	24 May 1821
Edward	40	M	Gentleman	England	England	Savannah	10 Jan 1828
Edward, Mr.	38	M	Merchant	Gt. Britain	Gt. Britain	Pacific	22 May 1826
Edwd.	24	M	Miner	Gt. Britain	U. States	Atlantic	17 May 1828
Eliza	6	F	None	England	New York	America	1 Aug 1828
Eliza	24	F		England	U. States	Mary	24 Jun 1824
Elizabeth	2	F	None	Wales	United States	Mentor	28 Apr 1824
Elizabeth	2	F		U. States	U. States	Nassau	13 Aug 1825
Elizabeth	40	F		England	England	Tontine	1 Jun 1826
Evan	35	M	Farmer	Wales	United States	Mentor	28 Apr 1824
Francis	56	M	Labour	U. States	U. States	Nassau	13 Aug 1825
Garretson	12	M	Labour	U. States	U. States	Nassau	13 Aug 1825
Geo. Francis	40	M	...	Gt. Britain	United States	Crisis	13 Nov 1824
Georgiana	14	F	Lady	England	Barbadoes	Jupiter	27 Jun 1828
Hugh	3	M		Wales	New York	Eliza Grant	29 Aug 1829
J.	27	M	Mechanic	England	U. States	Hanover	12 Oct 1822
James	20	M	Merchant	U. States	U. States	Fabius	30 Aug 1827
James	30	M	None	England		Marchioness	13 May 1828
James E.	36	M	Farmer	England	America	Meteor	21 Aug 1822
Jesse	3	M	Son	England	United States	Cambria	8 Oct 1828
John	7/12	M	None	Ireland	Uitica, U.S.	Angelica	18 Aug 1823
John	1	M		Wales	New York	Eliza Grant	29 Aug 1829
John	5	M	None	Wales	United States	Mentor	28 Apr 1824
John	20	M	Servant	Upper Canada	Upper Canada	Essex	24 Aug 1829
John	45	M	Laborer	England	United States	Indian Chief	16 Aug 1822
John A.	18	M	Merchant	England	America	Manhattan	23 May 1822

NAMES OF PASSENGERS	AGE	SEX	OCCUPATIONS	COUNTRY TO WHICH THEY BELONG	COUNTRY THEY INTEND TO INHABIT	SHIPS/DATES OF ARRIVAL	
JAMES (cont'd)							
John Pierre	4/12	M		U. States	U. States	Nassau	13 Aug 1825
Juba	8	F	None	England	New York	America	1 Aug 1828
Lydia	3	F	None	England	America	Meteor	21 Aug 1822
Lydia	34	F	None	England	America	Meteor	21 Aug 1822
Margaret	5	F	None	Ireland	Uitica, U.S.	Angelica	18 Aug 1823
Margaret	25	F		England	England	Tontine	1 Jun 1826
Marth	6	F		Wales	New York	Eliza Grant	29 Aug 1829
Martha	44	F		Wales	New York	Eliza Grant	29 Aug 1829
Mary	13	F		Wales	New York	Eliza Grant	29 Aug 1829
Mary	28	F		U. States	United States	Sarah G.	15 May 1828
Mary	30	F	Wife	England	United States	Cambria	8 Oct 1828
Mary	35	F	None	England	New York	America	1 Aug 1828
Mary Ann	1	F	None	England		Marchioness	13 May 1828
Mary Ann	7	F	None	England	New York	America	1 Aug 1828
N.	10	M		Great Brittain	United States	Sarah Ralston	27 Jan 1827
Nicholas	26	F	Labourer	Ireland	United States	Essex	23 May 1828
Peota	25	F	Servant	Upper Canada	Upper Canada	Essex	24 Aug 1829
Peter	26	M	Merchant	St. Croix	U. States	Chase	12 May 1826
Peter	29	M	Domestic	Denmark	Denmark	Chase	24 Aug 1822
Richard	7	M	None	Ireland	Uitica, U.S.	Angelica	18 Aug 1823
Richard	34	M	Taylor	Ireland	Uitica, U.S.	Angelica	18 Aug 1823
Sally	30	F	Labour	U. States	U. States	Nassau	13 Aug 1825
Sally Ann	4	F	Labour	U. States	U. States	Nassau	13 Aug 1825
Saloma	26	F				Belfast	28 Sep 1820
Samuel	5	M	Son	England	United States	Cambria	8 Oct 1828
Sarah	12	F		Wales	New York	Eliza Grant	29 Aug 1829
Sarah	33	F	None	Ireland	Uitica, U.S.	Angelica	18 Aug 1823
Silas Clemitson	27	M	Clerk	England	United States	Cambria	8 Oct 1828
Silas Josh.	7	M	Son	England	United States	Cambria	8 Oct 1828
Stephen	30	M	Gentleman	U. States	United States	Sarah G.	15 May 1828
Stephen	30	M	Merchant	U. States	U. States	Edwin	10 Feb 1829
T.	35	M	Carpenter	England	United States	Marmione	20 Nov 1821
Theador	26	M	None	Great Britain	United States	Washington	9 Apr 1821
Thomas	5	M	None	England	New York	America	1 Aug 1828
Thomas	30	M	Tailor	England	United States	Persia	19 Sep 1823
W.	40	M	Farmer	England	U. States	Diana	30 Apr 1824
W...	43	M	Shoe Maker	Wales	New York	Eliza Grant	29 Aug 1829
William	9	M		Wales	New York	Eliza Grant	29 Aug 1829
William	24	M	Clergyman	United States	United States	Dublin Packet	3 Sep 1822
William	43	M	Shoemaker	Wales	U. States	Eliza Grant	29 Aug 1829
William	50	M				Reuben & Eliza	21 Aug 1820
Wm.	5	M		England	U. States	Diana	30 Apr 1824
Wm.	30	M	Mechanic	England	U.S.A.	Peru	2 Oct 1827
Wm.	40	M	Cooper	...	United States	Minerva	30 Oct 1827
JAMESON, Andrew	34	F		Great Britain	United States	India	5 Sep 1827
James	28	M	Mariner	England	England	Franklin	26 May 1825
Jno.	30	M	Merchant	Scotland	Great Brittan	Florida	17 May 1825
John	40	M	Farmer	Ireland	America	Wilson	27 Nov 1826
John	42	M	Merchant	Gt. Britain	Canada	Manchester	15 Apr 1828
Margret	18	F	Servant	Ireland	United States	Carolina Ann	14 May 1827
Mille	50	M	Weaver	Scotland	United States	St. John	5 Oct 1829
Richd.	1	M	None	Great Britain	United States	Friends	13 Jun 1825
William	16	M	Labourer	Ireland	United States	Carolina Ann	14 May 1827
Wm.	30	M	Mariner	U. States	U. States	Emma	25 Oct 1825
JAMIES..., Mary	11		Laboring Class		United States	Atlantic	2 Apr 1827
JAMIESON, Adam	20	M	Farmer	Scotland	America	Friends	28 Sep 1822
Adam	29	M	Clerk	Great Britain	United States	Friends	13 Jun 1825
Ann	18	F	Dressmaker	Ireland	New York	Louisa	20 Jul 1826
Ann	24	F	his wife [Walter]	Great Britain	United States	Rosina	28 May 1827
Ann	30	F	None	Great Britain	United States	Friends	13 Jun 1825
Elisa	30	F	Waiter	U. States	U. States	Ranger	29 Jul 1824
James	6	M	None	Scotland	U. States	Camillus	27 Jun 1826
Jane	4/12	F	Daughter	Ireland	New York	Louisa	20 Jul 1826
Lettias	13	F	None	Scotland	U. States	Camillus	27 Jun 1826
Margaret	24 10/12	F	Wife	Ireland	New York	Louisa	20 Jul 1826
Mary	35	F	None	Scotland	U. States	Camillus	27 Jun 1826
Mary Ann	11	F	None	Scotland	U. States	Camillus	27 Jun 1826
Robert	8	M	None	Scotland	U. States	Camillus	27 Jun 1826

NAMES OF PASSENGERS	AGE	SEX	OCCUPATIONS	COUNTRY TO WHICH THEY BELONG	COUNTRY THEY INTEND TO INHABIT	SHIPS/DATES OF ARRIVAL	
JAMIESON (cont'd)							
Robert	25	M	Farmer	Great Britian	United States	Isaac Hicks	22 May 1826
Robt.	2	M	None	Great Britain	United States	Friends	13 Jun 1825
Thomas	24 10/12	M	Farmer	Ireland	New York	Louisa	20 Jul 1826
Thos.	29	M	Farmer	Great Britain	United States	Friends	13 Jun 1825
Walter	26	M	Stone cutter	Great Britain	United States	Rosina	28 May 1827
William	17	M	Clerk	Great Britain	United States	Friends	13 Jun 1825
JAMISEN, H.	18	M	Mechanic	England	U. States	Acasta	21 Jan 1825
JAMISON, Alexander	24	M	Weaver	Great Britain	United States	Manchester	12 Aug 1829
Andrew	26	M	Type Founder	Irereland	America	Carolina Ann	20 Jun 1825
Ann	20 4/12	F	Seamstress	Ireland	United States	Atlantic	21 Jul 1827
Dorathy D.	21	F	None	Gt. Brittian	Gt. Brittian	Manchester	17 Aug 1825
Duncan	28	M	Weaver	Scotland	U. States	Hector	18 Apr 1825
Evan	45	M	Mechanic	Norway	America	Wm. Tell	22 Sep 1828
James	38	M	Farmer	Scotland	U. States	Ben Lomond	3 Apr 1823
John	22	M	Labourer	Ireland		Robert Fulton	4 Jun 1828
John A.	26	M	Mariner	Scotland	U.S. of America	Camillus	16 Apr 1822
Mary	31	F		Ireland	United States	Mary	1 Jul 1829
Mary Ann	16 8/12	F	House Keeper	Irereland	America	Carolina Ann	20 Jun 1825
Oliver	19	M		Norway	America	Wm. Tell	22 Sep 1828
W.	33	M	Merchant	England	U. States	Pocahontas	18 May 1825
Wm.	1 9/12	M		Ireland	United States	Atlantic	21 Jul 1827
JAMISSON, James	26	M	Merchant	Scotland	United States	William Byrnes	15 Aug 1826
JAMISTON, Bridget	30	F	Spinster	Ireland	America	Dublin Packet	9 Oct 1820
JAMITON, Mary	65	F		Scotland	U. States	Camillus	17 Sep 1823
JAMMISON, ...n	35		Labourer	St. John	U. States	Lady Hunter	5 Jul 1823
Saml.	30		Labourer	St. John	U. States	Lady Hunter	5 Jul 1823
JAMROSE, Daniel				Virginia	Virginia	Meteor	19 Aug 1829
JANDON, —, Dr.	23	M	Surgeon U.S. Navy	United States	United States	India	24 Mar 1826
JANE, Hart	22	M	Labourer	Ireland	United States	Aurelia	7 Jun 1826
Maria	3/12	M	None	N. York	U. States	Ambuscade	6 Oct 1821
JANES, R.	28	M	Mercht.	England	U. States	Hiram	4 Sep 1824
JANETT, Joseph, Junr.	28	M	Merchant	Gt. Britain	Gt. Britain	Canada	4 Oct 1824
Joseph, Junr.	30	M	Merchant	G. Bt.	G. Bt.	Canada	13 Oct 1825
Noah	30	M	Merchant	U. States	U. States	Worromontogus	23 Jun 1823
JANICKE, F.	35	M	Merchant	United States	United States	Maria Elizabeth	2 Sep 1822
JANIE, Andr. Foster	20	M	Merchant	United States	United States	White Oak	30 Oct 1820
JANKEL, D.	50	M	Merchant	Jerusalem	Jerusalem	Venus	8 May 1826
JANNCEY, Joseph	18	M	Student Medicine	U.S. America	State New York	Columbia	24 Aug 1825
JANNER, Johann Wilhelim	21	M	Weaver	Germany	America	Falcon	28 Aug 1828
JANSAN, Georges	20	M	Farmer	Germany	United States	Oxford	14 Aug 1828
Jacob	22	M	Farmer	Germany	United States	Oxford	14 Aug 1828
JANSON, Henry	29	M	Laborer	Holland	U.N. States	Franklin	20 May 1828
JAQUES, Manuel	40	M	Merchant	Spain	Spain	Margaret	12 May 1823
William	19	M	Merchant	England	England	Earl of Liverpool	20 Aug 1825
JAQUET, Adeline	22	F	Servant	New York	New York	Frances Henrietta	25 Aug 1825
JARDON, J.	32	M	Merchant	Port Au Prince	Port Au Prince	Jean Baptist	5 Mar 1827
JARELS, Euslein	9	M		England		Fame	9 Dec 1826
Sereh	45	F	Dress Maker	England		Fame	9 Dec 1826
JARRATT, Jos.	26	M				Ann Maria	29 Nov 1821
JARRE, Louis	34	M	Merchant	France	U. States	Victoria	9 Sep 1828
JARREN, Ann	24	F	None	Great Brittan	U. States	Gem	26 Jul 1827
Mary	2	F	None	Great Brittan	U. States	Gem	26 Jul 1827
Thos.	25	M	Laborer	Great Brittan	U. States	Gem	26 Jul 1827
JARRETT, Henry	27	M	Baker	Ireland	New York	Atlantic	8 May 1828
JARRIT, John J.	30	M	Gentleman	England	England	Panthia	7 Feb 1822
JARVEY, John	22	M	Farmer	Scotland	United States	Samuel Robertson	5 Oct 1827
JARVIS, Edward	25	M	Farmer	England	United States	Jubilee	1 Oct 1828
Harriet M.	30	F	Lady	Saint John, N.B.	Saint John, N.B.	Sarah G.	28 Nov 1827
Hugh	27	M	Laborer	Ireland	United States	Sarah G.	11 Jan 1828
Mary	21	F	None	England	United States	Jubilee	1 Oct 1828
Mary	56	F		Great Britain	United States	Freak	14 oct 1828
Richard	37	M	Labourer	G.B.	America	Pacific	13 Jan 1827
Thomas	30	M	Bricklayer	England	United States	Jubilee	4 Mar 1829
Walter	25	M	Schoolmaster	United States	United States	Freak	14 oct 1828
JASCUR, Robert	11	F				Splendid	14 Aug 1829

NAMES OF PASSENGERS	AGE	SEX	OCCUPATIONS	COUNTRY TO WHICH THEY BELONG	COUNTRY THEY INTEND TO INHABIT	SHIPS/DATES OF ARRIVAL	
JASPAR, C.	25	M	Merchant	New York	U. States	Maria Elizabeth	9 Jun 1826
JASQUER, Y.	25	M	Merchant	Spain	U. States	Lucy Ann	6 Sep 1826
JASTAN, Tom	26	M	Coal miner	England	U.S. States	Splendid	14 Aug 1829
JATE, Elisabeth	14	F		Ireland	United States	Mary	1 Jul 1829
James	1	M	Laborer	Ireland	United States	Mary	1 Jul 1829
John	12	M	Laborer	Ireland	United States	Mary	1 Jul 1829
Mary Ann	5	F		Ireland	United States	Mary	1 Jul 1829
Mary Ann	37	F		Ireland	United States	Mary	1 Jul 1829
Rebecca	16	F		Ireland	United States	Mary	1 Jul 1829
William	2	M	Laborer	Ireland	United States	Mary	1 Jul 1829
William	52	M	Laborer	Ireland	United States	Mary	1 Jul 1829
JATHIM, Catherine	14	F	Farmer	Great Brit.	Ohio	Gov. Griswald	3 Jul 1820
Cristabella	41	F		Great Brit.	Ohio	Gov. Griswald	3 Jul 1820
John	21	M	Farmer	Great Brit.	Ohio	Gov. Griswald	3 Jul 1820
Joseph	20	M	Farmer	Great Brit.	Ohio	Gov. Griswald	3 Jul 1820
Pricilla	7	F		Great Brit.	Ohio	Gov. Griswald	3 Jul 1820
Samuel	12	M		Great Brit.	Ohio	Gov. Griswald	3 Jul 1820
Stephen	27	M	Farmer	Great Brit.	Ohio	Gov. Griswald	3 Jul 1820
JAUNERIER, John James, the Count's ...	32	M	...	...	...	Meteor	16 Aug 1824
JAUNTCHE, Peter	25	M	Merchant	France	U. States	Superb	9 Jul 1821
JAURIN, Owen	26	M	Labr.	Ireland	New York	Atlantic	8 May 1828
JAUROQUIA, C.	24	F		So. America	U. States	Eclipse	10 Jun 1823
N.	26	F		So. America	U. States	Eclipse	10 Jun 1823
JAVENS, Ann	8	F	None	Great Britain	United States	William Dawson	18 Jun 1827
Charles	17	M	Gardner	Great Britain	United States	William Dawson	18 Jun 1827
Edwd	4	M	None	Great Britain	United States	William Dawson	18 Jun 1827
Eliza	1	F	None	Great Britain	United States	William Dawson	18 Jun 1827
John	55	M	Gardner	Great Britain	United States	William Dawson	18 Jun 1827
Joseph	12	M	Gardner	Great Britain	United States	William Dawson	18 Jun 1827
Mary	6	F	None	Great Britain	United States	William Dawson	18 Jun 1827
Mary	42	F	None	Great Britain	United States	William Dawson	18 Jun 1827
Samuel	10	M	Gardner	Great Britain	United States	William Dawson	18 Jun 1827
Will	14	M	Gardner	Great Britain	United States	William Dawson	18 Jun 1827
JAVIN, L.	25	M		G. Britain	G. Britain	Brittania	17 Jul 1828
JAVIS, Eliza	3	M	None	N. York	U. States	Ambuscade	6 Oct 1821
Fransisco	1	M	None	N. York	U. States	Ambuscade	6 Oct 1821
John	3	M	None	N. York	U. States	Ambuscade	6 Oct 1821
JAY, Thomas	19		Gentleman	England	America	Florida	14 Oct 1829
JAYES, Thomas	21	M	Carpenter	England	New York	Lima	16 Mar 1829
JAYLER, John	25	M	Merchant	Scotland	Ama.	Expedition	19 May 1828
JAYNE, Charles	34		Mariner	U. States	Long Island	Ann Maria	31 Aug 1821
JE...INGS, ...	30	M	Farmer	Great Britian	United States	London	24 Jun 1823
JEACOCK, Ann	26	F	None	England	America	Francis & Henrietta	11 Jul 1823
Elizabeth	6	F	None	England	America	Francis & Henrietta	11 Jul 1823
Hannah	1	F	None	England	America	Francis & Henrietta	11 Jul 1823
Maria	2	F	None	England	America	Francis & Henrietta	11 Jul 1823
Mary Ann	4	F	None	England	America	Francis & Henrietta	11 Jul 1823
Thomas	26	M	Farmer	England	America	Francis & Henrietta	11 Jul 1823
Thos.	7	M	None	England	America	Francis & Henrietta	11 Jul 1823
JEAGER, Frederick	35	M	Merchant	Germany	to return to Germany	Aurora	1 May 1826
JEAGERS, John	37	M	Dyer	England	U.S.A.	Peru	2 Oct 1827
JEAN, Catherine	23	F				Henri IV	17 May 1828
Fredic.	22	M	Weaver			Henri IV	17 May 1828
Joseph	35	M	Merchant	France	to return to France	Aurora	1 May 1826
JEANIAN, Walter	30	M	Mariner	United States	United States	Edward	21 Apr 1821
JEANJAQUET, Chs. Frs.	30	M	Merchant	Neuchatel in Switzerland	U. States	Wyoming	21 Jan 1828
JEARRAK, David, M.D.	39		Surgeon	England		Hudson	5 Apr 1826
JEENS, John R.	28	M	Tailor	England	United States	Cosmo	21 Aug 1828

NAMES OF PASSENGERS	AGE	SEX	OCCUPATIONS	COUNTRY TO WHICH THEY BELONG	COUNTRY THEY INTEND TO INHABIT	SHIPS/DATES OF ARRIVAL	
JEENS (cont'd)							
Mary A.	9	F		England	United States	Cosmo	21 Aug 1828
Mary A.	26	F		England	United States	Cosmo	21 Aug 1828
Wm. M.	8	M		England	United States	Cosmo	21 Aug 1828
JEFFER, Catharine	27	F	Farmer	France	France	Sully	15 Jul 1829
Christina	22	F	Farmer	France	France	Sully	15 Jul 1829
Godfrey	29	M	Farmer	France	France	Sully	15 Jul 1829
JEFFEREY, Elizabeth	30	F	None	Great Britain	United States	Ganges	26 Oct 1826
James	3	M	None	Great Britain	United States	Ganges	26 Oct 1826
Richd.	5	M	None	Great Britain	United States	Ganges	26 Oct 1826
Robert	1	M	None	Great Britain	United States	Ganges	26 Oct 1826
Robert	32	M	Farmer	Great Britain	United States	Ganges	26 Oct 1826
Sally	6	F	None	Great Britain	United States	Ganges	26 Oct 1826
JEFFERSON, Eliza	13	F		Great Britain	Albany	Zodiac	14 Jun 1822
Eliza	26	F	Farmer	England	United States	Essex	23 May 1828
Elizabeth	52	F		Great Britain	Albany	Zodiac	14 Jun 1822
Richard	11	M		Great Britain	Albany	Zodiac	14 Jun 1822
Robert	60	M	Shoemaker	Great Britain	Albany	Zodiac	14 Jun 1822
Robert, Jr.	14	M	Shoemaker	Great Britain	Albany	Zodiac	14 Jun 1822
Wm.	24	M	Farmer	England	United States	Essex	23 May 1828
JEFFERY, Barbara	1/2			England	England	Thames	25 Oct 1821
Edward	3			England	England	Thames	25 Oct 1821
Grace	...	F	...	Ireland	United States	General Putnam	20 Jun 1825
Marren	19	M	Mariner	U. States	U. States	Florida	25 Apr 1825
Mary Ann	22			England	England	Thames	25 Oct 1821
Stephen	23		Farmer	England	England	Thames	25 Oct 1821
William	26		Laborer	Ireland	New York	Lady Hunter	19 Oct 1826
Wm.	...	M	...	Ireland	United States	General Putnam	20 Jun 1825
JEFFORD, Elizth.	22	M	Servant	England	U. States	Manhattan	12 Jun 1824
JEFFREY, Agnes	11	F		Scotland	United States	Camillus	9 May 1827
Ann	37	F		Scotland	United States	Camillus	9 May 1827
James	3	M		Scotland	United States	Camillus	9 May 1827
Janet	6	F		Scotland	United States	Camillus	9 May 1827
John	8	M		Scotland	United States	Camillus	9 May 1827
John	33			England	United States	Hugh Johnson	11 Jun 1828
William	12	M		Scotland	United States	Camillus	9 May 1827
Willim.	37	M	Gardner	St. John, N.B.	St. John, N.B.	St. Michael	28 Feb 1826
JEFFRY, John	37	M		Scotland	United States	Camillus	9 May 1827
Mary	15	F		Scotland	United States	Camillus	9 May 1827
JEFFY, Ann	3	F		Great Britain	United States	Grecian	24 Sep 1828
Myria	1	F		Great Britain	United States	Grecian	24 Sep 1828
Susan	29	F	Spinner	Great Britain	United States	Grecian	24 Sep 1828
Wm.	6	M		Great Britain	United States	Grecian	24 Sep 1828
JEHNSON, Robt., J.	40	M	Trader	Scotland	Gt. Britain	Friends	29 Apr 1822
JEHORICH, Chs.	24	M	Merchant	N. York	U. States	Lyon	5 Jul 1825
JEHOVITH, —, Mrs.	22	F		Gibraltar	U. States	Bordeaux	26 Nov 1824
Chas.	24	M	Mariner	Gibraltar	Gibraltar	Bordeaux	26 Nov 1824
Edward	5	M		Gibraltar	U. States	Bordeaux	26 Nov 1824
JEICUEL, Catherine	32	F	Spinster	Switzerland	United States	Andes	5 May 1828
Catherine	60	F	Spinster	Switzerland	United States	Andes	5 May 1828
Machqul	18	M	Farmer	Switzerland	United States	Andes	5 May 1828
JELLET, Thomas	22	M	Merchant	Ireland	United States	Fabius	4 Jun 1828
JELLIS, Jane	19	F	None			Amity	11 Sep 1820
Thos.	23	M	None			Amity	11 Sep 1820
JEMENEZ, Manuel, Don	24	M	Attached to the Mexican Legation	Mexico	United States	Mercid	21 Oct 1824
JEMMISON, Archib.	26	M	Cabinet Maker	Scotland	U.S.A.	Calliope	15 Aug 1827
JEMPERIER, Francis	27	M	Weaver	France	U. States	Sully	25 Jun 1828
JENBRAIT, Mariamne	23	F	Nurse	France	Louisiana	Sully	30 Oct 1827
JENCKER, Edwin T.	29	M	Supercargo	U. States	U.S.	Fame	22 Mar 1826
JENGER, Philipe	1	M	Farmer	Switzerland	United States	Olympia	12 Aug 1828
JENKIN, Juan	12	M	Boy	Cuba	Cuba	Franklin	14 Jul 1827
JENKINS, Aleander	45		Mariner	U. States	U. States	Maria	20 Jul 1820
Alexander	45		Farmer	Scotland	United States	Corinthian	30 May 1828
Amelia	1	F	None	Great Britain	United States	Fidelity	16 Oct 1820
Ann	5	F	None	Great Britain	United States	Fidelity	16 Oct 1820
Ann	11	F	None	England	United States	Oscar	24 Jul 1823
Ann	13	F	None	England	United States	Oscar	24 Jul 1823

NAMES OF PASSENGERS	AGE	SEX	OCCUPATIONS	COUNTRY TO WHICH THEY BELONG	COUNTRY THEY INTEND TO INHABIT	SHIPS/DATES OF ARRIVAL	
JENKINS (cont'd)							
Ann	35	F	None	Great Britain	United States	Fidelity	16 Oct 1820
Ann	44	F	None	England	United States	Oscar	24 Jul 1823
Betsey	2		Farmer	Scotland	United States	Corinthian	30 May 1828
Caroline	14	F		England	America	Plato	31 Oct 1829
Catharine	12	F	None	England	United States	Oscar	24 Jul 1823
Catharine	50	F		Wales	United States	Mount Vernon	9 Jun 1823
Cecil	2	F	None	England	United States	Oscar	24 Jul 1823
Charles	16	M		England	America	Plato	31 Oct 1829
Chester	13		Farmer	Scotland	United States	Corinthian	30 May 1828
David	13	M	None	England	United States	Oscar	24 Jul 1823
David	54	M	Mechanic	United States	United States	John Wells	22 Sep 1824
Edward	12	M		England	America	Plato	31 Oct 1829
Edward	20	M	Farmer	England	United States	Oscar	24 Jul 1823
Edward	47	M	Farmer	England	United States	Oscar	24 Jul 1823
Eliza	17	F		England	America	Plato	31 Oct 1829
Elizth.	10	F	None	England	United States	Oscar	24 Jul 1823
Fredk.	2	M		England	America	Plato	31 Oct 1829
George	1	M	None	England	United States	Oscar	24 Jul 1823
George	4	M	None	England	United States	Oscar	24 Jul 1823
Henry	6	M	None	Great Britain	United States	Fidelity	16 Oct 1820
Henry	42	M	Miner			Plato	31 Oct 1829
Ira	40	M	Merchant	U. States	U. States	Hesper	25 Apr 1828
James	21 11/12	M	Merchant	Great Britan	U. States	Carpenter	12 Aug 1828
James	24		Farmer			Amphion	31 May 1824
Jane	4	F	None	England	United States	Oscar	24 Jul 1823
Jane	6	F	None	England	United States	Oscar	24 Jul 1823
Jane	9		Farmer	Scotland	United States	Corinthian	30 May 1828
Jno.	25	M	Mariner	U. States	U. States	Florida	25 Apr 1825
John	12		Farmer	Scotland	United States	Corinthian	30 May 1828
John	16	M	None	Great Britain	United States	Fidelity	16 Oct 1820
John	16	M	Farmer	England	United States	Oscar	24 Jul 1823
John	37	M	...	Great Britain	United States	Fidelity	16 Oct 1820
John	43	M	Cooper	England	America	Plato	31 Oct 1829
John H.	6	M		England	America	Plato	31 Oct 1829
Joseph	20	M	Laborer	Ireland	United States	Belleville	13 Oct 1827
Joseph	23	M	Brazier	Great Britain	United States	Superior	31 Mar 1828
L., Miss	18	F	Matu maker	Gt. Britan	U. States	Earl of Liverpool	12 Apr 1825
M.	43	M	Merchant	Boston	N. Orleans	Eclipse	3 Aug 1824
Margaret	24	F	None	England	United States	Oscar	24 Jul 1823
Margaret	44	F	None	England	United States	Oscar	24 Jul 1823
Maria	19	F		England	America	Plato	31 Oct 1829
Marie	6/52	F	None	England	United States	Oscar	24 Jul 1823
Mary	6	F	None	England	United States	Oscar	24 Jul 1823
Mary	8	F	None	England	United States	Oscar	24 Jul 1823
Ostrand	8	M		England	America	Plato	31 Oct 1829
Rachael	11		Farmer	Scotland	United States	Corinthian	30 May 1828
Reuben	32	M	Mariner	United States	U. States	Rachel Ann	19 Oct 1827
Richd.	30	M	Merchant	England	New York	Amity	13 Sep 1821
Ruth	34		Farmer	Scotland	United States	Corinthian	30 May 1828
Sarah	43	F		England	America	Plato	31 Oct 1829
Thomas	11	M	None	England	United States	Oscar	24 Jul 1823
Thomas	28		Seaman	Rotherhith, E.	England	Packet	27 Aug 1822
William	4	M	None	Great Britain	United States	Fidelity	16 Oct 1820
William	4	M		England	America	Plato	31 Oct 1829
William	14		Farmer	Scotland	United States	Corinthian	30 May 1828
William	16	M	Farmer	England	United States	Oscar	24 Jul 1823
William	18	M	Farmer	England	United States	Oscar	24 Jul 1823
William	36	M		Great Brittan	U. States	Prince Leopold	2 Jul 1821
William	40	M	Farmer	Wales	United States	Mount Vernon	9 Jun 1823
JENKINSON, David	20	M	apprentice	Great Britain	United States	Diana	6 Jul 1829
John	19		Weaver	England	America	Sarah	18 Aug 1829
Mary	25	F	None	England	U. States	Montgomery	18 Oct 1828
Willm.	22		Weaver	England	America	Sarah	18 Aug 1829
JENNER, ...lyh.	23	M		Gt. Britain	P...	Betsey	18 Apr 1822
...nn	44			Gt. Britain	P...	Betsey	18 Apr 1822
Ann	9 2/12	F		Gt. Britain	P...	Betsey	18 Apr 1822
Charity	3 6/12	F		Gt. Britain	P...	Betsey	18 Apr 1822

NAMES OF PASSENGERS	AGE	SEX	OCCUPATIONS	COUNTRY TO WHICH THEY BELONG	COUNTRY THEY INTEND TO INHABIT	SHIPS/DATES OF ARRIVAL	
JENNER (cont'd)							
Charles	18	M	Farmer	Great Briton	uncertain	Mount Vernon	29 Aug 1828
Faith	16 4/12	F		Gt. Britain	P...	Betsey	18 Apr 1822
Hannah	11 4/12	F	None	Great Briton	uncertain	Mount Vernon	29 Aug 1828
Hope	14 1/12	F		Gt. Britain	P...	Betsey	18 Apr 1822
James	55	M	Farmer	Great Briton	uncertain	Mount Vernon	29 Aug 1828
John	18	M		Gt. Britain	P...	Betsey	18 Apr 1822
Mary	5 6/12	F		Gt. Britain	P...	Betsey	18 Apr 1822
Sarah	17	F	None	Great Briton	uncertain	Mount Vernon	29 Aug 1828
Sarah	19			Sussex, England		Cincinnatus	17 May 1823
Thos.	11 6/12	M		Gt. Britain	P...	Betsey	18 Apr 1822
Thos.	40	M	Farmer	Gt. Britain	P...	Betsey	18 Apr 1822
William	22 2/12	M	Farmer	Great Briton	uncertain	Mount Vernon	29 Aug 1828
William	30	M	Merchant	Great Britain	Savannah	James Cropper	14 Oct 1824
Wm.	32	M	Merchant	Great Britain	Great Britain	Columbia	24 Dec 1822
JENNERS, H. M.	29	M	Merchant	U. States	U. States	Tobasco	17 Aug 1825
JENNESTONE, Aaron	32	M	Collier	Great Britain	New Jersey	Zodiac	14 Jun 1822
JENNING, Joseph	25	M	Smith	England	U.S.	Acasta	11 May 1827
JENNINGS, Amelia	31	F	Seamstress	Great Britain	United States	Washington	22 Mar 1820
H.	16	M	Mariner	N. York	U. States	Jane	29 Jul 1823
John	27	M	Weaver	Ireland	U. States	Borneo	15 Apr 1828
John	30	M	Farmer	Ireland	United States	Samuel Robertson	9 Apr 1828
Jonah	54	M	Gentleman	U. States		Hudson	23 Jul 1828
Mathew	17	M	Farmer	England	United States	Cincinnatus	21 Nov 1821
Richard	23	M	Farmer	England	United States	Cincinnatus	21 Nov 1821
Richard	28	M	Law	Great Britain	United States	Columbia	9 Aug 1822
Thomas	15	M	Gardiner	England	Deleware	Indian Chief	19 Jun 1823
Thomas	26	M	Mechanic	Great Britain	United States	Washington	22 Mar 1820
Thos.	26	M	None	Great Britain	United States	Columbia	9 Aug 1822
JENNIS, Mariah	30	F	Servant	England	England	Tontine	1 Jun 1826
JEPHSON, William	40	M	Mercht.	United States	United States	Manchester	6 Dec 1825
JEPSON, Anna	5	F		England	America	Panthia	17 Sep 1821
Benjamin	32	M	Farmer	England	America	Panthia	17 Sep 1821
Edward	36	M	Weaver	Great Britain	United States	India	5 Sep 1827
Ellen	3	F		England	America	Panthia	17 Sep 1821
Ellen	26	F		England	America	Panthia	17 Sep 1821
Hannah	24	F		Great Britain	United States	India	5 Sep 1827
Rhoda	1	F		England	America	Panthia	17 Sep 1821
Saml.	1	M		Great Britain	United States	India	5 Sep 1827
Samuel	21	M	Merchant	U. States	U. States	Harriet	3 Mar 1828
JEQUE, Franois	30	M	Carpenter	Ireland	United States	Hannah Eliza	23 Sep 1826
JERAGO, Petro	38	M	Seaman	France		Enterprise	18 Sep 1820
JERGNOT, Charles	28	M	Merchant	United States	United States	Bayard	13 Nov 1823
JERIAHLOKE, Georg Heinrich, Mr.	44	M	Labourer	Hamburg	New York	Europa	12 Oct 1829
JERKERS, Wm.	25	M	Mechanic	U. States	U. States	Eliza Davidson	28 Jul 1828
JERMOCH, Louie	34	M	Merchant	Holland	U. States	Abby M.	7 Apr 1825
JERN, J.	1					Apollo	11 Jun 1828
JERN...G, James	30	M	Labourer			Hercules	25 Sep 1820
JEROME, J.	36	M	Servant	England	unknown	Robert Edwards	4 Jun 1824
JERRILS, H. B.	28	M	Seaman	U. States	U. States	Brothers	28 Apr 1823
JERRY, James	24	M		Gt. Britain	United States	Penelope	9 Sep 1828
JERT, Henry	20	M	f...	Germany	New York	Constitution	20 Aug 1825
JERVIS, Fanny	30	F	None	Gt. Britain	United States	Crisis	6 Apr 1825
Fanny	33	F		Switzerland	U. States	Robert Edward	2 Nov 1827
Mary	22 1/12	F	Domestic	England	United States	London	6 Feb 1829
William	24 3/12	M	Engineer	England	United States	London	6 Feb 1829
JESOP, Mary	40	F	Servant (free)	England	U. States	Little John	20 Aug 1822
JESS, Henrietta	32	F	Lady	United States	United States	Hanford	9 Oct 1829
William	6	M	Child	Great Britain	United States	Hanford	9 Oct 1829
JESSE, Henrietta	25	F	Lady	Great Brittain	St. John	Nancy	18 Jul 1821
John S.	30	M	Officer	Great Brittain	St. John	Nancy	18 Jul 1821
JESSERSIN, M. A.	26	M	Merchant	Curacoa	Curacoa	Independence	19 Aug 1825
JESSNER, Ann, Miss	23	F		St. Domingo	United States	Paquet des Cayes	26 May 1828
JESSOP, Arron	30	M	Merchant	G. Britain	U. States	Canada	19 Sep 1828
Thos.	35	M	Merchant	G. Britain	U. States	Canada	19 Sep 1828

NAMES OF PASSENGERS	AGE	SEX	OCCUPATIONS	COUNTRY TO WHICH THEY BELONG	COUNTRY THEY INTEND TO INHABIT	SHIPS/DATES OF ARRIVAL	
JESSOPP, Henry, Mr.	38	M	In his B. M. Customs	England	Canada	Cortes	23 Nov 1827
Henry, Mrs.	26	F		England	Canada	Cortes	23 Nov 1827
JESSUP, E.	28	M	Merchant	U. States	U. States	Emma	25 Feb 1826
JESUP, Wm.	60	M	Planter	U. States	U. States	Seine	27 Oct 1823
JETTE, Gurpanet	74	M	Laborer	Switzerland	U.S.	C. Amelia	30 Jun 1828
JEUNE, Chevre	30	M	Merchant	United States	United States	Don Quixote	18 Aug 1824
JEWELL, —, Mrs.	35	F		Brooklin	U. States	Agnes	1 Jul 1825
JEWETT, Betsey	35	F	Lady	U. States	U. States	Diana	18 Jul 1820
David	60	M	Mariner	U. States	U. States	Horatio	14 Mar 1829
Eleazer	28	M	Mechanic	Connecticutt	U. States	Howard	3 Mar 1828
Monk	32	M	Merchant	U. States	U. States	Diana	18 Jul 1820
Noah	42	M	Merchant	U. States	Bermuda	Rising Sun	24 May 1824
Saml.	14	M	Servant	U. States	U. States	Diana	18 Jul 1820
Xenophen	50	M	Merchant	St. John, N.B.	St. John, N.B.	Ann Maria	1 Apr 1826
JEWIS, Jos.	28	M	Mechanic	Connecticutt	U. States	Benjamin	1 Jun 1822
JEWITT, Elizabeth	7	F	Labourer	Great Britain	United States	Thomas Dickason	31 Jul 1829
Hannah	5	F	Labourer	Great Britain	United States	Thomas Dickason	31 Jul 1829
John	3	M	Labourer	Great Britain	United States	Thomas Dickason	31 Jul 1829
Mary	16	M	Labourer	Great Britain	United States	Thomas Dickason	31 Jul 1829
Mary	42	M	Labourer	Great Britain	United States	Thomas Dickason	31 Jul 1829
Robert	10	M	Labourer	Great Britain	United States	Thomas Dickason	31 Jul 1829
Thomas	8/12	M	Labourer	Great Britain	United States	Thomas Dickason	31 Jul 1829
Thomas	48	M	Labourer	Great Britain	United States	Thomas Dickason	31 Jul 1829
JEXIDO, M.	50	M	Mariner	U. States	U. States	Victory	12 Jul 1820
JI...WAS, ...mas	7	M		Great Britian	United States	London	24 Jun 1823
...no.	10	F		Great Britian	United States	London	24 Jun 1823
Ann	27	M	Farmer	Great Britian	United States	London	24 Jun 1823
Ann	40	M	Farmer	Great Britian	United States	London	24 Jun 1823
Eliza	6	M		Great Britian	United States	London	24 Jun 1823
Mary	11	M		Great Britian	United States	London	24 Jun 1823
JIBBERY, —	28	M	Gentleman	U. States	U. States	Columbia	7 Sep 1827
JILER, Jean	27	M	Mercht.	Switzerland	U.S.	Edward Quesnel	21 Apr 1827
JIMMON, Alfred	23	M	British Navy	England	England	Canton Packet	13 Oct 1829
JINKIN, Edward	22	M	Farmer	England	America	Hercules	10 Apr 1823
JINKINS, Cradon	52	M	Farmer	England	America	Hercules	10 Apr 1823
JINLING, Edward	52	M	Mason	England	U. States	Orient	20 May 1822
JINNINGAN, Micle	24	M	Labourer			Evergreen	28 Jul 1820
JISHIE, Edward	25	M	Labourer	Great Brittan	United States	Hanford	3 Aug 1829
JO...MES, Ann	21	F	Servant to Miss Kotch	G. Britain	U.S. America	Cincinnatus	31 Oct 1820
JO...SON, Thomas	23	M	Weaver	Ireland	U. States	Josephine	7 May 1827
JOANNEAU, Abigail	36	F		Germany	U. States	Isabella	10 Aug 1829
JOANNUEA, Abby	10	F		Germany	U. States	Isabella	10 Aug 1829
Antoinatte	3	F		Germany	U. States	Isabella	10 Aug 1829
August	9	M		Germany	U. States	Isabella	10 Aug 1829
Jacobus	4	M		Germany	U. States	Isabella	10 Aug 1829
Maria	6	F		Germany	U. States	Isabella	10 Aug 1829
Matthew	7	M		Germany	U. States	Isabella	10 Aug 1829
Matthew	40	M	Farmer	Germany	U. States	Isabella	10 Aug 1829
JOANNY, J.	18	M	Sailor	Portugal	Portugal	Jeune Antoinette	31 Oct 1829
JOAQUIM, —, Mr.	35	M	officer in the Portuguese Navy	Portugal	Portugal	Ariosto	12 Apr 1822
—, Servant, Negro Man	45	M	Servant	Gaudaloupe	U. States	Eliza	3 Jul 1820
JOBSON, William	29	M	Farmer	England	America	Francis & Henrietta	11 Jul 1823
JOCHY, Patrick	22	M	...	Ireland	U. States	Union	3 Jun 1822
Vimaldey	25	M	...	Ireland	U. States	Union	3 Jun 1822
JODRIDGE, Thos.	22	M	Merchant	U. States	United States	Combine	20 Nov 1824
JOE, Frs.	52	M	Farmer	Fayal	U. States	L. M. Pelham	3 Jan 1823

NAMES OF PASSENGERS	AGE	SEX	OCCUPATIONS	COUNTRY TO WHICH THEY BELONG	COUNTRY THEY INTEND TO INHABIT	SHIPS/DATES OF ARRIVAL	
JOELL, Saml.	25	M	Servant	Bermuda		Camden	14 May 1825
W.	12	M		Bermuda	Bermuda	Pacification	31 Aug 1822
JOESENS, L.	48	M	Clerk	Holland	U. States	Amos Palmer	17 Aug 1826
JOFF, Paul	31			Great Britain	U. States America	Maria	22 May 1822
JOFFROY, Mary	53	F		Germany	New York	Orient	25 Nov 1825
JOFFRY, Ferrant	25	M	Clerk	England	United States	Essex	23 May 1828
JOH..., C.	22	M	Baker	France	United States	New England	29 Aug 1828
JOHANDOTHER, Johanna	35	F	Farmer	Norway	United States	Salem	31 Aug 1829
JOHES, Catherine	19	F	Merchant	Bermuda	Great Britian	Two Brothers	6 Sep 1823
JOHN, Catherine	26	F	None	England	United States	Oscar	24 Jul 1823
Elinor	24			Wales	England	Rockingham	23 Aug 1822
Evan	16	M	None	Wales South	U. States	Oglethorpe	8 Jul 1824
Geor.	27		Mines	England	England	Triumph	23 Jul 1829
George	11	M	Farmer	France	France	Sully	15 Jul 1829
H.	17	F	None	Great Britain	U. States America	Columbia	15 Nov 1826
Heny.	7/12					Olympia	2 Sep 1823
Ignace	32	M	Farmer	France	France	Sully	15 Jul 1829
James	22	M	Mercht.	Gt. Britain	U.S. of America	Friends	25 Sep 1823
John F.	22			Wales	England	Rockingham	23 Aug 1822
Madelina	12	F	Farmer	France	France	Sully	15 Jul 1829
Marie	38	F	Farmer	France	France	Sully	15 Jul 1829
Marie, Jr.	6	F	Farmer	France	France	Sully	15 Jul 1829
Mike	23	M		Native of Switzerland	United States	Canaris	30 Jun 1827
Salomie	1	F	Farmer	France	France	Sully	15 Jul 1829
Thomas	55		Farmer	Wales	England	Rockingham	23 Aug 1822
JOHNAS, Catharine	7/12			France	U. States	Parachute	14 May 1828
Christian	38		Cooper	France	U. States	Parachute	14 May 1828
Christiene	25			France	U. States	Parachute	14 May 1828
JOHNISON, Stephen	29	M	Captain	U. States	U. States	Agness	30 Jul 1829
JOHNS, Elizabeth	24	F		America	America	Telegraph	18 May 1827
JOHNSON, —			child [of William]	Ireland	U. States	Xenophon	28 May 1822
—	9	M	Servt.	United States	United States	Bayard	13 Nov 1823
—, Miss	16	F	None	U. States	U. States	Surprize	1 Aug 1825
—, Mr.	40			G. Britain	America	Magnet	24 Sep 1824
—, Mrs.	24	F	None	England	America	Meteor	21 Aug 1822
—, Mrs.	30	F		G. Britain	Canada	Columbia	7 Sep 1827
—, Mrs.	32			G. Britain	America	Magnet	24 Sep 1824
—, Mrs.	35	F		U. States	U. States	Lark	11 Jun 1828
...	20 1/12	M	Merchant	Great Britton	Great Britton	Elias Burger	18 Sep 1821
...	22	M		Great Brittain	United States	Sarah Ralston	27 Jan 1827
Abn.	28	M		Scotland	U.S.	Curler	19 Jul 1828
Abraham	22	M	Merchant	Germany		Ariel	24 Sep 1827
Abraham	42	M	Mariner	Virginia	Slave	Hippomenes	5 Jul 1820
Agnes	24	F	Labourer	Ireland	U. States	Atlantic	19 Aug 1825
Alexander	10	M	Merchant	England	Canada	William Byrnes	11 Dec 1827
Alexander	14	M	None, Child	Ireland	United States	Phocian	5 Aug 1826
Andrew	25	M	Weaver	Ireland	United States	Trident	30 Sep 1826
Ann	...	F	None	England	United States	Baltic	21 Apr 1827
Ann	2	F	None	England	United States	Baltic	21 Apr 1827
Ann	5	F		G. Britain	U. States	London	23 Sep 1828
Ann	6	F	None, Child	Ireland	United States	Phocian	5 Aug 1826
Ann	22	F		England	United States	William Byrnes	15 Aug 1826
Ann	39	F		Great Brittain	America	Pacific	13 Jan 1827
Ann	40	F		Ireland	United States	Phocian	5 Aug 1826
Ann	77	F		England	America	Britannia	22 Jul 1829
Ann Maria	4	F	Laborer or Spinster	Ireland	United States	Sarah G.	15 Aug 1827
Archer	35	M	Labourer	Ireland	U. States	Sarah G	30 Jun 1828
Arthur	44	M	Farmer	Ireland	United States	James Cropper	26 Mar 1822
B. F.	24	M	Merchant	United States	United States	Elbe	30 Sep 1826
Benj.	53	M	Mariner	U. States	U. States	Ranger	29 Aug 1826
Benjamin	40	M	Farmer	Great Brittan	U.S.	Emulous	29 Jun 1827
Benjamin	52	M	Mariner	Freeport	U. States	Amazon	28 Nov 1821
Benjm.	52	M	Mariner	U. States	U. States	New York	19 Mar 1827
Benjn.	49	M	Mariner	U. States	U. States	Jane	16 Oct 1821
Benjn.	50	M	Merchant	U. States	U. States	Mount Hope	30 Sep 1822
Betsey	4	F	None, Child	Ireland	United States	Phocian	5 Aug 1826
Betsey	20	F		Ireland	U. States	Concordia	11 Jun 1823
Biddy	27 2/12	F		Ireland	America	Braganza	7 Oct 1823

NAMES OF PASSENGERS	AGE	SEX	OCCUPATIONS	COUNTRY TO WHICH THEY BELONG	COUNTRY THEY INTEND TO INHABIT	SHIPS/DATES OF ARRIVAL	
JOHNSON (cont'd)							
C.	28	M	Merchant	United States	U. States	Seneca	23 Oct 1826
C. H.	32	M	Mariner	Baltimore	U. States	Jane	13 Dec 1822
C. H.	38	M	Navy	U. States	U. States	Tampico	20 Jan 1825
Cahs.	35	M	Carpenter	New York	New York	Milo	8 May 1826
Charles	21	M	Captain, Officers & crew of the Brig George of New York (wrecked at Fayal)	U.S. America	U.S.A.	Gallego	13 Mar 1829
Charles	35	M	Gentleman	England	Canada	Acasta	14 Jun 1824
Charlotte	25	F		U. States	Maryland	James Cropper	21 Oct 1825
Charlotte	40	F		England	United States	Resign	7 Oct 1822
Chas. J.	28	M	Merchant	U. States	U. States	Rachel Ann	13 Jul 1826
Chs.	22	M	Mariner	England	U. States	Neptune	11 Jun 1822
E.	6	F		Ireland	U. States	Sarah G	30 Jun 1828
E.	21	F	None	G. Britain		Ann Maria	3 Jul 1820
E.	21	M	Servant	U. States	U. States	Cannon	25 Apr 1821
Edwd.	29	M	Spinner	England	U. States	Panthea	8 Apr 1826
Elisth.	23	F	Farmer			Splendid	14 Aug 1829
Eliza	7	F		Great Brittain	America	Pacific	13 Jan 1827
Eliza	18	F	None	England	United States	Orozimbo	11 Aug 1823
Elizabeth	28	F	None	Great Britain	Virginia	Globe	14 May 1822
Elizth.	30	F	None	Great Britain		Moro Castle	6 Jul 1827
Ellen	26	F	None	Great Britain	United States	Martha	22 Jul 1820
Ester	55	M		England	America	Britannia	22 Jul 1829
Frances	6	M		Great Brittain	America	Pacific	13 Jan 1827
Francis	2	M	None, Child	Ireland	United States	Phocian	5 Aug 1826
Francis	25	M	Labourer	Great Britain	United States	Colossus	5 Jun 1827
Francis	26	M	Merchant	Birmingham	New York	Leeds	26 Sep 1826
Francis	26	M	Merchant	Great Britain		Manhattan	7 Nov 1827
Francis	27	M	Merchant	Netherland	United States	Dawn	15 Oct 1827
Francis	32	M	Black Smith	Great Brittain	America	Pacific	13 Jan 1827
Francis	60	M		America	New York	Cincinnatus	5 Dec 1825
Geo.		M				Prudence	19 Apr 1826
*died							
Geo.	1	M		England	U. States	Unity	5 Sep 1828
Geo.	12			England	United States	Hugh Johnson	11 Jun 1828
George	30	M	Farmer	Scotland	Bueonos Ayres	Curler	7 Jul 1827
Grace	14	F	...	Scotland	unknown	Robert Edwards	4 Jun 1824
Grace	35		Wife [of William]	Ireland	U. States	Xenophon	28 May 1822
H.	50	F		England	U. States	Evelina	31 May 1825
Hannah	28	F		Great Britain	New York	Radius	7 Jul 1821
Harriet	25	F	Servant	U. States	U. States	Harmony	19 Aug 1822
Henry	3	F		U. States	U. States	Good Friends	20 May 1825
Henry	4	M		Demara	U. States	Sudan	6 Aug 1823
Henry	35	M	Merchant	New York	U. States	Carlo	6 Oct 1827
Herriet	12	F		Great Brittain	America	Pacific	13 Jan 1827
Hugh	16	M	None, Child	Ireland	United States	Phocian	5 Aug 1826
Hugh	20	M	Taylor	Great Britian	United States	Diamond	8 Nov 1824
Hugh	25	M	Mariner	United States	United States	John Wells	16 Feb 1824
J.						Athenian	3 Mar 1828
*put on board by American Consul @ Carthagena							
J.	40	M	Shoe Maker	G. Britain	Canada	Columbia	7 Sep 1827
James		M	Chiefly farmers		United States	Factor	8 Jul 1829
James	...	M	...	...	...	Braganza	8 Aug 1825
James	4		child [of William]	Ireland	U. States	Xenophon	28 May 1822
James	8	M	None, Child	Ireland	United States	Phocian	5 Aug 1826
James	16	M	Printer	Gt. Britain	United States	Grecian	24 Sep 1828
James	18	M	Labourer	Ireland	United States	William & George	14 May 1828
James	21	M	Labourer	Ireland	United States	Nancy Henrietta	3 Nov 1828
James	21 7/12	M	Merchant	United States	New York	Loire	9 Aug 1821
James	24	M	Gentleman	Ireland	United States	General Putnam	20 Jun 1825
James	24	M	Labourer	U. States	U. States	St. Croix	13 Sep 1827
James	27	M	Farmer	England	United States	Albion	7 Feb 1820
James	31	M	Farmer	Scotland	Canada	Abigail	23 Nov 1820
James	32	M	Farmer	U. States	U. States	Bellville	14 May 1827

NAMES OF PASSENGERS	AGE	SEX	OCCUPATIONS	COUNTRY TO WHICH THEY BELONG	COUNTRY THEY INTEND TO INHABIT	SHIPS/DATES OF ARRIVAL	
JOHNSON (cont'd)							
James	35	M	Taylor	Great Britten	U. States	Factor	27 Mar 1827
James	35	M	Merchant	New York	New York	Athenian	9 Jan 1829
James	35 1/12	M	Merchant	Great Britain	Great Britain	Hector	8 Jan 1820
James J.	28	M	Merchant	New Jersey	U. States	Venus	27 Dec 1824
James W.	32 8/12		Merchant	New York	New York	Agnes	27 Mar 1828
Jane	12	F	Seamstress	Gt. Britain	United States	Grecian	24 Sep 1828
Jane	21	F		U. States	U. States	Good Friends	20 May 1825
Jane	63	F	None	G. Britain		Ann Maria	3 Jul 1820
Jno.	25	M	Merchant	London	G. Brittain	Andrew Jackson	30 Oct 1821
Jno.	26	M	Merchant	Great Britain	United States	Cortes	19 Nov 1821
Jno.	32	M	Miner	G. Brittain	U. States	Pacific	23 Jan 1826
John	2	M		England	Canada	Acasta	14 Jun 1824
John	8	M		Gt. Britain	United States	Grecian	24 Sep 1828
John	10	M	None, Child	Ireland	United States	Phocian	5 Aug 1826
John	11	M		G. Britain	U. States	Dalhouse Castle	12 Sep 1828
John	14	M		Scotland	United States	Shakespeare	24 Jul 1828
John	17		Mariner			Logan	14 Aug 1820
John	18	M	Seaman	U. States	U. States	Boston	26 Sep 1820
John	19	M	Weaver	Ireland	U. States	Josephine	7 May 1827
John	21	M	...			Manhattan	8 Aug 1820
John	22	M	Farmer	Great Brittan	U.S.	Emulous	29 Jun 1827
John	22	M	Carpenter	America	America	Splendid	23 Mar 1829
John	23	M	Farmer	England	U. States	Commerce	28 May 1824
John	24	M	Farmer	England	America	Britannia	22 Jul 1829
John	25	M	Merchant	Ireland	America	Albion	4 Oct 1820
John	25	M	Clothier	Great Britain		Robert Fulton	8 Mar 1823
John	25	M	Gentleman	Ireland	U. States	Fame	15 Nov 1826
John	25		Farmer	Ireland	United States	Fabius	18 Mar 1829
John	26		Silk Weaver	Ireland	United States	Cambria	19 Oct 1829
John	27	M	Tailor	England	United States	Baltic	21 Apr 1827
John	28	M			U. States	Criterion at London	10 May 1821
John	28	M	Farmer	England	U. States	James Cropper	10 Jun 1823
John	28	M	Merchant	England	U. States	Amity	23 Sep 1823
John	28	M		G. Britain	U. States	George Clinton	10 Sep 1828
John	28	M	Carpenter	Great Britain	United States	Thomas Dickason	31 Jul 1829
John	29	M	Labourer	U. States	U. States	Robt. Reade	12 Apr 1825
John	30		Farmer	England	United States	Hugh Johnson	11 Jun 1828
John	30	M	Metalurgist	G. Britain	U. States	Canada	19 Sep 1828
John	32	M	Saddler	Sweden	United States	Elbe	22 Aug 1828
John	35		Gardiner	England		Corinthian	11 Mar 1829
John	38	M				Lady of the Lake	23 Aug 1828
*left ship							
John	60	M	Farmer	Scotland	America	Camillus	12 Sep 1822
John, Jr.	15	M	Son	Scotland	America	Camillus	12 Sep 1822
Jone	23	F		England	U. States	Unity	5 Sep 1828
Js.	12	M	Farmer	Great Brittan	U.S.	Emulous	29 Jun 1827
Juliana	30	F		England	U. States	Frances	4 Jun 1825
L.		M	Mercht.	U. States	U. States	Atlantic	13 Aug 1824
L. W., Mrs.	28	F	Lady	U. States	U. States	Jupiter	29 Jun 1825
M.	42	M	Farmer	England	United States	Delta	24 Oct 1829
M. B.	19	M	Merchant	N. York	N. York	Thrasher	3 Jul 1826
Ma...t...	24			Ireland	United States	Robert Burns	18 Jun 1822
Madaline	29	F		Sweden	U. States	Hamilton	22 Sep 1828
Mary		F	Merchant	St. John, N.B.	St. John, N.B.	Ann Maria	8 May 1826
Mary	22	F		U. States	U. States	Triton	4 Oct 1822
Mary	28	F		Great Brittain	America	Pacific	13 Jan 1827
Mary	30	F	Wife	Ireland	U. States	Sarah G	30 Jun 1828
Mary	36	F	Farmer	Great Brittan	U.S.	Emulous	29 Jun 1827
Mary	38	F				Lady of the Lake	23 Aug 1828
*left ship							
Mary, Miss	28	F	Lady	England	Canada	Brighton	24 Aug 1827
Mary Ann	4	F		England	Canada	Acasta	14 Jun 1824
Mary Ann	24	F	Wife	England	United States	Cambria	8 Oct 1828
Mary C.	21	F		Bahamas	Bahamas	Success	25 Jun 1825

NAMES OF PASSENGERS	AGE	SEX	OCCUPATIONS	COUNTRY TO WHICH THEY BELONG	COUNTRY THEY INTEND TO INHABIT	SHIPS/DATES OF ARRIVAL	
JOHNSON (cont'd)							
Mm.	25	M	Servant	U. States	U. States	Abeona	1 Oct 1823
Nicholas	23	M	Mariner	Sweden	U. States	Almira	18 Sep 1823
Ole	32	M	Carpenter	Sweden	U. States	Hamilton	22 Sep 1828
P.	25		Farmer	Cork	New York	Schuylkill	22 Aug 1825
Pat	31	M	Farmer	England	U.S. States	Splendid	14 Aug 1829
Paul	13	M	Boy	Ireland	United States	Dublin Packet	29 Jun 1825
Peggy	10	F		G. Britain	U. States	Dalhouse Castle	12 Sep 1828
R.	17 2/12	M	Gentleman	Scotland	New York	Cririe	2 Jul 1821
Rob.	36	M	Sadler	England	U. States	Frances	4 Jun 1825
Robert	6	M	None, Child	Ireland	United States	Phocian	5 Aug 1826
Robert	25	M	Farmer	England	United States	Maria	3 Oct 1822
Robert	25	M	Labourer	Scotland	United States	Mary & Susan	5 Aug 1828
Robert	35	M	None	England	England	William Thompson	19 Aug 1829
Robt.	24	M	Blacksmith	Great Britain	New York	Superior	5 Sep 1827
Robt.	28	M	Stocking Maker	England	U. States	Unity	5 Sep 1828
Rosana	30	F	Servant	Philadelphia	United States	Astrea	16 Nov 1825
Saml.	27	M	Mariner	U. States	U. States	Fourth of July	19 Oct 1824
Saml.	29	M	Merchant	U. States	Bahamas	Success	25 Jun 1825
Samuel	11	M	Boy	Ireland	United States	Dublin Packet	29 Jun 1825
Samuel	18 6/12	M	Weaver	Ireland	United States	Atlantic	21 Jul 1827
Samuel	37	M	Gent.	United States	United States	Cambria	16 Aug 1827
Samuel	45	M	Shoemaker	England	United States	Resign	7 Oct 1822
Sarah	19	F	Farmer	Ireland	United States	L. M. Pelham	25 Jun 1822
Sarah	20	F	Servant	England	New York	Cincinnatus	5 Dec 1825
Sarah	21	F		England	America	Britannia	22 Jul 1829
Sarah	25	F	Laborer or Spinster	Ireland	United States	Sarah G.	15 Aug 1827
Sarah	36	F	Lady	Ireland	United States	Dublin Packet	29 Jun 1825
Susan	27	F		England	Canada	Acasta	14 Jun 1824
Susan	37	F	Seam Stress	Gt. Britain	United States	Grecian	24 Sep 1828
Theodore	8	M		Great Brittain	America	Pacific	13 Jan 1827
Thomas	3	M		Great Brittain	America	Pacific	13 Jan 1827
Thomas	6		child [of William]	Ireland	U. States	Xenophon	28 May 1822
Thomas	29	M	Labourer	England	U. States	Ayrshire	12 May 1828
Thomas	33	M	Doctor	Great Brit.	Ohio	Gov. Griswald	3 Jul 1820
Thomas	40	M	Farmer	England	United States	Delta	24 Oct 1829
Thos	1 6/12	M		Gt. Britain	United States	Grecian	24 Sep 1828
Thos.	3	M	Farmer	Gt. Britain	U. States	Superior	20 Aug 1825
Thos.	17	M	Aprentice [?]	Ireland	United States	Dublin Packet	29 Jun 1825
Thos.	23	M	Joiner	Great Britain	United States	William Dawson	18 Jun 1827
Thos.	28	M	Manufacture	England	U. States	Favourite	2 Sep 1822
Thos.	30	M	Merchant	Great Britain	Virginia	Globe	14 May 1822
Thos. K.	28	M	Carpenter	Great Britain	New York	Radius	7 Jul 1821
W.	30	M	Farmer	Gt. Britain	U. States	Superior	20 Aug 1825
W. Cly.	60	M	Merchant	Ireland	United States	Abigail	25 Jun 1822
William	3	M		England	Canada	Acasta	14 Jun 1824
William	19	M	Merchant	England	America	Courier	24 Jul 1820
William	25	M	Shoe Maker	England	United States	Cambria	8 Oct 1828
William	26	M	Weaver	Ireland	United States	Trident	30 Sep 1826
William	27		Cotton Spinner	Cumberland	England	Great Britain	7 May 1827
William	30	M	Mechanic	U. States	U. States	Hesper	21 Sep 1827
William	40		Farmer	Ireland	U. States	Xenophon	28 May 1822
Wm.	18	M	None, Child	Ireland	United States	Phocian	5 Aug 1826
Wm.	21	M	Servant	Great Britain	United States	Washington	3 Sep 1827
Wm.	21	M	Mariner	England	U. States	Melantho	8 Sep 1827
Wm.	23	M	Servant	America	U. States	Hudson	26 Jan 1825
Wm.	26	F	Farmer			Splendid	14 Aug 1829
Wm.	30	M	Mechanic	Connecticutt	U. States	Henry	11 Apr 1823
Wm.	30	M	Farmer	Great Brittan	U.S.	Emulous	29 Jun 1827
Wm.	31	M	Farmer	Great Britain		Moro Castle	6 Jul 1827
Wm.	35		Labourer	England	United States	Hugh Johnson	11 Jun 1828
Wm.	36	M	Weaver	Gt. Britan	U. States	Sarah Skeafe	10 Sep 1827
Wm.	38	M	Merchant	Ireland	U. States	Concordia	11 Jun 1823
Wm.	39	M	Miller	Great Brittain	America	Pacific	13 Jan 1827
Wm.	45	M	Cooper	Bristol	New York	Cosmo	25 Sep 1827
Wm. H.	28	M	Architect	England	America	Level	8 Sep 1827
Wm. John	20 4/12	M	Shoemaker	Ireland	United States	Atlantic	21 Jul 1827
Z. F.	20	M	Navy	Maryland	U. States	Commerce	10 Nov 1823

NAMES OF PASSENGERS	AGE	SEX	OCCUPATIONS	COUNTRY TO WHICH THEY BELONG	COUNTRY THEY INTEND TO INHABIT	SHIPS/DATES OF ARRIVAL	
JOHNSONE, Nicholas	26	M	Merchant	U.S. America	U.S. America	James Cropper	29 Nov 1827
JOHNSTON, (see Armstrong)							
—			Servant	Ireland	U. States	Henrietta	7 Jul 1825
—, Midshipman	19	M	U.S. Navy	U. States	U. States	Brown	11 Jan 1825
—, Mrs.	35	F		U. States	U. States	Harmony	19 Aug 1822
—, Mrs.	35	F	None	U. States	U. States	Camillus	27 Jun 1826
...	20	M	Labourer	Blantyre	U.S. America	Camillus	10 Sep 1821
Agnes	10	F	None	Balfron, Scotland	Massachusetts	Eagle	10 Aug 1825
Agnes	37	M	None	Balfron, Scotland	Massachusetts	Eagle	10 Aug 1825
Alexander	29	M	Farmer	Ireland	America	Farmer	3 May 1824
Ann	15	F	Spinster	Blantyre	U.S. America	Camillus	10 Sep 1821
Ann	24	F		England	United States	William & Henry	19 Jul 1822
Arthur	3	M		Ware	United States	Carolina Ann	11 Jun 1824
B.	49	M	Mariner	U. States	U. States	Harmony	19 Aug 1822
Belle	30	M	Farmer	Scotland	United States	Broke	16 Jul 1829
Dorothy	11/12	F	child	Great Britain	United States	Minerva	28 Jul 1823
E.	36	F		Gt. Britain	United States	Robert Edwards	1 Jun 1826
E. W.	23	M	Merchant	United States	United States	Hannibal	27 May 1822
Edward	23	M	Mechanic	Ireland	United States	Concordia	25 Aug 1827
Elizabeth	22	F	None	Great Britain	United States	Friends	13 Jun 1825
Emelia	13	F		Ireland	United States	William & George	14 May 1828
Fanny	68	F		New York	United States	McDonough	3 Nov 1823
Geo.	50	M	Blacksmith	U. States	U. States	Jay	18 Apr 1823
Geo. G.	25	M	Merchant	Scotland	Great Brittan	Florida	17 May 1825
Geo. H.	22	M	Merchant	U. States	U. States	Robert Fulton	1 Nov 1822
George	12	M	Weaver	Great Britain	United States	Atlantic	8 Dec 1827
George	19	M	Merchant	Glasgow	Great Britan	Columbia	11 Aug 1823
George Greig	23	M	Merchant	Glasgow, Scotland	United States	James Cropper	7 Oct 1823
Helen	14	F	None	Balfron, Scotland	Massachusetts	Eagle	10 Aug 1825
Henry	7	M	None	England	United States	Huron	26 Dec 1827
Henry	8	M	None	England	Connecticut	Indian Chief	16 Aug 1822
Henry	19	M	Carpenter	England	U. States	Unity	5 Sep 1828
Henry	22	M	Farmer	England	United States	Roman	12 Jun 1826
Henry	23	M	Weaver	Ireland	United States	Meteor	19 Aug 1829
Hy.	55	M	None	U. States	U. States	Herald	7 Jul 1825
Isabella	18	F		Ireland	U. States	Nancy	16 Aug 1822
J.	8	M		Gt. Britain	United States	Robert Edwards	1 Jun 1826
J.	26	M	Merchant	U. States	U. States	Laveria	23 Jul 1828
J.	36		Lawyer	Great Britian	Halifax	America	28 Jul 1826
James	1	M		Ware	United States	Carolina Ann	11 Jun 1824
James	16	M	Labourer	Scotland	America	Mentor	21 Sep 1824
James	20	M	Labourer	Tyrone	United States	Carolina Ann	11 Jun 1824
James	21	M	Mercht.	Scotland	New York	Samuel Wright	12 Oct 1829
James	26	M	Blacksmith	Aberdeen	U. States	Gowan	28 Aug 1822
James	26	M	Baker	Scotland	U. States of Amer	Dale	14 Mar 1828
James	26	M	Lawyer	U. States	U. States	France	14 Mar 1828
James	30	M	Farmer	Scotland	United States	Broke	16 Jul 1829
James	40	M	Merchant	England	United States	Nancy	28 Oct 1822
Jane	4	F		Ware	United States	Carolina Ann	11 Jun 1824
Jane	22	F	Soldier	Great Britain	U.S.	Panthea	13 Nov 1823
Jane	28	F	his Wife [Wm.]	Great Britain	United States	Minerva	28 Jul 1823
Janes	13	M		Cobrain	United States	Carolina Ann	11 Jun 1824
Janet	2	F	Farmer	Scotland	United States	Broke	16 Jul 1829
Jas.	31	M	weaver	Scotland	New York	Joseph Hume	26 Oct 1829
Jno.	30	M	Weaver	Great Britain	U. States	Morning Star	9 Nov 1824
John	4	M	child	Great Britain	United States	Minerva	28 Jul 1823
John	11	M	None	Balfron, Scotland	Massachusetts	Eagle	10 Aug 1825
John	16	M	Cotton Spinner	Ireland	America	Hesperus	7 Jul 1820
John	17	M		Ireland	United States	William & George	14 May 1828
John	22	M	Joiner	Scotland	United States	Culloden	17 May 1828
John	22	M		U. States	U. States	Natchez	18 Aug 1828

NAMES OF PASSENGERS	AGE	SEX	OCCUPATIONS	COUNTRY TO WHICH THEY BELONG	COUNTRY THEY INTEND TO INHABIT	SHIPS/DATES OF ARRIVAL	
JOHNSTON (cont'd)							
John	25	M	Labourer	Ireland	United States	Concordia	25 Aug 1827
John	35	M	Mariner	U. States		Abigail	2 Oct 1820
John	50	M	Farmer	Ireland	United States	Phocian	5 Aug 1826
John G.	39	M	Ship Master	U. States	United States	Wabash	9 Feb 1827
Joseph	26	M	Taylor	England	United States	William & Henry	19 Jul 1822
Joseph	30	M	Mariner	England	United States	Trident	31 Mar 1827
Lloyd	12	M	Son	St. John, N.B.	United States	Sarah G.	11 Jan 1828
Lloyd	56	M	Surveyer	St. John, N.B.	United States	Sarah G.	11 Jan 1828
M.	22	M	Servant	Ireland	U. States	Henrietta	7 Jul 1825
Margaret	9	F	Child	Blantyre	U.S. America	Camillus	10 Sep 1821
Margt.	18	F		Cobrain	United States	Carolina Ann	11 Jun 1824
Maria	17	F	None	Balfron, Scotland	Massachusetts	Eagle	10 Aug 1825
Mary	11	F	None	England	Connecticut	Indian Chief	16 Aug 1822
Mary	24	F	None	England	U. States	Thomas Ritchie	2 Jul 1827
Mary	32	F	Seamstress	England	United States	Huron	26 Dec 1827
Mary Ann	26	F		Ware	United States	Carolina Ann	11 Jun 1824
Mary Jane	18	F	Spinster	Blantyre	U.S. America	Camillus	10 Sep 1821
Matilda	13	F	Spinster	Blantyre	U.S. America	Camillus	10 Sep 1821
Nancy	44	F	None	Ireland	America	Hesperus	7 Jul 1820
R. W.	22	M	None	U. States	U. States	John Jay	26 Jan 1829
Rachael	20	F	Wife	Ireland	United States	Henry Kneeland	7 Jun 1828
Robert	3	M	Farmer	Scotland	United States	Broke	16 Jul 1829
Robert	9	M	None	Balfron, Scotland	Massachusetts	Eagle	10 Aug 1825
Robert	10	M	Son	St. John, N.B.	United States	Sarah G.	11 Jan 1828
Robert	17	M		Cobrain	United States	Carolina Ann	11 Jun 1824
Robt.	22		Smith	Great Britain	United States	Camillus	12 Sep 1827
Samuel	21	M	Shoomaker	Ireland	U. States	Courier	17 Mar 1828
Sophia	24	M	U.S. Navy	U.S.A.	U.S.A.	Potomac	25 Jul 1829
Susan	3	F		U. States	United States	Wabash	9 Feb 1827
Thomas	11	M	Child	Blantyre	U.S. America	Camillus	10 Sep 1821
Thomas	32	M	Flax Dresser	England	Connecticut	Indian Chief	16 Aug 1822
Thos.	16	M	Labourer	England	U. States	Thomas Ritchie	2 Jul 1827
Thos.	30	M	Farmer	Ware	United States	Carolina Ann	11 Jun 1824
Tooler	22		...			Amphion	31 May 1824
W.	6	M		Gt. Britain	United States	Robert Edwards	1 Jun 1826
W.	30	M	Catler	With intention to become citizen		New York	18 Jul 1828
William	6	M	child	Great Britain	United States	Minerva	28 Jul 1823
William	9	M	None	England	United States	Huron	26 Dec 1827
William	18	M	Clerk	Great Britain	...	Hector	18 Jul 1822
William	18	M	Son	St. John, N.B.	United States	Sarah G.	11 Jan 1828
William	20	M	Clerk	United States	State of New York	Loire	3 Dec 1821
William	25	M	Gold Smith	America		Peruvian	28 Jul 1824
William	30	M	Canal Cutter	England	United States	Lord Wellington	14 Nov 1827
Wm.	17	M	Labourer	Scotland	United States	Tom	2 Jul 1827
Wm.	20		Farmer	Ireland	United States	John Dickinson	28 Jun 1822
Wm.	22		Farmer	England	America	Governor Griswold	6 Jun 1821
Wm.	23	M	Taylor	Scotland	U. States	Gleaner	22 Apr 1822
Wm.	24	M	Gentn.	Gt. Brittain	United States	York	6 Dec 1826
Wm.	27	M				Cassack	25 Jul 1820
Wm.	29	M	Farmer	Great Britain	United States	Minerva	28 Jul 1823
JOHNSTONE (see ...hnstone)							
James	13	M	None	Scotland	United States	Samuel Robertson	9 May 1827
James	20	M	Merchant	Great Britain	U. States	Hector	11 Oct 1824
James	31	M	Labourer	Great Britain	United States	Isaac Hicks	10 Jul 1827
James	32	M	Merchant	United States		General Marion	6 Oct 1828
John	21	M		Ireland	America	Carolina Ann	7 Aug 1826
Robert	36	M	Surgeon R.N.	England		General Marion	6 Oct 1828
W.	45	M	Farmer	England	U. States	Louisa Matilda	9 Jun 1823
JOHNTON, Elizabeth	23			Great Britian	Halifax	America	28 Jul 1826
Wm.	25	M	Farmer	New York	America	Carolina Ann	14 Feb 1825
JOHRSON, Andrew	32	M				Apollo	11 Jun 1828
JOHRSON, Ann	37	F		G. Britain	America	Quill	19 Jun 1828

NAMES OF PASSENGERS	AGE	SEX	OCCUPATIONS	COUNTRY TO WHICH THEY BELONG	COUNTRY THEY INTEND TO INHABIT	SHIPS/DATES OF ARRIVAL	
JOHRSON (cont'd)							
Geo.	37	M	Mechanic	G. Britain	America	Quill	19 Jun 1828
J.	38	M	Labourer	Ireland	U. States	Sarah G	30 Jun 1828
James	6	M		Ireland	U. States	Sarah G	30 Jun 1828
John	4	M		Ireland	U. States	Sarah G	30 Jun 1828
Mary	2	F		Ireland	U. States	Sarah G	30 Jun 1828
Mary	32	F		Ireland	U. States	Sarah G	30 Jun 1828
JOICE, Bridget	26		Farmer	Ireland	U. States	Schuylkill	22 Aug 1825
John	24		Farmer	Ireland	U. States	Schuylkill	22 Aug 1825
M.	30		Farmer	Ireland	U. States	Schuylkill	22 Aug 1825
P.	30		Farmer	Ireland	U. States	Schuylkill	22 Aug 1825
Thomas	27		Farmer	Ireland	U. States	Schuylkill	22 Aug 1825
Wm.	22	M	Weaver			John Dickinson	14 Sep 1820
JOILLET, Louis	32	M	Merchant	France	United States	Stephania	22 Apr 1822
JOIN, L. H.	22	M	Surgeon	U. States	U. States	United States	11 Sep 1828
JOIRE, P. L.	25	M	Merchant	France	France	Stephania	13 Sep 1821
JOIRE, Wm.	25	M	Farmer	Wales	United States	Orozimbo	11 Aug 1823
JOLIOET, J. M.	22	M	Jeweler	France		Montano	3 Jan 1823
JOLLER, Wm.	21	M	Farmer	Ireland	United States	Trident	30 Sep 1826
JOLLEY, Charles	32	M		G. Britain	New York	Brighton	26 Mar 1827
JOLLY, Gust.	29	M		Germany	U. States	Florida	2 Jun 1828
Henry	24	M	Weaver	England	New York	Xenophon	3 Oct 1829
James	24		Farmer	Combe	Ireland	Carolina Ann	21 May 1823
P., Miss	17	F		France	United States	Marmione	20 Nov 1821
Richard	21	M	Laborer	Great Brittan	U. States	Gem	26 Jul 1827
Robert	65	M	Farmer	Ireland	United States	John Dickinson	18 Feb 1822
JON, John	35	M	Rope Maker	Great Britain	U.S. of America	Gratitude	3 Oct 1829
Mary	19	F	Farmer			Splendid	14 Aug 1829
JONAN, A.	24	M	Merchant	U. States	U. States	Claudio	29 Dec 1827
JONAS, Geo.	15	M		G. Britain	U. States	Robt. Edwards	4 Sep 1828
JONCKE, Fredk.	33	M		England	America	Ann	3 Jul 1820
JONE, Charls. E.	41	M	Merchant	England	England	William Byrnes	14 Apr 1824
JONES, —, Infant				born on the ...	United States	Mary Howland	19 Jul 1827
—, Miss	12	F		Bristol	New York	Cosmo	25 Sep 1827
—, Miss	22			G. Britain	America	Magnet	24 Sep 1824
—, Mr.		M	Planter	Barbadoes	United States	Warren	10 Sep 1824
—, Mr.	18	M	Gentleman	Wales	U. States	William	28 Nov 1823
—, Mr.	22	M	Doctor	England	Barbadoes	Celia	15 Oct 1825
—, Mr., Junr.		M	Planter	Barbadoes	United States	Warren	10 Sep 1824
—, Mrs.	27	F	None	Ireland	United States	John Wells	22 Sep 1824
—, Mrs.	53			G. Britain	America	Magnet	24 Sep 1824
—, Servant	25	M	Servant	Baltimore	U. States	Commodore Porter	8 Sep 1823
A.	18	F	None	England	United States	Enterprize	19 Oct 1826
A.	22	M	Mariner	G. Brittain	U. States	Favorite	13 Jun 1821
A.	24	M	Doctor	U. States	U. States	Edward Quesnel	15 May 1826
Abrm.	30	M	Labourer	G. Britain	U. States	St. George	7 Jun 1828
Alexander	21	M	Labourer	Ireland	United States	Princess Charlotte	26 Apr 1827
Alfred	19	M	None	Great Britan	United States	Bolivar	21 May 1827
Alice	30		Farmer	Wales	Great Britain	Oglethorpe	25 Aug 1825
Amelia	19	F		G. Brittain	U. States	Cincinnatus	2 Oct 1822
Amy	4	F	Farmer	Gt. Britain	United States	Europa	20 Apr 1825
Anabella	20	F	Servant	Berlin	Berlin	Wanderer	4 Aug 1829
Andrew	2	M				Betsey	17 Aug 1820
Ann	1	F	Miner	Great Britain	United States	Thomas Dickason	31 Jul 1829
Ann	5	F	daughter [of Charls.]	Great Britain	United States	Wyton	12 May 1821
Ann	7	F		Europe	United States	Aspasia	5 Sep 1827
Ann	11	F	Child	Wales	U. States	William Thompson	27 May 1824
Ann	13	F	Farmer	Britain	U. States	Fame	3 Jun 1828
Ann	15	F		Ireland	U. States	William Byrnes	17 Jul 1825
Ann	18	F				Ocean	17 Aug 1820
Ann	22	F	Farmer	Ireland	United States	Justina	5 Aug 1823
Ann	27	F	None	Great Brittan	U.S.	Emulous	29 Jun 1827
Ann	35	F	None	Great Britain	United States	Washington	9 Apr 1821
Ann	35	F		England	United States	Cambria	16 Aug 1827

643

NAMES OF PASSENGERS	AGE	SEX	OCCUPATIONS	COUNTRY TO WHICH THEY BELONG	COUNTRY THEY INTEND TO INHABIT	SHIPS/DATES OF ARRIVAL
JONES (cont'd)						
Ann	38					Mount Vernon 26 Aug 1820
Ann	40	F	Spinster	G.B.	U.S.	Missouri 4 Aug 1825
Ann	40	F		Europe	United States	Aspasia 5 Sep 1827
Ann	43	F		Grate Brittan	Pennsylvania	Susquehanna 9 Jan 1824
Ann	47	F	None	England	United States	Enterprize 19 Oct 1826
Anne	4	F		Llannstyn	United States	Marquis of Anglesea 8 Jun 1827
Anne	23	F		Great Britain	Great Britain	Orozimbo 31 May 1824
Anne	27	F	Smith	G. Britain	Canada	Cosmo 25 Nov 1826
Anne	27	F		Gt. Britain	United States	Meteor 19 Aug 1829
Anne, Child [of William]	3	F	Labourer	Wales		Gomer 22 May 1827
Anne, Wife [of Griffith]	51	F	Labourer	Wales		Gomer 22 May 1827
Anthony	32	M	Physician	Scotland	Mississippia	Indian Chief 16 Aug 1822
Benj.	26	M		England	America	Ann 3 Jul 1820
Benj.	34	M	Labourer			Evergreen 28 Jul 1820
Benjamin	31 6/12	M	Farmer	Scotland	United States	Euphrates 25 Mar 1820
Betsey	19	F	Farmer	Britain	U. States	Fame 3 Jun 1828
Betsey	25	F	Spinster	Ireland	United States	St. Michaels 18 Jul 1826
Betty	24	F				Ocean 17 Aug 1820
Birbia	21	F	None	Scotland	United States	Roman 12 Jun 1826
Bridget	28		Laboring Class		United States	Atlantic 2 Apr 1827
Bridget	30	F		Ireland	United States	Princess Charlotte 26 Apr 1827
Bridget	31	F		England	U.S.A.	Mexico 9 Jul 1827
C., Esqr.	35	M	Gent. Traveller	England	England	Electra 17 Nov 1828
Caroline	10	F		Great Britain	U. States	Albert 1 Apr 1822
Casterine	50	F	None	Great Brittan	U.S.	Emulous 29 Jun 1827
Cath.	22	F		G. Britain	U. States	London 23 Sep 1828
Catharan	51	F		Great B.	U. States	William Neilson 26 Jul 1828
Catharine	22	F		G. Britain	U. States	William Thompson 30 Apr 1822
Catharine	22	F	Spinster	Wales		Gomer 22 May 1827
Catharine	26	F	Spinster	Great Britain	America	Lady Gallatin 21 Jun 1820
Catharine, Wife [of William]	27	F	Labourer	Wales		Gomer 22 May 1827
Cathe.	12			Wales		Anacreon 7 Sep 1827
Cathe.	21	F	Farmer	Britain	U. States	Fame 3 Jun 1828
Catherine	7	F	None			Evergreen 28 Jul 1820
Catherine	9	F	None	Ireland	United States	John Wells 22 Sep 1824
Catherine	16	F		G. Britain	U. States	Mary & Harriot 8 Sep 1828
Catherine	21	F	None	Wales	United States	Orozimbo 11 Aug 1823
Cathrinne	16	F	None	Great Brittan	U.S.	Emulous 29 Jun 1827
Charles	12	M	None	Great Britan	United States	Bolivar 21 May 1827
Charles	19		Joiner	England	United States	Hudson 5 Apr 1826
Charles	25	M	Blacksmith	Great Britan	United States	Dispatch 16 Jul 1827
Charles	25	M	pudler		uncertain	Mount Vernon 29 Aug 1828
Charles F.	26	M	Merchant	U. States	U. States	Harriet 2 Jan 1829
Charls.	45	F	None	Great Britain	United States	Wyton 12 May 1821
Chas.	3	M		England	U. States	Unity 5 Sep 1828
Chas. McClan	39	M	Farmer	Gt. Brittain	United States	York 6 Dec 1826
Clara	1	F		England	United States	John & Elizabeth 25 Sep 1827
Croasdelly	2	F	None	Ireland	United States	John Wells 22 Sep 1824
Cynor	26	M		North Wales	United States	Magnet 16 May 1823
Daniel	29 4/12	M	Farmer	England	U.S. America	Illinois 16 Oct 1822
David	6/12		Farmer	Wales	Great Britain	Oglethorpe 25 Aug 1825
David	2	M	Farmer	Britain	U. States	Fame 3 Jun 1828
David	6	M		G. Britain	U. States	Mary & Harriot 8 Sep 1828
David	8	M	None	Great Brittan	U.S.	Emulous 29 Jun 1827
David	9	M	Servant	England	U. States	Comet 28 Jul 1825
David	17	M	None	Wales South	U. States	Oglethorpe 8 Jul 1824
David	28	M	Baker	Ireland	United States	Trio 13 Jun 1827
David	31	M	Butler	England	America	Josephine 8 Jan 1827
David	50	M	Farmer	G. Britain	U. States	Mary & Harriot 8 Sep 1828

NAMES OF PASSENGERS	A G E	S E X	OCCUPATIONS	COUNTRY TO WHICH THEY BELONG	COUNTRY THEY INTEND TO INHABIT	SHIPS/DATES OF ARRIVAL	
JONES (cont'd)							
David, child							
[of John Davis]	6	M	Farmer	Wales		Gomer	22 May 1827
David W.	40	M	Minister	Great Britian	United States	Hamilton	21 Nov 1826
Deborah	4	F		England	United States	Cincinnatus	21 Nov 1821
Dolly	25	F	None	U. States	U. States	Almira	11 Dec 1826
Dora	24	M	Merchant	...d b..., Wales	Gt. Britain	Orozimbo	19 Oct 1822
Dorothy	45	F	Gentlwoman	England	America	Maine	16 Jul 1821
E.	1			Great Britain	United States	Gomer	21 May 1828
E.	25	M	Merchant	United States	South America	Hebe	18 Feb 1825
E.	62	F		G. Brittain	U. States	Favorite	13 Jun 1821
Ebenezer, child							
[of John Davis]	4	M	Farmer	Wales		Gomer	22 May 1827
Ebenr.	36	M	Laborer	Ireland	United States	Weser	29 Jul 1823
Edmd.	40	M	Seaman	United States	United States	Elizabeth & Mary	23 Nov 1820
Edmund	17	M		Gt. Britain	United States	Silas Richards	20 Jun 1826
Edward	4/12	M		England	United States	Nancy Henrietta	3 Nov 1828
Edward	2	M	None	Gt. Britain	United States	Union	9 Jan 1824
Edward	3	M	None	Great Brittan	U.S.	Emulous	29 Jun 1827
Edward	4	M		England	United States	Siroc	31 Oct 1829
Edward	21	M	Car...	Great Britain	United States	Mary Howland	19 Jul 1827
Edward	27	M	Labourer	Great Britain	U. States	Ganges	21 Jun 1827
Edward	27	M	Minor	England	United States	Siroc	31 Oct 1829
Edward	28	M	Miner	Hinchpaggot		Colossus	27 Mar 1828
Edward	49	M	Labourer	England	United States	Enterprize	19 Oct 1826
Edward J.	24	M	Merchant	Canada	Canada	St. George	16 Jan 1829
Eleanor	25	F	Spinster	Wales		Gomer	22 May 1827
Eleanor, Child							
[of Griffith]	6	F	Labourer	Wales		Gomer	22 May 1827
Eleanor, Wife							
[of Ellis]	24	F	Farmer	Wales		Gomer	22 May 1827
Elena	11	F	Farmer	Britain	U. States	Fame	3 Jun 1828
Elener	50	F	Farmer	Britain	U. States	Fame	3 Jun 1828
Elenor	5	F	None	England	United States	Orozimbo	1 Dec 1823
Elenor	20		Servant	Great Britain	United States	Gomer	21 May 1828
Elenor	29			Great Britain	United States	Gomer	21 May 1828
Eleseus	1			Great Britain	United States	Gomer	21 May 1828
Elias	2	M	Lad	Great Brittain	N. York	Leonidas	24 Jul 1824
Elinor	8	F	Female	Great Brittain	N. York	Leonidas	24 Jul 1824
Elisabeth	3	F		England	U.S. of America	Illinois	16 Jun 1821
Elisabeth	25	F		U.S.A.	U.S.A.	Silas Richards	28 Jun 1825
Elisabeth	28	F				Plato	31 Oct 1829
Elisabeth	32	F		England	United States	Nancy Henrietta	3 Nov 1828
Elisabeth	33	F		England	U.S. of America	Illinois	16 Jun 1821
Elisabeth	50	F		Great Britain	United States	Mary Howland	19 Jul 1827
Eliza	1	F		Ireland	United S.	Hanford	19 Aug 1828
Eliza	12/12	F	Merchant	...d b..., Wales	Gt. Britain	Orozimbo	19 Oct 1822
Eliza	2	F				Plato	31 Oct 1829
Eliza	3	F		G. Britain	U. States	London	23 Sep 1828
*Died on the Passage							
Eliza	12	F	None	England	U. States	Thomas Ritchie	2 Jul 1827
Eliza	20	F	Spinster	Ireland	United S.	Hanford	19 Aug 1828
Eliza	32	F		G. Britain	U. States	London	23 Sep 1828
Elizabeth	2	F	None	U. States	U. States	Almira	11 Dec 1826
Elizabeth	16	F	Servant	Great Britain	U.S. America	Chili	7 Jul 1827
Elizabeth	20	F	None	Wales	America	Minerva	31 May 1824
Elizabeth	24	F	Lady			Seine	10 Jun 1822
Elizabeth	24	F	Weaver	Great Britain	United States	Thomas Dickason	31 Jul 1829
Elizabeth	25	F	None	England	United States	Jubilee	12 May 1828
Elizabeth	28	F				Hesperus	2 Nov 1820
Elizabeth	28	F	None	England	United States	Great Britain	5 Sep 1827
Elizabeth	36	F	None	England		Manhattan	22 May 1827
Elizbth.	3			Great Britain	United States	Gomer	21 May 1828
Ellen	3	F		Europe	United States	Aspasia	5 Sep 1827
Ellen	5	F	None	Ireland	United States	John Wells	22 Sep 1824
Ellen	5	F		England	United States	John & Elizabeth	25 Sep 1827

NAMES OF PASSENGERS	AGE	SEX	OCCUPATIONS	COUNTRY TO WHICH THEY BELONG	COUNTRY THEY INTEND TO INHABIT	SHIPS/DATES OF ARRIVAL	
JONES (cont'd)							
Ellen	8	F		England	U.S. of America	Illinois	16 Jun 1821
Ellen	12	F		G. Britain	U. States	Mary & Harriot	8 Sep 1828
Ellen	13	F		U.S.A.	U.S.A.	Silas Richards	28 Jun 1825
Ellen	13	F	None	Great Brittan	U.S.	Emulous	29 Jun 1827
Ellen	30	F	None	Great Britain	United States	Martha	22 Jul 1820
Ellen	50	F		G. Britain	U. States	Mary & Harriot	8 Sep 1828
Ellen	51			Wales		Anacreon	7 Sep 1827
Ellis	3/12	M	None	England	United States	Great Britain	5 Sep 1827
Ellis	25	M	Farmer	Wales		Gomer	22 May 1827
Ellis, Child [of Griffith]	10	M	Labourer	Wales		Gomer	22 May 1827
Emma	25	F	None	Great Britian	United States	Hamilton	21 Nov 1826
Emy	17	F		Halifax	U. States	William Barker	29 Aug 1823
Evan	5		Farmer	Wales	Great Britain	Oglethorpe	25 Aug 1825
Evan	13	M		Llannstyn	United States	Marquis of Anglesea	8 Jun 1827
Evan	24	M	Farmer	England	U. States	Thomas Ritchie	2 Jul 1827
Evan	28	M	Farmer	Great Britan	United States	Clematis	8 May 1827
Evan	30	M	Labourer	Wales		Marchioness	13 May 1828
Evan	39	M	Con...lor	England	New York	Corinthian	5 May 1827
Evan	63	M	Labourer	Wales		Gomer	22 May 1827
Evan, Child [of Ellis]	1	M	Farmer	Wales		Gomer	22 May 1827
Even	18	M	Farmer	Ireland	United States	Justina	5 Aug 1823
Faulkner	4	M	Farmer	Gt. Britain	United States	Europa	20 Apr 1825
Frances	31	F	Married Woman	England	United States	Robert Edwards	3 Oct 1829
Frederick	10	M			U. States	William Thompson	27 May 1824
G.	15	F	Farmer	Britain	U. States	Fame	3 Jun 1828
G.	26	M	Shoemaker	Great Britain	United States	Mary	11 Jul 1820
G.	50	M	Carpenter	England	U. States	York	12 Jul 1825
Garnet	50		Farmer	England	United States	Hudson	5 Apr 1826
Garnet, Jr.	24		Farmer	England	United States	Hudson	5 Apr 1826
Garnett	53	M	Carpenter	United States		Marchioness	13 May 1828
Geo.	1	M		England	U. States	Unity	5 Sep 1828
Geo.	48	M	Farmer	U. States	U. States	New Packet	20 Sep 1826
Geo., Jr.	11	M	Child	Wales	U. States	William Thompson	27 May 1824
George	23	M	None	New York	U. States	New York	15 Nov 1823
George	29	M	Merchant	Great Britain	Great Britain	Orozimbo	31 May 1824
George	38	M		Wales	U. States	William Thompson	27 May 1824
Grace	21	F	Laboror	Great Brittian	United States	Perseverance	7 Aug 1826
Griffis	12	M	None	England	United States	Orozimbo	1 Dec 1823
Griffis	35	M	Farmer	England	United States	Orozimbo	1 Dec 1823
Griffith	6	M	Lad	Great Brittain	N. York	Leonidas	24 Jul 1824
Griffith	18			Wales		Anacreon	7 Sep 1827
Griffith	19	M	Labourer	Llannstyn	United States	Marquis of Anglesea	8 Jun 1827
Griffith	21			G. Britain	U. States	Mary & Harriot	8 Sep 1828
Griffith	23	M	Labourer	Wales		Gomer	22 May 1827
Griffith	30	M	Labourer	Wales		Gomer	22 May 1827
Griffith	36	M	Laborer	Ireland	United States	Weser	29 Jul 1823
Griffith	49	M	Labourer	Wales		Gomer	22 May 1827
Gwen	23		Farmer	Great Britain	United States	Gomer	21 May 1828
H.	58	M	Farmer	G. Brittain	U. States	Favorite	13 Jun 1821
Hannah	2 1/2	F		England	United States	Cincinnatus	21 Nov 1821
Hannah	7		Farmer	Wales	Great Britain	Oglethorpe	25 Aug 1825
Hannah	18 3/12	F		Ireland	U.S. of America	Douglass	6 Jul 1829
Harriet	6	F	None	England	U. States	Thomas Ritchie	2 Jul 1827
Henry	1	M	None	England	United States	Orozimbo	1 Dec 1823
Henry	20	M	Joiner	Newport	Monmouthshire	Howard Douglass	11 May 1827
Henry	27	M	Servant	U. States	U. States	Chase	17 Jan 1825
Henry	28	M	Gentleman	Great Britain	Great Britain	Sarah G	11 Sep 1827
Henry	29	M	Gentleman	Stapleton, England	Great Britain	James Cropper	7 Oct 1823
Henry	29	M	Merchant	Great Britten	United States	Cortes	6 Mar 1827

NAMES OF PASSENGERS	AGE	SEX	OCCUPATIONS	COUNTRY TO WHICH THEY BELONG	COUNTRY THEY INTEND TO INHABIT	SHIPS/DATES OF ARRIVAL	
JONES (cont'd)							
Henry	34		...	Great Britain	United States	Gomer	21 May 1828
Howard	6	M		Europe	United States	Aspasia	5 Sep 1827
Hugh	2	M	None	Great Brittan	U.S.	Emulous	29 Jun 1827
Hugh	14	M		Llannstyn	United States	Marquis of Anglesea	8 Jun 1827
Hugh	21	M		Great Britain	America	Lady Gallatin	21 Jun 1820
Hugh	22	M	Farmer	Wales	United States	John Wells	22 Sep 1824
Hy.	14	M		Gt. Britain	United States	Silas Richards	20 Jun 1826
Hy.	19	M	Shoemaker	G. Britain	Canada	Cosmo	25 Nov 1826
Isaac	4		Farmer	Wales	Great Britain	Oglethorpe	25 Aug 1825
Isaac	28	M	Blacksmith			Plato	31 Oct 1829
J.	1	M		Europe	United States	Aspasia	5 Sep 1827
J.	36	M	Mariner	U. States	U. States	Elias Burger	30 Nov 1822
J. J.	30	M	Gentleman	America	U. States	Catharine Rogers	6 Oct 1823
J. W.	13	M	Mariner	G. Brittain	U. States	Favorite	13 Jun 1821
J...	22	M	Labourer	Ireland	America	Wilson	27 Nov 1826
James	13	M	Brick Maker	Great Britan	United States	Bolivar	21 May 1827
James	22	M	Carver & Gilder	London	N. York	Manhattan	20 Sep 1821
James	23	M	Merchant	U. States	U. States	Fly	28 Jun 1824
James	27		Miller	England	United States	Acasta	16 Aug 1826
James	31	M	Accountant	United States	United States	Paez	5 Mar 1827
James G.	18	M	unknown	U. States	U. States	Mary	7 Nov 1822
Jane	5			Great Britain	United States	Gomer	21 May 1828
Jane	7	F	None	Great Britan	United States	Bolivar	21 May 1827
Jane	8	F	Farmer	Britain	U. States	Fame	3 Jun 1828
Jane	13	F	None	Great Brittan	U.S.	Emulous	29 Jun 1827
Jane	14	F	None			Evergreen	28 Jul 1820
Jane	22	F		England	U.S. America	Cortes	19 May 1826
Jane	23	F		America	America	Brittannia	28 Feb 1827
Jane	23	F		Aberdarorgen, Great Britain	United States	Marquis of Anglesea	8 Jun 1827
Jane	24	F		Gt. Britain	United States	Meteor	19 Aug 1829
Jane	26	F		Great Britain	United States	Meridian	2 Jul 1827
Jane	30			Great Britain	United States	Gomer	21 May 1828
Jane	40	F	None			Evergreen	28 Jul 1820
Jane	40	F	Farmer	Britain	U. States	Fame	3 Jun 1828
Jane	43	F	None	Great Britain	Great Britain	Nestor in Liverpool	29 Jul 1822
Jane	52	F		Aberdaron	United States	Marquis of Anglesea	8 Jun 1827
Jane	55	F		Great Britain	United States	Mary	11 Jul 1820
Jane	55	F	Farmer	Wales, Gt. Bn.	United States	Orozimbo	31 May 1824
Jane, child	6	F	None	England	United States	Great Britain	5 Sep 1827
Jane, Wife [of William]	33	F	Labourer	Wales		Gomer	22 May 1827
Jane, Wife [of Evan]	63	F	Labourer	Wales		Gomer	22 May 1827
Jane [crossed out]	32	F	None	Ireland	United States	Leonidas	3 Aug 1825
Jas.	13	M	None	England	U. States	Thomas Ritchie	2 Jul 1827
Jas.	22		Gentn.	England	U. States	New York	30 Oct 1827
Jas.	23	M	Laborer or Spinster	Ireland	United States	Sarah G	11 Sep 1827
Jeanet	28	F	None	Wales	United States	Orozimbo	11 Aug 1823
Jeffery	29	M	Farmer	Gt. Britain	United States	Europa	20 Apr 1825
Jeffery, Jr.	2	M	Farmer	Gt. Britain	United States	Europa	20 Apr 1825
Jemima	19	F		Great Britain	United States	Mary Howland	19 Jul 1827
*Died on the Voyage							
Jemmima	24	F	Farmer	Gt. Britain	United States	Europa	20 Apr 1825
Jereh.	31	M	Mercht.	U.S.	U.S.	Clarissa	23 May 1822
Jesse	40	M	Minister	England	U. States	New York	11 Jul 1823
Jno.	10	M	Lad	Great Brittain	N. York	Leonidas	24 Jul 1824
Jno.	25	M	Mariner	Baltimore	U. States	Decatur	3 May 1821
Jno.	34	M	Clerk	England	U.S. America	Cortes	19 May 1826
Job	6	M	Servant	England	U. States	Comet	28 Jul 1825
John		M	Merchant	N. York	U. States	Jane	22 Mar 1824
John	1	M		Aberdaron	United States	Marquis of Anglesea	8 Jun 1827
John	3			Great Britain	United States	Gomer	21 May 1828
John	6	M	None	Great Brittan	U.S.	Emulous	29 Jun 1827

647

NAMES OF PASSENGERS	AGE	SEX	OCCUPATIONS	COUNTRY TO WHICH THEY BELONG	COUNTRY THEY INTEND TO INHABIT	SHIPS/DATES OF ARRIVAL	
JONES (cont'd)							
John	8	M	Laborer	Ireland	United States	Weser	29 Jul 1823
John	8	M	None	England	United States	Orozimbo	1 Dec 1823
John	10	M	None			Evergreen	28 Jul 1820
John	11	M		Europe	United States	Aspasia	5 Sep 1827
John	13	M		G. Britain	G. Britain	Brittania	17 Jul 1828
John	16	M	Farmer			Hercules	25 Sep 1820
John	18	M	Servant	England	U. States	Comet	28 Jul 1825
John	18	M	Clothier	England	U.N. States	Jane	7 Oct 1826
John	19	M	Farmer	U.S.A.	U.S.A.	Silas Richards	28 Jun 1825
John	19	M	Farmer	Wales	U.N. States	William Byrnes	13 Aug 1829
John	20		...	Great Britain	United States	Gomer	21 May 1828
John	21	M				Ocean	17 Aug 1820
John	21	M	Surgeon	England	West Indies	Euphrates	12 May 1823
John	21	M	...	G. Britain	U. States	New England	28 Sep 1824
John	21	M	Gentleman	Scotland	United States	Roman	12 Jun 1826
John	22	M	Farmer	England	Great Brittan	Amity	11 May 1821
John	22	M	Glasgow	Glasgow	Glasgow	Howard Douglass	11 May 1827
John	22	M	Labourer	England	United States	Jubilee	12 May 1828
John	23	M	Iron Monger	Great Britan	United States	Bolivar	21 May 1827
John	23	M	None	Great Britan	United States	Isaac Hicks	10 Jul 1827
John	24	M	Miner	Great Britain	United States	Thomas Dickason	31 Jul 1829
John	25	M	Merchant	Great Britian	U. States	Orbit	29 Apr 1822
John	25	M	Farmer	Great Britain	United States	Mary & Harriet	3 Jul 1829
John	26	M	Labourer	Great Brittain	United States	Robert Fulton	13 Mar 1827
John	27	M	Labourer	Wales		Gomer	22 May 1827
John	28	M	Farmer	Great Brittan	U.S.	Emulous	29 Jun 1827
John	29	M	Farmer	England	New York	Thames	6 Oct 1820
John	30	M	Farmer	Gt. Britain	United States	Europa	20 Apr 1825
John	30	M	Smith	G. Britain	Canada	Cosmo	25 Nov 1826
John	30			Great Britan	U. States	Columbia	7 May 1828
John	35	M	...	G. Britain	U. States	New England	28 Sep 1824
John	35	M	Mariner	U. States	United States	Pionier	4 Mar 1828
John	35	M	Physician	Ireland	United States	Pallas	28 Oct 1828
John	38	M	Merchant	Canada	United States	William Byrnes	15 Aug 1826
John	40	M	Farmer	England	U. States	Birmingham	16 Jun 1828
John	41	M	Collier	Wales	U.S. States	Splendid	14 Aug 1829
John	41 1/12	M	Merchant	Great Brittain	U.S. America	Leeds	5 Feb 1827
John	44	M	Farmer	United States	United States	John Wells	22 Sep 1824
John	49	M	Labourer	Great Britain		Moro Castle	6 Jul 1827
John	56	M	Farmer			Hercules	25 Sep 1820
John	58	M	Grocer	G. Britain	U. States	America	17 Oct 1825
John	60	M	Farmer	Great Britain	United States	Mary Howland	19 Jul 1827
John, Boy	13	M	None	England	United States	Great Britain	5 Sep 1827
John, Child [of William]	3	M	Labourer	Wales		Gomer	22 May 1827
John, Jr.	2	M	Smith	G. Britain	Canada	Cosmo	25 Nov 1826
John, Jr.	22	M	Farmer	Great Britain	United States	Mary Howland	19 Jul 1827
John, Junr.	18	M	Collier	Wales	U.S. States	Splendid	14 Aug 1829
John [crossed out]	33	M	Farmer	Ireland	United States	Leonidas	3 Aug 1825
John A.	20	M	Merchant	Great Britan	Great Britan	Columbia	10 Mar 1824
John A.	36	M	Merchant	United States		General Marion	6 Oct 1828
John C.	50	M	Merchant	U.S. America	U.S. America	Commodore Preble	17 Dec 1825
John D.	26	M	Merchant	G. Brittain	Canada	Hercules	24 Oct 1821
Jonathan	21	M	Collier	Wales	U.S. States	Splendid	14 Aug 1829
Jos. P.	23	M	Ship Carpenter	N. York	U. States	Borneo	4 Dec 1824
Joseph	3	M	Child			Seine	10 Jun 1822
Joseph	11	M		Ireland	U. States	William Byrnes	17 Jul 1825
Joseph	13	M		England	United States	Siroc	31 Oct 1829
Joseph	19	M	Miner	Great Britain	United States	Thomas Dickason	31 Jul 1829
Joseph	24	M	Farmer			Seine	10 Jun 1822
Joseph	25	M	None	Great Brittian		Armadillo	15 Oct 1827
Joseph	30	M	Carpenter		New York	Hesperus	2 Nov 1820
Joseph	34	F	Servant			Cadmus	18 Aug 1828
L., Doctor	44	M	M.D.	U. States		Hudson	23 Jul 1828

NAMES OF PASSENGERS	A G E	S E X	OCCUPATIONS	COUNTRY TO WHICH THEY BELONG	COUNTRY THEY INTEND TO INHABIT	SHIPS/DATES OF ARRIVAL	
JONES (cont'd)							
Laura, Child							
[of Griffith]	12	F	Labourer	Wales		Gomer	22 May 1827
Lemach	26	M	Merchant	United States	United States	Atlantic	3 Dec 1821
Lewis	17	M	Farmer	Great Britain	United States	Mary Howland	19 Jul 1827
Liddy	17	F	None	England	U. States	Thomas Ritchie	2 Jul 1827
Liddy	48	F	None	England	U. States	Thomas Ritchie	2 Jul 1827
Loeis	23	M	Farmer	G. Britian	U. States	Messouri	17 Jun 1824
Lydia	4	F	None	U. States	U. States	Almira	11 Dec 1826
M.	16	F	None	England	United States	Enterprize	19 Oct 1826
M.	58	F	Brewer	England	U.S. States	Splendid	14 Aug 1829
Mairick	9	M	None			Evergreen	28 Jul 1820
Margaret	2		Farmer	Wales	Great Britain	Oglethorpe	25 Aug 1825
Margaret	3	F				Plato	31 Oct 1829
Margaret	5	F	None			Evergreen	28 Jul 1820
Margaret	17		Merch.	Havana	U. States	Courier	9 Feb 1829
Margaret	30	F		U. States		Leader	28 Mar 1822
Margaret	30	F	None	United States	United States	Leader	4 Oct 1824
Margaret	32	F		U. States		Leader	18 Apr 1823
Margaret	34	F	Female	Great Brittain	N. York	Leonidas	24 Jul 1824
Margaret	36	F		United States A.	United States A.	Elbe	13 Mar 1829
Margaret	40	F	None	England	U. States	Comet	28 Jul 1825
Margaret	60	F	Laboror	Great Brittian	United States	Perseverance	7 Aug 1826
Margaret, child							
[of John Davis]	12	F	Farmer	Wales		Gomer	22 May 1827
Margaret, Child							
[of Griffith]	13	F	Labourer	Wales		Gomer	22 May 1827
Margret	1			Great Britain	United States	Gomer	21 May 1828
Margrt.	19			Great Britain	United States	Gomer	21 May 1828
Margt.	5	F	None	England	United States	Great Britain	5 Sep 1827
Margt.	21	F		G. Britain	G. Britain	Brittania	17 Jul 1828
Margt.	30	F	None	England	United States	Great Britain	5 Sep 1827
Margt.	60	F	Spinner	Great Britain	United States	Atlantic	8 Dec 1827
Mark	20	M	Baker	Halifax	U. States	Greek	8 Mar 1828
Martha	4	F	None	England	U. States	Comet	28 Jul 1825
Martha	20	F	None	G. Britain		Casanda	5 Sep 1827
Mary	9/12	F	Weaver	Great Britain	United States	Thomas Dickason	31 Jul 1829
Mary	2	F	Laborer	Ireland	United States	Weser	29 Jul 1823
Mary	3	F	Farmer	Gt. Britain	United States	Europa	20 Apr 1825
Mary	6	F		England	United States	Siroc	31 Oct 1829
Mary	11	F				Ocean	17 Aug 1820
Mary	12	F	Calico Printer	England	United States	Amelia	20 Aug 1829
Mary	17			G. Britain	U. States	Mary & Harriot	8 Sep 1828
Mary	19	F	None	Great Brittan	U.S.	Emulous	29 Jun 1827
Mary	19	F		U. States	United States	Henri IV	14 Sep 1827
Mary	19 3/12	F	Servant	Ireland	United States	Wilson	27 Jun 1826
Mary	20	F		England	U. States	Emulous	22 Aug 1828
Mary	20	F		Gt. Britain	United States	Meteor	19 Aug 1829
Mary	21					Hudson	5 Apr 1826
Mary	21	F		Llannstyn	United States	Marquis of Anglesea	8 Jun 1827
Mary	21	F	Farmer	Britain	U. States	Fame	3 Jun 1828
Mary	22	F	Servant	England	United States	Comet	6 Mar 1823
Mary	24	F	Spinster	Great Britain	United States	Corinthian	29 Apr 1826
Mary	24	F		Llannstyn	United States	Marquis of Anglesea	8 Jun 1827
Mary	24	F	None	England	U. States	Thomas Ritchie	2 Jul 1827
Mary	24	F	Wife	Great Britain	United States	Washington	3 Sep 1827
Mary	24	F	Servant	Great Britain	United States	Manchester	12 Aug 1829
Mary	30	F		England	United States	Helen	17 Dec 1827
Mary	32	F		Gt. Britain	United States	Silas Richards	20 Jun 1826
Mary	34	F		England	United States	Cincinnatus	21 Nov 1821
Mary	35	F	None	England	United States	Orozimbo	1 Dec 1823
Mary	36	F	Merchant	England	United States	John & Elizabeth	25 Sep 1827
Mary	40	F	None	Gt. Britain	United States	Union	9 Jan 1824
Mary	40	F	Servant	Gt. Britain		Silas Richards	20 Jun 1826
Mary	50	F		England	U. States	Emulous	22 Aug 1828

NAMES OF PASSENGERS	AGE	SEX	OCCUPATIONS	COUNTRY TO WHICH THEY BELONG	COUNTRY THEY INTEND TO INHABIT	SHIPS/DATES OF ARRIVAL	
JONES (cont'd)							
Mary	60	F	Spinster	Ireland	United States	Dublin Packet	3 Sep 1822
Mary, (Wife [of Robert])	40	F		Ireland	New York	Brighton	24 Aug 1827
Mary, Child [of William]	1	F	Labourer	Wales		Gomer	22 May 1827
Mary, Mrs.	20			Great Britan	U. States	Columbia	7 May 1828
Mary, Mrs.	29	F				Betsey	17 Aug 1820
Matilda	1	F	None	Ireland	United States	John Wells	22 Sep 1824
Maurice	9	M	None	England	United States	Great Britain	5 Sep 1827
Maurice	24	M	Labourer	G. Britain	U. States	London	23 Sep 1828
Meredith	40	F		Europe	United States	Aspasia	5 Sep 1827
Merith	9	M		Europe	United States	Aspasia	5 Sep 1827
Morgan	13	M	Servant	England	U. States	Comet	28 Jul 1825
Morgan	21	M	Farmer	Great Britain	United States	Mary Howland	19 Jul 1827
Morris	5	M	None	Great Brittan	U.S.	Emulous	29 Jun 1827
Morris	11	M		England	U. States	Birmingham	16 Jun 1828
Moses	5	M	Farmer	Gt. Britain	United States	Europa	20 Apr 1825
Murden	6			Wales		Anacreon	7 Sep 1827
Nancy [crossed out]	14	F	None	Ireland	United States	Leonidas	3 Aug 1825
Naomi	9		Farmer	Wales	Great Britain	Oglethorpe	25 Aug 1825
O.	12	M	Mariner	G. Brittain	U. States	Favorite	13 Jun 1821
Onig	30	F	Sempstress	Great Britain	United States	Atlantic	8 Dec 1827
Owen	9	M		G. Britain	U. States	Mary & Harriot	8 Sep 1828
Owen	10	M		Llannstyn	United States	Marquis of Anglesea	8 Jun 1827
Owen *died on passage	20	M	Taylor	Great Britain	United States	Richmond	18 Feb 1820
Peggy	10	F		England	United States	Siroc	31 Oct 1829
Peggy	26	F		England	United States	Siroc	31 Oct 1829
Peter [crossed out]	12	M	None	Ireland	United States	Leonidas	3 Aug 1825
Peter L.	2	M	Infant	America	America	Telegraph	18 May 1827
Phebe	1	F	Child			Seine	10 Jun 1822
Philip	24	M	Labourer	England	United States	Young Phoenix	26 Jul 1824
R.	53	M	Cabinet Maker	England	U.S. States	Splendid	14 Aug 1829
R., Junr.	13	M	Cabinet Maker	England	U.S. States	Splendid	14 Aug 1829
R. K., Mr.	24	M	Merchant	Rhode Island	U. States	Lewis	11 Nov 1824
Ralph	45	M	...man	United States	United States	Silas Richards	27 Oct 1825
Rawban	23	M	Farmer	North Wales	United States	Magnet	16 May 1823
Rebacca	29		Hair Dresser	England	United States	Acasta	16 Aug 1826
Rebecca	26	F	Spinster	Great Britain	United States	Corinthian	29 Apr 1826
Ricd.	2	M	None	Great Brittan	U.S.	Emulous	29 Jun 1827
Richard	1	M		England	United States	Siroc	31 Oct 1829
Richard	5			Great Britain	United States	Gomer	21 May 1828
Richard	7	M	None	Wales	United States	Mentor	28 Apr 1824
Richard	12	M	Collier	Wales	U.S. States	Splendid	14 Aug 1829
Richard	22	M		Great Britain	United States	John Jay	8 May 1828
Richard	24 2/12	M	Carpenter	England	U.S. American	Criterion	7 Jul 1824
Richard	28 11/12	M	Farmer	England	U.S. of America	Illinois	16 Jun 1821
Richard	29 10/12	M	Farmer	England	U.S. of America	Illinois	16 Jun 1821
Richard	32		...	Great Britain	United States	Gomer	21 May 1828
Richard	36	M	Farmer			Seine	10 Jun 1822
Richard, Child [of William]	10	M	Labourer	Wales		Gomer	22 May 1827
Richard, Jr.	33	M	Farmer	Great Britain	United States	John Jay	8 May 1828
Richd.	25	M	Farmer	England	U. States	Unity	5 Sep 1828
Richd.	27	M	Farmer	England	U. States	New York	11 Jul 1823
Rob.	40	M	Mariner	U. States	U. States	Abigail	24 Mar 1825
Robert	3	M	None	Ireland	United States	John Wells	22 Sep 1824
Robert	13	M	None	Gt. Britain	United States	Union	9 Jan 1824
Robert	22	M	Glazier	Great Britain	United States	James Cropper	26 Mar 1822
Robert	25	M	Seaman	Sangr...	Boston	Young Phenix	17 Jan 1825
Robert	25		Farmer	Great Britain	United States	Gomer	21 May 1828
Robert	30	M	Farmer	Gt. Britain	United States	Meteor	19 Aug 1829
Robert	32	M	Penman	Ireland	U. States	Reaper	31 May 1824
Robert	36	M	Labourer	Gt. Britain	United States	Union	9 Jan 1824
Robert	36		Farmer	Wales	Great Britain	Oglethorpe	25 Aug 1825
Robert	45	M	Victualer	Ireland	New York	Brighton	24 Aug 1827
Robert	47	M	Shoemaker	Great Britain	U. States	Ganges	21 Jun 1827

NAMES OF PASSENGERS	AGE	SEX	OCCUPATIONS	COUNTRY TO WHICH THEY BELONG	COUNTRY THEY INTEND TO INHABIT	SHIPS/DATES OF ARRIVAL	
JONES (cont'd)							
Robert, Child							
[of Griffith]	16	M	Labourer	Wales		Gomer	22 May 1827
Robt.	5/12	M	None	Great Brittan	U.S.	Emulous	29 Jun 1827
Robt.	20	M	Painter	England	U.S. America	Cortes	19 May 1826
Robt.	24	M	Farmer	Great Brittan	U.S.	Emulous	29 Jun 1827
Robt.	48	M	Ship Master	United States	United States	Elbe	30 Sep 1826
Robt. J.	30	M	Mercht.	Gt. Brittian	United States	Manchester	17 Aug 1825
Roger	22		Laboring Class		United States	Atlantic	2 Apr 1827
Rogers	26	M	Farmer	Ireland		Ocean	17 Aug 1820
Ruth	11		Farmer	Wales	Great Britain	Oglethorpe	25 Aug 1825
S.	5	F	None	England	United States	Enterprize	19 Oct 1826
S.	62	M	Farmer	England	U.S. States	Splendid	14 Aug 1829
Saml.	26	M	Servant	United States	United States	Robert Read	10 Jan 1825
Saml. D.	28	M	Ship Master	New York	U. States	Flight	1 Oct 1829
Samuel	3	M				Betsey	17 Aug 1820
Samuel	28	M	Farmer	Great Britain		Ulysses	29 Oct 1822
Samuel	30 7/12	M	Merchant	U.S.A.	U. States	Silas Richards	27 Oct 1826
Samuel	59	M	Merchant	United States	South Carolina	Xenophon	3 Oct 1829
Samuell	24	M	Merchant	United States	United States	Florida	11 May 1822
Sarah	3		Child	England	United States	Cincinnatus	21 Nov 1821
Sarah	6	F	Farmer	Gt. Britain	United States	Europa	20 Apr 1825
Sarah	12	F	daughter				
[of Charls.]				Great Britain	United States	Wyton	12 May 1821
Sarah	13 5/12	F		England	U.S. American	Criterion	7 Jul 1824
Sarah	15	F		Gt. Britain	United States	Silas Richards	20 Jun 1826
Sarah	16	F	None	Great Britan	United States	Bolivar	21 May 1827
Sarah	20	F		England	U. States	York	12 Jul 1825
Sarah	23	F		England	U. States	Unity	5 Sep 1828
Sarah	24	F	Miner	Great Britain	United States	Thomas Dickason	31 Jul 1829
Sarah	25	F	Farmer	Gt. Britain	United States	Europa	20 Apr 1825
Sarah	27	M	Merchant	Gt. Britan	Gt. Britan	Canada	8 Jun 1826
Sarah	29	F		England	United States	Cincinnatus	21 Nov 1821
Sarah	43	F	None	Great Britan	United States	Bolivar	21 May 1827
Simeon	7	M	Collier	Wales	U.S. States	Splendid	14 Aug 1829
Simon	24	M	Coal Miner	Wales	New York	Indian Chief	19 Jun 1823
Sophia	21			England	England	Hudson	4 Sep 1823
Steph.	24		Royal Navy	Kensington	England	Elizabeth	8 Dec 1821
Susannah	16	F	Collier	Wales	U.S. States	Splendid	14 Aug 1829
Susannah, Mrs.	45	F	Lady	U. States	U. States	Acasta	21 Oct 1825
Sush.	5	F	None	England	U. States	Thomas Ritchie	2 Jul 1827
T.			Servant			Dromo	14 Aug 1829
Theodw.	26	M	Farmer	G. Britain	U. States	Mary & Harriot	8 Sep 1828
Thomas	1	M		Gt. Britain	United States	Meteor	19 Aug 1829
Thomas	4	M	None	Great Britan	United States	Bolivar	21 May 1827
Thomas	9	M		G. Britain	U. States	Mary & Harriot	8 Sep 1828
Thomas	20	M	None	Great Britain	United States	Roman	19 Dec 1825
Thomas	20	M	Fuller	Wales	U.S. America	Josephine	24 Jul 1826
Thomas	20	M	Collier	England	United States	Amelia	20 Aug 1829
Thomas	21	M	Farmer	G. Britain	U. States	Mary & Harriot	8 Sep 1828
Thomas	22	M	B...er	England	United States	William Byrnes	1 Dec 1824
Thomas	24	M	Labourer	Llannstyn	United States	Marquis of Anglesea	8 Jun 1827
Thomas	26	M	Weaver	Great Britain	United States	Thomas Dickason	31 Jul 1829
Thomas	27		Merchant	England	England	Hudson	4 Sep 1823
Thomas	28	M	Labourer	Great Britain	United States	Robert	15 Jul 1822
Thomas	30	M	Farmer	England	U.S.A.	Mexico	9 Jul 1827
Thomas	39	M	Cabinet Maker	Gt. Britain	United States	Silas Richards	20 Jun 1826
Thomas	50	M	Shoemaker	Great Britain	U. States	Ganges	21 Jun 1827
Thomas	52	M	Iron Monger	Great Brittan	United States	Bolivar	21 May 1827
Thomas	58	M	Farmer	Great Brittan	U.S.	Emulous	29 Jun 1827
Thomas, Mr.	22	M	Gent.	England	U.S.	Acasta	11 May 1827
Thomas Mercer	29	M	None	England	England	Britannia	23 Mar 1829
Thomas W.	23	M	Printer	America	America	Hannibal	28 May 1827
Thos.	10	M	Laborer	Ireland	United States	Weser	29 Jul 1823
Thos.	10	M	None	England	U. States	Thomas Ritchie	2 Jul 1827
Thos.	13	M	Servant	Great Britain	United States	Martha	3 May 1821

NAMES OF PASSENGERS	AGE	SEX	OCCUPATIONS	COUNTRY TO WHICH THEY BELONG	COUNTRY THEY INTEND TO INHABIT	SHIPS/DATES OF ARRIVAL	
JONES (cont'd)							
Thos.	24	M	Merchant	...d b..., Wales	Gt. Britain	Orozimbo	19 Oct 1822
Thos.	24	M	None	G. Britain		Casanda	5 Sep 1827
Thos.	30	M	None	United States	United States	James Cropper	14 Oct 1824
Thos.	33	M	Wheelwright	England	U. States	Hudson	8 Oct 1827
Thos.	34	M	Gentn.	England	United States	Robert Edwards	1 Jun 1826
Thos.	34	M	Farmer	Scotland	United States	Indus	5 Sep 1827
Thos.	51			Wales		Anacreon	7 Sep 1827
Ths.	11	M	None	Great Brittan	U.S.	Emulous	29 Jun 1827
Ths.	27	M	Compossiter	England	England	Venus	15 Apr 1822
Tom	26	M	Mariner	G. Brittain	U. States	Favorite	13 Jun 1821
W.	6	F	Farmer	Britain	U. States	Fame	3 Jun 1828
W.	6	M	Farmer	Britain	U. States	Fame	3 Jun 1828
W.	13	M		England	United States	Earl of Liverpool	28 Apr 1824
W.	13	M		Europe	United States	Aspasia	5 Sep 1827
W.	22	M	Farmer	Gt. Britan	U. States	Earl of Liverpool	12 Apr 1825
W.	24	M	Blacksmith	Bristol	New York	Cosmo	25 Sep 1827
W.	49	M	Manufacturer	Ireland	U. States	William Byrnes	17 Jul 1825
W. R.	25	M	Coachmaker	U. States	U. States	Georgetown Packet	24 Feb 1823
William	...			Great Britain	United States	Gomer	21 May 1828
William	11	M	Farmer	Great Britain	United States	Isaac Hicks	10 Jul 1827
William	14		Labourer	Manchester, England	Great Britain	Franklin	22 Jun 1827
William	16	M	Servant	England	U. States	Comet	28 Jul 1825
William	18	M	Grocer			Manhattan	20 Sep 1821
William	19	M	None	Great Britain	United States	Roman	19 Dec 1825
William	19	M	Painter	Ireland	United States	Thompson	12 Sep 1827
William	21	M	Farmer	Britain	U. States	Fame	3 Jun 1828
William	22	M	Carpenter	Bristol, Engl.	...	Warrior	19 May 1828
William	22	M	B. Smith	England	U. States	Josephine	23 Jan 1829
William	23	M	Labourer	Ireland	United States	Wanderer	1 Aug 1828
William	25	M	Farmer	Great Brittain	U. States	William Byrnes	23 Jul 1824
William	28	M	Gold & silver chaser	Great Britain	New York	Thames	16 May 1821
William	30	M	Gentleman	Great Britain	United States	Courier	13 Mar 1820
William	30	M	Labourer	United States	New York	John London	7 Apr 1824
William	30	M	Gentleman	England	Uncertain	John Wells	22 Sep 1824
William	30	M	Labourer	Wales		Gomer	22 May 1827
William	30	M	Cabinet maker	England	U. States	Emulous	22 Aug 1828
William	32	M	Farmer	Wales		Gomer	22 May 1827
William	37	M	Skinner	England	America	Britannia	22 Jul 1829
William	40	M	Sawyer	England	United States	Nancy Henrietta	3 Nov 1828
William	43	M	Pedlar	England	U. States	Comet	28 Jul 1825
William, Child [of William]	6/12	M	Labourer	Wales		Gomer	22 May 1827
William, Child [of William]	6	M	Labourer	Wales		Gomer	22 May 1827
William, Jr.	4	M		England	United States	Nancy Henrietta	3 Nov 1828
Willm.	32	M	Merchant	England	United States	Helen	17 Dec 1827
Winiper	11	F	None			Evergreen	28 Jul 1820
Wm.	5	M				Betsey	17 Aug 1820
Wm.	5	M	None	U. States	U. States	Almira	11 Dec 1826
Wm.	7		Child	England	United States	Cincinnatus	21 Nov 1821
Wm.	9	M	Collier	Wales	U.S. States	Splendid	14 Aug 1829
Wm.	12	M	Lad	Great Brittain	N. York	Leonidas	24 Jul 1824
Wm.	20	M	Calico ...	England	America	Hercules	2 Nov 1825
Wm.	22	M	Farmer	Donegal	United States	Solon	21 Jun 1824
Wm.	22	M	Carpenter	N. York		Swift	28 Jun 1828
Wm.	22	M		G. Britain	U. States	Canada	19 Sep 1828
Wm.	24	M	Merchant	Gt. Brittain	United States	Florida	23 Aug 1825
Wm.	26	M	Servant	England	Central America	Tampico	29 Apr 1826
Wm.	27	M	Joiner	Great Britain	U. St.	Manchester	7 Dec 1826
Wm.	29		Farmer	Great Britain	United States	Gomer	21 May 1828
Wm.	29		Farmer	Wicklow	Pensylvania	Peru	30 May 1828
Wm.	35	M	Farmer	Great Brittain	N. York	Leonidas	24 Jul 1824

NAMES OF PASSENGERS	AGE	SEX	OCCUPATIONS	COUNTRY TO WHICH THEY BELONG	COUNTRY THEY INTEND TO INHABIT	SHIPS/DATES OF ARRIVAL	
JONES (cont'd)							
Wm.	35	M	Labourer	England	England	Sir James Kempt	10 Dec 1827
Wm.	38	M	Merchant	Stockholm	America	Dromo	10 Sep 1827
Wm.	40	M	Merchant	England	United States	John & Elizabeth	25 Sep 1827
Wm.	45	M	Mason	U. States	U. States	Commodore Perry	9 Apr 1821
Wm.	52	F		Great Britain	U. States	Albert	1 Apr 1822
Wm.	54	M	Gentleman	Great Britain	United States	Corinthian	5 Jan 1824
Wm.	60	M	Farmer	America	N.Y.	Stephania	13 Mar 1820
Wm. F.	23	M	Merchant	U. States	U. States	Romulus	16 Feb 1824
Wm. S.	42	M	Linen Draper	England	New York	Bowditch	27 Apr 1826
Z.	6	M	Laborer	Ireland	United States	Weser	29 Jul 1823
Zachariah	24	M	Miner	Great Britain	United States	Thomas Dickason	31 Jul 1829
JONS, H.	32	M	Laboror	Great Brittian	United States	Perseverance	7 Aug 1826
JONSON, Thos.	30	M	Carpenter	Ireland	United States	Henry Kneeland	7 Jun 1828
JONTE, Catharine	18	F		France	U. States	Edward Bopnnaffe	30 Jul 1829
JOOST, Chrs.	20	M	Labourer	Germany	U. States	Hudson	26 Jan 1825
JOPPLE, Jos.	19	M	Shoe Maker	Germany	United States	Lydia	18 Jun 1828
JORDAN, —, Mr.	30	M	Gentn.	Gt. Brittain	United States	Robert Edwards	1 Jun 1826
—, Mrs.	23	F		United States	United States	Robert Edwards	1 Jun 1826
Ann	1...	F	Spinster	Ireland	Unt. St. America	Wilson	21 May 1827
Bathsheba	50	F		United States	United States	Nancy	28 Oct 1822
F., Miss	2	F		United States	United States	Robert Edwards	1 Jun 1826
Geo.	1	M		United States	United States	Robert Edwards	1 Jun 1826
George Colebrook	20		Gent.	London		Manhattan	20 Sep 1821
James	50	M	Merchant	Great Britain	United States	Cortes	19 Nov 1821
John	21	M	Labourer	Ireland, Great Britain	U.S. of Amer	Dublin	21 Feb 1826
John	25	M	Farmer	...ford		Mount Vernon	7 Jun 1824
John	47	M	Officer	England	Quebec	Lewis	25 Jun 1824
Margt.	20	F	Dressmaker	Ireland	United States	Carolina Ann	11 Dec 1826
Mary	18	F	None	Great Britain		Moro Castle	6 Jul 1827
P.	24	M		Ireland	United States	William Byrnes	6 Apr 1826
Pat	21	M		Ireland	U.S. of America	Douglass	6 Jul 1829
Stephen	23	M	Laborer	Gt. Britain		Dalhouse Castle	13 May 1828
Emily	28	F		England	United States	Cosmo	26 Aug 1829
John	28	M	Moulder	England	United States	Cosmo	26 Aug 1829
Mary	46	F	None	Great Britain	United States	Washington	9 Apr 1821
Simon	44	M	Labourer	Great Britain	United States	Washington	9 Apr 1821
William	25	M	Farmer	Ireland	United States	Justina	5 Aug 1823
Eliza	16	F	Spinster	Ireland	America	Wilson	16 May 1825
J.	32	M	Mariner	U. States	U. States	Caroline	17 Apr 1821
Jane	38	F	Wife	Ireland	United States	Meteor	27 Sep 1826
John	37	M	Weaver	Ireland	United States	Meteor	27 Sep 1826
Lawrence	13	M	Boy	Ireland	America	Wilson	16 May 1825
Mary Ann	20	F		Mayo	America	Margaret	31 Jul 1824
Rose	25	F		Great Britain	United States	Samuel Wright	12 Oct 1829
Rufus	21	M	Farmer	Portland	U. States	Sally	14 Jun 1823
JOREDAN, Patrick	30	M	Labourer	Ireland	United States	Princess Charlotte	26 Apr 1827
JORING, Haslott	44		Merchant	Ireland	Ireland	William Byrnes	25 Aug 1828
JORNDERS, Michl.	45	M	Shipmaster	U.S.	U.S.	Emma	7 Jul 1824
JOSAS, Patrick	27	M		Great Britain	United States	Mary Howland	19 Jul 1827
JOSELINE, George R.	25		Farmer	England	England	Hudson	4 Sep 1823
JOSEPH, —, Wife	31	F		Baden	United States	Cavalier	25 Jul 1828
Abm.	25	M	Labourer	G. Britain	U. States	London	23 Sep 1828
Barbara	10	F	Spinster	Switzerland	United States	Andes	5 May 1828
Benjamin	32	M	Gentleman	England	U. States	Robert Edwards	9 May 1827
C.	40	F	Milliner	Great Britain		Caravan	8 Sep 1828
Catherine	6	F	Spinster	Switzerland	United States	Andes	5 May 1828
Catherine	17	F	Spinster	Switzerland	United States	Andes	5 May 1828
Catherine	36	F	Spinster	Switzerland	United States	Andes	5 May 1828
Daniel	21	M	Servant to the above [Jose Lorenzo Billco]	Portugal	Havana	Margaret	22 Jun 1821

NAMES OF PASSENGERS	AGE	SEX	OCCUPATIONS	COUNTRY TO WHICH THEY BELONG	COUNTRY THEY INTEND TO INHABIT	SHIPS/DATES OF ARRIVAL	
JOSEPH (cont'd)							
E.	25	F	Seamstress	New York	United States	Falcon	16 Aug 1826
George	12	M	Merchant	England	To return to Eng.	Maine	16 Jul 1821
H.	27	M	Merchant	France	United States	Elizabeth	22 May 1822
Isaac	56	M	Merchant	England	To return to Eng.	Maine	16 Jul 1821
J.	27	M	Labourer	Baden	United States	Cavalier	25 Jul 1828
J. G.	24	M	Optician	England	U.S.A.	Hudson	21 Aug 1829
Jacob	41	M	Farmer	Switzerland	United States	Andes	5 May 1828
John	35	M	Servant	United States	United States	William Bayard	17 May 1825
Margaret	14	F	Spinster	Switzerland	United States	Andes	5 May 1828
Maria	12	F	Spinster	Switzerland	United States	Andes	5 May 1828
Mariane	0 3/12	F		Baden	United States	Cavalier	25 Jul 1828
Marie	50	F	Lady	Martinique	France	Alpha	27 Jul 1827
Mary	38	F	Servant	Barbadoes	Great Britain	Only Daughter	26 Apr 1826
P. L.	25	M	Merchant	Germany	U. States	Edward Bonaffe	11 Dec 1827
Peter	30	M	Mariner	U. States	U.S.	Ambuscade	14 Mar 1820
Sophia	7	F	Spinster	Switzerland	United States	Andes	5 May 1828
Va Vaux	25 5/12	M	Museseon [Musician?]	France	America	Edward Bonaffe	1 Mar 1825
Volburga	56	F		France	United States	Stephania	24 Mar 1828
Xolban	53	M	Agricultural	France	United States	Stephania	24 Mar 1828
JOSEPHENIA, Catharine	40	F	Servant	Great Brittain	Canada	Canada	5 Feb 1827
JOSEPHINE, —, Miss	17	F	Merchant	Hayti	U. States	Jean Baptiste	2 Dec 1826
—, Mrs.	30	F	Merchant	Hayti	U. States	Jean Baptiste	2 Dec 1826
JOSSEN, H.	12	F	Servant	Curacoa	U. States	Douglass	30 Oct 1826
JOST, Z.	18	M	Laborer	Hannover	United States	Constitution	6 Jul 1829
JOTED, William, ...42, 35, 12, etc.			(males & female) Laborer	England	Pitchford, N.Y. [Pittsford?]	Thames	6 Oct 1820
JOTT, Francis	21	M	Watch Maker	Germany	U. States	Rook	25 Jul 1827
JOTTE, Cath.	40	F		Switzerland	U.States	C. Amelia	30 Jun 1828
JOUAN, A.	20	M	Carpenter	Spain	U. States	Don Quixote	15 Apr 1825
A.	37	M	Merchant	France	France	Eliza	28 Apr 1827
Augustus	21		None	France		Bayard	10 Sep 1827
JOUAR, A.	18	M	Gentleman	France	U. States	Seine	30 Aug 1824
JOUBA, Devaur	24	M	Shoe Maker	France	United States	Virginia	31 May 1828
JOUCHIOM, Ghilione	40	M	Merchant	Italy	New York	Enterprize	3 Nov 1824
JOUGHIN, Ann E.	18	F	None	United States	United States	Euphrates	15 Nov 1824
Margaret	14	F	None	United States	United States	Euphrates	15 Nov 1824
Margaret	50	F	None	United States	United States	Euphrates	15 Nov 1824
Mary E.	12	F	None	United States	United States	Euphrates	15 Nov 1824
JOUGLIN, Maria	50	F	None	U. States	U. States	Louisa	21 Aug 1824
JOUGLING, Jno.	60	M	Merchant	U. States	U. States	Louisa	21 Aug 1824
JOUNG, William	20	M	Weaver	Ireland	United States	Asia	29 Jul 1829
JOUNGHIN, Eliza	20	F	None	U. States	U. States	Louisa	21 Aug 1824
JOUR, Abby	27	F		Germany	U. States	Isabella	10 Aug 1829
Elizabeth	1	F		Germany	U. States	Isabella	10 Aug 1829
Matthew	4	M		Germany	U. States	Isabella	10 Aug 1829
Matthew	28	M	Farmer	Germany	U. States	Isabella	10 Aug 1829
JOURDAN, Bridget	19	F	Spinster	Ireland	United States	Dublin Packet	22 Oct 1821
Joseph	29	M	Farmer	State of Mississippi		Casanda	5 Sep 1827
JOUREGAY, Francisco	40	M	Mercht.	Spain	Spain	Savannah	10 Jan 1828
JOURNEY, John	60	M	Farmer	St. Johns, N.B.	England	Nancy	4 Jun 1824
JOWINE, James	...7	M	Labourer	Ireland	United States	General Putnam	20 Jun 1825
JOY, Alexr.	32	M	Mariner	U. States	U. States	General Scott	7 May 1824
Charles L.	30	M	Merchant	U. States	U. States	Lucy Ann	6 Sep 1826
Fredrick	20	M	Printer	Ireland	United States	Carolina Ann	11 Dec 1826
Joseph	24	M	Farmer	Gt. Britain	U. States	Maria	22 May 1822
Levi	59	M	Mariner	United States	United States	George Clinton	10 Oct 1825
Rachel	10/12	F		Gt. Britain	U. States	Maria	22 May 1822
Sarah	22	F		Gt. Britain	U. States	Maria	22 May 1822
Sarah Ann	3	F		Gt. Britain	U. States	Maria	22 May 1822
JOYCE, —, Miss	35	F	Servant	Great Britain	United States	Mariner	21 Aug 1827
Bridget	21	F		Great Brittain	United States	Sarah Ralston	27 Jan 1827
Ewd.	24	M	Clerk	Great Britain	United States	Grecian	24 Sep 1828
John	11	M		Ireland	United States	Trio	31 Oct 1827
Julia	23	F		U.S.A.	U.S.A.	Potomac	25 Jul 1829

NAMES OF PASSENGERS	AGE	SEX	OCCUPATIONS	COUNTRY TO WHICH THEY BELONG	COUNTRY THEY INTEND TO INHABIT	SHIPS/DATES OF ARRIVAL	
JOYCE (cont'd)							
Mary	29	F		England	U. States of Amer	Dale	14 Mar 1828
Pat	39	M	Labourer	Great Brittain	United States	Sarah Ralston	27 Jan 1827
Thomas	35	M	Laborer	England	U. States of Amer	Dale	14 Mar 1828
JOYNT, G. C.	38	M	Farmer	England	Canada	Comet	24 Dec 1821
Mary	40	F	Farmer	England	Canada	Comet	24 Dec 1821
JUANA, A.	7	M		Spain	Spain	Circassian	13 Jun 1825
JUBB, Joseph	28	M	Mechanic	Ireland	United States	Pallas	28 Oct 1828
Mary	22	F		England		Fame	9 Dec 1826
William	30	M	Farmer	England		Fame	9 Dec 1826
JUBBINS, Michale	20	M	Coachmaker	Ireland	America	Parrington	9 Jun 1827
JUBERT, Adam	1	M	One Family [Henry]	France	United States	Henri IV	2 Oct 1828
Ann Maria	8	F	One Family [Henry]	France	United States	Henri IV	2 Oct 1828
Elizabeth	6	F	One Family [Henry]	France	United States	Henri IV	2 Oct 1828
Henry	46	M	Miller	France	United States	Henri IV	2 Oct 1828
Mader	11	F	One Family [Henry]	France	United States	Henri IV	2 Oct 1828
Philip	3	M	One Family [Henry]	France	United States	Henri IV	2 Oct 1828
Sophia	39	F	One Family [Henry]	France	United States	Henri IV	2 Oct 1828
JUDAH, S. N.	24	M	Merchant	U. States	U. States	Virginia	30 May 1827
S. N.	25	M	Merchant	U.S.	U.S.	Athenian	8 Feb 1827
JUDD, Jonathan	38	M	Clergyman	U. States	U. States	Charlotte Corday	15 Aug 1820
JUDEWICK, Andrew	36	M	Merchant	England	United States	Dalhouse Castle	6 Sep 1827
JUDGE, —, Mrs.	25	F		U. States	U. States	Lord Nelson	8 Nov 1826
Alice	22 5/12	F		Ireland	U.S. of America	Douglass	6 Jul 1829
Ann	24	F	None	Ireland	United States	John Wells	11 May 1827
G. R.	30	M	Clergyman	United States	United States	Langdon Cheeves	19 Mar 1827
James	21	M	Labourer	Ireland	United States	John Wells	11 May 1827
James	38	M	Farmer	United States	United States	Trident	30 Sep 1826
James Wm., Mr.	21	M	Gent.	England	New York	Cortes	23 Nov 1827
John	1	M	None	Ireland	United States	John Wells	11 May 1827
Louisa	5	F		U. States	U. States	Lord Nelson	8 Nov 1826
Mary	19 11/12	F		Ireland	U.S. of America	Douglass	6 Jul 1829
Mary	25	F		Ireland	U. States	Wanderer	30 Sep 1828
Wm.	3	F		U. States	U. States	Lord Nelson	8 Nov 1826
JUDSON, H. H.	32	F		Boston	U. States	Amity	25 Sep 1822
P. G.	17	M	Merchant	N. York	U. States	Martha	25 Sep 1822
P. G.	19	M	Mercht.	U. States	U. States	Martha	24 Jun 1822
P. G.	20	M	Mariner	U. States	U. States	Fourth of July	13 Jul 1825
Philo S.	20	M	Merch.	United States	United States	Mercator	10 Oct 1823
Sylvester A.	18	M	Mariner	United States	United States	Mary Ann	7 Jan 1829
JUEP, Chesapret	30	M	Farmer	Ireland		Quatre Freres	29 Jul 1828
JUITAR, —	55	F	Shop Keeper	U. States	U. States	Imperial	10 Dec 1821
JUKAIN, C.	26	M		France	France	Ann Elizabeth	24 Jun 1823
JUKEL, Cornelia, Miss	16	F		New York	U.S.	Bayard	30 Oct 1820
Cornelia, Mrs.	36	F		New York	U.S.	Bayard	30 Oct 1820
JUKERBOWSKI, —	47	M	...	...	United States	John London	20 Dec 1825
JULIAN, Moses	36	M	Merchant	Saint Thomas	Saint Thomas	Munroe	6 Aug 1825
Pierre	60	M	Merchant	France	United States	Paris	10 Sep 1823
JULIANO, A.	35	M	Merchant	France		Athenian	3 Sep 1827
JULIEN, N. F.	59	M	Mercht.	U. States	U. States	Caroline	21 Jun 1823
JULIET, Charles, Mr.	35	M	Merchant	France	U. States	Athenian	17 Jul 1829
JULIETT, C.	30	M	Merchant	France	U. States	Medina	23 Apr 1828
JULLUM, Luke	30	M		Great Brit.	Ohio	Gov. Griswald	3 Jul 1820
JULMI, Johanna B.	16	F		Germany	America	Falcon	28 Aug 1828
JUMEL, Nicholas A.	30	M	Merchant	France	U. States	Bayard	9 Nov 1825
Oliver	32	F	None	France	U. States	Bayard	9 Nov 1825
JUNE, Mary	15	F		New York	U. States	Manhattan	12 Jun 1824
JUNG, —, his Wife	46	F				New York Packet	19 Aug 1820
Catharina	13	F				New York Packet	19 Aug 1820
Dorothea	5	F				New York Packet	19 Aug 1820
Frederick	16	M	Taylor			New York Packet	19 Aug 1820
Frederika	2	F				New York Packet	19 Aug 1820
Johann Christ	9 6/12	M		Germany	America	Falcon	28 Aug 1828

NAMES OF PASSENGERS	A G E	S E X	OCCUPATIONS	COUNTRY TO WHICH THEY BELONG	COUNTRY THEY INTEND TO INHABIT	SHIPS/DATES OF ARRIVAL	
JUNG (cont'd)							
Johannes	3	M	Farmer			New York Packet	19 Aug 1820
John	22	M		Gt. Brittan		L'Esperance	6 Sep 1828
Maria Elizabeth	19	F				New York Packet	19 Aug 1820
Nicholas	48	M				New York Packet	19 Aug 1820
JUNGLING, John	7	M	Merchant	Great Britain	United States	Washington	3 Sep 1827
JUNIVALO, Wm. R.	18	M	Boy	Denmark	United States	Alfred	8 Jul 1822
JUNOD, Constantia H.	22	M	Watch maker	Switzerland	United States	Aurora	21 Jun 1824
JUNQUITO, Manuel	50	M	Spanish Offr.	Spain	Havana	Henry	11 Oct 1825
Polina	23	F	Lady	Spain	Havana	Henry	11 Oct 1825
JURGERSON, Wm. J.	28	M	Farmer	England	U.N. States	William Byrnes	13 Aug 1829
JURIER, Stephen	64	M	Merchant	France	U. States	Edward Bonaffe	23 Jul 1828
JURLWAY, Michael	30	M	Labourer	Great Brittan	United States	Hanford	3 Aug 1829
JURNAN, Bart.	26	M	Black Smith	England	United States	Essex	23 May 1828
JURNBRIDGE, Jno.	26	M	Painter	London		Robert Edwards	8 Nov 1825
JURVES, W.	32	M	Consul	Great Britain	United States	Don Quixote	18 Aug 1824
JUSCAR, Mary	13	F				Splendid	14 Aug 1829
JUSTICE, Archd., Mr.	34	M	Manufacturer	Scotland	New York	Broughty Castle	18 Dec 1826
Laurence	30	M	Printer	U. States	U. States	Emigrant	10 Feb 1827
JUSTIN, Hariaque	38	M	Merchant	Bayonne	U. States	Liberty	1 Nov 1823
JUTARO, Jno.	55	M	Mariner	France	France	Tuscaloosa	31 Oct 1825
JUTTING, H. L., Mrs.	24	F	Lady	Curracoa	U. States	Charleston	10 May 1825
J., Miss	3	F	Child	Curracoa	U. States	Charleston	10 May 1825
S. M., Miss	5	F	Child	Curracoa	U. States	Charleston	10 May 1825
T.	5	M	Child	Curracoa	U. States	Charleston	10 May 1825
JUTZE, Geo.	25	M	Farmer	Hessian-Germany	Canada	Caesar	8 Sep 1828
K..., —, Child	1	F		England	New York	Thames	6 Oct 1820
..., & 1 Servant	28	F	Actress	England	New York	Thames	6 Oct 1820
J...	...		...	...ld...a ...	England	Great Britain	7 May 1827
K...GAN, Bridget	16	F	Spinster	Ireland	Unt. St. America	Wilson	21 May 1827
K...LL, Robert	23	M	Baker	England	New York	Thames	6 Oct 1820
KAANAN, ...	11	M	None	England	United States	India	8 Jun 1827
Betty	18	F	None	England	United States	India	8 Jun 1827
Betty	40	F	None	England	United States	India	8 Jun 1827
Margt.	13	F	None	England	United States	India	8 Jun 1827
Michael	12	M	None	England	United States	India	8 Jun 1827
Michael	45	M	Butcher	England	United States	India	8 Jun 1827
KAB, Simon	39	M	Shoe Maker	France	United States	New England	29 Aug 1828
KACKER, Isaack	22	M	Farm	Ireland		Quatre Freres	29 Jul 1828
Isaack	46	M	Farm	Ireland		Quatre Freres	29 Jul 1828
John	18	M	Weaver	Ireland		Quatre Freres	29 Jul 1828
Maregaret	18	F	Farm	Ireland		Quatre Freres	29 Jul 1828
KADDEN, Ann	36	F		England	England	Amity	31 May 1822
D.	48	M		England	England	Amity	31 May 1822
KADMAN, John	25	M		Hamburg	U. States	Martha	4 Sep 1828
KAFER, Mather	26	M	Butcher	Germany	Pensylvania	James Noble	27 Aug 1827
KAFFE, Peter	17	M	Planter	Ireland	United States	William	20 Jul 1829
KAFFMAN, H.	23	M	Merchant	U. States	U. States	Virginia	25 Nov 1822
KAGG, Patrick	21	M	Labourer	England	U. States	Emulous	22 Aug 1828
KAHILL, James	23	M	Scholar	Ireland	U.S.A.	Dalhouse Castle	21 Aug 1829
James	23	M	Scholar	Ireland	United States	Dalhouse Castle	21 Aug 1829
KAHL, Frederick	23	M	Merchant	Switzerland	United States	Howard	14 May 1825
KAHLER, Catherine	21	F		England	U. States	Brighton	14 Apr 1828
John	1	M		England	U. States	Brighton	14 Apr 1828
John	35	M	Merchant	England	U. States	Brighton	14 Apr 1828
KAHN, Andres	39	M	Farmer	France	United States	New England	29 Aug 1828
Anton	7	M		France	United States	New England	29 Aug 1828
Catarina	12	F		France	United States	New England	29 Aug 1828
Floresy	4	M		France	United States	New England	29 Aug 1828
Ludwig	10	M		France	United States	New England	29 Aug 1828
Martin	1	M		France	United States	New England	29 Aug 1828
Rosina	2	F		France	United States	New England	29 Aug 1828
Sebastian	6	M		France	United States	New England	29 Aug 1828

NAMES OF PASSENGERS	AGE	SEX	OCCUPATIONS	COUNTRY TO WHICH THEY BELONG	COUNTRY THEY INTEND TO INHABIT	SHIPS/DATES OF ARRIVAL	
KAHO, D.	25	M	Brewer	Great Britain	United States	Greek	23 Jan 1828
KAHOA, Patrick	25	M	Labourer	Ireland	United States	Hope & Esther	27 Jul 1829
KAHOUGH, Garritt	35	M	Labourer	Great Britan	United States	Clematis	8 May 1827
John	13	M	Labourer	Great Britan	United States	Clematis	8 May 1827
Michael	11	M	Labourer	Great Britan	United States	Clematis	8 May 1827
KAILE, John	27	M	Weaver	Ireland	U. States	Belville	5 Jul 1827
KAIN, Barney	21	M	Blacksmith	Ireland	United States	Trident	17 May 1825
Elizabeth	32	M	Merchant	Ireland	N. Orleans	Ann Maria	4 Nov 1834
James	65	M	Labourer	Isle of Man		Ocean	13 Jul 1827
Jane	20	F	Farmer	England	U. States	Acasta	12 May 1825
Jane	65	F	None	Isle of Man		Ocean	13 Jul 1827
Jas.	29	M	Merchant	New York	New York	York	2 Dec 1828
John	20	M	Labourer	Ireland	United States	Sarah G.	15 May 1828
Martin	14	M	Wife, Farmer	England	U. States	Acasta	12 May 1825
Morris	33	M	Merchant	Ireland	N. Orleans	Ann Maria	4 Nov 1834
William	28	M	Merchant	St. John, N.B.	St. John, N.B.	St. Michaels	24 Mar 1825
Wm.	27	M	Statuary	United States		Edward Quesnel	17 Nov 1828
KAINS, Henry	46	M	Farmer	Pennsylvania	U. States	Martha	26 Dec 1823
Joseph	33	M	Joiner	United States	United States	Seine	21 Oct 1822
KAIRNEY, Ann	18	F		G. Britain	U. States	Camillus	8 Sep 1828
KAITLY, Jane	21	F	Spinster	Ireland	United States	Trident	17 May 1825
William	1	M	Child	Ireland	United States	Trident	17 May 1825
KALAHOOLE, Peggy	20	F	Farmer	Ireland	U. States	Virginia	20 Jun 1825
KALER, Bridget	28	F	Laborer or Spinster	Ireland	United States	Sarah G	11 Sep 1827
John	0 6/12	M	Laborer or Spinster	Ireland	United States	Sarah G	11 Sep 1827
John	30	M	Laborer or Spinster	Ireland	United States	Sarah G	11 Sep 1827
Mary	3	F	Laborer or Spinster	Ireland	United States	Sarah G	11 Sep 1827
KALKMAN, Chris F.	40	M	Planter	Spain	U. States	Brown	7 Jul 1826
KALLAHAN, William	19	M	Labourer	Ireland	United States	Catharine	22 Jul 1825
KALLENHAM, Herman	23		...	Breman	Germany	Hudson	14 Jun 1827
KAM, Anna Maria, (his wife [Jacob])	48	F		Germany	New York	James Noble	27 Aug 1827
Barbara, (his daughter [Jacob]	23	F		Germany	New York	James Noble	27 Aug 1827
Elizabeth, (his daughter [Jacob]	20	F		Germany	New York	James Noble	27 Aug 1827
Jacob	44	M	Blacksmith	Germany	New York	James Noble	27 Aug 1827
John	35	M	Gent	French	Switzerland	Charlemagne	19 Sep 1828
John, (his son [Jacob]	10	M		Germany	New York	James Noble	27 Aug 1827
Leonard, (his son [Jacob]	12	M		Germany	New York	James Noble	27 Aug 1827
Margereth, (his daughter [Jacob]	18	F		Germany	New York	James Noble	27 Aug 1827
KAMAGER, Wm., Doctor	25	M	Surgeon	Scotland	New York	Maine	16 Jul 1821
KAMMERER, Joseph	7 6/12	M		Switzerland	U. States	Hewes	30 Oct 1829
Joseph	30	M	Musician	Switzerland	U. States	Hewes	30 Oct 1829
KAMPMEYER, Henry	24	M	Merchant	Hamburgh	Canada	Silas Richards	3 Apr 1826
KAMROTH, A., wife	58	F		Brunswick	not known	Commodore Preble	17 Dec 1825
Jane	30	F		Brunswick	not known	Commodore Preble	17 Dec 1825
Wm.	13	M		Brunswick	not known	Commodore Preble	17 Dec 1825
KAMSHER, George	45	M	Weaver	England	America	Two Marys	24 Sep 1827
KANALY, Patrick	25	M	Labourer	Ireland	U. States	Combine	30 Nov 1825
William	26	M	Farmer	Great Britain	U.N. States	Reindeer	10 Dec 1827
KANAN, Bridget	20	F	None	England	United States	Jubilee	1 Oct 1828
Isabella	19	F	Farmer	Ireland	U. States	Dickinson	30 Jul 1825
KANCHER, Georg	12	M	Farm	Ireland		Quatre Freres	29 Jul 1828
KANCHMAN, Anna	38	F	Farmer	Switzerland		Charlemagne	20 Aug 1829
Armt	6	M	Farmer	Switzerland		Charlemagne	20 Aug 1829
Armt	40	M	Farmer	Switzerland		Charlemagne	20 Aug 1829
Jacob	10	M	Farmer	Switzerland		Charlemagne	20 Aug 1829
Mary	2	F	Farmer	Switzerland		Charlemagne	20 Aug 1829
Thomas	4	M	Farmer	Switzerland		Charlemagne	20 Aug 1829
KANDELL, Geo.	26	M	Farmer	England	United States	Acasta	15 Jul 1822
KANE, Catharan	6	F	Labourer	Ireland	United States	Hope	12 Jun 1828
Charles	35	M	Gentleman	Great Britain	United States	Camberwell	2 Oct 1828

NAMES OF PASSENGERS	AGE	SEX	OCCUPATIONS	COUNTRY TO WHICH THEY BELONG	COUNTRY THEY INTEND TO INHABIT	SHIPS/DATES OF ARRIVAL	
KANE (cont'd)							
Darreol	17 6/12	M	Labourer	Ireland	U. States	Courier	17 Mar 1828
Denis	32	M	Gentleman	Ireland	United States	Dublin Packet	13 Oct 1828
James	19	M	Farmer	Ireland	United States	Asia	29 Jul 1829
James	24	M	Farmer	Ireland	United States	Asia	29 Jul 1829
Jno. R.	22	M	Merchant	U. States	U. States	Georgetown Packet	24 Feb 1823
John	4	M	Labourer	Ireland	United States	Hope	12 Jun 1828
John	60	M	Farmer	Ireland	United States	Erin	25 Dec 1820
John R.	20	M	Merchant	N. York	U. States	Mohawk	15 Nov 1821
Julia	21	F		Great Britain	United States	Camberwell	2 Oct 1828
Lawrence	26		Farmer	England	United States	Corinthian	30 May 1828
Margaret	20	F		Gt. Britain		Dalhouse Castle	13 May 1828
Margeret	26 6/12	F	Spinster	Ireland	United States	Robert Fulton	24 Jul 1826
Margret	15	F	Farmer, Labourer or Spinster	Ireland	U. States	Meteor	4 Oct 1827
Mary	22	F	Spinster	Ireland	United States	St. Michaels	18 Jul 1826
O. G.	25	M	Merchant	U. States	U. States	General Saublette	14 Apr 1823
Owen	18	M	Labourer	Ireland	United States	Hope	12 Jun 1828
Pat	22		Farmer	Ireland		Westmoreland	1 Aug 1826
Patck.	19	M	Clerk	Belfast	United States	Minerva	30 Oct 1829
Perceval	30	M	Farmer	Aghan Co. Derry...		Gleaner	24 May 1823
Peter	20	M	Labourer	Ireland	United States	Hope	12 Jun 1828
Qurton	25	M	Labourer	Ireland	United States	Hope	12 Jun 1828
Richard M.	32	M	Merchant	England	U. States	Topaz	28 May 1827
Rose	24	F	Labourer	Ireland	United States	Hope	12 Jun 1828
Thomas	2	M	Labourer	Ireland	United States	Hope	12 Jun 1828
KANET, Abraham	32	M	Farmer	Switzerland	Switzerland	Edward Quesnel	3 Jul 1829
Ferdinand	3	M		Switzerland	Switzerland	Edward Quesnel	3 Jul 1829
James	8	M		Switzerland	Switzerland	Edward Quesnel	3 Jul 1829
Susanna	29	F		Switzerland	Switzerland	Edward Quesnel	3 Jul 1829
KANG, Christina	28	F	his Wife [Gotfrid]	Switzerland	U. States	Hewes	30 Oct 1829
Gotfrid	1	M		Switzerland	U. States	Hewes	30 Oct 1829
Gotfrid	34	M	Farmer	Switzerland	U. States	Hewes	30 Oct 1829
Henrich	10	M		Switzerland	U. States	Hewes	30 Oct 1829
KANIGAN, Bridget	19 2/12	F		England	United States	Rising States	16 Jan 1829
Thomas	23 3/12	M	Shoemaker	England	United States	Rising States	16 Jan 1829
KANN, Bernard	23	M	Labourer	Ireland	United States	Dalhouse Castle	8 May 1827
KANNER, John	30	M	Labourer	Werdenburg	United States	Xenophon	2 Jun 1824
KANOUSE, Geo.	29	M	Mechanic	U.S.	U.S.	Prometheus	30 Aug 1828
KANROTH, A.	62	M	Farmer	Brunswick	not known	Commodore Preble	17 Dec 1825
KANSNER, Nicolaos Christoffe, Mr.	22 7/12	M	Wine Cooper	Hamburg		Europa	12 Oct 1829
KANTZ, M... Heinr.	49	M	Butcher	Baden in Netherlands	New York	Louisa	6 Oct 1828
KAPACH, Francis	23	M	Merchant	Germany	U. States	Merchant	22 Oct 1821
KAPFFER, Joseph	27	M	Farmer	Germany	United States	Virginia	31 May 1828
KAPP, Johann Jacob	6	M		Germany	America	Falcon	28 Aug 1828
KAPPLER, Caroline	5	F	Black Smith	Germany	United States	Virginia	31 May 1828
Carterlene	9	F	Black Smith	Germany	United States	Virginia	31 May 1828
Henrey	2	M	Black Smith	Germany	United States	Virginia	31 May 1828
Henrey	41	M	Black Smith	Germany	United States	Virginia	31 May 1828
Margret	40	F	Black Smith	Germany	United States	Virginia	31 May 1828
Sophie	7	F	Black Smith	Germany	United States	Virginia	31 May 1828
KARCHER, —	35	M	Labourer	France	United States	Cavalier	25 Jul 1828
—, Wife	33	F		France	United States	Cavalier	25 Jul 1828
Christian	8	F		France	United States	Cavalier	25 Jul 1828
Elizabeth	7	F		France	United States	Cavalier	25 Jul 1828
Fred	5	M		France	United States	Cavalier	25 Jul 1828
Geo.	9	M		France	United States	Cavalier	25 Jul 1828
KARGHEN, Ann	1	F	None	Isle of Man		Ocean	13 Jul 1827
Ellen	26	F	None	Isle of Man		Ocean	13 Jul 1827
Luke	30	M	Shoemaker	Isle of Man		Ocean	13 Jul 1827
KARLAND, James	23 10/12	M	Mechanic	England	United States	John Wells	22 May 1826
KARN, Elizabeth	...	F	...ant	Ireland	United States	Carolina Ann	24 Oct 1825
Elizabeth	33	F	...	Ireland	United States	Carolina Ann	24 Oct 1825

NAMES OF PASSENGERS	AGE	SEX	OCCUPATIONS	COUNTRY TO WHICH THEY BELONG	COUNTRY THEY INTEND TO INHABIT	SHIPS/DATES OF ARRIVAL	
KARNWADE, —, Mrs.	51	F		Isle of Man	United States	Lunar	5 May 1828
Thomas	59	M	Farmer	Isle of Man	United States	Lunar	5 May 1828
KARR, Jane	18	F	Spinster	Ireland	United States	Catharine	22 Jul 1825
KARRAGAN, James	21	F		Ireland	United States	Mary	1 Jul 1829
KARRAN, Danl.	17		Labourer	Ireland	United States	Helen	5 Jul 1820
KARRICK, J.	43	M	Merchant	United States	United States	Tampico	27 Jun 1827
KARSHALL, Abm.	24	M	Farmer	England	America	Panthia	17 Sep 1821
KARTES, Cathrina	3/12	F	Daughter	Germany	United States	Elizabeth	4 Sep 1826
Cathrina	35	F	Wife	Germany	United States	Elizabeth	4 Sep 1826
John	2 1/12	M	Son	Germany	United States	Elizabeth	4 Sep 1826
Maria	6 6/12	F	Daughter	Germany	United States	Elizabeth	4 Sep 1826
Mathias	4 3/12	M	Son	Germany	United States	Elizabeth	4 Sep 1826
Nicholas	36	M	Farmer	Germany	United States	Elizabeth	4 Sep 1826
KARTONNE, D.	29	M		Bavaria	Bavaria	Edward Quesnel	3 Jul 1829
KARZIE, John ...	31	M	Merchant	Great Brittain	Montreal	Albion	11 Jun 1821
KASAN, Chas.	25	M	Merchant	Germany	Charleston	Maria Elizabeth	16 Feb 1826
KASEL, Andrew	15	M	Mason	New York	New York	Nancy	9 Oct 1820
Margart.	13	F	Mason	New York	New York	Nancy	9 Oct 1820
Nancy	40	F		New York	New York	Nancy	9 Oct 1820
Roberd	40	M	Mason	New York	New York	Nancy	9 Oct 1820
KASEMAKER, Charles	26	M	Mechanic	Prussia	U. States	Minerva	13 Sep 1827
KASSIDY, James	27	M	Mason	Ireland	U.S.A.	Dalhouse Castle	21 Aug 1829
James	27	M	Mason	Ireland	United States	Dalhouse Castle	21 Aug 1829
KATCHFORD, Margt.	18	F	None	Ireland	United States	Aurelia	7 Jun 1826
Richard	24	M	Farmer	Ireland	United States	Aurelia	7 Jun 1826
KATHMAN, Esther K.	24		Sugar Baker	Germany	U.S. of America	Mary	21 Sep 1821
KATTEL, Thos. O.	45	M	Merchant	U. States	U. States	Minerva	23 May 1825
KATY, William	34	M	Farmer	Great Britian	United States	Andes	19 Aug 1829
KAUFFERMANN, Xavier	32	M	Farmer	U.S.		Antioch	18 Aug 1829
KAUFFMAN, Christn. H.	54	M	Merchant	United States	United States	Romulus	13 Aug 1829
J.	35	M	Miller	Switzerland	U. States	Marmion	18 Oct 1824
KAUFMAN, —, Mr.	35	M	Papermaker	Germany	U. States	Orion	8 Oct 1823
—, Mrs.	28	F		Germany	U. States	Orion	8 Oct 1823
Carl	6/12	M		Germany	U. States	Orion	8 Oct 1823
Elizabeth	3	F	...	Baden	United States	Wade	29 Aug 1825
Judith	16	F	...	Baden	United States	Wade	29 Aug 1825
Maria Eva	20	F	...	Baden	United States	Wade	29 Aug 1825
Michael	63	M	Farmer	Baden	United States	Wade	29 Aug 1825
Tendny	13	F	...	Baden	United States	Wade	29 Aug 1825
KAUG, Barbara	18	F	Agriculture	Wirtemburg	United States	Henri IV	14 Oct 1829
Jacob	44	M	Agriculture	Wirtemburg	United States	Henri IV	14 Oct 1829
Johan	48	M	Agriculture	Wirtemburg	United States	Henri IV	14 Oct 1829
Jos.	7	M	Agriculture	Wirtemburg	United States	Henri IV	14 Oct 1829
Wallaug	47	F	Agriculture	Wirtemburg	United States	Henri IV	14 Oct 1829
KAUSLER, Wm. C.	36	M	Merchant	Germany	U. States	John Wells	16 May 1825
KAVANAGH, Andrew	22	M	Labourer	England	U. States	Hope & Esther	10 Jul 1827
KAVANNAH, Charles	13	M	None	England	U. States	Montgomery	18 Oct 1828
Daniel	5	M	None	England	U. States	Montgomery	18 Oct 1828
Michael	9	M	None	England	U. States	Montgomery	18 Oct 1828
Michael	39	M	Farmer	England	U. States	Montgomery	18 Oct 1828
Thomas	11	M	None	England	U. States	Montgomery	18 Oct 1828
KAVENAGH, Bridget	18	F	Matron	Ireland	America	Wilson	16 May 1825
Mary	20	F	Spinster	Ireland	United States	Dublin Packet	28 Apr 1824
Michael	24	M	Farmer	Ireland	United States	Dublin Packet	13 Oct 1828
Thomas	20	M	Taylor	Ireland	America	Wilson	16 May 1825
KAVENEGH,							
Joseph Henry	10	M	Child	Ireland	America	Farmer	15 Nov 1823
Theresa	7	F	Child	Ireland	America	Farmer	15 Nov 1823
KAY, —, Mrs.	29		None	England	New York	Albion	11 Oct 1821
Ann	13	F		England	U. States	Severn	12 Oct 1826
Ann	34	F		England	U. States	Severn	12 Oct 1826
Betty	4 6/12	F		England	U. States	Severn	12 Oct 1826
George	29	M	Weaver	Scotland	Ut. States	Courier	13 Jul 1826
Green	8	M		England	U. States	Severn	12 Oct 1826
Hales	35		Farmer	England	New York	Albion	11 Oct 1821
James	10		None	England	New York	Albion	11 Oct 1821
James	22	M	Taylor	Great Britain	United States	Colossus	1 Nov 1826
Jeremiah	5	M		England	U. States	Severn	12 Oct 1826
Jno.	11	M		England	U. States	Severn	12 Oct 1826

NAMES OF PASSENGERS	AGE	SEX	OCCUPATIONS	COUNTRY TO WHICH THEY BELONG	COUNTRY THEY INTEND TO INHABIT	SHIPS/DATES OF ARRIVAL	
KAY (cont'd)							
Jno.	30	M	Weaver	England	U. States	Severn	12 Oct 1826
John	8		None	England	New York	Albion	11 Oct 1821
Joshua	22	M	Shoemaker	England	U. States	Severn	12 Oct 1826
Maria	8	F		England	U. States	Severn	12 Oct 1826
Mary	9		None	England	New York	Albion	11 Oct 1821
Mary	10	F		England	U. States	Severn	12 Oct 1826
Mary	32	F		England	U. States	Severn	12 Oct 1826
Mary	40	F	None	Ireland	America	Dewitt Clinton	27 Jul 1824
Sarah	2	F		England	U. States	Severn	12 Oct 1826
Simon	11	M		England	U. States	Severn	12 Oct 1826
Sirus	6	F		England	U. States	Severn	12 Oct 1826
Thomas	67	M	Farmer	England	United States	Manhattan	11 Oct 1824
Wm.	14		None	England	New York	Albion	11 Oct 1821
KAYE, Ann	50	F	None	England	United States	Jubilee	1 Oct 1828
Elizabeth	1/4	F	None	England	United States	Jubilee	1 Oct 1828
George	27	M	Mason	Great Britain	United States	Mount Vernon	20 May 1822
James	28	M	Bleacher	England	United States	Jubilee	1 Oct 1828
Joshua	29	M	Mason	Great Britain	United States	Mount Vernon	20 May 1822
Richard	6	M	None	England	United States	Jubilee	1 Oct 1828
Sarah	22	F	None	England	United States	Jubilee	1 Oct 1828
KAYHAN, Eleanor	50	F	None	England	United States	Jubilee	1 Oct 1828
Elizabeth	13	F	None	England	United States	Jubilee	1 Oct 1828
James	11	M	None	England	United States	Jubilee	1 Oct 1828
Jane	25	F	None	England	United States	Jubilee	1 Oct 1828
John	20	M	Farmer	England	United States	Jubilee	1 Oct 1828
Mary	2	F	None	England	United States	Jubilee	1 Oct 1828
Phillip	12	M	None	England	United States	Jubilee	1 Oct 1828
Thomas	8	M	None	England	United States	Jubilee	1 Oct 1828
KE..., John	31		Tailor			Emulous	19 Feb 1822
KEA...Y, John	59	M	...	G. Britain	U. States	St. George	7 Jun 1828
KEAD, Michaell	25	M	Farier	Scotland	Ut. States	Courier	13 Jul 1826
KEAFE, Anthony	27	M	Farmer	France	America	La Grange	7 Aug 1828
KEAGAN, Margaret	14	F		Ireland	U.S. of America	Douglass	6 Jul 1829
KEALE, Sarah	36	F		Limerick	N. York	Thomas & William	25 May 1827
William	43	M	Surgeon & Dentist	Limerick	N. York	Thomas & William	25 May 1827
KEALER, Dennis	4	M	Child	Ireland	Ireland	Sarah G.	28 Nov 1827
James	1	M	Child	Ireland	Ireland	Sarah G.	28 Nov 1827
James	40	M	Labourer	Ireland	Ireland	Sarah G.	28 Nov 1827
Johannah	40	F	Wife	Ireland	Ireland	Sarah G.	28 Nov 1827
Patrick	8	M	Child	Ireland	Ireland	Sarah G.	28 Nov 1827
Timothy	6	M	Child	Ireland	Ireland	Sarah G.	28 Nov 1827
KEALY, Catharin	25	F		England	U. States	Severn	12 Oct 1826
Sarah	1 6/12	F		England	U. States	Severn	12 Oct 1826
KEAM, Catherine	27	F				Hibernia	15 Aug 1820
KEAMES, Jeremiah	32	M	Tailor	Great Brittan	Great Brittan	Orbit	30 Aug 1824
KEAN, —, Mrs.	29	F		Great Britain	New York	Dublin	21 Dec 1824
Catherine	50	F	None	Great Britain	United States	Mary & Harriet	3 Jul 1829
Christy	18	F	Servant	Ireland	America	Fairy	8 Aug 1821
Easter, Mrs.	20 10/12	F		Scotland	United States	Mobile	21 Aug 1827
Edmund	36	M	Gentleman	Ireland	United States	Silas Richards	27 Oct 1825
Francis	22	M	Labourer	Ireland	America	Plutarch	18 Jul 1826
James	24	M	Carver	Scotland	U.S.A.	Calliope	15 Aug 1827
James	24	M	Farmer	England	United States	Cosmo	26 Aug 1829
Jas.	5	M		Great Britain	New York	Dublin	21 Dec 1824
Joanna	6	F		Great Britain	New York	Dublin	21 Dec 1824
John	24		Laborer	Ireland	America	Parrington	9 Jun 1827
M.	28	M	Farmer	Ireland	United States	L. M. Pelham	25 Jun 1822
Margaret	3 2/12	F		Scotland	United States	Mobile	21 Aug 1827
Nancy	7	F		Great Britain	New York	Dublin	21 Dec 1824
Pat	4	M		Great Britain	New York	Dublin	21 Dec 1824
Pat	32	M	Smith	Ireland	United States	Essex	23 May 1828
Patk.	23	M	Labourer	England	United States	Aurelia	7 Jun 1826
Peggy	30	F		Ireland	United States	Mary	1 Jul 1829
Peter	2/12	M		Scotland	United States	Mobile	21 Aug 1827
Philip	50	M	Labourer	Great Britain	United States	Mary & Harriet	3 Jul 1829
Sarah	24	F		England	United States	Cosmo	26 Aug 1829

NAMES OF PASSENGERS	AGE	SEX	OCCUPATIONS	COUNTRY TO WHICH THEY BELONG	COUNTRY THEY INTEND TO INHABIT	SHIPS/DATES OF ARRIVAL	
KEAN (cont'd)							
Thomas	2 1/12	M		Scotland	United States	Mobile	21 Aug 1827
Thomas	23	M	Farmer	Bristol, Engl.	...	Warrior	19 May 1828
Thomas	24	M	Laborer	Gt. Britain		Dalhouse Castle	13 May 1828
KEANAN, George	27	M	Labourer	Ireland	United States	Princess Charlotte	26 Apr 1827
Robt.	...		Laboring Class		United States	Atlantic	2 Apr 1827
KEANARD, Hans	7	M	Farmer	France	United States	Crescent	12 Jul 1827
Margaret	6/12	F	Farmer	France	United States	Crescent	12 Jul 1827
Margaret	33	F	Farmer	France	United States	Crescent	12 Jul 1827
Phelp	10	M	Farmer	France	United States	Crescent	12 Jul 1827
Phelp	34	M	Farmer	France	United States	Crescent	12 Jul 1827
KEANE, Cathr.	38	F		Ireland	United States	Pallas	28 Oct 1828
Edmund	31	M	Professor	Great Britain	Great Britain	Martha	25 Nov 1820
Jer.	42	M	Labourer	Ireland	United States	Pallas	28 Oct 1828
John	16	M		Limerick	N. York	Thomas & William	25 May 1827
Mary	14			Waterford	Gt. Britain	Enterprize	19 Feb 1822
Thomas	21	M		Great Brittian	United States	Carolina Augusta	2 Dec 1828
Timothy, Senr.	60	M	Dy...	Limerick	N. York	Thomas & William	25 May 1827
Timy., Jnr.	18	M		Limerick	N. York	Thomas & William	25 May 1827
KEANGAN, James	33	M	Spinner	England	U. States	Panthea	22 Nov 1826
KEANLY, Bray	18	F		U. States	U. States	United States	11 Sep 1828
KEAR, James	35	M	Laborer	Ireland	United States	Mary	1 Jul 1829
Wm.	21	M	Laborer	Ireland	United States	Mary	1 Jul 1829
KEARHAULTS, Gabriel	30	M	Farmer	Germany	United States	Stephania	16 Aug 1827
Mary	46	F	Farmer	Germany	United States	Stephania	16 Aug 1827
KEARLY, Pat	30	M		Ireland	United States	Thompson	12 Sep 1827
KEARMAN, Biddy	1	F	None	Ireland	U.S.A.	Dalhouse Castle	21 Aug 1829
Biddy	1	F	None	Ireland	United States	Dalhouse Castle	21 Aug 1829
KEARNAN, Edward	22	M	Merchant	Great Britain	U. States America	Columbia	15 Nov 1826
Peggy	20	F		Gt. Britain		Dalhouse Castle	13 May 1828
KEARNEN, Bridget	8	F	Servant	Ireland	United States	Josephine	30 Apr 1828
James	3	M		Ireland	United States	Josephine	30 Apr 1828
Mary	5	F	Servant	Ireland	United States	Josephine	30 Apr 1828
Mary	40	F	Servant	Ireland	United States	Josephine	30 Apr 1828
Thomas	4	M	Child	Ireland	United States	Josephine	30 Apr 1828
KEARNEY, Ann	9	F	Child	Ireland	United States	Dublin Packet	23 May 1828
Anthony	26	M	Clerk	Ireland	United States	Dublin Packet	23 May 1828
Bridget	11	F	Child	Ireland	United States	Dublin Packet	23 May 1828
Catharine	20	F	Labourer	Ireland	United States	General Marion	6 Oct 1828
Catherine	2 1/2	F	Child	Ireland	United States	Wilson	27 Jun 1826
Catherine	30	F		England	United States	Danube	22 Aug 1825
Daniel	28	M	Gent.	New York	America	Wilson	27 Nov 1826
Dr.	37	M	Surgeon	U.S.A.	U.S.A.	Bayard	25 Aug 1829
E.	21	F		U. States	U. States	Hibernia	24 Aug 1820
Edward	25	M	Labourer	England	U. States	Ayrshire	12 May 1828
Frances	18	F	Lady	Ireland	United States	Dublin Packet	23 May 1828
Frances	48	F	Lady	Ireland	United States	Dublin Packet	23 May 1828
Francis	7/12	F		Ireland	United States	Wilson	27 Jun 1826
George	19	M	Clerk	Ireland	United States	Dublin Packet	23 May 1828
James	40	M	Farmer	West Wood, West Wood, Ireland	N. York	New Orleans	24 Aug 1827
Jane	14	F	Child	Ireland	United States	Dublin Packet	23 May 1828
Jno.	11	M		England	United States	Danube	22 Aug 1825
Jno.	40	M	Miner	England	United States	Danube	22 Aug 1825
John	2 6/12	M		Ireland	United States	Wilson	27 Jun 1826
John	8	M		Ireland	U. States	Nancy	1 Sep 1823
John	49	M	Gentleman	Ireland	United States	Dublin Packet	23 May 1828
John, Jr.	6	M	Child	Ireland	United States	Dublin Packet	23 May 1828
Lary	29	M	Labourer	Ireland	United States	Dalhouse Castle	26 Dec 1827
Margt.	22	F		Ireland	United States	Wilson	27 Jun 1826
Mary	20			Ireland	United States	John Dickinson	28 Jun 1822
Mary Ann	22	F	Lady	Ireland	United States	Dublin Packet	23 May 1828
Nancy	20	F	None	Ireland		Marchioness	13 May 1828

NAMES OF PASSENGERS	AGE	SEX	OCCUPATIONS	COUNTRY TO WHICH THEY BELONG	COUNTRY THEY INTEND TO INHABIT	SHIPS/DATES OF ARRIVAL	
KEARNEY (cont'd)							
Samuel	20	M	Labourer	Ireland	United States	William & George	14 May 1828
KEARNS, Ann	30	F	wife [James]	Ireland	United States	Dublin Packet	24 Sep 1823
Edward	20	M	Labourer	England	New York	America	1 Aug 1828
James	45	M	Farmer	Ireland	United States	Dublin Packet	24 Sep 1823
John	30	M	Farmer	Ireland	United States	Dublin Packet	24 Sep 1823
Mary	25	F	Spinster	Ireland	United States	Dublin Packet	24 Sep 1823
Mary Ann	2	F	Child	Ireland	United States	Dublin Packet	24 Sep 1823
Patrick	31	M	Farmer	Great Britian	United States	Silvanus Jenkins	6 Apr 1826
William	25	M	Farmer	Ireland	United States	Dublin Packet	29 Jun 1825
KEARNY, Bridget	24	F	None	Great Brittan	United States	America	24 Jul 1827
Ellen	36	F	None	Great Brittan	United States	America	24 Jul 1827
Ellen	50	F	None	Great Brittan	United States	America	24 Jul 1827
John W.	48	M	Merchant	United States	United States	New York	3 Apr 1826
Lawrence	10	M	None	Great Brittan	United States	America	24 Jul 1827
Lawrence	60	M	Farmer	Great Brittan	United States	America	24 Jul 1827
Mary	29	F	None	Great Brittan	United States	America	24 Jul 1827
Patt	24	M	Farmer	Ireland	United States	Dublin Packet	29 Jun 1825
Peter	27	M	Farmer	Great Brittan	United States	America	24 Jul 1827
Peter	28	M	Farmer	Great Brittan	United States	America	24 Jul 1827
Rose	17	F	None	Great Brittan	United States	America	24 Jul 1827
Sarah	20	F	None	Great Brittan	United States	America	24 Jul 1827
Thomas	32	M	Farmer	Great Brittan	United States	America	24 Jul 1827
Thos.	12	M	None	Great Brittan	United States	America	24 Jul 1827
Wm.	20	M	Farmer	Ireland	United States	Dublin Packet	22 Oct 1821
KEARSLEY, Jno.	18	M	Farmer	Gt. Britain	U. States	Superior	20 Aug 1825
KEART, Antonio	32	M	Merchant	Switzerland	United States	Cambridge	19 Sep 1828
KEARWAN, Hugh	0 6/12	M		Scotland	United States	Indus	5 Sep 1827
Mary	22	F		Scotland	United States	Indus	5 Sep 1827
Q.	24	M	...	Scotland	United States	Indus	5 Sep 1827
KEATES, George	28	M	Merchant	Great Britain	United States	Courier	13 Mar 1820
KEATING, Amelia	7	F		U. States	U. States	Florida	2 Jun 1828
B. H.	31	M	Merchant	Philada.	U. States	Milo	8 Mar 1824
Eliza	25	F		U. States	U. States	Florida	2 Jun 1828
James A.	22	M	Supercargo	America	America	Catherine & Jane	4 Nov 1820
John	43		Labourer	Ireland	United States	Corinthian	30 May 1828
John	60	M		U. States	U. States	Florida	2 Jun 1828
John, Mastr.	12		Labourer	Ireland	United States	Corinthian	30 May 1828
Lerome	26	M		U. States	U. States	Florida	2 Jun 1828
M.	26	M		England	United States	Yobah	26 Sep 1827
Michael	24	M	Labourer	Ireland	United States	Lunar	5 May 1828
Patrick	30	M	Labourer	Ireland	America	Wilson	16 May 1825
Thomas	23	M	Farmer	Ireland	America	Liverpool	31 Aug 1827
Thos.	24	M		England	United States	Yobah	26 Sep 1827
W.	40	M	Mariner	U. States	U. States	Caroline	17 Apr 1821
Walter	23	M	Labourer	Ireland	United States	Edwin	27 Oct 1828
William	5	M		U. States	U. States	Florida	2 Jun 1828
KEATLY, Samuel	25		Sawyer	Ireland	Great Britain	Robert Burns	14 Jun 1824
KEATS, —, Miss	9	F		America	America	Britannia	5 Nov 1828
—, Mrs.	30	F		England	America	Britannia	5 Nov 1828
John	1	F		America	America	Britannia	5 Nov 1828
KEAZ, Jean	34	F		Scotland	United States	Commerce	17 Jul 1823
KEBAN, Jean	43	M	Farmer	France	U. States	Montano	2 Sep 1828
KEBEL, Charlotta	9 9/12	F		Bavaria		François I	19 Nov 1828
Charlotte Fanlin	42	F		Bavaria		François I	19 Nov 1828
Wilhelm	43	M	Weaver	Bavaria		François I	19 Nov 1828
KEDNEY, Patrick	20	M	Weaver	Gt. Britain		Dalhouse Castle	13 May 1828
KEDRICK, Andrew	34		Carpenter			Charlotte Corday	11 Sep 1820
Don	32					Charlotte Corday	11 Sep 1820
KEDWALL, Ann	35		Farmer	England	United States	Corinthian	30 May 1828
Deborah	10		Farmer	England	United States	Corinthian	30 May 1828
Eliza	4		Farmer	England	United States	Corinthian	30 May 1828
George	8		Farmer	England	United States	Corinthian	30 May 1828
John	40		Farmer	England	United States	Corinthian	30 May 1828
William	13		Farmer	England	United States	Corinthian	30 May 1828

NAMES OF PASSENGERS	AGE	SEX	OCCUPATIONS	COUNTRY TO WHICH THEY BELONG	COUNTRY THEY INTEND TO INHABIT	SHIPS/DATES OF ARRIVAL	
KEE, Hugh	22	M	Labourer	Ireland	United States	Robert Fulton	24 Jul 1826
KEEBAS, Bernard	23	M	Farmer	Alsace in the Department of Upper and lower Rhine	United States	Carolina Augusta	16 May 1828
Henry	22	M	Farmer	Alsace in the Department of Upper and lower Rhine	United States	Carolina Augusta	16 May 1828
Jacob	24	M	Farmer	Alsace in the Department of Upper and lower Rhine	United States	Carolina Augusta	16 May 1828
KEEBROS, Christiana	32	M	Farmer	Alsace in the Department of Upper and lower Rhine	United States	Carolina Augusta	16 May 1828
KEEF, Derby	21		Labourer	Ireland	New York	Marcella	18 May 1827
John	24	M	Farmer	Great Britain	United States	Eliza Barker	3 Jul 1826
Thomas	18	M	Labourer	Ireland	United States	Euphrates	12 Mar 1824
Thomas	18	M	Sailor	America	U. States	Hiram	17 Jun 1826
KEEFE, Cornelius	28	M	Labourer	Ireland	United States	Combine	4 Jun 1825
Danl.	24	M	Laborer	Ireland	United States	Trio	13 Jun 1827
Jeremiah	21		Farmer & Labourer	Great Britain & Ireland	United States	Trio	8 Feb 1827
John	27		Draper	Ireland	U.S.	Union	20 Aug 1827
KEEFFE, Catherine	19	F		Ireland	United States	Trio	2 Oct 1828
James	60	M	Labourer	Ireland	United States	Pallas	28 Oct 1828
KEEFFEE, Arthur	10	M		Ireland	United States	Trio	2 Oct 1828
Catherine	14	F		Ireland	United States	Trio	2 Oct 1828
Cornelius	50	M	Farmer	Ireland	United States	Trio	2 Oct 1828
Eliza	12	F		Ireland	United States	Trio	2 Oct 1828
Margaret	16	F		Ireland	United States	Trio	2 Oct 1828
Mary	50	F		Ireland	United States	Trio	2 Oct 1828
KEEG, Arey	41	M	Farmer	France	United States	Crescent	12 Jul 1827
Elizabeth	37	F	Farmer	France	United States	Crescent	12 Jul 1827
Gereg	11	M	Farmer	France	United States	Crescent	12 Jul 1827
John	6	M	Farmer	France	United States	Crescent	12 Jul 1827
Margaret	8/12	F	Farmer	France	United States	Crescent	12 Jul 1827
KEEGAN, Catherine	24	F	None	Ireland	United States	Elizabeth	8 Jun 1827
James	3	M	None	Ireland	United States	Elizabeth	8 Jun 1827
James	28	M	Labourer	England	U. States	Ayrshire	12 May 1828
Michl.	21	M	Labourer	Co. Lougford	Co. Lougford	Howard Douglass	11 May 1827
KEELAN, Ann	48	F		Gt. Britain		Dalhouse Castle	13 May 1828
Betty	6	F		Gt. Britain		Dalhouse Castle	13 May 1828
Catherine	18	F		Gt. Britain		Dalhouse Castle	13 May 1828
Elizabeth	14	F		Gt. Britain		Dalhouse Castle	13 May 1828
Judith	8	F		Gt. Britain		Dalhouse Castle	13 May 1828
Margaret	10	F		Gt. Britain		Dalhouse Castle	13 May 1828
KEELEN, Henry P.	21	M	Labourer	Ireland	America	Wilson	16 May 1825
KEELER, Louiza	9	F	Farmer	Holland	U. States	Don Quixote	25 Oct 1828
KEELERT, James	38	M	Mariner	Jamaica	Jamaica	Dispatch	25 Apr 1825
KEELIN, Adeline	14	F	Farmer	Holland	U. States	Don Quixote	25 Oct 1828
Bernard	49	M	Farmer	Holland	U. States	Don Quixote	25 Oct 1828
KEELING, Edith	12 3/12	F		England	America, U.S.	Illinois	3 Jun 1822
Ellen	22 2/12	F		England	America, U.S.	Illinois	3 Jun 1822
Hannah	8 2/12	F		England	America, U.S.	Illinois	3 Jun 1822
Isaac	9 5/12	M		England	America, U.S.	Illinois	3 Jun 1822
Isaac	46 9/12	M		England	America, U.S.	Illinois	3 Jun 1822
Mary	15 8/12	F		England	America, U.S.	Illinois	3 Jun 1822
Olive	51 6/12	F		England	America, U.S.	Illinois	3 Jun 1822
Theopalus	19	M	Farmer	England	America, U.S.	Illinois	3 Jun 1822
William	13 3/12	M		England	America, U.S.	Illinois	3 Jun 1822
KEELSHER, Pat	22			Ireland	U.S.	Union	20 Aug 1827
KEEMAN, Ann	20	F	Servant	Ireland	United States	Josephine	30 Apr 1828
John	19	M	Student	Ireland		William Tell	24 Oct 1829
Michael	14	M	Mechanic	Ireland		William Tell	24 Oct 1829
KEEMBLE, William, Mr.	20	M	Mariner	U.S. of America		Brilliant	28 Jan 1828

NAMES OF PASSENGERS	AGE	SEX	OCCUPATIONS	COUNTRY TO WHICH THEY BELONG	COUNTRY THEY INTEND TO INHABIT	SHIPS/DATES OF ARRIVAL	
KEEN, Ann	20	F	Lady	Ireland	U. States	Howard	25 Jul 1823
Anthony	45	M		England	United States	Yobah	26 Sep 1827
John	9	M		England	United States	Yobah	26 Sep 1827
Maria	30	F		Spain	Spain	Montano	15 Jan 1829
R.	60	M	Military	Spain	Spain	Montano	15 Jan 1829
KEENAN, Catherine	18	F	Child	Ireland	New York	Louisa	20 Jul 1826
Dan	30	M	Labourer	Ireland	United States	Louisa	18 Apr 1827
Francis	33	M	Weaver	Ireland	United States	Meteor	27 Sep 1826
Frans.	20 3/12	M	Labourer	Ireland	United States	Atlantic	21 Jul 1827
Hugh	1 9/12	M	Child	Ireland	United States	Louisa	18 Apr 1827
John	26	M	Shomaker	Ireland	United States	Louisa	18 Apr 1827
Mary	25	F	Servant	Ireland	United States	Louisa	18 Apr 1827
Mary	40	F	Spinner	Ireland	New York	Louisa	20 Jul 1826
Owen	66	M	Superannuated	Ireland	New York	Louisa	20 Jul 1826
Patrick	20	M	Servant	Ireland	America	Carolina Ann	7 Aug 1826
Rose	16	F	Servant	Ireland	America	Carolina Ann	7 Aug 1826
Samuel	20	M	Laborer	Ireland	United States	Mary	1 Jul 1829
Thomas	30	M	Farmer	Ireland	U. States	Dickinson	30 Jul 1825
KEENE, Maria Theresa	29	F		United States	N... ...	Burdett	7 Dec 1827
Richard Raynal, Colonel	41	M	Lawyer	United States	N... ...	Burdett	7 Dec 1827
KEENEN, Lawrence	30	M	Fuller	England	America	Saluda	16 Oct 1824
KEENER, Adolph	51	M				Eliza Grant	6 Oct 1828
Ann	30	F				Eliza Grant	6 Oct 1828
Catharine	35	F	None	Germany	U. States	Pedler	20 Aug 1827
David	29	M	Physician	United States	United States	Cadmus	9 Dec 1825
Wm.	4	M				Eliza Grant	6 Oct 1828
KEENES, John	55	M	Merchant	Philada.	U. States	Martha	26 Nov 1825
KEENEY, James	20	M	Labourer	Ireland	United States	Henry Kneeland	7 Jun 1828
KEENING, Catherine	10	F	Agriculturist	Germany	U.S.	Helen	3 May 1828
Catherine	33	F	Agriculturist	Germany	U.S.	Helen	3 May 1828
Jacque	32	M	Agriculturist	Germany	U.S.	Helen	3 May 1828
Madelaine	3	F	Agriculturist	Germany	U.S.	Helen	3 May 1828
Margaret	7	F	Agriculturist	Germany	U.S.	Helen	3 May 1828
KEEP, Briget	22	F	Spinster	Great Brittan	United States	Hanford	3 Aug 1829
KEER, Ann Maria	16 3/12	F		Switzerland	U.S. America	Edward	28 Oct 1825
Jacob	18 1/12	M		Switzerland	U.S. America	Edward	28 Oct 1825
John	20	M	Blacksmith	Ireland	United States	Trident	16 May 1826
John R.	2 1/12	M		Switzerland	U.S. America	Edward	28 Oct 1825
Macina	5 2/12	F		Switzerland	U.S. America	Edward	28 Oct 1825
Marey	42 2/12	F		Switzerland	U.S. America	Edward	28 Oct 1825
Michiel	48 3/12	M	Farmer	Switzerland	U.S. America	Edward	28 Oct 1825
Queronick	10 1/12	F		Switzerland	U.S. America	Edward	28 Oct 1825
R.	18	M	Clerk	Ireland	United States	Josephine	30 Apr 1828
Susan	14 2/12	F		Switzerland	U.S. America	Edward	28 Oct 1825
KEERL, Wm.	25	M	Doctor	United States	United States	Britannia	29 Oct 1829
KEERLEY, Robt.	33	M	Labourer	England	U. States	Ayrshire	12 May 1828
KEERNON, Mathew	24	M	Farmer	G. Britain	U. States	America	17 Oct 1825
KEERSALE, William	27	M	Labourer	Great Britian	United States	George Clinton	13 Apr 1826
KEES, William	20	M	Weaver	Ireland	N. Jersey	Potomac	7 Aug 1827
KEESER, George	27	M	Merchant	United States	United States	Commerce	30 Apr 1821
KEEVER, Charles	18	M	Labourer	Ireland	U. States	Wanderer	1 Sep 1828
KEFFEN, Elizabeth	20	F	Servant	Gt. Britain	U. States	Caledonia	10 Sep 1828
KEGAN, Catharine	14			Cork	Philadelphia	Schuylkill	22 Aug 1825
Manuel	21		Weaver	Cork	Philadelphia	Schuylkill	22 Aug 1825
KEGEL, Christina	20	F	Maid Servant	Germany	United States	Helen	5 Sep 1828
KEGG, Denis	27	M	Labourer	Ireland	United States	Hope	12 Jun 1828
KEGHAN, Patrick	22	M	Labourer	Ireland	United States	Nancy Henrietta	3 Nov 1828
KEHOE, Daniel	20	M	Labourer	Ireland	Pennsylvania	Atlantic	6 Oct 1828
Dominick	23	M	Clerk	Great Britain	U.S.A.	Silas Richards	7 Mar 1825
Edwd.	24	M	Merchant	England	U. States	James Cropper	17 Jun 1825
John	9	M	Boy	Ireland	United States	Dublin Packet	22 Apr 1822
Margret	20	F	Wife	Ireland	Pennsylvania	Atlantic	6 Oct 1828
Pat	1 6/12	M	Son	Ireland	Pennsylvania	Atlantic	6 Oct 1828
Philip	11	M	Boy	Ireland	United States	Dublin Packet	22 Apr 1822
KEHOW, Ann	65	F	Spinster	Ireland	United States	St. Michaels	23 Dec 1826
Ellen	25	F	Wife	Ireland	United States	St. Michaels	23 Dec 1826
James	28	M	Shoemaker	Ireland	United States	St. Michaels	23 Dec 1826

NAMES OF PASSENGERS	AGE	SEX	OCCUPATIONS	COUNTRY TO WHICH THEY BELONG	COUNTRY THEY INTEND TO INHABIT	SHIPS/DATES OF ARRIVAL	
KEIB, Gasper	28	M	Farmer	Alsace in the Department of Upper and lower Rhine	United States	Carolina Augusta	16 May 1828
KEIFF, Betsy	24	F	Spinster	Ireland	United States	Dublin Packet	22 Oct 1821
KEIGH, Thos.	27	M	Labourer	Ireland	America	Manhattan	20 Mar 1820
KEIK, J. J.	25	M	Tailor	...	Canada	Columbia	7 Sep 1827
KEIL, J.	28	M	Merchant	U. States	U. States	Six Brothers	21 Nov 1822
KEILD, Thomas F.		M	Merchant	Jamaica		Antelope	22 Aug 1820
KEILEY, Thomas	30	M	Farmer	Ireland	United States	Dublin Packet	22 Aug 1829
KEILLY, Wm.	25	M	Labourer	Ireland		Ocean	13 Jul 1827
KEIM, Christina	22	F	Agriculture	Wirtemburg	United States	Henri IV	14 Oct 1829
Fred.	27	M	Agriculture	Wirtemburg	United States	Henri IV	14 Oct 1829
Rosine	1	F	Agriculture	Wirtemburg	United States	Henri IV	14 Oct 1829
KEIN, —, Colonel	50	M	Milatary Officer	Baltimore	Baltimore	Genl. Pike	15 Jan 1827
Ann	36	F	None	U. States	U. States	Signal	3 Jan 1827
Ann	56	F	Lady			Seine	10 Jun 1822
KEINAN, Patt	20	M	Labourer	Ireland	Pensylvania	Lima	5 Aug 1829
Patt	20	M	Labourer	Ireland	U. States	Lima	5 Aug 1829
KEINE, —	23	M		Swisse	United States	Deux Ernest	29 Dec 1827
*landed at Lewiston, Delw.							
—	23			Suisse		Deux Ernest	29 Dec 1827
KEINERN, Martin	17	M	White Smith	Ireland	New York	Amanda	23 May 1827
KEINEY, Rose	20	F	Servant	Ireland	New York	Atlantic	8 May 1828
KEIPER, Henneh	26	M	Candidate	Rhyn Bayden	United States	Jason	3 Nov 1828
KEIRAN, John	21	M	Labourer	Ireland	New York	Atlantic	8 May 1828
KEIRNAN, Margaret	24	F	Spinster	Ireland	United States	Dublin Packet	6 Dec 1827
Rose	17	F	Servant	Ireland	New York	Atlantic	8 May 1828
KEIS, Johannes	35	F		Germany	Pensylvania	James Noble	27 Aug 1827
KEISSA, Magadelina	40	F		France	United States	New England	29 Aug 1828
KEISSER, Johana	0 1/12	M		France	United States	New England	29 Aug 1828
*Died 12 July							
KEITH, Andrew	26	M	Joiner	Scotland	United States	Culloden	17 May 1828
D.	30	M	Servant	Ireland	U. States	Henrietta	7 Jul 1825
George	43	M	Merchant	Great Britain	Unknown	William Thompson	1 May 1827
J. Alexr.	30	M	Mariner	New York	New York	Robert Edwards	17 Mar 1828
James	46	M	Merchant	Gt. Britain	Canada	Manchester	15 Apr 1828
Thos. D.	20	M	None	England	Canada	Silas Richards	3 Apr 1826
W.	29	M	Merchant	Great Brittain	Great Brittain	Robert Fulton	2 Aug 1824
KEITHS, —			Servant	Ireland	U. States	Henrietta	7 Jul 1825
Catharine	29	F	Servant	Ireland	U. States	Henrietta	7 Jul 1825
KEITLEY, Francis	27	M	Sawyer	Great Brittan	U. States	John & Elizabeth	11 Dec 1826
KEIZER, T.	24	M	Clerk	Germany	Baltimore	Stephania	13 Mar 1820
KEKOL, Lawrence	22	M	Merchant	Ireland	U. States	Albion	23 Apr 1822
KELAN, John	28	M	Weaver	Ireland	U. States	Courier	17 Mar 1828
KELBY, Sarah	9	F		Gt. Britain		Corinthian	27 Oct 1829
Sarah	43	F		Gt. Britain		Corinthian	27 Oct 1829
Thomas	45	M	Master of Vessel	State Main	U. States	Paquet Des Cayes	11 Oct 1827
William	46	M	Painter	Gt. Britain		Corinthian	27 Oct 1829
KELDAY, Hugh	46	M	...	Ireland	U. States	Ann Maria	6 Jul 1824
James	3	M		Ireland	U. States	Ann Maria	6 Jul 1824
Mary	18	F	Wife	Ireland	U. States	Ann Maria	6 Jul 1824
KELEHER, Maurice	35	M	Clerk	Ireland	U.S. America	Traveller	10 Sep 1827
KELL, Hugh	37			Ireland		Anacreon	7 Sep 1827
KELLAGHER, Matthew	27	M	Labourer	Ireland	United States	Nancy Henrietta	3 Nov 1828
KELLAIN, Nabby	30	F	Servant	Ireland	United States	Josephine	30 Apr 1828
Sally	26	F	Servant	Ireland	United States	Josephine	30 Apr 1828
KELLARLAN, Thomas	27	M	Laborer	Ireland	U. States	Lady Hunter	8 Aug 1826
KELLBURY, W.	27	M	Farmer	Ireland	U. States	Mentor	5 Jul 1825
KELLEN, B.	26		Farmer	Ireland	United States	Courier	16 May 1825
T.	26		Farmer	Ireland	United States	Courier	16 May 1825
KELLER, —	31	M		France	United States	Cavalier	25 Jul 1828
—, Wife	36	F		France	United States	Cavalier	25 Jul 1828
Anabar	6	F	Framer	Switzerland	Ohio	Danube	20 Jul 1826
Anna	14	F	Framer	Switzerland	Ohio	Danube	20 Jul 1826
Caterinia	37	F	Framer	Switzerland	Ohio	Danube	20 Jul 1826

665

KELLER (cont'd)

NAMES OF PASSENGERS	AGE	SEX	OCCUPATIONS	COUNTRY TO WHICH THEY BELONG	COUNTRY THEY INTEND TO INHABIT	SHIPS/DATES OF ARRIVAL	
Christian	13	M	Framer	Switserland	Ohio	Danube	20 Jul 1826
Christian	25	M	Miller	Wirtemburg	United States	Wade	29 Aug 1825
Christian	41	M	Framer	Switserland	Ohio	Danube	20 Jul 1826
Elizabath	2	F	Framer	Switserland	Ohio	Danube	20 Jul 1826
Etienne	27	M	Farmer	France	U. States	France	14 Mar 1828
Eve	24	F	Single Woman	United States	United States	Globe	30 Aug 1828
Jacop	5	M	Framer	Switserland	Ohio	Danube	20 Jul 1826
Jh.	30		Charper. [carpenter]	Suisse		Deux Ernest	29 Dec 1827
John	11	M	Framer	Switserland	Ohio	Danube	20 Jul 1826
John	34	M	Framer	Switserland	Ohio	Danube	20 Jul 1826
Joseph	21	M	Schoolmaster	Germany	Pensylvania	James Noble	27 Aug 1827
Joseph	30	M	Carpenter	Swisse	United States	Deux Ernest	29 Dec 1827
*landed at Lewiston, Delw.							
Lorentz	6	F		France	United States	Cavalier	25 Jul 1828
Margeret	33	F	Framer	Switserland	Ohio	Danube	20 Jul 1826
Margt.	8	F		France	United States	Cavalier	25 Jul 1828
Mariane	9	F		France	United States	Cavalier	25 Jul 1828
Michael	7	M		France	United States	Cavalier	25 Jul 1828
KELLERAN, Thomas	4	F	None	England	United States	Jubilee	1 Oct 1828
KELLERIN, Dorothy	21	F	Maid Servant	Germany	United States	Helen	5 Sep 1828
KELLERING, Peter	26	M	Farmer	Bavarian	United States	American	27 Aug 1827
KELLETT, Robert	33	M	Weaver	Gt. Britain	United States	Eliza Barker	11 Jan 1826
KELLEY, Agnes	22	F	None	Great Britain	United States	William Dawson	18 Jun 1827
Ann	19	F	None	Great Britan	United States	Silvanus Jenkins	10 Mar 1827
Ann	25	F		Great Britain	U. States	Hope & Esther	13 Oct 1829
Ann	28		None			Emulous	19 Feb 1822
Bridget	26	F	Spinster	Ireland	United States	Wilson	4 Oct 1827
Bridget	35	F	Spiner	...aven	United States	Minerva	30 Oct 1829
Ch...s	...	M	Labourer	Ireland	Unt. St. America	Wilson	21 May 1827
Edward	23	M	Weaver	Ireland	United States	Enterprize	23 Jul 1827
Elisha	22	F	Spinster	Ireland	America	Wilson	16 May 1825
Eliza	...	F	Child	Queen County, Corkley, Ireland	N. York	New Orleans	24 Aug 1827
Esther	19	M	Female	England	U. States	Birmingham	16 Jun 1828
Fredk.	5	M	None	Great Britain	United States	William Dawson	18 Jun 1827
G.	40	M	Gass Lightman	Great Britain	United States	Isaac Hicks	6 Dec 1827
James	20	M	Merchant	G. Britain		Sarahs Delight	13 May 1823
James	27	M	Druggist	England	U.S. States	Splendid	14 Aug 1829
James	40	M	Labourer	Ireland	U.S. of America	Meteor	19 Mar 1828
Jno.	20	M	Farmer	England	United States	Essex	23 May 1828
John	11/12	M		Ireland	United States	Enterprize	23 Jul 1827
John	5	M	Joiner	Great Britain	U.S. America	Chili	7 Jul 1827
John	19	M	Joiner	Ireland	United States	Neury	27 Jan 1827
John	23	M	Piano Forte Maker	England	New York	Brighton	16 Nov 1826
John	26	M	...	...	...	Indian Chief	8 Sep 1824
John	34	M	Farmer	Great Britain	United States	William Dawson	18 Jun 1827
Maria	...	F	Child	Queen County, Corkley, Ireland	N. York	New Orleans	24 Aug 1827
Mary	4	F	None	Great Britain	United States	William Dawson	18 Jun 1827
Mary	20	F	Spinster	G. Britain	U. States	Hanford	18 Sep 1828
Mary	21	F		Ireland	United States	Enterprize	23 Jul 1827
Mary Ann	2	F		Great Britain	U. States	Hope & Esther	13 Oct 1829
Matthew	43	M	Mariner	United States	United States	Diamond	13 Nov 1823
Patrick	18	M	Servant	Ireland	United States	Sylvester Healy	19 Aug 1825
Patrick, Rt. Revd.	41	M	Gentleman	Ireland	United States	Erin	25 Dec 1820
Patt	...	M	Child	Queen County, Corkley, Ireland	N. York	New Orleans	24 Aug 1827
Plina	...	F	Child	Queen County, Corkley, Ireland	N. York	New Orleans	24 Aug 1827
Richard	20	M	Laborer	England	United States	Jubilee	1 Oct 1828
Robert	33	M	Labourer	Great Britain	U. States	Hope & Esther	13 Oct 1829
Rose	46	F	Matron	Ireland	America	Josephine	8 Dec 1827
Salley	20	F	Milaner	Ireland	United States	Wilson	4 Oct 1827
Thomas	32	M	Clerk	Ireland	Washington	Angelica	18 Aug 1823

NAMES OF PASSENGERS	AGE	SEX	OCCUPATIONS	COUNTRY TO WHICH THEY BELONG	COUNTRY THEY INTEND TO INHABIT	SHIPS/DATES OF ARRIVAL	
KELLEY (cont'd)							
Thos.	26	M	Farmer	England	U. States	Acasta	12 May 1825
William	1	M		Great Britain	U. States	Hope & Esther	13 Oct 1829
Wm.	31	M	Farmer	Ireland	United States	Trident	31 Mar 1827
KELLIAN, Martin	21	M	Farmer	Ireland	U. States	Edward	15 Jul 1825
KELLOG, Martin	40	M	Farmer	Switzerland	U. States	Bayard	9 Nov 1825
Silas	27	M	Super Cargo	U. States	U. States	Ben Alam	23 Dec 1826
KELLOGG, Silas	21	M	Merchant	New York	U. States	Mosquito	5 Dec 1821
Silas	22	M	Mercht.	U. States	U. States	Ben Alam	2 Aug 1827
Silas	24	M	Supercargo	New York	U. States	Morhey	3 Mar 1825
Silas	24	M	Merchant	United States	United States	Morkey	18 Aug 1825
KELLUM, John	30		Gentleman	England	United States	Cambria	19 Oct 1829
KELLUP, Jane	28	F		G. Britain	U. States	St. George	7 Jun 1828
Pat	26	M	Farmer	G. Britain	U. States	St. George	7 Jun 1828
KELLY, —, Mr.	25	M		Dublin	U. States	Hibernia	26 Oct 1826
—, Mr.	26	M	Farmer	Dublin	U. States	Hibernia	26 Oct 1826
—, Mrs.	24	F	Farmer	Dublin	U. States	Hibernia	26 Oct 1826
...	...	M	Laborer	England	United States	Lord Wellington	14 Nov 1827
Adam	6/12			Scotland	United States	Camillus	3 May 1828
Agnes	6			Scotland	United States	Camillus	3 May 1828
Alexr.	20	M	Farmer	Ireland	U. States	Dickinson	30 Jul 1825
Alice	0 3/12	F		England	U. States	Rising States	20 Sep 1828
Ana.	40	M	Merchant	Ireland	U. States	New Speculation	1 Mar 1823
Ann	9	F		Great Britain	United States	Meridian	2 Jul 1827
Ann	10	F	None	Great Britain	United States	Atlantic	28 May 1827
Ann	16	F	Spinster	Ireland	United States	Dublin Packet	3 Sep 1822
Ann	16	F		Great Britain	United States	Meridian	2 Jul 1827
Ann	18	F	Weaver	Gt. Britain	United States	Grecian	24 Sep 1828
Ann	22	F				Lady of the Lake	23 Aug 1828
Ann	24	F	Servant	Ireland	United States	Neury	27 Jan 1827
Ann	25	F		Ireland	U. States	St. Michael	27 Mar 1827
Ann	33	F	Weaver	Ireland	U. States	Atlantic	7 Aug 1823
Ann	73	F	Spinster	Ireland	United States	Henry Kneeland	7 Jun 1828
Arthur	27	M	Joiner	Ireland	United States	Essex	23 May 1828
B.	6	M	Labourer	Great Brittain	United States	Sarah Ralston	27 Jan 1827
Barny	37	M	Labourer	Ireland	U. States	Two Marys	20 Apr 1825
Barthw.	31	M	Clark	Ireland	United States	Aurora	9 Jul 1827
Betsey	2	F	None	Isle of Man	Isle of Man	Howard Douglass	11 May 1827
Betsy	6	F		Great Britain	United States	Meridian	2 Jul 1827
Bridget	5	F	Child	Ireland	America	Josephine	8 Dec 1827
Bridget	6	F		Dublin	U. States	Hibernia	26 Oct 1826
Bridget, Miss	22	F	Lady	Ireland	United States	Erin	25 Dec 1820
Bridgitt	35	F		Great Britain	United States	Samuel Wright	12 Oct 1829
C.	25	M	Labourer	...	U. States	Governor Tompkins	26 Jul 1824
Cate	32	F	None	Great Britain	United States	Atlantic	28 May 1827
Catharine	22	F	None	Great Britain		Casanda	5 Sep 1827
Catherine	9		Laboring Class		United States	Atlantic	2 Apr 1827
Catherine	20	F				John Dickinson	14 Sep 1820
Catherine	21	F		Gt. Britain		Dalhouse Castle	13 May 1828
Catherine	24	F		Isle of Mann	United States	Lord Wellington	14 Nov 1827
Catherine	37 6/12	F		England	United States	Rising States	16 Jan 1829
Catherine, Jr.	1	F		Isle of Mann	United States	Lord Wellington	14 Nov 1827
Catherine, Miss	27	F	Servant	Cork in Ireland	New York	Europa	12 Oct 1829
Cathn.	2	F	None	Great Britain	United States	Atlantic	28 May 1827
Cathr.	10	F	None	Isle of Man	Isle of Man	Howard Douglass	11 May 1827
Charles	25	M	Merchant	Ireland	U. States	Nancy	10 Jul 1822
Charles	27	M	Labourer	Ireland	Ireland	Sarah G.	28 Nov 1827
Connor	40		Laboring Class		United States	Atlantic	2 Apr 1827
Cothrel	18	M	Labourer	Great Britain	United States	William Dawson	18 Jun 1827
Danl.	25	M	Labourer	Ireland	U.S.	Oliver Wolcott	3 Nov 1827
Denis	34	M	Farmer	Ireland	United States	Dublin Packet	13 Oct 1828
Dennis	20	M	Clothier	U. States	U. States	United States	11 Sep 1828
Dennis	21		Laboring Class		United States	Atlantic	2 Apr 1827
Dennis	21	M	Labourer	Ireland		Marchioness	13 May 1828
Edward	24	M	Labourer	Ireland	United States	Atlantic	21 Jul 1827

NAMES OF PASSENGERS	AGE	SEX	OCCUPATIONS	COUNTRY TO WHICH THEY BELONG	COUNTRY THEY INTEND TO INHABIT	SHIPS/DATES OF ARRIVAL	
KELLY (cont'd)							
Edward	24	M	Laborer or Spinster	Ireland	United States	Sarah G.	15 Aug 1827
Edward	26 6/12	M	Labourer	Ireland	United States	Fabius	31 Jul 1829
Edward	28	M	Labourer	Ireland	New York	America	1 Aug 1828
Edwd.	14	M	Weaver	Ireland	U. States	Atlantic	7 Aug 1823
Edwd.	27	M	Farmer	Ireland	U. States	Wilson	22 Apr 1822
Edwd.	40	M	Weaver	Ireland	U. States	Atlantic	7 Aug 1823
Elenor	...0	F	Spinster	Ireland	U. States	Josephine	7 May 1827
Elenor	35	F	Wife	Ireland	United States	Dublin Packet	29 Jun 1825
Elisa	17	F		Great Britain	United States	Meridian	2 Jul 1827
Eliza	4	F		Isle of Man	America	Plutarch	18 Jul 1826
Eliza	16	F	Weaver	Ireland	U. States	Atlantic	7 Aug 1823
Elizabeth	...	...		Ireland	U. States	Nancy	16 Aug 1822
Elizabeth	43	F	Lady	U. States	U. States	Abeona	1 Oct 1823
Elizebath	18	F	None	Great Briton	United States	Mount Vernon	30 Dec 1828
Ellan	7		Laboring Class		United States	Atlantic	2 Apr 1827
Ellen	12	F	None	Isle of Man	Isle of Man	Howard Douglass	11 May 1827
Ellen	30 3/12	F	Servant	Ireland	United States	Atlantic	21 Jul 1827
Ellen	31	F		Isle of Man	America	Plutarch	18 Jul 1826
Esther	36	F		Great Britain	United States	Meridian	2 Jul 1827
Ewd.	24	M	Labourer	England	America	Two Marys	24 Sep 1827
Ezra	26	M	Watchmaker	U. States	United States	Cicero	19 Nov 1825
Francis	38	M	Joiner	Ireland	U. States	Calais Packet	7 Jul 1828
Geo.	40	M	Shoe Maker	Scotland	United States	Louisiana	3 Nov 1827
George	23	M	Painter	Ireland	United States	Trio	13 Jun 1827
George	39	M				Lady of the Lake	23 Aug 1828
*left ship							
Grace	40	F	None	England	U. States	Roman	1 Dec 1828
Heigle	10	M		Irereland	America	Carolina Ann	20 Jun 1825
Henry	18	M	Labourer	G. Britain	U. States	Mary & Harriot	8 Sep 1828
Honor	17	F		Ireland	United States	William	20 Jul 1829
Hugh	21	M	Bookkeeper	Ireland	U.S. of America	Hannibal	17 Dec 1823
Issabella	20	F		Great Britain	U. States	Lady Hunter	28 May 1823
James	1	M		England	New York	Curler	7 Jul 1827
James	6	M	None	Isle of Man	Isle of Man	Howard Douglass	11 May 1827
James	16	M	...	Ireland	United States	Carolina Ann	24 Oct 1825
James	18	M	Farmer	Ireland	United States	Dublin Packet	29 Jun 1825
James	21	M	Baker	Irereland	America	Carolina Ann	20 Jun 1825
James	22	M	Farmer	Ireland	United States	Curler	3 Mar 1828
James	22	M	Farmer	Ireland	United States	Dublin Packet	22 Aug 1829
James	23	M	Servant	Ireland	United States	Josephine	30 Apr 1828
James	24	M	Labourer	Ireland	United States	Robert Fulton	24 Jul 1826
James	26	M	Farmer	Ireland	United States	Trident	31 Mar 1827
James	27	M	Farmer	Ireland	New York	Curler	7 Jul 1827
Jane	12	F		Great Britain	United States	Meridian	2 Jul 1827
Jane	20	F		Mayo	America	Margaret	31 Jul 1824
Janus	2...	M	Son	Ireland	New York	Louisa	18 Apr 1827
Jas.	6	M	None	Great Britain	United States	Atlantic	28 May 1827
Jas.	19		Printer	U. States	United States	Roman	10 Sep 1827
Jas.	24	M	Labourer	Ireland	U. States	Two Marys	20 Apr 1825
Jas.	28	M	Cooper	Ireland	United States	William	20 Jul 1829
Jno.	8	M	None	Great Britain	United States	Atlantic	28 May 1827
Jno.	20	M	...	Great Britain	United States	Atlantic	28 May 1827
Jno.	20	M	Spinner	Great Britain	United States	Penelope	11 Jun 1827
Jno.	23	M	Farmer	Ireland	U. States	Meteor	11 Apr 1825
Jno.	24			England		Anacreon	7 Sep 1827
Jno.	30	M	Farmer	Great Britain	United States	Atlantic	28 May 1827
John	1	M	Labourer	Ireland	U. States	Two Marys	20 Apr 1825
John	2	M		Isle of Man	America	Plutarch	18 Jul 1826
John	4			Scotland	United States	Camillus	3 May 1828
John	14	M	...	Ireland	United States	Carolina Ann	24 Oct 1825
John	14	M	Labourer	England	U. States	Comet	23 Aug 1828
John	16	M	Labourer	G. Britain	U. States	Mary & Harriot	8 Sep 1828
John	18	M	Labourer	Great Britian	United States	Princess Charlotte	6 Sep 1828
John	20	M	Farmer	Ireland	United States	Trident	31 Mar 1827

NAMES OF PASSENGERS	AGE	SEX	OCCUPATIONS	COUNTRY TO WHICH THEY BELONG	COUNTRY THEY INTEND TO INHABIT	SHIPS/DATES OF ARRIVAL	
KELLY (cont'd)							
John	20	M	Labourer	England	U. States	Comet	23 Aug 1828
John	22		Labourer	Ireland	America	Sarah	18 Aug 1829
John	24	M	Laborer	Ireland	New York	Indian Chief	19 Jun 1823
John	24	M	Farmer	Ireland	U. States	Dickinson	30 Jul 1825
John	25		Laborer	Ireland	Great Britain	Robert Burns	14 Jun 1824
John	25	M	Taylor	Irereland	America	Carolina Ann	20 Jun 1825
John	25	M	Labourer	Ireland	United States	Borneo	14 Aug 1827
John	25	M	Labourer	Ireland	United States	Hope	12 Jun 1828
John	26	M	Mason	Gt. Britain	United States	Penelope	9 Sep 1828
John	26	M		G. Britain	U. States	London	23 Sep 1828
John	27	M	Servant	Jamaica	U. States	Milo	24 Jun 1824
John	28	M	Bricksetter	Ireland	New York	Louisa	18 Apr 1827
John	28	M	Carder	Great Britain	United States	Roanoak	19 Sep 1827
John	28	M	Mechanic	Ireland	U. States	Howard Douglass	29 Jan 1828
John	29	M	Farmer	Ireland	U. States	Dickinson	30 Jul 1825
John	30	M	Labaorent	Galway	U. States	Eliza Ann	30 Jul 1823
John	30	M	Labourer	England	New York	Curler	7 Jul 1827
John	30			Longford	Virginia	Peru	30 May 1828
John	30	M	Labourer			Lady of the Lake	23 Aug 1828
*left ship							
John	31	M	Watchmaker	Halifax	United States	Oliver Wolcott	3 Nov 1827
John	32	M	Mariner	New York	Boston, Mass.	Rubicon	22 May 1826
John	42	M		Ireland	U. States	Packet	23 Sep 1820
John	45	M	Farmer	Tyrone	...	Gleaner	24 May 1823
John	55	M	Farmer	Great Britain	United States	Meridian	2 Jul 1827
Johnan	20	F		England	U. States	Rising States	20 Sep 1828
Johrane...	29	F		G. Britain	U. States	London	23 Sep 1828
Jon.	12	M	None	Great Britain	United States	Atlantic	28 May 1827
Jos.	22	M	Labourer	Ireland	United States	Thomas	13 Dec 1827
Js.	25	M	Farmer	Great Brittan	U. States	John & Elizabeth	11 Dec 1826
Laina	27	M	Weaver	Ireland	New York	Louisa	18 Apr 1827
Lydia	24	F	Lady	England	U. States	Pacific	11 Sep 1824
M.	18	M	Farmer	Farmer	U. States	Wilson	2 Sep 1823
M.	22	M	Labourer	G. Britain	U. States	London	23 Sep 1828
M.	29	M	Merchant	Ireland	U. States	Annawan	3 Apr 1826
Manan	33	F		England	U. States	Rising States	20 Sep 1828
Margaret	2 1/12	F		England	United States	Rising States	16 Jan 1829
Margaret	11	F	Child	Ireland	America	Wilson	16 Nov 1824
Margaret	14	F	Farmer	Ireland	U. States	Dickinson	30 Jul 1825
Margaret	18 1/12	F	Servant	Ireland	New York	Louisa	20 Jul 1826
Margaret	24	F		Ireland	U. States	Packet	23 Sep 1820
Margt.	2	F		Ireland	United States	William Byrnes	6 Apr 1826
Margt.	18	F		Gt. Britain	U. States	St. George	20 Sep 1828
Margt.	19	F		Great Britain	United States	Meridian	2 Jul 1827
Margt.	40	F	None	Isle of Man	Isle of Man	Howard Douglass	11 May 1827
Maria	4	F		England	U. States	Rising States	20 Sep 1828
Maria	17		Maid Servant	Ireland	America	Sarah	18 Aug 1829
Mark	26	M	Labourer	Ireland	U. States	Sarah G	7 May 1827
Martha	9	F	Weaver	Ireland	U. States	Atlantic	7 Aug 1823
Mary	4	F	Labourer	Ireland	U. States	Two Marys	20 Apr 1825
Mary	4	F		Great Britain	United States	Meridian	2 Jul 1827
Mary	8			Scotland	United States	Camillus	3 May 1828
Mary	10	F	Child	Ireland	America	Josephine	8 Dec 1827
Mary	13	F	Spinster	Ireland	America	Wilson	16 Nov 1824
Mary	20	F	Wife	Great Britain	United States	Washington	3 Sep 1827
Mary	20	F		Gt. Britain		Dalhouse Castle	13 May 1828
Mary	21	F		Ireland	United States	Princess Charlotte	26 Apr 1827
Mary	22	F		Ireland	New York	Curler	7 Jul 1827
Mary	22	F		England	New York	Curler	7 Jul 1827
Mary	24	F	Spinster	Ireland	United States	Robert Fulton	24 Jul 1826
Mary	24	F		Gt. Britain		Dalhouse Castle	13 May 1828
Mary	27	F	Labourer	Ireland	U. States	Two Marys	20 Apr 1825
Mary	40	F	Wife	Ireland	New York	Louisa	18 Apr 1827

NAMES OF PASSENGERS	AGE	SEX	OCCUPATIONS	COUNTRY TO WHICH THEY BELONG	COUNTRY THEY INTEND TO INHABIT	SHIPS/DATES OF ARRIVAL	
KELLY (cont'd)							
Mary	54	M	Weaver	Gt. Britain	United States	Penelope	9 Sep 1828
Mary J.	18	F	Spinster	Ireland	U. States	Courier	17 Mar 1828
Mathew	40	M	Labourer	England	U. States	Comet	23 Aug 1828
May	20	F	Servant	Ireland	N. York	Trusty	12 Sep 1828
May	29	F	None	England	United States	India	8 Jun 1827
Mic	24	M		Gt. Britain	United States	Penelope	9 Sep 1828
Mich.	20	M	Laborer	Gt. Britain		Dalhouse Castle	13 May 1828
Mich.	28	M	Farmer	Ireland	United States	Curler	3 Mar 1828
Michael	...		Laboring Class		United States	Atlantic	2 Apr 1827
Michael	21	M	Painter	Mayo	America	Margaret	31 Jul 1824
Michael	21	M	Carpenter	Ireland	New York	Amanda	23 May 1827
Michael	25	M	Farmer	Great Brittan	U. States	John & Elizabeth	11 Dec 1826
Michael	26	M	Labourer	Ireland	U. States	Marcus	7 Apr 1825
Michl.	30	M	Farmer	Ireland	U. States	Dickinson	30 Jul 1825
Morto	31	M	Cooper	England	U. States	Rising States	20 Sep 1828
N.	25	F		France & Switzerland	U. States	Bayard	14 Jul 1826
Neil	14	M	Labourer	Ireland	United States	Robert Fulton	24 Jul 1826
Owen	23	M	Weaver	Ireland	United States	Romulus	24 Jun 1826
Pat	20	M				Hibernia	15 Aug 1820
Pat	21	M	Farmer	Great Britain	United States	Atlantic	28 May 1827
Pat	22	M	Farmer	G. Britain	U. States	Margaret Bogle	12 Jun 1828
Pat	23	M	Labourer	St. Johns, N.B.	United States	Antioch	21 Sep 1827
Pat	25	M				Lady of the Lake	23 Aug 1828
Pat	30	M	Labourer	Great Britain		Moro Castle	6 Jul 1827
Patrick	3	M		Dublin	U. States	Hibernia	26 Oct 1826
Patrick	4 10/12	M		England	United States	Rising States	16 Jan 1829
Patrick	11	F	Spinster	Ireland	United States	Dublin Packet	3 Sep 1822
Patrick	16	M		Irereland	America	Carolina Ann	20 Jun 1825
Patrick	19	M	Labourer	Ireland	New York	Lima	5 Aug 1829
Patrick	19	M		Ireland	N. York	Lima	5 Aug 1829
Patrick	20		None			Amphion	31 May 1824
Patrick	20	M		Ireland	United States	William & George	14 May 1828
Patrick	22		Laborer	Ireland	New York	Lady Hunter	19 Oct 1826
Patrick	24	M	Labourer	Ireland	United States	Hope	12 Jun 1828
Patrick	25	M	Weaver	Irereland	America	Carolina Ann	20 Jun 1825
Patrick	25	M	Farmer	Ireland	United States	Trident	30 Sep 1826
Patrick	28	M	Farmer	Ireland	New York	Curler	7 Jul 1827
Patrick	65	M	Scrivener	Newfoundland	Nfoundland.	Combine	22 May 1824
Patrick A.	22	M	...	St. Croix	New York	Jupiter	21 Nov 1825
Paul	28	M	Joiner	Isle of Mann	United States	Lord Wellington	14 Nov 1827
Peter	15	M	None	Ireland	United States	Mary & Harriet	3 Jul 1829
Philip	20	M	Shoemaker	Isle of Man	America	Plutarch	18 Jul 1826
Ric.	2...	M	Farmer	Great Britain	United States	Atlantic	28 May 1827
Robert	7	M		Great Britain	United States	Meridian	2 Jul 1827
Robert	33	M	Clerk	Great Britain	United States	Ocean	27 Jul 1825
Robt.	1	M	Weaver	Ireland	U. States	Atlantic	7 Aug 1823
Robt.	23	M	Farmer	Great Britain	United States	William Dawson	18 Jun 1827
Rosanna	12	F	Child	Ireland	United States	Dublin Packet	9 Jul 1827
Rosinna	20		Maid Servant	Ireland	America	Sarah	18 Aug 1829
Sally	23		Wife, Going to her husband	Scotland	United States	Camillus	3 May 1828
Sarah	16	F				John Dickinson	14 Sep 1820
Sarah	23	F		U. States	U. States	United States	11 Sep 1828
Sarah, Mrs.	28			St. John, N.B.	Great Britain	Henrietta	26 Nov 1825
Sarah Thomas	6			New York	U.S. America	Henrietta	26 Nov 1825
Simeon	23		Farmer	England	United States	Corinthian	30 May 1828
Simon	25	M	Farmer	Great Britain	United States	Ocean	27 Jul 1825
Sophia	30	F	Spinster	Queen County, Corkley, Ireland	N. York	New Orleans	24 Aug 1827
Stephen	22	M	Shop Keeper	U. States	U. States	United States	11 Sep 1828
Teresa	2	F		England	U. States	Rising States	20 Sep 1828
Terins	19	M	Taylor	Irereland	America	Carolina Ann	20 Jun 1825

NAMES OF PASSENGERS	AGE	SEX	OCCUPATIONS	COUNTRY TO WHICH THEY BELONG	COUNTRY THEY INTEND TO INHABIT	SHIPS/DATES OF ARRIVAL	
KELLY (cont'd)							
Thomas	13	M	None	Isle of Man	Isle of Man	Howard Douglass	11 May 1827
Thomas	18	M	Farmer	Ireland	U. States	Alexander	28 Jul 1821
Thomas	19	M	Labourer	Ireland	U. States	William & John	10 Jul 1824
Thomas	19 6/12	M	Carpenter	Ireland	United States	Fabius	31 Jul 1829
Thomas	20	M	Farmer	Ireland	United States	Dublin Packet	29 Jun 1825
Thomas	20	M	Farmer	Ireland	United States	Dublin Packet	23 May 1828
Thomas	27	M	Farmer	Ireland	United States	Curler	3 Mar 1828
Thomas	34	M	Farmer	Ireland	United States	Trident	31 Mar 1827
Thos.	1	M	Farmer	Great Britain	United States	Atlantic	28 May 1827
Thos.	5	M	Labourer	Ireland	U. States	Two Marys	20 Apr 1825
Thos.	24	M	Labourer	Ireland	United States	Thomas	13 Dec 1827
Thos.	26	M		Gt. Britain	United States	Penelope	9 Sep 1828
Timothy	33	F		Great Britain	United States	Samuel Wright	12 Oct 1829
W.	21	M	Farmer	Great Brittan	U. States	John & Elizabeth	11 Dec 1826
W.	28	M	Gentleman	America	America	Brittania	17 Jul 1828
Walker	25	M	Labourer	Great Britain	United States	Washington	3 Sep 1827
William	4	M		Gt. Britain		Dalhouse Castle	13 May 1828
William	13	M	Labourer	Isle of Man	Ohio	Curler	7 Jul 1827
William	14		Laboring Class		United States	Atlantic	2 Apr 1827
William	25	M	Merchant	United States	United States	Bunker Hill	16 Apr 1827
William	26	M	Labourer	Isle of Man	America	Plutarch	18 Jul 1826
William	26	M		U. States	U. States	United States	11 Sep 1828
William	28	M	Labourer	Ireland	United States	William	20 Jul 1829
William	30	M	Baker	Great Britain	United States	Samuel Wright	12 Oct 1829
William	40	M	Farmer	Great Britain	United States	Meridian	2 Jul 1827
William	45	M	Laborer	Ireland	United States	Dublin Packet	9 Jul 1827
Willm.	7	M	None	Isle of Man	Isle of Man	Howard Douglass	11 May 1827
Willm.	30	M	Shoemaker	Isle of Man	Lancaster	Howard Douglass	11 May 1827
Willm.	40	F	Farmer	Isle of Man	Isle of Man	Howard Douglass	11 May 1827
Wm.	2	M		U. States	U. States	United States	11 Sep 1828
Wm.	6	M		Great Britain	United States	Meridian	2 Jul 1827
Wm.	6	M		Great Britain	United States	Meridian	2 Jul 1827
Wm.	18 3/12	M	Weaver	Ireland	United States	Atlantic	21 Jul 1827
Wm.	22	M	Merchant	Ireland	U. States	William Barker	21 Apr 1823
Wm.	22	M	Merchant	Galway	U. States	Eliza Ann	30 Jul 1823
Wm.	25	M	Laborer	Great Britain	United States	Corinthian	5 Jan 1824
Wm.	25	M		St. Johns	U. States	Wanderer	30 Oct 1828
Wm.	26	M	Merchant	G. Britan	U. States	Canada	27 Sep 1826
Wm.	27			Dundock	N. York	Peru	30 May 1828
Wm.	43		Plumber & Glazer	England		Hudson	23 Jul 1828
Wm., & servant	27		Merchant	New York	United States	Triumph	23 Jul 1829
KELMURRY,							
Andrew	25	M	...	Ireland	United States	Wilson	22 Jun 1824
Edward	25 4/12	M	...	Ireland	United States	Wilson	22 Jun 1824
John	26	M	...	Ireland	United States	Wilson	22 Jun 1824
Patrick	30	M	...	Ireland	United States	Wilson	22 Jun 1824
KELRAY, Elizth.	7	...	...	...	...	Diamond	27 Jul 1824
Hugh	41	...	...	...	...	Diamond	27 Jul 1824
Isabela	4	...	...	...	...	Diamond	27 Jul 1824
Isabela	28	...	...	...	...	Diamond	27 Jul 1824
James	34	...	...	...	...	Diamond	27 Jul 1824
Margt.	6	...	...	...	...	Diamond	27 Jul 1824
Mary Ann	.../12	...	...	...	...	Diamond	27 Jul 1824
KELSALL, Sarah	23	F	None	Great Britain	United States	Roman	10 May 1828
KELSH, Ann	1	F		Ireland	United States	Danube	13 Jul 1827
John	3...	M	Farmer	Ireland	United States	Danube	13 Jul 1827
Margaret	3	F		Ireland	United States	Danube	13 Jul 1827
Mary	4	F		Ireland	United States	Danube	13 Jul 1827
Mary	3...	F		Ireland	United States	Danube	13 Jul 1827
KELSO, Chas.	29	M	Farmer	Saintfield	United States	Carolina Ann	11 Jun 1824
George	25	M	Weaver	Ireland	United States	Robert Fulton	10 Aug 1827
Margaret	20	F		Antrim	United States	Carolina Ann	11 Jun 1824
Marshall	25	M		Antrim	United States	Carolina Ann	11 Jun 1824

NAMES OF PASSENGERS	AGE	SEX	OCCUPATIONS	COUNTRY TO WHICH THEY BELONG	COUNTRY THEY INTEND TO INHABIT	SHIPS/DATES OF ARRIVAL	
KELSO (cont'd)							
Mary	22	F	Spinner	Ireland	Philad.	Triton	12 Jul 1823
William	20	M	Gentleman	Ireland	U. States	William & John	10 Jul 1824
KELSTER, M.	35	M	Merchant	Germany	Liverpool	Native	29 May 1824
KELVER, Barbaretta	22	F	Spinster	Switzerland	United States	Andes	5 May 1828
Madalena	7	F	Child	Switzerland	United States	Andes	5 May 1828
Margaret	31	F	Spinster	Switzerland	United States	Andes	5 May 1828
Mule	1	F	Child	Switzerland	United States	Andes	5 May 1828
Peter	4	M	Child	Switzerland	United States	Andes	5 May 1828
Peter	31	M	Farmer	Switzerland	United States	Andes	5 May 1828
KELZAL, Mary	21	F	Lady	United States	U.S.	Panthea	13 Mar 1823
KEMBER, T.	21	M	Doctor	Great Britan	Montreal	Cadmus	28 May 1821
KEMBLE, Charles	21	M			U. States America	Cambria	2 Jul 1821
Eliza	45	F			U. States America	Cambria	2 Jul 1821
Jesse	11	F			U. States America	Cambria	2 Jul 1821
Maria	16	F			U. States America	Cambria	2 Jul 1821
Peter	60	M	Gentleman	America	U. States America	Cambria	2 Jul 1821
Wm.	38	M	Farmer	U. States	U. States	Pleiades	9 Oct 1829
KEMETT, Charles	4	M		England	United States	Peru	23 May 1827
Charles	27	M	Farmer	England	United States	Peru	23 May 1827
Sarah	27	F		England	United States	Peru	23 May 1827
KEMGAN, John	20		Laborer	Ireland	United States	Robert Burns	18 Jun 1821
KEMMERSMAN, Eliz.	23	F		Switzerland	United States	Thetis	5 Jul 1821
KEMP, Aaron	16	M	Student	New York	New York	Sully	4 Mar 1828
Albert	2	M	Child	England	United States	Cambria	3 Jul 1829
Alfred	14			England	U. States	Corinthian	8 Oct 1828
Ann	6	F	Child	England	United States	Cambria	3 Jul 1829
Arthr	13			England	U. States	Corinthian	8 Oct 1828
Charles	25	M	Mechanic	England	U. States of Amer	Dale	14 Mar 1828
Charls	26	M	Farmer	England	U. States	Emily	25 Aug 1827
Edmund	2			England	U. States	Corinthian	8 Oct 1828
Edwd.	20	M	Labourer	Ireland	United States	Essex	23 May 1828
Elizabeth	44			England	U. States	Corinthian	8 Oct 1828
Ellice	5	F	Child	England	United States	Cambria	3 Jul 1829
Emmar	17			England	U. States	Corinthian	8 Oct 1828
Ethelinda	36	F	Wife	England	United States	Cambria	3 Jul 1829
George	4	M	Child	England	United States	Cambria	3 Jul 1829
George	38	M	Nail Maker	London	United States	Dalhousie Castle	27 Jul 1826
George	44		Farmer	England	U. States	Corinthian	8 Oct 1828
Harrot	16			England	U. States	Corinthian	8 Oct 1828
James	5	M	Child	England	United States	Cambria	3 Jul 1829
James	24	M	Weaver	Ireland		William Tell	24 Oct 1829
James	29	M	Tanner	Scotland	U. States	Camillus	27 Jun 1826
Jane	29	M	None	Scotland	U. States	Camillus	27 Jun 1826
John	22	M	Farmer	England	United States	William & Henry	19 Jul 1822
John	50	M		Scotland	United States	Camillus	9 May 1827
Martin	4			England	U. States	Corinthian	8 Oct 1828
Mary	21	F	Sempstress	Ireland		William Tell	24 Oct 1829
Thomas	15	M	boy	England	United States	Cambria	3 Jul 1829
Thomas	40	M	Sawyer	England	United States	Cambria	3 Jul 1829
KEMPE, Ashton	20	M	Labourer	Prussia		Constitution	20 Jun 1828
Nicholas S.	13 2/12	M	Student	England	Great Britian	Indian Chief	8 Feb 1822
KEMPIN, Maria	10	F		Ireland	United States	Essex	23 May 1828
KEMPMEYER, Johann	18	M	Merchant	Hamburgh	America	Zwey Brieder Johanes & Henerick	20 Mar 1820
KEMPSON, Rebecca	18	F	Servant	Ireland	America	Weser	26 Jun 1821
KEMPTON, Joseph	22	M	Merchant	Massachusetts	U. States	Tobasco	23 Jul 1827
Wm.	65	M	Mariner	U. States	U. States	General Jackson	24 Mar 1828
KEN, Hugh	24	M	Spiner	Great Britain	United States	Colossus	5 Jun 1827
KEN...ER..., Danl.	28	M	Painter	Manchester	Manchester	Howard Douglass	11 May 1827
Peter	21	M	Currier	...ll	...a...s	Howard Douglass	11 May 1827
KEN...ITT, M., Mrs.	25			Bermondsey	Great Brit.	London	13 Dec 1822
KENAGHAN, James	23	M	Farmer	Ireland	United States	Lord Strangford	20 Jun 1826
KENAH, Robert		M	Merchant	United States	United States	Samaritan	24 Nov 1820
KENAN, Patrick	32	M	Labourer	Ireland	New York	America	1 Aug 1828

NAMES OF PASSENGERS	AGE	SEX	OCCUPATIONS	COUNTRY TO WHICH THEY BELONG	COUNTRY THEY INTEND TO INHABIT	SHIPS/DATES OF ARRIVAL	
KENARY, John	30	M	Labourer	Ireland	United States	General Marion	20 Aug 1828
KENDALE, Wm.	40	M	Gentleman	England		Marchioness	13 May 1828
KENDALL, Sarah	27	F	None	Great Britain	United States	James Monroe	5 Apr 1820
Thomas B.	18	M	Merchant	United States	U. States	Saml. Smith	24 Jul 1826
KENDER, H.	35	M	Merchant	U. States	U. States	Mentor	26 Jul 1825
KENDRICK, Geo.	20	M	Farmer	England	U. States	Commerce	2 Oct 1823
KENEAR, John	30	M	Labourer	Ireland	United States	General Marion	6 Oct 1828
Letitia	1...	F	Lady	Great Britain	Great Britain	Ann Maria	17 Apr 1827
William D.	27	M	Planter	Great Britain	Great Britain	Ann Maria	17 Apr 1827
KENEBAR, H.	25	M	Labourer	Germany	U. States	Jane	26 Jul 1825
KENEDEY, Wm.	26	M	Sawyer	Ireland	Und. Stts of Amer	Alexander Mansfield	18 Aug 1826
KENEDY, Duncan	30	M	Merchant	U. States	U. States	Canada	6 Jun 1825
Fanny	20	F	Wife	Scotland	United States	Tom	2 Jul 1827
Francis	18	M	F. Dresser	Ireland	New York	Trusty	12 Sep 1828
James	25	M	F. Dresser	Ireland	New York	Trusty	12 Sep 1828
James	27	M	Blacksmith	Ireland	America	Josephine	8 Jan 1827
John	24	M	None	Great Britain	United States	Eliza Barker	3 Jul 1826
John	32	M	Merchant	U. States	U. States	Exchange	25 Sep 1826
John, Jr.	24	M	Merchant	U. States	U. States	Mary Ann	13 Mar 1826
Pat	24 6/12	M		Ireland	U.S. of America	Douglass	6 Jul 1829
KENEVELS, —, Mrs.	22	F	None	U. States	U. States	Agnes	29 Nov 1826
Isaac	2	M		U. States	U. States	Agnes	29 Nov 1826
Isaac A.	22	M	Gentleman	U. States	U. States	Agnes	29 Nov 1826
V.	4	F		U. States	U. States	Agnes	29 Nov 1826
KENEY, Elizabeth	3	F	Child	Switzerland	United States	Andes	5 May 1828
Margaretta	37	F	Spinster	Switzerland	United States	Andes	5 May 1828
Maria	7	F	Child	Switzerland	United States	Andes	5 May 1828
Nancy	5	F	Child	Switzerland	United States	Andes	5 May 1828
Nats.	32	M	Farmer	Switzerland	United States	Andes	5 May 1828
KENIDY, Elizabeth	4	F	Farmer	Ireland	United States	Julia Ann	24 Jul 1820
KENIFECK, Daniel	22	M	Farmer	Ireland	United States	Dublin Packet	22 Oct 1821
KENIN, Eliza	30	F	Spinster	Ireland		Robert Fulton	4 Jun 1828
KENJOY, Mary	27	F	None	England	U.N. States	William Byrnes	13 Aug 1829
KENKENAN, Benjn.	23	M	Plasterer	England	United States	Dalhouse Castle	6 Sep 1827
KENKINS, Thos.	28	M	Labourer	England	England	Sir James Kempt	10 Dec 1827
KENLEN, Danl.	6	M		Great Britain	United States	India	5 Sep 1827
Wm.	46	M	Shoe Maker	Great Britain	United States	India	5 Sep 1827
Wm., Jur.	9	M		Great Britain	United States	India	5 Sep 1827
KENMAN, R.	24			G. Britain	U. States	Great Britain	6 Sep 1828
KENMONT, Jas.	25	M	Teacher	Scotland	U. States	Dalmarnock	23 May 1823
KENMORE, Franklin	20	M	Servant	Great Britian	United States	Diamond	8 Nov 1824
Nelly	25	F	Servant	Great Britian	United States	Diamond	8 Nov 1824
William	29	M	Servant	Great Britian	United States	Diamond	8 Nov 1824
KENNA, Ann	1	M		England	U. States	Emulous	22 Aug 1828
Ann	10	F		Great Britain	United States	India	5 Sep 1827
Ann	32	F		Great Britain	Taunton, Mass.	Hesperus	13 Oct 1825
Betsey	13	F		Great Britain	United States	India	5 Sep 1827
Catherine	9/12	F		Great Britain	Taunton, Mass.	Hesperus	13 Oct 1825
Charlot	12	F		Great Britain	United States	India	5 Sep 1827
Fredk.	6/12	M		Great Britain	United States	India	5 Sep 1827
Jane	16	F		Great Britain	United States	India	5 Sep 1827
Jane	21	F		England	U. States	Emulous	22 Aug 1828
John	2	M		England	U. States	Emulous	22 Aug 1828
John	4	M		Great Britain	Taunton, Mass.	Hesperus	13 Oct 1825
John	6	M		Great Britain	United States	India	5 Sep 1827
John	24	M	Miner	England	U. States	Emulous	22 Aug 1828
John	28	M	Shoe Maker	Great Britain	United States	India	5 Sep 1827
Margaret	5	F		Great Britain	United States	India	5 Sep 1827
Margaret	16	F	None	Ireland		Marchioness	13 May 1828
Mary	17			Ireland	U.S.	Union	20 Aug 1827
Mary	40	F		Great Britain	United States	India	5 Sep 1827
Mary Ann	14	F		Great Britain	Taunton, Mass.	Hesperus	13 Oct 1825
Michael	16	M		Great Britain	Taunton, Mass.	Hesperus	13 Oct 1825
Michael	21	M	Labourer	Ireland		Marchioness	13 May 1828
Michael	38	M	Tradesman	England	U. States	York	7 Aug 1828
Owen	25	M	Labourer	Great Britain	United States	Penelope	11 Jun 1827
Richard	26	M	Mill wright	Great Britain	United States	India	5 Sep 1827

NAMES OF PASSENGERS	AGE	SEX	OCCUPATIONS	COUNTRY TO WHICH THEY BELONG	COUNTRY THEY INTEND TO INHABIT	SHIPS/DATES OF ARRIVAL	
KENNA (cont'd)							
Rose	23	F	...	Ireland	U. States	William	27 Jul 1824
Silvester	3	F		Great Britain	United States	India	5 Sep 1827
Terrisa	5	F		Great Britain	Taunton, Mass.	Hesperus	13 Oct 1825
Thomas	24	M	Labourer	Great Britain	United States	India	5 Sep 1827
Thos.	40	M	Farmer	Great Britain	United States	India	5 Sep 1827
William	38	M	Calico Printer	Great Britain	Taunton, Mass.	Hesperus	13 Oct 1825
KENNADY, Andrew T.	30	M	Stationer	Ireland	United States	Roman	17 Oct 1826
KENNAN, Bridget	50	F		G. Britain	U. States	London	23 Sep 1828
Edwd.	19	M	Labourer	Ireland	U. States	Marcus	7 Apr 1825
Ewd.	20	M		G. Britain	U. States	London	23 Sep 1828
Fr. M.	23	M	Farmer	Great Briton	United States	Erin	26 May 1821
Francis	26	F	None	Great Britain		Moro Castle	6 Jul 1827
John	21	M	Labourer	Ireland	U. States	Marcus	7 Apr 1825
Mary	20	F		G. Britain	U. States	London	23 Sep 1828
KENNARD, Albert	17	M	Mechanic	N. York	N. York	Tartar	14 Apr 1824
Alfred	23	M	Sailor	U. States	U. States	Sophia & Eliza	13 Jun 1828
Jesse	51		Farmer	England	U.S. America	Constitution	18 Jun 1827
KENNEDDY, Jno.	30	M	Weaver	Ireland	America	Mary	29 May 1827
KENNEDY, Alex.	30	M	Tailor	Scotland	United States	Tom	2 Jul 1827
Andrew	24	M	Labourer	Ireland	United States	Hannah Eliza	6 Jun 1826
Angel	26	M	Cooper	Ireland	America	Plutarch	18 Jul 1826
Ann	19	F	Spinster	Ireland		Robert Fulton	4 Jun 1828
Ann	22	F		Ireland	America	Corinthian	1 Sep 1827
Ann [crossed out]	20	F	None	Ireland	United States	Jubilee	1 Oct 1828
Bartholomew	13	M	Farmer	Ireland	United States	Dublin Packet	9 Jul 1827
Betsey	22	F	Spinster	Ireland	United States	Dublin Packet	22 Aug 1829
Bridget	17	F	None	Ireland	United States	Jubilee	12 May 1828
Catherine	21	F		Limerick	N. York	Thomas & William	25 May 1827
Catherine	23	F	None	Ireland	New York	Munroe	27 May 1825
Catherine	24	F	None	Ireland	New York	Munroe	27 May 1825
Cathr.	29	M	Farmer	Stackport	United States	Aurelia	7 Jun 1826
Charles	11 4/12	M	Son [of Esther]	Ireland	Pensylvania	Atlantic	8 May 1828
Christina	56	F	None	Great Britain	United States	Colossus	5 Jun 1827
Christopher	20	M	Farmer	Ireland	New York	Munroe	27 May 1825
Cornelius	24	M	Farmer	Gt. Britain	United States	Silas Richards	20 Jun 1826
D.	11	M	None	Great Britain	United States	Sarah	9 Nov 1820
David	21	M	Labourer	England	U. States	Comet	23 Aug 1828
David	23	M	Merchant	America	America	La Grange	7 Aug 1828
David	27	M	Planter	Jamaica	Ireland	Eliza Ann	2 May 1826
David	infant	F	Child	Scotland	United States	Tom	2 Jul 1827
David S.	31	M	Merchant	U. States Ame	New York	Ann Maria	29 Nov 1821
Dennis	20	M	Farmer	Ireland	America	Panthia	17 Sep 1821
Dennis	22	M	Woolenspinner	Ireland	United States	Meteor	19 Aug 1829
Duncan	36	M	Merchant	United States	New York	Cortes	7 Jul 1821
Duncan	37	M	Merchant	United States	United States	Robert Fulton	27 Jun 1822
Duncan	40	M	Merchant	U.S.A.		Silas Richards	20 Jun 1826
Duncan	41	M	Merchant	U. States	U. States	Silas Richards	27 Jun 1827
Duncan	43	M	Merchant	U.S.A.	U. States	Silas Richard	30 Jun 1828
Edward	23	M	Laborer	Ireland	United States	Mary	1 Jul 1829
Edward	24	M	Labourer	Ireland	United States	Jubilee	13 Jul 1829
Edward	28	M	Laborer	Ireland	America	Parrington	9 Jun 1827
Eliz.	30	F	Servant	Ireland	N. York	Trusty	12 Sep 1828
Eliza	1	F	Labourer	Ireland	U. States	Two Marys	20 Apr 1825
Eliza	25	F		Ireland	United States	Mary	1 Jul 1829
Eliza	60	F	None	Ireland	United States	Jubilee	12 May 1828
Eliza	66	F		Ireland	United States	Hannibal	25 Sep 1827
Esther	44	F	Spinster	Ireland	United States	Trident	17 May 1825
Esther	70	F		Ireland	Pensylvania	Atlantic	8 May 1828
Ewd.	15	M	Labourer	England	U. States	Thomas Ritchie	2 Jul 1827
Fanny	23	F	Servant	Ireland	N. York	Trusty	12 Sep 1828
Francis	18	M	Labourer	Ireland		Marchioness	13 May 1828
Francis	25	M	Farmer	Ireland	United States	Dublin Packet	9 Jul 1827
Gilbert	24	M	Farmer	Ireland	America	Farmer	4 Aug 1825
Hector	57 2/12	M	Merchant	New York	New York	Jas. Monroe	11 Aug 1823
Hector	59	M	Merchant	U. States	U. States	Marmion	7 May 1827
Henrietta	36	F		New York	U. States	Marmion	8 Sep 1828
Honora	18	F	Spinster	Ireland	America	Parrington	9 Jun 1827

NAMES OF PASSENGERS	AGE	SEX	OCCUPATIONS	COUNTRY TO WHICH THEY BELONG	COUNTRY THEY INTEND TO INHABIT	SHIPS/DATES OF ARRIVAL	
KENNEDY (cont'd)							
James	8	M	None	Ireland	United States	Jubilee	1 Oct 1828
James	14	M	Boy	Ireland	United States	Trident	17 May 1825
James	20	M	Farmer	Ireland	America	Farmer	4 Aug 1825
James	26	M	Farmer	Ireland	New York	Munroe	27 May 1825
James	28	M	Farmer	England	U. States	Commerce	2 Oct 1823
James	38	M		Gt. Britain	United States	Penelope	9 Sep 1828
James L.	26	M	Merchant	N. York	U. States	John	2 Feb 1824
James L.	30	M	Merchant	U. States	U. States	Merope	6 Dec 1825
Jean	13	F	None	Great Britain	United States	Colossus	5 Jun 1827
Jno.	30	M		Ireland		Lady Hunter	12 Apr 1823
Johanna	20	F	...	...	...	Braganza	8 Aug 1825
John	1/12	M		Limerick	N. York	Thomas & William	25 May 1827
John	8	M	Labourer	Ireland	U. States	Two Marys	20 Apr 1825
John	12	M	None	Ireland	United States	Jubilee	1 Oct 1828
John	18	M	Farmer	Ireland	United States	Dublin Packet	9 Jul 1827
John	32	M	Labourer	Ireland	U. States	Two Marys	20 Apr 1825
Joseph	14	M	Weaver	Ireland	United States	Hannibal	25 Sep 1827
Joseph	23	M	Farmer	Ireland	United States	Dublin Packet	9 Jul 1827
Lawe.	18	M	Labourer	England	U. States	Thomas Ritchie	2 Jul 1827
Margaret	28	F	None	Ireland	United States	Friends	21 Oct 1825
Margary	13	F	Servant	Ireland	N. York	Trusty	12 Sep 1828
Margerett	22	F	None	Ireland	New York	America	1 Aug 1828
Margret	26	F		Ireland	America	Plutarch	18 Jul 1826
Martin	19	M	Labourer	Ireland		Marchioness	13 May 1828
Martin	23	M	Painter	Ireland	America	John Adams	2 Aug 1827
Mary	16	F	Servant	Ireland	N. York	Trusty	12 Sep 1828
Mary	20	F		Ireland	America	John Adams	2 Aug 1827
Mary	21	F		G. Britain	U. States	London	23 Sep 1828
Mary	32	F	Labourer	Ireland	U. States	Two Marys	20 Apr 1825
Mary	32	F	Servant	Ireland	N. York	Trusty	12 Sep 1828
Michael	17	M	Farmer	Ireland	United States	Dublin Packet	9 Jul 1827
Michael	30	M	...erb...	England	U.S. States	Splendid	14 Aug 1829
Michal	20	M	Labourer	England	U. States	Comet	23 Aug 1828
Nancy	20	F	Servant	Ireland	N. York	Trusty	12 Sep 1828
Patk.	26	M	Cooper	Limerick	N. York	Thomas & William	25 May 1827
Patrick	23	M	Weaver	Ireland	America	Atlantic	8 May 1828
Patrick	30	M	Cooper	Ireland	United States	Jubilee	1 Oct 1828
Peter	20	M	Labourer	Ireland	United States	Friends	21 Oct 1825
Philip	22	M	Farmer	Ireland	United States	Dublin Packet	3 May 1823
Richd.	26	M	Labourer	Ireland	United States	Wilson	27 Jun 1826
Robert	60	M	Weaver	Great Britain	United States	Colossus	5 Jun 1827
Robt.	50		None	...	...	James Cropper	28 Jun 1824
Rose	24		Dress Maker	Ireland	America	Sarah	18 Aug 1829
Thomas	30 3/12	M	Merchant	Great Britain	United States	Atlantic	8 Dec 1827
Thos.	6	M	Labourer	Ireland	U. States	Two Marys	20 Apr 1825
Thos.	28	M	...	United States	United States	Loire	18 Oct 1820
Thos.	32	M	...			Manhattan	25 Dec 1820
Timothy	5	M	None	Ireland	United States	Jubilee	1 Oct 1828
W.	4	M	Labourer	Ireland	U. States	Two Marys	20 Apr 1825
William	5/12	M	None	Ireland	New York	Munroe	27 May 1825
William	25	M	Servant	Ireland	America	Carolina Ann	7 Aug 1826
KENNELL, Wm.	21	M	Draper	England	U. States	Corinthian	2 May 1823
KENNELLY, Stephen	40	M	Mercht.	U.S.	U.S.	Clarissa	23 May 1822
KENNELY, Jane	24	F	None	Canada	Canada	James Monroe	18 Apr 1821
KENNEN, Judith	26	F	Labourer	Ireland	New York	Bowditch	27 Apr 1826
KENNER, Andrew	22	M	Weaver	Europe	United States	Aspasia	5 Sep 1827
Witt. Carl Wilhelm	18	M	Shepherd	Saxony		Massasoit	3 Jul 1829
KENNETT, Thomas	23	M	Miller	England	New York	Brighton	29 Aug 1828
KENNEY, Catharn	25			Ireland		Lady Hunter	12 Apr 1823
D.	27	M	Mariner	U.S. of Amer	U.S. of Amer	Estrella de La Mañana	26 May 1825
D.	31	M	Gardner	Ireland	Upper Canada	Infant	21 Nov 1820
Ellen	12	F		Ireland		Lady Hunter	12 Apr 1823
J.	18	M				Lady of the Lake	23 Aug 1828
John	1 1/2	M	None	Ireland	New York	Commerce	24 Sep 1823

NAMES OF PASSENGERS	AGE	SEX	OCCUPATIONS	COUNTRY TO WHICH THEY BELONG	COUNTRY THEY INTEND TO INHABIT	SHIPS/DATES OF ARRIVAL	
KENNEY (cont'd)							
John	10	M		Ireland		Lady Hunter	12 Apr 1823
John	28	M	Cooper	Ireland	New York	Munroe	27 May 1825
Lawrence	22	M		Ireland	Pennsylvania	Lima	5 Aug 1826
Margaret	26	F	None	Ireland	New York	Commerce	24 Sep 1823
Martin	30	M	Farmer	Ireland	New York	Commerce	24 Sep 1823
Mary	8	F	None	Ireland	New York	Commerce	24 Sep 1823
Mary	28	F	None	Ireland	New York	Munroe	27 May 1825
Michel	30	M	Labourer	England	America	William	21 Sep 1821
Patrick	9/12	M	None	Ireland	New York	Munroe	27 May 1825
Peter	23	M	Laborer	Ireland	New York	Amanda	23 May 1827
W.	30	M				Lady of the Lake	23 Aug 1828
Wm.	26	M	Farmer	Ireland	United States	Eliza	29 Aug 1822
KENNI, M	60	M	Milliner	G. Britain		Caravan	8 Sep 1828
KENNIDY, Duncan	38	M	Merchant	United States	United States	Canada	20 Jun 1823
James	1	M		Ireland	United States	Julia Ann	24 Jul 1820
Nicholast	26	M	Farmer	Ireland	United States	Julia Ann	24 Jul 1820
Sarah	29	F	Farmer	Ireland	United States	Julia Ann	24 Jul 1820
KENNIFICK, Edward	2	M		Ireland	United States	Trio	31 Oct 1827
Morry	33	F		Ireland	United States	Trio	31 Oct 1827
KENNIGER, Briget	23	F	Spinster	England	United States	Hanford	3 Jul 1829
KENNING, Brian	24	M	Labourer	England	U.S.	Acasta	11 May 1827
John	35	M	Labourer	England	U.S.	Acasta	11 May 1827
Joseph	24	M	Merchant	Ireland	America	Carolina Ann	7 Aug 1826
KENNODE, Margt.	20	F	None	Isle of Man		Ocean	13 Jul 1827
Wm.	27	M	Labourer	Isle of Man		Ocean	13 Jul 1827
KENNON, F.	25	M		Ireland	U. States	Adno	5 Jul 1828
James	29	M	Laborer	Ireland	United States	Sarah G	19 Jun 1827
KENNY, —, Mrs.	23	F	Merchant	W. Indies	U. States	Alfred	17 Sep 1822
Ann	8/12	F	None	England	New York	Brighton	9 Dec 1828
Ann	20	F		Gt. Britain	United States	John & Elizabeth	25 Sep 1827
Ann	23	F	Servant	Ireland	United States	William	20 Jul 1829
Ann	30	F	Servant	Ireland	United States	Carolina Ann	14 May 1827
Betsey	23	F	Spinster	Ireland	United States	Dublin Packet	23 May 1828
Betty	24	F	Farmer	Ireland	America	Farmer	4 Aug 1825
Bridget	20	F		Ireland	Pensylvania	Lima	5 Aug 1829
Cap.	40	M	Mariner	England	U. States	Falcon	12 Oct 1822
Catherine	5...	F		Ireland	United States	Trio	31 Oct 1827
Edward	18	M	...	Ireland	United States	Carolina Ann	24 Oct 1825
Eliza	26	F	Dressmaker	England	United States	Manhattan	20 Feb 1826
Ellen	20	F	None	England	U. States	Roman	1 Dec 1828
Ellen	24	F		Ireland	United States	Trio	13 Jun 1827
Hugh	30	M	Labourer	Great Britian	United States	Princess Charlotte	6 Sep 1828
J.	25		Farmer	Ireland	United States	Courier	16 May 1825
James	20	M	Farmer	Ireland	United States	Justina	5 Aug 1823
John	18	M	Labourer	Ireland	N. York	Trusty	12 Sep 1828
John	22	M	Cooper	Ireland	United States	Trio	13 Jun 1827
John	26	M	Labourer	Ireland	Pensylvania	Lima	5 Aug 1829
Julia	30	F	None	England	New York	Brighton	9 Dec 1828
Laurence	22	M	Labourer	Ireland	Pensylvania	Lima	5 Aug 1829
Lawrence	31	M	Cooper	England	New York	Brighton	9 Dec 1828
Mary	3 6/12	F	None	England	U. States	Roman	1 Dec 1828
Mary	22	F		Gt. Britain	United States	John & Elizabeth	25 Sep 1827
Michael	13	M	Child	Ireland	United States	Dublin Packet	23 May 1828
Micheal	...	M	Labourer	Ireland	Unt. St. America	Wilson	21 May 1827
Nicholas	20	M		Gt. Britain	United States	John & Elizabeth	25 Sep 1827
Nicholas	43	M	Merchant	America	United States	John & Elizabeth	25 Sep 1827
Owen	19			Longford	Virginia	Peru	30 May 1828
Pat	22 1/12	M		Ireland	U.S. of America	Douglass	6 Jul 1829
Patrick	22	M		Gt. Britain	United States	John & Elizabeth	25 Sep 1827
Patrick, Mr.	28	M	Labourer	England	U.S.	Acasta	11 May 1827

676

NAMES OF PASSENGERS	AGE	SEX	OCCUPATIONS	COUNTRY TO WHICH THEY BELONG	COUNTRY THEY INTEND TO INHABIT	SHIPS/DATES OF ARRIVAL	
KENNY (cont'd)							
Peter	21	M	Farmer	America	United States	John & Elizabeth	25 Sep 1827
Robert	20	M		G. Britan	U. States	William Neilson	26 Jul 1828
T. F., Mr.	24	M	Merchant	United States	United States	Sally	26 Jun 1822
Tarquina, Miss	3	F	None	United States	United States	Sally	26 Jun 1822
Terence	30	M	Farmer	Ireland	United States	Dublin Packet	23 May 1828
Thomas	4	M	None	England	New York	Brighton	9 Dec 1828
Thos.	28	M	Farmer	Ireland	U. States	Orozimbo	7 Jul 1825
Wm.	44	M	Farmer	Ireland	New York	Carolina Ann	15 Oct 1824
KENRAD, Charles	37	M	Painter	England		Henri IV	17 May 1828
KENT, Ann	2 6/12	F		U.S. of Am.	New York	Louisa	10 Nov 1825
Charles J.	42	M	Shoemaker	France	New York	Louisa	10 Nov 1825
Edmund	5		Boy	London	England	London	13 Dec 1822
Eliza, Miss	7			London	G. Brit.	London	13 Dec 1822
Ellen, Miss	8			London	G. Brit.	London	13 Dec 1822
Henry	10		Boy	London	England	London	13 Dec 1822
James	3		None	London	England	London	13 Dec 1822
John	15		Boy	London	England	London	13 Dec 1822
John	18	M	Farmer	Ireland	America	Liverpool	31 Aug 1827
John	35		Commedian	England	England	Thames	25 Oct 1821
Mary	4	F		U.S. of Am.	New York	Louisa	10 Nov 1825
Mary	25	F	Spinster	Ireland	America	William	11 Nov 1825
Mary	29			...	...	James Cropper	28 Jun 1824
Mary, Mrs.	33			London	Great Brit.	London	13 Dec 1822
Michael	25		Labourer	Desmore	Gt. Britain	Enterprize	19 Feb 1822
Moss	55	M	Gentn.	United States	New York	Brighton	16 Nov 1826
Robert	27	M	Blacksmith	Great Britain	U. States	Great Britain	18 Mar 1828
Thomas	29		Merchant	...	...	James Cropper	28 Jun 1824
William	12		Boy	Scotland	England	London	13 Dec 1822
William	45		Ladies and Gentlemen	England	United States	Corinthian	7 Jul 1829
KENTAR, Jno.	26	M	Labourer	Ireland	United States	Thomas	13 Dec 1827
KENTLY, Willm.	23	M	Labourer	Ireland	United States	Trident	16 May 1826
KENTON, Thomas	30	M		Great Brittain	United States	Active	12 Sep 1828
KENTZING, Abm.	35	M	Merchant	U. States	U. States	Thule	29 Apr 1825
KENWALS, Isaac S.	48		Farmer	United States	United States	Alfred	8 Jul 1822
KENWARD, Elizabeth	5			England	U.S. America	Constitution	18 Jun 1827
Elizabeth	36			England	U.S. America	Constitution	18 Jun 1827
Jesse, Jr.	9			England	U.S. America	Constitution	18 Jun 1827
Martha	8/12			England	U.S. America	Constitution	18 Jun 1827
Mary Ann	7			England	U.S. America	Constitution	18 Jun 1827
Thomas	3			England	U.S. America	Constitution	18 Jun 1827
KENWARTHEY, Wm.	43	M	Merchant	England	England	Ann	11 Apr 1821
KENWAY, Cairns	19	M	Servant	Gt. Britan	America	Braganza	1 Dec 1824
KENWORTH, John	14	M		Great Britain	U.S. of America	Gratitude	3 Oct 1829
Robert	36	M	Clothier	Great Britain	U.S. of America	Gratitude	3 Oct 1829
Thos.	34	M	Weaver	Gt. Britan	U. States	Magnet	9 Apr 1825
KENWORTHY, Ann	30	F	Weaver	England	America	Franklin	3 Dec 1827
Francis, Jr.	21	M	Merchant	England	England	Manhattan	21 Sep 1822
George	3	M		Great Britain	United States	New York	19 Nov 1828
J. S.	22	M	Mercht.	England	U. States	Pacific	20 Aug 1825
James	1 3/12	M		Great Britain	United States	New York	19 Nov 1828
*Died							
James	35	M	Weaver	England	America	Franklin	3 Dec 1827
James	38	M	Weaver	Gt. Britain	United States	Meteor	19 Aug 1829
James, Junr.	20 3/12	M	Merchant	Great Britain	Great Britain	James Cropper	26 Mar 1822
Jane	6	F		England	America	Franklin	3 Dec 1827
Jas.	22	M	Weaver	Blakleer	Blakleer	Howard Douglass	11 May 1827
Jas.	30	M	Mercht	G. Britain	U. States	New York	6 Mar 1827
John	7	M		Great Britain	United States	New York	19 Nov 1828
John	10	M	Weaver	England	America	Franklin	3 Dec 1827
John	44	M	Weaver	Gt. Britain	United States	Meteor	19 Aug 1829
Jos.	26	M	Mercht.	G. Britain		Ann Maria	3 Jul 1820
Lazarus	8	M		Great Britain	United States	New York	19 Nov 1828
Lemuel	29	M	Carpenter	Great Britain, Ireland	New York	Britannia	3 Nov 1827
Mary	32	F		Great Britain	United States	New York	19 Nov 1828

NAMES OF PASSENGERS	AGE	SEX	OCCUPATIONS	COUNTRY TO WHICH THEY BELONG	COUNTRY THEY INTEND TO INHABIT	SHIPS/DATES OF ARRIVAL	
KENWORTHY (cont'd)							
Ricd.	4	M		England	America	Franklin	3 Dec 1827
Samuel	6	M		Great Britain	United States	New York	19 Nov 1828
William	40	M	Weaver	England	America	Franklin	3 Dec 1827
KENYAN, Ann	23	F		G. Britain	U. States	London	23 Sep 1828
Brgt.	62	F		G. Britain	U. States	London	23 Sep 1828
KENYGA, D.	27	F	Merchant	U. States	U. States	Columbia	20 Jul 1825
G. H.	35	M	Merchant	Hamburg	U. States	Columbia	20 Jul 1825
KENYON, John	22	M	Farmer	Longford		Mount Vernon	7 Jun 1824
Joseph	20	M	Clouthier	Ireland	Ut. States	Courier	13 Jul 1826
Margaret	24	F	Farmer	Longford		Mount Vernon	7 Jun 1824
Mary	20	F	Farmer	Longford		Mount Vernon	7 Jun 1824
Wm.	20	M	Turner	Great Britain		Moro Castle	6 Jul 1827
KEOGH, Ann	20	F	Spinster	Ireland	United States	Dublin Packet	23 May 1828
Jno.	28	M	Farmer	Great Britain	United States	Atlantic	28 May 1827
Laurence	28	M	Farmer	Ireland	United States	Lord Strangford	20 Jun 1826
KEOGHAN, Mat	24	M	Laborer	Ireland	United States	Thomas	13 Dec 1827
Terence	20	M	Labourer	Ireland	United States	Thomas	13 Dec 1827
KEOHAN, Jerh.	27	M	Farmer	England	United States	Ganges	10 May 1828
KEON, John	20	M	Laborer	Ireland	America	Parrington	9 Jun 1827
KEONAN, Fanny	25			Ireland	United States	Alexander Mansfield	23 Nov 1824
KEOUGH, Bridget	30	F	None	Ireland	United States	Jubilee	12 May 1828
Bryan	4	M	None	Ireland	United States	Jubilee	12 May 1828
Ellen	6	F	None	Ireland	United States	Jubilee	12 May 1828
John	24	M	Y. Man	Ireland	New York	Trusty	12 Sep 1828
KEOWEN, Ann	1	F	None	Great Britain	United States	William Dawson	18 Jun 1827
Jane	30	F	None	Great Britain	United States	William Dawson	18 Jun 1827
John	3 1/2	M	None	Great Britain	United States	William Dawson	18 Jan 1827
Matthew	40	M	Tailor	Great Britain	United States	William Dawson	18 Jun 1827
Will	2 1/2	M	None	Great Britain	United States	William Dawson	18 Jun 1827
KEPOE, Catherin	20	F		Ireland	United States	William Byrnes	6 Apr 1826
Jno.	30	M		Ireland	United States	William Byrnes	6 Apr 1826
KEPPAX, Saml.	37	M	Farmer	England	Canada	William	10 Dec 1823
KEPPLER, —, Miss	16	F	Comedienne	France	U. States	Queen Mab	16 Jun 1827
—, Mrs.	42	F	Lady	France	U. States	Queen Mab	16 Jun 1827
E., Miss	14	F		France		Henri IV	17 May 1828
KER, —, Mrs.	25	F		Virginia	U. States	Jane	29 Apr 1822
—, Mrs.	25	F				Genl. Urdaneta	19 Apr 1826
Ann B.	30	F	None	Great Britain	United States	Cortes	11 Dec 1822
Ann Blair	35	F	None	America	America	Hannibal	12 Oct 1826
Caroline M.	28	F		United States	United States	Rachel Ann	15 Jan 1827
Collins	18	M	Currier	Scotland	United States	Herald	7 Jun 1824
Edward A.	28	M	Gent.	U. States	U. States	Bayard	9 Jul 1824
Ellen		F	Chiefly farmers		United States	Factor	8 Jul 1829
Hannah M.	18/12	F		England	United States	Euphrates	18 Aug 1827
Jno. C.	41	M	Merchant	Great Britain	United States	Cortes	11 Dec 1822
John Cessford	43	M	Merchant	America	America	Hannibal	12 Oct 1826
Margret	22	F	Spinster	Ireland	United States	Fabius	4 Jun 1828
Mary	2	F		Virginia	U. States	Jane	29 Apr 1822
Mary	20	F	Servant	Ireland	United States	Henry Kneeland	7 Jun 1828
Mary	61	F	Spinster	Ireland	United States	Fabius	4 Jun 1828
Richard	26	M	Gentleman	England	United States	Euphrates	18 Aug 1827
Rob	45	M	Merchant	G. Britain	U. States	Diligence	29 Jul 1823
Rob.	32	M	Merchant	Virginia	U. States	Jane	29 Apr 1822
Sally	21	F	Spinster	Ireland	United States	Henry Kneeland	7 Jun 1828
Susanah	28	F		England	United States	Euphrates	18 Aug 1827
William	30	M	Shoemaker	Scotland	United States	Samuel Robertson	9 May 1827
William, Mr.	50	M	Gentleman	Scotland	New York	Astrea	21 Oct 1823
Wm.	45	M	Labourer	Ireland	United States	Henry Kneeland	7 Jun 1828
KERAND, Catharine	18	F	None	Gt. Britain	U. States	Isaac Hicks	18 Apr 1825
KERBY, Henry	24	M	Shoemaker	England	United States	Essex	23 May 1828
KERCKHOFF, Geo.	50	M	Miller	Germany		Ariel	24 Sep 1827
KERER, Elisa	20	F		Ireland	United States	Nancy R. Crowell	21 Sep 1822
Elisa	22	F		Ireland	United States	Nancy R. Crowell	21 Sep 1822

NAMES OF PASSENGERS	AGE	SEX	OCCUPATIONS	COUNTRY TO WHICH THEY BELONG	COUNTRY THEY INTEND TO INHABIT	SHIPS/DATES OF ARRIVAL	
KERIGAN, Ann	22	F		Ireland	United States	Carolina Ann	11 Dec 1826
Bridget	16	F		Ireland	United States	Carolina Ann	11 Dec 1826
Ellen	15	F	Servant	Ireland	United States	Carolina Ann	11 Dec 1826
Francis	21	M	Thread Maker	Ireland	United States	Fabius	31 Jul 1829
James	27	M	Labourer	Ireland	United States	Dalhouse Castle	8 May 1827
Mary	24	F	Servant	Ireland	America	Weser	26 Jun 1821
KERIGHAN, Sally	22	F	Spinster	Ireland		Dublin Packet	30 Apr 1821
KERIGON, John	30	M		Great Brittain	United States	Active	12 Sep 1828
*Died on the Passage							
KERKMAN, Andrias	18	M	Gardner	Great Britain		Caravan	8 Sep 1828
Catarina	16	F		G. Britain		Caravan	8 Sep 1828
Eliza	19	F		G. Britain		Caravan	8 Sep 1828
Halastika	38	M		Great Britain		Caravan	8 Sep 1828
Johram	8	M		G. Britain		Caravan	8 Sep 1828
M.	14	F		G. Britain		Caravan	8 Sep 1828
M.	42	M		G. Britain		Caravan	8 Sep 1828
Magdalina	11	F		G. Britain		Caravan	8 Sep 1828
Maria	5	F		Great Britain		Caravan	8 Sep 1828
Susana	4	F		Great Britain		Caravan	8 Sep 1828
Thos.	52	M	Joiner	G. Britain		Caravan	8 Sep 1828
KERLEY, Laurence	31	M	Mentor	Sligo	U. States	Panthea	8 Apr 1826
KERLIGAN, Rose	17	F	Servt. Md.	Sligo	New York	Susquehana	27 Jun 1823
KERLING, Wm.	23	M	Labourer	Ireland	United States	Hope	12 Jun 1828
KERLY, Thos.	22	M	Gentleman	Bermuda	U. States	Agnes	1 Jul 1825
KERMAGHAN, Jane	35	F	Labourer	Great Britain	U. States	Princess Charlotte	6 Sep 1828
KERMAHON, John	30	M	Farmer	Antrim	Ireland	Carolina Ann	11 Jun 1824
Joseph	infant	M		Antrim	Ireland	Carolina Ann	11 Jun 1824
KERMAHRINE, Thomas	23	M	...	Germany	New York	Constitution	20 Aug 1825
KERMIT, Henry	30	M	Merchant	United States	United States	Aurora	11 Dec 1824
Robt.	28	M	Merchant	United States	United States	Aurora	21 Jun 1824
KERMO, Andrew	18	M		Ireland	United States	Thompson	12 Sep 1827
Catharine	60	F		Ireland	United States	Thompson	12 Sep 1827
Fanny	20	F		Ireland	United States	Thompson	12 Sep 1827
KERNAHAN, Archibald	26	M	Farmer	Ireland	America	Superior	12 Jun 1824
Elizabeth	30	F		Antrim	United States	Carolina Ann	11 Jun 1824
Ellen	22	F	Farmer	Ireland	America	Superior	12 Jun 1824
Samuel	24	M	Farmer	Ireland	America	Superior	12 Jun 1824
Tim	26	M	Farmer	Antrim	United States	Carolina Ann	11 Jun 1824
William	28	M	Farmer	Ireland	America	Superior	12 Jun 1824
KERNAN, Cornelius	26	M	Farmer	Ireland	United States	Dublin Packet	9 Jul 1827
Elizabeth	33	F	Lady	Great Briton	United States	Erin	26 May 1821
John	21	M	Merchant	Great Briton	United States	Erin	26 May 1821
Mathew	3	M		Ireland	New York	Lima	5 Aug 1829
Mathew	3	M		England	U. States	Lima	5 Aug 1829
Michael	22	M	Miller	Great Britain	United States	Mount Vernon	17 Jun 1825
KERNEY, Anna	27	F		Great Britain	U. States	Columbia	22 Sep 1828
James	22		Labourer			Rufus King	7 Aug 1820
John	3	M		Great Britain	U. States	Columbia	22 Sep 1828
Nancey	22	F	Servant	Great Britain	U. States	Columbia	22 Sep 1828
Redman	4	M		Ireland	America	William	11 Nov 1825
KERNIEN, John	28	M		England	England	Tontin	13 Jun 1825
KERNON, Mary	23	F	None	Great Briton	United States	Mount Vernon	30 Dec 1828
KEROPUGH, Andrew	23	M	Hatter	Ireland	U. States	Franklin	7 Jul 1828
KEROSCK, Ferdinand	25	M	Farmer	Switzerland		Charlemagne	20 Aug 1829
KERPOLTS, Adam	18	M	Farmer	Bavarian	United States	American	27 Aug 1827
Adam	55	M	Farmer	Bavarian	United States	American	27 Aug 1827
Elizabeth	55	F	Farmer	Bavarian	United States	American	27 Aug 1827
Henry	8	M	Farmer	Bavarian	United States	American	27 Aug 1827
Jacob	7	M	Farmer	Bavarian	United States	American	27 Aug 1827
Johana	22	F	Farmer	Bavarian	United States	American	27 Aug 1827
John N.	14	M	Farmer	Bavarian	United States	American	27 Aug 1827
Michael	6	M	Farmer	Bavarian	United States	American	27 Aug 1827
Peter A.	23	M	Farmer	Bavarian	United States	American	27 Aug 1827
KERR, Alex	24	M	Labourer	Scotland	United States	Tom	2 Jul 1827
Andrew	8	M		Ireland	United States	General Putnam	20 Jun 1825
Andrew	48	M	Labourer	Scotland	United States	Friends	7 Jul 1827
Ann	15	F	None	Great Brittain	New York	Albion	11 Jun 1821
Charles	19	M	Taylor	Ireland	United States	Trident	17 May 1825

NAMES OF PASSENGERS	AGE	SEX	OCCUPATIONS	COUNTRY TO WHICH THEY BELONG	COUNTRY THEY INTEND TO INHABIT	SHIPS/DATES OF ARRIVAL	
KERR (cont'd)							
Daniel	33	M	Watch Maker	Germany	U. States	Rook	25 Jul 1827
Duncan	20	M	Labourer	Ireland	United States	Robert Fulton	10 Aug 1827
Eleanor	20	F	None	Great Brittain	New York	Albion	11 Jun 1821
Elizabeth	...	F		Ireland	United States	General Putnam	20 Jun 1825
Elizabeth	2	F		Scotland	United States	Samuel Robertson	5 Oct 1827
Elizth.	44	F	None	Great Brittain	New York	Albion	11 Jun 1821
G.	25	M	Labourer	Scotland	United States	Tom	2 Jul 1827
Geo.	10	M	None	Great Brittain	New York	Albion	11 Jun 1821
Grace	17	F	Servant	Ireland	United States	Henry Kneeland	7 Jun 1828
Hugh	24	M		Scotland	United States	Camillus	9 May 1827
Isabella	30	F	Spinster	Ireland	United States	Asia	29 Jul 1829
Isebella	22	F	Spinster	Ireland	United States	Robert Fulton	24 Jul 1826
James	6	M		Ireland	United States	General Putnam	20 Jun 1825
James	9	M	None	Great Brittain	New York	Albion	11 Jun 1821
James	18	M	Clerk	Glasgow	U. States	Ossian	18 Feb 1822
James	19	M		Scotland	United States	Camillus	9 May 1827
James	22	M	Spinster	Derry	...	Gleaner	24 May 1823
James	34	M	Farmer	Ireland	United States	General Putnam	20 Jun 1825
James	45	M	Farmer	Scotland	U. States	Cato	12 May 1828
James	59	M	Farmer	Scotland		Samuel Robertson	5 Oct 1827
*Dead							
Jane	12	F		Ireland	United States	General Putnam	20 Jun 1825
Jane	30	F	Spinster	Gt. Britain	U. States	Frances Henrietta	18 Apr 1825
Janet	60	F		Scotland		Samuel Robertson	5 Oct 1827
*Dead							
Jaque	40	M	Labourer	Gt. Britain	U. States	Frances Henrietta	18 Apr 1825
Jno. C.	45	M	Merchant	Scotland	U.S.	Florida	17 May 1825
John	1	M		Ireland	United States	General Putnam	20 Jun 1825
John	6	M		Gt. Britain	U. States	Frances Henrietta	18 Apr 1825
John	17	M	Weaver	Great Britain	United States	Colossus	5 Jun 1827
John	18	M	Labourer	Ireland	U. States	William & John	10 Jul 1824
John	23	F	Farmer	Scotland	U. States	Roger Stewart	9 Jun 1828
John	38	M	Merchant	Scotland	United States	Samuel Robertson	5 Oct 1827
John	40	M	Labourer	Scotland	United States	Samuel Robertson	5 Oct 1827
John	55	M	Farmer	Ireland	U. States	Dickinson	30 Jul 1825
Jos.	29	M	Baker	N. York	U. States	Ann Maria	6 Jul 1824
Jos.	44	M	Merchant	United States	America	Alexander	28 Jul 1821
Joseph	23		Mercht.	Dublin	America	Manhattan	20 Sep 1821
Josias	80	M	Merchant	Ireland	United States	Asia	29 Jul 1829
Lewis	12	M	Gentleman	Nassau	U.States	Venus	28 Jun 1825
Louisa	12	F		Nassau, N.P.	U. States	Jane	7 Dec 1821
Margaret	28	F	Spinster	Ireland	United States	Asia	29 Jul 1829
Maria	22	F		U. States	U. States	Silas Richards	27 Jun 1827
Mary	4	F		Ireland	United States	General Putnam	20 Jun 1825
Mary	21	F	Spinster	Ireland	United States	Robert Fulton	24 Jul 1826
Mary	22	F	Unknown	...	U. States	Nancy	11 Apr 1822
Mary	22	F	Farmer	Ireland	U. States	Dickinson	30 Jul 1825
Mary	28	F		Scotland	United States	Samuel Robertson	5 Oct 1827
Mary	32	F	Spinster	Ireland	United States	Asia	29 Jul 1829
Mary	35	F	Spinster	Grt. Britain	United States	Robert Fulton	8 Oct 1828
Mary Ann	22	F	Wife [of Robert J.]	England	England	William	2 Sep 1822
Mathew	2	M		Ireland	United States	General Putnam	20 Jun 1825
Michael	26	M	Labourer	Gt. Britain	U. States	Frances Henrietta	18 Apr 1825
Pam	22	F	Seamstress	Ireland	America	Caroline	25 Jul 1828
Patrick	17	M	...	Ireland	United States	Carolina Ann	24 Oct 1825
Peggy	38	F	Servant	Ireland	United States	Henry Kneeland	7 Jun 1828
Rialto	10	F		Ireland		Nancey	25 Jan 1823
Robert	21	M	Labourer	Ireland	United States	Robert Fulton	24 Jul 1826

NAMES OF PASSENGERS	AGE	SEX	OCCUPATIONS	COUNTRY TO WHICH THEY BELONG	COUNTRY THEY INTEND TO INHABIT	SHIPS/DATES OF ARRIVAL	
KERR (cont'd)							
Robert	28	M	Clerk	Scotland	Gt. Britain	Friends	29 Apr 1822
Robert J.	28	M	Gentleman	England	England	William	2 Sep 1822
Robt.	21	M	Farmer	Scotland	United States	Margaret Bogle	11 Jun 1824
Rose	50	F	None	Great Brittain	New York	Albion	11 Jun 1821
Rose	55	F	Farmer	Ireland	U. States	Dickinson	30 Jul 1825
Rose, Jr.	18	F	None	Great Brittain	New York	Albion	11 Jun 1821
Sarah	25	F	Unknown	...	U. States	Nancy	11 Apr 1822
Spear	27	M	Labourer	Ireland	United States	Fabius	31 Jul 1829
Susan	9	F		Scotland	United States	Samuel Robertson	5 Oct 1827
Susan	40	F		Scotland	United States	Samuel Robertson	5 Oct 1827
William	18	M	Farmer	Scotland	United States	Samuel Robertson	5 Oct 1827
William	20	M	Farmer	Ireland	U. States	Dickinson	30 Jul 1825
William	40	M	Farmer	Ireland		Nancey	25 Jan 1823
William	72	...	...	Ireland	United States	Carolina Ann	24 Oct 1825
Wm.	24	M	Bookkeeper	Scotland	New York	Margaret	18 May 1825
Wm.	25	M	Labourer	Ireland	U. States	William & John	10 Jul 1824
Wm.	32	M	Farmer	Carnavan, Wales	U. States	Elizabeth	11 Aug 1826
KERRE, Rebecca	15	F	Spinster	Ireland	United States	Robert Fulton	24 Jul 1826
KERRIAN, James	21	M	Laborer	Gt. Britain		Dalhouse Castle	13 May 1828
KERRIE, Antonio	24		Mechanic	France	U. States	Parachute	14 May 1828
Louis	2/12			France	U. States	Parachute	14 May 1828
Marie	25			France	U. States	Parachute	14 May 1828
KERRIGAN, Ann	13	F	Child			Commerce	22 Jun 1825
Martin	27	M	Mason	Ireland	Baltimore	Lima	5 Aug 1829
Martin	27	M	Mason	Ireland	U. States	Lima	5 Aug 1829
Mary	20	F		Ireland	Baltimore	Lima	5 Aug 1829
Ml.	24	M	Farmer	Ireland	U. States	Ohio	21 Mar 1825
Owen	22	M	Labourer	G. Britain	U. States	Dalhouse Castle	12 Sep 1828
Patrick	19	M	Spinter			Commerce	22 Jun 1825
William	25	M	Labourer	Ireland	United States	Robert Fulton	24 Jul 1826
KERRY, Ann	7	F	None	England	U. States	Dalhouse	23 Mar 1829
Catherine	20	F		Gt. Britain		Dalhouse Castle	13 May 1828
KERSER, William	18	M	Laborer	Ireland	United States	Nancey	8 Jun 1822
KERSEY, James	39	M	Farmer	Ireland	America	William	21 May 1825
Julia	36	F	Spinster	Ireland	America	William	21 May 1825
Patrick	28	M	Farmer	Ireland	America	William	21 May 1825
KERSHAM, Joseph	13	M	Carpenter	England	America	Ann	23 Jul 1821
Robert	71	M	Carpenter	England	America	Ann	23 Jul 1821
KERSHAW, ...hs.	75	M	Student	U.S.	U.S.	London	19 Dec 1823
Benjamin	27	M	Weaver	England	America	Josephine	8 Jan 1827
Edmund	24	M	Weaver	England	America	Josephine	8 Jan 1827
Eliza	0 8/12	F		England	U. States	Pacific	5 Sep 1827
Hannah	28	F		England	U. States	Pacific	5 Sep 1827
Thos.	22	M	Farmer	Gt. Britain	U. States	Superior	20 Aug 1825
Wm.	22	M	Gentleman	U.S.	U.S.	London	19 Dec 1823
KERSIGOUR, Jno.	27	M	Stone Mason	England		Fame	9 Dec 1826
KERSTEN, —	36	F	Wife	Germany	U. States	Ranger	2 Jul 1827
C.	44	M	Merchant	Germany	U. States	Ranger	2 Jul 1827
KERSTOW, Cr.	55	M		U. States	U. States	Seine	10 Jun 1822
KERVAL, Frederick	28	M	Sadler	Bavaria	United States	American	27 Aug 1827
KERVEY, Elizabeth	70 10/12	F	None	Scotland	America	Minerva	15 Jun 1825
KERWICK, John	16	M	Farmer	Ireland	U. States	Wilson	22 Apr 1822
KERWIN, Mary Ann	20	F	Servant	Ireland	U.States	Nancy	31 May 1823
KERZ, Peter	24	M	Carpenter			New York Packet	19 Aug 1820
KESLER, Ann	18 4/12	F		France	United States	Charles Carroll	16 Jan 1829
Catharine	9 4/12	F		France	United States	Charles Carroll	16 Jan 1829
Madeline	15 2/12	F		France	United States	Charles Carroll	16 Jan 1829
Madeline	44 6/12	F		France	United States	Charles Carroll	16 Jan 1829
Margaret	20 3/12	F		France	United States	Charles Carroll	16 Jan 1829
Marie	5 5/12	F		France	United States	Charles Carroll	16 Jan 1829
Nicholas	13	M		France	United States	Charles Carroll	16 Jan 1829
Pierre	49 7/12	M	Mechanic	France	United States	Charles Carroll	16 Jan 1829
KESSEN, Julia	20	F	Servant	England	United States	Manchester	15 Aug 1826

NAMES OF PASSENGERS	AGE	SEX	OCCUPATIONS	COUNTRY TO WHICH THEY BELONG	COUNTRY THEY INTEND TO INHABIT	SHIPS/DATES OF ARRIVAL	
KESSEY, Benedict	42	M	Farmer	Switzerland	United States	Don Quixote	7 May 1824
KESSLER, C.	18	M		France	U. States	Danube	21 Nov 1826
C.	44	M		France	U. States	Danube	21 Nov 1826
Catharine	18	F	None	Gt. Britain	U. States	Isaac Hicks	18 Apr 1825
George	19	M		France	U. States	Danube	21 Nov 1826
Joseph	7	M		France	U. States	Danube	21 Nov 1826
M.	49	F		France	U. States	Danube	21 Nov 1826
Madeline	16	F		France	U. States	Danube	21 Nov 1826
KETCHELMAN, Thomas	6	M		England	U. States	Pleiades	9 Oct 1829
Tomison	36	F		England	U. States	Pleiades	9 Oct 1829
KETCHEM, Isaac	30	M	Merchant	St. John, N.B.	St. John, N.B.	Ann Maria	1 Apr 1826
KETCHEN, Charles	19	M	Labourer			Lady of the Lake	23 Aug 1828
John	40	M	Labourer			Lady of the Lake	23 Aug 1828
KETCHEON, Susana	47	F		New York	United States	Potomac	28 Sep 1827
KETCHER, Isaac	20	M	Merchant	St. John	St. John	St. Michael	27 Mar 1827
KETCHIN, Thomas	25	M	Fur Maker	Ireland	New Orleans	Eliza Grant	29 Aug 1829
KETCHMAN, Barbary	18	F		England	England	Manchester Packet	30 Nov 1822
KETCHMIN, James	20	M	Farmer	England	England	Manchester Packet	30 Nov 1822
KETCHUM, James	25	M	Merchant	St. John	St. John	St. Michael	24 Jun 1824
KETCHUME, J.	30	M	Merchant	N. York	U. States	Hunter	1 Jul 1828
KETCHUR, Thos.	30	M	Teacher	Scotland	U. States	Domestic	31 Aug 1820
KETER, Anset	6	M		Germany	United States	Lydia	18 Jun 1828
George	5	M		Germany	United States	Lydia	18 Jun 1828
Jacob	3	M		Germany	United States	Lydia	18 Jun 1828
M.	3	M		Germany	United States	Lydia	18 Jun 1828
M.	8	M		Germany	United States	Lydia	18 Jun 1828
Margt.	1	F		Germany	United States	Lydia	18 Jun 1828
KETTELL, George A.	23 8/12	M	Merchant	United States	United States	France	6 Oct 1828
J.	34	M	Merchant	United States	United States	Sally	26 Jun 1822
KETTERELL, Jno.	30	M	Mariner	England	England	Wilson	8 Jan 1825
KETTLEWOOD, Maria	20	F	Wife [of Mathew]	Great Briton	United States	Orion	18 Jun 1821
Mathew	26	M	Labourer	Great Briton	United States	Orion	18 Jun 1821
KETZ, Jane	30	F		England	U. States	Amulet	9 Jan 1829
Thos.	27	M	Farier	England	U. States	Amulet	9 Jan 1829
KEVAN, Thomas	27	M	Farmer	Ireland	America	Josephine	24 Jul 1826
KEVIN, Ansel	23	M	Farmer	Alsace in the Department of Upper and lower Rhine	United States	Carolina Augusta	16 May 1828
George	51	M	Farmer	Alsace in the Department of Upper and lower Rhine	United States	Carolina Augusta	16 May 1828
Margaretta	22	F	Farmer	Alsace in the Department of Upper and lower Rhine	United States	Carolina Augusta	16 May 1828
Peter	10	M	Farmer	Alsace in the Department of Upper and lower Rhine	United States	Carolina Augusta	16 May 1828
KEVINS, Jane	18	F	Spinster	Ireland	America	William	11 Nov 1825
KEVON, Catherine	4	F	Farmer	Alsace in the Department of Upper and lower Rhine	United States	Carolina Augusta	16 May 1828
Catherine	24	F	Farmer	Alsace in the Department of Upper and lower Rhine	United States	Carolina Augusta	16 May 1828
George	27	M	Farmer	Alsace in the Department of Upper and lower Rhine	United States	Carolina Augusta	16 May 1828

NAMES OF PASSENGERS	AGE	SEX	OCCUPATIONS	COUNTRY TO WHICH THEY BELONG	COUNTRY THEY INTEND TO INHABIT	SHIPS/DATES OF ARRIVAL	
KEVON (cont'd)							
Yorick	2	M	Farmer	Alsace in the Department of Upper and lower Rhine	United States	Carolina Augusta	16 May 1828
KEW, Bernard	34	M	Labourer	Ireland		Marchioness	13 May 1828
Catherine	30	F	Labourer	Ireland		Marchioness	13 May 1828
Honora	2	F	Labourer	Ireland		Marchioness	13 May 1828
Mary	6	F	Labourer	Ireland		Marchioness	13 May 1828
Thomas	4	M	Labourer	Ireland		Marchioness	13 May 1828
William	26	M	Merchant	Scotland	U.S. of America	Friends	10 May 1823
William	30	M	Farmer	Great Britain	United States	Favorite	10 Dec 1822
KEWIN, Margt.	17	F	None	Isle of Man		Ocean	13 Jul 1827
KEWLEY, Ann	24	F	Labourer	England	U. States	Comet	23 Aug 1828
Cath.	28	F	Labourer	England	U. States	Comet	23 Aug 1828
Catharine	9	F	Labourer	England	U. States	Comet	23 Aug 1828
Esther	1	F	Labourer	England	U. States	Comet	23 Aug 1828
John	3	M	Labourer	England	U. States	Comet	23 Aug 1828
Margaret	14	F	Labourer	England	U. States	Comet	23 Aug 1828
Margaret	37	F	Labourer	England	U. States	Comet	23 Aug 1828
Pat	15	M	Labourer	England	U. States	Comet	23 Aug 1828
Thomas	6	M	Labourer	England	U. States	Comet	23 Aug 1828
Thomas	40	M	Labourer	England	U. States	Comet	23 Aug 1828
Wm.	20	M	Smith	Isle of Man		Ocean	13 Jul 1827
KEW MYRE, Robt.	24 2/12	M	Merchant	England	England	Leeds	29 May 1824
KEY, Gen.	35	M				Belfast	28 Sep 1820
John A.	2...	M	Merchant	...	United States	Horatio	26 Oct 1827
Maria	21	F	Farmer	England	United States	Siroc	31 Oct 1829
Moses	24	M	Farmer	England	United States	Siroc	31 Oct 1829
Sald.	19	M	Merchant	Spanish America	U. States	Endymion	22 May 1822
KEYDECKER,							
Joachim	29 10/12	M	Merchant	Germany	United States	France	6 Oct 1828
KEYLE, Rebecca	...	F	...	...	U. States	Louisiana	31 Oct 1827
Sarah	...	F	...	...	U. States	Louisiana	31 Oct 1827
KEYLER, Ann	30	F	Semstress	England	America	Franklin	19 Nov 1828
KEYLEY, Rodger	23	M	Blacksmith	St. Johns, N.B.	United States	Henrietta	17 Aug 1825
KEYS, Eez.	4	F	Spinster	Ireland	U. States	Meteor	19 Jul 1828
Fanny	24		Spinster	Ireland		Westmoreland	1 Aug 1826
George, Mr.	35	M	Gentn.	England	England	Acasta	3 Apr 1826
John	28	M	Labourer	Ireland	United States	Lady Hunter	27 Dec 1825
Thos.	3	M	Labourer	Ireland	U. States	Meteor	19 Jul 1828
KEYSER, J.	28	M	private	U. States	U. States	Enterprize	9 Aug 1825
KEYTE, W.	32	M	Laborer			Importer	30 Oct 1820
KHOUGH, Margt.	49	F	None	Whitehaven	Liverpool	Aldebaron	21 Jan 1826
Margt.	49	F	None	Whitehaven	Liverpool	Aldebaron	21 Jan 1826
KIAN, Robert	20	M	Farmer	Co. Darry	Co. Antrin	Aldebaron	21 Jan 1826
KIBEERS, Daniel	16	M	Farmer	Swis	United States	Iris	21 Sep 1821
Samuel	18	M	Farmer	Swis	United States	Iris	21 Sep 1821
KIBLIN, Jans	1 6/12	M	D. Maker	Ireland	N. York	Trusty	12 Sep 1828
KIBNIE, Joseph	26	M	None	Ireland	United States	Lord Wellington	28 May 1827
KICK, Catherine	31	F	Spinster	Switzerland	United States	Andes	5 May 1828
George	6	M	Child	Switzerland	United States	Andes	5 May 1828
Henry	1	M	Child	Switzerland	United States	Andes	5 May 1828
Philip	3	M	Child	Switzerland	United States	Andes	5 May 1828
Theofiler	8	M	Farmer	Switzerland	United States	Andes	5 May 1828
Theofiler	33	M	Farmer	Switzerland	United States	Andes	5 May 1828
Wm.	30	M	Laborer	...	United States	Combine	20 Nov 1824
KICKEY, Michl.	18	M	Labourer	England	U. States	Thomas Ritchie	2 Jul 1827
KICKUP, Simpson	35	M	Labourer	Great Britain	United States	Mary & Harriet	3 Jul 1829
KICMAN, Jno. P.	22	M	Merchant	Spain	U. States	Commerce	20 May 1823
KID, Mary, Mrs.	22	F	Lady	England	U.N. States	Ariel	9 Mar 1829
KIDD, Elizabeth, Miss	22			Hampshire/ Sussex, Eng.	England	Venus	12 Apr 1821
George	21	M	Mill Wright	Ireland	United States	Romulus	24 Jun 1826
John	29	M	Labourer	Lancaster	Lancaster	Howard Douglass	11 May 1827
Wm. Campbell	26	M	Gentleman	Scotland	U.S. of America	Camillus	16 Apr 1822

NAMES OF PASSENGERS	AGE	SEX	OCCUPATIONS	COUNTRY TO WHICH THEY BELONG	COUNTRY THEY INTEND TO INHABIT	SHIPS/DATES OF ARRIVAL	
KIDDE, John R.	55	M	Marriner	U. States	U. States	Eliza Barker	19 Dec 1825
KIDING, Charles	31	M	Servant	Great Britain	England	John Wells	29 Jan 1825
KIDNEY, Biddy	25	F				Trio	5 May 1828
Catharine	5	F		England	United States	Margaret	5 Sep 1827
Eliza	2	F		England	United States	Margaret	5 Sep 1827
Ellen		F	Spinster	Ireland	United States	Diana	1 May 1826
Hannah	8	F		England	United States	Margaret	5 Sep 1827
Hannah	20	F		Ireland	America	Liverpool	31 Aug 1827
Maria	12	F	Spinster	Ireland	United States	Diana	1 May 1826
Mary	11	F		Ireland	America	Liverpool	31 Aug 1827
Mary	35	F		Ireland	United States	Margaret	5 Sep 1827
Timothy	27	M	Farmer	Ireland	America	William	21 May 1825
KIDON, Judith	21	F	Spinster	Ireland	America	William	21 May 1825
KIDSON, Joseph	27 10/12	M	pudler		uncertain	Mount Vernon	29 Aug 1828
KIDWELL, Leaveritt	38	M	Merchant	United States	United States	Union Packet	10 Aug 1829
KIE, M.	2	M		France	United States	New England	29 Aug 1828
KIEFE, Michael	27	M	Shoe Maker	England	U. States	Rising States	20 Sep 1828
KIEFFER, Catharine, his wife [Jacob]	33	F	Seamstress	France	United States	William	31 Jul 1826
Catharine, his wiffe [Peter]	43	F	Seamstress	France	United States	William	31 Jul 1826
Elizabeth, his daughter [Jacob]	2	F		France	United States	William	31 Jul 1826
George, his son [Peter]	10	M		France	United States	William	31 Jul 1826
Jacob	32	M	Farmer	France	United States	William	31 Jul 1826
John, his son [Peter]	7	M		France	United States	William	31 Jul 1826
Margarita, his daughter [Jacob]	6	F		France	United States	William	31 Jul 1826
Margarita, his daughter [Peter]	19	F	Seamstress	France	United States	William	31 Jul 1826
Maria, his daughter [Peter]	2	F		France	United States	William	31 Jul 1826
Peter	42	M	Weaver	France	United States	William	31 Jul 1826
Peter, his son [Peter]	13	M		France	United States	William	31 Jul 1826
Pierre	19	M	Weaver	Switzerland	U. States	La Urania	3 Jul 1828
KIEFHABER, F.	25	M	Tailor	Germany	America	Falcon	28 Aug 1828
KIEKY, David	25	M	Mason	Ireland	United States	Trio	13 Jun 1827
KIELD, Eliza	30	F	Farmer	Great Britian	United States	Princess Charlotte	6 Sep 1828
John	16	M	Farmer	Great Britian	United States	Princess Charlotte	6 Sep 1828
John	33	M	Farmer	Great Britian	United States	Princess Charlotte	6 Sep 1828
KIELE, Andres	58			France	U. States	Parachute	14 May 1828
Christien	4			France	U. States	Parachute	14 May 1828
Christin	22			France	U. States	Parachute	14 May 1828
Christin	54			France	U. States	Parachute	14 May 1828
Jno. A.	9			France	U. States	Parachute	14 May 1828
Madeline	29			France	U. States	Parachute	14 May 1828
Petre	27			France	U. States	Parachute	14 May 1828
Philip	7			France	U. States	Parachute	14 May 1828
KIELLEY, Mathew	16	M	Labourer	England	United States	Jubilee	1 Oct 1828
KIERNAN, Bridget	20	F	Spinstress	Great Briton	United States	Erin	26 May 1821
Bryan	19	M	Weaver	Ireland	United States	Carolina Ann	11 Dec 1826
Ellen	18	F	Servant	Ireland	United States	Carolina Ann	11 Dec 1826
John	22	M	Farmer	Ireland	United States	Dublin Packet	28 Apr 1824
Margaret	19	F	Spinster	Ireland	United States	Dublin Packet	28 Apr 1824
Mary	22	F	Spinster	Ireland	America	Wilson	16 May 1825
William	22	M	Labourer	Ireland	America	Wilson	16 May 1825
KIERSULF, Libe, Mr.	30		Merchant	...	U. States	South Carolina Packet	30 May 1825
KIES, Catarina	15	F		France	United States	New England	29 Aug 1828
Christina	3	M		France	United States	New England	29 Aug 1828
Gottlieb	5	M		France	United States	New England	29 Aug 1828
Johann Geo.	17	F		France	United States	New England	29 Aug 1828
Johann Geo.	42	M	Farmer	France	United States	New England	29 Aug 1828
Julina	10	F		France	United States	New England	29 Aug 1828

NAMES OF PASSENGERS	AGE	SEX	OCCUPATIONS	COUNTRY TO WHICH THEY BELONG	COUNTRY THEY INTEND TO INHABIT	SHIPS/DATES OF ARRIVAL	
KIES (cont'd)							
Margaretta	13	F		France	United States	New England	29 Aug 1828
KIESTERING, Funguil	3	M	Farmer	Swizerland		Antioch	18 Aug 1829
Gusta	28	F	Farmer	Swizerland		Antioch	18 Aug 1829
Jacob	30	M	Farmer	Swizerland		Antioch	18 Aug 1829
Jacques	5	M	Farmer	Swizerland		Antioch	18 Aug 1829
Nicolus	4/12	M	Farmer	Swizerland		Antioch	18 Aug 1829
KIETH, William	27	M	Mercht.	England	U. States	Brown	8 Aug 1825
KIETING, Jeremiah	19	M	Labourer	Ireland	United States	Robert Edwards	3 Oct 1829
Michael	45	M	Labourer	Ireland	United States	Robert Edwards	3 Oct 1829
KIGHER, John	21	M	Labourer	Ireland	United States	William	20 Jul 1829
KILBERTON, Eliza	24			England		Anacreon	7 Sep 1827
Jno.	29			England		Anacreon	7 Sep 1827
Mary Ann	18			England		Anacreon	7 Sep 1827
KILBRED, Edwd.	18	M	Farmer	Ireland	America	Mary	29 May 1827
Ml.	20	M	Farmer	Ireland	America	Mary	29 May 1827
KILBRIDGE, Michael	25	M	Labourer	G. Britain	U. States	Dalhouse Castle	12 Sep 1828
KILBY, Thomas	34	M	Mariner	U. States	U. States	Fabius	9 Jul 1824
KILCULLEN, Catharine	21	F		Ireland	U.S. of America	Douglass	6 Jul 1829
KILDAY, John	23	M	Labourer	Ireland	United States	Henry Kneeland	7 Jun 1828
KILEY, ...an	6		Laboring Class		United States	Atlantic	2 Apr 1827
John	20	M	Merchant	Ireland	U. States	Albion	9 Aug 1826
Mary	8		Laboring Class		United States	Atlantic	2 Apr 1827
Patrick	22		Laboring Class		United States	Atlantic	2 Apr 1827
KILFEATHER, Farrel	30	M	Labourer	Ireland	United States	Robert Fulton	24 Jul 1826
KILHOLM, John	23	M	Labourer	Ireland	United States	Enterprize	23 Jul 1827
KILKENNY, Francis	16	M	None	Ireland	U.S.A.	Dalhouse Castle	21 Aug 1829
Francis	16	M	None	Ireland	United States	Dalhouse Castle	21 Aug 1829
KILKILLENE, Mary	20	F	Spinster	Ireland	United States	Wilson	6 Jun 1828
KILKINNY, Peter	22	M	Labourer	Sligo	New York	Susquehana	27 Jun 1823
KILLAN, Chas.	25	M	Labourer	Scotland	United States	Morning Star	25 Jun 1822
KILLCHRIST, Jane H.	18	F		Ireland	U. States	Nancy	2 May 1823
John	24	M	Labourer	Ireland	U. States	Nancy	2 May 1823
KILLDUFF, Mary	22	F	None	Great Britain	United States	Eliza Barker	3 Jul 1826
Patrick	1	M	None	Great Britain	United States	Eliza Barker	3 Jul 1826
Peter	22	M	Farmer	Great Britain	United States	Eliza Barker	3 Jul 1826
KILLEKELLY, Caroline J.	20	F	Lady	Barbados, U.S.	West Indies	Spartan	24 Jul 1826
KILLEN, J.	20		Farmer	Ireland	United States	Courier	16 May 1825
KILLERLAIN, Rose	21	F	Spinster	Ireland	United States	Wilson	4 Oct 1827
KILLEY, Catharne	18	F	None	Great Briton	United States	Mount Vernon	29 Aug 1828
Hy.	28	M	Weaver	Gt. Brittain	United States	Balaena	24 Aug 1825
KILLFEATHER, Winny	30	M				Ocean	17 Aug 1820
KILLIN, James	12	M	Taylor	Ireland	U. States	Josephine	27 Jul 1825
John	38	M	Taylor	Ireland	U. States	Josephine	27 Jul 1825
Mary	14	F	None	Ireland	U. States	Henry Kneeland	27 Jul 1825
KILLINGER, William	23	M	Carpenter	Germany	United States	Martha	30 Jun 1823
KILLKELLY, B. B.	20	M	Merchant	Barbadoes	Barbadoes	Rose in Bloom	10 Aug 1824
John B.	25	M	Merchant	Barbadoes	Barbadoes	Only Daughter	9 Nov 1825
KILLOCK, Ann	25	F	None	Gt. Britain	U.S. of America	Friends	25 Sep 1823
Jane	7	F	None	Gt. Britain	U.S. of America	Friends	25 Sep 1823
John	1	M	None	Gt. Britain	U.S. of America	Friends	25 Sep 1823
William	25	M	Laborer	Gt. Britain	U.S. of America	Friends	25 Sep 1823
KILLORAN, Elizabeth	20	F	None	England	United States	Jubilee	1 Oct 1828
John	36	M	Husbandman	Great Britan	United States	Bolivar	21 May 1827
Mary	30	F	None	Great Britan	United States	Bolivar	21 May 1827
Mary Ann	1	F	None	England	United States	Jubilee	1 Oct 1828
KILLPATRICK, Saml.	25	M	Labourer	Ireland	U.States	Nancy	31 May 1823
KILLRIDE, Catherine	20	F	None	Ireland	United States	John Wells	11 May 1827
KILLUN, Thomas	25		Labourer	Ireland	New York	Marcella	18 May 1827
KILLY, Ann	6	F		England		Anacreon	7 Sep 1827
Isabella	2	F		England		Anacreon	7 Sep 1827
Isabella	24	F		England		Anacreon	7 Sep 1827
Jane	10	F		England		Anacreon	7 Sep 1827
Jas.	30	M		England		Anacreon	7 Sep 1827
Margt.	4	F		England		Anacreon	7 Sep 1827
Maria	1	F		England		Anacreon	7 Sep 1827
Thos.	35	M		England		Anacreon	7 Sep 1827
Thos.	67	M		England		Anacreon	7 Sep 1827

NAMES OF PASSENGERS	AGE	SEX	OCCUPATIONS	COUNTRY TO WHICH THEY BELONG	COUNTRY THEY INTEND TO INHABIT	SHIPS/DATES OF ARRIVAL	
KILMURRY, Rose	2...	F	...	Ireland	United States	Wilson	22 Jun 1824
KILNER, John	42	M	Sleator	England	America	Plutarch	18 Jul 1826
KILPATRIC, Thos.	18	M	Labourer	Ireland		Robert Fulton	4 Jun 1828
KILPATRICK, Andw.	62	M		Ireland	New York	Atlantic	6 Oct 1828
Elisher	25	M	Gentleman	U. States	U. States	Hero	21 Jan 1825
Jane	61	F	Wife	Ireland	New York	Atlantic	6 Oct 1828
Jas.	27			Great Britan	United States	Newry	11 Jul 1827
Mary	21	F	Lady	Ireland	United States	Borneo	14 Aug 1827
Robert	26	M	Tallow Chandler	Ireland	United States	Borneo	9 Jul 1827
KILRIDE, Jane	23	F	Wife [of Patrick]	Great Briton	United States	Orion	18 Jun 1821
Patrick	25	M	Weaver	Great Briton	United States	Orion	18 Jun 1821
KILROY, Catherine	5	F		Ireland	U.S.	George Canning	26 Aug 1829
Larry	26	M	Farmer	Ireland	United States	Dublin Packet	23 May 1828
Patrick	26	M	Weaver	Ireland	U. States	Courier	17 Mar 1828
KILSEY, James	18	M	Weaver	Ireland	U. States of America	Courier	17 Mar 1827
KILVARY, Sally	20	F				Ocean	17 Aug 1820
KILVINGTON, Robert	24	M	Farmer	England	America	John Adams	2 Aug 1827
KIMBAL, Theodore	19	M	Merchant	U. States		Indian Chief	22 Aug 1822
KIMBALL, —, Mrs.		F		U. States	U. States	Fair Play	5 Jun 1823
—, Mrs.	36	F		U. States	U. States	Worromontogus	23 Jun 1823
Geo.	35	M	Merchant	U. States	U. States	Worromontogus	23 Jun 1823
Jno.	18	M	Laborer	Ireland	United States	Weser	29 Jul 1823
M.	27	M	Mariner	U. States	U. States	Fame	20 Feb 1822
Moses	21 9/12		Merchant	U. States	U. States	Jackin	15 May 1828
Nancy	10	F		U. States	U. States	Worromontogus	23 Jun 1823
KIMBELL, Henry	24	M	Baker	France	U. States	Comet	28 Jul 1825
KIMBLE, J. A., Miss	16	F	None	England	United States	Manchester	15 Aug 1826
Peter, Mr.	60	M	Mercht.	England	United States	Manchester	15 Aug 1826
KIMPBAL, Carolin	2	F	Farmer	Switzerland	U. States	Alfred	8 Jul 1828
F.	26	M	Farmer	Switzerland	U. States	Alfred	8 Jul 1828
Jos.	0 1/12	M	Farmer	Switzerland	U. States	Alfred	8 Jul 1828
M.	22	F	Farmer	Switzerland	U. States	Alfred	8 Jul 1828
Maria	26	F	Farmer	Switzerland	U. States	Alfred	8 Jul 1828
KIMPLE, Annette	5	F		France	U. States	Leonarde	29 Aug 1828
Genevieve J.	28	F		France	U. States	Leonarde	29 Aug 1828
Jean	32	M	Weaver	France	U. States	Leonarde	29 Aug 1828
Jean P.	2	M		France	U. States	Leonarde	29 Aug 1828
Margerite	7	F		France	U. States	Leonarde	29 Aug 1828
KINAR, Cathn.	20	F	Servant	Ireland	United States	William	20 Jul 1829
James	40	M	Laborer	Ireland	United States	Ann Maria	3 Jul 1827
Margabet	39	F	Wife	Ireland	United States	Ann Maria	3 Jul 1827
William	20	M	Laborer	Ireland	United States	Ann Maria	3 Jul 1827
KINCAID, E. T. Mr.	21	M	Merchant	England	America	Birmingham	16 Oct 1826
Eliza	3	F		G. Britain	U. States	Camillus	8 Sep 1828
James	35	M	Farmer	Scotland	U. States	Camillus	17 Sep 1823
Mary	1	F		G. Britain	U. States	Camillus	8 Sep 1828
Susan	25	F		G. Britain	U. States	Camillus	8 Sep 1828
KINCHLER, Ann	28	F	None	England	U. States	Thomas Ritchie	2 Jul 1827
Jno.	4	M	None	England	U. States	Thomas Ritchie	2 Jul 1827
Jno.	30	M	Farmer	England	U. States	Thomas Ritchie	2 Jul 1827
Mary A.	1	F	None	England	U. States	Thomas Ritchie	2 Jul 1827
Thos.	6	M	None	England	U. States	Thomas Ritchie	2 Jul 1827
KINDELINE, Utelle	17 4/12	F		France	United States	Charles Carroll	16 Jan 1829
KINDER, John	35	M	Hatter	Grate Brittan	New York	Susquehanna	9 Jan 1824
Peter	22	M	Farmer	Switzerland	United States	Andes	5 May 1828
KINDLE, Ann	34	F	None	England	U. States	Montgomery	18 Oct 1828
Betty	3	F	None	England	U. States	Montgomery	18 Oct 1828
Charles	1	M	None	England	U. States	Montgomery	18 Oct 1828
Henry	5	M	None	England	U. States	Montgomery	18 Oct 1828
James	38	M	Labourer	England	U. States	Montgomery	18 Oct 1828
Jonathan	7	M	None	England	U. States	Montgomery	18 Oct 1828
KINDRICK, Francis, Rev.	30	M	Clergyman	Ireland	Kentucky	Abigail	9 Aug 1821
KINE, Johannes	28	M	Farmer	Germany	U. States	Isabella	10 Aug 1829
KINEER, Ellen	40	F				Helicon	3 Aug 1826
Ether	10/12	F				Helicon	3 Aug 1826
Ether	25	F				Helicon	3 Aug 1826
Jane	62	F				Helicon	3 Aug 1826
John	22	M	Shoemaker	Isle of Man	Isle of Man	Helicon	3 Aug 1826
Magery	24	F				Helicon	3 Aug 1826

NAMES OF PASSENGERS	AGE	SEX	OCCUPATIONS	COUNTRY TO WHICH THEY BELONG	COUNTRY THEY INTEND TO INHABIT	SHIPS/DATES OF ARRIVAL	
KINEY, Martin	20	M	Farmer	Ireland		Cuba	24 Jun 1822
KING, —, Mr.	21	M	Miller	G. Britain	U.S.	Robert Edwards	11 Nov 1822
—, Mrs.	28	F			U. States	Cygnet	22 Jun 1821
...	7	F	None	Ireland	U.S.	Pacific	24 Oct 1828
...	9	M	None	Ireland	U.S.	Pacific	24 Oct 1828
Alfred	23	M	Merchant	Barbadoes	Barbadoes	Sudan	6 Aug 1823
Ann	16	F	None	Gt. Britain	United States	Eliza Barker	11 Jan 1826
Ann	20	F	Lady	U. States	U. States	Nancy	19 Oct 1821
Ann, Mrs.	35			England	U.S. of America	Mary	21 Sep 1821
Ann Marie	24	F	Spinster	Werdenburg	United States	Xenophon	2 Jun 1824
Anna	25	F	None	Great Britain	United States	Colossus	5 Jun 1827
Archibald	5	M		U. States	U.S.	Bayard	10 Nov 1824
Bernard	35	M	Gentleman	England	United States	Nimrod	31 Jul 1828
Caroline	9	F		U. States	U.S.	Bayard	10 Nov 1824
Charles V.	26	M	Slater	Scotland	United States	Meteor	27 Sep 1826
Chas.	25	M	Dyer	England	United States	Cosmo	26 Aug 1829
Chas.	40	M	Merchant	United States	United States	Orris	12 Mar 1825
Cornelia, Miss	3		Lady	United States	United States	Acasta	16 Aug 1826
Denis	20 3/12	M		Ireland	America	Carolina Ann	7 Apr 1826
Dorothy	30	F		Great Britain	United States	Grecian	24 Sep 1828
Duke	24	M	Labourer	Ireland, Great Britain	U.S. of America	Dublin	21 Feb 1826
Edward	9	M	Farmer	Great Britian	United States	Andes	19 Aug 1829
Edward	30	M	Farmer	Ireland	United States	Dublin Packet	28 Apr 1824
Eleanor	24	F				Splendid	14 Aug 1829
Elen	1	F				Splendid	14 Aug 1829
Eleonor	50 4/12	F	Lady	England	United States	Nimrod	28 Apr 1824
Eliz.	66	F	Servant	Ireland	N. York	Trusty	12 Sep 1828
Eliz., Miss	12		Lady	United States	United States	Acasta	16 Aug 1826
Eliza	1		his Daughter			Cambria	19 Oct 1829
Elizabeth	9/12	F		Ireland	United States	Meteor	27 Sep 1826
Elizabeth	20	F		England, Born in Barbadoes	U. States	Cannon	15 Jul 1822
*all the children have come under the care of Mrs. Fenwick for their education							
Ellen	3	F	None	Ireland	U.S.	Pacific	24 Oct 1828
Ellen	36	F	Wife	Ireland	U.S.	Pacific	24 Oct 1828
Ellen, Miss	1		Lady	United States	United States	Acasta	16 Aug 1826
Emily	19	F		U. States	U. States	Montano	2 Sep 1828
Ezra	10	M		England, Born in Barbadoes	U. States	Cannon	15 Jul 1822
*all the children have come under the care of Mrs. Fenwick for their education							
F. G.	22	M	Physician	United States	United States	Orris	12 Mar 1825
Finlay	21	M	Weaver	Great Britain	United States	Colossus	5 Jun 1827
Francis	30	M	Labourer	Ireland	U. States	William	27 Jul 1824
Fred., Mrs.	15		Lady	United States	United States	Acasta	16 Aug 1826
Fred. G., Dr.	26	M	Physician	U. States	U. States	Montano	2 Sep 1828
Fred. G., Esqre.	25		Physician	United States	United States	Acasta	16 Aug 1826
Frederick	25	M	Labourer	Werdenburg	United States	Xenophon	2 Jun 1824
Fredk.	50	M	Mariner	U. States	U. States	Jane	10 Jan 1824
Frs.	8	M		England, Born in Barbadoes	U. States	Cannon	15 Jul 1822
*all the children have come under the care of Mrs. Fenwick for their education							
George	5	M	Farmer	England	America	Thames	27 May 1822
George	21		Farmer	England	S. New York	Xenophon	25 Jul 1826
H.	30	M	Tailor	Germany		Ariel	24 Sep 1827
Hannah	19		None	Blackburn, England	Great Britain	Franklin	22 Jun 1827
Harriet	11	F		U. States	U.S.	Bayard	10 Nov 1824
Harriett	27			England	U.S. of America	Mary	21 Sep 1821
Henrietta	13	F	Farmer	Great Britian	United States	Andes	19 Aug 1829
Henry	32		Jeweller	England	United States	Cambria	19 Oct 1829
Henry	38	M	Mariner	United States	United States	Martha	29 May 1822
Hetty	22					Trio	5 May 1828
Hugh	20	M	Lawyer	Ireland	N. York	Trusty	12 Sep 1828
Hugh	28	M	...	Ireland	U. States	William	27 Jul 1824
Isabella	12	F	Farmer	England	America	Thames	27 May 1822
Isabella	21	F	None	Great Britain	United States	Colossus	5 Jun 1827

NAMES OF PASSENGERS	AGE	SEX	OCCUPATIONS	COUNTRY TO WHICH THEY BELONG	COUNTRY THEY INTEND TO INHABIT	SHIPS/DATES OF ARRIVAL	
KING (cont'd)							
James	9	M		England, Born in Barbadoes	U. States	Cannon	15 Jul 1822
*all the children have come under the care of Mrs. Fenwick for their education							
James	11	M	Farmer	Great Britian	United States	Andes	19 Aug 1829
James	15	M	Farmer	Great Britian	United States	Andes	19 Aug 1829
James	18	M	Labourer	Ireland	United States	Princess Charlotte	26 Apr 1827
James	18 6/12	M		Ireland	America	Carolina Ann	7 Apr 1826
James	40	M	Preacher	United States	U. States	Pacific	5 Sep 1827
James	41	M	E. J. Company Sons	G. Briton	G. Briton	James Monroe	14 Dec 1820
James	45	M	Sawyer	England	U. States	York	12 Jul 1825
James G.	6	M		U. States	U.S.	Bayard	10 Nov 1824
James G.	32	M	Merchant	New York, U. States	United States	James Cropper	7 Oct 1823
James G.	32	M	Merchant	U. States	U.S.	Bayard	10 Nov 1824
Jane	3	F	Farmer	England	America	Thames	27 May 1822
Janet	2...	F	Wife	Scotland	United States	Samuel Robertson	9 May 1827
Jas.	22	M	Farmer	Ireland	United States	Trident	16 May 1826
Jno.	1			England	U.S. of America	Mary	21 Sep 1821
Jno., Mr.	53		Farmer	England	U.S. of America	Mary	21 Sep 1821
John	5	M	Farmer	Great Britian	United States	Andes	19 Aug 1829
John	8	M		G. Britain	U. States	London	23 Sep 1828
John	14	M		England	England	Criterion	29 May 1822
John	14		Labourer	England	United States	Hudson	5 Apr 1826
John	15	M	None	Ireland	U.S.	Pacific	24 Oct 1828
John	24	M	Labourer	Ireland	United States	Princess Charlotte	26 Apr 1827
John	25					Splendid	14 Aug 1829
John	26 10/12	M	Accountant	England	United States	Nimrod	28 Apr 1824
John	27		Soap Boiler	England	U.S. of America	Mary	21 Sep 1821
John	30	M	Clerk	U. Kingdom Great Britain	United States	Cambria	7 May 1828
John	32	M	Weaver	Ireland	United States	Alexander Mansfield	16 Sep 1823
John	40	M	Farmer	Great Britian	United States	Andes	19 Aug 1829
John	45	M	Surgeon	U.S. America	U.S. America	Cincinnatus	31 Oct 1820
John	48		Mariner	England	England	Lafayette	3 Dec 1827
John, Mrs.	28		Lady	United States	United States	Acasta	16 Aug 1826
John T.	26		Gardener	Birmingham, Eng./Birmingham	New York	Venus	12 Apr 1821
Jolia	2	M	None	Great Britain	United States	Colossus	5 Jun 1827
Joseph	27	M	Iron Roller	Gt. Britain	U.S. America	James Cropper	14 Mar 1828
Louisa	23	F		Great Britain	United States	Nestor in Liverpool	29 Jul 1822
Lucy M.	26		his Wife			Cambria	19 Oct 1829
M... B...	36	M	Shoemaker	Steal...	Lancaster	Howard Douglass	11 May 1827
Margaret	12	F	Spinster	Ireland	United States	Fabius	31 Jul 1829
Mary	6	F	Child	Ireland	United States	Dublin Packet	28 Apr 1824
Mary	8	F				Splendid	14 Aug 1829
Mary	10	F	Farmer	England	America	Thames	27 May 1822
Mary	35	F	Farmer	Great Britian	United States	Andes	19 Aug 1829
Mary, Miss	16		Lady	United States	United States	Acasta	16 Aug 1826
Mary Ann	11/12	F	None	Ireland	New York	Indian Chief	19 Jun 1823
*died							
Mary Ann, Miss			None	U.S.	U.S.	Sully	26 Oct 1829
Nancy	2	F	Farmer	Great Britian	United States	Andes	19 Aug 1829
Nicholus	35					Splendid	14 Aug 1829
Patarick	30	M	Labourer	Ireland	U. States	Atlantic	19 Aug 1825
Robert	2	F				Splendid	14 Aug 1829
Robert	25	M	Labourer	Scotland	United States	Samuel Robertson	9 May 1827
Roswell A.	30	M		U. States	U. States	Cincinnatus	2 Oct 1822
Rufus	11	M	None	United States	United States	Orris	12 Mar 1825

NAMES OF PASSENGERS	AGE	SEX	OCCUPATIONS	COUNTRY TO WHICH THEY BELONG	COUNTRY THEY INTEND TO INHABIT	SHIPS/DATES OF ARRIVAL	
KING (cont'd)							
Rufus, Honble.	71		Ambassidor of the United States	United States	United States	Acasta	16 Aug 1826
Sam	9	M			U. States	Cygnet	22 Jun 1821
Sampson	4	M			U. States	Cygnet	22 Jun 1821
Samuel	21	M	Iron Roller	Gt. Britain	U.S. America	James Cropper	14 Mar 1828
Samuel	27	M	Labourer	Ireland	United States	Meteor	26 Jun 1827
Sarah	28	F	Wife	U. States	U.S.	Bayard	10 Nov 1824
Sarah J.	18	F	D. Maker	Ireland	N. York	Trusty	12 Sep 1828
Sariah	8	F	Farmer	England	America	Thames	27 May 1822
Solm.	29	M	Merchant	England	U. States	Cygnet	22 Jun 1821
Solm., Jr.	7	M			U. States	Cygnet	22 Jun 1821
Stephen	3/12	M			U. States	Cygnet	22 Jun 1821
Susannah	25	F	None	Ireland	New York	Indian Chief	19 Jun 1823
Thomas	20 1/12	M		Ireland	America	Carolina Ann	7 Apr 1826
Thomas	23 10/12	M	Accountent	England	United States	Nimrod	28 Apr 1824
Thos.	28	M	Farmer	G. Britain	U. States	Dalthousie Castle	2 Jan 1827
Thos.	30	M	Farmer	Great Britian	United States	Columbia	17 Apr 1827
Thos.	35	M	Mariner	United States	United States	Florida	23 Aug 1825
Walter	42	M	Farmer	England	America	Thames	27 May 1822
William	7	M	Farmer	Great Britian	United States	Andes	19 Aug 1829
William	21 5/12	M	Labourer	G. Britain	United States	Louisa	14 Jun 1825
William	23	M	Jeweller & Goldsmith	Ireland	New York	Indian Chief	19 Jun 1823
William	23	M	Iron Roller	Gt. Britain	U.S. America	James Cropper	14 Mar 1828
William	25	M	Labourer	Great Britan	United States	Bolivar	21 May 1827
William	30	M	Clerk	U. States	U. States	Alert	9 Jul 1824
Wm.	29	M	Weaver	Great Britain	United States	Colossus	5 Jun 1827
Wm.	36	M	Cotton Spinner	G. Britain	U. States	Camillus	8 Sep 1828
Wm.	40					Splendid	14 Aug 1829
Wm.	45	M	Inn Keeper			Robert Edwards	8 Nov 1825
Wm.	45	M	Navy Officer	Great Britain	Great Britain	John Jay	8 May 1828
Wm.	54	M	Merchant	Gt. B.	Gt. B.	Caledonia	20 Jan 1829
KINGAN, John	30	M		England	United States	Yobah	26 Sep 1827
Mary	1	F		England	United States	Yobah	26 Sep 1827
Mary	24	F		England	United States	Yobah	26 Sep 1827
KINGDOM, Elizabeth	29	F		Wales	United States	Mount Vernon	9 Jun 1823
Mary	9/12	F		Wales	United States	Mount Vernon	9 Jun 1823
William	29	M	Farmer	England	United States	Mount Vernon	9 Jun 1823
KINGE, John P.	24	M	Aug.	Augusta, Geoa.	U.S.	Cadmus	17 Aug 1824
KINGHORN, Thos.	23		Gentleman	Great Britain	U. States	Nile	30 Apr 1827
KINGINGER, A. N.	34	M	Mechanic	U.S.	U.S.	Edward Quesnel	17 Jan 1825
KINGSBERRY, E.		M	Mariner	United States	U. States	Perseverance	25 Jun 1821
KINGSBURY, E.	39	M	Mariner	U. States	U. States	Flight	2 Nov 1825
E., Capt.	40	M	Ship Master	United States	United States	Claudio	16 Oct 1827
Jno.	21	M	Mariner	U. States	U. States	Henry	3 Jun 1828
KINGSBY, —, Mr.	32	M	Merchant	Great Britain	Bermuda	Mary & Elizabeth	7 Sep 1824
KINGSINGER, J.	24	M	Farmer	Germany	America	Howard	27 Sep 1826
S.	26	M	Farmer	Germany	America	Howard	27 Sep 1826
KINGSLAND, George	24		Cooper	England	United States	Corinthian	30 May 1828
Jane	16	F	Lady			Charlotte Corday	15 Aug 1820
KINGSMITH, James	11	M	...	Ireland	United States	Carolina Ann	14 May 1827
Thomas	20	M	Weaver	Ireland	United States	Carolina Ann	14 May 1827
KINGSNOTH, William	26	M	farmer	England	Newyork	Cortes	16 Jul 1827
KINGSTON, Harriot	25	F		U.S.A.	U. States	Edward Bonnaffe	12 Oct 1826
Sally	25	F	Servant	Ireland	U. States	Marcus	7 Apr 1825
Stephen	55	M	Mercht.	U.S.A.	U. States	Edward Bonnaffe	12 Oct 1826
Wm. H.	29	M	Gentleman	G.B.	U. States	Silas Richard	30 Jun 1828
KINGSWORTH, Joh., Mr.	19	M	Farmer	England	U. States	Emily	25 Aug 1827
KINGWOOD, Robt.	27	M	Farmer	Scotland	United States	Orozimbo	5 Mar 1827
KINIAN, James	20	M	Cooper	England	America	Two Marys	24 Sep 1827
KINISTON, A.	50	F		Ireland	United States	Commerce	13 Jun 1828
Abagail	11	F		Ireland	United States	Commerce	13 Jun 1828
Agnes	18	F		Ireland	United States	Commerce	13 Jun 1828

NAMES OF PASSENGERS	AGE	SEX	OCCUPATIONS	COUNTRY TO WHICH THEY BELONG	COUNTRY THEY INTEND TO INHABIT	SHIPS/DATES OF ARRIVAL	
KINISTON (cont'd)							
Christopher	17	M	Farmer	Ireland	United States	Commerce	13 Jun 1828
Jane	25	F		Ireland	United States	Commerce	13 Jun 1828
Margt.	23	F		Ireland	United States	Commerce	13 Jun 1828
Mary	20	F		Ireland	United States	Commerce	13 Jun 1828
Rob.	50	M	Labourer	Ireland	United States	Commerce	13 Jun 1828
Wm.	26	M	Labourer	Ireland	United States	Commerce	13 Jun 1828
KINKERD, Andrew	2 6/12	M	Son	Ireland	New York	Louisa	20 Jul 1826
Esther	5	F	Daughter	Ireland	New York	Louisa	20 Jul 1826
Jeorge	7 10/12	M	Son	Ireland	New York	Louisa	20 Jul 1826
Margaret	37	F	Wife	Ireland	New York	Louisa	20 Jul 1826
KINKHEAD, Margaret	9			Ireland	United States	Robert Burns	30 May 1823
Margaret	28			Ireland	United States	Robert Burns	30 May 1823
Ths.	4		boy	Ireland	United States	Robert Burns	30 May 1823
KINKOCK, George	37		Merchant	England	U. States	Hudson	4 Sep 1823
KINLOCH, Francis	26	M	Merchant	United States	United States	Leeds	29 Sep 1823
KINLOCK, Barbara	3		Child	Great Britain	United States	Camillus	12 Sep 1827
Charlotte	22			U. States	U. States	Hudson	4 Sep 1823
Emma	1			U. States	U. States	Hudson	4 Sep 1823
George	5			U. States	U. States	Hudson	4 Sep 1823
Rachel	1/2			Great Britain	United States	Camillus	12 Sep 1827
KINLUCK, John	36	M	Comedian	Great Britain	Great Britan	United States	21 May 1827
KINMER, Aloas	24	M	Watchmaker	Switzerland	United States	Howard	27 Sep 1824
KINNA, John	5	M	Labourer	Ireland	United States	St. George	25 Aug 1829
Mary	13	F	None	Ireland	United States	St. George	25 Aug 1829
Michael	12	F	None	Ireland	United States	St. George	25 Aug 1829
KINNAN, Cora	20	F	Labourer	St. John	Great Britain	General Coffin	9 Mar 1827
Patrick	24	M	Weaver	St. John	Great Britain	General Coffin	9 Mar 1827
KINNAR, ...s	10	M	Child	Ireland	United States	Ann Maria	3 Jul 1827
Edward	15	M	Laborer	Ireland	United States	Ann Maria	3 Jul 1827
KINNARD, Albert	19	M	Mechanic	U. States		Patriot	31 May 1825
David	18	M	Shop Keeper	Ireland	U.S. of America	Hannibal	17 Dec 1823
KINNER, Ellen	18	F		England	America	Two Marys	24 Sep 1827
John	5	M	Labourer	Ireland	United States	St. George	25 Aug 1829
Mary	13	F	None	Ireland	United States	St. George	25 Aug 1829
Michel	12	M	None	Ireland	United States	St. George	25 Aug 1829
Wm.	24	M		England	America	Two Marys	24 Sep 1827
KINNERSLEY, Alfred	1			London/London	New York	Venus	12 Apr 1821
Edwin	4			London/London	New York	Venus	12 Apr 1821
Frederick, Master	9			London/London	New York	Venus	12 Apr 1821
Henry	6			London/London	New York	Venus	12 Apr 1821
Mary Ann, Miss	11			London/London	New York	Venus	12 Apr 1821
Mary Ann, Mrs.	33			.../London	New York	Venus	12 Apr 1821
Thomas	55		Printer	Surrey/London	New York	Venus	12 Apr 1821
Thomas, Master	14			London/London	New York	Venus	12 Apr 1821
KINNEY, —, Mrs.	28	F		England	U. States	Milton	6 Dec 1825
Edward	25	M	Labourer	Ireland	U.S.	Lady Hunter	10 Jul 1826
Elizabeth	28	F		Gt. Britain		Dalhouse Castle	13 May 1828
James	5	M		Gt. Britain		Dalhouse Castle	13 May 1828
James	18	M	Carpenter	Ireland	U. States	Josephine	7 May 1827
James	40	M	Merchant	Ireland	America	Weser	26 Jun 1821
John	7	M		Gt. Britain		Dalhouse Castle	13 May 1828
Mary	18	F	Labourer	England	U. States	Ayrshire	12 May 1828
Pat	20	M	Labourer	England	U. States	Ayrshire	12 May 1828
KINNICK, Michl.	27	M	Mechanic	Ireland	United States	Wm. Byrnes	30 Apr 1828
KINNIER, Ellen	34	F	None	Ireland	Baltimore	Angelica	18 Aug 1823
George	8	M	None	Ireland	Baltimore	Angelica	18 Aug 1823
George	40	M	Shoe Maker	Ireland	Baltimore	Angelica	18 Aug 1823
KINNION, Mary	2	F		England	Philadelphia	Curler	7 Jul 1827
Michael	4	M		England	Philadelphia	Curler	7 Jul 1827
Sarah	30	F		England	Philadelphia	Curler	7 Jul 1827
Thomas	30	M	Labourer	England	Philadelphia	Curler	7 Jul 1827
KINNOCHAN, Jas.	33	M	Merchant	United States	United States	Cortes	11 Dec 1822
KINNY, Edwd. L.	31	M	in the Navy—Lieut.	U. States	U. States	Day	6 Feb 1822
Mary	17	F	...	Ireland	United States	Carolina Ann	24 Oct 1825
KINO, Felix	34		Farmer	Mexico	Mexico	Othello	6 Nov 1823
KINSEY, Ann	45	F		Great Britain	America	Lady Gallatin	21 Jun 1820
Betsey	6	F		Great Britain	America	Lady Gallatin	21 Jun 1820
Chas.	4	M		Great Britain	America	Lady Gallatin	21 Jun 1820

NAMES OF PASSENGERS	AGE	SEX	OCCUPATIONS	COUNTRY TO WHICH THEY BELONG	COUNTRY THEY INTEND TO INHABIT	SHIPS/DATES OF ARRIVAL	
KINSEY (cont'd)							
David	infant	M		Great Britain	America	Lady Gallatin	21 Jun 1820
Edward	8	M		Great Britain	America	Lady Gallatin	21 Jun 1820
Evan	10	M		Great Britain	America	Lady Gallatin	21 Jun 1820
Hannah	12	F		Great Britain	America	Lady Gallatin	21 Jun 1820
Jane	20	F		Great Britain	America	Lady Gallatin	21 Jun 1820
Lydia	16	F		Great Britain	America	Lady Gallatin	21 Jun 1820
Stephen	18	M		Great Britain	America	Lady Gallatin	21 Jun 1820
Thos.	46	M	Farmer	Great Britain	America	Lady Gallatin	21 Jun 1820
KINSILER, Jas.	40	M	Farmer	Ireland	America	Mary	29 May 1827
KINSLOW, John	29	M	Pedlar	Great Britain	United States	Ann Maria	23 Jan 1826
KINTERBOTTOM,							
Abraham	27 4/12	M		England	United States	Mobile	21 Aug 1827
KINTZE, A.	16	M	Gent	French	Switzerland	Charlemagne	19 Sep 1828
Ann	14	M	Gent	French	Switzerland	Charlemagne	19 Sep 1828
F.	6	M	Gent	French	Switzerland	Charlemagne	19 Sep 1828
H.	8	M	Gent	French	Switzerland	Charlemagne	19 Sep 1828
L.	12	M	Gent	French	Switzerland	Charlemagne	19 Sep 1828
M.	20	F	Gent	French	Switzerland	Charlemagne	19 Sep 1828
KINTZING, Abm.	28	M	Merchant	United States	United States	Hannibal	27 May 1822
KINULFF, Catharine	2	F		St. Croix	America	South Carolina Packet	2 Aug 1825
Rosamond	4	M		St. Croix	America	South Carolina Packet	2 Aug 1825
Susanna	23	F		St. Croix	America	South Carolina Packet	2 Aug 1825
KINWARD, —, Mr.	50	M	Gentleman	Antigua	Antigua	Margaret	29 Oct 1825
KIPP, L., Miss	20	F		U.S.A.		François I	19 Nov 1828
KIPPAX, Charlotte	26	F		England	U. States	Hudson	10 Nov 1825
Elizabeth	9	F		England	U. States	Hudson	10 Nov 1825
Emma	6	F		England	U. States	Hudson	10 Nov 1825
Maria	11	F		England	U. States	Hudson	10 Nov 1825
Maria	38	F		England	U. States	Hudson	10 Nov 1825
William	14	M		England	U. States	Hudson	10 Nov 1825
KIPPIN, Thos.	25	M	Merchant	U. States	U. States	Columbia	7 Sep 1827
KIRBY, Jas.	41	M	Comedian	England	U. States	Pacific	20 Aug 1825
John		M	Mercht.	U. States	U. States	David	19 Apr 1824
Thomas	26	M	Labourer	Gr. Britain		Moro Castle	6 Jul 1827
KIRCHENBAUER,							
Geo. Martin	38	M	Wheelwright	France	United States	New England	29 Aug 1828
KIRCHENBAUR,							
George Martin	6	M		France	United States	New England	29 Aug 1828
Juliana	4	F		France	United States	New England	29 Aug 1828
Krast	8	M		France	United States	New England	29 Aug 1828
Madalena	10	F		France	United States	New England	29 Aug 1828
KIRCHHOLTES,							
Fredk. H.	28	M	Gentleman	Holland	Holland	Hudson	21 Aug 1829
KIRCKHAM, Jas.	26			Ireland	U.S.	Hibernia	27 Jun 1821
KIRK, Agness	7	F	None	Ireland	U. States	Josephine	27 Jul 1825
Alexander	23	M	Weaver	Codoun	Drumballyrons	Aldebaron	21 Jan 1826
Andrew	24 2/12	M	Tailor	Ireland	America	Farmer	3 May 1824
Ann	36	F	Weaver	Ireland	United States	William Thompson	19 Aug 1829
Ann Jane	11	F		Ireland	United States	Meteor	27 Sep 1826
Anna	4	F		Ireland	United States	Meteor	27 Sep 1826
Benjn.	5	M	Child	Great Britain	United States	Meteor	15 Apr 1823
Betsey	16	F	None	United States	United States	Hope	13 Jun 1822
Catharine	9	F	None	Ireland	U. States	Josephine	27 Jul 1825
D.	27	M	Farmer	scotland	U. States	Criterion	15 Oct 1822
Edward	5	M		Ireland	United States	Meteor	27 Sep 1826
Elisabeth	11	F		England	New York	Cincinnatus	5 Dec 1825
Elisabeth	33	F		Great Britain	United States	Meteor	15 Apr 1823
Eliza	8	F		Ireland	United States	Meteor	27 Sep 1826
Eliza	28	F	Wife	Ireland	United States	Meteor	27 Sep 1826
Elizabeth	34	F				Lady of the Lake	23 Aug 1828
*left ship							
Geo.	1	M		England	New York	Cincinnatus	5 Dec 1825
George	11	M	None	Ireland	U. States	Josephine	27 Jul 1825

691

NAMES OF PASSENGERS	AGE	SEX	OCCUPATIONS	COUNTRY TO WHICH THEY BELONG	COUNTRY THEY INTEND TO INHABIT	SHIPS/DATES OF ARRIVAL
KIRK (cont'd)						
Hannah	1	F	None	Ireland	U. States	Josephine	27 Jul 1825
Hannah	6	F	Child	Great Britain	United States	Meteor	15 Apr 1823
Hariet	41	F		England	New York	Cincinnatus	5 Dec 1825
Henry	23	M	...	Great Britain	United States	Robert Fulton	18 May 1825
James	19	M	Turner	Ireland	United States	Fabius	31 Jul 1829
James	20	M	Taylor	Scotland	U. States	Roger Stewart	9 Jun 1828
Jno.	25	M		Ireland		Lady Hunter	12 Apr 1823
John	8	M	Child	Great Britain	United States	Meteor	15 Apr 1823
John	9	M		England	New York	Cincinnatus	5 Dec 1825
John	22	M	Farmer	Ireland	U. States	Josephine	27 Jul 1825
John	26	M	Baker	England	United States	Nancy	15 Mar 1820
John	26	M	Miller	England	United States	Manhattan	11 Oct 1824
Joseph	10	M	Child	Great Britain	United States	Meteor	15 Apr 1823
Joseph	22 6/12	M	B...	...	United States	Wade	29 Aug 1825
Lawerence	3	M		Ireland	U. States	Josephine	27 Jul 1825
Margaret	15	F	None	Ireland	U. States	Josephine	27 Jul 1825
Mary	2	F		Ireland	United States	Meteor	27 Sep 1826
Mary	3	F		England	New York	Cincinnatus	5 Dec 1825
Mary	24	F	None	Ireland	U. States	Josephine	27 Jul 1825
Mary	40	F	None	Ireland	U. States	Josephine	27 Jul 1825
Matilda	14	F		England	New York	Cincinnatus	5 Dec 1825
Patrick	26			Great Britain	United States	Ocean	27 Jul 1825
Peggy	18	F	Labourer	England	U. States	Comet	23 Aug 1828
Peter	20	M	Labourer	Ireland	U.States	Nancy	31 May 1823
Rebecca	64	F	Weaver	Ireland	United States	William Thompson	19 Aug 1829
Richard	34	M	Labourer	England	U. States	Ayrshire	12 May 1828
Thomas	22	M	Merchant	Great Britain	Great Britain	Meteor	17 Jan 1825
Thomas	28	M				Lady of the Lake	23 Aug 1828
*left ship						
William	18	M	Farmer	Ireland	U. States	Josephine	27 Jul 1825
William	22	M	Coachman	England	New York	Cincinnatus	5 Dec 1825
William	60	M	Porter	Scotland	United States	Camillus	7 Mar 1825
Wm.	24		Labourer			Splendid	14 Aug 1829
Wm.	30	M	Mechanic	United States	United States	Ann Maria	23 Oct 1820
KIRKAM, Elizabeth	18	F		England, Born in Barbadoes	U. States	Cannon	15 Jul 1822
*all the children have come under the care of Mrs. Fenwick for their education						
KIRKBY, Richard	32	M	Servant	U. States	Great Britain	Thompson	26 Apr 1828
Robert	30	M	Weaver	England	United States	Colossus	26 Aug 1828
KIRKHAM, Richard	21	M	Collegian	Ireland, G.B.	United States	Orozimbo	31 May 1824
Watson	25		Mason	Great Britain	United States	Camillus	12 Sep 1827
KIRKHOFER, John	50 4/12	M	Tailor	Switzerland	U.S. America	Edward	28 Oct 1825
Mary	20 3/12	F		Switzerland	U.S. America	Edward	28 Oct 1825
KIRKLAND, Alexr.		M	Merchant	U. States	U. States	Saml. Smith	8 Jul 1823
Charles	44	M	Weaver	Great Britain	United States	Magnet	19 Aug 1822
Elizabeth	39	F	Farmer	Great Britain	New York	Eliza Grant	29 Aug 1829
Mary	12	F	Farmer	Great Britain	New York	Eliza Grant	29 Aug 1829
Peter	25	M	Mason	England	U. States	Montgomery	18 Oct 1828
William	10	M	Farmer	Great Britain	New York	Eliza Grant	29 Aug 1829
KIRKLEY, James	19	M	Weaver	Royton	Royton	Howard Douglass	11 May 1827
KIRKMAN, —, Mrs.	30	F	his wife [L.]	England	United States	Ganges	20 Aug 1825
E.	9/12	F	Child	England	United States	Ganges	20 Aug 1825
Elizabeth	50	F	None	United States	United States	Pacific	24 Oct 1828
Henry	18	M	None	United States	United States	Pacific	24 Oct 1828
James	25	M	Gentleman	United States	United States	Pacific	24 Oct 1828
Jane	19	F	None	United States	United States	Pacific	24 Oct 1828
Jno.	8	M	Child	England	United States	Ganges	20 Aug 1825
John	25	M	Painter	England	America	Plutarch	18 Jul 1826
L.	30	M	Planter	England	United States	Ganges	20 Aug 1825
Mary	22	F		England	America	Plutarch	18 Jul 1826
Rhechel	13	F		England	America	Plutarch	18 Jul 1826
W.	3	M	Child	England	United States	Ganges	20 Aug 1825
KIRKPALICK, James	20	M	Farmer	Ireland	U. States	Dickinson	30 Jul 1825
Martha	30	F	Farmer	Ireland	U. States	Dickinson	30 Jul 1825
Thomas	60	M	Farmer	Ireland	U. States	Dickinson	30 Jul 1825

NAMES OF PASSENGERS	AGE	SEX	OCCUPATIONS	COUNTRY TO WHICH THEY BELONG	COUNTRY THEY INTEND TO INHABIT	SHIPS	DATES OF ARRIVAL
KIRK PATRICK, John	27	M	Carpenter	Ireland	United States	Wanderer	1 Aug 1828
KIRKPATRICK (see Rickpatrick)							
Bernard L.	30	M	Merchant	Roteland [Scotland?]	St. John, N.B.	Frances Miller	27 Jul 1827
J. B.	30	M	Merchant	U. States	U. States	Tuscaloosa	19 Mar 1827
James	26			England		Anacreon	7 Sep 1827
James	41	M	Farmer	Ireland	United States	William & George	14 May 1828
Jean	20	F	Spinner	Great Britain	United States	Grecian	24 Sep 1828
John	25	M				Imperial	19 Jul 1820
Rob.	30	M	Farmer	England	U. States	Frances Henrietta	19 Feb 1823
Robt.	26	M	Gentleman	England	Canada	Hercules	21 Nov 1822
Sarah	23	F		England	U. States	Frances Henrietta	19 Feb 1823
Thos.	24		Weaver	Ireland	United States	John Dickinson	28 Jun 1822
KIRKS, Elizabeth	35	F	Labourer	England	U. States	Ayrshire	12 May 1828
KIRKSHAW, James	21	M	Joiner	Kastor	Lancaster	Howard Douglass	11 May 1827
KIRKWOOD, Alex.	22		Weaver			Zamoa	5 Nov 1828
Ann	28	F	None	Scotland	United States	Mary & Susan	5 Aug 1828
Ann	65	F	None	Scotland	United States	Mary & Susan	5 Aug 1828
Christie	20	F	Mechanic	England	Great Britain	Manchester Packet	30 Nov 1822
James	23	M	Mechanic	England	Great Britain	Manchester Packet	30 Nov 1822
Jane	37	F	None	Scotland	United States	Mary & Susan	5 Aug 1828
Joseph	1	M	Mechanic	England	Great Britain	Manchester Packet	30 Nov 1822
Robert	30	M	Preacher	Scotland	United States	Mary & Susan	5 Aug 1828
KIRMAN, Mary	25	F	None	Ireland	America	Minerva	31 May 1824
KIRNEY, Jarvis	19	M	Clerk	Ireland	United States	Dublin Packet	22 Apr 1822
KIRPATRICK, Jane	21	F	Seamstress	Ireland	America	Caroline	25 Jul 1828
Mary	23	F	Seamstress	Ireland	America	Caroline	25 Jul 1828
KIRTLAND, Wm.	27	M	A.M.	Utica	U. States	Electra	4 Sep 1827
KISHSAW, David	22	M	Weaver	England	U. States	Thomas Ritchie	2 Jul 1827
KISSACK, Samuel	17	M	Gentn.	England	America	James Cropper	3 Mar 1825
Thos.	30	M	Farmer	Great Britain	United States	William Dawson	18 Jun 1827
KISSAM, D. W., Dr.	32	M	Doctor	U. States	U. States	Don Quixotte	17 Jan 1825
KISSECKE, John	24	M	Weaver	Great Britain	United States	Mount Vernon	20 May 1822
KISTER, Franscisse	38	F	Farmer	Alsace in the Department of Upper and lower Rhine	United States	Carolina Augusta	16 May 1828
George	11	M	Farmer	Alsace in the Department of Upper and lower Rhine	United States	Carolina Augusta	16 May 1828
George	36	M	Farmer	Alsace in the Department of Upper and lower Rhine	United States	Carolina Augusta	16 May 1828
KITCHEN, A.	6	F		Germany	United States	Lydia	18 Jun 1828
Andrew	34	M	Weaver	Great Britain	United States	Courier	13 Mar 1820
Edward	28	M	Joiner	England	United States	Trident	30 Sep 1826
Eh.	26	F		Great Brittain	U.S.	Trafalgar	22 Jun 1821
Hannah		F		Germany	United States	Lydia	18 Jun 1828
Jacob	54	M		Germany	United States	Lydia	18 Jun 1828
John	31	M		Germany	United States	Lydia	18 Jun 1828
Margt.	8	F		Germany	United States	Lydia	18 Jun 1828
Maria	30	F	Wife	England	United States	Trident	30 Sep 1826
Maria	30	F		Germany	United States	Lydia	18 Jun 1828
Robt.	36		Farmer	Wa...l...y, England	Great Britain	Franklin	22 Jun 1827
Samis	74	M	Physician	U. States	U. States	Marmion	7 Jun 1824
Walter	34	M	Weaver	Great Britain	United States	Courier	13 Mar 1820
KITCHERY, George	35	M	None	G. Bt.	G. Bt.	Canada	13 Oct 1825
KITCHING, George	22		Farmer	Yorkshire		Mount Vernon	18 Oct 1822

NAMES OF PASSENGERS	AGE	SEX	OCCUPATIONS	COUNTRY TO WHICH THEY BELONG	COUNTRY THEY INTEND TO INHABIT	SHIPS/DATES OF ARRIVAL	
KITCHING (cont'd)							
John	26		Maltster	Albany		Mount Vernon	18 Oct 1822
William	28		Merchant	New York		Mount Vernon	18 Oct 1822
KITE, Elizabeth	50	F		England	England	Criterion	29 May 1822
James	25	M	Gentn.	England	United States	Trio	2 Oct 1828
John	48	M		England	England	Criterion	29 May 1822
KITSON, Daniel	12	M	None	Great Britain	United States	Aurora	10 Nov 1827
Elizth.	10	F	None	Great Britain	United States	Aurora	10 Nov 1827
Hannah	4	F	None	Great Britain	United States	Aurora	10 Nov 1827
Harriet	2	F	None	Great Britain	United States	Aurora	10 Nov 1827
Joseph	14	M	None	Great Britain	United States	Aurora	10 Nov 1827
Rachel	8	F	None	Great Britain	United States	Aurora	10 Nov 1827
KITTERA, Jno. M.	24	M	Merchant	Philada.	U. States	Antelope	9 Sep 1822
Jno. M.	28	M	Merchant	Philada.	U. States	William Henry	29 Dec 1823
KITTERSEN,							
Jno. M., Supercargo	35	M	Merchant	U. States	U. States	Forrest	16 May 1821
KITTY, James	17	M	Laborer	Gt. Britain		Dalhouse Castle	13 May 1828
KLAFFER, Danick	36	M	Shoe Maker	United States	United States	Martha	30 Jun 1823
KLARNY, —, Miss	17	F		Great Brittain	United States	Sarah Ralston	27 Jan 1827
KLAUZANG,							
C. F. Wilhelm	20	M	Merchant	Holland	U. States	Harmony	6 Jan 1823
KLEAK, Christopher	26	M	Shoemaker	Germany	U. States	Isabella	10 Aug 1829
Margaret	6/12	F		Germany	U. States	Isabella	10 Aug 1829
Margaret	26	F		Germany	U. States	Isabella	10 Aug 1829
KLEG, Robt.	22	M	Labourer	Isle of Man		Ocean	13 Jul 1827
KLEIN, Daniel, kinder [child of Jacob]	16	M		Limbach	United States	Juffraw Johanna	16 Oct 1821
Frederic	21	M	Saddler	United States	United States	Globe	30 Aug 1828
Jacob	34	M	Boer	Limbach	United States	Juffraw Johanna	16 Oct 1821
Jacob, kinder [child of Jacob]	1	M		Limbach	United States	Juffraw Johanna	16 Oct 1821
Johanna, kinder [child of Jacob]	12	F		Limbach	United States	Juffraw Johanna	16 Oct 1821
Louisa, kinder [child of Jacob]	4	F		Limbach	United States	Juffraw Johanna	16 Oct 1821
Lutwich, kinder [child of Jacob]	7	M		Limbach	United States	Juffraw Johanna	16 Oct 1821
Susanna, kinder [child of Jacob]	10	F		Limbach	United States	Juffraw Johanna	16 Oct 1821
KLEINE, Elizabeth, Zyn Vrouw [his wife, Ludwich Mondinger]	47	F		Limbach	United States	Juffraw Johanna	16 Oct 1821
KLENIM, —, Mr.	30	M	Merchant	Germany	Germany	Electra	4 Sep 1827
KLEPER, Jean A.	27	M	Clerk	France		Pallas	14 Jun 1828
KLERGKIST, Edwd.	24		Merchant	Germany	U. States	Silvanus Jenkins	30 Nov 1827
KLEVENHOUSEN, A.	35	M	Mariner	Bremen	U. States	Jay	28 May 1822
KLIDENSTERN, F.	33	M	Weaver	Switzerland	U. States	La Urania	3 Jul 1828
KLIEN, A.	21	M	...	Germany	U. States	L. Emilie Marie	12 Jul 1820
KLIMPEAU, Adolph	22	M	Farmer	Lubec	U.S. America	Sereno	31 Jul 1826
KLINE, Elenor	3 6/12	F	Farmer	France	U.S.	Cadmus	9 Dec 1826
Eve	23	F	Farmer	France	U.S.	Cadmus	9 Dec 1826
Henry	8/12	M	Farmer	France	U.S.	Cadmus	9 Dec 1826
John	28	M	Farmer	Ireland	America	William	21 May 1825
M.	19	M		Switzerland	U. States	La Urania	3 Jul 1828
Margaret						Olympia	12 Aug 1828
*After having been at Sea a Number of Days was ascertaining the quantity of Baggage to report found the under mentioned persons had secreted themselves away notwithstanding our searach with the Gendearmes at the of leaving the port							
Nicholas	2 6/12	M	Farmer	France	U.S.	Cadmus	9 Dec 1826
Nicholas	28	M	Farmer	France	U.S.	Cadmus	9 Dec 1826
KLINGEL, Georg	36	M	Taylor	Baden	United States	Wade	29 Aug 1825
Joseph	3 6/12	M		Baden	United States	Wade	29 Aug 1825
Louis	11	M		Baden	United States	Wade	29 Aug 1825
Margaretha	6	F		Baden	United States	Wade	29 Aug 1825
KLIPFEL, Elizabeth	9	F	there child [James & Elizabeth]	France	United States	Helen	5 Sep 1828

NAMES OF PASSENGERS	AGE	SEX	OCCUPATIONS	COUNTRY TO WHICH THEY BELONG	COUNTRY THEY INTEND TO INHABIT	SHIPS/DATES OF ARRIVAL	
KLIPFEL (cont'd)							
Elizabeth	36	F	his wife [James]	France	United States	Helen	5 Sep 1828
James	3	M	there child [James & Elizabeth]	France	United States	Helen	5 Sep 1828
James	36	M	Cooper	France	United States	Helen	5 Sep 1828
Louisa	4/12	F	there child [James & Elizabeth]	France	United States	Helen	5 Sep 1828
Magdelene	3	F	there child [James & Elizabeth]	France	United States	Helen	5 Sep 1828
Philip	5	M	there child [James & Elizabeth]	France	United States	Helen	5 Sep 1828
KLOPFANSTEIN, Ana	5	F	Farmer	France	United States	Elizabeth	27 Jul 1824
Barbara	11	F	Farmer	France	United States	Elizabeth	27 Jul 1824
Catharina	9	F	Farmer	France	United States	Elizabeth	27 Jul 1824
Catharina	36	F	Farmer	France	United States	Elizabeth	27 Jul 1824
Christian	4	M	Farmer	France	United States	Elizabeth	27 Jul 1824
Christian	36	M	Farmer	France	United States	Elizabeth	27 Jul 1824
Joseph	1	M	Farmer	France	United States	Elizabeth	27 Jul 1824
Maria	7	F	Farmer	France	United States	Elizabeth	27 Jul 1824
Peter	12	M	Farmer	France	United States	Elizabeth	27 Jul 1824
KLOPFENSTEIN,							
Barbara	3	F	Farmer	France	U. States	Lewis	6 Jul 1825
Barbara	20		Weaver	France	U. States	Elizabeth	9 Jul 1825
Barbary	35	F	Farmer	France	U. States	Lewis	6 Jul 1825
Barbary	48		Weaver	France	U. States	Elizabeth	9 Jul 1825
C.	40	M	Farmer	France	U. States	Lewis	6 Jul 1825
Henry	18	M	Farmer	France	U. States	Lewis	6 Jul 1825
Margt.	16	F	Farmer	France	U. States	Lewis	6 Jul 1825
Maria	18		Weaver	France	U. States	Elizabeth	9 Jul 1825
Peter	12	M	Farmer	France	U. States	Lewis	6 Jul 1825
Peter	45		Weaver	France	U. States	Elizabeth	9 Jul 1825
Susan	1	F	Farmer	France	U. States	Lewis	6 Jul 1825
Wm.	10	M	Farmer	France	U. States	Lewis	6 Jul 1825
P.	25	M	Baker	Germany	U. States	Edward Bonaffe	11 Dec 1827
KLOTZ, George Fredrik	24	M	Farmer	Wortenberg	Lancaster	Louisa	6 Oct 1828
KLUMPP, Francois	24	M	Taylor	Swizerland		Antioch	18 Aug 1829
KNAB, Simon	4	M		France	United States	New England	29 Aug 1828
KNABELE, Andrew	28	M	Labourer	Prussia		Constitution	20 Jun 1828
KNACHT, Adam	3	M				Golden Grove	6 Sep 1820
Catherine	33	F				Golden Grove	6 Sep 1820
Charles	9	M				Golden Grove	6 Sep 1820
Charles W.	33	M	Farmer			Golden Grove	6 Sep 1820
KNACKWOUST, G. F.	25	M	Merchant	Holland	Holland	James Cropper	29 Nov 1827
KNAPP, Charles	24	M	Ship Master	New York	America	South Carolina Packet	2 Aug 1825
Charles W.	25	M	Ship Master	United States		Sea Gull	27 Mar 1827
Thos.	40	M	Merchant	Aux Cayes	U. States	Milo	7 Jul 1823
William	20			...	...	Hudson	14 Jun 1827
KNEA, Harmon	25		Sugar Baker	Hanovurine	United States	Hudson	5 Apr 1826
KNEAL, —, Mrs.	21	F		Isle of Man	United States	Lunar	5 May 1828
Ann	3 3/12	F		Isle of Man	United States	Lunar	5 May 1828
Thomas	31	M	Joiner	Isle of Man	United States	Lunar	5 May 1828
KNEALE, Christn.	8	M	None	Isle of Man		Ocean	13 Jul 1827
Jane	21	F		England	U. States	Birmingham	16 Jun 1828
John	13	M	None	Isle of Man		Ocean	13 Jul 1827
Margt.	15	F	None	Isle of Man		Ocean	13 Jul 1827
Margt.	45	F	None	Isle of Man		Ocean	13 Jul 1827
Thos.	11	M	None	Isle of Man		Ocean	13 Jul 1827
Wm.	17	M	Joiner	Isle of Man		Ocean	13 Jul 1827
Wm.	42	M	Joiner	Isle of Man		Ocean	13 Jul 1827
KNEALL, Elinor	48	F		England	U. States	Birmingham	16 Jun 1828
John	36	M	Mechanic	England	U. States	Birmingham	16 Jun 1828
Thomas	44	M	Mechanic	England	U. States	Birmingham	16 Jun 1828
KNEELAND, Chas.	19	M	Gentleman	New York	New York	York	2 Dec 1828
Henry	20	M	Merchant	U. States	U. States	Don Quixotte	27 Jun 1827

NAMES OF PASSENGERS	AGE	SEX	OCCUPATIONS	COUNTRY TO WHICH THEY BELONG	COUNTRY THEY INTEND TO INHABIT	SHIPS/DATES OF ARRIVAL	
KNEEN, Jane	1 1/2	F		Isle of Man	America	Plutarch	18 Jul 1826
John	4	M		Isle of Man	America	Plutarch	18 Jul 1826
Mary	6	F		Isle of Man	America	Plutarch	18 Jul 1826
Mary	36	F		Isle of Man	America	Plutarch	18 Jul 1826
William	8	M		Isle of Man	America	Plutarch	18 Jul 1826
William	39	M	Labourer	Isle of Man	America	Plutarch	18 Jul 1826
KNEEN..., Anne	30	F	Wife	..., ..., Ireland	U. States	New Orleans	24 Aug 1827
Cathe.	8	F	Child	..., ..., Ireland	U. States	New Orleans	24 Aug 1827
Maria	12	F	Child	..., ..., Ireland	U. States	New Orleans	24 Aug 1827
Sophia	6	F	Child	..., ..., Ireland	U. States	New Orleans	24 Aug 1827
Susan	3	F	Child	..., ..., Ireland	U. States	New Orleans	24 Aug 1827
Wm.	1	M	Child	..., ..., Ireland	U. States	New Orleans	24 Aug 1827
Wm.	30	M	Farmer	..., ..., Ireland	U. States	New Orleans	24 Aug 1827
KNICK, Henry	23	M	Officer	England	U. States	Hiram	17 Jun 1826
KNIDEL, James	36	M	...	England	...lane	Colossus	2 Oct 1827
KNIES, Sebastian	23	M	Baker			New York Packet	19 Aug 1820
KNIFFER, George	42	M	Butcher			Golden Grove	6 Sep 1820
KNIGHT, —, Mrs.	30	F	Planter	U.S.	U.S.	New England	11 Jul 1827
Abraham	7	M				Robert Edwards	8 Nov 1825
Alexander	24	M	Slater	Great Britain	United States	Elizabeth & Mary	20 Mar 1828
Alfred	6	M	Child	England	U. States	Cincinnatus	24 May 1821
Ann	4	F		U.S.	U.S.	New England	11 Jul 1827
Anne	6	F	Farmer	Great Britain	Canada	Orozimbo	31 May 1824
Aphar	27	F		U.S.A.	U.S.A.	Reindeer	22 Aug 1827
Caroline	14	F		England	U. States	Criterion at London	10 May 1821
Daniel	45	M	Mariner	U. States	United States	Pionier	4 Mar 1828
Edward	19	M	Gentleman	Ireland	U. States	Dublin	21 Feb 1824
Edwd.	24	M	Gentn.	England	New York	Brighton	16 Nov 1826
Elizabeth	6	F				Hercules	25 Sep 1820
Elizabeth	34	F	Farmer	Great Britain	Canada	Orozimbo	31 May 1824
Emma	3	F		England	U. States	Cincinnatus	24 May 1821
Enoch	18	M	Boy	England		Boyer	9 May 1825
Faustin	5	M		England	U. States	Criterion at London	10 May 1821
Foster	10		Boy	England	United States	Acasta	16 Aug 1826
Geo.	52	M	Merchant	U. States	U. States	Trimmer	21 Jul 1825
George	30	M	Merchant	U. States	U. States	Dromo	27 Sep 1826
Hanah	50	F				Robert Edwards	8 Nov 1825
Henry W.	23	M	Merchant	England	United States	Florida	14 Sep 1827
Hester	48	F		England	U. States	Criterion at London	10 May 1821
Humphrey S.	20	M	Mercht.	Germany	Germany	Pacific	24 Oct 1828
Isaac	17	M	None	United States	United States	Trent	1 Oct 1823
James	6	M		England	U. States	Criterion at London	10 May 1821
James	10	M	None	England	United States	Brighton	11 Mar 1825
James	21	M	Gentleman	Ireland	U. States	Dublin	21 Feb 1824
James	32	M	Merchant	England	U. States	Cincinnatus	24 May 1821
James	43	M	Carpenter	England	Philadelphia	Thames	6 Oct 1820
James	45	M	Farmer	England	United States	Brighton	11 Mar 1825
Jessey	13	M				Robert Edwards	8 Nov 1825
Jno.	43	M	Planter	U.S.	U.S.	New England	11 Jul 1827
Joel	17	M				Robert Edwards	8 Nov 1825
John	20	M	Farmer	England	U. States	Criterion at London	10 May 1821
John	23	M	Servant	England	New York	Brighton	16 Nov 1826
John	25	M	Farmer	England	Upper Canada	Comet	6 Mar 1823
John B.	22	M	Merchant	U. States	U. States	Quill	26 Jun 1827
Lucinda	1	F		England	U. States	Cincinnatus	24 May 1821
Lucy	21	F				Robert Edwards	8 Nov 1825
*died 6 Oct in a decline							
Lucy	35	F	Lady	United States		Nancy	20 Sep 1821
Mary	21	F	Lady	England	New York	Brighton	16 Nov 1826
Rd. Walter	26 3/12	M	Callenderer	Great Britain	Pennsylvania	Venus	8 Sep 1820
Robert	2	M	Farmer	Great Britain	Canada	Orozimbo	31 May 1824

NAMES OF PASSENGERS	AGE	SEX	OCCUPATIONS	COUNTRY TO WHICH THEY BELONG	COUNTRY THEY INTEND TO INHABIT	SHIPS/DATES OF ARRIVAL	
KNIGHT (cont'd)							
Robert	18	M	Farmer	England	U. States	Criterion at London	10 May 1821
Saml.	30	M	Farmer	Great Britain	Canada	Orozimbo	31 May 1824
Sarah	30	F		England	U. States	Cincinnatus	24 May 1821
Simon	10	M				Robert Edwards	8 Nov 1825
Simon	47	M	Wheelwright			Robert Edwards	8 Nov 1825
Thos.	22	M	Farmer	Great Britain	United States	Mary & Harriet	3 Jul 1829
William	8	M	Farmer	Great Britain	Canada	Orozimbo	31 May 1824
William	12	M	Farmer	England	U. States	Criterion at London	10 May 1821
KNIGHTON, George	21 7/12	M	Mole Caste	Great Briton	United States	Mount Vernon	30 Dec 1828
Robt.	33	M	Baker	Great Britain		Casanda	5 Sep 1827
Saml.	7	M	None	Great Britain		Casanda	5 Sep 1827
Sarah	37	F	None	Great Britain		Casanda	5 Sep 1827
KNIVELLY, Henry	28	M	Planter	St. Croix	U. States	Chase	9 Aug 1827
KNOCK, Sarah	23	F		Nova Scotia	United States	McDonough	3 Nov 1823
Wm.	7/12	M		Nova Scotia	United States	McDonough	3 Nov 1823
KNOCKLER, H.	28	M		Germany		Apollo	11 Jun 1828
KNOLEY, Wm.	21	M	Tailor	Isle of Man		Ocean	13 Jul 1827
KNOPFF, Adam	20	M	Agriculturist	Germany	U.S.	Helen	3 May 1828
Anna	27	F	Agriculturist	Germany	U.S.	Helen	3 May 1828
Christiana	18	F	Agriculturist	Germany	U.S.	Helen	3 May 1828
Gadelaine	22	F	Agriculturist	Germany	U.S.	Helen	3 May 1828
Henry	11	M	Agriculturist	Germany	U.S.	Helen	3 May 1828
Henry	34	M	Agriculturist	Germany	U.S.	Helen	3 May 1828
Madalaine	7	F	Agriculturist	Germany	U.S.	Helen	3 May 1828
Margaret	5	F	Agriculturist	Germany	U.S.	Helen	3 May 1828
Michel	7	M	Agriculturist	Germany	U.S.	Helen	3 May 1828
Michel	27	M	Agriculturist	Germany	U.S.	Helen	3 May 1828
Peter	4	M	Agriculturist	Germany	U.S.	Helen	3 May 1828
Sarah	43	F	Agriculturist	Germany	U.S.	Helen	3 May 1828
KNOPP, Michl.	63	M	Farmer	Swiss	U. States	Montano	2 Sep 1828
KNORR, Chas.	23 2/12	M	Gentleman	Germany	U. States	Kanhawa	6 May 1828
KNOTT, Danl.	44	M	Weaver	Great Britain	United States	William Dawson	18 Jun 1827
James	55	M	Labourer	Mashton	U. States	Milton	21 May 1827
Ogden	23	M	Moulderer	Ashton	U. States	Milton	21 May 1827
W.	40	M	Mason	England	America	Two Marys	24 Sep 1827
KNOUD, Henry	28	M	Merchant	Hesler		Constitution	20 Jun 1828
KNOUT, Lewis	40	M	Merchant	Hanover	U. States	Perseverance	3 Aug 1822
KNOWL, Jane	20	F	Spinster	G. Britain	U. States	St. George	7 Jun 1828
KNOWLAN, Ann	25	F		Gt. Britain	United States	John & Elizabeth	25 Sep 1827
Elizabeth	13	F	None	England and Ireland	United States	Jubilee	12 May 1828
James	19	M	Labourer	England and Ireland	United States	Jubilee	12 May 1828
Jeremiah	52	M	Labourer	England and Ireland	United States	Jubilee	12 May 1828
Martha	12	F	None	England and Ireland	United States	Jubilee	12 May 1828
Mary	14	F	None	England and Ireland	United States	Jubilee	12 May 1828
Mary	50	F	None	England and Ireland	United States	Jubilee	12 May 1828
Michael	27	M	Laborer	Ireland	United States	Lord Wellington	14 Nov 1827
Sarah	18	F	None	England and Ireland	United States	Jubilee	12 May 1828
William	6	M	None	England and Ireland	United States	Jubilee	12 May 1828
KNOWLAND, —, Mrs.	42	F		Halifax	some to return & the others to Canada	Albert	14 May 1822
—, Rev. Mr.	50	M	Clergyman	Halifax	some to return & the others to Canada	Albert	14 May 1822
Emily	16	F		G. Britain	U. States	Armadello	22 Jun 1827
James	12	M		G. Britain	U. States	Armadello	22 Jun 1827
John	20	M		G. Britain	U. States	Armadello	22 Jun 1827

NAMES OF PASSENGERS	AGE	SEX	OCCUPATIONS	COUNTRY TO WHICH THEY BELONG	COUNTRY THEY INTEND TO INHABIT	SHIPS/DATES OF ARRIVAL	
KNOWLAND (cont'd)							
Mary	24	F	None	Great Britain	United States	Atlantic	28 May 1827
P.	9	M		Halifax	some to return & the others to Canada	Albert	14 May 1822
Rhoda	14	F		G. Britain	U. States	Armadello	22 Jun 1827
Richard	49	M	Farmer	G. Britain	U. States	Armadello	22 Jun 1827
Richard, Jr.	11	M		G. Britain	U. States	Armadello	22 Jun 1827
Sarah	6	F		G. Britain	U. States	Armadello	22 Jun 1827
Sarah	40	F		G. Britain	U. States	Armadello	22 Jun 1827
Susannah	11	F		G. Britain	U. States	Armadello	22 Jun 1827
KNOWLES, Ann Maria	26	F			New York	New York	31 Jul 1829
David	49	M	Weaver	England	America	Two Marys	24 Sep 1827
Elizth.	24	F		U. States	U. States	Eliza Jane	26 Oct 1829
George	6	M	None	England	United States	London	21 May 1828
J.	23	M	Carpenter	Gt. Britain	U. States	Camberwell	7 Apr 1828
John	16	M	Farmer	England	United States	London	21 May 1828
John A.	30	M	Mariner	America	America	Governor Von Schollen	7 Nov 1827
Mary	9	F	None	England	United States	London	21 May 1828
Mary	46	F	None	England	United States	London	21 May 1828
Norah	11	F	None	England	United States	London	21 May 1828
Seth, Mr.	42	M	Merchant	U.S.	U.S.	Cadmus	11 Jul 1827
Thomas	26	M	Labourer	G. Brittain	U.S. America	York	4 Aug 1826
William	13		Weaver	Cork	Philadelphia	Schuylkill	22 Aug 1825
William	26	M	Missionary		New York	New York	31 Jul 1829
Wm.	19	M		Scotland	United States	Concordia	25 Aug 1827
KNOX, Andrew	24	M	Farmer	Halifax	Great Britton	William	11 May 1821
Andrew	26	M	Weaver	G.B.	United States	Corinthian	29 Apr 1826
Ann	42	F		Great Britain	United States	Grecian	24 Sep 1828
E., Mrs.	20	F	Wife	G.B.	United States	Corinthian	29 Apr 1826
Ewd.	14			Great Britain	United States	Grecian	24 Sep 1828
Hugh	48	M	Farmer	Halifax	Great Britton	William	11 May 1821
Jane	48	F		Halifax	Great Britton	William	11 May 1821
Jas.	25	M	Laborer	Scotland	U. States	Czar	29 Aug 1829
John	7	M	Farmer	Halifax	Great Britton	William	11 May 1821
John	18		Laborer	Ireland	U. States	Robert Burns	18 Jun 1822
John	22	M	Weaver	G.B.	United States	Corinthian	29 Apr 1826
John	37 11/12	M	Minister of the Gospel	United States	United States	Four Sons	31 May 1828
Joseph	23	M	Weaver	G.B.	United States	Corinthian	29 Apr 1826
Margt.	12	F		Great Britain	United States	Grecian	24 Sep 1828
Robert	22	M	Weaver	Ireland	United States	Fabius	4 Jun 1828
Sarah, Miss	21	F	Lady	Halifax	U. States	Manchester	23 Jan 1826
Wm.	21	M	Farmer	Halifax	Great Britton	William	11 May 1821
Wm. J.	23	M	Gentleman	England	Great Britain	New York	22 Jul 1824
KOARK, Rose	19	F	None	Ireland	New York	America	1 Aug 1828
KOBBE, Henry	22	M	Labourer	Greenock, Mid [Parish], Renfrew [County]	New York	Hero	19 May 1828
*to look for Employment							
KOBLER, George	1	M	Farmer	France	France	Sully	15 Jul 1829
Madelina	8	F	Farmer	France	France	Sully	15 Jul 1829
Marie	35	F	Farmer	France	France	Sully	15 Jul 1829
Philip	33	M	Farmer	France	France	Sully	15 Jul 1829
KOCH, Caroline	4	F		Germany	Philadelphia	Falcon	21 Oct 1826
Gottleb	1	F		Germany	Philadelphia	Falcon	21 Oct 1826
John D.	29	M	Merchant	Brunwick	United States	Pioneer	28 Jun 1827
KOCHER, Elizabeth	39	F		Switzerland	America, U.N.S.	Great Britain	3 Aug 1829
Frederick	4	M		Switzerland	America, U.N.S.	Great Britain	3 Aug 1829
Jacob	8	M		Switzerland	America, U.N.S.	Great Britain	3 Aug 1829
John	11	M		Switzerland	America, U.N.S.	Great Britain	3 Aug 1829
Maria	1	F		Switzerland	America, U.N.S.	Great Britain	3 Aug 1829
Samuel	40	M	Wheelwright	Switzerland	America, U.N.S.	Great Britain	3 Aug 1829
KOCK,							
Christian Gottlob, Mr.	48 3/12	M	Farmer	Saxony	Saxony	Europa	12 Oct 1829
Patrick	36	M	Schoolmaster	Ireland	Ohio	Commerce	24 Sep 1823
KOCKHER, Bennis	60	M	Farmer	Switzerland	Ohio	Eugenie	20 Aug 1827

NAMES OF PASSENGERS	AGE	SEX	OCCUPATIONS	COUNTRY TO WHICH THEY BELONG	COUNTRY THEY INTEND TO INHABIT	SHIPS/DATES OF ARRIVAL	
KOCKHER (cont'd)							
Christian	9	F		Switzerland	Ohio	Eugenie	20 Aug 1827
Maria	13	F		Switzerland	Ohio	Eugenie	20 Aug 1827
Randolph	20	M		Switzerland	Ohio	Eugenie	20 Aug 1827
KODEN, Ann	35	F	None	Ireland	United States	Trident	18 Jul 1827
KOEBEL, Elizabeth	40	F	Farmer	Switzerland	United States	Olympia	12 Aug 1828
Martin	2	M	Farmer	Switzerland	United States	Olympia	12 Aug 1828
Martin	40	M	Farmer	Switzerland	United States	Olympia	12 Aug 1828
KOEBLY, Antoine	7	M	One Family [Joseph]	France	United States	Henri IV	2 Oct 1828
Cathrine	10	M	One Family [Joseph]	France	United States	Henri IV	2 Oct 1828
Geneveive	46	F	One Family [Joseph]	France	United States	Henri IV	2 Oct 1828
Jacques	4	M	One Family [Joseph]	France	United States	Henri IV	2 Oct 1828
John	19	F	One Family [Joseph]	France	United States	Henri IV	2 Oct 1828
Joseph	49	M	Carpenter	France	United States	Henri IV	2 Oct 1828
Madelaine	14	F	One Family [Joseph]	France	United States	Henri IV	2 Oct 1828
Maria	2	M	One Family [Joseph]	France	United States	Henri IV	2 Oct 1828
Michael	17	F	One Family [Joseph]	France	United States	Henri IV	2 Oct 1828
KOELE, Mary	40	M	Labourer	Ireland	U. States	Belville	5 Jul 1827
KOEN, Thos.	40	F		Great B.	U. States	William Neilson	26 Jul 1828
KOENING, George	20	M	Agriculturist	Germany	U.S.	Helen	3 May 1828
KOFLET, Angelique	6	F	Farmer	Swizerland		Antioch	18 Aug 1829
Antoine	3	M	Farmer	Swizerland		Antioch	18 Aug 1829
Carole	8	F	Farmer	Swizerland		Antioch	18 Aug 1829
Carole	40	F	Farmer	Swizerland		Antioch	18 Aug 1829
Eliza	5	F	Farmer	Swizerland		Antioch	18 Aug 1829
Frederick	40	M	Farmer	Swizerland		Antioch	18 Aug 1829
Jacob	16	M	Farmer	Swizerland		Antioch	18 Aug 1829
Veronique	10	F	Farmer	Swizerland		Antioch	18 Aug 1829
KOFMAN, Mary	16	F		Norfolk	U. States	Day	16 Aug 1826
KOHAELER, Andrew	28	M	Tailor	Baden		Constitution	20 Jun 1828
KOHAN, Bridget	25	F	Matron	Ireland	U. States	Courier	17 Mar 1828
KOHEN, Ann Maria	27	F		Switzerland	U.S.	Francois I	8 Aug 1829
KOHLER, Ann	22	F	Agriculture	Wirtemburg	United States	Henri IV	14 Oct 1829
G. F.	45	M	Skin dresser	Germany	U. States	Stephania	26 Apr 1824
George	3 6/12	M		Switzerland	America, U.N.S.	Great Britain	3 Aug 1829
Henri	7	M		Switzerland	America, U.N.S.	Great Britain	3 Aug 1829
Henri	34	M	Farmer	Switzerland	America, U.N.S.	Great Britain	3 Aug 1829
Henri	67	M	Farmer	France	America, U.N.S.	Great Britain	3 Aug 1829
Jacob	5 6/12	M		Switzerland	America, U.N.S.	Great Britain	3 Aug 1829
Madelina	1 6/12	F		Switzerland	America, U.N.S.	Great Britain	3 Aug 1829
Madelina	29	F		Switzerland	America, U.N.S.	Great Britain	3 Aug 1829
Magdelina	67	F		France	America, U.N.S.	Great Britain	3 Aug 1829
Michel	9	M		Switzerland	America, U.N.S.	Great Britain	3 Aug 1829
Peter	40	M	Joiner	France	America	Bayard	15 Dec 1828
Theos.	28	M	Farmer	Germany	United States	Helen	5 Sep 1828
KOHLHUND, Christian	5	M		Wertemberg	Wertemberg	Edward Quesnel	3 Jul 1829
Christina	11	F		Wertemberg	Wertemberg	Edward Quesnel	3 Jul 1829
Dorathia	46	F		Wertemberg	Wertemberg	Edward Quesnel	3 Jul 1829
Geo. J.	50	M	Potter	Wertemberg	Wertemberg	Edward Quesnel	3 Jul 1829
Matheus	9	M		Wertemberg	Wertemberg	Edward Quesnel	3 Jul 1829
William	13 6/12	M		Wertemberg	Wertemberg	Edward Quesnel	3 Jul 1829
KOHN, John H.	60	M	None	Halifax	England	Loire	7 Jun 1827
KOLER, George	23		Butcher	Germany	Germany	London	16 Aug 1824
KOLEREN, John	28	M	Tailor	Ireland	United States	Combine	4 Jun 1825
KOLLEN, Lewis	23	M	Merchant	U. States	U. States	Frances	22 May 1827
KOLLER, M.	62	M	Millwright	Germany	United States	Maria Theresa	28 Aug 1821
KOLLETT, J.	36	M	Merchant	U. States	U. States	Prudence	11 Jun 1825
KOLMAN, Catharine	...6	F	Wife	Great Britain	United States	Ann Maria	17 Apr 1827
Henry	37	M	Labourer	Great Britain	United States	Ann Maria	17 Apr 1827
KOMMER, John	26	M	Labourer	Ireland	United States	Robert Fulton	10 Aug 1827

NAMES OF PASSENGERS	AGE	SEX	OCCUPATIONS	COUNTRY TO WHICH THEY BELONG	COUNTRY THEY INTEND TO INHABIT	SHIPS/DATES OF ARRIVAL	
KONNICK, Hugh	19	M	Farmer	...than, ..., Ireland	Philadelphia	New Orleans	24 Aug 1827
Thomas	18	M	Farmer	...than, ..., Ireland	Philadelphia	New Orleans	24 Aug 1827
KONRAD, William	17	M	None	Great Britain	United States	George Clinton	27 Aug 1827
KONTSMAN, Frederick	32 7/12	M	Tanner	Germany	New York	Dawn	12 Jun 1826
KOOP, Anthony	47	M	Farmer	France	United States	Globe	30 Aug 1828
*landed at this Port, Custom House, Portland, Aug 19, 1828							
Anthony, Jur.	8	M		France	United States	Globe	30 Aug 1828
*landed at this Port, Custom House, Portland, Aug 19, 1828							
John	19	M	Laborer	Hannover	United States	Constitution	6 Jul 1829
Mary	44	F		France	United States	Globe	30 Aug 1828
*landed at this Port, Custom House, Portland, Aug 19, 1828							
KOOPER, S.	22	M	Merchant	America	America	Britannia	5 Nov 1828
KOPFENSTEIN, A., Mr.	43	M	Farmer	Switzerland		François I	19 Nov 1828
Abraham	12	M		Switzerland		François I	19 Nov 1828
Elisabetha	18	F		Switzerland		François I	19 Nov 1828
Johannes	9 6/12	M		Bavaria		François I	19 Nov 1828
KÖPLY, E.	21	M	Clerk	Guadaloupe		Alexander	18 Aug 1828
KOPPERTON, George	23	M	Farmer	England	...	America	25 Dec 1827
John	21	M	Butcher	England	...	America	25 Dec 1827
KOPT, Gulliame	58		Butcher	France	U. States	Parachute	14 May 1828
Louis	22			France	U. States	Parachute	14 May 1828
KORB, E.	25	F		Hamburg	U. States	Hope	18 Jun 1824
Jas.	3	M		Hamburg	U. States	Hope	18 Jun 1824
KORBELL, Jacob	29	M	Dyer	Switzerland	Switzerland	Edward Quesnel	3 Jul 1829
KORGAN, James	19	M	Labourer	Great Britain	U. States	Lady Hunter	26 Nov 1823
KORN, Friedrik	24	M	Farmer	Hamburg	United States	Maria Elizabeth	6 Jan 1823
KORNMILLER, Anna Maria	11	F		France	United States	New England	29 Aug 1828
Anna Maria	35	F		France	United States	New England	29 Aug 1828
Catarina	4	F		France	United States	New England	29 Aug 1828
Elizabeta	1	F		France	United States	New England	29 Aug 1828
Margaretta	5	F		France	United States	New England	29 Aug 1828
Martin	35	M	Tailor	France	United States	New England	29 Aug 1828
Michael	23	M	Tailor	France	United States	New England	29 Aug 1828
KORRNMILLER, Michael	32	M	Farmer	France	United States	New England	29 Aug 1828
KORT, Albert	20	M	Merchant	Germany		Ariel	24 Sep 1827
KORTRIGHT, Nicholas	62	M	Lieutenant in his Magisty's navy	England	United States	Robert Edwards	3 Oct 1829
KORTWRIGHT, —, Mr.	41	M	Merchant	St. Croix	St. Croix	Commerce	13 Nov 1823
—, Mrs.	32	F		St. Croix	St. Croix	Commerce	13 Nov 1823
KORY, John	21	M	Joiner	Scotland	United States	Tom	2 Jul 1827
KOTCH, Anna	25	F		U. States	U. States	Napolean	26 Sep 1828
Benjamin	50	M	Merchant	U.S. America	U.S. America	Cincinnatus	31 Oct 1820
Eliza	25	F	Spinster	U.S. America	U.S. America	Cincinnatus	31 Oct 1820
Francis	38	M	Merchant	U. States	U. States	Napolean	26 Sep 1828
Francis M.	6	M		U. States	U. States	Napolean	26 Sep 1828
KOTTMAN, J. D.	35	M	Merchant	Germany	America	Panthia	17 Sep 1821
KOVAN, Cathr.	22	F		U. States	U. States	United States	11 Sep 1828
KOVEL, Cathrina	4		One Family [George]	France	United States	Henri IV	2 Oct 1828
George	9	M	One Family [George]	France	United States	Henri IV	2 Oct 1828
George	39	M	Agriculturalist	France	United States	Henri IV	2 Oct 1828
Jack	8	M	One Family [George]	France	United States	Henri IV	2 Oct 1828
Madelaine	37	F	One Family [George]	France	United States	Henri IV	2 Oct 1828
Margretta	6	F	One Family [George]	France	United States	Henri IV	2 Oct 1828
KOVELL, John	36	M	Farmour	Trobotton	U.S. America	Camillus	10 Sep 1821
KOYLE, Ann	23	F		G. Britain	U. States	Camillus	8 Sep 1828
John	2	M		G. Britain	U. States	Camillus	8 Sep 1828
KRAFFTS, E. D.	35	M	...man	United States	United States	Silas Richards	27 Oct 1825
KRAFT, Antoine	4	M	Farmer	Germany	United States	Oxford	14 Aug 1828
Catherine	3	F	Farmer	Germany	United States	Oxford	14 Aug 1828
Derera	16	M	Merchant	France	United States	Ardelle	18 Jan 1828
Louis	6	M	Farmer	Germany	United States	Oxford	14 Aug 1828
Louis	40	M	Farmer	Germany	United States	Oxford	14 Aug 1828

NAMES OF PASSENGERS	A G E	S E X	OCCUPATIONS	COUNTRY TO WHICH THEY BELONG	COUNTRY THEY INTEND TO INHABIT	SHIPS/DATES OF ARRIVAL	
KRAFT (cont'd)							
Magdelain	10	F	Farmer	Germany	United States	Oxford	14 Aug 1828
Magdelaine	40	F	Farmer	Germany	United States	Oxford	14 Aug 1828
Marguerite	1	F	Farmer	Germany	United States	Oxford	14 Aug 1828
Marie	7	F	Farmer	Germany	United States	Oxford	14 Aug 1828
Mary	18	F		G. Britain	U. States	William Thompson	30 Apr 1822
Sophia	20	F		G. Britain	U. States	William Thompson	30 Apr 1822
KRAMER, Henry	34	M	Merchant	Germany	Pensylvania	James Noble	27 Aug 1827
Sibart	32	M	Clockmaker	Germany	U. States	Four Sons	30 Jul 1829
KRANESS, Fredk. Wilh.	21	M	Labourer	Germany	America	Falcon	28 Aug 1828
KRANIG,							
Christiana Catharina	22	F		Germany	U. States	Isabella	10 Aug 1829
Jacob	24	M	Shoemaker	Germany	U. States	Isabella	10 Aug 1829
KRAPES, Ann	26	F	Wife	Swiss	U. States	Comet	28 Jul 1825
Benedict	1	M	Son	Swiss	U. States	Comet	28 Jul 1825
Christian	7	M	Son	Swiss	U. States	Comet	28 Jul 1825
Christian	33	M	Farmer	Swiss	U. States	Comet	28 Jul 1825
Elisabeth	6	F	Daughter	Swiss	U. States	Comet	28 Jul 1825
John	5	M	Son	Swiss	U. States	Comet	28 Jul 1825
Mary	5	F	Daughter	Swiss	U. States	Comet	28 Jul 1825
KRATING, James H.	30	M	Merchant	Philada.	U. States	Fair Play	22 Feb 1823
KREBE, John	27	M	Farmer	Alsace in the Department of Upper and lower Rhine	United States	Carolina Augusta	16 May 1828
Joseph	1	M	Farmer	Alsace in the Department of Upper and lower Rhine	United States	Carolina Augusta	16 May 1828
Maria	28	F	Farmer	Alsace in the Department of Upper and lower Rhine	United States	Carolina Augusta	16 May 1828
Maria	40	F	Farmer	Alsace in the Department of Upper and lower Rhine	United States	Carolina Augusta	16 May 1828
KREBS, Catharine	48	F		Germany	Charlston	Cotton Plant	15 Nov 1823
Hannah	10	F		Germany	Charlston	Cotton Plant	15 Nov 1823
KREEALE, Wm.	50	M	Brickmaker	Isle of Man		Ocean	13 Jul 1827
KREHMER, G.	25		Secy Russian Legation	Russia		New York	18 Jul 1828
KREISS, Barbara	17		Farmer	France	U. States	Edward Quesnel	4 Aug 1828
Barbara	35		Farmer	France	U. States	Edward Quesnel	4 Aug 1828
Jacques	40		Farmer	France	U. States	Edward Quesnel	4 Aug 1828
Magdalina	15		Farmer	France	U. States	Edward Quesnel	4 Aug 1828
KRESGE, Mary	19	F	Agriculturist	France	U.S.	Helen	3 May 1828
KREUSER, Cristian	26	M	Weaver	Switzerland	America, U.N.S.	Great Britain	3 Aug 1829
John	18	M		Switzerland	America, U.N.S.	Great Britain	3 Aug 1829
KRI...I...DY, Thomas	26	M	...	Scotland	America	Nimrod	9 Jul 1827
KRIEG, George	12	M		Germany	United States	Samuel Robertson	8 Aug 1828
James	30	M	Labourer	Ireland	United States	Lord Wellington	28 May 1827
John	8	M		Germany	United States	Samuel Robertson	8 Aug 1828
John	44	M	Farmer	Germany	United States	Samuel Robertson	8 Aug 1828
Margaret	42	F		Germany	United States	Samuel Robertson	8 Aug 1828
Maria	18	F		Germany	United States	Samuel Robertson	8 Aug 1828
KRIEZER, Matthews	42	M	Farmer	Wortenberg	Lancaster	Louisa	6 Oct 1828
Vigina Margeratha	40	F	Farmer	Wortenberg	Lancaster	Louisa	6 Oct 1828
KRIGGLES, Abraham	40	M	Merchant	Great Britain	United States	Florida	2 Sep 1822
KRINDIG, Martin	22 4/12	M	Student in Bardstown's College	Switzerland	America	Henry	17 May 1828

NAMES OF PASSENGERS	AGE	SEX	OCCUPATIONS	COUNTRY TO WHICH THEY BELONG	COUNTRY THEY INTEND TO INHABIT	SHIPS/DATES OF ARRIVAL	
KRITZ, Cath.	6	F		Switzerland	U. States	La Urania	3 Jul 1828
Jean	9	F		Switzerland	U. States	La Urania	3 Jul 1828
Jean	46	F		Switzerland	U. States	La Urania	3 Jul 1828
Jos.	3	M		Switzerland	U. States	La Urania	3 Jul 1828
Maria Ann	11	F		Switzerland	U. States	La Urania	3 Jul 1828
Maria Ann	44	F		Switzerland	U. States	La Urania	3 Jul 1828
Marie	18	F		Switzerland	U. States	La Urania	3 Jul 1828
T.	17	F		Switzerland	U. States	La Urania	3 Jul 1828
KROAZENGER, Jacob	32	M	Taylor	Wittenburg	U. States	Comet	28 Jul 1825
Kitty	20	F	Wife	Wittenburg	U. States	Comet	28 Jul 1825
KROG, P. A.	27	M	Mariner	Denmark	U. States	Condor	22 Aug 1822
KROGH, Michl.	24	M	Labourer	Ireland	United States	Thomas	13 Dec 1827
KROK, G. E.	30	M	Merchant	Sweden	United States	India	8 Oct 1823
KROMILLER, Barbara	8	F		France	U. States	Edward Quesnel	4 Aug 1828
Barbara	34	F		France	U. States	Edward Quesnel	4 Aug 1828
Michael	2	M		France	U. States	Edward Quesnel	4 Aug 1828
Michael	35	M	Farmer	France	U. States	Edward Quesnel	4 Aug 1828
KRON, Francois J.	24	M	Professor of Languages	Prusia	U. States	Elizabeth	29 Sep 1823
M. Catharine	26	F		France	U. States	Elizabeth	29 Sep 1823
KRONCKER, Aug.	25	M	Merchant	United States		Montano	3 Jan 1823
KROOKEW, A.	25	M	Mariner	U. States	U. States	Doris	21 Jan 1826
KROPFS, Elisabeth	21	F		Germany	United States	Samuel Robertson	8 Aug 1828
Gotliff	1	M		Germany	United States	Samuel Robertson	8 Aug 1828
John	6	M		Germany	United States	Samuel Robertson	8 Aug 1828
John	41	M	Joiner	Germany	United States	Samuel Robertson	8 Aug 1828
KROSS, Harriott	3	F				James Monroe	8 Aug 1820
Joshua	19	M	Tailor			James Monroe	8 Aug 1820
Sarah	24	F	None			James Monroe	8 Aug 1820
Wm.	3	M				James Monroe	8 Aug 1820
KROUSSE, Henrietta	11	F		Danish	U. States	Mary & Nancy	7 Aug 1824
KROWAN, Patrick	25			Ireland	Philidelphia	General Marion	21 Nov 1828
KROWN, Jas. R.	27	M	Mercht.	U.S.	U.S.	Bruce	5 Jul 1827
KROZ, Christian	30	M	Farmer	Germany	U. States	Isabella	10 Aug 1829
Elizabeth	30	F		Germany	U. States	Isabella	10 Aug 1829
Jacob	2 6/12	M		Germany	U. States	Isabella	10 Aug 1829
Jean	1/12	M		Germany	U. States	Isabella	10 Aug 1829
KRUCKSHANKS, John	24	M	Clergyman	G. Britan	U. States	Dalmarnock	11 Dec 1828
KRUGAN, Barney	24	M	Labourer	Ireland	United States	Mary & Harriet	3 Jul 1829
KRUGER, George	21	M		New York	U. States	Maria Elizabeth	9 Jun 1826
KRUGLER, Ann M.	46		Farmer	France	U. States	Elizabeth	9 Jul 1825
Ann M.	63		Farmer	France	U. States	Elizabeth	9 Jul 1825
Annah	8		Farmer	France	U. States	Elizabeth	9 Jul 1825
Catharine	22		Farmer	France	U. States	Elizabeth	9 Jul 1825
Elizabeth	20		Farmer	France	U. States	Elizabeth	9 Jul 1825
John	57		Farmer	France	U. States	Elizabeth	9 Jul 1825
Madeline	16		Farmer	France	U. States	Elizabeth	9 Jul 1825
Maria	18		Farmer	France	U. States	Elizabeth	9 Jul 1825
KRUM, J. A.	40	M	Militaire	United States	United States	Columbia	16 Jan 1829
KU...A..., —	45	M	Fabricant	France	America	Henry	18 Oct 1826
KUCH, Anna Margareta	2	F		Germany	Philadelphia	Falcon	21 Oct 1826
F. Barbara	1	F		Germany	Philadelphia	Falcon	21 Oct 1826
Martha M.	6	M		Germany	Philadelphia	Falcon	21 Oct 1826
Martha M.	37	F		Germany	Philadelphia	Falcon	21 Oct 1826
Martin	8	M		Germany	Philadelphia	Falcon	21 Oct 1826
Michael	34	M	Farmer	Germany	Philadelphia	Falcon	21 Oct 1826
Michel	3	M		Germany	Philadelphia	Falcon	21 Oct 1826
KUDHIN, Elizabeth	50	F	None	England	New York	Brighton	29 Aug 1828
KUES, Saml.	32	M	Carpenter	Baltimore	U. States	Robt. Y. Hayne	27 Jun 1825
KUFFER, John	25	M	Labourer	Ireland		Marchioness	13 May 1828
KUGEL, Elizabeth	14	F	Taylor	Reikert	U.S. America	Superior	18 Jun 1825
Elizabeth	53	F	Taylor	Reikert	U.S. America	Superior	18 Jun 1825
Isaac M.	42	M	Taylor	Reikert	U.S. America	Superior	18 Jun 1825
Margaritte	16	F	Taylor	Reikert	U.S. America	Superior	18 Jun 1825
Sean S. A.	13	M	Taylor	Reikert	U.S. America	Superior	18 Jun 1825

NAMES OF PASSENGERS	AGE	SEX	OCCUPATIONS	COUNTRY TO WHICH THEY BELONG	COUNTRY THEY INTEND TO INHABIT	SHIPS/DATES OF ARRIVAL	
KUHM, Elizabeth	27	F		Germany	U. States	Isabella	10 Aug 1829
Jacob	1 6/12	M		Germany	U. States	Isabella	10 Aug 1829
Jane	2 6/12	F		Germany	U. States	Isabella	10 Aug 1829
Johannes	28	M	Farmer	Germany	U. States	Isabella	10 Aug 1829
Maria	6/12	F		Germany	U. States	Isabella	10 Aug 1829
KUHNER, Elizabeth	26	F	his Wife [John]	Germany	United States	Helen	5 Sep 1828
KUHNER, John	28	M	Farmer	Germany	United States	Helen	5 Sep 1828
KUIRSTON, Jasper	14	F		England	England	Venus	15 Apr 1822
KUKENMUTH, J.	30	M	Merchant	Hesler		Constitution	20 Jun 1828
KULIN, Barbara	16 10/12	F		France	United States	Charles Carroll	16 Jan 1829
Barbara	49 4/12	F		France	United States	Charles Carroll	16 Jan 1829
George	18 2/12	M		France	United States	Charles Carroll	16 Jan 1829
Henry	9 6/12	M		France	United States	Charles Carroll	16 Jan 1829
Henry	49 8/12	M	Farmer	France	United States	Charles Carroll	16 Jan 1829
KUMFORMAN, Jean	26	F		France		Pallas	14 Jun 1828
KUNAHAN, David	24	M	Farmer	Antrim	United States	Carolina Ann	11 Jun 1824
KUNAN, Hugh	24	M	Taylor	Ireland	United States	Catharine	22 Jul 1825
KUNBY, Sebastian	32	M	Baker	Germany	New York	Isabella	15 Sep 1828
KUNE, Gonfred	31	M	Farmer	Switzerland	U.S.	Francois I	8 Aug 1829
KUNEMANN,							
Catherine	5 1/12	F	Mechanic	Switzerland	United States	France	6 Oct 1828
Catherine	51 4/12	F	Mechanic	Switzerland	United States	France	6 Oct 1828
David	7 3/12	M	Mechanic	Switzerland	United States	France	6 Oct 1828
Enos	9 2/12	M	Mechanic	Switzerland	United States	France	6 Oct 1828
Joseph	17 5/12	M	Mechanic	Switzerland	United States	France	6 Oct 1828
Nicholas	53 7/12	M	Mechanic	Switzerland	United States	France	6 Oct 1828
KUNFRIND, Elizabeth	32	F		Baden	United States	Wade	29 Aug 1825
KUNIGER, Bridget	20	F	Servant	Ireland	America	Carolina Ann	7 Aug 1826
KUNLY, Christine	23	F	Taylor	Switzerland	U. States	Romulus	24 Sep 1828
Elizabeth	9	F	Taylor	Switzerland	U. States	Romulus	24 Sep 1828
Louis	31	M	Taylor	Switzerland	U. States	Romulus	24 Sep 1828
Margaret	11	F	Taylor	Switzerland	U. States	Romulus	24 Sep 1828
KUNNELASSE, H.	30	M	Merchant	Germany	U. States	Ranger	2 Jul 1827
KUNTZ, Ellen	32	F	Lady	United States	United States	New Packet	20 Oct 1827
Eve	50	F		France	U. States	Edward Quesnel	4 Aug 1828
George	30	M		France	U. States	Edward Quesnel	4 Aug 1828
George	47	M	Farmer	France	U. States	Edward Quesnel	4 Aug 1828
Micheal	18	M		France	U. States	Edward Quesnel	4 Aug 1828
KUNTZE, John G.	32	M	Weaver	Saxony	United States	Howard	6 Jul 1829
KUPHEL, Ruphel	20	M	Labourer	G. Britain	U. States	London	23 Sep 1828
KURINTZTEN, Jaques	8	M		France		Pallas	14 Jun 1828
Jaques F.	40	M	Farmer	France		Pallas	14 Jun 1828
Suzan	39	M		France		Pallas	14 Jun 1828
KURKINS, Partrick	28		Labourer	England	United States	Mary	15 Jul 1822
KURST, Arthur	27	M	Merchant	Great Britian	United States	Orbit	31 Dec 1821
KURTZ, Daniel L.	36	M	Ship Master	U. States	U. States	Sultana	6 Nov 1828
Margaretha	30	F	...	Wirtemburg	United States	Wade	29 Aug 1825
KURZ, Ana	1	F		Switzerland	United States	Elizabeth	27 Jul 1824
Barbara	5	F		Switzerland	United States	Elizabeth	27 Jul 1824
Dorathea	35	F	Taylor	Switzerland	United States	Elizabeth	27 Jul 1824
Elizabeth	3	F		Switzerland	United States	Elizabeth	27 Jul 1824
Johanes	42	M	Taylor	Switzerland	United States	Elizabeth	27 Jul 1824
KÜSTNER, A.	18	M	Merchant	Saxony	U.S.	Edward Quesnel	31 Jul 1827
H.	49	M	Merchant	Saxony	U.S.	Edward Quesnel	31 Jul 1827
KUSTSCHER,							
Margareta Barbara,							
kind [child of Frederik]		F		Amsterdam	United States	Juffraw Johanna	16 Oct 1821
KUTCH, John	32	M	Mert.	Boston	America	Mary	2 Oct 1820
KUTSCHER, Frederik	58	M	Boer	Hogtorf	United States	Juffraw Johanna	16 Oct 1821
Maria, Zyn Vrouw							
(his wife [Frederik])	40	F		Zweyberdinge	United States	Juffraw Johanna	16 Oct 1821
KUTTALL, Ann	47	F	None	England	United States	Aurelia	7 Jun 1826
Thomas	47	M	Slator	England	United States	Aurelia	7 Jun 1826
KUYPERS, —, Mrs.	45	F	Lady	Spain	U. States	Vigilant	14 Apr 1823
KWALE, Hugh	30	M	Wheelwright	Great Britain	United States	George Clinton	27 Aug 1827
Margaret	2	F	None	Great Britain	United States	George Clinton	27 Aug 1827
Mary	25	F	None	Great Britain	United States	George Clinton	27 Aug 1827
KYARS, William	26 10/12	M	Labourer	Ireland	United States	Bethlehem	18 Oct 1828
KYDER, Chariela	22	F		New York	New Jersey	Loire	11 Jun 1824

NAMES OF PASSENGERS	A G E	S E X	OCCUPATIONS	COUNTRY TO WHICH THEY BELONG	COUNTRY THEY INTEND TO INHABIT	SHIPS/DATES OF ARRIVAL	
KYLE, Alexr.	24	M	Weaver	Ireland	United States	General Marion	20 Aug 1828
David, Jr.	29	M	Merchant	Virginia	Virginia	New York	31 Jul 1829
Eliza	6	F		Ireland	United States	Romulus	24 Jun 1826
Elizabeth	22	F		Ireland	United States	General Marion	20 Aug 1828
Elizabeth	28	F		Virginia	Virginia	New York	31 Jul 1829
Francis	26	M	Yeoman	Ireland	United States	Borneo	9 Jul 1827
Geo.	30	M	Labourer			Hanford	17 Jul 1828
Hannah	20	F	Spinster			Commerce	22 Jun 1825
John	1	M		Ireland	United States	Romulus	24 Jun 1826
John	24	M	Yeoman	Ireland	United States	Borneo	9 Jul 1827
John	30	M	Weaver	Ireland	United States	Romulus	24 Jun 1826
L.	36	M	Farmer	N. Brunswick	New Brunswick	Abigale	9 Aug 1821
Margaret	4	F		Ireland	United States	Romulus	24 Jun 1826
Margt.	1 6/12	F	Spinster			Hanford	17 Jul 1828
Margt.	32	F				Hanford	17 Jul 1828
Mary	28	F		Ireland	United States	Romulus	24 Jun 1826
Sarah	20	F	Spinster			Hanford	17 Jul 1828
KYLES, Amee	24	F	Servant	Ireland	America	Weser	26 Jan 1821
KYNN, Crezane	1 6/12	F		Switzerland	America, U.N.S.	Great Britain	3 Aug 1829
Cristiana	6 2/12	F		Switzerland	America, U.N.S.	Great Britain	3 Aug 1829
Elizabeth	30	F		Switzerland	America, U.N.S.	Great Britain	3 Aug 1829
Johphin	3	F		Switzerland	America, U.N.S.	Great Britain	3 Aug 1829
Joseph	13	M		Switzerland	America, U.N.S.	Great Britain	3 Aug 1829
Joseph	48	M	Farmer	Switzerland	America, U.N.S.	Great Britain	3 Aug 1829
Lew	7 1/12	M		Switzerland	America, U.N.S.	Great Britain	3 Aug 1829
KYSER, Elizabeth	24	F	Maid Servant	Germany	United States	Helen	5 Sep 1828
L..., David	25	M	Labourer	Scotland	U. States	Sceptre	24 Jul 1822
Henry	20	M	Servant	Ireland	United States	Magnet	16 May 1823
J...s	...	...	...	...	...	William Thompson	30 Sep 1824
James	...	...	...	...	...	William Thompson	30 Sep 1824
Jane	25	F	Labourer	Ireland	United States	Meteor	26 Jun 1827
Sara	50	F		N. York	U. States	Nancy	29 Nov 1821
L...B...LL, Wm.	45	M	Gentleman	United States	United States	Britannia	29 Oct 1829
L...G, John	28	M	B...		U. States	Margaret	3 Jun 1822
L...LEY, Jno. James	43	M	...	...	Canada	Martha	22 Jul 1820
L...VILLA, Jose	45	M	None	Spain	U. States	Brown	7 Jul 1826
L..ON, H...or	28	M	Labourer	Ireland	United States	Meteor	26 Jun 1827
L'EGLE, George	45	M	Tailor	France		Henri IV	17 May 1828
Piere	12	M				Henri IV	17 May 1828
L'HOMME, —, Abbé	33	M	Priest	U.S.	U.S.	Edward Quesnel	31 Jul 1827
L'PEU, Robert	23	M	Gentleman	Great Britain	U. States	Lord Wellington	17 Mar 1823
LA..., Edward	27	M	Sailler	England	America	Comet	26 Jun 1822
Joseph	26	M	Merchant	Great Britain	U. States	Hector	11 Oct 1824
LA...IE, Ann	45	F		Ireland	U.S.	Oliver Wolcott	3 Nov 1827
LABADIER, —, Mr.	30	M	Merchant	U. States	U. States	Imperial	10 Dec 1821
—, Mrs.	18	F	Lady	U. States	U. States	Imperial	10 Dec 1821
Eliza	16	F	Servant	U. States	U. States	Imperial	10 Dec 1821
Manuel	18	M	Servant	U. States	U. States	Imperial	10 Dec 1821
Saml.	15	M	Servant	U. States	U. States	Imperial	10 Dec 1821
LABAGH, Abraham J.	22 11/12	M	Clergyman	United States	United States	Bellona	2 Jul 1828
LA BALLON, M.	14	F	None	U. States	U. States	Ardell	7 Jul 1827
T.	16	F	None	U. States	U. States	Ardell	7 Jul 1827
LABALMONDIERE, George	22	M	Gentleman	England	England	Jupiter	4 Aug 1829
LABAN, Ls.	53	M	Merchant	France	Newyork	Maria Theresa	16 Nov 1820
LA BANISSE, J. P.	20	M	Merchant	U.S. America	U.S. America	Claudio	22 Mar 1828
LABANURE, Felix	14	M	Mercht.	France	United States	Bayard	13 Nov 1823
LA BARBE, J.	32	M	Merchant	U. States	U. States	Edward Quesnel	15 May 1826
LABARINE, Jais.	28	M	Merchant	France	New York	Maria Theresa	16 Nov 1820
LABARRE, Jean Piere	29 6/12	M	Tanner	France	France	Edward Bonnaffe	13 Mar 1826
LABATER, J.	25	M	Servant	Switzerland	Boston	Howard	26 Aug 1823
LABATS, J. A.	35	M	Merchant	Portugal	U. States	Daphne	31 Aug 1822
LABB, J.	33	M	Blacksmith	Vera Cruz	U. States	Eliza	11 Apr 1826
LABBE, Francis C.	38	M	Professor	U. States	U. States	Elizabeth	20 Sep 1822
LABEAU, Jno., Don	26	M		U. States	U. States, Spain	Amos Palmer	9 Sep 1828

704

NAMES OF PASSENGERS	AGE	SEX	OCCUPATIONS	COUNTRY TO WHICH THEY BELONG	COUNTRY THEY INTEND TO INHABIT	SHIPS/DATES OF ARRIVAL	
LABERT, Jean Piere	38	M	Merchant	Bayonne	Trewilling	Richmond	2 May 1828
LABORDE, John	28	M		France	United States	Henri IV	2 Oct 1828
P.	29	M	Merchant	France	U. States	Elizabeth Malvina	6 Dec 1827
LABOUBE, Catherine	37	F		France	U. States	Edward Quesnel	4 Aug 1828
Joseph	4	M		France	U. States	Edward Quesnel	4 Aug 1828
Joseph	31	M	Labourer	France	U. States	Edward Quesnel	4 Aug 1828
Mary Ann	2	F		France	U. States	Edward Quesnel	4 Aug 1828
LABOUBERE, C.	27	M	Merchant	France	France	Perry	3 Jul 1827
LABOUCHE, Desire	28	F		England	U. States	Marmion	29 Sep 1823
LABOUCHERE, S. A.	20		Merchant	France	France	Silvanus Jenkins	30 Nov 1827
LABOURCHE, Henry	26	M	Gentleman	England	Great Britain	New York	22 Jul 1824
LA BOURDELE, Lewis	50	M	Doctor	France	U. States	Purrington	14 May 1827
LABOUROIS, Francis	34	M	Gardner	France		Pallas	14 Jun 1828
Joseph	46	M		France		Pallas	14 Jun 1828
LABOURSSE, John P.	20		Mercht.	U. States	New York	Director	11 Dec 1827
LABOUSE, Ann	3	F		Germany	United States	Samuel Robertson	8 Aug 1828
Ann	25	F		Germany	United States	Samuel Robertson	8 Aug 1828
Antony	21	M		Germany	United States	Samuel Robertson	8 Aug 1828
Ephraim	28	M	Farmer	Germany	United States	Samuel Robertson	8 Aug 1828
Francis	1 6/12	M		Germany	United States	Samuel Robertson	8 Aug 1828
George	32	M	Farmer	Germany	United States	Samuel Robertson	8 Aug 1828
Mareon	9	F		Germany	United States	Samuel Robertson	8 Aug 1828
Mareon	37	F		Germany	United States	Samuel Robertson	8 Aug 1828
Maria	5	F		Germany	United States	Samuel Robertson	8 Aug 1828
Moses	2	M		Germany	United States	Samuel Robertson	8 Aug 1828
Moses	2	M		Germany	United States	Samuel Robertson	8 Aug 1828
Seraphem	7	F		Germany	United States	Samuel Robertson	8 Aug 1828
LA BRANCHE, ...	28		Merchant	N. Orleans	N. Orleans	James Cropper	12 Jul 1822
A.	58		Merchant	N. Orleans	New Orleans	James Cropper	12 Jul 1822
LABRINEAR, G. M.	32	M	Merchant	Holland	Holland	Superb	18 Oct 1821
LABRO, Antoine	76	M	Merchant	France	Georgia	Cadmus	17 Apr 1823
LABROCETTE, Jose	50	M	Merchant	Spain	Spain	Virginia	8 Mar 1828
LABUNAN, A.			Servant			Dromo	14 Aug 1829
LABURTON, Alexander	65	M	Merchant	United States	United States	Enterprize	28 Aug 1828
LABY, Edward	25	M	Tailor		New York	Governor Clinton	3 Jul 1827
LABZELE, Jane	27	F	...	Ireland	U. States	Atlantic	19 Aug 1825
Mary S.	5	F	...	Ireland	U. States	Atlantic	19 Aug 1825
Saml.	3	M	...	Ireland	U. States	Atlantic	19 Aug 1825
Thos.	27	M	...	Ireland	U. States	Atlantic	19 Aug 1825
LACAY, James	45	M	Trader	Great Britain	United States	Thomas Dickason	31 Jul 1829
LACE, Betty	1	F	None	Isle of Man		Ocean	13 Jul 1827
Bridget	2			Ireland		Anacreon	7 Sep 1827
Cathe.	12	F	None	Isle of Man		Ocean	13 Jul 1827
Chas.	3	M	None	Isle of Man		Ocean	13 Jul 1827
Eliza	1/2	F	None	Great Brittan	U.S.	Emulous	29 Jun 1827
James	15	M		Ireland	United States	John Dickinson	18 Feb 1822
Jane	5	F	None	Isle of Man		Ocean	13 Jul 1827
Jno.	35			England		Anacreon	7 Sep 1827
John	4	M	None	Isle of Man		Ocean	13 Jul 1827
John	20	M	Smith	Isle of Man		Ocean	13 Jul 1827
Joseph	4	M	None	Great Brittan	U.S.	Emulous	29 Jun 1827
Margt.	3	F	None	Isle of Man		Ocean	13 Jul 1827
Margt.	4			Ireland		Anacreon	7 Sep 1827
Nancy	1	F	None	Isle of Man		Ocean	13 Jul 1827

NAMES OF PASSENGERS	AGE	SEX	OCCUPATIONS	COUNTRY TO WHICH THEY BELONG	COUNTRY THEY INTEND TO INHABIT	SHIPS/DATES OF ARRIVAL	
LACE (cont'd)							
Nelly	30	F	None	Isle of Man		Ocean	13 Jul 1827
Pat	6			Ireland		Anacreon	7 Sep 1827
Patk.	28	M	Farmer	Isle of Man		Ocean	13 Jul 1827
Peggy	20			Ireland		Anacreon	7 Sep 1827
Thos.	5	M	None	Isle of Man		Ocean	13 Jul 1827
LACEILE, Eulalie	24	F	Baroness	France	travellers	Desdemona	12 Jun 1826
LACEY, Geo.	35		Labourer	G. Britain		Casanda	5 Sep 1827
Jas.	35	M	...	Ireland	U. States	Atlantic	19 Aug 1825
Joshua	36	M	Inn Keeper	Gt. Britain		Corinthian	27 Oct 1829
LACH, Abm.	36	M	Weaver	Great Britain	United States	India	5 Sep 1827
LACKEY, Daniel	24	M		Ireland	U. States	Nancy	10 Jul 1822
Jas.	22	M	...er	...	United States	Combine	20 Nov 1824
LACKIE, Hugh	28	M	...	Scotland	United States	Camillus	27 Oct 1829
LACKIN, Margt.	20	F		Gt. Britain	United States	Penelope	9 Sep 1828
LACKINS, An	25	M				Lady of the Lake	23 Aug 1828
*left ship							
Ann	5	F				Lady of the Lake	23 Aug 1828
*left ship							
Mary	30	F				Lady of the Lake	23 Aug 1828
*left ship							
LACMIE, Charles	24		Baker	Somwiller	Switzerland	Ann	27 Nov 1820
LACORTE, —	45	M	Merchant	U. States	U. States	Imperial	10 Dec 1821
A., Miss	9	F		United States		Howard	17 Oct 1822
C.	46	M	Merchant	United States		Howard	17 Oct 1822
C., Miss	14	F		United States		Howard	17 Oct 1822
E., Mrs.	37	F		United States		Howard	17 Oct 1822
H.	7	M		United States		Howard	17 Oct 1822
S., Miss	12	F		United States		Howard	17 Oct 1822
LA COSTE, Emily	22	F				Stephania	22 Apr 1822
John	29	M	Merchant	France	United States	Stephania	22 Apr 1822
LACOSTE, Adolphus	19	M	Merchant	U. States	U. States	Sully	24 Oct 1828
Charles	18 2/12	M	...	...	U.S. America	Edward	28 Oct 1825
E., Mrs.	44	F	None	U. States	U. States	Sully	24 Oct 1828
LA COURE, Adolph	13	M		France	U. States	Superb	9 Jul 1821
LACY, Jno.	22	M	...	Switzerland	U. States	Robert Edward	2 Nov 1827
Patrick	16	M	Farmer	Farmer	U. States	Wilson	2 Sep 1823
Saml.	23	M	Butcher	England	America	Meteor	21 Aug 1822
LAD, John	22	M	Labourer	Ireland	U. States	Sarah G	7 May 1827
LADD, Isaac	12		Labourer	Cork	Gt. Britain	Enterprize	19 Feb 1822
J...	2...	M	Labourer	Ireland	Unt. St. America	Wilson	21 May 1827
Thomas	8		Labourer	Cork	Gt. Britain	Enterprize	19 Feb 1822
Thomas	30	M	Labourer	England	Ohio	Governor Fenner	23 Jul 1829
LADEN, Ann	26	F				Ocean	17 Aug 1820
Ann	30	F	Labourer	Ireland	U. States	Virginia	20 Jun 1825
Darby	20	M		Ireland	U.S. of America	Douglass	6 Jul 1829
Luke	10	M				Ocean	17 Aug 1820
Magaret	35	F	Seamstress	Sligo		Ocean	17 Aug 1820
Mary	3	F		Ireland	U. States	Virginia	20 Jun 1825
Micheal	7/12	M		Ireland	U. States	Virginia	20 Jun 1825
Pat	8	M				Ocean	17 Aug 1820
LADERMANN, Christian	...	M	...	...	U.S. America	Superior	18 Jun 1825
Jaques	32	M	Gardner	Laerperswyl	U.S. America	Superior	18 Jun 1825
Pauline	25	F	Gardner	Laerperswyl	U.S. America	Superior	18 Jun 1825
LADLOW, Robt.	18 2/12	M	Merchant	N. York	U. States	Charlotte Corday	15 Aug 1820
LADOWITCH, Mary	28	F	Spinster			Servant	30 Aug 1820
Mary, 2d.	5	F				Servant	30 Aug 1820
Solomon	2	M				Servant	30 Aug 1820
LADY, William	25	M	Baker	Germany	U.S.A.	Hudson	21 Aug 1829
LA FATE, Ralphel	18	M	Merchant	Spain	Havana	Robert Fulton	22 May 1824
LAFAYETTE, —, Genl.	67	M	Gent.	France	France	Cadmus	17 Aug 1824
Geo. Washington	43	M	Gent.	France	France	Cadmus	17 Aug 1824
LAFETTE, Edgar	16	M	Boy	United States	United States	New Packet	20 Oct 1827
Josephine	7	F	Child	United States	United States	New Packet	20 Oct 1827
Loise	28	F	Lady	United States	United States	New Packet	20 Oct 1827

NAMES OF PASSENGERS	AGE	SEX	OCCUPATIONS	COUNTRY TO WHICH THEY BELONG	COUNTRY THEY INTEND TO INHABIT	SHIPS/DATES OF ARRIVAL	
LA FEVER, —, Mr.	27	M	...man	England	U. States	Robert Edwards	11 Mar 1822
LAFFAN, Edwin	43	M	Labourer	England	New York	Brighton	19 Aug 1829
Edwin	43	F	Labourer			Brighton	19 Aug 1829
LAFFATTE, R.	19	M	Merchant	Spain	Havana	John and Edward	6 Jan 1824
LAFFERTY, Ellenor	25	F	Spinster	Ireland	United States	Trident	17 May 1825
Thomas	21	M	Farmer	Ireland	St. John	Lady Hunter	28 Apr 1824
LAFFIN, Samuel	35	M	Merchant	United States	United States	Hanford	3 Aug 1829
LAFIER, D.	44	M	Farmer	United States	United States	Seine	21 Oct 1822
LAFITTA, R.	19	M	Mercht.	Havana de Cuba		Brown	12 Oct 1824
LAFOATON, M.	28	M	Merchant	France	U. States	Waldo	19 Aug 1826
LA FOREST, —, Mr.	40	M	Barber	France	U. States	Neptune	11 Oct 1821
LAFOY, Cora	20	F		U. States	U. States	Montano	2 Sep 1828
Evelina	13	F		U. States	U. States	Montano	2 Sep 1828
Helen	35	F		U. States	U. States	Montano	2 Sep 1828
Jean B.	53	M	Barber	U. States	U. States	Montano	2 Sep 1828
Theodore	10	M		U. States	U. States	Montano	2 Sep 1828
LAFRENTZ, Peter T.	52		Merchant	U. States	U. States	Alfred	24 Jul 1828
LAFUNIERE, H.	28	M	Merchant	France	U. States	Edwd. Quesnel	30 Apr 1825
LAGARA, Louis	18	M	Servant	United States	United States	Only Daughter	29 Apr 1825
LAGHI, Michal	25	M		G. Britan	U. States	William Neilson	26 Jul 1828
LAGHY, Joseph	22	M	Weaver	Ireland	New York	Louisa	18 Apr 1827
LAGLE, Catherine	4	F	Agriculturist	France	U.S.	Helen	3 May 1828
Frederick	28	M	Agriculturist	France	U.S.	Helen	3 May 1828
John	44	M	Agriculturist	France	U.S.	Helen	3 May 1828
Margaret	19	F	Agriculturist	France	U.S.	Helen	3 May 1828
Margaret	46	F	Agriculturist	France	U.S.	Helen	3 May 1828
Maryann	8	F	Agriculturist	France	U.S.	Helen	3 May 1828
Susan	17	F	Agriculturist	France	U.S.	Helen	3 May 1828
LAGOREE, John	76	M	Gentleman	Great Britain	America, U.N.S.	Great Britain	3 Aug 1829
LA GRANGE, John	27	M	Merchant	America	America	La Grange	7 Aug 1828
LAGREE, Jacob	20	M	Tailor	United States	United States	Only Daughter	29 Apr 1825
LA GUDINE, Emanuel	51	M	Merchant	New Orleans	Philadelphia	Charleston	1 Jun 1826
LAGUEDOR, Jos. M.	25	M	Merchant	S. America	Philada.	Douglass	13 Feb 1824
LAGUENIER, Peter	36	M	Clerk	Baltimore	U. States	Robt. Y. Hayne	27 Jun 1825
LAHANCE, Lesabeth	30	F		United States	United States	Nancy	28 Oct 1822
LAHASADA, J. B.	48	M	Mercht.	Spain	U.S.	Emma	24 Jun 1825
LAHEY, Ann	2	F		Ireland	United States	St. George	25 Aug 1829
Ann	29	F	None	Ireland	United States	St. George	25 Aug 1829
Ann, Junr.	2	F	None	Ireland	United States	St. George	25 Aug 1829
Thomas	7	M	None	Ireland	United States	St. George	25 Aug 1829
LAHMAN, Diedrick	34	M	Laborer	Germany	U. States	Hannibal	12 Oct 1829
LAHORY, Ann	19	F	...	...	United States	Minerva	30 Oct 1827
LAHY, Joseph	17	M	Servant	Ireland	Pensylvania	Atlantic	8 May 1828
LAIGHT, W. E.	22	M	Merchant	U.S.	U.S.	Francois I	8 Aug 1829
LAIKE, D.	40	M	Labourer	G. Britain	U. States	Hanford	10 Jun 1828
Mary	30	F		G. Britain	U. States	Hanford	10 Jun 1828
LAIL, Wm.	57	M	Farmer	..., ..., England	N. York	New Orleans	24 Aug 1827
LAIMAR, M.	36	M	Mechanic	France	U. States	Harriet	3 Sep 1823
LAIMDEN, W.	24	M	Cordwinder	England	U. States	William Byrnes	17 Jul 1825
LAIN, Dennis	30	M	Labourer	Ireland	U. States	Bellville	14 May 1827
Hugh	10	M	None	Great Britain		Eliza Grant	29 Aug 1829
Hugh, Revd.	29	M	Clergyman	United States	United States	Meteor	27 Sep 1826
LAINE, Leon C.	11	M	Boy	France	U.S. America	Gibraltar	12 Oct 1829
LAING, James	25		of the Army	Scotland	Canada	James Cropper	12 Jul 1822
Jas., Capt.	30	M	British Army	U. States	U. States	Canada	27 Sep 1826
Mary	2	F		Ireland	New York	New York	5 May 1828
LAINIER, Robert	22	M		America	America	Ann	11 Apr 1821
LAINS, Hugh	10	M		G.B.	St. New York	Eliza Grant	29 Aug 1829
LAIR..., Nicholas, Mr.	23	M	Coach Maker	United States	United States	Dromo	9 Oct 1828
LAIRD, Eliza	16	F	Servant	G. Britain	U. States	Nimrod	31 Jul 1828
Hugh	3	M	Farmer	Ireland	U. States	Atlantic	19 Aug 1825
James	24	M	Carpenter	Scotland	United States	Shakespeare	24 Jul 1828
Jas.	5	M	Farmer	Ireland	U. States	Atlantic	19 Aug 1825
John	19	M	Spinter			Commerce	22 Jun 1825
Margt.	40	F		G. Britain	U. States	Nimrod	31 Jul 1828
Nancy	7	F	Farmer	Ireland	U. States	Atlantic	19 Aug 1825
P.	18	F	Servant	G. Britain	U. States	Nimrod	31 Jul 1828
Robert	30	M	Cotton Spinner	England	United States	Jubilee	4 Mar 1829
Samuel	20	M	Labourer	Blantier	U.S. America	Camillus	10 Sep 1821

NAMES OF PASSENGERS	AGE	SEX	OCCUPATIONS	COUNTRY TO WHICH THEY BELONG	COUNTRY THEY INTEND TO INHABIT	SHIPS/DATES OF ARRIVAL	
LAIRD (cont'd)							
Thos.	9	M	Farmer	Ireland	U. States	Atlantic	19 Aug 1825
LAITCHARD, Mary	67	F	Lady	England	New York	Brighton	16 Nov 1826
LAITHWORTH, Allen	20	F		G. Britan	U. States	William Neilson	26 Jul 1828
Ellen	34	F		G. Britan	U. States	William Neilson	26 Jul 1828
Thomas	40	M		G. Britan	U. States	William Neilson	26 Jul 1828
LAJORN, Joseph	24	F	Wood Sho.	Ireland		Quatre Freres	29 Jul 1828
LAKE, Edward	25	M	Merchant	St. Johns, N.B.	Great Britain	Sylvester Healy	23 Nov 1825
Jas.	13	M	None	Scotland	United States	Euphrates	8 Nov 1821
LAKELIN, George	28	M	Merchant	Great Britain	U. States	Birmingham	12 Oct 1829
LAKEMAN, J.	28	M	Merchant	U. States	U. States	Lewis	20 Feb 1824
LA KOKA, D.	65	M		Spain	Spain	Fabius	3 Jun 1825
LA LALAMOE, Arsene	22	F	Chambermaid	France	United States	Stephania	22 Apr 1822
LALAURA, —	26					Olympia	12 Aug 1828
LALER, Ann	5	F		Great Britain	New York	Dublin	21 Dec 1824
Fredk.	33	M	Labourer	Great Britain	New York	Dublin	21 Dec 1824
Mary	14	F		Great Britain	New York	Dublin	21 Dec 1824
Mary	33	F		Great Britain	New York	Dublin	21 Dec 1824
Michl.	7/12	M		Great Britain	New York	Dublin	21 Dec 1824
LALETUNO, Anthony	34	M	Merchant	U. States	United States	Dromo	22 Feb 1827
LALEU, Mil.	31			Laon [?]		Deux Ernest	29 Dec 1827
LA LIBERTY, M.	40	M	Merchant	Great Britain	Great Britain	Nancy	20 Mar 1820
LALLAN, Ann	20	F		Ireland	New York	Lady Hunter	5 Jun 1826
LALLARS, Patrick	30	M	Mechanic	United States	...	Mechanic	11 Apr 1826
LALLOT, Jos.	_/12	M		France	United States	Le Voltaire	19 Jul 1828
Joseph	34	M	Farmer	France	United States	Le Voltaire	19 Jul 1828
M. F.	27	F		France	United States	Le Voltaire	19 Jul 1828
M. J.	3	F		France	United States	Le Voltaire	19 Jul 1828
Rose	5	F		France	United States	Le Voltaire	19 Jul 1828
LALLY, Denis	25 4/12	M	Labourer	Ireland	America	Enterprize	29 Jun 1827
Frs.	35	M	Merchant	Aquin	U. States	Sarah Ann	25 Jun 1822
W.	20	M	Mercht.	United States	U. States	Hiram	4 Sep 1824
LALOR, Alice	18	F	Spinster	Ireland	United States	Dublin Packet	13 Oct 1828
Martin	26	M	Farmer	Ireland	United States	Dublin Packet	29 Jun 1825
LAMACKE, J. B.	21	M	Merchant	France		Howard	17 Oct 1822
LAMAIRE, J. D.	35	M	Merchant	France	U. States	Queen Mab	7 Apr 1826
LAMANE, A.	60	M		France	United States	La Flora	30 Jun 1828
LAMAR, —, Mr.	28	M	Mariner	U. States	U. States	Cadmus	12 Apr 1825
Charles	36	M	Printer	England	America	Plutarch	18 Jul 1826
Sarah	32	F		England	America	Plutarch	18 Jul 1826
LAMASURE, M., Mr.	36	M	Planter	U. States	U. States	Bayard	9 Jul 1824
LAMATRE, E.	16 5/12	M		France	France	Edward Bonnaffe	20 Jun 1826
Elizabeth	27 3/12	F		France	France	Edward Bonnaffe	20 Jun 1826
J. B.	25 4/12	M		France	France	Edward Bonnaffe	20 Jun 1826
LAMB, —, child	1 _/12	F		Ireland	U. States	Albion	11 May 1827
Agnes	29	F		Scotland	United States	Commerce	17 Jul 1823
Agnes	50	F		Scotland	United States	Commerce	17 Jul 1823
Allin	21	M	Farmer	Scotland	United States	Commerce	17 Jul 1823
Anna	16	F	Farmer	Alsace in the Department of Upper and lower Rhine	United States	Carolina Augusta	16 May 1828
C.	16	F		England	U. States	Seine	10 Jun 1822
Catherina	22	F	Farmer	Alsace in the Department of Upper and lower Rhine	United States	Carolina Augusta	16 May 1828
David	2	M	Boy	Scotland	U.S.	Panthea	22 Jul 1826
David	25	M	Farmer	Scotland	United States	Commerce	17 Jul 1823
David	55	M	Farmer	Scotland	United States	Commerce	17 Jul 1823
Eliza	1 6/12	F		Scotland	U. States	Dalmarnock	23 May 1823
Eliza	10	F	Farmer	Alsace in the Department of Upper and lower Rhine	United States	Carolina Augusta	16 May 1828
Elizabeth	6/12	F	Infant	Ireland	U. States	Josephine	7 May 1827

NAMES OF PASSENGERS	AGE	SEX	OCCUPATIONS	COUNTRY TO WHICH THEY BELONG	COUNTRY THEY INTEND TO INHABIT	SHIPS/DATES OF ARRIVAL	
LAMB (cont'd)							
Elizabeth	4	F	Lady	Scotland	U.S.	Panthea	22 Jul 1826
Ewd.	20	M	Labourer	Great Britain	United States	Penelope	11 Jun 1827
George	23	M	Stone Cutter	Ireland	U. States	Hanford	29 Dec 1828
George	27	M	Farmer	Scotland	United States	Commerce	17 Jul 1823
Henry	31	M	Stone Mason	Great Britain		Eliza Grant	29 Aug 1829
Henry	51	M	Stone Mason	G.B.	New York	Eliza Grant	29 Aug 1829
J. S.	40	M	Servant	G. Brittain	U. States	Canada	6 Jun 1825
J...	20	M	Clerk			John & Edward	25 Aug 1820
James	19	M	Farmer	Great Britian	United States	Andes	19 Aug 1829
James	28	M	Labourer	Ireland	United States	Trident	31 Mar 1827
James	33	M	Labourer	Great Britain	N. York	Josephine	10 Dec 1825
Jane	23		Merchant	Canada	Canada	Hudson	18 Jun 1825
Jane	24	F		Scotland	U. States	Dalmarnock	23 May 1823
Jane	24	F		Canada	Canada	Hudson	20 Nov 1828
Jeanette	26	F	Lady	Scotland	U.S.	Panthea	22 Jul 1826
John	2	M	Farmer	Alsace in the Department of Upper and lower Rhine	United States	Carolina Augusta	16 May 1828
John	47	M	Gentleman	United States		Howard	17 Oct 1822
Judith	22	F		Ireland	U. States	Albion	11 May 1827
M. C., Mrs.	21	F	Lady	United States		Howard	17 Oct 1822
Margaretta	23	F	Farmer	Alsace in the Department of Upper and lower Rhine	United States	Carolina Augusta	16 May 1828
Margaretta	36	F	Farmer	Alsace in the Department of Upper and lower Rhine	United States	Carolina Augusta	16 May 1828
Maria	18	F	Farmer	Alsace in the Department of Upper and lower Rhine	United States	Carolina Augusta	16 May 1828
Mary	8	F	Girl	Ireland	United States	Trident	17 May 1825
Mary	19	F		Scotland	United States	Commerce	17 Jul 1823
Mary	25	F	Matron	Ireland	U. States	Josephine	7 May 1827
Mary	26	F	Wife	Ireland	U. States	Hanford	29 Dec 1828
Mary A.	6	F	Child	England	U. States	Seine	10 Jun 1822
Mary Ann	20	F		G. Britain	U. States	Hanford	18 Sep 1828
Michael	8	M	Farmer	Alsace in the Department of Upper and lower Rhine	United States	Carolina Augusta	16 May 1828
Michael	36	M	Farmer	Alsace in the Department of Upper and lower Rhine	United States	Carolina Augusta	16 May 1828
P.	30	M	Labourer	Ireland	U. States	Albion	11 May 1827
Peter	17	M	Farmer	Great Britian	United States	Andes	19 Aug 1829
Richd.	22	M	Clerk			John & Edward	25 Aug 1820
Robert	30	M	Stone Cutter	Ireland	U. States	Hanford	29 Dec 1828
Robt.	12	M		England	U. States	Seine	10 Jun 1822
Salley	18	F	Spinster	Ireland	United States	Henry Kneeland	7 Jun 1828
Samuel	36	M	Merchant	United States		Howard	17 Oct 1822
Samuel	38	M	Merchant	U.S.	U.S.	Stephania	13 Sep 1821
Thomas		M	...	...	...	Indian Chief	8 Sep 1824
William	23	M	Farmer	Scotland	United States	Commerce	17 Jul 1823
Wm.	45	M	Farmer	England	U. States	Electra	7 Jul 1828
LAMBA, John	44	M	Mason	Great Britain		Caravan	8 Sep 1828
L.	9/12	M		Great Britain		Caravan	8 Sep 1828
M..	38	F		Great Britain		Caravan	8 Sep 1828
LAMBE, Agnes	45	F		Scotland	United States	Broke	16 Jul 1829
Alexander T.	3	M		Scotland	United States	Broke	16 Jul 1829
James	12	M		Scotland	United States	Broke	16 Jul 1829
Jas. Henry	35	M	Merchant	England	Canada	Manhattan	12 Jun 1824
Margaret	7	F		Scotland	United States	Broke	16 Jul 1829
Penelope	5	M		Scotland	United States	Broke	16 Jul 1829

NAMES OF PASSENGERS	AGE	SEX	OCCUPATIONS	COUNTRY TO WHICH THEY BELONG	COUNTRY THEY INTEND TO INHABIT	SHIPS/DATES OF ARRIVAL	
LAMBE (cont'd)							
William	10	M		Scotland	United States	Broke	16 Jul 1829
William	50	M	Weaver	Scotland	United States	Broke	16 Jul 1829
LAMBER, Eva	27	M		G. Britain		Caravan	8 Sep 1828
Jacob	1			G. Britain		Caravan	8 Sep 1828
Janet	16	F	None	Scotland	United States	Mary & Susan	5 Aug 1828
John	18	M	Farmer	Scotland	United States	Mary & Susan	5 Aug 1828
Peter	25	M	Tailor	G. Britain		Caravan	8 Sep 1828
Robin	20	F	None	Scotland	United States	Mary & Susan	5 Aug 1828
LAMBERRALT, Frs.	38	M	Farmer	Germany	United States	Stephania	16 Aug 1827
LAMBERT, —, Mrs.	29	F	None	U. States	U. States	Hercules	5 Sep 1826
Anne	29	F	None	Great Briton	United States	Mount Vernon	30 Dec 1828
Bab	3	F		Native of Switzerland	United States	Canaris	30 Jun 1827
Bab	24	F		Native of Switzerland	United States	Canaris	30 Jun 1827
C.	14	M	Labourer	...	U. States	Governor Tompkins	26 Jul 1824
C.	40	M	Merchant	Albany	U. States	Mary Hobin	29 May 1826
Chs.	23	M	Gentleman	Ireland	United States	Thomas	13 Dec 1827
Eli	36	M	Farmer	Bedford	England	Helicon	3 Aug 1826
Elija	13	F		St. Eustatia	U. States	Henry	26 May 1823
Ensebius	8	M		St. Eustatia	U. States	Henry	26 May 1823
Eugenius	3	M		St. Eustatia	U. States	Henry	26 May 1823
George	3 5/12	M	None	Great Briton	United States	Mount Vernon	30 Dec 1828
Jane	22	F		England	New York	Hudson	20 Nov 1828
Jane	26	F	Blacksmith	Great Britain	U. States	Princess Charlotte	6 Sep 1828
John	19	M	...tter	Great Britain	New York	Hesperus	13 Oct 1825
John	22	M		Ireland	United States	Thompson	12 Sep 1827
John	37	M	Farmer	Great Britain	United States	Ann Maria	12 Jul 1821
John F.	16	M		St. Eustatia	U. States	Henry	26 May 1823
Jos.	10	M		St. Eustatia	U. States	Henry	26 May 1823
Joseph	23	M	Mechanic	U. States	U. States	Mechanic	24 Mar 1823
Mary Anne	7 2/12	F	None	Great Briton	United States	Mount Vernon	30 Dec 1828
Michael	20	M				Eliza Grant	6 Oct 1828
Micheal	25	M	Wool Manufacturer	Ireland	United States	Delta	24 Oct 1829
Peter	1	M		Native of Switzerland	United States	Canaris	30 Jun 1827
Peter	24	M	Shoemaker	Native of Switzerland	United States	Canaris	30 Jun 1827
Richard	34	M	Printer	England	New York	Hudson	20 Nov 1828
Robt.	28	M	Blacksmith	Great Britain	U. States	Princess Charlotte	6 Sep 1828
Ursula	6	M		St. Eustatia	U. States	Henry	26 May 1823
William	22	M	Farmer	Ireland	United States	Dublin Packet	3 Sep 1822
LAMBERTON, Charles	4	M		Gt. Britain	United States	Columbia	7 Sep 1827
James	0 4/12	M		Gt. Britain	United States	Columbia	7 Sep 1827
Wm.	2	M		Gt. Britain	United States	Columbia	7 Sep 1827
LAMBIE, John	22		Slater	Scotland	United States	Camillus	3 May 1828
LAMBRIK, John	20	M	Servant	U. States	U. States	Weymouth	3 Apr 1821
LAMBS, James	26	M	Farmer	Ireland	United States	Princess Charlotte	6 Oct 1827
LAMBURTIS, Peir	30	M	Servant	Curacao	United States	General Paez	28 May 1828
LAMENT, Joseph	36 6/12	M	Merchant	U. States		Parnasson	1 Mar 1820
LAMERSON, Hugh	28	M	Farmer	Ireland	United States	Samuel Robertson	9 Apr 1828
LAMEYER, Fredk. W.	21		Merchant	Bremen	U. States	Princess Louise	10 Mar 1825
LAMEZO, —, Mrs.	35	F		France	France	Montano	15 Jan 1829
Victor	6	M	Merchant	France	France	Montano	15 Jan 1829
LAMI, Ernest	12	M		France	United States	Montano	5 May 1828
LAMIN, Frans.	40	M	Merchant	Spain	Spain	Victory	13 Oct 1823
LAMINER, Charles	36	M		New Orleans	New Orleans	Eliza Grant	6 Oct 1828
LAMMER, A.	20	F	Taylor	Hannover		Constitution	5 Jan 1829
C.	50		Gardener	Hannover		Constitution	5 Jan 1829
H.	18		Laborer	Hannover		Constitution	5 Jan 1829
Jos.	35	M	Merchant	N. York	U. States	Eagle	18 Jul 1822
LAMNITZ, Henry	21	M	Gentleman	Hamburg	U. States	La Fayette	7 Apr 1825
LAMON, Maurice	23	M	Druggist	G. Brittian	U. States	Pacific	19 Oct 1829

NAMES OF PASSENGERS	AGE	SEX	OCCUPATIONS	COUNTRY TO WHICH THEY BELONG	COUNTRY THEY INTEND TO INHABIT	SHIPS/DATES OF ARRIVAL	
LAMONAL, S.	12	F	None	U. States	U. States	Ardell	7 Jul 1827
LAMONT, Archd.	25	M	Farmer	Great Britain	United States	Friends	13 Jun 1825
Christiana	21	F		England	U. States	Alert	22 Sep 1821
Daniel	21	M	Cooper	Scotland	America	Concord	4 Jun 1821
Daniel	29	M	Farmer	Great Britain	United States	Friends	13 Jun 1825
Euphania	2	F	Farmer	Great Britain	United States	Friends	13 Jun 1825
Frs.	40	M	Merchant	France	U. States	Fame	20 Feb 1822
Geo.	25	M	Blacksmith	England	U. States	Alert	22 Sep 1821
Geo.	58	M	Blacksmith	Scotland	U. States	Alert	22 Sep 1821
H.	34	M	Merchant	France	U. States	Fame	20 Feb 1822
Issabella	22	F	Farmer	Great Britain	United States	Friends	13 Jun 1825
Jno.	42	M	Merchant	France	U. States	Fame	20 Feb 1822
John	2	M	Farmer	Great Britain	United States	Friends	13 Jun 1825
M.	58	F		England	U. States	Alert	22 Sep 1821
Margt.	24	F		England	U. States	Alert	22 Sep 1821
Mary	7	F	Farmer	Great Britain	United States	Friends	13 Jun 1825
S.	22	M	Mariner	American	S. America	Cleanthes	9 May 1825
LAMONTE, Alex	30	M	Merchant	Scotland	U. States	Atlantic	27 Aug 1827
LAMORE, Lucien	21	M		France	U. States	Canada	6 Jun 1825
LAMORY, Samuel	24	M	Mercher	U.S.	U.S.	Charleston Allen	15 Nov 1826
LAMOTH, Jno.	30	M	Merchant	France	America	Saluda	16 Oct 1824
LA MOTTE, Robert	32		Gold Smith	Le Rochelle	New York	Elba	9 May 1827
LAMOTTE, Guilliaume	23	M	Merchant	France	France	Neptune	22 Oct 1822
LAMOUNT, —	25	M	Farmer	Scotland	U.S.	James & Margaret	4 Aug 1823
LAMPHER, Betwel	30	M	Merchant	U. States	U. States	Dromo	4 May 1827
LAMPHTON, Jas.	50	M	Labourer	Ireland	United States	Trident	16 May 1826
LAMSON, —, Capt.	22	M	Mariner	U. States	U. States	Alexander Le Grand	9 Sep 1823
G. A.	26	M	Mariner	United States	United States	Tandem	8 Mar 1826
Geo. O.	22	M	Mariner	U. States	U. States	Hippomenes	22 Dec 1821
George O.	32	M	Merchant	U. States	U. States	Mary Livingston	14 May 1827
George O.	36	M	Merchant	U. States Amer.	U.S.A.	Robert Y. Hayne	21 Aug 1828
Z.	38	M	Mariner	U. States	U. States	Hesper	7 Oct 1823
Z. G.	35	M	Mariner	Boston	Boston	Lavinia	19 Aug 1824
LAMYON, Andrew	26	M	Merchant	Boston	Boston	Orient	9 Dec 1826
LAN..., J...s.	27	M	Butcher	Germany	United States	Robert Edwards	1 Jun 1826
LANAGAN, Andrew	1	M		G. Britain	U. States	London	23 Sep 1828
C.	24	M		G. Britain	U. States	London	23 Sep 1828
Catharine	6/12	F	Labourer	Ireland	United States	General Marion	6 Oct 1828
Catherine	1	F	Child	Ireland	America	Josephine	24 Jul 1826
Edmond	5	M	Child	Ireland	America	Josephine	24 Jul 1826
Edward	35	M	Surveyor	Ireland	America	Josephine	24 Jul 1826
Elizabeth	7	F	Child	Ireland	America	Josephine	24 Jul 1826
John	26	M	Labourer	G. Britain	U. States	London	23 Sep 1828
Joseph	13	M	Labourer	Ireland	America	Josephine	24 Jul 1826
Margaret	3	F	Child	Ireland	America	Josephine	24 Jul 1826
Margaret	30	F	Matron	Ireland	America	Josephine	24 Jul 1826
Mary	9	F	Child	Ireland	America	Josephine	24 Jul 1826
Mary	20	F	Labourer	Ireland	United States	General Marion	6 Oct 1828
Patrick	24	M	Labourer	Ireland	United States	General Marion	6 Oct 1828
Peter	11	M	Child	Ireland	America	Josephine	24 Jul 1826
LANAGHAN, Anthony	25	M	House Carpenter	Great Britain	U.S. of America	Gratitude	3 Oct 1829
LANAGUS, James	15	M		G. Britain	U. States	St. George	7 Jun 1828
Nancy	20	F		G. Britain	U. States	St. George	7 Jun 1828
LANARD, William [crossed out]	40	M	Mariner	Penna.	Phila.	South America	29 Aug 1826
LANARHAN, Edward	38	M		Great Britain	United States	Mary Howland	19 Jul 1827
LANART, Andrew	3	M	None	Scotland	United States	Friends	7 Jul 1827
Daniel	34	M	Labourer	Scotland	United States	Friends	7 Jul 1827
John	7	M	None	Scotland	United States	Friends	7 Jul 1827
Margaret	6/12	F	None	Scotland	United States	Friends	7 Jul 1827
Margret	34	F	Spinster	Scotland	United States	Friends	7 Jul 1827
Thomas	5	M	None	Scotland	United States	Friends	7 Jul 1827
LANAUGHAN, Alice	19	F	Spinster	Ireland	Unt. St. America	Wilson	21 May 1827
LANBAR, Georg	19	M	Black Smith	France	United States	Virginia	31 May 1828
LANCASHIRE, James	26	M	Weaver	Royton	Royton	Howard Douglass	11 May 1827
LANCASTER, Alendor	42	F	None	Great Britain	United States	Cambria	26 Dec 1827

NAMES OF PASSENGERS	AGE	SEX	OCCUPATIONS	COUNTRY TO WHICH THEY BELONG	COUNTRY THEY INTEND TO INHABIT	SHIPS/DATES OF ARRIVAL	
LANCASTER (cont'd)							
Ann	17	F	Farmer	England	U. States	Margarett Scott	22 Aug 1827
Betsy	11	F	Farmer	England	U. States	Margarett Scott	22 Aug 1827
Betty	57	F				Amity	11 Sep 1820
Edward	6	M	None	Great Britain	United States	Cambria	26 Dec 1827
Ephrim	4	M	None	Great Britain	United States	Cambria	26 Dec 1827
Fustin	11	M	None	Great Britain	United States	Cambria	26 Dec 1827
Geo.	27	M	Farmer	England	U. States	Foster	28 Aug 1822
Isaac	32	M	Weaver	England	Philadelphia	Indian Chief	16 Aug 1822
James	46	M	Farmer	Great Britain	United States	Cambria	26 Dec 1827
James, Jur.	19	M	Farmer	Great Britain	United States	Cambria	26 Dec 1827
John	44	M	Farmer	England	U. States	Margarett Scott	22 Aug 1827
John	57	M				Amity	11 Sep 1820
Joseph	24	M	Teaman	England	United States	Siroc	31 Oct 1829
Lydia	8	F	None	Great Britain	United States	Cambria	26 Dec 1827
Mary	40	F	Farmer	England	U. States	Margarett Scott	22 Aug 1827
Nancy	13	F	None	Great Britain	United States	Cambria	26 Dec 1827
Samuel	14	M	None	Great Britain	United States	Cambria	26 Dec 1827
Sophia	27	F	Lady	England	United States	Siroc	31 Oct 1829
Wm.	13	M	Farmer	England	U. States	Margarett Scott	22 Aug 1827
Wm.	42	...	...	...	United States	Minerva	30 Oct 1827
LANCASTLE, John	23	M	Gentleman	G. Britain	U. States	Cosmo	15 May 1827
LANCE, Solomon	32 3/12	M	Farmer	Switzerland	America	Henry	17 May 1828
LAND, Catherine	58	F		England	United States	Acosta	28 Jul 1823
David	22	M	Gentleman	England	England	Leo	30 Apr 1825
Margaret	34	F	...	Ireland	U. States	Atlantic	19 Aug 1825
William	60	M	Tradesman	England	United States	Acosta	28 Jul 1823
LANDALE, John	42	M	Farmer	Scotland	United States	Minerva	25 Aug 1823
LANDANELLO, Sophia	26	F	None	Stockholm	U. States	Roanoake	12 Oct 1826
LANDELY, George	56	M	Barber	Scotland	U. States	Roger Stewart	9 Jun 1828
LANDEN, John	33	M	Clerk	New Brunswick	Canada	Belleville	29 Aug 1827
LANDER, —	45	M	Labourer	France	United States	Cavalier	25 Jul 1828
—, Wife	36	F		France	United States	Cavalier	25 Jul 1828
Cathr.	3	F		France	United States	Cavalier	25 Jul 1828
Leonhard	9	F		France	United States	Cavalier	25 Jul 1828
M.	5	M		France	United States	Cavalier	25 Jul 1828
Maria	9	F		France	United States	Cavalier	25 Jul 1828
Michl.	7	M		France	United States	Cavalier	25 Jul 1828
W.	45	M	Merchant	U. States	U. States	Quesnel	6 Sep 1824
Wm.	23	M	Currier	Great Brittain	U.S.	Trafalgar	22 Jun 1821
LANDERING, Louisa, Zyn Vrouw [his wife, Jacob Luther]	27	F		Munster	United States	Juffraw Johanna	16 Oct 1821
LANDERKIN, James	33	M	Farmer	England	Canada	General Stark	12 Jun 1826
LANDERMAN,							
Adam	2 8/12	M	Farmer	Switzerland	America	Henry	17 May 1828
Catherine	30	F	Farmer	Switzerland	America	Henry	17 May 1828
John	32 4/12	M	Farmer	Switzerland	America	Henry	17 May 1828
C.	23		baker	Hannover		Constitution	5 Jan 1829
LANDERS, Catherine	25	F		Ireland	United States	Trio	2 Oct 1828
M. D.	21	M	Surveyor	Ireland	United States	Trio	2 Oct 1828
LANDFORD, Alexander	21	M	Brick Layer	Ireland	U. States	Courier	17 Mar 1828
LANDHAM, George	28	M	Farmer	Ireland		Cuba	24 Jun 1822
LANDIGAN, Patrick	24	M	Farmer	Ireland	United States	Diana	1 May 1826
LANDING, Charlotte	4			L...	England	Great Britain	7 May 1827
Elizh.	...			L...	England	Great Britain	7 May 1827
Francis	...			L...	England	Great Britain	7 May 1827
John	2...			L...	England	Great Britain	7 May 1827
Mary	6			L...	England	Great Britain	7 May 1827
LANDON, Francis	4	F	None	Great Britian	U. States	Henry Kneedland	7 Aug 1826
Richard M.	40	M	Seaman	United States	New York	Gleaner	30 Apr 1821
LANDRADA, R.	17	M	Servent	Spain	Spain	General Marion	12 Jul 1823
LANDRETH, Cuthbert	32	M	Labourer	Great Britain	United States	Courier	13 Mar 1828
LANDROY, Henry	30	M	Taylor	France	U. States	La Virginie	21 Sep 1826
LANDY, Desire	32	F		U. States	U. States	Bayard	16 May 1827
Nicholas	24	M	Labourer	Ireland	U.S.A.	Dalhouse Castle	21 Aug 1829
Nichs.	24	M	Labourer	Ireland	United States	Dalhouse Castle	21 Aug 1829
LANE, Andrew	54	M	Farmer			Importer	30 Oct 1820

NAMES OF PASSENGERS	AGE	SEX	OCCUPATIONS	COUNTRY TO WHICH THEY BELONG	COUNTRY THEY INTEND TO INHABIT	SHIPS/DATES OF ARRIVAL	
LANE (cont'd)							
Benjamin, Mr.	45	M	Gentln.	England	U. States	Corinthian	8 Oct 1828
Cathr.	35	F		Great Britain	U. States	St. Croix	13 Sep 1827
David	6	M	Laborer or Spinster	Ireland	United States	Sarah G.	15 Aug 1827
David	16	M	Labourer	Ireland	U. States	St. Michael's	10 Feb 1827
Denis	30	M	Laborer or Spinster	Ireland	United States	Sarah G.	15 Aug 1827
Edmund	12	M		Ireland	America	Liverpool	31 Aug 1827
Eliza	27	F	Comedian	England		Britannia	20 Jun 1827
James	26	M	Weaver	Wegan	United States	Dalhousie Castle	27 Jul 1826
Jeremiah	15	M	Labourer	Ireland	U.States	Nancy	31 May 1823
John	6	M	Child	Ireland	Ireland	Sarah G.	28 Nov 1827
John	8	M	Laborer or Spinster	Ireland	United States	Sarah G.	15 Aug 1827
John	20	M	Merchant	St. Johns	United States	Nancey	13 May 1822
John	20	M	Farmer	Ireland	United States	Fabius	4 Jun 1828
John	21	M	Ship Wright	Great Britain	U. States	St. Croix	13 Sep 1827
John	25	M	None	Great Britain	Unknown	William Thompson	1 May 1827
Josiah	25	M	Gentleman	Boston	U. States	Bayard	7 Mar 1825
Louisa	7	F	Comedian	England		Britannia	20 Jun 1827
Mary	10	F	Laborer or Spinster	Ireland	United States	Sarah G.	15 Aug 1827
Mary	30	F	Laborer or Spinster	Ireland	United States	Sarah G.	15 Aug 1827
Mary	40	F	Wife	Ireland	Ireland	Sarah G.	28 Nov 1827
Michael	22	M	Laborer or Spinster	Ireland	United States	Sarah G.	15 Aug 1827
Nancy	18			Ireland	New York	Marcella	18 May 1827
Norry	13	F		Ireland	America	Liverpool	31 Aug 1827
Pat	18	M	Farmer	Ireland	United States	Fabius	4 Jun 1828
Pat	30	M	Ship Wright	U. States	U. States	St. Croix	13 Sep 1827
Philip	17	M	Labourer	Ireland	United States	Ann Maria	4 Oct 1824
Reganold	30	M	France	France	France	Stephania	13 Sep 1821
Solomon	30		Mariner	United States		New Orleans	27 Feb 1829
Susan	31	F	None	Lincolnshire	United States	Dalhousie Castle	27 Jul 1826
Tedde	3	M	Laborer or Spinster	Ireland	United States	Sarah G.	15 Aug 1827
Thos.	19	M	Servant	Ireland	America	Liverpool	31 Aug 1827
William	19	M	Labourer	Ireland	United States	Ann Maria	4 Oct 1824
William	22	M	Farmer	Ireland	United States	Fabius	4 Jun 1828
LANEVOILE, E.	4	M	None	U. States	U. States	Patriot	23 May 1821
Louisa	40	F	None	U. States	U. States	Patriot	23 May 1821
LANFEAR, —, Mrs.	32	F		England	U.S.	York	1 Dec 1827
A., Mr.	40	M	Merchant	U.S.	U.S.	York	1 Dec 1827
Ambrose	32	M	Mercht.	G.B.	G.B.	London	19 Dec 1823
Ambrose	35	M	Merchant	Gt. Brittain	United States	York	6 Dec 1826
LANG, Agnes	3	F		Scotland	United States	Camillus	9 May 1827
Alexr.	23	M	None	America	U.S.	Panthea	13 Nov 1823
C.	8	F		Germany	U. States	Falcon	11 Jun 1827
C., Mrs.	30	F		Scotland	United States	Camillus	9 May 1827
Caroline	7	F	there child [George & Dorothy]	France	United States	Helen	5 Sep 1828
Cornelius	1/2	M		Scotland	United States	Camillus	9 May 1827
Dorothy	37	F	his wife [George]	France	United States	Helen	5 Sep 1828
Elizabeth, his child [Joseph]	7	F		Germany	United States	Rent	13 May
Favier G. V.	26	F		France	United States	Le Voltaire	19 Jul 1828
Frederick R.	29	M	Gentleman	United States	United States	Isaac Hicks	10 Jul 1827
George	4	M	there child [George & Dorothy]	France	United States	Helen	5 Sep 1828
George	40	M	tiler	France	United States	Helen	5 Sep 1828
H. N.	16	M	Farmer	Germany	U. States	Falcon	11 Jun 1827
Harmon	21	M	Blacksmith	Germany	U.S.A.	Hudson	21 Aug 1829
Jacob	13	M	Farmer	Germany	U. States	Falcon	11 Jun 1827
James	39 4/12	M	Weaver	Scotland	U. States	Hopes Delight	21 Apr 1828
Janet	6	F		Scotland	United States	Camillus	9 May 1827
Jno.	30	M	Mariner	Scotland	S. Croix	Nancy	7 Feb 1825
Joanna, his wife [Joseph]	20	F		Germany	United States	Rent	13 May
Joseph	30	M	Wheelwright	Germany	United States	Rent	13 May
Margaret	5	F		Scotland	United States	Camillus	9 May 1827
Margaretha	13	F		Germany	U. States	Falcon	11 Jun 1827
Marie	1/12	F		France	United States	Le Voltaire	19 Jul 1828

*born at Sea

713

NAMES OF PASSENGERS	AGE	SEX	OCCUPATIONS	COUNTRY TO WHICH THEY BELONG	COUNTRY THEY INTEND TO INHABIT	SHIPS/DATES OF ARRIVAL	
LANG (cont'd)							
Marie	3	F		France	United States	Le Voltaire	19 Jul 1828
Marie	26	F		France	United States	Le Voltaire	19 Jul 1828
Marie G. M.	3...	F		France	United States	Le Voltaire	19 Jul 1828
Mary	17	F	Lady	United States		Elias Burger	28 May 1821
Michael	1 6/12	M	there child [George & Dorothy]	France	United States	Helen	5 Sep 1828
Nancy	22		Spinster	Ireland	United States	Robert Burns	18 Jun 1821
Peter	28	M	Farmer	Germany	U. States	Falcon	11 Jun 1827
Pierre	47	M		France	United States	Le Voltaire	19 Jul 1828
Richard	26	M	Labourer	Ireland	United States	Jubilee	13 Jul 1829
Robert	29	M	Weaver	Great Britain		Dalmannock	24 Ocg 1826
Sarah	40	F	Lady	United States		Elias Burger	28 May 1821
William	46	M	Farmer	New York	New York	Hesperus	2 Nov 1820
LANGA, Joaquin, Don	22	M	Merchant	Columbia	Columbia	Enterprize	15 Nov 1825
LANGAN, Joseph	18	M	Labourer	Ireland	U. States	William Byrnes	17 Jul 1825
LANGANSTE, Antonio	25	M	Labourer	England	America	Two Marys	24 Sep 1827
J.	19	M		England	America	Two Marys	24 Sep 1827
LANGDAN, Michl.	30 2/12	M		Ireland	U.S. of America	Douglass	6 Jul 1829
LANGDEN, John	21	M	Miner	England	New York	America	1 Aug 1828
LANGDON, Ann	3	F	None	Great Britian	U. States	Henry Kneedland	7 Aug 1826
Catherine	32	F	None	Great Britian	U. States	Henry Kneedland	7 Aug 1826
Francis	30	M	None	Great Britian	U. States	Henry Kneedland	7 Aug 1826
Mary	28	F	Lady	N. York	N. York	Motion	11 Jan 1826
Mary S.	26	F		U. States	United States	Motion	15 Mar 1825
S.	15	F		U.S.	U.S.	Francois I	8 Aug 1829
LANGE, ...	36	F		Copenhagen, Denmark	going to reside in Clearfield, Pennsylvania	Friketon	7 Nov 1823
Carl	5	M		Copenhagen, Denmark	going to reside in Clearfield, Pennsylvania	Friketon	7 Nov 1823
Dorethea	9	F		Copenhagen, Denmark	going to reside in Clearfield, Pennsylvania	Friketon	7 Nov 1823
Frederica	5	F		Copenhagen, Denmark	going to reside in Clearfield, Pennsylvania	Friketon	7 Nov 1823
Johannas	2	M		Copenhagen, Denmark	going to reside in Clearfield, Pennsylvania	Friketon	7 Nov 1823
Peter	30 4/12	M	Goldsmith	Spane	Spane	Hesper	7 Dec 1827
LANGESTER, J.	30	M	Labourer	U. States		Cordelia	8 Sep 1820
LANGFORD, Sarah	17 9/12	F	Servant	Great Britain	United States	Thames	16 May 1821
LANGHAN, Michael	22 6/12	M	Taylor	Ireland	U. States	Virginia	20 Jun 1825
LANGIN, Daniel	30	M	Labourer	Ireland	United States	Catharine	22 Jul 1825
James	25	M	Labourer	Ireland	United States	Catharine	22 Jul 1825
LANGLADE, J.	28	M	Merchant	Mexico	Canada	Saltana	18 Apr 1825
Jno.	19	M	Merchant	Aquin	Aquin, St. Domingo	Emily	2 Jun 1824
LANGLANDS, Alexander	40	M	Farmer	Great Britain	United States	Natchez	17 Aug 1822
Janet	4	F		Great Britain	United States	Natchez	17 Aug 1822
Janet	27	F		Great Britain	United States	Natchez	17 Aug 1822
Sarah	2	F		Great Britain	United States	Natchez	17 Aug 1822
Sarah	16	F		Great Britain	United States	Natchez	17 Aug 1822
William	23	M	Farmer	Great Britain	United States	Natchez	17 Aug 1822
LANGLEN, Mary	18	F	Lady	Scotland	United States	Sarah G.	15 Aug 1827
LANGLEY, Ann	23 11/12	F	Domestic	Ireland	United States	London	6 Feb 1829
Ellen	17			Ireland	U.S.	Hibernia	27 Jun 1821
Ewd.	28	M	Labourer			Hanford	17 Jul 1828
Harriet	20	F	None	England	U. States	Hercules	6 Jul 1827
Jno.	16	M		U. States	U. States	Decatur	29 Nov 1825
Rose	26	F	Spinster			Hanford	17 Jul 1828
Thomas	28	M	Farmer	England	U. States	Hercules	6 Jul 1827

NAMES OF PASSENGERS	AGE	SEX	OCCUPATIONS	COUNTRY TO WHICH THEY BELONG	COUNTRY THEY INTEND TO INHABIT	SHIPS/DATES OF ARRIVAL	
LANGLEY (cont'd)							
Timothy	31	M	Merchant	Great Britain	United States	James Cropper	27 Sep 1821
William	23	M	Wheelright	England	United States	London	21 May 1828
LANGLOIS, Mary	32	F	None	France		Charlemagne	20 Aug 1829
LANGLY, Francis	21	M	Farmer	Ireland	United States	Dublin Packet	28 Apr 1824
LANGON, Mary	24	F	Farmer	Ireland	America	Farmer	4 Aug 1825
Patt	1	M	Farmer	Ireland	America	Farmer	4 Aug 1825
Peter	26	M	Farmer	Ireland	America	Farmer	4 Aug 1825
LANGRIDGE, Eliza	17	F		England	U. States	Acosta	28 Jul 1823
Frances	36	F		England	U. States	Acosta	28 Jul 1823
John L.	20	M	Clerk	U. Kingdom of Great Britain	United States	Cambria	7 May 1828
Stephen	41	M	Farmer	England	U. States	Acosta	28 Jul 1823
LANGSDALE, Edward	36	M	Stone Mason	England	U.S.A.	Lima	6 Dec 1826
LANGSDON, Wm.	33	M	Mercht.	England	Charleston	Canada	1 Nov 1823
LANGSDORFF, Louis	45	M	Counsellor	Grand Duchy of Baden		Howard	4 Feb 1826
LANGSTAFF, Biene	28	M	Laborer	Switzerland	U.S.	C. Amelia	30 Jun 1828
Cat.	3	F		Switzerland	U.S.	C. Amelia	30 Jun 1828
Geo.	47	M		Switzerland	U.S.	C. Amelia	30 Jun 1828
Jacob	19	M		Switzerland	U.S.	C. Amelia	30 Jun 1828
Jno.	25	M	Farmer	Ireland	America	Mary	29 May 1827
Mary	17	M	Laborer	Ireland	United States	Delta	24 Oct 1829
Mary	40	F	None	Ireland	United States	Jubilee	1 Oct 1828
LANGTON, Cath.	30	F		Gt. Britain	United States	Penelope	9 Sep 1828
Eliza	19	F	...	...	United States	Minerva	30 Oct 1827
Emma	31	F		England	United States	Cincinnatus	21 Nov 1821
Thomas	35	M	Taylor	Ireland	United States	Abigale	17 Jul 1822
William	40	M	Servant	England	England	Britannia	5 Nov 1828
LANGUILLE, —	20	M	Merchant	France	U. States	Maria Ann	29 Sep 1823
*landed at Balize [Biloxi?], Missippi							
LANGUNETTE, J. J.	20		Merchant	Great Britian	Halifax	America	28 Jul 1826
LANGWORTHY, S. S.	22	M	Merchant	Saratoga, N. York	U. States	General Jackson	25 Jun 1823
T. S.	21	M	Merchant	New York	Saratoga	Wilson	28 Aug 1822
LANIEER, Eugeine	22 4/12	M	Merchant	France	U.S. America	Edward Bonnaffe	20 Jun 1826
LANKFORD, John	28	M	Baker	G.B.	New York	Eliza Grant	29 Aug 1829
John	28	M	Baker	Great Britain		Eliza Grant	29 Aug 1829
LANKMAN, Clarisa	28	F				Cassack	25 Jul 1820
Cors.	28	M				Cassack	25 Jul 1820
LANKSTON, ...	12	M	Child	Great Britain	United States	Superior	31 Mar 1828
...	40	M	Engineer	Great Britain	United States	Superior	31 Mar 1828
...th	40	F	Spinster	Great Britain	United States	Superior	31 Mar 1828
John	11	M	Child	Great Britain	United States	Superior	31 Mar 1828
LANNEGAN, John	34	M	Labourer	England and Ireland	United States	Jubilee	12 May 1828
LANNITH, Geo.	40	M	Merchant	Great Britain	Great Britain	John Jay	8 May 1828
LANOIN, Francis	21	M		America	New York	Cincinnatus	5 Dec 1825
LA NOIR, Catherine	30	F				Henri IV	17 May 1828
Piere	39	M	Farmer			Henri IV	17 May 1828
LANSD, Gerold	18	M	Gent	Ireland	N. York	Trusty	12 Sep 1828
LANSDALE, Henry T.	19	M	Merchant	G. Britain	United States	Sarah G.	15 May 1828
LANSDON, Amanuel	20	M	Labourer	England	U.N. States	Earl of Liverpool	20 Aug 1825
LANSDOUN, Emanuel	27		Paper Harner	England	New York	Caroline	10 Mar 1828
LANSFIELD, —, Child	7	M	None	Great Britain	United States	Nimrod	5 Apr 1821
Wm.	40	M	Shoemaker	Great Britain	United States	Nimrod	5 Apr 1821
LANSING, J. B.	25	M	Merchant	Spain	U. States	Native	15 Apr 1826
LANSSAT, Alfred	32	M	Merchant	United States	United States	William	6 Oct 1828
LANTIER, Frans.	42	M	Baker		U. States	Petit Antoine	18 Jul 1827
Lazarria	15				U. States	Petit Antoine	18 Jul 1827
Victor	30	F	Wife		U. States	Petit Antoine	18 Jul 1827
LANTRON, Ts.	20	M	Gentleman	G. Brittain	U. States	Clarence	8 Dec 1821
LANTRY, Mary	18	F		Ireland	United States	Thompson	12 Sep 1827
LANUZA, Cayilano	42	M	Doctor	Spain	Cuba	Adonis	17 Aug 1824
Josa	9	M	Merchant	Spain	America	Rolla	9 Aug 1828
Juan Maria	35	M	Merchant	Spain	America	Rolla	9 Aug 1828
LANVEE, Charles	30	M	Hatter	France	United States	Hannibal	12 Oct 1829

NAMES OF PASSENGERS	AGE	SEX	OCCUPATIONS	COUNTRY TO WHICH THEY BELONG	COUNTRY THEY INTEND TO INHABIT	SHIPS/DATES OF ARRIVAL	
LANY, Catherine	29 6/12	F	Farmer	Switzerland	America	Henry	17 May 1828
George	6	M	Farmer	Switzerland	America	Henry	17 May 1828
George	36	M	Farmer	Switzerland	America	Henry	17 May 1828
Margaret	22 5/12	F	Farmer	Switzerland	America	Henry	17 May 1828
Peter	2 8/12	M	Farmer	Switzerland	America	Henry	17 May 1828
LANYAN, Thos. Jas.	20	M	Farmer	England	U. States	Commerce	2 Oct 1823
LAPARD, Patt., Mas.	9	M	None	Grate Britain	...	Courier	14 Jun 1825
Richard, Mas.	11	M	None	Grate Britain	...	Courier	14 Jun 1825
LAPHAM, W.	30	M	Merchant	Ireland	U. States	Howard	11 Jan 1827
LAPHANS, Bernerd	28	M	Cooper	Great Britain	U. States	Lady Hunter	28 May 1823
LAPIER, Jas.	25	M	Merchant	France	U. States	General A. Jackson	9 Apr 1822
LA PLACE, Theod.	45	M	Merchant	France		Columbia	30 Jul 1821
LAPONNE, D.	25	M	Merchant	France	France	Meta	5 Jun 1824
LAPP, Edward	1	M	None	Germany	U. States	Sully	24 Oct 1828
Ferdinand	8	M	None	Germany	U. States	Sully	24 Oct 1828
Louisa	3	F	None	Germany	U. States	Sully	24 Oct 1828
Mary	28	F	None	Germany	U. States	Sully	24 Oct 1828
Philip	30	M	Brazier	Germany	U. States	Sully	24 Oct 1828
Philip, Jr.	6 6/12	M	None	Germany	U. States	Sully	24 Oct 1828
William	4 6/12	M	None	Germany	U. States	Sully	24 Oct 1828
LAPPIN, Anne	36	F	None	Great Brittain	U. States	Louisa	11 Jun 1824
Bridget	1	M	None	Great Brittain	U. States	Louisa	11 Jun 1824
Mary	4	M	None	Great Brittain	U. States	Louisa	11 Jun 1824
Thos.	10	M	None	Great Brittain	U. States	Louisa	11 Jun 1824
Wm.	13	M	None	Great Brittain	U. States	Louisa	11 Jun 1824
Wm.	40	M	Labourer	Great Brittain	U. States	Louisa	11 Jun 1824
LAPPING, Dennis	24	M	Farmer	Great Brittain	United States	Active	12 Sep 1828
Margret	24	F		Great Brittain	United States	Active	12 Sep 1828
LAPPTHORN, Jane	23			England	England	Corinthian	8 Oct 1828
LAPSLEY, William	21	M	Printer	Canada		Fame	9 Dec 1826
LAPTHORN, Henry	48	M	Carpenter	England	U.S.A.	Brighton	21 Jan 1826
LARA, Arthur	...	M		Irland	United States	Nancy	28 Oct 1822
LARAGAR, John	40	M	Labourer	Ireland	United States	Borneo	14 Aug 1827
LARBER, Clb.	27	M	Merchant	Germany	U. States	Canada	6 Jun 1825
LARDEN, Charles	30	M		Ireland	U. States	Vermont	19 Jun 1827
LARDES, J. L.	25	M	Merchant	France	U. States	Boston	25 Apr 1825
LAREN, James	25	M	Carpenter	Ireland	U. States	Meteor	19 Jul 1828
LARENCE, T. E.	25	M	Merchant	Great Britain	America	Nancy	18 Aug 1821
LARGE, Christopher	25	M	Farmer	Gt. Britain	U. States	New York Packet	6 Aug 1824
D.	43	M	Merchant	U. States	U. States	Leader	17 Sep 1821
Eliza	21	F	Wife	Gt. Britain	U. States	New York Packet	6 Aug 1824
Wm.	30	M	Farmer	Gt. Britain	United States	Penelope	9 Sep 1828
LARGY, Barnard	29	M	Spinster	Ireland	U. States	Concordia	11 Jun 1823
Betsey	10	F		Ireland	U. States	Concordia	11 Jun 1823
Ellen	6	F		Ireland	U. States	Concordia	11 Jun 1823
Mary	30	F		Ireland	U. States	Concordia	11 Jun 1823
LARINA, John	27	M	Spanish Navy	Cadiz	Spain	General Brown	10 Dec 1823
LA RINAGA, A. G.	25	M	Merchant	Spain	Spain	Fabius	3 Jun 1825
LARING, Margaret	23	F		Ireland	New York	New York	5 May 1828
LARKEN, Edwd.	30	M	Farmers and Mechanics	Ireland	America	Constitution	1 Oct 1825
LARKEY, Andrew	22	M	Carpenter	Ireland	United States	General Putnam	20 Jun 1825
Eugine	18	M	Farmer	Ireland	United States	Asia	29 Jul 1829
Philip	30	M		Ireland		Lady Hunter	12 Apr 1823
LARKIN, Ann	40	F	Farmer	England	New York	Brighton	11 Dec 1827
Edmd.	30	M	Labourer	Ireland	New Orleans	Commerce	24 Sep 1823
Edward	25	M	Laborer	Great Britian	United States	Columbia	21 Jan 1828
Eliza	16	F	Farmer	England	New York	Brighton	11 Dec 1827
James	40	M	Farmer	Ireland	America	Josephine	8 Jan 1827
John	3	M		Ireland	America	Josephine	8 Jan 1827
John	21	M	Joiner	England	United States	Lord Wellington	14 Nov 1827
John	22 4/12	M	Labourer	Scotland	United States	London	6 Feb 1829
John	40	M	Farmer	England	New York	Brighton	11 Dec 1827
Joseph	30	M	Farmer	England	New York	Brighton	11 Dec 1827
Joseph J.	24	M	Mariner	U. States	U. States	Rice Plant	22 May 1827
Mary	7	F		Ireland	America	Josephine	8 Jan 1827

NAMES OF PASSENGERS	AGE	SEX	OCCUPATIONS	COUNTRY TO WHICH THEY BELONG	COUNTRY THEY INTEND TO INHABIT	SHIPS/DATES OF ARRIVAL	
LARKIN (cont'd)							
Mary	22	F		Gt. Britain	United States	Penelope	9 Sep 1828
Mary	28	F	Farmer	England	New York	Brighton	11 Dec 1827
Richard	5	M		Ireland	America	Josephine	8 Jan 1827
LARLEY, Ellen	18	F	None	Great Brittan	United States	America	24 Jul 1827
LARMOUR, Matthew	28	M		Antrim, Ireland	New York	Anthusa	24 Aug 1825
LARNED, Jno. S.	42	M	Merchant	U. States	U.S.	Fame	22 Mar 1826
LA ROCHE, Fanny	27	F		Jacmel	St. Domingo	Eliza Ann	17 Jul 1824
Luis Auguste	13	M	Mariner	France	Bordeaux	Rachel Ann	13 Mar 1829
LAROCHEL, Charles	22	M	Unknown	Hayti	Hayti	Chauncy	10 Jan 1820
LAROCHELE,							
Charles Adoleph	40	M	Mechanic	France	France	Splendid	31 Aug 1827
LAROCHELL, C.	25	M	Mercht.	Hayty	U. States	Pedler	2 Jul 1823
LA ROCHELLE, Chas.	29	M	Merchant	Aux Cayes	Aux Cayes	Eloise	30 Apr 1824
LA ROCQUE, F. A.	35	M	Merchant	Canada	Canada	William Byrnes	6 Apr 1826
LA ROGUE, Frs. A.	42	M	Merchant	Canada	Canada	Corinthian	5 May 1827
LAROQUE, Edward	26	M	Merchant	New York	America	Don Quixotte	2 Jun 1828
LA ROSER, F.	23	M	Gentleman	Spain	U. States for a time	Lucy Ann	17 Apr 1822
LAROUEL, Pierre	25			Switzerland	Interior	Desdemona	12 Jun 1826
LAROUGE, Edw.	28	M	Merchant	France	U. States	Amiable Matilda	28 Sep 1822
LARRADO, Jose	37	M	Merchant	Spain	Spain	Centurion	20 Aug 1828
Ygnacio	30	M	Merchant	Spain	Spain	Centurion	20 Aug 1828
LARRIA, Jose	55	M	Gentleman	Spain	S. America	Abeona	12 Oct 1825
LARRIEN, E.	23	M	Merchant	France	United States	Howard	20 Aug 1827
LARRIEU, Amédeé	23	M		France	France	Britannia	22 Jul 1829
Eugene	20	M	Merchant	France	U.S.	Edward Bonnaffe	20 Jun 1825
LARRY, Jos.	23	M	Farmer	Ireland	New York	New York	5 May 1828
LARS, A.	18	F	None	England	U. States	Birmingham	12 Oct 1827
R.	26	M	Merchant	England	U. States	Birmingham	12 Oct 1827
LARSEN, Christian	22	M	Mechanic	Denmark	U. States	Chase	5 Oct 1824
LARSON, Thos.	28	M	Labourer	Ireland	Pittsburgh	Orozimbo	8 Jun 1822
LARTCH, Jean	46	F	Spinster	Swtserland	America	Saluda	18 Jun 1825
Pat.	27	F	Weaver	Ireland	U. States	Adno	5 Jul 1828
LA RUE, Lewis, Mr., Junr.	22	M	Merchant	U. States	U. States	Lewis	11 Nov 1824
LARUE, Delia	30	F		St. Domingo	U. States	Fair Play	22 Feb 1823
Edward	21	M	Mercht.	France	Havre	Lewis	29 Oct 1825
L., Mr.	22	M	Gent.	France		Henri IV	7 May 1827
Wm.	24	M	Physician	Canada	Canada	London	19 Dec 1823
LARUSE, A.	4...	M	Master	France	France	Sloop Packet	5 Oct 1821
LARVETTAN,							
John Francis	44	M	Merchant	Hytia	U. States	Pedlar	17 Sep 1824
LARWELL, Abraham	47	M	Brazier	England	United States	Criterion	27 Oct 1820
Abrm.	12		None	Sussex	England	Elizabeth	8 Dec 1821
Ebnr.	14		None	Sussex	England	Elizabeth	8 Dec 1821
Edwin	11		None	Sussex	England	Elizabeth	8 Dec 1821
Eliza	18		None	Sussex	England	Elizabeth	8 Dec 1821
Elizabeth	41		None	Sussex	England	Elizabeth	8 Dec 1821
Henr.	3		None	Sussex	England	Elizabeth	8 Dec 1821
John	9		None	Sussex	England	Elizabeth	8 Dec 1821
Maria	8		None	Sussex	England	Elizabeth	8 Dec 1821
Sarah	6		None	Sussex	England	Elizabeth	8 Dec 1821
LARY, Helen	22	M	Servant	United States	United States	Only Daughter	29 Apr 1825
LARYE, E. F.	23	M	Hatter	Havre Towns	New York	Leeds	7 Nov 1828
LASA, S. S.	10	M	None	Spain	France & Spain	Native	24 Aug 1825
LASALA, A.	31	M	Merchant	Spain	Spain	Claudio	22 Mar 1828
LASALE, Jno.	38	M	Merchant	Germany	U. States	Sarah	5 Aug 1825
LASALLE, Joseph	34 6/12	M	Merchant	Germany	U.S.	Otho	2 Jan 1822
LASANAGH, Francis	38	M	Mariner	Spain	Spain	Abigail	19 May 1826
LA SAUBLER,							
Joseph	15 3/12	M	Bookkeeper	America, U.S.	America, U.S.	Illinois	3 Jun 1822
LASCANO, A.	12	M	Servent	Spain	United States	Enterprize	9 Aug 1825
J.	10	M	Servent	Spain	U. States	Enterprize	9 Aug 1825
LASH, George	6	M	Child	England	United States	Cambria	3 Jul 1829
Jane	38		Wife	England	United States	Cambria	3 Jul 1829
Martha	9	F	Child	England	United States	Cambria	3 Jul 1829
Richard	13	M	Child	England	United States	Cambria	3 Jul 1829
Richard	42	M	Farmer	England	United States	Cambria	3 Jul 1829
Susan	11	F	Child	England	United States	Cambria	3 Jul 1829

NAMES OF PASSENGERS	AGE	SEX	OCCUPATIONS	COUNTRY TO WHICH THEY BELONG	COUNTRY THEY INTEND TO INHABIT	SHIPS/DATES OF ARRIVAL	
LASH (cont'd)							
Thomas	1 3/12	M	Child	England	United States	Cambria	3 Jul 1829
LASHMAN, Francis	22	M	Farmer	Great Brittan	United States	Cambria	11 Feb 1829
LASPLEY, George	37	M	Gentleman	England	America	Hercules	10 Apr 1823
LASQUA, —, Mr.	45	M	Upholster	America	United States	Andrew Jackson	9 Jul 1822
—, Mrs.	30	F		America	United States	Andrew Jackson	9 Jul 1822
LASSAC, Adolph	30	M	Farmer	Ireland	United States	Jubilee	13 Jul 1829
LASSAL, Joseph	34	M	Doctor	Netherlands		Armadillo	13 Aug 1829
LASSERRE, Peter	27		Taylour, White Man	France	France	Argus	17 Aug 1826
LASTRANGE, Thomas	29	M	Farmer	Ireland	U.S.A.	Dalhouse Castle	21 Aug 1829
Thos.	29	M	Farmer	Ireland	United States	Dalhouse Castle	21 Aug 1829
LATASA, Juan	28	M	Merchant	Caracas	Caracas	Herald	21 Sep 1824
LATASTE, Victor	16	M	Merchant	France	N. Orleans	Desdemona	21 Oct 1825
LATCH, Carl	20	M	Brewer & wasser	Bardin	U. States	Bayard	5 Sep 1828
LATCHIZE, W.	32	M	Priest	France	U. States	Monroe	13 May 1823
LATERMANDER, A.	9	F		Spain	U. States	Monroe	13 May 1823
D.	19	M		Spain	U. States	Monroe	13 May 1823
De.	30	M	Consul to Florada	Spain	U. States	Monroe	13 May 1823
LATHAM, Catherine	6	F	None	England	U. States	Frances Henrietta	25 Oct 1824
Charles, Mr.	25	M	Merchant	Great Britain	Great Britain	Nestor	3 Nov 1820
Henry	9	M	None	England	U. States	Frances Henrietta	25 Oct 1824
James	26	M	Joeiner	England	America	Britannia	22 Jul 1829
Louisa	8	F	None	England	U. States	Frances Henrietta	25 Oct 1824
Mary	54	F	None	England	U. States	Frances Henrietta	25 Oct 1824
LATHELESI, —	35	M	Missionary	France	France	Rousseau	19 Apr 1825
LATHERMAN, John	43	M	Labourer	Germany	United States	Samuel Robertson	8 Aug 1828
Maria	52	F		Germany	United States	Samuel Robertson	8 Aug 1828
LATHROOP, J.	32	M	Merchant	U. States	U. States	Canada	2 Jun 1824
LATHWAITE, George	26	M	Labourer	Whipsey		Aurora	8 Jun 1827
LATIMER, Geo.	22	M	Merchant	U. States	U. States	Balize	29 Aug 1825
James	50	M	Merchant	United States	U. States	Superior	20 Aug 1824
Jno. R.	28	M	Merchant	Philada.	U. States	China	5 Apr 1822
John R.	29	M	Merchant	United States	United States	Superior	21 May 1823
LATIMOR, Geo.	22	M	Mariner	U. States	United States	Superior	14 Apr 1825
LATIRLIE, John	31	M	Weaver			Henri IV	17 May 1828
LATOUR, Ameda	28	M	Army	U. States	U. States	Superior Hope	27 Oct 1824
J. M.	28	M	Platner	France	New York	Herald	23 Jun 1827
LATRIE, Danl.	32	M	Wheelwright	Ireland	U.S.	Oliver Wolcott	3 Nov 1827
LA TROBRIANO,							
Jacques	46	M	Colonel	France	United States	Montano	8 May 1827
LATTA, Eliza	30			United States	United States	Hudson	14 Jun 1827
Robert	40		Merchant	Ireland	United States	Hudson	14 Jun 1827
Sarah E.	4			United States	United States	Hudson	14 Jun 1827
William A.	17			United States	United States	Hudson	14 Jun 1827
Wm.	45	M	Farmer	Pennsylvania	U. States	Antelope	23 Mar 1824
LATTAPY, John	25	M	Merchant	France	France	Hannah Elizabeth	14 Sep 1827
LATTER, George	27	M	Farmer	England	New York	Hercules	11 Feb 1822
Sarah	26	F	Lady	England	New York	Hercules	11 Feb 1822
LATTIMORE, Elisha	26	M	Carpenter	U. States	U. States	Radius	12 Jul 1825
Etesher	26	M	Carpenter	America, Connecticut	America	William	16 Apr 1823
LATTING, Wareing	17	M	Dentist	United States	United States	Bolivar	21 May 1827
LATZ, Jno.	23	M	Labourer	Germany	United States	Margarett Scott	22 Aug 1827
LAUB, Caroline	9	F	Ropemaker	...ia	Pennsylvania	Frances Henrietta	25 Aug 1825
John	10	M	Ropemaker	...ia	Pennsylvania	Frances Henrietta	25 Aug 1825
Joseph	15	M	Ropemaker	...ia	Pennsylvania	Frances Henrietta	25 Aug 1825
Joseph	45	M	Ropemaker	...ia	Pennsylvania	Frances Henrietta	25 Aug 1825

NAMES OF PASSENGERS	AGE	SEX	OCCUPATIONS	COUNTRY TO WHICH THEY BELONG	COUNTRY THEY INTEND TO INHABIT	SHIPS/DATES OF ARRIVAL	
LAUB (cont'd)							
Mary	3	F	Ropemaker	...ia	Pennsylvania	Frances Henrietta	25 Aug 1825
Mary Ann	5	F	Ropemaker	...ia	Pennsylvania	Frances Henrietta	25 Aug 1825
Mary Ann	40	F	Ropemaker	...ia	Pennsylvania	Frances Henrietta	25 Aug 1825
Richard	27	M	Merchant	U. States	U. States	York	10 Dec 1825
LAUCHAUTIN, —, Mr.	30			France	United States	Henri IV	14 Sep 1827
LAUDER, George	23	M	Merchant	Scotland		York	11 Apr 1827
LAUGHAN, M.	22	M	Weaver	Ireland	United States	Josephine	30 Apr 1828
Owen	29	M	Labourer	Great Britian	United States	Princess Charlotte	6 Sep 1828
Richd.	20	M	Merchant	New York	New York	New York Packet	8 May 1823
LAUGHERAN, Charles	28	M	Bricklayer	England	U. States	Hercules	6 Jul 1827
LAUGHLAN, Bryan	24	M	Black Smith	Ireland	U. States	Virginia	20 Jun 1825
John	24	M		Sligo	New York	Susquehana	27 Jun 1823
John	71	...	...	Ireland	United States	Carolina Ann	24 Oct 1825
LAUGHLAY, J. M.	34	M		Great Britain	Canada	James Monroe	25 Apr 1822
LAUGHLIN, James	28	M	Fer.	Wales	U. States	Franklin	7 Jul 1828
Martin	23	M	Labourer	Ireland	America	Weser	26 Jun 1821
Nancey	17	F	Spinster	Ireland	United States	Wilson	4 Oct 1827
Thomas	20	M	Farmer		New York	Robert Fulton	8 Mar 1823
LAUGHLON, David	26	M	Book Keeper	Scotland	United States	Orozimbo	11 Aug 1823
LAUGHRAM, Geo.	2	F	Labourer	Ireland	U. States	Atlantic	19 Aug 1825
LAUGRIDGE, Ann	2	F		G. Brittain	U. States	Cincinnatus	2 Oct 1822
James	3	M		G. Brittain	U. States	Cincinnatus	2 Oct 1822
John	35	M	Farmer	G. Brittain	U. States	Cincinnatus	2 Oct 1822
Lydia	27	F		G. Brittain	U. States	Cincinnatus	2 Oct 1822
Susan	6/12	F		G. Brittain	U. States	Cincinnatus	2 Oct 1822
LAUGSHAW, Saml.	35	M	Merchant	England	U. States	Rising Sun	1 May 1823
LAULE, Bridget	7	F		Ireland	New York	Xenophon	3 Oct 1829
LAUND, Alice	29	F	Farmer	England	United States	Siroc	31 Oct 1829
Isabella	1	F	Farmer	England	United States	Siroc	31 Oct 1829
Robert	30	M	Farmer	England	United States	Siroc	31 Oct 1829
LAUNDER, Mary	27	F	None	Great Britian	United States	Isaac Hicks	23 Aug 1825
William	29	M	Merchant	Great Britian	United States	Isaac Hicks	23 Aug 1825
LAUNDERS, James	40	M	Currier	England	United States	Cambria	3 Jul 1829
Sarah	33	F		England	United States	Cambria	3 Jul 1829
LAUNDREAU, P.	24	M	Gentleman	U. States	U. States	New York	22 Jul 1824
LAUNEY, Henry A.	30	M	Labourer	Great Britain	United States	Courier	13 Mar 1820
LAUR, Dorotha	50	F	Farmer	Switzerland	United States	Olympia	12 Aug 1828
LAUR..., —	24	M	Farmer	Switzerland	United States	Olympia	12 Aug 1828
LAURANCE, Jno.		M	None	U. States	U. States	South Carolina	22 Dec 1824
Wm.	21	M	W. Maker	Ireland	New York	Trusty	12 Sep 1828
LAURANSON, M.	37	M	Merchant	France	France	Ranger	3 May 1828
V.	35	M	Merchant	France	France	Ranger	3 May 1828
LAURAT, W.	40	M	Merchant	France	U. States	Arrington	14 Nov 1825
LAURÉ, Jilles	23	M	Apothecerry	Native of Niort	New York	Superiour	11 Oct 1828
LAURENCE, Boverton	50	M	None	G. Britton	U. States	Sully	25 Jun 1828
H.	26	M	Merchant	U. States	U. States	Gov. Clinton	1 Feb 1827
Isaac	70	M	Farmer	New Brunswick	St. John, N.B.	Nancy	15 Nov 1824
Nicholas	23	M	Coachmaker	New York	U. States	Lydia	7 Oct 1823
Peter P.	2	M	Mason	France	U. States	Sully	25 Jun 1828
S.	26	M		America	America	Corinthian	1 Sep 1827
Saml.	21	M	Farmer	England	United States	Earl of Liverpool	29 Sep 1823
LAURENS, Charles	23	M	Teacher	France	U. States	Sully	24 Oct 1828
LAURENSON, Mary	18	F		United States	United States	Robert Fulton	27 Jun 1822
LAURENT, Charles	28	M	Gunsmith	Swizerland		Antioch	18 Aug 1829
J. R.	21	M	Merchant	Switzerland	U. States	Lewis	20 Feb 1824
John	18	M	Farmer	France	U. States	Bayard	16 May 1827
John	35	M	Servant	France	France	Caledonia	10 Sep 1828
Joseph	3	M	Farmer	France	U. States	Bayard	16 May 1827
Joseph	65	M	Farmer	France	U. States	Bayard	16 May 1827
Louis B.	22	M	Farmer	France	U. States	Bayard	16 May 1827
Mary F.	24	F	Farmer	France	U. States	Bayard	16 May 1827
Peter F.	25	M	Farmer	France	U. States	Bayard	16 May 1827

NAMES OF PASSENGERS	AGE	SEX	OCCUPATIONS	COUNTRY TO WHICH THEY BELONG	COUNTRY THEY INTEND TO INHABIT	SHIPS/DATES OF ARRIVAL
LAURENTT, Henry	24	M	Weaver	France	U. States	Edward Quesnel 4 Aug 1828
LAUREY, Chas.	12	M	Mercht.	France	United States	Bayard 13 Nov 1823
LAURIE, Edwd.	40	M	Mechanic	N. York	N. York	Free Ocean 14 Feb 1824
Isabella	24	F	None	England	U.S.A.	Lima 6 Dec 1826
Thomas	38	M	Mercht.	England	U.S.A.	Lima 6 Dec 1826
Wm.	20	M	Gentleman	G. Britain		Diana 14 Sep 1820
LAUSON, Hannah	20	F		G. Britain	U. States	Nimrod 31 Jul 1828
Joseph	5	M		G. Britain	U. States	Nimrod 31 Jul 1828
LAUTESLOT, Maria	20	F	Farmer	Switzerland		Antioch 18 Aug 1829
LAUTRY, Ann	31	F		Ireland	United States	Thompson 12 Sep 1827
John	1	M		Ireland	United States	Thompson 12 Sep 1827
Pat	4	M		Ireland	United States	Thompson 12 Sep 1827
Pat	31	M		Ireland	United States	Thompson 12 Sep 1827
Timothy	3	M		Ireland	United States	Thompson 12 Sep 1827
Wm.	6	M		Ireland	United States	Thompson 12 Sep 1827
LAUXEN, Jose	42	M	Gentleman	Spain	Spain	Sabina 5 May 1826
LAVAGUE, A.	30	M	Merchant	France	New York	Queen Mab 20 Nov 1826
LAVALETTE, L.	25	M	Planter	Spain	U.S.	Radius 29 Jul 1823
LA VASSEUR, Auguste	28	M	Gent.	France	France	Cadmus 17 Aug 1824
LAVATER, Chas.	26	M	Gentleman	Germany	England	Leo 9 Jul 1825
LAVATY, John	25	M	Farmer	Ireland	United States	Leonidas 3 Aug 1825
LAVENDER, Eliza	30	F	None	England	U. States	Hercules 6 Jul 1827
Harriet	2	F	None	England	U. States	Hercules 6 Jul 1827
John	11	M	None	England	U. States	Hercules 6 Jul 1827
John	41	M	Farmer	England	U. States	Hercules 6 Jul 1827
Mary	8	F	None	England	U. States	Hercules 6 Jul 1827
Thomas	3	M	None	England	U. States	Hercules 6 Jul 1827
Thomas	38 7/12	M	Gentlman.	England	England	France 28 Mar 1829
LAVENGSTON, D.	35	M	Coachman	New York	United States	Falcon 16 Aug 1826
LAVEOLELLE, Charles	30	M	Upholsterer	France	United States	Howard 14 May 1825
J. B.	20	M	Upholsterer	France	United States	Howard 14 May 1825
L.	18	M	Portor	...	United States	Howard 14 May 1825
LAVERGNE, Ha.	40	M	Merchant	U. States	U. States	Silas Richards 29 Oct 1828
LAVERS, Mary	28			England	England	Corinthian 8 Oct 1828
LAVERSUSS, John	34	M	Farmer	Gt. Brittain	United States	Cortex 7 Mar 1823
LAVERTY, Daniel	34	M	Weaver	Scotland	United States	Princess Charlotte 26 Apr 1827
Mary	35	F	Spinster	Great Britain	United States	Rosina 28 May 1827
LAVERY, John	26	M	Baker	Ireland	America	Plutarch 18 Jul 1826
Margret	24	F		Ireland	United States	Aurora 9 Jul 1827
Patrick	20	M	Labourer	England	U. States	Hope & Esther 10 Jul 1827
LAVETTE, M.	30	F	Lady	France	United States	Exchange 16 Feb 1822
Prospere	2	M	None	France	United States	Exchange 16 Feb 1822
LAVIA, Christian	21	F	Spinster	Ireland	United States	Marmion 17 Jun 1825
LAVIER, —, Mrs.	34	F	Priestess	France	U.S.	Edward Quesnel 31 Jul 1827
LAVIEUVILLE, —	22	M	Gilder	france	U. States	Belle 28 Dec 1824
LAVIGNE, —	5	M		United States	United States	Robert Read 10 Jan 1825
Jacques, Mde.	30	F	Widow	United States	United States	Robert Read 10 Jan 1825
James	28	M	Gentleman	France	United States	Cicero 9 Nov 1825
Joseph	4	M		United States	United States	Robert Read 10 Jan 1825
Savary	1	M		United States	United States	Robert Read 10 Jan 1825
LAVINE, Sidney Lindo	21	M	Clerk	England	United States	Rebecca 11 Jan 1828
LAVINGTON, Mary Jane	22	F	Spinster	G. Britain	U. States	Hanford 18 Sep 1828
LAVIOTTE, Emile	6	M		Gaudaloupe	Morristown, N.J.	Horace 31 May 1822
LAVMEY, Henry	24	M	Sugar Baker	Germany	U.S. America	Cincinnatus 31 Oct 1820
LAVRE, —	49	M	Merchant	France	U. States	Charles 19 Dec 1822
LAW, —, Mrs.	33	F		G. Britain	U. States	Camillus 8 Sep 1828
Ann	23	F		Scotland	U.S.	Curler 19 Jul 1828
Anna	9	F				Cassack 25 Jul 1820
B.	24	M		Scotland	U.S.	Curler 19 Jul 1828
Cath.	1	F		Scotland	U.S.	Curler 19 Jul 1828
D...	44	M	Farmer	Scotland	United States	Samuel Robertson 9 May 1827
Da..., Junr.	18	M	Farmer	Scotland	United States	Samuel Robertson 9 May 1827
Daniel	8	M		G. Britain	U. States	Camillus 8 Sep 1828
Eliza	30	F	None	England	U. States	Hercules 6 Jul 1827
Elizabeth	22	F	Chamber maid	England		Stephania 22 Apr 1822
Frances	5	F	Child	Great Britain	U. States	Robert Fulton 3 Dec 1827

NAMES OF PASSENGERS	AGE	SEX	OCCUPATIONS	COUNTRY TO WHICH THEY BELONG	COUNTRY THEY INTEND TO INHABIT	SHIPS/DATES OF ARRIVAL	
LAW (cont'd)							
George	33	M	Merchant	U. States Amer		Ann Maria	29 Nov 1821
James	23	M	Merchant	England		Aspasia	19 Jul 1823
James	55	M	Farmer	England		Britannia	20 Jun 1827
Jemima	5	F				Cassack	25 Jul 1820
John	25		Weaver	Ballymore	Ireland	Carolina Ann	21 May 1823
John	30		Gardner	Scotland	United States	Camillus	3 May 1828
John	33	M	Carpenter	G. Britain	U. States	Wanderer	23 Jun 1828
John, Mrs.	23			Scotland	United States	Camillus	3 May 1828
John K.	21	M	Merchant	U.S. America	U.S. America	William Frederick	17 Mar 1825
Joseph	56	M	None	Great Britain		Moro Castle	6 Jul 1827
Martha	20	F	None	Great Britain		Moro Castle	6 Jul 1827
Mary	7	F				Cassack	25 Jul 1820
Mary	7	F	Child	Great Britain	U. States	Robert Fulton	3 Dec 1827
Mary	33	F	Matron	Great Britain	U. States	Robert Fulton	3 Dec 1827
Mary	38	F	None	Great Britain		Moro Castle	6 Jul 1827
Moses	40			England		Anacreon	7 Sep 1827
Peter	10	M		G. Britain	U. States	Camillus	8 Sep 1828
Thomas	1 6/12	M	Child	Great Britain	U. States	Robert Fulton	3 Dec 1827
Thomas	30	M	None	England	U. States	Hercules	6 Jul 1827
Thomas	30	M	Blacksmith	Great Britain	United States	Isaac Hicks	10 Jul 1827
Thomas	34	M	Farmer	Scotland	United States	Samuel Robertson	9 May 1827
Wallace	18	M	Farmer	Ireland	United States	John Dickinson	18 Feb 1822
Wm.	14	F				Cassack	25 Jul 1820
David	...	...	...	...	...	St. Michael	22 Sep 1824
LAWDEN, John	35	M	Weaver	Ireland	United States	Robert Fulton	10 Aug 1827
Susan	21	F	Matron	Ireland	United States	Robert Fulton	10 Aug 1827
LAWDER, George	25	M	Merchant	Scotland	New York, U.S.	New York	14 Mar 1828
LAWDOR, Ann	...	M	Labourer	Ireland	United States	Meteor	26 Jun 1827
LA WELCH, Thos.	20	M	Laborer	Gt. Britain		Dalhouse Castle	13 May 1828
LAWELL, Jane	62	F	None	Great Britain	United States	Mount Vernon	30 Dec 1828
Joseph	64	M	Wever	Great Briton	United States	Mount Vernon	30 Dec 1828
William	30	M	Labourer	Ireland	New York	Potomac	7 Aug 1827
LAWGAN, Catherine	32	F	Farmer	Ireland	U.S. States	Solon	25 Nov 1824
John	37	M	Farmer	Ireland	U.S. States	Solon	25 Nov 1824
LAWGUNG, Frederick	30	M	Merchant	France	U. States	Buck	7 Aug 1822
LAWKENER, Sarah	64	F	Widdow	United States	United States	Hanford	3 Jul 1829
LAWLARD, William	50		Spring Maker	England	U. States	Venus	4 Oct 1821
LAWLER, Anastatia	17	F	Servant	Ireland	United States	Wilson	27 Jun 1826
Catherine	25	F	Matron	Ireland	America	Josephine	24 Jul 1826
Edward	22	M	Weaver	Ireland	America	Josephine	24 Jul 1826
Eliza	9/12	F	Child	Ireland	America	Josephine	24 Jul 1826
John	3	M		Ireland	New York	Lima	5 Aug 1829
Judith	32	F		Ireland	New York	Lima	5 Aug 1829
Marthew	33	M	Tobacconist	Ireland	New York	Lima	5 Aug 1829
Mary	30	F	None	Ireland	Boston	Concordia	12 Oct 1826
Mathew	33	M	Tobacconist	Ireland	New York	Lima	5 Aug 1829
Patrick	30	M	Farmer	Ireland	Boston	Concordia	12 Oct 1826
Patrick	30	M	Laborer	Ireland	United States	Lord Wellington	14 Nov 1827
Thomas	4/12	M		Ireland	New York	Lima	5 Aug 1829
LAWLESS, Ann	26		Weaver	Ireland	America	Sarah	18 Aug 1829
James	22	M	Farmer	Ireland	U. States	Dickinson	30 Jul 1825
James	27		Weaver	Ireland	America	Sarah	18 Aug 1829
Mary	11	F	Child	Ireland	United States	Dublin Packet	22 Aug 1829
Mary	25	F	Spinster	Ireland	United States	Dublin Packet	22 Aug 1829
Mary	30	F	Wife	Ireland	United States	Dublin Packet	22 Aug 1829
Patrick	28	M	Farmer	Ireland	U. States	Henry Kneeland	27 Jul 1825
Patt	9	M	Child	Ireland	United States	Dublin Packet	22 Aug 1829
Thomas	34	M	Gentelman	Ierland		Jasper	30 May 1828
LAWLOR, Thomas	25	M	Labourer	Ireland	United States	Wilson	27 Jun 1826
LAWN, John	38	M	Farmer	Scotland	U. States	Roger Stewart	9 Jun 1828
Thomas	24	M	Clothier	Great Britain	United States	Frances Henrietta	17 Sep 1827
Wm.	35	M	Shop Keeper	Gt. Brittain	United States	Balaena	21 Aug 1824
LAWNDES, Thos.	22	M	Gent.	America	America	Panthea	18 Jul 1823
LAWNEY,							
Woliot C., Capt.	41	M	U.S. Navy	U. States	U. States Navy	Caledonia	20 Jan 1829

NAMES OF PASSENGERS	AGE	SEX	OCCUPATIONS	COUNTRY TO WHICH THEY BELONG	COUNTRY THEY INTEND TO INHABIT	SHIPS/DATES OF ARRIVAL	
LAWPOT, Ambrose	37	M	Supercargo	United States	U. States	Exchange	26 Jul 1824
LAWRANCE, John	30		Bricklayer	England		Corinthian	11 Mar 1829
Jona.	18	M	Merchant	U. States	U. States	Jane	30 Apr 1825
Mary A.	60	F	Lady	State New York	United States	Sarah G.	15 Aug 1827
LAWRANSON, Martha	78	F	Lady	England	America	Braganza	1 Dec 1824
LAWREN, Knieth	35	M	Mechanic	France	America	Mary Ann	7 Dec 1827
LAWRENCE, A. S.	25	M	Merchant	New York	U. States	Edward	6 May 1822
A. S.	30	M	Merchant	U. States	U. States	Leader	23 Jul 1827
Ann	13	F	None	Gt. Brittain	United States	Balaena	9 Oct 1823
Ann	43	F	None	Gt. Brittain	United States	Balaena	9 Oct 1823
Anne	27	F	Spinster	United States	United States	Hanford	3 Jul 1829
C.	20	M	Mercht.	United States	U. States	Hiram	4 Sep 1824
C. K.	38	M	Merchant	U. States	U. States	Tampico	20 Jan 1825
C. K.	40	M	Mariner	U. States	U. States	Prince Edward	23 Dec 1823
Caroline	21	F	Lady	S. Carolina	S. Carolina	Sully	30 Oct 1827
Charles K.	37	M	Merchant	U. States	U. States	Prince Edward	29 Jul 1823
Chas. J.	40	M	Merchant	United States	United States	Prince Edward	13 Apr 1824
David		M	White	United States	United States	Falcon	1 May 1824
David	10	M	None	Gt. Brittain	United States	Balaena	9 Oct 1823
David	43	M	Farmer	Gt. Brittain	United States	Balaena	9 Oct 1823
E., Mrs.	20	F		United States		Howard	17 Oct 1822
Elizabeth	11	F		England	U. States	Criterion at London	10 May 1821
Esther, Mrs.			Lady	U.S.	U.S.	Sully	15 Jul 1829
Gilbert	22	M	Miller	State New York	United States	Sarah G.	15 Aug 1827
Godfrey	5/12	M		Switzerland	America	Saluda	16 Oct 1824
Henry	25	M	Book Binder	England	United States	American	27 Aug 1827
Henry	25	M	Merchant	N. York	N. York	Governor Clinton	17 Oct 1828
Hy.	23	M	Merchant	U. States	U. States	Pacific	11 Sep 1824
Iac.	5	M		Switzerland	America	Saluda	16 Oct 1824
Isaac, Jr.	1	M	Child	U.S.	U.S.	Sully	15 Jul 1829
J. P.	40	M	Merchant	U. States	U. States	Topaz	2 Dec 1828
J. T., Mr.	34	M	Planter	Jamaica	U. States	Nile	15 Aug 1823
Joanna	12	F	None	Gt. Brittain	United States	Balaena	9 Oct 1823
John	20	M	Miller	England	United States	Cambria	16 Aug 1827
John	36	M	Merchant	Great Britain	Canada	Canada	20 Jun 1823
John B.	28	M	Gentleman	S. Carolina	S. Carolina	Sully	30 Oct 1827
John J.	9	M		U.S.	U.S.	Agenoria	15 Jun 1822
Louis	6	M		Switzerland	America	Saluda	16 Oct 1824
M.	45	M	Mercht.	France	United States	Nestor	14 Nov 1823
Margaret	17	F	None	Gt. Brittain	United States	Balaena	9 Oct 1823
Marry	... 4/12	F	...	United States	United States	Hopes Delight	26 Aug 1829
Mary C.	33	F		Switzerland	America	Saluda	16 Oct 1824
Mathew	35	M	Blacksmith	Switzerland	America	Saluda	16 Oct 1824
Nancy	20	F		N. York	U. States	Nancy	29 Nov 1821
R., Mr.	37		Merchant	U.S. of America	U.S. America	Mary	10 Mar 1826
Robt.	36	M	Merchant	U. States	U. States	Cortes	13 Aug 1825
Roger	5	M	None	Gt. Brittain	United States	Balaena	9 Oct 1823
Saml. A.	40	M	Merchant	Rhode Island	U. States	Brandt	20 Sep 1822
Thos.	44	M	Gentleman	G. Brittain	U. States	Rengal	9 Oct 1823
W. B.	22	M	Gentleman	United States		Howard	17 Oct 1822
Walter	8	M	None	Gt. Brittain	United States	Balaena	9 Oct 1823
William, Esq.			Chargé D'affaires at the court of St. James			Sully	15 Jul 1829
Wm.	3	M	None	Gt. Brittain	United States	Balaena	9 Oct 1823
Wm.	27	M	Farmer	New Brunswick	St. John, N.B.	Nancy	15 Nov 1824
Wm. B., Jr.	4	M	Child	U.S.	U.S.	Sully	15 Jul 1829
Wm. H.	32	M	Mariner	N. York	U. States	Frances Jarvis	11 May 1822
LAWRENS, Wm.	30	M	Seaman	U. States	U. States	Chase	19 Sep 1823
LAWRENSON, Margaret	15	F	Lady	America	America	Braganza	1 Dec 1824
LAWRIN, Gilbert	24	M	Merchant	United States	United States	Hanford	3 Aug 1829
LAWRSON, Joseph	35		Labourer	Manchester, England	Great Britain	Franklin	22 Jun 1827
LAWS, Edward	30	M	Merchant	England	Great Brittan	Amity	11 May 1821
James	28	M	Mariner	United States	United States	Harriet Smith	18 Oct 1821
Thos.	68	M	Gent.	England	U. States	Pacific	20 Aug 1825
LAWSON, —, Mrs.	23	F		G. Britain	U. States	Camillus	8 Sep 1828

NAMES OF PASSENGERS	AGE	SEX	OCCUPATIONS	COUNTRY TO WHICH THEY BELONG	COUNTRY THEY INTEND TO INHABIT	SHIPS/DATES OF ARRIVAL	
LAWSON (cont'd)							
—, Mrs.	32		Spinster	Great Britain	United States	Camillus	12 Sep 1827
Alex	45	M	Labourer	Scotland	United States	Samuel Robertson	5 Oct 1827
Alexr.	8	F		G. Britain	U. States	Camillus	8 Sep 1828
Andrew	35	M	Mariner	Germany	U.S.	Frances	21 Jul 1827
Catherin A.	20	F	Lady	Denmark	U.N. States	William Byrnes	23 Jul 1824
Charlotte, Mrs.	40	F	None	Great Britain	Great Britain	Nestor	3 Nov 1820
David	20	F				Splendid	14 Aug 1829
David	24	M	Baker	Scotland	United States	Confidence	5 Sep 1828
Edward	22	M	Merchant	Gt. B.	Gt. B.	Caledonia	20 Jan 1829
Eliza	1	F	None	England	U.S.	Pacific	24 Oct 1828
Emma	28	F				Euphrates	8 Aug 1820
Fenton	21		None			Euphrates	8 Aug 1820
Geo.	30	M	Carpenter	Scotland	U.S.	Curler	19 Jul 1828
George	70	M	Gentleman	Scotland	United States	Roman	12 Jun 1826
Henry	50	M	Merchant	Scotland	United States	Camillus	28 Apr 1824
James	23	M	Merchant	Scotland	United States	Camillus	6 Apr 1821
Janny	20	F	Spinster			Commerce	22 Jun 1825
Jas.	43	M	Gentleman	Jamaica	U. States	Plandome	12 Aug 1826
Jean	9	F		G. Britain	U. States	Camillus	8 Sep 1828
John	7	M		Scotland	America	Camillus	12 Sep 1822
John	8	M	None	Great Britain	Great Britain	Nestor	3 Nov 1820
John	22	M	Farmer	Isle of Man	Isle of Man	Howard Douglass	11 May 1827
Margt.	5	F		G. Britain	U. States	Camillus	8 Sep 1828
Martha	22	F	Wife	England	U.S.	Pacific	24 Oct 1828
P.	28	M	Merchant	United States	U. States	Native	8 Feb 1826
P.	30	M	Merchant	Spain	U. States	Native	15 Apr 1826
P.	35	M	Merchant	New York	America	Constitution	2 Apr 1828
Peter	17	M	Labourer	Scotland	United States	Samuel Robertson	5 Oct 1827
Peter	19	M	Shoemaker	England	U. States	Shallet	21 Apr 1821
Peter	28	M	Merchant	New York	New York	Rebecca	31 Oct 1825
Peter	35	M	Farmer	N. York	U. States	Burdett	11 Oct 1827
Peter	40	M	Mariner	American	United States	Conclusion	4 Feb 1829
R. W.	25	M	Officer	St. Thomas	U. States	Lady Tompkins	13 Apr 1824
Rd. W.	23	M	Army	England	G. Brittain	Chase	24 Aug 1822
Robert	6					Euphrates	8 Aug 1820
Robert	20	M	Farmer	Great Britain	United States	Rosina	28 May 1827
Robt.	2	M	None	England	U.S.	Pacific	24 Oct 1828
Robt., Mr.	20	M	Surgeon	Scotland	Scotland	Hector	11 May 1821
Samuel	25	M	Farmer	Great Britain	United States	Blakely	29 Sep 1826
Thomas	31		Merchant			Euphrates	8 Aug 1820
Thos.	23	M	Brazier	England	U.S.	Pacific	24 Oct 1828
William	27	M	Merchant	Scotland	America	Minerva	8 Oct 1824
William	72		Farmer	England	United States	Thomas Dickason	5 Jun 1827
LAWTH, S.	50	M	Mariner	Philada.	U. States	Abrona	1 Nov 1821
LAWTON, —, Mrs.	25	F		New York	U. States	General Vedaneta	25 Nov 1825
Alice	7	F	None	England	United States	Trident	18 Jul 1827
Alice	40	F	None	England	United States	Trident	18 Jul 1827
Ann	20	F	Servant	G. Britain	U. States	Nimrod	31 Jul 1828
Ann	24	F		England	Canada	York	31 Mar 1828
Betty, Miss, Daughter [of James]	16	F		England		Hercules	19 Jun 1821
Chas.	4/12	M		New York	U. States	General Vedaneta	25 Nov 1825
Danl.	50		None	Lancashire	England	Great Britain	7 May 1827
Edward	19	M	Shoemaker	Ireland	United States	Trio	2 Oct 1828
Eliza	22	F	Servant	G. Britain	U. States	Nimrod	31 Jul 1828
Geo.	6/12	M		England	Canada	York	31 Mar 1828
George	27	M	Shoe Maker	Stanley Bridge	U. States	Milton	21 May 1827
Hamman, Master, Son [of James]	14	M		England		Hercules	19 Jun 1821
Hannah	49	F		G. Britain	U. States	Nimrod	31 Jul 1828

NAMES OF PASSENGERS	AGE	SEX	OCCUPATIONS	COUNTRY TO WHICH THEY BELONG	COUNTRY THEY INTEND TO INHABIT	SHIPS/DATES OF ARRIVAL	
LAWTON (cont'd)							
Howing, Master, Son [of James]	12			England		Hercules	19 Jun 1821
James	12	M	None	England	United States	Trident	18 Jul 1827
James	34	M	Merchant	Great Britain	U.S. of Ama.	Robert Fulton	16 Aug 1824
James, Mr.	43		Farmer	England		Hercules	19 Jun 1821
Jas.	2	M		England	Canada	York	31 Mar 1828
Jas.	37	M	Farmer	England	Canada	York	31 Mar 1828
Jeremiah			Captain	United States	United States	William & Henry	19 Jul 1822
Job G.	28	M	Mariner	United States	United States	Diamond	12 Mar 1824
John	14	M	None	England	United States	Trident	18 Jul 1827
John	17	M	Servant	G. Britain	U. States	Nimrod	31 Jul 1828
John	27	M	Merchant	Great Britain	United States	James Monroe	5 Apr 1820
John	30	M	Merchant	England	United States	Minerva	25 Aug 1823
John	30	M	Farmer	England	United States	Montgomery	6 Mar 1829
John, Mr.	28	M	Merchant	England	England	Hector	20 Sep 1821
Jos.	21	M	Merchant	England	United States	Cortes	10 Apr 1822
Lewis	25	M		Great B.	U. States	William Neilson	26 Jul 1828
M.	28	M	Cooper	New York		Genl. Urdaneta	19 Apr 1826
Maria	32	F		England	United States	Yobah	26 Sep 1827
Mariah	25	F	None	Ireland	U. States	Franklin	7 Jul 1828
Mary	40	F		Great Britain	United States	Mary Howland	19 Jul 1827
Patrick	25	M	Labourer	...	U. States	St. Michael	21 Jul 1824
Peter	28	M	Farmer	England	United States	Montgomery	6 Mar 1829
Ruth	24			Lancashire	England	Great Britain	7 May 1827
S.	37	F	None	Grt. Brittain	United States	Euphrates	8 Nov 1821
Saml.	13	M	Servant	G. Britain	U. States	Nimrod	31 Jul 1828
Samuel	30	M	Farmer	England	United States	Meteor	16 Aug 1824
Samuel	52	M	Farmer	G. Britain	U. States	Nimrod	31 Jul 1828
Samuel N.	28	M	Cooper	New York	United States	Orion	27 Jul 1827
Sarah	26	F	Farmer	England	United States	Meteor	16 Aug 1824
Stephen	5	M	None	Ireland	U. States	Franklin	7 Jul 1828
Stephen	13	M	None	Manchester	Manchester	Howard Douglass	11 May 1827
Thomas	8	M	Servant	G. Britain	U. States	Nimrod	31 Jul 1828
Thomas	9	M	None	Manchester	Manchester	Howard Douglass	11 May 1827
Walter, Master, Son [of James]	11			England		Hercules	19 Jun 1821
Wm.	10	M	Servant	G. Britain	U. States	Nimrod	31 Jul 1828
Wm.	28	M		England	United States	Yobah	26 Sep 1827
LAYCOCK, Celia	28	F		England	United States	William Byrnes	11 Dec 1827
Edwin	3/12	M	Died	England	United States	William Byrnes	11 Dec 1827
Frederick	3	M		England	United States	William Byrnes	11 Dec 1827
James	28	M		England	United States	William Byrnes	11 Dec 1827
Mary	22	F		England	United States	William Byrnes	11 Dec 1827
Mary Ann	6	F		England	United States	William Byrnes	11 Dec 1827
Thomas	28	M	Farmer	Great Britain	United States	Diana	20 Nov 1828
William	5	M		England	United States	William Byrnes	11 Dec 1827
LAYFIELD, Robt.	27	M		England	England	Amity	31 May 1822
LAYMAN, Alex	16	M	Stone Cutter	G. Britain	U. States	St. George	16 Jan 1829
Ellen	7	F		G. Britain	U. States	St. George	16 Jan 1829
Francess	23	F	Farmer	France	United States	Crescent	12 Jul 1827
Jerald	34	M	Stone Cutter	G. Britain	U. States	St. George	16 Jan 1829
John	22	M	Farmer	France	United States	Crescent	12 Jul 1827
Mary	30	M	Stone Cutter	G. Britain	U. States	St. George	16 Jan 1829
LAYNAYASMANE, Graconio	35	M	Grocer	French	America	Britania	27 Mar 1820
LAYNE, Cath.	25	F		Gt. Britain	U. States	Tantiva	7 Jul 1828
LAYTON, Buxton	9	M	None	United States	United States	New York	12 Nov 1822
Thomas	8	M	None	United States	United States	New York	12 Nov 1822
LAZARO, Nicolas	60	M	Priest	Spain	Spain	Virginia	8 Mar 1828
LAZARUS, A.	24	M	Merchant	Jamaica	Jamaica	Hal	7 Jun 1824
A.	26	M	Merchant	Jamaica	U. States	Comet	10 Mar 1825
A.	30	M		Jamaica	England	Pleiades	13 Nov 1826
Abraham, Jr.	6	F	None	Jamaica	Jamaica	Hal	7 Jun 1824
Aron	20	M		Jamaica	England	Pleiades	13 Nov 1826
John	2	M		Jamaica	England	Pleiades	13 Nov 1826

NAMES OF PASSENGERS	AGE	SEX	OCCUPATIONS	COUNTRY TO WHICH THEY BELONG	COUNTRY THEY INTEND TO INHABIT	SHIPS/DATES OF ARRIVAL	
LAZARUS (cont'd)							
Mary	4	F		Jamaica	England	Pleiades	13 Nov 1826
P.	45	M	Merchant	South Carolina	U. States	Signa	9 Dec 1824
Peter	1	M		Jamaica	England	Pleiades	13 Nov 1826
Susan	3	F		Jamaica	England	Pleiades	13 Nov 1826
LAZENBY, Edward	22	M	Farmer	England	America	Manhattan	21 Sep 1822
Wm.	59	M	Farmer	England	America	Manhattan	21 Sep 1822
LE...NE, Napolean	25	M	Labourer	France	United States	Howard	20 Aug 1827
LEA, Charles	5	M	Son [of John]	Great Britain	United States	Wyton	12 May 1821
George	13	M		Ireland	America	Carolina Ann	7 Aug 1826
Harriet	26	F	Wife of Minister	Great Britain	United States	Wyton	12 May 1821
Hy.	1	M		Great Britain	United States	Wyton	12 May 1821
John	27	M	Minister	Great Britain	United States	Wyton	12 May 1821
William	27	M		Great Britain	U. States	Great Britain	18 Mar 1828
LEABAR, Phillip	40			England	England	Corinthian	8 Oct 1828
LEABOURGE, J.	24	M	Merchant	France	U. States	Bayard	25 Apr 1828
LEACH, —	25	M	Domestic	S. Eustatia	Holland	Chase	29 June 1821
Allis	11	F	None	England	U. States	Severn	12 Oct 1826
Amir	5	F	None	England	U. States	Severn	12 Oct 1826
Ann	10	F	Labourer	Ireland	United States	Meteor	26 Jun 1827
B. R.	27	M	Mariner	United States	United States	Mercator	12 Mar 1829
Bell	7	F	Labourer	Ireland	United States	Meteor	26 Jun 1827
Elizabeth	34	F	None	England	U. States	Severn	12 Oct 1826
Hariet	2/12	F	None	England	U. States	Severn	12 Oct 1826
Henry	15	M	None	England	U. States	Severn	12 Oct 1826
Isaac	35	M	Weaver	England	U. States	Severn	12 Oct 1826
James	5	M	Labourer	Ireland	United States	Meteor	26 Jun 1827
James	22	M	Labourer	Ireland	United States	Meteor	26 Jun 1827
James	27	M	Cotton Corder	G.B.	Massachusetts	Eliza Grant	29 Aug 1829
John	41	M	Farmer	Preson	United States	Dalhousie Castle	27 Jul 1826
John	46	M	Labourer	Ireland	United States	Meteor	26 Jun 1827
Mary	9	F	None	England	U. States	Severn	12 Oct 1826
Rebecca	30	F	Labourer	Ireland	United States	Meteor	26 Jun 1827
Sarah	7	F	None	England	U. States	Severn	12 Oct 1826
Thomas	31	M	Merchant	G.B.	U. States	Silas Richard	30 Jun 1828
Thomas	43	M	Weaver	England	U. States	Importer	24 Jul 1820
Thos.	13	M	None	England	U. States	Severn	12 Oct 1826
Thos.	23	M	Farmer	Scotland	United States	Camillus	7 Mar 1825
William	37	M	Merchant	U. States	U. States	Factor	9 Mar 1829
LEACHMAN, Jos.	30	M	Tailor	Germany	Brazils	Favorite	27 Dec 1825
LEAD, Herey	20	M		United States	United States	Nancey	8 Jun 1822
LEADBATER, Garrett	39	M	Farmer	Great Britain	United States	Favorite	10 Dec 1822
Rose	22	F	None	Great Britain	United States	Favorite	10 Dec 1822
LEADBEATER, Edwd.	46	M	Farmer	Gt. Brittain	United States	Balaena	21 Aug 1824
Sam.	25	M	Mechanic	England	U. States	Howard Douglass	29 Jan 1828
LEADBETTER,							
Sarah Ann	16	F	Farmer	England	U. States	Margarett Scott	22 Aug 1827
Thomas	13	M	Farmer	England	U. States	Margarett Scott	22 Aug 1827
Wm.	60	M	Farmer	England	U. States	Margarett Scott	22 Aug 1827
Wm., Jr.	25	M	Farmer	England	U. States	Margarett Scott	22 Aug 1827
LEADING, J. E.	25	M	Clerk	Breslaw	United States	Hector	29 Nov 1823
LEAF, Ann	16	F	Farmer	Great Brittain	U. States	Nancy	18 Jul 1821
Elzabeth	14	F	Farmer	Great Brittain	U. States	Nancy	18 Jul 1821
Hugh	20	M	Farmer	Great Brittain	U. States	Nancy	18 Jul 1821
James	40	M	Farmer	Great Brittain	U. States	Nancy	18 Jul 1821
LEAGBY, Dennis	26	M		Great Brittian	United States	Carolina Augusta	2 Dec 1828
LEAGLE, Jno.	22			England		Anacreon	7 Sep 1827
LEAGLEY, James	22	M	Gardner	Ireland	United States	Trio	2 Oct 1828
LEAHEY, Betty	27			Ireland	U.S.	Union	20 Aug 1827
John	28			Ireland	U.S.	Union	20 Aug 1827
LEAHY, Biddy, Junr.	15	F		Ireland	America	Liverpool	31 Aug 1827
Cathr.	26	F		Ireland	America	Liverpool	31 Aug 1827
Daniel	22	M	Farmer	Ireland	America	William	21 May 1825
Denis	40	M	Labourer	Great Britain	United States	Henrietta	19 Oct 1825
Mary	28	F	Seamstress	Great Britain	United States	Henrietta	19 Oct 1825
LEAK, Aron	23	M	Farmer	England	America	Hercules	2 Nov 1825
David	20	M	Farmer	England	America	Hercules	2 Nov 1825

NAMES OF PASSENGERS	AGE	SEX	OCCUPATIONS	COUNTRY TO WHICH THEY BELONG	COUNTRY THEY INTEND TO INHABIT	SHIPS/DATES OF ARRIVAL
LEAKE, —, Mrs.	44	F		U. States	U. States	Liverpool Packet 4 Aug 1825
Jonas	24	M	Surgeon	Gt. Britain		Dalhouse Castle 13 May 1828
Richd.	45	M	Lwyer	U. States	U. States	Liverpool Packet 4 Aug 1825
LEAKES, John	28	M	Merchant	Britain	Great Britain	Thompson 26 Apr 1828
LEAKY, Thomas	21		Carpenter	Cork	Philadelphia	Schuylkill 22 Aug 1825
LEAL, Ioao Gonsalvo		M		Portugal	U. States	Sarah Louisa 10 Oct 1822
LEAMAN, John	33	M	Boot Maker	Ireland	America	Manhattan 20 Mar 1820
LEAMAR, G., Jr.	25	M	Labourer	England	United States	Alicia 9 May 1827
Geo.	40	M	Labourer	England	United States	Alicia 9 May 1827
O.	70	F	Labourer	England	United States	Alicia 9 May 1827
LEAMER, Harman	21		Sugar boiler			Zamoa 5 Nov 1828
LEAMOS, Domingo	24	M	Merchant	Spain	Spain	Charlotte Corday 12 Apr 1821
LEAN, Catherine	30	F	None	Ireland	New York	America 1 Aug 1828
LEANIO, Antonio	25		Merchant	Spain	Spain	Hind 12 Jul 1820
LEAPER, Andrew	23	M	Servant	Ireland	U. States	Sarah G 30 Jun 1828
John	2	M	Child	Ireland	U. States	Sarah G 30 Jun 1828
LEAR, Francis	37	M	Dealer	England	England	Joseph 13 Oct 1823
James	26	M	Brick Layer	England	U. States	Florida 16 May 1827
LEARD, Alexr.	28	M	Merchant	France	New York	Ariadne 25 Sep 1820
Gover	40	M	Farmer	Ireland	United States	Helen 27 Jun 1821
LEARMONT, Anne	40	F	None	Scotland	United States	Washington 2 Oct 1828
James	40	M	Weaver	Scotland	United States	Washington 2 Oct 1828
Janet	1	F	None	Scotland	United States	Washington 2 Oct 1828
LEARNED, Samuel	35	M	Merchant	U. States	U. States	Edward 17 Aug 1820
LEARNER, Henry	22	M				Washington 15 Sep 1821
LEARY, Biddy	40	F		Ireland	America	Liverpool 31 Aug 1827
Bridget	26	F	Labourer	Ireland	United States	Essex 23 May 1828
Catherine	19	F		Gt. Britain		Dalhouse Castle 13 May 1828
Johanna	17	F	Servant	Ireland	America	Liverpool 31 Aug 1827
John	24	M	...	Ireland	United States	Nancey 8 Jun 1822
John	40	M	Weaver	Ireland	United States	Neury 27 Jan 1827
Lawrence	26	M	Farmer	Ireland	U. States	Mentor 5 Jul 1825
Mary	20	F		Ireland	United States	Princess Charlotte 26 Apr 1827
Michael	23	M	Tayler	Ireland	U. States	Hanford 29 Dec 1828
Michl.	20	M	Farmer	Ireland	America	Liverpool 31 Aug 1827
Patrick	18	M	Laborer	Gt. Britain		Dalhouse Castle 13 May 1828
Peggy	18	F		England	U. States	Rising States 20 Sep 1828
Wm.	30	M	Shoemaker	..., ..., Ireland	N. York	New Orleans 24 Aug 1827
LEAS, —, Madam	31	F		France	U. States	Ambuscade 6 Oct 1821
Aegert	5	F	Farmer	France	United States	Crescent 12 Jul 1827
Andre	57	M	Farmer	France	United States	Crescent 12 Jul 1827
Andrés	14	M	Farmer	France	United States	Crescent 12 Jul 1827
Barbery	7	F	Farmer	France	United States	Crescent 12 Jul 1827
Elizabeth	9	F	Farmer	France	United States	Crescent 12 Jul 1827
Lorenzo	2	M	None	N. York	U. States	Ambuscade 6 Oct 1821
Margaret	18	F	Farmer	France	United States	Crescent 12 Jul 1827
Marram	16	F	Farmer	France	United States	Crescent 12 Jul 1827
Marram	46	F	Farmer	France	United States	Crescent 12 Jul 1827
LEASH, James	27	M	Cotton Carder	Great Britain		Eliza Grant 29 Aug 1829
LEASHMEN, Archibald	10	M	Boy	Great Briton	United States	Orion 18 Jun 1821
Christian	3	M	Boy	Great Briton	United States	Orion 18 Jun 1821
Elizabeth	8	F	Girl	Great Briton	United States	Orion 18 Jun 1821
Margaret	5	F	Girl	Great Briton	United States	Orion 18 Jun 1821
Morehead	26	F	Spinstress	Great Briton	United States	Orion 18 Jun 1821
LEATHER, John	36	M	Merchant	England	Canada	Corinthian 20 Apr 1825
John	38	M	Mercht.	G.B.	Canada	George Canning 2 May 1828
LEATHERMAN, —	31	F		Switzerland	United States	Elbe 2 Aug 1822
LEATON, Abel	15	M	Farmer	Great Britain	United States	Magnet 28 Jun 1821
Ann	44	F	None	Great Britain	United States	Magnet 28 Jun 1821
Charles	16	M	Farmer	Great Britain	United States	Magnet 28 Jun 1821
Howard	14	M	Farmer	Great Britain	United States	Magnet 28 Jun 1821
John	26	M	Farmer	Ireland	U. States	William & John 10 Jul 1824
Mary	26	F	Wife to [John]	Ireland	U. States	William & John 10 Jul 1824
Samuel	8	M	None	Great Britain	United States	Magnet 28 Jun 1821
LEAVER,						
Prince Alexander	20	M		Great Brittain		Corinthian 9 Jan 1827

NAMES OF PASSENGERS	AGE	SEX	OCCUPATIONS	COUNTRY TO WHICH THEY BELONG	COUNTRY THEY INTEND TO INHABIT	SHIPS/DATES OF ARRIVAL
LEAVETT, Thomas	25	M	Merchant	Great Brittain	Great Britain	Loire 12 Dec 1820
Willm.	25	M	Merchant	St. Johns	St. Johns	Rambler 28 Oct 1822
LEAVEY, Cornelius	25	M	Carpenter	Ireland	America	Cincinnatus 22 May 1826
D. P.	33	M	Minister	Ireland	U. States	Saunders 16 May 1827
Eves	22	F		England	America	Cincinnatus 22 May 1826
LEAVITT, Daniel	42	M	Merchant	England	England	Hope 15 Oct 1821
Dd.	30	M	Merchant	U. States	U. States	Georgetown Packet 24 Feb 1823
Jane	25	F		G. Britain	U. States	Hanford 10 Jun 1828
Thoms.	35	M	Merchant	England	England	Hanford 3 Jul 1829
William	...	...	...	...	...	St. Michael 22 Sep 1824
William	35	M	Merchant	St. John, N.B.	St. John, N.B.	Ann Maria 21 May 1827
Wm.	38	M	Merchant	G. Britain	U. States	Hanford 10 Jun 1828
LEAVY, Danl.	29	M	Laborer	Gt. Britain		Dalhouse Castle 13 May 1828
Hugh	23	M	Mason	Ireland	U. States	Henry Kneeland 27 Jul 1825
William	24	M	Farmer	Ireland	United States	Dublin Packet 24 Sep 1823
LE BARRIER, J. M.	30	M	Mariner	Denmark	U. States	Alabama 21 May 1823
Lauretta	20	F	Servant	Denmark	U. States	Alabama 21 May 1823
Louisa	30	F	None	Denmark	U. States	Alabama 21 May 1823
LEBERIF, Marteal	18 4/12	M		U.S. America	U.S. America	Edward Bonnaffe 20 Jun 1826
LEBLANE, J.	20	M		Cuba	U. States	Industry 10 Mar 1825
LE BORGUE, John B.	43	M	Planter	Guadaloupe		Little John 4 Nov 1820
LE BOUTILLIN, Geo.	44	M	Merchant	England	United States	Margarett Scott 22 Aug 1827
LEBRA, Godfry	48	M	Brewer	France	U. States	Sully 25 Jun 1828
LE BRETON, A. S.	25	M	Merchant	France	U.S.	Comet 21 Aug 1820
Amont	28	M	Book Binder	France	United States	American 27 Aug 1827
Amos	60		Book Binder	United States	United States	American 27 Aug 1827
Catherine	52	F	Book Binder	United States	United States	American 27 Aug 1827
Joseph	21	M	Book Binder	United States	United States	American 27 Aug 1827
Juliana	30	F	Book Binder	United States	United States	American 27 Aug 1827
Mary	18	F	Book Binder	France	United States	American 27 Aug 1827
Simon	26	M	Merchant	France	United States	Nestor in Liverpool 29 Jul 1822
LE BRITON, Peter	30	M	Merchant	St. John, N.B.	United States	Edwin 29 Nov 1828
LE BRUN, Victor	49	M	Tobacconist	America	America	Portland 30 Mar 1820
LE CARAN, Chr.	26	M	Mercht.	France	France	Cadmus 26 Apr 1824
LE CARON, Charles	31	M	Merchant	France	U. States	Sully 24 Oct 1828
Chas.	32	M	Merchant	France	U.S.	Edward Quesnel 19 Oct 1827
LE CASIGRE, J.	19	M	Merchant	U. States	U. States	Fabius 30 Aug 1827
LECATAIR, S.	22	M	Merchant	France	U. States	Bayard 25 Apr 1828
LE CERF, Francis	31	M	Farmer	France	France	Sully 15 Jul 1829
LE CHARTIER, Plaude	42 6/12	M	Merchant	United States	United States	France 6 Oct 1828
LECHET, Thomas	29	M	Smith	Great Britain	United States	Frances Henrietta 17 Sep 1827
LECHTE, Jacob	23	M	Farmer			New York Packet 19 Aug 1820
LECHTENESS, Daniel	1	M		France	United States	New England 29 Aug 1828
Jacob	4	M		France	United States	New England 29 Aug 1828
LECKE, Frederick E.	25	M	Gentleman	U. States	U. States	Diana 18 Jul 1820
LECKER, Martha	40	F	None	Scotland	United States	Mary & Susan 5 Aug 1828
Mary Ann	10	F	None	Scotland	United States	Mary & Susan 5 Aug 1828
Robert	36	M	Cotton Spinner	Scotland	United States	Mary & Susan 5 Aug 1828
William	12	M	None	Scotland	United States	Mary & Susan 5 Aug 1828
LE CLUE, —	28	M	Seaman	France	France	Artibonite 9 Sep 1826
LE CONTE, Joseph	44	M	Capt. U.S. Navy	U. States	U. States	Montano 2 Sep 1828
Paul		M	Merchant	France	Marselles	Triton 30 Oct 1826
LE COSTA, —, Mr.	33	M	Merchant	United States	United States	Only Daughter 29 Apr 1825
LECOSTE, Virginia	22	F		New York	U. States	Congress 9 Mar 1829
LE COUSSIER, —	23	M	Seaman	France	France	Artibonite 9 Sep 1826
LECTENESS, Conrad	30	M	Farmer	France	United States	New England 29 Aug 1828
LECTON, Jane	26	F	Wife	Ireland	United States	Henry Kneeland 7 Jun 1828
Robt.	6/12	M	Child	Ireland	United States	Henry Kneeland 7 Jun 1828
William	36	M	Weaver	Ireland	United States	Henry Kneeland 7 Jun 1828
LEDAN, D. Felig	40	M	Merchant	Mexico	Mexico	Eliza 3 Jan 1826
LEDDEN, Bryan S.	41	M	Bricklayer	England	U.S.	Panthea 22 Jul 1826
Thomas	25	M	None	Great Britain	United States	Mary Howland 19 Jul 1827
William	50	M	None	Great Britain	United States	Mary Howland 19 Jul 1827

NAMES OF PASSENGERS	AGE	SEX	OCCUPATIONS	COUNTRY TO WHICH THEY BELONG	COUNTRY THEY INTEND TO INHABIT	SHIPS/DATES OF ARRIVAL	
LEDDER, Geo.	28	M	None	Great Britain	United States	Atlantic	28 May 1827
LEDDINGTON, Anna	27	F		Ireland	New York	Amanda	23 May 1827
LEDDY, James	26	M	Grocer	England	United States	William Byrnes	1 Dec 1824
Margt.	26	F	Spinster	Ireland	United States	Dublin Packet	22 Oct 1821
Mary	16	F	Spinster	Ireland	United States	Dublin Packet	29 Jun 1825
Patk.	22	M	Farmer	Ireland	United States	Dublin Packet	22 Apr 1822
Rose	...	...	...	Ireland	United States	Carolina Ann	24 Oct 1825
William	17	M	Farmer	Ireland	United States	Dublin Packet	29 Jun 1825
LEDENBURG, J. H.	31	F	Farmer	Germany	U. States	United States	3 Sep 1828
LEDERER, Adam	34	M	Merchant	Austria	Holland	Franklin	3 Jul 1820
Janger	39	M	Merchant	Austria	Holland	Franklin	3 Jul 1820
LEDFERD, ...	25	M	Laborer	Ireland	United States	Nancey	8 Jun 1822
LEDGET, John	38	M	Clothier	G.B.	New York	Eliza Grant	29 Aug 1829
LEDLEY, Owen	22	M	Farmer	Ireland	United States	Lord Strangford	20 Jun 1826
LE DORY, Mary	24	F	Milliner	U. States	U. States	Nassau	13 Aug 1825
LE DUC, Etienne	45		Physician	France	U. States	Almira	15 Jul 1822
LE DUIS, Julian	18		Tailor	France	U. States	Parachute	14 May 1828
M.	29		Dyer	France	U. States	Parachute	14 May 1828
LEDWELL, Peter	18	M	Farmer	France	Canada	Abby Jones	12 Jul 1827
LEDWICH, Ann	20	F	Spinster	Ireland	United States	Sarah Ann	18 Nov 1826
Patrik	26	M	Farmer	Gt. Britain	United States	Pacific	22 May 1826
LEDWITCH, Patric	26	M	Merct.	Ireland	America	Wilson	16 May 1825
LEDY, Barnard	35	M	Labourer	New York	United States	Trident	31 Mar 1827
Michael	20	M	Labourer	Ireland	United States	Trident	31 Mar 1827
LEE, —, Miss	20	F	None	America	America	Hercules	5 Sep 1826
Abigal	37	F	Lady	U.S.	U.S.	Panthea	22 Jul 1826
Alexr., Jr., Mr.	28	M		Scotland	New York	Joseph Hume	26 Oct 1829
Alexr., Mr.	52	M	Weaver	Scotland	New York	Joseph Hume	26 Oct 1829
Allen	45	M	Labourer	Kilbarhan	U.S. America	Camillus	10 Sep 1821
Allis	36	F	Semstress	England	America	Franklin	19 Nov 1828
Augustus	23	M	Gent.	England	U. States	Pacific	20 Aug 1825
B. T.	29	M	Merchant	U. States	U. States	Pacific	11 Sep 1824
Barbary	19	F		Great Britain	U. States	United States	8 Sep 1827
Benja. F.	30	M	Merchant	United States	New York, U.S.	Florida	2 Oct 1828
Benjamin ...	22 4/12	M	Gentleman	U.S.A.	U. States	Silas Richards	27 Oct 1826
Catherine	1	F	Farmer	France	United States	Crescent	12 Jul 1827
Cathn.	22	F	Servant	Ireland	United States	Wilson	27 Jun 1826
Cathrine	40	F	None	Great Brittan	U.S.	Emulous	29 Jun 1827
Charles	45	M	Merchant	United States	United States	Cincinnatus	21 Nov 1821
Chas.	35	M		U. States	U. States	Doris	2 Jun 1828
Clara	5	F		England	New York	Brighton	24 Aug 1827
Dennis	38	M	Soap Boiler	Ireland	United States	American	27 Aug 1827
Diana	1	F	Farmer	England	U. States	Margarett Scott	22 Aug 1827
E.	27	M		Great Britain	U. States	United States	8 Sep 1827
Edward	13	M	Merchant	England	America	Cincinnatus	19 Oct 1826
Eliza	2	F		Great Britain	U. States	United States	8 Sep 1827
Elizabeth, Mrs., & Infant	25	F	None	England	Philadelphia	Thames	6 Oct 1820
Francis	39	M	Merchant	Massachusetts	U. States	Columbia	7 Jul 1824
G. W.	45	M	Mariner	Connecticutt	U. States	Charles	5 Mar 1824
Geo.	5	M	None	Great Brittan	U.S.	Emulous	29 Jun 1827
Geo.	20	M	Gent.	England	U. States	Pacific	20 Aug 1825
Geo. W.	45	M	Merchant	America, U.S.A.	United States	Belle	3 Aug 1822
Geo. W.	47	M	Farmer	United States	United States	Flos	7 Apr 1826
George	...	...	...	...	...	St. Michael	22 Sep 1824
George	21	M	Farmer	France	United States	Crescent	12 Jul 1827
Hannah	35		None	Walbale	Great Britain	William Thompson	13 May 1823
Henrietta	19	F	Lady	United States	United States	Tampico	13 Oct 1825
Henrietta	35	F	Lady	England	New York	Brighton	24 Aug 1827
Henry	5	M	...	...	...	Indian Chief	8 Sep 1824
Hent.	12	F		England	New York	Brighton	24 Aug 1827
Isabela	26	F	Farmer	England	U. States	Margarett Scott	22 Aug 1827
James	11	M	Soap Boiler	Ireland	United States	American	27 Aug 1827
James	20	M	Gentleman	U. States	United States	Vermont	26 Aug 1824
James	20	M	Weaver	Ireland	N. York	Trusty	12 Sep 1828
James	23	M	None	Great Britain	United States	William Dawson	18 Jun 1827
James	28	M	Merchant	United States	New York	Corinthian	27 Apr 1824
James, Senior	5	M	None	United States	New York	Corinthian	27 Apr 1824
Jane	26	F		Great Britain	United States	Ann	22 Dec 1821

NAMES OF PASSENGERS	AGE	SEX	OCCUPATIONS	COUNTRY TO WHICH THEY BELONG	COUNTRY THEY INTEND TO INHABIT	SHIPS/DATES OF ARRIVAL	
LEE (cont'd)							
Jas.	24	M	Weaver	Great Brittain	United States	Nimrod	9 Jan 1827
Jeremiah	18	M	Slate Maker	G. Britain	U.S. America	Cincinnatus	31 Oct 1820
John	...	...	...	...	...	St. Michael	22 Sep 1824
John	2/12	M	Farmer	France	United States	Crescent	12 Jul 1827
John	0 6/12	M		Great Britain	U. States	United States	8 Sep 1827
John	2	M		Great Britain	United States	Ann	22 Dec 1821
John	4	M	Farmer	England	U. States	Margarett Scott	22 Aug 1827
John	27	M	Comedian	England	U. States	Pacific	11 Sep 1824
John	36	M	Farmer	Great Brittan	U.S.	Emulous	29 Jun 1827
John	53	M	Mechanic	U.S.	U.S.	Panthea	22 Jul 1826
Jonathan	46	M	Clothier	England		Marchioness	13 May 1828
Joseph	24	M	Watch Maker	England	New York	Frances Henrietta	3 Apr 1826
Joseph	29		Farmer	Ireland	United States	Fabius	18 Mar 1829
Julia	25	F	Unknown	U. States	U. States	Nancy	11 Apr 1822
Lucinda	20	F	Servant	Ireland	United States	Carolina Ann	14 May 1827
Margaret	26	F		Scotland	New York	Joseph Hume	26 Oct 1829
Margret	22	F		Irland	United States	Nancy	28 Oct 1822
Maria, Mrs.	30	F		England		Hercules	19 Jun 1821
Marie	24			Ireland	United States	Fabius	18 Mar 1829
Mark	5		None	Walbale	Great Britain	William Thompson	13 May 1823
Mary	8		None	Walbale	Great Britain	William Thompson	13 May 1823
Mary	10	F		Great Britian	United States	Columbia	21 Jan 1828
Mary	22	F	None	Great Britain	New York	Corinthian	27 Apr 1824
Mary	30	F		Great Britian	United States	Columbia	21 Jan 1828
Mary Ann	22	F	Farmer	France	United States	Crescent	12 Jul 1827
Mary Jane	20	F	Dress Maker	Ireland	United States	Carolina Ann	11 Dec 1826
Morris	30	M	Cooper	England	United States	Nancy	15 Mar 1820
P. H.	3	M	None	United States	New York	Corinthian	27 Apr 1824
Patrick	25	M	Labourer	Ireland		Marchioness	13 May 1828
Rebeca	13	F	Dress Maker	Ireland	United States	Carolina Ann	11 Dec 1826
Rebecca	7	F	Child	Ireland	United States	Trident	30 Sep 1826
Richard	9	M		Great Britian	United States	Columbia	21 Jan 1828
Richard	22	M				Lydia Adams	11 Sep 1824
Robert	32	M	Mechanic	England	United States	Hercules	24 Oct 1821
Saml.	10		None	Walbale	Great Britain	William Thompson	13 May 1823
Samuel	23 2/12	M	Wine & spirit Merchant	Great Britain	New York	Thames	16 May 1821
Sarah	16	F	None	Great Britain	New York	Corinthian	27 Apr 1824
Sophia	20	F	None	Gt. Britain	U. States	Importer	15 Sep 1821
Thomas	17	M		England	New York	Chelsea	16 May 1828
Thomas	23	M	Merchant	United States	United States	Atlantic	3 Dec 1821
Thomas	25	M	Shoemaker	Ireland	United States	Carolina Ann	11 Dec 1826
Thomas	27	M	Printer	Great Britain	United States	Ann	22 Dec 1821
Thos.	24	M		England	United States	Yobah	26 Sep 1827
Thos. N., Mr.	35	M	Mercht.	United States	United States	Manchester	16 Dec 1828
William	17	M	Farmer	Great Britian	United States	Ganges	8 Jul 1820
William	23	M	Silver Smith	England	Philadelphia	Debby & Eliza	20 Nov 1820
Wm.	35	M	Draper	Great Britain	New York	Orozimbo	2 Oct 1824
Wm. E.	39	M	Merchant	U. States	U. States	Cadmus	9 Apr 1825
LEEB, G.	19	M	Merchant	Germany	U. States	Ohio	2 May 1821
Jn.	45	M	Merchant	Germany	U. States	Ohio	2 May 1821
LEECE, Joseph	16	M	N	U. States	U. States	United States	11 Sep 1828
LEECH, Catharine	22	F	Spinster	Ireland	United States	Catharine	22 Jul 1825
David	22	M	Weaver	Ireland	United States	Trident	16 May 1826
Elinor	20		None	Ireland	Ireland	William Byrnes	25 Aug 1828
John	22 7/12	M	...	Ireland	United States	Lima	19 Jun 1824
John	25	M	Labourer	Ireland	United States	Catharine	22 Jul 1825
Jos.	25	M	Weaver	Ireland	United States	Trident	16 May 1826
Littia	15	F	None	Ireland	United States	Catharine	22 Jul 1825
Richard	17	M	Child	Ireland	United States	Marmion	17 Jun 1825
Thomas	25	M	...b...	...shire	U. States	Panthea	24 Mar 1825
LEEDER, Wm.	25	M	Miller	Amsterdam	U. States	Elizabeth	28 May 1822
LEEDS, A.	10		Farmer	Ireland	United States	Courier	16 May 1825
H.	4		Farmer	Ireland	United States	Courier	16 May 1825

NAMES OF PASSENGERS	AGE	SEX	OCCUPATIONS	COUNTRY TO WHICH THEY BELONG	COUNTRY THEY INTEND TO INHABIT	SHIPS/DATES OF ARRIVAL	
LEEDS (cont'd)							
J.	20		Farmer	Ireland	United States	Courier	16 May 1825
J.	45		Farmer	Ireland	United States	Courier	16 May 1825
M.	9		Farmer	Ireland	United States	Courier	16 May 1825
M.	42		Farmer	Ireland	United States	Courier	16 May 1825
T.	38		Farmer	Ireland	United States	Courier	16 May 1825
W.	2		Farmer	Ireland	United States	Courier	16 May 1825
LEELY, R.	24	F		Gt. Britain	United States	John & Elizabeth	25 Sep 1827
LEEMAIR, Francisco	63	M	Merchant	France		Claudio	21 Aug 1827
LEEMULIER, A. F.	35	M	Mariner	Germany	Germany	Eliza	22 Dec 1826
LEEN, John	11	M	Farmer	France	United States	Crescent	12 Jul 1827
John	45	M	Farmer	France	United States	Crescent	12 Jul 1827
John Adams	18	M	Farmer	France	United States	Crescent	12 Jul 1827
Margaret	15	F	Farmer	France	United States	Crescent	12 Jul 1827
LEENARD, Edwd.	29	M	Labourer	Great Britain	United States	William Dawson	18 Jun 1827
LEERY, Mary	28	F	Laborer	Ireland	U. States	Lady Hunter	14 Mar 1826
LEES, Alice	11	F	Spinner	England	U. States	Panthea	22 Nov 1826
Ann	5	F		Great Britain	United States	Atlantic	28 May 1827
Anne	8	F	None	England	U. States	Birmingham	12 Oct 1827
B.	40	M	Mariner	France	U. States	Tampico	14 Jul 1825
Elizabeth	6	F	None	England	U. States	Birmingham	12 Oct 1827
Elizabeth	35	F	Spinner	England	U. States	Panthea	22 Nov 1826
Geo.	3	M		Great Britain	United States	Atlantic	28 May 1827
James	...1		Joiner	Del...	England	Great Britain	7 May 1827
James	21	M	Artist			Importer	30 Oct 1820
Jane	1	F	None	England	U. States	Birmingham	12 Oct 1827
Jane	21	F		Great Britain	United States	Atlantic	28 May 1827
Jane	23	F		G. Britain	U. States	William Thompson	30 Apr 1822
John	...		Joiner	Del...	England	Great Britain	7 May 1827
John	22	M	Labourer	Laddleworth	Laddleworth	Howard Douglass	11 May 1827
John	40	M	Tailor	Great Britain	U. States	Great Britain	18 Mar 1828
John	56	M	Labourer	England	New York	York	8 Aug 1829
John, Mr.	23		Cotton Spinner	England		Hercules	19 Jun 1821
Jos.	9	M		U. States	U. States	United States	11 Sep 1828
Josef	31	M	Stone Mason	G.B.	New York	Eliza Grant	29 Aug 1829
Joseph	31	M	Stone Mason	Great Britain		Eliza Grant	29 Aug 1829
Mary	4	F	None	England	U. States	Birmingham	12 Oct 1827
Mary	13	F	Spinner	England	U. States	Panthea	22 Nov 1826
Mary	36	F	None	England	U. States	Birmingham	12 Oct 1827
Randall	26	M	Draper	Great Britain	United States	James Monroe	5 Apr 1820
Rob.	22	M	Manufacturer	England	U. States	Amity	25 Sep 1822
S. D.	27	M	Merchant	United States	United States	Potomac	8 Dec 1826
Saml.	41	M	Manufacturer	England	U. States	Birmingham	12 Oct 1827
Samuel D.	29	M	Mercht.	U. States	U. States	Sully	15 Jul 1829
Sarah *dead	1	F		Great Britain	United States	Atlantic	28 May 1827
Sarah	9	F	Spinner	England	U. States	Panthea	22 Nov 1826
Stanly	6	M		U. States	U. States	United States	11 Sep 1828
Wm.	23	M	Mason	Great Britain	United States	Atlantic	28 May 1827
Wm. L.	25	M	Merchant	Phila.	U. States	Pocahontas	28 Jun 1824
LEESON, John	5	M	None	Ireland		Marchioness	13 May 1828
Patrick	3	M	None	Ireland		Marchioness	13 May 1828
Peggy	24	F	None	Ireland		Marchioness	13 May 1828
Peter	29	M	Labourer	Ireland	United States	Jubilee	1 Oct 1828
LEESTER, Authur	10			England	United States	Hugh Johnson	11 Jun 1828
Eliz.	30			England	United States	Hugh Johnson	11 Jun 1828
Jane	17			England	United States	Hugh Johnson	11 Jun 1828
John	36		Labourer	England	United States	Hugh Johnson	11 Jun 1828
Mary	15			England	United States	Hugh Johnson	11 Jun 1828
Thos.	14			England	United States	Hugh Johnson	11 Jun 1828
Wm.	6			England	United States	Hugh Johnson	11 Jun 1828
LEEVES, George	34	M	Merchant	United States	United States	Pacific	11 Mar 1829
LEFEBIE, Anthony	23	M	Carpenter	Ireland	United States	Trio	31 Oct 1827
Henrietta	21	F		Ireland	United States	Trio	31 Oct 1827
LE FERRE, Ann C.	23	F		France	United States	Le Voltaire	19 Jul 1828
F. P.	7/12	M		France	United States	Le Voltaire	19 Jul 1828

NAMES OF PASSENGERS	AGE	SEX	OCCUPATIONS	COUNTRY TO WHICH THEY BELONG	COUNTRY THEY INTEND TO INHABIT	SHIPS/DATES OF ARRIVAL	
LE FERRE (cont'd)							
J. F.	23	M	Black smith	France	United States	Le Voltaire	19 Jul 1828
LE FEVER, Ancabat	85	F		England	U. States	Nymph	5 Jul 1820
Ann M.	10				U. States	Nymph	5 Jul 1820
Elizabeth	12				U. States	Nymph	5 Jul 1820
Peter	45	M	Mariner	England	U. States	Nymph	5 Jul 1820
Roxbey	35	F		U. States	U. States	Nymph	5 Jul 1820
Sarueli	2				U. States	Nymph	5 Jul 1820
LEFFT, Thomas	37		Mariner	Providence	United States	London	13 Dec 1822
LE FORT, —	30	M	Seaman	France	France	Artibonite	9 Sep 1826
LEGAL, Francis	10	F	Lady	France	U.S.	Montano	24 Jun 1823
Mary, Widow	60	F	Lady	France	U.S.	Montano	24 Jun 1823
LEGAN, Daniel	26	M	Labourer	Ireland	United States	Enterprize	23 Jul 1827
Mary	24	F		Ireland	United States	Enterprize	23 Jul 1827
LEGAR, Absenedensoste	35	M	Apothecary	France	New York	Frances Henrietta	25 Aug 1825
LEGARD, Edward	28	M	Merchant	U. States	U. States	President	25 Jul 1825
LEGARG, C.	24	M	Musician	Genoa	U. States	Nimrod	31 Jul 1828
F.	50	M	Musician	Genoa	U. States	Nimrod	31 Jul 1828
M.	27	M	Musician	Genoa	U. States	Nimrod	31 Jul 1828
LEGARY, Jese	49	M	Merchant	Spain	Spain	Jane	13 Mar 1829
LE GAVRA, Jno.	20	M		France	U. States	Henri IV	3 Feb 1829
LEGET, John	38	M	Cloth Maker	Great Britain		Eliza Grant	29 Aug 1829
LEGGATT, George	1 6/12	M		England	United States	Concordia	25 Aug 1827
Harriet	27	F		England	United States	Concordia	25 Aug 1827
James	11	M	Mechanic	England	United States	Concordia	25 Aug 1827
James	38	M	Mechanic	England	United States	Concordia	25 Aug 1827
John	7	M		England	United States	Concordia	25 Aug 1827
LEGGETT, Alex	15	M	Carpenter	St. Thomas	U. States	Jane	2 Nov 1826
Andw.	22	M	Whipmaker	G. Britain	United States	Ariel	21 May 1827
LEGGITT, Thomas H.	33	M	Merchant	United States	United States	Nestor	20 Nov 1821
LEGHORN, John	19	M		Italy	United States	Siroc	13 Sep 1828
LEGINET, Joseph	46 7/12	M	Farmer	France	U.S. America	Illinois	16 Oct 1822
LEGINY, Jorge	30	M	Mariner	U. States	U. States	Pedler	27 May 1825
LEGO, Jesse		M		England	America	Britannia	22 Jul 1829
John	6	M		England	America	Britannia	22 Jul 1829
Mary	2/12	M	Farmer	England	America	Britannia	22 Jul 1829
Mary	26	M	Farmer	England	America	Britannia	22 Jul 1829
Samuel	31	M	Farmer	England	America	Britannia	22 Jul 1829
LEGOMER, Felix	30	M	Merchant	Cuba	Cuba	William	18 Oct 1824
LE GOUILLER, George Francis	28	M	Merchant	Hesse	United States	Constitution	2 Aug 1826
LE GOUX, Jno. F.	60	M	Doctor	France	U. States	Velocipede	26 Jun 1823
LEGOUX, Ann	21	M	Merchant	France	America	Don Quixotte	2 Jun 1828
LEGRAN...A, —, Mrs.	48	F		France	U. States	India	8 Dec 1826
LEGRAND, J.	25	M	Merchant	France	United States	Joseph	11 Jul 1821
LEGRIN, Elisa	22	F	Lady	St. John	U.States	Nancy	31 May 1823
LEGRIX, Jean Antoine	33	M		France	U. States	Howard	22 Sep 1828
LE GUER, Emily	16		Lady	U. States	U. States	Brandt	14 Aug 1823
Josephine	17		Lady	U. States	U. States	Brandt	14 Aug 1823
Mary, Miss	15		Lady	U. States	U. States	Brandt	14 Aug 1823
Mary, Mrs.	40		Lady	U. States	U. States	Brandt	14 Aug 1823
LEGUERRIER, Peter	36	M	Merchant	New York	New York	Washington	19 Jun 1826
LEHAR, John	28	M	Plasterer	Great Britain	United States	Milton	21 Mar 1828
LEHE, —, Mrs.	33	F	Spouse	Prusia	U. States	Franklin	3 Jul 1820
LEHMAN, Abraham	35	M	Farmer	Switzerland	United States	Thetis	5 Jul 1821
Anne	10	F		Switzerland	United States	Thetis	5 Jul 1821
Anne	18	F		Switzerland	United States	Howard	11 Jun 1824
Barbara	26	F		Switzerland	United States	Howard	11 Jun 1824
Catharine	50	F		Switzerland	United States	Howard	11 Jun 1824
David	12	M	Boy	Switzerland	United States	Howard	11 Jun 1824
Elizabeth	15	F		Switzerland	United States	Howard	11 Jun 1824
George	21	M	Painter	Switzerland	United States	Howard	11 Jun 1824
Jacob	40	M	Merchant	Switzerland	United States	Howard	11 Jun 1824
John	27	M	Stone Cutter	Switzerland	United States	Howard	11 Jun 1824
Marie	35	F		Switzerland	United States	Thetis	5 Jul 1821
Mary	25	F		Switzerland	United States	Howard	11 Jun 1824
Samuel	52	M	Stone Cutter	Switzerland	United States	Howard	11 Jun 1824
Samuel, 2d	23	M	Stone Cutter	Switzerland	United States	Howard	11 Jun 1824

NAMES OF PASSENGERS	AGE	SEX	OCCUPATIONS	COUNTRY TO WHICH THEY BELONG	COUNTRY THEY INTEND TO INHABIT	SHIPS/DATES OF ARRIVAL	
LEHMAN (cont'd)							
Susan	28	F		Switzerland	United States	Howard	11 Jun 1824
Willm.	24	M	Mercht.	Germany	Philidelphia	Brighton	16 Nov 1826
LEHMANN, Abraham	6/12	M		Switzerland	United States	Thetis	5 Jul 1821
*died							
Barbary	23	F		Switzerland	United States	Thetis	5 Jul 1821
Christien	13	M		Switzerland	United States	Thetis	5 Jul 1821
Christien	20	M	Mason	Switzerland	United States	Thetis	5 Jul 1821
Christien	43	M	Carpenter	Switzerland	United States	Thetis	5 Jul 1821
Elizabeth	10	F		Switzerland	United States	Thetis	5 Jul 1821
Elizabeth	22	F		Switzerland	United States	Thetis	5 Jul 1821
Hans	44	M	Carpenter	Switzerland	United States	Thetis	5 Jul 1821
John	56	M	Farmer	Switzerland	United States	Thetis	5 Jul 1821
Jonas	7	M		Switzerland	United States	Thetis	5 Jul 1821
Magdalaine	5	F		Switzerland	United States	Thetis	5 Jul 1821
Magdalaine	33	F		Switzerland	United States	Thetis	5 Jul 1821
Peter	2	M		Switzerland	United States	Thetis	5 Jul 1821
Verena	19	F		Switzerland	United States	Thetis	5 Jul 1821
LEHMANOUSKEY, ...	27			Pensylvania	United States	Packet	27 Aug 1822
...etta	3			Philadelphia	United States	Packet	27 Aug 1822
J.	46		late officer of the French army	Warsau (Poland)	United States	Packet	27 Aug 1822
Lewis	1		Infant			Packet	27 Aug 1822
LEHR, Frederic	33	M	Sadler	Prusia	U. States	Franklin	3 Jul 1820
LEHTON, Jams	25	M	Labourer	England	America	William	21 Sep 1821
LEHUMMANN, —	28	M	Labourer	Brattain		L'Esperance	6 Sep 1828
Christine	6/12	F		Brattain		L'Esperance	6 Sep 1828
Julia	5	F		Brattain		L'Esperance	6 Sep 1828
Magdelene	36	F		Brattain		L'Esperance	6 Sep 1828
Martin	7	M		Brattain		L'Esperance	6 Sep 1828
Requin	3	M		Brattain		L'Esperance	6 Sep 1828
LEHWISTER, St. Cyr	17	M	Mechanic	U.S.	U.S.	Abeona	24 May 1822
LEIBER, —, Mrs.	48	F		Hanover	United States of Am.	Constitution	6 Jul 1829
Amalie	20	F		Hanover	United States of Am.	Constitution	6 Jul 1829
Andreas	18	M	Laborer	Hanover	United States of Am.	Constitution	6 Jul 1829
George	23	M	Carpenter	Hanover	United States of Am.	Constitution	6 Jul 1829
Hanna	25	F		Hanover	United States of Am.	Constitution	6 Jul 1829
Henrietta	13	F		Hanover	United States of Am.	Constitution	6 Jul 1829
Henry	15	M	Laborer	Hanover	United States of Am.	Constitution	6 Jul 1829
LEICESTER, Thomas	24		Farmer	Warrington		Mount Vernon	18 Oct 1822
LEICH, Samuel	30	M	Farmer	Ireland	United States	Meteor	27 Sep 1826
LEICHELY, Elizabeth	16		Farmer	France	U. States	Elizabeth	9 Jul 1825
Maria	18		Farmer	France	U. States	Elizabeth	9 Jul 1825
Nicholas	13		Farmer	France	U. States	Elizabeth	9 Jul 1825
LEICHLY, Joseph	20		Farmer	France	U. States	Elizabeth	9 Jul 1825
LEICHT, Christina	55	F		Germany	Penselvaney	Orient	25 Nov 1825
Forodas	25	F		Germany	Penselvaney	Orient	25 Nov 1825
LEICHTY, Verine	42	M	Farmer	Germany	United States	Origon	8 Jun 1824
LEIGH, Alich.	28	F	None	England	United States	Ann Maria	23 Oct 1820
Ann	27	F		Great Britain	United States	Saml. Wight	6 Sep 1827
E.	5	M		Great Britain	United States	Saml. Wight	6 Sep 1827
Eliza	3	F		Great Britain	United States	Saml. Wight	6 Sep 1827
Hanah Moat, Mrs.	34			England		Hercules	19 Jun 1821
Harriet, her Daughter [Hanah Moat]	8			England		Hercules	19 Jun 1821
Jane	23	F	Seamstress	England	United States	Essex	23 May 1828
John	6	M	None	G. Britan	U. States	Canada	27 Sep 1826
Mary, her Daughter [Hanah Moat]	3			England		Hercules	19 Jun 1821
Moses, her Son [Hanah Moat]	13	M		England		Hercules	19 Jun 1821
Oliver	26	M	Planter	Great Britain	United States	Saml. Wight	6 Sep 1827
Richard	36	M	Labourer	England	U. States	Emulous	22 Aug 1828
Saml.	22	M	Tinplater	England	United States	Essex	23 May 1828
Susan	18	F		England	America	Erin	7 Nov 1821
Thos.	25	M	Weaver	Great Britain	America	Lady Gallatin	21 Jun 1820
Thos.	31	M	Planter	Great Britain	United States	Saml. Wight	6 Sep 1827
Thos., Jr.	12	M		Great Britain	America	Lady Gallatin	21 Jun 1820

NAMES OF PASSENGERS	AGE	SEX	OCCUPATIONS	COUNTRY TO WHICH THEY BELONG	COUNTRY THEY INTEND TO INHABIT	SHIPS/DATES OF ARRIVAL	
LEIGH (cont'd)							
William, her Son							
[Hanah Moat]	10			England		Hercules	19 Jun 1821
Wm.	10/12	M		Great Britain	United States	Saml. Wight	6 Sep 1827
LEIGHTON, Cathr.	6	F	None	Edinburgh	U. States	Milton	21 May 1827
George	10	M	None	Edinburgh	U. States	Milton	21 May 1827
Hamilton	12	M	None	Edinburgh	U. States	Milton	21 May 1827
James	24	M	Glass Cutter	Edinburgh	U. States	Milton	21 May 1827
John	22	M	Glass Cutter	Edinburgh	U. States	Milton	21 May 1827
Margt.	16	F	None	Edinburgh	U. States	Milton	21 May 1827
Mary Ann		F	None	Edinburgh	U. States	Milton	21 May 1827
Peter	2	M	None	Edinburgh	U. States	Milton	21 May 1827
Robt.	4	M	None	Edinburgh	U. States	Milton	21 May 1827
Thos.	18	M	Glass Maker	Edinburgh	U. States	Milton	21 May 1827
Wm.	20	M	Glass Maker	Edinburgh	U. States	Milton	21 May 1827
LEIGHTOR, Thomas	40	M	Glass Maker	Great Britain	United States	United States	18 Oct 1826
LEIHRS, H.	26	M	Laborer	Hannover	United States	Constitution	6 Jul 1829
LEINER, Heinrich	30	M	Merchant	Frankfort	New York	Louisa	6 Oct 1828
Robert	16	M	Wever	Ireland	United States	Fabius	4 Jun 1828
LEINHART, Samuel	33	M	Mechanic	France	U. States	Edward Quesnel	4 Aug 1828
LEIPTON, Edward	24	M				Cassack	25 Jul 1820
LEISON, Margaret	20	F	Spinster	..., ..., Ireland	N. York	New Orleans	24 Aug 1827
LEITCH, Ann	16	F		G. Britain	U. States	Camillus	8 Sep 1828
Cathr.	15	F		G. Britain	U. States	Camillus	8 Sep 1828
Mary	50	F		G. Britain	U. States	Camillus	8 Sep 1828
LEITICAR, —	30	F	Servant	Bermuda	Bermuda	Improvement	6 Jun 1826
LEITTLE, F.	22	M	Labourer			Hanford	17 Jul 1828
LEIZ, Gustar	19	M	Brewer	Germany	Pensylvania	James Noble	27 Aug 1827
LEKSAR, Catharin	8	F	Child	Ireland	U. States	Meteor	19 Jul 1828
Edward	18	M	Labourer	Ireland	U. States	Meteor	19 Jul 1828
Margaret	7	F	Child	Ireland	U. States	Meteor	19 Jul 1828
LELAND, Francis,							
& Servant	20		Merchant	United States	Columbia	Bogota	25 Oct 1827
LELAZSAN, Dan C.	28	M	Merchant	Columbia	U. States	Dandy	22 Dec 1824
LELEN, Abel	31	M		Swisse	United States	Deux Ernest	29 Dec 1827
*landed at Lewiston, Delw.							
LELPER, John	18	M	Carpenter	Halifax, N.S.	New York	Citizen	1 Nov 1828
LE MAIRE, Celestin	30	M	Cabinet Maker	France	America	Mary	8 Feb 1827
LEMAIRE, Pepin	47	M	Merchant	U. States	U. States	Edward Bonnaffe	4 May 1827
LEMAITRE, Azemia	18	F	None	United States	United States	Montano	4 Nov 1823
Cecile V.	45	F	None	United States	United States	Montano	4 Nov 1823
John B., Jr.	22	F	Merchant	United States	United States	Montano	4 Nov 1823
LEMAN, Edward	29 5/12	M	Merchant	Sweden	Pensylvania, U.S.	Alfred	1 Dec 1827
Felix	30	M	Merchant	Spain	U. States	Amphion	24 Aug 1821
M.	34	M	Merchant	Hamburgh	U. States	Minerva	23 Aug 1824
M.	34	M	Merchant	Hamburg	U. States	Minerva	23 May 1825
LEMANT, M.	22	M	Merchant	Great Britan	Great Britan	Robert Read	25 Aug 1824
LEMEISTER, Jean	29	M	Mechanic	France	U.S.	Helen	3 May 1828
LE MESURER, H.	33	M	Merchant	England	Canada	Corinthian	20 Apr 1825
LE MESURIER, H.	31		Merchant	Guernsey	Great Britain	William Thompson	13 May 1823
W.	31	M	Merchant	Germany		London	29 Apr 1824
LEMETAIS, —	40	M	Mercht.	France	France	Don Quixote	3 Jan 1826
LEMMON, Eliza	23	F	Lady	England	United States	Cambria	8 Oct 1828
Hannah	19	F	Lady	England	United States	Cambria	8 Oct 1828
John	32	M	Merchant	Great Britain	Canada	Pacific	7 May 1827
M...	51	F	Lady	England	United States	Cambria	8 Oct 1828
Mary	19	F	Lady	England	United States	Cambria	8 Oct 1828
Wm.	1	M	Boy	England	United States	Cambria	8 Oct 1828
Wm. P.	30	M	Merchant		U. States	Eclipse	10 Jun 1823
LEMMONIER, Joseph	22	M	Gentleman	France	U. States	Rio	11 Sep 1827
LEMOINE, P.	42	M	Merchant	France	Hava.	Favourite	18 Aug 1823
Sean	19	M	Merchant	France	France	Montano	13 Jan 1826
LEMON, Cristol	34		Merchant	Spain	U. States	Alfred	24 Jul 1828
David	70	M	Farmer	Killinchey	United States	Carolina Ann	11 Jun 1824
Jabes	18	M	Laborer	England	U. States of America	Dale	14 Mar 1828
Jane	23	F	None	Ireland	United States	Lord Wellington	28 May 1827
John	31	M	Carpenter	Killinchey	United States	Carolina Ann	11 Jun 1824

NAMES OF PASSENGERS	A G E	S E X	OCCUPATIONS	COUNTRY TO WHICH THEY BELONG	COUNTRY THEY INTEND TO INHABIT	SHIPS/DATES OF ARRIVAL	
LEMON (cont'd)							
Leonard	40	M	Laborer	England	U. States of Amer	Dale	14 Mar 1828
Lewis	35	M	None	Germany	United States	Montgomery	6 Mar 1829
Thos.	37	M		Killinchey	United States	Carolina Ann	11 Jun 1824
William	26	M		Killinchey	United States	Carolina Ann	11 Jun 1824
Wm.	28	M	Labourer	Ireland	United States	Lord Wellington	28 May 1827
LEMONAL, H.	45	F	None	U. States	U. States	Ardell	7 Jul 1827
LEMONNER, Alexander	45	M	Merchant	U. States	U. States	Bayard	25 Apr 1828
D.	22	M	Merchant	Germany	U. States	Bayard	25 Apr 1828
LEMONT, Eliza	29	F		England	U. States	Alert	22 Sep 1821
LEMOT, Ann		F		Great Britain	United States	Active	25 Mar 1828
James	54	M		Great Britain	United States	Active	25 Mar 1828
Margt.	34	F		Great Britain	United States	Active	25 Mar 1828
LE MOYNE, Adolphe	24	M	Merchant	France	United States	Montano	5 May 1828
LEMPKE, Fred. Julius	20	M	Merchant	Hamburg	New York	Maria Elizabeth	18 Jun 1827
LEMPSON, John	24	M		Great Britain	Canada	James Monroe	25 Apr 1822
LENAGHEN, John	47	M	Gent	Ireland	United States	Paragon	12 Aug 1828
LENAIRD, Bridget	20	F	Spinster	Ireland	United States	Wilson	4 Oct 1827
LENARD, Diana	25	F	None	G. Britain	United States	Fairy	18 Feb 1825
James	21	M	Labourer	Ireland	U.S.	Lady Hunter	10 Jul 1826
Mary Ann	5	F	None	G. Britain	United States	Fairy	18 Feb 1825
Riby	29	M	Labourer	G. Britain	United States	Fairy	18 Feb 1825
LENARDA, —	48	F	Wife	Spain	Spain	Franklin	14 Jul 1827
—, Commandant	45	M	Officer of Customs	Spain	Spain	Franklin	14 Jul 1827
LENAS, D., & Son	22	F				Sarah Ann	5 Aug 1820
LENCK, Rosina	22	F		France	United States	New England	29 Aug 1828
LENES, A.	43	M	Merchant	U. States	U. States	Superior	25 Sep 1824
LENET, E.	20	F	Labourer	Ireland	United States	Combine	4 Jun 1825
LENETEAN, Peter	20	M	Spinster	G. Britain	U. States	Hanford	18 Sep 1828
LENEY, John	36			France	U. States	Parachute	14 May 1828
LENG, Kamnann, Mr.	27	M	Mercht.	France	New York	Cadmus	27 Aug 1822
LENGE, Johanna B.	19	F	Labourer	England	America	Two Marys	24 Sep 1827
LENGIS, —, Miss	18	F	Comedienne	France	U. States	Queen Mab	16 Jun 1827
—, Mrs.	45	F	Lady	France	U. States	Queen Mab	16 Jun 1827
LENGSTAFF, Ewd.	16	M	Farmer	Gt. Britain	United States	Penelope	9 Sep 1828
LENIARD, Jane	4/12	F	None	G. Britain	United States	Fairy	18 Feb 1825
LENIBURD, Rinney	25	M	Sailor	America	America	Antoinette	25 Jan 1828
LE NIEVE, Pepin	44	M	Mercht.	U.S.	U.S.	Cadmus	26 Apr 1824
LENKHURST, Ann	12	F	Farmer	Rye, England	United States	William	21 May 1828
Clark	6/12	M		Rye, England	United States	William	21 May 1828
Eliza	8	F		Rye, England	United States	William	21 May 1828
Susannah	35	F		Rye, England	United States	William	21 May 1828
Thomas	3	M		Rye, England	United States	William	21 May 1828
William	6	M	Farmer	Rye, England	United States	William	21 May 1828
William	37	M	Farmer	Rye, England	United States	William	21 May 1828
LENNIG, Chs.	19	M	Merchant	United States	United States	Lovinia	20 Nov 1828
LENNON, Agnis	32	F		Ireland	U. States	Alexander	28 Jul 1821
Elizabeth	30	F	Wife	Ireland	United States	Dublin Packet	9 Jul 1827
Elizth.	13	F	Spinner	Great Britain	United States	Atlantic	8 Dec 1827
F.	18	M	Weaver	Ireland	United States	Josephine	30 Apr 1828
James	4	M		Ireland	U. States	Alexander	28 Jul 1821
John	7	M		Ireland	U. States	Alexander	28 Jul 1821
John	20 3/12	M	Labourer	Ireland	United States	Louisa	27 Nov 1826
John	31	M	Farmer	Ireland	United States	Dublin Packet	9 Jul 1827
John, Jr.	22	M	Mason	Scotland	U. States	Exchange	25 Sep 1826
Mary	20	F	Spinner	Great Britain	United States	Atlantic	8 Dec 1827
Michael	5	M		Ireland	U. States	Alexander	28 Jul 1821
Patrick	24	M	Labourer	Ireland	United States	Hannah Eliza	6 Jun 1826
Sarah	18	F	Servant	Ireland	United States	Louisa	27 Nov 1826
Thos.	20	M	Baker	Ireland	United States	William	20 Jul 1829
Thos.	30	M	Farmer	Ireland	America	Mary	29 May 1827
Wm.	34	M	Baker	England		Hudson	23 Jul 1828
Wm. Douglass	24		Baker	Scotland	United States	Camillus	3 May 1828
LENNOX, J. S.	24	M	Merchant	U. States	U. States	Canada	6 Jun 1825
James	26	F	Farmer			Orion	21 Aug 1820
LENNY, Lionel	29	M	Mercht.	G.B.	Canada	George Canning	2 May 1828
LENO, Wm.	27	M		England	America	Birmingham	16 Oct 1826
LENOCK, Emmy	19	M	Labourer	Ireland	United States	Hope	12 Jun 1828
LENON, Mary	13	F	Spinster	Ireland	America	Mary	29 May 1827

NAMES OF PASSENGERS	AGE	SEX	OCCUPATIONS	COUNTRY TO WHICH THEY BELONG	COUNTRY THEY INTEND TO INHABIT	SHIPS/DATES OF ARRIVAL	
LENOX, ...	20	F	Sevant			Robert Burns	13 Jul 1820
...tha	15	F	Sevant			Robert Burns	13 Jul 1820
Fanny	11	F	Girl	Ireland	United States	Trident	17 May 1825
George	9	M	child	Ireland	U. States	Nancy	13 Dec 1822
Isaac	25	M	Farmer	Ireland	U. States	Nancy	13 Dec 1822
Isabella	51	F	Widow	Ireland	United States	Trident	17 May 1825
James	38		Writer			Rufus King	7 Aug 1820
John	27	M	Farmer	Ireland	U. States	Nancy	13 Dec 1822
Mary	16	F		Ireland	U. States	Nancy	13 Dec 1822
Robert	22	M	Farmer	Ireland	U. States	Nancy	13 Dec 1822
Samuel	18	M	Farmer	Ireland	U. States	Nancy	13 Dec 1822
Samuel	50	M	Farmer	Ireland	U. States	Nancy	13 Dec 1822
Sarah	12	F		Ireland	U. States	Nancy	13 Dec 1822
Sarah	50	F	Wife	Ireland	U. States	Nancy	13 Dec 1822
Wm.	10	M	Boy	Ireland	United States	Trident	17 May 1825
LENSE, Thomas	26	F		Great B.	U. States	William Neilson	26 Jul 1828
LENSEN, Geo. Henry	26	M	Merchant	Holland	U. States	Roseway	10 Jul 1820
LENT, Auby, Jr.	18	F		United States	United States	Mazzinghi	31 Mar 1826
LENTON, Saml.	36	M	Labourer	Gt. Britain	U. States	Frances Henrietta	18 Apr 1825
LENTZ, Catherine	48	F	Spinner	France	U.S.	Helen	3 May 1828
LENTZE, Agatha	26	F		Swis	United States	Iris	21 Sep 1821
Alexander	4	M		Swis	United States	Iris	21 Sep 1821
Antonia	33	M	Mason	Swis	United States	Iris	21 Sep 1821
Elizabeth	2	F		Swis	United States	Iris	21 Sep 1821
Godlob	9	M		Wirtemburg	United States	Wade	29 Aug 1825
Godlob	40	M	Gentleman	Wirtemburg	United States	Wade	29 Aug 1825
Henrich	19	M		Wirtemburg	United States	Wade	29 Aug 1825
Jacob	22	M		Wirtemburg	United States	Wade	29 Aug 1825
Louisa	4	F		Wirtemburg	United States	Wade	29 Aug 1825
Martin	5	M		Swis	United States	Iris	21 Sep 1821
Sebastian	23	M	Blacksmith	Swis	United States	Iris	21 Sep 1821
LENY, Catharine	2			France	U. States	Parachute	14 May 1828
Catherine	28			France	U. States	Parachute	14 May 1828
Christian	4			France	U. States	Parachute	14 May 1828
George	28		Mechanic	France	U. States	Parachute	14 May 1828
LEOMOS, Frans.	16	M	Merchant	Spain	Spain	Charlotte Corday	12 Apr 1821
LEON, A. M.	7	F		Bermuda	Bermuda	Magnet	10 Jul 1820
Arnard	39 4/12	M	Joiner	France	U. States	France	26 Jun 1828
Caroline	14 2/12	F	...	U.S. America	U.S. America	Edward	28 Oct 1825
Charles	19	M	Gentleman	Spain	Spain	Eliza Jane	11 Jul 1822
D., Mrs.	28	F		Bermuda	Bermuda	Magnet	10 Jul 1820
Daniel	34	M	Merchant	Bermuda	Bermuda	Magnet	10 Jul 1820
Elias	41 5/12	M	...	U.S. America	U.S. America	Edward	28 Oct 1825
Elisha	10 1/12	M	...	U.S. America	U.S. America	Edward	28 Oct 1825
Ezekiel	12 4/12	M	...	U.S. America	U.S. America	Edward	28 Oct 1825
Jacob	17 2/12	M	...	U.S. America	U.S. America	Edward	28 Oct 1825
Joseph	14 1/12	M	...	U.S. America	U.S. America	Edward	28 Oct 1825
Mo.	75	F		France	U. States	Danube	21 Nov 1826
R.	33	M	Minister	Havana	U. States	Mary Jane	2 Jul 1828
Saml.	23	M	Merchant	English	England	Prudence	19 Apr 1826
Sarah	47 2/12	F	...	U.S. America	U.S. America	Edward	28 Oct 1825
Wm., Mrs.	26	F		Bermuda	Bermuda	Magnet	10 Jul 1820
LEONAR, Zion Clouds	32	M	Clergman	France	Montreaul	Edward Bonaffe	23 Jul 1828
LEONARD, Ann	1	F	None	Ireland	United States	John Wells	11 May 1827
Ann	30	F	None	Great Britain	U.S. America	Mentor	22 Jul 1823
Biddy	8	F	None	Ireland	United States	John Wells	11 May 1827
Bridget	25	F	Servant	Ireland	United States	Sarah G.	15 May 1828
Denis	21	M	Farmer	Ireland	United States	Dublin Packet	3 Sep 1822
Edward	25	M	Weaver	Ireland		Fame	9 Dec 1826
Edward	32		Surgeon & Physician	Ireland	Great Britain	Henrietta	26 Nov 1825
Eliza	19	F		New York		Only Son	14 Jun 1827
Eliza	22	F	Spinster	Ireland	America	Farmer	15 Nov 1823
Geo. V. *Dead	22	M		N. York		Jane	27 Aug 1824
Henry	11	M		Ireland	United States	Fabius	4 Jun 1828
Hugh	20	M	Labourer	Ireland	United States	Robert Fulton	24 Jul 1826

NAMES OF PASSENGERS	AGE	SEX	OCCUPATIONS	COUNTRY TO WHICH THEY BELONG	COUNTRY THEY INTEND TO INHABIT	SHIPS/DATES OF ARRIVAL	
LEONARD (cont'd)							
Isabella	27	F	Spinster	Ireland	United States	Fabius	4 Jun 1828
Jno.	19	M	Farmer	Ireland	U. States	Margaret	19 Mar 1825
John	20			England	America	Robert Burns	8 Dec 1821
John	27	M	Farmer	St. Johns, N.B.	United States	Henrietta	17 Aug 1825
Kitty	5	F	None	Ireland	United States	John Wells	11 May 1827
Kitty	36	F	None	Ireland	United States	John Wells	11 May 1827
Martin	24	M	Labourer	Ireland	United States	Trident	18 Jul 1827
Mary	35	F		Great Brittian	United States	Carolina Augusta	2 Dec 1828
Michael	10	M	None	Ireland	United States	John Wells	11 May 1827
Richard, Jr.	11	M	None	Ireland	United States	John Wells	11 May 1827
Robert	15	M	Tailor	Ireland	United States	Carolina Ann	14 May 1827
Robert	30	M		Great Brittian	United States	Carolina Augusta	2 Dec 1828
Rueben	25	M	Gardner	G. Britain	U. States	Two Friends	22 May 1822
Simeon	22	M	Gardner	G. Britain	U. States	Two Friends	22 May 1822
Thomas	22	M	Stationor	Ireland	Great Britian	Florida	13 Feb 1826
Thomas	33	M	B. Smith	Great Britain	United States	Blakely	29 Sep 1826
William	29	M	Farmer	New Orleans	New Orleans	Hope Mary Ann	3 May 1824
Wm.	23	M	Mariner	Boston	U. States	St. Michaels	21 Apr 1824
LEOND, Joseph J.	27	M	Merchant		France	Packet Margaret	20 Sep 1824
LEONER, J.	45	M	Mariner	U. States	U. States	Helen	24 Apr 1827
LE PAGE, Lepold	26	M	None	France	U. States	Sully	25 Jun 1828
LEPER, Mattues	21	M	mecanick	German	America	William	12 Aug 1826
LE PETTELIER, M.	40	F	Lady	France	United States	Packet	10 Jul 1823
LEPHEL, Jno.	40	M	Merchant	St. Thomas	St. Thomas	Venus	12 Oct 1824
LERAU, A.	23	M	Butcher	Germany	United States	Robert Edwards	1 Jun 1826
LERNEY, Allici	46	F	None	Gt. Brittian	U. States	Catharine	7 Feb 1826
James	35	M	Cooper	U. States	U. States	Catharine	7 Feb 1826
Sarah	25	F	None	Gt. Brittian	U. States	Catharine	7 Feb 1826
LE ROUX, P.	31	M	Planter	France	gone to France	Diana	9 Aug 1823
LE ROY, Jerome	23	M	Cooper	France	United States	Seine	7 Dec 1821
Martha	45	F		United States		Britannia	20 Jun 1827
Narcisse	22	M	Merchant	France	New York	Sully	30 Oct 1827
LEROY, Narcisse	23 4/12	M	Traveller	France	United States	France	6 Oct 1828
LERRY, Jacob	56	M	Merchant	England	England	Bunker Hill	20 Sep 1827
LERUDE,							
Amante Adeline	1 4/12	F	Infant	France	America	Bayard	15 Dec 1828
Thérése Desirée	25	F	Same Trade [Painter & Gilder]	France	America	Bayard	15 Dec 1828
Victor Nicolas	29	M	Painter & Gilder	France	America	Bayard	15 Dec 1828
LESAGE, J.	65	M	...	...	United States	Abeona	26 Jun 1824
LESANDRA, A.	40	M	Merchant	France		William	16 Apr 1823
LESANGO, Harry	13	M	Boy	Point Petre	New Jersey	Proxy	20 Jul 1826
LESLEY, Magnes	29	M	Seaman	New Hampshire	Boston	Secretary	10 Aug 1829
LESLIE, Alexr.	16	M	Merchant	Gt. Britain	Canada	New York	15 Jul 1825
Anna, Miss	30	F		U. States	U. States	Hudson	10 Nov 1825
Anthony	38	M		Scotland	Scotland	Britannia	22 Jul 1829
B.	32	M	Merchant	Gt. Britain	Canada	New York	15 Jul 1825
George	20	M	Labourer	Ireland	United States	General Putnam	20 Jun 1825
James	16	M	Labourer	England	United States	Dalhouse Castle	8 May 1827
Jane	20	F	None	England	United States	Martha	17 Sep 1821
Jane	50	F		England	United States	Dalhouse Castle	8 May 1827
John	28	M	Merchant	Great Britain	Canada	Jean	17 Aug 1827
Jona.	28	M	Mason	Scotland	U. States	James & Margaret	15 Jul 1822
Joseph	20		...	Ireland	United States	Alexander Mansfield	23 Nov 1824
Robt.	30	M	Merchant	U. States	Petersburg	La Fayette	7 Apr 1825
LESLLEY, James	6	M	Labourer	England	U. States	Ayrshire	12 May 1828
John	40	M	Labourer	England	U. States	Ayrshire	12 May 1828
LE SOER, Chas.	22	M	Denmark	U. States	U. States	Columbia	1 Dec 1824
LESPONE, D.	22			Bayonne	New York	Manchester	30 May 1821
LESPY, Charles	48	M	Farmer	England	Pittsburg	Curler	7 Jul 1827
Mary	10	F		England	Pittsburg	Curler	7 Jul 1827
Oliver	19	M	Farmer	England	Pittsburg	Curler	7 Jul 1827
LESQUA, J.	25	M	Mechanic	France	U. States	Cannon	10 Dec 1821

NAMES OF PASSENGERS	AGE	SEX	OCCUPATIONS	COUNTRY TO WHICH THEY BELONG	COUNTRY THEY INTEND TO INHABIT	SHIPS/DATES OF ARRIVAL	
LESQUOYA, Ann	32	F	Upholsterer	United States	New York	Nassau	19 Aug 1823
Jas.	46	M	Upholsterer	United States	New York	Nassau	19 Aug 1823
LESSORGUES, John	48	M	Merchant	France	United States	Helen	5 Sep 1828
LESTER, Ann	35	F	Laborer or Spinster	Ireland	United States	Sarah G	11 Sep 1827
Caroline	3	F		United States	United States	Globe	30 Aug 1828
Catharine	44	F		United States	United States	Globe	30 Aug 1828
Charles	3/12	M		G. Britain	United States	Edward	21 Apr 1821
Claren.	17	F		United States	United States	Globe	30 Aug 1828
David	3	M	Laborer or Spinster	Ireland	United States	Sarah G	11 Sep 1827
George	6	M		United States	United States	Globe	30 Aug 1828
Gilbert	5	M	Laborer or Spinster	Ireland	United States	Sarah G	11 Sep 1827
John	25	M	Linnen Draper	G. Britain	United States	Edward	21 Apr 1821
Lesters	27	M	Mariner	America	U. States	Ambuscade	11 Jul 1821
Mary	40	F		England	U. States	Howard Douglass	29 Jan 1828
Michael	56	M	Farmer	United States	United States	Globe	30 Aug 1828
N. R.	44	M	Mariner	U. States	U. States	Sarah	11 Apr 1825
Robert	23	M	Weaver	Ireland	United States	Trio	31 Oct 1827
Sophia	13	F		United States	United States	Globe	30 Aug 1828
Theodore	8	M		United States	United States	Globe	30 Aug 1828
Thomas	7	M	Laborer or Spinster	Ireland	United States	Sarah G	11 Sep 1827
William	20	M	Carpenter	U. States	U. States	Julia	9 Jun 1825
Wm.	21		Farmer	G. Britain		Casanda	5 Sep 1827
Zachariah	10	M	Laborer or Spinster	Ireland	United States	Sarah G	11 Sep 1827
LESTOR, Ellen	21	F		G. Britain	United States	Edward	21 Apr 1821
Gilbert	42	M	Mariner	New York	U. States	Champion	26 Jul 1827
LESTRADE, John	32	M	M.D.	France	U. States	Marmion	29 Sep 1823
Mary	28	F		France	U. States	Marmion	29 Sep 1823
LESTY, Joseph	25	M	Farmer	France	United States	Crescent	12 Jul 1827
LETEVERE, Peter D.	24	M	Student in Bardstown's College	Netherland	America	Henry	17 May 1828
LETHGOW, William	33	M	Merchant	Boston, U.S.	Boston, U.S.	Brighton	21 Jan 1826
LETLER, Jame	24	M	Farmer	Great Brittan	U.S.	Emulous	29 Jun 1827
John	22	M	Farmer	Great Brittan	U.S.	Emulous	29 Jun 1827
LETOTHOUR, A.	28	M	Merchant	France	U. States	Canton	17 Aug 1824
LETTERS, Ellen	20	F	Farmer	Ireland	U. States	Dickinson	30 Jul 1825
LEUMETO, Juan, Don	36	M	Merchant	France	Cuba	Tontine	9 Jun 1827
LEURRING, Santimus	25	M	Merchant	United States	United States	John & William	20 Jul 1829
LEUTEL, Isabella	24	F				Lady of the Lake	23 Aug 1828
John	3	M				Lady of the Lake	23 Aug 1828
LEVAGO, Vincinta	39	M	Merchant	Spain	Spain	Galatea	20 Jul 1829
LEVANY, Elinor	19	F		G. Britain	United States	Louisa	14 Jun 1825
LEVAVASSEUR, Leon	47	M	Farmer	France	France	Sully	15 Jul 1829
LEVE, Henry	28	M	Merchant	United States	United States	Cambria	7 May 1828
Samuel	20	M	Servant to Mr. David Atties			William	12 Aug 1826
LEVECOMP, —	36	M	Hatter	France	U. States	Magnet	3 May 1826
LEVER, Frs.	35	M	Mechanic	France	U. States	Edward	12 Aug 1825
John	21	M	Farmer	Alsace in the Department of Upper and lower Rhine	United States	Carolina Augusta	16 May 1828
LEVERICH, Sacket	23	M	Mariner	United States	United States	Magnet	19 Aug 1822
LEVERING, Samuel	23	M	Labourer	Great Britain	United States	Frances Henrietta	17 Sep 1827
LEVERMAN, H., Mr.	26	M	Mariner	England		Boyer	9 May 1825
LEVERNG, John	50	M	Merchant	U. States	U. States	Asaph	23 Mar 1827
LEVERY, Hannah, Mrs.	10	F		England		Hudson	23 Jul 1828
LEVEY, Bridget	20	F	Spinster	Ireland	U.S. of America	Meteor	19 Mar 1828
Lemel S.	28	M	Merchant	Canada	Canada	Corinthian	5 May 1827
Thomas	20	M	Labourer	Ireland	U.S. of America	Meteor	19 Mar 1828
LEVI, Aaron	27	M	Farmer	Germany	United States	Stephania	16 Aug 1827
Catherine	16	F	Servant	Great Britain	United States	Sylvester Healy	23 Nov 1825
Ebben	20	M	Labourer	Great Britain	United States	Sylvester Healy	23 Nov 1825
H.	21	M	Mercht.	France	U. States	Catherine	4 Sep 1824
John	25	M	Merchant	England	Great Brittan	Amity	11 May 1821

NAMES OF PASSENGERS	AGE	SEX	OCCUPATIONS	COUNTRY TO WHICH THEY BELONG	COUNTRY THEY INTEND TO INHABIT	SHIPS/DATES OF ARRIVAL	
LEVILLA, —, Mrs.	30	F	Lady	Guadaloupe	U. States	Turner	8 Jun 1824
LEVILLIS, —, child of							
Mr. Levillis	2	M		Guadaloupe	U. States	Turner	8 Jun 1824
—, child of Mr. Levillis	5	M		Guadaloupe	U. States	Turner	8 Jun 1824
—, child of Mr. Levillis	7	M		Guadaloupe	U. States	Turner	8 Jun 1824
—, Mr.	35	M	Planter	Guadaloupe	U. States	Turner	8 Jun 1824
LEVIN, W.	12	M	Gentleman	England		Hudson	23 Jul 1828
LEVINE, James	22	M	Stone Mason	Ireland	United States	Asia	29 Jul 1829
John	47	M	Merchant	U.States	U. States	Patty & Sally	25 Apr 1821
LEVING, John	14	M		England	United States	Acasta	12 Dec 1823
LEVINGSTON, —, Mrs.	45	F	Lady	U. States	U. States	Wallace	12 Apr 1824
E., Miss	12	F	Lady	U. States	U. States	Wallace	12 Apr 1824
LEVINGTON, C., Miss	17	F	Lady	U. States	U. States	Wallace	12 Apr 1824
LEVIOR, Goerge	40	M	Labourer	Scotland	U. States	Czar	29 Aug 1829
LEVIS, Henry	19	M	Taylor	Charleston	United States	Brown	26 Apr 1826
LEVIT, Hannah, Miss	2	F	Farmer	England	U. States	Acasta	21 Oct 1825
LEVITT, Harriet	26	F	Farmer	England	U. States	Acasta	21 Oct 1825
William	32	M	Farmer	England	U. States	Acasta	21 Oct 1825
LEVITY, James	26	M		Ireland	U. States	Olive Branch	30 Oct 1823
John	1/12	M		Ireland	U. States	Olive Branch	30 Oct 1823
Nanny	2	F		Ireland	U. States	Olive Branch	30 Oct 1823
Nanny	23	F	Weaver	Ireland	U. States	Olive Branch	30 Oct 1823
LEVY, —, Mrs.	40	F		England	United States	Hiram	14 Aug 1829
Aaron	36	M	Furrier	Rusia	United States	Elizabeth	8 Jun 1827
Abraham	22	M	Trader	G. Britain	U. States	Robt. Edwards	4 Sep 1828
Aime, Misses	8	F		St. Croix	United States	Hiram	14 Aug 1829
Anne	10	F	Lady	England	U.S. America	Cortes	19 May 1826
Arthur L.	14	M		England	U.S. America	Cortes	19 May 1826
David	1	M		England	U.S. America	Cortes	19 May 1826
David	18	M	Merchant	United States	United States	Eliza	10 Jul 1827
David, Jr., Esqr.	40	M	Merchant	France	United States	Hiram	14 Aug 1829
Easter	33	F	Lady	England	U.S. America	Cortes	19 May 1826
Elias	19	M	Docter	England	United States	Maria	3 Oct 1822
Emma, Misses	8	F		St. Thomas	United States	Hiram	14 Aug 1829
Isabella	24	F	Tailoress	England	United States	Elizabeth	8 Jun 1827
Jacob	22	M	Merchant	Helimer	U.S. America	Superior	18 Jun 1825
Jno.	5	M		England	U.S. America	Cortes	19 May 1826
John		M	Farmer	Ireland	United States	Justina	5 Aug 1823
Jonas	25	M	Merchant	England	U.S.A.	Hudson	21 Aug 1829
Josephine, Misses	9	F		St. Croix	United States	Hiram	14 Aug 1829
L.	21	M	Merchant	France		Edward Quesnel	13 Mar 1828
M. E.	47	M	Planter	America	America	Britannia	5 Nov 1828
Moses Jacob	50	M	Mercht.	London, Eng.	U.S.A.	Orator	1 Oct 1829
Nathan	62	M	Consul of U.S. at St. Thos.	U. States	U. States	Cannon	25 Apr 1821
Peggy	20	F		Ballymopoly	...	Gleaner	24 May 1823
Phoebe	13	F	Lady	England	U.S. America	Cortes	19 May 1826
Rebecca	2	F		England	U.S. America	Cortes	19 May 1826
Sarah	4	F		England	U.S. America	Cortes	19 May 1826
Saul	7	M		England	U.S. America	Cortes	19 May 1826
Thomas	28	M	Labourer	Ireland	United States	William & Henry	19 Jul 1822
LEVYARD, Elizabeth	50	F		Switzerland	United States	Howard	11 Jun 1824
LEW, William	20	M	Labourer	Ireland	N. York	Trusty	12 Sep 1828
LEWELLIN, David	27	M	Fireman	England	United States	Amelia	20 Aug 1829
LEWERS, Sally	20	F	None	Ireland	United States	Lord Wellington	28 May 1827
William	21	M	Clergiman	Ireland	U. States	Josephine	7 May 1827
LEWFFORN, John Shaw	26					Plutarch	18 Jul 1826
LEWIGHT, J. E., Revd.	37	M	Divine	U. States	U. States	Pacific	20 Aug 1825
LEWIN, Jane	44	F		England	United States	Criterion	27 Oct 1820
Robert	41	M	Merchant	Great Britain	Great Britain	Columbia	1 Dec 1823
LEWIS, —, child	5/12	M		England	New York	Thames	6 Oct 1820
—, Miss	22	F	Lady	U. States	U. States	Paquet des Cayes	16 Aug 1828
—, Mr.	28	M	Carpenter	U. States	U. States	Rachel	14 Mar 1825
—, Mrs.	16	F		G. Britain	U. States	London	23 Sep 1828
—, Mrs.	30	F	None	U. States	U. States	White Oak	5 Apr 1828
... J.	35	M	Master	United States		Rebecca Ann	29 Nov 1820
A.	2	F	Girl	Philadelphia	Philadelphia	Inspector	26 May 1828

NAMES OF PASSENGERS	AGE	SEX	OCCUPATIONS	COUNTRY TO WHICH THEY BELONG	COUNTRY THEY INTEND TO INHABIT	SHIPS/DATES OF ARRIVAL	
LEWIS (cont'd)							
A., Mrs.	30	F	Lady	Philadelphia	Philadelphia	Inspector	26 May 1828
Abm.	45	M	Merchant	U. States		Mary	10 Aug 1820
Alfred	31 4/12		Merchant	England	U. States	Jackin	15 May 1828
Ann	14/12	F		Great Brittan	U. States	Prince Leopold	2 Jul 1821
Ann	16	F	Farmer	Wales, Gt. Bn.	United States	Orozimbo	31 May 1824
Ann	49			Cardigan		Mount Vernon	18 Oct 1822
B...	50	F				Eliza Grant	6 Oct 1828
Catherine	24 7/12			England	U. States	Jackin	15 May 1828
Cecelia	25	F		U. States	U. States	Jupiter	29 Jun 1825
D.	25	M	private	U. States	U. States	Enterprize	9 Aug 1825
Darah	50	F		England	England	Tontin	13 Jun 1825
David	22	M	Carpenter	Bristol, Engl.	...	Warrior	19 May 1828
Dixson	22	M	Farmer	Ireland	United States	Fabius	4 Jun 1828
Dorothy	7	F		Great Britain	U.S. of America	Gratitude	3 Oct 1829
Dorothy	27			Great Britain	United States	Gomer	21 May 1828
Drucella	40	F		United States	United States	William Byrnes	1 Dec 1824
E. ..., Mr.	28	M	Merchant	England	New York	Thames	6 Oct 1820
E. S.						Day	14 Jun 1822
Edward	4	M		Great Brittan	U. States	Prince Leopold	2 Jul 1821
Edward	40	M	Farmer	Great Brittan	U. States	Prince Leopold	2 Jul 1821
Elisha	34	M	Merchant	U.S. of America	U.S. of America	Canada	1 Oct 1827
Eliza	3	F		U. States	U. States	White Oak	5 Apr 1828
Eliza	9	F		Great Britain	U.S. of America	Gratitude	3 Oct 1829
Eliza	35	F		England	Great Britain	Albion	7 Feb 1820
Eliza	50	F		G. Britain	U. States	St. George	7 Jun 1828
Ellen	16	F		Great Britain	U.S. of America	Gratitude	3 Oct 1829
Evan	30	M	Carpenter	Younghall, Great Britain	United States	Union	24 Sep 1823
Ewd.	30	M	Farmer	G. Britain	U. States	St. George	7 Jun 1828
Fanny	4 8/12			England	U. States	Jackin	15 May 1828
Francis	30	F	None	United States	Virginia	Brighton	19 Aug 1829
Fredrick	23	M	Merchant	U. States	U. States	Canada	2 Jun 1824
Geo.	24	M	Doctor	Baltimore	U. States	Swift	31 Mar 1825
Geo. E.	25	M	Mariner	U. States	U. States	Andrew Jackson	16 Jun 1821
Geo. G., Lt. Col.	45	M	Royal Engineer	Great Britain	Great Britain	Roman	10 May 1828
George	7			Cardigan		Mount Vernon	18 Oct 1822
George	26	M	Merchant	England		Charlemagne	16 Jan 1829
George	68	M	Gentleman	United States	United States	William Byrnes	1 Dec 1824
Harvey	60	M	Farmer	Ireland	United States	Justina	5 Aug 1823
Henry	14	M	Farmer	Wales, Gt. Bn.	United States	Orozimbo	31 May 1824
Henry	21	M		England	United States	Acosta	28 Jul 1823
Hugh	18		Farmer	Cardigan		Mount Vernon	18 Oct 1822
Hugh	23	M		G. Britain	U. States	St. George	7 Jun 1828
Hugh	30	M	Farmer	G. Britain	U. States	St. George	7 Jun 1828
Israel H.	28		Gentleman	U. States	U. States	Venus	4 Oct 1821
J. S.	30	M	Merchant	Gt. Britain	U. States	Prince Edward	5 Jul 1825
James	39	M	None	Younghall, Great Britain	United States	Union	24 Sep 1823
James ..., Mr.	35	M	Gentleman	England	New York	Thames	6 Oct 1820
Jane	7	F		Great Brittan	U. States	Prince Leopold	2 Jul 1821
Jane	24	F		Great Britain	U. States	United States	8 Sep 1827
Jane	33	F		Great Britain	United States	Robert	15 Jul 1822
Jas.	18	M	Farmer	St. Johns	Canada	Nancy	29 Nov 1821
Jas. Jno.	3	M	Mercht.	Belfast	N. York	Favourite	8 Oct 1823
Jeremiah	23	M	Iron Roller	Gt. Britain	U.S. America	James Cropper	14 Mar 1828
Jno.	18	M	Draper	Great Britain	U.S. of America	Gratitude	3 Oct 1829
Jno.	19	M	Carpenter	Charleston	U. States	Robt. Y. Hayne	27 Jun 1825
Jno., Black	22	M	Servant	N. York	U. States	Endymion	12 Mar 1822
John	3			Great Britain	United States	Gomer	21 May 1828
John	9	M		Great Britain	United States	Robert	15 Jul 1822
John	20	M	Farmer	France	U. States	France	14 Mar 1828
John	22		Farmer	Cardigan		Mount Vernon	18 Oct 1822
John	22	M	Farmer	Wales, Gt. Bn.	United States	Orozimbo	31 May 1824
John	22	M	E. Cutter	G. Brittan	U. States	Henry	24 Oct 1828
John	24		Farmer	Great Britain	United States	Gomer	21 May 1828
John	25	M	Mechanic	United States	United States	Tampico	12 Mar 1827
John	33	M	Labourer	Great Britain	United States	Robert	15 Jul 1822
June	7	F		Great Britain	United States	Robert	15 Jul 1822

NAMES OF PASSENGERS	AGE	SEX	OCCUPATIONS	COUNTRY TO WHICH THEY BELONG	COUNTRY THEY INTEND TO INHABIT	SHIPS/DATES OF ARRIVAL	
LEWIS (cont'd)							
K.	22	M	Sugar Baker	Ireland	U. States	Frederick	2 Apr 1828
Lewis	10			Cardigan		Mount Vernon	18 Oct 1822
Lewis	14	M	Farmer	England	U. States	New York	11 Jul 1823
Louisa	2 6/12			England	U. States	Jackin	15 May 1828
Ludwig	25	M	Gentleman	Prussia	New York	Braganza	16 Apr 1825
Margaret	...		Laboring Class		United States	Atlantic	2 Apr 1827
Margaret	1			Great Britain	United States	Gomer	21 May 1828
Mary		F	Farmer	Ireland	United States	Justina	5 Aug 1823
Mary	6	F		Great Britain	United States	Robert	15 Jul 1822
Mary	21			Cardigan		Mount Vernon	18 Oct 1822
Mary	24	F		G. Britain	U. States	St. George	7 Jun 1828
Mary	35	F		Great Brittan	U. States	Prince Leopold	2 Jul 1821
Mary, Mrs.	26	F		England	New York	Thames	6 Oct 1820
Mary, of Baltimore	48	F		Wales	America	Mary Lord	26 Oct 1829
Mary Ann	23	F	None	Great Britain	Great Britain	Nestor in Liverpool	29 Jul 1822
Mathew R.	21	M	Merchant	Great Britain	United States	Washington	22 Mar 1820
May	12	F		Great Brittan	U. States	Prince Leopold	2 Jul 1821
Morris	24	M	Trader	Germany	U.S.	Missouri	4 Aug 1825
Richard	12			Cardigan		Mount Vernon	18 Oct 1822
Richard	40	M	Taylor	England	United States	Nimrod	31 Jul 1828
Rob.	32	M	Mariner	U. States	U. States	Nimrod	30 Jul 1823
Rob.	36	M	Mariner	U. States	U. States	Brazillian	18 Oct 1824
Robert	12	M	Farmer	Wales, Gt. Bn.	United States	Orozimbo	31 May 1824
Robert	55	M	Planter	Ireland	Ireland	Jupiter	4 Aug 1829
S. A.	20	M	Merchant	American	U. States	Frederick	27 Jan 1823
S. J.	39	M	Mariner	U. States	U. States	Othello	11 Jul 1825
Sam.	24	M	Painter	Great Britain	United States	Atlantic	28 May 1827
Saml.	29	M	Merchant	Ireland	New York	Carolina Ann	15 Oct 1824
Samuel	25		Merchant	England	New York	Europa	27 Dec 1827
Samuel A.	28	M	Merchante	United States	United States	Prudence	31 Oct 1827
Sarah E., Miss	25	F		England	New York	Thames	6 Oct 1820
Thomas	9			Cardigan		Mount Vernon	18 Oct 1822
Thomas	13	M		England	Great Britain	Albion	7 Feb 1820
Thomas	21	...	...	...	...	Pioneer	21 Jun 1825
Thomas	23	M	Cabinet Maker	Bristol, Engl.	...	Warrior	19 May 1828
Thomas	30	M	Merchant	U. States	U. States	Eliza Barker	25 Dec 1824
Thomas	30	M	Farmer	Great Britain	U. States	United States	8 Sep 1827
Thomas	40	M	Brewer	England	Great Brittan	Amity	11 May 1821
Thomas	40	M		United States	United States	Only Daughter	29 Apr 1825
Thomas	51 6/12	M	Merchant	United States	United States	Hector	8 Jan 1820
Thomas, of Baltimore	56	M	Farmer	Wales	America	Mary Lord	26 Oct 1829
Thompkins V.	27	M	Gentleman	America	America	Governor Von Schollen	7 Nov 1827
Thos.	19	M	Farmer	Wales	America	Farmer	4 Aug 1825
Thos.	22	M				Belfast	28 Sep 1820
Thos.	30	M	Merchant	Hayti	U. States	Curlew	16 Jun 1823
Thos., Revd.	30		Clergyman	England	United States	Mary	15 Jul 1822
William	7	M		Great Brittan	U. States	Prince Leopold	2 Jul 1821
William	14			Cardigan		Mount Vernon	18 Oct 1822
William	18	M	Labourer	Great Britain	United States	Robert	15 Jul 1822
William	20	M	Mason	Ireland	United States	Fabius	4 Jun 1828
William	26	M	Farmer	Wales	United States	Orozimbo	11 Aug 1823
William	34	M	Merchant	England	Great Britain	Albion	7 Feb 1820
William	53		Farmer	Cardigan		Mount Vernon	18 Oct 1822
William H.	25	M	...	England		Boyer	9 May 1825
Wm.	0 3/12	M		Great Britain	U. States	United States	8 Sep 1827
Wm.	26	M	Merchant	G. Brittain	U. States	Pacific	23 Jan 1826
Wm.	27	M	Servant	Ireland	United States	Trio	13 Jun 1827
Wm.	46	M	Blacksmith	England	United States	Margarett Scott	22 Aug 1827
Wm. L.	30	M	Merchant	America	U. States	James Monroe	14 Jan 1823
LEWSEY, Eliza	37	F		Great Britain		Moro Castle	6 Jul 1827
Joseph	6	M		Great Britain		Moro Castle	6 Jul 1827
LEYLAND, R.	35	M	Merchant	England	U. States	New York	4 Nov 1824
LEYS, Jacobus O.	7		None	St. Croix	United States	General Marion	18 Jul 1829
John	30		Professional	St. Croix	United States	General Marion	18 Jul 1829
LEYSTER, Wm.	24	M	Clergyman	Ireland	U.S. of America	Splendid	14 Aug 1829
LEZZARD, R.	40	M	Merchant	France	United States	Dawn	15 Oct 1827

NAMES OF PASSENGERS	AGE	SEX	OCCUPATIONS	COUNTRY TO WHICH THEY BELONG	COUNTRY THEY INTEND TO INHABIT	SHIPS/DATES OF ARRIVAL	
LHON, Wm.	12	M		Guersey	New York	Comet	19 Oct 1826
LIANO, Doloris, Dn.	40	F		Mexico	United States	General Warren	8 Jul 1829
Ramon Gomez, Dn.	55	M	Merchant	Spainard	United States	General Warren	8 Jul 1829
Ygnicia, Dn.	11	F		Mexico	United States	General Warren	8 Jul 1829
LIBBY, Wm.	3		None			Amphion	31 May 1824
LIBEAU, Charles A. F.	26	M		Hess Castle	U.S. America	Sereno	31 Jul 1826
LIBERIA, C. B.	25	M	Musician	Genoa	U. States	Nimrod	31 Jul 1828
LIBERTON, R.	24	M	Labourer	Ireland	U. States	Loire	6 Dec 1827
LIBOCK, Benjamin	34 2/12	M	Waiter	Great Britain	New York	Thames	16 May 1821
LIBOTTE, —, Mrs.	30	F	Wife	France	U. States	Sarah Ralston	20 Feb 1826
J.	40	M	Gunsmith	France	U. States	Sarah Ralston	20 Feb 1826
J., child [of J.]	3	M		France	U. States	Sarah Ralston	20 Feb 1826
Joseph, child [of J.]	9	M		France	U. States	Sarah Ralston	20 Feb 1826
S., child [of J.]	7	M		France	U. States	Sarah Ralston	20 Feb 1826
W., child [of J.]	5	M		France	U. States	Sarah Ralston	20 Feb 1826
LICA, Gottliep	23	M	Stone cutter	France	America, U.N.S.	Great Britain	3 Aug 1829
Joseph F.	35	M	Shipmaster	Portugal	St. Bartholomews	Andes	22 Oct 1821
LICESTER, Carlne.	20	F		England	U. States	Howard Douglass	29 Jan 1828
Jos.	40	M	Weaver	England	U. States	Howard Douglass	29 Jan 1828
Thomas	1	M		England	U. States	Howard Douglass	29 Jan 1828
LICIS, George	4/12	M		Great Britain	United States	Freake	25 Jun 1827
John	1 6/12	M		Great Britain	United States	Freake	25 Jun 1827
John	23	M	Tanner	Great Britain	United States	Freake	25 Jun 1827
Maria	24	F		Great Britain	United States	Freake	25 Jun 1827
LIDDEL, Eliza	12/365	F		Great Britain	U.S. of Ama.	Robert Fulton	16 Aug 1824
Francis	22	M	Farmer	Great Britain	U.S. of Ama.	Robert Fulton	16 Aug 1824
George	9	M	Farmer	Great Britain	U.S. of Ama.	Robert Fulton	16 Aug 1824
Harriet	17	F	Farmer	Great Britain	U.S. of Ama.	Robert Fulton	16 Aug 1824
Jane	4	F	Farmer	Great Britain	U.S. of Ama.	Robert Fulton	16 Aug 1824
Jane	21	F	Farmer	Great Britain	U.S. of Ama.	Robert Fulton	16 Aug 1824
Martha	19	F	Farmer	Great Britain	U.S. of Ama.	Robert Fulton	16 Aug 1824
Mary	55	F	Farmer	Great Britain	U.S. of Ama.	Robert Fulton	16 Aug 1824
Sarah	27	F	Farmer	Great Britain	U.S. of Ama.	Robert Fulton	16 Aug 1824
Theresa	12	F	Farmer	Great Britain	U.S. of Ama.	Robert Fulton	16 Aug 1824
Thomas	59	M	Farmer	Great Britain	U.S. of Ama.	Robert Fulton	16 Aug 1824
Thos.	28	M	Farmer	Great Britain	U.S. of Ama.	Robert Fulton	16 Aug 1824
Wm.	24	M	Farmer	Great Britain	U.S. of Ama.	Robert Fulton	16 Aug 1824
LIDDELL, Joh.	21	F	Farmer			Splendid	14 Aug 1829
Thos.	20	M	Merchant	Scotland	United States	Friends	13 Mar 1824
LIDDLE, Grace	5	F	None	Gr. Britain		Moro Castle	6 Jul 1827
James	36	M	Labourer	Gr. Britain		Moro Castle	6 Jul 1827
John	6	M	None	Gr. Britain		Moro Castle	6 Jul 1827
Mary	20	F				Splendid	14 Aug 1829
Mary	30	F	None	Gr. Britain		Moro Castle	6 Jul 1827
Robert	1	M	None	Gr. Britain		Moro Castle	6 Jul 1827
Robt.	27	M	Joiner	Great Britain		Moro Castle	6 Jul 1827
William	39	M	Merchant	...	United States	Nestor	20 Nov 1821
Wm.	18	F				Splendid	14 Aug 1829
LIDDOL, Stuart	23	M	Merchant	U. States	U. States	Eliza Jane	26 Oct 1829
LIDDY, Jno.	30	M	Labourer	England	U. States	Thomas Ritchie	2 Jul 1827
John	21			Carvan	N. York	Peru	30 May 1828
Margt.	24	F		Ireland	United States	Potomac	28 Sep 1827
Thomas	20			Carvan	N. York	Peru	30 May 1828
LIDFORD, ...mes	9/12		Boy	Gt. Britain	P...	Betsey	18 Apr 1822
...nn	23 4/12	F		Gt. Britain	P...	Betsey	18 Apr 1822
James	25 8/12	M	Farmer	Gt. Britain	P...	Betsey	18 Apr 1822
Mary	3		Girl	Gt. Britain	P...	Betsey	18 Apr 1822
Thos.	18 4/12	M		Gt. Britain	P...	Betsey	18 Apr 1822
Willm.	4 6/12		Boy	Gt. Britain	P...	Betsey	18 Apr 1822
LIDWELL, Barby	15	F		France	Canada	Abby Jones	12 Jul 1827
Frances	25	F		France	Canada	Abby Jones	12 Jul 1827
Mary	60	F		France	Canada	Abby Jones	12 Jul 1827
LIEBER, A. G.	51	M	Laborer	Hanover	United States of Am.	Constitution	6 Jul 1829
Francis	28	M	Professor	Germany		Britannia	20 Jun 1827
LIEBING, Andreas	43	M	Weaver	Baden	United States	Jason	3 Nov 1828
Catharina	5	F		Baden	United States	Jason	3 Nov 1828

NAMES OF PASSENGERS	AGE	SEX	OCCUPATIONS	COUNTRY TO WHICH THEY BELONG	COUNTRY THEY INTEND TO INHABIT	SHIPS/DATES OF ARRIVAL	
LIEBING (cont'd)							
Christine	20	F		Baden	United States	Jason	3 Nov 1828
Jacob	13	M		Baden	United States	Jason	3 Nov 1828
Martin	16	M		Baden	United States	Jason	3 Nov 1828
Sophia	45	F		Baden	United States	Jason	3 Nov 1828
LIEF, Gottel	27	M	Potter	France	United States	New England	29 Aug 1828
LIEKS, Martha	50	F		G. Britain	U. States	Mary & Harriot	8 Sep 1828
Saml.	49	M	Shoemaker	G. Britain	U. States	Mary & Harriot	8 Sep 1828
LIETH, James	7			Ireland	United States	Jno. Dickinson	21 Sep 1821
John	52			Ireland	United States	Jno. Dickinson	21 Sep 1821
Margaret	36			Ireland	United States	Jno. Dickinson	21 Sep 1821
LIEVEN, Paquin	28	M	Farmer	France	France	Sully	15 Jul 1829
LIEVIDEL, Matthew	30	M	Miller	Switzerland	U. States	Bayard	9 Jul 1824
LIFE, Richard	37	M	Merchant	England	U. States	Cincinnatus	24 May 1821
Sarah	29	F		England	U. States	Cincinnatus	24 May 1821
LIFFMAN, U. C. A.	20	M	Hatter	Havre Towns	New York	Leeds	7 Nov 1828
LIGHT, Jas.	35	M	Servant	Gt. Britain	Canada	Corks	3 Aug 1824
Thos.	31	M	Labourer	Ireland	U. States	Severn	12 Oct 1826
LIGHTBOURNE, John	42	M	Merchant	Bermuda	Bermuda	Emblem	25 Oct 1825
Nathl.	37	M	Merchant	Bermuda	Bermuda	Emblem	25 Oct 1825
LIGHTFOOT, Wm.	20			G. Britain	U. States	Hamilton	28 Apr 1828
LIGHTON, Jane	18	F	Seamstress	Great Britain	United States	Grecian	24 Sep 1828
LIGNARYS, Antonio	52	M	Merchant	United States		Orestelle	4 Oct 1828
LIGNIE, —, Mrs.	24	F		France	U. States	Edward Quesnel	15 May 1826
L.	23	M	Tailor	France	U. States	Edward Quesnel	15 May 1826
LIGOTER, Jean	25	M	Farmer	France	U. States	Edward Bopnnaffe	30 Jul 1829
LIKELY, Jane	37	F	Seamstress	Ireland	United States	Meteor	19 Aug 1829
LILEY, Mary	19	F	Servant	Ireland	United States	Wilson	27 Jun 1826
LILLIE, Charles	4	M	Child	England	United States	Cambria	3 Jul 1829
Charles	30	M	Surgeon	England	United States	Cambria	3 Jul 1829
George	1 6/12	M	Child	England	United States	Cambria	3 Jul 1829
Matilda	27	F	Wife	England	United States	Cambria	3 Jul 1829
LILLINGTON, N. D.	26	M	Merchant	Great Britain	Great Britain	Columbia	1 Dec 1823
LILLY, —, Mrs.	30	F		England	U. States	Cincinnatus	21 Feb 1825
James	19	M	Blacksmith	Ireland	United States	Louisa	18 Apr 1827
Margt.	45	F		Ireland	U. States	Wanderer	30 Sep 1828
LIMA, E.	22	F	Spinster	Ireland		Robert Fulton	4 Jun 1828
Joáo Francisco	17	M	Apothecary	Brazil	United States	Isabella	1 Aug 1829
Manuel	21	M	Gentleman	Cuba	U. States	Swan	23 Jun 1823
LIMBERG, A. G.	40	M	...	Denmark	U. States	South Carolina Packet	4 Sep 1822
LIMERICK, Henry	11	M	Child	Ireland	America States	Beaver	18 Aug 1827
James	28	M	Sleater	Ireland	America States	Beaver	18 Aug 1827
Martha	27	F	Mantumaker	Ireland	America States	Beaver	18 Aug 1827
Nancy	5	F	Child	Ireland	America States	Beaver	18 Aug 1827
LIMES, M.	30	M	Milatary	Spain	Spain	Atlantic	26 Jul 1825
LIMON, Marie, & two Children	37	F		Guadaloupe		Little John	4 Nov 1820
LIMSON, William	20	M	...	Ireland	United States	Nancey	8 Jun 1822
LIN, Hariet	30	F		Philadelphia	U. States	Plato	5 Nov 1821
Priscilla	8	F		Philadelphia	U. States	Plato	5 Nov 1821
LINCH, Ann	16	F	Servant	Ireland	United States	Carolina Ann	11 Dec 1826
David	28	M	Farmer	Ireland	U. States	Nancy	29 Nov 1821
Garrit	21	M	Labourer	England	United States	Essex	23 May 1828
J. B.	30	M	Gent	French	Switzerland	Charlemagne	19 Sep 1828
John	25	M	Labourer	England	United States	Enterprize	19 Oct 1826
John	50	M	Gent	French	Switzerland	Charlemagne	19 Sep 1828
M.	45	F	Gent	French	Switzerland	Charlemagne	19 Sep 1828
Patrick	24	M	Farmer	Ireland	Pennsylvania	Governor Fenner	23 Jul 1829
LINCOLN, —, Mrs.	30	F	None	United States	United States	Cuba	3 Jan 1823
Eliza	4	F	None	United States	United States	Cuba	3 Jan 1823
Ellenor	30	F	Labourer	England	U. States	Ayrshire	12 May 1828
Isaac	41	M	Mariner	United States	United States	Florida	13 Feb 1826
Jane	13	F	Labourer	England	U. States	Ayrshire	12 May 1828
Mary	7	F	None	United States	United States	Cuba	3 Jan 1823
Thomas	30	M	Labourer	England	U. States	Ayrshire	12 May 1828
LINCY, Ann	24	F	his wife [James]	Ireland	United States	Lady Hunter	29 Apr 1826

NAMES OF PASSENGERS	AGE	SEX	OCCUPATIONS	COUNTRY TO WHICH THEY BELONG	COUNTRY THEY INTEND TO INHABIT	SHIPS/DATES OF ARRIVAL	
LINCY (cont'd)							
Hugh	4	M	their Son [James & Ann]	Ireland	United States	Lady Hunter	29 Apr 1826
James	25	M	Shoemaker	Ireland	United States	Lady Hunter	29 Apr 1826
LIND, John	24	M	Blacksmith	England	United States	Siroc	31 Oct 1829
LINDAN, John L.	26	M		Great Brittain	United States	Nimrod	9 Jan 1827
LINDER, Geoe.	22		Farmer	Switzerland	United States	Henri IV	14 Sep 1827
Jno. Zimin	21		Merchant	Bavaria	Bavaria	Black Warrior	1 Nov 1827
LINDLEY, A.	26	M	Moulder	Gt. Britain	New York	Columbia	3 Apr 1826
Joab	28	M	Carpenter	United States	United States	George	25 May 1825
Mary	4	F		Great Brittian	United States	Carolina Augusta	2 Dec 1828
Wm.	32	M	Basketmaker	England	New York	America	1 Aug 1828
LINDLY, Hannah	27	F		Great Brittian	United States	Carolina Augusta	2 Dec 1828
LINDON, James	20	M	None	Great Britain	United States	Orozimbo	5 Mar 1827
LINDS, Antonio		M	Gentleman	Spaniard		Happy Return	23 Jul 1821
LINDSAY, —, Mrs.	23	F		G. Britain	U. States	Camillus	8 Sep 1828
Charles	5	M		...nbu...ge	United States	Carolina Ann	11 Jun 1824
David	9	M		...nbu...ge	United States	Carolina Ann	11 Jun 1824
Delly	30	F	Farmer	Ireland	U. States	Dickinson	30 Jul 1825
Edward	7	M		...nbu...ge	United States	Carolina Ann	11 Jun 1824
Harriet	24	F		...nbu...ge	United States	Carolina Ann	11 Jun 1824
James	20	M	Farmer	Scotland	U. States	Hannah	16 Sep 1823
James	25	M	Farmer	...nbu...ge	United States	Carolina Ann	11 Jun 1824
John	2	M		G. Britain	U. States	Camillus	8 Sep 1828
John, an infant		M		...nbu...ge	United States	Carolina Ann	11 Jun 1824
Maurice	3	M		...nbu...ge	United States	Carolina Ann	11 Jun 1824
Nathaniel, Capt.	32	M	Mariner	U.S. of Amer		Brilliant	28 Jan 1828
Samuel	18	M	Shoemaker			Robert Burns	13 Jul 1820
Thomas	26	M	Merchant	Great Britain	United States	Colossus	5 Jun 1827
Thos.	28	M	Paper Maker	Scotland	United States	Camillus	9 May 1827
LINDSEY, Ann	50	F	None	England	America	Bolivar	2 Oct 1826
David	28 6/12	M	Weaver	Scotland	United States	Mobile	21 Aug 1827
E.	48	F	None	England	U. States	Unity	27 Mar 1827
James	28	M	Carpenter	Scotland	Buenos Ayres	Factor	10 May 1821
Joseph	14	M	None	G. Britain		Ann Maria	3 Jul 1820
Joseph	20	M	Merchant	England	America	Bolivar	2 Oct 1826
Mary	3	F	daughter	Grt. Britain	United States	Henry Kneeland	5 Nov 1828
Moses	1	M	Son	Grt. Britain	United States	Henry Kneeland	5 Nov 1828
Sarah	27	F	Wife of [William]	Grt. Britain	United States	Henry Kneeland	5 Nov 1828
Thos.	2	M	Son	Grt. Britain	United States	Henry Kneeland	5 Nov 1828
William	27	M	Farmer	Grt. Britain	United States	Henry Kneeland	5 Nov 1828
Wm.	47	M	Mercht.	G. Britain		Ann Maria	3 Jul 1820
Wm.	50	M	Clothier	England	U. States	Unity	27 Mar 1827
LINDY, Jno.	50	M	Farmer	Scotland	United States	Commerce	17 Jul 1823
LINE, Andrew	20	M	Joiner	Scotland	United States	Culloden	17 May 1828
LINÉ, José Lalur	25	M	Servt.	Cuba	U. States	Brown	8 Aug 1825
LINEHAN, Mary	14	F		Ireland	United States	Trio	2 Oct 1828
LINEN, Elizabeth	6	F		Ireland	United States	Jubilee	13 Sep 1827
John	23	M	Labourer	Ireland	United States	Jubilee	13 Sep 1827
Patrick	26	M	Labourer	Ireland	United States	Jubilee	13 Sep 1827
Rose	20	F	Seamstress	Ireland	United States	Jubilee	13 Sep 1827
Wm.	25	M	Labourer	Ireland	United States	Jubilee	13 Sep 1827
LINER, Michel	25	M	...	Ireland	United States	Nancey	8 Jun 1822
LINERA, Frs. Lopez	15	M	Labourer	Spain	U. States	Mercid	10 Jul 1826
LINERD, Francis	25	M	...	Ireland	United States	Nancey	8 Jun 1822
LINGER...ON, Catlo	22	M	...	...	...	George	23 Sep 1824
LINGIN, F.	22	M	Gent	French	Switzerland	Charlemagne	19 Sep 1828
J.	42	M	Gent	French	Switzerland	Charlemagne	19 Sep 1828
R.	38	F	Gent	French	Switzerland	Charlemagne	19 Sep 1828
LINGNGER, Aner	25	M	Farmer	France	United States	Crescent	12 Jul 1827
Debolt	2	M	Farmer	France	United States	Crescent	12 Jul 1827
John	1	M	Farmer	France	United States	Crescent	12 Jul 1827
Margaret	25	F	Farmer	France	United States	Crescent	12 Jul 1827
LINGON, Francis	34	M	Black Smith	France	U. States	Edward Bonaffe	23 Jul 1828
LINGS, —, Mr.	23	M	Marriner	England	Canada	Mary Jane	7 Jan 1829
LININGER, Marie	48			France	United States	Parachute	14 May 1828
LINK, Jacob	17	M	Baker	Gt. Britain		Corinthian	27 Oct 1829

NAMES OF PASSENGERS	AGE	SEX	OCCUPATIONS	COUNTRY TO WHICH THEY BELONG	COUNTRY THEY INTEND TO INHABIT	SHIPS/DATES OF ARRIVAL	
LINKIN, Ralph T., Capt.	43	M	Ship Master	U. States	U.S.	Burdett	7 Dec 1827
LINLEY, John	26	M	Geoponiker	England	United States	Orbit	22 Apr 1824
Thomas	40	M	Clothier	Great Britain	United States	Silvanus Jenkins	16 Aug 1826
LINN, Catharine	1 4/12	F	daughter [of Sarah]	G. Brittian	United States	Louisa	14 Jun 1825
James	37	M	Labourer	Ireland	United States	Carolina Ann	14 May 1827
Joan	20	F	Servant	Ireland	U. States	St. Michael's	10 Feb 1827
John H.	38	M	Mercht.	America	America	Lima	11 Dec 1823
Mary	...6	M	Labourer	Ireland	United States	Carolina Ann	14 May 1827
Michael	25	M	Labourer	Ireland	U. States	St. Michael's	10 Feb 1827
Sarah	24	F	going to her Husband	G. Brittian	United States	Louisa	14 Jun 1825
Thomas	22	M	Farmer	G. Britain	U. States	Mary & Harriot	8 Sep 1828
LINNEL, John	40	M	Mechanic	Great Britain	U. States	Hannibal	12 Oct 1829
LINNER, John	18	M	Labourer	Ireland	United States	Hopes Delight	29 Nov 1827
LINNEY, John	29	M	Mechanic	England	United States	Hercules	24 Oct 1821
Sarah	25	F	Mechanic	England	United States	Hercules	24 Oct 1821
LINNOW, Henery	50	M	Mercht.	U.S.		Don Quixote	3 Jan 1826
LINNTE, Wm.	7	M	Merchant	Spain	U. States	Pocahontas	9 Jun 1823
LINSDAY, Joseph	11	M		England	America	John Wells	11 Jun 1823
Nancy	45	F	Widow	Ireland	U. States	William & John	10 Jul 1824
LINSEY, Alicia	...	...	...	Ireland	United States	Carolina Ann	24 Oct 1825
E.	2	M			United States	Sarah	9 Nov 1820
Felix	...	...	...	Ireland	United States	Carolina Ann	24 Oct 1825
Jane	25	F	Lady	U. States	U. States	Bunker Hill	9 Jan 1827
Joan	25	F			United States	Sarah	9 Nov 1820
Margt.	1	F			United States	Sarah	9 Nov 1820
Peter	55		Yeoman	England	United States	Acasta	16 Aug 1826
LINSIE, B. J.	34			Boston		Ocean	28 Jul 1820
LINSLEY, Ann	22	F	None	England	Pittsburgh	Orozimbo	8 Jun 1822
Hanah	26	F		G. Britain	U. States	Mary & Harriot	8 Sep 1828
James	4	M		G. Britain	U. States	Mary & Harriot	8 Sep 1828
William	32	M	Labourer	England	Pittsburgh	Orozimbo	8 Jun 1822
LINSMAISTER, Ann	2	F			United States	Spartan	21 Aug 1824
Ann	26	F			United States	Spartan	21 Aug 1824
Elizabeth	10	F			United States	Spartan	21 Aug 1824
Jacob	4	M			United States	Spartan	21 Aug 1824
John	6	M			United States	Spartan	21 Aug 1824
Nicholas	5	M			United States	Spartan	21 Aug 1824
Nicholas	35	M	Taylor	Switzerland	United States	Spartan	21 Aug 1824
LINSTED, ...artha	9		Child	Woodbridge, E.	England	Packet	27 Aug 1822
...ashingta	Infant		Child		England	Packet	27 Aug 1822
...ma	8		Child	Woodbridge, E.	England	Packet	27 Aug 1822
Eliaria	13			Woodbridge, E.	England	Packet	27 Aug 1822
Elizabeth	18			Woodbridge, E.	England	Packet	27 Aug 1822
John	3		Child	Woodbridge, E.	England	Packet	27 Aug 1822
Mary	6		Child	Woodbridge, E.	England	Packet	27 Aug 1822
Robert	...		...	...	England	Packet	27 Aug 1822
Robt., Junr.	10		Child	Woodbridge, E.	England	Packet	27 Aug 1822
Sarah	28			Woodbridge, E.	England	Packet	27 Aug 1822
William	5		Child	Woodbridge, E.	England	Packet	27 Aug 1822
LINTEN, Elizabeth	3/12		Child	Ireland		Westmoreland	1 Aug 1826
Mary	20		Wife	Ireland		Westmoreland	1 Aug 1826
Robert	25		Farmer	Ireland		Westmoreland	1 Aug 1826
LINTH, Mary	26	F		Ireland	U. States	Adno	5 Jul 1828
LINTON, Ann	33	F		England	U. States	Braganza	20 May 1823
Elizabeth	7	F		England	U. States	Braganza	20 May 1823
Jane	21	F	None	England	U. States	Roman	1 Dec 1828
Michael	28	M	Farmer	England	U. States	Roman	1 Dec 1828
Wm.	43	M	Farmer	England	U. States	Braganza	20 May 1823
LINWOOD, Richard	13		Wife	England	U.S. States	Splendid	14 Aug 1829
LINZ, John	25	M	Stocking Weaver	Nuremberg	United States	Howard	6 Jul 1829
Meldior	24	M	Farmer	Germany	U. States	Isabella	10 Aug 1829
LION, A. M.	31	M	Merchant	Scotland	U. States	Superior	25 Sep 1828
John	23	M	Slater	Great Britain	United States	Courier	26 Jun 1827
LIONLIN, ...on	26	M	Merchant	Great Britain	U. States	Hector	11 Oct 1824
LIPPETT, Edwin	21	M	Merchant	Providence	Providence	Virginia	1 Feb 1825
LIPSETT, Eliza	20	F		Ireland	United States	Sarah G.	15 May 1828
Mary	22	F		Ireland	United States	Sarah G.	15 May 1828
LIRTCH, Ann	32		Wife [of John]	Great Britain	United States	Camillus	12 Sep 1827

NAMES OF PASSENGERS	AGE	SEX	OCCUPATIONS	COUNTRY TO WHICH THEY BELONG	COUNTRY THEY INTEND TO INHABIT	SHIPS/DATES OF ARRIVAL	
LIRTCH (cont'd)							
Isabella	24		Sister [of John]	Great Britain	United States	Camillus	12 Sep 1827
John	29		Merchant	Great Britain	United States	Camillus	12 Sep 1827
LISBEN, Jose	22			England	U. States	Corinthian	8 Oct 1828
LISCY, L.	25	M	Merchant	France	U.S.	Edward Bonnaffe	20 Jun 1825
LISEBONA, Carim	37	M	Traveller	Jeruselam	U. States	Hudson	12 Mar 1824
LISEZ, L.	29		Merchant	France		Edward Bonnaffe	17 Mar 1828
LISHGOR, William	24	M	Sawyer	Great Britain	U. States	Great Britain	18 Mar 1828
LISHMAN, John	26 3/12	M	Printer	G. Britain	United States	Dutchess of Portland	30 Oct 1826
LISLE, Mary	12	F	None	Gt. Brittain	United States	Balaena	21 Aug 1824
LISLEY, James	16	M		G.B.	America	Pacific	13 Jan 1827
Jane	35	F		G.B.	America	Pacific	13 Jan 1827
LISLIE, David	28	M	Labourer	Ireland	U.States	Nancy	31 May 1823
LIST, Caroline, Mrs.	34	F		Wirtenberg	America	Henry	19 Jun 1825
Elisa, Daught.	2 6/12	F		Wirtenberg	America	Henry	19 Jun 1825
Emilie, Daughter	6	F		Wirtenberg	America	Henry	19 Jun 1825
F., Mr.	35	M	Profeser of letters	Wirtenberg	America	Henry	19 Jun 1825
Oscar, Son	5	M		Wirtenberg	America	Henry	19 Jun 1825
Wm.	25	M	Farmer	Gt. Britain	U. States	New York Packet	6 Aug 1824
LISTER, Elisabeth	38	F	None	Great Brittain	U. States	Louisa	11 Jun 1824
Hannah	10	F	None	Great Brittain	U. States	Louisa	11 Jun 1824
LISTRE, Martha	60	F	None			Euphrates	8 Aug 1820
LISTRE, Thomas	67	M	Farmer			Euphrates	8 Aug 1820
LITCHFORD, John	23		Laborer	Ireland	America	Parrington	9 Jun 1827
LITELL, S.	25		Docter	U.S.	U. States	Athenian	18 Oct 1826
LITHGOW, Arther	28	M	Master Mariner	U.S. States		Mary Ann	10 Oct 1820
LITNEY, John	32	M	Carpenter	Nova Scotia	Nova Scotia	Sarah Ann	18 Nov 1826
William	47	M	Carpenter	Nova Scotia	Nova Scotia	Sarah Ann	18 Nov 1826
LITSMAN, Maria S.	26	F		France	U.S. America	Huntress	6 Sep 1827
Mathew	30	M	Soap boiler	France	U.S. America	Huntress	6 Sep 1827
LITTELE, Archer	21	M	Labourer	Ireland	United States	Wilson	6 Jun 1828
Mary	19 6/12	F	Spinster	Ireland	United States	Wilson	6 Jun 1828
Sam	60	F	Spinster	Ireland	United States	Wilson	6 Jun 1828
LITTLE, Alexander	23	M	Laborer or Spinster	Ireland	United States	Sarah G.	15 Aug 1827
Alexr.	30	M	Chandler	Ireland	New York	Atlantic	6 Oct 1828
Ann	17	F	None	Ireland	United States	Trident	18 Jul 1827
Bridget	9	F	None	Ireland	United States	Trident	18 Jul 1827
Catharine	22	F	None	Great Britain	United States	Comet	9 Aug 1822
Catherine	3	F	Child	Switzerland	United States	Andes	5 May 1828
Catherine	27	F	Spinster	Switzerland	United States	Andes	5 May 1828
Charlotte	5			England	United States	Caspian	12 Jul 1821
Charlotte	40		Lady	England	United States	Caspian	12 Jul 1821
David	30	M	Farmer	Longford		Mount Vernon	7 Jun 1824
Eliza	22	F	Spinster	Ireland	United States	Fabius	4 Jun 1828
Elizabeth	26		None			Amphion	31 May 1824
George	9	M	Farmer	Switzerland	United States	Andes	5 May 1828
George	38	M	Farmer	Switzerland	United States	Andes	5 May 1828
Hugh	23	M	Labourer	Ireland	U. States	Josephine	7 May 1827
Isabella	24	F		Ireland	America	Carolina Ann	7 Apr 1826
James	26	M	Clerk & Joiner [?]	Great Britain	United States	Comet	9 Aug 1822
Jaquil	7	M	Spinster	Switzerland	United States	Andes	5 May 1828
John	5 2/12	M		Ireland	America	Carolina Ann	7 Apr 1826
John	20	M	Officer	U.S. America		Phoebe Ann	27 Dec 1825
John	24	M	Weaver	Gt. Britan	America	Braganza	1 Dec 1824
John	25	M	Stone Cutter	St. Johns, N.B.	New York	Nancy	26 Nov 1822
John	28	M	Stone cutter	Great Britain	United States	William Dawson	18 Jun 1827
John	31	M	Carpenter	Ireland	New York	Lima	5 Aug 1829
John	55		Farmer	Ireland	United States	Carolina Ann	12 Sep 1823
Kitty	42	F	None	Ireland	United States	Trident	18 Jul 1827
M. A., Miss	23	F	Lady	England	U. States	Acasta	21 Oct 1825
Margaret	8	F	Spinster	Switzerland	United States	Andes	5 May 1828
Margret	27	F	Wife	Ireland	New York	Atlantic	6 Oct 1828
Margt.	28		None	Blackburn, England	Great Britain	Franklin	22 Jun 1827
Maria	5	F	Child	Switzerland	United States	Andes	5 May 1828

NAMES OF PASSENGERS	AGE	SEX	OCCUPATIONS	COUNTRY TO WHICH THEY BELONG	COUNTRY THEY INTEND TO INHABIT	SHIPS/DATES OF ARRIVAL	
LITTLE (cont'd)							
Mary	4			England	United States	Caspian	12 Jul 1821
Mary	7	F		Ireland	America	Carolina Ann	7 Apr 1826
Mary	13	F	None	Ireland	United States	Trident	18 Jul 1827
Mary	32	F	None	Great Britain	United States	William Dawson	18 Jun 1827
Mary	50		Farmer	Ireland	United States	Carolina Ann	12 Sep 1823
Mary Ann	23 3/12	F		Ireland	America	Carolina Ann	7 Apr 1826
Mele	1	F	Child	Switzerland	United States	Andes	5 May 1828
Michael	12	M	None	Ireland	United States	Trident	18 Jul 1827
Patrick	43	M	Farmer	Ireland	United States	Trident	18 Jul 1827
Philip	13	M	Farmer	Switzerland	United States	Andes	5 May 1828
Robert	25	M	Planter	St. Croix	St. Croix	Betsey	20 Jun 1826
Thomas	11	M	None	Ireland	United States	Trident	18 Jul 1827
Thos.	36	M	Merchant	U. States		Charleston Packet	4 May 1821
William	7			England	United States	Caspian	12 Jul 1821
William	22		Farmer	Ireland	United States	Carolina Ann	12 Sep 1823
William	22	M	Farmer	Ireland	United States	Dublin Packet	9 Jul 1827
Wm.	21	M	Farmer	England	U. States	Elizabeth	29 Dec 1824
LITTLEFIELD, —, Mr.	21	M	Merchant	U. States	U. States	Centurion	20 Oct 1828
Jane	22 4/12	F		Ireland	U.S. of America	Douglass	6 Jul 1829
LITTLETON, Owen	32	M	Labourer	England	U. States	Hercules	24 Oct 1821
Wm.	17	M	Cutter	England	United States	Peru	23 May 1827
Wm.	29	M	Gent.	Ireland	U. States	Cincinnatus	5 Oct 1824
LITTLEWOOD, Edward	20	M	Hatter	England	United States	Peru	23 May 1827
George	63	M	Silver Plater	England	United States	Peru	23 May 1827
Hannah	27	F		England	United States	Peru	23 May 1827
Hannah	44	F		England	United States	Peru	23 May 1827
James	7	M		England	United States	Peru	23 May 1827
John	13	M		England	United States	Peru	23 May 1827
Jonas	22	M	Mason	Great Britain	United States	Mount Vernon	20 May 1822
Mary	11	M		England	United States	Peru	23 May 1827
LITZMAN, Eliza	3	F		France	U.S. America	Huntress	6 Sep 1827
Justine	1	F		France	U.S. America	Huntress	6 Sep 1827
Maria	4	F		France	U.S. America	Huntress	6 Sep 1827
Mathew	6	M		France	U.S. America	Huntress	6 Sep 1827
LIVELY, H.		M	Merchant	U. States	U. States	George	12 Jul 1821
T.	21		Nothing			William Neilson	26 Jul 1828
LIVEN, Thos.	35	M	Labour	England	U. States	Trident	8 Mar 1824
LIVENEY, Danl.	13	M	Boy	Ireland	United States	Trident	16 May 1826
John	15	M	Boy	Ireland	United States	Trident	16 May 1826
LIVER, Jno.	24	M				Belfast	28 Sep 1820
LIVERE, Hormia	17	F	Spinster	Ireland	United States	Wilson	6 Jun 1828
LIVERMORE, W. M.	23	M	Gentleman	England	United States	Corinthian	10 Jan 1826
LIVEROCK, John	14	M	Domestic	Saba	Holland	Chase	29 June 1821
LIVERSIDGE, Henry	12	M	None	England	United States	William Thompson	19 Aug 1829
Mary	47	F	None	England	United States	William Thompson	19 Aug 1829
Stephen	47	M	Merchant	England	United States	William Thompson	19 Aug 1829
Stephen, Jr.	9	M	None	England	United States	William Thompson	19 Aug 1829
Thomas	16	M	None	England	United States	William Thompson	19 Aug 1829
Walter	18	M	None	England	United States	William Thompson	19 Aug 1829
William	24	M	Servant	England	United States	William Thompson	19 Aug 1829
LIVESEN, Wm.	27	M	Carpenter	England	United States	Siroc	31 Oct 1829
LIVIA, Joseph S.	24 2/12	M	Merchant	Greece	America	Abeona	24 Feb 1827
LIVING, Elizabeth	17	F		England	United States	Acasta	12 Dec 1823
Elizabeth	44	F		England	United States	Acasta	12 Dec 1823
Hector	11	M		England	United States	Acasta	12 Dec 1823
Jane	14	F		England	United States	Acasta	12 Dec 1823
Jno.	40		Merchant	U.S.	U.S.	Monroe	29 Nov 1823
Robert	12	M		England	United States	Acasta	12 Dec 1823
LIVINGSTON, Anson	18	M		U. States	U. States	Pacific	17 Jun 1828
B., Jr.	25	M	Merchant	United States	United States	Ariadne	25 Jul 1822

NAMES OF PASSENGERS	AGE	SEX	OCCUPATIONS	COUNTRY TO WHICH THEY BELONG	COUNTRY THEY INTEND TO INHABIT	SHIPS/DATES OF ARRIVAL	
LIVINGSTON (cont'd)							
Carroll, Mr.	23	M	Gent	U. States	U. States	Sully	24 Oct 1828
Chas.						Hero	19 May 1828
Chas. L., Mr.	25	M	Gentleman	U.S. Am.	U.S. Am.	Henry IV	5 Feb 1827
Cornelia, Mrs.	20	F	None	U. States	U. States	Sully	24 Oct 1828
Daniel	40	M	Planter	G. Britain	G. Britain	Azores	20 Sep 1824
Danl.	35	M	Merchant	Jamaica	United States	Enterprize	15 Nov 1825
E.	22	M	Merchant	America	U. States	Victory	13 Oct 1823
Henry M.	23	M		U. States	U. States	James Monroe	18 Apr 1821
James	30	M	Merchant	Ireland		William Tell	24 Oct 1829
Jane	25	M		Great B.	U. States	William Neilson	26 Jul 1828
John	7	F		Great B.	U. States	William Neilson	26 Jul 1828
Schrdglin	30	M	Merchant	New York	United States	Edwin	29 Nov 1828
Walter	23	M	Gentleman	New York	U. States	William Thompson	6 Sep 1822
William	18	M	Laborer	Carrah Cayr, Derry	...	Gleaner	24 May 1823
LIVINGSTONE, James	22	M	Farmer	Scotland	United States	Natchez	22 Apr 1822
LIVINGTON, J.	22	M	Merchant	America	America	Brittannia	28 Feb 1827
LLANGO, Jos. A.	30	M	Gentleman	Spain	St. Domingo	Enterprize	27 Feb 1826
LLOYD, Ann	3		Child	Gt. Britain	U. States	New York Packet	6 Aug 1824
Ann	24	F		G. Britain	U. States	Dalhouse Castle	12 Sep 1828
Benjamin	32	M	Gentleman	Bridgeworth, England	New York	New York	31 Jul 1829
George P.	28		Druggist	Great Brittain	Great Brittain	Commerce	14 Mar 1823
Henry	22			England	U. States	Corinthian	8 Oct 1828
James	14	M	Labourer	England	America	Ulysses	1 May 1822
John	22 5/12	M	Tailor	England	America	Minerva	15 Jun 1825
John	24	M		England	United States	John & Elizabeth	25 Sep 1827
Mary	36	F	Servant	Gt. Britain	U. States	New York Packet	6 Aug 1824
Owen	43	M	Paper Maker	G. Britain	U. States	Dalhouse Castle	12 Sep 1828
Rob.	1	M		G. Britain	U. States	Dalhouse Castle	12 Sep 1828
Robert	21	M	Carpenter	County Salap		Colossus	27 Mar 1828
Wm., Capt.	24	M	the Sea Mariner	England	England	William Thompson	29 Jan 1824
LO...S, Geo.	23	M	Miner	England	England	Eliza	31 Jul 1826
LOADER, Robert	34	M	Farmer	England	America	Comet	26 Jun 1822
J.	21	M	Farmer	St. Johns	U. States	Isabella	28 Jun 1825
N.	18	F	Farmer	Ireland	U. States	Isabella	28 Jun 1825
LOAN, —	4	F		America	U. States	Good Return	12 Apr 1827
—	6	F		America	U. States	Good Return	12 Apr 1827
Mary	30	F	Baw...wife	America	U. States	Good Return	12 Apr 1827
Wm.	18	M	Labourer	Gt. Britain	U. States	Panthea	21 Jul 1825
LOCHRAN, Alexander	3	M	None	Gt. Britain	U. States	Frances Henrietta	18 Apr 1825
Bridget	35	F	Spinster	Gt. Britain	U. States	Frances Henrietta	18 Apr 1825
Ellen	5	F	None	Gt. Britain	U. States	Frances Henrietta	18 Apr 1825
Nancy	12	F	Spinster	Gt. Britain	U. States	Frances Henrietta	18 Apr 1825
LOCHW..., Thomas G.	25	M	Clothier	Great Britain	United States	Frances Henrietta	17 Sep 1827
LOCK, Betsey	16	F				Mount Vernon	9 Jun 1823
Betsey	23	F				Mount Vernon	9 Jun 1823
Jno.	23	M	Druggist	Gt. Britan	U. States	Earl of Liverpool	12 Apr 1825
John	2	M				Mount Vernon	9 Jun 1823
Wm.	28		Servant	England	England	Silvanus Jenkins	30 Nov 1827
LOCK..., William	24	M	Labourer	Scotland	United States	Samuel Robertson	9 May 1827
LOCKART, Alexander	25	M	Labourer	Scotland	United States	Friends	7 Jul 1827
Margret	6/12	F	None	Scotland	United States	Friends	7 Jul 1827
Margret	24	F	Spinster	Scotland	United States	Friends	7 Jul 1827
LOCKE, —, Mr.					U. States	Montgomery	18 Oct 1828
James	26	M	Farmer	Ireland	United States	Dublin Packet	9 Jul 1827

NAMES OF PASSENGERS	AGE	SEX	OCCUPATIONS	COUNTRY TO WHICH THEY BELONG	COUNTRY THEY INTEND TO INHABIT	SHIPS/DATES OF ARRIVAL	
LOCKE (cont'd)							
Thomas	30	M	Merchant	U.S.	New York	Brighton	24 Aug 1827
LOCKER, Frederick	26	M	Shoemaker	Switzerland	United States	Howard	11 Jun 1824
LOCKETT, Mary	22	F		Ireland	United States	Kleber	23 Jul 1827
LOCKHARD, Jane	12	F		Scotland	United States	Trent	10 Jul 1827
John	3	M		Scotland	United States	Trent	10 Jul 1827
M. A.	29	F		Scotland	United States	Trent	10 Jul 1827
LOCKHART, David	23	M	Merchant	G. Britain	U. States	James Monroe	18 Apr 1821
Edward	29	M	Taylor	Scotland	United States	Trent	10 Jul 1827
Elizabeth	22	F	Wife	Ireland	United States	St. Michaels	27 Nov 1824
John	25	M	Laborer	Ireland	United States	St. Michaels	27 Nov 1824
Rob.	40	M	Merchant	N. York	N. York	Solon	12 Jun 1826
Robt.	40	M	Merchant	U. States	U. States	Edward	26 Jun 1828
Wm.	26	M	Farmer	Great Brittain	U. States	Louisa	11 Jun 1824
LOCKLIR, Daniel	22	M	Farmer	Great Brittain	U. States	Nancy	18 Jul 1821
LOCKRAM, Wm.	20	M	Mason	Ireland	United States	York	31 Mar 1828
LOCKWOOD, Anna	32	F	None	England	U.N. States	William Byrnes	13 Aug 1829
Anthony	26		Sa...ezer	England	United States	Hudson	5 Apr 1826
Eliza, Mrs.	28	F	None	N. York	U. States	South Carolina Packet	31 Mar 1824
George	6	M	None	England	U.N. States	William Byrnes	13 Aug 1829
Henry	1 1/4	M	None	England	U.N. States	William Byrnes	13 Aug 1829
Isaac	28	M	Merchant	N. York	U. States	Edward Bonaffe	11 Dec 1827
Isaac J.	28	M	Merchant	U. States	U. States	Tampico	2 Aug 1828
John	4	M	None	England	U.N. States	William Byrnes	13 Aug 1829
Joseph	28	M	Clerk	England	U. States	Laburnum	10 Apr 1823
Martha	26			England	United States	Hudson	5 Apr 1826
Rachif	12	M	None	England	U.N. States	William Byrnes	13 Aug 1829
Sarah	8	F	None	England	U.N. States	William Byrnes	13 Aug 1829
Wm.	22	M	Mariner	United States	United States	Heroine	7 Jul 1829
Wm.	35	M	Farmer	England	U.N. States	William Byrnes	13 Aug 1829
LODDINGTON, ...							
and... Melwell	16/365	M		Great Britian	United States	London	24 Jun 1823
Bess... C.	2	F		Great Britian	United States	London	24 Jun 1823
Edwd. Clarence	3	M		Great Britian	United States	London	24 Jun 1823
Mar...llen	24	F		Great Britian	United States	London	24 Jun 1823
Thos.	27	M		Great Britian	United States	London	24 Jun 1823
LODGE, Aen	15	F	Spinster	Toddington	U. States	Panthea	8 Apr 1826
David	32	M	Stonemason	Great Brittain	United States	Robert Fulton	13 Mar 1827
Mary	47	F	Spinster	Toddington	U. States	Panthea	8 Apr 1826
Saml.	48	M	Spinster	Toddington	U. States	Panthea	8 Apr 1826
LODS, Catherina	12	F		France	France	Edward Quesnel	3 Jul 1829
Charles	3	M		France	France	Edward Quesnel	3 Jul 1829
Elizabeth	11	F		France	France	Edward Quesnel	3 Jul 1829
Elizabeth	48	F		France	France	Edward Quesnel	3 Jul 1829
Jaqual	7	M		France	France	Edward Quesnel	3 Jul 1829
Jean P.	59	F		France	France	Edward Quesnel	3 Jul 1829
Joseph	10	M		France	France	Edward Quesnel	3 Jul 1829
Louisa	1	F		France	France	Edward Quesnel	3 Jul 1829
Rose	5	F		France	France	Edward Quesnel	3 Jul 1829
Susanna	15	F		France	France	Edward Quesnel	3 Jul 1829
LODWIG, Gusta	26	M	Merchant	Germany	United States	Henri IV	14 Oct 1829
LODZEQUEZ, Juan	22	M	Merchant	Havana	Havana	Olive Branch	23 Nov 1827
LOES, Edward	19	M	Merchant	England	United States	Stephania	22 Apr 1822
LOEVE, P.	28	M	Merchant	France	U. States	Laveria	23 Jul 1828
LOFFLER, Joseph	27	M	Butcher	Switzerland	U. States	Hewes	30 Oct 1829
LOFGOIRT, C.	46	M	Gentleman	Sweden	U. States	Neptune	11 Jun 1822
LOFTUS, Joseph	24	M	Mechanic	Scotland	United States	Concordia	25 Aug 1827
LOGAN, —, Mrs.	30	F		Scotland	U.S.	Curler	19 Jul 1828
Bet	6	F	child	U. States	U. States	Nancy	19 Oct 1821
Catharine	8	F	child	U. States	U. States	Nancy	19 Oct 1821
Catherine	37	F	...	Scotland	America	Nimrod	9 Jul 1827
Christopher	24	M	Farmer	Great Britain	United States	Ocean	27 Jul 1825
David	26	M	Merchant	G. Bt.	Canada	Canada	12 May 1828
Edmond	23	M	Labourer	Ireland	United States	Hope & Esther	17 Oct 1827
Eleanor	23	F		Antrim, Ireland	New York	Anthusa	24 Aug 1825
Francis	45	M	Labourer	Ireland	United States	Silas Richards	27 Oct 1825
Geo.	16	M	Farmer			Commerce	22 Jun 1825
Hugh	36	M	Labourer	Ireland	United States	Phocian	5 Aug 1826

NAMES OF PASSENGERS	AGE	SEX	OCCUPATIONS	COUNTRY TO WHICH THEY BELONG	COUNTRY THEY INTEND TO INHABIT	SHIPS/DATES OF ARRIVAL	
LOGAN (cont'd)							
James	18	M	Labourer	Ireland	United States	William & George	14 May 1828
James	21	M	Butcher	Ireland	United States	William	20 Jul 1829
James	24	M	Merchant	Great Britain	Canada	Pacific	7 May 1827
James	29	M	Merchant	Canada	Canada	William Thompson	27 May 1824
Jane	1	F		Antrim, Ireland	New York	Anthusa	24 Aug 1825
John	...	...	...	...	...	St. Michael	22 Sep 1824
John	40	M	...	Ireland	United States	General Putnam	20 Jun 1825
Margaret	18	F	Spinster	Ireland	United States	Trident	17 May 1825
Mary	30	F		U. States	U. States	Nancy	19 Oct 1821
Patrick	1	M		Ireland	United States	Hope	12 Jun 1828
Peter W.	24	M	Farmer	Great Britain	United States	Ocean	27 Jul 1825
Rarler	48	F		France	U. States	Edward Bonaffe	23 Jul 1828
Thos.	21	M	Shoemaker	Great Britain	United States	Nimrod	5 Apr 1821
William	3...	M	...	Scotland	America	Nimrod	9 Jul 1827
William	30	M	Merchant	England	U. States	Danube	2 Sep 1828
Wm.	36 11/12	M	Merchant	America	United States	Hiram	31 Oct 1828
Wm. E.	29	M	Merchant	Great Britain	Montreal	Auritz	20 May 1823
Wm. John	3	M		Antrim, Ireland	New York	Anthusa	24 Aug 1825
LOGGIS, David	20	M	Weaver	Great Britan	United States	Franklin	15 Apr 1826
LOGNET, Michel.	25			Ireland	U.S.	Union	20 Aug 1827
LOGON, A.	36	M	Merchant	U. States	U. States	Laveria	23 Jul 1828
B. M.	34	F		U. States	U. States	Laveria	23 Jul 1828
LOGUE, Bridget	55			Ireland	Great Britain	Robert Burns	14 Jun 1824
Daniel	55		Laborer	Ireland	Great Britain	Robert Burns	14 Jun 1824
James	23			Ireland	Great Britain	Robert Burns	14 Jun 1824
LOHL, John P.	25	M	Farmer	Germany	United States	Helen	5 Sep 1828
LOHRMER, Chs.	31	M	Merchant	Germany	Pensylvania	James Noble	27 Aug 1827
LOHSE, F. A.	25	M	Merchant	U. States	United States	Cadmus	9 Apr 1825
LOID, James	38	M	Trader	Gt. Britain	United States	John & Elizabeth	25 Sep 1827
LOIENT, P. L.	23	M	Merchant	France	U. States	Canton	17 Aug 1824
LOIGES, —, Miss	20	F		France	France	Hesper	7 Oct 1823
M.	43	F		France	France	Hesper	7 Oct 1823
LOIRBIE, Jno.	28	M	Farmer	Germany	United States	Stephania	16 Aug 1827
LOIRD, Geo.	17	M	Labourer	Ireland	U. States	Wanderer	1 Sep 1828
LOKOLAWAY, Ewan	26	M	Sevant	Russia	U. States	Xenophon	15 Sep 1820
LOLLAN, James	22	M		Ireland	New York	Lady Hunter	5 Jun 1826
LOMAN, Caroline	9	F	Servant	England	United States	Nimrod	30 Aug 1824
Harriet	34	F	Servant	England	United States	Nimrod	30 Aug 1824
LOMAS, Robert	67	M	Farmer	Great Britain	United States	Atlantic	28 May 1827
Robt.	38	M	Farmer	England	U. States	Auritz	20 May 1823
LOMBARD, Richard	17	M	None	Ireland	United States	Trio	31 Oct 1827
LONA, Alexr.	21	M	Labourer	Ireland	United States	Trident	16 May 1826
LONCHAY, John	28	M	Merchant	France	France	Chalcedony	24 Oct 1829
LONDA, A.	26	M		Spain	Spain	Fabius	3 Jun 1825
LONDER, Elen	20	F		Ireland	U. States	Sarah G	30 Jun 1828
LONDLY, James	20	M	Labourer	Ireland	United States	Ann Maria	4 Oct 1824
LONDON, Margaret	28	F		Scotland	United States	Camillus	9 May 1827
William	30	M		Scotland	United States	Camillus	9 May 1827
LONERY, Caroline	20	F	Laborer, Spinster or Child	Ireland	United States	Ann Maria	4 Aug 1827
LONERY, Michael	18	M	Laborer, Spinster or Child	Ireland	United States	Ann Maria	4 Aug 1827
LONG, Ann	22	F	Labourer	Ireland	United States	Margarett Scott	22 Aug 1827
E.	71	M	Farmer	Scotland	U. States	Superior	25 Sep 1828
Geo.	25	M	Gt. Britain	U. States	U. States	Columbia	1 Dec 1824
George	22 3/12	M	Farmer	England	America	Nimrod	1 Dec 1827
James	18	M	Mariner	United States	U.S.	Missouri	30 May 1828
*put on board by consul							
James	21		Cooper		U. States	Aristides	7 Mar 1825
James	25	M	Labourer	Ireland	United States	Lord Wellington	28 May 1827
Jane	4	F	Labourer	Ireland	United States	Margarett Scott	22 Aug 1827
Jane	18	F	Wife	C. Down	Long Island	Nile	18 Aug 1829
Jas.	2	M	Labourer	Ireland	United States	Margarett Scott	22 Aug 1827
John	1	M	Labourer	Ireland	United States	Margarett Scott	22 Aug 1827
John	18	M	Farmer	Ireland	Philad.	Triton	12 Jul 1823

NAMES OF PASSENGERS	AGE	SEX	OCCUPATIONS	COUNTRY TO WHICH THEY BELONG	COUNTRY THEY INTEND TO INHABIT	SHIPS/DATES OF ARRIVAL	
LONG (cont'd)							
John	21	M	Farmer	...shire	Lancaster	Howard Douglass	11 May 1827
John	34	M	Miner	England	United States	Jubilee	12 May 1828
Joseph	25	M	Farmer	Great Britain	United States	Margaret Ann	3 Apr 1822
Joseph	28	M	Farmer	Switzerland	United States	Andes	5 May 1828
Joseph	32	M	Labourer	Ireland	United States	Margarett Scott	22 Aug 1827
Patrick	24	M	Laborer	...	United States	Combine	20 Nov 1824
Peter	26	M	Farmer	Switzerland	United States	Andes	5 May 1828
Rebecca	20	F		Ireland	U. States	Nancy	16 Aug 1822
Richd.	28		Carpenter	Ireland	United States	Geo. Canning	5 Jun 1828
Robert	28	M	Farmer	England	United States	Cosmo	26 Aug 1829
Robt.	20	M	Labourer	C. Down	Long Island	Nile	18 Aug 1829
Thos.	21	M		Ireland	United States	Thompson	12 Sep 1827
William	24	M	Servant	Ireland	United States	William & George	14 May 1828
William	27	M	Labourer	England	United States	Jubilee	12 May 1828
Wm.	5	M	Labourer	Ireland	United States	Margarett Scott	22 Aug 1827
LONGAN, Ann	45	F		Ireland	United States	Silas Richards	27 Oct 1825
LONGBERY, Grace	12	F		Ireland	United States	Gem	16 Jun 1824
Margt.	38	F	Spinster	Ireland	United States	Gem	16 Jun 1824
Patrick	7	M		Ireland	United States	Gem	16 Jun 1824
William	10	M		Ireland	United States	Gem	16 Jun 1824
LONGDON, Wm.	22	M	Farmer	Great Britain	America	Lady Gallatin	21 Jun 1820
LONGDUPLAN, Hugh	29	M	Merchant	France	United States	Lewis	30 May 1823
LONGE, Thos.	19	M		Great Britain	United States	Mary	11 Jul 1820
LONGFELLOW, Henry	22	M	Merchant	United States	United States	Manchester	12 Aug 1829
LONGLERE, Anthony	6	M	Family [of Joseph]	France	America	La Grange	7 Aug 1828
Eaf	36	F	Family [of Joseph]	France	America	La Grange	7 Aug 1828
Gertrude	4	F	Family [of Joseph]	France	America	La Grange	7 Aug 1828
Josep	8	M	Family [of Joseph]	France	America	La Grange	7 Aug 1828
Joseph	44	M	Farmer	France	America	La Grange	7 Aug 1828
Maria	10	F	Family [of Joseph]	France	America	La Grange	7 Aug 1828
Rosalia	14	F	Family [of Joseph]	France	America	La Grange	7 Aug 1828
Theresa	12	F	Family [of Joseph]	France	America	La Grange	7 Aug 1828
LONGLEY, Michael	18	M				Hibernia	15 Aug 1820
LONGMAN, —, Mrs.	19	F		England	U. States	Ann Maria	13 Mar 1823
R. M.	24	M	Mechanic	England	U. States	Ann Maria	13 Mar 1823
Saml.	2	M		England	U. States	Ann Maria	13 Mar 1823
LONGMEN, Gabriel	18	M	Farmer	Scotland	United States	Commerce	17 Jul 1823
John	30	M	Farmer	Scotland	United States	Commerce	17 Jul 1823
LONGSDALE, ...	22	M	Spinner	Great Brittain	United States	Sarah Ralston	27 Jan 1827
Joseph	20	M	Labourer	Great Brittain	United States	Active	12 Sep 1828
LONGSDON, Anna	18	F		Great Britain	U.S. of America	Gratitude	3 Oct 1829
Benjamin	43	M	Taylor	Great Britain	U.S. of America	Gratitude	3 Oct 1829
Francis	10	M		Great Britain	U.S. of America	Gratitude	3 Oct 1829
John	9/12	M		Great Britain	U.S. of America	Gratitude	3 Oct 1829
Rebecca	12	F		Great Britain	U.S. of America	Gratitude	3 Oct 1829
Sarah	7	F		Great Britain	U.S. of America	Gratitude	3 Oct 1829
Sarah	35	F		Great Britain	U.S. of America	Gratitude	3 Oct 1829
William	36	M	Merchant	Charleston	Charleston	New York	14 Nov 1826
Wm.	31	M	Merchant	G. Brittain	United States	Hercules	24 Oct 1821
LONGSDOWN, Wm.	35	M	Merchant	G. Bt.	G. Bt.	Canada	13 Oct 1825
LONGSOLOR, Wm.	32	M	Merchant	G. Britain	United States	New York	12 Nov 1822
LONGWORTH, Ann	21	F	None	England	United States	Great Britain	5 Sep 1827
Chas.	20	M	Iron Moulder	England	United States	Great Britain	5 Sep 1827
David M.	21 10/12	M	Weaver	Scotland	New York	Debby & Eliza	20 Nov 1820
Hannah, child	2/12	F	None	England	United States	Great Britain	5 Sep 1827
John	24	M	Iron Moulder	England	United States	Great Britain	5 Sep 1827
Thos.	2	M	None	England	United States	Great Britain	5 Sep 1827
LONICH, Valentine	20	M	Sadler	Prussia		Constitution	20 Jun 1828
LONINGER, George	25	M	Weaver	Native of Switzerland	United States	Canaris	30 Jun 1827
John	2	M		Native of Switzerland	United States	Canaris	30 Jun 1827
Margaret	30	F		Native of Switzerland	United States	Canaris	30 Jun 1827
LOOKERY, John	22	M	Shoe Maker	Ireland	United States	Kleber	23 Jul 1827
LOOMIS, Henry	27	M	Merchant	United States	United States	James Monroe	25 Apr 1822

NAMES OF PASSENGERS	AGE	SEX	OCCUPATIONS	COUNTRY TO WHICH THEY BELONG	COUNTRY THEY INTEND TO INHABIT	SHIPS/DATES OF ARRIVAL	
LOONEY, Ann	18	F	None	England	United States	Hercules	24 Oct 1821
Esther	1	F	None	Great Britain	United States	Penelope	11 Jun 1827
George	26	M	Labourer	England	U. States	Ayrshire	12 May 1828
Hugh	21	M	Labourer	England	U. States	Ayrshire	12 May 1828
Issabella	80	F	None	Great Britain	United States	Penelope	11 Jun 1827
Jane	6	F	None	Great Britain	United States	Penelope	11 Jun 1827
Margaret	56	F	None	England	United States	Hercules	24 Oct 1821
Mary	4	F	None	Great Britain	United States	Penelope	11 Jun 1827
Mary	31	F	None	Great Britain	United States	Penelope	11 Jun 1827
Patrick	20	M	Mercht.	Ireland	U. States	Albion	9 Aug 1826
Wilt	25	M	Labourer	England	U. States	Ayrshire	12 May 1828
LOONY, Nell	26	F				Hanford	17 Jul 1828
Nelly	22	F				Hanford	17 Jul 1828
R.	24	M	Labourer			Hanford	17 Jul 1828
LOOS, John A.	22	M	Farmer	Wertemberg	Wertemberg	Edward Quesnel	3 Jul 1829
LOOSMORE, Edwin	25	M	Archector	England	America	Mary Lord	26 Oct 1829
LOPE, Henry	21	M	Sugar baker	Hanover	New York	Thames	16 May 1821
LOPES, John	38	M	Merchant	Spain	United States	Charles	18 Aug 1826
Ls.	75		Merchant	Citizen of New York	U. States	Camille	31 Jul 1826
LOPEZ, A.	25	M	Merchant	U.S.	U.S.	Frances	28 Jan 1828
Antonio	49	M	Priest	Spain	Spain	Virginia	8 Mar 1828
Augustine, Dn.	38	M	Merchant	Mexico	United States	General Warren	8 Jul 1829
Francis	14	M	None	Spain	U. States	St. Croix	31 Jul 1827
J.	35	M	Merchant	U.S.	U.S.	Toison	15 Dec 1828
John	36	M	Merchant	Canary Isld.	U. States & Spain	Seneca	21 May 1825
John Magee	22	M	Mercht.	Spain	U. States	Fair American	16 Oct 1822
Lovy	2	F		Mexico	United States	General Warren	8 Jul 1829
Manuel	25	M	Servant	Island of Cuba	Cuba	James Monroe	21 May 1825
Manuel	25 2/12	M	Farmer	France	U.S. America	Erie	19 Oct 1829
Ramon	4	M		Mexico	United States	General Warren	8 Jul 1829
Rosa, Dn.	18	F		Mexico	United States	General Warren	8 Jul 1829
Sarah, Mrs.	9	F	None	Jamaica	U. States	Essex	20 May 1823
LOPKIN, Albert	26		Sugar Baker	Germany		Pomona	28 May 1822
LORA, Wm., Jr.	28	M	Mariner	U. States	United States	Superior	14 Apr 1825
LORALE, Elis.	50	M	Labourer	Halafax, N.S.	New York	Citizen	1 Nov 1828
LORD, —, Mrs.	20	M		American	United States	Exchange	16 Feb 1822
B., Capt.	48	M	Seaman	America	America	Samuel Robertson	26 Nov 1825
Benjn.	26	M	Merchant	American	United States	Exchange	16 Feb 1822
Edw.	22	M	Weaver	Great Brittain	United States	Nimrod	9 Jan 1827
Ellen	63	F	None	Great Britian	U. States	Pallas	17 Aug 1824
James	45	M	Carpenter	England	U.S.	Acasta	11 May 1827
Jane	22			England	United States	Hugh Johnson	11 Jun 1828
Jno.	35	M	Ship Master	U. States	U. States	Porcia	28 May 1827
John	21	M	Merchant	Great Britain	United States	James Monroe	5 Apr 1820
John	27	M	...	Ireland	United States	Colossus	30 May 1825
John	28			England	United States	Hugh Johnson	11 Jun 1828
Joseph	19	M	Cotton Spinner	England	America	Manhattan	21 Sep 1822
Josph.	19	M	Manufacturer	England	U. States	Exchange	4 Jan 1823
Maria	19	F	...	Ireland	United States	Colossus	30 May 1825
Mary	20	F		Great Britain	United States	John Jay	8 May 1828
Mary	22	F	None	England	America	Francis & Henrietta	11 Jul 1823
Mary	34	F	None	G.B.	U.S.A.	Silas Richard	30 Jun 1828
Mary, (Infant)	1	F		Great Britain	United States	John Jay	8 May 1828
R.	25	M	Clergman	Montreaul	Montreau	Edward Bonaffe	23 Jul 1828
Robert B.	40	M	Merchant	U. States		Rodney	6 Oct 1827
Samuel	22	M	Iron...lter	England	America	Constitution	1 Oct 1825
Samuel	24	M	Farmer	England	United States	Great Britain	5 Sep 1827
Samuel	62	M	Farmer	England	New York	Hercules	11 Feb 1822
Samuel, Junr.	21	M	Farmer	England	New York	Hercules	11 Feb 1822
Simon	22	M	Weaver	England	United States	Curler	3 Mar 1828
Wm.	12	M	Merchant	America	America	Silas Richard	24 Oct 1829
Wm.	29	M	Laborer	England	America	Francis & Henrietta	11 Jul 1823
Wm. B.	25	M	Mercht.	U. States	U.S.	Albany Packet	14 Nov 1826
Wm. B.	26	M	Merchant	England	West Indies	Union Packet	9 Feb 1827
LORDS, Georg	18	M	Clouthier	France	United States	Virginia	31 May 1828

NAMES OF PASSENGERS	AGE	SEX	OCCUPATIONS	COUNTRY TO WHICH THEY BELONG	COUNTRY THEY INTEND TO INHABIT	SHIPS/DATES OF ARRIVAL	
LORE, Jno.	18	M	Farmer	England	U.S. America	Cortes	19 May 1826
LOREMY, Saml.	20	M		England	England	Amity	31 May 1822
LORENTZ, Joseph	57	M	Sock Maker	France	United States	New England	29 Aug 1828
Stephan	20	M	Sock Maker	France	United States	New England	29 Aug 1828
LORENZO, Calalina	43	F	Theatrical Performer				
Foriosa			or Play Actor	France	U.S. America	Sicily	7 Oct 1829
LORES, Ann	2		Farmer	France	United States	Crescent	12 Jul 1827
Catherine	6	F	Farmer	France	United States	Crescent	12 Jul 1827
Catherine	32	F	Farmer	France	United States	Crescent	12 Jul 1827
Hans	36	M	Farmer	France	United States	Crescent	12 Jul 1827
Margaret	9	F	Farmer	France	United States	Crescent	12 Jul 1827
Yerouth	11	F	Farmer	France	United States	Crescent	12 Jul 1827
LORET, L.	41	M	Planter	Point Petre, Guadaloupe	United States	General Macombe	17 Jul 1827
LOREY, J.	21	F	Servant	Ireland	Canada	Ann Maria	7 Sep 1827
LORIAH, Severone	33 2/12	M	Consul Gnl.	Sweden	Philadelphia	Quito	9 Jul 1823
LORIMER, Wm.	28	M	Woolen draper	England	United States	Nancy	15 Mar 1820
LORING, A.	50	M	Mariner	U. States	U. States	Florida	25 Apr 1825
Anna	25	F		Great Britain	Canada	Columbia	22 Sep 1828
Davis	37	M	Mariner	U. States	U. States	Amazon	29 Aug 1825
Josep G.	9	M		Spain		Leander	18 May 1827
Robt. R.	35	M	British Army	Great Britain	Canada	Columbia	22 Sep 1828
LORNAN, Robert	25	M	Labourer	G. Brittain	U.S.	Olive Branch	28 Aug 1828
LORR, Elizabeth	12	F		England	England	Britannia	5 Nov 1828
Martha	38	F		England	England	Britannia	5 Nov 1828
LORREL, Esther	4	F	None	England	America	Francis & Henrietta	11 Jul 1823
Esther	28	F	None	England	America	Francis & Henrietta	11 Jul 1823
George, Jur.	1	M	None	England	America	Francis & Henrietta	11 Jul 1823
George, Sen.	27	M	Farmer	England	America	Francis & Henrietta	11 Jul 1823
LORRET, Lewis	25	M	Merchant	France	U. States	Canada	27 Sep 1826
LORRILLA, Juan T.	24	M	Merchant	Tampico	Tampico	Alto	8 Jun 1827
LORSBET, Charles O. E.	34	M	None	France	U. States	Sully	25 Jun 1828
LORTZ, Michel	18	M	Farmer	Switzerland	United States	Olympia	12 Aug 1828
LORY, George	22 4/12	M	Black Smith	America	America	Hiram	2 Apr 1828
LOS, Martin		M		Mexico		Joseph	20 Jul 1829
LOSENGARTEN, Babet	29	F		Netherlands	Philadelphia	Louisa	6 Oct 1828
LOSEY, Elezer L.	31	M	Merchant	United States	New York	Florida	22 May 1826
LOSHEN, John H.	24	M	Labourer	Hanover		Constitution	20 Jun 1828
LOSHON, Catherine	24	F	Spinster	Switzerland	United States	Andes	5 May 1828
LOSS, Louisa	55	F	Spinster	United States	United States	Howard	19 May 1826
Louisa H.	25	F	Spinster	United States	United States	Howard	19 May 1826
LOTEMER, Andrew	24	M	Labourer	Scotland	United States	Samuel Robertson	5 Oct 1827
LOTHER, Charlote	27	F		Halifax, N.S.	New York	Citizen	1 Nov 1828
Jhon	2	M		Halifax, N.S.	New York	Citizen	1 Nov 1828
William	25	M	Shoemaker	Halifax, N.S.	New York	Citizen	1 Nov 1828
LOUATE, Charles	26		Merchant			Carolina Ann	14 Feb 1824
LOUBAH, Alphonse	27	M	Merchant	France	United States	Henry	9 Jun 1826
LOUCHRAY, Dl.	30	M	Labourer	Scotland	United States	Morning Star	25 Jun 1822
LOUCUS, Paine	30	M	Farm	Ireland		Quatre Freres	29 Jul 1828
LOUD, Philogus	25		P. Forte Maker	United States	United States	Hudson	18 Jun 1825
Thomas	63		P. Forte Maker	United States	United States	Hudson	18 Jun 1825
LOUDER, Edwd., Mr.	40	M	Mercht.	United States	United States	Manchester	16 Dec 1828
LOUDERMAN, Frederick	25	M	Mariner	America	Baltimore	Rachel Ann	13 Mar 1829
LOUDERRI, Catharine	5			France	U. States	Parachute	14 May 1828
Chas.	9			France	U. States	Parachute	14 May 1828
Chas.	42		Carpenter	France	U. States	Parachute	14 May 1828
Godifor	3			France	U. States	Parachute	14 May 1828
Madeline	11			France	U. States	Parachute	14 May 1828
Madeline	46			France	U. States	Parachute	14 May 1828
Salome	6			France	U. States	Parachute	14 May 1828
LOUER, Mary	15	F		Ireland	United States	Trio	13 Jun 1827
Michael	14	M		Ireland	United States	Trio	13 Jun 1827
Saml.	45	M	Bootmaker	Ireland	United States	Trio	13 Jun 1827
LOUERWOOD, Jno.	27	M	Carpenter	Ireland	United States	Trio	13 Jun 1827

NAMES OF PASSENGERS	AGE	SEX	OCCUPATIONS	COUNTRY TO WHICH THEY BELONG	COUNTRY THEY INTEND TO INHABIT	SHIPS/DATES OF ARRIVAL	
LOUGE, M.	22	F		Ireland	U. States	Sarah G	7 May 1827
Margt.	18	F		Ireland	U. States	Sarah G	7 May 1827
Mary	2	F		Ireland	U. States	Sarah G	7 May 1827
LOUGENBILL, Mary	20	F	...	...	Ohio	Frances Henrietta	25 Aug 1825
Peter	30	M	...	...	Ohio	Frances Henrietta	25 Aug 1825
LOUGHEAD, Jas.	28	M	Farmer	Ireland	United States	General Putnam	20 Jun 1825
LOUGHHEAD, Wm.	26	M	Farmer	Ireland	United States	General Putnam	20 Jun 1825
LOUGHLAN, —, Mr.	36	M		Dublin	U. States	Hibernia	26 Oct 1826
LOUGHLIN, James	31	M	Shoemaker	Ireland	Pittsburgh	Indian Chief	19 Jun 1823
LOUGHMAN, Cathran	18	F		Ireland	Pennsylvania	Susquehanna	9 Jan 1824
Denis	23	M	Farmer	Ireland	Pennsylvania	Susquehanna	9 Jan 1824
John	4/12		child	Ireland	Pennsylvania	Susquehanna	9 Jan 1824
LOUGHNAN, Dennis	27	M	Farmer	England	U. States	Thomas Ritchie	2 Jul 1827
Michael	26	M	Labourer	Ireland	United States	Combine	4 Jun 1825
LOUGHREY, John	26		Farmer			Rufus King	7 Aug 1820
LOUGHRINE, Rose	16	F	Milliner	Irereland	America	Carolina Ann	20 Jun 1825
LOUGHRY, Daniel	35	M	Farmer	Ireland	United States	Dublin Packet	23 May 1828
Margaret	28	F	Lady	Ireland	United States	St. Michaels	12 Jun 1826
Michael	25	M	Farmer	Ireland	United States	Dublin Packet	9 Jul 1827
LOUIS, Isaac	23	M	Seaman	U. States	United States	Brilliant	24 Sep 1827
LOUISA, M.	15	F	Servant	St. Domingo	St. Domingo	Genl. Warren	10 Jul 1828
LOUISE, Edward	30	M	Farmer	Gt. Britain	U. States	Louisa Matilda	25 May 1825
LOULORK, Catharin	37	F		Switzerland		Pallas	14 Jun 1828
Fred	44	M		Switzerland		Pallas	14 Jun 1828
LOUNDS, H. O.	29	M	Gentleman	Great Brittan	U. States	Cadmus	5 Apr 1826
LOUNGE, Charles	35	M	Weaver	Ireland	United States	Sylvester Healy	14 Jun 1825
LOUPY, Victor	35	M	Merchant	Fernandina	America	Laurel	3 Jun 1828
LOURANT, Threbet	20	F	Carpenter	Ireland		Quatre Freres	29 Jul 1828
LOUSE, Richard	17	M	Clark	Ireland	U. States	Josephine	23 Jan 1829
LOUTHER, Wm.	18		Farmer	Ireland	United States	John Dickinson	28 Jun 1822
Wm., Jun.	3			Ireland	United States	John Dickinson	28 Jun 1822
LOUVEL, Eduard	29	M	Author	Cain	U.S. America	Superior	18 Jun 1825
LOUZARD, Robt.	40	M	Merchant	France	U. States	Bayard	9 Nov 1825
LOVE, Alaxander	37	M	Weaver	Great Britain	United States	Courier	26 Jun 1827
Christian	24	F		Scotland	United States	Camillus	27 Oct 1829
Eliza	25 3/12	F	Spinner	Ireland	Beaver Town	Triton	12 Jul 1823
H.	23	M	Mechani	Great Britten	U. States	Wm. & Henry	23 May 1826
Hugh	28	M	Farmer	Scotland	U.S. of America	Friends	10 May 1823
Isabella	30	F		Ireland	U. States	St. Michael	27 Mar 1827
James	20	M	Laborer	England	United States	London	21 May 1828
James	23		Planter	Ireland	Louisiana	Eliza Davidson	8 Aug 1829
John	20	M	Farmer	Gt. Britain	United States	Robert Edwards	1 Jun 1826
Lileas	25	F	None	Great Britain	United States	Courier	26 Jun 1827
Mary Ann	2	F		Ireland	U. States	St. Michael	27 Mar 1827
Nancey	60 4/12	F	Spinner	Ireland	Beaver Town	Triton	12 Jul 1823
Rebecca	18 2/12	F	Spinner	Ireland	Beaver Town	Triton	12 Jul 1823
Saml.	30	M	Farmer	Ireland	Beaver Town	Triton	12 Jul 1823
W.	34	M	Merchant	U. States	U. States	Eliza	20 Nov 1828
William	34		Planter	Ireland	Louisiana	Eliza Davidson	8 Aug 1829
Wm.	12		...	Ireland	United States	Robert Burns	18 Jun 1822
Wm.	27	M	Merchant	American born	U. States	Leontine	18 Mar 1825
LOVEGREEN, Andrew	29 10/12	M	Merchant	U. States	U. States	Elizabeth	11 Sep 1827
LOVEJOY, Ezekiel	24	M	Doctor	United States	United States	Matteawan	2 Feb 1829
LOVEL, Ann	5	F	Farmer	England	United States	Florida	1 Sep 1823
Elizth.	10	F	Farmer	England	United States	Florida	1 Sep 1823
Francis	7	M	Farmer	England	United States	Florida	1 Sep 1823
Francis	37	M	None	England	United States	Florida	1 Sep 1823
Jane	4	F	Farmer	England	United States	Florida	1 Sep 1823
John	11	M	Farmer	England	United States	Florida	1 Sep 1823
Martin	54	F	Bortour	France	U. States	Edward Bonaffe	23 Jul 1828
Peter	1	M	Farmer	England	United States	Florida	1 Sep 1823
Rhd.	8	M	Farmer	England	United States	Florida	1 Sep 1823
Vincent	13	M	Farmer	England	United States	Florida	1 Sep 1823
Vincent	37	M	Farmer	England	United States	Florida	1 Sep 1823
William	2	M	Farmer	England	United States	Florida	1 Sep 1823
LOVELAND, James R.	18		Sailor	Halifax	U. States	Almira	15 Jul 1822

NAMES OF PASSENGERS	AGE	SEX	OCCUPATIONS	COUNTRY TO WHICH THEY BELONG	COUNTRY THEY INTEND TO INHABIT	SHIPS/DATES OF ARRIVAL	
LOVELAND (cont'd)							
John	40	M	Mariner	Middleton	U. States	Washington	22 Apr 1825
S. B.	25	M	House Joiner	United States	United States	Deborah	3 Jul 1824
Saml.	16	M	Mariner	Middleton	U. States	Washington	22 Apr 1825
LOVELL, B. D.	21	M	Merchant	American born	U. States	Leontine	18 Mar 1825
Jno. M.	21	M	Gentleman	U. States	U. States	Mapocho	9 Jan 1824
Jnoson.	21	M	Farmer	England	United States	Euphrates	18 Aug 1827
Thos.	29	M	Cabinetmaker	England	America	Josephine	8 Jan 1827
LOVENTI, Annetto	33	M	Servant	France	U. States	Cincinnatus	24 May 1821
LOVER, Robt.	60	M	Farmer	Ireland	Beaver Town	Triton	12 Jul 1823
LOVETT, Alice	30	F		Gt. Britain	U. States	Camberwell	7 Apr 1828
Hannah	8 2/12	F		Gt. Britain	U. States	Camberwell	7 Apr 1828
Jabish	40	M	Merchant	New York	U. States	Romulus	26 Apr 1822
Josiah	35	M	Ship Master	United States	U. States	Day	11 Jun 1823
Mary Ann	10 9/12	F		Gt. Britain	U. States	Camberwell	7 Apr 1828
R.	1 9/12	F		Gt. Britain	U. States	Camberwell	7 Apr 1828
Ruth	3 8/12	F		Gt. Britain	U. States	Camberwell	7 Apr 1828
S.	37	M	Farmer	Gt. Britain	U. States	Camberwell	7 Apr 1828
Saml.	5 9/12	M		Gt. Britain	U. States	Camberwell	7 Apr 1828
Wm.	20		Farmer	England	United States	Hugh Johnson	11 Jun 1828
LOVIAT, Jean Franois	40	M	Merchant	France	U. States	Great Britain	6 Sep 1828
V. V.	14	F		France	U. States	Great Britain	6 Sep 1828
Victoria L.	35	F		France	U. States	Great Britain	6 Sep 1828
LOVINGIRTH, George	2	M		Native of Switzerland	United States	Canaris	30 Jun 1827
John G.	34	M	Weaver	Native of Switzerland	United States	Canaris	30 Jun 1827
Margaret	8	F		Native of Switzerland	United States	Canaris	30 Jun 1827
Margaret	40	F		Native of Switzerland	United States	Canaris	30 Jun 1827
Salome	6	M		Native of Switzerland	United States	Canaris	30 Jun 1827
LOW, ...	1	F		Great Britain	United States	Atlantic	28 May 1827
*dead							
Alexr.	58	M	Weaver	Scotland	United States	Broke	16 Jul 1829
Andrew	44	M	Merchant	United States	United States	New York	19 Nov 1828
Andw., Mr.	40	M	Merchant	England	England	Manchester	8 Dec 1827
Ann	12	F	None	England	United States	Dalhouse Castle	6 Sep 1827
Cath.	4	F		G. Britain	U. States	Camillus	8 Sep 1828
David	40		Merchant	U. States	U. States	Napoleon	10 Jan 1828
Eliza	5	F		Great Britain	United States	Atlantic	28 May 1827
George	16	M	None	Scotland	Ama.	Expedition	19 May 1828
George, Mr.	30	M	Seaman	England	U. States	Acasta	3 Apr 1826
Hannah	1 6/12			England	United States	Thomas Dickason	5 Jun 1827
Henry S.	31 4/12	M	Merchant	U.S. America	U.S. America	Erie	19 Oct 1829
Isaac	19	M	Gentleman	New York	U. States	Chase	6 Jun 1822
Isaac	21	M	Mercht.	United States	United States	Hannibal	6 Sep 1824
James	7	M	family [of Joseph]	England	U.N. States	Jane	7 Oct 1826
James	32		Butcher	England	United States	Thomas Dickason	5 Jun 1827
Jane	3	F		G. Britain	U. States	Camillus	8 Sep 1828
Jane	4	F		Great Britain	United States	Atlantic	28 May 1827
Jane	19	F	Maid to Mrs. Campbell	England	England	Bayard	30 Oct 1820
Jas.	38	M	Clothier	Great Britain	United States	Atlantic	28 May 1827
John	21	M	Shoemaker	Ireland	U. States	Calais Packet	7 Jul 1828
John	24		Gentleman	Scotland	Canada	Hudson	18 Jun 1825
John	41	M	Shoemaker	Ireland	U. States	Severn	12 Oct 1826
John A.	29	M	Merchant	New Hampshire	New York	Eliza Ann	12 Mar 1825
Joseph	8			England	United States	Thomas Dickason	5 Jun 1827
Joseph	30	M	Joiner	England	U.N. States	Jane	7 Oct 1826
Mary	6			England	United States	Thomas Dickason	5 Jun 1827
Mary	25	F	Lady	Ireland	United States	Borneo	9 Jul 1827
Mary	30			England	United States	Thomas Dickason	5 Jun 1827

NAMES OF PASSENGERS	AGE	SEX	OCCUPATIONS	COUNTRY TO WHICH THEY BELONG	COUNTRY THEY INTEND TO INHABIT	SHIPS/DATES OF ARRIVAL	
LOW (cont'd)							
Mary	31	F	family [of Joseph]	England	U.N. States	Jane	7 Oct 1826
Robert	29	M	Chair Maker	England	United States	Montgomery	6 Mar 1829
Sally	25	F	Lady	Ireland	United States	Borneo	9 Jul 1827
Saml.	19	M	Farmer	Gt. Britain	United States	Europa	20 Apr 1825
Sarah	32	F	None	England	United States	Dalhouse Castle	6 Sep 1827
Sophia	35	F		Ireland	U. States	Severn	12 Oct 1826
Susan	32	F		Scotland	United States	Broke	16 Jul 1829
V.	12	M		Columbia	U. States	Weymouth	16 Feb 1825
Violet	4			England	United States	Thomas Dickason	5 Jun 1827
Wm.	6	M		G. Britain	U. States	Camillus	8 Sep 1828
Wm. H.	32	M	Merchant	U. States	U. States	Florida	2 Jun 1828
Wm. H., Mr.	23	M	Gent.	U.S. America	U.S. America	James Cropper	2 Aug 1827
LOWBLET, Henry	24	M	Merchant	England	United States	Nimrod	30 Aug 1824
LOWDEN, Isabela B.	29	F		Ireland	United States	Kleber	23 Jul 1827
John	9	M		Ireland	United States	Kleber	23 Jul 1827
John	32	M	Labourer	Ireland	United States	Kleber	23 Jul 1827
Margaret	5	F		Ireland	United States	Kleber	23 Jul 1827
LOWDES, Josiah	26	M	Servant	Spain	Spain	Circassian	13 Jun 1825
LOWDON, Richard	22	M	Farmer	England	America	Thames	27 May 1822
LOWE, Ann	7	F			U. States	Manhattan	21 May 1821
Ann	35	F	None	Lankshire Sheffield	U. States	Manhattan	21 May 1821
George	35	M	Farmer	Darbayshire	U. States	Manhattan	21 May 1821
Jane	15	F				John Dickinson	14 Sep 1820
Janes	10	M				John Dickinson	14 Sep 1820
John	3	M				Cassack	25 Jul 1820
John	27 8/12	M	...	England	America, U.S.	Illinois	3 Jun 1822
John	37	M	Engineer	England	England	Sully	15 Jul 1829
Joseph	20		Shoe Maker	Manchester, England	Great Britain	Franklin	22 Jun 1827
Joseph	29		Merchant	W. Hampton	England	Great Britain	7 May 1827
Joseph, Mr.	26	M	Merchant	England	England	Acasta	12 May 1825
Joshua	39	M	Jeweller	Great Britain	U. St.	Manchester	7 Dec 1826
Marry	3	F			U. States	Manhattan	21 May 1821
Mary A.	24	F				Cassack	25 Jul 1820
Robert	40			England	U. States	Corinthian	8 Oct 1828
Robert, Jur.	17			England	U. States	Corinthian	8 Oct 1828
Wm. J.	21	M	Weaver			John Dickinson	14 Sep 1820
LOWEHELL, Chas.	27	M	Merchant	St. Domingo	St. Domingo	Leo	2 Oct 1822
LOWEL, Vincentz	34	M	Farmer			Amity	11 Sep 1820
LOWELL, —, Mr.	17	M	Merchant	Bermuda	Bermuda	Hiram	10 Mar 1827
Edmond	23	M	Lawyer	U. States	U. States	Sully	25 Jun 1828
LOWENSTEIN, Jacob	35	M		Germany	Ohio	Orient	25 Nov 1825
LOWER, David	4	M		Great Britain	America	Lady Gallatin	21 Jun 1820
Humphrey	36	M		Great Britain	America	Lady Gallatin	21 Jun 1820
Johannah	28	F	Wife	Ireland	New York, U. States	Combine	1 Aug 1825
Lenah	40	F		Great Britain	America	Lady Gallatin	21 Jun 1820
Maria	10	F		Great Britain	America	Lady Gallatin	21 Jun 1820
LOWERLEY, John	24	M	Labourer	G. Britain	U. States	Freak	9 Jun 1828
LOWERS, Jas.	22	M	Seaman	Great Britain	United States	Mary Howland	19 Jul 1827
LOWERSON, Peter S.	32	M	...	U. States	U. States	Charlemagne	19 Sep 1828
LOWERY, David	18	M	...	Ireland	United States	Nancey	8 Jun 1822
Edwd.	45	M	Merchant	U. States	U. States	Cobbosse Conte	18 Apr 1823
Fredrick	28	M	Farmer	Ireland		Quatre Freres	29 Jul 1828
J.	34		Farmer	Ireland	United States	Courier	16 May 1825
James	21	M	Baker	Scotland	United States	Curler	3 Mar 1828
N.	18	M	Farmer	Ireland	U. States	Isabella	28 Jun 1825
Peggy	12	F		Ireland	United States	Commerce	13 Jun 1828
Peter	12	M		Ireland	United States	Commerce	13 Jun 1828
Robert	20	M	...	Ireland	United States	Nancey	8 Jun 1822
Robert	28	M	Farmer	England	U. States	Lima	5 Aug 1829
Sarah	54	F		Ireland	United States	Commerce	13 Jun 1828
LOWEY, John	30	M	Farmer	Ireland	Ohio	Atlantic	8 May 1828
LOWIS, Jannette	23	F		New York	New York	Brighton	20 Aug 1825
LOWLY, James	30	M	Servant	Ireland	Ireland	Express	25 Sep 1827
LOWNDES, Elizabeth	40	F		America	United States	Marmion	13 Jun 1823
Rebecca	12	F		America	United States	Marmion	13 Jun 1823

NAMES OF PASSENGERS	AGE	SEX	OCCUPATIONS	COUNTRY TO WHICH THEY BELONG	COUNTRY THEY INTEND TO INHABIT	SHIPS/DATES OF ARRIVAL
LOWREY, Dennis	28	M	Labourer	Ireland	Boston	General Marion 12 Jan 1829
LOWRIE, Geo.	43		Mercht.	England	U. States	New York 30 Oct 1827
John	36	...	...	Scotland	America	Nimrod 9 Jul 1827
LOWRY, Ann Maria	25	F		Jamaica	England	Jay 13 Aug 1823
Edward	26	M	Butcher	America	America	Portland 30 Mar 1820
J. D.	21	M	Sadler	U. States	U. States	Phoebe 17 Apr 1821
James	26	M	Weaver			Hanford 17 Jul 1828
James	28	M	Farmer	Ireland	United States	Dublin Packet 9 Jul 1827
Jane	20	F	Servant	G. Brittian	United States	Louisa 14 Jun 1825
Jane	23	F				Hanford 17 Jul 1828
Jas.	30	M	Labourer	Ireland	United States	Thomas 13 Dec 1827
Jennet	20	F	None	Great Britain	United States	Courier 26 Jun 1827
Jno.	20	M	Weaver	Ireland	United States	Trident 16 May 1826
M	28	F				Hanford 17 Jul 1828
Mary	60	F		England	United States	Amelia 20 Aug 1829
Michl.	21		Farmer	Ireland	United States	Rufus King 4 Sep 1823
R.	21	M				Hanford 17 Jul 1828
Robert	28	M	Farmer	Ireland	New York	Lima 5 Aug 1829
Sarah	55	F				Hanford 17 Jul 1828
William	21	M		England	United States	Amelia 20 Aug 1829
Wm.	45		Cooper	Great Britain	United States	Comet 9 Aug 1822
LOWTHER, Chas.	17	M	teacher or Goldlace Maker	England	New York	Cortes 23 Nov 1827
Harriet	15	F	teacher or Goldlace Maker	England	New York	Cortes 23 Nov 1827
James	20	M	Bleacher	Rath...	United States	Carolina Ann 11 Jun 1824
Jane	15	F		Rath...	United States	Carolina Ann 11 Jun 1824
Mary	20	F	Spinster	Ireland	United States	Wilson 28 Nov 1828
Mary Anne	12	F	teacher or Goldlace Maker	England	New York	Cortes 23 Nov 1827
Robert	19 7/12	M	Labourer	G. Britain	United States	Louisa 14 Jun 1825
Sarah	6	F	teacher or Goldlace Maker	England	New York	Cortes 23 Nov 1827
Thomas	9	M	teacher or Goldlace Maker	England	New York	Cortes 23 Nov 1827
Thos.	23	M	Farmer	Ireland	New York	Triton 12 Jul 1823
William	45	M	teacher or Goldlace Maker	England	New York	Cortes 23 Nov 1827
LOY, An	6/12	F		Scotland	U. States	Superior 25 Sep 1828
B.	2	F		Scotland	U. States	Superior 25 Sep 1828
John Geo.	32	M	Black Smith	Germany	United States	Quito 16 Jun 1826
LOYD, Charlotte	30	F	None	Gt. Britain	United States	Crisis 6 Apr 1825
David	6	M		G. Britain	U. States	Mary & Harriot 8 Sep 1828
Elenor	23	F	Spinster	Ireland	United States	Dublin Packet 24 Sep 1823
Eliza	19	F	Farmer	Ireland	United States	Helen 27 Jun 1821
Francis	42	M	Farmer	Ireland	United States	Helen 27 Jun 1821
Hiram	25	M	Mariner	United States	United States	Leonora 3 Dec 1827
James, Jr.	8	M		Gt. Britain	United States	John & Elizabeth 25 Sep 1827
John	40	M	Joiner			William Neilson 26 Jul 1828
John	60	M	Farmer	Ireland	United States	Dublin Packet 24 Sep 1823
John, Jr.	25	M	Farmer	Ireland	United States	Dublin Packet 24 Sep 1823
M.	30	M	Merchant	U. States	U. States	Superior 16 Apr 1827
Maria	16	F	Farmer	Ireland	United States	Helen 27 Jun 1821
Martha	16	F	Spinster	Ireland	United States	Dublin Packet 24 Sep 1823
Mary	2	F		G. Britain	U. States	Mary & Harriot 8 Sep 1828
Mary Ann	17	F		England	U. States	Cincinnatus 21 Feb 1825
Maryan	50	F				William Neilson 26 Jul 1828
Michl.	50	M	Farmer	Ireland	United States	Helen 27 Jun 1821
Richard	30	M	Joiner	Wales	New York	Angelica 18 Aug 1823
Richd.	35	M	Last Maker	England		Fame 9 Dec 1826
Sophia	34	F				William Neilson 26 Jul 1828
Susan	9	F	Farmer	Ireland	United States	Helen 27 Jun 1821
Thomas	22	M	Farmer	Ireland	United States	Dublin Packet 24 Sep 1823
Thos.	33	M	Moulder	Gt. Britain	New York	Columbia 3 Apr 1826
William	11	M	Farmer	Ireland	United States	Helen 27 Jun 1821
LOZAIR, James	22	M	Gentleman	New York	U. States	Dispatch 12 Aug 1825
LOZENBERGER, Jacob	25	M	Tailor	Switzerland	U.S.	C. Amelia 30 Jun 1828
LUBBREN, F. M.	25	M	Merchant	Great Britain	U. States	Columbia 24 Dec 1822

NAMES OF PASSENGERS	AGE	SEX	OCCUPATIONS	COUNTRY TO WHICH THEY BELONG	COUNTRY THEY INTEND TO INHABIT	SHIPS/DATES OF ARRIVAL	
LUBE, William	17	M	Shoemaker	Great Briton	United States	Erin	26 May 1821
LUBY, Lawrence	25	M	Laborer	Ireland	United States	Justina	5 Aug 1823
LUCAROS, Francisco M.	50	M	Merchant	Spain	France	Fly	17 Jan 1824
LUCAS, Benjn.	...	M	Gentleman	Charleston	Charleston	Amity	13 Sep 1821
Edward	8	M	None	England	United States	Trident	18 Jul 1827
Elizabeth	19	F	None	England	United States	Trident	18 Jul 1827
Eve	22	F	Family [of Henry]	France	America	La Grange	7 Aug 1828
George	4	M	Family [of Henry]	France	America	La Grange	7 Aug 1828
George	6	M	None	England	United States	Trident	18 Jul 1827
Henry	28	M	Farmer	France	America	La Grange	7 Aug 1828
James	15	M	None	England	United States	Trident	18 Jul 1827
James	26	M	Farmer	England	Great Britain	Florida	26 Sep 1826
John	4	M	None	England	United States	Trident	18 Jul 1827
John	34	M	Farmer	England	United States	Richmond	4 Aug 1826
John	46	M	Labourer	England	United States	Trident	18 Jul 1827
Mary	10	F	None	England	United States	Trident	18 Jul 1827
Mary	43	F	None	England	United States	Trident	18 Jul 1827
Samuel	53	M	Merchant	England	England	Eliza	22 Dec 1826
Stephen	12	M	None	England	United States	Trident	18 Jul 1827
Susan	13	F	None	England	United States	Trident	18 Jul 1827
Susan	25	F		England	England	Eliza	22 Dec 1826
Thomas	17	M	None	England	United States	Trident	18 Jul 1827
William	22	M	None	England	United States	Trident	18 Jul 1827
William	36	M	Merchant	America	America	La Grange	7 Aug 1828
Wm. A.	21	M	Gent.	New York	New York	Panthea	22 Jul 1826
LUCCA, G.	32	M	Merchant	France	Porto Rico	Bellesarius	26 May 1828
LUCCHESE, Ferdinand	40	M	None	Naples	United States	New York	12 Nov 1822
LUCCHESS, Ferdinand, Count	42	M	Consul General	Sicily	Washington	Florida	22 May 1826
LUCE, L.	6	M	Merchant	Gaudaloupe	Gaudaloupe	Jane	13 Aug 1827
LUCHET, Carl	4	M		Bardin	U. States	Bayard	5 Sep 1828
Carl	42	M	B. Smith	Bardin	U. States	Bayard	5 Sep 1828
Christian	_/12	M		Bardin	U. States	Bayard	5 Sep 1828
Christian	34	M		Bardin	U. States	Bayard	5 Sep 1828
Englehard	12	M		Bardin	U. States	Bayard	5 Sep 1828
Fredrick	6	M		Bardin	U. States	Bayard	5 Sep 1828
Henny	2	M		Bardin	U. States	Bayard	5 Sep 1828
LUCHRAE, Margt.	20	F		G. Britain	U. States	Camillus	8 Sep 1828
Sarah	18	F		G. Britain	U. States	Camillus	8 Sep 1828
LUCHTY, John	67		Farmer	France	U. States	Elizabeth	9 Jul 1825
Madelina	52		Farmer	France	U. States	Elizabeth	9 Jul 1825
LUCIANE, Charles, Mr.	10	M	None	France	U.S.	Osprey	22 Nov 1824
LUCIANO, —, Mr.	20	M	Gent.	Spain	U. States	Cadmus	6 Oct 1825
LUCINNELLUS, Jose	46	M	Merchant	Spain	Havana	Robert Fulton	22 May 1824
Josea Iracena	13	M	Merchant	Spain	Havana	Robert Fulton	22 May 1824
LUCIOT, Frederick	23	M	Sugar Baker	Hamburg	U. States	Electra	28 Apr 1827
LUCK, Ann	2	F	Carpenter	England	United States	Euphrates	18 Aug 1827
Ann	34	F	Carpenter	England	United States	Euphrates	18 Aug 1827
Elizth.	35	F	None	Great Britain	United States	Orbit	23 Oct 1826
George	21	M	Carpenter	England	United States	Euphrates	18 Aug 1827
Harriet	8	F	None	Great Britain	United States	Orbit	23 Oct 1826
Henry	22		Farmer	Bremen	Germany	Hudson	14 Jun 1827
Isaac	9	M	Carpenter	England	United States	Euphrates	18 Aug 1827
Isaac	35	M	Carpenter	England	United States	Euphrates	18 Aug 1827
Lewis	13	M		Gt. Britain	United States	John & Elizabeth	25 Sep 1827
Phoebe	55	F	Carpenter	England	United States	Euphrates	18 Aug 1827
Samuel	3/12	M	None	Great Britain	United States	Orbit	23 Oct 1826
Thomas	5	M	Carpenter	England	United States	Euphrates	18 Aug 1827
Thomas	35	M	Victular	England	America	Plutarch	18 Jul 1826
Walter	18	M	Carpenter	England	United States	Euphrates	18 Aug 1827
Walter	60	M	Carpenter	England	United States	Euphrates	18 Aug 1827
William	14	M		England	America	Plutarch	18 Jul 1826
LUCKETT, F.	40	M	Mariner	U. States	U. States	Hopes Delight	6 Sep 1824
Feildear, Cpt.	45	M	Mariner	Virginia	Alexandria	South America	29 Aug 1826
LUCKLE, Joseph	30	M	Laborer	Ireland	United States	Ann Maria	12 Jun 1826
LUCKLEY, Thomas	24	M	Farmer	Great Britian	United States	Andes	19 Aug 1829
LUCKMAN, John	22	M	Carpenter	England	United States	Jubilee	1 Oct 1828
LUCQUE, Beau	22	M	Butcher	Swisse	United States	Deux Ernest	29 Dec 1827

NAMES OF PASSENGERS	A G E	S E X	OCCUPATIONS	COUNTRY TO WHICH THEY BELONG	COUNTRY THEY INTEND TO INHABIT	SHIPS/DATES OF ARRIVAL	
LUCUS, Ann	1			County of Carvan	Ohio	Peru	30 May 1828
Benjamin	6			County of Carvan	Ohio	Peru	30 May 1828
Bess	5			County of Carvan	Ohio	Peru	30 May 1828
Elizabeth	27			County of Carvan	Ohio	Peru	30 May 1828
Jane	7			County of Carvan	Ohio	Peru	30 May 1828
John	30		House Carpenter	County of Carvan	Ohio	Peru	30 May 1828
Letty	3 1/2			County of Carvan	Ohio	Peru	30 May 1828
R. T.	22	M	Printer	France	U.S.	Bayard	18 Oct 1826
LUCY, Bernard	21	M	Farmer	Ireland		Aurora	12 Mar 1827
Esther	4	F	Spinster	G. Britain	U. States	Hanford	18 Sep 1828
John	18	M	Farmer	Ireland		Aurora	12 Mar 1827
LUDDINGTON, Edd.	30	M	Laborer	England	U. States	Howard Douglass	29 Jan 1828
LUDE, Nicholas	33	M		Switzerland	U. States	London	13 Sep 1824
LUDEMAN, C.	30	M	Labourer	Germany	U. States	Brighton	14 Apr 1828
LUDEN, Hermen	24	M	Merchant	Holland		Louisa	12 Jun 1826
LUDGATE, Thos.	19	M	Baker	England		Marchioness	13 May 1828
LUDI, Barbara	27	F		Switzerland	America, U.N.S.	Great Britain	3 Aug 1829
Catharine	0 1/12	F		Switzerland	America, U.N.S.	Great Britain	3 Aug 1829
Jack	36	M	Farmer	Switzerland	America, U.N.S.	Great Britain	3 Aug 1829
Jaques	2 1/12	M		Switzerland	America, U.N.S.	Great Britain	3 Aug 1829
LUDLOW, Ann E.	13	F	None	N. York	U. States	Bayard	18 Jul 1823
Cornelia	9	F	None	N. York	U. States	Bayard	18 Jul 1823
E.	34	M	None	N. York	U. States	Bayard	18 Jul 1823
Eliza E.	15	F	None	N. York	U. States	Bayard	18 Jul 1823
Jane	20	F	None	U. States	U. States	Wicker	21 May 1827
Louisa	7	F	None	N. York	U. States	Bayard	18 Jul 1823
R. H.	22	M	Merchant	New York	U. States	Trimmer	30 Apr 1825
Rob.	22	M	Merchant	U. States	U. States	Edgar	1 Oct 1822
Rob. E.	17	M	None	N. York	U. States	Bayard	18 Jul 1823
Thos. W.	28	M	Lawyer	New York	U. States	New York	15 Nov 1823
LUDLUM, Androw S.	21	M	Clerk	U. States		Hudson	23 Jul 1828
Henry	21	M		Derbeyshire	U. States	Manhattan	21 May 1821
LUFERSHIRE, Anton	5	F	Child	France	U. States	Sally	14 May 1821
H.	28	F	Lady	U. States	U. States	Sally	14 May 1821
LUFF, Laura	7	F		U. States	U. States	Cincinnatus	24 May 1821
Sarah	47	F		U. States	U. States	Cincinnatus	24 May 1821
LUFFIN, Michael	35			England	U. States	Corinthian	8 Oct 1828
LUFIN, Joseph	26	M	Gent	French	U. States	Charlemagne	19 Sep 1828
LUFKIN, J., Capt. *Sick Dead	36	M	Mariner	America	America	Osprey	22 Nov 1824
LUGEBUL, Catherin	50	F	Framer	Switserland	Ohio	Danube	20 Jul 1826
Christian	20	M	Framer	Switserland	Ohio	Danube	20 Jul 1826
Maria	20	F	Framer	Switserland	Ohio	Danube	20 Jul 1826
LUGENBUHL, Ann	43		Farmer	France	U. States	Elizabeth	9 Jul 1825
Barbara	10		Farmer	France	U. States	Elizabeth	9 Jul 1825
Catharine	6		Farmer	France	U. States	Elizabeth	9 Jul 1825
Catharine	16		Farmer	France	U. States	Elizabeth	9 Jul 1825
Frederich	55		Farmer	France	U. States	Elizabeth	9 Jul 1825
Jannet	19		Farmer	France	U. States	Elizabeth	9 Jul 1825
John	4		Farmer	France	U. States	Elizabeth	9 Jul 1825
John	44		Gaker	France	U. States	Elizabeth	9 Jul 1825
Maria	41		Farmer	France	U. States	Elizabeth	9 Jul 1825
Marianne	21		Farmer	France	U. States	Elizabeth	9 Jul 1825
LUGERANE, Fournier, Doctr.	32	M	Phisician	France	United States	India	4 Aug 1826
LUGG, Ann	31	F	Farmer	Great Britain	United States	Asia	14 Jul 1829
Anthonn	4	M	Farmer	Great Britain	United States	Asia	14 Jul 1829
Charles	37	M	Farmer	Great Britain	United States	Asia	14 Jul 1829
Eliza	1	F	Farmer	Great Britain	United States	Asia	14 Jul 1829
Elizabeth	6	F	Farmer	Great Britain	United States	Asia	14 Jul 1829
Mary Ann	8	F	Farmer	Great Britain	United States	Asia	14 Jul 1829

NAMES OF PASSENGERS	AGE	SEX	OCCUPATIONS	COUNTRY TO WHICH THEY BELONG	COUNTRY THEY INTEND TO INHABIT	SHIPS/DATES OF ARRIVAL	
LUGG (cont'd)							
Sarah	10	F	Farmer	Great Britain	United States	Asia	14 Jul 1829
LUGGER, —, Mrs.	28	F		Gt. Britain	Canada	Columbia	7 Sep 1827
John	1	F		Gt. Britain	Canada	Columbia	7 Sep 1827
Julia	3	F		Gt. Britain	Canada	Columbia	7 Sep 1827
M.	35	M	Clergyman	Gt. Britain	Canada	Columbia	7 Sep 1827
Jude	35	M	Farmer	France	U. States	Sully	25 Jun 1828
LUGUESNE, Fs.	9	M		France	United States	Howard	20 Aug 1827
Mae.	28	F		France	United States	Howard	20 Aug 1827
LUGUINS, F. Ge.	23	M	Farmer	Switzerland	United States	Howard	11 Jun 1824
LUITZ, Albert	6	M		Germany	U. States	Exchange	28 Aug 1828
Charles	2	M		Germany	U. States	Exchange	28 Aug 1828
E.	38	M	Merchant	Germany	U. States	Exchange	28 Aug 1828
L.	36	F		Germany	U. States	Exchange	28 Aug 1828
Louisa	4	F		Germany	U. States	Exchange	28 Aug 1828
LUKE, C.	22	M	Labourer	Germany	U. States	Brighton	14 Apr 1828
George	19	M	Labourer	Prussia		Constitution	20 Jun 1828
LUMBAIRD, S.	27	M	Mariner	N. York	U. States	Flight	12 Dec 1825
LUMBY, John	20	M	Farmer	Great Britan	United States	Silvanus Jenkins	10 Mar 1827
LUMENSTROLL, Anna	4	F		Brattain		L'Esperance	6 Sep 1828
Catherine	1	F		Brattain		L'Esperance	6 Sep 1828
Christine	8	F		Brattain		L'Esperance	6 Sep 1828
Christine	29	F		Brattain		L'Esperance	6 Sep 1828
John	7	M		Brattain		L'Esperance	6 Sep 1828
John Geo.	32	M		Brattain		L'Esperance	6 Sep 1828
LUMETZ, Robert	22	M	Sculpture	Russia	U. States	Monument	22 Sep 1828
LUMLEE, James	26		Labourer	Queens County	N. York	Peru	30 May 1828
Mary	23			Queens County	N. York	Peru	30 May 1828
LUMLEY, James	20			Great Britain	U. States America	Maria	22 May 1822
James	20	M	Farmer	England	United States	William & Henry	19 Jul 1822
Leon	50	M	Merchant	England	America	John Dickinson	9 Oct 1828
Morris	24 4/12	M	Merchant	England	America	John Dickinson	9 Oct 1828
Wm.	20	M	None	Great Britian	Great Britian	Governor Hawkins	16 Mar 1826
LUMSDEN, Catherine	25	F	Spinster	Scotland	United States	Broke	16 Jul 1829
Christina	30	F		Scotland	United States	Broke	16 Jul 1829
Margaret	38	F	Spinster	Scotland	United States	Broke	16 Jul 1829
LUNCH, Rosana	21			Reading	England	Rockingham	23 Aug 1822
LUND, Geo.	53	M	Merchant	G. Britain		Ann Maria	3 Jul 1820
W.	30	M	Mechanic	U. States	U. States	Medina	23 Apr 1828
LUNDT, Henry N.	14	M	None	Great Britain	United States	Washington	9 Apr 1821
LUNDY, Thomas	37	M	Servant	England	U.S.A.	Brighton	21 Jan 1826
LUNE, John	30	M	Laborer	Great Britain	United States	Samuel Wright	12 Oct 1829
LUNEAU, Peter	45	M	Merchant	... Citizen		Otho	2 Jan 1822
LUNEN, Charles	18	M	Farmer	Mertingar		Mount Vernon	7 Jun 1824
LUNHAM, F. McDonald	22	M	Surveyor	Ireland		Eliza Grant	29 Aug 1829
Thos. McDonald	22	M	Surveyor	Scotland	New York	Eliza Grant	29 Aug 1829
LUNITA, Fredk.	37	M	Farmer	Sardania	U. States	Criterion	16 May 1825
LUNN, ...	30	M	Merch.	U. States	United States	Henri IV	14 Oct 1829
John	31	M	Weaver	G. Britain	U. States	Great Britain	6 Sep 1828
LUNNY, Meebe.	30	M		Ireland		Lady Hunter	12 Apr 1823
LUNT, George	21	M	Farmer	England	United States	Silas Richards	3 Apr 1826
Thomas	30	M	Farmer	England	United States	Silas Richards	3 Apr 1826
LUNTZINGER, Dorothy	23	F	Farmer	France	France	Sully	15 Jul 1829
LUPAN, Francis	31	M	Farm	Ireland		Quatre Freres	29 Jul 1828
LUPPLE, Pat	18	M	Labourer	Ireland	United States	Wilson	6 Jun 1828
LUPTON, Arthur	39	M	Merchant	England	America	Liverpool Packet	23 Mar 1822
Eliza.	9	F		England	U. States	Martha	1 Feb 1822
Jane	25	F		England	U. States	Martha	1 Feb 1822
Jno.	48	M	Mercht.	England	U. States	Martha	1 Feb 1822
John	50		Farmer	England	America	Robert Burns	8 Dec 1821
John, Junr.	25			England	America	Robert Burns	8 Dec 1821
Margt.	7	F		England	U. States	Martha	1 Feb 1822
LUPUCTUR, Agather	6	F	Carpenter	Ireland		Quatre Freres	29 Jul 1828
Maryan	32	F	Carpenter	Ireland		Quatre Freres	29 Jul 1828
Mayar	4	F	Carpenter	Ireland		Quatre Freres	29 Jul 1828
Nicolus	38	M	Carpenter	Ireland		Quatre Freres	29 Jul 1828

NAMES OF PASSENGERS	AGE	SEX	OCCUPATIONS	COUNTRY TO WHICH THEY BELONG	COUNTRY THEY INTEND TO INHABIT	SHIPS	DATES OF ARRIVAL
LURANDO, Jos. M.	19	M	Merchant	Pensacola	New York	Charleston	1 Aug 1825
LURASSCHI, Pietro	26	M	Mercht.	Italy	U. States	Aerial	10 Nov 1825
LURMANN, D.	28	M	Merchant	United States	United States	William	1 Jul 1828
LURNER, Wm.	31		Seaman	Baltimore		Hudson	18 Jun 1825

*Officers, Seamen and Passengers belonging to the Ship Jane of Boston and taken from on board the Schooner Olive of St. Johns , N.B. on the 4th June 1825, Lat. 41.30, Long 53.19, which ship foundered on the 31st ultimo in Lat. 41.44 Long 52.

NAMES OF PASSENGERS	AGE	SEX	OCCUPATIONS	COUNTRY TO WHICH THEY BELONG	COUNTRY THEY INTEND TO INHABIT	SHIPS	DATES OF ARRIVAL
LUSBEY, John	28	M	Labourer	Great Britan	U. States	Canada	2 Jun 1824
LUSCOMB, Henry	5			England	Maryland	Caroline	10 Mar 1828
James	50		Carpenter	England	Maryland	Caroline	10 Mar 1828
Jane	29			England	Maryland	Caroline	10 Mar 1828
John	9			England	Maryland	Caroline	10 Mar 1828
Philip	37		Millwright	England	Maryland	Caroline	10 Mar 1828
Susan	5			England	Maryland	Caroline	10 Mar 1828
LUSELEY, Abraham	13	M		G. Britain	U. States	Mary & Harriot	8 Sep 1828
Eleanor	16	F		G. Britain	U. States	Mary & Harriot	8 Sep 1828
Harriet	5	F		G. Britain	U. States	Mary & Harriot	8 Sep 1828
Joseph	17	M		G. Britain	U. States	Mary & Harriot	8 Sep 1828
Mary Ann	45	F		G. Britain	U. States	Mary & Harriot	8 Sep 1828
Saml.	3	M		G. Britain	U. States	Mary & Harriot	8 Sep 1828
Susan	7	F		G. Britain	U. States	Mary & Harriot	8 Sep 1828
LUSH, George	27	M	Dealer	England	United States	Warrior	6 Oct 1828
LUSHER, Ann	10	F	Farmer	Switzerland	United States	Factor	1 Sep 1823
Fredrick	9	M	Farmer	Switzerland	United States	Factor	1 Sep 1823
Hy.	7	M	Farmer	Switzerland	United States	Factor	1 Sep 1823
Jacob	13	M	Farmer	Switzerland	United States	Factor	1 Sep 1823
Martha	25	F		United States	United States	Globe	30 Aug 1828
Mary	22	F	Farmer	Switzerland	United States	Factor	1 Sep 1823
Mary	40	F	Farmer	Switzerland	United States	Factor	1 Sep 1823
Peter	30	M	Farmer	United States	United States	Globe	30 Aug 1828

*landed at this Port, Custom House, Portland, Aug 19, 1828

NAMES OF PASSENGERS	AGE	SEX	OCCUPATIONS	COUNTRY TO WHICH THEY BELONG	COUNTRY THEY INTEND TO INHABIT	SHIPS	DATES OF ARRIVAL
Rueby	20	M	Farmer	Switzerland	United States	Factor	1 Sep 1823
Saml.	46	M	Farmer	Switzerland	United States	Factor	1 Sep 1823
LUSKINGTON, —, Mr.	38	M	Trader	England	England	Robert Edwards	21 Sep 1821
LUSLON, Frances	30	F	Lady	U. States	U. States	Nancy	31 May 1823
LUSSID, Jno.	38	F	Lady	Bermuda	U. States	Mary & Elizabeth	10 Jul 1824
LUSSING, Morah	25	M		Bavaria	U. States	London	13 Sep 1824
LUSTER, Abraham	4	M				Euphrates	8 Aug 1820
Sarah	26	F	None			Euphrates	8 Aug 1820
LUSTRACE, Peter	24	M				Velocipede	20 Sep 1824
LUSTRE, William	35	M	Farmer			Euphrates	8 Aug 1820
LUSTRER, John	35	M	Sevant	Bermuda		Lancatter	5 Jul 1820
LUTCHNESS, Anna Maria	38	F		France	United States	New England	29 Aug 1828
LUTHER, George	4	M		France	United States	New England	29 Aug 1828
George	21	M	Clerk	U. States	U. States	Rodney	19 Jun 1827

*Passenger from the Wreck of Schooner Gen. Marion from Charleston to N.Y.

NAMES OF PASSENGERS	AGE	SEX	OCCUPATIONS	COUNTRY TO WHICH THEY BELONG	COUNTRY THEY INTEND TO INHABIT	SHIPS	DATES OF ARRIVAL
George, kinder [child of Jacob]	5	M		Limbach	United States	Juffraw Johanna	16 Oct 1821
Jacob	28	M		France	United States	New England	29 Aug 1828
Jacob	33	M	Schoemaker	Limbach	United States	Juffraw Johanna	16 Oct 1821
Jacob, kinder [child of Jacob]	6	M		Limbach	United States	Juffraw Johanna	16 Oct 1821
Johanna	30	M	Joiner	France	United States	New England	29 Aug 1828
Johann	6/12	M		France	United States	New England	29 Aug 1828
Magdalena, kinder [child of Jacob]	1	F		Limbach	United States	Juffraw Johanna	16 Oct 1821
Maria	2	F		France	United States	New England	29 Aug 1828
Niclas	6	M		France	United States	New England	29 Aug 1828
Paul	7	M		France	United States	New England	29 Aug 1828
Peter, kinder [child of Jacob]	3	M		Limbach	United States	Juffraw Johanna	16 Oct 1821
Richard	48	M	Chair Maker	England	America	Plutarch	18 Jul 1826
LUTLEY, Philip	28	M	Wool Comber	New York		Olive Branch	9 Oct 1829
LUTTER, Catharan	3	F	None	France	U. States	Sully	25 Jun 1828
Catharin	28	M	None	France	U. States	Sully	25 Jun 1828
Christian	30	M	Farmer	France	U. States	Sully	25 Jun 1828
Mary	28	F	None	France	U. States	Sully	25 Jun 1828
Peter	5	M	None	France	U. States	Sully	25 Jun 1828
Veronica	1	F	None	France	U. States	Sully	25 Jun 1828

NAMES OF PASSENGERS	AGE	SEX	OCCUPATIONS	COUNTRY TO WHICH THEY BELONG	COUNTRY THEY INTEND TO INHABIT	SHIPS/DATES OF ARRIVAL	
LUTTY, Jacques	38		Farmer	France	U. States	Elizabeth	9 Jul 1825
Madeline	53		Farmer	France	U. States	Elizabeth	9 Jul 1825
LUTY, John	21	M	Labourer	Ireland	United States	Jubilee	13 Jul 1829
LUTZ, —						Exchange	28 Aug 1828
*Born on the Passage							
Charles	23	M	Agriculturist	France	U.S.	Helen	3 May 1828
Christiana	34	F	Farmer	Alsace in the Department of Upper and lower Rhine	United States	Carolina Augusta	16 May 1828
Fred.	22	M	...wer	France	United States	Stephania	6 Dec 1827
Frederic	7	M	Farmer	Alsace in the Department of Upper and lower Rhine	United States	Carolina Augusta	16 May 1828
Frederic	36	M	Farmer	Alsace in the Department of Upper and lower Rhine	United States	Carolina	
				Department of Upper and lower Rhine	United States	Carolina	
Lewis	24	M	Tanner	France	United States	Augusta	16 May 1828
Michael	4	M	Farmer	Alsace in the Department of Upper and lower Rhine	United States	Stephania Carolina Augusta	6 Dec 1827 16 May 1828
Rudolph	32	M	Carpenter	Switzerland	United States	Aurora	21 Jun 1824
LUVIN, Ann	6	F	Labourer	England	U. States	Ayrshire	12 May 1828
Catharine	1	F	Labourer	England	U. States	Ayrshire	12 May 1828
Ellen	11	F	Labourer	England	U. States	Ayrshire	12 May 1828
Sarah	4	F	Labourer	England	U. States	Ayrshire	12 May 1828
Thomas	9	M	Labourer	England	U. States	Ayrshire	12 May 1828
LUX, Cathr.	6	F		Brattain		L'Esperance	6 Sep 1828
Christine	2_/12	F		Brattain		L'Esperance	6 Sep 1828
Christine	5	F		Brattain		L'Esperance	6 Sep 1828
Elizth.	3	F		Brattain		L'Esperance	6 Sep 1828
Elizth.	36	F		Brattain		L'Esperance	6 Sep 1828
George	7	M		Brattain		L'Esperance	6 Sep 1828
Jacques	41	M	Labourer	Brattain		L'Esperance	6 Sep 1828
Joseph	9	M		Brattain		L'Esperance	6 Sep 1828
Nicolas	16	M		Brattain		L'Esperance	6 Sep 1828
Salomie	24	F	Farmer	France	France	Sully	15 Jul 1829
LUYANDO, Salvadore	18	M	Gentleman	Columbia	Columbia	Gertrude	19 May 1826
LUYSTER, M. A., Miss	5	F	Lady	U. States	U. States	Acasta	21 Oct 1825
Mary, Mrs.	23	F	Lady	U. States	U. States	Acasta	21 Oct 1825
T. G. W., Master	3	M	Gentn.	U. States	U. States	Acasta	21 Oct 1825
William, Master	1	M	Gentn.	U. States	U. States	Acasta	21 Oct 1825
LY..., Francois	41		Weaver	France	U. States	Parachute	14 May 1828
LYALL, Alex.	20		Weaver	Great Britain	United States	Camillus	12 Sep 1827
LYDICK, Goefry	21 11/12	M	Farmer	England	America	Hope	12 Dec 1820
LYDON, —, Mr.	31	M	Merchant	Ireland	U. States	Convoy	14 Mar 1823
LYE, Poscon	19	M	Shoemaker	Germany	United States	Samuel Robertson	8 Aug 1828
LYLE, Ann	22	F	Matron	Ireland	U. States	Courier	17 Mar 1828
Henry M.	6	M		United States	Philadelphia	Gleaner	30 Apr 1821
Hugh	20	M	Farmer	Ireland	United States	Trident	16 May 1826
Hugh	22	M	Labourer	Ireland	U. States	Courier	17 Mar 1828
J.	13	M	Farmer	Ireland	U. States	Orozimbo	7 Jul 1825
John	28	M		Ireland	U. States	St. Michael	26 Oct 1824
M.	59	M	Farmer	Ireland	U. States	Orozimbo	7 Jul 1825
Margt.	10	F	Farmer	Ireland	U. States	Orozimbo	7 Jul 1825
Margt.	47	F	Farmer	Ireland	U. States	Orozimbo	7 Jul 1825
Samuel	46		Merchant	England	England	Bogota	25 Oct 1827
LYMAN, —, Miss	25	F		U. States	U.S.	Henri IV	14 Sep 1827
Chas.	22	M	None	United States	United States	Cortes	5 Aug 1822
Daniel	33	M	Glass Cutter	Ireland	New York	Governor Fenner	23 Jul 1829
Elizabeth	29	F	None	United States	United States	Cortes	5 Aug 1822
G. E.	35	M	None	United States	United States	Cortes	5 Aug 1822

NAMES OF PASSENGERS	AGE	SEX	OCCUPATIONS	COUNTRY TO WHICH THEY BELONG	COUNTRY THEY INTEND TO INHABIT	SHIPS/DATES OF ARRIVAL	
LYMAN (cont'd)							
Geo.	1/2	M	None	United States	United States	Cortes	5 Aug 1822
Geo.	27	M	Merchant	Massachusetts	U. States	Fly	9 Apr 1823
John	10	M	Servant	Ireland	United States	Carolina Ann	14 May 1827
John	19 3/12	M	Servant	France	United States	Hector	8 Jan 1820
Mar...	4/52	F		Ireland	United States	Carolina Ann	14 May 1827
Margret	...	F		Ireland	United States	Carolina Ann	14 May 1827
Patrick	14	M	Labourer	Ireland	United States	Carolina Ann	14 May 1827
Peleg	...	M	Servant	Ireland	United States	Carolina Ann	14 May 1827
Phillip	6	M		Ireland	United States	Carolina Ann	14 May 1827
Terence	5	M		Ireland	United States	Carolina Ann	14 May 1827
LYMBAUR, Matthew	60	M	Merchant	England	England	Amity	31 May 1822
LYME, Thos.	64	M	Farmer	Scotland	United States	Friends	16 Aug 1824
LYMN, John	27	M	Mason	Ireland	United States	Fabius	4 Jun 1828
LYMON, Thos.	26	M	Farmer	Ireland		Cuba	24 Jun 1822
LYNAL, Fredrick	26	M	T...	England	England	Electra	7 Jul 1828
Michal	23	F	T...	England	U. States	Electra	7 Jul 1828
LYNAR, Jno.	22	M				Hibernia	15 Aug 1820
LYNCH, Ann	18	F		Ireland	United States	Romulus	13 Aug 1829
Ann	24	F		Ireland	U. States	Virginia	20 Jun 1825
Ann	26	F				Lady of the Lake	23 Aug 1828
Ann	30	F	Matron	Ireland	America	Wilson	16 May 1825
Ann	50	F		Ireland	America	Plutarch	18 Jul 1826
Ann	60	F				Ocean	17 Aug 1820
Ann, Junior	13	F		Ireland	America	Plutarch	18 Jul 1826
Biddy	16	F	Spinster	Ireland	United States	Lord Strangford	20 Jun 1826
Bridget	21	F	Matron	Ireland	U. States	Courier	17 Mar 1828
Bridget	23	F	Spinster			Commerce	22 Jun 1825
Bryan	8	M	Farmer	Ireland	United States	Fabius	4 Jun 1828
Catharine	22	F	Servant	Ireland	New York	Atlantic	8 May 1828
Catherine	28	F		Ireland	United States	Enterprize	23 Jul 1827
Chas. M.	29	M	Merchant	England	U. States	Weser	24 Mar 1826
Danl.	28		Mason	Ireland		Cincinnatus	17 May 1823
Darby	18	M	Labourer	Ireland	America	Josephine	8 Jan 1827
Dominick	40	M	Merchant	U. States	U. States	Caledonia	10 Sep 1828
Dominick	42	M	Merchant	U.S. America	U.S. America	James Cropper	29 Nov 1827
Edward	22	M	Labourer	Ireland	U. States	Josephine	7 May 1827
Edwd.	22	M	Labourer	Ireland		Marchioness	13 May 1828
Edwd.	24	M	Labourer	Ireland	America	Dewitt Clinton	27 Jul 1824
Elizabeth	22	F	None	Great Britan	U. States	Ann Marria	6 Aug 1823
Honora	15	F	None	Ireland	United States	Jubilee	12 May 1828
Hugh	19	M	Labourer	Ireland	United States	Louisa	18 Apr 1827
Isabella	6	F	Child	Ireland	America	Wilson	16 May 1825
James	17	M	Labourer	Ireland	United States	Jubilee	12 May 1828
James	24			G. Britain	U. States	Great Britain	6 Sep 1828
James	25	M	Labourer	Ireland	United States	Enterprize	23 Jul 1827
James	44	M	Labourer	England		Marchioness	13 May 1828
Jno.	20	M	Farmer	England	U. States	Thomas Ritchie	2 Jul 1827
Jno.	30			Ireland	United States	Geo. Canning	5 Jun 1828
John	19	M	None	Ireland	United States	St. George	25 Aug 1829
John	20	M	Labourer	Ireland	U.S. of America	Hamilton	18 Jul 1827
John	24	M	Tradesman	Ireland	America	Samuel Robertson	26 Nov 1825
John	25	M	Labourer	England	United States	Aurelia	7 Jun 1826
John	26	M	Farmer	Ireland	United States	Diana	1 May 1826
John	40		Labourer	Ireland	New York	Atlantic	8 May 1828
John W.	21	M	Seaman	U. States	U. States	Louisa	7 Jun 1824
Margaret	21	M	Farmer	...ford, Ireland		Mount Vernon	7 Jun 1824
Mary	20	F	Spinster	Ireland	United States	Dublin Packet	22 Apr 1822
Mary	20	F	None	...th...ck	United States	Solon	21 Jun 1824
Mary	20	F	Spinster	Ireland	United States	Fabius	31 Jul 1829
Mary	22	F	Wife	Ireland	New York	Louisa	20 Jul 1826
Mary	25	F	Servant Maid	Ireland	America	Plutarch	18 Jul 1826
Mary	26	F	Seamstress	Great Britain	United States	Grecian	24 Sep 1828
Mary	55	F	None	Ireland	United States	Jubilee	12 May 1828
Mary	60	F	...	Ireland	United States	Carolina Ann	24 Oct 1825
Mary Ann	8	F	Child	Ireland	America	Wilson	16 May 1825
Michael	30	M	Labourer	Ireland	United States	Romulus	13 Aug 1829

NAMES OF PASSENGERS	AGE	SEX	OCCUPATIONS	COUNTRY TO WHICH THEY BELONG	COUNTRY THEY INTEND TO INHABIT	SHIPS/DATES OF ARRIVAL	
LYNCH (cont'd)							
Michal	26	M	Labourer	Ireland	New York	Louisa	20 Jul 1826
Michl.	26	M	Carpenter	Ireland	United States	Wilson	27 Jun 1826
P.	28	M	Labourer			Lady of the Lake	23 Aug 1828
Pat	22	M	Labourer	St. Johns, N.B.	United States	Antioch	21 Sep 1827
Patrick	29 6/12	M		Ireland	America	Carolina Ann	7 Apr 1826
Peter	30	M	Labourer	Ireland	America	Dewitt Clinton	27 Jul 1824
Peter	30	M	Labourer	Great Britain	United States	Penelope	11 Jun 1827
Rose	16	F	Spinster	Ireland	America	Wilson	16 May 1825
Thomas	1 6/12	M		Ireland	United States	Enterprize	23 Jul 1827
Thomas	23 6/12	M	Labourer	Ireland	U. States	Josephine	30 Aug 1828
Thomas	24	M	Farmer	Ireland	America	William	21 May 1825
Thos.	18	M	Weaver	Ireland	United States	Trio	13 Jun 1827
Thos.	22		Labourer	Ireland	United States	Courier	15 Oct 1827
Thos.	42	M	Planter	Guadaloupe	U. States	Ann Maria	18 May 1825
Timy.	27		Labourer	Ireland	United States	Geo. Canning	5 Jun 1828
Wm.	20	M	Labourer	Ireland	United States	Thomas	13 Dec 1827
Wm.	50		None	Suffolk	Great Britain	William Thompson	13 May 1823
Wm. F., Mr.	22		U.S. Navy	U.S. America	U.S. America	Mary	10 Mar 1826
LYNCK, James	17	M	Dyer	Cty. of Longford, Manchester, Ireland	N. York	New Orleans	24 Aug 1827
LYNE, Richd.	20	M	Mason	Ireland	United States	Trio	13 Jun 1827
Thomas	17	M	Seaman	Philadelphia	America	New York Packet	8 May 1823
Thos. A.	22	M	Gent		United States	Cosmo	21 Aug 1828
LYNETT, John	23 6/12	M	Labourer	Ireland	U. States	Josephine	30 Aug 1828
LYNN, Eleanor	20	F	None	Ireland	United States	Catharine	22 Jul 1825
George	30	M	Blacksmith	England	America	Ann	23 Jul 1821
Hugh	26	M	Farmer	Ireland	United States	Lord Strangford	20 Jun 1826
Margaret	25	F				John Dickinson	14 Sep 1820
Thos.	25	M	Farmer	G. Brittain	U. States	Rockingham	17 May 1821
LYOD, John	4	M		G. Britain	U. States	Mary & Harriot	8 Sep 1828
LYON, Alanson	30	M	Blacksmith	Connecticut	Connecticut	Governor Griswold	15 Jul 1826
Charles	29	M	Shoemaker	Great Briton	Ohio	Brighton	12 Jun 1826
Fras.	26	M		Co. ...th	United States	Java	9 Jul 1827
G. F.	30	M	Capn.	England	England	Brown	23 Dec 1826
George	41 1/12	M	Merchant	England	United States	Rebecca & Sally	21 Jun 1822
George	48	M		...land	U. States	Douglass	16 Jul 1824
James	25		Farmer	Ireland	U. States	Robert Burns	18 Jun 1822
James B.	3	M	Child	St. Johns	St. Johns	Nancy	3 Apr 1824
Jane	2	F	Butcher	Great Britain	United States	Dapper	21 Aug 1828
Jane	30	F	Butcher	Great Britain	United States	Dapper	21 Aug 1828
Jas.	26	M		N. Jersey	U. States	William	30 Jul 1824
John	20	M	Laborer	Ireland	United States	Nancy	15 Nov 1824
John	35	M	Butcher	Great Britain	United States	Dapper	21 Aug 1828
Joseph	48	M	Merchant	United States	United States	General Paez	28 May 1828
M.	22			Kerry	Philadelphia	Schuylkill	22 Aug 1825
Marian	32	F		Newmills, Louden [Parish], Dumbarton [County]	New York	Hero	19 May 1828
*going to her friends							
Mary	24	F		Co. ...th	United States	Java	9 Jul 1827
Peter	21	M		Ireland	United States	Commerce	13 Jun 1828
Philip	30	M	Gentleman	England	U. States	Milton	20 Aug 1827
Phoebe	50	F	Lady	Connecticut	United States	St. Michael	21 Aug 1824
Rachel	35	F	Butcher	Great Britain	United States	Dapper	21 Aug 1828
Saml.	31	M	Merchant	Curacoa	United States	Rebecca & Sally	18 Jul 1823
T.	32	M	Farmer	Ireland	U. States	Isabella	28 Jun 1825
Wm.	...	M		Newmills, Louden [Parish], Dumbarton [County]	New York	Hero	19 May 1828
*going to her friends							
LYONS, —, Mr.	21	M	Seaman	U. States	U. States	Suffolk	29 Apr 1828
Eliza, Miss	18	F		U.S. of America	U.S. of America	Canada	1 Oct 1827
Ellen	39	F	Dairy	Ireland	United States	Neury	27 Jan 1827

NAMES OF PASSENGERS	AGE	SEX	OCCUPATIONS	COUNTRY TO WHICH THEY BELONG	COUNTRY THEY INTEND TO INHABIT	SHIPS/DATES OF ARRIVAL	
LYONS (cont'd)							
George	39	M	Merchant			Washington	15 Sep 1821
Henry	20	M	Labourer	Ireland	United States	Josephine	30 Apr 1828
Henry	22	M	Tailor	England	United States	Richmond	4 Aug 1826
Henry	36			Ireland	United States	Robert Burns	30 May 1823
James	22 3/12	M	Baker	England	British North America	London	6 Feb 1829
James	30		Merchant	Ireland	Halifax, N.S.	Jane	9 Jul 1821
Jane	33	F	None	America	America	Hesperus	7 Jul 1820
Jno.	27	M	Farmer	Great Britain	America	Remittance	24 Aug 1825
John	10	M	Dairy	Ireland	United States	Neury	27 Jan 1827
John	25		...	Co...	...	Hudson	14 Jun 1827
Jonathan	8	M	Dairy	Ireland	United States	Neury	27 Jan 1827
Margt.	15	F	Servant	Ireland	United States	Henry Kneeland	7 Jun 1828
Mary Ann	17	F		England	U.S.A.	Hudson	21 Aug 1829
Matthew	24	M	Yeoman	England	Pittsburg	Hudson	20 Nov 1828
Robert	24	M	Merchant	Ireland	United States	James Monroe	14 Dec 1820
Robert	25	M	Merchant	England	England	Nestor	20 Nov 1821
William M., Mr.	28	M	Gentleman	England	New York	Hudson	10 Nov 1825
Wm.	13	M	Dairy	Ireland	United States	Neury	27 Jan 1827
Wm.	36	M	Mill Wright	America	America	Hesperus	7 Jul 1820
Z. S., of Baltimore	24	M	Gentleman	America	America	Mary Lord	26 Oct 1829
LYSHE, Stephen	31	M	Merchant	Scotland	United States	Euphrates	8 Nov 1821
LYTTLE, James	22	M	Labourer	Ireland	U. States	Virginia	20 Jun 1825
M..., Ebenr.	...	...	...	Ireland	United States	General Putnam	20 Jun 1825
Edward	22	M	Labourer	Ireland	Unt. St. America	Wilson	21 May 1827
George	...	...	...	...	...	St. Michael	22 Sep 1824
Isaac	30	M	Farmer	Great Britain	United States	Zodiac	29 Oct 1822
J...	17	M	Farmer	France	U. States	Bayard	16 May 1827
J...	37	M	Mason	Germany	United States	Montano	8 May 1827
John	30	M	F...	England	Cherrey Valley	Debby & Eliza	20 Nov 1820
John [crossed out]	33	M	Seaman	U. States		Columbia	17 Apr 1827
*Destitute American Seaman							
Mary	...	...	...	...	...	St. Michael	22 Sep 1824
Patrick	19 4/12	M	Chandler	Ireland	America	Carolina Ann	7 Apr 1826
Patrick	27	M	...	...	...	Braganza	8 Aug 1825
Sh...	...	...	...	Scotland	America	Nimrod	9 Jul 1827
M...AN, Charles	10	M	Labourer	Ireland	United States	Carolina Ann	14 May 1827
Eleanor	...	F	Spinster	Ireland	Unt. St. America	Wilson	21 May 1827
M...B...NIS, Sarah	30	F		Ireland	U. States	Nancy	16 Aug 1822
M...D, J...	21	M	Farmer	Great Britain	Susquehanah	Venus	8 Sep 1820
M...DAILE, Harvey	19		Miller	Bl...	England	Great Britain	7 May 1827
M...EN, William	5			Scotland	United States	Camillus	3 May 1828
M...GEN, J.	29		Farmer	Ireland	United States	Courier	16 May 1825
M.	1		Farmer	Ireland	United States	Courier	16 May 1825
M.	30		Farmer	Ireland	United States	Courier	16 May 1825
M...HAN, Bridget	21	F		Limerick	N. York	Thomas & William	25 May 1827
M...LSON, William	34	M	Farmer	Great Britian	United States	Robert Quayle	29 Jul 1822
M...ON, —, Count	25	M	...	...	...	Meteor	16 Aug 1824
M...SIAN, Alexander	3	M		Scotland	United States	Orion	15 Jan 1827
Elizabeth	8	F		Scotland	United States	Orion	15 Jan 1827
Margaret	1	F		Scotland	United States	Orion	15 Jan 1827
Margaret	26	F		Scotland	United States	Orion	15 Jan 1827
M...THER, John	40	M	...	Ireland	United States	Trident	18 Jul 1827
Margaret	4	F	None	Ireland	United States	Trident	18 Jul 1827
Margaret	3...	F	None	Ireland	United States	Trident	18 Jul 1827
Mary Ann	1	F	None	Ireland	United States	Trident	18 Jul 1827
Pat.	7	M	None	Ireland	United States	Trident	18 Jul 1827
Thomas	9	M	None	Ireland	United States	Trident	18 Jul 1827
M...WAN, Margaret	7			Scotland	United States	Camillus	3 May 1828
MA..., ...ose	...	F	Spinster	Ireland	Unt. St. America	Wilson	21 May 1827
Fredrico Ulysses	21	M	Merchant	Nancy	N. York	Stephania	29 Nov 1825
MA...WELL, Alex.	30	M	Merchant	Great Britain	Canada	James Monroe	5 Apr 1820
MA...Y..., ...	...	...	...	...	...	William Thompson	30 Sep 1824
MABEE, David	22	M	Labourer	G. Britain	U. States	Sarah G	5 Jun 1828
MABER, Jacob	34	M	Mechanic	U. States	U. States	Conveyance	15 Jan 1827

NAMES OF PASSENGERS	AGE	SEX	OCCUPATIONS	COUNTRY TO WHICH THEY BELONG	COUNTRY THEY INTEND TO INHABIT	SHIPS/DATES OF ARRIVAL	
MABERRY, Thomas	34	M	Iron Roller	Gt. Britain	U.S. America	James Cropper	14 Mar 1828
MABIN, Rose S.	20	F		France	U. States	Charlemagne	19 Sep 1828
MABUCK, John	21	M		United States	United States	Seine	21 Oct 1822
MACABE, B.	13	F		G. Britain	U. States	Great Britain	6 Sep 1828
MACADAM, John R. B.	21	M	Merchant	Scotland	U.S.	William Byrnes	11 Dec 1827
MACADEN, Elizabeth	23	F	Servant	Ireland	New York	Louisa	18 Apr 1827
Mathw.	21	M	Servant	Ireland	New York	Louisa	18 Apr 1827
MACALGIN, John	20	M		Ireland	United States	Nancy R. Crowell	21 Sep 1822
MACALISTER, Marion		F		Scotland	United States	Camillus	9 May 1827
MACALUSO, Antonio	50	M	None	Naples	United States	New York	12 Nov 1822
MACAM, Agnes	40	F		G. Britain	U. States	London	23 Sep 1828
Ebenr.	43	M	Mariner	Beverly, Mass.	U. States	Perseverance	18 Mar 1822
George	17	M	Mariner	Beverly, Mass.	U. States	Perseverance	18 Mar 1822
Pat	16	M		G. Britain	U. States	London	23 Sep 1828
MACANA, John	14	M	Labourer	G. Britain	U. States	Great Britain	6 Sep 1828
Mary	7	F		G. Britain	U. States	Great Britain	6 Sep 1828
MACARACA, John	18	M	Labourer	...	U. States	St. Michael	21 Jul 1824
MACARLNEY, Wm.	18	M	Farmer	Ireland	United States	L. M. Pelham	25 Jun 1822
MACARTY, John	30	M	Ostler	Great Britain	United States	Ann Maria	23 Jan 1826
Pat.	25	M	Labourer	Great Britain	United States	Atlantic	28 May 1827
MACARU, William	28	M	Laborer	Ireland	United States	St. Michaels	18 Jul 1826
MACATE, Kate	20	F	Weaver	Great Britain	United States	Colossus	5 Jun 1827
Thomas	28	M	Weaver	Great Britain	United States	Colossus	5 Jun 1827
MACAULAY, Thos.	39	M	Merchant	Ireland	United States	Atlantic	21 Jul 1827
MACAULY, James	28	M	Farmer	Scotland	U. States	Brilliant	19 Mar 1828
MACAVOY, Daniel	28	M	Labourer	Scotland, G.B.	United States	Orozimbo	31 May 1824
Sally	24	F	Labourer	Scotland, G.B.	United States	Orozimbo	31 May 1824
MACBREY, Mary	22	F	Housekeeper	Ireland	America	Alexander Mansfield	18 Jun 1821
MACCAY, Aleckander	20	M	None	Ireland	United States	Nancey	8 Jun 1822
Robert	22	M	None	Ireland	United States	Nancey	8 Jun 1822
MACCLAY, John	32	M	Farmer	Great Britain	United States	Colossus	5 Jun 1827
MACCRINDELL, George	32	M	Bookeeper	Great Britain	New York	Corinthian	27 Apr 1824
MACCULLUN, Achd.	2	M	None	Gt. Britain	United States	Minerva	12 Mar 1827
Dougle	4	M	None	Gt. Britain	United States	Minerva	12 Mar 1827
Elizabeth	28	F	None	Gt. Britain	United States	Minerva	12 Mar 1827
MACDERMOT, John	18	M	Labourer	England and Ireland	United States	Jubilee	12 May 1828
MACDONALD, Ronald	38	M	Merchant	England	United States	Brighton	9 Dec 1828
MACDOWELL, —, Mrs.	30	F		Halifax	U. States	Macdonough	5 Jul 1823
MACE, William	26	M	grocer	England	Newyork	Cortes	16 Jul 1827
MACEION, Geronimo	59	M	Merchant	Spain	Spain	Virginia	9 Feb 1829
MACEIRA, Carlota	3	F		Mexico	Spain	Virginia	9 Feb 1829
Conception	6/12	F		Mexico	Spain	Virginia	9 Feb 1829
Felicito	4	F		Mexico	Spain	Virginia	9 Feb 1829
Francisco	6	M		Mexico	Spain	Virginia	9 Feb 1829
Mariano	15	M		Mexico	Spain	Virginia	9 Feb 1829
MACELLE, Lydia Lambert	54	F		Boston	Connecticut	Jane	24 May 1828
MACEY, George	26	M		France	United States	Henri IV	2 Oct 1828
Louisa A.	21	F	Lady	N. York	N. York	Canada	1 Nov 1823
MACFALE, James	1	M	None	Great Britain	United States	Colossus	5 Jun 1827
James	40	M	Labourer	Great Britain	United States	Colossus	5 Jun 1827
Mary	26	F	None	Great Britain	United States	Colossus	5 Jun 1827
MACFARLAN, Robt.	30	M	Farmer			Servant	30 Aug 1820
MACFARLANE, ...	1	M	None	Great Britain	United States	Colossus	5 Jun 1827
Andrew	30	M	Farmer	Great Britain	United States	Colossus	5 Jun 1827
Christian	16	F	Spinster			Servant	30 Aug 1820
James	27	M	Miner	Great Britain	United States	Colossus	5 Jun 1827
Janet	33	F	None	Great Britain	United States	Colossus	5 Jun 1827
Malcolm	3	M	None	Great Britain	United States	Colossus	5 Jun 1827
Walter	31	M	Cotton Printer	Great Britain		Dalmannock	24 Ocg 1826
MACFEE, S.	23	M	Mechanic	Ireland	America	Howard	27 Sep 1826
MACFIL, Catherine	21			U. States	America	Florida	14 Oct 1829
James	29		Merchant	U. States	America	Florida	14 Oct 1829
MACGINGER, Mary	22	F	None		United States	Mount Vernon	29 Aug 1828
Patrick	63	M	Weaver		United States	Mount Vernon	29 Aug 1828
Thomas	21	M	Weaver		United States	Mount Vernon	29 Aug 1828

NAMES OF PASSENGERS	AGE	SEX	OCCUPATIONS	COUNTRY TO WHICH THEY BELONG	COUNTRY THEY INTEND TO INHABIT	SHIPS/DATES OF ARRIVAL	
MACGLOCHLIN, Dolly	20	F	None	Ireland	New York	America	1 Aug 1828
Patrick	20	M	Labourer	Ireland	New York	America	1 Aug 1828
MACGRATH, Peter	16	M	Labourer	Ireland	United States	Princess Charlotte	26 Apr 1827
MACGREGOR, Ann	26	F		Scotland	Unt. States	Robert Fulton	14 Mar 1829
Barbra	6	F	...f	Scotland	Unt. States	Robert Fulton	14 Mar 1829
Daniel	26	M	Merchant	Great Britain, Ireland	New York	Britannia	3 Nov 1827
Eliza	1	F	...f	Scotland	Unt. States	Robert Fulton	14 Mar 1829
James	4	M	...f	Scotland	Unt. States	Robert Fulton	14 Mar 1829
James	29	M	Merchant	Scotland	Unt. States	Robert Fulton	14 Mar 1829
MACGUDA, Jas.	34	M	Spinner	Scotland	New York	Joseph Hume	26 Oct 1829
MACGUIRE, Thomas	30	M	Farmer	Great Britain	U.S. of America	Gratitude	3 Oct 1829
MACH, Sam	24	M	Joiner	England	United States	Dalhouse Castle	8 May 1827
Sarah	25	F		England	United States	Dalhouse Castle	8 May 1827
MACHADO, Marian	30	M	Merchant	Island Cuba		Claudio	21 Aug 1827
Mariano	28	M	Merchant	Havana	Havana	Herald	21 Sep 1824
MACHALETTO, P.	50	M	Merchant	U. States	U. States	Panthea	12 Feb 1827
MACHAN, Ann	16	F		Ireland	U. States	Virginia	20 Jun 1825
John	35	M	Farmer	Europe	United States	Aspasia	5 Sep 1827
MACHAR, John, Revd. Mr.	30	M	Divine	Gt. Brittian	United States	Manchester	24 Aug 1827
MACHARD, M.	27	M	Merchant	Havana	U. States	Abeona	23 May 1823
MACHARE, —, Mrs.	30	F		Great Brittain	United States	Sarah Ralston	27 Jan 1827
MACHELETA, M.	48	M	Merch.	Italy	U. States	William Bayard	2 Mar 1824
MACHELL, Mary	15	F	Servant	Ireland	United States	Josephine	30 Apr 1828
MACHENS, Charlotte	22	F	None	Ilan...	U. States	Electra	7 Jul 1828
Roer	31	M		Ilan...	U. States	Electra	7 Jul 1828
MACHER, James	33	M	Merchant	St. John, N.B.	St. John, N.B.	Ann Maria	8 May 1826
MACHET, John V.	32	M	Merchant	United States	United States	Tampico	13 Oct 1825
Nicholas	47	M	Merchant	United States	United States	Elizabeth & Mary	23 Nov 1820
MACHETT, J.	22	M	Mason	Great Britain	United States	Isaac Hicks	6 Dec 1827
MACHETTS, Jno. V.	32	M	Mercht.	U. States	U. States	Emigrant	20 Sep 1823
MACHEY, Thomas	30	M	Mercht.	G.B.	Ireland	George Canning	2 May 1828
MACHIN, George	25	M	Tinman	England	United States	Andes	2 Oct 1828
Hannah	19	F	Child	Ireland	United States	Nancy	18 Oct 1824
Nichs.	22	M	Laborer	Gt. Britain		Dalhouse Castle	13 May 1828
MACHLIN, Cormick	23	F		Ireland	America	Carolina Ann	7 Aug 1826
MACHOT, Thomas	32	M	Mechanic	France		France	6 Feb 1829
MACHTLE, John	30	M	Farmer	Germany	United States	Helen	5 Sep 1828
MACHURST, Frederich	4	M		England	Ut. States	Courier	13 Jul 1826
MACILWAINE, Jno.	30	M	Mariner	Ireland	U. States	Iris	8 Jan 1824
MACIN, Ann	20	F		Ireland	United States	Princess Charlotte	26 Apr 1827
Arthur	40	M	Labourer	Ireland	United States	Princess Charlotte	26 Apr 1827
Bernard	6	M		Ireland	United States	Princess Charlotte	26 Apr 1827
James	14	M		Ireland	United States	Princess Charlotte	26 Apr 1827
Mary	13	F		Ireland	United States	Princess Charlotte	26 Apr 1827
Patrick	4	M		Ireland	United States	Princess Charlotte	26 Apr 1827
Peter	17	M	Labourer	Ireland	United States	Princess Charlotte	26 Apr 1827
Peter	18	M	Labourer	Ireland	United States	Princess Charlotte	26 Apr 1827
Sarah	18	F		Ireland	United States	Princess Charlotte	26 Apr 1827
Susan	10	F		Ireland	United States	Princess Charlotte	26 Apr 1827
MACINTIRE, Moses	48		Mayson	United States	United States	Iris	26 Jun 1821
Peter	18	M	Farmer			Servant	30 Aug 1820
MACINTYRE, ...n...s	...	...	...	Scotland	America	Nimrod	9 Jul 1827
Betsey	30	F		Great Britain	United States	Washington	3 Sep 1827
C...s	...	...	...	Scotland	America	Nimrod	9 Jul 1827
John	...	...	...	Scotland	America	Nimrod	9 Jul 1827
John	2	M	Child	Great Britain	United States	Washington	3 Sep 1827

NAMES OF PASSENGERS	AGE	SEX	OCCUPATIONS	COUNTRY TO WHICH THEY BELONG	COUNTRY THEY INTEND TO INHABIT	SHIPS/DATES OF ARRIVAL	
MACINTYRE (cont'd)							
Peter	24	M	Blacksmith	Great Britain	United States	Washington	3 Sep 1827
MACK, —, Mr.	38	M	Merchant	Germany	Baltimore	Elizabeth	5 Jul 1821
MACKA, Ann	25	F	Labourer	Great Britain	United States	Thomas Dickason	31 Jul 1829
Michael	34	M	Labourer	Great Britain	United States	Thomas Dickason	31 Jul 1829
Rose	20	F	Labourer	Great Britain	United States	Thomas Dickason	31 Jul 1829
MACKADY, John	22	M	Labourrer	Great Britan	U. States	Ann Marria	6 Aug 1823
John [crossed out]	22	M	Labourrer	G. Britan	U. States	Ann Marria	6 Aug 1823
MACKAN, Chas., Jr.	12	M	Servant	Ireland	United States	Josephine	30 Apr 1828
E.	18	F	Servant	Ireland	United States	Josephine	30 Apr 1828
M.	38	F	Servant	Ireland	United States	Josephine	30 Apr 1828
M., Jr.	8	F	Servant	Ireland	United States	Josephine	30 Apr 1828
MACKARSEL, —, Mr.	24	M	Stone Cutter	Scotland	U. States	Majestic	27 Jul 1829
MACKAVOY, Mary	12	F	Child	Ireland	U. States	Josephine	7 May 1827
MACKAY, Catherine	22	F		Switzerland	U. States	Robert Edward	2 Nov 1827
John	...	M	...	America	United States	London Packet	25 Dec 1820
Margaret	5	F		Great Britian	United States	Brok	29 Aug 1823
Margaret	38	F		Great Britian	United States	Brok	29 Aug 1823
Maria	2	F		Switzerland	U. States	Robert Edward	2 Nov 1827
Saml.	25	M	Farmer	Ireland	U. States	Francis	6 Sep 1827
Sarah	1	F		Switzerland	U. States	Robert Edward	2 Nov 1827
William	7	M		Great Britian	United States	Brok	29 Aug 1823
William	42	M	Schoolmaster	Great Britian	United States	Brok	29 Aug 1823
MACKDEAD, John	25	M		Ireland	United States	Nancy R. Crowell	21 Sep 1822
MACKDIVIT, Sarah	18	F		Ireland	U. States	Nancy	2 May 1823
MACKEE, Geo.	29	M	Merchant	Gt. Brittain	United States	Cortes	5 Aug 1822
MACKEFEE, Lydia	22	F		Ireland	U. States	Nancy	2 May 1823
Thomas	...	M	Labourer	Ireland	U. States	Nancy	2 May 1823
MACKEHOY, Jane	9	F	Merchant	Ireland	United States	Magnet	22 Aug 1822
MACKELWER, James	18	M		Ireland	United States	Nancy R. Crowell	21 Sep 1822
MACKEN, Biddy	17	F	Spinster	Ireland	United States	Dublin Packet	24 Sep 1823
Bridget	4	F		Ireland	United States	St. George	25 Aug 1829
Bridget	23	F		Ireland	United States	St. George	25 Aug 1829
H.	26		Farmer	Ireland	United States	Courier	16 May 1825
Marey	7	F		Ireland	United States	St. George	25 Aug 1829
Margaret	7	F		Ireland	United States	St. George	25 Aug 1829
Rose	21	F	Spinster	Ireland	U. States	Josephine	7 May 1827
MACKENER, Abety	25	M	Laborer	Ireland	U. States	Nancy	13 Dec 1822
MACKENEY, S.	38	M	Mechanic	Ireland	U. States	Birmingham	16 Jun 1828
MACKENNEY, Charles	9	M		England	U. States	Birmingham	16 Jun 1828
Joseph	5	M		England	U. States	Birmingham	16 Jun 1828
Lucy	26	F		England	U. States	Birmingham	16 Jun 1828
Luving	7	F		England	U. States	Birmingham	16 Jun 1828
Wm.	1	M		England	U. States	Birmingham	16 Jun 1828
MACKENTER, Burnard	27	M	Blacksmith	Ireland		Eliza Grant	29 Aug 1829
MACKENZIE, Edward	36	M	Mariner	Great Britian	Canada	Diamond	13 Nov 1823
George	19	M	Gentleman	British	Brittain	Govenor Lincoln	15 Feb 1827
John	44	M	Farmer	Scotland	United States	Belmont	30 Aug 1828
MACKER, —, Miss	22	F		Scotland	U. States	Aurora	18 Sep 1821
MACKERDEE, B...	27	M	Black Smith	Ireland	New York	Eliza Grant	29 Aug 1829
MACKETH, S. V.	30	M	Merchant	New York	N. York	Cadet	5 Dec 1824
MACKEY, Elizabeth	30	F		England	America	Ann	23 Jul 1821
Elizabeth	55	F		England	America	Ann	23 Jul 1821
Ellen	22	F	None	Ireland	United States	Lord Wellington	28 May 1827
Emily	6	F		America	America	Ann	23 Jul 1821
Francis	28	M	Labourer	Ireland	United States	Lord Wellington	28 May 1827
Jas.	23	M	Farmer	Ireland	Redstone	Triton	12 Jul 1823
Jennet	21	F		England	America	Ann	23 Jul 1821
John	32	M	Wheelwright	Ireland	U. States	Wanderer	30 Sep 1828
John	33	M	Farmer	Scotland	United States	Curler	3 Mar 1828
John	55	M	Farmer	England	America	Ann	23 Jul 1821
Judeth	24	F	None	Ireland	United States	Lord Wellington	28 May 1827
Judy	18	F		England	U. States	Emulous	22 Aug 1828
Lawa.	26	M	Labourer	Ireland	United States	Lord Wellington	28 May 1827

NAMES OF PASSENGERS	AGE	SEX	OCCUPATIONS	COUNTRY TO WHICH THEY BELONG	COUNTRY THEY INTEND TO INHABIT	SHIPS/DATES OF ARRIVAL	
MACKEY (cont'd)							
Mary	26	F		England	America	Ann	23 Jul 1821
Patrick	20	M	Labourer	England	U. States	Emulous	22 Aug 1828
Robert	20	M	Captain 79th Regt.	Colerain	Great Britain	Carolina Ann	11 Jun 1824
Robt.	32	M	Mariner	England	New York	William Byrnes	14 Apr 1824
Samuel	26	M	Merchant	Bermuda	Great Brittain	Victory	1 Sep 1820
Wm.	22	M	Tailor	England	America	Ann	23 Jul 1821
Wm. L.	20	M	Farmer	Colerain	United States	Carolina Ann	11 Jun 1824
MACKIE, Geo. D. L.	25	M	Merchant	Scotland	U. States	Edward Bonaffe	11 Dec 1827
George	30	M	Merchant	Great Britain	U.S. of America	Canada	1 Oct 1827
Jno.	36	M	Mechanic	Scotland		Domestic	31 Aug 1820
Jno. O.	12	M				Domestic	31 Aug 1820
Js.	18	M	Farmer	G. Britain	New York	Missouri	10 Apr 1821
Mary	8	F				Domestic	31 Aug 1820
Robt.	50	M	Farmer	G. Britain	New York	Missouri	10 Apr 1821
Wm.	40	M	Merchant	Great Britain	United States	Cortes	19 Nov 1821
MACKIN, Brid...t	23	F	None	Ireland	United States	St. George	25 Aug 1829
Bridget	4	F	None	Ireland	United States	St. George	25 Aug 1829
Edwd.	20 11/12	M		Ireland	America	Carolina Ann	7 Apr 1826
John	27	M	Laborer	Ireland	United States	Dublin Packet	9 Jul 1827
Margaret	7	F	None	Ireland	United States	St. George	25 Aug 1829
Margt.	17 10/12	F		Ireland	America	Carolina Ann	7 Apr 1826
Mary	7	F	None	Ireland	United States	St. George	25 Aug 1829
Mary	18	F		Ireland	United States	Aurora	9 Jul 1827
Patrick	23	M	Labourer	...	U. States	St. Michael	21 Jul 1824
Peter	13	M	Labourer	Ireland	United States	Baltic	21 Apr 1827
Sarah	28	F	Servant	Great Briten	U. States	Cortes	13 Aug 1825
MACKING, Sally	35	F	Lady	U. States	U. States	Nancy	19 Oct 1821
Tom	8	M	child	U. States	U. States	Nancy	19 Oct 1821
MACKINLY, Grace	28	F		Halifax		Domestic	31 Aug 1820
Jno.	7	M				Domestic	31 Aug 1820
Robt.	3	M				Domestic	31 Aug 1820
MACKINTOSH,							
Elizabeth	16	F	Lady	Ireland	United States	Nancy	20 Sep 1821
Margaret	18	F	Lady	Ireland	United States	Nancy	20 Sep 1821
MACKLARD, Bernard	24	M	Bookkeeper	Ireland	U.N. States	Jane	7 Oct 1826
MACKLEN, Cormak	23	M	Baker	Ireland	New York	America	1 Aug 1828
MACKLIFFE, Francis	32	M	Gentleman	Ireland	U. States	James Cropper	10 Jun 1823
MACKLIN, John	70	M	Labourer	Ireland	United States	Fabius	31 Jul 1829
*died							
Mary	60	F	Spinster	Ireland	United States	Fabius	31 Jul 1829
Mary, Miss	17	F	Spinster	Ireland	United States	Dublin Packet	13 Oct 1828
Mary Jane	16 6/12	F	Spinster	Ireland	U. States	Josephine	30 Aug 1828
Micheal	25	M	Farmers and Mechanics	Ireland	America	Constitution	1 Oct 1825
MACKLOT, L., Miss	8	F		New Jersey	New Jersey	Talma	23 Sep 1828
T., Mrs.	60	M		New Jersey	New Jersey	Talma	23 Sep 1828
MACKLY, Ann	21	F	Shoemaker	Great Britian	United States	Andes	19 Aug 1829
Robert	25	M	Shoemaker	Great Britian	United States	Andes	19 Aug 1829
MACKMULIN, William	25	M	Merchant	England	United States	Nancy	28 Oct 1822
MACKNEME, Matey	16	F	Servant	Ireland	United States	Ann Maria	5 May 1824
MACKNIE, Sarah	16	F				Comet	24 Dec 1821
Wm.	18	M				Comet	24 Dec 1821
MACKOLTER, Catherine	10	F	Daughter	Ireland	United States	Sylvester Healy	14 Jun 1825
Elizabeth	14	F	Daughter	Ireland	United States	Sylvester Healy	14 Jun 1825
Jane	3	F	Daughter	Ireland	United States	Sylvester Healy	14 Jun 1825
John	12	F	Daughter	Ireland	United States	Sylvester Healy	14 Jun 1825
Martha	1	F	Daughter	Ireland	United States	Sylvester Healy	14 Jun 1825
Robert	4	F	Daughter	Ireland	United States	Sylvester Healy	14 Jun 1825
William	45	M	Farmer	Ireland	United States	Sylvester Healy	14 Jun 1825
MACKONLD, Ann	20	F		Irland	U. States	Nancy	27 Jun 1823
Owen	2	M	Laber	Irland	U. States	Nancy	27 Jun 1823
Pat	22	M	Laber	Irland	U. States	Nancy	27 Jun 1823
MACKRAE, —,							
No name	6/12	M		England	New York	Frances Henrietta	3 Apr 1826
Arabella	35	F		England	New York	Frances Henrietta	3 Apr 1826
Colin	13	M	Boy	England	U. States	Amity	23 Sep 1823

NAMES OF PASSENGERS	AGE	SEX	OCCUPATIONS	COUNTRY TO WHICH THEY BELONG	COUNTRY THEY INTEND TO INHABIT	SHIPS/DATES OF ARRIVAL	
MACKRAE (cont'd)							
Colin	45	M	Gentleman	Demarara	U. States	Amity	23 Sep 1823
Henry	7	M		England	New York	Frances Henrietta	3 Apr 1826
Katharina	5	F		England	New York	Frances Henrietta	3 Apr 1826
Louisa	2	F		England	New York	Frances Henrietta	3 Apr 1826
Margaret	4	F		England	New York	Frances Henrietta	3 Apr 1826
Thomas	9	M		England	New York	Frances Henrietta	3 Apr 1826
MACKWELL, Jas.	25	M	Farmer	Suffolk	U. States	Criterion	15 Oct 1822
MACLARE, Barbara	18	F	Spinster	Switzerland	United States	Andes	5 May 1828
Catherine	20	F	Spinster	Switzerland	United States	Andes	5 May 1828
Jacob	9	M	Child	Switzerland	United States	Andes	5 May 1828
Madalena	24	F	Spinster	Switzerland	United States	Andes	5 May 1828
Margaret	22	F	Spinster	Switzerland	United States	Andes	5 May 1828
Margaret	52	F	Spinster	Switzerland	United States	Andes	5 May 1828
Mele	4	F	Child	Switzerland	United States	Andes	5 May 1828
Michel	13	M	Child	Switzerland	United States	Andes	5 May 1828
Michel	32	M	Farmer	Switzerland	United States	Andes	5 May 1828
MACLAVER, Henry	1	M	Child	Switzerland	United States	Andes	5 May 1828
Jacob	7	M	Child	Switzerland	United States	Andes	5 May 1828
Jacob	48	M	Farmer	Switzerland	United States	Andes	5 May 1828
Jeremiah	4	M	Child	Switzerland	United States	Andes	5 May 1828
Rosella	9	F	Spinster	Switzerland	United States	Andes	5 May 1828
Rosella	48	F	Spinster	Switzerland	United States	Andes	5 May 1828
Salina	18	F	Spinster	Switzerland	United States	Andes	5 May 1828
MACLENCAN, Geo.	30	M	Merchant	England	U. States	Panthea	8 Apr 1826
MACLENT, James	18	M	Labourer	Ireland	U. States	Wanderer	1 Sep 1828
MACLEOD, Daniel	19	M	Student	United States	Washington, U.S.	Florida	2 Oct 1828
MACLEY, Amros	29	M	Farmer	Ireland	United States	Nancy	16 Jul 1824
MACLOCKLAN, L.	22	M	Merchant	U. States	U. States	James	7 MKay 1823
MACMAHON, A.	35	M	Merchant	Gutamala	Spain	Swan	23 Jun 1823
MACMANNESS, Partrick	22	M	Shoemaker	Ireland	United States	General Marion	20 Aug 1828
MACMANUS, James	20	M	Labourer	Great Britian	U. States	St. Michael	3 Jan 1825
Mary	25	F	Wife	Great Britian	U. States	St. Michael	3 Jan 1825
MACMULLIN, Rose	20	F		Ireland	United States	Nancey	8 Jun 1822
William	24	M	...	Ireland	United States	Nancey	8 Jun 1822
MACMURDEE, John	27	M	Farmer	Great Britain	United States	Washington	3 Sep 1827
MACMURREY, Margt.	20	F	Labourer	Ireland	United States	Essex	23 May 1828
MACNALL, L., Mrs.	23	F	his Lady [William]	United States	United States	Potomac	8 Dec 1826
William	34	M	Ship Master	United States	United States	Potomac	8 Dec 1826
MACNAMARA, Ann	2	F	Merchant	Ireland	U. States	William Thompson	24 Aug 1827
Ann	32	F	Merchant	Ireland	U. States	William Thompson	24 Aug 1827
Ann	60	F	Merchant	Ireland	U. States	William Thompson	24 Aug 1827
Patrick	35	M	Merchant	Ireland	U. States	William Thompson	24 Aug 1827
MACNAMORA, Jno.	21	M	Mechanic	Boston	Boston	Leif	6 Sep 1824
MACOLIN, Smith	24	M	...	...	United States	Hanford	17 Oct 1828
MACOLM, Ann	22	F		Ireland	United States	Princess Charlotte	26 Apr 1827
MACOMB, —, Mrs.	35	F	Planter	Cuba	Cuba	Romulus	26 Apr 1822
Arita	8	F	Planter	Cuba	Cuba	Romulus	26 Apr 1822
Frances	2	F	Planter	Cuba	Cuba	Romulus	26 Apr 1822
George	4	M	Planter	Cuba	Cuba	Romulus	26 Apr 1822
James	3	M	None	United States	United States	Mary	23 Dec 1821
James	7	M	Planter	Cuba	Cuba	Romulus	26 Apr 1822
Stantaigo	40	M	Planter	Cuba	Cuba	Romulus	26 Apr 1822
Susan	24	F	Spinster	United States	United States	Mary	23 Dec 1821
William H.	25	M	Mechanic	United States	United States	Mary	23 Dec 1821
MACOMBE, John	24	M	Labourer	U. States	U. States	United States	11 Sep 1828
MACOME, John	21	M		Scotland	United States	Camillus	9 May 1827
MACON, Ebenezer	43	M	Mariner	Boston	Boston	Stephania	2 Jan 1824
MACONNIE, Jno.	24	M	Farmer	Great Britain	United States	Atlantic	28 May 1827

NAMES OF PASSENGERS	AGE	SEX	OCCUPATIONS	COUNTRY TO WHICH THEY BELONG	COUNTRY THEY INTEND TO INHABIT	SHIPS/DATES OF ARRIVAL	
MACORNISH, Thos.	22				United States	Robert Burns	18 Jun 1821
MACPHERIN, Hannah	35	F		Ireland	U. States	Nancy	29 Nov 1821
MACQUELAN, David	28	M	Farmer	U. States	U. States	United States	11 Sep 1828
MACRA, William	37	M	Cabinetmaker	Great Britain	U. States	Eclipse	26 Jun 1827
MACRADY, C. F., Mrs.	21	F	None	G. Britan	G. Britan	Canada	27 Sep 1826
L. M., Miss	29	F	None	G. Britan	G. Britan	Canada	27 Sep 1826
Wm. C.	33	M	Comedian	G. Britan	G. Britan	Canada	27 Sep 1826
MACRAE, Colin	45	M	Gentleman	Great Britain	U. States	Musidora	7 Jun 1821
MACREADY, Isabella	55	F	Lady	U. States	U. States	Wanderer	1 Sep 1828
William	56	M	Merchant	U. States	U. States	Wanderer	1 Sep 1828
MACROBB, Eliza	25	F	None	Canada	Canada	Nestor in Liverpool	29 Jul 1822
Robert	31	M	Merchant	Canada	Canada	Nestor in Liverpool	29 Jul 1822
MACROS, A.	19	M	Merchant	Spain	Spain	Swan	23 Jun 1823
MACSWINE, George	55		Farmer			Rufus King	7 Aug 1820
MACTIER, Alexander, Jr.	22	M	Merchant	United States	United States	Fair Play	22 May 1821
MACTON, Wm.	26	M	Labourer	Great Britian	U. States	St. Michael	3 Jan 1825
MACUNNELLY, Chas.	30	M	Labourer	...	U. States	St. Michael	21 Jul 1824
MACY, —, Mrs.		F	U. States			Stephania	18 Dec 1824
Cornelia, Miss	20	F	None	U. States	U. States	Sully	24 Oct 1828
Edward H., Capt.	27	M	Ship Master	United States	United States	Dromo	9 Oct 1828
M. H., Mrs.	28	F	None	U. States	U. States	Sully	24 Oct 1828
Mary H., Mrs.			None	U.S.	U.S.	Sully	26 Oct 1829
Mary H., Mrs.	26	F	Lady	New York	New York	Sully	4 Mar 1828
Robt. J.	30	M	Mariner	France	U. States	Bayard	11 Jul 1825
William A.	3 1/12	M	Child	New York	New York	Sully	4 Mar 1828
MADAGON, Patr.	40	M	Farmer	Ireland		L. M. Pelham	12 May 1823
MADAL, Margeal	43	M	Planter	Porto Rico		Sea Serpent	12 Jul 1828
MADALLETTO, P.	45	M	Merchant	U. States	U. States	Lady Tompkins	13 Apr 1824
MADAN, R. F.	24	M	Merchant	Havana	Spain	Seneca	21 May 1825
MADDEN, Amos	35	M	Merchant	United States	United S.	Ariel	1 Mar 1828
Bernard	20	M	Labourer	Ireland	U. States	Atlantic	19 Aug 1825
Bridget	28	F	Farmer	Great Briton	Canada	Brighton	12 Jun 1826
Catherine E., Mrs.	30	F	Lady	Ireland	United States	Dublin Packet	28 Apr 1824
David	30	M	Laborer	Ireland	United States	Trio	13 Jun 1827
Edward	30 1/12	M	Weaver	Ireland	United States	Atlantic	21 Jul 1827
Francis J.	7	F	Child	Ireland	United States	Dublin Packet	28 Apr 1824
Hubert	13	M	Boy	Great Britain	U. States	Robert Fulton	3 Dec 1827
James	19	M	Joiner	Ireland	New York	Amanda	23 May 1827
Johannah	23			Ireland	United States	Geo. Canning	5 Jun 1828
John	36 5/12	M	Merchant	U.S.	U.S.	Greyhound	10 Jan 1820
Lawrence	24	M	Joiner	Ireland	New York	Amanda	23 May 1827
Michael	21 3/12	M	Farmer			Cririe	18 Sep 1820
Michael	22	M	Weaver	Ireland	United States	Atlantic	21 Jul 1827
Michael	23	M	Laborer	Ireland	New York	Amanda	23 May 1827
William	30	M	Farmer	Great Briton	Canada	Brighton	12 Jun 1826
William H.	10	M	Child	Ireland	United States	Dublin Packet	28 Apr 1824
William H.	16	M	Gentleman	Ireland	United States	Dublin Packet	13 Oct 1828
MADDESON, G.	30	M	Farmer	England	U. States	Howard Douglass	29 Jan 1828
Mary	22	F		England	U. States	Howard Douglass	29 Jan 1828
MADDIGAN, Dennis	32	M	Clerk	Ireland	U.S. America	Traveller	10 Sep 1827
MADDIN, Ann	30	F	Labourer	Ireland	United States	Meteor	26 Jun 1827
John	3	M	Labourer	Ireland	United States	Meteor	26 Jun 1827
Margaret	2	F	Labourer	Ireland	United States	Meteor	26 Jun 1827
MADDOCK, Stephen	18	M	Bookseller	Great Brittain	Philadelphia	Albion	11 Jun 1821
MADDOX, Thomas H.	36		Mariner	New York	U. States	Lucy	16 Apr 1821
MADE, John	30	M	Sadler	England	United States	Acasta	25 Sep 1827
MADEGEN, Danl.	27	M	Farmer	Ireland		L. M. Pelham	12 May 1823
MADEN, —, Mrs.	20	F	None	England	U. States	Unity	27 Mar 1827
John	25	M	Clothier	England	U. States	Unity	27 Mar 1827
Moses	40	M	Clothier	England	U. States	Unity	27 Mar 1827
Wm.	28	M	Clothier	England	U. States	Unity	27 Mar 1827
MADERSON, John	21	M	Taylor	England	United States	Jubilee	1 Oct 1828
MADGALEN, Mary		F		St. Croix	St. Croix	Virginia	12 Jul 1820
MADISON, Gerrard	25	M	Taylor	Ireland	United States	Carolina Ann	11 Dec 1826
James	40	M	Farmer	United States	United States	Nancy Henrietta	3 Nov 1828

NAMES OF PASSENGERS	AGE	SEX	OCCUPATIONS	COUNTRY TO WHICH THEY BELONG	COUNTRY THEY INTEND TO INHABIT	SHIPS/DATES OF ARRIVAL	
MADOGAN, Paddy	20	M	Farmer	Ireland		L. M. Pelham	12 May 1823
MADOL, Mary	28	F	Servant	France	U. States	Pocahontas	28 Jun 1824
MADOLE, Wm., an Infant	1		Child	Ireland	United States	Eliza	29 Aug 1822
MADON, C.	14	M	None		Spain	Emma	24 Jun 1822
MADOR, —, Mr.	22	M	Silver Smith	England	U.S.	Robert Edwards	11 Nov 1822
—, Mrs.	20	F	Wife	England	U.S.	Robert Edwards	11 Nov 1822
MAEHR, —, Mrs.	50	F	Wife	U. States	U. States	Union	4 Sep 1824
G., Mr.	60	M	Clergyman	Germany	U. States	Union	4 Sep 1824
MAELZEL, Caroline	22	F		Austria		Howard	4 Feb 1826
John	46	M	Engineer	Austria		Howard	4 Feb 1826
John	48	M	Artist	Germany	New York	Sully	11 Mar 1829
MAEOR, Patric	30	M		Great Britain	United States	Thomas Dickason	31 Jul 1829
MAERLITO, P.	50	M	Mariner	Italy	U. States	Packet	26 Dec 1823
MAFFETT, James	33	M	Baker	Great Briton	uncertain	Mount Vernon	29 Aug 1828
MAFIRTH, Mary	22	F	Farmer	Great Britain	United States	Wanderer	14 May 1828
MAG..., John	24	M	Labourer	Ireland	United States	Princess Charlotte	26 Apr 1827
MAGA, Ann	25	F	Spinner	Great Britain	United States	Grecian	24 Sep 1828
Cath.	24	F	Servant	Ireland	United States	Louisa	18 Apr 1827
John	2...	M	Weaver	Ireland	United States	Louisa	18 Apr 1827
MAGAFFIN, John	20	M	Farmer	Ireland	America	Superior	12 Jun 1824
MAGAGIN, Edward	25	M		United States	United States	Crescent	12 Jul 1827
MAGAH, Joseph	28	M	Weaver	England	United States	Siroc	31 Oct 1829
MAGAHY, Francis	24	M	Laborer	Ireland	New York	Indian Chief	16 Aug 1822
MAGAINE, Charles	25	M	Farmer	U. States	U. States	Nancy	19 Oct 1821
Francis	22	M	Farmer	U. States	U. States	Nancy	19 Oct 1821
MAGALET, P.	49	M	Ship Master	America		Aspasia	19 Jul 1823
MAGALLY, Danl.	40	M	Tinman	England	U. States	Thomas Ritchie	2 Jul 1827
MAGAN, James	24	M	Weaver	Ireland	United States	Sarah Ann	11 Jan 1827
Jno.	37	M	Farmer	Ireland	America	Mary	29 May 1827
MAGANY, Joseph	32	M	Farmer	Switzerland	U. States	France	26 Jun 1828
MAGAR, Mary	30	F	Servant	Ireland	United States	Wanderer	31 Aug 1829
MAGAULLY, Biddy	11		None	G. Britain	United States	Roman	10 Sep 1827
Cathe.	1		None	G. Britain	United States	Roman	10 Sep 1827
Jno.	18		None	G. Britain	United States	Roman	10 Sep 1827
Mary	8		None	G. Britain	United States	Roman	10 Sep 1827
Mary	33		None	G. Britain	United States	Roman	10 Sep 1827
MAGEE, Ann	23	F		Ireland	America	Carolina Ann	7 Aug 1826
Barnard	19	M		Ireland	America	Carolina Ann	7 Aug 1826
Catharine	19	F	Spinster	Ireland	United States	Fabius	4 Jun 1828
Elizabeth	13	F	Spinster	Ireland	United States	Fabius	4 Jun 1828
Elizabeth	30	F				Silas Richards	20 Jun 1826
Hugh	20	M	Labourer	Ireland	U. States	Courier	17 Mar 1828
Hugh	27 2/12	M	Weaver	Ireland	U. States	Fabius	22 Sep 1828
James	22	M	Merchant	Ireland	America	Albion	4 Oct 1820
James	25	M	Merchant	Great Britian	U. States	Silas Richards	29 Oct 1828
James	50	M	Merchant	U.S.A.		Silas Richards	20 Jun 1826
Jane	25 6/12	F	Spinstress	Ireland	U. States	Fabius	22 Sep 1828
Jno.	30	M	Farmer	Ireland	America	Mary	29 May 1827
John	8	M	Child	Ireland	U. States	Josephine	30 Aug 1828
John	14		Boy	U. States	U. States	Waverly	5 Dec 1828
John	25 6/12	M	Weaver	Ireland	U. States	Courier	17 Mar 1828
Joseph	21	M	Labourer	Ireland	New York	Trusty	12 Sep 1828
Judah	40	M		G. Britan	U. States	William Neilson	26 Jul 1828
M.	25	M	Farmer	Ireland	America	Mary	29 May 1827
Margaret	16	F		G. Britan	U. States	William Neilson	26 Jul 1828
Margaret	22	F	Lady	St. John	U. States	St. Michaels	25 Apr 1825
Margeret Ann	6	F	Child	Ireland	U. States	Josephine	30 Aug 1828
Osia	12	F		G. Britan	U. States	William Neilson	26 Jul 1828
Patrick	25	M	Farmer	Ireland	America	Superior	12 Jun 1824
Rachel	2	F	Child	Ireland	U. States	Josephine	30 Aug 1828
Robart	25	M	Farmer	Great Britain	United States	Eliza Barker	3 Jul 1826
S. F.	10	M		G. Britan	U. States	William Neilson	26 Jul 1828
*drowned 16 June							
Sarah	17	F				Silas Richards	20 Jun 1826
MAGELLAN, William	32	...	...	Ireland	United States	Carolina Ann	24 Oct 1825
MAGERTY, Mary	18	F	Wife	Ireland	United States	St. Michaels	23 Dec 1826
Nancy	3	F	Child	Ireland	United States	St. Michaels	23 Dec 1826

NAMES OF PASSENGERS	AGE	SEX	OCCUPATIONS	COUNTRY TO WHICH THEY BELONG	COUNTRY THEY INTEND TO INHABIT	SHIPS/DATES OF ARRIVAL	
MAGESS, Nancy	20	F		Great Britain	United States	Atlantic	28 May 1827
MAGGART, James	34	M	...	...	...	Camillus	18 Nov 1824
MAGGRIDGE, Augustus	39		Merchant			Helen	4 Aug 1829
Emily	9					Helen	4 Aug 1829
Fredk.	13					Helen	4 Aug 1829
Joseph	14					Helen	4 Aug 1829
Mary	8					Helen	4 Aug 1829
MAGGS, —, Mr.	26	M	Clergyman	Great Britain	Great Britain	Mary & Elizabeth	7 Sep 1824
—, Mrs.	25	F		Great Britain	Great Britain	Mary & Elizabeth	7 Sep 1824
MAGHAGAHAN, Mary	19	F	None	Ireland	United States	Jubilee	13 Jul 1829
MAGHAN, Ann	25	F	Labourer	England	U. States	Comet	23 Aug 1828
John	17		Clerk	Ireland	United States	Courier	15 Oct 1827
John	30	M	Labourer	England	U. States	Comet	23 Aug 1828
Margt.	23	F		Great Britain	United States	Meridian	2 Jul 1827
MAGHER, John	28	M	Blacksmith	England	New York	America	1 Aug 1828
MAGILL, Ann	8	F	Child	Ireland	New York	Louisa	20 Jul 1826
Ann	25	F		Ireland	United States	Romulus	24 Jun 1826
Christiana	25	F	Labourer	Ireland	United States	Meteor	26 Jun 1827
Henry	20	M	Servant	Ireland	United States	John Wells	22 Sep 1824
Hugh, Junr.	22	M	Merchant	Ireland	United States	Herald	29 Oct 1825
Isabella	2	F	Child	Ireland	New York	Louisa	20 Jul 1826
James	21	M	Farmer	Ireland	U. States	William & John	10 Jul 1824
Janet	3	F	Labourer	Ireland	United States	Meteor	26 Jun 1827
Margaret	4 10/12	F	Child	Ireland	New York	Louisa	20 Jul 1826
Margaret	26 2/12	F	Wife	Ireland	New York	Louisa	20 Jul 1826
Mary	4	F	Child	Ireland	U. States	Josephine	30 Aug 1828
Mary	5 9/12	F	Child	Ireland	New York	Louisa	20 Jul 1826
Thomas	...	M	Labourer	Ireland	United States	Meteor	26 Jun 1827
William	50	M	Labourer	Ireland	United States	Meteor	26 Jun 1827
Wm.	23	M	Farmer	Ireland	U. States	Napolean	26 Sep 1828
MAGIN, John	24	M	Servant	Gt. Brittain	United States	Balaena	9 Oct 1823
Margaret	20	F		Ireland	United States	Princess Charlotte	26 Apr 1827
Patrick	20	M	Labourer	Ireland	United States	Princess Charlotte	26 Apr 1827
MAGINIS, Jacob	22	M	Hop Seller	England	U.S. America	Ganges	15 Dec 1826
Saml.	11	M		England	U.S. America	Ganges	15 Dec 1826
MAGINN, Hugh	19	M	Labourer	Ireland	United States	Princess Charlotte	26 Apr 1827
MAGINNES, Hugh	16	M	Labourer	Great Britian	United States	Princess Charlotte	6 Sep 1828
MAGINNIS, Bartholomew	24	M	Laborer	Great Britain	United States	Samuel Wright	12 Oct 1829
Katharine	11	...	...	Ireland	United States	Carolina Ann	24 Oct 1825
Thos.	30			England		Anacreon	7 Sep 1827
MAGINNISS, Ann	26	F		Ireland	United States	Princess Charlotte	26 Apr 1827
Catherine	3/12	F		Ireland	United States	Princess Charlotte	26 Apr 1827
Edward	22	M	Pedlar	Ireland	United States	Princess Charlotte	26 Apr 1827
MAGINNUS, Isabella	26	F	...	Ireland	United States	Carolina Ann	24 Oct 1825
James	7	...	...	Ireland	United States	Carolina Ann	24 Oct 1825
John	5	M	...	Ireland	United States	Carolina Ann	24 Oct 1825
Mary	3	...	...	Ireland	United States	Carolina Ann	24 Oct 1825
Richard	13	...	...	Ireland	United States	Carolina Ann	24 Oct 1825
MAGINUS, John	25	M	Weaver	Ireland	United States	Borneo	14 Aug 1827
MAGLOUGHLAN, Ann	22	F	Spinster	Ireland	U. States	Concordia	11 Jun 1823
John	24	M		Ireland	U. States	Concordia	11 Jun 1823
John	25	M	Shoemaker	Ireland	U. States	Concordia	11 Jun 1823
MAGNAR, D.	33	M	Merchant	France		Lucy Ann	5 Oct 1825
MAGNER, John	30	M		Gt. Britain	U. States	Tantiva	7 Jul 1828
MAGNES, Hiram	4	M		Jamaica	U. States	Active	11 Mar 1823
MAGNESS, Paulino	2	M				Leonidas	22 Jan 1829
Sarah	27 5/12	F		United States		Leonidas	22 Jan 1829
MAGNIER, Antonio	36	M	Gentleman	Mexico	Mexico	Lady Washington	31 Dec 1827
MAGNIMER, A.	35	M	Merchant	Spain	Mexico	Thacher	23 Sep 1828

NAMES OF PASSENGERS	AGE	SEX	OCCUPATIONS	COUNTRY TO WHICH THEY BELONG	COUNTRY THEY INTEND TO INHABIT	SHIPS/DATES OF ARRIVAL	
MAGNIN, David	51	M	Watchmaker	New York	New York	Sully	4 Mar 1828
James	25	M	Labourer	Europe	United States	Aspasia	5 Sep 1827
MAGNUS, Frederick	37	M	Merchant	St. Domingo	St. Domingo	Montano	24 Jun 1823
Margt.	20	F	None	Ireland		Aurora	12 Mar 1827
MAGONURE, Lewis	35	M	Merchant	France	U. States	Annawan	3 Apr 1826
MAGOR, Danial	43	M	Weaver	Great Britain	U. States	Robert Fulton	3 Dec 1827
Margeret	17	F	Spinster	Great Britain	U. States	Robert Fulton	3 Dec 1827
MAGOVARN, Edward	16	M	Mercht.	Ireland	N. York	George	10 Mar 1823
MAGOWEN, Patrick	26	M	Farmer	Ireland	U.S.A.	Dalhouse Castle	21 Aug 1829
Patrick	26	M	Farmer	Ireland	United States	Dalhouse Castle	21 Aug 1829
MAGOWN, David	36	M	Labourer	England	U. States	Montgomery	18 Oct 1828
MAGQUIRE, Ellen	22	F	Miliner	Ireland	United States	Nile	17 May 1827
MAGRA, Chas.	35	M	Mariner	U. States	U. States	Ajax	15 May 1822
MAGRAN, Edward	16		Labourer	Belfast	U. States	Carolina Ann	14 Feb 1824
John	13		Labourer	Belfast	U. States	Carolina Ann	14 Feb 1824
MAGRARD, Ferdinand	48	M	Merch.	U. States	United States	Henri IV	14 Oct 1829
MAGRATH, Ann	20	F	None	Ireland	U. States	Criterion	23 May 1826
B.	25	M	Farmer	Ireland	America	Mary	29 May 1827
Chas. [crossed out] *died 20 June						James Monroe	3 Jul 1824
John	26	M	Farmer	Ireland	U. States	Criterion	23 May 1826
John	26	M	Farmer	Ireland	U. States	Criterion	23 May 1826
Mary	20	F	Labourer	Ireland	United States	Essex	23 May 1828
Phillip	27	M	Farmer	Great Brittain	U. States	Hibernia	8 Jul 1823
Thos.	23	M	Stone Cutter	..., London, England	N. York	New Orleans	24 Aug 1827
MAGRAW, C.	19	F		Ireland	U. States	Alfred	7 Jun 1824
Eliza	13	F		Ireland	New York	Carolina Ann	15 Oct 1824
MAGREATH, John	...	M	Laborer	Irland	United States	Nancy	28 Oct 1822
MAGREGER, Grase	18	F		Ireland	United States	Nancey	8 Jun 1822
Nancey	24	F		Ireland	United States	Nancey	8 Jun 1822
MAGREW, Mary	26	F	None	Great Britain	United States	Mary & Harriet	3 Jul 1829
MAGRIDGE, Augustus P.	33	M	None	England	United States	Exchange	18 Nov 1822
MAGRIGALE, —	60	M	Gentleman	Italy	St. Domingo	Eliza Ann	17 Jul 1824
MAGRY, Nancy	23	F	Wife	Ireland	United States	Ann Maria	12 Jun 1826
Peter	23	M	Blacksmith	Ireland	United States	Ann Maria	12 Jun 1826
MAGUA, —, Mr.	28	M	None	Havana	U. States	Milo	15 May 1824
B.	23	M	Merchant	Spain	Havana	Tarantula	31 Oct 1823
MAGUE, Jemima	21	F	Spinster	Scotland	United States	St. Michaels	7 Jun 1827
MAGUIGEN, Brian	22	M	Weaver	Ireland	United States	Princess Charlotte	26 Apr 1827
MAGUIN, S.	22	M	Merchant	France	United States	Stephania	3 Oct 1822
MAGUIRE, Alice	25	F	Farmer	Scotland	U. States	Orozimbo	7 Jul 1825
Ann	23	F	Matron	Ireland	U. States	Courier	17 Mar 1828
Ann	30	F	Servant	Ireland	United States	Dublin Packet	28 Apr 1824
Aron E.	21	M	Merchant	United States	United States	Revenue	7 Oct 1829
Benjn.	28	M	Farmer	Scotland	U. States	Orozimbo	7 Jul 1825
Bridget	6	F	Farmer	Scotland	U. States	Orozimbo	7 Jul 1825
Briget	27	F	Taylor	Ireland	U. States	Virginia	20 Jun 1825
C.	4	F	Farmer	Scotland	U. States	Orozimbo	7 Jul 1825
Cathn.	24	F		Ireland	New York	Vigilant	6 May 1822
Cornelius	28	M	Navigator	Ireland	United States	Curler	7 Jul 1827
Daniel	24	M		Ireland	United States	William & George	14 May 1828
Dennis	21	M	Labourer	Great Britain	United States	Penelope	11 Jun 1827
Ellen	26	F		G. Britain	U. States	London	23 Sep 1828
Felix	30 1/12	M		Ireland	America	Carolina Ann	7 Apr 1826
Francis	20	M	Labourer	England and Ireland	United States	Jubilee	12 May 1828
Hannah	22	F		Ireland	United States	William & George	14 May 1828
Henry	30	M	Merchant	Great Britain	United States	Meridian	2 Jul 1827
Hugh	32	M	...	Ireland	United States	Carolina Ann	24 Oct 1825
James	30	M	Farmer	G. Britain	U. States	St. George	7 Jun 1828
Jas.	5	M		G. Britain	U. States	London	23 Sep 1828
John	24	M	Farmer	England	U. States	Oglethorpe	9 Nov 1824
Larry	25	M	Weaver	Ireland	United States	Princess Charlotte	26 Apr 1827
Lawrence	8	M	Farmer	Scotland	U. States	Orozimbo	7 Jul 1825

NAMES OF PASSENGERS	AGE	SEX	OCCUPATIONS	COUNTRY TO WHICH THEY BELONG	COUNTRY THEY INTEND TO INHABIT	SHIPS/DATES OF ARRIVAL	
MAGUIRE (cont'd)							
Lu...	22 6/12	M	Labourer	Ireland	U. States	Virginia	20 Jun 1825
M.	25	M	Merchant	United States	United States	Potomac	8 Dec 1826
Mathias	2	M	Farmer	Ireland	U. States	Orozimbo	7 Jul 1825
Michael	30	M	Farmer	Great Brittain	U. States	Hibernia	8 Jul 1823
Nancy	24	F		Great Brittain	U. States	Hibernia	8 Jul 1823
Owen	20	M	Weaver	Ireland	United States	Princess Charlotte	26 Apr 1827
Thomas	10	M	None	Ireland	United States	Trident	18 Jul 1827
Thomas	24	M	...	Ireland	United States	Carolina Ann	24 Oct 1825
Thos.	22	M	Farmer	Scotland	U. States	Orozimbo	7 Jul 1825
Unna	22	F		Ireland	New York	Vigilant	6 May 1822
MAGURE, Francis	43	M	Shoe Maker	G. Britain	U. States	London	23 Sep 1828
MAGWIRE,							
Catharin, Miss	20	F				Hercules	19 Jun 1821
Peter, her							
Brother [Peter]	12					Hercules	19 Jun 1821
MAHAD, Peggy	27	F		Great Brittian	United States	Carolina Augusta	2 Dec 1828
MAHADY, Bridget	20	M	Labourer	Ireland	United States	William & Henry	19 Jul 1822
Michael	22	M	Labourer	Ireland	United States	William & Henry	19 Jul 1822
MAHAFFEY, Joseph	22	M	Mason	Ireland	Ohio	Concordia	12 Oct 1826
MAHAFFY, John	30		Farmer	Ireland		Westmoreland	1 Aug 1826
MAHAN, Biddy	24	F	Labourer	Ireland	U. States	Wanderer	30 Sep 1828
Dennis	44	M	Paver	Great Britain	America	Remittance	24 Aug 1825
Eliza	1		Child	Great Britain	United States	Mount Vernon	17 Jun 1825
John	3		Child	Great Britain	United States	Mount Vernon	17 Jun 1825
John	18	M	Labourer	Ireland	United States	Trident	16 May 1826
John	27	M	Labourer	Great Britain	United States	Mount Vernon	17 Jun 1825
Martin	24	M	Farmer	Great Britain	United States	Eliza Barker	3 Jul 1826
Mary	26	F	None	Great Britain	United States	Mount Vernon	17 Jun 1825
Peter	36	M	Farmer	Great Britain	United States	Mount Vernon	17 Jun 1825
MAHAR, John	30	M	Labourer	Ireland	United States	Matvina	19 Oct 1826
MAHARG, James	30		Mariner	United States		John Dickinson	5 Apr 1821
*Died Jan. 15, 1821, in the Lough of Belfast							
MAHAVEN, Bridget	26	M	None	England	United States	India	8 Jun 1827
MAHEN, A.	22	M		Dublin	U. States	Hibernia	26 Oct 1826
Charles	1	M		France	United States	Montano	5 May 1828
Clovis	8	M		France	United States	Montano	5 May 1828
Eleanore	33	F		France	United States	Montano	5 May 1828
Elisa	9	F		France	United States	Montano	5 May 1828
Jean	40	M	Joiner	France	United States	Montano	5 May 1828
Marie	40	F		France	United States	Montano	5 May 1828
Nicolas	44	M	Joiner	France	United States	Montano	5 May 1828
MAHER, Bridget	23	F		Great Britain	United States	Mary Howland	19 Jul 1827
Eliza	18	F	Servant	Ireland	United States	Trio	31 Oct 1827
James	30	M	Labourer	Great Britain	United States	Mary Howland	19 Jul 1827
John	28	M	Blacksmith	Ireland	United States	Jubilee	1 Oct 1828
Margaret	11	F	Servant	Ireland	United States	Trio	31 Oct 1827
Martin	32 1/12	M	Saddler	Ireland	United States	London	6 Feb 1829
MAHEW, Ann	73	F		France	United States	India	4 Aug 1826
M.	61	M	Gardner	France	United States	India	4 Aug 1826
MAHIN, James	35		Farmer	Great Brittain	Great Brittain	Commerce	14 Mar 1823
MAHINS, Margaret	30	F	Merchant	Great Britain	U. States	William Thompson	1 May 1827
William	20	M	Merchant	Great Britain	U. States	William Thompson	1 May 1827
MAHLER, John R.	23	M	Mercht.	Switzerland	U. States	Sully	15 Jul 1829
Philip	29	M	Goldsmith	France	U. States	Edward Bopnnaffe	30 Jul 1829
MAHO, Timothy	22	M	Labourer	England	U. States	Rising States	20 Sep 1828
MAHOFFY, Henry	25			Great Britan	United States	Newry	11 Jul 1827
John	30			Great Britan	United States	Newry	11 Jul 1827
Saml.	27			Great Britan	United States	Newry	11 Jul 1827
MAHON, Biddy	20	F		Gt. Britain		Dalhouse Castle	13 May 1828
Catherine	22	F	None	Ireland	United States	Jubilee	13 Jul 1829
Hugh	20	M	Labourer	England	United States	John Wells	22 May 1826

NAMES OF PASSENGERS	AGE	SEX	OCCUPATIONS	COUNTRY TO WHICH THEY BELONG	COUNTRY THEY INTEND TO INHABIT	SHIPS/DATES OF ARRIVAL	
MAHON (cont'd)							
James	27	M	Farmer	Ireland	United States	Asia	29 Jul 1829
James	33	M	Farmer, Labourer or Spinster	Ireland	U. States	Meteor	4 Oct 1827
John	22	M	Farmer	Ireland	United States	Dublin Packet	22 Apr 1822
Luter	33	M	Labourer			Lady of the Lake	23 Aug 1828
Margt.	27	F	Spinster	St. Johns, N.B.	United States	Antioch	21 Sep 1827
Mary	19	F	None	Great Britain	United States	William Dawson	18 Jun 1827
Mary	20	F		Great Britain	United States	Robert Fulton	27 Jun 1822
Mary	34	F				Lady of the Lake	23 Aug 1828
Michael	21	M		G. Britain	U. States	Dalhouse Castle	12 Sep 1828
Pat	24	M	Labourer	Great Britain	United States	William Dawson	18 Jun 1827
Patrick	33	M	Labourer	Ireland	United States	Lord Wellington	28 May 1827
Patt	28	M	Labourer	Ireland	United States	Jubilee	13 Jul 1829
Walton	17	M	Hosler & Tailor	Great Britain	United States	Aspasia	16 Jul 1828
MAHONEY, Anne	30	F		Ireland	United States	Trio	13 Jun 1827
Catherine	12	F		Ireland	United States	Clothier	22 Nov 1827
Elen	8	F		Ireland	United States	Clothier	22 Nov 1827
Elr.	32	M	Laborer	Ireland	United States	Trio	13 Jun 1827
Joana	20	F		Ireland	United States	Trio	13 Jun 1827
John	2	M		Ireland	United States	Clothier	22 Nov 1827
Margt.		F		Ireland	United States	Trio	13 Jun 1827
Mary	5	F		Ireland	United States	Trio	13 Jun 1827
Mary	40	F		Ireland	United States	Clothier	22 Nov 1827
Patrick	40	M	Labourer	Ireland	United States	Clothier	22 Nov 1827
Timy.	35	M	Laborer	Ireland	United States	Trio	13 Jun 1827
William	37	M	Plaisterer	Ireland	U.S.A.	Hudson	21 Aug 1829
MAHONY, Abby	60	F	Wash Woman	Ireland	U. States	Albion	11 May 1827
Ann	25	F		County of Cork, Ireland	New York City	Thorny Close	3 May 1826
Catharine	18	F	Wash Woman	Ireland	U. States	Albion	11 May 1827
Ellen	16	F		Ireland	United States	Trio	2 Oct 1828
Francis	23	M	Laborer	Great Britain	United States	Samuel Wright	12 Oct 1829
James	11	M		Great Britian	United States	Columbia	21 Jan 1828
Jane	15	F		Ireland	United States	Trio	2 Oct 1828
Jeremiah	4	M		Ireland	U.S. America	Traveller	10 Sep 1827
Jeremiah	29	M	Weaver	County of Cork, Ireland	New York City	Thorny Close	3 May 1826
Joanna	4	F		Ireland	United States	Trio	2 Oct 1828
John	2	M		County of Cork, Ireland	New York City	Thorny Close	3 May 1826
John	10	M		Ireland	United States	Trio	2 Oct 1828
John	34	M	Gentleman	Ireland	America	Liverpool	31 Aug 1827
Judy	6	F		Ireland	United States	Trio	2 Oct 1828
Julia Ann	4	F		County of Cork, Ireland	New York City	Thorny Close	3 May 1826
Martin	2	M		Ireland	U.S. America	Traveller	10 Sep 1827
Mary	9	F		Ireland	United States	Trio	2 Oct 1828
Mary	14	F	Wash Woman	Ireland	U. States	Albion	11 May 1827
Mary	22	F		Ireland	U.S. America	Traveller	10 Sep 1827
Mary	30	F		Ireland	United States	Trio	2 Oct 1828
Mary	43	F		Ireland	U.S. America	Traveller	10 Sep 1827
Michael	7	M		Ireland	United States	Trio	2 Oct 1828
Norey	5	F		Ireland	United States	Trio	2 Oct 1828
Pat	27	M	Laborer	Ireland	United States	Trio	13 Jun 1827
Thady	2	M		Ireland	United States	Trio	2 Oct 1828
Thos.	25	M	Weaver	Ireland	U.S. America	Traveller	10 Sep 1827
Timothy	38	M	Labourer	Ireland	United States	Trio	2 Oct 1828
Timothy	40	M	Weaver	Ireland	U.S. America	Traveller	10 Sep 1827
MAHOON, Daniel	2/12	M	Child	Ireland	United States	St. Michael	21 Aug 1824
Johanna	28	F	Wife	Ireland	United States	St. Michael	21 Aug 1824
Thomas	30	M	Laborer	Ireland	United States	St. Michael	21 Aug 1824
MAHOWLY, W.	22	M		Ireland	U. States	St. Michael	26 Oct 1824
MAIBELLE, A.	20	M	Hair dresser	U.S.A.	U.S.A.	Bayard	25 Aug 1829
MAIER, Joseph	23	M	Shoemaker	Germany	Pensylvania	James Noble	27 Aug 1827
MAIGHAN, Edward	40	M	Weaver	England		Britannia	20 Jun 1827
James	35	M	Weaver	England		Britannia	20 Jun 1827

NAMES OF PASSENGERS	AGE	SEX	OCCUPATIONS	COUNTRY TO WHICH THEY BELONG	COUNTRY THEY INTEND TO INHABIT	SHIPS/DATES OF ARRIVAL	
MAIGHAN (cont'd)							
Mary	32	F		England		Britannia	20 Jun 1827
MAIKSINS, Mary	25	F	None	Great Britain		Moro Castle	6 Jul 1827
Wm.	29	M	Labourer	Great Britain		Moro Castle	6 Jul 1827
MAILLAN, Thomas H.	30	M	Sailor	United States	United States	New Packet	20 Oct 1827
*distressed Seaman							
MAILLARD, Edmond	20			France	New York	Desdemona	12 Jun 1826
Francis	88	M	French Officer	France	U. States	Stephania	24 Jul 1820
James	21	M		England	England	Pleiades	13 Nov 1826
M.	29	M	Merchant	France	U. States	Manchester Packet	23 May 1822
MAILLE, J. B.	50	M	Merchant	France	France	Savannah	24 Apr 1828
MAILLIARD, E.	27	M	Soldier	U. States	U. States	Quesnel	6 Sep 1824
M. A.	19	F	Wife	U. States	U. States	Quesnel	6 Sep 1824
MAIN, Betsey	42	F		Nova Scotia	U. States	Hope	9 Nov 1824
John	46	M	Stone Cutter	Nova Scotia	U. States	Hope	9 Nov 1824
Ruth	32	F	Nothing	G. Britan	U. States	William Neilson	26 Jul 1828
Thomas	22	M	Jeweller	Scotland	U.S.A.	Hudson	21 Aug 1829
William	25	M	Labourer	Scotland	United States	Mary & Susan	5 Aug 1828
MAINE, Wm.	22	M	Engraver			Hector	11 Sep 1820
MAINHARD, Frs.	25	M	Merchant	Germany	U. States	Louisa	21 Aug 1824
MAINON, C. J.	37	M	Basket Maker	France	United States	Howard	19 May 1826
Wm.	32	F	Basket Maker	France	United States	Howard	19 May 1826
MAINTAIN, John Stephen	24	M	Merchant	France	America	Mercury	2 Feb 1825
MAIR, Alexr.	25	M	Surgeon	Gt. Britain	U. States	Napolean	26 Sep 1828
Andrw.	40	M	...	England	Canada	William Thompson	10 May 1825
Emma	19	F		Gt. Britain	U. States	Napolean	26 Sep 1828
George	23	M	Stone cutter	Great Britain	United States	Rosina	28 May 1827
Hugh	30	M	Clergyman	Scotland		Zamoa	5 Nov 1828
Janet	12	F	None	Scotland	United States	Washington	2 Oct 1828
Janet	35	F	None	Scotland	United States	Washington	2 Oct 1828
John	4	M	None	Scotland	United States	Washington	2 Oct 1828
Matthw.	35	M	Comber	Scotland	United States	Washington	2 Oct 1828
MAIRET, Arnold	24 5/12	M	Gentleman	Swizerland		Hercules	15 Jul 1822
Chas.	28	M	Merchant	Switzerland	U. States	Seneca	14 May 1821
Hy.	27	M	Mercht.	Switzerland	U.S.	Edward Quesnel	21 Apr 1827
Julius	22	M	Mercht.	Switzerland	N. York	Canada	1 Nov 1823
Pierre	29	M	Farmer	France	France	Sully	15 Jul 1829
MAIRS, Levy	20	M	Merchant	Frankfort	U. States	Minerva	24 Sep 1821
MAIS, John C.	23	M	Gentleman	Isle of Jamaica	England	Canada	4 Oct 1824
MAISAT, Jno.	25	M	Printer	Massachusetts	U. States	Abigail	17 Sep 1822
MAISON, Augustine	16	M	Apprentice	America	U. States	Brutus	21 May 1824
John A., Mr.	40	M	Merchant	America	America	Henry	19 Jun 1825
Mary	25	F	Farmer	England	U. States	Lewis	1 Jul 1820
MAISSIN, A.	22	M	Merchant	France	U. States	Asia	5 Jul 1823
MAISTERY, Robt.	25	M	Mason	Scotland	U.S.	Curler	19 Jul 1828
MAITAN, Sarrah	15	F	Spinster	Ireland	United States	Fabius	4 Jun 1828
MAITEN, Eugene	19	M	Mechanic	Martinique	U. States	Govr. Von Scholten	23 Apr 1825
MAITHAIS, Jos.	2	M	Baker	Switzerland	U.S.	C. Amelia	30 Jun 1828
MAITIN, William	42	M	Plasterer	England	United States	Dalhouse Castle	6 Sep 1827
MAITINE, A.	14	M	Merchant	U. States	U.S.	Ambuscade	14 Mar 1820
MAITLAND, Alice	42		None	Manchester, England	Great Britain	Franklin	22 Jun 1827
Ann M.	24	F	None	U. States	U. States	Canada	6 Jun 1825
David	24 5/12	M	Merchant	America	America	Elias Burger	19 Dec 1820
E. S.	10	F	None	U. States	U. States	Canada	6 Jun 1825
E. S.	38	F	None	U. States	U. States	Canada	6 Jun 1825
Jane C.	23	F	None	U. States	U. States	Canada	6 Jun 1825
Jennet	8	F	None	U. States	U. States	Canada	6 Jun 1825
Jos.	20	M				Ann Maria	29 Nov 1821
L.	32	M	Merchant	England	England	Britannia	5 Nov 1828
Martha C.	18	F	None	U. States	U. States	Canada	6 Jun 1825
Robt.	58	M	Gent.	Gt. Brittain	U. States	Canada	6 Jun 1825
Robt. L.	7	M	None	U. States	U. States	Canada	6 Jun 1825
Sarah M.	21	F	None	U. States	U. States	Canada	6 Jun 1825
Wm., Mr.	58	M	Merchant	Gt. Britain	Gt. Britain	Pacific	22 May 1826
Wm. C.	17	M	None	U. States	U. States	Canada	6 Jun 1825

NAMES OF PASSENGERS	AGE	SEX	OCCUPATIONS	COUNTRY TO WHICH THEY BELONG	COUNTRY THEY INTEND TO INHABIT	SHIPS/DATES OF ARRIVAL	
MAITZOLF, Catharina	12	F		France	America, U.N.S.	Great Britain	3 Aug 1829
Elizabeth	48	F		France	America, U.N.S.	Great Britain	3 Aug 1829
Jaques	19	M	Wheelwright	France	America, U.N.S.	Great Britain	3 Aug 1829
Jaques	49	M	Carpenter	France	America, U.N.S.	Great Britain	3 Aug 1829
Michl.	14	M		France	America, U.N.S.	Great Britain	3 Aug 1829
MAJENNESS, Henry, Jur.	20	M	Labr.	Ireland	New York	Atlantic	8 May 1828
MAJILHURST, Richd.	25	M	Weaver	England	U. States	Severn	12 Oct 1826
MAJOHN, R., Jr.	18	M	Weaver	Ireland	United States	Josephine	30 Apr 1828
MAJOR, Alexander	13	...	...	Ireland	United States	Carolina Ann	24 Oct 1825
John	16	M	Labourer	Ireland	United States	Fabius	31 Jul 1829
Nathl.	15	M	Weaver	Armory	N. York	Favourite	8 Oct 1823
Robert	47	M	Butcher	England	Pensilvania	Angelica	18 Aug 1823
Saml.	37	M	Mercht.	England	U. States	Pacific	20 Aug 1825
Thomas	...0	M	Labourer	Ireland	U. States	Josephine	27 Jul 1825
MAKAY, Hugh	37		Clerk	Montreal		Buffalo	27 Mar 1820
MAKEL, Christiana	14	F	Farmer	Holland	U. States	Don Quixote	25 Oct 1828
MAKENZIE, J. J.	30	M	Merchant	Great Britain	Great Britain	John Jay	8 May 1828
MAKIN, Mary	18	F	Spinster	Ireland	United States	Dublin Packet	13 Oct 1828
MAL, John	25	M	Merchant	France	U.S.	Helen	3 May 1828
MALABEL, —	45	M	Merchant	France	U. States	Retrieve	10 Jan 1823
MALACHY, Joseph	35	M	Merchant	Gt. Britain	England	Excel	21 Apr 1828
MALADY, William	24	M	Labourer	Ireland	United States	Jubilee	12 May 1828
MALAGON, Elar	30	F	Wife	Ireland	U. States	Meteor	19 Jul 1828
Mary	6	F	Child	Ireland	U. States	Meteor	19 Jul 1828
MALALLY, Anna	38	F	his wiffe [Richard]	Ireland	New York	Lady Hunter	14 Mar 1826
John	13	M	their child [Richard and Anna]	Ireland	New York	Lady Hunter	14 Mar 1826
Michael	11	M	their child [Richard and Anna]	Ireland	New York	Lady Hunter	14 Mar 1826
Richard	48	M	Laborer	Ireland	New York	Lady Hunter	14 Mar 1826
Richd., Jur.	15	M	their child [Richard and Anna]	Ireland	New York	Lady Hunter	14 Mar 1826
MALAN, Francis	17	M	Farmer	Ireland	America	Farmer	4 Aug 1825
John	21	M	Sawyer	Ireland	U. States	Lima	5 Aug 1829
MALARCHY, Margt.	18		Spinster	Ireland	United States	Robert Burns	18 Jun 1821
MALAUGHTY, Mary	51			Longford	Boston	Peru	30 May 1828
MALAY, Edward	25	M	Labourer	Ireland	America	Otter	17 Mar 1828
MALBONE, Elizabeth	24	F		England	United States	Mount Vernon	9 Jun 1823
Michael	24	M	Gentleman	England	United States	Mount Vernon	9 Jun 1823
MALBY, Thos.	22	M	Weaver	G. Britain	U. States	Great Britain	6 Sep 1828
MALCHIN, Thomas	28	M		England	United States	Eliza Grant	6 Oct 1828
MALCOLM, James	28	M	Farmer	Ireland	New York	Governor Fenner	23 Jul 1829
Jno.	40			Scotland		Anacreon	7 Sep 1827
John	31	M	[Salver?]	Scotland	New York	Thames	6 Oct 1820
Robt.	30	M		Scotland	New York	Joseph Hume	26 Oct 1829
MALCOM, Andrew	28	M	Mill Wright	Great Britain	United States	Brutus	6 May 1828
Geo.	21	M	Labourer	Scotland	United States	Tom	2 Jul 1827
MALCOMSON, John	16	M	Clerk	Ireland	U. States	Josephine	7 May 1827
Josh.	24		Merchant	Ireland	United States	Carolina Ann	12 Sep 1823
MALCON, Agnes	5	F	Taylor	Argyle (Tedland) Scotland	United States	Jean Hastie	27 Jul 1829
Duncan	11	M	Taylor	Argyle (Tedland) Scotland	United States	Jean Hastie	27 Jul 1829
Eliza	17	F	Taylor	Argyle (Tedland) Scotland	United States	Jean Hastie	27 Jul 1829
Euphemia	5	F	Taylor	Argyle (Tedland) Scotland	United States	Jean Hastie	27 Jul 1829
James	9	M	Taylor	Argyle (Tedland) Scotland	United States	Jean Hastie	27 Jul 1829
Jno.	49	M	Labourer	Argyle (Tedland) Scotland	United States	Jean Hastie	27 Jul 1829
Margaret	16	F	Taylor	Argyle (Tedland) Scotland	United States	Jean Hastie	27 Jul 1829
Margaret	48	F	Labourer	Argyle (Tedland) Scotland	United States	Jean Hastie	27 Jul 1829
Peter	21	M	Taylor	Argyle (Tedland) Scotland	United States	Jean Hastie	27 Jul 1829
Will	7	M	Taylor	Argyle (Tedland) Scotland	United States	Jean Hastie	27 Jul 1829

NAMES OF PASSENGERS	AGE	SEX	OCCUPATIONS	COUNTRY TO WHICH THEY BELONG	COUNTRY THEY INTEND TO INHABIT	SHIPS/DATES OF ARRIVAL	
MALDEN, E.	20	F	Servant	Ireland	United States	Josephine	30 Apr 1828
MALE, Henry	21	M	Merchant	Netherlands	Netherlands	Columbia	3 Apr 1826
Henry W.	25	M	Gent	Netherland	U. States	Charlemagne	19 Sep 1828
MALEN, Ann	19	F	Servant	Ireland	United States	Carolina Ann	11 Dec 1826
MALENA, Pat	30		Labourer	Ireland	New York	Marcella	18 May 1827
MALEY, Michl.	18	M	Farmer	Great Britain	United States	Atlantic	28 May 1827
MALFRET, Anthony	47	M	Glazier	France	New York	Radius	7 Jul 1821
MALFRET, Elizabeth	53	F		Ireland	New York	Radius	7 Jul 1821
MALHILL, Ann	2	F		U. States	U. States	Canada	19 Sep 1828
David	8	M		U. States	U. States	Canada	19 Sep 1828
Joshua	4	M		U. States	U. States	Canada	19 Sep 1828
Rebecca, Mrs.	26	F		U. States	U. States	Canada	19 Sep 1828
Wm.	6	M		U. States	U. States	Canada	19 Sep 1828
MALHUE, Chas.	22	M	Tanner	France	United States	Stephania	24 Mar 1828
MALIBRAN, Charles	9	M	boy	Cuba	U. States	James Monroe	8 Sep 1824
Jos. Fernando	11	M	Gentleman	Trinidad in Cuba	United States	Mechanic	17 Aug 1822
MALIE, James	23	M	Labourer	Ireland	United States	Commerce	13 Jun 1828
MALIGH, Peter	30	M	None	Ireland	U. States	William Byrnes	24 Apr 1827
Thoms	3	M	None	Ireland	U. States	William Byrnes	24 Apr 1827
MALISS, R.	16	M	Merchant	England	U. States	Caseo	26 Apr 1828
MALISSIGER, Adolphan	31	F	Nurse	Holland	U. States	America	22 Sep 1826
MALKABLE, Margt.	17	F	None	Ireland	United States	Dalhouse Castle	21 Aug 1829
MALKIN, John	29		Baker & Druggist	Great Britain	United States	Thomas Dickason	29 Aug 1828
MALLAR, Jo...n	21	M	Sawyer	Ireland	New York	Lima	5 Aug 1829
MALLARD, Edward	28	M	Merchant	Great Britain		Robert Fulton	9 Jul 1823
Edward	32	M	Gent		United States	Cosmo	21 Aug 1828
Edwd.	27	M	Merchant	England	U. States	New York	4 Nov 1824
Edwd.	32	M	Merchant	England	U. States	New York	8 Mar 1825
Elizabeth	23	F		England	United States	Mount Vernon	9 Jun 1823
George	2 8/12	M	Farmer	Switzerland	America	Henry	17 May 1828
George	5 5/12	M	Farmer	Switzerland	America	Henry	17 May 1828
George	26 7/12	M	Farmer	Switzerland	America	Henry	17 May 1828
Mary	25 9/12	F	Farmer	Switzerland	America	Henry	17 May 1828
MALLAS, John	50	M	Merchant	N. Haven	U. States	Shepherdess	15 Jul 1824
MALLEAGH, John	20	M	Labourer	Great Britain		Moro Castle	6 Jul 1827
MALLEN, Jane	20	F	Servant	Dublin		Nimrod	21 Sep 1820
Mary	22	F	Servant	Ireland	United States	Josephine	30 Apr 1828
MALLER, Abrm.	29	M	Gentleman	Germany	New York	Mary Livingston	2 Nov 1826
MALLET, Mary Anne	36	F	Lady	France	U.S.	Montano	24 Jun 1823
William	35	M	Merchant	England	England	Buck	24 Jul 1821
Wm.	40	M	Merchant	England	U. States	Elizabeth	31 Dec 1821
MALLETS, Jean	23	M	Shoe Maker	Switzerland	U.S.	C. Amelia	30 Jun 1828
Salomn	27	M	Seamstress	Switzerland	U.S.	C. Amelia	30 Jun 1828
MALLETT, John	26	M	Gentleman	France	U. States	John London	26 Jun 1822
T.	26	M	Farmer	France	United States	Great Britain	18 Sep 1826
MALLIEW, Anne	20	F		Ireland	United States	Romulus	24 Jun 1826
MALLIGAN, Terry	50	M	Weaver	Ireland	United States	Carolina Ann	14 May 1827
MALLIN, Hugh	18	M	Spinster	Ireland	United States	Fabius	4 Jun 1828
Margret	20	F		Ireland	United States	Fabius	4 Jun 1828
Owen	25	M	Tanner	Ireland	United States	Fabius	4 Jun 1828
MALLINSON, Charles	33	M	Weaver	Yorkshire	Pennsylvania	Curler	7 Jul 1827
MALLON, Bridget	23	F	Spinster	Ireland	U. States	Josephine	7 May 1827
James	...0	...	...	...	United States	Criterion	27 Jun 1827
John	20 7/12	M	Labourer	Ireland	United States	Atlantic	21 Jul 1827
Owen	20 3/12	M	Labourer	Ireland	United States	Atlantic	21 Jul 1827
MALLONE, Jno. C.	24	M	Merchant	Martinique	Martinique	Jane	27 Aug 1824
MALLONY, Cathr.	40	F		England	U. States	Rising States	20 Sep 1828
Danl.	5	M		England	U. States	Rising States	20 Sep 1828
Elizabeth	54	F	Labourer	Ireland	U. States	Virginia	20 Jun 1825
H.	20	F		England	U. States	Rising States	20 Sep 1828
May	13	F		England	U. States	Rising States	20 Sep 1828
MALLOREY, Matthew	34	M	Bricklayer	Great Britain	United States	Penelope	11 Jun 1827
Rose	5	F	None	Great Britain	United States	Penelope	11 Jun 1827
Rose	34	F	None	Great Britain	United States	Penelope	11 Jun 1827
MALLORY, Lawrence	17		Labourer	Ireland	United States	Geo. Canning	5 Jun 1828
Wm.	21			Ireland	United States	Geo. Canning	5 Jun 1828

NAMES OF PASSENGERS	AGE	SEX	OCCUPATIONS	COUNTRY TO WHICH THEY BELONG	COUNTRY THEY INTEND TO INHABIT	SHIPS/DATES OF ARRIVAL	
MALLOW, Joshua	27	M	Clothier	Great Britain	United States	Colossus	1 Nov 1826
MALLOY, Caroline	6	F	Paper Maker	Ireland	U. States	Margarett Scott	22 Aug 1827
John	1	F	Paper Maker	Ireland	U. States	Margarett Scott	22 Aug 1827
Judah	25	F	Spinster	Ireland	United States	Sarah Ann	18 Nov 1826
Mary Ann	9	F	Paper Maker	Ireland	U. States	Margarett Scott	22 Aug 1827
Sophia	2	F	Paper Maker	Ireland	U. States	Margarett Scott	22 Aug 1827
Sophia	30	F	Paper Maker	Ireland	U. States	Margarett Scott	22 Aug 1827
Susan	5	F	Paper Maker	Ireland	U. States	Margarett Scott	22 Aug 1827
Willm.	34	M	Paper Maker	Ireland	U. States	Margarett Scott	22 Aug 1827
MALLVY, John	23	M	Farmer	Ireland	U. States	Henry Kneeland	27 Jul 1825
MALLY, John	20	M	Labourer	G. Britain	U. States	Mary & Harriot	8 Sep 1828
John	30	M	None	Great Britain	United States	Eliza Barker	3 Jul 1826
William	24	M	Butcher	Great Brit.	Ohio	Gov. Griswald	3 Jul 1820
MALON, Marge	18	F	Spinster			Commerce	22 Jun 1825
MALONE, Catharine	20	F	Labourer	Ireland	United States	Hope & Esther	17 Oct 1827
Edward	29			Ireland		Anacreon	7 Sep 1827
Jane	9/12			Ireland		Anacreon	7 Sep 1827
Jerremia	40	M				Ambuscade	1 Jul 1820
John	26	M	Labourer	Ireland	United States	Hope & Esther	17 Oct 1827
M.	25	M	Farmer	U. States	U. States	Infant	10 Jul 1821
Mary	23			Ireland		Anacreon	7 Sep 1827
Patty	25	F	Labourer	Ireland	United States	Hope & Esther	17 Oct 1827
Rosanna	21	F	Married	Ireland	America	Hannah	8 Nov 1821
W. H.	2	M		Ireland	America	Hannah	8 Nov 1821
Wm.	22	M	Laborer	Ireland	United States	Ann Maria	18 Dec 1827
MALONEY, Anastatia	5	F				John	16 Oct 1820
Charlotte	28	F				John	16 Oct 1820
Cornelius	30	M	Bluedyer	Ireland	United States	Meteor	19 Aug 1829
Jane	3/12	M		Ireland	United States	Meteor	19 Aug 1829
Jane	30	F		Ireland	United States	Meteor	19 Aug 1829
Jeremiah	32	M	Blacksmith	N. York		John	16 Oct 1820
John	3/12	M		Ireland	United States	Meteor	19 Aug 1829
John	12	M	Labourer	Ireland	United S.	Hanford	19 Aug 1828
Mary	4	F		Ireland	United States	Meteor	19 Aug 1829
Mary	10	F	Spinster	Ireland	United S.	Hanford	19 Aug 1828
Patrick	25	M		Ireland	U. States	Howard	25 Jul 1823
Philip	17	M	Labourer	Ireland	United S.	Hanford	19 Aug 1828
Thomas	5/12	M				John	16 Oct 1820
MALONY, Ann	15	F	Spinster	G. Britain	U. States	Hanford	10 Jun 1828
Ann	50	F		Ireland	United S.	Hanford	19 Aug 1828
Daniel	30	M	Farmer	England	U. States	Montgomery	18 Oct 1828
James	25	M	Carpenter	Great Britain	United States	Hopes Delight	26 Aug 1829
Jeremiah	40	M	Mill Whoright	U.S.	U.S.	Frances	21 Jul 1827
John	20	M	None	Ireland	U. States	Criterion	23 May 1826
Jonas	61	M	Laborer	Ireland	America	Parrington	9 Jun 1827
Nathaniel	16	M	Servant	Bermuda	Bermuda	Magnet	10 Jul 1820
MALOY, Bridget	30	F		Great Brittian	United States	Carolina Augusta	2 Dec 1828
Charles	3	M		Great Brittian	United States	Carolina Augusta	2 Dec 1828
John	12	M		Great Brittian	United States	Carolina Augusta	2 Dec 1828
John	30	M	Lawyer	U. States	U. States	United States	11 Sep 1828
Mary	50	F	Servant	Ireland	America	Josephine	24 Jul 1826
Sarah	8	F		Great Brittian	United States	Carolina Augusta	2 Dec 1828
MALRAIN, John	2	M	...	Ireland	United States	General Putnam	20 Jun 1825
Mary Ann	25	F	...	Ireland	United States	General Putnam	20 Jun 1825
MALREWS, Mary	6	F		Ireland	U. States	Nancy	16 Aug 1822
MALRICH, John	61	M	Merchant	Switzerland	United States	Osprey	2 Sep 1824
MALRONY, Nancy	13	F		Ireland	United States	Trio	2 Oct 1828
MALSEED, Jane	18	F	Spinster	Great Britain	United States	Agnes	12 Apr 1821
John	22	M	Merchant	Great Britain	United States	Agnes	12 Apr 1821
Wm.	18	M	None	Great Britain	United States	Agnes	12 Apr 1821
MALSLAY, Peter	28	M	Farmer	Ireland	New Orleans	Commerce	24 Sep 1823
MALSON, —, Mrs.	26	F	None	Vera Cruz	U. States	Eliza	11 Apr 1826
—, Mrs.	30	F		U. States	U. States	Ranger	15 Jan 1827
John	2	M		U. States	U. States	Ranger	15 Jan 1827
Morris	1	M		U. States	U. States	Ranger	15 Jan 1827

NAMES OF PASSENGERS	AGE	SEX	OCCUPATIONS	COUNTRY TO WHICH THEY BELONG	COUNTRY THEY INTEND TO INHABIT	SHIPS/DATES OF ARRIVAL	
MALT, —, his Wife & two Children	36	M	Shoemaker	Swisse	United States	Deux Ernest	29 Dec 1827
*landed at Lewiston, Delw.							
MALTAUR, Catrania	28	F		France	United States	New England	29 Aug 1828
MALTBY, Jos.	28	M	Manufacturer	England	U. States	Exchange	4 Jan 1823
MALTE, H.	30	M	Merchant	L'pool	N. York	James Cropper	4 Feb 1824
MALTIN, John J.	59	M	Planter	G. Britan	Antigua	Canada	27 Sep 1826
MALTITZ, D., Baron, Secy. of Russian Ligation	27	M	Secy. Rusian Legation	Rusia	Rusia	Robert Edwards	21 Sep 1821
MALURKEY, David	19	M	Weaver	Ireland	United States	Trident	17 May 1825
MALVAREZ, Domingo	27	M	Merchant	Spain	Spain	Dromo	28 Feb 1829
MALVEEN, Charles	11			Scotland	United States	Camillus	3 May 1828
Davd.	56		Mason	Scotland	United States	Camillus	3 May 1828
David	15		Mason	Scotland	United States	Camillus	3 May 1828
Jane	46			Scotland	United States	Camillus	3 May 1828
Saml.	14			Scotland	United States	Camillus	3 May 1828
MALVEL, Charles	32	M	Stone Cutter	Scotland	Scotland	Sarah G.	28 Nov 1827
James	30	M	Stone Cutter	Scotland	Scotland	Sarah G.	28 Nov 1827
MAN, John	45	M	Labourer	Gt. Britain	U. States	Panthea	21 Jul 1825
Jonathan	24	M	Merchant	G. Britain	U. States	Canada	19 Sep 1828
Mary	35	F		U. States	United States	Acasta	25 Sep 1827
Philip	19	M	Merchant	Europe	United States	Braganza	30 Nov 1827
Thos.	14	M	Glass blower	Gt. Britain	U. States	Panthea	21 Jul 1825
MANAGAR, Henry	28	M	Weaver			Catherine	19 Aug 1825
MANAGER, Margaret	24	F				Catherine	19 Aug 1825
MANAGH, James	24	M	Wever	Ireland	United States	Fabius	4 Jun 1828
MANAGHAN, Wm.	11	M	Merchant	America	America	David	4 May 1825
Wm.	23		Wheelwright	Ireland	United States	Courier	15 Oct 1827
MANAGIN, Mary		F		Ireland	United States	Trio	2 Oct 1828
Peggy	22	F		Ireland	United States	Trio	2 Oct 1828
MANAHAN, —, Miss	10	F		U. States	U. States	Industry	1 Sep 1824
Anthony	26	M	Merchant	Ireland	United States	Dublin Packet	30 Apr 1821
Bridget	1	F		England	United States	Ganges	10 May 1828
Jas.	35	M	Farmer	England	United States	Ganges	10 May 1828
Jas.	37	M	Farmer	England	United States	Ganges	10 May 1828
Mary	12	F		England	United States	Ganges	10 May 1828
Mary	50	F	None	England	United States	India	8 Jun 1827
Michl.	10	M		England	United States	Ganges	10 May 1828
Rose	18	F	Spinster	Ireland	United States	Dublin Packet	22 Apr 1822
S., Mrs.	40	F	Lady	U. States	U. States	Industry	1 Sep 1824
William	25	M	Farmer	Ireland	United States	Dublin Packet	3 Sep 1822
MANAS, Frandis	23	M	Merchant	Havana	Havana	Robert Reade	9 Feb 1822
MANAVAIL, J. L.	30	M	Merchant	France	Havana	Ardent	2 Nov 1826
MANCEE, A.	37	M	Mendlew Painter	Italy		Aspasia	19 Jul 1823
MAND, David	40	M	Weaver	England	United States	Essex	23 May 1828
Robt.	20	M	Weaver	England	United States	Essex	23 May 1828
MANDEBLE, Miechael	18	M	Laborer			Plato	31 Oct 1829
MANDERELLE, H. D.	35	M	Merchant	N. York	U. States	William & Jane	20 Feb 1823
MANEGUET, Pierre	28	M	Merchant	Gaudaloupe	Gaudaloupe	Jane	13 Aug 1827
MANELY, Edmund, Dctr.	22	M	Doctor	England	United States	Leeds	4 Jun 1827
MANENDEZ, Manwel	23	M	Merchant	Spain	United States	Otter	25 Feb 1822
MANES, Cayetano	30	M	Mercht.	Spain	United States	Georgetown Packet	15 Nov 1823
MANET, Henry	28	M	Merchant	France	United States	Bayard	23 Mar 1826
MANEY, Moses E.	26	M	Merchant	Hamburg	U. States	Martha	4 Sep 1828
MANGE, Fran_ois	22	M	Merchant	Switzerland	U. States	Queen Mab	16 Mar 1825
Saml.		M	Gentleman			Frederick	18 Feb 1822
Saml.	22	M	Mercht.	Switzerland	Philadea.	Canada	1 Nov 1823
MANGELS, Salsar	1...	M	Sugar Baker	Germany	New York	Constitution	20 Aug 1825
MANGEN, Maurice	22	M	Labourer	Ireland	America	Wilson	16 May 1825
MANGER, C.	32	M	Farmer	France	U. States	Bayard	25 Apr 1828
Daniel	11	M	Carpenter	England	United States	Helen	5 Sep 1828
Jack	67	M		France	United States	Henri IV	2 Oct 1828
L.	36	M	Farmer	France	U. States	Bayard	25 Apr 1828
Wm.	27	M	Farmer	Great Britain	United States	William Dawson	18 Jun 1827
MANGETOW, John	34	M	Merchant	Cadiz	Havana	Sally Ann	11 Dec 1824
MANGHAM, John	20	M	Farmer	Ireland	United States	Dublin Packet	23 May 1828
MANHEAD, Alexander	38	M		England	England	Pleiades	13 Nov 1826

NAMES OF PASSENGERS	AGE	SEX	OCCUPATIONS	COUNTRY TO WHICH THEY BELONG	COUNTRY THEY INTEND TO INHABIT	SHIPS/DATES OF ARRIVAL	
MANICAN, Mary	20	F		Ireland	United States	Borneo	28 Aug 1828
MANIGOLT, John	39 4/12	M	Carpenter	Switzerland	United States	France	6 Oct 1828
Madelin	33 1/12	F	Carpenter	Switzerland	United States	France	6 Oct 1828
Madeline	1 2/12	F	Carpenter	Switzerland	United States	France	6 Oct 1828
MANINAN, Mary M.	19	F	Farmer	Ireland	United States	L. M. Pelham	25 Jun 1822
MANING, Eliza, Mrs.	36	F	Lady	Ireland	United States	Dublin Packet	6 Dec 1827
MANIORT, John	26	M	Servant	United States	New York, U.S.	Amity	31 Jan 1822
MANJET, Jacob	25	M	Farmer	United States	United States	Seine	21 Oct 1822
Mary	26	F		United States	United States	Seine	21 Oct 1822
MANKS, James	40	M	Merchant	England	New York	James Monroe	23 Aug 1822
William	34	M	Mercht.	England	Leeds	William Byrnes	14 Apr 1824
William	36	M	Merchant	Great Britain	United States	Hamilton	21 Nov 1826
MANLEY, —, Miss	25	F	Lady	England	U.S.A.	Bayard	25 Aug 1829
Charles	5	M		England	United States	Maria	3 Oct 1822
Charles	27	M	Painter	England	United States	Maria	3 Oct 1822
Charlot	26	F		England	United States	Maria	3 Oct 1822
George	3	M		England	United States	Maria	3 Oct 1822
Mary	1	F		England	United States	Maria	3 Oct 1822
MANLOVE, Dd.	30	M	Merchant	U. States	U. States	General Paez	17 Aug 1825
Edward	26	M	Merchant	G. Brittian	U. States	Pacific	19 Oct 1829
MANLY, Briget	40	F	Woman	Ireland	America	Erin	14 Feb 1820
Eliza	22	F	Servant	Great Britan	U. States	Cortes	13 Aug 1825
Helen	17		Spinster/Woman	Ireland	America	Erin	14 Feb 1820
James	54	M	Weaver	Ireland	United States	Dalhouse Castle	8 May 1827
Jane	15		Spinster/Woman	Ireland	America	Erin	14 Feb 1820
Leonora	10		Spinster/Woman	Ireland	America	Erin	14 Feb 1820
Walter	24	M	M...	Great Britain	U. States	Panthea	24 Mar 1825
MANN, Amos	2	M		G. Britain	U. States	George Clinton	10 Sep 1828
Andes	32		Gentleman	Columbia	Columbia	Triumph	23 Jul 1829
Ann	30	F		Ireland	U. States	Phocion	19 Sep 1822
Henry	45	F	Merchant	Germany	U.S.	Bordeaux	17 Jun 1825
Jabez	22	M		G. Britain	U. States	George Clinton	10 Sep 1828
Jacob	28	M	...	Wirtemburg	United States	Wade	29 Aug 1825
James	24	M	Labourer	Ireland	United States	Fabius	31 Jul 1829
Mary	20	F		G. Britain	U. States	George Clinton	10 Sep 1828
Monjo Johern	62 6/12	M	Priest	Spain	Spain	Virginia	8 Mar 1828
Rob.	30	M	Merchant	England	England	Macdonough	5 Jul 1823
Saml.	42	M	General dealer	United States	United States	Robert Edwards	3 Oct 1829
Sarah	30	F		England	U. States	Criterion	20 Nov 1823
Thos.	35	M	Cordwainer	Gt. Britain	United States	Robert Edwards	1 Jun 1826
W. ...	2	M	Bricklayer	Great Britian	United States	London	24 Jun 1823
Wm.	35	M	Jewellry	England	U. States	Criterion	20 Nov 1823
MANNA, Roger Tafentoz	17	M	Gentleman	Trinidad	Spain	Free Ocean	10 May 1826
MANNAHAN, John	30	M	Mechanic	Ireland	St. John, N.B.	Ann Maria	7 Aug 1826
MANNEN, Daniel	5	M	Child	Ireland	United States	Sarah Ann	18 Nov 1826
Jeremiah	45	M	Farmer	Ireland	United States	Sarah Ann	18 Nov 1826
Margaret	10	F	Child	Ireland	United States	Sarah Ann	18 Nov 1826
Mary	30	F	Wife	Ireland	United States	Sarah Ann	18 Nov 1826
MANNERING, Daniel	45		Painter	England		Helen	4 Aug 1829
David	11	M				Helen	4 Aug 1829
Elizabeth	8	F				Helen	4 Aug 1829
George	5	M				Helen	4 Aug 1829
Holan	3	M				Helen	4 Aug 1829
Jacob	12	F				Helen	4 Aug 1829
Mary	10	F				Helen	4 Aug 1829
Mary	44	F				Helen	4 Aug 1829
MANNERS, Elisa	30	M	Farmer	England	U.S. States	Splendid	14 Aug 1829
Harrit	10	M	Farmer	England	U.S. States	Splendid	14 Aug 1829
James	30	M	Farmer	England	U.S. States	Splendid	14 Aug 1829
John	7	M	Farmer	England	U.S. States	Splendid	14 Aug 1829
Mary	9	M	Farmer	England	U.S. States	Splendid	14 Aug 1829
Robt.	19	M	Barber	Gt. Britain		Corinthian	27 Oct 1829
MANNESSER, Mary	21	M	None	Great Britain	United States	Aspasia	16 Jul 1828
MANNIN, J.	10	F	Labourer	Ireland	U. States	Bellville	14 May 1827
Patrick	22	M	Shoemaker	England	United States	William	4 Oct 1822
MANNING, Alfred	22	M	Painter	England	U. States	Unity	5 Sep 1828
Ann	4	F				Hudson	23 Jul 1828
Chas.	20	M		England	U. States	Unity	5 Sep 1828
Corns.	48	M	Farmer	England	United States	Ganges	10 May 1828

NAMES OF PASSENGERS	AGE	SEX	OCCUPATIONS	COUNTRY TO WHICH THEY BELONG	COUNTRY THEY INTEND TO INHABIT	SHIPS/DATES OF ARRIVAL	
MANNING (cont'd)							
Danl.	8	M		England	United States	Ganges	10 May 1828
David	2	M				Hudson	23 Jul 1828
David	12	M		England	United States	Ganges	10 May 1828
Dennis	10	M		England	United States	Ganges	10 May 1828
Elizabeth	11	F				Hudson	23 Jul 1828
Elizabeth	30			England	Boston	Xenophon	25 Jul 1826
Hannah	6	F		England	United States	Ganges	10 May 1828
Hannah	8	F				Hudson	23 Jul 1828
Jams	6	M				Hudson	23 Jul 1828
Jas.	4	M		England	United States	Ganges	10 May 1828
Jas.	16	M		England	United States	Ganges	10 May 1828
John	14	M		England	United States	Ganges	10 May 1828
M., Mrs.	40	F		England		Hudson	23 Jul 1828
Margt.	35	F		England	United States	Ganges	10 May 1828
Martha	17	F				Hudson	23 Jul 1828
Mary	19	F		Ireland	United States	Trio	2 Oct 1828
Rebecca	30	F	Servant	St. Croix	U. States	Carlo	6 Oct 1827
Rebecca	38		Servant	St. Croix	St. Croix	Emelia	26 Jun 1828
Robert, Don	33	M	Merchant	Great Britain	United States	Mercid	21 Oct 1824
Thomas	13	M				Hudson	23 Jul 1828
Thomas, Master	14	M	Boy	Ireland	United States	Dublin Packet	6 Dec 1827
Timo.	2	M		England	United States	Ganges	10 May 1828
William	23	M	Silver Smith	England	America	Comet	26 Jun 1822
MANNINGS,							
William	19 7/12	M	Baker	England	United States	London	6 Feb 1829
MANNION, Catharine	20	F		Ireland	U.S. of America	Douglass	6 Jul 1829
MANNON, John	30	M	Smith	Ireland	United States	Trio	31 Oct 1827
John	32	M	...er	Ireland	United States	Trio	31 Oct 1827
Mary	30	F	Servant	Ireland	United States	Josephine	30 Apr 1828
MANON, James	27 4/12	M	Farmer	England	U.S. of America	Illinois	16 Jun 1821
MANSARGH, —, Mrs.	20	F	Lady	Ireland	Ireland	Argus	12 Dec 1826
A.	24	M	Merchant	Ireland	Ireland	Argus	12 Dec 1826
MANSFIELD, —, Mr.	27	M	Mariner	U. States	U. States	Cadmus	12 Apr 1825
Ellen	20	F	Servant	Ireland	United States	Trio	31 Oct 1827
Ellen	20	F		Ireland	United States	Trio	2 Oct 1828
Geo.	20		Farmer	England	United States	Hugh Johnson	11 Jun 1828
George	26	M	Ship Wright	United States	State of New York	Loire	3 Dec 1821
James	15	M	Tailor	England	New York	Thames	6 Oct 1820
Jane	11 6/12	F		Ireland	U. States	Virginia	20 Jun 1825
John T.	25	M	Merchant	Salem	U. States	Neva	9 Oct 1824
Margrett	20	F	wife to [Thos.]	Great Brittan	United States	Hanford	3 Aug 1829
Margt.	25	F		Ireland	U. States	Phocion	19 Sep 1822
Maria	3	F		Ireland	U. States	Phocion	19 Sep 1822
Mary	8	F		Ireland	New York State	Manhattan	20 Jun 1826
Nancy	22	F		Ireland	U.S.	George Canning	26 May 1829
Patrick	27	M	Painter	Havannah	Havannah	Rising State	15 Dec 1820
Thomas	36		Farmer	Ireland	New York State	Manhattan	20 Jun 1826
Thos.	26	M	Labourer	Great Brittan	United States	Hanford	3 Aug 1829
William	10		Farmer	Ireland	New York State	Manhattan	20 Jun 1826
MANSFOLD, Richard	28	M	Farmer	...chl...		Mount Vernon	7 Jun 1824
MANSON, Betsey	37	F		State of N. York	State of N. York	Danube	20 Jul 1826
Eliza	13	F		State of N. York	State of N. York	Danube	20 Jul 1826
H. N.	30	M	Merchant	Sweden	St. Barts	Planter	15 Mar 1820
Harit	15	F		State of N. York	State of N. York	Danube	20 Jul 1826
Lewis	17	M		State of N. York	State of N. York	Danube	20 Jul 1826
MANSONI, John J.	33		Merchant	Leghorn (Florence & London)	United States	London	13 Dec 1822
MANSULTEN, Jacob	25	M	Farmer	Switzerland	United States	Andes	5 May 1828
MANTER, F.	45	M	Merchant	Spain		Aspasia	19 Jul 1823
MANTIER, Iresto	26	M	Merchant	Spain	Spain	Weymouth	13 Aug 1822
MANTIMAN, James	20	M	Labourer	Ireland	United States	Louisa	16 Mar 1826
MANTLE, Benjn. D.	5	M	None	Great Britain	United States	Orlando	8 Nov 1826
George S.	7	M	None	Great Britain	United States	Orlando	8 Nov 1826
Mary F.	6	F	None	Great Britain	United States	Orlando	8 Nov 1826
Mary F.	27	F	None	Great Britain	United States	Orlando	8 Nov 1826
Thomas W.	9	M	None	Great Britain	United States	Orlando	8 Nov 1826
MANTOBEN, A.	30	M	Merchant	Carraccas	Carracas	Robert Fulton	2 Aug 1824
MANTON, Alexr.	22	M	Clerk	Scotland	U. States	Magnet	22 Aug 1822

NAMES OF PASSENGERS	AGE	SEX	OCCUPATIONS	COUNTRY TO WHICH THEY BELONG	COUNTRY THEY INTEND TO INHABIT	SHIPS/DATES OF ARRIVAL	
MANTURE, Saml. [crossed out]	20	M	Mariner	Massa.	Nantucket	South America	29 Aug 1826
MANUEL, Jno.	18	M	Servant	St. Iago	U. States	Nancy	21 Jul 1825
MANUELL, James	21	M	Labourer	Ireland	United States	Commerce	13 Jun 1828
MANUS, John	14	M	Child	Ireland	United States	Sylvester Healy	14 Jun 1825
John	45	M	Farmer	Ireland	United States	Sylvester Healy	14 Jun 1825
MANVALL, Jesse	42	M	Farmer	England	United States	Richmond	4 Aug 1826
MANVILLE, Jesse	40	M	Farmer	Great Britton	U. States	Factor	27 Mar 1827
MANYTRICK, C. L.	35	M	Gentleman	Curaca	Curacoa	Douglass	27 Apr 1824
MANZANOS, Jos.	38	M	Mariner	America	U. States	Herald	21 May 1824
MANZEDO, Isabella	19	F	...	...	U. States	Francis	16 Sep 1824
J.	...	F	...	...	U. States	Francis	16 Sep 1824
Juan	1 6/12	M	...	...	U. States	Francis	16 Sep 1824
Miguel	4	M	...	...	U. States	Francis	16 Sep 1824
Teresa	33	F	...	...	U. States	Francis	16 Sep 1824
MANZINGER, Adam	64	M	there Grand father [Christine, Chas., Philip, Theobald & James]	Germany	United States	Helen	5 Sep 1828
Chas.	8	M	there child [Christian & Ever]	Germany	United States	Helen	5 Sep 1828
Christian	33	M	Farmer	Germany	United States	Helen	5 Sep 1828
Christine	9	M	there child [Christian & Ever]	Germany	United States	Helen	5 Sep 1828
Ever	35	F	his wife [Christian]	Germany	United States	Helen	5 Sep 1828
James	1 6/12	M	there child [Christian & Ever]	Germany	United States	Helen	5 Sep 1828
Philip	6	M	there child [Christian & Ever]	Germany	United States	Helen	5 Sep 1828
Theobald	3	M	there child [Christian & Ever]	Germany	United States	Helen	5 Sep 1828
MAOKIN, James	20 7/12	M	Cotton Printer	Ireland	U. States	Fabius	22 Sep 1828
MAPAEL, Charles	25	M	Labourer	Ireland	United States	Hope & Esther	17 Oct 1827
MAPHAEL, Mary	28	F	Labourer	Ireland	United States	Hope & Esther	17 Oct 1827
Thomas	1	F	Labourer	Ireland	United States	Hope & Esther	17 Oct 1827
MAPLES, Edward	4	M		England	United States	Siroc	31 Oct 1829
George	8	M		England	United States	Siroc	31 Oct 1829
George	30	M	Minor	England	United States	Siroc	31 Oct 1829
Hannah	3	F		England	United States	Siroc	31 Oct 1829
Hannah	36	F		England	United States	Siroc	31 Oct 1829
Henry	6	M		England	United States	Siroc	31 Oct 1829
Mary Ann	1	F		England	United States	Siroc	31 Oct 1829
MAPLESDEN, Elizabeth	28	F	Smith	England	America	Leeds	2 Aug 1828
John	26	M	Smith	England	America	Leeds	2 Aug 1828
Mary Ann	8	F	Smith	England	America	Leeds	2 Aug 1828
Richard	4	M	Smith	England	America	Leeds	2 Aug 1828
MAR, Jas.	12	M		Spain	Mexico	Sarah	23 Sep 1826
Reuben	36	M	Farmer	Gt. Britain	United States	Robert Edwards	1 Jun 1826
MARA, Ann	7	F	None	Ireland	New York	Margaret	18 May 1825
Anna	35	F	None	Ireland	New York	Margaret	18 May 1825
Anne	1	M		Ireland	America	Mary	29 May 1827
Daniel	7/12	M	None	Ireland	New York	Margaret	18 May 1825
Daniel	40	M	Farmer	Ireland	New York	Margaret	18 May 1825
Ellen	18	F		Ireland	America	Liverpool	31 Aug 1827
George	39 4/12	M	Farmer	Switzerland	America	Henry	17 May 1828
Jane	13	F	None	Ireland	New York	Margaret	18 May 1825
Jas.	4	M	None	Ireland	New York	Margaret	18 May 1825
Jeremiah	7	M	None	Ireland	New York	Margaret	18 May 1825
Johanah	21	F		Ireland	America	Liverpool	31 Aug 1827
Jos.	25	M	Farmer	Ireland	America	Mary	29 May 1827
Margaret	9	F	None	Ireland	New York	Margaret	18 May 1825
Mary	25	F		Ireland	America	Mary	29 May 1827
Norry	17	F		Ireland	America	Liverpool	31 Aug 1827

NAMES OF PASSENGERS	AGE	SEX	OCCUPATIONS	COUNTRY TO WHICH THEY BELONG	COUNTRY THEY INTEND TO INHABIT	SHIPS/DATES OF ARRIVAL	
MARA (cont'd)							
P.	50	M	Joiner	Ireland	U. States	Hope & Esther	27 Sep 1824
Patrick	2	M	None	Ireland	New York	Margaret	18 May 1825
MARALL, Ann	55	F				Belfast	28 Sep 1820
MARALLES, B.	33	M	Merchant	Spain	Teneriffe	Brown	30 Jan 1826
MARANAH, Patrick	26	M	Farmer	Ireland	United States	Mary Howland	19 Jul 1827
MARANDTLY, Cathr.	24	F		Great Britain	United States	Grecian	24 Sep 1828
Cathr.	74	F		Great Britain	United States	Grecian	24 Sep 1828
James	7	M		Great Britain	United States	Grecian	24 Sep 1828
John	26	M		Great Britain	United States	Grecian	24 Sep 1828
Mary	22	F		Great Britain	United States	Grecian	24 Sep 1828
Michael	77	M	Farmer	Great Britain	United States	Grecian	24 Sep 1828
Michl.	28	M		Great Britain	United States	Grecian	24 Sep 1828
MARAONNEAU, Alexd.	25	M	Taylor	France	U. States	Jane Blossom	28 Aug 1826
Alxr., Mrs.	30	F		France	U. States	Jane Blossom	28 Aug 1826
MARAR, Mary	20	F	Tayloress	Halifax	United States	Genl. Marion	4 Jun 1828
MARASTE, T.	28	M	Merchant	France	U. States	Ranger	2 Jul 1827
MARAY, Cate.	20	F	Farmer	England	United States	India	8 Jun 1827
MARBLE, W.	25	M	Mariner	U. States	United States	Superior	14 Apr 1825
MARBON, Jim	12	M	Farmer	Great Brittan	U.S.	Emulous	29 Jun 1827
John	4	M	Farmer	Great Brittan	U.S.	Emulous	29 Jun 1827
Wm.	2	M	Farmer	Great Brittan	U.S.	Emulous	29 Jun 1827
MARCEIL, Carlice	9	M	Servant	Martinique	France	Alpha	27 Jul 1827
MARCH, Abagail	1	F		England	United States	Lord Wellington	14 Nov 1827
Caroline	3	F		England	United States	Lord Wellington	14 Nov 1827
Christopher	1	M		England	United States	Lord Wellington	14 Nov 1827
Elizabeth	6	F		England	United States	Lord Wellington	14 Nov 1827
Elizabeth	11	F		England	United States	Lord Wellington	14 Nov 1827
Esther	8	F		England	United States	Lord Wellington	14 Nov 1827
Harriet	17	F		England	United States	Lord Wellington	14 Nov 1827
James	3	M		England	United States	Lord Wellington	14 Nov 1827
John	17	M	Weaver	England	United States	Lord Wellington	14 Nov 1827
John	34	M	Farmer	Germany	United States	Lydia	18 Jun 1828
Martha	40	F		England	United States	Lord Wellington	14 Nov 1827
Mary	40	F		England	United States	Lord Wellington	14 Nov 1827
Mary L.	1	F		Germany	United States	Lydia	18 Jun 1828
Richard	22	M	Farmer	England	U. States	Rockingham	29 Nov 1821
Samuel	5	M		England	United States	Lord Wellington	14 Nov 1827
Silas	21	M	Merchant	Great Britian	United States	Sarah	11 Jul 1829
Thomas	49	M	Weaver	England	United States	Lord Wellington	14 Nov 1827
Zacharias	14	M	Weaver	England	United States	Lord Wellington	14 Nov 1827
MARCHAIRD, —,							
Madam	25	F		France	United States	Henry	9 Jun 1826
MARCHALK, Henry	23	M	Shepherd	Germany	Germany	Albion	27 Jun 1827
MARCHAND, A.	20	M	officer of the King's guard	France	France	Howard	27 Sep 1826
Francoise	29	F	Farmer	France	United States	Le Voltaire	19 Jul 1828
G. F.	24	M	Mechanic	France	U.S.	Helen	3 May 1828
Joseph	3	M		France	United States	Le Voltaire	19 Jul 1828
Maria F.	42	F		France	United States	Le Voltaire	19 Jul 1828
Pierre M.	18	M		France	United States	Le Voltaire	19 Jul 1828
Susan	32	F	Spinster	Roche	U.S. America	Superior	18 Jun 1825
MARCHAY, John	30	M	Planter	West Indies	West Indies	Delia	26 Oct 1829
MARCHEL, Michel	20	M	Farmer	Germany	United States	Oxford	14 Aug 1828
MARCHELL, John	1 6/12	M	None	Liverpool	America	Evelina	10 Nov 1825
Joseph	38	M	Baker	Liverpool	America	Evelina	10 Nov 1825
Mary	28	F	None	Liverpool	America	Evelina	10 Nov 1825
Wm. C.	3 6/12	M	None	Liverpool	America	Evelina	10 Nov 1825
MARCHER, A.	32	F		St. Johns	U. States	Wanderer	30 Sep 1828
Anna Jane	7	F		Virginia	U. States	Wanderer	30 Sep 1828
Annebeler	30	F	Lady	St. Johns	St. Johns	Nancy	3 Apr 1824
Caroline	32	F	Spinster	United States	United States	Annah	21 Jun 1826
Geo. Q.	13	M		St. Johns	U. States	Wanderer	30 Sep 1828
MARCHMAN, Robt.	38	M	Dyer	England	United States	Cambria	8 Oct 1828
MARCKHAM, John	36	M	Mariner [?]	Great Britian	Canada	Silvanus Jenkins	6 Apr 1826
MARCKLAND, Eliza.	38	F		England	U. States	Spartan	21 Apr 1826
John	32	M	Shoemaker	England	U. States	Spartan	21 Apr 1826
MARCKS, Wm.	25	M	Carpenter	Ireland	America	Dublin Packet	9 Oct 1820
MARCOS, M.	32	M	Gentleman	Colombia	U. States	Birmingham	12 Oct 1827

NAMES OF PASSENGERS	AGE	SEX	OCCUPATIONS	COUNTRY TO WHICH THEY BELONG	COUNTRY THEY INTEND TO INHABIT	SHIPS/DATES OF ARRIVAL	
MARCUAT, Constant			Servant	France	U.S.	Sully	26 Oct 1829
MARCUS, James	27	M	Seaman	Spain	Spain	Hesper	21 Sep 1827
M.	34	M	Merchant	Mexico	U. States	John Jay	17 Sep 1828
MARDEN, Benjn.	57	M	Gentleman	Philad.	U. States	Desdemona	21 Oct 1825
Catharine	11	F	Farmer	Switzerland	America	Henry	17 May 1828
Catharine	36	F	Farmer	Switzerland	America	Henry	17 May 1828
Elisabeth	9 8/12	F	Farmer	Switzerland	America	Henry	17 May 1828
Jack	35 3/12	M	Farmer	Switzerland	America	Henry	17 May 1828
Margaret	3 5/12	F	Farmer	Switzerland	America	Henry	17 May 1828
Mary	10/12	F	Farmer	Switzerland	America	Henry	17 May 1828
Susan	7	F	Farmer	Switzerland	America	Henry	17 May 1828
MARDERNUTT, Henry	24	M	Labourer	Ireland	New York	America	1 Aug 1828
MARDINGER, Barbara	19	F		Germany	America	Falcon	28 Aug 1828
Elizabeth M.	27	F		Germany	America	Falcon	28 Aug 1828
Gottlieb W.	1 6/12	M		Germany	America	Falcon	28 Aug 1828
Johannes	29	M	Farmer	Germany	America	Falcon	28 Aug 1828
MARDLAW, Jno.	45	M	C...	Gt. Britain	Canada	Corks	3 Aug 1824
MARE, Eve	21	F	Farmer	Germany	United States	Oxford	14 Aug 1828
Frederic	6 6/12	M	Farmer	Germany	United States	Oxford	14 Aug 1828
Frederic	21	M	Farmer	Germany	United States	Oxford	14 Aug 1828
H.	30	M	Merchant	Gt. Britain	U. States	Tantiva	7 Jul 1828
Jno.	25	M	Farmer	Argyle (Tedland) Scotland	United States	Jean Hastie	27 Jul 1829
Mary	26	F		Argyle (Tedland) Scotland	United States	Jean Hastie	27 Jul 1829
MAREAN, John	30	M	Miner	Great Britain	Mexico	Corinthian	27 Apr 1824
MAREANO, Joseph	16	M	Merchant	Mexico	U. States	Tobasco	23 Jul 1827
MARENO, Santiago	47	M	Military	Spain	Spain	Virginia	9 Feb 1829
MAREOS, Manuel, Mr.	33	M	Merchant	Columbia	Columbia	Athenian	17 Jul 1829
MARES, Richard	21 3/12	M	Merchant	U.S. America	America	Erie	19 Oct 1829
MARETTA, P.	34	M				Atlanta	20 May 1822
MAREY, Ann	40	F	Wife	Ireland	United States	Ann Maria	3 Jul 1827
Brine	45	F	Laborer	Ireland	United States	Ann Maria	3 Jul 1827
Charles	17	M	Laborer	Ireland	United States	Ann Maria	3 Jul 1827
Fanny	4	F	Child	Ireland	United States	Ann Maria	3 Jul 1827
Geo.		M		Scotland	U.S.	Curler	19 Jul 1828
Nelly	15	F	Child	Ireland	United States	Ann Maria	3 Jul 1827
Patrick	7	M	Child	Ireland	United States	Ann Maria	3 Jul 1827
MARFIELD, Jno.	33	M	Labourer	Great Britain	U. States	Dominica	4 Jan 1823
MARGANT, Christian	44	M	Gardner	Prussia	U. States	Minerva	13 Sep 1827
Hannah	36	F	Wife [of Christian]	Prussia	U. States	Minerva	13 Sep 1827
MARGARD, Catharine	36	M	Mechanic	Prussia	Prussia	Florida	17 May 1825
Christian	40	M	Mechanic	Prussia	Prussia	Florida	17 May 1825
MARGARET, Ann	2 2/12	F		France	United States	Catharine	10 Sep 1827
MARGATROYD, Ellen	33	M	Farmer	Great Britain	United States	India	5 Sep 1827
William	34	F		Great Britain	United States	India	5 Sep 1827
MARGBOTHLIN,							
Margret	35			Ireland	Philidelphia	General Marion	21 Nov 1828
Mary	14			Ireland	Philidelphia	General Marion	21 Nov 1828
MARGELS, C.	23	M	Smith	Hannover	United States	Constitution	6 Jul 1829
MARGERUM, William	32	M	Moraca Dresser	America	America	Leeds	2 Aug 1828
MARGILL,							
Croisbie, Rvd.	24	M	Chaplin	Gt. Britian	Canada	Pacific	22 May 1826
MARGNES, Francis	45	M	Farmer	France	United States	Virginia	31 May 1828
Michell	40	F	Farmer	France	United States	Virginia	31 May 1828
Nicholas	15	M	Farmer	France	United States	Virginia	31 May 1828
MARGRAUGH,							
Thomas	27	M	Labourer	Ireland	U. States	Combine	30 Nov 1825
MARHAR, James	40 6/12	M	Labourer	Ireland	America	Rising States	7 Jul 1828
MARHER, Phillip	24	M	Labourer	Ireland	United States	Combine	4 Jun 1825
MARHON, John	30	M	Labourer	Ireland	United States	Potomac	28 Sep 1827
Thos.	34	M	Labourer	Ireland	United States	Potomac	28 Sep 1827
MARIA, Cathern. Elizat.	70	F		Germany	America	Falcon	28 Aug 1828
Francesco	26	M	Gentleman	U. States	U. States	Abeona	1 Oct 1823
MARIAN, John	...0	M	Hostler	England	United States	Lunar	5 May 1828
MARICE, P.	50	M	Merchant	Havana	U. States	Napolian	20 Nov 1828
MARICH, Francisco	14	M		Spain	Spain	Richmond Packet	13 Jun 1825
MARIDETH, Wm.	45	M	Mason	England	United States	William	5 Oct 1822

NAMES OF PASSENGERS	AGE	SEX	OCCUPATIONS	COUNTRY TO WHICH THEY BELONG	COUNTRY THEY INTEND TO INHABIT	SHIPS/DATES OF ARRIVAL	
MARIE, Francoise	27	F	Servt.	Africa	United States	Bayard	13 Nov 1823
P.	50	M	Mercht.	France	United States	Herald	25 Nov 1826
MARIÉ, John B.	52	M	Merchant	United States	United States	Packet Eliza	1 Jul 1829
MARIEN, Peter	25	M	Labourer	Ireland	United States	Wilson	6 Jun 1828
MARIER, Antonio	35	M	Merchant	Spain	Cuba	Clarissa	3 Sep 1824
MARIGNEY, Gustav	21	M	Merchant	U. States	U. States	Bayard	25 Apr 1828
MARILLA, Peter	10	M	Merchant	St. Domingo	St. Domingo	Blue Ey'd Man	23 Aug 1823
MARILLAS, —, Mrs.	30	F		St. Domingo	St. Domingo	Blue Ey'd Man	23 Aug 1823
MARIN, —, Mrs.	12	F		La Guayra	U.S.	Love	12 Oct 1827
Auguste	25	M	ex officer de Cavalrie	France	United States	Robert Edwards	3 Oct 1829
MARINER, A.	20	M	Servant	England	St. Johns	Silvanus Jenkins	24 Jul 1828
MARION, Andrew	25 11/12	M	...	France	United States	Criterion	13 Oct 1825
John	10	M	None	Ireland	New York	Sully	4 Mar 1828
Kitty	6	F	None	Ireland	New York	Sully	4 Mar 1828
Mary	4	F	None	Ireland	New York	Sully	4 Mar 1828
Nadey	37	F	None	Ireland	New York	Sully	4 Mar 1828
Patrick	15	M	None	Ireland	New York	Sully	4 Mar 1828
MARIOT, Joseph	20	M		France		Pallas	14 Jun 1828
MARIRA, William Frederick	20	M	Shoemaker	Great Britian	United States	Baltic	19 Mar 1824
MARIS, —	32	M	Merchant	France	U. States	Greyhound	31 May 1823
MARISON, —, Mr.	25	M	Mariner	Massachusetts	U. States	Amanda	19 Jan 1824
MARJORIBANKS, John	37	M	M...	Great Britain	U. States	Panthea	24 Mar 1825
MARK, Barbara	46	F		United States	United States	Globe	30 Aug 1828
*landed at this Port, Custom House, Portland, Aug 19, 1828							
Elisabeth	9	F		United States	United States	Globe	30 Aug 1828
*landed at this Port, Custom House, Portland, Aug 19, 1828							
Gabriel	18	M	Cutler	United States	United States	Globe	30 Aug 1828
*landed at this Port, Custom House, Portland, Aug 19, 1828							
Gilbert	24	M	Labourer			Hanford	17 Jul 1828
Godfrey	20	M	Tin Plate worker	United States	United States	Globe	30 Aug 1828
*landed at this Port, Custom House, Portland, Aug 19, 1828							
John Jacob	45	M	Catlen	United States	United States	Globe	30 Aug 1828
*landed at this Port, Custom House, Portland, Aug 19, 1828							
Louisa	7	F		United States	United States	Globe	30 Aug 1828
*landed at this Port, Custom House, Portland, Aug 19, 1828							
MARKELOTT, Ld.		M	Merchant	Spain	U. States	Lady Tompkins	31 Jan 1824
MARKER, Frederick	6	M	Farmer	Alsace in the Department of Upper and lower Rhine	United States	Carolina Augusta	16 May 1828
Jacob	19	M	Farmer	Alsace in the Department of Upper and lower Rhine	United States	Carolina Augusta	16 May 1828
Madelena	9	F	Farmer	Alsace in the Department of Upper and lower Rhine	United States	Carolina Augusta	16 May 1828
Madelina	48	F	Farmer	Alsace in the Department of Upper and lower Rhine	United States	Carolina Augusta	16 May 1828
Philip	17	M	Farmer	Alsace in the Department of Upper and lower Rhine	United States	Carolina Augusta	16 May 1828
Philip	43	M	Farmer	Alsace in the Department of Upper and lower Rhine	United States	Carolina Augusta	16 May 1828
Solomon	11	M	Farmer	Alsace in the Department of Upper and lower Rhine	United States	Carolina Augusta	16 May 1828
MARKESSE, J. B.	30	M	Merchant	Columbia	Columbia	William	1 Jul 1828
MARKEY, —, Mrs.	25	F				Neptunes Barge	23 Apr 1821
Ba.	3	F				Neptunes Barge	23 Apr 1821

NAMES OF PASSENGERS	AGE	SEX	OCCUPATIONS	COUNTRY TO WHICH THEY BELONG	COUNTRY THEY INTEND TO INHABIT	SHIPS/DATES OF ARRIVAL	
MARKEY (cont'd)							
Philip	25	M	Butcher	Ireland	United States	Essex	23 May 1828
Thomas	40	M	Sawyer	New York	United States	Grecian	24 Sep 1828
MARKLAND, Ann	4	F		Great Britain	U. States	Ganges	21 Jun 1827
Anna	30	F	Lady	Canada	Canada	Brighton	16 Nov 1826
George	34	M	Gentn.	Canada	Canada	Brighton	16 Nov 1826
Jane	12	F		Great Britain	U. States	Ganges	21 Jun 1827
John	6	M		Great Britain	U. States	Ganges	21 Jun 1827
Sarah	1	F		Great Britain	U. States	Ganges	21 Jun 1827
Susan	10	F		Great Britain	U. States	Ganges	21 Jun 1827
Susan	35	F		Great Britain	U. States	Ganges	21 Jun 1827
William	13	M		Great Britain	U. States	Ganges	21 Jun 1827
William	39	M		Great Britain	U. States	Ganges	21 Jun 1827
MARKLOT, —, Mrs.	34	F		Philada.	U. States	Manchester Packet	21 Aug 1823
John	56	M	Merchant	Philada.	U. States	Manchester Packet	21 Aug 1823
Louis	1 6/12	M		Philada.	U. States	Manchester Packet	21 Aug 1823
Louisa	3	F		Philada.	U. States	Manchester Packet	21 Aug 1823
V.	9	F		Philada.	U. States	Manchester Packet	21 Aug 1823
Z.	15	F		Philada.	U. States	Manchester Packet	21 Aug 1823
MARKOE, C.	12	M	None	Denmark	U. States	Chase	20 Jul 1826
F.	52	M	Merchant	Denmark	U. States	Chase	20 Jul 1826
H.	13	M	None	Denmark	U. States	Chase	20 Jul 1826
Peter	59		Planter	Denmark	St. Croix	Eliza Davidson	8 Aug 1829
MARKS, —, Mr.	65	M	Farmer	England	U. States	Robert Edwards	11 Mar 1822
A. J.	26	M	Commedian	England	United States	Amelia	20 Aug 1829
Diana	32	F		Philada.	Philada.	Chase	11 Mar 1826
Elisa	7	F		England	United States	Cosmo	26 Aug 1829
Eliza	19	F	Commedian	United States	United States	Amelia	20 Aug 1829
George	26	M	D...s...	G. Britain	U. States	Armadello	22 Jun 1827
Jacob	19	M	Merchant	United States	U. States	Horatio	21 Jan 1829
Martha	2			England	United States	Cosmo	26 Aug 1829
S.	27	M		Great Brittain	United States	Sarah Ralston	27 Jan 1827
Saml.	30	M	Butcher	England	United States	Cosmo	26 Aug 1829
Sarah	2	F	Commedian	United States	United States	Amelia	20 Aug 1829
Sarah	32	F		England	United States	Cosmo	26 Aug 1829
Virginia	1/4	F	Commedian	England	United States	Amelia	20 Aug 1829
MARKVEST, John	70	M	Doctor	Germany	America	Wm. Tell	9 Jan 1827
MARKWELL, Wm.	50	M	Smith	Great Britain	United States	Freake	25 Aug 1829
Wm., Junr.	13	M		Great Britain	United States	Freake	25 Aug 1829
MARKY, Ann	36	F	Farmer	Switzerland		Antioch	18 Aug 1829
Jacques	43	M	Farmer	Switzerland		Antioch	18 Aug 1829
Nichs.	24	M	Doctor	Grt. Britain	United States	Henry Kneeland	5 Nov 1828
Peter	22	M	Currier	Grt. Britain	United States	Henry Kneeland	5 Nov 1828
Thos.	19	M	Clerk	Grt. Britain	United States	Henry Kneeland	5 Nov 1828
MARLE, Pat	25	M	Labourer	G. Britain	U. States	Sarah G	5 Jun 1828
MARLEING, A.	50	M	Farmer	Ireland	United States	Commerce	13 Jun 1828
Anthony	24	M	Weaver	Ireland	United States	Commerce	13 Jun 1828
Ellen	8	F		Ireland	United States	Commerce	13 Jun 1828
Jane	20	F		Ireland	United States	Commerce	13 Jun 1828
John	18	M	Weaver	Ireland	United States	Commerce	13 Jun 1828
Mary	17	F		Ireland	United States	Commerce	13 Jun 1828
Mary	26	F		Ireland	United States	Commerce	13 Jun 1828
Sarah	12	F		Ireland	United States	Commerce	13 Jun 1828
Sarah	48	F		Ireland	United States	Commerce	13 Jun 1828
MARLEMESON, James	18	M	Weaver	Ireland	United States	Commerce	13 Jun 1828
MARLEY, Agnes	19	F	None	Ireland	United States	Lord Wellington	28 May 1827
Domc.	29		Farmer	Ireland		Westmoreland	1 Aug 1826
Nancey	20		Wife	Ireland		Westmoreland	1 Aug 1826
Patrick	23	M	Labourer	Ireland	United States	Lord Wellington	28 May 1827
William	1/12		Child	Ireland		Westmoreland	1 Aug 1826
MARLING, Fanny	22	F		England	United States	Danube	13 Jul 1827
MARLLORD, Jean J.	62	F	Farmer	France		Pallas	14 Jun 1828
MARLONE, James	28	M	Merchant	Ireland	U. States	Lucinda	11 Nov 1824

787

NAMES OF PASSENGERS	AGE	SEX	OCCUPATIONS	COUNTRY TO WHICH THEY BELONG	COUNTRY THEY INTEND TO INHABIT	SHIPS/DATES OF ARRIVAL	
MARLOW, Eliz.	28	M	Farmer	Great Brittan	U.S.	Emulous	29 Jun 1827
Richd.	30	M	Farmer	Great Brittan	U.S.	Emulous	29 Jun 1827
MARMAN, James	24	M	...	...	United States	Hanford	17 Oct 1828
MARMICHAEL, Mary	21	F	None	Ireland	United States	Friends	21 Oct 1825
MARMION, John	22	M	Joiner	Ireland	United States	Romulus	24 Jun 1826
MARMLE, Nelson	23	M	Seaman	U. States	United States	Brilliant	24 Sep 1827
MARNANE, John	24		Silk Manufactorer	West Indies		Union	20 Aug 1827
MARNEN, Charlotte	25	F	Lady	England	United States	Siroc	31 Oct 1829
MARO, —, Col.	31	M		Mexico	U. States	Laveria	23 Jul 1828
—, Col.	35	M		Mexico	U. States	Laveria	23 Jul 1828
MAROLF, —	6/12	F		France & Switzerland	U. States	Bayard	14 Jul 1826
A.	25	M		France & Switzerland	U. States	Bayard	14 Jul 1826
Anny Cath.	6	F		Switzerland	Ohio	Eugenie	20 Aug 1827
Anny Cath.	30	F		Switzerland	Ohio	Eugenie	20 Aug 1827
C.	24	M		France & Switzerland	U. States	Bayard	14 Jul 1826
C. M.	26	F		France & Switzerland	U. States	Bayard	14 Jul 1826
Jean Cath.	1	M		Switzerland	Ohio	Eugenie	20 Aug 1827
John	27	M	Farmer	Switzerland	Ohio	Eugenie	20 Aug 1827
M.	30	F		France & Switzerland	U. States	Bayard	14 Jul 1826
MAROTTE, Lewis	20	M	Merchant	United States	United States	Virginia	9 Feb 1829
Lewis	45	M	Merchant	U. States	U. States	Virginia	8 Mar 1828
MARQUER, M.	30	M	Merchant	Spain	France & Spain	Native	24 Aug 1825
MARQUET, Camille	20	M	Merchant	France	Great Britain	Stephania	24 Jul 1820
MARQUON, Paddy	27	M	Labourer	Gt. Britain	U. States	Sarah G.	14 Apr 1828
MARR, —, Miss	23	F		U. States	U.S.	Henri IV	14 Sep 1827
Ann M.	24	F		Ireland	U. States	Fame	15 Nov 1826
Barbara	1 1/12	F		France	America, U.N.S.	Great Britain	3 Aug 1829
Catharine	30	F		Halifax	U. States	Adoro	14 Apr 1828
H.	30	M	Farmer	France	America, U.N.S.	Great Britain	3 Aug 1829
Marguerite	23	F		France	America, U.N.S.	Great Britain	3 Aug 1829
Michl.	24	M	Farmer	France	America, U.N.S.	Great Britain	3 Aug 1829
Stephen	30	M	Weaver	Halifax	U. States	Adoro	14 Apr 1828
MARRAH, Anora	30	F		Ireland	America	Panthia	17 Sep 1821
James	34	M	Farmer	Ireland	America	Panthia	17 Sep 1821
Mary	1	F		Ireland	America	Panthia	17 Sep 1821
MARRAST, A.	22	M	None	U. States	U. States	Rival	25 May 1826
Francisco	26	M	Merchant	France	U. States	Emma	15 Dec 1824
MARRAW, Gorge	24	M		Irland	U. States	Nancy	27 Jun 1823
MARRIAN, Catherine	19	F		Derry	...	Gleaner	24 May 1823
Joaquim	57	M	Gentleman	Mexico	U. States	Bayard	19 Mar 1824
MARRIGOLD, Jaques	28	M	Spinner	France	United States	Alexander	2 Oct 1829
MARRINAL, F., Mde. (Thibaut)	27		None	Suisse	New York	Manchester	30 May 1821
MARRINGTON, M.	25	M	Chandler	G. Britain	U. States	Margaret Bogle	12 Jun 1828
MARRIOTT, J. R.	51	M	Physican	U. States	U. States	Pallas	17 Aug 1824
J. R.	53	M	Medical	U.S.	U.S.	Panthea	22 Jul 1826
MARRISON, Barrett	25	M	shoemaker	Great Britain	United States	Atlantic	8 Dec 1827
Jean	40 3/12	F	Spinner	G. Britain	United States	Dutchess of Portland	30 Oct 1826
MARRISS, Ruth	32	F	Wife	Ireland	United States	Ann Maria	18 Dec 1827
MARRON, Patrick	21	M	Reporter	Ireland	New York	Governor Fenner	23 Jul 1829
MARROW, Dens.	45			Great Britan	United States	Newry	11 Jul 1827
Ellen	22			Great Britan	United States	Newry	11 Jul 1827
John	20			Great Britan	United States	Newry	11 Jul 1827
Joseph	21	M	Farmer	Great Britain	United States	Eliza Barker	3 Jul 1826
Margaret	30 10/12	F	Servant	Ireland	United States	Atlantic	21 Jul 1827
Philip	22	M	Bleacher	Ireland	United States	Atlantic	21 Jul 1827
MARRY, James	24	M	Labourer	Ireland	United States	Meteor	26 Jun 1827
MARS, Ann	26	F	None	England	England	Sully	15 Jul 1829
Fras.	22	M	Mechanic	France	U. States	Olive & Sarah	27 Jan 1823
John	32	M	Engineer	England	England	Sully	15 Jul 1829
John, Jr.	10	M	None	England	England	Sully	15 Jul 1829
Mary	7	F	None	England	England	Sully	15 Jul 1829

NAMES OF PASSENGERS	AGE	SEX	OCCUPATIONS	COUNTRY TO WHICH THEY BELONG	COUNTRY THEY INTEND TO INHABIT	SHIPS/DATES OF ARRIVAL	
MARS (cont'd)							
Peter Joseph	60	M	Planter	U. States	U. States	Stephania	24 Jul 1820
Phillip	1 9/12	M	None	England	England	Sully	15 Jul 1829
William	5	M	None	England	England	Sully	15 Jul 1829
MARSBREA, George	7	M		France	Louisiana	Abby Jones	12 Jul 1827
Jacob	15	M		France	Louisiana	Abby Jones	12 Jul 1827
John	3	M		France	Louisiana	Abby Jones	12 Jul 1827
Maria	17	F		France	Louisiana	Abby Jones	12 Jul 1827
Maria	34	F		France	Louisiana	Abby Jones	12 Jul 1827
Mary Catharine	5	F		France	Louisiana	Abby Jones	12 Jul 1827
Mary Frances	10	F		France	Louisiana	Abby Jones	12 Jul 1827
Michael	46	M	Farmer	France	Louisiana	Abby Jones	12 Jul 1827
Nicholas	11	M		France	Louisiana	Abby Jones	12 Jul 1827
MARSCHAL, F.	28	M	Merchant	France	United States	Howard	20 Aug 1827
MARSDEN, Jacob	10	M		U.S.		Florenzo	23 Aug 1827
James	25	M	Farmer	Great Britian	United States	Andes	19 Aug 1829
Mary	52	F	None	Birmingham	America, New York	Washington	3 Mar 1828
Susan	32	F	Wife	U.S.		Florenzo	23 Aug 1827
Wm.	19	M	...			Importer	30 Oct 1820
Wm.	31		Cotton Spinner	Great Britain	United States	Roman	10 Sep 1827
MARSDIN, William	25	M	Clerk	Great Britain	U. States	Superb	28 May 1821
MARSDON, Jno.	24		Carpenter	England	U.S. of America	Mary	21 Sep 1821
MARSH, —, Mrs.	22	F	Wife	G.B.	United States	Corinthian	29 Apr 1826
A.	5	M		Nova Scotia	United States	Sarah	12 Jul 1828
A.	8	M		Nova Scotia	United States	Sarah	12 Jul 1828
A.	65	F		Nova Scotia	United States	Sarah	12 Jul 1828
Abraham	19	M	Labourer	Great Britain	U. States	Lady Hunter	26 Nov 1823
Ann	50	F	Lady	U.S.	U.S.	New England	27 Jul 1829
C.	10	F		Nova Scotia	United States	Sarah	12 Jul 1828
Charles	15	M	Lad	England	U. States	Cincinnatus	24 May 1821
Christien	11	M		Switzerland	U.S.	C. Amelia	30 Jun 1828
Daniel	33	M	Butcher	England	U.S.A.	Robin Hood	6 May 1828
E.	6/12	F		Nova Scotia	United States	Sarah	12 Jul 1828
E.	20	F		Nova Scotia	United States	Sarah	12 Jul 1828
Edward	11	M	Farmer	England	Pensylvania	Chelsea	16 May 1828
Elijah	21	M	Merchant	England	England	Loire	7 Apr 1821
Eliza	23	F	Mason	England	U. States	Acasta	21 Oct 1825
Geo.	47	M		Ireland	U. States	Fame	15 Nov 1826
George	5	M	Farmer	Bristol, Engl.	England	Warrior	19 May 1828
George	6	M		Ireland	U. States	Fame	15 Nov 1826
Harriet	7	F	Farmer	England	Pensylvania	Chelsea	16 May 1828
Henry	22	M	Merchant	Great Britian	United States	Sarah	11 Jul 1829
J.	5	M		Nova Scotia	United States	Sarah	12 Jul 1828
J.	6	M		Nova Scotia	United States	Sarah	12 Jul 1828
J.	16	F		Nova Scotia	United States	Sarah	12 Jul 1828
J.	18	M	Farmer	Nova Scotia	United States	Sarah	12 Jul 1828
J.	28	F		Nova Scotia	United States	Sarah	12 Jul 1828
J.	30	M	Farmer	Nova Scotia	United States	Sarah	12 Jul 1828
J.	35	M	Merchant	U. States	U. States	Seneca	7 Nov 1825
J.	35	F		Nova Scotia	United States	Sarah	12 Jul 1828
J.	38	M	Farmer	Nova Scotia	United States	Sarah	12 Jul 1828
J. A.	5	F		Nova Scotia	United States	Sarah	12 Jul 1828
J. A.	8	M		Nova Scotia	United States	Sarah	12 Jul 1828
James	9	M	Farmer	England	Pensylvania	Chelsea	16 May 1828
James	20	M	Weaver	England	United States	Delta	24 Oct 1829
Jas.	22	M		England		Anacreon	7 Sep 1827
John	3	M	Farmer	Bristol, Engl.	England	Warrior	19 May 1828
John	14	M		Porto Rico	Porto Rico	Hanna	3 Jun 1828
John	23	M	Farmer	England	Alexandria, U.S.	Roman	17 Oct 1826
John	35	M	Farmer	England	Pensylvania	Chelsea	16 May 1828
Joseph	60	M	Farmer	England	United States	William & Henry	19 Jul 1822
L.	35	F		Porto Rico	Porto Rico	Hanna	3 Jun 1828
Lydia	10	F		Ireland	U. States	Fame	15 Nov 1826
M.	7	F		Nova Scotia	United States	Sarah	12 Jul 1828
Maria	8	F	Farmer	Bristol, Engl.	England	Warrior	19 May 1828
Mary	2	F	Farmer	England	Pensylvania	Chelsea	16 May 1828
Mary	10	F	Farmer	Bristol, Engl.	England	Warrior	19 May 1828
Mary	25	F		England	U.S.A.	Robin Hood	6 May 1828

NAMES OF PASSENGERS	AGE	SEX	OCCUPATIONS	COUNTRY TO WHICH THEY BELONG	COUNTRY THEY INTEND TO INHABIT	SHIPS/DATES OF ARRIVAL	
MARSH (cont'd)							
Mary	30	F	Farmer	England	Pensylvania	Chelsea	16 May 1828
Mary Ann	18	F	None	England	U. States	Corinthian	20 Apr 1825
Nicholes	60	M	Farmer	Switzerland	U.S.	C. Amelia	30 Jun 1828
P.	12	F		Nova Scotia	United States	Sarah	12 Jul 1828
P.	36	M	Farmer	Nova Scotia	United States	Sarah	12 Jul 1828
Phoebe	12	F		Ireland	U. States	Fame	15 Nov 1826
R.	2	F		Nova Scotia	United States	Sarah	12 Jul 1828
R.	3	F		Nova Scotia	United States	Sarah	12 Jul 1828
S.	16	F		Nova Scotia	United States	Sarah	12 Jul 1828
Samuel	34	M	Merchant	United States	United States	Nestor in Liverpool	29 Jul 1822
Silas	25	M	Labourer	Great Britian	United States	Sarah	11 Jul 1829
Susanna	39	F	Farmer	Bristol, Engl.	England	Warrior	19 May 1828
Susanne	49	F		Ireland	U. States	Fame	15 Nov 1826
T.	22	M	Farmer	Nova Scotia	United States	Sarah	12 Jul 1828
Thos.	29	M	Mason	England	U. States	Acasta	21 Oct 1825
Thos., Master	1	M	Mason	England	U. States	Acasta	21 Oct 1825
Ward, Lt.	25	M	U.S. Navy	U.S.A.	U.S.A.	Potomac	25 Jul 1829
William	32	M	Merchant	Great Brittan	Great Brittan	Orbit	30 Aug 1824
William	38	M	Farmer	Bristol, Engl.	England	Warrior	19 May 1828
William	45	M	Clothier	England	United States	Aurora	9 Jul 1827
Wm.	17	M	Farmer	Great Britian	United States	Columbia	17 Apr 1827
MARSHAL, John	35	M	Merchant	England	United States	Stephania	22 Apr 1822
Thomas	10	M	Merchant	England	United States	Stephania	22 Apr 1822
MARSHALL, —, Miss	33	F	None	England	U. States	Don Quixotte	27 Jun 1827
—, Mrs.	20	F				Montano	3 Jan 1823
A.	52	M	Clergy	U. States	U. States	Six Brothers	21 Nov 1822
Ann	6	F		Barbados	United States	Cannon	18 Aug 1821
Bary, Mr.	37	M	Merchant	America	America	Albion	4 Oct 1820
Bary, Mrs.	31	F		America	America	Albion	4 Oct 1820
Benjamin	20	M		Ireland	U. States	Nancy	10 Jul 1822
Benjamin	41	M	Merchant	Great Britain	U. States	Canada	4 Oct 1824
Benjamin	42	M	Merchant	G. Bt.	U. States	Canada	13 Oct 1825
Charles, Mr.	18	M	Gent	England	New York	Governor Fenner	23 Jul 1829
D.	38	M	Mariner (Capt.)	United States	United States	India	24 Mar 1826
Diana	37	F		England	United States	John Wells	16 May 1825
E.	25	M	Gentleman	Ireland	U. States	Milton	20 Aug 1827
Edward	4/12			England	U.S. America	Constitution	18 Jun 1827
Eliza	2	F	None	American	U. States	James Cropper	17 Jun 1825
Elizabeth	15	F				Polly	26 May 1821
F.	25	M	Merchant	German	U. States	Minerva	23 May 1825
Fedelia	22	F	None	American	U. States	James Cropper	17 Jun 1825
Francis Dayrell	9	M		Barbados	United States	Cannon	18 Aug 1821
George		M	None	Great Britain	United States	Orbit	23 Oct 1826
George	29			England	U.S. America	Constitution	18 Jun 1827
George, Jr.	5			England	U.S. America	Constitution	18 Jun 1827
George Crook	11	M	None	Gt. Britain	U. States	Canada	4 Oct 1824
H. C.	38	M	Ship Master	United States		Montano	3 Jan 1823
Hannah	22	M		New York	New York	Talma	23 Sep 1828
Harriot	35	F	None	Gt. Britain	U. States	Canada	4 Oct 1824
Henry	12	M		Barbados	United States	Cannon	18 Aug 1821
Herbert	32	M	Parson	United States	United States	Rolla	8 May 1823
James	21	M	Joiner	Great Britain	United States	Colossus	5 Jun 1827
James	21	M	Cooper	England	United States	Acasta	25 Sep 1827
James	26	M	Weaver	Great Britain	United States	Orbit	23 Oct 1826
James	45	M	Gentleman	United States	United States	Hercules	21 Nov 1822
Jane	24	F	Spinster	Ireland	United States	Gem	16 Jun 1824
Janet	30	F	wife to Paper Manufr. [John]	G. Brittan	U. States	Trafalgar	4 Jun 1822
Jas.	20	M	Farmer	Scotland	U. States	Alert	22 Sep 1821
Jas.	22	M	Mariner	U. States	U. States	Florida	25 Apr 1825
Jno.	15	M		Barbados	United States	Cannon	18 Aug 1821
Jno.	27	M	Carpenter	St. Johns, N.B.	United States	Martha	23 Aug 1825
Jno. Worrell	41	M	Merchant	Barbados	United States	Cannon	18 Aug 1821
John	4/12	M	None	Great Britain	United States	Orbit	23 Oct 1826
John	9	M	None	U. States	U. States	Canada	13 Oct 1825
John	13	M		England	United States	John Wells	16 May 1825
John	21	M				Imperial	19 Jul 1820

790

NAMES OF PASSENGERS	AGE	SEX	OCCUPATIONS	COUNTRY TO WHICH THEY BELONG	COUNTRY THEY INTEND TO INHABIT	SHIPS/DATES OF ARRIVAL	
MARSHALL (cont'd)							
John	22	M	Farmer	England	U. States	Hercules	6 Jul 1827
John	27	M	Farmer	England	Pensylvania	Lima	5 Aug 1829
John	29	M	Labourer	Ireland	America	Minerva	15 Nov 1823
John	30	M	Merchant	U. States	U. States	Champion	1 Sep 1820
John	31	M	Cooper	Ireland	United States	Herald	7 Jun 1824
John	35	M	Bricklayer	Great Britain	United States	Diana	6 Jul 1829
John	40	M	Paper Manufr.	G. Brittan	U. States	Trafalgar	4 Jun 1822
John	54	M	Mechanic	England	U.S.	Panthea	22 Jul 1826
John H.	23	M	Mercht.	Manchr.	N. York	Canada	1 Nov 1823
John S.	2	M	None	U. States	U. States	Canada	4 Oct 1824
John S.	4	M		America	America	Albion	4 Oct 1820
Joseph	16	M	Clergy	U. States	U. States	Six Brothers	21 Nov 1822
Joseph	54	M		England	United States	Florida	14 Sep 1827
Margt.	25	F	None	Great Britain	United States	Orbit	23 Oct 1826
Mary	16	F		G. Brittan	U. States	Trafalgar	4 Jun 1822
Mary	28			England	U.S. America	Constitution	18 Jun 1827
Mary	35	F	Lady	United States	United States	Hercules	21 Nov 1822
Richard	22		Saddler	England	England	London	16 Aug 1824
Richard	28	M		G. Britain	U. States	Mary & Harriot	8 Sep 1828
Rinaldo	17	F	Servant	United States	United States	Hercules	21 Nov 1822
Robert	18	M	Baker	Scotland	United States	Tom	2 Jul 1827
Robert	37	M	Mechanic	England	United States	John Wells	16 May 1825
Saml., Esqr.	39	M	Merchant	U. States	U. States	Don Quixote	27 Jun 1827
Samuel	25 5/12	M	...	England	America, U.S.	Illinois	3 Jun 1822
Sarah	4	F		Barbados	United States	Cannon	18 Aug 1821
Sarah	36	F		Barbados	United States	Cannon	18 Aug 1821
Sarah	40	F	Spinster	Ireland	United States	William Byrnes	15 Aug 1826
T.	31	M	Merchant	London	England	Yamacraw	10 May 1821
Thomas	3			England	U.S. America	Constitution	18 Jun 1827
Thos.	32	M	Butcher	N. York	New York	General Paez	9 Dec 1825
Thos. C.	30	M	Merchant	U. States	U. States	Crawford	4 Jan 1826
W. T.	25	M	Merchant	Barbadoes	Barbadoes	William & Nancy	5 Jun 1823
William	14	M		G. Brittan	U. States	Trafalgar	4 Jun 1822
William	44	M	Barn...	G. Britian	Canada	William Byrnes	23 Aug 1827
Wm.	43	M	Barber	Great Britain	New York	Superior	5 Sep 1827
Wm. G.	40	M	Merchant	Great Britain	Great Britain	Mentor	26 Dec 1826
MARSHEL, —	12/12	M				Abby Jones	12 Jul 1827
Jane	32	F		Gt. Britain	U. States	Sarah G.	14 Apr 1828
John	1 6/12	M		Gt. Britain	U. States	Sarah G.	14 Apr 1828
Margaret	6	F		Gt. Britain	U. States	Sarah G.	14 Apr 1828
Mary	4	F		Gt. Britain	U. States	Sarah G.	14 Apr 1828
Samuel	35	M		Gt. Britain	U. States	Sarah G.	14 Apr 1828
William	2	M		Gt. Britain	U. States	Sarah G.	14 Apr 1828
MARSHELL, Catherine	18	F	Spinster	Ireland	United States	Wilson	28 Nov 1828
John	48	M	Gentleman	United States	United States	Orleans	14 Dec 1821
MARSHET, Sarah	38	F		Barbadoes	New York	Only Daughter	9 Nov 1825
MARSHURST, William	23	M	Weaver	Ireland	United States	St. Michaels	18 Jul 1826
MARSLAND, Joseph	29	M	Carder	England	U. States	York	4 Apr 1826
S.	28	M	Merchant	U. States	U.S.	Ambuscade	14 Mar 1820
Stephen	28	M	Merchant	G. Briton	United States	James Monroe	14 Dec 1820
MARSTEN, W.	34	M	Supercargo	U. States	U. States	Eunice & Wealthy	24 Jan 1829
MARSTON, Wm.	15	M	None	Birmingham	America, New York	Washington	3 Mar 1828
MART, Ann	36	F		G. Britain	United States	Edward	21 Apr 1821
MARTA, Mary	20	F		Gt. Britain		Dalhouse Castle	13 May 1828
MARTAGH, Patrick	20	M	Farmer	Ireland	United States	Dublin Packet	23 May 1828
MARTAIN, Thos.	50	M	Merchant	Spain	U. States	Fair American	24 Dec 1821
MARTALLER, Edward H.	...		Clerk	Great Brittian	Unknown	Armadillo	15 Oct 1827
MARTALY, P.	35	M	Merchant	France	France	Fancy	28 Apr 1824
MARTEL, Stephen	43	M	Merchant	France	Havana	Ellen	13 May 1824
MARTELLY, Louis	42	M	Merchant	France	United States	Robert Fulton	27 Jun 1822
MARTEMONE, Joseph	25	M	Mill Wright	Gt. Britain	U. States	Frances Henrietta	18 Apr 1825
MARTEN, —	8	F		Havana	U. States	Senica	17 Mar 1824
—	9	F		Havana	U. States	Senica	17 Mar 1824
Elisha	30	M	Merchant	Havana	U. States	Senica	17 Mar 1824
Thomas	57		Farmer	England	S. New York	Xenophon	25 Jul 1826

NAMES OF PASSENGERS	AGE	SEX	OCCUPATIONS	COUNTRY TO WHICH THEY BELONG	COUNTRY THEY INTEND TO INHABIT	SHIPS/DATES OF ARRIVAL	
MARTEN (cont'd)							
William	22					Xenophon	25 Jul 1826
MARTENUS, Betsey	5	F	Segar Maker	Island of Cuba	United States	Betsey	28 Oct 1825
Catharine	33	F	Segar Maker	Island of Cuba	United States	Betsey	28 Oct 1825
Eliza	13	F	Segar Maker	Island of Cuba	United States	Betsey	28 Oct 1825
Francis	10	F	Segar Maker	Island of Cuba	United States	Betsey	28 Oct 1825
John	11	M	Segar Maker	Island of Cuba	United States	Betsey	28 Oct 1825
Joseph	12	M	Segar Maker	Island of Cuba	United States	Betsey	28 Oct 1825
Joseph	45	M	Segar Maker	Island of Cuba	United States	Betsey	28 Oct 1825
MARTER, Humphrey	21		Printer	Great Briton	Canada	Manchester Packet	17 Dec 1827
James	19	M	Labourer	Ireland	United States	Hope	12 Jun 1828
Michael	25	M	Farmer	Ireland	U. States	William & John	10 Jul 1824
MARTIAL, Michael	24	M	Labourer	Ireland	U. States	Hanford	29 Dec 1828
Rose	30	F	Wife	Ireland	U. States	Hanford	29 Dec 1828
MARTIGNEY, B.	29	M	Consul	France	U. States	Cadmus	9 Apr 1825
MARTIGU...,							
Manuel, Don	21	M		Great Brittain		Corinthian	9 Jan 1827
MARTIME, Jos. R.	18	M	Servant	Mexico	United States	York	31 Mar 1828
MARTIN, —, Miss		F	None		U. States	Antelope	18 Dec 1822
—, Mr.	30	M	Merchant	France	U. States	Robert Edwards	11 Mar 1822
—, Mr.	32	M	Enigner	U. States	U. States	Milo	15 May 1824
—, Mrs.		F	None		U. States	Antelope	18 Dec 1822
...bert	19	M	Taylor		Philadelphia	Hesperus	2 Nov 1820
Adam	9 6/12	M		Bavaria		François I	19 Nov 1828
Agness	1	F	None	Scotland	United States	Elizabeth	8 Jun 1827
Alexander	28	M	Engineer	Ireland	New York	Trusty	12 Sep 1828
Alexdr.	30	M	Engineer	Ireland	Und. Stts	Alexander Mansfield	18 Aug 1826
Alexr.	6		Son [of Robert]	Great Britain	United States	Camillus	12 Sep 1827
Alexr.	23	M	...	G. Brittain	America	Robin Hood	20 Jul 1827
And.	28	M	Merchant	N. York	New York	Leonora	30 Sep 1826
Ann	2	F		England	U. States	Emulous	22 Aug 1828
Ann	18	F		England	U. States	Emulous	22 Aug 1828
Ann	20	F		England	U. States	Emulous	22 Aug 1828
Ann	25	F	Servant	Ireland	United States	Ann Maria	5 May 1824
Ann	25	F		England	U. States	Emulous	22 Aug 1828
Ann	30	F	None	Ireland	America	Dewitt Clinton	27 Jul 1824
Ann	34	F		England	United States	Nimrod	31 Jul 1828
Ann Maria	8 6/12	F		Bavaria		François I	19 Nov 1828
Anne	40	F		England	U. States	Emulous	22 Aug 1828
Antoine	10	F	None	France	U. States	Sully	25 Jun 1828
Antoine	15	M		France	U. States	Trumbell	26 Oct 1829
Antoine	36	F	None	France	U. States	Sully	25 Jun 1828
B.	39 6/12	M	Carpenter	France	United States	Catharine	10 Sep 1827
Barbara	13	F	None	Scotland	United States	Camillus	28 Apr 1824
Bernard	25	M	Labourer	Ireland	New York	Atlantic	8 May 1828
Bridget	16	F	Servant	Ireland	United States	Josephine	30 Apr 1828
Bridget	21	F	Wife	G. Britain	U. States	Wanderer	23 Jun 1828
Bridget	30	F	Spinster		United States	St. Michaels	23 Dec 1826
Briget	25	F	Farmer	Great Britan	United States	Clematis	8 May 1827
Bryant	32	M	Labourer	Ireland	America	Dewitt Clinton	27 Jul 1824
C.	24	M	Labourer	Ireland	U. States	Two Marys	20 Apr 1825
C. D. P.	30	M	Merchant	France	France	Athenian	8 Feb 1827
Cath.	3	F		G. Britain	U. States	Wanderer	23 Jun 1828
Catharine	9	F		Bavaria		François I	19 Nov 1828
Catharine	29	F				Governor Fenner	23 Jul 1829
Catherine	2	F	Child	St. John, N.B.	United States	St. Michaels	23 Dec 1826
Catherine	10	F	Milliner	Great Britain	United States	Atlantic	8 Dec 1827
Cathr.	40 9/12	F		France	United States	Catharine	10 Sep 1827
Cathr.	60	F		England	U. States	Emulous	22 Aug 1828
Charles	8 3/12	M		France	United States	Catharine	10 Sep 1827
Charlotte	2			Ireland	United States	Jno. Dickinson	21 Sep 1821
Charlotte	4	F		England	U. States	Emulous	22 Aug 1828
Christina	7	F	None	Scotland	United States	Camillus	28 Apr 1824
Chs.	27	M	Labourer	Gt. Britain	U. States	Panthea	21 Jul 1825
D.	20	M		Germany	United States	Lydia	18 Jun 1828
David	12	M	Sailor	England	England	New York	7 Jul 1828
David	24	M	Labourer	Ireland	United States	Hope	12 Jun 1828

NAMES OF PASSENGERS	AGE	SEX	OCCUPATIONS	COUNTRY TO WHICH THEY BELONG	COUNTRY THEY INTEND TO INHABIT	SHIPS/DATES OF ARRIVAL	
MARTIN (cont'd)							
Dorothy	20	F		Ireland	U. States	Olive Branch	30 Oct 1823
E.	40	M	Merchant	Switzerland	U. States	Bayard	5 Sep 1828
E. L.	22	F		Germany	United States	Lydia	18 Jun 1828
Edmund	24	M	Labourer	Ireland	United States	Josephine	30 Apr 1828
Edward	11	M	Farmer	England	In the country	Chelsea	16 May 1828
Edward	45	M	Gentleman	New York	New York	Emily Cook	10 Apr 1826
Edward	48 11/12	M	...	England	United States	Criterion	27 Oct 1820
Edward	52	M	Gentleman	England	U. States	Acasta	28 Jan 1823
Edward Francis	3 7/12	M	None	England	United States	Criterion	27 Oct 1820
Edwd.	28	M	Cook	France	U. States	Jane Blossom	28 Aug 1826
Elisa	2	F		England	U. States	Emulous	22 Aug 1828
Elisa	4	F	Farmer	Ireland	America	Superior	12 Jun 1824
Elisabeth	15	F		England	U. States	Emulous	22 Aug 1828
Eliza	7	F	Farmer	England	United States	Euphrates	18 Aug 1827
Eliza	18		Lady			Hibernia	15 Aug 1820
Eliza	26 4/12	F		France	U.S. America	Erie	19 Oct 1829
Elizabeth	21	F	...	Ireland	United States	Carolina Ann	24 Oct 1825
Elizabeth	23		Lady	England	U.N. States	Meteor	25 Aug 1823
Elizabeth	41	F		U. States	Philadelphia	Sicily	25 Apr 1828
Ellen	6	F	Child	Ireland	United States	Ann Maria	8 Jun 1824
Ellen	6	F		England	U. States	Emulous	22 Aug 1828
Ellen	24	F	None	Scotland	United States	Elizabeth	8 Jun 1827
Emma	13	F		England	U.S.A.	Robin Hood	6 May 1828
Eva	6	F		Bavaria		François I	19 Nov 1828
Ewd.	1	M	Child	Switzerland	U. States	Bayard	5 Sep 1828
Ewd.	24	M	Farmer	Germany	United States	Lydia	18 Jun 1828
Felix	6/12	M			United States	Java	9 Jul 1827
Feranz	4 1/2	F		Bavaria		François I	19 Nov 1828
Frances	14	M		Germany	United States	Lydia	18 Jun 1828
Francisca	48					Apollo	11 Jun 1828
Frederlin	6	M	None	France	U. States	Sully	25 Jun 1828
G. Barby	4 9/12	F		France	United States	Catharine	10 Sep 1827
George	28	M	Weaver	England	United States	Aurora	9 Jul 1827
George	28	M	Laborer	Ireland	United States	Belleville	13 Oct 1827
George	29	M	Labourer	Ireland	United States	Dalhouse Castle	26 Dec 1827
George Henry	22	M	Merchant	America		Silas Richards	19 Mar 1828
H.	30	M	Merchant	Cadiz	Tampico	Sally Ann	23 May 1825
Hannah	5	F	Farmer	England	United States	Euphrates	18 Aug 1827
Hannah L.	26	F	Lady	U.S.	U.S.	Agenoria	12 Oct 1822
Helen	20	F		Scotland	United States	Trent	10 Jul 1827
Henry	10	M	Farmer	England	In the country	Chelsea	16 May 1828
Henry	17	M	Weaver	England	United States	Aurora	9 Jul 1827
Henry	22	M	Merchant	England	England	Virginia	9 Feb 1829
Henry	24	M	Perfumer	France	United States	Elizabeth	13 Nov 1824
Henry	24	M	Laborer	Ireland	New York	Amanda	23 May 1827
Henry	62	M	Farmer	Switzerland	America	Henry	17 May 1828
Henry, & family	31	M	Farmer	England	In the country	Chelsea	16 May 1828
Hugh	18	M		Ireland	U. States	Constitution	24 Jun 1823
Isaac	31	M	Cooper	Marblehead	U. States	Prize	10 Jun 1824
Isabella	6	F	Farmer	Ireland	U. States	Atlantic	19 Aug 1825
J.	9	F		Germany	United States	Lydia	18 Jun 1828
J.	26		Farmer	Ireland	United States	Courier	16 May 1825
J.	57		Farmer	Ireland	United States	Courier	16 May 1825
James	3	M	Farmer	Ireland	America	Superior	12 Jun 1824
James	4	M		England	U. States	Emulous	22 Aug 1828
*Died on the Voyage							
James	5	M	Farmer	Ireland	U. States	Atlantic	19 Aug 1825
James	6	M				Governor Fenner	23 Jul 1829
James	8	M		England	U. States	Emulous	22 Aug 1828
James	14	M		Ireland	U. States	Constitution	24 Jun 1823
James	22	M	Weaver	Ireland	U. States	Olive Branch	30 Oct 1823
James	22	M	Carpenter	Scotland	United States	Trent	10 Jul 1827
James	24	M	Weaver	England	United States	Aurora	9 Jul 1827
James	25	M	Labourer	Ireland	America	Weser	26 Jun 1821
James	25	M	Farmer	Great Britan	United States	Clematis	8 May 1827
James	28	M	Weaver	England	United States	Dalhouse Castle	8 May 1827
James	33 8/12	M	Labourer	G. Britain	United States	Louisa	14 Jun 1825
James, Mr.	18		Army	England	Canada	Acasta	16 Aug 1826

793

NAMES OF PASSENGERS	AGE	SEX	OCCUPATIONS	COUNTRY TO WHICH THEY BELONG	COUNTRY THEY INTEND TO INHABIT	SHIPS/DATES OF ARRIVAL	
MARTIN (cont'd)							
Jamesson	25	M	Labourer	Scotland	United States	Samuel Robertson	5 Oct 1827
Jane	7	F		England	U. States	Emulous	22 Aug 1828
Jane	24	F	Spinster	Ireland	America	Liverpool	31 Aug 1827
Jane	60	F		England	United States	Aurora	9 Jul 1827
Jas.	2	M	Labourer	Ireland	U. States	Two Marys	20 Apr 1825
Jas.	19	M				Hibernia	15 Aug 1820
Jas.	19	M		England	United States	Loire	4 Oct 1824
Jas.	20		Weaver	Ireland	United States	John Dickinson	28 Jun 1822
Jas.	20	M	Labourer	Gt. Britain	U. States	Frances Henrietta	18 Apr 1825
Jas.	30		Baker	G. Britain	U. States	Hamilton	28 Apr 1828
Jean	27		Wife [of Robert]	Great Britain	United States	Camillus	12 Sep 1827
Jno.	19	M		Ireland	U. States	Alfred	7 Jun 1824
Jno.	27	M	Mechanic	G. Britian	U. States	William Byrnes	23 Aug 1827
Jno.	34	M	Saddler	Ireland	United States	Nancy Henrietta	3 Nov 1828
Jno.	35	M	Storekeeper	Guadaloupe	France	James Monroe	15 Oct 1821
Jno.	35	M	Merchants	Philada.	U. States	Hope	28 Feb 1822
Jno.	37	M	Merchant	N. York	N. York	Martha	23 Jun 1825
John	...	M	Millwright	York, Great Britain		Casanda	5 Sep 1827
John	1	M	Labourer	Ireland	U. States	Two Marys	20 Apr 1825
John	1	M	Farmer	England	United States	Euphrates	18 Aug 1827
John	4	M	Labourer	Ireland	United States	Meteor	26 Jun 1827
John	5	M	None	France	U. States	Sully	25 Jun 1828
John	7	M	Child	Ireland	United States	Ann Maria	8 Jun 1824
John	10	M		England	U. States	Emulous	22 Aug 1828
John	12	M		Great Brittain	America	Pacific	13 Jan 1827
John	16	M	Farmer	Ireland	U.S. of America	Hamilton	18 Jul 1827
John	19	M	None	G.B.	U.S.A.	Silas Richard	30 Jun 1828
John	20	M	Labourer	Ireland	United States	Josephine	30 Apr 1828
John	20	M		Glasgow, St. Johns [Parish], Lanark [County]	New York	Hero	19 May 1828
John	22	M	Merchant	U. States	U. States	Betsey	23 Jul 1824
John	22	M	Baker	Ireland		Fame	9 Dec 1826
John	26	M	Weaver	Ireland	United States	Jno. Dickinson	21 Sep 1821
John	26	M	Blacksmith	England	America	Hercules	10 Apr 1823
John	26	M	Weaver	Ireland	U. States	Ann Maria	6 Jul 1824
John	26	M	Weaver	England	United States	Aurora	9 Jul 1827
John	26	M	Weaver	Ireland	United States	Henry Kneeland	7 Jun 1828
John	29 8/12	M	Barber	France	U.S. America	Erie	19 Oct 1829
John	30	M	Merchant	England	New York	Brighton	11 Dec 1827
John	38	M	Farmer	France	U. States	Sully	25 Jun 1828
John	45	M	Farmer	Great Britain	United States	Spartan	25 Jul 1821
John	45	M	Mariner	U. States	U. States	Courier	9 Feb 1829
John	49	M	Laborer	Scotland	United States	Camillus	28 Apr 1824
John B.	29 1/12	M	Taylor	France	U.S. America	Sicily	7 Oct 1829
John L.	24	M	Grocer	America	New York	Rachel Ann	13 Mar 1829
Joseph	5	M		Germany	United States	Lydia	18 Jun 1828
Joseph	10 1/12	M		France	United States	Catharine	10 Sep 1827
Joseph	21	M	Labourer	Ireland	United States	Lady Hunter	29 Apr 1826
Josh.	17	M	Baker	Great Britain	United States	Penelope	11 Jun 1827
Joshua	20	M	Weaver	England	United States	Aurora	9 Jul 1827
Judith	24	F	Labourer	Gt. Britain	U. States	Panthea	21 Jul 1825
Julia	30	M	Lady	Switzerland	U. States	Bayard	5 Sep 1828
Julia A. M.	15 1/12	F	None	England	United States	Criterion	27 Oct 1820
Juliana	3	F		Bavaria		François I	19 Nov 1828
Katzal	30	M	Farmer	Switzerland		Charlemagne	20 Aug 1829
Lackey	22	M		Great Britain	New York	Philetus	21 Jul 1827
Lidia	30	F	Farmer	England	United States	Euphrates	18 Aug 1827
Louisa	17	F		England	U.S.A.	Robin Hood	6 May 1828
M.	2	F		France	United States	Catharine	10 Sep 1827
M.	6 3/12	F		France	United States	Catharine	10 Sep 1827
M.	19	M	Merchant	U. States	U. States	Brown	29 Apr 1825
M.	50		Farmer	Ireland	United States	Courier	16 May 1825
Manuele	45	M	Priest	Spain	U. States	Horatio	21 Jan 1829
Marcellus	1	M			United States	Java	9 Jul 1827

NAMES OF PASSENGERS	AGE	SEX	OCCUPATIONS	COUNTRY TO WHICH THEY BELONG	COUNTRY THEY INTEND TO INHABIT	SHIPS/DATES OF ARRIVAL	
MARTIN (cont'd)							
Margaret	2/12	F	None	France	U. States	Sully	25 Jun 1828
Margaret	10	F	Labourer	Ireland	United States	Meteor	26 Jun 1827
Margaret	16	F		Ireland	U. States	Constitution	24 Jun 1823
Margaret	22	M	Wife	Scotland	United States	Samuel Robertson	9 May 1827
Margaret	28	F	Farmer	Ireland	U. States	Atlantic	19 Aug 1825
Margaret	28	F	Spinster	Ireland	United States	Lord Strangford	20 Jun 1826
Margaret	35	F	Spinster	Ireland	United States	Ann Maria	8 Jun 1824
Margaret	55 7/12	F	Farmer	Switzerland	America	Henry	17 May 1828
Margaretha	7	F		Bavaria		François I	19 Nov 1828
Margaretha Wild	36	F		Bavaria		François I	19 Nov 1828
Margaretta S. D.	19 9/12	F	None	England	United States	Criterion	27 Oct 1820
Margaretta S. D.	37	F	None	England	United States	Criterion	27 Oct 1820
Margt.	28	F	Matron	Ireland	America	Josephine	8 Dec 1827
Margt. Ann	2	F	Infant	Ireland	America	Josephine	8 Dec 1827
Maria	4 6/12	F		France	U.S. America	Erie	19 Oct 1829
Maria	11	F		England	U. States	Emulous	22 Aug 1828
Maria A. D.	8 7/12	F	None	England	United States	Criterion	27 Oct 1820
Maria An	3	F		England	United States	Nimrod	31 Jul 1828
Martin	11 11/12	M		France	United States	Catharine	10 Sep 1827
Martin	22	M	Planter	Jamaica	Halifax	May Flower	7 Jun 1826
Mary	8	F		Ireland	U. States	Constitution	24 Jun 1823
Mary	11	F	Farmer	England	United States	Euphrates	18 Aug 1827
Mary	11	F		Germany	United States	Lydia	18 Jun 1828
Mary	15	F	Farmer	England	In the country	Chelsea	16 May 1828
Mary	15	F		Germany	United States	Lydia	18 Jun 1828
Mary	17	F	Servant	Ireland	New York	Louisa	18 Apr 1827
Mary	17	F		Ireland	U.S. of America	Douglass	6 Jul 1829
Mary	18	F				Hibernia	15 Aug 1820
Mary	18	F	Labourer	Ireland	U. States	Two Marys	20 Apr 1825
Mary	18	F	Spinster	Ireland	United States	Robert Fulton	24 Jul 1826
Mary	22			Ireland	United States	Jno. Dickinson	21 Sep 1821
Mary	23	F	Farmer	England	England	Criterion	29 May 1822
Mary	23	F	...	...	United States	Camillus	10 Dec 1825
Mary	25	F	Labourer	Ireland	U. States	Two Marys	20 Apr 1825
Mary	26	F			United States	Java	9 Jul 1827
Mary	27	F		Gt. Britain		Dalhouse Castle	13 May 1828
Mary	35	F	Farmer	England	In the country	Chelsea	16 May 1828
Mary	40	F	Labourer	Ireland	United States	Meteor	26 Jun 1827
Mary	40	F		Germany	United States	Lydia	18 Jun 1828
Mary	42	F		Ireland	U. States	Constitution	24 Jun 1823
Mary	48	F		Great Britain	United States	Spartan	25 Jul 1821
Mary	60	F		England	U.S.A.	Robin Hood	6 May 1828
Mary Ann	32	F	None	Great Britain	United States	Blakely	29 Sep 1826
Mary Jane	18			Ireland	United States	John Dickinson	28 Jun 1822
Mathew	30	M	Farmer	Ireland	U. States	Atlantic	19 Aug 1825
Matthew	17	M	Labourer	Ireland	America	Minerva	31 May 1824
Michael	2/12	M	None	Ireland	America	Dewitt Clinton	27 Jul 1824
Michal	28	M	Farmer	Ireland		Aurora	12 Mar 1827
Miles	25	M	Labourer	Ireland	United States	Alexander Mansfield	9 Jul 1829
Mosus	8	M		Down, Ireland	Rhode Island	Anthusa	24 Aug 1825
N. Gwen	48	M		Germany	United States	Lydia	18 Jun 1828
Nathaniel	6	M		Ireland	U. States	Constitution	24 Jun 1823
Owen	35		Labourer	England	United States	Mary	15 Jul 1822
P.	27	M		G. Britain	U. States	Great Britain	6 Sep 1828
Pat	24	M	Farmer	England	United States	Nimrod	31 Jul 1828
Patrick	2	M		Gt. Britain		Dalhouse Castle	13 May 1828
Patt	20	M		Great Brittain	United States	Active	12 Sep 1828
Peter	23	M	Farmer	France		France	28 Mar 1829
Peter	28	M	Farmer	Gt. Brittian	Gt. Brittian	Manchester	21 Apr 1827
Peter	35	M	Mariner	French	United States	Fox	9 Mar 1829
Peter	42	M	Farmer	Bavaria		François I	19 Nov 1828
Peter	45	M	Seaman	England	United States	Brilliant	24 Sep 1827
Philip	5	M		Gt. Britain		Dalhouse Castle	13 May 1828
Philip	20	M		Ireland	United States	Essex	23 May 1828
Phillip	24	M	Labourer	Ireland	Unt. St. America	Wilson	21 May 1827
Phillis	5	F	Farmer	England	In the country	Chelsea	16 May 1828

NAMES OF PASSENGERS	AGE	SEX	OCCUPATIONS	COUNTRY TO WHICH THEY BELONG	COUNTRY THEY INTEND TO INHABIT	SHIPS/DATES OF ARRIVAL	
MARTIN (cont'd)							
Rebeca	40	F	Farmer	England	England	Criterion	29 May 1822
Revalz Rayd.	30	M	Mariner	France	St. Thomas	Ospray	2 Apr 1824
Richard	32	M	Blacksmith	Schotland	Ohio	Governor Fenner	23 Jul 1829
Robert	20	M	Leb...master	Ireland	America	John Adams	2 Aug 1827
Robert	22	M	Weaver	England	United States	Aurora	9 Jul 1827
Robert	24	M	Labourer	Rathefreland	United States	Carolina Ann	11 Jun 1824
Robert	27		Spinner	Great Britain	United States	Camillus	12 Sep 1827
Robert	30	M	Servnat	U. States	U. States	Wallace	12 Apr 1824
Robt.	22	M	Dyer	Great Britain	U. States America	Ann Maria	29 Nov 1821
Rose	20	F	Farmer	Great Britan	United States	Clematis	8 May 1827
Samuel	15			Ireland	United States	Jno. Dickinson	21 Sep 1821
Samuel	22	M	Labourer	Ireland	United States	Catharine	22 Jul 1825
Samuel	67	M	Weaver	England	United States	Aurora	9 Jul 1827
Sarah	4			Ireland	United States	Jno. Dickinson	21 Sep 1821
Sarah	19	F		Ireland	U. States	Constitution	24 Jun 1823
Sarah	19 9/12	F	Servent	Ireland	United States	Louisa	16 Mar 1826
Sarah	25	F		England	United States	Aurora	9 Jul 1827
Sophia	3	F	Farmer	England	In the country	Chelsea	16 May 1828
Sophia	80	F		Germany	United States	Samuel Robertson	8 Aug 1828
Susan	25	F	Spinster	Ireland	United States	Dublin Packet	28 Apr 1824
Susan	27	F	Farmer	Ireland	America	Superior	12 Jun 1824
Theodore	34		Mariner	France	United States	General Marion	18 Jul 1829
Theresa	3	F	Farmer	England	United States	Euphrates	18 Aug 1827
Tho.	9	M	Farmer	England	United States	Euphrates	18 Aug 1827
Thomas	18	M	Weaver	England	United States	Aurora	9 Jul 1827
Thomas	20	M	Labourer	Ireland	United States	Alexander Mansfield	9 Jul 1829
Thomas	30	M	Farmer	England	United States	Euphrates	18 Aug 1827
Thomas	32	M	Shoe Maker	Ireland	United States	Gem	16 Jun 1824
Thomas	39	M	Carpenter	England	England	Virginia	26 May 1828
Thomas	45	M	Merchant	U. States	United States	Dromo	22 Feb 1827
Thomas	47	M	Merchant	U.S.	America	Wave	15 Aug 1821
Thomas	49	M	Merchant	Spain	U. States	Neptune	25 Jan 1823
Thomas	49	M	Merchant	Spain	U. States	Packet	26 Dec 1823
Thomas	51	M	Mercht.	U. States	U. States	Brown	7 Jul 1826
Thomas	57	M	Merchant	Spain	N. York	Brown	30 Jan 1826
Thos.	12	M		England	U. States	Emulous	22 Aug 1828
Thos.	17	M	Labourer	Ireland	U. States	Two Marys	20 Apr 1825
Thos.	20	M	Shoemaker	England	U. States	Emulous	22 Aug 1828
Thos.	26	M	Labourer	Isle of Man		Ocean	13 Jul 1827
Thos.	27	M	Servant	Great Britain	U. States	Columbia	22 Sep 1828
Thos.	28	M	Trader	England	U. States	Emulous	22 Aug 1828
Thos.	35	M	Labourer	Manchester	United States	Java	9 Jul 1827
Thos.	40	M	Merchant	U. States		Emerald	27 Mar 1822
Thos.	49	M	Cooper	Isle of Man		Ocean	13 Jul 1827
Thos.	50		Merchant			Victory	12 Jul 1820
Thos.	50	M	Shoemaker	England	U. States	Emulous	22 Aug 1828
Thos.	51	M	Merchant	U. States	U. States	Good Friends	20 May 1825
Walter	27	M	Labourer	Scotland	United States	Samuel Robertson	9 May 1827
William	1/12	M	Child	St. John, N.B.	United States	St. Michaels	23 Dec 1826
William	7	M		England	U. States	Emulous	22 Aug 1828
William	14	M	Boy	Ireland	to return	Lady Hunter	10 Jul 1826
William	30	M	W...	Ireland	United States	Carolina Ann	24 Oct 1825
William	33	M	Merchant	England	New York	Brighton	11 Dec 1827
William	45	M	Farmer	England	England	Criterion	29 May 1822
William	45	M	Planter	St. Croix	Ireland	Jupiter	6 Aug 1826
William Stephens Ogden	1 6/12	M	None	England	United States	Criterion	27 Oct 1820
Willian	1/2	M	Labourer	Ireland	United States	Meteor	26 Jun 1827
Willm.	38	M	Manufacturer	Ireland	America	Josephine	8 Dec 1827
Wm.	1	M		Ireland	U. States	Olive Branch	30 Oct 1823
Wm.	1 6/12	M		G. Britain	U. States	Wanderer	23 Jun 1828
Wm.	19	M	Tobacconist	Great Brittain	U.S.	Trafalgar	22 Jun 1821
Wm.	22	M	Servant			John & Edward	25 Aug 1820
Wm.	27	M	Farmer	Great Britain	United States	Ann	22 Dec 1821
Wm.	27	M	Labourer	Ireland	N. York	Trusty	12 Sep 1828

NAMES OF PASSENGERS	AGE	SEX	OCCUPATIONS	COUNTRY TO WHICH THEY BELONG	COUNTRY THEY INTEND TO INHABIT	SHIPS/DATES OF ARRIVAL	
MARTIN (cont'd)							
Wm.	28	M	Servant	U. States	U. States	Matilda	23 May 1826
Wm.	33		Merchant	Baltimore	U. States	Brown	11 Jun 1827
Zeperlein	3	M	None	France	U. States	Sully	25 Jun 1828
MARTINACKS, W.	40	M	Merchant	Spain	U.States	Sally	16 Apr 1821
MARTINAS,							
Joseph, Don	18	M				Mercid	21 Oct 1824
MARTINBOROUGH,							
John	39	M	Merchant	New York	U. States	Liberty	1 Nov 1823
MARTINCOURT,							
Magdeline	50	F		France	United States	Montano	5 May 1828
Nicholas	21	M	Tin Smith	France	United States	Montano	5 May 1828
Nicholas	55	M	Distiller	France	United States	Montano	5 May 1828
MARTINDALE, Jonan.	33	M	Teacher	Barbadoes	U. States	Ruth	1 Aug 1824
Thos.	28			Ireland		Agricola	1 Jul 1820
MARTINE, —	18	M	Servant	Havana	U. States	Evelina	31 May 1825
—	46	M	Merchant	Spain	United States	Rose in Bloom	12 Apr 1821
Antonia	40	M	Officer	Spain	U. States	Pomona	18 Aug 1824
James	19	M		G. Brittian	United States	Louisa	14 Jun 1825
M.	28	M		France	N. York	Queen Mabb	22 Nov 1824
MARTINER, Thos.	49	M	Merchant	Spain	U. States	Pocahontas	9 Jun 1823
MARTINES, A.	36	M	Merchant	Spain	U. States	Sally	4 Aug 1821
Miguel	31	M		Spain	Spain	Richmond Packet	13 Jun 1825
Simon	20	M	Merchant	Havana	Havana	Boon	26 Feb 1820
MARTINET, P. L.	34	M	Merchant	New York	U. States	Peter Remsen	30 Jun 1828
MARTINEZ, Andres	75	M	Merchant	Spain	Spain	Virginia	9 Feb 1829
Angelo	33		Mercht.			Corsair	2 Oct 1820
Jose V.	20	M	Gentleman	Columbia	U. States	Bunker Hill	12 Aug 1828
Juana	29	F		Mexico	Mexico	Virginia	9 Feb 1829
Leocada	40	F		Mexico	Mexico	Virginia	9 Feb 1829
Louise L.	25		Planter	France		Bayard	10 Sep 1827
Manuel	30 3/12	M	Comirainta	Spaniard	New York	Leonidas	22 Jan 1829
Pedro	48	M	Priest	Spain	Spain	Virginia	8 Mar 1828
MARTINGDALE, —, Mrs.	37	M	Planter	Barbadoes	Barbadoes	William & Nancy	5 Jun 1823
MARTINIS, Michael	34	M	Gentleman	Spain	Spain	Superior	9 Jun 1825
MARTINO, Jos.	27	M	Merchant	N. Orleans	Porto Rico	Concordia	8 Nov 1822
MARTINS,							
Antonio Constantino	16	M	Merchant	Portugeese	United States	Mary Elizabeth	15 Oct 1829
Jos.	34	M	Merchant	France	United States	Andrew Jackson	9 Jul 1822
MARTINUS, M. Domingo	31	M	Merchant	Porto Rico	Porto Rico	Flight	23 Sep 1826
MARTONES, M. A. R.		M	Officer	Portugal	Portugal	Diana	7 Jun 1823
MARTOUGH, Jane	25	F	None	England	New York	America	1 Aug 1828
Mary	24	F	None	England	New York	America	1 Aug 1828
MARTRAY, Catherine	16	F	Servant	Ireland	United States	Ann Maria	3 Jul 1827
James	30	M	Laborer	Ireland	United States	Ann Maria	3 Jul 1827
Rose	20	F	Servant	Ireland	United States	Ann Maria	3 Jul 1827
William	27	M	Laborer	Ireland	United States	Ann Maria	3 Jul 1827
MARTTY, Hugh	18	M		Scotland	Upper Canada	Exertion	9 Oct 1828
John	16	M		Scotland	Upper Canada	Exertion	9 Oct 1828
John	70	M		Scotland	Upper Canada	Exertion	9 Oct 1828
Margeret	65	F		Scotland	Upper Canada	Exertion	9 Oct 1828
MARTZ, Carteran	26	F	Farmer	Germany	United States	Virginia	31 May 1828
Carteran	50	F	Farmer	Germany	United States	Virginia	31 May 1828
Elizabeth	1 1/2	F	Farmer	Germany	United States	Virginia	31 May 1828
Elizabeth	24	F	Farmer	Germany	United States	Virginia	31 May 1828
Enoch	18	M	Farmer	Germany	United States	Virginia	31 May 1828
Ferazer	16	M	Farmer	Germany	United States	Virginia	31 May 1828
George	20	M	Farmer	Germany	United States	Virginia	31 May 1828
Margret	11	F	Farmer	Germany	United States	Virginia	31 May 1828
Michel	56	M	Farmer	Germany	United States	Virginia	31 May 1828
Michell	28	M	Farmer	Germany	United States	Virginia	31 May 1828
MARTZTOF, John	37 5/12	M	Baker	France	United States	France	6 Oct 1828
MARUROT,							
Elizabeth, Mrs.	53	F	Seamstress	France	Burlington (N.J.)	Cadmus	27 Aug 1822
MARVIN, John	30	M		Gt. Britain	U. States	Tantiva	7 Jul 1828
Mary	22	F	Lady	St. John, N.B.	United States	St. Michaels	25 May 1825
W.	25	M		Ireland	U. States	St. Michael	26 Oct 1824

NAMES OF PASSENGERS	AGE	SEX	OCCUPATIONS	COUNTRY TO WHICH THEY BELONG	COUNTRY THEY INTEND TO INHABIT	SHIPS/DATES OF ARRIVAL	
MARY, Heffolyte	20	M	Mechanic	France	U.S.	Edward Quesnel	17 Jan 1825
MARZE, J.	2	M		Martineco		Angenora	12 May 1826
MASARO, Manuel	11	M	Merchant	Columbia	U. States	Dandy	22 Dec 1824
MASCHEITTE, Pietre	33		Merchant	Italy	Italy	Silvanus Jenkins	30 Nov 1827
MASCORD, Edwd.	28	M	Bookbinder	England	United States	St. John	5 Oct 1829
Geo.	2	M		England	United States	St. John	5 Oct 1829
Harriet	28	F		England	United States	St. John	5 Oct 1829
MASELA, An Marguerite	23	F	Wife	Swiss	U. States	Comet	28 Jul 1825
David Lewis	32	M	Labourer	Swiss	U. States	Comet	28 Jul 1825
Henry Lewis	1	M	Son	Swiss	U. States	Comet	28 Jul 1825
MASEY, Mary	40	F	None	Gt. Brittian	Gt. Brittian	Manchester	21 Apr 1827
Robt.	50	M	Farmer	Gt. Brittian	Gt. Brittian	Manchester	21 Apr 1827
Wm.	14	M	Farmer	Gt. Brittian	Gt. Brittian	Manchester	21 Apr 1827
MASFIELD, Jas.	35	M	Mariner	U. States	U. States	Hope	29 Dec 1821
Nathaniel	30	M	Mariner	U. States	U. States	Mary Ann	9 Jan 1827
MASH, Mary	18	F	Lady	Ireland	U. States	Sarah G	7 May 1827
MASHMIAG, John	28	M	Merchant	Spain	Spain	Native	8 Feb 1826
MASLIN, M. M.	39	M	Merchant	America	America	Brittannia	28 Feb 1827
MASLON, George	33		Shoemaker	Northampton-shire	N. York	Peru	30 May 1828
MASON, —, Master	9	M		Halifax	some to return & the others to Canada	Albert	14 May 1822
—, Master	12	M		Halifax	some to return & the others to Canada	Albert	14 May 1822
—, Mrs.	28	F		Halifax	some to return & the others to Canada	Albert	14 May 1822
...	...	...	...	Scotland	America	Nimrod	9 Jul 1827
...	...	...	...	Scotland	America	Nimrod	9 Jul 1827
...	...	F	...	Scotland	America	Nimrod	9 Jul 1827
...aurila	40	F				Hesperus	2 Nov 1820
...mul	40	M	Baker	England	U.S.	Acasta	11 May 1827
...seph	52	M	Baker		Pensylvania	Hesperus	2 Nov 1820
A...	...	...	...	Scotland	America	Nimrod	9 Jul 1827
Abram	33	M	Farmer	France	Ohio	Abby Jones	12 Jul 1827
Ann	17	F	Spinster	Ireland	United States	Asia	29 Jul 1829
Ann	26	F	Matron	Great Britain	U. States	Robert Fulton	3 Dec 1827
Benjamin	9	M				Hesperus	2 Nov 1820
Benjm.	56	M	Planter	G. Britain	Jamaica	Mary Ann	28 Jun 1824
Catharine	26	F		France	Ohio	Abby Jones	12 Jul 1827
Catherine	2	F				St. Anna	8 Aug 1827
Ch.	9	M	Farmer	England	United States	Euphrates	18 Aug 1827
Christian	5	M		France	Ohio	Abby Jones	12 Jul 1827
Dennis	30	M	Farmer	Ireland	United States	Antioch	21 Sep 1827
E.	1/2	F	Brewer	Scotland	U.S. States	Splendid	14 Aug 1829
Easter	70	M	Lady	Ireland	U. States	Sarah G	7 May 1827
Eliza	34	F	Seamstress	United States	United States	New Packet	20 Oct 1827
Elizabeth	7	F		Gt. Britain	United States	Meteor	19 Aug 1829
Elizabeth	30	F		Gt. Britain	United States	Meteor	19 Aug 1829
Elizabeth	35	F		England		Boyer	9 May 1825
Ellen	12	F				Hesperus	2 Nov 1820
George	...	...	...	Scotland	America	Nimrod	9 Jul 1827
George	5	M				Hesperus	2 Nov 1820
Henry	26	M	Merchant	England		Boyer	9 May 1825
Henry	39	M	Farmer	Germany	United States	Origon	8 Jun 1824
J.	2	M	Brewer	Scotland	U.S. States	Splendid	14 Aug 1829
J.	7	F	Brewer	Scotland	U.S. States	Splendid	14 Aug 1829
Jabes	20 6/12	M	Boot Maker	Great Britain	U. States	Robert Fulton	3 Dec 1827
Jacob	1	M		France	Ohio	Abby Jones	12 Jul 1827
James	6/12	M				Hesperus	2 Nov 1820
James	4	M		Gt. Britain		Dalhouse Castle	13 May 1828
Jas.	29	M	Merchant	England	Canada	Acasta	14 Jun 1824
John	5	M	Boy	United States	United States	New Packet	20 Oct 1827
John	10	M		Gt. Britain	United States	Meteor	19 Aug 1829
John	40	M	Farmer	Ireland	U. States	Vermont	19 Jun 1827
Jonathan	29	M	Gent.	Boston	U.S.	Cadmus	17 Aug 1824
Joseph	3	M		France	Ohio	Abby Jones	12 Jul 1827

NAMES OF PASSENGERS	AGE	SEX	OCCUPATIONS	COUNTRY TO WHICH THEY BELONG	COUNTRY THEY INTEND TO INHABIT	SHIPS/DATES OF ARRIVAL	
MASON (cont'd)							
Joseph	11	M				Hesperus	2 Nov 1820
Judith	38	F	None	England	United States	Nestor	20 Nov 1821
L.	14	M	Apprentice	America	U. States	Brutus	21 May 1824
M.	12		child, Brewer	Scotland	U.S. States	Splendid	14 Aug 1829
Maraqueta	27	F				St. Anna	8 Aug 1827
Margt.	32	F	Lady	Ireland	U. States	Sarah G	7 May 1827
Margt.	50	F	Spinster	Ireland	United States	Antioch	21 Sep 1827
Mary	22	F		Canada	Canada	Thames	16 May 1821
Mary	25	F	Lady	Ireland	U. States	Sarah G	7 May 1827
Mary	30	F	Labourer	Ireland	United States	Hope	12 Jun 1828
Mary	36		Wife, Brewer	Scotland	U.S. States	Splendid	14 Aug 1829
Mary	40	F		Port au Prince	Spain	Harmony	16 Oct 1821
Mary Ann	5	F	Farmer	England	United States	Euphrates	18 Aug 1827
Mary Bluemwith, Miss	25 8/12	F	Spinster	England	U. States	William Thompson	25 Aug 1828
Pat.	30	M	Labourer	Ireland	United States	Antioch	21 Sep 1827
R.	10		child, Brewer	Scotland	U.S. States	Splendid	14 Aug 1829
Rob	28	M	Merchant	Antigua	G. Brittain	Elisa Pigott	17 Jan 1822
Robert	1	M		Gt. Britain	United States	Meteor	19 Aug 1829
Robert	21		Glass Cutter	England	Alexandria, U.S.	Roman	17 Oct 1826
Robert	38	M	Brewer	Scotland	U.S. States	Splendid	14 Aug 1829
Samuel	0 11/12	M	Child	Great Britain	U. States	Robert Fulton	3 Dec 1827
Samuel	24	M	Lapiderry	Great Britain	U. States	Robert Fulton	3 Dec 1827
Samuel	55	M	Mechanic	England	U. States	Birmingham	16 Jun 1828
Sarah	33	F	Farmer	England	United States	Euphrates	18 Aug 1827
Sidney	35	M	Mercht.	U. States	U. States	St. Anna	8 Aug 1827
T. H.	30	M	Merchant	N. Scotia	U. States	Infant	10 Jul 1821
Thomas	21	M	Farmer	Great Britain	U.S.A.	Silas Richards	7 Mar 1825
Thomas	45			Yorkshire, England	Great Britain	Frances Henrietta	31 May 1824
Thomas, Master	16	M	Clerk	New York	U. States	Manchester	23 Jan 1826
Thos.	27	M	Draper	Great Britain	U. States	United States	8 Sep 1827
Thos.	28	M	Weaver	Armagh, Ireland	New York	Anthusa	24 Aug 1825
Thos. H.	25	M	Merchant	Saint John	St. John	Nancy	11 Apr 1822
William	...	...	...	Scotland	America	Nimrod	9 Jul 1827
William	12	M		Gt. Britain	United States	Meteor	19 Aug 1829
William	19	M	Cordwainer	England	New York	Hudson	20 Nov 1828
William	31	M	Mason	Gt. Britain	United States	Meteor	19 Aug 1829
William	33	M	Jeweller	Great Britain	United States	Ganges	26 Oct 1826
William	35	M	Mariner	U. States	U. States	Oristello	19 Mar 1827
Wm.	10	M	Farmer	England	United States	Euphrates	18 Aug 1827
Wm.	26		Labourer	Halifax	U. States	Edwin	26 Sep 1828
MASQUELEZ, M.	53	M	Merchant	France	U. States	Heroine	19 Jun 1828
MASS, Mary	27	F		G. Britain		James Monroe	8 Aug 1820
MASSA, Ann Maria	23	F		Wertemberg	Wertemberg	Edward Quesnel	3 Jul 1829
Antonio	32	M	Servant	Swis	United States	Iris	21 Sep 1821
Catherine	51	F		Wertemberg	Wertemberg	Edward Quesnel	3 Jul 1829
Dorathia	18	F		Wertemberg	Wertemberg	Edward Quesnel	3 Jul 1829
Jacob	65	M	Farmer	Wertemberg	Wertemberg	Edward Quesnel	3 Jul 1829
John C.	27	M	Merchant	Porto Rico	Porto Rico	Francis Jarvis	30 Aug 1826
MASSE, —, Mrs.	17	F		Marseilles	U. States	Superior	30 Apr 1824
M. Antony	23	M	Gentleman	Marseilles	U. States	Superior	30 Apr 1824
MASSERWANDEL,							
Catharina	27	F	Farmer	Wortenberg	Lancaster	Louisa	6 Oct 1828
Geo.	34	M	Farmer	Wortenberg	Lancaster	Louisa	6 Oct 1828
Johann Fredrich	2	M	Farmer	Wortenberg	Lancaster	Louisa	6 Oct 1828
Johann Georg	0 2/12	M	Farmer	Wortenberg	Lancaster	Louisa	6 Oct 1828
Johann Jacob	3	M	Farmer	Wortenberg	Lancaster	Louisa	6 Oct 1828
MASSET, Joseph	34	M	Tailor	Native of Switzerland	United States	Canaris	30 Jun 1827
Mary	1	F		Native of Switzerland	United States	Canaris	30 Jun 1827
Mary	33	F		Native of Switzerland	United States	Canaris	30 Jun 1827
MASSEY, —, Mrs.	40	F	Merchant	U. States	Canada	Columbia	7 Sep 1827

NAMES OF PASSENGERS	AGE	SEX	OCCUPATIONS	COUNTRY TO WHICH THEY BELONG	COUNTRY THEY INTEND TO INHABIT	SHIPS/DATES OF ARRIVAL	
MASSEY, (cont'd)							
Amy	35	F	Servant	England	United States should they approve of it	Robert Edwards	20 Jan 1829
J. W.	25	M	Merchant	Maryland, U.S.	U. States	Moro	20 Oct 1826
James	3		Bleacher	Bolton	England	Great Britain	7 May 1827
John	13	M	None			Emulous	19 Feb 1822
John	26	M	Shoemaker	Ireland	United States	Nancy Henrietta	3 Nov 1828
Sarah	29	F	Wife	England	U. States	Emulous	19 Feb 1822
MASSIAN, Victor	30	M	Merchant	France	France	Virginia	26 May 1828
MASSIEN, Rosilla	37	F		America	America	Brittannia	28 Feb 1827
MASSINE, Jaquss	20	M	Servant	Rushia	England	Electra	7 Jul 1828
MASSOE, Stephans	32	M	Merchant	Swis	United States	Iris	21 Sep 1821
MASSON, J., Mr.	24	M	Merchant	G. Britain	Canada	Corinthian	29 Apr 1826
Thos.	25	M	Merchant	England	U. States	Orazimbo	7 Jan 1821
MASSY, Geo.	24	M		Great Britain	United States	Aspasia	16 Jul 1828
MASTAIN, Walter	34	M	Merchant	New York	New York	La Plata	29 Dec 1827
MASTER, ...	28	F		Scotland	New York	Joseph Hume	26 Oct 1829
..., Mrs.	60	F		Scotland	New York	Joseph Hume	26 Oct 1829
Alexander	18	M	Laborer	Gt. Britain	U.S. of America	Friends	25 Sep 1823
Joseph	17	M	Laborer	Gt. Britain	U.S. of America	Friends	25 Sep 1823
MASTERMAN, Elizath.	32		Servant	Ireland	United States	Rufus King	4 Sep 1823
John	30	M	Laborer	Ireland	United States	Justina	5 Aug 1823
MASTERS, Henry	45	M	Merchant	England	England	Vermont	29 Oct 1822
M.	23	M	Labourer	Ireland	U. States	Wanderer	1 Sep 1828
Martha C.	20	F		U. States		New York	19 Nov 1828
Philip	22	M	Mariner	U. States	U. States	Trimmer	3 Jan 1826
Thomas	47	M	Merchant	U. States		New York	19 Nov 1828
MASTERSON, Ann	8	F	Servant	Ireland	United States	Josephine	30 Apr 1828
Bridget	25	F	Spinster	Ireland	America	Wilson	16 May 1825
Cath.	25		Spinster	Ireland	United States	Courier	15 Oct 1827
Chas.	22	M	Farmer	Ireland	America	Farmer	4 Aug 1825
Ellen	2 6/12	F		Ireland	U. States	Fabius	22 Sep 1828
Henry	22	M	Labourer	Ireland	U. States	Hanford	29 Dec 1828
James	18	M	Labourer	Ireland	U. States	Fabius	22 Sep 1828
John	3	M		Ireland	U. States	Fabius	22 Sep 1828
John	30	M	Farmer	Great Britain	United States	Illinois	9 Oct 1820
M.	22	F	Servant	Ireland	United States	Josephine	30 Apr 1828
Margaret	18	F	None	Ireland	United States	Silas Richards	3 Apr 1826
Margt.	20		Spinster	Ireland	United States	Courier	15 Oct 1827
Mary	13	F	Servant	Ireland	United States	Josephine	30 Apr 1828
Michael	27	M	Laborer	Ireland	United States	Indian Chief	16 Aug 1822
Patric	20	M	Labourer	Ireland	America	Wilson	16 May 1825
Patrick	34	M	Laborer	Ireland	United States	Weser	29 Jul 1823
Rose	26	F	Servant	Ireland	United States	Josephine	30 Apr 1828
Susan	25 9/12	F		Ireland	U. States	Fabius	22 Sep 1828
MASTERSTAN, Bridget	25	F	Spinster	Ireland	America	Dublin Packet	9 Oct 1820
Nancy	22	F	Wife	Ireland	America	Dublin Packet	9 Oct 1820
Nancy, Junr.	1	F	Infant	Ireland	America	Dublin Packet	9 Oct 1820
MASTERTON, Andrew	21	M	Farmer	Ireland	United States	Elizabeth	8 Jun 1827
Bridget	11	F	None	Ireland	United States	Elizabeth	8 Jun 1827
Henry	35	M	B. N. C...	U.S.	U. States	America	17 Oct 1825
Mary	30	F			U. States	America	17 Oct 1825
MASTIER, —, Miss	27	F		U.S.	U.S.	York	1 Dec 1827
MASTRE, Louis	22	M	Saddler	Swiss	U. States	Montano	2 Sep 1828
MATADO, C. B.	28	M	Merchant	Spain	U. States	Margaretta	2 May 1826
MATCHET, Thomas	...	...	...	Ireland	U. States of America	Courier	17 Mar 1827
MATCHETT, Daud	24	M	Labourer	Grt. Britain	United States	Robert Fulton	8 Oct 1828
J. V.	35	M	Merchant	United States	United States	Bogota	16 Dec 1826
John	24	M	Labourer	Grt. Britain	United States	Robert Fulton	8 Oct 1828
Margret	20	F	Spinster	Grt. Britain	United States	Robert Fulton	8 Oct 1828
MATEL, —, one born at sea	Infant		Born at Sea	Bavaria	United States	American	27 Aug 1827
Elizabeth	36			Bavaria	United States	American	27 Aug 1827
Jacob	43	M	Farmer	Bavaria	United States	American	27 Aug 1827
MATELL, Jacob	7	M	Farmer	Bavaria	United States	American	27 Aug 1827
MATER, Cornelius	30	M	Shoe Maker	Ireland	United States	Jubilee	1 Oct 1828
MATERTEN, Chrs.	19	M	Labourer	Germany	U. States	Hudson	26 Jan 1825
MATEY, Constant	5	M	Farmer	France	United States	Crescent	12 Jul 1827

NAMES OF PASSENGERS	A G E	S E X	OCCUPATIONS	COUNTRY TO WHICH THEY BELONG	COUNTRY THEY INTEND TO INHABIT	SHIPS/DATES OF ARRIVAL	
MATEY (cont'd)							
Francis	29	M	Farmer	France	United States	Crescent	12 Jul 1827
James	2	M	Farmer	France	United States	Crescent	12 Jul 1827
Joseph	7	M	Farmer	France	United States	Crescent	12 Jul 1827
Marram	35	F	Farmer	France	United States	Crescent	12 Jul 1827
MATHAN, E.	50	F	None	U. States		Queen Mab	24 Sep 1827
H.	20	F	None	U. States		Queen Mab	24 Sep 1827
MATHEMER, Catherine	24	F	there child [Jas. & Christina]	Germany	United States	Helen	5 Sep 1828
Christian	17	M	there child [Jas. & Christina]	Germany	United States	Helen	5 Sep 1828
Christina	60	F	his wife [Jas.]	Germany	United States	Helen	5 Sep 1828
Frederick	20	M	there child [Jas. & Christina]	Germany	United States	Helen	5 Sep 1828
Jas.	60	M	Stone Cutter	Germany	United States	Helen	5 Sep 1828
John	33	M	there child [Jas. & Christina]	Germany	United States	Helen	5 Sep 1828
Rose	23	F	there child [Jas. & Christina]	Germany	United States	Helen	5 Sep 1828
Sophia	15	F	there child [Jas. & Christina]	Germany	United States	Helen	5 Sep 1828
MATHER, Agnes	2	F	Child	Scotland	United States	Ann Maria	18 Dec 1827
Agnes	23	F	Wife	Scotland	United States	Ann Maria	18 Dec 1827
Agnes	25	F	Wife	Holland	United States	Ann Maria	28 Jan 1828
Agnes	30	F	None	Scotland	U. States	Czar	29 Aug 1829
Agnes	53	F	Wife	Scotland	United States	Ann Maria	18 Dec 1827
Elizh.	10			Kamsbottom	England	Great Britain	7 May 1827
H. S.	27	M	Printer	N. York	U. States	General Scott	7 May 1824
Hannah	10			Kamsbottom	England	Great Britain	7 May 1827
J.	25	M	Labourer	Ireland	United States	Sarah G.	15 May 1828
J.	50	M	Farmer	U. States	U. States	Robt. Edwards	4 Sep 1828
James	3			Kamsbottom	England	Great Britain	7 May 1827
James	40		Calico Printer	Kamsbottom	England	Great Britain	7 May 1827
John	3	M	Child	Scotland	United States	Ann Maria	18 Dec 1827
John	14			Kamsbottom	England	Great Britain	7 May 1827
John	25	M	Son	Scotland	United States	Ann Maria	18 Dec 1827
John	65	M	Farmer	Scotland	United States	Ann Maria	18 Dec 1827
Lewis	26	M	Tailor	United States	United States	Gertrude	19 May 1826
Lewis	30	M	Gentleman	U.S.	U. States	Milton	20 Aug 1827
Martha	6			Kamsbottom	England	Great Britain	7 May 1827
Mary	1			Kamsbottom	England	Great Britain	7 May 1827
Mary	40			Kamsbottom	England	Great Britain	7 May 1827
Rachel	8			Kamsbottom	England	Great Britain	7 May 1827
Robt.	24	M	Merchant	G. Brittain	U. States	Hercules	24 Oct 1821
Sarah	5			Kamsbottom	England	Great Britain	7 May 1827
Sarah	35	F	Servant	United States	United States	Cortes	11 Dec 1822
Thomas	23	M	Joiner	Scotland	U. States	Czar	29 Aug 1829
Thomas	27	M	Farmer	Holland	United States	Ann Maria	28 Jan 1828
MATHERS, Catharine	35	F	Wife	Ireland	United States	William & George	14 May 1828
Edwd.	25	M	Labourer	Ireland	United States	Andes	2 Oct 1828
Hugh	21	M	Farmer	England	U. States	Commerce	2 Oct 1823
Joseph	35	M	Farmer	Ireland	United States	William & George	14 May 1828
Lawrence	29	M	Farmer	England	U. States	Commerce	2 Oct 1823
Lettice	18	F	Lady	Great Brittain	U. States	Nancy	18 Jul 1821
Petro	20	M	Merchant	Spain	Spain	Brillante	24 May 1822
MATHERSOLE,							
Wm. Austin	25	M	Merchant	Great Britain		Birmingham	11 Oct 1828
MATHERSON, Alexander	7	M	None	U. States	U. States	Camillus	27 Jul 1825
Eliza	32	F	None	U. States	U. States	Camillus	27 Jul 1825
Flora	3	F	None	Ireland	U. States	Josephine	27 Jul 1825
John	45	M	Farmer	Ireland	U. States	Josephine	27 Jul 1825

NAMES OF PASSENGERS	AGE	SEX	OCCUPATIONS	COUNTRY TO WHICH THEY BELONG	COUNTRY THEY INTEND TO INHABIT	SHIPS/DATES OF ARRIVAL	
MATHERSON, (cont'd)							
John P.	1	M	None	Ireland	U. States	Josephine	27 Jul 1825
Murdock	9	M	None	U. States	U. States	Camillus	27 Jul 1825
MATHES, Jacques	32	M	Tailor	Wirtemberg	United States	Thetis	5 Jul 1821
MATHESON, Ann	1 6/12	F		Scotland	United States	Mobile	21 Aug 1827
Ann, Mrs.	22 4/12	F		Scotland	United States	Mobile	21 Aug 1827
G. F.	23	M	Merchant	England	England	Citizen	7 Jul 1823
John	3 5/12	M		Scotland	United States	Mobile	21 Aug 1827
MATHEUS, David	...	...	...	...	...	St. Michael	22 Sep 1824
John	25	M		Great Brittian	United States	Carolina Augusta	2 Dec 1828
Patrick	23	M	Farmer	Ireland	United States	Lord Strangford	20 Jun 1826
Robt.	22	M	Farmer	Great Britain	United States	Grecian	24 Sep 1828
MATHEW, —, Mrs.	25		Spinster	Ireland	United States	Courier	15 Oct 1827
D.	45	M	Merchant	America	U. States	Mary Livingston	26 Jul 1824
George	30	M	Black Smith	Ireland		Quatre Freres	29 Jul 1828
J. M.	26	M	Farmer	Great Britain	United States	Isaac Hicks	6 Dec 1827
Newman	16		Farmer	Switzerland	United States	Henri IV	14 Sep 1827
Richard	22		Baker	London	England	Elizabeth	8 Dec 1821
MATHEWS, —	12	M	Servant	England	U. States	Sarah Thornton	13 Sep 1828
—, Mrs.	50	F		G Britian	U. States	Leader	20 Apr 1827
Abrm.	20		Merchant	Ireland	United States	Courier	15 Oct 1827
Ann	32 4/12	F	None	Ireland	America	Minerva	31 May 1824
Ann	40	F	None	England	United States	New Packet	7 Aug 1826
Benard	4 6/12	M	None	Ireland	America	Minerva	31 May 1824
Bernard	12	M		Ireland	United States	Princess Charlotte	26 Apr 1827
Bernard	20 10/12	M		Ireland	America	Carolina Ann	7 Apr 1826
Bridget	3	F		Ireland	United States	Princess Charlotte	26 Apr 1827
C.	24	M	Gentleman	G. Brittain	U. States	Clarence	8 Dec 1821
Charles	30	M	Merchant	Cayenne	England	Falcon	11 Oct 1824
Chas.	3					Mount Vernon	26 Aug 1820
Chas.	29		Clergyman	Grt. Britain	Uper Canada	Britannia	29 Oct 1829
Chas.	45	M	Comedian	London	G. Brittain	William Thompson	6 Sep 1822
Chs.	1	M		G Britian	U. States	Leader	20 Apr 1827
Edwd.	28	M	Joiner	Great Britain	United States	William Dawson	18 Jun 1827
Eleanor	23	F		...	United States	Dublin Packet	30 Apr 1821
Eliza	2	F	Daughter	Ireland	New York	Atlantic	6 Oct 1828
Eliza	29	F	Wife	Ireland	New York	Atlantic	6 Oct 1828
Elizabeth	38					Mount Vernon	26 Aug 1820
Elizabeth	50			England	United States	Thomas Dickason	5 Jun 1827
Elizabeth	64	F	None	Great Britian	U. States	Henry Kneedland	7 Aug 1826
Ellen	1 2/12	F	None	Ireland	America	Minerva	31 May 1824
Fras.	25	M	Farmer	Ireland	America	Mary	29 May 1827
George	8					Mount Vernon	26 Aug 1820
George	33	M	Carpenter	G Britian	U. States	Leader	20 Apr 1827
Harriet	10					Mount Vernon	26 Aug 1820
Harriot	24	F		G. Brittain	U. States	Clarence	8 Dec 1821
Henry	26	M	Tailorman	England	New York	Brighton	29 Aug 1828
Hugh	30 6/12	M	Farmer	Ireland	America	Minerva	31 May 1824
Isabella	21	F	Tailorman	England	New York	Brighton	29 Aug 1828
James	18	M		Ireland	America	Carolina Ann	7 Apr 1826
James	30	M	Physician	Ireland	New York	Atlantic	6 Oct 1828
James	35	M	Labourer	Ireland	United States	Princess Charlotte	26 Apr 1827
Jane	6	F	Daughter	Ireland	New York	Atlantic	6 Oct 1828
Jarvis	5					Mount Vernon	26 Aug 1820
Jas.	64	M	Laborer	Great Britian	U. States	Henry Kneedland	7 Aug 1826
Jno.	50	M	Farmer	Great Brittan	Canada	Florida	17 May 1825
John	10					Mount Vernon	26 Aug 1820
John	30	M	Servant	Great Britain	U. States	Birmingham	12 Oct 1829
John	32	M	Wright	Ireland		Dublin Packet	30 Apr 1821
Joseph	39	M	Merchant	Great Britain	United States	Martha	25 Nov 1820
Julia	8					Mount Vernon	26 Aug 1820

NAMES OF PASSENGERS	AGE	SEX	OCCUPATIONS	COUNTRY TO WHICH THEY BELONG	COUNTRY THEY INTEND TO INHABIT	SHIPS/DATES OF ARRIVAL	
MATHEWS (cont'd)							
Mary	2 3/12	F	None	Ireland	America	Minerva	31 May 1824
Mary	4	F	Daughter	Ireland	New York	Atlantic	6 Oct 1828
Mary	35					Mount Vernon	26 Aug 1820
Matthias	24	M	pudler		uncertain	Mount Vernon	29 Aug 1828
Peter	22	M		Great Britain	Baltimore	Philetus	21 Jul 1827
Richd.	28	M	Labourer	Ireland	United States	Essex	23 May 1828
Robt.	45	M	Merchant	England	United States	New Packet	7 Aug 1826
Thomas	35	M	Carpenter	Ireland	United States	Princess Charlotte	26 Apr 1827
W. P.	30	M	Merchant	U. States	U. States	Pacific	23 Jan 1826
Weg.	25	M	Labourer	Ireland	United States	Essex	23 May 1828
Wm. L.	5					Mount Vernon	26 Aug 1820
MATHEWSON, Ann	15	F	Spinster	Ireland	United States	Robert Fulton	10 Aug 1827
Asahel		M	None			Emily Cook	29 Aug 1825
*dead							
Eliza	17	F	Spinster	Ireland	United States	Robert Fulton	10 Aug 1827
Henry	45	M	Merchant	U. States	U. States	Porcia	28 May 1827
Jas.	21	M	Farmer	Scotland		Aurora	12 Mar 1827
Margeret	20	F	Spinster	Ireland	United States	Robert Fulton	10 Aug 1827
Mary	15	F	Spinster	Ireland	United States	Robert Fulton	10 Aug 1827
Mary	45	F	Matron	Ireland	United States	Robert Fulton	10 Aug 1827
Rob.	30	M	Merchant	England	U. States	Dart	3 Aug 1822
Serah	18	F	Spinster	Ireland	United States	Robert Fulton	10 Aug 1827
Susan	6	F	Child	Ireland	United States	Robert Fulton	10 Aug 1827
MATHEY, Adelaide	8		Husband in America	Somwiller	Switzerland	Ann	27 Nov 1820
C.	18	M	Mechanic	Switzerland	U. States	Don Quixote	14 Aug 1826
C. H.	19	M	Mechanic	Switzerland	U. States	Don Quixote	14 Aug 1826
Cahan	19	F	Spinster	Ireland	U. States	Meteor	19 Jul 1828
Eliza	10		Husband in America	Somwiller	Switzerland	Ann	27 Nov 1820
Francoise	5	F		France	U. States	Leonarde	29 Aug 1828
Joseph	18	M		France	U. States	Leonarde	29 Aug 1828
Louis	14		Husband in America	Somwiller	Switzerland	Ann	27 Nov 1820
Marianne	53		Husband in America	Somwiller	Switzerland	Ann	27 Nov 1820
Rose	48	F	Farmeress	France	U. States	Leonarde	29 Aug 1828
Therese	17	F		France	U. States	Leonarde	29 Aug 1828
MATHIAS, Jos.	30	M	Doctor	Holland	U. States	Jane	17 Jan 1825
MATHIESON,							
Nichl.	22 2/12	M	Spinner	Great Britain	United States	Amity	1 Dec 1826
MATHIS, ...arb...	21		Merchant	United States	America	Nancy	8 May 1821
Danl.	20	M	Labourer	Ireland	U. States	Meteor	19 Jul 1828
George, Mr.	26		Merchant	United States	America	Nancy	8 May 1821
Joseph	19	M	Artiste d'Agilite	Nancy	U.S. America	Superior	18 Jun 1825
Margaret	19	F	Spinster	Ireland	U. States	Meteor	19 Jul 1828
MATHISON, Margaret	38	F	None	Gt. Brittain	United States	Balaena	24 Aug 1825
Mary	3	F	None	Gt. Brittain	United States	Balaena	24 Aug 1825
MATHON, Mary	20	F	Farmer	Ireland	U. States	Champion	26 Jul 1827
MATHONE, Rose	32	F	Farmer	Ireland	U. States	Champion	26 Jul 1827
MATHYAS, Joseph	36	M	Merchant	Holland	Braziles	Tandem	30 Nov 1826
MATKABLE, Margaret	17	F	None	Ireland	U.S.A.	Dalhouse Castle	21 Aug 1829
MATKIS, Ann	20	F		Ireland	United States	Nancy R. Crowell	21 Sep 1822
MATLACK, A., Mrs.	35	M	None	United States	United States	Atlantic	3 Dec 1821
J. M., Miss	12	M	None	United States	United States	Atlantic	3 Dec 1821
R., Mr.	15	M	Gentleman	United States	United States	Atlantic	5 Jul 1821
MATO, Raphael	12	M	Gentleman	Columbia	Columbia	Gertrude	19 May 1826
Raymond Jose		M	Merchant	Spain	U. States	James	23 Oct 1824
MATOS, Raymond	18	M	Merchant	Spanish Maine	U. States	Diana	31 Oct 1822
MATOSE, Jacob	36		...	Switzerland	Switzerland	Bogota	25 Oct 1827
MATTER, Dolvicho	18	M	Artist	Italy	U. States	Eliza	24 Aug 1825
MATTERSHEAD, Ewd.	23	M	Calico Printer	England	United States	Amelia	20 Aug 1829
MATTERSON, Alexander	50	M	Merchant	U. States	U. States	Camillus	27 Jul 1825
MATTHAIE, Johannas	22	M	Merchant	Hamburgh	America	Zwey Brieder Johanes & Henerick	20 Mar 1820

NAMES OF PASSENGERS	A G E	S E X	OCCUPATIONS	COUNTRY TO WHICH THEY BELONG	COUNTRY THEY INTEND TO INHABIT	SHIPS/DATES OF ARRIVAL	
MATTHAIS, Joseph	38 4/12	M	Miller	France	United States	France	6 Oct 1828
MATTHERSON, F.	13	M		United States		Howard	17 Oct 1822
MATTHEW, Charles	21	M	Farmer	Great Britain	U. States	Ganges	21 Jun 1827
Michael	27	M	Carpenter	Ireland	United States	Siroc	31 Oct 1829
MATTHEWS, Ann		F	None		U. States	Antelope	18 Dec 1822
Ann	6	F	None	Ireland	United States	Lord Wellington	28 May 1827
Ann	20			Northampton	G. Brit.	London	13 Dec 1822
Ann	26	F	his Wife	England	United States	Delta	24 Oct 1829
Cath.	7	F	None	Great Britain	United States	Mary & Harriet	3 Jul 1829
Cath.	23	F	None	Great Britain	United States	Mary & Harriet	3 Jul 1829
Charlotte	19	F		Ireland	U. States	Alexander	28 Jul 1821
Daniel	6/12	M	None	Ireland	United States	Lord Wellington	28 May 1827
David	45	M	Mariner	America	America	Loire	7 Apr 1821
Eliza	3	F	son of Wm.	Ireland	United States	Trident	30 Sep 1826
Elizabeth	6	F		England	United States	Delta	24 Oct 1829
Harriet	3	F		England	United States	Delta	24 Oct 1829
Heny	8	M		England	United States	Delta	24 Oct 1829
Heny	30	M	Tailor	England	United States	Delta	24 Oct 1829
James	5	M	None	Great Britain	United States	Mary & Harriet	3 Jul 1829
Jane	14	F	None	Great Britain	United States	Mary & Harriet	3 Jul 1829
Jas.	33	M	Labourer	Great Britain	United States	Penelope	11 Jun 1827
John	8	M	son of Wm.	Ireland	United States	Trident	30 Sep 1826
John	13	M	None	Ireland	United States	Orozimbo	5 Mar 1827
John	19	M	Labourer	Ireland	United States	Lord Wellington	28 May 1827
John	22	M	Merchant	Philada.	U. States	Jane	9 Dec 1822
John	40	M	Farmer	England	U. States	Hercules	6 Jul 1827
John	42	M	Farmer	Ireland	United States	Trident	30 Sep 1826
Jos.	26	M	Laborer			Delta	24 Oct 1829
Joseph	21	M	Farmer	England		Manhattan	22 May 1827
Laurence	10	M	son of Wm.	Ireland	United States	Trident	30 Sep 1826
Luphin	7	M	Farmer	England	U. States	Hercules	6 Jul 1827
M.	17		Farmer	Ireland	United States	Courier	16 May 1825
M. Ann	15	F	daughter of Wm.	Ireland	United States	Trident	30 Sep 1826
Margaret	28	F	None	Ireland	United States	Lord Wellington	28 May 1827
Mary	6	M	Farmer	England	U. States	Hercules	6 Jul 1827
Mary	30	F	Wife	Ireland	United States	Trident	30 Sep 1826
Mathew	23	M	Merchant	United States	United States	James Monroe	14 Dec 1820
Michael	25	M	Labourer	Ireland	United States	Ann Maria	8 Jun 1824
Patrick	22	M	Labourer	Ireland	United States	Ann Maria	8 Jun 1824
Patt	19	M	Butcher	Ireland	United States	Meteor	19 Aug 1829
Peter	26	M	None	Ireland	New York	America	1 Aug 1828
R.	42	M	Manufacturer	England	U. States	Birmingham	12 Oct 1827
Ricd.	37	M	Farmer	G. Britain	New York	Radius	7 Jul 1821
Robert	39	M	Baker	Engd.	United States	Cosmo	21 Aug 1828
Samuel	20	M	Farmer	England	U. States	Hercules	6 Jul 1827
Sarah	24	M	Servant	U. States	United States	Seine	7 Dec 1821
Valentine	20	M	Farmer	Ireland	United States	Trident	30 Sep 1826
William	40	M	Weaver	Ireland	United States	Trident	30 Sep 1826
Wm.	24	M	Mariner	United States	U.S.	Missouri	30 May 1828
Wm.	35	M	Farmer	England	U. States	Hercules	6 Jul 1827
MATTHIEUS, Raymond	42	M	Merchant	Spain	Spain	Wallace	18 May 1825
MATTHISON, Frederick	30	M	Joiner	Hamburg	U. States	Mariana & Paulina	8 Sep 1827
MATTHYA, Joseph	37	M	Merchant	Germany	U. States	Lady Washington	9 Jun 1828
MATTIN, Peter	24	M	None	Great Britain	United States	Eliza Barker	3 Jul 1826
MATZACKER, Aloye	27		Carpenter	France	U. States	Elizabeth	9 Jul 1825
MAUCH, Johan	27	M	Goldsmith	Switzerland	U. States	Hewes	30 Oct 1829
MAUCHET, —	20	M	Servant	Port au Prince	Port au Prince	Nature	17 Aug 1824
MAUCK, Huns	31	M	Surgeon	Prussia	United States	Maria Elizabeth	6 Jan 1823
MAUDE, John	24	M	Merchant	G. Briton	United States	James Monroe	14 Dec 1820
MAUFFRAY, —, Miss	4	F		United States	U. States	Manchester Packet	9 Mar 1826
—, Miss	14	F		United States	U. States	Manchester Packet	9 Mar 1826
—, Mr.	11	M		United States	U. States	Manchester Packet	9 Mar 1826
—, Mr.	16	M		United States	U. States	Manchester Packet	9 Mar 1826

NAMES OF PASSENGERS	AGE	SEX	OCCUPATIONS	COUNTRY TO WHICH THEY BELONG	COUNTRY THEY INTEND TO INHABIT	SHIPS/DATES OF ARRIVAL	
MAUFFRAY (cont'd)							
—, Mrs.	30	F		United States	U. States	Manchester Packet	9 Mar 1826
MAUGER, Charles	22	M	Carpenter	Guersey	New York	Comet	19 Oct 1826
MAUGH, David	34	M	Labourer	Ireland	U. States	Josephine	30 Aug 1828
MAULD, Charles	40	M	Farmer	G. Britain	U. States	Stephania	24 Jul 1820
Harriet	30	F				Stephania	24 Jul 1820
M. H.	4	F				Stephania	24 Jul 1820
MAULE, Fox	20		Military	Scotland	Quebec	Albion	11 Oct 1821
MAULEY, Jacob	9	F	None	England	United States	Dalhouse Castle	6 Sep 1827
Sarah	49	F	None	England	United States	Dalhouse Castle	6 Sep 1827
Thomas	26	M	Labourer	Great Britain	United States	Mary & Harriet	3 Jul 1829
MAUNDER, Joseph	23	M	Merchant	England	P. A. Prince	Fancy	28 Apr 1824
MAUNE, Catherine	8	F		Ireland	U.S.A.	Hudson	21 Aug 1829
Margaret	20	F		Ireland	U.S.A.	Hudson	21 Aug 1829
Mary	10	F		Ireland	U.S.A.	Hudson	21 Aug 1829
MAURAN, Pat	20	M	Labourer	Great Britain		Moro Castle	6 Jul 1827
S.	35	M	Captain	Rhode Island	U. States	Empress	7 Jul 1827
MAURAT, Lucien	21	M	Gentleman	Germany	U. States	Hesper	28 Jun 1825
MAUREL, B.	38	M	Merchant	France	France	La Sophie	23 Dec 1824
MAURICE, ...	19	F				Belfast	28 Sep 1820
James	21	M	Grocer	Aberdeen	United States	James & Margaret	30 May 1825
Jane	25	F		Ireland	America	Carolina Ann	7 Aug 1826
Jane B.	20	F		Ireland	America	Carolina Ann	7 Aug 1826
N.	45	M		United States	United States	Topaz	14 Aug 1826
Ulysses	22	M	Merchant	France	United States	Stephania	27 Nov 1826
William	20	M		Ireland	America	Carolina Ann	7 Aug 1826
MAURIDGE, Charles	66	M	Silver Smith	England		Washington	15 Sep 1821
George	13	M				Washington	15 Sep 1821
Laura	9 1/12	F				Washington	15 Sep 1821
Mary	56	F				Washington	15 Sep 1821
MAUROT,							
Eleanor, Miss	13 6/12	F	Seamstress	France	Burlington (N.J.)	Cadmus	27 Aug 1822
Virginia, Miss	16	F	Seamstress	France	Burlington (N.J.)	Cadmus	27 Aug 1822
MAURRY, Charles	6	M	Child	Scotland	America	Ann	23 Jul 1821
Ellen	10	F	Child	Scotland	America	Ann	23 Jul 1821
Hugh	3	M	Child	Scotland	America	Ann	23 Jul 1821
Mary	5	F	Child	Scotland	America	Ann	23 Jul 1821
Mary	33	F	Wife	Scotland	America	Ann	23 Jul 1821
William	8	M	Child	Scotland	America	Ann	23 Jul 1821
MAURY, James	24	M	Merchant	Liverpool, England	Liverpool, England	Ann Maria	26 Apr 1822
Mathew	23	M	Merchant	G. Brittain	U. States	Canada	6 Jun 1825
W., Mr.	28		Coal Man	England	U.S.	Pacific	24 May 1824
William	23	M	Merchant	United States	United States	New York	12 Nov 1822
MAVAINEZ, Ann	21	F		Great Britain	U. States	Hamilton	28 Apr 1828
Jas.	18		Labourer	Great Britain	U. States	Hamilton	28 Apr 1828
MAVOR, C. L.	1	M		England		Edward Quesnel	17 Nov 1828
Emily E.	19	F		England		Edward Quesnel	17 Nov 1828
John Fr. St. C.	41	M	Gentleman	Upper Canada		Edward Quesnel	17 Nov 1828
MAVRE, Catharine	20	F	Labourer	England	U. States	Comet	23 Aug 1828
MAVRY, Elizabeth	23	F	Servant	Ireland	New York	Atlantic	6 Oct 1828
MAWL, John	27	M	Lace Weaver	England	United States	Euphrates	18 Aug 1827
MAWLEY, —, Mrs.	27	F	None	Great Britain	America	Magnet	13 Nov 1821
Geo.	2 1/12	M	None	Great Britain	America	Magnet	13 Nov 1821
William	25	M	Printer	England	U. States	Ann	29 Jan 1820
Wm.	7 7/12	M	None	Great Britain	America	Magnet	13 Nov 1821
MAWLF, Jacob	37	M	Carpenter	Switzerland	United States	Aurora	21 Jun 1824
Maria R.	45	F	Wife of [Jacob]	Switzerland	United States	Aurora	21 Jun 1824
MAWLY, Joseph	8 8/12	M	None	Great Britain	America	Magnet	13 Nov 1821
Mary	4 3/12	F	None	Great Britain	America	Magnet	13 Nov 1821
MAWN, Ann	6	F	None	England	U. States	Thomas Ritchie	2 Jul 1827
Bessey	4	F	None	England	U. States	Thomas Ritchie	2 Jul 1827
Godfrey	12	M	None	England	U. States	Thomas Ritchie	2 Jul 1827
Hannh.	17	F	None	England	U. States	Thomas Ritchie	2 Jul 1827
Jas.	13	M	None	England	U. States	Thomas Ritchie	2 Jul 1827
Mary	19	F	None	England	U. States	Thomas Ritchie	2 Jul 1827
Mary	42	F	None	England	U. States	Thomas Ritchie	2 Jul 1827
Wm.	46	M	Manufact.	England	U. States	Thomas Ritchie	2 Jul 1827

NAMES OF PASSENGERS	AGE	SEX	OCCUPATIONS	COUNTRY TO WHICH THEY BELONG	COUNTRY THEY INTEND TO INHABIT	SHIPS/DATES OF ARRIVAL	
MAWRET, Achaze	30	M	Turner	Raden	U. States	Comet	28 Jul 1825
MAWSER, Daniel	36	M	Mechanic	Switzerland	America	Anna Maria	22 Feb 1820
MAWSON, John	22	M	Farmer	Great Britain	United States	Blakely	29 Sep 1826
MAXAT, Fas.	25	M	Mariner	New York	U. States	Signal	12 Jul 1825
MAXFIELD, Benjamin	28	M	Mariner	Rhode Island	New York	Baltic	20 Aug 1821
Benjn.						Baltic	20 Aug 1821
MAXWELL,							
Archibald	2 2/12	M	None	England	America	Euphrates	26 Jun 1821
Barny	34	M	Labourer	England	U. States	Emulous	22 Aug 1828
Catharine	22	F		Great Britain	U. States	Great Britain	18 Mar 1828
Catherine	6	F	None	Ireland		Marchioness	13 May 1828
E.	22	F	wife	England	United States	Ganges	20 Aug 1825
Edward	31	M	Mechanic	G. Britain	U. States	Hercules	24 Oct 1821
Euphema	25	F		Scotland	United States	Orion	15 Jan 1827
F.	28	M	Shopman	England	United States	Ganges	20 Aug 1825
F., Jr.	1 7/12	M	Child	England	United States	Ganges	20 Aug 1825
James	18	M	Ropemaker	Ireland	America	Wilson	16 Nov 1824
James	22	M	Labourer	Ireland		Marchioness	13 May 1828
James	25	M	Merchant	Belfast	United States	Carolina Ann	11 Jun 1824
James	45	M	Shopkeeper	Great Britain	United States	Robert Fulton	22 Oct 1821
Jane	57		Husbandman	England	America	Sarah	18 Aug 1829
Jno.	3/12	M	Child	England	United States	Ganges	20 Aug 1825
John	...0	M	Laborer	Ireland	United States	Mary	1 Jul 1829
John	36	M	Bricklayer	Scotland	United States	Orion	15 Jan 1827
John	52	M	Gentleman	Ireland	Ireland	Erin	25 Dec 1820
Laurance	25	M	Farmer	Ireland	Pensylvania	Agenora	12 Jul 1828
Margaret	20	F	None			Amity	31 Jan 1822
Margaret	25	F	None	Ireland		Marchioness	13 May 1828
Marion	21	F	None	U. States	U. States	Pacific	20 Aug 1825
Mary	2	F	None	Ireland		Marchioness	13 May 1828
Mary	5 1/12	F	None	England	America	Euphrates	26 Jun 1821
Mary	6	F		England	U. States	Emulous	22 Aug 1828
Mary	25	F	None	Ireland	United States	Washington	2 Oct 1828
Mary	26	F	None	England	America	Euphrates	26 Jun 1821
Mary	30	F		England	U. States	Emulous	22 Aug 1828
Mary	40	F		Great Britain		Dalmannock	24 Ocg 1826
Matilda	18	F		Great Britain		Dalmannock	24 Ocg 1826
Michael	3	M		England	U. States	Emulous	22 Aug 1828
Patrick	21	M	Ropemaker	Ireland	America	Wilson	16 Nov 1824
Peter	56		Husbandman	England	America	Sarah	18 Aug 1829
Rachel	35			Ireland	United States	Alexander Mansfield	9 Nov 1822
Rebecca	25	F		Belfast	United States	Carolina Ann	11 Jun 1824
Robert	21	M	Carpenter	Scotland	United States	Nimrod	1 Jun 1821
Robt.	39	M	Merchant	Great Britain	Canada	Manhattan	18 Feb 1824
S.	26		Mariner	New Castle ... Delaware	Philadelphia	Albion	5 Feb 1822
Stewart	28	M	Labourer	Ireland	United States	Robert Fulton	10 Aug 1827
Thomas	32	M	Ship Master	Scotland	Canada	Silas Richards	3 Apr 1826
William	41			Ireland	United States	Alexander Mansfield	9 Nov 1822
Wm.	12 3/12	M	None	England	America	Euphrates	26 Jun 1821
MAY, Alexander	36	M	Merchant	Scotland	Unt. States	Robert Fulton	14 Mar 1829
Anne, his Wife and Infant)							
[Richard]	25	F				Criterion	27 Oct 1820
Betty	48	F	Spinstress			Orion	21 Aug 1820
Bridget	25	F		Ireland	U. States	Wanderer	30 Sep 1828
G.	22 3/12	M	Courier	England	Philadelphia	Cririe	2 Jul 1821
John	17	M	Farmer			Orion	21 Aug 1820
Marry	28	F	None	Great Britan	U. States	Ann Marria	6 Aug 1823
Mary	12	F	Spinstress			Orion	21 Aug 1820
Oliver, Capt.	28	M	Ship Master	New York	New York	Mazzinghi	27 Feb 1824
Patrick	25	M	Laborer	Ireland	United States	Ann Maria	12 Jun 1826
Richard	5	M				Orion	21 Aug 1820
Richard	27	M	Gardner	England	United States	Criterion	27 Oct 1820
Richard	50	M	Farmer	England	United States	Jubilee	1 Oct 1828
Robert	10	M				Orion	21 Aug 1820
Sarah	15	F	Spinstress			Orion	21 Aug 1820

NAMES OF PASSENGERS	AGE	SEX	OCCUPATIONS	COUNTRY TO WHICH THEY BELONG	COUNTRY THEY INTEND TO INHABIT	SHIPS/DATES OF ARRIVAL	
MAY (cont'd)							
Willm.	30	M	Shoe Maker	Great Britan	U. States	Ann Marria	6 Aug 1823
Wm.	52	M	Farmer			Orion	21 Aug 1820
MAYAR, Margaret						Olympia	12 Aug 1828

*After having been at Sea a Number of Days was ascertaining the quantity of Baggage to report found the under mentioned persons had secreted themselves away notwithstanding our searach with the Gendearmes at the of leaving the port

NAMES OF PASSENGERS	AGE	SEX	OCCUPATIONS	COUNTRY TO WHICH THEY BELONG	COUNTRY THEY INTEND TO INHABIT	SHIPS/DATES OF ARRIVAL	
MAYBEE, Mary	22	F	Servant	Ireland	United States	St. Michaels	18 Jul 1826
MAYBEN, Isaac	22		Gentleman	England	Boston	Xenophon	25 Jul 1826
MAYBORN, Wm.	33	M	Mason	Great Britian	United States	Mount Vernon	19 May 1823
MAYBREY, William	23	M	pudler		uncertain	Mount Vernon	29 Aug 1828
MAYCOCK, Ann	1	M	None	England	United States	Jubilee	1 Oct 1828
Martha	10	M	None	England	United States	Jubilee	1 Oct 1828
Mary	38	F	None	England	United States	Jubilee	1 Oct 1828
Samuel	18	F	None	England	United States	Jubilee	1 Oct 1828
MAYER, —	48	M	Soap Boiler	France	United States	Cavalier	25 Jul 1828
—, his wife	44	F		France	United States	Cavalier	25 Jul 1828
Austin	30	M	Shoemaker	England	Kentucky	Abigail	9 Aug 1821
Barbara	41	F		Germany	America	Falcon	28 Aug 1828
Bernard	9	M		France	United States	Cavalier	25 Jul 1828
Carol Fredk.	19	M		Germany	America	Falcon	28 Aug 1828
Carol Fredk.	44	M	Shoemaker	Germany	America	Falcon	28 Aug 1828
Dorothea	36	F		Wirtemberg	America, U.N.S.	Great Britain	3 Aug 1829
Elizabeth	30	F		Germany	United States	Belfast	21 Mar 1820
Eugene	25	M	Merchant	Leghorn	U.S. America	Leeds	6 Jun 1826
F.	67	M	Farmer	Swiss	U. States	Edwd. Quesnel	30 Apr 1825
George	15	M	None	England	America	William Thompson	18 Jan 1825
George	52	M	Farmer	Wirtemberg	America, U.N.S.	Great Britain	3 Aug 1829
Geteliep	2 6/12	F		Wirtemberg	America, U.N.S.	Great Britain	3 Aug 1829
Gustavus	20	M	Merchant	Germany	U. States	Edward Quesnel	4 Aug 1828
Joh. Fredk.	4/12	M		Germany	America	Falcon	28 Aug 1828
John	42	M	Gentleman	England	U. States	Milton	20 Aug 1827
John Jacob	27	M	Gardner	Germany	U. States	Falcon	11 Jun 1827
Lament	9	M		France	United States	Cavalier	25 Jul 1828
Leonard	21	M	Labourer	France	America, U.N.S.	Great Britain	3 Aug 1829
Lewis	3	M		France	United States	Cavalier	25 Jul 1828
Lewis	23	M	Mechanic	Wurtemburg	U. States	Minerva	13 Sep 1827
Lodvick	6	M		Wirtemberg	America, U.N.S.	Great Britain	3 Aug 1829
Louis	23	M	Black Smith	Germany	United States	Helen	5 Sep 1828
Louise	0 3/12	F		France	United States	Cavalier	25 Jul 1828
M	15	M		France	United States	Cavalier	25 Jul 1828
M.	7	M		France	United States	Cavalier	25 Jul 1828
Mary	20	F		France	United States	Cavalier	25 Jul 1828
Michel	37	M	Servant	Switzerland	America, U.N.S.	Great Britain	3 Aug 1829
Sonira	18	M		France	United States	Cavalier	25 Jul 1828
Thos.	26	M	Mercht.	England	England	Britannia	5 Nov 1828
Wilh. Gottlieb	10	M		Germany	America	Falcon	28 Aug 1828
Wilhelmina	11 1/12	F		Germany	America	Falcon	28 Aug 1828
William H.	28	M	Tin & Nedle maker	Germany	United States	Belfast	21 Mar 1820
MAYES, John	38	M	Merchant	Pennsylvania	U. States	Emigrant	9 Oct 1826
John Phillip	41	M	Merchant			New York Packet	19 Aug 1820
MAYEW, John	24	M	Labourer	England		Marchioness	13 May 1828
MAYFAIR, Charles	25	M	Shopkeeper			Manhattan	25 Dec 1820
Mary	23	F	Shopkeeper			Manhattan	25 Dec 1820
Wm.	1	M	Shopkeeper			Manhattan	25 Dec 1820
MAYLER, Patrick	30	M	Labourer	Ireland	United States	Jubilee	12 May 1828
MAYLES, Ann	16	F	Farmer	Switzerland		Antioch	18 Aug 1829
Anne	7	F	Farmer	Switzerland		Antioch	18 Aug 1829
Barbara	37	F	Farmer	Switzerland		Antioch	18 Aug 1829
Christian	3	M	Farmer	Switzerland		Antioch	18 Aug 1829
Christian	32	M	Farmer	Switzerland		Antioch	18 Aug 1829
Conrad	24	M	Farmer	Switzerland		Antioch	18 Aug 1829
Elizabeth	6	F	Farmer	Switzerland		Antioch	18 Aug 1829
Elizabeth	33	F	Farmer	Switzerland		Antioch	18 Aug 1829
Elizabeth	65	F	Farmer	Switzerland		Antioch	18 Aug 1829
Jean	32	M	Farmer	Switzerland		Antioch	18 Aug 1829
Verona	1	F	Farmer	Switzerland		Antioch	18 Aug 1829

NAMES OF PASSENGERS	AGE	SEX	OCCUPATIONS	COUNTRY TO WHICH THEY BELONG	COUNTRY THEY INTEND TO INHABIT	SHIPS/DATES OF ARRIVAL	
MAYN, Ann	18		Merchant	England	United States	Mary	15 Jul 1822
Henry	20		Merchant	England	United States	Mary	15 Jul 1822
MAYNARD,							
Andrew	45 3/12	M	Merchant	America	America	Hiram	2 Apr 1828
E.	25	M	Carpenter	New York	New York	Gertrude	6 May 1828
Eliz.	11	F	None	England	U. States	Hercules	6 Jul 1827
Hannah	7	F	None	England	U. States	Hercules	6 Jul 1827
Hannah	36	F	None	England	U. States	Hercules	6 Jul 1827
James	43	M	Baker	Gt. Britain	U. States	Panthia	13 Nov 1824
Joseph	13	M	Farmer	England	U. States	Hercules	6 Jul 1827
R.	35	M	Merchant	France	U. States	Independence	19 Oct 1826
Richard	9	M	None	England	U. States	Hercules	6 Jul 1827
Samuel	6	M	None	England	U. States	Hercules	6 Jul 1827
Stephen	2	M	None	England	U. States	Hercules	6 Jul 1827
Thomas	16	M	Farmer	England	U. States	Hercules	6 Jul 1827
Wm.	23	M	Farmer	England	U. States	Hercules	6 Jul 1827
Wm.	47	M	Farmer	England	U. States	Hercules	6 Jul 1827
MAYNE, —		F	Child born on the passage			John Dickinson	5 Apr 1821
—, Mrs.	33	F		Scotland	Columbia	Abigail	25 Feb 1826
H. G.	44	M	Doctor	Scotland	Columbia	Abigail	25 Feb 1826
Jane	18			Great Britain		John Dickinson	5 Apr 1821
Joseph	40	M	Farmer			Orion	21 Aug 1820
Rob. S. B.	31	M	Gentleman	England	U. States	Hudson	26 Jan 1825
Thomas	16 0/12	M		Ireland	United States	Josephine	30 Apr 1828
Wallace	26		Farmer	Great Britain		John Dickinson	5 Apr 1821
MAYNES, Isabella	18	F	Lady at Large	G. Britain	United States	Louisa	14 Jun 1825
John	21	M	Gentleman at Large	G. Britain	United States	Louisa	14 Jun 1825
Thos.	27	M	Mason	Great Britain	United States	Atlantic	8 Dec 1827
MAYO, —, Mrs.	17	F		U. States	U. States	Katharine	25 Aug 1828
O.	30	M	Merchant	North America	Different	Tampico	11 Jul 1826
MAYON, M. F.	35	M	Gentleman	France	U. States	Seneca	14 May 1821
MAYOTIN, James	19	M	Gentleman	Spanyard	U. States	Romulus	31 Jul 1823
MAYS, Abigail, Mrs.	68	F		United States	United States	Henri IV	14 Oct 1829
Ann	4	F	Shipcarpenter	England	United States	Resign	7 Oct 1822
Ann	26	F	Shipcarpenter	England	United States	Resign	7 Oct 1822
James	10	M		Ireland	U. States	Nancy	29 Nov 1821
John	25	M	Shipcarpenter	England	United States	Resign	7 Oct 1822
Margt.	30	F		Ireland	U. States	Nancy	29 Nov 1821
Mary Ann	5	F	Shipcarpenter	England	United States	Resign	7 Oct 1822
Peter	8	M		Ireland	U. States	Nancy	29 Nov 1821
MAYWARD, Caroline	21	F	None	Great Britain	United States	Eliza Barker	3 Jul 1826
MAYWOOD, Mary	8	F		United States	U. States	Pacific	5 Sep 1827
Robert	35	M	Player	United States	U. States	Pacific	5 Sep 1827
MAZAR, Peter	33		Farmer	England	United States	Corinthian	30 May 1828
MAZARD, Catherine	40	F		France	Ohio	Eugenie	20 Aug 1827
Cherry	16	M		France	Ohio	Eugenie	20 Aug 1827
Martin	40	M	Merchant	France	Ohio	Eugenie	20 Aug 1827
Semey	36	M	Smith	France	Ohio	Eugenie	20 Aug 1827
T.	48	M	Cabinet Maker	France	Ohio	Eugenie	20 Aug 1827
MAZARTINE, James	30	M	...	...	...	Dawn	19 Aug 1825
MAZEGAN, Joaran	12	M	Schollar	Spain	Spain	Wave	21 May 1821
MAZIA, Juan	23	M	Merchant	Spain		Alfred	20 Dec 1821
MAZIERE, A.	23	M	Merchant	Vera Cruz	U. States	Eliza	11 Apr 1826
MAZZLAND, Robt.	23	M	Turner	England	United States	Peru	23 May 1827
MC..., ...	4	F	Labourer			Robert Burns	13 Jul 1820
...	8	F	Labourer			Robert Burns	13 Jul 1820
...ph	22	M	Labourer			Robert Burns	13 Jul 1820
Bathers	36	M	Labourer	Great Britain	United States	Aspasia	16 Jul 1828
Cath.	17	F		Great Britain	United States	Aspasia	16 Jul 1828
Cathr.	12	F		Great Britain	United States	Aspasia	16 Jul 1828
Ellen	7	F		Great Britain	United States	Aspasia	16 Jul 1828
Evan	13	M		Great Britain	United States	Aspasia	16 Jul 1828
Harry	6	M		Great Britain	United States	Aspasia	16 Jul 1828
Jane	6/12	M		Great Britain	United States	Aspasia	16 Jul 1828
John	10	M		Great Britain	United States	Aspasia	16 Jul 1828
L.	51	F		Great Britain	United States	Aspasia	16 Jul 1828
Mary	3	F		Great Britain	United States	Aspasia	16 Jul 1828
Mary	15	F		Great Britain	United States	Aspasia	16 Jul 1828

NAMES OF PASSENGERS	AGE	SEX	OCCUPATIONS	COUNTRY TO WHICH THEY BELONG	COUNTRY THEY INTEND TO INHABIT	SHIPS/DATES OF ARRIVAL	
MC... (cont'd)							
Mary	36	F		Great Britain	United States	Aspasia	16 Jul 1828
Mick	20		...	Ireland		Westmoreland	1 Aug 1826
Patrick	...	...	...	...	...	St. Michael	22 Sep 1824
R. R.	46	M		Great Britain	United States	Aspasia	16 Jul 1828
Robert	4	M		Great Britain	United States	Aspasia	16 Jul 1828
Robert	11	M		Great Britain	United States	Aspasia	16 Jul 1828
Robert	50	M	Labourer			Robert Burns	13 Jul 1820
William	6	M		Great Britain	United States	Aspasia	16 Jul 1828
MC...AN, Bridget	2...	F	Spinster	Ireland	United States	Ann Maria	8 Jun 1824
MC...GH, ...l	20	M	Joiner			Robert Burns	13 Jul 1820
MC...HENY, Jno.	28		Farmer	Ireland	United States	Courier	16 May 1825
MC...K, Charles ...	26	M	...	Gt. Britain	United States	Crisis	13 Nov 1824
MC...N, Charlotte	...			...	England	Great Britain	7 May 1827
MC...NEY, C.	13		Farmer	Ireland	United States	Courier	16 May 1825
J.	37		Farmer	Ireland	United States	Courier	16 May 1825
MC...OY..., James	20	M	Labourer	...	United States	Baltic	21 Apr 1827
MC...RAN, James	30	M	Labourer	England	...	Braganza	8 Aug 1825
MC...STING, William	27	M	Labourer	Ireland	United States	Meteor	26 Jun 1827
MCA..., Thomas	23		Carpenter		United States	Atlantic	2 Apr 1827
MCADAM, Jno.	24	M	Merchant	Great Britain	United States	Cortes	19 Nov 1821
John	25	M	Farmer		United States	Sarah	9 Nov 1820
John	27	M	Merchant	Scotland	America	Camillus	9 Oct 1820
Patrick	20	M	Shoemaker	Ireland	New York	Louisa	20 Jul 1826
MCADAMS, Ann	22	F	...	Ireland	U. States of America	Courier	17 Mar 1827
James	25	M	Sailor	Ireland	New Orleans	Mentor	20 Oct 1825
Patk.	23	M	Flax dresser	Ireland	U. States of America	Courier	17 Mar 1827
Patrick	24	M	Farmer	Great Britain	United States	Mount Vernon	17 Jun 1825
Thomas	28	M	Sailor	Ireland	New Orleans	Mentor	20 Oct 1825
MCADONE, Mary	30	F	Farmer, Labourer or Spinster	Ireland	U. States	Meteor	4 Oct 1827
MCAFEE, Thomas	30	M	Farmer	Ireland	U. States	Dickinson	30 Jul 1825
MCAFFEE, James	26 1/12	M		America	America	Carolina Ann	7 Apr 1826
MCAFFEY, John	22	M	Laborer	Great Britain	United States	Hanford	9 Oct 1829
MCAFIE, Mathew	19	M	Labourer	Ireland	United States	Robert Fulton	10 Aug 1827
MCAGETY, Edward	24	M	Labourer	Ireland	United States	Ann Maria	4 Oct 1824
MCALAGAN, Ann	20	F	Spinster	Ireland	U.S. of America	Meteor	19 Mar 1828
MCALEAR, Elizabeth	24	F	Spinster	Ireland	United States	Asia	29 Jul 1829
Mary	20	F	Spinster	Ireland	United States	Asia	29 Jul 1829
MCALEER, Bridget	13			Great Britain		John Dickinson	5 Apr 1821
Catherine	45			Great Britain		John Dickinson	5 Apr 1821
Eliza	9			Great Britain		John Dickinson	5 Apr 1821
Francis	7			Great Britain		John Dickinson	5 Apr 1821
John	20			Great Britain		John Dickinson	5 Apr 1821
Mary	22	F		Ireland	America	Carolina Ann	7 Aug 1826
Michae	11			Great Britain		John Dickinson	5 Apr 1821
Sarah	15			Great Britain		John Dickinson	5 Apr 1821
MCALENDA, Rose	30	F	None	Ireland	United States	Lord Wellington	28 May 1827
MCALENDEN, Daniel	25	M	None	Ireland	United States	Lord Wellington	28 May 1827
MCALESTER, James	20	M	Labourer	Kilmarnock	U.S. America	Camillus	10 Sep 1821
Walter	54	M	Merchant	Scotland	U. States	Josephine	23 Jan 1829
Walter, Jr.	18	M	Merchant	Scotland	U. States	Josephine	23 Jan 1829
MCALEY, John	35		Schoolmaster	Halifax	U. States	Almira	15 Jul 1822
Margaret	43			Halifax	U. States	Almira	15 Jul 1822
MCALIER, Rosa	50	F	Maid	Ireland	U.S. of America	Meteor	19 Mar 1828
MCALISH, Mary Ann	30	F	None	United States	United States	Nestor	20 Nov 1821
MCALISTER, Alexr.	10 6/12	M		Ireland	United States	Josephine	30 Apr 1828
Archibald	45	M	Weaver	Scotland	United States	Elizabeth	8 Jun 1827
John	23 5/12	M	Merchant	Ireland	United States	Josephine	30 Apr 1828
Rose	18		Spinster	Ireland	United States	Courier	15 Oct 1827
MCALL, Alice	25	F	None	Ireland	United States	Trident	18 Jul 1827
MCALLESTER, Charles	33	M	Labourer	England	U. States	Ayrshire	12 May 1828
MCALLINDAW, Robert	30	M	Labourer	Ireland	United States	Princess Charlotte	26 Apr 1827
MCALLISTER, A.	9	M		G. Britain	U. States	Camillus	8 Sep 1828
Agness	35	F		G. Britain	U. States	Camillus	8 Sep 1828
Alex	60	M	Labourer	Argyle (Tedland) Scotland	United States	Jean Hastie	27 Jul 1829
Ellen	3 2/12	F		Ireland	U. States	Fabius	22 Sep 1828

NAMES OF PASSENGERS	AGE	SEX	OCCUPATIONS	COUNTRY TO WHICH THEY BELONG	COUNTRY THEY INTEND TO INHABIT	SHIPS/DATES OF ARRIVAL	
MCALLISTER (cont'd)							
G.	3	M		G. Britain	U. States	Camillus	8 Sep 1828
G.	5	M		G. Britain	U. States	Camillus	8 Sep 1828
Jane	13 7/12	F		Ireland	U. States	Fabius	22 Sep 1828
John	9 3/12	M		Ireland	U. States	Fabius	22 Sep 1828
Margt.	11	F		G. Britain	U. States	Camillus	8 Sep 1828
Mary	16	M		G. Britain	U. States	Camillus	8 Sep 1828
Mary	34 8/12	F	House Keeper	Ireland	U. States	Fabius	22 Sep 1828
Mary Ann	11 10/12	F		Ireland	U. States	Fabius	22 Sep 1828
Rose	7 4/12	F		Ireland	U. States	Fabius	22 Sep 1828
S.	20	M	Farmer	Ireland	United States	L. M. Pelham	25 Jun 1822
Thos.	1 9/12	M		Ireland	U. States	Fabius	22 Sep 1828
Walter	52	M	Merchant	Scotland	U.S. America	New Hampshire	28 Sep 1826
Wm.	5 1/12	M		Ireland	U. States	Fabius	22 Sep 1828
Wm.	7	M		G. Britain	U. States	Camillus	8 Sep 1828
MCALLSTER, Walter	16	M		England	U. States	Friends	31 Jan 1825
MCALONAN, John	20	M	Shoomaker	Ireland	U. States	Courier	17 Mar 1828
MCALPEN, Jno.	20	M	Clerk	Gt. Britain	United States	Baltic	11 Apr 1825
MCALPIN, Christian	40	F				Frances	17 Aug 1820
John C.	21 3/12	M	Clerk	Ireland	United States	Louisa	27 Nov 1826
MCALPINE, A. B.	30	M	Merchant	U. States	U. States	Geo. Canning	2 Sep 1828
John	34		Smith	Great Britain	United States	Camillus	12 Sep 1827
Wm.	29	M	Merchant	United States	United States	Manchester	12 Aug 1829
MCALROY, Alice	25	F	None	Ireland	U. States	Criterion	23 May 1826
J.	28	M	Farmer	Ireland	U. States	Criterion	23 May 1826
James	2	M	None	Ireland	U. States	Criterion	23 May 1826
Martin	5/12	M	None	Ireland	U. States	Criterion	23 May 1826
Peter	19	M	Spinner	England	United States	Trident	18 Jul 1827
MCALVEN, John	24 7/12	M	Bakker	G. Britain	United States	Louisa	14 Jun 1825
Margaret	18	F		G. Britain	United States	Louisa	14 Jun 1825
Rosana	11 6/12	F		G. Britain	United States	Louisa	14 Jun 1825
MCAMRY, John	24	M		Ireland	New York	Lady Hunter	5 Jun 1826
MCAN..., Daniel	22		Carpenter		United States	Atlantic	2 Apr 1827
MCANALLY, Barnard	22	M	Labourer	Ireland	U. States	Concordia	11 Jun 1823
MCA NANNY, Edward	28	M	Farmer	Ireland	United States	Asia	29 Jul 1829
MCANDREW, Biddy	25 6/12	F		Ireland	U.S. of America	Douglass	6 Jul 1829
MCANELIST,							
Bartholomew	13	M	Labourer	Ireland	U. States	William & John	10 Jul 1824
MCANLY, Patrick	35	M	Clergyman	Ireland	Gt. Britain	Friends	29 Apr 1822
MCANN, Elenor	22	F				Catherine	19 Aug 1825
MCANNALLY, Anne	23	F	Spinster	Ireland	America	Superior	12 Jun 1824
John	25	M	Farmer	Ireland	America	Superior	12 Jun 1824
MCANNENY, James	20	M	Labourer	Ireland	United States	William & George	14 May 1828
MCANONY, John	20	M	Labourer	Ireland	United States	Robert Fulton	10 Aug 1827
MCANSLAND, John	23	M	Labourer	Scotland	United States	Samuel Robertson	9 May 1827
MCANSLEY, John	25	M	Servant	England	U. States	Roman	1 Dec 1828
MCANTEY, Garrick	40	M	Labourer	Great Britain	U. States	Superb	28 May 1821
Mary	45	F	Spinster	Great Britain	U. States	Superb	28 May 1821
MCANULLY, Margret	21	F	Spinster	Ireland		Robert Fulton	4 Jun 1828
MCANULTEY, Mary	17	F	Spinster	Ireland	United States	Wilson	4 Oct 1827
Patrick	7	M	Labourer	Ireland	United States	Wilson	4 Oct 1827
MCANULTY, Peter	21		Farmer	Ireland		Westmoreland	1 Aug 1826
MCARDE, Margret	30	F		Ireland	United States	Fabius	4 Jun 1828
MCARDELL, Henry	20	M	Hawker	Ireland	America	Panthea	18 Jul 1823
Margaret	30 1/12	F	going to Husband	Ireland	United States	Atlantic	21 Jul 1827
Mary, Int.	2	F		Ireland	United States	Atlantic	21 Jul 1827
Nancy	25 2/12	F	going to Husband	Ireland	United States	Atlantic	21 Jul 1827
MCARDER, Arthur	22	M	Laborer	Ireland	United States	Nile	17 May 1827
MCARDLE, Bernard	24	M	Weaver	Ireland	United States	Romulus	24 Jun 1826
Ellen	9/12	F		Ireland	United States	Romulus	24 Jun 1826
James	25	M	Farmer	Ireland	United States	Dublin Packet	29 Jun 1825
Jas.	30			Great Britan	United States	Newry	11 Jul 1827
Margaret	20	F		Ireland	United States	Romulus	24 Jun 1826
Margaret	41		Farmer	Great Britan	United States	Newry	11 Jul 1827
Peter	2	M	Child	Ireland	U. States	Josephine	30 Aug 1828
Peter	21	M	Labourer	Ireland	United States	Trident	31 Mar 1827
Philip	56		Farmer	Great Britan	United States	Newry	11 Jul 1827
Sarah	25	...	Matron	Ireland	U. States	Josephine	30 Aug 1828

NAMES OF PASSENGERS	AGE	SEX	OCCUPATIONS	COUNTRY TO WHICH THEY BELONG	COUNTRY THEY INTEND TO INHABIT	SHIPS/DATES OF ARRIVAL	
MCARDLE (cont'd)							
Sarah	27		Farmer	Great Britan	United States	Newry	11 Jul 1827
MCARDNEY, Cathr.	20	F	Spinster	Ireland		Robert Fulton	4 Jun 1828
MCARTER, Bernard	25	M	Farmer	Great Britian	United States	Andes	19 Aug 1829
Peter	57	M	Bassfounder	Scotland	N. York	Mexico	19 Mar 1828
MCARTHUR (see McAuthur)							
Alexr.	49	M	Land Surveyor	Ireland	New York	Carolina Ann	15 Oct 1824
Amelia, Mrs.	44 2/12	F		Scotland	United States	Mobile	21 Aug 1827
Ann	47	F		Ireland	New York	Carolina Ann	15 Oct 1824
Cathrine	20	F		Ireland	New York	Carolina Ann	15 Oct 1824
David	22	M	Land Surveyor	Ireland	New York	Carolina Ann	15 Oct 1824
David	32	M	Farmer	Scotland	U.S. of America	Friends	10 May 1823
Francis, Child	12	M		Ireland	New York	Carolina Ann	15 Oct 1824
James	24 11/12	M	Clerk	Scotland	United States	Mobile	21 Aug 1827
John	18	M	Land Surveyor	Ireland	New York	Carolina Ann	15 Oct 1824
John	27	M	Seamstur	Scotland	U. States	Roger Stewart	9 Jun 1828
John	44 8/12	M	Weaver	Scotland	United States	Mobile	21 Aug 1827
Letitia, Child	14	F		Ireland	New York	Carolina Ann	15 Oct 1824
MCARTY, Slomen	40	M	Labourer	Great Brittan	United States	Hanford	3 Aug 1829
MCASTNEY, Bridget	21	F	Spinster	Ireland		Robert Fulton	4 Jun 1828
MCATEE, Bujet	21	M	Farmer	Great Britian	United States	Andes	19 Aug 1829
Ellen	20	F	Servant	Ireland	New York	Atlantic	8 May 1828
John	25	M		Ireland	New York	Lady Hunter	5 Jun 1826
Mary	20	F	Spinster	Ireland	United States	Fabius	4 Jun 1828
Mary	85	F	Spinster	Ireland	United States	Fabius	4 Jun 1828
MCATEER, Bridget	27 6/12	F	& family	Ireland	United States	Atlantic	21 Jul 1827
Burnett	4	M	& family	Ireland	United States	Atlantic	21 Jul 1827
Martha	2 5/12	F	& family	Ireland	United States	Atlantic	21 Jul 1827
Mary	24 4/12	F	Servant	Ireland	United States	Atlantic	21 Jul 1827
Pat	55	M	Labourer	Great Britain	United States	Atlantic	8 Dec 1827
Patrick	6 9/12	M	& family	Ireland	United States	Atlantic	21 Jul 1827
Peter	27 4/12	M	Labourer	Ireland	United States	Atlantic	21 Jul 1827
Sarah	55	F	Spinner	Great Britain	United States	Atlantic	8 Dec 1827
MCATSSON, John	28	M	...	G. Britain		Manhattan	8 Aug 1820
MCAUBREY, —, Mrs.	40	F	None	Gt. Brittian	Gt. Brittian	Manchester	24 Aug 1827
G., Mr.	45	M	Gentleman	Gt. Brittian	Gt. Brittian	Manchester	24 Aug 1827
MCAULEY, Anne	20	F	Spinster	Ireland	America	Superior	12 Jun 1824
Anne	20	F	Spinster	Ireland	America	Superior	12 Jun 1824
Daniel	16	M	Farmer	Ireland	United States	Dublin Packet	22 Aug 1829
Hugh	20 7/12	M		Ireland	America	Carolina Ann	7 Apr 1826
Jane	8	F	Spinster	Ireland	America	Superior	12 Jun 1824
Jane	8	F	Spinster	Ireland	America	Superior	12 Jun 1824
John	28	M	Mechanic	St. John, N.B.	United States	Henrietta	3 Jun 1825
Margaret	35	F	Servant	Ireland	United States	St. Michaels	12 Jun 1826
Mathew	30	M	Farmer	Ireland	America	Superior	12 Jun 1824
Mathew	30	M	Farmer	Ireland	America	Superior	12 Jun 1824
Sarah	26	F	None	Scotland	U. States	Camillus	27 Jul 1825
William	18	M	Farmer	Ireland	America	Superior	12 Jun 1824
William	18	M	Farmer	Ireland	America	Superior	12 Jun 1824
MCAULIFF, Bridget	27	F		England	United States	Ganges	10 May 1828
Mary	25	F		England	United States	Ganges	10 May 1828
Pat	22	M	Farmer	England	United States	Ganges	10 May 1828
Tim	37	M	Farmer	England	United States	Ganges	10 May 1828
MCAULIFFE, John	15			Ireland	United States	Geo. Canning	5 Jun 1828
Richd.	23		Labourer	Ireland	United States	Geo. Canning	5 Jun 1828
MCAULLY, —	33	M	Merct.	U. States	Canada	Camillus	7 Mar 1825
MCAULON, Agnes		F				Hero	19 May 1828
MCAUSLAND, Arch.	26	M	Farmer	Great Britain	New York	Intrepid	8 Aug 1822
MCAUTHUR, Saml.	33	M	Seaman	U. States	U. States	Boston	26 Sep 1820
MCAVERNON, John	30		Labourer	Great Britan	United States	Newry	11 Jul 1827
MCAVORY, John	28 8/12	M	Clerk	Ireland	U. States	Fabius	22 Sep 1828
MCAVOY, Ann	15	F		Ireland	United States	Princess Charlotte	26 Apr 1827
Arthur	12	M		Ireland	United States	Princess Charlotte	26 Apr 1827
Carl.	11 3/12	M	Labourer	Scotland, G.B.	United States	Orozimbo	31 May 1824
Catherine	8	F		Ireland	United States	Princess Charlotte	26 Apr 1827
Francis	25	M	Labourer	Ireland	United States	Wilson	28 Nov 1828

811

NAMES OF PASSENGERS	AGE	SEX	OCCUPATIONS	COUNTRY TO WHICH THEY BELONG	COUNTRY THEY INTEND TO INHABIT	SHIPS/DATES OF ARRIVAL	
MCAVOY (cont'd)							
Francis	38	M	Farmer	Scotland	United States	Delta	24 Oct 1829
Hugh	2	M	Labourer	Scotland, G.B.	United States	Orozimbo	31 May 1824
James	1	M		Ireland	United States	Princess Charlotte	26 Apr 1827
*Died on the Voyage							
Jno.	2	M	None	England	U. States	Thomas Ritchie	2 Jul 1827
John	45	M	Stone Mason	Ireland	United States	Princess Charlotte	26 Apr 1827
Mara.	4	F	None	England	U. States	Thomas Ritchie	2 Jul 1827
Margarett	26	F	Spinster	Ireland	United States	Wilson	28 Nov 1828
Maria	6	F	None	England	U. States	Thomas Ritchie	2 Jul 1827
Mary	6	F		Ireland	United States	Princess Charlotte	26 Apr 1827
Mary	28	F	None	England	U. States	Thomas Ritchie	2 Jul 1827
Patrick	2	M		Ireland	United States	Princess Charlotte	26 Apr 1827
*Died on the Voyage							
Robt.	1 6/12	M	Child	Ireland	United States	Wilson	28 Nov 1828
Rose	3	F		Ireland	United States	Princess Charlotte	26 Apr 1827
Sarah	6/12	F		Ireland	United States	Princess Charlotte	26 Apr 1827
Sarah	24	M	Sister	G. Britain	United States	Louisa	14 Jun 1825
Sarah	35	F		Ireland	United States	Princess Charlotte	26 Apr 1827
Sarah, & Infant	24	F	None	G. Briton	United States	James Monroe	14 Dec 1820
Thomas	18	M	Stone Mason	Ireland	United States	Princess Charlotte	26 Apr 1827
William	27	M	Farmer	G. Britain	United States	Louisa	14 Jun 1825
MCAYON, Edward	25	M	Labourer	Ireland	United States	Trident	31 Mar 1827
MCBANEN, Ellen	40	F	Farmer	Ireland	U. States	Dickinson	30 Jul 1825
Thomas	40	M	Farmer	Ireland	U. States	Dickinson	30 Jul 1825
MCBANNEN, Mary		F	Farmer	Ireland	U. States	Dickinson	30 Jul 1825
MCBARREN, Ann	12	F	Farmer	Ireland	U. States	Dickinson	30 Jul 1825
Ellen	2	F	Farmer	Ireland	U. States	Dickinson	30 Jul 1825
James	4	M	Farmer	Ireland	U. States	Dickinson	30 Jul 1825
James, an infant		M	Farmer	Ireland	U. States	Dickinson	30 Jul 1825
Margarette	6	F	Farmer	Ireland	U. States	Dickinson	30 Jul 1825
Owen	18	M	Farmer	Ireland	U. States	Dickinson	30 Jul 1825
Pat	2	M	Farmer	Ireland	U. States	Dickinson	30 Jul 1825
Patrick	8	M	Farmer	Ireland	U. States	Dickinson	30 Jul 1825
Patrick	38	M	Farmer	Ireland	U. States	Dickinson	30 Jul 1825
Rose	24	F	Farmer	Ireland	U. States	Dickinson	30 Jul 1825
MCBEAN, Alexr.	36	M	Shopkeeper			Belle Savage	15 Aug 1820
Jane, Miss	23	F	None	St. Croix	U. States	Chase	2 Oct 1826
William	38	M	Lawyer	England	England	Loyalist	17 Oct 1829
MCBEATH, John	42	M	Merchant	Scotland	United States	Friends	7 Jul 1827
MCBEILLE, Ann	4	F		Ireland	United States	William Byrnes	6 Apr 1826
Bridget	35	F		Ireland	United States	William Byrnes	6 Apr 1826
Rose	6	F		Ireland	United States	William Byrnes	6 Apr 1826
MCBENNET, Owen	24	M	Clerk	Ireland	New York	Atlantic	6 Oct 1828
MCBETH, Elizabeth	21	F	Spinster	Ireland	United States	Robert Fulton	24 Jul 1826
James	22	M	Farmer	Ireland	U.S. of America	Meteor	19 Mar 1828
John	21	M	Baker	Scotland	U. States	Othello	3 Dec 1828
Nancy	60	F	Spinster	Ireland	U.S. of America	Meteor	19 Mar 1828
MCBETT, William	22	M	Farmer	Ireland	United States	Marmion	17 Jun 1825
MCBIRNIE, Mary	25	F		Ireland	United States	Princess Charlotte	26 Apr 1827
MCBLAINE, Robert	25	M	Farmer	Ireland	U. States	Dickinson	30 Jul 1825
MCBOND, Thos.	30	M	unknown	U. States	U. States	Mary	7 Nov 1822
MCBOWER, Geo	27	M	Labourer	Ireland	U. States	Atlantic	19 Aug 1825
MCBOY, James	30	M	Wever	Ireland	United States	Fabius	4 Jun 1828
MCBREA, Hamilton	8	M	Farmer	Ireland	U. States	Dickinson	30 Jul 1825
MCBREARTY, Edward	21		Carpenter	Ireland	United States	Robert Burns	30 May 1823
MCBREW, Mary	35	F	Farmer	Ireland	U. States	Dickinson	30 Jul 1825
MCBRIDE, Agnes	22		Farmer	Ireland	United States	Carolina Ann	12 Sep 1823
Anne	25	F	Wife	Ireland	United States	Trident	16 May 1826
Biddy	22	F	Farmer	Ireland	U. States	Dickinson	30 Jul 1825

NAMES OF PASSENGERS	AGE	SEX	OCCUPATIONS	COUNTRY TO WHICH THEY BELONG	COUNTRY THEY INTEND TO INHABIT	SHIPS/DATES OF ARRIVAL	
MCBRIDE (cont'd)							
Danial	14 6/12	M	Labourer	Ireland	U. States	Josephine	30 Aug 1828
Ellen	20	F	Spinster	Ireland	United States	Robert Fulton	10 Aug 1827
Frances	66 7/12	M	Labourer	G. Brittian	United States	Louisa	14 Jun 1825
George	18	M	Servant	Canada	U. States	Mary Ann	22 Aug 1828
Henry	16	M	Labourer	Ireland	U. States	Josephine	30 Aug 1828
Hugh	30	M	Farmer	Ireland	U. States	Dickinson	30 Jul 1825
James	25	M	Cooper	U. States	U. States	St. Anna	1 Apr 1828
Jane	7	F	None	United States	United States	Importer	21 May 1821
Jas.	22	M	Cooper	U. States	U. States	Free Ocean	10 May 1826
Jas.	22	M	Labourer	Ireland	United States	Edwin	27 Oct 1828
John	14		Farmer	Ireland	United States	Carolina Ann	12 Sep 1823
John	15 2/12	M	Family	G. Brittian	United States	Louisa	14 Jun 1825
John	32	M	Merchant	U. States	New York	James Monroe	23 Aug 1822
Magaret	18	F	Labourer	Ireland	United States	Hope	12 Jun 1828
Margret	19	F	Servant	Ireland	United States	Carolina Ann	14 May 1827
Mary	13	F	Family	G. Brittian	United States	Louisa	14 Jun 1825
Mary	32	F	...	Ireland	Lower Canada	Crisis	13 Nov 1824
Mary	45	F	Family	G. Brittian	United States	Louisa	14 Jun 1825
Mattw.	17	M	Family	G. Brittian	United States	Louisa	14 Jun 1825
Nancy	10 5/12	F	Family	G. Brittian	United States	Louisa	14 Jun 1825
Owen	20	M	Carpenter	Gt. Britain		Dalhouse Castle	13 May 1828
Patk.	24	M	servant	Ireland	United States	Trident	16 May 1826
Patrick	17	M	None	Great Britain	United States	Isaac Hicks	27 Sep 1826
Patrick	28	F	Labourer	Ireland	United States	Hope	12 Jun 1828
Patrick	30		Merchant			Amphion	31 May 1824
Peter	19	M	Cooper	U. States	U. States	Julia	22 May 1827
Sarah	4	F	Farmer	Ireland	U. States	Dickinson	30 Jul 1825
Susy	26	F	Spinster	Ireland	United States	William & George	14 May 1828
Terence	60	M	Farmer	Ireland	U. States	Dickinson	30 Jul 1825
Thomas	20 5/12	M		Ireland	America	Carolina Ann	7 Apr 1826
Thos.	22	M	Baker	Ireland	New York	Atlantic	6 Oct 1828
MCBRIEN, Arthur	25	M	Labourer	Ireland	America	Weser	26 Jun 1821
Catherine	14	F	Servant	Ireland	America	Weser	26 Jun 1821
Danl.	18	M	Weaver	England	United States	India	8 Jun 1827
Denis	16	M	Labourer	Ireland	America	Weser	26 Jun 1821
Micle	25	M	Labourer	England	...	Braganza	8 Aug 1825
MCBRIES, Jane	21	F	Servant	Ireland	America	Weser	26 Jun 1821
MCBRINE, Owen	2...	M	...	Ireland	United States	General Putnam	20 Jun 1825
MCBRIOH, John	20	M	Labourer	Ireland	United States	Robert Fulton	10 Aug 1827
MCBROMELL, Mary	3	F	Farmer	Great Britain	U. States	Princess Charlotte	6 Sep 1828
MCBRYAN, Bridget	...8	F	Spinster	Ireland	United States	Ann Maria	8 Jun 1824
MCBRYDE, Jas.	28	M	Merchant	United States	United States	Britannia	29 Oct 1829
MCBUELL, Jas.	19	M		Ireland	U. States	Fame	15 Nov 1826
MCBURNEY, Alex	24		Farmer	Ireland	U. States	Xenophon	28 May 1822
Isabella	50	F	Wife	Ireland	New York	Louisa	20 Jul 1826
Jane	22 3/12	F	Daughter	Ireland	New York	Louisa	20 Jul 1826
Joseph	29	M	Weaver	England	Philadelphia	Curler	7 Jul 1827
Mary	19 4/12	F	Daughter	Ireland	New York	Louisa	20 Jul 1826
Robert	20	M	Jailor	G. Brittian	United States	Louisa	14 Jun 1825
Samuel	12 8/12	M	Son	Ireland	New York	Louisa	20 Jul 1826
Samuel	66	M	Farmer	Ireland	New York	Louisa	20 Jul 1826
Thomas	24 3/12	M	Son	Ireland	New York	Louisa	20 Jul 1826
William	21 2/12	M	Son	Ireland	New York	Louisa	20 Jul 1826
MCC...EARE, Peter	25	M	Labourer	Dunblane	U.S. America	Camillus	10 Sep 1821
MCC...FEE, Biddy	...	F	...	Ireland	United States	General Putnam	20 Jun 1825
MCCA..., Job	26...	M	Labourer	Ireland	Unt. St. America	Wilson	21 May 1827
Ma...	21		Laboring Class		United States	Atlantic	2 Apr 1827
MCCAB, Catherine	18	F	Spinster	Ireland	United States	Lady Hunter	27 Dec 1825
MCCABA, Charles	30	M	Labourer	Great Britain	United States	Frances Henrietta	17 Sep 1827
MCCABE, Andrew	20			b. County of Carvan, last of Longford	Newyork	Peru	30 May 1828
Ann	20	F	Servant	Ireland	N. York	Trusty	12 Sep 1828
Bridget	18	F	Spinster	Ireland	United States	Ann Maria	8 Jun 1824
Bryan	23	M	Labourer	England	U. States	Comet	23 Aug 1828

NAMES OF PASSENGERS	AGE	SEX	OCCUPATIONS	COUNTRY TO WHICH THEY BELONG	COUNTRY THEY INTEND TO INHABIT	SHIPS/DATES OF ARRIVAL	
MCCABE (cont'd)							
Catherine	26	F	Servant	Ireland	United States	Carolina Ann	14 May 1827
Cathr.	40	F	Labourer	Great Britian	United States	Princess Charlotte	6 Sep 1828
Charles	24	M	Weaver	Ireland	United States	Silas Richards	3 Apr 1826
Edward	36	M	Cleark	Ireland	America	Ann	2 Nov 1820
Edwd.	18	M	Labourer	Ireland	United States	William	20 Jul 1829
Eliza	22	F	None	Ireland	United States	Lord Wellington	28 May 1827
Eliza	30	M	None/Farmer	Mertingar		Mount Vernon	7 Jun 1824
Ellen	20	F	Servant	Great Britain	United States	Ganges	26 Oct 1826
Hugh	14	M	Labourer	Ireland	U.S. of America	Meteor	19 Mar 1828
James	18		Labourer	Ireland	United States	Courier	15 Oct 1827
James	26	M	None	Ireland	United States	Lord Wellington	28 May 1827
James	31	M	Labourer	Great Britian	United States	Princess Charlotte	6 Sep 1828
Jas.	21	M	Mechanic	Ireland	United States	Wm. Byrnes	30 Apr 1828
Jno.	20	M		Ireland	United States	Essex	23 May 1828
John	18	M	...	...	...	Frances Henrietta	30 Jun 1827
John	22	M	Laborer	Ireland	Pennsylvania	Indian Chief	16 Aug 1822
John	25	M	Farmer	Ireland	United States	Dublin Packet	9 Jul 1827
Mary	20	F	Dressmaker	Ireland	United States	Carolina Ann	11 Dec 1826
Mary	22	F	Spinster	Ireland	United States	Dublin Packet	24 Sep 1823
Mary	30	F		Ireland	United States	Neury	27 Jan 1827
Mary Ann	3	F		Gt. Britain	U. States	Lima	22 Sep 1828
Michael	24	M	Servant	Great Britain	United States	Ganges	26 Oct 1826
Pat	34	M	Farmer	Great Britain	United States	William Dawson	18 Jun 1827
Patrick	21	M	Weaver	Ireland	United States	Silas Richards	3 Apr 1826
Patrick	22	M	Laborer	Ireland	United States	Weser	29 Jul 1823
Patrick	24	M	Weaver	Ireland	United States	Neury	27 Jan 1827
Patrick	27	M	Laborer	Ireland	Pennsylvania	Indian Chief	16 Aug 1822
Patt	18	M	Labourer	Ireland	U.S. of America	Meteor	19 Mar 1828
Peter	28	M	Labourer	Ireland	Pennsylvania	Curler	7 Jul 1827
Rose	15	F	Spinster	Ireland	U. States	Josephine	7 May 1827
Rose	17	F	Spinster	Ireland	United States	Dublin Packet	29 Jun 1825
Rose	22	F	None	England	United States	London	21 May 1828
Sally	19	F	Servant	Ireland	United States	Carolina Ann	14 May 1827
Susan	23	F		Gt. Britain	U. States	Lima	22 Sep 1828
Thomas	19	M	Laborer	England	United States	London	21 May 1828
Thomas	24	M	Weaver	Ireland	U. States	Josephine	30 Aug 1828
Wm.	19 7/12	M	Tailor	Ireland	United States	Atlantic	21 Jul 1827
MCCABIE, Patt	36	M	Farmer	Ireland	U. States	Lady Hunter	8 Aug 1826
MCCADDEN, Alice	27	F	Spinster	Ireland	Unt. St. America	Wilson	21 May 1827
MCCAFERTY, Fanny	31	F	Spinster	Ireland	United States	Gem	16 Jun 1824
George	32	M	Labourer	Scotland	Unt. States	Robert Fulton	14 Mar 1829
James	30	M	Labourer	Scotland	Unt. States	Robert Fulton	14 Mar 1829
John	20	M	Labourer	Ireland	United States	Gem	16 Jun 1824
MCCAFFARTY, Sarah	22		Spinster	Ireland		Westmoreland	1 Aug 1826
MCCAFFERTY, Elizabeth	2	F	None	Scotland	United States	Camillus	27 Oct 1829
Hugh	22	M	Farmer	Ireland	United States	Catharine	22 Jul 1825
James	6	M	None	Scotland	United States	Camillus	27 Oct 1829
John	21	M	Labourer	Ireland	United States	Catharine	22 Jul 1825
John	23	M	Labourer	Ireland	United States	Hope	12 Jun 1828
Mary	3	F	None	Scotland	United States	Camillus	27 Oct 1829
Mary	26	F	None	Scotland	United States	Camillus	27 Oct 1829
Patrick	24	M	Labourer	Ireland	United States	Hope	12 Jun 1828
MCCAFFERY, Rose	26	F	Labourer	Ireland	U. States	Two Marys	20 Apr 1825
MCCAFFETY, Mary	24	F	Laborer or Spinster	Ireland	United States	Sarah G.	15 Aug 1827
MCCAFFRAY, John	20	M	Labourer	Great Britain	U. States	Princess Charlotte	6 Sep 1828
John	23	M	Blacksmith	Ireland	New York	Louisa	20 Jul 1826
Mary	24	F	Wife	Ireland	New York	Louisa	20 Jul 1826
Mary, Jr.	10/12	F	Child	Ireland	New York	Louisa	20 Jul 1826
MCCAFFREY, Patrick	29		Farmer	Ireland	United States	Asia	29 Jul 1829
Thomas	28	M	Weaver	Irereland	America	Carolina Ann	20 Jun 1825
MCCAFFRY, James	22	M	Shoe Maker	Ireland	United States	Fabius	31 Jul 1829
MCCAGHY, James	21	M	Labourer	Ireland	Pensylvania	Atlantic	8 May 1828
MCCAHAN, Terence	22	M	Flax Hackler	Ireland	New York	Atlantic	8 May 1828

NAMES OF PASSENGERS	AGE	SEX	OCCUPATIONS	COUNTRY TO WHICH THEY BELONG	COUNTRY THEY INTEND TO INHABIT	SHIPS/DATES OF ARRIVAL	
MCCAHEY, James	19	M	Labourer	Great Britian	United States	Princess Charlotte	6 Sep 1828
MCCAHILL, Mathew	22	M	Laboror	Ireland	United States	Wilson	27 Jun 1826
Philip	27	M	Labourer	Ireland	United States	Jubilee	1 Oct 1828
MCCAIG, Fanny	...0	F		Ireland	United States	Mary	1 Jul 1829
Henry	25	M	Laborer	Ireland	United States	Mary	1 Jul 1829
James	16	M	Laborer	Ireland	United States	Mary	1 Jul 1829
Mick	11	M	Laborer	Ireland	United States	Mary	1 Jul 1829
Sally	80	F		Ireland	United States	Mary	1 Jul 1829
Susana	50	F		Ireland	United States	Mary	1 Jul 1829
Thomas	13	M	Laborer	Ireland	United States	Mary	1 Jul 1829
MCCAIN, Bernard	8	M		Ireland	New York	Lima	5 Aug 1829
Bernard	8	M		Ireland	New York	Lima	5 Aug 1829
Bridget	16	F		Ireland	United States	Jubilee	13 Sep 1827
Bridget	40	F		Ireland	New York	Lima	5 Aug 1829
Daniel	10	M	Labourer	Ireland	New York	Lima	5 Aug 1829
Ellen	6	F		Ireland	United States	Jubilee	13 Sep 1827
Henry	3 6/12	M		Ireland	New York	Lima	5 Aug 1829
Hugh	19	M	Labourer	Ireland	New York	Lima	5 Aug 1829
Hugh	19	M	Labourer	Ireland	New York	Lima	· 5 Aug 1829
John	4	M		Ireland	United States	Jubilee	13 Sep 1827
Margt.	8	F		Ireland	United States	Jubilee	13 Sep 1827
Maria	14	F	Tayloress	Ireland	United States	Jubilee	13 Sep 1827
Owen	40	M	Taylor	Ireland	United States	Jubilee	13 Sep 1827
Winfred	15	F	Tayloress	Ireland	United States	Jubilee	13 Sep 1827
MCCAIRACK, Patrick	30	M	Servant	Ireland	U.S.	Francois I	8 Aug 1829
MCCALE, Hugh	28	M	Merchant	Ireland	United States	Fabius	4 Jun 1828
W.	38	M	Merchant	England	U. States	Favourite	2 Sep 1822
MCCALECK, James	14	M	Child	Ireland	United States	Ann Maria	3 Jul 1827
Jane	4	F	Child	Ireland	United States	Ann Maria	3 Jul 1827
Margaret	29	F	Wife	Ireland	United States	Ann Maria	3 Jul 1827
Saml.	50	M	Laborer	Ireland	United States	Ann Maria	3 Jul 1827
Samuel	9	M	Child	Ireland	United States	Ann Maria	3 Jul 1827
Samuel	30	M	Laborer	Ireland	United States	Ann Maria	3 Jul 1827
William	11	M	Child	Ireland	United States	Ann Maria	3 Jul 1827
MCCALER, James	32	M	Farmer	Ireland	United States	L. M. Pelham	25 Jun 1822
MCCALISTER, Archibald	28	M		Ireland	U. States	Nancy	16 Aug 1822
William	17	M	Merchant	Irereland	America	Carolina Ann	20 Jun 1825
MCCALL, A.	32	M	Merchant	Scotland	U. States	Elias Burger	11 Jul 1822
Alexr.	23	M	Farmer	England	U. States	Thomas Ritchie	2 Jul 1827
Alexr.	35	M	Merchant	Great Britain	Canada	Manhattan	18 Feb 1824
Ann	20	F	None	England	U. States	Thomas Ritchie	2 Jul 1827
Edward	23	M	Labourer	Ireland	U. States	Borneo	15 Apr 1828
Edward R.	35	M	U.S.N.	United States	United States	Ardelle	18 Jan 1828
James	22	M	Accountant	Great Britain	United States	Aurora	5 Sep 1826
James	23	M	Labourer	Scotland	United States	Samuel Robertson	5 Oct 1827
James	25	M	Taylor	G. Britain	U. States	George Clinton	10 Sep 1828
Jean	13	F		Scotland	United States	Margaret Bogle	11 Jun 1824
Jno.	30	M	Farmer	Ireland	U. States	Emigrant	23 Jul 1822
John	52	M	Merchant	England	U. States	Comet	24 Dec 1821
Mary	20	F		Ireland	U. States	Emigrant	23 Jul 1822
Wm. C.	26	M	Merchant	Philada.	U. States	China	5 Apr 1822
MCCALLA, Francis L.	27	M	Officer	U.S. America		Phoebe Ann	27 Dec 1825
MCCALLEN, James	26	M	Labourer	Ireland	U.S. of America	Meteor	19 Mar 1828
MCCALLION, Eleanor	26	F	his wife [Patrick]	Ireland	United States	Asia	29 Jul 1829
Patrick	30	M	Stone Mason	Ireland	United States	Asia	29 Jul 1829
MCCALLISTER, Jno.	20	M		Ireland	United States	William & George	14 May 1828
Richard	28	M	Law	U. States	U. States	Birmingham	12 Oct 1829
Robt.	25	M	Labourer	Ireland	United States	Louisa	7 Oct 1824
MCCALLUM, Thomas	27 7/12	M	Sheet Maker	Scotland	United States	Mobile	21 Aug 1827
MCCALLVER, Andw.	21	M	Clerk	Great Britain	United States	Friends	13 Jun 1825
MCCALRA, Betsey	10	F	Child	Scotland	Canada	Ann Maria	7 Sep 1827
James	23	M	Child	Scotland	Canada	Ann Maria	7 Sep 1827
Margt.	16	F	Child	Scotland	Canada	Ann Maria	7 Sep 1827
Mary	39	F	Child	Scotland	Canada	Ann Maria	7 Sep 1827

NAMES OF PASSENGERS	AGE	SEX	OCCUPATIONS	COUNTRY TO WHICH THEY BELONG	COUNTRY THEY INTEND TO INHABIT	SHIPS/DATES OF ARRIVAL	
MCCALRA (cont'd)							
Mary Ann	6	F	Child	Scotland	Canada	Ann Maria	7 Sep 1827
Nancy	21	F	Child	Scotland	Canada	Ann Maria	7 Sep 1827
Robt.	4	M	Child	Scotland	Canada	Ann Maria	7 Sep 1827
Robt.	45	M	Wheelwright	Scotland	Canada	Ann Maria	7 Sep 1827
Sally	12	F	Child	Scotland	Canada	Ann Maria	7 Sep 1827
William	2	M	Child	Scotland	Canada	Ann Maria	7 Sep 1827
MCCALSAR, John	25	M	Gentleman	Mexico	Mexico	Howard	21 May 1827
MCCAM, Cathrin	16	F		Great Britain	United States	Atlantic	28 May 1827
Eliza	23	F		G.B.	America	Pacific	13 Jan 1827
MCCAMER, Jno.	2			Ireland		Anacreon	7 Sep 1827
MCCAMLY, John	22	M	Weaver	Ireland	United States	Commerce	13 Jun 1828
MCCAMM, Edward	26 1/12	M	Weaver	Ireland	America	Carolina Ann	7 Apr 1826
MCCAMPBELL, Dennis	27			England	United States	Hugh Johnson	11 Jun 1828
MCCAN, John	27	M	Carpenter	Ireland	United States	Lady Hunter	27 Dec 1825
Margaret	20	F	Spinster	Ireland	United S.	Hanford	19 Aug 1828
Mary	27	F	Spinster	Ireland	Unt. St. America	Wilson	21 May 1827
Peter	23	M	Farmer	Ireland	United States	Dublin Packet	29 Jun 1825
Roger	33	M	Labourer	Ireland	Unt. St. America	Wilson	21 May 1827
MCCANAGHAN, Alice	...	F	...	Ireland	United States	General Putnam	20 Jun 1825
Jane	16	F	...	Ireland	United States	General Putnam	20 Jun 1825
John	11	M	...	Ireland	United States	General Putnam	20 Jun 1825
Mat.	13	M	...	Ireland	United States	General Putnam	20 Jun 1825
Robt.	18	M	...	Ireland	United States	General Putnam	20 Jun 1825
Thos.	3	M	...	Ireland	United States	General Putnam	20 Jun 1825
Wm.	...	M	...	Ireland	United States	General Putnam	20 Jun 1825
MCCANARTY, Mary	20	F		Ireland	Baltimore	Lima	5 Aug 1829
Mary	20	F		Ireland	U. States	Lima	5 Aug 1829
MCCANDLE, Dennis	17	M	Weaver	Ireland	New York	Trusty	12 Sep 1828
James	13	M	Labourer	Ireland	U. States	Two Marys	20 Apr 1825
Rebecca	3	F	Labourer	Ireland	U. States	Two Marys	20 Apr 1825
Rebecca	38	F	Labourer	Ireland	U. States	Two Marys	20 Apr 1825
Robt.	8	M	Labourer	Ireland	U. States	Two Marys	20 Apr 1825
MCCANDLER, Henry	30	M	Weaver	Ireland	New York	Trusty	12 Sep 1828
MCCANE, Briget	36	F	Fer.	Wales	U. States	Franklin	7 Jul 1828
Catharar	3	F	Fer.	Wales	U. States	Franklin	7 Jul 1828
Mathew	18	M	Tin Smith	Great Britain	United States	Atlantic	8 Dec 1827
MCCANEY, Bernard	23		Laboring Class		United States	Atlantic	2 Apr 1827
MCCANN, —	30	M	Weaver	Ireland	America	Mary	29 May 1827
Ann	12	F	Servant	Ireland	United States	Carolina Ann	14 May 1827
Ann	22	F	Farmer	Ireland	U. States	Dickinson	30 Jul 1825
Ann	26			Great Britan	United States	Newry	11 Jul 1827
Ann	28	F	Wife	Ireland	New York	Atlantic	6 Oct 1828
B.	30	M	Merchant	Canada	U. States	Francis	6 Sep 1827
C. A.	20	F		Canada	U. States	Francis	6 Sep 1827
Caughlin	21	M	Servant	Ireland	United States	Trident	16 May 1826
Edwd.	37		Labourer	Great Britan	United States	Newry	11 Jul 1827
Eliza	4/12	F	Daughter	Ireland	New York	Atlantic	6 Oct 1828
Esther	8	F	Daughter	Ireland	New York	Atlantic	6 Oct 1828
Favel	24	M	Weaver	Ireland	N. Jersey	Potomac	7 Aug 1827
Felix	24	M	Joiner	Great Britain	United States	Mary Howland	19 Jul 1827
Francis	22	M	Laborer	Ireland	United States	Justina	5 Aug 1823
George	19		Farmer	Ireland	United States	John Dickinson	28 Jun 1822
Hugh	14	M	Servant	Ireland	United States	Carolina Ann	14 May 1827
James	25	M	Merchant	Ireland	Rhode Island	Atlantic	6 Oct 1828
James	33	M	Labourer	Great Britian	United States	Princess Charlotte	6 Sep 1828
James	35	M	Gentleman	St. Croix	Great Britain	Chase	4 Sep 1821
John	3	M	Son	Ireland	New York	Atlantic	6 Oct 1828
John	22	M	Butcher	Ireland	United States	William & Henry	19 Jul 1822
John	23	M	Weaver	Ireland	Rhode Island	Atlantic	6 Oct 1828
John	32	M	Labourer	Ireland	United States	Carolina Ann	14 May 1827
John, Mr.	22	M	Watch Maker	Grate Britain	...	Courier	14 Jun 1825
Kitty	25	F		Antrim, Ireland	New York	Anthusa	24 Aug 1825
M.	29	M	Doctor	Ireland	Demerara	Hannah & Jane	20 Jun 1825
Margaret	6			Great Britan	United States	Newry	11 Jul 1827
Margaret	20	F	Spinster	Ireland	U. States	Meteor	19 Jul 1828

NAMES OF PASSENGERS	AGE	SEX	OCCUPATIONS	COUNTRY TO WHICH THEY BELONG	COUNTRY THEY INTEND TO INHABIT	SHIPS/DATES OF ARRIVAL	
MCCANN (cont'd)							
Margt.	24	F	Labourer	Great Britian	United States	Princess Charlotte	6 Sep 1828
Mary	9/12	F		Antrim, Ireland	New York	Anthusa	24 Aug 1825
Mary	36	F	Servant	Ireland	United States	Carolina Ann	14 May 1827
Patrick	20	M	Farmer	Great Brittain	United States	Nimrod	9 Jan 1827
Patrick	30	M	Farmer	Ireland	U. States	Dickinson	30 Jul 1825
Petr.	30			Great Britan	United States	Newry	11 Jul 1827
Robt.	25	M	Dresser	Ireland	Rhode Island	Atlantic	6 Oct 1828
Thos.	1			Great Britan	United States	Newry	11 Jul 1827
Ths.	35	M	Confectioner	Ireland	New York	Infant	21 Nov 1820
MCCANNA, Bridjet	1	F		Great Britain	New York	Philetus	21 Jul 1827
Bridjet	30	F		Great Britain	New York	Philetus	21 Jul 1827
Catharine	19	F	None	Great Britain		Moro Castle	6 Jul 1827
Chas.	23	M		Great Britain	New York	Philetus	21 Jul 1827
Francis	22	M	None	Great Britain		Moro Castle	6 Jul 1827
Owen	32	M	Labourer	England	U. States	Thomas Ritchie	2 Jul 1827
Rose	28	F	Spinster	Ireland	United S.	Hanford	19 Aug 1828
MCCANNO, Philip	16	M	Labourer	Ireland		Robert Fulton	4 Jun 1828
MCCANNON, Charles	13	M	Labourer	Sligo	New York	Susquehana	27 Jun 1823
Giles	22	M	Servant	Ireland	United States	William & George	14 May 1828
Jamus	25	M		Irland	United States	Nancy	2 Jan 1824
Judith	23	F		Irland	United States	Nancy	2 Jan 1824
Mary	6/12	F		Irland	United States	Nancy	2 Jan 1824
Patrick	9	M	Labourer	Sligo	New York	Susquehana	27 Jun 1823
MCCANNY, Anne	26	F	Spinster	Ireland	United States	Asia	29 Jul 1829
John	28	M	Farmer	Ireland	United States	Justina	5 Aug 1823
Margaret	24	F	Spinster	Ireland	United States	Asia	29 Jul 1829
MCCANON, Mary	28	F			U. States	Abigail	11 Apr 1823
MCCANY, Elizabeth	34	F	Wife	Ireland	U. States	Meteor	19 Jul 1828
Mary An	1 6/12	F	Child	Ireland	U. States	Meteor	19 Jul 1828
MCCARA, Henrietta	37	F		Scotland	U. States	Lady Hunter	8 Aug 1826
William	37	M	Doctor	Scotland	U. States	Lady Hunter	8 Aug 1826
MCCARDLE,							
Edward	29 5/12	M	Weaver	Ireland	United States	Atlantic	21 Jul 1827
John	26	M	Labourer	Ireland	State of New York	Curler	7 Jul 1827
Philip	20	M	Labourer	Great Britain	United States	Martha	6 Feb 1822
MCCARDY, Lewis	25		Merch.	Cuba		Artibonett	21 Nov 1826
May	30	F	Servant	Ireland	U. States	Sarah G	30 Jun 1828
MCCARELL, Mary	18	F	Spinster	England	United States	Euphrates	18 Aug 1827
MCCARGO, Robert		M	Farmer	Ireland	U. States	Dickinson	30 Jul 1825
MCCARMELL, Jno.	39	M	Merchant	America	U. States	Tampico	14 Jul 1825
MCCARMEN, Cathr.	1	F		Gt. Britain	United States	Penelope	9 Sep 1828
MCCARN, Mary	20	F	Laborer or Spinster	Ireland	United States	Sarah G	11 Sep 1827
MCCARNEY, J.	24	M	Labourer	Gt. Brittain	United States	Balaena	24 Aug 1825
MCCARNON, Ann	30	F		Gt. Britain	United States	Penelope	9 Sep 1828
Barcella	6	F		Gt. Britain	United States	Penelope	9 Sep 1828
John	30	M		Gt. Britain	United States	Penelope	9 Sep 1828
Mic.	4	M		Gt. Britain	United States	Penelope	9 Sep 1828
MCCARNORCON, Patr.	55		Labourer	Ireland	Ireland	Dewitt Clinton	26 Aug 1825
MCCARR, Alixander	3	M	Sawyer	Scotland	Canada	Swift	16 Jul 1827
Ann	20	F		Ireland	New York	Lady Hunter	5 Jun 1826
Bernard	22	M		Ireland	New York	Lady Hunter	5 Jun 1826
Cathren	9	F	Sawyer	Scotland	Canada	Swift	16 Jul 1827
Elixander	36	M	Sawyer	Scotland	Canada	Swift	16 Jul 1827
John	28	M	Labourer			Evergreen	28 Jul 1820
Kat	37	M	Sawyer	Scotland	Canada	Swift	16 Jul 1827
Margret	6	F	Sawyer	Scotland	Canada	Swift	16 Jul 1827
Mary	12	F	Sawyer	Scotland	Canada	Swift	16 Jul 1827
Nanna	13	F	Sawyer	Scotland	Canada	Swift	16 Jul 1827
MCCARRAN, Hugh	46	M	Weaver	Ireland	United States	Clothier	22 Nov 1827
Jane	14	F		Ireland	United States	Clothier	22 Nov 1827
Jane	40	F		Ireland	United States	Clothier	22 Nov 1827
Katey	21	F		Ireland	United States	Borneo	28 Aug 1828
MCCARROL, Mary	12	F		Gt. Britain	U. States	Panthea	21 Jul 1825
MCCARROLL, Ann	3	F	Labourer	Ireland	U. States	Two Marys	20 Apr 1825
Catharin	1	F	Labourer	Ireland	U. States	Two Marys	20 Apr 1825
Ellen	25	F		Ireland	United States	Marmion	17 Jun 1825

NAMES OF PASSENGERS	AGE	SEX	OCCUPATIONS	COUNTRY TO WHICH THEY BELONG	COUNTRY THEY INTEND TO INHABIT	SHIPS/DATES OF ARRIVAL	
MCCARROLL (cont'd)							
G.	21		Farmer	Ireland	United States	Courier	16 May 1825
Mary	23	F	Labourer	Ireland	U. States	Two Marys	20 Apr 1825
Mary	35	F	Labourer	Ireland	U. States	Two Marys	20 Apr 1825
Michael	6	M	Labourer	Ireland	U. States	Two Marys	20 Apr 1825
Michael	30	M	Stone Mason	Ireland	United States	Asia	29 Jul 1829
Owen	8	M	Labourer	Ireland	U. States	Two Marys	20 Apr 1825
Pat	40	M	Labourer	Ireland	U. States	Two Marys	20 Apr 1825
Rose	4	F	Labourer	Ireland	U. States	Two Marys	20 Apr 1825
Terrence	22	M	Labourer	Ireland	U. States	Two Marys	20 Apr 1825
MCCARRON, James	24	M	Labourer	Grt. Britain	United States	Robert Fulton	8 Oct 1828
MCCARRY, Sally	14	F	Spinster	Gt. Britain	U. States	Frances Henrietta	18 Apr 1825
MCCARTA, Martha	24	F	Founder	Ireland	U. States	Meteor	19 Jul 1828
MCCARTEE, Banery	22	M	Laborer	Ireland	United States	Sarah G	19 Jun 1827
MCCARTELEY, Fras.	60	M	Farmer	Ireland	U. States	Atlantic	19 Aug 1825
Mary	50	F	Farmer	Ireland	U. States	Atlantic	19 Aug 1825
MCCARTEN, Bridget	4	F	Spinster	Ireland	United States	Dublin Packet	22 Apr 1822
Bryan	23	M	Baker	Ireland	United States	Princess Charlotte	26 Apr 1827
Maria	11	F	Spinster	Ireland	United States	Dublin Packet	22 Apr 1822
Mary	35	F	Spinster	Ireland	United States	Dublin Packet	22 Apr 1822
Miles	13	F	Spinster	Ireland	United States	Dublin Packet	22 Apr 1822
MCCARTER, Alex	25	M	Farmer	England	U. States	Emulous	22 Aug 1828
Bernard	47		Gentleman	United States	United States	Hudson	14 Jun 1827
Dodey	19	M	Labourer	Ireland		Robert Fulton	4 Jun 1828
John	24	M	Farmer	England	U. States	Emulous	22 Aug 1828
MCCARTHEN, Amelia	28	F	None	Ireland	New York	Eliza Grant	29 Aug 1829
Mary	20	F	Servant	Ireland	United States	Trident	30 Sep 1826
MCCARTHEY, Patrick	19	F		Ireland	America	Carolina Ann	7 Aug 1826
Timohty	25		Farmer	Cork	New York	Schuylkill	22 Aug 1825
MCCARTHIE, Amelia	28	F	None	Ireland		Eliza Grant	29 Aug 1829
Partrick	30	M	Cooper	Great Britain	U. States	Fontine	4 Oct 1824
MCCARTHY, C.	23	M	Labourer	G. Britain	U. States	Hanford	10 Jun 1828
Catherine	21	F	Spinster	Ireland	America	William	21 May 1825
Charles	25 9/12	M	Taylor	Great Briton	United States	Erin	26 May 1821
Chas.	25	M	Farmer	England	United States	Siroc	31 Oct 1829
Corls.	21		...	Ireland	U.S.	Union	20 Aug 1827
Daniel				St. Croix	New York	Virginia	12 Jul 1820
Daniel	23		Stone Mason	Ireland	U.S.	Union	20 Aug 1827
Den.	47	M	Merchant	New York	U. States	Lewis	11 Nov 1824
Elizabeth	38	F	None	N. York	U. States	South Carolina Packet	21 May 1824
Ellen	26			Cork	Gt. Britain	Enterprize	19 Feb 1822
Ellen	36	F		Ireland	United States	Trio	13 Jun 1827
Fanny	18	F		Ireland	United States	Trio	2 Oct 1828
Felix	20		Farmer	Cork	New York	Schuylkill	22 Aug 1825
Francis	22		Farmer	Ireland	United States	Geo. Canning	5 Jun 1828
J., Miss	17	F		New York	U. States	Lewis	11 Nov 1824
Jane	17	F	None	N. York	U. States	South Carolina Packet	21 May 1824
Jas.	19	M		Ireland	United States	Trio	13 Jun 1827
Jeremiah	20	M	Labourer	Ireland	United States	Trio	2 Oct 1828
Jno.	30	M	Labourer	Ireland	U.S. America	Traveller	10 Sep 1827
John	11	M	Smith	Ireland	United States	Trio	13 Jun 1827
John	21	M	Farmer	Ireland	America	William	21 May 1825
John	24	M	Farmer	Ireland	America	William	21 May 1825
John	26	M	Cabinet Maker	Ireland	United States	Trio	31 Oct 1827
John	32	M	Farmer	Ireland	America	Liverpool	31 Aug 1827
Juliana	16	F		Ireland	United States	Trio	2 Oct 1828
Justin	22	M	Laborer	Ireland	United States	Trio	13 Jun 1827
Mary	10	F	Servt.	Ireland	U.S. America	Traveller	10 Sep 1827
Mary	17	F		Ireland	United States	Trio	2 Oct 1828
Mary	39	F		Ireland	United States	Trio	13 Jun 1827
Mary, Jnr.	46	F		Ireland	United States	Trio	13 Jun 1827
Michl.	25		Labourer	Ireland	United States	Geo. Canning	5 Jun 1828
Ml.	35	M	Farmer	Ireland	United States	Trio	13 Jun 1827
Owen	20	M	Farmer	England	U. States	Oglethorpe	9 Nov 1824
Philip	21	M	Getl.	Ireland	U. States	Camillus	27 Jul 1825

NAMES OF PASSENGERS	AGE	SEX	OCCUPATIONS	COUNTRY TO WHICH THEY BELONG	COUNTRY THEY INTEND TO INHABIT	SHIPS/DATES OF ARRIVAL	
MCCARTHY (cont'd)							
Thos.	26	M	Shoemaker	Great Briton	New York	Brighton	12 Jun 1826
Timothy	56	M	Carpenter	Ireland	United States	Trio	2 Oct 1828
MCCARTHYUNDER, —,							
Twin Infants on breast				Ireland	United States	Trio	13 Jun 1827
Jno.	11	M	Laborer	Ireland	United States	Trio	13 Jun 1827
Margt.	—	F		Ireland	United States	Trio	13 Jun 1827
MCCARTLE, D.	36	M	Farmer	N. Brunswick	New Brunswick	Abigale	9 Aug 1821
M.	11	M	Farmer	N. Brunswick	New Brunswick	Abigale	9 Aug 1821
MCCARTLEY, Bridget	30	F	None	Ireland	United States	Jubilee	13 Jul 1829
Catherine	8	F	None	Ireland	United States	Jubilee	13 Jul 1829
Charles	10	M	None	Ireland	United States	Jubilee	13 Jul 1829
Ellnor	4	F	None	Ireland	United States	Jubilee	13 Jul 1829
John	1	M	None	Ireland	United States	Jubilee	13 Jul 1829
John	12	M	None	Ireland	United States	Jubilee	13 Jul 1829
Michiel	6	M	None	Ireland	United States	Jubilee	13 Jul 1829
Patt	35	M	Farmer	Ireland	United States	Jubilee	13 Jul 1829
MCCARTNEY, Ann	11	F		Ireland	United States	Marion	25 Nov 1825
Ann	30	F	Labourer	Ireland	United States	Meteor	26 Jun 1827
Eliza	17	F	Farmer	Ireland	U. States	Atlantic	19 Aug 1825
Geo.	22	M	Weaver	Gt. Britain	U. States	Frances Henrietta	18 Apr 1825
Hugh	21	M	Farmer	Ireland	United States	Marion	25 Nov 1825
Hugh	31	M	Farmer	Ireland	United States	Concordia	25 Aug 1827
James	29	M	Merchant	Scotland	Scotland	Virginia	26 May 1828
Mary Anne	19	F	Farmer	Ireland	U. States	Atlantic	19 Aug 1825
Michael	28	M	Clerk	Ireland	United States	Marion	25 Nov 1825
MCCARTY, Aaron M.	29	M	Carpenter	U. States	U. States	Cobbosse Conte	18 Apr 1823
Anaes	28			United States	United States	Thomas Dickason	5 Jun 1827
Ann	3/12	F		Great Britain	U. States	Great Britain	18 Mar 1828
*Died the 1st March							
Ann	30	F		Gt. Britain		Dalhouse Castle	13 May 1828
Daniel	26	M	Laborer	Ireland	United States	St. Michaels	23 Dec 1826
Ellen	25	F		England	United States	Ganges	10 May 1828
Eugene	22	M	Farmer	Great Britain	U. States	Eclipse	26 Jun 1827
Eugene C.	30	M	Merchant	France	United States	Lewis	30 May 1823
James	21	M	Mason	Great Britain	United States	Mount Vernon	17 Jun 1825
James	23	M	Farmer	Ireland	U. States	William & John	10 Jul 1824
Jeremiah	17	M	Farmer	Ireland	South America	Josephine	24 Jul 1826
Joanna	30	F	Wife	Ireland	United States	Nancy	15 Nov 1824
John	14	M	Farmer	Ireland	South America	Josephine	24 Jul 1826
John	22	M	Labourer	Great Britain	U. States America	Maria	22 May 1822
John	28	M	Labourer	Ireland	United States	Robert Fulton	24 Jul 1826
John	35	M	Laborer	Ireland	United States	Nancy	15 Nov 1824
Margt.	25	F		Gt. Britain	U. States	St. George	20 Sep 1828
Mary	17	F	Spinster	Ireland	United States	Dublin Packet	22 Apr 1822
Matrick	27	M		Ireland	United States	John & Adam	21 Sep 1822
Owen	23	M	Farmer	Ireland	South America	Josephine	24 Jul 1826
Owen	25	M	Laborer	Ireland	United States	St. Michaels	18 Jul 1826
P.	25	M	Merchant	Ireland	U. States	Franklin	27 May 1825
Patrick	18	M	None	Great Britain	United States	Mount Vernon	17 Jun 1825
Peter	26	M	Farmer	England	United States	Ganges	10 May 1828
Sarah	25	F		Great Britain	U. States	Great Britain	18 Mar 1828
T. S.	22	M	Merchant	U. States		Queen Mab	24 Sep 1827
Thomas	25	M	Taylor	Ireland	United States	Dublin Packet	29 Jun 1825
Thos.	17	M	Merchant	New York	New York	Hope Mary Ann	19 Jan 1825
Thos.	30		Mason	Ireland	U. States	Sall & Hope	12 Jul 1820
W.	19	F				Hibernia	15 Aug 1820
W.	29	M	Labourer	Ireland	U. States	Albion	11 May 1827
MCCARVILLE, Mary	22	F	Spinster	Ireland	United States	Catharine	22 Jul 1825
Thomas	26	M	Labourer	Ireland	United States	Catharine	22 Jul 1825
MCCARY, James	26	M	Stone Cutter	Ireland	U. States	Hanford	29 Dec 1828
Jas.	30	M	Labour	Ireland	U. States	Atlantic	19 Aug 1825
Pat	25	M	Labourer	Ireland	United States	Sarah G.	15 May 1828
MCCASH, John	40	M	Weaver	Ireland	New York	Louisa	18 Apr 1827
MCCASKEE, Francis	40	M	Farmer	Ireland	U. States	Dickinson	30 Jul 1825
MCCASKEL, Mary	26	F	None	Ireland	United States	Silas Richards	3 Apr 1826
MCCASKER, ...	2...		Laboring Class		United States	Atlantic	2 Apr 1827

NAMES OF PASSENGERS	AGE	SEX	OCCUPATIONS	COUNTRY TO WHICH THEY BELONG	COUNTRY THEY INTEND TO INHABIT	SHIPS/DATES OF ARRIVAL	
MCCASKER (cont'd)							
Margaret	25		Laboring Class		United States	Atlantic	2 Apr 1827
Robt.	32	M	Butcher	Great Britain	United States	Atlantic	8 Dec 1827
MCCASKEY, Mary	18		Spinster			Rufus King	7 Aug 1820
MCCASTER, Patrick	7		Laboring Class		United States	Atlantic	2 Apr 1827
MCCATCHIN, A.	30	M	Gentleman	Great Britain	United States	Jupiter	14 Sep 1827
MCCATTIE, John	47	M	Merchant	Scotland		Helen	13 May 1822
MCCAUDLE, Peter	25	M	Labourer	Ireland	U. States	Atlantic	19 Aug 1825
Philip	30	M	Labourer	Ireland	U. States	Atlantic	19 Aug 1825
MCCAUGE, Mary	23	F	Seamstress	Great Britain	United States	Grecian	24 Sep 1828
MCCAUGHAN, Henry	38	M	Weaver	Derry, Ireland	New York	Anthusa	24 Aug 1825
John	2 6/12	M		Derry, Ireland	New York	Anthusa	24 Aug 1825
Mary	20	F		Derry, Ireland	New York	Anthusa	24 Aug 1825
MCCAUGHY, Owen	24	M	Labourer	England	U. States	Ayrshire	12 May 1828
MCCAULEY, Jno.	31	M	Weaver	Great Britain	New York	Superior	5 Sep 1827
MCCAULIFE, John	25	M	Laborer	Ireland	United States	Belleville	13 Oct 1827
MCCAULLEY, Robt.	30	M	Mercht.	England	U. States	Trident	8 Mar 1824
MCCAULLY, William	24	M	Labourer	Ireland	U. States	Nancy	1 Sep 1823
MCCAULT, Archibald	52	M	Mariner	U. States	U. States	Hesperus	29 Sep 1827
MCCAUN, Michl.	20	M	Laborer	Ireland	United States	Thomas	13 Dec 1827
MCCAUSLAND, Jane	15	F		Ireland	United States	Mary	1 Jul 1829
Sarah	17	F		Ireland	United States	Mary	1 Jul 1829
MCCAUSTAND, Margt.	18	F		Ireland	United States	William & George	14 May 1828
MCCAVE, Patrick	26		Labourer	Ireland	America	Sarah	18 Aug 1829
MCCAVEN, Philip	21		Servant	Ireland	United States	Fabius	18 Mar 1829
MCCAVILLE, Charles	26	M	Weaver	Ireland	United States	Asia	29 Jul 1829
Jane	24	F	his Wife [Charles]	Ireland	United States	Asia	29 Jul 1829
John	23	M	Farmer	Ireland	United States	Asia	29 Jul 1829
Michael	3/52	M	his child [John]	Ireland	United States	Asia	29 Jul 1829
*died on the passage							
MCCAWL, Patt	28	M	Nailer	Ireland	Albany	Potomac	7 Aug 1827
MCCAWLEY, Clara	25		Lady	United States	United States	Corinthian	30 May 1828
James	29	M	Navy	U. States	U. States	Zephyr	21 Feb 1825
John	37		Gentleman	United States	United States	Corinthian	30 May 1828
Margt.	23	F		Ireland	U. States	Wanderer	30 Sep 1828
Pat	2	M		Ireland	U. States	Wanderer	30 Sep 1828
MCCAWN, William	22	M	Labourer	Ireland	United States	William & George	14 May 1828
MCCAY, A.	22	M	Merchant	Baltimore	Baltimore	Levant	20 Sep 1824
*Landed at Cape May							
A.	26	M	Weaver			Hanford	17 Jul 1828
D.	22	M	Labourer	Ireland	U. States	Wanderer	1 Sep 1828
Fanny	22	F	his wife [James]	Ireland	United States	Asia	29 Jul 1829
Georg	23	M	Carpenter	Pictue, N.S.	New York	Swift	19 Aug 1828
George	40	M	Tailor	Great Britain	United States	Courier	26 Jun 1827
James	24	M		Ireland	New York	Lady Hunter	5 Jun 1826
James	24	M	Farmer	Ireland	United States	Asia	29 Jul 1829
John	24	M	Farmer	England	United States	Mary & Harriet	9 Mar 1827
John	56	M	Farmer	Ireland	United States	Trident	17 May 1825
Patrick	26	M	Farmer	Ireland	United States	Asia	29 Jul 1829
Peggy	16	F	Spinster	Ireland	United States	Trident	17 May 1825
Saml.	20	M	Weaver	Ireland	United States	Trident	17 May 1825
W.	26	M	Carpenter	Savannah	Savannah	Robert Y. Haynes	7 Nov 1825
MCCELLAN, —, Mr.	22	M	Carpenter	Bermuda	Bermuda	Mary & Elizabeth	7 Sep 1824
MCCENLY, James	21	M	Labourer	Great Britain	U. States	Lady Hunter	28 May 1823
MCCHERKIN, James	37	M	Planter	Ireland	St. Croix	Chase	2 Oct 1823
MCCHORY, Joseph	19	M	Labourer	Ireland	United States	Hope	12 Jun 1828
MCCILUFF, Corns.	40	M	Clerk	Ireland	U. States	Hunter	1 Sep 1824
James	24	M	Clerk	Ireland	U. States	Hunter	1 Sep 1824
Timothy	22	M	Clerk	Ireland	U. States	Hunter	1 Sep 1824
MCCIRA, Elizabeth	23	F	Servant	Ireland	N. York	Trusty	12 Sep 1828
MCCIUMBER, Garge	1 8/12	M		Novocotia	Lower Canaday	America	1 Aug 1829
Gavelin		M	Yoman	Novocotia	Lower Canaday	America	1 Aug 1829
Hannah	19 2/12	F		Novocotia	Lower Canaday	America	1 Aug 1829
MCCLAIN, W.	25	M	Planter	Scotland	Matanzes	Betsey	2 May 1825
MCCLAMMER, Danial	27	M	Cotton Dresser	G. Britain	New York	Hesperus	13 Oct 1825

NAMES OF PASSENGERS	AGE	SEX	OCCUPATIONS	COUNTRY TO WHICH THEY BELONG	COUNTRY THEY INTEND TO INHABIT	SHIPS/DATES OF ARRIVAL	
MCCLANE, Joseph	19	M	Weaver	Ireland	United States	Henry Kneeland	7 Jun 1828
Patrick	33	M	Farmer	Great Britain	United States	Colossus	5 Jun 1827
MCCLARE, Archd.	25	M	Farmer	England	U. States	Thomas Ritchie	2 Jul 1827
John	26	M				Splendid	14 Aug 1829
MCCLARISON, Margt.	18	F	Spinster	Ireland	America	Josephine	8 Dec 1827
Mary	44	F	Matron	Ireland	America	Josephine	8 Dec 1827
MCCLATCHEY, David	30	M	Labourer	Ireland	United States	Lord Wellington	28 May 1827
Eliza	3/12	F	None	Ireland	United States	Lord Wellington	28 May 1827
Mary	26	F	None	Ireland	United States	Lord Wellington	28 May 1827
MCCLAUGHEY, Andrew, Mr.	24	M	...	Grate Britain	...	Courier	14 Jun 1825
MCCLAVY, Patrick	22		Laboring Class		United States	Atlantic	2 Apr 1827
MCCLAY, Elizabeth	2	F	None	Great Britain	United States	Courier	26 Jun 1827
Hennery	28	M	Dark	Ireland	New Yourk	Jane Ann	29 May 1826
Jane	23	F	None	Great Britain	United States	Courier	26 Jun 1827
John	23		Blacksmith	Ireland	Great Britain	Robert Burns	14 Jun 1824
Joseph	23	M	Smith	Ireland	United States	Robert Fulton	10 Aug 1827
Mary	3	F	None	Great Britain	United States	Courier	26 Jun 1827
Robert	27	M	Smith	Ireland	United States	Robert Fulton	10 Aug 1827
MCCLEAN, Ann	14	F	...	Ireland	United States	Carolina Ann	24 Oct 1825
Ann	30	F		Down, Ireland	Boston	Anthusa	24 Aug 1825
Eliza	13	F		Down, Ireland	Boston	Anthusa	24 Aug 1825
Henry	25	M	...	...	...	Dawn	19 Aug 1825
J.	24	F	...	Ireland	U.S. America	Columbia	26 Nov 1825
James	20 9/12	M	Weaver	Ireland	America	Carolina Ann	7 Apr 1826
James	36	M	Soldier	U. States	U. States	Virginia	3 Dec 1827
James	45			Great Britan	United States	Newry	11 Jul 1827
James, Jr.	27		Carpenter	Great Britan	United States	Newry	11 Jul 1827
Jane	9	F	...	Ireland	United States	Carolina Ann	24 Oct 1825
John	14	M	Gentleman	Ireland	U. States	Meteor	4 Oct 1827
John	17	M	...	Ireland	United States	Carolina Ann	24 Oct 1825
John	22	M		Ireland	America	Carolina Ann	7 Apr 1826
John	24	M	...	Ireland	United States	Carolina Ann	24 Oct 1825
Margaret	17	F	...	Ireland	United States	Carolina Ann	24 Oct 1825
Mary	10	F		Down, Ireland	Boston	Anthusa	24 Aug 1825
Matilda	30	F	Spinster	Ireland	United States	Fabius	31 Jul 1829
Sarah	23	...	...	Ireland	United States	Carolina Ann	24 Oct 1825
William	40	M	Labourer	Ireland	United States	Fabius	31 Jul 1829
Wm.	40	M	Gentleman	Down, Ireland	Boston	Anthusa	24 Aug 1825
MCCLEAR, T. [crossed out]						Enterprize	19 Oct 1826
MCCLEARY, Chas.	1 6/12	M	None	England	U. States	Thomas Ritchie	2 Jul 1827
David	19	M	Labourer	Ireland	U. States	Josephine	30 Aug 1828
Rose	7	F	Child	Ireland	United States	Dublin Packet	22 Apr 1822
MCCLEEN, Nancy	20	F	Spinster	Ireland	United States	Wilson	6 Jun 1828
Robert	23		...	Ireland	United States	Alexander Mansfield	23 Nov 1824
MCCLELLAND, ...	2...		Weaver	Ireland	Great Britain	Robert Burns	14 Jun 1824
Ann	...1	F	Labourer	Ireland	United States	Meteor	26 Jun 1827
Barbara	5	F	None	Ireland	United States	Princess Charlotte	6 Oct 1827
Eliza	9	F	None	Ireland	United States	Princess Charlotte	6 Oct 1827
Jackson	20		Gent	Ireland	United States	Fabius	18 Mar 1829
Jane	1	F	Labourer	Ireland	United States	Meteor	26 Jun 1827
Jane	38	F	None	Ireland	United States	Princess Charlotte	6 Oct 1827
Jas.	21	M	Farmers and Mechanics	Ireland	America	Constitution	1 Oct 1825
John	3	M	None	Ireland	United States	Princess Charlotte	6 Oct 1827
Margaret	16	F	None	Ireland	United States	Princess Charlotte	6 Oct 1827
Robert	22	M	Farmer	Ireland	United States	Princess Charlotte	6 Oct 1827
Saml.	30	M	Labourer	Ireland	United States	Meteor	26 Jun 1827
Sarah	17 9/12	F	Servant	Ireland	United States	Louisa	27 Nov 1826
Susan	25	F	Labourer	Ireland	United States	Meteor	26 Jun 1827
William	21	M	Farmer	Ireland	United States	Princess Charlotte	6 Oct 1827

NAMES OF PASSENGERS	AGE	SEX	OCCUPATIONS	COUNTRY TO WHICH THEY BELONG	COUNTRY THEY INTEND TO INHABIT	SHIPS/DATES OF ARRIVAL	
MCCLELLAND (cont'd)							
Wm.	12			Great Britain		John Dickinson	5 Apr 1821
MCCLELLY, Sarah	22 1/12	F	Servant	Ireland	United States	Atlantic	21 Jul 1827
MCCLEMAND, Ann	22	F	Spinster	Ireland	United States	Gem	16 Jun 1824
James	26	M	Labourer	Ireland	United States	Gem	16 Jun 1824
Jane	24	F	...maker	Ireland	United States	Gem	16 Jun 1824
Jane	65	F	Spinster	Ireland	United States	Gem	16 Jun 1824
MCCLENCHAY, Neil	23	M		Ireland	U. States	St. Michael	26 Oct 1824
MCCLENN, James	20	M	Weaver	Ireland	United States	Josephine	30 Apr 1828
MCCLEOD, James	51	M	Gentleman	U.S.	U.S.	Stephania	13 Sep 1821
MCCLERA, Jams	_/12	M	D. Maker	Ireland	N. York	Trusty	12 Sep 1828
MCCLESTER, Alexander	21	M	C. Maker	Ireland	New York	Trusty	12 Sep 1828
James	20	M	Labourer	Ireland	New York	Trusty	12 Sep 1828
MCCLEUNG, Rob	28	M	Farmer	England	U. States	Thomas Ritchie	2 Jul 1827
MCCLEURE, Margaret	23	F		Great Britain	U. States	Lady Hunter	28 May 1823
MCCLEW, Francis	21	M	Clerk	G. Britain	U. States	George Clinton	10 Sep 1828
MCCLIN...LEY, N.	22	M	Merchant	Ireland	United States	Sarah G.	15 May 1828
MCCLINCH, John	21	M	House Carpenter	Great Brittan	United States	Hanford	3 Aug 1829
Mary	20	F	wife to [John]	Great Brittan	United States	Hanford	3 Aug 1829
Nicls.	22	M	Pedlar	Great Brittan	U. States	St. Michael	3 Jan 1825
MCCLINCHY, James	30	F	Farmer	Ireland	United States	Sarah Ann	6 Mar 1827
MCCLINCKEY, Jane	1	M		Ireland	United States	Concordia	25 Aug 1827
Mary	25	F		Ireland	United States	Concordia	25 Aug 1827
Michael	30	M	Farmer	Ireland	United States	Concordia	25 Aug 1827
MCCLING, James	40	M	F. Dresser	Ireland	New York	Trusty	12 Sep 1828
MCCLINTOC, Mathew	21	M	Labourer	England	U. States	Ayrshire	12 May 1828
MCCLOCKLIN, Patrick	40	M	Labourer	Great Britan	United States	Silvanus Jenkins	10 Mar 1827
MCCLOEY, Neill	29	M	Labourer	Ireland	U. States	Josephine	7 May 1827
MCCLONE, Danl.	23	M		Ireland	America	Carolina Ann	7 Apr 1826
James	28	M	Labourer	Ireland	United States	Hope	12 Jun 1828
MCCLOSKEY, Anne	7	F		Ireland	United States	Fabius	4 Jun 1828
Catharine	11	F		Ireland	United States	Fabius	4 Jun 1828
Francis	14	M		Ireland	United States	Fabius	4 Jun 1828
Francis	18	F	Laborer	Ireland	United States	Fabius	4 Jun 1828
John	24	M	Labourer	Ireland	United States	Catharine	22 Jul 1825
John	26		Laborer	Ireland	Great Britain	Robert Burns	14 Jun 1824
Mary	20			Ireland	Great Britain	Robert Burns	14 Jun 1824
Michael	20	M	Labourer	Ireland	United States	Borneo	2 Oct 1827
Patrick	16	M	Laborer	Ireland	United States	Fabius	4 Jun 1828
Patrick	43	F		Ireland	United States	Fabius	4 Jun 1828
Sally	4	F	Spinster	Ireland	United States	Fabius	4 Jun 1828
Susan	18	F	Spinster	Ireland	United States	Fabius	4 Jun 1828
MCCLOSKY, James	24	M	Farmer	Ireland	United States	Asia	29 Jul 1829
Philip	25		Labourer	Ireland	England	Emulous	26 Jul 1821
MCCLOUD, Alexander	24	M	Carpenter	England	New York	Swift	19 Aug 1828
Daniel	27	M	Domestic	G. Britian	U. States	Chase	5 Oct 1824
John	27	M	Farmer	Great Britian	United States	Andes	19 Aug 1829
Letis	18	F				Nancy	12 Aug 1820
Mary	25	F		Ireland	United States	Enterprize	23 Jul 1827
Norman	55	M	Clergyman	Great Britain	Great Britain	Reindeer	29 Jun 1827
Samuel	20	M				Nancy	12 Aug 1820
MCCLOUTH, Jame	30	M		Great B.	U. States	William Neilson	26 Jul 1828
MCCLOY, H.	4	M		Ireland	U. States	Emigrant	23 Jul 1822
Jno.	6	M		Ireland	U. States	Emigrant	23 Jul 1822
Margaret	1	F		Ireland	U. States	Emigrant	23 Jul 1822
Margaret	33	F		Ireland	U. States	Emigrant	23 Jul 1822
Mary	10	F		Ireland	U. States	Emigrant	23 Jul 1822
Wm.	38	M	Weaver	Ireland	U. States	Emigrant	23 Jul 1822
MCCLUCIS, Archey	39	M	Laborer	Ireland	United States	Mary	1 Jul 1829
MCCLUE, William	20	M	Labourer	England	U.N. States	Reindeer	20 Aug 1828
Wm.	37	M	Draper	Great Britain	U. States	Cadmus	26 Oct 1821
MCCLUNE, James	38	M	Labourer	Grt. Britain	United States	Robert Fulton	8 Oct 1828
MCCLUNG, Anna	6/12	F	None	Ireland	United States	Lord Wellington	28 May 1827
Anthony	14	M	None	Ireland	United States	Lord Wellington	28 May 1827
Ellen	7	F	None	Ireland	United States	Lord Wellington	28 May 1827
James	10	M	None	Ireland	United States	Lord Wellington	28 May 1827
John	38	M	Labourer	Ireland	United States	Lord Wellington	28 May 1827
Margaret	4	F	None	Ireland	United States	Lord Wellington	28 May 1827
Samuel	12	M	None	Ireland	United States	Lord Wellington	28 May 1827

NAMES OF PASSENGERS	AGE	SEX	OCCUPATIONS	COUNTRY TO WHICH THEY BELONG	COUNTRY THEY INTEND TO INHABIT	SHIPS/DATES OF ARRIVAL	
MCCLURE, Charles	21	M		England	U. States	Cowper	8 Jan 1827
Dorthea	23	F	Servant	Ireland	New York	Carolina Ann	15 Oct 1824
Francis	24	M	Cotton Machine Maker	G. Britain	U. States	Camillus	8 Sep 1828
Isabella	20	F	Spinster	Ireland	United States	Trident	17 May 1825
John, Col.	28	M	Merchant	Tennessee	United States	Nancy Henrietta	3 Nov 1828
Mary	20	F		G. Britain	U. States	Camillus	8 Sep 1828
Sally	33	F	Cook	Ireland	New York	Carolina Ann	15 Oct 1824
W.	62	M	Gentleman	U. States	U. States	Bayard	11 Jul 1825
William	15	M	Youth	Ireland	United States	Romulus	24 Jun 1826
Wm.	29	M	Mariner	Great Britain	Great Britain	Hannibal	12 Oct 1829
MCCLURG, John	20		Taylor	Ireland	United States	John Dickinson	28 Jun 1822
MCCLURKIN, James	32	M	Gentleman	Ireland	U. States	Tidal	28 Oct 1824
MCCLUSKER, Chatharin	21	F	Labourer	Ireland	United States	Hope	12 Jun 1828
MCCLUSKEY, John	...	...	...	Ireland	United States	Carolina Ann	24 Oct 1825
Peter	34	M	Laborer	Ireland	Pittsburgh	Indian Chief	16 Aug 1822
Sarah	26	...	...	Ireland	United States	Carolina Ann	24 Oct 1825
MCCOAKLEY, George	11	M	Servant	St. Croix	U. States	Chase	9 Aug 1827
MCCOAMM, John	18	M	Laborer	Ireland	United States	St. Michaels	12 Jun 1826
MCCOAN, John	28	M	Labourer	G. Britain	U. States	St. George	7 Jun 1828
MCCOAST, Mary	20	F				Hanford	17 Jul 1828
MCCOBIE, John	25	M	Taylor	Ireland	U. States	Sarah G	30 Jun 1828
MCCOCHRAN, Andw.	33	M	Gentleman	England	Canada	York	12 Jul 1825
MCCOFFRY, Catherine	33	F	Matron	Ireland	U. States	Josephine	30 Aug 1828
Catherine, Jr.	1 4/12	F	Child	Ireland	U. States	Josephine	30 Aug 1828
James	11	M	Boy	Ireland	U. States	Josephine	30 Aug 1828
John	13	M	Boy	Ireland	U. States	Josephine	30 Aug 1828
Mary	9	F	Child	Ireland	U. States	Josephine	30 Aug 1828
Thomas	5	M	Child	Ireland	U. States	Josephine	30 Aug 1828
MCCOIL, Moses	22	M	Labourer	Ireland	United States	Hope	12 Jun 1828
MCCOLE, Catherine	1	F	Child	Ireland	United States	Sarah Ann	18 Nov 1826
Catherine	27	F	Wife	Ireland	United States	Sarah Ann	18 Nov 1826
John	3	M	Child	Ireland	United States	Sarah Ann	18 Nov 1826
Thimothy	27	M	White Smith	Ireland	United States	Sarah Ann	18 Nov 1826
MCCOLGA, Celey	24	F	Servt.	Ireland	United States	St. Michaels	23 Dec 1826
MCCOLGAN, Charles	27	M	Mechanic	Great Britain	United States	Grecian	24 Sep 1828
Danl.	10	M	Boy	Ireland	United States	Trident	16 May 1826
Esther	22	F	Spinner	Ireland	America	Fairy	8 Aug 1821
Michl.	22	M	Labourer	Ireland	United States	General Putnam	20 Jun 1825
Nancy	17		...	Ireland	United States	Robert Burns	18 Jun 1822
Owen	20		Labourer	Ireland	United States	Robert Burns	18 Jun 1822
Own	23	M	...	Ireland	United States	General Putnam	20 Jun 1825
Peggy	21	F	Spinster	Ireland	United States	Trident	16 May 1826
Sarah	20	F	Spinster	Ireland	United States	Asia	29 Jul 1829
Sarah	21	F	Child	Ireland	United States	Trident	16 May 1826
Sarah	25	F	Spinner	Ireland	America	Fairy	8 Aug 1821
Shan	26	M	Labourer	Ireland	United States	Henry Kneeland	7 Jun 1828
MCCOLGER, Mark	25	M	Laborer	Ireland	United States	Sylvester Healy	17 Oct 1825
MCCOLGIN, Michael	30	M	Labourer	Ireland	United States	William & George	14 May 1828
MCCOLLAM, Barnard	20	M	Servant	Ireland	America	Carolina Ann	7 Aug 1826
MCCOLLESTER, Saml.	22	M	Labourer	Great Britian	United States	Sarah	11 Jul 1829
MCCOLLEY, George	17		Farmer	Ireland	United States	Robert Burns	18 Jun 1822
George	65		Farmer	Ireland	United States	Robert Burns	18 Jun 1822
Hugh	...0	M	Farmer	Ireland	United States	General Putnam	20 Jun 1825
Jane	2			Ireland	United States	Robert Burns	18 Jun 1822
Jane	21			Ireland	United States	Robert Burns	18 Jun 1822
Jane	53			Ireland	United States	Robert Burns	18 Jun 1822
Joseph G.	35		Farmer	Ireland	United States	Robert Burns	18 Jun 1822
Mary	27			Ireland	United States	Robert Burns	18 Jun 1822
Roberta	30			Ireland	United States	Robert Burns	18 Jun 1822
Susanna	27			Ireland	United States	Robert Burns	18 Jun 1822
Wm.	12		Farmer	Ireland	United States	Robert Burns	18 Jun 1822
MCCOLLIE, Elizabeth	5...			Galaway	Albany	Peru	30 May 1828
James	29			Galaway	Albany	Peru	30 May 1828
Jo Elexander	55		Labourer	Galaway	Albany	Peru	30 May 1828
MCCOLLIGAN, Jno.	27	M	Merchant	Great Britain	U. States	Dominica	4 Jan 1823
MCCOLLIN, Chas.	17	M	...	Ireland	United States	General Putnam	20 Jun 1825
MCCOLLINS, James	27	M	Labourer	Tyrone, Ireland	New York	Anthusa	24 Aug 1825

NAMES OF PASSENGERS	AGE	SEX	OCCUPATIONS	COUNTRY TO WHICH THEY BELONG	COUNTRY THEY INTEND TO INHABIT	SHIPS/DATES OF ARRIVAL	
MCCOLLOCK, Robert	25			b. Galawa, last of Longford	Newyork	Peru	30 May 1828
MCCOLLOGH, Jane	22	F	Labourer	Dunnacon	United States	Minerva	30 Oct 1829
MCCOLLOM, Aaron	22 6/12	M	Tanner	Ireland	U. States	Josephine	30 Aug 1828
MCCOLLOUGH, Margt.	20	F		Ireland	America	Carolina Ann	7 Apr 1826
MCCOLLUM, James	18	M	Labourer	Ireland	United States	Robert Fulton	24 Jul 1826
Jane	24	F	Spinster	Ireland	United States	Robert Fulton	24 Jul 1826
John	22	M	Labourer	Great Britain	U. States	Lady Hunter	28 May 1823
Susan	17 6/12	F	Spinster	Ireland	United States	Robert Fulton	24 Jul 1826
MCCOLSON, Jno.	24	M	Mariner	U. States		Cumberland	5 May 1828
MCCOM, E.	20	F	D. Maker	Ireland	N. York	Trusty	12 Sep 1828
J.	55	F	D. Maker	Ireland	N. York	Trusty	12 Sep 1828
Jane	13	F	D. Maker	Ireland	N. York	Trusty	12 Sep 1828
Robert [crossed out]	24	M	Farmer	Ireland	United States	Leonidas	3 Aug 1825
MCCOMB, Alexander	15	M	Child			Commerce	22 Jun 1825
Alexander	21	M	Farmer, Labourer or Spinster	Ireland	U. States	Meteor	4 Oct 1827
Elizabeth	21	F q	Farmer, Labourer or Spinster	Ireland	U. States	Meteor	4 Oct 1827
Ellen	16	F	Spinster			Commerce	22 Jun 1825
George	32	M	Mearcht.	United States	United States	Planter	26 Jul 1822
Jam	40	F	Servant	Ireland	N. York	Trusty	12 Sep 1828
James	17	M	Labourer	Ireland	United States	Gem	16 Jun 1824
John	1/2	M	Farmer, Labourer or Spinster	Ireland	U. States	Meteor	4 Oct 1827
John	19	F	Spinster	Ireland	U.S. of America	Meteor	19 Mar 1828
Margaret	9	F	Child			Commerce	22 Jun 1825
Mary	19	F	Spinster	Ireland	United States	Gem	16 Jun 1824
Mary	21	F	Spinster	Ireland	United States	Catharine	22 Jul 1825
Matilda	11	F	Child			Commerce	22 Jun 1825
Nancy	55	M	Wife	Ireland	United States	Marmion	17 Jun 1825
Thomas	50	M	Farmer	Ireland	United States	Marmion	17 Jun 1825
William	2	M	Farmer, Labourer or Spinster	Ireland	U. States	Meteor	4 Oct 1827
William	24	M	Labourer	Ireland	United States	Catharine	22 Jul 1825
MCCOMERICK, Bridget	22	F	Labourer	Ireland	U.S. of America	Hamilton	18 Jul 1827
MCCOMICK, Catharine	25	F	Servant	Ireland	United States	Edwin	29 Nov 1828
MCCOMO, Thos.	31	M	Weaver	Ireland	U. States	Courier	17 Mar 1828
MCCONACHY, Ann	34 3/12	F	family [of Thomas]	Ireland	United States	Atlantic	21 Jul 1827
Patrick	3 5/12	M	family [of Thomas]	Ireland	United States	Atlantic	21 Jul 1827
Thomas	33	M	Doctor	Ireland	United States	Atlantic	21 Jul 1827
MCCONAGHY, —	0 6/12		Child	Ireland	United States	Atlantic	21 Jul 1827
MCCONAHY, John	26	M	Labourer	Ireland	U. States	William	27 Jul 1824
MCCONALOGUE, Jno.	24	M	Labourer	Ireland	United States	Trident	16 May 1826
Jno.	26	M	Labourer	Ireland	United States	Trident	16 May 1826
MCCONDREY, Cattenia	20	F	Wife	C. Down	Ohione	Nile	18 Aug 1829
Jane	3	F	Daughter	C. Down	Ohione	Nile	18 Aug 1829
John	22	M	Weaver	C. Down	Ohione	Nile	18 Aug 1829
MCCONE, Michael	27	M	Butcher	G. Britain	U. States	America	17 Oct 1825
MCCONEGA, Neil	23	M	Weaver	Ireland	United States	St. Michaels	18 Jul 1826
MCCONEGAL, John	65	M	Farmer	Ireland	United States	St. Michaels	18 Jul 1826
Mary	28	F	Daughter	Ireland	United States	St. Michaels	18 Jul 1826
Mary	70	F	Wife	Ireland	United States	St. Michaels	18 Jul 1826
MCCONEL, Height	24	M	Farmer	Ireland	New York	Trusty	12 Sep 1828
MCCONELEY, Saml.	21	M	Weaver	Ireland	United States	Carolina Ann	11 Dec 1826
MCCONIGAN, Betsey	25	F		Ireland	U. States	Nancy	12 Aug 1820
MCCONKEY, Eliza	20	F	going to her Brother	G. Brittian	United States	Louisa	14 Jun 1825
MCCONKY, Wm.	18	M	Farmer	Ireland	United States	Alex. Mansfield	17 May 1823
MCCONLIE, Eliza	6	F	Clerk	Belfast	United States	Minerva	30 Oct 1829
Mary Jane	1 6/12	F	Clerk	Belfast	United States	Minerva	30 Oct 1829
Sarah	26	F	Clerk	Belfast	United States	Minerva	30 Oct 1829
Theophilus	4	M	Clerk	Belfast	United States	Minerva	30 Oct 1829
Theophilus	30	M	Clerk	Belfast	United States	Minerva	30 Oct 1829
MCCONN, Josep	46	M	Labour	U. States	U. States	Georgetown Packet	12 Mar 1825
MCCONNAL, Forbes	15	M	Weaver	Ireland	U. States	Josephine	30 Aug 1828
MCCONNEL, Ellen	6/12	F	Daughter	Ireland	New York	Louisa	18 Apr 1827
James	24	M	Labourer	Ireland	New York	Louisa	18 Apr 1827
Jane	24	F	Wife	Ireland	New York	Louisa	18 Apr 1827

NAMES OF PASSENGERS	AGE	SEX	OCCUPATIONS	COUNTRY TO WHICH THEY BELONG	COUNTRY THEY INTEND TO INHABIT	SHIPS/DATES OF ARRIVAL	
MCCONNEL (cont'd)							
John	26	M	Labourer	Great Britain	United States	William Dawson	18 Jun 1827
MCCONNELE, Ellen	18		Labourer	Belfast	U. States	Carolina Ann	14 Feb 1824
MCCONNELL, Adam	30	M		Ireland	United States	William & George	14 May 1828
Bernard	40 1/12	M	Tailor	Ireland	America	Carolina Ann	7 Apr 1826
David	27	M	Cabinet Maker	Scotland	U.S.A.	Calliope	15 Aug 1827
Jane	25	F		Down, Ireland	Boston	Anthusa	24 Aug 1825
Jas.	25		Surveyor	Ireland	Great Britain	Robert Burns	14 Jun 1824
Jas.	35	M	Laborer	Ireland	United States	Nancy	15 Nov 1824
John	29	M	Labourer	Ireland	New York	Wilson	28 Aug 1822
Margaret	28	F	None	Great Britain		Moro Castle	6 Jul 1827
Michl.	34	M	Labourer	Great Britain		Moro Castle	6 Jul 1827
Nancy	27			Ireland	Great Britain	Robert Burns	14 Jun 1824
Patrick	5	M	Child	Ireland	United States	Nancy	15 Nov 1824
Peter	1	M	None	Great Britain		Moro Castle	6 Jul 1827
Rose	35	F	Wife	Ireland	United States	Nancy	15 Nov 1824
William	10	M	None	Great Britain		Moro Castle	6 Jul 1827
MCCONNEY, Joseph R.	32	M	Merchant	Barbados	Supposition is he will return	Superb	7 Jul 1823
MCCONNORHY, John	29	M	Merchant	Scotland	Scotland	Lively Hope	31 Oct 1822
MCCONNULE, J. S.	29	M	Gent.	G. Britain	United States	Fairy	18 Feb 1825
MCCONNY, J.		M		Ireland	U. States	Wanderer	1 Sep 1828
P.		F		Ireland	U. States	Wanderer	1 Sep 1828
MCCONOLOGG, Bidget	16	F	Labourer	Ireland	United States	Hope	12 Jun 1828
James	22	M	Labourer	Ireland	United States	Hope	12 Jun 1828
MCCONOLOGUE,							
Patrick	26	M	Labourer	Ireland	United States	Hope	12 Jun 1828
MCCONOUGHY, Archd.	25	M	Labourer	Ireland	United States	Hesperus	14 Feb 1820
MCCONVILL, Charles	21	M	Labourer	Ireland	United States	Lord Wellington	28 May 1827
John	23	M	Labourer	Ireland	United States	Lord Wellington	28 May 1827
MCCOOK, Edwd.	21	M		Great Britain	New York	Philetus	21 Jul 1827
MCCOOL, Ann	18	F	Laborer or Spinster	Ireland	United States	Sarah G	11 Sep 1827
Mary	16	F	Servant	Ireland	United States	Carolina Ann	11 Dec 1826
MCCOON, —, Miss	21	F		N. York	U. States	Emigrant	9 Oct 1826
MCCORD, Jane	2	F	Farmer, Labourer or Spinster	Ireland	U. States	Meteor	4 Oct 1827
John	28	M	Farmer, Labourer or Spinster	Ireland	U. States	Meteor	4 Oct 1827
Mary	22 3/12	F		Ireland	America	Carolina Ann	7 Apr 1826
Wm.	20	M	Gentleman	Canada	Canada	London	19 Dec 1823
MCCORKER, Catherine	17	F	Spinster	Ireland	U. States	Josephine	7 May 1827
MCCORMACK,							
Charles	26 3/12	M	Joiner	Ireland	United States	Lunar	5 May 1828
Edward	19	M	None	Ireland	United States	St. George	25 Aug 1829
Eliza	24	F		G. Britain	U. States	St. George	16 Jan 1829
James	24	M	Labourer	Ireland	United States	Lady Hunter	27 Dec 1825
Mary	23	F		Ireland	New York	Lady Hunter	5 Jun 1826
MCCORMAN, John	18	M	Labourer	England	United S.	Hanford	19 Aug 1828
MCCORMEH, James	21	M		G. Britain	U. States	Mary & Harriot	8 Sep 1828
MCCORMIC, Bridget	19	F		Ireland	U.S. of America	Douglass	6 Jul 1829
MCCORMICK, —, Mr.	36	M		Dublin	U. States	Hibernia	26 Oct 1826
...s	24	M	Traveler	Ireland	America	Plutarch	18 Jul 1826
Alexr.	20	M		Ireland	United States	Neury	27 Jan 1827
Alexr. *Dead	45	M	School Master	Ireland	United States	Neury	27 Jan 1827
Ann	17	F	Servant	Ireland	United States	Carolina Ann	11 Dec 1826
Ann	21	F	Spinster	Ireland	United States	Lord Strangford	20 Jun 1826
Ann	22		Spinster	Ireland	United States	Courier	15 Oct 1827
Ann	24	F		Ireland	Massachusetts	Eliza Grant	29 Aug 1829
Ann	26	F		England	United States	Camillus	27 Oct 1829
Ann	30		Spinster	Ireland	U. States	Xenophon	28 May 1822
Ann	60		Spinster	Ireland	United States	Courier	15 Oct 1827
Bridget	25	F		Ireland	U. States	Wilson	2 Sep 1823
Christopher	18	M		Ireland	U. States	Ganges	21 Jun 1827
D.	50	M	Mariner	U. States	U. States	Lycurgus	3 Dec 1821
D., Jr.	18	M	Mariner	U. States	U. States	Lycurgus	3 Dec 1821
David	22	M	Labourer	Ireland	U. States	Josephine	7 May 1827
Ellen	13	F		Ireland	United States	Neury	27 Jan 1827
Ellen	30	F	Wife	Ireland	New York	Atlantic	6 Oct 1828

NAMES OF PASSENGERS	AGE	SEX	OCCUPATIONS	COUNTRY TO WHICH THEY BELONG	COUNTRY THEY INTEND TO INHABIT	SHIPS/DATES OF ARRIVAL	
MCCORMICK (cont'd)							
Francis	17	M	Farmer	Ireland	United States	Elizabeth	8 Jun 1827
Hugh	24	M		Gt. Britain	United States	Penelope	9 Sep 1828
J.	24	M	Labourer	Ireland		Marchioness	13 May 1828
James	22	M	...	...	Ireland	Indian Chief	8 Sep 1824
James	37	M	Wever	Ireland	United States	Nile	17 May 1827
Jane	17	F		Ireland	United States	Neury	27 Jan 1827
John	17	M	Labourer	Ireland	U. States	Courier	17 Mar 1828
John	23	M	Labourer	Ireland	United States	William & George	14 May 1828
John	24	M		Irereland	America	Carolina Ann	20 Jun 1825
John	24	M	Weaver	Ireland	U. States	Courier	17 Mar 1828
John	32	M	Black Smith	Ireland	Massachusetts	Eliza Grant	29 Aug 1829
Judy	20	F		Ireland	U. States	Wilson	2 Sep 1823
Luke	22	M	Farmer	Ireland	United States	Lord Strangford	20 Jun 1826
Magt. A.	2	F		England	United States	Camillus	27 Oct 1829
Margaret	19	F	None	Ireland	United States	Elizabeth	8 Jun 1827
Margaret	20	F		Ireland	U. States	Ganges	21 Jun 1827
Mary	4/12	F		Ireland	Massachusetts	Eliza Grant	29 Aug 1829
Mary	1	F		England	United States	Camillus	27 Oct 1829
Mary	20	F	Spinster	Ireland	United States	Fabius	31 Jul 1829
Mary	40	F		Ireland	United States	Neury	27 Jan 1827
Michael	44	M	...	...	...	Indian Chief	8 Sep 1824
Michal	30	M	Labourer	England	U. States	Comet	23 Aug 1828
Nancy	23	F	Spinster	Ireland	United States	Sarah Ann	18 Nov 1826
Neill	1 8/12	M	Son	Ireland	New York	Atlantic	6 Oct 1828
Owen	16	M	Laborer	Gt. Britain		Dalhouse Castle	13 May 1828
Owen	23	M	Tailor	Ireland	New York	Louisa	20 Jul 1826
P. Rose	16	F	Spinster	Ireland	United States	Fabius	4 Jun 1828
Pat	20	M	Labourer	Great Britain		Moro Castle	6 Jul 1827
Pat	27	M	...	Ireland	United States	Trident	18 Jul 1827
Pat	27	M	...	Ireland	United States	Trident	18 Jul 1827
Patrick	18	M	Labourer	Ireland	U. States	Marcus	7 Apr 1825
Patrick	23		Farmer			Amphion	31 May 1824
Patt	18	M		Ireland	United States	William Byrnes	6 Apr 1826
Rose	17	F	Labourer	Ireland	U. States	Marcus	7 Apr 1825
Sarah	18		Spinster	Ireland	United States	Courier	15 Oct 1827
Thomas	26	M	Merchant	Tyrone	United States	Carolina Ann	11 Jun 1824
Thos.	15	M	Mechanic	Ireland	United States	Wm. Byrnes	30 Apr 1828
Thos.	23	M	Labourer	Ireland	U. States	Two Marys	20 Apr 1825
W.	18	M	Labourer	Great Britain		Moro Castle	6 Jul 1827
Wm.	40	M	Merchant	Upper Canada	Great Britan	Carolina Ann	14 Feb 1825
MCCORMIK, Issabella	31		Spinster	Ireland	U. States	Xenophon	28 May 1822
Sarah	11		child	Ireland	U. States	Xenophon	28 May 1822
MCCORNIELL, Thomas	21	M	Farmer	Great Britain	U. States	Yamacraw	4 Sep 1822
MCCORNY, Polly	50	F				Hudson	23 Jul 1828
MCCORRY, Edward	22	M	Farmer	Ireland	United States	Dublin Packet	22 Oct 1821
MCCORTY, Edward	27	M	Taylor	Great Britain	United States	Mount Vernon	17 Jun 1825
MCCORY, Kitey	25	F		Ireland	United States	Nancy R. Crowell	21 Sep 1822
MCCOSGREENE,							
Patrick	44	M	Farmer	England	U. States	Hercules	6 Jul 1827
MCCOSKEY, Eliza	1 8/12	F	Lady	England	United States	Hanford	19 Aug 1828
Fanny	26	F	Lady	England	United States	Hanford	19 Aug 1828
MCCOSLINE, Andrew	11	M		Irereland	America	Carolina Ann	20 Jun 1825
MCCOUCHY, John	19	M	Black Smith			Hanford	17 Jul 1828
MCCOUGH, Michal	22	M	Weaver	Ireland	New York	Louisa	20 Jul 1826
Peter	26	M	Baker	Dublin	New York	New York	31 Jul 1829
MCCOUL, David	28	M	Mechanic	St. John, N.B.	United States	Henrietta	3 Jun 1825
MCCOUN, John T.	17	M		United States	United States	Acasta	15 Jul 1822
Margaret	38	F		United States	United States	Acasta	15 Jul 1822
Samuel	49	M	Merchant	United States	United States	Acasta	15 Jul 1822
MCCOURBLIN,							
Anthony	50	M	Farmer	Ireland	U. States	Atlantic	19 Aug 1825
Anthony, Jur.	16	M	Farmer	Ireland	U. States	Atlantic	19 Aug 1825
MCCOURLAND, C.	40	M	Clerk	N. York	U. States	Robt. Y. Hayne	27 Jun 1825
MCCOURLIN, Nancy	30	F	Farmer	Ireland	U. States	Atlantic	19 Aug 1825
MCCOURT, Alice	23	F	Servant	Great Britain	United States	Atlantic	8 Dec 1827

NAMES OF PASSENGERS	AGE	SEX	OCCUPATIONS	COUNTRY TO WHICH THEY BELONG	COUNTRY THEY INTEND TO INHABIT	SHIPS/DATES OF ARRIVAL	
MCCOURT (cont'd)							
Danl.	14	M	Labourer	Gt. Britain	U. States	Frances Henrietta	18 Apr 1825
John	24	M	Carpenter	Great Britain	United States	Atlantic	8 Dec 1827
May	30			Great Britan	United States	Newry	11 Jul 1827
MCCOURTNEY, James	25	M		Ireland	United States	Sarah G.	20 Jul 1827
Martha	23	F		Ireland	United States	Sarah G.	20 Jul 1827
MCCOUT, J. G.	34	M	Merchant	Scotland	U. States	Elias Burger	12 Sep 1822
MCCOUTTEY, William	25	M	Mason			Carrier	31 Aug 1820
MCCOVEOLL, Fogey	35	M	Surver	Ireland	New York	Potomac	7 Aug 1827
MCCOW, Rose	20	F	Matron	Ireland	United States	Robert Fulton	10 Aug 1827
MCCOWEN, Andrew	22	M	Labourer	Argyle (Tedland) Scotland	United States	Jean Hastie	27 Jul 1829
MCCOWIN, William	18	M	Laborer	Ireland	United States	Nancey	8 Jun 1822
MCCOWLEY, John	35	M		U. States	U. States	York	10 Dec 1825
MCCOY, Cathr.	24	F		G. Britain	G. Britain	Brittania	17 Jul 1828
Elizabeth	18	F		Ireland	United States	Mary	1 Jul 1829
John	27	M	Saddlier	Ireland	St. John, N.B.	Ann Maria	7 Aug 1826
Mary	21	M	Wife	Ireland	St. John, N.B.	Ann Maria	7 Aug 1826
MCCRA, Patrick	35	M	Labourer	Ireland	United States	Belleville	13 Oct 1827
MCCRAB, John	20		Farmer			Rufus King	7 Aug 1820
MCCRABE, James	24	M	Weaver	St. Johns, N.B.	United States	Antioch	21 Sep 1827
Mary	20	F		St. Johns, N.B.	United States	Antioch	21 Sep 1827
MCCRACKAN, John	47	M		United States	United States	Columbia	9 Aug 1822
MCCRACKEN, Jno.	50	M	Merchant	U. States	U. States	Columbia	20 Jul 1825
Saml.	26	M	Merchant	U. States	U. States	Lady Tompkins	13 Apr 1824
Saml.	27	M	Shoemaker	G. Britain	U. States	Eliza	20 Aug 1824
Saml.	30	M	Shoemaker	U. States	U. States	Free Ocean	10 May 1826
Samuel	36		Laboring Class		United States	Atlantic	2 Apr 1827
Wm.	30	M	Labourer	Ireland	United States	Hope	12 Jun 1828
MCCRACKON, Hopkins	25	M	None	France	U. States	Sully	25 Jun 1828
MCCRADY, James	19	M	Black...	Ireland	United States	Robert Fulton	10 Aug 1827
Sally	12	F	Child	Ireland	United States	Henry Kneeland	7 Jun 1828
MCCRAG, Wm.	26	M	Labourer	Ireland	United States	Hannah Eliza	6 Jun 1826
MCCRALL, Mathew	30	M	Labourer	Ireland	United States	Catharine	22 Jul 1825
MCCRATH, John	24	M	Labourer	Ireland	America	Franklin	13 Aug 1827
MCCRAY, Carsty	13	F	Sawyer	Scotland	Canada	Swift	16 Jul 1827
Danker	6	M	Sawyer	Scotland	Canada	Swift	16 Jul 1827
Elixander	9	M	Sawyer	Scotland	Canada	Swift	16 Jul 1827
Elixander	40	M	Sawyer	Scotland	Canada	Swift	16 Jul 1827
Nanna	35	F	Sawyer	Scotland	Canada	Swift	16 Jul 1827
Rorry	11	M	Sawyer	Scotland	Canada	Swift	16 Jul 1827
William	11	M	Sawyer	Scotland	Canada	Swift	16 Jul 1827
MCCREA, Ann	6/12	F		Ireland	America	Alexander	28 Jul 1821
C.	48	M	Planter	Scotchman	London	Industry	31 Jul 1826
Jane	30	F		Ireland	America	Alexander	28 Jul 1821
Jas.	20	M	Farmer			Commerce	22 Jun 1825
Jas.	30	M	Farmer	Ireland	America	Alexander	28 Jul 1821
Margaret	18	F	Spinster	Great Britain	United States	Colossus	5 Jun 1827
Margaret	30	M	Lady	U. States		Hebe	14 Jun 1825
Sarah	2 3/12	F		Ireland	America	Alexander	28 Jul 1821
Walter	20	M	Labourer	Ireland	United States	William & George	14 May 1828
MCCREADY, Catherine	31	F	None	Great Brittain	United States	Active	12 Sep 1828
Ellen	30	F		Great Brittain	United States	Active	12 Sep 1828
J.	39	F	Labourer	England	England	Sir James Kempt	10 Dec 1827
Jane	31	F		Great Brittain	United States	Active	12 Sep 1828
John	5	M		Great Brittain	United States	Active	12 Sep 1828
John	35	M	Farmer	Great Brittain	United States	Active	12 Sep 1828
Wm.	44	M	Labourer	England	England	Sir James Kempt	10 Dec 1827
MCCREAN, Margaret	2		Laboring Class		United States	Atlantic	2 Apr 1827
MCCREARY, John	20	M	Farmer	Ireland	America	Superior	12 Jun 1824
Mark	20	M	Farmers and Mechanics	Ireland	America	Constitution	1 Oct 1825
MCCREDIE, Agnes	13	F	Child	Scotland	United States	Samuel Robertson	9 May 1827
Archd.	22	M	Merchant	Scotland	United States	Samuel Robertson	9 May 1827

NAMES OF PASSENGERS	AGE	SEX	OCCUPATIONS	COUNTRY TO WHICH THEY BELONG	COUNTRY THEY INTEND TO INHABIT	SHIPS/DATES OF ARRIVAL	
MCCREDIE (cont'd)							
Grace	17	F	Spinster	Scotland	United States	Samuel Robertson	9 May 1827
Harriot	6 6/12	F	Child	Scotland	United States	Samuel Robertson	9 May 1827
Jean	8 6/12	F	Child	Scotland	United States	Samuel Robertson	9 May 1827
Jean	45	F	Spinster	Scotland	United States	Samuel Robertson	9 May 1827
William	20	M	Miller	Scotland	United States	Samuel Robertson	9 May 1827
MCCREE, Wm.	38	M	Millwright	York, Great Britain		Casanda	5 Sep 1827
MCCREED, Joseph	11	M	None	Ireland	America	Hesperus	7 Jul 1820
MCCREEDY, Eliza	17			Great Britain		John Dickinson	5 Apr 1821
John	70			Great Britain		John Dickinson	5 Apr 1821
Margaret	38			Great Britain		John Dickinson	5 Apr 1821
William	15			Great Britain		John Dickinson	5 Apr 1821
MCCREEKAN, Solomon	19	M	Laborer	Ireland	United States	Mary	1 Jul 1829
MCCREESH, Pat	22	M	Weaver	Ireland	United States	Commerce	13 Jun 1828
MCCRELER, Willm.	25	M	Taylor	Great Britan	U. States	Ann Marria	6 Aug 1823
MCCRERY, Andrew	26	M	Labourer	Ireland	United States	Catharine	22 Jul 1825
MCCROCKEN, ...	23	M	Labourer	G. Britain	U. States	America	17 Oct 1825
MCCROLIN, Wm.	12	M	Child	Ireland	New York	Atlantic	8 May 1828
MCCRORY, Danl.	21	M	Weaver	Ireland	U. States	Josephine	7 May 1827
Saml.	24		Weaver	Ireland	United States	Courier	15 Oct 1827
MCCROSCKEY, Gawn	19	M	Laborer	Ireland	United States	Carolina Ann	11 Dec 1826
MCCROSSON, James	23	M	Farmer	Ireland	United States	Clothier	22 Nov 1827
MCCROW, Wm.	6	M	Labourer	Ireland	United States	Hope	12 Jun 1828
MCCROY, James	22 7/12			Ireland	America	Carolina Ann	7 Apr 1826
MCCUE, Anne	30	F	Spinster	Ireland	Unt. St. America	Wilson	21 May 1827
Biddy	5	F		Ireland	U. States	Wanderer	30 Sep 1828
Bridget	25	F		Ireland	U. States	Wanderer	30 Sep 1828
Jos.	21	M	Labourer	Ireland	United States	Lord Wellington	28 May 1827
Margt.	21	F		Ireland		Robert Fulton	4 Jun 1828
Mary	28	F	Labourer	Ireland	U. States	Wanderer	30 Sep 1828
O.	20	M	Labourer	Ireland		Robert Fulton	4 Jun 1828
Roderic	17	M	Labourer	Ireland		Robert Fulton	4 Jun 1828
Sarah	19	F	Spinster	Ireland	United States	Wilson	4 Oct 1827
MCCUIE, Nall	25	M	Labourer	Ireland		Robert Fulton	4 Jun 1828
MCCULLA, Jno.	35	M	...	...	U. States	Governor Tompkins	26 Jul 1824
S.	1	M	None	...	U. States	Governor Tompkins	26 Jul 1824
Sarah	30	F	None	...	U. States	Governor Tompkins	26 Jul 1824
MCCULLAGAN, Elizth.	...	F	...	Ireland	U. States of	Courier	17 Mar 1827
MCCULLEN, A.	40	F				Hanford	17 Jul 1828
Ellen	30	F				Hanford	17 Jul 1828
Mary Ane	2	F				Hanford	17 Jul 1828
MCCULLER, Alexander	30	M	Carpender	Great Britain	United States	Richmond	24 Aug 1829
MCCULLIN, Catharine	27	M	Barber	Scotland	U. States	Roger Stewart	9 Jun 1828
David	20	M	Barber	Scotland	U. States	Roger Stewart	9 Jun 1828
Marther	24	M	Farmer	Scotland	U. States	Roger Stewart	9 Jun 1828
Thos.	42	M		Scotland	U. States	Roger Stewart	9 Jun 1828
MCCULLION, James	21	M	Weaver			Hanford	17 Jul 1828
John	47	M	Gardner			Hanford	17 Jul 1828
Mary	15	F				Hanford	17 Jul 1828
MCCULLOCH, J. W.	34	M	Doctor	England	United States	Ann Maria	5 Nov 1821
Janett, & infant	45	F		Scotland	Great Britain	Camillus	28 Apr 1823
Patk.	30	M	Stonemason	...th...ck	United States	Solon	21 Jun 1824
Susan	20	F	Spinster	Ireland	United States	Asia	29 Jul 1829
Wm. S.	23	M	Merchant	...	U. States	Douglass	16 Jul 1824
MCCULLOCK, Alexr.	...	M	None	Isle of Man	Albany	Amity	13 Sep 1821
Elizabeth	30	F	Farmer, Labourer or Spinster	Ireland	U. States	Meteor	4 Oct 1827
Henry	23	M	Labourer	Ireland	United States	Hope	12 Jun 1828
John	24	M	Weaver	Gt. Britain	U. States	Frances Henrietta	18 Apr 1825

NAMES OF PASSENGERS	AGE	SEX	OCCUPATIONS	COUNTRY TO WHICH THEY BELONG	COUNTRY THEY INTEND TO INHABIT	SHIPS/DATES OF ARRIVAL	
MCCULLOCK (cont'd)							
Margt.	12	F		Great Britian	United States	Brok	29 Aug 1823
Robert	10	M	Farmer, Labourer or Spinster	Ireland	U. States	Meteor	4 Oct 1827
Thos.	27	M	Labourer	Ireland	U. States	Balaena	29 Apr 1825
MCCULLOGH, W.	46	M	Indian Department	Great Britain	United States	Isaac Hicks	6 Dec 1827
MCCULLON, Serah	55	F	House Keeper	Ireland	United States	Carolina Ann	11 Dec 1826
MCCULLOUGH, John	28	M	Engineer	Gt. Britain	United States	Meteor	19 Aug 1829
Mary	21	F	Sempstress	Ireland		William Tell	24 Oct 1829
Mary	22	F	Spinster	Ireland	United States	Fabius	31 Jul 1829
MCCULLUM, Elizabeth	21	F	...	Ireland	United States	General Putnam	20 Jun 1825
Jos.	20	M	Mechanic	Glasgow	U. States	Hercules	8 Jan 1827
MCCULLY, James	28	M	Merchant	Ireland	United States	Carolina Ann	24 Oct 1825
MCCUNAGHY, —	24	M	Labourer	Great Britain	United States	Thomas Dickason	31 Jul 1829
MCCUNLIN, Alexr.	35	M	Mechanic	Ireland	United States	Concordia	25 Aug 1827
MCCURADY, Andrew	35	M	Cooper	Bermuda	Montreal	Orlando	1 Aug 1826
MCCURDY, James	25	M	Farmer	Ireland	U. States	Francis	6 Sep 1827
John	40 8/12	M	Mariner	U. States	U. States	Fabius	22 Sep 1828
John	42	M	Mariner	Great Britain	U. States	Eclipse	26 Jun 1827
William	38	M	Labourer	Scotland	United States	Samuel Robertson	5 Oct 1827
MCCURIE, Hugh	27	M	Labourer	Ireland	U. States	Two Marys	20 Apr 1825
MCCURLY, Jane	23	M				Hanford	17 Jul 1828
MCCURRY, William	25	M	Surgeon	United States		Exchange	11 Jul 1823
Wm.	23	M	Labourer	Gt. Britain	U. States	Frances Henrietta	18 Apr 1825
MCCUSK, Thomas	25	M		Ireland	U. States	Nancy	16 Aug 1822
MCCUSKEE, An	18	F	None	Ireland	United States	Catharine	22 Jul 1825
Mary	20	F	Spinster	Ireland	United States	Catharine	22 Jul 1825
Patrick	12	M	None	Ireland	United States	Catharine	22 Jul 1825
MCCUSKER, Biddy	22	F	Spinster	Ireland	United States	Asia	29 Jul 1829
Edward	24	M	Farmer	Ireland	United States	Asia	29 Jul 1829
Fugus	25	M		Ireland	U. States	Nancy	16 Aug 1822
Mary	20	F	Spinster	Ireland	United States	Asia	29 Jul 1829
MCCUSTER, Patrick	24	M	Labourer	Ireland	U. States	Two Marys	20 Apr 1825
MCCUTCHEN, Catharine	9	F		Ireland	United States	Lincoln	10 Dec 1823
James	5	M		Ireland	United States	Lincoln	10 Dec 1823
Margaret	31	F		Ireland	United States	Lincoln	10 Dec 1823
Mary Ann	7	F		Ireland	United States	Lincoln	10 Dec 1823
Nancy	2	F		Ireland	United States	Lincoln	10 Dec 1823
Robt.	32	M	Weaver	Ireland	United States	Lincoln	10 Dec 1823
MCCUTCHEON, Robert	26	M	Farmer, Labourer or Spinster	Ireland	U. States	Meteor	4 Oct 1827
MCCUTCHIN,							
Mary	31 5/12	F	Servant	Ireland	New York	Louisa	20 Jul 1826
Mary Anne	6 1/12	F		Ireland	New York	Louisa	20 Jul 1826
MCCWEE, Mary	20	F	Spinster	Ireland		Robert Fulton	4 Jun 1828
MCDADE, Dominick	18	M	Labourer	Ireland	United States	Robert Fulton	10 Aug 1827
John	22	M	Millwright	Great Britain	New York	Hesperus	13 Oct 1825
MCDAED, Henry	26	M	Labourer	Ireland	United States	Trident	16 May 1826
MCDAID, Sally	16		Spinster	Ireland		Westmoreland	1 Aug 1826
MCDANALD, Bridget	17	F	Spinster	Ireland	U. States	Josephine	30 Aug 1828
MCDANIEL, Alexr.	65	M	Merchant			Ben & James	15 Aug 1820
Danl.	60	M	Merchant			Ben & James	15 Aug 1820
David	24	M	Farmer	England	United States	Ganges	10 May 1828
Ellen	1	F		England	United States	Ganges	10 May 1828
Fanny	5	F		England	America	Two Marys	24 Sep 1827
Jerh.	3	M		England	United States	Ganges	10 May 1828
John	32	M	Farmer	England	United States	Ganges	10 May 1828
Margt.	40	F		England	America	Two Marys	24 Sep 1827
Mary	20	F	Servant	Ireland	United States	Dublin Packet	28 Apr 1824
Mary	23	F		England	United States	Ganges	10 May 1828
Mary Ann	8	F		England	America	Two Marys	24 Sep 1827
Thos.	3	M	Carpenter	England	America	Two Marys	24 Sep 1827
Thos.	40	M	Carpenter	England	America	Two Marys	24 Sep 1827
Wm.	4	M	Farmer	Ireland	United States	Justina	5 Aug 1823
MCDANIELS, James	21	M	Merchant	...	America	Columbia	6 Oct 1825
Thos.	27	M	Labourer	England	United States	John Wells	22 May 1826

NAMES OF PASSENGERS	AGE	SEX	OCCUPATIONS	COUNTRY TO WHICH THEY BELONG	COUNTRY THEY INTEND TO INHABIT	SHIPS/DATES OF ARRIVAL	
MCDANLINE, Curl	30	M	Labourer	Ireland	Philadelphia	General Marion	12 Jan 1829
MCDANNOLD, Susanah	30	F	Spinster	Ireland	U. States	Josephine	30 Aug 1828
MCDANOLD, Wilands	20	M	Labourer	Ireland	United States	Robert Fulton	10 Aug 1827
MCDANOUGH, William	9	M	Labourer	Ireland	United States	Robert Fulton	10 Aug 1827
MCDARDLY, Briget	16	F	...	...	United States	Hanford	17 Oct 1828
Margrett	18	F	...	...	United States	Hanford	17 Oct 1828
Patrick	55	M	...	...	United States	Hanford	17 Oct 1828
MCDAVETT, Geo.	29	M	Servant	Ireland	U. States	Henrietta	7 Jul 1825
MCDAVID, Mary	24	F	his wife [Thomas]	Ireland	United States	Asia	29 Jul 1829
Michael	/12		child	Ireland	United States	Asia	29 Jul 1829
Thomas	26	M	Taylor	Ireland	United States	Asia	29 Jul 1829
MCDAVITT, Ann	18	F	Spinster	Ireland	United States	Trident	17 May 1825
Daniel	23	M	Farmer	Ireland	United States	Trident	17 May 1825
Edward	14	M	Farmer	Ireland	United States	Trident	17 May 1825
Eliza	17	F	Spinster	Ireland	United States	Trident	17 May 1825
Ellenor	15	F	Spinster	Ireland	United States	Trident	17 May 1825
Ellinor	42	F	Spinster	Ireland	United States	Trident	17 May 1825
Giles	21	F	Spinster	Ireland	United States	Trident	17 May 1825
Henry	18	M	Farmer	Ireland	United States	Trident	17 May 1825
John	20	M	Farmer			Commerce	22 Jun 1825
Margt.	22	F	Spinster	Ireland	United States	Trident	17 May 1825
Michl.	20	M	Farmer	Ireland	United States	Trident	17 May 1825
Rosanna	16	F	Spinster	Ireland	United States	Trident	17 May 1825
MCDAY, William, Mr.	30	M	Farmer	Grate Britain	...	Courier	14 Jun 1825
MCDEARMOND,							
Francis	28	M	Farmer	Great Britain	United States	Mount Vernon	17 Jun 1825
James	30	M	Farmer	Great Britain	United States	Mount Vernon	17 Jun 1825
MCDEMROTH, Hugh	78	M	Farmer	Ireland	America	Hesperus	7 Jul 1820
Wm.	24	M	Farmer	Ireland	America	Hesperus	7 Jul 1820
MCDENINTO, Mary	24	F	Spinster	Ireland	America	Superior	12 Jun 1824
MCDERMAT, Catharine	18	F	Servant	Ireland	United States	Wanderer	1 Aug 1828
MCDERMEDE, Michl.	27	M		Ireland	United States	William Byrnes	6 Apr 1826
MCDERMIT, Catharine	22	F	Labourer	Ireland	U. States	Bellville	14 May 1827
Margaret	50	F	Servant	Ireland	U. States	Edwin	1 Jul 1829
MCDERMON, Luke	11	M	None	England	United States	India	8 Jun 1827
MCDERMOT, Danl.	20	M	Weaver	Ireland	U. States	Ann Maria	6 Jul 1824
E.	42	M	Weaver	Ireland	U. States	Ann Maria	6 Jul 1824
Francis	24	M	Labourer	Ireland	United States	Fabius	31 Jul 1829
James	20	M	Labourer			Splendid	14 Aug 1829
John	6	M		Gt. Britain	United States	Penelope	9 Sep 1828
John	22	M	Taylor	Ireland	U. States	Virginia	20 Jun 1825
John	25	M	Labourer	Ireland	United States	William & George	14 May 1828
John	40	M	Y. Man	Ireland	New York	Trusty	12 Sep 1828
Joseph	6	M	Child	Ireland	United States	Fabius	31 Jul 1829
Margt.	35	F		Gt. Britain	United States	Penelope	9 Sep 1828
Mary	2	F		Gt. Britain	United States	Penelope	9 Sep 1828
Mary Ann	18	F	Spinster	Ireland	U.S. of America	Meteor	19 Mar 1828
May	30	F	Servant	Ireland	N. York	Trusty	12 Sep 1828
Mich	1	M		Gt. Britain	United States	Penelope	9 Sep 1828
Michael	27	F	Laborer	Ireland	U. States	Nancy	13 Dec 1822
Michd.	20 3/12	M		Ireland	U.S. of America	Douglass	6 Jul 1829
Michl.	30	M	Laboror	Ireland	United States	Wilson	27 Jun 1826
Minny	17	F	Servant	Gt. Brittain	United States	Balaena	9 Oct 1823
Olivar	17	M	Labourer	Ireland	United States	Fabius	31 Jul 1829
P. J.	27	M	Merchant	Philad.	U. States	General Paez	30 Jun 1827
Pat	4	M		Gt. Britain	United States	Penelope	9 Sep 1828
Pat	37	M	Weaver	Gt. Britain	United States	Penelope	9 Sep 1828
R.	19	F	Servant	G. Britain	U. States	Wanderer	23 Jun 1828
Richard	16	M	Labourer	Ireland	United States	Fabius	31 Jul 1829
Robert	26		Cartmaker	Ireland	Great Britain	Robert Burns	14 Jun 1824
Samuel	20	M	Clerk	Ireland	United States	Dublin Packet	22 Aug 1829
MCDERMOTT, Anne	20		Laboring Class		United States	Atlantic	2 Apr 1827
Betty	9	F	Girl	Ireland	United States	Trident	17 May 1825
Catherine	11	F		Gt. Britain		Dalhouse Castle	13 May 1828
Jane	30	F	Spinster	Ireland	United States	Robert Fulton	10 Aug 1827
John	9	M		Gt. Britain		Dalhouse Castle	13 May 1828
John	24	M	Farmer	Ireland	United States	Andes	2 Oct 1828
Margaret	16	F	None	Ireland	United States	Mary & Harriet	3 Jul 1829

NAMES OF PASSENGERS	AGE	SEX	OCCUPATIONS	COUNTRY TO WHICH THEY BELONG	COUNTRY THEY INTEND TO INHABIT	SHIPS/DATES OF ARRIVAL
MCDERMOTT (cont'd)						
Margaret	50	F		Gt. Britain		Dalhouse Castle 13 May 1828
Margaret, Sen.	46	F	None	Ireland	United States	Mary & Harriet 3 Jul 1829
Michael	20	M	Mechanic	Ireland	United States	Mary & Harriet 3 Jul 1829
Michl.	26	M	Weaver	Ireland	United States	Wilson 27 Jun 1826
William	18	M	Mechanic	Ireland	United States	Mary & Harriet 3 Jul 1829
MCDERMUT, Patrick	28	M	Farmer	Ireland	U. States	Henry Kneeland 27 Jul 1825
MCDERNOTT, James	20	M	Labourer	Ireland	United States	Mary & Harriet 3 Jul 1829
MCDEVIT, Hugh	20	M	Labourer	Ireland	United States	Catharine 22 Jul 1825
John	27	M	Labourer	Ireland	United States	William & George 14 May 1828
Thomas	25	M	Labourer	Ireland	United States	William & George 14 May 1828
MCDEVITT, Bridget	61	F	Dressmaker	Ireland		William Tell 24 Oct 1829
Bridget, Junr.	19	F	Sempstress	Ireland		William Tell 24 Oct 1829
Catharine	14	F	Spinster	Ireland		William Tell 24 Oct 1829
Elizabeth	24	F	Spinster	Ireland	United States	Asia 29 Jul 1829
Patrick	26	M	Weaver	Ireland	United States	Robert Fulton 10 Aug 1827
MCDEVNEL, Patt	34	M	Labourer	Great Britain	United States	Thomas Dickason 31 Jul 1829
MCDEVOTT, Ed.	20	M	Weaver	Ireland	United States	Trident 16 May 1826
MCDILL, Easter	24	F		Irereland	America	Carolina Ann 20 Jun 1825
Thomas	25	M	Farmer	Irereland	America	Carolina Ann 20 Jun 1825
MCDIVETT, Mary	20		Servant	Ireland	United States	Robert Burns 30 May 1823
Sally	19			Ireland	United States	Robert Burns 30 May 1823
MCDIVITT, Jas.	27		Painter	Ireland	United States	Robert Burns 30 May 1823
John	24	M	Labourer	Ireland	United States	Robert Fulton 10 Aug 1827
Mary	19			Ireland	United States	Robert Burns 30 May 1823
MCDOLAND, John	42	M	Brewer	Great Britan	United States	Clematis 8 May 1827
MCDOMNELL, James	20	M	Labourer	England	United States	Nimrod 31 Jul 1828
MCDONAGH, John	28	M	Weaver	Ireland	U. States	Josephine 7 May 1827
MCDONAL, Helen	26	M	Store Keeper	Ireland	U. States	Milo 8 Sep 1828
James	30	M	Store Keeper	Ireland	U. States	Milo 8 Sep 1828
Julia, Child	8	F	Store Keeper	Ireland	U. States	Milo 8 Sep 1828
Mary Ann, Child	6	F	Store Keeper	Ireland	U. States	Milo 8 Sep 1828
MCDONALD, —, Mrs.	26	F		Great Britain	U. States	Finchel 3 Dec 1821
A.	35	M		G. Britann		Manchester 29 Aug 1828
Agnes	8	F	Farmer, Labourer or Spinster	Ireland	U. States	Meteor 4 Oct 1827
Agnes	19	F		Kirkintalloch, Kirkintalloch [Parish], Dumbarton [County]	New York	Hero 19 May 1828
*going to her friends						
Alexander	24	M	Farmer	Scotland	United States	Broke 16 Jul 1829
Alexander	63	M	Bishop	Great Britain	Canada	Roman 19 Dec 1825
Alexd.	28	M	Mason	Great Britian	G. Britain	Enterprize 3 Jul 1826
Alexd.	30	M	Shoemaker	Scotland	United States	Trent 10 Jul 1827
Alexr.	23	M		Scotland	United States	Camillus 9 May 1827
Alexr.	24	M	Labourer	Scotland	United States	Tom 2 Jul 1827
Alexr.	25	M	Farmer	Scotland	U. States	Camillus 27 Jun 1826
Alice	3	F	...	Ireland	United States	Colossus 30 May 1825
Andrew	26	M	Labourer	Ireland	United States	Trident 18 Jul 1827
Angus	35	M	Farmer		U. States	Camillus 29 Jan 1829
Ann	19	F	Servant	Ireland	New York	Atlantic 8 May 1828
Ann	28	F	Spinster	Greece	Greece	Bayard 23 Mar 1826
Ann	38	F	Spinster	Ireland	U. States	William & John 10 Jul 1824
Archd.	25	M	Farmer	Great Britain	America	Samuel Robertson 26 Nov 1825
Bridget	24	F	None	York, Great Britain		Casanda 5 Sep 1827
Cathe.	30	F	Spinster	Great Britain	U. States	Superb 28 May 1821
Catherine	15 4/12	F		England	United States	Rising States 16 Jan 1829
Catherine	33	F	Servant	Great Britain	New York	Intrepid 8 Aug 1822
Chas.	23	M	Brick Layer	England	U. States	Rising States 20 Sep 1828
Columbus	18	M	Seaman	United States		Orozimbo 8 Mar 1826
*distressed Seaman						
D.	22	M	Letter Maker	Scotland	U. States	Superior 25 Sep 1828

NAMES OF PASSENGERS	AGE	SEX	OCCUPATIONS	COUNTRY TO WHICH THEY BELONG	COUNTRY THEY INTEND TO INHABIT	SHIPS/DATES OF ARRIVAL	
MCDONALD (cont'd)							
D.	25	M	Silver Smith	Halifax	U. States	Hope & Esther	22 Jul 1825
Daniel	26	M	Silver Smith	Halifax	New York	Hope & Esther	25 Aug 1827
Dillon	16	M	Clerk	Ireland	New York	Amanda	23 May 1827
Don	45	M	Planter	Scotchman	don't Know	Industry	31 Jul 1826
Donald	22	M	Mercht.	Scotland	U. States	Rebecca	6 Jul 1829
Donald	26	M	Farmer	Scotland	United States	Broke	16 Jul 1829
Donald	30	M	Mason	Scotland	U. States	Roger Stewart	9 Jun 1828
Donald	37	M	None	England	U. States	New York	4 Nov 1824
Edward	23	M	Labourer	Ireland	United States	Lunar	5 May 1828
Elenor	18	F	Farmer, Labourer or Spinster	Ireland	U. States	Meteor	4 Oct 1827
Elijah	2	M		York, Great Britain		Casanda	5 Sep 1827
Eliza	26		Servant	St. Croix	United States	Emelia	10 Dec 1827
Elizabeth	22	F	Farmer, Labourer or Spinster	Ireland	U. States	Meteor	4 Oct 1827
Elizabeth	72	F	Brewer	Great Britan	United States	Clematis	8 May 1827
Felic	20	M	Labourer	Ireland	U. States	Atlantic	19 Aug 1825
Geo.	20	M	Coal Miner	G. Britain	U. States	Camillus	8 Sep 1828
George	11	M	Carpenter	England	England	Hudson	13 Jan 1827
H.	26	M	Merchant	Great Britain	U. States	Finchel	3 Dec 1821
Hannah	28			Scotland	United States	Camillus	3 May 1828
Henry	11	M		Great Britain	U.S. of America	Gratitude	3 Oct 1829
Henry	19	M	Labourer	Ireland	U.S. of America	Meteor	19 Mar 1828
Hery	11	M	Servant	Ireland	Colombia, South America	Hiram	14 Aug 1829
Hugh	17	M		Ireland	New York	Carolina Ann	15 Oct 1824
J.	26	M	Merchant	New York	United States	Excel	26 Apr 1827
James	13 1/12	M	Merchant	England	United States	Rising States	16 Jan 1829
James	23	M	Farmer	Great Britain	United States	Rosina	28 May 1827
James	24 8/12	M	Papermaker	Scotland	United States	Mobile	21 Aug 1827
James	30	M	Laborer	Scotland	United States	Tom	2 Jul 1827
James	33	M	Glass Cutter	Great Britain	U.S. of America	Gratitude	3 Oct 1829
Jane	20	F		Gt. Britain	U. States	Tantiva	7 Jul 1828
Jane	21			Ireland	United States	John Dickinson	28 Jun 1822
Jane	27			Ireland	Great Britain	Robert Burns	14 Jun 1824
Jane	27	F		Scotland	United States	Trent	10 Jul 1827
Janes	23	M	Labourer	Ireland		Robert Fulton	4 Jun 1828
Jas.	6/12	M		York, Great Britain		Casanda	5 Sep 1827
Jas.	22	M	Bookeeper	Kedrth County, Scotland	Gt. Britain	Orozimbo	19 Oct 1822
Jas.	26	M	Farmer	Scotland	United States	Samuel Robertson	5 Oct 1827
Jas.	40	M	Carpenter	England	England	Hudson	13 Jan 1827
Jno.	19	M	Taylor	Great Britain	U.S. of America	Gratitude	3 Oct 1829
Jno.	24	M	Merchant	Montreal	G. Britain	Catharine	22 Jan 1822
John	8 8/12	M		England	United States	Rising States	16 Jan 1829
John	14	M	None	Scotland	United States	Camillus	28 Apr 1824
John	15	M	Labourer	Ireland	U. States	William & John	10 Jul 1824
John	2...	M	...	Scotland	America	Nimrod	9 Jul 1827
John	22		Farmer	Great Britain	United States	Camillus	12 Sep 1827
John	22		Joiner	Scotland	United States	Camillus	3 May 1828
John	25	M	Farmer	U. States	U. States	Euphrates	8 Aug 1820
John	25	M	None	Scotland	U. States	Camillus	27 Jun 1826
John	25	M	Joiner	York, Great Britain		Casanda	5 Sep 1827
John	28	M	Labourer	...	N. York	New Orleans	24 Aug 1827
John	28	M	Labourer	Scotland	U. States	Czar	29 Aug 1829
John	30	M		Great Britain	New York	Philetus	21 Jul 1827
John, Mr.	25	M	Merchant	New York	U. States	Manchester	23 Jan 1826
M.	21	F		Scotland	U. States	Superior	25 Sep 1828
Maria	25	F	Minister	Providence	U. States	Hope & Hester	27 Jun 1823
Mary	11	F	...	Ireland	United States	Colossus	30 May 1825
Mary	20	F	...	Ireland	United States	Colossus	30 May 1825
Mary	22	F	None	Ireland		John Dickinson	14 Sep 1820
Mary	24	F	Spinster	Ireland	U. States	William & John	10 Jul 1824
Mary	24	F		Great Britain	U.S. of America	Gratitude	3 Oct 1829

NAMES OF PASSENGERS	AGE	SEX	OCCUPATIONS	COUNTRY TO WHICH THEY BELONG	COUNTRY THEY INTEND TO INHABIT	SHIPS/DATES OF ARRIVAL	
MCDONALD (cont'd)							
Mary	26	F		Great Britain	New York	Philetus	21 Jul 1827
Michael	27	M	Farmer	Ireland	America	Dewitt Clinton	27 Jul 1824
Patrick	... 1/12	M	...	Ireland	United States	Colossus	30 May 1825
Paul	32		Labourer	Ireland	Great Britain	Henrietta	26 Nov 1825
Phillip	20	M	Labourer	Ireland	U. States	Nancy	1 Sep 1823
R.	33	M		G. Brittain	U. States	Hope & Esther	26 Nov 1822
Randall	30	M	Labourer	Ireland	Ireland	Sarah G.	28 Nov 1827
Ronald	30	M		Ireland	U. States	Nancy	16 Aug 1822
Rosanna	20	F		Great Britain	U. States	Lady Hunter	28 May 1823
Saml.	36	M	Farmer	Ireland	U. States	William & John	10 Jul 1824
Saml.	84	M	Farmer	Ireland	U. States	William & John	10 Jul 1824
Thomas	25	M	Butcher	Ireland	New York	Lima	5 Aug 1829
Thos.	30		Labourer	Ireland	United States	Courier	15 Oct 1827
Timothy	30	M	Labourer	England	United States	Acasta	14 Jun 1824
W.	24	M	Paper Maker	Scotland	U. States	Czar	29 Aug 1829
William	25	M		Ireland	United States	William & George	14 May 1828
Wm.	7	M		England	America	Silas Richard	24 Oct 1829
Wm.	21	M	...	Ireland	U. States	William & John	10 Jul 1824
Wm.	49	M	Labourer	Greenock, Mid [Parish], Renfrew [County]	New York	Hero	19 May 1828
*to follow his occupation							
MCDONALND, Ael	20	M	Brass Bornier [?]	Ireland	United States	Fabius	4 Jun 1828
MCDONANGER,							
Thomas	24	M	Labourer	Ireland	America	Plutarch	18 Jul 1826
MCDONEGAN, Hugh	20	M	Labourer	Ireland	U. States	Nancy	1 Sep 1823
Mary	24	F		Ireland	U. States	Nancy	1 Sep 1823
MCDONELL, Alexr.	43	M	Farmer	Great Britain	Canada	James Monroe	5 Apr 1820
John	34	M	Labourer	Great Britain		Moro Castle	6 Jul 1827
MCDONELLS, Jane	22	F	Labourer	Ireland	U. States	Two Marys	20 Apr 1825
MCDONGALD, Robert	22	M	Blacksmith	Scotland	United States	Andes	2 Oct 1828
MCDONNALD,							
Alexander	21	M	Farmer	Ireland	U. States	Josephine	7 May 1827
Henry	25	M	Seaman	New York	New York	Mary & Elizabeth	7 Sep 1824
James	22	M	Officer	Canaday	Canaday	Loire	22 Jul 1820
James	35	M	Weaver	Great Britain	United States	Courier	26 Jun 1827
Jane	30	F	None	Great Britain	United States	Courier	26 Jun 1827
Mary Ann	14	F	Spinster	Ireland	United States	Dublin Packet	6 Dec 1827
Mathw.	39	M		Great Britain	Baltimore	Philetus	21 Jul 1827
Michael	30	M	Labourer	Ireland	Ohio	Curler	7 Jul 1827
Roderick	22	M	Gentleman	Ireland	United States	Dublin Packet	13 Oct 1828
Thomas	21	M	Labourer	Grt. Britain	United States	Robert Fulton	8 Oct 1828
MCDONNALL, Randall	...	...	...	...	...	St. Michael	22 Sep 1824
MCDONNAND, Margaret	16	F	Spinster	Ireland	United States	Dublin Packet	6 Dec 1827
MCDONNELL, A.	22	M	Mechanic	Great Britain	United States	Hannibal	12 Oct 1829
Angus	32		Lieutenant	Scotland	England	London	16 Aug 1824
Anthony, Mr.	50	M	Merchant	United States	United States	Dublin Packet	24 Sep 1823
Catherine	25	F		Limerick	N. York	Thomas & William	25 May 1827
Edmond	38	M				Trio	5 May 1828
Ellen	8	F	None	Gt. Brittain	United States	Balaena	8 Jan 1825
Ellen	32	F	None	Gt. Brittain	United States	Balaena	8 Jan 1825
Ellenor	22	F		Ireland	America	Plutarch	18 Jul 1826
Etty	17	F	Spinster	Ireland	United States	Dublin Packet	24 Sep 1823
George	20	M	Weaver	Irereland	America	Carolina Ann	20 Jun 1825
George	27	M	Cotton Spinner	Irereland	America	Carolina Ann	20 Jun 1825
Gerald	11	M	None	Gt. Brittain	United States	Balaena	8 Jan 1825
Jas.	21	M	Farmer	England	U. States	Thomas Ritchie	2 Jul 1827
Jerry	24	F	Labourer	Ireland	United States	Sylvester Healy	17 Oct 1825
John	1/2	M		Ireland	America	Plutarch	18 Jul 1826
John	9	M	None	Gt. Brittain	United States	Balaena	8 Jan 1825
John	26	M	Farmer	Ireland	United States	Dublin Packet	29 Jun 1825
John	28	M	Farmer	Ireland	United States	Dublin Packet	24 Sep 1823
John	29	M	Trader	England	United States	Jubilee	1 Oct 1828
Maria	7	F	None	Gt. Brittain	United States	Balaena	8 Jan 1825
Mary	20	F	Servant	Ireland	United States	William	20 Jul 1829

NAMES OF PASSENGERS	AGE	SEX	OCCUPATIONS	COUNTRY TO WHICH THEY BELONG	COUNTRY THEY INTEND TO INHABIT	SHIPS/DATES OF ARRIVAL	
MCDONNELL (cont'd)							
Michael	20	M	Clark	Ireland	New York	Virginia	7 May 1824
Michael	30	M	Smith or Farmer	Limerick	N. York	Thomas & William	25 May 1827
Michl.	30	M	Farmer	Great Brittan	U. States	Gem	26 Jul 1827
Park	21	M	Blacksmith	Ireland	United States	William	20 Jul 1829
Peter	23	M	Servant	Ireland	United States	Carolina Ann	14 May 1827
Rose	24	F	Spinster	Ireland	United States	Asia	29 Jul 1829
Susan	30 6/12	F		Irereland	America	Carolina Ann	20 Jun 1825
Thomas	31	M	Carpenter	U. States	U. States	Frances	22 May 1827
Thos.	27	M				Trio	5 May 1828
MCDONNELLE, Thos.	40	M	Labourer	Great Britain	United States	Penelope	11 Jun 1827
MCDONNOUGH, Henry	3	M				Imperial	19 Jul 1820
Isabella	30	F				Imperial	19 Jul 1820
Jane S.	7	M				Imperial	19 Jul 1820
John	12	M				Imperial	19 Jul 1820
Michael	9	M				Imperial	19 Jul 1820
MCDONOGH, Andrew	25	M	Farmer	Ireland	New York	Susquehanna	9 Jan 1824
Mary	35	M	Farmer	G.B.	U.S.A.	Silas Richard	30 Jun 1828
MCDONOLD, James	30	M	Farmer	Great Britain	United States	Mount Vernon	17 Jun 1825
MCDONOLL, Alexander	19	M	Farmer	Scotland	Canada	Swift	16 Jul 1827
Allin	10	M	Farmer	Scotland	Canada	Swift	16 Jul 1827
Ann	41	F	Farmer	Scotland	Canada	Swift	16 Jul 1827
Hugh	52	M	Farmer	Scotland	Canada	Swift	16 Jul 1827
Janes	17	M	Farmer	Scotland	Canada	Swift	16 Jul 1827
Jemima	6	M	Farmer	Scotland	Canada	Swift	16 Jul 1827
Margeret	15	F	Farmer	Scotland	Canada	Swift	16 Jul 1827
MCDONOUGH, —	10/12	F		Ireland	New York	Amanda	23 May 1827
—	24	F		Ireland	New York	Amanda	23 May 1827
...	2	F	None	Ireland	United States	St. George	25 Aug 1829
...	13	M	None	Ireland	United States	St. George	25 Aug 1829
...	14	F	None	Ireland	United States	St. George	25 Aug 1829
Alice	21	F	None	Ireland	United States	St. George	25 Aug 1829
Ann	5			b. County of Sligo, last of London	N. York	Peru	30 May 1828
Ann	21	F		Ireland	United States	St. George	25 Aug 1829
Biddy	19	F	Laborer or Spinster	Ireland	United States	Frances Miller	27 Jul 1827
Bridget	24	F	None	Ireland	United States	St. George	25 Aug 1829
Charles	30	M	Merchant	Ireland	New York	Amanda	23 May 1827
Eliza	28			b. County of Sligo, last of London	N. York	Peru	30 May 1828
Francis	29	M	Weaver	England	U. States	Roman	1 Dec 1828
Francis	31		Painter	b. County of Sligo, last of London	N. York	Peru	30 May 1828
Hon...	60	F	None	Ireland	United States	St. George	25 Aug 1829
James	7			b. County of Sligo, last of London	N. York	Peru	30 May 1828
James	13	M		Ireland	United States	St. George	25 Aug 1829
James	25	M	Weaver	Ireland	United States	St. George	25 Aug 1829
Jane	24	F	None	England	U. States	Roman	1 Dec 1828
John	20	M	None	Ireland	United States	St. George	25 Aug 1829
John	40	M	Merchant	G. Britain	U. States	Hercules	24 Oct 1821
Mary	2	F		Ireland	United States	St. George	25 Aug 1829
Mary	3			b. County of Sligo, last of London	N. York	Peru	30 May 1828
Mary	14	F	None	Ireland	United States	St. George	25 Aug 1829
Mary	25	F		Derry, Ireland	Philadelphia	Anthusa	24 Aug 1825
Mary	25	F	Laborer or Spinster	Ireland	United States	Frances Miller	27 Jul 1827
Owin	20	M	Labourer	Ireland	United States	Fabius	31 Jul 1829
Pat	23	M				Ocean	17 Aug 1820
Philip	23	M	None	Ireland	United States	St. George	25 Aug 1829
Philip	60	M	None	Ireland	United States	St. George	25 Aug 1829
Sarah	22	F		Derry, Ireland	Philadelphia	Anthusa	24 Aug 1825

NAMES OF PASSENGERS	AGE	SEX	OCCUPATIONS	COUNTRY TO WHICH THEY BELONG	COUNTRY THEY INTEND TO INHABIT	SHIPS/DATES OF ARRIVAL	
MCDONOUGH (cont'd)							
Susannah	6/12	F		Derry, Ireland	Philadelphia	Anthusa	24 Aug 1825
Thomas	22	M	Labourer	Ireland	United States	Wilson	4 Oct 1827
Thos.	33			Great Britan	United States	Newry	11 Jul 1827
MCDONUGH, Honor	60	F		Ireland	United States	St. George	25 Aug 1829
Philip	60	M	Ireland	Ireland	United States	St. George	25 Aug 1829
MCDONWELL, Henry	20	M	Labourer	Ireland	United States	Lunar	5 May 1828
MCDOOLE, Thos.	19	M	Laborer	Gt. Britain		Dalhouse Castle	13 May 1828
MCDORMOND, Jams	24	M	Labourer	Scotland	U. States	Superior	25 Sep 1828
MCDOUGAL, David	31	M	Farmer	Great Britain	United States	Rosina	12 Aug 1823
Duncan	14	M	Merchant	U. States	New York	Howard	11 Jan 1827
G. G.	36	M	Merchant	St. Croix	St. Croix	Emilia	19 Jan 1829
George	8	F	Farmer	Scotland	U. States	Roger Stewart	9 Jun 1828
Henry	30	M	Wheelwright	Ireland	United States	Catharine	22 Jul 1825
John	37	M	Servt.	Ireland	America	Josephine	8 Dec 1827
Patrick	40	M		Ressina	U. States	William Neilson	26 Jul 1828
Robert	22	M	Wheelwright	Ireland	United States	Catharine	22 Jul 1825
Sally	6	F	Lady	Ireland	United States	Lord Strangford	20 Jun 1826
Sarah	60	F	Lady	Ireland	United States	Lord Strangford	20 Jun 1826
Terance	24	M	Blacksmith	Gt. Britain	U. States	Frances Henrietta	18 Apr 1825
MCDOUGALL, Andw.	50	M	Labourer	Scotland	U. States	Camillus	27 Jul 1825
Christian	12	F	Spinster	Great Britain	United States	Roanoak	19 Sep 1827
James	18	M	Weaver	Great Britain	United States	Roanoak	19 Sep 1827
Jenuth	22	F		Scotland	U.S.A.	Calliope	15 Aug 1827
John	48	M	Labourer	Scotland	U.S.A.	Calliope	15 Aug 1827
Mary	20	F	Lady	U. States	U. States	Osgood	9 Dec 1826
S.	25	M	Merchant	England	England	Virginia	9 Feb 1829
Susan	48	F		Scotland	U.S.A.	Calliope	15 Aug 1827
MCDOUGUL, John	30	M	Imports Goods	England		Robert Edwards	8 Nov 1825
MCDOVERT, John	19	M	Weaver	Ireland	United States	Kleber	23 Jul 1827
MCDOWALL, Robt.	27	M	Farmer	Ireland	New York	Commerce	24 Sep 1823
Samuel	15	M	Cotton	Newton Stewart, Shinnegall [Parish], Kirkcudbright [County]	New York	Hero	19 May 1828
*to look for employment							
William	19	M	Labourer	Ireland	United States	William & George	14 May 1828
MCDOWD, Andw.	34	M	Merchant	G. Brittain	G. Brittain	Franklin	28 Feb 1825
MCDOWEL, Abigail	26	F	Spinster	Ireland	United States	Trident	16 May 1826
Ann	3	F	Farmer	Ireland	United States	Justina	5 Aug 1823
Archibald	23	M	Farmer	Ireland	United States	Justina	5 Aug 1823
Elizabeth	6	F	Farmer	Ireland	United States	Justina	5 Aug 1823
George	20	M	Farmer	Ireland	United States	Justina	5 Aug 1823
Jane	20	F	Farmer	Ireland	United States	Justina	5 Aug 1823
Jane	50	F	Farmer	Ireland	United States	Justina	5 Aug 1823
John	36	M	Farmer	Ireland	United States	Justina	5 Aug 1823
Jos.	24	M	Labourer	Ireland	United States	Trident	16 May 1826
Martha	4	F	Farmer	Ireland	United States	Justina	5 Aug 1823
Martha	20	F	Farmer	Ireland	United States	Justina	5 Aug 1823
Mary Ann	18	F	Wife	Ireland	United States	Trident	16 May 1826
Wm.	24	M	Farmer	Ireland	United States	Justina	5 Aug 1823
MCDOWELL, Bernd.	30		Labourer	Great Britan	United States	Newry	11 Jul 1827
Chas.	21	M	Merchant	France	France	Zephyr	17 Mar 1825
James	28		Farmer	Combe	Ireland	Carolina Ann	21 May 1823
Jane	24	F	...	Ireland	U. States	William	27 Jul 1824
John	24	M	Labourer	Ireland	United States	Alex. Mansfield	17 May 1823
Margaret	25	F	...	Ireland	United States	Wilson	22 Jun 1824
Martha		F	Farmer	Ireland	United States	Justina	5 Aug 1823
Mary	49	F		Ireland	United States	Romulus	24 Jun 1826
Patrick	24	M	Labourer	Ireland	America	Wilson	16 May 1825
Samuel	15		Farmer	Combe	Ireland	Carolina Ann	21 May 1823
Sarah	22	F		Ireland	United States	Alex. Mansfield	17 May 1823
MCDOWET, John	26	M	Labrer	Ireland	U. States	Edwin	1 Jul 1829
MCDOWNY, John	15	M	Labourer	Ireland	New York	Trusty	12 Sep 1828
MCDOY, Daniel	21	M	Laborer	Ireland	United States	Mary	1 Jul 1829

NAMES OF PASSENGERS	AGE	SEX	OCCUPATIONS	COUNTRY TO WHICH THEY BELONG	COUNTRY THEY INTEND TO INHABIT	SHIPS/DATES OF ARRIVAL	
MCDUGAL, Wm.	27	M	Labourer	England	England	Sir James Kempt	10 Dec 1827
MCDUGALL, Sarah	50			St. Croix	United States	Emelia	10 Dec 1827
MCEACHAN, Malcolm	24	M	Farmer	Scotland	United States	Belmont	30 Aug 1828
MCEAGAN, Charles	28	M	Laborer	Ireland	United States	St. Michaels	18 Jul 1826
MCEARVIL, Jas.	25	M	Gentleman	Ireland	U. States	Ohio	21 Mar 1825
MCEHEE, Michl.	30	M	Farmer	Ireland	U. States	Dickinson	30 Jul 1825
MCEHENERY, George	33	M	Clergyman	U. States	U. States	Brighton	14 Apr 1828
MCEHWAY, Grizzy, Mrs.	61 3/12	F	Lady	New York	United States	Bethlehem	18 Oct 1828
MCELDIN, James	24	M	Sadler	Ireland	United States	Clothier	22 Nov 1827
MCELGIN, Ann	19		Farmer	Ireland	United States	Courier	16 May 1825
James	8		Farmer	Ireland	United States	Courier	16 May 1825
M.	20		Farmer	Ireland	United States	Courier	16 May 1825
Mary	50		Farmer	Ireland	United States	Courier	16 May 1825
Samuel	50		Farmer	Ireland	United States	Courier	16 May 1825
Sarah	17		Farmer	Ireland	United States	Courier	16 May 1825
MCELHINEY, Bryan	26	M	Labourer	Ireland	United States	Trident	16 May 1826
Catherine	2	F	Child	Ireland	United States	Trident	16 May 1826
Nancy	27	F	Wife	Ireland	United States	Trident	16 May 1826
Sawn	1	M	Child	Ireland	United States	Trident	16 May 1826
Shelah	27	F	Spinster	Ireland	United States	Trident	16 May 1826
MCELHINNEY, Cathr.	17	F		Ireland	United States	William & George	14 May 1828
Charles	18	M		Ireland	United States	William & George	14 May 1828
Robt.	15	M		Ireland	United States	William & George	14 May 1828
Sarah	20	F		Ireland	United States	William & George	14 May 1828
Wm.	21	M		Ireland	United States	William & George	14 May 1828
MCELINN, Francis	23	M	Brick setter	Ireland	America	Plutarch	18 Jul 1826
MCELKINNEY, Robert	30	M	Weaver	Ireland	United States	Catharine	22 Jul 1825
MCELLIC, James	24	M	Gentleman	Great Britain		Charlotte Corday	7 Mar 1820
MCELLREY, James	33	M	Labourer	Ireland	New York	Trusty	12 Sep 1828
MCELRA, Felix	25	M	Farmer	Ireland	United States	Leonidas	3 Aug 1825
MCELREE, Amelia	16			Ireland	United States	John Dickinson	28 Jun 1822
Fanny Jane	19			Ireland	United States	John Dickinson	28 Jun 1822
MCELREY, Cochram	22	M	Labourer	Ireland	New York	Trusty	12 Sep 1828
MCELROY, F. B.	25	M	Navy	Philadelphia	Philadelphia	Independence	25 Oct 1828
James	23 3/12		E. Clk.	Great Britain	United States	Thomas Dickason	29 Aug 1828
Maria	20 4/12			Great Britain	United States	Thomas Dickason	29 Aug 1828
Mary	21	F	Spinster	Ireland	United States	Dublin Packet	29 Jun 1825
MCELVANNA, Susan	21	F		Ireland	United States	Romulus	24 Jun 1826
MCELVY, Conur	23	M	Labourer	Ireland	United States	Hope	12 Jun 1828
MCELWAIN, Thomas	13			Ireland	Great Britain	Robert Burns	14 Jun 1824
MCELWAYNE, J.	19	M	Farmer	Ireland	U. States	Isabella	28 Jun 1825
MCENANY, John	1	M		Ireland	United States	Princess Charlotte	26 Apr 1827
Mary	23	F		Ireland	United States	Princess Charlotte	26 Apr 1827
Thomas	25	M	Tin Smith	Ireland	United States	Princess Charlotte	26 Apr 1827
MCENENY, Catherine	31	F	Wife	Ireland	New York	Louisa	20 Jul 1826
Nancy	3	F	Child	Ireland	New York	Louisa	20 Jul 1826
Patrick	21	M	Labourer	Ireland	New York	Louisa	20 Jul 1826
Peter	29	M	Mason	Ireland	New York	Louisa	20 Jul 1826
MCENERMY, Anne	18	F		Ireland	U.S. America	Traveller	10 Sep 1827
Donero	8	M		Ireland	U.S. America	Traveller	10 Sep 1827
Mary	53	F		Ireland	U.S. America	Traveller	10 Sep 1827
Mathew	40	M	Hosier	Ireland	U.S. America	Traveller	10 Sep 1827
MCENEROE, John, Mr.	26	M	Clergyman	Ireland	United States	Dublin Packet	3 Sep 1822
MCENTER, Mary C.	38	F		America	America	Eliza Ann	2 May 1826
MCENTYRE, B.	26	M		Ireland	United States	Commerce	13 Jun 1828
Martha	2	F		Ireland	United States	Commerce	13 Jun 1828

NAMES OF PASSENGERS	AGE	SEX	OCCUPATIONS	COUNTRY TO WHICH THEY BELONG	COUNTRY THEY INTEND TO INHABIT	SHIPS/DATES OF ARRIVAL	
MCENUTH, Mary	20	F		Ireland	U. States	Olive Branch	30 Oct 1823
MCENZY, James	25	M	Labourer	Ireland	America	Franklin	13 Aug 1827
MCEROY, Jarves	23	M	Weaver	Ireland	New York	Trusty	12 Sep 1828
MCESAY, Jno.	30	M	Cooper	Great Britain	U. States	Dominica	4 Jan 1823
MCETHUMERY, James	25		Planter	United States		Bayard	10 Sep 1827
MCEVAISE, John	29	M	Farmer	Ireland	New York	Robert Edwards	17 Mar 1828
MCEVER, Ellen	23	F	Labourer	Great Britian	United States	Princess Charlotte	6 Sep 1828
Francis	27	M	Labourer	Great Britian	United States	Princess Charlotte	6 Sep 1828
Terence	26	M	Farmer	Ireland	America	Superior	12 Jun 1824
MCEVIN, Robert	50	M	Seaman	Ireland	America	Francis & Henrietta	11 Jul 1823
MCEVOY, Ann	4 9/12	F	Daughter	Ireland	United States	Louisa	16 Mar 1826
Ann	24	F		Ireland	United States	Princess Charlotte	26 Apr 1827
Bernard	29	M	Tailor	Ireland	United States	Princess Charlotte	26 Apr 1827
James	2	M		Ireland	United States	Princess Charlotte	26 Apr 1827
James	24	M	Weaver	Ireland	United States	Princess Charlotte	26 Apr 1827
John	4	M		Ireland	United States	Princess Charlotte	26 Apr 1827
Laurence	2/12	M		Ireland	United States	Princess Charlotte	26 Apr 1827
*Died on the Voyage Margaret	.../12	F		Ireland	United States	Princess Charlotte	26 Apr 1827
*Died on the Voyage Margret	25 6/12	F	Wife	Ireland	United States	Louisa	16 Mar 1826
Mary Ann	2	F		Ireland	United States	Princess Charlotte	26 Apr 1827
*Died on the Voyage Patrick	23	M	Labourer	Ireland	United States	Princess Charlotte	26 Apr 1827
Sarah	24	F		Ireland	United States	Princess Charlotte	26 Apr 1827
Sarah	29	F		Ireland	United States	Princess Charlotte	26 Apr 1827
Thomas	3 3/12	M	son	Ireland	United States	Louisa	16 Mar 1826
Thomas	22	M	Labourer	Ireland	United States	Princess Charlotte	26 Apr 1827
MCEWAN, Barney	45	M	Laborer	Ireland	U. States	Albion	9 Aug 1826
John	30		Wife, going to her husband	Scotland	United States	Camillus	3 May 1828
Kitty	45	F	Wife	Ireland	U. States	Albion	9 Aug 1826
Rosa	18	F		Ireland	U. States	Albion	9 Aug 1826
MCEWEN, —, Mrs.	60	F		Scotland	United States	Camillus	9 May 1827
Catharine	4			Scotland	United States	Camillus	3 May 1828
Duncan	20 2/12	M	Printer	G. Britain	United States	Dutchess of Portland	30 Oct 1826
Duncan	60	M		Scotland	United States	Camillus	9 May 1827
Hugh	30		Weaver	Great Britain	United States	Camillus	12 Sep 1827
Isabella	20	F		Scotland	United States	Camillus	9 May 1827
James	25	M	Merchant	Scotland	United States	Commerce	17 Jul 1823
Janet	19	F		Scotland	United States	Camillus	9 May 1827
Janet	30	F		Scotland	United States	Camillus	27 Oct 1829
John	3/12			Scotland	United States	Camillus	3 May 1828
John	28	M	Farmer	Scotland	U.S. of America	Friends	10 May 1823
Robt.	21	M	Farmer	Scotland	U.S. of America	Friends	10 May 1823
T. S., Mr.	35	M	Merchant	England	England	Manchester	8 Dec 1827
MCEWINE, John	27 11/12	M	Printcutter	Scotland	United States	Mobile	21 Aug 1827
MCEWING, James	23	M	Farmer	Scotland	U. States	Roger Stewart	9 Jun 1828
MCFA..., Wm.	23	M	Weaver	Ireland	U. States of Amer	Courier	17 Mar 1827
MCFADDAN, John	20	M	Merchant	Ireland	United States	Carolina Ann	24 Oct 1825
MCFADDEN, Childs	22	M	Labourer	Ireland		Robert Fulton	4 Jun 1828
David	12 1/12	M	her children [Isabella]	G. Brittian	United States	Louisa	14 Jun 1825

NAMES OF PASSENGERS	AGE	SEX	OCCUPATIONS	COUNTRY TO WHICH THEY BELONG	COUNTRY THEY INTEND TO INHABIT	SHIPS/DATES OF ARRIVAL	
MCFADDEN (cont'd)							
David	35		...			Amphion	31 May 1824
Eleanor	20		Spinster	Ireland		Westmoreland	1 Aug 1826
Geo.	50	M	Hostler	N. York	U. States	Hope Return	6 Oct 1824
Isabella	30 2/12	F	going to her Mother with her children	G. Brittian	United States	Louisa	14 Jun 1825
Jane	45	F		Ireland	America	Alexander	28 Jul 1821
Jno.	21	M	Farmer	Ireland	America	Alexander	28 Jul 1821
John	5	M	her children [Isabella]	G. Brittian	United States	Louisa	14 Jun 1825
Roseanna	20	F	Spinstress			Orion	21 Aug 1820
Samuel	24	M	Farmer	Ireland	United States	Dublin Packet	24 Sep 1823
Wm.	30	M	Farmer	Ireland	U. States	Dickinson	30 Jul 1825
MCFADDON, A.	29	M	Goldsmith	Scotland	U. States	Alert	22 Sep 1821
MCFADEN, Jno.	25	M	Merchant	U. States	U. States	Marcellus	26 Feb 1824
John	26	M	Farmer	Scotland	United States	Commerce	17 Jul 1823
MCFADGIN, —, Mrs.	26	M	Planter	Scotland	U. States	Exchange	19 Aug 1822
MCFADIN, H.	25	M	Shopkeeper	G. Britain	U. States	Panthia	23 Apr 1824
MCFADOTER, Ellen	19	F	Labourer	Ireland	United States	Hope	12 Jun 1828
MCFADYEN, Archd.	28	M	Painter	Scotland	United States	Broke	16 Jul 1829
MCFALEIN, Con.	18	M	Labourer	Ireland		Robert Fulton	4 Jun 1828
MCFALL, Danl.	18	M	White Smith	Ireland	United States	Genl. Marion	4 Jun 1828
George	25		...o...			Amphion	31 May 1824
Patrick	46 4/12	M	Farmer	Ireland	America	Farmer	3 May 1824
MCFALUNE, William	25	M	Clerk	Glasgow		Herald	1 Apr 1828
MCFANDER, Wm.	22	M	Labourer	Ireland	United States	Hope	12 Jun 1828
MCFAQUA, James	40	M	Merchant	Scotland	Scotland	Athenian	8 Jul 1828
MCFARLAN, Agnes	14		Family [of Alexr.]	Great Britain		Camillus	12 Sep 1827
Alexr.	21		Family [of Alexr.]	Great Britain	United States	Camillus	12 Sep 1827
Alexr.	52		Spinner	Great Britain	United States	Camillus	12 Sep 1827
Christian	48		Wife [of Alexr.]	Great Britain	United States	Camillus	12 Sep 1827
Daniel	2	M	None	England		Exchange	11 Jul 1823
Danul	4	M		England		Exchange	11 Jul 1823
Dl., Mr.	60	M	Merchant	Scotland	U. States	Chase	2 Oct 1826
Elizabeth	8		Family [of Alexr.]	Great Britain	United States	Camillus	12 Sep 1827
Francis	22	M	Labour	England		Exchange	11 Jul 1823
James	4	M	None	England		Exchange	11 Jul 1823
James	22	M	Merchant	Great Brittan	U. States	British King	4 Apr 1827
Jane	13		Family [of Alexr.]	Great Britain	United States	Camillus	12 Sep 1827
Jane	36	F	None	Great Britain	United States	Ann Maria	23 Oct 1820
John	11		Family [of Alexr.]	Great Britain	United States	Camillus	12 Sep 1827
John	29	M	Labourer	Great Britain	United States	Ann Maria	23 Oct 1820
Margaret	30	F	None	England		Exchange	11 Jul 1823
Mary	1/12	F		England		Exchange	11 Jul 1823
Mary	26	F	None	England		Exchange	11 Jul 1823
Michael	2	M		England		Exchange	11 Jul 1823
Michael	34	M	Carpenter	England		Exchange	11 Jul 1823
Owen	6	M	None	England		Exchange	11 Jul 1823
Owen	30	M	Labour	England		Exchange	11 Jul 1823
Patrick	40	M	Labor	England		Exchange	11 Jul 1823
Peter	6	M	None	England		Exchange	11 Jul 1823
Robt.	35	M	Merchant	England	England	Arthenian	28 Apr 1827
Rose	20	F	None	England		Exchange	11 Jul 1823
Thos.	26	M	Weaver	Scotland	America	Eyder	7 Aug 1826
Walter	22	M	Merchant	U. States	U.S.	Franklin	10 Jan 1825
MCFARLAND,							
Alexander	19	M	Wheel Wright	Ireland	United States	Romulus	24 Jun 1826
Andrew	30	M	Laborer	Great Britain	United States	Courier	26 Jun 1827
Daniel	25	M	Gardner	England	United States	Hamlet	25 Aug 1825
Eliza J.	5	F		Great Britain	United States	Grecian	24 Sep 1828
Ester	3	F		Great Britain	United States	Grecian	24 Sep 1828
Ester	50	F	Spinner	Great Britain	United States	Grecian	24 Sep 1828
Huldah	19	F		America	U. States	Active	28 Aug 1829
James	30	M	Seaman	Great Britain	United States	Favorite	10 Dec 1822
John	24	M	Weaver	Tyrone, Ireland	Pennsylvania	Anthusa	24 Aug 1825
Lydia	12	F		Great Britain	United States	Grecian	24 Sep 1828
Margt.	24	F	Spinner	Great Britain	United States	Grecian	24 Sep 1828
Mary	24		Spinster	Ireland	United States	Courier	15 Oct 1827
Owen	35		Weaver	Ireland	United States	Courier	15 Oct 1827

NAMES OF PASSENGERS	AGE	SEX	OCCUPATIONS	COUNTRY TO WHICH THEY BELONG	COUNTRY THEY INTEND TO INHABIT	SHIPS/DATES OF ARRIVAL	
MCFARLAND (cont'd)							
Sally	26	F		America	U. States	Active	28 Aug 1829
Serah	20	F	Spinster	Ireland	United States	Robert Fulton	10 Aug 1827
MCFARLANE, ...y	19	M	None	United States	United States	Dalhouse Castle	21 Aug 1829
Alexr.						Hero	19 May 1828
Christin	2	M		Scotland	America	Eyder	7 Aug 1826
Danl.	25	M	Shoemaker	Scotland	U. States	Czar	29 Aug 1829
David	3	M		Scotland	United States	Samuel Robertson	5 Oct 1827
Eliza	26	F	Spinster	Scotland	United States	Friends	7 Jul 1827
Ellen	26	F		Scotland	America	Eyder	7 Aug 1826
Geo.	26	M	Merchant	Scotland	America	Hector	11 Oct 1822
Henry	19	M	None	United States	U.S.A.	Dalhouse Castle	21 Aug 1829
Hugh	20	M	Clerk	England	United States	Hannibal	25 Sep 1827
James	5	M		Scotland	United States	Samuel Robertson	5 Oct 1827
James	28	M	Laborer	Scotland	America	Eyder	7 Aug 1826
Jane	35	F		Scotland	United States	Samuel Robertson	5 Oct 1827
Janet	6/12	F		Scotland	United States	Samuel Robertson	5 Oct 1827
Jno.	20	M	Dyer	England	U. States	Thomas Ritchie	2 Jul 1827
John	17	M	Merchant	England	England	Pacific	17 Jun 1828
John Cameron	30	M	Merchant	America		Silas Richards	19 Mar 1828
Malcom	28	M	Farmer			Frances	17 Aug 1820
Margaret	6/12	F		Scotland	United States	Samuel Robertson	5 Oct 1827
Marian	4	F		Scotland	America	Eyder	7 Aug 1826
Mary	20	F	None	Scotland	U. States	Camillus	27 Jun 1826
Mungo	14	M	Servant	G.B.	G.B.	Sally	19 Sep 1821
R.	30	M	Merchant	Carthagena	England	Bunker Hill	11 Mar 1826
Robert	5	M	None	Scotland	United States	Friends	7 Jul 1827
Walter	20 10/12	M	Merchant	United States	New York, U. States	Cadmus	12 Dec 1823
Walter	45	M	Mariner	U. States	U. States	Lycurgus	3 Dec 1821
Wm.	35	M	Merchant	G.B.	G.B.	Sally	19 Sep 1821
MCFARLANIE, Willm.	34	M	Labourer	New Brunswick	U. States	Lady Hunter	22 Aug 1825
MCFARLANN, Duncan	24	M	Laborer	Scotland	America	Camillus	12 Sep 1822
Duncan	39	M	Gardiner	Scotland	America	Camillus	12 Sep 1822
MCFARLEN, Dennis	25	M	Farmer	Ireland	America	Alexander	28 Jul 1821
MCFARLIN, Andrew	23	M	Mechanic	England	Great Britain	Manchester Packet	30 Nov 1822
MCFARLON, Walter	22	M	Merchant	United States	United States	Louisiana	9 Aug 1826
MCFAUL, Daniel	24	M	Farmer	Ireland	U. States	Josephine	7 May 1827
Martha	64	F	Widow	Ireland	U. States	Josephine	7 May 1827
Mary	17	F	Spinster	Ireland	U. States	Josephine	7 May 1827
Rosannah	40	F	Spinster	Ireland	U. States	Josephine	7 May 1827
MCFAVISH, Jno. G.	36	M	Merchant	Great Britain	Canada	James Monroe	5 Apr 1820
MCFEELER, Charles	8	M		Ireland	United States	Huldah & Judah	30 Jul 1822
Daniel	6	M		Ireland	United States	Huldah & Judah	30 Jul 1822
Dennis	5	M		Ireland	United States	Huldah & Judah	30 Jul 1822
Mary	30	F		Ireland	United States	Huldah & Judah	30 Jul 1822
MCFEELEY, John	23	M	Labourer	Ireland	U.S.	Lady Hunter	10 Jul 1826
MCFEELY, Eliza	24	F		Ireland	United States	William & George	14 May 1828
James	26	M		Ireland	United States	William & George	14 May 1828
MCFELLEN, Robt.	22	M	Labourer	G. Britain	U. States	Sarah G	5 Jun 1828
MCFIE, Patrick	25	M	Clerk	Ireland	St. Johns	Ann Maria	7 Sep 1827
MCFIER, Terrill	27	M	Labourer	Ireland	U. States	Two Marys	20 Apr 1825
MCFILLOP, Alex	23		Merchant	Ireland	U. States	Xenophon	28 May 1822
MCFINLY, Ann	2 7/12	F		G. Britain	United States	Louisa	14 Jun 1825
Mary	30	F	going to her Husband	G. Britain	United States	Louisa	14 Jun 1825
MCFINNY, Patrick	25	M	Labourer	Ireland	United States	Hope	12 Jun 1828
MCFORLEY, Alice	...		Laboring Class		United States	Atlantic	2 Apr 1827
MCFURSON, Alexander	23	M	Labourer	Ireland		Robert Fulton	4 Jun 1828
MCG..., Pat	27	M	Labourer	Ireland	Unt. St. America	Wilson	21 May 1827
MCG...G..., Hugh	22		Laboring Class		United States	Atlantic	2 Apr 1827
MCG...GER, Wm.	25	M	Farmer	Scotland	U. States	Roger Stewart	9 Jun 1828

NAMES OF PASSENGERS	AGE	SEX	OCCUPATIONS	COUNTRY TO WHICH THEY BELONG	COUNTRY THEY INTEND TO INHABIT	SHIPS/DATES OF ARRIVAL	
MCG...HAM, Saml.	25	F	Seamstress	Ireland	U. States	Atlantic	19 Aug 1825
MCG...S, Rose	20	F	Servant	Ireland	United States	Carolina Ann	14 May 1827
MCGA...EY, Jno.	24	M	Labourer	Great Britian	United States	Sarah	11 Jul 1829
MCGADDY, Patrick	30	M	School Master	England	United States	Hannibal	25 Sep 1827
MCGAFFRY, Margaret	25	F	Seamstress	Great Britain	United States	Henrietta	19 Oct 1825
MCGAGHAM, John	30	M	Labourer	Ireland	U. States	Atlantic	19 Aug 1825
MCGAGHAN, John	19	M	Laborer	Ireland	United States	Delta	24 Oct 1829
Roger	30	M	Lady		Newburgh	Betsy	4 Sep 1820
MCGAHEY, Wm.	17	M	Labourer	Ireland		Robert Fulton	4 Jun 1828
MCGAIEL, Peter	15	M	Traveler	Great Britain	United States	Thomas Dickason	31 Jul 1829
MCGAILE, Bryne	32	M	Farmer	Ireland	United States	Romulus	24 Jun 1826
Catherine	32	F		Ireland	United States	Romulus	24 Jun 1826
Mary	3	F		Ireland	United States	Romulus	24 Jun 1826
Simon	25	M	Weaver	Ireland	United States	Romulus	24 Jun 1826
MCGAIN, John	23	M	Labourer	Ireland		Robert Fulton	4 Jun 1828
MCGALER, John	22	M		G. Britan	U. States	William Neilson	26 Jul 1828
MCGALLAGER, Rose	22	F	Servant	Ireland	United States	Louisa	18 Apr 1827
MCGALLAGHER,							
Charles	6		Laboring Class		United States	Atlantic	2 Apr 1827
George	...0		Laboring Class		United States	Atlantic	2 Apr 1827
Margaret	19		Laboring Class		United States	Atlantic	2 Apr 1827
Owen	2...		Laboring Class		United States	Atlantic	2 Apr 1827
MCGALLIGHER,							
Catherine	29		Laboring Class		United States	Atlantic	2 Apr 1827
MCGALLPEN, Sally	23	F	Servant	Ireland	United States	Carolina Ann	14 May 1827
MCGALPEN, John	21	M	...an...	Ireland	United States	Carolina Ann	14 May 1827
MCGALRICH, Mary	16	F	Spinster	Ireland	United States	Lima	19 Jun 1824
MCGAN, William	35	M	Farmer	Lundarry	United States	Minerva	30 Oct 1829
MCGANEY, Bernard	30	M	Labourer	Ireland	United States	Princess Charlotte	26 Apr 1827
MCGANN, Pat	20	M	Labourer	Ireland	America	Weser	26 Jun 1821
MCGANNETY, R.	20		Farmer	Ireland	United States	Courier	16 May 1825
MCGANTY, Cathrine	20	F	None	Great Britain	United States	Penelope	11 Jun 1827
Elizabeth	28	F	None	Great Britain	United States	Penelope	11 Jun 1827
MCGAR, Bridget	25	F	Widow	Ireland	U. States	William & John	10 Jul 1824
Patk.	30	M	Farmer	Ireland	U. States	William & John	10 Jul 1824
MCGARERTY, Catharine	24	F	Labourer	Ireland	U. States	Two Marys	20 Apr 1825
Mary	30	F	Labourer	Ireland	U. States	Two Marys	20 Apr 1825
MCGAREY, Andrew	19	M	Farmer	Ireland	United States	Princess Charlotte	6 Oct 1827
Patrick	23 8/12	M	Musician	Ireland	United States	London	6 Feb 1829
MCGARGE, Joseph	21	M	Clerk	G. Britain	New York	Hesperus	13 Oct 1825
MCGARNEY, Catherine	7	F	Child	Ireland	United States	Dublin Packet	22 Apr 1822
Peter	9	M	Child	Ireland	United States	Dublin Packet	22 Apr 1822
MCGARRAGH, Mary	15	F	Ma...maker	Irereland	America	Carolina Ann	20 Jun 1825
MCGARRAH, Thomas	23	M	Taylor	Ireland	New York	Brighton	24 Aug 1827
MCGARRAN, Ada	2	F		Ireland	United States	Dalhouse Castle	8 May 1827
Elizabeth	6	F		Ireland	United States	Dalhouse Castle	8 May 1827
Francis	23	F	Carpenter	Ireland	United States	Dalhouse Castle	8 May 1827
J.	33	M	Labourer	Ireland	United States	Dalhouse Castle	8 May 1827
Mary	31	F		Ireland	United States	Dalhouse Castle	8 May 1827
Mary Ann	4	F		Ireland	United States	Dalhouse Castle	8 May 1827
MCGARRITY, Ann	20	F		Ireland	United States	William & George	14 May 1828
Bryan	26	M	Labourer	Ireland	United States	William & George	14 May 1828
MCGARRY, Biddy	50	F		Ireland	America	Carolina Ann	7 Apr 1826
Denis	19	M	Labourer	Ireland	United States	Fabius	31 Jul 1829
Mary	16 3/12	F		Ireland	America	Carolina Ann	7 Apr 1826
MCGARTER, James	34	M	Grocer	..., ..., Ireland	N. York	New Orleans	24 Aug 1827
Sarah	20	F	Wife	..., ..., Ireland	N. York	New Orleans	24 Aug 1827
MCGARVEN, David	30	M	Laborer	Ireland	United States	Sarah G	19 Jun 1827
MCGARVEY, Alex.	14	M	Labourer	Ireland	United States	Trident	16 May 1826
Giles	12	F	Spinster	Ireland	United States	Trident	16 May 1826
John	19	M	Blacksmith	Ireland	United States	Trident	16 May 1826
John	35	M	Laborer or Spinster	Ireland	United States	Sarah G	11 Sep 1827
Sally	32	F	Laborer or Spinster	Ireland	United States	Sarah G	11 Sep 1827
Wm.	12	M	Laborer or Spinster	Ireland	United States	Sarah G	11 Sep 1827

NAMES OF PASSENGERS	AGE	SEX	OCCUPATIONS	COUNTRY TO WHICH THEY BELONG	COUNTRY THEY INTEND TO INHABIT	SHIPS/DATES OF ARRIVAL	
MCGARVEY (cont'd)							
Wm.	20					Zamoa	5 Nov 1828
MCGARVIN, Mary	28	F		Ireland	U. States	Sarah G	7 May 1827
MCGARVY, Alexander	45	M	Labourer	Ireland	United States	Meteor	26 Jun 1827
Elanor	20	F	Labourer	Ireland	United States	Meteor	26 Jun 1827
Mathew	24	M	Labourer	Ireland	United States	Meteor	26 Jun 1827
MCGAUFEY, E.	20	M	Labourer	England	America	Two Marys	24 Sep 1827
MCGAUGE, Pat	30	M	Labourer	Ireland	United States	Josephine	30 Apr 1828
MCGAUGHAN, Ann	9	...	...	Ireland	United States	Carolina Ann	24 Oct 1825
Mary	...	...	...	Ireland	United States	Carolina Ann	24 Oct 1825
MCGAUGHAY, Edward	...	...	...	Ireland	United States	Carolina Ann	24 Oct 1825
MCGAUGHRAN, Philip	30	M	Labourer	Ireland	United States	Ann Maria	8 Jun 1824
MCGAULEY, Peter	22	M	Farmer	Ireland	United States	Dublin Packet	22 Aug 1829
MCGAUVERN, Hugh	15	M	Boy	Ireland	United States	Dublin Packet	29 Jun 1825
Mary	22	F	Spinster	Ireland	United States	Dublin Packet	29 Jun 1825
MCGAVERN, Francis	21	M	Labourer	Ireland	New York	Lima	5 Aug 1829
Franis	21	M		Ireland	U. States	Lima	5 Aug 1829
Philip	20	M	Labourer	Great Britain	United States	Ganges	26 Oct 1826
MCGAVOY, Pat	30	M	Shoemaker	Great Britain	United States	William Dawson	18 Jun 1827
MCGAWAN, Anthy.	9	M	Labourer	Sligo	New York	Susquehana	27 Jun 1823
MCGAYGAN, Rebecca	21	F	Servant	Ireland	United States	Trident	16 May 1826
MCGEARY, Owen	10	M		Ireland	U.S. of America	Meteor	19 Mar 1828
MCGEAUGH, James	22	M	weaver	Ireland	United States	Josephine	30 Apr 1828
MCGEE, Alexr.	20	M	Mariner	England	England	Esperanza	7 Jul 1823
Hugh	23	M	Blacksmith	Great Britain	United States	Mount Vernon	17 Jun 1825
James	23		Labourer	Ireland	Great Britain	Robert Burns	14 Jun 1824
John	22	M		Ireland	United States	William & George	14 May 1828
John	24	M	Labourer	Ireland	United States	Asia	29 Jul 1829
John	25		Farmer	Ireland		Westmoreland	1 Aug 1826
Mary	18	F		Ireland	U. States	Nancy	16 Aug 1822
Mary	24		Spinster	Ireland		Westmoreland	1 Aug 1826
Mathew, Mr.	27	M	Laborer	Grate Britain	...	Courier	14 Jun 1825
Patrick	25	M	...	Ireland	U. States	William	27 Jul 1824
Thomas	...	...	...	...	...	St. Michael	22 Sep 1824
Thos.	20	M	Laborer	Ireland	U. States	Albion	9 Aug 1826
Willm.	34	M	Phasician	Ireland	America	Josephine	8 Dec 1827
MCGELDISH, H.	40	F		G. Britain	U. States	Hanford	18 Sep 1828
MCGELEVARY, J.	30	M	Merchant	Montreal	U. States	Pacific	16 Apr 1825
MCGELL, John	24	M	Farmer	Scotland	U.S.	Curler	19 Jul 1828
MCGENNIS, Patrick	28	M	Black Smith	Ireland	United States	Princess Charlotte	26 Apr 1827
MCGEOGH, Andrew	24 9/12	M	Labourer	Ireland	U. States	Fabius	22 Sep 1828
Ellen	20 3/12	F		Ireland	U. States	Fabius	22 Sep 1828
John	25 7/12	M	Labourer	Ireland	U. States	Fabius	22 Sep 1828
Owen	20 5/12	M	Labourer	Ireland	U. States	Fabius	22 Sep 1828
MCGEORGE, Eben	25	M	Taylor	G. Britain	United States	Ariel	21 May 1827
Harriet	2 6/12	F	None	Great Britain	United States	Milton	21 Mar 1828
MCGERITY, John	27	M	Weaver	Ireland	United States	Atlantic	21 Jul 1827
MCGERRES, Andw.	23	M	Weaver	Gt. Britan	U. States	Magnet	9 Apr 1825
Ann	26	F		Gt. Britan	U. States	Magnet	9 Apr 1825
MCGERTY, Cathrine	28	F	Spinster	Ireland	United States	Gem	16 Jun 1824
Philip	9	M		Ireland	United States	Gem	16 Jun 1824
MCGESENNIS, Patrick	32	M	Farmer	Ireland	U. States	Mentor	5 Jul 1825
MCGETTIGAN, Margrett	29	F	Spinster	Ireland	United States	Robert Fulton	10 Aug 1827
MCGHURTEN, Richard	17	M	Clerck	United States	St. John, N.B.	Ann Maria	7 Aug 1826
MCGIBBEN, Wm.	48	M	Weaver	Scotland	U. States	Camillus	27 Jun 1826
MCGIBBON, Agnes	28	F		Scotland	United States	Commerce	17 Jul 1823
David D.	25	M	Gentn.	G.B.	G.B.	George Canning	20 Jan 1829
Jno.	38	M	Miller	Scotland	United States	Commerce	17 Jul 1823
Thomas	31	M	Weaver	England	United States	Jubilee	4 Mar 1829
MCGIBBY, Dougale	49	M	Farmer	Scotland	New York	Concordia	12 Oct 1826
Marina	29	F	None	Scotland	New York	Concordia	12 Oct 1826
MCGIBNEY, Elad., Mrs.	20			Ireland	U.S.	Hibernia	27 Jun 1821
Jno.	32		Clerk	Ireland	U.S.	Hibernia	27 Jun 1821
MCGIEVER, Catherine	30	F	Spinster	Ireland	United States	Robert Fulton	24 Jul 1826
MCGIFFIGAR, Dennis	8	M	Boy	Ireland	United States	Trident	17 May 1825
MCGIFFORD, Jos.	20	M	Farmer	Ireland	United States	Alex. Mansfield	17 May 1823
Wm.	19		Labourer	Ireland	United States	John Dickinson	28 Jun 1822

NAMES OF PASSENGERS	AGE	SEX	OCCUPATIONS	COUNTRY TO WHICH THEY BELONG	COUNTRY THEY INTEND TO INHABIT	SHIPS/DATES OF ARRIVAL	
MCGIG, David	28	M	Tailor	Ireland	United States	Ann Maria	4 Oct 1824
Sarah	19	F	Wife	Ireland	United States	Ann Maria	4 Oct 1824
MCGILKIN, Andrew	60	M	Miller	Ireland		William Tell	24 Oct 1829
MCGILL, —,							
Six Children	40, 41			St. John	Canada	Henrietta	7 Jul 1825
...	30	M	Merchant	Lower Canada	Canada	Manhattan	21 May 1821
Andrew	22	M	Merchant	Great Britan	Canada	Canada	2 Jun 1824
Andrew	25	M	Merchant	Canada	Canada	Corinthian	5 May 1827
Andrew H.	26	M	Merchant	Britain	Great Britain	Thompson	26 Apr 1828
Biddy	15	F	Spinster	Ireland	United States	Trident	16 May 1826
Bill	10	M	Child	Ireland	U. States	William & John	10 Jul 1824
David	28	M	Labourer	Scotland	United States	Mary & Susan	5 Aug 1828
Elizabeth	30	F		Scotland	America	Wilson	27 Nov 1826
Frederic	31	M	Merchant	Ireland	United States	Manchester	12 Aug 1829
James	17	M	Labourer	Ireland	United States	General Putnam	20 Jun 1825
Jane	26	F	Farmer	St. John	Canada	Henrietta	7 Jul 1825
Jas.	32	M	Labourer	Ireland	United States	Neury	27 Jan 1827
John	30	M	Servant	Ireland	U. States	Henrietta	7 Jul 1825
Michael	30	M	Labourer	Ireland	United States	Lord Wellington	28 May 1827
Nancy	20	F	Spinster	Ireland	U. States	William & John	10 Jul 1824
Peter	30	M	Merchant	England	Canada	Florida	11 May 1822
Peter, Mr.	50		Merchant	Scotland	G.B.	Pacific	24 May 1824
Saml.	25	M	Farmer	Ireland	U. States	William & John	10 Jul 1824
Thos.	23	M	Farmer	St. John	Canada	Henrietta	7 Jul 1825
John	...	...	...	...	...	...	26 Mar 1823
MCGILLAN, John	19	M	Weaver	Ireland	United States	Meteor	19 Aug 1829
MCGILLERAY, Simon	35	M	Merchant	Holland	Canada	Manhattan	21 May 1821
MCGILLEY, James	38	M	Miner	England	England	Virginia	26 May 1828
MCGILLIOREY, Joseph	27	M	None	Canada	Canada	Britannia	23 Mar 1829
MCGILLIVAY, William	50	M	Merchant	Inverness		Hannibal	28 Jul 1823
MCGILLIVRAY, Anne	18	F	None	Montreal		Hannibal	28 Jul 1823
Magdalen	15	F	None	Montreal		Hannibal	28 Jul 1823
Simon	38	M	Merchant	Great Britain	United States	Robert Fulton	27 Jun 1822
MCGILLON, Nancy	30	M	Wife	Ireland	United States	Nancy	15 Nov 1824
MCGILLONY, Brine	24	M	Labourer	Ireland	United States	Hope	12 Jun 1828
MCGILLVERAY, Simon	30	M	Merchant		Canada	Columbia	11 Apr 1822
MCGILVARY, F.	40	M	Planter	Great Briton	U. States	Chase	24 Jul 1823
MCGILVRAE, Neil	28	M	Farmer	Scotland	United States	Belmont	30 Aug 1828
MCGIMSEY, Robt.	25	M	Laborer or Spinster	Ireland	United States	Sarah G	11 Sep 1827
MCGIN, John	21		Farmer	Ireland		Westmoreland	1 Aug 1826
Mary	24	F	Servant	Ireland	United States	William & George	14 May 1828
Patk.	18	M	Labourer	Ireland	United States	Meteor	26 Jun 1827
MCGINLAY, Ellen	28	F	Lady		New York	Betsy	4 Sep 1820
Ellen	28	F	Lady		N. York	Betsy	4 Sep 1820
Roger	30				New York	Betsy	4 Sep 1820
MCGINN, Margerett	20	F	Matron	Ireland	United States	Robert Fulton	10 Aug 1827
MCGINNES, Henry	18	M	Labourer	Ireland	United States	Fabius	31 Jul 1829
Robert	27		Weaver	Ireland	G. Britain	Robert Burns	14 Jun 1824
William	30	M	Labourer	Ireland	United States	Jubilee	4 Mar 1829
MCGINNESS, Barnd.	30	M	Farmer	Ireland	United States	Concordia	25 Aug 1827
Dorethy	44	F	Widow	Ireland	United States	Dublin Packet	22 Aug 1829
Eleanor	54	F	Wife [of Henry]	Ireland	New York	Atlantic	8 May 1828
Henry	56	M	Labourer	Ireland	New York	Atlantic	8 May 1828
John [crossed out]	19	M	Farmer	Ireland	United States	Leonidas	3 Aug 1825
Peter [crossed out]	10	M	None	Ireland	United States	Leonidas	3 Aug 1825
MCGINNIS, Francis	23	M	Weaver	Ireland	United States	Borneo	2 Oct 1827
Margaret	26	F	Servant	Ireland		France	6 Feb 1829
MCGINNISS, Grace	28	F	Spinster	Ireland	United States	Robert Fulton	24 Jul 1826
MCGINNITY, Owen	22	M	Servant	Ireland	New York	Atlantic	8 May 1828
MCGINSON, Jno.	21	M	Farmer	Babryrdan	N. York	Favourite	8 Oct 1823
MCGINTY, Bridget	5	F		Great Britain		Robert Fulton	8 Mar 1823
Francis	9	M		Great Britain		Robert Fulton	8 Mar 1823
Mary	29	F		Great Britain		Robert Fulton	8 Mar 1823
MCGINTZ, Mary	22	F	Spinster	Ireland	United States	Asia	29 Jul 1829
MCGIRNEY, Wm.	10	M	None	Gt. Britain	U.S. America	James Cropper	2 Aug 1827
MCGITHEN, John	19	M	Painter	Ireland	United States	Trident	17 May 1825
MCGIVEN, Bridget	30	F		Irereland	America	Carolina Ann	20 Jun 1825
MCGIVENN, Michl.	23	M				Ocean	17 Aug 1820

NAMES OF PASSENGERS	AGE	SEX	OCCUPATIONS	COUNTRY TO WHICH THEY BELONG	COUNTRY THEY INTEND TO INHABIT	SHIPS/DATES OF ARRIVAL	
MCGIVONY, Michl.	26	M		Ireland	United States	William Byrnes	6 Apr 1826
MCGLACHLAN, —, Child		F		Ireland	United States	Loore	9 Sep 1822
Brye	20	M	Farmer	Ireland	United States	Loore	9 Sep 1822
Danl.	19	M		Ireland	United States	Loore	9 Sep 1822
Nancy	17	F		Ireland	United States	Loore	9 Sep 1822
Nancy	19	F		Ireland	United States	Loore	9 Sep 1822
MCGLAINE, Patrick	22	M	Farmer	Ireland	United States	Lima	19 Jun 1824
MCGLANCY, Ann	21	F		Ireland	United States	Mary	1 Jul 1829
Michael	19	M	Laborer	Ireland	United States	Mary	1 Jul 1829
MCGLANERY, —, Mrs.	35	F		U. States	U. States	Paragon	4 Oct 1824
Henry	1 6/12	M		U. States	U. States	Paragon	4 Oct 1824
John	7/12	M		U. States	U. States	Paragon	4 Oct 1824
MCGLARGHLIN, Biddy	26	F	...	Ireland	United States	General Putnam	20 Jun 1825
MCGLATHERY, Arthur	28	M	Weaver	Ireland	America	Josephine	8 Dec 1827
MCGLAUGHAN, Ann	4	F	Labourer	England	U. States	Ayrshire	12 May 1828
Mary	1	F	Labourer	England	U. States	Ayrshire	12 May 1828
MCGLAUGHLEN, C.	30		Farmer	Ireland	United States	Courier	16 May 1825
M.	1		Farmer	Ireland	United States	Courier	16 May 1825
M.	20		Farmer	Ireland	United States	Courier	16 May 1825
M.	45		Farmer	Ireland	United States	Courier	16 May 1825
Pat	5		Farmer	Ireland	United States	Courier	16 May 1825
R. A.	2		Farmer	Ireland	United States	Courier	16 May 1825
MCGLAUGHLIN,							
Charles	20	M	Farmer	Ireland	United States	Romulus	24 Jun 1826
Grace	26	F	Farmer	Ireland	Canada	Lady Hunter	26 May 1825
John	25	M	Weaver	Ireland	United States	Romulus	24 Jun 1826
Margaret	6/12	F		Ireland	United States	Romulus	24 Jun 1826
Mary	2	F	Farmer	Ireland	Canada	Lady Hunter	26 May 1825
Mary	20	F		Ireland	United States	Romulus	24 Jun 1826
Mary	39	F	Spinster	Ireland	United States	Lima	19 Jun 1824
Patrick	26	M	Farmer	Ireland	Canada	Lady Hunter	26 May 1825
Peter	4	M	Farmer	Ireland	Canada	Lady Hunter	26 May 1825
Sarah	4/12	F	Farmer	Ireland	Canada	Lady Hunter	26 May 1825
MCGLEN, John	29	M	Labourer	Ireland	U. States	Belville	5 Jul 1827
MCGLENCHY,							
Eleanor	_/12	F	daughter of [Nancy]	Ireland	United States	Asia	29 Jul 1829
Nancy	25	F	sent for by her husband	Ireland	United States	Asia	29 Jul 1829
MCGLENN, Mary	20	F	Labourer	Ireland	United States	Essex	23 May 1828
MCGLENNAN, John	24	M	Reedmaker	Ireland	U. States	Josephine	7 May 1827
MCGLILAN, May	23	F		G. Britan	U. States	William Neilson	26 Jul 1828
MCGLIN, Ann	6	F		Ireland	United States	Gem	16 Jun 1824
Bridget	7	F		Ireland	United States	Gem	16 Jun 1824
Katr.	54	F	House Keper	Ireland	United States	Carolina Ann	11 Dec 1826
Mary	27	F	...	Ireland	United States	Gem	16 Jun 1824
Pat	25	M	Labourer	Ireland	N. York	Trusty	12 Sep 1828
MCGLINCHY, Neal	24	M	Merchant	St. John, N.B.	St. John, N.B.	St. Michaels	24 Mar 1825
P.	40	M	Farmer	Ireland	U. States	William & John	10 Jul 1824
MCGLINN, Peter	25	M	Labourer	Ireland	U. States	Marcus	7 Apr 1829
MCGLOAN, John	22	M	Farmer	Ireland	U. States	Champion	26 Jul 1827
John	22	M	Farmer	Ireland	U. States	Champion	26 Jul 1827
MCGLOCHLIN, John	30	M	Laborer or Spinster	Ireland	United States	Sarah G.	15 Aug 1827
MCGLOCKLIN, Isabella	25	F	Wife	Ireland	United States	St. Michael	21 Aug 1824
John	30	M	Laborer	Ireland	United States	St. Michael	21 Aug 1824
MCGLOCLIN, Catherine	28	F	Wife	Ireland	United States	St. Michaels	15 Feb 1825
Mary	1	F	Child	Ireland	United States	St. Michaels	15 Feb 1825
MCGLOIN, Cathr.	38			Great Britan	United States	Newry	11 Jul 1827
Geo.	40			Great Britan	United States	Newry	11 Jul 1827
James	20	M	Farmer	Ireland	United States	Helen	27 Jun 1821
M.	27	M	Taylor			Hanford	17 Jul 1828
Mary	22	F	Servant	Ireland	America	Weser	26 Jun 1821
Mary	28	F				Hanford	17 Jul 1828
MCGLOIRE, Ann	22	F	Spinster			Ocean	17 Aug 1820
MCGLON, John	20	M	Gentleman	Ireland	United States	Nancy	16 Jul 1824
MCGLONE, —	15			Great Britan	United States	Newry	11 Jul 1827
MCGLOTHIN, James	28	M	Joiner	Ireland	United States	Borneo	28 Aug 1828
MCGLOTHRIN, Owen	20	M	Labourer	Ireland	United States	William	20 Jul 1829
Thos.	13	M		Ireland	United States	William	20 Jul 1829

NAMES OF PASSENGERS	AGE	SEX	OCCUPATIONS	COUNTRY TO WHICH THEY BELONG	COUNTRY THEY INTEND TO INHABIT	SHIPS/DATES OF ARRIVAL	
MCGLOULDING, James	26	M	Farmer	G. Britain	United States	Louisa	14 Jun 1825
MCGLOVER, John	25	M	Servant	Ireland	U. States	Henrietta	7 Jul 1825
MCGLOWAN, John	24 5/12	M		Ireland	U.S. of America	Douglass	6 Jul 1829
MCGLOWN, Bridget	18	F	Spinster	Ireland	United States	Robert Fulton	10 Aug 1827
Jane	13	F	Spinster	Ireland	United States	Wilson	4 Oct 1827
Thomas	17	M	Labourer	Ireland	United States	Robert Fulton	10 Aug 1827
MCGLOYSTINE, G.	35	M	Merchant	United States	United States	Nestor	16 Aug 1824
MCGLUE, Cat.	27	F		Ireland	United States	Curler	3 Mar 1828
Hugh	26	M	Farmer	Ireland	United States	Curler	3 Mar 1828
Lawce.	30	M	Farmer	Ireland	United States	Curler	3 Mar 1828
Mary	28	F		Ireland	United States	Curler	3 Mar 1828
MCGOFFIN, Alexr.	25	M	Weaver	Ireland	New York	Carolina Ann	15 Oct 1824
MCGOLDOWNEY,							
Charles	18		Farmer	Great Britain		John Dickinson	5 Apr 1821
MCGOLDRICH, Jno.	41	M	Merchant	N. York	U. States	Thomas Wilson	16 Sep 1822
MCGOLDRICK, Catharan	3	F		Scotland	U. States	Superior	25 Sep 1828
Cattarar	3	F		Scotland	U. States	Superior	25 Sep 1828
Charles	4	M		Scotland	U. States	Superior	25 Sep 1828
Danl.	30 7/12	M	Labourer	Ireland	U. States	Fabius	22 Sep 1828
Edward	5	M		Scotland	U. States	Superior	25 Sep 1828
Edwd.	5	M		Scotland	U. States	Superior	25 Sep 1828
Felix	2	M		Scotland	U. States	Superior	25 Sep 1828
Mary	24	F		Scotland	U. States	Superior	25 Sep 1828
Mary	28	F		Scotland	U. States	Superior	25 Sep 1828
May	25	M		Scotland	U. States	Superior	25 Sep 1828
Patrick	17	M		Ireland	America	Carolina Ann	7 Apr 1826
MCGOLICH, E.	11	F		G. Britain	U. States	Hanford	18 Sep 1828
Hugh	14	M		G. Britain	U. States	Hanford	18 Sep 1828
Rose	16	F		G. Britain	U. States	Hanford	18 Sep 1828
Wm.	5	M		G. Britain	U. States	Hanford	18 Sep 1828
MCGOLICK, Catherina	25	F	Servant	Ireland	U. States	Edwin	1 Jul 1829
MCGOLRICK, Bell			his wife [Charles]	Ireland	United States	Asia	29 Jul 1829
Charles	26	M	Farmer	Ireland	United States	Asia	29 Jul 1829
Ellen	20	F	Spinster	Ireland	United States	Asia	29 Jul 1829
Wency	20	F	Servt.	Sligo	New York	Susquehana	27 Jun 1823
MCGONETH, John	27	M	Labr.	Ireland	New York	Atlantic	8 May 1828
MCGONIGAL, Mary	19	F	Servant			Superb	18 Jul 1820
MCGONIGLE, Arthur	27	M	Weaver	Ireland	N. York	Salem	15 Mar 1828
MCGONLEY, Hugh	21	M	Labourer	Ireland	United States	Robert Fulton	24 Jul 1826
MCGONNAL, Dennis	26	M	Labourer	Ireland	United States	Belleville	13 Oct 1827
Mary	24	F	Lady	Ireland	United States	Belleville	13 Oct 1827
Patrick	0 4/12	M	Child	Ireland	United States	Belleville	13 Oct 1827
MCGONNESS, John	21	M	Farmer	Ireland	United States	William	5 Oct 1822
MCGONNOGHAN, May	25	F		Great Britain	U. States	Lady Hunter	28 May 1823
MCGONNOLL, James	...	...	...	Ireland	United States	General Putnam	20 Jun 1825
MCGOOWN, Bernard	20	M	Miller	Ireland	United States	Carolina Ann	14 May 1827
MCGORAN, Michael	22	M	Labourer	Ireland	N. York	Trusty	12 Sep 1828
Patrick	20	M	Labourer	Great Brittan	U. States	John & Elizabeth	11 Dec 1826
MCGORAR, Ann	22	F	Child	Ireland	N. York	Trusty	12 Sep 1828
MCGOREGAN, Thomas	18	M	Taylor	Ireland	United States	Fabius	31 Jul 1829
MCGORIRAN, Eliza	18 7/12	F		Ireland	U.S. of America	Douglass	6 Jul 1829
Ellen	16	F		Ireland	U.S. of America	Douglass	6 Jul 1829
MCGORMICK, Ann	18	F	Spinster	Ireland		Robert Fulton	4 Jun 1828
MCGORNEGLE,							
Michl.	19 6/12	M		Ireland	U.S. of America	Douglass	6 Jul 1829
MCGORRAN, Danl.	25	M	Labourer	Great Brittain	United States	Active	12 Sep 1828
MCGORTICK, Barnard	35	M	Labourer	Ireland	United States	Meteor	26 Jun 1827
MCGORVAN, Biddy	26	F	Spinster	Ireland	United States	Sarah Ann	18 Nov 1826
MCGOTTERY, Mary	24	F	Servant	Ireland	U. States	Sarah G	30 Jun 1828
MCGOUGH, Alexr.	20			Great Britan	United States	Newry	11 Jul 1827
Ann	30	F	None	Ireland	United States	Lord Wellington	28 May 1827
Anne	25			Great Britan	United States	Newry	11 Jul 1827
James	24	M	Labourer	Ireland	United States	Lord Wellington	28 May 1827
Jas.	28		Labourer	Great Britan	United States	Newry	11 Jul 1827
John	26		Labourer	Great Britan	United States	Newry	11 Jul 1827
John	30	M	Stone Mason	Ireland	United States	Princess Charlotte	26 Apr 1827
Mary	24			Great Britan	United States	Newry	11 Jul 1827

NAMES OF PASSENGERS	AGE	SEX	OCCUPATIONS	COUNTRY TO WHICH THEY BELONG	COUNTRY THEY INTEND TO INHABIT	SHIPS/DATES OF ARRIVAL	
MCGOUGH (cont'd)							
Rose	24	F		Ireland	United States	Princess Charlotte	26 Apr 1827
MCGOULDING, Francis	19	M	Taylor	G. Britain	United States	Louisa	14 Jun 1825
MCGOUNAGLE, Ann	1 6/12	F		St. Johns, N.B.	United States	Henrietta	17 Aug 1825
Catharine	25	F		St. Johns, N.B.	United States	Henrietta	17 Aug 1825
Daniel	28	M	Farmer	St. Johns, N.B.	United States	Henrietta	17 Aug 1825
Grace	29	F	Farmer	St. Johns, N.B.	United States	Henrietta	17 Aug 1825
MCGOURAN,							
Margaret	32 7/12	F		Ireland	U.S. of America	Douglass	6 Jul 1829
MCGOVAN, Allice	23	F	None	Ireland	U. States	Erin	5 Jul 1820
Ann	23		Labourer	Halifax	U. States	Edwin	26 Sep 1828
MCGOVERAN,							
Ellen	9 7/12	F		Ireland	U. States	Fabius	22 Sep 1828
MCGOVERN, Ann	21	F		England	America	Two Marys	24 Sep 1827
Bernard	24 1/12	M		Ireland	America	Carolina Ann	7 Apr 1826
Bridget	...	F	...	Ireland	U. States of Amer	Courier	17 Mar 1827
Catherine	29	F	Spinster	Ireland	United States	Robert Fulton	24 Jul 1826
Chas.	30	M	Farmers and Mechanics	Ireland	America	Constitution	1 Oct 1825
Eleanor	25	F	Spinster	Ireland	United States	Wilson	22 Jun 1824
Elizabeth	16	F		Ireland	America	Wilson	27 Nov 1826
Elizabeth	19	F	Spinster	Ireland	America	Wilson	16 May 1825
J.	24	M	Weaver	Ireland	United States	Josephine	30 Apr 1828
Maria	26	F	Spinster	Ireland	United States	Wilson	22 Jun 1824
Mary	15	F		Ireland	America	Wilson	27 Nov 1826
Owen	...	M	...	Ireland	U. States of Amer	Courier	17 Mar 1827
Patk.	...	...	...	Ireland	U. States of Amer	Courier	17 Mar 1827
MCGOVORN, Michel	24	M	Labourer	Ireland	United States	Hope	12 Jun 1828
MCGOWAN, Agnes	28	M	Farmer	Ireland	U. States	Atlantic	19 Aug 1825
Alexr.	14	M		Ireland	New York	Atlantic	6 Oct 1828
Andrew	15	M	Labour	Sligo	New York	Susquehana	27 Jun 1823
Andrew	18		Merchant	Ireland	United States	Robert Burns	18 Jun 1821
Ann	12	F		Ireland	U. States	Virginia	20 Jun 1825
Ann	14		girl	Ireland	United States	Robert Burns	30 May 1823
Ann	23	F		Ireland	U. States	Virginia	20 Jun 1825
Ann	26	F		Ireland	U. States	Balaena	29 Apr 1825
Ann	35	F	Farmers wife	United States		Aurora	4 Sep 1823
Betty	14	F	Laborer	Ireland	United States	Weser	29 Jul 1823
Bridget	6	F		England	United States	Yobah	26 Sep 1827
Bridget	25		Wife	Ireland	G. Britain	Robert Burns	14 Jun 1824
Bridget	26	F	None	Ireland	United States	Dalhouse Castle	21 Aug 1829
Bryan	16	M	Labourer	Sligo	New York	Susquehana	27 Jun 1823
Catharine	20	F	Servant	Ireland	United States	Josephine	30 Apr 1828
Catharine	25			Ireland	Great Britain	Robert Burns	14 Jun 1824
Cathrine	18	F		Ireland	U. States	Virginia	20 Jun 1825
Cathrine	21	F		Ireland	U. States	Virginia	20 Jun 1825
Charles	20	M	Farmer	Ireland	United States	Trident	17 May 1825
Chas.	5	M	Farmer	Ireland	U. States	Atlantic	19 Aug 1825
D.	38	M	Merchant	Scotland	U. States	Isabella	21 May 1825
Daniel	18 9/12	M	Black Smith	Ireland	U. States	Virginia	20 Jun 1825
Ellen	...0	F	Wife	Ireland	New York	Louisa	18 Apr 1827
Hen.	28	M	Labourer	Ireland	New York	Louisa	18 Apr 1827
Henry	30	M	Mason	Ireland	New York	Louisa	18 Apr 1827
James	22	M	Carpenter	Ireland	United States	Clothier	22 Nov 1827
James	22 6/12	M	Weaver	Ireland	United States	Atlantic	21 Jul 1827
James	24	M	Weaver	Ireland	United States	Kleber	23 Jul 1827
James	25		Tanner & Currier	Ireland	Great Britain	Robert Burns	14 Jun 1824
James	28	M	Servant	Canada	Canada	New York	5 Jul 1826
Jas.	8/12	M	Farmer	Ireland	U. States	Atlantic	19 Aug 1825
Jas.	23		Farmer	Ireland	G. Britain	Robert Burns	14 Jun 1824
John	3			Ireland	G. Britain	Robert Burns	14 Jun 1824
John	18		Laborer	Ireland	United States	Robert Burns	30 May 1823
John	18 6/12	M	Labourer	Ireland	U. States	Virginia	20 Jun 1825
John	25	M	Labourer	Ireland	U. States	Panthea	8 Apr 1826
Mark	20		Merchant	Ireland	United States	Robert Burns	18 Jun 1821
Mary	9	F		England	United States	Yobah	26 Sep 1827
Mary	12	F	Servt. Md.	Sligo	New York	Susquehana	27 Jun 1823
Mary	21 6/12	F		Ireland	U.S. of America	Douglass	6 Jul 1829

NAMES OF PASSENGERS	AGE	SEX	OCCUPATIONS	COUNTRY TO WHICH THEY BELONG	COUNTRY THEY INTEND TO INHABIT	SHIPS/DATES OF ARRIVAL	
MCGOWAN (cont'd)							
Mary	30	F	Mantuamaker	Ireland	New York	Atlantic	6 Oct 1828
Michael	21 6/12	M	Labourer	Ireland	U. States	Virginia	20 Jun 1825
Michael	24	M	Labourer	Ireland	United States	Josephine	30 Apr 1828
Nancy	25			Ireland	Great Britain	Robert Burns	14 Jun 1824
Owen	20	M	Laborer	Ireland	United States	Weser	29 Jul 1823
Pat	16	M				Ocean	17 Aug 1820
Patk.	16	M		Ireland	New York	Atlantic	6 Oct 1828
Patrick	20	M	Labourer	...	United States	Hanford	17 Oct 1828
Patrick	20 3/12	M	Weaver	Ireland	United States	Atlantic	21 Jul 1827
Peter	30	M		England	United States	Yobah	26 Sep 1827
Phillip	1	M	Laborer	Ireland	United States	Weser	29 Jul 1823
Rachel	26	F		Scotland	U. States	Isabella	21 May 1825
Robt.	2 1/2	M	Farmer	Ireland	U. States	Atlantic	19 Aug 1825
Robt. B.	21	M	Merchant	Scotland	New York	Atlantic	6 Oct 1828
Roger	22	M	Weaver	Ireland	United States	Trident	17 May 1825
Rose	23	F	Servant	Ireland	United States	Josephine	30 Apr 1828
Rose	26	F	Laborer	Ireland	United States	Weser	29 Jul 1823
Rose	40	F		Ireland	U. States	Virginia	20 Jun 1825
Susanah	1			Ireland	G. Britain	Robert Burns	14 Jun 1824
Thos.	30	M	Farmer	Ireland	U. States	Atlantic	19 Aug 1825
Thos., Jur.	8	M	Farmer	Ireland	U. States	Atlantic	19 Aug 1825
William	27	M	Weaver	Ireland	U. States	Virginia	20 Jun 1825
William	30	M	Merchant	Scotland	England	St. Michael	21 Aug 1824
Wm.	22	M	Nailer	Ireland	United States	Eliza	29 Aug 1822
MCGOWEN, John	19	F	Spinster	Ireland	United States	Wilson	6 Jun 1828
MCGOWIN, Bridget	26	F	None	Ireland	U.S.A.	Dalhouse Castle	21 Aug 1829
Cathrin	30	F	...	...	United States	Hanford	17 Oct 1828
MCGOWN, Bridget	4	F	Spinster	Ireland	United States	Wilson	4 Oct 1827
David	40	M	Merchant	Scotland	St. John	Lady Hunter	28 Apr 1824
James	17	M	Farmer	Great Britain	United States	Loire	12 Dec 1820
Wm.	23	M	Shoemaker	Great Britain	United States	Courier	26 Jun 1827
MCGOWON, James	28	M	Weaver	Ireland	United States	Princess Charlotte	26 Apr 1827
Sarah	20	F		Ireland	United States	Princess Charlotte	26 Apr 1827
MCGRADY, Jas.	22	M	Labourer	Down, Ireland	New York	Anthusa	24 Aug 1825
Nancy	60	F		Down, Ireland	New York	Anthusa	24 Aug 1825
MCGRAEL, Thomas	30	M	Weaver	Ireland	U. States	Josephine	7 May 1827
MCGRAGAN, Henry	11	M	Farmer	Ireland	U. States	Dickinson	30 Jul 1825
Hugh	13	M	Farmer	Ireland	U. States	Dickinson	30 Jul 1825
Rachel	14	F	Farmer	Ireland	U. States	Dickinson	30 Jul 1825
MCGRAGHAN, Ellen	17	F	Spinster	Ireland	U. States	Josephine	30 Aug 1828
MCGRAITTE, Terrance	26	M	Tailor	Ireland	U.N. States	Jane	7 Oct 1826
MCGRALEY, James	17	M	Servant	Ireland	United States	General Putnam	20 Jun 1825
MCGRAMEC, Catherine	25	F	Labourer	Ireland	United States	Meteor	26 Jun 1827
Patk.	22	M	Labourer	Ireland	United States	Meteor	26 Jun 1827
MCGRANAGHAN,							
Thomas	19	M	Tailor	Ireland	United States	Louisa	27 Nov 1826
MCGRANAHEN, James	35	M	Labourer	Ireland	United States	Robert Fulton	24 Jul 1826
MCGRAND, Betsey	27	F	Spinster	Ireland	United States	Ann Maria	21 May 1827
Charles	30	M	Laborer	Ireland	United States	Ann Maria	21 May 1827
Jacob	26	M	Laborer	Ireland	United States	Ann Maria	21 May 1827
Mary	20 3/12	F	Servant	Ireland	United States	Atlantic	21 Jul 1827
MCGRANOHON,							
Mary	29	F	Spinster	Ireland	United States	Robert Fulton	24 Jul 1826
MCGRATH, Allan		M	Child	Halifax	United States	Dodge Healy	14 Oct 1828
B.	23	M	Laborer	Gt. Britain		Dalhouse Castle	13 May 1828
B.	30	F		G. Britain	U. States	London	23 Sep 1828
Bridget	16	M	going to [his] Brother	G. Britain	United States	Louisa	14 Jun 1825
D.	20	M	Labourer	Ireland	U. States	Loire	6 Dec 1827
Dl.	22	M	Cartwright	Ireland	United States	Trio	13 Jun 1827
Jno.	19	M	Labourer	Great Britain	United States	Penelope	11 Jun 1827
John		M	Child	Halifax	United States	Dodge Healy	14 Oct 1828
John	23 2/12	M	Labourer	Ireland	U. States	Virginia	20 Jun 1825
Margaret	9	F	going to [her] Brother	G. Britain	United States	Louisa	14 Jun 1825
Owen	20	M	Bricklayer	Great Britain		Moro Castle	6 Jul 1827

NAMES OF PASSENGERS	AGE	SEX	OCCUPATIONS	COUNTRY TO WHICH THEY BELONG	COUNTRY THEY INTEND TO INHABIT	SHIPS/DATES OF ARRIVAL	
MCGRATH (cont'd)							
Paschal		F	Child	Halifax	United States	Dodge Healy	14 Oct 1828
Pat	24	M	Grocer	England	U. States	Mary Howland	22 Sep 1828
Patrick	26	M	Laborer	Ireland	United States	Lord Wellington	14 Nov 1827
Thomas		M	Joiner	Halifax	United States	Dodge Healy	14 Oct 1828
Timothy	26	M	Labourer	Ireland	U. States	Lady Hunter	9 Oct 1825
William		M	Child	Halifax	United States	Dodge Healy	14 Oct 1828
William	20	M	Farmer	Ireland	America	William	21 May 1825
MCGRAVE, Susanna	7	F		Great Britain	United States	Thomas Dickason	31 Jul 1829
MCGRAVES, B.	20		Labourer	Halifax	U. States	Edwin	26 Sep 1828
Owen	22		Labourer	Halifax	U. States	Edwin	26 Sep 1828
MCGRAW, Ann	12	F		St. John	Great Britain	General Coffin	9 Mar 1827
Biddy	21	F		Ireland	U.S. of America	Douglass	6 Jul 1829
James	26	M		Great Brittian	United States	Carolina Augusta	2 Dec 1828
John	2	M		Great Brittian	United States	Carolina Augusta	2 Dec 1828
Mary	9	F		St. John	Great Britain	General Coffin	9 Mar 1827
Mary	26	F		Great Brittian	United States	Carolina Augusta	2 Dec 1828
Rose	40	M	Labourer	St. John	Great Britain	General Coffin	9 Mar 1827
Thomas	28	M		Great Brittian	United States	Carolina Augusta	2 Dec 1828
MCGRAY, Dominick	24	M	Labourer	Ireland	United States	Edwin	27 Oct 1828
MCGREAGAN, Owen	30	M	Labourer	Ireland	United States	Margarett Scott	22 Aug 1827
MCGREAR, M.	28		Farmer	Ireland	United States	Courier	16 May 1825
MCGREELY, Cathr.	18	F	Spinster			Commerce	22 Jun 1825
MCGREENAHAN, Ann	21	F	Spinster	Ireland		Robert Fulton	4 Jun 1828
MCGREENUP, W.	24	M	Merchant	England	N. York	James Monroe	29 Apr 1823
MCGREGAN, Auther	27	M	Merchant	Ireland	St. John, N.B.	Ann Maria	7 Aug 1826
MCGREGER, James	23	M	Labourer	Paisley, Renfrew [County]	New York	Hero	19 May 1828
*to look for employment							
John	26	M	Joiner	Kinglassy, Kinglassy [Parish], Fife [County]	New York	Hero	19 May 1828
*to follow his occupation							
Simon	24	M	Farmer	Scotland	United States	Friends	13 Mar 1824
MCGREGOR, —, Mrs.	29	F	None	U. States	United States	New York	12 Nov 1822
A.	24		Merchant	Glasgow		New York	18 Jul 1828
Alex	9	M		Scotland	United States	Camillus	27 Oct 1829
Alexr.	19	M	Labourer	Ireland	U. States	Loire	6 Dec 1827
Alexr.	19	M	Farmer	Scotland	United States	Belmont	30 Aug 1828
Anthony	32	M	Carpenter	England	United States	Trident	31 Mar 1827
D.	36	M	Captain	U.S.	U.S.	Porcia	4 Jan 1828
George	18	M	Gunmaker	Scotland	Alexandria, U.S.	Roman	17 Oct 1826
George	30	M	Merchant	U. States	U. States	Bayard	8 Mar 1825
Hugh	18	M	Merchant	Scotland	United States	Commerce	17 Jul 1823
Hugh	45	M	in the Army	Scotland	United States	Margaret Bogle	11 Jun 1824
J., Jr.	40	M	Merchant	U. States	United States	New York	12 Nov 1822
James	11	M		Scotland	United States	Camillus	27 Oct 1829
James	22	M	Gentleman	America	New York	Hercules	10 Apr 1823
James	28	M	Mechanic	Great Britain, Ireland	Ohio	Britannia	3 Nov 1827
Jno.	30	M	Cook	Scotland	U. States	Albert	2 Oct 1823
John	18	M	Labourer	Scotland	U. States	Czar	29 Aug 1829
John	27	M	Calico Printer	England	America	Hercules	2 Nov 1825
John	30	M	Farmer	England	U. States	Emulous	22 Aug 1828
John	36	M	Merchant	Britain	America	Camillus	9 Oct 1820
Margt.	1	F		England	U. States	Emulous	22 Aug 1828
Margt.	20	F		England	U. States	Emulous	22 Aug 1828
Margt.	36	F		Scotland	United States	Camillus	27 Oct 1829
Mary	20	F		Great Britain, Ireland	Ohio	Britannia	3 Nov 1827
P.	35		Gentleman	England	U.S.	Monroe	29 Nov 1823
R.	22	M	Laborer	Scotland	U. States	Magnet	22 Aug 1822
Richard	23	M	Mechanic	Scotland	United States	Concordia	25 Aug 1827

NAMES OF PASSENGERS	AGE	SEX	OCCUPATIONS	COUNTRY TO WHICH THEY BELONG	COUNTRY THEY INTEND TO INHABIT	SHIPS/DATES OF ARRIVAL	
MCGREGOR (cont'd)							
Simon	21	M	Merchant			Frances	17 Aug 1820
Wm.	3	M		Scotland	United States	Camillus	27 Oct 1829
MCGREGORY, A.	10	F	No	Campeache	U. States	Doris	22 May 1826
A.	11	M	No	Campeache	U. States	Doris	22 May 1826
Elisha	1	F		Ireland	America	Mary	29 May 1827
J.	13	M	No	Campeache	U. States	Doris	22 May 1826
MCGREIGER, Alexander	7	M		Scotland	U. States	Superior	25 Sep 1828
Catharan	15	F		Scotland	U. States	Superior	25 Sep 1828
David	1	M		Scotland	U. States	Superior	25 Sep 1828
John	10	M		Scotland	U. States	Superior	25 Sep 1828
Margaret	12	F		Scotland	U. States	Superior	25 Sep 1828
Mary	38	F		Scotland	U. States	Superior	25 Sep 1828
Peter	4	M		Scotland	U. States	Superior	25 Sep 1828
Peter	40	M	Labourer	Scotland	U. States	Superior	25 Sep 1828
MCGRENNY, James	45	M	Farmer	Ireland	U. States	Francis	6 Sep 1827
Thos.	30	M	Farmer	Ireland	U. States	Francis	6 Sep 1827
MCGROGEN, Eliza	20	F		Ireland	New York	Phoenix	29 Apr 1826
Thos.	27	M	Carpenter	Ireland	New York	Phoenix	29 Apr 1826
MCGRORTY, Dennis	21		Laborer	Ireland	Great Britain	Robert Burns	14 Jun 1824
MCGROTH, Biddy	...	F	...	Ireland	United States	General Putnam	20 Jun 1825
Biddy	45	F	...	Ireland	United States	General Putnam	20 Jun 1825
John	...	M	...	Ireland	United States	General Putnam	20 Jun 1825
John	...7	M	...	Ireland	United States	General Putnam	20 Jun 1825
Margt.	...	F	...	Ireland	United States	General Putnam	20 Jun 1825
Nancy	...	F	...	Ireland	United States	General Putnam	20 Jun 1825
MCGRUIN, Betsey	19	F	Tayloress	Great Britain	United States	Enterprize	18 Jul 1829
MCGUEN, B.	27		Farmer	Ireland	United States	Courier	16 May 1825
MCGUGHY, William	25	M		Ireland	U. States	Nancy	16 Aug 1822
MCGUIBBY, Rosanna	18	F	Servant	Ireland	U. States	Sarah G	7 May 1827
MCGUIDE, Mary	21	F	None	Longford		Mount Vernon	7 Jun 1824
MCGUIGAN, Biddy	21	F	Servant	Ireland	United States	Josephine	30 Apr 1828
MCGUIGGAN, Pat	23		Laboring Class		United States	Atlantic	2 Apr 1827
MCGUILL, Andw.	30	M	Farmer	Ireland	U. States	Mentor	5 Jul 1825
MCGUINIS, Margret	25	F		Ireland	N. Jersey	Potomac	7 Aug 1827
MCGUIR, Andrew	21	M	Merchant	Gt. Brittain	Canada	Leeds	19 May 1823
MCGUIRE, A.	10	F		G. Britain	U. States	Dalthousie Castle	2 Jan 1827
Alice	19	F	None	Ireland	U.S.A.	Dalhouse Castle	21 Aug 1829
Ann	34	F				Governor Fenner	23 Jul 1829
B.	37	M	Farmer	Gt. Britain	United States	Penelope	9 Sep 1828
Barney	28	M	Laborer	Ireland	United States	Sylvester Healy	17 Oct 1825
Bernard	2	M		Gt. Britain	United States	Penelope	9 Sep 1828
C.	3	F		G. Britain	U. States	Dalthousie Castle	2 Jan 1827
Catharine	15	F		Ireland	U. States	Nancy	16 Aug 1822
Catharine	28	F		G. Britain	U. States	Dalthousie Castle	2 Jan 1827
Catherine	5	F	Farmer	Ireland	America	Farmer	4 Aug 1825
Eliza	1	F	Farmer	Ireland	America	Farmer	4 Aug 1825
Eliza	6	F				Governor Fenner	23 Jul 1829
Ewd.	6	M		Gt. Britain	United States	Penelope	9 Sep 1828
Felix	15		Boy, Labourer	Ireland	U. States	Josephine	7 May 1827
James		M	Chiefly farmers		United States	Factor	8 Jul 1829
James	12	M				Governor Fenner	23 Jul 1829
James	20	M	Labourer	Ireland	New York	Trusty	12 Sep 1828
James	22	M	Labourer	Ireland	United States	Trident	31 Mar 1827
Jane	23	F	None	Ireland	United States	Essex	23 May 1828
Jas.	23	M	Farmer	Great Brittain	United States	Nimrod	9 Jan 1827
Jas.	32	M	Laborer	Ireland	U. States	Lady Hunter	8 Aug 1826
Jno.	23	M	None	Ireland	United States	Essex	23 May 1828
Jno.	35	M	Gardner	Scotland	St. Johns, N.B.	Isabella	10 Mar 1825
John	16	M	Labourer	Ireland	U. States	Josephine	7 May 1827
John	22	M	Taylor	Halifax	U. States	Combine	30 Nov 1825
John	24	M	...	...ford	...	Frances Henrietta	30 Jun 1827

NAMES OF PASSENGERS	AGE	SEX	OCCUPATIONS	COUNTRY TO WHICH THEY BELONG	COUNTRY THEY INTEND TO INHABIT	SHIPS/DATES OF ARRIVAL	
MCGUIRE (cont'd)							
John	24	M	Labourer	Great Britain	United States	Thomas Dickason	31 Jul 1829
John	28	M		G. Britain	U. States	Mary & Harriot	8 Sep 1828
John	30	M	Smith	Great Brittain	United States	United States	16 Feb 1827
John	30	M	Weaver	Ireland	United States	Baltic	21 Apr 1827
Judith	24	F	None	...ford	...	Frances Henrietta	30 Jun 1827
M.	25	M	Student	Great Britian	U. States	Pallas	17 Aug 1824
Margaret	2	F		Scotland	U. States	Isabella	10 Mar 1825
Margaret	12	F	Child	Ireland	U. States	Josephine	7 May 1827
Margaret	19	F	Spinster	Ireland	New York	Governor Fenner	23 Jul 1829
Margret	16	F	Spinster	Ireland	United States	Wilson	4 Oct 1827
Margt.	12	F		G. Britain	U. States	Dalthousie Castle	2 Jan 1827
Mary	4	F		Gt. Britain	United States	Penelope	9 Sep 1828
Mary	13	F	Farmer	Ireland	America	Farmer	4 Aug 1825
Mary	19	F	Spinster	Ireland	United States	Wilson	6 Jun 1828
Mary	27	F		Ireland	U. States	Nancy	13 Dec 1822
Mary	30	F		Scotland	U. States	Isabella	10 Mar 1825
Mary	30	F	Farmer	Ireland	America	Farmer	4 Aug 1825
Mathew	7	M	Farmer	Ireland	America	Farmer	4 Aug 1825
Michael	10/12	M				Governor Fenner	23 Jul 1829
Michael	9	M	Farmer	Ireland	America	Farmer	4 Aug 1825
Michael	26	M	Weaver	Ireland	America	Plutarch	18 Jul 1826
Nancy	30	F	Laborer	Ireland	U. States	Lady Hunter	8 Aug 1826
Nath.	27 3/12	M		Ireland	U.S. of America	Douglass	6 Jul 1829
P.	25	M	Labourer			Hanford	17 Jul 1828
Patrick	16	M	Farmer	Ireland	America	Farmer	4 Aug 1825
Patrick	21	M	Laborer	Ireland	New York	Indian Chief	16 Aug 1822
Patrick	21	M	Labourer	Great Britain	United States	Aurora	10 Nov 1827
Patrick	32	M	Farmer	Ireland	United States	Champion	27 Dec 1827
Peter	16	M	Labourer	Ireland	New York	Atlantic	8 May 1828
R.	37	M	Shoe Maker	Gt. Britain	United States	Penelope	9 Sep 1828
Richd.	30	M	Farmer	Gt. Britain	United States	Penelope	9 Sep 1828
Sarah	9/12	F		Scotland	U. States	Isabella	10 Mar 1825
Thomas	4	M	Laborer	Ireland	U. States	Lady Hunter	8 Aug 1826
Thomas, Jr.	3	M	Farmer	Ireland	America	Farmer	4 Aug 1825
Thos.	26	M	Merchant	Great Britain	U. States	Birmingham	12 Oct 1829
Thos.	40	M	Farmer	Ireland	America	Farmer	4 Aug 1825
Timothy, Revd.	38	M	Clergyman	Ireland	United States	Silas Richards	3 Apr 1826
William	34	M	Farmer	Ireland	New York	Governor Fenner	23 Jul 1829
MCGUIRIE, Catherine	19	F	Spinster	Ireland	United States	Gem	16 Jun 1824
MCGUIRK, John	35			Great Britan	United States	Newry	11 Jul 1827
Margaret	30			Great Britan	United States	Newry	11 Jul 1827
MCGUIRY, John	28	M	Laborer	Ireland	United States	St. Michaels	12 Jun 1826
MCGULL, Addam	19	M	Labourer	Ireland	New York	Trusty	12 Sep 1828
MCGULLERN, Thomas	20	M	Labourer	Ireland	United States	Lord Wellington	28 May 1827
MCGUNNER, John	27	M	Servant	Ireland	U. States	Henrietta	7 Jul 1825
MCGUNNISS, Patrick	20	M	Labourer	Ireland	United States	Robert Fulton	24 Jul 1826
MCGURE, John	42	M	Callo Pewter	Botton	Bolon	Aldebaron	21 Jan 1826
MCGURGAN, Edward	20	M	...	Ireland	United States	Carolina Ann	24 Oct 1825
MCGURK, Mary	40	F	Farmer	Ireland	U. States	Francis	6 Sep 1827
MCGURLICK, Bridget	26	F	Servant	Ireland	New York	Louisa	18 Apr 1827
James	20	M	Weaver	Ireland	New York	Louisa	18 Apr 1827
MCGURLIE, Mary	22	F	Servant	Ireland	United States	Louisa	18 Apr 1827
MCGURRIGH, Ann	35	F	Lady		Goshen	Betsy	4 Sep 1820
Catherine	18	F	Lady			Betsy	4 Sep 1820
Dennis	18	M	Gent			Betsy	4 Sep 1820
Edward	8	M	Gent			Betsy	4 Sep 1820
John	10	M	Gent			Betsy	4 Sep 1820
John	40	M	Gent		Goshen	Betsy	4 Sep 1820
Thos.	16	M	Gent			Betsy	4 Sep 1820
MCGUZZIN, Margret	19	F	Spinster	Ireland		Robert Fulton	4 Jun 1828
MCGWIN, Pat	35	M	Labourer	Great Britain	United States	Penelope	11 Jun 1827
Thomas	28	M	Weaver	Ireland	United States	Borneo	28 Aug 1828

NAMES OF PASSENGERS	AGE	SEX	OCCUPATIONS	COUNTRY TO WHICH THEY BELONG	COUNTRY THEY INTEND TO INHABIT	SHIPS/DATES OF ARRIVAL	
MCGWIRE, Ellen	16	F		Ireland	U. States	Nancy	16 Aug 1822
MCGWYRE, B.	30	M				Lady of the Lake	23 Aug 1828
*left ship							
Mary	2	F				Lady of the Lake	23 Aug 1828
*left ship							
R.	20	F				Lady of the Lake	23 Aug 1828
*left ship							
MCHAFFETY, Mary	23	F	Spnster	Ireland	United States	General Marion	20 Aug 1828
MCHAN, D.	19	M	Labourer	Great Britain	United States	Frances Henrietta	17 Sep 1827
MCHARRE, John	23	M	Weaver	Ireland	United States	Robert Fulton	10 Aug 1827
MCHATTIN, John	28	M	Labourer or Spinster	Ireland	United States	Champion	3 Nov 1827
MCHAY, John	4	M		Derry, Ireland	Philadelphia	Anthusa	24 Aug 1825
Margt.	27	F		Derry, Ireland	Philadelphia	Anthusa	24 Aug 1825
Mary	16	F		Derry, Ireland	Philadelphia	Anthusa	24 Aug 1825
Sarah	1 6/12	F		Derry, Ireland	Philadelphia	Anthusa	24 Aug 1825
MCHEELEY, Geo.	30	M	Merchant	U. States	U. States	Albert	1 Apr 1822
MCHELLEN, Catherine	27	F	Servant	St. John, N.B.	United States	St. Michaels	11 May 1826
MCHENRY, Jas.	18	M	Farmer	Ireland	U. States	William & John	10 Jul 1824
Mary	19	F	...	...	United States	Hanford	17 Oct 1828
MCHERRIN, Pat	28	M	Labourer	Ireland	United States	Hope	12 Jun 1828
MCHERRY, Thos.		M	Chiefly farmers		United States	Factor	8 Jul 1829
Wm.	32	M	Clergyman	U. States	U. States	Eugene	15 Dec 1828
MCHONE, Bernard	26	M	Shoe Maker	Irereland	America	Carolina Ann	20 Jun 1825
MCHUGH, Angus	50	M	Servant	Great Brittan	Great Brittain	Florida	17 May 1825
Ann	20	F		Great Britain	United States	Mary Howland	19 Jul 1827
Briget	25	M	Servant	G. Britain	United States	Louisa	14 Jun 1825
Chs.	32	M	Labourer	Ireland	U. States	Marcus	7 Apr 1825
James	28	M	Blacksmith	Great Britain	United States	Mary Howland	19 Jul 1827
Michael	1	M		Great Britain	United States	Mary Howland	19 Jul 1827
MCHUN, Danl.	33	M	Farmer	Scotland	U. States	Marcellus	2 Sep 1820
MCHUW, Mary	23	F		Gt. Britain	U. States	Panthea	21 Jul 1825
MCIELROW, Felix	24	M	Labourer	Ireland	United States	Hope	12 Jun 1828
MCIL..., ...	24	M	Farmer			Robert Burns	13 Jul 1820
MCILDOUNY, Pat	20	M	Labourer	Ireland	United States	Trident	16 May 1826
MCILEWAIN, Jos.	22	M	Farmer	Ireland	Pittsburg	Triton	12 Jul 1823
MCILHAN..., Rose	30	F	...	Ireland	United States	General Putnam	20 Jun 1825
MCILHENEY,							
Bridget	20 7/12	F	Seamstress	Ireland	United States	Atlantic	21 Jul 1827
Mary	18 4/12	F	Seamstress	Ireland	United States	Atlantic	21 Jul 1827
Thomas	50 3/12	M	Weaver	Ireland	United States	Atlantic	21 Jul 1827
MCILROY, Betsey	22	F		Clonis	United States	Carolina Ann	11 Jun 1824
James	20	M	Labour	Ireland	New York	Amanda	23 May 1827
Jane	20	F	Spinster	Ireland	United States	Fabius	4 Jun 1828
Judith	55	F		Clonis	United States	Carolina Ann	11 Jun 1824
Matthew	24	M		Clonis	United States	Carolina Ann	11 Jun 1824
Pat.	60	M	Farmer	Clonis	United States	Carolina Ann	11 Jun 1824
Patrick	23	M		Ireland	America	Carolina Ann	7 Apr 1826
Paul	20	M	Barber	Great Britain	United States	Atlantic	8 Dec 1827
Peter	22 1/12	M		Ireland	America	Carolina Ann	7 Apr 1826
William	25	F	Farmer	Ireland	United States	Fabius	4 Jun 1828
MCILSEE, Daniel	31	M	Merchant	America	America	Carolina Ann	7 Apr 1826
MCILVAINE, D.	33	M	Merchant	Philada.	U. States	General Brown	10 Dec 1823
J. R.	33	M	Merchant	U. States	U. States	Alabama	21 May 1823
Jos. B.	32	M	Merchant	United States	United States	Susquehanna	23 Nov 1822
MCILVENA, Elizabeth	20	F	Spinster	Ireland	U.S. of America	Meteor	19 Mar 1828
MCILVINE, Bridget	20	F	Servant	Ireland	U. States	Fabius	22 Sep 1828
MCILVOGUE,							
Catharine	20 8/12	F	Sister [of Terry]	G. Britain	United States	Louisa	14 Jun 1825
Terry	22 7/12	F	Bricklayer	G. Britain	United States	Louisa	14 Jun 1825
MCILVOY, Jas.	28		Labourer	Halifax	U. States	Edwin	26 Sep 1828
MCILWAIN, Robert	20	M	Farmer	Ireland	United States	William & George	14 May 1828
MCILWAINE, James	20	M	Weaver	Ireland	United States	Trident	17 May 1825
Joseph	27	M	Weaver	Ireland	United States	Trident	17 May 1825

NAMES OF PASSENGERS	AGE	SEX	OCCUPATIONS	COUNTRY TO WHICH THEY BELONG	COUNTRY THEY INTEND TO INHABIT	SHIPS/DATES OF ARRIVAL	
MCIN...LLY, Owen	28	M	None	Great Britain	United States	Eliza Barker	3 Jul 1826
MCINDOE, Mather	57	M	Merchant	America	America	Albion	4 Oct 1820
MCINLEY, John	20	M	Baker	Scotland	U. States	Othello	3 Dec 1828
MCINNERY, Catherine	20	F	Laborer	Ireland	America	Parrington	9 Jun 1827
Denis	22		Victualer	Ireland	America	Parrington	9 Jun 1827
James	18	M	Glozier	Ireland	America	Parrington	9 Jun 1827
Mary	22	F	Glozier	Ireland	America	Parrington	9 Jun 1827
Patrick	25	M	Laborer	Ireland	America	Parrington	9 Jun 1827
MCINTAGGART, Patk.	20	M	Labourer	Ireland	United States	Trident	16 May 1826
MCINTIRE, Ann	18	F	Spinster	Ireland	United States	Robert Fulton	24 Jul 1826
Ann	25	F	Spinster	Ireland	United States	Robert Fulton	10 Aug 1827
C.	24	F	Farmer	Ireland	U. States	Isabella	28 Jun 1825
Catharine	16	F	Servant	Ireland	United States	Wilson	27 Jun 1826
Catherine	17			Great Britain		John Dickinson	5 Apr 1821
Danl.	25	M	Cabinet Maker	Scotland	U.S.A.	Calliope	15 Aug 1827
David	19	M	Farmer	Great Brittain	U. States	William Byrnes	23 Jul 1824
Donald	29	M	Bookeeper	Glasgow	Glasgow	Howard Douglass	11 May 1827
Eliza	20		Servant	Ireland	Great Britain	Robert Burns	14 Jun 1824
George	38	M	Marble Cutter	New York		Olive Branch	9 Oct 1829
Hannah	12	F	Child	Ireland	United States	St. Michaels	25 May 1825
Hugh	1 5/12	M	None	Scotland	United States	Friends	7 Jul 1827
James	23	M	Labourer	Ireland	United States	Robert Fulton	10 Aug 1827
James	32	M	Farmer	Great Brittain	U. States	William Byrnes	23 Jul 1824
James	50	M	Laborer	Ireland	United States	St. Michaels	25 May 1825
Jane	19	F	Spinster	Ireland	United States	Robert Fulton	10 Aug 1827
John	21	M	Weaver	Ireland	United States	Robert Fulton	10 Aug 1827
M.	22	M	Farmer	Ireland	U. States	Isabella	28 Jun 1825
Martin	40	M		Ireland	United States	William	5 Oct 1822
Mary	18	F	Child	Ireland	United States	St. Michaels	25 May 1825
Mary	26	F	Wife [of James]	United States	New York	Intrepid	8 Aug 1822
Mavnes	16	F	Child	Ireland	United States	St. Michaels	25 May 1825
Peter	23	M	Shoe Maker	Scotland	U.S.A.	Calliope	15 Aug 1827
Rose	21	F	Child	Ireland	United States	Nancy	18 Oct 1824
Thos.	30	M	Laborer	Ireland	America	Francis & Henrietta	11 Jul 1823
W.	21	M	Laborer	Ireland	United States	Mary	1 Jul 1829
W. H.	26	M		England		Ann	17 May 1822
MCINTOS, Thos.	29	M	Flisher	Scotland	U. States	Superior	25 Sep 1828
MCINTOSH, —, Mrs.	19	F		U. States	U. States	Good Friends	20 May 1825
Agnes	28	F		Scotland	United States	Broke	16 Jul 1829
Alexr.	20	M	Dyer	Scotland	U. States	Camillus	27 Jun 1826
Alexr.	33	M	Carpenter	Scotland	United States	Belmont	30 Aug 1828
Andrew	30	M	Blacksmith	Scotland	United States	Leda	30 Aug 1828
Ann	20	F	Farmer	Scotland	U.S. States of Am.	Camillus	17 Sep 1823
Ann	30	F		Scotland	United States	Leda	30 Aug 1828
Anna	4	F		England	United States	Alexander Mansfield	9 Jul 1829
Barbara	5	F	Dyer	Scotland	U. States	Camillus	27 Jun 1826
Barbara	69	F	Dyer	Scotland	U. States	Camillus	27 Jun 1826
Betsey	8	F		England	United States	Alexander Mansfield	9 Jul 1829
Charles	6	M		England	United States	Alexander Mansfield	9 Jul 1829
Christina	14	F	Farmer	Scotland	U.S. States of Am.	Camillus	17 Sep 1823
Daniel	1	M	None	Scotland	U. States	Camillus	27 Jun 1826
David	4	M		Scotland	United States	Broke	16 Jul 1829
David	28	M		Scotland	United States	Broke	16 Jul 1829
Donald	15	M	Farmer	Scotland	U.S. States of Am.	Camillus	17 Sep 1823
Donald	30	M	Dyer	Scotland	U. States	Camillus	27 Jun 1826
Elizabeth	2	F		Scotland	United States	Broke	16 Jul 1829
Geo.	22	M	None	United States	United States	Brown	26 Apr 1826
George	18	M	Gentleman	America	United States	Euphrates	25 Jun 1824
George	19	M	Farmer	Scotland	U.S. States of Am.	Camillus	17 Sep 1823
James	21	M	Farmer	Scotland	U.S. States of Am.	Camillus	17 Sep 1823
James	31	M	Caddler [?]	Great Britain	U. States	Brutus	5 Sep 1827
James	36	M	Tailor	G. Britain	U. States	Dalthousie Castle	2 Jan 1827
James	36	M	Engineer	Scotland	United States	Broke	16 Jul 1829

NAMES OF PASSENGERS	AGE	SEX	OCCUPATIONS	COUNTRY TO WHICH THEY BELONG	COUNTRY THEY INTEND TO INHABIT	SHIPS/DATES OF ARRIVAL	
MCINTOSH (cont'd)							
James	42	M	Labourer	Great Britain	United States	Colossus	5 Jun 1827
Janet	35	F	None	Great Britain	United States	Colossus	5 Jun 1827
John	10	M		England	United States	Alexander Mansfield	9 Jul 1829
John	17	M	Labourer	Scotland	United States	Coquet	6 Jun 1827
John D.	11	M	Farmer	Scotland	U.S. States of Am.	Camillus	17 Sep 1823
Margaret	17	F	Farmer	Scotland	U.S. States of Am.	Camillus	17 Sep 1823
Margaret	28	F	Dyer	Scotland	U. States	Camillus	27 Jun 1826
Margaret	50	F	Farmer	Scotland	U.S. States of Am.	Camillus	17 Sep 1823
Mathew	3	M		Scotland	United States	Broke	16 Jul 1829
Selina	30	M		England	United States	Alexander Mansfield	9 Jul 1829
W. C.	24	M	Mechanic	New York	New York	Leif	6 Sep 1824
William	3	M	Dyer	Scotland	U. States	Camillus	27 Jun 1826
MCINTREE, George	28		Laborer	Ireland	Great Britain	Robert Burns	14 Jun 1824
MCINTYRE, —, Mrs.	50			Scotland	United States	Camillus	3 May 1828
...	20	F		Scotland	New York	Joseph Hume	26 Oct 1829
...l.	30	M	Labourer	Great Britain		Casanda	5 Sep 1827
And.	20	M	Laborer	England	U. States	Lady Hunter	14 Mar 1826
Archd.	7	M		Scotland	United States	Belmont	30 Aug 1828
Barney	4	F		St. Johns	U. States	Wanderer	30 Oct 1828
Barney	36	M	Farmer	St. Johns	U. States	Wanderer	30 Oct 1828
Catharine	18		Spinster	Scotland	United States	Camillus	3 May 1828
Catherine	15	F		Scotland	United States	Belmont	30 Aug 1828
Donald	29	M	Labourer	Scotland	United States	Friends	7 Jul 1827
Dond.	3	M	None	United States	New York	Intrepid	8 Aug 1822
Dugold	5	M		Scotland	United States	Belmont	30 Aug 1828
Eliza	13	F		Scotland	United States	Belmont	30 Aug 1828
Flora	17	F		Scotland	United States	Belmont	30 Aug 1828
George	14	M		Scotland	United States	Belmont	30 Aug 1828
J. J.	26	M	Merchant	Gt. Britain	United States	Prince Edward	1 Apr 1825
James	1	M	None	United States	New York	Intrepid	8 Aug 1822
James	36	M	Farmer	United States	New York	Intrepid	8 Aug 1822
Jas.	21	M	Labourer	Ireland	United States	Trident	16 May 1826
Jean	24	F	Spinster	Scotland	United States	Friends	7 Jul 1827
Jean	33	F		St. Johns	U. States	Wanderer	30 Oct 1828
John	40	M	Merchant	Great Britain	United States	Elizabeth & Mary	20 Mar 1828
M. S.	50	M		Scotland	New York	Joseph Hume	26 Oct 1829
Mary	24	F	Servant	G. Britain	U. States	Wanderer	23 Jun 1828
Mary	30	F		Scotland	United States	Belmont	30 Aug 1828
Neal	40	M		Scotland	United States	Belmont	30 Aug 1828
Peter	2	M	None	United States	New York	Intrepid	8 Aug 1822
Robt.	25	M	Labourer	Ireland	United States	Asia	29 Jul 1829
Wm.	16	M	Laborer	Scotland	America	Camillus	12 Sep 1822
Wm.	26	M		Scotland	New York	Joseph Hume	26 Oct 1829
MCINVOY, Margrt.	19	F	Spinster	Ireland		Robert Fulton	4 Jun 1828
Patrick	4	M	Labourer	Ireland		Robert Fulton	4 Jun 1828
MCIRILLA, Patrick	20	M	Weaver	Ireland	U. States	Josephine	30 Aug 1828
MCISAAC, Hugh	45	M	Merchant			Lady of the Lake	23 Aug 1828
MCITTIRE, John	28	M	Merchant	G. Britain	G. Britain	Brittania	17 Jul 1828
MCJANVERAN, John	19	M	Labourer	Ireland		Marchioness	13 May 1828
MCJENINGS, Rebecca	27	F	Servant	Ireland	U. States	Henrietta	7 Jul 1825
MCJERSON, E.	28	M	Shoemaker	Great Britain	United States	Isaac Hicks	6 Dec 1827
MCJOHN, John	30	M	Farmer	Great Britain	U. States	Columbia	22 Sep 1828
MCJOURNIGAN, Eunia	20	F	Taylor	Ireland	U. States	Virginia	20 Jun 1825
MCJOY, Arthur	24			Ireland	U.S.	Union	20 Aug 1827
MCK...LL, Francis	...	...	...	Scotland	America	Nimrod	9 Jul 1827
MCKAHELL, Biddy	26	F		Ireland	United States	Curler	3 Mar 1828
MCKAIG, —	1	F		Ireland	United States	Mary	1 Jul 1829
—	4	F		Ireland	United States	Mary	1 Jul 1829
—	6	M		Ireland	United States	Mary	1 Jul 1829
—	26	M		Ireland	United States	Mary	1 Jul 1829
MCKALLA, Wm.	50	M	Naval Officer	England	England	John Wells	14 Oct 1823
MCKALVENETSH, Solomon	38	M	Merchant	Prussia	United States	Orozimbo	28 Jun 1827
MCKANE, Betsey	35	F	Farmer	Ireland	U. States	Edward	15 Jul 1825
MCKARRAN, Phillip	21		Labourer	Ireland	United States	Helen	5 Jul 1820

NAMES OF PASSENGERS	AGE	SEX	OCCUPATIONS	COUNTRY TO WHICH THEY BELONG	COUNTRY THEY INTEND TO INHABIT	SHIPS/DATES OF ARRIVAL	
MCKAY, —, Mr.	34	M	Merchant	G. Britain	Canada	Corinthian	29 Apr 1826
Alexdr.	20	F		England	U.N. States	Helen	17 Dec 1827
Daniel	19	M	Labourer	Ireland	New York	Governor Fenner	23 Jul 1829
Donald	28	M	Uppolsterer	Great Britain	United States	Minerva	28 Jul 1823
Elizabeth	56	F	Baker	Great Britain	New York	Superior	5 Sep 1827
Hugh	24	M	Labourer	Ireland	United States	Princess Charlotte	26 Apr 1827
Isabella	24	F	...	Ireland	United States	General Putnam	20 Jun 1825
James	28	M	Shoe Maker	Scotland	America	Eyder	7 Aug 1826
James	40	M	Farmer	Scotland	U. States	Camillus	27 Jun 1826
Janeth	70	M	None	Scotland	U. States	Camillus	27 Jun 1826
Mary	26	F	None	Scotland	U. States	Camillus	27 Jun 1826
Patt	22	M	Weaver	Great Britain	United States	Magnet	19 Aug 1822
Richd.	20	M	Farmer	Hill Hale	N. York	Favourite	8 Oct 1823
Robt.	30	M	Baker	Great Britain	New York	Superior	5 Sep 1827
Sam	60	M	Army	England	U. States	Foster	28 Aug 1822
Wm.	9	M	Baker	Great Britain	New York	Superior	5 Sep 1827
MCKEA, Andrew	32	M	Labourer	Ireland	United States	Mary & Harriet	3 Jul 1829
MCKEAG, Robt.	22	M	Farmer	C. Down	Philedelphia	Nile	18 Aug 1829
MCKEAN, James	18	M	Labourer	Scotland	United States	Samuel Robertson	5 Oct 1827
James	50	M	Butcher	Scotland	United States	Samuel Robertson	5 Oct 1827
Jas.	20	M	Farmer	Ireland	United States	Alex. Mansfield	17 May 1823
M.	27	M	Carpenter	U. States	U. States	Palestine	1 May 1821
MCKEARNAN, James	18		None			Amphion	31 May 1824
Patrick	22		None			Amphion	31 May 1824
MCKEARNY, Henry	20	M	Farmer	Ireland	U. States	Dickinson	30 Jul 1825
Henry	infant	M	Farmer	Ireland	U. States	Dickinson	30 Jul 1825
Peggy	20	F	Farmer	Ireland	U. States	Dickinson	30 Jul 1825
MCKECHNIE, Janet	28	F	None	Great Britain	United States	Colossus	5 Jun 1827
John	1/2	M	None	Great Britain	United States	Colossus	5 Jun 1827
John	27	M	Miner	Great Britain	United States	Colossus	5 Jun 1827
MCKEE, Agnes	8	F		Ireland	United States	Princess Charlotte	26 Apr 1827
Agnes	21	F		Ireland	United States	Princess Charlotte	26 Apr 1827
Ann	0 9/12	F				Hanford	17 Jul 1828
Brian	40	M	Carpenter	Ireland	America	Josephine	8 Dec 1827
Catharine	4	F		Saintfield	United States	Carolina Ann	11 Jun 1824
Catherine	36	F		Saintfield	United States	Carolina Ann	11 Jun 1824
Charles	20 6/12	M	Weaver	Ireland	U. States	Courier	17 Mar 1828
Daniel	21	M	Bricklayer	Ireland		Fame	9 Dec 1826
David	6	M		Saintfield	United States	Carolina Ann	11 Jun 1824
David	14	M	Labourer	Bally Banah	United States	Minerva	30 Oct 1829
Duncan	18	M	Marriner	Scotland	United States	Liverpool Trader	24 Oct 1825
Eliza	13	F		Saintfield	United States	Carolina Ann	11 Jun 1824
Elizabeth	35	F	Matron	Ireland	America	Josephine	8 Dec 1827
George	25	M	Farmer			Superb	18 Jul 1820
H.	20		Farmer	Ireland	United States	Courier	16 May 1825
Isabella	17	F		Saintfield	United States	Carolina Ann	11 Jun 1824
Jane	15	F		Saintfield	United States	Carolina Ann	11 Jun 1824
Jane	20	F				Superb	18 Jul 1820
Jane	21	F		Ireland	United States	Princess Charlotte	26 Apr 1827
Jane	23	F		Ireland	United States	Princess Charlotte	26 Apr 1827
Jane	30	F		Ireland	Philadelphia	Carolina Ann	15 Oct 1824
John	21	M	Watch Maker	Ireland	New York	Trusty	12 Sep 1828
John	25	M	Labourer	Killinchey	United States	Carolina Ann	11 Jun 1824
John	32	M	Labourer	England	America	Manhattan	20 Mar 1820
John	46	M	Mariner	Younghall, Great Britain	United States	Union	24 Sep 1823
Mary	2	F		Ireland	United States	Princess Charlotte	26 Apr 1827
*Died on the Voyage							
Mary	3	F				Hanford	17 Jul 1828
Mary	10	F		Saintfield	United States	Carolina Ann	11 Jun 1824

NAMES OF PASSENGERS	AGE	SEX	OCCUPATIONS	COUNTRY TO WHICH THEY BELONG	COUNTRY THEY INTEND TO INHABIT	SHIPS/DATES OF ARRIVAL	
MCKEE (cont'd)							
Mary	10	F	Child	Ireland	America	Josephine	8 Dec 1827
Mary	24	F	Servant	Ireland	United States	Carolina Ann	14 May 1827
Matthew	26	M	Weaver	Banbridge	United States	Carolina Ann	11 Jun 1824
Patrick	8	M	Boy	Ireland	America	Josephine	8 Dec 1827
Richard	2	M		Saintfield	United States	Carolina Ann	11 Jun 1824
Richd.	40	M	Farmer	Saintfield	United States	Carolina Ann	11 Jun 1824
Robert	23	M	Weaver	Ireland	United States	Princess Charlotte	26 Apr 1827
Robert	24	M	Weaver	Ireland	United States	Princess Charlotte	26 Apr 1827
Rose	34	F	None	Younghall, Great Britain	United States	Union	24 Sep 1823
Rossanna	19	F	Spinster	Ireland	United States	Lady Hunter	27 Dec 1825
Saml.	8	M		Saintfield	United States	Carolina Ann	11 Jun 1824
Thomas	9	M	Boy	Ireland	America	Josephine	8 Dec 1827
Thomas	26	M	Weaver	Ireland	United States	Princess Charlotte	26 Apr 1827
Thos.	13	M	Carpenter	Ireland	United States	Lady Hunter	27 Dec 1825
Thos.	17	M	Labourer	Ireland	United States	Meteor	26 Jun 1827
MCKEEF, B.	30	F				Hanford	17 Jul 1828
E.	38	M				Hanford	17 Jul 1828
MCKEEN, John	32 4/12	M	Carpenter	New York	New York	Harriot	1 May 1822
MCKEERNAN, Thomas	18		Laboring Class		United States	Atlantic	2 Apr 1827
MCKEEVOR, Thomas	22	M	Labourer	Ireland	United States	Robert Fulton	24 Jul 1826
MCKEG, Julia	20	F		Gt. Britain	U. States	St. George	20 Sep 1828
MCKEIL, Mathew	24	M	Labourer	Gt. Britain	U. States	Frances Henrietta	18 Apr 1825
MCKEINE, Archibald	34	M	Labourer	Kilmarnock	U.S. America	Camillus	10 Sep 1821
MCKELLER, Peter	25	M	Merchant	U. States	U. States	Eliza Jane	26 Oct 1829
MCKELLY, Janes	25	M	Farmer	Scotland	U.S.	Curler	19 Jul 1828
MCKENDRICK, Betty	24	F		Scotland	United States	Samuel Robertson	5 Oct 1827
Peter	27	M	Labourer	Scotland	United States	Samuel Robertson	5 Oct 1827
MCKENLY, Jane	40	F	Dressmaker	Ireland	America	Carolina Ann	7 Aug 1826
MCKENNA, ...	23	M	Labourer	Ireland	U. States	Josephine	30 Aug 1828
Bemd.	24	M	Farmer	Ireland	U. States	Dickinson	30 Jul 1825
Brid...	21	...	Spinster	Ireland	U. States	Josephine	30 Aug 1828
Catharine	4	F	Daughter	Ireland	New York	Atlantic	6 Oct 1828
Cathn.	1	F	None	Great Britain	America	Remittance	24 Aug 1825
Cathr.	26	F	None	Great Britain	America	Remittance	24 Aug 1825
Eliza	2	F	None	Great Britain	America	Remittance	24 Aug 1825
Ellen	25	F	Sempstress	Great Britain	United States	Atlantic	8 Dec 1827
Hannah	32	F	Wife	Ireland	New York	Atlantic	6 Oct 1828
James	21	M	Farmer	Ireland	United States	Leonidas	3 Aug 1825
Jas.	21	M	Farmer	England	U. States	Oglethorpe	9 Nov 1824
John	12	M	Weaver	Ireland	New York	Atlantic	6 Oct 1828
John	20 5/12	M	Weaver	Ireland	New York	Atlantic	8 May 1828
John	33	M	Weaver	Ireland	United States	Delta	24 Oct 1829
Lawr.	35	F	Farmer	England	United States	Danube	22 Aug 1825
Louisa	3	F	None	Great Britain	America	Remittance	24 Aug 1825
Margeret	21 6/12	...	Spinster	Ireland	U. States	Josephine	30 Aug 1828
Mary	4	F	None	Great Britain	America	Remittance	24 Aug 1825
Mary	9	F	Daughter	Ireland	New York	Atlantic	6 Oct 1828
Mary	50	F	Spinster	Ireland	United States	Dublin Packet	3 Sep 1822
Nancy	19 0/12	F	Servant	Ireland	New York	Atlantic	8 May 1828
Owen	33		Marbler Pols	Ireland		Hudson	23 Jul 1828
Owen	35	M	Farmer	Great Britain	America	Remittance	24 Aug 1825
Owen C.	4	M	None	Great Britain	America	Remittance	24 Aug 1825
Patk.	14	M	Weaver	Ireland	New York	Atlantic	6 Oct 1828
Philip	40	M	Farmer	Ireland	U. States	Dickinson	30 Jul 1825
Susan	60	...	Matron	Ireland	U. States	Josephine	30 Aug 1828
Terence	25	M	Blacksmith	Great Britain	United States	Atlantic	8 Dec 1827
MCKENNAN, Jas.(Surgeon)						Thomas Ritchie	2 Jul 1827
Mary	60	F	Spinster	Ireland	United States	Fabius	31 Jul 1829
Mary, Jr.	25	F	Spinster	Ireland	United States	Fabius	31 Jul 1829
Susan	25	F	Spinster	Ireland	United States	Fabius	31 Jul 1829
William	18	M	Labourer	Ireland	United States	Fabius	31 Jul 1829

NAMES OF PASSENGERS	AGE	SEX	OCCUPATIONS	COUNTRY TO WHICH THEY BELONG	COUNTRY THEY INTEND TO INHABIT	SHIPS/DATES OF ARRIVAL	
MCKENNE, Andrew	5	M	None	Scotland	United States	Mary & Susan	5 Aug 1828
Elisebeth	15	F	None	Scotland	United States	Mary & Susan	5 Aug 1828
Jane	13	F	None	Scotland	United States	Mary & Susan	5 Aug 1828
John	2	M	None	Scotland	United States	Mary & Susan	5 Aug 1828
Peter	45	M	Farmer	Scotland	United States	Mary & Susan	5 Aug 1828
Thomas	22	M	Farmer	Scotland	United States	Mary & Susan	5 Aug 1828
MCKENNEL, Robert	22	M	Clerk	Scotland	United States	Lord Wellington	14 Nov 1827
MCKENNER, H.	28	M	Brewer	Ireland	U. States	Elizabeth	5 Oct 1822
Jas.	22		Farmer	Ireland		Westmoreland	1 Aug 1826
MCKENNERDY, Wm.	23	M	Engineer	Great Britten	England	Cortes	6 Mar 1827
MCKENNEY, Jas.	27	M	Labourer	England	U. States	Magnet	6 Feb 1823
Neill	24	M	Labourer	Ireland	U. States	Josephine	7 May 1827
William	29	M	Weaver	Ireland	New York	Lima	5 Aug 1829
MCKENNING,							
Elizabeth	2	F		Ireland		Eliza Grant	29 Aug 1829
James	25	M	Cotton Spinner	Ireland		Eliza Grant	29 Aug 1829
MCKENNON, Hugh	40	M	Farmer	Scotland	United States	Belmont	30 Aug 1828
John	30	M	Labourer	Lochcarron, Lochcarron [Parish], Ross [County]	New York	Hero	19 May 1828
*to look for Employment							
Mary	30	F		Scotland	United States	Belmont	30 Aug 1828
Meysie	3	F		Scotland	United States	Belmont	30 Aug 1828
Neil	10	M		Scotland	United States	Belmont	30 Aug 1828
MCKENNY, ...n	18		Laboring Class		United States	Atlantic	2 Apr 1827
Andrew	30	M	Dyer	Ireland	America	Josephine	8 Dec 1827
Ann	15	F		G. Britain	U. States	St. George	7 Jun 1828
Cathr.	28	F		G. Britain	U. States	St. George	7 Jun 1828
Elizabeth	60	F	Widow	Ireland	America	Josephine	8 Dec 1827
James	32	M	Farmer	Ireland	U. States	Mentor	5 Jul 1825
Jane	17	F	Spinster	Ireland	America	Josephine	8 Dec 1827
John	21	M	Labourer	Ireland	Unt. St. America	Wilson	21 May 1827
John	22	M	Weaver	Ireland	America	Josephine	8 Dec 1827
M.	20	M		G. Britain	U. States	St. George	7 Jun 1828
Mary	20	F		G. Britain	U. States	St. George	7 Jun 1828
Mary	25	F	Spinster	Ireland	United States	Fabius	31 Jul 1829
Pat.	25	M	Weaver	Ireland	America	Meteor	26 Dec 1825
MCKENRIE, John, Mr.	28	M	Labourer	Scotland	U. States	Majestic	27 Jul 1829
MCKENY, Margret	30	F	Spinster	Ireland		Robert Fulton	4 Jun 1828
MCKENZIE, James	43	M	Merchant	Scotland	New York, U.S.	New York	14 Mar 1828
Jane	19	F	Milliner	Ireland	United States	Wanderer	1 Aug 1828
Jno.	26	M	Carpenter	Halifax	U. States	Hope & Esther	22 Jul 1825
Peter	34	M	Labourer	G. Britain	U. States	Mary & Harriot	8 Sep 1828
Willm. Alex.	16	M	Farmer	England	United States	Concordia	25 Aug 1827
Wm.	45	M	Merchant	Scotland	U. States	America	20 Sep 1821
MCKEON, Bernard	60	M	Farmer	Ireland	U. States	Dickinson	30 Jul 1825
E.	19		Farmer	Ireland	United States	Courier	16 May 1825
Edward	26	M	Farmer	Ireland	United States	Leonidas	3 Aug 1825
James	19	M	Farmer	Ireland	United States	Dublin Packet	22 Apr 1822
James	25	M	Farmer	Ireland	United States	General Putnam	20 Jun 1825
Robert	21	M	Weaver	Ireland	United States	Asia	29 Jul 1829
MCKEOUGH, Michl.	28	M	Labourer	Ireland	United States	Baltic	21 Apr 1827
MCKEOUR, Alexander	24	M		Ireland	America	Carolina Ann	7 Aug 1826
Daniel	20	M		Ireland	America	Carolina Ann	7 Aug 1826
Eliza				Ireland	America	Carolina Ann	7 Aug 1826
Eliza	16	M		Ireland	America	Carolina Ann	7 Aug 1826
Robert	50	M	Servant	Ireland	America	Carolina Ann	7 Aug 1826
Samuel	19	M		Ireland	America	Carolina Ann	7 Aug 1826
William	22	M		Ireland	America	Carolina Ann	7 Aug 1826
William	50	M	Servant	Ireland	America	Carolina Ann	7 Aug 1826
MCKEOWN, Catherine	27	F	Farmer, Labourer or Spinster	Ireland	U. States	Meteor	4 Oct 1827
Eliza	20	F	Manumaker	Irereland	America	Carolina Ann	20 Jun 1825
Francis	15 4/12	M		Ireland	America	Carolina Ann	7 Apr 1826
James	9	M	Farmer, Labourer or Spinster	Ireland	U. States	Meteor	4 Oct 1827
Jane	16	F				Imperial	19 Jul 1820
Jane	16	F	Servant	Ireland	United States	Carolina Ann	14 May 1827

NAMES OF PASSENGERS	AGE	SEX	OCCUPATIONS	COUNTRY TO WHICH THEY BELONG	COUNTRY THEY INTEND TO INHABIT	SHIPS/DATES OF ARRIVAL	
MCKEOWN (cont'd)							
Martha	25	F	Spinster	Ireland	America	Wilson	16 May 1825
Mary Ann	2...	F	Labourer	Ireland	United States	Carolina Ann	14 May 1827
Michl.	18	M		Ireland	America	Carolina Ann	7 Apr 1826
Robert	7	M	...	Ireland	United States	Carolina Ann	24 Oct 1825
Rodger	...	M	Farmer, Labourer or Spinster	Ireland	U. States	Meteor	4 Oct 1827
Rose	11	F	Farmer, Labourer or Spinster	Ireland	U. States	Meteor	4 Oct 1827
Samuel	25	M	...	Ireland	United States	Carolina Ann	24 Oct 1825
Sarah	20	F		Ireland	America	Carolina Ann	7 Apr 1826
William	25	M	Mason	Darry	Ohione	Nile	18 Aug 1829
MCKER, Thomas	21	M	Carpenter	Ireland	America	William	11 Nov 1825
MCKERN, May	20	F	Servant	Ireland	N. York	Trusty	12 Sep 1828
MCKERNAN, Francis	23	M	Farmer	Ireland	United States	Dublin Packet	29 Jun 1825
Jane	19	F	Spinster	Ireland	United States	Fabius	31 Jul 1829
Rose	20	F	Servant	Ireland	United States	Josephine	30 Apr 1828
MCKERNEY, Jno.	20	M	Carpenter	Great Britain	New York	Superior	5 Sep 1827
MCKERNY, X. F.	10	M		U. States	U. States	Olympia	19 Jun 1828
MCKERR, Elizabeth	24	F		Ireland	Ohio	Curler	7 Jul 1827
John	34	M	Farmer	Ireland	Ohio	Curler	7 Jul 1827
Sarah	50	F		Ireland	Ohio	Curler	7 Jul 1827
William	22	M	Farmer	Ireland	Ohio	Curler	7 Jul 1827
MCKERRON, Wm.	30	M	Attorney	Gt. Britain	Gt. Britain	Canada	4 Oct 1824
MCKERWEN, Jno.	28	M	Labourer	Gt. Britain	U. States	Isaac Hicks	18 Apr 1825
MCKESEY, Margaret	26	F	None	Ireland	U. States	Erin	5 Jul 1820
MCKET, Matias	35	M	Merchant	Italy	Italy	Athenian	8 Feb 1827
MCKEVER, Grace	.../12	F		Ireland	United States	Mary	1 Jul 1829
Mary	32	F	Wife	Ireland	United States	St. Michaels	15 Feb 1825
Roderick	30	M	Laborer	Ireland	United States	St. Michaels	15 Feb 1825
MCKEW, Jno.	20	M	Farmers and Mechanics	Ireland	America	Constitution	1 Oct 1825
MCKEWAN, John	21	M	Carpenter	G. Britain	New York	Brighton	26 Mar 1827
MCKEY, Bryan	20	M	Labourer	Ireland	America	Weser	26 Jun 1821
Daniel	15		Clerk	Scotland	United States	Rufus King	4 Sep 1823
Elisabeth	20	F	Servant	America	America	Pacific	13 Jan 1827
Hy.	5	M	Child	Ireland	U. States	Meteor	19 Jul 1828
James	25		Farmer			Rufus King	7 Aug 1820
James	28		Clerk	Scotland	United States	Rufus King	4 Sep 1823
John	3	M	Child	Ireland	U. States	Meteor	19 Jul 1828
Mary	24	F	Spinster	Ireland	U. States	Meteor	19 Jul 1828
MCKIBBEN, Eliza	4		...	Ireland	United States	Alexander Mansfield	23 Nov 1824
Jane	6		...	Ireland	United States	Alexander Mansfield	23 Nov 1824
Jane	35		...	Ireland	United States	Alexander Mansfield	23 Nov 1824
Jas.	8		...	Ireland	United States	Alexander Mansfield	23 Nov 1824
Robert	2		...	Ireland	United States	Alexander Mansfield	23 Nov 1824
MCKIBBIN, Ann	8	F	Daughter of Shoemaker [Jas.]	Ireland	United States	James Monroe	26 Aug 1822
Catharine	2	F		Irereland	America	Carolina Ann	20 Jun 1825
Elizh.	34	F	Wife of Shoemaker [Jas.]	Ireland	United States	James Monroe	26 Aug 1822
Jane	6	F		Irereland	America	Carolina Ann	20 Jun 1825
Jas.	36	M	Shoemaker	Ireland	United States	James Monroe	26 Aug 1822
Jas., Jr.	3/12	M	Son of Shoemaker [Jas.]	Ireland	United States	James Monroe	26 Aug 1822
John	6	M	Son of Shoemaker [Jas.]	Ireland	United States	James Monroe	26 Aug 1822
Mary	4	F		Irereland	America	Carolina Ann	20 Jun 1825
Rachel	28	F	House Keeper	Irereland	America	Carolina Ann	20 Jun 1825
Sarah	11	F	Daughter of Shoemaker [Jas.]	Ireland	United States	James Monroe	26 Aug 1822
Wm.	3	M	Son of Shoemaker [Jas.]	Ireland	United States	James Monroe	26 Aug 1822
MCKIBBON, Ann	55	F	Seamstress	Ireland	U. States	Atlantic	19 Aug 1825

NAMES OF PASSENGERS	AGE	SEX	OCCUPATIONS	COUNTRY TO WHICH THEY BELONG	COUNTRY THEY INTEND TO INHABIT	SHIPS/DATES OF ARRIVAL	
MCKIE, Ann	20	F	None	England	United States	Baltic	21 Apr 1827
Catherine, & infant	24	F	Laborer	Ireland	U. States	Albion	9 Aug 1826
Elizh.	38	F		Gt. Britain	America	Ariel	20 Jul 1822
Elizth.	22	F		Gt. Britain	America	Ariel	20 Jul 1822
James	22	M	Blacksmith	England	United States	Baltic	21 Apr 1827
John F.	13	M				Domestic	31 Aug 1820
Martha	18 6/12	F	Spinster	Ireland	United States	Fabius	31 Jul 1829
Mary Fletcher	38	M				Domestic	31 Aug 1820
Thos.	30	M	Laborer	Ireland	U. States	Albion	9 Aug 1826
MCKIERNAN, Ann	20	F		Ireland	America	Carolina Ann	7 Apr 1826
MCKIGZON, Owen	30	M	Labourer	Ireland	U. States	Atlantic	19 Aug 1825
MCKILBIN, James	26	M	weaver	Irereland	America	Carolina Ann	20 Jun 1825
MCKILLIP, Edwd.	30	M	Mariner	Scotland	Great Brittan	Ranger	9 Jan 1824
MCKILLOP, Euphemia	18	F	Servant	Scotland	America	Camillus	12 Sep 1822
MCKILROY, Barthw.	31 8/12	M	Farmer	Ireland	America	Euphrates	26 Jun 1821
MCKINDLEY, Margt.	23	F		Scotland	United States	Culloden	17 May 1828
MCKINEY, Jane	33	F	Labourer	Ireland	United States	Meteor	26 Jun 1827
MCKINLAY, M.	30	M	Weaver	Ireland	U. States	Lady Hunter	18 Jul 1825
MCKINLEY, Edward	29	M	Labourer	Argyle (Tedland) Scotland	United States	Jean Hastie	27 Jul 1829
James	23	M	Labourer	Ireland	America	Minerva	15 Nov 1823
James	30	M	Merchant	Scotland	United States	Friends	7 Jul 1827
James	49	M	Carpenter	Scotland	United States	Trident	31 Mar 1827
John	24	M	Farmer	Scotland	U. States	Camillus	27 Jun 1826
John	25	M	Farmer	Ireland	United States	General Putnam	20 Jun 1825
John	25	M	Carpenter	Scotland	United States	Trident	31 Mar 1827
P.	50	M	Merchant	Scotland	New York	Lady Tompkins	25 Aug 1824
Peter	50	M	Merchant	Scotland	U. States	Azora	18 Apr 1825
MCKINLY, George	2	M				Domestic	31 Aug 1820
John	28	M	Blacksmith	Ireland	New York	Louisa	20 Jul 1826
MCKINNA, Rose	18	F	Spinster	Ireland	United States	Fabius	31 Jul 1829
MCKINNAN, P.	25	M		G. Britain	U. States	Camillus	8 Sep 1828
MCKINNER, Cath.	4	F	Daughter	Ireland	United States	Louisa	18 Apr 1827
Dugal	37	M	Farmer	Argyle (Tedland) Scotland	United States	Jean Hastie	27 Jul 1829
Ellen	28	F	Wife	Ireland	United States	Louisa	18 Apr 1827
MCKINNEY, Catherin	22	F	None	Ireland	America	Braganza	8 Aug 1825
Elizabeth	20		Farmer	Ireland	United States	Carolina Ann	12 Sep 1823
John	27	M	Farmer	Ireland	U. States	Francis	6 Sep 1827
May	20	F	Spinster	Ireland		Robert Fulton	4 Jun 1828
Samuel	7	M	Weaver	Ireland	United States	Carolina Ann	14 May 1827
MCKINNING, Edward	23	M	Labourer	Ireland	United States	Catharine	22 Jul 1825
John	30	M	Labourer	Ireland	United States	Catharine	22 Jul 1825
MCKINNON, Mary	10	F		Lochcarron, Lochcarron [Parish], Ross [County]	New York	Hero	19 May 1828
MCKINSIE, David	25	M	Baker	Scotland	U. States	Roger Stewart	9 Jun 1828
MCKINSLEY, Peter	45	M	Merchant	U.S.	America	Wave	15 Aug 1821
MCKINSTRY, —, Mr.	46	M	Merchant	U.S.	U.S.	Radius	9 May 1823
...	60	M	Clergyman	United States	United States	London	24 Jan 1823
J.	56	M	Merchant	U.S.	U.S.	Radius	27 Apr 1824
MCKINZEY, Elizabeth	2	F		G.B.	Philad.	Eliza Grant	29 Aug 1829
James	25	M	Cotton Spinner	G.B.	Philad.	Eliza Grant	29 Aug 1829
MCKINZIE, Alaxander	46	M	Farmer	England	United States	Jubilee	1 Oct 1828
D. C.	39	M	Navy	England	Canada	Congress	21 Nov 1823
James	16	M	Farmer	England	United States	Jubilee	1 Oct 1828
Jno. M.	27	M	Carpenter	Halifax	U. States	Hope & Esther	4 Oct 1825
MCKIRAN, John	40	M	Tailor	Great Britain	United States	Courier	26 Jun 1827
MCKIRK, Lawrence	34		Lock Smith	England	United States	Mary	15 Jul 1822
Thos.	36		Lock Smith	England	United States	Mary	15 Jul 1822
MCKIRKAN, Jane	22	F	Spinster	Ireland	America	Josephine	8 Dec 1827
MCKITTRICK, Elizabeth	27			Great Britan	United States	Newry	11 Jul 1827
John	34			Great Britan	United States	Newry	11 Jul 1827
MCKIVER, Wm.	19	M	Labourer	Glasgow, Barony [Parish], Lanark [County]	New York	Hero	19 May 1828
*to follow his occupation							
MCKLEAN, Henry	30	M	Priest	Ireland	U.S.	Panthea	13 Nov 1823

NAMES OF PASSENGERS	AGE	SEX	OCCUPATIONS	COUNTRY TO WHICH THEY BELONG	COUNTRY THEY INTEND TO INHABIT	SHIPS/DATES OF ARRIVAL	
MCKLIN, Ann	17	F	Farmers and Mechanics	Ireland	America	Constitution	1 Oct 1825
MCKLOCKLEN, A.	23		Labourer	Halifax	U. States	Edwin	26 Sep 1828
MCKNIGHT, Catherine	9	F	Girl	Ireland	United States	Trident	17 May 1825
Cathr.		F		Scotland	U.S.	Curler	19 Jul 1828
James	32	M	Farmer	Ireland	United States	Trident	17 May 1825
Jane	50	F	Widow	Ireland	United States	Trident	17 May 1825
John	13	M	Farmer	Ireland	United States	Trident	17 May 1825
Margt.	31	F	Spinster	Ireland	United States	Trident	17 May 1825
Mary	18	F	Spinster	Ireland	United States	Trident	17 May 1825
Patrick	11	M	Farmer	Ireland	United States	Trident	17 May 1825
Robert	23		Cooper	Ireland	United States	Fabius	18 Mar 1829
Robert	24	M	Farmer	Scotland	United States	Camillus	28 Apr 1824
Robt.		M		Scotland	U.S.	Curler	19 Jul 1828
Saml.	5	M	Child	Ireland	United States	Dublin Packet	22 Apr 1822
Thomas	8	M	Boy	Ireland	United States	Trident	17 May 1825
MCKNOLLY, Partrick	18	M	Labourer	Ireland	United States	Colossus	26 Aug 1828
MCKNOWN, Pat	20	M	Labourer	G. Britain	U. States	London	23 Sep 1828
MCKOINY, Elisabeth	25	F	Farmer	Ireland	U. States	Dickinson	30 Jul 1825
MCKOINY, Jane	22	F	Farmer	Ireland	U. States	Dickinson	30 Jul 1825
MCKONALD, Wm.	36	M	Gent.	Ireland	U. States	Howard Douglass	29 Jan 1828
MCKONE, Arthur	19	M	Laborer	Ireland	United States	Mary	1 Jul 1829
James	1	M	None	Ireland	United States	Princess Charlotte	6 Oct 1827
Kitty	25	F	None	Ireland	United States	Princess Charlotte	6 Oct 1827
Michael	28	M	Farmer	Ireland	United States	Princess Charlotte	6 Oct 1827
MCKOUN, Rose	21	F	None	Great Britain	United States	Roman	10 May 1828
MCKOWAN, John	16	M	Carpenter	Ireland	N. York	Trusty	12 Sep 1828
John	80	M	Carpenter	Ireland	N. York	Trusty	12 Sep 1828
MCKOWEN, James	23	M	Labourer	Ireland	United States	Wilson	28 Nov 1828
MCKOWN, M.	20	F	Servant	Ireland	United States	Josephine	30 Apr 1828
MCKREZZ, Thened. 25 4/12		M	Merchant	England	Mexico	Alfred	12 Oct 1827
MCKUE, —, Capt.	37	M		American	United States	Louisa	18 Apr 1827
MCKUTCHIN, Alexander	1	M	None	Scotland	United States	Mary & Susan	5 Aug 1828
Elisebeth	23	F	Weaver	Scotland	United States	Mary & Susan	5 Aug 1828
MCL...S..., William	32	M	Labourer	Scotland	United States	Samuel Robertson	9 May 1827
MCLA...LIN, Cathrin	9			Longford	Newyork	Peru	30 May 1828
MCLACHLAN, Bernard	54	M	Labourer	Scotland	United States	Samuel Robertson	9 May 1827
Da...i...	23	M	Labourer	Scotland	United States	Samuel Robertson	9 May 1827
Frances	...	F	Child	Scotland	United States	Samuel Robertson	9 May 1827
Martha	23	F	Spinster	Scotland	United States	Samuel Robertson	9 May 1827
Mary	1	F	Child	Scotland	United States	Samuel Robertson	9 May 1827
Mary	50	M	Wife	Scotland	United States	Samuel Robertson	9 May 1827
MCLAFFEY, Samuel	20	M	Labourer	Ireland	United States	Catharine	22 Jul 1825
MCLAIN, Andrew	24		Smith	Ireland	United States	Fabius	18 Mar 1829
Helen	20	F	Spinster	Scotland	United States	Friends	7 Jul 1827
Mathew	22		Farmer			Rufus King	7 Aug 1820
MCLAINE, Cathr.	22	M	Labourer	U. States	U. States	Wm. Penn	18 Sep 1827
Jane	29	F	None	England		Exchange	11 Jul 1823
Neal	33	M	Labourer	England		Exchange	11 Jul 1823
MCLAIRN, John	23	M	Paper Maker	Scotland	U. States	Superior	25 Sep 1828
MCLALLEN, David	30	M	Mason	Great Britain	United States	Roanoak	19 Sep 1827
MCLAMEE, James	18	M	Weaver	Ireland	United States	Wanderer	1 Aug 1828
MCLANAGH, James	38	M	Farmer	Ireland	U. States	Dickinson	30 Jul 1825
MCLANE, Agnes	22	F			U. States	Rockingham	29 Nov 1821
Charles	18/12	M			U. States	Rockingham	29 Nov 1821
James	25	M	Farmer	England	U. States	Rockingham	29 Nov 1821
MCLANGLAN, Mica	24	F	Labourer	Ireland	United States	Hope	12 Jun 1828
Peggy	18	F	Labourer	Ireland	United States	Hope	12 Jun 1828

NAMES OF PASSENGERS	AGE	SEX	OCCUPATIONS	COUNTRY TO WHICH THEY BELONG	COUNTRY THEY INTEND TO INHABIT	SHIPS/DATES OF ARRIVAL	
MCLANGLAN (cont'd)							
Mical	24	M	Labourer	Ireland	United States	Hope	12 Jun 1828
MCLANGTIN, Wm.	19	M	Labourer	Ireland	United States	Hope	12 Jun 1828
MCLAREN, Alexander	2	M	None	Scotland	U.S. of America	Friends	12 May 1826
Charles	19	M	Clerk	Ireland	United States	Friends	21 Oct 1825
Helen	19	F		Scotland	U. States	Percival	16 May 1821
Janet	29	F	None	Scotland	U.S. of America	Friends	12 May 1826
Jno.	20	M	Gardner	Scotland	U. States	Percival	16 May 1821
Margt.	22	F	None	Ireland	United States	Friends	21 Oct 1825
Mary	25	F	None	Scotland	U.S. of America	Friends	12 May 1826
Peter	27	M		Great Britain	United States	Active	25 Mar 1828
Peter	34	M	Cabinet Maker	Scotland	United States	Belmont	30 Aug 1828
Robert	27	M	Gardner	Scotland	U.S. of America	Friends	12 May 1826
MCLARIGIN, Patrick	23	M	Labourer	Ireland	United States	Hope	12 Jun 1828
MCLARON, Alex.	24	M	Carpenter	Scotland	United States	Louisiana	3 Nov 1827
MCLARTY, Benjn.	24	M	Mechanic	Gt. Britain	U. States	Combine	9 Sep 1824
MCLARY, ...abold	20	M	Labourer	G. Brittian	United States	Louisa	14 Jun 1825
MCLASKEY, Phillip	26	M	Weaver	Ireland	U.S.	Lady Hunter	10 Jul 1826
MCLASS, William	24	M		Great Britain	United States	Active	25 Mar 1828
MCLAUCHLAN, Isabela	14	F		Ireland	United States	Nancy	16 Jul 1824
John	18	M	Clerk	G. Brittan	U. States	Trafalgar	4 Jun 1822
Ann	28	F	Seamstress	England	United States	Essex	23 May 1828
Catherine	50	F	Matron	Ireland	United States	Robert Fulton	24 Jul 1826
Daniel	8	M	...	Ireland	United States	Carolina Ann	24 Oct 1825
Daniel	24	M	Merchant	Ireland	America	Hesperus	7 Jul 1820
Danl.	27	M	Laborer	Gt. Britain		Dalhouse Castle	13 May 1828
Grace	20	F		Ireland	U. States	Olive Branch	30 Oct 1823
Hugh	45	M	Labourer	Ireland	United States	Carolina Ann	24 Oct 1825
James	20	M		Ireland	U. States	William Barker	29 Aug 1823
Jas.	27	M	Mechanic	St. John, N.B.	United States	Henrietta	3 Jun 1825
Jno.	20	M	Farmers and Mechanics	Ireland	America	Constitution	1 Oct 1825
John	27	M	Farmer	Ireland	United States	L. M. Pelham	25 Jun 1822
Margaret	30	F	...	Ireland	United States	Carolina Ann	24 Oct 1825
Mary	16	F	Servant	Ireland	United States	Sarah G.	15 May 1828
Sarah	22	F	Spinster	Ireland	U. States	Josephine	7 May 1827
T.	30	M	Farmer	Ireland	U. States	Martha	28 Jan 1826
Walter	2	M	...	Ireland	United States	Carolina Ann	24 Oct 1825
MCLAUGHLEN, Ann	13			Ireland	Great Britain	Robert Burns	14 Jun 1824
Betsey	14			Ireland	Great Britain	Robert Burns	14 Jun 1824
Cornlius	11	M	children	G. Britain	United States	Louisa	14 Jun 1825
Jas.	11			Ireland	Great Britain	Robert Burns	14 Jun 1824
John	25 4/12	M	Shoe Maker	G. Britain	United States	Louisa	14 Jun 1825
Peggy	40			Ireland	Great Britain	Robert Burns	14 Jun 1824
Phillip	20 7/12	M	children	G. Britain	United States	Louisa	14 Jun 1825
MCLAUGHLIN, Allen	28	M	Laborer or Spinster	Ireland	United States	Sarah G	11 Sep 1827
Ann	18	F		Ireland	New York	Carolina Ann	15 Oct 1824
Anne	26	F	None	Ireland	United States	Mary & Harriet	3 Jul 1829
Barnard	24	M	Blacksmith			Commerce	22 Jun 1825
Bernard	22 2/12	M	Labourer	Ireland	New Jersey	Louisa	20 Jul 1826
Biddy	16	F		Lo...g..., Ireland	New York	Anthusa	24 Aug 1825
Bridget	17	M		Gt. Britain	U. States	St. George	20 Sep 1828
Bridget	30	F	None	Ireland	United States	Jubilee	13 Jul 1829
Catherine	5	F	None	Ireland	United States	Trident	18 Jul 1827
Charles	20	M	Labourer	Ireland	United States	Robert Fulton	24 Jul 1826
Charles	30		Labourer	Ireland	Great Britain	Henrietta	26 Nov 1825
Charles	55	M	Weaver	Ireland	New York	Carolina Ann	15 Oct 1824
Chas.	20	M	...	Ireland	United States	General Putnam	20 Jun 1825
Danl.	14	M		Ireland	United States	Gem	16 Jun 1824
Danl.	21	M	Carpenter	St. John, N.B.	United States	Lady Hunter	27 Dec 1825
Danl.	21	M	Labourer	Ireland	United States	Trident	16 May 1826
Danl.	30	M		Ireland	United States	William & George	14 May 1828
Dennis	21		Clerk	Ireland	Great Britain	Robert Burns	14 Jun 1824
Edward	17	M	Merchant	Ireland	U. States	Purrington	14 May 1827
Edward	29	M	Printer	United States	U. States	Saml. Smith	24 Jul 1826
Edwd.	13	M		Ireland	United States	Gem	16 Jun 1824
Eliza	11	F		Ireland	United States	Gem	16 Jun 1824

NAMES OF PASSENGERS	AGE	SEX	OCCUPATIONS	COUNTRY TO WHICH THEY BELONG	COUNTRY THEY INTEND TO INHABIT	SHIPS/DATES OF ARRIVAL	
MCLAUGHLIN (cont'd)							
Eliza	24	F		Ireland	United States	William & George	14 May 1828
Eliza	30	F	Seamstress	Great Britain	United States	Grecian	24 Sep 1828
Ellen	18	F	...	Ireland	United States	Gem	16 Jun 1824
Ellen	23	F	Spinster	Ireland		Robert Fulton	4 Jun 1828
Ellen	42	F	...	Ireland	United States	Gem	16 Jun 1824
George	23		Laborer	Ireland	Great Britain	Robert Burns	14 Jun 1824
George	44	M	Hatter	U. States	U. States	Abigail	10 May 1821
Hugh	39	M	Joiner	Great Britain	United States	Orbit	23 Oct 1826
J. M.	35	M	Merchant	Canada	Great Brittan	Amity	11 May 1821
James	1/12	M		Ireland	United States	William & George	14 May 1828
James	7	M	Child			Commerce	22 Jun 1825
James	22	M		Ireland	United States	William & George	14 May 1828
James	26		Labourer	Ireland	United States	Courier	15 Oct 1827
James	50	M	...	Ireland	United States	Gem	16 Jun 1824
Jane	24	F	Spinster	Ireland	United States	Trident	16 May 1826
Jno.	26	M	Laborer or Spinster	Ireland	United States	Sarah G	11 Sep 1827
Jno.	29	M	Labourer	Entrim	England	Flora	3 May 1825
John	12	M	Labourer	Ireland	United States	Robert Fulton	24 Jul 1826
Joseph	1	M		Great Britain	United States	Grecian	24 Sep 1828
Joseph	25	M		Gt. Britain	U. States	St. George	20 Sep 1828
Kitty	12	F		Lo...g..., Ireland	New York	Anthusa	24 Aug 1825
Mable	34	F	Wife			Commerce	22 Jun 1825
Margaret	12	F	None	Ireland	United States	Trident	18 Jul 1827
Maria	6	F	None	Great Britain	United States	Orbit	23 Oct 1826
Mary	...	F	...	Ireland	United States	General Putnam	20 Jun 1825
Mary	3/12	F	None	Great Britain	United States	Orbit	23 Oct 1826
Mary	10	F		Lo...g..., Ireland	New York	Anthusa	24 Aug 1825
Mary	11	F	Child			Commerce	22 Jun 1825
Mary	16	F	None	Ireland		Marchioness	13 May 1828
Mary	20	F	Servant	Ireland		William Tell	24 Oct 1829
Mary	22	F	Spinster	Ireland	United States	Gem	16 Jun 1824
Mary	22			Ireland	Great Britain	Henrietta	26 Nov 1825
Mary	26	F	Servant	Ireland	United States	General Putnam	20 Jun 1825
Mary	29	F	None	Great Britain	United States	Orbit	23 Oct 1826
Mary	45	F		Lo...g..., Ireland	New York	Anthusa	24 Aug 1825
Mary A.	8	F		Ireland	United States	Gem	16 Jun 1824
Matthew	8	M		Lo...g..., Ireland	New York	Anthusa	24 Aug 1825
Michael	1	M	None	Ireland	United States	Jubilee	13 Jul 1829
Michael	10	M	None	Ireland	United States	Trident	18 Jul 1827
Michl.	26	M	Farmer	Ireland	Ireland	Trident	17 May 1825
P.	24	M	Labourer	Entrim	England	Flora	3 May 1825
Peter	28	M	Labourer	Ireland	United States	Jubilee	13 Jul 1829
Phillip	13	M	Boy	Ireland	United States	Trident	17 May 1825
Robert	6	M		Ireland	United States	Gem	16 Jun 1824
Rose	6	F		Lo...g..., Ireland	New York	Anthusa	24 Aug 1825
Rose	40	F	None	Ireland	United States	Trident	18 Jul 1827
Sarah	18		Spinster	Ireland	United States	Courier	15 Oct 1827
Stephen	4	F		Ireland	United States	Gem	16 Jun 1824
Thomas	24	M	Weaver	Great Britan	United States	Franklin	15 Apr 1826
Thomas	34	M	Storekeeper	Ireland	New York	Louisa	20 Jul 1826
William	4	M	None	Ireland	United States	Trident	18 Jul 1827
William	45	M	Chandler	Ireland	United States	Trident	18 Jul 1827
Wm.	4	M	Child			Commerce	22 Jun 1825
Wm.	13	M		Lo...g..., Ireland	New York	Anthusa	24 Aug 1825
Wm.	22		Labourer	Ireland	G. Britain	Robert Burns	14 Jun 1824
Wm.	28	M	Farmer	Ireland	U. States	William & John	10 Jul 1824
MCLAUGHLINE, Owen	24	M	Farmer	Ireland	United States	Henry Kneeland	7 Jun 1828
Thomas	25	M	Distiller	Irereland	America	Carolina Ann	20 Jun 1825
MCLAUGHTON, W.	24	M	Servant	Great Britain	United States	Nestor	3 Nov 1820
MCLAUGLIN, Danl.	24	M	Merchant	Scotland	New York	Ariel	22 Feb 1823
John S.	41	M	Farmer	St. Johns	U. States	Isabella	28 Jun 1825
Michael	21	M	None	Ireland	U. States	Criterion	23 May 1826
Z. C.	29	M		Boston (U. States)	Boston, Mass.	Napoleon	7 Jul 1829
MCLAUVIN, —, Mrs.	30	F	Farmer	Scotland	U. States	Roger Stewart	9 Jun 1828

NAMES OF PASSENGERS	AGE	SEX	OCCUPATIONS	COUNTRY TO WHICH THEY BELONG	COUNTRY THEY INTEND TO INHABIT	SHIPS/DATES OF ARRIVAL	
MCLAUVIN (cont'd)							
Catharine	27	F		Scotland	U. States	Roger Stewart	9 Jun 1828
David	44	M		Scotland	U. States	Roger Stewart	9 Jun 1828
Janet	4	F		Scotland	U. States	Roger Stewart	9 Jun 1828
MCLAVIN, Jemima	20	M	Smith	England	U. States	York	4 Apr 1826
Peter	28	M	Smith	England	U. States	York	4 Apr 1826
MCLAW, John	24	M	Farmer	Ireland	America	Superior	12 Jun 1824
MCLE...ME, Rose	18	F	house maid	Ireland	United States	William	20 Jul 1829
MCLEA, —, Mrs.	30	F		Scotland	United States	Friends	13 Mar 1824
Arch.	25	M	Farmer	Scotland	U. States	Czar	29 Aug 1829
Margaret	4	F	child			Friends	13 Mar 1824
William	3	M	child			Friends	13 Mar 1824
William	30	M	Merchant			Importer	30 Oct 1820
MCLEAN, Alex	41	M	Farmer	Scotland	United States	Camillus	27 Oct 1829
Andrew	35	M	Labourer	Ireland	United States	Meteor	26 Jun 1827
Andrew	69	M	Weaver	Ireland	N. Jersey	Potomac	7 Aug 1827
Archd.	20	M	Labourer	Great Britain	United States	Frances Henrietta	17 Sep 1827
Archd.	34	M	Barrister at Law	Canada	Canada	Silas Richards	3 Apr 1826
Arthur	26	M	Weaver	G. Britain	United States	Dutchess of Portland	30 Oct 1826
Daniel, Mr.	45		Planter	Cuba		Hesper	9 Jun 1827
Donald	35	M	Farmer	Scotland	America	Mentor	21 Sep 1824
Geo.	27	M	Labourer	Scotland	United States	Samuel Robertson	5 Oct 1827
Hugh	18	M	None	Ireland	United States	Friends	21 Oct 1825
Hugh	40	M	Weaver	Scotland	U.S. of America	Camillus	16 Apr 1822
J.	23	F		Scotland	U.S.	Curler	19 Jul 1828
Janet	29	F	his wife [Arthur]	G. Britain	United States	Dutchess of Portland	30 Oct 1826
Jno.	23	M	Brick Maker	G. Britain	United States	Ariel	21 May 1827
John	7	M		Scotland	United States	Samuel Robertson	5 Oct 1827
John	26	M	Labourer	Scotland	U. States	Czar	29 Aug 1829
Mary	18	F	Spinster	Ireland	United States	Trident	17 May 1825
Mary	18	F		Ireland	N. Jersey	Potomac	7 Aug 1827
Mary	21	F		Great Britain		Ulysses	29 Oct 1822
Mary	30	F		Ireland	N. Jersey	Potomac	7 Aug 1827
Mary	30 2/12	F				Washington	15 Sep 1821
Pat.	30	M	None	Gt. Britan	U. States	Magnet	9 Apr 1825
Peter	3		Boy	Ireland	N. Jersey	Potomac	7 Aug 1827
Peter	32	M	Labourer	Great Britain	United States	Ganges	26 Oct 1826
Richard	7		Boy	Ireland	N. Jersey	Potomac	7 Aug 1827
Robt., Revd.	38 4/12	M	Minister of the Gospel	England	America	Washington	15 Sep 1821
Thomas	9		Boy	Ireland	N. Jersey	Potomac	7 Aug 1827
Thomas	28	M	Weaver	Ireland	N. Jersey	Potomac	7 Aug 1827
Wm.	30	M	Farmer	Scotland	United States	Camillus	27 Oct 1829
MCLEAR, Hugh	21	M	Merchant	St. Johns, N.B.	U. States	Mary Ann	11 Apr 1827
MCLEDSON, William	25		Laboring Class		United States	Atlantic	2 Apr 1827
MCLEECK, Hariet	26	F		Great Britain	New York	Philetus	21 Jul 1827
Jas.	36	M		Great Britain	New York	Philetus	21 Jul 1827
MCLEER, Hugh	60	M	Flax Dryer	Ireland	New York	Louisa	18 Apr 1827
Jane	20	F	Spintress	Ireland	New York	Louisa	18 Apr 1827
MCLEIRE, B.	40	M		Great Britain	United States	Mary	11 Jul 1820
MCLELLAN, Ann	54	F	Seamstress	Scotland	U. States	Camillus	27 Jun 1826
Farquer	27	M	Farmer	Great Britain	America	Samuel Robertson	26 Nov 1825
Jas.	22	M	Collier	Scotland	U. States	Czar	29 Aug 1829
John	24	M	Mason	Scotland	United States	Camillus	27 Oct 1829
Thos.	23	M	Artist	United States	United States	Louisiana	9 Aug 1826
MCLELLAND, Jamar	32	M	Farmer	Scotland	United States	William & Henry	19 Jul 1822
MCLEMME, Judith	16	F	house maid	Ireland	United States	William	20 Jul 1829
MCLENAN, Anne	3	F		G. Britain	U. States	Leavitts	25 Aug 1828
Barney	30	M	Labourer	G. Britain	U. States	Leavitts	25 Aug 1828
Kitty	8	F		G. Britain	U. States	Leavitts	25 Aug 1828
Mary	5	F		G. Britain	U. States	Leavitts	25 Aug 1828
MCLENAYHIN, Mary	18	F	Spinster	Ireland	America	Hesperus	7 Jul 1820

NAMES OF PASSENGERS	AGE	SEX	OCCUPATIONS	COUNTRY TO WHICH THEY BELONG	COUNTRY THEY INTEND TO INHABIT	SHIPS/DATES OF ARRIVAL	
MCLENNIN, Donald	34	M	Baker	Scotland	America	Maine	16 Jul 1821
MCLENSID, Michael	30	M	Laborer	Ireland	U. States	Albion	9 Aug 1826
MCLEOD, Alex.	32	M	Farmer	Scotland	United States	Belmont	30 Aug 1828
Alexander	24	M	Engineer	G. Britain	U. States	Armadello	22 Jun 1827
Barbara	4	F	None	Great Britain	United States	Purrington	8 Dec 1827
Donald	38	M	Mason	Scotland	United States	Belmont	30 Aug 1828
Donald	53	M	Farmer	Scotland	United States	Belmont	30 Aug 1828
George	1	M	None	Great Britain	United States	Purrington	8 Dec 1827
George	40	M	Taylor	Great Britain	United States	Purrington	8 Dec 1827
John		M	infant	Scotland	United States	Belmont	30 Aug 1828
John	27	M	Painter	Great Brittan	U.S.	Emulous	29 Jun 1827
Margaret	15	F	None	Great Britain	United States	Purrington	8 Dec 1827
Margt.	31	F		Scotland	United States	Belmont	30 Aug 1828
Violet	7	F	None	Great Britain	United States	Purrington	8 Dec 1827
Violet	39	F	None	Great Britain	United States	Purrington	8 Dec 1827
William	12	M	None	Great Britain	United States	Purrington	8 Dec 1827
Wm.	24	M	Merchant	U. States	U. States	Columbia	24 Dec 1822
MCLERIM, Janes	25	M		Scotland	U.S.	Curler	19 Jul 1828
MCLESE, Daniel	30	M	Laborer, Spinster or Child	Ireland	United States	Ann Maria	4 Aug 1827
Mary	6	F	Laborer, Spinster or Child	Ireland	United States	Ann Maria	4 Aug 1827
Peggy	19	F	Laborer, Spinster or Child	Ireland	United States	Ann Maria	4 Aug 1827
MCLESTER, M.	25 5/12	M	Labourer	Ireland	U. States	Fabius	22 Sep 1828
MCLEYMONT, G.	28	M		Scotland	U.S.	Curler	19 Jul 1828
MCLIERTE, Alexander	30	M	Joiner	Scotland	United States	Lunar	5 May 1828
MCLISTER, Sarah	25	F	Farmer	Ireland	U. States	Dickinson	30 Jul 1825
MCLOCKLIN, Dennis	22		Farmer			Rufus King	7 Aug 1820
Petre	23	M	Stone Cutter	U. States	United States	Neptune	5 Jul 1820
MCLOED, Janet	35	F	Spinster	Scotland	America	Camillus	12 Sep 1822
MCLOGHLIN, Jane	20		None	Dros...da, Ireland	Great Britain	Franklin	22 Jun 1827
Mary Anne	22		None	Dros...da, Ireland	Great Britain	Franklin	22 Jun 1827
P.	27		Labourer	Dros...da, Ireland	Great Britain	Franklin	22 Jun 1827
P.	30		None	Dros...da, Ireland	Great Britain	Franklin	22 Jun 1827
MCLOGHLING, Maria	25	F	None	Ireland	New York	Concordia	12 Oct 1826
MCLOGHLLON, John	25	M	Servant	Ireland	U. States	Henrietta	7 Jul 1825
MCLOON, Arthur	30	M	Farmer	Ireland	United States	Asia	29 Jul 1829
MCLORMAN, Chas.	23	M	Weaver	Antrim, Ireland	New York	Anthusa	24 Aug 1825
Eleanor	20	F		Antrim, Ireland	New York	Anthusa	24 Aug 1825
Sarah	6/12	F		Antrim, Ireland	New York	Anthusa	24 Aug 1825
MCLOSKEY, Patrick	28	M	Merchant	U. States	U. States	Birmingham	12 Oct 1829
MCLOUGHLAN, Henry	20	M	Shoemaker	Ireland	United States	Aurora	27 Apr 1825
Michael	37	M	...	Ireland	U. States	William	27 Jul 1824
MCLOUGHLIN,							
Bryan	23	M	Labourer			Ocean	17 Aug 1820
Henry	22 6/12	M	Labourer	Ireland	United States	Robert Fulton	24 Jul 1826
John	10	M		Ireland	New York	Amanda	23 May 1827
John	23	M	Doctor	Ireland	Ireland	Wilson	22 Jun 1824
Mary	8	F	Child	Ireland	United States	Robert Fulton	24 Jul 1826
Mary	16	F	Spinster	Ireland	United States	Robert Fulton	24 Jul 1826
Mary	24	F	Dress Maker	Ireland	United States	Princess Charlotte	26 Apr 1827
Own	28	M	Labourer	Ireland	United States	Robert Fulton	24 Jul 1826
Susan	22	F	Spinster	Ireland	United States	Robert Fulton	10 Aug 1827
MCLOUGHLON, John	25	M	Shoemaker	Ireland	United States	Aurora	27 Apr 1825
MCLOWAN, Brady	20	M	Labourer	Ireland	United States	Hope	12 Jun 1828
MCLOWERY, Wm.	21	M	Laborer	Ireland	United States	Ann Maria	18 Dec 1827
MCLOWTHER, Sarah	...	...	...	Ireland	United States	General Putnam	20 Jun 1825
MCLUCAN, John	23	M	...	Ireland	United States	General Putnam	20 Jun 1825
MCLUCAS, Alex.	6	M	Boy	Ireland	United States	Trident	16 May 1826
Geo.	2	M	Boy	Ireland	United States	Trident	16 May 1826
Jane	46	F	Wife	Ireland	United States	Trident	16 May 1826
Jas.	8	M	Boy	Ireland	United States	Trident	16 May 1826
Jno.	48	M	Farmer	Ireland	United States	Trident	16 May 1826

NAMES OF PASSENGERS	A G E	S E X	OCCUPATIONS	COUNTRY TO WHICH THEY BELONG	COUNTRY THEY INTEND TO INHABIT	SHIPS/DATES OF ARRIVAL	
MCLUCAS (cont'd)							
Mary	10	F	Child	Ireland	United States	Trident	16 May 1826
Mary	25	F	Spinster	Ireland	United States	Trident	16 May 1826
Robt.	16	M	Boy	Ireland	United States	Trident	16 May 1826
Walter	12	M	Boy	Ireland	United States	Trident	16 May 1826
Willm.	14	M	Boy	Ireland	United States	Trident	16 May 1826
MCLUGLEY, H.	20	M	Weaver	Ireland	New York	Trusty	12 Sep 1828
MCLUNE, —				G. Britain	U. States	Camillus	8 Sep 1828
MCLUNIN, J.	37	M	Merchant	Scotland	U. States	Climax	19 Apr 1828
MCLURE, Charles	35					Charlotte Corday	11 Sep 1820
Jane	24					Charlotte Corday	11 Sep 1820
MCM..., Bridget	27	F	None	England	United States	India	8 Jun 1827
MCMACKIN, Ann	34	M		Jamaica	U. States	Active	11 Mar 1823
MCMADAN, Andre	18	M	Notary	France	U. States	Montano	2 Sep 1828
MCMAGUIRE, Thomas	20	M	Glue Maker	Irereland	America	Carolina Ann	20 Jun 1825
MCMAHAIN, Anne	16	F		Ireland	United States	Washington	2 Oct 1828
MCMAHAN, Andrew	22	M	Labourer	Ireland	Ireland	Helicon	3 Aug 1826
Charles	9	M		Great Britain	United States	Ann	24 Sep 1822
Denis	20	M		Limerick	N. York	Thomas & William	25 May 1827
Jno.	19	M		Limerick	N. York	Thomas & William	25 May 1827
John	11	M		Great Britain	United States	Ann	24 Sep 1822
Margrat	22	F	Chandler	Ireland	New York	Virginia	7 May 1824
Mary	20		Spinster	Ireland	United States	Courier	15 Oct 1827
Mary	31	F		G. Britain	U. States	Wanderer	23 Jun 1828
Richard	33	M	Farmer	Great Britain	United States	Ann	24 Sep 1822
Sarah	20		Seamstress	Scotland	Great Britain	Henrietta	26 Nov 1825
Thomas	32	M	Chandler	Ireland	New York	Virginia	7 May 1824
MCMAHON, —, Mr.	35	M	None	Havana	U. States	Milo	15 May 1824
And.	28	M	Farmer	Ireland		L. M. Pelham	12 May 1823
Ann	16 10/12	F		Ireland	America	Carolina Ann	7 Apr 1826
Ann	28		Labourer	Ireland	New York	Marcella	18 May 1827
Archd.	23	M	Labourer	Ireland	United States	Mary & Harriet	3 Jul 1829
B.	11	F	Servant	Ireland	United States	Josephine	30 Apr 1828
B.	13 4/12	F		G. Britain	U. States	Wanderer	23 Jun 1828
Bridget	6	F	None	Great Britain	United States	Ocean	27 Jul 1825
Bridget	27	F	None	Ireland	U.S.A.	Dalhouse Castle	21 Aug 1829
E.	20	M	Labourer	G. Britain	U. States	St. George	7 Jun 1828
Edwd.	21	M	Clerk	Gt. Brittain	United States	Balaena	21 Aug 1824
Francis	27	M	Farmer	Ireland		L. M. Pelham	12 May 1823
George	25	M	Joiner	Ireland	United States	Andes	2 Oct 1828
Henry	30	M	None	Ireland	U.S.A.	Dalhouse Castle	21 Aug 1829
James	3/12	M				Governor Fenner	23 Jul 1829
James	23	M	Farmer	Drumballyrons	Drumballyrons	Aldebaron	21 Jan 1826
James	26	M	Labourer	Ireland	Rhode Island	Governor Fenner	23 Jul 1829
James	54	M	Farmer	England	United States	Dalhouse Castle	6 Sep 1827
John	4	M		G. Britain	U. States	Wanderer	23 Jun 1828
John	35		Labourer	Ireland	New York	Marcella	18 May 1827
M.	14	F	Servant	Ireland	United States	Josephine	30 Apr 1828
Margt.	10	F		G. Britain	U. States	Wanderer	23 Jun 1828
Martin	11 5/12	M		G. Britain	U. States	Wanderer	23 Jun 1828
Mary	2	F		Ireland		L. M. Pelham	12 May 1823
Mary	6	F		G. Britain	U. States	Wanderer	23 Jun 1828
Mary	16 1/12	F		Ireland	America	Carolina Ann	7 Apr 1826
Mary	17	F				Governor Fenner	23 Jul 1829
Mary	29	F		Ireland		L. M. Pelham	12 May 1823
Mary	50 6/12	F	Domestic	Ireland	United States	London	6 Feb 1829
Mary Ann	21	F				Governor Fenner	23 Jul 1829
Owen	23	M	Farmer	Ireland	America	Superior	12 Jun 1824
Patrick	5	M	None	Great Britain	United States	Ocean	27 Jul 1825
Patrick	31	M	Mason	Ireland	New York	Louisa	20 Jul 1826
Philip	28	M	Weaver	Great Britain	United States	Ocean	27 Jul 1825
Robert	20 2/12	M	Weaver	Ireland	United States	Atlantic	21 Jul 1827
Rosa	25	F	None	Great Britain	United States	Ocean	27 Jul 1825
Thomas	25		Labourer	Ireland	New York	Marcella	18 May 1827
Timy.	26	M	Labourer	Ireland	Newyork	Cortes	16 Jul 1827

NAMES OF PASSENGERS	AGE	SEX	OCCUPATIONS	COUNTRY TO WHICH THEY BELONG	COUNTRY THEY INTEND TO INHABIT	SHIPS/DATES OF ARRIVAL	
MCMAHON (cont'd)							
William	2	M				Governor Fenner	23 Jul 1829
MCMALIN, C.	25	F	Child	Ireland	N. York	Trusty	12 Sep 1828
MCMALSON, John	32	M	Labourer	Great Britain	U. States America	Ann Maria	29 Nov 1821
Patrick	36	M	Labourer	Great Britain	U. States America	Ann Maria	29 Nov 1821
MCMAMAN, Danl.	24	M		Ireland	United States	John & Adam	21 Sep 1822
MCMANAMAN, Neil	28	M	Labourer	Gt. Britain	U. States	Sarah G.	14 Apr 1828
MCMANAMUM, Betty	22	F		Ireland	U. States	Nancy	1 Sep 1823
Margaret	25	F		Ireland	U. States	Nancy	1 Sep 1823
MCMANAMY, James	18	M	Labourer	Ireland	United States	Robert Fulton	24 Jul 1826
Michal	6	M	Labourer	Ireland	United States	Robert Fulton	24 Jul 1826
MCMANCIS, Peter	30	M	Labourer	Ireland	U.N. States	Jane	7 Oct 1826
MCMANE, Francis	22	M	Labourer or Spinster	Ireland	United States	Champion	3 Nov 1827
MCMANEN, Eliza	25	F		Great Britain	U. States	Lady Hunter	28 May 1823
MCMANERS, Mary	19	F	Servant	Ireland	New York	Atlantic	6 Oct 1828
Sarah	20	F	Servant	Ireland	New York	Atlantic	6 Oct 1828
MCMANEY, Ellen	6	F	Child	Ireland	America	Wilson	16 May 1825
Terry	22	M	Labourer	Ireland	America	Wilson	16 May 1825
MCMANICE, Jas.	9	M	Labourer	Ireland	United States	Essex	23 May 1828
MCMANIHAN, John	25	M	Labourer	Ireland	United States	Ann Maria	21 May 1827
MCMANINAN, Edwd.	12	M	Labourer	Ireland	United States	Ann Maria	21 May 1827
Peggy	22	F	Spinster	Ireland	United States	Ann Maria	21 May 1827
MCMANIS, Catharine	18	F	going to her Husband	G. Britain	United States	Louisa	14 Jun 1825
Elanor	12	F		G. Britain	United States	Louisa	14 Jun 1825
John	22	F	Shoemaker	Ireland	United States	Wilson	6 Jun 1828
MCMANN, Barry	25	M	Weaver	Ireland	United States	Jubilee	13 Jul 1829
MCMANNA, Danl.	20	M	Farmer	Ireland	United States	Samuel Robertson	9 Apr 1828
MCMANNAMAN, James	16	M	Baker	Ireland	United States	Catharine	22 Jul 1825
Patrick	22	M	Blacksmith	Ireland	United States	Catharine	22 Jul 1825
MCMANNENEY, Wm.	27	M	Carpenter	U. States	U. States	Jason	25 May 1822
MCMANNIS, John	2	M		G. Britain	U. States	Mary & Harriot	8 Sep 1828
John	10 7/12	M		G. Britain	United States	Louisa	14 Jun 1825
John	19	M	Taylor	G. Britain	United States	Louisa	14 Jun 1825
John	20	M	Labourer	G. Britain	United States	Louisa	14 Jun 1825
John	22	M	Labourer	G. Britain	U. States	Mary & Harriot	8 Sep 1828
Judith	19	F	Wife	G. Britain	United States	Louisa	14 Jun 1825
Mary	20	F		Great Britain	United States	Lady Hunter	26 Nov 1823
Ormer	50	M		G. Britain	United States	Louisa	14 Jun 1825
Phillip	14	M		G. Britain	United States	Louisa	14 Jun 1825
MCMANNUS, Ellen	17	F	Labourer	Ireland	U. States	Two Marys	20 Apr 1825
Mary	20	F	Labourer	Ireland	U. States	Two Marys	20 Apr 1825
MCMANOR, Mary	19	F	Servant	Ireland	United States	Sylvester Healy	17 Oct 1825
MCMANUS, Andrew	24	M	Farmer	Ireland	United States	Dublin Packet	6 Dec 1827
Bridget	26		Spinster	Ireland	United States	Courier	15 Oct 1827
Catharine	24	F	Spinster	Ireland	America	Farmer	15 Nov 1823
Daniel	28	M	Farmer	Ireland	United States	Asia	29 Jul 1829
Dennis	26	M	Farmer	Ireland	United States	Dublin Packet	3 Sep 1822
James	26	M	Shoemaker	U. States	U. States	Cobbosse Conte	18 Apr 1823
James, Mr.	30	M	Merchant	U.S.	U.S.	Hesper	2 May 1826
Jas.	1 1/2	M	None	Great Britian	U. States	Henry Kneedland	7 Aug 1826
John	7	M	None	Great Britian	U. States	Henry Kneedland	7 Aug 1826
John	22	M	Labourer	Ireland	United States	Robert Fulton	24 Jul 1826
John	22	M	Weaver	Ireland	United States	Fabius	4 Jun 1828
Judith	2	F		Ireland	U. States	Alfred	7 Jun 1824
Margret	30	F	None	Great Britian	U. States	Henry Kneedland	7 Aug 1826
Mary	29	F		Ireland	U. States	Alfred	7 Jun 1824
Nicholas	5	M	None	Great Britian	U. States	Henry Kneedland	7 Aug 1826
Pat.	21	M	Schoolmaster	British ...	American States	Loyalty	9 Sep 1822
Patrick	22	M	Merchant	Ireland	United States	Fabius	4 Jun 1828
Philip	24	M	Labourer	Ireland	United States	Robert Fulton	24 Jul 1826
T.	7	M		Ireland	U. States	Alfred	7 Jun 1824

NAMES OF PASSENGERS	AGE	SEX	OCCUPATIONS	COUNTRY TO WHICH THEY BELONG	COUNTRY THEY INTEND TO INHABIT	SHIPS/DATES OF ARRIVAL	
MCMANUS (cont'd)							
William	18	M	Labourer	Ireland	United States	Robert Fulton	24 Jul 1826
MCMARAH, Danl.	22	M		Ireland	U. States	Howard	25 Jul 1823
MCMARKETY, Michl.	19	M	Labourer	Ireland	United States	Essex	23 May 1828
MCMARTIN, John	30	M	Labourer	Ireland	United States	Robert Fulton	24 Jul 1826
MCMASTER, Agnus, Capn.	27	M	Mariner	England	England	Helen	17 Dec 1827
Ann	47	F	None	England	Philiadelphia	Brighton	16 Nov 1826
Charles	18	M	Marble Cutter	C. Armannar [Armagh or Farmanagh?]	Boston	Nile	18 Aug
Hugh Adair	25	M	Watch Maker	Ireland	United States	Fabius	31 Jul 1829
John	13	M	None	England	Philiadelphia	Brighton	16 Nov 1826
John	45	M	Currier	England	Philiadelphia	Brighton	16 Nov 1826
Peter	22	M		Scotland	United States	Camillus	9 May 1827
MCMASTERS, John	30	M	Merchant	America	America	Brittannia	28 Feb 1827
MCMATHERS, Elizabeth	25	F				John Dickinson	14 Sep 1820
MCMAUGHTON, —,							
Miss	22	F	Lady	England	U. States	Cincinnatus	5 Oct 1824
MCMAVY, Francis	35	M	Butcher	Ireland	United States	William & Henry	19 Jul 1822
MCMEARY, Elivira	18	F	Spinster	Ireland		Robert Fulton	4 Jun 1828
MCMEE, Ann	23	F		Ireland	U. States	William	27 Jul 1824
James	28	M	Labourer	Ireland	U. States	William	27 Jul 1824
Michael	3	M		Ireland	U. States	William	27 Jul 1824
MCMELLEN, Alexander	22	M	Weaver	Ireland	United States	Loore	9 Sep 1822
Helen	30	F		United States	United States	Loore	9 Sep 1822
James	16	M	Copper Smith	United States	United States	Loore	9 Sep 1822
MCMEMMON, Mary	22	F	Labourer	Ireland	United States	Hope	12 Jun 1828
MCMENOMEN, Charles	25	M	Shoe Maker	Ireland	United States	Enterprize	23 Jul 1827
MCMENOMY, Margery	30	F	Servant	Ireland	United States	General Putnam	20 Jun 1825
MCMEURY, John	36	M	Gentleman	Ireland	United States	Nancy	15 Nov 1824
MCMIACKLE, Alexr.	2	M	None	Gt. Brittain	United States	Balaena	21 Aug 1824
Elizth.	6/12	F	None	Gt. Brittain	United States	Balaena	21 Aug 1824
Geo.	30	M	Farmer	Gt. Brittain	United States	Balaena	21 Aug 1824
Mary	28	F	None	Gt. Brittain	United States	Balaena	21 Aug 1824
MCMICHEL, Ann	2 2/12	F		Irereland	America	Carolina Ann	20 Jun 1825
Elizabeth	23	F	Servant	Irereland	America	Carolina Ann	20 Jun 1825
John	23	M	Labourer	Irereland	America	Carolina Ann	20 Jun 1825
Mary Ann	19	F		Irereland	America	Carolina Ann	20 Jun 1825
MCMIL, Archd.	26	M	Blacksmith	Great Britain	United States	Colossus	5 Jun 1827
MCMILLAN, Bid	22	F		Bridgetown, Barony [Parish], Lanark [County]	New York	Hero	19 May 1828
*going with her husband							
Bind	20	M	Stone Mason	Great Britain	United States	Samuel Wright	12 Oct 1829
Daniel	20	M	Block Maker	St. John	Great Britain	General Coffin	9 Mar 1827
Danl.	25	M	Weaver	Great Britain	United States	Roanoak	19 Sep 1827
David	22	M	Labourer	Glasgow, Barony [Parish], Lanark [County]	New York	Hero	19 May 1828
*to look for employment							
George	19	M	Farmer, Labourer or Spinster	Ireland	U. States	Meteor	4 Oct 1827
James	19	M	Printer	New Brunswick	United States	Hanford	19 Aug 1828
James	24	M	Labourer	Drummore	United States	Carolina Ann	11 Jun 1824
James	30	M	Farmer, Labourer or Spinster	Ireland	U. States	Meteor	4 Oct 1827
John	22	M	Baker	Scotland	United States	Curler	3 Mar 1828
John	25	M	Laborer	Ireland	United States	Carolina Ann	11 Dec 1826
John	45	M	Merchant	England	U. States	William Thompson	17 Dec 1827
John	50	M	Merchant	United States	United States	New York	19 Nov 1828
Peter	19	M	Labour	Great Britain	United States	Samuel Wright	12 Oct 1829
Thos.	26 3/12	M	Farmer	Wales	America	Minerva	15 Jun 1825
MCMILLEN, Alexander	21	M	Farmer, Labourer or Spinster	Ireland	U. States	Meteor	4 Oct 1827
Ann	17	F	Servant	Ireland	United States	Louisa	27 Nov 1826

NAMES OF PASSENGERS	AGE	SEX	OCCUPATIONS	COUNTRY TO WHICH THEY BELONG	COUNTRY THEY INTEND TO INHABIT	SHIPS/DATES OF ARRIVAL	
MCMILLEN (cont'd)							
Martha	34	F	Farmer, Labourer or Spinster	Ireland	U. States	Meteor	4 Oct 1827
Samuel	18	M	Farmer, Labourer or Spinster	Ireland	U. States	Meteor	4 Oct 1827
William	21 2/12	M	Weaver	Ireland	United States	Louisa	27 Nov 1826
MCMILLER, James	34	M	Mechanic	Great Britain	United States	Birmingham	15 Jun 1827
Wm.	36	M	...	Ireland	U. States of Amer	Courier	17 Mar 1827
MCMILLIN, James	20	M	Merchant	England	America	William	21 Sep 1821
Mona	30	F	Merchant	England	America	William	21 Sep 1821
MCMILLON, Patrick	35	M	Gentleman	Scotland	Scotland	Emily Cook	10 Apr 1826
MCMILLS, T.	20	M	Farmer	Ireland	U. States	Isabella	28 Jun 1825
MCMILWAS, Williams	15	M				Imperial	19 Jul 1820
MCMIMMONY, Jams	28	M	Labourer	Ireland	United States	Hope	12 Jun 1828
MCMIMS, Geo.	22	M	Labourer	England	United States	Essex	23 May 1828
MCMIN, P.	12	M		U. States	U. States	St. Croix	13 Sep 1827
Sarah	29	F		U. States	U. States	St. Croix	13 Sep 1827
MCMINER, Bridget	30	F		Ireland	U. States	Adno	5 Jul 1828
John	40	M		Ireland	U. States	Adno	5 Jul 1828
MCMINERNY, Jas.	19	M	Clerk	Ireland	United States	Trident	16 May 1826
Martin	44	M	shoemaker	Ireland	United States	Trident	16 May 1826
MCMINN, Robert	50	M	Planter	Great Britain	Nashville, U.S.	Florida	2 Oct 1828
Thos. B.	30	M	Merchant	Gt. Brittain	United States	York	6 Dec 1826
MCMINNE, James	20	M	Labourer	Ireland	N. York	Trusty	12 Sep 1828
MCMINSTY, Jas.	50	M	Gentleman	U. States	U. States	Radius	12 Jul 1825
MCMIRRAH, Michl.	24	M	Labourer	Ireland	United States	Hopes Delight	29 Nov 1827
MCMONAGLE, James	25	M	Farmer	Ireland	United States	Eliza	29 Aug 1822
MCMONMAN, John	16	M	Laborer, Spinster or Child	Ireland	United States	Ann Maria	4 Aug 1827
MCMORAN, Robt.	10			Ireland		Anacreon	7 Sep 1827
Robt.	30			Ireland		Anacreon	7 Sep 1827
MCMORELAND, Agness	25	F	Spinster	Glasgow	U.S. America	Camillus	10 Sep 1821
MCMORLAND, Peter	27	M	Shoe Maker	Great Britain	U. States	Great Britain	18 Mar 1828
MCMORRIS, Pat	26	M	Doctor	England	U. States	Thomas Ritchie	2 Jul 1827
R.	36	M	None	Ireland	U. States	Criterion	23 May 1826
MCMORRY, Patrick	40	M	Labourer	U. States	U. States	Wm. Penn	18 Sep 1827
MCMUILA..., Sarah	...	...	Servant	Ireland	United States	Edwin	29 Nov 1828
MCMULION, James	30		Farmer			Rufus King	7 Aug 1820
MCMULLAN, ...wn	...0		Laboring Class		United States	Atlantic	2 Apr 1827
A.	6	M		Scotland	U. States	Superior	25 Sep 1828
C.	2	M		Scotland	U. States	Superior	25 Sep 1828
Eliza	19 4/12	F		Ireland	U. States	Fabius	22 Sep 1828
H.	30	M	Weaver	Scotland	U. States	Superior	25 Sep 1828
Jane	...		Laboring Class		United States	Atlantic	2 Apr 1827
John	7		Laboring Class		United States	Atlantic	2 Apr 1827
M.	30	F		Scotland	U. States	Superior	25 Sep 1828
Michael	3		Laboring Class		United States	Atlantic	2 Apr 1827
Michael	15	M		Ireland	United States	William & George	14 May 1828
Patrick	2		Laboring Class		United States	Atlantic	2 Apr 1827
Rob.	8	M		Scotland	U. States	Superior	25 Sep 1828
Rosanna	6		Laboring Class		United States	Atlantic	2 Apr 1827
MCMULLEN, Alex.	14	M	Boy	Ireland	United States	Trident	16 May 1826
Alexr.	1/2			Ireland	Great Britain	Robert Burns	14 Jun 1824
Alexr.	19			Ireland	Great Britain	Robert Burns	14 Jun 1824
Biddy	18	F		Ireland	U. States	Olive Branch	30 Oct 1823
James	30	M	Labourer	Ireland	United States	Hesperus	14 Feb 1820
Jas.	18	M	Grocer	U. States	U. States	Jupiter	29 Jun 1825
John	25		Labourer	Ireland	Great Britain	Robert Burns	14 Jun 1824
John	26	M	Labourer	Ireland	United States	Robert Fulton	24 Jul 1826
Mary Ann	19	F	Farmer	Ireland	United States	L. M. Pelham	25 Jun 1822
Moore	20	M	Labourer	Ireland	United States	Borneo	14 Aug 1827
Richard	4 3/12	M		Irereland	America	Carolina Ann	20 Jun 1825
Robert	18		Labourer	Ireland	United States	Courier	15 Oct 1827
Sarah	19		Wife	Ireland	Great Britain	Robert Burns	14 Jun 1824
MCMULLER, Elizabeth	27	F	Lady	Ireland	United States	Borneo	2 Oct 1827
MCMULLIN, John	35	M	Farmer	Great Britain	United States	Colossus	5 Jun 1827

NAMES OF PASSENGERS	AGE	SEX	OCCUPATIONS	COUNTRY TO WHICH THEY BELONG	COUNTRY THEY INTEND TO INHABIT	SHIPS/DATES OF ARRIVAL	
MCMULLIN (cont'd)							
Nancy	22		Lady		U. States	Charlotte Corday	15 Jul 1820
Patrick	23	M	Farmer	Ireland	New York	Essex	6 Jul 1829
Susan	40	F	Spinster	Ireland	United States	Fabius	31 Jul 1829
William	35	M	Labourer	Ireland	United States	Fabius	31 Jul 1829
MCMULLON, Lucy	52	F		Ireland	America	Carolina Ann	14 Feb 1825
MCMULON, Malcolm	20	M	Merchant	Great Britain	United States	Friends	13 Jun 1825
MCMUMMIGLE, Josph.	17	M	Labourer	Ireland		Robert Fulton	4 Jun 1828
MCMUNN, Bridget	15	F	Spinster	Ireland	United States	Wilson	4 Oct 1827
MCMURCHY, Annabella	18	F		Great Britain	United States	Natchez	17 Aug 1822
Catherine	14	F		Great Britain	United States	Natchez	17 Aug 1822
Eliza	10	F		Great Britain	United States	Natchez	17 Aug 1822
Jean	12	F		Great Britain	United States	Natchez	17 Aug 1822
Jean	44	F		Great Britain	United States	Natchez	17 Aug 1822
John	16	M	Farmer	Great Britain	United States	Natchez	17 Aug 1822
Marion	1	F		Great Britain	United States	Natchez	17 Aug 1822
Mary	20	F		Great Britain	United States	Natchez	17 Aug 1822
Nelly	3	F		Great Britain	United States	Natchez	17 Aug 1822
Peter	50	M	Farmer	Great Britain	United States	Natchez	17 Aug 1822
Sarah	6	F		Great Britain	United States	Natchez	17 Aug 1822
MCMURDOCH, Thos.	21	M	Engineer	Gt. Britain	U.S. America	James Cropper	2 Aug 1827
MCMURDOCK, Gilbert	22	M	Merchant	Glasgow	U. States	Duchess of Gloucester	1 Dec 1823
MCMURRAN, John	20	M	Taylor	Ireland	New York	Carolina Ann	15 Oct 1824
MCMURRAY, Andrew	41	M	Merchant	Great Britain	United States	Orbit	23 Oct 1826
Edwd.	35		Farmer	Great Britan	United States	Newry	11 Jul 1827
Esther	28	F	Family	G. Brittian	United States	Louisa	14 Jun 1825
George	30	M	None	Scotland	United States	William Thompson	19 Aug 1829
Henry	18	M	Family	G. Brittian	United States	Louisa	14 Jun 1825
Hutchinson	60	F	Family	G. Brittian	United States	Louisa	14 Jun 1825
Jane	28	F	Family	G. Brittian	United States	Louisa	14 Jun 1825
John	23	M	Labourer	Ireland	America	Wilson	27 Nov 1826
John	51	M	Farmer	Belfast	United States	Minerva	30 Oct 1829
John	60	M	Weaver	G. Brittian	United States	Louisa	14 Jun 1825
Rose	27		Farmer	Great Britan	United States	Newry	11 Jul 1827
Wm.	24	M	Weaver	Ireland	United States	Atlantic	21 Jul 1827
MCMURREY, Augs.	20	M	Labourer	Ireland	United States	Essex	23 May 1828
James	24	M	Labourer	Ireland	Unt. St. America	Wilson	21 May 1827
MCMURRY, Bridget	23	F	Matron	Ireland	U. States	Josephine	30 Aug 1828
Daniel	7	M		Great Brittain	United States	Active	12 Sep 1828
Joseph	1	M		Great Brittain	United States	Active	12 Sep 1828
Lindsey	30	M	Farmer	Ireland	America	Wilson	27 Nov 1826
Margret	4	F		Great Brittain	United States	Active	12 Sep 1828
Sophia	26	F		Great Brittain	United States	Active	12 Sep 1828
Wm.	5	M		Great Brittain	United States	Active	12 Sep 1828
MCMURTERY, Thomas	20	M		Ireland	U. States	Nancy	16 Aug 1822
MCMURTREY, Sarah	21	F	Servant	Ireland	N. York	Trusty	12 Sep 1828
MCNA, Duncan	29	M	Farmer	Scotland	U. States	Camillus	27 Jul 1825
MCNAB, Alaxander	3 1/2	M	None	Great Britain	United States	Courier	26 Jun 1827
John	2	M	None	Great Britain	United States	Courier	26 Jun 1827
John	25	M	Merchant	Scotland	U.S.A.	Calliope	15 Aug 1827
John	30	M	Carpenter	Scotland	United States	Broke	16 Jul 1829
Malcolm	37	M	Farmer		U. States	Camillus	29 Jan 1829
Margaret	27	F	None	Great Britain	United States	Courier	26 Jun 1827
Primrose	20	F		Scotland	United States	Culloden	17 May 1828
Thomas	27	M	Smith	Great Britain	United States	Courier	26 Jun 1827
MCNAGLIN, Owen	20	M	Labourer	Ireland	N. York	Trusty	12 Sep 1828
MCNAIR, Catherine	30	F	Farmer	Scotland	America	Mentor	21 Sep 1824
James	22	M	Stone Mason	Scotland	New York	Indian Chief	19 Jun 1823
MCNALE, Auncan	24 9/12	M	Mason	England	America	John Dickinson	15 Oct 1826
John	21	M	Farmer	Great Britain	United States	Colossus	5 Jun 1827
MCNALLY, Barnd.	22	M	Labourer	Ireland	United States	Mary & Harriet	3 Jul 1829
Henry	24	M	Baker	Scotland	Gt. Britain	Friends	29 Apr 1822
Pat	25	M				Eliza Grant	6 Oct 1828
MCNALS, —, Mr.	40	M	Carpenter	U. States	U. States	Robert Edwards	11 Mar 1822
MCNAMAR, Owen	35	M	Carpenter	Ireland	United States	Silas Richards	3 Apr 1826

NAMES OF PASSENGERS	AGE	SEX	OCCUPATIONS	COUNTRY TO WHICH THEY BELONG	COUNTRY THEY INTEND TO INHABIT	SHIPS/DATES OF ARRIVAL	
MCNAMARA,							
Bernard, Doctor	53	M	Surgeon	Ireland	United States	Dublin Packet	28 Apr 1824
Dan	28	M	Farmer	Ireland	America	Liverpool	31 Aug 1827
MCNAME, James	18	M	Farmer	Great Britain	United States	Grecian	24 Sep 1828
MCNAMEE, Eliza	2	F	Labourer	Ireland	United States	Essex	23 May 1828
Jos.	35	M	Labourer	Ireland	United States	Essex	23 May 1828
Kitty	30	F	None	Longford		Mount Vernon	7 Jun 1824
Mary	23	F	Spinster	Ireland	U. States	Hibernia	29 Nov 1821
Mary	38	F	Labourer	Ireland	United States	Essex	23 May 1828
May	15	F	Labourer	Ireland	United States	Essex	23 May 1828
Michael	6	M	None	Longford		Mount Vernon	7 Jun 1824
Michael	22	M	None	Longford		Mount Vernon	7 Jun 1824
MCNAMER, Nancy	18	F		Ireland	U. States	Nancy	16 Aug 1822
MCNAMIER, Robert	30	M	Farmer	Ireland	U. States	Nancy	16 Aug 1822
MCNAMIS, William	18	...		Ireland	U. States	Nancy	16 Aug 1822
MCNANARNY, Jos.	25	M	Farmers and Mechanics	Ireland	America	Constitution	1 Oct 1825
MCNANCE, James	35		Farmer	Ireland, G.B.		London	29 Apr 1824
Mary	24	F		Great Britain		London	29 Apr 1824
MCNANEY, John	23	M	Farmer	Gt. Britan	America	Braganza	1 Dec 1824
MCNANNY, Willm.	20	M	Shoemaker	Ireland	United States	Wilson	27 Jun 1826
MCNAUGHAN, —, Mrs.	30	F		G. Britain	U. States	Camillus	8 Sep 1828
Arch.	6	M		G. Britain	U. States	Camillus	8 Sep 1828
Archibold	34	M	Type Founder	G. Britain	U. States	Camillus	8 Sep 1828
Christian	4	M		G. Britain	U. States	Camillus	8 Sep 1828
Jas.	9	M		G. Britain	U. States	Camillus	8 Sep 1828
John	12	M	Type Founder	G. Britain	U. States	Camillus	8 Sep 1828
MCNAUGHLIN, Helen	40	F		Scotland	United States	Shakespeare	24 Jul 1828
MCNAUGHT, Mal	90	M	Farmer	Great Britain	U.S. America	Prince Madoc	24 Sep 1821
MCNAUGHTON,							
Alexander	31 11/12	M	Dr. of Medicine	Scotland	Albany	Cadmus	27 Aug 1822
Jas.	28	M	Physician	Gt. Britain	U. States	Canada	4 Oct 1824
John	25	M	Gentleman	England	New York	Robert Edwards	17 Mar 1828
MCNAUGHTY, Catherin	70	F	None	G. Briton	United States	James Monroe	14 Dec 1820
MCNAUGLIN, Helen	3	F		Scotland	United States	Shakespeare	24 Jul 1828
Margt.	1	F		Scotland	United States	Shakespeare	24 Jul 1828
Mary	5	F		Scotland	United States	Shakespeare	24 Jul 1828
MCNEAGH, Rose	24	F	Farmer, Labourer or Spinster	Ireland	U. States	Meteor	4 Oct 1827
MCNEAL, Andrew	19	M	Labourer	Ireland	United States	Hope	12 Jun 1828
Catherine	23	F	Servt.	South Carolina	South Carolina	Hector	30 Dec 1820
F.	22	M	Mariner	U. States	U. States	Atlas	24 Jun 1828
John	19	F	Labourer	Ireland	United States	Hope	12 Jun 1828
Mary	6	F	Labourer	Ireland	United States	Hope	12 Jun 1828
Patrick	33	M	Labourer	Ireland	United States	Hope	12 Jun 1828
Sally	22	F	Labourer	Ireland	United States	Hope	12 Jun 1828
MCNEALE, Anne	3	F	None	Gt. Britain	U.S. America	James Cropper	2 Aug 1827
Anne	24	F	None	Gt. Britain	U.S. America	James Cropper	2 Aug 1827
MCNEAREY, Ann	28		Farmer	England	United States	Mary	15 Jul 1822
Ann	30		Farmer	England	United States	Mary	15 Jul 1822
Arthur	6		Farmer	England	United States	Mary	15 Jul 1822
Catharine	8		Farmer	England	United States	Mary	15 Jul 1822
Catharine	35		Farmer	England	United States	Mary	15 Jul 1822
Lawrence	60		Farmer	England	United States	Mary	15 Jul 1822
Owen	30		Farmer	England	United States	Mary	15 Jul 1822
MCNEARREY, Patrick	24	M	Labourer	G. Brittian	United States	Louisa	14 Jun 1825
MCNEEL, Alexander	27	M	Merchant	Scotland	United States	Nimrod	1 Jun 1821
Ann	1	F		Scotland	United States	Nimrod	1 Jun 1821
Elizabeth	18	F		Scotland	United States	Nimrod	1 Jun 1821
MCNEENEY, George	12	M		Irereland	America	Carolina Ann	20 Jun 1825
MCNEENY, Ann	34	F	House Keeper	Irereland	America	Carolina Ann	20 Jun 1825
MCNEFF, Cathr.	35	F	Servant	G. Britain	U. States	Wanderer	23 Jun 1828
Philip	18	M	Labourer	Ireland	United States	Wilson	6 Jun 1828
MCNEIDER, A. L.	37	M	Merchant	Gt. Britan	Gt. Britan	Canada	8 Jun 1826
MCNEIL, Christina	16	F		Scotland	United States	Hope	5 Dec 1827
Esabella	18	F	Spinster	Scotland	New York	Xenophon	3 Oct 1829
George	15	M		U.S. of Amer	U.S. of Amer	Canada	1 Oct 1827
George	19	M	Labourer	Argyle (Tedland) Scotland	United States	Jean Hastie	27 Jul 1829

NAMES OF PASSENGERS	AGE	SEX	OCCUPATIONS	COUNTRY TO WHICH THEY BELONG	COUNTRY THEY INTEND TO INHABIT	SHIPS/DATES OF ARRIVAL
MCNEIL (cont'd)						
James	22	M	Merchant	Halifax	Halifax	Greyhound 20 Mar 1820
John	30	M	Laborer	Scotland	United States	Mercator 18 Aug 1825
John	37	M	Paper Maker	Scotland	United States	Hope 5 Dec 1827
John	40	M	Labourer			Hanford 17 Jul 1828
Laurence	30	M	Clerk	Gt. Britain	United States	Neptune 23 Jan 1826
M. B., Mr.	28	M	Mercht.	U. States	U. States	Joseph Eastburn 6 Feb 1826
Sarah	29	F	Governess	England	U. States	York 12 Jul 1825
Sue	19	F		G. Brittain	U. States	York 10 Dec 1825
MCNEILL, Jany	26	M	Farmer	Scotland	U. States	Roger Stewart 9 Jun 1828
Peter	30	M	Weaver	Drumg...	Co. Down	Howard Douglass 11 May 1827
Samuel	24	M	Weaver	Ireland	U. States	Courier 17 Mar 1828
MCNEILLEDGE, Colin	29	M	Merchant	England	Canada	William Byrnes 11 Dec 1827
Duncan	39	M	Farmer	Inverness	New York	Hero 19 May 1828
*to follow his occupation						
MCNEILLY, Rose	25	F		Irereland	America	Carolina Ann 20 Jun 1825
MCNELEY, Francis	30	F	Farmer	Ireland	United States	Fabius 4 Jun 1828
MCNELLAN, Robert	29	M	Farmer	Ireland	United States	William & Henry 19 Jul 1822
MCNELLEDGE, D.	64	M	Mariner	Greenock	Scotland	Yamacraw 10 May 1821
MCNELLON, D.	25	M	Servant	Ireland	U. States	Henrietta 7 Jul 1825
MCNELLY, Eliza	32	F	None	U. States	U. States	Signa 6 Apr 1827
J.	30	M	Doctor	Great Britain	United States	Courier 26 Jun 1827
Michl.	28		Labourer	Ireland	America	Sarah 18 Aug 1829
MCNERNEY, Patrick	25	M		Irereland	America	Carolina Ann 20 Jun 1825
MCNESTRY, Pat	22		Farmer	Ireland		Westmoreland 1 Aug 1826
MCNEUGH, John	14	M	Farmer, Labourer or Spinster	Ireland	U. States	Meteor 4 Oct 1827
Robert	16	M	Farmer, Labourer or Spinster	Ireland	U. States	Meteor 4 Oct 1827
MCNEVIN, Thos.	27	M	Sadler	Ireland	America	Colossus 22 Aug 1829
MCNEY, John	34	M	Weaver	England	United States	Delta 24 Oct 1829
Peter	31	M	Weaver	England	United States	Delta 24 Oct 1829
MCNICHOLS, John	30	M	Merchant	Connecticut	U. States	Lyon 5 Jul 1825
MCNICKEL, Mary	18		Spinster	Ireland	United States	Robert Burns 18 Jun 1821
MCNICKLE, Robt.	19	M	Weaver	Ireland	United States	Henry Kneeland 7 Jun 1828
MCNICKOLS, Agnes	30	F	None	Great Britain	United States	Mary & Harriet 3 Jul 1829
Alexr.	28	M	Farmer	Great Britain	United States	Mary & Harriet 3 Jul 1829
Alexr., Junr.	4	M	None	Great Britain	United States	Mary & Harriet 3 Jul 1829
Peter	2	M	None	Great Britain	United States	Mary & Harriet 3 Jul 1829
MCNIEL, Daniel	26	M	Gunsmith	Scotland	Buenos Ayres	Factor 10 May 1821
John	23	M	Weaver	Ireland	United States	Louisa 18 Apr 1827
Peter	21	M	Farmer			Importer 30 Oct 1820
MCNIGHT, Ellen	20	F	Servant	Ireland	United States	Onion 1 Nov 1821
Robert	25	M	Farmer	Ireland	United States	Romulus 24 Jun 1826
MCNILLAN, James	1			Scotland	United States	Camillus 3 May 1828
Sarah	28		Wife, Going to her Husband	Scotland	United States	Camillus 3 May 1828
MCNIN, Robt.	30	M	Musician	U. States	U. States	St. Croix 13 Sep 1827
MCNINN, Catharine	26	F		Great Britian	United States	Mount Vernon 19 May 1823
Mary	7	F		Great Britian	United States	Mount Vernon 19 May 1823
Michael	5	M		Great Britian	United States	Mount Vernon 19 May 1823
Robt.	34	M		Great Britian	United States	Mount Vernon 19 May 1823
MCNIRE, Jane	18	F		Ireland	United States	Kleber 23 Jul 1827
MCNOBY, Christian	30	M	Servant	St. Croix	St. Croix	Ludwig 10 Aug 1825
MCNOLTY,						
Catharine	12 9/12	F		Ireland	U.S. of America	Douglass 6 Jul 1829
Ellen	45 11/12	F		Ireland	U.S. of America	Douglass 6 Jul 1829
MCNOME, Margaret	24	M	Labourer	Ireland	United States	Hope 12 Jun 1828
MCNONCE, John	30	M	Labourer	Ireland	United States	Hope 12 Jun 1828
MCNORTLAND, James	22	M	Labourer	Ireland	New York	Louisa 18 Apr 1827
MCNULLY, Bridget	36	F	Servant	Ireland	America	Weser 26 Jun 1821
MCNULTY, Anne	40	F	Servt.	Sligo	New York	Susquehana 27 Jun 1823
Biddy	22	F	Spinster	Ireland	United States	Asia 29 Jul 1829
Catherine	4	F	Servt.	Sligo	New York	Susquehana 27 Jun 1823
Catherine	8	F	Servt.	Sligo	New York	Susquehana 27 Jun 1823
Cathrine	20 3/12	F	Labourer	Ireland	U. States	Virginia 20 Jun 1825

NAMES OF PASSENGERS	AGE	SEX	OCCUPATIONS	COUNTRY TO WHICH THEY BELONG	COUNTRY THEY INTEND TO INHABIT	SHIPS/DATES OF ARRIVAL	
MCNULTY (cont'd)							
Eliza	27	F				Lady of the Lake	23 Aug 1828
Henry	25	M	Farmer	Ireland	United States	Meteor	19 Aug 1829
Jane	22	F	Matron	Ireland	United States	Robert Fulton	10 Aug 1827
John	27	M	Carpenter			Lady of the Lake	23 Aug 1828
John	40	M	Merchant	U. States	U. States	Josephine	30 Aug 1828
Mary	5	F	Servt.	Sligo	New York	Susquehana	27 Jun 1823
Mathies	24	M	Black Smith	Ireland	U. States	Virginia	20 Jun 1825
Robert	4	M				Lady of the Lake	23 Aug 1828
Seraha	30	F	Servt.	Sligo	New York	Susquehana	27 Jun 1823
William	22	M	Labourer	Ireland	United States	Robert Fulton	10 Aug 1827
MCNUMEE, Mary	25		Spinster	Ireland		Westmoreland	1 Aug 1826
MCNURNEY, Catherine	18	F	Spinster	Ireland	U. States	Courier	17 Mar 1828
MCNUTLY, Catharine		F		Halifax	United States	Dodge Healy	14 Oct 1828
James		M	Laborer	Halifax	United States	Dodge Healy	14 Oct 1828
James		M	Child	Halifax	United States	Dodge Healy	14 Oct 1828
MCNUTT, G. S.	29	M	Mariner	United States	United States	William	19 Jan 1820
Richd.	20	M		Ireland	United States	William & George	14 May 1828
MCNUTTEN, J.	24	F				Belfast	28 Sep 1820
MCNUTTY, Dennis	16	M		G. Britain	U. States	Camillus	8 Sep 1828
Hugh	16	M		G. Britain	U. States	Camillus	8 Sep 1828
Hugh	26	M	Labourer	Ireland	United States	Louisa	18 Apr 1827
Jean	28	F		G. Britain	U. States	Camillus	8 Sep 1828
John	12	M		G. Britain	U. States	Camillus	8 Sep 1828
Pat	20	M	Weaver	Ireland	United States	Louisa	18 Apr 1827
W.	34	M	Labourer	Ireland	United States	Robert Fulton	24 Jul 1826
MCOWEN, Bridget	2	F	None	Ireland	United States	Elizabeth	8 Jun 1827
Bridget	25	F	None	Ireland	United States	Elizabeth	8 Jun 1827
John	22	M	Weaver	Ireland	United States	Trident	17 May 1825
Mary	3	F	None	Ireland	United States	Elizabeth	8 Jun 1827
Patrick	1	M	None	Ireland	United States	Elizabeth	8 Jun 1827
Thomas	30	M	Farmer	Ireland	United States	Elizabeth	8 Jun 1827
MCOWENLY, Hugh	24	M	Labourer	Ireland	N. York	Trusty	12 Sep 1828
MCPAITLAND, John	19	M	Labourer	Ireland	U. States	Josephine	7 May 1827
MCPARLIN, Ann	3/12	F	Labourer	Barley Armagh, Scotland	Gt. Britain	Orozimbo	19 Oct 1822
Ann	20	F	Labourer	Barley Armagh, Scotland	Gt. Britain	Orozimbo	19 Oct 1822
Bernard	25	M	Lawyer	Ireland	New York	Trusty	12 Sep 1828
John	23	M	Labourer	Barley Armagh, Scotland	Gt. Britain	Orozimbo	19 Oct 1822
Wm.	12	M	Labourer	Barley Armagh, Scotland	Gt. Britain	Orozimbo	19 Oct 1822
MCPARLON, John	35	M	Millwight	Ireland	U. States	Josephine	30 Aug 1828
MCPARTAN, Andrew	24	M	Shoemaker	C. Armannar [Armagh or Farmanagh?]	Philedelphia	Nile	18 Aug 1829
Patt	28	M	Blacksmith	C. Armannar [Armagh or Farmanagh?]	Philedelphia	Nile	18 Aug 1829
MCPARTIN, May	21	F	Servant	Ireland	N. York	Trusty	12 Sep 1828
MCPARTLEN, Patt	26	M	Weaver	Ireland	America	Plutarch	18 Jul 1826
MCPARTNEY, Mary	27	F	Spinster	Ireland	U. States	Josephine	30 Aug 1828
MCPEAK, Allis	60	F	Matron	Ireland	United States	Robert Fulton	10 Aug 1827
Elizabeth	17	F	Spinster	Ireland	U. States	Josephine	7 May 1827
James	3	M	...	Ireland	United States	Robert Fulton	10 Aug 1827
John	32	M	Weaver	Ireland	United States	Robert Fulton	10 Aug 1827
Patrick	4	M	...	Ireland	United States	Robert Fulton	10 Aug 1827
Polly	6	F	...	Ireland	United States	Robert Fulton	10 Aug 1827
Rachel	32	F	Matron	Ireland	United States	Robert Fulton	10 Aug 1827
Thomas	0 6/12	M	...	Ireland	United States	Robert Fulton	10 Aug 1827
MCPECK, Esther	22	F	Wife	G. Britain	U. States	Wanderer	23 Jun 1828
James	28	M	Farmer	G. Britain	U. States	Wanderer	23 Jun 1828
MCPERTOCK, Esible	53	F	None	Scotland	United States	John Dickinson	12 Aug 1824
MCPHAA, Alixander	6	M	Sawyer	Scotland	Canada	Swift	16 Jul 1827

NAMES OF PASSENGERS	AGE	SEX	OCCUPATIONS	COUNTRY TO WHICH THEY BELONG	COUNTRY THEY INTEND TO INHABIT	SHIPS/DATES OF ARRIVAL	
MCPHAA (cont'd)							
Archible	52	M	Sawyer	Scotland	Canada	Swift	16 Jul 1827
Dolil	21	M	Sawyer	Scotland	Canada	Swift	16 Jul 1827
Dunkin	17	M	Sawyer	Scotland	Canada	Swift	16 Jul 1827
John	19	M	Sawyer	Scotland	Canada	Swift	16 Jul 1827
Kathren	40	M	Sawyer	Scotland	Canada	Swift	16 Jul 1827
Sarah	12	F	Sawyer	Scotland	Canada	Swift	16 Jul 1827
MCPHADAN, Cany	20	M	Labourer			Catherine	19 Aug 1825
MCPHAIL, Ann	8		Lady			Betsy	4 Sep 1820
John	34	M	Merchant	Great Britain	U. States	Indiana	11 Sep 1827
Pat	12		Gent			Betsy	4 Sep 1820
MCPHERSON, Ann	11	F	Daughter	Scotland	America	Camillus	12 Sep 1822
Duncan	18	M	Sadler	New Brunswick	United States	New Packet	15 Nov 1828
Easter	18	F	None	Great Britain	United States	Friends	13 Jun 1825
Edward	17	M	Farmer	United States	United States	Nestor	20 Nov 1821
Eliza	37	F	Spinster	Scotland	America	Camillus	12 Sep 1822
James	12	M	Son	Scotland	America	Camillus	12 Sep 1822
John	24	M	Farmer	United States	United States	Nestor	20 Nov 1821
John	40	M	Planter	England	England	Tontine	1 Jun 1826
John	45	M	Shoemaker	Scotland	U.S. of America	Friends	12 May 1826
Louisa	22	F		England	U. States	Elias Burger	12 Sep 1822
Orin	22	M	Currier	Great Brittain	U.S.	Trafalgar	22 Jun 1821
P.	47	M	Army	Scotland	Great Brittain	Jane	31 Jan 1827
Sam.	40	M	Mariner	U. States	U. States	Volant	30 Mar 1824
Saml.	17	M	Labourer	Alvey Invonsshire, Scotland	Gt. Britain	Orozimbo	19 Oct 1822
Wm.	17	M	Son	Scotland	America	Camillus	12 Sep 1822
Wm. L.	21	M	Merchant	U. States	U. States	Bayard	19 Mar 1824
MCPHINNEY, John	25	M		Jamaica	England	Pleiades	13 Nov 1826
MCPOO..., Ann	65	F	Servant	Ireland	United States	Carolina Ann	14 May 1827
Edward	60	M	Labourer	Ireland	United States	Carolina Ann	14 May 1827
MCQUAD, Ann	25	F	Spinster	Ireland	United States	Sarah G	19 Jun 1827
MCQUADE, Ann	3	F		Gt. Britain		Dalhouse Castle	13 May 1828
Betty	25	F	Spinster	Ireland	U. States	Josephine	7 May 1827
Bridget	24	F	Spinster	Ireland	U. States	Josephine	7 May 1827
Catharine	30	F		Gt. Britain		Dalhouse Castle	13 May 1828
Charles	6	M		Gt. Britain		Dalhouse Castle	13 May 1828
Eliz.	1			England	United States	Hugh Johnson	11 Jun 1828
Eliz.	22			England	United States	Hugh Johnson	11 Jun 1828
Felix	22	M	Farmer	Ireland	United States	Asia	29 Jul 1829
Isabella	4			England	United States	Hugh Johnson	11 Jun 1828
James	14 2/12	M	None	Ireland	United States	London	6 Feb 1829
Margt.	6			England	United States	Hugh Johnson	11 Jun 1828
Mary	2	F		Gt. Britain		Dalhouse Castle	13 May 1828
Mary	25	F	Spinster	Ireland	United States	Fabius	31 Jul 1829
Mary Jane	7			England	United States	Hugh Johnson	11 Jun 1828
Owen	30	M	Labourer	Ireland	America	Plutarch	18 Jul 1826
P. J., Revd.	41 3/12	M	Priest	Ireland	United States	London	6 Feb 1829
Patrick	17 6/12	M	Labourer	Ireland	United States	Fabius	31 Jul 1829
Thomas	22	M	Labourer	Ireland	United States	Catharine	22 Jul 1825
Thos.	22			England	United States	Hugh Johnson	11 Jun 1828
MCQUADLE, Elen	6	F	Labourer	Ireland	United States	Hope	12 Jun 1828
MCQUAID, Ann	26	F	Spinster	Ireland	U.S. of America	Meteor	19 Mar 1828
John	20		Laboring Class		United States	Atlantic	2 Apr 1827
Jos.	23	M	Labourer	Ireland	United States	Lord Wellington	28 May 1827
William	24	M	Labourer	Ireland	U.S. of America	Meteor	19 Mar 1828
MCQUAIDE, Biddy	18	F		Ireland	America	Carolina Ann	7 Aug 1826
Mary	19	F		Ireland	America	Carolina Ann	7 Aug 1826
MCQUAIL, Edward	23	M	Labourer	Ireland	United States	Hope	12 Jun 1828
John	24	M	Labourer	Ireland	United States	Hope	12 Jun 1828
Lawrence	40	M	Labourer	Ireland	United States	Dalhouse Castle	8 May 1827
Owen	22	M	Labourer	Ireland	United States	Hope	12 Jun 1828
MCQUALTEL, D.	35	M	Stonemason	Great Britain	United States	Britannia	29 Oct 1829
MCQUAY, Jas.	32	M		G. Britain	U. States	St. George	7 Jun 1828
MCQUEDLE, Mary	26	F	Labourer	Ireland	United States	Hope	12 Jun 1828
MCQUEEN, Agnes	5	F	None	Scotland	U. States	Camillus	27 Jul 1825
Alex	24	M	Laborer	Scotland	United States	Camillus	27 Oct 1829
An	40	F	None	Scotland	U. States	Camillus	27 Jul 1825

NAMES OF PASSENGERS	AGE	SEX	OCCUPATIONS	COUNTRY TO WHICH THEY BELONG	COUNTRY THEY INTEND TO INHABIT	SHIPS/DATES OF ARRIVAL	
MCQUEEN (cont'd)							
Ann	25	F		Scotland	U. States	Camillus	27 Jul 1825
Donald	3	M	None	Ireland	U. States	Josephine	27 Jul 1825
James	24	...	...	Scotland	America	Nimrod	9 Jul 1827
John	7	M	None	Scotland	U. States	Camillus	27 Jul 1825
John	24	M	Clerk	America	U. States	Camillus	29 Jan 1829
John	40	M	Farmer	Scotland	U. States	Camillus	27 Jul 1825
Lachlan	25	M	Farmer	Scotland	U. States	Camillus	27 Jul 1825
M.		M		Scotland	U.S.	Curler	19 Jul 1828
Malcolm				Scotland	U. States	Camillus	27 Jul 1825
Mary	20	F	Spinster	Scotland	U. States	Hector	18 Apr 1825
Murdock	12	M	None	Scotland	U. States	Camillus	27 Jul 1825
Peggy	6	F	None	Ireland	U. States	Josephine	27 Jul 1825
Peggy	14	F	None	Ireland	U. States	Josephine	27 Jul 1825
Roderick	28	M	Laborer	Scotland	United States	Mercator	18 Aug 1825
W.	35	M	Farmer	Scotland	U. States	Hector	18 Apr 1825
Wm.	27	M	Merchant	New York	U. States	Fly	9 Apr 1823
MCQUEERY, M.	18	F				Hanford	17 Jul 1828
MCQUETEN, Jas.	24	M	Shoemaker	United States	Philadelphia	Hope	2 Jul 1824
MCQUID, Andw.	15	M	Servant	Ireland	United States	Carolina Ann	11 Dec 1826
MCQUIDD, John	20	M	Carpenter	Ireland	United States	St. Michaels	23 Dec 1826
MCQUIDLE, Allen	25	M	Laborer, Spinster or Child	Ireland	United States	Ann Maria	4 Aug 1827
James	7	M	Laborer, Spinster or Child	Ireland	United States	Ann Maria	4 Aug 1827
Mackil	21	M	Laborer, Spinster or Child	Ireland	United States	Ann Maria	4 Aug 1827
MCQUILLAN, Jas.	30	M	Labourer	Great Britain		Moro Castle	6 Jul 1827
Richard	23	M	Labourer	Ireland	United States	William & Henry	19 Jul 1822
MCQUIN, James	40	M	Weaver	Ireland	U. States	Ann Maria	6 Jul 1824
Ml.	8	M	Laborer	Ireland	United States	Trio	13 Jun 1827
Nicholas	20	M	Weaver	Gt. Britain		Dalhouse Castle	13 May 1828
MCQUINN, Mary	30	F	Spinster	Ireland	U.S. of America	Meteor	19 Mar 1828
MCQUIRK, Andrew	30	M	Farmer	Gt. Britain	United States	Penelope	9 Sep 1828
Margt.	30	F		Gt. Britain	United States	Penelope	9 Sep 1828
Pat	28	M		Gt. Britain	United States	Penelope	9 Sep 1828
MCQUNON, Thos.	33	M	Labourer	Ireland	United States	Hope	12 Jun 1828
MCQUOID, Cathrine	20	F	...	Ireland	United States	General Putnam	20 Jun 1825
John	22	M	Weaver	Ireland	United States	Meteor	27 Sep 1826
John	25	M	...	Ireland	United States	General Putnam	20 Jun 1825
MCQUONE, Patrick	18	M	Labourer	Ireland	United States	Hope	12 Jun 1828
MCQURERY, —, Mr.	32	M	Gentleman	Great Britain	Great Britain	Visitor	30 Jun 1825
MCQUWNE, Mary	36	F	Labourer	Ireland	United States	Hope	12 Jun 1828
MCRAE, Harriet	20	F		England	United States	Richmond	4 Aug 1826
Jane	18	F	Dressmaker	England	United States	Richmond	4 Aug 1826
MCRAY, John	35	M	Labourer	Scotland	United States	Samuel Robertson	9 May 1827
MCREA, —, Mrs.	18	F		U. States	U. States	Constitution	17 Mar 1823
Wm.	18	M	None	U. States	U. States	Hippomenes	29 Nov 1822
MCREARNEY, Henry	21	M	Labourer	Ireland	United States	William & George	14 May 1828
MCREE, Andw.	26	M	Farmer	Ireland	United States	Marmion	17 Jun 1825
B.	18	M	Labourer	Ireland	United States	Josephine	30 Apr 1828
Thos.	20	M	Farmer	Ireland	United States	Marmion	17 Jun 1825
MCREEVE, James	24	M	Merct.	Ireland	U. States	Josephine	7 May 1827
MCREGAN, Thomas	18	M	Farmer	Ireland	U. States	Dickinson	30 Jul 1825
MCREHAN, Bernard	40	M	Labourer	Ireland	United S.	Hanford	19 Aug 1828
MCREILEY, Wm.	33	M	Merchant	England	U. States	Hudson	8 Oct 1827
MCREILY, Samuel	40	M	Farmer	United States	United States	Sarah G.	11 Jan 1828
MCRENOLDS, Pat	65	M	Labourer	Ireland	United States	Meteor	26 Jun 1827
MCREY, Wm.	20		Merchant	England	U. States	Alfred	24 Jul 1828
MCREYNOLDS, Rosy	23	F	Farmer	Ireland	U. States	Dickinson	30 Jul 1825
Sally	25	F	Farmer	Ireland	U. States	Dickinson	30 Jul 1825
MCRINNON, Wm.	30	M	Black Smith	U. States	U. States	Nature	2 Jun 1828
MCRITCHIE, Robert	23	M	Tailor	Scotland	United States	Camillus	9 May 1827
MCROBBIN, Sa.	22	F	D. Maker	Ireland	N. York	Trusty	12 Sep 1828
Thos.	24	M	Sergant	Ireland	N. York	Trusty	12 Sep 1828
MCROBLIE, Janet	42	F		Scotland	United States	Camillus	27 Oct 1829

NAMES OF PASSENGERS	AGE	SEX	OCCUPATIONS	COUNTRY TO WHICH THEY BELONG	COUNTRY THEY INTEND TO INHABIT	SHIPS/DATES OF ARRIVAL	
MCRODDEN, Sarah	22			St. John	U. States	Lady Hunter	5 Jul 1823
MCRORIE, Ann	22	F		Scotland	U.S.A.	Calliope	15 Aug 1827
Augusta	24	F		Scotland	U.S.A.	Calliope	15 Aug 1827
Bill	20	F		Scotland	U.S.A.	Calliope	15 Aug 1827
Duncen	2	M	None	Scotland	U.S.A.	Calliope	15 Aug 1827
E.	35	F		Scotland	U.S.A.	Calliope	15 Aug 1827
Elizabeth	18	F		Scotland	U.S.A.	Calliope	15 Aug 1827
John	55	M	Farmer	Scotland	U.S.A.	Calliope	15 Aug 1827
John, Jur.	6	M	None	Scotland	U.S.A.	Calliope	15 Aug 1827
Margaret	28	F		Scotland	U.S.A.	Calliope	15 Aug 1827
MCRORY, A.	48	M	Gent	French	Switzerland	Charlemagne	19 Sep 1828
C.	40	F	Gent	French	Switzerland	Charlemagne	19 Sep 1828
MCROW, Andrew	20	M	Labourer	Ireland	United States	Hope	12 Jun 1828
Jane	18	F	Labourer	Ireland	United States	Hope	12 Jun 1828
Wm.	16	M	Labourer	Ireland	United States	Hope	12 Jun 1828
MCRUTH, James	28	M	Farmer	Ireland	U.S. States	Splendid	14 Aug 1829
MCSADDER, James	14	M	Farmer	Ireland	America	Superior	12 Jun 1824
MCSAIGHT, Owen	30	M	Labourer	Ireland	United States	Trident	16 May 1826
MCSASTY, Margrtt.	17	F	Servant	Ireland	United States	Louisa	18 Apr 1827
MCSEAGERRY, Hugh	...	...	...	Ireland	United States	Carolina Ann	24 Oct 1825
MCSHADRICK, Ann	20	F	Traveler	England	U. States	Electra	7 Jul 1828
MCSHAFFEY, Ann	6	F			New York	Leader	18 Aug 1823
Danil. J.	7	M			New York	Leader	18 Aug 1823
John	35	M	Tobacconist	Ireland	New York	Leader	18 Aug 1823
Mary	5	F			New York	Leader	18 Aug 1823
Mary	36	F			New York	Leader	18 Aug 1823
MCSHAN, John	25	M	Labourer	...	U. States	St. Michael	21 Jul 1824
MCSHEAFE, Mark	29	M	Merchant	United States		Hannah	27 Dec 1827
MCSHEE, May	23	F	Seamstress	Great Britain	United States	Grecian	24 Sep 1828
Patrick	20	M	Labourer	Ireland	United States	Wanderer	1 Aug 1828
MCSHEFFERY, Patr.	21	M		Ireland	United States	William & George	14 May 1828
MCSHEFFEY, Charles	22	M		Ireland	United States	William & George	14 May 1828
MCSHIFFERY, John	37	M	Labourer	Great Brittan	U. States	John & Elizabeth	11 Dec 1826
MCSHIFFEY, Margaret	63	F	Spinster	Celdoffborough	...	Gleaner	24 May 1823
MCSONSKY, Pat	30	M	Bleacher of Linnen	Ireland	United States	Andes	2 Oct 1828
MCSORLEY, James	26	M	Farmer	Ireland	New York	Louisa	20 Jul 1826
MCSORLY, Patrick	25		Labourer	Ireland	United States	Robert Burns	18 Jun 1822
MCSORRELL, Patrick	29	M	Labourer	Tyrone, Ireland	Philadelphia	Anthusa	24 Aug 1825
MCSTEER, Thos.	20	M	Bleacher	Ireland	New York	Atlantic	6 Oct 1828
MCSULLY, Bridget	28	F	Spinster	Ireland	United States	Sarah G.	15 May 1828
Hug	25	M	Labourer	Ireland	United States	Sarah G.	15 May 1828
MCSULON, John	22	M	Labourer	Ireland	U. States	Sarah G	30 Jun 1828
MCSWEENEY, Jas.	24	M	Farmer	Ireland	U. States	Gem	28 Dec 1824
Margt.	21	F	Servant	England	U. States	York	12 Jul 1825
MCSWEENY, John	7	M		Ireland	America	William	21 May 1825
MCSWEGAN, Thos.	21		Weaver	Ireland	G. Britain	Robert Burns	14 Jun 1824
MCSWENEY, Catharine	17	F	House Servant	England	New York	Robert Edwards	17 Mar 1828
John	23	M	Mason	England	New York	Robert Edwards	17 Mar 1828
MCTAGGART, William	24	M	Sailor	Scotland		Marchioness	13 May 1828
MCTAGUE, P.	30	M		Ireland	United States	William Byrnes	6 Apr 1826
MCTAVISH, Jas.	32	M	Merchant		Canada	Columbia	11 Apr 1822
MCTEAR, Alexander	18	M	Shoe Maker	Ireland	New York	Atlantic	8 May 1828
MCTIVERMON, Edwin	25	M	...	G. Brittain	...	Robin Hood	20 Jul 1827
MCTUCK, Patt.	30	M	Farmer	Ireland		Cuba	24 Jun 1822
MCTULLY, John	21	M	Labourer	G. Britain	U. States	Hanford	18 Sep 1828
MCTUTTERS, Joseph	24	M	Baker	Ireland	United States	Catharine	22 Jul 1825
MCURDLE, Patrick	21	M	Farmer	Ireland	United States	Romulus	24 Jun 1826
MCUWEN, Daniel	33 9/12	M	Baker	U. States	U. States	Hiram	31 Oct 1828
MCVANE, Peter	55	M	Farmer	America	America	Samuel Robertson	26 Nov 1825
Peter, Jr.	28	M	Farmer	America	America	Samuel Robertson	26 Nov 1825
MCVAY, James	20	M	Weaver	Gt. Britain	U. States	Frances Henrietta	18 Apr 1825
Sally	16	F	Spinster	Gt. Britain	U. States	Frances Henrietta	18 Apr 1825

NAMES OF PASSENGERS	AGE	SEX	OCCUPATIONS	COUNTRY TO WHICH THEY BELONG	COUNTRY THEY INTEND TO INHABIT	SHIPS/DATES OF ARRIVAL	
MCVEAGH, James	22	M	Tailor	...	United States	Carolina Ann	11 Jun 1824
MCVEAL, Thomas	26	M	Labourer	Ireland	United States	Robert Fulton	10 Aug 1827
MCVEAN, Janet	26	F		Scotland	United States	Camillus	9 May 1827
John	1 1/2	M		Scotland	United States	Camillus	9 May 1827
William	3	M		Scotland	United States	Camillus	9 May 1827
MCVEIGH, Peggy	22	F	Spinster	Ireland	America	Superior	12 Jun 1824
MCVEY, James	21	M	Cordwaner	Ireland	America	Franklin	13 Aug 1827
William	35	M	Cotton Spinner	Great Britain	U.S. of America	Gratitude	3 Oct 1829
MCVICAR, Benjamin	25	M	...icar	U. States	U. States	Canada	13 Oct 1825
Mary	8	M		Denny, Denny [Parish], Stirling [County]	New York	Hero	19 May 1828
*going with her Father							
Peter	30	M	Labourer	Denny, Denny [Parish], Stirling [County]	New York	Hero	19 May 1828
*to look for Employment							
MCVICKAR, Elizabeth	12	F	Child	Britain	America	Camillus	9 Oct 1820
Elizabeth	35	F	Going to her Husband	Britain	America	Camillus	9 Oct 1820
Frances	6	F	Child	Britain	America	Camillus	9 Oct 1820
John	16	M	Child	Britain	America	Camillus	9 Oct 1820
MCVINA, John	31		Farmer	England	United States	Mary	15 Jul 1822
MCVINAR, Donald	22	M	Shoemaker	Scotland	U.S. of America	Camillus	16 Apr 1822
John	24	M	Shoemaker	Scotland	U.S. of America	Camillus	16 Apr 1822
MCWATERS, S.	24	F	his wife [Thos.]	United States	United States	India	24 Mar 1826
Thos.	29	M	Mariner, U.S.N.	United States	United States	India	24 Mar 1826
MCWATLY, Ja...	14	F	Dress Maker	Ireland	United States	Carolina Ann	14 May 1827
Thomas	20	M	Tailor	Ireland	United States	Carolina Ann	14 May 1827
MCWATSON, Jany	20	F	Spinster	Ireland	U. States	Meteor	19 Jul 1828
MCWHORTER, Andrew	32	M	Gentelman	Scotland		Jasper	30 May 1828
MCWILLIAM, Arthur	24	M	Weaver	Ireland	United States	Catharine	22 Jul 1825
MCWILLIAMS, Andrew		M	Chiefly farmers		United States	Factor	8 Jul 1829
Elizabeth		F	Chiefly farmers		United States	Factor	8 Jul 1829
Hugh	32	M	Weaver	Ireland	United States	Nancy	15 Dec 1824
Robert		M	Chiefly farmers		United States	Factor	8 Jul 1829
MCWRIGHT, Pred.	34	M	Lawyer	U. States		Quill	11 May 1825
MCYONCER, Mary	25	F	None	Scotland	U. States	Camillus	27 Jun 1826
Robert	27	M	Farmer	Scotland	U. States	Camillus	27 Jun 1826
MCZIGNAY, Francis	18	M	Merchant	Portugal	St. Bartholomews	Andes	22 Oct 1821
ME...G...N, L., Mr.	30	M	Musician	France		François I	19 Nov 1828
MEA, Ferdinand	28	M	Basket Maker	France	United States	Acasta	15 Jul 1822
MEACAULAY, Saml.	25 7/12	M	Gentleman	Canada	Canada	Leeds	29 May 1824
MEAD, Ann	25	F		England	United States	Cosmo	26 Aug 1829
Cathe.	20	F	Labourer	Ireland	United States	Trio	5 May 1828
Elizabeth	38	F		Great Britain	United States	Freak	14 oct 1828
Frances	5			England	United States	Cosmo	26 Aug 1829
Gabriel	26	M	Merchant	U. States	U.S.	Florida	17 May 1825
Gabriel	28	M	Merchant	U. States	U. States	Caledonia	10 Sep 1828
George	22	M	Labourer	Germany	U. States	Hudson	26 Jan 1825
James	40	M	Shoe Maker	Great Britain	United States	Freak	14 oct 1828
Jeremiah, Mr.	30	M	Labourer	England	U.S.	Acasta	11 May 1827
Marian	9/12	F		Great Britain	United States	Freak	14 oct 1828
Michl.	25	M	Labourer	England	United States	Loire	26 May 1828
Patt	22	M	Labourer	Ireland	United States	Jubilee	13 Jul 1829
Richard W.	42	M	Merchant	U. States	U. States	Edward	17 Aug 1820
Richard W., Jr.	14	M	Lad	U. States	U. States	Edward	17 Aug 1820
MEADE, Andw.	30	M	Farmer	Ireland	United States	Trio	13 Jun 1827
E.	32	M	Merchant	U. States	U. States	Worromontogus	23 Jun 1823
Garratt	19	M	Labourer	Ireland	United States	Trio	2 Oct 1828
Irana	22	F		Ireland	United States	Trio	13 Jun 1827
John				Ireland	United States	Trio	13 Jun 1827
M.	22	M	Labourer	Ireland	U. States	Greenhow	10 Mar 1823
Margaret	16	F		Ireland	United States	Trio	2 Oct 1828
Stephen	18					Trio	5 May 1828
MEADOW, William	34	M	Mariner	U.S. America	U.S. America	Ganges	15 Dec 1826
*Destitute Seaman put on board by the American Consul in London							
MEADOWCRAFT, Betty	12	F	None	England	United States	Hercules	24 Oct 1821
John	9	M	None	England	United States	Hercules	24 Oct 1821

NAMES OF PASSENGERS	AGE	SEX	OCCUPATIONS	COUNTRY TO WHICH THEY BELONG	COUNTRY THEY INTEND TO INHABIT	SHIPS/DATES OF ARRIVAL	
MEADOWCRAFT (cont'd)							
Mary	34	F	None	England	United States	Hercules	24 Oct 1821
MEADOWCROFF, Jno.	55	M	Printer	England	New York	Phoenix	29 Apr 1826
MEADOWCROFT, Alice	26	F	None	England	United States	Trident	18 Jul 1827
Alice	53	F	None	England	United States	Trident	18 Jul 1827
Harriet	19	F	None	England	United States	Trident	18 Jul 1827
John	15	M	None	England	United States	Trident	18 Jul 1827
Margaret	1	F	None	England	United States	Trident	18 Jul 1827
Martha	8	F	None	England	United States	Trident	18 Jul 1827
Robert	25	M	Calico Printer	England	United States	Trident	18 Jul 1827
MEADOWS, Mary,							
(his wife) [William]	27	F	Wife	Ireland	United States	Ann Maria	8 Jun 1824
William	28	M	Servant	Ireland	United States	Ann Maria	8 Jun 1824
MEAGER, Grace	43	F	Miner	G. Britain	U. States	Mary & Harriet	8 Sep 1828
James	13	M		G. Britain	U. States	Mary & Harriet	8 Sep 1828
Joseph	17	M	Miner	G. Britain	U. States	Mary & Harriet	8 Sep 1828
Wm.	45	M		G. Britain	U. States	Mary & Harriet	8 Sep 1828
MEAGHER, Jno.	33	M	Farmer	Ireland	United States	Trio	13 Jun 1827
MEAGUIN, John	6	M	Labourer	Ireland	United States	Edwin	27 Oct 1828
MEAGURES, Jas.	30	M	Labourer	Ireland	United States	Edwin	27 Oct 1828
MEAKELL, James	26	M	Millwright	Dun...	...	Howard Douglass	11 May 1827
MEAKINGS, B. H.	22	M	Merchant	U. States	U. States	L. M. Pelham	23 Aug 1823
MEAL, John	34	M	Lawyer	U. States	U. States	Don Quixotte	27 Jun 1827
MEAN, Brigtet	60	M	Servant	Ireland	United States	Edwin	29 Nov 1828
Ellen	3	F	Child	Ireland	United States	Edwin	29 Nov 1828
Patrick	60	M	Labourer	Ireland	United States	Edwin	29 Nov 1828
Peter	18	M	Labourer	Ireland	United States	Edwin	29 Nov 1828
Thomas	3	M	Child	Ireland	United States	Edwin	29 Nov 1828
William	52	M	Merchant	Great Britain	Great Britain	Martha	25 Nov 1820
MEANANS, E.	21	M	Merchant	South America		Haitien	10 Jun 1822
MEANETT, Joshua	30	M	Laborer or Spinster	Ireland	United States	Sarah G	11 Sep 1827
MEANS, Isaac, Mr.	30		Merchant	United States	United States	Alexander Mansfield	9 Nov 1822
MEARA, John	26	M	Laborer	Ireland	United States	Trio	13 Jun 1827
MEARDER, Barnabas	30	M	Linnen weaver	Ireland	America	Franklin	13 Aug 1827
MEARES, Ann	5/12	F		Great B.	U. States	William Neilson	26 Jul 1828
Ann	30	F		Great B.	U. States	William Neilson	26 Jul 1828
Charles	5	M		Great B.	U. States	William Neilson	26 Jul 1828
Francis	35	M		Great B.	U. States	William Neilson	26 Jul 1828
Richard	11	M		Great B.	U. States	William Neilson	26 Jul 1828
Wm.	2	M		Great B.	U. States	William Neilson	26 Jul 1828
MEARHAN, James	23	M	Yeoman	Ireland	United States	Borneo	9 Jul 1827
MEARL, Eliza	25	F		Great Britain	U. States	Lady Hunter	28 May 1823
MEARRIN, James	22	M	Farmer	Ireland	United States	Leonidas	3 Aug 1825
MEARS, Isaac	31	M		U. States	U. States	Robt. Edwards	4 Sep 1828
John	25	M		G. Britain	U. States	Robt. Edwards	4 Sep 1828
John G.	22	M	Officer	England	U. States	Bayard	9 Jul 1824
Thomas	30	M	Servant	London		Hannibal	28 Jul 1823
MEARTE, Blas	19	M	None	Spain	United States	Patriot	21 Nov 1820
MEARTIN, John D.	20	M	Laborer	Hannover	New York	Constitution	12 Jul 1827
O. Henry	19	M	Cabinet Maker	Hannover	New York	Constitution	12 Jul 1827
MEAS, Chas.	36	M	Shipmaster	U. States	U. States	Sisters	7 Jul 1826
MEASE, Thomas	43	M	Baker	England	U.S.A.	Robin Hood	6 May 1828
Thomas R., Jr.	14	M	Farmer	England	U.S.A.	Robin Hood	6 May 1828
MEASHAM, Jno.	34	M	Butcher	England	U. States	William & Jane	4 Apr 1825
MEBAN, P.	24	M	Farmer	Ireland	U. States	Isabella	28 Jun 1825
MECH, M.	27	M	Merchant	France	U. States	Edward Quesnel	3 Sep 1826
MECHALLITTER, P.	51	M	Trader	Italy	U. States	Frances	7 Aug 1826
MECHAN, Danl.	30	M	Farmer	England	U. States	Thomas Ritchie	2 Jul 1827
MECHELINE, Francisco	24	M	Merchant	Colombia	United States	Bogota	16 Dec 1826
MECHIN, Luce	29	F	his wife [Reynold]	France	United States	Helen	5 Sep 1828
Reynold	32	M	Painter	France	United States	Helen	5 Sep 1828
MECHNELLETH,							
Lewis	43 2/12	M	Spectulator	Sicaly	U.S.A.	Hesper	7 Dec 1827
MECKER, Jacob							
Frederick	47	M	Baker	Switzerland	United States	Elizabeth	27 Jul 1824
MECKLEHAM, Robt.	21		Farmer	Great Britain	United States	Camillus	12 Sep 1827
MECKLIN, —, Mrs.	26	M	Lady	Ireland	Ireland	William Byrnes	14 Apr 1824
MECUNIA, —, Mrs.	18	F	Weaver	Ireland	U. States	Atlantic	7 Aug 1823
Wm.	24	M	Weaver	Ireland	U. States	Atlantic	7 Aug 1823

NAMES OF PASSENGERS	AGE	SEX	OCCUPATIONS	COUNTRY TO WHICH THEY BELONG	COUNTRY THEY INTEND TO INHABIT	SHIPS/DATES OF ARRIVAL	
MEDCALF, Elizabeth	1	F		Great Britain	United States	Diana	30 Oct 1827
George	30 8/12	M	Brewer	England	United States	London	6 Feb 1829
Hannah	22	F		Great Britain	United States	Diana	30 Oct 1827
Thomas	34	M	Farmer	Great Britain	United States	Diana	30 Oct 1827
MEDDOWCROFT, B. B.	34	M	Labourer	Great Britain	United States	Cortes	18 Oct 1820
MEDDOWS, Joseph	18	M	Farmer	Great Britian	United States	London	24 Jun 1823
MEDEAD, Jack	20	M		Ireland	United States	Nancy R. Crowell	21 Sep 1822
MEDEN, Hernande	25		Merchant	Columbia	Columbia	Bogota	25 Oct 1827
MEDER, E., Mr.	30	M	Merchant	U. States		Florida	3 Jun 1824
MEDERNCOT, Patric	24		Labourer	County of Westmouth	N. York	Peru	30 May 1828
MEDFORD, William	23	M	M.D.	Great Britain	United States	Thomas Dickason	31 Jul 1829
MEDIAVILLA, Dionessus	24	M	Merchant	Spain	U. States	Eliza	20 Aug 1824
MEDLAN, Ann	21	F	None	Great Britain	United States	Comet	9 Aug 1822
Benj.	19	M	Farmer	Great Britain	United States	Comet	9 Aug 1822
Frink	12	M	Farmer	Great Britain	United States	Comet	9 Aug 1822
Jane	13	F	None	Great Britain	United States	Comet	9 Aug 1822
Jno.	25	M	Farmer	Great Britain	United States	Comet	9 Aug 1822
Mary	26	F	None	Great Britain	United States	Comet	9 Aug 1822
Matthew	17	M	Farmer	Great Britain	United States	Comet	9 Aug 1822
Saml.	23	M	Farmer	Great Britain	United States	Comet	9 Aug 1822
Susana	54	F	None	Great Britain	United States	Comet	9 Aug 1822
Thos.	27	M	Farmer	Great Britain	United States	Comet	9 Aug 1822
MEDLAR, James	25	M	Farmer	Great Briton	United States	Erin	26 May 1821
MEDLEN, Thos.	49	M	Farmer	Great Britain	United States	Comet	9 Aug 1822
MEDOLE, Catharine	28	F	Seamster	Ireland	United States	Eliza	29 Aug 1822
James	28	M	Farmer	Ireland	United States	Eliza	29 Aug 1822
Jane	5	F		Ireland	United States	Eliza	29 Aug 1822
Phoebe	3	F		Ireland	United States	Eliza	29 Aug 1822
MEDRA, John	26	M	Gentleman	England	United States	Hercules	21 Nov 1822
MEDWOOD, Jas.	25	M	Merchant	England	England	James Cropper	16 Oct 1826
MEDZGER, Andrew	16	M	Merchant	Ireland		Quatre Freres	29 Jul 1828
MEE, Pat	25		Carpenter	Great Britan	United States	Newry	11 Jul 1827
MEEGHAM, Mary	21	M	Spinster	Ireland	United States	Leonidas	3 Aug 1825
MEEHAN, Henry	22	M	Labourer	Ireland	U. States	Josephine	7 May 1827
Michael	25	M	Farmer	Great Britian	United States	Andes	19 Aug 1829
Polly	24	F		Great Britian	United States	Andes	19 Aug 1829
MEEK, Edward	24	M	pudler		uncertain	Mount Vernon	29 Aug 1828
Newburn	28		Farmer	Great Britian	Halifax	America	28 Jul 1826
MEEKER, Chs.	23	M	Merchant	U. States	U. States	New York	15 Jul 1825
J. W.	25	M	Merchant	New York	U. States	Paulina Julia	19 Dec 1823
MEEKIN, Henry	25	M	Labourer	Ireland	United States	Ann Maria	8 Jan 1824
MEEKS, Jno.	24	M	Merchant	N. York	U. States	Jane	17 Jan 1825
John	40	M	Seaman	Scotland	Pennsylvania	Psyche	16 May 1821
MEELEVY, Patrick	17	M	Labourer	Ireland	United States	Princess Charlotte	26 Apr 1827
MEEPS, Fanney	26	F	Spinster	New York	U. States	Chase	29 Apr 1825
MEERT, J. M.	38	M	Merchant		Holland	Hippomenes	7 Jan 1820
MEESER, N.	18	F		France & Switzerland	U. States	Bayard	14 Jul 1826
MEGAN, John	27	M		G. Britain	U. States	London	23 Sep 1828
MEGARY, Catharine	6	F		Ireland	U.States	Nancy	31 May 1823
Emily	8	F		Ireland	U.States	Nancy	31 May 1823
Fanny	30	F		Ireland	U.States	Nancy	31 May 1823
MEGEE, Cela	30	F	Spinster	Ireland	United States	Wilson	6 Jun 1828
MEGERS, Betty	34	F		Germany	U. States	Constitution	25 Jul 1823
MEGGINSON, Wm.	22		None	G. Britain	United States	Roman	10 Sep 1827
MEGGOT, Alexr.	38	M		Scotland	United States	Camillus	9 May 1827
MEGHETEET, L.	39	M	Merchant	Havan	U. States	Greek	3 Mar 1825
MEGIVERIN, Hugh	22	M	Flax Draper	Ireland	America	Hesperus	7 Jul 1820
Hugh, Jur.	13	M	...man	Ireland	America	Hesperus	7 Jul 1820
Nancy	9	F	...	Ireland	America	Hesperus	7 Jul 1820
MEGLONE, Catharine	20	F		Ireland	New York	Four Sisters	25 Sep 1823
MEGLOW, James	20	M	Farmer	Ireland	United States	Leonidas	3 Aug 1825
MEGNARD, Maurice	45	M	Merchant	France	America	Saluda	18 Jun 1825
MEGNE, Jose	40	M	Priest	Spain	Spain	Virginia	8 Mar 1828

NAMES OF PASSENGERS	AGE	SEX	OCCUPATIONS	COUNTRY TO WHICH THEY BELONG	COUNTRY THEY INTEND TO INHABIT	SHIPS/DATES OF ARRIVAL	
MEGNON, Jaques	43	M	Poet	Bardin	U. States	Bayard	5 Sep 1828
MEGOWIN, Beatey	18	F		Ireland	United States	Nancy R. Crowell	21 Sep 1822
Mary	20	F		Ireland	United States	Nancy R. Crowell	21 Sep 1822
MEGRAFF, Francis	45		Gentleman	Germany	U. States	Caledonian	16 Aug 1820
MEGRATH, Edwd.	11	M	Cabin boy	Ireland	United States	William	20 Jul 1829
H. J.	23		Merchant	England	England	Hopes Return	6 Sep 1823
John	19	M	Clother	Manchester	United States	Nile	17 May 1827
Pat	19	M	Weaver	Ireland	United States	Commerce	13 Jun 1828
MEGUE, Ellie	27	F	Spinster	Ireland	United States	St. Michaels	7 Jun 1827
MEGUIRE, Bernard	33	M	Merchant	Philada.	Philada.	Mary & Susan	27 Aug 1825
MEHAGAN, Mary	23	F		Ireland	United States	Trio	13 Jun 1827
MEHAN, Bridget	18	F	Spinster	Ireland		Robert Fulton	4 Jun 1828
C.	20	M	Farmer	Ireland	U. States	Isabella	28 Jun 1825
J.	24	M	Farmer	Ireland	U. States	Isabella	28 Jun 1825
J.	25	M	Farmer	Ireland	U. States	Isabella	28 Jun 1825
Patrick	30	M	Labourer	Ireland	United States	Robert Fulton	10 Aug 1827
MEHARA, Elisbath	4	F	Child	Ireland	United States	Fabius	31 Jul 1829
Elisbath	60	F	Spinster	Ireland	United States	Fabius	31 Jul 1829
Rebecca	26	F	Spinster	Ireland	United States	Fabius	31 Jul 1829
MEHER, Andrew	3 6/12	M		France	America	France	28 Mar 1829
Jane	27 4/12	F		France	America	France	28 Mar 1829
MEHGER, Lowely	20	M		Switzerland	U.S.	Francois I	8 Aug 1829
MEIDA, Antonio	21		Servant	Spain	Spain	Hind	12 Jul 1820
MEIER, —, Mrs.	28	F	Teacher	Great Britain	United States	Mariner	21 Aug 1827
Ann Catharine	9			Kingdom of Hanover	U. States	Princess Louise	10 Mar 1825
Ann Catharine	39			Dukedom of Aldenburg	U. States	Princess Louise	10 Mar 1825
Ann Margaret	6			Kingdom of Hanover	U. States	Princess Louise	10 Mar 1825
Ann Margaret	11			Kingdom of Hanover	U. States	Princess Louise	10 Mar 1825
C. H.		M	Merchant	U. States	U. States	Constitution	6 Jun 1822
Fredk. Wm.	15	M	Mercht.	Germany	United States	Hannibal	6 Sep 1824
Gesof Margaret	11			Kingdom of Hanover	U. States	Princess Louise	10 Mar 1825
Jacob	26	M		Bade	United States	Thetis	5 Jul 1821
John	42		Farmer	Kingdom of Hanover	U. States	Princess Louise	10 Mar 1825
John Henry	19			Kingdom of Hanover	U. States	Princess Louise	10 Mar 1825
John Herman	14			Kingdom of Hanover	U. States	Princess Louise	10 Mar 1825
Julius	33	M	Professor	Great Britain	United States	Mariner	21 Aug 1827
Martin	18	M		Bade	United States	Thetis	5 Jul 1821
Mathias	16	M		Bade	United States	Thetis	5 Jul 1821
Mathias	57	M	Farmer	Bade	United States	Thetis	5 Jul 1821
Olivia	1/12	F	None	Great Britain	United States	Mariner	21 Aug 1827
Wm.	1	M	None	Great Britain	United States	Mariner	21 Aug 1827
MEIN, Edward	26	M	Mechanic	Burmingham	U. States	Plato	18 Apr 1826
Sarah	26	F		Burmingham	U. States	Plato	18 Apr 1826
MEINADIER, A.	28	M	Supercargo	U. States	U. States	Haytie	2 Jul 1827
MEINHALT, Francis	27	M	Merchant	Germany		Ariel	24 Sep 1827
MEINKE, Joh. Wilh.	19	M	Joiner	Hamburg	New York	Maria Elizabeth	18 Jun 1827
MEIR, D. A.	22	M	Merchant	Germay	Germany	Caledonia	20 Jan 1829
George	8	M		England	U. States	Emily	25 Aug 1827
Jares, Jr.	10	M		England	U. States	Emily	25 Aug 1827
Jares, Mr.	31	M	Farmer	England	U. States	Emily	25 Aug 1827
John	4	M		England	U. States	Emily	25 Aug 1827
Margaret Adelbert	22			Kingdom of Hanover	U. States	Princess Louise	10 Mar 1825
Sarah	11/12	F		England	U. States	Emily	25 Aug 1827
Sarah, Mrs.	28	F		England	U. States	Emily	25 Aug 1827
MEIS, Samuel	60	M	Labourer	England	U. States	Ann	29 Jan 1820
MEITZER, Eva	23	F		Switzerland	U. States	Hewes	30 Oct 1829
Gotlip	11	M		Switzerland	U. States	Hewes	30 Oct 1829
Maria	52	F	Farmer	Switzerland	U. States	Hewes	30 Oct 1829

NAMES OF PASSENGERS	AGE	SEX	OCCUPATIONS	COUNTRY TO WHICH THEY BELONG	COUNTRY THEY INTEND TO INHABIT	SHIPS/DATES OF ARRIVAL	
MEITZER (cont'd)							
Sichmond	60	M	Farmer	Switzerland	U. States	Hewes	30 Oct 1829
MEKER, James	20	M	Labourer	England	U. States	Hope & Esther	10 Jul 1827
MELANO, Pedro	28	M	Merchant	Spain	Spain	Claudio	22 Mar 1828
MELBERING, Patrick	26	M	Labourer	Ireland	U. States	Harriet Frances	10 May 1827
MELDINTIEN, Jacob	48	M	Planter	Cuba	Spain	Ariel	30 Jun 1828
MELDON, Jane	20	F		United States	United States	Cortes	11 Aug 1823
MELDRAN, —	18	M	Lad	Scotland	U.S.	James & Margaret	4 Aug 1823
MELECK, John	52	M	Merchant	St. John, N.B.	St. John, N.B.	St. Michaels	27 Nov 1824
Mary	45	F	Wife	St. John, N.B.	St. John, N.B.	St. Michaels	27 Nov 1824
MELEN, John	20	M	Labourer	Ireland		Robert Fulton	4 Jun 1828
MELENS, Bess	22	F	Spinster	Ireland	United States	Sarah G	19 Jun 1827
MELFORD, Elizabeth	34	F				Amity	11 Sep 1820
Samuel	32	M	Merchant			Amity	11 Sep 1820
MELICK, Henery	24		Merchant	St. John, N.B.		Catherine	28 Dec 1820
James G.	18	M	Merchant	St. John, N.B.	St. John, N.B.	Ann Maria	1 Apr 1826
Mary	21	F	Lady	St. John, N.B.	St. John, N.B.	St. Michaels	18 Jul 1826
MELINT, L. G.	30	M	Merchant	America	America	Silas Richard	24 Oct 1829
MELISSANT, Victor		M	Merchant	France		Frederick	18 Feb 1822
MELISSENS, Ann	18	F		Philada.	U. States	Brandt	20 Sep 1822
MELIZET, —, Mrs.	35	F		France	U. States	Ellen	13 May 1824
Amelia	7	F		France	U. States	Ellen	13 May 1824
Cornelius	14	M		France	U. States	Ellen	13 May 1824
J. M.	37	M	Merchant	France	U. States	Ellen	13 May 1824
Sophia	8	F		France	U. States	Ellen	13 May 1824
MELLA, Ed.	22	M	Farmer	Great Britain	United States	Mary & Harriet	3 Jul 1829
MELLADY, Mary	28			Ireland	Ohio	Peru	30 May 1828
MELLAN, William, Mr.	40	M	Farmer	Grate Britain	...	Courier	14 Jun 1825
MELLEN, Thomas	20	M	Tailor	Ireland	United States	Hannah Eliza	23 Sep 1826
MELLENGER, David	72	M	Farmer	Citizen of United States	United States	Acasta	14 Jun 1824
MELLIN, Edward	30 4/12	M	Farmer	Ireland	United States	Atlantic	16 Dec 1825
Lawrence	25	M	Weaver	Ireland	United States	Robert Fulton	10 Aug 1827
MELLING, Thomas	23	M	...	...	...	Frances Henrietta	30 Jun 1827
MELLIS, Anthony	25	M	Merchant	Switzerland	U. States	Edward Quesnel	4 Aug 1828
MELLON, Hannah	36	F	None	G. Britain	U. States	James Monroe	18 Apr 1821
Henry	10	M	None	G. Britain	U. States	James Monroe	18 Apr 1821
John	12	M	None	G. Britain	U. States	James Monroe	18 Apr 1821
John	60	M	Grocer	Ireland	United States	Louisa	7 Oct 1824
Joseph	3	M	None	G. Britain	U. States	James Monroe	18 Apr 1821
Levi	6	M	None	G. Britain	U. States	James Monroe	18 Apr 1821
Margarett	59	F		Great Britain	United States	Corinthian	2 Sep 1824
William	35	M	Farmer	Great Britain	United States	Corinthian	2 Sep 1824
Wm.	34	M	Farmer	Great Britain	U. States	Birmingham	11 Oct 1828
MELLONY, Mary	24	F		Gt. Britain	United States	Penelope	9 Sep 1828
Peter	24	M	Farmer	Gt. Britain	United States	Penelope	9 Sep 1828
MELLOR, Abam	45	M	Farmer	Lancashire, England	United States	Aurelia	7 Jun 1826
Benjamin	27	M	Clothier	England	United States	Aurora	9 Jul 1827
Henry	1 6/12	M		England	United States	Aurora	9 Jul 1827
John	12	M	None	England	United States	Aurelia	7 Jun 1826
Judith	23	F		England	United States	Aurora	9 Jul 1827
Thos.	28	M	Brick Layer	England	United States	Aurelia	7 Jun 1826
MELLOW, Mark	24	M	Weaver	Ireland	United States	Catharine	22 Jul 1825
Mary	18	F	Spinster	Ireland	United States	Catharine	22 Jul 1825
MELLS, S.	23	M	Shoe Maker	Port au Prince	New York	Jean Baptiste	11 Aug 1828
MELLUMANN, E.	20	M	None	Germany	U. States	Louise	28 Jul 1823
MELLY, Ferdinand	20		Merchant	Geneva	New York	Don Quixote	19 Aug 1825
Winifred	20	F	Spinster	Ireland	United S.	Hanford	19 Aug 1828
MELNER, B.	40	M	Mariner	New York	U. States	Signal	12 Jul 1825
MELOCK, —, Mr.	22	M	Merchant	St. John, N.B.	St. John, N.B.	Nancy	16 Aug 1822
MELOR, Robert	26	M	Farmer	Scotland	New York	Lima	5 Aug 1829
Robert	26	M	Farmer	Scotland	New York	Lima	5 Aug 1829
MELORLY, Jos.	24	M	Labourer	England	United States	Nimrod	31 Jul 1828
MELRANI, J. F.	23	M	Merchant	Spain	Spain	Sarah Ann	8 May 1822
MELRILL, —, Mr.			Merchant	England	England	Henrietta	18 Aug 1829
MELSON, Benjamin	35	M	Merchant	U. States	U. States	Lord Wellington	17 Mar 1823

NAMES OF PASSENGERS	AGE	SEX	OCCUPATIONS	COUNTRY TO WHICH THEY BELONG	COUNTRY THEY INTEND TO INHABIT	SHIPS/DATES OF ARRIVAL	
MELSON (cont'd)							
Elizabeth	26	F	...	Ireland	United States	Wilson	22 Jun 1824
Joseph	30	M	...	Ireland	United States	Wilson	22 Jun 1824
MELTHROSS, George	34	M	Merchant	Denmark	U. States	Catherine	3 Jul 1820
Maria	27	F	Lady	Denmark	U. States	Catherine	3 Jul 1820
MELTZER, C.	24	M	Butcher	Germany	United States	Howard	15 Jun 1825
MELVILLE, Isabella	1	F		Scotland	United States	Culloden	17 May 1828
Isabella	38	F		Scotland	United States	Culloden	17 May 1828
John	38	M	Joiner	Scotland	United States	Culloden	17 May 1828
Peter	8	M		Scotland	United States	Culloden	17 May 1828
William	6	M		Scotland	United States	Culloden	17 May 1828
MEMBEDRING, Barbe	2	F	his family [Jean]	Germany	United States	Wm. Osborne	16 Sep 1828
Catherine	40	F	his family [Jean]	Germany	United States	Wm. Osborne	16 Sep 1828
Francis	1	M	his family [Jean]	Germany	United States	Wm. Osborne	16 Sep 1828
Jean	42	M	Cooper	Germany	United States	Wm. Osborne	16 Sep 1828
Joseph	4	M	his family [Jean]	Germany	United States	Wm. Osborne	16 Sep 1828
MEMDISH, Mathew	40	M	Gentleman	Ireland	United States	Sarah Ann	11 Jan 1827
MEME, G. H.	41	M	Merchant	Germany	U. States	James M	15 Sep 1828
MENARDIE, P.	53	M	Merchant	W. Indies	U. States	Cadmus	28 May 1821
MENCHAL, Andrew	6/12			St. John	U. States	Lady Hunter	5 Jul 1823
Hannah	26			St. John	U. States	Lady Hunter	5 Jul 1823
James	28	M	Farmer	St. John	U. States	Lady Hunter	5 Jul 1823
MENCHEL, James	2			St. John	U. States	Lady Hunter	5 Jul 1823
MENDE, Wm.		M	Cooper	...	United States	Minerva	30 Oct 1827
MENDES, J. M.	45	M	Curate	Mexico	Mexico	General Brown	10 Dec 1823
MENDEZ, Sarah, Miss	27	F		England	United States	Hiram	14 Aug 1829
MENDIA, Josea	25	M	Merchant	Spain	Havana	Robert Fulton	22 May 1824
Joseph	32	M	Merchant	France	U. States	Victoria	9 Sep 1828
MENDOZE, Catherine	30	F	Lady	Naturalized U.S.	New York	Robert Fulton	22 May 1824
MENDS, Charlotte Ann	3			England	Canada	Venus	4 Oct 1821
Charlotte Ann	29			London	Canada	Venus	4 Oct 1821
John D.	7/12			England	Canada	Venus	4 Oct 1821
Mary Ann	2			England	Canada	Venus	4 Oct 1821
Mathew Bowen	31		Navl Offer.	Pembroke	Canada	Venus	4 Oct 1821
Mathew Thos.	5		Child	England	Canada	Venus	4 Oct 1821
MENENDEZ, Ballazer	25	M	Merchant	Spain	United States	Montano	4 Nov 1823
MENEY, Robt.	24	M	Labourer	Ireland	U. States	Hudson	26 Jan 1825
MENEZZO, Antonio	43	M	Merchant	Italy	U.S.	Edward Quesnel	19 Oct 1829
MENFENN, John	25	M	Labourer	Ireland	U. States	Bellville	14 May 1827
MENG, Wm.	30	M	Joiner	Bermuda	U. States	Agnes	1 Jul 1825
MENGAL, Jan Hendrick	36	M	Bakker	Hoofgeismar	United States	Juffraw Johanna	16 Oct 1821
MENGIBAR, Manl.	31	M	Merchant	Caracas	Caracas	Herald	21 Sep 1824
MENIATURE, James	25	M	Laborer	St. John, N.B.	United States	St. Michaels	11 May 1826
MENLY, Mary	21	F		G. Britain	U. States	Mary & Harriot	8 Sep 1828
MENNCHEN, Johanna	6	F	Child	Ireland	United States	Edwin	27 Oct 1828
Julia	30	F	Servant	Ireland	United States	Edwin	27 Oct 1828
Michael	3	M	Child	Ireland	United States	Edwin	27 Oct 1828
MENNENER, Ann	25	F	Servant	Ireland	U. States	Henrietta	7 Jul 1825
Peter	27	M	Servant	Ireland	U. States	Henrietta	7 Jul 1825
MENNING, Gerald	40	M	Labourer	Ireland	United States	Thomas	13 Dec 1827
MENNT, E.	40	M	Mariner	U. States	U. States	Georgiana	25 Jun 1824
MENOGE, Jno.	25	M	Merchant	Spain	Spain	Packet	10 Jul 1823
MENON, D., The Count	38	M	Of the French Legation	France	French	Howard	4 May 1827
MENSCH, Frederick Augustus, Esq.	31	M	Merchant	New York	New York	Europa	12 Oct 1829
Henriette, his lady [Frederick Augustus]	21 9/12	F		New York	New York	Europa	12 Oct 1829
MENSES, F.	13	M		Mexico	U. States	Laveria	23 Jul 1828
MENSLEY, Jesse	30	M	Cotton Spinner	Hepton Brige		Aurora	8 Jun 1827
MENTON, Martin	26	M	Merchant	France	U. States	Cadmus	28 May 1821
MENTRAL, B.	38	M	Slingman	Havre	U. States	Edward Bonaffe	23 Jul 1828
MENZIE, David	27			Kilpatric	N. York	Peru	30 May 1828
MENZIES, —	50	F		Glasgow, St. Johns [Parish], Lanark [County]	New York	Hero	19 May 1828

NAMES OF PASSENGERS	AGE	SEX	OCCUPATIONS	COUNTRY TO WHICH THEY BELONG	COUNTRY THEY INTEND TO INHABIT	SHIPS/DATES OF ARRIVAL	
MENZIES (cont'd)							
Alexr., Jr.		M		Glasgow, St. Johns [Parish], Lanark [County]	New York	Hero	19 May 1828
Alexr., Sr.	18	M		Glasgow, St. Johns [Parish], Lanark [County]	New York	Hero	19 May 1828
Ann	4	F		Glasgow, St. Johns [Parish], Lanark [County]	New York	Hero	19 May 1828
Ann	9	F	Child	Kenross	U.S. America	Camillus	10 Sep 1821
Christian	2	F		Glasgow, St. Johns [Parish], Lanark [County]	New York	Hero	19 May 1828
Christian	35	F	Wife	Kenross	U.S. America	Camillus	10 Sep 1821
Janet	10	F		Glasgow, St. Johns [Parish], Lanark [County]	New York	Hero	19 May 1828
Jean	13	F		Glasgow, St. Johns [Parish], Lanark [County]	New York	Hero	19 May 1828
John	8	M		Glasgow, St. Johns [Parish], Lanark [County]	New York	Hero	19 May 1828
Margt.	15	F		Glasgow, St. Johns [Parish], Lanark [County]	New York	Hero	19 May 1828
Mary		F		Glasgow, St. Johns [Parish], Lanark [County]	New York	Hero	19 May 1828
Robert	40	M	Farmer	Kenross	U.S. America	Camillus	10 Sep 1821
MEOR, Dollen	20	M	Labourer	Isle of Man	Ohio	Curler	7 Jul 1827
MERACY, Jos.	24	M		Gt. Britain	U. States	Tantiva	7 Jul 1828
MERAN, M.	32	M		England	United States	Yobah	26 Sep 1827
MERAUD, Louise	28	F	Spinster	France	United States	Aurora	11 Dec 1824
MERCADA, Felix, Don	4	M		Mexico	United States	Mercid	21 Oct 1824
Joanna, Don	25	F	A Lady	Mexico	United States	Mercid	21 Oct 1824
Leano, Don	6	F		Mexico	United States	Mercid	21 Oct 1824
Sebastian, Don	42	M	Attached to the Mexican Legation	Mexico	United States	Mercid	21 Oct 1824
MERCARD, A.	65	M	Farmer	France	France	Edward Quesnel	3 Jul 1829
Claude Josephine	65	F		France	France	Edward Quesnel	3 Jul 1829
MERCELLI, Bernard	40	M	Merchant	Germany	U. States	Roseway	10 Jul 1820
MERCELLO, John	22	M	Merchant	Havana	U. States	Greek	17 May 1825
MERCEN, James	19		Farmer	England	United States	Hudson	5 Apr 1826
Joseph	23		Farmer	England	United States	Hudson	5 Apr 1826
MERCER, Daniel	26	M	Carpenter	G.B.	St. New York	Eliza Grant	29 Aug 1829
Daniel	26	M	Carpenter	Great Britain		Eliza Grant	29 Aug 1829
Eunice	30	F		G. Britain	U. States	Mary Howland	22 Sep 1828
Henrietta	3	F		G. Britain	U. States	Mary Howland	22 Sep 1828
James	20	M				Lady of the Lake	23 Aug 1828
James	27	M	Baker	Scotland	U. States	Teio	5 Jun 1826
Jos.	30	M	Tailor	G. Britain	U. States	Mary Howland	22 Sep 1828
Mary	1	F		G. Britain	U. States	Mary Howland	22 Sep 1828
Stephen	28	M	Farmer			Brighton	19 Aug 1829
Steven	28	M	Farmer	England	New York	Brighton	19 Aug 1829
Thomas	30	M	Papermaker	Ireland	United States	Nancy Henrietta	3 Nov 1828
Thos.	32		Weaver	Ireland	United States	John Dickinson	28 Jun 1822

NAMES OF PASSENGERS	AGE	SEX	OCCUPATIONS	COUNTRY TO WHICH THEY BELONG	COUNTRY THEY INTEND TO INHABIT	SHIPS/DATES OF ARRIVAL	
MERCER (cont'd)							
Walter	32	M	Farmer	Great Britain	United States	Ann Maria	12 Jul 1821
MERCERNE, Daniel S.	46	M	Merchant	London	New York, U.S.	New York	14 Mar 1828
Frederick	14	M	Son [of Daniel S.]	London	New York, U.S.	New York	14 Mar 1828
MERCERON,							
Caroline Brooks	10		Lady	England	United States	Corinthian	30 May 1828
Catherine Allison	2		Lady	England	United States	Corinthian	30 May 1828
Cecelia Amant	4		Lady	England	United States	Corinthian	30 May 1828
Charles Augustus	8		Gentn.	England	United States	Corinthian	30 May 1828
Louisa	35		Lady	England	United States	Corinthian	30 May 1828
Maria Louisa	12		Lady	England	United States	Corinthian	30 May 1828
Napoleon Alexander	6		Gentn.	England	United States	Corinthian	30 May 1828
MERCHANT, Lewis	49	M	Carpenter	Swtserland	America	Saluda	18 Jun 1825
MERCHARD, Agart	2	M	Boy	Switserland	America	Saluda	18 Jun 1825
MERCHEAD, L.	25	M	Merchant	Holland	U. States	Pallas	15 Jul 1822
MERCHERY, James	21 7/12	M	Merchant	Scotland	Scotland	Nimrod	9 Jul 1827
MERCIER, —, Mde.	26	F	Lady	France	U. States	Imperial	10 Dec 1821
Fredk.	23		Farmer	France	U. States	Parachute	14 May 1828
Theodore	21	M	Shoemaker	Belfoit	U.S. America	Superior	18 Jun 1825
MERCKIN, John C.	25	M	Gentleman	Philidelphia	America	Carlo	28 Nov 1828
MERCOME, B.	7		Child	Great Britain	United States	Isaac Hicks	6 Dec 1827
B.	9		Child	Great Britain	United States	Isaac Hicks	6 Dec 1827
E.	3		Child	Great Britain	United States	Isaac Hicks	6 Dec 1827
E.	30	F		Great Britain	United States	Isaac Hicks	6 Dec 1827
F.	1		Child	Great Britain	United States	Isaac Hicks	6 Dec 1827
J.	1		Child	Great Britain	United States	Isaac Hicks	6 Dec 1827
J.	11		Child	Great Britain	United States	Isaac Hicks	6 Dec 1827
M.	5		Child	Great Britain	United States	Isaac Hicks	6 Dec 1827
MERCUR, Georg	24	M	Slater	Ireland		Quatre Freres	29 Jul 1828
MERDANT, Mary R.	30	F	None	France		Charlemagne	20 Aug 1829
MERDITH, William	29		Servant	England		Cincinnatus	29 Apr 1822
MEREDITH, John	16 9/12	M	Farmer	Wales	America	Minerva	15 Jun 1825
John	48 4/12	M	Farmer	Wales	America	Minerva	15 Jun 1825
MEREID, John, Jr.	12	M		Ireland	U. States	Nancy	16 Aug 1822
MERENA, Edwd.	50	M	Taylor	Ireland	U. States	Hibernia	3 Dec 1823
MERENO, Felix		M		Mexico		Joseph	20 Jul 1829
MERES, Elias	24	M		Great B.	U. States	William Neilson	26 Jul 1828
MERGENTALER,							
Catharin	39	F		Wirtemberg	America, U.N.S.	Great Britain	3 Aug 1829
Catharina	3 6/12	F		Wirtemberg	America, U.N.S.	Great Britain	3 Aug 1829
Cristian	7	M		Wirtemberg	America, U.N.S.	Great Britain	3 Aug 1829
D.	43	M	Farmer	Wirtemberg	America, U.N.S.	Great Britain	3 Aug 1829
Dorothea	0 3/12	F		Wirtemberg	America, U.N.S.	Great Britain	3 Aug 1829
Gettliep	4 6/12	F		Wirtemberg	America, U.N.S.	Great Britain	3 Aug 1829
Jacob	12	M		Wirtemberg	America, U.N.S.	Great Britain	3 Aug 1829
Michel	10	M		Wirtemberg	America, U.N.S.	Great Britain	3 Aug 1829
MERGG, Francios	4	M	his family [Joseph]	Germany	United States	Wm. Osborne	16 Sep 1828
Joseph	6	M	his family [Joseph]	Germany	United States	Wm. Osborne	16 Sep 1828
Joseph	40	M	Wheelwright	Germany	United States	Wm. Osborne	16 Sep 1828
Magdelene	5	F	his family [Joseph]	Germany	United States	Wm. Osborne	16 Sep 1828
Maria	40	F	his family [Joseph]	Germany	United States	Wm. Osborne	16 Sep 1828
Sopha	7	F	his family [Joseph]	Germany	United States	Wm. Osborne	16 Sep 1828
Theresa	2	F		Germany	United States	Wm. Osborne	16 Sep 1828
MERGGER, John	22	M	Artist	Germany	America	Saluda	18 Jun 1825
MERHAFER, Catherine	12	F		United States	United States	Globe	30 Aug 1828
Elizabeth	62	F		United States	United States	Globe	30 Aug 1828
Jacob	60	M	Farmer	United States	United States	Globe	30 Aug 1828
Jacob, Jur.	17	M		United States	United States	Globe	30 Aug 1828
Mary	3	F		United States	United States	Globe	30 Aug 1828
MERHAUX, Augts.	24	M	Gentleman	Netherlands		Margaret	20 Dec 1827
Ferdinand	26	M	Gentleman	Netherlands		Margaret	20 Dec 1827
MERIA, Ann	18	F	Spinster	Bavarian	United States	American	27 Aug 1827
MERIDEN, Ballaza	25	M	Mercht.	Havama	United States	Brown	26 Apr 1826
MERIDITH, Elizabeth	5	F	None	Wales	America	Hercules	2 Nov 1825
James	22 5/12	M		Ireland	U.S. of America	Douglass	6 Jul 1829
Jane	9	F	None	Wales	America	Hercules	2 Nov 1825
Jane	40	F	None	Wales	America	Hercules	2 Nov 1825
John	16	M	Farmer	Wales	America	Hercules	2 Nov 1825
John	27	M	Farmer	Great Britian	United States	Silvanus Jenkins	6 Apr 1826

NAMES OF PASSENGERS	AGE	SEX	OCCUPATIONS	COUNTRY TO WHICH THEY BELONG	COUNTRY THEY INTEND TO INHABIT	SHIPS/DATES OF ARRIVAL	
MERIDITH (cont'd)							
Joseph	26 6/12	M		Ireland	U.S. of America	Douglass	6 Jul 1829
Mary	13	F	None	Wales	America	Hercules	2 Nov 1825
Richard	10	M	None	Wales	America	Hercules	2 Nov 1825
Sarah	1	F	None	Wales	America	Hercules	2 Nov 1825
Susan	3	F	None	Wales	America	Hercules	2 Nov 1825
Thomas	25	M	Farmer	Great Britian	United States	Silvanus Jenkins	6 Apr 1826
MERIED, John	30	M	Farmer	Ireland	U. States	Nancy	16 Aug 1822
MERILL, J.	24	M	Commerce		United States	New York	5 Nov 1828
MERINAGH, Edward	36	M	Farmer	Ireland	U. States	Dickinson	30 Jul 1825
MERINDALE, A.	30	M	Merchant	Island Cuba	U. States	Havana Packet	27 Jul 1827
MERING, Benj. A.	32	M	Clergyman	U. States	U. States	Eugene	15 Dec 1828
MERIS, Mary J.	26			Switzerland	U. States	Parachute	14 May 1828
MERISE, Jos.	21		Mechanic	Switzerland	U. States	Parachute	14 May 1828
MERIT, George	16	M	None	United States	United States	Nancey	8 Jun 1822
Nehemiah	50	M	Merchant	United States	United States	Nancey	8 Jun 1822
MERLE, Anthony	2	M		United States	United States	Globe	30 Aug 1828
C.	30	M	Merchant	Switzerland	U. States	Henry	11 Oct 1824
Catharine	8	F		United States	United States	Globe	30 Aug 1828
Louis Edmund, Mr.	42	M	Planter	Guadaloupe	France	Elizabeth	17 Jul 1823
Maren	4	F		United States	United States	Globe	30 Aug 1828
Marica	34	F		United States	United States	Globe	30 Aug 1828
Michael	6	M		United States	United States	Globe	30 Aug 1828
Michael	35	M	Farmer	United States	United States	Globe	30 Aug 1828
MERLOT, Robert	26	M	Merchant	France	U. States	Queen Mab	31 Jul 1826
Robert	27	M	Merchant	France		Edward Quesnel	17 Nov 1828
MERNIN, Jeremiah	21	M	Labourer	England	U. States	Hope & Esther	10 Jul 1827
MERO, T.	40	M	Merchant	Spain	U. States	Native	15 Apr 1826
MERPHY, Michel.	24	M	Labourer	Ireland	N. Jersey	Potomac	7 Aug 1827
MERREL, J.	39	M	Mercht.	France	France	Fabius	19 Mar 1825
MERRERO, —, Mrs.	27	F	Lady	U. States	U. States	Vigilant	14 Apr 1823
Augustin	36	M	Gentleman	Spain	U. States	Vigilant	14 Apr 1823
MERRICK, John	22	M	Merchant	U.S. America	U.S. America	Columbia	31 Jul 1826
John	23	M	Merchant	England	U. States	Martha	7 Nov 1825
John	28	M	Merchant	New York	New York, U.S.	New York	14 Mar 1828
M.	29	M	Farmer	Ireland	N. York	Elizabeth	20 Jun 1828
R.	36	M	Farmer	Ireland	N. York	Elizabeth	20 Jun 1828
MERRIHEW, Jas.	45	M	Mariner	U. States	U. States	Phoebe	17 Apr 1821
MERRILL, Mary	30	F	None	Great Britain	Great Britain	Galaxy	9 Sep 1826
Wiggin	30	M	Mariner	American	U. States	Frederick	27 Jan 1823
MERRIMAN, Patrick	30	M	Farmer	Ireland	United States	Dublin Packet	9 Jul 1827
MERRIT, —, Mrs.	60	F	None	St. John, N.B.	United States	Edwin	29 Nov 1828
Fanny	25	F	Domestic	Ireland	U. States	Teio	5 Jun 1826
Isabella	17	F	...	England	United States	Danube	1 Nov 1827
Julia	16	F	None	St. John, N.B.	United States	Edwin	29 Nov 1828
Mary	18	F	None	St. John, N.B.	United States	Edwin	29 Nov 1828
Willm.	24	M	Marchant	N. York	U. States	Commodore Perry	9 Apr 1821
MERRITS, Peter	36	M	Merchant	Switzerland	U. States	Musidora	20 Feb 1823
MERRITT, —, Mrs.		F		U. States	U. States	Angelina	25 Nov 1822
—, Mrs.	38	F		St. Johns, N.B.	St. John, N.B.	Loire	9 Aug 1821
David	63	M	Merchant	St. John, N.B.	St. John, N.B.	Ann Maria	8 May 1826
Nehamiah	50	M	Merchant	St. Johns, N.B.	St. John, N.B.	Loire	9 Aug 1821
Nehemiah	...	...	...	...	...	St. Michael	22 Sep 1824
Nehemiah	64	M	Merchant	Province, N.B.	New Brunswick	Edwin	27 Oct 1828
Robert	45	M	Merchant	England	U. States	Tilton	28 Jun 1826
Saml.	27	M	Merchant	U. States	U. States	Napolean	26 Sep 1828
Thomas	33	M	Merchant	Great Britain		Sarah G.	20 Jul 1827
Thomas	60	M	Officer	Cannada	Canada	St. Michael	21 Aug 1824
Thos.	32	M	Merchant	St. John, N.B.	Canada	Henrietta	3 Jun 1825
William	15	M		St. Johns, N.B.	St. John, N.B.	Loire	9 Aug 1821
Wm. H.	34	M		Gt. Britain	U. States	Napolean	26 Sep 1828
MERRY, Arthur	22	M	Farmer	Ireland	United States	Romulus	24 Jun 1826
Daniel	19	M	Labourer	Ireland	United States	Meteor	26 Jun 1827
Jean	37	M	Gentleman	Holland	United States	Isaac Hicks	10 Jul 1827
Rose	25	F		Ireland	United States	Romulus	24 Jun 1826
T. H.	47	M	Mariner	Massachusetts	U. States	Henry	24 Apr 1821
Wm.	20	M	Mariner	N. York	U. States	Henry	24 Apr 1821
Wm.	20		Labourer	Great Britain	United States	Camillus	12 Sep 1827

NAMES OF PASSENGERS	AGE	SEX	OCCUPATIONS	COUNTRY TO WHICH THEY BELONG	COUNTRY THEY INTEND TO INHABIT	SHIPS/DATES OF ARRIVAL	
MERRYWEATHER,							
Francis	40	M	Farmer	England	U. States	Howard Douglass	29 Jan 1828
Martha	6	F		England	U. States	Howard Douglass	29 Jan 1828
Martha	39	F		England	U. States	Howard Douglass	29 Jan 1828
Richd.	18	M		England	U. States	Howard Douglass	29 Jan 1828
MERSEN, Barbara	32	F		France	United States	New England	29 Aug 1828
MERSSE, Gustave	9	M		France	United States	Montano	8 May 1827
MERTEEN, Sarah	40	F		Hayti	Hayti	Aurora Alcide	8 Jul 1826
MERTETIM, Thos.	21	M	Labourer	G. Britain	U. States	Hanford	18 Sep 1828
MERTON, Matthew	25	M	Brewer	England	United States	Siroc	31 Oct 1829
Saml. Geo.	25		Doctor	...	...	James Cropper	28 Jun 1824
Thomas	25	M	Farmer	Hudd...sfield	...	Frances Henrietta	30 Jun 1827
MERTY, James	26	M		Ireland	U. States	Belville	5 Jul 1827
James, 2d	24	M	Labourer	Ireland	U. States	Belville	5 Jul 1827
John	28	M	Carpenter	Ireland	U. States	Belville	5 Jul 1827
Robert	22		Laboring Class...		United States	Atlantic	2 Apr 1827
Rose	20		Laboring Class		United States	Atlantic	2 Apr 1827
MERVA, James	30	M	Bricklayer	England	United States	Jubilee	4 Mar 1829
MERVAIER, Aren	6	M	Farmer	France	United States	Great Britain	18 Sep 1826
Zerhob	4	M	Farmer	France	United States	Great Britain	18 Sep 1826
MERVIN, Henry C.	24	M	...	United States	United States	John London	20 Dec 1825
MERVOCK, Alexr. P.	38	M	Merchant	America	unknown	Juanita	13 Oct 1829
MESBAUMER, Nicholas	34	M	Farmer	Switzerland	U. States	Sully	15 Jul 1829
MESKLE, John J.	28	M	Carpenter	Switzerland	U.S.	Francois I	8 Aug 1829
MESMER, Anthony	14	M		France	U. States	Edward Quesnel	4 Aug 1828
Anthony	45	M		France	U. States	Edward Quesnel	4 Aug 1828
Catherine	21	F		France	U. States	Edward Quesnel	4 Aug 1828
Elizabeth	7	F		France	U. States	Edward Quesnel	4 Aug 1828
Gaspard	1	M		France	U. States	Edward Quesnel	4 Aug 1828
Joseph	5	M		France	U. States	Edward Quesnel	4 Aug 1828
Mary Ann	9	F		France	U. States	Edward Quesnel	4 Aug 1828
Rawan	46	M		France	U. States	Edward Quesnel	4 Aug 1828
MESMUR, Catherine	40	F		France	U. States	Edward Quesnel	4 Aug 1828
Gaspard	40	M	Farmer	France	U. States	Edward Quesnel	4 Aug 1828
Joseph	8	M		France	U. States	Edward Quesnel	4 Aug 1828
Mars	16	M		France	U. States	Edward Quesnel	4 Aug 1828
Michael	7	M		France	U. States	Edward Quesnel	4 Aug 1828
MESNUR, Anthony	2	M		France	U. States	Edward Quesnel	4 Aug 1828
Barbar	6	M		France	U. States	Edward Quesnel	4 Aug 1828
Theresa	4	F		France	U. States	Edward Quesnel	4 Aug 1828
MESSANT,							
Lewis D.	20 3/12	M	...	...	U.S. America	Edward	28 Oct 1825
MESSANTE, Saul	30	M	Merchant	Italy	U. States	Saltana	18 Apr 1825
MESSENERS, N.	19	M	Labourer	Germany	U. States	Harriet	20 Oct 1824
MESSENGER, Edward	4	M				Betsey	17 Aug 1820
Elizabeth	7	M				Betsey	17 Aug 1820
James	27	M	Farmer	England	United States	Siroc	31 Oct 1829
Jane	1	F				Betsey	17 Aug 1820
John	37	M	Brewer	G. Britain	U. States	Betsey	17 Aug 1820
John F.	10	M				Betsey	17 Aug 1820
Joseph	24	M	Labourer	America	America	Josephine	8 Jan 1827
Maria	3	F				Betsey	17 Aug 1820
Maria	38	F				Betsey	17 Aug 1820
Rosa	5	F				Betsey	17 Aug 1820
Thomas	9	M				Betsey	17 Aug 1820
William	4	M				Betsey	17 Aug 1820
MESSEN SMIT, Conrad	27	M	Boer	Bleicheim	United States	Juffraw Johanna	16 Oct 1821
Eliza, Zyn Vrouw [his wife, Conrad]	27	F		Bleicheim	United States	Juffraw Johanna	16 Oct 1821
Magdalen, Kind [child of Conrad]	4	F		Bleicheim	United States	Juffraw Johanna	16 Oct 1821
MESSER, John	21	M	Farmer	Switzerland	U. States	Sully	15 Jul 1829
Nicholas	22	M	Farmer	Switzerland	U. States	Sully	15 Jul 1829
William	25	M	Seaman	United States	United States	Ceres	13 Dec 1827
MESSHONS, Henry	30	M	B. Smith	Great Britain	United States	Blakely	29 Sep 1826

NAMES OF PASSENGERS	AGE	SEX	OCCUPATIONS	COUNTRY TO WHICH THEY BELONG	COUNTRY THEY INTEND TO INHABIT	SHIPS/DATES OF ARRIVAL	
MESSIER, Jacques	30	M	Gardner	France	United States	American	27 Aug 1827
MESSMER, Fois.	40			Suisse		Deux Ernest	29 Dec 1827
MESSNER, Francis	40	M		Swisse	United States	Deux Ernest	29 Dec 1827
*landed at Lewiston, Delw.							
METCALF, Ann	25	F		Ireland	United States	Abigale	17 Jul 1822
Catharine	4	F		Ireland	United States	Abigale	17 Jul 1822
Catharine	19	F		Ireland	United States	Abigale	17 Jul 1822
Dorrathia	17	F		Ireland	United States	Abigale	17 Jul 1822
Elizabeth	22	F		Ireland	United States	Abigale	17 Jul 1822
Isaac	24	M	Carpenter	Ireland	United States	Abigale	17 Jul 1822
James	6	M		Ireland	United States	Abigale	17 Jul 1822
Jane	20	F		Ireland	United States	Abigale	17 Jul 1822
Jane	50	F		Ireland	United States	Abigale	17 Jul 1822
John	23	M	Labourer	England	Pittsburgh	Orozimbo	8 Jun 1822
Murphy	36	M	Lathe ...aler	England		Exchange	11 Jul 1823
Samuel	1	M		Ireland	United States	Abigale	17 Jul 1822
METCALFE, Emma	16	F	None	G...	United States	Solon	21 Jun 1824
Henry	2	M	None	G...	United States	Solon	21 Jun 1824
Isabella	9	F	None	G...	United States	Solon	21 Jun 1824
Mary	47	F	None	G...	United States	Solon	21 Jun 1824
Richd.	14	M	None	G...	United States	Solon	21 Jun 1824
Richd.	45	M	Labourer	G...	United States	Solon	21 Jun 1824
Rowland	18	M	Labourer	G...	United States	Solon	21 Jun 1824
Thos.	5	M	None	G...	United States	Solon	21 Jun 1824
Wm.	12	M	None	G...	United States	Solon	21 Jun 1824
METCHERS, Hy.	21	M	Mechanic	Bremen	U. States	Caesar	18 Mar 1829
METHIERS, John	30	M	Merchant	Brazil	United States	Georgetown Packet	6 May 1824
METHUEN, Jas.	26	M	Farmer	Gt. Britan	U. States	Magnet	9 Apr 1825
METHURST, William	12	M		England	U.S.A.	Hudson	21 Aug 1829
METS, Perrier	54	M	Farmer	Switzerland	U.States	C. Amelia	30 Jun 1828
METUTEY, F.	40	M	Merchant	United States	U. States	Prince Edward	26 Mar 1827
METZ, Edmund	23	M	Musician	...	U. States	Emily	19 Apr 1825
METZLER, Philip	19	M		Switzerland	U. States	La Urania	3 Jul 1828
MEUR, Henry	30	M	Sugar Bakers	Germany	U.S. America	Cincinnatus	31 Oct 1820
MEURHOFF, Martin	17	M	Labourer	Germany	United States	Constitution	2 Aug 1826
MEVIGO, Joseph	28	M	Farmer	Switserland	U.S.	C. Amelia	30 Jun 1828
MEW, Wm.	24	M	Weaver	Gt. Britain	United States	Penelope	9 Sep 1828
MEYBURN, Elizabeth	35			England	England	London	16 Aug 1824
Joseph	4		Child	England	England	London	16 Aug 1824
Julia	6		Child	England	England	London	16 Aug 1824
Mary	9		Child	England	England	London	16 Aug 1824
Selina	2		Child	England	England	London	16 Aug 1824
William	11		Child	England	England	London	16 Aug 1824
MEYER, —	40	M	Merchant	Bremen	Philadelpia	Louisa	16 May 1826
Adelle		F	Child	France	U. States	Fair Trader	25 Jul 1820
Anthony	28	M	Pianomaker	France	U. States	Sully	25 Jun 1828
August	17	M		Wirtemburg	U.S.	Francois I	8 Aug 1829
C.	25	M	Waiter	Germany		Ariel	24 Sep 1827
Charles	5	M		Wirtemburg	U.S.	Francois I	8 Aug 1829
D.	30		Laborer	Hannover		Constitution	5 Jan 1829
Daniel	22 7/12	M	Farmer	Germany	Germany	France	28 Mar 1829
David	29 4/12	M	Farmer	France	United States	France	6 Oct 1828
Elizabeth	50	F		Wirtemburg	U.S.	Francois I	8 Aug 1829
Frances	40	F		United States	at Baltimore	Homer	28 Aug 1829
Francis		F	Child	France	U. States	Fair Trader	25 Jul 1820
Fred	30	M	Brewer	France	United States	New England	29 Aug 1828
Fredericka	17	F		Wirtemburg	U.S.	Francois I	8 Aug 1829
George	45	M	Merchant	U. States	U. States	Columbia	24 Dec 1822
George	50	M	Shoemaker	Wirtemburg	U.S.	Francois I	8 Aug 1829
George V.	44		Merchant	New York	New York	Weser	24 Jul 1820
H.	26		Merchant	Hannover		Constitution	5 Jan 1829
Helaise	8	F	Girl			Weser	24 Jul 1820
Hendrick	30	M	Bricklayer	France	America	Saluda	16 Oct 1824
Henrich	28		Mason	Germany	U. States	Columbia	7 May 1828
Henry	5 6/12	M	Boy			Weser	24 Jul 1820
Henry, Mr.	41		Mercht.	London		Hercules	19 Jun 1821
Ignace	22	M	Tanner	Wertemberg	U. States	Sully	15 Jul 1829
Jacob	21	M		Germany	Maryland	Orient	25 Nov 1825

NAMES OF PASSENGERS	AGE	SEX	OCCUPATIONS	COUNTRY TO WHICH THEY BELONG	COUNTRY THEY INTEND TO INHABIT	SHIPS/DATES OF ARRIVAL	
MEYER (cont'd)							
Jacob	28	M	Black Smith	France	U. States	Sully	25 Jun 1828
Jean	30	M	Cooper	Swiss	United States	Elizabeth	4 Sep 1826
Jean B.	21	M	Merchant	France	U. States	Edward Quesnel	16 Nov 1827
Jno. G.	36	M	Merchant	Switzerland	N. York	Queen Mab	20 Nov 1826
Johan	25	M	Kleermaker	Rees	United States	Juffraw Johanna	16 Oct 1821
Johanna	36					Weser	24 Jul 1820
John	25	M	Cultivator	Brattain		L'Esperance	6 Sep 1828
John L.	47	M	Merchant	United States	at Baltimore	Homer	28 Aug 1829
Joseph	17	M	Farmer	France	U. States	Edward Bopnnaffe	30 Jul 1829
Josephine	12	F		United States	at Baltimore	Homer	28 Aug 1829
Julian	3	F	Girl			Weser	24 Jul 1820
Louisa		F	Child	France	U. States	Fair Trader	25 Jul 1820
M.	50	F	School Mis.	France	U. States	Fair Trader	25 Jul 1820
O.	23	M	Labourer	Hamburg	United States	Brilliant	24 Sep 1827
P. S.	38	M	Mariner	U. States	U. States	Dionesio	28 Jan 1828
T.	50	M	Merchant	U.S.	U.S.	Francois I	8 Aug 1829
Theodore	19	M		Germany	U. States	Edward Bonaffe	11 Dec 1827
W. H.	22	M	Mariner	U. States	U. States	New Packet	20 Sep 1826
William	1 2/12	M	Boy			Weser	24 Jul 1820
William F.	45	M	Merchant	United States	United States	Foster	12 Dec 1821
MEYERS, John	30	M	Mariner	U. States	U. States	Sally Ann	27 Oct 1825
W.	20	M	Gentleman	Hamburg	U. States	Morning Star	28 Apr 1824
Wm.	16	M		England	New York	York	2 Dec 1828
MEYR, Catharina	48	F		Wirtemburg	United States	Wade	29 Aug 1825
MEYRELES, M.	35	M	Merchant	St. Domingo	St. Domingo	Blue Ey'd Man	23 Aug 1823
MEYRICK, Ellen	40	F	None	England	United States	Jubilee	1 Oct 1828
Mary	9	F	None	England	United States	Jubilee	1 Oct 1828
Philip	12	M	None	England	United States	Jubilee	1 Oct 1828
MEZA, Matias	34	M	Lawyer	Island Cuba		Claudio	21 Aug 1827
MI..., ...et	28	F	Spinster	Ireland	United States	Wilson	6 Jun 1828
MIALL, Sarah	20	F		England	United States	Cambria	16 Aug 1827
MICHAEL, J.	24	M	Labourer	U. States	U. States	Robt. Reade	12 Apr 1825
L.	45	M	Merchant	U. States	U. States	Prudence	11 Jun 1825
Peter	40	M		Scotland	U.S.	Curler	19 Jul 1828
Wm.	12	M	None	Isle of Man		Ocean	13 Jul 1827
Wm., Mrs.	23	M	Merchant	England	New York	Maine	16 Jul 1821
MICHAELL, Samuel	25	M	Carpenter	G. Brittan	England	Frances	23 Mar 1827
MICHAELLETTI, P.	52	M	Merchant	U. States	U. States	Claudio	29 Dec 1827
MICHALBRIGHT, John	33	M	Engineer	England	United States	Amelia	20 Aug 1829
MICHALETT, R.	48	M	Merchant	Spain	U. States	Brown	29 Apr 1825
MICHALETTE, P.	33	M	Merchant	Spain	U. States	Mary Jane	2 Jul 1828
P.	50	M	Mariner	United States	United States	Agricola	19 Jul 1824
P.	51	M	Mercht.	U. States	United States	Herald	25 Nov 1826
P.	56	M	Merchant	U. States	U. States	Emblem	14 May 1827
Paranal, (Esq)	18 6/12	M	Merchant	United States	United States	Mary Jane	7 Jan 1829
MICHALETTI, P. B.	50	M	Merchant	Spain	United States	Burdett	30 Apr 1828
MICHALL, James W.	27	M	Mariner	United States	U. States	Saml. Smith	24 Jul 1826
MICHAN, Henry	24		Labourer			Rufus King	7 Aug 1820
James	22		Labourer			Rufus King	7 Aug 1820
Mary	20	F	Spinster	Ireland	United States	Wilson	6 Jun 1828
Peggy	15	F	Spinster	Ireland	United States	Trident	17 May 1825
MICHANDOR, J.	28	M	Military	Lima, Peru		Brown	12 Oct 1824
MICHEIL, John	30	M	Jeweller	Scotland	United States	Cambria	3 Jul 1829
MICHEL, Bridget	22	F	Spinster	Ireland		Robert Fulton	4 Jun 1828
Francis ...	28		Merchant	Switzerland	Switzerland	London	16 Aug 1824
Jac.	26	M	Agriculture	France	United States	Henri IV	14 Oct 1829
Laurens						Olympia	12 Aug 1828

*After having been at Sea a Number of Days was ascertaining the quantity of Baggage to report found the under mentioned persons had secreted themselves away notwithstanding our searach with the Gendearmes at the of leaving the port

MICHELETTE, Lewis	27	M	Merchant	Itally	America	Commodore Chauncy	19 Jan 1826
P.	44	M	Merchant	U. States	U. States	Cadmus	27 Jul 1825
MICHELL, Andw.	24	M	Labourer	Ireland	America	Wilson	27 Nov 1826
John	20	F	Spinster	Ireland	United States	Wilson	6 Jun 1828
Thos.	9	M	Child	St. John	U. States	Agnes	29 Nov 1826
MICHELLETTA, P.	50	M	Merchant	U. States	U. States	Hesper	28 Dec 1825

NAMES OF PASSENGERS	AGE	SEX	OCCUPATIONS	COUNTRY TO WHICH THEY BELONG	COUNTRY THEY INTEND TO INHABIT	SHIPS/DATES OF ARRIVAL	
MICHELLETTE,							
Louis, Mr.	38 6/12	M	Trader	Italy	U.S.	Hesper	2 May 1826
P.	50	M	Merchant	U.S.	U.S.	Hesperus	13 Mar 1826
MICHELON, A.	25	M	Barber	France	United States	Marmione	20 Nov 1821
MICHIGAN, Jas.		M	Carpenter	U. States	U. States	David	19 Apr 1824
MICHLATTE, Lewis	44	M	Merchant	U. States	U. States	Sarah	17 Mar 1829
MICHOLTTE, Pasquel	50	M	Merchant	New York	New York	Milo	8 May 1826
MICHRO, Mary S.	14	F	Lady	Connecticut	United States	St. Michaels	12 Jun 1826
MICK, Owen	18	M	Boy	Ireland	N. York	Trusty	12 Sep 1828
MICKIE, Robt.	30	M	Mariner	Gt. Britain	British America	Cortes	6 Apr 1825
MICKLE, George	28	M	Weaver	Great Britain	United States	Courier	26 Jun 1827
MICKLES, Robt.	35	M	Sailor			Evergreen	28 Jul 1820
MICKLEY, William	21	M	Farmer	England	U.S. America	Cortes	19 May 1826
MICKLIN, Jane	29	F		Gt. Britain	United States	John & Elizabeth	25 Sep 1827
Joseph	29	M		Gt. Britain	United States	John & Elizabeth	25 Sep 1827
Thos.	32	M	Merchant	England	England	William Byrnes	14 Apr 1824
MICKS, Wm.	9	M	Shoemaker	England	United States	Euphrates	12 May 1823
MICLAN, E. S.	27	M	Merchant	Havana	U. States	Greek	3 Aug 1825
MICOUD, Francis	25		Merchant	France	New York	Don Quixote	19 Aug 1825
Francis	28	M	Merchant	United States	United States	Don Quixote	12 Feb 1829
MICTCHELL, Letitia	24	F	None	Ireland	United States	Leonidas	3 Aug 1825
Robert	30	M	Farmer	Ireland	United States	Leonidas	3 Aug 1825
MIDDESON, Saml.	25	M				Eliza Grant	6 Oct 1828
MIDDLETON, A.	26	M	Merchant	Charleston	United States	Marmione	20 Nov 1821
Elizth.	26	F	...	Great Brittain	N. York	Albion	11 Jun 1821
Francis	28	M	Farmer	England	United States	Resign	7 Oct 1822
John	6	M				Lady of the Lake	23 Aug 1828
*left ship							
John	22	M	Cooper	England	America	Comet	26 Jun 1822
Lucy	12	F				Lady of the Lake	23 Aug 1828
*left ship							
Mary Ann	8	F				Lady of the Lake	23 Aug 1828
*left ship							
William	38	M	Gunsmith	England	United States	Siroc	31 Oct 1829
MIDDLETOWN, Jane	1	F		Ireland	U. States	Wanderer	1 Sep 1828
John	3	M		Ireland	U. States	Wanderer	1 Sep 1828
Kreir	23	M		Ireland	U. States	Wanderer	1 Sep 1828
Mary	17	F		Ireland	U. States	Wanderer	1 Sep 1828
MIDGLEY, Charles	21 9/12	M	Machine Maker	England	Massachusetts	Concordia	12 Oct 1826
Elizabeth	12	F	None	England	New York	Indian Chief	16 Aug 1822
MIDLER, Jacob	60	M	Farmer	U. States	U. States	Exertion	14 Dec 1822
MIDMER, —				Suisse		Deux Ernest	29 Dec 1827
—	25	M		Swisse	United States	Deux Ernest	29 Dec 1827
*landed at Lewiston, Delw.							
MIDWOOD, James, Jur.	28	M	Merchant	Yorkshire	New York, U.S.	New York	14 Mar 1828
MIECHOLETTE, Peter	50	M	Merchant	U. States	U. States	Ambuscade	15 Dec 1824
MIEDZA, George	43	M	Farmer	Switzerland		Antioch	18 Aug 1829
Maria Theresa	30	F	Farmer	Switzerland		Antioch	18 Aug 1829
MIEGS, Ephraim			Seaman	U.S.A.	U.S. America	Sereno	31 Jul 1826
*works his passage							
MIENS, Robt.	27	M	Merchant	New York	United States	Fabius	31 Jul 1829
MIERT, John M.	39	M	Merchant	Brussels	U.S.	Montano	24 Jun 1823
MIESSON, R. S., Mr.	26	M		Bermuda	Missouri	Camden	14 May 1825
MIEVRE, J. G., Mr.	46	M	Merchant	France	France	Cadmus	11 Jul 1827
MIEZ, J. E.	26	M	Merchant	Spain	Havana	Robert Fulton	11 Jan 1825
MIGAN, Bernard	18	M	Farmer	Ireland	U. States	Dickinson	30 Jul 1825
MIGERICH, ...	20	M	Farmer	Ireland	America	Mary	29 May 1827
MIGHT, George	28	M	Mechanic	Great Britain		Birmingham	11 Oct 1828
Jno.	22	M	Tanner	Argyle (Tedland) Scotland	United States	Jean Hastie	27 Jul 1829
MIGNOW, H.	32	M	Watchmaker	French	U. States	Topaz	23 Jul 1828
MIGUERAS, Jose	54	M	Merchant	Spain	Mexico	Four Sons	4 Jun 1827
MIHAN, Peggy	19	F	Spinster	Ireland	United States	Wilson	6 Jun 1828
MIIRDAR, Mary	21		Servant	England	England	Silvanus Jenkins	30 Nov 1827

NAMES OF PASSENGERS	AGE	SEX	OCCUPATIONS	COUNTRY TO WHICH THEY BELONG	COUNTRY THEY INTEND TO INHABIT	SHIPS/DATES OF ARRIVAL	
MIKENNY, Cathrine	21	F		Ireland	United States	Aurora	9 Jul 1827
MIKHAEL, ...	10			England	United States	Hugh Johnson	11 Jun 1828
Agness	4			England	United States	Hugh Johnson	11 Jun 1828
Ellison	8			England	United States	Hugh Johnson	11 Jun 1828
Henry	6			England	United States	Hugh Johnson	11 Jun 1828
Is...lla	28			England	United States	Hugh Johnson	11 Jun 1828
Isabella	2			England	United States	Hugh Johnson	11 Jun 1828
MILAN, Mary	22	F		Gt. Britain		Dalhouse Castle	13 May 1828
Mary	24					Trio	5 May 1828
Patrick	25	M	Laborer	Gt. Britain		Dalhouse Castle	13 May 1828
MILAY, Archd.	24	M	Schoolmaster	Scotland	United States	Commerce	17 Jul 1823
Mary	30	F		Scotland	United States	Commerce	17 Jul 1823
MILBURGH, Saml.	35	M	Army	G. Brittain	U. States	Canada	6 Jun 1825
MILCOMANN, Patrick	18	M	Carpenter	Ireland	United States	Jubilee	13 Sep 1827
MILDEBERGER, John	28	M	Merchant	U. States	U. States	Charles	13 May 1823
MILDENSTIEN, C.	10	M	None	Cuba	U. States	Betsey	31 Jul 1826
J.	14	M	None	Cuba	U. States	Betsey	31 Jul 1826
J.	45	M	Merchant	Cuba	U. States	Betsey	31 Jul 1826
M., Miss	18	F	None	Cuba	U. States	Betsey	31 Jul 1826
T.	7	M	None	Cuba	U. States	Betsey	31 Jul 1826
T., Mrs.	35	F	None	Cuba	U. States	Betsey	31 Jul 1826
W.	12	M	None	Cuba	U. States	Betsey	31 Jul 1826
MILDERS, John	25	M	Merchant	Scotland	...	Corks	3 Aug 1824
MILDEWATERS, Mary	1 1/2	F	Family [of Joseph]	England	United States	Comet	6 Mar 1823
MILDEY, Elizebeth	56	F		Great B.	U. States	William Neilson	26 Jul 1828
John	25	M		Great B.	U. States	William Neilson	26 Jul 1828
Joseph	60	M		Great B.	U. States	William Neilson	26 Jul 1828
Samuel	19	M		Great B.	U. States	William Neilson	26 Jul 1828
Thomas	29	M		Great B.	U. States	William Neilson	26 Jul 1828
MILDRIDEZE, Eliz.	18	F		Great B.	U. States	William Neilson	26 Jul 1828
Eliz.	29	F		Great B.	U. States	William Neilson	26 Jul 1828
Isable	16	F		Great B.	U. States	William Neilson	26 Jul 1828
Maryan	4/12	F		Great B.	U. States	William Neilson	26 Jul 1828
Mem.	17	F		Great B.	U. States	William Neilson	26 Jul 1828
MILDWATERS, —	Infant	F	born at sea	England	United States	Comet	6 Mar 1823
Charlotte	28	F	Family [of Joseph]	England	United States	Comet	6 Mar 1823
MILEAR, Richd.	45	M	Servant	Great Britain	Great Britain	Martha	25 Nov 1820
MILES, Arna	20	F		St. Johns	U. States	Nancy	10 Jul 1822
Benj.	7	M		G. Britain	G. Britain	Brittania	17 Jul 1828
D. M.	39	M	Mariner	U. States	U. States	New Packet	27 Jul 1822
Daniel	29	M	Druggist	U. States	U. States	Morning Star	28 Apr 1824
Han	36	F		G. Britain	G. Britain	Brittania	17 Jul 1828
Henry	20	M	Printer	England	United States	Cosmo	26 Aug 1829
Henry	31	M	Merchant	New York	New York	Brighton	20 Aug 1825
Jacob	10	M		G. Britain	G. Britain	Brittania	17 Jul 1828
Josiah	25	M	Engineer	Great Britain	United States	Penelope	11 Jun 1827
Mary	60	F	Lady	St. John, N.B.	United States	Sarah G	19 Jun 1827
Sarah E., Mrs.	34	F		England	New York	Thames	6 Oct 1820
Thomas	13	M		G. Britain	G. Britain	Brittania	17 Jul 1828
MILEWOOD, Luke	25		Clerk	England	United States	Rufus King	4 Sep 1823
MILFORD, Samuel	36	M	Dentist	Philadelphia	United States	New York	14 Jul 1827
Wm.	26	M	Merchant	Great Britan	United States	Hamilton	19 Mar 1827
MILGATE, Mary, Mrs.	32			Rye.../Rye	New York	Venus	12 Apr 1821
William	22		Farmer	Rye.../Rye	New York	Venus	12 Apr 1821
MILGROVE, Mary	18		Servant	Frome, E.	England	Packet	27 Aug 1822
MILHAIR, John	28	M	Gent.	Baltimore	U.S.	Cadmus	17 Aug 1824
MILIA, M. A.	25	F		Gottenburgh	U. States	Alexander	4 Oct 1822
MILIGAN, J.	22	M	Sadler	Scotland	U. States	Superior	25 Sep 1828
Pat	20	M	Painter	Ireland	U. States	Wanderer	1 Sep 1828
MILIKEN, Owen	25	M	Labourer	Ireland	Unt. St. America	Wilson	21 May 1827
MILKHAM, James	20	F	Farmer	England	U. States	Unity	5 Sep 1828
MILL, John	20	M	Farmer	England	U. States	Emulous	22 Aug 1828
Robert	21	M	Labourer	Ireland	America	Josephine	8 Dec 1827
Robt.	26	M	Farmer	Scotland	United States	Minerva	29 Oct 1822
Thomas A.	38	M	Clerk			John & Edward	25 Aug 1820
William	60	M	Farmer	England	U. States	Emulous	22 Aug 1828
MILL..., Lawrence	26	M	Labourer	Ireland	Unt. St. America	Wilson	21 May 1827
MILLAGAIN, Thomas	20	M	Labourer	Ireland	N. York	Trusty	12 Sep 1828

NAMES OF PASSENGERS	AGE	SEX	OCCUPATIONS	COUNTRY TO WHICH THEY BELONG	COUNTRY THEY INTEND TO INHABIT	SHIPS/DATES OF ARRIVAL	
MILLAM, Thos.	13			Sussex, England		Cincinnatus	17 May 1823
*died							
MILLAN, Cathr.	4	F		G. Britain	U. States	Camillus	8 Sep 1828
Christian	23	M		G. Britain	U. States	Camillus	8 Sep 1828
David	0 3/12	M		G. Britain	U. States	Camillus	8 Sep 1828
Eliza	1	F		Ireland	United States	Thompson	12 Sep 1827
James David	26	M	Gardiner	England	Philadelphia	Concordia	12 Oct 1826
John	25	M		Ireland	United States	Thompson	12 Sep 1827
Jose	38	M		Spain	Spain	Fabius	3 Jun 1825
M.	18	F		Great Britain	United States	Isaac Hicks	6 Dec 1827
Mary	20	F		Ireland	United States	Thompson	12 Sep 1827
Patrick	22	M	Dealer	Ireland	Philadelphia	Cadmus	22 Mar 1822
Thomas	22	M	Tailor	New Brunswick to return thither		Lady Hunter	14 Mar 1826
MILLAR, Agnes	9	F		Great Britain		Dalmannock	24 Ocg 1826
Agnes	23	F		Great Britain		Dalmannock	24 Ocg 1826
Alexr.	5	M		Great Britain		Dalmannock	24 Ocg 1826
Benjamin G.	41	M	Labourer	U. States	U. States	Josephine	30 Aug 1828
Catharine	52	F		Germany	United States	Samuel Robertson	8 Aug 1828
Eliza	22	F		Germany	United States	Samuel Robertson	8 Aug 1828
Elizabeth	17	F	Spinster	Ireland	U. States	Josephine	30 Aug 1828
Frederick	19	M		Germany	United States	Samuel Robertson	8 Aug 1828
Fredrick	53	M	Butcher	Germany	United States	Samuel Robertson	8 Aug 1828
Helen	32	F		Great Britain		Dalmannock	24 Ocg 1826
James	27	M		G. Britain	U. States	Camillus	8 Sep 1828
Jean	7	F		Great Britain		Dalmannock	24 Ocg 1826
John	21		Farmer	Isle of Wight	England	London	13 Dec 1822
John	28	M	Farmer	Ireland	New York	Carolina Ann	15 Oct 1824
John	28	M	Farmer	Great Britain		Dalmannock	24 Ocg 1826
Joseph	13	M	Weaver	Great Britain	U. States	Ganges	21 Jun 1827
Joseph	34		Weaver	Great Britain	United States	Thomas Dickason	29 Aug 1828
Leaze	21	F		Germany	United States	Samuel Robertson	8 Aug 1828
Margaret	3	F		Great Britain		Dalmannock	24 Ocg 1826
Rose	44	F	None	England	America	Dewitt Clinton	27 Jul 1824
William	1	M		Great Britain		Dalmannock	24 Ocg 1826
William	40	M	Manufacr.	Great Britain		Dalmannock	24 Ocg 1826
Wm.	22	M	Cotton Spinner	Scotland	United States	Tom	2 Jul 1827
MILLARD, John	23	M	Black Smith	England	U. States	Pacific	17 Jun 1828
MILLBURN, Thos.	20	M		Great Britain	U. States	Hamilton	28 Apr 1828
MILLBURY, William	20	M	Miller	Great Brittan	U. States	Gem	26 Jul 1827
MILLE, Andrew	45	M	Merchant	Philedelphia	United States	Eliza Grant	18 Aug 1826
MILLEAR, Wm.	22	M	...	Ireland	United States	General Putnam	20 Jun 1825
MILLEN, Jno.	19	M	Clerk	France	U. States	Alonzo	16 Jul 1821
Mary	19	F	Labourer	Ireland	United States	Hope	12 Jun 1828
Thomas	22	M	Merchant	United	U. States	Sarah G	30 Jun 1828
William	20	M	Labourer	Ireland	Unt. St. America	Wilson	21 May 1827
MILLENBERG, Anne	20	F	Farmer	Switzerland		Antioch	18 Aug 1829
Anne	40	F	Farmer	Switzerland		Antioch	18 Aug 1829
Elizabeth	25	F	Farmer	Switzerland		Antioch	18 Aug 1829
Jean	12	M	Farmer	Switzerland		Antioch	18 Aug 1829
Joseph	50	M	Farmer	Switzerland		Antioch	18 Aug 1829
MILLER, —	23	M		Germany	United States	Lydia	18 Jun 1828
—	36	M	Gentleman	U. States	U. States	Imperial	10 Dec 1821
—, Master	1 2/12	M		Scotland	U. States	Eliza	23 Dec 1822
—, Mr.	28	F		New Jersy	New Jersy	General Warren	6 Mar 1829
—, Mr.	33	M	Merchant	Norwegian	United States	Swift	13 Jan 1827
—, Mrs.	25	F		Scotland	U. States	Eliza	23 Dec 1822
—, Revd. Mr.	20	M		Halifax	some to return & the others to Canada	Albert	14 May 1822
...	36	F		G. Britain	U. States	Mary & Harriot	8 Sep 1828

888

NAMES OF PASSENGERS	A G E	S E X	OCCUPATIONS	COUNTRY TO WHICH THEY BELONG	COUNTRY THEY INTEND TO INHABIT	SHIPS/DATES OF ARRIVAL	
MILLER (cont'd)							
Adam	36	M	Miller	Germany	United States	Helen	5 Sep 1828
Adolph	24		...	...	Germany	Hudson	14 Jun 1827
Agnes	...			Roxbrookshire	Delaware	Peru	30 May 1828
Alex	19	M	Blockmaker	Scotland	U. States	Czar	29 Aug 1829
Alexr.	12			Ireland	United States	Jno. Dickinson	21 Sep 1821
Andrais	4	M		Germany	U. States	Isabella	10 Aug 1829
Andrew	6	M		Great Britain	U. States	St. Croix	13 Sep 1827
Ann	2			England	United States	Hugh Johnson	11 Jun 1828
Ann	3	F	None	England	United States	Jubilee	1 Oct 1828
Ann	7			Ireland	United States	Jno. Dickinson	21 Sep 1821
Ann	14 8/12	F		Ireland	United States	Atlantic	16 Dec 1825
Ann	20	F	None	England	United States	Jubilee	1 Oct 1828
Ann	22	F	None	Great Britain		Olive Branch	9 Oct 1829
Ann	49	F	Wife	Manchester	United States	Nile	17 May 1827
Anne	30	F		Ireland	America	Wilson	27 Nov 1826
Anne Maria	40	F	Spinster	Germany	U. States	Isabella	10 Aug 1829
Austin	31	F	Stone Mason	England	U. States	Electra	7 Jul 1828
B.	26	F	Farmer	Switzerland	U. States	Alfred	8 Jul 1828
Barbara	1 6/12	F	Child	Switzerland	United States	Andes	5 May 1828
Barbary	26	F	Lady	England	United States	Nimrod	30 Aug 1824
Barnard	25	M		Gt. Britain	United States	Penelope	9 Sep 1828
Benjamin	28	M	Machine Maker	Great Britain		Olive Branch	9 Oct 1829
Bridget	30	F	Farmer, Labourer or Spinster	Ireland	U. States	Meteor	4 Oct 1827
C.	20	M	Mechanic	Massachusetts	U. States	Clarissa	14 Jul 1821
C., Miss	17	F	Lady	St. Croix	on a Visit	Carlo	27 Aug 1829
Carolina	16	F	Farmer	Germany	United States	Elizabeth	27 Jul 1824
Carolina	38	F	Farmer	Germany	United States	Elizabeth	27 Jul 1824
Casper	1 6/12	F		Germany	U. States	Isabella	10 Aug 1829
Catharine	2			France	U. States	Parachute	14 May 1828
Catharine	43			France	U. States	Parachute	14 May 1828
Catherina	29	F	Farmer	Alsace in the Department of Upper and lower Rhine	United States	Carolina Augusta	16 May 1828
Catherine	27		Farmer	German	America	Romulus	15 May 1828
Charles	19	M	Painter	Great Britain	United States	William Dawson	18 Jun 1827
Charles	24	M	Gentleman	Scotland	Jamaica	Sanford William	26 Jul 1824
Charles	30	M	Labourer	England	United States	Jubilee	1 Oct 1828
Charlotte	12			England	United States	Hugh Johnson	11 Jun 1828
Chatharina	8	F	Farmer	Germany	United States	Elizabeth	27 Jul 1824
Christian	4	M	Farmer	Germany	U. States	Bayard	16 May 1827
Christiana	16	F	Farmer	Germany	United States	Lydia	18 Jun 1828
Christina	5	F	Child	Switzerland	United States	Andes	5 May 1828
Christina	13	F	Farmer	Germany	United States	Elizabeth	27 Jul 1824
Christina	30	F	Spinster	Switzerland	United States	Andes	5 May 1828
Chs.	29	M	Merger	Bristol	New York	Cosmo	25 Sep 1827
Cristian	22	M		Germany	Pelselvaney [Pennsylvania?]	Orient	25 Nov 1825
Daniel	1	M		Swis	United States	Iris	21 Sep 1821
David	31	M	Farmer	Great Britain	United States	Richmond	18 Feb 1820
David	35	M	Baker	St. Andrews	U. States	Sally	14 Jun 1823
David	43 6/12	M	Mariner	United States		Orestelle	4 Oct 1828
Dorothea	32	F	Weaver	Germany	U. States	Isabella	10 Aug 1829
Dorothy	8	F	Spinster	Switzerland	United States	Andes	5 May 1828
E. L.	25	M	Merchant	U. States	U. States	Silas Richards	29 Oct 1828
E. M.	24	M	Merchant	U. States	U. States	Ann Marie	22 May 1827
Ebenezer	20	M	Labourer	Ireland	United States	Lord Wellington	28 May 1827
Edmond	7 8/12	M		United States	United States	Brighton	12 Jun 1826
Elinor	10			Ireland	United States	Jno. Dickinson	21 Sep 1821
Elisabeth	2	F		Great Britain	United States	Mary Howland	19 Jul 1827
Eliza	6	F	Lady	England	New York	Brighton	11 Dec 1827
Eliza	8	F	Farmer	Germany	United States	Lydia	18 Jun 1828
Eliza	28	M		Great Britain	U. States	St. Croix	13 Sep 1827
Eliza	28	F	Farmer	Germany	United States	Lydia	18 Jun 1828
Elizabeth	3	F		Germany	U. States	Isabella	10 Aug 1829
Elizabeth	20	F	Spinster	Ireland	United States	Dublin Packet	9 Jul 1827
Elizabeth	28			St. John	U. States	Lady Hunter	5 Jul 1823

NAMES OF PASSENGERS	AGE	SEX	OCCUPATIONS	COUNTRY TO WHICH THEY BELONG	COUNTRY THEY INTEND TO INHABIT	SHIPS/DATES OF ARRIVAL	
MILLER (cont'd)							
Elizabeth	30	F		Germany	U. States	Isabella	10 Aug 1829
Ellen	2			Ireland	United States	Geo. Canning	5 Jun 1828
Ellen	8		None	Great Brittain	U. States America	James Cropper	23 Mar 1827
Ellen	28		None	Great Brittain	U. States America	James Cropper	23 Mar 1827
Euphemia	4	F		G. Britain	U. States	Eliza	9 May 1827
Euphemia	30	F		G. Britain	U. States	Eliza	9 May 1827
Frances	10	F	Lady	England	New York	Brighton	11 Dec 1827
Francis	3			England	United States	Hugh Johnson	11 Jun 1828
Frederic	3		Farmer	German	America	Romulus	15 May 1828
Frederic	27			German	America	Romulus	15 May 1828
Frena	24	F		Swis	United States	Iris	21 Sep 1821
Friderick	5	M	Farmer	Germany	United States	Elizabeth	27 Jul 1824
Geo.	15	M	None	England	America	Dewitt Clinton	27 Jul 1824
Geo.	18			Ireland	United States	Jno. Dickinson	21 Sep 1821
George	5			France	U. States	Parachute	14 May 1828
George	24	M	Clothier	Great Britain	United States	Atlantic	28 May 1827
George	24	M	Shoemaker	Engd.	United States	Cosmo	21 Aug 1828
George	27	M	Weaver	Gt. Britan	America	Braganza	1 Dec 1824
George	27	M		Great Brittian	United States	Carolina Augusta	2 Dec 1828
George	49	M	Block Maker	England	America	Two Marys	24 Sep 1827
George	50	M	Farmer	G. Britain	U.S.A.	Silas Richards	29 Oct 1827
Gilbert	35	M	Mechanic	N. York	U. States	Dispatch	22 Mar 1822
Gottleb	11	M	Farmer	Germany	United States	Elizabeth	27 Jul 1824
H.	35	M	Farmer	Germany	United States	Lydia	18 Jun 1828
Hanah	8	F		G. Britain	U. States	Mary & Harriot	8 Sep 1828
Hannah	9	F	None	England	America	Dewitt Clinton	27 Jul 1824
Hannah	23	F		England	United States	Earl of Liverpool	28 Apr 1824
Hannah	26	F		Great Britain	United States	Mary Howland	19 Jul 1827
Hariot	1	F	None	England	United States	Jubilee	1 Oct 1828
Harriet	2	F	Farmer	Germany	U. States	Bayard	16 May 1827
Harry	3		Farmer	Jerman	America	Romulus	15 May 1828
Helen	19 6/12	F	Matron	Great Britain	State of N. York	Robert Fulton	30 Dec 1824
Henery	23		Shoe Maker	Hanovurine	United States	Hudson	5 Apr 1826
Henry	11	M	Farmer	Germany	United States	Lydia	18 Jun 1828
Henry	30		Farmer	Jerman	America	Romulus	15 May 1828
Henry	40	M	Gentleman	Philadelphia	Philadelphia	Inspector	26 May 1828
Henry	50	M	Planter	England	U. States	Elias Burger	12 Sep 1822
Henry	58	M	Farmer	United States	United States	Nancy	16 Jul 1824
Hugh	29	M	Farmer		United States	Sarah	9 Nov 1820
Humphry	12	M	None	Gt. Britan	America	Braganza	1 Dec 1824
J.	25	M		England	United States	Earl of Liverpool	28 Apr 1824
J.	40	M		Ireland	U. States	Josephine	27 Jul 1825
Jacen	40			France	U. States	Parachute	14 May 1828
Jacob	1	M	None	Holland	U. States	United States	7 Jul 1827
Jacob	6	M		Germany	U. States	Isabella	10 Aug 1829
Jacob	7			France	U. States	Parachute	14 May 1828
Jacob	7	M		Germany	U. States	Isabella	10 Aug 1829
Jacob	38	M	Farmer	Switzerland	United States	Andes	5 May 1828
James	18	M	Servant	England	England	Emulation	12 Mar 1825
James	18	M	Farmer	Lundarry	United States	Minerva	30 Oct 1829
James	20		Labourer			Rufus King	7 Aug 1820
James	21	M	Halle	Manchester	United States	Nile	17 May 1827
James	24	M	Farmer	Ireland	U. States	Francis	6 Sep 1827
James	24	M	Shoemaker	Scotland	United States	Mary & Susan	5 Aug 1828
James	25	M	Merchant	Great Britain	State of N. York	Robert Fulton	30 Dec 1824
James	37	M	Doctor	Scotland	Halifax, N.S.	Hunter	2 Aug 1822
James	51 4/12	M	Farmer	Ireland	America	Euphrates	26 Jun 1821
Jane	2	F	None	Ireland	United States	Lord Wellington	28 May 1827
Jane	3			Roxbrookshire	Delaware	Peru	30 May 1828
Jane	4	F	None	England	America	Dewitt Clinton	27 Jul 1824
Jane	4	F	None	Ireland	United States	Lord Wellington	28 May 1827
Jane	7			England	United States	Hugh Johnson	11 Jun 1828
Jane	30			England	United States	Hugh Johnson	11 Jun 1828
Jane	31	F		England	U. States	Lima	5 Aug 1829
Jas.	26	M	Farmer	United States	United States	Loire	18 Oct 1820

NAMES OF PASSENGERS	AGE	SEX	OCCUPATIONS	COUNTRY TO WHICH THEY BELONG	COUNTRY THEY INTEND TO INHABIT	SHIPS/DATES OF ARRIVAL	
MILLER (cont'd)							
Jas.	26	M	Mason	G. Britain	U. States	Eliza	9 May 1827
Jas.	32	M	Weaver	G. Britain	U. States	Eliza	9 May 1827
Jean	28	M	Weaver	Germany	U. States	Isabella	10 Aug 1829
Jean	35		Farmer	France	U. States	Parachute	14 May 1828
Jean	35	M	Weaver	Germany	U. States	Isabella	10 Aug 1829
Jeremiah	44	M	None	America		Manhattan	7 Nov 1827
Jno.	30	M	Merchant	U. States	U. States	Tampico	20 Apr 1825
Johanes	3	M	Farmer	Germany	United States	Elizabeth	27 Jul 1824
Johanes	42	M	Farmer	Germany	United States	Elizabeth	27 Jul 1824
Johannes	34	M	Farmer	Germany	U. States	Isabella	10 Aug 1829
John			Distressed Seaman	New York	U. States	Mary & Eliza	2 Jul 1829
John	1	M	Farmer	Alsace in the Department of Upper and lower Rhine	United States	Carolina Augusta	16 May 1828
John	10	M		Germany	U. States	Isabella	10 Aug 1829
John	13	M	None	England	America	Dewitt Clinton	27 Jul 1824
John	19	M	Halle	Manchester	United States	Nile	17 May 1827
John	21 2/12	M		England	U.S. of America	Illinois	30 Apr 1823
John	22	M	Farmer	Native of Switzerland	United States	Canaris	30 Jun 1827
John	22	M	Labourer	G. Britain	U. States	Mary & Harriot	8 Sep 1828
John	23	M	Taylor	G. Britain	U. States	George Clinton	10 Sep 1828
John	24	M		England	England	Amity	31 May 1822
John	24	M	Clothier	Great Britain	United States	Frances Henrietta	17 Sep 1827
John	24	M	Millwright	Amfield	U. States	Milton	21 May 1827
John	25	M	Carpenter	Britain	America	Camillus	9 Oct 1820
John	26	M	Labourer	Ireland	United States	Lord Wellington	28 May 1827
John	26	M	Farmer	Switzerland	U. States	Romulus	24 Sep 1828
John	27	M	Ship Wright	Ireland	U. States	Wanderer	1 Sep 1828
John	28	M	Merchant	Gt. Britain	United States	Neptune	23 Jan 1826
John	30	F	Carpenter	France	U. States	Edward Bonaffe	23 Jul 1828
John	34	M				Golden Grove	6 Sep 1820
John	34	M	Moulder	Great Brittain	U. States America	James Cropper	23 Mar 1827
John	35	M	Weaver	Ireland	United States	Atlantic	16 Dec 1825
John	50 3/12	M	Farmer	United States	United States	Louisa	16 Mar 1826
John, Mr.	36	M	Servant to the Bishop	Gt. Britain	Canada	Pacific	22 May 1826
John Rogers	51	M		England	England	Britannia	22 Jul 1829
Jon.	33	M	Labourer	Great Britain	United States	Atlantic	28 May 1827
Jos.	3		None	Great Brittain	U. States America	James Cropper	23 Mar 1827
Joseph	11	M	None	England	America	Dewitt Clinton	27 Jul 1824
Joseph	18	M	Weaver	Gt. Britan	America	Braganza	1 Dec 1824
Joseph	45	M	Farmer	England	America	Dewitt Clinton	27 Jul 1824
M.	19	F		Hessen		Constitution	20 Jun 1828
M.	39	M	Farmer	Switzerland	U. States	Alfred	8 Jul 1828
Maango	26	M	Phisician	Kentucky		Secretary	10 Aug 1829
Macy	5			England	United States	Hugh Johnson	11 Jun 1828
Madalena	21	F	Spinster	Switzerland	United States	Andes	5 May 1828
Mara	10			France	U. States	Parachute	14 May 1828
Marey	24	F	None	Holland	U. States	United States	7 Jul 1827
Margaret	16	F	Spinster	Ireland	United States	Dublin Packet	22 Aug 1829
Margaret	24	F	Wife & Child	Manchester	United States	Nile	17 May 1827
Margaret	35	F	Farmer	Germany	U. States	Bayard	16 May 1827
Margret	30			Ireland	United States	Geo. Canning	5 Jun 1828
Margret	40	F	None		New York	Governor Clinton	3 Jul 1827
Margt.	20	F		Gt. Britain	United States	Penelope	9 Sep 1828
Maria	14	F	Lady	England	South Carolina	Brighton	11 Dec 1827
Maria	14	F		Germany	U. States	Isabella	10 Aug 1829
Marie Eliz.	18			France	U. States	Parachute	14 May 1828
Marie Rose	11			France	U. States	Parachute	14 May 1828
Mark	4	M	None	Great Britain		Olive Branch	9 Oct 1829
Martha	30	F	None	Gt. Britan	America	Braganza	1 Dec 1824
Mary	6/12	F		Great Britain	United States	Mary Howland	19 Jul 1827
Mary	1			England	United States	Hugh Johnson	11 Jun 1828
Mary	14	F		Ireland	United States	General Putnam	20 Jun 1825

NAMES OF PASSENGERS	AGE	SEX	OCCUPATIONS	COUNTRY TO WHICH THEY BELONG	COUNTRY THEY INTEND TO INHABIT	SHIPS/DATES OF ARRIVAL	
MILLER (cont'd)							
Mary	18	F		Great Britian	United States	Isaac Hicks	22 May 1826
Mary	19	F	Millenner	Ireland	United States	Trident	17 May 1825
Mary	20	F		Barbadoes	Barbadoes	Elias Burger	24 Jul 1820
Mary	21		Labourer	Roxbrookshire	Delaware	Peru	30 May 1828
Mary	27	F	Wife	Ireland	United States	Sylvester Healy	11 May 1825
Mary	30	F		United States	United States	Brighton	12 Jun 1826
Mary	35					Agricola	1 Jul 1820
Mary	58	F	Farmer	Germany	United States	Lydia	18 Jun 1828
Mary A.	13	F	None	Honaghan	U. States	Milton	21 May 1827
Mary A.	41	F	None	Honaghan	U. States	Milton	21 May 1827
Mathew	18	M	Cooper	Switzerland	United States	Elbe	2 Aug 1822
Michael	26	M	Farmer	Holland	U. States	United States	7 Jul 1827
Micle	23	M	Labourer	Wittenburg	U. States	Comet	28 Jul 1825
Nancy	1	F		G. Britain	U. States	Eliza	9 May 1827
Nancy	18	F	Farmer	Germany	United States	Lydia	18 Jun 1828
Nicholas	8	M	Farmer	Germany	U. States	Bayard	16 May 1827
Nicholas	40	M	Farmer	Germany	U. States	Bayard	16 May 1827
P. V. C.	23	M		New York		Leander	18 May 1827
Patrick	14	M	Labourer	Ireland	United States	William & George	14 May 1828
Patrick	20	M	Weaver	Ireland	U. States	Josephine	7 May 1827
Peter	6	M	Farmer	Germany	U. States	Bayard	16 May 1827
Pierre	48		Farmer	France	U. States	Parachute	14 May 1828
Polly	59 6/12	F		New York	U. States	Wanderer	1 Sep 1828
R.	65	M	Glass Cutter	Great Britain	United States	Saml. Wight	6 Sep 1827
R. K.	6/12	F		New Jersy	New Jersy	General Warren	6 Mar 1829
Regina	6/12	F	Farmer	Germany	United States	Elizabeth	27 Jul 1824
Richd.	13			England	United States	Hugh Johnson	11 Jun 1828
Richd.	38		Carpenter	England	United States	Hugh Johnson	11 Jun 1828
Robert	18	M	Labourer	G. Britain	U. States	Mary & Harriot	8 Sep 1828
Robert	22	M	Labourer	Ireland	United States	Catharine	22 Jul 1825
Robert	38	...	...	Scotland	America	Nimrod	9 Jul 1827
Robt.	8	M		Great Britain	U. States	St. Croix	13 Sep 1827
Robt.	17	M		Great Britain	United States	Atlantic	28 May 1827
Robt.	40	M	Farmer	Great Britain	U. States	St. Croix	13 Sep 1827
Romulus	30/365		Farmer	born at Sea	America	Romulus	15 May 1828
Rosey	16	F	None	Gt. Britan	America	Braganza	1 Dec 1824
Rosina	38	F				Golden Grove	6 Sep 1820
Rudolph	22	M	Farrier	Swis	United States	Iris	21 Sep 1821
Saml.	4	M		Great Britain	U. States	St. Croix	13 Sep 1827
Samuel	38	M	Hatter	Great Britain	United States	Mary Howland	19 Jul 1827
Sarah	2	F	None	Great Britain		Olive Branch	9 Oct 1829
Sarah	15			Ireland	United States	Jno. Dickinson	21 Sep 1821
Sarah	17	F	None	England	America	Dewitt Clinton	27 Jul 1824
Sarah	17	F	Miliner	England	United States	Trident	30 Sep 1826
Sarah	22	F		France	United States	Catharine	10 Sep 1827
Sarah	35 6/12	F		Ireland	United States	Atlantic	16 Dec 1825
Shaw	21		Labourer	Roxbrookshire	Delaware	Peru	30 May 1828
Sophia	4		Farmer	Jerman	America	Romulus	15 May 1828
Sophia	27		Farmer	Jerman	America	Romulus	15 May 1828
Susan	25	F	None	Ireland	United States	Lord Wellington	28 May 1827
Tabathy	6/12	F		Germany	U. States	Isabella	10 Aug 1829
Thomas	1... 7/12	M	...	Ireland	United States	Lima	19 Jun 1824
Thomas	15	M	Labourer	G. Britain	U. States	Mary & Harriot	8 Sep 1828
Thomas	22	M	Miller	Ireland	United States	Andes	2 Oct 1828
Thomas	25	M	Labourer	Ireland	United States	Lord Wellington	28 May 1827
Thomas	36	M	Lithographer	Great Britten	United States	Cortes	6 Mar 1827
Thomas	40	M	Farmer	Scotland	U.S.	Curler	19 Jul 1828
Thomas	46	M	Labourer	G. Britain	U. States	Mary & Harriot	8 Sep 1828
Thos.	22	M	Labourer	England	United States	Bolivar	15 Jun 1826
William	4/12	M	Child	Ireland	United States	Sylvester Healy	11 May 1825
William	10	M	None	Gt. Britan	America	Braganza	1 Dec 1824
William	17		Labourer	Ireland	Great Britain	Robert Burns	14 Jun 1824
William	25	M	Shoemaker	England	United States	Trident	30 Sep 1826
William	27	M	Coachman	Ireland	United States	Sylvester Healy	11 May 1825
William	29	M	Merchant	Great Britain	United States	Jean	17 Aug 1827
William	32	M	Clerk	Great Britain	United States	Robert Fulton	22 Oct 1821

NAMES OF PASSENGERS	AGE	SEX	OCCUPATIONS	COUNTRY TO WHICH THEY BELONG	COUNTRY THEY INTEND TO INHABIT	SHIPS/DATES OF ARRIVAL	
MILLER (cont'd)							
William	40	M	Labourer		New York	Governor Clinton	3 Jul 1827
Wm.	6		None	Great Brittain	U. States America	James Cropper	23 Mar 1827
Wm.	9			England	United States	Hugh Johnson	11 Jun 1828
Wm.	10	M		Great Britain	U. States	St. Croix	13 Sep 1827
Wm.	26	M	Merchant	Scotland	U. States	Eliza	23 Dec 1822
Wm.	26	M	Labourer	Ireland		Marchioness	13 May 1828
Wm.	27	M		Scotland	United States	Trent	10 Jul 1827
Wm.	30		Weaver	Ireland	United States	Geo. Canning	5 Jun 1828
Wm.	45		Mason			Agricola	1 Jul 1820
MILLERET, Louis	50		Merchant	France	France	London	16 Aug 1824
MILLERMAN, Bridgt.	12	F	Labourer	Ireland	United States	Essex	23 May 1828
MILLERR, Hy.	54	M	Gent.	Baltimore	U. States	Chase	5 Oct 1824
MILLERS, Jno.	36	M	Mechanic	England	U. States	Cygnet	22 Jun 1821
MILLES, John	24	M	Clerk	England	America	Braganza	1 Dec 1824
MILLETS, Z. S.	38	M	Merchant	New York	U. States	Crisis	26 May 1824
MILLETT, N. M.	25	M	Labourer	Ireland	U. States	Sarah G	30 Jun 1828
MILLIAN, Andrew	26	M	Stone Cutter	Scotland	Scotland	Sarah G.	28 Nov 1827
Thomas	30	M	Laborer	Ireland	Pittsburgh	Indian Chief	16 Aug 1822
MILLIER, Adolphe	21		Mercht.	France	United States	Cadmus	24 Oct 1827
Arnold	22		Engraver	France	United States	Cadmus	24 Oct 1827
MILLIGAN, Ellen	25	F	House Keeper	Ireland	United States	Carolina Ann	14 May 1827
James	3	M		Ireland	United States	Carolina Ann	14 May 1827
James	30	M	Cooper	Anthrem	Baltimore	Nile	18 Aug 1829
James	36	M	Labourer	Ireland	United States	Carolina Ann	14 May 1827
John	35	M	Farmer	G. Britain	U. States	Wanderer	23 Jun 1828
Mary	1	F		Ireland	United States	Carolina Ann	14 May 1827
Mary	18	F		Ireland	New York	Lady Hunter	5 Jun 1826
Mary	29		his wife [Thomas]	England	U. States	Rufus King	3 Sep 1822
Mary	29		Wife [of Wm. Ror.]	Great Britain	United States	Camillus	12 Sep 1827
Mary	60		Spinster	Scotland	United States	Camillus	3 May 1828
Peter	...		their child [Thomas and Mary]	England	U. States	Rufus King	3 Sep 1822
Thomas	47		Iron Founderer	England	U. States	Rufus King	3 Sep 1822
William	5	M		Ireland	United States	Carolina Ann	14 May 1827
William	26	M	Gentleman	Scotland	United States	Richmond	4 Aug 1826
Wm.	10		Son [of Wm. Ror.]	Great Britain	United States	Camillus	12 Sep 1827
Wm. Ror.	34		Weaver	Great Britain	United States	Camillus	12 Sep 1827
MILLIHAN, J.	40	M		Ireland	United States	Sarah G.	15 May 1828
James	30	M		Ireland	United States	Sarah G.	15 May 1828
MILLIN, S.	40	M	Gentleman	United States	United States	Betsey	1 Apr 1828
MILLINGTON, —, Mrs.	26	F		England	United States	Earl of Liverpool	28 Apr 1824
Mathew	34	M	Mechanic	Gt. Britain	United States	John & Elizabeth	25 Sep 1827
MILLMAN, Jacob(Milleman)	18	M	Laborer	United States	United States	Globe	30 Aug 1828
*landed at this Port, Custom House, Portland, Aug 19, 1828							
MILLMORE, Bridget	18 7/12	F		Ireland	U.S. of America	Douglass	6 Jul 1829
MILLNER, J. P., Mrs.	20	F	None	U. States	U. States	Canada	2 Jun 1824
Thos. P.	2	M	None	U. States	U. States	Canada	2 Jun 1824
MILLOR, Alexander	19		Weaver	Scotland	America	Sarah	18 Aug 1829
Ellen	10	F		England	New Jersey	Lima	5 Aug 1829
James	36	M	Labourer	England	New Jersey	Lima	5 Aug 1829
James	36	M	Labourer	England	U. States	Lima	5 Aug 1829
Jane	31	F		England	New Jersey	Lima	5 Aug 1829
MILLS, —, Mr.	40	M	Merchant	Dublin	U. States	Hibernia	26 Oct 1826
—, Mrs.	27	F	Farmer	Gt. Britain	U. States	Constitution	19 Jul 1825
Abraham	32	F	Weaver	England		Aurora	12 Mar 1827
Alexr.	5	M		G. Britain	U. States	Camillus	8 Sep 1828
Ann	8	F		Ireland		Lady Hunter	12 Apr 1823
Ann	30	F		Ireland		Lady Hunter	12 Apr 1823
Ann	30		None	Great Britain	United States	Roman	10 Sep 1827
Benja.	34	M	Farmer	Great Brittan	U. States	Prince Leopold	2 Jul 1821
Benjamin	24	M	Miner	Great Britain	U.S. of America	Gratitude	3 Oct 1829
Betsey	8	F		Great Britain	U. States	Prince Leopold	2 Jul 1821
Betty	24	F		Great Britain	United States	John Jay	8 May 1828
C.	33	M	Merchant	Montreal, L.C.	Montreal, L.C.	New York	14 Jul 1827

NAMES OF PASSENGERS	AGE	SEX	OCCUPATIONS	COUNTRY TO WHICH THEY BELONG	COUNTRY THEY INTEND TO INHABIT	SHIPS/DATES OF ARRIVAL	
MILLS (cont'd)							
C.	36	M	Merchant	England	U. States	New York	8 Mar 1825
Cathe.	8		None	Great Britain	United States	Roman	10 Sep 1827
Charles	24	M	Farmer	England	U. States	Electra	7 Jul 1828
Christian	6	F		Scotland	United States	Camillus	27 Oct 1829
E.	21 7/12	M	Merchant	London	U. States	Hopes Delight	21 Apr 1828
E.	35	M	Merchant	G. Britain	U. States	St. George	7 Jun 1828
Edwd.	26	M	Farmer	Great Britain	U. States	Columbia	22 Sep 1828
Elisha	4	M		G. Britain	U. States	St. George	7 Jun 1828
Eliza	4	F		Scotland	United States	Camillus	27 Oct 1829
Elizabeth	1	F		Great Britain	United States	John Jay	8 May 1828
Elizabeth	36	F		Scotland	United States	Camillus	27 Oct 1829
Euphemia	19	F	Spinster	Ireland	U. States	William & John	10 Jul 1824
Geo.	26	M	Carpenter	Scotland	United States	Louisiana	3 Nov 1827
George	2/12	M		Ireland		Lady Hunter	12 Apr 1823
Grace	24	F	None	England	United States	Jubilee	12 May 1828
Grace, Jr.	2	F	None	England	United States	Jubilee	12 May 1828
Hannah	12	F		England	U. States	Cincinnatus	24 May 1821
Hannah	43	F		England	U. States	Cincinnatus	24 May 1821
Harriot	2	F		Great Brittan	U. States	Prince Leopold	2 Jul 1821
Harriot	9	F		England	U. States	Cincinnatus	24 May 1821
James	18	M		Ireland	U. States	Nancy	16 Aug 1822
James	25	M	Mechanic	Philada.	Philada.	Four Sons	23 Mar 1825
James	60	M	Merchant	Great Brittan	United States	Orbit	31 Dec 1821
Jane	1	F		England	U. States	Cincinnatus	24 May 1821
Jane	10	F		Ireland		Lady Hunter	12 Apr 1823
Jean	2	F		Scotland	United States	Camillus	27 Oct 1829
Jefrey	42 6/12	M	Farmer	Scotland	United States	Euphrates	25 Mar 1820
Joh. H.	25	M	Gent.	Great Britain	United States	Atlantic	28 May 1827
John	10	M		Scotland	United States	Camillus	27 Oct 1829
John	21	M	Labourer	Ireland	United States	Hope	12 Jun 1828
John	22	M	Labourer	Ireland	U. States	William & John	10 Jul 1824
John	26	M	Labourer	England	Newyork	Cortes	16 Jul 1827
John	30	M	Joiner	Scotland	United States	Culloden	17 May 1828
Joseph	12	M	None	England	Philada.	Colossus	2 Oct 1827
Margaret	8	F		Scotland	United States	Camillus	27 Oct 1829
Margarett	30	F		Great Brittan	U. States	Prince Leopold	2 Jul 1821
Margret	15		Spinster			Charlotte Corday	11 Sep 1820
Margt.	28	F		G. Britain	U. States	Camillus	8 Sep 1828
Martha	7/12	F		Great Britain	U.S. of America	Gratitude	3 Oct 1829
Mary	5	F		Great Brittan	U. States	Prince Leopold	2 Jul 1821
Mary	27	F		Great Brittan	U.S. of America	Gratitude	3 Oct 1829
Moses	35	M	Mariner	U. States	U. States	Fox	5 Sep 1821
Rhoda	4	F		England	U. States	Cincinnatus	24 May 1821
Robert	18	M	Labourer	Ireland	U. States	William & John	10 Jul 1824
Robert	80	M	Farmer	Ireland	U. States	William & John	10 Jul 1824
Saml.	27	M	Farmer	Gt. Brittian	Gt. Brittian	Manchester	21 Apr 1827
Saml.	30	M	Farmer	Ireland	U. States	William & John	10 Jul 1824
Samuel	23	M	Clothier	England	Alexandria, U.S.	Roman	17 Oct 1826
Sarah	2	F		Ireland		Lady Hunter	12 Apr 1823
Sarah	24	F		Great Britain	United States	Atlantic	28 May 1827
Sarah	25	F		G. Britain	U. States	St. George	7 Jun 1828
Sarah	51	F	None	England	New York	Brighton	9 Dec 1828
Stephen F.	33	M	Merchant	U. States	U. States	Virginia	26 May 1828
T. R.	10		None	Great Britain	United States	Roman	10 Sep 1827
Thomas	29	M	Miller	England	America	Colossus	22 Aug 1829
Thos.	25	M	Blacksmith	Great Britain	United States	Washington	3 Sep 1827
Thos. J.	25	M	Glass Blower	England	U. States	Orazimbo	7 Jan 1821
William	33	M	Mechanic	Ireland	United States	Concordia	25 Aug 1827
William	34	M	Hatter	England	New York	Brighton	9 Dec 1828
William	46	M	Farmer	England	U. States	Cincinnatus	24 May 1821
Wm.	1 6/12	M		Great Britain	U.S. of America	Gratitude	3 Oct 1829
Wm.	12	M		Ireland		Lady Hunter	12 Apr 1823
Wm.	25	M	Sadler	Ireland		Lady Hunter	12 Apr 1823
Wm. H.	1		None	Great Britain	United States	Roman	10 Sep 1827
MILLSON, John	64	M	Farmer	United States	United States	Acosta	28 Jul 1823
Martha	52	F		United States	United States	Acosta	28 Jul 1823
William	30	M	Farmer	Great Britain	United States	Freake	25 Aug 1829

NAMES OF PASSENGERS	AGE	SEX	OCCUPATIONS	COUNTRY TO WHICH THEY BELONG	COUNTRY THEY INTEND TO INHABIT	SHIPS/DATES OF ARRIVAL	
MILLTONER, Johanna	50	F		Germany	America	Falcon	28 Aug 1828
MILLWOOD, Eliza	23	F	None	Great Brittan	U. States	Gem	26 Jul 1827
Jas.	21	M	Joiner	Great Brittan	U. States	Gem	26 Jul 1827
MILLY, James	37	M	Labourer	Ireland	United States	Robert Fulton	24 Jul 1826
MILN, David	55	M	Planter	S. Croix	S. Croix	Jupiter	29 Jun 1825
Geo.	28	M	Merchant	Scotland	U. States	Resign	1 May 1822
Hugh	21	M	Shoe Maker	Ireland	United States	Kleber	23 Jul 1827
MILNE, A.	22	M	Farmer	Scotland	U. States	Exchange	19 Aug 1822
Andw.	36	M	Merchant	America	U. States	James Monroe	14 Jan 1823
Helen	40	F		Scotland	United States	Louisiana	3 Nov 1827
Isabella	14	F		Scotland	United States	Louisiana	3 Nov 1827
James	17	M	Merchant	Scotland	United States	Louisiana	3 Nov 1827
James	18	M	Merchant	Great Britain	United States	Atlantic	3 Dec 1821
James	25	M	Merchant	Great Britain	Savannah	James Cropper	14 Oct 1824
Jas.	20	M	Merchant	England	England	John Wells	14 Oct 1823
John	30	M	Merchant	Europe	United States	Aspasia	5 Sep 1827
Jos.	25	M	Merchant	England	England	John Wells	14 Oct 1823
Joshua	23	M	Merchant	Great Britain	Great Britain	Nestor	3 Nov 1820
Joshua	24	M	Merchant	Great Britain	United States	Atlantic	3 Dec 1821
Joshua	25	M	Merchant	Great Britain	Savannah	James Cropper	14 Oct 1824
Robert	43	M	Merchant	Great Britain	America	Samuel Robertson	26 Nov 1825
Rosina	9	F		Great Britain	Canada	Marmion	13 Jun 1823
Sarah	40	F		Great Britain	Canada	Marmion	13 Jun 1823
William	36	M	Physician	England	Canada	Brighton	9 Dec 1828
Willm.	35	M	Merchant	Scotland	Havana	Amity	13 Sep 1821
MILNER, Jno.	29	M	Merchant	U. States	U. States	Lewis	20 Feb 1824
Rob.	26	M	Merchant	U. States	U. States	Nassau	6 Sep 1824
MILNEY, John	37					William	17 Aug 1820
MILNOR, Isaac	25	M	Merchant	Philada.	U. States	Paulina Julia	19 Dec 1823
Samuel	30	M	Servant			John Wills	21 May 1824
MILROY, P.	25	M	Merchant	Great Britan	U. States	Aspasia	23 Nov 1825
MILTA, Juan	10	M	Servant	Republic of Columbia		Ductile	30 Nov 1822
MILTIMORE, Andrew W., Capt.	34			New Hampshire		Hudson	18 Jun 1825

*Officers, Seamen and Passengers belonging to the Ship Jane of Boston and taken from on board the Schooner Olive of St. Johns , N.B. on the 4th June 1825, Lat. 41.30, Long 53.19, which ship flounderd on the 31st ultimo in Lat. 41.44 Long 52.

NAMES OF PASSENGERS	AGE	SEX	OCCUPATIONS	COUNTRY TO WHICH THEY BELONG	COUNTRY THEY INTEND TO INHABIT	SHIPS/DATES OF ARRIVAL	
MILTON, J.	30	M	Sailor	America	U. States	Hiram	17 Jun 1826
Margt.	32	F	Spinster	Gt. Britain	New York	Columbia	3 Apr 1826
MILWAIN, John	21	M	Labourer	England	America	Alexander Mansfield	16 Nov 1821
MIMNING, George	23	M	Planter	United States	United States	Richmond	2 May 1828
MINARDI, Jos.	12	M	Farmer	France	U. States	Ohio	18 Jul 1821
Jos.	45	M	Farmer	France	U. States	Ohio	18 Jul 1821
Louisa	8	F		France	U. States	Ohio	18 Jul 1821
MINCHIN, Ellen, Miss	8	F	Child	Ireland	United States	Dublin Packet	6 Dec 1827
Maria, Mrs.	30	F	Lady	Ireland	United States	Dublin Packet	6 Dec 1827
Mary, Miss	7	F	Child	Ireland	United States	Dublin Packet	6 Dec 1827
MINDER, Anne	40	F	Farmer	Hietwyss	U.S. America	Superior	18 Jun 1825
Antoine	5	M	Farmer	Hietwyss	U.S. America	Superior	18 Jun 1825
Francois S.	9	M	Farmer	Hietwyss	U.S. America	Superior	18 Jun 1825
Jean	40	M	Farmer	Hietwyss	U.S. America	Superior	18 Jun 1825
Jean E.	12	M	Farmer	Hietwyss	U.S. America	Superior	18 Jun 1825
Nicolas	33	M	Farmer	Hietwyss	U.S. America	Superior	18 Jun 1825
Susanne	15	F	Farmer	Hietwyss	U.S. America	Superior	18 Jun 1825
MINEKIN, T.	26	M	Labourer	Ireland	United States	Sarah G.	15 May 1828
MINER, B. F., Capt.	35	M	Mariner	United States	United States	Columbia	21 Jan 1828
MINERLY, Robert	28	M	Labourer	Ireland	United States	William & George	14 May 1828
MINES, Mary	21	F	Servant	Ireland	America	Carolina Ann	7 Aug 1826
MINGRAND, L.	46	M	Super Cargo	France	return in the vessel	Andreas	20 Aug 1821
MINIEL, E.	36	F		Philad.	U. States	Hero	17 May 1825
MINIER, —, child	4	M	None	France	United States	Marmione	20 Nov 1821
—, Mrs.	34	F	None	France	United States	Marmione	20 Nov 1821
MINK, Alexander	26	M	Clergyman	Scotland	U.S. of America	Camillus	16 Apr 1822
Philip	22	M	Mariner	U. States	U. States	Atlas	24 Jun 1828
MINKIN, John Jacob	22		Baker	England	United States	Acasta	16 Aug 1826
MINLOVE, Edwd.	27		Merchant	England	England	Silvanus Jenkins	30 Nov 1827

895

NAMES OF PASSENGERS	AGE	SEX	OCCUPATIONS	COUNTRY TO WHICH THEY BELONG	COUNTRY THEY INTEND TO INHABIT	SHIPS/DATES OF ARRIVAL	
MINMAGH, Bridget	26	F	Spinster	Ireland	United States	Robert Fulton	24 Jul 1826
Margeret	24	F	Spinster	Ireland	United States	Robert Fulton	24 Jul 1826
MINN, Edward	23	M	Carpenter	England	United States	Cincinnatus	21 Nov 1821
MINNEY, Jane	55	F	Servant	America	U.S. America	Cortes	19 May 1826
MINNIS, Hugh	3	M	None	United States	U. States	Gem	26 Jul 1827
Susan	30	F	Laborer	United States	U. States	Gem	26 Jul 1827
MINNY, Jane	50	F	Servant	England	England	Tontin	13 Jun 1825
MINOCH, Agusta	30	M	Merchant	Germany	U. States	Bayard	9 Jul 1824
MINOGH, Ann	18	F	Servant	Ireland	America	Atlantic	8 May 1828
MINOHAN, Catherine	21			Ireland	United States	Geo. Canning	5 Jun 1828
John	21		Labourer	Ireland	United States	Geo. Canning	5 Jun 1828
Wm.	1			Ireland	United States	Geo. Canning	5 Jun 1828
MINOR, William	26	M	Farmer	Ireland	United States	Dublin Packet	23 May 1828
MINSE, James	18	M	Farmer	Ireland	United States	Asia	29 Jul 1829
MINSHALL, Ann	1	F		Great Britain	United States	Mary Howland	19 Jul 1827
Anne	46	F		Great Britain	United States	Mary Howland	19 Jul 1827
Henry	4	M		Great Britain	United States	Mary Howland	19 Jul 1827
James	9	M		Great Britain	United States	Mary Howland	19 Jul 1827
Joseph	14	M		Great Britain	United States	Mary Howland	19 Jul 1827
Joshua	22	M	Farmer	Great Britain	United States	Mary Howland	19 Jul 1827
Margaret	16	F		Great Britain	United States	Mary Howland	19 Jul 1827
Samuel	6	M		Great Britain	United States	Mary Howland	19 Jul 1827
Thos.	12	M		Great Britain	United States	Mary Howland	19 Jul 1827
Thos.	44	M	Farmer	Great Britain	United States	Mary Howland	19 Jul 1827
MINTIER, Zephinin	20	M	Shoemaker	France	U.S.	Edward Quesnel	19 Oct 1829
MINTUN, Charles	28		Planter	United States		Bayard	10 Sep 1827
MINTURN, —, Mrs.	48	F		New York	New York	Camden	14 May 1825
B. G., Jr.	23	M	Merchant	U. States	U. States	Cincinnatus	3 Sep 1827
Mary	18	F		America	America	Silas Richard	24 Oct 1829
MINUGH, Ann	50	F	Spinster	Ireland	United States	Dublin Packet	22 Apr 1822
MINUTOLI, Philipo	19	M	Gentleman	Messina	Messina	Sofia	17 May 1828
MIRANDOLE, Edward	28	M	Mercht.	Italy	U. States	Eugene	15 Dec 1828
MIRBRAN, Thos.	30	M	Labourer	Ireland	United States	Mary & Harriet	3 Jul 1829
MIRDIE, John, Mr.	23	M	Weaver	Scotland	U. States	Majestic	27 Jul 1829
MIRE, Jeremiah	42 7/12	M	Farmer	France	America	Henry	17 May 1828
Judaith	24	F	Wife	Ireland	New York	Louisa	18 Apr 1827
MIRHALETTE, Lewis	46	M	Merchant	New York	New York	Romulus	9 Oct 1828
MIRMAN, Jno.	35	M	Coachman	Ireland	United States	Essex	23 May 1828
MIRNA, Martha	18	F		Great Britain	New York	Dublin	21 Dec 1824
MIRO, Blais	30	M	Cabinet Maker	Cuba	Cuba	Clio	8 Apr 1828
MIROL, Andrew	19	M	Labourer	Ireland	United States	Hope	12 Jun 1828
MIRONA, Francis	26	M	Merchant	France	U. States	France	14 Mar 1828
MIRSIER, Frederick	21	M	Hoabmaker [?]	France	U. States	Edward Bopnnaffe	30 Jul 1829
MISOGARS, C. H.	25	M	Merchant	Germany	U. States	Dido	26 Apr 1825
MISSERLI, Abraham	3	M	Son	Swiss	United States	Elizabeth	4 Sep 1826
Abraham	25	M	Tailor	Swiss	United States	Elizabeth	4 Sep 1826
Anna	30	F	Wife	Swiss	United States	Elizabeth	4 Sep 1826
John	5	M	Son	Swiss	United States	Elizabeth	4 Sep 1826
Madelina	2	F	Daughter	Swiss	United States	Elizabeth	4 Sep 1826
MITCHEAL, John	63	M	Weaver	Great Britain	United States	Courier	26 Jun 1827
MITCHEL, A.	16	M		France	U. States	Topaz	2 Oct 1828
Agns	10	F	Spinster	Ireland	U. States	Meteor	19 Jul 1828
Ann	25	F	Spinster	Ireland	U. States	Meteor	19 Jul 1828
Armstrong	20		Weaver	Ireland	Great Britain	Robert Burns	14 Jun 1824
Eliz.	19	F	Spinster	Ireland	U. States	Meteor	19 Jul 1828
George	56	M	Farmer	Ireland	U. States	Meteor	19 Jul 1828
Isabella	4	F	Child	Ireland	U. States	Meteor	19 Jul 1828
Jane	12	F	Spinster	Ireland	U. States	Meteor	19 Jul 1828
Jane	46	F	Spinster	Ireland	U. States	Meteor	19 Jul 1828
John	14	M	Farmer	Great Britain	U. States America	Ann Maria	29 Nov 1821
John	40	M	Merchant	Ireland	Und. Stts of Amer	Alexander Mansfield	18 Aug 1826
Margaret	7	F	Spinster	Ireland	U. States	Meteor	19 Jul 1828
Mary	23	F	Spinster	Ireland	U. States	Meteor	19 Jul 1828
Robt.	15	M	Farmer	Ireland	U. States	Meteor	19 Jul 1828
Samuel	50	M	Merch.	U. States	U. States	Brown	11 Jan 1825
Seney	27			Great Britain	United States	Comet	9 Aug 1822
Wm.	22	M	Farmer	Ireland	U. States	Meteor	19 Jul 1828

NAMES OF PASSENGERS	AGE	SEX	OCCUPATIONS	COUNTRY TO WHICH THEY BELONG	COUNTRY THEY INTEND TO INHABIT	SHIPS/DATES OF ARRIVAL	
MITCHELAULES, Louis	28	M	Merchant	U. States	U. States	Frances	27 Dec 1826
MITCHELL (see Mictchell)							
Alex.	66	M	Farmer	Great Britain	United States	Aurora	5 Sep 1826
Alexander	21	M	Engineer	Great Britain	United States	Ganges	26 Oct 1826
Alexander, Jr.	30	M	...ackman	Ireland	United States	Carolina Ann	14 May 1827
Alexander, Senr.	82	M	Farmer	Ireland	United States	Carolina Ann	14 May 1827
*died							
Alexr.	30	M	Parson	Scotland	U. States	Brilliant	19 Mar 1828
Alexr.	31	M	Merchant	U. States	U. States	Jay	18 Apr 1823
Andrew	20	M	Merchant	United States	U. States	Manhattan	25 Dec 1820
Andrew	27	M	Merchant	Great Britain	U.S. of America	Canada	1 Oct 1827
Andrew	30 10/12	M	Clergyman	Ireland	United States	Atlantic	21 Jul 1827
Andw.	23		Merchant	Glasgow	Great Britain	William Thompson	13 May 1823
Ann		F	Chiefly farmers		United States	Factor	8 Jul 1829
Ann	18	F	Servant	Ireland	United States	Josephine	30 Apr 1828
Archd.	25	M	Cooper	Ireland	United States	Alex. Mansfield	17 May 1823
Archibald	37	M	Farmer	Scotland	Canada	Ann	11 Sep 1827
Benjin. T.	23	M	Merchant	United States	U.S.	William Byrnes	11 Dec 1827
Benjn. F. B.	26	M	Merchant	U. States	U. States	Talma	20 Nov 1828
C.	22	M	Gentleman	U. States	U. States	Robert Lenox	6 Jun 1821
Daniel	40	M	Printer	England	United States	Nancy Henrietta	3 Nov 1828
Eliza	20	F		Ireland	United States	Romulus	24 Jun 1826
Elizabeth	25	F		Ireland	United States	Mary	1 Jul 1829
Elizabeth	33	F	Matron	Great Britain	U. States	Robert Fulton	3 Dec 1827
Geo.		M	Chiefly farmers		United States	Factor	8 Jul 1829
Geo.	26	M	Merchant	U.S.	U.S.	Agenoria	15 Jun 1822
Geo.	32	M	Carpenter	U. States	Cuba	Magnet	18 Aug 1825
Isabella	70	F	None	Langholm	U. States	New York	11 Jul 1823
J.	20	M	Labourer	Ireland		Robert Fulton	4 Jun 1828
J.	23	M	Sailor	England	U. States	Hiram	17 Jun 1826
J. C.	24	M	Merchant	United States	United States	Bunker Hill	16 Apr 1827
James		M	Chiefly farmers		United States	Factor	8 Jul 1829
James		M	Chiefly farmers		United States	Factor	8 Jul 1829
James	1 6/12	M	Child	Great Britain	U. States	Robert Fulton	3 Dec 1827
James	20	M	Shoe Maker	Great Britain	United States	Aurora	5 Sep 1826
James	26	M	Merchant	Great Britain	U. States	Ganges	21 Jun 1827
James	27		Labourer	Scotland	United States	Isabella	5 Jul 1826
James	28	M	Laborer	Ireland	United States	Mary	1 Jul 1829
James	68	M	Labourer	Ireland	United States	Robert Fulton	10 Aug 1827
Jane	23	F		G. Britain	United States	Siroc	13 Sep 1828
Jas.	21	M	Farmer		United States	Sarah	9 Nov 1820
Jno.	23	M	Merchant	Gibraltar	U. States	Leontine	10 Jul 1826
John	...3	...	...	...	United States	Criterion	27 Jun 1827
John	8 6/12	M	Child	Great Britain	U. States	Robert Fulton	3 Dec 1827
John	22	M		England	United States	Yobah	26 Sep 1827
John	30	M	Weaver	Ireland	United States	Robert Fulton	10 Aug 1827
M.			Merchant	America		Columbus	20 Aug 1828
Margeret	60	F	Matron	Ireland	United States	Robert Fulton	10 Aug 1827
Margret	83	F	Housekeeper	Ireland	United States	Carolina Ann	14 May 1827
Margret, Jr.	21	F	Servant	Ireland	United States	Carolina Ann	14 May 1827
Margrett		F	Chiefly farmers		United States	Factor	8 Jul 1829
Martha	1	F		Ireland	United States	Mary	1 Jul 1829
Martha	37	...	...	...	United States	Criterion	27 Jun 1827
Mary		F	Chiefly farmers		United States	Factor	8 Jul 1829
Mary	22	F	Child	Great Britain	United States	Aurora	5 Sep 1826
Mary	24	F	Servant	England	New York	Brighton	29 Aug 1828
Mary	64	F	Wife of [Alex.]	Great Britain	United States	Aurora	5 Sep 1826
Mary Ann	10	F	Child	Great Britain	U. States	Robert Fulton	3 Dec 1827
Nancy	20	F		Ireland	United States	Mary	1 Jul 1829
Nathaniel	22	M	Merchant	U. States		Fanny	14 Mar 1820
Pat	22	M	Weaver	Ireland	New York	Louisa	18 Apr 1827
Paul	20		Servant	Pesardy, France	France	Frances Henrietta	31 May 1824
R.	24	M		G. Britain	United States	Siroc	13 Sep 1828
R.	25	M	Labourer	Great Britain	United States	Frances Henrietta	17 Sep 1827
R. G.	32	M	Merchant	U. States	U. States	Tobasco	17 Aug 1825
R. G.	34	M	Merchant	Havana	U. States	Empress	7 Jul 1827

NAMES OF PASSENGERS	AGE	SEX	OCCUPATIONS	COUNTRY TO WHICH THEY BELONG	COUNTRY THEY INTEND TO INHABIT	SHIPS/DATES OF ARRIVAL	
MITCHELL (cont'd)							
Robert	20	M	Weaver	Ireland	United States	Robert Fulton	10 Aug 1827
Robert	30	M	Brewer	Great Britain	United States	Isaac Hicks	27 Sep 1826
Robert	60	M	Merchant	U.S.A.	U.S.A.	Silas Richards	7 Mar 1827
Robt. G.	30	M	Merchant	United States	United States for 2 Months	Diana	9 Aug 1823
Robt. G.	34	M	Merchant	U. States	U. States	Dromo	24 Jul 1826
Rose	21	F		Scotland	United States	Indus	5 Sep 1827
S.	50	M	Merchant	U. States	U. States	Superion	30 Apr 1825
Sam	52	M	Marchant	N. York	U. States	Commodore Perry	9 Apr 1821
Samuel	28	M	Miner	Great Britain	Great Britain	Sisters	10 Jan 1826
Samuel	50	M	Merchant	France	U. States	Spermo	18 Sep 1823
Sarah	32	F	Commedian	England		Britannia	20 Jun 1827
Schuster	22	M	Baker	Germany	United States	Virginia	31 May 1828
Thomas	6	M	Comedian	England		Britannia	20 Jun 1827
Thomas	6	M	Child	Great Britain	U. States	Robert Fulton	3 Dec 1827
Thomas	29	M	Iron Founder	England	New York	Corinthian	5 May 1827
Thomas	34	M	Commedian	England		Britannia	20 Jun 1827
Thos.		M	Chiefly farmers		United States	Factor	8 Jul 1829
Thos. H.	30	M	Merchant	Richmond	U. States	Fly	9 Apr 1823
Thos. H.	30	M	Surgeon	Virginia	U. States	Concord	10 Nov 1824
Tousand	28	M	Merchant	France	U. States	Julia	16 Nov 1824
William	3 6/12	M	Child	Great Britain	U. States	Robert Fulton	3 Dec 1827
William	16	M	Printer	England	United States	Nancy Henrietta	3 Nov 1828
William	25	M	Mechanic	Great Britain	United States	Florida	2 Oct 1828
William	37	M	Farmer	Scotland	U.S. of America	Friends	10 May 1823
Wm.	20	F	Farmer	Great Brittan	U. States	Gem	26 Jul 1827
Wm.	35	M	Farmer	Scotland	U. States	Spartan	11 Mar 1823
Wm.	73	M	Carpenter	England	U.S.	Acasta	11 May 1827
MITCHELTREE,							
William, Junr.	26	M	Gentleman	Ireland	United States	Liverpool Trader	24 Oct 1825
MITCHER, John	17	M	Farm	Ireland	U. States	Meteor	19 Jul 1828
John	80	M	Carpenter	U. States	U. States	Meteor	19 Jul 1828
MITHAM, Francis	29	M	R. Navy	Great Britain	Great Britain	Columbia	24 Dec 1822
MITHIL, Moses D. *Distressed Seaman				America	America	Medina	4 Sep 1828
MITIJANS, Jesse	25	M	Merchant	Havana	U. States	Courier	9 Feb 1829
MITRA, Anthony	28	M	Carpenter	France	United States	Nile	13 Aug 1828
MITTLE, John	42	M	Carpenter	United States	United States	Greyhound	20 Mar 1820
MITTON, John	17	M	Labourer	Great Britain	United States	Atlantic	8 Dec 1827
MIX, Chas. A. *died on passage	25		Carpenter	U. States		Maria	23 Aug 1824
E. H.	46	M	Mariner	U. States	U. States	Seneca	15 Apr 1822
William	23	M	Clerk	United States	United States	Bellona	2 Jul 1828
MIZEN, ...	6	F	Child	Switzerland	United States	Andes	5 May 1828
Jacob	1	M	Child	Switzerland	United States	Andes	5 May 1828
Lena	4	F	Child	Switzerland	United States	Andes	5 May 1828
Philip	35	M	Farmer	Switzerland	United States	Andes	5 May 1828
Sophia	35	F	Spinster	Switzerland	United States	Andes	5 May 1828
MJOBERG, J. U.	30	M	Mercht.	Sweden	Mexico	Florida	8 Nov 1826
MO...T, Thomas	...4	...	...	Ireland	United States	Carolina Ann	24 Oct 1825
MOANET, James	20	M	Weaver	Ireland	U. States	Wanderer	1 Sep 1828
MOAT, Bryan	20	M	Labourer	England	United States	Jubilee	12 May 1828
MOATS, Henry	25	M	Carpenter	Ireland	United States	Ann Maria	4 Oct 1824
MOBBS, Ann	15	F	None	Great Britain		Olive Branch	9 Oct 1829
Betsey	11	F	None	Great Britain		Olive Branch	9 Oct 1829
Francis	43	M	Labourer	Great Britain		Olive Branch	9 Oct 1829
George	17	M	Stockingweaver	Great Britain		Olive Branch	9 Oct 1829
John	7	M	None	Great Britain		Olive Branch	9 Oct 1829
Mark	1	M	None	Great Britain		Olive Branch	9 Oct 1829
Mary	40	F	None	Great Britain		Olive Branch	9 Oct 1829
Sarah	19	F	None	Great Britain		Olive Branch	9 Oct 1829
Thomas	4	M	None	Great Britain		Olive Branch	9 Oct 1829
William	9	M	None	Great Britain		Olive Branch	9 Oct 1829
MOCH, P. M.	50	M	Merchant	St. Thomas	St. Thomas	Douglass	29 Apr 1828
MOCK, Samuel S.	18		Bewer	Halifax	U. States	Almira	15 Jul 1822
MOCKALDSON, Henry	30	M	Soap Boiler	Great Britain	U. States	St. Croix	13 Sep 1827

NAMES OF PASSENGERS	AGE	SEX	OCCUPATIONS	COUNTRY TO WHICH THEY BELONG	COUNTRY THEY INTEND TO INHABIT	SHIPS/DATES OF ARRIVAL	
MOCKLY, Edmond	28	M	Gardner	Ireland	United States	Potomac	28 Sep 1827
MOCOL, G. F.	25	M	Merchant	U. States	U. States	Leopard	23 Nov 1820
MODENBIEN, J.	25	M	Butcher	German	America	Wm. Henry	25 Sep 1827
MODEST, —	32	M	Dentist	Martinico	U. States	Comet	28 Jul 1825
MODGE, Thomas	25	M	Servant	England	United States	Silas Richards	27 Oct 1825
MOE, Michael	30	M	Farmer	Ireland		Cuba	24 Jun 1822
MOEN, Arthur	18		Miller	Ireland	United States	Fabius	18 Mar 1829
Polly	20		Spinster	Ireland	United States	Fabius	18 Mar 1829
MOES, M.	47		Mercht.	France		Artibonett	21 Nov 1826
MOETLY, John H.	32	M	Farmer	Switzerland	United States	Ospray	2 Sep 1824
William	49	M	Silk Manufacturer	Switzerland	United States	Ospray	2 Sep 1824
MOFFAT, Andw.	25 2/12	M	Farmer	Ireland	Philad.	Triton	12 Jul 1823
Christn.	36	F	Farmer	Ireland	Philad.	Triton	12 Jul 1823
Fras.	3/12		infant	Ireland	Pittsburg	Triton	12 Jul 1823
James	50	M	Mercht.	Great Britain	N. Scotia	Ann	10 Jan 1825
Jas.	2		infant	Ireland	Pittsburg	Triton	12 Jul 1823
John	36	M	Farmer	Ireland	Philad.	Triton	12 Jul 1823
John G.	22	M	Gentleman	England	England	William	2 Sep 1822
Th...	24	M	Teacher	U. States	U. States	Queen Mab	16 Jun 1827
MOFFATT, Margaratt	22	F	None	England	New York	Indian Chief	19 Jun 1823
William	23	M	Weaver	England	New York	Indian Chief	19 Jun 1823
MOFFET, James	16	M	Farmer	Great Brittain	U. States	Nancy	18 Jul 1821
John	40	M	Farmer	Great Brittain	U. States	Nancy	18 Jul 1821
Rial	40	F	Farmer	Great Brittain	U. States	Nancy	18 Jul 1821
Samuel	18	M	Farmer	Great Brittain	U. States	Nancy	18 Jul 1821
William	12	M	Farmer	Great Brittain	U. States	Nancy	18 Jul 1821
MOFFETT, David	32	M	Mariner	United States	U. States	South Carolina Packet	5 Nov 1821
Elizabeth	20	F	Farmer	Great Brittain	U. States	Nancy	18 Jul 1821
Robert	18	M	Weaver	Ireland	United States	Asia	29 Jul 1829
MOFFORD, John	25	M	Farmer	G. Britain	U. States	Mary & Harriot	8 Sep 1828
MOGELEY, Thomas	21 11/12	M	Watch Maker	England	U.S. of America	Illinois	16 Jun 1821
MOGER, H.	34	M	Mariner	U. States	U. States	Atlas	24 Jun 1828
MOGGIA, Augestino	26	M	Barber	Italy	United States	Neptune	29 Oct 1821
MOGIER, —	30	M	Mercht.	France	France	Don Quixote	3 Jan 1826
A.	25		Merchant	Lyon	France	Brown	11 Jun 1827
MOGINER, Ann	3	F	Spinster	Ireland	United States	Sarah G.	20 Jul 1827
Margary	23	F		Ireland	United States	Sarah G.	20 Jul 1827
MOGRIDGE, Joseph	32	M	Seaman	Massachusetts	U. States	Velocipede	24 May 1824
MOHAN, Michael	23	M	Labourer	Ireland	America	Atlantic	8 May 1828
MOHIEN, Pat	34	M	Labourer	Great Britian	United States	Princess Charlotte	6 Sep 1828
MOHL, Gottlob Adolph	21	M	Merchant	Germany	United States	Elizabeth	27 Jul 1824
MOHLAR, Matthias	25 3/12	M	Mechanic	Switzerland	United States	France	6 Oct 1828
MOHN, Patrick	22	M	Labourer	...	U. States	St. Michael	21 Jul 1824
MOHNS, Jesse	25	M	Merchant	France	Mexico	Eliza	14 Mar 1825
MOHOFFY, John	22	M	Weaver	Ireland	United States	Robert Fulton	10 Aug 1827
MOHONY, Denis	23	M	Glozier	Ireland	America	Parrington	9 Jun 1827
MOHR, Henry	35	M	Merchant	Germany	United States	Ann	22 Dec 1821
MOHRE, Henry	40	M	Merchant	Charleston, N.C.	Charleston, N.C.	Caesar	8 Oct 1827
MOHRHENNE, F. A.	21	M	Merchant			Franklin	8 Jun 1827
MOHRING, M. E.	34	M	Merchant	Hamburg	U. States	Minerva	18 Oct 1828
MOILA, J., Jr.	60	M	Merchant	Jamaica	N. York	Cadet	5 Dec 1824
M., Miss	20	F		Jamaica	N. York	Cadet	5 Dec 1824
MOILES, Cathe.		F		Spain	U. States	Madison	22 May 1822
MOILET, J., Mr.	26			France	United States	Henri IV	14 Sep 1827
MOILS, —	28	M	Mariner	Spain	U. States	Maria Ann	29 Sep 1823
*landed at Balize [Biloxi?], Missippi							
MOING, Gott.	25	M	Docter	Prussia	U. States	Minerva	13 Sep 1827
Sophia	22	F	Wife	Prussia	U. States	Minerva	13 Sep 1827
MOIR, Robert	27	M	Gentleman	Scotland	U. States	Emblem	18 Jun 1825
MOLAS, Antonio	17	M	Merchant	Russia	U. States	Balance	28 Sep 1822
MOLATTONA, H. L.	16	M		Demerara	U. States	South Carolina	2 Aug 1822
MOLAY, E.	30	F		Great Britain	United States	Isaac Hicks	6 Dec 1827
G.	7			Great Britain	United States	Isaac Hicks	6 Dec 1827
M.	5			Great Britain	United States	Isaac Hicks	6 Dec 1827
M.	27	M	Farmer	Great Britain	United States	Isaac Hicks	6 Dec 1827

NAMES OF PASSENGERS	AGE	SEX	OCCUPATIONS	COUNTRY TO WHICH THEY BELONG	COUNTRY THEY INTEND TO INHABIT	SHIPS/DATES OF ARRIVAL	
MOLEMEAUX, Edmd., Jr.	28	M	Merchant	Great Britian	U. States	Silas Richards	29 Oct 1828
MOLETTER, John	29	M	Custom Officer	Sicily	America	Ivanhoe	10 Mar 1827
MOLINA, F. X.	12	M	Merchant	Mexico	U. States	Desdemona	15 Jun 1827
Jose Joaquim	12	M	Merchant	Mexico	U. States	Desdemona	15 Jun 1827
P. A.	11	M	Servant to the Agent [J. M. Espardo]	... [Spain?]	U. States	Favourite	18 Aug 1823
MOLINARD, Josephine	55	F	Merchant	France	Newyork	Cortes	16 Jul 1827
Laura	28	F		France	Newyork	Cortes	16 Jul 1827
Peter	30	M	Merchant	France	Newyork	Cortes	16 Jul 1827
MOLINDER, Joseph	...		Weaver	Bl...	England	Great Britain	7 May 1827
MOLINEUX, William	66	M	Farmer	England		Manhattan	22 May 1827
MOLISSAR, M. M., Mrs.	26	F	Lady	U.S.	U.S.	Cadmus	23 Mar 1827
MOLL, Charles	29	M	Wheel right	Germany	United States	Virginia	31 May 1828
MOLLAN, Susannah	25	F		Derry, Ireland	Philadelphia	Anthusa	24 Aug 1825
William	30	M	Weaver	Ireland	United States	Romulus	24 Jun 1826
MOLLAY, John	40	M	Shoemaker	England	U. States	Howard Douglass	29 Jan 1828
MOLLEN, Thomas	24	M	Merchant	Ireland	United States	St. Michaels	23 Dec 1826
MOLLER, Fredrick	4	M	Son	Swiss	United States	Elizabeth	4 Sep 1826
Janna	30	F	Wife	Swiss	United States	Elizabeth	4 Sep 1826
John	5	M	Son	Swiss	United States	Elizabeth	4 Sep 1826
John Jacob	32	M	Turner	Swiss	United States	Elizabeth	4 Sep 1826
MOLLES, Jean Leopold	13	M	Nephew	Swiss	United States	Elizabeth	4 Sep 1826
Marianne	46	F	Spinster	Swiss	United States	Elizabeth	4 Sep 1826
MOLLETERT, Bler	18	M	Farmer	France	United States	Virginia	31 May 1828
MOLLETT, Louis Wm.	27	M	Teacher of Languages	Havre	New York	Leeds	7 Nov 1828
Louisa	2	F		Gt. Britain	New York	Leeds	7 Nov 1828
Mary Ann	21	F		Gt. Britain	New York	Leeds	7 Nov 1828
MOLLEY, C.	19	M		Germany	U. States	Louisa Matilda	4 Dec 1821
MOLLISON, A. F.	20	M	Merchant	G. Brittain	U. States	Sanford William	14 Dec 1824
MOLLONEY, Betsey	1	F		Ireland	United States	Silas Richards	3 Apr 1826
Charlotte	26	F		Ireland	U.S.A.	Silas Richards	28 Jun 1825
Jeremiah	35	M	Blacksmith	Ireland	U.S.A.	Silas Richards	28 Jun 1825
John	24	M	Blacksmith	Ireland	U.S.A.	Silas Richards	28 Jun 1825
Samuel	3 2/12	M		Ireland	U.S.A.	Silas Richards	28 Jun 1825
Thomas	4 6/12	M		Ireland	U.S.A.	Silas Richards	28 Jun 1825
MOLLONY, Mary	21	F		Ireland	United States	Silas Richards	3 Apr 1826
Morris	48	M	Carpenter	Ireland	United States	Silas Richards	3 Apr 1826
MOLLOY, Chas.	28	M	Merchant	Ireland	G. Brittain	Planter	17 Sep 1821
James	24	M	Labourer	England	U. States	Panthea	8 Apr 1826
Jas.	35	M	Gentleman	St. John	St. John	St. Michaels	25 Apr 1825
Mary	32	F	Lady	St. John	St. John	St. Michaels	25 Apr 1825
Thos.	11	M			G. Brittain	Planter	17 Sep 1821
MOLLRING, Christopher	25 3/12	M	Smith	Hanover	United States	Robert Edwards	3 Oct 1829
Henry G.	28 6/12	M	Sugar Baker	Hanover	United States	Robert Edwards	3 Oct 1829
MOLLY, Charles	45	M	Labourer	England	United States	Dalhouse Castle	8 May 1827
Thos.	19	M	Labourer	Ireland	United States	Essex	23 May 1828
MOLLYNEUX, Giles	34	M	Farmer	England	United States	Mary & Harriet	9 Mar 1829
MOLLZ, Jh.	38		Cordonnier [shoemaker]	Suisse		Deux Ernest	29 Dec 1827
*son épouse, son pere & 2 enfans [his wife, his father and two children]							
MOLOGHAN, Roger	21	M	Labourer	Ireland	United States	Ann Maria	8 Jun 1824
MOLONE, Martin	22	M	Laborer	Ireland	United States	Dublin Packet	9 Jul 1827
MOLONG, James	24	M	Labourer	Limerick	N. York	Thomas & William	25 May 1827
MOLONY, Henry	24	M	Draper	Ireland	America	Parrington	9 Jun 1827
MOLOVER, Christian	42	M	Merchant	Halifax, N.S.	State of Ohio	Adno	25 Aug 1828
MOLOY, Mary	18	F	None	G.B.	U.S.A.	Silas Richard	30 Jun 1828
Michel	32	M	Clerk	Ireland	America	Josephine	24 Jul 1826
Michl.	22	M	Labourer	Ireland	U. States	Josephine	7 May 1827
MOLSOIN, John	32	M	Merchant	Great Britain	United States	Courier	13 Mar 1820
MOLSOM, Jno., Jr.	37	M	Mercht.	Canada	Canada	Manchester	6 Dec 1825
MOLSON, Thomas, Mr.	30	M	Merchant	Canada	Montreal	Hannibal	28 Apr 1824
MOLTEE, Vincent	35	M	Italy	U. States	U. States	Columbia	1 Dec 1824
MOLYNEAUX, E., Jr.	75	M	Merchant	England	America	Silas Richard	24 Oct 1829

NAMES OF PASSENGERS	A G E	S E X	OCCUPATIONS	COUNTRY TO WHICH THEY BELONG	COUNTRY THEY INTEND TO INHABIT	SHIPS/DATES OF ARRIVAL	
MOLYNEUX,							
Edmund, Jr.	32	M	Merchant	G.B.		Silas Richards	29 Oct 1827
W. W.	21	M	Merchant	U. States	U. States	Dromo	13 Dec 1826
Wilf.	27	M	Merchant	Ireland	United States	Silas Richards	27 Oct 1825
MOMP...SSON, James, Lt.	27	M	Lt. Army	England	England	Meteor	22 Apr 1822
MONADELLO, John	23	M	Merchant	U.S. of America	U.S. of America	Harmony	20 Nov 1820
MONAGAN, Louisa	23	F		Great Britain	United States	Frances Henrietta	17 Sep 1827
Richard	27	M	Joiner	Great Britain	United States	Frances Henrietta	17 Sep 1827
MONAGER, ...	36 5/12	M	Farmer	Switzerland	U. States	France	26 Jun 1828
MONAGH, Mary	17	F	Mantuamaker	Ireland	United States	Trident	16 May 1826
MONAGHAN, Catherine	18	F	Spinster	Ireland	U.S. of America	Meteor	19 Mar 1828
Catherine	18	F	Spinster	Ireland	United States	Dublin Packet	23 May 1828
Charles	28	M	Weaver	Ireland	U.S. of America	Meteor	19 Mar 1828
Edward	31	M	Merchant	Great Britain	U. States	William Thompson	29 Jan 1823
Patk.	23	M	Labourer	Ireland		Marchioness	13 May 1828
Patrick	12	M	boy	Ireland	United States	Abigail	25 Jun 1822
Patt	20	M	Farmer	Ireland	New York	Margaret	18 May 1825
Patt.	52	M	Labourer	Ireland	U. States	Josephine	27 Jul 1825
Peggy	10	F	Spinster	Ireland	U.S. of America	Meteor	19 Mar 1828
Richard	20	M	Labourer	Ireland	U.S. of America	Meteor	19 Mar 1828
Richard	50	M	Labourer	Ireland	U.S. of America	Meteor	19 Mar 1828
MONAGY, ...a...n	9/12	M	Farmer	Switzerland	U. States	France	26 Jun 1828
Ande	46 5/12	M	Farmer	Switzerland	U. States	France	26 Jun 1828
Buttena	15 3/12	F	Farmer	Switzerland	U. States	France	26 Jun 1828
Floren	17 4/12	F	Farmer	Switzerland	U. States	France	26 Jun 1828
Francis	13 4/12	M	Farmer	Switzerland	U. States	France	26 Jun 1828
Jese	19 5/12	M	Farmer	Switzerland	U. States	France	26 Jun 1828
Josephine	7/12	F	Farmer	Switzerland	U. States	France	26 Jun 1828
Lorence	1 2/12	F	Farmer	Switzerland	U. States	France	26 Jun 1828
Mariah	44 4/12	F	Farmer	Switzerland	U. States	France	26 Jun 1828
Marian	5 2/12	F	Farmer	Switzerland	U. States	France	26 Jun 1828
MONAHAM, Sarah	27	F	Semstr	Trinidad	America	Edward	10 Aug 1820
MONAHAN, Ann	3...	F		Great Britain	United States	Atlantic	28 May 1827
Bernard	35	F	Servant	Great Brittan	United States	America	24 Jul 1827
Beth	6	F		Great Britain	United States	Atlantic	28 May 1827
Jno.	5	M		Great Britain	United States	Atlantic	28 May 1827
Mary	1	F		Great Britain	United States	Atlantic	28 May 1827
Mary	32	M	Labourer	Ireland	United States	Wilson	6 Jun 1828
Thos.	34	M	...er	Great Britain	United States	Atlantic	28 May 1827
MONAHE, Eliz.	2	F	Farmer	Ireland		Quatre Freres	29 Jul 1828
Eliz.	28	M	Farmer	Ireland		Quatre Freres	29 Jul 1828
George	5	M	Farmer	Ireland		Quatre Freres	29 Jul 1828
Isaach	28	M	Farmer	Ireland		Quatre Freres	29 Jul 1828
MONAHEN, Mary	17	F	house maid	Ireland	United States	William	20 Jul 1829
MONARTY, Thomas	41	M	Master Mariner	United States	United States	Roanoke	21 May 1828
MONASON, Thos.	17 11/12	M	Clerk	U. States	U. States	Champion	2 Feb 1829
MONATHAN, Margt.	21	F		Gt. Britain	U. States	St. George	20 Sep 1828
May *Died				Gt. Britain	U. States	St. George	20 Sep 1828
Pat	23	M	Labourer	Gt. Britain	U. States	St. George	20 Sep 1828
MONAY...AN, Anne	20		Laboring Class		United States	Atlantic	2 Apr 1827
MONCADO, Guadalupe	30	M	Gentleman	Mexico	England	Brown	23 Dec 1826
MONCE, Alaxander	21	M	Cotton Spiner	Great Britain	United States	Courier	26 Jun 1827
Daniel	23	M	Laborer	Great Britain	United States	Courier	26 Jun 1827
MONCHARD, John	26	M	Carpenter	France	United States	Henri IV	2 Oct 1828
MONCREIFF, D.	28	M	Merchant	United States	United States	Eliza Pigott	27 Mar 1820
MONCURE, William	22	M	Mason	Great Britain	United States	Colossus	5 Jun 1827
MONDAY, Catharine	31	F		Ireland	U.S. of America	Douglass	6 Jul 1829
MONDILLE, Adolph	22	M	Merchant	Holland	France	Athenian	8 Jul 1828
MONDINGER, Barbarra, kinder [child of Ludwich]	8	F		Limbach	United States	Juffraw Johanna 16 Oct 1821	
Jacob, kinder [child of Ludwich]	11	M		Limbach	United States	Juffraw Johanna 16 Oct 1821	

NAMES OF PASSENGERS	AGE	SEX	OCCUPATIONS	COUNTRY TO WHICH THEY BELONG	COUNTRY THEY INTEND TO INHABIT	SHIPS/DATES OF ARRIVAL
MONDINGER (cont'd)						
Ludwich	50	M	Boer	Stutgard	United States	Juffraw Johanna 16 Oct 1821
Maria, kinder [child of Ludwich]	18	F		Limbach	United States	Juffraw Johanna 16 Oct 1821
Susanna, kinder [child of Ludwich]	15	F		Limbach	United States	Juffraw Johanna 16 Oct 1821
MONES, J. B.	22	M	Merchant	U. States	U. States	Fair Play 5 Nov 1821
MONEY, Andrés	30	M	Farmer	France	United States	Crescent 12 Jul 1827
Catherine	3	F	Farmer	France	United States	Crescent 12 Jul 1827
John	43	M	Turner	England	United States	Robert Edwards 3 Oct 1829
Josephine	2	F	Farmer	France	United States	Crescent 12 Jul 1827
Margaret	30	F	Farmer	France	United States	Crescent 12 Jul 1827
Mary	6	F	Farmer	France	United States	Crescent 12 Jul 1827
P. K.	22	M	Gentleman	U. States	U. States	William Tell 3 Dec 1825
MONEYPENNEY, Wm.	24	M	Merchant	Ireland	Ireland	Sarah 25 Oct 1825
MONGAHAN, Ann	27	F		G. Britan	U. States	William Neilson 26 Jul 1828
Catharan	2	F		G. Britan	U. States	William Neilson 26 Jul 1828
*D[ied] 5th July Decline						
Ellen	7/12	F		G. Britan	U. States	William Neilson 26 Jul 1828
Ryan	30	M		G. Britan	U. States	William Neilson 26 Jul 1828
MONGAN, Alexander	21	M	Farmer	Ireland	United States	Wilson 22 Jun 1824
MONGE, John	24	M	Merchant	Spain	U. States	Eliza 20 Aug 1824
MONGES, J. A.	23	M	Mercht.	Philad.	U. States	Catherine 4 Sep 1824
MONGOMREY, Joseph	20	M	Labourer	Ireland		Robert Fulton 4 Jun 1828
MONHALL, Jno.	24	M	Labourer	Great Britain	United States	Penelope 11 Jun 1827
Mary	20	F	None	Great Britain	United States	Penelope 11 Jun 1827
Pat.	1	M	None	Great Britain	United States	Penelope 11 Jun 1827
MONHAM, Anne, Mrs.	30	F		Canada	Canada	Hudson 10 Nov 1825
MONHOF, Francis	5	M	Tanner	France		Pallas 14 Jun 1828
Georg	7	F	Tanner	France		Pallas 14 Jun 1828
Joseph	3	M	Tanner	France		Pallas 14 Jun 1828
Magalar	16	M	Tanner	France		Pallas 14 Jun 1828
Margaret	...	F	Tanner	France		Pallas 14 Jun 1828
Marjan	11	F	Tanner	France		Pallas 14 Jun 1828
Monin	35	M	Black Smith	France		Pallas 14 Jun 1828
Nicolus	49	M	Watch	France		Pallas 14 Jun 1828
MONHOLLON, Merrit	30	M	Carpenter	Ireland	United States	Alex. Mansfield 17 May 1823
MONHOLM, Mary	11	F	Spinner	Great Britain	United States	Atlantic 8 Dec 1827
MONHUT, Joseph	19	M	Farmer	Native of Switzerland	United States	Canaris 30 Jun 1827
MONIEL, Etien	32	M	Mechanic	France	U. States	Emblem 15 Apr 1826
MONIER, David H.	21	M	Shoemaker	Framclans	U.S. America	Superior 18 Jun 1825
Isaac P.	25	M	Farmer	Belfoit	U.S. America	Superior 18 Jun 1825
J. P. A.	29		Farmer	France	U. States	Elizabeth 9 Jul 1825
Maria	6		Carpenter	France	U. States	Elizabeth 9 Jul 1825
Maria	44		Carpenter	France	U. States	Elizabeth 9 Jul 1825
MONIHUE, James	30		Farmer	England	United States	Mary 15 Jul 1822
MONILAWS, Mary	40	F	None	Great Britain	United States	Ann Maria 9 Mar 1820
Thomas	40	M	Shop Keeper	Great Britain	United States	Ann Maria 9 Mar 1820
MONIN, Catherine	42	M	Book Binder	France	United States	American 27 Aug 1827
Charles	18	F	Book Binder	France	United States	American 27 Aug 1827
Francis	17	F	Book Binder	France	United States	American 27 Aug 1827
John Peter	6	M	Book Binder	France	United States	American 27 Aug 1827
Nicholas	42	M	Book Binder	France	United States	American 27 Aug 1827
MONIOT, N.	45	M	Clergyman	Granade at Spain	Cincinati, U.S. of America	Charles Miller 31 May 1825
MONISEY, Thomas	35	M	Joiner	G. Britain	U. States	Margaret Bogle 12 Jun 1828
MONISS, John	27		Gardner	Ireland	United States	Geo. Canning 5 Jun 1828
MONK, Agnes	2			Manchester		Mount Vernon 18 Oct 1822
Agnes	27			Manchester		Mount Vernon 18 Oct 1822
George	35	M	Merchant	United States	United States	Seine 21 Oct 1822
William	3			Manchester		Mount Vernon 18 Oct 1822
William	27		Clerk	Manchester		Mount Vernon 18 Oct 1822
MONKEATH, A.	19		None	Scotland	Baltimore	Albion 11 Oct 1821
MONKEY, James	23	M	Labourer	Great Britain	United States	Ocean 27 Jul 1825
Michael	25	M	Weaver	Great Britain	United States	Ocean 27 Jul 1825
MONKMAN, Thomas	23	M	Farmer	England	New York	Indian Chief 19 Jun 1823
Thos.	24	M	Merchant	England	England	Gulnard 24 Mar 1825
MONKS, James	22			England	United States	Hugh Johnson 11 Jun 1828

NAMES OF PASSENGERS	AGE	SEX	OCCUPATIONS	COUNTRY TO WHICH THEY BELONG	COUNTRY THEY INTEND TO INHABIT	SHIPS/DATES OF ARRIVAL	
MONKS (cont'd)							
John	35	M	Joiner	England	United States	Delta	24 Oct 1829
Saml. P.	22	M	Merchant	Ireland	United States	Dublin Packet	3 Sep 1822
MONKTON, John	25	M	Farmer	Ireland	New York	Susquehanna	9 Jan 1824
MONLAUGRO, G.	10	M	No	Spain	U. States	Dromo	22 May 1826
MONLY, L.	38	M	Merchant	France	U. States	Neptune	20 Apr 1825
MONMETERS, Gabriel	17	M	Farmer	Switzerland	United States	Olympia	12 Aug 1828
MONMETS, John	22	M	Farm	Ireland		Quatre Freres	29 Jul 1828
MONNER, Peter	39		Farmer	France	U. States	Elizabeth	9 Jul 1825
MONNIERE, Jacques	24		Wheelwright	France	U. States	Elizabeth	9 Jul 1825
MONNIN, Peter F.	32	M	Framer	Switserland	Ohio	Danube	20 Jul 1826
MONOCKE, James	23	M	Labourer	Gt. Britain	U. States	Sarah G.	14 Apr 1828
MONREAU, P. A.	27		Chemest	France	U. States	Elizabeth	9 Jul 1825
MONRO, Agnes	21	F	Artist			Servant	30 Aug 1820
Andrew	35	M	Farmer			Servant	30 Aug 1820
Henrietta	4	F				Servant	30 Aug 1820
Margaret	1	F				Servant	30 Aug 1820
MONROE, —, Miss	19	F		U. States	U. States	Matilda	16 Aug 1822
—, Miss	24	F		U. States	U. States	Matilda	16 Aug 1822
Chas.	26	M	Se[r]vant	G. Briten	G. Britan	Isabella	26 Nov 1825
Geo.	27	M	Mariner	U. States	U. States	Hunter	4 Aug 1824
Geo.	31	M	Merchant	Scotland	Jamaica	Azora	22 Oct 1824
Harriet	28	F	None	Cuba	United States	Ariel	30 Jun 1828
John	5	M	None	Cuba	United States	Ariel	30 Jun 1828
Margerie		F	None	Great Britain	United States	Colossus	5 Jun 1827
Thos.	25	M	Carpenter	U. States	U. States	Wicker	21 May 1827
William	35	M	Labourer	Ireland	United States	Roman	12 Jun 1826
Wm.	26	M	Baker	Europe	United States	Aspasia	5 Sep 1827
MONROW, Charly	24 2/12	M	Joiner	France	U. States	France	26 Jun 1828
George	27	M	Farmer	Scotland	U. States	Roger Stewart	9 Jun 1828
James	25	M	Smith	Scotland	U. States	Superior	25 Sep 1828
Janet	22	F		Scotland	U. States	Superior	25 Sep 1828
MONS, Theresa, Miss	20	F	Lady	Ireland	United States	Dublin Packet	23 May 1828
MONSEVILL, H. M.	32	M	Merchant	Spain	Bordeaux	Emelia	21 Sep 1826
MONSO, Diego	38	M	Merchant	Spain	Spain	Sciot	12 Mar 1828
MONSON, S. H.	21	M	Merchant	United States	United States	Amphion	5 Jul 1822
MONT. ARANT, Jonquin	22	M	Merchant	Spain	Havana	Commodore Chauncy	28 Nov 1825
MONTADEVERT, Jas. L.	32	M	Merchant	New York	New York, U. States	Rose in Bloom	30 Jul 1823
MONTAGH, Anne	20	F	Spinster	Ireland	America	Mary	29 May 1827
MONTAGUE, E.	23	M	Doctor	American	United States	Exchange	16 Feb 1822
Henry	23	M		Gt. Britain	G. Britain	Silvanus Jenkins	24 Jul 1828
R.	48	M	Merchant	England	G. Brittain or her Collonies	Etheldred	17 Oct 1822
MONTAIGRO, L.	11	M	No	Spain	U. States	Dromo	22 May 1826
MONTAIN, William	21	M	Farmer	Ireland	America	William	21 May 1825
MONTALAN, Gabriel	16	M	Student	America	America	Henry	11 Oct 1825
MONTANDON, Eugene	22	M	Watchmaker	Switzerland	United States	Eliza Grant	18 Aug 1826
MONTANDOR, Edward	24		Engraver	Switzerland	United States	Cadmus	24 Oct 1827
MONTANIA, Josh.	22	M	None	Great Britain		Casanda	5 Sep 1827
Lawe.	28	M	None	Great Britain		Casanda	5 Sep 1827
MONTANT, Augustus	20	M	Merchant	Philada.	United States	Henri IV	2 Oct 1828
MONTARO, Allonso H.	8	M		Portugal	United States	William Byrnes	1 Dec 1824
Angela E.	34	F		Portugal	United States	William Byrnes	1 Dec 1824
Duarte	1	M		Portugal	United States	William Byrnes	1 Dec 1824
Emilia C.	12	F		Portugal	United States	William Byrnes	1 Dec 1824
Eudora	4	F		Portugal	United States	William Byrnes	1 Dec 1824
Francisco J.	15	M		Portugal	United States	William Byrnes	1 Dec 1824
Francisco X.	45	M	Gentleman	Portugal	United States	William Byrnes	1 Dec 1824
Henrique X.	6	M		Portugal	United States	William Byrnes	1 Dec 1824
Joze J.	17	M	Servant	Portugal	United States	William Byrnes	1 Dec 1824
MONTATANT, Gustave	15	M	None	France	U. States	Bayard	9 Jul 1824
MONTE, Peter	42	M	Mechanic	Switzerland	U. States	Thomas	3 Sep 1822
MONTEETH, —, Mrs.	60	F	Labourer	Glasgow	U. States	Florenzo	29 Jun 1826
Wm.	35	M	Labourer	Glasgow	U. States	Florenzo	29 Jun 1826
MONTEGUE, S. E.	30	M	Merchant	Havana	U. States	Courier	9 Feb 1829
MONTEITH, Agnes	4			Scotland	United States	Camillus	3 May 1828
Ann	40	F	None	Ireland	United States	Friends	21 Oct 1825
Helen	19			Scotland	United States	Camillus	3 May 1828

NAMES OF PASSENGERS	AGE	SEX	OCCUPATIONS	COUNTRY TO WHICH THEY BELONG	COUNTRY THEY INTEND TO INHABIT	SHIPS/DATES OF ARRIVAL	
MONTEITH (cont'd)							
Isabella	40			Scotland	United States	Camillus	3 May 1828
John	8			Scotland	United States	Camillus	3 May 1828
Mary	10			Scotland	United States	Camillus	3 May 1828
Walter	22		Farmer	Scotland	United States	Camillus	3 May 1828
Walter	60		Farmer	Scotland	United States	Camillus	3 May 1828
William	10	M	None	Ireland	United States	Friends	21 Oct 1825
MONTELEGER, Jose M.	11	M	Merchant	England	England	Bunker Hill	20 Sep 1827
Marina	12	M	Merchant	England	England	Bunker Hill	20 Sep 1827
MONTENDEVERT,							
Jas. L.	29	M	Merchant	U. States	U. States	Ductile	11 Feb 1822
MONTER, Twier	18	M	Joiner	France	United States	Virginia	31 May 1828
MONTERE, P. D.	23	M	Shoe Maker	France	U. States	Edward Bonaffe	11 Dec 1827
MONTERI, D.	27	M	Merchant	Spain	U. States	Mary Jane	29 Mar 1828
MONTERO, Dionisio	24	M	Merchant	Spain	U. States	Fabius	7 Dec 1825
MONTERS, L. J.	14	M		Brazil	America	Quill	19 Jun 1828
MONTFORD, Jno.	35	M	Merchant	G. Brittain	U. States	Pacific	23 Jan 1826
MONTGOMERY, Adam	45	M	Blacksmith	Great Britain	United States	Roanoak	19 Sep 1827
Alexr.	26	M	Farmer	England	U. States	Commerce	2 Oct 1823
Ann	17	F	None	Great Britain	United States	Orbit	23 Oct 1826
Charles	10/365			...	United States	Erin	25 Dec 1820
Elijah	12	M		Great Britain	United States	Roanoak	19 Sep 1827
Elizabeth	59	F	Spinster	Ireland	New York	Atlantic	6 Oct 1828
Geo.	27	M	Weaver	U. States	U. States	United States	11 Sep 1828
George	34	M	Farmer	...	United States	Erin	25 Dec 1820
Henry	22	M	Tailor	Great Britain	United States	Orbit	23 Oct 1826
Henry	30	M	Plaisterer	Great Britain	United States	Meridian	2 Jul 1827
James	6	M		Great Britain	United States	Roanoak	19 Sep 1827
James C.	34	M	Gentleman	United States	United States	Richmond	4 Aug 1826
Jane	50	F		Great Britain	United States	Roanoak	19 Sep 1827
Job	20	M	Engineer	Great Britain	United States	Samuel Wright	12 Oct 1829
John	3	M		...	United States	Erin	25 Dec 1820
John	9	M	Labourer	U. States	U. States	Robt. Reade	12 Apr 1825
John	16				Brooklyn	Betsy	4 Sep 1820
John	21	M	Sawyer	Ireland	U. States	Josephine	30 Aug 1828
John	22	M	Labourer	Ireland	United States	Catharine	22 Jul 1825
John	25	M	Farmer	Ireland	United States	Asia	29 Jul 1829
John	30	M	Tailor	Ireland	New York	Atlantic	6 Oct 1828
John	35	M	Merchant	Great Britian	United States	Diamond	13 Nov 1823
Jos.	25	M	Labourer			Hanford	17 Jul 1828
Letitia	30	F	Spinster	...	United States	Erin	25 Dec 1820
Margaret	19	F		Ireland	New York	Lima	5 Aug 1829
Margurita	19			Ireland	U. States	Lima	5 Aug 1829
Mary Ann	10	F		Great Britain	United States	Roanoak	19 Sep 1827
Michael	23	M	Farmer	Ireland	U. States	Henry Kneeland	27 Jul 1825
Mr.		M	Merchant	Great Britain	United States	Ann Maria	12 Jul 1821
Nathan	21	M	Weaver	Ireland	U. States	Josephine	7 May 1827
Robert	25		Farmer			Rufus King	7 Aug 1820
Robt.	24	M	Labourer	Ireland	United States	General Putnam	20 Jun 1825
Robt.	25	M	Farmer	Ireland	U. States	William & John	10 Jul 1824
Sarah	34	F		Ireland	Philadelphia	Curler	7 Jul 1827
Thomas	28	M	Labourer	Ireland	U. States	Erin	5 Jul 1820
Thomas	28	M	Weaver	Ireland	Philadelphia	Curler	7 Jul 1827
William	19	M	Sawyer	Ireland	U. States	Josephine	30 Aug 1828
William	22	M	Farmer	Ireland	United States	Dublin Packet	24 Sep 1823
Wm.	20	M	Labourer	Ireland	United States	General Putnam	20 Jun 1825
MONTGOMORIE, John	21	M	Joiner	Glasgow, Barony [Parish], Lanark [County]	New York	Hero	19 May 1828
*to follow his occupation							
MONTIETH, Walter	18	M	Labourer	Scotland	United States	Friends	7 Jul 1827
MONTINARD, —,							
Madam	23	F		France	United States	Henry	9 Jun 1826
Alexander	31	M	Merchant	France	United States	Henry	9 Jun 1826
MONTOGA, Jose, Don	40	M	Attached to the Mexican Legation	Mexico	United States	Mercid	21 Oct 1824

NAMES OF PASSENGERS	AGE	SEX	OCCUPATIONS	COUNTRY TO WHICH THEY BELONG	COUNTRY THEY INTEND TO INHABIT	SHIPS/DATES OF ARRIVAL	
MONTORRO, Jos.	49	M		Spain	U. States	Rampart	28 Nov 1823
MONTOTO, Eusibie	22	M	Gentn.			Silas Richards	20 Jun 1826
MONTREG, Elizabeth	35	F	Labourer	England	U. States	Ayrshire	12 May 1828
Isaac	34	M	Labourer	England	U. States	Ayrshire	12 May 1828
James	6	M	Labourer	England	U. States	Ayrshire	12 May 1828
John	3	M	Labourer	England	U. States	Ayrshire	12 May 1828
Thoma	1	M	Labourer	England	U. States	Ayrshire	12 May 1828
William	12	M	Labourer	England	U. States	Ayrshire	12 May 1828
MONTROS, C.	19	M	Merchant	U. States	U. States	Hetta	11 Apr 1826
MONTZEIL, Jean P.	5	M		France	U. States	Leonarde	29 Aug 1828
Leonard	2_/12	M		France	U. States	Leonarde	29 Aug 1828
*born on the passage							
Marie J. D.	30	F		France	U. States	Leonarde	29 Aug 1828
Maurice	32	M	Carpenter	France	U. States	Leonarde	29 Aug 1828
Rose	4	F		France	U. States	Leonarde	29 Aug 1828
Rose E. D.	26	F		France	U. States	Leonarde	29 Aug 1828
MONVALD, John	29	M	Farmer	Bardin	U. States	Bayard	5 Sep 1828
MOODES, Roger	34	M	Farmer	England	America	Thames	27 May 1822
MOODWAR, Jesse	60	M	Mercht.	N. York	U. States	St. Michael	21 Jul 1824
MOODY, David	26	M	Farmer	England	U. States	Commerce	2 Oct 1823
Henry	25	M	Shoemaker	Great Britain	United States	Britannia	29 Oct 1829
James	38	M	Labourer	Great Britain	U. States	Princess Charlotte	6 Sep 1828
James A.	21	M	Merchant	Halifax, N.S.		General Marion	12 Jan 1829
Jane	18	F	Spinster	Ireland	United States	Sarah Ann	11 Jan 1827
John	38		Printer	Ireland	United States	Courier	15 Oct 1827
Major	42	M	Army	London	England	South Carolina Packet	16 Sep 1823
Robert	21	M	Student	Ireland	America	Francis & Henrietta	11 Jul 1823
William	30	M	Farmer	Great Britian	United States	Andes	19 Aug 1829
MOOERS, John W.	21 6/12	M	Officer U.S.N.	New York	New York	Potosi	28 May 1825
MOOLLY, William	21	M	Farmer	England	United States	Young Phoenix	26 Jul 1824
MOON, Charles	40	F	None	Great Britain	United States	Eliza Barker	3 Jul 1826
David	2		Farmer	England	United States	Corinthian	7 Jul 1829
James	22		Labourer	England	United States	Corinthian	7 Jul 1829
John	22	M	Labourer	Ireland	New York	Trusty	12 Sep 1828
Mary	20	F	Servant	England	U. States	William Thompson	25 Aug 1828
Mary	26		Farmer	England	United States	Corinthian	7 Jul 1829
Mary Ann	6		Farmer	England	United States	Corinthian	7 Jul 1829
Peter	28	M	Farmer	Ireland	United States	Dublin Packet	24 Sep 1823
Richard	1		Farmer	England	United States	Corinthian	7 Jul 1829
Richard	18		Labourer	England	United States	Corinthian	7 Jul 1829
Richard	32	M	None	Great Britain	United States	Eliza Barker	3 Jul 1826
William	4		Farmer	England	United States	Corinthian	7 Jul 1829
William	27		Farmer	England	United States	Corinthian	7 Jul 1829
Wm.	38	M	Merchant	U. States	U. States	America	17 Oct 1825
MOONE, Joseph	21	M	Farmer	Alsace in the Department of Upper and lower Rhine	United States	Carolina Augusta	16 May 1828
MOONEY, —, Mr.	32	M	Farmer	Gt. Britain	U. States	Constitution	19 Jul 1825
—, Mrs.	30	F	Farmer	Gt. Britain	U. States	Constitution	19 Jul 1825
Ann	25	F		Scotland	United States	Samuel Robertson	5 Oct 1827
Austia	8	F	None	England	United States	Bolivar	15 Jun 1826
Bridget	20	F	Spinster	Ireland	U. States	Josephine	30 Aug 1828
David	14	M		Ireland	United States	Dalhouse Castle	26 Dec 1827
Esther	7	F		Ireland	United States	Dalhouse Castle	26 Dec 1827
Felix	24	M	Labourer	Ireland	United States	Atlantic	21 Jul 1827
Florence	23	M	Servant	Ireland	United States	Sylvester Healy	19 Aug 1825
John	1	M		Scotland	United States	Samuel Robertson	5 Oct 1827
John	28	M	Labourer	Ireland	United States	Lord Wellington	28 May 1827
John	30	M	Cooper	U. States	U. States	Brothers	7 Aug 1820
John	32	M	Labourer	Scotland	United States	Samuel Robertson	5 Oct 1827
Joseph	10	M		Ireland	United States	Dalhouse Castle	26 Dec 1827

NAMES OF PASSENGERS	AGE	SEX	OCCUPATIONS	COUNTRY TO WHICH THEY BELONG	COUNTRY THEY INTEND TO INHABIT	SHIPS/DATES OF ARRIVAL	
MOONEY (cont'd)							
Margaret	6	F	None	England	United States	Bolivar	15 Jun 1826
Margaret	33	F	None	England	United States	Bolivar	15 Jun 1826
Maria	13	F		Ireland	United States	Dalhouse Castle	26 Dec 1827
Mary	24	F	Servant	Ireland	United States	Carolina Ann	11 Dec 1826
Mary	37	F		Ireland	United States	Dalhouse Castle	26 Dec 1827
Mary	40	F	Spinster	Ireland	U. States	Josephine	30 Aug 1828
Michael	18	M		Ireland	U. States	St. Michael	26 Oct 1824
Michael	35	M	Joiner	England	United States	Bolivar	15 Jun 1826
P.	16		Farmer	Ireland	United States	Courier	16 May 1825
Pat	15 6/12	M		Ireland	U.S. of America	Douglass	6 Jul 1829
Pat	20	M	Labourer	Great Britain		Moro Castle	6 Jul 1827
Patk.	22	M	Labourer	Ireland	U.S.	Oliver Wolcott	3 Nov 1827
Robert	23	M	Labourer	Great Britain	United States	Richmond	24 Aug 1829
Rose	9	F		Ireland	United States	Dalhouse Castle	26 Dec 1827
Theresa	5	F		Ireland	United States	Dalhouse Castle	26 Dec 1827
Willm.	25	M	Turner	England	United States	Robert Edwards	3 Oct 1829
MOONY, David	31	M	Merchant	England	U. States	Trident	1 Dec 1824
Duncan	10	M		Scotland	Great Britain	Camillus	28 Apr 1823
MOOR, Cash	60	F	None	England	U. States	Dalhouse	23 Mar 1829
John	16	M	Labourer	England	America	Constitution	1 Oct 1825
Thos.	25			England	United States	Acasta	16 Aug 1826
MOORAN, Allen	10	M	Labourer	Co. L...th	United States	Java	9 Jul 1827
Wm.	20	M	Labourer	Co. L...th	United States	Java	9 Jul 1827
MOORE, —			an Infant of Mrs. Mary Moore			Commerce	24 Sep 1823
*died 20 Aug, aged 2 days							
—, Miss	20	F				Hibernia	15 Aug 1820
—, Mr.	50	M	Merchant	Barbados	Barbados	Margaret	29 Oct 1825
—, Mrs.	40	F		Ireland	U. States	Hope & Esther	19 Aug 1824
Abendigo	35	M	Grocer	Great Brit.	Ohio	Gov. Griswald	3 Jul 1820
Alexande	1	M		Ireland	United States	Fabius	4 Jun 1828
Alexander	25	M	Weaver	Ireland	United States	Fabius	4 Jun 1828
Allex.	30	M	Labourrer	Great Britan	U. States	Ann Marria	6 Aug 1823
Andrew	7	M	Taylor	Great Britain	U. States	Columbia	22 Sep 1828
Andrew	18	M	Farmer	Ireland	United States	Dublin Packet	23 May 1828
Ane	4	F	Wife	England	U.S. States	Splendid	14 Aug 1829
Ann	3	F		Ireland	United States	Fabius	4 Jun 1828
Ann	9	F	None	U. States	U. States	Patriot	23 May 1821
Ann	13	F	Child	Ireland	America	Wilson	16 May 1825
Ann	16	F		Ireland	N. York	Eliza Grant	29 Aug 1829
Ann	21	F	Farmer	Great Britain	United States	Weser	9 May 1822
Ann	23	F	Spinster	Ireland	America	Wilson	16 May 1825
B.	35	M	Merchant	N. York	N. York	Queen Mab	20 Nov 1826
Brid.	11	F		Great Britain	New York	Dublin	21 Dec 1824
Bridget	3			Great Britan	United States	Newry	11 Jul 1827
Bridget	22	F	None	England	United States	India	8 Jun 1827
Bridget	33	F	Taylor	Great Britain	U. States	Columbia	22 Sep 1828
Bridget	43	F	Matron	Ireland	America	Wilson	16 May 1825
Briget	12	F	Servant	Ireland	United States	Wilson	27 Jun 1826
C.	21	M				Hibernia	15 Aug 1820
Cath.	30	F		G. Britain	U. States	St. George	7 Jun 1828
Catherine	9	F	Child	Ireland	America	Wilson	16 May 1825
Clarissa	18	F		Ireland	U. States	Xenophon	13 Jun 1823
Connett	25	M	Labourer	England	U. States	Comet	23 Aug 1828
David	30	M	Labourer	Ireland	U. States	Albion	11 May 1827
E...	60	F		G. Britain	U. States	St. George	7 Jun 1828
Edward	29	M	Weaver	Ireland	U. States	William	27 Jul 1824
Edward	30		Merchant	N. York	United States	Robert Burns	18 Jun 1821
Edward	30	M	Tanner & dier	Ireland	New York, U.S.	Angelica	18 Aug 1823
Elisabeth	25	F	Spinner	Ireland	Newark	Triton	12 Jul 1823
Eliza	7	F	Child	Ireland	America	Wilson	16 May 1825
Elizabeth	7	F	...	Ireland	United States	Carolina Ann	24 Oct 1825
Elizabeth	20	F	Dressmaker	Ireland	U. States	Josephine	7 May 1827
Elizabeth	20		Seamster	Scotland	United States	Camillus	3 May 1828
Elizabeth	24	F		Ireland	United States	Fabius	4 Jun 1828
Elizabeth	27	F	Lady	Scotland	United States	Sarah G.	15 Aug 1827
Elizabeth	62	F	Lady	Ireland	Ireland	Britannia	14 Mar 1828
Ellen	...	...	...	Ireland	U. States of Amer	Courier	17 Mar 1827

NAMES OF PASSENGERS	AGE	SEX	OCCUPATIONS	COUNTRY TO WHICH THEY BELONG	COUNTRY THEY INTEND TO INHABIT	SHIPS/DATES OF ARRIVAL	
MOORE (cont'd)							
Ewd.	29	M	Labourer	G. Britain	U. States	Margaret Bogle	12 Jun 1828
Francis	6	M	Wife	England	U.S. States	Splendid	14 Aug 1829
Francis	46	M		Great Brittain	United States	Sarah Ralston	27 Jan 1827
Geo.	25	M	Cabinet Maker	England	U. States	Pallas	15 Jul 1822
Geo.	26	M	Sadler	Great Britain	U. States	United States	8 Sep 1827
George	13	M	Farmer	Great Britain	United States	Diana	20 Nov 1828
George	25	M	Tobacconist	Great Britain	United States	Corinthian	2 Sep 1824
George	43	M	Merchant	G. Britain	U. States	New York	11 Mar 1823
Grizzey	9	F	Child	Ireland	U. States	Courier	17 Mar 1828
Hannah	2	F		Great Britain	United States	Diana	20 Nov 1828
Hannah	13	F	Wife	England	U.S. States	Splendid	14 Aug 1829
Hannah	30	F		Ireland	N. York	Eliza Grant	29 Aug 1829
Henry	7	M		Ireland	United States	Thomas	13 Dec 1827
Henry	19	M	Joiner	Great Britain	U. States	United States	8 Sep 1827
Henry	20		Laborer	Ireland	United States	Robert Burns	18 Jun 1822
Henry	30	M	Merchant	England	United States	Brighton	11 Mar 1825
Henry	40	M	Farmer	England	U.S. States	Splendid	14 Aug 1829
Henry	60	M	Farmer	G. Britain	U. States	St. George	7 Jun 1828
Henry, Mr.	25	M	Mercht.	Gt. Brittian	Gt. Brittian	Manchester	21 Apr 1827
Honora	17 5/12	F	Servant	Ireland	United States	Wilson	27 Jun 1826
Hosea	21	M	Carpenter	U. States	U. States	Almira	18 Sep 1823
Hugh	26	M	Farmer	G. Brittian	United States	Louisa	14 Jun 1825
Isabella	15	F		U. States	U. States	New York	11 Mar 1823
Isabella	21	F	Spinner	Ireland	Newark	Triton	12 Jul 1823
J.	13	M	None	U. States	U. States	Patriot	23 May 1821
J.	40	M	Merchant	U.S.	U.S.	Radius	1 May 1822
J. B.	26	M	Mercht.	America	America	Gertrude	8 Aug 1821
James	19	M	Labourer	Ireland	U. States	Marcus	7 Apr 1825
James	21		Laborer	Ireland	United States	Robert Burns	18 Jun 1821
James	21	M	Servant	England	United States	India	8 Jun 1827
James	22	M	Weaver	Ireland	United States	Wilson	27 Jun 1826
James	22	M	Laborer	Great Britain	United States	Foster	23 Mar 1829
James	23	M	Labourer	Ireland	United States	Meteor	26 Jun 1827
James	25	M	Sailor	Ireland	New Orleans	Mentor	20 Oct 1825
James	25	M	Farmer	Ireland	United States	Lord Strangford	20 Jun 1826
James	30	M	Weaver	England	United States	Jubilee	4 Mar 1829
James	33	M	Labourer	Ireland	United States	Wilson	28 Nov 1828
James	35	M	Labourer	Great Britain		Moro Castle	6 Jul 1827
James	35	M	Labourer	England	United States	Siroc	31 Oct 1829
James	45	M	Mason	U. States	U. States	Magnet	18 Aug 1825
James	45			Great Britan	United States	Newry	11 Jul 1827
Jane	3	F	Taylor	Great Britain	U. States	Columbia	22 Sep 1828
Jane	11	F	Wife	England	U.S. States	Splendid	14 Aug 1829
Jane	16	F	Farmer	England	U. States	Acasta	12 May 1825
Jane	17	F	Spinster	Ireland	U. States	Courier	17 Mar 1828
Jane	20			Ireland	United States	Robert Burns	18 Jun 1822
Jane	23	F	Labourer	Ireland	United States	Meteor	26 Jun 1827
Jane	25	F	Matron	Ireland	United States	Robert Fulton	10 Aug 1827
Jas.	19	M	Carpenter	Ireland	United States	William	20 Jul 1829
Jere, Capt.	64	M	Ship Master	U. States	U.S.	Burdett	7 Dec 1827
John	2	M	None	England	New Jersey	Commerce	24 Sep 1823
John	16	M	Labourer	Ireland	U. States	Lady Hunter	9 Oct 1825
John	17	M	Farmer	Ireland	U. States	Globe	14 Jul 1821
John	18	M	Farmer	Bristol, Engl.	...	Warrior	19 May 1828
John	19	M	Iron Founder	Great Britain	United States	Roanoak	19 Sep 1827
John	19	M	Labourer	Ireland	United States	Courier	17 Mar 1828
John	20	M	Farmer	Killinchey	United States	Carolina Ann	11 Jun 1824
John	20	M	Weaver	Ireland	United States	Fabius	4 Jun 1828
John	20 6/12	M	Farmer	Ireland	United States	Wilson	22 Jun 1824
John	22	M	Farmer, Labourer or Spinster	Ireland	U. States	Meteor	4 Oct 1827
John	24	M	Taylor	Great Britain	United States	Samuel Wright	12 Oct 1829
John	25	M	Servant to Mr. Whittock	U. States	U. States	Quill	26 Jun 1827
John	26 3/12	M	Laborer	Great Briton	United States	Mount Vernon	30 Dec 1828
John	27	M	Laboror	Ireland	United States	Wilson	27 Jun 1826
John	28	M	Labourer	Ireland	U. States	William & John	10 Jul 1824
John	28	M	Farmer	Great Britain	United States	Diana	20 Nov 1828

NAMES OF PASSENGERS	AGE	SEX	OCCUPATIONS	COUNTRY TO WHICH THEY BELONG	COUNTRY THEY INTEND TO INHABIT	SHIPS/DATES OF ARRIVAL	
MOORE (cont'd)							
John	29	M	Brass Founder	Great Britian	United States	Mount Vernon	19 May 1823
John	30	M		England	United States	Yobah	26 Sep 1827
John	30	M	Cooper	England	America	England	23 Jun 1828
John	35		Carpenter	Great Britan	United States	Newry	11 Jul 1827
John	40	M	Taylor	Great Britan	U. States	Columbia	22 Sep 1828
John	42	M	Baker	United States	United States	Comet	6 Mar 1823
John J.	4	M			U. States	New York	11 Mar 1823
Joseph	4	M		Great Brit.	Ohio	Gov. Griswald	3 Jul 1820
Joseph	5	M	None	England	New Jersey	Commerce	24 Sep 1823
Joseph	20		Taylor	England	United States	Hudson	5 Apr 1826
Julia	31	F	None	Great Brittan	U.S.	Emulous	29 Jun 1827
Julia	31	F	Wife	England	U.S. States	Splendid	14 Aug 1829
Julia	36	F	house keeper	Ireland	United States	William	20 Jul 1829
Lewis	22	M	Farmer	Ireland	U. States	Wilson	22 Apr 1822
Louis	28	M	Merchant	France	U.S.	Bayard	30 Oct 1820
Louisa	25	F	Lady	Ireland	U. States	Howard	25 Jul 1823
Lucy	26	F		G. Britain	U. States	St. George	7 Jun 1828
M.	38	M	Clerk	Ireland	S.C.	Hope & Esther	19 Aug 1824
Margret	25	F		Ireland	America	Plutarch	18 Jul 1826
Martha	21	F	Spinster	Ireland	U. States	Courier	17 Mar 1828
Martha	40	F	Wife	Blantier	U.S. America	Camillus	10 Sep 1821
Martha	52		Spinster	Ireland	United States	Courier	15 Oct 1827
Mary	1			Scotland	United States	Camillus	3 May 1828
Mary	1	F	Wife	England	U.S. States	Splendid	14 Aug 1829
Mary	4			Great Britan	United States	Newry	11 Jul 1827
Mary	5	F		Great Britain	United States	Diana	20 Nov 1828
Mary	11	F	Child	Ireland	America	Wilson	16 May 1825
Mary	15	F	Spinster	Ireland	America	Wilson	16 May 1825
Mary	20	M	Labourer	Ireland, Great Britain	U.S. of America	Dublin	21 Feb 1826
Mary	21	F	Spinster	Ireland	U. States	Globe	14 Jul 1821
Mary	27	F		England	United States	Yobah	26 Sep 1827
Mary	31	F	None	England	New Jersey	Commerce	24 Sep 1823
Mary	34			Ireland	U.S.	Union	20 Aug 1827
Mary	40			Great Britan	United States	Newry	11 Jul 1827
Mary Ann	5	F	Taylor	Great Britain	U. States	Columbia	22 Sep 1828
Mathew	10			Great Britan	United States	Newry	11 Jul 1827
Michal	21	M	Labourer	Ireland	United States	Robert Fulton	24 Jul 1826
Moses	18	M	...	Ireland	United States	General Putnam	20 Jun 1825
Nicholous	26	M	Laborer or Spinster	Ireland	United States	Frances Miller	27 Jul 1827
Pat	20	M	Farmer	Great Britain	New York	Dublin	21 Dec 1824
Patrick	6	M	Child	Ireland	America	Wilson	16 May 1825
Patrick	7	M	Taylor	Great Britain	U. States	Columbia	22 Sep 1828
Patrick	50 4/12	M	Farmer	Ireland	United States	Wilson	22 Jun 1824
Peggy	66	F		Ireland	United States	Dalhouse Castle	26 Dec 1827
Penelope	45	F	Matron	Ireland	U. States	Courier	17 Mar 1828
Peter	14	M	Farmer	Ireland	U. States	Globe	14 Jul 1821
Richard	19	M	Farmer	Great Britain	United States	Diana	20 Nov 1828
Robert			Farmer			Amphion	31 May 1824
Robert	1	M	...	Ireland	United States	Carolina Ann	24 Oct 1825
Robert	8	M	Wife	England	U.S. States	Splendid	14 Aug 1829
Robert	13	M	Labourer	Ireland	U. States	Courier	17 Mar 1828
Robert	21	M	Labourer	Ireland	United States	Robert Fulton	10 Aug 1827
Robt.	21	M	Labourer	Ireland	United States	Wilson	28 Nov 1828
Robt.	35	M	Farmer	Great Brittan	U.S.	Emulous	29 Jun 1827
Sally	48	F		England	America	John Adams	2 Aug 1827
Samuel	10	M		Irereland	America	Carolina Ann	20 Jun 1825
Samuel	16	M	Labourer	Ireland	U. States	Courier	17 Mar 1828
Samuel	28	M	Mariner	U.S.	U.S.	Alpha	4 Feb 1829
Sarah	15	F		Great Britain	United States	Corinthian	2 Sep 1824
Sarah	31	F		G. Britain	U. States	New York	11 Mar 1823
Sarah	35	F		Great Brit.	Ohio	Gov. Griswald	3 Jul 1820
Sarah	51	F		Great Britain	United States	Corinthian	2 Sep 1824
Sophia	24	F	Spinster	Ireland	United States	Thomas	13 Dec 1827
T. W. C.	32	M	Merchant	New York	U. States	Natchez	7 Feb 1825
Thomas	8	M	Child	Ireland	U. States	Courier	17 Mar 1828
Thomas	18	M	Labourer			Evergreen	28 Jul 1820
Thomas	18	M	Farmer	Ireland	United States	Dublin Packet	29 Jun 1825

NAMES OF PASSENGERS	AGE	SEX	OCCUPATIONS	COUNTRY TO WHICH THEY BELONG	COUNTRY THEY INTEND TO INHABIT	SHIPS/DATES OF ARRIVAL	
MOORE (cont'd)							
Thomas	19	M	Labourer	Ireland	United States	Meteor	26 Jun 1827
Thomas	25	M	Sawyer	England	Ohio	Concordia	12 Oct 1826
Thomas	28	M	Farmer	Ireland	United States	Lord Strangford	20 Jun 1826
Thomas	58	M	Farmer	Great Britain	United States	Diana	20 Nov 1828
Thos.	25	M	Farmer	Ireland	U. States	Xenophon	13 Jun 1823
Thos.	29	M	Labourer	Ireland	U. States	Marcus	7 Apr 1825
Thos. W.	26	M	Merchant	U. States	U. States	Blooming Rose	2 Apr 1821
Thos. W. C.		M	Merchant	U. States	U. States	Nimrod	19 Jan 1822
William	6	M		Great Brit.	Ohio	Gov. Griswald	3 Jul 1820
William	17	M	Farmer	Great Britain	United States	Diana	20 Nov 1828
William	20	M	Butcher	New York	New York	Florida	28 Jun 1825
William	20	M	Mill Wright	Ireland	United States	Romulus	24 Jun 1826
William	20	M	Labourer	Grt. Britain	United States	Robert Fulton	8 Oct 1828
William	24	M	Labourer	Ireland	United States	Meteor	26 Jun 1827
William	24	M	Labourer	Ireland	America	Franklin	13 Aug 1827
William	26	M	Plaisterer	Ireland	New York	Lima	5 Aug 1829
William	27	M	Labourer	Irereland	America	Carolina Ann	20 Jun 1825
William	27	M	...	Ireland	United States	Carolina Ann	24 Oct 1825
William	38	M	Joiner	Scotland		Zamoa	5 Nov 1828
Wm.		Prisoner taken by the U.S. Ship Cyane and sent by the Consul at St. Iago				Maria	20 Jul 1820
Wm.	1			Great Britan	United States	Newry	11 Jul 1827
Wm.	5	M	Gentleman	Ireland	United States	Thomas	13 Dec 1827
Wm.	8	M	None	England	New Jersey	Commerce	24 Sep 1823
Wm.	20 9/12	M	House Carpenter	Ireland	Kentucky	Atlantic	6 Oct 1828
Wm.	21	M	Hatter	Ireland	U. States	Union	10 Mar 1823
Wm.	22	M	Mechanic	Ireland	U. States	Martha	28 Jan 1826
Wm.	25	M	F...	Ireland	West Indies	Courier	17 Mar 1827
Wm.	25	M	Turner	G. Britain	U. States	Nimrod	31 Jul 1828
Wm.	29	M	Farmer	Ireland	New York	Louisa	18 Apr 1827
Wm.	39			Great Britan	United States	Newry	11 Jul 1827
Wm.	40		Stone Mason	Ireland	U.S.	Union	20 Aug 1827
Wm.	50		Gilder	Essex	United States	Elizabeth	8 Dec 1821
Wm. B.	18	M	Cabinetmaker	U. States	U. States	Sarah	4 Aug 1825
MOOREE, William	26	M	Plasterur	Ireland	New York	Lima	5 Aug 1829
MOOREHEAD, John	38	M	Merchant	United States	United States	Nestor	20 Nov 1821
Matilda C.	4	F	None	United States	United States	Nestor	20 Nov 1821
Rebecca	21	F	None	United States	United States	Nestor	20 Nov 1821
Thomas	44	M	Clothier	England	America	Plutarch	18 Jul 1826
MOOREHOUSE, Thomas	38	M	Labourer	Haddersfield		Aurora	8 Jun 1827
MOORELAND, Margret	14	F	Spinster	Grt. Britain	United States	Robert Fulton	8 Oct 1828
MOORELEY, Wm.	23		Labourer	England	United States	Hugh Johnson	11 Jun 1828
MOORER, Irvin	10	M		Ireland	U. States	Adno	5 Jul 1828
MOORET, Fredk. W.	29	M	Mariner	America	America	Mercury	2 Feb 1825
MOORFIELD, James	47	M	Merchant	U. States	U. States	Centurion	20 Aug 1828
MOORHEA..., Henry	20	M	Weaver	Ireland	United States	Enterprize	23 Jul 1827
MOORHEAD, Alexander	1	M		Ireland	United States	Lord Wellington	14 Nov 1827
Hugh	11	M		Ireland	United States	Lord Wellington	14 Nov 1827
James	29	M	Canal Cutter	Ireland	United States	Lord Wellington	14 Nov 1827
Margaret	25	F		Ireland	United States	Lord Wellington	14 Nov 1827
Mary	9	F		Ireland	United States	Lord Wellington	14 Nov 1827
Robbert, Doctor	27	M	Doctor	Ireland	United States	Dublin Packet	24 Sep 1823
Robinson	24		Weaver	Ireland	United States	Robert Burns	30 May 1823
Robt.	30	M	Physician	U.S.	U.S.	Pacific	24 Oct 1828
MOORI..., Jno.	28	M	Labourer	Great Britain	New York	Dublin	21 Dec 1824
MOORICY, Jane	24	F	Lady	Great Britain	United States	Sylvester Healy	23 Nov 1825
MOORIS, John	21		Mechant	Wittshire	England	London	13 Dec 1822
MOORN, Sampson	17	M	Grocer	England	England	William Byrnes	14 Apr 1824
MOORSTER, Chatarina, Kinder (child [Christiaan Forgo])	2 6/12	F		Hechgen	United States	Juffraw Johanna	16 Oct 1821
Chatarina, Zyn Vrouw (his wife [Christiaan Forgo])	26	F		Breidenbach	United States	Juffraw Johanna	16 Oct 1821
Chaterina, Kinder (child [Christiaan Forgo])	12 6/12	F		Hechgen	United States	Juffraw Johanna	16 Oct 1821

NAMES OF PASSENGERS	AGE	SEX	OCCUPATIONS	COUNTRY TO WHICH THEY BELONG	COUNTRY THEY INTEND TO INHABIT	SHIPS/DATES OF ARRIVAL
MOORSTER (cont'd)						
Elizabeth, Kinder						
(child [Christiaan						
Forgo])	4	F		Hechgen	United States	Juffraw Johanna 16 Oct 1821
MOPPIN,						
Benjamin, Junr.	20 3/12	M	Merchant	United States	United States	London Trader 29 Mar 1824
MOQUE, Andrew	1			France	U. States	Parachute 14 May 1828
Eliza	7			France	U. States	Parachute 14 May 1828
Eliza	26			France	U. States	Parachute 14 May 1828
John	4 1/2			France	U. States	Parachute 14 May 1828
Philip	3			France	U. States	Parachute 14 May 1828
Philip	29		Mechanic	France	U. States	Parachute 14 May 1828
MOR, Saml.	42	M	Merchant	G. Britain	U. States	Canada 19 Sep 1828
MORA, Antonio	32	M	Merchant	Spain	Spain	Ambuscade 1 Jul 1820
MORA, Jose Domingo	25	M	Sugur Planter	Cuba	Cuba	Hesper 16 Jun 1828
MORAGER, Eliza	18	F	Servant	S. Croix	S. Croix	Jupiter 29 Jun 1825
MORAL, Juan	21	M	Merchant	Spain	U. States	Anne 20 Jun 1828
MORALES, B.	25	M	Merchant	Island Cuba	U. States	Havana Packet 27 Jul 1827
Jose Tomas	30	M	Sadler	Columbia	Columbia	William 31 Mar 1828
MORAN, Ann	41	F		Ireland	U. States	Howard Douglass 29 Jan 1828
Annette	4	F			U. States	Roseway 10 Jul 1820
Antonio	7	M		Spain	Spain	Paquebot Bordeaux 25 May 1828
Catharine	3	F	None	United States	United States	Foster 12 Dec 1821
Catherine	3	F	Capt. Child	France	United States	American 27 Aug 1827
Charles	8	M			U. States	Roseway 10 Jul 1820
Daniel	40	M	... & Currier	England	U. States	Roseway 10 Jul 1820
Eliza	30	F	Spinster	United States	United States	Foster 12 Dec 1821
Eliza W.	35	F	Captain's Wife	France	United States	American 27 Aug 1827
Ignacio	3	M		Spain	Spain	Paquebot Bordeaux 25 May 1828
James	30	M	Leather Dresser	United States		Panthea 15 Jun 1822
James Lewis	1	M			U. States	Roseway 10 Jul 1820
Joaquin	6	M		Spain	Spain	Paquebot Bordeaux 25 May 1828
John	14	M	Farmer	Ireland	U. States	Hibernia 29 Nov 1821
John	23	M		Ireland	New York	Lady Hunter 5 Jun 1826
John	35	M	Mechanic	Ireland	U. States	Malabar 3 Apr 1823
Jori	60	M	Military	Spain	Spain	Paquebot Bordeaux 25 May 1828
Mary Ann	40	F		Holland	U. States	Roseway 10 Jul 1820
Mathew	20	M	Farmer	Ireland	United States	Dublin Packet 13 Oct 1828
Mathew	68	M	Merchant	Ireland	New York	Wilson 10 Apr 1823
Michael	21	M	Labourer	Ireland	U. States	Marcus 7 Apr 1825
Michl.	30	M	Farmer	Stackport	United States	Aurelia 7 Jun 1826
Monica	4	F		Spain	Spain	Paquebot Bordeaux 25 May 1828
Patr.	20	M	Labourer	Ireland	Unt. St. America	Wilson 21 May 1827
Patt	10	M	Joiner	Ireland	New York	Amanda 23 May 1827
Rose	6	F			U. States	Roseway 10 Jul 1820
Theodoria	5	F		Spain	Spain	Paquebot Bordeaux 25 May 1828
Victorina	10	F			U. States	Roseway 10 Jul 1820
MORANES, Joseph	50	M	Merchant	Hayti	U. States	Curlew 16 Jun 1823
MORANGAS, Antonio	41	M	Mariner	Spain	Spain	Richmond Packet 13 Jun 1825
MORANGE, Amelie	20	F	Spinster	France	U. States	Trident 1 Dec 1824
Bella	37	F	Spinster	France	U. States	Trident 1 Dec 1824
Benjamin	45	M	Merchant	France	U. States	Trident 1 Dec 1824
Betsey	14	F	Spinster	France	U. States	Trident 1 Dec 1824
Desire	6	F		U. States	U. States	Trident 1 Dec 1824
Eliza	9	F		France	U. States	Trident 1 Dec 1824
Fanny	15	F		France	U. States	Trident 1 Dec 1824
Gallathee	12	M		France	U. States	Trident 1 Dec 1824
Henrietta	3	F		U. States	U. States	Trident 1 Dec 1824
Lambert	18	M		France	U. States	Trident 1 Dec 1824
MORANO, Ramon	19	M	Servant	Mexico	U. States	Virginia 3 Dec 1827
MORATTE, —, Mrs.	45	F		France	U.S.	Osprey 22 Nov 1824

NAMES OF PASSENGERS	AGE	SEX	OCCUPATIONS	COUNTRY TO WHICH THEY BELONG	COUNTRY THEY INTEND TO INHABIT	SHIPS/DATES OF ARRIVAL	
MORATTE (cont'd)							
J., Mr.	35	M	Carpenter	France	U.S.	Osprey	22 Nov 1824
MORAW, Michael	29	M	Carpenter	Mayo	America	Margaret	31 Jul 1824
MORAY, Rebecca	45	F		Jamaica	U. States	Active	11 Mar 1823
MORCELES, A.	15	M		Spain	Spain	Cadmus	27 Jul 1825
MORDICAI, M.	46	M	Merchant	Jamaica	U. States	Comet	10 Mar 1825
MORDOCK, Danl.	1	M	None	Ireland	United States	Washington	2 Oct 1828
Jane	4	F	None	Ireland	United States	Washington	2 Oct 1828
Jane	30	F	None	Ireland	United States	Washington	2 Oct 1828
MORE, Ann	32			Ireland	Great Britain	Robert Burns	14 Jun 1824
Anton	24	M	Taylor	Switzerland	U. States	Hewes	30 Oct 1829
Cayitan	28	M	Gentleman	Italy	U. States	Sally Ann	6 Nov 1824
Constant	5 6/12	M	None	Netherlands	U. States	Sully	25 Jun 1828
David	55		Farmer	Ireland	Great Britain	Robert Burns	14 Jun 1824
Eliza	6	F	Traveller	Great Britian	United States	Andes	19 Aug 1829
Eliza	19	F		N. York	U. States	New Speculation	29 Jun 1824
Elizabeth	5	F	Traveller	Great Britian	United States	Andes	19 Aug 1829
Elizabeth	26	F	Traveller	Great Britian	United States	Andes	19 Aug 1829
Ellen	5	F	Spinster	Ireland	U. States	Lady Hunter	18 Jul 1825
Felix	20		Cordwainer	St. John	U. States	Lady Hunter	5 Jul 1823
George	6 6/12	M	None	Netherlands	U. States	Sully	25 Jun 1828
Henry	30			Ireland	Great Britain	Robert Burns	14 Jun 1824
Hezekiah	1	M	Traveller	Great Britian	United States	Andes	19 Aug 1829
J.	42	M	Gentleman	U.S.	U.S	Radius	18 Feb 1823
Jere	17	M		N. York	U. States	New Speculation	29 Jun 1824
Jere	55	M	Merchant	U.S.	U. States	New Speculation	29 Jun 1824
John	22			Ireland	Great Britain	Robert Burns	14 Jun 1824
John	27	M	Paper Maker	Scotland	Baltimore	Eunice	13 Dec 1827
John	28	M	Merchant	Switzerland		Rose in Bloom	30 Jul 1823
John	40	M	Merchant	U.S.	U.S.	Radius	8 Feb 1822
Levers	2	F	None	Netherlands	U. States	Sully	25 Jun 1828
Margaret	15	F	...	Ireland	United States	Wilson	22 Jun 1824
Margaret	18	F		Ireland	U. States	Wilson	2 Sep 1823
Mary	20	F		N. York	U. States	New Speculation	29 Jun 1824
Mary	20	F	Domestic	Scotland	New York	Eunice	13 Dec 1827
Moriah, Mrs.	29	F	None	Netherlands	U. States	Sully	25 Jun 1828
Nancy	20	F	Spinster	Ireland	U. States	Lady Hunter	18 Jul 1825
Patrick	22	M	Labourrer	Great Britan	U. States	Ann Marria	6 Aug 1823
Richard	25	M	Labourer	Ireland	U. States	Lady Hunter	18 Jul 1825
Rogmer	4	F	None	Netherlands	U. States	Sully	25 Jun 1828
Samuel	13	M	Traveller	Great Britian	United States	Andes	19 Aug 1829
Sarah	2	F	Traveller	Great Britian	United States	Andes	19 Aug 1829
Sarah	19	F	Lady	Scotland	New York	Eunice	13 Dec 1827
Thomas	20	M	Painter	Ireland	U. States	Union	3 Jun 1822
Thomas	20	M	Farmer	Ireland	America	Carolina Ann	14 Feb 1825
Thos.	20	M	Seaman	Charlestown	United States	Venus	8 Sep 1820
Thos.	50		Farmer	Ireland	Great Britain	Robert Burns	14 Jun 1824
William	4	M	Traveller	Great Britian	United States	Andes	19 Aug 1829
Wm.	28	M	Baker	G. Brittan	U. States	Trafalgar	4 Jun 1822
MOREAH, Nicolus	41	M		Switzerland		Pallas	14 Jun 1828
MOREAN, John	1	M		England	England	Ranger	15 Jan 1827
Nancy	25	F		England	England	Ranger	15 Jan 1827
Wm.	23	M	Miner	England	England	Ranger	15 Jan 1827
MOREAU, George	26	M		Canada	Great Brittain	Frances	21 Jul 1827
James	35	M	Mercht.	Haiti	U. States	Moreau	21 Jun 1827
John, Mr.	37	M	Merchant	France	America	Henry	19 Jun 1825
MOREFIELD, James	27	M	Merchant	U. States	U. States	Fabius	30 Aug 1827
MOREHAM, William	16	M	Farmer	England	America	Comet	26 Jun 1822
MOREHEAD, Alexr.	20	M	Shoemaker	Ireland	U. States	Nancy	25 Nov 1823
Danl.	30			England		Anacreon	7 Sep 1827
Eliza	27			England		Anacreon	7 Sep 1827
Henry	30	M	Laborer or Spinster	Ireland	United States	Sarah G	11 Sep 1827
John	16			England		Anacreon	7 Sep 1827
John	20			England		Anacreon	7 Sep 1827
John	20	M	Labourer	Ireland	United States	Wilson	4 Oct 1827

NAMES OF PASSENGERS	AGE	SEX	OCCUPATIONS	COUNTRY TO WHICH THEY BELONG	COUNTRY THEY INTEND TO INHABIT	SHIPS/DATES OF ARRIVAL	
MOREHEAD (cont'd)							
Mary	3	F	Laborer or Spinster	Ireland	United States	Sarah G	11 Sep 1827
Mary Ann	13			England		Anacreon	7 Sep 1827
Nancy	1	F	Laborer or Spinster	Ireland	United States	Sarah G	11 Sep 1827
Robt.	5			England		Anacreon	7 Sep 1827
Robt.	22			England		Anacreon	7 Sep 1827
Sarah	28	F	Laborer or Spinster	Ireland	United States	Sarah G	11 Sep 1827
MOREHOUSE, E.	25	M	Merchant	U. States	U. States	Aria	16 Jan 1829
MOREL, G. A.	24	M	Farmer or Mechanic	Switzerland	U.S.	Edward Quesnel	31 Jul 1827
John	32	M	Servant	U. States	U. States	Amphion	24 Aug 1821
Louis	25	M	Mechanic	France	U.S.	Helen	3 May 1828
MORELAND, Francis	20	M	Farmer	Ireland	U. States	Dickinson	30 Jul 1825
J.	48	M	Merchant	U.S.	U.S.	Mordicae	24 Nov 1828
MORELL, Christian	30	M	Wheelright	France	U. States	Sully	25 Jun 1828
Dorothy	28	F	None	France	U. States	Sully	25 Jun 1828
MORELLA, John	24	M				Amos Palmer	9 Sep 1828
MORELLO, Peter	45	M	Merchant	France	U. States	Leontine	10 Jul 1826
MOREMAN, ...lla	4	M				Venus	15 Apr 1822
Ann	9	F	Printer	England	England	Venus	15 Apr 1822
Elizabeth	32	F		England	England	Venus	15 Apr 1822
James	7	M		England	England	Venus	15 Apr 1822
Mary	11	F		England	England	Venus	15 Apr 1822
William	13	M				Venus	15 Apr 1822
MOREN, —, Mr.	30	M	Mechanic	Ireland	U. States	Peter Francisco	7 Jun 1822
—, Mrs.	20	F		Ireland	U. States	Peter Francisco	7 Jun 1822
MORENA, J.	35	M	Soldier	Spain	Spain	Prince Edward	22 Jul 1824
MORENBECK,							
Dorathea	40	F	Farmer	Switzerland		Charlemagne	20 Aug 1829
Eliza	7	F	Farmer	Switzerland		Charlemagne	20 Aug 1829
Jacob	45	M	Farmer	Switzerland		Charlemagne	20 Aug 1829
John	10	M	Farmer	Switzerland		Charlemagne	20 Aug 1829
MORENIER, Eliza	27	F	None	France	U. States	Marmion	7 Jun 1824
MORENO, Felix	25	M	Merchant	Truxello	Truxello	Adeline	16 Aug 1827
R.	42	M	Merchant	England	U. States	Caseo	26 Apr 1828
MORESON, Ann	22	F	Wife	Ireland	U. States	Nancy	14 Jan 1822
William	25	M	Farmer	Ireland	U. States	Nancy	14 Jan 1822
MORETON, Calbeck	20	M	Baker	Prince Edwd. Island	United States	General Marion	20 Aug 1828
Samuel	38	M	Dyer	England	U.S. America	Samuel Wright	9 Jan 1829
Thomas	15	M	None	England	U.S. America	Samuel Wright	9 Jan 1829
MORG, D.	2	F				Hanford	17 Jul 1828
D.	22	F	Spinster			Hanford	17 Jul 1828
Ellen	6	F	Spinster			Hanford	17 Jul 1828
Mary Jane	4	F				Hanford	17 Jul 1828
R.	0 4/12	M				Hanford	17 Jul 1828
Saml.	29	M	Weaver			Hanford	17 Jul 1828
MORGAN, —	21	M	Mercht.	United States	U. States	Hiram	4 Sep 1824
—, Mrs.	25	F		New York	New York	Huntress	15 Oct 1823
...	45		Servant	New Jersey	Halifax	America	28 Jul 1826
Andie	62	M	Farmer	Alsace in the Department of Upper and lower Rhine	United States	Carolina Augusta	16 May 1828
Andrew W.	22	M	Mercht.	U.S.		Charlemagne	16 Jan 1829
Ann	6/12	F		Wales	America	John Adams	2 Aug 1827
Ann	5	F		Great B.	U. States	William Neilson	26 Jul 1828
Ann	21	F		U. States	U. States	Cincinnatus	24 May 1821
Ann	22	F	None	Gt. Britain	United States	Pacific	22 May 1826
Ann	28	F	Farmer	Bristol, Engl.	England	Warrior	19 May 1828
Ann	40	F		England	U.N. States	Earl of Liverpool	20 Aug 1825
Ann	60	F	None	Great Britain	United States	Ocean	27 Jul 1825
B.	30	M	Labourer	Ireland	United States	Princess Charlotte	6 Oct 1827
Bernard	18	M	Taylor	Ireland	United States	Orozimbo	5 Mar 1827

NAMES OF PASSENGERS	AGE	SEX	OCCUPATIONS	COUNTRY TO WHICH THEY BELONG	COUNTRY THEY INTEND TO INHABIT	SHIPS/DATES OF ARRIVAL	
MORGAN (cont'd)							
Bridget	19	F	Spinster	Ireland	America	Wilson	16 May 1825
Bridget	21	F	None	Great Britain	United States	Ocean	27 Jul 1825
Bridget	24	F		Great Britain	United States	Isaac Hicks	10 Jul 1827
Catharan	30	F		Great B.	U. States	William Neilson	26 Jul 1828
Catharine	22	F		England	United States	Siroc	31 Oct 1829
Catherine	25	F	Spinster	Switzerland	United States	Andes	5 May 1828
Catherine	61	F	Farmer	Alsace in the Department of Upper and lower Rhine	United States	Carolina Augusta	16 May 1828
Cathr.	21	F		Ireland	United States	Commerce	13 Jun 1828
Celia	30	F	Servant	U. States	U. States	Canada	4 Oct 1824
Charles	12	M	None	Great Britain	United States	Penelope	11 Jun 1827
Charles	36 10/12	M	Calico Printer	England	U.S. America	Illinois	16 Oct 1822
Charles W.	32	M	Officer	U.S. America		Phoebe Ann	27 Dec 1825
Charlotte	16	F	None	Great Britain	United States	Penelope	11 Jun 1827
Daniel	22	M	Farmer	England	United States	William Byrnes	1 Dec 1824
Daniel	28	M	Plasterer	Ireland		Eliza Grant	29 Aug 1829
David	21	M	Farmer	England	America	Comet	26 Jun 1822
David	37	M	Weaver	Wales	America	John Adams	2 Aug 1827
E.	4	F		New York	New York	Huntress	15 Oct 1823
E.	26	M	Carpenter	England	U. States	William	17 Jun 1823
Edward	25	M	Merchant	Barbados	Supposition is he will return	Superb	7 Jul 1823
Edward	29	M	Skin...	Great Britain	United States	Roman	19 Dec 1825
Eliza	2 7/12	F	Farmer	Bristol, Engl.	England	Warrior	19 May 1828
Eliza	4					Xenophon	25 Jul 1826
Eliza	9	M		England	U.N. States	Earl of Liverpool	20 Aug 1825
Elizabeth	6	F		Wales	America	John Adams	2 Aug 1827
Elizabeth	26	F		Ireland		Eliza Grant	29 Aug 1829
Elizabeth	35					Xenophon	25 Jul 1826
Elizabeth	65	F		England	U. States	Amity	23 Sep 1823
Ellenor	4	F		Irereland	America	Carolina Ann	20 Jun 1825
Eunice *Deceased		F		U. States		Huntress	20 Aug 1824
Euphrahs	2/52	M	None	Born on the Passage	America	Euphrates	26 Jun 1821
Evan	42	M	Cordwinder	Wales	America	John Adams	2 Aug 1827
Francis	17	M		U. States	U. States	Cincinnatus	24 May 1821
Francis	24	M	Labourer	Ireland	United States	Princess Charlotte	26 Apr 1827
G. L.	21	M	Merchant	American	U. States	Monroe	13 May 1823
Geo. W.	47	M	Gent.	U. States	U. States	Cadmus	28 May 1821
Hannah	12	F		England	United States	William Byrnes	1 Dec 1824
Hannah	48	F		U. States	U. States	Cincinnatus	24 May 1821
Hugh	22	M	Labourer	Great Britain	United States	Mary & Harriet	3 Jul 1829
Humprey	40	M		Great B.	U. States	William Neilson	26 Jul 1828
Isaac	12	M	Weaver	Great Britain	United States	Spartan	25 Jul 1821
J. B.	22	M	Weaver	France	United States	Le Voltaire	19 Jul 1828
Jacob	19	M	Farmer	Gt. Britan	U. States	Earl of Liverpool	12 Apr 1825
James	20	M		Great Britain		Corinthian	27 Oct 1829
James	21	M	Farmer	England	America	Dewitt Clinton	27 Jul 1824
James	23	M		Scotland	United States	Camillus	9 May 1827
James	24	M	Weaver	England	United States	Siroc	31 Oct 1829
James	25	M	Merchant	United States	United States	Columbia	17 Apr 1827
James	32	M	Mariner	U. States	U. States	Copernican	7 Jan 1823
James, Mr.	28	M	Farmer	Grate Britain	...	Courier	14 Jun 1825
Jane	2	F		Wales	America	John Adams	2 Aug 1827
Jane	19	F	None	Great Britain	United States	Mary & Harriet	3 Jul 1829
Jno.	30	M	Seamen	U. States	U. States	Eunice	17 Jul 1828
John	2 1/12	M	None	England	America	Euphrates	26 Jun 1821
John	6	M	Farmer	England	United States	Essex	23 May 1828
John	13	M		Wales	America	John Adams	2 Aug 1827
John	18	M		U. States	U. States	Cincinnatus	24 May 1821
John	19	M	...	...	...	Braganza	8 Aug 1825
John	20	M		Gt. Britain	United States	Penelope	9 Sep 1828

NAMES OF PASSENGERS	AGE	SEX	OCCUPATIONS	COUNTRY TO WHICH THEY BELONG	COUNTRY THEY INTEND TO INHABIT	SHIPS/DATES OF ARRIVAL	
MORGAN (cont'd)							
John	21	M	Dyer	Ireland	United States	Romulus	24 Jun 1826
John	22	M	Seaman	New York	United States	Minerva	30 Oct 1829
John	23	M	...	...	U. States	New England	28 Sep 1824
John	25	M	Gentleman	U.S.A.	America	Helen	4 Aug 1829
John	28	M	Mechanic	England	U. States	Nestor	4 Jun 1824
John	28	M	Farmer	Alsace in the Department of Upper and lower Rhine	United States	Carolina Augusta	16 May 1828
John	28	M	Farmer	Bristol, Engl.	England	Warrior	19 May 1828
John	30		Farmer	England	S. New York	Xenophon	25 Jul 1826
John	35	M	Servant	Great Britain	United States	Manchester	12 Aug 1829
John	40	M	Merchant	London	U. States	Milton	21 May 1827
John	44	M	Labourer	Wales	Uitica, U.S.	Angelica	18 Aug 1823
John	45	M	Planter	Bermuda	Bermuda	Orlando	1 Aug 1826
Joseph	2					Xenophon	25 Jul 1826
Josepha	17	F	Farmer	Alsace in the Department of Upper and lower Rhine	United States	Carolina Augusta	16 May 1828
Judeth	22	F	None	Ireland	United States	Lord Wellington	28 May 1827
Margaret	2 6/12	F	None	Great Britain	United States	Mary & Harriet	3 Jul 1829
Margaret	23	F		Wales	U. States	Pilot	11 Apr 1828
Margt.	36	F		England	United States	William Byrnes	1 Dec 1824
Maria	13	F		England	U. States	Amity	23 Sep 1823
Mary	...	F		Great B.	U. States	William Neilson	26 Jul 1828
Mary	5	F		Wales	America	John Adams	2 Aug 1827
Mary	5	F	Farmer	Bristol, Engl.	England	Warrior	19 May 1828
Mary	18/12	F		Great Britain	U. States	Great Britain	18 Mar 1828
Mary	21	F		Great Britain	U. States	Great Britain	18 Mar 1828
Mary	32 9/12	F	None	England	America	Euphrates	26 Jun 1821
Mary	38	F		England	U. States	Amity	23 Sep 1823
Mary	57	F	None	Great Britain	United States	Penelope	11 Jun 1827
Mary Ann	12 9/12	F		England	America	Cincinnatus	22 May 1826
Mary Ann	19	F	Spinster	Ireland	United States	Fabius	4 Jun 1828
Mary Anne	5/12	F	None	Great Britain	United States	Mary & Harriet	3 Jul 1829
Michael	9/12	M		Ireland		Eliza Grant	29 Aug 1829
Michael	17	M	Weaver	Ireland	New York	Atlantic	8 May 1828
Morgan		M	Miner	England		Iris	7 Dec 1827
Morgan	45	M	Weaver	Great Britain	United States	Spartan	25 Jul 1821
Pat	30	M	Labour	Great Britian	United States	Andes	19 Aug 1829
Patrick	20	M	Carpenter	Ireland	United States	Princess Charlotte	26 Apr 1827
Patrick	22 7/12	M		Ireland	America	Carolina Ann	7 Apr 1826
Patrick	25	M	Labourrer	Great Britan	U. States	Ann Marria	6 Aug 1823
Patrick	31	M	Labourer	Great Britain	United States	Ocean	27 Jul 1825
Patrick	40 7/12	M	Tailor	England	America	Euphrates	26 Jun 1821
Ralph	35	M	Merchant	Scotland	United States	Indus	5 Sep 1827
Rebecca	4	F	Farmer	England	United States	Essex	23 May 1828
Saml.	32	M	Farmer	N. Brunswick	New Brunswick	Abigale	9 Aug 1821
Sarah	7/12	F		England	U. States	Amity	23 Sep 1823
Sarah	7	F		Great B.	U. States	William Neilson	26 Jul 1828
Sarah	14	F		Wales	America	John Adams	2 Aug 1827
Sarah	19	F		U. States	U. States	Cincinnatus	24 May 1821
Sarah	30	F		Irereland	America	Carolina Ann	20 Jun 1825
Sarah	37	F		Wales	America	John Adams	2 Aug 1827
Susan	26	F	Farmer	England	United States	Essex	23 May 1828
Susan, Jr.	8	F	Farmer	England	United States	Essex	23 May 1828
Thomas	7	M	Farmer	Bristol, Engl.	England	Warrior	19 May 1828
Thomas	13 2/12	M		England	U.S. America	Illinois	16 Oct 1822
Thomas	21	M	Labourer	Ireland	United States	Lord Wellington	28 May 1827
Thomas	25	M	Farmer	England	America	Dewitt Clinton	27 Jul 1824
Thomas	25	M	Taylor	Great Britain	U. States	Great Britain	18 Mar 1828
Thos.	18		Labourer	Denbyh, England	Great Britain	Franklin	22 Jun 1827
Thos.	41	M	...	Ireland	U. States	Margarett Scott	22 Aug 1827
Thos.	50	M	Farmer	England	United States	Essex	23 May 1828
William	1 6/12	M		Irereland	America	Carolina Ann	20 Jun 1825

NAMES OF PASSENGERS	AGE	SEX	OCCUPATIONS	COUNTRY TO WHICH THEY BELONG	COUNTRY THEY INTEND TO INHABIT	SHIPS/DATES OF ARRIVAL
MORGAN (cont'd)						
William	22	M	Farmer	England	America	Comet 26 Jun 1822
Wm.	1	M	Farmer	England	United States	Essex 23 May 1828
Wm.	2	M		Great B.	U. States	William Neilson 26 Jul 1828
Wm.	4	M		England	U. States	Amity 23 Sep 1823
Wm.	27	M	Farmer	England	United States	Essex 23 May 1828
Wm.	59	M	Labourer	Great Britain	United States	Penelope 11 Jun 1827
MORGANSTER, Adam	20	M	Cleermaker	Breidenbach	United States	Juffraw Johanna 16 Oct 1821
MORGHAN, Anne	6	F		Ireland	United States	Fabius 4 Jun 1828
Sally	4	F		Ireland	United States	Fabius 4 Jun 1828
MORGUES, Antonio	41	M	Mercht.	Spain	Spain	Richmond Packet 28 Oct 1825
MORIA, John	25	M	Mercht.	U.S.	U.S.	Toison 6 May 1828
MORICE, J. P.	26	M	Male	France	France	William Bayard 21 Feb 1823
Nancy	26	F		G. Britain	Upper Canada	Perseverance 9 Jun 1827
MORIE, —	20	F	Servant	Portugal	U. States	Deligence 21 Mar 1825
MORILLO, Antonio	24	M	Merchant	Italy	United States	Pegasus 17 May 1828
MORIN, Bony	18	F	Servant	Ireland	United States	William 20 Jul 1829
James	50	M	Shoemaker	Ireland	U. States	Albion 23 Apr 1822
John	23 2/12	M	Engineer	Switzerland	U.S. America	Edward 28 Oct 1825
P.	25	M	Merchant	U. States	U. States	John London 20 Jan 1823
P., colored	22	M	Doctor	N. Orleans	U. States	John London 26 Mar 1822
Peter	22	M	Gentleman	France	U. States	John London 26 Jun 1822
MORINER, Phillip	25	M	Watch Maker	Germany	America	Orozimbo 1 Oct 1827
MORIS, Alran	25	M	Farmer	England	U. States	Unity 5 Sep 1828
Ellen	3	F		England	U. States	Unity 5 Sep 1828
Hannah	34	F		England	U. States	Unity 5 Sep 1828
Harriet	5	F		England	U. States	Unity 5 Sep 1828
James	7	M		England	U. States	Unity 5 Sep 1828
Mary	40			Ireland	Philidelphia	General Marion 21 Nov 1828
Peter	20	M	Farmer	Ireland	U. States	Erin 5 Jul 1820
R. K.	24	M	U.S. Service	U. States	U. States	Potosi 2 Jun 1828
Saml.	31	M	Merchant	Gt. Brittain	United States	Balaena 8 Jan 1825
Thos.	15			Ireland	Philidelphia	General Marion 21 Nov 1828
Thos.	20	M	Laborer	Gt. Britain		Dalhouse Castle 13 May 1828
William	1	M		England	U. States	Unity 5 Sep 1828
MORISON, A.	11	F		Scotland	U. States	Superior 25 Sep 1828
B.	4	F		Scotland	U. States	Superior 25 Sep 1828
George	35	M	Baker			Helen 4 Aug 1829
J.	2	M		Scotland	U. States	Superior 25 Sep 1828
Jno.	42	M	Merchant	U. States	U. States	Brazillian 18 Oct 1824
N.	9	M		Scotland	U. States	Superior 25 Sep 1828
N.	33	F	Farmer	Scotland	U. States	Superior 25 Sep 1828
Simon	20	M	Merchant	America		Manhattan 7 Nov 1827
Thomas	46	M	Merchant	St. Thomas	New York	St. Pierre 16 Oct 1827
MORITS, James	40	M	Koopman	Mermeltaum	United States	Juffraw Johanna 16 Oct 1821
MORLAND, Janet	40	F		Great Britian	United States	Brok 29 Aug 1823
Jno.	34	M	Merchant	American	U. States	Romulus 31 Jul 1823
MORLOT, Robert	24	M	Merchant	France	N. York	Charlemagne 20 Aug 1829
MORMAN, Joshua	40	M	Trader	U. States	U. States	Rodney 19 Jun 1827
*Passenger from the Wreck of Schooner Gen. Marion from Charleston to N.Y.						
MORNE, Cathrane	5	F		Germany	United States	Samuel Robertson 8 Aug 1828
Cathrine	40	F		Germany	United States	Samuel Robertson 8 Aug 1828
Margaret	3	F		Germany	United States	Samuel Robertson 8 Aug 1828
Peter	35	M	Farmer	Germany	United States	Samuel Robertson 8 Aug 1828
Wm.	21	M				Eliza Grant 6 Oct 1828
MORO, Gaetano	25	M	Engineer	Italy	Mexico	Corinthian 27 Apr 1824
J.	36	M	Merchant	Spain	U. States	Native 15 Apr 1826
Jose Antonia	32	M	Labourer	Spain	U. States	Mercid 10 Jul 1826
MOROLAU, John	22	M	Farmer	Great Britain	United States	Frances Henrietta 17 Sep 1827
MOROW, David	35	M	Farmer	Ireland	United States	Nancy 16 Jul 1824
Jane	35	F		Ireland	United States	Nancy 16 Jul 1824
Margaret	2	F		Scotland	U. States	Superior 25 Sep 1828
*Died 14th August, Dropsie In Chest						

NAMES OF PASSENGERS	AGE	SEX	OCCUPATIONS	COUNTRY TO WHICH THEY BELONG	COUNTRY THEY INTEND TO INHABIT	SHIPS/DATES OF ARRIVAL	
MORPENGO, —, Mrs.	38	F	School Master	Amsterdam	New York	Richard Meade	27 Apr 1822
Ben	12	M				Richard Meade	27 Apr 1822
Eliza	7	F			New York	Richard Meade	27 Apr 1822
Hannah	4	F			New York	Richard Meade	27 Apr 1822
Jane	18/12	M			New York	Richard Meade	27 Apr 1822
John	10	M			New York	Richard Meade	27 Apr 1822
Moses	40	M	School Master	Amsterdam	New York	Richard Meade	27 Apr 1822
MORR, Saml. D.	27	M	Merchant	Scotland	Virginia	Globe	3 Dec 1821
MORRALL, John C.	19	M	Merchant	England	England	Hannibal	28 May 1827
MORRAN, Ellen	20	F	Lady	Ireland	New York	Betsy	4 Sep 1820
Silas	44	M	Merchant	U. States	Martinique	Jane	27 Aug 1824
MORRE, John	15	M	Labourer	Ireland		Robert Fulton	4 Jun 1828
MORREL, Mary	17	F	Servant	Barbadoes	Great Britain	Only Daughter	26 Apr 1826
Sarah D.	30	F		Barbadoes	United States	Only Daughter	26 Apr 1826
Wm.	40	M	Merchant	Barbadoes	United States	Only Daughter	26 Apr 1826
MORRELL, Elizabeth A.	11	F		Barbadoes	United States	Only Daughter	26 Apr 1826
L.	36	F		Jamaica		Topaz	14 Aug 1826
Robt.	33	M	Doctor	Louisiana	U. States	Venus	26 Jun 1822
MORRET, —, Mrs.	25	F		Great Britian	United States	London	24 Jun 1823
MORREY, E. W.	22	M	Merchant	New York	America	Mary	2 Oct 1820
Margaret	30	F	None	...	New York	Frances Henrietta	30 Jun 1827
Mary Ann	1	F	None	...	New York	Frances Henrietta	30 Jun 1827
MORRI, Louis	18	M		Paris	Philadelphia	Falcon	10 Sep 1823
MORRICE, Catherine	19	F	Farmer	France	United States	Crescent	12 Jul 1827
Jacob	45	M	Farmer	France	United States	Crescent	12 Jul 1827
Magdalen	7	F	Farmer	France	United States	Crescent	12 Jul 1827
Margaret	45	F	Farmer	France	United States	Crescent	12 Jul 1827
Margeret	18	F	Farmer	France	United States	Crescent	12 Jul 1827
Mary	10	F	Farmer	France	United States	Crescent	12 Jul 1827
MORRIN, Ann	2	F		Ireland	New York	Rambler	31 Aug 1829
Elisha	4	F		Ireland	New York	Rambler	31 Aug 1829
James	22	M	Taylor	Ireland	New York	Rambler	31 Aug 1829
Lawrence	32	M	Labourer	Ireland	New York	Rambler	31 Aug 1829
Mary	26	F		Ireland	New York	Rambler	31 Aug 1829
MORRINS, Manuel F.	32	M	Shoemaker	U. States	U. States	Cobbosse Conte	18 Apr 1823
MORRIS, —, Captain	42	M	U.S. Navy	United States	United States	Corinthian	29 Apr 1826
—, Mrs.	36	F		Scotland	Pennsylvania	Psyche	16 May 1821
Alice	12	F	Spinster	Ireland	America	Josephine	8 Jan 1827
Alice	26	F	Spinster	England	United States	Hannibal	25 Sep 1827
Andrew	18	M	Labourer	Ireland	America	Wilson	16 May 1825
Ann	2 3/12	F		G. Britain	U. States	Wanderer	23 Jun 1828
Ann	15	F		England	U. States	Frances Henrietta	9 Dec 1823
Ann	21	F		Gt. Britain		Dalhouse Castle	13 May 1828
Ann	24	F	Labourer	Ireland	United States	Hope	12 Jun 1828
B.	22	M	Merchant	France	France	Eliza	28 Apr 1827
Benj.	22	M	Farmer	England		Marchioness	13 May 1828
Benj. H.	21	M	Merchant	Vera Cruz	U. States	Eliza	11 Apr 1826
Benjm.	36	M	Merchant	U. States	U. States	Martha	20 Jun 1825
Betty	45	F		England	United States	Hannibal	25 Sep 1827
Biddy	7	F		G. Britain	U. States	Wanderer	23 Jun 1828
Cath.	20		Spinster	Ireland	United States	Courier	15 Oct 1827
Catharin	24		Spinster	Ireland		Westmoreland	1 Aug 1826
Catharine	25	F	Servant	Wales	U. States	Mary Stewart	12 May 1827
Catherine	23	F	Spinster	Ireland	America	Wilson	16 May 1825
Cathr.	4	F		G. Britain	U. States	Wanderer	23 Jun 1828
Cathrn.	3	F		Scotland	Pennsylvania	Psyche	16 May 1821
David	8	M		Scotland	Pennsylvania	Psyche	16 May 1821
David	30	M		Ireland	U. States	Fame	15 Nov 1826
Dennis	22		Farmer	Ireland		Westmoreland	1 Aug 1826
Duepray	25	M	Farmer	France	United States	Crescent	12 Jul 1827
E.	10	M		G. Britain	U. States	St. George	7 Jun 1828
E. B.	22	M	Watchmaker	United States		Mentor	23 May 1821
Edwd.	37	M	...	...	...	Diamond	27 Jul 1824
Eleanor	44	F	Matron	Ireland	America	Josephine	8 Jan 1827
Eliz.	27	F		Gt. Britain	Canada	Friends	25 Sep 1823

NAMES OF PASSENGERS	AGE	SEX	OCCUPATIONS	COUNTRY TO WHICH THEY BELONG	COUNTRY THEY INTEND TO INHABIT	SHIPS/DATES OF ARRIVAL	
MORRIS (cont'd)							
Eliza	19	F		England	U. States	Frances	
						Henrietta	9 Dec 1823
Elizabeth	1	F		Scotland	Pennsylvania	Psyche	16 May 1821
Elizabeth	35	F	None	Great Britain	United States	Friends	13 Jun 1825
Ellen	5	F		Ireland	America	Josephine	8 Jan 1827
Ellen	7	F		Great Britain	U.S. of America	Gratitude	3 Oct 1829
Emily	12	F		England	U. States	Frances	
						Henrietta	9 Dec 1823
Enoch	3		Child	England	England	London	16 Aug 1824
Ephraim	22	M	Farmer	England	America	Comet	26 Jun 1822
Esther	28	F				Comet	24 Dec 1821
Ewd.	11	M		G. Britain	U. States	St. George	7 Jun 1828
Ewd.	17	M		England	United States	Hannibal	25 Sep 1827
Frans.	13	M		England	U. States	Frances	
						Henrietta	9 Dec 1823
Geo.	36	M		G. Britain	U. States	St. George	7 Jun 1828
George	48	M	Farmer	France	United States	Stephania	16 Aug 1827
Henry	20	M	Merchant	Philada.	U. States	New Priscilla	22 Aug 1823
Henry, Mr.	35		Taylor	England		Hercules	19 Jun 1821
Hugh	26	M	Farmer	Ireland	United States	William &	
						George	14 May 1828
Is...	9	M		Scotland	Pennsylvania	Psyche	16 May 1821
J. H.	25	M	Officer U.S. Navy	U. States	U. States	Greek	1 Oct 1825
Jacob W.	24	M	None	U. States	U. States	Canada	27 Sep 1826
James	19	M	Labourer	Ireland	United States	Hope	12 Jun 1828
James	22	M	Tailor	Ireland	United States	Loore	9 Sep 1822
James	22	M	Labourer	Ireland	United States	Catharine	22 Jul 1825
James	26	M	Farmer	Ireland	United States	William &	
						George	14 May 1828
James	28	M	Merchant	Ireland	U. States	Decatur	2 Jan 1822
James	51	M	Furnace Keeper	G. Britain	U. States	Great Britain	6 Sep 1828
Jane	1	F		England	United States	Hannibal	25 Sep 1827
Jesiah	28	M	Carder	England	United States	Trident	30 Sep 1826
John	4	M		G. Britain	U. States	St. George	7 Jun 1828
John	5	M		Scotland	Pennsylvania	Psyche	16 May 1821
John	12	M	Boy	America	America	Wilson	16 Nov 1824
John	23	M	Farmer	England	New York	Cincinnatus	16 Apr 1824
John	23	M	Farmer	Ireland	United States	Dublin Packet	23 May 1828
John	26	M	Farmer	England	United States	Concordia	25 Aug 1827
John	28	M	Shoemaker			Comet	24 Dec 1821
John	29 4/12	M	Shoe Maker	Ireland	America	Rising States	7 Jul 1828
John	37		Cotton Manufr.	England	America	Sarah	18 Aug 1829
John	50	M	Wheelwright	Ireland	United States	Hannibal	25 Sep 1827
John	60	M	Labourer	England	U.S. America	Ganges	15 Dec 1826
Jos.	12	M	Blacksmith	G. Britain	Canada	Cosmo	25 Nov 1826
Josiah	18	M	Farmer	England	U.S.A.	Brighton	21 Jan 1826
Margaret	24	F	Farmer	France	United States	Crescent	12 Jul 1827
Margaret	30	F	Wife	Ireland	United States	William &	
						George	14 May 1828
Margaret	37	F		Great Britain	U.S. of America	Gratitude	3 Oct 1829
Marge	17	F	Servant	Ireland	New York	Atlantic	6 Oct 1828
Mark	16	M	Farmer	England	U.S.A.	Brighton	21 Jan 1826
Mary	17	F		England	U. States	Frances	
						Henrietta	9 Dec 1823
Mary	26	F		Ireland	United States	Loore	9 Sep 1822
Mary	26		Wife of [Thos.]	England	England	London	16 Aug 1824
Mary	27	F	Servant	G. Britain	U. States	Wanderer	23 Jun 1828
Mary	30	F		Ireland	America	Wilson	27 Nov 1826
Mary	30	F	Labourer	Ireland	United States	Hope	12 Jun 1828
Mary Ann	1		Child	England	England	London	16 Aug 1824
Michael	8	M		Ireland	America	Josephine	8 Jan 1827
Michael	20	M	Laborer	Ireland	United States	Sylvester Healy	17 Oct 1825
Michal	24	M	Labourer	Ireland	New York	Louisa	20 Jul 1826
Michl.	2...	M	Labourer	Ireland	America	Wilson	16 May 1825
Mores	23	M	Pencil Mr.	England	U. States	Dalhouse	23 Mar 1829
Nancy	37	F		G. Britain	U. States	St. George	7 Jun 1828
Neary	24	F			New York	New York	31 Jul 1829

NAMES OF PASSENGERS	A G E	S E X	OCCUPATIONS	COUNTRY TO WHICH THEY BELONG	COUNTRY THEY INTEND TO INHABIT	SHIPS/DATES OF ARRIVAL	
MORRIS (cont'd)							
Nelly	42	F		England	U. States	Frances Henrietta	9 Dec 1823
Pat	27	M	Planter	Gt. Britain	United States	Eagle	26 Jul 1828
Patrick	2/52	M	Son	Ireland	United States	William & George	14 May 1828
Peter	28	M	Farmer	France	United States	American	27 Aug 1827
Priscilla	17	F	None	Great Britain	United States	Friends	13 Jun 1825
R.	23	M	Farmer	United States	U. States	Reindeer	29 Jun 1827
R.	33	M	Weaver	Wales		Eliza Jane	12 Sep 1820
Rebrick	45	M	Gentm.	U.S.	U.S.	Anita	5 May 1821
Redmond	18					Trio	5 May 1828
Reuben	19		Farmer	England	S. New York	Xenophon	25 Jul 1826
Richard	7	M		Ireland	America	Josephine	8 Jan 1827
Richard	20	M	Carpenter	U. Kingdom of Great Britain	United States	Cambria	7 May 1828
Richard	26	M		Gt. Britain	U.S. America	James Cropper	14 Mar 1828
Robert	16	M		Scotland	Pennsylvania	Psyche	16 May 1821
Robert	48	M	Merchant	Ireland	America	Josephine	8 Jan 1827
Robt.	14	M		England	United States	Hannibal	25 Sep 1827
Robt.	24	M	Store Keeper	Gt. Britain		Corinthian	27 Oct 1829
Rosa	9	F			U. States	Silas Richards	29 Oct 1828
Rose	6/52	F	Daughter	Ireland	United States	William & George	14 May 1828
Sally	3_/52	F	Daughter	Ireland	United States	William & George	14 May 1828
Sally	20	F	Labourer	England	U. States	Ayrshire	12 May 1828
Samuel	24	M	Turner	Great Britain	United States	India	5 Sep 1827
Sarah	3	F		England	United States	Hannibal	25 Sep 1827
Sarah	6	F		G. Britain	U. States	St. George	7 Jun 1828
T. B. C.	30	M	Gentleman	America	America	Britannia	5 Nov 1828
Thomas	21	M	Manufacturer	Great Britain	U. States	Elizabeth	20 Mar 1824
Thomas	22	M	Joiner	Scotland	United States	Marion	25 Nov 1825
Thomas	23	M	Missionary		New York	New York	31 Jul 1829
Thomas	25	M	Merchant	U.S.		Stephania	22 Apr 1822
Thomas	35	M	...	St. Johns, N.B.	United States	Henrietta	17 Aug 1825
Thos.	4		Child	England	England	London	16 Aug 1824
Thos.	8	M		G. Britain	U. States	St. George	7 Jun 1828
Thos.	26	M	Joiner	Great Britain	United States	Penelope	11 Jun 1827
Thos.	30		Farmer	England	England	London	16 Aug 1824
Tobin	24	M	Collier	Wales	U.S. States	Splendid	14 Aug 1829
W.	22	M	Silver Smith	U. States	U. States	Helicon	26 Jul 1822
W.	22	M	Weaver	Ireland	United States	Antioch	21 Sep 1827
William	22	M	Farmer	England	New York	Cincinnatus	16 Apr 1824
William	36	M	Merchant	Gt. Britain		Friends	25 Sep 1823
Wm.	2	M		G. Britain	U. States	St. George	7 Jun 1828
Wm.	18	F	Farmer	England	U. States	Frances Henrietta	9 Dec 1823
Wm.	25	M	Labourer	England	United States	Nestor	25 Jul 1823
Wm.	28	M	Farmer	G. Britain	U. States	Nimrod	31 Jul 1828
Wm. P.	48	M	Farmer	England	U. States	Frances Henrietta	9 Dec 1823
Zachariah	40	M	Farmer	Great Britain	U.S. of America	Gratitude	3 Oct 1829
MORRISEY, Margt.	22					Trio	5 May 1828
Thomas	27					Trio	5 May 1828
MORRISON (see Marrison)							
—, Mrs.	32	F		Scotland	U.S.	Curler	19 Jul 1828
And.	15	M	Servant	U. States	Great Britain	Thompson	26 Apr 1828
Ann	32			Scotland	United States	Camillus	3 May 1828
Catherine	16	F		Ireland	United States	Trio	2 Oct 1828
David	19	M	Farmer	Ireland	U. States	William & John	10 Jul 1824
Eleanor	11	F	Child	Ireland	U. States	William & John	10 Jul 1824
Elisabeth	33	F		Perth	Noagards	Robert	28 Aug 1829
Eliza	20	F		G. Britain	U. States	St. George	7 Jun 1828
Eliza	37	F	Spinner	Great Britain	United States	Grecian	24 Sep 1828
Elizabeth	3			Scotland	United States	Camillus	3 May 1828
H...	28	M	Farmer	Antrim	Ireland	Carolina Ann	11 Jun 1824
Helen	24	F	Labourer	Argyle (Tedland) Scotland	United States	Jean Hastie	27 Jul 1829

NAMES OF PASSENGERS	AGE	SEX	OCCUPATIONS	COUNTRY TO WHICH THEY BELONG	COUNTRY THEY INTEND TO INHABIT	SHIPS/DATES OF ARRIVAL
MORRISON (cont'd)						
Henry	22	M	...	Ireland	United States	General Putnam 20 Jun 1825
Isabella	5	F		Great Britain	United States	Grecian 24 Sep 1828
Isabella	23	F	Spinster	Ireland	U. States	William & John 10 Jul 1824
Isabella	23	M	Farmer	Great Britain	United States	Grecian 24 Sep 1828
J.	40	M	Mechanic	England	U. States	Hanover 12 Oct 1822
J.	45	M	Merchant	England	Great Britain	Ranger 3 May 1828
James	11	M		Great Britain	United States	Grecian 24 Sep 1828
James	13	M		Scotland	U. States	Hector 18 Apr 1825
James	17	M	Farmer	Ireland	U. States	William & John 10 Jul 1824
James	23	M	Labourer		New York	Prince Madore 28 Aug 1820
James	26	M	Farmer	Argyle (Tedland) Scotland	United States	Jean Hastie 27 Jul 1829
James	28	M	Cabinet Maker	Scotland	United States	Belmont 30 Aug 1828
James	33	M	...	...	...	Laurel 16 Nov 1824
James	66	M	Farmer	Ireland	U. States	William & John 10 Jul 1824
Jane	4/12			Scotland	United States	Camillus 3 May 1828
Jane	22	F	Spinster	Ireland	U. States	William & John 10 Jul 1824
Janet	4	F		Perth	Noagards	Robert 28 Aug 1829
Jno.	26	M	Mechanic	N. York	U. States	Hippomenes 25 Mar 1822
John	2	M		Perth	Noagards	Robert 28 Aug 1829
John	4	M		Great Britain	United States	Grecian 24 Sep 1828
John	7					Xenophon 25 Jul 1826
John	9	M		Scotland	U. States	Hector 18 Apr 1825
John	21	M	Farmer	Ireland	U. States	William & John 10 Jul 1824
John	22	M	Labourer	Ireland		William Tell 24 Oct 1829
John	25	M	Chairmaker	New York	U.S.	McDonough 21 May 1821
John	27		Mechanic	...	...	James Cropper 28 Jun 1824
John	30	M	Pattern Drawer	Paseley, Paisley, Scotland	U. States	New Orleans 24 Aug 1827
John	36	M	Farmer	Scotland	U.S.	Curler 19 Jul 1828
John	40		Farmer & Labourer	Great Britain & Ireland	United States	Trio 8 Feb 1827
Joseph	7	M	Child	Ireland	U. States	William & John 10 Jul 1824
Leonard	40	M	Labourer	Hananna		Orozimbo 16 Apr 1821
Margaret	2	F		Scotland	U. States	Hector 18 Apr 1825
Margaret	22	F	None	Great Britain	United States	Manchester 12 Aug 1829
Margaret	28	F	Spinster	Scotland	U. States	Hector 18 Apr 1825
Margt.	6			Scotland	United States	Camillus 3 May 1828
Martha	9	F	Child	Ireland	U. States	William & John 10 Jul 1824
Martha	50	F	wife to [James]	Ireland	U. States	William & John 10 Jul 1824
Mary	5					Xenophon 25 Jul 1826
Mary	33			Ireland	S. New York	Xenophon 25 Jul 1826
Mary Ann	11		Spinster	Scotland	United States	Camillus 3 May 1828
Mathew	30	M	Farmer	Ireland	U. States	Dickinson 30 Jul 1825
Michael	35		Shoemaker	Ireland	United States	Antioch 3 Dec 1827
Nancy	13	F	Child	Ireland	U. States	William & John 10 Jul 1824
Patrick	20	M	Gentleman	Ireland	Albany	Betsy 4 Sep 1820
Peter	2	M		Scotland	U.S.	Curler 19 Jul 1828
Peter	4	M		Scotland	U. States	Hector 18 Apr 1825
Rebecca	20 6/12	F		Ireland	U.S. of America	Douglass 6 Jul 1829
Richard	20	M		Ireland	United States	Trio 2 Oct 1828
Thomas	4/12	M		Perth	Noagards	Robert 28 Aug 1829
Thomas	15	M	Farmer	Ireland	U. States	William & John 10 Jul 1824
Thomas	20	M	Weaver	Scotland	United States	Culloden 17 May 1828
Thomas	31	M	Farmer	Perth	Noagards	Robert 28 Aug 1829
Thos.	27	M				Trio 5 May 1828
W.	7	M		Scotland	U. States	Hector 18 Apr 1825
W.	40	M	Farmer	Scotland	U. States	Hector 18 Apr 1825
William	6	M		Perth	Noagards	Robert 28 Aug 1829
William	18	M	Shoemaker	Scotland	United States	Culloden 17 May 1828
William	19	M	Blacksmith	Ireland		William Tell 24 Oct 1829
Wm.	24	M	Merchant	Scotland	U. States	Martha 1 Feb 1822
Wm.	56	M	...	U. States		Mattrawan 7 Jul 1824
Wm., Mrs.	25	F		U. States	U. States	Vigilant 25 Nov 1822
MORRISSEY, Catherine	2	F	Labourer	Ireland	Boston	General Marion 12 Jan 1829
Catherine	18	F	Labourer	Ireland	New York	General Marion 12 Jan 1829
Hannah	8	F	Labourer	Ireland	Philadelphia	General Marion 12 Jan 1829
Margaret	16	F	Labourer	Ireland	New York	General Marion 12 Jan 1829

NAMES OF PASSENGERS	AGE	SEX	OCCUPATIONS	COUNTRY TO WHICH THEY BELONG	COUNTRY THEY INTEND TO INHABIT	SHIPS/DATES OF ARRIVAL	
MORRISSEY (cont'd)							
Margt.	30	F	Labourer	Ireland	Boston	General Marion	12 Jan 1829
Mary Ann	12	F	Labourer	Ireland	Philadelphia	General Marion	12 Jan 1829
Patrick	10	F	Labourer	Ireland	New York	General Marion	12 Jan 1829
Thomas	14	F	Labourer	Ireland	New York	General Marion	12 Jan 1829
Thomas	57	M	Labourer	Ireland	New York	General Marion	12 Jan 1829
MORRISSON, Ann	51	F				Belfast	28 Sep 1820
E.	10	F				Belfast	28 Sep 1820
Jane	12	F				Belfast	28 Sep 1820
William	29	M	Merchant	United States	United States	Cyno	8 Dec 1827
MORROW, —, Mr.	25	M	Labourer	England	U. States	Ann Maria	13 Mar 1823
...ry	...	F	Wife	...	... States	Louisa	18 Apr 1827
Agness	50	F	Spinster	Gt. Britain	U. States	Frances Henrietta	18 Apr 1825
Ann	18	F	Labourer	Ireland	United States	William & George	14 May 1828
Ann, Miss	20	F		U.S.	U.S.	Frances	21 Jul 1827
Eliz.	22		Labourer	England	United States	Hugh Johnson	11 Jun 1828
Geo.	22	M	Farmer	Brittain	U. States	Ann Maria	5 Aug 1824
Geo.	35	M	Merchant	St. Johns	U. States	Wanderer	30 Sep 1828
James	19		Labourer			Rufus King	7 Aug 1820
Jane	8		Child			Rufus King	7 Aug 1820
John	22	M	Laborer	Ireland	United States	St. Michaels	27 Nov 1824
Joseph	18	M	Weaver	Gt. Britain	U. States	Frances Henrietta	18 Apr 1825
Joseph	40			England	United States	Hugh Johnson	11 Jun 1828
Lewis	26	M	Carpenter	France	United States	Nile	13 Aug 1828
Margaret	2 5/12	F	Daughter	Ireland	United States	Louisa	27 Nov 1826
Margt.	19	F	Servant	Ireland	U. States	St. Michaels	25 Apr 1825
Maria	18	F	Matron	Ireland	U. States	Courier	17 Mar 1828
Mary	20	F	Wife	Ireland	United States	St. Michaels	27 Nov 1824
Mary	26		Housewife			Rufus King	7 Aug 1820
Michael	26	M	Farmer	Ireland	United States	Dublin Packet	9 Jul 1827
Nancy	26	F	Wife	Ireland	United States	Louisa	27 Nov 1826
Saml.	50	M	Labourer	Gt. Britain	U. States	Frances Henrietta	18 Apr 1825
William	20	M	Carpenter	Gt. Britain	U. States	Frances Henrietta	18 Apr 1825
William	20	M	Sadler	Ireland	U. States	Courier	17 Mar 1828
Wm.	20	M	Weaver	Banbirdge	United States	Carolina Ann	11 Jun 1824
Wm.	20	M	Saddler	Great Britain	United States	Atlantic	8 Dec 1827
MORSE, E.	30	M		G. Britain	U. States	Canada	19 Sep 1828
Geo. W.	18	M	Mariner	U.S. of America	U.S. of America	Estrella de La Mañana	26 May 1825
James	30 3/12	M	Merchant	United States	United States	France	6 Oct 1828
James	37	M	Mechanic	England	Canada	Hogarth	12 Oct 1829
Jane	28	F	Servant	Gt. Brittain	U. States	Robert Fulton	1 Nov 1822
Jese, Jr.	21	M	Gentleman	U. States	U. States	Ambuscade	15 Dec 1824
S.	13	M		U. States		Maria	24 Oct 1829
Sophia	11		None	England	New Jersey	Albion	11 Oct 1821
MORSIN, Peter	40	M	Mechanick	Spain	Spain	Wave	21 May 1821
MORSING, G.	25	M	Lawyer	Stockholm	U. States	Commerce	29 Jul 1822
MORSOT, A. S.	20	M	C. Maker	France	U. States	C. Amelia	30 Jun 1828
MORT, David	22	M	Carpenter	England	United States	Cosmo	26 Aug 1829
MORTES, J. L.	29	M	Merchant	N. York	U. States	Panther	9 Jul 1825
J. L.	38	M	Merchant	Aux Cayes	U. States	Marshall	12 Jun 1824
MORTIMER, —	30	M	Merchant	U. States	U. States	Imperial	10 Dec 1821
—, Mrs.	24	F		U.S.	U.S.	York	1 Dec 1827
Anne	25	F	Wife	Ireland	New York	Louisa	18 Apr 1827
Anne Jane	2	F	Dayrie	Ireland	New York	Louisa	18 Apr 1827
Charles E.	21	M	Merchant	U. States	U. States	Canada	27 Sep 1826
Charlotte	12	F		G. Britain	America	Spring	12 Oct 1821
Charlotte, Miss	23 6/12	F		United States	Philadelphia	Cadmus	27 Aug 1822
Chas.	23		Gentleman	New Bedford	U. States	Pettrell	15 Sep 1826
Edmund	18	M	Blacksmith	England	United States	Maria	12 May 1823
Edwd.	21	M	Blacksmith	G. Britain	Canada	Cosmo	25 Nov 1826
Ellen	23	F	Servant	Ireland	New York	Louisa	18 Apr 1827
J.	28	M	Merchant	U.S.	U.S.	York	1 Dec 1827
J. H.	5	M		U.S.	U.S.	York	1 Dec 1827

NAMES OF PASSENGERS	AGE	SEX	OCCUPATIONS	COUNTRY TO WHICH THEY BELONG	COUNTRY THEY INTEND TO INHABIT	SHIPS/DATES OF ARRIVAL	
MORTIMER (cont'd)							
John	20	M	Weaver	Ireland	United States	Trident	16 May 1826
John	22	M	Merchant	Great Britain	Great Britain	Magnet	28 Jun 1821
John	24	M	Labourer	Ireland	New York	Louisa	18 Apr 1827
John, Mr.	47 10/12	M	Gentleman	United States	Philadelphia	Cadmus	27 Aug 1822
Joseph	25	M	Labourer	Ireland	New York	Louisa	18 Apr 1827
Martha	6	F		G. Britain	America	Spring	12 Oct 1821
Mary	4	F		G. Britain	America	Spring	12 Oct 1821
Mary	17	F	None	Great Britain	Great Britain	Magnet	28 Jun 1821
Mary	20	F	Blacksmith	G. Britain	Canada	Cosmo	25 Nov 1826
Mary	41	F		G. Britain	America	Spring	12 Oct 1821
Rob.	6	M	Son	Ireland	New York	Louisa	18 Apr 1827
Robt.	21	M	Weaver	Ireland	United States	Trident	16 May 1826
Sarah	24	F	None	Great Britain	Great Britain	Magnet	28 Jun 1821
Sarah, Mrs.	45 8/12	F		United States	Philadelphia	Cadmus	27 Aug 1822
Saraph	21	F	Servant	Ireland	New York	Louisa	18 Apr 1827
Simeon	14	M	Blacksmith	G. Britain	America	Spring	12 Oct 1821
Sybil	8	F		G. Britain	America	Spring	12 Oct 1821
Willm.	47	M	Blacksmith	G. Britain	Canada	Cosmo	25 Nov 1826
Wm.	17	M	Labourer	Ireland	New York	Louisa	18 Apr 1827
Wm.	42	M	Blacksmith	G. Britain	America	Spring	12 Oct 1821
MORTIMORE, William	34	M	Clerk	Great Britain	United States	Cambria	26 Dec 1827
MORTIS, J. L.	28	M	Merchant	St. Domingo	St. Domingo	Charlotte Corday	8 Nov 1823
MORTIZEN, Jno.	55	M	Merchant	Copenhagen	U. States	Chase	12 May 1826
MORTON, ...	24 2/12	M	...	England	America, U.S.	Illinois	3 Jun 1822
Alex	9	M	None	Scotland	U. States	Czar	29 Aug 1829
Alfred	20	M		United States	U. States	Corinthian	2 Sep 1824
Antonio	25	M	Merchant	Spain	U. States	Fabius	7 Dec 1825
Chs. F.	25		Farmer	Halifax	U. States	Edwin	26 Sep 1828
Elizabeth	2	F	None	England	U. States	Montgomery	18 Oct 1828
Elizabeth	4	F	None	Scotland	U. States	Czar	29 Aug 1829
Emeline	28	F	Lady	U. States	U. States	Rodney	19 Jun 1827
*Passenger from the Wreck of Schooner Gen. Marion from Charleston to N.Y.							
Eslen	20	F	Spinster	Ireland	United States	William	5 Oct 1822
Euphema	15	F	None	Scotland	U. States	Czar	29 Aug 1829
Geo.	25	M	Merchant	Scotland	United States	Oscar	21 Oct 1822
George	54	M	Farmer	G.B.	Ohio	Eliza Grant	29 Aug 1829
Harriet	5/12	F	None	England	U. States	Montgomery	18 Oct 1828
Henrietta	1	F	None	Rayton	Lancaster	Howard Douglass	11 May 1827
James	1 6/12	M	None	England	U. States	Montgomery	18 Oct 1828
James	11	M	None	Scotland	U. States	Czar	29 Aug 1829
James	27	M	Merchant	Great Britian	U. States	Calliope	20 Mar 1824
Jane	17	F	None	Scotland	U. States	Czar	29 Aug 1829
Janet	2	F	None	Scotland	U. States	Czar	29 Aug 1829
Jeremiah	26	M	Attorney at Law	United States	United States	New York	3 Apr 1826
John	17	M	Labourer	Ireland	U. States	Meteor	19 Jul 1828
John	25	M	Labourer	Ireland	United States	Fabius	31 Jul 1829
John	30	M	Glass Cutter	Great Britain	U. States	Great Britain	18 Mar 1828
John A.	53	M	Merchant	United States	U. States	Corinthian	2 Sep 1824
John A., Mr.	54	M	Merchant	U. States		Henri IV	7 May 1827
John W.	20	M	Merchant	France	France	Lovinia	20 Nov 1828
Joseph	9	M		Great Britain	U. States	Great Britain	18 Mar 1828
Martha	8	F		England	United States	William Byrnes	1 Dec 1824
Mary	7	F	None	Scotland	U. States	Czar	29 Aug 1829
Mary	38	F	None	Scotland	U. States	Czar	29 Aug 1829
Mary Ann	24	F	None	England	U. States	Montgomery	18 Oct 1828
Noah	7	M	None	England	U. States	Montgomery	18 Oct 1828
Peter	35	M	Mechanic	Scotland	U. States	Howard Douglass	29 Jan 1828
Richard	22	M	Cotton Spinner	Great Britain	United States	Roman	19 Dec 1825
Robert	29	M		Scotland	United States	Camillus	9 May 1827
Robert	32 7/12	M	Merchant	Great Britain	United States	Courier	23 Feb 1824
Robt.	36	M	Merchant	England	U. States	Calais Packet	3 Sep 1827
Robt.	40	M	Blacksmith	Scotland	U. States	Czar	29 Aug 1829
Samuel	5	M	None	England	U. States	Montgomery	18 Oct 1828
Samuel	38	M	Seaman	United States	United States	Port Captain	17 May 1825

NAMES OF PASSENGERS	AGE	SEX	OCCUPATIONS	COUNTRY TO WHICH THEY BELONG	COUNTRY THEY INTEND TO INHABIT	SHIPS/DATES OF ARRIVAL	
MORTON (cont'd)							
Sarah	23	F	None	Rayton	Lancaster	Howard Douglass	11 May 1827
Stephen	25	M	Merchant	U. States	U. States	Dromo	28 Feb 1829
Thomas		M	Carpenter	Ireland		Eliza Grant	29 Aug 1829
Thomas	10	M		Great Britain	U. States	Great Britain	18 Mar 1828
Thomas	20	M	Grocer	England	United States	William Byrnes	1 Dec 1824
Thomas	24	M	Carder	G.B.	Philad.	Eliza Grant	29 Aug 1829
Thomas	40	M	Grocer	England	United States	William Byrnes	1 Dec 1824
Thos.	18	M	Farmer	Scotland	United States	Commerce	17 Jul 1823
Thos.	23	M	Stone Mason	Great Brittain	United States	Nimrod	9 Jan 1827
Thos. C.	19	M	None	U. States	U. States	Rachel Ann	13 Jul 1826
Washington	46	M		United States	U. States	Corinthian	2 Sep 1824
Wm.	26	M	Farmer	Stackport	United States	Aurelia	7 Jun 1826
MORTORDEAU, Julian	33	M	Watchmaker	Switzerland	U. States	Dolphin	15 Apr 1822
MORTUN, Richard	40	M	Merchant	New Brunswic	N. Brunsweick	Loire	22 Jul 1820
MORVIELL, Bartolomo	13	M	Lad	Mexico	U. States	Virginia	3 Dec 1827
MORY, Ann	40	F	Farmer	...	Ohio	Frances Henrietta	25 Aug 1825
Anna	10	F	Farmer	...	Ohio	Frances Henrietta	25 Aug 1825
Benedict	5	M	Farmer	...	Ohio	Frances Henrietta	25 Aug 1825
Christian	2	M	Farmer	...	Ohio	Frances Henrietta	25 Aug 1825
John	14	M	Farmer	...	Ohio	Frances Henrietta	25 Aug 1825
Rodolphe	8	M	Farmer	...	Ohio	Frances Henrietta	25 Aug 1825
Rodolphe	40	M	Farmer	...	Ohio	Frances Henrietta	25 Aug 1825
MOSE, Marie	42	F		Switzerland	United States	Thetis	5 Jul 1821
MOSEL, Aggustus	29	M	Black Smith	Switzerland	United States	Virginia	31 May 1828
MOSELY, John	25	M	Labourer	Ireland	Ireland	Sarah G.	28 Nov 1827
Seneca, Capt.	40	M	Shipmaster	United States	United States	James Monroe	12 Aug 1828
Wm.	30	M	Mercht.	U. States	U. States	Betsey	23 Jul 1824
MOSEN, Catharine	68	F			United States	Spartan	21 Aug 1824
Jean Michel	59	M		Watchmaker	United States	Spartan	21 Aug 1824
John	9	M			United States	Spartan	21 Aug 1824
Ulisses	13	M			United States	Spartan	21 Aug 1824
MOSER, Annah	...		...	France	U. States	Elizabeth	9 Jul 1825
Benedick	20	M	Framer	Switserland	Ohio	Danube	20 Jul 1826
Catharinn	20		...	France	U. States	Elizabeth	9 Jul 1825
Elizabath	10	F	Framer	Switserland	Ohio	Danube	20 Jul 1826
Elizabath	18	F	Framer	Switserland	Ohio	Danube	20 Jul 1826
Francois	22	F		Switserland	United States	Thetis	5 Jul 1821
Frans.	48	F	Framer	Switserland	Ohio	Danube	20 Jul 1826
Jacob	24		Farmer	France	U. States	Elizabeth	9 Jul 1825
Jacob	28	M	Weaver	Switzerland	United States	Thetis	5 Jul 1821
John	23	M	Framer	Switserland	Ohio	Danube	20 Jul 1826
Madeline	18		...	France	U. States	Elizabeth	9 Jul 1825
Margret	40	F	Framer	Switserland	Ohio	Danube	20 Jul 1826
Marie	1	F	Weaver	Switzerland	United States	Thetis	5 Jul 1821
Nickolas	13	M	Framer	Switserland	Ohio	Danube	20 Jul 1826
Peter	13		...	France	U. States	Elizabeth	9 Jul 1825
Samuel	16	M	Framer	Switserland	Ohio	Danube	20 Jul 1826
Ulrich	33		Farmer	France	U. States	Elizabeth	9 Jul 1825
MOSES, Alexr.	27	M	Merchant	France	United States	Prince Edward	1 Apr 1825
L.	34	M	Carpenter	Connecticut	U. States	Planter	28 Apr 1823
MOSEY, Richd.	50	M	Merchant	G. Britain	G. Britain	Brothers	27 Jun 1828
MOSHER, Archable	6 1/12	M		Novocotia	Lower Canaday	America	1 Aug 1829
Braselen	3 10/12	M		Novocotia	Lower Canaday	America	1 Aug 1829
Daniel	42 10/12	M	Yoman	Novocotia	Lower Canaday	America	1 Aug 1829
Elisabeth	14	F		Novocotia	Lower Canaday	America	1 Aug 1829
Jehu	17	M		Novocotia	Lower Canaday	America	1 Aug 1829
Levinea	39 8/12	F		Novocotia	Lower Canaday	America	1 Aug 1829
Matilda	10 9/12	F		Novocotia	Lower Canaday	America	1 Aug 1829
Reuben	8 1/12	M		Novocotia	Lower Canaday	America	1 Aug 1829
Sally	8/12	F		Novocotia	Lower Canaday	America	1 Aug 1829

NAMES OF PASSENGERS	AGE	SEX	OCCUPATIONS	COUNTRY TO WHICH THEY BELONG	COUNTRY THEY INTEND TO INHABIT	SHIPS/DATES OF ARRIVAL	
MOSHERSETT, Robt.	32	M	Planter	Ireland	U. States	Acasta	21 Jan 1825
MOSIER, Abm.	5		Farmer	France	U. States	Elizabeth	9 Jul 1825
Annah	41		Farmer	France	U. States	Elizabeth	9 Jul 1825
Christ.	35		Farmer	France	U. States	Elizabeth	9 Jul 1825
MOSLEY, A.	20	F		G. Britain	U. States	Robt. Edwards	4 Sep 1828
Jos.	32	M	Mechanic	England	U. States	Howard Douglass	29 Jan 1828
Mary	25	F		England	U.S.A.	Peru	2 Oct 1827
Wm.	5	M		England	U.S.A.	Peru	2 Oct 1827
MOSNIER, Frances	31	F	Spinster	France	U. States	Elizabeth	20 Mar 1824
John	10	M	None	France	U. States	Elizabeth	20 Mar 1824
Lewis	32	M	Farmer	France	U. States	Elizabeth	20 Mar 1824
MOSOWE, Mathew	10	M	Labourer	Ireland	United States	Wilson	4 Oct 1827
MOSQUART, Thos.	37	M	Merchant	France	United States	Howard	27 Sep 1824
MOSS, —, Miss	15					Prometheus	30 Aug 1828
—, Mrs.	21	F		G. Britain	Canada	Columbia	7 Sep 1827
—, Mrs.	35	M	Mechanic	U.S.	U.S.	Prometheus	30 Aug 1828
—, Mrs.	38	F		Nova Scotia	United States	Superior	14 Apr 1825
Edward	45	M	Cordwainer	England	U.S. America	Josephine	24 Jul 1826
Eliza	21	F	Child	England	United States	Cambria	3 Jul 1829
George	10	M	Child	England	U.S. America	Josephine	24 Jul 1826
J.	21	M	Manufacturer	G. Britain	Canada	Columbia	7 Sep 1827
James	24	M	Merchant	Great Britain	United States	Milton	21 Mar 1828
Jas.	45	M	Gentleman	Nassau	United States	Superior	14 Apr 1825
John	18/12					Prometheus	30 Aug 1828
John	13	M	None	Great Britain	United States	William Dawson	18 Jun 1827
John	18	M	teacher or Goldlace Maker	England	New York	Cortes	23 Nov 1827
John	23	M	Labourer	England	U. States	Ayrshire	12 May 1828
John	60	M	Shoemaker	Manchester	Manchester	Howard Douglass	11 May 1827
Joseph	24	M	Labourer	Great Britain	United States	William Dawson	18 Jun 1827
Mary	1	F	Labourer	England	U. States	Ayrshire	12 May 1828
Mary	19	F	Labourer	England	U. States	Ayrshire	12 May 1828
Saul	24	M		Jamaica	England	Pleiades	13 Nov 1826
Stephen	40	M	Mechanic	U.S.	U.S.	Prometheus	30 Aug 1828
Thos.	5	M	None	Great Britain	United States	William Dawson	18 Jun 1827
William	8	M	Child	England	U.S. America	Josephine	24 Jul 1826
MOSSELL, John	26	M				Amity	11 Sep 1820
MOSSET, John	50	M	Farmer	Switzerland	United States	Howard	11 Jun 1824
MOST, Wm.	23	M	Brewer	Germany	U. States	Sully	25 Jun 1828
MOTIN, Peter	32	M	Whitesmith	France	U. States	Sully	24 Oct 1828
MOTLES, J. S.	12	F	Farmer	Barbadoes	U. States	Azores	2 Jun 1824
MOTT, Benjamin, Mr.	27	M	Farmer	England	U. States	Emily	25 Aug 1827
C.	18	M	Farmer	Gt. Britain	U. States	Columbia	7 Sep 1827
J.	25		Ship Master	America	New York	Cicero	18 Aug 1829
Jane	18	F	None	England	United States	Nestor	20 Nov 1821
Jno.	43	M		Switzerland	U. States	London	13 Sep 1824
Margt. C.	25	F	25	U. States	U. States	Fabius	30 Aug 1827
Mary	6	F		England	U. States	Emily	25 Aug 1827
Mary Ann	24	F	None	England	United States	Brighton	11 Mar 1825
Sarah	18/12	F		England	U. States	Emily	25 Aug 1827
Sarah, Mrs.	28	F		England	U. States	Emily	25 Aug 1827
William	27	M	Painter	G. Brittain	U. States	Cincinnatus	2 Oct 1822
Willm.	18	M	Merchant	New York	U. States	Lady Hunter	22 Aug 1825
Wm.	4	M		England	U. States	Emily	25 Aug 1827
Wm. H.	24	M	Farmer	New York	U. States	Ann Maria	7 Sep 1827
MOTTERAM, Thomas	30	M	Farmer	England	United States	Aurora	9 Jul 1827
MOTTIER, John Emanuel	19	M	Domestic	Switzerland	United States	Thetis	5 Jul 1821
MOTTIN, Patrick	23	M	Laborer	...	United States	Combine	20 Nov 1824
MOTZ, Barbara	31	F		France	U. States	Edward Quesnel	4 Aug 1828
Barbara	54	F		France	U. States	Edward Quesnel	4 Aug 1828
Diedrich	26	M	Merchant	Bremen	United States	Howard	6 Jul 1829
Soafrey	18	M		France	U. States	Edward Quesnel	4 Aug 1828
MOUGLAR, Saloma	24	F		France	United States	Stephania	24 Mar 1828
MOULET, —, Miss	5	F	None	France	New York	Gleaner	17 Jan 1820
—, Miss	6	F	None	France	New York	Gleaner	17 Jan 1820
—, Miss	7	F	None	France	New York	Gleaner	17 Jan 1820
—, Mrs.	32	F	None	France	New York	Gleaner	17 Jan 1820

NAMES OF PASSENGERS	AGE	SEX	OCCUPATIONS	COUNTRY TO WHICH THEY BELONG	COUNTRY THEY INTEND TO INHABIT	SHIPS/DATES OF ARRIVAL	
MOULET (cont'd)							
A.	28	M	Mechanic	France	United States	Gleaner	17 Jan 1820
MOULLIN, Francis	2	M				Henri IV	17 May 1828
Francois	33	M	Farmer	France		Henri IV	17 May 1828
Jaqui	20	M				Henri IV	17 May 1828
Mary	39	F		France		Henri IV	17 May 1828
Mary Ann	6	F				Henri IV	17 May 1828
Nicolas	4	M				Henri IV	17 May 1828
MOULT, Martin	33 6/12	M	Merchant	England	Philadelphia	Hercules	11 Feb 1822
Martin	35	M	Mercht.	Manchr.	Charleston	Canada	1 Nov 1823
Wm.	17	M	Clerk	Manchest.	Charleston	Canada	1 Nov 1823
MOULTON, C. F.		M	Printer	U. States	U. States	David	19 Apr 1824
C. J., Mrs.	18	F	None	U. States	U. States	Sully	25 Jun 1828
Charles F.	31	M	None	U. States	U. States	Sully	25 Jun 1828
MOULVEY, John	16	M	Labourer	Ireland		Robert Fulton	4 Jun 1828
MOUNSFIELD, Arthur	3	F		Ireland	United States	Sarah G.	15 May 1828
Jane	8	F		Ireland	United States	Sarah G.	15 May 1828
Mary	6	F		Ireland	United States	Sarah G.	15 May 1828
Patrick	30	M	Shoe Maker	Ireland	United States	Sarah G.	15 May 1828
MOUNT, Barbara	9	F	Seamstress	Ireland	United States	Eliza	29 Aug 1822
Catharine	30	F	Seamstress	Ireland	United States	Eliza	29 Aug 1822
Catherin	16	F	Spinster	Great Brittan	United States	Hanford	3 Aug 1829
Dolly	14	F	Spinster	Great Brittan	United States	Hanford	3 Aug 1829
James	30	M	Farmer	Ireland	United States	Eliza	29 Aug 1822
Jane	40			England	England	Hudson	4 Sep 1823
Louiza P. H.	3			England	England	Hudson	4 Sep 1823
Margaret	15	F	Seamstress	Ireland	United States	Eliza	29 Aug 1822
Mary Ann	17	F	Lady	Great Britain	United States	Washington	22 Mar 1820
Mary Ann, an Infant	1		Child	Ireland	United States	Eliza	29 Aug 1822
Matilda	16			England	England	Hudson	4 Sep 1823
Roswell	30	M	Surveyor	Upper Canada	United States	Danube	13 Jul 1827
MOUNTAIN, Joseph	22	M				Eliza Grant	6 Oct 1828
MOUNTCASTLE, John	26	M	Tin plate Worker	London	Indiana	Ann Maria	24 Feb 1824
MOUNTFORD, John	38	M	Merchant	G. Brittain	United States	Hercules	24 Oct 1821
John	40	M	Surgeon			Helen	4 Aug 1829
MOUNTRANFILS,							
—, Mrs.	22	M	Merchant	Hayti	Hayti	Pedler	15 Dec 1824
MOURA..., John	25	M	Butcher	Co. La...gford	La...gford	Howard Douglass	11 May 1827
MOUREAUR, Carroline	13		Husband in America	Somwiller	Switzerland	Ann	27 Nov 1820
Fleurine	9		Husband in America	Somwiller	Switzerland	Ann	27 Nov 1820
Julie	7		Husband in America	Somwiller	Switzerland	Ann	27 Nov 1820
Justine	11		Husband in America	Somwiller	Switzerland	Ann	27 Nov 1820
Louis	4		Husband in America	Somwiller	Switzerland	Ann	27 Nov 1820
Marrianne	37		Husband in America	Somwiller	Switzerland	Ann	27 Nov 1820
Rosalie	1		Husband in America	Somwiller	Switzerland	Ann	27 Nov 1820
MOURHEAD, John	21	M	Weaver	England	U. States	Franklin	7 Jul 1828
MOURITZON, Johanas	51	M	Gentleman	Denmark	Denmark	Chase	24 Aug 1822
MOURLIN, Ellen	30	F		England	U. States	Electra	7 Jul 1828
Humphry	28	M		England	U. States	Electra	7 Jul 1828
MOURNE, John	25	M	Cabinet Maker	Dublin, Dublin, Scotland	N. York	New Orleans	24 Aug 1827
Mary	25	F	Wife	Dublin, Dublin, Scotland	N. York	New Orleans	24 Aug 1827
Owen	26	M	Blacksmith	Ireland	United States	Jubilee	12 May 1828
MOURTUCK, James	25	M	Gent.	...	U. States	Cadmus	6 Oct 1825
MOUSE, Nathan	24	M		Switzerland	U. States	Henri IV	7 May 1827
MOW, Martin	40	M	Merchant	United States	United States	Ardelle	18 Jan 1828
MOWATT, Charles	22	M	Merchant	United States	United States	Orbit	29 Aug 1821
Frans.	23	M	Planter	England	U. States	Genl. Marion	9 Jan 1827
MOWHY, Joseph	27	M	Cooper	Gt. Britan	U. States	Sarah Skeafe	10 Sep 1827
MOXEY, J.	22	M	Carpenter	Massachusetts	U. States	Planter	28 Apr 1823

NAMES OF PASSENGERS	AGE	SEX	OCCUPATIONS	COUNTRY TO WHICH THEY BELONG	COUNTRY THEY INTEND TO INHABIT	SHIPS/DATES OF ARRIVAL	
MOXSTE, Jaques	24	M	Farmer	Germany	United States	Oxford	14 Aug 1828
MOYER, Antonio	7	M	his family [Mark]	Germany	Pensylvania	Isabella	15 Sep 1828
Bangina	5	M	his family [Mark]	Germany	Pensylvania	Isabella	15 Sep 1828
Benharty	15	M	his family [Jacob]	Germany	Pensylvania	Isabella	15 Sep 1828
Christian	25 1/12	M	Farmer	France	United States	France	6 Oct 1828
Ernest	3	F	his family [Mark]	Germany	Pensylvania	Isabella	15 Sep 1828
Fanny	9	F	his family [Mark]	Germany	Pensylvania	Isabella	15 Sep 1828
Jacob	21	M	his family [Jacob]	Germany	Pensylvania	Isabella	15 Sep 1828
Jacob	51	M	Weaver	Germany	Pensylvania	Isabella	15 Sep 1828
Josephine	9	F	his family [Jacob]	Germany	Pensylvania	Isabella	15 Sep 1828
Margret	1	F	his family [Mark]	Germany	Pensylvania	Isabella	15 Sep 1828
Margret	41	F	his family [Mark]	Germany	Pensylvania	Isabella	15 Sep 1828
Marian	53	F	his family [Jacob]	Germany	Pensylvania	Isabella	15 Sep 1828
Mark	12	M	his family [Mark]	Germany	Pensylvania	Isabella	15 Sep 1828
Mark	45	M	Weaver	Germany	Pensylvania	Isabella	15 Sep 1828
Paviser	18	M	his family [Jacob]	Germany	Pensylvania	Isabella	15 Sep 1828
MOYES, Harriet	17	F	None	Great Britain	United States	Ganges	26 Oct 1826
J. M.	35	M	Mariner	U. States	U. States	Venus	27 Jun 1821
MOYLAN, Patrick	20					Trio	5 May 1828
MOYLOR, John	20	M	Farmer	England		Marchioness	13 May 1828
MOYNEY, William	23	M	Farmer	Ireland	United States	Dublin Packet	23 May 1828
MOYOLI, Diago	21	M	Mercht.	Spain	U. States	Brown	7 Jul 1826
MOZINO, Antonio		M	Prisoner charged with Piracy			Oswego	12 Apr 1824
MUADIE, A.	23	M	Merchant	French	U. States	Topaz	23 Jul 1828
MUARRY, Martin	40	M	Joiner	Ireland	New York or Boston	Concordia	12 Oct 1826
MUCH, Francis	35	M	Merchant	U. States	U. States	John Laird	16 Jun 1827
MUCHIN, J.	26	M	Farmer	With intention to become citizen		New York	18 Jul 1828
MUCIA, M.	20	M	Merchant	Cuba	U. States	Brown	29 Apr 1825
MUCKLE JOHN, William	40	M	Farmer	Scotland	United States	Broke	16 Jul 1829
MUCKLETON, Bridget	44			Ireland		Anacreon	7 Sep 1827
Owen	11			Ireland		Anacreon	7 Sep 1827
Peter	39			Ireland		Anacreon	7 Sep 1827
MUDEY, Peter	32	M	Shoemaker	England	United States	Copernicus	3 Aug 1829
MUDGE, Zachariah	27	M	Military	England	Canada	Hudson	20 Nov 1828
MUELER, Griten	25	M	Laborer	Ireland	United States	St. Michaels	23 Dec 1826
MUGET, M.	44	M	Merchant	France	U. States	Waldo	19 Aug 1826
MUGHAN, Bridget	19	F	None	Great Britain	United States	Aurora	10 Nov 1827
Francis	36	M	Merchant	Ireland	America	Panthea	18 Jul 1823
MUGNUS, D., Mr.	31	M	Merchant	France	France	Stephania	28 Jul 1823
MUHE, Frank	28	M	Butcher	Germany	America	Falcon	28 Aug 1828
MUHENY, Wm.	22	M				Trio	5 May 1828
MUHLENBERG, F. A.	23	M	Doctor	U. States	U. States	Edward Quesnel	15 May 1826
MUHOVY, William	18	M	Servant	Ireland	United States	Sylvester Healy	19 Aug 1825
MUIR, David	30	M	Labourer	Scotland	United States	Tom	2 Jul 1827
Helen	18	F	Labourer	Scotland	United States	Tom	2 Jul 1827
J.	28	M	Merchant	France	France	Eliza	28 Apr 1827
James	16	M	Labourer	Scotland	United States	Tom	2 Jul 1827
James	44	M	Labourer	Scotland	United States	Tom	2 Jul 1827
Janet	11	F	Labourer	Scotland	United States	Tom	2 Jul 1827
John	19	M	Farmer	Gt. Britain	U. States	Camberwell	7 Apr 1828
John	27	M	Gentleman	United States	U. States	Emblem	18 Jun 1825
Mary	56	F	None	U. States	U. States	Camillus	27 Jul 1825
William	25	M	Butler	Scotland	United States	Camillus	7 Mar 1825
William	36	M	Baker	Scotland	U. States	Camillus	27 Jul 1825
MUIRHEAD, Francis	25	M	Mason	Scotland	United States	Culloden	17 May 1828
James	6	M		Scotland	U.S.	Curler	19 Jul 1828
Janet	4	F		Scotland	U.S.	Curler	19 Jul 1828
Wm.	33	M	Farmer	Scotland	U.S.	Curler	19 Jul 1828
MULAGAN, Mariah	19	F	Spinster	Ireland	U. States	Josephine	7 May 1827
MULANPHY, Bryan	17	M	Merchant	Great Britain	United States	Thomas Dickason	14 Sep 1827
MULANY, John	26	M	Farmer	Ireland	United States	Dublin Packet	23 May 1828
Maria	22	F	Wife	Ireland	United States	Dublin Packet	23 May 1828
MULBERRY, George	24		Farmer	Ireland	United States	Robert Burns	30 May 1823
MULBNER, Mary	26	F	Spinster	Ireland		Robert Fulton	4 Jun 1828
MULBOUCH, Augine	24	M	Merchant	France	United States	Factor	1 Sep 1823

NAMES OF PASSENGERS	AGE	SEX	OCCUPATIONS	COUNTRY TO WHICH THEY BELONG	COUNTRY THEY INTEND TO INHABIT	SHIPS/DATES OF ARRIVAL
MULCAHY, John	27					Trio 5 May 1828
MULCHALY, J.	21		Labourer	Ireland	United States	Geo. Canning 5 Jun 1828
MULCHANECK, Catherine	12	F		Ireland	America	Liverpool 31 Aug 1827
Ellen	36	F		Ireland	America	Liverpool 31 Aug 1827
Michl.	38	M	Mason	Ireland	America	Liverpool 31 Aug 1827
Patrick	6	M		Ireland	America	Liverpool 31 Aug 1827
Thos.	8	M		Ireland	America	Liverpool 31 Aug 1827
William	4	M		Ireland	America	Liverpool 31 Aug 1827
MULDARRY, Bridget	15			Ampor, Ireland	Ireland	Hudson 18 Jun 1825

*Officers, Seamen and Passengers belonging to the Ship Jane of Boston and taken from on board the Schooner Olive of St. Johns , N.B. on the 4th June 1825, Lat. 41.30, Long 53.19, which ship foundered on the 31st ultimo in Lat. 41.44 Long 52.

NAMES OF PASSENGERS	AGE	SEX	OCCUPATIONS	COUNTRY TO WHICH THEY BELONG	COUNTRY THEY INTEND TO INHABIT	SHIPS/DATES OF ARRIVAL
James, Jr.	9/12			Ampor, Ireland	Ireland	Hudson 18 Jun 1825

*Officers, Seamen and Passengers belonging to the Ship Jane of Boston and taken from on board the Schooner Olive of St. Johns , N.B. on the 4th June 1825, Lat. 41.30, Long 53.19, which ship foundered on the 31st ultimo in Lat. 41.44 Long 52.

NAMES OF PASSENGERS	AGE	SEX	OCCUPATIONS	COUNTRY TO WHICH THEY BELONG	COUNTRY THEY INTEND TO INHABIT	SHIPS/DATES OF ARRIVAL
Mary	18			Ampor, Ireland	Ireland	Hudson 18 Jun 1825

*Officers, Seamen and Passengers belonging to the Ship Jane of Boston and taken from on board the Schooner Olive of St. Johns , N.B. on the 4th June 1825, Lat. 41.30, Long 53.19, which ship foundered on the 31st ultimo in Lat. 41.44 Long 52.

NAMES OF PASSENGERS	AGE	SEX	OCCUPATIONS	COUNTRY TO WHICH THEY BELONG	COUNTRY THEY INTEND TO INHABIT	SHIPS/DATES OF ARRIVAL
Mary	35			Ampor, Ireland	Ireland	Hudson 18 Jun 1825

*Officers, Seamen and Passengers belonging to the Ship Jane of Boston and taken from on board the Schooner Olive of St. Johns , N.B. on the 4th June 1825, Lat. 41.30, Long 53.19, which ship foundered on the 31st ultimo in Lat. 41.44 Long 52.

NAMES OF PASSENGERS	AGE	SEX	OCCUPATIONS	COUNTRY TO WHICH THEY BELONG	COUNTRY THEY INTEND TO INHABIT	SHIPS/DATES OF ARRIVAL
Patrick	5			Ampor, Ireland	Ireland	Hudson 18 Jun 1825

*Officers, Seamen and Passengers belonging to the Ship Jane of Boston and taken from on board the Schooner Olive of St. Johns , N.B. on the 4th June 1825, Lat. 41.30, Long 53.19, which ship foundered on the 31st ultimo in Lat. 41.44 Long 52.

NAMES OF PASSENGERS	AGE	SEX	OCCUPATIONS	COUNTRY TO WHICH THEY BELONG	COUNTRY THEY INTEND TO INHABIT	SHIPS/DATES OF ARRIVAL
Peter	35			Ampor, Ireland	Ireland	Hudson 18 Jun 1825

*Officers, Seamen and Passengers belonging to the Ship Jane of Boston and taken from on board the Schooner Olive of St. Johns , N.B. on the 4th June 1825, Lat. 41.30, Long 53.19, which ship foundered on the 31st ultimo in Lat. 41.44 Long 52.

NAMES OF PASSENGERS	AGE	SEX	OCCUPATIONS	COUNTRY TO WHICH THEY BELONG	COUNTRY THEY INTEND TO INHABIT	SHIPS/DATES OF ARRIVAL
MULDARY, Ann	2			Ampor, Ireland	Ireland	Hudson 18 Jun 1825

*Officers, Seamen and Passengers belonging to the Ship Jane of Boston and taken from on board the Schooner Olive of St. Johns , N.B. on the 4th June 1825, Lat. 41.30, Long 53.19, which ship foundered on the 31st ultimo in Lat. 41.44 Long 52.

NAMES OF PASSENGERS	AGE	SEX	OCCUPATIONS	COUNTRY TO WHICH THEY BELONG	COUNTRY THEY INTEND TO INHABIT	SHIPS/DATES OF ARRIVAL
Mary	17			Ampor, Ireland	Ireland	Hudson 18 Jun 1825

*Officers, Seamen and Passengers belonging to the Ship Jane of Boston and taken from on board the Schooner Olive of St. Johns , N.B. on the 4th June 1825, Lat. 41.30, Long 53.19, which ship foundered on the 31st ultimo in Lat. 41.44 Long 52.

NAMES OF PASSENGERS	AGE	SEX	OCCUPATIONS	COUNTRY TO WHICH THEY BELONG	COUNTRY THEY INTEND TO INHABIT	SHIPS/DATES OF ARRIVAL
MULDOON, James	18	M	Servant	England		Marchioness 13 May 1828
John	20	M	Servant	England		Marchioness 13 May 1828
MULDOWNEY, Pat	28	M	Labourer	Great Britain	United States	Penelope 11 Jun 1827
MULDRONE, Mary	22	F	None	Great Brittan	United States	America 24 Jul 1827
Michael	26	M	Labourer	Great Brittan	United States	America 24 Jul 1827
Patrick	5/52	M	None	Great Brittan	United States	America 24 Jul 1827
Peter	30	M	Labourer	Great Brittan	United States	America 24 Jul 1827
Thomas	20	M	Labourer	Great Brittan	United States	America 24 Jul 1827
MULE, Frederick	19	M	Joiner	G. Britain	U. States	Armadello 22 Jun 1827
MULEGAN, James	24	M	Labourer	Grt. Britain	United States	Robert Fulton 8 Oct 1828
John	16			County of Carvan	Ohio	Peru 30 May 1828
MULER, Eliza, Mrs.	24	F	None	Netherlands	New York	Sully 11 Mar 1829
Hector	34	M	Artist	Netherlands	New York	Sully 11 Mar 1829
Wm.	32	M	Book Keeper	G.B.	America	Pacific 13 Jan 1827
MULGREW, Felix	20	M	Farmer	Ireland, G.B.	United States	Orozimbo 31 May 1824
MULHAN, Catherine	22	F	None	Great Britain	United States	Eliza Barker 3 Jul 1826
MULHEAR, Ann	50	F	Labourer	Ireland	United States	Essex 23 May 1828
Barny	12	M	Labourer	Ireland	United States	Essex 23 May 1828
Bryan	55	M	Labourer	Ireland	United States	Essex 23 May 1828
Chas.	17	M	Labourer	Ireland	United States	Essex 23 May 1828
Jas.	10	M	Labourer	Ireland	United States	Essex 23 May 1828
Mary	8	F	Labourer	Ireland	United States	Essex 23 May 1828
Owen	16	M	Labourer	Ireland	United States	Essex 23 May 1828
Pat	20	M	Labourer	Ireland	United States	Essex 23 May 1828
MULHN, C.	40	F	Gent	French	Switzerland	Charlemagne 19 Sep 1828
Christopher	20	M	Gent	French	Switzerland	Charlemagne 19 Sep 1828
Christopher	50	M	Gent	French	Switzerland	Charlemagne 19 Sep 1828
Jacob	18	M	Gent	French	Switzerland	Charlemagne 19 Sep 1828
MULHOLAND, James	23	M	Labourer	Ireland	United States	Lord Wellington 28 May 1827
MULHOLLAND, Catherine	24	F	Spinster	Ireland	United States	Fabius 31 Jul 1829
Jno.	12	M		Ireland	United States	Thomas 13 Dec 1827
Thomas	28	M	Labourer	Grt. Britain	United States	Robert Fulton 8 Oct 1828
MULHOLLON, Ann	30	F		Ireland	United States	Princess Charlotte 26 Apr 1827
MULIGAN, Mich.	19	M	Weaver	Ireland	United States	Fabius 4 Jun 1828
MULINEUX, Charles	25	M	Labourer	England	U. States	Ayrshire 12 May 1828

NAMES OF PASSENGERS	AGE	SEX	OCCUPATIONS	COUNTRY TO WHICH THEY BELONG	COUNTRY THEY INTEND TO INHABIT	SHIPS/DATES OF ARRIVAL	
MULKERON, Hugh	21		Laborer	Ireland	United States	Robert Burns	18 Jun 1821
Margaret	18		Spinster	Ireland	United States	Robert Burns	18 Jun 1821
Sally	40		Wife	Ireland	United States	Robert Burns	18 Jun 1821
MULLAGAN, Matthew	20	M	Laborer	Gt. Britain		Dalhouse Castle	13 May 1828
MULLAIN, F.	22			Cork	New York	Schuylkill	22 Aug 1825
J.	24		Farmer	Cork	New York	Schuylkill	22 Aug 1825
MULLAN, Anne	19		Laboring Class		United States	Atlantic	2 Apr 1827
Catharine	26	...	...	...	...	Alexander Mansfield	18 Jun 1821
Catherine	18	F	Laborer	Ireland	U. States	Lady Hunter	14 Mar 1826
Francis	26		Laboring Class		United States	Atlantic	2 Apr 1827
James	19 7/12	M	Weaver	Ireland	U. States	Fabius	22 Sep 1828
James	31	M	Labourer	Great Britain	United States	Penelope	11 Jun 1827
James	32	...	...	...	...	Alexander Mansfield	18 Jun 1821
Jane, & wife	26	...	...	...	...	Alexander Mansfield	18 Jun 1821
John	...	...	...	...	...	Alexander Mansfield	18 Jun 1821
John	22	M	Labourer	Ireland	United States	Gem	16 Jun 1824
Mary	18		Laboring Class		United States	Atlantic	2 Apr 1827
Mary	50	F	Spinster	Ireland	United States	Gem	16 Jun 1824
Michael	26 11/12	M	Carpenter	G. Britain	United States	Louisa	14 Jun 1825
Wm.	Child	...	...	...	...	Alexander Mansfield	18 Jun 1821
MULLANS, Alice	13		Laboring Class		United States	Atlantic	2 Apr 1827
Hannack	...		Laboring Class		United States	Atlantic	2 Apr 1827
MULLAR, Garey	33	M	Farmer	France	United States	Great Britain	18 Sep 1826
Mayhed	35	M	Laborer	Ireland	United States	St. Michaels	18 Jul 1826
MULLARDY, Patc.	20		Labourer	Longford	Boston	Peru	30 May 1828
MULLAY, Ellen	14	F	None	Ireland	United States	St. George	25 Aug 1829
John	4	M	None	Ireland	United States	St. George	25 Aug 1829
John	41	M	Printer	Pennsylvania	Pennsylvania	Meteor	19 Aug 1829
Nancy	14	F	None	Ireland	United States	St. George	25 Aug 1829
Nancy	40	F	None	Ireland	United States	St. George	25 Aug 1829
MULLDGY, Thomas	34	M	Clergyman	U. States	U. States	Eugene	15 Dec 1828
MULLEN, ...	20	M	Farmer			Robert Burns	13 Jul 1820
...ap...	19	M	Gentleman	Ireland	United States	Thomas	13 Dec 1827
Ann	20	F	Servant	Ireland	United States	Josephine	30 Apr 1828
Ann	46	F	Farmer, Labourer or Spinster	Ireland	U. States	Meteor	4 Oct 1827
Ann	46	F		Ireland	United States	Mary	1 Jul 1829
Biddy	8	F		Ireland	United States	Mary	1 Jul 1829
Biddy	10	F		Ireland	United States	Mary	1 Jul 1829
Bridchy	48	F		Ireland	United States	Mary	1 Jul 1829
Catharine	14	F		Ireland	United States	Mary	1 Jul 1829
Catherine	40	F	Spinster	Ireland	United States	Dublin Packet	3 Sep 1822
Edward	19		Labourer	Ireland	England	Emulous	26 Jul 1821
Eleanor	27		Spinster	Ireland	England	Emulous	26 Jul 1821
Eliza	5	F		Ireland	United States	Mary	1 Jul 1829
Ellen	14	F		Ireland	America	Corinthian	1 Sep 1827
George	18	M	Agriculture	Wirtemburg	United States	Henri IV	14 Oct 1829
Isaac	13	M	Laborer	Ireland	United States	Mary	1 Jul 1829
Isaac	18	M	Laborer	Ireland	United States	Mary	1 Jul 1829
James	11	M	Laborer	Ireland	United States	Mary	1 Jul 1829
James	12		Labourer	Ireland	England	Emulous	26 Jul 1821
Jane	24	F	Spinster	Ireland	New York	Louisa	20 Jul 1826
Jno., Jur.	10	M	Laborer or Spinster	Ireland	United States	Sarah G	11 Sep 1827
John	...	...	...	...	...	St. Michael	22 Sep 1824
John	7	M	Laborer	Ireland	United States	Mary	1 Jul 1829
John	21	M	Mercht.	Switzerland	America	Henry	11 Oct 1825
John	22	M				Imperial	19 Jul 1820
John	24	M	Labourer	Ireland	U. States	Sarah G	30 Jun 1828
John	30	M	Laborer or Spinster	Ireland	United States	Sarah G	11 Sep 1827
John	52		Labourer	Ireland	England	Emulous	26 Jul 1821
John	53	M	Laborer	Ireland	United States	Mary	1 Jul 1829
John	54	M	Farmer	Ireland	United States	Herald	29 Oct 1825
John, Junr.	25	M	Farmer	Ireland	United States	Herald	29 Oct 1825
Margt.	17	F		Ireland	America	Corinthian	1 Sep 1827

NAMES OF PASSENGERS	AGE	SEX	OCCUPATIONS	COUNTRY TO WHICH THEY BELONG	COUNTRY THEY INTEND TO INHABIT	SHIPS/DATES OF ARRIVAL	
MULLEN (cont'd)							
Mary	...	...	...	...	...	St. Michael	22 Sep 1824
Mary	16	F	Servant	Ireland	United States	Josephine	30 Apr 1828
Mary	17	F		Ireland	United States	Mary	1 Jul 1829
Mary	19	F	Servant	Gt. Britain	U. States	Sarah G.	14 Apr 1828
Mary	22	F	Wife	Ireland	United States	Dublin Packet	9 Jul 1827
Mary	30	F	Spinster	Ireland		Robert Fulton	4 Jun 1828
Mary	67	F	Spinster	Ireland	Und. Stts of Amer	Alexander Mansfield	18 Aug 1826
Mich.	27	M	Musician	England	United States	Siroc	31 Oct 1829
Michael	20	M	Labourer	Great Britain	United States	Atlantic	8 Dec 1827
Moses	26	M	Weaver	Ireland	U. States	Josephine	30 Aug 1828
Nancy	4		Child	Ireland	England	Emulous	26 Jul 1821
Nancy	18	F		Ireland	United States	Mary	1 Jul 1829
Pat	19	M	Labourer	Ireland	U.S.A.	Dalhouse Castle	21 Aug 1829
Patrick	6	M	Laborer or Spinster	Ireland	United States	Sarah G	11 Sep 1827
Patrick	21	M	Laborer	Ireland	United States	Mary	1 Jul 1829
Patrick	28	M	Laborer or Spinster	Ireland	United States	Frances Miller	27 Jul 1827
Peggy	14	F		Ireland	United States	Mary	1 Jul 1829
Peter	19	M	Servant	Ireland	America	Corinthian	1 Sep 1827
Robert	25	M	Labourer	Ireland	United States	Robert Fulton	10 Aug 1827
Rose	9	F		Ireland	United States	Mary	1 Jul 1829
Rose	25	F	None	Great Britan	U. States	Ann Marria	6 Aug 1823
Sarah	30	F	Laborer or Spinster	Ireland	United States	Sarah G	11 Sep 1827
Sarah, Jur.	8	F	Laborer or Spinster	Ireland	United States	Sarah G	11 Sep 1827
Sul.	22	M	Agriculture	Bavaria	United States	Henri IV	14 Oct 1829
T...	3 6/12	F		Ireland		Robert Fulton	4 Jun 1828
Thomas	30	M	Farmer	Ireland	United States	Dublin Packet	9 Jul 1827
Thomas	51	M	Laborer	Ireland	United States	Mary	1 Jul 1829
Thomas	68	M	Laborer	Ireland	United States	Mary	1 Jul 1829
Thos.	6		Child	Ireland	England	Emulous	26 Jul 1821
Thos.	9	M	Laborer	Ireland	United States	Mary	1 Jul 1829
Thos.	17	M	Labourer	Ireland	United States	Louisa	18 Apr 1827
MULLENDER, S., Mr.	26	M	Mercht.	United States	United States	Manchester	6 Apr 1826
MULLENS, John	19	M	Farmer	Ireland	U.S. States	Splendid	14 Aug 1829
MULLER, —, Mrs.	20	F		Denmark	U. States	Elias Burger	18 Apr 1823
—, Mrs.	57	F	Shoemaker	Switzerland	U. States	Seine	30 Aug 1824
— (Infant)	7/12	F		Denmark	U. States	Elias Burger	18 Apr 1823
Abraham	14	M	Baker	Switzerland	New York	Frances Henrietta	25 Aug 1825
Alberst	27	M	Doctor	Switzerland	U. States	Sully	25 Jun 1828
Anna Maria	48	F	Farmer	Baden	United States	Jason	3 Nov 1828
Anne	49	F		Brattain		L'Esperance	6 Sep 1828
Caspar	6	M		Baerns	United States	Constitution	2 Aug 1826
Catharine	12	F			United States	Constitution	2 Aug 1826
Conrad	20	M	Farmer	Baden	United States	Jason	3 Nov 1828
Daniel	25	M	Agriculturist	France	U.S.	Helen	3 May 1828
David	27	M	Merchant	France	United States	Cavalier	25 Jul 1828
Elizabeth	2	F	Daughter	Swiss	United States	Elizabeth	4 Sep 1826
Elizabeth	48	F	Baker	Switzerland	New York	Frances Henrietta	25 Aug 1825
Estella	33	F		Brattain		L'Esperance	6 Sep 1828
Francis	4	M		Denmark	U. States	Elias Burger	18 Apr 1823
Frederic	25	M	Farmer	Germany	United States	Oxford	14 Aug 1828
G.	6	M		Denmark	U. States	Elias Burger	18 Apr 1823
Geoa.	40	M	Shoemaker	Switzerland	U. States	Seine	30 Aug 1824
J.	25	M	Gentleman	Germany	U. States	Deux Freres	27 Nov 1824
J. H.	22	M	Tailor	New York	U. States	Maria Elizabeth	9 Jun 1826
Jacob	3/12	M	Son	Swiss	United States	Elizabeth	4 Sep 1826
Jacob L.	40	M	Merchant	Denmark	U. States	Elias Burger	18 Apr 1823
Johan	2 6/12	M			United States	Constitution	2 Aug 1826
Johan	9	M		Saxony	United States	Constitution	2 Aug 1826
Johannes Martin	56	M	Farmer	Baden	United States	Jason	3 Nov 1828
John	8	M	Baker	Switzerland	New York	Frances Henrietta	25 Aug 1825
John	8	M		Brattain		L'Esperance	6 Sep 1828
John	20	M	None	Switzerland	U. States	Sully	25 Jun 1828
John	26	M	Black Smith	Brattain		L'Esperance	6 Sep 1828
John	28	M	Potter	Germany	U. States	Falcon	11 Jun 1827

NAMES OF PASSENGERS	A G E	S E X	OCCUPATIONS	COUNTRY TO WHICH THEY BELONG	COUNTRY THEY INTEND TO INHABIT	SHIPS/DATES OF ARRIVAL	
MULLER (cont'd)							
John	33	M				Lady of the Lake	23 Aug 1828
John	38	M	Taylor		United States	Constitution	2 Aug 1826
John Abraham	41	M	Baker	Switzerland	New York	Frances Henrietta	25 Aug 1825
Julia	7	F	Baker	Switzerland	New York	Frances Henrietta	25 Aug 1825
Margretta	30	F			United States	Constitution	2 Aug 1826
Maria	34	F	Wife	Swiss	United States	Elizabeth	4 Sep 1826
Maria	65	F		Swis	United States	Iris	21 Sep 1821
Marinet	27	F	Book Binder	France	United States	American	27 Aug 1827
Mary M.	30	...	...	...	United States	Criterion	27 Jun 1827
Michl.	16		Porter	Ireland	United States	Geo. Canning	5 Jun 1828
P.	5	F		Brattain		L'Esperance	6 Sep 1828
Patk.	25	M	Weaver	Ireland		Aurora	12 Mar 1827
Peter	24		Weaver	France	U. States	Elizabeth	9 Jul 1825
Peter	27		Mercht.	Switzerland	U. States	New York	30 Oct 1827
R. F.		M	Merchant	Holland	U. States	Elisa Pigott	24 Apr 1822
Rosalie	13	F	Baker	Switzerland	New York	Frances Henrietta	25 Aug 1825
Samuel	4	M	Son	Swiss	United States	Elizabeth	4 Sep 1826
Samuel	35	M	Turner	Swiss	United States	Elizabeth	4 Sep 1826
Wilh. Henr.	20	M	Weaver	Germany	America	Falcon	28 Aug 1828
MÜLLER, Daniel	32	M	Labourer	Switzerland	United States	Thetis	5 Jul 1821
MULLERON, Ellen	20	M	Labourer	Ireland	United States	Essex	23 May 1828
Jno.	22	M	Labourer	Ireland	United States	Essex	23 May 1828
MULLET, —, Miss	19	F	Spinster	France	U. States	Othello	31 Aug 1824
MULLEY, Dennis	26	M	Servant	Ireland	United States	Sylvester Healy	19 Aug 1825
MULLHERON, Peter	26	F	Labourer	Ireland	United States	Essex	23 May 1828
MULLHOLLAND, Pat	22	M	Labourer	Ireland	United States	Aurelia	7 Jun 1826
Pat.	20	M	Labourer	Ireland	United States	Aurelia	7 Jun 1826
MULLICAN, Patrick	27	M	Labourer	Ireland	United States	Mary & Harriet	3 Jul 1829
MULLIGAN, Ann	20	F	Farmer, Labourer or Spinster	Ireland	U. States	Meteor	4 Oct 1827
Barney	23	M	Farmer	Ireland	U. States	Edward	15 Jul 1825
Bridget	19	F		U. States	U. States	New England	4 Jun 1828
Bridget	21	F	Spinster	Ireland	U. States	Josephine	7 May 1827
Bridjet	25	F	None	Ireland	U. States	Henry Kneeland	27 Jul 1825
Cathe.	18	F	Spinster	Ireland	United States	Dublin Packet	29 Jun 1825
Fairly	20	M	Farmer	Ireland	U. States	Edward	15 Jul 1825
Francis	26	M	Farmer	Ireland	United States	Eliza	29 Aug 1822
James, Mr.	25			Great Britain		John Dickinson	5 Apr 1821
John	1 6/12	M	None	Ireland	U. States	Henry Kneeland	27 Jul 1825
John	17	M	Farmer	Ireland	United States	Dublin Packet	22 Oct 1821
John	23	M	Farmer	Ireland	United States	Dublin Packet	29 Jun 1825
John	23	M	Labourer	Ireland	United States	Josephine	30 Apr 1828
Mary	20	F		Great Britain	Philadelphia	Philetus	21 Jul 1827
Mary	22	F	Servant	Ireland	United States	Josephine	30 Apr 1828
Mary	26	F	Seamster	Ireland	United States	Eliza	29 Aug 1822
Mary	60	F	None	England	U. States	Montgomery	18 Oct 1828
Mary, an Infant	1		Child	Ireland	United States	Eliza	29 Aug 1822
Michl.	20	M	Farmer	Ireland	United States	Aurora	9 Jul 1827
Pat	3	M	Child	Ireland	United States	Dublin Packet	29 Jun 1825
Patrick	27	M	Labourer	Ireland	U. States	Nancy	1 Sep 1823
Patrick	28	M	Labourer	Ireland	U.N. States	Jane	7 Oct 1826
Samuel	25	M	Farmer	Ireland	United States	Leonidas	3 Aug 1825
Sarah	3	F	None	Ireland	U. States	Henry Kneeland	27 Jul 1825
Thomas	25	M	Farmer	Ireland	U. States	Henry Kneeland	27 Jul 1825
William	30	M	Bricklayer	Ireland	United States	Baltic	21 Apr 1827
Wm.	5	M	Farmer	Great Britain	United States	Zodiac	29 Oct 1822
Wm.	19	M	Farmer	Ireland	United States	Leonidas	3 Aug 1825
MULLIGHAN, Pat	20	M	Labourer	Great Britain		Moro Castle	6 Jul 1827
MULLIN, Andrew	40	M	Bootmaker	Gt. Britain		Corinthian	27 Oct 1829
Bridget	14	F		Ireland	United States	Aurora	9 Jul 1827
Bridget	26	F	Spinster	Ireland	United States	Robert Fulton	24 Jul 1826
Edwd.	38 5/12	M		Ireland	America	Carolina Ann	7 Apr 1826
Mary	33	F		Gt. Britain		Corinthian	27 Oct 1829
Owen	24 3/12	M	Weaver	Ireland	America	Carolina Ann	7 Apr 1826

NAMES OF PASSENGERS	AGE	SEX	OCCUPATIONS	COUNTRY TO WHICH THEY BELONG	COUNTRY THEY INTEND TO INHABIT	SHIPS/DATES OF ARRIVAL	
MULLIN (cont'd)							
Pat	30	M	Farmer	Ireland	U. States	Dickinson	30 Jul 1825
Sary	18	F		Ireland	United States	Borneo	28 Aug 1828
Thos.	22	M	Merchant	St. John	St. John	St. Michael	27 Mar 1827
MULLINDER, Samuel	18	M	...	England	United States	London Packet	25 Dec 1820
MULLINS, Aaron	5	M		England	United States	Cosmo	26 Aug 1829
Catherine	38	F		Ireland	United States	Copernicus	3 Aug 1829
Danl.	18	M	Farmer	Ireland	United States	General Putnam	20 Jun 1825
Edward	24	M	Merchant	Gt. Britan	Gt. Britan	Canada	8 Jun 1826
Hannah	17			England	United States	Cosmo	26 Aug 1829
Henry	23	M	Laborer	Ireland	United States	Fabius	4 Jun 1828
Hugh	25	M	Carpenter	Ireland	United States	Fabius	4 Jun 1828
Joanna	40	F		England	United States	Cosmo	26 Aug 1829
John	13	M		England	United States	Cosmo	26 Aug 1829
John	27	M	Merchant	Great Britian	U. States	Orbit	29 Apr 1822
John	36	M	Merchant	Canada	Canada	Thames	16 May 1821
John	42	M	Labourer	Ireland	United States	Copernicus	3 Aug 1829
Jos.	15	M		England	United States	Cosmo	26 Aug 1829
Michel	30	M	Laborer	Ireland	United States	Belleville	13 Oct 1827
Moses	10	M		England	United States	Cosmo	26 Aug 1829
MULLMAN, Eliza	8	F	Labourer	England	U. States	Comet	23 Aug 1828
John	10	M	Labourer	England	U. States	Comet	23 Aug 1828
John	34	M	Labourer	England	U. States	Comet	23 Aug 1828
Mary	32	F	Labourer	England	U. States	Comet	23 Aug 1828
Mary Ann	1	F	Labourer	England	U. States	Comet	23 Aug 1828
Thomas	3	M	Labourer	England	U. States	Comet	23 Aug 1828
William	6	M	Labourer	England	U. States	Comet	23 Aug 1828
MULLOCK, Charles	36	M	Labourer	Great Britain	United States	Washington	3 Sep 1827
MULLON, Barney	32	M	Laborer	Ireland	United States	Nancy	18 Oct 1824
Biddy	1	F	Child	Ireland	United States	Nancy	18 Oct 1824
Catharine	27	F	Spinster	Ireland	United States	Catharine	22 Jul 1825
Joseph	3	M	Child	Ireland	United States	Nancy	18 Oct 1824
MULLON, Mary	32	F	Child	Ireland	United States	Nancy	18 Oct 1824
MULLONY, Jeremiah	31	M	Blacksmith	United States	Havana	Halecon	12 Feb 1820
MULLOWNEY, Ellen	20	F	Spinster	Great Britain	United States	Wanderer	11 Jul 1826
MULLOY, Ellen	14	F		Ireland	United States	St. George	25 Aug 1829
John	4	M		Ireland	United States	St. George	25 Aug 1829
Maney	40	F		Ireland	United States	St. George	25 Aug 1829
Nancy	14	F		Ireland	United States	St. George	25 Aug 1829
MULLRAIN, Marrey	19	F	Spinster	Ireland		Robert Fulton	4 Jun 1828
MULLTON, Pat.	25	M	Farmer	Great Britain	United States	Atlantic	28 May 1827
MULLY, Bryan	26	M	Manufacturer	Ireland	U. States	William Byrnes	17 Jul 1825
MULNEY, Ann	20	F		Ireland	United States	William Byrnes	15 Aug 1826
MULOCK, Francis	25	M	Clerk	Halifax	U. States	Hercules	4 Oct 1824
MULQUENEY, Mary	13	F		Ireland	U. States	Liverpool	25 Mar 1828
Michael	10	M		Ireland	U. States	Liverpool	25 Mar 1828
MULREADY, Wm.	26	M	Labourer	Great Britain	United States	Penelope	11 Jun 1827
MULROONY, Ricd.	33	M	Labourer	Ireland	United States	Wilson	6 Jun 1828
MULVANY, Patrick	30	M	Farmer	Ireland	United States	Dublin Packet	28 Apr 1824
MULVAY, Ann 24 5/12		F	Seamstress	Ireland	United States	Atlantic	21 Jul 1827
John	23	M	Farmer	Ireland	N. York	Elizabeth	20 Jun 1828
John 23 2/12		M	Merchant	Scotland	U. States	Hopes Delight	21 Apr 1828
MULVEHILL, Ellen	18	F		Gt. Britain	United States	John & Elizabeth	25 Sep 1827
Wm.	20	M		Gt. Britain	United States	John & Elizabeth	25 Sep 1827
MULVILLE, Elizabeth	22	F	Labourer	Ireland	United States	General Marion	6 Oct 1828
James 1 6/12		M	Labourer	Ireland	United States	General Marion	6 Oct 1828
Michael	24	M	Labourer	Ireland	United States	General Marion	6 Oct 1828
MULVINE, Jno.	23	M	Labourer	Gt. Britain	U. States	Panthia	13 Nov 1824
MUM, Samuel	20	M	Shoemaker	England	United States	Euphrates	18 Aug 1827
MUMFORD, James	34	M	Broker	New York		Robert Edwards	8 Nov 1825
Thos.	24	M	Joiner	England	New York	Robert Edwards	17 Mar 1828
MUMLEY, Robert	32	M	Baker	England	America	James Cropper	3 Mar 1825
MUNCH, Cath	6	F	Farmer	Switzerland	U. States	Alfred	8 Jul 1828
Christine	25	F		France	U.S. America	Huntress	6 Sep 1827
Geo.	8	M	Farmer	Switzerland	U. States	Alfred	8 Jul 1828
H.	1	F	Farmer	Switzerland	U. States	Alfred	8 Jul 1828
Henry	55	M	Farmer	Switzerland	U. States	Alfred	8 Jul 1828

NAMES OF PASSENGERS	AGE	SEX	OCCUPATIONS	COUNTRY TO WHICH THEY BELONG	COUNTRY THEY INTEND TO INHABIT	SHIPS/DATES OF ARRIVAL	
MUNCH (cont'd)							
Joseph	17	M	Farmer	Switzerland	U. States	Alfred	8 Jul 1828
M	4	F	Farmer	Switzerland	U. States	Alfred	8 Jul 1828
M.	15	M	Farmer	Switzerland	U. States	Alfred	8 Jul 1828
Maria	11	F	Farmer	Switzerland	U. States	Alfred	8 Jul 1828
Philip	2	M		France	U.S. America	Huntress	6 Sep 1827
Philip	18	M		France	U.S. America	Huntress	6 Sep 1827
Sophia	20	F		France	U.S. America	Huntress	6 Sep 1827
T.	5	F	Farmer	Switzerland	U. States	Alfred	8 Jul 1828
MUNCLAIR, J. B.	28	M	Currier	French	French	Howard	4 May 1827
MUNDAY, James	25	M	Labourer	Glasgow	U. States	Florenzo	29 Jun 1826
MUNDIGER, Barbara	44	F	Farmer	Coburg	Ohio	Caesar	24 Aug 1829
Catharine	10	F	Farmer	Coburg	Ohio	Caesar	24 Aug 1829
Jacob	18	M	Farmer	Coburg	Ohio	Caesar	24 Aug 1829
Jacob	49	M	Farmer	Coburg	Ohio	Caesar	24 Aug 1829
John	20	M	Farmer	Coburg	Ohio	Caesar	24 Aug 1829
Margareth	10	F	Farmer	Coburg	Ohio	Caesar	24 Aug 1829
Peter	12	M	Farmer	Coburg	Ohio	Caesar	24 Aug 1829
MUNDOR, —, Miss	17	F		England	United States	Lewis	30 May 1823
—, Mr.	31	M	Shoemaker	England	United States	Lewis	30 May 1823
—, Mrs.	30	F		England	United States	Lewis	30 May 1823
David	9	M		England	United States	Lewis	30 May 1823
Jane	1	F		England	United States	Lewis	30 May 1823
Jeremiah	10	M		England	United States	Lewis	30 May 1823
William	5	M		England	United States	Lewis	30 May 1823
MUNG, Sarah, Miss	23		None	Gt. Britan	Portauprince	James Monroe	11 Dec 1821
MUNGER, J.	33	M	Clockmaker	Great Britain	United States	Isaac Hicks	6 Dec 1827
MUNHALL, Kitty	8	F		Newfoundland	U. States	Combine	30 Nov 1825
Larence	50	M	Labourer	Ireland	U. States	Combine	30 Nov 1825
Sally	30	F		Newfoundland	U. States	Combine	30 Nov 1825
William	3	M		Newfoundland	U. States	Combine	30 Nov 1825
MUNN, Ann	19	F	None	England	United States	London	21 May 1828
Arthur	30	M	Servent	England	U. States	Henri IV	7 May 1827
D.	18	M		Scotland	U.S.	Curler	19 Jul 1828
D.	23	M		Scotland	U.S.	Curler	19 Jul 1828
Elizabeth	6	F	daughter	England	United States	Robert Edwards	3 Oct 1829
George	8	M	Son	England	United States	Robert Edwards	3 Oct 1829
George	28	M	Labourer	Great Britan	United States	Clematis	8 May 1827
George	50	M	Carpenter	England	United States	Euphrates	18 Aug 1827
James	4	F	daughter	England	United States	Robert Edwards	3 Oct 1829
James	9	M	Carpenter	England	United States	Euphrates	18 Aug 1827
Jane	10	F	daughter	England	United States	Robert Edwards	3 Oct 1829
John	23		Farmer	England	United States	Hudson	5 Apr 1826
Louisa	28	F	Wife	England	United States	Robert Edwards	3 Oct 1829
Pat.	30	M	Farmer	Ireland	America	Mary	29 May 1827
Rebecca	18		None	London	England	Elizabeth	8 Dec 1821
Sarah	34	F	Carpenter	England	United States	Euphrates	18 Aug 1827
Thomas	1 6/12	M	None	England	United States	London	21 May 1828
Willm.	31	M	Weelwright	England	United States	Robert Edwards	3 Oct 1829
Wm.	24		Baker	London	England	Elizabeth	8 Dec 1821
MUNOZ, Francisco	17	M	Lad	Mexico	Mexico	Virginia	30 Oct 1828
MUNRO, Ann	16	F	None	Scotland	America	Minerva	8 Oct 1824
Barbary	10	F	None	Scotland	America	Minerva	8 Oct 1824
Isabella	11	F	None	Scotland	America	Minerva	8 Oct 1824
John	25	M	Mechanic	England	United States	Panthea	11 Nov 1825
Mary	23	F		Scotland	United States	Commerce	17 Jul 1823
Robina	8	F	None	Scotland	America	Minerva	8 Oct 1824
Will	26	M	Miller	Scotland	United States	Commerce	17 Jul 1823
MUNROE, —, Capt.	30	M	Seaman	U. States	U. States	Corinthian	20 Apr 1825
George	16	M	Farmer	Scotland	United States	Belmont	30 Aug 1828
James	24	M	Mechanic	New York	New York	Dandy	17 May 1825
John	18	M	Farmer	Scotland	United States	Belmont	30 Aug 1828
Robert	23	M	Joiner			Lady of the Lake	23 Aug 1828
Rowland	21	M	None	Scotland	U. States	Camillus	27 Jun 1826
MUNSON, Benjn.	29	M	Farmer	United States	United States	Ann Maria	23 Oct 1820
MUNUSARE, E.	40	M	Merchant	Spain	Spain	Hesperus	13 Mar 1826
MUNY, James	23	M	Mason	Scotland	U.S.	Curler	19 Jul 1828
MUR, Anon	45	M	Farmer	Scotland	U. States	Roger Stewart	9 Jun 1828

NAMES OF PASSENGERS	AGE	SEX	OCCUPATIONS	COUNTRY TO WHICH THEY BELONG	COUNTRY THEY INTEND TO INHABIT	SHIPS/DATES OF ARRIVAL	
MUR (cont'd)							
Mary	17	F	Farmer	Scotland	U. States	Roger Stewart	9 Jun 1828
Mary	24	F	Farmer	Scotland	U. States	Roger Stewart	9 Jun 1828
Sarah	21	M	Farmer	Scotland	U. States	Roger Stewart	9 Jun 1828
MURAT (see Poza)							
A., H.R.H. Prince	22	M	Gentleman	Italy	United States	Daphne	20 May 1823
Betsey	11	F	None	Scotland	U. States	Magnet	22 Aug 1822
Elizabeth	40	F	None	Scotland	U. States	Magnet	22 Aug 1822
J. P.	33	M	Musician	France	U. States	Queen Mab	22 Jul 1825
Jno.	13	M	None	Scotland	U. States	Magnet	22 Aug 1822
Thos.	6	M	None	Scotland	U. States	Magnet	22 Aug 1822
Walter	18	M	None	Scotland	U. States	Magnet	22 Aug 1822
MURCHEE, Robt.	32	M	Mercht.	United States	United States	Manchester	6 Dec 1825
MURCUCIA, D.	22	M	Merchant	France	U. States	Velocipede	26 Jun 1823
MURDEN, Edward	27	M	Merchant	New York	New York	Brighton	20 Aug 1825
MURDOCH, James	21	M	Merchant	U. States	U. States	Persia	24 Mar 1828
Jas.	33	M	Publican	Great Britain	United States	Atlantic	8 Dec 1827
John	16	M	Groom to the Honorable Chipman	Province of New Brunswick	to return to New Brunswick	Loire	23 May 1821
John	23	M	Farmer	Great Britain	United States	Friends	13 Jun 1825
MURDOCK, Ann	3	F	None	Scotland	America	Minerva	8 Oct 1824
Deborah	33	F		Ireland	United States	Clothier	22 Nov 1827
Grace	25	F	Servant	Killiloage	United States	Carolina Ann	11 Jun 1824
James	4	M	None	Scotland	America	Minerva	8 Oct 1824
John	8/12	M	None	Scotland	America	Minerva	8 Oct 1824
John	6	M		Ireland	United States	Carolina Ann	11 Dec 1826
Margaret	7	F	None	Scotland	America	Minerva	8 Oct 1824
Margt.	28	F	Servant	Ireland	United States	Carolina Ann	11 Dec 1826
Mary	28	F	None	Scotland	America	Minerva	8 Oct 1824
Mary Sally	2	F		Ireland	United States	Carolina Ann	11 Dec 1826
Mathew	30	M	Laborer	Ireland	U. States	Albion	9 Aug 1826
Nancy	4	F		Ireland	United States	Carolina Ann	11 Dec 1826
Richard	6	M		Ireland	United States	Clothier	22 Nov 1827
Samuel	25	M	Labourer	Ireland	United States	Fabius	31 Jul 1829
Thos.	13	M	Laborer	Ireland	U. States	Albion	9 Aug 1826
William	28	M	Farmer	Scotland	America	Minerva	8 Oct 1824
MURE, M.	40	M	Farmer	Scotland	United States	Curler	3 Mar 1828
Margaritta	11	F	Farmer	Switzerland		Pallas	14 Jun 1828
Mollany	5	F		Switzerland		Pallas	14 Jun 1828
Morant	37	F		Switzerland		Pallas	14 Jun 1828
Moriah E.	14	F		Switzerland		Pallas	14 Jun 1828
MUREAU, —, Madam	40	F	None	France	U. States	Columbia	9 Aug 1822
MUREN, Parker	45	M	Mariner	New Hampshire	U. States	William	28 Nov 1823
MURET, Charles		M	Farmer			Frederick	18 Feb 1822
MURFORD, John	25	M	Labourer	Gt. Britain	U. States	Sarah G.	14 Apr 1828
MURFRY, Saml.	30	M	Carpenter	Ireland	United States	Potomac	28 Sep 1827
MURFY, Mary	30	F		Ireland	United States	Potomac	28 Sep 1827
Thos.	30	M	Truckman	Ireland	United States	Potomac	28 Sep 1827
MURGATHROYD, Jno.	25	M	Manufaturer	England	United States	Dalhouse Castle	6 Sep 1827
MURGETROID, Elizabeth	3	F	None	England	New York	Indian Chief	16 Aug 1822
Hannah	26	F	None	England	New York	Indian Chief	16 Aug 1822
Mary Anna	6	F	None	England	New York	Indian Chief	16 Aug 1822
Thomas	1 3/12	M	None	England	New York	Indian Chief	16 Aug 1822
MURGETROYE, E.	16	F	Servant	England	Pennsylvania	York	8 Aug 1829
MURGITROYD, Benj.	26	M	Farmer	England	United States	Baltic	21 Apr 1827
Richd.	30	M	Stone Mason	England	United States	Baltic	21 Apr 1827
Saml.	36	M	Farmer	England	United States	Baltic	21 Apr 1827
MURHAR, Michael	25	M	Labourer	Ireland	United States	Combine	4 Jun 1825
MURIEN, Dolly	29	F	None	Philadelphia	U. States	Burdett	11 Oct 1827
MURLEY, John	26			England		Margarett	2 Mar 1820
MUROE, C.	23	M	Merchant	France		Queen Mab	24 Sep 1827
J.	24	F		France		Queen Mab	24 Sep 1827
MURON, Catharine P.	29	F	Farmer	Scotland	United States	Minerva	29 Oct 1822
MURPHEY, Charles	26	M	Laborer	Ireland	United States	St. Michaels	18 Jul 1826
James	20	M	Farmer	Ireland		L. M. Pelham	12 May 1823
John	28	M	Labourer	England	U.S.	Acasta	11 May 1827
Pat	27	M	Butcher	Gt. Britain	United States	Penelope	9 Sep 1828

NAMES OF PASSENGERS	AGE	SEX	OCCUPATIONS	COUNTRY TO WHICH THEY BELONG	COUNTRY THEY INTEND TO INHABIT	SHIPS/DATES OF ARRIVAL
MURPHEY (cont'd)						
Peter	23		Farmer	Ampor, Ireland	Ireland	Hudson 18 Jun 1825

*Officers, Seamen and Passengers belonging to the Ship Jane of Boston and taken from on board the Schooner Olive of St. Johns , N.B. on the 4th June 1825, Lat. 41.30, Long 53.19, which ship foundered on the 31st ultimo in Lat. 41.44 Long 52.

NAMES OF PASSENGERS	AGE	SEX	OCCUPATIONS	COUNTRY TO WHICH THEY BELONG	COUNTRY THEY INTEND TO INHABIT	SHIPS/DATES OF ARRIVAL
Thomas	25		Farmer	Ireland		Nancy 11 Sep 1820
W.	44	M	Sawyer	Great Britain	United States	Washington 9 Apr 1821
MURPHY, —	22	M	Shoemaker	Ireland	U. States	Hazard 27 Aug 1821
—, Infant	1	M		England	United States	Siroc 31 Oct 1829
—, Mrs.	25	F		Ireland	United States	Alex. Mansfield 17 May 1823
—, Mrs.	35	F		New York	U. States	Ambuscade 12 Nov 1823
A.	18		Farmer	Ireland	United States	Courier 16 May 1825
A.	29	M	Merchant	U. States	U. States	Sully 24 Oct 1828
Adam	26	M	Labourer	Ireland	United States	Hope 12 Jun 1828
Allen	19	M	Laborer	Ireland	United States	Ann Maria 18 Dec 1827
Andrew	12	M	Boy	Ireland	United States	Lord Strangford 20 Jun 1826
Andrew	20	M	Labourer	Great Britain	United States	Aurora 5 Sep 1826
Ann	10	F	Girl	Ireland	United States	Lord Strangford 20 Jun 1826
Ann	19	F	Seamstress	England	United States	Brighton 11 Mar 1825
Ann	20	F	None	Great Britain	United States	William Dawson 18 Jun 1827
Ann	20	F	Spinster	Ireland	United States	Dublin Packet 23 May 1828
Ann	24	F	Weaver	England	United States	India 8 Jun 1827
Ann	30	F	Lady	Ireland	United States	Lord Strangford 20 Jun 1826
Ann	30			Ireland	U.S.	Union 20 Aug 1827
Ann	35	F		England	U. States	Emulous 22 Aug 1828
Ann, Mrs.	26	F	Labourer	England	U.S.	Acasta 11 May 1827
B. J.	25	M	Plasterer			Lady of the Lake 23 Aug 1828
Bartle	27	M	Farmer	Ireland	United States	Dublin Packet 29 Jun 1825
Bernard	30	M	Labourer	Ireland		Marchioness 13 May 1828
Biddy	6	F	Child	Ireland	United States	Edwin 27 Oct 1828
Biddy	20	F		Ireland	United States	Thompson 12 Sep 1827
Biddy	25	F	None	England	U. States	Thomas Ritchie 2 Jul 1827
Bridget	18	F	Spinster	Ireland	America	Josephine 8 Dec 1827
Bridget	31	F		Ireland	United States	Kleber 23 Jul 1827
Bridy	2	F	None	Dublin	Dublin	Howard Douglass 11 May 1827
C.	17		Farmer	Ireland	United States	Courier 16 May 1825
Catharine	10/12	F		New York	U. States	Ambuscade 12 Nov 1823
Catharine	3	F		England	United States	Siroc 31 Oct 1829
Catharine	17	F	None	...	New York	Frances Henrietta 30 Jun 1827
Cathe.	2	F	None	Great Britain	United States	William Dawson 18 Jun 1827
Catherine	20	F	Spinster	Ireland	America	Josephine 8 Dec 1827
Catherine	21	F	None	Gt. Britain	U. States	Swift 25 Apr 1828
Catherine	22	F	Dress Maker	Ireland	United States	Princess Charlotte 26 Apr 1827
Catherine	50	F	None	England	United States	London 21 May 1828
Catherine	70	F	Widow	Ireland	United States	Dublin Packet 22 Aug 1829
Cathr.	19	F		Ireland	United States	Commerce 13 Jun 1828
Cecelia	21	F	Servant	Ireland	United States	Henry Kneeland 7 Jun 1828
Chas.	9	M	None	Great Britain	United States	Washington 9 Apr 1821
Con.	21	M	Farmer	Ireland	U. States	Edward 15 Jul 1825
Con.	22			Ireland	U.S.	Union 20 Aug 1827
Cornelius	7	M	None	Great Britain	United States	Washington 9 Apr 1821
Cornelius	26	M		Ireland	United States	John & Adam 21 Sep 1822
Corns.	11	M	None	Great Britain	United States	Washington 9 Apr 1821
Daniel	27	M	Labourer	Ireland	U. States	Josephine 23 Jan 1829
Daniel	30	M		Ireland	United States	William Byrnes 6 Apr 1826
Daniel	32	M	Labourer	Ireland	United States	Jubilee 1 Oct 1828
Danl.	2	M		G. Britain	U. States	Mary Howland 22 Sep 1828
Danl.	6			Ireland	America	Liverpool 31 Aug 1827
David	22	M	Blacksmith	Ireland	New York	William 27 Aug 1827
David	50	M	Laborer	Ireland	United States	Trio 13 Jun 1827
Dennis	24	M	Laborer	Great Britain	U. States	Gem 26 Jul 1827
E.	20		Farmer	Ireland	United States	Courier 16 May 1825
Edmond	1	M		G. Britain	U. States	Mary Howland 22 Sep 1828
Edmund	8	M	Boy	Ireland	United States	Lord Strangford 20 Jun 1826
Edward	24	M				Lady of the Lake 23 Aug 1828

NAMES OF PASSENGERS	AGE	SEX	OCCUPATIONS	COUNTRY TO WHICH THEY BELONG	COUNTRY THEY INTEND TO INHABIT	SHIPS/DATES OF ARRIVAL	
MURPHY (cont'd)							
Edward	30	M	Clerk	Great Briton	United States	Erin	26 May 1821
Edward	31	M	Tailor	Ireland	U.S.	Oliver Wolcott	3 Nov 1827
Edwd	2	M	None	Great Britain	United States	Washington	9 Apr 1821
Edwd.	7	M	Child	Ireland	U. States	Hibernia	3 Dec 1823
Edwd.	22	M	Black Smith	Ireland	United States	Wilson	27 Jun 1826
Edwd.	26	M	Apothicary	Ireland	N. York	Salem	15 Mar 1828
Eleanor	16	F	Servant	Ireland	United States	Josephine	30 Apr 1828
Elisabeth	26	F	Wife	Ireland	New York	Louisa	20 Jul 1826
Eliza	9	F		G. Britain	U. States	Mary Howland	22 Sep 1828
Elizabeth	26	F	Labourer	England	U. States	Comet	23 Aug 1828
Elizth.	8	F		New York	U. States	Ambuscade	12 Nov 1823
Ellen		F	None	...	United States	Minerva	30 Oct 1827
Ellen	20 3/12	F		England	America, U.S.	Illinois	3 Jun 1822
Ellen	25	M			U. States	Greyhound	19 Aug 1820
Ellen	26	F		Ireland	United States	Trio	13 Jun 1827
Ellen	30	F		Ireland	U. States	Alexander	28 Jul 1821
Ellen	30 2/12	F	Domestic	Ireland	United States	London	6 Feb 1829
Ellen	40	F		G. Britain	U. States	London	23 Sep 1828
Francis	20	M	Labourer	Ireland	United States	Catharine	22 Jul 1825
Francis	26	M	Labourer	Ireland	U. States	Sarah G	30 Jun 1828
Geo.	26	M	Miner	U. States	U. States	Martha	20 Jun 1825
Georg	26	M	Labourer	Ireland	United States	Hope	12 Jun 1828
Helen	14	F				Lady of the Lake	23 Aug 1828
Henry	4	M	None	Great Britain	United States	Washington	9 Apr 1821
Henry	23 1/12	M	Farmer	Great Briton	United States	Mount Vernon	30 Dec 1828
Henry	33	M	Privt. Gentlemn.	Ireland	United States	William	20 Jul 1829
Hetty	17	F	None	England	United States	London	21 May 1828
Hugh	18	M	Labourer	Ireland	United States	Wilson	28 Nov 1828
Hugh	25	M	Labourer	Ireland	United States	Wilson	28 Nov 1828
Hugh	38	M	Labourer	Dublin	Dublin	Howard Douglass	11 May 1827
Hugh	40 7/12	M	Labourer	Ireland	United States	London	6 Feb 1829
J.	50	M	Labourer			Lady of the Lake	23 Aug 1828
James						Venus	12 Apr 1821
James	2	M		Ireland	U. States	Alexander	28 Jul 1821
James	4 6/12	M	Son	Ireland	New York	Louisa	20 Jul 1826
James	6	M	None	Great Britain	United States	Washington	9 Apr 1821
James	21	M	Farmer	Ireland	United States	Princess Charlotte	26 Apr 1827
James	24	M	Weaver	Ireland	United States	Kleber	23 Jul 1827
James	25	M	Labourer	Ireland	New York	Louisa	20 Jul 1826
James	27	...	...	...	...	Diamond	27 Jul 1824
James	28	M	Mercht.	U. States	U. States	Astrea	3 Jul 1822
James	30	M	Labourer	Ireland	United States	Trident	18 Jul 1827
James	30	M	Chandler	G. Britain	U. States	Margaret Bogle	12 Jun 1828
James	36	M		Dublin	U. States	Hibernia	26 Oct 1826
James	44	M	Machaine Maker	Great Britan	United States	Clematis	8 May 1827
Jane	10 5/12	F		Ireland	United States	Silas Richards	27 Oct 1825
Jane	26	F	None	Dublin	Dublin	Howard Douglass	11 May 1827
Jane	33	F		G. Britain	U. States	Mary Howland	22 Sep 1828
Jas.	24	M	Farmer			Robert Fulton	8 Mar 1823
Jas.	27	M	None	Great Brittan	Great Brittan	Tuscarora	26 Jan 1827
Jas. D.	34	M	Doctor	Ireland	U. States	Champion	26 Jul 1827
Jeremiah	32	M	Farmer	Gt. Britain	United States	Silas Richards	20 Jun 1826
Jerh.	3	M	None	Great Britain	United States	Washington	9 Apr 1821
Jerh.	10	M	Laborer	Ireland	United States	Trio	13 Jun 1827
Jerh.	14	M	Laborer	Ireland	United States	Trio	13 Jun 1827
Jerh.	20		Farmer	Ireland	America	Liverpool	31 Aug 1827
Jerh.	38	M		Ireland	U. States	Howard	25 Jul 1823
Jerry	6	M		Ireland	United States	Potomac	28 Sep 1827
Jno.	25	M	Farmer	England	U. States	Orazimbo	7 Jan 1821
Jno.	30	M	None	Great Britain	United States	Penelope	11 Jun 1827
Johanna	24	F		Ireland	U. States	Hercules	4 Oct 1824
John	1	M	Child	...	United States	Hanford	17 Oct 1828

NAMES OF PASSENGERS	AGE	SEX	OCCUPATIONS	COUNTRY TO WHICH THEY BELONG	COUNTRY THEY INTEND TO INHABIT	SHIPS/DATES OF ARRIVAL	
MURPHY (cont'd)							
John	9	M	Laborer, Spinster or Child	Ireland	United States	Ann Maria	4 Aug 1827
John	11	M	None	...	New York	Frances Henrietta	30 Jun 1827
John	13	M	None	Great Britain	United States	Washington	9 Apr 1821
John	14	M	Son	Ireland	United States	Louisa	18 Apr 1827
John	19	M	Clerk	Ireland	United States	Dublin Packet	22 Oct 1821
John	20	M		Ireland	United States	Thompson	12 Sep 1827
John	20	M	Weaver	Ireland	United States	Jubilee	1 Oct 1828
John	20	M	Labourer	Ireland	United States	Mary & Harriet	9 Mar 1829
John	22	M	Laborer	Gt. Britain	U. States	Combine	9 Sep 1824
John	22	M	Taylor	Ireland	U. States	Virginia	20 Jun 1825
John	22	M	Saddlier	Ireland	United States	Ann Maria	1 Apr 1826
John	22	M	Laborer	Gt. Britain		Dalhouse Castle	13 May 1828
John	23	M		Great B.	U. States	William Neilson	26 Jul 1828
John	24	M	Farmer	England		Exchange	11 Jul 1823
John	25	M	Laborer, Spinster or Child	Ireland	United States	Ann Maria	4 Aug 1827
John	25	M	Sawyer	Irish	United States	Patriots Eagle	30 Oct 1829
John	26	M	Laborer	Ireland	New York	Munroe	27 May 1825
John	27	M	Farmer	Gt. Britain	United States	Penelope	9 Sep 1828
John	28	M	Labourer	Ireland	United States	Princess Charlotte	26 Apr 1827
John	40	M		Ireland	British Amera.	William & George	14 May 1828
John	50			Ireland	U.S.	Union	20 Aug 1827
Jos.	27	M	Labourer	Ireland	N. York	Trusty	12 Sep 1828
Joseana	4	F	None	Spain	Mexico	Sarah	23 Sep 1826
Joseph	40	M	Labourer	England	America	William	21 Sep 1821
Joseph	41	M	Labourer	Ireland	America	Wilson	16 May 1825
Judith	24	...	...	...	...	Diamond	27 Jul 1824
Julian	12	F		Ireland	America	Liverpool	31 Aug 1827
Julian	31			Ireland	America	Liverpool	31 Aug 1827
Laurence	19					Trio	5 May 1828
Lawrence	20	M	Labourer	Ireland	Philadelphia	General Marion	12 Jan 1829
M.	11		Farmer	Ireland	United States	Courier	16 May 1825
M.	18	M		G. Britain	U. States	London	23 Sep 1828
M.	28	F		Great Britain	United States	Isaac Hicks	6 Dec 1827
M.	30	M		Ireland	U. States	St. Michael	26 Oct 1824
M. C.	37	F	None	Spain	Mexico	Sarah	23 Sep 1826
Mag.	15	F				Lady of the Lake	23 Aug 1828
Marg.	27	F	None	Great Britain	U. States	Gem	26 Jul 1827
Margaret	18	F	Spinster	Ireland	United States	Dublin Packet	29 Jun 1825
Margaret	22	F	Spinster	Ireland	United States	Dublin Packet	13 Oct 1828
Margaret	25					Trio	5 May 1828
Margaret	36	F	None	Great Britain	United States	Washington	9 Apr 1821
Margaret	40	F	Laborer, Spinster or Child	Ireland	United States	Ann Maria	4 Aug 1827
Margarett	25	F	Clerk	...	United States	Minerva	30 Oct 1829
Margarette	18	F		Gt. Britain	United States of Ama.	Silas Richards	20 Jun 1826
Margrett	5	F	Child	...	United States	Hanford	17 Oct 1828
Maria, Miss	1	F	Labourer	England	U.S.	Acasta	11 May 1827
Marrey	20	F	None	England	U. States	Thomas Ritchie	2 Jul 1827
Martin	15	M	None	...	New York	Frances Henrietta	30 Jun 1827
Mary	6/12	F	None	Ireland		Marchioness	13 May 1828
Mary	1	F	None	Great Britain	United States	William Dawson	18 Jun 1827
Mary	2	F		New York	U. States	Ambuscade	12 Nov 1823
Mary	4	F		Ireland	United States	Potomac	28 Sep 1827
Mary	14	F	Lady	Ireland	United States	Lord Strangford	20 Jun 1826
Mary	17	F	Spinster	Ireland	United States	Fabius	31 Jul 1829
Mary	18	F	Spinster	Ireland	America	Wilson	16 May 1825
Mary	20	F	Labourer	Ireland	United States	Josephine	30 Apr 1828
Mary	22	F	None	Great Britain	United States	Washington	9 Apr 1821
Mary	24	F	Wife	...	United States	Hanford	17 Oct 1828
Mary	25	F		Ireland	United States	Potomac	28 Sep 1827

NAMES OF PASSENGERS	AGE	SEX	OCCUPATIONS	COUNTRY TO WHICH THEY BELONG	COUNTRY THEY INTEND TO INHABIT	SHIPS/DATES OF ARRIVAL	
MURPHY (cont'd)							
Mary	26	F		Ireland	America	Panthia	17 Sep 1821
Mary	26	F		Great Brittain	United States	Sarah Ralston	27 Jan 1827
Mary	26	F	Servant	Ireland	United States	Edwin	27 Oct 1828
Mary	30	F		England	United States	Siroc	31 Oct 1829
Mary	35	F	Servant	Ireland	U. States	Nancy	13 Dec 1822
Mary	40	F	Seamstress	England	United States	Brighton	11 Mar 1825
Mary	55	F	Woman	Ireland	United States	Dublin Packet	9 Jul 1827
Mary Ann	25	F	None	Ireland		Marchioness	13 May 1828
Michael	11	M	Boy	Ireland	America	Josephine	8 Dec 1827
Michael	20	M	Printer	Gt. Britain	United States	Silas Richards	20 Jun 1826
Michael	26			Ireland		Anacreon	7 Sep 1827
Michael	28	M	Leather dresser	Great Britain	United States	Birmingham	15 Jun 1827
Michael	29	M	Labourer	Ireland	United States	Hope & Esther	17 Oct 1827
Michael	32		Cement Manufr.	Ireland	United States	Cambria	19 Oct 1829
Michal	11	M	Boy	Ireland	America	Wilson	16 May 1825
Michiel	20	M	Farmer	Ireland	United States	Jubilee	13 Jul 1829
Michl.	22	M	Farmer	Great Britain	United States	Ann Maria	12 Jul 1821
Nancy	20	F	None	Ireland	United States	Jubilee	1 Oct 1828
Nony	38	F		Ireland	United States	Trio	2 Oct 1828
Norey	18	F	None	Great Britain	United States	Washington	9 Apr 1821
O.	20		Farmer	Ireland	United States	Courier	16 May 1825
Owen	24	M	Labourer	Ireland	United States	Hannah Eliza	23 Sep 1826
P.	5		Farmer	Ireland	United States	Courier	16 May 1825
P.	40	M	Taylor	Ireland	St. Johns, N.B.	Isabella	10 Mar 1825
P.	48		Farmer	Ireland	United States	Courier	16 May 1825
Partrick	25	M	Labourer	Ireland	United States	General Marion	20 Aug 1828
Pat	22	M		Ireland	United States	Thompson	12 Sep 1827
Pat	26	M	Laborer	Great Britain	U. States	Gem	26 Jul 1827
Pat	27	M	Labourer	Great Britain		Moro Castle	6 Jul 1827
Pat	29	M		G. Britain	U. States	London	23 Sep 1828
Pat.	24	M	Farmer	Ireland	United States	Curler	3 Mar 1828
Patk.	34			Great Britan	United States	Newry	11 Jul 1827
Patrick	3/12	M		Ireland	U. States	Alexander	28 Jul 1821
Patrick	17	M	Farmer	England	United States	Trident	30 Sep 1826
Patrick	21	M	Labourer	Ireland	America	Josephine	8 Dec 1827
Patrick	22	M	Laborer	Great Britain	United States	Hanford	9 Oct 1829
Patrick	25	M	Farmer	Ireland	America	Panthia	17 Sep 1821
Patrick	28	M	Labourer	Ireland	United States	Borneo	2 Oct 1827
Patrick	30	M	Farmer	Ireland	U. States	Alexander	28 Jul 1821
Patrick	30	M	Farmer	England	Alexandria, U.S.	Roman	17 Oct 1826
Patrick	30 1/12	M	...	England	America, U.S.	Illinois	3 Jun 1822
Patrick	40	M	Labourer	...	United States	Hanford	17 Oct 1828
Pattrick	20	M	Weaver	England	United States	India	8 Jun 1827
Peggy	50	F		Ireland	United States	Trio	13 Jun 1827
Peter	20	M	Labourer	Ireland	United States	Commerce	13 Jun 1828
Peter	25	...	Labourer	...	...	Diamond	27 Jul 1824
Peter	28	M	Labourer	England	U. States	Thomas Ritchie	2 Jul 1827
Peter	45	M	None	...	New York	Frances Henrietta	30 Jun 1827
R. O. N.	24	M	Gentleman	Ireland	United States	Siroc	31 Oct 1829
Richard	13	M		Ireland	United States	Thompson	12 Sep 1827
Richard	30	M	Laborer	Ireland	United States	St. Michaels	25 May 1825
Richard	32	M	Labourer	Ireland	United States	Silas Richards	27 Oct 1825
Robert	9	M	Boy	Ireland	United States	Lord Strangford	20 Jun 1826
Robert	20	M	Farmer	Ireland	U. States	Dickinson	30 Jul 1825
Robert	32	M	Laborer	Great Britain	U. States	Gem	26 Jul 1827
Robt.	2	M	Joiner	Ireland	United States	St. John	5 Oct 1829
Rose	23	F		Ireland	United States	Aurora	9 Jul 1827
S.	48		Farmer	Ireland	United States	Courier	16 May 1825
Sally	15	F	Lady	Ireland	United States	Lord Strangford	20 Jun 1826
Saml.	6	M		New York	U. States	Ambuscade	12 Nov 1823
Samuel	17 3/12	M	...	England	America, U.S.	Illinois	3 Jun 1822
Sarah	4	F	None	Dublin	Dublin	Howard Douglass	11 May 1827
Sarah	16	F	None	Great Britain	United States	Washington	9 Apr 1821
Sarah	18	F	Spinster	Ireland	America	Wilson	16 Nov 1824
Stephen	4	M		G. Britain	U. States	Mary Howland	22 Sep 1828
Susan	4	F		New York	U. States	Ambuscade	12 Nov 1823

NAMES OF PASSENGERS	AGE	SEX	OCCUPATIONS	COUNTRY TO WHICH THEY BELONG	COUNTRY THEY INTEND TO INHABIT	SHIPS/DATES OF ARRIVAL	
MURPHY (cont'd)							
T.	28	M	Smith	Great Britain	United States	Isaac Hicks	6 Dec 1827
Teresa	24	F	None	Spain	Mexico	Sarah	23 Sep 1826
Tern	5	M		England	United States	Siroc	31 Oct 1829
Terrance	22	M	Labourer	Great Britain	United States	Penelope	11 Jun 1827
Thomas	8	M	Servant	Ireland	U. States	Nancy	13 Dec 1822
Thomas	10	M	Boy	Ireland	United States	Dublin Packet	3 Sep 1822
Thomas	13	M	Gentleman	Jamaica	Jamaica	Emily Cook	10 Apr 1826
Thomas	14	M	None	...	New York	Frances Henrietta	30 Jun 1827
Thomas	21	M	Labourer	England	U. States	Comet	23 Aug 1828
Thomas	25 3/12	M	Farmer	Great Briton	United States	Mount Vernon	30 Dec 1828
Thomas	30	M	Farmer	G. Britain	U. States	Mary Howland	22 Sep 1828
Thos.	6	M		Spain	Mexico	Sarah	23 Sep 1826
Thos.	11	M	Laborer	Ireland	America	Parrington	9 Jun 1827
Thos.	30	M	Labourer	Great Britain	United States	William Dawson	18 Jun 1827
Thos.	30			Great Britan	United States	Newry	11 Jul 1827
Tim	8			Ireland	America	Liverpool	31 Aug 1827
Timothy, Mr.	25	M	Labourer	England	U.S.	Acasta	11 May 1827
Timy.	33	M	Farmer	Ireland	U. States	Hercules	4 Oct 1824
Walter	22	M		G. Britain	U. States	London	23 Sep 1828
William	11	M	Farmer	G. Britain	U. States	Mary Howland	22 Sep 1828
*Died							
William	13	M	Boy	Ireland	United States	Lord Strangford	20 Jun 1826
William	25	M		Limerick	N. York	Thomas & William	25 May 1827
Wm.	16	M	None	Great Britain	United States	Washington	9 Apr 1821
Wm.	22	M		Ireland	United States	Clothier	22 Nov 1827
Wm.	23	M	Labourer	Ireland	United States	Hannah Eliza	23 Sep 1826
Wm.	25	M	Farmer	Ireland	America	Liverpool	31 Aug 1827
Wm.	26	M		Great B.	U. States	William Neilson	26 Jul 1828
Wm.	30	...	...	...	...	Diamond	27 Jul 1824
Wm.	30	M	Labourer	...	United States	Minerva	30 Oct 1827
Wm.	35	F	Wormculler	England	U.S. States	Splendid	14 Aug 1829
Wm. J.	40	M	Gentleman	Jamaica	Jamaica	Emily Cook	10 Apr 1826
MURPY, Fras.	20	M	Labourer	Ireland	United States	Commerce	13 Jun 1828
Sarah	18	F		Ireland	United States	Commerce	13 Jun 1828
MURR, James	23	M	Mercht.	U.S.	U.S.	Toison	6 May 1828
MURRAY, —, Mrs.	26	F	Lady	St. Croix	on a Visit	Catharine	3 Sep 1821
...	...	...	...	Scotland	America	Nimrod	9 Jul 1827
Agnes	9	F				Governor Fenner	23 Jul 1829
Alex., Mr.	45		Gent.	England	returns to England	Mary	21 Sep 1821
Alexander	18/12	M				Governor Fenner	23 Jul 1829
Alexander Oliver	25		Taylor	Scotland	United States	Camillus	3 May 1828
Alexr.	22	M	Potter	Great Britain	United States	Atlantic	8 Dec 1827
Andrew	23	M	Merchant	Great Britian	New York	Diamond	13 Nov 1823
Ann	34	F	Wife	Scotland	America	Nimrod	9 Jul 1827
Ann, Mrs.	41	F	None	England	U. States	Radius	16 Mar 1822
Arthur	22	M	Labourer	Ireland	United States	William & George	14 May 1828
Barnard	38	M	...	Ireland	United States	Colossus	30 May 1825
Bridget	...6		Laboring Class		United States	Atlantic	2 Apr 1827
Bridget	19	F	Servant	Ireland	United States	Wilson	27 Jun 1826
Bridget	23	F	Seamstress	Great Britain	United States	Henrietta	19 Oct 1825
C.	20	M	Farmer	Ireland	U. States	Napolean	26 Sep 1828
Catharine	4	F				Governor Fenner	23 Jul 1829
Catharine	30	F				Governor Fenner	23 Jul 1829
Catharine	56 7/12	F	None	Scotland	America	Minerva	15 Jun 1825
Cathe.	35	F	Wife	...	U. States	New Orleans	24 Aug 1827
Catherine	30	F	Spinster	Ireland	United States	St. Michaels	7 Jun 1827
Charles	1	M	Child	...	U. States	New Orleans	24 Aug 1827
Charles	13	M	None	England	U. States	Radius	16 Mar 1822
Charles	28	M	Merchant	United States	United States	New Packet	20 Oct 1827
Chas.	26	M	Merchant	U. States	U. States	Ann	3 Oct 1826
Cornelius	34	M	Weaver	Ireland	United States	Catharine	22 Jul 1825
Danl.	23	M	Teacher	Ireland	United States	Trio	13 Jun 1827
Dolly	35	F		Ireland	U. States	Wanderer	1 Sep 1828
E.	21	M	Farmer	Ireland	U. States	New England	12 Apr 1825
E.	30	F		G. Britain	U. States	Hanford	10 Jun 1828

NAMES OF PASSENGERS	AGE	SEX	OCCUPATIONS	COUNTRY TO WHICH THEY BELONG	COUNTRY THEY INTEND TO INHABIT	SHIPS/DATES OF ARRIVAL	
MURRAY (cont'd)							
Edward	20	M	Labourer	Ireland	United S.	Hanford	19 Aug 1828
Edward	21 1/12	M		Ireland	America	Carolina Ann	7 Apr 1826
Edward	29	M	Weaver	England	United States	Bolivar	15 Jun 1826
Edward	29	M	Labourer	Ireland	United States	Hope	12 Jun 1828
Edwin	35	M	Musician	Great Britain	U. States	Columbia	22 Sep 1828
Elizabeth	2 6/12	F	None	Ireland	New York or Boston	Concordia	12 Oct 1826
Elizabeth	45	F	None	Ireland	New York or Boston	Concordia	12 Oct 1826
Geo.	30			Great Britan	United States	Newry	11 Jul 1827
Geo. W.	65	M	Merchant	New York	New York	Hudson	21 Aug 1829
George	11	M	None	England	U. States	Radius	16 Mar 1822
Gorge	23 5/12		Merchant	New York	U.S. of America	Helen	8 Feb 1822
Hannah	4	F	Servant	Ireland	U. States	Sarah G	7 May 1827
Henry	17	M	None	England	U. States	Radius	16 Mar 1822
Hugh	7	M	...	Scotland	America	Nimrod	9 Jul 1827
Hugh	29	M	Labourer	Great Britain	U. States	Superb	28 May 1821
J. B.	27	M	Whitesmith	France	U. States	Sully	24 Oct 1828
J. T.	28	M	Gent.	New Brunswick	New Brunswick	Columbia	31 Jul 1826
James		M	Miner	England		Iris	7 Dec 1827
James	21	M	Labourer	Ireland	United States	Clothier	22 Nov 1827
James	23	M	Merchant	Scotland	America	Minerva	8 Oct 1824
James	32	M	Carpenter	Ireland	United States	Cambria	3 Jul 1829
James	40	M	Weaver	Ireland	United States	Louisa	18 Apr 1827
Jane	19	F	Spinster	Ireland	United States	Trident	17 May 1825
Jane	20			Scotland	United States	Camillus	3 May 1828
Jas.	24	M	Labourer	Ireland	U. States	Two Marys	20 Apr 1825
Jess	19			Scotland	United States	Camillus	3 May 1828
Jno.	25	M	Merchant	Jenava	U. States	Mazzinghi	19 Feb 1823
John	...	...	...	Scotland	America	Nimrod	9 Jul 1827
John	19	F	None	England	U. States	Radius	16 Mar 1822
John	22	M		Ireland	U. States	St. Michael	27 Mar 1827
John	25 6/12	M	Shoe Maker	Scotland	America	Minerva	15 Jun 1825
John	26	M	Merchant	Scotland	U. States	Zepher	20 Oct 1827
John	27	M	Carpenter	Scotland	U. States	Camillus	17 Sep 1823
John	28	M	...	...	U.S. America	Columbia	26 Nov 1825
John	30	M	Weaver	England	Alexandria, U.S.	Roman	17 Oct 1826
John	32	M	Merchant	St. Johns	Great Britain	St. Michael	5 Jan 1826
John	61	M	...	Scotland	America	Nimrod	9 Jul 1827
Joseph	26 3/12	M	...	Ireland	Ireland	Wilson	16 Nov 1824
Katy	5	F	Child	Ireland	United States	St. Michaels	7 Jun 1827
Malcom	2	M	Labourer	Great Britain	U. States	Superb	28 May 1821
Margaret	22			Scotland	United States	Camillus	3 May 1828
Margaret	25	F	None	Ireland	United States	Trident	18 Jul 1827
Mary	6/12	F	Labourer	Great Britain	U. States	Superb	28 May 1821
Mary	9	F	Child	Ireland	United States	St. Michaels	7 Jun 1827
Mary	20	F	Spinster	Gt. Britain	U. States	Frances Henrietta	18 Apr 1825
Mary	22	F	Labourer	Great Britain	U. States	Superb	28 May 1821
Mary	24	F	None	Ireland	United States	Trident	18 Jul 1827
Mary Ann	1	F	None	Ireland	United States	Trident	18 Jul 1827
Mary Ann	16	F	Seamstress	Mayo	America	Margaret	31 Jul 1824
Mary Ann	16	F	Servant	Ireland	Ireland	Sarah G.	28 Nov 1827
Mary Ann	22	F	None	Ireland	New York or Boston	Concordia	12 Oct 1826
Michael	27	M		Ireland	United States	Thompson	12 Sep 1827
Michael	27	M	...conist	New York	New York	Colossus	2 Oct 1827
Michael	40	M	Farmer	...	U. States	New Orleans	24 Aug 1827
Ml.	19	M	Laborer	Ireland	United States	Trio	13 Jun 1827
O. C.	27	M	Mariner	U. States	U. States	Mohawk	18 Jun 1821
P.	20	M	Labourer	G. Britain	U. States	Hanford	18 Sep 1828
Pat	30	M	Labourer	G. Britain	U. States	Hanford	10 Jun 1828
Patk.	24					Trio	5 May 1828
Patric	28		Chandler	Carvan	N. York	Peru	30 May 1828
Patrick	7	M	Child	Ireland	United States	St. Michaels	7 Jun 1827
Patrick	18	M	Labourer	England	U. States	Hope & Esther	10 Jul 1827
Patrick	20	M	Laborer	Gt. Britain		Dalhouse Castle	13 May 1828
Patrick	27	M	Carpenter	Great Britain	United States	Mary Howland	19 Jul 1827
Peggy	22	F		G. Britain	U. States	Hanford	10 Jun 1828
Peter	21 4/12	M	School Master	Scotland	America	Minerva	15 Jun 1825
Peter	25	M	Farmer	Ireland	United States	Herald	7 Jun 1824

NAMES OF PASSENGERS	AGE	SEX	OCCUPATIONS	COUNTRY TO WHICH THEY BELONG	COUNTRY THEY INTEND TO INHABIT	SHIPS/DATES OF ARRIVAL	
MURRAY (cont'd)							
Phelix	24	M	Labourer	Great Britain	United States	Henrietta	19 Oct 1825
Robert	30	M	Baker	Scotland	New York	Governor Fenner	23 Jul 1829
Rose	25	F	Farmer	Ireland	U. States	Dickinson	30 Jul 1825
Susannah	2	F	Servant	Ireland	U. States	Sarah G	7 May 1827
Tereance	3	M	Child	...	U. States	New Orleans	24 Aug 1827
Thomas	4	M	None	Ireland	United States	Trident	18 Jul 1827
Thomas	30	M	Waiter	Ireland		Marchioness	13 May 1828
Thomas	34	M		Ireland	United States	William & George	14 May 1828
Thomas	35	M	Farmer	England	United States	Trident	18 Jul 1827
Thos.	20	M	Labourer	Great Britain	New York	Dublin	21 Dec 1824
Thos.	24	M	Blacksmith	Great Britain	United States	Aurora	5 Sep 1826
Thos.	33	M	Merchant	Scotland	on a Visit	Catharine	3 Sep 1821
W.	21	M	Sailor	Ireland	U. States	Prince Edward	5 Dec 1821
W. C.	30	M	Merchant	England	America	Silas Richard	24 Oct 1829
Walter	8	M	None	England	U. States	Radius	16 Mar 1822
William	...	M	...	Scotland	America	Nimrod	9 Jul 1827
William	23 2/12	M	Shoe Maker	Scotland	America	Minerva	15 Jun 1825
William	25	M	Mason	Scotland	New York	Governor Fenner	23 Jul 1829
William	29	M	Stone Mason	Ireland	U. States	Josephine	27 Jul 1825
Wm.	22		Sugar boiler			Zamoa	5 Nov 1828
MURREY, John	22	M	Labourer	Scotland	New York	Margaret	18 May 1825
MURRKRUN, Geo.	30	M	Butcher	Gt. Britain		Corinthian	27 Oct 1829
MURRON, Anto.	25	M	Merchant	Spain	Havana	Commodore Chauncy	28 Nov 1825
MURROW, James	40	M	Weaver	Great Britain	United States	Courier	26 Jun 1827
John	12	M	None	Great Britain	United States	Courier	26 Jun 1827
MURRY, —, Mr.				...	...	Laurel	16 Nov 1824
Alexander	22	M	Saddler	Sligo	Ireland	Helicon	3 Aug 1826
Ann	47	F	None	Ireland	New York	Angelica	18 Aug 1823
Bernard	20	M	Laborer	Ireland	United States	Fabius	4 Jun 1828
Bridget	3	F		G. Britan	U. States	William Neilson	26 Jul 1828
Catharine	30	F	Servant	Ireland	U. States	Sarah G	7 May 1827
Charles S.	28 4/12	M	Merchant	Scotland	Canada	Globe	3 Dec 1821
Daniel	25	M	Labourer	Ireland	United States	Enterprize	23 Jul 1827
Edward	26	M	Farmer	Ireland	United States	Trident	17 May 1825
Ellen	26	F		Ireland	U. States	Union	3 Jun 1822
James	1	M		Ireland	United States	Edwin	27 Oct 1828
John	3	M	Labourer	Ireland	United States	Edwin	27 Oct 1828
John	10	M	...	England	United States	Milton	20 Oct 1827
John	15	M	Labourer	Sligo	New York	Susquehana	27 Jun 1823
John	26	M	...	Ireland	U. States	Union	3 Jun 1822
John	36	M	Marener	U.N. States		Orient	9 Dec 1826
*sent Home by the Marican Counsell							
Louvana	5	M		G. Britan	U. States	William Neilson	26 Jul 1828
Margaret	1	F		G. Britan	U. States	William Neilson	26 Jul 1828
Margaret	22	F	None	Ireland	New York	Angelica	18 Aug 1823
Martha	26	F		G. Britan	U. States	William Neilson	26 Jul 1828
Mary	27	F		G. Britan	U. States	William Neilson	26 Jul 1828
Mary Ann	25 6/12	F	Houskeeper	England	United States	Manhattan	20 Feb 1826
Michael	7/12	M		England	United States	Manhattan	20 Feb 1826
Ned	30	M	Labourer	Ireland	United States	Edwin	27 Oct 1828
Patrick	14	M	None	Ireland	New York	Angelica	18 Aug 1823
Patrick	28	M	Labourer	Ireland	United States	Lord Wellington	28 May 1827
Patrick	50	M	Blacksmith	Ireland	New York	Angelica	18 Aug 1823
Richd.	25	M	Labourer	Ireland	United States	Edwin	27 Oct 1828
Robt.	16	M	Blacksmith	Ireland	New York	Angelica	18 Aug 1823
Rose	20	F	None	Ireland	New York	Angelica	18 Aug 1823
Rose	20	F	...	Ireland	United States	General Putnam	20 Jun 1825
Samuel	20	M	Farmer	Ireland	United States	Trident	17 May 1825
Thomas	20	M	Laboror	Ireland	United States	Wilson	27 Jun 1826
William	18	M	Blacksmith	Ireland	New York	Angelica	18 Aug 1823
William	24	M	Labourer	Scotland	New York	Eunice	13 Dec 1827
MURSAL, Robt.	14	M	Fishmonger			Comet	24 Dec 1821
MURTAGH, Daniel	25	M	Labourer	Ireland	United States	Ann Maria	8 Jun 1824
MURTAUGH, James	20	M	Farmer	Ireland	United States	Lord Strangford	20 Jun 1826
Mathew	35	M	Labourer	Ireland	U. States	Globe	14 Jul 1821
Patrick	20	M	Labourer	England	New York	America	1 Aug 1828

NAMES OF PASSENGERS	AGE	SEX	OCCUPATIONS	COUNTRY TO WHICH THEY BELONG	COUNTRY THEY INTEND TO INHABIT	SHIPS/DATES OF ARRIVAL	
MURTER, John	25	M	Labourer	Ireland	U. States	St. Michael	27 Mar 1827
MURTHA, Elisa	10	F	Child	Ireland	New York	Louisa	20 Jul 1826
Ellen	20	F	Dress Maker	Ireland	United States	William	20 Jul 1829
MURTOCK, Mary	8	F		Ireland	America	Mary	29 May 1827
MURTON, Jno.	22	M	Laborer	Ireland	United States	Weser	29 Jul 1823
John	19	M	Merchant	England	U. States	Cincinnatus	24 May 1821
Thos.	30	M		England		Henri IV	17 May 1828
MURTOUGH, Mary	20	F	Spinster	Ireland	United States	Dublin Packet	22 Apr 1822
MURTS, Joseph	35	M	Merchant	France	U. States	Bayard	9 Nov 1825
MURTUCGH, Owen	20	M	Labourer	Ireland	U. States	Loire	6 Dec 1827
MURY, James	26	M				Lady of the Lake	23 Aug 1828
*left ship							
MUSBAWMER, Jean Bets.	20	M	Weaver	Switzerland	U.S.	C. Amelia	30 Jun 1828
MUSE, John	52	M	Mariner	U. States	U. States	Atlas	24 Jun 1828
MUSEGANY, Diedrick	26	M	Baker	Bremen	U. States	Franklin	23 Sep 1828
MUSGANE, John	20	M	Merchant	G. Britain	U. States	Canada	19 Sep 1828
MUSGEON, Elizabeth	62	F	None	U.S.A.	U.S.A.	Silas Richards	29 Oct 1827
MUSGRAVE,							
Fredk. William	17	M	Gentleman	Great Brittain	U.S. America	York	4 Aug 1826
MUSHGROVE, —, Mr.	30	M		Massachusetts		York	8 Aug 1829
MUSNIEN, Oliver	30	M	Surgeon	France	France	Athenian	8 Jul 1828
MUSON, Sam. G.	31	M	Joiner	N. York	U. States	William	1 Apr 1822
MUSSEN, S. P.	30	M	Merchant	Bermuda	Bermuda	Sally Ann	11 Dec 1826
MUSSER, Sabinna	23	F		ober ambt Kenky	United States	Juffraw Johanna	16 Oct 1821
MUSSON, —, Miss	21 3/12	F		Bermuda	Bermuda	Florida	27 Aug 1825
—, Mrs.	27	F		Bermuda	U. States	Susan	2 Aug 1822
A.	14	M	Mercht.	Bermuda	U. States	Susan	2 Aug 1822
E. H.	16	F	Lady	Great Britain	U. States of Amer	Junius	5 Jul 1820
James	32	M	Mercht.	Bermuda	U. States	Susan	2 Aug 1822
James	60	M	Merchant	Great Britain	U. States of Amer	Junius	5 Jul 1820
James	64 11/12	M	Merchant of B...d.	Bermuda	Bermuda	Florida	27 Aug 1825
James	65	M	Merchant	Bermuda	Bermuda	Improvement	6 Jun 1826
S., Mrs.	40	F	Lady	Great Britain	U. States of Amer	Junius	5 Jul 1820
S., Mrs.	49	F		Bermuda	Bermuda	Florida	27 Aug 1825
MUSSOR, E. M., Miss	6	F		Bermuda		Friends Delight	5 Dec 1825
F. D., Miss	5	F		Bermuda		Friends Delight	5 Dec 1825
R. S., Mrs.	23	F		Bermuda		Friends Delight	5 Dec 1825
Rob. S.	27	M	Merchant	Bermuda		Friends Delight	5 Dec 1825
MUSTER, Elizabeth	8	F		England	U. States	Cincinnatus	24 May 1821
Francis	30	M		G. Britan	U. States	William Neilson	26 Jul 1828
Jane	7	F		England	U. States	Cincinnatus	24 May 1821
Laurance	26	M		G. Britan	U. States	William Neilson	26 Jul 1828
Robert	41	M	Physician	England	U. States	Cincinnatus	24 May 1821
Sarah	29	F		England	U. States	Cincinnatus	24 May 1821
Thomas	23	M		G. Britan	U. States	William Neilson	26 Jul 1828
Thos.	10	M	Lad	England	U. States	Cincinnatus	24 May 1821
MUSTERSON, Bridget	24	F	Servant	Ireland	United States	Josephine	30 Apr 1828
MUTCHEAD, Edwd.	50	M	Laborer	Brittain	U. States	Manhattan	25 Dec 1820
MUTER, Ann	6	F		England	U. States	Cincinnatus	24 May 1821
Elen	3	F		England	U. States	Cincinnatus	24 May 1821
Robt.	1	M		England	U. States	Cincinnatus	24 May 1821
Sarah	5	F		England	U. States	Cincinnatus	24 May 1821
MUTHARNN, Ann		F	Chiefly farmers		United States	Factor	8 Jul 1829
MUTHWILL, Philip	53	M	Confectionary	Germany	United States	Germania	29 Aug 1828
MUTILLA, —	32	F		Bermuda	U. States	Agnes	1 Jul 1825
MUTLER, Josannes	26	M	Labourer	France	America, U.N.S.	Great Britain	3 Aug 1829
MUTTER, Edward	47	M	Farmer	England	U. States	Cincinnatus	24 May 1821
John	22	M	Baker	Argyle (Tedland) Scotland	United States	Jean Hastie	27 Jul 1829
Thos.	20	M	Labourer	Argyle (Tedland) Scotland	United States	Jean Hastie	27 Jul 1829
MUTTON, Ann	30	F		Great Brit.	Ohio	Gov. Griswald	3 Jul 1820
Caroline	2	F		Great Brit.	Ohio	Gov. Griswald	3 Jul 1820
Mary	6	F		Great Brit.	Ohio	Gov. Griswald	3 Jul 1820
Samuel	30	M		Great Brit.	Ohio	Gov. Griswald	3 Jul 1820
MUTZGER, John	18	M	Merchant	Ireland		Quatre Freres	29 Jul 1828
Joseph	50	M	Merchant	Ireland		Quatre Freres	29 Jul 1828

NAMES OF PASSENGERS	AGE	SEX	OCCUPATIONS	COUNTRY TO WHICH THEY BELONG	COUNTRY THEY INTEND TO INHABIT	SHIPS/DATES OF ARRIVAL	
MUTZGER (cont'd)							
Susan	53	M	Merchant	Ireland		Quatre Freres	29 Jul 1828
MUXLON, Agnes	9/12	F		Great Britain	United States	Diana	30 Oct 1827
Eliz. Mary	27	F		Great Britain	United States	Diana	30 Oct 1827
Mary	2 6/12	F		Great Britain	United States	Diana	30 Oct 1827
Thomas	26	M	Mason	Great Britain	United States	Diana	30 Oct 1827
William Tyler	3	M		Great Britain	United States	Diana	30 Oct 1827
MYATT, Joseph	42	M	Potter	England	United States	Andes	2 Oct 1828
MYCOCK, George	27	M	Tailor	England	United States	Lord Wellington	14 Nov 1827
MYER, Frest	35	F		France	U. States	Edward Bonaffe	23 Jul 1828
Hy.	8	M	Farmer	United States	United States	Seine	21 Oct 1822
Jaleph	29	M	Farmer	France	U. States	Edward Bonaffe	23 Jul 1828
James J.	18	M	Merchant	United States	U.S. of America	Friends	25 Sep 1823
John	6	M		France	U. States	Edward Bonaffe	23 Jul 1828
John	36	M	Farmer	France	U. States	Edward Bonaffe	23 Jul 1828
Joseph	21	M		Great Brittian	United States	Carolina Augusta	2 Dec 1828
Mariah L.	1 5/12	F	Farmer	Switzerland	U. States	France	26 Jun 1828
Maryon	9	F		France	U. States	Edward Bonaffe	23 Jul 1828
Mathias	45	M	Farmer	Holland	U. States	Don Quixote	25 Oct 1828
Mathis	35 4/12	M	Farmer	Switzerland	U. States	France	26 Jun 1828
Nicolie	4 5/12	M	Farmer	Switzerland	U. States	France	26 Jun 1828
Sopha	3 5/12	F	Farmer	Switzerland	U. States	France	26 Jun 1828
Theo	7 3/12	M	Farmer	Switzerland	U. States	France	26 Jun 1828
Theo	24 5/12	M	Farmer	Switzerland	U. States	France	26 Jun 1828
MYERS, Angel	2	M		England	U. States	Hudson	21 Aug 1829
Anne	25	F				Imperial	19 Jul 1820
Antony	8	M		France	Canada	Abby Jones	12 Jul 1827
Antony	38	M	Farmer	France	Canada	Abby Jones	12 Jul 1827
Briget	9	F	Farmer, Labourer or Spinster	Ireland	U. States	Meteor	4 Oct 1827
Catharine	28	F		France	Canada	Abby Jones	12 Jul 1827
Chas. G.	26	M	Gentleman	G. Britain	U. States	Nassau	30 Jun 1824
Christian	26 8/12	M	Sugar Refiner	Germany	U.S. American	Criterion	7 Jul 1824
Christian	46	M	Servant	France	U. States	Lewis	6 Jul 1825
D.	42	M	Mariner	Charleston, S.C.	U. States	Elba	21 May 1825
Eliza	4	F		England	U. States	Hudson	21 Aug 1829
Eliza	17	F		Charleston, S.C.	U. States	Elba	21 May 1825
Elizabeth	25	F	Lady my Wife [David, Master of Amiable Matilda]	U.S.	U. States	Amiable Matilda	28 Sep 1822
Hester	24	F		England	U. States	Hudson	21 Aug 1829
Hy.	27	M	Mariner	Pensylvania	New York	Charleston	1 Aug 1825
James	38	M	Farmer			Imperial	19 Jul 1820
John	1	M		France	Canada	Abby Jones	12 Jul 1827
John	12	M		Philadelphia	U. States	Howard	25 Jul 1823
John	20	M	Glass Cutter	England	New York	Hudson	20 Nov 1828
John	21	M	Merchant	England	Canada	Brighton	11 Mar 1825
John	30		Gent.	England	America	Cosmo	17 Mar 1828
Joseph	6	M		France	Canada	Abby Jones	12 Jul 1827
Lawrence	19		Merchant	England	England	Hudson	18 Jun 1825
Lawrence	21	M	Gentn.	England	New York	Brighton	16 Nov 1826
Lawrence	22	M	Merchant	England	U. States	Hudson	8 Oct 1827
Lazarus	29	M	Jeweller	Germany	United States	Meteor	19 Aug 1829
Nelly	23	F		Ireland	United States	Sarah G.	15 May 1828
Stephen	45	M	Farmer			Imperial	19 Jul 1820
Thos.	26		Gent.			Cosmo	17 Mar 1828
Wolfe Solomon	19	M	Gent.	England	New York	Cortes	23 Nov 1827
MYETT, Richard	37	M	Moulder	England	U.S. America	New Hampshire	28 Sep 1826
MYGUER, Mary	28	F	Labourer	Ireland	U. States	Bellville	14 May 1827
MYHALFY, John	30	M	Shoemaker	Ireland	New York	Colossus	2 Oct 1827
MYLCON, Price	30	M		Ireland	United States	Nancy R. Crowell	21 Sep 1822
MYLNE, Joseph	21 11/12	M	Taylor	England	New York	Concordia	12 Oct 1826
Mary Ann	19 1/12	F	None	England	New York	Concordia	12 Oct 1826
William	22	M	Merchant	England	England	Britannia	5 Nov 1828
MYNER, John	25	M	Weaver	Ireland	United States	Trident	18 Jul 1827
MYRA, A. R.	27	M	Gentleman	Goverment of Columbia	U. States	Charles	15 Oct 1822

NAMES OF PASSENGERS	A G E	S E X	OCCUPATIONS	COUNTRY TO WHICH THEY BELONG	COUNTRY THEY INTEND TO INHABIT	SHIPS/DATES OF ARRIVAL	
MYRA (cont'd)							
Maria A.	7	F		Goverment of Columbia	U. States	Charles	15 Oct 1822
MYRICH, J.	28	M	Seaman	U. States	U. States	Ranger	2 Jul 1827
MYRICK, Charles	30	M	Merchant	United States	United States	Otter	25 Feb 1822
Chas.		M	Mariner	Nantucket	U. States	Nancy	16 May 1823
Chas.	33	M	Mercht.	New York	U. States	Catherine	4 Sep 1824
Freeman	20	M	Mariner	United States	United States	Tandem	8 Mar 1826
J.	53	M	Mariner	Philada.	U. States	Henry	24 Apr 1821
Saml.	40	M	Mariner	U. States	U. States	New York	14 Feb 1826
MYS, Horae	21	F	None	France	U. States	Sully	25 Jun 1828
M.	24	M	Farmer	France	U. States	Sully	25 Jun 1828
N..., David	...	...	...	Ireland	United States	General Putnam	20 Jun 1825
Henry	32	M	Physician	U.S.	U.S.	Cadmus	9 Dec 1826
Peter	21	M	Labourer	Great Britain	United States	Atlantic	28 May 1827
Susan ...	...			F.../London	Newjersey	Venus	12 Apr 1821
N...AUR, Ulrich	26	M	Weaver	Switzerland	United States	Elbe	2 Aug 1822
NA...LE, Christopher	28	M	Farmer	Great Britain	United States	Freake	25 Jun 1827
NAAR, David	28	M	Merchant	St. Thomas	Denmark	Chase	5 Jul 1825
NAB, Carl	11	M		France	United States	New England	29 Aug 1828
Madam	8	F		France	United States	New England	29 Aug 1828
NABB, Sarah, Mrs.	21	F		Maryland, Bal. Cy.	U. States	Imperial	23 Oct 1826
NABE, Larenza	29	M	Mercht.	Havama	United States	Brown	26 Apr 1826
NADEN, Mary	63	F		G. Brittain	U. States	Rockingham	17 May 1821
Sarah	14	F		G. Brittain	U. States	Rockingham	17 May 1821
NADOLES, Gomez	30	M	Gent.	Spain	Havana	Olive Branch	28 Aug 1828
NAEFF, Jn.	28	M	Distiller	Holland	United States	Wilmot	14 Mar 1820
NAFF, Barbara	3	F		France	United States	Globe	30 Aug 1828
Barbara	28	F		France	United States	Globe	30 Aug 1828
Catharine	5	F		France	United States	Globe	30 Aug 1828
Jacob	38	M	Weaver	France	United States	Globe	30 Aug 1828
Marian	6	F		France	United States	Globe	30 Aug 1828
NAFNIGER, Danl.	25	M	Farmer	Hessian-Germany	Canada	Caesar	8 Sep 1828
NAGEL, —, Mr.	28	M	Farmer	Germany	U. States	Anna Doreatha	5 Mar 1822
NAGELY, James	22	M	Laborer	Ireland	United States	St. Michael	21 Aug 1824
NAGHEL, Francis	42	M	Mariner	United States	United States	Bordeaux	25 Mar 1823
George	40	M	Merchant	N. York	U. States	Ann Maria	6 Jul 1824
John C.	15	M	Student	U.S.	U.S.	Edward Quesnel	3 Jul 1829
NAGLE, Bridget	11			Ireland	United States	Geo. Canning	5 Jun 1828
Edmond	9					Trio	5 May 1828
Ja...	...	M	Labourer	...	U. States	New Orleans	24 Aug 1827
Margt.	19		Farmer	Ireland	U. States	Schuylkill	22 Aug 1825
Mary	15		Farmer	Ireland	U. States	Schuylkill	22 Aug 1825
P.	22	M	Gentleman	Cork	U. States	Justina	29 Jul 1822
Wm.	24	M	Farmer	Ireland	America	Liverpool	31 Aug 1827
NAGTON, Andrew	37	M	Merchant	Ireland	U. States	Jefferson	7 Aug 1820
NAHAN, Ellen	4	F		Ireland	United S.	Hanford	19 Aug 1828
John	3/12	M		Bluenase	United S.	Hanford	19 Aug 1828
Margaret	25	F		Ireland	United S.	Hanford	19 Aug 1828
Mary	3/12	F		Bluenase	United S.	Hanford	19 Aug 1828
NAIL, Dennis	13	M		England	United States	Ganges	10 May 1828
Mary	8	F		England	United States	Ganges	10 May 1828
Michl.	10	M		England	United States	Ganges	10 May 1828
Thos.	6	M		England	United States	Ganges	10 May 1828
Thos.	40	M	Blacksmith	England	United States	Ganges	10 May 1828
NALBER, P.	49	M	Planter	France	France	Circassian	13 Jun 1825
NALES, Ellen	30	F		Great Britain	America	Lady Gallatin	21 Jun 1820
George	24	M	Clerk	Great Britain	America	Lady Gallatin	21 Jun 1820
Sarah	10	F		Great Britain	America	Lady Gallatin	21 Jun 1820
NALIS, Thomas	20	M	Labourer	Ireland	U.S.	Lady Hunter	10 Jul 1826
NALLERLY, James	28	M	Soap Boiler	U. States	U. States	St. Croix	13 Sep 1827
NANAHAN, Wm.	30	M	Farmer	England	United States	Ganges	10 May 1828
NANCE, James	15	M	Tailor	Ireland	United States	Josephine	30 Apr 1828
NANCY, Margarete	28	F	Farmer	Ireland	U. States	Dickinson	30 Jul 1825
NANGUINE, John	35	M	Mariner	Great Brittan	United States	Euphrates	12 Mar 1824
NANKINS, George	23	M	Sugar Baker	Germany	U.S.	Robert Edwards	11 Nov 1822

NAMES OF PASSENGERS	AGE	SEX	OCCUPATIONS	COUNTRY TO WHICH THEY BELONG	COUNTRY THEY INTEND TO INHABIT	SHIPS/DATES OF ARRIVAL	
NANNNY, William	18	M	Labourer	Ireland	United States	Nancy Henrietta	3 Nov 1828
NANOMAN, James	22	M	Butcher	G. Britain	U. States	Dalhouse Castle	12 Sep 1828
NANTZ, Joseph	34	M	Sevant	Flanders	Great Britan	Columbia	11 Aug 1823
NAPFLE, Balthasar	25	M	Farmer	Swisserland	United States	Montano	13 Jan 1826
NAPIER, —, Mr.	34	M	Mariner	U. States	U. States	Laura Ann	25 May 1822
Geo.	26	M	Slater	England	U. States	Pacific	17 Jun 1828
George	25	M	Farmer	Scotland	U. States of America	Dale	14 Mar 1828
John, Mr.	39	M	Merchant	U.S. America	U.S. America	James Cropper	14 Mar 1828
Wm.	40	M	Mariner	U. States	United States	Swiftsure	14 Apr 1828
Wm. Brydie	25	M	Merchant	United States	United States	Cortes	11 Aug 1823
NAPTHA, Jno., Jr.	25	M	Merchant	U. States	U. States	Robert Edwards	25 Apr 1821
NAPWORTH, Joseph	23	M	Weaver			Eliza Jane	12 Sep 1820
NARD, M.	30	M	Labourer	Ireland	U. States	Sarah G	30 Jun 1828
NAREVILL, Thoms.	25	M	Merchant	United States	U. States	Ann Marria	6 Aug 1823
NARMAN, R.	22	F		U. States	U. States	Alfred	26 Apr 1828
NARR, R.	26	M	Merchant	England	U. States	Caseo	26 Apr 1828
Sarrah Maria	5	F		C...	U. States	Agness	23 Jun 1827
NARRANTOS, M. Vallez	23	M	Merchant	Colombia	U. States	Athenian	18 Oct 1826
NASACA, J.	36	M		Spain	U. States	Napolean	2 Sep 1828
NASEARE, Gaetano	28	M	Domestic	Switzerland	U. States	Edward Quesnel	4 Aug 1828
NASH, Agathe	20	F		France	U. States	Danube	21 Nov 1826
Elisabeth	35	F		Great Britain	U. States	Ganges	21 Jun 1827
Hannah	4 6/12	F	Child	England	United States	Cambria	3 Jul 1829
John	3	M		Great Britain	U. States	Ganges	21 Jun 1827
John	3 6/12	M	Child	England	United States	Cambria	3 Jul 1829
Joseph	28	M	Cloth dresser	England	United States	Maria	12 May 1823
Joseph	34	M	Manufacturer	Great Britain	U. States	Ganges	21 Jun 1827
Joshua	32	M	Gentleman	United States	United States	Brighton	12 Jun 1826
Lewis	22	M		France	U. States	Danube	21 Nov 1826
Mary	20		Laborer	Ireland	America	Parrington	9 Jun 1827
Mary	32	F	Farmer	England	U. States	Acasta	21 Oct 1825
Maryann	6	F		Great Britain	U. States	Ganges	21 Jun 1827
Richd.	2	M	Child	England	United States	Cambria	3 Jul 1829
Robart	...		Sheomaker	America	New York	Rufus King	3 Sep 1822
Sarah	30	F	Wife	England	United States	Cambria	3 Jul 1829
Stephen	35	M	Farmer	England	United States	Cambria	3 Jul 1829
William	6/12	M	Child	England	United States	Cambria	3 Jul 1829
NASHE, Henry	25	M	Farmer	England	England	Venus	15 Apr 1822
James	40	M	Farmer	England	England	Venus	15 Apr 1822
NAST, Wilhelm	20 6/12	M	Labourer	Germany	America	Falcon	28 Aug 1828
NASTLAND, Benjamin	16	M	Army			Amity	11 Sep 1820
NATERA, A.	31	M	Mercht.	Spain	Spain	Juliana	2 Sep 1826
NATHAN, Daniel	27	M	Currier			Plato	31 Oct 1829
NAUNCE, Poer	33	M	Sugar Refiner	France	United States	Cortes	18 Oct 1820
NAVARRO, Bernardo M.	22	M	Merchant	Spain	New York	Abeona	20 Dec 1823
NAVELSMITH, Francisco	30	M	Smith	Germany	United States	Samuel Robertson	8 Aug 1828
George	23	M	Smith	Germany	United States	Samuel Robertson	8 Aug 1828
Maria	1	F		Germany	United States	Samuel Robertson	8 Aug 1828
NAVES, A.	18	M	Servant	G. Britain	U. States	La Plata	6 Jun 1828
NAY, Jane, Mis	24	F		England		Hudson	23 Jul 1828
NAYLOR, —, Capt.	40	M	...:	...	...	Cuba	25 Mar 1823
Ben	1	M	None	England	U. States	Thomas Ritchie	2 Jul 1827
Chs.	21	M	Farmer	Great Brittan	U. States	Gem	26 Jul 1827
George	30	M				Lady of the Lake	23 Aug 1828
*left ship							
Jno.	32	M	Sawyer	England	U. States	Thomas Ritchie	2 Jul 1827
Love	4	F				Lady of the Lake	23 Aug 1828
*left ship							
Maria	30	F	None	England	U. States	Thomas Ritchie	2 Jul 1827
Sampson	20 10/12	M	Carpenter	England	United States	London	6 Feb 1829
Susan	2	F				Lady of the Lake	23 Aug 1828
*left ship							

NAMES OF PASSENGERS	AGE	SEX	OCCUPATIONS	COUNTRY TO WHICH THEY BELONG	COUNTRY THEY INTEND TO INHABIT	SHIPS/DATES OF ARRIVAL	
NAYLOR (cont'd)							
Susan	30	F				Lady of the Lake	23 Aug 1828
*left ship							
Wm.	2	M	None	England	U. States	Thomas Ritchie	2 Jul 1827
NAYTON, Etienne	21	M	Merchant	France	Neworleans	Danube	20 Jul 1826
NAZDEY, William	30	M	Farmer	Great Britian	United States	Andes	19 Aug 1829
NAZER, Jno.	7	M		Switzerland	America	Saluda	16 Oct 1824
Joseph	8	M		Switzerland	America	Saluda	16 Oct 1824
Joseph	40	M	Weaver	Switzerland	America	Saluda	16 Oct 1824
Tracy	28	F		France	America	Saluda	16 Oct 1824
NE..., Jacob	20	M	Farmer	Switzerland	United States	Elbe	2 Aug 1822
NE...LL, John	23	M	Shoemaker	Ireland	U. States	Josephine	7 May 1827
Peter	18	M	Labourer	Ireland	U. States	Josephine	7 May 1827
NEAGAL, Rhoda	30	F	Lady	St. John	St. John	Ann Maria	5 May 1824
NEAGLE, R.	20		Farmer	Cork	New York	Schuylkill	22 Aug 1825
NEAL, Allen	26		Labourer	England	United States	Hugh Johnson	11 Jun 1828
Ann	20	F	Spinster	Ireland	United States	Fabius	4 Jun 1828
Chas.	30		Labourer	England	United States	Hugh Johnson	11 Jun 1828
Elenaner	24	F	Servant	Ireland	America	Carolina Ann	7 Aug 1826
Francis	30	M	Mariner	U. States		General Brewer	9 Dec 1825
Henry	24	M	Cabinet Maker	England	United States	Andes	2 Oct 1828
James	3/12	M	Servant	Ireland	America	Carolina Ann	7 Aug 1826
James	16			England	United States	Hugh Johnson	11 Jun 1828
James	24	M	Servant	Ireland	America	Carolina Ann	7 Aug 1826
John	2			W...	...	Hudson	14 Jun 1827
John	5		Labourer	England	United States	Hugh Johnson	11 Jun 1828
John	27		Painter	W...	...	Hudson	14 Jun 1827
John	30	M	Merchant	Irish	United States	Patriots Eagle	30 Oct 1829
M.	24	F	Servant	Ireland	U. States	Courier	31 Jul 1828
M.	34	M	Servant	Ireland	U. States	Courier	31 Jul 1828
Patrick	2	M	Child	Ireland	United States	Robert Fulton	24 Jul 1826
Rachael	27			W...	...	Hudson	14 Jun 1827
Thomas	28		Labourer	England	United States	Hugh Johnson	11 Jun 1828
W. H.	30	M	Merchant	U.S.A.	U.S.A.	Bayard	25 Aug 1829
NEALE, Ann	15		Child	London	England	London	13 Dec 1822
Ann	23	F		Ireland	U.S.A.	Hudson	21 Aug 1829
Biddy	15	F		U. States	U. States	United States	11 Sep 1828
Caroline	6		Child	London	England	London	13 Dec 1822
Charles	2	M	None	Great Britain	United States	John	6 Oct 1820
Charles	9		Child	London	England	London	13 Dec 1822
Charles	46	M	Engine Maker	Great Britain	United States	John	6 Oct 1820
George	21		Gardiner	London	England	London	13 Dec 1822
Hannah	1			W...	...	Hudson	14 Jun 1827
Hannah	2		Child	London	England	London	13 Dec 1822
Harriett	12		Child	London	England	London	13 Dec 1822
Henry	7	M	None	Great Britain	United States	John	6 Oct 1820
James	32 2/12	M	Farmer	England	United States	Nimrod	28 Apr 1824
John	8	M	None	Great Britain	United States	John	6 Oct 1820
Mary	28	F	None	United States	Virginia	Brighton	19 Aug 1829
Matilda	12	F		England	New Jersey	Hudson	20 Nov 1828
Richard	4		Child	London	England	London	13 Dec 1822
Robert	14		Child	London	England	London	13 Dec 1822
Sarah	36	F	None	Great Britain	United States	John	6 Oct 1820
Sarah	40			Southwalk	England	London	13 Dec 1822
Susan	5	F	None	Great Britain	United States	John	6 Oct 1820
William	40		Gardiner	Hertford	England	London	13 Dec 1822
NEALES, Frances	18	M	Family [of Frances]	G. Brittian	United States	Louisa	14 Jun 1825
Frances	50	M	Gentleman	G. Brittian	United States	Louisa	14 Jun 1825
John	5 7/12	M	Family [of Frances]	G. Brittian	United States	Louisa	14 Jun 1825
Margaret	24	F	Family [of Frances]	G. Brittian	United States	Louisa	14 Jun 1825
Mary	40	F	Family [of Frances]	G. Brittian	United States	Louisa	14 Jun 1825
NEALY, George W.	30	M	Labourer	Ireland	United States	Hesperus	14 Feb 1820
NEAN, Stephan	34	M	Labourer	England	U. States	Ayrshire	12 May 1828
NEARVERCELT, John George	24 8/12	M	Sugar Baker	Zurig	United States	Mercury	8 Jun 1825
NEARY, B.	14	F		Ireland	U. States	Wanderer	30 Sep 1828
John	20	M		Ireland	United States	Thompson	12 Sep 1827
P.	29	M	Farmer	Farmer	U. States	Wilson	2 Sep 1823

944

NAMES OF PASSENGERS	AGE	SEX	OCCUPATIONS	COUNTRY TO WHICH THEY BELONG	COUNTRY THEY INTEND TO INHABIT	SHIPS/DATES OF ARRIVAL	
NEAVEN, Patk.	45	M	Farmer	Scotland	United States	Loire	26 May 1828
NEBLOCK, A.	6		Farmer	Ireland	United States	Courier	16 May 1825
A.	48		Farmer	Ireland	United States	Courier	16 May 1825
J.	9		Farmer	Ireland	United States	Courier	16 May 1825
J.	11		Farmer	Ireland	United States	Courier	16 May 1825
M.	...		Farmer	Ireland	United States	Courier	16 May 1825
M.	49		Farmer	Ireland	United States	Courier	16 May 1825
W.	13		Farmer	Ireland	United States	Courier	16 May 1825
NEBOR, H.	26	M	Sugar Baker	Ireland	U. States	Frederick	2 Apr 1828
NECED, James	26	M	Labourer	Ireland	United States	William & Henry	19 Jul 1822
NEDLET, —, Mrs.	75	F		France	France	Henri IV	14 Sep 1827
NEEDES, Richd.	32		Merchant			Cincinnatus	17 May 1823
NEEDHAM, John	34	M	Gentleman	Ireland	England	Athenian	8 Jul 1828
John, of Baltimore	25	M	Printer	England	America	Mary Lord	26 Oct 1829
NEEDS, Elizabeth	24	F	None	England	New York	Brighton	16 Nov 1826
*Died on Board							
Thomas	3/12	M	None	England	New York	Brighton	16 Nov 1826
William	3	M	None	England	New York	Brighton	16 Nov 1826
NEELEN, Jos.	25	M	Brewer	Germany	United States	Lydia	18 Jun 1828
NEELLY, William	23	M	Labourer	Ireland	U. States	Atlantic	19 Aug 1825
NEESAM, Bridget	34	F	None	Ireland	United States	Jubilee	13 Jul 1829
Charles	5	M	None	Ireland	United States	Jubilee	13 Jul 1829
Elizabeth	12	F	None	Ireland	United States	Jubilee	13 Jul 1829
Hugh	4	M	None	Ireland	United States	Jubilee	13 Jul 1829
James	34	M	Farmer	Ireland	United States	Jubilee	13 Jul 1829
Mary	6	F	None	Ireland	United States	Jubilee	13 Jul 1829
Patrick	9	M	None	Ireland	United States	Jubilee	13 Jul 1829
William	1	M	None	Ireland	United States	Jubilee	13 Jul 1829
NEF, Nicolas	28	M	Merchant	France	U. States	Edward Bopnnaffe	30 Jul 1829
NEGASIA, Padro Lucas	20	M	Merchant	Havana	Havana	Mercator	24 Mar 1826
NEGLIS, Fraz Joseph	46	M	Farmer	France	United States	New England	29 Aug 1828
NEGMEIGER, Adrian	1 6/12	M		Switzerland	U. States	Hewes	30 Oct 1829
Anton	7	M		Switzerland	U. States	Hewes	30 Oct 1829
Catharine	23	F	Wife	Switzerland	U. States	Hewes	30 Oct 1829
Christopher	26	M	Weaver	Switzerland	U. States	Hewes	30 Oct 1829
Elizabeth	15	F		Switzerland	U. States	Hewes	30 Oct 1829
Gabriel	3	M		Switzerland	U. States	Hewes	30 Oct 1829
Gorch	9	M		Switzerland	U. States	Hewes	30 Oct 1829
Ingnathe	10	M		Switzerland	U. States	Hewes	30 Oct 1829
Jacob	4	M		Switzerland	U. States	Hewes	30 Oct 1829
Johannes	8	M		Switzerland	U. States	Hewes	30 Oct 1829
Joseph	5	M		Switzerland	U. States	Hewes	30 Oct 1829
Lioborld	1	M		Switzerland	U. States	Hewes	30 Oct 1829
Marian	3	F		Switzerland	U. States	Hewes	30 Oct 1829
Philip	44	M	Weaver	Switzerland	U. States	Hewes	30 Oct 1829
Ragina	38	F	his Wife [Philip]	Switzerland	U. States	Hewes	30 Oct 1829
NEGRA, A. P.	54	M	Merchant	Rio Grande	Rio Grande	Wm. Tell	22 Jul 1828
NEGRUN, Josephine	32	F	Nurse	France	San Domingo	Victory	29 May 1821
NEGUS, Edw.	40	M	Gentleman	England	United States	Robert Edwards	3 Oct 1829
NEIDHURT, Charles	16	M		Wirtenberg	America	Henry	19 Jun 1825
NEIL, A. F.	38	M	Merchant	Port au Prince	New York	Jean Baptiste	11 Aug 1828
Ann	34	F		County of Cork, Ireland	New York City	Thorny Close	3 May 1826
Con.	26	M	Farm	Ireland	U. States	Meteor	19 Jul 1828
Elisabeth	28	F		England	United States	Nancy Henrietta	3 Nov 1828
Elizabeth	36	F		Switzerland	U. States	Robert Edward	2 Nov 1827
Eugine	18					Trio	5 May 1828
Frances	32	F		Switzerland	U. States	Robert Edward	2 Nov 1827
Frederich	35	M	Mariner	United States	United States	Delta	24 Oct 1829
Henry D.	35	M	Surgeon	England	United States	Nancy Henrietta	3 Nov 1828
Hugh	25	M	Farmer	Scotland	United States	Commerce	17 Jul 1823
James	21	M	Farmer	Ireland	United States	Fabius	4 Jun 1828
James	30	M	Mason	Ireland	United States	Hannah Eliza	23 Sep 1826
James	34 2/12	M	Merchant	Ireland	Ireland	Express	25 Sep 1827
Jas.	20	M	Farmer	Switzerland	U. States	Robert Edward	2 Nov 1827
John B.	32	M	Merchant	U. States	U. States	Fabius	30 Aug 1827
Timothy	30	M	Weaver	England	United States	Roman	12 Jun 1826

NAMES OF PASSENGERS	AGE	SEX	OCCUPATIONS	COUNTRY TO WHICH THEY BELONG	COUNTRY THEY INTEND TO INHABIT	SHIPS/DATES OF ARRIVAL	
NEIL (cont'd)							
Wm. H.	26	M	Merchant	U. States	U. States	York	10 Dec 1825
NEILL, David	28	M	Mason	Scotland	U. States	Camillus	27 Jun 1826
NEILLY, James	17	M	Farmer	G.B.	U.S.A.	Silas Richard	30 Jun 1828
Martha	38	F	Spinster	Ireland	United States	Trident	17 May 1825
Owen	18	M	Farmer	G.B.	U.S.A.	Silas Richard	30 Jun 1828
Saml.	13	M	Boy	Ireland	United States	Trident	17 May 1825
Wm.	17	M	Tailor	Great Britain	United States	William Dawson	18 Jun 1827
NEILSON, Alexander	26	M	Labourer	Scotland	United States	Mary & Susan	5 Aug 1828
Alexander	34	M	Merchant	Scotland		Edward Quesnel	17 Nov 1828
E. H.	21	M	Merchant	New York	New York	Herald	13 Mar 1826
Eliza	22	F	Wife	Scotland	America	Camillus	12 Sep 1822
John	47	M		United States	United States	Canada	20 Jun 1823
Margaret	1	F	Child	Scotland	America	Camillus	12 Sep 1822
Peter	26	M	Merchant	Scotland	America	Camillus	12 Sep 1822
William D.	37	M	Physian	Scotland	U. States	York	4 Apr 1826
William S.	30		Merchant	United States	United States	Emilia	25 Aug 1828
Wm.	46	M	Merchant	England	U. States	New York	11 Jul 1823
NEILY, Robt.	23	M	Watch Maker	Ireland	New York	Trusty	12 Sep 1828
NEINE, Elizabeth	54	F		England	United States	Acosta	28 Jul 1823
Hannah E.	21	F		England	United States	Acosta	28 Jul 1823
NEISDALE, Mary	20	F		Ireland	U. States	Adno	5 Jul 1828
NEITHARLING,							
Caroline Elisab.	12	F	Farmer	Wortenberg	Lancaster	Louisa	6 Oct 1828
Christine Frederica	3 2/12	F	Farmer	Wortenberg	Lancaster	Louisa	6 Oct 1828
John Tobin	0 10/12	M	Farmer	Wortenberg	Lancaster	Louisa	6 Oct 1828
Margaretha							
Magdalena	5	F	Farmer	Wortenberg	Lancaster	Louisa	6 Oct 1828
NEITO, A.	20	M	Servant	Scotland	Columbia	Abigail	25 Feb 1826
NEIVES, Marie	34	F	Lady	New York	New York	Native	30 Jun 1826
NEKELE, Margt.	30	F		France	United States	New England	29 Aug 1828
NELIS, Bridget	23	F	Spinster	Ireland	United States	Robert Fulton	24 Jul 1826
NELLA, Giovanni	32	M	Mercht.	Italy	U. States	Aerial	10 Nov 1825
NELLAFURTE, Jos.	28	M	Merchant	Spain	Spain	Iris	3 Jul 1828
NELLING, —, Mrs.	22	F		England	United States	Loire	6 Jul 1821
NELLIS, Jno.	20	M	Weaver	Ireland	U. States	Atlantic	7 Aug 1823
NELLY, Louis C. L.	31	M	Merchant	Gaudaloupe	Gaudaloupe	Henry	10 Oct 1820
NELM, Susan	77	F	...	Ireland	United States	Carolina Ann	24 Oct 1825
NELMASS, Saml.	25	M	Merchant	Turks Island		Mary	3 Aug 1825
NELSON, —, Mr.	50	M	Gentleman	Great Britain	Great Britain	Visitor	30 Jun 1825
Agness	20	F	Wife	Glasgow	U.S. America	Camillus	10 Sep 1821
Alexander	20	M	Labourer	Ireland	United States	Fabius	31 Jul 1829
Allan	2	M		Scotland	United States	Camillus	9 May 1827
Ann	6	F		Scotland	United States	Camillus	9 May 1827
Ann	36	F		Scotland	United States	Camillus	9 May 1827
B. D.		M	Merchant	Gt. Britain	England	Agenoria	27 Jun 1823
C.	28	M	Mariner	U. States	U. States	Florida	25 Apr 1825
Catharine, (Wife							
[of Thomas])	23	F		Ireland	New York	Brighton	24 Aug 1827
Cathrine	20	F	Servant	Portugal	U. States	Agenoria	17 Sep 1821
David	32	M	Joiner	England	United States	Jubilee	1 Oct 1828
Dorothy	1	F	None	England	United States	Trident	31 Mar 1827
Eben	38	M	Mariner	U.S. America	U.S. America	Ganges	15 Dec 1826
*Destitute Seaman put on board by the American Consul in London							
Edward	44	M	Farmer	Great Britian	United States	London	24 Jun 1823
Hannah	26	F	None	England	United States	Trident	31 Mar 1827
Henry	28	M	Smith	England	United States	Trident	31 Mar 1827
Henry	30	M	Labourer	Ireland	United States	Hannah Eliza	6 Jun 1826
James	44	M	Sawyer	England	America	Josephine	24 Jul 1826
James	61	M	Labourer	Ireland	America	Franklin	13 Aug 1827
Jane	21	F		Ireland	New York	Carolina Ann	15 Oct 1824
John	1	M		Scotland	United States	Camillus	9 May 1827
John	20	M	Servant	Portugal	U. States	Agenoria	17 Sep 1821
John	21	M	Mechanic	England	U.S. of America	Splendid	14 Aug 1829
John	28	M	Labourer	England	United States	Nancy Henrietta	3 Nov 1828
John	30	M		Argyle (Tedland)			
				Scotland	United States	Jean Hastie	27 Jul 1829
John	33	M	...	Scotland	United States	Camillus	9 May 1827
John	35	M	Baker	Scotland	United States	Delta	24 Oct 1829

NAMES OF PASSENGERS	AGE	SEX	OCCUPATIONS	COUNTRY TO WHICH THEY BELONG	COUNTRY THEY INTEND TO INHABIT	SHIPS/DATES OF ARRIVAL	
NELSON (cont'd)							
John	52	M	Merchant	Gt. Britain	Canada	Caledonia	10 Sep 1828
John, Child	4	M		Ireland	New York	Carolina Ann	15 Oct 1824
Joseph	20	M	S. Maker	Ireland	N. York	Trusty	12 Sep 1828
Joseph	30	M	Farmer	England		Marchioness	13 May 1828
Liddy	40	F	Wife	Ireland	United States	Dublin Packet	13 Oct 1828
M. J.	23	M	Gentleman	England	U. States	Hudson	26 Jan 1825
Margaret	33	F		Scotland	United States	Camillus	9 May 1827
Mary	22	F	Servant	St. John, N.B.	United States	St. Michaels	11 May 1826
Mary	25	F	Wife	Ireland, C. Barry	Pensylvany	Nile	18 Aug 1829
Mary	30	F	his Wife	Scotland	United States	Delta	24 Oct 1829
Michael	45	M	Merchant	Great Britain	G.B.	Orozimbo	31 May 1824
Moses	25	M	Labourer	Ireland	U. States	Sarah G	7 May 1827
Peter	42 3/12	M	...	England	America, U.S.	Illinois	3 Jun 1822
Robt., Child	2	M		Ireland	New York	Carolina Ann	15 Oct 1824
Saml., Servt. Boy	13	M	Lad	Philada.	United States	Harriet & Lucy	3 Oct 1823
Sarah	1	F	Servant	Ireland	U. States	Sarah G	7 May 1827
Thomas	23	M	Bookbinder	Ireland	New York	Brighton	24 Aug 1827
Thomas	36	M	Farmer	Ireland	United States	Dublin Packet	13 Oct 1828
Thos.	23 1/12	M	Farmer	Ireland	Red Stone	Triton	12 Jul 1823
W.	23	M	Labourer	Ireland	United States	Princess Charlotte	6 Oct 1827
Wilbart	23	M	Labourer	Ireland	U. States	Sarah G	7 May 1827
William	4	M		Scotland	United States	Camillus	9 May 1827
William	26	M	House Carpenter	Ireland, C. Barry	Pensylvany	Nile	18 Aug 1829
Wm.	25	M	Servant	Portugal	U. States	Agenoria	17 Sep 1821
Wm.	40	M	Merchant	Glasgow	U.S. America	Camillus	10 Sep 1821
Wm., Jr.	20	M	Merchant	Glasgow	U.S. America	Camillus	10 Sep 1821
NENNER, Henrietta	24	F		England	U. States	St. Michael	5 May 1827
John Lander	4 11/12	M		England	U. States	St. Michael	5 May 1827
Richd. Wm.	11	M		England	U. States	St. Michael	5 May 1827
Samuel James	55	M	Merchant	England	U. States	St. Michael	5 May 1827
NEPLOMACEMO, Cesario	34	M	Merchant	Spain	U. States	Enterprize	2 Jun 1828
NEPOMNEINO, C.	30	M	Merchant	Spain	S.	Frances	15 Jun 1825
NEPOMUERNO, Cesarea	29	M	Merchant	Teneriffe	Teneriffe	Merury	14 Dec 1824
NERRENT, Robert	31	M	Merchant	United States	United States	Aurora	5 Sep 1826
NERROLD, Lieho.	25	M	Sugar Baker	Germany	U. States	Constitution	21 Jun 1824
NERVEER, N., Genl.	46	M		Netherlands	Netherlands	Talma	23 Sep 1828
W., Miss	18	F		Netherlands	U. States	Talma	23 Sep 1828
NESBETT, James	21	M	Farmer	Ireland	America	Superior	12 Jun 1824
Jno.	24	M	Merchant	England	England	Corinthian	2 May 1823
S.	18		Farmer	Ireland	United States	Courier	16 May 1825
NESBIT, E.	27	M	Mariner (Capt.)	United States	United States	India	24 Mar 1826
Eleanor	30	F	Wife [of Nathaniel]	Ireland	Pensylvania	Atlantic	8 May 1828
Jane	5	F	Daughter [of Nathaniel]	Ireland	Pensylvania	Atlantic	8 May 1828
Jas. J.	45	M	Mercht.	U. States	U. States	Olive Branch	12 Aug 1822
John	7	M	Son [of Nathaniel]	Ireland	Pensylvania	Atlantic	8 May 1828
Nathaniel	72	M		Ireland	Pensylvania	Atlantic	8 May 1828
Sarah	2	F	Daughter [of Nathaniel]	Ireland	Pensylvania	Atlantic	8 May 1828
Sarah	19	F		Halifax, N.S.	United States	Hopes Delight	29 Nov 1827
NESBITT, Agness	20			England	United States	Hugh Johnson	11 Jun 1828
Samuel	30	M	Farmer	Ireland	United States	Fabius	4 Jun 1828
William	27	M	Labourer	Ireland	United States	Lord Wellington	28 May 1827
NESBOT, Elenor	30	F	Privt. Lady	Ireland	United States	William	20 Jul 1829
NESBTE, John	22	M	Butcher	Ireland	America	Sarah	18 Aug 1829
NESCHER, Luke	34	M	Merchant	France	United States	Lewis	30 May 1823
NESMITH, James	33	M	Merchant	U. States	U. States	Tobasco	14 Apr 1828
NESS, Cathr.	38	F		France	U. States	Montano	2 Sep 1828
NESSAMUCENO, C. Y.	31	M	Merchant	U. States	U. States	St. Croix	31 Jul 1827
NESTNER, Jacob	17	M	Weaver	Switzerland	U. States	Hewes	30 Oct 1829
NESTOR, Ann, Miss	22	F		Nova Scotia	United States	Hopes Delight	31 May 1828
NESTRIS, Carolin	26	F	Artist	Italy	U. States	Edward Quesnel	4 Aug 1828
Charles	31	M	Artist	Prussia	U. States	Edward Quesnel	4 Aug 1828
NESTY, A.	27	M	Merchant	France	U. States	Neptune	20 Apr 1825

NAMES OF PASSENGERS	AGE	SEX	OCCUPATIONS	COUNTRY TO WHICH THEY BELONG	COUNTRY THEY INTEND TO INHABIT	SHIPS/DATES OF ARRIVAL
NETCALF, John	24	M	Draper	Great Britain	United States	Washington	3 Sep 1827
Wm.	27	M	Slater	Great Britain	United States	Washington	3 Sep 1827
NETMAS, —, Miss	19	F		G. Britain	U. States	Hope Success	16 Jul 1828
—, Mrs.	48	F		G. Britain	U. States	Hope Success	16 Jul 1828
S.	28	M	Merchant	G. Britain	U. States	Hope Success	16 Jul 1828
NETSHRAP, George	40		Merchant	Denmark	St. Croix	Eliza Davidson	8 Aug 1829
NETTELS, J.	36	M		U. States	U. States	Larch	18 Jul 1828
M.	6	F		U. States	U. States	Larch	18 Jul 1828
M.	8	F		U. States	U. States	Larch	18 Jul 1828
R.	11	F		U. States	U. States	Larch	18 Jul 1828
R.	38	F		U. States	U. States	Larch	18 Jul 1828
NETTLESON, Ann	27	F		Great Britain	U. States	United States	8 Sep 1827
John	33	M	Farmer	Great Britain	U. States	United States	8 Sep 1827
NETTLETON, Edward	35	M	Farmer	Great Britain	U. States	Columbia	22 Sep 1828
NEUF, James	38	M	Builder	England	United States	Dalhouse Castle	8 May 1827
NEUGASS, Henry	25	M	Merchant	Germany	United States	Plato	25 Aug 1829
NEUHAM, —, Mrs.	38	F	Lady	Great Britain	Canada	Manhattan	18 Feb 1824
J., Revd.	33	M	Clergy	Great Britain	Canada	Manhattan	18 Feb 1824
Jane	6	F	Child	Great Britain	Canada	Manhattan	18 Feb 1824
John	3	M	Child	Great Britain	Canada	Manhattan	18 Feb 1824
Susan	8	F	Child	Great Britain	Canada	Manhattan	18 Feb 1824
NEUMAN, Charles	23	M	Glazer	Germany	United States	Plato	25 Aug 1829
NEUNAN, Anne	18	F		Limerick	N. York	Thomas & William	25 May 1827
NEUSCHANDER, Barbe	1	F	Farmer	Langnan	U.S. America	Superior	18 Jun 1825
Catherine	10	F	Farmer	Langnan	U.S. America	Superior	18 Jun 1825
Catherine	45	F	Farmer	Langnan	U.S. America	Superior	18 Jun 1825
Christage	13	M	Farmer	Langnan	U.S. America	Superior	18 Jun 1825
David	16	M	Farmer	Langnan	U.S. America	Superior	18 Jun 1825
Elisabeth	6	F	Farmer	Langnan	U.S. America	Superior	18 Jun 1825
Isaac	4	M	Farmer	Langnan	U.S. America	Superior	18 Jun 1825
Isaac	14	M	Farmer	Langnan	U.S. America	Superior	18 Jun 1825
Jean	49	M	Farmer	Langnan	U.S. America	Superior	18 Jun 1825
NEUSCHERANDER, Christ.	42		Weaver	France	U. States	Elizabeth	9 Jul 1825
NEUSCHWANDER, Christ.	51		Farmer	France	U. States	Elizabeth	9 Jul 1825
Magdelaine	13	F		Switzerland	United States	Thetis	5 Jul 1821
NEUSINGER, Jac.	38	M	Agriculture	Wirtemburg	United States	Henri IV	14 Oct 1829
NEUTHE, —, Mr.	52	M	Gent.	England	United States	Warrior	6 Oct 1828
NEUVIS, A.	25	M	Merchant	Havana	Havana	Crusader	23 Apr 1827
NEVAN, John	19	M	Labourer	U. States	U. States	United States	11 Sep 1828
NEVELL, Priscilla	30	F	None	Gt. Britain	U. States	Panthia	13 Nov 1824
NEVEN, Hugh	24	M		England	United States	Loire	4 Oct 1824
Martin	18	M	Labourer			Ocean	17 Aug 1820
NEVER, Ellen	30	F	None	Great Briton	uncertain	Mount Vernon	29 Aug 1828
NEVERIGOUR, Patrick	23	M	Labourer	Ireland	United States	Robert Fulton	24 Jul 1826
NEVES, Henry	21		Labourer	England	U.S. America	Constitution	18 Jun 1827
NEVETT, Robert	34	M	Cabinet Maker	United States	United States	William Thompson	19 Aug 1829
NEVIL, —, Mr.	33	M	Farmer	Gt. Britain	U. States	Constitution	19 Jul 1825
NEVILL, James	20	M	Labourer	G. Britain	U. States	Nimrod	31 Jul 1828
Thomas	24			Planter	West Indies	Union	20 Aug 1827
NEVILLE, Elizabeth	23	F		England	U. States	Mary Ann	2 Jan 1829
John	4 2/12	M		England	U. States	Mary Ann	2 Jan 1829
Marey	3/12	F		Nova Scotia	U. States	Mary Ann	2 Jan 1829
Noah	2 4/12	M		England	U. States	Mary Ann	2 Jan 1829
NEVIN, Ann	21	F		Ireland	United States	Trio	2 Oct 1828
Edward	1	M		Ireland	United States	Trio	2 Oct 1828
Geo.	38	M	Farmer		United States	Sarah	9 Nov 1820
James N.	21	M	Merchant	U. States	U. States	Amity	23 Sep 1823
Jane	70	F	House Keeper	Irereland	America	Carolina Ann	20 Jun 1825
Perald	29	M	Clerk	Gt. Britain	U.S. America	James Cropper	14 Mar 1828
NEVINS, Bridget	7	F	Farmer	Ireland	U. States	Champion	26 Jul 1827
Lewis	24	M	Servant	Russia	Russia	New York	11 Mar 1823
R. H., Mr.	36	M				Henri IV	17 May 1828
NEVIRT, Samuel	31	M	Merchant	United States	United States	Nestor	20 Nov 1821
NEVIS, William	22	M	Gentn.	U. States	U. States	Manhattan	20 Jun 1825
NEW, John	18	M	Farmer	Great Britain	United States	Mount Vernon	20 May 1822

NAMES OF PASSENGERS	AGE	SEX	OCCUPATIONS	COUNTRY TO WHICH THEY BELONG	COUNTRY THEY INTEND TO INHABIT	SHIPS/DATES OF ARRIVAL	
NEW (cont'd)							
Judith	22	F		England	America	Two Marys	24 Sep 1827
William	45	M	Farmer	Great Britain	United States	Mount Vernon	20 May 1822
NEWBEGGING, James	24	M	Merchant	Scotland	United States	St. George	25 Aug 1829
James	24	M	Merchant	Scotland	United States	St. George	25 Aug 1829
NEWBERRY, Benjamin	30	M	Mariner	American		John & Edward	18 Oct 1828
NEWBOLD, Anna, Mrs.	22 4/12		Lady	United States	United States	Meteor	25 Aug 1823
Jos.	31	M	Merchant	Bermudas	U. States	Prince Edward	3 Apr 1826
Thomas	27	M	Mercht.	United States	United States	Manchester	6 Dec 1825
Thos.	24	M	Merchant		United States	Columbia	11 Apr 1822
Thos.	26		Merchant	England	England	Meteor	25 Aug 1823
NEWBOULD, A.	20	M	Merchant	England	U. States	Ocean	8 Jun 1826
Arthur	16	M	Merchant	England	America	Manhattan	23 May 1822
Arthur, Mr.	21	M	Mercht.	Gt. Brittian	New York	Manchester	21 Apr 1827
Geo. H.	38	M	Merchant	United States	U. States	Manhattan	25 Dec 1820
George H.	41	M	Merchant	England	America	Orbit	22 Apr 1824
Thos.	26	M	Merchant	U.S.		Pacific	29 Dec 1824
Wm.	22	M	Gentleman	England	G. Britain	Eliza Jane	11 Jul 1822
NEWBY, Harriet	23			England		Hudson	5 Apr 1826
Martha	1	F	None	England	United States	Jubilee	1 Oct 1828
Martha	45	F	None	England	United States	Jubilee	1 Oct 1828
Nathan	3	M	None	England	United States	Jubilee	1 Oct 1828
Nathan	48	M	Farmer	England	United States	Jubilee	1 Oct 1828
Robert	8	M	None	England	United States	Jubilee	1 Oct 1828
Samuel	26	M	Grocer	G.B.	U.S.	London	19 Dec 1823
William	6	M	None	England	United States	Jubilee	1 Oct 1828
NEWCOMB, Charles	23	M	Merchant	New York	U. States	Orleans	10 Sep 1822
E.	35	M	Weaver	Canada	U. States	Ann Maria	5 Aug 1824
E.	36	M	Merchant	Nova Scotia	U. States	Leader	17 Sep 1821
E. H.	21	M	Merchant	Norfolk	U. States	Three Brothers	27 Apr 1825
Eliakim	38 5/12	M	Farmer	United States	New York	Loire	9 Aug 1821
Emanuel	26	M	Farmer	England	United States	William Howland	5 Jul 1821
O.	34	M	Carpenter	N. York	U. States	Ambuscade	12 Jan 1822
S. S.	28	M	Merchant	St. Andrews	St. Andrews	Thomas	29 Jun 1824
William	45	M		England	England	Britannia	22 Jul 1829
NEWCOMBE, Fred.	9	M	Artist	United States	United States	Columbia	16 Jan 1829
Geo.	40	M	Artist	United States	United States	Columbia	16 Jan 1829
Nane	35	F	Artist	United States	United States	Columbia	16 Jan 1829
Tobias	26	M	Gentleman	England	United States	Helen Mar	29 Jun 1827
NEWEL, Henry	18	M	Mason	Nova Scotia	U. States	Beaver	27 Oct 1828
Theodore	25	M	Carpenter	America, Massachusets	America	William	16 Apr 1823
NEWELL, A.	23		Farmer	Ireland	United States	Courier	16 May 1825
Alexander	14	M	Youth	Ireland	United States	Romulus	24 Jun 1826
Francis	7	F		U. States	U. States	Cincinnatus	2 Oct 1822
George	32	M	Seaman	America	America	Pleiades	13 Nov 1826
James	5		Labourer	Downpersmith	U. States	Carolina Ann	14 Feb 1824
James	22	M	Gent	Ireland	N. York	Trusty	12 Sep 1828
John	8		Labourer	Downpersmith	U. States	Carolina Ann	14 Feb 1824
L. C.	22	M	Merchant	New York	U. States	Edward	6 May 1822
Mary	27		Labourer	Downpersmith	U. States	Carolina Ann	14 Feb 1824
Mary Ann	2		Labourer	Downpersmith	U. States	Carolina Ann	14 Feb 1824
Sarah	30	F		U. States	U. States	Cincinnatus	2 Oct 1822
NEWGENT, Mary	20	F	Servant	Ireland	United States	Edwin	29 Nov 1828
Mary	21	M	Yeoman	Ireland	United States	Borneo	9 Jul 1827
NEWGER, Ellen	22	F		Ireland	U. States	Balaena	29 Apr 1825
NEWHALL, G. G.	25	M	Merchant	U.S. States	U. States	Mary Jane	23 Mar 1829
NEWLAND, C., Mrs.	28	F		Scotland	U. States	Camillus	17 Sep 1823
Christina	7	F		Scotland	U. States	Camillus	17 Sep 1823
Henry	35	M	Farmer	England	New York	Brighton	20 Aug 1825
John	3	M		Scotland	U. States	Camillus	17 Sep 1823
John	40	M	Farmer	New York	New York	Brighton	20 Aug 1825
NEWLORE, John	25	M	Mechanic	England	U. States	John Wells	16 May 1825
NEWMAN, Anne	20	F	None	Ireland	United States	Jubilee	12 May 1828
Eliza	21	F	None	Great Britain	United States	Atlantic	28 May 1827
G. W.	23	M	Clerk	Baltimore	U. States	Robt. Y. Hayne	27 Jun 1825
Geo.	21	M	Merchant	U. States	U. States	Emily	10 Sep 1824
Geo.	30	M	Merchant	Brittain	U. States	Ann Maria	5 Aug 1824

NAMES OF PASSENGERS	AGE	SEX	OCCUPATIONS	COUNTRY TO WHICH THEY BELONG	COUNTRY THEY INTEND TO INHABIT	SHIPS/DATES OF ARRIVAL	
NEWMAN (cont'd)							
James	20	M	Farmer	England	United States	India	8 Jun 1827
Jane	5		her Daughter			Cambria	19 Oct 1829
Jane	34	F		England	U. States	Wanderer	1 Sep 1828
Jane	34	F	Lady	New Brunswick	New Brunswick	Wanderer	31 Aug 1829
Jane	40	F		Gt. Britain	United States	Penelope	9 Sep 1828
Jno.	25		Farmer	England	U.S. of America	Mary	21 Sep 1821
John	1	M		Gt. Britain	United States	Penelope	9 Sep 1828
John	24	M	Labourer	Ireland	United States	William & Henry	19 Jul 1822
John	31	M	Labourer	Ireland	America	Cincinnatus	22 May 1826
Mary	3	F		Gt. Britain	United States	Penelope	9 Sep 1828
Mary	20	F	None	Ireland		Marchioness	13 May 1828
Mary	28			England	United States	Cambria	19 Oct 1829
Mary Ann	3		her Daughter			Cambria	19 Oct 1829
Michl.	26	M	Labourer	Ireland	United States	Essex	23 May 1828
Pat	5	M		Gt. Britain	United States	Penelope	9 Sep 1828
Pat	40	M	Farmer	Gt. Britain	United States	Penelope	9 Sep 1828
Peter	35	M	Mariner	U. States	U. States	Ellen	2 Aug 1822
Peter	46	M	Ship Master	U. States	U. States	Nassau	30 Jun 1824
S.	52		Mariner	U. States	U. States	Acosta	28 Jul 1823
Thomas	8		her Son			Cambria	19 Oct 1829
Thomas	18	M	Merchant	France	U. States	Great Britain	6 Sep 1828
William	28	M	Labourer	Ireland		Marchioness	13 May 1828
Wm.	23	M	Labourer	England	U. States	Thomas Ritchie	2 Jul 1827
NEWNHAM, James	10	M	Farmer	England	America	Comet	26 Jun 1822
William	18	M	Servant	England	United States	Comet	6 Mar 1823
NEWPORT, Thomas	42	M	Silversmith	England	U. States	Montgomery	18 Oct 1828
NEWSCHERANDER,							
Catharine	21			France	U. States	Elizabeth	9 Jul 1825
Isaac	35		Carpenter	France	U. States	Elizabeth	9 Jul 1825
NEWSCHEWANDER,							
Elizabeth	18		Farmer	France	U. States	Elizabeth	9 Jul 1825
NEWSCHWANDER,							
Catharine	51		Farmer	France	U. States	Elizabeth	9 Jul 1825
NEWSHAM, Eli	19	M	Labourer	Great Britain	U. States	Great Britain	18 Mar 1828
Thomas	21	M	Labourer	Great Britain	U. States	Great Britain	18 Mar 1828
NEWSOM, Betsey	24	F	None	Great Britain	America	Remittance	24 Aug 1825
NEWSON, Joseph	24	M	Hatter	Great Britain	U.S. of America	Gratitude	3 Oct 1829
NEWSWANDER,							
Emanual	33	M	Gentleman	United States	U. States	Martha	24 Aug 1829
NEWTON, —, Mrs.	41	F	Lady	England	U. States	William	28 Nov 1823
A. C.	23	M	Merchant	U. States	U. States	Zephyr	18 Oct 1824
Anne	75	F		Gt. Britain	Gt. Britain	Silvanus Jenkins	24 Jul 1828
Arabella	14	F		U. States	U. States	Montano	2 Sep 1828
Chris	24	M	Mechanic	Great Britain	United States	Mary & Harriet	3 Jul 1829
Edward	40	M	Mercht.	U.S.	U.S.	Envoy	4 Jan 1826
Frances	5			England	U.S. States	Splendid	14 Aug 1829
Francis	29	M	Farmer	Great Britain	United States	Rebecca	20 Mar 1824
George	26	M	Merchant	United States	United States	Montano	31 May 1824
Gorge *[died] May 22	27	M	Merchant	New York		Packet	31 May 1826
H. C.	26	M	U. Navy	U. States	U. States	Balize	29 Aug 1825
Hannah	6	F	None	Gt. Brittain	United States	Balaena	21 Aug 1824
Hannah	12	F	Mason	England	U.S. States	Splendid	14 Aug 1829
Hannah	32	F	Wife	England	U.S. States	Splendid	14 Aug 1829
J. E.	19	F	Spinster	U.S.	U.S.	Emma	24 Jun 1825
James	27		Labourer	England	United States	Hugh Johnson	11 Jun 1828
James	64	M	Weaver	Gt. Britain	Gt. Britain	Silvanus Jenkins	24 Jul 1828
Jane	8	F	Mason	England	U.S. States	Splendid	14 Aug 1829
Jas.	32	M	Labourer	England	U. States	Dalhouse	23 Mar 1829
John	8	M			U. States	William	28 Nov 1823
John	9	M	None	Gt. Brittain	United States	Balaena	21 Aug 1824
John	22	M	Merchant	England	New York	James Monroe	23 Aug 1822
John	28	M	Labourer	Ireland, Great Britain	U.S. of America	Dublin	21 Feb 1826
John	40	M	Mason	England	U.S. States	Splendid	14 Aug 1829
John, Junr.	16	M	Mason	England	U.S. States	Splendid	14 Aug 1829
Joseph	45	M	Weaver	England	United States	London	21 May 1828

NAMES OF PASSENGERS	AGE	SEX	OCCUPATIONS	COUNTRY TO WHICH THEY BELONG	COUNTRY THEY INTEND TO INHABIT	SHIPS/DATES OF ARRIVAL	
NEWTON (cont'd)							
Leah	27	F	None	Gt. Brittain	United States	Balaena	21 Aug 1824
Louisa	35	F	Servant	St. Croix	St. Croix	Jupiter	21 Nov 1825
Robert	29	M	Weaver	Great Britain	United States	Amelia	20 Aug 1829
Robt.	22	M	Farmer	England	United States	Peru	23 May 1827
Robt.	24	M	Labourer	England	U. States	Dalhouse	23 Mar 1829
Sarah	35	F		U.S.	U.S.	Envoy	4 Jan 1826
William	32	M	Currier	Great Britain	United States	Ganges	26 Oct 1824
Wm.	23	M	Taylor	Great Britain	U. States	Laburnum	12 Dec 1821
NEWTZ, Ellin	1	F		America	America	Ann	3 Jul 1820
Emily	7	F		America	America	Ann	3 Jul 1820
Emily	30	F		England	America	Ann	3 Jul 1820
Margaret	2	F		America	America	Ann	3 Jul 1820
Seabert	10	M		America	America	Ann	3 Jul 1820
Sophia	8	F		America	America	Ann	3 Jul 1820
NEWTZGER,							
Edward	21 3/12	M	Cotton Spinner	Great Briton	uncertain	Mount Vernon	29 Aug 1828
NEWWARK, Jno.	35	M	Shoemaker	England	America	Saluda	16 Oct 1824
Mary	33	F		England	America	Saluda	16 Oct 1824
NEX, Geo.	25		Soap Boiler	England	U.S. of America	Mary	21 Sep 1821
Sophia	6/12			England	U.S. of America	Mary	21 Sep 1821
Sophia	18			England	U.S. of America	Mary	21 Sep 1821
NEY, Ada	31	M	Farmer	Bavarian	United States	American	27 Aug 1827
Adalina	5	F	Spinster	Bavarian	United States	American	27 Aug 1827
Eva	30	M	Farmer	Bavarian	United States	American	27 Aug 1827
Henry	2	M	Farmer	Bavarian	United States	American	27 Aug 1827
Nicholas	6	M	Farmer	Bavarian	United States	American	27 Aug 1827
Peter	24/365	M	Farmer	Bavarian	United States	American	27 Aug 1827
NEYBERGHT,							
Elizabeth	35	F		France	United States	Lewis	30 May 1823
NEYSTER, Robert G. L.	26	M	Merchant	United States	United States	Virginia	24 Jul 1821
NIAGRA, Fras.	31	M	Merchant	Italy	United States	Cambridge	19 Sep 1828
Margt.	22	F		America	United States	Cambridge	19 Sep 1828
NIBB, William	26	M	Tavernkeeper	America	United States	London Packet	25 Dec 1820
NIBBS, Jane, Mrs.	40	F	Lady	Jamaica	Jamaica	Wallace	12 Apr 1824
NIBCOCK, Alexr.	33	M	Weaver	Ireland	U. States of America	Courier	17 Mar 1827
NICHEOL, M.	35	M	Merchant	Germany	U. States	Aspasia	23 Nov 1825
NICHILSON, Nancy	15 6/12	F		Ireland	U.S. of America	Douglass	6 Jul 1829
NICHLES, Mary	...	F	...	Ireland	United States	General Putnam	20 Jun 1825
Wm.	...0	M	...	Ireland	United States	General Putnam	20 Jun 1825
NICHOL, Allan	42	F	Lady	Scotland	United States	Siroc	31 Oct 1829
Danl.	40	M	Schoe Maker	Great Britian	United States	Brok	29 Aug 1823
Ebe, Servant	19	M	Servant	U.S.	U.S.	Howard	4 May 1827
Henry W.	38	M	Merchant	U.S.	U.S.	Howard	4 May 1827
J. G.	25	M	Farmer	England	U. States	Lord Gambier	3 Apr 1827
James	20	M	Farmer	Ireland	America	Carolina Ann	14 Feb 1825
John	25	M	Weaver	Great Britain	United States	Washington	3 Sep 1827
Margt.	12	F		Great Britian	United States	Brok	29 Aug 1823
Robert	40	M	Gentleman	Scotland	United States	Siroc	31 Oct 1829
Robt.	22	M	Weaver	Gt. Britain	U. States	Frances Henrietta	18 Apr 1825
NICHOLAS, Antonae	6	M	Son	France	U. States	Comet	28 Jul 1825
David	24	M	Carpenter	London	America	Evelina	10 Nov 1825
Elisabeth	Infant	F	Daughter	Swiss	U. States	Comet	28 Jul 1825
Elizabeth	25	F	Tailoress	a confectioner	France, U.S. America	Sicily	7 Oct 1829
Faver	38	M	Baker	France	U. States	Comet	28 Jul 1825
Frace	4	F	Daughter	France	U. States	Comet	28 Jul 1825
Francis	29	M	Farmer	Swiss	U. States	Comet	28 Jul 1825
Gabriel	58	M	Merchant	France	U. States	Edward Quesnel	16 Nov 1827
Jean Marie Aubert	75	F	Has a Son in Boston, a confectioner	France	U.S. America	Sicily	7 Oct 1829
Joseph	infant	M	Son	France	U. States	Comet	28 Jul 1825
Julain	2	M	Son	France	U. States	Comet	28 Jul 1825
Mary An	2	F	Daughter	Swiss	U. States	Comet	28 Jul 1825
Mary An	29	F	Wife	Swiss	U. States	Comet	28 Jul 1825
R.	24 3/12	M	Tailor	France	United States	Catharine	10 Sep 1827
Rowsall	41	F	Wife	France	U. States	Comet	28 Jul 1825
Smith	27	M	Blacksmith	Switzerland	U.S.	C. Amelia	30 Jun 1828

NAMES OF PASSENGERS	AGE	SEX	OCCUPATIONS	COUNTRY TO WHICH THEY BELONG	COUNTRY THEY INTEND TO INHABIT	SHIPS/DATES OF ARRIVAL	
NICHOLASON, John	13	M	None	Great Britian	United States	George Clinton	21 Oct 1826
NICHOLES, Wm.	30	M	Locksmith	Great Britten	U. States	Magnet	29 Sep 1823
NICHOLET, Abraham	43	M	Coach Maker	Switzerland	U. States	Don Quixote	25 Oct 1828
S.	36	M	Merchant	Switzerland	N. Orleans	Desdemona	21 Oct 1825
NICHOLETTE, L.	42	M	Merchant	U. States	U. States	Dromo	4 May 1827
Theod.	36	M	Merchant	Switzerland	N. Orleans	Queen Mab	20 Nov 1826
Winthrop	12	M	Merchant	U. States	U. States	Dromo	4 May 1827
NICHOLLS, Jno.	25	M	Seaman	Philadelphia	United States	Venus	8 Sep 1820
John	29	M	Gentleman	Great Britain	United States	Isaac Hicks	6 Dec 1827
Margaret	24	F	Servant	England	United States	Aurelia	7 Jun 1826
NICHOLOS, Eliza	33	F	Matron	Great Britain	U. States	Robert Fulton	3 Dec 1827
NICHOLS, Agness	28	F	...	...	...	Dawn	19 Aug 1825
Aikin	22		Shoe maker	Northampton-shire	N. York	Peru	30 May 1828
Ann	1			Northampton-shire	N. York	Peru	30 May 1828
Ann	18/12	F	Laborer	Ireland	United States	Weser	29 Jul 1823
Ann	17	F	None	Great Britain	United States	Atlantic	28 May 1827
Ann	25	F		U. States	U. States	United States	11 Sep 1828
Catherine	42		Lady			Charlotte Corday	11 Sep 1820
Charles	6	M	None	Great Britain	United States	Atlantic	28 May 1827
Charlotte	1	F		U. States	U. States	United States	11 Sep 1828
Edward H.	23 10/12	M	Mercht.	New York	New York	Panthea	22 Jul 1826
Edwd.	25	M	Laborer	Ireland	United States	Weser	29 Jul 1823
Eliza	65	F	Wife	Great Britain	United States	Washington	3 Sep 1827
Elizabeth	21			Northampton-shire	N. York	Peru	30 May 1828
Ellenor	22	F		England	America, U.S.	Illinois	3 Jun 1822
Esther	13	F	None	Great Britain	United States	Atlantic	28 May 1827
G.	0 3/12	F		France	United States	Catharine	10 Sep 1827
George	25 ...	M	Farmer	England	America, U.S.	Illinois	3 Jun 1822
Hannah	0 5/12	F	Child	Great Britain	United States	Washington	3 Sep 1827
Hannah	30	F	Wife	Great Britain	United States	Washington	3 Sep 1827
Isaac	15	M	None	Great Britain	United States	Atlantic	28 May 1827
James	10	M	Boy			Baltic	21 Apr 1827
John	44	M	...	Great Britain	United States	Atlantic	28 May 1827
Joseph	6	M	Child	Great Britain	United States	Washington	3 Sep 1827
Joseph	30	M	...	...	...	Dawn	19 Aug 1825
Joseph	69	M	Teacher	Great Britain	United States	Washington	3 Sep 1827
Joseph, Jr.	32	M	Engineer	Great Britain	United States	Washington	3 Sep 1827
Joseph, Jur.	6/12	M	...	...	...	Dawn	19 Aug 1825
Lawrence	41	M		U. States	U. States	Bayard	16 May 1827
Lyman	14	M	Mariner	U.S.	U.S.	Agenoria	7 Jan 1822
Margt.	22 2/12	F		France	United States	Catharine	10 Sep 1827
Peter J.	29	M	Surveyor	England	U. States	Acosta	28 Jul 1823
Saml.	3	M	None	United States	United States	Orozimbo	1 Dec 1823
Saml.	42 3/12	M	Mason	Gt. Britain	New York	Betsey	18 Apr 1822
Samuel	22 8/12	M	Weaver	Ireland	United States	Atlantic	21 Jul 1827
Samuel	41		Merchant	England	U. States	Charlotte Corday	11 Sep 1820
Samuel C.	42	M	Mariner	United States	United States	Genl. Brown	3 Dec 1821
Sarah	29	F	None	United States	United States	Orozimbo	1 Dec 1823
Sarah	39	F	None	Great Britain	United States	Atlantic	28 May 1827
Thomas B.	21	M	Merchant	U. States	U. States	Betsey	29 Aug 1829
Thos.	19 5/12	M	Mason	Gt. Britain	New York	Betsey	18 Apr 1822
NICHOLSON (see ...icholson)							
—, Mrs.	18	F		U. States	U. States	Rachel	14 Mar 1825
Ann	50	F	None	Gt. Britain	U.S.A.	Dalhouse Castle	21 Aug 1829
Betsey	12	F		Great Britain	United States	Dalhouse Castle	21 Aug 1829
Betsy	12	F	Shipwright	Gt. Britain	U.S.A.	Dalhouse Castle	21 Aug 1829
Catherine	5	F	their child [Patrick & Peggy]	Ireland	United States	Asia	29 Jul 1829
Christopher	25	M	Miner	England	U.S. States	Splendid	14 Aug 1829
David	22	M	Trader	Scotland	United States	Jubilee	13 Jul 1829
Edward	74	M	Merchant	G. Bt.	G. Bt.	Canada	13 Feb 1826
Elizabeth	17	F		Scotland	United States	Morning Star	25 Jun 1822
George	27	M	Trader	Scotland	United States	Jubilee	13 Jul 1829
Johanna	9	F	Shipwright	Gt. Britain	U.S.A.	Dalhouse Castle	21 Aug 1829

NAMES OF PASSENGERS	AGE	SEX	OCCUPATIONS	COUNTRY TO WHICH THEY BELONG	COUNTRY THEY INTEND TO INHABIT	SHIPS/DATES OF ARRIVAL
NICHOLSON (cont'd)						
Johanna	9	F		Great Britain	United States	Dalhouse Castle 21 Aug 1829
John	25	M	Shipwright	Gt. Britain	U.S.A.	Dalhouse Castle 21 Aug 1829
John	30	M	Merchant	Scotland	America	Ann 23 Jul 1821
John	35	M	Labourer	Scotland	United States	Samuel Robertson 5 Oct 1827
Joseph	10	M	Shipwright	Gt. Britain	U.S.A.	Dalhouse Castle 21 Aug 1829
Josh.	10	M		Great Britain	United States	Dalhouse Castle 21 Aug 1829
Libby	26	F	Taylor	New York	U. States	Virginia 20 Jun 1825
M. R.	23	F		Maryland	U. States	Garonne 24 Jul 1821
Margaret	26			Great Britain		John Dickinson 5 Apr 1821
Mary	18	F	Shipwright	Gt. Britain	U.S.A.	Dalhouse Castle 21 Aug 1829
Meadows T.	14	M	Lad	England	U. States	Cincinnatus 24 May 1821
Patrick	40	M	Farmer	Ireland	United States	Asia 29 Jul 1829
Peggy	36	F	his wife [Patrick]	Ireland	United States	Asia 29 Jul 1829
Peter	28	M	Merchant	Halifax	Halifax	Emeline 4 Sep 1827
Rachael	16	F	Shipwright	Gt. Britain	U.S.A.	Dalhouse Castle 21 Aug 1829
Rachel	16	F		Great Britain	United States	Dalhouse Castle 21 Aug 1829
S.	24	M	Merchant	Ireland	U. States	Xenophon 13 Jun 1823
Sarah	23	F		England	U. States	York 12 Jul 1825
Thomas	24	M	Weaver	Scotland	United States	Camillus 27 Oct 1829
Thomas	29	M	Miller	G. Brittain	U. States	Cincinnatus 2 Oct 1822
Thomas	37	M	Weaver	Great Britian	United States	George Clinton 21 Oct 1826
Thomas	45	M	Farmer	Scotland	United States	Trident 18 Jul 1827
William	1_/12	M	their child [Patrick & Peggy]	Ireland	United States	Asia 29 Jul 1829
Wm.	29	M	Farmer	Gt. Britain	United States.	Silas Richards 20 Jun 1826
Wm.	42	M	Farmer	Great Britain	United States	Diana 6 Jul 1829
NICKELS, Solomon	30	M	Merchant	St. Johns	England	Nancy 2 Jan 1824
NICKERSON, Joseph	23	M	Mariner	U. States	U. States	Aurora 22 May 1827
Joshua	39	M	Mariner	U. States	U. States	Florida 25 Apr 1825
NICKLES, Samul	40	M	Merchant	St. Johns	U. States	Nancy 27 Jun 1823
NICKLEY, J. L.	35	M	Merchant	America	U. States	Gen. A. Jackson 10 Sep 1821
John	35	M	Merch't.	U. States	Rhode Island	Mercator 10 Apr 1823
Thomas	37	M	Farmer	Great Britian	United States	Andes 19 Aug 1829
NICKLIN, Edward	50	M	Joiner	England	U. States	Balaena 29 Apr 1825
NICKOL, James	2	M	Child	Ireland	United States	Sylvester Healy 14 Jun 1825
James	35	M	Laborer	Ireland	United States	Sylvester Healy 14 Jun 1825
Jane	5	M	Child	Ireland	United States	Sylvester Healy 14 Jun 1825
Mary	32	F	Wife	Ireland	United States	Sylvester Healy 14 Jun 1825
William H.	33	M	Mariner	U. States	U. States	Rambler 26 Jul 1824
NICKOLS, John	36	M	Mariner	America	America	Wilson 16 Nov 1824
NICKS, —, Mrs.	12	F	None	Great Britain	Gt. Britain	Emeline 6 Jul 1824
Lucy	25	F	None	Great Britain	Gt. Britain	Emeline 6 Jul 1824
William	28	M	Merchant	Great Britain	Gt. Britain	Emeline 6 Jul 1824
NICKSEN, Floid	30	M		Ireland	U. States	St. Michael 26 Oct 1824
NICOL, A., Mr.	36	M		Scotland	Missouri	Camden 14 May 1825
Edward	37	M		New York	New York	Amity 31 May 1822
James	33	M	Masin	Scotland	United States	Friends 13 Mar 1824
John		M	Printer	Scotland	G. Brittain	Catharine 23 Jun 1821
Mary	32	F		New York	New York	Amity 31 May 1822
Wm.	22	M			New York	Hero 19 May 1828
NICOLE, John	22	M	Servant	St. Martins	St. Martins	Matilda 10 Sep 1821
NICOLES, Isaac	30		Merchant	N. York	New York	James Cropper 12 Jul 1822
NICOLET, Ja. Theodore	32	M	Merchant	France	America	Hannibal 4 Apr 1823
NICOLL, ...	21	F	Spinster	Great Britain	United States	Superior 31 Mar 1828
...	21	F	Spinster	Great Britain	United States	Superior 31 Mar 1828
...	30	M	Bricklayer	Great Britain	United States	Superior 31 Mar 1828
Chs. A.	34	M	Merchant	...	U. States	Emily 19 Apr 1825
Florentine	24	M	Servant	England	U. States	New York 11 Jul 1823
Jno. C.	22	M	Lawyer	N. Brunswick	U. States	Diana 1 Jun 1822
John	26	M	Shoemaker	U. States	U. States	Virginia 26 May 1828
Samuel	40	M	Merchant	St. John, N.B.	United States	Nancy 20 Sep 1821
Thomas	29	M	Farmer	Great Britain	United States	Ann Maria 12 Jul 1821
NICOLLE, Jaques 22 6/12		M	Merchant	France	United States	Deux Ernest 29 Dec 1827
*landed at Lewiston, Delw.						
Jques. 22 1/2			Commis [Clerk]	Colombia		Deux Ernest 29 Dec 1827
NICOLLS, Chas. H.	35	M	Clergyman	Holland	U. States	Elizabeth 5 May 1826
Elsebella	35	F		St. John	St. John	Nancy 16 Aug 1822

NAMES OF PASSENGERS	AGE	SEX	OCCUPATIONS	COUNTRY TO WHICH THEY BELONG	COUNTRY THEY INTEND TO INHABIT	SHIPS/DATES OF ARRIVAL	
NICOLLS (cont'd)							
Hannah	39	F	Spinner	Great Britain	United States	Unity	20 Oct 1829
John	7	M	Spinner	Great Britain	United States	Unity	20 Oct 1829
Mary	10	F	Spinner	Great Britain	United States	Unity	20 Oct 1829
Robt.	25	M	Farmer	Great Brittain	United States	Active	12 Sep 1828
Samuel	15	M	Spinner	Great Brittain	United States	Unity	20 Oct 1829
NICOLN, Jacob	25	M	Weaver	Germany	U. States	Isabella	10 Aug 1829
NICOLS, Sarah	31	F	Surveyor	England	U. States	Acosta	28 Jul 1823
NICOLSON, Elizabeth	28	M	Farmer	Scotland	U. States	Roger Stewart	9 Jun 1828
John	32	F	Mason	Scotland	U. States	Roger Stewart	9 Jun 1828
NIDELE, J. F.	23	M	Black Smith	France	U. States	Canning	18 Jul 1828
NIEGUS, Henry	21	M	Merchant	Germany	United States	Concordia	25 Aug 1827
NIELE, John	28	M	Carpenter	Scotland	U. States	Brilliant	19 Mar 1828
NIELSON, —, Mr.	25	M	Farmer	Ireland	New York	Carolina Ann	15 Oct 1824
E. P.	21	M	Merchant	U.S.	U. States	Athenian	18 Oct 1826
Thos.	40	M	...	...	U.S. America	Columbia	26 Nov 1825
NIENDISTA, A.	32	M	Merchant	Spain	U. States	James	29 Jul 1820
NIGA, Laurent	28	M	Merchant	England	U.S.	Maria Caroline	12 Jul 1820
NIGAL, Eliza	26	F		Germany	United States	Lydia	18 Jun 1828
L.	20	M		Germany	United States	Lydia	18 Jun 1828
Philip	3	M		Germany	United States	Lydia	18 Jun 1828
Philip	27	M	Cooper	Germany	United States	Lydia	18 Jun 1828
NIGHT, Elizabeth	24			St. John	U. States	Lady Hunter	5 Jul 1823
James	16	M	Servant	England	England	Tontine	1 Jun 1826
NIGHTINGALE, Robert	15	M	Servant	U. States	United States	Pionier	4 Mar 1828
NIGLE, Lawrence	27	M	Mechanic	Great Britain	U.S. Am.	Eliza	12 May 1828
NILEY, Thomas	26	M	Merchant			Hercules	25 Sep 1820
NILLEAURA, J. E., Don	45	M	Gentleman	Curaca	Curacoa	Douglass	27 Apr 1824
NINNE, Ann	5/12	F	Child	England	United States	Cambria	3 Jul 1829
Harriot	3	F	Child	England	United States	Cambria	3 Jul 1829
Jane	20	F	Wife	England	United States	Cambria	3 Jul 1829
William	30	M	Farmer	England	United States	Cambria	3 Jul 1829
NINNIS, —	25	M	Sailor	England	U. States	Hiram	17 Jun 1826
NIPE, Adam	7	M	Farm	Holland	U. States	Edward Bonaffe	23 Jul 1828
Allen	10	F	Farm	Holland	U. States	Edward Bonaffe	23 Jul 1828
Catharar	36	F	Farm	Holland	U. States	Edward Bonaffe	23 Jul 1828
Henry	3	M	Farm	Holland	U. States	Edward Bonaffe	23 Jul 1828
Jacob	9	M	Farm	Holland	U. States	Edward Bonaffe	23 Jul 1828
Jacob	41	M	Farm	Holland	U. States	Edward Bonaffe	23 Jul 1828
NIPPER, —, Mrs.	30	F		Glasgow	U. States	Florenzo	29 Jun 1826
Geo.	35	M	Labourer	Glasgow	U. States	Florenzo	29 Jun 1826
NIRLIN, Thomas McA.	25	M		Ireland	United States	William & George	14 May 1828
NIRSON, Martha	50	F	None	England	America	Ann	2 Nov 1820
NIS, Barbara	11	F		France	America, U.N.S.	Great Britain	3 Aug 1829
Barbara	13	F		France	America, U.N.S.	Great Britain	3 Aug 1829
Barbara	30	F		France	America, U.N.S.	Great Britain	3 Aug 1829
Bernard	4	M		France	America, U.N.S.	Great Britain	3 Aug 1829
Bernard	38	M	Farmer	France	America, U.N.S.	Great Britain	3 Aug 1829
Effa	6	F		France	America, U.N.S.	Great Britain	3 Aug 1829
Effa	9	F		France	America, U.N.S.	Great Britain	3 Aug 1829
George	12	M		France	America, U.N.S.	Great Britain	3 Aug 1829
Marguerita	7	F		France	America, U.N.S.	Great Britain	3 Aug 1829
Marguerita	10	F		France	America, U.N.S.	Great Britain	3 Aug 1829
Marguerita	34	F		France	America, U.N.S.	Great Britain	3 Aug 1829
Michl.	13	M		France	America, U.N.S.	Great Britain	3 Aug 1829
Wealter	38	M	Farmer	France	America, U.N.S.	Great Britain	3 Aug 1829
NISBETT, Maria	46	F	None	United States	United States	William Thompson	19 Aug 1829
NISH, Alexr.	40	M	Farmer	Scotland	U. States	Camillus	27 Jun 1826
Alice	8	F	None	Scotland	U. States	Camillus	27 Jun 1826
James	12	M	None	Scotland	U. States	Camillus	27 Jun 1826
Janett	1	F	None	Scotland	U. States	Camillus	27 Jun 1826
Janette	40	F	None	Scotland	U. States	Camillus	27 Jun 1826
John	10	M	None	Scotland	U. States	Camillus	27 Jun 1826
Mary	6	F	None	Scotland	U. States	Camillus	27 Jun 1826
NITSON, Thos.	43	M	Farmer	Gt. Brittian	Gt. Brittian	Manchester	21 Apr 1827
NIVEN, David	36	M	Merchant	England	England	Trimmer	19 Nov 1824
NIVIN, John	19	M	Baker	Scotland	United States	Camillus	9 May 1827

NAMES OF PASSENGERS	AGE	SEX	OCCUPATIONS	COUNTRY TO WHICH THEY BELONG	COUNTRY THEY INTEND TO INHABIT	SHIPS/DATES OF ARRIVAL	
NIVIN (cont'd)							
William	21	M	Baker	Scotland	United States	Camillus	9 May 1827
NIXCEN, Thomas	29	M		St. Johns	U. States	Wanderer	30 Oct 1828
NIXLAR, Joshua	30	M	Merchant	Ireland	United States	Silas Richards	27 Oct 1825
NIXON, Andrew	14	M	Farmer	Ireland	U. States	Josephine	7 May 1827
Andrew	20	M	Farmer	Ireland	United States	Asia	29 Jul 1829
Bridget	38	F	None	Gt. Britain	United States	Pacific	22 May 1826
Bridget	58	F	None	Gt. Britain	United States	Pacific	22 May 1826
Charity	29	F		England	U. States	John Wells	16 May 1825
Eliza	17			Ireland	United States	Robert Burns	30 May 1823
Elizabeth	1	F		England	U. States	John Wells	16 May 1825
Geo.	19	M	Shoe Maker	England	America	Two Marys	24 Sep 1827
Isabella	26	F	None	Gt. Britain	United States	Pacific	22 May 1826
Jane	26	F	Agriculture	England	United States	Hercules	24 Oct 1821
Mary	7	F	Agriculture	England	United States	Hercules	24 Oct 1821
Robt.	17	M	Labourer	Ireland	United States	Wilson	6 Jun 1828
Thomas	19	M	Farmer	Ireland	United States	Asia	29 Jul 1829
Wm.	13			Ireland	United States	Robert Burns	30 May 1823
Wm.	30	M	Gentleman	England	U. States	John Wells	16 May 1825
Wm., Mr.	72	M	Farmer	Gt. Britain	United States	Pacific	22 May 1826
NO...OOD, David	22	M	Weaver	Ireland	U. States	Josephine	7 May 1827
NOAD, Homer	21	M	Labourer	Ireland	U. States	Marcus	7 Apr 1825
NOAH, Saml.	36	M	Army	England (U. States)	U. States	Foster	28 Aug 1822
NOAL, William	25	M	Laborer	Ireland	United States	St. Michaels	23 Dec 1826
NOB, Catarina	4	F		G. Britain		Caravan	8 Sep 1828
Catraa.	40	F		G. Britain		Caravan	8 Sep 1828
Eliza	11	F		G. Britain		Caravan	8 Sep 1828
Mark	40	M	Black Smith	G. Britain		Caravan	8 Sep 1828
Martin	10	M		G. Britain		Caravan	8 Sep 1828
NOBELS, Robert	22	M	Laborer	Ireland	United States	Nancey	8 Jun 1822
NOBHER, Catherine	22	F		Ireland	United States	Romulus	24 Jun 1826
NOBLE, D. P.	34	M	Mariner	U. States	U. States	Nassau	30 Mar 1824
Dl.	32	M	Mariner	N. York	U. States	Aurilla	8 Jul 1823
Elisabeth	58	F		Dundee	Phildelphia	Robert	28 Aug 1829
George	22	M	Laborer	England	United States	Lord Wellington	14 Nov 1827
James, Jr., Mr.	19		U.S. Navy	U.S. America	U.S. America	Mary	10 Mar 1826
Jane	22	F	Spinster	Ireland	United States	Trident	17 May 1825
John	17		Weaver	Ireland	United States	Robert Burns	30 May 1823
Mericy	23	F		Great Britain	New York	Radius	7 Jul 1821
Richard	20	M	Farmer	Ireland	United States	Trident	17 May 1825
NOBLY, J. Betheo	32	M	Milatary	Perambuco	Brazil	Jane	17 Jan 1825
NOCK, Edward	18	M		Savannah	United States	Juno	26 Nov 1821
Edward	20	M	Gentleman	Great Britan	Great Britan	Columbia	10 Mar 1824
Elizebeth, Mrs.	32	F		Savannah	United States	Juno	26 Nov 1821
James	33	M		Savannah	United States	Juno	26 Nov 1821
John	5	M		Savannah	United States	Juno	26 Nov 1821
Oswold	28	M	Merchant	New Jersey	U. States	Venus	27 Dec 1824
NOE, Ann	25	F	None	Halifax	U. States	Loire	7 Jul 1827
Edward	7	M	None	Halifax	U. States	Loire	7 Jul 1827
James	40	M	Labourer	Halifax	U. States	Loire	7 Jul 1827
John	5	M	None	Halifax	U. States	Loire	7 Jul 1827
Michael	10	M	None	Halifax	U. States	Loire	7 Jul 1827
Patrick	2	M	None	Halifax	U. States	Loire	7 Jul 1827
George	23	M	Farmer	Swizerland		Antioch	18 Aug 1829
NOEL, Alphonsus	15	M	None	France	America, U.N.S.	Great Britain	3 Aug 1829
Charlotte, Zyn Vrouw (his wife [Michel]	24	F		Homberg	United States	Juffraw Johanna	16 Oct 1821
Claude	23	M	Butcher	France	New York	Sully	11 Mar 1829
James L.	50	M	Gentleman	France	America, U.N.S.	Great Britain	3 Aug 1829
Jane A.	34	F	Lady	France	America, U.N.S.	Great Britain	3 Aug 1829
Michel	28	M	Boer	Homberg	United States	Juffraw Johanna	16 Oct 1821
NOFTER, Joseph	25	M	...	G. Britain	U. States	New England	28 Sep 1824
Nicholas	32	M	...	G. Britain	U. States	New England	28 Sep 1824
NOGUEIRA, Leus	54	M	Merchant	France	United States	Prince Edward	1 Apr 1825
NOHE, Jane	10	F		Gt. Brittain	U. States	Courier	30 Dec 1824
Jane	30	F	None	Gt. Brittain	U. States	Courier	30 Dec 1824
NOLAN, B.	38	M	Army	G. Brittain	U. States	Elizabeth	29 Sep 1823

NAMES OF PASSENGERS	AGE	SEX	OCCUPATIONS	COUNTRY TO WHICH THEY BELONG	COUNTRY THEY INTEND TO INHABIT	SHIPS/DATES OF ARRIVAL	
NOLAN (cont'd)							
Bridget	60	F	Wife	Ireland	United States	Dublin Packet	13 Oct 1828
Colane	27	F	Labourer	England	U. States	Ayrshire	12 May 1828
W. B.	37	M	Seaman	British ...	Upper Canada	Loyalty	9 Sep 1822
NOLAND, Marcia	38	F	Spinster	Ireland	United States	Fabius	31 Jul 1829
NOLES, John	25	M	Farmer	Grt. Britain	United States	Henry Kneeland	5 Nov 1828
Mical	50	M	Labourer	Halifax, N.S.	New York	Citizen	1 Nov 1828
NOLIN, Numan	32	M	Merchant	Hamburgh	Uncertain	Ocean	23 Oct 1820
NOLLES, C.	23	F		G. Brittain	U. States	Hope & Esther	26 Nov 1822
NOLLEY, Robt.	23	M	Merchant	Scotland	Scotland	Agness	7 Jan 1828
NOLOLIN, Anne	19	F		G. Britain	U. States	Great Britain	6 Sep 1828
NOLON, Ann	38	F	Matron	Ireland	America	Wilson	16 Nov 1824
Thomas	43	M	Gentleman	Ireland	America	Wilson	16 Nov 1824
NOLTE, Herman	37	M	Merchant	Mexico	Mexico	Canada	13 Feb 1826
John	30	M	Servent	United States	United States	Nestor	20 Nov 1821
Vincent	47	M	Merchant	Leghorn	United States	Nestor	20 Nov 1821
NONAN, John	30	M	Mariner	U. States	U. States	Worromontogus	23 Jun 1823
NONBLOCH, Caroline	9/12	F	Farmer	Switzerland	America	Henry	17 May 1828
Catharine	29 7/12	F	Farmer	Switzerland	America	Henry	17 May 1828
Frederick	3	M	Farmer	Switzerland	America	Henry	17 May 1828
Frederick	30	M	Farmer	Switzerland	America	Henry	17 May 1828
Jack	20 5/12	M	Farmer	Switzerland	America	Henry	17 May 1828
NONES, B.	22	M	Merchant	Spain	U. States	Joseph S. Lewis	6 Dec 1822
Dd. B.	41	M	Mcht.	U. States	U. States	Nassau	24 Nov 1824
J. B.	26	M	Merchant	Philada.	U. States	Elisa Pigott	24 Apr 1822
Jefferson B.	27	M	Merchant	United States	United States	Ceres	7 Aug 1826
Q. B.	32	M	Mariner	U. States	U. States	Henry	24 Nov 1828
NOONAN, Bridget	32	F		Ireland	United States	Pallas	28 Oct 1828
Catherine	27			Ireland	U.S.	Union	20 Aug 1827
John	28			Ireland	U.S.	Union	20 Aug 1827
Mary Ann	4/12			Ireland	U.S.	Union	20 Aug 1827
NOONIN, Ewd.	28 7/12	M	Brick Layer	Ireland	America	Rising States	7 Jul 1828
NOR..., Mary Ann	31	F	...	...	...	Camillus	18 Nov 1824
William	34	M	...	...	...	Camillus	18 Nov 1824
NORCOTT, John	20	M	Farmer	Ireland	America	William	21 May 1825
NORDMANN, Bernhard	12	M	Farmer	Germany	Pensilvania	Maria Elizabeth	24 Mar 1828
Emil	6	M	Farmer	Germany	Pensilvania	Maria Elizabeth	24 Mar 1828
Ernst Stoebing	28	M	Farmer	Germany	Pensilvania	Maria Elizabeth	24 Mar 1828
Franciska	21	F	Farmer	Germany	Pensilvania	Maria Elizabeth	24 Mar 1828
Gotlob	50	M	Farmer	Germany	Pensilvania	Maria Elizabeth	24 Mar 1828
Heinrich	11	M	Farmer	Germany	Pensilvania	Maria Elizabeth	24 Mar 1828
Maria	47	F	Farmer	Germany	Pensilvania	Maria Elizabeth	24 Mar 1828
Thusnelda	15	F	Farmer	Germany	Pensilvania	Maria Elizabeth	24 Mar 1828
NORE, Betty	19	F		G. Britain	U. States	Dalhouse Castle	12 Sep 1828
Judith	20	F		G. Britain	U. States	Dalhouse Castle	12 Sep 1828
NORFOR, R. W.	38	M	Mariner	England	England	Importer	10 Sep 1823
NORIS, Ann	6	F	None	Ireland	United States	Trident	31 Mar 1827
Deborah	21	F		England	U.N.S.	Helen	16 Mar 1829
James	28	M	Farmer	England	U.N.S.	Helen	16 Mar 1829
Jane	26	F	None	Ireland	United States	Trident	31 Mar 1827
Joseph	25	M	Farmer	Ireland	United States	Trident	31 Mar 1827
Margaret	4	F	None	Ireland	United States	Trident	31 Mar 1827
William	1	M	None	Ireland	United States	Trident	31 Mar 1827
Wm.	21	M	Stone Cutter	England	U.N.S.	Helen	16 Mar 1829
NORMAN, Ann	24	F				Reuben & Eliza	21 Aug 1820
B. M.	18	M	Merchant	United States	U. States	Havana Packet	27 Jul 1827
E.	20	F		Great Britain	United States	Isaac Hicks	6 Dec 1827
Elizabeth	25	F		Great Britain	United States	Samuel Wright	12 Oct 1829
Esther	7	F				Reuben & Eliza	21 Aug 1820
G.	20	M	Baker	Great Britain	United States	Isaac Hicks	6 Dec 1827
Jeremiah	20	M	Gardener	Great Britain	United States	Dapper	29 Jan 1829
John	3	M	None	Great Britain		Casanda	5 Sep 1827
John	25	M	Farmer	Great Britain	United States	Samuel Wright	12 Oct 1829
Mary Ann	9	F				Reuben & Eliza	21 Aug 1820
Sarah	4/12	F				Reuben & Eliza	21 Aug 1820
Sarah	35	F				Reuben & Eliza	21 Aug 1820
NORMAND, F.	24	M	Merchant	U. States	U. States	Howard	14 Apr 1823
NORMINGTON, John	45	M	Weaver	England	U. States	Panthea	8 Apr 1826
NORRAWAY, Grace	32	F	Farming	England	America	Maine	16 Jul 1821

NAMES OF PASSENGERS	AGE	SEX	OCCUPATIONS	COUNTRY TO WHICH THEY BELONG	COUNTRY THEY INTEND TO INHABIT	SHIPS/DATES OF ARRIVAL	
NORRAWAY (cont'd)							
Richard	39	M	Farming	England	America	Maine	16 Jul 1821
Robert	3	M	Farming	England	America	Maine	16 Jul 1821
Sarah	5	F	Farming	England	America	Maine	16 Jul 1821
NORRIS, —, Mr.	22	M		Ireland	U. States	Howard	25 Jul 1823
—, Mrs.		F		Ireland	U. States	Howard	25 Jul 1823
Auron B.	24	M	Merchant	U. States	U. States	Ann Elizabeth	24 Jun 1823
Benjm.	1	M		Ireland	U. States	Alex Mansfield	1 Jun 1822
Bridget	3	F		Ireland	United States	Dublin Packet	30 Apr 1821
Elizabeth	22	F		New York	U. States	Falcon	4 May 1826
Henry	28	M	Merchant	Ireland	United States	Sarah G.	11 Jan 1828
John	36	M	Merchant	Ireland	United States	Dublin Packet	30 Apr 1821
Jos. B.	26	M	Merchant	U. States	U. States	Ann Elizabeth	24 Jun 1823
Jos. B.	30	M	Merchant	U. States	U. States	Mattrawan	1 Oct 1822
Lewis And.	18		...	...	...	Hudson	14 Jun 1827
Margaret	65	F	Lady	Ireland	United States	Dublin Packet	3 Sep 1822
Patience	23	F		...	United States	Dublin Packet	30 Apr 1821
Polly	22	F		England	U.N.S.	Helen	16 Mar 1829
R.	41		Merchant	U. States		New York	18 Jul 1828
Rob.	60	M	Manufacturer	Ireland	U. States	Alex Mansfield	1 Jun 1822
Robert	2	M		Ireland	United States	Dublin Packet	30 Apr 1821
Stephen	33	M	Tailor	England	America	Two Marys	24 Sep 1827
Thomas	25	M	Labourer	Ireland	U. States	Combine	30 Nov 1825
Thomas	25	M	Mason	New York	U. States	Falcon	4 May 1826
Thos.	29		Weaver	Bolton	England	Great Britain	7 May 1827
Walter	38	M	Mariner	New York	New York	Charleston	1 Aug 1825
NORTEN, Wm.	26	M	Seaman	U.S. America	United States	Orozimbo	11 Aug 1823
NORTH, Abel	20	M	Gentleman	Ireland	America	Hannah	8 Nov 1821
Benj.	22	M	Cloth Dripers	Great Britain	America	Lady Gallatin	21 Jun 1820
Benjamin	28	M	Farmer	Yorkshire	United States	Dalhousie Castle	27 Jul 1826
Betsey	27	F	None	Yorkshire	United States	Dalhousie Castle	27 Jul 1826
Harriot	4	F	None	England		Manhattan	22 May 1827
Jabez	26	M	Merchant	G. Brittain	United States	Hercules	24 Oct 1821
James	25		Clothier	England	America	Sarah	18 Aug 1829
John	9	M	None	England		Manhattan	22 May 1827
Joseph	26		Labourer	Haddersfield		Aurora	8 Jun 1827
M.	9	F		France	United States	Cavalier	25 Jul 1828
Mary	21	F		United States	United States	Euphrates	2 Sep 1823
Mary Jane	6	F	None	England		Manhattan	22 May 1827
Sarah	2	F	None	England		Manhattan	22 May 1827
Sarah	28	F	None	Haddersfield		Aurora	8 Jun 1827
Sarah	32	F	None	England		Manhattan	22 May 1827
Thomas	32	M	Farmer	England		Manhattan	22 May 1827
Thos.	20	M	Farmer	England	United States	Euphrates	2 Sep 1823
William	9	M	None	Yorkshire	United States	Dalhousie Castle	27 Jul 1826
Wm.	21	M	Mercht.	G. Britain		Ann Maria	3 Jul 1820
Wm.	51	M	Farmer	United States	United States	Isaac Hicks	22 Aug 1828
NORTHAM, J. D.	17	M	Gentleman	United States	United States	Mary	1 May 1828
S. T., Jr.	22	M	Merchant	U. States	U. States	Frances	7 Aug 1826
NORTHCOAT, Richard	30			England	England	Corinthian	8 Oct 1828
NORTHIT, Mary	24	F	Spinster	Ireland	United States	Erin	25 Dec 1820
NORTHLY, George	45	M	Miner	England	England	Eliza	31 Jul 1826
NORTHRUP, Job	38	M	Seaman	U. States	U. States	Ductile	4 Oct 1825
NORTON, ...	35 4/12	M	...	England	America, U.S.	Illinois	3 Jun 1822
A.	23	M	Carpenter	U. States		Emeline	24 Apr 1828
Bernard	28	M	Gentn.	England	N. Orleans	Cortes	23 Nov 1827
Catherine Jane	10	F	Girl	Ireland	United States	Trident	17 May 1825
Ellen	38	F	Servant	England	America	William	21 Sep 1821
Eve	24	F	Baker	England	United States	Comet	6 Mar 1823
Jas.	25					Trio	5 May 1828
John	39	M	Baker	England	United States	Comet	6 Mar 1823
Mary	21					Trio	5 May 1828
Saml.	45	M	Merchant	U. States	U. States	Rebecca	20 Dec 1822
Thomas	26	M	Labourer	Ireland	New York	Brighton	24 Aug 1827
NORTT, P., Master	13	M	Boy	Denmark	United States	Alfred	8 Jul 1822
NORVY, John	34	M	...	England	U.N. States	William Byrnes	23 Jul 1824
NORWOOD, Carlisle	17	M	Merchant	United States		France	6 Feb 1829
Emiley	12 6/12	F		America	America	France	28 Mar 1829
Jane	24 5/12	F		America	America	France	28 Mar 1829

NAMES OF PASSENGERS	AGE	SEX	OCCUPATIONS	COUNTRY TO WHICH THEY BELONG	COUNTRY THEY INTEND TO INHABIT	SHIPS/DATES OF ARRIVAL	
NORWOOD (cont'd)							
Rebecka	51 6/12	F		America	America	France	28 Mar 1829
NOT, Andrew	22	M	Weaver	Ireland	United States	Fabius	4 Jun 1828
John	25	M	Weaver	Ireland	United States	Fabius	4 Jun 1828
NOTHINGER, Gabriel A.	36	M	Carpenter	Berne	U.S. America	Superior	18 Jun 1825
NOTHINGHAM, Ann	8			U. States		Manhattan	8 Aug 1820
Eliza	...	F	None	U. States		Manhattan	8 Aug 1820
Eliza	4			U. States		Manhattan	8 Aug 1820
Lovina	7			U. States		Manhattan	8 Aug 1820
Rebecca	9	F		U. States		Manhattan	8 Aug 1820
Sarah	1			U. States		Manhattan	8 Aug 1820
Wm.	36	M	...	U. States		Manhattan	8 Aug 1820
NOTMAN, William	16	M	Mercht.	United States	United States	Importer	21 May 1821
NOTRE, Vin.	47	M	Merchant	U.S. of America	U.S. of America	Canada	1 Oct 1827
NOTT, —, Mrs.	18	F		S. Carolina	U. States	Stephania	18 Dec 1824
A.	3/12	F		S. Carolina	U. States	Stephania	18 Dec 1824
Henry G.	27	M	Lawyer	S. Carolina	U. States	Stephania	18 Dec 1824
Thos. J.	24	M	Artist	Philadelphia	U.S. America	Lafayette	3 Dec 1827
NOTTE, Jacques	19	M	Farmer	Swizerland		Antioch	18 Aug 1829
NOTTEERE, John	24	M	Merchant	Antwerp	U. States	Hornillus	13 Aug 1827
NOTTINGHAM, W.	43	M	Merchant	Great Britain	United States	Dapper	24 Aug 1827
Wm.	40	M	Merchant	United States	United States	Euphrates	12 Mar 1824
NOTZER, Catharine	45	F	Agriculturist	Germany	U.S.	Helen	3 May 1828
Catherine	5	F	Agriculturist	Germany	U.S.	Helen	3 May 1828
Frederick	13	M	Agriculturist	Germany	U.S.	Helen	3 May 1828
Jean	7	M	Agriculturist	Germany	U.S.	Helen	3 May 1828
Jean	32	M	Agriculturist	Germany	U.S.	Helen	3 May 1828
Rosaly	4	F	Agriculturist	Germany	U.S.	Helen	3 May 1828
NOUDAY, B.	80	M		Ireland	U. States	Sarah G	30 Jun 1828
Susana	78	F		Ireland	U. States	Sarah G	30 Jun 1828
NOUTHEIR, John F.	20	M	Merchant	France	U. States	Montano	2 Sep 1828
NOVES, James	18	M	Husbandman	England	America	Criterion	27 Oct 1821
NOVET, Edward, Mr.	24	M	Mercht.	U.S.	U.S.	Cadmus	26 Apr 1824
NOVIA, Manuel	27	M	Merchant	Mexico	Mexico	Brown	30 Nov 1827
NOVIER, Anthony	18	M	Farmer	France	U. States	Edward Quesnel	4 Aug 1828
Catherine	2	F	Farmer	France	U. States	Edward Quesnel	4 Aug 1828
Elisabeth	8	F	Farmer	France	U. States	Edward Quesnel	4 Aug 1828
Francis	13	F	Farmer	France	U. States	Edward Quesnel	4 Aug 1828
Jane	44	F	Farmer	France	U. States	Edward Quesnel	4 Aug 1828
Jaques	4	M	Farmer	France	U. States	Edward Quesnel	4 Aug 1828
Jaques	47	M	Farmer	France	U. States	Edward Quesnel	4 Aug 1828
John P.	6	M	Farmer	France	U. States	Edward Quesnel	4 Aug 1828
Maria	15	F	Farmer	France	U. States	Edward Quesnel	4 Aug 1828
NOWELL, Harriett	13	F	None	Great Britain		Moro Castle	6 Jul 1827
John				Great Britain		Moro Castle	6 Jul 1827
John	3	M	None	Great Britain		Moro Castle	6 Jul 1827
John	32	M	Shoemaker	Great Britain		Moro Castle	6 Jul 1827
Maria	10	F	None	Great Britain		Moro Castle	6 Jul 1827
Maria	30	F	None	Great Britain		Moro Castle	6 Jul 1827
Mary Ann	6	F	None	Great Britain		Moro Castle	6 Jul 1827
S. C.	22	M	Merchant	Charleston	U. States	William & Henry	13 Mar 1823
William	1	M	None	Great Britain		Moro Castle	6 Jul 1827
William	34	M	Blacksmith	Great Britain	U. States	Ganges	21 Jun 1827
NOWLAN, John	12	M		Ireland	United States	St. John	5 Oct 1829
John	20		Carpenter	Ireland	United States	Geo. Canning	5 Jun 1828
John	26		Labourer	Manchester		Mount Vernon	18 Oct 1822
Margaret	35	F		Ireland	United States	Pallas	28 Oct 1828
Miles	35	M	Mariner	United States		France	6 Feb 1829
Owen	32	M	Tobacconist	Ireland	United States	St. John	5 Oct 1829
Tim	20		Labourer	Ireland	United States	Geo. Canning	5 Jun 1828
NOWLAND, Andrew	22	M	Labourer	England	U. States	Hope & Esther	10 Jul 1827
C. W. B.	21	M	Merchant	U. States	U. States	John & Edward	8 Feb 1827
NOWLIN, Moses	24	M		G. Brittain	U. States	Hope & Esther	26 Nov 1822
NOWLING, John	25	M	Labourer	Ireland	United States	Hopes Delight	29 Nov 1827
NOYES, —, Mrs.	25	F		U. States	St. Johns, N.B.	Borneo	26 Apr 1824
Amos	25	M	Merchant	U. States	U. States	New Packet	20 Sep 1826
J. M.	33	M	Merchant	U. States	U. States	Mary	22 May 1822
Jacob	29	M	Merchant	United States	United States	Hanford	3 Jul 1829

NAMES OF PASSENGERS	AGE	SEX	OCCUPATIONS	COUNTRY TO WHICH THEY BELONG	COUNTRY THEY INTEND TO INHABIT	SHIPS/DATES OF ARRIVAL	
NOYES (cont'd)							
John	1 1/12	M				Borneo	26 Apr 1824
Mary	9	F	Lady	United States	United States	Sylvester Healy	17 Oct 1825
Mary Jane	18	F	Lady	U. States	U.States	Nancy	31 May 1823
Saml.	22	M	Merchant	New York	New York	Borneo	27 Oct 1824
Wm.	18	M	Merchant	America	United States	Sarah G.	15 May 1828
NOYS, C. W.	39	M	Mariner	United States	United States	Diamond	12 Mar 1824
NOYSE, Henry	25	M	Gentln.	U. States	U. States	Eunice	12 Mar 1829
Mary T.	20	F		United	U. States	Sarah G	30 Jun 1828
NUCIER, John	17	M	Merchant	Spain		Eliza Ann	29 Sep 1820
NUDON, Isaac	35	M		Cheshire Hule	U. States	Manhattan	21 May 1821
NUGENT, Amy	24	F		England	New York	Cincinnatus	5 Dec 1825
Ane	40	F		G. Britain	G. Britain	Brittania	17 Jul 1828
Ann	15	F	None	Ireland	United States	Jubilee	12 May 1828
Ann Maria	23	F		Great Britain	United States	Washington	3 Sep 1827
Catharin	4/12	F		St. Thomas	U. States	May Flower	11 Oct 1826
Catherine	1/2	F		Scotland	United States	Camillus	9 May 1827
Cathrine	37	F	Spinster	Grt. Britain	United States	Robert Fulton	8 Oct 1828
Edmund	1	M		England	New York	Cincinnatus	5 Dec 1825
Edward	30	M	Labourer	Ireland	Ireland	Sarah G.	28 Nov 1827
Emily	2	F		England	New York	Cincinnatus	5 Dec 1825
G.	45	F				Hibernia	15 Aug 1820
George	32	M	Merchant	U. States	Great Britain	Thompson	26 Apr 1828
James	21	M	Labourer	England	U. States	Ayrshire	12 May 1828
James	40	M	Merchant	England	France	Stephania	24 Jul 1820
James	40	M	Labourer	Grt. Britain	United States	Robert Fulton	8 Oct 1828
Johannah	28	F		St. Thomas	U. States	May Flower	11 Oct 1826
John	35	M	Planter	St. Thomas	U. States	May Flower	11 Oct 1826
M.	20					Hibernia	15 Aug 1820
Margaret	4	F		St. Thomas	U. States	May Flower	11 Oct 1826
Margaret	25	F		England	U. States	Indian Queen	5 Dec 1825
Mark	15					Hibernia	15 Aug 1820
Martin	27	M	Engineer	United States	United States	Rapid	24 Oct 1823
Martin	30	M	Engineer	England	U. States	Indian Queen	5 Dec 1825
Mary	3	F		England	New York	Cincinnatus	5 Dec 1825
Mary	19	F	Labourer	England	U. States	Ayrshire	12 May 1828
Mary	23	M		England	United States	Nancy Henrietta	3 Nov 1828
Michael	19		Shoemaker	Ireland	Great Britain	Robert Burns	14 Jun 1824
Patrick	3 6/12	M	Labourer	Grt. Britain	United States	Robert Fulton	8 Oct 1828
Peter	30	M	Labourer	Ireland	New York	Cincinnatus	5 Dec 1825
Sarah	1 6/12	F	Infant	Grt. Britain	United States	Robert Fulton	8 Oct 1828
Susanna	30	F		Scotland	United States	Camillus	9 May 1827
T.	22	M	Merchant	America	America	Nancy	18 Aug 1821
Thomas	12	M		St. Thomas	U. States	May Flower	11 Oct 1826
Thos.	24	M	Labourer	Great Britain	United States	Atlantic	8 Dec 1827
Thos.	27	M		Great Britain	United States	Washington	3 Sep 1827
Thos.	45	M	Planter	Ireland	U. States	Elias Burger	12 Sep 1822
NUGINT, Cathrin	28	F		Great Britain	U. States	Lady Hunter	28 May 1823
NUHOTH, David	25	M	Merchant	United States	United States	Abeona	31 Oct 1820
NUIMAN, Richd.	33	M	Merchant	Jamaica	England	Desdemona	24 Feb 1827
NULL, Margaret	20	F	Servant	Ireland	N. York	Trusty	12 Sep 1828
Mary	20	M	Barber	Scotland	U. States	Roger Stewart	9 Jun 1828
NULLING, T.	22	F		Wurtemburg		Constitution	20 Jun 1828
NUMBER, Rump	28	M	Seaman	U. States	U. States	Boston	26 Sep 1820
NUMER, Frederick	35	M	Miner	Germany	Germany	Virginia	26 May 1828
NUMIONS, M. J., Mr.	25	M	Mariner	Portugal	Portugal	Hesper	2 May 1826
NUMON, M.	11	M	No	Campeache	U. States	Doris	22 May 1826
NUN, Thomas	35	M	Mason	Ireland	U. States	Borneo	15 Apr 1828
NUNAN, Bridget	11	F		Limerick	N. York	Thomas & William	25 May 1827
Catherine	14	F		Limerick	N. York	Thomas & William	25 May 1827
Corns.	9	M		Limerick	N. York	Thomas & William	25 May 1827
Danl.		M	Farmer	Limerick	N. York	Thomas & William	25 May 1827
James	24	M	Farmer	Limerick	N. York	Thomas & William	25 May 1827

959

NAMES OF PASSENGERS	AGE	SEX	OCCUPATIONS	COUNTRY TO WHICH THEY BELONG	COUNTRY THEY INTEND TO INHABIT	SHIPS/DATES OF ARRIVAL	
NUNAN (cont'd)							
James Ths.	22	M	Labourer	Limerick	N. York	Thomas & William	25 May 1827
Maria	4/12	F		Limerick	N. York	Thomas & William	25 May 1827
Mary	40	F		Limerick	N. York	Thomas & William	25 May 1827
Michael	7	M		Limerick	N. York	Thomas & William	25 May 1827
Michael	19	M	Gentleman	Ireland	America	Parrington	9 Jun 1827
Patk.	17	M	Farmer	Limerick	N. York	Thomas & William	25 May 1827
Thomas	20	M	Farmer	Limerick	N. York	Thomas & William	25 May 1827
NUNES, Jose	40	M	Merchant	Spaine	Cuba	Rubicon	7 Oct 1826
W.	45	M	Merchant	France	United States	Phoebe Ann	6 Sep 1826
NUNIS, A. J.	37	M	Merchant	England	U. States	Governor Lincoln	10 Jul 1827
NUNMAKER, John	19	M	Butcher	France	U. States	Sully	25 Jun 1828
NUNN, Jos.	32	M	Farmer	Suffolk	U. States	Criterion	15 Oct 1822
O...	20	F		Great Britian	United States	London	24 Jun 1823
NUNNING, Charles	6	M	None	England		Marchioness	13 May 1828
Mary	30	F	None	England		Marchioness	13 May 1828
Mathew	5	M	None	England		Marchioness	13 May 1828
Nathl.	39	M	Slater	England		Marchioness	13 May 1828
NUNNS, Elenor	24	F		England		Cincinnatus	29 Apr 1822
Elizabeth	5	F		England		Cincinnatus	29 Apr 1822
Elizabeth	20			England	England	Hudson	4 Sep 1823
John	15	M		England		Cincinnatus	29 Apr 1822
Joseph	22		Mechanic	England	England	Hudson	4 Sep 1823
Maria	14		Lady	England	England	London	16 Aug 1824
Mary	21	F		England		Cincinnatus	29 Apr 1822
Mary	56		Lady	England	England	London	16 Aug 1824
Robert	3	M		England		Cincinnatus	29 Apr 1822
Robert	30	M	Merchant	England		Cincinnatus	29 Apr 1822
Sarah	13		Lady	England	England	London	16 Aug 1824
Thomas	24		Mechanic	England	England	Hudson	4 Sep 1823
Wm.	1	M		England		Cincinnatus	29 Apr 1822
Wm. J.	27	M	Merchant	England	United States	Cincinnatus	21 Nov 1821
NUNUNES, Pedro	40	M	Merchant	Spain	Spain	Sciot	12 Mar 1828
NUNZIATE, Cleafide	30	F	Lady	Italy	United States	White Oak	9 Oct 1828
NUPPER, Richard	36	M	Merchant	England	United States	Bogota	16 Dec 1826
NUSBAUMER, Christien	21	M	Shoemaker	Switzerland	United States	Thetis	5 Jul 1821
John	20	M	Weaver	Switzerland	United States	Thetis	5 Jul 1821
Peter	18	M	Labourer	Switzerland	United States	Thetis	5 Jul 1821
NUSGRAVE, Thomas	22	M	Weaver			Eliza Jane	12 Sep 1820
NUSON, Erastus	25	M	Seaman	New York	New York	Charleston	1 Jun 1826
NUTAL, Robt.	32	M	Farmer	England	U.N.S.	Helen	16 Mar 1829
NUTALL, Mary	9	F	Spinster	Toddington	U. States	Panthea	8 Apr 1826
NUTH, John	14	M	Carpenter	England	United States	Cosmo	26 Aug 1829
Mary	24		Spinster	Ireland	United States	Fabius	18 Mar 1829
William	18		Labourer	Ireland	United States	Fabius	18 Mar 1829
NUTT, Jas.	23	M	Carpenter	Antrim, Ireland	Pennsylvania	Anthusa	24 Aug 1825
Sarah	19	F		Antrim, Ireland	Pennsylvania	Anthusa	24 Aug 1825
W. C.	24	M	Supercargo	U.S.	U.S.	Porcia	4 Jan 1828
NUTTALL, Allice	32	F	Mason	Manchester	United States	Nile	17 May 1827
Ann	4	F	Spinster	Toddington	U. States	Panthea	8 Apr 1826
Edward	44	M	Painter	Manchester	United States	Nile	17 May 1827
Ellis	1	F	Spinster	Toddington	U. States	Panthea	8 Apr 1826
Jno.	40	M	Bleacher	Toddington	U. States	Panthea	8 Apr 1826
John	38	M	Weaver	Manchester	United States	Nile	17 May 1827
Sarah	30	F	Spinster	Toddington	U. States	Panthea	8 Apr 1826
Thomas	25	M	Calico Printer	Great Britain	United States	Roman	19 Dec 1825
Thos.	7	M	Spinster	Toddington	U. States	Panthea	8 Apr 1826
NUTTER, Benjamin	28		Tailor	England	United States	Corinthian	30 May 1828
Benjamin, Master	2		Tailor	England	United States	Corinthian	30 May 1828
Henry	4		Tailor	England	United States	Corinthian	30 May 1828
Mary	30		Tailor	England	United States	Corinthian	30 May 1828
William	1		Tailor	England	United States	Corinthian	30 May 1828

NAMES OF PASSENGERS	AGE	SEX	OCCUPATIONS	COUNTRY TO WHICH THEY BELONG	COUNTRY THEY INTEND TO INHABIT	SHIPS/DATES OF ARRIVAL	
NUTTLE, John	21	M	Taylor	England	United States	Siroc	31 Oct 1829
Joseph	31	M	Weaver	England	U. States	Severn	12 Oct 1826
NUZER, Christian	30	M	Miller	France	U. States	Sully	25 Jun 1828
NYE, Adam	20	M	Taylor	Germany	United States	Samuel Robertson	8 Aug 1828
Ann	28	F		Germany	United States	Samuel Robertson	8 Aug 1828
Anna M.	5	F		Germany	United States	Samuel Robertson	8 Aug 1828
Ezra	29	M	Mariner	U. States	U. States	Agness	7 Jan 1828
Frederick	26	M	Weaver	Germany	United States	Samuel Robertson	8 Aug 1828
James	20	M	Wool Assorter	England	U.S.A.	Robin Hood	6 May 1828
Mariline	9	M		Germany	United States	Samuel	
Michael	56	M	Labourer	Germany	United States	Samuel Robertson	8 Aug 1828
NYMAN, Benjamin	24	M	Atizan	England	United States	Jubilee	1 Oct 1828
Jemina	22	F	None	England	United States	Jubilee	1 Oct 1828
NYMEYER (see Negmeiger)							
O..., Bartlet	25	M	Farmer	Ireland	U. States	Nancy	29 Nov 1821
O'BOUHE, Biddy	19	F	None	Great Britain	United States	Florida	10 Dec 1823
O'BOYLE, B.	50	M	Merchant	Great Britain	United States	Atlantic	8 Dec 1827
Ellin	23	F	Gentleman	Ireland	New York	Betsy	4 Sep 1820
Felix, Jr.	16	M	Gentleman	Ireland	New York	Betsy	4 Sep 1820
Hugh	16	M	Labourer	Great Britain	United States	Atlantic	8 Dec 1827
Jane	7	F	Spinner	Great Britain	United States	Atlantic	8 Dec 1827
Philip	50	M	Masn.	America	New York	Betsy	4 Sep 1820
Thos.	18	M	Gentleman	Ireland	New York	Betsy	4 Sep 1820
O'BR...N, J.	37		Farmer	Ireland	United States	Courier	16 May 1825
O'BREGAN, B.	45	M	Deputy to Cortes	Mexico	Mexico	General Brown	10 Dec 1823
O'BRENT, Daniel	25	M	Laborer	Ireland	United States	St. Michaels	18 Jul 1826
O'BRIAN, —		F	Spinster	Ireland	U. States	Panthea	8 Apr 1826
Bridget	4		Laboring Class		United States	Atlantic	2 Apr 1827
Bridget	23	F	Spinster	Ireland	U. States	Panthea	8 Apr 1826
Hanah	28		Laboring Class		United States	Atlantic	2 Apr 1827
Hezek.	33		Laboring Class		United States	Atlantic	2 Apr 1827
Honora	25	F	Wife	..., ..., ...land	U. States	New Orleans	24 Aug 1827
Hugh	9		Laboring Class		United States	Atlantic	2 Apr 1827
James	12		Laboring Class		United States	Atlantic	2 Apr 1827
Jas.	22	M	Farmer	England	U. States	Commerce	2 Oct 1823
Johana	20	F		Ireland	U. States	Howard	25 Jul 1823
John	13		Laboring Class		United States	Atlantic	2 Apr 1827
M.	25	M	Grocer	Great Brittain	U. States	Louisa	11 Jun 1824
M.	25		Farmer	Limerick	New York	Schuylkill	22 Aug 1825
Mary	29	F	Farmer	England	U. States	Commerce	2 Oct 1823
Phillip	12		Laboring Class		United States	Atlantic	2 Apr 1827
Thos.	6	M	Farmer	England	U. States	Commerce	2 Oct 1823
Thos.	20	M		Ireland	U. States	Howard	25 Jul 1823
O'BRIAR, C.	24	M	Labourer	G. Britain	U. States	Hanford	18 Sep 1828
O'BRIDE, Rose	22	F	Servant	Ireland	United States	Josephine	30 Apr 1828
O'BRIEN, —, Mr.	40	M	Blacksmith	Ireland	U. States	Favourite	2 Sep 1822
Ann	20	F	Seampstress	Scotland		Zamoa	5 Nov 1828
Ann	27	F		Gt. Britain		Dalhouse Castle	13 May 1828
Bartholomew	27	M	Laborer	Ireland	New York	Indian Chief	19 Jun 1823
Bridget	45	F	Matron	Ireland	America	Parrington	9 Jun 1827
Bridget, Mrs.	24	F	None	Grate Britain	...	Courier	14 Jun 1825
Catharine	5/12	F	None	Ireland	U. States	Criterion	23 May 1826
Catherine	44	F	Wife	Ireland	United States	Sarah Ann	18 Nov 1826
Dl.	27	M	Supercargo	Ireland	U. States	Clarissa	14 Jul 1821
Edward	22	M	Farmer	Ireland	United States	Dublin Packet	22 Aug 1829
Edwd.	21	M	Stone Mason	Great Britain	United States	Blakely	29 Sep 1826
Edwd.	30	M	Gentleman	England	U.S.	Corinthian	11 Mar 1829
Eliza	16	F	None	U. States	U. States	Loire	7 Jun 1827
Ellen	19	F	Mechanic	G.B.	U.S.A.	Silas Richard	30 Jun 1828
Ellen	40	F	Wife	Ireland	United States	Dublin Packet	23 May 1828
Ester	30	F		Ireland	U. States	Favourite	2 Sep 1822
George	13		Merchant	Ireland	United States	Florida	11 Mar 1829

NAMES OF PASSENGERS	AGE	SEX	OCCUPATIONS	COUNTRY TO WHICH THEY BELONG	COUNTRY THEY INTEND TO INHABIT	SHIPS/DATES OF ARRIVAL	
O'BRIEN (cont'd)							
H. E.	23	M	Merchant	U. States	U. States	Glenthorne	25 Jul 1821
H. E.	23	M	Merchant	United States	United States	Amphion	5 Jul 1822
Hannah	20	F		G. Britain	U. States	Sarah G	5 Jun 1828
Henry	30		Labourer	Great Britan	United States	Newry	11 Jul 1827
Jacob	24		Shoe Maker	Ireland	Great Britain	Henrietta	26 Nov 1825
James	19		Taylor	Ireland	Great Britain	Henrietta	26 Nov 1825
James	21	M	Clerk	Ireland	United States	Gem	16 Jun 1824
James	27	M	Laborer	Ireland	America	Parrington	9 Jun 1827
James, Mas.	7/12	M	None	Grate Britain	...	Courier	14 Jun 1825
Jarret	28	M	Labourer	Ireland	United States	Combine	4 Jun 1825
Jno.	21	M	Laborer	Ireland	United States	Thomas	13 Dec 1827
John	18	M	Boy	Ireland	United States	Dublin Packet	6 Dec 1827
John	21		Shoe Maker	Ireland	Great Britain	Henrietta	26 Nov 1825
John	24	M	Farmer	Ireland	United States	Dublin Packet	23 May 1828
John	29	M	Laborer	Ireland	America	Parrington	9 Jun 1827
John	35					Copernicus	3 Aug 1829
Joseph	7	M		Gt. Britain		Dalhouse Castle	13 May 1828
Joseph	34	M	Stone Mason	Ireland	U. States	Josephine	27 Jul 1825
Judith	20	F	None	Ireland	U. States	Criterion	23 May 1826
K.	36	M	None	Ireland	U. States	Criterion	23 May 1826
Margaret	2	F	Child	Ireland	United States	Dublin Packet	22 Aug 1829
Margaret	22	M	Labourer	Limerick	Baltimore	Thomas & William	25 May 1827
Mary	3 6/12	F		Ireland	Pensylvania	Lima	5 Aug 1829
Mary	3 6/12	F		England	U. States	Lima	5 Aug 1829
Mary	8	F		Gt. Britain		Dalhouse Castle	13 May 1828
Mary	19	F		Gt. Britain	United States	Penelope	9 Sep 1828
Mary	20	F	Servant	Ireland, Great Britain	U.S. of America	Dublin	21 Feb 1826
Mary	20	F	None	England	U. States	Thomas Ritchie	2 Jul 1827
Mary, Mrs.	25	F	Wife	Ireland	United States	Dublin Packet	22 Aug 1829
Mary Ann	22	F	Farmer	Ireland	U. States	Atlantic	19 Aug 1825
Mathew	30	M	Farmer	Ireland	U. States	Atlantic	19 Aug 1825
Matthew	12	M	None	Ireland	U. States	Criterion	23 May 1826
Michael	22	M	Merchant	Gt. Britain	U. States	Swift	25 Apr 1828
Michael	22	M	Farmer	Ireland	United States	Dublin Packet	23 May 1828
Michael	44	M	Merchant	Ireland	United States	Sarah Ann	18 Nov 1826
Morgan	25	M	Laborer	Ireland	America	Parrington	9 Jun 1827
Nelly	22	F		Ireland	Pensylvania	Lima	5 Aug 1829
Nelly	22	F		England	U. States	Lima	5 Aug 1829
Nicholas	27	M	Farmer	Ireland	United States	Dublin Packet	13 Oct 1828
Nicholas	38	M	Labourer	Ireland	United States	Potomac	28 Sep 1827
Ns.	28	M	Farmer	Ireland	U. States	Hercules	4 Oct 1824
P.	3	F	None	Ireland	U. States	Criterion	23 May 1826
P.	30	F	None	Ireland	U. States	Criterion	23 May 1826
Patrick	2	M	None	Ireland	U. States	Criterion	23 May 1826
Patrick	23	M	Farmer	Ireland	United States	Dublin Packet	13 Oct 1828
Peter, Mr.	27	M	Farmer	Grate Britain	...	Courier	14 Jun 1825
Redmun	29	M	Farmer	Great Britain	England	Jay	18 Apr 1823
Rose T.	18	F	Spinster	Ireland	United States	Gem	16 Jun 1824
T.	0 5/12	M	Mechanic	Gt. Britain	U. States	Swift	25 Apr 1828
Thomas	22	M	Labourer	Limerick	N. York	Thomas & William	25 May 1827
Thomas	23	M	Merchant	Ireland	U. States	Arrington	9 Oct 1826
Thos.	3	M		Gt. Britain		Dalhouse Castle	13 May 1828
Thos.	30	M	Labourer	England	U. States	Thomas Ritchie	2 Jul 1827
Thos.	35		Labourer	Great Britan	United States	Newry	11 Jul 1827
Timothy	17	M	Tailor	Halifax	United States	Josephine	13 Oct 1829
Timothy	22	M	Laborer	Ireland	United States	St. Michaels	18 Jul 1826
William	30	M	Labourer	Ireland	Philadelphia	General Marion	12 Jan 1829
O'BRIM, Charles	14	M	Son	Ireland	United States	William & George	14 May 1828
Edward	10/12	M	Son	Ireland	United States	William & George	14 May 1828
Nancy	52	F		Ireland	United States	William & George	14 May 1828
Robert	7/12	M	Son	Ireland	United States	William & George	14 May 1828

NAMES OF PASSENGERS	AGE	SEX	OCCUPATIONS	COUNTRY TO WHICH THEY BELONG	COUNTRY THEY INTEND TO INHABIT	SHIPS/DATES OF ARRIVAL	
O'BRINE, Peggy	18	F	Spinster	Ireland	United States	Trident	17 May 1825
O'BRION, Admiral	5	M	Child	Ireland	United States	Nancy	15 Nov 1824
Bridget	18	F	Spinster	Ireland	United States	Nancy	15 Nov 1824
Bridget	22	F		Great Britain	United States	Mount Vernon	17 Jun 1825
Joanna	30	F	Wife	Ireland	United States	Nancy	15 Nov 1824
John	3	M	Child	Ireland	United States	Nancy	15 Nov 1824
Martin	31	M	Schoolmaster	Great Britain	United States	Mount Vernon	17 Jun 1825
Michael	32	M	Laborer	Ireland	United States	Nancy	15 Nov 1824
Norah	9	F	Child	Ireland	United States	Nancy	15 Nov 1824
O'BRYAN, Charles	13	M	Merchant	N. York	United States	Huntress	25 Mar 1822
Charles	13	M		N. York	U. States	Prize	20 Sep 1823
Grace	21	F		N. York	U. States	Prize	20 Sep 1823
J.	20	F	Labourer	Ireland	United States	Combine	4 Jun 1825
Jane	25	F		U. States	U. States	Abeona	5 Jul 1822
Jane	28	F	None	U. States	U. States	Adze	24 Jul 1820
Jane	45	F		N. York	U. States	Prize	20 Sep 1823
Jno.	50	M	Planter	New York	U.S.	Radius	21 Jul 1824
John	52	M	Shipmaster	N. York	U. States	Prize	20 Sep 1823
John, Jr.	24	M	Merchant	United States	United States	Hope	19 Jan 1820
Julia	8	F		N. York	U. States	Prize	20 Sep 1823
Melvina	15	F		N. York	U. States	Prize	20 Sep 1823
Rosina	17	F		N. York	U. States	Prize	20 Sep 1823
Thomas	11	M		N. York	U. States	Prize	20 Sep 1823
Thomas	35	M	Farmer	Great Britain	U. States	Balance	19 Jun 1824
Thomas	60	M	Merchant	U. States	U. States	Zepher	20 Oct 1827
Wm.	8	M		N. York	U. States	Prize	20 Sep 1823
O'BRYON, Edward	35	M	Merchant	England	England	Leonora	29 Nov 1826
O'BUCKEL, Thomas	34		Labourer	St. John	U. States	Lady Hunter	5 Jul 1823
O'BUCKLE, Jane	22			St. John	U. States	Lady Hunter	5 Jul 1823
O'CALLAGHAN, Jer., Revd.	40	M		Ireland	New York	William	26 Apr 1823
Mich	22	M	Merchant	Ireland	U. States	Emma	15 Dec 1824
O'CALLAGHER, Eliza	22	F	Spinster	Great Britain	U.S. of Ama.	Robert Fulton	16 Aug 1824
O'CONMER, William	28	M	Merchant	United States	United States	George Clinton	13 Apr 1826
O'CONNELL, Agnes	1	F	Lady	Denmark	U. States	Catherine	3 Jul 1820
Lawrence	27	M	Farmer	Ireland	United States	Meteor	19 Aug 1829
Mary	40	F	Lady	Denmark	U. States	Catherine	3 Jul 1820
Patrick	31	M	Merchant	Ireland	United States	Meteor	19 Aug 1829
O'CONNER, Arthur	10	M		Ireland	United States	Jubilee	13 Sep 1827
M.	47	M	Reed Maker	Ireland	United States	Jubilee	13 Sep 1827
Mary	20	F		Ireland	United States	Jubilee	13 Sep 1827
Micheal	13	M	None	Gt. Brittain	United States	Balaena	21 Aug 1824
Patrick	6	M		Ireland	United States	Jubilee	13 Sep 1827
Peter	8	M		Ireland	United States	Jubilee	13 Sep 1827
Wm.	4	M		Ireland	United States	Jubilee	13 Sep 1827
O'CONNOR, Bridget	24	F	Servant	Ireland	America	Weser	26 Jun 1821
Ch.	38	M	Weaver	Ireland	United States	Trident	30 Sep 1826
Daniel	28	M	Clerk	Ireland	United States	Pallas	28 Oct 1828
Denis	20	M	School Master	Sligo	New York	Susquehana	27 Jun 1823
Jas.	22	M	Merchant	Halifax	U. States	Tiger	21 Jul 1825
Joanna	30	F	Wife	Ireland	United States	Nancy	15 Nov 1824
John	19			United States		John Dickinson	5 Apr 1821
John	25	M	Talor	Ireland	Amarica	United States	22 Mar 1824
John	66	M	Teacher	Ireland	America	Dewitt Clinton	27 Jul 1824
M.	46	M	Merchant	St. Thomas	New York	St. Pierre	16 Oct 1827
Mary	6	F	...	Ireland	United States	Carolina Ann	24 Oct 1825
Michael	33	M	Laborer	Ireland	United States	Nancy	15 Nov 1824
Mickiel	28 2/12	M	Hatter	Ireland	U.S. America	Illinois	16 Oct 1822
Patrick	2	M	Child	Ireland	United States	Nancy	15 Nov 1824
Sarah	10/12	F	...	Ireland	United States	Carolina Ann	24 Oct 1825
William	32	M	Carpenter	Ireland	U. States	Union	3 Jun 1822
Wm.	37	M	Carpenter	Ireland	U. States	Swift	28 Jan 1828
O'DANIEL, Hugh	23	M	Butcher	Ireland	U. States	Wanderer	1 Sep 1828
Mary	17	F		Ireland	U. States	Wanderer	1 Sep 1828
O'DOAN, Frederic	23	M	Butcher	England	United States	Nimrod	30 Aug 1824
O'DOLLIN, Patrick	18	M	Labourer	Ireland	U. States	Nancy	1 Sep 1823
O'DONALD, Dennis	20	M	Labourer	Gt. Britain	U. States	Sarah G.	14 Apr 1828
James	27	M	Labourer	Ireland	United States	Hannah Eliza	23 Sep 1826

NAMES OF PASSENGERS	AGE	SEX	OCCUPATIONS	COUNTRY TO WHICH THEY BELONG	COUNTRY THEY INTEND TO INHABIT	SHIPS/DATES OF ARRIVAL	
O'DONALD (cont'd)							
Patrick	14	M	None	Great Britian	U. States	Henry Kneedland	7 Aug 1826
O'DONELL, Mary	20	F	Sevt.	Sligo	New York	Susquehana	27 Jun 1823
O'DONNALD, R. M.	25 6/12	M	Dr. Divinity	Ireland	United States	Potomac	29 Oct 1828
O'DONNALL, Edward	30	M	Mechanic	U. States	U. States	Alabama	21 May 1823
O'DONNEL, Bernard	26	M	Carpenter	Great Britain	United States	Agnes	12 Apr 1821
Bryan	55		Farmer	Ireland		Westmoreland	1 Aug 1826
Daniel	25	M	Farmer	Ireland	United States	Eliza	29 Aug 1822
Edwd.	18	M	Farmer	Ireland	Redstone	Triton	12 Jul 1823
Edwd.	24		Farmer	Ireland		Westmoreland	1 Aug 1826
Elizabeth	64	F	None			Importer	30 Oct 1820
Jonnes	27		Farmer	Ireland		Westmoreland	1 Aug 1826
Mary	5		Spinster	Ireland		Westmoreland	1 Aug 1826
Mary	50		Wife	Ireland		Westmoreland	1 Aug 1826
Nancy	18		Spinster	Ireland		Westmoreland	1 Aug 1826
Rose	20		Spinster	Ireland		Westmoreland	1 Aug 1826
W...l	15	M	Boy	Ireland	United States	Trident	16 May 1826
O'DONNELE, Mary	25	F	None	Ireland		Marchioness	13 May 1828
Thomas	2	M	None	Ireland		Marchioness	13 May 1828
Thomas	19	M	Farmer	Ireland	America	William	21 May 1825
O'DONNELL, Ann	19	F	Servant	Ireland	United States	Henry Kneeland	7 Jun 1828
Anthony	22 6/12	M	Clerk	Ireland	Baltimore	Debby & Eliza	20 Nov 1820
Cathe.	18	F		Limerick	N. York	Thomas & William	25 May 1827
Catherine	27	F		Gt. Britain		Dalhouse Castle	13 May 1828
Charles	20	M	Weaver	Rath...land	United States	Carolina Ann	11 Jun 1824
Conelia	40	F	Labourer	Great Britian	United States	Princess Charlotte	6 Sep 1828
Coun	20	M	Clerk	Great Britain	U. States	Dominica	4 Jan 1823
Darby	16	M		Limerick	N. York	Thomas & William	25 May 1827
E.	22	M	Physician	Baltimore	America	Hannibal	4 Oct 1822
H...	...	M	...			Importer	30 Oct 1820
Isaac	70		...	Ireland	United States	Robert Burns	18 Jun 1822
James	8	M	Youth	Ireland	United States	Romulus	24 Jun 1826
James	23	M	Labourer	Ireland	United States	Asia	29 Jul 1829
Jas.	18	M				Imperial	19 Jul 1820
Jas.	20		Farmer	Ireland	United States	Robert Burns	18 Jun 1822
Jas.	21	M	Farmer	Ireland	United States	Trio	13 Jun 1827
M.	28		Labourer	Halifax	U. States	Edwin	26 Sep 1828
Margaret	18	F	Spinster	Great Britain	United States	Agnes	12 Apr 1821
Margaret	24	F		Ireland	United States	Romulus	24 Jun 1826
Mary	25	F		Ireland	United States	Mary	1 Jul 1829
Matilda	15	F	Spinster	Ireland	United States	Robert Fulton	24 Jul 1826
Patrick	23	M	Labourer	Ireland	United States	William & George	14 May 1828
S. M.	20	F	None	Ireland	America	Hannibal	4 Oct 1822
Wm.	66		...	Ireland	United States	Robert Burns	18 Jun 1822
O'DONNOR, Michael	4	M	Child	Ireland	United States	St. Michaels	15 Feb 1825
O'DONOHOO, Ann	20	F		Gt. Britain		Dalhouse Castle	13 May 1828
O'DONOUGHUE,							
Henry H.	19	M		Ireland	Ohio	Debby & Eliza	20 Nov 1820
Mary	14	F		Ireland	Ohio	Debby & Eliza	20 Nov 1820
Patrick	45	M	Merchant	Ireland	Ohio	Debby & Eliza	20 Nov 1820
O'DONVILLE, Patrick		M	Miner	America		Iris	7 Dec 1827
O'DOUGHERTY, Danl.	27	M	Labourer	Ireland	United States	Henry Kneeland	7 Jun 1828
O'DUNOHUE, Fs.	30	M	Clergyman	Ireland	U. States	Romeo	10 Aug 1821
O'FERRALL, Edward M.	19	M	Merchant	Porto Rico	U. States	Commerce	29 Jul 1824
O'FLAHERTY, Wm.	58	M	Mercht.	G. Britain	U. States	America	17 Oct 1825
O'FLANAGAN, Bridget	19	F		Ireland	U.S. of America	Douglass	6 Jul 1829
O'FLING, Charles	35	M	Teacher	Ireland	Canada	Nancy	12 Aug 1820
O'GILLEY, George	40	M	Merchant	Jamaica	U. States	Packet	18 Sep 1826
O'GRADY, Ann	34	F		Ireland	U. States	Courier	31 Jul 1828
Corns.	3	M		Ireland	U. States	Courier	31 Jul 1828
Wm.	5	M		Ireland	U. States	Courier	31 Jul 1828
Wm.	38	M	Priest	Ireland	U. States	Courier	31 Jul 1828
O'GREADY, Alexander	6	M		Ireland	United States	Aurora	27 Apr 1825
Bernard	10	M		Ireland	United States	Aurora	27 Apr 1825

NAMES OF PASSENGERS	AGE	SEX	OCCUPATIONS	COUNTRY TO WHICH THEY BELONG	COUNTRY THEY INTEND TO INHABIT	SHIPS/DATES OF ARRIVAL	
O'GREADY (cont'd)							
Edwin	34	M	Farmer	Ireland	United States	Aurora	27 Apr 1825
Francis	8	M		Ireland	United States	Aurora	27 Apr 1825
Thomas	23	M	Gentleman	Ireland	America	Parrington	9 Jun 1827
O'HAIN, B.	40	M	Weaver	Ireland	United States	Josephine	30 Apr 1828
O'HANLEN, Matthew	23	M	Farmer	Ireland	United States	Dublin Packet	22 Oct 1821
O'HANLON, Bernard	30	M	Labourer	Great Britain	U. States	Lord Wellington	17 Mar 1823
O'HARA, Alice	22	F	Wife	Ireland	United States	Dublin Packet	22 Aug 1829
Ann	5	F		Scotland	United States	Camillus	9 May 1827
Catherine	2 1/2	F		Scotland	United States	Camillus	9 May 1827
Danl.	21	M	Laborer	Ireland	United States	Trio	13 Jun 1827
Elanor	20	F	Wife	Ireland	United States	Meteor	27 Sep 1826
Ellen	20	F	Laborer or Spinster	Ireland	United States	Sarah G.	15 Aug 1827
Hugh	3 1/2	M		Scotland	United States	Camillus	9 May 1827
John	20	M	Farmer	Ireland	United States	Meteor	27 Sep 1826
John	28	M	Labourer	Ireland	United States	Asia	29 Jul 1829
John	32	M		Scotland	United States	Camillus	9 May 1827
Mary	1	F		Scotland	United States	Camillus	9 May 1827
Mary	27	F		Scotland	United States	Camillus	9 May 1827
Ml.	24	M	Farmer	Ireland	United States	Trio	13 Jun 1827
Peter	22	M	Labourer	Ireland	U.States	Nancy	31 May 1823
Thomas	22	M	Labourer	Ireland	America	Weser	26 Jun 1821
O'HARDY, Richard	24		Honble. Company & Service	England	England	Hudson	4 Sep 1823
O'HARE, Edward	23	M	None	Ireland	United States	Lord Wellington	28 May 1827
Elice	2	F		Ireland	America	Ann	3 Jul 1820
Ellin	23	F		Ireland	America	Ann	3 Jul 1820
James	4	M		Ireland	America	Ann	3 Jul 1820
John	18	M	Labourer	Great Britain	United States	Isaac Hicks	10 Jul 1827
John	22	M	Labourer	Great Britain	United States	Isaac Hicks	10 Jul 1827
John	23	M	Labourer	Ireland	United States	Lord Wellington	28 May 1827
Mary	22	F	None	Ireland	United States	Lord Wellington	28 May 1827
Michael	24	M	Labourer	Ireland	United States	Lord Wellington	28 May 1827
O'HARO, Michl.	23	M	Labourer	Ireland	United States	Wilson	6 Jun 1828
O'HARRA, A.	37	M	Lawyer	U. States	U. States	Mary Ann	30 Aug 1824
James	54	M	Servant	Ireland	United States	Wanderer	31 Aug 1829
Peter	29	M	Pedler	Scotland		Zamoa	5 Nov 1828
O'HARRIS, Richd.	54	M		Gt. Britain	United States	Penelope	9 Sep 1828
O'HEAR, Nicholas	24	M	Weaver	Drumg...	Co. Down	Howard Douglass	11 May 1827
O'HENLY, David	44	M	Child	Ireland	United States	Sarah Ann	18 Nov 1826
O'KEEF, Elizabeth	20	F	Spinster	Ireland	United States	Diana	1 May 1826
O'KEEFE, John	40	M	Merchant	United States	United States	John Wells	18 Sep 1826
O'KELLEY, Ann	15	F		Gt. Britain	U. States	Panthea	21 Jul 1825
Mary	32	F		Ireland	U. States	Calais Packet	7 Jul 1828
Pat	6	M		Ireland	U. States	Calais Packet	7 Jul 1828
Patrick	33	M	Labourer	Ireland	U. States	Calais Packet	7 Jul 1828
O'LEARY, Alexr.	30	M	Labourer	Ireland	United States	Neury	27 Jan 1827
Danl.	28	M	Candidate	Ireland	Kentucky	Abigail	9 Aug 1821
Honora	45			Cork	Gt. Britain	Enterprize	19 Feb 1822
James	20	M		Gt. Britain	United States	Penelope	9 Sep 1828
Jas.	30	M	Merchant	Great Britain	United States	Ann Maria	23 Oct 1820
Juli Ann	28	F	Servant	Ireland	New Jersy	General Warren	6 Mar 1829
Mary	30	F		Ireland	America	Liverpool	31 Aug 1827
Redmond	30	M	Gentleman	Ireland	America	Liverpool	31 Aug 1827
Wm.	24	M		Ireland	United States	John & Adam	21 Sep 1822
O'LESLY, Saml.	21	M		American	United States	Louisa	18 Apr 1827
O'MAHER, Peter	25	M	Gentleman	Ireland	U. States	Erin	5 Jul 1820
O'MALY, Thomas	27	M	Farmer	Ireland	Massachusetts	Munroe	27 May 1825
O'MEARA, Catharine	8	F		England	United States	Manhattan	22 Sep 1823
Jane	10	F		England	United States	Manhattan	22 Sep 1823
Jeremiah	14	M		England	United States	Manhattan	22 Sep 1823
Judith	12	F		England	United States	Manhattan	22 Sep 1823
Mary	28	F		England	United States	Manhattan	22 Sep 1823
Thos.	30	M	Farmer	England	United States	Manhattan	22 Sep 1823
O'MEARE, Michael	30	M	Labourer	Ireland	United States	Trio	2 Oct 1828
O'MOLLAY, ...no.	17			Ireland	U.S.	Hibernia	27 Jun 1821
O'MULLEN, Anna Villa	20			Ireland	United States	Alexander Mansfield	9 Nov 1822

NAMES OF PASSENGERS	AGE	SEX	OCCUPATIONS	COUNTRY TO WHICH THEY BELONG	COUNTRY THEY INTEND TO INHABIT	SHIPS/DATES OF ARRIVAL	
O'NAIL, James	24	M	Labourer	Ireland	United States	William & George	14 May 1828
O'NEAL, Ann	17	F	None	Gt. Brittain	United States	Balaena	8 Jan 1825
Barney	13	M	None	Gt. Brittain	United States	Balaena	8 Jan 1825
Bridget	25	M		Ireland	U. States	Concordia	11 Jun 1823
Catherin	30	F		Great Britain	U. States	Lady Hunter	28 May 1823
Darius	23	M	Labourer	Ireland	United States	Edwin	27 Oct 1828
James	22	F	Blacksmith	Ireland	U. States	Adno	5 Jul 1828
James	24 6/12	M	Farmer	Ireland	U.S. America	Illinois	16 Oct 1822
James	72	M	Farmer	Ireland	United States	Jubilee	13 Jul 1829
John	3	M	Labourer	Ireland	United States	Edwin	27 Oct 1828
John	4	M		Great Britain	U. States	Lady Hunter	28 May 1823
John	16	M	Labourer	Ireland	United States	Lady Hunter	29 Apr 1826
John	23	M	Weaver	Ireland	New York	Trusty	12 Sep 1828
Mary	20	F		Ireland	U. States	Adno	5 Jul 1828
May	2	F		Great Britain	U. States	Lady Hunter	28 May 1823
Owen	32	M	Cooper	Great Britain	U. States	Lady Hunter	28 May 1823
Patrick	32	M	Labourer	Ireland	United States	Hope	12 Jun 1828
Robert H.	32	M	Shipmaster	U. States	U. States	Quill	26 Jun 1827
Thomas	21	M	Labourer	Limerick	N. York	Thomas & William	25 May 1827
O'NEALE, Bridget	28	F	None	Great Britain	United States	Aurora	5 Sep 1826
Thos.	6/12	M	Child of [Bridget]	Great Britain	United States	Aurora	5 Sep 1826
O'NEIL, Arthur	47	M	Labourer	Ireland	United States	Trident	30 Sep 1826
Bernard	20	M	Labourer	Ireland		Marchioness	13 May 1828
Bernard	30	M	Merchant	Gt. Britain	U. States	Frances Henrietta	18 Apr 1825
Bethsey	11	F	Child	Ireland	United States	Trident	30 Sep 1826
Danil	20	M	Labourer	Ireland	U. States	Atlantic	19 Aug 1825
Elisabeth	47	F	Wife	Ireland	United States	Trident	30 Sep 1826
Ellenor	18	F	Spinster	Ireland	Ireland	Trident	17 May 1825
James	19	M	Farmer	Ireland	Ireland	Trident	17 May 1825
James	26	M	Labourer	Ireland	New York	Vigilant	6 May 1822
James	36	M	House Carpenter	Ireland	United States	Nancy Henrietta	3 Nov 1828
Mary	16	F	Child	Ireland	United States	Trident	30 Sep 1826
Mary	20	F	Labourer	Ireland	U. States	Atlantic	19 Aug 1825
Mary	21	F	None	Ireland		Marchioness	13 May 1828
P.	18	F	Servant	Gt. Britain	U. States	Sarah G.	14 Apr 1828
Patrick	11	M	Labourer	Great Britain	United States	Atlantic	8 Dec 1827
Patrick	21	M	Labourer	County of Cork, Ireland	New York City	Thorny Close	3 May 1826
Patrick	22	M	Weaver	Ireland	Und. Stts of Amer	Alexander Mansfield	18 Aug 1826
Peggy	8	F	Child	Ireland	United States	Trident	30 Sep 1826
Robert	7	M	Child	Ireland	United States	Trident	30 Sep 1826
Thomas	23	M	Labourer	Ireland	America	Wilson	27 Nov 1826
William	25	M	Wheelright	Ireland	Ireland	Trident	17 May 1825
O'NEILE, Joseph	3	M	Child of [Bridget]	Great Britain	United States	Aurora	5 Sep 1826
O'NEILL, Bernard	20	M		Irereland	America	Carolina Ann	20 Jun 1825
Biddy	3	F		Gt. Britain		Dalhouse Castle	13 May 1828
Catherine	22	F	Spinster	Ireland	United States	Robert Fulton	10 Aug 1827
Elleia	26	F		Ireland	U. States	Howard Douglass	29 Jan 1828
H.	31	M	Weaver	Ireland	U. States	Howard Douglass	29 Jan 1828
James	25	M	Labourer	Ireland	United States	Robert Fulton	10 Aug 1827
James	25	M	Labourer	England	U. States	Ayrshire	12 May 1828
Jane	30	F	Matron	Ireland	United States	Robert Fulton	10 Aug 1827
John	22	M	Laborer	Gt. Britain		Dalhouse Castle	13 May 1828
Judh.	25	F	None	Ireland	United States	Essex	23 May 1828
Mary	16		Spinster	Ireland	United States	Courier	15 Oct 1827
Mary	21	F	Servant	Ireland	New York	Atlantic	8 May 1828
Mathew	15	M	Labourer	Ireland	United States	Robert Fulton	10 Aug 1827
Michl.	26	M	None	Ireland	United States	Essex	23 May 1828
Owen	27	M	Labourer	Ireland	United States	Lord Wellington	28 May 1827
P.	40	M	Bricklayer	Ireland	U. States	Panthea	8 Apr 1826
Rose	18		Spinster	Ireland	United States	Courier	15 Oct 1827
William	0 6/12	M	Child	Ireland	United States	Robert Fulton	10 Aug 1827
O'NEILLE, Tarrence	20	M	Labourer	Ireland	U. States	Atlantic	19 Aug 1825

NAMES OF PASSENGERS	AGE	SEX	OCCUPATIONS	COUNTRY TO WHICH THEY BELONG	COUNTRY THEY INTEND TO INHABIT	SHIPS/DATES OF ARRIVAL	
O'NIEL, Biddy	10 5/12	F		Ireland	U.S. of America	Douglass	6 Jul 1829
Charles	20	M	Labourer	Ireland	United States	Louisa	18 Apr 1827
Jno.		M	Merchant	England	U. States	Hesperus	16 Feb 1822
John	24	M	Labourer	Ireland	United States	Meteor	26 Jun 1827
Mary	5 4/12	F		Ireland	U.S. of America	Douglass	6 Jul 1829
Mary	18	F	Miliner	Ireland	United States	Nile	17 May 1827
Matthew B.	25	M	Merchant	United States	United States	Leonora	3 Dec 1827
Michael	18	M	Clerk	Ireland	United States	Dublin Packet	22 Apr 1822
Rose	40 2/12	F		Ireland	U.S. of America	Douglass	6 Jul 1829
Sally	7 5/12	F		Ireland	U.S. of America	Douglass	6 Jul 1829
Terrance	45 6/12	M		Ireland	U.S. of America	Douglass	6 Jul 1829
O'NIELE, Arthur	35	M	Merchant	Ireland	Ireland	Havana Packet	13 May 1824
O'RAFFERTY, B.	2...	M	Labourer	England	United States	Enterprize	19 Oct 1826
Bernard [crossed out]						Enterprize	19 Oct 1826
O'REALEY, Patrick	22	M	Farmer	Ireland	United States	Clothier	22 Nov 1827
O'REEL, Jos.	45	M	Merchant	N. York	U. States	Hopes Delight	16 Feb 1825
O'REILLEY, Edward	29	M	Labourer	Great Britain	U. States	Great Britain	18 Mar 1828
O'REILLY, Bernard	19	M	Farmer	Great Britain	U.S.A.	Silas Richards	7 Mar 1825
Eliza, Miss	6	F	Child	Ireland	United States	Dublin Packet	6 Dec 1827
Henry Willm.	39	M	Military Off.	Great Britain	Great Britain	Lawson	31 Aug 1825
James	33	M	Printer	Irishman	W. Indies	Congress	21 Nov 1823
John	27	M	Farmer	Ireland	United States	Elizabeth	8 Jun 1827
Joseph	22	M	Planter	Ireland	Ireland	Jupiter	12 May 1827
Philip	24	M	Weaver	Gt. Britain		Dalhouse Castle	13 May 1828
Robt.	16	M	Planter	Ireland		Hope Mary Ann	3 May 1824
Robt.	18	M	Farmer	Great Britain	America	Remittance	24 Aug 1825
Thos.	26	M	Shoemaker	England	U. States	Thomas Ritchie	2 Jul 1827
O'RIED, Thomas	19	M	Farmer	Glasgow	United States	Henry Clay	25 Apr 1822
O'ROMNY, Ann	19	F		Ireland	U.S. of America	Douglass	6 Jul 1829
Nancy	14	F		Ireland	U.S. of America	Douglass	6 Jul 1829
O'ROURKE, Owen	26	M	Labourer	Ireland	U. States	Hope & Esther	22 Jul 1825
O'SALAVENT, Lawrena	25	F	Se[r]vant	Ireland	United States	Sylvester Healy	17 Oct 1825
Mary	18	F	Se[r]vant	Ireland	United States	Sylvester Healy	17 Oct 1825
O'SHAUGNESSY,							
Catherine	21	F		Limerick	N. York	Thomas & William	25 May 1827
John	11/12	M		Limerick	N. York	Thomas & William	25 May 1827
O'SHAUNESSY,							
Edmond	24	M	Butcher	Limerick	N. York	Thomas & William	25 May 1827
O'SULIVAN, John	37	M	Farmer	Ireland	United States	Huron	26 Dec 1827
O'SULLIVAN (see Addicks)							
Adelaide	9	F		U. States	U. States	Hudson	8 Oct 1827
Ellen	22	F		Ireland	America	Liverpool	31 Aug 1827
Jno.	40	M	Merchant	N. York	U. States	General Brown	10 Dec 1823
John	7	M		U. States		Sarah & Louisa	7 Dec 1820
John	13	M		U. States	U. States	Hudson	8 Oct 1827
John	35	M	Merchant	U. States	U. States	Sarah & Louisa	7 Dec 1820
John	37	M	Lawyer	Canada	United States	Corinthian	10 Jan 1826
John, & son	40	M		Ireland	U. States	Howard	25 Jul 1823
Martha	13	M		Philadelphia	U. States	Howard	25 Jul 1823
Mary	11	F		U. States	U. States	Hudson	8 Oct 1827
Mary	30	F		U. States	U. States	Hudson	8 Oct 1827
Robert	2	M		U. States	U. States	Hudson	8 Oct 1827
Thos.	7	M		U. States	U. States	Hudson	8 Oct 1827
Thos.	24	M	Carpenter	Ireland	America	Liverpool	31 Aug 1827
William	8	M		U. States	U. States	Sarah & Louisa	7 Dec 1820
Wm.	17	M		United States	United States	Hudson	17 Mar 1828
O'TEVILL, Michael	34	M	Black Smith	Gt. Britain	U. States	Diana	28 Apr 1828
OADWELL, Daniel K.	27	M	Printer	U.S. America	U.S. America	Cincinnatus	31 Oct 1820
OAKES, Gideon	33	M	Mariner	U.S.	U.S.	Trimmer	28 Nov 1826
OAKEY, Daniel	33	M	Merchant	New York	New York	New York	14 Nov 1826
William F.	18	M	Gentleman	United States	United States	Panthea	11 Nov 1825
OAKLEY, Arabella, Miss	20	F		England	England	Acasta	12 May 1825
Deama, Miss	22	F		England	England	Acasta	12 May 1825
Francis	45	M	Farmer	United States	United States	Brighton	11 Mar 1825
Francis	60	M	Merchant	England	U. States	Cincinnatus	5 Oct 1824
George	27	M	Merchant	England	America	Julius Seesar	29 Jul 1820

NAMES OF PASSENGERS	AGE	SEX	OCCUPATIONS	COUNTRY TO WHICH THEY BELONG	COUNTRY THEY INTEND TO INHABIT	SHIPS/DATES OF ARRIVAL	
OAKLEY (cont'd)							
George, Mr.	32	M	Merchant	U. States	U. States	Acasta	12 May 1825
Louisa, Miss	25	F		England	England	Acasta	12 May 1825
Robert J.	33	M	Gentleman	U. States	U. States	Edward Quesnel	16 Nov 1827
Robt. W.		M	Gentmn.	America	America	Mary & Susan	5 Oct 1829
Thomas	46	M	Farmer	United States	United States	Brighton	11 Mar 1825
OAKWELL, George	21		Labourer	England	United States	Corinthian	7 Jul 1829
OAKYARD, John	42	M	Miner	England	England	Virginia	26 May 1828
OALEFIELD, James	16			London	England	Rockingham	23 Aug 1822
OATES, Ann	23	F		Ireland	N. York	Eliza Grant	29 Aug 1829
Ann	23	F		Ireland		Eliza Grant	29 Aug 1829
George	7	M	None	Great Britan		Colossus	27 Mar 1828
Henry	5	M	None	Great Britan		Colossus	27 Mar 1828
Joseph	35	M	Mariner	England	England	Enterprize	14 Oct 1828
Thomas	25	M	Laborer	Ireland	N. York	Eliza Grant	29 Aug 1829
OATLY, William	25	M	Gentleman	England	U. States	George Canning	13 Jun 1826
OATS, John	20	M	Labourer	England	U. States	Emulous	22 Aug 1828
OAXBY, Robt.	19	M	Farmer	Great Britain	United States	Ann Maria	12 Jul 1821
OBART, Alase	21		Mulatto, Hatter	New York	New York	Fortuna	13 Nov 1827
OBBERLY, ...n	46 5/12	M	Farmer	Switzerland	U. States	France	26 Jun 1828
OBBERRY, James	20	M	Joiner	England	United States	Curler	3 Mar 1828
OBENSFORD, B.	16	M	Servant	France	U. States	Bayard	11 Jul 1825
OBER, Geo.	1	M		Switzerland	U. States	La Urania	3 Jul 1828
Piere	24	M	Mason	Switzerland	U. States	La Urania	3 Jul 1828
T.	3	F		Switzerland	U. States	La Urania	3 Jul 1828
T.	25	F		Switzerland	U. States	La Urania	3 Jul 1828
OBERKAN, Pat	26	M	Labourer	Ireland	United States	Louisa	18 Apr 1827
OBERN, A.	30	M	Doctor	France	U. States	Artibonite	2 Jul 1827
OBERT, Matthias	21	M	Shoemaker	Switzerland	U. States	Hewes	30 Oct 1829
OBERTON, Ann	20	F		England	U.N. States	William Byrnes	23 Jul 1824
Jane	10	F		England	U.N. States	William Byrnes	23 Jul 1824
Jane	31	F		England	U.N. States	William Byrnes	23 Jul 1824
OBEYS, Edward	23	M	Farmer	England	United States	Cambria	3 Jul 1829
OBREGON, Pablo, Don	38	M	Ambassador	Mexico	United States	Mercid	21 Oct 1824
OBRIAN, Mary	20	F		Ireland	U. States	Balaena	29 Apr 1825
Michael	25	M	Farmer	...., ..., ...land	U. States	New Orleans	24 Aug 1827
Patrick	27	M		Ireland	U. States	Balaena	29 Apr 1825
Rebecca	42	F	Milliner	United States	U. States	Mary Ann	22 Aug 1828
OBRIEN, Bridget, Wife [of Micheal]	22	F	Labourer	Ireland	New York	Brighton	24 Aug 1827
Micheal	26	M	Labourer	Ireland	New York	Brighton	24 Aug 1827
Ths.	27	M	Labourer	Great Brittan	U. States	John & Elizabeth	11 Dec 1826
OBRINE, Ricd.	20	M	None	Great Britain	United States	Penelope	11 Jun 1827
OBURN, John	18	M	Miller	England	United States	Cosmo	26 Aug 1829
OCHARDARENO, F.	15	M	Merchant	Spain	Spain	Brown	15 Nov 1825
OCHENDEN, Thos.	61	M	Farmer	England	Gt. Britain	Electra	4 Sep 1827
OCHENDER, Anna	69	F		England	Gt. Britain	Electra	4 Sep 1827
Saml.	30	M	Farmer	England	Gt. Britain	Electra	4 Sep 1827
OCHEO, Yosidoro, Don	27	M	Merchant	Spain	Spain	Lovinia	20 Nov 1828
OCHSNER, G.	23	M		Switzerland		Manchester	29 Aug 1828
OCKER, Michael	36	M	Farmer	Switzerland	U.S.	Francois I	8 Aug 1829
OCONNELL, James	40	M	Farmer	Ireland	United States	Huron	26 Dec 1827
OCONNOR, Andrew	33	M	Farmer	Ireland	U.S.A.	Silas Richards	28 Jun 1825
Dennis	24	M	Farmer	Ireland	U.S.A.	Silas Richards	28 Jun 1825
Joseph	18	M	Farmer	Ireland	United States	Dublin Packet	13 Oct 1828
Maurice	17	M	Farmer	Ireland	United States	Dublin Packet	13 Oct 1828
ODAM, John	50	M	Captain	America	America	Nestor	13 Jul 1829
ODBERT, Robert	30 6/12	M	Stone Cutter	N. Yorke	America	Henry	15 Feb 1826
ODDY, —, Mr.	21	M	Merchant	England	England	Edgar	1 Aug 1823
Andrew	23	M	Farmer	Great Britain	United States	James Cropper	27 Sep 1821
ODELL, Mary	40			England	United States	Hugh Johnson	11 Jun 1828
William F.	46	M	H. B. M. Surveyor under the same article	Province of New Brunswick	to return to New Brunswick	Loire	23 May 1821
ODENHEINER, Frederick	35	M	Carpenter	Switzerland	U. States	Hewes	30 Oct 1829
ODENINGHAR, William	24	M	...	England	United States	Hamilton	13 Nov 1827
ODIN, George	30		Merchant	Boston	United States	London	13 Dec 1822
George	33	M	Merchant	United States	United States	Ann Maria	23 Oct 1820

NAMES OF PASSENGERS	AGE	SEX	OCCUPATIONS	COUNTRY TO WHICH THEY BELONG	COUNTRY THEY INTEND TO INHABIT	SHIPS/DATES OF ARRIVAL	
ODLE, Matilda	17	F		Great Britain	United States	Aspasia	16 Jul 1828
ODLING, Chas.	29	M	Butcher	Great Britain	United States	Freake	25 Aug 1829
Edna	26	F		Great Britain	United States	Dapper	24 Aug 1827
Elizabeth	7	F		Great Britain	United States	Dapper	24 Aug 1827
James	8	M		Great Britain	United States	Dapper	24 Aug 1827
S., wife	22	F		Great Britain	United States	Freake	25 Aug 1829
Thomas	2	M		Great Britain	United States	Dapper	24 Aug 1827
William	4	M		Great Britain	United States	Dapper	24 Aug 1827
ODLUN, Thomas	24	M	...	...	America	Farmer	4 Aug 1825
ODONNEL, Marrus	35		Farmer	Ireland		Westmoreland	1 Aug 1826
ODONOR, Grace	30	F		Ireland	U. States	Nancy	2 May 1823
OFALL, Seth	28	M	Mariner	U. States	U. States	Worromontogus	23 Jun 1823
OFENHOUSLE, Joseph	41 5/12	M	Farmer	Switzerland	United States	France	6 Oct 1828
OFF, J.	22	M	Shoemaker	Germany	America	Falcon	28 Aug 1828
OFFEN, Abraham	18	M	Shoemaker	G. Brittain	U. States	Cincinnatus	2 Oct 1822
Benjamin	51 4/12	M	Shoemaker	England	United States	Nimrod	28 Apr 1824
Charles	16	M	Farmer	Great Brittian	U. States	Hudson	12 Mar 1824
Jannes	12		Farmer	England	England	Hudson	18 Jun 1825
Lydia	50		Farmer	England	England	Hudson	18 Jun 1825
Maria	38		Farmer	England	England	Hudson	18 Jun 1825
OFFENSANDT, C. A.	22	M	Merchant	Germany	Germany	Virginia	30 Oct 1828
OFFER, Anne	17	F	Daughter	Swiss	U. States	Comet	28 Jul 1825
Anne	46	F	Wife	Swiss	U. States	Comet	28 Jul 1825
Caroline	7	F	Daughter	Swiss	U. States	Comet	28 Jul 1825
Christian	3	M	Son	Swiss	U. States	Comet	28 Jul 1825
Christian	48	M	Farmer	Swiss	U. States	Comet	28 Jul 1825
Margaret	2	F	Daughter	Swiss	U. States	Comet	28 Jul 1825
Mary Ann	14	F	Daughter	Swiss	U. States	Comet	28 Jul 1825
Peter	12	M	Son	Swiss	U. States	Comet	28 Jul 1825
Sophia	5	F	Daughter	Swiss	U. States	Comet	28 Jul 1825
William	Infant					Comet	28 Jul 1825
*Died on the 11th day of July 1825							
OFFINE, Benjamin	25	M	Mechanic	England	U.N. States	Helen	17 Dec 1827
OFFLEY, David W.	21	M	Gent.	United States	United States	Seaman	24 Jul 1826
OFFORD, George	5	M				Helen	4 Aug 1829
Mary	40	F				Helen	4 Aug 1829
William	35		Chair Maker			Helen	4 Aug 1829
OFINDIN, George	28	M	Stone Mason	England		Fame	9 Dec 1826
OFISTER, Elizabeth	5	F	Farmer	Switzerland		Antioch	18 Aug 1829
Jean	12	M	Farmer	Switzerland		Antioch	18 Aug 1829
Jean	40	M	Farmer	Switzerland		Antioch	18 Aug 1829
Maria	7	F	Farmer	Switzerland		Antioch	18 Aug 1829
Maria	34	F	Farmer	Switzerland		Antioch	18 Aug 1829
Sarah	10	M	Farmer	Switzerland		Antioch	18 Aug 1829
Verena	2	F	Farmer	Switzerland		Antioch	18 Aug 1829
OG, Geo. A.	26	M	Student	France	U. States	Edward Quesnel	16 Nov 1827
OG...N, A.	40	M	Merchant	New York	New York	Nancy	16 Aug 1822
OGAN, Isaac	22	M	Mason	England	United States	Siroc	31 Oct 1829
Mary	30	F	None	Ireland	America	Evelina	10 Nov 1825
Patrick	21	M		Ireland	U. States	Balaena	29 Apr 1825
OGBERT, Ann	2	F		England	U. States	Unity	5 Sep 1828
John	7	M		England	U. States	Unity	5 Sep 1828
John	32	M	Farmer	England	U. States	Unity	5 Sep 1828
Mary	27	F		England	U. States	Unity	5 Sep 1828
Stephen	5	M		England	U. States	Unity	5 Sep 1828
OGBURN, James G.	35 6/12	M	Clergyman	United States	United States	Cambria	7 May 1828
OGDEN, —, Mr.	22	M	Seaman	U. States	U. States	Mazinghi	15 Jan 1827
... ...	20	M	Merchant		U. States	Edward Quesnel	3 Sep 1826
Amelia	6	F	None	U. States	U. States	Queen Mab	26 Nov 1825
Anna	8	F	None	U. States	U. States	Queen Mab	26 Nov 1825
Anne	20	F		U. States	U. States	United States	11 Sep 1828
Charles	16	M	None	U. States	U. States	Queen Mab	26 Nov 1825
Charles	33	M	...	Gt. Britain	Lower Canada	Crisis	13 Nov 1824
Chas.	24	M	Merchant	Gt. Brittain	United States	Cortes	7 Dec 1825
Eliza	35	F	Wife	U. States	U. States	Queen Mab	26 Nov 1825
Governier	49	M	Gentn.	United States	United States	York	6 Dec 1826
Henry	22	M	Mariner	United States	U. States	Jones	28 Aug 1826
Henry	41	M	Merchant	United States	United States	Bunker Hill	16 Apr 1827

NAMES OF PASSENGERS	AGE	SEX	OCCUPATIONS	COUNTRY TO WHICH THEY BELONG	COUNTRY THEY INTEND TO INHABIT	SHIPS/DATES OF ARRIVAL	
OGDEN (cont'd)							
Isaac	37	M	Merchant	U. States	United States	New York	12 Nov 1822
Isaac	55	M	Carpenter	N. York	U. States	Rodman	4 Apr 1825
James	25	M	Spinner	U. States	U. States	United States	11 Sep 1828
James D.	33	M	Merchant	New York	U. States	New York	15 Nov 1823
James D. P., Mr.	40	M	Mercht.	United States	United States	Manchester	16 Dec 1828
John	4	M		U. States	U. States	United States	11 Sep 1828
John	24		Rat Catcher	England	United States	Corinthian	7 Jul 1829
John	28		Weaver	S... ...h	England	Great Britain	7 May 1827
John	28		Hatter	England	United States	Thomas Dickason	5 Jun 1827
John	42	M	Farmer	Manchester	Manchester	Colossus	27 Mar 1828
Jonay, Mrs.	20	F	None	Gt. Britain	Lower Canada	Crisis	13 Nov 1824
Jos.	1	M		U. States	U. States	United States	11 Sep 1828
Josh.	30	M	Turner	Great Britain		Moro Castle	6 Jul 1827
L., Mrs.	46	F	None	Gt. Britain	Canada	Corks	3 Aug 1824
Levinia	14	F	None	U. States	U. States	Queen Mab	26 Nov 1825
Lewis	12	M	None	U. States	U. States	Queen Mab	26 Nov 1825
Louisa	13	F	None	U. States	U. States	Queen Mab	26 Nov 1825
M. L.	15	M	Merchant	United States	United States	Don Quixote	7 May 1824
Margaret	10	F	None	Manchester	Manchester	Colossus	27 Mar 1828
Margaret	35	F	None	Manchester	Manchester	Colossus	27 Mar 1828
Mary	3	F	None	U. States	U. States	Queen Mab	26 Nov 1825
Mary	17	F		England	U.N. States	Earl of Liverpool	20 Aug 1825
Mary	30	F	None	Gt. Britain	Canada	Corks	3 Aug 1824
Matilda	9	F	None	U. States	U. States	Queen Mab	26 Nov 1825
P.	35	M	Merchant	Canada	Canada	James Monroe	29 Apr 1823
Saml. G., Mr.	48	M	Merchant			Henri IV	17 May 1828
Samuel G.	44	M	Merchant	United States	United States	Don Quixote	7 May 1824
Samul. G.	45	M	Merchant	U. States	U. States	Queen Mab	26 Nov 1825
T.	50	M	Labourer	G. Britann		Manchester	29 Aug 1828
T., Jr.	19	M	Labourer	G. Britann		Manchester	29 Aug 1828
Wallace	23	M	...	United States	U. States	Seine	20 Dec 1825
Wm.	2	M		U. States	U. States	United States	11 Sep 1828
OGDIN, David	27	M	Merchant	America	America	Silas Richard	24 Oct 1829
OGDON, A., Mr.	40	M	Merchant	America	America	Nancy	18 Aug 1821
Daniel	22	M	Iron Turner	Great Britain	U.S. of America	Gratitude	3 Oct 1829
OGGARD, Anthony	24	M	Laborer	United States	United States	Globe	30 Aug 1828
OGILVY, Jno. N.	17	M	Merchant	Canada	Canada	Silas Richards	7 Mar 1825
OGIN, J. L.	17	M		U.S.	U.S.	York	1 Dec 1827
OGLAND, B.	30	M	Tile Maker	Great Britain	United States	Freake	25 Aug 1829
OGLESBY, Samuel	24	M	...	England	America, U.S.	Illinois	3 Jun 1822
OGSBURY, Charles	10	M		New York	U. States	Thomas & Sarah	18 Sep 1822
Henry	12	M		New York	U. States	Thomas & Sarah	18 Sep 1822
Hy. A.	18	M	Clark	N. York	U. States	Frances Miller	1 May 1826
John	10	M		New York	U. States	Thomas & Sarah	18 Sep 1822
Lucy, Mrs.	39	F		New York	U. States	Thomas & Sarah	18 Sep 1822
OHAIR, Jno.	30	M		England	United States	Loire	4 Oct 1824
Margaret	28	F		England	United States	Loire	4 Oct 1824
OHARE, B. F.	39	M	Cook	France	France	Fabius	19 Mar 1825
OHARRY, Betty	25	F	Mechanic	Great Britain	United States	Thomas Dickason	31 Jul 1829
OHL, Johanna	10	F	Merchant	U. States		Ariel	24 Sep 1827
Sophia	37	F	Merchant	U. States		Ariel	24 Sep 1827
OHM, Albrecht	25	M	Botanist	Bremen	United States	Howard	6 Jul 1829
OHOULES, John	23	M	Baptist preacher	England	U. States	Frances Henrietta	25 Oct 1824
OHRESSEL, Felux	55	M	House Carpenter	Germany	United States	Virginia	31 May 1828
OKEEFFE, George	28	M	Preacher	Ireland	United States	Trio	31 Oct 1827
OLAND, Henry	20		Laborer	Great Britan	U. States	Columbia	7 May 1828
OLARA, Augustin	42	M	Merchant	Spain	U. States	Tobasco	23 Jul 1827
OLAVARIA, G.	17	M	Gentleman	Colombia	United States	General Jackson	12 Aug 1824
OLAY, John	27	M	Miller	Great Britten	United States	Cortes	6 Mar 1827
OLCOTT, Henry W.	26	M	Merchant	United States	United States	New York	19 Nov 1828

NAMES OF PASSENGERS	AGE	SEX	OCCUPATIONS	COUNTRY TO WHICH THEY BELONG	COUNTRY THEY INTEND TO INHABIT	SHIPS/DATES OF ARRIVAL	
OLD, Benjm. Hide	11	M	Gentleman	England	New York	William	2 Sep 1822
Jonah	15	M	Sailor	England	United States	Warrior	6 Oct 1828
OLDEN, Eliza	3	F	Spinster	United States	United States	Abaco	20 Oct 1829
Susannah	20	F	Spinster	United States	United States	Abaco	20 Oct 1829
OLDFIELD, ...	19	M	Gentl.	Great Britian	United States	London	24 Jun 1823
George	11		None	Great Britain	United States	Roman	10 Sep 1827
J. P.	20	M	Merchant	England	England	Brittannia	28 Feb 1827
Mary	48		None	Great Britain	United States	Roman	10 Sep 1827
V. P.	29	M	Merchant	England	U. States	Birmingham	23 Feb 1829
Wm.	10		None	Great Britain	United States	Roman	10 Sep 1827
Wm.	44		Weaver	Great Britain	United States	Roman	10 Sep 1827
OLDREW, Edward	26	M	Courier	England	New York	Lima	5 Aug 1829
Edward	26	M	Caurier	England	U. States	Lima	5 Aug 1829
OLDRIDGE, Alphea	15	M		Great Britain	America	Lady Gallatin	21 Jun 1820
Cyrus	17	M		Great Britain	America	Lady Gallatin	21 Jun 1820
Esther	24	F		Great Britain	America	Lady Gallatin	21 Jun 1820
John	49	M	Farmer	Great Britain	America	Lady Gallatin	21 Jun 1820
John	55	M	Chemist	Great Britain	United States	Diana	6 Jul 1829
OLEBIRO, Franscisco	23	M	Comb Maker	Porto Cabello	New York	Transport	19 Aug 1829
OLEO, José	46	M	Mercht.	Spain	U.S.	Emma	24 Jun 1825
OLIFER, Susan	14	F	W...t...	Jamaica	U. States	Sanford William	26 Jul 1824
OLIFFE, J.	24	M	Labourer	England	United States	Alicia	9 May 1827
OLIO, D.	57	M	Planter	Italy	Spain	Circassian	13 Jun 1825
OLIPHANT, D. W. C.	35	M	Merchant	New York	U. States	Importer	10 Sep 1823
D. W. C.	42	M	Merchant	United States		Beaver	9 Jul 1829
OLIVAR, H.	25	M	Sugar baker	Germany	U. States	Jane	26 Jul 1825
OLIVE, Jose	40	M	Mercht.	Spain	Spain	Clarissa	28 Apr 1824
OLIVER, Andes	28	M	Seaman	U. States	U.S.	Radius	22 Aug 1820
Brinley	28	M	Mariner	N. Scotia	U. States	Francis Miller	22 May 1822
Charles	27 4/12	M	Gentleman	U. States	U. States	France	26 Jun 1828
Francis	26	M	Merchant	England	United States	Rebecca	21 Dec 1827
George	10		Gardiner	England	United States	Corinthian	7 Jul 1829
Henry	28	M	Gentleman	U. States	U. States	New York	13 Mar 1824
James	17		Gardiner	England	United States	Corinthian	7 Jul 1829
James	21	M	Weaver	Ireland	United States	Romulus	24 Jun 1826
Jane	22	F		Ireland	United States	Romulus	24 Jun 1826
John	14		Gardiner	England	United States	Corinthian	7 Jul 1829
John	44		Gardiner	England	United States	Corinthian	7 Jul 1829
Jos.	32	M	Merchant	France	France	Atlanta	20 May 1822
Jos.	35	M	Merchant	Spain	Matanzas	Edgar	11 Feb 1824
José	28	M	Servant	Spain	U. States	Zephyr	18 May 1825
Joseph	24		Farmer	England	England	Hudson	4 Sep 1823
M.	16	F	No	Campeache	U. States	Doris	22 May 1826
Margaret	35	F	Mechanic	England	U. States	Charles Hamilton Aberdeen	24 Oct 1825
Mary	8		Gardiner	England	United States	Corinthian	7 Jul 1829
Mary	46		Gardiner	England	United States	Corinthian	7 Jul 1829
Peggy	21	F		Ireland	U. States	Xenophon	13 Jun 1823
Penfield	19	M	Shoemaker	Great Britain	United States	Fame	26 May 1828
Sarah	3		Gardiner	England	United States	Corinthian	7 Jul 1829
Stephen	32	M	None	Great Britain	United States	Eliza Barker	3 Jul 1826
W.	35	M	Merchant	U. States	U. States	Gazette	27 Jul 1824
Wm.	20	M	Laborer	Great Britain	United States	Diana	6 Jul 1829
Wm.	30	M	Merchant	Great Britain	United States	Martha	3 May 1821
Wm.	35	M	Mechanic	England	U. States	Charles Hamilton Aberdeen	24 Oct 1825
OLIVIAR, T.	40	M	Baker	France	U. States	North Star	27 Oct 1828
OLIVIER, Agathe	35	F	Servant	Colombia	Colombia	Sully	15 Jul 1829
Francoise X.	2	M		France	U. States	Leonarde	29 Aug 1828
Jean B.	36	M	Cabinet Maker	France	U. States	Leonarde	29 Aug 1828
Jenevive B.	34	F		France	U. States	Leonarde	29 Aug 1828
Marie T. C.	7	F		France	U. States	Leonarde	29 Aug 1828
OLLAWAY, Mary	22			...	...	Hudson	14 Jun 1827
OLLIVER, —, Mr.	45	M	Merchant	France	U. States	Robert Edwards	11 Mar 1822
George	23		Black Smith	England	England	Thames	25 Oct 1821
OLLMAN, Lucy	27	F		Hanoveras	United States	Constitution	2 Aug 1826
OLMAN, Maria Louse	3	F			United States	Constitution	2 Aug 1826
OLMOND, Caleb	24	M	Farmer	Ireland	United States	Loore	9 Sep 1822
OLMSTEAD, D.	19	M	Merchant	Eastport	U. States	Columbia	27 Dec 1822

NAMES OF PASSENGERS	AGE	SEX	OCCUPATIONS	COUNTRY TO WHICH THEY BELONG	COUNTRY THEY INTEND TO INHABIT	SHIPS/DATES OF ARRIVAL	
OLMSTED, Edmond T.	17	M	Merchant	New York	New York	Genl. Pike	15 Jan 1827
Francis	36	M	Merchant	United States	United States	Britannia	29 Oct 1829
Jno.	25	M	Merchant	U. States	United States	Burdett	30 Apr 1828
M. A.	33	F		United States	United States	Britannia	29 Oct 1829
OLOFIELD, Robert	28		...	...	...land	Hudson	14 Jun 1827
OLSON, Christian	27	M	Farmer	Norway	United States	Salem	31 Aug 1829
Maria	16	F		Great Britian	United States	London	24 Jun 1823
OLTMANS, Eneke J.	40	F	Mantuamaker	Holland	United States	James Noble	12 Oct 1829
OLVINE, Mary	13	F	Labourer	Ireland	United States	Borneo	28 Aug 1828
Philip	18	M	Labourer	Ireland	United States	Borneo	28 Aug 1828
OLWAY, Frans.	42	M	Merchant	South Americ	South America	Margaret	13 Mar 1826
OLWELL, Mathew	18	M	Labourer	Ireland	U. States	Courier	17 Mar 1828
OMANOA, Lewis, Esqr.	30	M	Gentleman	Columbia	France	Athenian	1 Dec 1827
OMBORNS, Girton	42	M	Merchant	Switzerland	United States	Ann Maria	9 Mar 1820
OMER, Thomas	27	M	Merchant	U. States	U. States	Sarah	24 Mar 1828
OMIRSTER, John	30	M	Farmer	Scotland	United States	Commerce	17 Jul 1823
OMSTIN, Elizabeth	1	M	Child	Ireland	U. States	Hanford	29 Dec 1828
Ellen	25	F	Darymaid	Ireland	U. States	Hanford	29 Dec 1828
ONAEL, Catherine	60	F	Spinster	Ireland	United States	Wilson	4 Oct 1827
ONEAL, Bridget	28	F	Spinster	Ireland	United States	Sarah G	19 Jun 1827
Charles	23		Wheelwright	County Carvan	N. York	Peru	30 May 1828
Francis	20	M	Black Smith	Ireland	U. States	Virginia	20 Jun 1825
Henry	27	M	Sugar Baker	Prussia	United States	Richmond	4 Aug 1826
Hugh	30	M	Labourer	Ireland	United States	Fabius	31 Jul 1829
Jeremiah	32	M	Dyer	England	New York	Brighton	29 Aug 1828
Mary	16	F	Spinster	Ireland	United States	Fabius	31 Jul 1829
Mary	22			County Carvan	N. York	Peru	30 May 1828
Mary	26	F	Farmer	Ireland	U. States	Virginia	20 Jun 1825
Owen	26	M	Farmer	Ireland	U. States	Virginia	20 Jun 1825
ONEHEO, T.	36	M	Merch.	Spain	U. States	William Bayard	2 Mar 1824
ONEIL, Catherine	23	F	None	Ireland	U. States	Erin	5 Jul 1820
James	22	M	Currier	Ireland	U. States	Erin	5 Jul 1820
John	25	M	...	...	United States	Hanford	17 Oct 1828
Joseph	6	M		Ireland	United States	St. John	5 Oct 1829
Mary	30	F		Ireland	United States	St. John	5 Oct 1829
Thos.	8	M		Ireland	United States	St. John	5 Oct 1829
ONEILL, Briget	22	F	None		United States	Mount Vernon	29 Aug 1828
Daniel	28	M	Labourer	Ireland	United States	William	20 Jul 1829
Hiram	24	M	Carpenter	Serry	Ireland	Carolina Ann	11 Jun 1824
James	19	M	Weaver		uncertain	Mount Vernon	29 Aug 1828
John	24	M	Farmer	Ireland	United States	Dublin Packet	23 May 1828
John	25	M	Chandler	Ireland	United States	Courier	15 Oct 1827
Margaret	22	F	Wife	Ireland	United States	Dublin Packet	23 May 1828
Mary	2	F	Child	Ireland	United States	Dublin Packet	23 May 1828
Michael	24	M	Labourer	England	U. States	Comet	23 Aug 1828
ONGEE, Uban	32	M	military officer	France	South America	Cortes	16 Jul 1827
ONSLEY, John	26	M	Merchant	Great Britain	Great Britain	Sylvester Healy	23 Nov 1825
Selina	18	F	Lady	France	Great Britain	Sylvester Healy	23 Nov 1825
OPPENHEIM, Adolph	18	M	Merchant	Germany	New York	Maria Elizabeth	16 Mar 1829
OPPENSHAW, John	43	M	Weaver	Harts	Yorkshire	Howard Douglass	11 May 1827
OPPERLANDER, Adam	27	M	Farmer	Germany	United States	Helen	5 Sep 1828
OPPIMUS, Antioch	1/12	M				Antioch	18 Aug 1829
*Born on Voyage							
George	4	F	Farmer	Swizerland		Antioch	18 Aug 1829
Joseph	33	M	Farmer	Swizerland		Antioch	18 Aug 1829
Magdeline	6	F	Farmer	Swizerland		Antioch	18 Aug 1829
Maria	30	F	Farmer	Swizerland		Antioch	18 Aug 1829
OPPLIGER, Cristian	27	M	Weaver	Switzerland	America, U.N.S.	Great Britain	3 Aug 1829
Jean	11	F		Switzerland	America, U.N.S.	Great Britain	3 Aug 1829
Jean	33	M		Switzerland	America, U.N.S.	Great Britain	3 Aug 1829
Marguerita	12	F		Switzerland	America, U.N.S.	Great Britain	3 Aug 1829
Marguerita	35	F		Switzerland	America, U.N.S.	Great Britain	3 Aug 1829
OR...LY, M.	26		Farmer	Ireland	United States	Courier	16 May 1825
ORA, George	40	M	...	United States	Philadelphia	Albion	11 Jun 1821
ORAGO, J. Meg	22	M	Gentleman	Mexico	Mexico	Governor Von Schollen	7 Nov 1827
ORAM, Jas.	19	M	Clothier	Great Britain	United States	John	6 Oct 1820
ORANGE, Aimé	17	F		France	United States	Henri IV	2 Oct 1828

NAMES OF PASSENGERS	AGE	SEX	OCCUPATIONS	COUNTRY TO WHICH THEY BELONG	COUNTRY THEY INTEND TO INHABIT	SHIPS/DATES OF ARRIVAL	
ORANGE (cont'd)							
Lewis	32	M	Merchant	France	U. States	Comet	28 Jul 1825
ORANGO, Manuel	25	M	Merchant	Spain	Spain	Topaz	25 Mar 1826
ORD, Elizabeth	27	F		England	United States	Cambria	16 Aug 1827
Jane	21			England		Hudson	5 Apr 1826
Jas. Brigas, Mr.	16 4/12	M		United States	Philadelphia	Cadmus	27 Aug 1822
John	35	M	Cordwainer	England	United States	Cambria	16 Aug 1827
Meary	67	F		England	United States	Cambria	16 Aug 1827
ORDARZA, J. M.	28	M	Merchant	Spain	U. States	Mary Jane	2 Jul 1828
ORDERSON, D. A.	50	F		Barbadoes	Barbadoes	Elias Burger	24 Jul 1820
J. H.	45	M	Clergamin	Barbadoes	Barbadoes	Elias Burger	24 Jul 1820
ORDIERA, Joseph	33	M	Merchant	Spain	United States	Howard	14 May 1825
ORDINANCE, Domingo	12	M	Merchant	Columbia	U. States	Tampico	19 Oct 1826
Hosea	11	M	Merchant	Columbia	U. States	Tampico	19 Oct 1826
ORDRINAUX, John	54	M	Merchant	U. States	U. States	Perseverance	28 Apr 1828
OREYTY, Ann, Miss	15	F		Ireland	United States	Henry	9 Jun 1826
ORFORD, Robert	21	M	Farmer	England	United States	Richmond	4 Aug 1826
Thomas	35	M	Merchant	England		Athenian	3 Sep 1827
ORGAN, Betty	27			Ireland	U.S.	Union	20 Aug 1827
Edward	42	M	Labourer	United States	United States	Euphrates	12 Mar 1824
John	26		Labourer	Ireland	U.S.	Union	20 Aug 1827
Royal	21	M	Shoemaker	Ireland	United States	Euphrates	12 Mar 1824
ORGE, Frs.	42	M	Merchant	France	Hayti	Aurora	11 Aug 1824
ORICLE, William	24		Farmer	Bolton	England	Great Britain	7 May 1827
ORIGEN, Mary	23	F		Ireland	New York State	Manhattan	20 Jun 1826
ORILY, Charles	20	M	Laborer	Ireland	United States	St. Michaels	12 Jun 1826
ORKNEY, Elize	19	F	Spinster	Scotland	Canada	Camillus	6 Apr 1821
Isabella	1	F	Child	Scotland	Canada	Camillus	6 Apr 1821
Jane	3	F	Child	Scotland	Canada	Camillus	6 Apr 1821
John	20	M	Gentleman	British	Brittain	Govenor Lincoln	15 Feb 1827
Robert	25	M	Merchant	Scotland	Canada	Camillus	6 Apr 1821
Robert	30	M	Gentleman	British	Brittain	Govenor Lincoln	15 Feb 1827
ORLAC, Lydia	12	F		St. Thomas	Havre	Mary Hobin	29 May 1826
ORLANDO, J. P.	30	M	Merchant	U. States	U. States	Brown	29 Apr 1825
ORLIAC, D. L.	60	M	Doctor	England	Havre	Mary Hobin	29 May 1826
ORMAN, Elizabeth	31					Xenophon	25 Jul 1826
Henry	22		Farmer	England	S. New York	Xenophon	25 Jul 1826
James	30		Farmer	England	S. New York	Xenophon	25 Jul 1826
John	9					Xenophon	25 Jul 1826
Richard	4					Xenophon	25 Jul 1826
William	2					Xenophon	25 Jul 1826
William	30		Farmer	England	S. New York	Xenophon	25 Jul 1826
ORME, Edward	25	M	...	...	...	Indian Chief	8 Sep 1824
Hannah	60	F	...	...	...	Indian Chief	8 Sep 1824
Joseph	21	M	...	...	...	Indian Chief	8 Sep 1824
Wm.	25	M	Mechanic	England	U.S.	Panthea	22 Jul 1826
ORMELLO,							
Norbert Antoine	40	M	Merchant	Portugal	U. States	Minos	24 Oct 1828
ORMERVED, Ann	2	F	None	Great Britain	United States	William Dawson	18 Jun 1827
Ann	28	F	None	Great Britain	United States	William Dawson	18 Jun 1827
Geo.	6	M	None	Great Britain	United States	William Dawson	18 Jun 1827
Geo.	33	M	Weaver	Great Britain	United States	William Dawson	18 Jun 1827
Peter	8	M	None	Great Britain	United States	William Dawson	18 Jun 1827
Sarah	10	F	None	Great Britain	United States	William Dawson	18 Jun 1827
ORMOND, Amelia, Miss	21	F	Spinster	Ireland	United States	Dublin Packet	13 Oct 1828
Elizabeth, Miss	18	F	Spinster	Ireland	United States	Dublin Packet	13 Oct 1828
Hannah	27	F	Milliner	England	United States	Siroc	31 Oct 1829
Jno.	15	M		Ireland	U. States	Alex Mansfield	1 Jun 1822
Rebecah, Mrs.	54	F	Wife	Ireland	United States	Dublin Packet	13 Oct 1828
ORMSBY, Jas.	25		Smith	Ireland	United States	Fabius	18 Mar 1829
ORMSTER, James	23		Merchant	Scotland	State New York	Rufus King	3 Sep 1822
James	37		Merchant	Scotland	City New York	Rufus King	3 Sep 1822
Janis	24		his wife [James]	America	New York	Rufus King	3 Sep 1822
Nancy	...		their child [James and Janis]	America	New York	Rufus King	3 Sep 1822
Robart	...		their child [James and Janis]	America	New York	Rufus King	3 Sep 1822

NAMES OF PASSENGERS	AGE	SEX	OCCUPATIONS	COUNTRY TO WHICH THEY BELONG	COUNTRY THEY INTEND TO INHABIT	SHIPS/DATES OF ARRIVAL	
ORMSTON, Grace	19	F		America	U. States	Camillus	29 Jan 1829
Samuel	22	M	Mason	America	U. States	Camillus	29 Jan 1829
ORN, Dorothy	23	F	Spinster	Switzerland	United States	Andes	5 May 1828
ORNE, W.	23	M	Merchant	America	United States	Marmion	13 Jun 1823
ORNELL, W., Capt.	45	M	Merchant	U. States	U. States	Sea Nymph	7 Jul 1827
ORNOLD, Catherine	24	F		Switzerland	United States	Thetis	5 Jul 1821
Mariane Elizabeth	26	F		Switzerland	United States	Thetis	5 Jul 1821
ORPHEN, Edward	20					Trio	5 May 1828
ORR, —, Mrs.		F		Scotland	New York	Joseph Hume	26 Oct 1829
...ph	16	M	Farmer			Robert Burns	13 Jul 1820
...rt	22	M	Joiner			Robert Burns	13 Jul 1820
Adam	7	M	Child	Ireland	United States	Trident	16 May 1826
Adam	45	M	Blacksmith	Ireland	United States	Trident	16 May 1826
Allen	40	M	Labourer	England	America	Manhattan	20 Mar 1820
Ann	9	F	...	Ireland	United States	General Putnam	20 Jun 1825
Ann	22		Spinster	Ireland	United States	Courier	15 Oct 1827
Anne	2	F	Child	Ireland	United States	Trident	16 May 1826
Anne	40	F	Wife	Ireland	United States	Trident	16 May 1826
Cath.	33	F	None	England	America	Manhattan	20 Mar 1820
Catherine	9	F	Girl	Ireland	United States	Trident	16 May 1826
Catherine	38	F	None	England	America	Manhattan	20 Mar 1820
Christian	12	F	Child	Ireland	U. States	Courier	17 Mar 1828
David	2	M		Scotland	New York	Joseph Hume	26 Oct 1829
Elisabeth	34			Ireland	United States	Antioch	3 Dec 1827
Eliza	4	F	Child	Ireland	United States	Trident	16 May 1826
Eliza W.	10	F		Great Britian	United States	London	24 Jun 1823
Elizabeth	13	F	...	Ireland	United States	General Putnam	20 Jun 1825
Esther	16	F	Spinster	Ireland	United States	Trident	16 May 1826
Francis	10	M	Child	Ireland	U. States	Courier	17 Mar 1828
Francis	20		Servant	Salem, Masst.	U. States	Sarah Lee	29 May 1826
Hugh	31	M	Weaver	Ireland	U. States	Courier	17 Mar 1828
James	28		Merchant	Ireland	United States	Robert Burns	18 Jun 1821
Jane	21	F	Servant	Ireland	United States	Carolina Ann	11 Dec 1826
Jane	26 5/12	F		Ireland	U. States	Fabius	22 Sep 1828
Jane	Dead		Dead	Ireland	United States	Courier	15 Oct 1827
*Died							
Jann	15	F	Spinster	United States	United States	York	31 Mar 1828
Jas.	8	M		Scotland	New York	Joseph Hume	26 Oct 1829
Jas.	35		Labourer	Ireland	United States	Antioch	3 Dec 1827
Jno.	14			Ireland	U. States	Robert Burns	18 Jun 1822
John	1 1/12	M	Child	Ireland	U. States	Courier	17 Mar 1828
John	3	M	Spinster	Glasgow	United States	Henry Clay	25 Apr 1822
John	12	M	...	Ireland	United States	General Putnam	20 Jun 1825
John	17	M	Mercht.	England	U. States	Perseverance	18 Nov 1824
John	18	M				Czar	29 Aug 1829
John	19	M	Merchant	Ireland	United States	Fabius	31 Jul 1829
John	21	M	Baker	Ireland	United States	Carolina Ann	11 Dec 1826
John	21	M	Labourer	Ireland	New York	Trusty	12 Sep 1828
John	21 9/12	M	Merchant	U. States	U. States	Fabius	22 Sep 1828
John	30	M	Gentleman	Ireland	America	Superior	12 Jun 1824
John, Mr.	31	M	Farmer	Grate Britain	...	Courier	14 Jun 1825
Margarett	8	F	...	Ireland	United States	General Putnam	20 Jun 1825
Margt.	14	F	Spinster	Ireland	United States	Trident	16 May 1826
Mary	2/12			Glasgow	United States	Henry Clay	25 Apr 1822
Mary	1	F	None	England	America	Manhattan	20 Mar 1820
Mary	34	F	Spinster	Glasgow	United States	Henry Clay	25 Apr 1822
Mary J.	3 6/12	F	Child	Ireland	U. States	Courier	17 Mar 1828
Matthew	...0	M	...	Ireland	United States	General Putnam	20 Jun 1825
Rachel	31	F	Matron	Ireland	U. States	Courier	17 Mar 1828
Robert	20		Weaver	Ireland	Great Britain	Robert Burns	14 Jun 1824
Robert	26	M	Merchant	Holand	Holland	South Carolina	14 Aug 1823
Robert	27	M	Farmer	U. States	U. States	Trident	17 May 1825
Robert	30	M	Merchant	G.B.		Silas Richards	29 Oct 1827
Robt.	5	M	Spinster	Glasgow	United States	Henry Clay	25 Apr 1822
Robt.	26	M	Ma...			Abigail	10 May 1821
S. C.	31			England	U. States	New York	30 Oct 1827
Saml.	12	M	Boy	Ireland	United States	Trident	16 May 1826
Samuel	20	M	Labourer	Ireland	New York	Trusty	12 Sep 1828
Sarah	10	F	...	Ireland	United States	General Putnam	20 Jun 1825

NAMES OF PASSENGERS	AGE	SEX	OCCUPATIONS	COUNTRY TO WHICH THEY BELONG	COUNTRY THEY INTEND TO INHABIT	SHIPS/DATES OF ARRIVAL	
ORR (cont'd)							
Sarah	28	F	Servant	Ireland	N. York	Trusty	12 Sep 1828
William	5 6/12	M	Child	Ireland	U. States	Courier	17 Mar 1828
William	20	M	Labourer	Ireland	United States	Catharine	22 Jul 1825
William	21	M	Farmer	G. Britain		Robert Burns	13 Jul 1820
William	21	...	...	Ireland	United States	Carolina Ann	24 Oct 1825
William	30	M	Coal Miner	Scotland	New York	Joseph Hume	26 Oct 1823
Willm.	18	M	Blacksmith	Ireland	United States	Trident	16 May 1826
Wm.	...	...	...	Ireland	U. States of America	Courier	17 Mar 1827
Wm.	1/12	F	D. Maker	Ireland	N. York	Trusty	12 Sep 1828
Wm.	26		Farmer	Ireland	United States	Courier	15 Oct 1827
ORRAN, Judy	22	F	None	Ireland	U.S.A.	Dalhouse Castle	21 Aug 1829
Judy	22	F	None	Ireland	United States	Dalhouse Castle	21 Aug 1829
ORREL, Marrron	19	F	Dress Maker	Scotland	United States	Liverpool Trader	24 Oct 1825
ORRELL, Ann	14	F	None	England	Philadelphia	Indian Chief	16 Aug 1822
Ann	56	F	None	England	Philadelphia	Indian Chief	16 Aug 1822
Catherine	20	F	None	England	Philadelphia	Indian Chief	16 Aug 1822
Edward	15	M	Grocer	England	Philadelphia	Indian Chief	16 Aug 1822
Mary	18	F	None	England	Philadelphia	Indian Chief	16 Aug 1822
Robert	19	M	Mechanick	England	Philadelphia	Indian Chief	16 Aug 1822
Sarah	16	F	None	England	Philadelphia	Indian Chief	16 Aug 1822
ORSBAND, —, Mr.	28	M	Labourer	St. John, N.B.	United States	Edwin	29 Nov 1828
John	2	M	Child	St. John, N.B.	United States	Edwin	29 Nov 1828
Julia	26	F	Wife	St. John, N.B.	United States	Edwin	29 Nov 1828
Thoms.	6/12	M	Child	St. John, N.B.	United States	Edwin	29 Nov 1828
ORSBORN, William	26	M	Theatrical	Great Britain	United States	Bolivar	21 May 1827
ORTGIES, Cartlen	21	M	Labourer	Germany	United States	Constitution	2 Aug 1826
ORTICHEN, A. J.	24	M	Merchant	Cadez	U. States	Helen	24 Apr 1827
ORTIQ, Eligio	24	M	Merchant	Spain	Spain	Virginia	9 Feb 1829
ORTOJUS, Cloun	19	F		Gt. Britain	United States	Europa	20 Apr 1825
ORTON, Jane	26	F		Ireland	United States	Loore	9 Sep 1822
Mariah	16	F		Ireland	United States	Loore	9 Sep 1822
ORYBEADE, C.	25	M	Merchant	Spain	United States	Sisters	24 Jan 1820
OSBORN, A. K.	23	M	Merchant	United States	U. States	Franklin	3 Feb 1825
Abner	Infant	F		England	U. States	Commerce	28 May 1824
E. F.	21	M	Merchant	U. States	U. States	Columbia	4 Jun 1824
E. F.	28	M	Merchant	U. States	U. States	Natchez	18 Aug 1828
Eliza	14		their Child [Samuel and Mary]	Great Britain	United States	Rufus King	4 Sep 1823
Elizabeth	2	F		England	U. States	Commerce	28 May 1824
Emery	12		their Child [Samuel and Mary]	Great Britain	United States	Rufus King	4 Sep 1823
Francis	27	M	Labourer	Ireland	U. States	Nancy	1 Sep 1823
Fredk. J.	39 5/12	M	Clerk	England	America	Cincinnatus	22 May 1826
Isaac	3	M		England	U. States	Commerce	28 May 1824
John	13	M		England	U. States	Commerce	28 May 1824
John	43	M	Husbandman	England	U. States	Commerce	28 May 1824
Joseph	3		their Child [Samuel and Mary]	Great Britain	United States	Rufus King	4 Sep 1823
Joseph	9	M		England	U. States	Commerce	28 May 1824
Joseph	20		Merchant	Ireland	United States	Robert Burns	18 Jun 1822
Maria	5/12		their Child [Samuel and Mary]	Great Britain	United States	Rufus King	4 Sep 1823
Mary	8		their Child [Samuel and Mary]	Great Britain	United States	Rufus King	4 Sep 1823
Mary	34	F		England	U. States	Commerce	28 May 1824
Mary	37		his Wife [Samuel]	Great Britain	United States	Rufus King	4 Sep 1823
Robert	7	M		England	U. States	Commerce	28 May 1824
Robt.	35	M	Musician	U. States	U. States	New Packet	20 Sep 1826
Samuel	5		their Child [Samuel and Mary]	Great Britain	United States	Rufus King	4 Sep 1823
Samuel	11	M		England	U. States	Commerce	28 May 1824
Samuel	36		Farmer	Great Britain	United States	Rufus King	4 Sep 1823
William	10		their Child [Samuel and Mary]	Great Britain	United States	Rufus King	4 Sep 1823
OSBORNE, Charles F., Mr.	26	M	Merchant	U. States	U. States	Hudson	10 Nov 1825
Charls	3	M		England	U. States	Pleiades	9 Oct 1829
Charls	29	M	Miller	England	U. States	Pleiades	9 Oct 1829
Dianah	28	F		England	U. States	Pleiades	9 Oct 1829

NAMES OF PASSENGERS	AGE	SEX	OCCUPATIONS	COUNTRY TO WHICH THEY BELONG	COUNTRY THEY INTEND TO INHABIT	SHIPS/DATES OF ARRIVAL	
OSBORNE (cont'd)							
Elizabeth	15	F	None	England	United States	Colossus	26 Aug 1828
Elizabeth	40	F	None	England	United States	Colossus	26 Aug 1828
Henry	18	M	Labourer	Ireland	United States	Trident	16 May 1826
Jethro	4	M	None	England	United States	Colossus	26 Aug 1828
Jno.	12	M	Boy	Ireland	United States	Trident	17 May 1825
John	28		Joiner	England	United States	Hudson	5 Apr 1826
Mary	1	F		England	U. States	Pleiades	9 Oct 1829
Mary	30					Hudson	5 Apr 1826
Owen	10	M	None	England	United States	Colossus	26 Aug 1828
Rebecca	2	F	None	England	United States	Colossus	26 Aug 1828
Robert	21	M	Farmer	Ireland	U. States	William & John	10 Jul 1824
Samuel	28		Merchant	N. York	United States	Robert Burns	18 Jun 1821
Sarah	6	F		England	U. States	Pleiades	9 Oct 1829
Sophia	7	F	None	England	United States	Colossus	26 Aug 1828
William	12	M	None	England	United States	Colossus	26 Aug 1828
William	39	M	Farmer	England	United States	Colossus	26 Aug 1828
OSBOROUGH, Wan.	27	M	Sadler	Great Britain	United States	John	6 Oct 1820
OSBURN, —	20	M	Servant	British	Brittain	Govenor Lincoln	15 Feb 1827
John	24	M		Ireland	United States	William & George	14 May 1828
OSCAR, Joseph	24	M	Weaver	Switzerland	America	Saluda	16 Oct 1824
OSGODLY, Ann	31	F	Farmer	Great Britan	United States	Clematis	8 May 1827
George	6/52	M	Farmer	Great Britan	United States	Clematis	8 May 1827
Harrison	31	M	Farmer	Great Britan	United States	Clematis	8 May 1827
John	6	M	Farmer	Great Britan	United States	Clematis	8 May 1827
John	25		Labourer	England	United States	Hugh Johnson	11 Jun 1828
OSGOOD, Elizabeth	16	F	None	U. States	U. States	Dromo	24 Jul 1826
Emma	43	F	None	U. States	U. States	Dromo	24 Jul 1826
Hazen	30 1/12	M	Farmer	United States	United States	Sicily	16 Feb 1829
J.	30	M	Mercht.	United States	United States	Manchester	6 Dec 1825
OSIOS,							
Fredrick Wilhelm	28	M		Germany	Vermont	Orient	25 Nov 1825
OSITA, J. A.	23	M	Merchant	Mexico	Mexico	Washington	29 Apr 1826
OSIZ, Valantine	30	M	Doctor of Law	Columbia	U. States	Bunker Hill	12 Aug 1828
OSMUNDSON,							
Gudmund	42	M	Farmer	Norway	United States	Salem	31 Aug 1829
OSNEY, Robt.	27	M	Weaver	St. Johns, N.B.	United States	Antioch	21 Sep 1827
OSSESTON, Samuel	25	M	Miller	England	United States	Criterion	27 Oct 1820
OSTER, John	26	M	Weaver	Native of Switzerland	United States	Canaris	30 Jun 1827
OSTERBRIDGE,							
William	23	M	Mariner	U. States	N. York	Mercator	10 Apr 1823
OSTERTAG, Christina	3	F		Germany	America	Falcon	28 Aug 1828
Doratha	1	F		Germany	America	Falcon	28 Aug 1828
Eva Funk	33	F		Germany	America	Falcon	28 Aug 1828
Henry	4	M		Germany	America	Falcon	28 Aug 1828
Jno.	31	M	Farmer	Germany	America	Falcon	28 Aug 1828
Johann George	7	M		Germany	America	Falcon	28 Aug 1828
Johann Jacob	6	M		Germany	America	Falcon	28 Aug 1828
OSTON, Fredrick	22	M	Carpenter	Germany	Newyork	Cortes	16 Jul 1827
Henry	26	M	Blacksmith	Germany	Newyork	Cortes	16 Jul 1827
OSTWALDT, Balthazar	7	M		France	America, U.N.S.	Great Britain	3 Aug 1829
Catharina	3/12	F		France	America, U.N.S.	Great Britain	3 Aug 1829
Catharina	27	F		France	America, U.N.S.	Great Britain	3 Aug 1829
Frederick	5	M		France	America, U.N.S.	Great Britain	3 Aug 1829
George	3	M		France	America, U.N.S.	Great Britain	3 Aug 1829
Martin	8 6/12	M		France	America, U.N.S.	Great Britain	3 Aug 1829
Michel	36	M	Wheelwright	France	America, U.N.S.	Great Britain	3 Aug 1829
OSWALD, Elizabeth	24	F	Farmer	France	France	Sully	15 Jul 1829
George	17	M	Laborer	Scotland	America	Camillus	12 Sep 1822
OSWALL, Sarah	36	F		United States	United States	Romulus	13 Aug 1829
OSWELD, Cathr.	13 9/12	F		France	United States	Catharine	10 Sep 1827
Eliza	16 1/12	F		France	United States	Catharine	10 Sep 1827
Hannah	60	M	Farmer	France	United States	Catharine	10 Sep 1827
Henry	17 3/12	M	Farmer	France	United States	Catharine	10 Sep 1827
Maria	26 2/12	F	Farmer	France	United States	Catharine	10 Sep 1827
Maria	30	F	Farmer	France	United States	Catharine	10 Sep 1827

NAMES OF PASSENGERS	AGE	SEX	OCCUPATIONS	COUNTRY TO WHICH THEY BELONG	COUNTRY THEY INTEND TO INHABIT	SHIPS/DATES OF ARRIVAL	
OSWELL, John N.	23	M	Gentleman	England	U. States	La Fayette	7 Apr 1825
OSZARD, Robt.	35	M	Mechanic	England	United States	Columbia	16 Jan 1829
OTARO, Frs.	30	M	Merchant	Havana	Havana	New Packet	12 Dec 1825
OTCHEL, Francois						Olympia	12 Aug 1828

*After having been at Sea a Number of Days was ascertaining the quantity of Baggage to report found the under mentioned persons had secreted themselves away notwithstanding our searach with the Gendearmes at the of leaving the port

OTERO, A.	25	M	Taylor	Spain	Spain	Betsey Ann	22 Dec 1821
Ignacio, Señor Don	19	M	Gentn.	Mexico	Mexico	Acasta	21 Oct 1825
OTES, Charlotte	20	F		United States	United States	Thames	16 May 1821
H.		M	Mercht.	U. States	U. States	Atlantic	13 Aug 1824
Helen	18	F		United States	United States	Thames	16 May 1821
Thomas	46	M	Merchant	United States	United States	Thames	16 May 1821
OTIGNON, M.	40	M	Merchant	France	United States	Howard	19 May 1826
OTIS, Charles	20	M	Clerk	U. States	U. States	Julia	9 Jun 1825
David	50	M	Merchant	Maine	U. States	Diana	4 Sep 1827
Harrison G.	33	M	Navy	U.S.	U.S.	Edward Bonnaffe	20 Jun 1825
Isaac	30	M	Cabinet Maker	United States	United States	Pilot	27 Feb 1826
OTLEY, B. W., Col.	55	M	Col. 70th Regiment	Great Britain	Great Britain	Nestor	3 Nov 1820
OTT, Anna Barbara	5	F		Germany	America	Falcon	28 Aug 1828
Anna Maria	9	F		Germany	America	Falcon	28 Aug 1828
Ant.	46	M	Merchant	Germany	New York	Orient	25 Nov 1825
Barbara E.	40	F		Germany	America	Falcon	28 Aug 1828
Elizabath C.	3 6/12	F		Germany	America	Falcon	28 Aug 1828
Gottlob Fredk.	12	M		Germany	America	Falcon	28 Aug 1828
Jno.	39	M	Farmer	France	France	Edward Quesnel	3 Jul 1829
Johann Fredk.	6	M		Germany	America	Falcon	28 Aug 1828
Johann Fredk.	40	M	Farmer	Germany	America	Falcon	28 Aug 1828
M.	30	M	Farmer	Germany	U. States	Minerva	9 Jan 1827
Philliptna	2	F		Germany	America	Falcon	28 Aug 1828
OTTEN, Henry	25	M				Cassack	25 Jul 1820
OTTERBURN, Hannah	18					Mount Vernon	26 Aug 1820
William	21		Farmer			Mount Vernon	26 Aug 1820
OTTIGNON, Claudius	54	M	Merchant	U. States	U. States	Bayard	25 Apr 1828
Fermen	48	M	Merchant	France	United States	Montano	29 Apr 1826
Peter	16	M	Merchant	U. States	U. States	Bayard	25 Apr 1828
OTTING, Peter	19	M	Merchant	Spain—Curacoa	Spain	Swan	23 Jun 1823
OTTINGNON, Claudius	53	M	Merchant	United States	United States	Montano	31 May 1824
Nicolas	19	M	Merchant	France	United States	Montano	31 May 1824
OTTLEY,							
Maria Ann, misess	9	F				Armadillo	15 Oct 1827
Martha, wife of ...	4...	F				Armadillo	15 Oct 1827
Matthew	4...	M	Gent.	Great Brittian	Canada	Armadillo	15 Oct 1827
OTTO, Johannis	21	M	fynochilder	Amsterdam	United States	Juffraw Johanna	16 Oct 1821
Philip	40	M	Apothecary	Hassan	United States	Xenophon	2 Jun 1824
OTWAY, L. H.	22	M	Merchant	Grenada	U. States	Columbia	14 Oct 1824
OTWELL, Mary Ann	24	F		Scotland, Great Britain	America	Superb	11 Oct 1821
OUEN, Geo. A.	22	M	Merchant	U. States	U. States	Pacific	28 Mar 1822
OUNE, Maria	17	F		France	U. States	Danube	21 Nov 1826
OUORAR, F.	30	M	Coachmaker	France	U. States	North Star	27 Oct 1828
OURPER, Robert	35	M	Merchant	Great Britain	United States	Florida	2 Sep 1822
OUSELEY, Wm. G.	27	M	Gentleman	England	United States	Corinthian	10 Jan 1826
OUTRIDGE, Jane	11	F		Great Britain	U. States	Columbia	22 Sep 1828
Wm.	28	M	Cooper	Great Britain	U. States	Columbia	22 Sep 1828
OUTWIN, John	30		Farmer	Yorkshire		Mount Vernon	18 Oct 1822
OVECOUX, Peter	30	M	Mariner	Brostol, N.B.	Bristol	St. Helena	18 Feb 1823

*Invalid from the U.S. Ship Cayenne, to be received in the Maine Hospital

OVENS, Cathr.	18	F	Servant	G. Britain	U. States	Wanderer	23 Jun 1828
OVER..., James	44	M	Merchant	Yorkshire	N. York	Manhattan	21 May 1821
OVERALL, Joseph	34	M		Great Britain	United States	Active	25 Mar 1828
OVEREND, A.	32	F	Spinster	G. Britain	U. States	St. George	7 Jun 1828
Ewd.	9	M		G. Britain	U. States	St. George	7 Jun 1828
Joseph	19	M	Merchant	Yorkshire	America	Hannibal	4 Apr 1823
Joseph	21	M	Merchant	England	America	James Cropper	3 Mar 1825
OVERENT, John	32	M	Carpenter	England	United States	India	8 Jun 1827
OVERHALL, Alxr.	1	M	Butcher	Great Britain	United States	Thomas Dickason	31 Jul 1829

NAMES OF PASSENGERS	AGE	SEX	OCCUPATIONS	COUNTRY TO WHICH THEY BELONG	COUNTRY THEY INTEND TO INHABIT	SHIPS/DATES OF ARRIVAL
OVERHALL (cont'd)						
Amelia	5	F	Butcher	Great Britain	United States	Thomas Dickason 31 Jul 1829
Henry	10	M	Butcher	Great Britain	United States	Thomas Dickason 31 Jul 1829
James	3 6/12	M	Butcher	Great Britain	United States	Thomas Dickason 31 Jul 1829
Joseph	41	M	Butcher	Great Britain	United States	Thomas Dickason 31 Jul 1829
Joseph, Junr.	8 4/12	M	Butcher	Great Britain	United States	Thomas Dickason 31 Jul 1829
Maria	7	F	Butcher	Great Britain	United States	Thomas Dickason 31 Jul 1829
Maria	28	F	Butcher	Great Britain	United States	Thomas Dickason 31 Jul 1829
Mary	11 6/12	F	Butcher	Great Britain	United States	Thomas Dickason 31 Jul 1829
OVERTON, Catherine	30	F	Seamstress			Splendid 14 Aug 1829
Charles	26	M	Mechanic	England	Great Britain	Manchester Packet 30 Nov 1822
Eliza	21	F		England	Great Britain	Manchester Packet 30 Nov 1822
James	21	M	farmer	England	Great Britain	Manchester Packet 30 Nov 1822
James	32	M	Brass founder	England	United States	Jubilee 12 May 1828
Thomas	1	M		England	Great Britain	Manchester Packet 30 Nov 1822
OWANS, John	25	M	Farmer	Great Britan	United States	Clematis 8 May 1827
Wm.	27	M	Farmer	Glasgow	Glasgow	Howard Douglass 11 May 1827
OWEN, —, Miss	30	F	None	Great Britan		Colossus 27 Mar 1828
—, Mrs.	20	F		Scotland	U.S.	Curler 19 Jul 1828
Charlotte	10	F	None	Great Britain	United States	Isaac Hicks 27 Sep 1826
Eleanor	9	F	None	Wales	United States	Orozimbo 11 Aug 1823
Eliza	13	F	None	Wales	United States	Orozimbo 11 Aug 1823
Elizabeth	17	F	None	Great Britain	United States	Isaac Hicks 27 Sep 1826
Evan	14	M	Labourer	Wales	United States	Orozimbo 11 Aug 1823
Griffith	47	M	Weaver	England	United States	Bolivar 15 Jun 1826
Harry	16	M	Labourer	Wales	United States	Orozimbo 11 Aug 1823
James	20	M	Laborer	Gt. Britain		Dalhouse Castle 13 May 1828
John	1 11/12	M		Scotland	United States	Indus 5 Sep 1827
John	11	M	Labourer	Wales	United States	Orozimbo 11 Aug 1823
John	30	M	Mariner	U. States	United States	Fox 9 Mar 1829
John	32	M		Scotland	U.S.	Curler 19 Jul 1828
John	44	M	Glassmaker	Great Britain	United States	Isaac Hicks 27 Sep 1826
Joseph	2 6/12	M	None	Great Britain	United States	Isaac Hicks 27 Sep 1826
M.	21	M	Gentleman	England	U. States	Radius 12 Sep 1822
M.	49	M	Farmer	Anglesea	U. States	Favorite 13 Jun 1821
Margt.	36 7/12	M		Scotland	United States	Indus 5 Sep 1827
Mary	14	F	None	Great Britain	United States	Isaac Hicks 27 Sep 1826
Mary	16	M		Scotland	United States	Indus 5 Sep 1827
Mary	21		Spinner	Rochall, England	Pleasant Valley	Albion 5 Feb 1822
Mary	40	F	None	Great Britain	United States	Isaac Hicks 27 Sep 1826
Mary	45	F		Philadelphia	U. States	Peter Remsen 30 Jun 1828
Robert	17		Tailor	Great Britain	United States	Gomer 21 May 1828
Robt.	53	M	Merchant	England	U. States	New York 4 Nov 1824
Samuel	5	M	None	Great Britain	United States	Isaac Hicks 27 Sep 1826
Thomas	20	M	Merchant	U. States	U. States	Phoebe 17 Apr 1821
Thomas	21	M	Mechanic	England	United States	John Wells 16 May 1825
Thomas	23	M	Mercht.	U. States	U. States	Gleaner 18 Jul 1822
Thomas	29	M	Merchant	N. York	U. States	Sarah 12 Dec 1828
Thos.	22	M	Merchant	N. London	U. States	Romeo 23 Jun 1823
William	11	M	None	Great Britain	United States	Isaac Hicks 27 Sep 1826
William	22	M	Merchant	England	U. States	New York 4 Nov 1824
OWENES, Thos.	26	M		Great B.	U. States	William Neilson 26 Jul 1828
OWENS, ...	40	M	Merchant	Great Britain	United States	John Wells 18 Sep 1826
Alexr.	12	M	Son	Ireland	New York	Atlantic 6 Oct 1828
Ann	20	F	None			Evergreen 28 Jul 1820

NAMES OF PASSENGERS	AGE	SEX	OCCUPATIONS	COUNTRY TO WHICH THEY BELONG	COUNTRY THEY INTEND TO INHABIT	SHIPS/DATES OF ARRIVAL	
OWENS (cont'd)							
Anne	3	F		Ireland	U. States	Fame	15 Nov 1826
Bridget	12	F	Child	Ireland	U. States	Josephine	7 May 1827
Catharine	6	F		Ireland	U. States	Fame	15 Nov 1826
Catherine	11	F	...	...	...	Indian Chief	8 Sep 1824
David W.	24	M	Coach Driver	United States	United States	Brown	30 Nov 1827
Edward	7	M	...	...	...	Indian Chief	8 Sep 1824
Edward	27	M	Merchant	America		Hope	27 Aug 1821
Edwd.	1	M	Son	Ireland	New York	Atlantic	6 Oct 1828
Eliza	15	F		Great Britain	United States	Saml. Wight	6 Sep 1827
Frans.	9	M	Son	Ireland	New York	Atlantic	6 Oct 1828
Griffeth	26	M	Farmer	Great Britan	United States	Clematis	8 May 1827
Hannah	18	F	None	England	United States	Martha	17 Sep 1821
Hugh	48	M	Farmer	U.S.A.	U.S.A.	Silas Richards	28 Jun 1825
Jane	6/12	F		Ireland	U. States	Fame	15 Nov 1826
Jane	30	F	None	Gt. Brittain	United States	Balaena	8 Jan 1825
Jane	41	F		Ireland	U. States	Fame	15 Nov 1826
John	3/12	M	...	...	...	Indian Chief	8 Sep 1824
John	16	M	Farmer	Mer...	...thshire	Howard Douglass	11 May 1827
Mary	11	F		Great Britain	United States	Saml. Wight	6 Sep 1827
Mary	13	F	Daughter	Ireland	New York	Atlantic	6 Oct 1828
Mary	16	F	...	...	...	Indian Chief	8 Sep 1824
Mary	18	F		Ireland	U. States	Fame	15 Nov 1826
Mary	44	F	...	...	...	Indian Chief	8 Sep 1824
Matthew	25	M	Farmer	Great Brittain	U. States	Hibernia	8 Jul 1823
Michael	38	M	Apothicary	Sligo	U. States	Panthea	8 Apr 1826
Michael, Jr.	21	M	Labourer	England	U. States	Panthea	8 Apr 1826
Owan	50	M	...	...	...	Indian Chief	8 Sep 1824
Owen	15	M	...	...	...	Indian Chief	8 Sep 1824
Owen	23	M	Engineer	England	U.S. America	Samuel Wright	9 Jan 1829
Owen	30	M	Labourer	G. Britain	U. States	London	23 Sep 1828
Owen	32	M	Farmer	G. Britain	U. States	St. George	7 Jun 1828
Pat	25	M	Labourer	Great Britain	United States	Penelope	11 Jun 1827
Patk.	30	M	Butcher	Ireland	New York	Atlantic	6 Oct 1828
Peggy	12	F	Clerk	...	United States	Minerva	30 Oct 1829
Robert	22	M	None	Wales	America	Hannibal	4 Apr 1823
Susan	28	F	Wife	Ireland	New York	Atlantic	6 Oct 1828
Thos.	23	M	Farmer	G. Britian	U. States	Messouri	17 Jun 1824
W.	50	M	Weaver			Lady of the Lake	23 Aug 1828
Wm.	19	M	Labourer	Co. Wicklow	United States	Java	9 Jul 1827
Wm.	27	M	Lab.	Glasgow	Glasgow	Howard Douglass	11 May 1827
OWER, John	45	M	Weaver	Perth	New York	Gratitude	25 Jun 1828
OWING, —, Child	7/12	F		U.S. America	U.S. America	Robert Y. Haynes	3 Jul 1827
Hannah	37	F	Wash Woman	U.S. America	U.S. America	Robert Y. Haynes	3 Jul 1827
OWINS, Peter	22	M	Laborer	Scotland	New York	Indian Chief	19 Jun 1823
OWNES, Ann	20	F		Great Britain	Philadelphia	Philetus	21 Jul 1827
OWR, Joseph	17	M	Taylor	France	U. States	India	8 Dec 1826
OWREM, John	24	M	Farmer	St. Johns	U. States	St. Michael	26 Oct 1824
OXCANTAR, Felix G.	39	M	Clergyman	Spain	Spain	Corsair	2 Oct 1820
OXEDA, J.	25	F	Merchant	France	France	Eliza	28 Apr 1827
Jane	36	F	Merchant	France	France	Eliza	28 Apr 1827
OXLEY, Jane	13	F		Gt. Britain		Dalhouse Castle	13 May 1828
Wm., Mr.	30	M	Mercht.	England	England	Manchester	6 Apr 1826
OYLER, Alfred	4	M		Great Britain	United States	Fame	26 May 1828
Danl.	8	M		Great Britain	United States	Fame	26 May 1828
Elizabeth	25	F		Great Britain	United States	Fame	26 May 1828
George	12	M		Great Britain	United States	Fame	26 May 1828
George	31	M	Farmer	Great Britain	United States	Fame	26 May 1828
John	23	M	Farmer	Great Britain	United States	Fame	26 May 1828
Samuel	6	M		Great Britain	United States	Fame	26 May 1828
Sarah	34	F		Great Britain	United States	Fame	26 May 1828
Wm.	10	M		Great Britain	United States	Fame	26 May 1828
OZAM, Ann	25	F		England	United States	Earl of Liverpool	29 Sep 1823

NAMES OF PASSENGERS	AGE	SEX	OCCUPATIONS	COUNTRY TO WHICH THEY BELONG	COUNTRY THEY INTEND TO INHABIT	SHIPS/DATES OF ARRIVAL	
OZAM (cont'd)							
Betsey	20	F		England	United States	Earl of Liverpool	29 Sep 1823
Bettey	48	F		England	United States	Earl of Liverpool	29 Sep 1823
George	6	M		England	United States	Earl of Liverpool	29 Sep 1823
John	10	M		England	United States	Earl of Liverpool	29 Sep 1823
Martha	24	F		England	United States	Earl of Liverpool	29 Sep 1823
Mary	17	F		England	United States	Earl of Liverpool	29 Sep 1823
Sarah	18	F		England	United States	Earl of Liverpool	29 Sep 1823
William	16	M		England	United States	Earl of Liverpool	29 Sep 1823
William	50	M	Farmer	England	United States	Earl of Liverpool	29 Sep 1823
OZOMBES, Mauric	26	M	Merchant	France		Lucy Ann	5 Oct 1825
P..., J. O.	...	M	...	...	Canada	Martha	22 Jul 1820
Mary Ann	33		None	..., England	Great Britain	Frances Henrietta	31 May 1824
Thankful	16	M		Great Britain	U. States	Boston	28 Aug 1821
Thomas	5		None	New York	America	Frances Henrietta	31 May 1824
PABENATT, C	26	F		Italy	U. States	Canning	18 Jul 1828
M.	53	F		Italy	U. States	Canning	18 Jul 1828
PABLO, Pedro	14	M		Columbian Republic	Columbian Republic	Meta	5 Jun 1824
PACE, Wm.	25		Miller	England		Hudson	23 Jul 1828
PACHAL, Benjn., Jr.	33	M	Farmer	U. States	U. States	Robt. Reade	12 Apr 1825
Deborah	31	F	Farmer	U. States	U. States	Robt. Reade	12 Apr 1825
Jane	26	F	Wife	Ireland	United States	Sarah G	19 Jun 1827
Julia	18	F	Farmer	U. States	U. States	Robt. Reade	12 Apr 1825
Lavina	3	F	Farmer	U. States	U. States	Robt. Reade	12 Apr 1825
PACHARD, Isaac	55	M	Merchant	U. States	U. States	Orono	21 May 1827
PACHARETTA, F.	30	M	Merchant	Italy	U. States	Protector	2 Jul 1824
PACHEL, Andrew	28	M	Laborer	Ireland	United States	Sarah G	19 Jun 1827
PACHELL, Mary F.	3	F	Child	Ireland	United States	Sarah G	19 Jun 1827
PACHET, Edward	21	M	Merchant	France	United States	William Byrnes	1 Dec 1824
PACHWOOD, Robert	35	M	Waiter	Bermuda	Bermuda	Samuel	23 Aug 1824
PACK, Rob.	27	M	Mechanic	Dunbarton	U. States	Ann	11 Feb 1822
William	28	M	Ship Master	G.B.	U.S.	Silvanus Jenkins	27 Jul 1829
PACKARD, Isaac	...	M	...	Switzerland	United States, the State of Ohio	Florian	28 Sep 1824
Isaac	45		Merchant	Massachusetts	Philadelphia	James Cropper	12 Jul 1822
Isaac	45	M	Merchant	New York	U. States	Zephyr	18 May 1825
Isaac	46	M	Gentleman	U. States	New York	Sully	30 Oct 1827
Isac	38	M	Planter	Boston	U. States	Circassian	3 Jun 1826
Louisa E.	18	F	Lady	U. States	New York	Sully	30 Oct 1827
Mary A.	18	F		Massachusetts	Philadelphia	James Cropper	12 Jul 1822
Mary A.	18	F		New York	U. States	Zephyr	18 May 1825
Polly	22	F	...	Switzerland	United States, the State of Ohio	Florian	28 Sep 1824
Susan	14	F		New York	U. States	Zephyr	18 May 1825
PACKE, Jose	18	M	Merchant	France	U. States	Joseph S. Lewis	6 Dec 1822
PACKER, Jas. H.	23 4/12	M	Accountant	Ireland	New York	Triton	12 Jul 1823
Mathew	36	M	Mariner	Philadelphia	U. States	Mary Jane	29 Dec 1821
Perez	34	M	Physician	New York	U. States	Crisis	26 May 1824
PACKSON, B.	34	M		Ireland	America	Corinthian	1 Sep 1827
PACKWOOD, Robt.	28	M	Servant	U. States	U. States	Worromontogus	23 Jun 1823
PACY, John	20	M	Wheelwright	England	United States	Jubilee	1 Oct 1828
PADDIE, Wm.	34	M	Merchant	Gt. Brittain	Canada	Leeds	19 May 1823
PADDON, Jas.	21	M	Merchant	England	United States	Montano	4 Nov 1823
John	48	M	Merchant	England	United States	Montano	4 Nov 1823
John S.	24	M	Merchant	England	United States	Montano	4 Nov 1823

NAMES OF PASSENGERS	AGE	SEX	OCCUPATIONS	COUNTRY TO WHICH THEY BELONG	COUNTRY THEY INTEND TO INHABIT	SHIPS/DATES OF ARRIVAL	
PADFIELD, R.	10	M	Farmer	Great Britton	U. State	Earl of Liverpool	16 Aug 1826
PADGET, John	55	M	Farmer	Great Britain	United States	Florida	10 Dec 1823
PADGETT, John	28	M	Tanner	Gt. Britain	U. States	Camberwell	7 Apr 1828
PADGUIN, Harriet	21	F		France	New York	Isabella	15 Sep 1828
PADILLO, Gabriel	35	M	Priest	Central America	Central America	Robert Y. Haynes	2 Oct 1829
PADRO, Pelor	21	M	Merchant	Spain	Mexico	Sarah	23 Sep 1826
PADRON, Jos.	20	M	Merchant	Spain	U. States	Native	16 Nov 1825
PAETER, Chatarina, kinder [child of Adam]	13	F		Limbach	United States	Juffraw Johanna	16 Oct 1821
Elizabeth, kinder [child of Adam]	9	F		Limbach	United States	Juffraw Johanna	16 Oct 1821
Jacob, kinder [child of Adam]	1	M		Limbach	United States	Juffraw Johanna	16 Oct 1821
Louisa, kinder [child of Adam]	11	F		Limbach	United States	Juffraw Johanna	16 Oct 1821
PAEY, Mary Ann	26	F		Switzerland	Switzerland	Edward Quesnel	3 Jul 1829
PAEZ, Manuel Antonia	7			S. America	U. States	Endymion	2 Jul 1821
Thomas	9			S. America	U. States	Endymion	2 Jul 1821
PAGAN, James	27	M		Scotland	Jamaica	Little Cherub	11 Aug 1825
PAGE, Ann	31	F	None	France	U. States	Marmion	7 Jun 1824
E. P.	40	M				Velocipede	20 Sep 1824
Elizabeth	30	F		England	Boston	Cortes	16 Jul 1827
Hannah	36	F	Female	Russia	United States	Baltic	17 Aug 1824
J.	33	M	Commerce	U. States	United States	New York	5 Nov 1828
James	25	M	Farmer	Great Britian	United States	London	24 Jun 1823
John	9	M	None		U. States	Marmion	7 Jun 1824
John	52	M	Gentleman	United States	United States	Assiduous	30 Jul 1822
John	56	M	Music master	England	Boston	Cortes	16 Jul 1827
Lewis	49	M	Confectioner	United States	United States	Eugene	25 Aug 1829
Mary	55	F		Gt. Brittain	U. States	Courier	30 Dec 1824
Mary Ann	2	F	None	Russia	United States	Baltic	17 Aug 1824
Richd.	33	M	None	France	U. States	Marmion	7 Jun 1824
Richd.	35	M	None	Great Britain	United States	Cambria	26 Dec 1827
Samuel	4	M	None	Russia	United States	Baltic	17 Aug 1824
Silas	10	M	Farmer	Great Britian	U. States	Marmion	7 Jun 1824
Thomas	25	M	Labourer	England	America	Sarah	18 Aug 1829
Thomas	54	M	Farmer	Gt. Brittain	U. States	Courier	30 Dec 1824
W.	28	M	Ship Master	U. States	U. States	Morning Star	28 Apr 1824
William	6	M	None		U. States	Marmion	7 Jun 1824
Wm.	35	M	Merchant	Bath	U. States	Milo	8 Mar 1824
Wm. P.	34	M	Merchant	United States	United States	Baltic	17 Aug 1824
PAGGI, Ann	19	F		England	U.S. America	Magnet	17 Aug 1825
PAGSEED, —	30	M	Merchant	Spain	U. States	Anne	20 Jun 1828
Francis	50	M	Merchant	Spain	U. States	Anne	20 Jun 1828
PAHLEY, George	64	M	Merchant	England	Uncertain	John Wells	22 Sep 1824
PAIGNER, Mary Ann, Servant	24	F	Farmer	France	United States	Crescent	12 Jul 1827
PAILAND, Michael M.	22 2/12		Labourer	Ireland	United States	Helen	5 Jul 1820
PAILLARD, Henrietta	19	F		France	United States	New England	29 Aug 1828
PAILLET, Hy., Mr.	23		Mercht.	U.S.	France	Brandt	7 Feb 1822
PAILLETTE, Alexander	29	M	Carpenter	France	United States	Montano	5 May 1828
PAIN, Ann	45	F		Great Britain	United States	Atlantic	28 May 1827
P... Ann	13	F		Great Britain	United States	Atlantic	28 May 1827
Ths.	45	M	Farmer	Great Britain	United States	Atlantic	28 May 1827
PAINAT, P.	21	M	Merchant	France	U. States	Bayard	25 Apr 1828
PAINBOFF, Eliza	40	F	Merchant	U. States	U. States	Purrington	14 May 1827
Lewis	55	M	Merchant	U. States	U. States	Purrington	14 May 1827
Virginia	36	F	Merchant	U. States	U. States	Purrington	14 May 1827
PAINE, Alfred	4	M	Farmer	Rye, England	United States	William	21 May 1828
Charles	8	M	Farmer	Rye, England	United States	William	21 May 1828
Eliza	5	F		Rye, England	United States	William	21 May 1828
Elizabeth	8	F	Farmer	England	United States	Joseph	13 Oct 1823
Elizabeth	37	F	Farmer	England	United States	Joseph	13 Oct 1823
Frances	31	M	Cordwainer	England	U.S.A.	Robin Hood	6 May 1828
Hannah	12	F		Rye, England	United States	William	21 May 1828

NAMES OF PASSENGERS	AGE	SEX	OCCUPATIONS	COUNTRY TO WHICH THEY BELONG	COUNTRY THEY INTEND TO INHABIT	SHIPS/DATES OF ARRIVAL	
PAINE (cont'd)							
Jedh.	30	M	Mariner	U. States	U. States	Bolina	9 May 1822
John	17	M	Farmer	Rye, England	United States	William	21 May 1828
John	44	M	Mechanic	Great Britain	U.S. Am.	Eliza	12 May 1828
Louisa	5	F		England	U.S.A.	Robin Hood	6 May 1828
Mary	6	F		England	U.S.A.	Robin Hood	6 May 1828
Mary	19	F		Rye, England	United States	William	21 May 1828
Mary	20	M	None	Ireland	New York	America	1 Aug 1828
Mary	35	F		United States	United States	Only Son	14 Jan 1828
Mary Ann	15	F	None	Great Britain	U.S. Am.	Eliza	12 May 1828
Nathaniel	36	M	Farmer	England	United States	Joseph	13 Oct 1823
Peggy	35	F	None	Great Britain	U.S. Am.	Eliza	12 May 1828
Saraah	29	F		England	U.S.A.	Robin Hood	6 May 1828
Sarah	45	F		Rye, England	United States	William	21 May 1828
Thomas	46	M	Farmer	Rye, England	United States	William	21 May 1828
Thomas, Jr.	15	M	Farmer	Rye, England	United States	William	21 May 1828
Thos.	4/12	M	None	Great Britain	U.S. Am.	Eliza	12 May 1828
William	10	M	Farmer	Rye, England	United States	William	21 May 1828
Wm.	14	M	None	Great Britain	U.S. Am.	Eliza	12 May 1828
PAINSEY, Veren	1	F		Germany	United States	Origon	8 Jun 1824
PAINTER, Tlexes	25	M	Gentleman	New Haven, Connecticut	New Haven, Connecticut	Hercules	11 Feb 1822
PAIRARAY, Mich.	25	M	Merchant	Spain	U. States	Abigail	16 Jul 1824
PAIRÉ, Theodore	17 3/12	M		France	France	France	28 Mar 1829
PALACOOZ, C.	31	M	Marchant	Nassau	New Providence	Sea Flower	24 Jun 1824
PALAFEE, H.	25	M	Grocer	Hayti		Ranger	29 Jul 1828
PALANEO, J. Antonia	12			S. America	U. States	Endymion	2 Jul 1821
PALE, James	25	M				Eliza Grant	6 Oct 1828
PALELLI, Antonio	20	M	Shoemaker	Italy	Kentucky	Abigail	9 Aug 1821
PALENER, Richard	20	M		Ireland	U. States	Nancy	16 Aug 1822
PALET, Hycinthe	32	F		France	United States	Henri IV	2 Oct 1828
Louis	18	M	Mechanic	France	U.S.	Helen	3 May 1828
PALFREYMAN, Charles	25 6/12	M	Merchant	England	England	New York	3 Apr 1826
PALIMEN, David	21	M	Farmer	Scotland	United States	Camillus	27 Oct 1829
PALIMENO, L.	11	M	Student	Spain	United States	Diana	9 Aug 1823
PALINER, Charles	21		Farmer	Somerset	England	London	13 Dec 1822
PALING, Ann	25	F	Lady	England	U. States	Radius	16 Mar 1822
Maria	8	F	None	England	U. States	Radius	16 Mar 1822
Thomas	32	M	Gentleman	England	U. States	Radius	16 Mar 1822
William	4	M	None	England	U. States	Radius	16 Mar 1822
PALINGRE, Henry M.	30	F		France	U. States	Leonarde	29 Aug 1828
Joseph	8/12	M		France	U. States	Leonarde	29 Aug 1828
Judin	4	M		France	U. States	Leonarde	29 Aug 1828
Pierre N.	42	M	Distiller	France	U. States	Leonarde	29 Aug 1828
PALISTER, George	22	M	Currier	United States	United States	Josephine	22 Aug 1829
PALLAIS, A.	20	M	Merchant	Spain	Havana	Rolla	10 Feb 1824
D.	40	M	Gentleman	Mexico	England	Brown	23 Dec 1826
M.	14	M		Italy	U. States	George	9 Jul 1825
PALLEN, Bineto	32	M	Segar Maker	Island of Cuba	United States	Betsey	28 Oct 1825
PALLESTER, J. H.	18	M		Halifax	U. States	Hope & Esther	12 May 1826
PALLETT, Edmund	58	M	Porter	Scotland		Zamoa	5 Nov 1828
PALLIS, Pobe	15	M	Gentleman	Mexico	England	Brown	23 Dec 1826
PALLISTAR, —, Mrs.	38	F		Halifax	some to return & the others to Canada	Albert	14 May 1822
PALLISTER, Geo.	15	M		N. York	United States	Loire	4 Oct 1824
Mary	20	F		Halifax	United States	Loire	4 Oct 1824
PALLON, Pierre	44	M		France	U. States	Courier	31 Jul 1828
PALMA, G.	22	M	Mariner	France	Honduras or South America	Alabama	3 Dec 1823
PALMER, —, Mr.	31	M		Halifax	U. States	Borneo	26 Apr 1824
—, Mr.	35	F		U. States	Canada	Columbia	7 Sep 1827
—, Mrs.	36	F		Germany	Germany	Benjamin	10 Aug 1821
Ag.	17	F	Lady	Boston	Boston	Howard	26 Aug 1823
Alexr.	38	M	Gentleman	Germany	Germany	Benjamin	10 Aug 1821
Betsey	8	F		Gt. Britain	United States	Robert Edwards	1 Jun 1826
C., Mrs.	39	F	Gentleman	Boston	Boston	Howard	26 Aug 1823
C. C.	21	M	Gentleman	Boston	Boston	Howard	26 Aug 1823

NAMES OF PASSENGERS	AGE	SEX	OCCUPATIONS	COUNTRY TO WHICH THEY BELONG	COUNTRY THEY INTEND TO INHABIT	SHIPS/DATES OF ARRIVAL	
PALMER (cont'd)							
Daniel	35	M	Labourer	Bristol	U. States	Latona	7 Jul 1827
E.	20	M	Merchant	France	U. States	Howard	27 Feb 1824
E.	28	M	Laborer	Switzerland	U.S.	C. Amelia	30 Jun 1828
Eliza	2			D...	England	Great Britain	7 May 1827
Eliza	3	F		United	U. States	Sarah G	30 Jun 1828
Elizabeth	32	F		Gt. Britain	United States	Robert Edwards	1 Jun 1826
Elizh.	15	F		Boston	Boston	Howard	26 Aug 1823
F.	7	M		Boston	Boston	Howard	26 Aug 1823
Francis	22	M	Mechanic	Maine	U. States	Orlando	5 May 1826
Francis	31	M	Servant to Mr. Atkinson	England	Quebec	Robert Edwards	3 Oct 1829
Frederick	60	M	Farmer	United States	United States	St. Michaels	23 Dec 1826
Geo.	23	M	Merchant	Great Brittain	G. Brittain	Bordeaux	13 Oct 1821
Georg	9	M	Labourer	England	U.N. States	Earl of Liverpool	20 Aug 1825
Gideon	74	M	Farmer	U. States	U. States	Thomas	30 Aug 1824
H.	1	M		Gt. Britain	United States	Robert Edwards	1 Jun 1826
H.	33	M	Farmer	Gt. Britain	United States	Robert Edwards	1 Jun 1826
James	...		Bricklayer	L...	England	Great Britain	7 May 1827
James	21	M	Farmer	England	United States	Siroc	31 Oct 1829
James	22	M	Farmer	England	England	Criterion	29 May 1822
Jeremiah	15	M	Labourer	Bristol	U. States	Latona	7 Jul 1827
Jno. H.	35	M	Schoolmaster	Great Britain	U. States	Dominica	4 Jan 1823
Job	25	M	Merchant	U. States		John Dickinson	14 Sep 1820
John	20	M	Cabinet Maker	Great Britain	United States	Albion	18 Feb 1823
John	21	M	Labourer	England	U.N. States	Earl of Liverpool	20 Aug 1825
Joseph, Dr.	28	M	Doctor	U. States	Boston, Mass.	Rubicon	22 May 1826
Lucretia	3	F	None	Halifax	U. States	Loire	7 Jul 1827
M.	0 6/12	M		United	U. States	Sarah G	30 Jun 1828
Mary	27	F	None	Halifax	U. States	Loire	7 Jul 1827
Mary Ann	13	F		Gt. Britain	United States	Robert Edwards	1 Jun 1826
Philip	25	M	Labourer	G. Britain	U. States	Nimrod	31 Jul 1828
Sapphire	4			L...	England	Great Britain	7 May 1827
Sarah	35	F	None	Great Briton	United States	Mount Vernon	30 Dec 1828
Sophia	10	F		Gt. Britain	United States	Robert Edwards	1 Jun 1826
Thomas	20	M	Labourer	England	U.N. States	Earl of Liverpool	20 Aug 1825
Thomas	21	M	Merchant	Ireland		John Dickinson	14 Sep 1820
Thomas	27	M	Shoemaker	Great Briton	United States	Mount Vernon	30 Dec 1828
W. L.	47	M	Gentleman	Boston	Boston	Howard	26 Aug 1823
William	...			L...	England	Great Britain	7 May 1827
William N.	28	M	Harness Maker	New York	U.S.	Lydia	7 Oct 1823
Wm.	5	M		Boston	Boston	Howard	26 Aug 1823
Wm.	32	M	Baker	Halifax	U. States	Washington	8 Oct 1825
Wm.	34	M	Gentleman	U. States	U. States	Martha	20 Jun 1825
PALMIERI, Giuseppe	17	M		Roma	Philadelphia	Falcon	10 Sep 1823
PALOMA, Menuela	22	F	Merchant	Spain	Havana	Commodore Chauncy	28 Nov 1825
PALOMINE, J.	13	M	Boy	Spain	France	Caravan	1 May 1824
L.	16	M	Boy	Spain	France	Caravan	1 May 1824
PALORCE, Felix	23		Gardener	Paris	France	Ann	27 Nov 1820
Vincent	32		Gardener	Paris	France	Ann	27 Nov 1820
PALTON, W. D.	19	M	Merchant	U. States	U. States	Superb	18 Oct 1821
PAMMET, Charles *died	1	M		England	United States	Acasta	14 Jun 1824
Martha	8	F		England	United States	Acasta	14 Jun 1824
Mary Ann	3	F		England	United States	Acasta	14 Jun 1824
Sarah	4	F		England	United States	Acasta	14 Jun 1824
Sarah	34	F		England	United States	Acasta	14 Jun 1824
Stephen	9	M		England	United States	Acasta	14 Jun 1824
William	40	M	Labourer	England	United States	Acasta	14 Jun 1824
PANBRUN, A.	33	M	Merchant	France	U. States	Ann Eliza Jane	7 Feb 1825
Anty.	38	M	Merchant	France	New York	Enterprize	3 Nov 1824
PANCES, Pierre	36	M	Mason	Germany	United States	Wm. Osborne	16 Sep 1828
PANCHAL, Susan	60	F	Wash	France	U. States	C. Amelia	30 Jun 1828
PANCHON, Francis	16	M	Servant	U. States	U. States	Cadmus	28 May 1821
PANDY, James	19	M	Labourer	Ireland	U. States	Hope & Esther	9 Jun 1827

NAMES OF PASSENGERS	AGE	SEX	OCCUPATIONS	COUNTRY TO WHICH THEY BELONG	COUNTRY THEY INTEND TO INHABIT	SHIPS/DATES OF ARRIVAL	
PANE, Jno. Wm.	25	M	Merchant	United States	Charlstown	Martha	4 Oct 1822
PANET, Philip	36	M	Merchant	Canada	U. States	Edward Bonaffe	11 Dec 1827
Wm.	20	M	...	Switzerland	U. States	Robert Edward	2 Nov 1827
PANGBUN, Richd.	35	M	Mercht.			General Coffin	9 Mar 1827
PANNALL, R. A.	36	F		Spain	Havana	Liberty	31 Jan 1826
PANNEL, Ann	17		her Daughter	England	United States	Cambria	19 Oct 1829
Ann	60			England	United States	Cambria	19 Oct 1829
Charles	22		Cooper	England	United States	Cambria	19 Oct 1829
Eliza	19		her Daughter	England	United States	Cambria	19 Oct 1829
Rachael	15		her Daughter	England	United States	Cambria	19 Oct 1829
PANPILLION, Ned	12	M	Servant			Ductile	4 Oct 1825
PANSIN, E.	18	M	Merchant	France	United States	Belle	3 Aug 1822
PANSORBO, Maria	25	F	Nurse	Mexico	Mexico	Virginia	9 Feb 1829
PANTER, J.	28	M	Merchant	Spain	United States	Enterprize	9 Aug 1825
PANTON, —, Mrs.	30	F		England	U. States	Seneca	7 Nov 1825
Ann	2	F		England	U. States	Seneca	7 Nov 1825
J.	45	M	Merchant	England	U. States	Seneca	7 Nov 1825
Samuel	5	M		England	U. States	Seneca	7 Nov 1825
PANVERT, E.	21	M	Merchant	New York	U. States	Andrew Jackson	29 Aug 1823
PAPE, C. Lewis	32	M	Sadler	Sweden	U. States	Cadmus	28 May 1821
PAPENEAU, Lewis J.	36	M	Advocate	Montreal	U. States	New York	15 Nov 1823
PAPINO, L.	23	M	Farmer	G. Brittain	U. States	General Jackson	15 Jan 1829
PAPPAR, Thomas	22	M	Framer	Ireland	U. States	Globe	14 Jul 1821
PAR, Douglass	10	M		Great Britain	U. States of Amer	Junius	5 Jul 1820
PARADIN, Dennis	6	M	Labourer or Spinster	Ireland	United States	Champion	3 Nov 1827
PARAL, Laban	23	M	Sugar Baker	Prussia	United States	Richmond	4 Aug 1826
PARARA, Domi	32	M	Merchant	U. States	U. States	Superion	30 Apr 1825
Domingo	37	M	Mariner	Portugal	U. States	Ambuscade	12 Jan 1822
PARAVIA, Domingo	35	M	Merchant	U. States	U. States	Eliza Ann	29 Sep 1820
PARCALES, Peter	24	M	Milwright	New York	U. States	Nancy	7 Sep 1824
PARCE, Jane	18	F	Servant	Bahamas	Bahamas	Success	25 Jun 1825
PARDO, J.	30	M	Merchant	Holland	Holland	Prudence	11 Jun 1825
PARDOW, George	14		Gentleman	U. States	America	Florida	14 Oct 1829
Julia	16	F	None	New York	America	William Thompson	18 Jan 1825
Robt.	17	M	Student	United States	United States	Manhattan	22 Sep 1823
PARERO, E.	26	M	Merchant	Spain	Spain	Emma	26 May 1827
J.	22	M	Merchant	Spain	U. States	Emma	26 May 1827
PARETER, Adam	34	M	Boer en weever	Schonbach	United States	Juffraw Johanna	16 Oct 1821
PARFAIT, Jose	29	M	Mercht.	Carthagena	U. States	Polly & Eliza	23 Mar 1826
PARIS, Albert	30	M		Brucelles	Philadelphia	Falcon	10 Sep 1823
Charles	29		Artist	Italy	Italy	London	16 Aug 1824
Peter	25	M	Merchant	France	Honduras or South America	Alabama	3 Dec 1823
PARISE, Jerome	28	M	Mercht.	Italy	America	Henry	11 Oct 1825
PARISH, George	42	M	None	Great Britan	Great Britan	Columbia	11 Aug 1823
George	44	M	Gentleman	Bath, England	New York	New York	31 Jul 1829
Heny.	18	M		Porto Rico	N. York	Hanna	3 Jun 1828
John	23	M	Mercht.	Hamburg	Hamburg	George Canning	2 May 1828
Lomen	38	F		Porto Rico	N. York	Hanna	3 Jun 1828
PARISOT, Antoni	18	F		France	United States	Le Voltaire	19 Jul 1828
Chas. C.	61	M	Farmer	France	United States	Le Voltaire	19 Jul 1828
Eliz.	44	F		France	United States	Le Voltaire	19 Jul 1828
Jean	4	F		France	United States	Le Voltaire	19 Jul 1828
Judith	2 3/12	F		France	United States	Le Voltaire	19 Jul 1828
PARK, —, Mrs.	28	F		G. Brittain	U. States	Clarence	8 Dec 1821
Agnes	1	F		G. Brittain	U. States	Clarence	8 Dec 1821
Alexander	16 6/12	M		Ireland	U. States	Virginia	20 Jun 1825
David	6/12	M	None	Scotland	United States	Mary & Susan	5 Aug 1828
Elizabeth	17	F	Spinster	Ireland	America	Josephine	8 Dec 1827
Em.	45	F	Widow	Ireland	U. States	William & John	10 Jul 1824
George	25	M	Shoemaker	England	United States	Danube	13 Jul 1827
Hanlin	20	M	Labourer	Scotland	United States	Mary & Susan	5 Aug 1828
Henry	70		Weaver	Ireland	United States	Courier	15 Oct 1827
James	17	M	None	Great Britain	United States	Ann Maria	9 Mar 1820
Jane	18	F	Spinster	Paisley	U.S. America	Camillus	10 Sep 1821
Jane	20	F		Ireland	U. States	Nancy	2 May 1823
John	9	M	Child	Paisley	U.S. America	Camillus	10 Sep 1821

984

NAMES OF PASSENGERS	AGE	SEX	OCCUPATIONS	COUNTRY TO WHICH THEY BELONG	COUNTRY THEY INTEND TO INHABIT	SHIPS/DATES OF ARRIVAL	
PARK (cont'd)							
John	29	M	Labourer	New Castle, New Castle [Parish], Edinr. [County]	New York	Hero	19 May 1828
*to follow his occupation							
John	60	M	Labourer	Paisley	U.S. America	Camillus	10 Sep 1821
Joseph	50	M	Labourer	England	United States	Alexander Mansfield	16 Sep 1823
Letitia	3	F	Child	Paisley	U.S. America	Camillus	10 Sep 1821
Letitia	45	F	Labourer	Paisley	U.S. America	Camillus	10 Sep 1821
Margreth	12	F		Ireland	U. States	Virginia	20 Jun 1825
Margt.	24	F	Spinster	Ireland	America	Josephine	8 Dec 1827
Martha	16	F	Spinster	Paisley	U.S. America	Camillus	10 Sep 1821
Mary	17	F		England	United States	Alexander Mansfield	16 Sep 1823
Robert	22	M	Joiner	Scotland	America	John Adams	2 Aug 1827
Robert	37		Farmer	Ireland		Westmoreland	1 Aug 1826
Ruth	24	F		Halifax	Great Britton	William	11 May 1821
Samuel	11	M	Child	Paisley	U.S. America	Camillus	10 Sep 1821
Sarah	21	F	None	Scotland	United States	Mary & Susan	5 Aug 1828
W., Jr.	6	M		G. Brittain	U. States	Clarence	8 Dec 1821
Walter	30	M	Joiner	G. Brittain	U. States	Clarence	8 Dec 1821
PARKALL, —	25	M	Merchant	United States	United States	Aurora	10 Nov 1827
PARKE, George	7 3/12	M		England	United States	Dalhouse Castle	26 Dec 1827
Sarah	20	F		England	United States	Dalhouse Castle	26 Dec 1827
William	18	M	Glazer	Sligo	New York	Susquehana	27 Jun 1823
Wm.	40	M	Farmer	Great Britian	U. States	Orbit	29 Apr 1822
PARKER, —, Miss	7	F		United States	Curacao	Anna Elizabeth	14 Jun 1824
—, Mrs.	30	F	Lady	United States	Curacao	Anna Elizabeth	14 Jun 1824
A. E.	36	F		P. Amboy	U. States	General Paez	30 Jun 1827
Abm.	50	M	Farmer			Splendid	14 Aug 1829
Albert	24	M	Merchant	United States	U.S.	Jane	18 Oct 1828
Alchason	46	M	Farmer	Gt. Brittain	United States	Balaena	8 Jan 1825
Bridjet	35	F	None	Ireland	U. States	Henry Kneeland	27 Jul 1825
Catherine	50	F	Collier	Wales	U.S. States	Splendid	14 Aug 1829
Edward	26	M	Merchant	Gt. Britain	U. States	Margaret	26 Jul 1828
Eliza	22	F	Child	Ireland	United States	Dublin Packet	23 May 1828
Ellen	27	F		Great Britain	United States	Freake	25 Jun 1827
Ellen M.	7	F	Farmer	Shelburn	U. States	Loire	28 Aug 1824
F., Miss	15	F				Auritz	20 May 1823
Francis	19	F	Spinster	Ireland	United States	Trident	16 May 1826
Geo.	10	M		England	U. States	Hudson	8 Oct 1827
George	19		Baker	Northampton-shire	N. York	Peru	30 May 1828
George	20					Cincinnatus	29 Apr 1822
George	45	M	Farmer			Manhattan	25 Dec 1820
H...dia	22	F	None	Great Britain	United States	Martha	22 Jul 1820
Isaac	28	M	Mariner	Boston	Boston	Comet	1 Jun 1826
James		M	Merchant	Spain	U. States	James	23 Oct 1824
James	12	M	None	United States	United States	General Paez	21 Jun 1826
James, Jr.	20	M	Merchant	United States	United States	General Paez	14 Apr 1826
James F.	26	M	...	New York	United States	Gem	16 Jun 1824
James H.	27	M	Accountant	United States	U.S.	Trident	17 May 1825
Jane	25	F		Ireland	United States	Delta	24 Oct 1829
Jane	35	F	None	Ireland	America	Orbit	1 Sep 1823
Jane S.	27	F				Imperial	19 Jul 1820
Jessey	26	F	None	Gt. Britain	United States	Pacific	22 May 1826
John	10	M		P. Amboy	U. States	General Paez	30 Jun 1827
John	23	M	Miner			Splendid	14 Aug 1829
John	25	M	Merchant	United States	United States	Otter	25 Feb 1822
John	30	M	Seaman	United States	United States	William	7 Jan 1828
John	33	M	Mason	Ireland	U. States	Henry Kneeland	27 Jul 1825
John	33	M	Merchant	Great Britain		Howard	4 Feb 1826
John A.	23	M	Merchant	U. States	U. States	Echo	22 Apr 1823
Jonathan	54	M	Farmer	England	United States	Danube	13 Jul 1827
Joseph	9					Splendid	14 Aug 1829
Joseph	21	M	Farmer	Ireland	United States	Henry Kneeland	7 Jun 1828
M.	26	M	Shoemaker	Connecticutt	U. States	Ann	21 May 1824

NAMES OF PASSENGERS	AGE	SEX	OCCUPATIONS	COUNTRY TO WHICH THEY BELONG	COUNTRY THEY INTEND TO INHABIT	SHIPS/DATES OF ARRIVAL	
PARKER (cont'd)							
Margaret	23	F	his Wife	Ireland	United States	Delta	24 Oct 1829
Martha	2/12	F	None	Ireland	U. States	Henry Kneeland	27 Jul 1825
Martha	2	F	Child	Ireland	United States	Dublin Packet	23 May 1828
Martha	18	F		Holland	Holland	Lydia	30 Apr 1821
Mary	6/12	F		Great Britain	United States	Freake	25 Jun 1827
Mary	1 4/12	F	None	Ireland	U. States	Henry Kneeland	27 Jul 1825
Mary	11	F	Collier	Wales	U.S. States	Splendid	14 Aug 1829
Mary	52	F				Splendid	14 Aug 1829
Mary G.	16	F	None	United States	United States	General Paez	21 Jun 1826
Nicholas	21	M	Miller	Germany	United States	Montano	8 May 1827
Pat	20	M	Labourer	G. Britain	U. States	Nimrod	31 Jul 1828
Richard	25	M	Miner			Splendid	14 Aug 1829
Robert	4	M				Splendid	14 Aug 1829
Robert	24	M	Joiner	Gt. Britain	United States	Eliza Barker	11 Jan 1826
Robert	25	M	Farmer	Ireland	United States	Delta	24 Oct 1829
Robert	26	M	Farmer	Great Britain	United States	Natchez	17 Aug 1822
Robert	26	M	Mason	Manchester	United States	Nile	17 May 1827
Samuel	40	M	Traveller	Ireland	America	Orbit	1 Sep 1823
Sarah	13	F				Splendid	14 Aug 1829
Serah	3 6/12	F	Child	Ireland	U. States	Courier	17 Mar 1828
Sophia P.	21	F	Farmer	Shelburn	U. States	Loire	28 Aug 1824
Susannah	54	M	Farmer	England	United States	Danube	13 Jul 1827
Thom.	7					Splendid	14 Aug 1829
Thomas	...	...	...	...	...	St. Michael	22 Sep 1824
Thomas	30	M	Calico Printer	England	U. States	Florida	13 Jan 1827
W. L.	9	M		P. Amboy	U. States	General Paez	30 Jun 1827
William	4	M		Great Britain	United States	Freake	25 Jun 1827
William	21	M		Ireland	United States	John Dickinson	18 Feb 1822
William	22	M	Florist	England	U. States	Acasta	28 Jan 1823
William	23	M	...	Ireland	United States	Gem	16 Jun 1824
William	24	M	Cooper	United States	United States	St. Anna	16 Aug 1828
William	25	M	Blacksmith	England	America	John Adams	2 Aug 1827
William	25	M	Farmer	Ireland	United States	Dublin Packet	23 May 1828
William	28	M	Brickmaker	Great Britain	United States	Freake	25 Jun 1827
William	44	M	Cloathier	Great Britain		Olive Branch	9 Oct 1829
William	46	M	Seaman	United States	United States	Comet	6 Mar 1823
Willm.	60	M	Mechanic	England	United States	Concordia	25 Aug 1827
Wm.	11	F				Splendid	14 Aug 1829
Wm.	22		Shoemaker	Ireland	United States	Geo. Canning	5 Jun 1828
Wm.	24	M	...	England	United States	Margarett Scott	22 Aug 1827
Wm.	36	M	Farmer	Great Brittan	U. States	John & Elizabeth	11 Dec 1826
PARKES, Edward	2	M	None	England	United States	Bolivar	15 Jun 1826
Edwd.	20	M	Butcher	England	United States	Essex	23 May 1828
Frederick	7	M	None	England	United States	Bolivar	15 Jun 1826
Frederick	35	M	Blaise Dr...	Great Britain	New York	Zodiac	14 Jun 1822
Henry	4	M	None	England	United States	Bolivar	15 Jun 1826
Henry	19	M	Carpenter	Great Britian	United States	Isaac Hicks	22 May 1826
Jane	21	F		Great Britian	United States	Isaac Hicks	22 May 1826
Jemima	11	F	None	England	United States	Bolivar	15 Jun 1826
John	20	M	Blaise Dr...	Great Britain	New York	Zodiac	14 Jun 1822
Mary	15	F	None	England	United States	Bolivar	15 Jun 1826
Mary	19	F	Spinster	Ireland	United States	Gem	16 Jun 1824
Richard	24	M	Glassmaker	Great Britian	United States	Isaac Hicks	22 May 1826
Susan	40	F	None	England	United States	Bolivar	15 Jun 1826
Thos.	42	M	Bricklayer	England	United States	Bolivar	15 Jun 1826
Thos., Jr.	19	M	None	England	United States	Bolivar	15 Jun 1826
Zachariah	28	M	Merchant	England	United States	Manhattan	11 Oct 1824
PARKIN, Eliza	9	F	None	Great Britain	U. States	Ann Marria	6 Aug 1823
Jane	8	F	None	Great Britain	U. States	Ann Marria	6 Aug 1823
Wm.	42	M	Miller	Great Britain	U. States	Ann Marria	6 Aug 1823
PARKINS, Alice	13	F	None	Great Britain		Moro Castle	6 Jul 1827
Eliz.	35	F	daughter	England	U.S. States	Splendid	14 Aug 1829
Elizabeth	1	F	None	Great Britain		Moro Castle	6 Jul 1827
Ellen	6	F	None	Great Britain		Moro Castle	6 Jul 1827
John	6	M	daughter	England	U.S. States	Splendid	14 Aug 1829
John	24	M	Miner	England	U.S. States	Splendid	14 Aug 1829
Joseph	11	M	daughter	England	U.S. States	Splendid	14 Aug 1829

NAMES OF PASSENGERS	AGE	SEX	OCCUPATIONS	COUNTRY TO WHICH THEY BELONG	COUNTRY THEY INTEND TO INHABIT	SHIPS/DATES OF ARRIVAL	
PARKINS (cont'd)							
Joseph	52	M	Labourer	Great Britain		Moro Castle	6 Jul 1827
Mary	11	F	None	Great Britain		Moro Castle	6 Jul 1827
Mary	42	F	None	Great Britain		Moro Castle	6 Jul 1827
Richard	2	M	daughter	England	U.S. States	Splendid	14 Aug 1829
Robert	4	M	None	Great Britain		Moro Castle	6 Jul 1827
William	21	M	Labourer	Great Britain		Moro Castle	6 Jul 1827
PARKINSON, Ben	28	M	Bead Maker	G.B.	New York	Eliza Grant	29 Aug 1829
Benjamin	28	M	Baker	Great Britain		Eliza Grant	29 Aug 1829
Edward	48	M	Farmer	Ireland	America	Braganza	8 Aug 1825
Geo.	27	M	Sadler	England	England	Gulnard	24 Mar 1825
Henry	22	M	Farmer	Great Britain	United States	Birmingham	15 Jun 1827
James	30	M	Farmer	England	New York	Curler	7 Jul 1827
Jane	20	F	None	England	America	Braganza	8 Aug 1825
John	24	M	Calico Printer	Great Britain	United States	Aurora	5 Sep 1826
John	27	M	Weaver	Great Britain	United States	Birmingham	15 Jun 1827
Mary	40	F	None	England	America	Braganza	8 Aug 1825
Robert	9	M	None	England	America	Braganza	8 Aug 1825
Thomas	12	M	None	England	America	Braganza	8 Aug 1825
Wm.	23	M	Joiner	G. Brittian	U. States	Pacific	19 Oct 1829
PARKISON, Ezith.	6	F	None	England	America	Braganza	8 Aug 1825
PARKMAN, Wm.	20	M	Labourer	Great Brittain	United States	Active	12 Sep 1828
PARKS, —, Miss	38			G.B.	G.B.	Pacific	24 May 1824
Auburn	...	...	...	Switzerland	U. States	Robert Edward	2 Nov 1827
Benjamin	2	M	None	Great Britain		Moro Castle	6 Jul 1827
Daniel	5	M	None	Great Britain		Moro Castle	6 Jul 1827
David	22	M	Farmer	England	New York	Chelsea	16 May 1828
David	49	...	...	Switzerland	U. States	Robert Edward	2 Nov 1827
Edwd.	28	M	Labourer	Ireland	United States	Wilson	6 Jun 1828
Eliza	20	F	Farmer	England	New York	Chelsea	16 May 1828
Elizabeth	17	...	...	Switzerland	U. States	Robert Edward	2 Nov 1827
Hannah	4	F	Farmer	England	New York	Chelsea	16 May 1828
Harriet	...	...	...	Switzerland	U. States	Robert Edward	2 Nov 1827
Harriet	13	...	...	Switzerland	U. States	Robert Edward	2 Nov 1827
Henry	1...	...	...	Switzerland	U. States	Robert Edward	2 Nov 1827
Hester	28	...	...	Switzerland	U. States	Robert Edward	2 Nov 1827
Isaac	6	M	None	Great Britain		Moro Castle	6 Jul 1827
Isaac	31	M	Labourer	Great Britain		Moro Castle	6 Jul 1827
Isabella	32	F	None	Great Britain		Moro Castle	6 Jul 1827
Jas.	...	...	...	Switzerland	U. States	Robert Edward	2 Nov 1827
Jas.	...	...	...	Switzerland	U. States	Robert Edward	2 Nov 1827
Jno.	31	...	...	Switzerland	U. States	Robert Edward	2 Nov 1827
John	13	M	None	England	United States	Bolivar	15 Jun 1826
Jonah	1...	...	...	Switzerland	U. States	Robert Edward	2 Nov 1827
Joseph	1...	...	...	Switzerland	U. States	Robert Edward	2 Nov 1827
Joseph	11	M	None	Great Britain		Moro Castle	6 Jul 1827
Josiah	...	...	...	Switzerland	U. States	Robert Edward	2 Nov 1827
Levi	1	M	Farmer	England	New York	Chelsea	16 May 1828
Levi, and family	26	M	Farmer	England	New York	Chelsea	16 May 1828
Mary	13	F	Spinster	Paisley	U.S. America	Camillus	10 Sep 1821
Mary	25	F	Farmer	England	New York	Chelsea	16 May 1828
Mary	30	F	Spinster	Ireland	United States	Wilson	6 Jun 1828
Philip	1...	...	...	Switzerland	U. States	Robert Edward	2 Nov 1827
Rebecca	48	...	...	Switzerland	U. States	Robert Edward	2 Nov 1827
Ruth	10	...	...	Switzerland	U. States	Robert Edward	2 Nov 1827
Saml.	19	...	...	Switzerland	U. States	Robert Edward	2 Nov 1827
Sarah	9	F	None	Great Britain		Moro Castle	6 Jul 1827
William	1	M	None	Great Britain		Moro Castle	6 Jul 1827
William	6	M	Farmer	England	New York	Chelsea	16 May 1828
PARLANE, Alexr.	40	M	Merchant	Montreal	U. States	New York	15 Nov 1823
PARLANS, Alexander	26	M	Merchant	Scotland	Canada	Nestor	20 Nov 1821
PARLEY, William	38	M	Weaver	G.B.	Connecticut	Eliza Grant	29 Aug 1829
William	38	M	Weaver	Great Britain		Eliza Grant	29 Aug 1829
PARMENTIER, Adele	8	F	child	Netherlands	United States	Montano	31 May 1824
Andrew	43	M	Botaniste	Netherlands	United States	Montano	31 May 1824
Leon	4	M	child	Netherlands	United States	Montano	31 May 1824
Sylvie	30	F	wife	Netherlands	United States	Montano	31 May 1824
PARMIER, Chas.	50	M	Merchant	France	Jacquemel	Stranger	10 Aug 1824
PARMLY, Eleazer	23	M	Artist	United States	United States	Cincinnatus	21 Nov 1821

NAMES OF PASSENGERS	AGE	SEX	OCCUPATIONS	COUNTRY TO WHICH THEY BELONG	COUNTRY THEY INTEND TO INHABIT	SHIPS/DATES OF ARRIVAL	
PARMLY (cont'd)							
George W.	2	...	Child	England	United States	Cincinnatus	21 Nov 1821
J.	21	M	Artist	United States	United States	Cincinnatus	21 Nov 1821
PARMOMTIN, Chs.	21	M	Negotient	France	U. States	Montano	23 Apr 1825
PARMONSTALL, P.	23	M	Merchant	France	U. States	New Packet	5 May 1823
PARNEL, Levy	58	M	Cooper	England	United States	Cambria	3 Jul 1829
PARNELL, Richd.	21	M	Farmer	England	United States	America	25 Dec 1827
Thomas	23	M	Farmer	England	United States	America	25 Dec 1827
PARNETT, Edward	26	M	Merchant	Nassau	Nassau	Leo	31 Jul 1826
PARNIER, Wm.	40	M	Farmer	Great Britain	United States	Asia	14 Jul 1829
PARONETT, Lewis	24	M	Planter	Hayti	Hayti	Reunion	28 Sep 1821
PAROS, Matis	38	M	Mercht.	Spain	Spain	Albany Packet	14 Nov 1826
PAROT, Anne	37	F		France	United States	Montano	5 May 1828
Catherine	4	F		France	United States	Montano	5 May 1828
Frederick	12	M		France	United States	Montano	5 May 1828
George	10	M		France	United States	Montano	5 May 1828
George	36	M		France	United States	Montano	5 May 1828
Louis	1 7/12	M		France	United States	Montano	5 May 1828
Pierre	8	M		France	United States	Montano	5 May 1828
PARQUET, C.	52	M	Merchant	France	France	Reunion	28 Sep 1821
PARR, John	27	M	Farmer	Ireland	America	Superior	12 Jun 1824
Malinda	25	F	None	England	United States	Montgomery	6 Mar 1829
Martha	56	F	None	England	United States	Montgomery	6 Mar 1829
Mary	10	F	Labourer	England	U. States	Comet	23 Aug 1828
P.	25	M	Labourer	Great Britain	U. States America	Ann Maria	29 Nov 1821
Samuel	62	M	Hatter	Great Britain	United States	Roman	10 May 1828
PARRAN, Thomas	25	M	Farmer	Scotland	Gt. Britain	Friends	29 Apr 1822
PARRASENT, Peter L.	46	M	Merchant	U.S.	U.S.	Montano	24 Jun 1823
PARRELL, Eliza	20	F	None	Great Britain	United States	Aspasia	16 Jul 1828
John	26	M	Lamp Maker	Great Britain	United States	Aspasia	16 Jul 1828
PARRILL, Hugh	16	M	Merchant	U. States	U. States	Josephine	30 Aug 1828
PARRIN, Theops.	26	M	Clerical	U. States	U. States	William Tell	3 Dec 1825
PARRITT, Obadiah	24	M	Farmer	Great Britain	United States	Ann Maria	9 Mar 1820
Theodosia	23	F	None	Great Britain	United States	Ann Maria	9 Mar 1820
PARROT, Mary	18		Weaver	Cork	Philadelphia	Schuylkill	22 Aug 1825
Richd.	57		Weaver	Cork	Philadelphia	Schuylkill	22 Aug 1825
Sarah	58			Cork	Philadelphia	Schuylkill	22 Aug 1825
Thomas	19		Weaver	Cork	Philadelphia	Schuylkill	22 Aug 1825
PARROTT, Jas.	25	M		Ireland	United States	Essex	23 May 1828
John	26	M	None	United States	United States	Ann Maria	23 Oct 1820
Peter	23	M	None	United States	United States	Ann Maria	23 Oct 1820
PARRVIS, W.	21	M	Merchant	Port au Prince	United States	Artibonite	9 Sep 1826
PARRY, ...l...	2 1/2	F	None		New York	Governor Clinton	3 Jul 1827
Catharine	22	F	Spinster	Wales		Gomer	22 May 1827
Charlot	33	F	None		New York	Governor Clinton	3 Jul 1827
David	22	M	Farmer	Great Brittan	U.S.	Emulous	29 Jun 1827
Elihu	21	M	Carpenter	England	United States	Warrior	6 Oct 1828
Elizabeth	6	F		Wales	United States	Lord Wellington	14 Nov 1827
Evan	23	M	Farmer	Wales	United States	Orozimbo	11 Aug 1823
George	7/12	M	None		New York	Governor Clinton	3 Jul 1827
George	37	M	Farmer		New York	Governor Clinton	3 Jul 1827
Hugh	25	M				Eliza Grant	6 Oct 1828
James	1	M		Wales	United States	Lord Wellington	14 Nov 1827
Jane	21	F	None	Wales	United States	Orozimbo	11 Aug 1823
Jno.	29	M	Sadler	Germany	Philada.	Mary	1 Nov 1824
John	25	M	Joiner	Ireland	New York	Brighton	24 Aug 1827
John	28	M	Farmer	Wales	United States	Lord Wellington	14 Nov 1827
John	35	M	Ship wright	Ireland	New York	William	26 Apr 1823
John, Jr.	3	M		Wales	United States	Lord Wellington	14 Nov 1827
Laura	15	F	Spinster	Wales		Gomer	22 May 1827
Mayinia	18	F		Wales	United States	Lord Wellington	14 Nov 1827
Una	19	M	Farmer	England	United States	Warrior	6 Oct 1828
William	25	M	Paper Maker	England	U. States	Brighton	14 Apr 1828
PARSARICE, Francisco	24	M	Gentleman	Spain	U. States	Exploit	19 Apr 1828
PARSAT, Maura	40	M	Army	France	France	Columbia	1 Mar 1825

NAMES OF PASSENGERS	AGE	SEX	OCCUPATIONS	COUNTRY TO WHICH THEY BELONG	COUNTRY THEY INTEND TO INHABIT	SHIPS/DATES OF ARRIVAL	
PARSE, Susan	26	F		England	U. States	Diana	27 Aug 1822
PARSENS, Amanda	6	F	None	Cuba	United States	Ariel	30 Jun 1828
James	9	M	None	Cuba	United States	Ariel	30 Jun 1828
Margaret	35	F	None	Cuba	United States	Ariel	30 Jun 1828
Mary	1	F	None	Cuba	United States	Ariel	30 Jun 1828
PARSHALL, James	23	M	Cabinet Maker	U. States	U. States	Othello	11 Jul 1825
PARSIN, Joseph	14	M	Clerk	France	U. States	Annawan	26 Apr 1824
PARSON,							
J. Rieplipp	74 5/12	F	Farmer	Switzerland	U. States	France	26 Jun 1828
S. G.	36	M	Merchant	U. States	U. States	Silvia	10 Sep 1827
PARSONS, —, Mr.	17	M	Clerk	Great Brittain	Great Brittain	Acasta	13 Feb 1822
A.	7	M	None	St. Croix	U. States	Martha	13 Jul 1826
C., Miss	13	F	None	St. Croix	U. States	Martha	13 Jul 1826
Catharinna		F	Chiefly farmers		United States	Factor	8 Jul 1829
E., Miss	32	F	Merchant	U. States	U. States	Mattewan	20 Oct 1827
E. H.	24	M	Gentleman	U. States	U. States	New York	22 Jul 1824
Edward	19	M	Merchant	G. Britian	United States	Diamond	12 Mar 1824
Elizabeth, Mrs.	...	F				Rufus King	27 Jun 1821
Fredk.	11	M	None	St. Croix	U. States	Martha	13 Jul 1826
Henry	57	M	Ship Master	U. States	U. States	Sultana	6 Nov 1828
Hy.	9	M	None	St. Croix	U. States	Martha	13 Jul 1826
Isaac	23	M	Farmer	Great Britain	America	Remittance	24 Aug 1825
J. C., Revd.	29	M	Clergyman	U. States	U. States	Rufus King	27 Jun 1821
Jaspher	4	M	None	St. Croix	U. States	Martha	13 Jul 1826
L., Miss	8	F	None	St. Croix	U. States	Martha	13 Jul 1826
Lucia, Miss	1 2/12	F	None	St. Croix	U. States	Martha	13 Jul 1826
M., Mrs.	38	F	None	St. Croix	U. States	Martha	13 Jul 1826
Matilda		F	Chiefly farmers		United States	Factor	8 Jul 1829
Michael A.	26	M	Mariner	United States	United States	Orient	17 Feb 1829
Sherlock	31	M	Mariner	St. John, N.B.	St. John, N.B.	St. Michael	28 Feb 1826
Thomas	28	M		Ireland	New York	Cincinnatus	5 Dec 1825
William	22	M	Farmer	England	United States	Young Phoenix	26 Jul 1824
Wm.		M	Chiefly farmers		United States	Factor	8 Jul 1829
Wm.	32	M	Carpenter	United States	United States	Augusta	27 Aug 1829
PARSTON, Edward	4	M		Ireland	U. States	Eliza Grant	29 Aug 1829
George	15	M		Ireland	U. States	Eliza Grant	29 Aug 1829
Hannah	1	F	None	England	U. States	Franklin	7 Jul 1828
Hannah	21	F		Ireland	U. States	Eliza Grant	29 Aug 1829
John	19	M		Ireland	U. States	Eliza Grant	29 Aug 1829
Joseph	13	M		Ireland	U. States	Eliza Grant	29 Aug 1829
Maria	9	F		Ireland	U. States	Eliza Grant	29 Aug 1829
Mary	22	F	None	England	U. States	Franklin	7 Jul 1828
Mary	41	F		Ireland	U. States	Eliza Grant	29 Aug 1829
Sarah	17	F		Ireland	U. States	Eliza Grant	29 Aug 1829
Thomas	11	M		Ireland	U. States	Eliza Grant	29 Aug 1829
PARTAGE,							
Saml. Steward	24	M	Merch.	England	England	William Thompson	18 Jan 1825
PARTELOPE, William	34	M	Shoemaker	England	United States	Delta	24 Oct 1829
PARTER, Henry	22	M		England	America	Ann	3 Jul 1820
PARTIANO, Thos.	40	M	...	England	Canada	William Thompson	10 May 1825
PARTIES, John	45	M	Servant	Antigua	U. States	South Carolina	2 Aug 1822
PARTIMER, C.	5	F	Farmer	Switzerland	U. States	Alfred	8 Jul 1828
J.	30	F	Farmer	Switzerland	U. States	Alfred	8 Jul 1828
PARTLOW, Mathew	20	M	Blockmaker	Ireland	United States	Ann Maria	2 Nov 1827
Wm.	40	M	Mariner	U. States	U. States	Genl. Victoria	7 Apr 1828
PARTNELLO, G., Don	36	M	Gentleman	Curaca	Curacoa	Douglass	27 Apr 1824
PARTNER, John	32	M	Gentleman	America	America	La Grange	7 Aug 1828
PARTON, J.	40	M	Merchant	Cuba	U.S.	Richmond Packet	3 Aug 1829
T.	26	M	Merchant	Havan	U. States	Greek	3 Mar 1825
PARTOR, J.	28	M	Mercht.	Spain	Spain	Richmond Packet	10 Dec 1828
PARTRICK, Rosa	27	F	...	...	...	Dawn	19 Aug 1825
PARTRIDGE, Alfred	8	M		England	United States	William Howland	5 Jul 1821
David	36	M	Blacksmith	England	America	John Adams	2 Aug 1827
Diana	32	F	None	England	United States	Euphrates	12 May 1823

NAMES OF PASSENGERS	A G E	S E X	OCCUPATIONS	COUNTRY TO WHICH THEY BELONG	COUNTRY THEY INTEND TO INHABIT	SHIPS/DATES OF ARRIVAL	
PARTRIDGE (cont'd)							
Henry	20	M	Gardener	Great Britain	United States	Meteor	17 Jan 1825
Jabez	15	M		England	America	John Adams	2 Aug 1827
James	13	M		England	America	John Adams	2 Aug 1827
James	21	M	Labourer	England and Ireland	United States	Jubilee	12 May 1828
John	10	M		England	America	John Adams	2 Aug 1827
John	21	M	Farmer	England	Upper Canada	Comet	6 Mar 1823
John	40	M		England	America	John Adams	2 Aug 1827
Joseph	12	M		England	United States	William Howland	5 Jul 1821
Margery	21	F	None	Ireland		Marchioness	13 May 1828
Mary	23	F		England	United States	William Howland	5 Jul 1821
Mary	40	F		England	America	John Adams	2 Aug 1827
Mary Ann	7	F		England	America	John Adams	2 Aug 1827
Sarah	10	F	None	England	United States	Euphrates	12 May 1823
Sarah	18	F		England	United States	William Howland	5 Jul 1821
William	23	M	Farmer	England	United States	William & Henry	19 Jul 1822
William	24	M	Labourer	Ireland		Marchioness	13 May 1828
William	25	M	Merchant	England	United States	William Howland	5 Jul 1821
Wm.	29	M		Great Britain	United States	Active	25 Mar 1828
Wm., Jr.	8	M	None	England	United States	Euphrates	12 May 1823
Wm. T.	52	M	Grocer	England	United States	Euphrates	12 May 1823
PASARA, Domingo	37	M	Merchant	U.S.	America	Wave	15 Aug 1821
PASAVILLOSO, Pdr.	28	M	Merchant	S. America	U. States	Milo	20 Feb 1826
PASCALL, Chas. E.	26	M	Confectioner	Matanzas	U. States	Mary & Emily	23 Mar 1825
PASCHAL, Benjm.	63	M	Farmer	U. States	U. States	Robt. Reade	12 Apr 1825
Betty	54	F	Farmer	U. States	U. States	Robt. Reade	12 Apr 1825
PASCOW, R.	28	M	Mechanic	G. Britain	U. States	Mary Howland	22 Sep 1828
PASGINE, James	35	M				Hudson	23 Jul 1828
Monah	35	M				Hudson	23 Jul 1828
PASIMON, Mary	18	F		England	United States	Richmond	4 Aug 1826
PASLER, Catharine	5	F	Farmer	Switzerland		Charlemagne	20 Aug 1829
Fredr.	2	F	Farmer	Switzerland		Charlemagne	20 Aug 1829
Fredr.	45	M	Farmer	Switzerland		Charlemagne	20 Aug 1829
Jacob	8	M	Farmer	Switzerland		Charlemagne	20 Aug 1829
John	10	M	Farmer	Switzerland		Charlemagne	20 Aug 1829
Mary	40	F	Farmer	Switzerland		Charlemagne	20 Aug 1829
PASQUAL, Jon A.	25	M	Merchant	Spain	America	Port Captain	6 Dec 1825
Juan	22		Servant	Manilla	U. States	Cadet	11 Jan 1826
N.	25	M	Merchant	Spain	U. States	Mary Jane	29 Mar 1828
PASQUEL, L.	19	M	Merchant	France	United States	Elizabeth	22 May 1822
PASQUIL, Jose Anto.	24	M	Merchant	Spain	Spain	Hope	29 Dec 1821
PASSAGE, —, Mrs.	26	F		U. States	U. States	Charles Hays	28 Mar 1825
A.	42	M	Fencing Master	U. States	U. States	Charles Hays	28 Mar 1825
John	2	M		U. States	U. States	Charles Hays	28 Mar 1825
PASSERDU, —, Madam	45	F		St. Domingo, Hayti	Hayti	Illinois	18 Jun 1821
PASSEVAN, John	32	M	Merchant	France	America	Liverpool Packet	23 Mar 1822
PASSEVENCE, A. F.	59	F		France	U. States	Six Brothers	21 Nov 1822
PASTOR, James	25	M	Merchant	Spain	Spain	Richmond Packet	30 Oct 1827
James	26	M	Mercht.	Spain	Spain	Richmond Packet	13 Jun 1825
James	26	M	Mercht.	Spain	Spain	Richmond Packet	28 Oct 1825
James	28	M	Merchant	Spain	U. States	Richmond Packet	15 Jun 1826
James	36	M	Merchant	Catatona	Matanzes	Richmond Packet	27 Nov 1826
Jas.	30	M	Mercht.	Spain	Spain	Richmond Packet	11 Jul 1827
Jas.	30	M	Mercht.	Spain	Spain	Richmond Packet	29 Mar 1828

NAMES OF PASSENGERS	AGE	SEX	OCCUPATIONS	COUNTRY TO WHICH THEY BELONG	COUNTRY THEY INTEND TO INHABIT	SHIPS/DATES OF ARRIVAL	
PASTOR (cont'd)							
Jayme	27	M	Merchant	Cuba	Cuba	Richmond Packet	25 Feb 1826
Jayme	28	M	Merchant	Catalonia	Cuba	Richmond Packet	23 Feb 1827
Loranzo	35	M	Mariner	Spain	Teneriffe	Hannah	16 Nov 1822
PATALUGU, A.	30	M	Merchant	Gibralter	U. States	Mary Jane	8 Dec 1826
PATCHELL, Eliza	20	F	Seamstress	Great Britain	United States	Grecian	24 Sep 1828
PATE, Henry	23	M	Merchant	England	Baltimore	Corinthian	5 May 1827
PATELIN, George	40	M	Merchant	St. John	St. John	Nancy	16 Aug 1822
PATEN, Thomas	20		Merchant	Great Britain	United States	Camillus	12 Sep 1827
Thos.	27	M	Artist	G. Britain	New York	Radius	7 Jul 1821
PATENGUELA, Ramon	12	M	Merchant	St. Domingo	New York	Curlew	1 Mar 1824
PATENT, Petrie	30	F	Spinster	Swtserland	America	Saluda	18 Jun 1825
PATEOR, F.	25	M	Merchant	Spain	U. States	Independence	2 Sep 1824
PATER, Theophlus	40	M	Farmer	Scotland	United States	Commerce	17 Jul 1823
PATERSON, —, Mrs.	40	F			U. States	Greyhound	19 Aug 1820
Ann	18	F	None			Trent	1 Oct 1823
Ballidge	30	F		Great B.	U. States	William Neilson	26 Jul 1828
David	25	M	Gentleman	England	United States	Cortex	4 Dec 1824
David	27	M	Labourer	Ireland	United States	Fabius	31 Jul 1829
Delph	50	M		Great B.	U. States	William Neilson	26 Jul 1828
George	21	M	Merchant	Denmark	United States	India	8 Oct 1823
Isaac	25	M	Farmer	Gt. Brittain	United States	Trent	1 Oct 1823
James	17	M	Weaver	Argyle (Tedland) Scotland	United States	Jean Hastie	27 Jul 1829
Jane	6	F		Ireland	U. States	Nancy	1 Sep 1823
John	5	M		Great B.	U. States	William Neilson	26 Jul 1828
John	17	M	Labourer	Kincardine, Tillalair [Parish]	New York	Hero	19 May 1828
*to follow occupation							
John	27	M	Baker	England	U. States	Franklin	7 Jul 1828
Margaret	29	F		Ireland	U. States	Nancy	1 Sep 1823
Mary	10/12	F	None	Ireland	America, New York	Washington	3 Mar 1828
Mary	14	F			U. States	Greyhound	19 Aug 1820
Mary	29		Child			Rufus King	7 Aug 1820
Mathew	34	M	Merchant	Dominica	Dominica	Adno	7 Apr 1823
R. H. L.	22	M	Mariner	New York	U. States	Dromo	24 Sep 1827
Robert	10	M	Child	Scotland	America	Concord	4 Jun 1821
Sam	...	...	...	Ireland	United States	General Putnam	20 Jun 1825
Thomas	4	M		Ireland	U. States	Nancy	1 Sep 1823
William	1	M		Ireland	U. States	Nancy	1 Sep 1823
William	32	M	Labourer	Ireland	U. States	Nancy	1 Sep 1823
PATISON, Mary Ann	19	F	Servant	Ireland	United States	Carolina Ann	11 Dec 1826
PATIT, Henry D.	27	M	Merchant	France	U. States	Lewis	10 Sep 1823
PATON, John	25	M		Scotland	United States	Camillus	9 May 1827
Marion	26	F		Scotland	United States	Camillus	9 May 1827
Mathew	24	M	Weaver	Ireland	U. States	Ann Maria	6 Jul 1824
PATOZ, George	24	M	Merchant	Great Britain	United States	Orozimbo	5 Mar 1827
PATREILLO, Gerard	54	M	Merchant	United States	United States	Montano	5 May 1828
PATRICK (see Ptrick)							
Alexr.	28	M	Weaver	Scotland	U. States	Josephine	27 Jul 1825
Alexr.	30	M	Weaver	Great Britain	U. States	Hamilton	28 Apr 1828
Alexr., Jr.	11	M		Great Britain	U. States	Hamilton	28 Apr 1828
Ann	26	F		Great Britain	U. States	Hamilton	28 Apr 1828
Daniel T.	22	M	Laborer	Ireland	United States	Sarah G	19 Jun 1827
Geo.	27	M	Optician	England	Gt. Britain	Electra	4 Sep 1827
J.	31	M	Merchant	U. States	U. States	Tobasco	17 Aug 1825
Louisa	28	F	None	Gt. Britain	U. States	Panthia	13 Nov 1824
Mary	33	F	Lady	England	United States	Cambria	8 Oct 1828
Mary Anne	1 6/12	F	Girl	England	United States	Cambria	8 Oct 1828
Patrick	4			Great Britain	U. States	Hamilton	28 Apr 1828
Peter	21	M	Merchant	Italy	U. States	Charles	21 Jul 1825
Thos.	6	M	None	Gt. Britain	U. States	Panthia	13 Nov 1824
Walter	8			Great Britain	U. States	Hamilton	28 Apr 1828
PATRIDGE, Ann	33	F		England	U.S. America	Cortes	19 May 1826
Ann M.	12	F		England	U.S. America	Cortes	19 May 1826
B.	18	M		Ireland	United States	William Byrnes	6 Apr 1826

NAMES OF PASSENGERS	AGE	SEX	OCCUPATIONS	COUNTRY TO WHICH THEY BELONG	COUNTRY THEY INTEND TO INHABIT	SHIPS/DATES OF ARRIVAL	
PATRIDGE (cont'd)							
Charlotte	3	F		England	U.S. America	Cortes	19 May 1826
Chas.	23	M	Tailor	Switzerland	U. States	Robert Edward	2 Nov 1827
Eliza	19	F		Switzerland	U. States	Robert Edward	2 Nov 1827
Jno.	31	M	Farmer	England	U.S. America	Cortes	19 May 1826
May	2	F		England	U.S. America	Cortes	19 May 1826
R.	17	M		Ireland	United States	William Byrnes	6 Apr 1826
Ruth	1	F		England	U.S. America	Cortes	19 May 1826
Saml.	34	M	Cutler	Gt. Britain	U. States	Isaac Hicks	18 Apr 1825
PATS, Frans, haar Kinder							
[her child, Marger]	22	M		Lauderbach	United States	Juffraw Johanna	16 Oct 1821
Johannis, haar Kinder							
[her child, Marger]	2	M		Lauderbach	United States	Juffraw Johanna	16 Oct 1821
Ludovich, haar Kinder							
[her child, Marger]	29	M		Lauderbach	United States	Juffraw Johanna	16 Oct 1821
Margaretta, haar Kinder							
[her child, Marger]	16	F		Lauderbach	United States	Juffraw Johanna	16 Oct 1821
Marger, de weduwe							
[the widow]	48	F	Boerim	Lauderbach	United States	Juffraw Johanna	16 Oct 1821
Maria, haar Kinder							
[her child, Marger]	26	F		Lauderbach	United States	Juffraw Johanna	16 Oct 1821
PATTEN, Andw.	19	M	Mechanic	Scotland	U. States	Herald	21 May 1824
G.	29	M	Merchant	U. States	U. States	Elias Burger	30 Nov 1822
Geo.	18	M	Clerk	Ireland	U. States	Hibernia	29 Nov 1821
George	25	M	Gentleman	Ireland	U. States	Howard	25 Jul 1823
Jas.	18			Ireland	United States	John Dickinson	28 Jun 1822
John	22	M	Joiner	England	United States	Paul Jones	14 Oct 1829
Margaret	25	F	Farmer	Ireland	America	Superior	12 Jun 1824
Robert	27	M	Joiner	England	United States	Paul Jones	14 Oct 1829
Robt. B.	27	M	Prof. Langes.	United States	New York	Radius	7 Jul 1821
Sally	30	F	Joiner	England	United States	Paul Jones	14 Oct 1829
Theophilus	27	M	Farmer			Frances	17 Aug 1820
Thomas	4	M	Joiner	England	United States	Paul Jones	14 Oct 1829
William	19 6/12	M	Merchant	U. States	U.S.	Adrianna	8 Aug 1822
Wm. D.	20	M	Merchant	America	America	Live Oak	16 Oct 1823
PATTER, Henry	40	M	Carpenter	Swtserland	America	Saluda	18 Jun 1825
PATTERSON, —, Miss	18	F		United States	United States	William	11 Dec 1820
—, Mr.	6	M		Scotland	U.S.	Curler	19 Jul 1828
—, Mr.	40	M	Merchant	United States	U. States	Manchester Packet	9 Mar 1826
—, Professor	33	M	...icar	G. Bt.	U. States	Canada	13 Oct 1825
Agnes	1	F	Farmer	Scotland	United States	Minerva	29 Oct 1822
Andrew	25	M	Weaver	Ireland	United States	Borneo	28 Aug 1828
Ann	5			Ireland	United States	John Dickinson	28 Jun 1822
Ann	15	F		England	U. States	Edward Bonaffe	11 Dec 1827
Ann	20	F		Germany	U. States	Edward Bonaffe	11 Dec 1827
Ann	24			Ireland	United States	John Dickinson	28 Jun 1822
Christian	23	F	Spinster	Ireland	United States	Trident	16 May 1826
David	18	M	Spinner	Scotland	U. States	Brilliant	19 Mar 1828
Duncan D.	41	M	Merchant	Jamaica	England	Albert	19 Apr 1823
E.	28	M	Merchant	United States		William Byrnes	6 Apr 1826
Edward	36	M	Merchant	United States	United States	Cortes	7 Dec 1825
Eliza	3			Ireland	United States	John Dickinson	28 Jun 1822
Elizabeth	20	F	Spinner	Ireland	America	Hesperus	7 Jul 1820
Elizabeth	36	F		United States	United States	Don Quixote	18 Aug 1824
Elizabeth	56			Ireland	United States	John Dickinson	28 Jun 1822
Fanny	29	F		Ireland	United States	Mary	1 Jul 1829
George	2 6/12	M				Hector	17 Aug 1825
Grace	17	F	None	Great Britain	Canada	James Monroe	25 Apr 1822
H.	25 6/12	M	Merchant	U. States	U. States	Circassian	26 Jun 1823
Henry	23	M	Merchant	United States	United States	Don Quixote	18 Aug 1824
Isaac	20	M	Weaver	Ireland	United States	Commerce	13 Jun 1828
Isibella	11	F	None		United States	Mount Vernon	29 Aug 1828
J. F.	23	M	Merchant	Dresden, Maine	U. States	Eastern Star	7 May 1824
James	1			Ireland	United States	John Dickinson	28 Jun 1822
James	16	M	None	Ireland	United States	Lord Wellington	28 May 1827
James	20	M	Clerk	Ireland	United States	Josephine	30 Apr 1828
James	23 3/12	M	Farmer	G. Britain	United States	Louisa	14 Jun 1825
James	24	M	Farmer	Ireland	America, New York	Washington	3 Mar 1828

NAMES OF PASSENGERS	AGE	SEX	OCCUPATIONS	COUNTRY TO WHICH THEY BELONG	COUNTRY THEY INTEND TO INHABIT	SHIPS/DATES OF ARRIVAL	
PATTERSON (cont'd)							
James	25		Labourer	England	United States	Hudson	5 Apr 1826
James	28	M	Blacksmith	Scotland	United States	Mary & Susan	5 Aug 1828
James	30	M	Farmer	U. States	U. States	Corinthian	4 Jan 1825
James	30	M	Weaver	Ireland	United States	Catharine	22 Jul 1825
James	31	M	Labourer	United States	U. States	Great Britain	18 Mar 1828
James	32	M	Farmer	Scotland	America	Minerva	15 Nov 1823
Jane	8	F	Girl	Ireland	United States	Trident	17 May 1825
Jane	22		Housewife			Rufus King	7 Aug 1820
Jane	25	F		Great Britian	U. States	Hector	17 Aug 1825
Jane	28	F	None	Scotland	United States	Mary & Susan	5 Aug 1828
Jane	30	F	Spinster	Ireland	U. States	Josephine	30 Aug 1828
Jane	35	F	Lady	St. John, N.B.	St. John, N.B.	Nancy	2 May 1823
Jannet	25	F		Great Britain	United States	Ann	22 Dec 1821
Jannt	20	F		Scotland	U.S.	Curler	19 Jul 1828
Jas.	22	M	Merchant	U. States	U. States	Leader	17 Sep 1821
Jas.	30		Farmer	Ireland		Westmoreland	1 Aug 1826
Jno.	20	M	Teacher	Scotland	U. States	Domestic	31 Aug 1820
Jno.	23	M	Labourer	Ireland	U. States	Atlantic	19 Aug 1825
John	10	M			U. States	Greyhound	19 Aug 1820
John	17	M	Labourer	Ireland	U. States	Josephine	30 Aug 1828
John	18		Farmer	Ireland	U. States	Xenophon	28 May 1822
John	20	M	Chandler	Great Britain	United States	Washington	3 Sep 1827
John	21	M	Clerk	Ireland	United States	Josephine	30 Apr 1828
John	21	M	Traveler	Great Britain	United States	Thomas Dickason	31 Jul 1829
John	22	M	Labourer	Ireland	United States	Sylvester Healy	17 Oct 1825
John	22	M		Scotland	New York	Joseph Hume	26 Oct 1829
John	23	M	Soap Boiler	Ireland	Pittsburgh	Indian Chief	19 Jun 1823
John	23	M	Mercht.	England	England	Pacific	24 Oct 1828
John	26	M	Farmer	Ireland	U. States	William & John	10 Jul 1824
John	27	M	Stone Cutter	Scotland	Scotland	Sarah G.	28 Nov 1827
John	30	M	Weaver	Ireland	United States	Trident	17 May 1825
John	30	M	Laborer	Ireland	United States	Mary	1 Jul 1829
John	49	M	Labourer	Ireland	United States	Lord Wellington	28 May 1827
Letitia	15	F	Milliner	Ireland	Und. Stts of Amer	Alexander Mansfield	18 Aug 1826
Margaret	28	F		Sligo	Kentucky	Susquehana	27 Jun 1823
Margeret	6	F	Child	Ireland	U. States	Josephine	30 Aug 1828
Margt.	10/12	F	Child [of Samuel]	G. Britain	United States	Louisa	14 Jun 1825
Margt.	45	F	Spinster	Ireland	United States	Trident	17 May 1825
Martha	3	F		Scotland	U.S.	Curler	19 Jul 1828
Mary	23	F	None	Ireland	America, New York	Washington	3 Mar 1828
Mary	26	F	Spinster	Ireland	United States	Ann Maria	8 Jun 1824
Mary	27	F	None	Scotland	United States	John Dickinson	12 Aug 1824
Mary	50	F	None	Ireland	United States	Lord Wellington	28 May 1827
Mary Ann, Mrs.	30	F	None	United States	United States	Nestor	3 Nov 1820
Mary Jane	10	F	Child	Ireland	U. States	Josephine	30 Aug 1828
Mathew	4	M	None	Scotland	United States	John Dickinson	12 Aug 1824
Matthew	22	M	Labourer	Ireland	United States	Ann Maria	8 Jun 1824
May	19	F	Labourer	Ireland	U. States	Atlantic	19 Aug 1825
Ohne	50	M		Scotland	U.S.	Curler	19 Jul 1828
Patrick	30	M	Labourer			Superb	18 Jul 1820
Peggy	19	F	Wife [of Samuel]	G. Britain	United States	Louisa	14 Jun 1825
Peter	30	M	Weaver	England	United States	Peru	23 May 1827
Peter	52	M	Merchant	Canada	Canada	James Monroe	18 Apr 1821
Peter	52		Merchant	England	N. America	Hudson	4 Sep 1823
R.	35		Farmer	Ireland	United States	Courier	16 May 1825
Rebecca	17	F	Spinster	Ireland	U. States	William & John	10 Jul 1824
Rob.	23	M	Mercht.	U. States	U. States	Olive Branch	12 Aug 1822
Robert	6	M		Great Britain	United States	Ann	22 Dec 1821
Robert	8	M	Child	Ireland	U. States	Josephine	30 Aug 1828
Robert	12	M			U. States	Greyhound	19 Aug 1820
Robert	28	M	Merchant	Sligo	Kentucky	Susquehana	27 Jun 1823
Robert	30	M	Merchant	Scotland	Great Brittan	Amity	11 May 1821
Robert	31	M		Great Britain	Canada	James Monroe	25 Apr 1822
Robert	35	M	None	United States	United States	Nestor	3 Nov 1820
Robt.	25	M	...	...	U.N. States	William Byrnes	23 Jul 1824
Robt.	28		Farmer	Ireland	United States	John Dickinson	28 Jun 1822

NAMES OF PASSENGERS	AGE	SEX	OCCUPATIONS	COUNTRY TO WHICH THEY BELONG	COUNTRY THEY INTEND TO INHABIT	SHIPS/DATES OF ARRIVAL	
PATTERSON (cont'd)							
Samuel	24 5/12	M	Farmer	G. Britain	United States	Louisa	14 Jun 1825
Samuel	28	M	Labourer	Ireland	United States	Meteor	26 Jun 1827
Stephen	11	M	Farmer	Ireland	United States	Trident	17 May 1825
Stewart	20	M	Merchant	Ireland	United States	Catharine	22 Jul 1825
Susannah	28	F	Lady	Scotland	New York	Eunice	13 Dec 1827
T.	39	M	Soldier	Kentucky	U. States	Greek	3 Mar 1825
Thomas	4	M				Hector	17 Aug 1825
Thomas	11	M		Sligo	Kentucky	Susquehana	27 Jun 1823
Thomas	14	M	None	Ireland	United States	Lord Wellington	28 May 1827
Thomas	26	M	Farmer	England	United States	London	21 May 1828
Thomas	28	M	Surgeon	Scotland	United States	Camillus	9 May 1827
Thos.	1 3/12	M	Child	Ireland	United States	Ann Maria	8 Jun 1824
Thos.	19	M	Labourer	Ireland	U. States	William & John	10 Jul 1824
Thos.	23	M	Farmer	Ireland	United States	Washington	2 Oct 1828
Thos.	29		Merchant	Surrey	England	Great Britain	7 May 1827
Ths.	28	M	Mercht.	Ireland	United States	St. John	5 Oct 1829
W. D.	50	M	Merchant	Pennsylvania	New York	Alto	8 Jun 1827
William	4	M	Child	Ireland	U. States	Josephine	30 Aug 1828
William	8	M			U. States	Greyhound	19 Aug 1820
William	18	M	Farmer	Scotland	United States	Commerce	17 Jul 1823
William	19	M	Shoomaker	Ireland	U. States	Josephine	30 Aug 1828
Wm.	6	M	Boy	Ireland	United States	Trident	17 May 1825
Wm.	24	M	Farmer	Ireland	U. States	Hibernia	29 Nov 1821
Wm.	24	M	Paper Maker	Scotland	U. States	Superior	25 Sep 1828
Wm.	27	M	Manufacturer	Great Britain	United States	Ann	22 Dec 1821
Wm.	32		Seaman	Boston		Hudson	18 Jun 1825

*Officers, Seamen and Passengers belonging to the Ship Jane of Boston and taken from on board the Schooner Olive of St. Johns , N.B. on the 4th June 1825, Lat. 41.30, Long 53.19, which ship foundered on the 31st ultimo in Lat. 41.44 Long 52.

NAMES OF PASSENGERS	AGE	SEX	OCCUPATIONS	COUNTRY TO WHICH THEY BELONG	COUNTRY THEY INTEND TO INHABIT	SHIPS/DATES OF ARRIVAL	
Wm., Jr.	21	M	Merchant	Havana	U. States	Hesper	28 Dec 1825
Wm. G.	18		Merchant	Ireland	United States	John Dickinson	28 Jun 1822
PATTESON, Godfrey	21	M	Merchant	Gt. Britain		Dalhouse Castle	13 May 1828
Jno.	30	M	Weaver	Gt. Britain		Dalhouse Castle	13 May 1828
R. T.	18	M	Merchant	Great Britain	America	Samuel Robertson	26 Nov 1825
PATTET, —, Mrs.	24	F		France	U. States	Lewis	10 Sep 1823
PATTISON, F. H.		M		Scotland	U.S.	Curler	19 Jul 1828
J.	25	M		Great Brittain	United States	Active	12 Sep 1828
Patt	23	M	Farmer	Great Brittain	United States	Active	12 Sep 1828
Wm.	26	M	Labourer	Great Britain	United States	Washington	3 Sep 1827
PATTON, —, Mr.	35	M	Carpenter	Scotland	Spain	Hind	11 Jun 1820
Andrew	37	M	Farmer	England	United States	Acosta	28 Jul 1823
Ann	11	F	None	Great Britain	United States	Florida	10 Dec 1823
E., Servant	27	F	Servant	England	U.S. America	Leeds	6 Jun 1826
Henry	9	M	None	Great Britain	United States	Florida	10 Dec 1823
Isaac	25		Merchant	...	...	James Cropper	28 Jun 1824
Jane	16	F	None	Great Britain	United States	Florida	10 Dec 1823
John	21	M	Farmer	Ireland	United States	Asia	29 Jul 1829
John	32	M	Clerk	Britain	America	Camillus	9 Oct 1820
Mary	7	F	None	Great Britain	United States	Florida	10 Dec 1823
Nancy	37	F	None	Great Britain	United States	Florida	10 Dec 1823
Pat.	3...	M	Labourer	Ireland	United States	General Putnam	20 Jun 1825
W.	22	M	Mason	Scotland	U. States	Superior	25 Sep 1828
William	25		Merchant	United States	United States	Carolina Ann	12 Sep 1823
William	30	M	Clergyman	United States	New York, U.S.	Florida	2 Oct 1828
William	42	M	Farmer	Great Britain	United States	Florida	10 Dec 1823
Wm.	13	M	None	Great Britain	United States	Florida	10 Dec 1823
Wm.	26		Clergyman	United States	United States	Hudson	18 Jun 1825
Wm. D.	17	M	Merchant	U. States	U. States	Superb	9 Jul 1821
PATTS, Henry	19	M	Merchant	France	U. States	La Virginie	6 Aug 1828
Thos.	21	M	Farmer	England	America	Ann	11 Apr 1821
PATY, Wm.	32	M	Mariner	Plymouth	Massachusetts	Constitution	9 Dec 1824
PAUGA, Domingo	21	M	Segar Maker	Island of Cuba	United States	Betsey	28 Oct 1825
PAUGH, George	12	M	Labourer	England	U. States	Comet	23 Aug 1828
Maria	10	F	Labourer	England	U. States	Comet	23 Aug 1828
Timothy	48	M	Labourer	England	U. States	Comet	23 Aug 1828
PAUKE, —, Capt.	39	M	Mariner	U. States	U. States	Eagle	17 Jun 1826
PAUL, —, Mrs.	29	F		St. Andrews	U. States	Mary Louisa	6 Mar 1827
Anna Maria	35	F		Germany	America	Falcon	28 Aug 1828

NAMES OF PASSENGERS	AGE	SEX	OCCUPATIONS	COUNTRY TO WHICH THEY BELONG	COUNTRY THEY INTEND TO INHABIT	SHIPS/DATES OF ARRIVAL	
PAUL (cont'd)							
Catherine	12	F		Germany	America	Falcon	28 Aug 1828
Dunbar	36		Merchant	U. States	U. States	Silvanus Jenkins	30 Nov 1827
Geo.	20	M	Mariner	U. States	U. States	Florida	25 Apr 1825
J.	18	M	Servant	St. Domingo	St. Domingo	Genl. Warren	10 Jul 1828
Jacob	4	M	Labourer	Germany	America	Falcon	28 Aug 1828
Jacob	42	M	Farmer	Germany	America	Falcon	28 Aug 1828
Johann George	9	M		Germany	America	Falcon	28 Aug 1828
John	23	M		Gt. Britain	G. Britain	Silvanus Jenkins	24 Jul 1828
Pierre	32	M	Farmer	France	U. States	France	14 Mar 1828
Rosina	10	F		Germany	America	Falcon	28 Aug 1828
Thomas L.	22	M	None	Gr. Britan	United States	Courier	12 Mar 1827
Thos.	37		Brgs Tinker			Hudson	23 Jul 1828
PAULA, —	10/12	M		Spain	Spain	Fabius	3 Jun 1825
—	2	M		Spain	Spain	Fabius	3 Jun 1825
—	3	M		Spain	Spain	Fabius	3 Jun 1825
Francisca	1	M		Spain	Spain	Fabius	3 Jun 1825
PAULENS, Joaquen	45	M	Merchant	Madeira	Madeira	Howard	18 Sep 1828
PAULINO, Joaquim	45	M	Merchant	Portugal	U. States	Howard	11 Apr 1826
PAULIUS, Anthony	9/12	M		France	U. States	Edward Quesnel	4 Aug 1828
Catherine	30	F		France	U. States	Edward Quesnel	4 Aug 1828
Clare	7	F		France	U. States	Edward Quesnel	4 Aug 1828
Martin	3	M		France	U. States	Edward Quesnel	4 Aug 1828
Martin	32	M	Butcher	France	U. States	Edward Quesnel	4 Aug 1828
Nicholas	5	M		France	U. States	Edward Quesnel	4 Aug 1828
PAULS, Paul	30	M	Merchant	Germany	U. States	Six Brothers	21 Nov 1822
PAUPE, Fredrick	30	M	Farmer	France	United States	Montano	5 May 1828
PAUSS, Catherine	5	F	Child	Switzerland	United States	Andes	5 May 1828
John	17	M	Farmer	Switzerland	United States	Andes	5 May 1828
John	32	M	Farmer	Switzerland	United States	Andes	5 May 1828
Margaret	1 6/12	F	Child	Switzerland	United States	Andes	5 May 1828
Margaret	30	F	Spinster	Switzerland	United States	Andes	5 May 1828
Morgan	7	M	Child	Switzerland	United States	Andes	5 May 1828
PAUTET, G.	31	M	Merchant	France	Geneva	Medina	17 Dec 1828
PAVOY, James	31	M		U. States	United States	Exchange	18 Nov 1822
PAWEL, John	42	M	Officer	England	England	Nelson	14 Mar 1823
PAWLER, John	20	M	Labourer	Ireland	U. States	Josephine	30 Aug 1828
PAXTEN, James	30	M	Labourer	England	U. States	Ayrshire	12 May 1828
PAXTON, Hannah, Mrs.	55	F	Lady	Ireland	America	Dublin Packet	9 Oct 1820
Jos. R.	33	M	Merchant	United States	United States	Cortes	10 Apr 1822
PAY, Amanda	4		Girl	America	America	Saluda	18 Jun 1825
Maraet	56	F		France		Pallas	14 Jun 1828
Martha	23	F	Labourer	England	U. States	Comet	23 Aug 1828
Mary L.	5	M	Tanner	France		Pallas	14 Jun 1828
Maryar	26	M	Tanner	France		Pallas	14 Jun 1828
Oscar	6		boy	America	America	Saluda	18 Jun 1825
Rhoda	38	F	Spinster	America	America	Saluda	18 Jun 1825
Thomas	35	M	Labourer	England	U. States	Comet	23 Aug 1828
Treckin	27	M	Tanner	France		Pallas	14 Jun 1828
William	19	M	Labourer	England	U. States	Comet	23 Aug 1828
William	47	M	Merchant	America	America	Saluda	18 Jun 1825
Wm.	5		boy	America	America	Saluda	18 Jun 1825
PAYNE, Ann	1 1/2	F		G. Britain	U. States	St. George	7 Jun 1828
Barnard	28	M	Mariner	U. States	U. States	Rambler	26 Jul 1824
Benjn.	16			England		Anacreon	7 Sep 1827
Charles	6	M	None	England		Manhattan	22 May 1827
Eliza	10			England		Anacreon	7 Sep 1827
Elizabeth	22	F		England	United States	Peru	23 May 1827
Frederick W.	33	M	Merchant	United States	United States	Cincinnatus	21 Nov 1821
Geo.	7	M		G. Britain	U. States	St. George	7 Jun 1828
Hannah	1	F	None	England		Manhattan	22 May 1827
Hannah	29	F	None	England		Manhattan	22 May 1827
Harriet	22			England		Anacreon	7 Sep 1827
Harriet	36	F		G. Britain	U. States	St. George	7 Jun 1828
James	6	M		G. Britain	U. States	St. George	7 Jun 1828
John	3	M	None	England		Manhattan	22 May 1827
John	31	M	Farmer	England	United States	Peru	23 May 1827
Joseph	4	M		G. Britain	U. States	St. George	7 Jun 1828
Mary	23			England		Anacreon	7 Sep 1827

NAMES OF PASSENGERS	AGE	SEX	OCCUPATIONS	COUNTRY TO WHICH THEY BELONG	COUNTRY THEY INTEND TO INHABIT	SHIPS/DATES OF ARRIVAL	
PAYNE (cont'd)							
Mary	54			England		Anacreon	7 Sep 1827
Mary Ann	1			England		Anacreon	7 Sep 1827
T. W., Mr.	38	M	Merchant	America	America	Birmingham	16 Oct 1826
Thos.	24			England		Anacreon	7 Sep 1827
W., Mrs.	30	F	None	Canada	U. States	Bayard	9 Jul 1824
William	30	M	Weaver	England		Manhattan	22 May 1827
Wm.	12	M		G. Britain	U. States	St. George	7 Jun 1828
Wm.	35	M	Mariner	United States	United States	Edward	21 Apr 1821
Wm.	40	M	Labourer	G. Britain	U. States	St. George	7 Jun 1828
Wm.	61			England		Anacreon	7 Sep 1827
PAYNER, Charles	4	M	None	Great Britain	United States	Cambria	26 Dec 1827
Henery	7	M	None	Great Britain	United States	Cambria	26 Dec 1827
James	3	M	None	Great Britain	United States	Cambria	26 Dec 1827
John	16	M	Carpenter	Great Britain	United States	Cambria	26 Dec 1827
Nancy	34	F	None	Great Britain	United States	Cambria	26 Dec 1827
William	13	M	None	Great Britain	United States	Cambria	26 Dec 1827
PAYS, Eliza	6	F	None	France	America, U.N.S.	Great Britain	3 Aug 1829
Theybout	27	M	None	France	America, U.N.S.	Great Britain	3 Aug 1829
PAYSON, Jane	32	F		Great Britain	United States	Margaret Ann	3 Apr 1822
John	31	M	Cordwainer	Great Britain	United States	Margaret Ann	3 Apr 1822
PAYTON, Craven	15 7/12	M	Student	U.N. States	U.N. States	Ariel	9 Mar 1829
Robert	38	M	Merchant	U. States	United States	New York	12 Nov 1822
PAZE, Charles	27	M	Merchant	France	travelling	Desdemona	12 Jun 1826
PE..., George	24 10/12	M	Merchant	U.S.A.	U. States	Silas Richards	27 Oct 1826
PE...H...FERMOY, Matilda	3	F		Gaudaloupe	Morristown, N.J.	Horace	31 May 1822
PE...S, John	20	M	Gentleman	Great Britain	United States	Isaac Hicks	6 Dec 1827
PEABODY, Geo.	32	M	Merchant	U. States	U. States	Geo. Canning	2 Sep 1828
P.	30	M	Merchant	U. States	U. States	Ann Maria	5 Feb 1822
PEACH, Richard, Mr.	50	M	Jewler	State of New Jersy	Lizahott town New Jersy	Mary	28 Sep 1822
Sally, Mrs.	45	F		State of New Jersy	Lizahott town New Jersy	Mary	28 Sep 1822
PEACHY, William	20		Shepherd	England	England	London	16 Aug 1824
PEACOCK, Agnes	3...	F	...	Scotland	America	Nimrod	9 Jul 1827
Ann	1	F	None	England	Albany	Indian Chief	19 Jun 1823
Ann	30	F	None	England	United States	Trident	18 Jul 1827
Ann	36	F	None	England	Albany	Indian Chief	19 Jun 1823
Elisa	4	F		England	U. States	Manhattan	12 Jun 1824
Eliza	9	F	None	England	United States	Trident	18 Jul 1827
Elizibeth	30	F	None	England	Albany	Indian Chief	19 Jun 1823
George	10	M	None	England	United States	Trident	18 Jul 1827
George	32	M	Planter	England	United States	Nimrod	30 Aug 1824
George	35	M	M...	Great Britian	United States	Diamond	8 Nov 1824
James	32		Laborer	Ireland	New York	Lady Hunter	19 Oct 1826
Jane	7	F	None	England	Albany	Indian Chief	19 Jun 1823
John	22	M	Clerk	England	United States	Cosmo	26 Aug 1829
John	32	M	Taylor	England	Albany	Indian Chief	19 Jun 1823
John	43	M	Mariner	England	Unknown	Vulcan	22 Nov 1824
Martha	...	F	...	Scotland	America	Nimrod	9 Jul 1827
Mary	16	F	...	Scotland	America	Nimrod	9 Jul 1827
Mary	18	F	Tailor	G. Britain	U. States	Perseverance	9 Jun 1827
Mary	22	F	None	Cob Kirby, Yorshire		Hannibal	28 Jul 1823
Mary	30	F	None	Great Britian	United States	Diamond	8 Nov 1824
Mathew	5	M	None	England	Albany	Indian Chief	19 Jun 1823
R. W.	22	M	Merchant	New York	U. States	Natchez	7 Feb 1825
Robert	10	M	...	Scotland	America	Nimrod	9 Jul 1827
Thomas	3	M	None	England	Albany	Indian Chief	19 Jun 1823
Thomas	5	M	None	England	Albany	Indian Chief	19 Jun 1823
Thomas	30	M	Farmer	England	Albany	Indian Chief	19 Jun 1823
William	5	M	None	England	United States	Trident	18 Jul 1827
William	19	M	Glass Cutter	Scotland	United States	Orion	15 Jan 1827
William	29	...	...	Scotland	America	Nimrod	9 Jul 1827
William	30	M	Manufacturer	England	U. States	Manhattan	12 Jun 1824
William	36	M	Merchant	Demeaton, Yorshire		Hannibal	28 Jul 1823
Wm.	20	M	Labourer	England	England	Hudson	13 Jan 1827

NAMES OF PASSENGERS	AGE	SEX	OCCUPATIONS	COUNTRY TO WHICH THEY BELONG	COUNTRY THEY INTEND TO INHABIT	SHIPS/DATES OF ARRIVAL	
PEAK, Thomas	30	M	Plumber & ...	England	New York, U.S.	Angelica	18 Aug 1823
Wm.	33	M	Merchant	France	U. States	Ann Eliza Jane	19 Dec 1825
PEAL, Robt.	24	M	Cabinetmaker	England	United States	Resign	7 Oct 1822
PEALL, Mary	38	F		United States		Nestor	20 Oct 1827
PEAN, B.	27	M	Merchant	France	U. States	General A. Jackson	9 Apr 1822
Thomas	24	M	Labourer	England	United States	Nimrod	31 Jul 1828
PEAON, Jas.	19	M	Mechanic	Connecticutt	U. States	Benjamin	1 Jun 1822
PEAR, John	Infant	M	Son	Swiss	U. States	Comet	28 Jul 1825
Mary	29	F	Wife	Swiss	U. States	Comet	28 Jul 1825
Walter	30	M	Farmer	Swiss	U. States	Comet	28 Jul 1825
PEARCE, Alfred	4			Madd.../London	Pittsburgh	Venus	12 Apr 1821
Ambrose	6			Madd.../London	Pittsburgh	Venus	12 Apr 1821
Ann	37	F		U. States	U. States	Tampico	19 Oct 1826
David	5	M		Columbia	U. States	Tampico	19 Oct 1826
Frederick	3			London	Pittsburgh	Venus	12 Apr 1821
Giles	45	M	Carpenter	U.S.	U.S.	Pactolus	19 Aug 1823
John	...	...	...		United States	London Packet	25 Dec 1820
Maria	1			London	Pittsburgh	Venus	12 Apr 1821
Nathl.	27	M	Merchant	United States	U.S.	Pacific	22 May 1826
Richard	30		Farmer	B...ham, Eng./ London	Pittsburgh	Venus	12 Apr 1821
Susannah, Mrs.	28			Madd.../London	Pittsburgh	Venus	12 Apr 1821
Thos.	33	M	Mariner	U. States	U. States	Florida	25 Apr 1825
William	9	M		Columbia	U. States	Tampico	19 Oct 1826
Wm.	31	M	Weaver	Gt. Britain	United States	Penelope	9 Sep 1828
PEARCY, James	19 4/12	M	Silktwister	Wales	United States	London	6 Feb 1829
John	19 6/12	M	Groom	Wales	United States	London	6 Feb 1829
PEARE, Wm.	19	M		England	U. States	Frances Henrietta	9 Dec 1823
PEARER, A.	1	M		G. Britain		Caravan	8 Sep 1828
Alfred	5	M		G. Britain		Caravan	8 Sep 1828
L.	29	M		G. Britain		Caravan	8 Sep 1828
Lyde	17	M		G. Britain		Caravan	8 Sep 1828
U.	3	M		G. Britain		Caravan	8 Sep 1828
PEARL, James	23	M	Farmer	United States	United States	Magnet	19 Aug 1822
Mich.	25	M	Farmer	Ireland	U. States	Edward	15 Jul 1825
PEARMAN, James	40	M	Farmer	Great Britain	United States	Zodiac	29 Oct 1822
Wm.	27	M	Comedian	England	England	Canada	1 Nov 1823
Wm. P.	33	M	Th. R.C.G.	England	New York	Cortes	23 Nov 1827
PEARNE, Hannah	28 4/12	F	Wife of Nath. Bearne	Great Britain	Red Hook	Venus	8 Sep 1820
Nathaniel	2 3/12	M	Son of Nath. Bearne	Great Britain	Red Hook	Venus	8 Sep 1820
Tom	1 1/12	M	Son of Nath. Bearne	Great Britain	Red Hook	Venus	8 Sep 1820
PEARSE, Eliza	40	F		Ireland	United States	Thomas	13 Dec 1827
Jno.	40	M	Labourer	Ireland	United States	Thomas	13 Dec 1827
PEARSON, Arden	8	M		England	United States	Delta	24 Oct 1829
Betty	15	F	None	Great Britain	New York	Superior	5 Sep 1827
Brian	40	M	Glass Cutter	Great Britain	United States	Aurora	5 Sep 1826
Christopher	10	M		England	United States	Delta	24 Oct 1829
Elizabeth	28	F	Wife of [Brian]	Great Britain	United States	Aurora	5 Sep 1826
Ellen	8	F	None	Great Britain	New York	Superior	5 Sep 1827
Enoch	22	M	Joiner	Great Britain		Moro Castle	6 Jul 1827
Ephraim	25	M	Mariner	Philada.	U. States	Stanford	19 Mar 1829
James	26		Miner	Scotland	United States	Camillus	3 May 1828
Jane	6	F	None	Great Britain	New York	Superior	5 Sep 1827
Jane	6	M		G. Britain	U. States	Freak	9 Jun 1828
Jane	49	F		G. Britain	U. States	Freak	9 Jun 1828
John	12	M		G. Britain	U. States	Freak	9 Jun 1828
John	19	M	Hair Dres...	England	U. States	Franklin	7 Jul 1828
John	20	M	Laborer	England	America	Francis & Henrietta	11 Jul 1823
Martha	36	F	his Wife	England	United States	Delta	24 Oct 1829
Mary	12	F	None	Great Britain	New York	Superior	5 Sep 1827
Peter	12	M	None	England	U. States	Franklin	7 Jul 1828
Rebecca	37	F	None	Great Britain	New York	Superior	5 Sep 1827
Sarah	9	F	None	Great Britain	New York	Superior	5 Sep 1827

NAMES OF PASSENGERS	AGE	SEX	OCCUPATIONS	COUNTRY TO WHICH THEY BELONG	COUNTRY THEY INTEND TO INHABIT	SHIPS/DATES OF ARRIVAL	
PEARSON (cont'd)							
Sydney	17	M	Weaver	Great Britain	New York	Superior	5 Sep 1827
Thes.	42	M	Gardner	England	U. States	Franklin	7 Jul 1828
Thomas	3	M		England	United States	Delta	24 Oct 1829
Thomas	26	M		Great Brittan	U. States	Prince Leopold	2 Jul 1821
Thomas	30	M	Farmer	Great Brittain	United States	Active	12 Sep 1828
Thomas	56	M	Farmer	G. Britain	U. States	Freak	9 Jun 1828
Thos.	40	M	Farmer	England	U. States	Caius	11 Jun 1824
Thurston	1	M		England	United States	Delta	24 Oct 1829
William	22	M	Gentleman	Scotland	U. States	Camillus	29 Jan 1829
William	28	M	Basket Maker	England	United States	London	21 May 1828
Wm.	9	M		G. Britain	U. States	Freak	9 Jun 1828
Zachas.	34	M	Farmer	Great Briton	New York	Brighton	12 Jun 1826
PEARY, Eliza	24	F	Spinster	Ireland	United States	Asia	29 Jul 1829
PEASE, Edwd.	17	M		Ireland	America	Mary	29 May 1827
PEASON, Christopher	40	M	Cabinet maker	England	United States	Delta	24 Oct 1829
George	15	M		England	United States	Delta	24 Oct 1829
PEAT, —, Mrs.	40	F		United States	United States	Don Quixote	18 Aug 1824
Jas.	20	M	Butcher	Ireland	United States	William	20 Jul 1829
PEATERS, Samul	32	M	Merchant	St. Johns	U. States	Nancy	27 Jun 1823
PECAN, Pedro	14	M		Columbia	U. States	Tampico	19 Oct 1826
PECK, Chloe, Mrs.	35	F	None	United States	United States	Manchester	15 Aug 1826
Edward	4	M	None	United States	United States	Manchester	15 Aug 1826
Elisha	41	M	Merchant	U.S.	U.S.	George Canning	26 Aug 1829
Elisha, Mr.	38	M	Mercht.	United States	United States	Manchester	15 Aug 1826
George, Jr.	27	M	Mr. [Master?] Stone Cutter	Great Britain	United States	Meteor	15 Apr 1823
Harriot	8	F	None	United States	United States	Manchester	15 Aug 1826
Jonathan	1 4/12	M	family of [Margaret]	U. Kingdom of Great Britain	United States	Cambria	7 May 1828
Jos.	52	M	Mechanic	U.S.	U.S.	Prometheus	30 Aug 1828
Margaret	33	F		U. Kingdom of Great Britain	United States	Cambria	7 May 1828
Mary Ann	3	F	None	United States	United States	Manchester	15 Aug 1826
Mary Ann	19	F	None	U. States	U. States	Loire	7 Jun 1827
P.	32	M	Farmer	France	U. States	Bayard	25 Apr 1828
R.	32	M	Mechanic	Gt. Brittain	U. States	Robert Fulton	1 Nov 1822
Richard	3	M	family of [Margaret]	U. Kingdom of Great Britain	United States	Cambria	7 May 1828
Samuel	7	M	family of [Margaret]	U. Kingdom of Great Britain	United States	Cambria	7 May 1828
Sarah Ann	10	F	family of [Margaret]	U. Kingdom of Great Britain	United States	Cambria	7 May 1828
Shubeal	13	M	Gent.	America	America	Napoleon	26 May 1828
Virgil	25	M	Merchant	U. States	U. States	Combine	12 Nov 1821
PECKAN, Helen	20		Servant	Great Britain	United States	Camillus	12 Sep 1827
PECKEEP, Aaron	30	M	Weaver	Great Britain	U.S. America	Chili	7 Jul 1827
Ann	1	F	Weaver	Great Britain	U.S. America	Chili	7 Jul 1827
Eliza	4	F	Weaver	Great Britain	U.S. America	Chili	7 Jul 1827
James	3	M	Weaver	Great Britain	U.S. America	Chili	7 Jul 1827
Martha	30	F	Weaver	Great Britain	U.S. America	Chili	7 Jul 1827
PECKHAM, Eldridge	35	M	Butcher	Great Britain	New York	Radius	7 Jul 1821
PECKIN, Piere	19	M	Professor			Henri IV	17 May 1828
Piere	20	M	Farmer			Henri IV	17 May 1828
PEDDER, Wm., Mr.	36		Merchant	Scotland	G.B.	Pacific	24 May 1824
PEDDON, James	20	M	Labourer	England	U. States	Comet	23 Aug 1828
PEDES, Augustes	2 6/12	M	Farmer	France	United States	Crescent	12 Jul 1827
Eugene	8/12	M	Farmer	France	United States	Crescent	12 Jul 1827
Francis	9	M	Farmer	France	United States	Crescent	12 Jul 1827
George	38	M	Farmer	France	United States	Crescent	12 Jul 1827
Joseph	7	M	Farmer	France	United States	Crescent	12 Jul 1827
Mary	36	F	Farmer	France	United States	Crescent	12 Jul 1827
Victor	11	M	Farmer	France	United States	Crescent	12 Jul 1827
Xavier	4	M	Farmer	France	United States	Crescent	12 Jul 1827
PEDLICA, John M.	50	M	Sugar Baker	Holland	Canada	United States	7 Jul 1827
PEDMONTE, Sidney	34	M	Merchant	Guadeloupe	New York	Notre Dame	6 Oct 1827
PEDRAGO, —	42	M	Barker	Spain	U. States	Maria Ann	29 Sep 1823
*landed at Balize [Biloxi?], Missippi							
PEDRO, —, Don	10	M			U. States	Trimmer	3 Jan 1826

NAMES OF PASSENGERS	AGE	SEX	OCCUPATIONS	COUNTRY TO WHICH THEY BELONG	COUNTRY THEY INTEND TO INHABIT	SHIPS/DATES OF ARRIVAL	
PEDRO (cont'd)							
C.	35	M	Servant	U. States	U. States	Douglass	27 Jul 1825
Pedro Martior	29	M	Merchant	Spain	U. States	Pocahontas	9 Jun 1823
PEDROD, Easter	35	F		Irland	U. States	Nancy	27 Jun 1823
Haner	18	F		Irland	U. States	Nancy	27 Jun 1823
Hary	14	F		Irland	U. States	Nancy	27 Jun 1823
Jane	10	F		Irland	U. States	Nancy	27 Jun 1823
Suser	8	F		Irland	U. States	Nancy	27 Jun 1823
PEEL, David	36	M	Weaver	Great Britian	United States	George Clinton	21 Oct 1826
PEENE, Samuel	30	M	Gentleman	Great Brittian	Great Brittian	Governor Von Schollen	7 Nov 1827
PEERONSE, John	55	M	Merchant	United States	New York	Britannia	3 Nov 1827
PEETFIELD, James	24	M	Smith	England	United States	Curler	7 Jul 1827
PEGBONE, Edward	39	M	Servant	England	United States	Comet	6 Mar 1823
PEGET, Anthony	7/12	M	Farmer	France	United States	Crescent	12 Jul 1827
Francess	18	F	Farmer	France	United States	Crescent	12 Jul 1827
Francis	27	M	Farmer	France	United States	Crescent	12 Jul 1827
Franciss Zeffe	55	M	Farmer	France	United States	Crescent	12 Jul 1827
Joan	43	F	Farmer	France	United States	Crescent	12 Jul 1827
John Lewis	5	M	Farmer	France	United States	Crescent	12 Jul 1827
John Peter	8	M	Farmer	France	United States	Crescent	12 Jul 1827
Josephine	22	F	Farmer	France	United States	Crescent	12 Jul 1827
Mary	11	F	Farmer	France	United States	Crescent	12 Jul 1827
PEGHAM, Thomas	38	M	Coachman	G. Britain	U. States	Mary & Harriot	8 Sep 1828
PEIFREIR, Morant	24	M	Joiner	Germany	United States	Samuel Robertson	8 Aug 1828
PEIGNET, Emmeline	22	F		France	New York	Desdemona	12 Jun 1826
Hyacinth	32	M		France	New York	Desdemona	12 Jun 1826
PEIMSTON, Jane	26	F	Spinster	Ireland	U. States	Josephine	30 Aug 1828
Margeret	26	F	Spinster	Ireland	U. States	Josephine	30 Aug 1828
PEINE, Jno. M.	23	M	Baker	France	U. States	Hyperion	7 Aug 1826
PEIRCE,							
Cinthy, (Mulatto)	35	F	Servant	America	United States	South Carolina Packet	25 Mar 1820
Francis	4	M		England	United States	Copernicus	3 Aug 1829
Hugh, Capt.	27	M	Mariner	United States	United States	Columbia	21 Jan 1828
Isaac	22	M	Backer	United States	United States	Only Daughter	29 Apr 1825
James	1	M		England	United States	Copernicus	3 Aug 1829
Jane	33	F		England	United States	Copernicus	3 Aug 1829
John	11	M		England	United States	Copernicus	3 Aug 1829
Mary	13	F		England	United States	Copernicus	3 Aug 1829
Philo	7	F		England	United States	Copernicus	3 Aug 1829
Richard	25	M	Merant.	Barbadoes	Halifax, N.S.	Salumith	17 Nov 1826
Weldern	6	M		England	United States	Copernicus	3 Aug 1829
William	24	M	Seaman	U. States	U. States	Golden Age	6 Jul 1821
Wm.	36	M	Labourer	England	United States	Copernicus	3 Aug 1829
PEIRCIE, Jos.	30	M	Laman	United States	United States	Ann Maria	23 Oct 1820
PEIRCY, Jos.	27	M	Engineer	U. States	U. States	Wave	27 Jul 1822
PEIROT, John B.	32	M	Merchant	France	U. States	Ann Eliza Jane	1 May 1823
PEIRSON, Poole	45	M	Gentleman	United States	U.S.	Robert Fulton	7 Nov 1823
PEITZ, Anna	6	F	Agriculturist	France	U.S.	Helen	3 May 1828
Antoine	3	M	Agriculturist	France	U.S.	Helen	3 May 1828
Catherine	36	F	Agriculturist	France	U.S.	Helen	3 May 1828
Lamont	11	M	Agriculturist	France	U.S.	Helen	3 May 1828
Samuel	40	M	Agriculturist	France	U.S.	Helen	3 May 1828
PEIXOTTE, Samuel	35	M		America	America	Pleiades	13 Nov 1826
PELAGO, A.	22	M	Merchant	Spain	Spain	Packet	10 Jul 1823
PELBA, Sarah	40		Servant	England	U.S.	Corinthian	11 Mar 1829
PELBY, William	29 10/12	M	Gentleman	United States	United States	Brighton	12 Jun 1826
PELELLOT, Francis	44 ...	M	...	...	U.S. America	Edward	28 Oct 1825
PELER, Jno.	26	M	Servent	America	U. States	Circassian	13 Jun 1825
PELHAM, Joh., Mr.	56	M	Gentleman	England	U. States	Emily	25 Aug 1827
John	40	M	Ship Builder	Gt. Britain	U. States	Columbia	7 Sep 1827
PELIN, James	26 1/12	M	Clerk	Ireland	British North America	London	6 Feb 1829
PELL, Alfred	25	M	Mercht.	America	America	Savannah	10 Jan 1828
Alfred	25	M	Mercht.	U. States	U. States	Sully	15 Jul 1829
Eliza, Mrs.	19	F	Lady	U. States	U. States	Sully	15 Jul 1829
Jno.	28	M	Miller	Great Brittan	U. States	Gem	26 Jul 1827

NAMES OF PASSENGERS	AGE	SEX	OCCUPATIONS	COUNTRY TO WHICH THEY BELONG	COUNTRY THEY INTEND TO INHABIT	SHIPS/DATES OF ARRIVAL	
PELL (cont'd)							
Stephen	16	M	Farmer	N. York	U. States	Ann Maria	6 Jul 1824
Thos.	31	M		England	America	Corinthian	1 Sep 1827
PELLET, —	45	M	Merchant	France	France	Asparia	1 Sep 1824
PELLETEW, James A.	32	M	Upholsterer	France	United States	Edward Quesnel	3 Jul 1829
PELLETIER, A. L.	13 3/12	M	Sugar Baker	Netherlands	U. States	Louisa	7 Jun 1824
H. A.	15 1/12	F	Sugar Baker	Netherlands	U. States	Louisa	7 Jun 1824
J. J. A.	20 1/12	M	Sugar Baker	Netherlands	U. States	Louisa	7 Jun 1824
J. T.	43	M	Sugar Baker	Netherlands	U. States	Louisa	7 Jun 1824
M. T.	39 4/12	F		Netherlands	U. States	Louisa	7 Jun 1824
PELLETIN, Rosalie	34		Hair dresser	France		Bayard	10 Sep 1827
PELLICET, F.	31	M	Spanish Offr.	Spain	Havana	Henry	11 Oct 1825
PELLING, Ephraim	22	M	Clothier	England	U. States	Montgomery	18 Oct 1828
James	24	M	Laborer	Ireland	U. States	Dale	14 Mar 1828
Jos.	22	M		Ireland	U. States	Fame	15 Nov 1826
Joseph	22	M	Miller	England	U. States	Severn	12 Oct 1826
PELLINGER, M...	42			L...	England	Great Britain	7 May 1827
Mary	...			L...	England	Great Britain	7 May 1827
PELLISSIER, Joseph	18	M	Clergiman	France	N. York	Charlemagne	20 Aug 1829
PELLNERER, George	30	M	Merchant	England	Great Britian	Florida	24 Jul 1826
PELLOT, Andrew P.	31	M	Merchant	U. States	S. Carolina	Sully	30 Oct 1827
PELLY, Jos.	24	M	Mercher	U.S.	U.S.	Charleston Allen	15 Nov 1826
PELTIER, Lucien	25	M	Merchant	France	U. States	Sully	24 Oct 1828
Pauline, Mrs.	42	F	None	France	U. States	Sully	25 Jun 1828
PELTIN, —, Mr.	22	M	Mercht.	France	U. States	Hamlet	4 Aug 1823
PELVRE, A.	32	M	Merchant	France	America	Saluda	18 Jun 1825
PEMA, C.	20	M	Merchant	Havana	Havana	Crusader	23 Apr 1827
PEMBERTON, George	21	M	...	England	Canada	William Thompson	10 May 1825
James	35	M	Gardner	England	New York	Indian Chief	16 Aug 1822
Maria	33	F	Wife	England	U.N. States	Corinthian	1 Sep 1823
Thomas	18	M	Gardner	England	New York	Indian Chief	16 Aug 1822
Thos.	45	M	Merchant	England	U.N. States	Corinthian	1 Sep 1823
Wm.	32	M		Great Britain	Canada	James Monroe	25 Apr 1822
PEMBLY, Edward	46	M	Calico Printer	England	United States	Andes	2 Oct 1828
PEMITERT, Luke	41	M	Docter	France	U. States	Rebecca & Sally	12 Nov 1821
PEMLEY, George	22	M	Calico Printer	Great Britain	United States	Aurora	5 Sep 1826
PEN, Ann	40	M		Great Britain	United States	Mary	11 Jul 1820
Ann, Junior	2	F		Great Britain	United States	Mary	11 Jul 1820
John	40	M	Labourer	Great Britain	United States	Mary	11 Jul 1820
Mary	6	F		Great Britain	United States	Mary	11 Jul 1820
Moris, Mr.	45	M	Carpenter	England	U. States	Acasta	11 Dec 1826
Thomas	5	M		Great Britain	United States	Mary	11 Jul 1820
PENA, Ausinta	12	M	None	Colombia	Colombia	Cornelia	12 Mar 1825
PENALBER, N.	32	M	Planter	Havana	Cuba	Quesnel	6 Sep 1824
PENALROZ, Fernando	50	M	Doctor of Law	Columbia	U. States	Bunker Hill	12 Aug 1828
PENAN, John	20	M	M...	France	U. States	Little Cherub	8 Sep 1824
PENANCAS, Joseph	29	M	Merchant	Havana	Havana	Robert Reade	9 Feb 1822
PENARREDONDA, Jose	21	M	Merchant	Aux Cayes	United States	Paquet Des Cayes	9 Jul 1827
PENBROOK, Nichovas	25			Ireland	Philidelphia	General Marion	21 Nov 1828
Wm.	18			Ireland	Philidelphia	General Marion	21 Nov 1828
PENDAGAST, Edward	23	M	Bookkeeper	Great Britain	U. States	Cadmus	26 Oct 1821
Michl.	21		Carpenter	Ireland	United States	Geo. Canning	5 Jun 1828
Mark	8	M		Mayo	America	Margaret	31 Jul 1824
PENDEGRASS, Bridget	6	F		Ireland		Fame	9 Dec 1826
Ellen	29	F		Ireland		Fame	9 Dec 1826
Geo. C.	40	M	Merchant	U. States	U. States	Chase	19 Sep 1823
John	34	M		England	United States	Yobah	26 Sep 1827
Michl.	30	M	Servant	Ireland		Fame	9 Dec 1826
Patt	7/12	M		Ireland		Fame	9 Dec 1826
Thomas	4	M		Ireland		Fame	9 Dec 1826
Willm.	8	M		Ireland		Fame	9 Dec 1826
PENDEGROVE, Mary	1	F				Eliza Grant	6 Oct 1828
Mary	24	F				Eliza Grant	6 Oct 1828
Sarah	3	F				Eliza Grant	6 Oct 1828
Wm.	25	M				Eliza Grant	6 Oct 1828
PENDER, Jno.	26	M	Merchant	Massachusetts	U. States	Childe Harold	21 Feb 1825

NAMES OF PASSENGERS	AGE	SEX	OCCUPATIONS	COUNTRY TO WHICH THEY BELONG	COUNTRY THEY INTEND TO INHABIT	SHIPS/DATES OF ARRIVAL	
PENDERGAST, Jno.	25	M	Farmer	Great Britain	America	Remittance	24 Aug 1825
PENDERGRASS, Allin	36	M	Merchant	America	America	Hope	15 Oct 1821
Edwd.	22	M	Labourer	Ireland		Marchioness	13 May 1828
John	12	M	...	Ireland	United States	Colossus	30 May 1825
PENDERGST, C. Flinn	27	M	Merchant	Ireland	U. States	Hunter	24 Jul 1821
PENDERHATH, —, Major	45	M	Merchant	Great Britain	Canada	Columbia	7 Sep 1827
PENDLEATH, —, Mrs.	42	F		U. States	Canada	Columbia	7 Sep 1827
PENDLEBURY, Thos.	27		Bleacher	Bolton	England	Great Britain	7 May 1827
PENDLETON, —, Mr.	24	M	Carpenter	U. States	U. States	Cadmus	12 Apr 1825
Agnes	4	F	Child	Scotland	United States	Samuel Robertson	9 May 1827
Isabella	3	F	Child	Scotland	United States	Samuel Robertson	9 May 1827
J., Mr.	30	M	Merchant	Boston	U. States	Imperial	23 Oct 1826
Margaret	6/12	F	Child	Scotland	United States	Samuel Robertson	9 May 1827
Sarah	25	F		Scotland	United States	Samuel Robertson	9 May 1827
William	21	M	Farmer	Ireland	U. States	Dickinson	30 Jul 1825
PENEGERT, Cozie	29	M	Mariner	France	France	Charlotte Corday	8 Nov 1823
PENELA, Susana	30	F	None	U. States	U. States	Betsey	6 May 1826
PENETT, Wm.	30	M	Labourer	Bristol	U. States	Latona	7 Jul 1827
PENEVYAR, Charles	36	M	Merchant	France	U. States	Queen Mab	16 Mar 1825
PENEYRME, C.	27	M	Merchant	Philadelphia	U. States	Don Quixote	14 Aug 1826
PENFIELD, Elisabeth	24		None	United States	United States	William Byrnes	25 Aug 1828
Josiah	44		Merchant	United States	United States	William Byrnes	25 Aug 1828
PENFOLD, John	39	M	Merchant	U. States	N. York	James Cropper	21 Oct 1825
PENICE, Francis	45	M	Nothing			William Neilson	26 Jul 1828
PENISTON, A. J.	35	M	Merchant	Norfolk	U. States	Dirigo	24 Mar 1828
Francis F.	28	M	Merchant	Bermuda	Bermuda	Samuel	23 Aug 1824
R., Mr.	21	M	Merchant	Bermuda	Canada	Camden	14 May 1825
PENLY, Mary	20	F		England	U. States	Emulous	22 Aug 1828
PENMAN, Alexander	7	M	None	Scotland	United States	Mary & Susan	5 Aug 1828
David	5	...		Scotland	America	Nimrod	9 Jul 1827
Elisebeth	50	F	None	Scotland	United States	Mary & Susan	5 Aug 1828
Elizabeth	...	...	...	Scotland	America	Nimrod	9 Jul 1827
Isabella	12	F	None	Scotland	United States	Mary & Susan	5 Aug 1828
James	16	M	Labourer	Scotland	United States	Mary & Susan	5 Aug 1828
John	...	...	...	Scotland	America	Nimrod	9 Jul 1827
John	29	M	...	Scotland	America	Nimrod	9 Jul 1827
Margaret	28	F	None	Scotland	United States	Mary & Susan	5 Aug 1828
Mary	30	F	...	Scotland	America	Nimrod	9 Jul 1827
Robert	4	M	None	Scotland	United States	Mary & Susan	5 Aug 1828
PENN, B.	13	M	Boy	Mexico	United States	Saluda	14 May 1827
G.	14	M	Boy	Mexico	United States	Saluda	14 May 1827
Isaac	22	M	Merchant	U. States	U. States	Noble	9 Jan 1824
PENNELL, G.	20	M	Servant	Switzerland	Boston	Howard	26 Aug 1823
PENNEVEYRE, Moses	35	M	Labourer	Sweden	United States	Brighton	11 Mar 1825
PENNEYVERT, Adrianne Susanne, Mrs.	30	F		Switzerland	Switzerland	Bayard	30 Oct 1820
PENNIN, Charles	35	M	Mercht.	England	England	Pacific	24 Oct 1828
PENNINGTON, —, Mrs.	26	F		England	U. States	Venus	1 Apr 1828
Ann	40			England	United States	Hugh Johnson	11 Jun 1828
Edward, Jr.	23 1/12	M	Merchant	United States	Philadelphia, U. States	Cadmus	12 Dec 1823
Harriot	4	F		England	U. States	Venus	1 Apr 1828
J.	34	M	Gentleman	England	U. States	Venus	1 Apr 1828
Mary	4			England	United States	Hugh Johnson	11 Jun 1828
Michael	16	M	None	Ireland	United States	Trio	31 Oct 1827
Sarah	1			England	United States	Hugh Johnson	11 Jun 1828
Wm.	6			England	United States	Hugh Johnson	11 Jun 1828
PENNISTON, Francis	35	M	Merchant	Bermuda	Bermuda	Worromontogus	23 Jun 1823
PENNY, Hannah	16	F	None	Great Britain	United States	Cortes	18 Oct 1820
James	42	M	Cordwainer	Great Britain	United States	Cortes	18 Oct 1820
John	29	M	Farmer	Great Britian	U. States	Orbit	29 Apr 1822
Josh.	5	M	None	Great Britain	United States	Cortes	18 Oct 1820
Lucier	12	M		Port au Prince	Haytia	Atalanta	28 Aug 1822

NAMES OF PASSENGERS	AGE	SEX	OCCUPATIONS	COUNTRY TO WHICH THEY BELONG	COUNTRY THEY INTEND TO INHABIT	SHIPS/DATES OF ARRIVAL	
PENNY (cont'd)							
Mary Ann	7	F	None	Great Britain	United States	Cortes	18 Oct 1820
P. B.	30	M	Merchant	United States	United States	Four Sons	1 Sep 1827
Saml.	24	M	Labourer	England	U. States	Comet	23 Aug 1828
T. H.	26	M	...	England	U. States	Chase	26 Jul 1824
Ths.	21			England	America	Robert Burns	8 Dec 1821
W. K.	26	M	Merchant	America	United States	South Carolina	14 Aug 1823
PENORIA, D.	40	M	Mariner	U. States	U.S.	Ambuscade	14 Mar 1820
PENOT, Catharar	39	F		France	U. States	Edward Bonaffe	23 Jul 1828
Jam	49	M	Carpenter	Holland	U. States	Edward Bonaffe	23 Jul 1828
PENROSE, George	30	M	Labourer	England	U. States	Comet	23 Aug 1828
James	1	M	Labourer	England	U. States	Comet	23 Aug 1828
Mary	20	F	Labourer	England	U. States	Comet	23 Aug 1828
Sarah	2	F	Labourer	England	U. States	Comet	23 Aug 1828
PENRY, Ellen	19	F		England	United States	Danube	13 Jul 1827
Hannah	14	F		England	United States	Danube	13 Jul 1827
James	20	M		Scotland	U.S.	Curler	19 Jul 1828
John	54	M	Laborer	England	United States	Danube	13 Jul 1827
John Oldham	23	M	Laborer	England	United States	Danube	13 Jul 1827
Martha	43	F		England	United States	Danube	13 Jul 1827
Mary	1	F		England	United States	Danube	13 Jul 1827
PENSELL, Pendope	50	F	Servant	Jamaica	Jamaica	Ambuscade	12 Nov 1823
PENTARD, Morriston	20	M	Laborer	New York	United States	St. Michaels	15 Feb 1825
PENTCLOW, Wm.	32	M	...	Great Britain	N. York	Josephine	10 Dec 1825
PENTFIELD, Joseph	46	M	Gardner	England	America	John Adams	2 Aug 1827
PENTLAND, Jane	17	M	Fema	Ireland	United States	Dublin Packet	3 Sep 1822
William	19	M	Farmer	Ireland	United States	Dublin Packet	3 Sep 1822
PENTO, A.	18	M	None	Jamaica	Jamaica	Hal	7 Jun 1824
A.	30	M	Merchant	Jamaica	U. States	Hal	7 Jun 1824
PENTON, ...	37	F		Ireland	America	Carolina Ann	7 Aug 1826
...	40	M	Merchant	Ireland	America	Carolina Ann	7 Aug 1826
Ann	17	F		Ireland	America	Carolina Ann	7 Aug 1826
David	1	M		Ireland	America	Carolina Ann	7 Aug 1826
Eliza	19	F		Ireland	America	Carolina Ann	7 Aug 1826
Ellen	11	F		Ireland	America	Carolina Ann	7 Aug 1826
Isabella	15	F		Ireland	America	Carolina Ann	7 Aug 1826
Josar	8	M		Ireland	America	Carolina Ann	7 Aug 1826
Margaret	13	F		Ireland	America	Carolina Ann	7 Aug 1826
Mary	14	F		Ireland	America	Carolina Ann	7 Aug 1826
Olivia	3	F		Ireland	America	Carolina Ann	7 Aug 1826
Richard	7	M		Ireland	America	Carolina Ann	7 Aug 1826
Septania	9	F		Ireland	America	Carolina Ann	7 Aug 1826
Thomas	5	M		Ireland	America	Carolina Ann	7 Aug 1826
William	6	M		Ireland	America	Carolina Ann	7 Aug 1826
PENZITON, Richd.	18	M	Merchant	England	Bermuda	Rising Sun	24 May 1824
PEOLI, John G.	44		...	...	Columbia	Bogota	25 Oct 1827
PEON, Jose M.	25	M	Merchant	Mexico	U. States	Frances	22 May 1827
PEOPLES, John	20	M	Labourer	Ireland	United States	Trident	16 May 1826
John	24	M	Farmer	Ireland	United States	Asia	29 Jul 1829
Rebaccah	22	F	Spinster	Ireland	United States	Asia	29 Jul 1829
PEPHALL, Alfred	6	M	None	Gt. Brittain	United States	Balaena	24 Aug 1825
Bridget	35	F	None	Gt. Brittain	United States	Balaena	24 Aug 1825
Deborah	4	F	None	Gt. Brittain	United States	Balaena	24 Aug 1825
Frederick	17	M	None	Gt. Brittain	United States	Balaena	24 Aug 1825
Geo.	2	M	None	Gt. Brittain	United States	Balaena	24 Aug 1825
Margaret	10	F	None	Gt. Brittain	United States	Balaena	24 Aug 1825
Miro	14	F	None	Gt. Brittain	United States	Balaena	24 Aug 1825
Thos.	11/12	M	None	Gt. Brittain	United States	Balaena	24 Aug 1825
PEPLON, Mary	24	F		Dudley	U. States	Plato	18 Apr 1826
Robt.	26	M	Mechanic	Dudley	U. States	Plato	18 Apr 1826
PEPPARD, Wm.	21	M	C...	...	...	Diamond	27 Jul 1824
PEPPER, Christian G.	11	M	Boy	Ireland	United States	Dublin Packet	23 May 1828
Ellen	8	F	Child	Ireland	United States	Dublin Packet	23 May 1828
George	45	M	Mercht.	G.B.	G.B.	George Canning	2 May 1828
Margaret	30	F	Wife	Ireland	United States	Dublin Packet	23 May 1828
Napolian	5	M	Boy	Ireland	United States	Dublin Packet	23 May 1828
Thomas	3	M	Boy	Ireland	United States	Dublin Packet	23 May 1828
PEPPERDINE, Mary	28	F	Labourer	Great Britan	United States	Clematis	8 May 1827
Thomas	30	M	Labourer	Great Britan	United States	Clematis	8 May 1827

NAMES OF PASSENGERS	AGE	SEX	OCCUPATIONS	COUNTRY TO WHICH THEY BELONG	COUNTRY THEY INTEND TO INHABIT	SHIPS/DATES OF ARRIVAL	
PEPPERDINE (cont'd)							
William	1 6/12	M	Labourer	Great Britan	United States	Clematis	8 May 1827
PEPPIT, Chas.	20	M	Bricklayer	England		Marchioness	13 May 1828
PEPRIAN, Jean C.	25	F	Farmer	Switzerland		Pallas	14 Jun 1828
PERACHET, Clod	30		Coper Smith	United States	United States	Iris	26 Jun 1821
PERAL, Adolph	27 6/12	M	Merchant	France	U. States	France	26 Jun 1828
PERASO, Jno.	18	M	Merchant	France	U. States	Transit	26 Apr 1823
PERAULT, Louis	21	M	Merchant	Montreal	Montreaul	Edward Bonaffe	23 Jul 1828
PERCEDER, M.	33	M	Soldier	New York	U. States	Greek	3 Mar 1825
PERCH, Ann	6	F		United States	United States	Globe	30 Aug 1828
Danl.	31	M	Farmer	United States	United States	Globe	30 Aug 1828
Eve	30	F		United States	United States	Globe	30 Aug 1828
George	14	M		United States	United States	Globe	30 Aug 1828
Marian	3	F		United States	United States	Globe	30 Aug 1828
PERCHERON, —	23	M		France	United States	Howard	20 Aug 1827
PERCIVAL, ...	4	M	Wife	Wales	U.S. States	Splendid	14 Aug 1829
Bercy	35	M	Merchant	Wales	U.S. States	Splendid	14 Aug 1829
Cathe.	1			England		Anacreon	7 Sep 1827
Charles	10	M	Wife	Wales	U.S. States	Splendid	14 Aug 1829
Isaac	42	M	Mariner	U. States	U. States	London	23 Sep 1828
James	41	M	Mariner	Great Britian	U. States	Hudson	12 Mar 1824
Jane	7	F	Wife	Wales	U.S. States	Splendid	14 Aug 1829
Jane	26			England		Anacreon	7 Sep 1827
Jane	30	F	Wife	Wales	U.S. States	Splendid	14 Aug 1829
John	30	M	Wife	Wales	U.S. States	Splendid	14 Aug 1829
Joseph	8	M	Wife	Wales	U.S. States	Splendid	14 Aug 1829
Mary	28	F	Wife	Wales	U.S. States	Splendid	14 Aug 1829
Wm.	3	F	Wife	Wales	U.S. States	Splendid	14 Aug 1829
Wm.	6	M	Wife	Wales	U.S. States	Splendid	14 Aug 1829
Wm.	30			England		Anacreon	7 Sep 1827
PERCY, —, Mrs.		F		Maine	U. States	Four Sisters	11 Aug 1823
PERDLIGEON, Arsine	35	M		Havre	N. York	Stephania	29 Nov 1825
PERDOMO, Antonio	42	M	Mariner	Spain	Mexico	Sarah	23 Sep 1826
M.	8	M	None	Spain	Mexico	Sarah	23 Sep 1826
PERELLO, Pearr	27	M	Merchant	Mayorca	Havana	Britannia	23 Mar 1829
Peter	20	M	Merchant	Spain	Spain	Native	8 Feb 1826
PERERA, Eugenio	21	M	Gentleman	Spain	Havana	United States	13 Dec 1824
PERES, Diego	35	M	Merchant	Spain	U. States	Mount Vernon	18 Dec 1824
Pedro	55	M	Mariner	Spain	Spain	Abigail	19 May 1826
Pedro, Don	52	M	Gentleman	Spain	Spain	Abigail	18 Aug 1826
PEREZ, A.	50	M	Merchant	Spain, Teneriffe	Spain	Volant	30 Oct 1821
Anna	18	F		Spain	U. States	Mount Vernon	18 Dec 1824
Antonio	8	M		Mexico	Mexico	Virginia	9 Feb 1829
Antonio, Don	50	M	Merchant	Spain	U. States	Packet	24 Apr 1823
Asension	30	F	Servant	Spain	Spain	Franklin	14 Jul 1827
Bernardo	7	M	Child	Spain	U. States	Virginia	8 Mar 1828
Delores	25	F		Spain	U. States	Mount Vernon	18 Dec 1824
Dolores	6/12	F		Spain	U. States	Mount Vernon	18 Dec 1824
Gabriel	25	M	Mariner	Spain	U. States	Packet	24 Apr 1823
J.	25	M	Trader	Spain	U. States	Patriot	23 May 1821
James	30	M	Servant	Spain, Teneriffe	Spain	Volant	30 Oct 1821
Jos., Mastr.	11	M	Merchant	Mexico	U. States	Sea Nymph	7 Jul 1827
Jos. M.	3	M		Spain	U. States	Mount Vernon	18 Dec 1824
José Ma.	6	M		Mexico	Mexico	Virginia	9 Feb 1829
Joseph R.	20	M	Merchant	Spain		Liberty	3 Sep 1827
Juana	1	F	Child	Spain	Spain	Franklin	14 Jul 1827
Leonardo	5	M		Spain	U. States	Mount Vernon	18 Dec 1824
Leonardo	35	M	Surgeon	Spain	U. States	Virginia	8 Mar 1828
Lewis	22	M	Merchant	Spain		Liberty	3 Sep 1827
PEREZE, C.	40	M	Rope Dancer	Mexico	U. States	Aurora	11 Aug 1824
PERIA, John B.	26	M	Gentleman	Bordeaux	U. States	Smyrna	30 Apr 1825
P.	25	M	Clerk	Spain	Matanzes	New England	5 Feb 1827
PERILLIAT, F. M.	42	M	Merchant	United States	United States	Howard	19 May 1826
PERISON, F.	24	M	Merchant	Spain		Radius	21 Jul 1824
PERIT, Pelatiah	40	M	Merchant	America	N. York	James Cropper	13 Mar 1826
PERKIN, Charles	6	M	Baker	France		Pallas	14 Jun 1828
Eliz.	14	F		France		Pallas	14 Jun 1828
Lousia	2	F		France		Pallas	14 Jun 1828
Margaretta	18	F		France		Pallas	14 Jun 1828

NAMES OF PASSENGERS	AGE	SEX	OCCUPATIONS	COUNTRY TO WHICH THEY BELONG	COUNTRY THEY INTEND TO INHABIT	SHIPS/DATES OF ARRIVAL	
PERKIN (cont'd)							
Moriah	41	F		France		Pallas	14 Jun 1828
Susan	9	F		France		Pallas	14 Jun 1828
Wm.	36		Clothier	Great Britain	United States	Roman	10 Sep 1827
PERKINS, —, Mrs.	35	F		Boston, U.S.		Robert Edwards	8 Nov 1825
Ambrose	22	M	Merchant	St. John	St. John	St. Michael	27 Mar 1827
Chs.	25		Seaman	New York		Hudson	18 Jun 1825

*Officers, Seamen and Passengers belonging to the Ship Jane of Boston and taken from on board the Schooner Olive of St. Johns , N.B. on the 4th June 1825, Lat. 41.30, Long 53.19, which ship foundered on the 31st ultimo in Lat. 41.44 Long 52.

Ebenezer	25	M	Artist	United States	United States	Columbia	22 Sep 1828
Geo. C.	23	M	Mercht.	U.S.A.	U. States	Edward Bonnaffe	12 Oct 1826
Henry	23	M	Merchant	United States	United States	Bunker Hill	16 Apr 1827
J. H.	51	M	Merchant	United States	United States	Richmond	4 Aug 1826
Jos.	36		Mariner	America	U. States	Edward	24 Oct 1827
S. H.	24	M	Merchant	U. States	U. States	Bayard	25 Apr 1828
Saml. G.	65	M	Merchant	U. States	U. States	Bayard	19 Mar 1824
Thos. W.	55	M	Merchant	United States	U. States	Ann Maria	23 Oct 1820
Wm.	40	M	Miller	England	United States	Manhattan	11 Oct 1824
PERKS, Wm.	36	M	Army	France	U. States	Native	31 Jan 1825
PERLEY, Louisa	18	F	Spinster	U.S.	U.S.	Minerva	3 Dec 1821
Thos.	42	M	Spinner	Great Britian	U. States	Henry Kneedland	7 Aug 1826
PERLY, Charles	25	M	Laborer	Ireland	United States	Ann Maria	12 Jun 1826
PERMERADA, B.	60	M	Merchant	Spain	France & Spain	Native	24 Aug 1825
PERNET, Daniel Saml.	58	M	Labourer	Switzerland	United States	Thetis	5 Jul 1821
David Emanuel	9	M		Switzerland	United States	Thetis	5 Jul 1821
David Emanuel	23	M	Teacher	Switzerland	United States	Thetis	5 Jul 1821
Henrietta Paulina	2	F		Switzerland	United States	Thetis	5 Jul 1821
John David	16	M	Labourer	Switzerland	United States	Thetis	5 Jul 1821
John David Saml.	31	M	Teacher	Switzerland	United States	Thetis	5 Jul 1821
John Emanuel	7	M		Switzerland	United States	Thetis	5 Jul 1821
Susanna Maria	58	F	Labourer	Switzerland	United States	Thetis	5 Jul 1821
Suzane Marie	32	F	Labourer	Switzerland	United States	Thetis	5 Jul 1821
PERNIE, Geo.	20	M	Clerk		United States	Sarah	9 Nov 1820
James	64	M	None	Scotland	U. States	Camillus	27 Jun 1826
Mary	20	F	Seamstress	Scotland	U. States	Camillus	27 Jun 1826
PERNIRA, Domingos	37	M	Trader	New York	New York	Harriot	1 May 1822
PERNON, —, Mr.	27	M	Merchant	France	Marseilles	Cadmus	12 Apr 1825
PERNOY, F.	1	M		So. America	U. States	Eclipse	10 Jun 1823
Is.	2	F		So. America	U. States	Eclipse	10 Jun 1823
J. B.	10	F		So. America	U. States	Eclipse	10 Jun 1823
Josepha	4	F		So. America	U. States	Eclipse	10 Jun 1823
N.	5	F		So. America	U. States	Eclipse	10 Jun 1823
Rosa	6	F		So. America	U. States	Eclipse	10 Jun 1823
PERNRADESA, A. Joze	21	M	Merchant	Portugal	U. States	Frederick	27 Jan 1823
PERO, —	18	M	Servant	Spain	Spain	Sabina	5 May 1826
David	22	M	Farmer	Great Britain	United States	John Jay	8 May 1828
PEROHN, Constant	35	M	Merchant	France	United States	India	4 Aug 1826
PEROILL, Edward	27	M		Ireland	United States	John & Adam	21 Sep 1822
PERON, Aldave	5	M		Point Petre	New Jersey	Proxy	20 Jul 1826
Eliza	8	F		Point Petre	New Jersey	Proxy	20 Jul 1826
Fanny	0 9/12	F		Point Petre	New Jersey	Proxy	20 Jul 1826
Nancy	25	F		Point Petre	New Jersey	Proxy	20 Jul 1826
Rosa	3	F		Point Petre	New Jersey	Proxy	20 Jul 1826
PERONA, Lewis	25	M	Musician	Genoa	U. States	Nimrod	31 Jul 1828
PEROT, —	30	M	Merchant	France	U. States	Ann Eliza Jane	19 Dec 1825
A., Mr.	36			France	France	Henri IV	14 Sep 1827
Christof	5	M		France	U. States	Edward Bonaffe	23 Jul 1828
Jams	2	M		France	U. States	Edward Bonaffe	23 Jul 1828
Jno. B.		M	Mercht.	France	U. States	Ann Eliza Jane	24 Sep 1823
Mary	3	F		France	U. States	Edward Bonaffe	23 Jul 1828
PERRATO, John	40	M	Mercher	U.S.	U.S.	Charleston Allen	15 Nov 1826
PERREAU, Anna M.	17	F		America	U. States	Dawn	8 Jun 1827
Charles J.	31	M		America	U. States	Dawn	8 Jun 1827
PERRECHOLAT, Augustis	31	M	Watch	France		Pallas	14 Jun 1828
Delphin	37	M	Watch	France		Pallas	14 Jun 1828
PERRERA, D.	40	M	Merchant	Portugal	New York	John and Edward	6 Jan 1824

NAMES OF PASSENGERS	AGE	SEX	OCCUPATIONS	COUNTRY TO WHICH THEY BELONG	COUNTRY THEY INTEND TO INHABIT	SHIPS/DATES OF ARRIVAL	
PERRET, A. S.	31 5/12	M	Lawyer	U.S. America	America	Erie	19 Oct 1829
PERRI, David	19	M	Shoemaker	Great Britain	U. States	Balance	19 Jun 1824
PERRIJO, Anton	35	M	Merchant	Cololumbia	Columbia	Ann	4 Mar 1826
PERRILIAT, M.	27	M	Baker	N. Orleans	N. Orleans	Stephania	7 Aug 1824
PERRIN, Paul	20	M	Gentn.	England	U. States	Trident	8 Mar 1824
Phillibert	44	M	Merchant	France	N. York	France	29 Nov 1827
Philobert	29	M	Merchant	United States	United States	Bayard	13 Nov 1823
PERRING, John	25	M	Baker	England		Marchioness	13 May 1828
PERRIT, Edwd.	21	M	Watchmaker	France	U. States	Benlomond	20 Sep 1822
John	26	M	Merchant	Scotland, Great Britain	America	Superb	11 Oct 1821
PERRO, Adel	8	F	Farmer	Corgernon	U.S. America	Superior	18 Jun 1825
Cecil	34	F	Farmer	Corgernon	U.S. America	Superior	18 Jun 1825
Ferdinand	21	M	Farmer	Corgernon	U.S. America	Superior	18 Jun 1825
Francois F.	36	M	Farmer	Corgernon	U.S. America	Superior	18 Jun 1825
Jule	3	M	Farmer	Corgernon	U.S. America	Superior	18 Jun 1825
PERRONE, Ferdinand	38	M	Merchant	Sicily		Felecita	11 Apr 1828
PERROSSIER, J.	24	M	Mariner	United States	United States	Mary	1 May 1828
PERROT, —, Mr.	36	M	Merchant	France	Halifax	La Guadaloupe	26 May 1823
—, Mrs.	23	F				La Guadaloupe	26 May 1823
Antoine S.	28	M	Merchant	France	U. States	Queen Mab	31 Jul 1826
F.	30	M	Mechanic	France	U. States	Bayard	25 Apr 1828
J. W.	27	M	Merchant	U. States	United States	Sarah G.	15 May 1828
Jno. B.	34	M	Merchant	France	U. States	Ann Eliza Jane	7 Feb 1825
Jno. W.	21	M	Merchant	United States	United States	Abigail	23 Nov 1820
John	25	M	Merchant	United States	United States	Sylvester Healy	17 Oct 1825
John	30	M	Merchant	United States	St. John, N.B.	Sylvester Healy	14 Jun 1825
John H.	26	M	Merchant	New York	New York	St. Michael's	10 Feb 1827
John W.	25	M	Merchant	New York	Great Britain	St. Michaels	12 Apr 1826
Manuel	30	M	Merchant	Guatemala	Guatemala	Favorite	9 Oct 1823
Mary	65	F	Lady	United States	United States	Sylvester Healy	17 Oct 1825
PERROTT, —, Mr.	25	M	Merchant	France	U. States	Rolla	24 Apr 1824
PERRY, —, Mrs.	27	F		England		New York	14 Jul 1827
A., Miss	22	F		Nova Scotia	U. States	William	25 Sep 1821
Ann	2			...der	England	Great Britain	7 May 1827
Benj.	32	M	Seaman	U. States	U. States	Sarah Thornton	13 Sep 1828
Benjamin	27	M	Minor	England	America	Minerva	31 May 1824
Bluss	20	M	Segar Maker	Island of Cuba	United States	Betsey	28 Oct 1825
Daniel	25	M	Farmer	Gt. Britain	U. States	Louisa Matilda	25 May 1825
Elizh.	2	F		Great Britain	United States	Ann	22 Dec 1821
James	12		boy	Ireland	United States	Abigail	25 Jun 1822
Jane	39	F	Married Woman	United States	United States	Robert Edwards	3 Oct 1829
Jas.	8	M		G. Braitan	U. States	Cosmo	29 Jun 1826
John	22	M	Farmer			Seine	10 Jun 1822
John	26	M	Merchant	Great Britain	United States	Ann	22 Dec 1821
John	27	M	Farmer	England	U.S. States	Splendid	14 Aug 1829
Joseph	4		Spinner	...der	England	Great Britain	7 May 1827
Louiza	2	F		G. Braitan	U. States	Cosmo	29 Jun 1826
Margt.	28	F		Great Britain	United States	Ann	22 Dec 1821
Megan	27	M	Weaver	France	U. States	Edward Bonaffe	23 Jul 1828
Priscilla	4	F		G. Braitan	U. States	Cosmo	29 Jun 1826
Robert	45	M	Carpenter	England	New York	Brighton	11 Dec 1827
Sarah	30	F		G. Braitan	U. States	Cosmo	29 Jun 1826
Sarah Ann	6	F		G. Braitan	U. States	Cosmo	29 Jun 1826
Wm.	9/12	M		England		New York	14 Jul 1827
Wm.	21	M	Ironworker	G. Britian	U. States	Howard	27 Jan 1825
PERRYRA, Cipriano	33	M	Sea faring man	Portugal	unknown	Juanita	13 Oct 1829
PERSAN, Cath.	30	F		France	United States	Le Voltaire	19 Jul 1828
Francoise	40	M	Farmer	France	United States	Le Voltaire	19 Jul 1828
Jean	10	F		France	United States	Le Voltaire	19 Jul 1828
Joseph	8	M		France	United States	Le Voltaire	19 Jul 1828
Marie	6	F		France	United States	Le Voltaire	19 Jul 1828
PERSER, Francis B.	16 2/12	F			New York	Marcella	18 May 1827
PERSSE, N.	13	M		Galway	U. States	Eliza Ann	30 Jul 1823
PERTER, Balthazar	1 3/12	M		France	America, U.N.S.	Great Britain	3 Aug 1829
Elizabeth	12	F		France	America, U.N.S.	Great Britain	3 Aug 1829
Elizabeth	38	F	Farmer	France	America, U.N.S.	Great Britain	3 Aug 1829
Frederick	7	M		France	America, U.N.S.	Great Britain	3 Aug 1829
G. M.	52	M	Farmer	France	America, U.N.S.	Great Britain	3 Aug 1829

NAMES OF PASSENGERS	AGE	SEX	OCCUPATIONS	COUNTRY TO WHICH THEY BELONG	COUNTRY THEY INTEND TO INHABIT	SHIPS/DATES OF ARRIVAL	
PERTER (cont'd)							
Jaquim	4	M		France	America, U.N.S.	Great Britain	3 Aug 1829
Martin	9	M		France	America, U.N.S.	Great Britain	3 Aug 1829
PERTULA, Jno.	50	M	Gentleman	U. States	U. States	Douglass	27 Jul 1825
PERUJO, Joseph H.	35	M	Merchant	Mexico	Mexico	Splendid	11 Jul 1826
PERVIS, Alexr.	66	M	Gentn.	Scotland	U. States	Silas Richards	29 Oct 1828
PERWIL, Frances	8	F		Scotland, Great Britain	America	Superb	11 Oct 1821
Helen	22	F		Scotland, Great Britain	America	Superb	11 Oct 1821
Susan	1 1/2	F		Scotland, Great Britain	America	Superb	11 Oct 1821
PERZER, Francis	23	M	Weaver	Scotland	United States	Washington	2 Oct 1828
Francis	54	M	Weaver	Scotland	United States	Washington	2 Oct 1828
Fredk.	6/12	M	Weaver	Scotland	United States	Washington	2 Oct 1828
James	23	M	Weaver	Scotland	United States	Washington	2 Oct 1828
Millecent	60	F	None	Scotland	United States	Washington	2 Oct 1828
PESARO, M.	16	M	Servant	Spain	Spain	Carpenter	3 Sep 1821
PESCATORA, Joseph	25	M	Gentleman	Prusia	Prusia	Mercator	21 Feb 1820
PESSE, —, Madam	40	F	Farmer	France	U. States	Ohio	18 Jul 1821
A., Miss	18	F		France	U. States	Ohio	18 Jul 1821
Frs. Jos.	53	M	Farmer	France	U. States	Ohio	18 Jul 1821
PESSON, Lewis	36	M	Watchmaker	France	New York	Rebecca	17 Aug 1824
Wm.	23	M		G. Britain	U. States	Canada	19 Sep 1828
PESTANA, Manuel	52	M	Taylor	Portugal	U. States	General Scott	7 May 1824
PESTEN, Christian	29	M	Farmer	Wertemberg	Wertemberg	Edward Quesnel	3 Jul 1829
John G.	2	M		Wertemberg	Wertemberg	Edward Quesnel	3 Jul 1829
Louisa Rosine	4	F		Wertemberg	Wertemberg	Edward Quesnel	3 Jul 1829
Regina	23	F		Wertemberg	Wertemberg	Edward Quesnel	3 Jul 1829
Rosina M.	1	F		Wertemberg	Wertemberg	Edward Quesnel	3 Jul 1829
PESTER, ...ward	35	M	Farmer	Great Britian	United States	Andes	19 Aug 1829
PESTINA, M.	49	M	Taylor, Merchant	Portugal	Portugal	Pomona	26 Jul 1821
PETE, Christopher	22	M		France		Pallas	14 Jun 1828
PETEL, Bernard	20	M	Farmer	France	U. States	Bayard	25 Apr 1828
PETER, Mary	40	F		G. Britain	U. States	St. George	7 Jun 1828
N.	24	M	Rope Maker	Germany	United States	Lydia	18 Jun 1828
Peter	49	M	Farmer	G. Britain	U. States	St. George	7 Jun 1828
PETERGUN, Cath.	19	F	None	France		Pallas	14 Jun 1828
Eliz.	48	M		France		Pallas	14 Jun 1828
Geo.	22	M		France		Pallas	14 Jun 1828
Jean P.	50	F	Labour	France		Pallas	14 Jun 1828
Susan		F		France		Pallas	14 Jun 1828
PETERKIN, Geo. W.	22	M	Merchant	U. States	U. States	Horatio	9 Jun 1828
PETERQUA, Jno.	22	M	Merchant	Spain	Havana	Tuscaloosa	31 Oct 1825
PETERS, Alcie	20	F	Nurse	Point Petre	New Jersey	Proxy	20 Jul 1826
Ann	35	F	Lady	Philadelphia	Philadelphia	Inspector	26 May 1828
Benjn. L.	30	M	Esquire	Saint John	St. John	Nancy	11 Apr 1822
Catharine	7	F		Switzerland	U. States	Hewes	30 Oct 1829
Catharine	32	F	His Wife [Hans]	Switzerland	U. States	Hewes	30 Oct 1829
Charles J.	54	M	Attorney General	St. Johns	St. Johns	Silvanus Jenkins	24 Jul 1828
Daniel	21	M	Cabinetmaker	Holland	U. States	Franklin	3 Jul 1820
E.	19	F		St. Johns	St. Johns	Silvanus Jenkins	24 Jul 1828
Edward John, (Sevt.)	14	M	Sevanet	Columbia	Columbia	Athenian	14 Oct 1828
George	4	M		Switzerland	U. States	Hewes	30 Oct 1829
George	24	M		France	United States	Stephania	6 Dec 1827
Ha.		M	Mariner	U. States	U. States	Atlanta	5 Jul 1821
Hans	8	M		Switzerland	U. States	Hewes	30 Oct 1829
Hans	30	M	Farmer	Switzerland	U. States	Hewes	30 Oct 1829
Harriett	23		Professor in Music	England	U.S. of America	Mary	21 Sep 1821
Henry	28	M	Painter	Prussia	United States	Montano	5 May 1828
J.	45	M	Mariner	U.S.	U. States	Diana	8 Aug 1822
James	23	M	Merchant	New Brunswick	New Brunswick	Columbia	15 Nov 1826
James	38	M	Farmer	England	New York	Brighton	9 Dec 1828
Jane	19	F	Lady	St. John	St. John	Ann Maria	19 Apr 1825
Jane	35	F		Wales	United States	Mount Vernon	9 Jun 1823
Jas.	25		Professor in Music	England	U.S. of America	Mary	21 Sep 1821
Jas., Jr.	30	M	Gentleman	St. John	St. John	Ann Maria	19 Apr 1825
John, Mast.	6	M	Smith	England	U.S.	Acasta	11 May 1827
John, Mr.	36	M	Carpenter	England	U.S.	Acasta	11 May 1827

NAMES OF PASSENGERS	AGE	SEX	OCCUPATIONS	COUNTRY TO WHICH THEY BELONG	COUNTRY THEY INTEND TO INHABIT	SHIPS/DATES OF ARRIVAL
PETERS (cont'd)						
Jos.	40	M	Gentleman	Great Brittian	Great Brittian	Governor Von Schollen 7 Nov 1827
M.	3	F		St. Johns	St. Johns	Silvanus Jenkins 24 Jul 1828
M.	27	F		St. Johns	St. Johns	Silvanus Jenkins 24 Jul 1828
Margaret	1	F		Switzerland	U. States	Hewes 30 Oct 1829
Mary	18	F	...	Switzerland	U. States	Robert Edward 2 Nov 1827
Mary, Miss	9	F	Carpenter	England	U.S.	Acasta 11 May 1827
Michael	22	M	Labourer	Ireland	United States	General Marion 6 Oct 1828
Rachel	50	F	Servant	United States	United States	James Monroe 14 Dec 1820
Sarah, Miss	12	F	Carpenter	England	U.S.	Acasta 11 May 1827
Sarah, Mrs.	3	F	Carpenter	England	U.S.	Acasta 11 May 1827
Simon	40	M	Farmer	Wales	United States	Mount Vernon 9 Jun 1823
William	32	M	Merchant	United States	United States	Elizabeth 1 Jul 1829
Wm.	21	M	Mariner	U.S.	U. States	Diana 8 Aug 1822
Wm.	32	M	Merchant	U. States	U. States	Prudence 5 Dec 1828
Wm. C.	20	M	Merchant	Great Britain	United States	Mount Vernon 17 Jun 1825
PETERSDOTER, Maria	33	F	Farmer	Norway	United States	Salem 31 Aug 1829
PETERSON, Betsey	11	F		St. Croix	U. States	Elias Burger 19 Mar 1822
Edward	28	M	Gentleman	Northumberland	La Guira	Swift 7 Apr 1827
Elizabeth	40	F	None		U. States	Hannibal 12 Oct 1829
Hy.	40	M	Mariner	U. States	U. States	Exchange 4 May 1826
J. F.	40	M	Merchant	Germany	N. Orleans	Mary 1 Nov 1824
John	28	M	Merchant	Germany	South Carolina	Arab 10 Nov 1826
Lewis	45	M	Mariner	U. States	U. States	Florida 25 Apr 1825
N. M.	36	M	Merchant	England	U. States	New York 4 Nov 1824
Olof	1 10/12	M	None		U. States	Hannibal 12 Oct 1829
Olof	45	M	Laborer	Sweden	U. States	Hannibal 12 Oct 1829
Peter	29	M	Coach Maker	Sweden	New York	Concordia 20 Oct 1829
Peter	33		Cook	Portland		Hudson 18 Jun 1825

*Officers, Seamen and Passengers belonging to the Ship Jane of Boston and taken from on board the Schooner Olive of St. Johns , N.B. on the 4th June 1825, Lat. 41.30, Long 53.19, which ship foundered on the 31st ultimo in Lat. 41.44 Long 52.

NAMES OF PASSENGERS	AGE	SEX	OCCUPATIONS	COUNTRY TO WHICH THEY BELONG	COUNTRY THEY INTEND TO INHABIT	SHIPS/DATES OF ARRIVAL
William	25	M	Merchant	Philada.	U. States	Brandt 20 Sep 1822
PETICOLE, Edward	35	M	Merchant	France	U. States	Bayard 9 Nov 1825
Jane	25	F	None	England	U. States	Bayard 9 Nov 1825
PETICOLLAS, Adolphus	30	M	Merchant	U. States	U. States	Edward Bonnaffe 4 May 1827
PETIT, A.	38	M	Merch.	France	U. States	William Bayard 2 Mar 1824
P.	37	M	Merchant	U. States	U. States	Emma 24 Jun 1822
PETITE, —, Miss	10	F	None	France	France	Caravan 1 May 1824
—, Mrs.	40	F	None	France	France	Caravan 1 May 1824
Juli	8		Husband in America	Hodbouis	Switzerland	Ann 27 Nov 1820
Margerite	45		Husband in America	Hodbouis	Switzerland	Ann 27 Nov 1820
Victor	10		Husband in America	Hodbouis	Switzerland	Ann 27 Nov 1820
PETIT JEAN,						
Amelia, & Infant	18	F		Havre	N. York	Stephania 29 Nov 1825
Auguste	33	M		Havre	N. York	Stephania 29 Nov 1825
PETITT, Bridget	20	F	None	Great Britain	United States	Eliza Barker 3 Jul 1826
PETO, A.	30	F	Merchant	Spain	Cuba	Quesnel 6 Sep 1824
Joseph	22	M	Builder	England	United States	Caspian 12 Jul 1821
Mary	23	F		England	United States	Caspian 12 Jul 1821
PETON, Placido	24	M	Hatter	France	France	Cadmus 26 Apr 1824
PETRE, Fredk.	11/12			France	U. States	Parachute 14 May 1828
George	2			France	U. States	Parachute 14 May 1828
Jacquis	6			France	U. States	Parachute 14 May 1828
Jacquis	30		Carpenter	France	U. States	Parachute 14 May 1828
John W.	52 6/12	M	Clerk	Guernsey	America	Cincinnatus 22 May 1826
Madeline	32			France	U. States	Parachute 14 May 1828
Richard	16 7/12	M	Clerk	England	America	Cincinnatus 22 May 1826
William	12 6/12	M		England	America	Cincinnatus 22 May 1826
PETREE, Andrew	19	M	Farmer	Great Britan	U. States	Ann Marria 6 Aug 1823
George	25	M	M...t	Great Britain	United States	Robert Fulton 18 May 1825
PETRI, Caroline	4 6/12	F		Baden	United States	Jason 3 Nov 1828
Magdalena	5 6/12	F		Baden	United States	Jason 3 Nov 1828
Magdalene	29	F		Baden	United States	Jason 3 Nov 1828
Michael	36	M		Baden	United States	Jason 3 Nov 1828
PETRIE, John	18	M	Gardner	Scotland	America	Eyder 7 Aug 1826
PETTEGREW, John	20	M	Baker	Halifax	U. States	Greek 8 Mar 1828
PETTEN, John	34	M		United States	United States	General Jackson 22 May 1826

NAMES OF PASSENGERS	AGE	SEX	OCCUPATIONS	COUNTRY TO WHICH THEY BELONG	COUNTRY THEY INTEND TO INHABIT	SHIPS/DATES OF ARRIVAL	
PETTES, D.	7			England	U. States	Unity	5 Sep 1828
Harriet	14	F		England	U. States	Unity	5 Sep 1828
J.	16			England	U. States	Unity	5 Sep 1828
James	3	M		England	U. States	Unity	5 Sep 1828
Jason	32	F		England	U. States	Unity	5 Sep 1828
Jesse	40	M	Farmer	England	U. States	Unity	5 Sep 1828
John	19	M		England	U. States	Unity	5 Sep 1828
Levi	1	M		England	U. States	Unity	5 Sep 1828
Philli	9	M		England	U. States	Unity	5 Sep 1828
William	11	M		England	U. States	Unity	5 Sep 1828
PETTET, James	26	M	Farmer	Great Britain	United States	Washington	3 Sep 1827
Michl.	18	M	Farmer	Great Britain	United States	Washington	3 Sep 1827
PETTICHEW, John	22	M	Gardener	Scotland	United States	Samuel Robertson	9 May 1827
PETTIE, —, Mr.	21	M	None	G. Britain	Canada	Corinthian	29 Apr 1826
PETTIGREW, George R.	20	M	Merchant	Belfast	United States	Nancy Henrietta	3 Nov 1828
PETTIGROW, Robt.	22	M	Joiner	Scotland	United States	Tom	2 Jul 1827
PETTINOS, P.	32	M	Merchant	Philadelphia	U. States	Don Quixote	14 Aug 1826
Peter	31	M	Merchant	United States		Cincinnatus	29 Apr 1822
PETTIS, John	25	M	Merchant	England	United States	Columbia	16 Jan 1829
Thos.	25	M		England	United States	Columbia	16 Jan 1829
PETTIT, Angelio	21 5/12	F	Joiner	France	U. States	France	26 Jun 1828
Cathr.	2	F		G. Britain	U. States	Leavitts	25 Aug 1828
Charles	28	M	Merchant	Philada.	U. States	Catharine	22 Jan 1822
Chas.	30	M	Mercht.	United States	United States	Eliza	12 Jul 1822
Elizabeth	38	F	Lady	England	England	Manhattan	12 May 1823
James	32	M	Labourer	G. Britain	U. States	Leavitts	25 Aug 1828
John	27	M	Merchant	U.S. of Am.	United States	Silas Richards	20 Jun 1826
Mary	16	F		Gt. Britain		Dalhouse Castle	13 May 1828
Mary	28	F		G. Britain	U. States	Leavitts	25 Aug 1828
Richard	35	M	Merchant	England	England	Manhattan	12 May 1823
Thos.	1	M		G. Britain	U. States	Leavitts	25 Aug 1828
PETZHORN, —, Child	1	F		Hamburg	N. York	Howard	18 Jan 1826
Johan Christofer	24	M	Blacksmith	Hamburg	N. York	Howard	18 Jan 1826
Johana Honrila Mariane	18	F		Hamburg	N. York	Howard	18 Jan 1826
PEUGNET, Jean G.	60	M	None	France	U. States	Sully	15 Jul 1829
L., Mr.	35	M	Instructor	France		François I	19 Nov 1828
Lewis D.	30	M	Formerly Officer of the French Armey	France	Canada	Olympia	2 Sep 1823
Natalie	55	F	Lady	France	U. States	Sully	15 Jul 1829
T.	25	M	Farmer	France	U. States	Quesnel	6 Sep 1824
Theophile	29	M	Teacher	France	U. States	Sully	15 Jul 1829
PEW, Thomas	28	M	Farmer	Ireland	United States	Dublin Packet	6 Dec 1827
PEWART, William, Mr.	25	M	Merchant	Great Britain	Great Britain	Nestor	3 Nov 1820
PEWE, J. H.	36	M	Tradesman	Germany	Uncertain	Ocean	30 Jun 1821
PEWER, Richd.	37	M	Labourer	Great Britain	United States	William Dawson	18 Jun 1827
PEWLING, Betty	1	F	None	England	United States	Trident	18 Jul 1827
John	2	M	None	England	United States	Trident	18 Jul 1827
Jonathan	27	M	Farmer	England	United States	Trident	18 Jul 1827
Martha	24	F	None	England	United States	Trident	18 Jul 1827
Nancy	4	M	None	England	United States	Trident	18 Jul 1827
PEXOTTO, —, Dr.	23	M	Physician	New York	U. States	Cleo	22 May 1822
PEXTON, Edward	1	M		Great Britain	United States	Freake	25 Aug 1829
Elizabeth	30	F		Great Britain	United States	Freake	25 Aug 1829
Henry	6/52	M		Great Britain	United States	Freake	25 Aug 1829
William	29	M	Farmer	Great Britain	United States	Freake	25 Aug 1829
PEYTIM, Phillipe	25	M	Merchant	Switzerland	United States	Olympia	20 Aug 1829
PEYTON, Alexr.	30	M	Manufacturer	Ireland	U. States	William Byrnes	17 Jul 1825
Ann V., Miss	11 6/12	F		U. States	U. States	Circassian	26 Jun 1823
Craven	9 10/12	M		U. States	U. States	Circassian	26 Jun 1823
M.	1	F		Ireland	U. States	John Jay	17 Sep 1828
M.	29	F		Ireland	U. States	John Jay	17 Sep 1828
Margt.	20	F		Ireland	U. States	William Byrnes	17 Jul 1825
Walter	30	M	Merchant	Ireland	U. States	John Jay	17 Sep 1828
PEZE, Charles	37	M	Merchant	France	U. States	Edward Bonnaffe	4 May 1827
PFEIFFER, Charles	29 2/12	M	Planter	Germeny	Mexico	Native	19 Sep 1826
PFISTER, Alex W.	56	M	Merchant	U. States	U. States	Marmion	30 Apr 1828

NAMES OF PASSENGERS	AGE	SEX	OCCUPATIONS	COUNTRY TO WHICH THEY BELONG	COUNTRY THEY INTEND TO INHABIT	SHIPS/DATES OF ARRIVAL	
PFISTER (cont'd)							
Chas. A. V.	20	M	Merchant	U. States	U. States	Marmion	30 Apr 1828
PFREANIGLE, John	18	M	Agriculturist	France	U.S.	Helen	3 May 1828
PHA...ON, Michael	26	M	None	Great Britain	United States	Eliza Barker	3 Jul 1826
PHALAN, Chrisr.	23	M	Labourer	Ireland	U. States	Hope & Esther	22 Jul 1825
Michl.	25	M	Labourer	Ireland	U. States	Hope & Esther	22 Jul 1825
PHALEN, Richd.	18	M	Labourer	Ireland	U. States	Lady Hunter	9 Oct 1825
PHALIN, John	29	M	Carpenter	Ireland	United States	Lady Hunter	27 Dec 1825
PHARSON, Wm.	21	M	Labourer	Ireland	United States	General Putnam	20 Jun 1825
PHE..., —	12	F	Servent	New York	New York	Native	30 Jun 1826
PHEABEN, Mary	22	F		England	U. States	Pacific	17 Jun 1828
PHEHELE, An	18	F				Superb	18 Jul 1820
PHELAN, ...	...	F		Ireland	U.S.	Hibernia	27 Jun 1821
...	9	M		Ireland	U.S.	Hibernia	27 Jun 1821
...n.	16	F		Ireland	U.S.	Hibernia	27 Jun 1821
Catherine	3	F	Farmer	Ireland		Manhattan	20 Jun 1826
Catherine	26	F	Spinster	Ireland	United States	Dublin Packet	28 Apr 1824
Daniel	30	M	Gardner	Ireland	United States	Dublin Packet	28 Apr 1824
James	2	M	Child	Ireland	United States	Dublin Packet	28 Apr 1824
John	3	M	Farmer	Ireland	New York State	Manhattan	20 Jun 1826
John	7	M		Great Brittian	United States	Carolina Augusta	2 Dec 1828
John	22	M	Labourer	Ireland	United States	Robert Fulton	24 Jul 1826
Judith	45	F	Servant	Ireland	America	Josephine	24 Jul 1826
Lawrence	46	M	Labourer	Ireland	America	Dewitt Clinton	27 Jul 1824
Margaret	26	F	Matron	Great Britain	United States	Wilson	26 Feb 1824
Margaret	30	F	Farmer	Ireland	New York State	Manhattan	20 Jun 1826
Maria	5	F		Great Brittian	United States	Carolina Augusta	2 Dec 1828
Mary	30	F		Great Brittian	United States	Carolina Augusta	2 Dec 1828
Mary	infant	F	infant	Ireland	United States	Dublin Packet	28 Apr 1824
Patt	28	M	Mason	Ireland	New York	Hope & Esther	21 Dec 1827
Timothy	23	M	Farmer	Ireland	U. States	Hibernia	29 Nov 1821
PHELANY, Dennis	22	M	Merchant	France	U. States	Traveller	2 Jun 1822
PHELEGA, And.	25	M	Merchant	Spain	Havana	Tuscaloosa	31 Oct 1825
PHELP, Ann	22	F		England	United States	Dalhouse Castle	8 May 1827
PHELPS, —, Mrs.	32	F		America	U. States	Florida	13 Feb 1823
Charles	30	M	Planter	Boston	Boston	Admittance	8 Mar 1826
Henrietta Persom	18	F		United States	United States	Romulus	13 Aug 1829
Henry	35	M	Merchant	U. States	U. States	Bunker Hill	25 Jun 1827
J.	12	M	Merchant	St. Domingo	U. States	Rover	11 Jun 1823
James	32	M	Merchant	Connecticutt	U. States	Mark	14 Oct 1824
John	9	M		America	U. States	Florida	13 Feb 1823
Maria, Mrs.	26	F	Lady	U. States	New York	Robert Fulton	22 May 1824
Royal, Jr.	20	M	Merchant	U. States	U. States	Milton	20 Aug 1827
Saml. B., Lieut.	25	M	Lieutenant	U. States	U. States	Brutus	3 Feb 1827
Sarah	17	F	Servt. to Mrs. Candler	United States	United States	Venus	8 Sep 1820
Susan	7	F		America	U. States	Florida	13 Feb 1823
Timothy	18	M	Merchant	U. States	U. States	Bunker Hill	25 Jun 1827
Wm.	56	M	Merchant	England	England	Albion	4 Oct 1820
PHENEY, Betsey	3	F		Ireland	U. States	Wanderer	1 Sep 1828
Biddy	40	F		Ireland	U. States	Wanderer	1 Sep 1828
Debly	30	F		Ireland	U. States	Wanderer	1 Sep 1828
Eliza	14	F		Ireland	U. States	Wanderer	1 Sep 1828
Ellen	17	F		Ireland	U. States	Wanderer	1 Sep 1828
John	8	M		Ireland	U. States	Wanderer	1 Sep 1828
John	57	M	Barber	Ireland	U. States	Wanderer	1 Sep 1828
Patrick	16	M		Ireland	U. States	Wanderer	1 Sep 1828
Rosana	19	F		Ireland	U. States	Wanderer	1 Sep 1828
PHERIDSOD, Lawrence	27	M	Surgeon	New York	U. States	Pacific	20 Aug 1825
PHERNMAN, Jacob Fredk.	23	M		Germany	America	Falcon	28 Aug 1828
PHEWLES, George	23	M	Gardner	England	America	Panthia	17 Sep 1821
PHEYAN, Thomas	20	M	Brazier	England	America	Two Marys	24 Sep 1827
PHIAL, Ann	20	F	Wife	Ireland	United States	Ann Maria	21 May 1827
Matthew	26	M	Wheelwright	Ireland	United States	Ann Maria	21 May 1827
Wm.	9	M	Child	Ireland	United States	Ann Maria	21 May 1827

NAMES OF PASSENGERS	AGE	SEX	OCCUPATIONS	COUNTRY TO WHICH THEY BELONG	COUNTRY THEY INTEND TO INHABIT	SHIPS/DATES OF ARRIVAL	
PHIBBOY, John	45		Farmer	England	United States	Hudson	5 Apr 1826
PHIBBS, James	40	M	carpenter	Ireland	U. States	Champion	26 Jul 1827
PHIBURY, D.	30	M	Merchant	Paris	Jacqumel	Orion	30 Mar 1825
PHIELS, Pat	30	M		Gt. Britain	United States	Penelope	9 Sep 1828
PHILAGRET, Jos.	19	M	Jewellry	Marseilles	U. States	Conveyance	9 Feb 1825
PHILAN, Jno.	21	M	Farmer	Great Britain	New York	Dublin	21 Dec 1824
PHILARY, —	25	M	Merchant	France	U. States	Ductile	11 Feb 1822
PHILBERY, Caroline	21			England	England	Hudson	14 Jun 1827
PHILIBERT, M.	35	F	Merchant	France	U. States	Edward Quesnel	15 May 1826
PHILIP, —	26	M	Hairdresser	U. States	U. States	Imperial	10 Dec 1821
Ann	50	F	Servant	Ireland	U. States	Henrietta	7 Jul 1825
George	18	M	Agricultural	France	United States	Stephania	24 Mar 1828
Jane	29	F	Servant	Ireland	U. States	Henrietta	7 Jul 1825
Jean	32	M	his family [Amst. Godefman]	Germany	United States	Wm. Osborne	16 Sep 1828
PHILIPE, —,							
Wife [of Y.]	35	F		France	United States	Cavalier	25 Jul 1828
—, Wife [of B.]	45	F		France	United States	Cavalier	25 Jul 1828
B.	56	M	Labourer	France	United States	Cavalier	25 Jul 1828
Catherine	3	F		France	United States	Cavalier	25 Jul 1828
Cathr.	12	F		France	United States	Cavalier	25 Jul 1828
Jacob	22	M	Farmer	Switzerland	United States	Olympia	12 Aug 1828
Joseph	5	M		France	United States	Cavalier	25 Jul 1828
Louisa	18	F	Farmer	Switzerland	United States	Olympia	12 Aug 1828
Louise	1	F		France	United States	Cavalier	25 Jul 1828
Magdelina	18	F		France	United States	Cavalier	25 Jul 1828
Mariane	9	F		France	United States	Cavalier	25 Jul 1828
Michael	5	M		France	United States	Cavalier	25 Jul 1828
Philip	15	M		France	United States	Cavalier	25 Jul 1828
Philipe	7	F		France	United States	Cavalier	25 Jul 1828
Threse	1	F		France	United States	Cavalier	25 Jul 1828
Threse	9	F		France	United States	Cavalier	25 Jul 1828
Y.	37	M	Labourer	France	United States	Cavalier	25 Jul 1828
PHILIPPE, Leon	31	M	Architect	France	United States	Galaxy	17 Feb 1824
Masse	24	M	Baker	France	U. States	Howard	21 Aug 1826
Michael	32	M	Painter	France	United States	American	27 Aug 1827
PHILIPPEANE, John Francois	26	M		France	United States	Stephania	4 Aug 1826
PHILIPPS, Catharine	26		None	Ireland	New York	Albion	11 Oct 1821
Isaac	28 2/12	M	distressed seaman	Philadelphia	United States	Florida	27 Aug 1825
Thos.	41		Professor Music	England	New York	Albion	11 Oct 1821
PHILIPS, Alexander	32	M	Merchant	Germany	Baltimore	Stephania	13 Mar 1820
Ann	28	F		G. Britain	U. States	Mary & Harriot	8 Sep 1828
Caroline	11	F		G. Britain	U. States	Mary & Harriot	8 Sep 1828
Edward	25	M	Glass Blower	England	United States	Justina	5 Aug 1823
James	...	...	...	...	...	St. Michael	22 Sep 1824
Jno., Junr.	27	M	Mercht.	U. States	U. States	Henri IV	3 Feb 1829
John	30	F	Farmer	G. Britain	U. States	Mary & Harriot	8 Sep 1828
Lydia	6	F	...	...	...	St. Michael	22 Sep 1824
Margaret	4...	...	...	...	...	St. Michael	22 Sep 1824
Margret	22	F	Servant	Ireland	United States	Henry Kneeland	7 Jun 1828
Michael	36	M	Fiddler	United States	United States	Globe	30 Aug 1828
Nancy	22	F	Spinster	Ireland	United States	St. Michaels	23 Dec 1826
Philip	9	M		G. Britain	U. States	Mary & Harriot	8 Sep 1828
Saml. R.	32	M	Merchant	England	Great Brittan	Amity	11 May 1821
Thomas	...	...	...	...	...	St. Michael	22 Sep 1824
Thos.	27	M	Mariner	U. States	U. States	Prince Edward	5 Jul 1825
Wh.	5	M		G. Britain	U. States	Mary & Harriot	8 Sep 1828
PHILIP SON, G. T.	37	M	Slingman	Havre	Montreale	Edward Bonaffe	23 Jul 1828
PHILIPSON, A.	19	M	Merchant	Holland	U. States	Resign	20 Oct 1821
A.	25 4/12	M	Merchant	United States	United States	Potomac	29 Oct 1828
Abraham	24	M	Merchant	U.S. of A.	U.S. of A.	Monmouth	17 Nov 1826
Jacob	46	M	Merchant	Germany	United States	Brandt	26 Jun 1826
PHILLIP, Anna	32	F		Germany	United States	Samuel Robertson	8 Aug 1828
Anna M.	7	F		Germany	United States	Samuel Robertson	8 Aug 1828
Charles	44		Farmer	America	America	Courier	24 Jul 1820
Francis F.	38	M	hair Dresser	France	U. States	Bayard	19 Mar 1824

NAMES OF PASSENGERS	AGE	SEX	OCCUPATIONS	COUNTRY TO WHICH THEY BELONG	COUNTRY THEY INTEND TO INHABIT	SHIPS/DATES OF ARRIVAL	
PHILLIP (cont'd)							
Johanas	3	F		Germany	United States	Samuel Robertson	8 Aug 1828
Johannas	6	F		Germany	United States	Samuel Robertson	8 Aug 1828
Joseph	13	M		Germany	United States	Samuel Robertson	8 Aug 1828
Joseph	34	M	Wheelwright	Germany	United States	Samuel Robertson	8 Aug 1828
M., Mr.	8	M	None	France	U. States	Bayard	9 Jul 1824
Magdalain	5	F		Germany	United States	Samuel Robertson	8 Aug 1828
Maria	36	F		Germany	United States	Samuel Robertson	8 Aug 1828
Marian	6/12	F		Germany	United States	Samuel Robertson	8 Aug 1828
Raky	10	M		Germany	United States	Samuel Robertson	8 Aug 1828
Wm.	30	M	Merchant	England	England	Pacific	17 Jun 1828
PHILLIPE,							
Pauline Anestana	34 8/12	F	Seamstress	France	Philadelphia	Cadmus	27 Aug 1822
PHILLIPOTTS, Thomas	36	M	Merchant	Great Britain	Jamaica	Nestor	6 Jul 1821
PHILLIPPOW, Henry	30	M	Mercht.	France	France	Manchester	17 Aug 1825
PHILLIPS, —	12	M	Moulder	Gt. Britain	New York	Columbia	3 Apr 1826
—, Miss	12	F	None	America	America	Hercules	5 Sep 1826
—, Mr.	31	M	Merchant	England	U.S.A.	Bayard	25 Aug 1829
—, Mrs.	30	F	Lady	England	U.S.A.	Bayard	25 Aug 1829
A., Miss	12	F	None	France	U. States	Bayard	9 Jul 1824
Addey, Mrs.	27	F	Lady	Gt. Britain		Corinthian	27 Oct 1829
Alex	17	F	Servant	Ireland	United States	Carolina Ann	14 May 1827
Amelia		F	Servant	England	England	Tontine	1 Jun 1826
Ann	7	F				Cassack	25 Jul 1820
Ann	7	F		Gt. Britain		Corinthian	27 Oct 1829
Anthony	15	M		United States	United States	Globe	30 Aug 1828
Catharine	10		her child [Nancy]	Ireland	U. States	Xenophon	28 May 1822
Catharine	30	F	None	Great Britian	United States	Diamond	8 Nov 1824
Catherine	16	F	Servant	Ireland	United States	Carolina Ann	14 May 1827
Charles	11	M	her son [Elizabeth]	Great Britain	United States	Assiduous	30 Jul 1822
Daniel	35	M	Stock Broker	England	United States	Acasta	14 Jun 1824
Danl.	45	M	Shoemaker			John Dickinson	14 Sep 1820
Davis	8	M		Wales	United States	William & Henry	19 Jul 1822
E., Mr.	20	M	Merchant	London	U. States	United States	29 Nov 1823
Eliza	16	F		Gt. Britain		Corinthian	27 Oct 1829
Eliza	23	F		Great Britton	U. State	Earl of Liverpool	16 Aug 1826
Elizab.	5	F				Cassack	25 Jul 1820
Elizabeth	17	F	Servant to Miss Kotch	G. Britain	U.S. America	Cincinnatus	31 Oct 1820
Elizabeth	38	F		Gt. Britain		Corinthian	27 Oct 1829
Elizabeth	45	F	Farmers wife	Great Britain	United States	Assiduous	30 Jul 1822
Esthr.	26	F				Cassack	25 Jul 1820
F., Mrs.	32	F	None	France	U. States	Bayard	9 Jul 1824
Fanny	2	F				Cassack	25 Jul 1820
Geor.	39	M	Gentleman	England	U.S. America	Criterion	27 Oct 1821
George	5	M		Gt. Britain		Corinthian	27 Oct 1829
George	17	M		Gt. Britain		Corinthian	27 Oct 1829
Hardman	37	M	Farmer	Great Britain	United States	Cortes	19 Nov 1821
Hugh	40	M	Moulder	Gt. Britain	New York	Columbia	3 Apr 1826
Isaac	23	M	Merchant	England	America	Ann	3 Jul 1820
Israel	22	M	Merchant	Germany	U. States	Birmingham	16 Jun 1828
James	1	M		Gt. Britain		Corinthian	27 Oct 1829
James	20	M	Merchant	England	U. States	Trimmer	10 Jul 1824
James	32	M	Mechanic	U. States	U. States	Tampico	2 Aug 1828
James Wm.	30	M	D.D.	England	U.S.A.	Orator	1 Oct 1829
John	6	M	None	Great Britian	United States	Diamond	8 Nov 1824
John	9	M		England	U.S. America	Criterion	27 Oct 1821
John	13	M		Gt. Britain		Corinthian	27 Oct 1829
John	26	M	Labourer	Wales		Marchioness	13 May 1828

NAMES OF PASSENGERS	AGE	SEX	OCCUPATIONS	COUNTRY TO WHICH THEY BELONG	COUNTRY THEY INTEND TO INHABIT	SHIPS/DATES OF ARRIVAL	
PHILLIPS (cont'd)							
John	40	M	Clerk	Great Britian	United States	Diamond	8 Nov 1824
John	40	M	Farmer	Ireland	United States	Josephine	30 Apr 1828
John W.	30		U.N.S. Army	U.N.S.		Hudson	5 Apr 1826
Joseph	18			London/London	New York	Venus	12 Apr 1821
Joseph	29	M	Mariner	Ireland	U. States	Champion	26 Jul 1827
Judas	15	F	Servant	Ireland	United States	Carolina Ann	14 May 1827
Lyon	36 4/12	M	Merchant	United States	Philadelphia	Venus	8 Sep 1820
Margaret	4		her child [Nancy]	Ireland	U. States	Xenophon	28 May 1822
Margaret	22	F	None	Wales		Marchioness	13 May 1828
Maria	24	F		Wales	United States	William & Henry	19 Jul 1822
Martha	30	F		Ireland	United States	Josephine	30 Apr 1828
Mary	4	F	None	Great Britian	United States	Diamond	8 Nov 1824
Mary	12		her child [Nancy]	Ireland	U. States	Xenophon	28 May 1822
Mary	14	F		England	U.S. America	Criterion	27 Oct 1821
Mary	25	F		Irereland	America	Carolina Ann	20 Jun 1825
Mary	30	F	Labourer	Gt. Britain	U. States	Panthea	21 Jul 1825
Mary	30	F	Seamstress	United States	United States	Globe	30 Aug 1828
Mary	33	F		England	U.S. America	Criterion	27 Oct 1821
Mary Ann	17	F	her daughter [Elizabeth]	Great Britain	United States	Assiduous	30 Jul 1822
Michael	12	M	...	Ireland	United States	Carolina Ann	14 May 1827
Nancy	36		Spinster	Ireland	U. States	Xenophon	28 May 1822
P., Mr.	6	M	None	France	U. States	Bayard	9 Jul 1824
Patk.	25	M	Laboror	Ireland	United States	Wilson	27 Jun 1826
Peggy	20	F	Servant	Wales	U. States	Harmony	12 Jul 1821
Phillip	19	M	Labourer	Ireland	United States	Carolina Ann	14 May 1827
R.	37	M	Mercht.	England	U. States	Pacific	20 Aug 1825
Robert	8		her child [Nancy]	Ireland	U. States	Xenophon	28 May 1822
Robert	40	M	Merchant	Philadelphia	Philadelphia	New York	31 Jul 1829
Robt.	34	M		America	America	Manhattan	12 May 1823
Sarah	11	F		Gt. Britain		Corinthian	27 Oct 1829
Sarah	26	F	None	Wales		Marchioness	13 May 1828
Sharlotte	5	F		England	U.S. America	Criterion	27 Oct 1821
Simeon	26	M	Brickmaker	Great Britain	U. States	Great Britain	18 Mar 1828
Sophia	20	F		G. Britain	U. States	John Jay	17 Sep 1828
Sophia	34	F	None	Great Britain	United States	Cortes	19 Nov 1821
Susan	4	F	her daughter [Elizabeth]	Great Britain	United States	Assiduous	30 Jul 1822
Susanah	68	F		Wales	United States	William & Henry	19 Jul 1822
Thomas	7/12	M	Labourer	England	United States	Dalhouse Castle	8 May 1827
Thomas	6	M	her son [Elizabeth]	Great Britain	United States	Assiduous	30 Jul 1822
Thomas	9	M		Gt. Britain		Corinthian	27 Oct 1829
Thomas	22	M	Labourer	Wales		Marchioness	13 May 1828
Thomas	25	M	Farmer	Ireland	United States	Asia	29 Jul 1829
Thomas	29	M	Mariner	U. States	U. States	Fourth of July	19 Oct 1824
Thomas	29	M	Loom Maker	Great Britain	U.S. of America	Gratitude	3 Oct 1829
Thomas	30	M	Mariner	U. States	U. States	Agenora	23 Aug 1827
Thos.	22	M	Carpenter	U. States	U. States	Rodman	28 May 1825
Thos.	25	M	Plumber	England	New York	James Cropper	16 Oct 1826
William	26		no occupation	London/London	New York	Venus	12 Apr 1821
William	44	M	Teacher (arts &c)	Gt. Britain		Corinthian	27 Oct 1829
William	72	M	Stone Cutter	Wales	United States	William & Henry	19 Jul 1822
Wm.	9	M				Cassack	25 Jul 1820
Wm.	27	M				Cassack	25 Jul 1820
Wm.	40	M	Merchant	U. States	U. States	Emblem	14 May 1827
PHILLIPSON, James	21	M	Merchant	Boston	U. States	Franklin	6 May 1828
PHILLY, Charles, Mr.	18	M	Painter	England	U. States	Acasta	11 Dec 1826
PHILPOT, Jno.	65	M	Mechanic	N. Scotia	U. States	Infant	10 Jul 1821
Wm.	31	M	Merchant	Great Britain	United States	John Jay	8 May 1828
PHILPS, Saml. B.	25	M	U.S. Navy	U. States	U. States	Nancy	5 Sep 1821
PHILTRAM, John	32	M	Servant	Colombia	St. Domingo	Bogota	28 Mar 1827
PHINEY, —, Mrs.	25	F		U. States	Cuba	Criterion	9 Aug 1826
Wm.	22	M	Labourer			Hanford	17 Jul 1828
Wm. T.	50	M	Planter	U. States	Cuba	Criterion	9 Aug 1826
PHINNEY, D.	3	F		U. States	Cuba	Criterion	9 Aug 1826

NAMES OF PASSENGERS	AGE	SEX	OCCUPATIONS	COUNTRY TO WHICH THEY BELONG	COUNTRY THEY INTEND TO INHABIT	SHIPS/DATES OF ARRIVAL	
PHINNEY (cont'd)							
M.	5	F		U. States	Cuba	Criterion	9 Aug 1826
S.	1	F		U. States	Cuba	Criterion	9 Aug 1826
PHIPPS, Hira	21	M	Farmer	England	America	Francis & Henrietta	11 Jul 1823
PHIQUEPAL, Wm.	44	M	Professor	France	U.S.	Cadmus	20 Dec 1824
PHOENIX, J. P.	27	M	Merchant	New York	U. States	William Thompson	6 Sep 1822
PHYTHEAN, John B.	25	M	Surgeon	Great Britain	United States	Robert Fulton	22 Oct 1821
PIBMAN, Jean	25	M		France	United States	La Flora	30 Jun 1828
PICA, Pedro	48	M	Merchant	Spain	Spain	Angelina	17 Sep 1827
PICABIA, Bartolomo	22	M	Mercht.	Campeache	Campeache	Emma	14 Oct 1825
B. P.	23	M	Merchant	Spain	United States	Burdett	30 Apr 1828
PICABRA, Bw.	22	M	Merchant	Spain	France	Greek	19 May 1826
PICALEZ, B. M.	23	M	Merchant	Spain	U. States	Dromo	19 Jul 1827
PICARD, —, Mr.	23	M	Merchant	Spain	U. States	Cadmus	12 Apr 1825
F.	25	M	Merchant	America		Spark	17 Sep 1821
Jno. R.	25 1/12	M	M...	...	...	Quito	9 Jul 1823
P. H.	19	M	Negotient	France	U. States	Montano	23 Apr 1825
W.	22	M	Merchant	Spain	France & Spain	Native	24 Aug 1825
PICE, Thos. L.	19	M	Mechanics	England	United States	Yobah	26 Sep 1827
PICEO, Jos.	23	M	Merchant	Spain	Spain	Native	8 Feb 1826
PICHARDO, Esteban	26		Lawyer	Havana	Havana	Don Quixote	19 Aug 1825
PICHARRY, John	34	M	Mercht.	France	United States	Rapid	24 Oct 1823
PICKARD, Felix	23	M	Marchant	N. York	U. States	Commodore Perry	9 Apr 1821
PICKENPACK, James	27	M	Brewer	Hanoverran	United States	Constitution	2 Aug 1826
PICKERING, ...	32	M				Eliza Grant	6 Oct 1828
Ann	17	F		England	United States	Hudson	17 Mar 1828
Jas.	18	M	Paper Maker	Great Brittain	United States	Nimrod	9 Jan 1827
John	24	M	Merchant	Great Britain	United States	Mary & Harriet	3 Jul 1829
PICKFORD, Mary	28	F		New York	New York	Cincinnatus	5 Dec 1825
PICKLE, Paul	25	M	Labourer	G. Britain	U. States	Sarah G	5 Jun 1828
PICKRESS, Henry	33	M	Farmer	England	England	William Thompson	19 Aug 1829
PICKWICK, L.	40	M	Clothier	G. Britain	Canada	Cosmo	25 Nov 1826
PICOLET, Allustine	8	F		France		Roanoke	21 May 1828
Julia	26	F		France		Roanoke	21 May 1828
Ruguel	30	M	Merchant	France		Roanoke	21 May 1828
PICOT,							
Ch. M. Jr. Laurot	29	M	Clergman	France	U. States	Edward Bonaffe	23 Jul 1828
PICQUOT, Octavia	1 2/12	F	None	France	France	Monroe	18 May 1827
PIDERAN, M., Mr.	37	M	Farmer	Marseilles	N. Orleans	Superior	30 Apr 1824
PIDGEON, Bridget	4			Ireland		Anacreon	7 Sep 1827
Cathe.	38			Ireland		Anacreon	7 Sep 1827
George	30	M	Merchant	England	United States	Hanford	3 Aug 1829
James	6/12			Ireland		Anacreon	7 Sep 1827
Michael	2			Ireland		Anacreon	7 Sep 1827
Pat	6			Ireland		Anacreon	7 Sep 1827
Pat	35			Ireland		Anacreon	7 Sep 1827
Thos.	10			Ireland		Anacreon	7 Sep 1827
Wm.	32	M	Merchant	U. States	U. States	Gertrude	12 Aug 1826
PIERA, Domengos	40	M	Merchant	Portugal	U. States	Richard	26 Jun 1823
PIERCE, Daniel H.	25		Surgeon	U.N.S.		Hudson	5 Apr 1826
Elizabeth	31	F	...	England	U. States	Radius	16 Mar 1822
Hannah	50	F	Lady	United States	United States	Sarah	31 Oct 1829
Jno. A., Captn.	23	M	...	... York	United States	Abeona	26 Jun 1824
John	23	M	Sculptor	England	United States	Manhattan	24 Oct 1825
John	23	M	Farmer	G. Britain	G. Britain	Brittania	17 Jul 1828
John	30	M	Labourer	England	Pittsburgh	Orozimbo	8 Jun 1822
Stephen	38		Attorney At Law	New York	New York	Albion	11 Oct 1821
Thos.	25	M	Labourer	England	Pittsburgh	Orozimbo	8 Jun 1822
PIERCEY, John	27	M	Farmer	Great Britain	United States	Ann Maria	12 Jul 1821
PIERCY, Isabella	24	F	Spinster	Ireland	New Jersey	Carolina Ann	15 Oct 1824
Margaret, Child	1	F		Ireland	New Jersey	Carolina Ann	15 Oct 1824
Robert, Child	2	M		Ireland	New Jersey	Carolina Ann	15 Oct 1824
PIERIS, Joseph	40	M	Merchant	Switzerland		Charlemagne	20 Aug 1829
PIEROT, Jh.	34			Suisse		Deux Ernest	29 Dec 1827

*son épouse & 3 enfans [his wife and three children]

NAMES OF PASSENGERS	AGE	SEX	OCCUPATIONS	COUNTRY TO WHICH THEY BELONG	COUNTRY THEY INTEND TO INHABIT	SHIPS/DATES OF ARRIVAL	
PIERRA, Sarason	25	M	Merchant	Vera Cruz	France	Independence	25 Oct 1828
PIERRAR, Pedro	35	M	Musician	Spain	United States	Georgetown Packet	15 Nov 1823
PIERRE, C.	32	M	Gentleman	Frances	United States	Maria Theresa	28 Aug 1821
Leroy Jean	30	M	Mariner	France	France	Ann Eliza	2 May 1828
Mignot J.	25	M	Merchant	France	United States	Reaper	31 Aug 1826
O.	34	M	Lock Smith	G. Britain		Caravan	8 Sep 1828
Royal	23		Merchant	New York	United States	Triumph	23 Jul 1829
PIERRET, Jean	17	M	Merchant	Paris	France	Bayard	30 Oct 1820
Jean	18		Mercht.	U.S.	France	Brandt	7 Feb 1822
Louis	18	M	Merchant	Paris	France	Bayard	30 Oct 1820
PIERROT, Eugene *landed in New York	7	M		Swisse	United States	Deux Ernest	29 Dec 1827
Joseph *landed in New York	34	M		Swisse	United States	Deux Ernest	29 Dec 1827
Julia *landed in New York	5	F		Swisse	United States	Deux Ernest	29 Dec 1827
Julina 2 6/12 *landed in New York		M		Swisse	United States	Deux Ernest	29 Dec 1827
Veronique 3.18/365 *landed in New York		F		Swisse	United States	Deux Ernest	29 Dec 1827
Veroniquy *landed in New York	27	M		Swisse	United States	Deux Ernest	29 Dec 1827
PIERS, Alexander	25	M	Miller	Hollingsgreen	Hollingsgreen	Howard Douglass	11 May 1827
Thos. M.	16	M		...	U. States	Governor Tompkins	26 Jul 1824
PIERSON, A. J.	30	M	Merchant	England	U. States	Falcon	12 Oct 1822
Ann Marston	29	F		United States	United States	Maria	12 May 1823
Charles E.	33	M	Physician	United States	United States	Maria	12 May 1823
Christian	3		Child of Janet Pierson	Aberdeen, Scotd.	State of New York	Albion	5 Feb 1822
Clara Ann	5	F		United States	United States	Maria	12 May 1823
Eleanor	20	F	Servant	England	United States	Euphrates	18 Aug 1827
J.	19	M	Seamen	U. States	U. States	Lexington	8 Jul 1828
James	27	M	Smith			Eliza Jane	12 Sep 1820
Janet	10		Child of Janet Pierson	Aberdeen, Scotd.	State of New York	Albion	5 Feb 1822
Janet	36		Spinner	Pasley, Scotland	State of New York	Albion	5 Feb 1822
John	1	M		United States	United States	Maria	12 May 1823
John	25	M	Grocer	Great Britian	United States	Andes	19 Aug 1829
William	36	M	Mechanic	United States	United States	Centurion	22 Dec 1828
Wm.	15		Child of Janet Pierson	Aberdeen, Scotd.	State of New York	Albion	5 Feb 1822
PIFER, Deuvis	31	M	Labourer	France	United States	Cavalier	25 Jul 1828
Fred.	0 6/12	M		Baden	United States	Cavalier	25 Jul 1828
PIFFARD, David	27		Gentleman	London	England	London	13 Dec 1822
David	29	M	Gentleman	Great Britan	Great Britan	Columbia	10 Mar 1824
PIGIN, Peater	21	M		Newbrunsick	Newbrunsick	Nancy	23 Oct 1823
PIGON, Mary A.	17	M	Farmer	England	U. States	Severn	12 Oct 1826
PIGOT, Joel	49		Merchant	Connecticut	New York	James Cropper	12 Jul 1822
PIGOTT, Robert	45	M	Gentelman	Ierland		Jasper	30 May 1828
PIKE, Benjamin	45		Optician	London	United States	London	13 Dec 1822
James	33	M	Cooper	U. States	United States	Neptune	5 Jul 1820
PILBRAN, Edward	24		Farmer	England	United States	Corinthian	30 May 1828
PILGRIM, Philip	36	M	Merchant	U. States	U. States	Columbia	24 Dec 1822
PILKIN, James	30	M	Weaver	England		Britannia	20 Jun 1827
PILKINGTON, Margaret Ann	12	F	Lady	Great Brittain	U. States	Nancy	18 Jul 1821
Saly, Mrs.	30	F		Great Britain	America	Nancy	18 Aug 1821
Sarah	35	F	Lady	Great Brittain	U. States	Nancy	18 Jul 1821
PILKINTON, Richd.	21	M	Weaver	England	U. States	Severn	12 Oct 1826
PILLAWIN, Alexr.	66	M	Consul at Baltimore	France	U. States	Howard	27 Feb 1824
PILLERO, P.	30	M	Merchant	France	United States	Sisters	24 Jan 1820
Peter	40	M	Marchant	N. York	U. States	Commodore Perry	9 Apr 1821
PILLING, Abraham	40	M	Stone Mason		Perien [?]	Governor Clinton	3 Jul 1827

NAMES OF PASSENGERS	AGE	SEX	OCCUPATIONS	COUNTRY TO WHICH THEY BELONG	COUNTRY THEY INTEND TO INHABIT	SHIPS/DATES OF ARRIVAL	
PILLING (cont'd)							
Betty	67	F	None		Perien [?]	Governor Clinton	3 Jul 1827
Charles	40	M	Weaver	England	United States	Lord Wellington	14 Nov 1827
Elizabeth	28	F		England	United States	Lord Wellington	14 Nov 1827
Hannagh	20	F	None		Perien [?]	Governor Clinton	3 Jul 1827
John	24	M	P...oner	England		Britannia	20 Jun 1827
Margaret	1	F		England	United States	Lord Wellington	14 Nov 1827
Mary	7	F		England	United States	Lord Wellington	14 Nov 1827
PILLIP, John	40	M	Labourer	G. Britain	U. States	Nimrod	31 Jul 1828
PILLOW, Alfred Perton	9	M	Son	England	United States	Robert Edwards	3 Oct 1829
Ann	29 10/12	F	Wife	England	United States	Robert Edwards	3 Oct 1829
Ann P.	6	F	daughter	England	United States	Robert Edwards	3 Oct 1829
Francis	5/12	F	daughter	England	United States	Robert Edwards	3 Oct 1829
James P.	7	M	Son	England	United States	Robert Edwards	3 Oct 1829
Mary P.	3	F	daughter	England	United States	Robert Edwards	3 Oct 1829
Peter	30	M	Merchant	United States	United States	Abeona	31 Oct 1820
Wm. Henry	28 11/12	M	Bookbinder	England	United States	Robert Edwards	3 Oct 1829
PIMTIN, Antonio	35	M	Merchant	Spain	Spain	Admittance	22 Sep 1823
PIN, James	26	M	Blacksmith	Great Britain	United States	Exertion	17 Jul 1829
PINA, Victor	9	M		Island of Cuba	Cuba	James Monroe	21 May 1825
PINCE, Antonis	12		Lad	Portugal	St. Iago	Maria	20 Jul 1820
PINCKEY, —, Col.	45	M	Collector of the Port Key West	U. States	U. States	Eagle	17 Jun 1826
PINCKNEY, Edwd. C.	28	M	Merchant	Baltimore	U. States	Rehoboth	27 Dec 1826
PINDALL, George	27	M	Farmer	England	America	Panthia	17 Sep 1821
PINDER, Biddy	23	F		England	America	Two Marys	24 Sep 1827
PINDON, John	21	M	Labourer	Great Britain	United States	Frances Henrietta	17 Sep 1827
PINEL, Jose	25 5/12	M	Segar Maker	Havanna	U. States	Nestor	15 Dec 1828
PINERO, José	33	M	Servant	Spain	Mexico	Virginia	9 Feb 1829
PINETTA, M. A.	39	M		Spain	Spain	Fabius	3 Jun 1825
PINGROT, Perre	25	F	Farmer	France		Pallas	14 Jun 1828
PINKCOMBE, Henry	28 6/12	M	Surgeon	England	Hayti	Gleaner	6 Jun 1828
PINKERTON, Bridget	26	F		Ireland	United States	Fabius	4 Jun 1828
Francis	6	M		Ireland	United States	Fabius	4 Jun 1828
Henry	7	M		Ireland	United States	Fabius	4 Jun 1828
Janes	3	M		Ireland	United States	Fabius	4 Jun 1828
John	1	M		Ireland	United States	Fabius	4 Jun 1828
John	30	M	Weaver	Ireland	United States	Fabius	4 Jun 1828
PINKUS, Henry	23	M	Merchant	U. States	U. States	Andrew Jackson	16 Jun 1821
PINNET, Jacques	38	M	Mercht.	France	France	Fontine	4 Oct 1824
PINTADOR, Joseph M.	35	M	Merchant	Spain		Dolphin	6 Sep 1822
PINTE, William	50	M	Merchant	England	U. States	Patty & Sally	30 Aug 1820
PINTO, —, Mr.	55	M	Merchant	America	U. States	Exchange	19 Aug 1822
Abraham, Jur.	25	M	Merchant	Jamaica	Jamaica	Tontine	25 Sep 1826
Antonio	30	M	Merchant	Brazil	Brazil	Zepher	20 Oct 1827
PIPER, Edward	24	M	Brick Layer	Great Britain	United States	Orbit	23 Oct 1826
Elizabeth	4	F		Great Britain	United States	India	5 Sep 1827
Ema	2	M		Great Britain	United States	India	5 Sep 1827
James	24		Shoemaker	b. County of Sligo, last of Cambrige	N. York	Peru	30 May 1828
Margaret	28	F		Great Britain	United States	India	5 Sep 1827
William	6	M		Great Britain	United States	India	5 Sep 1827
PIPERSON, Alexander	19	M	Mechanic	France	U.S.	Helen	3 May 1828
PIPPEY, Jane	35	F	Spinster	Ireland	United States	Sarah Ann	6 Mar 1827
PIQUET, Charles	28	M	Merchant	France	U. States	Don Quixote	20 Mar 1827
PIRETEAU, —, Mrs.	42	F	Priestess	France	U.S.	Edward Quesnel	31 Jul 1827
PIRNIE, Duncan	23		Farmer	Scotland	United States	Camillus	3 May 1828
PIRON, Anthon, Kinder (his Son [Tobald])		M			United States	Juffraw Johanna	16 Oct 1821
Chatarina, Kinder (his Son [Tobald])		F			United States	Juffraw Johanna	16 Oct 1821
Frans, Kinder (his Son [Tobald])		M		Kehrborg	United States	Juffraw Johanna	16 Oct 1821
Jacob, Kinder (his Son [Tobald])	15	M			United States	Juffraw Johanna	16 Oct 1821

NAMES OF PASSENGERS	AGE	SEX	OCCUPATIONS	COUNTRY TO WHICH THEY BELONG	COUNTRY THEY INTEND TO INHABIT	SHIPS/DATES OF ARRIVAL	
PIRON (cont'd)							
Johan, Kinder							
(his Son [Tobald])	13	M			United States	Juffraw Johanna	16 Oct 1821
Margareta, Kinder							
(his Son [Tobald])	3	F			United States	Juffraw Johanna	16 Oct 1821
Margareta, Zyn Vrouw							
(his wife [Tobald])	40	F		Kehrborg	United States	Juffraw Johanna	16 Oct 1821
Thobald Johan, Kinder							
(his Son [Tobald])		M			United States	Juffraw Johanna	16 Oct 1821
Tobald	44	M	Boer	Kehrborg	United States	Juffraw Johanna	16 Oct 1821
PISANCAS, —	30	M	Merchant	Spain	Spain	Commodore Perry	24 Nov 1820
PISGA, Manuel	37 7/12	M	Merchant	Spain	Spain	Brillante	24 May 1822
PISLEY, Geo.	23	M	Farmer	Great Britain	United States	Penelope	11 Jun 1827
PISOLE, P.	29	M	Merchant	U.S.	America	Wave	15 Aug 1821
PISTON, Philip	14	M		Germany	U. States	Cadmus	28 May 1821
PITCAIRN, Joseph	60	M	Merchant	U.S. of America		Canada	1 Oct 1827
Robt.	25	M	Blacksmith	Scotland	United States	Camillus	27 Oct 1829
PITCHE, Robert	24	M	Teacher	Scotland	U. States	Cicero	13 Jan 1827
PITCHER, Catherine	29	F	Miller	Great Briton	New York	Brighton	12 Jun 1826
Matilda	1 6/12	F	Miller	Great Briton	New York	Brighton	12 Jun 1826
William	33	M	Miller	Great Briton	New York	Brighton	12 Jun 1826
PITELLOW, F.	30	M		Dundee	U. States	Hind	12 May 1823
PITFIELD, Amelia	8		None	Great Britain	United States	Roman	10 Sep 1827
Ann	25		Weaver	Great Britain	United States	Roman	10 Sep 1827
Ann	46		None	Great Britain	United States	Roman	10 Sep 1827
Isabella	6		None	Great Britain	United States	Roman	10 Sep 1827
Margaret			None	Great Britain	United States	Roman	10 Sep 1827
Mary	4		None	Great Britain	United States	Roman	10 Sep 1827
Richard	22		None	Great Britain	United States	Roman	10 Sep 1827
PITKIN, James, Jr.	26	M	Supercargo	United States	United States	Prize	15 May 1822
PITMAN, Allen	38	M		Ireland	U. States	Howard	25 Jul 1823
Timy. G.	29	M	Merchant	U. States	U. States	Savannah	18 May 1822
PITON, Michel	24	M	Servt.	Saxony	United States	Bayard	13 Nov 1823
PITT, Joseph F.	50	M	Merchant	Great Britain	United States	Dapper	21 Aug 1828
PITTALAGO, John	30		Merchant	Spain	Spain	Hind	12 Jul 1820
PITTFIELD, Richard	23	M	Weaver	England	America	Sarah	18 Aug 1829
PITTING, James	34	M	Joiner	England		Britannia	20 Jun 1827
Mary Ann	33	F		England		Britannia	20 Jun 1827
Robert	1	M		England		Britannia	20 Jun 1827
PITTS, Sarah	60	F	None	Great Britain	New York	Corinthian	27 Apr 1824
Thomas	...1	M	Merchant	Great Britain	New York	Zodiac	14 Jun 1822
PIX, Thomas	23	M	Labourer	Ireland	New York	America	1 Aug 1828
PIZAM, Josi	12	M	None	Spain	U. States	Brown	7 Jul 1826
PL...M, Edward	31	M	Labourer		New York	Governor Clinton	3 Jul 1827
PL...T, James	23	M	Labourer	Ireland	U. States	Ganges	21 Jun 1827
PLACE, Jas.	7	M	None	Switzerland	United States	Ospray	2 Sep 1824
PLACKET, John	45		Planter	Great Britain	St. Croix	South Carolina Packet	7 Jul 1821
PLAGTIENE, Pastime	25	M	Miller	Germany	United States	Rent	13 May
PLAIN, Wm.	22	M	Merchant	N. York	U. States	Caravan	1 May 1824
PLANARD, Anne Brunn	39	F	Milliner	France	United States	Olympia	20 Aug 1829
Jean	55	M	Manufacturer	France	U. States	Isabella	10 Aug 1829
Paulina	17	F	Milliner	France	United States	Olympia	20 Aug 1829
Pictor	35	M	Milliner	France	United States	Olympia	20 Aug 1829
Virginia	19	F		France	U. States	Isabella	10 Aug 1829
PLANCHARD, Thomas	33	M	...	...	...	Indian Chief	8 Sep 1824
PLANIGAN, Bridget	30	F	Spinster	Ireland	Unt. St. America	Wilson	21 May 1827
Edward	19	M	Labourer	Ireland	Unt. St. America	Wilson	21 May 1827
PLANT, H. U.	25	M		New Brunswick	New Brunswick	Abigale	9 Aug 1821
Henery	26	M	Merchant	United States	United States	Nancey	25 Jan 1823
Henry U.	25	M	Merchant	Great Brittain	St. John, N.B.	Nancy	16 Aug 1822
Rd.	40	M	Planter	St. Croix	St. Croix	Telegraph	5 Aug 1824
Thos.	22	M		Gt. Britain	United States	Penelope	9 Sep 1828
PLANTON, A.	50	M	Physician	U. States		Antioch	18 Aug 1829
PLARSEAU, Antoine	48		Surgeon	Philadelphia	Philadelphia	Desdemona	12 Jun 1826
PLASAOLA, Andrew	25	M	Merchant	Spain	Spain	Jane	6 Apr 1826

NAMES OF PASSENGERS	AGE	SEX	OCCUPATIONS	COUNTRY TO WHICH THEY BELONG	COUNTRY THEY INTEND TO INHABIT	SHIPS/DATES OF ARRIVAL	
PLASHET, W.	28	M	Seamen	U. States	U. States	Eunice & Wealthy	24 Jan 1829
PLASKET, John	22	M	Planter	Cumberland	St. Croix	South Carolina Packet	16 Sep 1820
John	28		Planter	St. Croix	United States	Emelia	10 Dec 1827
Joshua	31	M		U. States	U. States	Criterion	29 May 1822
Wm.	23	M	Planter	Cumberland	St. Croix	South Carolina Packet	16 Sep 1820
PLASKETH, Timy.	45	M	Planter	St. Croix	St. Croix	Admittance	8 Mar 1826
PLASKETT, Thomas	21	M	Merchant	Great Britain	United States	Freake	25 Jun 1827
PLAT, E. M.	26	M	Merchant	G. Britan	U. States	Canada	27 Sep 1826
Fredr.	33	M	Blockmaker	Curacoa	U. States	Vigilant	13 Oct 1821
Louis	25	M	Servant	U. States	U. States	Jasper	17 Jul 1826
PLATAN, Alexr.	2	M				Stephania	24 Jul 1820
Clemence	4 3/12	M				Stephania	24 Jul 1820
Francoise Olymph	32	F		France	Great Britain	Stephania	24 Jul 1820
Josephine	8					Stephania	24 Jul 1820
Julia	4 6/12	M				Stephania	24 Jul 1820
Victoire	6					Stephania	24 Jul 1820
PLATE, John Frederick	28	M	Merchant	Hannover	U. States	Warren	7 Jul 1826
PLATS, —, Child	1 10/12	F		N. York	U. States	Hippomenes	30 Aug 1821
Maria, Mrs.	22	F		N. York	U. States	Hippomenes	30 Aug 1821
PLATT, —, Mr.	22	M	Mechanic	N. York	N. York	Wilson	3 Jan 1826
...mon	12	M				Hesperus	2 Nov 1820
Abigale	14	F				Hesperus	2 Nov 1820
Abrm.	20	M	Merchant	N. York	N. York	Independence	10 May 1825
Ann	6	F		Great Britan	United States	Clematis	8 May 1827
Ann	6	F	Miner	Great Britain	United States	Thomas Dickason	31 Jul 1829
Ann	24	F	Miner	Great Britain	United States	Thomas Dickason	31 Jul 1829
Betsey	9/12	F		Great Britan	United States	Clematis	8 May 1827
Betsey	32	F	Clothier	Great Britan	United States	Clematis	8 May 1827
Charles	2 6/12	M	None	England	United States	London	6 Feb 1829
D. Fk.	30	M	Physician		U. States	Chase	6 Jun 1822
David	30	M	Clothier	Great Britain	United States	Colossus	1 Nov 1826
Dianna	1 6/12	F	Miner	Great Britain	United States	Thomas Dickason	31 Jul 1829
Edmund	21	M	Manufacturer	England	U. States	Birmingham	12 Oct 1827
Edward	28	M	Miner	Great Britain	United States	Thomas Dickason	31 Jul 1829
Eliza	4 1/12	F	Domestic	England	United States	London	6 Feb 1829
Eliza	14		Spinster	Ireland	United States	Robert Burns	18 Jun 1821
Eliza	43	F	Tayloress	England	Pennsylvania	Governor Fenner	23 Jul 1829
Eunice	13	F	Farmer	Novascotia	Canada	Pedlar	2 Sep 1823
F.	21	M	Clerk	Gt. Brittain	United States	Cortes	5 Aug 1822
Francis	47	M	Merchant			Hercules	25 Sep 1820
Francis	51	M	Merchant	...	United States	Cortes	10 Apr 1822
Fredk.	28	M	Merchant	America	U. States	Magnolia	29 Apr 1822
Fredk.	33	M	Merchant	Curacoa	U. States	Logan	10 May 1821
Hannah	1 6/12	F	Miner	Great Britain	United States	Thomas Dickason	31 Jul 1829
Hannah	34	F	Miner	Great Britain	United States	Thomas Dickason	31 Jul 1829
Harriet	4	F		Great Britan	United States	Clematis	8 May 1827
J.	30	M		Vera Cruz	U. States	Eliza	11 Apr 1826
Jacob S.	28	M	Merchant	New York, U.S.	New York, U. States	Ann Maria	26 Apr 1822
James	15	M				Hesperus	2 Nov 1820
James	20	M		England	New York	Hesperus	2 Nov 1820
James	20	M	Weaver	England	United States	Siroc	31 Oct 1829
James	25	M	Weaver	Ireland	United States	Jubilee	13 Jul 1829
Jane	16	F				Hesperus	2 Nov 1820
Jane	34		Wife	Ireland	United States	Robert Burns	18 Jun 1821
Jno.	23	M	Mechanic	G. Britian	U. States	William Byrnes	23 Aug 1827
John	24	M	Dyer	Great Britain		Moro Castle	6 Jul 1827
John	34	M	Clothier	Great Britan	United States	Clematis	8 May 1827
John	34	M	Miner	Great Britain	United States	Thomas Dickason	31 Jul 1829

NAMES OF PASSENGERS	AGE	SEX	OCCUPATIONS	COUNTRY TO WHICH THEY BELONG	COUNTRY THEY INTEND TO INHABIT	SHIPS/DATES OF ARRIVAL	
PLATT (cont'd)							
John	39	M	Dyer	England	United States	Amelia	20 Aug 1829
Jonah	3 6/12	M	Miner	Great Britain	United States	Thomas Dickason	31 Jul 1829
Joseph	12		boy	Ireland	United States	Robert Burns	18 Jun 1821
Mary	26 10/12	F	Domestic	England	United States	London	6 Feb 1829
Mary	47	F				Hesperus	2 Nov 1820
Mary Jane	9		child	Ireland	United States	Robert Burns	18 Jun 1821
N.	30	M	...an...	C...	U. States	Agness	23 Jun 1827
Rebecca	4		child	Ireland	United States	Robert Burns	18 Jun 1821
Robert	32	M	Labourer	England	U. States	Panthea	8 Apr 1826
Saml.	25	M	Laborer	Great Brittan	U. States	Gem	26 Jul 1827
Sarah	11	F	Miner	Great Britain	United States	Thomas Dickason	31 Jul 1829
Thomas	25	M	Laborer	England	United States	Danube	13 Jul 1827
Thomas	25	M	Merchant	U. States	Great Britain	Thompson	26 Apr 1828
Thomas	30	M	Miner	Great Britain	United States	Thomas Dickason	31 Jul 1829
Thos.	22	M	Labourer	Great Britain	United States	Mary & Harriet	3 Jul 1829
Wm.	7		child	Ireland	United States	Robert Burns	18 Jun 1821
PLATTS, John	38	M		Parwick	U. States	Manhattan	21 May 1821
PLAY, Simon	24	M	...	...	...	Frances Henrietta	30 Jun 1827
PLAYER, Simon	27	M	Merchant	Spain	Spain	Napoleon	26 May 1828
PLAYFORD, Horatia	51	F	None	England	U. States	Hercules	6 Jul 1827
Hugh	51	M	None	England	U. States	Hercules	6 Jul 1827
James	32		Farmer	England	S. New York	Xenophon	25 Jul 1826
Jos.	19	M	None	England	U. States	Hercules	6 Jul 1827
King	6					Xenophon	25 Jul 1826
Mary	1					Xenophon	25 Jul 1826
Mary	15	F	None	England	U. States	Hercules	6 Jul 1827
Philip	17	M	None	England	U. States	Hercules	6 Jul 1827
Ruth	3					Xenophon	25 Jul 1826
Sarah	30					Xenophon	25 Jul 1826
Stephen	5					Xenophon	25 Jul 1826
Thomas	13	M	None	England	U. States	Hercules	6 Jul 1827
PLAZASTA, Andrew	25	M	Merchant	Spain	Spain	Commodore Chauncy	19 Jan 1826
PLEARY, Jeremiah	25	M	Hatter	U.S.A.	U.S.A.	Enterprize	30 Aug 1821
PLEASANT, J. P.	30	M	Merchant	U. States	U. States	La Plata	6 Jun 1828
John H.	26	M	Lawyer	United States	United States	Manhattan	24 Oct 1825
PLERA, —, Mrs.	35	F	None	Gt. Britain	U. States	Union	21 Jul 1825
Michael	54	M	Doctor	Gt. Britain	U. States	Union	21 Jul 1825
PLESENGER, F.	20	M		Germany	United States	Lydia	18 Jun 1828
PLESSY, Carlos	41	M	Baker	Colombia		Edward Quesnel	17 Nov 1828
Joseph	14/12	M		Colombia		Edward Quesnel	17 Nov 1828
PLETE, Lewis	26	M	Merchant	American	U. States	Mont Parnassus	31 Jan 1828
PLEYA, Carlos	44	M	Merchant	Columbia	Columbia	Tampico	20 Apr 1825
PLIFFIN, Catherine	11	F		France	United States	American	27 Aug 1827
Dominique	14	M		France	United States	American	27 Aug 1827
George	8	M		France	United States	American	27 Aug 1827
Gertrude	41	F	Wife of [Jacob G.]	France	United States	American	27 Aug 1827
Jacob G.	39	M	Carpenter	France	United States	American	27 Aug 1827
John G.	5	M		France	United States	American	27 Aug 1827
Maria Ursulla	1	F		France	United States	American	27 Aug 1827
PLIMMAN, W.	26	M	Merchant	U. States	U. States	Dandy	22 Dec 1824
PLINET, Elizabeth	18	F	Farmer	Switzerland		Antioch	18 Aug 1829
Elizabeth	38	F	Farmer	Switzerland		Antioch	18 Aug 1829
James	21	M	Farmer	Switzerland		Antioch	18 Aug 1829
Jean	40	M	Farmer	Switzerland		Antioch	18 Aug 1829
PLISANT, T. P., Mr.	27		Merchant	U.S. of America	U.S. America	Mary	10 Mar 1826
PLISTER, Hans Ulrich	43	M	Joiner	Switzerland	New York	Frances Henrietta	25 Aug 1825
Mary	19	F	Joiner	Switzerland	New York	Frances Henrietta	25 Aug 1825
PLITCHARD, Hannah	34	F	None	United States	United States	William Thompson	16 Jan 1826
PLITT, Philip	19 6/12	M	Painter	Germany	U. States	Wm. Penn	1 Sep 1828
PLOHL, Cath.	0 6/12	F		France	United States	La Flora	30 Jun 1828

NAMES OF PASSENGERS	AGE	SEX	OCCUPATIONS	COUNTRY TO WHICH THEY BELONG	COUNTRY THEY INTEND TO INHABIT	SHIPS/DATES OF ARRIVAL	
PLOHL (cont'd)							
Cath.	36	F		France	United States	La Flora	30 Jun 1828
J.	38	M		France	United States	La Flora	30 Jun 1828
Jacob	2 6/12	M		France	United States	La Flora	30 Jun 1828
PLOMNER, Thomis	30	M	Merchant	United States	United States	Nancey	25 Jan 1823
PLOTTARD, T.	24	M	Merchant	France	United States	Stephania	3 Oct 1822
PLOTTERY, John	17	M	Labourer	Ireland	U. States	Josephine	30 Aug 1828
PLOUGH, J. C. F.	22	M	Surgeon	Hamburg	United States	Maria Elizabeth	2 Sep 1822
PLOWMAN, Eliza, Mrs.	26	F	Servant	England	U. States	Pacific	5 Sep 1827
John	2	M		England	U. States	Pacific	5 Sep 1827
PLOWS, William	28	M	Printer	Great Britain	United States	William	12 Oct 1827
PLUCKER, R. C.	25	M	Clerk	Prusia	U. States	Cumberland	10 Nov 1823
PLUMB, —, Mrs.	45	F	Farmer	United States	United States	Atlantic	5 Jul 1821
Eliza Auga.	5	F	Farmer	United States	United States	Atlantic	5 Jul 1821
Isabella	9	F	Farmer	United States	United States	Atlantic	5 Jul 1821
Mary Ann	7	F	Farmer	United States	United States	Atlantic	5 Jul 1821
R.	11	M	Farmer	United States	United States	Atlantic	5 Jul 1821
S.	12	M	Farmer	United States	United States	Atlantic	5 Jul 1821
S.	57	M	Farmer	United States	United States	Atlantic	5 Jul 1821
Thomas	50	M	Farmer	Great Britain	United States	Colossus	1 Nov 1826
PLUMBER, Edward	5		Grocer	England	England	Hudson	18 Jun 1825
Elizabeth	32		Grocer	England	England	Hudson	18 Jun 1825
Francis	10		Grocer	England	England	Hudson	18 Jun 1825
Fredrick	1		Grocer	England	England	Hudson	18 Jun 1825
Henry	7		Grocer	England	England	Hudson	18 Jun 1825
John	38		Grocer	England	England	Hudson	18 Jun 1825
Mary	12		Grocer	England	England	Hudson	18 Jun 1825
PLUMER, —, Miss	1 1/12	F				Borneo	26 Apr 1824
—, Mrs.	26	F		U. States	St. Johns, N.B.	Borneo	26 Apr 1824
Edward	40	M	Labourer	Scotland	United States	Ann Maria	8 Jun 1824
Joseph	8			Ireland	United States	Jno. Dickinson	21 Sep 1821
William, (his Son)							
[Edward]	11	M	Boy	Scotland	United States	Ann Maria	8 Jun 1824
Wm. G.	28	M	Musician	Great Britain	U. States	Columbia	22 Sep 1828
PLUMMER, Jno.	2	M	Child	U. States	U. States	St. Michaels	25 Apr 1825
Mary	30	F	Lady	U. States	U. States	St. Michaels	25 Apr 1825
Thomas	32	M	Merchant	United States	St. John, N.B.	Sylvester Healy	14 Jun 1825
PLUMONDON, Janet	23	M	Merchant	U. Canada	Laguira	Gertrude	16 May 1827
PLUMP, F.	22	M	Merchant	Germany	U. States	Sophia	17 Jun 1823
PLUNCK, Wm.	21	M	Mercht.	Germany	U.S.	Sarah Thornton	9 Sep 1826
PLUNCKET, J.	21	M	Nailor	Ireland	New York	Infant	21 Nov 1820
PLUNCKETT, Catherine	14	F	Spinster	Ireland	U. States	Josephine	30 Aug 1828
Maria	52	F	Matron	Ireland	U. States	Josephine	30 Aug 1828
PLUNDERT, John	...		Labourer	Bolton	England	Great Britain	7 May 1827
PLUNKET, Thomas	18	M	Farmer	Ireland	United States	Dublin Packet	29 Jun 1825
Thos.	30	M	Farmer	Ireland	U. States	Greenhow	10 Mar 1823
PLUNKETT, Anne	5	F		G. Britain	U. States	Great Britain	6 Sep 1828
Edwd.	18	M	Labourer	Longford	United States	Solon	21 Jun 1824
John	19	F		G. Britain	U. States	Great Britain	6 Sep 1828
Mary	17	F	None	Longford	United States	Solon	21 Jun 1824
Robert	20	M	Calico Printer	Great Britain	U.S. of America	Gratitude	3 Oct 1829
PLUPINSKI, Adelbert	8	M	None	Prussia	America	John Dickinson	9 Oct 1828
Adelrade	1 6/12	F	None	Prussia	America	John Dickinson	9 Oct 1828
Antonio	42 4/12	M	Brewer	Prussia	America	John Dickinson	9 Oct 1828
Louisa S.	55 3/12	F	None	Prussia	America	John Dickinson	9 Oct 1828
PO...ERS, Eliza				G. Britain	U. States	Cosmo	15 May 1827
POA, John	20	M	Gentleman	Spain	Spain	Brilliant	29 Nov 1826
Joseph	21	M	Gentleman	Spain	Spain	Brilliant	29 Nov 1826
POAFREY, Desmolin	28	M	Farmer	France	United States	Euphrates	12 Mar 1824
POCHON, —	60	M	Doctor	U. States	U. States	Cadmus	28 May 1821
Irma	22	F	Lady	France	United States	Montano	5 May 1828
Josiah	6/12	M		France	United States	Montano	5 May 1828
POCKER, Georg	30	M		Switzerland		Pallas	14 Jun 1828
POCKET, Louis Francios	27	M	Merchant	France	United States	York	6 Dec 1826
POCOCK, Francis	35	M	Farmer	England	U.S.A.	Brighton	21 Jan 1826
James	21		Farmer	Isle of Wight	England	London	13 Dec 1822
Jno.	11/12	M	her Son [Rebecca]	Great Britain	Utica Onida	Venus	8 Sep 1820
John	24 8/12	M	Tinman	Great Britain	Utica Onida	Venus	8 Sep 1820
Rebecca	34	F	his Wife [John]	Great Britain	Utica Onida	Venus	8 Sep 1820

NAMES OF PASSENGERS	AGE	SEX	OCCUPATIONS	COUNTRY TO WHICH THEY BELONG	COUNTRY THEY INTEND TO INHABIT	SHIPS/DATES OF ARRIVAL	
PODRLAS,							
Menuela Garcia, Da.	41	F	Merchant	Spain	Havana	Commodore Chauncy	28 Nov 1825
POGSLY, Daniel	4	M	Farmer	St. John, N.B.	St. John, N.B.	St. Michael	21 Aug 1824
POGUE, Betsey	18	F	Spinster	Ireland		Dublin Packet	30 Apr 1821
Eliza	74	F	Servant	Ireland	United States	Josephine	30 Apr 1828
Isabella	16	F	Spinster	Ireland		Dublin Packet	30 Apr 1821
William	25	M	Mariner	United States	United States	Orozimbo	21 May 1821
POINES, Henry	20	M	...	England	United States	Hamilton	13 Nov 1827
POINGDESTER, James	21	M	Merchant	England	Guatemala	Helen Mar	29 Jun 1827
POINSITT, J. R.	40	M	Gentleman	United States	United States	Cortes	19 Nov 1821
POINT, Sarah	40	F		U. States	U. States	Criterion	20 Nov 1823
POIRÉRE, Julian	18	M	Weaver	France	United States	Bayard	23 Mar 1826
POIRIER, E.	22	M	Merchant	France	U. States	Queen Mab	16 Jun 1827
POISSON, Julia			Nurse	France	U.S.	Sully	26 Oct 1829
POITSELL, Fred.	18	M		Hamburg	U. States	Martha	4 Sep 1828
POLAND, Daniel	26		Blacksmith	England	U. States	Venus	4 Oct 1821
POLANTRE, Adolph	20	M	Gentleman	Germany	United States	Daphne	20 May 1823
POLCHAU, Chas.	42	M	Merchant	Hanover	U. States	John Wells	8 Sep 1897
POLDEN, A. J.	33	M	Merchant	England	Great Britain	Ranger	3 May 1828
POLE, Frederick	30	M	Brewer	Germany	America	Orozimbo	1 Oct 1827
POLHAMUS, Nelson	22	M	Cooper	New York	United States	Orion	27 Jul 1827
POLHILL, John	22	M	Farmer	Rye, England	United States	William	21 May 1828
POLIERS, Patrick	28	M	Labourer	Ireland	United States	Combine	4 Jun 1825
POLIN, —, Mrs.	40	F	Lady	Portugal	U. States	Deligence	21 Mar 1825
B.	4	F	Lady	Portugal	U. States	Deligence	21 Mar 1825
POLKINHOUR, Francis	32	M	Miner	England	England	Eliza	31 Jul 1826
POLLARD, A.	35	M	Sailor	U. States	U. States	Prince Edward	5 Dec 1821
Betsy	43		Calico Printer	England	America	Florida	14 Oct 1829
Elizth	23		Calico Printer	England	America	Florida	14 Oct 1829
F.		M	Merchant	U. States	U. States	Olympia	16 May 1822
Fred	23 5/12	M	Farmer	Switzerland	U. States	France	26 Jun 1828
George	24	M	Merchant	Virginia, U.S.	Virginia, U. States	Ann Maria	26 Apr 1822
George	27	M	Silk weaver & dyer	Ireland	United States	Robert Edwards	3 Oct 1829
Henry	14		Calico Printer	England	America	Florida	14 Oct 1829
Jane	6	F	None	United States	United States	Ann Maria	9 Mar 1820
John	45		Calico Printer	England	America	Florida	14 Oct 1829
John D.	25	M		London	United States	Jane	17 Jul 1821
Mary	9		Calico Printer	England	America	Florida	14 Oct 1829
Mary	20	F	None	Great Britain	United States	Hannibal	12 Oct 1829
Michl.	30	M	Farmer	Ireland	U.S. America	Columbia	31 Jul 1826
Rachael	2			England	America	Florida	14 Oct 1829
Robert	19	M	Cutter	Great Britan	United States	Hamilton	19 Mar 1827
Sarah	1	F	None	Great Britain	United States	Hannibal	12 Oct 1829
POLLAY, Richard	22	M		Ireland	U. States	St. Michael	26 Oct 1824
POLLETT, Cathr.	24	F		G. Britain	U. States	George Clinton	10 Sep 1828
Margt.	50	F		G. Britain	U. States	George Clinton	10 Sep 1828
Maria	18	F		G. Britain	U. States	George Clinton	10 Sep 1828
POLLICK, Robert	18 10/12		Farmer	Scotland	U.S. of America	Helen	8 Feb 1822
Susannah	10 10/12		Spinster	Scotland	U.S. of America	Helen	8 Feb 1822
POLLOCK, David	36		Farmer			Rufus King	7 Aug 1820
George	49	M	Paper Maker	Scotland	United States	Hope	5 Dec 1827
John	6/12	M	Child	Ireland	United States	Ann Maria	18 Dec 1827
Jos.	18	M		Ireland	U. States	Nancy	10 Jul 1822
Margaret	30	F	Wife	Ireland	United States	Ann Maria	18 Dec 1827
Mary Ann	11	F		Ireland	U.S. of America	Friends	10 May 1823
Mathew	21	M	Weaver	Great Britain	United States	Roanoak	19 Sep 1827
Robert	12	M	Boy	Ireland	United States	Dublin Packet	22 Aug 1829
Samuel	14	M	Farmer	Ireland	U.S. of America	Friends	10 May 1823
Samuel	28	M		U. States		Petril	14 Mar 1826
Thomas	3	M	Child	Ireland	United States	Ann Maria	18 Dec 1827
Thos.	42	M	Farmer	Ireland	U.S. of America	Friends	10 May 1823
Walter	28	M	Laborer	Ireland	United States	Ann Maria	18 Dec 1827
POLLY, Francis	43	M	Shoe Maker	L...dley, ..., England	N. York	New Orleans	24 Aug 1827
POLSON, Elizabeth	10	F	Child	Scotland	United States	Samuel Robertson	9 May 1827
Helen	6 6/12	F	Child	Scotland	United States	Samuel Robertson	9 May 1827

NAMES OF PASSENGERS	AGE	SEX	OCCUPATIONS	COUNTRY TO WHICH THEY BELONG	COUNTRY THEY INTEND TO INHABIT	SHIPS/DATES OF ARRIVAL	
POLSON (cont'd)							
Hugh	29	M	Miner	England	England	Eliza	29 Dec 1827
John	42	M	Labourer	Scotland	United States	Samuel Robertson	9 May 1827
POMEROY, B.	38	M	Lawyer	Connecticutt	Connecticutt	Florida	3 Jan 1826
E. B.	24	M	Merchant	N. York	U. States	George	9 Jul 1825
E. W.	21	M	Gentleman	U. States	U. States	Chase	22 May 1827
J.	20	M	Labourer	England	United States	Alicia	9 May 1827
William	70	M	Merchant	England	United States	Lord Wellington	14 Nov 1827
POMMER, Wm.	24	M	Cabinetmaker	Hamburg	U. States	Rebecca & Sally	12 Nov 1821
PON, Paul	40	M	Merchant	Spain	United States	Saluda	14 May 1827
PONCE, J. C.	24	M	Lawyer	Spain	Havana	Robert Fulton	22 May 1824
PONCE LION, Manuel	15		Gentleman	Spain	Spain	Florida	1 Dec 1828
PONCRENO, B.	55	M	Merchant	Havana	U. States	Greek	17 May 1825
PONELL, Ann	23	F		England	U.S. America	Cortes	19 May 1826
Chas.	4	M		England	U.S. America	Cortes	19 May 1826
David	27	M	Blacksmith	England	U.S. America	Cortes	19 May 1826
David, Jr.	6	M		England	U.S. America	Cortes	19 May 1826
James	2	M		England	U.S. America	Cortes	19 May 1826
PONES, R.	30	M		Ireland	America	Corinthian	1 Sep 1827
PONIN, Jean Baptiste P.	44	M	Officer in the French Army	France	United States	Nile	5 Oct 1827
PONNET, C.	50	M	Servant	Barbadoes	U. States	South Carolina	2 Aug 1822
James	9	M		St. Thomas	U. States	South Carolina	2 Aug 1822
John	11	M		St. Thomas	U. States	South Carolina	2 Aug 1822
PONSFORD, James	45	M	Gentleman	Dalwich, England	United States	James Cropper	7 Oct 1823
PONTE, Christoval	16	M	None	Spain	U. States	St. Croix	31 Jul 1827
Fran	42	M	Merchant	Spain	Spain	Alfred	12 Oct 1827
Francis	15	M	None	Spain	U. States	St. Croix	31 Jul 1827
PONTHIER, Stephen	25	M	Merchant	France	San Domingo	Victory	29 May 1821
PONTILIO, R.	40		Servant	Spain	Cuba	Draper	17 Dec 1823
PONTO, Antonio	48	M	Mercht.	Portugal	U. States	Liberty	20 Sep 1826
PONTON, E.	18	M	Merchant	Havana	U. States	Natchez	10 Apr 1823
J.	20	M	Merchant	Havana	U. States	Natchez	10 Apr 1823
PONVERT, E.	26	M	Merchant	St. Domingo	U. States	James Monroe	20 Sep 1826
POOK, Henry	28	M	Mason	England	U. States	Hudson	8 Oct 1827
POOKER, James	23	M	Printer	Ireland	United States	Neury	27 Jan 1827
POOL, David	45	M	Farmer			John & Edward	25 Aug 1820
Edward	28		Merchant	England	United States	Mary	15 Jul 1822
Eliza	3	F		England	U.S. America	Criterion	27 Oct 1821
Elizabeth	16	F		England	U.S. America	Criterion	27 Oct 1821
John, Mr.	35	M		England	U. States	Corinthian	8 Oct 1828
Martha	5	F		England	U.S. America	Criterion	27 Oct 1821
Richd.	9	M		England	U.S. America	Criterion	27 Oct 1821
Rubin	12 6/12	M	None	Great Briton	United States	Mount Vernon	30 Dec 1828
Samuel	33	M	Iron Founder	England	New York	Corinthian	5 May 1827
Thomas	28	M	Brass Founder	Great Brittain	United States	Nimrod	9 Jan 1827
Ths.	48	M	Instrument Maker			Washington	16 Sep 1820
POOLE, A.	50	M	Merchant	Great Britain		Midas	6 Oct 1823
*died							
Allice	45	F		England	U.S. America	Criterion	27 Oct 1821
Andw. R.	25	M	Merchant	England	U. States	Radius	28 May 1823
Ann	35	F	None	England	New York	Brighton	19 Aug 1829
Anne	39	F	None	England	Philada.	Colossus	2 Oct 1827
Brighton	3/365	M	None			Brighton	19 Aug 1829
Eddina	7 1/12	F	None	Great Briton	United States	Mount Vernon	30 Dec 1828
Elisha, Mr.	32	M	Merchant	United States	United States	Nestor	3 Nov 1820
Henry	9	M	None	Great Briton	United States	Mount Vernon	30 Dec 1828
Henry	12	M	None	England	Philada.	Colossus	2 Oct 1827
Henry	40	M	Miner	Englishman	Amemerica	Arcadia	5 May 1828
John	16		None	Leicester, England	Great Britain	Franklin	22 Jun 1827
John	36	M	Farmer	Gt. Britain	United States	Penelope	9 Sep 1828
John A.	21	M	Merchant	U. States	U. States	Georgetown Packet	27 Oct 1824
Joseph	24	M	Labourer	England	New York	Governor Fenner	23 Jul 1829
Lezatter	5 1/12	F	None	Great Briton	United States	Mount Vernon	30 Dec 1828

NAMES OF PASSENGERS	AGE	SEX	OCCUPATIONS	COUNTRY TO WHICH THEY BELONG	COUNTRY THEY INTEND TO INHABIT	SHIPS/DATES OF ARRIVAL	
POOLE (cont'd)							
Mary	36	F	None	Great Briton	United States	Mount Vernon	30 Dec 1828
Mary Anne	16	F	None	England	Philada.	Colossus	2 Oct 1827
Oswald	3 2/12	M	None	Great Briton	United States	Mount Vernon	30 Dec 1828
Robert	52	M	Turner	England	New York	Brighton	19 Aug 1829
Sieguett	20	M	Sculpter	France		Edward Quesnel	17 Nov 1828
Thomas	1	M	None	England	New York	Brighton	19 Aug 1829
Thomas	10	M	None	England	Philada.	Colossus	2 Oct 1827
Thomas	31	M	Cordwainer	England	New York	Governor Fenner	23 Jul 1829
Thos.	46	M	Mathematical Instrument Maker	England	U.S. America	Criterion	27 Oct 1821
William	18	M	...	England	Philada.	Colossus	2 Oct 1827
Wm. F.	24	M	Gold Smith	G. Britain	U.S. America	Cincinnatus	31 Oct 1820
POOLER, Robert W.	28	M	Gentleman	American	U. States	Factor	10 May 1821
POOLEY, Ann	3	F		England	America	John Wells	11 Jun 1823
Edward	8	M		England	America	John Wells	11 Jun 1823
George	6	M		England	America	John Wells	11 Jun 1823
Hen.	19	M	Merchant	G. Brittain	U. States	Pacific	23 Jan 1826
Maria	4	F		England	America	John Wells	11 Jun 1823
Nathan	1	M		England	America	John Wells	11 Jun 1823
POOLOY, Edward	40	M	Farmer	England	America	John Wells	11 Jun 1823
Maria	33	F		England	America	John Wells	11 Jun 1823
POOLS, John	30	M	Clothier	Great Britain	United States	Frances Henrietta	17 Sep 1827
Maria	32	F		England	U. States	Pacific	17 Jun 1828
May Ann	4	F		England	U. States	Pacific	17 Jun 1828
Saml.	7	M		England	U. States	Pacific	17 Jun 1828
Wm.	1	M		England	U. States	Pacific	17 Jun 1828
POOR, Charles *Died	34	M	Merchant	United States	United States	Only Daughter	29 Apr 1825
David	37	M	Merchant	America	U. States	John London	1 Sep 1823
David	40	M	Merchant	United States	United States	Only Daughter	29 Apr 1825
Thos.	35	M	Laborer	Ireland	United States	Nancy	15 Dec 1824
W.	19	M	Mariner	U. States	U. States	Florida	25 Apr 1825
POORE, David	30	M	Merchant	U. States	U. States	Union	22 Jul 1820
James	34	M		G. Britain	United States	United States	11 Sep 1828
POORY, Catherine	10	F	Farmer	Alsace in the Department of Upper and lower Rhine	United States	Carolina Augusta	16 May 1828
Christianea	7	F	Farmer	Alsace in the Department of Upper and lower Rhine	United States	Carolina Augusta	16 May 1828
George	2	M	Farmer	Alsace in the Department of Upper and lower Rhine	United States	Carolina Augusta	16 May 1828
George	42	M	Farmer	Alsace in the Department of Upper and lower Rhine	United States	Carolina Augusta	16 May 1828
Louise	33	F	Farmer	Alsace in the Department of Upper and lower Rhine	United States	Carolina Augusta	16 May 1828
Sophia	4	F	Farmer	Alsace in the Department of Upper and lower Rhine	United States	Carolina Augusta	16 May 1828
POPE, Chas.	36	M	Military	France	U. States	Montano	3 Jan 1825
Danl. W.	28	M	Merchant	U. States	U. States	Elizabeth	23 Oct 1828
George O.	6	M	Newphew of [Mary Burt]	England	Canada	General Stark	12 Jun 1826
H. W.	8	M		Stafford	United States	Java	9 Jul 1827
Jno.	26		Sugar boiler	Germany	Germany	Hudson	18 Jun 1825
Jonathan D.	30		Merchant	U. States	U. States	Empress	12 Jul 1827
Martha	45	F		Stafford	United States	Java	9 Jul 1827

NAMES OF PASSENGERS	AGE	SEX	OCCUPATIONS	COUNTRY TO WHICH THEY BELONG	COUNTRY THEY INTEND TO INHABIT	SHIPS/DATES OF ARRIVAL	
POPE (cont'd)							
Mora	29	M	Mercht.	U. States	U. States	Mary Livingston	6 Dec 1827
William	21	M	Merchant	Great Britain	Great Britain	Nestor	3 Nov 1820
Wm.	24	M	Merchant	Bermingham	U. States	New York	15 Nov 1823
POPHAM, J.	30	M	Merchant	U. States	U. States	Birmingham	12 Oct 1827
John	25		Merchant	England	...	James Cropper	28 Jun 1824
Richd. D.	52	M	Labourer			Evergreen	28 Jul 1820
POPP, Alexr.	27	M	Merchant	Mexico	England	Trimmer	30 Apr 1825
POPPLEIN, Andrew	60		Merchant	Frankfort	Baltimore	Don Quixote	19 Aug 1825
Mary	18			Frankfort	Baltimore	Don Quixote	19 Aug 1825
POR..., John	20	M	Farmer	Ireland	United States	Trident	30 Sep 1826
PORABOO, Bridget	30	F	None	Ireland	United States	Jubilee	1 Oct 1828
PORCHER, Francse.	14	F		France	United States	Le Voltaire	19 Jul 1828
Josh.	46	M	Lock Smith	France	United States	Le Voltaire	19 Jul 1828
Madeline	3	F		France	United States	Le Voltaire	19 Jul 1828
Marie	43	F		France	United States	Le Voltaire	19 Jul 1828
Marin	8	M		France	United States	Le Voltaire	19 Jul 1828
Pierre	11	M		France	United States	Le Voltaire	19 Jul 1828
POREE, B.	22	M	Merchant	U. States	U. States	Nancy Treat	6 Aug 1825
POREOUS, Andrew	38	M	Merchant	Great Britain	Montreal	Corinthian	27 Apr 1824
PORES, A.	20	M	Gentleman	France	France	Maine	30 Jun 1823
PORLLOCK, Daniel	30	M	Labourer	England	U.N. States	Earl of Liverpool	20 Aug 1825
PORONE, George	26	M	Toy Maker	Ireland		Quatre Freres	29 Jul 1828
Peter	28	M	Farmer	Ireland		Quatre Freres	29 Jul 1828
PORRINGTON, John	28	M	Weaver	England	United States	Lord Wellington	14 Nov 1827
PORTEOUS, Andrew	36	M	Merchant	Montreal	Montreal	Meteor	22 Apr 1822
Andrew	40	M	Merchant	Canada	Canada	James Monroe	18 Apr 1821
David	35	M	Tallow Chandler	Scotland	New York	Governor Fenner	23 Jul 1829
PORTER, (see Parter)							
—, Mr.	35	M	Merchant	U. States	U. States	Laura Ann	25 May 1822
Ann, Mrs.	18	F	Lady	New York	New York	Sully	4 Mar 1828
David C.	27	M	Merchant	New York	New York	Sully	4 Mar 1828
Elizabeth	18	F	Spinster	Ireland	United States	Robert Fulton	10 Aug 1827
Elizabeth	20	M				Splendid	14 Aug 1829
Hannah	5	F		G. Britain	U. States	Mary & Harriot	8 Sep 1828
Helen	6/12	F				James Margaret	17 May 1827
Helen	24	F				James Margaret	17 May 1827
Horace	26	M	...	...	U.S. America	Columbia	26 Nov 1825
Isabella	2	F				James Margaret	17 May 1827
James	18	M	Miner	G. Britain	U. States	Mary & Harriot	8 Sep 1828
James	28	M	Laborer	Aberdeen	New York	James Margaret	17 May 1827
John	18	M	Labourer	Ireland		Robert Fulton	4 Jun 1828
John	21	M	Merchant	Great Britain	Canada	New York	19 Nov 1828
John	26	M	Farmer	Ireland	United States	Princess Charlotte	26 Apr 1827
John	27	M	Miner	G. Britain	U. States	Mary & Harriot	8 Sep 1828
John	31	M	Farmer	England	United States	Milton	20 Oct 1827
John D. L.	22	M	Merchant	U.S.	America	Wave	15 Aug 1821
Joseph	28	M	Farmer	Great Britain	United States	Mary & Harriet	3 Jul 1829
Kenery	20	M	Merchant	England	United States	Nancy	28 Oct 1822
Manuel	35	M	Merchant	England	Mexico	Edward Quesnel	16 Nov 1827
Margert	17	F	Spinster	Ireland	United States	Robert Fulton	10 Aug 1827
Mary	20	F		G. Britain	U. States	Mary & Harriot	8 Sep 1828
Mathew	21	M	Labourer	Ireland		Robert Fulton	4 Jun 1828
Matthew	...	...	...	...	...	Alexander Mansfield	18 Jun 1821
Richd.	3	M		G. Britain	U. States	Mary & Harriot	8 Sep 1828
Thomas	27	M	Weaver	Ireland	United States	Atlantic	21 Jul 1827
William	18	M		G. Britain	U. States	Mary & Harriot	8 Sep 1828
William	22	M	Laborer	Ireland	U. States	Nancy	13 Dec 1822
William	24	M	Lace Maker	England		Edward Quesnel	17 Nov 1828
Wm.	68		Farmer	Ireland	U.S. America	Lafayette	3 Dec 1827
Wm., Mr.	28	M	Mason	England	U. States	Acasta	3 Apr 1826
PORTERIES, William	22	M	Mason	Scotland	United States	Culloden	17 May 1828
PORTERS, —, Miss	5	F	None	England	Canada	Corinthian	20 Apr 1825
A., Miss	16	F	None	England	Canada	Corinthian	20 Apr 1825
A., Mrs.	36	F	None	England	Canada	Corinthian	20 Apr 1825

NAMES OF PASSENGERS	AGE	SEX	OCCUPATIONS	COUNTRY TO WHICH THEY BELONG	COUNTRY THEY INTEND TO INHABIT	SHIPS/DATES OF ARRIVAL	
PORTERS (cont'd)							
Andw.	43	M	Merchant	England	Canada	Corinthian	20 Apr 1825
PORTES, A.	30	M		Mexico	U. States	Laveria	23 Jul 1828
PORTEUS, Peter	30	M		Great Brittain	United States	United States	16 Feb 1827
PORTH, James	35	M	Labourer	Ireland	United States	Princess Charlotte	6 Oct 1827
Nicolas	24	M	Tailor	France	U. States	Leonarde	29 Aug 1828
PORTHAMUS, Nelson	24	M	Cooper	U.S.	U.S.	Richmond Packet	3 Aug 1829
PORTIE, John	19	M	Mechanic	U. States	U. States	Rodney	19 Jun 1827
*Passenger from the Wreck of Schooner Gen. Marion from Charleston to N.Y.							
PORTILLA, Francis		M	Consular agent of the U. States at Guatemala			United States	
Joseph							20 Jul 1829
*died 5th July on the voyage							
PORTLOCK, Daniel	24 11/12	M	Shear Grinder	Great Britain	Upper Canada	Venus	8 Sep 1820
PORTMAN, Jacob	22	M	Cabinet Maker	United States	United States	Globe	30 Aug 1828
Peter (Porteman)	24	M	Nail Maker	United States	United States	Globe	30 Aug 1828
*landed at this Port, Custom House, Portland, Aug 19, 1828							
PORTO, Jose Anto	48	M		Spain		Apollo	11 Jun 1828
Manuel	32	M	Merchant	Mexico	Mexico	Virginia	26 May 1828
Michael	30	M	Merchant	Mexico	Mexico	Virginia	26 May 1828
PORTSMOUTH, John	19	M	Gentleman	Gt. Britain		Corinthian	27 Oct 1829
POSEE, Alphonse	22	M	Gentleman	Havre	France	Maine	21 May 1822
POSESE, Antonae	24	M	Mason	France	U. States	Comet	28 Jul 1825
POSHING,							
John Betest Fercorda	50	M	Merchant	France	Canada	Active	29 Nov 1820
POSSOL, Richard	21	M	Ironworker	G. Britian	U. States	Howard	27 Jan 1825
POST, Alfred C.	23 7/12	M	Physician	United States	United States	Isaac Hicks	22 Aug 1829
Cath.	8	F	Farmer	Switzerland	U. States	Alfred	8 Jul 1828
Cath.	39	F	Farmer	Switzerland	U. States	Alfred	8 Jul 1828
Charles Conr.	23		Gentn.	German	United States	Corinthian	30 May 1828
E.	6	F	Farmer	Switzerland	U. States	Alfred	8 Jul 1828
F.	2	F	Farmer	Switzerland	U. States	Alfred	8 Jul 1828
Francis	40	M	Farmer	Switzerland	U. States	Alfred	8 Jul 1828
Henry A. V.	22	M	Gentn.	N. York	N. York	Cadmus	16 Aug 1826
J. H.	34	M	Mariner	United States	United States	Leeds	19 May 1823
Jotham W.	22	M	M.D.	N. York	U. States	Marmion	29 Sep 1823
L. Hr.	22	M	Merchant	Bremen	U. States	Constitution	15 Nov 1822
Matthew	18	M	...	Ireland	United States	Borneo	2 Oct 1827
Sissily	16	F	Lady	Ireland	United States	Borneo	2 Oct 1827
POSTHAM, Hy.	30	M	Tailor	Germany	United States	Robert Edwards	1 Jun 1826
POSTLEY, Jane	28	F	Spinster	United States	United States	Wilson	28 Nov 1828
POSTNER, Anna Maria	15	F	Daughter	Swiss	United States	Elizabeth	4 Sep 1826
Christian	5	M	Son	Swiss	United States	Elizabeth	4 Sep 1826
Christian	17	M	Son	Swiss	United States	Elizabeth	4 Sep 1826
Christian	40	F	Wife	Swiss	United States	Elizabeth	4 Sep 1826
Daniel	12	M	Son	Swiss	United States	Elizabeth	4 Sep 1826
Daniel	40	M	Carpenter	Swiss	United States	Elizabeth	4 Sep 1826
David	3	M	Son	Swiss	United States	Elizabeth	4 Sep 1826
Jacob	6/12	M	Son	Swiss	United States	Elizabeth	4 Sep 1826
John	6	M	Son	Swiss	United States	Elizabeth	4 Sep 1826
POSTRIGUS, J.	30	M	Merchant	Spain	U. States	Laura Ann	2 Feb 1820
POTANNIA, Pietro	37	M	Merchant	Italy	United States	Cambridge	19 Sep 1828
POTS, Stephen	25	M	Farmer	Rye, England	United States	William	21 May 1828
POTTACKE,							
George Martin	48	M	Distiller	Wirtemburg, Germany	Pennsylvania	Frances Henrietta	25 Aug 1825
POTTER, —, Mrs.	28	F		G. Britain	U. States	Geo. Canning	2 Sep 1828
Ann		F		Ireland	America	Carolina Ann	7 Aug 1826
Ann	33	F	Married Lady	United States	United States	Robert Edwards	3 Oct 1829
Anne	3	F	his child [George]	Ireland	United States	Asia	29 Jul 1829
Anne	40	F	his wife [George]	Ireland	United States	Asia	29 Jul 1829
Betsey		M		Ireland	America	Carolina Ann	7 Aug 1826
Betty	33	F	None	England		Exchange	11 Jul 1823
C.	40	M	Merchant	Massachusetts	Massachusetts	York	8 Aug 1829
Charles	38	M	Merchant	United States	United States	John Jay	8 May 1828
Cyrus	38	M	...	Rhode Island	U. States	Ocean	23 Oct 1820
Eliza	3	F		G. Britain	U. States	Geo. Canning	2 Sep 1828
Emily	14	F	daughter	United States	United States	Robert Edwards	3 Oct 1829

NAMES OF PASSENGERS	AGE	SEX	OCCUPATIONS	COUNTRY TO WHICH THEY BELONG	COUNTRY THEY INTEND TO INHABIT	SHIPS/DATES OF ARRIVAL	
POTTER (cont'd)							
Geo.	50		Land Steward			Zamoa	5 Nov 1828
George	36	M	Weaver	Great Britain	New York	Superior	5 Sep 1827
George	50	M	Farmer	Ireland	United States	Asia	29 Jul 1829
Hannah	19	F	Spinster	Ireland	U. States	Courier	17 Mar 1828
Harriet	28	F		United States	United States	Cortes	11 Aug 1823
Henry		M		Ireland	America	Carolina Ann	7 Aug 1826
Henry	1 6/12	M		United States	United States	Cortes	11 Aug 1823
James	22	M	Labourer	Carlisle	United States	Carolina Ann	11 Jun 1824
Jane	3	F		United States	United States	Cortes	11 Aug 1823
Jane	8	F		G. Britain	U. States	Geo. Canning	2 Sep 1828
Jane	15	F	his child [George]	Ireland	United States	Asia	29 Jul 1829
Jno., Jr.	5	M		United States	United States	Cortes	11 Aug 1823
John	26	M	Weaver	Great Britain	United States	Ganges	26 Oct 1826
John	37	M	Merchant	United States	United States	Cortes	11 Aug 1823
John	42	M	Merchant	G. Britain	U. States	Geo. Canning	2 Sep 1828
John, Jr.	10	M		G. Britain	U. States	Geo. Canning	2 Sep 1828
Margaret	5	F	his child [George]	Ireland	United States	Asia	29 Jul 1829
Mary	6	M		G. Britain	U. States	Geo. Canning	2 Sep 1828
Mary	20 10/12	F	Servant	Ireland	United States	Atlantic	21 Jul 1827
Mary	28			England	England	Thames	25 Oct 1821
Robert	33	M	Labor	England		Exchange	11 Jul 1823
Robert	34	M	Farmer	Great Britian	United States	Andes	19 Aug 1829
Samuel W.	25	M	Merchant	America	America	Meteor	22 Apr 1822
Thomas	8	M	his child [George]	Ireland	United States	Asia	29 Jul 1829
Thomas	28	M	Weaver	Great Britain	United States	Ganges	26 Oct 1826
Thomas	35		Farmer	England	England	Thames	25 Oct 1821
Woodbern	18	M	Merchant	U. States	U. States	Tobasco	17 Aug 1825
POTTIER, Charles	32	M	Traveller	France	United States	Montano	8 May 1827
POTTS, Betsey	38	F	Seamstress	Scotland	U. States	Camillus	27 Jun 1826
Eliza	14	F		Ireland	United States	Romulus	24 Jun 1826
G.	14			Bermuda		Ocean	28 Jul 1820
George	10	M	None	Scotland	U. States	Camillus	27 Jun 1826
Isabella	8	F	None	Scotland	U. States	Camillus	27 Jun 1826
James	29	M	Labourer			Lady of the Lake	23 Aug 1828
John	2	M	None	Scotland	U. States	Camillus	27 Jun 1826
John	16	M	Cooper	Ireland	United States	Romulus	24 Jun 1826
Joseph	34	M	Weaver	England	United States	Aurora	9 Jul 1827
R. H.	30	M	Merchant	U.S.	New York	Auritz	20 May 1823
Thos., Mr.	59	M	Merchant	Great Britain	Great Britain	Nestor	3 Nov 1820
William	22	M	Milwright	England	New Jersey	Lima	5 Aug 1829
POTUS, Wm.	28	M	Cordwinder	Ireland	United States	William	5 Oct 1822
POU, Juste	30	M	Merchant	Spain	New York	Sully	4 Mar 1828
POUCARD, Charles	41	M	Gentleman	Marseilles	U. States	Herald	18 Apr 1827
POUGE, Samuel	28	M	Mariner	America	America	Peruvian	11 Mar 1822
Tory L.	42	M	Merchant	America	America	Peruvian	11 Mar 1822
POUGLE, Mary A.	60	M	Mercht.	U.S.	U.S.	Toison	6 May 1828
POUISIN, Joseph	26	M	Farmer	France	United States	American	27 Aug 1827
POUJARDHIEU, Nicolas J.	36	M	Merchant	Bordeau	United States	Henri IV	2 Oct 1828
POULAIN, Jacob	30	M	Baker	France	United States	Virginia	31 May 1828
POULINO, Joaquim	47		Merchant	Portugal	St. Iago	Maria	20 Jul 1820
POUND, Ann	12	F	Farmer	Ireland	U. States	Sabina	29 Apr 1825
Danl.	45	M	Farmer	Ireland	U. States	Sabina	29 Apr 1825
Elizabeth	7	F		England	U.S.A.	Hudson	21 Aug 1829
Harriet	3	F		England	U.S.A.	Hudson	21 Aug 1829
Jane	5	F		England	U.S.A.	Hudson	21 Aug 1829
Jesse	34	M	Tailor	England	U.S.A.	Hudson	21 Aug 1829
John	3	M	Farmer	Ireland	U. States	Sabina	29 Apr 1825
John	14	M		England	U.S.A.	Hudson	21 Aug 1829
Joseph	4/12	M		England	U.S.A.	Hudson	21 Aug 1829
Julia	10	F	Farmer	Ireland	U. States	Sabina	29 Apr 1825
Margaret	5	F	Farmer	Ireland	U. States	Sabina	29 Apr 1825
Margaret	40	M	Farmer	Ireland	U. States	Sabina	29 Apr 1825
Richard S.	11	M		England	U.S.A.	Hudson	21 Aug 1829
Sophia	33	F		England	U.S.A.	Hudson	21 Aug 1829
W.	15	M	Farmer	Ireland	U. States	Sabina	29 Apr 1825
POUNDER, John T.	52	M	Planter	Barbados, U.S.	West Indies	Spartan	24 Jul 1826

NAMES OF PASSENGERS	AGE	SEX	OCCUPATIONS	COUNTRY TO WHICH THEY BELONG	COUNTRY THEY INTEND TO INHABIT	SHIPS/DATES OF ARRIVAL	
POUNTANY, Ann	20			Ireland	United States	Alexander Mansfield	9 Nov 1822
POUNTAR, Jas.	22	M	Labourer	Great Britain	United States	Atlantic	28 May 1827
POURCHAND, Frederick	21	M	Weaver	France	United States	Montano	5 May 1828
POURSEY, Catherine	20	F	Spinster	Ireland	America	William	21 May 1825
POUSEN, Michael	28	M	Farmer	Bavarian	United States	American	27 Aug 1827
POVEY, John	28	M	Gent.	Great Brittain	Great Brittain	James Cropper	23 Mar 1827
POVIE, C.	46	M	Merchant	American	U. States	John London	1 Sep 1823
POVRE, David	45	M	Gentleman	America	America	Ranger	13 Mar 1829
POW, P.	37	F	Drugist	Spain	U. States	Brown	29 Apr 1825
POWEL, James	36		Plaister Manfr.	Ireland	United States	Cambria	19 Oct 1829
Nowel	35	M	Farmer	England	United States	William Howland	5 Jul 1821
Thos.	21		Gent.	America	America	Cosmo	17 Mar 1828
POWELL, —, child born on board	20/365					Manhattan	23 May 1822
—, Mr.	25	M	Printer	United States	United States	Cadmus	9 Dec 1825
Abigail	4	F		Great Britain	America	Lady Gallatin	21 Jun 1820
Ann	9	F		Ireland		L. M. Pelham	12 May 1823
Ann	74	F		Upper Canada	Upper Canada	Hudson	21 Aug 1829
B., Mrs.	63	F	None	Gt. Britan	U. States	Earl of Liverpool	12 Apr 1825
Benj.	30	M	Minister	Great Britain	America	Lady Gallatin	21 Jun 1820
Broget	30	F		Ireland		L. M. Pelham	12 May 1823
Charles	3	M		Ireland		L. M. Pelham	12 May 1823
Ed. M.	33	M	Farmer	Ireland	America	James Cropper	10 Feb 1823
Eliza	7	F				Hudson	23 Jul 1828
Eliza	35	F		Upper Canada	Upper Canada	Hudson	21 Aug 1829
Esther	6	F	Tailor	England	America	Manhattan	23 May 1822
George	50	M	Weaver	Great Britain		Manhattan	7 Nov 1827
H.	21	M	Musician	England	England	Virginia	9 Feb 1829
John	20	M	Clerk			Comet	24 Dec 1821
John	21	M	Farmer	Ireland	United States	Lord Strangford	20 Jun 1826
John	22	M	Gentleman	Canada	Upper Canada	Camillus	29 Jan 1829
John	23	M	Carpenter	Bristol, Engl.	...	Warrior	19 May 1828
Mary	27	F		Great Britain	America	Lady Gallatin	21 Jun 1820
Mary Ann	4	F	Tailor	England	America	Manhattan	23 May 1822
Maryan	37	F				Hudson	23 Jul 1828
Mathew	24	M	Farmer	Ireland	United States	Lord Strangford	20 Jun 1826
Micl.	1/2	M		Ireland		L. M. Pelham	12 May 1823
North	3	F		Great Britain	America	Lady Gallatin	21 Jun 1820
P.	19	M	Maunfacturer	Ireland	U. States	John Wells	8 Sep 1897
Sarah	28	F	Tailor	England	America	Manhattan	23 May 1822
Selina	infant	F		Great Britain	America	Lady Gallatin	21 Jun 1820
Susan	7	F				Hudson	23 Jul 1828
Thomas	40	M	Merchant	England	U. States	Hudson	8 Oct 1827
Thos.	28	M	Merchant	England	U. States	Venus	4 Oct 1824
Thos. S.	1	M				Hudson	23 Jul 1828
W. D.	74	M	Judge	Upper Canada	Upper Canada	Hudson	21 Aug 1829
William	2	M	Tailor	England	America	Manhattan	23 May 1822
William	27	M	Tailor	England	America	Manhattan	23 May 1822
William J.	13	M	None	New York	New York	Indian Chief	19 Jun 1823
William T.	20	M	Doctor	United States	United States	Hanford	9 Oct 1829
Willis J.	35 10/12	M	Cotton Planter	Louisiana	Louisiana	Harriot	1 May 1822
Wm. D.	66	M	Chief Justice	Gt. Brittain	U. Canada	Cortes	5 Aug 1822
POWER, Ann	18	F		England	United States	William Byrnes	15 Aug 1826
Ann	19	F	Spinster	Great Britain	U. States	Boston	28 Aug 1821
Ann	24	F		Great Britain	United States	Samuel Wright	12 Oct 1829
Catherine	29	F		Ireland	United States	William Byrnes	11 Dec 1827
Charles	22	M	Merchant	Germany	America	Saluda	18 Jun 1825
Conrad	25	M	Farmer	France	United States	American	27 Aug 1827
Ellen	3/12	F		England	United States	William Byrnes	11 Dec 1827
Francis	28	M	Tallow Chandler	G.B.	St. New York	Eliza Grant	29 Aug 1829
James	27	M		England	United States	William Byrnes	15 Aug 1826
John	1	M		Gt. Britain	United States	Penelope	9 Sep 1828
John	4	M	Boy	Ireland	United States	Dublin Packet	22 Aug 1829
John	25	M	Labourer	Ireland	U. States	Combine	30 Nov 1825
John	25			Ireland	New York	General Marion	21 Nov 1828
Lucy	20	F	Spinster	Great Britain	U. States	Boston	28 Aug 1821

NAMES OF PASSENGERS	AGE	SEX	OCCUPATIONS	COUNTRY TO WHICH THEY BELONG	COUNTRY THEY INTEND TO INHABIT	SHIPS/DATES OF ARRIVAL	
POWER (cont'd)							
Martha	24	M	Farmer	Gt. Britain	U. States	Lima	22 Sep 1828
Martin	36	M	Farmer	Ireland	United States	Dublin Packet	22 Aug 1829
Mary	1	F	Child	Ireland	United States	Dublin Packet	22 Aug 1829
Mary Ane	25	F	Seamstress	Halifax	New York	Hope & Esther	21 Dec 1827
Michael	31	M	Farmer	Great Britain	U.S. of America	Gratitude	3 Oct 1829
Michal	24	M	Labourer	Ireland	U. States	Combine	30 Nov 1825
Nancy	30	F	Wife	Ireland	United States	Dublin Packet	22 Aug 1829
Pat	2	M	Boy	Ireland	United States	Dublin Packet	22 Aug 1829
Pat	40	M	Maunfacturer	Ireland	U. States	John Wells	8 Sep 1897
Patrick	28	M	Blacksmith	Ireland	U.S.A.	Silas Richards	28 Jun 1825
Patrick	29	M		Ireland	United States	William Byrnes	11 Dec 1827
Patrick	30	M	Shoemaker	Great Britain	United States	Samuel Wright	12 Oct 1829
Richard	13	M	Boy	Ireland	United States	Dublin Packet	22 Aug 1829
Richard	30	M	Labourer	Great Britain	United States	Hopes Delight	26 Aug 1829
Richard	35	M	Gentleman	Barbadoes	Barbadoes	Falcon	4 Jun 1825
Richd.	35	M	Merchant	Barbadoes	Barbadoes	Rose in Bloom	4 Apr 1826
Thomas	26	F	Farmer	Great Britain	U. States	Boston	28 Aug 1821
Thos. A.	28	M	Merchant	United States	United States	Manhattan	22 Sep 1823
William	23	M	Labourer	Ireland	U. States	Combine	30 Nov 1825
Wm.	25	M		Ireland	U. States	Howard	25 Jul 1823
Wm. M.	50	M	Military	Ireland	United States	Exchange	16 Feb 1822
POWERS, —, Mrs.	35		Servant	Great Britain	United States	Camillus	12 Sep 1827
—, Mrs.	37	F	Spinster	U. States	U. States	Constitution	8 Sep 1823
Burras	27	M	Laborer	Ireland	United States	Sylvester Healy	17 Oct 1825
Edward			Laborer	Ireland	England	General Starke	17 Jul 1827
Francis	22	M	Servant	Great Britain	United States	Ganges	26 Oct 1826
J.	28	M	Mariner	U. States	U. States	Bolivar Liberator	3 Jul 1828
James H.	22 3/12	M	Merchant	U. States	U. States	Patty & Sally	10 Jul 1821
Nicholas	35	M	Sailor	St. John, N.B.	United States	Edwin	29 Nov 1828
S. A.	30	M	Merchant	United States	United States	Abigail	25 Jun 1822
Thomas	25	M	Farmer	Great Britain	U. States	Yamacraw	4 Sep 1822
Thomas	40		...	...fford	...	Hudson	14 Jun 1827
W.	45	M	Planter	Cuba	Cuba	Franklin	14 Jul 1827
POWES, Charles	9			Esher	England	London	13 Dec 1822
George	14		None	Esher	England	London	13 Dec 1822
Henry	16		None	Greenwich, England	England	London	13 Dec 1822
Louisa, Miss	3			London	G. Brit.	London	13 Dec 1822
S., Mrs.	30			London	Great Brit.	London	13 Dec 1822
Sophia, Miss	2			London	G. Brit.	London	13 Dec 1822
POWLES, Samuel C.	28	M	Merchant	London	England	Velocipede	24 May 1824
POYNER, John	30	M	Merchant	England	New York	Brighton	11 Dec 1827
POYNTON, Ellen	19	F	None	G.B.	New York	Eliza Grant	29 Aug 1829
Ellen	19	F	None	Great Britain		Eliza Grant	29 Aug 1829
POYSER, George	50	M	Farmer	Great Britain	New York	Eliza Grant	29 Aug 1829
George	50	M		Great Britain	U. States	Eliza Grant	29 Aug 1829
POYSON, John	28	M	None	England	United States	Jubilee	12 May 1828
Mary	33	F	None	England	United States	Jubilee	12 May 1828
Mary Anne	4	F	None	England	United States	Jubilee	12 May 1828
Sarah Maria	6/12	F	None	England	United States	Jubilee	12 May 1828
POZA, Jules, alias Prince Murat	21	M	Merchant	Holland	United States	Cortes	28 Nov 1823
POZANCAS, Jos.	32	M	Merchant	Spain	Spain	Swan	23 Jun 1823
POZANEOS, J.	29	M	Merchant	Spain	Havana	Rolla	10 Feb 1824
PRACHE, Andrew	2	M		Switzerland	U. States	Romulus	24 Sep 1828
Andrew	30	M	Carpenter	Switzerland	U. States	Romulus	24 Sep 1828
Freekling	4	M		Switzerland	U. States	Romulus	24 Sep 1828
Mary	5	F		Switzerland	U. States	Romulus	24 Sep 1828
Mary	24	F	Carpenter	Switzerland	U. States	Romulus	24 Sep 1828
PRADELL, James D.	17	M	None	United States	United States	Paez	5 Mar 1827
PRADEY, James	3	M		England	United States	St. John	5 Oct 1829
James	30	M	Cordwaner	England	United States	St. John	5 Oct 1829
Jno.	5	M		England	United States	St. John	5 Oct 1829
Mary	29	F		England	United States	St. John	5 Oct 1829
William	6/12	M		England	United States	St. John	5 Oct 1829
PRADLEY, John	25	M	Labourer	Gt. Britain	America	Ariel	20 Jul 1822
PRADO, Deb.	2	F	Merchant	Mexico	Mexico	Washington	29 Apr 1826

NAMES OF PASSENGERS	AGE	SEX	OCCUPATIONS	COUNTRY TO WHICH THEY BELONG	COUNTRY THEY INTEND TO INHABIT	SHIPS/DATES OF ARRIVAL	
PRADO (cont'd)							
Francisco	14	M	Servant	Columbia	U. States	Exchange	25 Sep 1826
Frans.	14	F	Merchant	Mexico	Mexico	Washington	29 Apr 1826
Jos.	6	M	Merchant	Mexico	Mexico	Washington	29 Apr 1826
Jose	14	M	Mercht.	Guatemela	Central America	Savannah	22 May 1827
M.	15	M	Merchant	Mexico	Mexico	Washington	29 Apr 1826
M. R.	12	F	Merchant	Mexico	Mexico	Washington	29 Apr 1826
M. T.	8	F	Merchant	Mexico	Mexico	Washington	29 Apr 1826
Manuel	16	M	Mercht.	Guatemela	Central America	Savannah	22 May 1827
P.	10	M	Merchant	Mexico	Mexico	Washington	29 Apr 1826
P.	65	M	Merchant	Mexico	Mexico	Washington	29 Apr 1826
PRADY, John	22	M	Farmer	Brittian	U. States	Acasta	28 Jan 1823
PRALL, John	25	M		Ireland	U. States	Nancy	10 Jul 1822
PRAME, Joseph	13	M	None	Gt. Britain	U.S. of America	Friends	25 Sep 1823
PRANDARGRET, Morris	23	M	Labourer	Ireland	Amarica	United States	22 Mar 1824
PRASAS, J. L.	35	M	Mercht.	Spain	Spain	Richmond Packet	11 Jul 1827
PRATE, DeSal	33	M	Seaman	U. States	U. States	Boston	26 Sep 1820
Thomas	24	M	Farmer	G. Britian	U. States	Leader	14 Apr 1826
PRATT, Alexander J., Mr.	2	M	Merchant	Savannah	Savannah	Amazon	30 Jul 1827
Ann	5	F		Engd.	United States	Cosmo	21 Aug 1828
Ann	37	F		Engd.	United States	Cosmo	21 Aug 1828
Daniel	30 4/12	M	Mariner	Boston	Boston	Florida	2 Oct 1828
Edward	12	M		Engd.	United States	Cosmo	21 Aug 1828
Elizabeth	9	F		Engd.	United States	Cosmo	21 Aug 1828
Elizabeth B.	16	F	Lady	United States	United States	John Jay	8 May 1828
Francis	1	M		Engd.	United States	Cosmo	21 Aug 1828
Henry	3	M		Engd.	United States	Cosmo	21 Aug 1828
James	27	M	Mariner	England	England	Elbe	13 Jun 1827
John	24	M	Farmer	Scotland	United States	Andes	2 Oct 1828
Mary	10	F		Engd.	United States	Cosmo	21 Aug 1828
Mary Ann	21			England	United States	Hugh Johnson	11 Jun 1828
Noah	50	M	Mercht.	Great Britain	U. States	Hamilton	28 Apr 1828
Pierce	18	M		Ireland	United States	John & Adam	21 Sep 1822
Richard	36	M	Cabinet Maker	Engd.	United States	Cosmo	21 Aug 1828
Richd.	7	M		Engd.	United States	Cosmo	21 Aug 1828
Robert	14	M		Engd.	United States	Cosmo	21 Aug 1828
T.	27	M	Mechanic	England	Massachusetts	York	8 Aug 1829
Wm.	26	M	Gent.	Great Britian	U. States	Hudson	12 Mar 1824
PRAY, James O.	24	M	Farmer	Ireland	Meriland	General Jackson	31 Oct 1820
Joseph	25	M	Gentleman	United States	United States	Elbe	19 Apr 1826
PRDEOUX, Henry	22		Shoemaker	England	United States	Mary	15 Jul 1822
PREAD, Joseph S.	24	M	Merchant	U.N. States		Orient	9 Dec 1826
*sent Home by the Marican Counsell							
PREBLE, —, Mrs.	39			United States	U. States	South Carolina Packet	30 May 1825
William P.	41		...dge	United States	U. States	South Carolina Packet	30 May 1825
PRECCE, Lois	19	F	None	Ilan...	U. States	Electra	7 Jul 1828
PREDOLIN, Angnst	1 2/12	M		Switzerland	Ohio	Eugenie	20 Aug 1827
Ann	4	F		Germany	Ohio	Eugenie	20 Aug 1827
Ann Marie	8	F		Germany	Ohio	Eugenie	20 Aug 1827
Anny	8	F		Switzerland	Ohio	Eugenie	20 Aug 1827
Eugenie	1/12	M		Switzerland	Ohio	Eugenie	20 Aug 1827
John	3 6/12	M		Switzerland	Ohio	Eugenie	20 Aug 1827
John	12	M		Germany	Ohio	Eugenie	20 Aug 1827
John George	6	M		Germany	Ohio	Eugenie	20 Aug 1827
Joseph	5	M		Switzerland	Ohio	Eugenie	20 Aug 1827
Maria	43	F		Germany	Ohio	Eugenie	20 Aug 1827
Marie	32	F		France	Ohio	Eugenie	20 Aug 1827
Martin	6	M		Switzerland	Ohio	Eugenie	20 Aug 1827
Teudove	36	M	Turner	Germany	Ohio	Eugenie	20 Aug 1827
Wetsel	9	M		France	Ohio	Eugenie	20 Aug 1827
Wetsel	48	M	Servant	Switzerland	Ohio	Eugenie	20 Aug 1827
PREDRAS, Pedro	25	M	Merchant	Spain	U. States	Lucy Ann	4 Sep 1822
PREEL, Dorothy	19	F			U. States	Rockingham	29 Nov 1821
PREEVIT, G.	33			France	United States	Columbus	25 Jun 1825
M.	43			France	United States	Columbus	25 Jun 1825

NAMES OF PASSENGERS	A G E	S E X	OCCUPATIONS	COUNTRY TO WHICH THEY BELONG	COUNTRY THEY INTEND TO INHABIT	SHIPS/DATES OF ARRIVAL
PRELL, J. N.	26	M	Farmer	not to Remain in the U. States	U. States	Maria Elizabeth 9 Jun 1826
J. N.	35	M	Farmer	not to Remain in the U. States	U. States	Maria Elizabeth 9 Jun 1826
PRELLY, William	19	M	Weaver	Ireland	U. States	Josephine 30 Aug 1828
PRENDEGRAST, David	21	M	Accountant	Mayo	America	Margaret 31 Jul 1824
Patt	19	M	Accountant	Mayo	America	Margaret 31 Jul 1824
PRENDERGRASS, Catherine, Miss	17	F	Lady	Ireland	United States	Dublin Packet 9 Jul 1827
PRENDERGAST, Thomas	17	M	Farmer	G.B.	U.S.A.	Silas Richard 30 Jun 1828
PRENGENEF, Francois	32	M	Farmer	Alsace in the Department of Upper and lower Rhine	United States	Carolina Augusta 16 May 1828
PRENTICE, —		M		Scotland	U.S.	Curler 19 Jul 1828
—, Mrs.	26	F		Scotland	U.S.	Curler 19 Jul 1828
John	57	M	Mason	Glasgow, Barony [Parish], Lanark [County]	New York	Hero 19 May 1828
*to follow his occupation						
John, Mr.	25	M	Farmer	England	United States	Maria 29 Sep 1823
L.	34	M	Mariner	U. States	U. States	Planter 7 May 1822
Thomas	42		Mariner	America	America	Commerce 14 Mar 1823
PRENTIS, James	21	M	Cotton Spinner	England	United States	Jubilee 4 Mar 1829
PRENTISS, Arch.	19		Moulder			Zamoa 5 Nov 1828
Mary	25		Spinster	Ireland	United States	Fabius 18 Mar 1829
PRERO, Francis	48	M	Merchant	Porto Rico	Porto Rico	Eliza 10 Jul 1827
PRESCOTT, Calvin	26	M	M.D.	United States	United States	Brighton 11 Mar 1825
Charles	9	M	None	England	U. States	Montgomery 18 Oct 1828
Charles	32	M	Labourer	England	America	Minerva 31 May 1824
George	12	M	None	England	U. States	Montgomery 18 Oct 1828
Nathan	24	M	Mariner	U.S. America	U.S. America	Ganges 15 Dec 1826
*Destitute Seaman put on board by the American Consul in London						
Reuben	7	M	None	England	U. States	Montgomery 18 Oct 1828
PRESLOW, ...	6	M	None	Great Britain	United States	Dalhouse Castle 21 Aug 1829
...	24	M	Miller	Great Britain	United States	Dalhouse Castle 21 Aug 1829
...	40	F	None	Great Britain	United States	Dalhouse Castle 21 Aug 1829
Ann	40	F	None	Great Britain	U.S.A.	Dalhouse Castle 21 Aug 1829
James	24	M	Miller	Great Britain	U.S.A.	Dalhouse Castle 21 Aug 1829
William	6	M	None	Great Britain	U.S.A.	Dalhouse Castle 21 Aug 1829
PRESLY, Jas.	24	M	Labourer	Great Britain	New York	Dublin 21 Dec 1824
PRESPARD, Peter	48 7/12	M	Seaman	U. States	Boston	Minerva 25 Sep 1820
PRESSER, Alexr.	22	M	G...	Great Britain	Great	Amazon 8 Dec 1820
PRESSLY, Abraham	50	M	Merchant	U. States	United States	Young Phoenix 26 Jul 1824
PRESSUN, Hannah	30	F		Liverpool	U. States	New York 11 Jul 1823
Mary Ann	20/12	F		Liverpool	U. States	New York 11 Jul 1823
PREST, Charles	14	M	Labourer	Ireland	United States	Nancy Henrietta 3 Nov 1828
PRESTAN, Caster	4	M		Great Britain	United States	Mary 11 Jul 1820
John	52	M	Carpenter	Great Britain	United States	Mary 11 Jul 1820
Joseph	8	M		Great Britain	United States	Mary 11 Jul 1820
Margaret	44	F		Great Britain	United States	Mary 11 Jul 1820
Robt.	6	M		Great Britain	United States	Mary 11 Jul 1820
PRESTEN, M.	20	M	Merchant	G. Brittain	U. States	Little Cherub 15 Dec 1824
PRESTON, —	35	M	Merchant	Hayti		Ranger 29 Jul 1828
Ann	2	F	None	England	United States	Orozimbo 11 Aug 1823
D., Mr.						Dromo 14 Aug 1829
D., Mrs.						Dromo 14 Aug 1829
F.	19	M	Bookkeeper	G. Britain	U. States	Panthia 23 Apr 1824
James	26	M	Miller	England	United States	Colossus 26 Aug 1828
Janet	26	F	None	England	United States	Orozimbo 11 Aug 1823
M.	27	M	Merchant	Philada.	Jamaica	Little Cherub 15 Dec 1824
Margt.	15	F	None	Gt. Britain	U.S. America	James Cropper 2 Aug 1827
Robert	9/12	M	None	England	United States	Orozimbo 11 Aug 1823
Saml.	4	M		Great Britain	United States	Mary 11 Jul 1820
Thomas	33	M	Farmer	England	United States	Orozimbo 11 Aug 1823
Thomas	40 10/12	M	Farmer	England	New York	Concordia 12 Oct 1826
Thos.	1	M		Great Britain	United States	Mary 11 Jul 1820
PRESTRIDGE, E.	6		Child	Great Britain	United States	Isaac Hicks 6 Dec 1827

NAMES OF PASSENGERS	AGE	SEX	OCCUPATIONS	COUNTRY TO WHICH THEY BELONG	COUNTRY THEY INTEND TO INHABIT	SHIPS/DATES OF ARRIVAL	
PRESTRIDGE (cont'd)							
E.	26	F		Great Britain	United States	Isaac Hicks	6 Dec 1827
S.	6		Child	Great Britain	United States	Isaac Hicks	6 Dec 1827
PRESTWICK, James	30	M	Clerk	Gt. Britain	United States	Silas Richards	20 Jun 1826
John	39	M	Clerk	Gt. Britain	United States	Silas Richards	20 Jun 1826
PRETERRÉ, Apoline	8	M		France		François I	19 Nov 1828
Eugene	10	M		France		François I	19 Nov 1828
Pierre	16	M		France		François I	19 Nov 1828
Pierre Abram	45	M	Grocer	France		François I	19 Nov 1828
Pierre Napoleon	14	M		France		François I	19 Nov 1828
PREW, Jacob	31	M	Tobacconist	Bristol	New York	Cosmo	25 Sep 1827
PREY, G.	27	M	Labourer	France	America, U.N.S.	Great Britain	3 Aug 1829
Philip	20	M	Shoemaker	France	America, U.N.S.	Great Britain	3 Aug 1829
PREYSLER, G.	30	F	One Family [J. C. Vanden Brach]	Netherlands	New York	Louisa	6 Oct 1828
PREYTH, Jane	25	F		G. Britain	United States	Louisa	14 Jun 1825
PRIAGO, Santiago	34	M		Spain		Boyer	9 May 1825
PRIBLE, Ed.	30	M	Sailor	U. States	U. States	Prince Edward	5 Dec 1821
John	30		Merchant	U. States		Amazon	7 Jul 1820
PRICE, —, Mr.	38	M	Docter	U. States	U. States	Desdemonia	9 Jun 1825
—, Mrs.	30	F		Philada.	U. States	Desdemonia	9 Jun 1825
...	6	M	Child	Great Britain	United States	Superior	31 Mar 1828
...bel	36	F	Spinster	Great Britain	United States	Superior	31 Mar 1828
...g...	5/12	F	None	Great Britain	United States	Penelope	11 Jun 1827
Allan	29	M	Gentleman	Ireland	United States	Hogarth	12 Oct 1829
Amelia	7	F	Farmer	England	United States	Euphrates	18 Aug 1827
Amelia	30	F	Farmer	England	United States	Euphrates	18 Aug 1827
Ann	30	F	None	Great Britain	United States	Penelope	11 Jun 1827
Bengamin	4	F	Merchant	England	U. States	Electra	7 Jul 1828
Betty	30	F		Great Britain	United States	John Jay	8 May 1828
Caroline	4	F	Farmer	England	United States	Euphrates	18 Aug 1827
Charles	6	M	None	Great Britain	United States	Penelope	11 Jun 1827
Chas. C.	35	M	Merchant	England	Great Britain	Rodman	19 Dec 1825
D.	40	M	Mariner	U. States	U. States	Neptune	30 Nov 1821
Dav.	38	M	Farmer	England	United States	Euphrates	18 Aug 1827
E. K.	29	M	Lawyer	United States	United States	Cincinnatus	21 Nov 1821
Eleanor	22	M		Antrim, Ireland	New York	Anthusa	24 Aug 1825
Eliza	1	F	Merchant	England	U. States	Electra	7 Jul 1828
Elizabeth	8	F	Farmer	England	United States	Euphrates	18 Aug 1827
Evan	50	M	Surgeon	Great Britain	United States	Samuel Wright	12 Oct 1829
Geo.	41	M	Labourer	Ireland	United States	Copernicus	3 Aug 1829
Henry	7 4/12	M	Boy	Great Britain	U. States	Robert Fulton	3 Dec 1827
Henry	24	M	Merchant	New York	U. States	Mary & Agnes	26 Jun 1824
James	24	M	Farmer	Ireland	United States	Lord Strangford	20 Jun 1826
James	40	M		Ireland	United States	Clothier	22 Nov 1827
James	40	M	Merchant	England	U. States	Electra	7 Jul 1828
Jane	2	F	None	Great Britain	United States	Penelope	11 Jun 1827
Jane	13	F	None	Great Britain	United States	Penelope	11 Jun 1827
Jane	45	F		Ireland	United States	Copernicus	3 Aug 1829
Jas.	26	M		Ireland	United States	Thompson	12 Sep 1827
Jno.	11	M	Farmer	England	United States	Euphrates	18 Aug 1827
Jno.	38	M	Merchant	England	U. States	William	6 May 1824
John	21	M	Servant	Jamaica	England	Venus	15 Apr 1822
John	24	M	Cordwainer	Ireland	U.S.A.	Dalhouse Castle	21 Aug 1829
John	29	M	Farmer	England	United States	William & Henry	19 Jul 1822
John	31	M	Carpenter	Bristol	New York	Cosmo	25 Sep 1827
John	40	M	Labourer	Wales	U. States	Greenhow	10 Mar 1823
Joseph	33	M	Mechanic	England	U.S.	George Canning	26 Aug 1829
Josephine	22	F	Servant	Island of Cuba	Cuba	James Monroe	21 May 1825
Louis	28	M	Merchant	Island of Cuba	Cuba	James Monroe	21 May 1825
Margaret	1	F		Ireland	United States	Clothier	22 Nov 1827
Margret	21	F		England	U.S. of America	Illinois	16 Jun 1821
Martha	30	F		Ireland	United States	Clothier	22 Nov 1827
Mary	10	F	None	Great Britain	United States	Penelope	11 Jun 1827
Mary	27	F	Matron	Great Britain	U. States	Robert Fulton	3 Dec 1827
Mary Ann	10	F		Great Britain	United States	Samuel Wright	12 Oct 1829
Polly	3	F		Switzerland	U. States	Desdemonia	9 Jun 1825
R. B.	19	M	Merchant	U.S. America	U.S. America	Columbia	31 Jul 1826

NAMES OF PASSENGERS	AGE	SEX	OCCUPATIONS	COUNTRY TO WHICH THEY BELONG	COUNTRY THEY INTEND TO INHABIT	SHIPS/DATES OF ARRIVAL	
PRICE (cont'd)							
Richard	26	M	Horses dealer	Great Britain	United States	Exertion	17 Jul 1829
Sally	3 6/12	F		Switzerland	U. States	Desdemonia	9 Jun 1825
Sarah	8	F		Great Britain	United States	Samuel Wright	12 Oct 1829
Sarah	9	F	None	Great Britain	United States	Penelope	11 Jun 1827
Sarah	28	F			U. States	Rockingham	29 Nov 1821
Step.	40	M	Gentleman	U. States	U. States	Pacific	11 Sep 1824
Stephen	39	M	Gentleman	New York	U. States	William Thompson	6 Sep 1822
Susan	38	F	Merchant	England	U. States	Electra	7 Jul 1828
Thomas	34	M	Sawyer	Gt. Britain	United States	Meteor	19 Aug 1829
Thos.	5	M	None	Great Britain	United States	Penelope	11 Jun 1827
W.	38	M	Labourer	Wales	U. States	Greenhow	10 Mar 1823
W.	45	M	Miner	Philadelphia	United States	Brown	30 Nov 1827
William	31	M	Merchant	Canada	Canada	Thames	16 May 1821
William	34	M	Carpenter	England	America	New York Packet	8 May 1823
Wm.	11	M	None	Great Britain	United States	Penelope	11 Jun 1827
Wm.	23	M	Traveler	England	England	Electra	7 Jul 1828
Wm.	36	M	Miner	Great Britain	United States	Superior	31 Mar 1828
Wm.	40	M	Labourer	Great Britain	United States	Penelope	11 Jun 1827
PRICES, A.	25	M	Mariner	Spain	Spain	Lady Tompkins	9 Feb 1825
PRICHARD, ...	30	F		Aberdarorgen, Great Britain	United States	Marquis of Anglesea	8 Jun 1827
...ay...	23	F		Aberdarorgen, Great Britain	United States	Marquis of Anglesea	8 Jun 1827
Ann	32	F		England	United States	Friends	9 Aug 1827
Anne	1	F		Aberdarorgen, Great Britain	United States	Marquis of Anglesea	8 Jun 1827
Catherine	5	F	None	Wales	United States	Orozimbo	11 Aug 1823
David	4	M		Aberdarorgen, Great Britain	United States	Marquis of Anglesea	8 Jun 1827
Ebenr.	2	M		England	United States	Friends	9 Aug 1827
Ellen	1	F	None	Wales	United States	Orozimbo	11 Aug 1823
Gaynor	23	F		Aberdarorgen, Great Britain	United States	Marquis of Anglesea	8 Jun 1827
Harry	6	M		Aberdarorgen, Great Britain	United States	Marquis of Anglesea	8 Jun 1827
Henry	11	M		England	United States	Friends	9 Aug 1827
Jane	11	F		Aberdarorgen, Great Britain	United States	Marquis of Anglesea	8 Jun 1827
John	10	M	None	Wales	United States	Orozimbo	11 Aug 1823
John	14	M		England	United States	Friends	9 Aug 1827
John	30	M	Labourer	Aberdarorgen, Great Britain	United States	Marquis of Anglesea	8 Jun 1827
Louisia	40	F	None	Wales	United States	Orozimbo	11 Aug 1823
Lowry	28	F		Aberdarorgen, Great Britain	United States	Marquis of Anglesea	8 Jun 1827
M. W.	24	M	Drugist	America	New York	James Cropper	16 Oct 1826
Margaret	20	F		Aberdarorgen, Great Britain	United States	Marquis of Anglesea	8 Jun 1827
Margaret	29	F		Aberdaron, Great Britain	United States	Marquis of Anglesea	8 Jun 1827
Mary	14	F		Aberdarorgen, Great Britain	United States	Marquis of Anglesea	8 Jun 1827
Mary	40	F		Aberdarorgen, Great Britain	United States	Marquis of Anglesea	8 Jun 1827
Richard	21	M	Labourer	Aberdarorgen, Great Britain	United States	Marquis of Anglesea	8 Jun 1827
Robert	19	M	Labourer	Aberdarorgen, Great Britain	United States	Marquis of Anglesea	8 Jun 1827
Robt.	15	M		Aberdarorgen, Great Britain	United States	Marquis of Anglesea	8 Jun 1827
Robt.	29	M	Farmer	Bal...	United States	Leader	4 Oct 1824
Thomas	11	M	None	Wales	United States	Orozimbo	11 Aug 1823
William	12	M		Aberdarorgen, Great Britain	United States	Marquis of Anglesea	8 Jun 1827
William	40	M	Farmer	Wales	United States	Orozimbo	11 Aug 1823

NAMES OF PASSENGERS	AGE	SEX	OCCUPATIONS	COUNTRY TO WHICH THEY BELONG	COUNTRY THEY INTEND TO INHABIT	SHIPS/DATES OF ARRIVAL	
PRICHARD (cont'd)							
William	56	M	Labourer	Aberdarorgen, Great Britain	United States	Marquis of Anglesea	8 Jun 1827
Wm.	8	M	None	Wales	United States	Orozimbo	11 Aug 1823
Wm.	36	M	Farmer	England	United States	Friends	9 Aug 1827
Wm., Jr.	6	M		England	United States	Friends	9 Aug 1827
PRICHARDS, Wm.	24	M	Farmer	North Wales	United States	Magnet	16 May 1823
PRICHIN, Catharin	24	F		France		Pallas	14 Jun 1828
Charles	3	M		France		Pallas	14 Jun 1828
Fred	9	F		France		Pallas	14 Jun 1828
Fred	40	M		France		Pallas	14 Jun 1828
George	20	M		France		Pallas	14 Jun 1828
Jacob	5	M		France		Pallas	14 Jun 1828
Jacob C.	1	M		France		Pallas	14 Jun 1828
Louisa	11	F		France		Pallas	14 Jun 1828
Perre	6	M	Farmer	France		Pallas	14 Jun 1828
Perree	48	M		France		Pallas	14 Jun 1828
Suzan	13	F		France		Pallas	14 Jun 1828
PRIDE, Geo. Ludlow	23	M	Mercht.	United States	United States	Manchester	17 Aug 1825
George	21	M	Merchant	N. York	United States	Huntress	25 Mar 1822
PRIER, Ellen	22	F	Spinster	Ireland	United States	Dublin Packet	9 Jul 1827
H. P.	27	M	Mariner	Virginia	U. States	Eliza Jane	29 Oct 1821
Judith	18	F	Spinster	Ireland	United States	Dublin Packet	9 Jul 1827
Mary	20	F	Spinster	Ireland	United States	Dublin Packet	9 Jul 1827
PRIEST, Betsey	31	F	Miner	Great Britain	United States	Enterprize	18 Jul 1829
John	5	M	Miner	Great Britain	United States	Enterprize	18 Jul 1829
John	25	M	Labourer	Great Britain		Moro Castle	6 Jul 1827
W. M.	22		Surgeon	Great Britain	United States	Comet	9 Aug 1822
William	38	M	Miner	Great Britain	United States	Enterprize	18 Jul 1829
Wm. H.	32	M	asst. Supercargo	U. States	U. States	Adonis	23 Jan 1822
PRIESTLEY, Elizabeth	39	F	Matron	Great Britain	U. States	Robert Fulton	3 Dec 1827
Frederick	1 10/12	M	Child	Great Britain	U. States	Robert Fulton	3 Dec 1827
Henry	5	M	Child	Great Britain	U. States	Robert Fulton	3 Dec 1827
James	20	M	Labourer	Ireland	U. States	Josephine	30 Aug 1828
John	48	M	Mechanic	Great Britain	United States	Mary & Harriet	3 Jul 1829
Joseph R.	32	M	Merchant	United States	United States	William Thompson	16 Jan 1826
Thomas	39 5/12	M	Cabinet Maker	Great Britain	U. States	Robert Fulton	3 Dec 1827
PRIESTLY, Elizabeth	7	F	Child	Great Britain	U. States	Robert Fulton	3 Dec 1827
James	13 4/12	M	Boy	Great Britain	U. States	Robert Fulton	3 Dec 1827
John	11 6/12	M	Boy	Great Britain	U. States	Robert Fulton	3 Dec 1827
Sarah	16 6/12	F	Girl	Great Britain	U. States	Robert Fulton	3 Dec 1827
William	9 4/12	M	Boy	Great Britain	U. States	Robert Fulton	3 Dec 1827
William	26	M	Shop Keeper	Yorkshire	U. States	Atlantic	13 Jul 1824
PRIESTMAN, Ann Elisa	12		Lady	United States	United States	Corinthian	30 May 1828
Emma, Mrs.	30		Lady	United States	United States	Corinthian	30 May 1828
PRIGNER, R.	47 3/12	M	Brazier	England	United States	Acasta	25 Sep 1827
Sophia	35 1/12	F		England	United States	Acasta	25 Sep 1827
PRIME, F.	20		Mercht.	United States	U. States	New York	30 Oct 1827
PRIMROSE, F. W.	37	M	Barrister	England		Howard	17 Oct 1822
M.	26	M	Cooper	Scotland	United States	Camillus	27 Oct 1829
PRINCE, Ann	7	F	None	Ilan...	U. States	Electra	7 Jul 1828
Benjm. E.	32	M	Shoemaker	U. States	U. States	Union	9 Aug 1824
Christopher	31	M	Farmer	Novascotia	New York	Leader	18 Aug 1823
E.	23			United States	U. States	New York	30 Oct 1827
Elizabeth, Mrs.	40	F	Servant	England	Canada	Brighton	24 Aug 1827
George	45	M	Mariner	U. States	U. States	Comet	24 Dec 1821
Henry	13	M	None	Ilan...	U. States	Electra	7 Jul 1828
Jams	17	M	None	Ilan...	U. States	Electra	7 Jul 1828
John	25 4/12	M	Painter	England	America	Euphrates	26 Jun 1821
John Dyneley	46 9/12		Merchant	England	Boston on the Brig ...o...brad	Manhattan	20 Jun 1826
Mary	15	F	None	Ilan...	U. States	Electra	7 Jul 1828
Susen	10	F	None	Ilan...	U. States	Electra	7 Jul 1828
W. G., Mr.	25	M	Merchant	U.S.A.		François I	19 Nov 1828
Wm. A.	30	M	Merchant	U. States	U. States	South Boston	15 Sep 1821
PRINCELY, Philip	60	M	Farmer	Ireland	United States	Dublin Packet	23 May 1828
PRINCES, —	25	M	None	United States	United States	Annah	21 Jun 1826
PRINDALL, C.	25	F	Farmer	St. Johns	U. States	Isabella	28 Jun 1825

NAMES OF PASSENGERS	AGE	SEX	OCCUPATIONS	COUNTRY TO WHICH THEY BELONG	COUNTRY THEY INTEND TO INHABIT	SHIPS/DATES OF ARRIVAL	
PRINEULT, Christmas	55	M	Merchant	St. Thomas	U. States	Agness	30 Jul 1829
Elisa	23	F		St. Thomas	U. States	Agness	30 Jul 1829
William	28	M	Merchant	St. Thomas	U. States	Agness	30 Jul 1829
PRINGLE, Alexander	12	M	None	Scotland	New York	Margaret	18 May 1825
Elizabeth	40	F	None	Scotland	New York	Margaret	18 May 1825
Elizebeth, Mrs.	40	F		Canada	United States	Juno	26 Nov 1821
Isabella	12	F	None	Great Britain	United States	Courier	26 Jun 1827
Issabella	20	F	None	Scotland	New York	Margaret	18 May 1825
James	7	M	None	Scotland	New York	Margaret	18 May 1825
James	30	M	Weaver	Great Britain		Dalmannock	24 Ocg 1826
James	56	M	Stone Cutter	Scotland	New York	Margaret	18 May 1825
John	25	M	Cabinet Maker	Ireland	U.S.A.	Dalhouse Castle	21 Aug 1829
Mark W.	38	M	Merchant	United States	United States	Fair Play	22 May 1821
R., Mr.	30	M	Planter	U.S.A.		François I	19 Nov 1828
Robert	47	M	Gentleman	Great Britain	U. States	Silas Richard	30 Jun 1828
Robt.	30	M	Millwright	Dun...	...	Howard Douglass	11 May 1827
Thos.	42		Merchant	Ireland	United States	Courier	15 Oct 1827
Will	20	M	Flisher	Scotland	U. States	Superior	25 Sep 1828
Wm.	8/12	M	None	Scotland	New York	Margaret	18 May 1825
Wm.	32	M	Clergyman	Scotland	United States	Samuel Robertson	5 Oct 1827
PRINSTON, Olif	25	M	Gentleman	Gt. Britain	U. States	William Howland	27 Jul 1824
PRIOR, Biddy *died	13	F		G. Britain	United States	Louisa	14 Jun 1825
Charles	33	M	Gentn.	England	Canada	Brighton	16 Nov 1826
J. S.	9	M	Child	Ireland	U. States	Atlantic	19 Aug 1825
James	20	M	Labourer	Great Brittain	United States	Active	12 Sep 1828
Thomas	4	M	Child	Ireland	United States	Dublin Packet	9 Jul 1827
Thomas	20	M	Labourer	Great Brittain	United States	Active	12 Sep 1828
Wm.	32	M	Miner	England	United States	Trident	30 Sep 1826
PRITCHARD, —, Lt.	35	M	Soldier (Off.)	England	England	Hudson	21 Aug 1829
Eleanor	9/12	F		Great Britain	United States	Aspasia	16 Jul 1828
Elizabeth, Wife [of Owen]	27	F	Labourer	Wales		Gomer	22 May 1827
Ellen	32	F		England	America	Two Marys	24 Sep 1827
James, Mr.	33	M	Gentleman	America	America	Atlantic	11 Oct 1822
Jane	3	F		Great Britain	United States	Aspasia	16 Jul 1828
Jane	5	F		England	America	Two Marys	24 Sep 1827
John	18	M	Smith	England	America	Two Marys	24 Sep 1827
Margaret, Child [of Owen]	2 1/2	F	Labourer	Wales		Gomer	22 May 1827
Mary	10	F		Great Britain	United States	Aspasia	16 Jul 1828
Mary	26	F	Nurse	England	U.S. America	New Hampshire	28 Sep 1826
Mary	35	F		Great Britain	United States	Aspasia	16 Jul 1828
Mary, Child [of Owen]	1 1/2	F	Labourer	Wales		Gomer	22 May 1827
Mary Jane, Mrs.	30	F		England	New York, U.S.	Amity	31 Jan 1822
Owen	25	M	Labourer	Wales		Gomer	22 May 1827
Richd.	7	M		Great Britain	United States	Aspasia	16 Jul 1828
Thomas	28	M	Taylor	England	U.S. America	New Hampshire	28 Sep 1826
Thos.	50	M	Smith	England	America	Two Marys	24 Sep 1827
Wm.	6	M		Great Britain	United States	Aspasia	16 Jul 1828
Wm.	38	M	Labourer	Great Britain	United States	Aspasia	16 Jul 1828
PROCHET, Cladan	35	M	Coppersmith	France	U. States	Fair American	24 Dec 1821
PROCTER, Charles	25	M	Printer	England	United States	Robert Edwards	3 Oct 1829
Nicholas	26	M	Merchant	Gt. Britain	England	Excel	21 Apr 1828
P.	45	M	Mariner	United States	United States	Daphne	20 May 1823
Thorndike	30	M	Mariner	United States	United States	Daphne	20 May 1823
PROCTOR, Amos	27	M	Butcher	Great Britain	United States	Camberwell	2 Oct 1828
Geo.	27	M	Merchant	England	Canada	York	12 Jul 1825
Wm.	23	M	Mechanic	Great Britain	United States	Washington	3 Sep 1827
Wm.	25 1/12	M	Farmer	Ireland	Newark	Triton	12 Jul 1823
PROFFIT, Ann	8	F			United States	Delta	24 Oct 1829
Catharine	30	F	his wife	England	United States	Delta	24 Oct 1829
Henry	6	M			United States	Delta	24 Oct 1829
Jane	4	F			United States	Delta	24 Oct 1829
John	30	M	Tailor	England	United States	Delta	24 Oct 1829

NAMES OF PASSENGERS	AGE	SEX	OCCUPATIONS	COUNTRY TO WHICH THEY BELONG	COUNTRY THEY INTEND TO INHABIT	SHIPS/DATES OF ARRIVAL	
PROH, Luding	35	M		Poland	U. States	London	13 Sep 1824
PROLL, James	28	M	Laborer	Ireland	United States	Sarah G	19 Jun 1827
PRONGERS, W.	22	M	Farmer	England	U. States	Acasta	12 May 1825
PROSCH, Josophina	22	F		Germeny	New York	Louisa	6 Dec 1827
Theor	32	M	Doctor	Germeny	New York	Louisa	6 Dec 1827
PROSSER, Joseph	21	M	Farmer			Emulous	19 Feb 1822
Phebe	40	F				Plato	31 Oct 1829
Robert	24	M	Shoemaker	Scotland	U.S. of America	Camillus	16 Apr 1822
Thomas	43	M	Coker			Plato	31 Oct 1829
PROUDFIR, John H.	27	M	Merch.	America	America	William Thompson	18 Jan 1825
PROUDFOOT, James	47		Labourer	Ireland	United States	Courier	15 Oct 1827
John	31		None	Great Britain	United States	Roman	10 Sep 1827
Wm.	30	M	Merchant	G.B.	U. States	Silas Richard	30 Jun 1828
PROUDHOMME, —, Mrs.	56	F		Louisiana	U. States	Six Brothers	4 Jun 1822
Jno. B.	37	M	Merchant	Louisiana	U. States	Six Brothers	4 Jun 1822
PROUL, Peter	64	M	U.S. Navy	U. States	U. States	L. M. Pelham	3 Jan 1823
PROVENCE, Ths.	25	M	Coachman	Ireland	N. York	Salem	15 Mar 1828
PROYBY, Edward	53	M	Farmer	England	United States	Exchange	18 Nov 1822
PRUDHOMME,							
Emmanuel	64	M	Gentleman	U. States	Louisiana	Sully	30 Oct 1827
John E.	20	M	Gentleman	U. States	Louisiana	Sully	30 Oct 1827
Narcisse	20	M	Gentleman	U. States	Louisiana	Sully	30 Oct 1827
Pierre P.	20	M	Gentleman	U. States	Louisiana	Sully	30 Oct 1827
St. Anne	20	M	Gentleman	U. States	Louisiana	Sully	30 Oct 1827
PRUGUAL, Peter	52	M	Gentleman	Germany	U. States	Perseverance	28 Apr 1828
PRUIT, William	20	M	Weaver	Blackburn	United States	Dalhousie Castle	27 Jul 1826
PRULL, Margaret	5/12	F				Harmony	15 Jul 1820
PRUMER, Barbara	36	F	Family [of George]	France	America	La Grange	7 Aug 1828
Fraturtle	6	M	Family [of George]	France	America	La Grange	7 Aug 1828
Frederick	16	M	Family [of George]	France	America	La Grange	7 Aug 1828
George	10	M	Family [of George]	France	America	La Grange	7 Aug 1828
George	40	M	Farmer	France	America	La Grange	7 Aug 1828
PRYCE, Edward	22	M	Druggist	England	U.S. States	Splendid	14 Aug 1829
PRYOR, Robert	53	M	Farmer	England	U.S. of America	Hannibal	17 Dec 1823
Wm.	25	M	Merchant	Halifax	Halifax, N.S.	Decatur	5 May 1825
PSALZAR, Jques.	24			Suisse		Deux Ernest	29 Dec 1827
PTRICK, John	40	M	Miner	England	England	Eliza	31 Jul 1826
PUCKWOOD, Robt.	31 1/12	M	Servant to Jas. Musson	Bermuda	Bermuda	Florida	27 Aug 1825
PUFFENWAIT, M.	35	M	Gentn.	Canada	Canada	Howard	26 Aug 1823
PUGADO, T.	40	M		Spain	Spain	Montano	15 Jan 1829
PUGET, —, Mr.	32	M	Merchant	Spain	U. States	Monroe	13 May 1823
PUGH, Griffith	26	M	Farmer	Britain	U. States	Fame	3 Jun 1828
Henry	37		Gentleman	United States	United States	Cambria	19 Oct 1829
James	1	M		England	England	William Byrnes	14 Apr 1824
John	23	M	Farmer	Britain	U. States	Fame	3 Jun 1828
L.	27	M	Mechanic	U. States	U. States	Abeona	11 Mar 1823
Mary	21	F	None	England	England	William Byrnes	14 Apr 1824
Steph.	28	M	Farmer	England	England	William Byrnes	14 Apr 1824
Stephen	28	M	Farmer	Great Britain	U.S.A.	Silas Richards	7 Mar 1825
PUGLEY, Jas.	38	M	Carpenter	Scotland	U. States	Isabella	10 Mar 1825
PUGNER, Jane	30			Cumberland	England	Great Britain	7 May 1827
John	6			Cumberland	England	Great Britain	7 May 1827
Joseph	2			Cumberland	England	Great Britain	7 May 1827
Robt.	4			Cumberland	England	Great Britain	7 May 1827
Robt.	32		Cotton Spinner	Cumberland	England	Great Britain	7 May 1827
PUGNET, Hyacinth	29	M	Formerly Officer of the French Armey	France	Canada	Olympia	2 Sep 1823
PUGOT, Virginia	24	F		France	U. States	Lewis	10 Sep 1823
PUGSLEY, James	3	M	Farmer	Novascotia	Canada	Pedlar	2 Sep 1823
PUILER, Fredk.	60	M	None	Germany	U. States	Sully	24 Oct 1828
PULL, F. A.	22	M	Merchant	Baltimore	U. States	Pocahontas	18 May 1825
Francis	25	M		Germany		Robert Edwards	8 Nov 1825
PULLAM, James	22	M	Gent.	U.S. America	U. States	William Thompson	25 Aug 1828
PULLAN, Eliza	6	F		England	Great Brittan	Amity	11 May 1821
James	14	M		England	Great Brittan	Amity	11 May 1821
John	4	M		England	Great Brittan	Amity	11 May 1821

NAMES OF PASSENGERS	AGE	SEX	OCCUPATIONS	COUNTRY TO WHICH THEY BELONG	COUNTRY THEY INTEND TO INHABIT	SHIPS/DATES OF ARRIVAL	
PULLAN (cont'd)							
Joseph	1	M		England	Great Brittan	Amity	11 May 1821
M.	39	F		England	Great Brittan	Amity	11 May 1821
Mary	13	F		England	Great Brittan	Amity	11 May 1821
Richard	2	M		England	Great Brittan	Amity	11 May 1821
Sarah	8	F		England	Great Brittan	Amity	11 May 1821
Thomas	11	M		England	Great Brittan	Amity	11 May 1821
William	9	M		England	Great Brittan	Amity	11 May 1821
PULLAR, James	24	M	Merchant	Scotland		Helen	13 May 1822
PULLART, L.	41	M	Merchant	G. Brittain	U. States	Canada	6 Jun 1825
PULLIN, Robt.	50	M	Merchant	U. States	U. States	Columbia	22 Sep 1828
PULVERMEHER,							
Harriette	9	F		Germany	U. States	Columbia	22 Sep 1828
Janette	30	F		Germany	U. States	Columbia	22 Sep 1828
PUNCH, Betsey	26	F		England	America	Two Marys	24 Sep 1827
Ellen	2	F		England	America	Two Marys	24 Sep 1827
Thos.	27	M	Labourer	England	America	Two Marys	24 Sep 1827
PUNDALL, Josiah	56	M	Super Cargo	U. States	U. States	Fanny	15 Aug 1826
PUNDER, J. K.	15	M	Gentleman	England		Hudson	23 Jul 1828
PUNER, Thomas	50	M	Merchant	United States	United States	Atlantic	3 Dec 1821
PUNK, P.	25	M	Mariner	U. States	U. States	Cincinnatus	3 Sep 1827
PUNNELL, James	39	M	Shoe Maker	U. States	United States	Eagle	26 Jul 1828
PUNNETT, Elizabeth	22	F	None	U. States	U. States	Rice Plant	22 May 1827
John	16	M	None	U. States	U. States	Rice Plant	22 May 1827
Waller	8	M	None	U. States	U. States	Rice Plant	22 May 1827
PUNNITT, Christmas	58	M	Servant	Denmark	St. Thomas	Four Sons	31 May 1828
Jane	19 5/12	F	None	Denmark	St. Thomas	Four Sons	31 May 1828
William	52 11/12	M	Merchant	Denmark	St. Thomas	Four Sons	31 May 1828
PUNTEE, Wm.	24	M	Farmer	Scotland	Baltimore	Cadmus	22 Mar 1822
PUNTELOS, Julius	51	M	Shipwright	Sweden	Curacoa	Rebecca Ann	13 Aug 1821
PUQUOT, Gilberta F	21 6/12	F	None	France	France	Monroe	18 May 1827
PURBECK, Wm.	30		Mariner	United States		New Orleans	27 Feb 1829
PURCALL, Paterich	24	M	Farmer	Great Brittan	U. States	John & Elizabeth	11 Dec 1826
PURCELL, —, Abbé	27	M	Priest	U.S.	U.S.	Edward Quesnel	31 Jul 1827
Mary	35	F		Great Britain	New York	Dublin	21 Dec 1824
Michael	25	M	Traveller	U. States	U. States	John	16 Oct 1820
Thos.	33	M	Farmer	Great Britain	New York	Dublin	21 Dec 1824
PURCET, Peter	55	M	Mariner	Germany	U. States	Banian	19 Dec 1823
PURCHASE, Amy	33	F		G. Britain	U. States	Cadmus	28 May 1821
James	3	F		G. Britain	U. States	Cadmus	28 May 1821
John	10	M		G. Britain	U. States	Cadmus	28 May 1821
Richard	8	M		G. Britain	U. States	Cadmus	28 May 1821
Richard	34	M	Butcher	G. Britain	U. States	Cadmus	28 May 1821
Thomas	6	M		G. Britain	U. States	Cadmus	28 May 1821
William	2	M		G. Britain	U. States	Cadmus	28 May 1821
PURDIE, James, Jun.	27	M	Weaver	England		Manhattan	22 May 1827
James, Sen.	60	M	Weaver	England		Manhattan	22 May 1827
Jane	8	F	None	England		Manhattan	22 May 1827
John	13	M	None	England		Manhattan	22 May 1827
John	26	M	Tailor	Scotland	United States	Shakespeare	24 Jul 1828
Margaret	19	F	None	England		Manhattan	22 May 1827
Marion, Sen.	54	F	None	England		Manhattan	22 May 1827
Marrion	11	F	None	England		Manhattan	22 May 1827
Priscilla	15	F	None	England		Manhattan	22 May 1827
Samuel	21	M	Weaver	England		Manhattan	22 May 1827
Thomas	24	M	Weaver	England		Manhattan	22 May 1827
PURDY, Alexander	5	M		England	U.S.A.	Hudson	21 Aug 1829
Alexander	35	M	Basketmaker	England	U.S.A.	Hudson	21 Aug 1829
Edward			Distressed Seaman			Boston	28 Aug 1821
Harriet	6	F		England	U.S.A.	Hudson	21 Aug 1829
Jacob G.	34	M	Merchant	St. John, N.B.	St. John, N.B.	St. Michaels	24 Mar 1825
Lovel	22	M	Merchant	New York	N. York	Queen Mabb	22 Nov 1824
Lovell	25	M	Gentleman	United States	United States	Robert Edwards	3 Oct 1829
Mary	24		Farmer	Ireland	United States	Carolina Ann	12 Sep 1823
Parfaite	16	F	Wife	United States	United States	Robert Edwards	3 Oct 1829
Sorell	22	M	Gentn.	U.S.A.		Silas Richards	20 Jun 1826
Stephen	38	M	Ship Wright	United States	State of New York	Loire	3 Dec 1821
Thomas	20	M	...	Ireland	United States	Carolina Ann	24 Oct 1825

NAMES OF PASSENGERS	AGE	SEX	OCCUPATIONS	COUNTRY TO WHICH THEY BELONG	COUNTRY THEY INTEND TO INHABIT	SHIPS/DATES OF ARRIVAL	
PURDY (cont'd)							
Wm.	46	M	Gentleman	England	England	Hudson	21 Aug 1829
PURFIN, Augustus	42	M	Merchant	France	St. Thomas	Genl. Pike	15 Jan 1827
PURIERE, Augustus	24		None	France		Bayard	10 Sep 1827
PURNDELL, James	21	M	Merchant	England	America	Panthia	17 Sep 1821
PURNET, Henry	20	M	Merchant	St. Thomas	St. Thomas, U. States	Signal	11 Jul 1826
Mary	11	F		St. Thomas	St. Thomas, U. States	Signal	11 Jul 1826
Sarah	24	F		St. Thomas	St. Thomas, U. States	Signal	11 Jul 1826
PURREY, —, Mr.	28	M	Merchant	France	U. States	Greyhound	31 May 1823
PURRINGTON, A.	35	M	Mariner	Bath	U. States	Milo	8 Mar 1824
PURRIS, S.	17	M	Servant	Spain	U. States	New York	8 Mar 1825
PURROY, S. S.	40	M	Merchant	Spain	Spain	General Marion	12 Jul 1823
PURSEGLOVE, George	1	M	None	England	U. States	Montgomery	18 Oct 1828
John	28	M	Clothier	England	U. States	Montgomery	18 Oct 1828
PURSIL (see Perwil)							
PURSON, Saml. S.	28	M	Mercht.	Philadelphia	U. States	Catherine	4 Sep 1824
PURTLE, Denis	35	M	Labourer	Ireland	United States	Dalhouse Castle	21 Aug 1829
PURVIANCE, Wilson						Day	14 Jun 1822
PURVILL, Michl.	20	M	Labourer	England	United States	London	21 May 1828
PURVIS, —, Mrs.	25			Scotland	United States	Camillus	3 May 1828
Bess	19	F	Servant	Ireland	New York	Atlantic	8 May 1828
John	26		Taylor	Scotland	United States	Camillus	3 May 1828
Robert	1 1/2			Scotland	United States	Camillus	3 May 1828
William	62	M	Merchant	U. States	S. Carolina	James Cropper	21 Oct 1825
PUSFAUX, L.	19	M	Merchant	Hayti	Hayti	Pedler	15 Dec 1824
PUSSARD, Barby	5	F		France	Canada	Abby Jones	12 Jul 1827
Catharine	8	F		France	Canada	Abby Jones	12 Jul 1827
Catharine	40	F	Farmer	France	Canada	Abby Jones	12 Jul 1827
Christian	3	M		France	Canada	Abby Jones	12 Jul 1827
Christian	40	M	Farmer	France	Canada	Abby Jones	12 Jul 1827
Mary	10	F		France	Canada	Abby Jones	12 Jul 1827
PUSTOR, —	20	M	Servant	Columbia	Columbia	William Bayard	6 Aug 1825
PUTLY, Charles	22	M	Weaver	England	United States	Delta	24 Oct 1829
PUTMAN, J.	30	M	Shipmaster	U. States	U. States	Topaz	2 Oct 1828
S. R.	26	M	Merchant	United States	United States	Cortes	28 Nov 1823
PUTNAM, Allen	34	M	Master Mariner	United States	United States	Roanoke	21 May 1828
PUTTUM, John L.	30	M	Sea Captain	Hallifax, N.V.	Hallifax, Norcroft...	Hercules	10 Apr 1823
PUVEES, H. C.	21	M	Merchant	U. States	U. States	Bengal	30 Jun 1823
PUXEAO, Paschal			Servant	Italy	Italy	Dewitt Clinton	26 Aug 1825
PYBOCK, Elizabeth	52	F		G.B.	Boston	Eliza Grant	29 Aug 1829
John Wm.	3	M		G.B.	Boston	Eliza Grant	29 Aug 1829
Mary	26	F		G.B.	Boston	Eliza Grant	29 Aug 1829
William John	2	M		G.B.	Boston	Eliza Grant	29 Aug 1829
PYBORN, Edward	34	M	Labourer	U.S.	New York	Brighton	24 Aug 1827
PYE, John	20	M				Splendid	14 Aug 1829
Richard	19	M	Mechanic	Gt. Britain	U.S. America	James Cropper	2 Aug 1827
PYKE, —, Mr.	35	M	Merchant	England	Havana	Centurion	20 Oct 1828
M.	27	M	Merchant	Cuba dependan Spain	Cuba	Robert Fulton	2 Aug 1824
Morris	25	M	Supercargo	England	U. States	Ann	18 May 1825
Wm.	43	M	Gentleman	G. Britain	U. States	Cosmo	25 Nov 1826
PYLE, Mary	40	F	Wife			Commerce	22 Jun 1825
Robt.	62	M	Weaver			Commerce	22 Jun 1825
PYLOCK, Elizabeth	52	F	Carder	Ireland		Eliza Grant	29 Aug 1829
John Wm.	3	M	None	Ireland		Eliza Grant	29 Aug 1829
Mary	26	F	Carder	Ireland		Eliza Grant	29 Aug 1829
William John	2	M	None	Ireland		Eliza Grant	29 Aug 1829
PYNE, E.	33	F		France	United States	Howard	20 Aug 1827
G.	8	M		France	United States	Howard	20 Aug 1827
H.	4	F		France	United States	Howard	20 Aug 1827
J. A.	31	M	Mechanic	France	United States	Howard	20 Aug 1827
J. A., Jr.	9	M		France	United States	Howard	20 Aug 1827
L.	2	F		France	United States	Howard	20 Aug 1827
S.	6	F		France	United States	Howard	20 Aug 1827
PYRMAN, John	30	M		Germany	United States	Lydia	18 Jun 1828

NAMES OF PASSENGERS	AGE	SEX	OCCUPATIONS	COUNTRY TO WHICH THEY BELONG	COUNTRY THEY INTEND TO INHABIT	SHIPS/DATES OF ARRIVAL	
QUA, C. Val	45	F	Lady	Mexico	Mexico	Brown	29 Apr 1825
QUACKERS, J.	1	M	Farmer	Switzerland	U. States	Alfred	8 Jul 1828
J.	2	M	Farmer	Switzerland	U. States	Alfred	8 Jul 1828
J.	40	M	Farmer	Switzerland	U. States	Alfred	8 Jul 1828
Maria	30	F	Farmer	Switzerland	U. States	Alfred	8 Jul 1828
QUADRADO,							
Joaquim Jose	18	M	Gentleman	S. America	S. America	American	18 Oct 1824
QUAGLE, Ellenor	54	F		Great Britain	United States	India	5 Sep 1827
QUAID, Mary	30	F	...	G. Britain	U. States	New England	28 Sep 1824
QUAIFE, Abraham	29	M	Farmer	England	United States	Acosta	28 Jul 1823
Ann	2					Xenophon	25 Jul 1826
Ann	26			Sussex	...	Hudson	14 Jun 1827
Eliza	26	F				Acosta	28 Jul 1823
Ezibella	4			Sussex	...	Hudson	14 Jun 1827
Grace	36			England	S. New York	Xenophon	25 Jul 1826
Harriot	28	F				Acosta	28 Jul 1823
John	7					Xenophon	25 Jul 1826
Joseph	3			Sussex	...	Hudson	14 Jun 1827
Stephen	1			Sussex	...	Hudson	14 Jun 1827
Susannah	6/12	F				Acosta	28 Jul 1823
Tamar	10	F				Xenophon	25 Jul 1826
Thomas	68	M	Farmer	England	United States	Acosta	28 Jul 1823
Walker	8					Xenophon	25 Jul 1826
William	4					Xenophon	25 Jul 1826
William	28		B...	Sussex	...	Hudson	14 Jun 1827
QUAIL, Ann	5	F	Labourer	England	U. States	Ayrshire	12 May 1828
Ann	23	F	None	Great Britain	United States	William Dawson	18 Jun 1827
Ann	36	F	Labourer	England	U. States	Ayrshire	12 May 1828
John	16	M	Labourer	England	U. States	Ayrshire	12 May 1828
Mary	1	F	Labourer	England	U. States	Ayrshire	12 May 1828
Matthew	26	M	Weaver	Great Britain	United States	William Dawson	18 Jun 1827
Philip	40	M	Labourer	England	U. States	Ayrshire	12 May 1828
Phillip	19	M	Labourer	England	U. States	Ayrshire	12 May 1828
QUAILE, Ann	3	F	Farmer	Great Britain	U.S. America	Chili	7 Jul 1827
Catharine	6	F	Farmer	Great Britain	U.S. America	Chili	7 Jul 1827
Catharine	40	F	Farmer	Great Britain	U.S. America	Chili	7 Jul 1827
Jane	12	F	Farmer	Great Britain	U.S. America	Chili	7 Jul 1827
Jno.	30	M		Ireland		Anacreon	7 Sep 1827
John	18	M	Farmer	Great Britain	U.S. America	Chili	7 Jul 1827
John	50	M	Farmer	Great Britain	U.S. America	Chili	7 Jul 1827
Thos.	16	M	Farmer	Great Britain	U.S. America	Chili	7 Jul 1827
Wm.	21	M	Farmer	Great Britain	U.S. America	Chili	7 Jul 1827
QUAIN, Patrick	33	M	Smith	U. States	U. States	Wm. Penn	18 Sep 1827
Robert	23	M		Ireland	Jamaica	Little Cherub	11 Aug 1825
QUAMPP, Anthony	22	M	Button Maker	Germany	United States	Ohio	10 Jul 1820
QUARDIEN, Joseph	30	M	Merchant	France	U. States	Don Quixote	20 Mar 1827
QUARDRATTO, Francis	34	M	Secretary Spanish Legation	Spain		Eliza	22 Oct 1828
QUARE, James	5	M		Isle of Man	Ohio	Curler	7 Jul 1827
James	34	M	Tailor	Isle of Man	Ohio	Curler	7 Jul 1827
Jane	6	F		Isle of Man	Ohio	Curler	7 Jul 1827
Jane	30	F		Isle of Man	Ohio	Curler	7 Jul 1827
John	1	M		Isle of Man	Ohio	Curler	7 Jul 1827
QUARQUE, Chay	37	M	Merchant	New York	New York	John London	8 May 1823
QUART, Thomas	32			Kent, England		Cincinnatus	17 May 1823
QUARTERMAN, Edward	22	M	Lamp Maker	England	United States	Nimrod	30 Aug 1824
John	22	M	Labourer	England	United States	Nimrod	30 Aug 1824
QUAY, Ann	24	F		England		Anacreon	7 Sep 1827
Richard	18	M	Machanic	England	U. States	Emulous	22 Aug 1828
QUAYLE, Catherine	21	F	Milliner	England	United States	Essex	23 May 1828
Charles	27	F		Great Britain	United States	India	5 Sep 1827
Emme	18	F	Milliner	England	United States	Essex	23 May 1828
John	18	M	Ser...	Great Britain	United States	George Clinton	27 Aug 1827
John	34	M	Labourer	England	U. States	Ayrshire	12 May 1828
Joseph	13	M	None	England	United States	Jubilee	12 May 1828
Robt.	6	M	None	Great Britain	United States	Penelope	11 Jun 1827
William	21		Shoe Maker	Great Britain	United States	Thomas Dickason	29 Aug 1828

NAMES OF PASSENGERS	AGE	SEX	OCCUPATIONS	COUNTRY TO WHICH THEY BELONG	COUNTRY THEY INTEND TO INHABIT	SHIPS/DATES OF ARRIVAL	
QUEEN, Catherine	4/12	F		Ireland	United States	Kleber	23 Jul 1827
Fanny	22	F		Ireland	United States	Kleber	23 Jul 1827
John	25	M	Labourer	Ireland	United States	General Marion	6 Oct 1828
Mary Ann	24	F	Servant	Ireland	U. States	Henrietta	7 Jul 1825
Mathew	23	M	C...t	Ireland	United States	Kleber	23 Jul 1827
QUEG, Betsey	20	F		Ireland	United States	Huldah & Judah	30 Jul 1822
QUEHANNO, John	30	M	Merchant	Cuba	Cuba	Exploit	3 Nov 1827
QUEL, Thomas	20	M		England	U. States	Emulous	22 Aug 1828
QUENTANA, J.	21	M	Merchant	Mexico	Mexico	Hannah Elizabeth	19 Mar 1827
QUENTIN, Margt.	24		Spinster	Scotland	United States	Camillus	3 May 1828
QUERIFEL, Mary		F		Guersey	New York	Comet	19 Oct 1826
Mary	20	F		Guersey	New York	Comet	19 Oct 1826
Mary	26	F		Guersey	New York	Comet	19 Oct 1826
Samuel	28	M	Painter & Glazier	Guersey	New York	Comet	19 Oct 1826
QUERPOISSON, —, Mrs.	48	F	Lady	France	U. States	Queen Mab	16 Jun 1827
QUERTIER, Amand	29	M	Merchant	United States	United States	Robert Fulton	13 Mar 1827
QUESNEL, Walter, Mr.			None	U.S.	U.S.	Sully	26 Oct 1829
QUESTEAD, William	30	M	Cooper	England	New York	Brighton	19 Aug 1829
QUESUDER, A.	21	M	Merchant	Island Cuba	U. States	Havana Packet	27 Jul 1827
QUIBBLE, William	25	M	Farmer	Great Britain	United States	Mary & Harriet	3 Jul 1829
QUICH, Thomas	20	M	Labourer	England	U. States	Ayrshire	12 May 1828
QUICK, —, Mr.	40		Sevt.	G. Britain	America	Magnet	24 Sep 1824
Bridget	20	F	Spinster	Ireland	America	William	21 May 1825
Elizh.	13	F	None	Isle of Man		Ocean	13 Jul 1827
James	9	M	None	Isle of Man		Ocean	13 Jul 1827
Jane	11	F	None	Isle of Man		Ocean	13 Jul 1827
Jerry	25	M	Baker	Ireland	United States	Combine	4 Jun 1825
John	1	M	None	Isle of Man		Ocean	13 Jul 1827
Margt.	16	F	None	Isle of Man		Ocean	13 Jul 1827
Margt.	43	F	None	Isle of Man		Ocean	13 Jul 1827
Margt.	60	F	None	Isle of Man		Ocean	13 Jul 1827
Patrick	34	M	Shoemaker	England	United States	Jubilee	12 May 1828
Philip	39	M	Farmer	Isle of Man		Ocean	13 Jul 1827
Saml.	38	M	Labourer	Isle of Man		Ocean	13 Jul 1827
Thos.	3	M	None	Isle of Man		Ocean	13 Jul 1827
Willm.	6	M	None	Isle of Man		Ocean	13 Jul 1827
QUID, Jno. Moore	26	M	Servant	Ireland	U. States	Xenophon	13 Jun 1823
Sarah T.	25	F	Servant	Ireland	U. States	Xenophon	13 Jun 1823
QUIG, Martha	28	F		Ireland	U. States	Nancy	16 Aug 1822
Philip	28	M	Servant	Ireland	U. States	Wormontogus	17 May 1822
QUIGAN, Ann	2	M	None	...	...	Frances Henrietta	30 Jun 1827
Catherine	28	M	None	...	...	Frances Henrietta	30 Jun 1827
Christian	.../12	M	None	...	...	Frances Henrietta	30 Jun 1827
Robert	30	M	...	...	...	Frances Henrietta	30 Jun 1827
QUIGGON, Thomas	32			Ireland	Ohio	Peru	30 May 1828
QUIGLAN, Hugh	30	M	Labourer	Gr. Britain		Moro Castle	6 Jul 1827
QUIGLEY, ...	5	F	Girl	Ireland	United States	Trident	17 May 1825
Ann	25		Shoemaker	England	United States	Mary	15 Jul 1822
Cathr.	11	F	Girl	Ireland	United States	Trident	17 May 1825
Henry	30	M	Farmer	Ireland	United States	Trident	17 May 1825
James	26	M		Ireland	United States	William & George	14 May 1828
John	24	M	Butcher	England	U. States	Rising States	20 Sep 1828
John	27	M	Labourer	Ireland	United States	Montgomery	6 Mar 1829
Mary	20	F	Farmer	Ireland	U. States	Champion	26 Jul 1827
Mary	30	F	Spinster	Ireland	United States	Trident	17 May 1825
Nancy	8	F	Girl	Ireland	United States	Trident	17 May 1825
Twins	30		Shoemaker	England	United States	Mary	15 Jul 1822
QUIGLY, Anor	9			Ireland	New York	Marcella	18 May 1827
Bernard	30	M	Labourer	Ireland	United States	Asia	29 Jul 1829
John	10	M	Boy	Ireland	United States	Trident	17 May 1825
Mary	10			Ireland	New York	Marcella	18 May 1827
QUIGNO, D.	39	M	Merchant	Spain	Spain	Hero	11 May 1824

NAMES OF PASSENGERS	AGE	SEX	OCCUPATIONS	COUNTRY TO WHICH THEY BELONG	COUNTRY THEY INTEND TO INHABIT	SHIPS/DATES OF ARRIVAL	
QUIIN, Dorothy	28	F	None			Manhattan	8 Aug 1820
QUILLET, Augustus	21	M	Servant	France	U. States	Edward Quesnel	17 Mar 1829
QUILLS, William	22	M		Scotland	United States	Camillus	9 May 1827
QUILT, Ann	22	F	None	Scotland	United States	Mary & Susan	5 Aug 1828
QUILY,							
Rosomond, Black	25	F	Servant	U.S.	U.S.	Frances	21 Jul 1827
QUIMBY, John	24	M	Black Smith	Sussex		Aurora	8 Jun 1827
QUIME, Robert	20	M	Wever	Ireland	United States	Fabius	4 Jun 1828
QUIN, Anne	20	F		Ireland	America	Liverpool	31 Aug 1827
Arthur	24	M	Labourer	Ireland	United States	Catharine	22 Jul 1825
Biddy	10	F		Ireland	United States	Trio	13 Jun 1827
Bridget	12	F	Labourer	Ireland	New York	Mary	13 Dec 1821
Bridget	18	F	None	England	Pittsburgh	Orozimbo	8 Jun 1822
Bridget	18	F	Farmer	Longford		Mount Vernon	7 Jun 1824
Catharine	16	F	Servant	Ireland	United States	Wilson	27 Jun 1826
Catharine	18	F	Labourer	Ireland	U.S.A.	Dalhouse Castle	21 Aug 1829
Catharine	40	F		Ireland	America	Liverpool	31 Aug 1827
Catherin	18	F		Ireland	United States	Nancy R. Crowell	21 Sep 1822
Catherine	1 3/12	F		Ireland	America	Liverpool	31 Aug 1827
Cathr.	18	F	Wife	Ireland	Canada	Ann Maria	7 Sep 1827
Cathr.	25	F	Farmer	Ireland	U. States	Francis	6 Sep 1827
Charles	14	M		Ireland	America	Liverpool	31 Aug 1827
Charles	17		Laborer	Ireland	United States	Robert Burns	18 Jun 1821
Chas.	20	M	Clerk	Ireland	United States	Trident	16 May 1826
Chas.	56	M	Farmer	Ireland	America	Liverpool	31 Aug 1827
D.	26		Farmer	Ireland	United States	Courier	16 May 1825
Daniel	15	M	Labourer	Ireland	New York	Mary	13 Dec 1821
Dennis	24	M	Laborer	Ireland	U. States	Lady Hunter	8 Aug 1826
Edward	51	M	Farmer	England	Pittsburgh	Orozimbo	8 Jun 1822
Edwd.	23	M	Shoemaker	Ireland	United States	Trident	16 May 1826
Elenor		F	Farmer	Ireland	U. States	Dickinson	30 Jul 1825
Eliza	19	F		Ireland	America	Liverpool	31 Aug 1827
Elizabeth	20	F		Ireland	U. States	Lady Hunter	8 Aug 1826
Elizth	...	...	...	Ireland	U. States	Courier	17 Mar 1827
Ellen	15	F		Ireland	United States	Trio	13 Jun 1827
Ellen	38		Farmer	Great Britain		John Dickinson	5 Apr 1821
Felix	32	M	Labourer			Manhattan	8 Aug 1820
Francis	17		Farmer	Great Britain		John Dickinson	5 Apr 1821
Geo.	23	M	Labourer	Ireland		Robert Fulton	4 Jun 1828
Harriet	20	F	Labourer	England	U. States	Comet	23 Aug 1828
Hugh	18	M	Labourer	Ireland	Canada	Ann Maria	7 Sep 1827
Hugh	18	M	Weaver	Ireland	U. States	Josephine	30 Aug 1828
Isable	27	F	Labourer	Ireland	United States	Borneo	2 Oct 1827
James	7	M	None	England	Pittsburgh	Orozimbo	8 Jun 1822
James	12	M		Ireland	America	Liverpool	31 Aug 1827
James	21	M	Servant	Ireland	New York	Louisa	20 Jul 1826
James	48		Farmer	Great Britain		John Dickinson	5 Apr 1821
Jane	18	F	None			Manhattan	8 Aug 1820
Jas.	23					Hibernia	15 Aug 1820
Jno.	30	M	Shop Keeper	Gt. Britain	U.S. America	James Cropper	29 Nov 1827
Joana	12	F		Ireland	United States	Trio	13 Jun 1827
John	4		Laborer	Ireland	New York	Lady Hunter	19 Oct 1826
John	18	M		Ireland	U. States	St. Michael	26 Oct 1824
John	23	M	Labourer	Ireland	U. States	Josephine	7 May 1827
John	23	M	Laborer	Ireland	United States	Trio	13 Jun 1827
John	28	M	Labourer	New Brunswick	New Brunswick	Lady Hunter	22 Aug 1825
John	40	M		Great Britain	U. States	Lady Hunter	26 Nov 1823
John	48	M	Farmer	Pennsylva.	Pennsylva.	Commerce	24 Sep 1823
John	55	M	Stonemason	Ireland	New York	Louisa	20 Jul 1826
Kitty	7	F				Manhattan	8 Aug 1820
Lawrence	31	M	Labourer	Ireland	U. States	Josephine	7 May 1827
M.	21	M	Labourer	Ireland	Canada	Ann Maria	7 Sep 1827
Margaret	10	F	Labourer	Ireland	New York	Mary	13 Dec 1821
Margaret	16	F		Ireland	U. States	St. Michael	26 Oct 1824
Margarett	3		Farmer	Great Britain		John Dickinson	5 Apr 1821
Maria	10		Farmer	Great Britain		John Dickinson	5 Apr 1821
Martin	24	M	Farmer	Ireland	United States	Dublin Packet	22 Apr 1822
Mary	17	F		Ireland	America	Liverpool	31 Aug 1827

NAMES OF PASSENGERS	AGE	SEX	OCCUPATIONS	COUNTRY TO WHICH THEY BELONG	COUNTRY THEY INTEND TO INHABIT	SHIPS/DATES OF ARRIVAL	
QUIN (cont'd)							
Mary	23	F		Ireland	U. States	Lady Hunter	8 Aug 1826
Mary	23		Laborer	Ireland	New York	Lady Hunter	19 Oct 1826
Mary	23	F	Spinner	Great Britain	United States	Atlantic	8 Dec 1827
Mary	25	F	Lady	Great Britain	United States	Hanford	9 Oct 1829
Mary	30	F		Ireland	U. States	Fame	15 Nov 1826
Mary, his wife [Miles]	19	F		United States	New York	Rambler	14 Oct 1824
Michl.	16	M		Ireland	America	Liverpool	31 Aug 1827
Miles	25	M	Carpenter	United States	New York	Rambler	14 Oct 1824
Pat	4	M		Ireland	United States	Commerce	13 Jun 1828
Pat	28	M	Laborer	Ireland	United States	Trio	13 Jun 1827
Patrick	29	M	Farmer	Ireland	United States	Lord Strangford	20 Jun 1826
Peter	24		Farmer	Great Britain		John Dickinson	5 Apr 1821
Phillip	13		Farmer	Great Britain		John Dickinson	5 Apr 1821
Robt.	6	M		Ireland	America	Liverpool	31 Aug 1827
Rosanna	8		Farmer	Great Britain		John Dickinson	5 Apr 1821
Rosanna	17	F		G.B.	America	Pacific	13 Jan 1827
Rose	33	F	None	Great Brittain	New York	Albion	11 Jun 1821
Sally	6		Farmer	Great Britain		John Dickinson	5 Apr 1821
Terence	18	M	Laborer	Ireland	U. States	Lady Hunter	8 Aug 1826
Thomas	24	M	Labourer	England	U. States	Comet	23 Aug 1828
Thos.	25	M	Farmer	Ireland	America	Liverpool	31 Aug 1827
Turner	25	M				Lady of the Lake	23 Aug 1828
*left ship							
William	20	M	Tailor	U. States	U. States	Nancy	11 Apr 1822
Wirth	20	M		Ireland	U. States	St. Michael	26 Oct 1824
QUINAN, Martin	22	M	Farmer	Ireland	United States	Lima	19 Jun 1824
Unity	24	F	Sevnt.	Ireland	United States	Lima	19 Jun 1824
QUINDER, Antonio	28	M	Merchant	Spain	U. States	Tobasco	23 Jul 1827
QUINDES, A.	30	M	Merchant	United States	U. States	Prince Edward	26 Mar 1827
QUINLAN, David	32	M	Farmer	St. Johns, N.B.	United States	Henrietta	17 Aug 1825
Edmond	52	M	Farmer	Ireland	New York, U.S.	Angelica	18 Aug 1823
QUINLEY, Daniel	22	M	Laborer	Ireland	United States	Sylvester Healy	17 Oct 1825
QUINLIN, Thomas	27 3/12	M	Labourer	England	United States	John Wells	22 May 1826
QUINN, A.	25		Farmer	Ireland	United States	Courier	16 May 1825
Ann	...	F	Spinster	Ireland	United States	General Putnam	20 Jun 1825
Ann	24 7/12	F	Seamstress	Ireland	United States	Atlantic	21 Jul 1827
Ann	25	F	Matron	Ireland	U. States	Josephine	30 Aug 1828
Bernard	24	M	Weaver	U. States	U. States	St. Croix	13 Sep 1827
Cath.	20	F		Ireland	United States	Thomas	13 Dec 1827
Catharine	18	F	Labourer	Ireland	U. States	Two Marys	20 Apr 1825
Chas.	20		Carpenter	Great Britan	United States	Newry	11 Jul 1827
Dennis	38	M	...	Co. Wicklow	United States	Java	9 Jul 1827
Elisabeth	22	F		Great Britain	United States	Mary Howland	19 Jul 1827
Elizabeth	25	F	Weaver	Ireland	Ireland	Sarah G.	28 Nov 1827
Ewd.	23	M	Labourer	Ireland	United States	Josephine	30 Apr 1828
F.	22	M	Labourer	Ireland	United States	Josephine	30 Apr 1828
Fanny	26	F		Ireland	United States	Curler	3 Mar 1828
Felix	14	M	family [of Onas]	Ireland	United States	Atlantic	21 Jul 1827
Francis	28	M	Laborer or Spinster	Ireland	United States	Sarah G	11 Sep 1827
Garret	24	M		Great Britain	United States	Mary Howland	19 Jul 1827
Hugh	20	M	Labourer	Ireland	U.S. of America	Meteor	19 Mar 1828
James	19		Farmer	England	United States	Mary	15 Jul 1822
James	24	M	Labourer	Ireland	United States	Catharine	22 Jul 1825
James	32	M	Smith	Isle of Man		Ocean	13 Jul 1827
John	6/12	M	Infant	Ireland	Ireland	Sarah G.	28 Nov 1827
John	11	M	family [of Onas]	Ireland	United States	Atlantic	21 Jul 1827
John	25	M	Farmer	Ireland	America	Superior	12 Jun 1824
John	27	M	Labourer	Ireland	Ireland	Sarah G.	28 Nov 1827
John	30	M	Labourer	Great Britain		Moro Castle	6 Jul 1827
John	30	M	Farmer	Ireland	U. States	Francis	6 Sep 1827
Joseph	25	M	...	England	U.N. States	William Byrnes	23 Jul 1824
L.	36	F		Ireland	United States	Commerce	13 Jun 1828
Margt.	30	F		Ireland	United States	Commerce	13 Jun 1828
Mary	0 6/12	F	Laborer or Spinster	Ireland	United States	Sarah G	11 Sep 1827
Mary	1	F	Labourer	Ireland	U. States	Two Marys	20 Apr 1825
Mary	12	F	Servant	Ireland	United States	Josephine	30 Apr 1828
Mary	13	F	...	Co. Wicklow	United States	Java	9 Jul 1827

NAMES OF PASSENGERS	AGE	SEX	OCCUPATIONS	COUNTRY TO WHICH THEY BELONG	COUNTRY THEY INTEND TO INHABIT	SHIPS/DATES OF ARRIVAL	
QUINN (cont'd)							
Mary	20	F	Labourer	Ireland	U. States	Two Marys	20 Apr 1825
Mary	20	F		Ireland	United States	Lord Wellington	14 Nov 1827
Mary	24	F	Farmer	Ireland	America	Superior	12 Jun 1824
Mary	27	F		Ireland	United States	Romulus	24 Jun 1826
Mary	30		None	Great Britain	United States	Roman	10 Sep 1827
Michl.	24	M	Farmer	N. Brunswick	New Brunswick	Abigale	9 Aug 1821
Onas	60 3/12	M	Dealer	Ireland	United States	Atlantic	21 Jul 1827
Pat	22	M	Baker	Great Britain	United States	Wanderer	11 Jul 1826
Pat	23	M	Labourer	Ireland	United States	Josephine	30 Apr 1828
Patrick	25	M	Baker	Ireland		Marchioness	13 May 1828
Patrick	25 6/12	M	Labourer	Ireland	U. States	Courier	17 Mar 1828
Patrick	40	M	Labourer	Ireland	U. States	Atlantic	19 Aug 1825
Peter	20	M	Labourer	Ireland	United States	Josephine	30 Apr 1828
Peter	24	M	Labourer	Ireland	U. States	William	27 Jul 1824
Rose	22	F	Laborer or Spinster	Ireland	United States	Sarah G	11 Sep 1827
Rose	23	F	Labourer	Ireland	U. States	Two Marys	20 Apr 1825
Sally	20	F	Spinster	Ireland	U.S. of America	Meteor	19 Mar 1828
Sarah	20	F	Wife	Ireland	U.S. of America	Meteor	19 Mar 1828
Sarah	20 3/12	F	family [of Onas]	Ireland	United States	Atlantic	21 Jul 1827
Sarah	50 4/12	F	family [of Onas]	Ireland	United States	Atlantic	21 Jul 1827
Thomas	24	M	Farmer	Ireland	United States	Elizabeth	8 Jun 1827
Thos.	20	M	Labourer	Ireland	United States	Essex	23 May 1828
William	18	M	Labourer	Ireland	U. States	Atlantic	19 Aug 1825
Wm.	24	M	Servant	Ireland	U. States	Sarah G	30 Jun 1828
QUINOULLY, —	45	M	Merchant	France	France	Clio	7 Aug 1826
QUINS, Cathr.	34	F	None	Ireland	New York	Concordia	12 Oct 1826
QUINSBY, Fanny	25	F	Servant	Ireland	United States	Edwin	27 Oct 1828
QUINSEY, L.	22	M	Clerk	G. Britain	U. States	St. George	7 Jun 1828
QUINSY, Ewd.	40	M	Carpenter	G. Britain	U. States	Mary Howland	22 Sep 1828
Hannah	5	F		G. Britain	U. States	Mary Howland	22 Sep 1828
John	17	M	Carpenter	G. Britain	U. States	Mary Howland	22 Sep 1828
Mary	38	F		G. Britain	U. States	Mary Howland	22 Sep 1828
Mary Ann	9	F		G. Britain	U. States	Mary Howland	22 Sep 1828
Robt.	13	M	Carpenter	G. Britain	U. States	Mary Howland	22 Sep 1828
Saml.	20	M	Carpenter	G. Britain	U. States	Mary Howland	22 Sep 1828
Thomas	19	M	Carpenter	G. Britain	U. States	Mary Howland	22 Sep 1828
William	12	M	Carpenter	G. Britain	U. States	Mary Howland	22 Sep 1828
QUINTAIN, Mary	20			Ireland	United States	Geo. Canning	5 Jun 1828
QUINTANA, Peter	22	M	Merchant	Havana	Havana	Robert Reade	9 Feb 1822
QUINTANO, Clemento	23	M	Servant	Spain	Spain	Wallace	18 May 1825
QUINTERRE, A.	30	M	Merchant	Spain	U. States	Sea Nymph	30 Apr 1828
QUINTYNE, Elenor F.	19	F	Servant	England	U. States	New York	11 Jul 1823
QUIR, James	23	M	Farmer	Ireland	America	William	21 May 1825
QUIRCK, Cathr.	18	F		Ireland	United States	William Byrnes	6 Apr 1826
QUIREAN, Ph. J.	30	M	Mariner	American	U. States	Factor	10 May 1821
QUIRIE, Alex.	24	M	Mason	Great Britain	United States	Colossus	5 Jun 1827
Anne	6	F	None	Great Britain	United States	Colossus	5 Jun 1827
Anne	52	F	None	Great Britain	United States	Colossus	5 Jun 1827
Ephraim	14	M	None	Great Britain	United States	Colossus	5 Jun 1827
George	52	M	Mason	Great Britain	United States	Colossus	5 Jun 1827
Joseph	17	M	Mason	Great Britain	United States	Colossus	5 Jun 1827
William	9	M	None	Great Britain	United States	Colossus	5 Jun 1827
QUIRIPAL, Csine	2	F	Mechanic	Germany	U. States	Bayard	16 May 1827
Mary	27	F	Mechanic	Germany	U. States	Bayard	16 May 1827
QUIRK, Charles	19	M		Ireland	United States	William Byrnes	6 Apr 1826
Jane	22	F		Isle of Man	Ohio	Curler	7 Jul 1827
Jerh.	20	M	Farmer	Ireland	America	Liverpool	31 Aug 1827
John	1	M		Isle of Man	Ohio	Curler	7 Jul 1827
John	23	M	Weaver	Isle of Man	Ohio	Curler	7 Jul 1827
Margaret	26	F		Isle of Man	Ohio	Curler	7 Jul 1827
Nancy	26	F	Servant	G. Britain	U. States	Margaret Bogle	12 Jun 1828
Thomas	26	M	Labourer	G. Britain	U. States	Margaret Bogle	12 Jun 1828
QUIROPAL, John	34	M	Mechanic	Germany	U. States	Bayard	16 May 1827
QUISADA, Josia	28	M	Merchant	Spain	U. States	Virginia	8 Mar 1828
QUITLIAN, Betsey	13	F		Great Britain	United States	Meridian	2 Jul 1827
Cathe.	11	F		Great Britain	United States	Meridian	2 Jul 1827
Cathe.	36	F		Great Britain	United States	Meridian	2 Jul 1827
Elisa	4	F		Great Britain	United States	Meridian	2 Jul 1827

NAMES OF PASSENGERS	AGE	SEX	OCCUPATIONS	COUNTRY TO WHICH THEY BELONG	COUNTRY THEY INTEND TO INHABIT	SHIPS/DATES OF ARRIVAL	
QUITLIAN (cont'd)							
John	10	M		Great Britain	United States	Meridian	2 Jul 1827
John	44	M	Farmer	Great Britain	United States	Meridian	2 Jul 1827
Joseph	1	M		Great Britain	United States	Meridian	2 Jul 1827
Mary	13	F		Great Britain	United States	Meridian	2 Jul 1827
Thos.	6	M		Great Britain	United States	Meridian	2 Jul 1827
QUNN, Peter	26	M	...loc Dresser	Great Britain	U. States	St. Croix	13 Sep 1827
QUNS, Charles	40	M	Printer	Ireland	New York	Concordia	12 Oct 1826
QUYANNO, Rafael	27	M	Merchant	Spain	Spain	Claudio	16 Oct 1827
QWYE, Janne M.	45	F		France	U. States	C. Amelia	30 Jun 1828
R..., ...	...	F	Servant	Ireland	United States	Carolina Ann	14 May 1827
Janes	...	...	C...	Ireland	United States	Fabius	4 Jun 1828
M...	...	F	Servant	Ireland	United States	Carolina Ann	14 May 1827
R...ODER, ...	27			Ireland	U.S.	Hibernia	27 Jun 1821
R...ON, ...	...			...	England	Great Britain	7 May 1827
RA..., ...	...			...	England	Great Britain	7 May 1827
RA...DERT, ...	40	F				Eliza Grant	6 Oct 1828
RA...SON, Eliza	20	F	Housekeeper	Ireland	United States	Carolina Ann	14 May 1827
John	...0	M	Labourer	Ireland	United States	Carolina Ann	14 May 1827
RABERG, Chas. H.	21	M	Merchant	Holland	U. States	Ariadne	12 Dec 1822
RABIN, Rosina	24	F	Spinster	Werdenburg	United States	Xenophon	2 Jun 1824
RABOLT, —	48	M	Domestic	France	United States	Cavalier	25 Jul 1828
Eliza	19	F	Domestic	France	United States	Cavalier	25 Jul 1828
M.	14	F		France	United States	Cavalier	25 Jul 1828
Maria	16	F		France	United States	Cavalier	25 Jul 1828
RABOT, Mary	25	F	Nurse			Cadmus	18 Aug 1828
RABY, Jno.	19	M	Miner	U. States	U. States	Martha	20 Jun 1825
RACHAEL, H.	21	M			United States	Elizabeth	22 May 1822
RACHEL, —	50	M	Domestic	Africa		Chase	5 Jul 1825
RACHUE, John	30	M	...	Ireland	U.S. of America	Hamilton	18 Jul 1827
RACINAT, M. H., Hon.	46	M	Collection of Quebeck	England	Canada	Auritz	20 May 1823
RADBONE, Thomas	60	M	Farmer	Great Britain	United States	Illinois	9 Oct 1820
RADCLEF, Jane	19	F	Servant	Ireland	United States	Wilson	27 Jun 1826
RADCLIFF, Ann	23	F	None	Isle of Man		Ocean	13 Jul 1827
Jane	44	F	None	Isle of Man		Ocean	13 Jul 1827
Wm.	1	M	None	Isle of Man		Ocean	13 Jul 1827
Wm.	32	M	Labourer	Isle of Man		Ocean	13 Jul 1827
RADCLIFFE, Ann	9	F	None	Great Britain		Casanda	5 Sep 1827
Betty	8	F	None	England	U. States	Birmingham	12 Oct 1827
Eliza	36	F	Wife	Ireland	United States	Dublin Packet	23 May 1828
Frances	28	F		England	United States	William Byrnes	15 Aug 1826
Hester	5	F	None	England	U. States	Birmingham	12 Oct 1827
Jas.	44	M	Cabinet Maker	Great Britain		Casanda	5 Sep 1827
Jas. C.	13	M	None	Great Britain		Casanda	5 Sep 1827
John	16	M	Farmer	Ireland	United States	Dublin Packet	23 May 1828
John	18	M	Joiner	Isle of Man		Ocean	13 Jul 1827
Jos.	1	M	None	England	U. States	Birmingham	12 Oct 1827
Mary	3	F	None	England	U. States	Birmingham	12 Oct 1827
Nancy	34	F	None	England	U. States	Birmingham	12 Oct 1827
R.	30	M	Weaver	England	United States	Dalhouse Castle	8 May 1827
Samuel	19	M	Farmer	Ireland	United States	Dublin Packet	23 May 1828
Tho.	31	M		England	United States	William Byrnes	15 Aug 1826
Thos.	15	M	Joiner	Isle of Man		Ocean	13 Jul 1827
Thos.	54	M	Joiner	Isle of Man		Ocean	13 Jul 1827
Wm.	24	M	Taylor	Isle of Man		Ocean	13 Jul 1827
RADDEN, Michael	24	M	Labourer	Ireland	United States	Nancy	16 Jul 1824
RADDIAK, James	17	M	Weaver	Ireland	U. States	Wanderer	1 Sep 1828
RADDY, Joseph	6	M	None	Great Britain	United States	Eliza Barker	3 Jul 1826
Martha	30	F	Farmer	Ireland	U. States	Dickinson	30 Jul 1825
RADEKER, John	20	M	Labourer	...	United States	Hanford	17 Oct 1828
RADESON, Charles	28/12	M		France	United States	Stephania	6 Dec 1827
*Died on the Voyage, Oct.							
Joseph	7/12	M		France	United States	Stephania	6 Dec 1827
*Died on the Voyage, Nov.							
Louisa	4	F		France	United States	Stephania	6 Dec 1827
Marian	30	F		France	United States	Stephania	6 Dec 1827
Mich.	31	M	Weaver	France	United States	Stephania	6 Dec 1827

NAMES OF PASSENGERS	AGE	SEX	OCCUPATIONS	COUNTRY TO WHICH THEY BELONG	COUNTRY THEY INTEND TO INHABIT	SHIPS/DATES OF ARRIVAL	
RADFIELD, G.	42	M	Farmer	Great Britton	U. State	Earl of Liverpool	16 Aug 1826
RADFORD, Ann	36	F		Great Britain	United States	Ganges	8 Jul 1820
George	42	M	Farmer	Great Britain	United States	Ganges	8 Jul 1820
RADSER, Ab.	50	F		England	United States	Curler	3 Mar 1828
RAE, Alexr.	2	M		G. Brittain	U. States	Huldah & Judah	21 Jun 1822
Elizabeth	30	F		G. Brittain	U. States	Huldah & Judah	21 Jun 1822
Jno.	4	M		G. Brittain	U. States	Huldah & Judah	21 Jun 1822
Mathew	25	M	Farmer	G. Brittain	U. States	Huldah & Judah	21 Jun 1822
Wm.	30	M	Farmer	G. Brittain	U. States	Huldah & Judah	21 Jun 1822
Wm., Jr.	3/12	M		G. Brittain	U. States	Huldah & Judah	21 Jun 1822
RAEL, Antonio	22	M	Merchant	Spain	unknown	Juanita	13 Oct 1829
RAFELYE, Wm. E.	23	M	Gentleman	Fiskill	Fishkill	Jupiter	27 May 1826
RAFERTY, A.	36	M	Labourer	Scotland	United States	Indus	5 Sep 1827
E.	30	F		Scotland	United States	Indus	5 Sep 1827
Harvey	1 7/12	M		Scotland	United States	Indus	5 Sep 1827
John	4	M		Scotland	United States	Indus	5 Sep 1827
Peter	6	M		Scotland	United States	Indus	5 Sep 1827
RAFFERTY, —, Mr.	25	M	Priest	U.S.	U.S.	Robert Edwards	11 Nov 1822
Catherine	9	F	Farmer	Great Brittain	U. States	William Byrnes	23 Jul 1824
Catherine	24	F	Farmer	Great Brittain	U. States	William Byrnes	23 Jul 1824
Elisabeth	17	F		Great Britain	United States	Mary Howland	19 Jul 1827
Felix	22	M	Bleacher	Ireland	United States	Princess Charlotte	26 Apr 1827
Francis	22	M	Farmer	Great Britain	United States	Mary Howland	19 Jul 1827
James	23		None			Amphion	31 May 1824
Joh...	2...	M	Labourer	Ireland	United States	Princess Charlotte	26 Apr 1827
Margaret	28	F	Spinster	Ireland	U. States	Globe	14 Jul 1821
Mary	19	F		Ireland	America	Plutarch	18 Jul 1826
Mary	24	F		Ireland	United States	Princess Charlotte	26 Apr 1827
Mary	30	...	...	...	...	Alexander Mansfield	18 Jun 1821
Maryan	9	...	...	...	...	Alexander Mansfield	18 Jun 1821
Matilda	5	...	...	...	...	Alexander Mansfield	18 Jun 1821
Pattrick	11	M	Farmer	Great Brittain	U. States	William Byrnes	23 Jul 1824
Peter	21	M	Farmer	Ireland	U. States	Francis	6 Sep 1827
Peter	27	M	Labourer	Ireland	America	Wilson	27 Nov 1826
Rose	4	F	Farmer	Great Brittain	U. States	William Byrnes	23 Jul 1824
Rose	32	F	Farmer	Great Brittain	U. States	William Byrnes	23 Jul 1824
Sarrah	16/12	F	Farmer	Great Brittain	U. States	William Byrnes	23 Jul 1824
Stewart	7	...	...	...	...	Alexander Mansfield	18 Jun 1821
Wm.	11	...	...	...	...	Alexander Mansfield	18 Jun 1821
RAFFO, M.	17	M	Gentleman	U. States	U. States	Perseverance	28 Apr 1828
RAFFORTY, Peter	32	M	Farmer	Great Brittain	U. States	William Byrnes	23 Jul 1824
RAFITIFF, Charls	24	M	Labourer	Ireland	United States	Edwin	29 Nov 1828
RAFLEN, Francois	42	M	Bake	Switzerland	United States	Calliope	20 Mar 1824
RAGE, John	55	M	Architect	Italy	U. States	Ann	11 Dec 1822
RAGG, Ann	13	F	None	England	United States	Great Britain	5 Sep 1827
RAGMONS, Stephn.	23	M	Merchant	U. States	U. States	Exertion	14 Dec 1822
RAGNET, Conely	40	M	Gentn.			Florida	1 Jun 1827
RAGONS, James	18	M	Farmer	Ireland	United States	Gem	16 Jun 1824
RAHIDLY, Mary	20	F	None	Ireland	U. States	Union	3 Jun 1822
RAIDY, Margt.	21 7/12	F	Servant	Ireland	United States	Atlantic	21 Jul 1827
RAIER, Felix	17	M	Farmer	Switzerland	United States	Elizabeth	27 Jul 1824
RAIN, Thomas	24	M	Master Book Binder	England	America	Erin	7 Nov 1821
RAINEBEAUX, A. C.	25	M	Merchant	N. York	U. States	Elias Burger	18 Apr 1823
RAINEY, Rob.	45	M	Merchant	Scotland	U. States	Amity	25 Sep 1822
Robert	45	M	Merchant	Scotland	United States	Amity	11 May 1821
RAINFORD, Benjn.	25	M	Malster	England	America	Franklin	19 Nov 1828
RAINFORTH, Thomas	24	M	Farmer	Yorkshire	New York	New York	31 Jul 1829
William	37	M	Farmer	Yorkshire	New York	New York	31 Jul 1829
RAINGEARD, —	30	M	Merchant	France	U. States	L'Adelee	22 Aug 1820
RAINIE, Alaxander	18	M	Weaver	Great Britain	United States	Courier	26 Jun 1827

NAMES OF PASSENGERS	AGE	SEX	OCCUPATIONS	COUNTRY TO WHICH THEY BELONG	COUNTRY THEY INTEND TO INHABIT	SHIPS/DATES OF ARRIVAL	
RAINIE (cont'd)							
George	60	M	Weaver	Great Britain	United States	Courier	26 Jun 1827
James	28	M	Weaver	Great Britain	United States	Courier	26 Jun 1827
Margaret	21	F	None	Great Britain	United States	Courier	26 Jun 1827
Margaret	50	F	None	Great Britain	United States	Courier	26 Jun 1827
Margaret	55	F	None	Great Britain	United States	Courier	26 Jun 1827
Marion	20	F	None	Great Britain	United States	Courier	26 Jun 1827
RAINS, ... W.	32	F		...	United States	Rufus King	27 Jun 1821
Alfred	7	M	Nothing	Great Britain	New York	Radius	7 Jul 1821
Elizabeth	5	F		...	United States	Rufus King	27 Jun 1821
Jane	7	F		...	United States	Rufus King	27 Jun 1821
John	3	M		...	United States	Rufus King	27 Jun 1821
John	16		Gentleman	England	England	Hudson	18 Jun 1825
John	36	M	...	...	United States	Rufus King	27 Jun 1821
Joseph	12	M		...	United States	Rufus King	27 Jun 1821
Nathaniel	40	M	Merchant	Great Britain	New York	Radius	7 Jul 1821
Thos.	1	M		...	United States	Rufus King	27 Jun 1821
Wm.	14	M		...	United States	Rufus King	27 Jun 1821
RAINY, —, Mr.	27	M	Planter	Dominico		Adams	11 Nov 1824
—, Mrs.	25	F		Dominico		Adams	11 Nov 1824
RAIRNON, James	30	M	Pedler	England	U. States	Roman	1 Dec 1828
RAISER, C. Margarita	18	F		Switzerland	United States	India	4 Aug 1826
F. E.	12	F		Switzerland	United States	India	4 Aug 1826
F. Lewis	6	M		Switzerland	United States	India	4 Aug 1826
G. B.	56	M	Tailor	Switzerland	United States	India	4 Aug 1826
J. A.	5	M		Switzerland	United States	India	4 Aug 1826
J. F.	9	M		Switzerland	United States	India	4 Aug 1826
L. Caroline	17	F		Switzerland	United States	India	4 Aug 1826
M.	47	F		Switzerland	United States	India	4 Aug 1826
S. Elizabeth	15	F		Switzerland	United States	India	4 Aug 1826
S. R.	3	F		Switzerland	United States	India	4 Aug 1826
RAITZ, Carl	10	M		Bardin	U. States	Bayard	5 Sep 1828
Carl	40	M	Farmer	Bardin	U. States	Bayard	5 Sep 1828
Cath.	10	M		Bardin	U. States	Bayard	5 Sep 1828
Christian	41	M		Bardin	U. States	Bayard	5 Sep 1828
Eliz.	13	M		Bardin	U. States	Bayard	5 Sep 1828
G. A.	15	M		Bardin	U. States	Bayard	5 Sep 1828
Lous	5	M		Bardin	U. States	Bayard	5 Sep 1828
Magdaline	7	M		Bardin	U. States	Bayard	5 Sep 1828
RAIVINGER, Anthony	4	M		Gt. Brittan		L'Esperance	6 Sep 1828
Caroline	37	F		Gt. Brittan		L'Esperance	6 Sep 1828
Jean	39	M	Tin man	Gt. Brittan		L'Esperance	6 Sep 1828
John	9	M		Gt. Brittan		L'Esperance	6 Sep 1828
Josephine	3	F		Gt. Brittan		L'Esperance	6 Sep 1828
Madeline	40	F		Gt. Brittan		L'Esperance	6 Sep 1828
RAKER, Jane	32	F		G. Britain	U. States	William Thompson	30 Apr 1822
RALAUSKI, J. C.	24	M	Merchant	Prussia	Prussia	Savannah	24 Apr 1828
RALERSTINE, C. Dono.	24	M	Merchant	Spain	U. States	Margaretta	2 May 1826
RALLEY, George	20	M		Great B.	U. States	William Neilson	26 Jul 1828
RALLY, James	33	M	Gentleman	Denmark		Chase	13 Apr 1821
RALPH, Edward	...	M	...	England	United States	London Packet	25 Dec 1820
Michal	38	M	None	Ireland	U. States	Franklin	7 Jul 1828
Samuel	45	M	Farmer	England	United States	Euphrates	18 Aug 1827
RALSTON, A. G.	25	M	Merchant	America	America	Panthea	18 Jul 1823
Gavin	25	M	Clerk	Schotland		New England	7 Jul 1826
George	48	M	Merchant	Great Britain	U.S. of America	Canada	1 Oct 1827
H., Mr.	23	M	Lawyer	U.S.A.		François I	19 Nov 1828
Samuel	17	M	Labourer	Ireland	South America	Robert Fulton	24 Jul 1826
RAM..., Christian	19	M	Farmer	Switzerland	United States	Elbe	2 Aug 1822
Joseph	20	M	Wheaver	Switzerland	United States	Elbe	2 Aug 1822
RAMAGE, —, Captn.	39	M	Captn. U.S. Navy	U.S.A.	U.S.A.	Bayard	25 Aug 1829
Barbara	1	F	Farmer	France	France	Sully	15 Jul 1829
Dorothy	8	F	Farmer	France	France	Sully	15 Jul 1829
George	40	M	Farmer	France	France	Sully	15 Jul 1829
George, Jr.	18	M	Farmer	France	France	Sully	15 Jul 1829
Justina	3	F	Farmer	France	France	Sully	15 Jul 1829
Maddina	15	F	Farmer	France	France	Sully	15 Jul 1829
Mary	10	F	Farmer	France	France	Sully	15 Jul 1829

NAMES OF PASSENGERS	AGE	SEX	OCCUPATIONS	COUNTRY TO WHICH THEY BELONG	COUNTRY THEY INTEND TO INHABIT	SHIPS/DATES OF ARRIVAL	
RAMAGE (cont'd)							
Salomie	40	F	Farmer	France	France	Sully	15 Jul 1829
Salomie, Jr.	13	F	Farmer	France	France	Sully	15 Jul 1829
W. J.	31	M	Doctor	United States	Jamaca	Active	25 Jun 1823
RAMAZIER, Lewis, Mr.	27	M	Merchant	Matanzes	Matanzes	Merced	23 Mar 1824
RAMBEY, C.	23	M	Merchant	France	Spain	Circassian	13 Jun 1825
RAMBIN, Arnaud	50	M	Merchant	U. States	U. States	Exchange	25 Sep 1826
RAMBURGER, Jno. J.	40	M	Mariner	Philada.	U. States	Exchange	20 Nov 1823
RAMFORD, Jane	15	F	None	Great Britan	United States	Hamilton	19 Mar 1827
RAMIENES, Sinforiam	25	M	Merchant	Central America	Central America	Robert Y. Haynes	2 Oct 1829
RAMIREZ, Jose	10	M	Servant	Spain	Spain	Franklin	14 Jul 1827
RAMKER, Ann	36	F		England	America	Birmingham	16 Oct 1826
John	27	M	Whitesmith	England	America	Birmingham	16 Oct 1826
Wm.	40	M	Cutter	England	America	Birmingham	16 Oct 1826
RAMMAGE, C.	35	M	Merchant	France	U. States	Jane	11 Dec 1827
RAMON, John	22	M	Locksmith	United States	United States	Globe	30 Aug 1828
RAMOS, A. V.	22	M	Watch Maker	Spain	Spain	Ambuscade	11 Jul 1821
RAMSAY, Alex	32	M	Bookbinder	Scotland	United States	Tom	2 Jul 1827
Eliza	45	F		Scotland	United States	Indus	5 Sep 1827
Hanna	4	F		Scotland	United States	Indus	5 Sep 1827
James	18	M		Scotland	United States	Indus	5 Sep 1827
James	30	M	Joiner	Scotland	United States	Scotsman	22 Aug 1828
Jean	21	F		Scotland	United States	Indus	5 Sep 1827
John	...	...	...		United States	London Packet	25 Dec 1820
John	0 6/12	M		Scotland	United States	Indus	5 Sep 1827
John	23	M	...	Scotland	United States	Indus	5 Sep 1827
John	25	M	Labourer	Ireland	United States	Catharine	22 Jul 1825
John	40	M	Farmer			Imperial	19 Jul 1820
Maria	22	F		United States	United States	Henri IV	14 Oct 1829
Martha	1	F		Scotland	United States	Indus	5 Sep 1827
Mary	1	F		Scotland	United States	Indus	5 Sep 1827
Mary	20	F		Scotland	United States	Indus	5 Sep 1827
Mary	25	F	Wife	Scotland	United States	Tom	2 Jul 1827
Nancy	16	F		Scotland	United States	Indus	5 Sep 1827
Richd.	27	M	Engraver	Great Briton	New York	Brighton	12 Jun 1826
Sarah	13	F		Scotland	United States	Indus	5 Sep 1827
William L.	22	M	Farmer	Great Britain	United States	Freak	14 oct 1828
RAMSBOTTOM, Richard	18	M	Farmer	Great Britain	New York	Superior	5 Sep 1827
RAMSBOTTON, Richard	21	M	Labourer	Great Britain	United States	Thomas Dickason	31 Jul 1829
RAMSDALE, Ann	35	F	None	Gr. Britain		Moro Castle	6 Jul 1827
Francis	37	M	Labourer	Gr. Britain		Moro Castle	6 Jul 1827
George	6	M	None	Gr. Britain		Moro Castle	6 Jul 1827
John	13	M	None	Gr. Britain		Moro Castle	6 Jul 1827
Mary	5	F	None	Gr. Britain		Moro Castle	6 Jul 1827
Sarah	3	F	None	Gr. Britain		Moro Castle	6 Jul 1827
RAMSER, Fredk.	20	M	Farmer	Switzerland	U. States	Sully	15 Jul 1829
John	19	M	Farmer	Switzerland	U. States	Sully	15 Jul 1829
RAMSEY, Ann	1	F	Farmer	Great Britain	U. States	Princess Charlotte	6 Sep 1828
Betty	10	F	Farmer	Great Britain	U. States	Princess Charlotte	6 Sep 1828
Ellen	7	F	Farmer	Great Britain	U. States	Princess Charlotte	6 Sep 1828
James	8	M	Farmer	Great Britain	U. States	Princess Charlotte	6 Sep 1828
James	25	M	Mason	Scotland	United States	Tom	2 Jul 1827
John	35	M	Farmer	Great Britain	U. States	Princess Charlotte	6 Sep 1828
John	38	M	Merchant	American born	U. States	Leontine	18 Mar 1825
John, The Honorable Colonel	46	M	Col. in his B. M. army	Great Britain		Birmingham	15 Jun 1827
Margret	30	F	Farmer	Great Britain	U. States	Princess Charlotte	6 Sep 1828
Margt.	5	F	Farmer	Great Britain	U. States	Princess Charlotte	6 Sep 1828

NAMES OF PASSENGERS	AGE	SEX	OCCUPATIONS	COUNTRY TO WHICH THEY BELONG	COUNTRY THEY INTEND TO INHABIT	SHIPS/DATES OF ARRIVAL	
RAMSEY (cont'd)							
Mary	3	F	Farmer	Great Britain	U. States	Princess Charlotte	6 Sep 1828
Mary	36	F	Spinster	Ireland	New York	Wilson	10 Apr 1823
Matthew	18	M		Ireland	U. States	Nancy	10 Jul 1822
Sarah, Servant	18	F	Servant	England	U. States	Acasta	11 Dec 1826
William	26	M	Farmer	Ireland	New York	Wilson	10 Apr 1823
RAMSEYER, Jacob	48	M		Wheelwright	United States	Spartan	21 Aug 1824
RAMSON, Gorton	14	M	Labourer	Gt. Britain	U. States	Sarah G.	14 Apr 1828
RANALL, W. P.	21	M	Merchant	Gibralter	U. States	White Oak	5 Apr 1828
RANARD, Jno.	37	M	Brewer	Germany	U. States	Ann	19 Aug 1824
RANCHE, J. R.	40	M	Merchant	France	Island St. Domingo	Juno	4 Sep 1824
RANCLIFF, Annice	1	F	None	England	U.N. States	William Byrnes	13 Aug 1829
Mary Ann	3	F	None	England	U.N. States	William Byrnes	13 Aug 1829
Nancy	32	F	None	England	U.N. States	William Byrnes	13 Aug 1829
Wm.	39	M	Farmer	England	U.N. States	William Byrnes	13 Aug 1829
RAND, Isaac	22 10/12	M	Mariner	Massachusetts	Massachusetts	Baltic	20 Aug 1821
Joseph	22	M	Brickmaker	England	U. States	Mary Ann	2 Jan 1829
RANDAL, B.	6		Farmer	Ireland	United States	Courier	16 May 1825
B.	25		Farmer	Ireland	United States	Courier	16 May 1825
J.	23		Farmer	Ireland	United States	Courier	16 May 1825
J.	35		Farmer	Ireland	United States	Courier	16 May 1825
Jacob	16	M	Capt.	Orange County	U. States	Lady Washington	16 Oct 1821
Jacob	45	M	Capt.	Orange County	U. States	Lady Washington	16 Oct 1821
K.	5		Farmer	Ireland	United States	Courier	16 May 1825
S.	10		Farmer	Ireland	United States	Courier	16 May 1825
T.	7		Farmer	Ireland	United States	Courier	16 May 1825
RANDALL, Anna	40	F	None	Great Britain	United States	Hannibal	12 Oct 1829
James	10	M	None	Great Britain	United States	Hannibal	12 Oct 1829
James	48	M	Farmer	Great Britain	United States	Hannibal	12 Oct 1829
James, Mr.	25	M	Gentn.	England	Mexico	Acasta	21 Oct 1825
Jos. C.	24	M	Mercht.	U. States	U. States	Emma	12 Aug 1824
R.	30	M	Mercht.	U.S.	U.S.	Shepherdess	17 May
Robt.	50	M	Merchant	Gt. Britain	Gt. Britain	Exchange	19 Sep 1827
William	7	M	None	Great Britain	United States	Hannibal	12 Oct 1829
RANDALLS, Thomas	28	M	Labourer	Ireland	America	Minerva	31 May 1824
RANDEL, —, Mr.	24	M	Doctor	Novascotia	U. States	Mohawk	15 Nov 1821
—, Mrs.	20	F		Novascotia	U. States	Mohawk	15 Nov 1821
RANDLE, Eber	9	M	Farmer	New York	United States	Mount Hope	10 Aug 1822
Henry	4	M	Farmer	New York	United States	Mount Hope	10 Aug 1822
Isabella	15	F	Farmer	New York	United States	Mount Hope	10 Aug 1822
Isabella	49	F	Farmer	New York	United States	Mount Hope	10 Aug 1822
Jos.	28	M	Farmer	New York	United States	Mount Hope	10 Aug 1822
Mordoch	12	M	Farmer	New York	United States	Mount Hope	10 Aug 1822
RANDOLPH, J. F.	45	M	Merchant	America	America	James Cropper	14 Oct 1822
Jeremiah F.	43	M	Merchant	United States	United States	Cortes	18 Oct 1820
John	31	M	Surgeon	United States	United States	Emulation	17 Dec 1825
John	48	M	None	United States	United States	New York	12 Nov 1822
John	53	M	Planter	United States	United States	York	6 Dec 1826
John, Dr.	30	M	Merchant	U. States	U. States	Tampico	19 Oct 1826
John, Hon.	51	M	Planter	United States	United States	Cortex	4 Dec 1824
Joseph	40	M	Labourer	U. States	U. States	Robt. Reade	12 Apr 1825
M.	26	M	U.S. Navy	U. States	U. States	Brown	29 Apr 1825
Midgley	25	M	Merchant	United States	U.S. of America	Hannibal	17 Dec 1823
RANEY, William Sh...	24	M	Weaver	Ireland	U. States	Josephine	7 May 1827
RANEYBURGES, Rakan						Olympia	12 Aug 1828

*After having been at Sea a Number of Days was ascertaining the quantity of Baggage to report found the under mentioned persons had secreted themselves away notwithstanding our searach with the Gendearmes at the of leaving the port

RANGE, Heny	20	M	Carpenter	Ireland	U. States	Meteor	19 Jul 1828
RANGELY, Hannah	8	F		England	America	John Wells	11 Jun 1823
James	16	M		England	America	John Wells	11 Jun 1823
James	50	M	Merchant	England	America	John Wells	11 Jun 1823
John	12	M		England	America	John Wells	11 Jun 1823
Mary	11	F		England	America	John Wells	11 Jun 1823
Mary	40	F		England	America	John Wells	11 Jun 1823
Sarah	14	F		England	America	John Wells	11 Jun 1823
RANGILY, Daniel	48	M	Merchant	...	United States	Cortes	10 Apr 1822

NAMES OF PASSENGERS	AGE	SEX	OCCUPATIONS	COUNTRY TO WHICH THEY BELONG	COUNTRY THEY INTEND TO INHABIT	SHIPS/DATES OF ARRIVAL	
RANIAR, Robert	16	M	Laborer	Ireland	United States	Ann Maria	3 Jul 1827
RANK, Richd.	39	M	Gun Maker	England	U. States	Acasta	28 Jan 1823
RANKANE, Robt.	22	M	Cooper	U. States	U. States	Julia	22 May 1827
RANKEN, —, Mr.	24	M		Dublin	U. States	Hibernia	26 Oct 1826
Geo.	23	M	Labourer	Gt. Britain	U. States	Frances Henrietta	18 Apr 1825
RANKIN, Ann	5	F	Spinster	Ireland	United States	Dublin Packet	13 Oct 1828
B.	28	M	Seaman	England	U. States	Sarah Thornton	13 Sep 1828
Barbara	24	F		Scotland	United States	Commerce	17 Jul 1823
Catharin	25	F	Spinster	Ireland	United States	Thomas	13 Dec 1827
Daniel	3	M	Child	Ireland	United States	Dublin Packet	13 Oct 1828
James	24		Farmer			Rufus King	7 Aug 1820
James	25	M	Military	Great Britain	Great Britain	Fontine	4 Oct 1824
Jno.	28	M	Laborer	Ireland	United States	Thomas	13 Dec 1827
Jno.	34	M	Merchant	Great Britain	United States	Leeds	29 Sep 1823
Jno.	46	M	Carpenter	Ireland	U. States	Edward	15 Jul 1825
John	25	M	Labourer	Ireland	U. States	William & John	10 Jul 1824
John C.	7	M	Child	Ireland	United States	Dublin Packet	13 Oct 1828
N.	20	M		Gt. Britain	U. States	Tantiva	7 Jul 1828
Robert	29	M	Mercht.	Scotland	America	Friends	24 Sep 1821
Robt.	28	M	Farmer	Great Britain	United States	Grecian	24 Sep 1828
Sarah	33	F	Spinster	Ireland	United States	Dublin Packet	13 Oct 1828
Thomas	24	M	Farmer	Ireland	U. States	William & John	10 Jul 1824
Thomas	45	M	Tanner	Scotland	U. States	Alert	22 Sep 1821
Wm.	39	M	Mariner	U. States	U.S.	Ambuscade	14 Mar 1820
RANKINS, Alexd.	27		Merchant	Scotland		Cincinnatus	17 May 1823
Janett	30		Merchant	Scotland		Cincinnatus	17 May 1823
RANKSON, Ann	17	F		Scotland	United States	Margaret Bogle	11 Jun 1824
Ann	23	F		Scotland	United States	Margaret Bogle	11 Jun 1824
Elizabeth	20	F		Scotland	United States	Margaret Bogle	11 Jun 1824
Jane	6	F		Scotland	United States	Margaret Bogle	11 Jun 1824
Margaret	9	F		Scotland	United States	Margaret Bogle	11 Jun 1824
Margaret	25	F		Scotland	United States	Margaret Bogle	11 Jun 1824
Margaret	50	F		Scotland	United States	Margaret Bogle	11 Jun 1824
Peter	70	M	Farmer	Scotland	United States	Margaret Bogle	11 Jun 1824
Robert	20	M	Farmer	Scotland	United States	Margaret Bogle	11 Jun 1824
RANNER, Susan	23			United States	United States	Planter	26 Jul 1822
RANNO, Charlotte	20	F		Switzerland	U. States	Robert Edward	2 Nov 1827
RANO, Leif	27	M	Servant	Germany	N. York	France	29 Nov 1827
RANOLD, Thomas	10 6/12	M	...	Ireland	U. States	Union	3 Jun 1822
RANSDALE, George	20	M	Labourer	England	U. States	Ayrshire	12 May 1828
RANSOM, Abraham	6	M		England	United States	Acasta	12 Dec 1823
Celia	13	F		England	United States	Acasta	12 Dec 1823
George	36	M	Farmer	Ireland	New York	Margaret	18 May 1825
Robt.	29		Labourer	G. Britian	G. Britian	Dewitt Clinton	26 Aug 1825
RANSON, Amy	11	F		England	United States	Acasta	12 Dec 1823
Jane	4	F		England	United States	Acasta	12 Dec 1823
Mary	22	F		Great Britain	United States	Diana	20 Nov 1824
RAOERTY, John	26	M	Labourer	England	United States	Aurelia	7 Jun 1826
RAPHIEL, Joseph	35	M	Servant to Mr. Butter	United States	United States	Robert Fulton	27 Jun 1822
RAPP, Catarina	36	F		France	United States	New England	29 Aug 1828
RARATY, Pat	20	M	Laborer	Ireland	United States	Thomas	13 Dec 1827
RARDON, James	21	M	Yeoman	Ireland	United States	Borneo	9 Jul 1827
RARN, George	22	M	...	Wirtemburg	United States	Wade	29 Aug 1825
RARTLEY, John	28	M	Labourer	Ireland	United States	Nancy Henrietta	3 Nov 1828
RASCH, August	48 6/12	M	Farmer	France	United States	Catharine	10 Sep 1827
Caroline	5 1/12	M	Farmer	France	United States	Catharine	10 Sep 1827
Josephine	12 6/12	M	Farmer	France	United States	Catharine	10 Sep 1827
Maria A.	46 3/12	F	Farmer	France	United States	Catharine	10 Sep 1827
RASIER, S. Anthony	7	M		Switzerland	United States	India	4 Aug 1826
RASINIONERS, Francis	9	M	Wheelright	France	U. States	Sully	25 Jun 1828
RASKILE, Nicholls	23		Merchant	Liverpool	New York	Albion	11 Oct 1821
RASMUSDOTER, Silva	50	F	Farmer	Norway	United States	Salem	31 Aug 1829
RASNE, Robert	16	M	Sailor	England	United States	Siroc	31 Oct 1829
RASNIE, Juan A.	13	M	None	Havana	U. States	Hesper	28 Dec 1825
RASON, Sarah	37	F		England	United States	Acasta	12 Dec 1823
RASPELLE, Nicholas	22	M	Black Smith	Switzerland	U.S.	C. Amelia	30 Jun 1828
RASSART, H.	33	M	Merchant	France	United States	Stephania	3 Oct 1822

NAMES OF PASSENGERS	AGE	SEX	OCCUPATIONS	COUNTRY TO WHICH THEY BELONG	COUNTRY THEY INTEND TO INHABIT	SHIPS/DATES OF ARRIVAL	
RASSEY, Grace	4	M	Cloth W.	England	U. States	Franklin	7 Jul 1828
Jams	44	M	Cloth W.	England	U. States	Franklin	7 Jul 1828
Joshea	2	M	Cloth W.	England	U. States	Franklin	7 Jul 1828
Martha	6	M	Cloth W.	England	U. States	Franklin	7 Jul 1828
Mary	2	M	Cloth W.	England	U. States	Franklin	7 Jul 1828
Morriadack	9	M	Cloth W.	England	U. States	Franklin	7 Jul 1828
RASSMUSSON, Call	44	M	Gentleman	Denmark	Denmark	Chase	24 Aug 1822
RATBURNE, John J.	38		Planter	St. Croix	St. Croix	South Carolina Packet	4 Mar 1822
RATCEFFE, Ann	29	F	None	Great Britain	United States	William Dawson	18 Jun 1827
RATCLIFF, Betsy	49	F	None	Great Brittan	U.S.	Emulous	29 Jun 1827
Cathrine	28	F	None	Great Brittan	U.S.	Emulous	29 Jun 1827
Chs.	18	M	None	Great Brittan	U.S.	Emulous	29 Jun 1827
Elizabeth	28	F		England	United States	William & Henry	19 Jul 1822
George	1	M		England	United States	William & Henry	19 Jul 1822
J.	55	M	Merchant	England	U.S.	York	1 Dec 1827
John	25	M	None	Great Brittan	U.S.	Emulous	29 Jun 1827
Mary Anne	3	F		England	United States	William & Henry	19 Jul 1822
T.	23	M	Shoemaker	England	U.S.	York	1 Dec 1827
Thomas	23	M	Brick Layer	Great Britain	United States	Frances Henrietta	17 Sep 1827
Thomas	26	M	Wheelwright	England	United States	William & Henry	19 Jul 1822
Thomas	29	M		Great Britain	United States	Active	25 Mar 1828
Ths.	23	M	None	Great Brittan	U.S.	Emulous	29 Jun 1827
William	21	M	Taylor	England	United States	William & Henry	19 Jul 1822
Wm.	50	M	Farmer	Great Brittan	U.S.	Emulous	29 Jun 1827
RATCLIFFE, James	36	M	Cotton Printer	England	America	Hercules	2 Nov 1825
Jane	10	F		U. States	U. States	United States	11 Sep 1828
Jane	40	F		U. States	U. States	United States	11 Sep 1828
RATCLIFFEE, Cathr.	1	F		England	U. States	Birmingham	16 Jun 1828
Cathr.	34	F		England	U. States	Birmingham	16 Jun 1828
Jane	7	F		England	U. States	Birmingham	16 Jun 1828
John	5	M		England	U. States	Birmingham	16 Jun 1828
John	37	M		England	U. States	Birmingham	16 Jun 1828
RATESHAW, Benjamin	39 5/12	M	Miller	Ireland	United States	Lunar	5 May 1828
RATFORD, Joseph	10	M	Mason	England	America	Two Marys	24 Sep 1827
Thomas	24	M	Mason	England	America	Two Marys	24 Sep 1827
RATGEN, Bruin, Mr.	24	M	Sugar Refnr.	England	U. States	Acasta	3 Apr 1826
RATHAY, Jno.	37	M	Weaver	Scotland	N. Orleans	Ann Maria	4 Nov 1834
RATHBON, Josh.	53	M	Mariner	U. States	U. States	L. M. Pelham	7 Mar 1822
RATHBONE, —, Mrs.	24		lady	U. States	U. States	Emma	17 Nov 1824
John	45	M	Gent.	U. States	U. States	Cadmus	28 May 1821
RATHERHOVEN, John	43	M	Gentleman	France	France	Jas. Monroe	11 Aug 1823
RATHERNS, Ricd.	19	M	None	Great Britain	United States	Atlantic	28 May 1827
RATHVILLE, Therese	30	F	Lady	France	U.S.	Bayard	10 Nov 1824
RATISH, Jno.	22	M		Spain	U. States	Monroe	13 May 1823
RATRAY, John	26	M	Merchant	Scotland	America	Mentor	21 Sep 1824
RATTAIN, A.	8	M		Great Britain		Caravan	8 Sep 1828
H.	36	M	Shoe Maker	Great Britain		Caravan	8 Sep 1828
M.	3	M		Great Britain		Caravan	8 Sep 1828
M.	5	M		Great Britain		Caravan	8 Sep 1828
Rosina	7	M		Great Britain		Caravan	8 Sep 1828
T.	0 6/12	M		Great Britain		Caravan	8 Sep 1828
RATTENBERG, Anna Maria	28 8/12	F		England	England	Venus	15 Apr 1822
Joseph Freeman	35 2/12	M	Barrister	England	England	Venus	15 Apr 1822
RATTENBURG, Joseph F.	38	M	Planter	U. States	U.S.	Edward Quesnel	19 Dec 1826
RATTRAY, Wm.	27	M	Blacksmith	Scotland	United States	Coquet	6 Jun 1827
RATZ, Adam	46	M		Bardin	U. States	Bayard	5 Sep 1828
Carl	20	M	Butcher	Bardin	U. States	Bayard	5 Sep 1828
Catharan	49	M		Bardin	U. States	Bayard	5 Sep 1828
Eliz.	22	M		Bardin	U. States	Bayard	5 Sep 1828

NAMES OF PASSENGERS	AGE	SEX	OCCUPATIONS	COUNTRY TO WHICH THEY BELONG	COUNTRY THEY INTEND TO INHABIT	SHIPS/DATES OF ARRIVAL	
RATZ (cont'd)							
Lousia	15	M		Bardin	U. States	Bayard	5 Sep 1828
Valentine	30	M	Farmer	Hessian-Germany	Canada	Caesar	8 Sep 1828
RAUL, J., Doct.	40	M	Doctor	France	New York	Rebecca	31 Oct 1825
RAUN, Regina	10	F		Wirtemburg	United States	Wade	29 Aug 1825
RAVAGO, B.	25	M	Merchant	Columbia	Columbia	Britannia	5 Nov 1828
Thos.	25	M	Merchant	Colombia	Colombia	Edgar	4 Jan 1828
RAVAHIS, A.	26	F	Servant	U. States	U. States	Chase	20 Jul 1826
RAVENCROFT, F.	15	M	Mariner	Ireland	United States	Euphrates	2 Sep 1823
RAVEND, Desforge	27	M	Merchant	Maragalante	U. States	Mary	29 Dec 1823
RAVENEL, Edmund	30	M	Physician	United States	New York	Britannia	3 Nov 1827
RAVERLY, Jane	27	F	Servant	Ireland	United States	Trident	30 Sep 1826
RAVERS, Peter	35	M	Servant	England	Great Brittan	Amity	11 May 1821
RAVERTY, Eliza	20 4/12	F	Seamstress	Ireland	United States	Atlantic	21 Jul 1827
RAVESIES, E.	25	M	Merchant	France	Philadelphia	Maria Theresa	16 Nov 1820
RAVIN, Ann Maria	6	F	Spinster	Bavarian	United States	American	27 Aug 1827
Catherine	8	F	Spinster	Bavarian	United States	American	27 Aug 1827
Catherine	38	F	Farmer	Bavarian	United States	American	27 Aug 1827
Elizabeth	4	F	Spinster	Bavarian	United States	American	27 Aug 1827
Henry	58	M	Farmer	Bavarian	United States	American	27 Aug 1827
Michael	1 6/12	M	Infant	Bavarian	United States	American	27 Aug 1827
Michael	42	M	Farmer	Bavarian	United States	American	27 Aug 1827
RAVINO, ...cterous	21 6/12	F	Joiner	France	U. States	France	26 Jun 1828
...lonzer	19 5/12	F	Joiner	France	U. States	France	26 Jun 1828
Adel	25 5/12	F	Joiner	France	U. States	France	26 Jun 1828
Castell	19 4/12	F	Joiner	France	U. States	France	26 Jun 1828
Ester	11 4/12	F	Joiner	France	U. States	France	26 Jun 1828
Louisia	17 7/12	F	Joiner	France	U. States	France	26 Jun 1828
RAW, Ellen	30 6/12	F	Servant	Ireland	United States	Atlantic	21 Jul 1827
RAWLE,							
Samuel Bruge	36 4/12	M	Merchant	United States	Philadelphia, U. States	Cadmus	12 Dec 1823
RAWLEY, Ellen	2	F		Ireland	United States	Trio	2 Oct 1828
James	35	M	Farmer	Ireland	United States	Trio	2 Oct 1828
Margaret	32	F		Ireland	United States	Trio	2 Oct 1828
RAWSON, Chas.	28	M	Mariner	Nantuck	United States	Henri IV	2 Oct 1828
William	48	M	Farmer	England	United States	Jubilee	12 May 1828
Wm. S.	26	M	Mariner	U. States	U. States	Adonis	23 Jan 1822
James	30		Labourer	England	United States	Hugh Johnson	11 Jun 1828
Jane	38			England	United States	Hugh Johnson	11 Jun 1828
Thos.	20		Labourer	England	United States	Hugh Johnson	11 Jun 1828
RAY, Ann	13		Grazier	England	United States	Corinthian	7 Jul 1829
Cornelia	27			United States	U. States	New York	30 Oct 1827
D. P.	38 3/12	M	Merchant	American	Port au Prince	William	28 Feb 1826
Daniel	40	M	Merchant	St. John, N.B.	St. John, N.B.	Sylvester Healy	17 Oct 1825
David	26	M	Farmer	Scotland	Baltimore	Cadmus	22 Mar 1822
David Hy.	3		Grazier	England	United States	Corinthian	7 Jul 1829
Elizabeth	26	F	None	Gt. Brittian	Gt. Brittian	Manchester	21 Apr 1827
Emanuel	17	M	Merchant	W. Indies	U. States	Matilda	27 Apr 1822
Emily	30	F	Wife	Great Britain	Great Britain	Ann Maria	17 Apr 1827
J.	39	M	Farmer	Philadelphia	Phila.	Sarah Herrick	10 Aug 1827
J. B.	24	M	Commerce		United States	New York	5 Nov 1828
James	22	M	Labourer			Hanford	17 Jul 1828
James	24	M				Eliza Grant	6 Oct 1828
James H.	20	M	Mercht.	Great Britain	Great Britan	Nancy	13 Dec 1822
James H.	45	M	Atty.	England	U. States	New York	4 Nov 1824
John	18	M	Tailor	Scotland	New York	Margaret	18 May 1825
Liddy	11		Grazier	England	United States	Corinthian	7 Jul 1829
Margery	18	F	Milener	Ireland	America	Franklin	13 Aug 1827
Michael	23	M	Shoe Maker	England	U.N.S.	Helen	16 Mar 1829
Rachel	60	F		St. Johns	St. Johns	St. Michael	26 Oct 1824
Ratchard	71	M	...	United States	United States	Hanford	17 Oct 1828
Richard	35		Grazier	England	United States	Corinthian	7 Jul 1829
Richard T.	7		Grazier	England	United States	Corinthian	7 Jul 1829
Robert	33		Mercht.	United States	U. States	New York	30 Oct 1827
Robert	40	M	Planter	Great Britain	Great Britain	Ann Maria	17 Apr 1827
Robt.	28	M	Farmer	Gt. Brittian	Gt. Brittian	Manchester	21 Apr 1827
Sally M.	22	F		Ireland	U. States	Nancy	13 Dec 1822

NAMES OF PASSENGERS	AGE	SEX	OCCUPATIONS	COUNTRY TO WHICH THEY BELONG	COUNTRY THEY INTEND TO INHABIT	SHIPS/DATES OF ARRIVAL	
RAY (cont'd)							
Samuel	1		Grazier	England	United States	Corinthian	7 Jul 1829
Sarah	30		Grazier	England	United States	Corinthian	7 Jul 1829
Thomas M.	25	M	Laborer	Ireland	U. States	Nancy	13 Dec 1822
Wm.	22	M	Merchant	Canada	Canada	Julia	13 Sep 1827
RAYARDON, Daniel	7			England	U. States	Corinthian	8 Oct 1828
Ellen	25			England	U. States	Corinthian	8 Oct 1828
RAYDEN, W.	24	M	Mariner	American	U. States	Sarah Ann	5 Aug 1820
RAYLEY, John	22	M	Farmer	Ireland	U. States	Francis	6 Sep 1827
RAYLLY, John	35	M	Taylor	Ireland	U. States	Adno	5 Jul 1828
RAYMOND, —	40	M	Merchant	Guadaloupe	Guadaloupe	Belle	10 Sep 1824
Augustus	18	M	Merchant		United States	London Packet	25 Dec 1820
Cathr.	28	F		England	U. States	Rising States	20 Sep 1828
George B.	54	M		United States	United States	John Wells	22 May 1826
Hannah, Child [of Prudence]	16	F	None		United States	London Packet	25 Dec 1820
Jno.	34	M	Merchant	Greek	U. States	Planter	7 May 1822
Martha, Child [of Prudence]	8	F			United States	London Packet	25 Dec 1820
Prudence	50	F			United States	London Packet	25 Dec 1820
William, Child [of Prudence]	11	M			United States	London Packet	25 Dec 1820
RAYNA, Wm.	23	M	Merchant	England	United States	Dalhouse Castle	6 Sep 1827
RAYNARD, George	5	M		Native of Switzerland	United States	Canaris	30 Jun 1827
James	2	M		Native of Switzerland	United States	Canaris	30 Jun 1827
John	12	M		Native of Switzerland	United States	Canaris	30 Jun 1827
John	40	M	Twister	Native of Switzerland	United States	Canaris	30 Jun 1827
Margaret	19	F		Native of Switzerland	United States	Canaris	30 Jun 1827
Margaret	40	F		Native of Switzerland	United States	Canaris	30 Jun 1827
Salome	9	M		Native of Switzerland	United States	Canaris	30 Jun 1827
RAYNEIR, Auguste	30	M	Merchant	France	U. States	Rufus	15 Dec 1828
RAYNER, Eliza	32	F	Farmer	England	U. States	Electra	7 Jul 1828
Francis	7	M	Farmer	England	U. States	Electra	7 Jul 1828
James	23	M	None	England	U. States	Criterion	20 Nov 1823
John	1	M	Farmer	England	U. States	Electra	7 Jul 1828
John	22	M	Merchant	Gt. Brittain	U. States	Robert Fulton	1 Nov 1822
Mary	11	M	Farmer	England	U. States	Electra	7 Jul 1828
Phebe	9	M	Farmer	England	U. States	Electra	7 Jul 1828
Robt.	38	M	Farmer	England	U. States	Electra	7 Jul 1828
Wm.	13	M	Farmer	England	U. States	Electra	7 Jul 1828
RAYNOLDS, Francis	27	M	...	Ireland	U.S. of America	Hamilton	18 Jul 1827
John	26	M	Farmer	England	America	Hercules	10 Apr 1823
Michael	20	M	Labourer	Ireland	New York	Lima	5 Aug 1829
RAYNOLS, Edward	32	M	Farmer	England	United States	Justina	5 Aug 1823
RAYOLLE, S., Miss	14	F		United States		Howard	17 Oct 1822
RAYONE, Jane	20	F		Great Britian	United States	Andes	19 Aug 1829
John	26	M	Preacher	Great Britian	United States	Andes	19 Aug 1829
RAYSON, Jas.		M	Merchant	England	England	Laurel	31 Mar 1828
RAYTH, Ja...	13	M		Wirtemburg	United States	Wade	29 Aug 1825
Joseph	26	M	Labourer	Wirtemburg	United States	Wade	29 Aug 1825
Paulina	27	F		Wirtemburg	United States	Wade	29 Aug 1825
RAZOR, Cathe.	13	F		France	U.S. America	Huntress	6 Sep 1827
Cathe.	46	F		France	U.S. America	Huntress	6 Sep 1827
Philip	5	M		France	U.S. America	Huntress	6 Sep 1827
Philip	11	M		France	U.S. America	Huntress	6 Sep 1827
RE...D, Eliza	20	F	Dressmaker	Ireland	United States	Carolina Ann	11 Dec 1826
RE...DING, John	28	M	Wheelwright	England	U. States	Montgomery	18 Oct 1828
RE...LEY, William	33 1/12	M	Surgeon	Great Britain		Silas Richards	27 Oct 1826
REA, —	30	F	...	Ireland	U.S. America	Columbia	26 Nov 1825
Edward	13	M	Labourer	Ireland	United States	Wilson	4 Oct 1827
James	8	M		Nova Scotia	Pittsburge	Hunter	25 May 1824
John	33	M	Weaver	Nova Scotia	Pittsburge	Hunter	25 May 1824

NAMES OF PASSENGERS	AGE	SEX	OCCUPATIONS	COUNTRY TO WHICH THEY BELONG	COUNTRY THEY INTEND TO INHABIT	SHIPS/DATES OF ARRIVAL	
REA (cont'd)							
John	36	M	Merchant	Spain	Spain	Brown	15 Nov 1825
Mary	35	F	Weaver	Nova Scotia	Pittsburge	Hunter	25 May 1824
William	4	M			Pittsburge	Hunter	25 May 1824
Willm.	19	M	Labourer	Ireland	U. States	Josephine	7 May 1827
REA..., —	25	F		Switzerland	United States	Elbe	2 Aug 1822
REACH, John	25	M	Merchant	Scotland	Ama.	Expedition	19 May 1828
REACHISON, John	20	M		Ireland	United States	Nancy R. Crowell	21 Sep 1822
READ, Alexander	14	M	Farmer	Scotland	Canada	Swift	16 Jul 1827
Ann	24	F	None	England	U. States	Unity	27 Mar 1827
Ann	50	F	None	England	U. States	Unity	27 Mar 1827
Arora	16	F	Farmer	Scotland	Canada	Swift	16 Jul 1827
Benjn.	28	M	Accoantant	England	America	Franklin	19 Nov 1828
Charles	10 4/12	M				Washington	15 Sep 1821
E. C.	25	M	Merchant	United States	U. States	Pacific	5 Sep 1827
Edward	...6	...	...	...	United States	John London	3 Aug 1824
Emma	4/12	F	None	England	U. States	Unity	27 Mar 1827
George	7	M	Farmer	Scotland	Canada	Swift	16 Jul 1827
Henry	40	M	Joiner	England	United States	Mount Vernon	9 Jun 1823
J. Hamilton	22		Planter	So. Carolina	Charleston	Albion	11 Oct 1821
James	24	M	Surgeon	England	United States	Joseph	13 Oct 1823
John	9	M	Child [of Mary]	Ireland	United States	Erin	25 Dec 1820
John	23	M	Clothier	England	U. States	Unity	27 Mar 1827
John	23	M	Labourer	Great Britain	U. States	Robert Fulton	3 Dec 1827
John	28	M	Mechanic	U.S.	U.S.	Comet	6 Dec 1827
John	39	M	Farmer	Scotland	Canada	Swift	16 Jul 1827
John G.	25	M	Joiner	Gt. Britain	United States	Eliza Barker	11 Jan 1826
Kravan	12	M	Child [of Mary]	Ireland	United States	Erin	25 Dec 1820
Laura	9	F				Washington	15 Sep 1821
Mary	10	F	Farmer	Scotland	Canada	Swift	16 Jul 1827
Mary	38	F	Spinster	Ireland	United States	Erin	25 Dec 1820
Mary D.	32	F		England		Washington	15 Sep 1821
Robert L.	35	M	Mercht.	U. States	U. States	Four Brothers	28 Jun 1825
Saml.	47	M	Merchant	New York	United States	Hammond	9 Feb 1820
T.	25	M	Mariner	U. States	U. States	Rose in Bloom	9 Apr 1827
Thomas	30	M	Gentleman	England	United States	Martha	21 Mar 1820
Thos.	50	M	Read Maker	Gt. Howard	U. States	Milton	21 May 1827
Wm.	50	M	Clothier	England	U. States	Unity	27 Mar 1827
Wm., Jr.	26	M	Clothier	England	U. States	Unity	27 Mar 1827
READAN, Michl.	32	M				Trio	5 May 1828
READE, Abel	26	M	Labourer	U. States	U. States	Robt. Reade	12 Apr 1825
Charles	26	M	Merchant	N. York	N. York	Andrew Jackson	23 Mar 1822
Charles	50	M	Merchant	N. York	N. York	Andrew Jackson	23 Mar 1822
READER, Elizabeth	1	F	None	England	America	Dewitt Clinton	27 Jul 1824
Elizabeth	20	F	None	England	America	Dewitt Clinton	27 Jul 1824
Guogue, Mr.	7	M	Tanner	France	United States	Martha	20 May 1825
John	22	M	Farmer	England	America	Dewitt Clinton	27 Jul 1824
READING, Jane	30	F	...	Gt. Britain	United States	Crisis	13 Nov 1824
READMOND, B.	24	F	Labourer	Ireland	U. States	Loire	18 Jul 1828
M.	27	M	Labourer	Ireland	U. States	Loire	18 Jul 1828
READY, Thomas	32	M	Labourer	Ireland	United States	Trio	2 Oct 1828
REAGAN, Daniel	19	M	Labourer	Ireland	N. York	Trusty	12 Sep 1828
William	9			Cork	Philadelphia	Schuylkill	22 Aug 1825
REAGGON, Tiimothy	22	M	Labourer	Ireland	United States	General Marion	6 Oct 1828
REAL, Ann	23	F	None	Great Britain	United States	Pacific	7 May 1827
Betsey	1	F	None	Great Britain	United States	Pacific	7 May 1827
Cathn.	30	F	Lady	Ireland	United States	William	20 Jul 1829
Dago, Don		M	Merchant	Teneriff	Spain	Cabbasso Conta	23 Aug 1824
Diego	51	M	Merchant	Spain	Tenerrif	Port Captain	6 Dec 1825
Heny	3	M	None	Great Britain	United States	Pacific	7 May 1827
James	23	M	Labourer	Gt. Britain	U. States	Panthea	21 Jul 1825
John	3	M		Ireland	United States	William	20 Jul 1829
John	6	M	None	Great Britain	United States	Pacific	7 May 1827
Jos.	35	M	Mariner	Spain	U. States	Mary Ann	30 Aug 1824
Maria	17	M	Gentleman	Spain	Spain	Governor Von Schollen	7 Nov 1827
Saml.	5	M	None	Great Britain	United States	Pacific	7 May 1827

NAMES OF PASSENGERS	AGE	SEX	OCCUPATIONS	COUNTRY TO WHICH THEY BELONG	COUNTRY THEY INTEND TO INHABIT	SHIPS/DATES OF ARRIVAL	
REAL (cont'd)							
Thomas, Don	31	M	Gentleman	Spain	Spain	Governor Von Schollen	7 Nov 1827
Thos.	6	M		Ireland	United States	William	20 Jul 1829
Thos.	28	M	Off. in B. Navy	England	United States	Manhattan	22 Sep 1823
REALE, Peter Leopold	18		Gentleman	Florence	Tuscany	London	13 Dec 1822
REALLY, Thomas	33	M	Labourer	Great Britain		Moro Castle	6 Jul 1827
REALUGE, D. Cladio	50	M	Mariner	Genoa	South America	Packet	24 Mar 1824
REANEY, Isabella	18	F	...	...	United States	Hanford	17 Oct 1828
REANGER, Jacob	46	M	Cobler	Swtserland	America	Saluda	18 Jun 1825
REANSCOUR, N.	45	M	Farmer	N. York	Canada	Nancy	29 Nov 1821
REARDAN, Cathr.	34	F		Ireland	United States	Pallas	28 Oct 1828
Mary	25	F		Ireland	United States	Pallas	28 Oct 1828
REARDEN, Elizabeth	22	F		Ireland	United States	Clothier	22 Nov 1827
Johannah	7	F		Ireland	America	William	21 May 1825
Margret	13	F		Ireland	America	William	21 May 1825
William	14	M		Ireland	America	William	21 May 1825
William	22	M	Farmer	Ireland	United States	Clothier	22 Nov 1827
REARDON,							
Hannah, Miss	1 6/12	F	Yeoman	England	U. States	Acasta	11 Dec 1826
Hannah, Mrs.	28	F	Yeoman	England	U. States	Acasta	11 Dec 1826
REAT, Bernard	30	M	Servant	Ireland	U. States	Josephine	27 Jul 1825
REAVES, Frs.	23	M		New Orlrsnd		Amazon	8 Dec 1820
REBALD, L.	40	M	Mercht.	Italy	U. States	Patty & Sally	23 Feb 1822
REBB, Adam	37	M	Shoe Maker	United States	United States	Globe	30 Aug 1828
Andrew	6	M		United States	United States	Globe	30 Aug 1828
Margaret	36	F		United States	United States	Globe	30 Aug 1828
REBEL, F. L.	22	M	Confectioner	Saxony	U. States	Minerva	13 Sep 1827
REBER, Ama	15	F	Framer	Switserland	Ohio	Danube	20 Jul 1826
Anna	41	F	Framer	Switserland	Ohio	Danube	20 Jul 1826
Catrena	9	F	Framer	Switserland	Ohio	Danube	20 Jul 1826
Christian	40	M	Framer	Switserland	Ohio	Danube	20 Jul 1826
John	2	M	Framer	Switserland	Ohio	Danube	20 Jul 1826
Luna	8	F	Framer	Switserland	Ohio	Danube	20 Jul 1826
RECH, Jacob	22	M	Farmer	Switzerland	U. States	Romulus	24 Sep 1828
RED, Alexander	41	M	Farmer	Scotland	Canada	Swift	16 Jul 1827
REDBURN, Jane	15	F	None	Great Britan	United States	Bolivar	21 May 1827
William	33	M	Mechanic	Great Britan	United States	Bolivar	21 May 1827
REDDER, Jas.	26	M	Clerk		U. States	Margaret	3 Jun 1822
REDDIE, David	40	M	Mechanic	Scotland	U.S.	Hiram	21 Jul 1823
REDDIN, Barbee	25	M	Farmer	Great Britain	United States	Weser	9 May 1822
James	58	M	Labourer	Ireland	America	Fairy	8 Aug 1821
Mary	2	F	Farmer	Great Britain	United States	Weser	9 May 1822
Nancy	20	F	Spinner	Ireland	America	Fairy	8 Aug 1821
Pat	30	M	Farmer	Great Britain	United States	Weser	9 May 1822
REDDINDT, J.	2	M		Scotland	U. States	Superior	25 Sep 1828
J.	28	M	Merchant	Scotland	U. States	Superior	25 Sep 1828
M.	21	F		Scotland	U. States	Superior	25 Sep 1828
REDDING, M.	18	F		England	U. States	Charlotte	19 Feb 1822
Michael	40	M	Farmer	Great Britain	United States	Magnet	19 Aug 1822
REDDINGTON, Michael	30	M	Saddler	Ireland	New York	Amanda	23 May 1827
REDDINS, Hannah	20	F		United States	Boston	Halecon	12 Feb 1820
*died 29 Jan 1820							
Louisa	7/12	F		United States	Boston	Halecon	12 Feb 1820
REDDISH, Thomas	49	M	Merchant	United States	U. States	Indiana	11 Sep 1827
REDDRICH, Richard Wm.	23		Doctor	United States	United States	Hudson	18 Jun 1825
REDDY, Bridget	23	F	Labourer	Ireland	U.S. of America	Hamilton	18 Jul 1827
John	28	M	Laborer	Ireland	United States	St. Michaels	23 Dec 1826
Nelly	50	F	Wife	Ireland	United States	Dublin Packet	22 Apr 1822
REDENDOR, Jose P.	21	M	Merchant	Colombia	St. Domingo	Bogota	28 Mar 1827
REDER, Joseph	19	M	Taylor	Austria	America, U.N.S.	Great Britain	3 Aug 1829
Simon T.	23	M	Mechanick	United States	United States	Gertrude	19 May 1826
Wm.	30	M	Gentleman	Jersey	United States	Nancy	15 Nov 1824
REDEWALD, Henry	30	M	Merchant	Bremen	U.S. America	Columbia	31 Jul 1826
REDFIELD, S. B.	40	M	Mercht.	United States	U. States	Lady Tompkins	9 Feb 1825
REDFORD, Joseph Holem	18	M	Taylor	England	United States	St. John	5 Oct 1829
REDICH, Thomas	50	M	Mercht.	United States	Cincinnati, Ohio	Samuel Wright	12 Oct 1829
REDINAN, Michael	31	M	Distiller	England		Venus	11 Aug 1820
REDINGER, Christien	29	F		Switzerland	U.S.	C. Amelia	30 Jun 1828

NAMES OF PASSENGERS	AGE	SEX	OCCUPATIONS	COUNTRY TO WHICH THEY BELONG	COUNTRY THEY INTEND TO INHABIT	SHIPS/DATES OF ARRIVAL	
REDINGER (cont'd)							
Geo.	6/12	M		Switzerland	U.S.	C. Amelia	30 Jun 1828
Nicholas	3	F		Switzerland	U.S.	C. Amelia	30 Jun 1828
REDMAN, Joseph	19	M	Labourer	Ireland	United States	Carolina Ann	14 May 1827
Ludwig	38	M	Joiner	Wurtemburg	United States	Jason	3 Nov 1828
REDMAYER, Charles	16	M	Gent	French	Switzerland	Charlemagne	19 Sep 1828
Francis	46	M	Gent	French	Switzerland	Charlemagne	19 Sep 1828
George	20	M	Gent	French	Switzerland	Charlemagne	19 Sep 1828
Mariah	40	F	Gent	French	Switzerland	Charlemagne	19 Sep 1828
REDMON, William	24		Merchant	Ireland	America	Florida	14 Oct 1829
REDMOND, —, Mr.	30	M	Merchant	Ireland	Matanzes	James Monroe	11 May 1824
—, Mrs.	26	F		Ireland	Matanzes	James Monroe	11 May 1824
Hawland	18	M	Gentleman	Ireland	U. States	Meteor	4 Oct 1827
William, Mr.	22	M	Merchant	Ireland	Charleston, S.C.	Birmingham	16 Oct 1826
Wm.	35	M	Merchant	U. States	U. States	Silas Richards	29 Oct 1828
REDONA, Jas.	20	M	Manufacturer	Italy	U. States	Hope Return	9 Oct 1827
REDORDO, Benita	15	F	Servant	Mexico	Mexico	Virginia	9 Feb 1829
Julian	45	M	Servant	Spain	Mexico	Virginia	9 Feb 1829
REDWOOD, S.	48	M	Mercht.	Gt. Brittian	United States	Manchester	17 Aug 1825
Sanford	40	M	Gentleman	England	U. States	Radius	12 Sep 1822
REEB, Catherine	15	F	Farmer	France	U.S.	Cadmus	9 Dec 1826
Catherine	39	F	Farmer	France	U.S.	Cadmus	9 Dec 1826
Nicholas	44	M	Farmer	France	U.S.	Cadmus	9 Dec 1826
Sophia	2 6/12	F	Farmer	France	U.S.	Cadmus	9 Dec 1826
REECE, Anne	24		None	Cheshire, England	Great Britain	Franklin	22 Jun 1827
George B.	21	M	Clerk	U. States	U. States	Abalino	13 Sep 1820
Owen	4		None	Cheshire, England	Great Britain	Franklin	22 Jun 1827
Richard, The Revd.	56	M	Minister of the Gospel	Great Britan	Great Britan	Columbia	10 Mar 1824
Robert	22	M	Pattern Maker	England	U. States	Montgomery	18 Oct 1828
Thomas	30	M	Joiner	England	United States	Colossus	26 Aug 1828
REED, —, Capt.	35	M	Gentleman	England	Great Britain	New York	22 Jul 1824
Agness	40	F	None	Scotland	United States	Washington	2 Oct 1828
Anna Maria	6	F	Lady	Island Jamaca	Island Jamaca	Agenora	19 Jun 1826
Betsey	18	F	None	Ireland	U. States	Denny McCobb	26 Jul 1827
Betty	48	F	None	England	U. States	Montgomery	18 Oct 1828
Cath.	40	F		England	America	Silas Richard	24 Oct 1829
Catharine	1_/12	F	Daughter	Ireland	United States	William & George	14 May 1828
Charles	20	M	Gentleman	America	America	Parrington	9 Jun 1827
Crowford	54	M	Weaver	Scotland	U. States	Superior	25 Sep 1828
E.	12	F		Scotland	U. States	Superior	25 Sep 1828
Elisbath	23	F	Spinster	Ireland	United States	Fabius	31 Jul 1829
Elizabeth	14	F	Daughter	Ireland	United States	William & George	14 May 1828
Elizabeth	25	F	None	London	America	Evelina	10 Nov 1825
Elizabeth O.	10	F	Lady	Island Jamaca	Island Jamaca	Agenora	19 Jun 1826
Emma	5	F	None	England	U. States	Montgomery	18 Oct 1828
Frs.	25	M		Ireland	U. States	Alex Mansfield	1 Jun 1822
George	14	M	Farmer	Great Britton	U. State	Earl of Liverpool	16 Aug 1826
George	29	M	Labourer	Ireland	United States	Fabius	31 Jul 1829
H.	20	M		Scotland	U. States	Superior	25 Sep 1828
Hannah	5	F		England	America	Josephine	8 Jan 1827
Herriot	29	F	Matron	England	America	Josephine	8 Jan 1827
Hiran	25	M	Sailor	United States	United States	New Packet	20 Oct 1827
*distressed Seaman							
Hugh	4/12	M	None	Great Britain	United States	Courier	26 Jun 1827
Hugh	24	M	Joiner	Great Britain	United States	Courier	26 Jun 1827
J.	11	M	Farmer	Great Britton	U. State	Earl of Liverpool	16 Aug 1826
J.	24		Merchant	Philadelphia	U. States	Brown	11 Jun 1827
James	16	M	None	Scotland	United States	Washington	2 Oct 1828
James	20	M	Black Smith			Hanford	17 Jul 1828
James	23	M	Merchant	U. States	U. States	Herald	4 Oct 1824
James	31	M	Gentleman	London	America	Evelina	10 Nov 1825
James	40	M	Farmer	Scotland		Ocean	17 Aug 1820

NAMES OF PASSENGERS	AGE	SEX	OCCUPATIONS	COUNTRY TO WHICH THEY BELONG	COUNTRY THEY INTEND TO INHABIT	SHIPS/DATES OF ARRIVAL	
REED (cont'd)							
James	40	M	Weaver	Scotland	United States	Washington	2 Oct 1828
Jams	35	M	Labourer	Ireland	United States	Hope	12 Jun 1828
Jane	11/12	F	Daughter	Ireland	United States	William & George	14 May 1828
Jane	24	F	None	Great Britain	United States	Courier	26 Jun 1827
Jane Mary	8/12	F	Daughter	Ireland	United States	William & George	14 May 1828
Janet	18	F	None	Scotland	United States	Washington	2 Oct 1828
Jas.	...	...	Merchant	...	United States	Minerva	30 Oct 1827
Jas.	28	M	Labourer	...	U. States	St. Michael	21 Jul 1824
Jer.	9	F	Farmer	Great Britton	U. State	Earl of Liverpool	16 Aug 1826
Jno. N.	35	M	Mercht.	St. Croix	U. States	Condor	22 Aug 1822
John	2	M	Farmer			Ocean	17 Aug 1820
John	4	M	None	Scotland	United States	Washington	2 Oct 1828
John	26	M	Tailor	Ireland	United States	Orozimbo	11 Aug 1823
John	28	M	Cloth Dresser	England	United States	Peru	23 May 1827
John	42	M	Spinner	Great Britain	United States	Hamilton	21 Nov 1826
John, Jr.	30	M	Officer	England	U. States	Hope & Esther	27 Sep 1824
John A.	24	M	Merchant	U. States	U. States	William Tell	3 Dec 1825
Joseph	3		...	Ireland	United States	Robert Burns	18 Jun 1822
Joshua	7	M		England	America	Josephine	8 Jan 1827
M.	54	M	Weaver	Scotland	U. States	Superior	25 Sep 1828
Margaret	37	F		Ireland	United States	William & George	14 May 1828
Margret	20	F	Spinster	Ireland	United States	Wilson	6 Jun 1828
Margt.	26	F	Farmer			Ocean	17 Aug 1820
Mary	26	F	None	Great Britain	United States	Illinois	9 Oct 1820
Mary	57	F		England	United States	Peru	23 May 1827
Mary Ann	1		...	Ireland	United States	Robert Burns	18 Jun 1822
Matilda	20	F	Daughter	Ireland	United States	William & George	14 May 1828
Mollian	24	M	Gardner	Scotland	United States	St. John	5 Oct 1829
Nancy	25	F	Labourer or Spinster	Ireland	United States	Champion	3 Nov 1827
Ninuan	21	M	Weaver	Scotland	United States	Washington	2 Oct 1828
Patrick		M		Ireland	U. States	Alex Mansfield	1 Jun 1822
R.	3	M	Farmer	Great Britton	U. State	Earl of Liverpool	16 Aug 1826
R. L.	50	M	Merchant	U. States	U. States	Bolivar Liberator	3 Jul 1828
Richard	21	M	Seaman	England	United States	Aurora	9 Jul 1827
Robt.	45	M	Mariner	U. States	U. States	Boston Packet	5 Jul 1825
Saml.	50	M	Labourer	Ireland	United States	Hope	12 Jun 1828
Samuel	18	M	Son	Ireland	United States	William & George	14 May 1828
Samuel	42	M	Merchant	England	America	Mary	20 Dec 1820
Sarah	21	F	None	Great Britain	United States	Illinois	9 Oct 1820
Sarah	27	F		Ireland	America	Wilson	27 Nov 1826
Sarah	40	F		Great Britton	U. State	Earl of Liverpool	16 Aug 1826
Sarah	48	F	None	Great Britain	United States	Courier	26 Jun 1827
Terrance	14	F	None	Scotland	United States	Washington	2 Oct 1828
Thomas	6	M				Ocean	17 Aug 1820
Thomas	21	M	Merchant	England	U. States	Lord Gambier	3 Apr 1827
Thos.	24		Farmer	Ireland		Westmoreland	1 Aug 1826
Thos.	26	M	Mechanic	United States	United States	Ann Maria	23 Oct 1820
W. A.	32	M	Merchant	U. States	U. States	Swiftsure	14 Apr 1828
William	5/52	M	Son	Ireland	United States	William & George	14 May 1828
William	3	M		England	America	Josephine	8 Jan 1827
William	25			Great Britain		John Dickinson	5 Apr 1821
William	36	M	Weaver	C. Down	Philedelphia	Nile	18 Aug 1829
William	57	M	Cloth Dresser	England	United States	Peru	23 May 1827
Wm.	20		Slater	Birmingham	Delaware	Peru	30 May 1828
Wm.	25	M	Grocer	England	United States	Manhattan	22 Sep 1823
Wm.	32	M	Farmer	Ireland	U. States	Francis	6 Sep 1827
REEF, Mathias	26	M	Turner	France	United States	La Flora	30 Jun 1828
REELE, George	45	M	Mariner	U. States	U. States	Martha	7 Nov 1825

NAMES OF PASSENGERS	AGE	SEX	OCCUPATIONS	COUNTRY TO WHICH THEY BELONG	COUNTRY THEY INTEND TO INHABIT	SHIPS/DATES OF ARRIVAL	
REELY, Charles	43	M	Locksmith	U.S. America	U.S. America	Commodore Preble	17 Dec 1825
REEN, Nancy	20	F		Co. ...th	United States	Java	9 Jul 1827
William	23	M	Merchant	Ireland	United States	Sylvester Healy	11 May 1825
REENNY, Francis	32	M	Farmer	Ireland	America	Mary	29 May 1827
REERDON, John	26	M		Great Britain	United States	Wilson	26 Feb 1824
REES, Ann	20	F		Wales	United States	New York Packet	14 Oct 1823
Eliza	1	F	None	Wales	United States	Orozimbo	11 Aug 1823
Evan	4	M	None	Wales	United States	Orozimbo	11 Aug 1823
Evan	27	M	Farmer	Wales	United States	New York Packet	14 Oct 1823
Evan	34	M	Shoemaker	Wales	United States	Orozimbo	11 Aug 1823
Jane	6	F	None	Wales	United States	Orozimbo	11 Aug 1823
John	5	M	None	Wales	United States	Orozimbo	11 Aug 1823
Marry	36	F	None	Wales	United States	Orozimbo	11 Aug 1823
Mary	8	F	None	Wales	United States	Orozimbo	11 Aug 1823
William	...	M	...	Great Britain	United States	Aurora	10 Nov 1827
Wm.	30	M	Comedian	England	United States	Dalhouse Castle	6 Sep 1827
Wm.	35	M	Mariner	U. States	U. States	Constitution	29 Dec 1821
REESE, Ann	27 0/12	F		United States	U.S.	Ontario	27 Jun 1821
C. R., Miss	19	F	None	U.S. America	U.S. America	James Cropper	29 Nov 1827
Charles M.	30 5/12	M	Doctor	United States	U.S.	Ontario	27 Jun 1821
G. B., Mrs.	26	M	Merchant	U.S. America	U.S. America	James Cropper	29 Nov 1827
H. B.	24	M	Merchant	United States	Philadelphia	Corinthian	27 Apr 1824
M., Mrs.	21	F	None	U.S. America	U.S. America	James Cropper	29 Nov 1827
Manuel	27	M	Gentn.	Naturalized U.S.	New York	Robert Fulton	22 May 1824
William M.	3	M		United States	U.S.	Ontario	27 Jun 1821
REESS, J. D.	25	M	Physician	Massachusetts	Massachusetts	Cadmus	16 Aug 1826
REEVE, Charles	36	M	Mariner	United States	U. States	Nimrod	24 Jan 1826
H. B.	25	M	Merchant	U. States	U. States	Columbia	20 Jul 1825
John	35	M	Seaman	United States	United States	Port Captain	17 May 1825
REEVEL, Catherine	4/12	F	Farmer	France	United States	Crescent	12 Jul 1827
Catherine	26	F	Farmer	France	United States	Crescent	12 Jul 1827
Margaret	3	F	Farmer	France	United States	Crescent	12 Jul 1827
Peter	28	M	Farmer	France	United States	Crescent	12 Jul 1827
REEVES, Ann	44	F	Weaver	Great Britain	New York	Superior	5 Sep 1827
Cathr.	40	F		St. Johns	U. States	Wanderer	30 Oct 1828
James	24	M	Farmer	England	America	Sarah	18 Aug 1829
Jno.	24	M	Black Smith	England	United States	Essex	23 May 1828
Jno.	65	M	Carman	N. York	N. York	Hope & Esther	19 Aug 1824
L.	35	M	Labourer	St. Johns	U. States	Wanderer	30 Oct 1828
Prael	24	M	Merchant	U. States	U. States	Fabius	30 Aug 1827
Rd.	40	M	Merchant	England	U. States	Nestor	9 Dec 1822
Robt.	44	M	Weaver	Great Britain	New York	Superior	5 Sep 1827
REEZ, T., Mr.	26	M	Mercht.	Spain	Spain	Henri IV	14 Sep 1827
REFOLL, H., Mr.	21	M	Gentleman	Columbia	Columbia	Athenian	17 Jul 1829
REFORCE, Saml.	25	M	Merchant	Ireland	U. States	Ospray	27 Aug 1822
REFORD, Joseph	32	M	Merchant	Ireland	United States	Herald	29 Oct 1825
REFUGIR, Marindale	21	F		Mexico		Apollo	11 Jun 1828
REG, Jose Manuel, Dr.	16	M	Merchant	Havana	U. States	Senica	17 Mar 1824
REGALAS, Jose, Don	27	M	Merchant	Spain	Spain	Vigilant	25 Nov 1822
REGAN, —, Mrs.	36	F	None	New York		Industry	11 Jun 1821
Ann	6	F	Farmers and Mechanics	America	America	Constitution	1 Oct 1825
Ann	22	F		Ireland	U. States	Fame	15 Nov 1826
Bridgt.	12	F	Farmers and Mechanics	America	America	Constitution	1 Oct 1825
Eliza	4	F	Farmers and Mechanics	America	America	Constitution	1 Oct 1825
Honora	6		Farmer & Labourer	Great Britain & Ireland	United States	Trio	8 Feb 1827
J.	33	M		Ireland	U. States	Fame	15 Nov 1826
James	25	M	Labourer	Ireland	United States	Baltic	21 Apr 1827
Jno.	25	M		G. Brittain	U. States	Canada	6 Jun 1825
Jno.	38	M	Farmers and Mechanics	America	America	Constitution	1 Oct 1825
Laurence	24	M	Laborer	Ireland	United States	Trio	13 Jun 1827

NAMES OF PASSENGERS	AGE	SEX	OCCUPATIONS	COUNTRY TO WHICH THEY BELONG	COUNTRY THEY INTEND TO INHABIT	SHIPS/DATES OF ARRIVAL	
REGAN (cont'd)							
Margaret	4		Farmer & Labourer	Great Britain & Ireland	United States	Trio	8 Feb 1827
Mary	2		Farmer & Labourer	Great Britain & Ireland	United States	Trio	8 Feb 1827
Mary	8	F	Farmers and Mechanics	America	America	Constitution	1 Oct 1825
Mary	26	F	Farmers and Mechanics	Ireland	America	Constitution	1 Oct 1825
Micheal	2	M	Farmers and Mechanics	Ireland	America	Constitution	1 Oct 1825
Michl.	29	M	Laborer	Ireland	United States	Trio	13 Jun 1827
Norris	32		Farmer & Labourer	Great Britain & Ireland	United States	Trio	8 Feb 1827
Pat.	10	M	Farmers and Mechanics	America	America	Constitution	1 Oct 1825
Thomas	16	M	Tailor	Ireland	United States	Carolina Ann	11 Dec 1826
Wm.	32	M	Laborer	Ireland	United States	Trio	13 Jun 1827
REGANO, Anthy.	25	M	Doctor	France	U. States	Bellona	1 Oct 1822
REGERA, D.	25	M	Merchant	Spain		Liberty	3 Sep 1827
REGGISER, Barbara	65	F	Farmer	Wortenberg	Lancaster	Louisa	6 Oct 1828
REGGON, Anthony	55	M	Servant	G. Britain	U. States	New York	11 Mar 1823
REGIART, Peter	64	M	Merchant	N. York	U. States	Ann Maria	5 Feb 1822
REGINA, Catharina	35	F		Germany	Philadelphia	Falcon	21 Oct 1826
January	30 4/12	M	Nopolitan Consul Genr.	Italy	America	France	28 Mar 1829
REGISTER, Susan, his wife [Thos.]	24	F		England	New York	Robert Edwards	17 Mar 1828
Thos.	24	M	Farmer	England	New York	Robert Edwards	17 Mar 1828
REGNEY, Patt	18	M	Laborer	Ireland	New York	Amanda	23 May 1827
REGUERO, B.	50	M	Mercht.	Havana	U. States	Evelina	31 May 1825
REGULAS, —, Mrs.	20	F		Havana	U. States	Herald	21 May 1824
J.	33	M	Merchant	Havana	U. States	Herald	21 May 1824
REGULEZ, Jose	28	M	Merchant	Spain	U. States	Emma	15 Dec 1824
REGULUS, A. D.	22	M	Mechanic	American	U. States	Mont Parnassus	31 Jan 1828
Jose, Don	28	M	Merchant	Spain	Spain	Vigilant	15 Feb 1823
REHER, Ch. Pat	35	M	Merchant	United States	United States	Neptunes Barge	23 Apr 1821
REICHARD, Geoe.	24	M	Agricultur	France	United States	Stephania	24 Mar 1828
REICHART, Barbara	6 6/12	F		Baden	United States	Jason	3 Nov 1828
Barbara	46	F		Baden	United States	Jason	3 Nov 1828
Cresentia	18	F		Baden	United States	Jason	3 Nov 1828
Ernestine	3	F		Baden	United States	Jason	3 Nov 1828
Françoise	24	F		Baden	United States	Jason	3 Nov 1828
Johan Adam	53	M	Cooper	Baden	United States	Jason	3 Nov 1828
Johannes	5	M		Baden	United States	Jason	3 Nov 1828
Joseph	22	M	Cooper	Baden	United States	Jason	3 Nov 1828
Karolina	12	F		Baden	United States	Jason	3 Nov 1828
Maddoneh	15	F		Baden	United States	Jason	3 Nov 1828
Manane	1 6/12	F		Baden	United States	Jason	3 Nov 1828
Matheldis	9	F		Baden	United States	Jason	3 Nov 1828
REICHHALT, Ormond	23	M	Labourer	Germany	Newyork	Cortes	16 Jul 1827
REICK, Joh.	24	M	Agriculture	Wirtemburg	United States	Henri IV	14 Oct 1829
REICTCLIFT, Chrish.	48	M	Farmer	England	U.S.A.	Lima	6 Dec 1826
REID, —, Mrs.	24	F		G. Britain	U. States	Camillus	8 Sep 1828
Agnes	15	F		Glasgow, St. Marys [Parish], Lanark [County]	New York	Hero	19 May 1828
*going with their friends							
Alexander	25	M	Farmer	Great Britain	United States	Natchez	17 Aug 1822
Alexr.	31	M	Clerk & Joiner [?]	Great Britain	United States	Comet	9 Aug 1822
Alexr.	54	F	Taylor	Glasgow, St. Marys [Parish], Lanark [County]	New York	Hero	19 May 1828
*Tailor to follow his occuation							
Andrew	1	M		G. Britain	U. States	Camillus	8 Sep 1828

NAMES OF PASSENGERS	AGE	SEX	OCCUPATIONS	COUNTRY TO WHICH THEY BELONG	COUNTRY THEY INTEND TO INHABIT	SHIPS/DATES OF ARRIVAL	
REID (cont'd)							
Ann	30	F	one family [William]	Ireland	Und. Stts of Amer	Alexander Mansfield	18 Aug 1826
Ann, Junr.	8		one family [William]	Ireland	Und. Stts of America	Alexander Mansfield	18 Aug 1826
Arthur	11	M	None	Great Britain	United States	Comet	9 Aug 1822
Arthur	27	M	Joiner	Great Britain	United States	Colossus	5 Jun 1827
Charlotte	25	F	Servant	Scotland	Scotland	New York	5 Jul 1826
Christina	18	F		France	United States	New England	29 Aug 1828
Crawford	20	M		Great Britain	United States	Birmingham	15 Jun 1827
David	26	M	Farmer	Ireland	Redstone	Triton	12 Jul 1823
David	28	M	Labourer	Scotland	United States	Friends	7 Jul 1827
Edward Jas.	37	M	Planter	Jamaica		Indus	19 Jun 1822
Eliza	32	F	None	Great Britain	United States	Comet	9 Aug 1822
Eliza	83	F	None	Great Britain	United States	Comet	9 Aug 1822
Elizabeth	15	F		Great Britain	United States	Natchez	17 Aug 1822
Ellen	13	F	None	Great Britain	United States	Comet	9 Aug 1822
Geo.	22	M	Mechanic	Rhode Island	U. States	Columbia	24 Mar 1823
George	43	M	Merchant	Scotland	America	Mentor	21 Sep 1824
Henry	4	M		England	United States	Earl of Liverpool	29 Sep 1823
Hy.	33	M	Sailor	America	U. States	Hiram	17 Jun 1826
James	3	M		G. Britain	U. States	Camillus	8 Sep 1828
James	20	M		Glasgow, St. Marys [Parish], Lanark [County]	New York	Hero	19 May 1828
*going with their friends							
James	25		Merchant	Ireland	United States	Robert Burns	30 May 1823
Jane	1		one family [William]	Ireland	Und. Stts of America	Alexander Mansfield	18 Aug 1826
Janet	7	F		Scotland	New York	Joseph Hume	26 Oct 1829
Jno.	11	M		England	United States	Earl of Liverpool	29 Sep 1823
Jno.	24	M	Joiner	England	U. States	Thomas Ritchie	2 Jul 1827
Jno.	48	M	Farmer	England	United States	Earl of Liverpool	29 Sep 1823
John	14	M	None	England	America	Courier	24 Jul 1820
John	23	M	Dresser	Great Britain	United States	Birmingham	15 Jun 1827
John	45	M	None	Ireland	America	Hesperus	7 Jul 1820
John H.	25	M	Merchant	England	U. States	Amity	25 Sep 1822
Margaret	17	F		Great Britain	United States	Natchez	17 Aug 1822
Margaret	25	F		Glasgow, St. Marys [Parish], Lanark [County]	New York	Hero	19 May 1828
*going with their friends							
Margaret	52	F		Great Britain	United States	Natchez	17 Aug 1822
Margaretta	24	F		France	United States	New England	29 Aug 1828
Margt.	49	F		Glasgow, St. Marys [Parish], Lanark [County]	New York	Hero	19 May 1828
*going with their friends							
Mary	4		one family [William]	Ireland	Und. Stts of America	Alexander Mansfield	18 Aug 1826
Mary	9	F	None	Great Britain	United States	Comet	9 Aug 1822
Mary	9	F		England	United States	Earl of Liverpool	29 Sep 1823
Mary	46	F		England	United States	Earl of Liverpool	29 Sep 1823
Mary, Mrs.	26	F	Lady	Ireland	United States	Dublin Packet	9 Jul 1827
Matthew	60	M	Farmer	Great Britain	United States	Natchez	17 Aug 1822
Peggy	20	F	Spinster	Kilmudar Donegal	...	Gleaner	24 May 1823
Robert	24	M		Glasgow, St. Marys [Parish], Lanark [County]	New York	Hero	19 May 1828

NAMES OF PASSENGERS	AGE	SEX	OCCUPATIONS	COUNTRY TO WHICH THEY BELONG	COUNTRY THEY INTEND TO INHABIT	SHIPS/DATES OF ARRIVAL	
REID (cont'd)							
Sam C.	38	M	Mariner	U. States	U. States	Jane	29 Jul 1823
Shepd.	35	M	Farier	Great Britain	U. States	Dominica	4 Jan 1823
Will	26	M	Baker	Great Britain	United States	William Dawson	18 Jun 1827
William	7	M		England	United States	Earl of	
						Liverpool	29 Sep 1823
William	33	M	Weaver	Ireland	Und. Stts of		
					America	Alexander	
						Mansfield	18 Aug 1826
William	37	M	Labourer	Scotland	United States	Friends	7 Jul 1827
William, Mr.	30	M	Gentleman	Ireland	United States	Dublin Packet	9 Jul 1827
Wm.	25	M	Sailor	England	U. States	Alert	22 Sep 1821
Wm.	25	M	Merchant	Virginia	Virginia	Hetta	15 Dec 1823
Wm.	28	M	Merchant	England	Canada	Bolina	16 Mar 1826
Wm.	36		Farmer	Great Britain	United States	Camillus	12 Sep 1827
Wm., Junr.	6		one family		Und. Stts of	Alexander	
			[William]	Ireland	America	Mansfield	18 Aug 1826
REIDER, P.	25	M	Distiller	United States	United States	Seine	21 Oct 1822
REIDINGER,							
Francois	1 6/12	M		Switzerland	U.S.	C. Amelia	30 Jun 1828
REIF, J. N.	24	M	Turner	France	United States	La Flora	30 Jun 1828
Jacob	3	M		France	United States	La Flora	30 Jun 1828
Jean	31	F		France	United States	La Flora	30 Jun 1828
M.	0 6/12	M		France	United States	La Flora	30 Jun 1828
Madelina	21	F	Taylor	France	United States	La Flora	30 Jun 1828
REIFFLER, Jacob	22	M	Sadler	Germany	U. States	Isabella	10 Aug 1829
REIGERT, Jacob	1 1/2	M	Farmer	Germany	United States	Virginia	31 May 1828
Jacob	23	M	Farmer	Germany	United States	Virginia	31 May 1828
Materlane	20	F	Farmer	Germany	United States	Virginia	31 May 1828
REIGHTON, P. T., Captn.	26	M	Mariner	United States	U. States	Pocahontas	11 Aug 1829
REIGNOT, Peter	60		Merchant	America	America	Sea Serpent	3 Jul 1820
REIL, Fred	26	M		G. Britan	U. States	William Neilson	26 Jul 1828
James	25	M	...	...	...	Frances	
						Henrietta	30 Jun 1827
REILE, John	35	M	Director of Mines	Great Britain	Mexico	Corinthian	27 Apr 1824
REILEY, Alexander	32	M	Farmer	England	New York	Concordia	12 Oct 1826
Ann	26	M	None	Ireland	U. States	William Byrnes	24 Apr 1827
Bernard	20	M	Labourer	Ireland	U. States	Lima	5 Aug 1829
Bridget	25	F		Ireland	United States	Thompson	12 Sep 1827
Eleanor	3	F	Clerk	...	United States	Minerva	30 Oct 1829
Eliza	10/12			Scotland	United States	Camillus	3 May 1828
Elizabeth	32	F	Clerk	...	United States	Minerva	30 Oct 1829
Hugh	21	M	Labourer	Ireland	United States	Trident	31 Mar 1827
James	8	M	Clerk	...	United States	Minerva	30 Oct 1829
John	19	M	None	Ireland	U. States	William Byrnes	24 Apr 1827
John	20		Laboring Class		United States	Atlantic	2 Apr 1827
John	40			England		Agricola	1 Jul 1820
John P.	21	M	Clerk	Canada	U. States	Commerce	24 Dec 1821
Margarett	7	F	Clerk	...	United States	Minerva	30 Oct 1829
Mary	16		Laboring Class		United States	Atlantic	2 Apr 1827
Maryann	5	F	Clerk	...	United States	Minerva	30 Oct 1829
Michael	19	M	Labourer	Ireland	U. States	Lima	5 Aug 1829
Owen	21		Laboring Class		United States	Atlantic	2 Apr 1827
Patrick	6	M	None	Ireland	U. States	William Byrnes	24 Apr 1827
Thomas	20	M	Blacksmith	Ireland	U. States	Josephine	30 Aug 1828
William	25	M		Irland	United States	Nancy	28 Oct 1822
Wm., Mrs.	24		Spinster	Scotland	United States	Camillus	3 May 1828
Wm. Wyles	29		Labourer	Scotland	United States	Camillus	3 May 1828
REILING, Eugenie	40	F	...	Baden	United States	Wade	29 Aug 1825
REILLEY, Mary	40	F		Ireland	United States	Essex	23 May 1828
Pat	7	M		Ireland	United States	Essex	23 May 1828
Philip	25	M		Ireland	United States	Essex	23 May 1828
Philip	47	M	Labourer	Ireland	United States	Essex	23 May 1828
REILLS, Bridget	16	F	Spinster	Ireland	United States	Fabius	4 Jun 1828
REILLY, Ann	17	F	Farmer	Ireland	U. States	Dickinson	30 Jul 1825
Ann	24	F		Ireland	U. States	Josephine	27 Jul 1825
B.	24	F		Great Britain	United States	Washington	3 Sep 1827
Bernard	21	M	Labourer	Ireland	U. States	Josephine	27 Jul 1825
Bridget	1	F	Labourer	Ireland	United States	Essex	23 May 1828

NAMES OF PASSENGERS	AGE	SEX	OCCUPATIONS	COUNTRY TO WHICH THEY BELONG	COUNTRY THEY INTEND TO INHABIT	SHIPS/DATES OF ARRIVAL	
REILLY (cont'd)							
Bridget	46	F	Spinster	Ireland	United States	Dublin Packet	3 May 1823
Bridjet	24	F	Farmer	Ireland	U. States	Dickinson	30 Jul 1825
Catharine	20	F	Farmer	Ireland	U. States	Dickinson	30 Jul 1825
Cathe.	20	F	Labourer	Ireland	United States	Essex	23 May 1828
Catherine	17	F	Spinster	Ireland	United States	Dublin Packet	22 Apr 1822
Catherine	17	F	Spinster	Ireland	United States	Dublin Packet	9 Jul 1827
Charles	29	M	Laborer	Ireland	United States	Lord Wellington	14 Nov 1827
Charles P.	32		Planter	Ireland	Ireland	Emilia	25 Aug 1828
Cornelius	17	M	Farmer	Ireland	United States	Alex. Mansfield	17 May 1823
E. O.	23	M	Farmer	Great Brittain	United States	Nimrod	9 Jan 1827
Edmond	40	M	Merchant	U. States		Emeline	24 Apr 1828
Edwd.	35	M	Mechanic	Ireland		Marchioness	13 May 1828
Ellen	11	F	Spinster	Ireland	United States	Dublin Packet	3 May 1823
Ellen	24	F	Servant	Ireland	United States	Josephine	30 Apr 1828
Francis	11	M	Labourer	Ireland	New York	America	1 Aug 1828
G. W.	22	M	Gentleman	United States	United States	Howard	19 May 1826
Honora	2	F	Labourer	Ireland	United States	Essex	23 May 1828
Hugh	23	M	Farmer	Great Britain	United States	William Dawson	18 Jun 1827
Hugh	26	M	Distiller	Ireland	United States	Asia	29 Jul 1829
J.	24	M	Labourer	England	U. States	Comet	23 Aug 1828
James	...	M	...	Ireland	United States	General Putnam	20 Jun 1825
James	20	M	Farmer	Ireland	United States	John Dickinson	18 Feb 1822
James	20	M	Labourer	Great Britain	United States	Ganges	26 Oct 1826
Jno.	25	M	Labourer	Ireland	United States	Essex	23 May 1828
John	1 1/2			Great Britan	United States	Newry	11 Jul 1827
John	14	M	Boy	Ireland	United States	Dublin Packet	3 May 1823
John	22	M	Farmer	Ireland	United States	Dublin Packet	9 Jul 1827
John	23		Labourer	Great Britan	United States	Newry	11 Jul 1827
John	27	M	Farmer	Ireland	United States	Dublin Packet	29 Jun 1825
Judith	25	F	Spinster	Ireland	United States	Dublin Packet	22 Aug 1829
Judy	24 5/12	F	Spinstress	Ireland	U. States	Fabius	22 Sep 1828
Law.	23		Labourer	Ireland	United States	Courier	15 Oct 1827
Lawrence	24	F		G. Britain	U. States	Hynd	12 Jul 1820
Lawrence	27	M	Currier	Ireland	United States	Meteor	19 Aug 1829
Manrie	28	M	Labourer	Ireland	United States	Jubilee	1 Oct 1828
Margt.	20	F	Spinster	Ireland	United States	Thomas	13 Dec 1827
Mary	1	F	None	Great Britain	United States	William Dawson	18 Jun 1827
Mary	13	F	Spinster	Ireland	United States	Dublin Packet	29 Jun 1825
Mary	16	F	None	Ireland	United States	Mary & Harriet	3 Jul 1829
Mary	17	F	Spinster	Ireland	America	Wilson	16 May 1825
Mary	18	F	Spinster	Ireland	Rhode Island	Governor Fenner	23 Jul 1829
Mary	20	F		Ireland	United States	Thompson	12 Sep 1827
Mary	25			Great Britan	United States	Newry	11 Jul 1827
Mary	25	F	Sempstress	Great Britain	United States	Atlantic	8 Dec 1827
Mary	27	F	None	Ireland	United States	Orozimbo	11 Aug 1823
Michael	22	M	Weaver	Ireland		Fame	9 Dec 1826
Michael	24	M	Labourer	Ireland	N. York	Lima	5 Aug 1829
Michael	25	M	Farmer	Ireland	United States	Trident	18 Jul 1827
Michl.	28	M	Carpenter	Ireland	United States	William	20 Jul 1829
Miles	21	M	gent. Servant	Ireland	United States	Meteor	19 Aug 1829
Nelly	20	F	None	Great Britain	United States	William Dawson	18 Jun 1827
P. C.	40	M	Planter	St. Martins	U. States	Matilda	23 May 1826
Pat	26	M	Farmer	Ireland	United States	Dublin Packet	22 Aug 1829
Pat	28			Great Britan	United States	Newry	11 Jul 1827
Pat	35	M	...	Ireland	United States	General Putnam	20 Jun 1825
Patk.	25		Labourer	Ireland	United States	Geo. Canning	5 Jun 1828
Patrick	22	M	Farmer	Ireland	United States	Dublin Packet	23 May 1828
Patrick	23	M	Laborer	Ireland	United States	Lord Wellington	14 Nov 1827
Patrick	28	M	Trader	Great Briton	United States	Erin	26 May 1821
Patrick	36	M	Labourer	Ireland	United States	Orozimbo	11 Aug 1823
Peggy	28	F	...	Ireland	United States	General Putnam	20 Jun 1825
Philip	22	M	Farmer	Ireland	United States	Dublin Packet	22 Aug 1829
Rose	18	F	Spinster	Ireland	America	Wilson	16 May 1825
Rose	20	F	Spinster	Ireland	United States	Dublin Packet	29 Jun 1825
Sarah	11	...	...	Ireland	United States	Carolina Ann	24 Oct 1825
T. O. C. O.	25		Traveller	Ireland	U. States	Nimrod	21 Sep 1820
Thomas	50	M	Mercht.	U. States	U. States	Emma	12 Aug 1824

NAMES OF PASSENGERS	AGE	SEX	OCCUPATIONS	COUNTRY TO WHICH THEY BELONG	COUNTRY THEY INTEND TO INHABIT	SHIPS/DATES OF ARRIVAL	
REILLY (cont'd)							
Thoms.	3			Great Britan	United States	Newry	11 Jul 1827
Thos.	30	M	Labourer	Ireland	United States	Essex	23 May 1828
REILY, Ann	26	F		Great Britain	United States	Isaac Hicks	10 Jul 1827
Caward	32	M	Mason	Great Britain	United States	Isaac Hicks	10 Jul 1827
Ed.	50	M	Drover	England	U. States	Foster	28 Aug 1822
James	1	M		Great Britain	United States	Isaac Hicks	10 Jul 1827
John	26		Laboring Class		United States	Atlantic	2 Apr 1827
Margaret	26	F	Spinster	Montross	U.S. America	Camillus	10 Sep 1821
Mary	19	F	Farmers and Mechanics	Ireland	America	Constitution	1 Oct 1825
Patk.	20	M	Farmers and Mechanics	Ireland	America	Constitution	1 Oct 1825
Philip	20	M	Farmer	Great Britain	United States	Colossus	5 Jun 1827
Saml.	28	M	None	Great Brittan	U. States	Gem	26 Jul 1827
REIN, Anna	1	F	Child of [John]	Switzerland	United States	Aurora	21 Jun 1824
Catharina	26	F	Wife of [John]	Switzerland	United States	Aurora	21 Jun 1824
Elizabeth	3	F	Child of [John]	Switzerland	United States	Aurora	21 Jun 1824
John	53	M	Fisherman	Switzerland	United States	Aurora	21 Jun 1824
REINDER, Dorothy	6	F	Agriculturist	France	U.S.	Helen	3 May 1828
Elizabeth	46	F	Agriculturist	France	U.S.	Helen	3 May 1828
Lament	25	M	Agriculturist	France	U.S.	Helen	3 May 1828
Madalaine	1 6/12	F	Agriculturist	France	U.S.	Helen	3 May 1828
Michel	18 6/12	M	Agriculturist	France	U.S.	Helen	3 May 1828
Michel	40	M	Agriculturist	France	U.S.	Helen	3 May 1828
Solomon	20	M	Agriculturist	France	U.S.	Helen	3 May 1828
Sophia	8	F	Agriculturist	France	U.S.	Helen	3 May 1828
Therese	9	F	Agriculturist	France	U.S.	Helen	3 May 1828
REINHART, A., Mr.	25	M	Musician	Bavaria		François I	19 Nov 1828
REINHOLD, Frederick	26	M	Weaver	Germany	United States	Brandt	26 Jun 1826
REINTEAUX, A. C.	26	M	Merchant	New York	U. States	Chase	18 Dec 1821
REISDIDGE, Magdalena Christine	16	F	Farmer	Wortenberg	Lancaster	Louisa	6 Oct 1828
REISESTOIN, A., Mr.	30	M	Musician	Bavaria		François I	19 Nov 1828
REISS, Michael	26	M	Mechanic	Switzerland	America	Anna Maria	22 Feb 1820
REIZ, —	47	M	Farmer	Germany	U.S.	Stephania	27 Nov 1826
Elizah.	43	F		Germany	U.S.	Stephania	27 Nov 1826
Francois T.	19	M		Germany	U.S.	Stephania	27 Nov 1826
RELF, Catharine	25	F	None	England	U. States	Hercules	6 Jul 1827
Eliza	1	F	Farmer	England	U. States	Hercules	6 Jul 1827
George	18	M	Farmer	England	U. States	Hercules	6 Jul 1827
George	33	M	None	England	U. States	Hercules	6 Jul 1827
Henry	6	M	None	England	U. States	Hercules	6 Jul 1827
Mary	2	F	None	England	U. States	Hercules	6 Jul 1827
RELFORD, Saml.	25	M	Weaver	England	United States	Siroc	31 Oct 1829
RELIN, Cristopher Fred.	28	M	Shoe Maker	Germany	America	Falcon	28 Aug 1828
RELL, Bridget	24	F		G. Britan	U. States	William Neilson	26 Jul 1828
Mariah		F		G. Britan	U. States	William Neilson	26 Jul 1828
Naly	26	F		G. Britan	U. States	William Neilson	26 Jul 1828
Rose	21	F		G. Britan	U. States	William Neilson	26 Jul 1828
RELLEFIELD, Perre	22	M	Watch	France		Pallas	14 Jun 1828
RELLEGAN, Dennis	22	M	Weaver	Ireland	United States	St. Michaels	18 Jul 1826
RELLET, John	34	M	Labourer	Whipsey		Aurora	8 Jun 1827
RELLEY, Margt.	26		Labourer	England	United States	Hugh Johnson	11 Jun 1828
RELPH, Frances	13	F		England	Albany	Cortes	16 Jul 1827
Geo.	33	M	Merchant	England	U. States	Amity	23 Sep 1823
RELSTEN, Solomon	31	M	Farmer	Boston	U. States	Zephyr	18 May 1825
RELY, Isaac M.	32	M	None	U. States	United States	New York	12 Nov 1822
REMAIRES, J.	13	M	School Boy	Columbia	U. States	Exchange	26 Jul 1824
REMAZIER, Juan	25	M	Merchant	England	England	Native	30 Jun 1826
M...on	23	M	Merchant	England	England	Native	30 Jun 1826
Sonier	17	M	Merchant	England	England	Native	30 Jun 1826
REMICK, Lydia Eliza	28	F	Domestic	St. John	Brooklyn	William	27 Aug 1827
REMING, Susan	25	F	Spinster	Ireland		Robert Fulton	4 Jun 1828
REMINGTON, Jno.	24	M	Mariner	U. States	U. States	Packet	25 May 1824
REMIS, John P.	39	M	Mercht.	America	America	Silvanus Jenkins	17 Nov 1828
REMSEN, Caroline	44	F		U. States	U. States	Carlo	19 Jun 1828
REN..., Hy.	49	M	Gentleman	England	U. States	Unity	27 Mar 1827
RENAERE, Lewis, Mr.	31	M	Merchant	France	U. States	Olive & Sarah	27 Jan 1823

NAMES OF PASSENGERS	AGE	SEX	OCCUPATIONS	COUNTRY TO WHICH THEY BELONG	COUNTRY THEY INTEND TO INHABIT	SHIPS/DATES OF ARRIVAL	
RENAND, Pediney	31	F	his Wife [Samuel F.]	France	U.S. America	Gibraltar	12 Oct 1829
RENARD, Lewis	35	M	Merchant	France	U. States	Velocipede	26 Jun 1823
Philippe	36	M	Planter	Point Peter	France	Pacific	14 May 1827
RENART, Jose A.	21	M	Merchant	Spain		Aspasia	19 Jul 1823
RENAUD, J.	30	M	Merchant	France	U. States	Washington	2 Oct 1822
Ll.	38	M	Merchant	France	France	Abigail	6 May 1822
Samuel F.	31	M	Musician	France	U.S. America	Gibraltar	12 Oct 1829
RENAULT, John	42	M	Merchant	France	United States	Stephania	22 Apr 1822
RENBORIGHT, Madelena	22	F	None	France	U. States	Sully	25 Jun 1828
Peter	28	M	Farmer	France	U. States	Sully	25 Jun 1828
RENCAKA, John	47	M	Merchant	United States	United States	Frances	19 Feb 1829
RENCH, David	12	M	Farmer	Great Britian	United States	Andes	19 Aug 1829
Elizabeth	40	F		Great Britian	United States	Andes	19 Aug 1829
Jessee	21	M	Farmer	Great Britian	United States	Andes	19 Aug 1829
Johnathan	15	M	Farmer	Great Britian	United States	Andes	19 Aug 1829
Thomas	8	M	Farmer	Great Britian	United States	Andes	19 Aug 1829
Thomas	44	M	Farmer	Great Britian	United States	Andes	19 Aug 1829
RENCHENUR, Jaques	22	M	Carpenter	France		Pallas	14 Jun 1828
RENDELL, Stephen W.	36	M	Mariner	U.S.	U.S.	Anita	5 May 1821
RENDERAL, A.	39	M	Merchant	France	France	Prize	10 Jun 1824
RENEAUX, Peter	60	M	Merchant	U. States	U. States	Leontine	19 May 1825
RENEFFEE, John	40	M	Farmer	Germany	United States	Wm. Osborne	16 Sep 1828
RENFREW, John	19	M	Clerk	Paisley, Renfrew [Parish], Abby [County]	New York	Hero	19 May 1828
*Clerk to look for Employt.							
John	19	M	Carpenter	Ireland	United States	Wilson	28 Nov 1828
RENGEN, Latge	47	M	Sugar Baker	England	New York	Cortes	23 Nov 1827
RENGUERER, Dorothie	14	F	Farmer	Switzerland	United States	Olympia	12 Aug 1828
Dorothie	40	F	Farmer	Switzerland	United States	Olympia	12 Aug 1828
Georges	6	M	Farmer	Switzerland	United States	Olympia	12 Aug 1828
Georges	40	M	Farmer	Switzerland	United States	Olympia	12 Aug 1828
Jacob	8	M	Farmer	Switzerland	United States	Olympia	12 Aug 1828
Marie	10	F	Farmer	Switzerland	United States	Olympia	12 Aug 1828
Phillipe	4	M	Farmer	Switzerland	United States	Olympia	12 Aug 1828
RENHMANN, Jacob F.	15	M	Shoemaker	Wertemberg	Wertemberg	Edward Quesnel	3 Jul 1829
RENIA, John	20	M	Weaver	Ireland	United States	Lord Wellington	14 Nov 1827
RENIL, Edward B.	6 3/12	M	Has a Father in New York, a Merchant	France	U.S. America	Sicily	7 Oct 1829
RENIS, Edwd.	27	M	Farmer	Ireland	U. States	Teio	5 Jun 1826
RENN, Anna Betty Dorathea, Miss	25	F	Servant	Hamburg	U. States	Minerva	24 Sep 1821
RENNER, Wm.	35	M	Farmer	Gt. Brittain	United States	Robert Edwards	1 Jun 1826
RENNEY, Mary	...	F	...	...	United States	Hanford	17 Oct 1828
RENNIE, James	27	M		Scotland	United States	Camillus	9 May 1827
RENNOLD, —, Mr.	26	M	Merchant	U.S.	U.S.	George Canning	26 Aug 1829
RENNY, Edward	24	M	Farmer	Ireland	U.S. America	Columbia	31 Jul 1826
RENOLDS, E.	25	M	Merchant	England	U. States	New York	4 Nov 1824
James	22	M	Labourer	Ireland	United States	Nile	17 May 1827
RENSEN, H. W.	20	M		U. States	U. States	Carlo	19 Jun 1828
RENSHAW, B.	30	M	Merchant	Philada.	United States	Harriet & Lucy	3 Oct 1823
Benjn.	4	F	Gentleman	U. States	United States	Vermont	26 Aug 1824
Emily	6	F	Lady	U. States	United States	Vermont	26 Aug 1824
Frances	25	F	Lady	U. States	United States	Vermont	26 Aug 1824
Francis	1	M	Gentleman	U. States	United States	Vermont	26 Aug 1824
James	35	M	Navy	U. States	U. States	Abeona	1 Oct 1823
RENSS, —	26	F	Wife	England	U. States	Ranger	2 Jul 1827
—	35	M	Merchant	Germany	U. States	Ranger	2 Jul 1827
RENTON, A., Mrs.	25	F		G. Britain	U. States	Camillus	8 Sep 1828
Alexr.	7	M		G. Britain	U. States	Camillus	8 Sep 1828
David	2	M		G. Britain	U. States	Camillus	8 Sep 1828
James	36	M		G. Britain	U. States	Camillus	8 Sep 1828
John	9	M		G. Britain	U. States	Camillus	8 Sep 1828
Mary	20	F	None	Scotland	U. States	Magnet	22 Aug 1822
RENTZ, S.	24	M	Baker	Bavaria	U.S.	Shepherdess	17 May

NAMES OF PASSENGERS	AGE	SEX	OCCUPATIONS	COUNTRY TO WHICH THEY BELONG	COUNTRY THEY INTEND TO INHABIT	SHIPS/DATES OF ARRIVAL	
RENWEEKS, David	24	M	Carpenter	U. States	U. States	Harriet Frances	10 May 1827
RENWICH, John	23	M		Scotland	U.S.	Curler	19 Jul 1828
RENZALL, F.	24	M	Merchant	Vera Cruz	U. States	Eliza	11 Apr 1826
REORDEN, Timothy	20		Painter	Ireland	United States	Geo. Canning	5 Jun 1828
REPE, Jane	22	F	None	Ireland	United States	Lord Wellington	28 May 1827
John	25	M	Labourer	Ireland	United States	Lord Wellington	28 May 1827
Martha	2	F	None	Ireland	United States	Lord Wellington	28 May 1827
Nancy	3	F	None	Ireland	United States	Lord Wellington	28 May 1827
REPER, —	45	F		Switzerland	United States	Elbe	2 Aug 1822
REPTON, Benjn.	30	M	Farmer	Derbeyshire	U. States	Manhattan	21 May 1821
Dorreythey	26	F		Derbeyshire	U. States	Manhattan	21 May 1821
RERFER, M.	14	M	Merchant	New York	U. States	Betsey	31 Jul 1826
RES, Christian	10	M		Bardin	U. States	Bayard	5 Sep 1828
Christian	42	M	Farmer	Bardin	U. States	Bayard	5 Sep 1828
Eliz.	45	F		Bardin	U. States	Bayard	5 Sep 1828
F.	20	M		Bardin	U. States	Bayard	5 Sep 1828
Jacob	18	M		Bardin	U. States	Bayard	5 Sep 1828
RESA, Janes	38	M	Labourer	Ireland	U. States	Meteor	19 Jul 1828
RESCHA, Harman	60	M		Hamburg	U. States	Martha	4 Sep 1828
RESENAI, Marcelino	30	M	Servant	Spain	Spain	Paquebot Bordeaux	25 May 1828
RESKEY, James	24	M	Merchant	England	U. States	Foster	28 Aug 1822
RESTREPO, F. M.	29	M	Merchant	Columbia	Columbia	Hudson	13 Jan 1827
REUDD, Antonio		M		Mexico		Joseph	20 Jul 1829
REUEL, Joseph	16	M	Segar Maker	Island of Cuba	United States	Betsey	28 Oct 1825
REUSS, ...	25	F	None	England	Mexico	Trident	30 Sep 1826
...	35	M	Merchant	England	Mexico	Trident	30 Sep 1826
Carl	26	M	Merchant	Germany	New York	Louisa	10 May 1828
REVANS, Sarah	28	F		United States	United States	Charles Sidney	9 Oct 1829
REVARRO, Joseph	34	M	Merchant	Spain	U. States	Virginia	3 Dec 1827
REVEL, James	32	M	Laborer	England	U.S.	Sisters	7 Jul 1826
REVELER, Edward	23	M	Taylor	France	United States	Bayard	15 Feb 1827
REVENOR, Francis	32	M	Merchant	Germany		Mary & Nancy	5 Oct 1829
REVERIEL, Pape	24	M	Segar Maker	Island of Cuba	United States	Betsey	28 Oct 1825
REVERO, Cap	28	M	Mariner	Spain	Spain	Vigilant	15 Feb 1823
REVES, Catharine	48	F	Labourer	Ireland	United States	Hope & Esther	17 Oct 1827
Martha S.	12	F	Labourer	Ireland	United States	Hope & Esther	17 Oct 1827
REVIE, Adam	16	M	Farmer	Bavarian	United States	American	27 Aug 1827
Adam	24	M	Farmer	Bavarian	United States	American	27 Aug 1827
Margaret	23	F	Spinster	Bavarian	United States	American	27 Aug 1827
REVIERD, Anecetto	7	M		Spain	United States	Georgetown Packet	15 Nov 1823
Juan	40	M	Merchant	Spain	United States	Georgetown Packet	15 Nov 1823
REVINASON, H. J.	38	M	Merchant	United States	United States	Orion	1 Feb 1820
REVOLO, Filipe	30	M	Servant	Italy	Italy	Centurion	22 Dec 1828
REVORIO, Peter, Capt.	25	M	Mariner	U.S.A.	New Orleans	Huntress	11 Dec 1821
REWATER, Cormack	20	M	Labourer	Ireland	United States	Thomas	13 Dec 1827
REWLEY, Ann	50		Farmer	England	United States	Hugh Johnson	11 Jun 1828
Wm.	20		Labourer	England	United States	Hugh Johnson	11 Jun 1828
REWZ, Fernando	10	M		Mexico	U. States	Cato	9 Aug 1823
REY, —	45	M	Mercht.	France	France to return to his native country	Don Quixote	3 Jan 1826
Alexander, son [of Gypolite]	9	M	Merchant	Harleille		Belle	13 Jul 1821
Chas.	23	M	Gentleman	State New York		Industry	28 Jul 1823
Gypolite	37	M	Merchant	Harleille	to return to his native country	Belle	13 Jul 1821
Jos. M.	19	M	...	...	U. States	Francis	16 Sep 1824
REYBURN, James	21	M	Merchant	U. States	U. States	Sarah	17 Mar 1829
REYER, John	30	M		England	U. States	Birmingham	16 Jun 1828
REYHLANS, Elenor	20 6/12	F	Labourer	Ireland	America	Enterprize	29 Jun 1827
REYHOLDS, Biddy	36	F	Labourer	Great Britian	United States	Princess Charlotte	6 Sep 1828
REYLEY, Cathrin, Mrs.	45	F	Labourer	England	U.S.	Acasta	11 May 1827
Jno.	35	M	Merchant	England	gone to Lipool.	Mary Ann	27 Sep 1822
John, Mr.	56	M	Labourer	England	U.S.	Acasta	11 May 1827
REYLY, Wm., Mast.	10	M	Labourer	England	U.S.	Acasta	11 May 1827
REYNAL, Garnier	17	M		Guadeloupe	New York	Notre Dame	6 Oct 1827
REYNARD, James	20	M	Smith	England	U.S. States	Splendid	14 Aug 1829

NAMES OF PASSENGERS	AGE	SEX	OCCUPATIONS	COUNTRY TO WHICH THEY BELONG	COUNTRY THEY INTEND TO INHABIT	SHIPS/DATES OF ARRIVAL	
REYNER, J.	33	M	Gentleman	U. States	U. States	New York	22 Jul 1824
REYNOLD, Charles	22	M	Labourer	England	New York	Curler	7 Jul 1827
Henry	32	M	Labourer	England	U. States	Comet	23 Aug 1828
Mary Ann	30	F	Labourer	England	U. States	Comet	23 Aug 1828
Thom.	29	M		Ireland	United States	William Byrnes	6 Apr 1826
REYNOLDS, —, Miss	22	M	Merchant	U. States	U. States	Zephyr	2 Oct 1826
—, Miss	27	M	Merchant	U. States	U. States	Zephyr	2 Oct 1826
Ann	8	F		Gt. Britain		Dalhouse Castle	13 May 1828
Ann	11	F		England	America	Hudson	20 Nov 1828
Ann	20	F		Ireland	United States	Alex. Mansfield	17 May 1823
Ann	35	F		England	America	Hudson	20 Nov 1828
B.	20			G. Britain	U. States	Great Britain	6 Sep 1828
Barney	6	M		Gt. Britain		Dalhouse Castle	13 May 1828
Bernard	38	M	Tailor	St. John, N.B.	St. John, N.B.	St. Michaels	11 May 1826
Biddy	24	F	Wife	Ireland	United States	Sarah Ann	18 Nov 1826
Bridget	18	F		Ireland	U. States	William Byrnes	17 Jul 1825
Cath.	16	F		Ireland	U. States	William Byrnes	17 Jul 1825
Catherine	18	F	Wife	Ireland	U.S. of America	Meteor	19 Mar 1828
Cathr.	22	F	Servant	Ireland	United States	Josephine	30 Apr 1828
Charlotte	2	F		England	America	Hudson	20 Nov 1828
Edward	24	M	Goldsmith	England	Great Britain	Florida	26 Sep 1826
Eliza	20	F	Milliner	England	United States	Siroc	31 Oct 1829
Emanuel	19	M	Mercht.	England	United States	Hannibal	6 Sep 1824
Frances	30	F	None	England	United States	Mary & Harriet	9 Mar 1829
Garret	27	M	Labourer	Great Britian	United States	Princess Charlotte	6 Sep 1828
Geo.	28	M	Merchant	W. Indies	U. States	Matilda	27 Apr 1822
Henry	1			England		Anacreon	7 Sep 1827
Henry	29	M	Accountant	England	U.S.A.	Hudson	21 Aug 1829
Hy. J.	25	M	Merchant	Great Britian	U. States	Hudson	12 Mar 1824
J. G.	32	M	None	U. States	U. States	Hippomenes	29 Nov 1822
James	11			England	U. States	Corinthian	8 Oct 1828
James	20	M	Farmer	Ireland	United States	Dublin Packet	23 May 1828
James	26 3/12	M	Labourer	Ireland	United States	Atlantic	21 Jul 1827
James	47	M	Labourer	Great Britian	United States	Princess Charlotte	6 Sep 1828
Jno.	26	M	Manufacturer	Ireland	U. States	William Byrnes	17 Jul 1825
John	16	M	Labourer	Great Britian	United States	Princess Charlotte	6 Sep 1828
John	20	M				Betsey	17 Aug 1820
John	22	M	Labourer	Ireland	U.S. of America	Meteor	19 Mar 1828
John	36	M	Clergyman	England	America	Hudson	20 Nov 1828
John	50		Labourer	Dundock	N. York	Peru	30 May 1828
M. A.	35 6/12	M	Merchant	An American	American	Boon	26 Feb 1820
Margarett	15					Amphion	31 May 1824
Martha	20	F	Servant	Ireland	United States	Josephine	30 Apr 1828
Mary	4	F	Laborer	Gt. Britain		Dalhouse Castle	13 May 1828
Mary	18	F	...	England	United States	Milton	20 Oct 1827
Mary	18	F	Labourer	Great Britian	United States	Princess Charlotte	6 Sep 1828
Mary	25			England		Anacreon	7 Sep 1827
Mary	32	F		Great Britain	America	Lady Gallatin	21 Jun 1820
Mary	infant	M		Great Britain	America	Lady Gallatin	21 Jun 1820
Mary Ann	30	F	Spinster	Ireland	United States	Trident	16 May 1826
Michael	20	M	Labourer	Ireland	New York	Lima	5 Aug 1829
Monica	50	F		Ireland	U. States	William Byrnes	17 Jul 1825
Mortimer	5	M		England	America	Hudson	20 Nov 1828
Owen	27			Dundock	N. York	Peru	30 May 1828
Pat	21	M	Labourer	Great Britain	United States	William Dawson	18 Jun 1827
Patrick	24	M		Ireland	U. States	William Byrnes	17 Jul 1825
Patrick	26	M	Farmer	Ireland	United States	Aurora	9 Jul 1827
Peter	27	M	Diker	Ireland	United States	Sarah Ann	18 Nov 1826
Richd.	19	M	Farmer	England	New York	Governor Fenner	23 Jul 1829
Robert	16	M	Mercht.	England	United States	Hannibal	6 Sep 1824
Roland, Master	9	M	Boy	United States	United States	Dublin Packet	6 Dec 1827
Rose	30	F		Ireland	United States	Lord Wellington	14 Nov 1827
Sally	14	F	Spinster	Ireland	U.S. of America	Meteor	19 Mar 1828
Saml.	36	M		Great Britain	America	Lady Gallatin	21 Jun 1820

NAMES OF PASSENGERS	AGE	SEX	OCCUPATIONS	COUNTRY TO WHICH THEY BELONG	COUNTRY THEY INTEND TO INHABIT	SHIPS/DATES OF ARRIVAL	
REYNOLDS (cont'd)							
Samul	32			England	U. States	Corinthian	8 Oct 1828
Sarah, Mrs.	25	F	Lady	United States	United States	Dublin Packet	6 Dec 1827
T. H.	33	M	Merchant		U. States	William Thompson	6 Sep 1822
Thos.	4	M		Great Britain	America	Lady Gallatin	21 Jun 1820
Thos.	26	M	Teacher	Gt. Britain	U. States	St. George	20 Sep 1828
William	25	M	Merchant	Grt. Britain	United States	Zamoa	5 Nov 1828
William	28	M	Gentleman	Ireland	United States	Dublin Packet	22 Apr 1822
William	30	M	Laborer	Gt. Britain		Dalhouse Castle	13 May 1828
William, Master	3	M	Boy	United States	United States	Dublin Packet	6 Dec 1827
Zack	3	M	Child	Ireland	United States	Sarah Ann	18 Nov 1826
REYOT, Alexander	13	M		France	United States	Helen	5 Sep 1828
Frederick	29	M	Farmer	France	United States	American	27 Aug 1827
Louisa	15	F		France	United States	Helen	5 Sep 1828
REYS, Antonio	14	M		Porto Rico	United States	St. Anna	16 Aug 1828
RHAME, Antoine	19	M				Henri IV	17 May 1828
Francois	4	M				Henri IV	17 May 1828
Francoise	11	F				Henri IV	17 May 1828
Francoise	44	F				Henri IV	17 May 1828
Louis	54	M	Farmer			Henri IV	17 May 1828
Lowis	17	M				Henri IV	17 May 1828
Mary Ann	9	F				Henri IV	17 May 1828
RHEINHOLT, Casper	33	M	Engraver	Germany	United States	Howard	15 Jun 1825
RHIGAS, Fidrit	28	M	Artist	Palras	U.S. America	Superior	18 Jun 1825
RHILIGWAN, John	18	M	Laborer	Great Britian	U. States	Henry Kneedland	7 Aug 1826
RHINES, Lanring	25	M	Carpenter	America	America	Splendid	23 Mar 1829
RHOADES, James	27	M	Merchant	England	United States	Amelia	20 Aug 1829
RHOD, Catharine	11	F		France	Canada	Abby Jones	12 Jul 1827
John	4	M		France	Canada	Abby Jones	12 Jul 1827
Mary	2/12	F		France	Canada	Abby Jones	12 Jul 1827
Matilda	7	F		France	Canada	Abby Jones	12 Jul 1827
Matilda	33	F		France	Canada	Abby Jones	12 Jul 1827
Michael	37	M	Farmer	France	Canada	Abby Jones	12 Jul 1827
RHODES, A. B.	23	M	Merchant	U. States	U. States	Cadmus	28 May 1821
Ann	47	F		Great Britain	United States	Freake	25 Aug 1829
C. D.	28	M	Merchant	Connecticutt	U. States	Chase	18 Dec 1821
C. D.	28	M	Merchant	Boston	U. States	Alfred	17 Sep 1822
Charlotte	23	F	None	Great Britain	United States	Richmond	18 Feb 1820
Chrs.	23	M	Mcht.	U. States	U. States	Nassau	24 Nov 1824
Francis	1 6/12	M	None	Great Britain	United States	Richmond	18 Feb 1820
Francis B.	21	M	Merchant	United States	Boston	Cadmus	27 Aug 1822
Francis B.	23	M	Mercht.	U.S.	U.S.	Cadmus	26 Apr 1824
Francis B.	28	M	Merchant	U. States		Charlemagne	16 Jan 1829
Frs.	25	M	Merchant	England	U.N. States	Corinthian	1 Sep 1823
James	25	M	Mechanic	Rhode Island	U. States	Columbia	24 Mar 1823
James	25	M	Merchant	Great Britain	Unknown	William Thompson	1 May 1827
Jas.	24	M	Mechanic	Connecticutt	U. States	Benjamin	1 Jun 1822
Jerimiah	30	M	Merchant	Great Britain	United States	Florida	2 Sep 1822
John	22	M		Great Britain	United States	Freake	25 Aug 1829
John	27	M	Merchant	Great Britain	United States	Corinthian	2 Sep 1824
John	44	M	Farmer	Great Britain	United States	Freake	25 Aug 1829
Joseph	22		None	England	New York	Albion	11 Oct 1821
Mary	9	F		France	Canada	Abby Jones	12 Jul 1827
Mary	10	F		Great Britain	United States	Freake	25 Aug 1829
Mary	29	F		France	Canada	Abby Jones	12 Jul 1827
Poster	33	M	Carpenter	New York	New York	Florida	1 Jun 1827
R. B.	24	M	Merchant	U. States	U. States	Howard	14 Apr 1823
R. B.	30	M	Merchant	U. States	U. States	Desdemonia	9 Jun 1825
Robert	26	M	Weaver	Great Britain	United States	Richmond	18 Feb 1820
Rudolft	28	M	Farmer	France	Canada	Abby Jones	12 Jul 1827
Saml.	35	M	Merchant	England	U. States	Pacific	5 Sep 1827
Samuel, Mr.	24	M	Merchant	Gt. Britain	U.S. America	James Cropper	14 Mar 1828
Thomas	16	M		Great Britain	United States	Freake	25 Aug 1829
Thomas	24	M	Stone Mason	England	U. States America	Electra	17 Nov 1828
William	37	M	Weaver	Great Britain	United States	Birmingham	15 Jun 1827
William	45	M	Merchant	England	United States	Concordia	25 Aug 1827

NAMES OF PASSENGERS	AGE	SEX	OCCUPATIONS	COUNTRY TO WHICH THEY BELONG	COUNTRY THEY INTEND TO INHABIT	SHIPS/DATES OF ARRIVAL
RHODES (cont'd)						
Wm. W.	23	M	Gentleman	U. States		Charleston Packet 4 May 1821
Wright	...1	M	Merchant	Great Britain	Unknown	William Thompson 1 May 1827
RHODIER, C. S.	25	M	Gent.	Canada	Canada	Columbia 3 Apr 1826
RHODS, Fernandi	36	M	Merchant	New York	U. States	Venus 26 Jun 1822
RIBBEY, Alexander	46	M	Farmer	Scotland	United States	Commerce 17 Jul 1823
RIBBY, Elizabeth	40	F		Scotland	United States	Commerce 17 Jul 1823
Iasabella	7	F		Scotland	United States	Commerce 17 Jul 1823
Peggy	9	F		Scotland	United States	Commerce 17 Jul 1823
RIBEIRO, L'Oranjo	29	M	Charge d'Affares de la Majeste Empr. de Bresil	Rio de Janeiro	Washington	New York 31 Jul 1829
RIBEY, Mary	4 2/12	F	None	Great Briton	United States	Mount Vernon 30 Dec 1828
Mary	30	F	None	Great Briton	United States	Mount Vernon 30 Dec 1828
Patrick	22 9/12	M	Laboer	Great Briton	United States	Mount Vernon 30 Dec 1828
Rose	2 5/12	F	None	Great Briton	United States	Mount Vernon 30 Dec 1828
Rose	55	F	None	Great Briton	United States	Mount Vernon 30 Dec 1828
RIBOAM, B.	19	M		Gt. Britain	U. States	Tantiva 7 Jul 1828
John	20	M		Gt. Britain	U. States	Tantiva 7 Jul 1828
RIC..., ...	25	M		France	U. States	Edward Quesnel 3 Sep 1826
RICARD, E.	25	F		U. States	U. States	Edward Quesnel 3 Sep 1826
N.	9	F		U. States	U. States	Edward Quesnel 3 Sep 1826
RICARDO, P.	34	M	Mechanic	U. States	U. States	Betsey 23 Jul 1824
RICARDS, —, Mrs.	32	F		France	United States	Ariadne 25 Jul 1822
Pascal	35	M	Jeweller	France	United States	Ariadne 25 Jul 1822
RICAWY, Genevive E.	15	F	Gentleman	Malta	U.S. America	Superior 18 Jun 1825
Jean B.	52	M	Gentleman	Malta	U.S. America	Superior 18 Jun 1825
Julie V.	38	F	Gentleman	Malta	U.S. America	Superior 18 Jun 1825
Marie T.	9	F	Gentleman	Malta	U.S. America	Superior 18 Jun 1825
RICE, —,						
Lady [James P.]	22	F		England	U. States	Lewis 11 Nov 1824
...	30	M	Mechanic	Great Briton	U. States	Leontine 10 Jul 1826
Ann	16	F	Servant	Ireland	U. States	Sarah G 7 May 1827
Christ. C.	2...	M		Limerick	Augusta	Thomas & William 25 May 1827
Edmund	21	M	Farmer	Ireland	America	Liverpool 31 Aug 1827
Henry	35	M	Labourer	Ireland	United States	Josephine 30 Apr 1828
J.	12	M		Havana	So. America	Hesperion 28 Oct 1823
James P., Mr.	24	M	Gentleman	England	U. States	Lewis 11 Nov 1824
Jane	17	F	Servant	United States	United States	Only Daughter 29 Apr 1825
John	23	M	Dealler	C. Armannar [Armagh or Farmanagh?]	Boston	Nile 18 Aug 1829
John N.	21	M	Merchant	Ireland	Georgey	Virginia 7 May 1824
Latitia F.	18 1/12	F		Limerick	Augusta	Thomas & William 25 May 1827
Mary	23	F		Ireland	America	Liverpool 31 Aug 1827
Mary	25	F	Servant	Ireland	United States	Sylvester Healy 19 Aug 1825
Michael	20	M	Tailor	Great Britain	United States	Sylvester Healy 23 Nov 1825
Patrick	26	M	Merchant	Ireland	U. States	Alex Mansfield 1 Jun 1822
Peter	22			Ireland	United States	Sarah G. 20 Jul 1827
Peter	31	M	Master			Amity 11 Sep 1820
Richd.	47	M	Farmer	Great Britain	U. States	United States 8 Sep 1827
S. B.	28	M	Merchant	N. Carolina	U. States	St. Clair 26 Apr 1826
Sarah Ann	16 2/12	F		Limerick	Augusta	Thomas & William 25 May 1827
Stephen C.	25	M	Student	Ireland	Georgey	Virginia 7 May 1824
Susan	30	F		Ireland	U. States	Howard 25 Jul 1823
Thomas	18	M	Mariner	U. States	U. States	Hopes Delight 6 Sep 1824
Thos.	8	M		Ireland	America	Liverpool 31 Aug 1827
Thos.	23	M	Gentleman	G. Britain	U. States	Cosmo 15 May 1827
Thos.	50	M	Carpenter	Ireland	America	Liverpool 31 Aug 1827
W.	35	M	Labourer	Great Britain		Moro Castle 6 Jul 1827
Wm., Captn.	40	M	Ship Master	U. States	U.S.	Burdett 7 Dec 1827
RICENE, Joseph	28	M	Confectioner	France	U. States	Sully 25 Jun 1828
RICEPES, E.	28	M	Gentleman	France	U. States	Six Brothers 6 Jul 1824
RICERS, G.	28	M	Farmer	France	U. States	Bayard 25 Apr 1828

NAMES OF PASSENGERS	AGE	SEX	OCCUPATIONS	COUNTRY TO WHICH THEY BELONG	COUNTRY THEY INTEND TO INHABIT	SHIPS/DATES OF ARRIVAL	
RICH, —, Miss	3	F		G Britian	U. States	Leader	20 Apr 1827
—, Mrs.	22	F		G Britian	U. States	Leader	20 Apr 1827
Ann	8	F		England	America	Erin	7 Nov 1821
C.	2	M	Farmer	Switzerland	U. States	Alfred	8 Jul 1828
Eliza	13	F		England	America	Erin	7 Nov 1821
F.	5	M	Farmer	Switzerland	U. States	Alfred	8 Jul 1828
F.	37	M	Farmer	Switzerland	U. States	Alfred	8 Jul 1828
Jacob	22	M	Farmer	Switzerland	U. States	Romulus	24 Sep 1828
John	6	M		England	America	Erin	7 Nov 1821
Joseph	11	M		England	America	Erin	7 Nov 1821
Joseph	19	M	Minor	England	United States	Siroc	31 Oct 1829
Marian	9	F		United States	United States	Globe	30 Aug 1828
Mary	16	F		England	Canada	Trimmer	13 Sep 1823
Mary	40	F		England	America	Erin	7 Nov 1821
N.	24	M	Carpenter	England	Canada	Trimmer	13 Sep 1823
R.	20	F		England	Canada	Trimmer	13 Sep 1823
Rachel Eliza	5	F	Child	United States	United States	Wanderer	31 Aug 1829
S.	16	M	Carpenter	England	Canada	Trimmer	13 Sep 1823
Samuel	11	M		England	America	Erin	7 Nov 1821
Theresa	47	F	Widow	United States	United States	Globe	30 Aug 1828
Thos.	1	M		G Britian	U. States	Leader	20 Apr 1827
Thos.	21	M	Carpenter	England	Canada	Trimmer	13 Sep 1823
Thos.	24	M	Carpenter	G Britian	U. States	Leader	20 Apr 1827
W.	6	M	Farmer	Switzerland	U. States	Alfred	8 Jul 1828
RICHARD, Abrh.	21	M				Henri IV	17 May 1828
Ann	11	F	Spinster	Ireland	United States	Fabius	31 Jul 1829
Archibald	47	M	Labourer	Ireland	United States	Fabius	31 Jul 1829
Bastain	25	M	Miner	England	England	Eliza	31 Jul 1826
Catharine	35 7/12	F	Farmer	Switzerland	America	Henry	17 May 1828
Charlotte	11/12	F	Farmer	Switzerland	America	Henry	17 May 1828
D.	30	M	Merchant	Aux Cayes	Aux Cayes	Nestor	12 Jul 1827
Elisbath	17	F	Spinster	Ireland	United States	Fabius	31 Jul 1829
Elisebeth	8 3/12	F	Farmer	Switzerland	America	Henry	17 May 1828
Ellen	3	F	Child	Ireland	United States	Fabius	31 Jul 1829
Etienne	29	M	Mechanic	France	United States	Henri IV	2 Oct 1828
Frederick	20	M	Servant to Mr. Campbell	Switzerland	Switzerland	Bayard	30 Oct 1820
Giles	45	M	Spinster	Ireland	United States	Fabius	31 Jul 1829
Hugh	5	M	Child	Ireland	United States	Fabius	31 Jul 1829
J. D.	29	M	Grocer	Great Britain	United States	Purrington	8 Dec 1827
James A.	1	M		Switzerland	U. States	La Urania	3 Jul 1828
Jane	13	F	Spinster	Ireland	United States	Fabius	31 Jul 1829
Jno.	18	M	Clerk	France	United States	Henri IV	14 Oct 1829
John	19	M	Labourer	Ireland	United States	Fabius	31 Jul 1829
Joseph, Mr.	19	M	Gentleman	France	United States	Montano	18 Dec 1827
Mary	9	F	Spinster	Ireland	United States	Fabius	31 Jul 1829
Mary	18	F				Henri IV	17 May 1828
Nancy	7		Child, Spinster	Ireland	United States	Fabius	31 Jul 1829
Owen	43	M	Labourer	Aberdaron	United States	Marquis of Anglesea	8 Jun 1827
Philip	37 5/12	M	Farmer	Switzerland	America	Henry	17 May 1828
S. D.	30	M	Gentleman	England	U. States	Washington	7 Jul 1824
Sally	15	F	Spinster	Ireland	United States	Fabius	31 Jul 1829
William	21	M	Carpenter	Ireland	United States	Fabius	31 Jul 1829
RICHARDO, Felix, Don	42	M	Watch Maker	Switzerland	Switzerland	Hesperus	13 Mar 1826
RICHARDS, —	45	M	Mechanic	Switzerland	Havana	Lady Tompkins	9 Feb 1825
—, Child	6/12	F		La Guayra	Colombia, South America	Hiram	14 Aug 1829
—, Child	2	F		La Guayra	Colombia, South America	Hiram	14 Aug 1829
—, Mrs.	24	F		St. Croix	Colombia, South America	Hiram	14 Aug 1829
...	...	M	Merchant	France	U. States	Edward Quesnel	3 Sep 1826
...	8	F			U. States	Edward Quesnel	3 Sep 1826
Abm.	30	M	Merchant	United States	United States	Leeds	29 Sep 1823
Affa, his daughter [Phillip]	1 6/12	F		France	United States	William	31 Jul 1826
Ann	17	F		England	America	Britannia	22 Jul 1829
Ann	22	F	Lady	St. John, N.B.	St. John, N.B.	Sylvester Healy	19 Aug 1825

NAMES OF PASSENGERS	AGE	SEX	OCCUPATIONS	COUNTRY TO WHICH THEY BELONG	COUNTRY THEY INTEND TO INHABIT	SHIPS/DATES OF ARRIVAL	
RICHARDS (cont'd)							
Ann	28	F	Gent		United States	Cosmo	21 Aug 1828
Anna, his daughter							
[Phillip]	4	F		France	United States	William	31 Jul 1826
Anne	45	F	None	Great Britain	United States	Mary & Harriet	3 Jul 1829
Augustus	36	M	Merchant	United States	United States	Brighton	11 Mar 1825
B.	35	M	Mariner	U. States	U. States	Holly	8 Feb 1827
Bartholomew W.	30		Gentleman	Ireland	Mexico	Hudson	18 Jun 1825
Catharina, his daughter							
[Phillip]	6	F		France	United States	William	31 Jul 1826
Catherine	24	F	None	Wales	United States	Orozimbo	11 Aug 1823
Constant	2...	F			U. States	Edward Quesnel	3 Sep 1826
Elias	28	M	Farmer	Younghall, Great Britain	United States	Union	24 Sep 1823
Eliza	7	F		N. York	U. States	Edward Quesnel	3 Sep 1826
Elizabeth	13	F		England	U. States	Hudson	26 Jan 1825
Elizabeth	38	F	Farmer	England	U. States	Hudson	26 Jan 1825
Elizabeth, his daughter							
[Phillip]	9	F		France	United States	William	31 Jul 1826
Emily	6	F			U. States	Edward Quesnel	3 Sep 1826
Emma	4	F	Gent		United States	Cosmo	21 Aug 1828
F.	44	M	Watchmaker	Switzerland	U. States	Queen Mab	22 Jul 1825
F., Junr.	8	M	None	Cuba	Cuba	Dover	17 Aug 1821
Faney	21	F	Servant	England	U.S. America	Cortes	19 May 1826
Francis	17	M		Spain	N. York	France	29 Nov 1827
Fred	6	M	Gent		United States	Cosmo	21 Aug 1828
Geo.	30		Gardiner	England		Corinthian	11 Mar 1829
George	2	M		England	U. States	Hudson	26 Jan 1825
H.	33	F	Nurse	Ireland	Canada	Edwin	1 Jul 1829
Harriet	21	F		England	America	Britannia	22 Jul 1829
Henry	27	M	Farmer	Great Brittan	U.S.	Emulous	29 Jun 1827
Henry	50	M	Mariner	U. States	U. States	Abeona	11 Mar 1823
Hugh	50	M		U. States	U. States	Cowper	8 Jan 1827
J.	23	M	Carpenter	U. States	U. States	Signal	3 Jan 1826
J.	24	M	Merchant	Boston	U. States	Nestor	7 Jan 1825
J.	28	M	Gentleman	U. States	U. States	Columbia	7 Sep 1827
James	14		Gentleman	England	Mexico	Hudson	18 Jun 1825
James	21	M	Merchant	U.S.A.		Silas Richards	20 Jun 1826
Jane	20	F	None	Wales	United States	Orozimbo	11 Aug 1823
Jane	21	F	Farmer	Wales, Gt. Bn.	United States	Orozimbo	31 May 1824
Jno. H., Dr.	24	M	M.D.	America	America	Napoleon	26 May 1828
Jno. S.	20	M	Merchant	United States	United States	Corks	3 Aug 1824
John	12	M		Aberdaron	United States	Marquis of Anglesea	8 Jun 1827
John	16		None	England	New York	Albion	11 Oct 1821
John	34	M	Gentleman	England	England	William	2 Sep 1822
John	50	M	Merchant	U. States	U. States	Queen Mab	16 Jun 1827
John	53	M	Merchant	Great Britain	United States	Cincinnatus	21 Nov 1821
John L.	21	M	Merchant	U. States	U. States	Birmingham	12 Oct 1827
Jos.	36	M	Merchant	France	U. States	Courier	31 Jul 1828
Lewis	33	M	Leather Dresser	Wales	Utica, U.S.	Angelica	18 Aug 1823
Lowry	4	F		Aberdaron	United States	Marquis of Anglesea	8 Jun 1827
Magaret	6	F		Aberdaron	United States	Marquis of Anglesea	8 Jun 1827
Margarita, his daughter							
[Phillip]	15	F	Seamstress	France	United States	William	31 Jul 1826
Maria, his daughter							
[Phillip]	13	F		France	United States	William	31 Jul 1826
Maria, his wife							
[Phillip]	40	F	Seamstress	France	United States	William	31 Jul 1826
Martha	6	F		England	U. States	Hudson	26 Jan 1825
Martha	36	F	None	Wales	United States	Orozimbo	11 Aug 1823
Mary	8	F		England	U. States	Hudson	26 Jan 1825
Mary	20	F	None	Great Britain	United States	Mary & Harriet	3 Jul 1829
Mary	40	F	Farmer	Wales, Gt. Bn.	United States	Orozimbo	31 May 1824
Phillip	38 6/12	M	Cooper	France	United States	William	31 Jul 1826
Richard	9	M		Aberdaron	United States	Marquis of Anglesea	8 Jun 1827

NAMES OF PASSENGERS	AGE	SEX	OCCUPATIONS	COUNTRY TO WHICH THEY BELONG	COUNTRY THEY INTEND TO INHABIT	SHIPS/DATES OF ARRIVAL	
RICHARDS (cont'd)							
Richard, Esqr.	30	M	Merchant	Ireland	Colombia, South America	Hiram	14 Aug 1829
Saffore	19	M	Clockmaker	Germany	America	Saluda	18 Jun 1825
Saml.	35	M	Merchant	United States	United States	Iris	30 Aug 1824
Samuel	28	M	Gent		United States	Cosmo	21 Aug 1828
Sarah	4	F		England	U. States	Hudson	26 Jan 1825
Sarah	50	F		U. States	U. States	Silas Richards	27 Jun 1827
Simon	23	M	Farmer	Great Britain	United States	Cambria	26 Dec 1827
T.	40	M	Slingman	Havre	Montreale	Edward Bonaffe	23 Jul 1828
Thomas	20	M		America	New York	Cincinnatus	5 Dec 1825
V.	27	M	Merchant	Ireland	England	Emulation	12 Mar 1825
W.	12	M		England	U. States	Hudson	26 Jan 1825
Wm.	23	M	Farmer	Wales	U. States	Mary Stewart	12 May 1827
Wm.	34	M	Farmer	England	U. States	Hudson	26 Jan 1825
RICHARDSON, —, Mr.	30	M	Tailor	England	United States	Robert Edwards	21 Sep 1821
—, Mrs.	25	F		G. Britain	U. States	Camillus	8 Sep 1828
Andrew	20	M	Merchant	England	U.S.	Pacific	24 Oct 1828
Ann	37	F	None	Ireland	U. States	Franklin	7 Jul 1828
Benjn.	34	M	File Smith	England	Philadelphia	Debby & Eliza	20 Nov 1820
C.	53	M	Merchant	Scotland	U. States	Mary Livingston	26 Jul 1824
Catherine	5	F	None	England	America	Colossus	22 Aug 1829
Daniel	24					Copernicus	3 Aug 1829
E. P.	13	M		U. States	U. States	Adeline	25 Sep 1827
Eliza	4	F		G. Britain	U. States	Camillus	8 Sep 1828
Eliza	29	F	Farmer	Great Britain	U. States	Yamacraw	4 Sep 1822
Elizabeth	32	F	None	Scotland	U. States	Aristides	7 Mar 1825
Elizabeth	63	F	Lady	England	United States	Cambria	8 Oct 1828
F. A.	25	M	Gentleman	America	U. States	Leo	30 Apr 1825
Geo.	41	M	Merchant	Great Britian	United States	Brok	29 Aug 1823
Geo., Jr.	10	M		Great Britian	United States	Brok	29 Aug 1823
Geo. J.	30	M	Merchant	U. States	U. States	Osgood	9 Dec 1826
Hugh	42	M	Ship Master	U. C.		Silas Richards	7 Mar 1827
Isaac	33	M	Farmer	Great Britain	U. States	Yamacraw	4 Sep 1822
J.	38	M	Farmer	England	U.S. States	Splendid	14 Aug 1829
J.	38	F	Farmer	England	U.S. States	Splendid	14 Aug 1829
J. P.	28	M	Mercht.	U. States	U. States	Savannah	22 May 1827
James	23	M	Weaver	Ireland	United States	Romulus	24 Jun 1826
James	27	M	Labourer	Scotland	U.S.	Curler	19 Jul 1828
Jane	19					Copernicus	3 Aug 1829
Jane	30	F	None	England	America	Colossus	22 Aug 1829
Jas.	1	M	Child	U. States	U. States	Osgood	9 Dec 1826
Jas.	6	M		G. Britain	U. States	Camillus	8 Sep 1828
Jas.	25	M	Labourer			Harmony	15 Jul 1820
Jas.	25	M	Phisician	Gt. Brittain	United States	Cortex	7 Mar 1823
Jerry	36	M	Farmer	Great Britain	U. States	Yamacraw	4 Sep 1822
Jno.	38	M	Gentleman	England	England	York	7 Aug 1828
John	...0	M	Clerk	Great Britian	United States	Brok	29 Aug 1823
John	8	M	None	England	America	Colossus	22 Aug 1829
John	19	M	Labourer	Great Britain	U. States America	Maria	22 May 1822
John	23	M	Gardener	Great Britain	United States	Diana	6 Jul 1829
John	26	M	...	Scotland	America	Nimrod	9 Jul 1827
Jos.	25	M	Planter	United States	United States	Laurel	20 Apr 1826
Joseph	24	M	Gentleman	England	U. States	Cyno	22 Jul 1826
Margaret	10	F	None	Ireland	U. States	Franklin	7 Jul 1828
Mary	4	F	None	Ireland	U. States	Franklin	7 Jul 1828
Mary	34	F		Great Britain	United States	Diana	6 Jul 1829
Mary Ann	3	F	None	England	America	Colossus	22 Aug 1829
N. T.	8	M		Great Britian	United States	Brok	29 Aug 1823
Richan	6	F	None	Ireland	U. States	Franklin	7 Jul 1828
Richard	8	M	None	Ireland	U. States	Franklin	7 Jul 1828
Robert	...1	M	Clerk	Great Britian	United States	Brok	29 Aug 1823
Robert	6/12	M		Great Britain	United States	Diana	6 Jul 1829
Ruth	6/12	F	Farmer	Great Britain	U. States	Yamacraw	4 Sep 1822
Sarah Ann	24	F	Lady	U. States	U. States	Osgood	9 Dec 1826
T.	23	M	Gentleman	England	Lower Canada	Amity	13 Sep 1821
Thomas	23		Husbandman	England	America	Sarah	18 Aug 1829
Thomas G.	20	M	Gentleman	St. Martins		Mary Ann	10 Oct 1820
Thomas S.	13	M	Mariner	United States	United States	Salem	31 Aug 1829

NAMES OF PASSENGERS	AGE	SEX	OCCUPATIONS	COUNTRY TO WHICH THEY BELONG	COUNTRY THEY INTEND TO INHABIT	SHIPS/DATES OF ARRIVAL	
RICHARDSON (cont'd)							
Thos. L.	30	M	Servant	G. Britain	Jamaica	Mary Ann	28 Jun 1824
W.	52	M	Bricklayer	Great Britain	United States	Diana	6 Jul 1829
William	14	M	File Smith	England	Philadelphia	Debby & Eliza	20 Nov 1820
William	30		Weaver	Great Britain	United States	Thomas Dickason	29 Aug 1828
Wm.	2	M	None	Ireland	U. States	Franklin	7 Jul 1828
Wm.	2	M		Great Britain	United States	Diana	6 Jul 1829
Wm.	22	M		England		Ann	17 May 1822
Wm.	23	M	Gent.	Great Britain	U. States	Hudson	12 Mar 1824
Wm.	35	M	Weaver	England	United States	Trident	30 Sep 1826
Wm.	36	M	Farmer	Great Britain	United States	Diana	6 Jul 1829
RICHART, Isaack	25	M	Farm	Ireland		Quatre Freres	29 Jul 1828
Jacob	3	M	Farm	Ireland		Quatre Freres	29 Jul 1828
Margaret	28	F	Farm	Ireland		Quatre Freres	29 Jul 1828
RICHAUX, Elen	26		Miller	Switzerand	U. States	Parachute	14 May 1828
RICHE, Jno. B.	21	M	Mechanic	France	U. States	Edward Quesnel	11 Jan 1826
RICHÉ, Francis	46	M	Farmer	France	France	Sully	15 Jul 1829
RICHEL, Daniel	26	M	Farmer	Germany	America	Falcon	28 Aug 1828
RICHER, —, Mr.	17	M	Accountant	U. States	U. States	Margaret Mercer	21 Dec 1825
Cristopher	35	M	Farmer	Germany	United States	Oxford	14 Aug 1828
Geo.	20	M	Clockmaker	Germany	America	Saluda	18 Jun 1825
Therese	3	F	Farmer	Germany	United States	Oxford	14 Aug 1828
Therese	35	F	Farmer	Germany	United States	Oxford	14 Aug 1828
RICHES, Richard	12	M		Gt. Britain		Corinthian	27 Oct 1829
Richard	38	M	Farmer	Gt. Britain		Corinthian	27 Oct 1829
RICHEY, Cathn.	36	F		Halifax	U. States	William Barker	29 Aug 1823
Nathaniel	26	M	Gentleman	Great Britain		Charlotte Corday	7 Mar 1820
Wm.	18	M	Merchant	St. Johns	Great Britain	St. Michael	5 Jan 1826
RICHFORD, John	30	M	Grocer	Great Brittain	U. States	William Byrnes	23 Jul 1824
RICHIE, Alexr.	24	M	None	Gt. Britan	U. States	Magnet	9 Apr 1825
Robt.	25	M	Carpenter	America	New York	Eliza	8 Mar 1827
Willm.	62	M	Weaver	Ireland	U. States	Josephine	7 May 1827
RICHINGS, Eliza	20	F	None	Great Britain	United States	Orbit	29 Aug 1821
Peter	23	M	Clerk	Great Britain	United States	Orbit	29 Aug 1821
RICHLER, Joseph	22	M	Gentlen.	U.S.	U.S.	Bayard	18 Oct 1826
RICHLIN, Catherin	20	F	Farmer	Switzerland	United States	Olympia	12 Aug 1828
Cristini	20	F	Farmer	Switzerland	United States	Olympia	12 Aug 1828
RICHMOND, —, Miss					U. States	Montgomery	18 Oct 1828
James	20	M	Clerk	Scotland	United States	Camillus	27 Oct 1829
John F.	22	M	Farmer	Great Britain		Robert Fulton	8 Mar 1823
RICHSON, Jane	24	F		Nfoundland	U. States	Hercules	4 Oct 1824
Jno.	28	M	Labourer	Nfoundland	U. States	Hercules	4 Oct 1824
Mary	4	F		Nfoundland	U. States	Hercules	4 Oct 1824
RICHTEN, —, Miss	20	F	Spinster	Germany	Charleston	Orion	24 Mar 1825
—, Mr.	24	M	Baker	Germany	Charleston	Orion	24 Mar 1825
RICHTER, John J.	18	M	Taylor	Coburg		Caesar	24 Aug 1829
Paul	30	M	Merchant	Germany	Charleston	Maria Elizabeth	16 Feb 1826
RICHU, May, Mrs.	25	F	Nurse	United States	United	Greyhound	27 Nov 1820
RICHY, Eliza	23	F	Domestic	France	United States	Cavalier	25 Jul 1828
RICKALLS, Caspar	27	M	Mercher	U.S.	U.S.	Charleston Allen	15 Nov 1826
RICKE, Gerd.	19	M	Shoe maker	Germany		Robert Edwards	8 Nov 1825
RICKEBOCK, A.	27	F	Farmer	United States	United States	Seine	21 Oct 1822
Farina	22	F	Farmer	United States	United States	Seine	21 Oct 1822
Hy.	54	M	Farmer	United States	United States	Seine	21 Oct 1822
RICKENS, John Henry	22	M	Labourer	Hanover		Constitution	20 Jun 1828
RICKERS, C.	23	M	Sugar Baker	Germany	U. States	Constitution	25 Jul 1823
Claus	25	M	Labourer	Germany	United States	Constitution	2 Aug 1826
Rebecca	18	F		Germany	U. States	Constitution	25 Jul 1823
RICKES, J. A.	36	M	Merchant	Martinique	St. Thomas	Remittance	18 Feb 1825
RICKETS, Ann	19	F				Cassack	25 Jul 1820
RICKETSON, Jos.	24	M	Mariner	U. States	U. States	Hunter	4 Aug 1824
RICKETT, B. F.	22	F	Farmer	Germany	U. States	United States	3 Sep 1828
Johnann	57	F	Farmer	Germany	U. States	United States	3 Sep 1828
M.	4	F	Farmer	Germany	U. States	United States	3 Sep 1828
RICKETTS, Harriett	17	F		Philadelphia	American	Midas	9 May 1827
Jacobs, Jur.	28	M	Merchant	U. States	U. States	Union	22 Jul 1820
Philip	33 4/12	M	Merchant	U.S.	U.S.	Greyhound	10 Jan 1820

NAMES OF PASSENGERS	AGE	SEX	OCCUPATIONS	COUNTRY TO WHICH THEY BELONG	COUNTRY THEY INTEND TO INHABIT	SHIPS/DATES OF ARRIVAL
RICKEY, Ann	25	M		Great B.	U. States	William Neilson 26 Jul 1828
Eliza	14			Ireland	United States	Robert Burns 30 May 1823
Jane	16			Ireland	United States	Robert Burns 30 May 1823
RICKKOM, Edward	6	M	Farmer	Gt. Britain	United States	Europa 20 Apr 1825
Jeremiah	31	F	Farmer	Gt. Britain	United States	Europa 20 Apr 1825
Judith	27	F	Farmer	Gt. Britain	United States	Europa 20 Apr 1825
Margaret	4	F	Farmer	Gt. Britain	United States	Europa 20 Apr 1825
RICKLES, Catharin	6	F	None	France	U. States	Sully 25 Jun 1828
Catharin	30	F	None	France	U. States	Sully 25 Jun 1828
Domer	40	M	Farmer	France	U. States	Sully 25 Jun 1828
Theresa	4	F	None	France	U. States	Sully 25 Jun 1828
RICKPATRICK, James	21	M	Labourer	Ireland	United States	Hope 12 Jun 1828
RICKS, Jane	16 3/12	F	Spinster	...	...	Spartan 14 Oct 1825
Thomas	47 2/12	M	...	...	...	Spartan 14 Oct 1825
RICKWITH, Ann	20	F	Milliner	England	United States	Siroc 31 Oct 1829
RICORD, Eliza, Madam	30	F	Lady	New Jersey	New Jersey	Margaret & Sarah 31 Oct 1822
Frederick	3	M	Boy, her child [Eliza]	New Jersey	New Jersey	Margaret & Sarah 31 Oct 1822
John	9	M	Boy, her child [Eliza]	New Jersey	New Jersey	Margaret & Sarah 31 Oct 1822
Peter	11	M	Boy, her child [Eliza]	New Jersey	New Jersey	Margaret & Sarah 31 Oct 1822
Philip	1	M	Boy, her child [Eliza]	New Jersey	New Jersey	Margaret & Sarah 31 Oct 1822
RID, Thos.	28	M		G. Britain	U. States	Canada 19 Sep 1828
RIDAGER, Jno. Keate	14			France	U. States	Parachute 14 May 1828
John	46		Farmer	France	U. States	Parachute 14 May 1828
Margaret	12			France	U. States	Parachute 14 May 1828
Mary	40			France	U. States	Parachute 14 May 1828
RIDDEN, Bernard	17	M	Farmer	Ireland	United States	Dublin Packet 28 Apr 1824
Catherine	21	F	Spinster	Ireland	United States	Dublin Packet 28 Apr 1824
RIDDLE, —, Mrs.	20	F		New York	America	Wilson 27 Nov 1826
...	3	F		Ireland	America	Wilson 27 Nov 1826
Alexander	19 0/12	M		Ireland	America	Carolina Ann 7 Apr 1826
Geo.	17	M		Ireland	United States	Essex 23 May 1828
Henk.	5	M	Child	Ireland	U. States	Atlantic 19 Aug 1825
Isabella	24	F	...	Ireland	U. States	Atlantic 19 Aug 1825
J.	39	M	Farmer	G. Britain	U. States	St. George 7 Jun 1828
James	23	M	Labourer	Ireland	America	Franklin 13 Aug 1827
James	30	M				Ann Maria 29 Nov 1821
Jane	2	F	Child	Ireland	U. States	Atlantic 19 Aug 1825
Jane	45	F		Ireland	United States	Essex 23 May 1828
Jno.	18	M		Ireland	United States	Essex 23 May 1828
John	22	M	Labourer	Ireland	U. States	Grand Turk 3 Dec 1821
Jos.	45	M	Butcher	Ireland	United States	Essex 23 May 1828
Rob.	20	M	Joiner	Ireland	United States	Essex 23 May 1828
Sarah	15	F		Ireland	United States	Essex 23 May 1828
Thos. R.	22	M	Bookkeeper	Gt. Britain	United States	Eliza Barker 11 Jan 1826
W.	28	M	Mariner	U. States	U. States	Artibonite 19 Apr 1827
RIDDLESBERG, Catherine	18	F	his family [Joseph]	Germany	United States	Wm. Osborne 16 Sep 1828
RIDDY, Hugh	30	M	None	Gt. Britan	U. States	Magnet 9 Apr 1825
RIDE, Ellen	9	F		England	United States	Danube 13 Jul 1827
Esther	66	F		England	United States	Danube 13 Jul 1827
George	70	M		England	United States	Danube 13 Jul 1827
RIDER, Geo.	32	M	Merchant	U.S.	U.S.	Iris 3 Jul 1828
Geo.	33	M	Merchant	U.S.	U.S.	Richmond Packet 3 Aug 1829
Moses	45	M	Brewer	England	U.S. of Amer	Hannibal 17 Dec 1823
Samuel	40	M	Shoemaker	U. States Amer		Charlotte Corday 7 Mar 1820
RIDEY, David	23	M	Farmer	France	United States	Montano 5 May 1828
RIDGE, Susan	22	F		England	U. States	Diana 30 Apr 1824
RIDGELY, John	33	M	None	Baltimore	U. States	New York 15 Nov 1823
Stephen	44	M	Fele cutter	England	United States	Robert Edwards 3 Oct 1829
RIDGEWAY, D. W.	35	M	Merchant	U. States	U. States	Echo 22 Apr 1823
James	18	M	Merchant	U. States	U. States	Elias Burger 21 Jun 1823
Joseph	43	M	Gentleman	U. States	U. States	Chase 17 Jan 1825

NAMES OF PASSENGERS	AGE	SEX	OCCUPATIONS	COUNTRY TO WHICH THEY BELONG	COUNTRY THEY INTEND TO INHABIT	SHIPS/DATES OF ARRIVAL	
RIDGEWAY (cont'd)							
William	33	M	Manufacturer	Great Britain	United States	Courier	13 Mar 1820
RIDGLER, David	28	M	Farmer	U. States	U. States	York	13 Aug 1827
RIDGWAY, James	22	M	Gentleman	U. States	U. States	Carlo	26 May 1827
James L.	23		Gentleman	U. States	U. States	Jupiter	11 Feb 1829
Jas.	41	M	Mariner	N. York	U. States	Chase	18 Dec 1821
Joseph	40	M	Mariner	America		Chase	11 Sep 1820
Joseph, Master	10/12		Lady	U. States	U. States	Jupiter	11 Feb 1829
Sarah, Mrs.	20		Lady	U. States	U. States	Jupiter	11 Feb 1829
RIDIN, John	25	M	Labourer	Ireland	U. States	Combine	30 Nov 1825
RIDING, Elizabeth	12	F	None	England	United States	Trident	18 Jul 1827
Ellen	1	F	None	England	United States	Trident	18 Jul 1827
Frederick	27	M	Turner	England	U. States	Pleiades	9 Oct 1829
Mary	3	F	None	England	United States	Trident	18 Jul 1827
RIDIOLI, Giuseppe	48	M		Roma	Philadelphia	Falcon	10 Sep 1823
RIDLEY, Ann	26	F		England	United States	Acosta	28 Jul 1823
Ann	60	F				Cassack	25 Jul 1820
Joseph	26	M	Planter	St. Croix	America	South Carolina Packet	2 Aug 1825
Thomas	22	M	Bootmaker	London	New York	Ann Maria	24 Feb 1824
RIDSHALL, Benjm.	33	M	Labourer	England	U. States	James Monroe	14 Jan 1823
RIECE, Hannah	3	F		Great Brit.	Ohio	Gov. Griswald	3 Jul 1820
John	30	M	Farmer	Great Brit.	Ohio	Gov. Griswald	3 Jul 1820
John	36	M	Farmer	Great Brit.	Ohio	Gov. Griswald	3 Jul 1820
Martha	27	F		Great Brit.	Ohio	Gov. Griswald	3 Jul 1820
RIECHERT, John	44	M	Farmer	United States	United States	Martha	30 Jun 1823
RIECHMULLER, John	29	M	Farmer	Switzerland		Antioch	18 Aug 1829
RIED, Alexr.	2	M		Scotland	United States	Camillus	9 May 1827
Ann	30	F		Scotland	United States	Camillus	9 May 1827
Edwn.	50	M	Shoemaker	G. Britain	U. States	Mary & Harriot	8 Sep 1828
Ellen	10	F		G. Britain	U. States	Mary & Harriot	8 Sep 1828
Ely	20	F	Reed Maker	England		Aurora	12 Mar 1827
Francis	13	M		G. Britain	U. States	Mary & Harriot	8 Sep 1828
James	1 1/2	M		Scotland	United States	Camillus	9 May 1827
Jane	26		Labourer	Great Britan	United States	Newry	11 Jul 1827
John	7	M		Scotland	United States	Camillus	9 May 1827
Martha	48	F		G. Britain	U. States	Mary & Harriot	8 Sep 1828
Mary	18	F		G. Britain	U. States	Mary & Harriot	8 Sep 1828
Robert	21	M	Weaver	Ireland	United States	Trident	16 May 1826
Robert	29	M		Scotland	United States	Camillus	9 May 1827
Saml.	8	M		G. Britain	U. States	Mary & Harriot	8 Sep 1828
Sarah	32	F		Scotland	United States	Camillus	9 May 1827
Thomas	3	M		Scotland	United States	Camillus	9 May 1827
Thos.	30		Labourer	Great Britan	United States	Newry	11 Jul 1827
William	1/2	M		Scotland	United States	Camillus	9 May 1827
RIEF, M.	33	M	Taylor	France	United States	La Flora	30 Jun 1828
RIEKHURD, Cathr. S.	38	F		Switzerland	U. States	La Urania	3 Jul 1828
Jean	9	M		Switzerland	U. States	La Urania	3 Jul 1828
M.	4	F		Switzerland	U. States	La Urania	3 Jul 1828
Marie L.	12	F		Switzerland	U. States	La Urania	3 Jul 1828
P.	40	M	Stone Cutter	Switzerland	U. States	La Urania	3 Jul 1828
RIELDY, Mary	5	F		Ireland	United States	Nile	17 May 1827
RIELET, J. G.	6	F	Farmer	Germany	U. States	United States	3 Sep 1828
J. S.	17	M	Farmer	Germany	U. States	United States	3 Sep 1828
N. E.	7	M	Farmer	Germany	U. States	United States	3 Sep 1828
RIELEY, Barnard	20	M	Labourer	Ireland	Baltimore	Lima	5 Aug 1829
Catherine	50	F	Matron	Ireland	United States	Robert Fulton	24 Jul 1826
John	7	M		Ireland	United States	Nile	17 May 1827
Mary	15	F	Spinster	Ireland	United States	Robert Fulton	24 Jul 1826
May	33	F	Labourer	Ireland	U. States	Virginia	20 Jun 1825
Michael	19	M	Labourer	Ireland	Baltimore	Lima	5 Aug 1829
Michl.	3	M	Child	Ireland	United States	Nile	17 May 1827
Philip	34	M	Mason	Ireland	United States	Nile	17 May 1827
Rose	29	F		Ireland	United States	Nile	17 May 1827
RIELLEY, Mary	20	F	Labourer	England	U. States	Comet	23 Aug 1828
RIELLIGER, Jean	11	M		Switzerland	U. States	La Urania	3 Jul 1828
M. A.	35	F		Switzerland	U. States	La Urania	3 Jul 1828
RIELLY, Ann	16	F	Servant	Ireland	United States	Josephine	30 Apr 1828
Ann	16	F	Servant	Ireland	United States	Josephine	30 Apr 1828

NAMES OF PASSENGERS	AGE	SEX	OCCUPATIONS	COUNTRY TO WHICH THEY BELONG	COUNTRY THEY INTEND TO INHABIT	SHIPS/DATES OF ARRIVAL	
RIELLY (cont'd)							
Ann	30	F	None	Great Britain	United States	Roman	10 May 1828
B.	19	F	Servant	Ireland	United States	Josephine	30 Apr 1828
Charles	11	M	None	Great Britain	United States	Roman	10 May 1828
Edward	3/12	M	Clangford [crossed out]	England	United States	India	8 Jun 1827
Edward	20	M	Weaver	Ireland	United States	Josephine	30 Apr 1828
Ellen	23	F	None	Ireland	U.S. of America	Hamilton	18 Jul 1827
Ewd.	23	M	Labourer	U. States	U. States	United States	11 Sep 1828
John	9	M	None	Great Britain	United States	Roman	10 May 1828
John	17	M	Labourer	Ireland	United States	Josephine	30 Apr 1828
John	25	M	Labourer	Ireland	U.S. of America	Hamilton	18 Jul 1827
Joseph	3	M	None	Great Britain	United States	Roman	10 May 1828
Judith	25	F	None	Ireland	U.S. of America	Hamilton	18 Jul 1827
Letta	0 6/12	F	None	Great Britain	United States	Roman	10 May 1828
M.	20	M	Labourer	Ireland	United States	Josephine	30 Apr 1828
Michl.	20	M	Labourer	Ireland		Marchioness	13 May 1828
Owen	25 10/12	M	Labourer	Ireland	U. States	Fabius	22 Sep 1828
RIELY, Catharn	18	F		Great B.	U. States	William Neilson	26 Jul 1828
Elisabeth	30	F	...	...	United States	Camillus	10 Dec 1825
Florence	31	F	...	...	United States	Camillus	10 Dec 1825
Heugh	28	M	Farmer	Ireland	United States	Fabius	4 Jun 1828
James	12	M	...	...	United States	Camillus	10 Dec 1825
Julia	20	F		Great Britain	Philadelphia	Philetus	21 Jul 1827
Michael	24	M	Labourer	Ireland	New York	Lima	5 Aug 1829
Patrick	18	M	Stone Cutter	Ireland	United States	Robert Fulton	24 Jul 1826
Richd.	27	M	Spinner	Ireland	United States	Orozimbo	5 Mar 1827
Thomas	18	M	Laborer	Ireland	United States	Fabius	4 Jun 1828
Thomas	23 6/12	M	Stone Cutter	Ireland	United States	Robert Fulton	24 Jul 1826
RIEMAN, F. C.	24	M	Joiner	Brunswick	United States	Howard	6 Jul 1829
RIENT, John						Francois I	8 Aug 1829
RIEPLER, Angeler	4	F	Farmer	Germany	United States	Virginia	31 May 1828
Angener	28	F	Farmer	Germany	United States	Virginia	31 May 1828
Geary	2	M	Farmer	Germany	United States	Virginia	31 May 1828
Henrey	21	M	Baker	Germany	United States	Virginia	31 May 1828
Jacob	6	M	Farmer	Germany	United States	Virginia	31 May 1828
Jacob	30	M	Farmer	Germany	United States	Virginia	31 May 1828
RIER, Bill	20	M		Ireland	United States	William & George	14 May 1828
John	22	M	Merchant	...	America	Columbia	6 Oct 1825
Joseph	26		Merchant	Havannah		Helen	4 Aug 1829
Ventura	28	M	...	...	America	Columbia	6 Oct 1825
RIERDAN, Michl.	20	M	Farmer			Robert Fulton	8 Mar 1823
RIERE, Henry B.	26	M	Merchant	U.S.	U. States	Canada	5 Feb 1827
RIERNDHAN,							
Catharine	6 3/12	F		G. Britain	United States	Louisa	14 Jun 1825
Fras.	24	M		G. Britain	United States	Louisa	14 Jun 1825
Michael	7 4/12	M		G. Britain	United States	Louisa	14 Jun 1825
Patrick	10	M		G. Britain	United States	Louisa	14 Jun 1825
Susan	4 5/12	F		G. Britain	United States	Louisa	14 Jun 1825
Susanah	30	F	going to her Husband	G. Britain	United States	Louisa	14 Jun 1825
RIETER, John	46	M	Farmer	Germany	New York	Lewis	29 Oct 1825
RIEZU, Thomas	44	M	Miner	England	U. States	Laveria	23 Jul 1828
RIFFENIGHT, Jacob	26	M	Laborer	United States	United States	Globe	30 Aug 1828
*landed at this Port, Custom House, Portland, Aug 19, 1828							
RIFFORD, Anna	2		child	Ireland	U. States	Xenophon	28 May 1822
Joseph	30		Merchant	Ireland	U. States	Xenophon	28 May 1822
Lewis	4		child	Ireland	U. States	Xenophon	28 May 1822
Mary	30		his wife [Joseph]	Ireland	U. States	Xenophon	28 May 1822
RIGALAN, —, child	1	M			U. States	Elias Burger	11 Jul 1822
M.	30	F			U. States	Elias Burger	11 Jul 1822
RIGALUS, A. D.	16	M	Servant	N. York	U. States	Alfred	17 Sep 1822
RIGAN, Pat	28	M	Duck Dresser	Scotland	United States	Indus	5 Sep 1827
RIGBY, Amelia	14	F		England	New York	Corinthian	5 May 1827
Betty	39	F	Gentleman	England	United States	Jubilee	1 Dec 1827
Eleanor	8/12	F	Gentleman	England	United States	Jubilee	1 Dec 1827
Elizabeth	30	F		Great Britain	United States	Mary	11 Jul 1820
Ellen	26	F		England	New York	Corinthian	5 May 1827

NAMES OF PASSENGERS	AGE	SEX	OCCUPATIONS	COUNTRY TO WHICH THEY BELONG	COUNTRY THEY INTEND TO INHABIT	SHIPS/DATES OF ARRIVAL	
RIGBY (cont'd)							
Ester	51	F	None	Ireland	U. States	Franklin	7 Jul 1828
F.	29	M		Great Britain	United States	Mary	11 Jul 1820
Hannah	4	F		Great Britain	United States	Mary	11 Jul 1820
James	6	M	Gentleman	England	United States	Jubilee	1 Dec 1827
Joseph	1	M		Great Britain	United States	Mary	11 Jul 1820
Mary	5	F	Gentleman	England	United States	Jubilee	1 Dec 1827
Rachel	60	F		England	New York	Corinthian	5 May 1827
Richard	18	M		England	New York	Corinthian	5 May 1827
Sarah	10	F	Gentleman	England	United States	Jubilee	1 Dec 1827
Thomas	3	M	Gentleman	England	United States	Jubilee	1 Dec 1827
Thomas	20	M	Weaver	England	New York	Corinthian	5 May 1827
Thomas	39	M	Gentleman	England	United States	Jubilee	1 Dec 1827
RIGG, Margaret	21	F	Servant	G. Bt.	G. Bt.	Canada	13 Oct 1825
RIGGS, Margaret	22	F	None	Gt. Britain	Gt. Britain	Canada	5 Jun 1827
RIGH, Thomas	30	M	Carpenter	Great Britain	U. States	Lady Hunter	26 Nov 1823
RIGHARD, C. T.	22	M		France	America	Saluda	16 Oct 1824
RIGHLEY, Jno.	28	M	Labourer	Ireland	U.S.	Ann	10 Jan 1825
RIGHT, Isabella	17	F		Ireland	U. States	Nancy	16 Aug 1822
Margaret Jane	18	F		Ireland	U. States	Nancy	16 Aug 1822
RIGLER, Jacob	42	M	Farmer	Germany	United States	Virginia	31 May 1828
RIGLEY, —	2	F		Europe	United States	Aspasia	5 Sep 1827
Betty	20	F		Europe	United States	Aspasia	5 Sep 1827
Jno.	34	M	Labourer	Great Britain	United States	Atlantic	28 May 1827
John	57	M	Clothier	England	U. St.	Manchester	7 Dec 1826
Peter	26	M	Labourer	G. Brittain	U.S. America	York	4 Aug 1826
Sarah	34	F		Europe	United States	Aspasia	5 Sep 1827
RIGNART, Peter	60	M	Merchant	Naturalized in U. States	U. States	Sea Serpent	21 Apr 1821
RIGNEY, Martin	24	M	Paper Maker	Scotland	United States	Belmont	30 Aug 1828
RIGULAS, Jos.	30	M	Merchant	Spain	U. States	Packet	24 Apr 1823
RIKER, Nancy	56	F		N. York	U. States	Prize	20 Sep 1823
RILARD, James	26	M	T Labourer	Sheffield	Sheffield	Howard Douglass	11 May 1827
RILEY, ...thers	26		Laboring Class		United States	Atlantic	2 Apr 1827
Allan	20	M	Seamstress	Ireland	U.S. States	Splendid	14 Aug 1829
Ann	22	F		Ireland	Jamaica	Huntress	15 Oct 1823
Ann	29	M		Great Britain	U. States	Lady Hunter	26 Nov 1823
B.	23	M				Hanford	17 Jul 1828
B.	26	F				Hanford	17 Jul 1828
B. C.	33	M	Gardner	America	U. States	David	5 Oct 1824
Benjamin	26	M	Shoemaker	Ireland	United States	Carolina Ann	14 May 1827
Bernard	25	M	Labourer	Ireland	U.N. States	Jane	7 Oct 1826
Biddy	20	F		Gt. Britain		Dalhouse Castle	13 May 1828
Biddy	20	F	None	Ireland	U.S.A.	Dalhouse Castle	21 Aug 1829
Bridget	10	F	...	Ireland	United States	Wilson	22 Jun 1824
Bridget	16	F	Spinster	Great Briton	United States	Erin	26 May 1821
Bridget, (her Child)							
[Mary]	6	F	Child	Ireland	United States	Ann Maria	8 Jun 1824
Catharine	15	F		Ireland	U. States	Nancy	16 Aug 1822
Catharine	23	F	Servant	Ireland	New York	Atlantic	8 May 1828
Catharine	26	F	Labourer	Ireland	U.S.A.	Dalhouse Castle	21 Aug 1829
Catharine, Junr.	8	F	Servant	Ireland	New York	Atlantic	8 May 1828
Cathe.	20	F	Spinster	G. Britain	U. States	St. George	7 Jun 1828
Catherine	19	F	...	Ireland	United States	Wilson	22 Jun 1824
Catherine	26	F	Labourer	Ireland	United States	Dalhouse Castle	21 Aug 1829
Catherine	31	F	Servant	Ireland	United States	Nancy	18 Oct 1824
Charles	22	M	Mason	Great Britain	U. States	Lady Hunter	26 Nov 1823
Charles	25 1/12	M	Weaver	Ireland	America	Carolina Ann	7 Apr 1826
Chrisr.	20		Pedler	Ireland	United States	Rufus King	4 Sep 1823
Christopher	19	M	Farmer	Great Britain	U. States	Boston	28 Aug 1821
Daniel	28	M	Labourer	Ireland	U.S.A.	Dalhouse Castle	21 Aug 1829
Edward	...	M	Labourer	Ireland	United States	Carolina Ann	14 May 1827
Edward	12	M	Child	Ireland	U. States	Josephine	7 May 1827
Elisabeth	18	F	Spinster	Ireland	U. States	Josephine	30 Aug 1828
Elizabeth	20	F	None	Ireland	New York	Margaret	18 May 1825
Elizabeth	20	F	None	Great Brittan	U. States	John & Elizabeth	11 Dec 1826
Elizth.	17	F	Servant	Ireland	United States	Wilson	27 Jun 1826

NAMES OF PASSENGERS	AGE	SEX	OCCUPATIONS	COUNTRY TO WHICH THEY BELONG	COUNTRY THEY INTEND TO INHABIT	SHIPS/DATES OF ARRIVAL	
RILEY (cont'd)							
Ellen	22	F		Ireland	United States	Princess Charlotte	26 Apr 1827
Ellen	23	F		Ireland	U. States	Fame	15 Nov 1826
Ellen	30	F	Spinster	Ireland	U. States	Hibernia	29 Nov 1821
Fanny	26	F		Ireland	U. States	William Barker	29 Aug 1823
Francis	20	M	Labourer	Ireland	United States	Princess Charlotte	26 Apr 1827
Garret	2...		Laboring Class		United States	Atlantic	2 Apr 1827
Hannah	11	F		Great Brit.	Ohio	Gov. Griswald	3 Jul 1820
Hue	26	M	Labourer	Ireland	America	Wilson	16 May 1825
J., Mr.	26	M	Merchant	U.S.	U.S.	Radius	9 May 1823
J. M.	38	M	Gentleman	Ireland		Hudson	23 Jul 1828
J. W.	24	M	Blacksmith	Norfolk	U. States	William	23 Jun 1821
James	6	M		Ireland	New York	Atlantic	8 May 1828
James	16	M	Labourer	Ireland	U.S. of America	Meteor	19 Mar 1828
James	18	M	Labourer	Ireland	U.S. of America	Meteor	19 Mar 1828
James	19	M	Laborer	United States	United States	Nancy	18 Oct 1824
James	20	M	None	Ireland	U.S.A.	Dalhouse Castle	21 Aug 1829
James	24	M	Labourer	Ireland	U. States	Josephine	7 May 1827
James	26	M	Merchant	U.S.	U.S.	Radius	8 Feb 1822
James	27	M	Jeweler	United States	U. States	Francis Jarvis	10 Jan 1825
James A.	18	M	Servant	England	U. States	Pacific	5 Sep 1827
Jane	22	F		St. Johns	U. States	Hope	9 Nov 1824
John	17	M	Labourer	G. Britain	U. States	St. George	7 Jun 1828
John	19	M	Laboror	Ireland	United States	Wilson	27 Jun 1826
John	21	M	Hatter	Ireland	America	Carolina Ann	7 Apr 1826
John *Drowned	22	M				Nancy	18 Oct 1824
John	22	M	Farmer	Ireland	U. States	Meteor	19 Jul 1828
John	23	M	Weaver	County Renagh, Ireland	United States	Hanford	15 May
John	24	M	Bricklayer	U. Kingdom Great Britain	United States	Cambria	7 May 1828
John	25	M	Tailor	Great Britain	United States	Sylvester Healy	23 Nov 1825
John	27	M	Farmer	Ireland	United States	William & Henry	19 Jul 1822
John	27	M	Silk Weaver	England	United States	Siroc	31 Oct 1829
John	28	M	Farmer	Ireland	United States	Lord Strangford	20 Jun 1826
Justus, Jr.		M	Mercht.	U. States	U. States	Governor Griswold	18 Jun 1821
Kitty	22	F	Spinster	Ireland	United States	Sarah G	19 Jun 1827
M.	26	M	Weaver			Hanford	17 Jul 1828
Margaret	23	F		Gt. Britain		Dalhouse Castle	13 May 1828
Marget	24	F	Servant	Great Britain	United States	Sylvester Healy	23 Nov 1825
Margt.	19	F	Servant	Ireland	United States	Wilson	27 Jun 1826
Maria	5	F		Great Brit.	Ohio	Gov. Griswald	3 Jul 1820
Maria	20	F		Gt. Britain		Dalhouse Castle	13 May 1828
Mary	8	F		Great Brit.	Ohio	Gov. Griswald	3 Jul 1820
Mary	14	F	Spinster	Ireland	U.S. of America	Meteor	19 Mar 1828
Mary	17	F	Matron	Ireland	America	Wilson	16 May 1825
Mary	17	F	Servant	Ireland	United States	Wanderer	1 Aug 1828
Mary	18	F	Servant	Ireland	New York	Atlantic	8 May 1828
Mary	19	M		G. Britain	U. States	Great Britain	6 Sep 1828
Mary	20 1/12	F		Ireland	America	Carolina Ann	7 Apr 1826
Mary	22	F	Farmer	Ireland	U. States	Dickinson	30 Jul 1825
Mary	22	F	Servant	Ireland	United States	Carolina Ann	14 May 1827
Mary	23	F	Labourer	Ireland	U.S.A.	Dalhouse Castle	21 Aug 1829
Mary	25	F		Great Brit.	Ohio	Gov. Griswald	3 Jul 1820
Mary	25	F	Spinster	Ireland	United States	Ann Maria	8 Jun 1824
Mary ...	20	F	Spinster	Great Briton	United States	Erin	26 May 1821
Mary Ann	14	F	Spinster	Ireland	U. States	Hibernia	29 Nov 1821
Mary Ann	27	F	...	Ireland	United States	Wilson	22 Jun 1824
Michael	19	M	Labourer	Ireland	U. States	Panthea	8 Apr 1826
Michael	33	M	Farmer	St. Johns	U. States	Hope	9 Nov 1824
Michal	24	M	Farmer	Scotland	U. States	Mentor	5 Jul 1825
Michal	30	M	Farmer	Ireland	U. States	Mentor	5 Jul 1825
Micheal	27 3/12			Ireland	America	Carolina Ann	7 Apr 1826
Micheal	33	M	Laborer	Scotland	United States	Delta	24 Oct 1829

NAMES OF PASSENGERS	AGE	SEX	OCCUPATIONS	COUNTRY TO WHICH THEY BELONG	COUNTRY THEY INTEND TO INHABIT	SHIPS/DATES OF ARRIVAL	
RILEY (cont'd)							
Nicholas	21	M	Labourer	Ireland	U.S.A.	Dalhouse Castle	21 Aug 1829
Owen	20	M	Farmer	Ireland	U. States	Dickinson	30 Jul 1825
Pat	20	M	Farmer	Ireland	U. States	Meteor	19 Jul 1828
Patk.	26	M	Labourer	Ireland	U.S. of America	Meteor	19 Mar 1828
Patric	25	M	Sevant	Ireland	Great Britan	Columbia	11 Aug 1823
Patric	25	M	Labourer	Ireland	America	Wilson	16 May 1825
Patrick	16		Pedler	Ireland	United States	Rufus King	4 Sep 1823
Patrick	18 6/12	M	Labourer	Ireland		Robert Fulton	4 Jun 1828
Patrick	24	M	Farmer	Ireland	U. States	Edward	15 Jul 1825
Patrick	35	M	Labourer	Ireland	United States	Wanderer	1 Aug 1828
Peter	36	M	...	Ireland	United States	Carolina Ann	14 May 1827
Philip	25	M	Farmer	Ireland	U. States	Florida	16 May 1827
Polly	30	F	...	...	...	Dawn	19 Aug 1825
Rose	14	F	...	Ireland	United States	Wilson	22 Jun 1824
Rose	19	F	None	Ireland	New York	Margaret	18 May 1825
Rosey	21	F	None	Ireland	New York	Margaret	18 May 1825
Terance	26	M	Labourer	Ireland	U. States	Concordia	11 Jun 1823
Thomas	20	M		Ireland	U. States	Nancy	16 Aug 1822
Thomas	28	M	Farmer	Gt. Britain	United States	Silas Richards	20 Jun 1826
Thos.	14	M	Farmer	Ireland	U. States	Hibernia	29 Nov 1821
Thos.	22	M	Weaver	G. Britain	U. States	Great Britain	6 Sep 1828
Thos.	30	M		Great Brit.	Ohio	Gov. Griswald	3 Jul 1820
Thos.	36	M		Great Brit.	Ohio	Gov. Griswald	3 Jul 1820
Ths.	27	M	Farmer	Great Brittan	U. States	John & Elizabeth	11 Dec 1826
William	34	M	Stone Cutter	Ireland	United States	Carolina Ann	11 Dec 1826
RILF, Elizabeth	6	F		Great Britian	United States	Columbia	17 Apr 1827
Frances	8	F		Great Britian	United States	Columbia	17 Apr 1827
Frances	20	F		Great Britian	United States	Columbia	17 Apr 1827
George	9	M		Great Britian	United States	Columbia	17 Apr 1827
Isaac	...	M		Great Britian	United States	Columbia	17 Apr 1827
John	16	M		Great Britian	United States	Columbia	17 Apr 1827
Joseph	14	M		Great Britian	United States	Columbia	17 Apr 1827
Wm.	52	M	Farmer	Great Britian	United States	Columbia	17 Apr 1827
RILKER, Peter	22	F		Scotland	United States	Belmont	30 Aug 1828
RILLER, Eliza	40	F	Seamstres	G. Brittain	America	Atlantic	11 Oct 1822
William	45	M	Farmer	G. Brittain	America	Atlantic	11 Oct 1822
RILLEY, Ana	19	F				Hibernia	15 Aug 1820
Biddy	20	F	None	Ireland	United States	Dalhouse Castle	21 Aug 1829
Hugh	25	M	Labourer	Ireland	America	Sarah	18 Aug 1829
James	20	M	None	Ireland	United States	Dalhouse Castle	21 Aug 1829
Margareth	20	M	Labourer	Ireland	America	Sarah	18 Aug 1829
Mary	18 3/12	F	Servant	Ireland	New York	Atlantic	6 Oct 1828
Mary	23	F	None	Ireland	United States	Dalhouse Castle	21 Aug 1829
Nichs.	21	M	Labourer	Ireland	United States	Dalhouse Castle	21 Aug 1829
Peter	21 9/12	M	Weaver	Irereland	America	Carolina Ann	20 Jun 1825
RILLING, Jacob	31	M	None	Great Britain	U. States	Hannibal	12 Oct 1829
RILLY, Ellen	25	F	Servant	Ireland	New York	Atlantic	8 May 1828
James	26	M	Carpenter	Ireland	United States	Eliza	29 Aug 1822
Jane	11	F	Servant	Ireland	New York	Atlantic	8 May 1828
William	14	M	Labourer	Ireland	New York	Atlantic	8 May 1828
RILPH, Geo.	35	M	Merchant	U. States	U. States	St. George	20 Sep 1828
M.	20	F		U. States	U. States	St. George	20 Sep 1828
RILY, Bridget	20	F		Ireland	U. States	Balaena	29 Apr 1825
Francis	17	M	Y. Man	Ireland	New York	Trusty	12 Sep 1828
Francis	19	M	Y. Man	Ireland	New York	Trusty	12 Sep 1828
Jas.	29	M	Mercht.	U. States	U. States	Savannah	22 May 1827
John	25	M		England	United States	William Byrnes	11 Dec 1827
Mary	20	F	Spinster	Ireland		Robert Fulton	4 Jun 1828
Patrick	25	M	Mason	England	United States	Euphrates	18 Aug 1827
Rose	24	F		Ireland	United States	Potomac	28 Sep 1827
Rose	25	F	Spinster	Ireland	U. States	Josephine	7 May 1827
RIMAN, Henry	44	M	Farmer	Prussia	U. States	Minerva	13 Sep 1827
RIMLER, Catherine	4	F	his family [Christe]	Germany	United States	Wm. Osborne	16 Sep 1828
Chata.	3	F	his family [Christe]	Germany	United States	Wm. Osborne	16 Sep 1828
Christe	32	M	Farmer	Germany	United States	Wm. Osborne	16 Sep 1828
Elizabeth	8	F	his family [Christe]	Germany	United States	Wm. Osborne	16 Sep 1828
Elizabeth	20	F	his family [Christe]	Germany	United States	Wm. Osborne	16 Sep 1828

NAMES OF PASSENGERS	AGE	SEX	OCCUPATIONS	COUNTRY TO WHICH THEY BELONG	COUNTRY THEY INTEND TO INHABIT	SHIPS/DATES OF ARRIVAL	
RIMLER (cont'd)							
Elizabeth	30	F	his family [Christe]	Germany	United States	Wm. Osborne	16 Sep 1828
Jacob	1	M	his family [Christe]	Germany	United States	Wm. Osborne	16 Sep 1828
Magdeline	7	F	his family [Christe]	Germany	United States	Wm. Osborne	16 Sep 1828
Pierie	6	M	his family [Christe]	Germany	United States	Wm. Osborne	16 Sep 1828
RINALDI, Jos.	42	M	Mercht.	Spain	Spain	Anna	23 May 1822
RINCK, —	24	M	Cooper	Brattain		L'Esperance	6 Sep 1828
RINE, Martin	30	M	Clerk	England	United States	Danube	22 Aug 1825
RINET, Jose A.	21	M	Mercht.	Spain	Spain	Clarissa	28 Apr 1824
RINFORD, Stillman	24	M	Mariner	Boston, U.S.A.	Boston, U.S.A.	Mary	7 Jan 1820
RING, Chas.	2	M		England	United States	Cosmo	26 Aug 1829
Edward	40	M	Coachman	England	United States	Cosmo	26 Aug 1829
Elisabeth	30	F		England	United States	Cosmo	26 Aug 1829
M.	22	M	Labourer	G. Britain	U. States	Hanford	10 Jun 1828
RINGERBERG, Jean	24	M	Farmer	France	U.S.	Edward Quesnel	19 Oct 1829
Joseph	26	M	Farmer	France	U.S.	Edward Quesnel	19 Oct 1829
RINGERS, Jacob	21	M	Kleermaker	Waltmohr	United States	Juffraw Johanna	16 Oct 1821
RINGLAND, James	20	M	Labourer	Ireland	U. States	Josephine	7 May 1827
RINGLEY, George	29	M	Merchant	Warwick, England	Great Britain	James Cropper	7 Oct 1823
RINGOLD, —, Mr.	24	M	Gentn.	United States	United States	Robert Edwards	1 Jun 1826
RINGWOOD, Joseph	22	M	Farmer	Ireland	United States	Lord Strangford	20 Jun 1826
RINK, H.	20	F		Ireland	United States	Indus	5 Sep 1827
RINLOCK, David	5		Weaver	Great Britain	United States	Camillus	12 Sep 1827
James	18			Great Britain	United States	Camillus	12 Sep 1827
Robruce	25			Great Britain	United States	Camillus	12 Sep 1827
RINNAR, Mary	26	F	Servant	G. Britain	U. States	St. George	7 Jun 1828
RINNIN, Pat	22	M	Weaver	Ireland	United States	Commerce	13 Jun 1828
RINSGORA, J.	22	F	Servant	St. Domingo	U. States	Brown	29 Apr 1825
RINSON, Henry A.	29	M	Merchant	England	United States	Nimrod	31 Jul 1828
RIOLING, Peter	22	M	Iron Founder	G. Britain		Caravan	8 Sep 1828
RION, Timothy	25	M				Splendid	14 Aug 1829
RIOR...ON, John	25	M	Mason	G. Britain	U. States	Eliza	9 May 1827
RIORDAN, Pat	24	M	Farmer	Ireland	United States	Trio	13 Jun 1827
RIORDEN, Timothy	26	M	Dyer	Ireland	U.S.A.	Hudson	21 Aug 1829
RIPLEY, Agnes	32	F		England	America	Panthia	17 Sep 1821
Agnes	66	F		England	America	Panthia	17 Sep 1821
Dorothy	60	F	None	Great Britan	United States	Great Britain	18 Sep 1826
Dorothy, Mrs.	42	F	None	Great Britan	Gt. Britan	Great Britain	16 Mar 1829
Dorthy	60			Whitbey	England	Great Britain	7 May 1827
Hannah	24	F		England	America	Panthia	17 Sep 1821
Jane	27	F		England	America	Panthia	17 Sep 1821
Jas. W.	30	M	Military	American	United States	Exchange	16 Feb 1822
Mary	22	F		England	America	Panthia	17 Sep 1821
Noah	22	M	Gentleman	America	U. States	Sarah Herrick	11 Jun 1825
Thos.	33	M	Farmer	England	America	Panthia	17 Sep 1821
Thos.	61	M	Farmer	England	America	Panthia	17 Sep 1821
RIPMANTI, Andw.	25	M	Merchant	Italy	U. States	Nestor	3 Apr 1822
RIPPE, Anna D. F., Miss	21 8/12	F	Servant	Hamburg	New York	Europa	12 Oct 1829
RIPPING, Robert, Mrs.	42	F		London	United States	Juno	26 Nov 1821
RIPPON, John	34	M	Joiner	England	America	John Adams	2 Aug 1827
Mary	51	F		Great Britain	United States	Hannibal	27 May 1822
Sarah	14	F		Great Britain	United States	Hannibal	27 May 1822
RISCOLL, Phillip	28		Labourer	England	America	Sarah	18 Aug 1829
RISEL, John	12	M	Merchant	Spain	U. States	Thomas Wilson	16 Sep 1822
RISH, Wm.	23	M	Joiner	Great Britain	United States	Washington	3 Sep 1827
RISI, Gaspard	29	M	Farmer	Swisserland	United States	Montano	13 Jan 1826
RISK, Jane	8			Ireland	U. States	Robert Burns	18 Jun 1822
Jas.	12			Ireland	U. States	Robert Burns	18 Jun 1822
John	9		Family [of Rachel]	Great Britain	United States	Camillus	12 Sep 1827
Martha	35			Ireland	U. States	Robert Burns	18 Jun 1822
Rachel	45		Spinster	Great Britain	United States	Camillus	12 Sep 1827
Robert	6			Ireland	U. States	Robert Burns	18 Jun 1822
Robert	40		...	Ireland	U. States	Robert Burns	18 Jun 1822
Wm.	12		Family [of Rachel]	Great Britain	United States	Camillus	12 Sep 1827
RITCHARDS, Alfred	4	M		Great Brittan	United States	Lewis	13 Jan 1827
Emily	12	F		Great Brittan	United States	Lewis	13 Jan 1827
George	10	M		Great Brittan	United States	Lewis	13 Jan 1827

NAMES OF PASSENGERS	AGE	SEX	OCCUPATIONS	COUNTRY TO WHICH THEY BELONG	COUNTRY THEY INTEND TO INHABIT	SHIPS/DATES OF ARRIVAL	
RITCHARDS (cont'd)							
Henry	34	M	Millwright	Great Brittan	United States	Lewis	13 Jan 1827
Louisa	8	F		Great Brittan	United States	Lewis	13 Jan 1827
Mary	6	F		Great Brittan	United States	Lewis	13 Jan 1827
Sarah	31	F		Great Brittan	United States	Lewis	13 Jan 1827
RITCHE, Andrew	40	M	Gentleman	U. States	U. States	Jupiter	27 Jun 1828
RITCHEY, Kenedy	21	M	Labourer	Derry	United States	Carolina Ann	11 Jun 1824
RITCHIE, Agness	21	F	Spinster	Ireland	U. States	Josephine	30 Aug 1828
Andw.	36	M	Gentleman	St. Croix	U. States	South Carolina Packet	16 Feb 1826
Archd.	24	M	Servant	Great Britain	United States	Cortes	18 Oct 1820
Charles	9	M		Scotland	United States	Camillus	9 May 1827
Christian	5	F		Scotland	United States	Camillus	9 May 1827
Christina	27	F	None	Great Britain	United States	Colossus	5 Jun 1827
Dugerlo	25	M	Weaver	Scotland	United States	Camillus	27 Oct 1829
George	25	M	Surgeon	Scotland	America	Camillus	9 Oct 1820
James *Died	3	M	None	Great Britain	United States	Colossus	5 Jun 1827
John	29	M		Scotland	United States	Camillus	9 May 1827
John, Mr.	26	M	Labourer	Scotland	U. States	Majestic	27 Jul 1829
Wm.	22	M	Labourer	Scotland	New York	Joseph Hume	26 Oct 1829
RITHEN, Robt.	21	M	Mechanic	Gt. Britain	United States	John & Elizabeth	25 Sep 1827
RITO, Cavil	22	M	Priest	Italy	U.S.	Francois I	8 Aug 1829
RITTER, Christine	44	F	Farmer	Switzerland		Charlemagne	20 Aug 1829
Jane	40	F	Farmer	Switzerland		Charlemagne	20 Aug 1829
Johannes	45	M	Shoe Maker	Germany	U. States	Wm. Penn	1 Sep 1828
Thomas	12	M	Farmer	Switzerland		Charlemagne	20 Aug 1829
William	46	M	Painter	Ireland	America	Atlantic	29 Jun 1822
Wm.	8	M	Farmer	Switzerland		Charlemagne	20 Aug 1829
RIVEN, James R.	31	M	Merchant	U. States	Georgia	James Cropper	21 Oct 1825
RIVENS, John	21	M	Mason	Ireland	America	Liverpool	31 Aug 1827
RIVER, Jos	30	M	Merchant	U. States	U. States	Spartan	7 Jan 1829
RIVERAU, D.	35	M	Merchant	Isld. Cuba	I. Cuba	Blue Ey'd Mary	26 Jun 1823
RIVERE, Peter	29	M	Merchant	Spain	Havana	Rolla	10 Feb 1824
RIVERO, Cap	29	M	Master	U. States	U. States	Amphion	24 Aug 1821
RIVERS, Chs.	40	M	Mercht.	England	Quebec	Canada	1 Nov 1823
Eliz.	24	F	Lady	England	Quebec	Canada	1 Nov 1823
Peter	26	M	Merchant	N. Orleans	U. States	William	1 Apr 1822
RIVERSA, R.	26	M	Merchant	Havana	U. States	Abeona	23 May 1823
RIVES, Eliza	22	F	his Wife	Ireland	United States	Delta	24 Oct 1829
Thomas	25	M	Musician	Ireland	United States	Delta	24 Oct 1829
RIVOUR, Jno. J.	24	M	Sadler	America	U. States	Magnolia	29 Apr 1822
RIX, David	27	M	Farmer	England	America	William	21 Sep 1821
David	50	M	Farmer	England	America	William	21 Sep 1821
Elizabeth	30	F	Farmer	England	America	William	21 Sep 1821
Elizabeth	50	F	Farmer	England	America	William	21 Sep 1821
Ellen	25	F	Farmer	England	America	William	21 Sep 1821
James	20	M	Farmer	England	America	William	21 Sep 1821
William	17	M	Farmer	England	America	William	21 Sep 1821
RIZENDE, Henriques	40	M	Smith	Brasil	New York	Constitution	9 Dec 1824
RO..., James	24	M	Merchant	England	New York	Hesperus	2 Nov 1820
Patrick	22		C...t...		United States	Atlantic	2 Apr 1827
ROACH, —, Miss	8	F		Barbadoes	Barbadoes	Rose in Bloom	10 Aug 1824
—, Mrs.	24	F		Barbadoes	Barbadoes	Rose in Bloom	10 Aug 1824
Ann	12	F		Ireland	U. States	Wilson	2 Sep 1823
Benj. W.	22	M	Merchant	N. York	U. States	Royal Oak	16 Oct 1820
Bridget	4	F		Ireland	United States	Concordia	25 Aug 1827
Catharine	8	F	Merchant	Ireland	U. States	Nancy	25 Nov 1823
Catherine	20	F	Servant	England	United States	Manhattan	24 Oct 1825
Cathne.	33	F		Ireland	United States	Concordia	25 Aug 1827
Cornelus	25	M	Farmer	Ireland	America	William	21 May 1825
Eliza Ann	3	F	None	Ireland		Birmingham	11 Oct 1828
Elizabeth	18	F	Servant	Ireland	United States	Wilson	27 Jun 1826
Elizabeth	25	F	None	Ireland	U. States	Birmingham	11 Oct 1828
Fanny	18	F		Ireland	United States	Concordia	25 Aug 1827
Fredk.	25	M	Sailor	America	America	Antoinette	25 Jan 1828
Helena	38	F	Merchant	Ireland	U. States	Nancy	25 Nov 1823
Henry	22		Sugar Baker	Germany	U.S. of America	Mary	21 Sep 1821

NAMES OF PASSENGERS	AGE	SEX	OCCUPATIONS	COUNTRY TO WHICH THEY BELONG	COUNTRY THEY INTEND TO INHABIT	SHIPS/DATES OF ARRIVAL	
ROACH (cont'd)							
James	6	M		Ireland	United States	Concordia	25 Aug 1827
James	12	M	Merchant	Ireland	U. States	Nancy	25 Nov 1823
Jane	8	F	Lady	Barbados, U.S.	West Indies	Spartan	24 Jul 1826
Jno.	26	M	Farmer	Ireland	United States	Aurora	27 Apr 1825
John	10	M	Merchant	Ireland	U. States	Nancy	25 Nov 1823
Lewis	40	M	Merchant	Ireland	U. States	Nancy	25 Nov 1823
Margaret	20	F		Ireland	United States	Aurora	27 Apr 1825
Mary	18	F	Spinster	Great Brittan	United States	Hanford	3 Aug 1829
Mary	26	F		Ireland	United States	John Wells	18 Sep 1826
Mary	51	F	None	England	United States	Hamilton	13 Nov 1827
Mary Ann	7	F	Merchant	Ireland	U. States	Nancy	25 Nov 1823
Patt	1	M		Ireland	United States	Concordia	25 Aug 1827
Patt	33	M	Mechanic	Ireland	United States	Concordia	25 Aug 1827
Paul	11	M		Ireland	United States	Concordia	25 Aug 1827
Philip	5	M	Merchant	Ireland	U. States	Nancy	25 Nov 1823
Susanna	12	F	Servant	Ireland	United States	Wilson	27 Jun 1826
Thomas	4	M	Merchant	Ireland	U. States	Nancy	25 Nov 1823
Thomas	40	M	Stone Cutter	..., ..., Ireland	U. States	New Orleans	24 Aug 1827
Waller	19	M	Labourer	Ireland	United States	Jubilee	12 May 1828
William	22	M	Farmer	England	United States	Hamilton	13 Nov 1827
William	30	M	Farmer	Ireland	America	William	21 May 1825
William M.	38	M	Baker	Barbadoes	St. Thomas	John London	8 Dec 1823
Wm.	6	M	Boy	Great Brittan	United States	Hanford	3 Aug 1829
Wm.	20	M	Merchant	Ireland	United States	Borneo	2 Oct 1827
ROACHE, Thomas	24	M	Farmer	Ireland	N. York	Elizabeth	20 Jun 1828
ROACK, Cathr.	18	F		Ireland	U. States	Wilson	2 Sep 1823
H., Mrs.	24	F	Lady	Barbados, U.S.	West Indies	Spartan	24 Jul 1826
ROACKES, A.	18	M	None	Colombian	U. States	Prince Edward	29 Jul 1823
ROAD, —, Mrs.	32	F		United States	United States	Seine	21 Oct 1822
Johanah	7	F		United States	United States	Seine	21 Oct 1822
Lidia	3	F		United States	United States	Seine	21 Oct 1822
Wm.	27	M	Mechanic	United States	United States	Seine	21 Oct 1822
ROADS, —, Mrs.	23	F		England	United States	Peru	23 May 1827
Thos.	33	M	Spinner	England	United States	Peru	23 May 1827
ROAG, John	35	M	Farmer	Scotland	America	Friends	24 Sep 1821
Paula	16	F	Spinster	Scotland	America	Friends	24 Sep 1821
ROAK, Bridget	28 4/12	F		England	United States	John Wells	22 May 1826
James	1 6/12	M		England	United States	John Wells	22 May 1826
M...s...	34		None	Ma...ter, England Great Britain		Frances Henrietta	31 May 1824
Mary Ann	5		None	London, England Great Britain		Frances Henrietta	31 May 1824
Michael	4 6/12	M		England	United States	John Wells	22 May 1826
Patrick	28	M	Labourer	England	United States	John Wells	22 May 1826
Wm.	3/12	M		England	United States	John Wells	22 May 1826
ROAKES, John	18	M	Farmer	Brittian	U. States	Acasta	28 Jan 1823
ROAL, Diego	40	M	Gentleman	U. States	U. States	Abeona	1 Oct 1823
ROAN, Ann	19	F	Spinster	Ireland	U. States	Courier	17 Mar 1828
John	28	M	Black Smith	Ireland	America	Rising States	7 Jul 1828
Michol	17 6/12	M	Labourer	Ireland	U. States	Courier	17 Mar 1828
ROARKE, Mary	25	F	Spinster	Ireland	United States	Dublin Packet	22 Apr 1822
ROARS, Mary	50	F	Cook	Ireland	America	Fairy	8 Aug 1821
ROASTAN, Thomas	28	M	Farmer	England	United States	Panthia	7 Feb 1822
ROATH, H.	28	M	Blacksmith	United States	U.S.	Frances	15 Jun 1825
ROAULY, James	28	M	Farmer	England	United States	India	8 Jun 1827
ROB..., William	2...		Weaver	C...tla...	England	Great Britain	7 May 1827
ROBACHER, —	28	M	Labourer	France	United States	Cavalier	25 Jul 1828
ROBALTS, Thos.	20	M	Seaman	Malaga	Malaga	Pleiades	5 Nov 1828
ROBART, Christopher	72		Farmer	United States	United States	Alfred	8 Jul 1822
ROBARTS, John	23	M	Tailor	England	Kentucky	Brighton	14 Oct 1824
Walter	25		Merchant	England	Philadelphia	Xenophon	25 Jul 1826
ROBB, Anler	27	M	Farmer	France	United States	Great Britain	18 Sep 1826
Cathr.	25	F	Wife	Great Britain	United States	Roanoak	19 Sep 1827
Geo.	28	M	Blacksmith	Great Britain	United States	Roanoak	19 Sep 1827
George	23	M	Supercargo	United States	United States	Roxana	30 Apr 1823
James	32	M	Carpenter	Great Britain	United States	Colossus	5 Jun 1827

NAMES OF PASSENGERS	AGE	SEX	OCCUPATIONS	COUNTRY TO WHICH THEY BELONG	COUNTRY THEY INTEND TO INHABIT	SHIPS/DATES OF ARRIVAL	
ROBB (cont'd)							
James	34	M	Carpenter	Great Britain	United States	Courier	13 Mar 1820
John	32	M	Merchant	Great Britain	Quebec	Auritz	20 May 1823
John	36		Farmer	Great Britain	United States	Camillus	12 Sep 1827
ROBBENSON, N.	30	M	Merchant	United	U. States	Sarah G	30 Jun 1828
ROBBINS, Allen	28	M	Merchant	U. States	U. States	Pacific	11 Sep 1824
Allen	30	M	Merchant	United States	New York	Britannia	3 Nov 1827
Allen	33	M	Merchant	United States	New York, U.S.	Florida	2 Oct 1828
Chauncey	27	M	Merchant	Connecticut	U. States	John Wells	8 Sep 1897
E.	14	M	Gentleman	Great Britain	United States	Isaac Hicks	6 Dec 1827
Foreman C.	26 4/12	M	Merchant	United States	United States	Isaac Hicks	22 Aug 1829
J. B.	28	M	Merchant	Jamaica	U. States	Protector	2 Jul 1824
Wm.	24	M	Painter & Glaser	England	Maryland	Eliza	8 Mar 1827
ROBCULLEN, Patrick	...	M	Labourer	Great Britain	United States	Ann Maria	17 Apr 1827
ROBE, Jas.	35	M	Planter	England	on a Visit	Catharine	3 Sep 1821
ROBELIN, Toward	26	M	Doctor	Cannada	G. Brittain	Stephania	13 Sep 1821
ROBERSON, John	21			Westmoreland	Ohio	Peru	30 May 1828
John	33	M	Seaman	Philadelphia	United States	Venus	8 Sep 1820
ROBERSTON,							
George W.	25 10/12	M	...ar...	U. States	New York	Wilson	10 Apr 1823
John	22	M	Weaver	Ireland	U. States	Champion	26 Jul 1827
ROBERT, Abel	33	M	Doctor	France	United States	Emulous	7 Oct 1822
Alexr.	70	M	Merchant	France	United States	Bayard	13 Nov 1823
Angel	35	M	Mercht.	Spain	Spain	Richmond Packet	28 Oct 1825
Angel	35	M	Merchant	Spain	Spain	Richmond Packet	15 Jun 1826
Angel	37	M	Merchant	Spain	unknown	Juanita	13 Oct 1829
Antionette	32	F		Holland	United States	Martha	30 Jun 1823
C. D.	28	M	Planter	Dominico	Dominico	Orra Maria	18 Oct 1823
Calestin	4	M		France	France	Edward Quesnel	3 Jul 1829
Claude	38	M		France	France	Edward Quesnel	3 Jul 1829
Francois	10	M		France	France	Edward Quesnel	3 Jul 1829
Frederick L.	24	M	Carpenter	Neufehatel	U.S. America	Superior	18 Jun 1825
Jose	20	M	Gentleman	Spain	United States	Georgetown Packet	15 Nov 1823
Joseph	22	M	Gentleman	England	U. States	Acasta	28 Jan 1823
Juan	14	M	Student	U. States	U. States	Altamira	31 Jan 1828
Rick.	21	M	Mariner			Superior	27 Jun 1825
Shopie, her Daughter							
[Antionette]	7	F		Holland	United States	Martha	30 Jun 1823
Theodore	25	M	Merchant	France	U.S.A.	Gallego	13 Mar 1829
Wm.	25	M	Clerk	G. Brittain	U. States	Rengal	9 Oct 1822
Wm.	31	M	Joiner	Great Britain	United States	Penelope	11 Jun 1827
ROBERTS, —	32	M	Mercht.	France	France	Don Quixote	3 Jan 1826
—, Child	2				U.S. America	Camillus	10 Sep 1821
—, Miss	26	F		Gt. Britain	United States	Columbia	7 Sep 1827
—, Mrs.	59			England	U. States	Elizabeth	5 Oct 1822
A.	28	M	Farmer	England	U. States	York	12 Jul 1825
A.	32	M	Merchant	Havana	U. States	Abeona	23 May 1823
Alice	26	F		G. Britain	U.S.A.	Silas Richards	29 Oct 1827
Alinter	8	M	Painter	England		Antioch	18 Aug 1829
Amos	5	M		England	U. States	York	12 Jul 1825
Angle	35	M	Merchant	Spain	Spain	Weymouth	13 Aug 1822
Ann	0 6/12	F		G. Britain	G. Britain	Brittania	17 Jul 1828
Ann	1	F				Hercules	24 Oct 1821
*died at sea							
Ann	1	F	None	England	United States	Jubilee	1 Oct 1828
Ann	2			Great Britain	United States	Gomer	21 May 1828
Ann	3	F	None	Wales	United States	Orozimbo	11 Aug 1823
Ann	9	F		England	United States	Amelia	20 Aug 1829
Ann	13	F	Spinster	United States	United States	Elbe	19 Apr 1826
Ann	20	F	None	Great Britain	U. St.	Manchester	7 Dec 1826
Ann	21	F				Lady of the Lake	23 Aug 1828
*left the ship b...							
Ann	22	F		Great Britain	America	Lady Gallatin	21 Jun 1820
Ann	24	F	Spinster	Ireland	United States	Ann Maria	2 Nov 1827
Ann	27	F		G. Britain	U. States	Leavitts	25 Aug 1828

NAMES OF PASSENGERS	AGE	SEX	OCCUPATIONS	COUNTRY TO WHICH THEY BELONG	COUNTRY THEY INTEND TO INHABIT	SHIPS/DATES OF ARRIVAL	
ROBERTS (cont'd)							
Ann	31	F	Farmer	Britain	U. States	Fame	3 Jun 1828
Ann	34 2/12	F		England	U.S. of America	Illinois	16 Jun 1821
Ann	38	F	Painter	U. States		Antioch	18 Aug 1829
Ann	41	F				Lady of the Lake	23 Aug 1828
*left the ship b...							
Ann	42	F	None	England	United States	Jubilee	1 Oct 1828
Ann	50	F	None	England	U. States	Franklin	7 Jul 1828
Barbara	1	F		England	United States	Amelia	20 Aug 1829
Benj.	22	M	Wire Drawer	G. Britain	U. States	Margaret Bogle	12 Jun 1828
Betsey	25	F	None			Evergreen	28 Jul 1820
Betsey	25	F	Weaver	England	United States	Baltic	21 Apr 1827
Betty	13	F	in Factory	England	U. States	Franklin	7 Jul 1828
C.	45	M	Planter	Cuba	Cuba	Andromache	18 May 1825
C. R.	21	M	Merchant	U. States	U. States	Andromache	13 Nov 1822
Catharine	5			Great Britain	United States	Gomer	21 May 1828
Catharine	10	F	Spinster	United States	United States	Elbe	19 Apr 1826
Catharine	20	M	Merchant	Great Britain	U. States	William Thompson	1 May 1827
Catharine, Wife [of John Griffith]	60	F	Farmer	Wales		Gomer	22 May 1827
Catherine	13	F	Daughter	G.B.	U.S.	Missouri	4 Aug 1825
Catherine	24	F	None	Wales	United States	Orozimbo	11 Aug 1823
Catherine	26	F	None	Wales	United States	Mentor	28 Apr 1824
Catherine	36	F	Wife	G.B.	U.S.	Missouri	4 Aug 1825
Catherine	45	F	Spinster	United States	United States	Elbe	19 Apr 1826
Charles	4	M		G. Britain	U.S.A.	Silas Richards	29 Oct 1827
Charles	24	M	Smith	Great Britian	United States	Baltic	5 Apr 1826
Daniel	46	M		Great Britain	United States	Amelia	20 Aug 1829
David	1 1/2	F		G. Britain	U. States	Leavitts	25 Aug 1828
David	4	M	Son	G.B.	U.S.	Missouri	4 Aug 1825
David	33	M	Mariner	U. States	U. States	Jasper	24 Feb 1826
Dorothy	48			Great Britain	United States	Gomer	21 May 1828
Doud	26	M	Labourer	Wales	United States	Orozimbo	11 Aug 1823
Ebenn	4	M				Lady of the Lake	23 Aug 1828
*left the ship b...							
Edmond		M	Merchant	U. States	U. States	Mary Ann	6 May 1828
Edward	3	M		England	United States	Amelia	20 Aug 1829
Edwd.	1	M	None	Wales	United States	Orozimbo	11 Aug 1823
Edwd.	20	M	Merchant	N. York	U. States	Pomona	18 Aug 1824
Edwd.	53	M	Surgeon	Pevllhely	United States	Marquis of Anglesea	8 Jun 1827
Eleanor, Wife [of John]	23	F	Farmer	Wales		Gomer	22 May 1827
Elenor	51			Great Britain	United States	Gomer	21 May 1828
Elinor	36	F		Great Britain	United States	Gomer	21 May 1828
Eliza	14	F		G. Britain	U. States	Leavitts	25 Aug 1828
Eliza	15 1/12	F	Servant	G. Britain	U. States	Wanderer	23 Jun 1828
Eliza	22	F	None	Wales	United States	Orozimbo	11 Aug 1823
Eliza	35	F	None	England	United States	John Dickinson	30 Sep 1823
Eliza	40	F	None	Great Britain	United States	Atlantic	28 May 1827
Elizabeth	8			Great Britain	United States	Gomer	21 May 1828
Elizabeth	9	F	Farmer	Great Britain	United States	Asia	14 Jul 1829
Elizabeth	16	F	None	England	United States	Jubilee	1 Oct 1828
Elizabeth	29	F	None	England	New York	America	1 Aug 1828
Elizabeth	33	F		England	United States	Comet	6 Mar 1823
Elizabeth	35	F	None	United States	United States	Brighton	12 Jun 1826
Elizabeth	35	F	Farmer	Great Britain	United States	Asia	14 Jul 1829
Elizabeth	38			Great Britain	United States	Gomer	21 May 1828
Elizabth.	16		Servant	Great Britain	United States	Gomer	21 May 1828
Ellen	1	F	None	Great Britain	United States	Atlantic	28 May 1827
*dead							
Ellen	5	F	None	Wales	United States	Orozimbo	11 Aug 1823
Ellen	30	F	None	England	United States	John Dickinson	30 Sep 1823
Ellen	37	F		Aberdarorgen, Great Britain	United States	Marquis of Anglesea	8 Jun 1827
Ellis	8	M	Son	G.B.	U.S.	Missouri	4 Aug 1825

NAMES OF PASSENGERS	AGE	SEX	OCCUPATIONS	COUNTRY TO WHICH THEY BELONG	COUNTRY THEY INTEND TO INHABIT	SHIPS/DATES OF ARRIVAL	
ROBERTS (cont'd)							
Ellis	38	M	Farmer	G.B.	U.S.	Missouri	4 Aug 1825
Ellis	47	M	Farmer	Great Brittan	U.S.	Emulous	29 Jun 1827
Elza	5	M		Great Britian	United States	Baltic	5 Apr 1826
Evan	11	M	None	England	United States	John Dickinson	30 Sep 1823
Evan	26 7/12	M	Farmer	England	U.S. of America	Illinois	16 Jun 1821
Evan	29	M	Joiner	G. Britain	U. States	St. George	7 Jun 1828
Evan	47	M	Labourer			Lady of the Lake	23 Aug 1828
*left the ship b...							
Evan, Child [of John]	1	M	Farmer	Wales		Gomer	22 May 1827
Evaner	21	M	Labourer			Lady of the Lake	23 Aug 1828
*left the ship b...							
Ewd.	3	M	None	Great Britain	United States	Atlantic	28 May 1827
Ewd.	3	F		G. Britain	U. States	Leavitts	25 Aug 1828
Ewd. S.	20	M	Labourer	England	America	Two Marys	24 Sep 1827
Frances	24	M	Gardiner	France	United States	Stephania	24 Mar 1828
Frances	38	F	Lady	England	New York	Brighton	16 Nov 1826
Franklin	33	M	Cabinet Maker	U. States	U. States	Telegraph	14 Jun 1828
Frederick	2	M	None	Ireland	United States	Jubilee	13 Jul 1829
George	5	M	Farmer	Great Britain	United States	Asia	14 Jul 1829
George	5 3/12	M		G. Britain	U.S.A.	Silas Richards	29 Oct 1827
George	18	M	None	England	U. States	Franklin	7 Jul 1828
George	24	M	Cloth Manfacturer	England	U.S. of America	Illinois	16 Jun 1821
George	25	M	Labourer	England	Rochester	Chelsea	16 May 1828
George	57	M	Farmer	Great Britain	U. St.	Manchester	7 Dec 1826
Griffith	5	M	Labourer	Wales		Gomer	22 May 1827
Griffith	10	M	Labourer	Wales		Gomer	22 May 1827
Griffith	22	M	Labourer	Aberdaron	United States	Marquis of Anglesea	8 Jun 1827
Griffith	43		Farmer	Great Britain	United States	Gomer	21 May 1828
Griffith	53	M	Tailor	Aberdaron	United States	Marquis of Anglesea	8 Jun 1827
Gwen	6			Great Britain	United States	Gomer	21 May 1828
H. J.	23	M	Mercht.	Cadiz	U. States	Romulus	7 Oct 1822
Hannah	12	F		England	United States	Amelia	20 Aug 1829
Hannah	21	F	in Factory	England	U. States	Franklin	7 Jul 1828
Hannah	22	F	Spinster	Carnarvon	U. States	Melantho	26 Mar 1827
Harriot	2/12	F		England	U. States	York	12 Jul 1825
Harry	6	M	None	England	United States	Jubilee	1 Oct 1828
Henry	10	M	Painter	England		Antioch	18 Aug 1829
Henry	12	M	Labourer	Wales		Gomer	22 May 1827
Henry	18	M	Clerk	Great Britain	United States	Florida	2 Oct 1828
Henry	22	M	Labourer	England	Pittsburgh	Orozimbo	8 Jun 1822
Hugh	1	M	Farmer	Britain	U. States	Fame	3 Jun 1828
Hugh	10	M	None	England	United States	Jubilee	1 Oct 1828
Hugh	13	M	Farmer	Great Britain	United States	Atlantic	28 May 1827
Hugh	20	M	Labourer	Wales	America	Minerva	31 May 1824
Hugh	21	M	Black Smith	Wales	U.S. America	Sereno	18 Jun 1827
Hugh	22	M	Farmer	England	United States	Concordia	25 Aug 1827
Hugh	30	M	Gentleman	Great Britain	England	John Wells	29 Jan 1825
Hugh	48	M	Farmer	Great Brittain	United States	Nimrod	9 Jan 1827
Isaac	13	M	Labourer	Wales		Gomer	22 May 1827
J.	22	M	Carpenter	England	United States	Earl of Liverpool	28 Apr 1824
James	2	M	None	England	U. States	Franklin	7 Jul 1828
James	4	M	Farmer	Great Britain	United States	Asia	14 Jul 1829
James	14	M	Mariner	Boston	U. States	Amphion	14 Mar 1823
James	15	M	Labourer			Lady of the Lake	23 Aug 1828
*left the ship b...							
James	34	M	Brick Layer	Great Britain	United States	Blakely	29 Sep 1826
James L.	33	M	Mainer	N. York	U. States	Herald	6 Feb 1824
Jane	9	F	None	Great Britain	United States	Atlantic	28 May 1827
Jane	20	F	None	Great Britain	America	Lady Gallatin	21 Jun 1820
Jane	21	F		Great Britain	United States	John Jay	8 May 1828
Jane	30	F	...	...	...	Indian Chief	8 Sep 1824
Jno.	18	M	Farmer	Great Britain	United States	Atlantic	28 May 1827

NAMES OF PASSENGERS	AGE	SEX	OCCUPATIONS	COUNTRY TO WHICH THEY BELONG	COUNTRY THEY INTEND TO INHABIT	SHIPS/DATES OF ARRIVAL	
ROBERTS (cont'd)							
Jno.	35	M	Mariner	U. States	U. States	Florida	25 Apr 1825
Jno.	37	M	Merchant	Boston	U. States	Packet	24 Mar 1824
Jno.	60	M	Farmer	Great Britain	United States	Atlantic	28 May 1827
*dead							
John	2			Great Britain	United States	Gomer	21 May 1828
John	3	M		Great Britian	United States	Baltic	5 Apr 1826
John	6	M	Boy	U. States	U. States	Francis Jarvis	17 Oct 1822
John	6	M	Labourer	Wales		Gomer	22 May 1827
John	14	M	Painter	England		Antioch	18 Aug 1829
John	16	M	Labourer			Lady of the Lake	23 Aug 1828
*left the ship b...							
John	21	M	None	England	U. States	Franklin	7 Jul 1828
John	22	M	Farmer	Wales		Gomer	22 May 1827
John	24	M	Ireland	G. Brittain	U. States	Calypso	1 Jun 1821
John	24	M	Merchant	America	U. States	Florida	13 Feb 1823
John	25	M	Farmer	Donegal	United States	Solon	21 Jun 1824
John	26	M	Labourer	Ireland	United States	Jubilee	13 Jul 1829
John	26		Mines	England	England	Triumph	23 Jul 1829
John	26 3/12	M	Farmer	England	U.S. of America	Illinois	16 Jun 1821
John	27	M	Butcher	England	U.S.	Panthea	22 Jul 1826
John	29	M	Engineer	England	U. States	Messenger	10 Jul 1829
John	30			England	U. States	Corinthian	8 Oct 1828
John	34	M	None	Great Britain	United States	Gomer	21 May 1828
John	35	M	Mercht.	U. States	U. States	Packet	6 Aug 1822
John	38	M	Farmer	Wales		Gomer	22 May 1827
John	40	M	Painter	England		Antioch	18 Aug 1829
John	50	M	Mecht.	Quebec	Quebec	Otter	30 Oct 1826
John	52	M		G. Britain	U. States	Leavitts	25 Aug 1828
John, Mr.	22	M	Brush Maker	England	U.S.	Acasta	11 May 1827
John T.	34	M	Farmer	America	America	Brittania	17 Jul 1828
Jonathan	7	M	None	Great Britain	U. St.	Manchester	7 Dec 1826
Jone	7	F	in Factory	England	U. States	Franklin	7 Jul 1828
Joseph	1	M		Gt. Britain	United States	Columbia	7 Sep 1827
Joseph	16	M	in Factory	England	U. States	Franklin	7 Jul 1828
Joseph	16	M	in Factory	England	U. States	Franklin	7 Jul 1828
Joseph	21 6/12	M	Farmer			Cririe	18 Sep 1820
Joseph	29 5/12	M	Merchant	France	America	Erie	19 Oct 1829
Joseph, Mr.	24	M	Merchant	New York	New York	Hannibal	28 Apr 1824
L.	55	M	Merchant	U. States	U. States	Eliza	28 Apr 1827
Laura, Wife [of John]	41	F	Farmer	Wales		Gomer	22 May 1827
Lewis	6	M	Son	G.B.	U.S.	Missouri	4 Aug 1825
Lewis	19	M	Labourer			Lady of the Lake	23 Aug 1828
*left the ship b...							
Lewis	25	M	Dyer	France	United States	Criterion	27 Oct 1820
Lydia	23	F	in Factory	England	U. States	Franklin	7 Jul 1828
Margaret	2	M	Painter	England		Antioch	18 Aug 1829
Margt.	6	F		U. States	U. States	George Clinton	10 Sep 1828
Margt.	27	F		G. Britain	G. Britain	Brittania	17 Jul 1828
Maria	6	F	None	Great Britain	United States	Atlantic	28 May 1827
Martha	22	F	None	England	United States	Hercules	24 Oct 1821
Martha	31	F	None	Great Britain	United States	Pacific	7 May 1827
Mary	2	F		England	U. States	York	12 Jul 1825
Mary	6	M		Great Britain	United States	Gomer	21 May 1828
Mary	7	F		England	United States	Amelia	20 Aug 1829
Mary	8	F				Lady of the Lake	23 Aug 1828
*left the ship b...							
Mary	12	F	None	Great Britain	U. St.	Manchester	7 Dec 1826
Mary	14	F	Spinster	United States	United States	Elbe	19 Apr 1826
Mary	14	F	None	England	United States	Jubilee	1 Oct 1828
Mary	16	F		England	United States	Manhattan	22 Sep 1823
Mary	16	F	Spinster	Great Britain	United States	Superior	31 Mar 1828
Mary	19	F	in Factory	England	U. States	Franklin	7 Jul 1828
Mary	25	F	Lady	U. States	U. States	Francis Jarvis	17 Oct 1822
Mary	25	F		U. States	U. States	George Clinton	10 Sep 1828
Mary	28	F	None	Ireland	United States	Jubilee	13 Jul 1829

NAMES OF PASSENGERS	AGE	SEX	OCCUPATIONS	COUNTRY TO WHICH THEY BELONG	COUNTRY THEY INTEND TO INHABIT	SHIPS/DATES OF ARRIVAL	
ROBERTS (cont'd)							
Mary	34	F	Traveller	England	West Indies	Conestoga	23 Nov 1825
Mary	65	F	Labourer	Wales		Gomer	22 May 1827
Mary, Child [of John]	17	F	Farmer	Wales		Gomer	22 May 1827
Mary, Wife [of William]	50	F	Farmer	Wales		Gomer	22 May 1827
Mary Ann	4	M	Painter	England		Antioch	18 Aug 1829
Mary Ann	25			W...	...	Hudson	14 Jun 1827
May	28	F		G. Britain	U. States	Leavitts	25 Aug 1828
May	44	F		Gt. Britain	U. States	St. George	20 Sep 1828
Mitchell	24	M	Farmer	Rye, England	United States	William	21 May 1828
N. L.	27	M	Merchant	England	U. States	Swift	11 May 1824
Nehemiah	28	M	Mariner	United States	United States	Mary Ann	7 Jan 1829
Owen	8	M	None	England	United States	Jubilee	1 Oct 1828
Phillis	31	F		England	U. States	York	12 Jul 1825
Phoebe	36	F		England	United States	Amelia	20 Aug 1829
R.	30	M	Merchant	England	United States	York	31 Mar 1828
Reese	32	M	Farmer	England	United States	John Dickinson	30 Sep 1823
Richard	1	M	...	...	...	Indian Chief	8 Sep 1824
Richard	22	M	Merchant	England	U. States	York	13 Aug 1827
Richard	27	M	Carpenter	England	New York	America	1 Aug 1828
Richard	34	M	...	...	...	Indian Chief	8 Sep 1824
Robert	1	M				Lady of the Lake	23 Aug 1828
*left the ship b...							
Robert	3	M	...	...	...	Indian Chief	8 Sep 1824
Robert	4	M	None	Wales	United States	Orozimbo	11 Aug 1823
Robert	4	M		Great Britain	United States	Gomer	21 May 1828
Robert	7	M		England	United States	Comet	6 Mar 1823
Robert	10	M	Son	G.B.	U.S.	Missouri	4 Aug 1825
Robert	12 6/12	M	None	United States	United States	Brighton	12 Jun 1826
Robert	18	M	None	England	United States	Jubilee	1 Oct 1828
Robert	27		...ler	W...	...	Hudson	14 Jun 1827
Robert	32	M	Cabinetmaker	England	United States	Comet	6 Mar 1823
Robert, Child [of John]	13	M	Farmer	Wales		Gomer	22 May 1827
Robert, Child [of William]	19	M	Labourer	Wales		Gomer	22 May 1827
Robert L.	32	M	Mariner	United States	United States	Tandem	8 Mar 1826
Robt.	14	M	Farmer	Great Britain	United States	Atlantic	28 May 1827
Robt.	24	M	Farmer	Great Brittan	U.S.	Emulous	29 Jun 1827
Robt.	25	M	Weaver	England	United States	Baltic	21 Apr 1827
Robt., Jr.	23	M	Sadler	United States	United States	Elbe	19 Apr 1826
S...	30	F			U.S. America	Camillus	10 Sep 1821
Sally	17	F	None	Great Britain	U. St.	Manchester	7 Dec 1826
Sally	53	F	None	Great Britain	U. St.	Manchester	7 Dec 1826
Sarah	17	F	Farmer	Britain	U. States	Fame	3 Jun 1828
Sarah	24	F	Spinster	Wales		Gomer	22 May 1827
Sarah	24	F	None	England	U. States	Franklin	7 Jul 1828*
Sarah	25	F		Great Britian	United States	Baltic	5 Apr 1826
Sarah	55	F	None	England	U. States	Franklin	7 Jul 1828
Sary Ann	2 4/12	F		G. Britain	U.S.A.	Silas Richards	29 Oct 1827
Sophia	5	F		G. Britain	U. States	Leavitts	25 Aug 1828
Stephen	6	M	Painter	England		Antioch	18 Aug 1829
Thomas	6	M	...	...	...	Indian Chief	8 Sep 1824
Thomas	9	M		England	U. States	York	12 Jul 1825
Thomas	21	F	Labourer	Ireland	United States	Carolina Ann	14 May 1827
Thomas	25	M	Farmer	Great Britain	United States	John Jay	8 May 1828
Thos.	7	M	Farmer	Great Britain	United States	Asia	14 Jul 1829
Thos.	24	M	Seaman	United States	United States	Augusta	27 Aug 1829
Thos.	30	M	Labourer	Great Britain	United States	Pacific	7 May 1827
Thos.	40	M	Farmer	Great Britain	United States	Asia	14 Jul 1829
Thos. W.	15	M	Clerk	England	U.S.A.	Silas Richards	7 Mar 1827
Ths.	20	M	Spinster	Great Brittain	United States	Corinthian	9 Jan 1827
Vincent	10	M	Farmer	Britain	U. States	Fame	3 Jun 1828
Walter	31	M	None	England	England	Britannia	23 Mar 1829
William	10	M	None	England	United States	Jubilee	1 Oct 1828
William	12	M	Painter	England		Antioch	18 Aug 1829
William	14	M	Tailor	England	Kentucky	Brighton	14 Oct 1824

NAMES OF PASSENGERS	AGE	SEX	OCCUPATIONS	COUNTRY TO WHICH THEY BELONG	COUNTRY THEY INTEND TO INHABIT	SHIPS/DATES OF ARRIVAL	
ROBERTS (cont'd)							
William	23	M	Labourer	Wales	United States	Orozimbo	11 Aug 1823
William	26	M	Filler up	Great Britian	United States	Baltic	5 Apr 1826
William	33	M	Farmer	Britain	U. States	Fame	3 Jun 1828
William	36	M	Merchant	Great Britain	United States	James Cropper	27 Sep 1821
William	40		Farmer	Great Britain	United States	Gomer	21 May 1828
William	52	M	Farmer	Wales		Gomer	22 May 1827
William, Child [of William]	21	M	Labourer	Wales		Gomer	22 May 1827
Willm. S.	16	M	Gentn.	England	New York	Brighton	16 Nov 1826
Winifred	31	F		Great Britain	America	Lady Gallatin	21 Jun 1820
Wm.	6	M	in Factory	England	U. States	Franklin	7 Jul 1828
Wm.	8	M	Farmer	Great Britain	United States	Atlantic	28 May 1827
Wm.	10	M	Farmer	Great Britain	United States	Asia	14 Jul 1829
Wm.	26	M	Shoemaker	G. Britain	America	Spring	12 Oct 1821
Wm.	27	M	Shoemaker	Great Britain	Manhattan, N.Y.	Zodiac	14 Jun 1822
Wm.	31	M	Labourer	Wales	United States	Orozimbo	11 Aug 1823
Wm.	60	M	Carpenter	England	U. States	Elizabeth	5 Oct 1822
Wm., Mr.	18	M	Brush Maker	England	U.S.	Acasta	11 May 1827
Wm. B.	27	M	Gardner	G. Britain	U. States	St. George	7 Jun 1828
ROBERTSON, —,							
Child [Mrs.]	11	F		United States	United States	William	11 Dec 1820
—, Child [Mrs.]	11	F		United States	United States	William	11 Dec 1820
—, Mr.	22	M	No	Dundee	U. States	Bolivar	19 May 1826
—, Mrs.	20	F		Scotland	U.S.	Curler	19 Jul 1828
—, Mrs.	30	F	None	U. States	U. States	Sea Nymph	7 Jul 1827
—, Mrs.	36	F		United States	United States	William	11 Dec 1820
...	33	M	Merchant	Gt. Britain		Dalhouse Castle	13 May 1828
...	67	M	Merchant	Denmark		Elias Burger	26 Jul 1821
Adaline	1/12	F	None	U. States	U. States	Sea Nymph	7 Jul 1827
Agnes	4	F		Scotland	U.S.	Curler	19 Jul 1828
Alexander	33	M	Merchant	Gt. Britain		Dalhouse Castle	13 May 1828
Amelias	3	M	None	Scotland	U.S. of America	Friends	12 May 1826
Andrew	19	M	Tinsmith	Scotland	United States	Culloden	17 May 1828
Ann	12	F	Child	Ireland	U. States	Courier	17 Mar 1828
Catherine	1	F				Washington	16 Sep 1820
Chaguet	21	F	Labourer	Ireland	United States	Hope	12 Jun 1828
Charlotte	31	M				Washington	16 Sep 1820
Christian	20	F		Scotland	United States	Camillus	9 May 1827
Colin	38	M	Gentleman	Canada	Canada	Thames	16 May 1821
Daniel	3	M		Scotland	U.S. of America	Friends	10 May 1823
Danl.	60	M	Mercht.	St. Croix	U. States	Argo	11 Aug 1824
David	1			Scotland	United States	Camillus	3 May 1828
David	4	M		Argyle (Tedland) Scotland	United States	Jean Hastie	27 Jul 1829
David	17	M	Farmer	Scotland	United States	Broke	16 Jul 1829
Donald	29		Spinner	Great Britain	United States	Camillus	12 Sep 1827
Donald McG.	17	M	Merchant	Scotland	United States	Commerce	17 Jul 1823
Duncan	20	M	Merchant	England	United States	Minerva	26 May 1821
Duncan	28	M	Farmer	Great Britain	America	Samuel Robertson	26 Nov 1825
Elenor	3	F	None	Great Britan	United States	Silvanus Jenkins	10 Mar 1827
Elisabeth	17		Labourer	G. Britain	U. States	Hamilton	28 Apr 1828
Eliza	8	F		Argyle (Tedland) Scotland	United States	Jean Hastie	27 Jul 1829
Eliza	40	F		Argyle (Tedland) Scotland	United States	Jean Hastie	27 Jul 1829
Elizabeth	17 5/12	F		England	U.S. America	Illinois	16 Oct 1822
Elizabeth	17 11/12	F		England	America, U.S.	Illinois	3 Jun 1822
Elizabeth	20	F	Spinster	Scotland	U. States	Phocion	8 May 1824
Elizabeth	50	F		America	America	James Cropper	14 Oct 1822
Ellen	14 8/12	F		England	U.S. America	Illinois	16 Oct 1822
Emily	9	F	Child	Ireland	U. States	Courier	17 Mar 1828
Emma	22 3/12	F		England	America, U.S.	Illinois	3 Jun 1822
Eugene	25	M	Aeronaut	Paris	U.S. America	Superior	18 Jun 1825
Ewd.	14	M	Boy	N. Orleans	U. States	Circassian	3 Jun 1826
George	24	M	Mercht.	Great Britain	Great Britain	Nancy	13 Dec 1822
George	28	M	Farmer	Great Britian	United States	Diamond	8 Nov 1824
George	30	M	Merchant	Ireland	United States	Edwin	27 Oct 1828

NAMES OF PASSENGERS	AGE	SEX	OCCUPATIONS	COUNTRY TO WHICH THEY BELONG	COUNTRY THEY INTEND TO INHABIT	SHIPS/DATES OF ARRIVAL	
ROBERTSON (cont'd)							
George	67	M		Scotland	U. States	Camillus	17 Sep 1823
Gilbert	60	M	...	Great Brittain	Philadelphia	Albion	11 Jun 1821
Hannah	21		Wife, going to her husband	Scotland	United States	Camillus	3 May 1828
Hety	18	F	Labourer	Ireland	United States	Hope	12 Jun 1828
Hugh	15	M	Labourer	Ireland	U. States	Courier	17 Mar 1828
J. J.	23	M	Merchant	U. States		Prince Madore	28 Aug 1820
James	5	M	None	Great Britan	United States	Silvanus Jenkins	10 Mar 1827
James	10	M		Argyle (Tedland) Scotland	United States	Jean Hastie	27 Jul 1829
James	12 3/12	M		England	America, U.S.	Illinois	3 Jun 1822
James	17	M	Carpenter	G. Britain	Upper Canada	Perseverance	9 Jun 1827
James	18	M	Clerk	Scotland	Great Britain	Camillus	28 Apr 1823
James	19	M	Labourer	Scotland	United States	Morning Star	25 Jun 1822
James	22	M	Weaver	Yorkshire	Boston	Curler	7 Jul 1827
James	24	M	Labourer	Argyle (Tedland) Scotland	United States	Jean Hastie	27 Jul 1829
James	26	M	Engineer	Great Britain	United States	Courier	26 Jun 1827
James	31		Merchant	England	U. States	Venus	4 Oct 1821
James	33	M	None	Great Britain	United States	Friends	13 Jun 1825
James	33	M	Glasgow	Glasgow	Glasgow	Howard Douglass	11 May 1827
James	34	M	Gentleman	Scotland	U.S. of America	Friends	12 May 1826
James	35	M	Farmer	Great Britan	United States	Silvanus Jenkins	10 Mar 1827
James	37	M	Farmer	Scotland	U. States	Roger Stewart	9 Jun 1828
James	38	M	Labourer	Scotland	United States	Samuel Robertson	5 Oct 1827
James	38	M		Scotland	U.S.	Curler	19 Jul 1828
James	40	M	Gardiner	Argyle (Tedland) Scotland	United States	Jean Hastie	27 Jul 1829
James	51	M	Tenner	Great Briton	uncertan	Mount Vernon	30 Dec 1828
James, Jur.	11	M	None	Scotland	U.S. of America	Friends	12 May 1826
Jane	10	F		Scotland	U.S. of America	Friends	10 May 1823
Jannet	2	F		Scotland	U.S.	Curler	19 Jul 1828
Jas.	20	M	Merchant	St. John	U. States	St. Michaels	25 Apr 1825
Jean	22	F	Baker	Great Britain	United States	Colossus	5 Jun 1827
Jessie	34	F	None	Scotland	U.S. of America	Friends	12 May 1826
Jno.	24	M	Merchant	L'pool	Canada	James Cropper	4 Feb 1824
John	... 1/12	M		England	America, U.S.	Illinois	3 Jun 1822
John	1	M		Scotland	U.S.	Curler	19 Jul 1828
John	7	M	None	Great Britan	United States	Silvanus Jenkins	10 Mar 1827
John	19	M	Labourer	Ireland	United States	Hope	12 Jun 1828
John	20 5/12	M	Weaver	England	U.S. America	Illinois	16 Oct 1822
John	24	M		Scotland	United States	Camillus	9 May 1827
John	24	M	Farmer	Scotland	U.S.	Curler	19 Jul 1828
John	25	M	Merchant	Great Britian	U. States	Dalhouse Castle	28 Feb 1826
John	25	M	Farmer	England	United States	Mary & Harriet	9 Mar 1829
John	28	M	Baker	Great Britain	United States	Colossus	5 Jun 1827
John	28	M	Merchant	Great Britain	United States	Milton	20 Oct 1827
John	29	M	Farmer	Great Britain	U.S.	Trafalgar	22 Jun 1821
John	30	M	Labourer	Great Brittain	United States	Sarah Ralston	27 Jan 1827
John	32	M	Mechanic	England	United States	John Wells	15 Jan 1827
John	32	M		England	England	Birmingham	16 Jun 1828
John	34	M	Glass Blower	England	United States	Justina	5 Aug 1823
John	36	M	Merchant		U. States	Washington	16 Sep 1820
John	60		Weaver	Scotland	United States	Camillus	3 May 1828
John D.	7	M	None	Scotland	U.S. of America	Friends	12 May 1826
Jone	23	F	Labourer	Ireland	United States	Hope	12 Jun 1828
Joseph	28	M	Farmer	Great Britain	U.S. America	Chili	7 Jul 1827
Joseph	54 11/12	M		England	America, U.S.	Illinois	3 Jun 1822
Lawrence	26 10/12	M	Merchant	America	United States	Pegasus	17 May 1828
Luke Frazer	2	M	None	Scotland	U.S. of America	Friends	12 May 1826
Magt.	59		Spinster	Scotland	United States	Camillus	3 May 1828
Margaret	42	F		Scotland	U.S. of America	Friends	10 May 1823
Margaret, Jur.	18	F		Scotland	U.S. of America	Friends	10 May 1823
Margret	5	F	None	Scotland	U.S. of America	Friends	12 May 1826
Martha	11			G. Britain	U. States	Hamilton	28 Apr 1828
Martha	24	F	Labourer	Ireland	United States	Hope	12 Jun 1828

NAMES OF PASSENGERS	AGE	SEX	OCCUPATIONS	COUNTRY TO WHICH THEY BELONG	COUNTRY THEY INTEND TO INHABIT	SHIPS/DATES OF ARRIVAL	
ROBERTSON (cont'd)							
Mary	1	F	None	Great Britan	United States	Silvanus Jenkins	10 Mar 1827
Mary	6			G. Britain	U. States	Hamilton	28 Apr 1828
Mary	16	F		Scotland	U.S. of America	Friends	10 May 1823
Mary	30	F	None	Great Britan	United States	Silvanus Jenkins	10 Mar 1827
Mary	40	F	Labourer	Ireland	United States	Hope	12 Jun 1828
Mary	53	M	Wife	Great Britain	U.S. America	Prince Madoc	24 Sep 1821
Mary	58	F	...	Great Britain	Mississippa	Josephine	10 Dec 1825
Mary Ann	19 7/12	F		England	America, U.S.	Illinois	3 Jun 1822
Michael	30	M	Gardener	Glasgow, Barony [Parish], Lanark [County]	New York	Hero	19 May 1828
*to follow his occupation							
Mt.	29	F		Great Brittain	U.S.	Trafalgar	22 Jun 1821
Rith	8	M		Scotland	U.S.	Curler	19 Jul 1828
Robert	20	M		Argyle (Tedland) Scotland	United States	Jean Hastie	27 Jul 1829
Robert	22	M	Mill Wright	Ireland	U. States	Courier	17 Mar 1828
Robert	31	M	Labourer	Scotland	United States	Samuel Robertson	5 Oct 1827
Robert	33	M	School Master	United States	New York	Rambler	31 Aug 1829
Ross	17	M		Scotland	United States	Camillus	9 May 1827
S.	14	F		Scotland	U.S.	Curler	19 Jul 1828
Saml.	30	M	Gent.	Scotland	New York	Panthea	22 Jul 1826
Sarah	9 1/12	F		England	America, U.S.	Illinois	3 Jun 1822
Thomas	6	M		Argyle (Tedland) Scotland	United States	Jean Hastie	27 Jul 1829
W.	13			G. Britain	U. States	Hamilton	28 Apr 1828
William	12			Argyle (Tedland) Scotland	United States	Jean Hastie	27 Jul 1829
William	16 4/12	M		England	U.S. America	Illinois	16 Oct 1822
William	16 9/12	M	Farmer	England	America, U.S.	Illinois	3 Jun 1822
William	18	M	Mill Wright	Ireland	U. States	Courier	17 Mar 1828
William	38		Farmer	G. Britain	U. States	Hamilton	28 Apr 1828
William	44	M	Merchant	Scotland	United States	New York	5 Jul 1826
Wm.	9	M	None	Great Britan	United States	Silvanus Jenkins	10 Mar 1827
Wm.	12	M		Scotland	U.S.	Curler	19 Jul 1828
Wm.	20	M	Teacher	Scotland	U. States	Phocion	8 May 1824
Wm.	35	M	Builder	Great Britan	United States	Silvanus Jenkins	10 Mar 1827
Wm.	36	M	Labourer	Ireland	United States	Hope	12 Jun 1828
Wm.	60	M	Clergeman	Great Britain	U.S. America	Prince Madoc	24 Sep 1821
Wm., Jr.	18	M	Tracker	Great Britain	U.S. America	Prince Madoc	24 Sep 1821
Wyndham	24		None	United States	United States	Bayard	17 Dec 1827
ROBINETT, Rob. W. C.	17	M	Gentleman	Philada.	U. States	Ann	21 May 1824
ROBINS, Ann	28	F		United States	United States	Howard	27 Sep 1824
Catherin	42	F	None	United States	United States	Pacific	11 Mar 1829
E.	50	M	Gentleman	Great Britton	U. State	Earl of Liverpool	16 Aug 1826
Edmund	22	M	Merchant	G. Britain	U. States	Kennebeck Trader	16 Jul 1822
Edmward	33	M	Physician	United States	United States	Howard	27 Sep 1824
Emma	5	F	None	Great Britain	United States	Atlantic	28 May 1827
Hannah	30	F	None	Great Britain	United States	Atlantic	28 May 1827
James	27	M	Merchant	America	United States	Marmion	13 Jun 1823
Jno.	27	M	Clothier	Great Britain	United States	Atlantic	28 May 1827
John	22	M	Accountant	G. Britain	New York	Brighton	26 Mar 1827
Mary	40	F	Spinster	England	United States	Orozimbo	5 Mar 1827
Mary	48	F		Great Britton	U. State	Earl of Liverpool	16 Aug 1826
Oliver R.	30	M				Lady of the Lake	23 Aug 1828
*left ship							
Philip	40	M	Merchant	U. States	U. States	Ann Elizabeth	24 Jun 1823
Rob.	4	M	None	Great Britain	United States	Atlantic	28 May 1827
Sarah	20	F	Lady	G. Britain	U. States	Kennebeck Trader	16 Jul 1822
William	21	M	Merchant	Great Britain	United States	Marmion	13 Jun 1823
Wm.	1 6/12	M	None	Great Britain	United States	Atlantic	28 May 1827

NAMES OF PASSENGERS	AGE	SEX	OCCUPATIONS	COUNTRY TO WHICH THEY BELONG	COUNTRY THEY INTEND TO INHABIT	SHIPS/DATES OF ARRIVAL	
ROBINS (cont'd)							
Wm.	22	M	None	Great Britain	United States	Atlantic	28 May 1827
Wm.	35	M	Mariner	U. States	U. States	Adno	29 Apr 1825
ROBINSON, —, Mrs.	40	F	Lady	New Brunswick	Great Brittain	Nancy	9 Jun 1821
...ne	22	M	Baker	England	U.S.	Acasta	11 May 1827
...y	...9	M	Stone Mason	Ashert...h..., L...f...d		Aurora	8 Jun 1827
A.	35	M	Merchant	England	America	Meteor	21 Aug 1822
Agnes	28	F	Farmer	Scotland	Canada	Swift	16 Jul 1827
Alexander	24	M	Farmer	Ireland	United States	Asia	29 Jul 1829
Alexdr.	22	M	Accountant	Ireland	United States	Trident	17 May 1825
Alfred	30		Merchant	...	...	James Cropper	28 Jun 1824
Alfred	38	M	Merchant	London	America	Hannibal	4 Apr 1823
Alice	45	F		England	England	Gulnard	24 Mar 1825
Amela	12	F	Farmer	Scotland	Canada	Swift	16 Jul 1827
Ann	2	F	None	England	United States	Jubilee	1 Oct 1828
Ann	17	F	Labourer	Ireland	United States	Meteor	26 Jun 1827
Ann	34	F	Gentleman	America	U. States	Bayard	11 Jul 1825
Ann	78	F	Lady	Ireland	United States	Borneo	2 Oct 1827
Betsey	20	F	None	England	Troy	Indian Chief	19 Jun 1823
Betsy	5	F	Farmer	Scotland	Canada	Swift	16 Jul 1827
C.	15	F		England	U. States	Sarah Thornton	13 Sep 1828
C. S., Captane	28	M	Capt. British Navy	England	U. States	Sarah Thornton	13 Sep 1828
Catherine	19 6/12	F	Servant	Ireland	United States	Louisa	27 Nov 1826
Chas.	40	M	Collector of Demara	England	U. States	Sarah Thornton	13 Sep 1828
Chas. S.	29	M	Miller	G. Britain	U.S. America	Cincinnatus	31 Oct 1820
David	22	M	Weaver	Ireland	United States	Trident	16 May 1826
David	26		Farmer	Ireland	Great Britain	Robert Burns	14 Jun 1824
David	26 3/12	M	Weaver	Ireland	United States	Louisa	27 Nov 1826
E.	16	F		England	U. States	Sarah Thornton	13 Sep 1828
E.	21	M	Printer	Bristol	New York	Cosmo	25 Sep 1827
E.	29	M		Great Britain	Canada	Canada	20 Jun 1823
Eleanor	52 5/12	F	Wife	Ireland	United States	Louisa	27 Nov 1826
Eleanor, Jr.	12 9/12	F	Servant	Ireland	United States	Louisa	27 Nov 1826
Elen	9	F	Farmer	Scotland	Canada	Swift	16 Jul 1827
Eliza, Mrs.	25	F	Lady	Ireland	United States	Dublin Packet	22 Aug 1829
Elizabeth	15 9/12	F	Servant	Ireland	United States	Louisa	27 Nov 1826
Elizabeth	20	F		G. Britain	U. States	Mary & Harriot	8 Sep 1828
Elizth.	1	F	None	Great Britain	America	Remittance	24 Aug 1825
Ellen	12	F	Labourer	Ireland	United States	Meteor	26 Jun 1827
Ellen	20	F		England	America	Erin	7 Nov 1821
Ellen	45	M	Farmer	Great Britain	United States	Ann Maria	12 Jul 1821
Emma	20	F	None	Great Britain	America	Remittance	24 Aug 1825
Enoch	16	M	Smith	G. Britain	U. States	Mary Howland	22 Sep 1828
Francis	18	M	None	England	United States	London	21 May 1828
Gannen	12	F	Labourer	Ireland	United States	Hope	12 Jun 1828
Geo.	28	M	Merchant	Ireland	U. States	Nancy	25 Nov 1823
George	21	M	Mechanic	England	United States	Concordia	25 Aug 1827
George	24	M	Labourer	England	United States	Eliza Grant	6 Oct 1828
George	28	M	Merchant	St. Johns	Great Britain	St. Michael	5 Jan 1826
George	29	M	Merchant	Great Britain	United States	Zodiac	29 Oct 1822
George	30		Victler	Ireland	Great Britain	Franklin	22 Jun 1827
George J.	20	M	Gentleman	New Brunswick	Great Brittain	Nancy	9 Jun 1821
Henery	24	M	Curier	England	United States	Jubilee	4 Mar 1829
Henry	39	M	Mariner	U. States	U. States	Bayard	19 Mar 1824
Isabella	1	F	None	Great Britain	America	Remittance	24 Aug 1825
Israel	20	M	Cap maker	...	United States	Carolina Ann	11 Jun 1824
J.	35		Merchant	Virginia	U. States	Eliza Barker	9 Jun 1823
J. K.	19	M	Mechanic	U. States	France	Montano	15 Jan 1829
James	20	M	Weaver	England	U.N. States	Jane	7 Oct 1826
James	28	M	...	England		Chase	29 Dec 1820
James	34	M	...	...	United States	Camillus	10 Dec 1825
James	40	M	Farmer	G. Britain	U. States	Panthia	23 Apr 1824
James, Mrs.	38	F	Lady	England	American	Acasta	3 Apr 1826
Jane	27	F	Spinster	Ireland	U. States	Courier	17 Mar 1828
Jane	40	F	None	Great Britain	United States	Wyton	12 May 1821
Jeremiah	32	M	Bookkeeper	Great Brittain	U. States	William Byrnes	23 Jul 1824
Jno.	21	M	Farmer	England	U. States	Mentor	5 Jul 1825

NAMES OF PASSENGERS	AGE	SEX	OCCUPATIONS	COUNTRY TO WHICH THEY BELONG	COUNTRY THEY INTEND TO INHABIT	SHIPS/DATES OF ARRIVAL	
ROBINSON (cont'd)							
Jno.	22	M	Merchant	England	England	William Byrnes	17 Jul 1825
Jno.	25	M	...	Helgay	United States	Solon	21 Jun 1824
Jno.	25	M	Merchant	G. Britain	Great Britain	Thompson	26 Apr 1828
Jno.	27	M	Ship Master	England		Dionisio	30 Oct 1827
Jno.	31	M	Farmer			Amity	11 Sep 1820
John					U. States	Montgomery	18 Oct 1828
John	7	M	Farmer	Scotland	Canada	Swift	16 Jul 1827
John	18	M	Farmer	Ireland	Ireland	Trident	17 May 1825
John	19	M	Merchant	Gt. Britain	U. States	Importer	15 Sep 1821
John	19	M	Carpenter	Great Britain	United States	Saml. Wight	6 Sep 1827
John	20	M	Weaver	Ireland	U. States	Courier	17 Mar 1828
John	21	M	Laborer	Ireland	United States	Indian Chief	16 Aug 1822
John	22		Merchant	Beverley	Great Britain	William Thompson	13 May 1823
John	22	M	Weaver	Ireland	United States	Louisa	27 Nov 1826
John	24	M	Merchant	Scotland, Great Britain	America	Superb	11 Oct 1821
John	24	M	Calico Printer	England	United States	Amelia	20 Aug 1829
John	25	M	Mercht.	Great Britiann	United States	Nestor	13 Mar 1824
John	25	M	Mercht.	United States	United States	Manchester	17 Aug 1825
John	25	M	Merchant	Gt. Britan	Gt. Britan	Canada	8 Jun 1826
John	26	M	Joiner	England	United States	Jubilee	4 Mar 1829
John	26	M	Brush Maker	England	United States	Amelia	20 Aug 1829
John	27	M	Merchant	Great Britain	Unknown	William Thompson	1 May 1827
John	27	M	Mill Wright	Ireland	U. States	Courier	17 Mar 1828
John	28	M	Merchant	Britain	U.S. America	Cincinnatus	31 Oct 1820
John	28	M	shoemaker	Great Britain	United States	Superior	31 Mar 1828
John	28	M	Merchant	Great Britain	Great Britain	Pacific	11 Mar 1829
John	29	M	Merchant	United States		Montano	3 Jan 1823
John	30	M	Mariner	United States	United States	Aurora	5 Sep 1826
John	32	M	Butcher	England	Troy	Indian Chief	19 Jun 1823
John	36	M	Farmer	Scotland	United States	Cambria	8 Oct 1828
John	39	F	None	Great Britain	United States	Ann Maria	12 Jul 1821
John	41	M	Master Mariner	United States	United States	Oswego	12 Apr 1824
John	45	M	Farmer	Scotland	Canada	Swift	16 Jul 1827
John	55	M	Boot Maker	Great Britain		Casanda	5 Sep 1827
John B.	31	M	Chief Justice Canada	Great Britain	Canada	Canada	20 Jun 1823
John F.	23	M	...	U.S.		Pacific	29 Dec 1824
Jose M.	30	M		England	United States	Amelia	20 Aug 1829
Joseph	5/12	M	Farmer	Laguyra	Canada	Swift	16 Jul 1827
Joseph	3	M	None	England	United States	Jubilee	4 Mar 1829
Joseph, Mr.	20		Farmer	England		Hercules	19 Jun 1821
Joshua	21 7/12	M	Dyer	England	America U. States	La Grange	27 Sep 1826
July	20	F		St. Johns	St. Johns	St. Michael	26 Oct 1824
Lucy	18	F		St. Johns	St. Johns	St. Michael	26 Oct 1824
Lucy	25	F	None	Great Britain	America	Remittance	24 Aug 1825
Lydia	30	F				Amity	11 Sep 1820
M.	26	M	Civil Engineer	U.S.	U.S.	York	1 Dec 1827
M.	34	F		Great Britain	United States	Isaac Hicks	6 Dec 1827
M. Henry	26	M	Merchant	Baltimore	Boston	Gertrude	6 Mar 1827
Major	34	M	Gent.	Gt. Britain	Nova Scotia	Columbia	3 Apr 1826
Margaret	15	F	Child	Ireland	United States	Dublin Packet	23 May 1828
Margaret	40	F	Wife	Ireland	United States	Dublin Packet	23 May 1828
Maria	18	F	Lady	Ireland	United States	Dublin Packet	29 Jun 1825
Martha	6	F	Labourer	Ireland	United States	Hope	12 Jun 1828
Martha	21	F		Great Britain	United States	Diana	6 Jul 1829
Martha	30	F	None	England	America	Manhattan	20 Mar 1820
Martha	45	F	Matron	Ireland	U. States	Courier	17 Mar 1828
Mary	3/12	F				Amity	11 Sep 1820
Mary	2	F		Great Britain	United States	Diana	6 Jul 1829
Mary	12	F	Lady	Ireland	United States	Borneo	2 Oct 1827
Mary	16	F	Labourer	Ireland	United States	Hope	12 Jun 1828
Mary	28	F	None	England	United States	Jubilee	1 Oct 1828
Mary	30	F	None	Great Brittain	U. States	William Byrnes	23 Jul 1824
Mary	30 3/12	F	Servant	Ireland	United States	Louisa	27 Nov 1826
Mary Ann, Miss	15	F	Lady	England	American	Acasta	3 Apr 1826

NAMES OF PASSENGERS	AGE	SEX	OCCUPATIONS	COUNTRY TO WHICH THEY BELONG	COUNTRY THEY INTEND TO INHABIT	SHIPS/DATES OF ARRIVAL	
ROBINSON (cont'd)							
Mary J.	17	F	Lady	U. States	U. States	Charleston	10 May 1825
Maryann	8	F	Labourer	Ireland	United States	Meteor	26 Jun 1827
Matilda	10	F	Child	Ireland	United States	Borneo	2 Oct 1827
Nancy	5	F	None	Great Britain	America	Remittance	24 Aug 1825
Nancy	30	M	Labourer	Ireland	United States	Josephine	30 Apr 1828
Nancy	47	F	Labourer	Ireland	United States	Meteor	26 Jun 1827
Normand	23	M	Distiller	United States	United States	Prize	23 Sep 1822
Nunn	19	F	Spinster	Ireland	United States	Erin	25 Dec 1820
P.	42	M	Merchant	St. Maria	Curacoa	Eclipse	20 Jul 1825
Peter	21	M	Carpenter	Ireland	United States	Fabius	31 Jul 1829
Peter	30	M	Governor of Upper Canada	Gt. Britain	York up C.	Panthea	21 Jul 1825
Peter	30	M	Gentn.	Great Britian	United States	Columbia	21 Jan 1828
Robert	4	M	Child	Ireland	U. States	Courier	17 Mar 1828
Robert	10	M	Labourer	Ireland	United States	Meteor	26 Jun 1827
Robert	35	M	Bleacher	Ireland	U. States	Courier	17 Mar 1828
Robt.	21	M		England	United States	Exchange	18 Nov 1822
Robt.	26	M	Labourer	Ireland	United States	Fabius	31 Jul 1829
Ruth	2	F				Amity	11 Sep 1820
Saml.	8	M	None	Great Britain	United States	Ann Maria	12 Jul 1821
Samuel	21	M	Weaver	Belfast	United States	Minerva	30 Oct 1829
Samuel	25	M	Weaver	Ireland	New York	Atlantic	8 May 1828
Samuel	40	M	Merchant	G. Bt.	G. Bt.	Canada	13 Feb 1826
Sarah	7	F	None	England	United States	Jubilee	1 Oct 1828
Sarah	13	F		England	America	Two Marys	24 Sep 1827
Sarah	26	F	None	England	United States	Jubilee	4 Mar 1829
Susan	48	F	None	England	United States	Jubilee	4 Mar 1829
Susan Ann	27	F	Wife	Scotland	United States	Cambria	8 Oct 1828
Susana	4	F	None	Great Britain	America	Remittance	24 Aug 1825
T.	24	M	Merchant	Virginia	Virginia	Chasseur	17 Aug 1824
T.	25	M	Carman			Lady of the Lake	23 Aug 1828
Theresa	11	F	Child	Ireland	United States	Dublin Packet	23 May 1828
Thomas	40	M	Mariner	U. States	U. States	Glenthorn	12 Aug 1822
Thomas	45	M	Labourer	England	United States	Jubilee	1 Oct 1828
Thomas, Mr.	32	M	Merchant	Great Britain	Great Britain	Roman	10 May 1828
Thomas, Mrs.	32	F	None	Great Britain	Great Britain	Roman	10 May 1828
Thos.	21	M	Gentl.	England	U. States	Thomas Ritchie	2 Jul 1827
Thos.	48	M	Farmer	England	U. States	Thomas Ritchie	2 Jul 1827
Thos., Mr.	28	M	Merchant	Gt. Britain	Gt. Britain	Pacific	22 May 1826
W.	36	M	Mechani	Great Britten	U. States	Wm. & Henry	23 May 1826
W.	48	M	Cloth Cutter	Great Britain	United States	Saml. Wight	6 Sep 1827
W. D.	50	M	Merchant	U. States	U. States	Trimmer	10 Jul 1824
William	5	M	None	England	United States	Jubilee	4 Mar 1829
William	21	M	Laborer	England	New York	Indian Chief	19 Jun 1823
William	21	M	Cotton Printer	England	United States	Delta	24 Oct 1829
William	26	M	Engeneer	England	America	Mary Lord	26 Oct 1829
William	29	M	Curier	England	United States	Jubilee	4 Mar 1829
William	38	M	Farmer	Gt. Britain	U. States	Maria	22 May 1822
William [crossed out]	21	M	Mariner	Halifax	United States	Manchester	23 Jan 1826
William C.	22	M	Gentleman	U. States	U. States	Jupiter	31 Mar 1826
Wm.	14	M	Carpenter	Great Britain	United States	Saml. Wight	6 Sep 1827
Wm.	22	M	Farmer	Halifax	U. States	Perserverance	21 Jul 1827
Wm.	25	M	Farmer	Ireland	United States	Asia	29 Jul 1829
Wm.	26	M	Labourer	Great Britain	America	Remittance	24 Aug 1825
Wm.	28	M	Farmer	Great Britain	America	Remittance	24 Aug 1825
Wm.	35	M	Joiner	Great Britain	United States	Wyton	12 May 1821
Wm.	49	M	Labourer	Ireland	United States	Meteor	26 Jun 1827
Wm. R.	26	M	Labourer	Scotland	United States	Morning Star	25 Jun 1822
ROBLARTS, Joseph	32	M	Mariner	Boston	U. States	Douglass	7 Aug 1827
ROBRTS, Owen	23	M		Great B.	U. States	William Neilson	26 Jul 1828
ROBSON, A.	5	F		U. States	U. States	New England	4 Jun 1828
Agness	30	M	Shepherd	England	America	Sarah	18 Aug 1829
Ann	2	F	None	Great Britain	United States	Magnet	28 Jun 1821
Ann	4	F	None			Evergreen	28 Jul 1820
Ann	40	F	None			Evergreen	28 Jul 1820
Barbara	44	F		England	U. States	Favourite	2 Sep 1822
Dinah	36	F	None	Great Britain	United States	Magnet	28 Jun 1821

NAMES OF PASSENGERS	AGE	SEX	OCCUPATIONS	COUNTRY TO WHICH THEY BELONG	COUNTRY THEY INTEND TO INHABIT	SHIPS/DATES OF ARRIVAL	
ROBSON (cont'd)							
Domigo	1	F		U. States	U. States	New England	4 Jun 1828
Elizabeth	22	F	Gentlm.	England	America	James Cropper	13 Mar 1826
Fredk.	68	M	Cook	America	America	Cincinnatus	22 May 1826
Henry	35	M	Gentlm.	England	America	James Cropper	13 Mar 1826
James	32	M	Farmer	G. Britain	U. States	Evergreen	28 Jul 1820
James	46	M	Minister	Halifax	Halifax	Hope & Hester	27 Jun 1823
Jane	8	F	None			Evergreen	28 Jul 1820
Jno.	59	M	Farmer	England	U. States	Favourite	2 Sep 1822
John	29	M	Block Maker	Great Britain	United States	Magnet	28 Jun 1821
Mary	28	F		U. States	U. States	New England	4 Jun 1828
Sarah	26	F		Great Britain	Philadelphia	Zodiac	14 Jun 1822
Wm.	6	F	None			Evergreen	28 Jul 1820
Wm.	28	M	Farmer	Great Britain	Philadelphia	Zodiac	14 Jun 1822
ROBUORA, Jose	25	M	Marchant	Nassau	New Providence	Sea Flower	24 Jun 1824
ROBY, Joseph, Jr.	30	M	Merchant	United States	United States	Leeds	6 Feb 1826
Thos.	55	M	Merchant	U. States	U. States	London	23 Sep 1828
ROCA, Rafael	25	M	Mercht.	Spain		Union	6 Nov 1826
ROCEE, Rd.	22	M	Merchant	Spain	Spain	Circassian	13 Jun 1825
ROCH, Garrit	25	M	Farmer	Ireland	U. States	Howard	25 Jul 1823
Willam	20	M	Labourer	Halifax, N.S.	New York	Citizen	1 Nov 1828
ROCHA, John	27	M	Labourer	Ireland	U. States	Ann Maria	13 Dec 1824
ROCHE, Bridget	29	F	None	England	United States	Dalhouse Castle	6 Sep 1827
Ellen	17	F		Ireland	United States	Trio	2 Oct 1828
Ellen	19	F	Spinster	Ireland	United States	Diana	1 May 1826
Harper	31 2/12	M	Gentleman	England	America	Nimrod	1 Dec 1827
James	25	M	Farmer	Ireland	New Jersey	Lima	5 Aug 1829
John, Mr.	22	M	Merchant	England	United States	Dublin Packet	23 May 1828
Joseph	24	M	Gentleman	England	United States should they approve of it	Robert Edwards	20 Jan 1829
Nicholas	25		Sadler	Ireland	U.S.	Union	20 Aug 1827
Pat	17	M	Planter	Ireland	United States	William	20 Jul 1829
Patrick	28	M	Carpenter	Ireland	New York	Indian Chief	19 Jun 1823
Sarah	28 1/12	F	Wife	England	America	Nimrod	1 Dec 1827
William	21	M	Turner	Ireland	United States	Trio	31 Oct 1827
Wm.	30	M	Waiter	Ireland	U. States	Albion	11 May 1827
ROCHELL, Anna C.	19	F		Hannover	U. States	Constitution	15 Nov 1822
H.	32	M	Grocer	Hannover	U. States	Constitution	15 Nov 1822
ROCHENSPAGER,							
Catharina	30	F		France	America, U.N.S.	Great Britain	3 Aug 1829
George	6	M		France	America, U.N.S.	Great Britain	3 Aug 1829
George	29	M	Farmer	France	America, U.N.S.	Great Britain	3 Aug 1829
Henri	3	M		France	America, U.N.S.	Great Britain	3 Aug 1829
Magdalina	2	F		France	America, U.N.S.	Great Britain	3 Aug 1829
Magdalina	60	F		France	America, U.N.S.	Great Britain	3 Aug 1829
ROCHERE, Derah	50		None	France		Bayard	10 Sep 1827
ROCHESTER, Anna	3	F		England	U. States	Cincinnatus	24 May 1821
Elizabeth	Infant	F		England	U. States	Cincinnatus	24 May 1821
John	25	M	Farmer	England	U. States	Cincinnatus	24 May 1821
Joseph	2	M	Child	England	U. States	Cincinnatus	24 May 1821
Mary Ann	24	F		England	U. States	Cincinnatus	24 May 1821
ROCK, Bernard	19	M	Labourer	Ireland	U. States	Ganges	21 Jun 1827
Nicholas	24	M	Farmer			New York Packet	19 Aug 1820
ROCKER, C.	22	M	Labourer	Germany	U. States	Hudson	26 Jan 1825
ROCKMAN, Joseph	25	M	Talor	Switzerland	U. States	La Urania	3 Jul 1828
ROCKWELL, C. W.	24	M	Merchant	U. States	U. States	Amity	23 Sep 1823
ROCTANT, —, Mrs.	32	F		U. States	U. States	Ann Maria	10 Sep 1828
Manuel	2	M		U. States	U. States	Ann Maria	10 Sep 1828
RODDEN, Homer	27		Carpenter	Kilpatric	N. York	Peru	30 May 1828
Nail	22	M	Labourer	Ireland		Nancy	1 Sep 1823
RODDERAGO, Gregory		M	Merchant	Teneriff	Spain	Cabbasso Conta	23 Aug 1824
RODDICAN, Mary	22	F	Wife	Ireland	U. States	Hanford	29 Dec 1828
RODDIN, John	23	M	Farmer	Great Britain	United States	Grecian	24 Sep 1828
RODDY, Anne	18	F	Spinster	Ireland	United States	Wilson	6 Jun 1828
Brian	26	M	Labourer	Great Britain	United States	William Dawson	18 Jun 1827
John	22	M	Farmer	Ireland	United States	Lima	19 Jun 1824
Martha	23	F	None	Great Britain	United States	William Dawson	18 Jun 1827
Owen	22	M	Labourer	Great Britain	United States	William Dawson	18 Jun 1827

NAMES OF PASSENGERS	AGE	SEX	OCCUPATIONS	COUNTRY TO WHICH THEY BELONG	COUNTRY THEY INTEND TO INHABIT	SHIPS/DATES OF ARRIVAL	
RODDY (cont'd)							
Robert	14	M	None	Ireland	America	Carolina Ann	7 Aug 1826
Thos.	1	M	None	Great Britain	United States	William Dawson	18 Jun 1827
Will	2	M	None	Great Britain	United States	William Dawson	18 Jun 1827
RODE,							
Carolina Frederica	22	F	Wife	Hamburg	U. States of Amer	Europa	6 Oct 1828
Edward J. Hancock	6/12	M	Child	Hamburg	U. States of Amer	Europa	6 Oct 1828
Frederick Gustaf	30	M	Seaman	Hamburg	U. States of Amer	Europa	6 Oct 1828
RODEN, Nale	50	M	Pedler	Ireland	United States	St. Michael	21 Aug 1824
RODEREGO, C.	21	M	Merchant	Spain	Spain	Prince Edward	25 Feb 1822
RODERICK, Braham	55	M	Merchant	U. States	U. States	Hope	7 Jul 1823
Patrick	18					Trio	5 May 1828
RODERIGUEZ, Santiago	30	M	Doctor of Law	Columbia	U. States	Bunker Hill	12 Aug 1828
RODERIGUO, Ramon	50	M	Gentn.	Spain	Spain	Fabius	2 Oct 1826
RODERIQUES, C.	26	M	Merchant	Spain	Havana	John and Edward	6 Jan 1824
Jno.	40	M	Merchant	Cuba	U. States	Industry	10 Mar 1825
M.	43	M	Merchant	Spain	U. States	Farmer	16 Feb 1825
RODEWALD, Eliza	20	F	None	U.S. America	U.S. America	Columbia	31 Jul 1826
RODEY, Ellen	16	F	Servant	Ireland	United States	Josephine	30 Apr 1828
RODGER, Elizabeth	30	F				Harmony	15 Jul 1820
John	27	M	Sadler	Irereland	America	Carolina Ann	20 Jun 1825
Margt.	26	F		Scotland	United States	Belmont	30 Aug 1828
Michl.	25	M	Weaver	Gt. Britain		Dalhouse Castle	13 May 1828
RODGERS, Alexd.	20	M	Merchant	United States	New York	Intrepid	8 Aug 1822
Elizabeth	18	F	Spinster	Ireland	U.S. of America	Meteor	19 Mar 1828
George	35 6/12	M	Merchant	Ireland	United States	Wilson	28 Nov 1828
Isaac	30	M	Farmer	England	United States	Concordia	25 Aug 1827
Jame	17	M	Farm	Ireland	U. States	Meteor	19 Jul 1828
James	6 5/12		Labourer	Ireland	United States	Helen	5 Jul 1820
John	20		Surgeon	Ireland	Great Britain	Robert Burns	14 Jun 1824
John	25	M		Gt. Britain	United States	Columbia	7 Sep 1827
Letetia	27 3/12		Spinster	Ireland	United States	Helen	5 Jul 1820
Maria	20	F	Spinster	Ireland	United States	Robert Fulton	10 Aug 1827
Nathan	24	M	Weaver	Ireland	United States	Robert Fulton	10 Aug 1827
William	2 1/12		Child	Ireland	United States	Helen	5 Jul 1820
RODGES, Ross	22	F	Milinar	Ireland	U. States	Reindeer	15 Aug 1820
RODIE, Clemant	24	M	Merchant	Cuba	U. States	James Monroe	8 Sep 1824
RODIER, Chs. S., Mr.	28	M	Merchant	Canada	Montreal	Hannibal	28 Apr 1824
RODIN, Betty	17	F	Wife	Ireland	St. John, N.B.	Ann Maria	7 Aug 1826
Charles	24	M	Merchant	Montreal, Canada	Montreal, Canada	Ann Maria	26 Apr 1822
Michael	20	M	Servant	Ireland	St. John, N.B.	Ann Maria	7 Aug 1826
Michael	30	M	Servant	Ireland	St. John, N.B.	Ann Maria	7 Aug 1826
RODLEY, —, Mrs.	40	F		Gt. Britain	New York	Betsey	18 Apr 1822
Richd.	42 4/12	M	Mason	Gt. Britain	New York	Betsey	18 Apr 1822
RODMAN, Wm. W.	30	M	Merchant	Stonnington	U. States	George	12 Mar 1825
RODNEY, George	15	M		United States	United States	Romulus	13 Aug 1829
Mary Louisa	35	F	Milliner	U. States	U. States	Nassau	13 Aug 1825
RODREGAS, Joseph	28	M	Merchant	Spain	America	Wave	15 Aug 1821
RODREGERS, Falcon	74	M	Gentleman	Spain	Spain	Governor Von Schollen	7 Nov 1827
RODRIGEZ, M.	35	M	Merchant	Spain	U. States	Packet	24 Apr 1823
RODRIGUES, B.	25	M	Merchant	Spain	Spain	Colossus	21 Apr 1827
G.	25	M	Merchant	Havana	U. States	United States	7 Dec 1827
Joaque	25	M	Merchant	Andelusia	Cuba	Richmond Packet	23 Feb 1827
Martin	14	M	Boy	Teneriffe	Teneriffe	Wanderer	6 Oct 1827
Merchor	12	M		Havana	U. States	Greek	3 Aug 1825
Ramon	25	M	Merchant	Spainard		Alifair	11 Jul 1821
RODRIGUEZ, Bientu	39	M	Mercht.	Teneriffe		Marcella	15 Mar 1827
Diego	23	M	Merchant	Teneriffe	Teneriffe	Nile	18 Oct 1828
Fernando	12	M		Mexico	Spain	Virginia	9 Feb 1829
Gregorio	37	M	Merchant	Spain	Spain	Sciot	12 Mar 1828
Manl.	34	M	Merchant	Spain	Havana	Herald	21 Sep 1824
Manuel	30	M	Sailor	Portugal	Portugal	Jeune Antoinette	31 Oct 1829
RODRIQUE, W.	24	M	Merchant	France	U. States	Othello	3 Jun 1823
RODY, Jane	22	F		Gt. Britain	U. States	St. George	20 Sep 1828

NAMES OF PASSENGERS	AGE	SEX	OCCUPATIONS	COUNTRY TO WHICH THEY BELONG	COUNTRY THEY INTEND TO INHABIT	SHIPS/DATES OF ARRIVAL	
ROE, Anna	12		their Child [Thomas and Anna]	Great Britain	United States	Rufus King	4 Sep 1823
Anna	38		his Wife [Thomas]	Great Britain	United States	Rufus King	4 Sep 1823
Barnet	10		their Child [Thomas and Anna]	Great Britain	United States	Rufus King	4 Sep 1823
Charles	14		their Child [Thomas and Anna]	Great Britain	United States	Rufus King	4 Sep 1823
Edward	40	M	Servant	England	United States	Manhattan	22 Sep 1823
Gilbert	43	M	Merchant	New York	America	Don Quixotte	2 Jun 1828
James	27	M	Baker	G. Britain	U. States	Camillus	8 Sep 1828
Joseph	5		their Child [Thomas and Anna]	Great Britain	United States	Rufus King	4 Sep 1823
Joseph	28	M	Farmer	Ireland	United States	Dublin Packet	13 Oct 1828
Mark	3		their Child [Thomas and Anna]	Great Britain	United States	Rufus King	4 Sep 1823
Mary Ann	1		their Child [Thomas and Anna]	Great Britain	United States	Rufus King	4 Sep 1823
Thomas	42		Farmer	Great Britain	United States	Rufus King	4 Sep 1823
Willm.	7		their Child [Thomas and Anna]	Great Britain	United States	Rufus King	4 Sep 1823
ROEBACH, William	24	M	Clothmaker	Ireland		Eliza Grant	29 Aug 1829
ROEBEL, Margaret	3	F	Farmer	Switzerland	United States	Olympia	12 Aug 1828
Margaret	50	F	Farmer	Switzerland	United States	Olympia	12 Aug 1828
Michel	11	M	Farmer	Switzerland	United States	Olympia	12 Aug 1828
Michel	50	M	Farmer	Switzerland	United States	Olympia	12 Aug 1828
Philiphe	7	M	Farmer	Switzerland	United States	Olympia	12 Aug 1828
Salina	20	F	Farmer	Switzerland	United States	Olympia	12 Aug 1828
ROEBUCK, William	24	M	Clothier	G.B.	New York	Eliza Grant	29 Aug 1829
ROEHE, Vincenta	25	M	A...	Colombia	Colombia	Bunker Hill	10 Dec 1825
ROEN, Edwd.	23	M	Labourer	Ireland	United States	Wilson	27 Jun 1826
ROEY, Joseph	23	M	Gentleman	Spain	U. States	Madison	22 May 1822
ROFFERTY, Hitty	29	F	Matron	Ireland	U. States	Josephine	30 Aug 1828
Hugh	23	M	Weaver	Ireland	U. States	Josephine	30 Aug 1828
James	1	M	Child	Ireland	U. States	Josephine	30 Aug 1828
Margeret	6	F	Child	Ireland	U. States	Josephine	30 Aug 1828
Peter	36	M	Flax Dresser	Ireland	U. States	Josephine	30 Aug 1828
ROG, —	5	F		America	America	Paragon	22 Sep 1827
—	10	M		America	America	Paragon	22 Sep 1827
—	12	M		America	America	Paragon	22 Sep 1827
July	20	F		America	America	Paragon	22 Sep 1827
ROGAN, Clon	23		Sugar Baker	Hanovurine	United States	Hudson	5 Apr 1826
Owen	20	M	Labourer	Ireland		Robert Fulton	4 Jun 1828
ROGER, Saml.	26	M	Child	Ireland	United States	Marmion	17 Jun 1825
Thomas	24	M	Merchant	France	United States	Bayard	13 Nov 1823
William	25	M	weaver	Irereland	America	Carolina Ann	20 Jun 1825
ROGEREO, A.	45	M	Merchant	France	United States	Paris	10 Sep 1823
ROGERRETTE, Maria	36	F		America	Charleston	James Monroe	24 Feb 1826
ROGERS, —	27	F	None	United States	United States	Orris	12 Mar 1825
—, Miss	11	F		St. Croix	United States	Excel	26 Apr 1827
...	18	M	Farmer			Robert Burns	13 Jul 1820
...ah	55	F				Robert Burns	13 Jul 1820
...me	58	F	None	Gt. Britain	U. States	Panthia	13 Nov 1824
A. B.	30 2/12	M	Merchant	Porto Rico	Doubtful	Victor	3 Jul 1829
Abel	21	M	Blockmaker	Ireland	United States	Ann Maria	2 Nov 1827
Abell.	22	M	Seaman	United States		Orozimbo	8 Mar 1826
*distressed Seaman							
Agness	17	F	None	Ireland	United States	Colossus	26 Aug 1828
Alex.	21	M	Miller	Ireland	United States	Gem	16 Jun 1824
Alfred	19	M	Merchant	Hayti	Liverpool	Native	29 May 1824
Andrew	12	M	Farmer	Ireland	United States	Asia	29 Jul 1829
Ann	1	F	Child	Ireland	United States	Sarah G	19 Jun 1827
Ann	2	F	None	England	U. States	Roman	1 Dec 1828
Ann	2 1/2	F	Child of Thos. Rogers	Ireland	United States	Asia	29 Jul 1829
Ann	22	F	Spinster			Robert Burns	13 Jul 1820
Anne	3			Great Britan	United States	Newry	11 Jul 1827
Anne	45			Great Britan	United States	Newry	11 Jul 1827
B. R.	47	M	Merchant	New Orleans	New York	Superiour	11 Oct 1828
Benj.	23	M	Baker	England		Marchioness	13 May 1828

NAMES OF PASSENGERS	AGE	SEX	OCCUPATIONS	COUNTRY TO WHICH THEY BELONG	COUNTRY THEY INTEND TO INHABIT	SHIPS/DATES OF ARRIVAL	
ROGERS (cont'd)							
Benjn.	30	M	Mechanic	England		Suffolk	12 Jan 1826
Catherine	26			Great Britain		John Dickinson	5 Apr 1821
Chas.	21		Labourer	Great Britan	United States	Newry	11 Jul 1827
Chas.	26	M	Farmer			Robert Burns	13 Jul 1820
Chs. C.	32	M	Gentleman	U. States	U. States	Enterprize	20 Apr 1825
D. R.	21	M	Merchant	Portsmouth, N.H.	U. States	Atalanta	13 Oct 1821
Daniel	25	M	Labourer			Lady of the Lake	23 Aug 1828
Danl.	27			Great Britan	United States	Newry	11 Jul 1827
David	22	M	Weaver	Ireland	United States	Commerce	13 Jun 1828
David	50	M	Gentleman	England	England	John Wills	21 May 1824
David	51	M	Merchant	U. States, N. York	U. States	Jupiter	4 Mar 1828
Davis	25	M	Labour	Livpool	U.S.	Samuel Wright	12 Oct 1829
Edward	28	M	Labourer	England	U. States	Roman	1 Dec 1828
Elenor	27	F	Laborer	Ireland	United States	Weser	29 Jul 1823
Eliza	26	F		G. Britain	U. States	Cosmo	15 May 1827
Elizabeth	9/12	F	Laborer	Ireland	United States	Weser	29 Jul 1823
Elizabeth	28	F	Spinster	Ireland	United States	Sarah G	19 Jun 1827
Elizabeth	30	F	None	England	U. States	Roman	1 Dec 1828
Elizabeth	40	F		England	United States	Cambria	16 Aug 1827
Ellen	24	F		Gt. Britain		Dalhouse Castle	13 May 1828
Ellen	25			Great Britan	United States	Newry	11 Jul 1827
Emily S.	25	F	None	United States	United States	Cortes	11 Dec 1822
Emma	3	F		England	United States	Cambria	16 Aug 1827
Ester	15	F		England	United States	Cambria	16 Aug 1827
Fanny	9	F	Child of Thos. Rogers	Ireland	United States	Asia	29 Jul 1829
Francis	16	M		England	United States	Cosmo	26 Aug 1829
George		M		England	United States	Cambria	16 Aug 1827
H.	28		Merchant	Providence, R.I.	U. States	Brown	11 Jun 1827
Harriet M.	22	F		Gt. Britain	U. States	Caledonia	10 Sep 1828
Henry	25			Great Britan	United States	Newry	11 Jul 1827
Henry B.	25	M	Merchant	United States	U. States	Pacific	5 Sep 1827
Henry F.	35	M	Merchant	United States	United States	Cortes	11 Dec 1822
Hessy	30	F	Spinster	Ireland	United States	Fabius	31 Jul 1829
Hugh	31	M	Farmer	Glasgow, Scotland	U. States	New Orleans	24 Aug 1827
J. K.		M	Doctor	U. States	U. States	James	28 Jul 1823
James	1	M	None	England	U. States	Roman	1 Dec 1828
James	3	M	Child	Ireland	United States	Sarah G	19 Jun 1827
James	4	M	None	Gt. Britain	U. States	Frances Henrietta	18 Apr 1825
James	16	M	Farmer	Ireland	United States	Asia	29 Jul 1829
James	18	M	Farmer	Ireland	United States	Dublin Packet	9 Jul 1827
James, Mr.	21	M	Sugar Refnr.	England	U. States	Acasta	3 Apr 1826
Jane	7	F		England	United States	Cambria	16 Aug 1827
Jane	8	F	Laborer	Ireland	United States	Weser	29 Jul 1823
Jane	27	F	Laborer	Ireland	United States	Weser	29 Jul 1823
Jane	40	M	Gentleman	St. Cruz	U. States	Manchester Packet	29 Jan 1825
Janet	42	F		G. Britain	U. States	Camillus	8 Sep 1828
Janie	20	F	Spinster			Commerce	22 Jun 1825
Jas.	30			Great Britan	United States	Newry	11 Jul 1827
Jason	26	M	U.S. Army	U. States	U. States Army	Caledonia	20 Jan 1829
Jer.	14	M	Merchant	United States	United States	Three Brothers	22 Mar 1825
Jno.	24		Labourer			Harmony	15 Jul 1820
John	8	M		England	United States	Cosmo	26 Aug 1829
John	12	M	Laborer	Ireland	United States	Marmion	17 Jun 1825
John	13	M	None	Ireland	America	Manhattan	20 Mar 1820
John	15	M		Philadelphia	U. States	Howard	25 Jul 1823
John	23	M	Labourer	Drogheda	Drogheda	Howard Douglass	11 May 1827
John	28	M	Weaver	Gt. Britain	U. States	Frances Henrietta	18 Apr 1825
John	32	M	Seaman	U.S.	U.S.	New York	20 Jun 1825
John	34	M	Carpenter	England	United States	Cosmo	26 Aug 1829

NAMES OF PASSENGERS	AGE	SEX	OCCUPATIONS	COUNTRY TO WHICH THEY BELONG	COUNTRY THEY INTEND TO INHABIT	SHIPS/DATES OF ARRIVAL	
ROGERS (cont'd)							
John	34	M	Rider	England	United States	Cosmo	26 Aug 1829
John	45	M	Planter	U. States	U.S.	Bayard	10 Nov 1824
Lewis	30	M	Merchant	United States		Britannia	20 Jun 1827
Lewis	30 6/12	M	Merchant	U.S. Amer.	U.S. America	Edward Bonnaffe	20 Jun 1826
Lewis	32	M	Merchant	U.S.A.	U. States	Silas Richard	30 Jun 1828
Lewis	35	M	Merchant	U. States	U. States	Queen Mab	16 Mar 1825
Louis	33	M		America	America	Britannia	22 Jul 1829
Marg. [crossed out]	...	F	St...	England	U. States	Franklin	7 Jul 1828
Margaret	5	F		England	United States	Cambria	16 Aug 1827
Margaret	36	F	Clerk	Ireland	U. States	Howard	25 Jul 1823
Margaret	36	F	wife to Wm. Rogers	Ireland	United States	Asia	29 Jul 1829
Margt.	8	F	Spinster	Ireland	United States	Fabius	31 Jul 1829
Marie	30	F	None	U.S.	U.S.	Canada	2 Jun 1824
Marth	50	F	Spinster	Ireland	United States	Fabius	31 Jul 1829
Mary	5			Great Britan	United States	Newry	11 Jul 1827
Mary	21	F	Wife	Glasgow, Glasgow, Scotland	U. States	New Orleans	24 Aug 1827
Mary	22	F	Spinster	Ireland	United States	Fabius	31 Jul 1829
Mary	24	F	Spinster	Gt. Britain	U. States	Frances Henrietta	18 Apr 1825
Mary	25			Great Britan	United States	Newry	11 Jul 1827
Mary	27	F	Mechanic	England		Suffolk	12 Jan 1826
Mary	41	F		England	United States	Cosmo	26 Aug 1829
Mary	60	F		Belfast	United States	Minerva	30 Oct 1829
Mary Ann	3	F				Suffolk	12 Jan 1826
Mary Ann	4	F		England	United States	Cosmo	26 Aug 1829
Matilda	20	F	None	England	United States	Hamilton	13 Nov 1827
Nancy	24	F	his Wife [Thomas]	Ireland	United States	Asia	29 Jul 1829
Oliver G.	37	M	Machinist	U.S.	United States	Josephine	24 Jul 1826
Owen	4			Great Britan	United States	Newry	11 Jul 1827
P. R. D.	21	M	Clerk	United States	United States	Bramin	20 May 1826
R., Miss	24	F		St. Croix	U. States	South Carolina Packet	4 Sep 1822
R., Mrs.	56	F		St. Croix	U. States	South Carolina Packet	4 Sep 1822
Richard	22	M	Merchant	Denmark	New York	South Carolina Packet	22 Jul 1820
Robert	1	M	None	Gt. Britain	U. States	Frances Henrietta	18 Apr 1825
Robert	1 1/2	M	Child of Thos. Rogers	Ireland	United States	Asia	29 Jul 1829
Robert	6	M		England	United States	Cosmo	26 Aug 1829
Robert	20 1/12	M	Distiler	Ireland	New York	Decatur	12 Dec 1820
Robt.	4	M	Laborer	Scotland	United States	Weser	29 Jul 1823
Robt.	35	M	Laborer	Ireland	United States	Weser	29 Jul 1823
S.	33	M	Mariner	United States	United States	Orris	12 Mar 1825
Sam	55	M		England	United States	Curler	3 Mar 1828
Saml.	23	M	Labourer	Ireland	United States	Gem	16 Jun 1824
Samuel	18	M	Farmer	Ireland	United States	Asia	29 Jul 1829
Sarah	6	F	Laborer	Ireland	United States	Weser	29 Jul 1823
Sarah	7	F	None	England	United States	Hamilton	13 Nov 1827
Susan	12	F	None	U.S.	U.S.	Canada	2 Jun 1824
Susan M.	16	F		U. States	U. States	Caledonia	10 Sep 1828
Thomas	1			Great Britan	United States	Newry	11 Jul 1827
Thomas	24	M	Clerk	Great Britain	U. States	Great Britain	18 Mar 1828
Thomas	26	M	Farmer	Ireland	United States	Asia	29 Jul 1829
Thomas	30		Black Smith	Great Britan	United States	Newry	11 Jul 1827
Thos.	56	M	Mariner	U. States	U. States	Hesper	6 Oct 1825
Thos. M.	40 4/12	M	Supercargo	United States	United States	America	18 Jan 1820
Timothy	20	M	Mariner	Middleton	U. States	Washington	22 Apr 1825
Tobothey	50	M	Mariner	U. States	U. States	Mary Ann	9 Jan 1827
Willa	26	M	Smith	Engd.	United States	Cosmo	21 Aug 1828
William	1 1/2	M		England	United States	Cambria	16 Aug 1827
William	5	M	Child of Thos. Rogers	Ireland	United States	Asia	29 Jul 1829
William	9	M		England	United States	Cambria	16 Aug 1827

NAMES OF PASSENGERS	AGE	SEX	OCCUPATIONS	COUNTRY TO WHICH THEY BELONG	COUNTRY THEY INTEND TO INHABIT	SHIPS/DATES OF ARRIVAL	
ROGERS (cont'd)							
William	10	M		England	United States	Cosmo	26 Aug 1829
William	25	M	Labourer	Ireland	United States	Lord Wellington	28 May 1827
William	30	M	Painter	England	United States	Hamilton	13 Nov 1827
William	40	M	his Wife	Ireland	United States	Asia	29 Jul 1829
Wm.	24	M	Gentleman	Ireland	America	Liverpool	31 Aug 1827
Wm.	46	M	Clerk	Ireland	U. States	Howard	25 Jul 1823
Wm.	57	M	Farmer			Robert Burns	13 Jul 1820
ROGERSON, —, Mrs.	22	F	Wife	England	U. States	Corinthian	20 Apr 1825
Thomas	30	M	Reed Maker	Great Britain	United States	Corinthian	2 Sep 1824
Thos.	6	M	None	England	U. States	Corinthian	20 Apr 1825
Wm.	4	M	None	England	U. States	Corinthian	20 Apr 1825
Wm.	21		None	Great Britain	United States	Roman	10 Sep 1827
ROGET, Aaron	19	M	Merchant	France	United States	Seine	7 Dec 1821
Moses	54	M	Merchant	France	United States	Seine	7 Dec 1821
ROGG, Benj.	24	M	Labourer	G. Britain	U. States	St. George	7 Jun 1828
ROGGERS, Mary	24			C...selsh.., Eng./ London	Susquehannah P	Venus	12 Apr 1821
William	30	M	Weaver	C. Anthrem	Philedelphia	Nile	18 Aug 1829
ROGIER, F.	40	M	Merchant	France	U. States	Bayard	9 Nov 1825
Warner	52	M	Planter	St. Thomas	St. Thomas	Jane	28 May 1827
ROGNAUD DE LA CHEINEYE, A. L.	36	M	Consul at Aux Cayes	France	France	Topaz	27 May 1828
ROHD, Wm.	20	M	Glass Cutter	G. Britain	U. States	Mary & Harriot	8 Sep 1828
ROHIN, Gh.	20	M	Turner	Gt. Brittan		L'Esperance	6 Sep 1828
ROHM, Johannes	26	M	Weaver	Germany	America	Falcon	28 Aug 1828
ROHMER, Peter	22	M	Farmer	France	France	Sully	15 Jul 1829
ROHNKE, Christian F.	28	M	Seilmakar	Germany	U.S.A.	Robert Wilson	2 Dec 1828
ROHR, Catharine	42	F		France	America, U.N.S.	Great Britain	3 Aug 1829
Marguerita	19	F		France	America, U.N.S.	Great Britain	3 Aug 1829
Peter	13	M		France	America, U.N.S.	Great Britain	3 Aug 1829
Peter	44	M	Labourer	France	America, U.N.S.	Great Britain	3 Aug 1829
ROHROR, Ana	13	F		Switzerland	United States	Elizabeth	27 Jul 1824
Ana	40	F		Switzerland	United States	Elizabeth	27 Jul 1824
Catharina	5	F		Switzerland	United States	Elizabeth	27 Jul 1824
Elizabeth	1/12	F		Switzerland	United States	Elizabeth	27 Jul 1824
Jacob	8	M		Switzerland	United States	Elizabeth	27 Jul 1824
Jacob	36	M	Weaver	Switzerland	United States	Elizabeth	27 Jul 1824
ROIBOL, Barbara	10	F		G. Britain		Caravan	8 Sep 1828
Caspar	8	M		G. Britain		Caravan	8 Sep 1828
Caspar	37	M	Farmer	G. Britain		Caravan	8 Sep 1828
Catrina	2	M		G. Britain		Caravan	8 Sep 1828
Donnide	37	F		G. Britain		Caravan	8 Sep 1828
Eliza	11	F		G. Britain		Caravan	8 Sep 1828
Jacob	5	M		G. Britain		Caravan	8 Sep 1828
John	7	M		G. Britain		Caravan	8 Sep 1828
Joseph	9	M		G. Britain		Caravan	8 Sep 1828
Margaret	0 2/12	M		G. Britain		Caravan	8 Sep 1828
ROIBUN, Margarete	21	F	Seamstress	Switzerland	U. States	Isaac Hicks	22 Aug 1829
ROINE, Eliza	30	F	Lady	England	United States	Siroc	31 Oct 1829
ROINERS, Nedro	15	M	Army	America	America	Medina	4 Sep 1828
ROIRDON, John	31	M	Mariner	United States	United States	Edward	21 Apr 1821
ROLA, W.	19	M	Mechanic	N. Orleans	U. States	Columbia	24 Mar 1823
ROLAND, Geo.	24	M	Miner	G. Brittain	U. States	Pacific	23 Jan 1826
ROLANDO, Carlos	24	M	Merchant	Spain	U. States	Anne	20 Jun 1828
ROLERS, ...z...	...	M	Labourer	Ireland	Unt. St. America	Wilson	21 May 1827
ROLEY, Biddy	9/12	F		England	United States	William Byrnes	15 Aug 1826
Rose	20	F	Spinster	Ireland	United States	Ann Maria	8 Jun 1824
ROLFE, John	24	M	Stationer	Great Britain	United States	Hannibal	12 Oct 1829
Robert	21	M	Gold Beater	Great Britain	United States	Hannibal	12 Oct 1829
ROLIN, Amelia	30	F	Lady	France	France	Tampico	13 May 1828
Frances	32	M	Surgeon	France	France	Tampico	13 May 1828
John, Esqr.	47	M	Merchant	Sweden	U. States	Leader	13 Sep 1826
ROLINS, William	19	M	Farmer	England	United States	Jubilee	13 Jul 1829
ROLL, F.	40	M	Mariner	U. States	U. States	John London	20 Jan 1823
ROLLA, Robert	21	M	Merchant	Great Britain	The Island of St. Thomas	Phoebe Ann	27 Dec 1825
ROLLE, William	26	M	Farmer	Derby	Derby	Howard Douglass	11 May 1827

NAMES OF PASSENGERS	AGE	SEX	OCCUPATIONS	COUNTRY TO WHICH THEY BELONG	COUNTRY THEY INTEND TO INHABIT	SHIPS/DATES OF ARRIVAL	
ROLLERAN, ...t	26 3/12	M	Farmer	Switzerland	U. States	France	26 Jun 1828
ROLLESTON, James	33	M	Farmer	Ireland	U. States	William & John	10 Jul 1824
Mary	30	F	Spinster	Ireland	U. States	William & John	10 Jul 1824
ROLLIN, F. H.	33	F		U. States	U. States	Caledonia	10 Sep 1828
Joseph	23	M	Farmer	France	U. States	Bayard	16 May 1827
L.	22	M	Merchant	U. States	U. States	Edward Quesnel	15 May 1826
Lewis	24	M	Merchant	U. States	United States	Burdett	30 Apr 1828
ROLLINS, Eben.	45	M	Merchant	U. States	U. States	Caledonia	10 Sep 1828
Elisha	27	M	Planter	United States	United States	Ductile	30 Nov 1822
Wm.	23	M	Mariner	Baltimore, U.S.	U. States	Fortuna	11 Oct 1827
ROLLINSON, John	28	M	Tailor	England	America	Two Marys	24 Sep 1827
ROLLOPE, —, Miss	15	F		Halifax	some to return & the others to Canada	Albert	14 May 1822
ROLLSTIN, Isabella Jane	3			Ireland	United States	Antioch	3 Dec 1827
John	31		Labourer	Ireland	United States	Antioch	3 Dec 1827
Sarah	2			Ireland	United States	Antioch	3 Dec 1827
ROLLY, Jacob	24	M	Weaver	U. States	U. States	Wm. Penn	18 Sep 1827
ROLPH, Charles	17	M	Farmer	Great Briton	New York	Brighton	12 Jun 1826
George	24	M	Farmer	Great Briton	New York	Brighton	12 Jun 1826
George	30	M	Barrister	England	Canada	Cincinnatus	16 Apr 1824
George	40	M	Farmer	Great Briton	New York	Brighton	12 Jun 1826
Harriet	22	F	Farmer	Great Briton	New York	Brighton	12 Jun 1826
John	28	M	Barrister at law	England	British America	Maine	16 Jul 1821
Lidia	40	F	Farmer	Great Briton	New York	Brighton	12 Jun 1826
R., Reverend	30	M	Clergiman	England	Canada	Robert Edwards	20 Jan 1829
Thomas	17	M	Student	England	British America	Maine	16 Jul 1821
William	5	M	Farmer	Great Briton	New York	Brighton	12 Jun 1826
ROLSTON, Alexr.	23	M	Labourer	Ireland	United States	William & George	14 May 1828
ROMAN, M.	35	M	Farmer	Switzerland	U. States	Romulus	24 Sep 1828
ROMANA, ...y	24 6/12	M	Farmer	Switzerland	U. States	France	26 Jun 1828
ROMANS, Wm.	25	M	Farmer	England	United States	Panthia	7 Feb 1822
ROMANSIO, Christopher	40	M	Mariner	Russia	United States	Nestor	20 Nov 1821
Mary	20	F	None	London	United States	Nestor	20 Nov 1821
ROMBART, G.	39	M	Taylor	France	U.S.	Francois I	8 Aug 1829
ROME, Jane	6	F	Farmer			Manhattan	25 Dec 1820
John	5	M	Farmer			Manhattan	25 Dec 1820
Mary Ann	30	F	Farmer			Manhattan	25 Dec 1820
ROMENELA, Jean	18	M	Farmer	Switzerland	United States	Olympia	12 Aug 1828
ROMEO, Raphael	34	M	Merchant	Spain	United States	Juliana	25 Jan 1820
ROMER, C. F.	45	M	Lawyer	Curacoa	U. States	Hippomenes	30 Aug 1821
ROMERO, John	9	M	Mercht.	Spain	Spain	Juliana	2 Sep 1826
Luis	40	M	Mercht.	Spain	Spain	Juliana	2 Sep 1826
ROMLEZ, George	25	M	Baker	Great Brittain	U. States	Florenzo	20 Mar 1827
ROMMAGE, C.	26	M	Merchant	U. States	U. States	Prudence	11 Jun 1825
RON, Henry	28	M	Labourer	Ireland	United States	Catharine	22 Jul 1825
RON..., Joel	30	M	Weaver	Switzerland	United States	Elbe	2 Aug 1822
Joseph	27	M	Farmer	Switzerland	United States	Elbe	2 Aug 1822
RONALDSON, John	20	M	Farmer	Scotland	United States	Culloden	17 May 1828
RONALEE, John J.	24	M	Farmer	France	U. States	Bayard	16 May 1827
RONAULT, Amoury	14			France	U. States	Magnet	24 Jun 1822
Hypolette	7			France	U. States	Magnet	24 Jun 1822
Joseph	58		Musician	France	U. States	Magnet	24 Jun 1822
Ulysse	4			France	U. States	Magnet	24 Jun 1822
RONEY, T.	18	M	Merchant	St. Domingo	U. States	John London	26 Mar 1822
RONIE, Patk.	18	M	Labourer	Ireland, Great Britain	U.S. of America	Dublin	21 Feb 1826
RONOLDS, Geo. W.	27	M	Gentleman	Gt. Britain	United States	Crisis	6 Apr 1825
RONOLDSON, Ann	25	F		Great Britain	United States	Samuel Wright	12 Oct 1829
RONTSTANT, George	24	M	Labourer	Ireland	United States	Hope	12 Jun 1828
ROOD, Patrick	20	M	Labourer	Ireland	United States	Dalhouse Castle	8 May 1827
ROODHOUSE, Miler	48		Farmer	England	United States	Mary	15 Jul 1822
ROODY, James	30	M	Schoolmaster	Ireland	United States	Andes	2 Oct 1828
ROOFE, Dianah	3	F				Acosta	28 Jul 1823
Hanah	15	F				Acosta	28 Jul 1823
James	7	M				Acosta	28 Jul 1823
Jane	9	F				Acosta	28 Jul 1823
Phillis	11	F				Acosta	28 Jul 1823

NAMES OF PASSENGERS	AGE	SEX	OCCUPATIONS	COUNTRY TO WHICH THEY BELONG	COUNTRY THEY INTEND TO INHABIT	SHIPS/DATES OF ARRIVAL	
ROOFE (cont'd)							
Sarah	31	F				Acosta	28 Jul 1823
Thomas	35	M	Farmer	England	United States	Acosta	28 Jul 1823
ROOK, Abby	13	F		Germany	U. States	Isabella	10 Aug 1829
Abby	35	F		Germany	U. States	Isabella	10 Aug 1829
August	7	M		Germany	U. States	Isabella	10 Aug 1829
Conrad	9	M		Germany	U. States	Isabella	10 Aug 1829
Elizabeth	5	F		Germany	U. States	Isabella	10 Aug 1829
Jacob	11	M		Germany	U. States	Isabella	10 Aug 1829
Jean	36	M	Weaver	Germany	U. States	Isabella	10 Aug 1829
Mary	20	F		Great Britian	United States	Andes	19 Aug 1829
William	25	M	Joiner	Great Britian	United States	Andes	19 Aug 1829
ROOKE, Tim	22	M	Farmer	Ireland	America	Plutarch	18 Jul 1826
ROOLPH, Mary	36	F	...	Ireland	New York	Wilson	10 Apr 1823
ROOM, Lydia, her servant [Caroline Coupland]	20	F		...	United States	Dawn	15 Oct 1827
ROOME, Ns.	15	M	Clerk	U. States	U. States	Hannah	19 Jul 1822
William	23	M	Farmer	Great Britian	United States	George Clinton	13 Apr 1826
ROOMEY, Bridget	20	F	Mercht.	Ireland	U. States	Albion	9 Aug 1826
ROOMY, Dolly	11 6/12	F	Spinster	Ireland	United States	Wilson	6 Jun 1828
ROONEY, —, Mrs.	30		Wife of Wm.	Ireland	United States	Mexico	1 Jun 1821
Alex.	34	M	Laborer	Ireland	U. States of America	Dale	14 Mar 1828
Andrew	20	M	Labourer	Ireland	Unt. St. America	Wilson	21 May 1827
Ann	4		Child [of Wm.]	Ireland	United States	Mexico	1 Jun 1821
Ann	9	F	None	England	U. States	Hercules	6 Jul 1827
Ann	20	F		Ireland	Baltimore	Curler	7 Jul 1827
Ann	28	F	...	Ireland	United States	Trident	18 Jul 1827
Ann	36	F	None	England	U. States	Hercules	6 Jul 1827
Bernard	13	M	None	England	U. States	Hercules	6 Jul 1827
Bernard	20	M	Labourer	Ireland	Baltimore	Curler	7 Jul 1827
Bernard	23	M	Labourer	Ireland	United States	Jubilee	13 Jul 1829
Bryan	28 9/12	M	Tailor	Great Briton	uncertain	Mount Vernon	29 Aug 1828
Cath.	30	F		Ireland	U. States of Amer	Dale	14 Mar 1828
Catharine	7	F	None	England	U. States	Hercules	6 Jul 1827
Catharine	19	F	None	England	U. States	Hercules	6 Jul 1827
Charles	27	M	Measurer	St. Johns	United States	Antioch	21 Sep 1827
Hugh	1/2	M	None	England	U. States	Hercules	6 Jul 1827
Hugh	18	M	Labourer	Ireland	America	Weser	26 Jun 1821
James	1		Child [of Wm.]	Ireland	United States	Mexico	1 Jun 1821
James	32	M	...	Ireland	United States	Trident	18 Jul 1827
Jane	6		Child [of Wm.]	Ireland	United States	Mexico	1 Jun 1821
John	2	M	None	England	U. States	Hercules	6 Jul 1827
John	22		Shoemaker			William	17 Aug 1820
John	36	M	Bricklayer	England	U. States	Hercules	6 Jul 1827
Margaret	28	F		Ireland	Baltimore	Curler	7 Jul 1827
Pat	24	M	Weaver	Ireland	United States	Commerce	13 Jun 1828
Pat.	15	M	Labourer	Ireland	America	Weser	26 Jun 1821
Patrick	23	M	Labourer	Ireland	United States	Silas Richards	3 Apr 1826
Patrick	26	M	Weaver	Ireland	Baltimore	Curler	7 Jul 1827
Peter	20		Cooper	Great Britan	United States	Newry	11 Jul 1827
Peter	23 6/12	M	Labourer	Ireland	United States	Robert Edwards	3 Oct 1829
William	8		Child [of Wm.]	Ireland	United States	Mexico	1 Jun 1821
William	45		Weaver	Ireland	United States	Mexico	1 Jun 1821
Wm., Mr.	21	M	Weaver	Scotland	U. States	Majestic	27 Jul 1829
ROONY, Peter	18	M	Labourer	Ireland	United States	Dalhouse Castle	8 May 1827
ROOP, Argel	19	M	Barber	Island Cuba	U.S.	Burdett	7 Dec 1827
ROORK, Patk.	27	M	Farmers and Mechanics	America	America	Constitution	1 Oct 1825
ROOS, Wm. H.	36	M	Painter	Sweden	U. States	Echo	13 Nov 1824
ROOFE, Anna	2	F	Farmer	Alsace in the Department of Upper and lower Rhine	United States	Carolina Augusta	16 May 1828
Catherinna	4	F	Farmer	Alsace in the Department of Upper and lower Rhine	United States	Carolina Augusta	16 May 1828

NAMES OF PASSENGERS	AGE	SEX	OCCUPATIONS	COUNTRY TO WHICH THEY BELONG	COUNTRY THEY INTEND TO INHABIT	SHIPS/DATES OF ARRIVAL	
ROOFE (cont'd)							
George	18	M	Farmer	Alsace in the Department of Upper and lower Rhine	United States	Carolina Augusta	16 May 1828
George	50	M	Farmer	Alsace in the Department of Upper and lower Rhine	United States	Carolina Augusta	16 May 1828
Jacob	8	M	Farmer	Alsace in the Department of Upper and lower Rhine	United States	Carolina Augusta	16 May 1828
Margaretta	5	F	Farmer	Alsace in the Department of Upper and lower Rhine	United States	Carolina Augusta	16 May 1828
Maria	10	F	Farmer	Alsace in the Department of Upper and lower Rhine	United States	Carolina Augusta	16 May 1828
Maria	44	F	Farmer	Alsace in the Department of Upper and lower Rhine	United States	Carolina Augusta	16 May 1828
ROOSEVELT, Nicholas, Mr.	29	M	...	U.S.	U.S.	Cadmus	11 Jul 1827
ROOT, ...ick	10	M		France	America, U.N.S.	Great Britain	3 Aug 1829
Elizabeth	34	F		France	America, U.N.S.	Great Britain	3 Aug 1829
George M.	12	M		France	America, U.N.S.	Great Britain	3 Aug 1829
Jaques	35	M	Blacksmith	France	America, U.N.S.	Great Britain	3 Aug 1829
Magdalina	5	F		France	America, U.N.S.	Great Britain	3 Aug 1829
Tim..	25	M	Merchant	U. States	U. States	Elisa	1 May 1821
ROOUSE, John	22	M	Cabinet Maker	Gt. Britain	U. States	Sarah G.	14 Apr 1828
ROPALY, Geo.	51	M	None	United States	United States	Cortes	11 Dec 1822
ROPELYE, Paul	27	M	Merch.	N. York	N. York	Wm. Thompson	13 Sep 1823
ROPER, Ann	33	F	None	Derbeyshire	U. States	Manhattan	21 May 1821
John	8	M	None	Derbeyshire	U. States	Manhattan	21 May 1821
John	39	M	Blacksmith	Derbeyshire	U. States	Manhattan	21 May 1821
Marry	6	F	None	Derbeyshire	U. States	Manhattan	21 May 1821
ROPES, Henry	32	M	Merchant	America	America	Orbit	31 Dec 1823
ROPINE, A. C.	36	M	Merchant	Switzerland	U. States	Six Brothers	21 Nov 1822
ROPP, F.	25	M	Clerk		U. States	Patriot	13 Nov 1823
ROPPER, Hannah	10	F	None	Derbeyshire	U. States	Manhattan	21 May 1821
ROQUES, Adele	4 6/12	M	Child	U. States	Louisiana	Sully	30 Oct 1827
Adeline	24	F	Lady	U. States	Louisiana	Sully	30 Oct 1827
Hypolite	7 3/12	M	Child	U. States	Louisiana	Sully	30 Oct 1827
John	40	M	Gentleman	U. States	Louisiana	Sully	30 Oct 1827
Leonce	1 4/12	M	Child	U. States	Louisiana	Sully	30 Oct 1827
ROR, Michael	22	M	Farmer	Alsace in the Department of Upper and lower Rhine	United States	Carolina Augusta	16 May 1828
RORCH, John Danl.	48	M	Merchant	France	U.S.	Edward Quesnel	19 Oct 1829
RORDRIGUES, Manuel	29	M	Merchant	Spain	Spain	Montano	2 Sep 1828
RORKE, John	29	M	Labor	England		Exchange	11 Jul 1823
RORRY, James	22	M	Labourer	Ireland	United States	Josephine	30 Apr 1828
ROSA, Fran...	50	M	Taylor	Spain	United States	Georgetown Packet	15 Nov 1823
ROSALA, Hosa	38	M	Meriner	Spain	Spain	Florida	30 Jun 1826
ROSAN, S.	4	M		Europe	United States	Aspasia	5 Sep 1827
ROSCAN, Jenny	28	M		Europe	United States	Aspasia	5 Sep 1827
Peter	30	M	Carver	Europe	United States	Aspasia	5 Sep 1827
Solomon	1	M		Europe	United States	Aspasia	5 Sep 1827
ROSE, —, Revd.	25	M	Revd.	France	U. States	Othello	31 Aug 1824
Bell	44	F	Farmer	Scotland	Canada	Swift	16 Jul 1827
F.	27	F	Svt.	France	United States	Cortes	5 Aug 1822
George	30	M	Surgeon	U. States	U. States	Louisa Matilda	25 May 1825

NAMES OF PASSENGERS	AGE	SEX	OCCUPATIONS	COUNTRY TO WHICH THEY BELONG	COUNTRY THEY INTEND TO INHABIT	SHIPS/DATES OF ARRIVAL	
ROSE (cont'd)							
George	34 3/12	M	Gentleman	England	U. States	Florida	13 Jan 1827
Isaac	34	M	Farmer	Great Britain	United States	Colossus	1 Nov 1826
James	25	M	Farmer	Great Britain	United States	William Dawson	18 Jun 1827
James	41	M		England	England	Tontin	13 Jan 1825
John	21	M	Labourer	Ireland		Robert Fulton	4 Jun 1828
John	24		Surgeon	England	United States	Cambria	19 Oct 1829
John	25	M	Farmer	Scotland	New York	Susquehanna	9 Jan 1824
M.	28	M	Sailor	America	U. States	Hiram	17 Jun 1826
Patrick	26	M	Labourer	Ireland	United States	Lord Wellington	28 May 1827
Robert	23	M	Butcher	England	United States	Cosmo	26 Aug 1829
S.	32	M	shoemaker	U. States	United States	Crisis	6 Apr 1825
Susan	24	F	Matron	Ireland	United States	Robert Fulton	10 Aug 1827
William	4	M	Child	Ireland	United States	Robert Fulton	10 Aug 1827
Wm.	27	M	Merchant	England	U. States	Amity	23 Sep 1823
ROSEMARY, Elisabeth	25	F	Segar Maker	Island of Cuba	United States	Betsey	28 Oct 1825
Francis	30	M	Segar Maker	Island of Cuba	United States	Betsey	28 Oct 1825
John	20	M	Segar Maker	Island of Cuba	United States	Betsey	28 Oct 1825
Magel	38	M	Segar Maker	Island of Cuba	United States	Betsey	28 Oct 1825
ROSENBERG, Frs.	29	M	Sugar Baker	Germany	United States	Robert Edwards	1 Jun 1826
ROSENBOON, Joh. Hein.	19	M	Sugar Baker	Germany	U. States	Constitution	21 Jun 1824
ROSENBURN, M.	33	M	Farmer	Hamburg	U. States	Martha	4 Sep 1828
ROSENDALE, Jane	28	F	Lady	St. John	U. States	St. Michaels	25 Apr 1825
ROSENORN, —, Mrs.		F		St. Croix	St. Croix	Ludwig	10 Aug 1825
Julius	3	M		St. Croix	St. Croix	Ludwig	10 Aug 1825
Matilda	1	F		St. Croix	St. Croix	Ludwig	10 Aug 1825
P., Counsellor	42	M		St. Croix	St. Croix	Ludwig	10 Aug 1825
ROSER, Andrew	20	M	None	Germany	U. States	Sully	24 Oct 1828
Catharine	6	F	None	Germany	U. States	Sully	24 Oct 1828
Christina	4	F	None	Germany	U. States	Sully	24 Oct 1828
James	13	M	None	United States	Albany	Albion	11 Jun 1821
Maria	38	F	None	Germany	U. States	Sully	24 Oct 1828
Richard	46	M	B...	United States	Albany	Albion	11 Jun 1821
Simon	35	M	Farmer	Germany	U. States	Sully	24 Oct 1828
ROSEVELT, H.	21			New York	U. States	Brown	11 Jun 1827
*Died on the passage							
ROSIBIN, —, Mrs.	20	F	Lady	Guadaloupe	U. States	Turner	8 Jun 1824
ROSICH, Julia	2	F	None	Great Britian	U. States	Dalhouse Castle	28 Feb 1826
Mary	25	F	None	Great Britian	U. States	Dalhouse Castle	28 Feb 1826
ROSIER, Jacob	28	M	Carpenter	Germany	U. States	Exchange	28 Aug 1828
Job	25	M	Farmer	Great Britain	United States	Spartan	25 Jul 1821
L...a	25	F		Great Britain	United States	Spartan	25 Jul 1821
ROSINBURGH, Henry	23		Sugar Baker	Germany		Pomona	28 May 1822
ROSKELL, Ns.	22	M	Merchant	England	U. States	Seneca	14 May 1821
ROSNER, Charles	35	M	Carpenter	Italy	U. States	Aspasia	23 Nov 1825
ROSS, —, Mr.						Martha	4 Sep 1828
*sent out by the Consul							
—, Mr.	21	M		England	U. States	Perseverance	18 Nov 1824
...y	25	F	Spinster	Ireland	United States	Henry Kneeland	7 Jun 1828
Alex	27	M		U. States	U. States	Jay	18 Apr 1823
Alexander	9	M		Ireland	United States	Pallas	28 Oct 1828
Alexander	33	M	Merchant	Halifax	Halifax	Hope & Esther	27 Jul 1829
Alexr.	26	M	Merchant	U. States	U. States	Albert	1 Apr 1822
Alexr.	27	M	Merchant	Halifax	U. States	Hope Return	20 Mar 1824
Alexr.	45	M	Farmer	Ireland	United States	Pallas	28 Oct 1828
Archibd.	30	M	Labourer	Great Brittain	United States	Active	12 Sep 1828
Arthur	25	M	Gentleman	England	Canada	Brighton	24 Aug 1827
Bridget	45	F	Spinster	Ireland	United States	Henry Kneeland	7 Jun 1828
Catharine	10	F	Family [of Jacob]	France	America	La Grange	7 Aug 1828
Catherine	20	F	on a visit to N. York	C. Down	N. York	Nile	18 Aug 1829
Cathr.	17	F		Ireland	United States	Pallas	28 Oct 1828
Charles	2	M	Family [of Jacob]	France	America	La Grange	7 Aug 1828
Coleswick	32	M	...	Scotland	America	Nimrod	9 Jul 1827
David	16	M	...	Scotland	America	Nimrod	9 Jul 1827
David	80	M	Farmer	Ireland	United States	Herald	29 Oct 1825
Eleanor	9	F	W...	Jamaica	U. States	Sanford William	26 Jul 1824
Elizh.	18	F	Spinster	Ireland	United States	Trident	16 May 1826
G. M.	28	M	Merchant	England	Canada	Corinthian	20 Apr 1825

NAMES OF PASSENGERS	AGE	SEX	OCCUPATIONS	COUNTRY TO WHICH THEY BELONG	COUNTRY THEY INTEND TO INHABIT	SHIPS/DATES OF ARRIVAL	
ROSS (cont'd)							
George	8	M	Family [of Jacob]	France	America	La Grange	7 Aug 1828
George	20	M	Weaver	Ireland	United States	Fabius	4 Jun 1828
Hugh	23		Farmer	Ireland		Westmoreland	1 Aug 1826
Isabella	17	F	Spinster	Scotland	America	Concord	4 Jun 1821
Jacob	19	M	Family [of Jacob]	France	America	La Grange	7 Aug 1828
Jacob	50	M	Farmer	France	America	La Grange	7 Aug 1828
James	...0	M	Labourer	New Brunswick [?]	U. States	St. Michael	5 May 1827
James	17	M	None	Great Britain	United States	Magnet	28 Jun 1821
James	25	M	Labourer	Ireland	U.S. of America	Meteor	19 Mar 1828
James	36	M	Labourer	Great Britain	U. States	Lord Wellington	17 Mar 1823
Jane	15	F		Ireland	United States	Pallas	28 Oct 1828
Jane	45	F		Great Britain	United States	Ann	22 Dec 1821
Janet	35 1/12	F	...	Scotland	America	Nimrod	9 Jul 1827
Jas.	15		Boy	Ireland		Westmoreland	1 Aug 1826
Jas.	40		Farmer	Ireland		Westmoreland	1 Aug 1826
Jas.	46		Farmer	Ireland		Westmoreland	1 Aug 1826
Jno.	40	M	Farmer	England	U. States	Orazimbo	7 Jan 1821
Jno.	42	M	Merchant	Bahama	Bahama	Lively	23 Jul 1825
John	10	M		Ireland	United States	Pallas	28 Oct 1828
John	16	M	Family [of Jacob]	France	America	La Grange	7 Aug 1828
John	22		Farmer	Ireland		Westmoreland	1 Aug 1826
John	23	M	Labourer	Ireland	New York	Atlantic	8 May 1828
John	24		Farmer	Ireland		Westmoreland	1 Aug 1826
John	25	M	Labourer	Ireland	United States	Commerce	13 Jun 1828
John	25	M	Farmer	Great Britian	United States	Andes	19 Aug 1829
John	26	M	Farmer	Scotland	United States	Hope	5 Dec 1827
John	30		Plumber	England	United States	Corinthian	7 Jul 1829
John	32	M	Merchant	United States	U. States	Baltic	29 Jul 1829
Joseph	20	M	Laborer	Ireland	United States	Mary	1 Jul 1829
Joseph	24	M	Farmer	Ireland	United States	Herald	29 Oct 1825
Joseph	24	M	Cleark	Ireland	New York	Eliza Grant	29 Aug 1829
Margaret	12	F	Family [of Jacob]	France	America	La Grange	7 Aug 1828
Margaret	40	F	Family [of Jacob]	France	America	La Grange	7 Aug 1828
Maria	4	F	Family [of Jacob]	France	America	La Grange	7 Aug 1828
Mary	38	F		Ireland	United States	Pallas	28 Oct 1828
Michael	14	M	Family [of Jacob]	France	America	La Grange	7 Aug 1828
Rob.	23	M	Merchant	England	U. States	Sanford William	16 Feb 1822
Robert	22	M	Cotton Printer	Great Britain		Dalmannock	24 Ocg 1826
Robert	35		Mason	Rosshein, Scotland	Great Britain	Iris	15 Jun 1822
Saml.	30	M	Capmaker	Germany	United States	Andes	2 Oct 1828
Syl...	3 8/12	F	...	Scotland	America	Nimrod	9 Jul 1827
Thomas	12	M		Ireland	United States	Pallas	28 Oct 1828
William	1	M		Ireland	United States	Pallas	28 Oct 1828
William	24	M	Weaver	Ireland	United States	Josephine	30 Apr 1828
Wm.	16	M	Sailor	England	U. States	Hiram	17 Jun 1826
Wm.	47	M	Carpenter	England	U. States	Hudson	8 Oct 1827
ROSSALENE, E.	25	M	Merchant	Havana	U. States	Greek	17 May 1825
ROSSEAU, F.	45	M	Merchant	Bordeaux	Cuba	Pacific	15 Apr 1824
ROSSITER, Jas.	35	M	Farmer	U. States	U. States	Martha	20 Jun 1825
RÖSSLE, Fritz	24	M	...	Wirtemburg	United States	Wade	29 Aug 1825
ROSSLERE, Barbara	18	F		Germany	Ohio	James Noble	27 Aug 1827
ROSTAING, S.	30	M	Labourer	G. Britann		Manchester	29 Aug 1828
ROSTER, James	29	M	Founder	U. States	U. States	John Jay	26 Jan 1829
ROSTERN, Thos.	33	M	Farmer	Gt. Brittian	Gt. Brittian	Manchester	21 Apr 1827
ROSTON, Alice	8	F		England	Philadelphia	Curler	7 Jul 1827
Betty	6	F		England	Philadelphia	Curler	7 Jul 1827
Richmond	28	F		England	Philadelphia	Curler	7 Jul 1827
William	30	M	Weaver	England	Philadelphia	Curler	7 Jul 1827
ROTCH, Wm. B.	25	M	Manufacture	Wales	U. States	York	4 Apr 1826
ROTH, C. E.	24	M	Miner	Germany	Virginia	Orion	24 Mar 1825
Catherine	31	F	Weaver	France	U.S.	Helen	3 May 1828
Jacob	9	M	Weaver	France	U.S.	Helen	3 May 1828
Jean	18	M	Weaver	France	U.S.	Helen	3 May 1828
Jean	48	M	Weaver	France	U.S.	Helen	3 May 1828
M.	40	M	Secretary of the French Legation	France	United States	St. Martin	10 Feb 1820

NAMES OF PASSENGERS	AGE	SEX	OCCUPATIONS	COUNTRY TO WHICH THEY BELONG	COUNTRY THEY INTEND TO INHABIT	SHIPS/DATES OF ARRIVAL	
ROTH (cont'd)							
Margaret	20	F	Weaver	France	U.S.	Helen	3 May 1828
Nicholas	49	M	Gentleman	Ireland	United States	Dublin Packet	29 Jun 1825
Peter	32	M	Barber			New York Packet	19 Aug 1820
ROTHCHILD, S.	28	M	Merchant	Germany	Philada.	Orion	30 Mar 1825
ROTHERY, Wm., Mr.	27	M	Mercht.	England	England	Manchester	6 Apr 1826
ROTHFORD, Alphius	28	M		Scotland	Canada	Braganza	16 Apr 1825
Chs.	35	M	Farmer	Scotland	Canada	Braganza	16 Apr 1825
ROTHMER, Wm.	22	M	Labourer	England	United States	Essex	23 May 1828
ROTHSCHILD, Fritz Sugesmunt	26	M	Merchant	Germany	U. States	Constitution	21 Jun 1824
ROTTER, George	34	M	Merchant	Scotland	United States	Nestor	20 Nov 1821
Margret	36	F	Farmer	Germany	United States	Virginia	31 May 1828
Materlane	9	F	Farmer	Germany	United States	Virginia	31 May 1828
Nicholas	40	M	Farmer	Germany	United States	Virginia	31 May 1828
ROTTIER, John	26	M	Merchant	Holland	U. States	Marmion	7 Jun 1824
ROTZINGER, Joseph	22	M	Butcher	Switzerland	U. States	Hewes	30 Oct 1829
ROUBOTTOM, Eli	24 2/12	M	Cottonspinner	Ireland	United States	London	6 Feb 1829
ROUCH, Bridget	32	F	None	England	U. States	Hercules	6 Jul 1827
John	38	M	Cooper	England	U. States	Hercules	6 Jul 1827
ROUD, John	...	M	Laborer	Irland	United States	Nancy	28 Oct 1822
ROUE, Henry	18	M	Labourer	Prussia		Constitution	20 Jun 1828
ROUGAL, Berre	6	F	Farmer	France		Pallas	14 Jun 1828
Catharin	9	F	Farmer	France		Pallas	14 Jun 1828
Mariah	28	F	Farmer	France		Pallas	14 Jun 1828
Perre F.	5	M	Farmer	France		Pallas	14 Jun 1828
Susan	2	F	Farmer	France		Pallas	14 Jun 1828
ROUGEMILHORT, Catharen	33	F	Farm	Ireland		Quatre Freres	29 Jul 1828
Henri	1	M	Farm	Ireland		Quatre Freres	29 Jul 1828
Joseph	2	M	Farm	Ireland		Quatre Freres	29 Jul 1828
Joseph	38	M	Farm	Ireland		Quatre Freres	29 Jul 1828
ROUGON, Michal	46		Marriner	New Orleans	New Orleans	Elba	9 May 1827
ROUK, Catharine	11	F	None	Great Britain		Moro Castle	6 Jul 1827
Ellen	40	F	None	Great Britain		Moro Castle	6 Jul 1827
James	50	M	Labourer	Great Britain		Moro Castle	6 Jul 1827
John	13	M	None	Great Britain		Moro Castle	6 Jul 1827
ROUKE, Ann	23	F	Labourer	Great Britian	United States	Princess Charlotte	6 Sep 1828
Patrick	30	M	Feather dealer	Gt. Britn.	United States	Union	9 Jan 1824
ROULAND, Wm.	28	M		Great Britain	United States	Active	25 Mar 1828
ROULSTAN, John	25	M	Farmer	Ireland	United States	Robert Fulton	10 Aug 1827
ROULSTON, Geo.	22	M	Mason	England	United States	Amelia	20 Aug 1829
John	46	M	Merchant	United States	United States	Diamond	13 Nov 1823
Robert	16	M	Farmer	Ropha	...	Gleaner	24 May 1823
ROUMAGE, C.	40	M	Merchant	France	United States	Marmion	13 Jun 1823
ROUMAGER, C.	40	M	Merchant	U. States	U. States	Zipporah	13 Jun 1828
ROUNALDS, Thomas	25	M	None	Ireland	United States	St. George	25 Aug 1829
ROUND, Joseph	20	M	Mason	England	New York	Exertion	3 Dec 1828
ROUNDHYAN, Peter	25	M		Ireland	U. States	Balaena	29 Apr 1825
ROUNDLEY, Stephen	32	M	Merchant	Salem	Salem, U. States	Apollo	23 Oct 1826
ROUNEY, John	10 5/12	M		Ireland	U.S. of America	Douglass	6 Jul 1829
ROURKE, Christopher	30	M	Farmer	Ireland	America	Farmer	4 Aug 1825
Edwd.	1	M	Farmer	Ireland	America	Farmer	4 Aug 1825
Elinor	2...	F	Farmer	Ireland	America	Farmer	4 Aug 1825
James	17	M	Carpenter	Ireland	United States	Jubilee	12 May 1828
John	26	M		England	United States	Danube	22 Aug 1825
John	27	M	Farmer	Ireland	United States	Samuel Robertson	9 Apr 1828
Joseph	37	M	Carpenter	Ireland	United States	Jubilee	12 May 1828
Maria, his wife [Peter]	30	F	Housekeeper	Ireland	United States	Andes	2 Oct 1828
Mary	3	F	Farmer	Ireland	America	Farmer	4 Aug 1825
Mary, their child [Peter & Maria]	2	F	Child	Ireland	United States	Andes	2 Oct 1828
Owen	24	M	Gentleman	Ireland	United States	Margarett Scott	22 Aug 1827
Peter	30	M	Sawyer	Ireland	United States	Andes	2 Oct 1828
Thomas	22	M	Labourer	England	U. States	Comet	23 Aug 1828
ROURT, Jane	22	F		G. Britain	Canada	Nancy	12 Aug 1820

NAMES OF PASSENGERS	AGE	SEX	OCCUPATIONS	COUNTRY TO WHICH THEY BELONG	COUNTRY THEY INTEND TO INHABIT	SHIPS/DATES OF ARRIVAL	
ROURT (cont'd)							
Thos.	25	M	Farmer	G. Britain	Canada	Nancy	12 Aug 1820
ROUSEAU, H.	24	M	Mercht.	Frenchman	France	Sisters	7 Jul 1826
ROUSSEAU, —, child		F		France	France	Bayard	30 Oct 1820
—, Mrs.	26	F		United States	United States	Don Quixote	18 Aug 1824
Adele	7	F		United States	United States	Don Quixote	18 Aug 1824
Edmund	40 6/12	M	Merchant	France	Traveler	Cadmus	12 Dec 1823
Edré	10			New York	New York	Desdemona	12 Jun 1826
Julia, Mrs.	30	F		France	France	Bayard	30 Oct 1820
ROUSSEL,							
Fredk. Wm., Mr.	37 6/12	M	Blacksmith	Swiss	New York	Cadmus	27 Aug 1822
ROUSSELIENE, F.	35		Clerk	France	U. States	Elizabeth	9 Jul 1825
ROUSSETT, M.	50	M	Farmer	England	U. States of Amer	Dale	14 Mar 1824
ROUT, Christine	15	F		France	United States	Le Voltaire	19 Jul 1828
Margret F.	43	F		France	United States	Le Voltaire	19 Jul 1828
Margt.	13	F		France	United States	Le Voltaire	19 Jul 1828
Philip	19	M		France	United States	Le Voltaire	19 Jul 1828
Philip	43	M	Tailor	France	United States	Le Voltaire	19 Jul 1828
ROUTELEDGE, Richard	29		Weaver	England	United States	Thomas Dickason	5 Jun 1827
ROUTH, A. M. J.	28	F		Great Brittain	Canada	Canada	5 Feb 1827
Henry	5	M		Great Brittain	Canada	Canada	5 Feb 1827
James	24	M	Labourer	Ireland	United States	Borneo	14 Aug 1827
Julius	4	M		Great Brittain	Canada	Canada	5 Feb 1827
L.	6	M		Great Brittain	Canada	Canada	5 Feb 1827
Randolph	7	M		Great Brittain	Canada	Canada	5 Feb 1827
Randolph J.	40	M	Commissary General	Great Brittain	Canada	Canada	5 Feb 1827
ROUVERT, Edmund	55	M	Merchant	France	U. States	Malabar	3 Apr 1823
ROUX, C. F. L.	35	M	Mercht.	Switzerland	America	Lima	11 Dec 1823
ROVALL, Ernest	19	M	Farmer or Mechanic	France	U.S.	Edward Quesnel	31 Jul 1827
ROVARS, Thomas	30	M	Mariner	U. States	U. States	Rose in Bloom	9 Apr 1827
ROVER, Henry	21	M	Gentleman	England	U. States	La Fayette	7 Apr 1825
ROVERE, August	25	M	Merchant	Italy	U. States	Circassian	3 Jun 1826
ROVERTS, Walter	19	M	Grocer			Plato	31 Oct 1829
ROW, Ann	4	F	None	England	United States	St. George	25 Aug 1829
Elizabeth	13	F	None	England	United States	St. George	25 Aug 1829
Jane	2	F	None	England	United States	St. George	25 Aug 1829
John	30	M	None	Ireland	U. States	Criterion	23 May 1826
John	40	M	Joiner	England	United States	St. George	25 Aug 1829
John, Jr.	19	M		England	United States	St. George	25 Aug 1829
Joseph Ring	42	M	Merchant	Great Britain	United States	Orbit	23 Oct 1826
Margaret	15	F	None	England	United States	St. George	25 Aug 1829
Margaret	45	F	None	England	United States	St. George	25 Aug 1829
Robert	10	M	None	England	United States	St. George	25 Aug 1829
William	17	M	Joiner	England	United States	St. George	25 Aug 1829
ROWAN, Ann	18	F	Labourer	Ireland	United States	Essex	23 May 1828
Danes	21	M	Labourer	Great Britain	United States	India	5 Sep 1827
Jas. N.	18	M	Navy	U. States	U. States	Helen	20 Jan 1825
Jno.	20	M	Labourer	Ireland	United States	Essex	23 May 1828
John	1 6/12	M		England	U.S.A.	Hudson	21 Aug 1829
Martin	5/12	M		England	U.S.A.	Hudson	21 Aug 1829
Martin	27	M	Turner	Ireland	U.S.A.	Hudson	21 Aug 1829
Mary	27	F		England	U.S.A.	Hudson	21 Aug 1829
Nancy	40	F	Labourer	Ireland	United States	Essex	23 May 1828
Stephen N.	41	M	Theologian	U.S.	U.S.	George Canning	26 Aug 1829
William	20	M	Sadler	Ireland	U. States	Josephine	7 May 1827
William	28	M	Framer	Ireland	U. States	Globe	14 Jul 1821
ROWARCH, John	27	M	Ca... Dealer	...aeland	United States	Baltic	21 Apr 1827
ROWBOTTOM,							
Catharine, Mrs.	20			Great Britan	U. States	Columbia	7 May 1828
Henry	30		Gentn.	Great Britan	U. States	Columbia	7 May 1828
Margaret	50	F	None	England	United States	Dalhouse Castle	6 Sep 1827
Robert	29	M	Farmer	Great Britian	United States	Andes	19 Aug 1829
Thos.	50	M	Sezer	England	United States	Dalhouse Castle	6 Sep 1827
ROWE, Catharine	4	F		Ireland	United States	Thompson	12 Sep 1827
Elisah	30	M	Painter	England	United States	Trident	30 Sep 1826

NAMES OF PASSENGERS	AGE	SEX	OCCUPATIONS	COUNTRY TO WHICH THEY BELONG	COUNTRY THEY INTEND TO INHABIT	SHIPS/DATES OF ARRIVAL	
ROWE (cont'd)							
Eliza	26	F		Ireland	United States	Thompson	12 Sep 1827
John	21	M		Ireland	United States	Thompson	12 Sep 1827
John	29		Tailor	England	United States	Helen	17 Dec 1827
John O.	40	M	Gentleman	United States	United States	Meteor	27 Sep 1826
Lewis, Mr.	33	M	Mercht.	America	United States	Andrew Jackson	9 Jul 1822
Mary	6	F		Ireland	United States	Thompson	12 Sep 1827
Robert W.	28		Clerk	England	United States	Rufus King	4 Sep 1823
Thomas	35	M	Merchant	Great Briton	U. States	Leontine	10 Jul 1826
William	2	M		Ireland	United States	Thompson	12 Sep 1827
Wm.	28	M		Ireland	United States	Thompson	12 Sep 1827
ROWELL, Jno.	27		Taylor	England	England	Gulnard	24 Mar 1825
ROWEN, Catherine	3	F	Child	Great Britain	United States	Wilson	26 Feb 1824
Elizth.	29	F	Matron	Great Britain	United States	Wilson	26 Feb 1824
Mary	7	F	Child	Great Britain	United States	Wilson	26 Feb 1824
ROWETT, Ann	26	F	Farmer	Great Britain	U. States America	Ann Maria	29 Nov 1821
Caroline	8/12	F	Farmer	Great Britain	U. States America	Ann Maria	29 Nov 1821
Harriet	2	F	Farmer	Great Britain	U. States America	Ann Maria	29 Nov 1821
John	44	M	Farmer	Great Britain	U. States America	Ann Maria	29 Nov 1821
Stephen	4	M	Farmer	Great Britain	U. States America	Ann Maria	29 Nov 1821
ROWLAN, James	21	M	Labourer	Ireland	United States	Aurelia	7 Jun 1826
Mary	21	F	None	Ireland	United States	Aurelia	7 Jun 1826
ROWLAND, Catherine	1	F				Henri IV	17 May 1828
G. G.	40	M	Merchant	America	America	Britannia	5 Nov 1828
George	25	M	Farmer			Henri IV	17 May 1828
Hellen	1	F	Hatter	Ireland	United States	Margarett Scott	22 Aug 1827
Henry	27	M	Farmer	Great Brittan	U.S.	Emulous	29 Jun 1827
Maria		F	None	Great Britain	United States	Hamilton	21 Nov 1826
Mary	26	F				Eliza Grant	6 Oct 1828
Mary Ann	10	F	None	Great Britain	United States	Hamilton	21 Nov 1826
Peter	25	M	Tailor	Isle of Man	United States	Aurelia	7 Jun 1826
Priscilla	34	F	None	Great Britain	United States	Hamilton	21 Nov 1826
R.	34	M	Planter	G. Britain	U. States	Hanford	10 Jun 1828
Richard	3	M				Eliza Grant	6 Oct 1828
Sarah	1	F				Eliza Grant	6 Oct 1828
Sarh.	1	F	Hatter	Ireland	United States	Margarett Scott	22 Aug 1827
Susan	25	F				Henri IV	17 May 1828
Thos.	26	M	Hatter	Ireland	United States	Margarett Scott	22 Aug 1827
W.	30	M				Eliza Grant	6 Oct 1828
Wm.	5	M				Eliza Grant	6 Oct 1828
Wm.	20	M	Mariner	England	U. States	Atlantic	26 Aug 1820
Wm.	25	M	Carpenter	England	U. States	William	17 Jun 1823
Wm.	38	M	Merchant	Staten Island	U. States	James Lawrence	3 Sep 1821
ROWLAW, Michael	20	M	Labourer	Ireland, Great Britain	U.S. of America	Dublin	21 Feb 1826
ROWLET, Elinor	40	F	Servant	Ireland	United States	Wanderer	1 Aug 1828
ROWLEY, Jone	7	F	in Factory	England	U. States	Franklin	7 Jul 1828
Sarah	26	F	in Factory	England	U. States	Franklin	7 Jul 1828
ROWLING, John	30	M	Miner	England	England	Eliza	31 Jul 1826
Thomas	25	M	Baker	Great Britain	United States	Mary Howland	19 Jul 1827
ROWLINGS, C.	32	M	Mariner	U. States	U. States	Jasper	22 Sep 1827
ROWLINS, Elizabeth	38	F		Staten Island	U. States	James Lawrence	3 Sep 1821
ROWN, R.	27	M	Tailor	U. States	U. States	Telegraph	14 Jun 1828
ROWNSLY, Joshua	22	M	Clothier	York Shire	England	Helicon	3 Aug 1826
Peter	23	M	Clothier	Great Britain	United States	Frances Henrietta	17 Sep 1827
ROY, Coll.	74	M	Farmer	Scotland	America	Mentor	21 Sep 1824
Jas.	20	M	Merchant	Scotland	U. States	Czar	29 Aug 1829
ROYCROSS, Thomas	16	M	None	Great Britain	United States	Eliza Barker	3 Jul 1826
ROYLE, James	18	M		Ireland	United States	St. George	25 Aug 1829
Janes	18	M	None	Ireland	United States	St. George	25 Aug 1829
Joseph	30	M	...	Great Brittain	On a tour of pleasure	Albion	11 Jun 1821
Mary	40	F	None	Ireland	United States	St. George	25 Aug 1829
Rose	8	F	None	Ireland	United States	St. George	25 Aug 1829
ROYSTON, Thos.	32		Merchant	Harwood, England	Great Britain	Franklin	22 Jun 1827
ROZELLI, Giovanni	48	M		Roma	Philadelphia	Falcon	10 Sep 1823
ROZZAOLIA, Liugi R.		M	Gentn.	Naples	New York, U.S.	Romp	12 Sep 1823

NAMES OF PASSENGERS	AGE	SEX	OCCUPATIONS	COUNTRY TO WHICH THEY BELONG	COUNTRY THEY INTEND TO INHABIT	SHIPS/DATES OF ARRIVAL	
RUALA, J. M.	23	M	Merchant	Matanzas	U. States	New England	23 Apr 1827
RUAN, John	18	M	Servant	St. Croix	U. States	Chase	9 Aug 1827
RUBEN, Hy.	21	M	Binder	Rotterdam	United States	New Packet	7 Aug 1826
RUBENY, Thomas	38	M	Wool Spinner	Great Britain	U.S. of America	Gratitude	3 Oct 1829
RUBES, Franswa	40	M	Merchant	France	France	Great Britain	16 Mar 1829
RUBIGO, D.	45	M	Merchant	Cuba	U. States	Ductile	12 May 1826
RUBIO, Jose	25	M	Musician	Portugal	Boston, Mass.	Rubicon	22 May 1826
RUBURY, Wm.	18	M			United States	William	5 Oct 1822
RUBY, Barbara	10	F	Family [of Mical]	France	America	La Grange	7 Aug 1828
Barbara	36	F	Family [of Mical]	France	America	La Grange	7 Aug 1828
Clarissa, & 2 small children	23	F		United States	United States	Mazzinghi	31 Mar 1826
Effa	40	F		France	America, U.N.S.	Great Britain	3 Aug 1829
George	32	M	T...	Brattain		L'Esperance	6 Sep 1828
Matin	38	M	Farmer	France	America, U.N.S.	Great Britain	3 Aug 1829
Michael	4	M	Family [of Mical]	France	America	La Grange	7 Aug 1828
Michal	40	M	Farmer	France	America	La Grange	7 Aug 1828
Salmon	6	M	Family [of Mical]	France	America	La Grange	7 Aug 1828
RUCH, Ann Maria	11	F	Farmer	France	United States	American	27 Aug 1827
Casper	1	M	Farmer	France	United States	American	27 Aug 1827
Catherine	8	F	Agriculturist	France	U.S.	Helen	3 May 1828
Catherine	38	M	Farmer	France	United States	American	27 Aug 1827
Catherine	47	F	Agriculturist	France	U.S.	Helen	3 May 1828
Christin	42		Farmer	France	United States	Parachute	14 May 1828
George M.	42	M	Agriculturist	France	U.S.	Helen	3 May 1828
Jacque	11	M	Agriculturist	France	U.S.	Helen	3 May 1828
James	12	M	Boy	St. Croix	U. States	Excel	26 Apr 1827
John	6	M	Farmer	France	United States	American	27 Aug 1827
Joseph	17	M	Farmer	France	United States	American	27 Aug 1827
Margaret	18	F	Agriculturist	France	U.S.	Helen	3 May 1828
Margaret	41			France	United States	Parachute	14 May 1828
Marian	4	F	Farmer	France	United States	American	27 Aug 1827
Michel	20	M	Agriculturist	France	U.S.	Helen	3 May 1828
Philip	22		Mechanic	France	United States	Parachute	14 May 1828
Sebastian	15	M	Farmer	France	United States	American	27 Aug 1827
Sebastian	46	M	Farmer	France	United States	American	27 Aug 1827
RUCHTI, Abram	23	M	Gardner	Beeren	U.S. America	Superior	18 Jun 1825
RUCKE, Paul	20		Farmer	Great Britain	United States	Comet	9 Aug 1822
RUCKEL, Agnes	6	F	Farmer	Great Britain	United States	Weser	9 May 1822
Catharine	28	F	Farmer	Great Britain	United States	Weser	9 May 1822
George	8	M	Farmer	Great Britain	United States	Weser	9 May 1822
Henry	30	M	Farmer	Great Britain	United States	Weser	9 May 1822
John	10	M	Farmer	Great Britain	United States	Weser	9 May 1822
Margt.	4	F	Farmer	Great Britain	United States	Weser	9 May 1822
Thomas	1	M	Farmer	Great Britain	United States	Weser	9 May 1822
Thos.	6	M	Farmer	Great Britain	United States	Weser	9 May 1822
RUCKER, Henry	33	M	Merchant	Hanseatic		Silas Richards	20 Jun 1826
RUCKETTS, James	28	M	Gentleman			Cassack	25 Jul 1820
RUCTON, Thoms.	29	M	Farmer	Great Britan	U. States	Ann Marria	6 Aug 1823
RUDAL, William	29 5/12	M	Merchant	Germany	Germany	France	28 Mar 1829
RUDD, James	2	M		Great Britian	United States	Isaac Hicks	13 Jan 1826
Mary	23	F		Great Britian	United States	Isaac Hicks	13 Jan 1826
RUDDAL, Sabra	43	M		Willshire, Bollington, York	U. States	Manhattan	21 May 1821
Thomas	35	M	Gardiner	Willshire, Bolington, York	U. States	Manhattan	21 May 1821
RUDDER, Febby	17	F	Servant	Ireland	New York	Atlantic	8 May 1828
RUDDIGHAM, Ann	3	F	None	Longford	Longford	Howard Douglass	11 May 1827
Chas.	2	M	None	Longford	Longford	Howard Douglass	11 May 1827
RUDDUCK, George Oxford	16	M	Tailor	England	U. States America	Electra	17 Nov 1828
Susan	35	M	Milliner	England	U. States America	Electra	17 Nov 1828
Wm.	56	M	Tailor	England	U. States America	Electra	17 Nov 1828
RUDDY, Rose	22	F	Servant	Ireland	N. York	Trusty	12 Sep 1828
RUDE, J. J.	28	M	Tobacconist	Denmark	U. States	Jane	11 Jul 1828
John N.	40	M	Merchant	St. Croix	St. Croix	General Paez	18 Aug 1828

NAMES OF PASSENGERS	AGE	SEX	OCCUPATIONS	COUNTRY TO WHICH THEY BELONG	COUNTRY THEY INTEND TO INHABIT	SHIPS/DATES OF ARRIVAL	
RUDE (cont'd)							
William	25	M	Baker	England	New York	Hudson	20 Nov 1828
RUDEN, Alexander, Jr., Mr.	23	M	Merchant	U. States	U. States	Athenian	17 Jul 1829
Alexander, Junr.	22 9/12	M	Merchant	New York	New York	Seraph	2 Jan 1828
Jaques	20	M	...	U. States	U. States	Hippomenes	4 Nov 1820
Jaques	23	M	Mercht.	America	America	Fox	21 Dec 1821
S.	24	M	Merchant	New York	U. States	Signa	9 Dec 1824
V., Mr.	21	M	Merchant	United States	United States	Sally	26 Jun 1822
RUDFORD, George	32	M	Gardner	England	Philadelphia	Indian Chief	16 Aug 1822
RUDGE, John	39	M	Shoe Maker	Great Britain	United States	Columbia	1 Dec 1823
RUDGER, Henry	21	M				Betsey	17 Aug 1820
RUDINGER, Fred W.	27	M	Weaver	Germany	U. States	Falcon	11 Jun 1827
RUDLAND, Cath.	22	F		G. Britain	U. States	Dalhouse Castle	12 Sep 1828
RUDOLPHUS, Amelia	18	F		Germany	U. States	Harriet	20 Oct 1824
W. G.	28	M	Musician	Germany	U. States	Harriet	20 Oct 1824
RUDY, Hugh	21	M	Labourer	Ireland	N. York	Trusty	12 Sep 1828
RUDYARD, Emma, Miss	20	F	None	New Brunswick	United States	Howard	14 May 1825
Harriet	16	F	None	New Brunswick	United States	Howard	14 May 1825
L., Mrs.	42	F	None	New Brunswick	United States	Howard	14 May 1825
RUE, A., Miss	15	F		France	U. States	Manchester Packet	23 May 1822
R.	20	F	Labourer	Ireland		Robert Fulton	4 Jun 1828
RUEBY, Charles	15	M	Servant	England	U. States	Manhattan	12 Jun 1824
RUES, Francisco, Don	27	M	Planter	Spain	Havana	Robert Fulton	22 May 1824
RUEZ, E.	16	M	No	Campeache	U. States	Doris	22 May 1826
RUF, Barbara	55	F		France	United States	Stephania	6 Dec 1827
RUFF, Barbara	27	F		France	United States	Stephania	6 Dec 1827
Eliza	22	F	None	Great Brittan	U. States	Gem	26 Jul 1827
Madaline	24	F		France	United States	Stephania	6 Dec 1827
Margaret	21	F		France	United States	Stephania	6 Dec 1827
Mich.	20	M	Blk. Smith	France	United States	Stephania	6 Dec 1827
Michl.	44	M	Shoe Maker	France	United States	Stephania	6 Dec 1827
Oliver	29	M	...on	Great Brittan	U. States	Gem	26 Jul 1827
Sarah	1	F	None	Great Brittan	U. States	Gem	26 Jul 1827
RUFFENSTEIN, J. C.	45	M	Merchant	Great Britain	Unknown	William Thompson	1 May 1827
RUFFERTY, John C.	20	M	Laborer	Ireland	United States	Fabius	4 Jun 1828
Thomas	18	M	Laborer	Ireland	United States	Fabius	4 Jun 1828
RUFFIORA, —	5	M		Bragils		Calypso	1 Jun 1821
RUFFY, George	36	M	Farmer	France	U. States	Edward Quesnel	4 Aug 1828
RUGAL, Catharan	19	F	Carpenter	France		Pallas	14 Jun 1828
Jean	18	F	Farmer	France		Pallas	14 Jun 1828
Jean D.	52	F	Watch	France		Pallas	14 Jun 1828
Jean G.	2	F	Sadler	France		Pallas	14 Jun 1828
Jean S.	28	F	Tanner	France		Pallas	14 Jun 1828
RUGAN, Charles	30	M	Merchant	America	America	Louisiana	20 Sep 1822
RUGER, Hannah	24	F	Farmer	Switzerland	United States	Olympia	12 Aug 1828
Jean Pierre	28	M	Farmer	Switzerland	United States	Olympia	12 Aug 1828
RUGERT, G.	28	M	Officer	U. States	U. States	Patriot	23 May 1821
RUGGLAND, Christian	20	M	Tailor	Switzerland	United States	Eliza Grant	18 Aug 1826
John	19	M	Baker	Switzerland	United States	Eliza Grant	18 Aug 1826
RUGGLES, L.	45	M	Merchant	New York	U. States	John London	26 Mar 1822
Timothy	45	M	Merchant	New Brunswick	Great Brittain	Nancy	9 Jun 1821
Timothy	45		Merchant	Halifax	U. States	Edwin	26 Sep 1828
RUIMOND, James	24	M	Labourer	Switzerland	United States	Helen	5 Sep 1828
RUIN, Philip	19	M	Rope Maker	Bardin	U. States	Bayard	5 Sep 1828
RUISSED, —	32	M	Labourer	France	United States	Cavalier	25 Jul 1828
Cath.	14	F		France	United States	Cavalier	25 Jul 1828
Francis	36	M	Labourer	France	United States	Cavalier	25 Jul 1828
Jean	16	F		France	United States	Cavalier	25 Jul 1828
Maria...	75	F		France	United States	Cavalier	25 Jul 1828
Michael	1	M		France	United States	Cavalier	25 Jul 1828
RULE, George, Capt.	34	M	Master	America		Washington	15 Sep 1821
RULEO, Frans.	30	F	Merchant	Mexico	Mexico	Washington	29 Apr 1826
RULHMEN, John Henrich	24	M	Sugar baker	Holland	America	Martha	13 Oct 1828
RULIO, V.	27	M		Spain	Spain	Fabius	3 Jun 1825
RULKLEY, Carle	39	M	Looking Glass Maker	Italy	United States	Acasta	15 Jul 1822

NAMES OF PASSENGERS	AGE	SEX	OCCUPATIONS	COUNTRY TO WHICH THEY BELONG	COUNTRY THEY INTEND TO INHABIT	SHIPS/DATES OF ARRIVAL	
RULLEY, Bernard	16	M	Labourer	Ireland	New York	America	1 Aug 1828
RUM, Edgar	33	M	Plater	England	United States	Siroc	31 Oct 1829
RUMCARD, T.	4	F		France	United States	New England	29 Aug 1828
RUMELHARD,							
Jean Joseph	18	M		France	United States	New England	29 Aug 1828
Joseph	51	M	Rope Maker	France	United States	New England	29 Aug 1828
RUMMEL, Dorothea	37	F		France	America, U.N.S.	Great Britain	3 Aug 1829
Frederick	16 1/12	M		France	America, U.N.S.	Great Britain	3 Aug 1829
George	11	M		France	America, U.N.S.	Great Britain	3 Aug 1829
Jacob	14	M		France	America, U.N.S.	Great Britain	3 Aug 1829
Jaques	40	M	Farmer	France	America, U.N.S.	Great Britain	3 Aug 1829
Martin	32	M	Farmer	Switzerland		Charlemagne	20 Aug 1829
RUMMELHARD, Agata	6	F		France	United States	New England	29 Aug 1828
Anna	16	F		France	United States	New England	29 Aug 1828
Gregor	2	M		France	United States	New England	29 Aug 1828
Marina	8	F		France	United States	New England	29 Aug 1828
RUMMER, Chs.	43	M	Shephard	Saxony	United States	Howard	28 Aug 1828
RUMNEY, Eliza	28	F	None	Great Britain	United States	Penelope	11 Jun 1827
Elizabeth	73	F	None	Great Britain	United States	Penelope	11 Jun 1827
G. H.	32	M	Marriner	Great Britain	United States	Penelope	11 Jun 1827
Jno.	5	M	None	Great Britain	United States	Penelope	11 Jun 1827
RUMPFF, Eliza	25			U. States		Bayard	10 Sep 1827
Vincent	35		Diplomatic	Germany		Bayard	10 Sep 1827
RUMWELL, Chas.	26	M	Mechanic	U. States	U. States	Rodman	22 Mar 1825
RUNAGHAN, S.	28	F				Hibernia	15 Aug 1820
RUNALDS, Thos.	30	M	Farmer	N. Brunswick	New Brunswick	Abigale	9 Aug 1821
RUNAN, Bridget	18	F	Spinster	Ireland	U. States	Josephine	7 May 1827
RUNBAR, Mary	23	F	None	Great Britain	United States	Cortes	11 Dec 1822
RUNBERRY, Abraham	23	M	Merchant	England	Canada	Ann	3 Jul 1820
RUNDELL, John	25	M	Baker			Sarah G.	20 Jul 1827
RUNDLS, Elinor	32	F	Servant	Ireland	N. York	Trusty	12 Sep 1828
Elizabeth	36	F	Servant	Ireland	N. York	Trusty	12 Sep 1828
RUNE, George	27	M	Servant to Sir Rupert [George]	England	England	William Thompson	29 Jan 1824
RUNELAR, Jane	16	F	Labourer	Ireland	U. States	Two Marys	20 Apr 1825
RUNESS, D.	26	M	Farmer	France	U. States	Bayard	25 Apr 1828
RUNKER, Frederick E.	27	M	Merchant	United States	United States	Bogota	28 Mar 1827
RUNNELLS, Bengamin	25	M	Labourer	Ireland	N. York	Trusty	12 Sep 1828
John	30	M	Labourer	Ireland	N. York	Trusty	12 Sep 1828
RUNNELS, Holland	21	M	Coach Maker	Nova Scotia	U. States	Hope & Esther	30 Apr 1827
RUNNEY, Jno.	42	M	Physician	Spain	U. States	Emeline	5 Jul 1823
RUNSSADER, Michael	30	M	Shoe Maker	France	United States	New England	29 Aug 1828
RUOPP, Frederica	7	F		Wertemburg	America, U.N.S.	Great Britain	3 Aug 1829
Frederica	40	F		Wertemburg	America, U.N.S.	Great Britain	3 Aug 1829
Jacob	28	M	Weaver	Wertemburg	America, U.N.S.	Great Britain	3 Aug 1829
Jacob	61	M	Weaver	Wertemburg	America, U.N.S.	Great Britain	3 Aug 1829
Marguerita	3	F		Wertemburg	America, U.N.S.	Great Britain	3 Aug 1829
Wilhemina	9	F		Wertemburg	America, U.N.S.	Great Britain	3 Aug 1829
RUPERT, Alexander	2	M	Farmer	United States	United States	Wanderer	14 May 1828
Catharine	28	F	Farmer	United States	United States	Wanderer	14 May 1828
Christopher	28	M	Farmer	United States	United States	Wanderer	14 May 1828
Elizabeth	13	F	Farmer	United States	United States	Wanderer	14 May 1828
Elizabeth	43	F	Farmer	United States	United States	Wanderer	14 May 1828
Henry	11	M	Farmer	United States	United States	Wanderer	14 May 1828
Henry	53	M	Farmer	United States	United States	Wanderer	14 May 1828
John D.	5	M	Farmer	United States	United States	Wanderer	14 May 1828
Margaret	16	F	Farmer	United States	United States	Wanderer	14 May 1828
Sarah	22	F	Farmer	United States	United States	Wanderer	14 May 1828
William	24	M	Farmer	United States	United States	Wanderer	14 May 1828
RUPFOE, Jacob	25	M	Weaver	Germany	United States	Origon	8 Jun 1824
RUPHER, Christopher	32	M	Farmer	Germany	United States	Origon	8 Jun 1824
RUPP, Abby	5	F		Germany	U. States	Isabella	10 Aug 1829
Jacob	2	M		Germany	U. States	Isabella	10 Aug 1829
Jean	3	M		Germany	U. States	Isabella	10 Aug 1829
Jean George	38	M	Farmer	Germany	U. States	Isabella	10 Aug 1829
Jos.	30	M	Agriculture	Wirtemburg	United States	Henri IV	14 Oct 1829
Maria Ann	35	F		Germany	U. States	Isabella	10 Aug 1829
RUPRECHT, John	28	M	Shoe Maker	Swiss	United States	Elizabeth	4 Sep 1826

NAMES OF PASSENGERS	AGE	SEX	OCCUPATIONS	COUNTRY TO WHICH THEY BELONG	COUNTRY THEY INTEND TO INHABIT	SHIPS/DATES OF ARRIVAL	
RURA, Francisco	26	M	Merchant	Vera Cruz	gone to Philadelphia	Milo	8 May 1826
RUSBEY, Edmund	21	M	Gentleman	Great Britain	United States	Thomas Dickason	31 Jul 1829
RUSCH, C.	2	M		Switzerland	U. States	La Urania	3 Jul 1828
Eliza S.	26	F		Switzerland	U. States	La Urania	3 Jul 1828
Geo.	5	M		Switzerland	U. States	La Urania	3 Jul 1828
Geo.	31	M		Switzerland	U. States	La Urania	3 Jul 1828
RUSCHOR, Ann	6	F	En.	England	U. States	Franklin	7 Jul 1828
Catharan	4	F	En.	England	U. States	Franklin	7 Jul 1828
Hannah	9	F	En.	England	U. States	Franklin	7 Jul 1828
Mary	46	F	En.	England	U. States	Franklin	7 Jul 1828
Paul	15	M	En.	England	U. States	Franklin	7 Jul 1828
Thomas	12	M	En.	England	U. States	Franklin	7 Jul 1828
RUSELL,							
James G., Gent.	28		Gent	Ireland	United States	Fabius	18 Mar 1829
RUSH, Benjm.	14	M		U. States	U. States	York	12 Jul 1825
Catharine	2	F		U. States	U. States	York	12 Jul 1825
Catharine	37	F		U. States	U. States	York	12 Jul 1825
Henry	6/12	M		U. States	U. States	York	12 Jul 1825
James	12	M		U. States	U. States	York	12 Jul 1825
John	20	M	Weaver	Ireland	U. States	Concordia	11 Jun 1823
John	28	M	Merchant	U.S.		Bliss	28 Jul 1821
Madison	4	M		U. States	U. States	York	12 Jul 1825
Maria	5	F		U. States	U. States	York	12 Jul 1825
Richard	10	M		U. States	U. States	York	12 Jul 1825
Richd.	44	M	Ambasador	U. States	U. States	York	12 Jul 1825
Wm.	25	M	Merchant	U. States	U. States	General Paez	17 Aug 1825
RUSHER, Ann	8	F	Seamstress			John & Edward	25 Aug 1820
Charles	21 7/12	M	Farmer	Switzerland	U. States	France	26 Jun 1828
Elizabeth	32	F	Seamstress			John & Edward	25 Aug 1820
Elizth.	5	F				John & Edward	25 Aug 1820
John	7	M				John & Edward	25 Aug 1820
John	30	M	Farmer			John & Edward	25 Aug 1820
Mary	4	F	Seamstress			John & Edward	25 Aug 1820
RUSHTON, Ann	35	F	...	...	...	Dawn	19 Aug 1825
Benjamin	14	M	...	...	...	Dawn	19 Aug 1825
Ester	12	F	...	...	...	Dawn	19 Aug 1825
Francis	8	M	...	...	...	Dawn	19 Aug 1825
Jacob	40	M	Farmer	Novascotia	...	Dawn	19 Aug 1825
James	45	M	Merchant	United States	U. States	Hercules	24 Oct 1821
Jane	6	F	...	...	...	Dawn	19 Aug 1825
John	4	M	...	...	...	Dawn	19 Aug 1825
Thomas	10	M	...	...	...	Dawn	19 Aug 1825
RUSIAR, Catharine	11	F		Native of Switzerland	United States	Canaris	30 Jun 1827
Elizabeth	36	F		Native of Switzerland	United States	Canaris	30 Jun 1827
George	17	M		Native of Switzerland	United States	Canaris	30 Jun 1827
John G.	48	M	Farmer	Native of Switzerland	United States	Canaris	30 Jun 1827
Margaret	9	F		Native of Switzerland	United States	Canaris	30 Jun 1827
Peter	2	M		Native of Switzerland	United States	Canaris	30 Jun 1827
Philip	13	M		Native of Switzerland	United States	Canaris	30 Jun 1827
RUSIL, Nancey	18	F		Ireland	United States	Nancey	8 Jun 1822
RUSK, Robert	20	M	Farmer	Ireland	U. States	Josephine	7 May 1827
RUSLED, John	22	M		United States	United States	Nancey	8 Jun 1822
RUSLOO, C. F.	22	M	Merchant	U. States	U. States	Nile	12 May 1823
RUSLOW, Chas.	30	M	Mechanic	United States	United States	Mary	1 May 1828
RUSS, Eva Barbara	35	F		France	United States	New England	29 Aug 1828
George	18	M	Farmer	Switzerland	United States	Olympia	12 Aug 1828
Hank	20	M	Labourer	Germany	Newyork	Cortes	16 Jul 1827
RUSSEL, ...	33 5/12	F	Farmer	Switzerland	U. States	France	26 Jun 1828
Archd.	12	M		Great Britian	United States	Brok	29 Aug 1823
Benjiman	45	M	Ship Master	United States	United States	Pilot	27 Feb 1826
C. H.	25	M	Merchant	United States	United States	Columbia	9 Aug 1822

NAMES OF PASSENGERS	AGE	SEX	OCCUPATIONS	COUNTRY TO WHICH THEY BELONG	COUNTRY THEY INTEND TO INHABIT	SHIPS/DATES OF ARRIVAL	
RUSSEL (cont'd)							
Catherine	18	F		Ireland	United States	Trio	13 Jun 1827
Chas.	13		boy	Ireland	United States	Robert Burns	30 May 1823
Elizabeth	4/12	F	Farmer	England	In the Country	Chelsea	16 May 1828
Elizabeth	37	F	Farmer	Ireland	United States	Jubilee	1 Dec 1827
Ellen	7/12	F		Great Britain	New York	Dublin	21 Dec 1824
Harriet	24	F	Farmer	England	In the Country	Chelsea	16 May 1828
James	25	M	Merchant	United States	New York	Intrepid	8 Aug 1822
Jane	12	F	Farmer	Ireland	United States	Jubilee	1 Dec 1827
Jas.	22	M	Merchant	G. Britain	U.S. America	Cincinnatus	31 Oct 1820
John	18	M	Farmer	Ireland	United States	Jubilee	1 Dec 1827
John	20	M	Farmer	Great Britain	United States	Colossus	5 Jun 1827
Peter	16	M	Farmer	Ireland	United States	Jubilee	1 Dec 1827
Robert	40		Laborer	Ireland	Great Britain	Robert Burns	14 Jun 1824
Teressa	11	F	Farmer	Ireland	United States	Jubilee	1 Dec 1827
Thomas	25	M	Plasterrer	Scotland	U.S.	Curler	19 Jul 1828
William	...	M	Farmer	England	In the Country	Chelsea	16 May 1828
William	24	M	Farmer	Ireland	United States	Trio	13 Jun 1827
William, & family	24	M	Farmer	England	In the Country	Chelsea	16 May 1828
RUSSELL, —, Mrs.	21	F	Farmer	Scotland	U. States	Roger Stewart	9 Jun 1828
—, Mrs.	27	F		N. York	U. States	Fame	3 Mar 1823
Abrahan	18 5/12	M	Farmer	Switzerland	U. States	France	26 Jun 1828
Alexr.	18	M	Labourer	Ireland	U. States	William & John	10 Jul 1824
Ann	40		Wife	Ireland	Great Britain	Robert Burns	14 Jun 1824
Ann, Mrs.	30	F	Farming	England	America	Maine	16 Jul 1821
B. M.	30	M	Merchant	U. States		Hope & Polly	17 Aug 1827
Catherine	10	F	Child	U. States	U. States	General Paez	3 Aug 1829
Charles	32	M	Mariner	United States	United States	Cambria	26 Dec 1827
Charles F.	9	M		...	U.S. America	Magnet	17 Aug 1825
Charles Frederick	3 3/12	M	Child			Criterion	27 Oct 1820
Cornelius	4	M		U. States	U. States	Fame	3 Mar 1823
Diane	30	F	Spinster	Ireland	U. States	William & John	10 Jul 1824
Edward	25	M	Labourer	Ireland	United States	Robert Fulton	24 Jul 1826
Edwd. A.	30	M	Mercht.	U. States	United States	Franklin	18 May 1827
Elias, Mr.	46	M	Farming	England	America	Maine	16 Jul 1821
Eliza	37	F	Lady	U. States	U. States	General Paez	3 Aug 1829
F.	22	M	Servt.	Cuba	U. States	Betsey	31 Jul 1826
Florena	50	F	wife to [Saml.]	Ireland	U. States	William & John	10 Jul 1824
George	3		Farmer	England	U. States	Venus	4 Oct 1821
Harriot	13	F	Farming	England	America	Maine	16 Jul 1821
Hellen	22	F	Farmer	Scotland	U. States	Roger Stewart	9 Jun 1828
Honora	23	F	None	Ireland	New York	America	1 Aug 1828
James	19	M	Farmer	Ireland	United States	Dublin Packet	22 Aug 1829
James	22		Weaver	Ireland	Great Britain	Robert Burns	14 Jun 1824
James	23	M	Labourer	Ireland	United States	General Putnam	20 Jun 1825
James	23	M	Farmer	Scotland	U. States	Roger Stewart	9 Jun 1828
James	25	M	Shoemaker	Argyle (Tedland) Scotland	United States	Jean Hastie	27 Jul 1829
James	26	M	Shop Keeper	Gt. Britain	United States	Elbe	8 Jun 1824
James	50	M	Builder	United States	United States	New York	12 Nov 1822
James, Mr.	19	M	Farming	England	America	Maine	16 Jul 1821
Jane	4	F	Farming	England	America	Maine	16 Jul 1821
Jane	22		Merchant	U. States	U. States	Alfred	24 Jul 1828
Jno.	8	M		Great Britain	New York	Dublin	21 Dec 1824
Jno.	25	M	Mercht.	Philad.	U. States	Leno	21 May 1822
John	3	M	None	Ireland	New York	America	1 Aug 1828
John	18			Ireland	U. States	Robert Burns	18 Jun 1822
John	18	M	Merchant	England	England	Gulnard	24 Mar 1825
John	19	M	Labourer	Ireland		Robert Fulton	4 Jun 1828
John	20		Farmer	England	Albany	Xenophon	25 Jul 1826
John	26	M	Farmer	Scotland	America	Friends	24 Sep 1821
Jos.	53	M	Merchant	United States	United States	Acasta	15 Jul 1822
Joseph	2	M		U. States	U. States	Fame	3 Mar 1823
Joseph	3		Blacksmith	England	U. States	Venus	4 Oct 1821
Joseph	47		Farmer	England	U. States	Venus	4 Oct 1821
L.	45	M	Mariner	America	U. States	William Byrnes	17 Jul 1825
Laban	9 8/12	M	Child			Criterion	27 Oct 1820
Lousia	22	F	Servant	London		Hannibal	28 Jul 1823
Margaret	15	F		Scotland	United States	Camillus	9 May 1827

NAMES OF PASSENGERS	AGE	SEX	OCCUPATIONS	COUNTRY TO WHICH THEY BELONG	COUNTRY THEY INTEND TO INHABIT	SHIPS/DATES OF ARRIVAL	
RUSSELL (cont'd)							
Maria	15	F	Farming	England	America	Maine	16 Jul 1821
Mary	9	F	None	Ireland	New York	America	1 Aug 1828
Mary	18 3/12	F	Spinster	Scotland	United States	Morning Star	25 Jun 1822
Mary	19			Ireland	G. Britain	Robert Burns	14 Jun 1824
Mary	35	F	None	America	U. States	William Byrnes	17 Jul 1825
Mary	35 8/12	F		America	United States	Criterion	27 Oct 1820
Mary Ann	25	F		England	U. States	Laburnum	10 Apr 1823
Mathew	27		Farmer	Ireland	United States	Robert Burns	18 Jun 1822
Michael	21	M	Labourer	Limerick	N. York	Thomas & William	25 May 1827
Ml.	4	M		Great Britain	New York	Dublin	21 Dec 1824
Patrick	28		Labourer	G. Britain	United States	Roman	10 Sep 1827
Peter, Mr.	30		Merchant	France	France	Hesper	9 Jun 1827
Phillip	25	M	Labourer	England	America	Sarah	18 Aug 1829
R.	25	M	Farmer	Great Britton	U. State	Earl of Liverpool	16 Aug 1826
Robert	40 2/12	M	Blacksmith	United States	United States	Dutchess of Portland	30 Oct 1826
Robert	56		Farmer	Ireland	United States	Robert Burns	18 Jun 1822
Salina	37		Farmer	England	U. States	Venus	4 Oct 1821
Saml.	45	M	Farmer	Ireland	U. States	William & John	10 Jul 1824
Sarah	11	F	Farming	England	America	Maine	16 Jul 1821
Sarah	20	F	Spinster	Ireland	America	Superior	12 Jun 1824
Stefher	13		Merchant	U. States	U. States	Alfred	24 Jul 1828
Sylvester P.	22	M	Merchant	New London	New London	Governor Griswold	15 Jul 1826
Thos.	24	M	Farmer	Scotland	U. States	Roger Stewart	9 Jun 1828
Thos.	25		Carpenter	England		Corinthian	11 Mar 1829
W. H.	28	M	Merchant	U.S. America	U.S. America	Columbia	15 Nov 1826
William	22	M	Farmer	Great Britain	United States	Colossus	5 Jun 1827
William	35	M	Planter	G. Britain	G. Britain	Azores	20 Sep 1824
Wm.	9	M		Great Britain	New York	Dublin	21 Dec 1824
Wm. H.	20	M		...	U.S. America	Magnet	17 Aug 1825
Wm. H.	30	M	Merchant	U. States	U. States	Caledonia	10 Sep 1828
RUSSIER,							
Carl Agust	0 3/12	M		France	United States	New England	29 Aug 1828
Irang Joseph	6	M		France	United States	New England	29 Aug 1828
Ludwig Joseph	7	M		France	United States	New England	29 Aug 1828
Maria Phillipe	3	F		France	United States	New England	29 Aug 1828
RUSSITER,							
Claude Joseph	38	M	Black Smith	France	United States	New England	29 Aug 1828
RUSSOOD, L. A.	21	M	Mariner	Germany	U. States	Dromo	24 Sep 1827
RUSSWORM, B.	26	M		England	New York	Cincinnatus	5 Dec 1825
RUST, Luder	22	M	Labourer	Greenock, Mid [Parish], Renfrew [County]	New York	Hero	19 May 1828
*to look for Employment							
Thos.	25		Labourer	Halifax	U. States	Edwin	26 Sep 1828
RUSTAN, J. T.	50	M	Gentleman	France	France	Dromo	22 Feb 1827
John	9	M		France	France	Dromo	22 Feb 1827
Louisa	7	F		France	France	Dromo	22 Feb 1827
Louisa	42	F		France	France	Dromo	22 Feb 1827
RUSTLAND, Agness	22	F		Ireland	U. States	Concordia	11 Jun 1823
RUTCLIFF, James	36	M	Merchant	England	America	Manhattan	23 May 1822
RUTGERS, Henry	26	M	Merchant	U. States	U. States	Cyno	18 Sep 1827
W. J.	26	M	Merchant	Holland	U. States	Hippomenes	12 Sep 1822
RUTH, James	29	M	Labourer	Ireland		Marchioness	13 May 1828
RUTHERFORD, Alexr.	30	M		Scotland	United States	Camillus	9 May 1827
Ann	22	F	Spinster	Ireland	U. States	Globe	14 Jul 1821
Chris, Jr.	10	M				Polly	26 May 1821
Christopher	45	M	Merchant	Great Britain	United States	Polly	26 May 1821
Collingwood	5	M				Polly	26 May 1821
Dinah	13	F				Polly	26 May 1821
Elizabeth	5	F		England, Born in Barbadoes	U. States	Cannon	15 Jul 1822

*all the children have come under the care of Mrs. Fenwick for their education

NAMES OF PASSENGERS	AGE	SEX	OCCUPATIONS	COUNTRY TO WHICH THEY BELONG	COUNTRY THEY INTEND TO INHABIT	SHIPS/DATES OF ARRIVAL	
RUTHERFORD (cont'd)							
Elizabeth	30	F		England, Born in Barbadoes	U. States	Cannon	15 Jul 1822
George	2	M				Polly	26 May 1821
Hamilton	1 6/12	M		Ireland	United States	Carolina Ann	11 Dec 1826
Isabella	25	F	None	...ingsham		Mount Vernon	7 Jun 1824
James	15	M				Polly	26 May 1821
Jane	40	F		England	England	Tontine	1 Jun 1826
Jas.	24	F	Framer	Ireland	U. States	Globe	14 Jul 1821
John	8	M				Polly	26 May 1821
John	10	M	Merchant	Great Britain		Birmingham	11 Oct 1828
John	38	M	Labourer	Gt. Britain	America	Ariel	20 Jul 1822
John	40	M	Miller	England	U.S.A.	Hudson	21 Aug 1829
Margaret	18	F	Spinster	Ireland	United States	Dublin Packet	24 Sep 1823
Margaret	20	F	Spinster	Ireland	America	Josephine	8 Dec 1827
Margaret	38	F	Spinster	Ireland	U. States	Globe	14 Jul 1821
Mary	24	F		Gt. Britain	America	Ariel	20 Jul 1822
Mary	28	F		Ireland	United States	Carolina Ann	11 Dec 1826
Mary	40	F				Polly	26 May 1821
N. H.	27	M	Merchant	Ireland	Ireland	James Monroe	8 Aug 1820
Orlando F.	3	M		England, Born in Barbadoes	U. States	Cannon	15 Jul 1822
*all the children have come under the care of Mrs. Fenwick for their education							
Robert	30	M	Weaver	Ireland	United States	Carolina Ann	11 Dec 1826
Thos. F.	6	M		England, Born in Barbadoes	U. States	Cannon	15 Jul 1822
*all the children have come under the care of Mrs. Fenwick for their education							
William	12	M				Polly	26 May 1821
Wm. P.	8	M		England, Born in Barbadoes	U. States	Cannon	15 Jul 1822
*all the children have come under the care of Mrs. Fenwick for their education							
RUTHERFURD, ...	...	M	daughter	England	U.S. States	Splendid	14 Aug 1829
...	...	M	daughter	England	U.S. States	Splendid	14 Aug 1829
...eth	...	F	daughter	England	U.S. States	Splendid	14 Aug 1829
Caroline	3	F	daughter	England	U.S. States	Splendid	14 Aug 1829
Jane	19	F	daughter	England	U.S. States	Splendid	14 Aug 1829
John	1	M	daughter	England	U.S. States	Splendid	14 Aug 1829
John	45	F	Tailor	England	U.S. States	Splendid	14 Aug 1829
Joseph	5	M	daughter	England	U.S. States	Splendid	14 Aug 1829
Rosella	40	F	Wife	England	U.S. States	Splendid	14 Aug 1829
Wm.	7	M	daughter	England	U.S. States	Splendid	14 Aug 1829
RUTHFORD, J. H.	25	M	Merchant	U. States	U. States	Columbia	20 Jul 1825
RUTHKIN, Saml. N.	21	M	Clerk	England	United States should they approve of it	Robert Edwards	20 Jan 1829
RUTHLAND, Samuel	22	M	Labourer	Ireland	United States	Jubilee	13 Jul 1829
RUTHLIDGE, Jane	12 6/12	F	Spinster	Ireland	United States	Robert Fulton	24 Jul 1826
RUTLAND, John	50	M	Baker	U. States	U. States	Greek	8 Mar 1828
RUTLEDGE, E. C.	24	M	Navy	America	U. States	Catharine Rogers	6 Oct 1823
Frederick	22			U. States	U. States	Hudson	4 Sep 1823
R. C.	28		Gentleman	U. States	U. States	Amazon	7 Jul 1820
RUTLEY, John	26	F	Merchant	England	England	Venus	15 Apr 1822
RUTLIDGE, Catherine	14 6/12	F	Spinster	Ireland	United States	Robert Fulton	24 Jul 1826
RUTLIFF, Jane	20	M	Shoe Maker	G. Britain	U. States	St. George	7 Jun 1828
RUTLY, Ths.	1 3/12	F	Merchant	England	England	Venus	15 Apr 1822
RUTTAD, Andrias	18	M		Great Britain		Caravan	8 Sep 1828
H.	15	M		Great Britain		Caravan	8 Sep 1828
RUTTEN, John	23	M	Farmer	Ireland	America	Minerva	31 May 1824
Wm.	25	M	Cotton Spinner	Great Britain	United States	India	5 Sep 1827
RUTTER, J.	32	M	Gentleman	England	U. States	Milton	6 Dec 1825
RUTZLER, Maria O.	25	F		Switzerland	U. States	La Urania	3 Jul 1828
Marie	2	F		Switzerland	U. States	La Urania	3 Jul 1828
RYAN, —	24		Linnen Draper	Ireland	U.S.	Union	20 Aug 1827
...ard	20	M	Labourer	Ireland	United States	Eliza Grant	6 Oct 1828
A.	19	M		Ireland	U. States	Alex Mansfield	1 Jun 1822
Alice	17	F		England	United States	Hannibal	6 Sep 1824
Ann	28	F		Ireland	America	Plutarch	18 Jul 1826
B.	27	F		Scotland	United States	Indus	5 Sep 1827

NAMES OF PASSENGERS	AGE	SEX	OCCUPATIONS	COUNTRY TO WHICH THEY BELONG	COUNTRY THEY INTEND TO INHABIT	SHIPS/DATES OF ARRIVAL	
RYAN (cont'd)							
Bergroth	20	M				Eliza Grant	6 Oct 1828
Biddy	13	F	None	Ireland	U.S.A.	Dalhouse Castle	21 Aug 1829
Brdget	25			England	U. States	Corinthian	8 Oct 1828
Bridget	27	F		Great Britain	U.S. of America	Gratitude	3 Oct 1829
Caggey	2	F	None	Ireland	America	Evelina	10 Nov 1825
Caggey	35	F	None	Ireland	America	Evelina	10 Nov 1825
Catharine	5	F		Ireland	America	Plutarch	18 Jul 1826
Catherine	13	F		Ireland	United States	Trio	2 Oct 1828
Catherine	20	F	Child	Ireland	United States	Dublin Packet	23 May 1828
Charles	24	M	Weaver	Great Britain	United States	Isaac Hicks	10 Jul 1827
D.	28	M	Labourer	Ireland	United States	Combine	4 Jun 1825
Daniel	3	M	Shoemaker	Ireland		Marchioness	13 May 1828
Daniel	30	M	Farmer	England	United States	Ganges	10 May 1828
Danl.	26	M	Shoemaker	Ireland	U. States	Severn	12 Oct 1826
David	21	M	Labourer	Gt. Britain	U. States	St. George	20 Sep 1828
David	24	M	Farmer	Ireland	America	Manhattan	20 Mar 1820
Denis	28	M	Labourer	Ireland	United States	Combine	4 Jun 1825
Denis	37	M	Mechanic	United States	U. States	Angenora	22 Dec 1826
Dennis	30	M	Farmer	England	U.S. States	Splendid	14 Aug 1829
Dorothy	25		his Wife [James]	Ireland	United States	Rufus King	4 Sep 1823
Edward	33	M	None	England	United States	Mary & Harriet	9 Mar 1829
Edwd.	26	M	Labourer	Ireland	United States	Matvina	19 Oct 1826
Eliza	7/12	F		Great Britain	U.S. of America	Gratitude	3 Oct 1829
Elizath.	8/12		their Child [James and Dorothy]	Ireland	United States	Rufus King	4 Sep 1823
Ellen	14	F		Ireland	United States	Trio	13 Jun 1827
Ellen	17	F	Matron	Ireland	America	Josephine	24 Jul 1826
Ellen	23	F	Shoemaker	Ireland		Marchioness	13 May 1828
Francis	29	F				Lady of the Lake	23 Aug 1828
*left ship							
Hannah	30	F		G. Britain	New York	Hesperus	13 Oct 1825
James	21	M	Gentleman	Ireland	U. States	Hibernia	3 Dec 1823
James	28		Brick Layer	Ireland	United States	Rufus King	4 Sep 1823
James	30	M	C...	Ireland	United States	Potomac	28 Sep 1827
James	30	M	Shoemaker	Ireland		Marchioness	13 May 1828
James	35	M	Laborer	Ireland	U. States	Lady Hunter	14 Mar 1826
Jas.	22	M	Mechanic	Ireland	United States	Wm. Byrnes	30 Apr 1828
Jas.	26	M	Laborer	Ireland	United States	Trio	13 Jun 1827
Jas.	30	M	Shoe Maker	England	U. States	Thomas Ritchie	2 Jul 1827
Jeremiah	25	M	Labourer	Ireland	United States	Eliza Grant	6 Oct 1828
Jno.	20	M	Farmer	Ireland	America	Mary	29 May 1827
Jno.	25	M	Mechanic	Ireland	U. States	Martha	28 Jan 1826
Johanah	4	F		Ireland	America	Plutarch	18 Jul 1826
John	1 6/12	M		Ireland	America	William	21 May 1825
John	21	M	Weaver	Great Britain	United States	Isaac Hicks	10 Jul 1827
John	27	M	Farmer	..., ..., Ireland	N. York	New Orleans	24 Aug 1827
John	36	M	Labourer	Ireland	United States	Trio	2 Oct 1828
Jones	32			England	U. States	Corinthian	8 Oct 1828
Joseph	24	M	Currier	Ireland	America	John Adams	2 Aug 1827
Kysan	22	M	Weaver	Great Britain	United States	Isaac Hicks	10 Jul 1827
Lennie	9	F	Taylor	Great Britain	U. States	Columbia	22 Sep 1828
Lydia	28	F	Farmer	England	United States	Mary & Harriet	9 Mar 1829
Mac Law	26	M	Diere	Great Britain	United States	Isaac Hicks	10 Jul 1827
Margret	6	F		Ireland	America	William	21 May 1825
Martin	29	M				Lady of the Lake	23 Aug 1828
*left ship							
Mary	7/12	F	Child	Ireland	America	Josephine	24 Jul 1826
Mary	3	F		Scotland	United States	Indus	5 Sep 1827
Mary	3 6/12	F		Great Britain	U.S. of America	Gratitude	3 Oct 1829
Mary	4	F	None	Ireland	America	Evelina	10 Nov 1825
Mary	17	F	Spinster	Ireland	America	Josephine	24 Jul 1826
Mary	26	F	Labourer	Ireland	New York	Bowditch	27 Apr 1826
Mary	26	F		England	America	Two Marys	24 Sep 1827
Mary	39	F	Matron	Great Britain	U. States	Robert Fulton	3 Dec 1827
Michl.	37 4/12	M	Merchant	England	Barbadoes	Falcon	19 Sep 1823
Monica	60	M	Weaver	Great Britain	United States	Isaac Hicks	10 Jul 1827

NAMES OF PASSENGERS	AGE	SEX	OCCUPATIONS	COUNTRY TO WHICH THEY BELONG	COUNTRY THEY INTEND TO INHABIT	SHIPS/DATES OF ARRIVAL	
RYAN (cont'd)							
N. W.	35	M	Merchant	U. States	U. States	Hannibal	12 Oct 1829
Pat	1	M				Lady of the Lake	23 Aug 1828
*left ship							
Patrick	22	M	Farmer	Ireland	United States	Dublin Packet	9 Jul 1827
Patrick	25	M	Taylor	Great Britain	U. States	Columbia	22 Sep 1828
Patrick	51	M	Schoolmaster	Ireland	Baltimore	Indian Chief	16 Aug 1822
Patt	27	M	Spinner	Great Britain	United States	Isaac Hicks	10 Jul 1827
Patt.	25	M	Mathematician	Kill, Kill, Ireland	N. York	New Orleans	24 Aug 1827
Peter	20	M	Laborer	Gt. Britain		Dalhouse Castle	13 May 1828
Peter	21 1/12	M	Labourer	Ireland	America	Enterprize	29 Jun 1827
R.	28	M	Farmer	England	America	Two Marys	24 Sep 1827
Rd.	7	M				Lady of the Lake	23 Aug 1828
*left ship							
Richd.	20	M	Farmer	Ireland	United States	Diana	1 May 1826
Stephen V. R.	24	M	Am. Army	U.S.	U.S.	Cadmus	23 Mar 1827
Thomas	34	M	Labourer	Ireland	America	Plutarch	18 Jul 1826
Thomas	35	M	Farmer	Great Britain	U.S. of America	Gratitude	3 Oct 1829
Thomas Tayler, Mr.	24		Merchant	Great Britain	U.S. America	Mary	10 Mar 1826
Thos.	20	M	Farmer	Ireland	America	Liverpool	31 Aug 1827
Wililliam	21	M	Labourer	Limerick	N. York	Thomas & William	25 May 1827
William	19	M	Farmer	Ireland		Manhattan	20 Jun 1826
William	24	M	Labourer	Ireland	U. States	Combine	30 Nov 1825
William	32	M	Sargeant	Ireland	America	Josephine	24 Jul 1826
William	40	M	Shoemaker	Ireland		Dublin Packet	30 Apr 1821
Wm.	15	M	Mason	Ireland	U. States	Alex Mansfield	1 Jun 1822
RYANS, Ann	17	F	Servant	Ireland	America	Carolina Ann	7 Aug 1826
Bridget	12	F	Spinster	Great Britain	U. States	Robert Fulton	3 Dec 1827
Catherine	14	F	Spinster	Great Britain	U. States	Robert Fulton	3 Dec 1827
Margeret	10 6/12	F	Child	Great Britain	U. States	Robert Fulton	3 Dec 1827
Margret	20	F	Servant	Ireland	America	Carolina Ann	7 Aug 1826
Mary	17	F	Spinster	Great Britain	U. States	Robert Fulton	3 Dec 1827
RYANT, Hippolitz	30	M	Watch Maker	France	San Domingo	Victory	29 May 1821
RYCARFT, John	30	M	Shipmaster	New York	America	Mary	2 Oct 1820
RYCKMAN, Cornelia	21	F		New York	U. States	Marmion	8 Sep 1828
RYDOR, Ann Hill, Miss	40	F	None	G. Bt.	G. Bt.	Canada	13 Oct 1825
RYEA, Catharine	29	F	...	G. Brittain		York	10 Dec 1825
RYEN, John	28		Husbandman	England	America	Sarah	18 Aug 1829
Mary	28		Husbandman	England	America	Sarah	18 Aug 1829
RYERDON, Elen	2			England	U. States	Corinthian	8 Oct 1828
Margat	3			England	U. States	Corinthian	8 Oct 1828
RYERSON, G. W.	38	M		G. Britain	U. States	Robt. Edwards	4 Sep 1828
RYLAND, George, Mr.	26	M	None	G. Britian	Canada	Corinthian	4 Jan 1825
RYLE, Ann	18	F		Great Britain	United States	Mary	11 Jul 1820
Ellen	22	F		Great Britain	United States	Mary	11 Jul 1820
John	24	M		Great Britain	United States	Mary	11 Jul 1820
RYLEY, Charles	21	M	...ler	...	U. States	New Orleans	24 Aug 1827
John	21	M	daughter	England	U.S. States	Splendid	14 Aug 1829
John	26	M	Butcher	Great Britain		Manhattan	7 Nov 1827
John	30	F	Shoemaker	England	U.S. States	Splendid	14 Aug 1829
Joseph	18	M	Physician	...	U. States	New Orleans	24 Aug 1827
Margett	25	F	Spinster	County Renagh, Ireland	United States	Hanford	15 May
Nancy	20	F		Great Britain		Manhattan	7 Nov 1827
Patrick	30	M	Labourer	England	United States	Dalhouse Castle	8 May 1827
RYLIN, Wm.	20	M	Wheelwright	G. Britain	U. States	Freak	9 Jun 1828
RYNE, Bridget	24	F	Lady	Ireland	United States	Nancy	15 Dec 1824
Pat	1	M		U. States	U. States	Wanderer	30 Oct 1828
Patrick	23	M	Labourer	England	U.N. States	Reindeer	20 Aug 1828
William	6	M	Child	Ireland	United States	Nancy	15 Dec 1824
RYNER, Daniel	25			England	U. States	Corinthian	8 Oct 1828
RYNER, Sarah	25			England	U. States	Corinthian	8 Oct 1828
RYNNDON, W.	35	M	Merchant	France	United States	Neptunes Barge	23 Apr 1821
RYON, Jas.	24	M	Farmer	Ireland	New York	Phoenix	29 Apr 1826
John	24	M	Carpenter	Ireland	America	Parrington	9 Jun 1827
John	25	M	Laborer	Ireland	America	Parrington	9 Jun 1827

NAMES OF PASSENGERS	AGE	SEX	OCCUPATIONS	COUNTRY TO WHICH THEY BELONG	COUNTRY THEY INTEND TO INHABIT	SHIPS/DATES OF ARRIVAL	
RYON (cont'd)							
Lysebeth	24	F	Servant	St. Johns	St. Johns	Nancy	3 Apr 1824
Michael	24	M	Glozier	Ireland	America	Parrington	9 Jun 1827
Patrick	18	M		Ireland	United States	Magnet	16 May 1823
RYOTT, John	16	M	Cooper	England	United States	Jubilee	1 Oct 1828
Thomas	33	M	Labourer	England	United States	Jubilee	1 Oct 1828
RYRE, John	17	M	Clerk	Great Brittain	U. States	Hibernia	8 Jul 1823
RYSANDER, Neils	24	M	Gentleman	Sweden	Sweden	William Howland	20 Jul 1829
S..., Sally	22	F		Gt. Britain	U. States	Sarah G.	14 Apr 1828
Willi...	7	M	Child	Ireland	United States	Robert Fulton	24 Jul 1826
S...ATON, Mathew	24	M	Laborer	Scotland	U. States	Magnet	22 Aug 1822
S...G, Gardiner	37		Minister	Newburyport	United States	London	13 Dec 1822
S...ITT, Gottlieb	42	M	Farmer	Wertemberg	Wertemberg	Edward Quesnel	3 Jul 1829
S...L, Joseph	23	M	S...	...	Canada	Martha	22 Jul 1820
S...LL..., ...	28	F		Gt. Britain	U. States	Sarah G.	14 Apr 1828
S...SON, John	20		Farmer	U. States		Caledonian	16 Aug 1820
S...TH, Wm.	...	...	...	...	...	William Thompson	30 Sep 1824
SA...D..., ..., Mr.	23		Farmer	England		Hercules	19 Jun 1821
SA...TON, Helen F., Miss	36	F	Seamstress	Low Countries	N. York	Cadmus	27 Aug 1822
SABECK, C. D.	29	M	Sugar Baker	Germany	U. States	Constitution	25 Jul 1823
SABOWINER, C.	46		Farmer	France	U. States	Elizabeth	9 Jul 1825
F.	20		Farmer	France	U. States	Elizabeth	9 Jul 1825
F.	46		Farmer	France	U. States	Elizabeth	9 Jul 1825
Jaques	17		Farmer	France	U. States	Elizabeth	9 Jul 1825
Joseph	10		Farmer	France	U. States	Elizabeth	9 Jul 1825
Lewis	6		Farmer	France	U. States	Elizabeth	9 Jul 1825
Peter	15		Farmer	France	U. States	Elizabeth	9 Jul 1825
X.	24		Farmer	France	U. States	Elizabeth	9 Jul 1825
SACKET, Jos.	65	M	Mariner	U. States	U. States	Minerva	30 Jun 1824
SACKMEISTER, Charles	33	M	Mechanic	Germany	New York	Orient	25 Nov 1825
SACO, Josea Antoneo	23	M	Lawyer	Spain	Havana	Robert Fulton	22 May 1824
SACRATI, Maximelian Arozze, Marquis	27	M	Gentleman	Italy	Italy	New York	14 Nov 1826
SADAY, Peter	13	...	...	...	United States	John London	3 Aug 1824
SADDEN, Anna	50	F	Farmer	Ireland	Ohio	Virginia	7 May 1824
Anna, Junr.	8	F	Farmer	Ireland	Ohio	Virginia	7 May 1824
George	10	M	Farmer	Ireland	Ohio	Virginia	7 May 1824
John	21	M	Farmer	Ireland	Ohio	Virginia	7 May 1824
Mary	14	F	Farmer	Ireland	Ohio	Virginia	7 May 1824
Michal	50	M	Farmer	Ireland	Ohio	Virginia	7 May 1824
Michal, Junr.	12	M	Farmer	Ireland	Ohio	Virginia	7 May 1824
SADERS, Charles	34	M	Physician	U.S.	U.S.	Cadmus	9 Dec 1826
SADIER, John C.	25	M	Mechanic	Germany	U. States	Indian Queen	20 Sep 1826
SADLER, Adam	20	M		Ireland	United States	Commerce	13 Jun 1828
Adam	28	M	Labourer	Ireland	United States	Commerce	13 Jun 1828
Agnes	30	F		Ireland	United States	Commerce	13 Jun 1828
Ann	21	F	Wife	Great Britain	United States	Washington	3 Sep 1827
Ann	28	F		Ireland	United States	Commerce	13 Jun 1828
Elenn	13	F	None	England		Manhattan	22 May 1827
Eliza	6	F		Ireland	United States	Commerce	13 Jun 1828
Elizabeth	48	F	Lady	Ireland	England	Manhattan	12 May 1823
Ewd.	6	M	Child	Great Britain	United States	Washington	3 Sep 1827
Ewd.	21	M	Engineer	Great Britain	United States	Washington	3 Sep 1827
J.	58	F		...	United States	Rufus King	27 Jun 1821
Jane	16	F	None	England		Manhattan	22 May 1827
Jane E.	1 6/12	F		Ireland	United States	Commerce	13 Jun 1828
John	2	M		Great Britain	United States	Washington	3 Sep 1827
John	4	M		Ireland	United States	Commerce	13 Jun 1828
John	5	M		Ireland	United States	Commerce	13 Jun 1828
John	32	M	Labourer	Ireland	United States	Commerce	13 Jun 1828
John	51	M	Gentleman	Ireland	England	Manhattan	12 May 1823
Mary	4	F		Great Britain	United States	Washington	3 Sep 1827
Mary	8	F		Ireland	United States	Commerce	13 Jun 1828
Mary	45	F	None	England		Manhattan	22 May 1827
Richd. M.	24	M	Merchant	U. States	U. States	Francis Jarvis	17 Oct 1822
Samuel	1	M		Great Britain	United States	Washington	3 Sep 1827

NAMES OF PASSENGERS	AGE	SEX	OCCUPATIONS	COUNTRY TO WHICH THEY BELONG	COUNTRY THEY INTEND TO INHABIT	SHIPS/DATES OF ARRIVAL	
SADLER (cont'd)							
Thomas	26	M	Weaver	Ireland	United States	Commerce	13 Jun 1828
William	2	M		Ireland	United States	Commerce	13 Jun 1828
SADLUIER, C.	45 1/12	M	Merchant	France	U. States	Jaine Louis	24 Aug 1820
SADOR, Michal	30		Nothing	Poland	Warsaw	Ann	27 Nov 1820
SADROON, Natividad	30	F	Servant	Island of Cuba	Cuba	James Monroe	21 May 1825
SAFAS, Alex.	23	M	Merchant	Havana	Havana	Robert Reade	9 Feb 1822
SAFERRIERE, A. Dua	26	M	Clerk	France		Montano	3 Jan 1823
SAFF, James	21	M	Shoe Maker	G. Britain	U.S. America	Cincinnatus	31 Oct 1820
SAFRANQUE, M.	6	M	Student	St. Martins	U. States	Matilda	16 Aug 1822
SAGAR, Maller	26	M	Carpenter	France	America	Saluda	18 Jun 1825
SAGE, Eben. W.	36	M	Merchant	Boston	U. States	Zephyr	18 May 1825
Ed. W.	31	M	Merchant	U. States	U. States	Emma	15 Apr 1822
Henry B.	40	M	Printer	U. States	U. States	Minerva	13 Sep 1827
Hepsy	24	F		Boston	U. States	Zephyr	18 May 1825
L. H.	33	M	Mercht.	U. States	U. States	Rambler	16 Jul 1829
Mary	32	F	Wife	U. States	U. States	Minerva	13 Sep 1827
W. M.	30	M	Planter	U. States	U. States	Venus	27 Jun 1821
SAGENDORF,							
Julia Ann	25	F		United States	United States	Frances	19 Feb 1829
Julia Sarah	1 10/12	F		United States	United States	Frances	19 Feb 1829
SAGER, Jan M.	37	F	None	France	U. States	Sully	25 Jun 1828
Peter	11	M	None	France	U. States	Sully	25 Jun 1828
Peter	37	M	Shoe Maker	France	U. States	Sully	25 Jun 1828
Philip	39	M	Painter	France	U. States	Sully	25 Jun 1828
SAGERDOLPH, Jerm.	27	M	Carpenter	U. States	U. States	Dart	5 Apr 1822
SAGGITT, Richd.	26	M	Farmer	Great Britain	United States	Diana	6 Jul 1829
SAGGOT, Christian	33		Baker			Caledonian	16 Aug 1820
SAGNISCH, G. W.	28	M	Physician	Germany	U. States	Lewis	6 Jul 1825
SAGORG, Charles	29	M	Merchant	France	U.S.	Bayard	30 Oct 1820
SAGUÉ, Theodore	22	M	Student	France	France	Stephania	13 Sep 1821
SAICKY, Jean	26	M	Farmer	Germany	United States	Oxford	14 Aug 1828
SAID, Jno.	28	M	Merchant	Greenock	Scotland	Yamacraw	10 May 1821
SAIDLER, —, Mr.	25	M	Merchant	U. States	U. States	Constitution	8 Sep 1823
Alexander	25	M	Farmer	Scotland	America	Friends	24 Sep 1821
SAIN, —, Mr.			Servant	St. Vincent	West Indies	Henrietta	18 Aug 1829
ST. ARMANT, —	21	M	Mariner	France	U. States	Maria Ann	29 Sep 1823
*landed at Balize [Biloxi?], Missipi							
ST. AUBYN, E.	20	F	Gentleman	England	U. States	Bayard	11 Jul 1825
ST. BENOIT, Jean	47	M	Merchant	France	France	Cadmus	11 Jul 1827
ST. CIN, Cornette	45	M	Planter	Gaudaloupe	U. States	Eliza	3 Jul 1820
Cornette, Madam	35	F	Planter	Gaudaloupe	U. States	Eliza	3 Jul 1820
ST. CROIX, Euphemia	12		Farmer	Halifax	U. States	Edwin	26 Sep 1828
Thomas	16		Farmer	Halifax	U. States	Edwin	26 Sep 1828
ST. GEORGE, Honora	40	F	None	Gallway	United States	Dalhousie Castle 27 Jul 1826
John	10	M	None	Gallway	United States	Dalhousie Castle 27 Jul 1826
Mary	8	F	None	Gallway	United States	Dalhousie Castle 27 Jul 1826
Michl.	3	M	Farmer	England	United States	Danube	22 Aug 1825
Monrat	10/12	M	None	Gallway	United States	Dalhousie Castle 27 Jul 1826
Patk.	2	M	None	Gallway	United States	Dalhousie Castle 27 Jul 1826
William	6	M	None	Gallway	United States	Dalhousie Castle 27 Jul 1826
Wm.	30	M	Farmer	England	United States	Danube	22 Aug 1825
ST. JATZ, J.	18	M	Merchant	France	New York	Nancy	17 Nov 1823
ST. JEAN, —	30	M	Servant	France	France	Clio	7 Aug 1826
ST. JOHN, Augustus	25	F	None	G. Bt.	G. Bt.	Canada	13 Feb 1826
Fredk. W.	28	M	None	G. Bt.	G. Bt.	Canada	13 Feb 1826
Jas.	2	M	None	G. Bt.	G. Bt.	Canada	13 Feb 1826
Saml., Junr.	32	M	Merchant	Mobile	Mobile	New York	14 Nov 1826
ST. LAGER, Margaret	2	F	None	Duckinfield	U. States	Milton	21 May 1827
S.	4	M	None	Duckinfield	U. States	Milton	21 May 1827
Susan	29	F	None	Duckinfield	U. States	Milton	21 May 1827
ST. MICHEAL, Micheal	35	M	Weaver	Germany	Pensylvania	Brighton	14 Oct 1824
ST. OLAN, Peter	28	M	Rope Maker	Scotland	United States	Euphrates	12 Mar 1824
SAINZ, Mateo	30	M	Merchant	Spain	Spain	Frances	21 Mar 1827
SAJA, Sacarius	33	M	Merchant	Spain	United States	John & William 20 Jul 1829
SALAIGNOE, Geo. P.	25 2/12	M	Merchant	United States	Philadelphia	Cadmus	27 Aug 1822
SALAJAR, John	48	M	Mercht.	Spain	U. States	Hippomenes	23 Jun 1823
SALAMAN, Abraham	30	M	Merchant	Georgetown	U. States	Alligator	15 Aug 1820
SALANO, Joseph M.	11	M	Army	America	America	Medina	4 Sep 1828

NAMES OF PASSENGERS	AGE	SEX	OCCUPATIONS	COUNTRY TO WHICH THEY BELONG	COUNTRY THEY INTEND TO INHABIT	SHIPS/DATES OF ARRIVAL	
SALASDELASISA,							
Josede Bairas	49	M	Milatary	Perambuco	Brazil	Jane	17 Jan 1825
SALATO, Joseph	42 2/12	M	Servent	Sardigna	United States	Potomac	29 Oct 1828
SALAZAR, Alexander		M	Prisoner charged with Piracy			Oswego	12 Apr 1824
Bernado	15	M	Servant	Vara Cruz	U. States	Fly	9 Apr 1823
C.	40	M	Merchant	Madree	U. States	Don Quixote	14 Aug 1826
C.	41	M	Merchant	Spain	Spain	Superior	25 Sep 1824
M.	21	M	Merchant	Madree	U. States	Don Quixote	14 Aug 1826
SALDANA, A. T.	50	M	Merchant	Spain	U. States	Mary Jane	23 Mar 1829
SALDANBRA, —, Senhor	30	M	Lawyer	Brasil	New York	Constitution	9 Dec 1824
SALDANO, A. J.	50	M	Merchant	Naturalized U.S.	New York	Robert Fulton	22 May 1824
Ambroze	30	F	Nurse	Naturalized U.S.	New York	Robert Fulton	22 May 1824
Charlotte	5	F	Child	Naturalized U.S.	New York	Robert Fulton	22 May 1824
Lonso	2	M	Child	Naturalized U.S.	New York	Robert Fulton	22 May 1824
Seraphina	1	F	Child	Naturalized U.S.	New York	Robert Fulton	22 May 1824
SALDONO, Antonio	50	M	Merchant	United States	United States	Cambria	8 Oct 1828
SALE, Alexr.	3	M		Great Brittain	United States	Active	12 Sep 1828
Ann	49	F		Great Brittain	United States	Active	12 Sep 1828
Cathr.	20	F		G. Britain	U. States	George Clinton	10 Sep 1828
Charles	48	M	Labourer	Great Brittain	United States	Active	12 Sep 1828
Charles, Jnr.	21	M	Labourer	Great Brittain	United States	Active	12 Sep 1828
Charlotte	10	F		Great Brittain	United States	Active	12 Sep 1828
Danl.	13	M		Great Brittain	United States	Active	12 Sep 1828
Jane	8	F		Great Brittain	United States	Active	12 Sep 1828
Jane	10	F		Great Brittain	United States	Active	12 Sep 1828
Jane	50	F		Great Brittain	United States	Active	12 Sep 1828
Sarah	8	F		Great Brittain	United States	Active	12 Sep 1828
Thomas	4	M		Great Brittain	United States	Active	12 Sep 1828
Thomas	6	M		Great Brittain	United States	Active	12 Sep 1828
Thomas	50	M	Farmer	Great Brittain	United States	Active	12 Sep 1828
Thos.	22	M	Shoe Maker	G. Britain	U. States	George Clinton	10 Sep 1828
Wm.	1	M		Great Brittain	United States	Active	12 Sep 1828
SALES, Eliza	18	F		U. States	U. States	New England	4 Jun 1828
Wm.	26	M	Merchant	U. States	U. States	New England	4 Jun 1828
SALEVEZ, Juan	28	M	Mercht.	Spain	Spain	Albany Packet	14 Nov 1826
SALEZDO,							
Deborah, Miss	24	F		St. Thomas	United States	Hiram	14 Aug 1829
SALFFENGIN, Catharan	28	F	Farmer	France	U. States	Edward Bonaffe	23 Jul 1828
Fred	36	M	Farmer	France	U. States	Edward Bonaffe	23 Jul 1828
SALGODO, R.	33	M	Military	Lima, Peru		Brown	12 Oct 1824
SALHELK, Thomas	53	M	Shoemaker	G. Britain	U. States	Mary & Harriot	8 Sep 1828
SALKS, Santiage		M	Gentleman	Spaniard		Happy Return	23 Jul 1821
SALLAMOND, Chs.	47	M	Gentleman	France	France	Meteor	11 Apr 1825
SALLEN, Thomas	46	M	Farmer	England	United States	Cambria	3 Jul 1829
Thos.	20	M	None	Great Britain	United States	Aurora	10 Nov 1827
SALLENBIER, Francois	42	M	Grocer	Hollins		François I	19 Nov 1828
Francoise	2	M		France		François I	19 Nov 1828
Margarette	26	F		Ireland		François I	19 Nov 1828
Mary Louise	4	F		U.S.A.		François I	19 Nov 1828
SALLICUM, Maffy	63	M	Farmer	Great Britain	United States	Meridian	2 Jul 1827
SALLIE, —, Mrs.		F		Hayti	Hayti	Speculator	12 Feb 1827
SALLIECE,							
Augustus	22 3/12	M	Merchant	Lexington	Lexington	Florida	2 Oct 1828
SALLY, Martha	13	F	Labourer	G. Britain	U. States	St. George	16 Jan 1829
SALMAN, F.	23	M	Merchant	U. States	U.S.	Ambuscade	14 Mar 1820
James	55		Priest	Ireland	United States	Rufus King	4 Sep 1823
R. D.	30	M	Merchant	U. States	U. States	Zephyr	2 Oct 1826
SALMON, —, Mrs.	26	F		G. Britain	Canada	Columbia	7 Sep 1827
Ann						Philetus	21 Jul 1827
Biddy	20	F	None	Ireland	U.S.A.	Dalhouse Castle	21 Aug 1829
F.	25	M	Merchant	United States		Howard	17 Oct 1822
F.	28	M	Mercht.	N. York	New York	Lewis	29 Oct 1825
Francis	24	M	Mercht.	France	France	Stephania	13 Sep 1821
Francis	24		None	France		Bayard	10 Sep 1827
H.	28	F		G. Britain	Canada	Columbia	7 Sep 1827
H.	28	M		G. Britain	Canada	Columbia	7 Sep 1827
James	26	M	Gentn.	England	Returning to St. Johns	Matvina	19 Oct 1826

NAMES OF PASSENGERS	AGE	SEX	OCCUPATIONS	COUNTRY TO WHICH THEY BELONG	COUNTRY THEY INTEND TO INHABIT	SHIPS/DATES OF ARRIVAL	
SALMON (cont'd)							
Jas.	2	M		Great Britain	New York	Philetus	21 Jul 1827
John	30	M		Great Britain	New York	Philetus	21 Jul 1827
John	61 6/12	M	Gentleman	England	Kentucky	Chelsea	16 May 1828
Lackey	5	M		Great Britain	New York	Philetus	21 Jul 1827
Louisa	20	F	None	England	United States	Montgomery	6 Mar 1829
M.	28	M	Secretary to the Ambassador	Spain	Spain	James Monroe	5 Apr 1820
Margt.	25	F		Great Britain	New York	Philetus	21 Jul 1827
R.	53	M	Artist	With intention to become citizen		New York	18 Jul 1828
Thomas	22	M	Labourer	Ireland		Marchioness	13 May 1828
W.	8	M	Artist	With intention to become citizen		New York	18 Jul 1828
SALMOND, P. R.	20	M	Merchant	U. States	U. States	Mary	19 May 1823
Sam.	35	M	Merchant	U. States	U. States	Rodman	28 May 1825
Saml.	34	M	Merchant	U. States	U. States	Mary	19 May 1823
SALMONE, Ellen	40	F		Great Britain	U. States	Columbia	22 Sep 1828
Wm.	45	M	Watchmaker	Great Britain	U. States	Columbia	22 Sep 1828
SALOMONS, Joachim	48	M	Mercht.	St. Thomas	St. Thomas	Esther	9 May 1825
SALON, Henry	35	M	Merchant	U.S. America, Augusta, Georgia		Martha	15 Oct 1825
SALOUN, C.	35	M	Mariner	France	U. States	Transit	26 Apr 1823
SALS, Ellen	40		Merchant	Halifax	U. States	Edwin	26 Sep 1828
SALSBURY,							
Elizabeth, Miss	6	F	None	Grate Britain	...	Courier	14 Jun 1825
Graspy	4	M		G. Britain	U. States	Freak	9 Jun 1828
Hannah	1	F		G. Britain	U. States	Freak	9 Jun 1828
Hugh	20	M	Farmer	Ireland	United States	Loore	9 Sep 1822
Joseph	36	M	Labourer	G. Britain	U. States	Freak	9 Jun 1828
Mary	36	F		G. Britain	U. States	Freak	9 Jun 1828
Robert	6	M		G. Britain	U. States	Freak	9 Jun 1828
SALSEDA, Jacob	26	M	Merchant	Curacoa	Curacoa	William Prince	30 May 1825
SALSLEY, William	48	M	Tailor	England	America	Plutarch	18 Jul 1826
SALT, William	55	M	Farmer	Gt. Britain	U.S. of America	Friends	25 Sep 1823
SALTEMAHIER, A.	45	M	Farmer	France	United States	Le Voltaire	19 Jul 1828
J. Lorn.	24	M	Cooper	France	United States	Le Voltaire	19 Jul 1828
SALTENSTALL, Wm. U.	30	M	Merchant	U. States	U. States	Perseverance	11 Jun 1824
SALTER, James	56	M	Printer & Binder	Dartmouth, England	N. York	Resolution	6 Jun 1822
Jane	30	F		England	America	Brittannia	28 Feb 1827
Saml.	30	M	Shoe Maker	England	Boston, U.S.	Angelica	18 Aug 1823
SALTINSTALL, W. W.	28	M	Merchant	United States	U. States	Blue Ey'd Mary	26 Jun 1823
SALTONSALL, W.	23	M	Merchant	U. States	U. States	Emma	24 Jun 1822
SALTUS, Wm.	30	M	Merchant	Bermuda	U. States	Wormontagus	11 Apr 1823
SALVE, Susan	46	F	Cook	France	U. States	Spartan	16 Feb 1825
SAM..., Da...	...	...	...	...	...	William Thompson	30 Sep 1824
SAMARAN, Lewis	45	M	Doctor	I[sland] Cuba	Spain	Abigail	21 Mar 1825
SAMAT, Jno.	27	M	Merchant	United States	U. States	Native	8 Feb 1826
John	28	M	Merchant	New York	New York	Rebecca	31 Oct 1825
John	30	M	Merct.	Havana	U. States	Greek	3 Aug 1825
SAMB, Wm.	40	F	Lady	England	U. States	Seine	10 Jun 1822
SAMER, John	14	M	Farmer	Alsace in the Department of Upper and lower Rhine	United States	Carolina Augusta	16 May 1828
SAMFORD, Francis	24	M	Machine Maker	England	U.S. America	New Hampshire	28 Sep 1826
SAMMATRON, Bridget	28	F	None	Great Britain	United States	Mount Vernon	17 Jun 1825
SAMMONS, Mary	23	F	Spinster	United States	United States	James Monroe	12 Aug 1828
SAMO, Charles	28	M		America	New York	Cincinnatus	5 Dec 1825
SAMOND, Sam	24	M	Merchant	Great Britain	United States	Atlantic	8 Dec 1827
SAMPANAD, Victor	18	M	Merchant	U. States	Alexandria	Howard	11 Jan 1827
SAMPELLO, M.	23	M		Spain		Apollo	11 Jun 1828
SAMPEY, John	22	M	Labourer	Ireland	United States	Louisa	7 Oct 1824
SAMPLE, Francis	30	M	Carpenter	Ireland	United States	St. Michaels	23 Dec 1826
James R.	37	M	Merchant	Barbados	Rover [?]	Cannon	18 Aug 1821
Samuel	30	M	Mason	Ireland	United States	Robert Fulton	24 Jul 1826

NAMES OF PASSENGERS	AGE	SEX	OCCUPATIONS	COUNTRY TO WHICH THEY BELONG	COUNTRY THEY INTEND TO INHABIT	SHIPS/DATES OF ARRIVAL	
SAMPSON, Angelica	20	F		England	U. States	Cincinnatus	24 May 1821
David	28	M	Taylor	Scotland	New York	Joseph Hume	26 Oct 1829
Francis	60	M	...	Ireland	United States	General Putnam	20 Jun 1825
Hy.	20	M	None	Great Britian	U. States	Pallas	17 Aug 1824
J. H., Mr.	28	M	Merchant	Great Britain	Great Britain	Roman	10 May 1828
J. H., Mrs.	27	F	None	Great Britain	Great Britain	Roman	10 May 1828
Jane	40	F	dress Maker	Great Britain	United States	Exertion	17 Jul 1829
John	22	M	Merchant	Scotland	United States	Commerce	17 Jul 1823
John	60	M	...	Ireland	United States	General Putnam	20 Jun 1825
Jos. W.	28	M	Merchant	Gt. Brittane	United States	Cortes	28 Nov 1823
Mungo	22	M	Taylor	Scotland	New York	Joseph Hume	26 Oct 1829
Samuel	54	M	Merchant	Gt. Britain	Canada	Corks	3 Aug 1824
Samuel	58	M		England	U. States	Adams	23 Jun 1828
Sandy	22	M	Shoemaker	Scotland	United States	John Dickinson	12 Aug 1824
Sarah	60	F	...	Ireland	United States	General Putnam	20 Jun 1825
Wm.	...	M	...	Ireland	United States	General Putnam	20 Jun 1825
Wm.	26	M	Carpenter	Great Britain	United States	Exertion	17 Jul 1829
SAMSEY, James	25	M	Mason	Ireland	America	William	21 May 1825
Hy.	26	M	Merchant	England	U. States	Six Brothers	4 Jun 1822
John	33	M	Merchant	United States	United States	Howard	27 Sep 1826
SAMUEL, —			their children [Jno. & An], ages 3, 7 & 12, 2 females & 1 male	England		New York Packet	20 Mar 1824
Albert	21	M	Merchant	United States	U. States	Brighton	14 Apr 1828
An	35	F		England		New York Packet	20 Mar 1824
David	18	M	Farmer	Wales	Uncertain	John Wells	22 Sep 1824
David	20	M	Mercht.	Gt. Brittian	United States	Nestor	14 Nov 1823
David	24	M	Merchant	Great Britain	United States	New York	19 Nov 1828
Edwd.	26	M		Halifax	some to return & the others to Canada	Albert	14 May 1822
Frederick	22	M	Mercht.	Gt. Brittian	United States	Nestor	14 Nov 1823
Frederick	24	M	Merchant	United States	U. States	Brighton	14 Apr 1828
Jno.	40	M		England		New York Packet	20 Mar 1824
SAMUELS, Fred.	22		Merchant	England	England	Hudson	14 Jun 1827
Nathan	19	M		Great Brittian	United States	Carolina Augusta	2 Dec 1828
SAN..ELER, Richard	26	M	Leather Dresser	Great Britten	America	Cortes	6 Mar 1827
SAN ANTONIA, —, Mrs.	18	F		La Guayra	U.S.	Love	12 Oct 1827
SANAPH, Joseph	29	M	Merchant	Switzerland	U. States	Canada	4 Oct 1824
SANBURGH, M.	25 6/12	F		Ireland	U. States	Alex Mansfield	1 Jun 1822
SANBURN, Amos	28	M	Seaman	Boston, Mass.	U. States	Pioneer	6 May 1828
SANCHER, Dier	41	M	Laborer	Hannover	New York	Constitution	29 Aug 1821
SANCHES, Maria Josefa *died 11th March at 10 P.M.	38	F		Mexico	Spain	Sciot	12 Mar 1828
Pedro M.	16	M	Student	Cuba	Spain	Jane	29 Jul 1823
SANCHEZ, —	14			Spain	U. States	Lucy Ann	4 Sep 1822
—, Mrs.	22	F		Havana	U. States	Hesperion	28 Oct 1823
—, Mrs.	35	M		Spain	U. States	Lucy Ann	4 Sep 1822
Jas.	45	M	Merchant	Spain	Spain	Lucy Ann	4 Sep 1822
Jose	46	M	Merchant	Havana	U. States	Hesperion	28 Oct 1823
Rapheal	19	M	Gent.	Spain	Cuba	Fabius	24 Oct 1825
Rd. Grabier	28	M	Merchant	Spain	non Resident	Charleston Packet	25 Jul 1821
Santiogo	38	M	Merchant	Spain	Spain	Sciot	12 Mar 1828
SANCHYEZ, Ealogio	15	M	Gent.	Spain	Cuba	Fabius	24 Oct 1825
SANCKES, Laurence	30	M	Merchant	U. States	United States	Dromo	22 Feb 1827
SAND, Henri	26	M	Merchant	U. States	U. States	Martha	18 Oct 1824
SANDARK, John	35	M	Trader	United States	United States	Elbe	22 Aug 1828
SANDBACH, Eliz.	30	F	Lady	Philadea.	Philadea.	Wm. Thompson	13 Sep 1823
SANDBACK, H. R.	22	M	Merchant	England	U. States	General Jackson	14 Jul 1829

NAMES OF PASSENGERS	AGE	SEX	OCCUPATIONS	COUNTRY TO WHICH THEY BELONG	COUNTRY THEY INTEND TO INHABIT	SHIPS/DATES OF ARRIVAL
SANDERING, Wilhemina, Zyn Vrouw [his wife, Adam Pareter]	26	F		Otweilder	United States	Juffraw Johanna 16 Oct 1821
SANDERN, Mary Ann	10	F	None	Great Britain	United States	Columbia 1 Dec 1823
SANDERS, Albert	25	M	Mariner	New providence	U. States	Cicero 16 May 1823
Benjamin	7	M		England	United States	St. John 5 Oct 1829
Geo.	25	M	Merchant	America	U. States	Magnolia 29 Apr 1822
Hannah	23	F	Servant	Ireland	U. States	Edwin 1 Jul 1829
Isiaiah	28	M	pudler		uncertain	Mount Vernon 29 Aug 1828
John	25	M	Mechanic	U. Kingdom Great Britain	United States	Cambria 7 May 1828
John	37	M	Engineer	England	U. States	Messenger 10 Jul 1829
Joseph	32	M	Merchant	U. States	U. States	Sultana 6 Nov 1828
M.	52	M	Mariner	United States	U. States	Hiram 8 Jul 1828
M.	52	M	Mariner	United States	United States	Hiram 8 Jul 1829
N., Mrs.	36	F		Vienna	U. States	Minerva 24 Sep 1821
Richd.	23	M	Labourer	Ireland	U. States	Sarah G 30 Jun 1828
Sarah	18	F		England	United States	St. John 5 Oct 1829
Thomas	73	M	Farmer	England	United States	Acosta 28 Jul 1823
Thos.	50	M	Mechanic	England	United States	St. John 5 Oct 1829
William	25	M	Labrer	Ireland	U. States	Edwin 1 Jul 1829
William	35	M	Shoe Maker	England	Great Britian	Florida 13 Feb 1826
SANDERSON, Charles	20	M	Printer	Gt. Britain	United States	Meteor 19 Aug 1829
Edward	20	M	Merchant	England	England	Albion 4 Oct 1820
Edward F.	26	M	Merchant	Gt. Britain	Gt. Britain	New York 5 Jul 1826
Edwd.	25	M	Gt. Britin	U. States	U. States	Columbia 1 Dec 1824
Edwd. F.	26		Mercht.	England	U. States	New York 30 Oct 1827
Eliza	2	F	child [of Margrat]	G. Britain	United States	Louisa 14 Jun 1825
James	21	M	child [of Margrat]	G. Britain	United States	Louisa 14 Jun 1825
James	35	M	Merchant	England	England	Albion 4 Oct 1820
Jane	26			United States	U. States	New York 30 Oct 1827
Jas.	38	M	Merchant	England	U. States	New York 11 Jul 1823
John	23	M	Clothier	Scotland	U. States	Reaper 31 May 1824
Margrat	23	F	going to her Husband	G. Britain	United States	Louisa 14 Jun 1825
Mary Ann	9	F	child [of Margrat]	G. Britain	United States	Louisa 14 Jun 1825
Robert	25	M	Farmer	Scotland	United States	Commerce 17 Jul 1823
S., Capt.	42	M	Mariner	America	America	Atlantic 29 Jun 1822
William	6	M	child [of Margrat]	G. Britain	United States	Louisa 14 Jun 1825
SANDERSTON, Elizabeth	38	F	None	Great Britain	United States	Blakely 29 Sep 1826
Wm.	35	M	...	Great Britain	United States	Blakely 29 Sep 1826
SANDFORD, Cathrine	2 3/12	F		England	U.S. of America	Illinois 30 Apr 1823
Elisabeth	8 2/12	F		England	U.S. of America	Illinois 30 Apr 1823
Elisabeth	30 5/12	F		England	U.S. of America	Illinois 30 Apr 1823
John	4 1/12	M		England	U.S. of America	Illinois 30 Apr 1823
John	36 3/12	M	Farmer	England	U.S. of America	Illinois 30 Apr 1823
Joseph	1	M		England	U.S. of America	Illinois 30 Apr 1823
SANDHUM, Andrew	20	M	None	Ireland	U. States	Henry Kneeland 27 Jul 1825
SANDIFORD, William	26 2/12	M	Merchant	Great Britain	United States	Cambria 26 Dec 1827
SANDILAND, Daniel	20	M		Scotland	United States	St. John 5 Oct 1829
Janet	10	F		Scotland	United States	St. John 5 Oct 1829
John	1	M		Scotland	United States	St. John 5 Oct 1829
John, Mrs.	60	F		Scotland	United States	St. John 5 Oct 1829
Margaret	4	F		Scotland	United States	St. John 5 Oct 1829
Mary	7	F		Scotland	United States	St. John 5 Oct 1829
Mary	26	F		Scotland	United States	St. John 5 Oct 1829
Thos.	30	M	Manufacturer	Scotland	United States	St. John 5 Oct 1829
SANDLAND, Catharine	6	F		Great Britain	U. States	Great Britain 18 Mar 1828
Henry	8	M		Great Britain	U. States	Great Britain 18 Mar 1828
Thomas	28	M	Button Maker	Great Britain	U. States	Great Britain 18 Mar 1828
SANDLOT, —	4	M	Infant	France	gone to France	Diana 9 Aug 1823
J. C.	60	M	Planter	France	gone to France	Diana 9 Aug 1823
SANDOZ, Henry	29	M	Watchmaker	Suisse	United States	Montano 5 May 1828
SANDRA, F.	28	M	Barber	France	United States	Marmione 20 Nov 1821
SANDS, —, Mrs.	28	F		N. York	U. States	Little Cherub 12 Apr 1825

NAMES OF PASSENGERS	AGE	SEX	OCCUPATIONS	COUNTRY TO WHICH THEY BELONG	COUNTRY THEY INTEND TO INHABIT	SHIPS/DATES OF ARRIVAL	
SANDS (cont'd)							
A.	35	M	Captain	U. States	U. States	Fornax	14 Mar 1829
Abra.	26	M	Farmer	Great Britain	United States	Mary & Harriet	3 Jul 1829
Ferdinand	22	M	Gentleman	U. States	U. States	Susquehanna	16 May 1827
Fr.	30	M	Merchant	England	England	Albion	4 Oct 1820
Francis	28	M	Mariner	U. States	U.S.	Ambuscade	14 Mar 1820
James	36	M	Merchant	St. Johns	U. States	Isabella	28 Jun 1825
Jane	3/52	F	None	Great Britain	United States	Mary & Harriet	3 Jul 1829
John	32	M				Betsey	17 Aug 1820
John	62	M	Farmer			Acosta	28 Jul 1823
John	66			Sussex	...	Hudson	14 Jun 1827
Joseph	26	M	Merchant	Great Britain	United States	Florida	2 Sep 1822
Margaret	24	F	None	Great Britain	United States	Mary & Harriet	3 Jul 1829
Mary	7	F				Betsey	17 Aug 1820
Mary	23			United States	U. States	New York	30 Oct 1827
Mary	26	F				Betsey	17 Aug 1820
Sarah	4	F				Betsey	17 Aug 1820
Sarah	28	F	None	England	United States	Martha	17 Sep 1821
Sophia	2	F				Betsey	17 Aug 1820
Susanna	1 6/12	F	None	England	United States	Martha	17 Sep 1821
Thomas	30	M	Merchant	England	United States	Martha	17 Sep 1821
Thomas	42	M	Merchant	U.S. America	U.S. America	Columbia	3 Apr 1826
Thos.	33	M	Merchant	U. States	U. States	Amity	23 Sep 1823
Thos. B.	6	M	None	United States	United States	Martha	17 Sep 1821
SANDY, Margaret	18	F		U. States	U. States	Bayard	16 May 1827
Saml.	24	M	Tailor	Gt. Britain	U. States	Henry Kneeland	25 Sep 1827
SANEN, Peter	17	M	Farmer	Alsace in the Department of Upper and lower Rhine	United States	Carolina Augusta	16 May 1828
SANER, Madelina	13	F	Farmer	Alsace in the Department of Upper and lower Rhine	United States	Carolina Augusta	16 May 1828
SANFOOT, William	35	M	Doctor	Ireland	U. States	Wanderer	1 Sep 1828
SANGES, Adaline	3/12	F		Havana	United States	Lucinda	29 Jun 1825
Adolphe	7	M	None	Havana	United States	Lucinda	29 Jun 1825
Amelia	5	M	None	Havana	United States	Lucinda	29 Jun 1825
Anton	3	F	Lady	Havana	United States	Lucinda	29 Jun 1825
Wokar	30	F	Lady	Havana	United States	Lucinda	29 Jun 1825
SANLEY, C.	24	F		Great Brittain	United States	Sarah Ralston	27 Jan 1827
Thomas	24	M	Labourer	Great Brittain	United States	Sarah Ralston	27 Jan 1827
SANMIRHELE, G.	26	M	Merchant	Rome	Denmark	Betsey	5 Jul 1823
SANS, Francisco, Don	35	M	Seaman	Malaga	Malaga	Pleiades	5 Nov 1828
SANSAIS, Henri	12	M	Farmer	Germany	United States	Oxford	14 Aug 1828
SANSDRICK, Danl.	19	M		Wirtemburg	United States	Wade	29 Aug 1825
SANSOM, Saml.	40	M	Merchant	Great Britain	United States	Nimrod	5 Apr 1821
SANTANNA, Carlos	40	M	Servant	Cuba	Cuba	Andromache	18 May 1825
SANTANNO, C.	10	M		So. America	U. States	Eclipse	10 Jun 1823
Marcos	11	M		So. America	U. States	Eclipse	10 Jun 1823
SANTER, Jean Jacques	18	M	Merchant	U. States	U. States	Queen Mab	16 Mar 1825
SANTEREAU, Alexis D.	32	M	Merchant	France	U.S.	Edward Bonnaffe	20 Jun 1825
SANTESBOWNE, John	42		Farmer	Switzerland		Charlemagne	20 Aug 1829
SANTO,							
Joaquim Frs. Esperto	19	M	Gentleman	S. America	S. America	American	18 Oct 1824
SANZE, Marteo	27	M	Mercht.	Havanna	Havanna	Silvanus Jenkins	17 Nov 1828
SANZUS, Alexr.	9	M		Cuba	Spain	Transit	13 Nov 1823
Jos. M.	11	M		Cuba	Spain	Transit	13 Nov 1823
SAPE, Joseph	27	M	Jeweller	England	United States	Great Britain	5 Sep 1827
SAPOLMA, M.		M			U. States	Jane Maria	12 Aug 1829
SAPPAN, Bernard	10	M	Boy	Ireland	United States	Fabius	31 Jul 1829
Catherine	45	F	Spinster	Ireland	United States	Fabius	31 Jul 1829
Eleninor	14	F	Spinster	Ireland	United States	Fabius	31 Jul 1829
Mary	5	F	Child	Ireland	United States	Fabius	31 Jul 1829
Owen	18	M	Labourer	Ireland	United States	Fabius	31 Jul 1829
SAR ROMAN, Jose	35	M	Merchant	Spain	Matanzes	Emma	25 Oct 1825
SARA, Anthony	32	M	Merchant	Corsica	U. States	Tartar	13 Aug 1823
SARAGEN, Lucretia	35	F		America	New York	Queen Mab	20 Nov 1826

NAMES OF PASSENGERS	AGE	SEX	OCCUPATIONS	COUNTRY TO WHICH THEY BELONG	COUNTRY THEY INTEND TO INHABIT	SHIPS/DATES OF ARRIVAL	
SARANAC, Margaret	31	M	Servant	France	U. States	Mary Ann	30 Aug 1824
SARAZEN, Josephine	36	F	None	Cuba	Spain	Ariel	30 Jun 1828
SARCIA, Manuel, Don	40	M	Servant	Mexico		Mercid	21 Oct 1824
SARDONET, —	32	M	Carpenter	Port Au Prince	Port Au Prince	Jean Baptist	5 Mar 1827
SARGANT, Edwin	1 9/12	M		England	America	Criterion	27 Oct 1821
Mary	5	F		England	America	Criterion	27 Oct 1821
Mary	26	F		England	America	Criterion	27 Oct 1821
Wm.	8	M		England	America	Criterion	27 Oct 1821
Wm.	43	M	Husband Man	England	America	Criterion	27 Oct 1821
SARGEANT, Elisabeth	35	F		Great Britain	U. States	Ganges	21 Jun 1827
Jas., Jun.	30	M	Planter	U.S.	U.S.	New England	11 Jul 1827
M. H.	25	M	Mariner	United States	U. States	Harmony	12 Sep 1823
Samuel	6	M		Great Britain	U. States	Ganges	21 Jun 1827
Thomas	10	M		Great Britain	U. States	Ganges	21 Jun 1827
Thomas	35	M	Surveyor	Great Britain	U. States	Ganges	21 Jun 1827
SARGENT, Caroline	2		Co... Keeper	England	United States	Corinthian	7 Jul 1829
Jas., Jr.	25	M	Mercht.	Spain	U.S.	Emma	24 Jun 1825
L., Mrs.	30	F		Gaudaloupe	Morristown, N.J.	Horace	31 May 1822
Lambert S.	7	M		Gaudaloupe	Morristown, N.J.	Horace	31 May 1822
Mary	26		Co... Keeper	England	United States	Corinthian	7 Jul 1829
Peter	59	M	Merchant	England	Cuba	James Cropper	12 Jul 1822
Sarah Ann	5		Co... Keeper	England	United States	Corinthian	7 Jul 1829
Thos.		M				Chasseur	17 Aug 1824
William	29		Co... Keeper	England	United States	Corinthian	7 Jul 1829
SARGLE, Joshua	28	M	Merchant	Ireland	U. States	Pacific	16 Apr 1825
SARGONTON, Alphonse	27	M	Merchant	St. Thomas	France	Wanderer	4 Aug 1829
SARGRAVE, Patk.	28	M	Farmer	England	United States	Orozimbo	5 Mar 1827
SARI, —, Madam	22	F		U.S.	U.S.	Cadmus	11 Jul 1827
Alexander, Mr.	33	M	...	U.S.	U.S.	Cadmus	11 Jul 1827
Emanuel	3	M		U.S.	U.S.	Cadmus	11 Jul 1827
Joseph	1	M		U.S.	U.S.	Cadmus	11 Jul 1827
SARIAGLAZ, Uglin	38	M	Merch.	U. States	United States	Henri IV	14 Oct 1829
SARICE, —, Mrs.	60	F		Ireland	Pensylvania	Lima	5 Aug 1829
—, Mrs.	60	F		England	U. States	Lima	5 Aug 1829
Edmond	10	M		Ireland	Pensylvania	Lima	5 Aug 1829
Edmond	10	M		England	U. States	Lima	5 Aug 1829
SARIGRUN, J.	20	M	Weaver	Ireland	United States	Josephine	30 Apr 1828
SARJEANT, Thomas	27	M	Merchant	Great Britain	United States	Thames	16 May 1821
Thomas	30	M	Merchant	Great Britain	United States	Laurel	20 Apr 1826
SARNELL, John	26	M	Merchant	Spain	Spain	Commodore Chauncy	19 Jan 1826
SARNOL, D.	18	M	Merchant	Spain	U.S.	Richmond Packet	15 Jun 1826
SARON, Phinis	41		Merchant	France	France	Hopes Return	6 Sep 1823
SARR, George	37	M	...	England	U. States	York	10 Dec 1825
SARRAH, Nicholas	30	M	Mearcht.	United States	United States	Planter	26 Jul 1822
SARRINGTON, Gilbert	27	M	Labourer	U. States	U. States	Robt. Reade	12 Apr 1825
SARSFIELD, John	34	M	Labourer	Ireland	U. States	Albion	11 May 1827
SARTON, John	52	M	Gent	U. States	U. States	Charlemagne	19 Sep 1828
SARTOR, Antoney	32	M	Merchant	Italy	United States	White Oak	9 Oct 1828
SARVAINET, Caroline	27	F		American	U. States	Circassian	13 Jun 1825
SARY, Bernardine, Miss	29 11/12	F	Teacher	Nederland	America	Henry	17 May 1828
SASPORTOS, H.	25	M	Merchant	American	U. States	Brunswick	14 Feb 1829
SATCHEFF, Abrm.	22	M		G. Britain	U. States	Mary & Harriot	8 Sep 1828
SATER, Jos.	27			England		Anacreon	7 Sep 1827
SATHWELL, L.	24	M	Merchant	L'pool	N. York	James Cropper	4 Feb 1824
SATON, Henry	50	M	Gentleman	Great Britain	United States	Jupiter	14 Sep 1827
SATTEROL, Jeane Pere	22	F		England	U. States	Elizabeth	20 Sep 1822
SATTERTHWAITE, Thos. W.	27	M	Merchant	Canada	Canada	John Wells	16 May 1825
SATTERWAITE, Mary	19	F	Servant	Great Britain	Canada	Florida	2 Oct 1828
SATTLER, Catharine	22	F		France	America, U.N.S.	Great Britain	3 Aug 1829
Jaques	22	M	Shoemaker	France	America, U.N.S.	Great Britain	3 Aug 1829
SATZYR, George	34	M	Carpenter	Saxony	United States	Wade	29 Aug 1825
Johann	15	M		Saxony	United States	Wade	29 Aug 1825
SAUBEN, Nathaniel	56	M	Mariner	U. States	U. States	Sarah Herrick	15 Apr 1823
SAUCH, Miguel	50	M	Doctor	Spain	Spain	Catharine Rogers	6 Oct 1823

NAMES OF PASSENGERS	AGE	SEX	OCCUPATIONS	COUNTRY TO WHICH THEY BELONG	COUNTRY THEY INTEND TO INHABIT	SHIPS/DATES OF ARRIVAL	
SAUER, J. F.	43	M	Farmer	Germany	America	Howard	27 Sep 1826
J. P.	14	M	Farmer	Germany	America	Howard	27 Sep 1826
T. G.	18	M	Farmer	Germany	America	Howard	27 Sep 1826
W.	17	M	Farmer	Germany	America	Howard	27 Sep 1826
SAUFFER, Elizabeth	17	F		Switzerland	U.S.	Francois I	8 Aug 1829
John	20	M		Switzerland	U.S.	Francois I	8 Aug 1829
Margarita	12	F		Switzerland	U.S.	Francois I	8 Aug 1829
Maria	17	F		Switzerland	U.S.	Francois I	8 Aug 1829
Maria	20	F		Switzerland	U.S.	Francois I	8 Aug 1829
Maria	55	F		Switzerland	U.S.	Francois I	8 Aug 1829
Saml.	45	M	Labourer	Switzerland	U.S.	Francois I	8 Aug 1829
Samuel	24	M		Switzerland	U.S.	Francois I	8 Aug 1829
SAUL, Thomas	37	M	Mariner	U. States	U. States	Doris	21 Jan 1826
Thomas	39	M	Shipmaster	U. States	U. States	Mary Livingston	6 Dec 1827
Thos.	26	M		Galway	U. States	Eliza Ann	30 Jul 1823
SAULET, —, Mr.	42	M	Gentn.	France	Louisiana	Cadmus	16 Aug 1826
Madam	19	F		France	Louisiana	Cadmus	16 Aug 1826
SAUMANN, A.	40	M	Farmer	Switzerland	U.S.	Bayard	18 Oct 1826
SAUMETZ, D.	40	M	Store Keeper	United States		Howard	4 Feb 1826
SAUNBY, —, Mrs.	34	F		New York	New York	Hope	7 Oct 1825
Edwd.	48	M	Hatter	New York	New York	Hope	7 Oct 1825
Eliza	3	F		New York	New York	Hope	7 Oct 1825
SAUNDERS, —, Mrs.	40	F		England	America	Britannia	5 Nov 1828
...	...	M		England	America	Britannia	5 Nov 1828
Adam	11	M		England	America	Britannia	5 Nov 1828
Albert	29	M	Mariner	Bahamas	Bahamas	Fourth of July	19 Oct 1824
D.	21	M	Carpenter	England	United States	Earl of Liverpool	28 Apr 1824
D.	40	M	Merchant	Great Britain	United States	Isaac Hicks	6 Dec 1827
Danl.	27	M	Merchant	Ireland	U. States	Hector	18 Apr 1825
Edwd.	29	M	Merchant	Ireland	U. States	Hector	18 Apr 1825
Eliza	24	F	None	Ireland	U. States	Hector	18 Apr 1825
Elizabeth	19			Warwickshire	G. Brit.	London	13 Dec 1822
Ellen	6	F		England	America	Britannia	5 Nov 1828
Emma	5	F	Farmer	England		Marchioness	13 May 1828
G.	0 7/12	F	Daughter	Qubec	U. States	Columbia	12 Sep 1827
Geo.	40	M	Mechanic	England	America	Britannia	5 Nov 1828
George	6	M	Farmer	England		Marchioness	13 May 1828
Jas.	30	M	Merchant	Gt. Britain	Quebec	Isaac Hicks	18 Apr 1825
Jno.	5/12	M		U. States	U. States	New Packet	20 Sep 1826
John	9	M		England	America	Britannia	5 Nov 1828
John	22 5/12	M	Farmer	Scotland	United States	London	6 Feb 1829
John James, Mr.	35	M	Mercht.	England	United States	Manchester	15 Aug 1826
John L.	26	M	Lieutenant	U. States	U. States	Factor	9 Mar 1829
Joseph	1	M		England	America	Britannia	5 Nov 1828
Joseph	48	M	H. Carpenter	New York, U.S.	New York, U. States	Ann Maria	26 Apr 1822
Lydia, Miss	23	F	Servant	G. Britan	G. Britan	Canada	27 Sep 1826
Martha	23	F	None	Great Britain	United States	William & Jane	22 Aug 1820
Mary	3	F	Farmer	England		Marchioness	13 May 1828
Mary	38	F	Farmer	England		Marchioness	13 May 1828
Mary Ann	21	F	Lady	Qubec	U. States	Columbia	12 Sep 1827
Robert, Junr.	32	M	Gentleman	U. States	U. States	Edward Quesnel	16 Nov 1827
Samuel	5	M		England	America	Britannia	5 Nov 1828
Sarah	5	F		U. States	U. States	New Packet	20 Sep 1826
Simon	16	M		England	America	Britannia	5 Nov 1828
Susan	27	F		U. States	U. States	New Packet	20 Sep 1826
Thomas	4	M	Farmer	England		Marchioness	13 May 1828
Thomas	34	M	Farmer	England		Marchioness	13 May 1828
W.	33	M	Hatter	U. States	U. States	New Packet	20 Sep 1826
William	26 3/12	M	Farmer	Scotland	United States	London	6 Feb 1829
Wm.	14	M		U. States	U. States	New Packet	20 Sep 1826
Wm.	14	M		England	America	Britannia	5 Nov 1828
Wm.	24	M	Clerk	Great Britain	United States	William & Jane	22 Aug 1820
SAUNTER, William	23 1/12	M	Farmer	U. Kingdom of Great Britain	United States	Cambria	7 May 1828
SAURAGE, J.	21	M	Weaver			Henri IV	17 May 1828
SAURINT, J. B. V.	26	M	Plaisterer	France	U. States	Montano	23 Apr 1825
SAUVALLE, Alfred	12	M	None	United States	United States	Montano	4 Nov 1823

NAMES OF PASSENGERS	AGE	SEX	OCCUPATIONS	COUNTRY TO WHICH THEY BELONG	COUNTRY THEY INTEND TO INHABIT	SHIPS/DATES OF ARRIVAL	
SAUVALLE (cont'd)							
Anna C., Mrs.	30	F	None	United States	United States	Montano	4 Nov 1823
Wm.	10	M	None	United States	United States	Montano	4 Nov 1823
SAUVAT, E.	14	M			U. States	Elizabeth Malvina	6 Dec 1827
SAUX, Thomas	46	M	Surveyor	U. Kingdom, G. Britain & Ireland	Pensylvania	James Cropper	21 Oct 1825
SAVAGE, —, Mistress	38	F	Woman	England	U. States	George Canning	13 Jun 1826
Ann L.	24	F	None	United States	United States	Charles Amburger	16 Aug 1826
Anna L.	28	F	Lady	U. States	U. States	Charles Amburger	11 Oct 1827
Augustus	4	M		United States	United States	Gem	24 Oct 1825
C.	27	M	Merchant	U. States	United States	Florida	14 Sep 1827
C.	35	M		England		Ann	17 May 1822
C., Esq.	40	M	Cl. General of Guatamala	U.S.	U.S.	Frances	21 Mar 1827
Caroline	14	F		United States	United States	Gem	24 Oct 1825
Charles	8	M		United States	United States	Gem	24 Oct 1825
Charles	48		American Consul, white	Gautemalia & Omoa		Martha	10 Mar 1829
Crafield	31	M	Carpenter	England	United States	Illinois	26 Dec 1821
Croffield	29	M	Mechanic	U. States	United States	Neptune	5 Jul 1820
Gordon	22	M	Journeyman of Shoemaker [Jas. McKibbin]	Ireland	United States	James Monroe	26 Aug 1822
H.	28	M		U. States	U. States	Horatio	9 Jun 1828
H. R.	27	M	Mercht.	U.S.	U.S.	Camden	24 Aug 1827
Henry	23	M	Merchant	Jamaica	U. States	Forest	15 Dec 1827
Hugh	30	M	Laborer			Czar	29 Aug 1829
James	24	M	Farmer	St. John	United States	Lingan	16 Jul 1822
James	40	M	Lawyer	United States	United States	Cuba	3 Jan 1823
Jno.	32	M	Planter	Jamacica	U. States	Nile	15 Aug 1823
John	21	M	Gentleman	U. States	U. States	Hero	21 Jan 1825
John	28	M	Clergyman	Cork	Philada.	Debby & Eliza	29 Jul 1824
John	28	M	Yeoman	Ireland	United States	Borneo	9 Jul 1827
John Y.	37	M	Watchmaker	United States	United States	Cortes	7 Dec 1825
Kitty	26	F	Lady	Ireland	United States	Borneo	9 Jul 1827
Margaret	50	F		U. States	U. States	Bayard	16 May 1827
Mary	4	F		Jamaica	U. States	Nile	15 Aug 1823
Osborne	20	M	Cabinet Maker	England	New York	Brighton	16 Nov 1826
Philip	24	M	Farmer	Ireland	America	Superior	12 Jun 1824
Robt.	26	M	Labourer	Great Britain		Moro Castle	6 Jul 1827
Sarah	32	F		United States	United States	Gem	24 Oct 1825
Sarah	50	F	Confectioner	Ireland	New York	Carolina Ann	15 Oct 1824
W.	22	M	Farmer	Great Brit.	U. States	George	31 Jul 1820
William	24	M	...	Ireland	United States	Trident	18 Jul 1827
William	50	M	Gentleman	United States	United States	General Warren	5 May 1828
Wm.	23	M	Laborer	Great Brittan	U. States	Gem	26 Jul 1827
Wm.	30	M	Carpenter	Connecticutt	U. States	Romulus	26 Apr 1822
SAVALIA, Bacento	40	M	Merchant	Cuba	Havanna, Cuba	Robert Read	8 Dec 1826
SAVANT, Carmill	14	M		France	U. States	Ann Celia	29 Aug 1826
SAVERTY, Peter	30	M	Labourer	G. Britain	U. States	London	23 Sep 1828
SAVIGNAE, Peter	23	M	Merchant	U. States	U. States	Commodore Perry	9 Apr 1821
SAVILL, Robert	25	M	Weaver	Ireland	United States	Enterprize	23 Jul 1827
SAVILLE, Ellen	2	F		G. Britain	U. States	St. George	7 Jun 1828
Esther	28	F	None	Great Britain	United States	Atlantic	28 May 1827
Ira	26	M	Merchant	U. States	U. States	Signal	5 Oct 1825
Joseph	1	M	None	Great Britain	United States	Atlantic	28 May 1827
Joseph	30	M	Clothier	Great Britain	United States	Atlantic	28 May 1827
Lucy	5	F	None	Great Britain	United States	Atlantic	28 May 1827
Mary Ann	6	F	None	Great Britain	United States	Atlantic	28 May 1827
SAVISNEER, James	23	M	Farmer	England	U. States	Acasta	11 Dec 1826
SAVON, Augustus ...	23		Gentleman	Brazil	United States	Cambria	19 Oct 1829
SAWDDON, James	22	M	Mechanic	England	England	John Wells	29 Jan 1825
SAWDON, John	31	M	Farmer	Lowerthorp	U. States	Manhattan	21 May 1821
Wm.	29	M	Shoemaker	England	U. States	Commerce	28 May 1824
SAWER, William	19	M	...	England	America	Cincinnatus	22 May 1826

NAMES OF PASSENGERS	AGE	SEX	OCCUPATIONS	COUNTRY TO WHICH THEY BELONG	COUNTRY THEY INTEND TO INHABIT	SHIPS/DATES OF ARRIVAL	
SAWLER, James	27 5/12	M	Labourer	Ireland	United States	Wilson	22 Jun 1824
SAWOOD, Saml.	20		Labourer	Rualon, England	Great Britain	Franklin	22 Jun 1827
SAWVELL, William	25	M	...	Ireland	United States	Nancey	8 Jun 1822
SAWYER, Agnass	10	F	Daughter	Scotland	America	Camillus	12 Sep 1822
B.	26	M	Merchant	U. States		Charleston Packet	4 May 1821
Camillus	8/365	F	Daughter	Born at Sea	America	Camillus	12 Sep 1822
Chatrine	30	F	Wife	Scotland	America	Camillus	12 Sep 1822
Edmund	23	M	Merchant	U. States	U. States	Acasta	27 Aug 1821
Elizabeth	9	F	Daughter	Scotland	America	Camillus	12 Sep 1822
Frances	21	F	Child	Ireland	United States	Dublin Packet	23 May 1828
Fredk.	20	M	Mariner	New providence	U. States	Cicero	16 May 1823
O...	22	M	Pilot	N. York	N. York	Andrew Jackson	23 Mar 1822
Ri.	4	M	Son	Scotland	America	Camillus	12 Sep 1822
Scott	33	M	Laborer	Scotland	America	Camillus	12 Sep 1822
William	28	M	Servant to Mr. McGillivray	Great Britain	United States	Robert Fulton	27 Jun 1822
SAWYERS, Ewd.	50	M	Farmer	G. Britain	Canada	Columbia	7 Sep 1827
SAXON, ...	23	M	Farmer	G. Britain	U. States	America	17 Oct 1825
Catharine	8	F		Great Britain		Robert Fulton	8 Mar 1823
Charl...	48	F		Great Britain		Robert Fulton	8 Mar 1823
Chr...	19	F		Great Britain		Robert Fulton	8 Mar 1823
John	52	M	Farmer	Great Britain		Robert Fulton	8 Mar 1823
SAXTON, Samuel	21	M	Farmer	England	U. States	Montgomery	18 Oct 1828
Thomas	30	M	Laborer, Spinster or Child	Ireland	United States	Ann Maria	4 Aug 1827
SAYER, Ann	38	F		England	U.S.A.	Hudson	21 Aug 1829
William	42	M	Merchant	U. States	U. States	Mary Ann	27 Feb 1824
SAYERS, Arch.	28	M	Merchant	U. States	U. States	Worromontogus	23 Jun 1823
Ewd., Jr.	24	F		G. Britain	Canada	Columbia	7 Sep 1827
John	7	M		Gt. Britain	United States	Columbia	7 Sep 1827
Sarah	23	F		G. Britain	Canada	Columbia	7 Sep 1827
Sarah	48	F		G. Britain	Canada	Columbia	7 Sep 1827
SAYLE, Cathe.	58	F	None	Isle of Man		Ocean	13 Jul 1827
Elizh.	14	F	None	Isle of Man		Ocean	13 Jul 1827
John	16	M	Farmer	Isle of Man		Ocean	13 Jul 1827
John	61	M	Preacher	Isle of Man		Ocean	13 Jul 1827
Thos.	21	M	Farmer	Isle of Man		Ocean	13 Jul 1827
SAYNER, John	21 8/12	M	Glass Manufacturer	England	U.S. American	Criterion	7 Jul 1824
Thomas	23 10/12	M	Glass Manufacturer	England	U.S. American	Criterion	7 Jul 1824
SAYNON, Roger	27	M	Labourer	Ireland		Marchioness	13 May 1828
SAYNS, Juan	25	M	Mercht.	Spain	United States	Conclusion	4 Feb 1829
SAYRE, William H.	26	M	Captain, Officers & crew of the Brig George of New York (wrecked at Fayal)	U.S. America	U.S.A.	Gallego	13 Mar 1829
Wm.	36	M	Merchant	U. States	U. States	Abby M.	7 Apr 1825
SAYRELL, Jno.	42	M	Farmer	England	U. States	Aolus	1 Aug 1823
SAYRES, Betsey	24	F		Ireland	America	Ann	11 Apr 1821
Edward	22	M	Mercht.	England	United States	Hannibal	6 Sep 1824
Gerald	3	F		Ireland	America	Ann	11 Apr 1821
Margaret	19					Mount Vernon	26 Aug 1820
Margaret	52	F		Ireland	America	Ann	11 Apr 1821
Mary	8	F		Gt. Britain	United States	Columbia	7 Sep 1827
Sarah	19	F		Ireland	America	Ann	11 Apr 1821
SAYRLES, ...	26	M				Eliza Grant	6 Oct 1828
SAYWARD, Hy.	49	M	Mariner	U. States	U. States	Florida	25 Apr 1825
SC..., J...	20	M	Servant	Denmark	Denmark	Gleaner	31 Jul 1821
SCAINBOROUGH, Elinor	19	M		Ireland	U. States	Climax	6 Aug 1822
Jno.	11	M		Ireland	U. States	Climax	6 Aug 1822
SCAINSBOROUGH, D.	25	M	Shoemaker	Ireland	U. States	Climax	6 Aug 1822
Hanah	22	F		Ireland	U. States	Climax	6 Aug 1822
SCAITH, Catharine	38	F		U. States	U. States	William Thompson	27 May 1824
Thos.	38	M	Merchant	U. States	U. States	William Thompson	27 May 1824
SCALES, Pat	...	M	Labourer	Ireland	Unt. St. America	Wilson	21 May 1827

NAMES OF PASSENGERS	AGE	SEX	OCCUPATIONS	COUNTRY TO WHICH THEY BELONG	COUNTRY THEY INTEND TO INHABIT	SHIPS/DATES OF ARRIVAL	
SCALINO, Abindio	23	M	Merchant	Italy	New York	Corinthian	27 Apr 1824
SCALLON, —, Dr.	55	M	Doctor	Newfoundland	Newfoundland	Mariner	11 Jul 1823
Jno.	16	M	Clerk	Ireland	United States	Dublin Packet	6 Dec 1827
SCAMMEL, M., Mrs.	35	F		U.S.	U.S.	York	1 Dec 1827
SCANDELL, Louis	16	M	Gentleman	Mexico	England	Brown	23 Dec 1826
SCANLAN, Ann	19	F	Spinster	Ireland	United States	Gem	16 Jun 1824
Elesay	1	F	Child	Ireland	United States	Sarah G	19 Jun 1827
James	19	M	Farmer	Ireland	United States	Trident	17 May 1825
Nicholas	20		Labourer			Rufus King	7 Aug 1820
P. N.	26	M	Surgeon	Demerara	Demerara	William Frederick	17 Mar 1825
Patrick	24	M	Servant	Great Britian	U. States	Pallas	17 Aug 1824
SCANLIN, Allen	28	M	Laborer	Ireland	United States	Sarah G	19 Jun 1827
John	30	M	Labourer	Ireland	U. States	Hanford	29 Dec 1828
Peter	30	M	Laborer	Ireland	United States	Sarah G	19 Jun 1827
SCANLON, Libby	24	F	Farmer	Ireland	U. States	Virginia	20 Jun 1825
SCANLOW, Bridget	13	F	Spinster	Ireland	United States	Wilson	6 Jun 1828
Ellen	7	F		Ireland	U. States	Wanderer	30 Sep 1828
SCANNEL, John	22	M	Shoemaker	Ireland	America	Liverpool	31 Aug 1827
SCANNELL, D.	22	M	Engraver	Ireland	U. States	Albion	11 May 1827
David	22	M	Farmer	England	United States	Ganges	10 May 1828
James	9	M		England	United States	Ganges	10 May 1828
Joana	3	F		England	United States	Ganges	10 May 1828
Joana	44	F		England	United States	Ganges	10 May 1828
John	17	M	Farmer	England	United States	Ganges	10 May 1828
Mary	19	F		England	United States	Ganges	10 May 1828
Peter	7	M		England	United States	Ganges	10 May 1828
Thos.	48	M	Farmer	England	United States	Ganges	10 May 1828
Tim	11	M		England	United States	Ganges	10 May 1828
Tom	10	M		England	United States	Ganges	10 May 1828
SCANTLEBURY, Joseph	29		Farmer	Sheffield		Mount Vernon	18 Oct 1822
Samuel	22		Farmer	Sheffield		Mount Vernon	18 Oct 1822
SCARBOROUGH, John	22		Painter	England	England	Thames	25 Oct 1821
SCARBROUGH, William	45	M	Merchant	Savannah, Georgia	Savannah, Georgia	Hector	11 Oct 1822
SCARLET, John	20	M	Dealer	F... Amah	United States	Minerva	30 Oct 1829
Prudentia	23	F	Spinster	Ireland	United States	Dublin Packet	3 May 1823
SCARTS, Catharine	2	F		France	Canada	Abby Jones	12 Jul 1827
Christian	30	M	Farmer	France	Canada	Abby Jones	12 Jul 1827
John	9	M		France	Canada	Abby Jones	12 Jul 1827
Mary	7	F		France	Canada	Abby Jones	12 Jul 1827
Matilda	33	F		France	Canada	Abby Jones	12 Jul 1827
Sapling	3	M		France	Canada	Abby Jones	12 Jul 1827
SCARVILL, Gearing	22	M	Mechanic	Great Britain	United States	Hannibal	12 Oct 1829
SCH..., ...	60 5/12	M	Farmer	America	U. States	France	26 Jun 1828
J. T. P.	26	M	None	England	United States	London Packet	25 Dec 1820
SCHA...LY, Christian	35	M	...	Germany	United States	Elizabeth	4 Sep 1826
SCHAAFSHALE, John Peter	48	M	brosier	Holland	United States	Plato	25 Aug 1829
Rudolph Jacob, his son [John Peter]	17	M	none	Holland	United States	Plato	25 Aug 1829
SCHACHERVEN, Agate	9	F		Switzerland	U. States	La Urania	3 Jul 1828
Cath. H.	34	F		Switzerland	U. States	La Urania	3 Jul 1828
Cathr.	11	F		Switzerland	U. States	La Urania	3 Jul 1828
J.	2	M		Switzerland	U. States	La Urania	3 Jul 1828
J.	6	M	Butcher	Switzerland	U. States	La Urania	3 Jul 1828
J.	37	M	Tailor	Switzerland	U. States	La Urania	3 Jul 1828
T.	4	M		Switzerland	U. States	La Urania	3 Jul 1828
T.	8	F		Switzerland	U. States	La Urania	3 Jul 1828
SCHACK, G.	8	M	Farmer	Switzerland	U. States	Alfred	8 Jul 1828
Jean	9	M	Farmer	Switzerland	U. States	Alfred	8 Jul 1828
M.	55	M	Farmer	Switzerland	U. States	Alfred	8 Jul 1828
T.	7	M	Farmer	Switzerland	U. States	Alfred	8 Jul 1828
SCHAEFFER, John Geo.	37	M	Shoemaker	France	U. States	Edward Quesnel	4 Aug 1828
SCHAEFTER, Anne M.	49	F	Farmer or Mechanic	Switzerland	U.S.	Edward Quesnel	31 Jul 1827
Henry C.	48	F	Farmer or Mechanic	Switzerland	U.S.	Edward Quesnel	31 Jul 1827
SCHAFFER, Herman	29		None	Germany	United States	Bayard	17 Dec 1827
V. F.	26	M	Gentleman	Germany	United States	Origon	8 Jun 1824

NAMES OF PASSENGERS	AGE	SEX	OCCUPATIONS	COUNTRY TO WHICH THEY BELONG	COUNTRY THEY INTEND TO INHABIT	SHIPS/DATES OF ARRIVAL	
SCHAFFNER, George	57	M	Doctor on Medicine St. Helliers		United States	Henri IV	2 Oct 1828
SCHAINE, Christien	30	F		Switzerland	U.S.	C. Amelia	30 Jun 1828
SCHALL, John	39	M	Gardiner	Switzerland	U.S.	Francois I	8 Aug 1829
Rob.	28	M	Gardiner	Switzerland	U.S.	Francois I	8 Aug 1829
SCHALLIG, Cathr.	5	F		Switzerland	U. States	La Urania	3 Jul 1828
Cathr.	33	F		Switzerland	U. States	La Urania	3 Jul 1828
F.	12	F		Switzerland	U. States	La Urania	3 Jul 1828
Geo.	40	M	Labourer	Switzerland	U. States	La Urania	3 Jul 1828
Jacque	4	M		Switzerland	U. States	La Urania	3 Jul 1828
Jeane	9	M		Switzerland	U. States	La Urania	3 Jul 1828
Joseph	15	M		Switzerland	U. States	La Urania	3 Jul 1828
Juan	2	F		Switzerland	U. States	La Urania	3 Jul 1828
M.	37	F		Switzerland	U. States	La Urania	3 Jul 1828
SCHANBACHER,							
Catharina	16	F	Farmer	Germany	United States	Elizabeth	27 Jul 1824
Christianne	2	F	Farmer	Germany	United States	Elizabeth	27 Jul 1824
Christina	9	F	Farmer	Germany	United States	Elizabeth	27 Jul 1824
Christina	48	F	Farmer	Germany	United States	Elizabeth	27 Jul 1824
Friderico	13	M	Farmer	Germany	United States	Elizabeth	27 Jul 1824
Georg	4	M	Farmer	Germany	United States	Elizabeth	27 Jul 1824
Jacob	19	M	Farmer	Germany	United States	Elizabeth	27 Jul 1824
Leonhard	18	M	Farmer	Germany	United States	Elizabeth	27 Jul 1824
Leonhard	48	M	Farmer	Germany	United States	Elizabeth	27 Jul 1824
SCHANLY, Joseph	2	M	his family [Joseph]	Germany	United States	Wm. Osborne	16 Sep 1828
Joseph	36	M	Miller	Germany	United States	Wm. Osborne	16 Sep 1828
Magdelene	6	F	his family [Joseph]	Germany	United States	Wm. Osborne	16 Sep 1828
Maria	4	F	his family [Joseph]	Germany	United States	Wm. Osborne	16 Sep 1828
Maria	36	F	his family [Joseph]	Germany	United States	Wm. Osborne	16 Sep 1828
SCHANTZ, Christn.	22	M		Switzerland	United States	Stephania	6 Dec 1827
SCHAPER, Adolphine			Servant	U.S.	U.S.	Sully	26 Oct 1829
H.	32	M	Merchant	Hamburg	Hamburg	Minerva	17 May 1828
SCHARDT, K.	21	M	Gentn.	Germany	United States	Robert Edwards	1 Jun 1826
SCHARK, Joh.	25	M	Agriculture	Wirtemburg	United States	Henri IV	14 Oct 1829
SCHARKE, John	22	M	Labourer	Gt. Brittan		L'Esperance	6 Sep 1828
Maurice	18	M	Taylor	Gt. Brittan		L'Esperance	6 Sep 1828
SCHARPENTIER,							
Jacob, kinder							
[child of Marten]	11	M		Nieder aurburg	United States	Juffraw Johanna	16 Oct 1821
Johan, kinder							
[child of Marten]	1	M		Limbach	United States	Juffraw Johanna	16 Oct 1821
Lourents, kinder							
[child of Marten]	17	M		Limbach	United States	Juffraw Johanna	16 Oct 1821
Marten	45	M	Boer	Courons	United States	Juffraw Johanna	16 Oct 1821
SCHARTSCAPIN,							
Dorothia	50	F	Farmer	Switzerland		Charlemagne	20 Aug 1829
Thomas	55	M	Farmer	Switzerland		Charlemagne	20 Aug 1829
SCHASSLER, Nics.	23	M	Laborer	Hannover	New York	Constitution	12 Jul 1827
SCHAUFFER, Fried.	40	M	Farmer	Switzerland		Charlemagne	20 Aug 1829
Mary	40	F	Farmer	Switzerland		Charlemagne	20 Aug 1829
SCHAUFORER, Cathrine	21	F		France	United States	Henri IV	2 Oct 1828
George	25	M	Shoemaker	France	United States	Henri IV	2 Oct 1828
SCHAUNDER, Adolphus	38	M	Farmer	Switzerland	U. States	Bayard	9 Nov 1825
SCHAVER, C.	6	M		Switzerland	U. States	La Urania	3 Jul 1828
C.	16	F		Switzerland	U. States	La Urania	3 Jul 1828
C. G.	46	F		Switzerland	U. States	La Urania	3 Jul 1828
H.	14	F		Switzerland	U. States	La Urania	3 Jul 1828
Hy.	51	M	Tailor	Switzerland	U. States	La Urania	3 Jul 1828
M.	9	F		Switzerland	U. States	La Urania	3 Jul 1828
SCHAZZACHELLE,							
Samuel	22	M	Priest	Italy		Edward Quesnel	17 Nov 1828
SCHEATON, E.	30	M	Merchant	Italy	United States	Cambridge	19 Sep 1828
SCHEDAGER, John	24	M	Servant	Switzarland		Armadillo	13 Aug 1829
SCHEFER, Adam	17	M	...	...		George	23 Sep 1824
Christian	22	M	...	...	...	George	23 Sep 1824
SCHEFFELIN, J.	27	M	Merchant	U. States	U. States	Abeona	11 Mar 1823
Jacob	32	M	Merchant	N. York	N. York	Altamira	16 May 1825
SCHEFIELD, John	48	M	Gardner	Scotland	United States	Orozimbo	5 Mar 1827
SCHEICH, Cath.	2	F	Farmer	Switzerland	U. States	Alfred	8 Jul 1828
J.	6	M	Farmer	Switzerland	U. States	Alfred	8 Jul 1828

NAMES OF PASSENGERS	AGE	SEX	OCCUPATIONS	COUNTRY TO WHICH THEY BELONG	COUNTRY THEY INTEND TO INHABIT	SHIPS/DATES OF ARRIVAL	
SCHEICH (cont'd)							
Maria	5	F	Farmer	Switzerland	U. States	Alfred	8 Jul 1828
Maria	44	F	Farmer	Switzerland	U. States	Alfred	8 Jul 1828
SCHEISER, Elizabeth	22	F	Farmer	Switzerland	U. States	Sully	15 Jul 1829
Justus	22	M	Farmer	Switzerland	U. States	Sully	15 Jul 1829
SCHEISS, Saphhire	28	M	Farmer	France	U. States	Edward Quesnel	4 Aug 1828
SCHEIZINGER,							
Catherine	45	F	Agriculturist	France	U.S.	Helen	3 May 1828
SCHELLINGER, Andrew	32	M	Weaver	Switzerland	U. States	Romulus	24 Sep 1828
Anna Maria	8	F		Switzerland	U. States	Romulus	24 Sep 1828
Christiana	2 6/12	F		Switzerland	U. States	Romulus	24 Sep 1828
Christiana	22	F		Switzerland	U. States	Romulus	24 Sep 1828
Eliza	34	F		Switzerland	U. States	Romulus	24 Sep 1828
SCHENCK, Abraham	50	M	Merchant	U. States	U. States	Canada	13 Oct 1825
Ann	35	F	Spinster	Ireland	United States	Diana	1 May 1826
Edward	1 2/12	M	None	Ireland	United States	Diana	1 May 1826
James	3	M	None	Ireland	United States	Diana	1 May 1826
John	14	M	None	Ireland	United States	Diana	1 May 1826
Paul R.	26	M	Merchant	Italy	U. States	Thomas Wilson	16 Sep 1822
Richard	8	M	None	Ireland	United States	Diana	1 May 1826
Thos.	11	M	None	Ireland	United States	Diana	1 May 1826
SCHENERMANN,							
Matthew	45	M	Distiller	Germany	U. States	Sully	24 Oct 1828
SCHENFELE, Ann Maria	1	F	Agriculture	Wirtemburg	United States	Henri IV	14 Oct 1829
Ann Maria	14	F	Agriculture	Wirtemburg	United States	Henri IV	14 Oct 1829
Ann Maria	28	F	Agriculture	Wirtemburg	United States	Henri IV	14 Oct 1829
Ann Maria	30	F	Agriculture	Wirtemburg	United States	Henri IV	14 Oct 1829
Catherine	67	F	Agriculture	Wirtemburg	United States	Henri IV	14 Oct 1829
George	3	M	Agriculture	Wirtemburg	United States	Henri IV	14 Oct 1829
George	6	M	Agriculture	Wirtemburg	United States	Henri IV	14 Oct 1829
Gulliel	5	M	Agriculture	Wirtemburg	United States	Henri IV	14 Oct 1829
Gulliel	38	M	Agriculture	Wirtemburg	United States	Henri IV	14 Oct 1829
Johanes	1	M	Agriculture	Wirtemburg	United States	Henri IV	14 Oct 1829
Johanus	3	M	Agriculture	Wirtemburg	United States	Henri IV	14 Oct 1829
John	30	M	Agriculture	Wirtemburg	United States	Henri IV	14 Oct 1829
John	71	M	Agriculture	France	United States	Henri IV	14 Oct 1829
SCHENKE, Christian	35	M	Servant	Switzarland		Armadillo	13 Aug 1829
SCHENLY, Catherine	18	F	his family [Joseph]	Germany	United States	Wm. Osborne	16 Sep 1828
Margret	20	F	his family [Joseph]	Germany	United States	Wm. Osborne	16 Sep 1828
SCHERBERGER,							
Catharine	4	F	None	Germany	U. States	Sully	24 Oct 1828
Christina	32	F	None	Germany	U. States	Sully	24 Oct 1828
Christina, Jr.	20	F	None	Germany	U. States	Sully	24 Oct 1828
John G.	34	M	Farmer	Germany	U. States	Sully	24 Oct 1828
John G., Jr.	8	M	None	Germany	U. States	Sully	24 Oct 1828
Madelina	2	F	None	Germany	U. States	Sully	24 Oct 1828
Mary	6	F	None	Germany	U. States	Sully	24 Oct 1828
SCHERMERHORN,							
Abm. M.	36	M		United States		Corinthian	27 Oct 1829
Mary K.	26	F		United States		Corinthian	27 Oct 1829
Susan	2	F		United States		Corinthian	27 Oct 1829
SCHETTLER,							
Wm. Edwd.	35	M	Merchant	Prussia	U. States	Chase	28 Sep 1826
SCHEVAL, Geswog	7	M	Agriculture	Wirtemburg	United States	Henri IV	14 Oct 1829
SCHIAFF, Jaques	19	F	Baker	France		Pallas	14 Jun 1828
Phillip	17	M		France		Pallas	14 Jun 1828
SCHICK, John	2	M		Great Britain	United States	Rosina	12 Aug 1823
Magt.	28	F		Great Britain	United States	Rosina	12 Aug 1823
Thomas	1	M		Great Britain	United States	Rosina	12 Aug 1823
Thos.	26	M	Labrour	Great Britain	United States	Rosina	12 Aug 1823
SCHICKLER, Adolphe	3	M	Weaver	Germany	Canada	Virginia	31 May 1828
Adolphe	29	M	Weaver	Germany	Canada	Virginia	31 May 1828
Aresile	36	F	Weaver	Germany	Canada	Virginia	31 May 1828
Bardon	8	F	Weaver	Germany	Canada	Virginia	31 May 1828
Carterrene	19	F	Weaver	Germany	Canada	Virginia	31 May 1828
Carterrene	40	F	Weaver	Germany	Canada	Virginia	31 May 1828
Cleater	9 1/2	F	Weaver	Germany	Canada	Virginia	31 May 1828
Frances	21	F	Weaver	Germany	Canada	Virginia	31 May 1828
Mariah	1	F	Weaver	Germany	Canada	Virginia	31 May 1828

NAMES OF PASSENGERS	AGE	SEX	OCCUPATIONS	COUNTRY TO WHICH THEY BELONG	COUNTRY THEY INTEND TO INHABIT	SHIPS/DATES OF ARRIVAL	
SCHIDER, Jacques	28	M	Shoe Maker	Switzerland	U.States	C. Amelia	30 Jun 1828
SCHIDT, George	52	M	Taylor	France	United States	Stephania	6 Dec 1827
SCHILB, Joachim	26	M	Kuikerbaker	gut acht beg Walkirch	United States	Juffraw Johanna	16 Oct 1821
SCHIMMON, Wm.	6	M		England	U. States	Emulous	22 Aug 1828
SCHINDLECKER, —, Mr.	45	M	Musician	Bavaria		François I	19 Nov 1828
SCHINDLER, Adolpha	48	M	Merchant	Germany	N. York	Stephania	29 Nov 1825
Ann Maria	36	F	Book Binder	France	United States	American	27 Aug 1827
Catherine	16	F	Farmer	France	United States	American	27 Aug 1827
Christian	15	M	Book Binder	France	United States	American	27 Aug 1827
John	16	M	Farmer	France	United States	American	27 Aug 1827
Joseph	15	M	Farmer	France	United States	American	27 Aug 1827
Maria A.	52	F	Farmer	France	United States	American	27 Aug 1827
Peter	13	M	Farmer	France	United States	American	27 Aug 1827
Peter	42	M	Farmer	France	United States	American	27 Aug 1827
SCHINDLEY, C.	15	M	Farmer	Swiss	U. States	Montano	2 Sep 1828
SCHIRER, Auguste	30			Germany	Interior	Desdemona	12 Jun 1826
SCHIULKLER, Agath	5	F	Farmer	Germany	United States	Oxford	14 Aug 1828
Agath	40	F	Farmer	Germany	United States	Oxford	14 Aug 1828
Cristini	9	F	Farmer	Germany	United States	Oxford	14 Aug 1828
John	50	M	Farmer	Germany	United States	Oxford	14 Aug 1828
Margaret	7	F	Farmer	Germany	United States	Oxford	14 Aug 1828
Osean	3	M	Farmer	Germany	United States	Oxford	14 Aug 1828
SCHLAFH, Benedict	40	M	Wheelright	Switzerland	United States	Cavalier	25 Jul 1828
SCHLAMBERGER, W.	27	M	Mechanic	France	France	Howard	27 Sep 1826
SCHLECHT, J. Martin	26	M	Gentleman	Rusia	In the Servis of the Rusian minister	William	12 Aug 1826
SCHLESINGER, Friedr. Salis.	31	M	Merchant	Germany	U. States	Canada	27 Sep 1826
SCHLESSINGER, P.	26	M	Merchant	Germany		Ariel	24 Sep 1827
SCHLEUB, J.	24	M	Farmer	France & Switzerland	U. States	Bayard	14 Jul 1826
SCHLIEP, Wm.	35	M	Merchant	Germany	U. States	Louisa Matilda	4 Dec 1821
SCHLITTLER, R.	25	M	Straw hat manufacturer	Switzerland	U. States	North Star	27 Oct 1828
SCHLONUGGER, Barbara	21	F		Germany	United States	Origon	8 Jun 1824
Christopher	13	M	Farmer	Germany	United States	Origon	8 Jun 1824
Jacob	12	M	Farmer	Germany	United States	Origon	8 Jun 1824
Jean	14	M	Farmer	Germany	United States	Origon	8 Jun 1824
Maria	18	F		Germany	United States	Origon	8 Jun 1824
Peter	20	M	Farmer	Germany	United States	Origon	8 Jun 1824
SCHLOSSEN, A.	35	M	Merchant	Germany	U. States	Panthea	8 Apr 1826
SCHMALTZHATT, Jacob	21	M	Weaver	Germany	U. States	Falcon	11 Jun 1827
SCHMANN, Isaac	3	M		Switzerland	United States	Thetis	5 Jul 1821
SCHMAT, Chas.	34	M	...	Sweden	N. York	Albion	11 Jun 1821
SCHMEDING, Chr.	44	F		Germany	U. States	Falcon	11 Jun 1827
SCHMELING, Jane	28	F		England	U. States	Agenora	18 Aug 1826
Peter A.	39	M	Music Master	France	U. States	Agenora	18 Aug 1826
SCHMENDERNER, Francis	34	F	Laborer	Switzerland	U.S.	C. Amelia	30 Jun 1828
SCHMICK, C.	34	M	Labourer	Switzerland	United States	India	4 Aug 1826
SCHMID, A.	17	M		Switzerland	U.S.	Francois I	8 Aug 1829
Alicia	2	F		Switzerland	U.S.	Francois I	8 Aug 1829
Catherine	4	F		Switzerland	U.S.	Francois I	8 Aug 1829
Catherine	27	F		Switzerland	U.S.	Francois I	8 Aug 1829
Eunice	6	F		Switzerland	U.S.	Francois I	8 Aug 1829
George	38	M	Farmer	Switzerland	U.S.	Francois I	8 Aug 1829
Maria	2	F		Switzerland	U.S.	Francois I	8 Aug 1829
Michel	52	M	Labourer	Switzerland	United States	Thetis	5 Jul 1821
SCHMIDT, Amelia	20	F	Wife	Switzerland	United States	Cambria	11 Feb 1829
Ballager	22	M	Agriculturist	France	U.S.	Helen	3 May 1828
Barbara	24	F	Farmer	France	France	Sully	15 Jul 1829
Catharine	13	F	Farmer	France	France	Sully	15 Jul 1829
Cathr.	4	F		France	United States	New England	29 Aug 1828
*Died 16 July Charles F.	1 1/12	M	Child	Switzerland	United States	Cambria	11 Feb 1829
Christian	21	M	Farmer	France	France	Sully	15 Jul 1829
Christr.	39	M	Cooper	France	United States	Pioneer	28 Jun 1827

NAMES OF PASSENGERS	AGE	SEX	OCCUPATIONS	COUNTRY TO WHICH THEY BELONG	COUNTRY THEY INTEND TO INHABIT	SHIPS/DATES OF ARRIVAL	
SCHMIDT (cont'd)							
F.	24	M	Merchant	Germany	United States	Prince Edward	1 Apr 1825
F.	25	M	Schoolmaster	Switzerland	U. States	Romulus	24 Sep 1828
F.	28	M	Farmer	France	France	Sully	15 Jul 1829
Fredk., Jr.	6	M	Farmer	France	France	Sully	15 Jul 1829
Fredk. W.	27	M	Merchant	U. States	New York	Sully	11 Mar 1829
Fredk. Wm.	25	M	Merchant	Germany	U. St.	Manchester	7 Dec 1826
G.	20	M	Farmer	Germany	U. States	United States	3 Sep 1828
George	5/12	M	Farmer	France	France	Sully	15 Jul 1829
George	6	M		France	United States	Stephania	6 Dec 1827
George	30	M	Farmer	France	France	Sully	15 Jul 1829
George, Jr.	4	M	Farmer	France	France	Sully	15 Jul 1829
George B.	9	M		York, Penna.	United States	Howard	6 Jul 1829
H.	26	M	Labourer	Switzerland	U. States	La Voltiquer	23 Jul 1822
James	27	M	Farmer	Switzerland	United States	Cambria	11 Feb 1829
Jeannette	29	F	Farmer	France	France	Sully	15 Jul 1829
Johan	6	M		France	United States	New England	29 Aug 1828
*Died 12 July							
Johann Andrew	17	M		France	United States	New England	29 Aug 1828
Johann Geo.	46	M	Joiner	France	United States	New England	29 Aug 1828
John	45	M	Cashier of York Bank	York, Penna.	United States	Howard	6 Jul 1829
John G.	60	M	Farmer	France	France	Sully	15 Jul 1829
M.	24	F		Switzerland	U. States	Romulus	24 Sep 1828
Madaline	1 7/12	F	Farmer	France	France	Sully	15 Jul 1829
Madelina	36	F	Farmer	France	France	Sully	15 Jul 1829
Margaret	20	F		France	United States	Stephania	6 Dec 1827
Margaret	44	F		France	United States	Stephania	6 Dec 1827
Maria Barbara	10	F		France	United States	New England	29 Aug 1828
Marie	7	F	Farmer	France	France	Sully	15 Jul 1829
Marie	58	F	Farmer	France	France	Sully	15 Jul 1829
P.	23	M	Waggon Maker	Switzerland	U. States	Romulus	24 Sep 1828
Philip Jacob	31	M	Farmer	Germany	America	Falcon	28 Aug 1828
T.	22	M	Merchant	Germany	U. States	Amity	21 Feb 1823
SCHMIDTEN, Godfrey	37	M	Gentleman	Denmark	Denmark	Chase	24 Aug 1822
SCHMIDTZ, H. G. D.	32	M	Gentleman	Germany	belongs to the Portugues legation	Debby & Eliza	12 Aug 1822
SCHMIEZER, Christian	22	M	Watchmaker	Switzerland	United States	Don Quixote	7 May 1824
SCHMIT, Anne	2	F	Farmer	Switzerland	United States	Olympia	12 Aug 1828
C.	4	F		France	United States	La Flora	30 Jun 1828
Cath.	5 6/12	F		France	United States	La Flora	30 Jun 1828
Cath.	8	F		France	United States	La Flora	30 Jun 1828
Cathr.	35	F		France	United States	La Flora	30 Jun 1828
Christine	5	F	Farmer	Switzerland	United States	Olympia	12 Aug 1828
D.	32	M	Servant	France	America, U.N.S.	Great Britain	3 Aug 1829
David	9	M	Farmer	Switzerland	United States	Olympia	12 Aug 1828
David	36	M	Farmer	Switzerland	United States	Olympia	12 Aug 1828
F.	1	F		France	United States	La Flora	30 Jun 1828
F.	40	M		France	United States	La Flora	30 Jun 1828
Frederich	7	M	Farmer	Switzerland	United States	Olympia	12 Aug 1828
Jacob	9	M		France	United States	La Flora	30 Jun 1828
Jean	3	M	Farmer	Switzerland	United States	Olympia	12 Aug 1828
Jean	7 6/12	M		France	United States	La Flora	30 Jun 1828
Jean	34	M	Jorney man	France	United States	La Flora	30 Jun 1828
M.	36	F		France	United States	La Flora	30 Jun 1828
P.	1 6/12	M		France	United States	La Flora	30 Jun 1828
Sophia	30	F	Farmer	Switzerland	United States	Olympia	12 Aug 1828
SCHMITH,							
Barbara, his wife [Gothard]	41	F		France	United States	William	31 Jul 1826
Caroline, his daughter [Gothard]	7 5/12	F		France	United States	William	31 Jul 1826
Charles, his son [Gothard]	1 6/12	M		France	United States	William	31 Jul 1826
Eve, his wife [Thiebould]	33	F		France	United States	William	31 Jul 1826
Frederick	6	M	Farmer	Bavarian	United States	American	27 Aug 1827
Frederick	46	M	Farmer	Bavarian	United States	American	27 Aug 1827

NAMES OF PASSENGERS	AGE	SEX	OCCUPATIONS	COUNTRY TO WHICH THEY BELONG	COUNTRY THEY INTEND TO INHABIT	SHIPS/DATES OF ARRIVAL	
SCHMITH (cont'd)							
Frederick, his son [Gothard]	4	M		France	United States	William	31 Jul 1826
George, his son [Gothard]	3	M		France	United States	William	31 Jul 1826
George, his son [Thiebould]	4	M		France	United States	William	31 Jul 1826
Gothard	37 2/12	M	Shoe Maker	France	United States	William	31 Jul 1826
Gothard, his son [Gothard]	9 5/12	M		France	United States	William	31 Jul 1826
Jacob, his son [Thiebould]	3	M		France	United States	William	31 Jul 1826
Jacob, his son [Gothard]	5 3/12	M		France	United States	William	31 Jul 1826
John, his son [Thiebould]	6	M		France	United States	William	31 Jul 1826
Michael	3	M	Farmer	Bavarian	United States	American	27 Aug 1827
Thiebould	34	M	Weaver	France	United States	William	31 Jul 1826
Thiebould, his son [Thiebould]	9	M		France	United States	William	31 Jul 1826
SCHMITT, Christian	20	F	Spinster	Switzerland	U. States	Hewes	30 Jul 1829
George	18	M	Agriculturist	France	U.S.	Helen	3 May 1828
Jacob	28	M	Mason	Germany	New York	Orient	25 Nov 1825
Jean	28	M	Agriculturist	France	U.S.	Helen	3 May 1828
SCHMOLDT, —, Mrs.	32	F		Hannover	United States	Constitution	6 Jul 1829
Adolphus	2	M		Hannover	United States	Constitution	6 Jul 1829
Amandus	6	M		Hannover	United States	Constitution	6 Jul 1829
Augusta	12	F		Hannover	United States	Constitution	6 Jul 1829
Minna	4	F		Hannover	United States	Constitution	6 Jul 1829
Rudolph	8	M		Hannover	United States	Constitution	6 Jul 1829
SCHMURES, Francis	28		Farmer	France	U. States	Elizabeth	9 Jul 1825
Lewis	18		Labourer	France	U. States	Elizabeth	9 Jul 1825
SCHNABEL, Catharine	56	F		Prusia	U. States	Harmony	6 Jan 1823
SCHNAUMBURGER,							
Barbara	24	F		Wirtemburg	United States	Wade	29 Aug 1825
Catharina	22	F		Wirtemburg	United States	Wade	29 Aug 1825
Christiana	8	F		Wirtemburg	United States	Wade	29 Aug 1825
Christina	20	F		Wirtemburg	United States	Wade	29 Aug 1825
Conrad	19	M		Wirtemburg	United States	Wade	29 Aug 1825
J. S.	45	M	Farmer	Wirtemburg	United States	Wade	29 Aug 1825
Johanna	15	F		Wirtemburg	United States	Wade	29 Aug 1825
Johannes	11	M		Wirtemburg	United States	Wade	29 Aug 1825
SCHNEBERGER, Anna	35	F	Framer	Switserland	Ohio	Danube	20 Jul 1826
Peter	38	M	Framer	Switserland	Ohio	Danube	20 Jul 1826
SCHNECK, Christopher	1	M		Germany	United States	Origon	8 Jun 1824
Marie	25	F		Germany	United States	Origon	8 Jun 1824
Peter	43	M	Weaver	Germany	United States	Origon	8 Jun 1824
SCHNEEDER,							
F..., his Wife & Six Children	46	M	Weaver	Swisse	United States	Deux Ernest	29 Dec 1827
*landed at Lewiston, Delw.							
SCHNEIDER, Catarine	19	F		France	United States	New England	29 Aug 1828
Catharine	3	F		Germany	U. States	Falcon	11 Jun 1827
Catharine	25	F		Germany	U. States	Falcon	11 Jun 1827
Christian B.	10	M	Farmer	Germany	U. States	United States	3 Sep 1828
E. V.	39	F	Farmer	Germany	U. States	United States	3 Sep 1828
F. G.	25	M	Merchant	Prusia	U. States	Diana	1 Jun 1822
Frederick	20	M	...	...	United States	Wade	29 Aug 1825
Geo.	45	F		France	United States	New England	29 Aug 1828
Heinr.	20	M	...	Wirtemburg	United States	Wade	29 Aug 1825
Jacob	12	M		France	United States	New England	29 Aug 1828
Jacob	27	M	Farmer	Germany	U. States	Falcon	11 Jun 1827
Jane Eliza	28	F	Farmer	Germany	U. States	United States	3 Sep 1828
Johnam	8	M	Farmer	Germany	U. States	United States	3 Sep 1828
Johnam K.	39	F	Farmer	Germany	U. States	United States	3 Sep 1828
Johan G.	21	M	Farmer	Germany	U. States	United States	3 Sep 1828
Katharina	4	F	Farmer	Germany	U. States	United States	3 Sep 1828
Madalena	20	F		France	United States	New England	29 Aug 1828
Magdalena	1	F		Germany	U. States	Falcon	11 Jun 1827

NAMES OF PASSENGERS	AGE	SEX	OCCUPATIONS	COUNTRY TO WHICH THEY BELONG	COUNTRY THEY INTEND TO INHABIT	SHIPS/DATES OF ARRIVAL	
SCHNEIDER (cont'd)							
Maria	16	F		France	United States	New England	29 Aug 1828
Maria	21	F		France	United States	New England	29 Aug 1828
Peter	4	M		France	United States	New England	29 Aug 1828
Peter	6	M		France	United States	New England	29 Aug 1828
V.	8	F		France	United States	New England	29 Aug 1828
Wendeliner	20	F	Agriculturist	France	U.S.	Helen	3 May 1828
SCHNEISS, Philipe	26	M	Farmer	Switzerland	United States	Olympia	12 Aug 1828
SCHNELLER, J. L.	27	M	Merchant	Austria	New York	Louisa	6 Dec 1827
SCHNERDER, Adam	47	M		Switzerland	U.S.	C. Amelia	30 Jun 1828
Cath	9	F		Switzerland	U.S.	C. Amelia	30 Jun 1828
Justine	3	M	Farmer	Switzerland	U.S.	C. Amelia	30 Jun 1828
Mar.	7	F		Switzerland	U.S.	C. Amelia	30 Jun 1828
Pervin	5	F		Switzerland	U.S.	C. Amelia	30 Jun 1828
SCHNIDER, Ann Maria	37	F	One Family [George]	France	United States	Henri IV	2 Oct 1828
Charlotte	18	F	None	Switzerland	U. States	Isaac Hicks	22 Aug 1829
Christian	3	M	One Family [George]	France	United States	Henri IV	2 Oct 1828
Frederick	0 6/12	M	One Family [George]	France	United States	Henri IV	2 Oct 1828
George	5	M	One Family [George]	France	United States	Henri IV	2 Oct 1828
George	42	M	Carpenter	France	United States	Henri IV	2 Oct 1828
Jacob	13	M	One Family [George]	France	United States	Henri IV	2 Oct 1828
John Frederick	32	M	Taylor	Wertemberg	Wertemberg	Edward Quesnel	3 Jul 1829
Madeline	23	F		Wertemberg	Wertemberg	Edward Quesnel	3 Jul 1829
Margretta	7	F	One Family [George]	France	United States	Henri IV	2 Oct 1828
Michael	16	M	None	Switzerland	U. States	Isaac Hicks	22 Aug 1829
S.	24	M		France & Switzerland	U. States	Bayard	14 Jul 1826
SCHNIEDER,							
Britiana, his daughter [Jacob]	14	F				Martha	30 Jun 1823
Danick, his son [Jacob]	21	M	Farmer			Martha	30 Jun 1823
Fois.	46		Cisseraux [?]	Suisse		Deux Ernest	29 Dec 1827
*son épouse & 6 enfans [his wife and six children]							
Frederic, his son [Jacob]	11	M				Martha	30 Jun 1823
Jacob	36	M	Carpenter			Martha	30 Jun 1823
Magdalena, his daughter [Jacob]	19	F				Martha	30 Jun 1823
Magdalena, his wife [Jacob]	32	F				Martha	30 Jun 1823
SCHNURR, Barbara	22	F		France	United States	New England	29 Aug 1828
SCHOAL, Louis	2	M	Tailor	Ireland		Quatre Freres	29 Jul 1828
Louis	36	M	Tailor	Ireland		Quatre Freres	29 Jul 1828
Margaret	28	F	Tailor	Ireland		Quatre Freres	29 Jul 1828
Perre	8	M	Tailor	Ireland		Quatre Freres	29 Jul 1828
SCHOALES, Thomas	40	M	Farmer	Belleany	...	Gleaner	24 May 1823
SCHOALS, Ann	15	M		England	United States	Hannibal	25 Sep 1827
Betty	13	M		England	United States	Hannibal	25 Sep 1827
G.	11	F		England	United States	Hannibal	25 Sep 1827
James	18	M		England	United States	Hannibal	25 Sep 1827
M.	9	F		England	United States	Hannibal	25 Sep 1827
Maria	7	F		England	United States	Hannibal	25 Sep 1827
R.	22	M	Calico Printer	England	United States	Hannibal	25 Sep 1827
SCHOCH, Daniel	27	M	Cabinet Maker	United States	United States	Globe	30 Aug 1828
SCHOEHARD, Fred.	32	M	...		United States	London Packet	25 Dec 1820
Maria	20	F	None		United States	London Packet	25 Dec 1820
SCHOELLHERMAN, Ed.	22	M	Artiste	France	U. States	Henri IV	3 Feb 1829
SCHOENBURGER,							
Hermann Robert	24 2/12	M		New York	United States	Howard	28 Aug 1828
SCHOERRER, —, Mrs.	30	F	Farmer	Piedemont	U. States	Ohio	18 Jul 1821
Jaques	30	M	Farmer	Piedemont	U. States	Ohio	18 Jul 1821
SCHOFFER, John	20	M	Black Smith	Bevier		Constitution	20 Jun 1828

NAMES OF PASSENGERS	AGE	SEX	OCCUPATIONS	COUNTRY TO WHICH THEY BELONG	COUNTRY THEY INTEND TO INHABIT	SHIPS/DATES OF ARRIVAL	
SCHOFFILED, John	28	M	Farmer	England	United States	Aurelia	7 Jun 1826
SCHOFIELD, Adam	7/12	M	None	England	Philada.	Colossus	2 Oct 1827
Clement	23	M	Merchant	Great Britain	U. States	New York	19 Nov 1828
Daniel	3	M	None	England	Philada.	Colossus	2 Oct 1827
Hannah	24	F	None	England	Philada.	Colossus	2 Oct 1827
Hellen	67	F	None	England	Philada.	Colossus	2 Oct 1827
Hiram	7	M	None	England	Philada.	Colossus	2 Oct 1827
Isaiah	16	M	Weaver	England	Philada.	Colossus	2 Oct 1827
James	27	M	Farmer	Great Britian	United States	Robert Quayle	29 Jul 1822
James	27	M	...	England	Philada.	Colossus	2 Oct 1827
James	40	M	Labourer	England	America	Two Marys	24 Sep 1827
Jane	3	F		England	United States	Hannibal	25 Sep 1827
Jno.	42	M	Merchant	Great Britain	New York	Superior	5 Sep 1827
John	0 7/12	M		England	United States	Hannibal	25 Sep 1827
John	11/12	M	None	England	Philada.	Colossus	2 Oct 1827
John	24	M	Weaver	England	Philada.	Colossus	2 Oct 1827
John	35	M	Wollen Manufacturer	Great Britain	United States	Aurora	5 Sep 1826
John	41	M	Merchant	England	United States	Amelia	20 Aug 1829
John	42	M	Carman	United States	United States	Florida	26 Sep 1826
Joseph	50	M	Clothier	England	U.N. States	Jane	7 Oct 1826
Maria	5	F	None	England	Philada.	Colossus	2 Oct 1827
Maria	24	F	None	England	Philada.	Colossus	2 Oct 1827
Mary	20	F	None	Great Brittan	U. States	John & Elizabeth	11 Dec 1826
Mary	24	F		England	United States	Hannibal	25 Sep 1827
Saml.	22	M	Merchant	Gt. Britain	United States	Corks	3 Aug 1824
Samuel	35	M	Merchant	England	America	Silas Richards	19 Mar 1828
Walter	23	M	Blacksmith	England	America	Cincinnatus	19 Oct 1826
Wm.	32	M	Black Smith	England	America	Franklin	19 Nov 1828
SCHOITZ, F., Mr.	38	M	Merchant	Cuba	U. States	Star	4 Oct 1826
SCHOLEFIELD, S. Matilda	20 6/12	F	None	United States	United States	Manchester	12 Aug 1829
William	22	M	Merchant	Great Britain	United States	Manchester	12 Aug 1829
Wm.	18		Mercht.	England	U. States	New York	30 Oct 1827
SCHOLES, James	26	M	Plaisterer	Bolton	Bolton	Howard Douglass	11 May 1827
SCHOLFIELD, Clement, Mr.	18	M		Gt. Britain	Gt. Britain	Pacific	22 May 1826
SCHOLL, Adam	33	M	Artist	Germany	United States	Virginia	31 May 1828
SCHONLUB, Jacob	44 2/12	M	Tailor	America	America	John Dickinson	9 Oct 1828
SCHOOLER, Ann	16	F	Taylor	St. John	Canada	Henrietta	7 Jul 1825
SCHOOLLY, John	30	M	Labourer	Ireland	U. States	Two Marys	20 Apr 1825
SCHRE, Jacob	24	M	Farmer	Switzerland	Swizland	Le Voltaire	19 Jul 1828
SCHREVE, Fr. Wm.	25	M	Clerk	Prussia	U.N. States	Franklin	20 May 1828
SCHRIEFER, Henry	40	M	Sugar Baker	Hanover	United States	Richmond	4 Aug 1826
Sarah	34	F		England	United States	Richmond	4 Aug 1826
SCHRIEN, J.	32	M	Mechanic	Germany	U. States	Minerva	23 Aug 1824
SCHRODER, —, Mrs.	35	F	Merchant	Germany		Maria Elizabeth	16 Feb 1826
Jacob Christ	36	M	Merchant	Germany	U. States	Kanhawa	6 May 1828
Wm. T.	35	M	Merchant	Germany		Maria Elizabeth	16 Feb 1826
SCHROEDER, —, his Wife	40	F				New York Packet	19 Aug 1820
Anna	15	F				New York Packet	19 Aug 1820
Augustus	13	M		Germany	United States	Maria Elizabeth	6 Jan 1823
Catherina	2	F				New York Packet	19 Aug 1820
Christ. H.	37	M	Merchant	Germany	United States	Maria Elizabeth	6 Jan 1823
Daniel	17	M				New York Packet	19 Aug 1820
Fredk. Henry	25		Farmer	Kingdom of Hanover	U. States	Princess Louise	10 Mar 1825
G.	34	M	Merchant	Germany	United States	Franklin	11 Oct 1827
Johannes	5	M				New York Packet	19 Aug 1820
Johannes	50	M	Farmer			New York Packet	19 Aug 1820

NAMES OF PASSENGERS	AGE	SEX	OCCUPATIONS	COUNTRY TO WHICH THEY BELONG	COUNTRY THEY INTEND TO INHABIT	SHIPS/DATES OF ARRIVAL
SCHROEDER (cont'd)						
John	11	M				New York Packet 19 Aug 1820
Maria	3	F				New York Packet 19 Aug 1820
Regina	8	F				New York Packet 19 Aug 1820
Theodor	12	M		Germany	United States	Maria Elizabeth 6 Jan 1823
SCHRONIDER, Margaret	50	F	Farmer	Switzerland	United States	Olympia 12 Aug 1828
SCHROODER,						
W. T., Esqr.	28	M	Merchant	America	Charleston	Orion 24 Mar 1825
SCHRUDER, Geo.	26	M	Sugar Baker	Bremen	U. States	Huntress 29 May 1822
SCHRUDERE, G. F.	29	M	Merchant	Germany	Germany	Autumn 1 Aug 1828
SCHU, James	38	M	Merchant	Philadelphia		Robert Edwards 8 Nov 1825
SCHUCH, P. C.	50	M	Merchant	Germany	U. States	Amphibious 4 Aug 1827
SCHUCHAETT, —, Mrs.	30	F	None	Amsterdam	U. States	Margaret 29 Oct 1822
SCHUDLIN, Daniel A.	32		Agriculturist	France		Bayard 10 Sep 1827
George C.	35		Physician	France		Bayard 10 Sep 1827
John A.	62		Agriculturist	France		Bayard 10 Sep 1827
Magdalina	57		Agriculturist	France		Bayard 10 Sep 1827
Magdaline	28		Agriculturist	France		Bayard 10 Sep 1827
Sarah	26		Agriculturist	France		Bayard 10 Sep 1827
SCHUESTER, Maria	30	F	Lady	St. Cruz	U. States	Manchester Packet 29 Jan 1825
SCHUGAUR, —	26	M	Brewer	France	United States	Cavalier 25 Jul 1828
SCHULLER, Anna	7	F		Brattain		L'Esperance 6 Sep 1828
Ignan	33	M	Shoemaker	Brattain		L'Esperance 6 Sep 1828
John	36	M	Mariner	Germany	United States	Crisis 13 Nov 1824
Joseph	19	M	Labour	France		Pallas 14 Jun 1828
Magdelene	10	F		Brattain		L'Esperance 6 Sep 1828
Magdelene	32	F		Brattain		L'Esperance 6 Sep 1828
Theresa	8	F		Brattain		L'Esperance 6 Sep 1828
SCHULLY, James	30	M	Mason	Great Britain	United States	Mount Vernon 17 Jun 1825
Mary	27	F	Labourer	Ireland	U. States	Two Marys 20 Apr 1825
Michael	28	M	Mason	Great Britain	United States	Mount Vernon 17 Jun 1825
SCHULTE,						
August George Adam	34	M	Gent.	Prussia	United States	Orozimbo 28 Jun 1827
SCHULTS, H.	30	M	Storekeeper	Germany		Robert Edwards 8 Nov 1825
SCHULTZ, Elisabeth	23	F	None	Switzerland	United States	Ospray 2 Sep 1824
G.	32	M	Mechanic	Germany	United States	Two Marys 12 Feb 1820
George	21	M	Farmer	Switzerland	United States	Ospray 2 Sep 1824
Henry	60	M	Farmer	Switzerland	United States	Ospray 2 Sep 1824
Jacob	15	M	None	Switzerland	United States	Ospray 2 Sep 1824
Jno. M.	30	M	Meckanic	Prussia	United States	Maria Elizabeth 2 Sep 1822
Joh.	36	M	Weaver			Elizabeth 5 Jul 1821
Johana	13	F	None	Switzerland	United States	Ospray 2 Sep 1824
Madalina	19	F	None	Switzerland	United States	Ospray 2 Sep 1824
SCHUMAKER, Albert	24	M	Merchant	Bremen	United States	Constitution 2 Aug 1826
SCHUNDER, Louis	27	M	Mechanic	Switzerland	U. States	Queen Mab 7 Apr 1826
SCHUR, Barbara	19	F		Germany	United States	Samuel Robertson 8 Aug 1828
Elizabeth	36	F		Germany	United States	Samuel Robertson 8 Aug 1828
Jacob	1	M		Germany	United States	Samuel Robertson 8 Aug 1828
Jacob	9	M		Germany	United States	Samuel Robertson 8 Aug 1828
Magdalana	10	F		Germany	United States	Samuel Robertson 8 Aug 1828
Michael	59	M	Farmer	Germany	United States	Samuel Robertson 8 Aug 1828
Phillip	17	M		Germany	United States	Samuel Robertson 8 Aug 1828
Sophia	15	F		Germany	United States	Samuel Robertson 8 Aug 1828
SCHURAN, P.	22	M	Mercht.	Germany	U. States	Protection 5 Feb 1822
SCHURCH, Christian	31	M	Farmer	Switzerland	United States	Aurora 21 Jun 1824
Jacob	1 6/12	M	Child of [Christian]	Switzerland	United States	Aurora 21 Jun 1824
John	2 6/12	M	Child of [Christian]	Switzerland	United States	Aurora 21 Jun 1824

NAMES OF PASSENGERS	AGE	SEX	OCCUPATIONS	COUNTRY TO WHICH THEY BELONG	COUNTRY THEY INTEND TO INHABIT	SHIPS/DATES OF ARRIVAL	
SCHURCH (cont'd)							
Magdalen	23	F	Wife of [Christian]	Switzerland	United States	Aurora	21 Jun 1824
SCHUREMBURG, Philip	58	M	Merchant	Jersey	Jersey	Columbia	5 Oct 1824
SCHURLKIN,							
Carol Friedk.	2	M		Germany	America	Falcon	28 Aug 1828
Cathar. Barbara	40	F		Germany	America	Falcon	28 Aug 1828
Catherina B.	7	F		Germany	America	Falcon	28 Aug 1828
Karolina	4	F		Germany	America	Falcon	28 Aug 1828
Reich. Fredk.	39	M	Farmer	Germany	America	Falcon	28 Aug 1828
SCHUSLER, Fredk.	22	M	Sugar Baker	Germany	U. States	Constitution	25 Jul 1823
J.	20	M	Mechanic	Germany	U. States	Condstitution	21 Mar 1825
SCHUTE, M.	35	F		Switzerland	U. States	La Urania	3 Jul 1828
SCHUTZ, Margaret	20	F	Agriculturist	France	U.S.	Helen	3 May 1828
SCHUZENBACH, J.	34	M	Gentleman	Germany	U. States	Queen Mab	22 Jul 1825
SCHWABIN, Barbara	28	F		Wirtemburg	United States	Wade	29 Aug 1825
SCHWABLT, Joseph	29	M	Shoemaker	Germany	Cincanatti	Isabella	15 Sep 1828
SCHWAN, C.	34	F		France	United States	La Flora	30 Jun 1828
Jean	5	F		France	United States	La Flora	30 Jun 1828
Joseph	34	M	Cartright	France	United States	La Flora	30 Jun 1828
SCHWANDER, A.	32	M	Merchant	Germany	U. States	Cadmus	28 May 1821
SCHWANDES, T.	39	M	Merchant	Germany	America	Orozimbo	1 Oct 1827
SCHWARTRAUBE,							
John	24	M	Farmer	Hessian-Germany	Canada	Caesar	8 Sep 1828
SCHWARTS, Michal	22	M	Labourer	Germany	America	Falcon	28 Aug 1828
Moses	40	M	Merchant	Hamburg	Hamburg	Venus	8 May 1826
SCHWARTZ, Caroline	6	F	Farmer	Swizerland		Antioch	18 Aug 1829
Catherine	17	F	Farmer	Swizerland		Antioch	18 Aug 1829
Francis	16	M	Farmer	France	France	Sully	15 Jul 1829
Geo.	50	M	Butcher	Switzerland	U. States	La Urania	3 Jul 1828
George	1	M	Farmer	France	France	Sully	15 Jul 1829
Jacob	29	M	Butcher	France	U. States	Edward Quesnel	4 Aug 1828
Joseph	3	M	Farmer	France	France	Sully	15 Jul 1829
Lewis	46	M	Farmer	Swizerland		Antioch	18 Aug 1829
Louisa	17	M		Switzerland		La Urania	3 Jul 1828
Louisa	26	F	Farmer	France	France	Sully	15 Jul 1829
Marianne	22	F	Farmer	France	France	Sully	15 Jul 1829
Michael	12	M	Farmer	France	France	Sully	15 Jul 1829
Rosalie	19	F	Farmer	France	France	Sully	15 Jul 1829
Theresa	40	F	Farmer	France	France	Sully	15 Jul 1829
Victor	9	M	Farmer	France	France	Sully	15 Jul 1829
Wilhelmina	9	F	Farmer	Swizerland		Antioch	18 Aug 1829
Wilhelmine	44	F	Farmer	Swizerland		Antioch	18 Aug 1829
SCHWARZENTRAUB,							
Chr.	55	M	Farmer	Hessian-Germany	Canada	Caesar	8 Sep 1828
John	25	M	Farmer	Hessian-Germany	Canada	Caesar	8 Sep 1828
SCHWATZ, Barbara	7	F	Farmer	Switzerland	United States	Olympia	12 Aug 1828
Catherine	4	F	Farmer	Switzerland	United States	Olympia	12 Aug 1828
Catherine	5	F	Farmer	Switzerland	United States	Olympia	12 Aug 1828
Catherine	36	F	Farmer	Switzerland	United States	Olympia	12 Aug 1828
Philipe	38	M	Farmer	Switzerland	United States	Olympia	12 Aug 1828
SCHWERDFEGER, C.	23	M	Gardiner	Hannover	United States	Constitution	6 Jul 1829
SCHWERTZER, Hannah	32	F	his Wife [Jean]	Holland	U. States	Xenophon	15 Sep 1820
Jean	36	M	Farmer	Holland	U. States	Xenophon	15 Sep 1820
Salomie	8	F	Daughter [Jean]	Holland	U. States	Xenophon	15 Sep 1820
SCHWERTZIG, Antonie	42 3/12	M	Carpenter	Switzerland	United States	France	6 Oct 1828
Mary							
	1	F	Carpenter	Switzerland	United States	France	6 Oct 1828
Mary	30 1/12	F	Carpenter	Switzerland	United States	France	6 Oct 1828
SCHWINITZ, L.	45	M	...	U.S. America	U.S. America	Columbia	26 Nov 1825
SCHWIRB, Anna Maria	21	F		Germany	America	Falcon	28 Aug 1828
SCHWISTER (see Lehwister)							
SCIDEL, John	39	M	Merchant	United States	Citizen	Pioneer	28 Jun 1827
SCIPIO, —	22	M	Servant	U. States	U. States	Emma	15 Apr 1822
SCOASH, —	...	F		Switzerland	United States	Elbe	2 Aug 1822
SCOBALL, Richard	7	M		U. States	U.S.A.	Hudson	21 Aug 1829
Richard	33	M	Dealer	England	U.S.A.	Hudson	21 Aug 1829

NAMES OF PASSENGERS	AGE	SEX	OCCUPATIONS	COUNTRY TO WHICH THEY BELONG	COUNTRY THEY INTEND TO INHABIT	SHIPS/DATES OF ARRIVAL	
SCOBIE, George	23	M		Scotland	United States	Camillus	9 May 1827
James	23	M	Clerk	Scotland	U. States	Camillus	27 Jun 1826
Jean	31	F		Gt. Britain	America	Ariel	20 Jul 1822
SCOFF, Andrew	60	M	Weaver	Ireland	United States	Henry Kneeland	7 Jun 1828
SCOFFIELD, Henry	77	M	Merchant	N. Haven	U. States	Lewis	7 Aug 1821
SCOFIELD, Betty	27	F	None	Great Britain	United States	William Dawson	18 Jun 1827
Eliza	3	F	None	Great Britain	United States	William Dawson	18 Jun 1827
Elizabeth	28	F		England	United States	Dalhouse Castle	26 Dec 1827
Frances	1	F	None	Great Britain	United States	William Dawson	18 Jun 1827
James	2	M		England	United States	Dalhouse Castle	26 Dec 1827
James	28	M	Merchant	Great Britain	United States	Blakely	29 Sep 1826
Jesse	50	M	Clothier	U. States	U. States	Nancy	19 Oct 1821
Joseph	2	M	Clothier	Great Britain	United States	William Dawson	18 Jun 1827
Mary	5	F	None	Great Britain	United States	William Dawson	18 Jun 1827
Sarah	25	F	None	Halifax	U. States	Borneo	23 Jun 1826
W.	82	M	Gentleman	U. States	U. States	St. Michael	26 Oct 1824
SCOLES, Bart. P.	47	M	Engraver	Gt. Britain	U.S. America	Canada	30 Jan 1829
SCOLION, John	22	M	Weaver	Ireland	N. Jersey	Potomac	7 Aug 1827
SCOOLER, Ann	18	F	None	St. Johns	St. Johns	Sarah G	7 May 1827
Elizabet	4	F	None	St. Johns	St. Johns	Sarah G	7 May 1827
Elizabeth	40	F	None	St. Johns	St. Johns	Sarah G	7 May 1827
SCOOTT, Hugh	42	M	Seaman	U. States	U. States	Boston	26 Sep 1820
SCORKIN, James	22	M	Labourer	Ireland	United States	Jubilee	13 Jul 1829
SCOTO, W.	24	M	Mason	Great Britain	United States	Isaac Hicks	6 Dec 1827
SCOTT, —,							
General, U.S.A.			General	U.S.	U.S.	Sully	26 Oct 1829
Alexander	22	M	Farmer	Great Britain		Robert Fulton	9 Jul 1823
Alexr.	22	M	Shoemaker	Great Britain	United States	Colossus	5 Jun 1827
Andrew	25 3/12	M	Weaver	G. Britain	United States	Dutchess of Portland	30 Oct 1826
Andrew	38	M	Mariner	U. States	U. States	Ann	4 Mar 1826
Ann	4		Family [of Peter]	Great Britain	United States	Camillus	12 Sep 1827
Ann	20			Ireland	U. States	Robert Burns	18 Jun 1822
Ann	22	F		Scotland	United States	Broke	16 Jul 1829
Ann	34			Ireland	United States	Jno. Dickinson	21 Sep 1821
Anne	18	F		Ireland	U. States	Fame	15 Nov 1826
B.	21	F		G. Britain	U. States	Camillus	8 Sep 1828
Betsy	27	F	Spinster	Ireland	United States	Trident	17 May 1825
Catharine	2	F		England	New York	Joseph Hume	26 Oct 1829
Catharine	31	F		Great Britian	United States	Isaac Hicks	13 Jan 1826
Cornelia, Miss	8		None	U.S.	U.S.	Sully	26 Oct 1829
Cornelius	35	M	Brewer	G. Britain	U. States	Eliza	31 Jul 1828
David	25	M	Seaman	America		Hope	27 Aug 1821
David	28	M	Labourer		New York	Prince Madore	28 Aug 1820
David	28	M	Clergiman	Argyle (Tedland) Scotland	United States	Jean Hastie	27 Jul 1829
Dl.	40	M	Taylor	Scotland	U. States	Isabella	10 Mar 1825
E., Miss	11	F	Lady	Great Britain	U. States of Amer	Junius	5 Jul 1820
Ebenezer	16	M		N. Brunswick	New Jersey	Rambler	31 Aug 1829
Edward	20		Bookseller	United States	United States	Corinthian	7 Jul 1829
Eliza	17	F		Ireland	New York	Triton	12 Jul 1823
Elizabeth	30	F	Spinster	Ireland	United States	Wilson	6 Jun 1828
Elizabeth	40	F		Denmark	Denmark	Gleaner	31 Jul 1821
Fras.	21	M	Merchant	Gibraltar	Gibraltar	Balize	29 Aug 1825
G. H.	50	M	Lawyer	North America	Different	Tampico	11 Jul 1826
Geo.	28	M	Farmer	Scotland	Canada	Braganza	16 Apr 1825
George	5	M	None	Great Britain	United States	Friends	13 Jun 1825
George	19	M	Baker	Great Britain	United States	Marshal Wellington	3 May 1822
George	22	M	Farmer	Ireland	Ireland	Trident	17 May 1825
Gideon	40	M	Mercht.	Scotland	Charleston	Canada	1 Nov 1823
Hans	20	M	Cooper	Great Britain	United States	Superior	31 Mar 1828
Harriet	10	F		Great Britian	United States	Isaac Hicks	13 Jan 1826
Helen	45	F		U. States	United States	Britannia	29 Oct 1829
Henry	2	M		Great Britian	United States	Isaac Hicks	13 Jan 1826
Herit	1	F		Irland	United States	Nancy	2 Jan 1824
Isaiah	16	M		Ireland	U. States	Fame	15 Nov 1826
J.	21	M	Gentleman	U. States	England	Brown	23 Dec 1826

NAMES OF PASSENGERS	AGE	SEX	OCCUPATIONS	COUNTRY TO WHICH THEY BELONG	COUNTRY THEY INTEND TO INHABIT	SHIPS/DATES OF ARRIVAL	
SCOTT (cont'd)							
James	3	M	Labourer	Glasgow, Scotland	Gt. Britain	Orozimbo	19 Oct 1822
James	5	M	Labourer	Glasgow, Scotland	Gt. Britain	Orozimbo	19 Oct 1822
James	25		Merchant	Glasgow	Great Britain	William Thompson	13 May 1823
James	25	M	Farmer	Scotland	United States	Commerce	17 Jul 1823
James	36	M	Farmer	Kendal	United States	Dalhousie Castle	27 Jul 1826
James	43	M	Merchant	U. States	U. States	Canada	13 Feb 1826
James	50	M	Farmer	Scotland	U. States	Richmond Packet	8 Apr 1822
James	50	M	Farmer	Scotland	U. States	Orozimbo	7 Jul 1825
Jane	6	F		Great Britian	United States	Isaac Hicks	13 Jan 1826
Jane	24		Family [of Peter]	Great Britain	United States	Camillus	12 Sep 1827
Jas.	21	M	Mechanic	U. States	U. States	Infant	10 Jul 1821
Jas.	28	M	Merchant	England	Canada	Corinthian	20 Apr 1825
Jas.	38	M	Labourer	Glasgow, Scotland	Gt. Britain	Orozimbo	19 Oct 1822
Jessie	10	M		Scotland	United States	Broke	16 Jul 1829
John	9	M	Labourer	Glasgow, Scotland	Gt. Britain	Orozimbo	19 Oct 1822
John	20	M				Lady of the Lake	23 Aug 1828
John	20 3/12	M	Weaver	Ireland	America	Carolina Ann	7 Apr 1826
John	22	M	Labourer	Great Britain	U. States America	Maria	22 May 1822
John	23	M	Labourer	Ireland	U. States	Ann Maria	1 Jun 1824
John	23	M	Labourer	Ireland	United States	General Marion	20 Aug 1828
John	24	M	Blacksmith	Great Britain	United States	Roman	19 Dec 1825
John	26	M	Cooper	Great Britain	United States	Superior	31 Mar 1828
John	29	M	Labourer	Great Britain	U.S. of Ama.	Robert Fulton	16 Aug 1824
John	34	M	Linen Draper	England	New York	Bowditch	27 Apr 1826
John	35	M	Weaver	England	United States	Roman	12 Jun 1826
John	35	M	Merchant	Ireland	United States	St. Michaels	18 Jul 1826
John	35	M	Tailor	England	United States	Trident	30 Sep 1826
John	60	M	Merchant	Scotland	New York	Joseph Hume	26 Oct 1829
John B.	23	M	Weaver	Great Britain	United States	Colossus	5 Jun 1827
Johns	19		Labourer	Manchester, England	Great Britain	Franklin	22 Jun 1827
Letitia	23 2/12	F		Ireland	New York	Triton	12 Jul 1823
Marey Ann	22	F		Irland	United States	Nancy	2 Jan 1824
Margaret	5		Child	Halifax	United States	Josephine	13 Oct 1829
Margaret	30			Ireland	Great Britain	Robert Burns	14 Jun 1824
Margret	11	F	Spinster	Ireland	United States	Wilson	6 Jun 1828
Maria, Miss			None	U.S.	U.S.	Sully	26 Oct 1829
Maria, Mrs.			None	U.S.	U.S.	Sully	26 Oct 1829
Marie	1		Child	Halifax	United States	Josephine	13 Oct 1829
Marshall	14			Ireland	Great Britain	Robert Burns	14 Jun 1824
Martha	45	F	Farmer	Scotland	U. States	Orozimbo	7 Jul 1825
Mary	2	F		Ireland	U. States	Fame	15 Nov 1826
Mary	7	F	None	Great Britain	United States	Friends	13 Jun 1825
Mary	13	F	Spinster	Ireland	United States	Trident	17 May 1825
Mary	21	F		Ireland	U. States	Ann Maria	1 Jun 1824
Mary	24	F	None	England		Marchioness	13 May 1828
Mary	35	F	None	England	United States	Roman	12 Jun 1826
Mary Ann	1	F	None	England		Marchioness	13 May 1828
Mary Jane	10		Child	United States	United States	Josephine	13 Oct 1829
Michael	22	M	Labourer	Great Britain	United States	Thomas Dickason	31 Jul 1829
N.	25	M	Farmer	England	America	James Cropper	10 Feb 1823
P. H.	22	M	Merchant	U. States	U. States	St. George	20 Sep 1828
Peter	24		Weaver	Great Britain	United States	Camillus	12 Sep 1827
Philip	21	M	Laborer	Gt. Britain		Dalhouse Castle	13 May 1828
Richard	...	M	...	Scotland	America	Nimrod	9 Jul 1827
Richard	20	M		Ireland	U. States	Fame	15 Nov 1826
Rob.	55	M	Planter	Jamaica	U. States	Packet	18 Sep 1826
Robert	6	M		Scotland	United States	Broke	16 Jul 1829
Robert	7			Ireland	Great Britain	Robert Burns	14 Jun 1824
Robert	7			Ireland	Great Britain	Robert Burns	14 Jun 1824

NAMES OF PASSENGERS	AGE	SEX	OCCUPATIONS	COUNTRY TO WHICH THEY BELONG	COUNTRY THEY INTEND TO INHABIT	SHIPS/DATES OF ARRIVAL	
SCOTT (cont'd)							
Robert	30	M	Weaver	Scotland	United States	John Dickinson	12 Aug 1824
Robt.	26 4/12	M	Mechanic	England	United States	John Wells	22 May 1826
Sarah	12	F		Ireland	U. States	Fame	15 Nov 1826
Sarah	14	F	None	England	United States	Roman	12 Jun 1826
Sarah	40	F	Labourer	Glasgow, Scotland	Gt. Britain	Orozimbo	19 Oct 1822
Sarah Ann	7		Child	United States	United States	Josephine	13 Oct 1829
Stephen	45	M	Carpenter	England	New York	Brighton	19 Aug 1829
Susan	55	F		Ireland	U. States	Fame	15 Nov 1826
Susana	10	F		Ireland	U. States	Fame	15 Nov 1826
Theodore	33	F	Lady	United States	United States	Josephine	13 Oct 1829
Tho.	29	M	Farmer	Ireland	N. Jersey	Triton	12 Jul 1823
Thomas	4	M		Scotland	United States	Broke	16 Jul 1829
Thomas	9	M	None	Great Britain	United States	Friends	13 Jun 1825
Thomas	13	M	Carpenter	England	New York	Brighton	19 Aug 1829
Thomas	26	M	Joiner	Wol..., H..., Scotland	U. States	New Orleans	24 Aug 1827
Thomas, Senr.	43	M	Farmer	Great Britain	United States	Friends	13 Jun 1825
Thos.	3	M		Ireland	U. States	Fame	15 Nov 1826
Thos.	22		Labourer	Ireland	United States	John Dickinson	28 Jun 1822
Thos.	26	M	Carpenter	England		Marchioness	13 May 1828
Thos.	29	M		Scotland	U.S.	Curler	19 Jul 1828
Thos.	55	M	Labourer	Ireland	U. States	Fame	15 Nov 1826
Virginia, Miss	12		None	U.S.	U.S.	Sully	26 Oct 1829
Walter	27	M				Lady of the Lake	23 Aug 1828
*left ship							
Walter	28	M		Scotland		Ann	17 May 1822
William	8	M	None	Great Britain	United States	Friends	13 Jun 1825
William	16	M		Scotland	United States	Broke	16 Jul 1829
William	20	M	Carpenter	England		Marchioness	13 May 1828
William	24	M		Scotland	United States	Camillus	9 May 1827
Wm.	2	M	Labourer	Glasgow, Scotland	Gt. Britain	Orozimbo	19 Oct 1822
Wm.	18	M	Doctor			Manhattan	25 Dec 1820
Wm.	22	M	Physician	United States	United States	Samuel Robertson	5 Oct 1827
Wm.	24	M	Merchant	England	England	Hudson	13 Jan 1827
Wm.	48	M	Gentleman	Denmark	Denmark	Gleaner	31 Jul 1821
Wm. H., Mrs.	32	F		England	New York	Joseph Hume	26 Oct 1829
Wm. S.	28	M	Surgeon	Great Britain	Canada	Robert Fulton	7 Nov 1823
SCOVEL, E.	21	M	Physician	United States	United States	Tampico	29 Apr 1826
SCOVELL, E.	22	F		England	Montreal, Canada	Cleveland	1 May 1821
J.	25	M	Merchant	England	Montreal, Canada	Cleveland	1 May 1821
James	31			England	America	Thames	25 Oct 1821
SCOVILLE, C.	35	M	Merchant	New York	U. States	William Henry	29 Dec 1823
SCRANTON, Noah	34	M	Mechanic	United States	United States	Centurion	22 Dec 1828
SCRASEN, Thos.	23	M	Phisician	Great Britian	U. States	Silas Richards	29 Oct 1828
SCREECH, B.	35		Weaver	Cork	Philadelphia	Schuylkill	22 Aug 1825
Catharine	5			Cork	Philadelphia	Schuylkill	22 Aug 1825
Edward	29		Weaver	Cork	Philadelphia	Schuylkill	22 Aug 1825
Edward	35		Weaver	Cork	Philadelphia	Schuylkill	22 Aug 1825
Ellen	25			Cork	Philadelphia	Schuylkill	22 Aug 1825
SCRYMGEOUR, James	...	M	...	England	United States	London Packet	25 Dec 1820
SCRYMYCOUR, John	32	M	Clerk	Scotland	U. States	Mentor	21 Mar 1825
SCUHEY, Jno.	28	M	Farmer	England	U. States	Thomas Ritchie	2 Jul 1827
SCULION, James	25	M	Weaver	Ireland	N. Jersey	Potomac	7 Aug 1827
SCULL, Jas.	38	M	Gentleman	United States	United States	Sarah Herrick	24 Oct 1825
SCULLEY, William	27	M	Merchant	Ireland	Great Britain	Nancy	13 Dec 1822
SCULLY, Jas.	32 6/12	M	Labourer	England	United States	John Wells	22 May 1826
John	25	M	Labourer	Ireland	America	Plutarch	18 Jul 1826
M.	25	M	Farmer	Ireland	U. States	Alex Mansfield	1 Jun 1822
Margaret	18	F		Ireland	America	Plutarch	18 Jul 1826
Mathew	20	M	Weaver	Ireland	United States	Hannibal	25 Sep 1827
Peter	18	M	Labourer	Ireland	America	Plutarch	18 Jul 1826
SCUNNETT, Patt	22	M	...	Ireland	U. States	Union	3 Jun 1822
SE...INY, Daniel	21	M	Labourer	Ireland	United States	Wanderer	1 Aug 1828
SEABOROUGH, Fanny	25	F				Hercules	25 Sep 1820

NAMES OF PASSENGERS	AGE	SEX	OCCUPATIONS	COUNTRY TO WHICH THEY BELONG	COUNTRY THEY INTEND TO INHABIT	SHIPS/DATES OF ARRIVAL	
SEABURN, —, Mr.	36	M	Mariner	U. States	U. States	Vigilant	14 Apr 1823
SEADON, John	1	M		Great Brittain	United States	Corinthian	9 Jan 1827
Mary	10	F	Spinster	Great Brittain	United States	Corinthian	9 Jan 1827
Samuel	30	M	Spinster	Great Brittain	United States	Corinthian	9 Jan 1827
Sarah	30	F	Spinster	Great Brittain	United States	Corinthian	9 Jan 1827
Wm.	23	M	Farmer	Great Britain	United States	Ganges	8 Jul 1820
SEAFIELD, Chas.	31	M	Gentn.	Austria	St. Croix	Stephania	16 Aug 1827
SEAGREN, John	24		...	Dorset	...	Hudson	14 Jun 1827
SEAL, Henry	24		Labourer	England	United States	Hugh Johnson	11 Jun 1828
J.	44	M	Cooper	United States	United States	Seine	21 Oct 1822
SEALE, William	33	M	Blacksmith	America	U. States	Criterion at London	10 May 1821
SEALY, Carlton W.	22	M	Shoemaker	U. States	U. States	St. Michael	26 Oct 1824
Jane	26	F	Lady	St. Johns	St. Johns	Nancy	3 Apr 1824
Sarah	22	F		U. States	U. States	Shamrock	17 Jun 1822
SEAMAN, B.	28	M	Mariner	U. States		Star	7 Jan 1827
Henry, his son [Timothy]	16	M	Labourer	United States	New York	John London	7 Apr 1824
Jno.	23	M	Miller	Amsterdam	U. States	Elizabeth	28 May 1822
Timothy	49	M	Labourer	United States	New York	John London	7 Apr 1824
W.	38	M	Mariner	U. States	U. States	Henry	3 Jun 1828
SEAMENS, Sam. T.	25	M	Merchant	U. States	U. States	Hero	20 Aug 1821
SEAMOUR, Robt.	30	M	Farmer	Steers	Yorkshire	Howard Douglass	11 May 1827
SEANLER, Hugh	20	M	Farmer	Great Britain	U. States	Yamacraw	4 Sep 1822
SEAR, Thos.	13	M	Servant	U. States	Great Britain	Thompson	26 Apr 1828
SEARCE, Diana	23	F	None	England	Pittsburgh	Orozimbo	8 Jun 1822
Edgar	4	M	None	England	Pittsburgh	Orozimbo	8 Jun 1822
SEARES, Jas.	25	M	Gardiner			Trent	1 Oct 1823
SEARL, Eliza	31	F	None	Great Britain	United States	Friends	13 Jun 1825
Hugh	37	M	Carpenter	Great Britain	United States	Friends	13 Jun 1825
Jane	21	F	None	Great Britain	United States	Friends	13 Jun 1825
SEARLE, —, Mrs.	30	F		U. States	U. States	Agenoria	17 Sep 1821
A. M.	28	M	Merchant	London	U. States	Decatur	2 Jan 1822
Catharine	4	F		U. States	U. States	Agenoria	17 Sep 1821
Jas. R.	9	M		U. States	U. States	Agenoria	17 Sep 1821
Jno.	35	M	Merchant	U. States	U. States	Agenoria	17 Sep 1821
Jno., Jr.	9	M		U. States	U. States	Agenoria	17 Sep 1821
John	40	M	Merchant	America	U. States	Cincinnatus	21 Feb 1825
Mary	2	F		U. States	U. States	Agenoria	17 Sep 1821
Thos.	26	M	Merchant	United States	Boston	Cadmus	27 Aug 1822
Wm.	5	M		U. States	U. States	Agenoria	17 Sep 1821
SEARLS, Caleb	20	M	Stone Layer	England	U. States	Electra	7 Jul 1828
SEARS, James	25	M	Printer	St. Johns	U. States	Nancy	10 Jul 1822
Lawrence	45	M	Preacher			Eliza Jane	12 Sep 1820
Richard	44	M	Mariner	U.S.	U.S.	Julia	26 Jun 1827
Sam.	16	M	Gentleman	Bermuda	U. States	Ann	11 Feb 1822
Susan	17					Borneo	28 Aug 1828
William	28	M	Merchant	St. John, N.B.	Great Britain	St. Michaels	12 Apr 1826
SEARTH, Samuel	30	M	Merchant	Great Britain	Great Britain	Magnet	28 Jun 1821
SEARY, Michael	20	M	Labourer	Ireland	U. States	Ganges	21 Jun 1827
SEATON, —, Miss	18	F		St. Croix	St. Croix	Carlo	19 Apr 1828
—, Mrs.	40	F		St. Croix	St. Croix	Carlo	19 Apr 1828
Alexr.	30	M	Painter	Great Britian	United States	Columbia	21 Jan 1828
H.	16	F		St. Croix	St. Croix	Carlo	19 Apr 1828
H.	18	M	Merchant	St. Croix		Chase	5 Jul 1825
Henery	50	M	Gentleman	Pennsylvania	Philadelphia	Carlo	1 Jul 1829
SEAVEN, Pat	9 5/12	M		Ireland	U. States	Fabius	22 Sep 1828
SEAVER, —, Mrs.	20	F		Germany	U. States	Louisa Matilda	4 Dec 1821
Frs.	29	M	Drugist	Germany	U. States	Louisa Matilda	4 Dec 1821
SEAVILL, Amos	34	M	Merchant	United States	United States	Maria	3 Oct 1822
SEAWARD, Jno. H., Captn.	65	M	Mariner	United States	New Hamshire	Astrea	21 Oct 1823
SEBASTIEN, Jaclard	28	M	Hair dresser	France	U. States	Lewis	16 Mar 1826
SEBLING, Anna Maria	24	F		Switzerland	U. States	Romulus	24 Sep 1828
C.	32	M	Farmer	Switzerland	U. States	Romulus	24 Sep 1828
C. F.	0 6/12			Switzerland	U. States	Romulus	24 Sep 1828
SECHEY, Elizabeth	23	F		Ireland	United States	Julia Ann	24 Jul 1820
SECKEL, L. D.	27		Merchant	Philadelphia	United States	William Thompson	13 May 1823

NAMES OF PASSENGERS	AGE	SEX	OCCUPATIONS	COUNTRY TO WHICH THEY BELONG	COUNTRY THEY INTEND TO INHABIT	SHIPS/DATES OF ARRIVAL	
SECKER, Ann	12	F	None	Great Britain	New York	Superior	5 Sep 1827
Benjn.	1	M	None	Great Britain	New York	Superior	5 Sep 1827
Betty	8	F	None	Great Britain	New York	Superior	5 Sep 1827
Joseph	10	M	None	Great Britain	New York	Superior	5 Sep 1827
Maria	31	F	None	Great Britain	New York	Superior	5 Sep 1827
Nancy	2	F	None	Great Britain	New York	Superior	5 Sep 1827
Sarah	4	F	None	Great Britain	New York	Superior	5 Sep 1827
SECKLES, J.	16	...	...	...	United States	John	London 3 Aug 1824
SECREOF, —, Mr.		M	Merchant	Charleston		Genl. A. Jackson 15 Jul 1820	
SEDANE, Felix	30	M	Gentleman	Spain	Spain	Lucinda	11 Mar 1825
SEDDON, Ely	11	M		Great Britain	United States	Ganges	8 Jul 1820
Hannah	20	F		Great Britain	United States	Ganges	8 Jul 1820
James	9	M		Great Britain	United States	Ganges	8 Jul 1820
John	18	M	Farmer	Great Britain	United States	Ganges	8 Jul 1820
John	18	M		Great Britain	United States	Ganges	8 Jul 1820
Margaret	14	F		Great Britain	United States	Ganges	8 Jul 1820
Mary	16	F		Great Britain	United States	Ganges	8 Jul 1820
Mary Ann	11	F		Great Britain	United States	Ganges	8 Jul 1820
Thomas	60	M	Farmer	Great Britain	United States	Ganges	8 Jul 1820
Wm.	Infant	M		Great Britain	United States	Ganges	8 Jul 1820
SEDERBERG, Magnus	22	M	Cooper	U. States	U. States	Orono	21 May 1827
SEDGWICK, Elisabeth	75	F		England	United States	Cosmo	26 Aug 1829
Hannah	5	F	None			John & Edward	25 Aug 1820
Leonan	28	M	Shoemaker	G. Britain		Ann Maria	3 Jul 1820
Sarah	38	F	Seamstress			John & Edward	25 Aug 1820
SEDLY, Isabella	3	F	Child	Great Britain	United States	Washington	3 Sep 1827
Isabella	21	F	Wife	Great Britain	United States	Washington	3 Sep 1827
Wm.	26	M	Chandler	Great Britain	United States	Washington	3 Sep 1827
SEDON, Mary	46	F		Great Britain	United States	Ganges	8 Jul 1820
SEEDS, Margt.	25	F		G. Britain	U. States	Mary Howland	22 Sep 1828
SEELLY, Dennis	45	M	Carpenter	U. States	U. States	Josephine	30 Aug 1828
SEEMON, George Henry	27	M	Merchant	Hesse	United States	Constitution	2 Aug 1826
SEEMS, N.	20	M	Seaman	Hanover	U. States	Minerva	9 Jan 1827
SEENER, Joseph	19	M	Farmer	Alsace in the Department of Upper and lower Rhine	United States	Carolina Augusta	16 May 1828
Maria	36	F	Farmer	Alsace in the Department of Upper and lower Rhine	United States	Carolina Augusta	16 May 1828
SEENEY, Catherine	40	F	Farmer	Alsace in the Department of Upper and lower Rhine	United States	Carolina Augusta	16 May 1828
Catherinne	17	F	Farmer	Alsace in the Department of Upper and lower Rhine	United States	Carolina Augusta	16 May 1828
Joseph	8	M	Farmer	Alsace in the Department of Upper and lower Rhine	United States	Carolina Augusta	16 May 1828
Joseph	44	M	Farmer	Alsace in the Department of Upper and lower Rhine	United States	Carolina Augusta	16 May 1828
Madelina	4	F	Farmer	Alsace in the Department of Upper and lower Rhine	United States	Carolina Augusta	16 May 1828
Madelina	9	F	Farmer	Alsace in the Department of Upper and lower Rhine	United States	Carolina Augusta	16 May 1828
Maria	5	F	Farmer	Alsace in the Department of Upper and lower Rhine	United States	Carolina Augusta	16 May 1828

NAMES OF PASSENGERS	AGE	SEX	OCCUPATIONS	COUNTRY TO WHICH THEY BELONG	COUNTRY THEY INTEND TO INHABIT	SHIPS/DATES OF ARRIVAL	
SEENEY (cont'd)							
Maria	38	F	Farmer	Alsace in the Department of Upper and lower Rhine	United States	Carolina Augusta	16 May 1828
Mariana	6	F	Farmer	Alsace in the Department of Upper and lower Rhine	United States	Carolina Augusta	16 May 1828
Maryabetta	66	F	Farmer	Alsace in the Department of Upper and lower Rhine	United States	Carolina Augusta	16 May 1828
Peter	3	M	Farmer	Alsace in the Department of Upper and lower Rhine	United States	Carolina Augusta	16 May 1828
SEER, Gaspard	20	M	Baker	France	U. States	Edward Quesnel	4 Aug 1828
SEERS, Haldah	50	F	None	United States	United States	James Monroe	27 Jul 1821
SEERY, John	1	M		G. Britain	U. States	Hanford	18 Sep 1828
Thos.	28	M	Farmer	Ireland	New York	Bowditch	27 Apr 1826
SEFER, John	22	M	Farmer	Switzerland	U. States	France	26 Jun 1828
SEFTON, John	21	M	Commedian	England		Britannia	20 Jun 1827
SEGEER, C.	9	F		U. States	U. States	Lewis	10 Sep 1823
SEGER, Lewis C.	26	M	Navy	U. States	U. States	Pacification	27 Apr 1824
SEGMALLIN, E.	50	F	Gent	French	Switzerland	Charlemagne	19 Sep 1828
Ja.	22	M	Gent	French	Switzerland	Charlemagne	19 Sep 1828
T.	58	M	Gent	French	Switzerland	Charlemagne	19 Sep 1828
SEGONNE, Victor	39	M	Mercht.	Spain	France	Richmond Packet	28 Oct 1825
SEGUE, Augustus	26	M	Merchant	France	U. States	Montano	19 Feb 1824
SEGUETIN, P. E.	31	M	Physician	France	U. States	Industry	29 Jan 1828
SEGUIN, Francis J.	34	M	Prof. of Medicin	England	Quebec	Cadmus	27 Aug 1822
SEHMES, Christian	37	M	Mason	Germany	United States	Wm. Osborne	16 Sep 1828
Jacob	3	M	his family [Christian]	Germany	United States	Wm. Osborne	16 Sep 1828
Louisa	2/12	F	his family [Christian]	Germany	United States	Wm. Osborne	16 Sep 1828
Maria	7	F	his family [Christian]	Germany	United States	Wm. Osborne	16 Sep 1828
Susanah	30	F	his family [Christian]	Germany	United States	Wm. Osborne	16 Sep 1828
SEIBERT, Adam	2/12	M	there Child [James & Elizabeth]	Germany	United States	Helen	5 Sep 1828
Elizabeth	30	F	his wife [James]	Germany	United States	Helen	5 Sep 1828
James	5	M	there Child [James & Elizabeth]	Germany	United States	Helen	5 Sep 1828
James	28	M	Joiner	Germany	United States	Helen	5 Sep 1828
SEIDER, O.	28	M	...	Wirtemburg	United States	Wade	29 Aug 1825
SEIDS, Mary, Mrs.	25	F		Ireland	Ireland	Athenian	17 Jul 1829
SEIFANG, Rosina	68	F		Germany	America	Falcon	28 Aug 1828
SEIFLIER, John U., Mr.	34	M	Gent.	England	U. States	Acasta	11 Dec 1826
SEIGLE, Antoinette	40	F		Germany	U. States	Isabella	10 Aug 1829
Conrad	17	M		Germany	U. States	Isabella	10 Aug 1829
Conrad	44	M	Carpenter	Germany	U. States	Isabella	10 Aug 1829
Elizabeth	50	F		Germany	U. States	Isabella	10 Aug 1829
George	24	M	Farrier	Germany	United States	Elizabeth	4 Sep 1826
Johannes	65	M	Shoemaker	Germany	U. States	Isabella	10 Aug 1829
Margaret	11	F		Germany	U. States	Isabella	10 Aug 1829
SEIGNETTE, Azac P.	2		None	United States	United States	Bayard	17 Dec 1827
Camille L.	4		None	United States	United States	Bayard	17 Dec 1827
Catharine A.	27		None	United States	United States	Bayard	17 Dec 1827
Francis	9		None	United States	United States	Bayard	17 Dec 1827
Swiran T.	6		None	United States	United States	Bayard	17 Dec 1827
SEINCE, R.	27	M		Cuba	Cuba	Radius	12 Jul 1825
SEINSS, —, Mr.	25	M	Merchant	Cattatonia	Havana	Mary Jane	7 Jan 1829
SEIRA, Barth.		M			U. States	Jane Maria	12 Aug 1829

NAMES OF PASSENGERS	AGE	SEX	OCCUPATIONS	COUNTRY TO WHICH THEY BELONG	COUNTRY THEY INTEND TO INHABIT	SHIPS/DATES OF ARRIVAL	
SEITZ, Barbara	8	F		Germany	America	Falcon	28 Aug 1828
Catharin E. F.	42	F		Germany	America	Falcon	28 Aug 1828
Fredk.	8	M		Germany	America	Falcon	28 Aug 1828
Johan G.	20	M		Germany	America	Falcon	28 Aug 1828
Johannes	15	M		Germany	America	Falcon	28 Aug 1828
Jurie George	46	M	Farmer	Germany	America	Falcon	28 Aug 1828
Margareth	11	F		Germany	America	Falcon	28 Aug 1828
Michael	17	M		Germany	America	Falcon	28 Aug 1828
SEIVERS, Charles	40	M	Sugar Bacler [Baker]	Germany	U. States	Emma	13 Oct 1824
SEKAWA, Jac.	30	M	Agriculture	Wirtemburg	United States	Henri IV	14 Oct 1829
SELANOR, Aristides	26	M	Gentleman	France	U. States	Bayard	8 Mar 1825
SELAR, Christain	22	M	Butcher	Germany	United States	Robert Edwards	1 Jun 1826
SELARD, John	25	M	Labourer			Henri IV	17 May 1828
SELDEN, Chas.	40	M	Mariner	N. York	N. York	Motion	11 Jan 1826
Hercules	26		Labourer	England	United States	Corinthian	7 Jul 1829
John *Dead	19	M	Merchant	U. States	U. States	Hopes Delight	21 Nov 1825
Richard	19		Labourer	England	United States	Corinthian	7 Jul 1829
Stephen	21		Labourer	England	United States	Corinthian	7 Jul 1829
SELF, James	23	M	Labourer	Great Britain	United States	Fidelity	16 Oct 1820
Wm. H.	21	M	Auctioneer	Great Britain	United States	Unity	20 Oct 1829
SELFAIR, Edmund	40	M	Merchant	U. States	U. States	Nymph	17 Jan 1822
SELFE, Abraham	27	M	Farmer	England	U.S.A.	Brighton	21 Jan 1826
SELINEY, John	30	F	Farmer	Switzerland	U. States	India	8 Dec 1826
SELL, Geo.	35	M	Pedler	Ireland	United States	Sarah Ann	11 Jan 1827
Janes	25	M	Servant	England	England	Eliza	28 Apr 1827
SELLANDER, Louis	20 3/12	M	Confectioner	France	United States	Catharine	10 Sep 1827
SELLAR, Sarah	20	F	None	Scotland	U.S.	Olive Branch	28 Aug 1828
Thos.	40	M	Mason	Scotland	U.S.	Olive Branch	28 Aug 1828
SELLEY, Hellen	25	M	Wife	G. Brittan	U. States	Henry	24 Oct 1828
James	21	M	Butcher	G. Brittan	U. States	Henry	24 Oct 1828
SELLICK, Charlotte	16	F		U. States	U. States	L. M. Pelham	7 Mar 1822
SELLON, Anna Maria	3	F				Criterion	27 Oct 1820
Benjamin	2	M				Criterion	27 Oct 1820
Edward	5	M				Criterion	27 Oct 1820
Henry	4	M				Criterion	27 Oct 1820
SELMAN, Betsey	40	F		England	U. States	Unity	5 Sep 1828
Melia	11	F		England	U. States	Unity	5 Sep 1828
Thomas	38	M	Shoe Maker	England	U. States	Unity	5 Sep 1828
SELMES, Spencer	46	M	Farmer	England	U. States	Bayard	11 Mar 1823
SELMS, Spencer	21	M	Farmer	England	U. States	Acasta	28 Jan 1823
SELMTH, ef E.	23	M	Merchant	Bremen	U. States	Constitution	10 Jan 1827
SELSTON, John C.	27	M	Merchant	U. States	U. States	Mattrawan	31 Jan 1823
SEM, Wm.	23	M	Stone Cutter	Scotland	New York	Hope & Esther	21 Dec 1827
SEMLY, J.	35	M	Merchant	Gaudaloupe	Gaudaloupe	Jane	13 Aug 1827
SEMPLE, Betsey	9		girl	Ireland	United States	Robert Burns	18 Jun 1821
Elizbith	19	F		Great Britian	United States	Brok	29 Aug 1823
Helen	17	F		Great Britian	United States	Brok	29 Aug 1823
James	20	M	Farmer	Great Britian	United States	Brok	29 Aug 1823
SEMPNEZ, Anthony	36	M	Carpenter	France	U. States	Sully	25 Jun 1828
Magaret	43	F	None	France	U. States	Sully	25 Jun 1828
Molann	7	F	None	France	U. States	Sully	25 Jun 1828
SENGLAND, Catherine	25		Merchant			Charlotte Corday	11 Sep 1820
SENGNEOTT, J.	33	M	Mechanic	Italy	United States	Cambridge	19 Sep 1828
SENIOR, A. H.	23	M		Netherlands	Netherlands	Hippomenes	9 Jun 1821
Catharine	4	F	Child	England	United States	Maria	29 Sep 1823
Catharine, Mrs.	28	F	Lady	England	United States	Maria	29 Sep 1823
Edward	5	M	Child	England	United States	Maria	29 Sep 1823
Edwd.	23 8/12	M	Stone cutter	Ireland	America	Carolina Ann	7 Apr 1826
George	1 6/12	M	Child	England	United States	Maria	29 Sep 1823
Louisa	10	F	Child	England	United States	Maria	29 Sep 1823
William	7	M	Child	England	United States	Maria	29 Sep 1823
William, Mr.	30	M	Gentleman	England	United States	Maria	29 Sep 1823
SENMAN, Heanor	8	F	None	Scotland	U. States	Czar	29 Aug 1829
Sarah	2	F	None	Scotland	U. States	Czar	29 Aug 1829
SENNETT, Bridgit	30			Ireland	United States	Geo. Canning	5 Jun 1828

NAMES OF PASSENGERS	AGE	SEX	OCCUPATIONS	COUNTRY TO WHICH THEY BELONG	COUNTRY THEY INTEND TO INHABIT	SHIPS/DATES OF ARRIVAL	
SENNETT (cont'd)							
Ellen	16		Cabinet Maker	Ireland	United States	Geo. Canning	5 Jun 1828
Francis	6			Ireland	United States	Geo. Canning	5 Jun 1828
John	35		Cabinet Maker	Ireland	United States	Geo. Canning	5 Jun 1828
Thos.	12			Ireland	United States	Geo. Canning	5 Jun 1828
SENOR, Olantin	46	M	Gardner	Italy	United States	Ospray	2 Sep 1824
SEONARD, Richard	47	M	Labourer	Ireland	United States	John Wells	11 May 1827
SEPLUPH, Anna	32	F		Switzerland	America, U.N.S.	Great Britain	3 Aug 1829
Anna M.	8	F		Switzerland	America, U.N.S.	Great Britain	3 Aug 1829
Barbara	4	F		Switzerland	America, U.N.S.	Great Britain	3 Aug 1829
Elizabeth	10	F		Switzerland	America, U.N.S.	Great Britain	3 Aug 1829
Maria	6	F		Switzerland	America, U.N.S.	Great Britain	3 Aug 1829
Nicholas	46	M	None	Switzerland	America, U.N.S.	Great Britain	3 Aug 1829
Nicolas	9	M		Switzerland	America, U.N.S.	Great Britain	3 Aug 1829
SEPSON, John	21	M	Taylor	England	U. States	Unity	5 Sep 1828
SEQUI, Ernest	24	M	Planter	France	U. States	Andromache	30 Jul 1823
SEQUIN, Nathl.	39	M	Cook	American	United States	Stephania	24 Mar 1828
SERANAGE, Chs.	21	M	Seaman	France		Enterprise	18 Sep 1820
SERANS, L. S., Don	28		Gentleman	Spain	Cuba	Draper	17 Dec 1823
SERANT, A.	18	F	Servant	Denmark	Denmark	Agness	23 Jun 1828
SERAY, Catherine	1	F	Farmer	Switzerland	United States	Olympia	12 Aug 1828
Constine	7	F	Farmer	Switzerland	United States	Olympia	12 Aug 1828
Hannah	5	F	Farmer	Switzerland	United States	Olympia	12 Aug 1828
Jacob	8	M	Farmer	Switzerland	United States	Olympia	12 Aug 1828
Jacob	37	M	Farmer	Switzerland	United States	Olympia	12 Aug 1828
Margaret	38	F	Farmer	Switzerland	United States	Olympia	12 Aug 1828
SERFTY, Jane	20		Farmer	Ireland	United States	Courier	16 May 1825
SERGANT, Thomas	22	M	Farmer	England	United States	Concordia	25 Aug 1827
SERLIE, Margt.	12	F		Ireland	United States	Gem	16 Jun 1824
SERQUET, Peter	24	M	Nail Maker	Switzerland	United States	Thetis	5 Jul 1821
SERRAY, M.	30	M	Labourer	G. Britain	U. States	Hanford	18 Sep 1828
SERRION, Ew.	20	M	None	Great Britain	United States	Atlantic	28 May 1827
SERRY, Ann		F	Spinster	G. Britain	U. States	Hanford	18 Sep 1828
Eliza	25	F	Spinster	G. Britain	U. States	Hanford	18 Sep 1828
SERS, Abel	18	M	Merchant	France	Alexandria	Howard	11 Jan 1827
SERTH, Wm.	34	M		G. Britain	U. States	Mary & Harriot	8 Sep 1828
SERVANT, Salina	20	F	Farmer	Switzerland	United States	Olympia	12 Aug 1828
SERVANTES, Marcela	25	F	Nurse	Mexico	Mexico	Virginia	9 Feb 1829
SERVE, Catharine	13	F		Native of Switzerland	United States	Canaris	30 Jun 1827
Catharine	45	F		Native of Switzerland	United States	Canaris	30 Jun 1827
Gertrude	8	F		Native of Switzerland	United States	Canaris	30 Jun 1827
Marice	5	M		Native of Switzerland	United States	Canaris	30 Jun 1827
Peter	15	M		Native of Switzerland	United States	Canaris	30 Jun 1827
Peter	50	M	Carpenter	Native of Switzerland	United States	Canaris	30 Jun 1827
SERVICE, David	17	M	...	Ireland	U.S. America	Columbia	26 Nov 1825
John	18	M	Farmer	Lundarry	United States	Minerva	30 Oct 1829
Jos.	18	M	Labourer	Gt. Britain	U.S. America	James Cropper	2 Aug 1827
Robert	17	M	Farmer	Lundarry	United States	Minerva	30 Oct 1829
Thos.	11	M	...	Ireland	U.S. America	Columbia	26 Nov 1825
SERVITOR, Lydia	26	F		Gt. Britain		Silas Richards	20 Jun 1826
Mary	3/12	F		Gt. Britain		Silas Richards	20 Jun 1826
Thomas	25	M	Surgeon	Gt. Britain		Silas Richards	20 Jun 1826
SESHEW, John, Capt.	36	M	Late of the Richmond	New York	New York	Hercules	11 Feb 1822
SESIN, F. Lavy	30	F	Min	France		Antioch	18 Aug 1829
SESLER, Andres	28	M	Fabricant	France	United States	New England	29 Aug 1828
SESSING, Jacob, Mr.			Missionary	Germany	Liberia	Sully	26 Oct 1829
T., Mrs.			None	Germany	Liberia	Sully	26 Oct 1829
SESTARS, Jos.	47	M	Merchant	U. States	U. States	Morgiana	31 Dec 1821
SESTORN, Ann	6	F		Great Britain	United States	Diana	6 Jul 1829
Ann	38	F		Great Britain	United States	Diana	6 Jul 1829
Elizabeth	13	F		Great Britain	United States	Diana	6 Jul 1829
James	9	M		Great Britain	United States	Diana	6 Jul 1829

NAMES OF PASSENGERS	AGE	SEX	OCCUPATIONS	COUNTRY TO WHICH THEY BELONG	COUNTRY THEY INTEND TO INHABIT	SHIPS/DATES OF ARRIVAL	
SESTORN (cont'd)							
John	14	M		Great Britain	United States	Diana	6 Jul 1829
Joseph	1 6/12	M		Great Britain	United States	Diana	6 Jul 1829
Judith	4	F		Great Britain	United States	Diana	6 Jul 1829
Mary	15	F		Great Britain	United States	Diana	6 Jul 1829
Susannah	3	F		Great Britain	United States	Diana	6 Jul 1829
Thos.	42	M	Farmer	Great Britain	United States	Diana	6 Jul 1829
Wm.	12	M		Great Britain	United States	Diana	6 Jul 1829
SETFORD, John	1	M	Farmer	England	U. States	Acasta	12 May 1825
Sarah	5	F	Farmer	England	U. States	Acasta	12 May 1825
Sarah	26	F	Farmer	England	U. States	Acasta	12 May 1825
Thos.	36	M	Farmer	England	U. States	Acasta	12 May 1825
SETLEY, William	18	F		England	United States	Danube	22 Aug 1825
SETON, —, Mrs.		F		New York	New York	United States	15 Jul 1824
—, one Child (Infant)		F		New York	New York	United States	15 Jul 1824
A.		M	Merchant	New York	New York	United States	15 Jul 1824
Alfred		M	Merchant	U. States	U. States	Swan	13 Nov 1821
Alfred	25	M	Merchant	U. States	U. States	Edgar	1 Oct 1822
Alfred	30	M	Merchant	N. York	U. States	Charleston Packet	21 Oct 1823
Alfred	31	M	Merchant	U. States	United States	Florida	14 Sep 1827
Alfred	35	M	Merchant	U. States	U. States	Edgar	4 Jan 1828
Eliza	15	F		G. Britain	U. States	Camillus	8 Sep 1828
Ethelinda		F		New York	New York	United States	15 Jul 1824
SETTER, J.	28	M	Farmer	G. Britain	U. States	St. George	7 Jun 1828
SEVANT, Juan Tarnquird	46		Gentleman	Spain	Spain	Florida	1 Dec 1828
Regina Diaz	40		Gentleman	Spain	Spain	Florida	1 Dec 1828
SEVENDER, Mathew	24	M	Weaver	Great Britan	United States	Silvanus Jenkins	10 Mar 1827
SEVER, Robt.	22	M	Farmer	England	U.S.A.	Lima	6 Dec 1826
SEVERN, James	35	M	Servant	England	America	William	21 Sep 1821
Jas. P.	23	M	Physician	United States	United States	Cortes	11 Dec 1822
John	34	M	Servant	England	America	William	21 Sep 1821
SEVERY, Eliz.	2	F	None	U. States	U. States	Bunker Hill	9 Jan 1827
Henry	1	M	None	U. States	U. States	Bunker Hill	9 Jan 1827
SEVIER, Sarah	34		Farmer	England	England	Hudson	18 Jun 1825
SEVILLE, James	21	M	Farmer	Gt. Britain	United States	Silas Richards	20 Jun 1826
SEVRES, C.	21	M	Glass Cutter	France	U. States	Stephania	18 Dec 1824
SEWARD, Amos	35	M	Mechanic	Connecticutt	U. States	Robert Reade	23 Jul 1823
John	26	M	Farmer	England	United States	John Dickinson	30 Sep 1823
Nancy	30	F	Spinster			Orion	21 Aug 1820
SEWART, James	21	M	Merchant	England	England	Loire	7 Apr 1821
SEWELL, Ann	11 9/12	F	Daughter of Wm. Sewell	United States	Kentucky	Venus	8 Sep 1820
Elizabeth	34 9/12	F	Wife of Wm. Sewell	United States	Kentucky	Venus	8 Sep 1820
George	19		Yeoman	England	United States	Cambria	19 Oct 1829
Henry	2 11/12	M	Son of Wm. Sewell	United States	Kentucky	Venus	8 Sep 1820
John	21	M	Cooper	Great Britain	United States	Orozimbo	5 Mar 1827
Mary	40	F	Servant	United States	United States	William Bayard	17 May 1825
Thos.	5 2/12	M	Son of Wm. Sewell	United States	Kentucky	Venus	8 Sep 1820
Wm.	9 11/12	M	Son of Wm. Sewell	United States	Kentucky	Venus	8 Sep 1820
SEXTON, Francis	24	M	Labourer	Gt. Britain	U. States	Isaac Hicks	18 Apr 1825
Harvey	22	M	Farmer	United States	United States	Meteor	17 Jan 1825
Mary	24	F		Great Britain	Philadelphia	Philetus	21 Jul 1827
SEYARS, James	19	M	Labourer	Ireland	United States	Fabius	31 Jul 1829
SEYBOUT, Henry	27	M	Gentleman	U. States	U. States	Montano	2 Sep 1828
SEYMOUR, Chas.	36	M	Merchant	England	U. States	Criterion	6 Dec 1824
Henry	24	M	Grocer	England	United States	Marion	25 Nov 1825
Henry	25	M	Merchant	England	U. States	Criterion	6 Dec 1824
Joseph	25	F	Clerk	U. States	U. States	Alabama	21 May 1823
S. J.	24	M	Merchant	Great Britain	Great Britain	Harriet	11 Jan 1820
Sarah	25	F		Ireland	United States	Romulus	24 Jun 1826
Susan, A.		M	family [of George D. Tucker]	Turks Island	U. States	Gold Hunter	24 Oct 1829
William	27	M	Weaver	Ireland	United States	Romulus	24 Jun 1826
SEYS, Ann	25	F		West Indies	America	Delia	26 Oct 1829
George	3	M		West Indies	America	Delia	26 Oct 1829
John	11/12	M		West Indies	America	Delia	26 Oct 1829
John	30	M	Minister	West Indies	America	Delia	26 Oct 1829

NAMES OF PASSENGERS	AGE	SEX	OCCUPATIONS	COUNTRY TO WHICH THEY BELONG	COUNTRY THEY INTEND TO INHABIT	SHIPS/DATES OF ARRIVAL	
SEYS (cont'd)							
Mary	4	F		West Indies	America	Delia	26 Oct 1829
SH..., John	24	M	Farmer	Great Britain	United States	Isaac Hicks	10 Jul 1827
SH...ACK, ...nry	...1		K...	...on	England	Great Britain	7 May 1827
Mary	...1			...on	England	Great Britain	7 May 1827
SH...IGHT, Joseph	35	M	Farmer	Great Britain	U. States	Hector	11 Oct 1824
SH...SON, William	24	M	Labourer	Great Britain	New York	Intrepid	8 Aug 1822
SHAAFF, Arthur	18	M	Merchant	Maryland	America	Manhattan	23 May 1822
SHAALEY, Ann	40	F		Ireland, Citizen of the United States	United States	Cambria	16 Aug 1827
William	56	M	Glover	Ireland, Citizen of the United States	United States	Cambria	16 Aug 1827
SHAATZ, David S.	33	M	Merchant	United States	U.S.	Robert Fulton	7 Nov 1823
SHACHAN, John	55	M	Merchant			Frances	17 Aug 1820
SHACKAN, John	20	M				Frances	17 Aug 1820
SHACKLETON, Thos.	40	M	...	England	United States	Danube	1 Nov 1827
SHACKLEY, Sarah	50	F	Servant	U.S.A.		Silas Richards	20 Jun 1826
SHADDON, Jane	1	F		Ireland	U. States	Balaena	29 Apr 1825
Mary	20	F		Ireland	U. States	Balaena	29 Apr 1825
Thomas	18	M	Labourer	Ireland	New York	Atlantic	8 May 1828
SHADDY, Martin	23 4/12	M	Mason	Ireland	United States	Cyno	1 Apr 1828
SHADFORD, John	40	M	Butcher	G. Britain	U. States	Freak	9 Jun 1828
SHADON, James	30	M		Ireland	U. States	Balaena	29 Apr 1825
SHADWICH, Martha	20	F	Farmer	England	United States	Euphrates	18 Aug 1827
SHAFE, Jno., Jur.	33	M	Merchant	England	U.S.	Florida	17 May 1825
SHAFFER, Aadam	57	M	Farm	Ireland		Quatre Freres	29 Jul 1828
C.	10/12	M	None	Switzerland	United States	Howard	14 May 1825
C.	28	M	Cooper	Switzerland	United States	Howard	14 May 1825
C., Mrs.	40	M	None	Switzerland	United States	Howard	14 May 1825
Eshart	6	M	Farmer	Switzerland		Charlemagne	20 Aug 1829
Eshart	40	M	Farmer	Switzerland		Charlemagne	20 Aug 1829
Geo.	21	M	Merchant	Germany	U. States	Ohio	2 May 1821
Magdalen	8	F	Farmer	Switzerland		Charlemagne	20 Aug 1829
Mary	32	F	Farmer	Switzerland		Charlemagne	20 Aug 1829
Nancy W.	19	F	Spinster	Ireland		Robert Fulton	4 Jun 1828
Thomas	10	M	Farmer	Switzerland		Charlemagne	20 Aug 1829
SHAFFLEY, Jas.	28	M	Farmer	Ireland	U. States	Globe	14 Jul 1821
SHAIN, Ben. J.	42 9/12	M	Ship Master	Philadelphia	Philadelphia	Florida	27 Aug 1825
SHALER, Owen	14	M		Ireland	U. States	Concordia	11 Jun 1823
Wm.	...	...	...	...	...	Ontario	25 Mar 1823
SHALLAR, Wm.	26	M	Farmer	Native of Switzerland	United States	Canaris	30 Jun 1827
SHALLEN, Andrew	52	M	Stone Mason	France	United States	Bolivar	30 Nov 1827
Marian	8	F		France	United States	Bolivar	30 Nov 1827
Marian	46	F		France	United States	Bolivar	30 Nov 1827
Marty	14	M		France	United States	Bolivar	30 Nov 1827
SHALLER, —, Mr.	30	M	Lawyer	United States	U. States	Manchester Packet	9 Mar 1826
SHAN, J. S., Mr.	26	M	Merchant	Bermuda	Canada	Camden	14 May 1825
J. W.	28	F		R. Island	America	Jupiter	8 Apr 1828
SHANAGHEY, Peter	25 6/12	M	Labourer	Ireland	United States	Fabius	31 Jul 1829
SHANAHAN, Alice	5	F	None	Ireland	United States	Roman	12 Jun 1826
Ann	6/12	F	None	Ireland	United States	Roman	12 Jun 1826
Catherine	14	F	None	Ireland	United States	Roman	12 Jun 1826
Elizabeth	35	F	None	Ireland	United States	Roman	12 Jun 1826
John	23	M	Labourer	Ireland	U.S.	Lady Hunter	10 Jul 1826
John	40	M	Carpenter	Ireland	United States	Roman	12 Jun 1826
Joseph	10	M	None	Ireland	United States	Roman	12 Jun 1826
Mary	7	F	None	Ireland	United States	Roman	12 Jun 1826
William	20	M	Farmer	Ireland	U. States	Combine	30 Nov 1825
SHANDY, William	21	M	Farmer	Ireland	United States	Dublin Packet	23 May 1828
SHANKS, James	20	M	Labourer	Ireland	United States	Meteor	26 Jun 1827
Mathew	33	M	Labourer	Scotland	United States	Samuel Robertson	5 Oct 1827
Robert	20	M	Merchant	Argyle (Tedland) Scotland	United States	Jean Hastie	27 Jul 1829

NAMES OF PASSENGERS	AGE	SEX	OCCUPATIONS	COUNTRY TO WHICH THEY BELONG	COUNTRY THEY INTEND TO INHABIT	SHIPS/DATES OF ARRIVAL	
SHANLY, Ellenor	16	F		Ireland	U. States	Nancy	16 Aug 1822
SHANNASHY, Betty	23	F	Servant	Ireland	New York	Atlantic	8 May 1828
SHANNE, R. G.	25	M	Watchman	Gt. Britain	United States	Robert Edwards	1 Jun 1826
SHANNEN, Owen	33 2/12	M	Distiller	Ireland	United States	London	6 Feb 1829
SHANNON, —	30	M	Blacksmith	Irish	United States	Patriots Eagle	30 Oct 1829
—, Mr.	38	M	Accountant	New York	U. States	Planet	26 May 1824
—, Mrs.	19	F		U.S.	U.S.	Radius	11 Dec 1824
—, Mrs.	21	F		Irish	United States	Patriots Eagle	30 Oct 1829
—, Mrs.	28	F	Accountant	New York	U. States	Planet	26 May 1824
A.	11	M	Accountant	New York	U. States	Planet	26 May 1824
Allen	2	F		Belfast	United States	Minerva	30 Oct 1829
Ann	13	F	house maid	Ireland	United States	William	20 Jul 1829
Anne	7			Great Britan	United States	Newry	11 Jul 1827
Augustius	9	M	Accountant	New York	U. States	Planet	26 May 1824
B.	13	M	Accountant	New York	U. States	Planet	26 May 1824
C.	7	F	Accountant	New York	U. States	Planet	26 May 1824
Edwd.	19	M	Gentleman	United States	United States	Georgetown Packet	15 Nov 1823
Elizabeth	9			Great Britan	United States	Newry	11 Jul 1827
Geo.	1			Great Britan	United States	Newry	11 Jul 1827
J. N.	36	M	Merchant	Gt. Britain	United States	Seeds	29 Sep 1824
James	4	M		Belfast	United States	Minerva	30 Oct 1829
James	24	M		Great Britain	U. States	Lady Hunter	26 Nov 1823
Jane	35			Great Britan	United States	Newry	11 Jul 1827
Janes	5			Great Britan	United States	Newry	11 Jul 1827
John	15			Great Britan	United States	Newry	11 Jul 1827
John	20	M	Merchant	England	Quebec	Rising States	20 Sep 1828
John	28			Great Britan	United States	Newry	11 Jul 1827
John	36			Great Britan	United States	Newry	11 Jul 1827
Joseph	8	M		Belfast	United States	Minerva	30 Oct 1829
Joseph	27	M	Mechanic	U.S.	U.S.	Radius	11 Dec 1824
Margarett	6/12	F		Belfast	United States	Minerva	30 Oct 1829
Margt.	20		Spinster	Ireland	United States	Fabius	18 Mar 1829
Mary	12	F		Belfast	United States	Minerva	30 Oct 1829
Mary	22	F	Spinster	Ireland	United States	Dublin Packet	23 May 1828
Maryann	35	F		Belfast	United States	Minerva	30 Oct 1829
Peter	6	M		Belfast	United States	Minerva	30 Oct 1829
Peter	43	M	Merchant	Belfast	United States	Minerva	30 Oct 1829
Richd.	3			Great Britan	United States	Newry	11 Jul 1827
Rob.	11			Great Britan	United States	Newry	11 Jul 1827
Robert	16	M		Belfast	United States	Minerva	30 Oct 1829
Saml.	70	M	Labourer	New York	U. States	Atlantic	19 Aug 1825
Sarah	10	F		Belfast	United States	Minerva	30 Oct 1829
Stanhope	14	M		Belfast	United States	Minerva	30 Oct 1829
William	22	M	Labourer	Ireland	U. States	Atlantic	19 Aug 1825
William	34	M	Merchant	United States	New York	John London	8 Dec 1823
Wm.	5	M	Accountant	New York	U. States	Planet	26 May 1824
Wm.	13			Great Britan	United States	Newry	11 Jul 1827
SHANON, Hannah	12	F	...	...	United States	Minerva	30 Oct 1827
Livingston	50	M	Mariner	U. States	U. States	Douglass	22 May 1823
SHANSTON, Wm. C.	27	M	Missionary	Great Britain	Canada	Lord Gambier	4 Feb 1829
SHANTON, James	32	M	Mason	England	America	Erin	7 Nov 1821
SHAPEL, —, Mr.		M	Merchant	St. Thomas	St. Thomas	Warren	10 Sep 1824
SHAPLY, Amos	6	M		England	America	Sarah	18 Aug 1829
Hannah	8	M		England	America	Sarah	18 Aug 1829
Hannah	40	M		England	America	Sarah	18 Aug 1829
Joseph	15	M		England	America	Sarah	18 Aug 1829
Martha	2	M		England	America	Sarah	18 Aug 1829
Mary	9	M		England	America	Sarah	18 Aug 1829
Priscilla	4	M		England	America	Sarah	18 Aug 1829
Ralph	43	M	Sail maker	England	America	Sarah	18 Aug 1829
Sarah	11	M		England	America	Sarah	18 Aug 1829
SHAPPER, Salvador	35	M	Merchant	United States	United States	Native	1 Dec 1826
SHAPSHANK, Dawson	21	M	Gentleman	United States	United States	Napoleon	28 Jan 1829
SHARDAN, Kitty	23	F		Ireland	U. States	William Byrnes	17 Jul 1825
SHARDON, Jas.	20	M	Labourer	Ireland	United States	William	20 Jul 1829
SHARER, Nicolus	24	M	Black Smi.	Holland	U. States	Edward Bonaffe	23 Jul 1828
SHARHEY, Henry	21	M	Labourer	England	U. States	Comet	23 Aug 1828

NAMES OF PASSENGERS	AGE	SEX	OCCUPATIONS	COUNTRY TO WHICH THEY BELONG	COUNTRY THEY INTEND TO INHABIT	SHIPS/DATES OF ARRIVAL	
SHARKERS, John		M		U. States	U. States	Eliza Davidson	28 Jul 1828
*Died on the passage							
SHARKEY, Ann	18	F	None	Ireland	United States	Aurelia	7 Jun 1826
Charles	23	M	Mercht.	Ireland	United States	Aurelia	7 Jun 1826
George	20	M	Laborer	Great Britain	United States	Hanford	9 Oct 1829
Jane	21	F		Ireland	U. States	Virginia	20 Jun 1825
Pat.	27	M	Labourer	England	United States	Aurelia	7 Jun 1826
Sarah	20	F	None	Ireland	United States	Aurelia	7 Jun 1826
Thomas	21	M	Traveler	Great Britain	United States	Thomas Dickason	31 Jul 1829
SHARKS, Ambrosel	3	M		France	U.S. America	Huntress	6 Sep 1827
Anthon	5 2/12	M		France	U.S. America	Huntress	6 Sep 1827
Argad	11 5/12	M		France	U.S. America	Huntress	6 Sep 1827
Catherine Y.	46	F		France	U.S. America	Huntress	6 Sep 1827
Francis	14	M		France	U.S. America	Huntress	6 Sep 1827
J. D.	47 4/12	M	Farmer	France	U.S. America	Huntress	6 Sep 1827
Jno. Geo.	12	M		France	U.S. America	Huntress	6 Sep 1827
Peter	9	M		France	U.S. America	Huntress	6 Sep 1827
Tarasea	7	M		France	U.S. America	Huntress	6 Sep 1827
SHARKY, John	26	M	...	Ireland	United States	Lima	19 Jun 1824
SHARON, James	46 2/12	M	...	America	America	Wilson	16 Nov 1824
SHARP, —		F	infant	Scotland	United States	Belmont	30 Aug 1828
Alexdr.	50	M	Setler	Scotland	Southern States	Maine	16 Jul 1821
Andrew	29	M	Navigator	Ireland	United States	Curler	7 Jul 1827
Bridget	10/12	F	Child	Ireland	U. States	Josephine	23 Jan 1829
Christian	40	F		Scotland	United States	Belmont	30 Aug 1828
Edward	27	M	Laborer	England	United States	London	21 May 1828
Edward, Jr.	1 2/12	M	None	England	United States	London	21 May 1828
Eliza	21	F	None	England	United States	London	21 May 1828
Elizabeth	27	F				Cassack	25 Jul 1820
G.	19	M				Lady of the Lake	23 Aug 1828
Geo	25	M				Cassack	25 Jul 1820
George	25	M	Farmer	Woodlands, Tellecoulty, [Parish], Clackmannan [County]	New York	Hero	19 May 1828
*to follow their occupation							
H.	10	M		Great Brittain	United States	Sarah Ralston	27 Jan 1827
Helen	8	F	Setler	Scotland	Southern States	Maine	16 Jul 1821
Henry D.	20	M	Merchant	Scotland	America	Camillus	9 Oct 1820
Henry D., Mr.	26	M	Mercht.	Gt. Brittian	New York	Manchester	21 Apr 1827
Henry J.	25	M	Merchant	England	United States	Panthia	7 Feb 1822
J. R.	25	M				Lady of the Lake	23 Aug 1828
James	4	M		Scotland	United States	Belmont	30 Aug 1828
James	27 6/12	M	Weaver	Ireland	U. States	Josephine	23 Jan 1829
James	38	M	Blacksmith	Scotland	United States	Belmont	30 Aug 1828
James	45	M	Stocking frame maker			Lady of the Lake	23 Aug 1828
Jane	66	F	Gentleman	England	England	Manhattan	12 May 1823
Janet	12	F				Lady of the Lake	23 Aug 1828
John	2	M		G. Britain	U. States	George Clinton	10 Sep 1828
John	13	M				Lady of the Lake	23 Aug 1828
John	22	M	Labourer	...	U. States	St. Michael	21 Jul 1824
John	22	M	Taylor	Ireland		Fame	9 Dec 1826
John	23		Merchant	England	New York	James Cropper	12 Jul 1822
John	25	M	Farmer	G. Britain	U. States	George Clinton	10 Sep 1828
John	35	M	Merchant	United States	United States	Pacific	7 May 1827
John	65	M	Gentleman	England	England	Manhattan	12 May 1823
Joseph	28	M	Chemist	United States	United States	Cambria	7 May 1828
K.	39	M	Farmer	Great Brittain	United States	Sarah Ralston	27 Jan 1827
Lydia A.	30	F	Setler	Scotland	Southern States	Maine	16 Jul 1821
M.	0 2/12	M		G. Britain	U. States	George Clinton	10 Sep 1828

NAMES OF PASSENGERS	AGE	SEX	OCCUPATIONS	COUNTRY TO WHICH THEY BELONG	COUNTRY THEY INTEND TO INHABIT	SHIPS/DATES OF ARRIVAL	
SHARP (cont'd)							
M.	21	M				Lady of the Lake	23 Aug 1828
Margt.	25	F		G. Britain	U. States	George Clinton	10 Sep 1828
Mary	22	F		England	New York	James Cropper	12 Jul 1822
Mary	45	F				Lady of the Lake	23 Aug 1828
N.	13	M		Great Brittain	United States	Sarah Ralston	27 Jan 1827
S.	28	F		Great Brittain	United States	Sarah Ralston	27 Jan 1827
Samuel	1	M				Cassack	25 Jul 1820
Susan	15	F	Servant	England	New York	James Cropper	12 Jul 1822
Susan	40	F	Matron	Ireland	U. States	Josephine	23 Jan 1829
Thomas	10	M		Scotland	United States	Belmont	30 Aug 1828
William	3 10/12	M	Child	Ireland	U. States	Josephine	23 Jan 1829
William	8	M		Scotland	United States	Belmont	30 Aug 1828
William	25	M	Laborer	Ireland	United States	St. Michaels	12 Jun 1826
William	32	M	Mason	Great Britain	United States	Colossus	5 Jun 1827
Wm.	16	M	Boy	G. Britain	U.S.	Robert Edwards	11 Nov 1822
Wm.	27	M	...	United States	United States	Loire	18 Oct 1820
Wm.	40	M	Merchant	America	U. States	Pacification	31 Aug 1822
SHARPE, ...	26	F		Great Britian	United States	London	24 Jun 1823
George	25	M	Chemist	England	United States	Cambria	8 Oct 1828
Hannah	27	F	None	Leeds, England	Great Britain	James Cropper	7 Oct 1823
James, Mr.	30		Merchant	England	returns to England	Mary	21 Sep 1821
Joseph	29	M	Merchant	York, England	Great Britain	James Cropper	7 Oct 1823
Mary	22	F	None	Great Britain	United States	Aurora	10 Nov 1827
Sarah	25	F	Wife	England	United States	Cambria	8 Oct 1828
Sophia	8	F	Girl	England	United States	Cambria	8 Oct 1828
Sophia	26	F	Lady	England	United States	Cambria	8 Oct 1828
William	3	M	None	Great Britain	United States	Aurora	10 Nov 1827
SHARPLES, John	32	M	Printer	Great Britain	United States	Blakely	29 Sep 1826
SHARPLESS, T.	34	M		America	America	Corinthian	1 Sep 1827
SHARRA..., Patrick	18	M	Farmer, Labourer or Spinster	Ireland	U. States	Meteor	4 Oct 1827
SHARS, —, Mrs.	40	F		U. States	U.S.	Henri IV	14 Sep 1827
SHARTON, Richard	25	M	Labourer	England	U. States	Comet	23 Aug 1828
SHARWOOD, John	29	M	Merchant	G. Bt.	G. Bt.	Canada	13 Feb 1826
SHAULTZ, Fredk.	36	M		Holland	U. States	Brutus	3 Feb 1827
SHAUNGHESSY,							
Catherine	32	F		Ireland	United States	Trio	13 Jun 1827
Nancy	11	F		Ireland	United States	Trio	13 Jun 1827
Pat	40	M	Laborer	Ireland	United States	Trio	13 Jun 1827
SHAUSEN, Walter	27 5/12	M	Merchant	Germany	Germany	France	28 Mar 1829
SHAVES, J.	17	M	Sailor	America	U. States	Hiram	17 Jun 1826
SHAW, —	45	M	Labourer	England	United States	Alicia	9 May 1827
—, Child	4	M	Labourer	England	United States	Alicia	9 May 1827
—, Child	5	M	Labourer	England	United States	Alicia	9 May 1827
—, Child	6	M	Labourer	England	United States	Alicia	9 May 1827
—, Child	7	M	Labourer	England	United States	Alicia	9 May 1827
—, Child	9	M	Labourer	England	United States	Alicia	9 May 1827
—, Wife	2...	F	Labourer	England	United States	Alicia	9 May 1827
Abel	34	M	Merchant	Gt. Britain	United States	Corks	3 Aug 1824
Alexander	13	M	Mariner	St. Martins	United States	Sally Ann	9 Oct 1828
Alexr.	30	M	Labourer	Scotland	United States	Margaret Bogle	11 Jun 1824
Alexr. H.	21	M	Gentleman	Great Britain		Andromache	7 Feb 1820
Alfred	2	M		Ireland	United States	Lord Wellington	14 Nov 1827
Alice	23	F		Ireland	United States	Kleber	23 Jul 1827
Allison	38	F		Great Britain	United States	Samuel Wright	12 Oct 1829
Andrew	25 7/12	M	Baker	Ireland	U. States	Fabius	22 Sep 1828
Ann	8	F				Governor Fenner	23 Jul 1829
Ann	20	F	Farmer, Labourer or Spinster	Ireland	U. States	Meteor	4 Oct 1827
Ann	22	F	Cotton Reeler	Ireland	U.S.A.	Dalhouse Castle	21 Aug 1829
Ann	22	F	Cotton Reeler	Ireland	United States	Dalhouse Castle	21 Aug 1829
Ann	30	F		England	United States	Copernicus	3 Aug 1829
Anna	3	F		Ireland	United States	Lord Wellington	14 Nov 1827
Anna	22	M	Spinster	Ireland	United States	Leonidas	3 Aug 1825
Belinda	5	F	None	Gt. Britain	United States	Union	9 Jan 1824

NAMES OF PASSENGERS	AGE	SEX	OCCUPATIONS	COUNTRY TO WHICH THEY BELONG	COUNTRY THEY INTEND TO INHABIT	SHIPS/DATES OF ARRIVAL	
SHAW (cont'd)							
Benjn.	21	M	Doctor	England	U. States	Oglethorpe	9 Nov 1824
Betsey	38	F	Lady	England	U.S.	Panthea	22 Jul 1826
C. J.	33	F	Wife	England	America	Corinthian	1 Sep 1827
Caroline	16	F	None	Gt. Brittain	United States	Euphrates	15 Jul 1822
Catherine	26	F	None	Dublin, Ireland	U. States	Manhattan	21 May 1821
Chales	28	M	Wever	Ireland	United States	Fabius	4 Jun 1828
Charles B.	22	M	Merchant	U. States	U. States	Fanny	24 Oct 1822
Danl. John	32			...	...	James Cropper	28 Jun 1824
David	6	M				Governor Fenner	23 Jul 1829
David	22	M	Weaver	Great Britain		Dalmannock	24 Ocg 1826
Deborah	39	F	None	Gt. Britain	United States	Union	9 Jan 1824
Eliza	2			Great Britan	United States	Newry	11 Jul 1827
Eliza	4	F				Governor Fenner	23 Jul 1829
Eliza	26	F				Governor Fenner	23 Jul 1829
Eliza	28	F				Governor Fenner	23 Jul 1829
Elizabeth	12	F		Great Britain	United States	Samuel Wright	12 Oct 1829
Elizabeth	24	F	Weaver	England	New York	Xenophon	3 Oct 1829
Elizabeth	70			Great Britan	United States	Newry	11 Jul 1827
Ellen	25	F		Ireland	U. States	Fabius	22 Sep 1828
Ellin	57	F	Weaver	England	New York	Xenophon	3 Oct 1829
G. H.	18	M	None	Gt. Britain	United States	Union	9 Jan 1824
George	1		Carver & Gilder	England	United States	Corinthian	7 Jul 1829
George	16	M	Laborer	Great Britain	United States	Comet	9 Aug 1822
George	23	M	...	...	...	Meteor	16 Aug 1824
George	25	M	Merchant	England	United States	York	31 Mar 1828
George	60		Farmer	Great Britain	United States	Comet	9 Aug 1822
Hannah	3	F	None	Great Britain	United States	Comet	9 Aug 1822
Hannah	8	F	Girl	England	U.S.	Panthea	22 Jul 1826
Harriet	4	F	None			Importer	30 Oct 1820
Henry	3	M	None	Gt. Britain	United States	Union	9 Jan 1824
Hinson	6/12	F		Great Britain	United States	Samuel Wright	12 Oct 1829
Hugh	17	M	Farmer	Ireland	United States	Trident	17 May 1825
Hugh	20	M	Farmer	Ireland	United States	William & George	14 May 1828
Isabella	28	F	None			Importer	30 Oct 1820
J. S.	32	M	Merchant	England	Great Britain	Ranger	3 May 1828
J. W.	26	M	Merchant	U. States	U. States	Prudence	11 Jun 1825
James	10	M		England	America	Corinthian	1 Sep 1827
James	26 4/12	M	Mechanic	England	United States	John Wells	22 May 1826
James	40	M		England	United States	Copernicus	3 Aug 1829
Jance	20			Great Britan	United States	Newry	11 Jul 1827
Jane	20		Carver & Gilder	England	United States	Corinthian	7 Jul 1829
Jane	21	F	Weaver	England	New York	Xenophon	3 Oct 1829
Jane	27	F	None	Great Britain	United States	Comet	9 Aug 1822
Jane	34	F	Spinster	Ireland	United States	Dublin Packet	9 Jul 1827
Jas.	20	M	Labourer	Ireland	U. States	Atlantic	19 Aug 1825
Jno.	22	M	Butcher	Scotland	U. States	Hunter	30 May 1827
Jno.	25	M	Comedian	America	U. States	General A. Jackson	9 Apr 1822
Johanna	60	F	None	Great Britain	United States	Hannibal	12 Oct 1829
John	1 2/12	M		Ireland	U. States	Fabius	22 Sep 1828
John	2	F	None			Importer	30 Oct 1820
John	12	M	None	England	United States	India	8 Jun 1827
John	12	M	None	England	America	Corinthian	1 Sep 1827
John	17	M	Boy	England	U.S.	Panthea	22 Jul 1826
John	19		Shoemaker	Ireland	Great Britain	Robert Burns	14 Jun 1824
John	22			G. Britain	U. States	Hamilton	28 Apr 1828
John	26	M	Weaver	Ireland	U. States	Courier	17 Mar 1828
John	32	M	Carpenter	England	Ohio	Governor Fenner	23 Jul 1829
John	35	M	Farmer	Great Britain	United States	Comet	9 Aug 1822
John	37	M	Stone Mason	England	United States	Hamilton	13 Nov 1827
John	38	M	Merchant	England		Hudson	23 Jul 1828
John	50	M	Manufacturer	England	U. States	Birmingham	12 Oct 1827

NAMES OF PASSENGERS	AGE	SEX	OCCUPATIONS	COUNTRY TO WHICH THEY BELONG	COUNTRY THEY INTEND TO INHABIT	SHIPS/DATES OF ARRIVAL	
SHAW (cont'd)							
John	50	M	Black & W. Smith	England	New York	Xenophon	3 Oct 1829
John B.	24	M	Merchant	England	England	William Byrnes	14 Apr 1824
John H.	52	M	Mariner	Philadelphia	U.S.	Lydia	7 Oct 1823
Jonathan	32	M	Weaver	England	United States	Peru	23 May 1827
Jos.	41	M	Grocer	England	U. States	Mary Howland	22 Sep 1828
Joseph	28	M	Farmer	Great Britain	United States	Robert Fulton	1 Apr 1824
Joseph	28			Westmoreland	Ohio	Peru	30 May 1828
Joseph	39	M	Weaver	England	U. States	Panthea	8 Apr 1826
Joseph	46	M	Weaver	...	United States	Minerva	30 Oct 1827
Joseph	50			G. Britain	U. States	Hamilton	28 Apr 1828
Marry	3	F	None	Dublin, Ireland	U. States	Manhattan	21 May 1821
Martha	18			Great Britan	United States	Newry	11 Jul 1827
Mary	4	F		England	America	Corinthian	1 Sep 1827
Mary	6	F	Child	England	New York	Xenophon	3 Oct 1829
Mary	10	F	Girl	England	U.S.	Panthea	22 Jul 1826
Mary	19	F	Weaver	England	New York	Xenophon	3 Oct 1829
Mary	20	F	Farmer	Ireland	U. States	Dickinson	30 Jul 1825
Mary D.	1	F	None	Gt. Britain	United States	Union	9 Jan 1824
Mathew	13			Great Britan	United States	Newry	11 Jul 1827
Mathew	14	M	Farmer	Ireland	United States	William & George	14 May 1828
Matthew	36	M	Collier	Scotland	New York	Joseph Hume	26 Oct 1829
Moses	62	M	Trader	England	England	Hanford	15 May
Philedelphia	24		Carver & Gilder	England	United States	Corinthian	7 Jul 1829
Rebecca	3		Carver & Gilder	England	United States	Corinthian	7 Jul 1829
Rob.	10	M	Boy	England	U.S.	Panthea	22 Jul 1826
Robert	21 7/12		Merchant	Washington	U.S. of America	Helen	8 Feb 1822
Robert	25	M	C...t	Ireland	United States	Kleber	23 Jul 1827
Saml.	20	M	Doctor			Robert Burns	13 Jul 1820
Saml.	23	M	Merchant	Scotland	United States	Louisiana	3 Nov 1827
Saml.	26			Great Britan	United States	Newry	11 Jul 1827
Saml.	28		Farmer	Great Britain	United States	Comet	9 Aug 1822
Saml.	29	M	Dyer	Great Britain		Moro Castle	6 Jul 1827
Samuel	7	M		Great Britain	United States	Samuel Wright	12 Oct 1829
Sarah	4	F	Cotton Reeler	Ireland	U.S.A.	Dalhouse Castle	21 Aug 1829
Sarah	4	F	Cotton Reeler	Ireland	United States	Dalhouse Castle	21 Aug 1829
Sarah	18	F	None	Gt. Brittain	United States	Euphrates	15 Jul 1822
Sarah	30	F		Ireland	United States	Lord Wellington	14 Nov 1827
Sarah	48	F	None	Gt. Brittain	United States	Euphrates	15 Jul 1822
Solina	8	F	None	Gt. Britain	United States	Union	9 Jan 1824
Susanna	3	F	None			Importer	30 Oct 1820
Thomas	5		Carver & Gilder	England	United States	Corinthian	7 Jul 1829
Thomas	27		Carver & Gilder	England	United States	Corinthian	7 Jul 1829
Thomas	38		Woollen Weaver	Marsden		Aurora	8 Jun 1827
Thomas	39	M	Taylor	Great Britain	United States	Samuel Wright	12 Oct 1829
Thos.	8	M		England	America	Corinthian	1 Sep 1827
Thos.	20	M	Farmer	G. Britain	U. States	George Clinton	10 Sep 1828
Thos.	30	M	Gentleman	Ireland	U. States	Hibernia	22 Feb 1823
Thos.	30	M	Labourer	Ireland	U. States	Fame	15 Nov 1826
Thos.	30	M	Cotton Twister	U. States	U. States	United States	11 Sep 1828
W.	23	M	Plumber	G. Britain	U. States	Cosmo	15 May 1827
William	2	M				Governor Fenner	23 Jul 1829
William	9	M		Great Britain	United States	Samuel Wright	12 Oct 1829
William	21		Carver & Gilder	England	United States	Corinthian	7 Jul 1829
William	25	M	Spinner	Great Britain		Moro Castle	6 Jul 1827
William	27	M	Farmer			Importer	30 Oct 1820
William	29	M	Weaver	Great Britain	United States	Courier	26 Jun 1827
William	32	M	Weaver	Ireland	United States	Lord Wellington	14 Nov 1827
William	33	M	Taylor	England	U.S. America	Franklin	2 Feb 1824
William	42	M	Mechanic	England	United States	Herald	29 Oct 1825
William	49	M	Merchant	U.S.	United States	Hamilton	21 Nov 1826
William, Mr.	34	M	Merchant	Philadelphia	Philada.	Governor Fenner	23 Jul 1829
William M.	30	M	Stone Mason	U. States	United States	Courier	23 Feb 1824
Willm.	47	M	Gent.	U. States	U. States	New York	6 Mar 1827
Wm.	5		None	Great Britain	United States	Comet	9 Aug 1822
Wm.	6	M	Boy	England	U.S.	Panthea	22 Jul 1826

NAMES OF PASSENGERS	AGE	SEX	OCCUPATIONS	COUNTRY TO WHICH THEY BELONG	COUNTRY THEY INTEND TO INHABIT	SHIPS/DATES OF ARRIVAL	
SHAW (cont'd)							
Wm.	7	M		England	America	Corinthian	1 Sep 1827
Wm.	25	M	Labourer			Lady of the Lake	23 Aug 1828
Wm.	26	M	Plowman	Scotland	United States	Essex	23 May 1828
Wm.	55	M	Merchant	North Carolina	United States	Hogarth	12 Oct 1829
Wm. C.	35	M	Mariner	England	U. States	Fame	21 Aug 1822
SHAWNER, Ellen	18	F	Spinstress	Ireland	Ut. States	Courier	13 Jul 1826
SHAWSON, Thomas	25 8/12	M	...	England	America, U.S.	Illinois	3 Jun 1822
SHAY, Daniel	24	M	Laborer or Spinster	Ireland	United States	Sarah G.	15 Aug 1827
Daniel	27	M	Laborer	Ireland	United States	Ann Maria	3 Jul 1827
Hannah	26	F	Laborer or Spinster	Ireland	United States	Sarah G.	15 Aug 1827
James	20	M		Ireland	U. States	Wanderer	1 Sep 1828
John	25	M	Laborer	Ireland	United States	Ann Maria	3 Jul 1827
Patick	25	M	Laborer	Ireland	United States	Sylvester Healy	11 May 1825
SHAZEL, S. S.	40	M	None	New York	U. States	Perry	16 Aug 1825
SHCHORTOR, John	29	M	Cord weaver	England	U. States	Electra	7 Jul 1828
SHE..., John	28	M	Bricklayer	Ireland	U. States	Josephine	7 May 1827
Martha	22	F		Great Britain	United States	Britannia	29 Oct 1829
SHEA, Daniel	22			Ireland	U.S.	Union	20 Aug 1827
Denis	30	M	Labourer	Great Britain	United States	Henrietta	19 Oct 1825
Emily	5	F		Ireland	United States	Pallas	28 Oct 1828
George	3	M		Ireland	United States	Pallas	28 Oct 1828
Jno.	30		Master Mariner	Ireland	U.S. of America	Mary	21 Sep 1821
John	18	M	Farmer	Ireland	United States	Diana	1 May 1826
Leonora	25	F		Gt. Britain		Corinthian	27 Oct 1829
Mary	26	F		Ireland	United States	Pallas	28 Oct 1828
Roland	1	M		Ireland	United States	Pallas	28 Oct 1828
Wm.	19	M	Labourer	England	U. States	Ayrshire	12 May 1828
SHEAD, Joseph	27	M	Weaver			Lady of the Lake	23 Aug 1828
SHEADOCK, Joseph	21	M	Tailor	Ireland		Quatre Freres	29 Jul 1828
SHEAFE, J. E.	18	M		America	America	Britannia	22 Jul 1829
SHEAHAN, Elizabeth	26	F		Ireland	New York	William	26 Apr 1823
Patrick	4	M		Ireland	New York	William	26 Apr 1823
SHEAK, Jno.	35	M	Gardner	Germany	U. States	Fanny	23 Apr 1822
SHEAL, Mical	22	M				Nancey	25 Jan 1823
SHEALEY, John	23	M	Farmer	Ireland	United States	Diana	1 May 1826
SHEALS, Patk.	14	M		Ireland	New York	Atlantic	6 Oct 1828
Samuel	21	M	Clothyer	Ireland	America	Franklin	13 Aug 1827
SHEAN, James	23	M	Farmer	England	United States	Ganges	10 May 1828
SHEAR, Geo.	34	M	None	Great Britain	United States	Washington	9 Apr 1821
SHEARD, John	25	M				Splendid	14 Aug 1829
SHEARDON, Dennis	14	M		Ireland		Nancey	25 Jan 1823
John	16	M	Laborer	Ireland		Nancey	25 Jan 1823
Rose	40	F		Ireland		Nancey	25 Jan 1823
SHEAREN, D.	35	M				Lady of the Lake	23 Aug 1828
*left ship							
Pat	30	M				Lady of the Lake	23 Aug 1828
*left ship							
SHEARER, Gavin	16	M		Scotland	United States	Camillus	9 May 1827
James	23		Farmer	England	America	Governor Griswold	6 Jun 1821
John	18		Weaver	Scotland	United States	Camillus	3 May 1828
Thomas	20	M	Labourer	Ireland	United States	Fabius	31 Jul 1829
SHEARMAN, Francis	24	M	Gentleman	Ireland		James Cropper	26 Mar 1822
John	29	M	Farmer	Great Britain	United States	Ann	22 Dec 1821
Maria	4	F	None	England	United States	Jubilee	13 Jul 1829
Timothy	40	M	Joiner	England	United States	Jubilee	13 Jul 1829
SHEARON, Joseph	29	M	Labourer			Lady of the Lake	23 Aug 1828
SHEARS, Jane	3...	F	...	...	...	Antioch	8 Oct 1827
Timothy	3...	M	...	...	...	Antioch	8 Oct 1827
SHEASER, Andrew	25	M	Labourer	Scotland	United States	Friends	7 Jul 1827
SHEATHER, James	50	M	Baker	England	United States	Cambria	3 Jul 1829
SHEAVER, John	25	M	Farmer	Great Britain	U. States	Columbia	22 Sep 1828
SHEAVES, John	30	M	Mariner	Bermuda		Lancatter	5 Jul 1820

NAMES OF PASSENGERS	AGE	SEX	OCCUPATIONS	COUNTRY TO WHICH THEY BELONG	COUNTRY THEY INTEND TO INHABIT	SHIPS/DATES OF ARRIVAL	
SHEBELSKA, Achilles	25	M	Prusia	U. States	U. States	Columbia	1 Dec 1824
SHECKLETON, Eliza	29	F	None	Great Britain	United States	Atlantic	28 May 1827
Issabella	6	F	None	Great Britain	United States	Atlantic	28 May 1827
Mattw.	2	M	None	Great Britain	United States	Atlantic	28 May 1827
Wm.	1	M	None	Great Britain	United States	Atlantic	28 May 1827
Wm.	36	M	Farmer	Great Britain	United States	Atlantic	28 May 1827
SHED, Abraham A.	35	M	Mariner	U. States	U. States	Pacification	27 Apr 1824
Mary	22					Trio	5 May 1828
SHEDD, William	28	M	Clergiman	U.S.	United States	Josephine	24 Jul 1826
SHEDDON, —, Mrs.	24	F				Czar	29 Aug 1829
A.	57	M	Merchant	Scotland	Bermuda	Columbia	20 Jul 1825
Christian	3	F				Czar	29 Aug 1829
Patrick	24 11/12	M	Labourer	Ireland	United States	Atlantic	21 Jul 1827
SHEDON, Mary	23	F		England	United States	John Wells	22 May 1826
SHEDWICK, John	32	M	Turner	Great Brittain	United States	United States	16 Feb 1827
SHEEBEL, Betty	15	F	Labourer	New York	New York	Meteor	16 Aug 1824
Marg.	38	F	Labourer	New York	New York	Meteor	16 Aug 1824
SHEED, —, Mrs.,							
(wife of A. A. Steed)	25	F		U. States	U. States	Amazon	29 Aug 1825
A.	33	M	Merchant	Charleston	U. States	Orion	30 Mar 1825
A. A.	34	M	Mariner	U. States	U.S.	Robert Y. Haynes	13 Mar 1826
A. A.	35	M	Merchant	U. States	U. States	Perry	21 Mar 1827
Abraham A.	33	M	Merchant	U. States	U. States	Amazon	29 Aug 1825
George, The Reverend	35	M	Clergyman	Great Britain	an Inhabitant of Upper Canada	Birmingham	15 Jun 1827
SHEEDON, Bryon	23	M		Ireland	U. States	Balaena	29 Apr 1825
SHEEGEN, Ann	11	F	Farmer	France	United States	Crescent	12 Jul 1827
Catherine	17	F	Farmer	France	United States	Crescent	12 Jul 1827
Hans	27	M	Farmer	France	United States	Crescent	12 Jul 1827
Margaret	6	F	Farmer	France	United States	Crescent	12 Jul 1827
Margaret	25	F	Farmer	France	United States	Crescent	12 Jul 1827
Margaret	49	F	Farmer	France	United States	Crescent	12 Jul 1827
Peter	20	M	Farmer	France	United States	Crescent	12 Jul 1827
SHEEHAN, Ellen	18	F	Milliner	Ireland	United States	Trio	2 Oct 1828
James	25		Farmer	Cork	New York	Schuylkill	22 Aug 1825
John	26	M	Labourer	Limerick	Philadelphia	Thomas & William	25 May 1827
Michael	22	M	Farmer	Ireland	United States	Dublin Packet	9 Jul 1827
Richard	28	M	Labourer	Ireland	U. States	Combine	30 Nov 1825
SHEEHEY, John	34	M	Farmer	Ireland	United States	Lord Strangford	20 Jun 1826
SHEEHY, Ellen	25	F			New York	Robert Fulton	8 Mar 1823
John	24	M	Butcher		New York	Robert Fulton	8 Mar 1823
SHEEN, John	35		... Dresser	Ireland	Ireland	Hudson	14 Jun 1827
Phillip	26	M	Military	G. Britain		Happy Return	11 Jul 1820
SHEENY, Paul	20	M	Farmer	Ireland	U. States	Meteor	19 Jul 1828
SHEEPSHANKS, Thos.	38	M	Merchant	England	America	Hannibal	4 Oct 1822
SHEERLEY, Abm.	35	M				Splendid	14 Aug 1829
SHEFFELD, Chas. H.	30	M	Miner	G. Brittain	U. States	Pacific	23 Jan 1826
SHEFFIELD, Harriet	23	F	None	England		Marchioness	13 May 1828
Js.	21	M	Mariner	England	U. States	Commerce	10 Nov 1823
Wm.	25	M	Mariner	U. States	U. States	Belvidere	31 Jul 1822
Wm.	27	M	Carpenter	England		Marchioness	13 May 1828
SHEFLER, Peter	40	M	Baker	France	U. States	Edward Bonaffe	23 Jul 1828
SHEHAN, Michl.	20	M		Ireland	U. States	Howard	25 Jul 1823
SHEIL, Andrew	21	M	Labourer	England and Ireland	United States	Jubilee	12 May 1828
Edward	34	M	Merchant	U. States	U. States	Sanford William	28 Jan 1823
SHEILDS, Jno.	30	M		Ireland	United States	Thomas	13 Dec 1827
Saml.	22	M	Farmer	Ireland	U. States	Francis	6 Sep 1827
SHEILL, John	5	M	Child	Ireland	U. States	Albion	9 Aug 1826
John	34	M	Laborer	Ireland	U. States	Albion	9 Aug 1826
Mary, & infant	30	F	his wife [John]	Ireland	U. States	Albion	9 Aug 1826
Ned	12	M	Child	Ireland	U. States	Albion	9 Aug 1826
Wm.	9	M	Child	Ireland	U. States	Albion	9 Aug 1826
SHEILS, John	21	M		Ireland	United States	William & George	14 May 1828

NAMES OF PASSENGERS	AGE	SEX	OCCUPATIONS	COUNTRY TO WHICH THEY BELONG	COUNTRY THEY INTEND TO INHABIT	SHIPS/DATES OF ARRIVAL	
SHEILS (cont'd)							
Michael	25	M	Labourer	Ireland	United States	General Marion	20 Aug 1828
SHEIMICK, Richd.	25	M	Laborer	Ireland	United States	Trio	13 Jun 1827
SHEIRA Y COBA, M. Jose	40	F	Lady	Spain	U. States	Greek	1 Oct 1825
SHEIRON, Pat	11	M	Boy	Ireland	U. States	Wanderer	30 Sep 1828
Sally	7	F		Ireland	U. States	Wanderer	30 Sep 1828
SHEKELFORD, W.	32	M	Merchant	Charleton	U. States	Alpha	15 Jul 1823
SHEL..., Robert	4...	...	...	...	...	Pioneer	21 Jun 1825
SHELAN, Micher	22	M		France		Pallas	14 Jun 1828
SHELBOURN, Michael	20	M		England	America	Thames	27 May 1822
William	30	M		England	America	Thames	27 May 1822
SHELDON, A. A.	25	M	Mercht.	Massachusetts	U. States	Six Brothers	4 Jun 1822
Absolam	40	M		Great Britain	United States	Active	25 Mar 1828
Eliza	3/12	F	None	U. States	U.S.	Queen Mab	26 Nov 1825
Eliza	26	F	Wife	U. States	U.S.	Queen Mab	26 Nov 1825
H. W.	30	M	Merchant	U. States	U.S.	Queen Mab	26 Nov 1825
Henry	32	M	Merchant	U. States	U. States	Lewis	25 Jun 1824
Henry	35	M		Gt. Britain	Gt. Britain	Caledonia	10 Sep 1828
John			Distressed Seaman			Boston	28 Aug 1821
Joseph	23	M	Iron Roller	Gt. Britain	U.S. America	James Cropper	14 Mar 1828
Lewis	2	M	None	U. States	U.S.	Queen Mab	26 Nov 1825
SHELDS, Pat	27	M	Labourer	Ireland	United States	Thomas	13 Dec 1827
SHELLABER, John	37	M	Merchant	New York	New York, U.S.	New York	14 Mar 1828
SHELLEY, Mary	22	F		Great Britain	U. States	Columbia	22 Sep 1828
Richard	25	M	Farmer	Great Britain	U. States	Columbia	22 Sep 1828
SHELLY, Catherine	28	F	Lady	Ireland	United States	Dublin Packet	23 May 1828
Elizabeth	20	F	Servant	Ireland	United States	Wilson	27 Jun 1826
Margaret	26	F	Spinster	Ireland	America	Wilson	16 May 1825
Martha	60	F	Lady	Ireland	United States	Dublin Packet	23 May 1828
Patrick	28	M	Merchant	Newfoundland	Newfoundland	Mariner	11 Jul 1823
William	25	M	Labourer	Ireland	America	Wilson	16 May 1825
William	25	M	Farmer	Ireland	United States	Baltic	21 Apr 1827
SHELMIRE, Elizabeth	23	F	Mason	Chandford	U.S. America	Superior	18 Jun 1825
Joseph	23	M	Mason	Chandford	U.S. America	Superior	18 Jun 1825
SHELSHORN, Ann	30	F				Lady of the Lake	23 Aug 1828
Thomas	31	M	Shoemaker	E...		Lady of the Lake	23 Aug 1828
SHELSTONE, ...	21	M	Merchant	England	U. States	New York	8 Mar 1825
SHELTER, Stephen S.	24	M	Merchant	U. States	U. States	Centinel	11 Oct 1820
SHELTERS, Henry	30	M	Merchant	New York	New York	Jupiter	27 May 1826
SHELTON, Francis	27	M	Labourer	...	United States	Minerva	30 Oct 1827
Stephen S.	30	M	Merchant	Cuba	Cuba	Sicily	24 Oct 1827
Wm.	23	M	...	...	United States	Minerva	30 Oct 1827
SHEM, James, Jr.	26	M	Labourer	England	United States of Am.	Helen	17 Dec 1827
SHENE, John	28	M	Labourer	England	New York	Hudson	20 Nov 1828
SHENOHAN, Mary	13	F		England	America	Silas Richard	24 Oct 1829
SHENON, John	25	M	Laborer or Spinster	Ireland	United States	Sarah G.	15 Aug 1827
SHENRICH, —	33	F		Switzerland	United States	Elbe	2 Aug 1822
SHEPARD, —, Mrs.	30	F		New York	U.S. America	Lafayette	3 Dec 1827
John	1	M		New York	U.S. America	Lafayette	3 Dec 1827
Richd.	25	M	Servant	Ireland	New York	Louisa	18 Apr 1827
Wm.	7	M		New York	U.S. America	Lafayette	3 Dec 1827
SHEPERD, Rebbecca	24	F	Servant	Irereland	America	Carolina Ann	20 Jun 1825
William	20	M	Weaver	Irereland	America	Carolina Ann	20 Jun 1825
SHEPERNIN, Wm.	10		Merchant	Austria		Constitution	5 Jan 1829
SHEPHARD, Ann Jane	27	F	Spinster	Ireland	U. States	Josephine	7 May 1827
G. A.	30	M	Mercht.	Wiscassett	Wiscassett	Wm. Thompson	13 Sep 1823
Geo. H.	9	M	Attorney	England	U. States	Bee	18 Dec 1821
Henry	25	M	Farmer	Ireland	U. States	Josephine	7 May 1827
John	21	M	Labourer	Ireland	United States	Meteor	26 Jun 1827
John	30	M	Merchant	Scotland	United States	Siroc	31 Oct 1829
Mary	20	F	Merchant	Scotland	United States	Siroc	31 Oct 1829
R., Jr.	45	M	Attorney	England	U. States	Bee	18 Dec 1821
Thos. J.	24	M	Merchant	U. States	U. States	Emma	15 Dec 1824
SHEPHARDS, Isaac	25	M	Labourer	G. Britain	U. States	St. George	7 Jun 1828
SHEPHEARD, Nicholas	25	M	Farmer	Ireland	U. States	Josephine	30 Aug 1828
SHEPHERD (see Shipherd)							
—, Capt.	43	M	Mariner	U. States	U. States	Exchange	4 Jan 1823

NAMES OF PASSENGERS	A G E	S E X	OCCUPATIONS	COUNTRY TO WHICH THEY BELONG	COUNTRY THEY INTEND TO INHABIT	SHIPS/DATES OF ARRIVAL	
SHEPHERD (cont'd)							
Ann	50	F		Great Britain	United States	Florida	2 Oct 1828
C.	38	M	Weaver	G. Britain	U. States	St. George	7 Jun 1828
Catharine	6	F	Lady	G. Britain	U. States	Kennebeck Trader	16 Jul 1822
Catharine	38	F	Lady	G. Britain	U. States	Kennebeck Trader	16 Jul 1822
Charles	2	M		England	U. States	Criterion at London	10 May 1821
E.	30	M	Smith	Great Britain	United States	Isaac Hicks	6 Dec 1827
Eliza	8	F	Lady	G. Britain	U. States	Kennebeck Trader	16 Jul 1822
Eliza, Sister [of John]	21	F		Ireland	New York	Brighton	24 Aug 1827
Emily, (daughter [of John or Eliza?])	7	F		Ireland	New York	Brighton	24 Aug 1827
Jno.	29			England		Anacreon	7 Sep 1827
John	4	M		England	U. States	Criterion at London	10 May 1821
John	30	M	Professor of Music	Ireland	New York	Brighton	24 Aug 1827
John	35	M	Merchant	U. States	U. States	Henrietta	13 Nov 1822
John	35	M	Farmer	Great Britain	United States	Diana	30 Oct 1827
Judith	29	F		England	U. States	Criterion at London	10 May 1821
Lewis	25	M	Servant to Ad. Graves	England	America	Liverpool Packet	23 Mar 1822
Mary	20	F	Servant	G. Britain	U. States	Kennebeck Trader	16 Jul 1822
Mary	20	F	None	Great Britain	New York	Corinthian	27 Apr 1824
Mathew Hercules	22		Doctor	England	England	Venus	4 Oct 1821
Nathl.	30	M	Watchmaker	U. States	United States	Cicero	19 Nov 1825
R. M.	24	M	Mechanic	Philada.	U. States	Sarah Herrick	7 Oct 1826
Robert	31	M	Merchant	United States	United States	New York	12 Nov 1822
Sarah	9	F	Lady	G. Britain	U. States	Kennebeck Trader	16 Jul 1822
Sarah	32	F	Servant	G. Britain	U. States	Kennebeck Trader	16 Jul 1822
Sarah Ann		F	Lady	Barbados	unknown	Superb	23 Apr 1823
Thos.	30	M	Farmer	England	U. States	Criterion at London	10 May 1821
Thos., Mr.	35	M	Merchant	Great Britain	Great Britain	Nestor	3 Nov 1820
W.	35	M	Merchant	England	America	Meteor	21 Aug 1822
William	23	M	Farmer	England		Manhattan	22 May 1827
William	30	M	Mercht.	G.B.	Canada	George Canning	2 May 1828
William	34	M	Merchant	Great Britain	United States	James Monroe	5 Apr 1820
William Thos.	33	M	Merchant	Great Britain	United States	Meteor	15 Apr 1823
Wm.	37	M	Merchant	Great Britan	Great Britan	Columbia	11 Aug 1823
SHEPHERDSON,							
E. Isabella	16	F		Great Britain	U. States	Ann Marria	6 Aug 1823
Eliza	42	F	None	Great Britain	U. States	Ann Marria	6 Aug 1823
Elizabeth	1	F		Great Britain	U. States	Ann Marria	6 Aug 1823
Francis	12	M		Great Britain	U. States	Ann Marria	6 Aug 1823
Marry	13	F	None	United States	U. States	Ann Marria	6 Aug 1823
Marry	20	F		Great Britain	U. States	Ann Marria	6 Aug 1823
Richd.	15	M		Great Britain	U. States	Ann Marria	6 Aug 1823
Richd.	50	M	Farmer	United States	U. States	Ann Marria	6 Aug 1823
Thomas	23	M	Cabinet Maker	Bristol, Engl.	...	Warrior	19 May 1828
Wm.	10	M		Great Britain	U. States	Ann Marria	6 Aug 1823
Wm.	32	M	Shoe M.	England	U. States	Franklin	7 Jul 1828
Wm.	44	M	Farmer	Great Britain	U. States	Ann Marria	6 Aug 1823
SHEPPARD, Charles	40	M	Farmer	England	United States	Acasta	14 Jun 1824
Edward	18	M	Laborer	Ireland	United States	Carolina Ann	11 Dec 1826
Edward	22	M	Tailor	England	New York	Brighton	29 Aug 1828
Eleanor	60	F		Ireland	United States	Carolina Ann	11 Dec 1826
Elizabeth	34	F	None	Great Britain	United States	Silvanus Jenkins	16 Aug 1826
Fanny	17	F		England	United States	Acasta	14 Jun 1824
George	3	M		England	United States	Acasta	14 Jun 1824
James	6	M	Cloth Dresser	England	United States	Acasta	14 Jun 1824
James	40	M	Cloth Dresser	England	United States	Acasta	14 Jun 1824

NAMES OF PASSENGERS	A G E	S E X	OCCUPATIONS	COUNTRY TO WHICH THEY BELONG	COUNTRY THEY INTEND TO INHABIT	SHIPS/DATES OF ARRIVAL	
SHEPPARD (cont'd)							
John	9	M	Cloth Dresser	England	United States	Acasta	14 Jun 1824
Mary	40	F		England	United States	Acasta	14 Jun 1824
Mary, Miss	6/12	F	Gentln.	England	U. States	Corinthian	8 Oct 1828
Robt.	20	M	Farmer	Ireland	United States	Julia Ann	24 Jul 1820
Sarah	11	F		England	United States	Acasta	14 Jun 1824
Thomas	60	M	Laborer	Ireland	United States	Carolina Ann	11 Dec 1826
Thomas, Mrs.	21	F	Gentln.	England	U. States	Corinthian	8 Oct 1828
William	32	M	...	...	...	Meteor	16 Aug 1824
SHEPPERD, Ann	21	F		Great Britain	State of Maine	Philetus	21 Jul 1827
Jane	11	F		Great Britain	State of Maine	Philetus	21 Jul 1827
John	12	M		Great Britain	State of Maine	Philetus	21 Jul 1827
Mary	44	F		Great Britain	State of Maine	Philetus	21 Jul 1827
Paul	26	M	Farmer	England	U.S. America	Cortes	19 May 1826
Serah	16	F		Great Britain	State of Maine	Philetus	21 Jul 1827
Thos.	45	M		Great Britain	State of Maine	Philetus	21 Jul 1827
SHER, Owen	28	M	Farmer	Great Britian	United States	Columbia	17 Apr 1827
SHERBA, Emely	25	F	Framer	Switzerland	Ohio	Danube	20 Jul 1826
SHERBETH, Stephen	25		Merchant	England	United States	Caspian	12 Jul 1821
SHERDAN, Jas.	25	M	Labourer	Ireland	U. States	Two Marys	20 Apr 1825
SHERDEN, Nancy	24	F		Irland	United States	Nancy	28 Oct 1822
Rose	18	F		Irland	United States	Nancy	28 Oct 1822
SHERDINE, James	18	M	Mason	England	United States	Euphrates	18 Aug 1827
SHERDON, Ann	16	F		Ireland	U. States	Nancy	16 Aug 1822
Ann	20	F	Labourer	Ireland	U. States	Two Marys	20 Apr 1825
Jane	23	F	Labourer	Ireland	U. States	Two Marys	20 Apr 1825
Margt.	22	F	Labourer	Ireland	U. States	Two Marys	20 Apr 1825
Mary	18	F		Ireland	U. States	Nancy	16 Aug 1822
Richard	18	M	Labourer	Ireland	America	Wilson	16 May 1825
Wm.	23	M	Tailor	Great Britain	U. States	Lady Hunter	26 Nov 1823
SHERGOULD, James	30	M	Iron Roller	Gt. Britain	U.S. America	James Cropper	14 Mar 1828
SHERIDAN, Ann	9	F		G. Britain	U. States	Leavitts	25 Aug 1828
Ann	16		Spinster	Ireland	United States	Courier	15 Oct 1827
Ann	30	F		G. Britain	U. States	Leavitts	25 Aug 1828
Bridget	18		Spinster	Ireland	United States	Courier	15 Oct 1827
Bridget	23	F	Farmer	Ireland	U. States	Edward	15 Jul 1825
Catharine	17	F	Servant	Ireland	United States	Josephine	30 Apr 1828
Catharine	20 3/12	F		Ireland	America	Carolina Ann	7 Apr 1826
Cathr.	4	F		G. Britain	U. States	Leavitts	25 Aug 1828
Chas.	21	M	Labourer	Ireland	United States	Wilson	27 Jun 1826
Ellen	18	F	Spinster	Ireland	U. States	Josephine	30 Aug 1828
Ewd.	25	M	Labourer	G. Britain	U. States	Hanford	18 Sep 1828
F.	25	M	Labourer	Ireland	United States	Josephine	30 Apr 1828
Hugh	28	M	Weaver	Ireland	U. States	Josephine	30 Aug 1828
James	19	M	Labourer	Ireland	United States	Jubilee	4 Mar 1829
James	23	M	Farmer	Ireland	U.S. America	Cincinnatus	31 Oct 1820
James	27	M	Weaver	Great Britain	United States	Frances Henrietta	17 Sep 1827
James	27	M	Labourer	Ireland	United States	Potomac	28 Sep 1827
James	28	M	Weaver	Ireland	United States	Josephine	30 Apr 1828
James	53	M		G. Britain	U. States	Leavitts	25 Aug 1828
Jno.	24	M		Ireland	United States	William Byrnes	6 Apr 1826
John	19	M	Servant	Ireland	United States	Josephine	30 Apr 1828
John	24	M	Store Keeper	Great Britain	U. States	Ann Maria	26 Apr 1822
John	26	M	Farmer	Ireland	America	Farmer	4 Aug 1825
M.	20	F		Ireland	United States	Josephine	30 Apr 1828
Margaret	20	F	Farmer	Ireland	America	Farmer	4 Aug 1825
Margaret	20	F		Gt. Britain		Dalhouse Castle	13 May 1828
Margeret	22	F	Spinster	Ireland	U. States	Josephine	30 Aug 1828
Mary	9	F		G. Britain	U. States	Leavitts	25 Aug 1828
Michael	25	M	Weaver	Ireland	New York	Atlantic	8 May 1828
Patrick	12	M	Boy	Ireland	U. States	Josephine	7 May 1827
Patrick	19	M	Labourer	Ireland	U. States	Josephine	7 May 1827
Patrick	24	M	Farmer	Ireland	America	Minerva	31 May 1824
Peter	17	M	Labourer	Ireland	New York	Atlantic	8 May 1828
Rich	27	M	Smith	Ireland	United States	Diana	1 May 1826
Thomas	19	M	Labourer	Ireland	United States	Wilson	27 Jun 1826
Thomas	24	M	Labourer	Great Britain	United States	Frances Henrietta	17 Sep 1827

NAMES OF PASSENGERS	A G E	S E X	OCCUPATIONS	COUNTRY TO WHICH THEY BELONG	COUNTRY THEY INTEND TO INHABIT	SHIPS/DATES OF ARRIVAL	
SHERIDAN (cont'd)							
Thos.	10	M		Ireland	U. States	Fabius	22 Sep 1828
William	18	M	Surveyor	England	United States	Herald	7 Jun 1824
SHERIDEN, Bridget	28	F	Labourer	England	U. States	Comet	23 Aug 1828
Frances	28	M	Labourer	England	U. States	Comet	23 Aug 1828
Mary	1	F	Labourer	England	U. States	Comet	23 Aug 1828
SHERIDON, John	34	M	Labourer	Great Brittan	U. States	John & Elizabeth	11 Dec 1826
Mary	25	F	None	Great Brittan	U. States	John & Elizabeth	11 Dec 1826
SHERIFF, George	12	M	None	Great Britain	United States	Orbit	23 Oct 1826
John	17	M	None	England	United States	Orozimbo	5 Mar 1827
Richard	31	M	Brick Layer	Great Britain	United States	Orbit	23 Oct 1826
Richard, Jr.	13	M	None	Great Britain	United States	Orbit	23 Oct 1826
Richd.	21	M	Bricklayer	England	United States	Orozimbo	5 Mar 1827
SHERIGAN, Morris	19		Weaver	Ireland	United States	Robert Burns	30 May 1823
SHERIMAN, Jacob	25	M	Farmer	Switzerland	United States	Ospray	2 Sep 1824
SHERINGTON, Robt.	45	M	Merchant	England	U. States	Emulous	22 Aug 1828
SHERINS, Bridgit	30	F	House Keeper	Ireland	United States	Carolina Ann	11 Dec 1826
SHERLIN, Mary	22	F	Servant	Ireland	America	Carolina Ann	7 Aug 1826
SHERLOCK, Edward	4	F	Child	Ireland	United States	Abigail	25 Jun 1822
Mary	23	F	Spinster	Ireland	United States	Abigail	25 Jun 1822
Michael	25	M	...	Ireland	United States	Abigail	25 Jun 1822
Nancy	57			Ireland	United States	Geo. Canning	5 Jun 1828
Richard	10	M	Farmer	Ireland	United States	Dublin Packet	13 Oct 1828
William	50	M	Currier	England	U. States	Montgomery	18 Oct 1828
Wm.	28	M	Labourer	G. Briton	United States	James Monroe	14 Dec 1820
SHERLY, Patrick	30	M	Labourer	G. Britain	U. States	Mary & Harriot	8 Sep 1828
SHERMAN, Catherine	16	F	None	England	United States	Jubilee	13 Jul 1829
James	23	M	Merchant	England	U. States	Manhattan	12 Jun 1824
N.	22	M	Servant	Ireland	U. States	Henrietta	7 Jul 1825
Rose	30	F		Ireland	New York	Lima	5 Aug 1829
Rose	50	F		England	U. States	Lima	5 Aug 1829
SHERMINTON, Wm.	33	M	Baker	England	United States	Hudson	17 Mar 1828
SHEROT, Josh	22	M	Labourer	England		Marchioness	13 May 1828
SHERRE, Casper	52	M	Farmer	Germany	United States	Ohio	10 Jul 1820
SHERREFF, Wm. H.	42	M	Royal Navy	England	U. States	Brighton	14 Apr 1828
SHERRIDAN, Bridget	25	M		Great Britain		London	29 Apr 1824
Peter	35	M	Glazier	Great Britian	U. States	Pallas	17 Aug 1824
Thomas	20	M	Labourer	Ireland	United States	Princess Charlotte	26 Apr 1827
SHERRIDEN, Michael	20	M		Ireland	America	Carolina Ann	7 Aug 1826
SHERRIDENS, Wm.	18	M	Laborer	Ireland	United States	Weser	29 Jul 1823
SHERRIF, Richard	18	M	...	G. Britain	U. States	New England	28 Sep 1824
SHERRIFF, Elizabeth	20	F	wife to Laborer [Selby]	Scotland	U. States	Magnet	22 Aug 1822
Selby	36	M	Laborer	Scotland	U. States	Magnet	22 Aug 1822
SHERRY, ...	9 2/12	F		Denmark	Denmark	Elias Burger	18 Sep 1821
John	21 6/12	M	Supercargo	New York	New York	Aurilla	28 Oct 1824
John	27	M	Merchant	U.S.	U.S.	Pomona	20 Dec 1825
Michal	23	M	Shoemaker	Ireland	U. States	Franklin	7 Jul 1828
Norah	29	F	None	Ireland	New York	Sully	4 Mar 1828
Norah, Jr.	10	F	None	Ireland	New York	Sully	4 Mar 1828
Patrick	8	M	None	Ireland	New York	Sully	4 Mar 1828
SHERTEN, Patrick	25	M	Laborer or Spinster	Ireland	United States	Frances Miller	27 Jul 1827
SHERTER, Leonard	18	M	Tanner	Wittenburg	U. States	Comet	28 Jul 1825
SHERWEN, George	29	M	Organ builder	Scotland		Zamoa	5 Nov 1828
John	42	M	Merchant	G. Britain	U. States	America	21 Aug 1820
Mary	25		Wife	Scotland		Zamoa	5 Nov 1828
SHERWIN, John	45	M	Merchant	United States	United States	Isaac Hicks	27 Sep 1826
SHERWOOD, Hy.	23	M	Baker	Ireland	New York	Commerce	24 Sep 1823
John W.	20	M	Acct.	U. States	U. States	Agenora	19 Mar 1823
SHERWOOL, William	24	M	Laborer	England	United States	Danube	13 Jul 1827
SHERY, Ann	23	F		G. Britain	U. States	Mary & Harriot	8 Sep 1828
Francis	27	M	Teacher	G. Britain	U. States	Mary & Harriot	8 Sep 1828
Mary	30	F		G. Britain	U. States	Mary & Harriot	8 Sep 1828
SHETTLAND, Jno.	46	M	Shoemaker	France	United States	Stephania	24 Mar 1828
SHEVER, Constantine	2	M	his family [Martin]	Germany	Pensylvania	Isabella	15 Sep 1828
Josephine	3	F	his family [Martin]	Germany	Pensylvania	Isabella	15 Sep 1828

NAMES OF PASSENGERS	AGE	SEX	OCCUPATIONS	COUNTRY TO WHICH THEY BELONG	COUNTRY THEY INTEND TO INHABIT	SHIPS/DATES OF ARRIVAL	
SHEVER (cont'd)							
Marian	23	F	his family [Martin]	Germany	Pensylvania	Isabella	15 Sep 1828
Martin	28	M	Carpenter	Germany	Pensylvania	Isabella	15 Sep 1828
SHEVIE, Eliza	7			France	U. States	Parachute	14 May 1828
Louisa	6			France	U. States	Parachute	14 May 1828
Margaret	4 1/2		Farmer	France	U. States	Parachute	14 May 1828
Margaret	34			France	U. States	Parachute	14 May 1828
Philip	44		Farmer	France	U. States	Parachute	14 May 1828
Richard	18			France	U. States	Parachute	14 May 1828
SHEVROLET, Genoure	30	F	Boat Maker	Ireland		Quatre Freres	29 Jul 1828
Joseph	41	M	Boat Maker	Ireland		Quatre Freres	29 Jul 1828
Margaret	46	F	Boat Maker	Ireland		Quatre Freres	29 Jul 1828
Rosalie	5	F	Boat Maker	Ireland		Quatre Freres	29 Jul 1828
Theacon	7	M	Boat Maker	Ireland		Quatre Freres	29 Jul 1828
SHEWEL, Geo.	40	M	Farmer	Germany	United States	Lydia	18 Jun 1828
Jowl	40	M	Farmer	Germany	United States	Lydia	18 Jun 1828
SHEWER, S. F.	16	M	Mariner	U. States	United States	Eclipse	26 Feb 1827
SHEWINSON, Henry	23	M	Merchant	England	United States	St. George	25 Aug 1829
SHEWLIES, Danl.	19	M	Laborer	Great Britian	U. States	Henry Kneedland	7 Aug 1826
SHIAL, Wm.	18	M	Farmer	Ireland	America	Mary	29 May 1827
SHIBZMANN, George	30	M	Clockmaker	Germany	U. States	Hudson	10 Nov 1825
SHIEALES, Edwd.	23	M	Labourer	Ireland	United States	Henry Kneeland	7 Jun 1828
SHIEL, Jane	24	F	None	Gt. Brittain	United States	York	6 Dec 1826
SHIELD, Bridget	19	F	None	Ireland	U.S.A.	Dalhouse Castle	21 Aug 1829
Bridgit	19	F	None	Ireland	United States	Dalhouse Castle	21 Aug 1829
Richard	40	M	Merchant	Ireland	N. York	William	29 Jun 1827
SHIELDES, Thomas, Mr.	40	M	Carpenter	England	U.S.	Acasta	11 May 1827
SHIELDS, Ann	20	F	None	Great Britain	U. States	Roman	10 May 1828
Ann	20	F	None	Ireland	U. States	Franklin	7 Jul 1828
Ann	21 11/12	F	Servant	Ireland	New York	Louisa	20 Jul 1826
Betty	28	F		Great Brittain	United States	Active	12 Sep 1828
Catharine	16	F	Spinster	Ireland	United States	Fabius	4 Jun 1828
Christopher, Sr.	60	M	Gardener	Ireland	United States	Wilson	27 Jun 1826
Danil	20	M	Labourer	Ireland	Charles Town	Rambler	31 Aug 1829
Elisa	25	F	None	Great Briton	New York	Brighton	12 Jun 1826
Elizabeth	24	F	...	Ireland	United States	Carolina Ann	24 Oct 1825
Ellen	39	M	Wife	Ireland	United States	Ann Maria	4 Oct 1824
Francis H.	14	M	Gentleman	Ireland	United States	Dublin Packet	13 Oct 1828
George	18	M		Great Brittain	United States	Active	12 Sep 1828
George	25	M	Labourer	Ireland	United States	Catharine	22 Jul 1825
Jas.	40	M	Blacksmith	Great Britian	U. States	Dalhouse Castle	28 Feb 1826
John	9 6/12	M	son [of John]	Ireland	United States	Louisa	16 Mar 1826
John	17	M	Farmer	Ireland	United States	Dublin Packet	28 Apr 1824
John	20	M	Labourer	Ireland	U. States	Belville	5 Jul 1827
John	34	M	Farmer	Ireland	United States	Louisa	16 Mar 1826
John	38	M	Blacksmith	Great Britian	U. States	Dalhouse Castle	28 Feb 1826
Joseph	29	M	Labourer	Great Brittain	United States	Active	12 Sep 1828
Mary	7 5/12	F	Daughter [of John]	Ireland	United States	Louisa	16 Mar 1826
Mary	28	F	wife [of John]	Ireland	United States	Louisa	16 Mar 1826
Mgt.	40	F		Ireland	United States	Thomas	13 Dec 1827
Micheal	17	M		Ireland	United States	Fabius	4 Jun 1828
Nancy	2	F		Great Brittain	United States	Active	12 Sep 1828
Nicholas	25	M	Plumber	Edinburgh	Edinburgh	Alto	8 Jun 1827
Patrick	3...	M	...	Ireland	United States	Carolina Ann	24 Oct 1825
Patrick	37	M	Cooper	Ireland	United States	Ann Maria	4 Oct 1824
Robt.	28		Merchant	United States	United States	John Dickinson	28 Jun 1822
Sarah	4	F		Great Brittain	United States	Active	12 Sep 1828
Sarah	24	F	None	Ireland	U. States	Franklin	7 Jul 1828
Thomas	29	M	Joiner	Great Briton	New York	Brighton	12 Jun 1826
Thos.	20	M	Merchant	England	United States	Brilliant	24 Sep 1827
William	12	M	son [of John]	Ireland	United States	Louisa	16 Mar 1826
William	26	M	Sadler	England	United States	Acasta	14 Jun 1824
SHIELS, Anne	5	F	Child	United States	United States	Trident	16 May 1826
Anne	24	F	Wife	Ireland	United States	Trident	16 May 1826
Anne	30	F	Wife	Ireland	New York	Louisa	18 Apr 1827
Bridget	2	F	Daughter	Ireland	New York	Louisa	18 Apr 1827
James	21	M	Weaver	Ireland	United States	Princess Charlotte	26 Apr 1827

NAMES OF PASSENGERS	AGE	SEX	OCCUPATIONS	COUNTRY TO WHICH THEY BELONG	COUNTRY THEY INTEND TO INHABIT	SHIPS/DATES OF ARRIVAL	
SHIELS (cont'd)							
Mary	16		Laboring Class		United States	Atlantic	2 Apr 1827
Michal	20		Laboring Class		United States	Atlantic	2 Apr 1827
Neil	8/12	M		Ireland	United States	William & George	14 May 1828
Pat	6	M	Son	Ireland	New York	Louisa	18 Apr 1827
Pat.	21	M	Farmer	Ireland	United States	General Putnam	20 Jun 1825
Patrick	21	M	Weaver	Ireland	United States	Princess Charlotte	26 Apr 1827
Peter	...0		Laboring Class		United States	Atlantic	2 Apr 1827
Peter	4	M	Child	Ireland	New York	Louisa	18 Apr 1827
SHIER, Danl.	25	M	...	Scotland	United States	Indus	5 Sep 1827
Margt.	20	F		Scotland	United States	Indus	5 Sep 1827
Thos.	22	M	...	Scotland	United States	Indus	5 Sep 1827
SHIGGATT, William	34	M	Mariner	England	England	Enterprize	14 Oct 1827
SHIGGUTT, John		M	Miner	England	England	Iris	7 Dec 1827
SHILDS, Christopher, Jr.	19	M	Servant	Ireland	United States	Wilson	27 Jun 1826
SHILEDS, John	23	M	Cooper	Ireland	United States	Ann Maria	4 Oct 1824
SHILL, Henry	48	M		United States	New York	William Penn	20 Jan 1829
SHILLABER, G.	25	M	Mariner	America	America	Romulus	27 Nov 1821
SHILLADAY, George	22	M	Weaver	Ireland	United States	Princess Charlotte	26 Apr 1827
Thomas	18	M	Weaver	Ireland	United States	Princess Charlotte	26 Apr 1827
SHILLETTOE, Chas.	26	M	Merchant	G. Britan	G. Britan	Isabella	26 Nov 1825
SHILLING, Adam	49	M	Carpenter			Golden Grove	6 Sep 1820
Christopher	2	M				Golden Grove	6 Sep 1820
Julia Ann	4	F				Golden Grove	6 Sep 1820
Leonard	9	M				Golden Grove	6 Sep 1820
Maria	4	F				Golden Grove	6 Sep 1820
Maria	12	F				Golden Grove	6 Sep 1820
Maria	46	F				Golden Grove	6 Sep 1820
SHIMONDS, Ann	26	F		Great Britain	United States	India	5 Sep 1827
James	2	M		Great Britain	United States	India	5 Sep 1827
Jno.	20	M	Farmer	Great Britain	United States	India	5 Sep 1827
SHIN, Ann	50	F		Germany	United States	Lydia	18 Jun 1828
Geo.	51	M	Farmer	Germany	United States	Lydia	18 Jun 1828
SHINE, John	30	M	Farmer	Ireland	United States	Dublin Packet	23 May 1828
SHINELL, Julia	14	F		Ireland	U. States	William Byrnes	17 Jul 1825
SHING, Mary	23	F	Lady	Ireland	United States	Borneo	2 Oct 1827
SHINGHAM, Philip	26	M		Great B.	U. States	William Neilson	26 Jul 1828
SHINKS, Eliza	10			S... ...h	England	Great Britain	7 May 1827
Fanny	12			S... ...h	England	Great Britain	7 May 1827
George	30		Weaver	S... ...h	England	Great Britain	7 May 1827
George	30		Weaver	S... ...h	England	Great Britain	7 May 1827
SHINN, Detrich	22	M	Sugar Refiner	England	U.S.	Acasta	11 May 1827
James			Merchant	France	France	Columbus	20 Aug 1828
SHINTON, Alex	24	M		Scotland	U.S.	Curler	19 Jul 1828
Cath.	24	F		Scotland	U.S.	Curler	19 Jul 1828
Jane	3	F		Scotland	U.S.	Curler	19 Jul 1828
Wm.	24	M		Scotland	U.S.	Curler	19 Jul 1828
SHIPENTER, Louis D.	27	M	Agriculturist	U. States	U. States	Stephania	4 Apr 1826
SHIPHERD, William	28	M	Merchant	England	Great Brittan	Amity	11 May 1821
SHIPHERDSON, Marry	47	F	None	United States	U. States	Ann Marria	6 Aug 1823
SHIPLEY, Ann	27	F		England	U. States	Hudson	8 Oct 1827
Eliza	12	F		England	U. States	John Jay	26 Jan 1829
Elizabeth	40	F		England	U. States	John Jay	26 Jan 1829
Jos.	41	M	Carpenter	England	U. States	Howard Douglass	29 Jan 1828
Joseph	1 6/12	M		England	U. States	John Jay	26 Jan 1829
Joseph	27	F	Cloth Dresser	England		Aurora	12 Mar 1827
Joseph	29 3/12	M	Gentleman	U.S.A.	U. States	Silas Richards	27 Oct 1826
Sarah	4	F		England	U. States	John Jay	26 Jan 1829
SHIPMAN, Chas. P.	23	M	Mariner	U. States	U. States	Trimmer	3 Jan 1826
SHIPPEN, Ewen	23	M	Weaver	Great Britain	United States	India	5 Sep 1827
SHIPPISON, Ann	7	F		Great Britain	United States	Diana	6 Jul 1829
Charlotte	9	F		Great Britain	United States	Diana	6 Jul 1829
Hannah	5	F		Great Britain	United States	Diana	6 Jul 1829
Jabus	1 6/12	M		Great Britain	United States	Diana	6 Jul 1829

NAMES OF PASSENGERS	AGE	SEX	OCCUPATIONS	COUNTRY TO WHICH THEY BELONG	COUNTRY THEY INTEND TO INHABIT	SHIPS/DATES OF ARRIVAL	
SHIPPISON (cont'd)							
John	3	M		Great Britain	United States	Diana	6 Jul 1829
Mary	20	F		Great Britain	United States	Diana	6 Jul 1829
SHIRAN, Mary	16	F	Spinster	Ireland	United States	St. Michaels	7 Jun 1827
Mary	40	M	Spinster	Ireland	United States	St. Michaels	7 Jun 1827
William	6	M	Child	Ireland	United States	St. Michaels	7 Jun 1827
SHIRBY, C.	31	M	Merchant	England	U. States	Balaena	29 Apr 1825
SHIRE, Eliza	19	F	None	England	United States	India	8 Jun 1827
Hugh	25	M	None	England	United States	India	8 Jun 1827
SHIRES, Joseph	23		Weaver	Great Britain	United States	Thomas Dickason	29 Aug 1828
SHIRIDEN, Barbara	18	F	None	Germany	America	Orozimbo	1 Oct 1827
Charles	10	M	None	Germany	America	Orozimbo	1 Oct 1827
Jacob	8	M	None	Germany	America	Orozimbo	1 Oct 1827
John	30	M	Butcher	Germany	America	Orozimbo	1 Oct 1827
Marian	14	F	None	Germany	America	Orozimbo	1 Oct 1827
Rosalie	3	F	None	Germany	America	Orozimbo	1 Oct 1827
Susan	37	F	None	Germany	America	Orozimbo	1 Oct 1827
SHIRIM, Ellen	18	F	Spinster	Ireland		Robert Fulton	4 Jun 1828
SHIRLEY, ...ham	4	M		Gt. Britain	U. States	Maria	22 May 1822
Edward	6	M		Gt. Britain	U. States	Maria	22 May 1822
Edward	31	M	Farmer	Gt. Britain	U. States	Maria	22 May 1822
Eliza	1 6/12	F		Gt. Britain	U. States	Maria	22 May 1822
Esther	27	F		Gt. Britain	U. States	Maria	22 May 1822
Jesse	38	M	Mercht.	England	U.S.	Lewis	29 Oct 1825
John	13	M	teacher or Goldlace Maker	England	New York	Cortes	23 Nov 1827
Mary	24	F	Spinster	Ireland	U. States	Hibernia	29 Nov 1821
Wm.	14	M	teacher or Goldlace Maker	England	New York	Cortes	23 Nov 1827
SHIRWIN, Wm.	45	M	Marchant	N. York	U. States	Commodore Perry	9 Apr 1821
SHISTER, Joseph, Mr.	40		Merchant	Canada	G.B.	Pacific	24 May 1824
SHITTON, Thomas	29	M	Blacksmith	England	United States	St. George	25 Aug 1829
SHIZE, Ann	42	F	Farmer	Ireland	United States	Helen	27 Jun 1821
Audrich	8	F	Farmer	Ireland	United States	Helen	27 Jun 1821
Cabel	5	F	Farmer	Ireland	United States	Helen	27 Jun 1821
Cable	16	F	Farmer	Ireland	United States	Helen	27 Jun 1821
Eleanor	30	F	Farmer	Ireland	United States	Helen	27 Jun 1821
George	2	M	Farmer	Ireland	United States	Helen	27 Jun 1821
James	7	M	Farmer	Ireland	United States	Helen	27 Jun 1821
James	49	M	Farmer	Ireland	United States	Helen	27 Jun 1821
Jane	17	F	Farmer	Ireland	United States	Helen	27 Jun 1821
John	5	M	Farmer	Ireland	United States	Helen	27 Jun 1821
Mary Ann	12	F	Farmer	Ireland	United States	Helen	27 Jun 1821
Michl.	2	M	Farmer	Ireland	United States	Helen	27 Jun 1821
Thomas	9	M	Farmer	Ireland	United States	Helen	27 Jun 1821
Thomas	10	M	Farmer	Ireland	United States	Helen	27 Jun 1821
William	14	F	Farmer	Ireland	United States	Helen	27 Jun 1821
Wm.	30	M	Farmer	Ireland	United States	Helen	27 Jun 1821
SHOAC, Thomas	37	M		England	England	Eliza	22 Dec 1826
SHOBERT, S. F.	22			St. Croix	United States	Bruce	30 Apr 1827
SHOCKART, John	23	M	Gentleman	United States	U.S.	Fanny	31 Mar 1825
SHOELAND, Hanah	26	F	Servant	Ireland	United States	Henry Kneeland	7 Jun 1828
SHOEMAKER, Caroline	9	F		Germany	Missouri	Isabella	15 Sep 1828
Felix	17	M	Bricklayer	Germany	Missouri	Isabella	15 Sep 1828
John	46	M	Farmer	Germany	Missouri	Isabella	15 Sep 1828
Mathas	10	M		Germany	Missouri	Isabella	15 Sep 1828
Ragina	48	F		Germany	Missouri	Isabella	15 Sep 1828
SHOESSTER, Carl F. Gottfried	31 1/12	M	Gardner	Germany	America	John Dickinson	9 Oct 1828
SHOFFIELD, Joshua	21	M	Clothier	Great Britain		Robert Fulton	8 Mar 1823
SHOFRER, James	35	M	Joiner	Germany	United States	Samuel Robertson	8 Aug 1828
SHOLLOO, William	20	M	Carpenter	Ireland	Pensylvania	Lima	5 Aug 1829
William	20	M	Carpenter	England	U. States	Lima	5 Aug 1829
SHOOLER, Andrew	19	M	Taylor	St. John	Canada	Henrietta	7 Jul 1825
James	50	M	Taylor	St. John	Canada	Henrietta	7 Jul 1825
SHOOT, John	26	M	Sailor	U. States	U. States	Horatio	10 Feb 1827

NAMES OF PASSENGERS	AGE	SEX	OCCUPATIONS	COUNTRY TO WHICH THEY BELONG	COUNTRY THEY INTEND TO INHABIT	SHIPS/DATES OF ARRIVAL	
SHORE, Elinor	26	F	Spinster	Ireland	United States	Wilson	22 Jun 1824
Joseph, Junr.	28	M	...	Great Brittain	On a tour of pleasure	Albion	11 Jun 1821
SHORNE, Mary	21	F		England	Canada	Hudson	20 Nov 1828
SHORT, B. D., Mrs.	20	F	Labourer	Ireland	U. States	Marcus	7 Apr 1825
Bryan	22	M	Laborer	Ireland	America	Francis & Henrietta	11 Jul 1823
Jason	24	M	Laborer	Ireland	America	Francis & Henrietta	11 Jul 1823
John	18	M	Student	St. John, N.B.	United States	St. Michaels	25 May 1825
Michael	30	M	Laborer	Ireland	America	Francis & Henrietta	11 Jul 1823
SHORTALL, Ellen	20	F	Spinster	Ireland	United States	Dublin Packet	22 Aug 1829
Simon	25	M	Cooper	Ireland	United States	Ann Maria	8 Jun 1824
SHORTER, Elisabeth	1	F		U. States	U. States	Nassau	13 Aug 1825
Nancy	30	F	Labour	U. States	U. States	Nassau	13 Aug 1825
Robert	5	M	Labour	U. States	U. States	Nassau	13 Aug 1825
SHORTHOUSE, Thos.	49	M	Merchant	U. States	United States	New York	12 Nov 1822
SHORTLAND, Grace	45	F	None	England	United States	St. George	25 Aug 1829
Grace	45	M	None	England	United States	St. George	25 Aug 1829
SHORTON, Mary	25	F	Spinster	Ireland	United States	Fabius	4 Jun 1828
SHOUGHERREY, John	10	M	Child	..., ..., Ireland	N. York	New Orleans	24 Aug 1827
SHOURER, Elizabeth	24	F		Germany	U. States	Isabella	10 Aug 1829
Elizabeth	56	F		Germany	U. States	Isabella	10 Aug 1829
Jean	20	M	Farmer	Germany	U. States	Isabella	10 Aug 1829
Johanny	55	M	Farmer	Germany	U. States	Isabella	10 Aug 1829
SHOWIN, John	20	M	Labourer	G. Britain	U. States	Mary & Harriot	8 Sep 1828
SHREVE, Saml.	36	M	Farmer	U. States	U. States	Jane	10 Jan 1824
SHRIGLEY, Mary	40	M	Merchant	U. States		Charleston Packet	4 May 1821
SHRINE, Margaretha	22	F	None	England	America	Hercules	2 Nov 1825
Samuel	25	M	Baker	England	America	Hercules	2 Nov 1825
SHRON, D. J.	18	M	Servant	Ireland	U. States	Sarah G	30 Jun 1828
SHUAND, William	21 9/12	M	Taylor		Pennsylvania	Decatur	12 Dec 1820
SHUCKLER, Maurice	39	M		Gt. Brittan		L'Esperance	6 Sep 1828
SHUDDER, John	20	M		Ireland	U. States	Nancy	16 Aug 1822
SHUIRER, George	18	M	Merchant	United States	United States	New Been	18 Jan 1820
SHULBY, Thos.	21			Great Britain	U. States America	Maria	22 May 1822
SHULL, Joseph	26	M	Servant	Dublin	U. States	Hibernia	26 Oct 1826
SHULLEY, John	5	M	Labourer	Ireland	U. States	Two Marys	20 Apr 1825
SHULT, Joseph	22	M	...	Great Britian	United States	Diamond	8 Nov 1824
SHULTZ, Gustavus	20	M	Mechanic	Germany	United States	Two Marys	12 Feb 1820
SHUMANN, Charles H.	30	M	Manufacturer of White Lead	Saxony	United States	Xenophon	2 Jun 1824
SHURR, George	21	M	Farmer	Switzerland	United States	Andes	5 May 1828
SHUTE, Wm.	16	M	Wheelwright			Evergreen	28 Jul 1820
SHUTT, John	38	M	Merchant	England	America	Comet	26 Jun 1822
SHUTTLEWOOD, Ann	10	F	None	Great Britain	United States	Aurora	10 Nov 1827
J.	15	M	Clothier	Great Britain	United States	Aurora	10 Nov 1827
Mary	...	F	None	Great Britain	United States	Aurora	10 Nov 1827
Susan	6	F	None	Great Britain	United States	Aurora	10 Nov 1827
Thomas	13	M	None	Great Britain	United States	Aurora	10 Nov 1827
SHUTTLEWORTH, C.	4	M	Labourer	Great Brittain	United States	Sarah Ralston	27 Jan 1827
J.	30	F		Great Brittain	United States	Sarah Ralston	27 Jan 1827
John	36	M	Butcher	England	Great Britain	Florida	26 Sep 1826
S.	24	F		Great Brittain	United States	Sarah Ralston	27 Jan 1827
SHWARK, Fredk.	9	M	None	Gt. Britain	United States	Seeds	29 Sep 1824
Peter	39	M	Farmer	Gt. Britain	United States	Seeds	29 Sep 1824
SIBACH, A.	40 9/12	M	Farmer	France	United States	Catharine	10 Sep 1827
Andos	6	M	Farmer	France	United States	Catharine	10 Sep 1827
E.	38 6/12	F	Farmer	France	United States	Catharine	10 Sep 1827
Jacob	12 3/12	M	Farmer	France	United States	Catharine	10 Sep 1827
N.	5	M	Farmer	France	United States	Catharine	10 Sep 1827
Peter	8 1/12	M	Farmer	France	United States	Catharine	10 Sep 1827
Philip	10 2/12	M	Farmer	France	United States	Catharine	10 Sep 1827
SIBBALD, Joseph	28	M	Bookeeper	Ireland	U.S. of America	Hannibal	17 Dec 1823
SIBBERIN, Thomas	28	M	Currier	England	United States	John Wells	11 May 1827
SIBBORN, Eliza F.	34	F		U. States	U. States	Cincinnatus	24 May 1821
Joshua	46	M	Merchant	U. States	U. States	Cincinnatus	24 May 1821
SIBELL, Joseph	36	M	Merchant	United States	United States	Cortex	7 Mar 1823

NAMES OF PASSENGERS	AGE	SEX	OCCUPATIONS	COUNTRY TO WHICH THEY BELONG	COUNTRY THEY INTEND TO INHABIT	SHIPS/DATES OF ARRIVAL	
SIBERHORN, C. F.	7	M		Bardin	U. States	Bayard	5 Sep 1828
C. H.	9	M		Bardin	U. States	Bayard	5 Sep 1828
Carl W.	3/4	F		Bardin	U. States	Bayard	5 Sep 1828
Sophia H.	5	F		Bardin	U. States	Bayard	5 Sep 1828
T. W.	3	F		Bardin	U. States	Bayard	5 Sep 1828
SICKESS, John	18	M	Farmer	Great Brittian		Merchant	22 Apr 1822
SICKLES, Simeon	22	M	Gentleman	U. States	U. States	Velocipede	20 Sep 1824
SICKLET, Augustus	35	M	Merchant	Gwadaloupe	New York	John London	7 Apr 1824
SICLEIF, A.	36	M	Hair Dresser	U. States	U. States	Orra Maria	18 Oct 1823
SIDDEL, Abm.	9	M	None	Great Britain	United States	Atlantic	28 May 1827
Abm.	40	M	Clothier	Great Britain	United States	Atlantic	28 May 1827
Ann	1	F	None	Great Britain	United States	Atlantic	28 May 1827
Ann	40	F	None	Great Britain	United States	Atlantic	28 May 1827
Jane	3	F	None	Great Britain	United States	Atlantic	28 May 1827
Mary	7	F	None	Great Britain	United States	Atlantic	28 May 1827
Robt.	5	M	None	Great Britain	United States	Atlantic	28 May 1827
Sarah	16	F	None	Great Britain	United States	Atlantic	28 May 1827
SIDEBOTHAM, John	35	M	Farmer	Great Britain	U. States	Columbia	22 Sep 1828
SIDEBOTHAN, John	23	M	Labourer			Splendid	14 Aug 1829
SIDEBOTTOM, A.	30	M	Calico Printer	England	United States	Amelia	20 Aug 1829
SIDES, John	23	M	Labourer	Great Britain		Olive Branch	9 Oct 1829
William	27	M	Labourer	Great Britain		Olive Branch	9 Oct 1829
SIDNEY, P.	30	M	Mechanic	U. States	U. States	John London	20 Jan 1823
P.	35	M	Merchant	United States	New York	John London	7 Apr 1824
P.	35	M	Gentleman	U. States	U. States	Native	31 Jan 1825
P.	40	M	Mercht.	United States	U. States	Harmony	12 Sep 1823
Peter	28	M	Taylor	America	America	Buck	2 Feb 1822
Peter	35	M	Merchant	New York	New York	John London	8 May 1823
Peter	37	M	Merchant	Bourbon	U. States	Nassau	2 Nov 1825
Robert	23	M	Merchant	Great Britain	America	Washington	2 Oct 1828
SIDWICH, Rose	22	F	...	...	United States	Minerva	30 Oct 1827
SIEGLING,							
Frederick, Mr.	15	M	Merchant	Germany	U. States	Hudson	10 Nov 1825
John, Mr.	33	M	Merchant	Germany	U. States	Hudson	10 Nov 1825
SIEMEN, Jacob	55	M	Merchant	United States	United States	Don Quixote	18 Aug 1824
SIENA, J. F.	29	M	Mercht.	Havana de Cuba		Brown	12 Oct 1824
SIERRA, Amb.	20	M	Merchant	Havana	U. States	Senica	17 Mar 1824
B.	30	M	Merchant	Italy	U. States	Napolean	2 Sep 1828
Damasio	36	M	Merchant	Spain	Spain	Virginia	8 Mar 1828
SIEVER, Peter	36		Weaver	G. Britain	U. States	Grand Turk	10 Jul 1820
SIFFRIES, Hannah	50	F		U. States	U. States	Columbia	22 Sep 1828
SIGG, J. J.	30	M	Merchant	Switzerland	U. States	Bellona	1 Oct 1822
T. G.	33	M	Merchant	Galpere, Jermany	United States	Robert Fulton	2 Aug 1824
SIGNAEGO, Guicamo	36	M	Merchant	Italy	Italy	Buck	24 Jul 1821
SIGOND, Charles	36	M	Nothing			William Neilson	26 Jul 1828
SIGRIS, Joseph	35	M	Boer	Nimbach	United States	Juffraw Johanna	16 Oct 1821
Joseph, Kinder (child [of Joseph])		M		Nimbach	United States	Juffraw Johanna	16 Oct 1821
Maria, Zyn Vrouw (his wife [Joseph])	30	F		Holleyn	United States	Juffraw Johanna	16 Oct 1821
Martiny, Kinder (child [of Joseph])	3	F		Nimbach	United States	Juffraw Johanna	16 Oct 1821
Nicholas, Kinder (child [of Joseph])	2	M		Nimbach	United States	Juffraw Johanna	16 Oct 1821
SIGSWORTH, John	26	M	Carpenter	Great Britain	United States	Diana	6 Jul 1829
SIHON, —, Mr.	25	M	Cabinet Maker	Copenhagen, Denmark	going to reside in Clearfield, Pennsylvania	Friketon	7 Nov 1823
SILBERTORN, J. H.	42	M	Butcher	Bardin	U. States	Bayard	5 Sep 1828
SILCOCK, Hannah	30	F	None	England	United States	Roman	12 Jun 1826
James	30	M	Gentleman	England	United States	Roman	12 Jun 1826
Sarah	4	F	None	England	United States	Roman	12 Jun 1826
SILCOCKS, Ann	22			...	...	Hudson	14 Jun 1827
Dan	48		...	...	...	Hudson	14 Jun 1827
Elizabeth	16			...	...	Hudson	14 Jun 1827
James	12			...	...	Hudson	14 Jun 1827
Malcolm	2			...	...	Hudson	14 Jun 1827
Mary	44			...	...	Hudson	14 Jun 1827

NAMES OF PASSENGERS	AGE	SEX	OCCUPATIONS	COUNTRY TO WHICH THEY BELONG	COUNTRY THEY INTEND TO INHABIT	SHIPS/DATES OF ARRIVAL	
SILCOCKS (cont'd)							
Mary M.	6			...	...	Hudson	14 Jun 1827
Thomas	8			...	...	Hudson	14 Jun 1827
SILCOX, Daniel	37	M		England	Canada	Acosta	28 Jul 1823
John	18	M	Farmer	Engd.	United States	Cosmo	21 Aug 1828
SILDER, George	7/12	M	Farmer	Switzerland	America	Henry	17 May 1828
John	20 8/12	M	Farmer	Switzerland	America	Henry	17 May 1828
Margaret	22 5/12	F	Farmer	Switzerland	America	Henry	17 May 1828
Mary	43 2/12	F	Farmer	Switzerland	America	Henry	17 May 1828
Peter	28 7/12	M	Farmer	Switzerland	America	Henry	17 May 1828
SILK, Alice	25		Farmer	England	United States	Corinthian	30 May 1828
Mathew	24	M	Labourer	Ireland	United States	Trio	2 Oct 1828
Thomas	25		Farmer	England	United States	Corinthian	30 May 1828
SILKO, Joseph	28	M	Brick Maker	Great Britain	United States	Frances Henrietta	17 Sep 1827
SILL, Arnny	3 6/12	F		Germany	United States	Samuel Robertson	8 Aug 1828
Catherine	26	F		Germany	United States	Samuel Robertson	8 Aug 1828
George	32	M	Farmer	Germany	United States	Samuel Robertson	8 Aug 1828
Horace L.	32	M	Merchant	U. States	U. States	Brazillian	21 May 1827
Joseph	6/12	M		Germany	United States	Samuel Robertson	8 Aug 1828
Nicholas	23	M	None	England	America	William Byrnes	22 Dec 1828
P.	20	M	Servent	Long Island	U. States	Sally Ann	29 Mar 1824
SILLEY, Francis	31	M	Merchant Sailer	England	America	Criterion	27 Oct 1821
SILLIMAN,							
John H., Capt.	45	M	Mariner	United States	United States	Francis	12 Jun 1826
SILLON, Betty	20	F	...	...	United States	Minerva	30 Oct 1827
SILLS, Jos.	28	M	Merchant	England	United States	Acasta	15 Jul 1822
SILLY, William	19	M	Farmer, Labourer or Spinster	Ireland	U. States	Meteor	4 Oct 1827
SILON, Joseph	50	M	Merchant	U. States	U.S.	Fair American	9 May 1825
SILSBEE, N...	22		Mercht.	England	U. States	New York	30 Oct 1827
SILVA, —	12	F	Servant	Portugal	U. States	Deligence	21 Mar 1825
—	50	M	Merchant	Portugal	U. States	Orion	23 Apr 1825
J. P. M.	20	M	Merchant	Portugal	Portugal	Pomona	26 Oct 1823
Jos.	51	M	Seaman	America	U. States	David	5 Oct 1824
Juan Francesco	40	M	Mariner	Portugal	U. States	Union	21 Nov 1822
T. S.	23	M		Brazil	Brazil	Halcyon	26 Sep 1828
Victorino Alvares, Esq.		M		Portugal	U. States	Sarah Louisa	10 Oct 1822
SILVER, M.	32	M	Merchant	Porto Rico	U. States	Martha	7 Jul 1826
SILVERSIDES,							
Elizabeth	33	F	None	England	United States	Great Britain	5 Sep 1827
Eunice	10	F	None	England	United States	Great Britain	5 Sep 1827
George	35	M	Farmer	England	United States	Great Britain	5 Sep 1827
Hannah	7	F	None	England	United States	Great Britain	5 Sep 1827
James B.	2	M	None	England	United States	Great Britain	5 Sep 1827
Mary B.	13	F	None	England	United States	Great Britain	5 Sep 1827
SILVESTER, —	65	F		Austria	U. States	Garonne	24 Jul 1821
Nathaniel	25	M	Merchant	Gt. Brittain	United States	Cortes	23 Mar 1824
T. B.	25	M	Laborer	Hanover	United States	Constitution	6 Jul 1829
William	21 7/12	M	Bricklayer	Ireland	British North America	London	6 Feb 1829
SILVYRA, Isaac	38	M	None	France	France	Canada	27 Sep 1826
SIM, Adam	35	M	Merchant	England	Halifax	Mary Ann	24 Feb 1827
David	26	M	Baker	Scotland	U. States	Hector	18 Apr 1825
Michal	21	M	Labourer	Ireland	United States	Hope	12 Jun 1828
SIMCOI, George	33	M	Farmer	Great Britain	Canada	Orozimbo	31 May 1824
SIMCOX, Fercrick	15	M	None	Great Britain	United States	Silvanus Jenkins	10 Mar 1827
Mary Ann	38	F	None	Great Britan	United States	Silvanus Jenkins	10 Mar 1827
Thomas	40	M	Wiredrawer	Great Britan	United States	Silvanus Jenkins	10 Mar 1827
SIMER, John	35	M	Weaver	Scotland	New York	Joseph Hume	26 Oct 1829
Mary	18	F		France	Canada	Abby Jones	12 Jul 1827
SIMERA, Fidelpe, Don	30	M	Merchant	Mexico	Tampico, Mexico	Nancy	15 Apr 1824
SIMERSIN, J.		M	Merchant	United States	United States	Tampico	27 Jun 1827
SIMERTON, Jno. W.	45	M	Merchant	U. States	U. States	Chase	19 Sep 1823
SIMES, John	10	M	None	Scotland	Ut. States	Courier	13 Jul 1826

NAMES OF PASSENGERS	AGE	SEX	OCCUPATIONS	COUNTRY TO WHICH THEY BELONG	COUNTRY THEY INTEND TO INHABIT	SHIPS/DATES OF ARRIVAL	
SIMLORT, Betsy	30	F		Ireland	United States	Fabius	4 Jun 1828
SIMM, Hugh	20	M	Weaver	Ireland	United States	Princess Charlotte	26 Apr 1827
James	25	M	Carpenter	Ireland	United States	Princess Charlotte	26 Apr 1827
SIMMIC, Wm.	18	M				Comet	24 Dec 1821
SIMMONS, —	30		None	Great Brittain	U. States America	James Cropper	23 Mar 1827
Ann, Mrs.	47	F		England	United States	Eliza Grant	7 Jun 1827
Cathr.	19	F		Ireland	U. States	Adno	5 Jul 1828
E., Jr.		M	Merchant	United States	United States	Samaritan	24 Nov 1820
Elazer	30			England	U. States	Corinthian	8 Oct 1828
Eliza	27 11/12	F		United States	United States	Brighton	12 Jun 1826
George	34	M	Merchant	England	New York	Brighton	11 Dec 1827
Isaac	28	M	Shoemaker	England	America	Saluda	18 Jun 1825
James	25	M		Ireland	U. States	Adno	5 Jul 1828
James	26			Yarmarnagh	Boston	Peru	30 May 1828
Jane	21		Farmer	England	England	Hudson	18 Jun 1825
Jas. W.	26		Gentleman	United States	United States	Hudson	14 Jun 1827
Jno.	28	M	Engineer	England	N. York	Salem	15 Mar 1828
John	40	M	Merchant	England	England	Virginia	26 May 1828
John A.	37	M	Merchant	U. States	U. States	Sarah	17 Mar 1829
Jonana	36	F	Merchant	St. Croix	U. States	Chase	12 May 1826
Maria	4 6/12	F		United States	United States	Brighton	12 Jun 1826
Richard	47	M	Stone Mason	England	United States	Eliza Grant	7 Jun 1827
William	26	M	Bookeeper	Great Britain	Mexico	Corinthian	27 Apr 1824
SIMMS, Alex.	29	M	Millwright	Glasgow	Glasgow	Howard Douglass	11 May 1827
Andw.	22	M	Baker	Glasgow	Glasgow	Howard Douglass	11 May 1827
Robert	33	M	Merchant	Ireland	U.S. of America	Hannibal	17 Dec 1823
SIMON, Alexandar	8	M		Switzerland	United States	Elizabeth	27 Jul 1824
Charles	29	M	Mercht.	Pensylvania		George	10 Mar 1823
Elis.	...	...	...	Ireland	United States	General Putnam	20 Jun 1825
Gottbel	11	M		Switzerland	United States	Elizabeth	27 Jul 1824
Gottfried	5	M		Switzerland	United States	Elizabeth	27 Jul 1824
Johanas	40	M	Cutlar	Switzerland	United States	Elizabeth	27 Jul 1824
John Frederick	10	M		Switzerland	United States	Elizabeth	27 Jul 1824
Leistle	12	F		Switzerland	United States	Elizabeth	27 Jul 1824
Louis Stanislas	35	M	Merchant	France	United States	Stephania	22 Apr 1822
M.	34	M	Gentleman	Netherlands	Netherlands	Jasper	22 Sep 1827
Margaretha	6	F		Switzerland	United States	Elizabeth	27 Jul 1824
Maria Ana	13	F		Switzerland	United States	Elizabeth	27 Jul 1824
Marinna	35	F		Switzerland	United States	Elizabeth	27 Jul 1824
R.	40	M	Butcher	G. Britain	G. Britain	Brittania	17 Jul 1828
Wm.	31	M	Baker	England	United States	Hannibal	25 Sep 1827
SIMONDS, William	25	M	Merchant	Germany	New York	Sully	4 Mar 1828
SIMONS, Benjamin H.	8	M		England	Cincinati	Hudson	20 Nov 1828
Catherine	8	F	Spinster	Switzerland	United States	Andes	5 May 1828
Eliza	12	F	Spinster	Ireland	United States	Dublin Packet	13 Oct 1828
Elnor	15	F				Betsey	17 Aug 1820
George	24	M	Farmer	Switzerland	United States	Andes	5 May 1828
George	47	M	Farmer	Switzerland	United States	Andes	5 May 1828
Henrietta	10	F		England	Cincinati	Hudson	20 Nov 1828
Jacob	22	M	Farmer	Switzerland	United States	Andes	5 May 1828
John	26	M	Glass Cutter	G.B.	St. New York	Eliza Grant	29 Aug 1829
Joseph	1	M		England	Cincinati	Hudson	20 Nov 1828
Julia	6	F		England	Cincinati	Hudson	20 Nov 1828
Louisa	38	F		England	Cincinati	Hudson	20 Nov 1828
Margaret	18	F	Spinster	Switzerland	United States	Andes	5 May 1828
Maryan	43	F	Spinster	Switzerland	United States	Andes	5 May 1828
Mazell	16	F	Farmer	Switzerland	United States	Andes	5 May 1828
Michel	16	M	Farmer	Switzerland	United States	Andes	5 May 1828
Philip	4	M		England	Cincinati	Hudson	20 Nov 1828
Rebecca	12	F		England	Cincinati	Hudson	20 Nov 1828
Ricd.	23	M	Miner	England	England	Eliza	31 Jul 1826
Samuel	12	M	Farmer	Switzerland	United States	Andes	5 May 1828
Simon	50	M	Merchant	England	Cincinati	Hudson	20 Nov 1828
Stephen	14	M	Mariner	St. Johns, N.B.	England	Peruvian	7 Oct 1825
W.	51	M	Merchant	France	U. States	Heroine	19 Jun 1828

NAMES OF PASSENGERS	AGE	SEX	OCCUPATIONS	COUNTRY TO WHICH THEY BELONG	COUNTRY THEY INTEND TO INHABIT	SHIPS/DATES OF ARRIVAL	
SIMONS (cont'd)							
William	30	M	Merchant	United States	United States	Union Packet	10 Aug 1829
Wm.	28		Farmer	Yarmarnagh	Boston	Peru	30 May 1828
SIMPLE, Jane	5	F	Child	Ireland	United States	Robert Fulton	24 Jul 1826
John	6	M	Child	Ireland	United States	Robert Fulton	24 Jul 1826
Robert	35	M	Stonemason	Ireland	U. States	Virginia	20 Jun 1825
Serah	35	F	Matron	Ireland	United States	Robert Fulton	24 Jul 1826
SIMPLOT, Charles	5	M	Farmer			Stephania	24 Jul 1820
John Henry	12	M	Farmer			Stephania	24 Jul 1820
Joseph	10	M	Farmer			Stephania	24 Jul 1820
SIMPSON, ...			child	Ireland	United States	Asia	29 Jul 1829
A., Mr.	37	M	Hudson Bay Co.	Gt. Brittian	North Brittian		6 Apr 1826
Agnes;F			...	Scotland	America	Nimrod	9 Jul 1827
Alexr.	20	M	Merchant	Gt. Britain	Canada	Manchester	15 Apr 1828
Andr.	24	M		Ireland	U. States	John Dickinson	13 May 1823
Ann	35	F	his Wife [William]	Ireland	United States	Asia	29 Jul 1829
C.	60	M	Merchant	U. States	U. States	Infant	10 Jul 1821
Catharan	22	F	wife	G. Brittan	U. States	Henry	24 Oct 1828
Catherine	17	F	Spinster	Ireland	United States	Trident	17 May 1825
Christian	17	F	Servant	Ireland	United States	Carolina Ann	14 May 1827
Daniel	7/12	M	Son	G. Brittan	U. States	Henry	24 Oct 1828
Daniel	2...	...	Capt.	State of Maine	N. Carolina	William & Frederick	16 Jun 1827
Edward	21	M	Weaver	Ireland	U. States	Josephine	30 Aug 1828
Eliza	1	F	None	Ireland	America	Hesperus	7 Jul 1820
Eliza	20	F		Ireland	U. States	John Dickinson	13 May 1823
Eliza [crossed out]	3/52	F		Ireland	United States	Asia	29 Jul 1829
Geo.	28	M	unknown	U. States	U. States	Mary	7 Nov 1822
Geo.	31	M	Merchant	Great Britain	United States	James Monroe	5 Apr 1820
Geo., Mr.	40	M	Hudson Bay Co.	Gt. Brittian	North Brittian		6 Apr 1826
George		M	Farmer	Great Britian	United States	Isaac Hicks	22 May 1826
Henry	2 2/12	M	Son	G. Brittan	U. States	Henry	24 Oct 1828
J. H.	27	M	Merchant	England	U. States	Martha	3 Aug 1824
Jacob	40	M	Hair dresser	Ireland	United States	Andes	2 Oct 1828
James	15	M	Labourer	Great Britain	United States	Henrietta	19 Oct 1825
James	20	M	Servant	Ireland	United States	Carolina Ann	14 May 1827
James	21		Shoemaker	Cove	Gt. Britain	Enterprize	19 Feb 1822
James	22	M	Wool Comber	Great Britian	United States	Isaac Hicks	22 May 1826
James	27	M	Merchant	Denmark	St. Croix	Henry	30 Aug 1826
James	28	M	Farmer	Scotland	New York	Susquehanna	9 Jan 1824
James	30	M	Cooper	England	U. States	Dalmarnock	17 May 1822
Jane	3/12	F	child	Ireland	United States	Asia	29 Jul 1829
Jane	27	F	None			Belle Savage	15 Aug 1820
Jane	29	F		Scotland	U. States	Sceptre	24 Jul 1822
Jane	60	F	widow of Wm. Simpson	Ireland	United States	Asia	29 Jul 1829
Janie	12	F	None	England	America	Meteor	19 Aug 1825
Jno.	22	M	Labourer	England	United States	Mary & Harriet	9 Mar 1829
Jno.	24	M	Planter	England	England	Mary Washington	14 Jan 1824
Jno.	32	M	Blacksmith	Manchester	United States	Java	9 Jul 1827
John	3/52	M	child	Ireland	United States	Asia	29 Jul 1829
John	8	M	None	Ireland	America	Hesperus	7 Jul 1820
John	17	M	Weaver	G. Britain	United States	Louisa	14 Jun 1825
John	25	M	Lawyer	Great Britain	United States	Henrietta	19 Oct 1825
John	27	M	Sawyer	Ireland	United States	Robert Fulton	10 Aug 1827
John	31	M	Merchant	United States	United States	Tampico	13 Oct 1825
John	40	M	Servant	Ireland	United States	Abigail	25 Jun 1822
John	60	M	Labourer	Ireland	United States	Carolina Ann	14 May 1827
Joseph	30	M	None	Ireland	America	Hesperus	7 Jul 1820
Lusick	23	M	Merchant	G. Brittan	U. States	Henry	24 Oct 1828
M. H.	20	M	Merchant	United States	United States	Matteawan	2 Feb 1829
Margaret	...	...	...	...	...	St. Michael	22 Sep 1824
Margaret	13			Cove	Gt. Britain	Enterprize	19 Feb 1822
Margaret	22	F	Seamstress	Great Britain	United States	Henrietta	19 Oct 1825
Margt.	...	F	Servant	Ireland	United States	Carolina Ann	14 May 1827
Maria Louisa	25	F		Liverpool	U. States	Panthea	24 Mar 1825
Martha	48	F	Seamstress	Great Britain	United States	Henrietta	19 Oct 1825
Mary	14	F	Servant	Ireland	United States	Carolina Ann	14 May 1827

1162

NAMES OF PASSENGERS	AGE	SEX	OCCUPATIONS	COUNTRY TO WHICH THEY BELONG	COUNTRY THEY INTEND TO INHABIT	SHIPS/DATES OF ARRIVAL	
SIMPSON (cont'd)							
Mary	15			Cove	Gt. Britain	Enterprize	19 Feb 1822
Mary	25	F		Great Britain	United States	Dapper	24 Aug 1827
Mary	60	F	House Keeper	Ireland	United States	Carolina Ann	14 May 1827
N.	28	M	Sailor	America	U. States	Hiram	17 Jun 1826
Paul	30	M		Ireland	United States	Hannibal	6 Sep 1824
Peter	18	M	Wood Cutter	France	U.S. America	Huntress	6 Sep 1827
Robert	24	M		Ireland	U. States	John Dickinson	13 May 1823
Robert	25		Merchant	U.S.	N. York	Little William	14 Jun 1823
Robert	28	M	Merchant	Canada	Canada	Bowditch	27 Apr 1826
Robt.	28	M	Merchant	Scotland	G. Brittain	L. M. Pelham	18 Jun 1821
Samuel	12	M		Great Britain	United States	Henrietta	19 Oct 1825
Samuel	40	M		England	England	Pleiades	13 Nov 1826
Samuel	56	M	Labourer	Great Britain	United States	Henrietta	19 Oct 1825
Sarah	23		Spinner	Ireland	America	Hesperus	7 Jul 1820
Sarah	30	F	Milliner	England	United States	Delta	24 Oct 1829
Thomas	31	M	Farmer			Belle Savage	15 Aug 1820
Thomas	38 2/12	M	Gentleman	England	United States	Eagle	20 Mar 1824
Thomas	41	M	Mariner	United States		Commerce	3 Nov 1820
Thomas	53	M	Clerk	England	United States	Criterion	27 Oct 1820
Thos.	24	M	Mechanic	Great Britain	United States	Mary & Harriet	3 Jul 1829
Thos.	35	M	Cabinet Maker	England	U. States	Cowper	8 Jan 1827
W.	25	M	Tailor	Great Britain	United States	Dapper	24 Aug 1827
Wilfred	40	M	Mercht.	U. States	U. States	Nancy	13 Dec 1822
Wilfred	40	M	Merchant	U. States	U.States	Nancy	31 May 1823
William	20	M		Ireland	United States	Sarah G.	20 Jul 1827
William	40	M	...	...	U. States	Panthea	24 Mar 1825
William	40	M	Farmer	Ireland	United States	Asia	29 Jul 1829
Wm.	3	M	None	Ireland	America	Hesperus	7 Jul 1820
Wm.	20	M	Farmer	Gt. Brittain	United States	Balaena	21 Aug 1824
Wm.	21	M	Farmer	Scotland	America	Friends	24 Sep 1821
Wm.	25	M	Stone Cutter	Scotland	U. States	Loire	18 Jul 1828
Wm.	30	M		Great Britian	United States	London	24 Jun 1823
Wm.	36		Brazier	Lincolnshire	England	Elizabeth	8 Dec 1821
SIMS, Ann	29	F		Scotland	Ut. States	Courier	13 Jul 1826
C.	36	M	Merchant	England	U. States	Sea Bird	8 Feb 1827
Charles	42	M	Merchant	England	Canada	Euphrates	12 May 1823
Geo. W.	22	M	Navy	U. States	U. States	American	28 Sep 1822
John	23		Servant	Russia	Russia	New York	11 Mar 1823
Wm.	32	M	Book Keeper	Scotland	Ut. States	Courier	13 Jul 1826
SIMSON, Isaac	30	M	Cotton Spinner	England	Boston	Curler	7 Jul 1827
Sarah	32	F	None	St. Thomas	St. Thomas	Jane	28 May 1827
SIMSPON, James	5	F		Scotland	U. States	Sceptre	24 Jul 1822
SIMSPSON, Ellson	10	F		Scotland	U. States	Sceptre	24 Jul 1822
Peter	8	F		Scotland	U. States	Sceptre	24 Jul 1822
SINCLAIR, Agnes	8	F	None	Great Britain	United States	Ann Maria	12 Jul 1821
Alexr.	8	M	None	Great Britain	United States	Ann Maria	12 Jul 1821
Alexr.	40		Weaver	Great Britain	United States	Camillus	12 Sep 1827
Betsey	4	F	None	Great Britain	United States	Ann Maria	12 Jul 1821
Eliza	28	F		England	U. States	Elias Burger	21 Aug 1823
Francis	23	M	Merchant	Spain		Star	7 Jan 1827
Geo.	26	M	Farmer	Glasgow	United States	Aurelia	7 Jun 1826
George	24	M	Butcher	Scotland	New York	Angelica	18 Aug 1823
Graham	26		Grocer	Great Britain	United States	Camillus	12 Sep 1827
Isababe.	2	F	None	Great Britain	United States	Ann Maria	12 Jul 1821
James	28	M	Merchant	Spain	U. States	Pocahontas	9 Jun 1823
James, Mr.	17	M		Ireland	United States	Alex. Mansfield	17 May 1823
Jane	12	F	None	Great Britain	United States	Ann Maria	12 Jul 1821
Janet	40	F		Scotland	U. States	Percival	16 May 1821
Jennet	2	F	None	Great Britain	United States	Ann Maria	12 Jul 1821
Jennet	34	F	None	Great Britain	United States	Ann Maria	12 Jul 1821
Jno.	22	M	Baker	Scotland	United States	Morning Star	25 Jun 1822
Jno.	33	M	Taylor	Scotland	U. States	Percival	16 May 1821
John	6	M	None	Great Britain	United States	Ann Maria	12 Jul 1821
John	10	M	None	Great Britain	United States	Ann Maria	12 Jul 1821
John	14	F	None	Great Britain	United States	Ann Maria	12 Jul 1821
John	43	M	Merchant	Great Britain	United States	Ann Maria	12 Jul 1821
Joseph	26		Farmer	Great Britain	United States	Camillus	12 Sep 1827
Margt.	1	F	None	Great Britain	United States	Ann Maria	12 Jul 1821

NAMES OF PASSENGERS	AGE	SEX	OCCUPATIONS	COUNTRY TO WHICH THEY BELONG	COUNTRY THEY INTEND TO INHABIT	SHIPS/DATES OF ARRIVAL	
SINCLAIR (cont'd)							
Mary	12	F	None	Great Britain	United States	Ann Maria	12 Jul 1821
Mary	38	F	None	Great Britain	United States	Ann Maria	12 Jul 1821
Rob.	40	M	Gentleman	Greenock	England	Francis	17 May 1824
Thomas	25	M	Stationer	Great Britain	United States	Samuel Wright	12 Oct 1829
Willm.	12	M	None	Great Britain	United States	Ann Maria	12 Jul 1821
Wm.	6	F	None	Great Britain	United States	Ann Maria	12 Jul 1821
SINCLANE, Wm.	20	M		England	United States	Essex	23 May 1828
SINCLAR, Joanas	7	F		Germany	United States	Samuel Robertson	8 Aug 1828
Magdalana	39	F		Germany	United States	Samuel Robertson	8 Aug 1828
Margaret	8	F		Germany	United States	Samuel Robertson	8 Aug 1828
Sam	51	M	Farmer	Germany	United States	Samuel Robertson	8 Aug 1828
SINCOE, Betsey	4	F		Great Britain	United States	Active	25 Mar 1828
Elisa	5	F		Great Britain	United States	Active	25 Mar 1828
George	34	M		Great Britain	United States	Active	25 Mar 1828
Harriet	2	F		Great Britain	United States	Active	25 Mar 1828
Harriet	31	F		Great Britain	United Stated	Active	25 Mar 1828
SINDLE, Wm.	36	M	Farmer	Great Brittan	U. States	Gem	26 Jul 1827
SINDLEY, James	77	M	Gardner	England	U. States	Josephine	23 Jan 1829
SINE, James	14					Mexico	1 Jun 1821
SINGER, Henry	20	M	Farmer	England	U. States	Hercules	6 Jul 1827
SINGEY, John	30	M	Black Smith	Ireland	Canada	Ann Maria	7 Sep 1827
SINGLE, Wm.	28	M	Farmer	Ireland	U. States	Orozimbo	7 Jul 1825
SINIGER, Sarah	18			France	United States	Parachute	14 May 1828
SININGER, Georte	60		Mechanic	France	United States	Parachute	14 May 1828
SINMONS, Wm.	24 8/12	M	Clerk	Ireland	U. States	Fabius	22 Sep 1828
SINN, Catharine	12 7/12	F		Irereland	America	Carolina Ann	20 Jun 1825
Hannah Maria	8 9/12	F		Irereland	America	Carolina Ann	20 Jun 1825
Matilda	30	F	House Keeper	Irereland	America	Carolina Ann	20 Jun 1825
SINNER, —, Mr.						Martha	4 Sep 1828
*sent out by the Consul							
SINNET, James	27	M	Tailor	Ireland	United States	Combine	4 Jun 1825
SINONS, Harriet, Mrs.	35	F	Dressmaker	England	United States	Maria	29 Sep 1823
SIOMMONS, Mercy	39		Farmer	England	England	Hudson	18 Jun 1825
SIPKINS, Spke. V.	40	M	Mariner	Holland	U. States	Prince Edward	23 Dec 1823
SIPPER, John	21	F	Labourer			Hanford	17 Jul 1828
SIPPLE, Richard	34		Tanner	England	U. States	Corinthian	8 Oct 1828
William	21 2/12	M	distressed seaman	Philadelphia	United States	Florida	27 Aug 1825
SIRAMION, Jno.	20	M	Merchant	England	England	John Wells	14 Oct 1823
SIREN, Ann	25	F		Ireland	United States	Mary	1 Jul 1829
SIRLE, John	48	M	Cabinet Maker	Ireland	U. States	Albion	11 May 1827
SIRRO, Jno.	25	M	Merchant	Spain	Spain	Native	8 Feb 1826
SIRSOVINS, J. C.	26	M	Merchant	Denmark	U.S. of America	Canada	1 Oct 1827
SISK, James	6	M		Ireland	America	William	21 May 1825
SISON, Roswell	40	M	Ship Master	United States	United States	Rook	2 Oct 1829
SISSON, R.	31	M	Mariner	U. States	U. States	Orra Maria	18 Oct 1823
Roswell	27 8/12	M	Mariner	Connecticut	Massachusetts	Baltic	20 Aug 1821
SISTARE, Leonard	24	M	Mariner	U. States	U. States	Hippomenes	29 Nov 1822
SIXSMITH, John	30	M	Glassmaker	Great Britain	United States	Isaac Hicks	27 Sep 1826
R.	26	M	Labourer	Ireland		Marchioness	13 May 1828
Sarah	20	F	None	Great Britain	United States	Isaac Hicks	27 Sep 1826
SKASK, Thos.	35	M	Labourer	..., ...ley, England	U. States	New Orleans	24 Aug 1827
SKEART, James	17		...	Middlsex	...	Hudson	14 Jun 1827
SKEEN, Ann	27	F		England	U. States	Hudson	8 Oct 1827
Carolilions	28	M	Clerk	Irishman	U.S.A.	Lima	6 Dec 1826
SKEENY, Susan	24	M	Spinster	Ireland	U. States	Meteor	19 Jul 1828
SKEHEN, Jane	23	F	Wife [of Richard]	Ireland	United States	Erin	25 Dec 1820
Richard	25	M	Farmer	Ireland	United States	Erin	25 Dec 1820
SKEIL, Ed.	27	M	Merchant	Ireland	G. Britain	Chase	18 Dec 1821
SKELLEY, Ann	2	F	Child	Ireland	United States	Sarah Ann	6 Mar 1827
Ann	30	F	Spinster	Ireland	United States	Sarah Ann	6 Mar 1827
John	1	M	Child	Ireland	United States	Sarah Ann	6 Mar 1827
SKELTON, John	35		Smith	England		Corinthian	11 Mar 1829
Thos. L.	45	M	None	G. Bt.	G. Bt.	Canada	13 Feb 1826

NAMES OF PASSENGERS	AGE	SEX	OCCUPATIONS	COUNTRY TO WHICH THEY BELONG	COUNTRY THEY INTEND TO INHABIT	SHIPS/DATES OF ARRIVAL	
SKENFF, Alexd.	24	M	Farmer	England	U. States	Oglethorpe	9 Nov 1824
SKERROW, Ann	25	F	None	England	United States	Orozimbo	11 Aug 1823
Ann	59	F	None	England	United States	Orozimbo	11 Aug 1823
James	31	M	Farmer	England	United States	Orozimbo	11 Aug 1823
Wm.	26	M	Farmer	England	United States	Orozimbo	11 Aug 1823
SKERWING, Wm.	28	M	Doctor	Scotland	Jamaica	Rolla	16 Nov 1824
SKETCHLEY, ...ah	39	F		U. States	U. States	William Thompson	27 May 1824
Sarah P.	16	F		U. States	U. States	William Thompson	27 May 1824
SKETENTZ, —, Mrs.	34	F	None	United States	United States	Martha	17 Sep 1821
Penelope	13	F	None	United States	United States	Martha	17 Sep 1821
SKIBELSKEE, Michael R.	30	M		Poland	U. States	Corinthian	2 Sep 1824
SKIDDY, Francis	14	M	Student	New York	New York	Lewis	29 Oct 1825
Rosetta, Mrs.	47	F		U. States	U. States	Lewis	11 Nov 1824
SKIGGINS, Jas.	23	M	Labourer	Ireland	U. States	Marcus	7 Apr 1825
SKILLEN, James	24	M	Tailor	Ireland	N. York	Salem	15 Mar 1828
Matha	20	F		England	N. York	Salem	15 Mar 1828
Wm.	1	M		England	N. York	Salem	15 Mar 1828
SKILLEY, Pat	30	M	Farmer	Ireland	America	Mary	29 May 1827
SKILLON, Moses	25	M	Weaver	Ireland	United States	Princess Charlotte	26 Apr 1827
SKILLY, John	30	M	Labourer	Ireland	New York	Curler	7 Jul 1827
SKIN, Thomas	20	M	Labourer	Ireland	United States	Josephine	30 Apr 1828
SKINMETZ, Otto W.	41	M	Scrivener	Cuxhaven	United States	Howard	6 Jul 1829
SKINNER, Ann	7	F	Labourer	England	U. States	Comet	23 Aug 1828
Ann	13	F	None	Isle of Man		Ocean	13 Jul 1827
Betty	5	F	Labourer	England	U. States	Comet	23 Aug 1828
Danl.	5	M	None	Isle of Man		Ocean	13 Jul 1827
Danl.	38	M	Labourer	Isle of Man		Ocean	13 Jul 1827
Eliza.	11	F	Spinster	G. Britain	U. States	Hynd	12 Jul 1820
Eliza.	30	F	Spinster	G. Britain	U. States	Hynd	12 Jul 1820
Elizh.	36	F	None	Isle of Man		Ocean	13 Jul 1827
Ellen	9	F	None	Isle of Man		Ocean	13 Jul 1827
Ellen	50	F	Labourer	England	U. States	Comet	23 Aug 1828
Esther	24	F	Labourer	England	U. States	Comet	23 Aug 1828
Frederick	1	M	Labourer	England	U. States	Comet	23 Aug 1828
James	11	M	Labourer	England	U. States	Comet	23 Aug 1828
Jane	1	F	None	Isle of Man		Ocean	13 Jul 1827
Jane	4	F	Labourer	England	U. States	Comet	23 Aug 1828
Janet	40	F	Spinster	G. Britain	U. States	Hynd	12 Jul 1820
John	75	M	Labourer	G. Britain	U. States	Hynd	12 Jul 1820
John A.	31	M	Marriner	Great Britian	United States	George Clinton	21 Oct 1826
Matthew	26	M	Farmer	Great Britian	United States	George Clinton	21 Oct 1826
Philip	9	M	Labourer	England	U. States	Comet	23 Aug 1828
Phillip	26	M	Labourer	England	U. States	Comet	23 Aug 1828
Thos. P.	22	M	Farmer	N. Jersey	U. States	Romeo	23 Jun 1823
Tomas	24	M	Merchant	U.S.	U.S.	William	18 Oct 1824
William	45	M	Labourer	Ireland	America	Josephine	8 Dec 1827
Wm.	1	M	Labourer	England	U. States	Comet	23 Aug 1828
Wm.	3	M	None	Isle of Man		Ocean	13 Jul 1827
Wm.	50	M	Labourer	England	U. States	Comet	23 Aug 1828
SKINNEY, John	27	M	Ploterin	Ireland	America	Parrington	9 Jun 1827
SKISKUR, Mary	20	F	Labourer	Ireland	United States	Hope	12 Jun 1828
SKITTING, H.	22	M	Labourer	Europe	United States	Aspasia	5 Sep 1827
SKORTKE, Louis	30	M	Merchant	Prussia	U. States	Marmion	7 Jun 1824
SKRIVING, Walter	25	M	Labourer	Scotland	U. States	Hunter	30 May 1827
SKY, Margt.	25		Niece [of John Lirtch]	Great Britain	United States	Camillus	12 Sep 1827
SLABBE, Louis	46	M	Merchant	Canada	Unknown	William Thompson	1 May 1827
SLACK, Joseph	59	M	Farmer	England	U. States	Camillus	27 Jul 1825
June	20	F	None			Manhattan	8 Aug 1820
Mary	40	F		England	U. States	Camillus	27 Jul 1825
Robert	28	M	Blacksmith	Great Britain	United States	Amelia	20 Aug 1829
Seth	23	M	Butcher			Manhattan	8 Aug 1820
SLADE, Jacob T.	35	M	Gentleman	America	U. States	Orazimbo	7 Jan 1821
W.	24	M	Cabnet Maker	U. States	United States	Baltic	11 Apr 1825
SLAIGLE, Barbara	4	F		Belfoit	U.S. America	Superior	18 Jun 1825

NAMES OF PASSENGERS	AGE	SEX	OCCUPATIONS	COUNTRY TO WHICH THEY BELONG	COUNTRY THEY INTEND TO INHABIT	SHIPS/DATES OF ARRIVAL	
SLAIGLE (cont'd)							
Catherine	7	F		Belfoit	U.S. America	Superior	18 Jun 1825
Catherine	32	F		Belfoit	U.S. America	Superior	18 Jun 1825
Christian	6	F		Belfoit	U.S. America	Superior	18 Jun 1825
Christian	33	M	Farmer	Belfoit	U.S. America	Superior	18 Jun 1825
Elizabeth	3	F		Belfoit	U.S. America	Superior	18 Jun 1825
Pierre	1	M		Belfoit	U.S. America	Superior	18 Jun 1825
SLAIMETH, A.	8	M	Farmer	Switzerland	U. States	Alfred	8 Jul 1828
Cath.	8	F	Farmer	Switzerland	U. States	Alfred	8 Jul 1828
Clara	30	F	Farmer	Switzerland	U. States	Alfred	8 Jul 1828
F.	39	F	Farmer	Switzerland	U. States	Alfred	8 Jul 1828
J.	7	M	Farmer	Switzerland	U. States	Alfred	8 Jul 1828
Jacob	12	M	Farmer	Switzerland	U. States	Alfred	8 Jul 1828
Louis	15	M	Farmer	Switzerland	U. States	Alfred	8 Jul 1828
M.	10	F	Farmer	Switzerland	U. States	Alfred	8 Jul 1828
SLAMMIN, John	21	M	Labourer	Ireland	United States	Jubilee	12 May 1828
SLANE, Danl.	30	M	Gardner	Ireland	New York	Atlantic	6 Oct 1828
SLANES, Mateo	34	M	Merchant	Mexico	Mexico	Cambria	8 Oct 1828
SLANTY, Allis	30	F	None	Great Britain	United States	Atlantic	28 May 1827
Ann	5/12	F	None	Great Britain	United States	Atlantic	28 May 1827
Eliza	4	F	None	Great Britain	United States	Atlantic	28 May 1827
James	2 6/12	M	None	Great Britain	United States	Atlantic	28 May 1827
James	5	F	None	Great Britain	United States	Atlantic	28 May 1827
Ker.	30	M	Joiner	Great Britain	United States	Atlantic	28 May 1827
Mary	25	F	None	Great Britain	United States	Atlantic	28 May 1827
Mattw.	6	M	None	Great Britain	United States	Atlantic	28 May 1827
Robt.	3	M	None	Great Britain	United States	Atlantic	28 May 1827
SLATER, A.	43	M	Merchant	United States	United States	Hannibal	27 May 1822
Ann	40	F		G. Britain	U. States	George Clinton	10 Sep 1828
Eliza	19	F	None	England	Pittsburgh	Orozimbo	8 Jun 1822
Isabella	25	F		United States	United States	Hannibal	27 May 1822
J.	40	M	Merchant	Jerusalem	Jerusalem	Venus	8 May 1826
James	29 6/12	M	Carver	Ireland	United States	Robert Edwards	3 Oct 1829
John	10	M	None	England	Pittsburgh	Orozimbo	8 Jun 1822
John	24	M	Taylor	England	United States	Andes	2 Oct 1828
Joseph	14	M	None	England	New York	Orozimbo	8 Jun 1822
Joseph	23	M	Clothier	England	U. St.	Manchester	7 Dec 1826
Margarett	2 6/12	F	Daughter	Ireland	United States	Robert Edwards	3 Oct 1829
Margt., Mrs.	24	F	Carpenter	England	U.S.	Acasta	11 May 1827
Mary Ann, his wife [John]	20	F	Taylor	England	United States	Andes	2 Oct 1828
Mathew	7	M	None	England	New York	Orozimbo	8 Jun 1822
Richard	30	M	Harnessmaker	G. Britain	U. States	Armadello	22 Jun 1827
Sarah	35	F	Servant	England	America	Britannia	5 Nov 1828
Thomas	3	M		United States	United States	Hannibal	27 May 1822
Thomas	20	M	None	England	New York	Orozimbo	8 Jun 1822
Thomas	30	M	Merchant	England	United States	St. George	25 Aug 1829
William D.	20	M	Clerk	England	United States	Magnet	16 May 1823
Wm., Mr.	28	M	Carpenter	England	U.S.	Acasta	11 May 1827
SLATERY, Pane	48	M	Clouthier	Ireland	Ut. States	Courier	13 Jul 1826
SLATLON, Thomas	28 0/12	M	Farmer	America	America	Hiram	2 Apr 1828
SLATOR, Alba	35	F		Great B.	U. States	William Neilson	26 Jul 1828
Allice	7	F		Great B.	U. States	William Neilson	26 Jul 1828
George	5	M		Great B.	U. States	William Neilson	26 Jul 1828
Kely	2	F		Great B.	U. States	William Neilson	26 Jul 1828
Luth	35	M		Great B.	U. States	William Neilson	26 Jul 1828
Mary	18	F		Great B.	U. States	William Neilson	26 Jul 1828
Mary	20	F	Spinster	Ireland	United States	Dublin Packet	28 Apr 1824
Michol	9	M		Great B.	U. States	William Neilson	26 Jul 1828
SLATTARY, Ann	40	F		Gt. Brittan	America	Reindeer	3 Aug 1827
SLATTERY, Ann	22	F	Labourer	England	U. States	Ayrshire	12 May 1828
Roger	24	M	Land Surveyor	Thurlis	Co. Tippereray	Howard Douglass	11 May 1827
Wm.	30	M	Farmer	Great Britain	United States	Weser	9 May 1822
SLATTREY, Ellen	25			Ireland	U.S.	Union	20 Aug 1827
M...	24			Ireland	U.S.	Union	20 Aug 1827
SLAVEN, Bernard	30	M	Farmer	Ireland	United States	General Putnam	20 Jun 1825
Daniel	22	M	Labourer	Ireland	United States	New Packet	15 Nov 1828
Joseph	22	M	Labourer	Ireland	United States	Marchioness	13 May 1828

1166

NAMES OF PASSENGERS	AGE	SEX	OCCUPATIONS	COUNTRY TO WHICH THEY BELONG	COUNTRY THEY INTEND TO INHABIT	SHIPS/DATES OF ARRIVAL	
SLAVEN (cont'd)							
Larrence	22	M	Farmer	Ireland	United States	General Putnam	20 Jun 1825
Michael	24	M	Farmer	Ireland	United States	New Packet	15 Nov 1828
Rose	26	F		Ireland	United States	General Putnam	20 Jun 1825
SLAVIN, Andrew	18	M	Labourer	Ireland	United States	Meteor	26 Jun 1827
Betty	19	F	Spinster	Ireland	United States	Trident	17 May 1825
SLAYDING, Wm.	46	M	Smith	Yorkshire		Ocean	13 Jul 1827
SLEAVEN, Susan	16 9/12	F	Spinstress	Ireland	U. States	Fabius	22 Sep 1828
SLEE, John	21	M	Cordwainer	England	U.S. States	Splendid	14 Aug 1829
Joseph	22	M	Cordwainer	England	U.S. States	Splendid	14 Aug 1829
L.	1	M	Cordwainer	England	U.S. States	Splendid	14 Aug 1829
SLEETH, Geo.	26	M	Sadler	U. States	U. States	Swift	11 May 1824
SLEGE, J.	2...	M	Labourer	England	United States	Alicia	9 May 1827
SLENSON, Edwin	15	M		Halifax	U. States	Hope & Esther	12 May 1826
SLEODLY, John	24	M	...	Ireland	United States	Carolina Ann	24 Oct 1825
SLERE, Christen	8	M	his family [Christen]	Germany	United States	Wm. Osborne	16 Sep 1828
Christen	50	M	Optician	Germany	United States	Wm. Osborne	16 Sep 1828
Maria	40	F	his family [Christen]	Germany	United States	Wm. Osborne	16 Sep 1828
SLETH, Margaret	30	F		U. States	U. States	Golconda	14 May 1823
SLICKS, J. C.	31	M	Merchant	U. States	U. States	Oglethorpe	9 Nov 1824
SLIGHT, Jane	31	F	None	U. States	U. States	Martha	20 Jun 1825
Thos.	39	M	Farmer	U. States	U. States	Martha	20 Jun 1825
SLIGLER, Johannes	28	M	Brewer	Germany	U. States	Isabella	10 Aug 1829
SLIMMER, Christiaan	18	M	Boer	Tornberg	United States	Juffraw Johanna	16 Oct 1821
SLINKEN, G.	22	M	Laborer	Hannover	United States.	Constitution	6 Jul 1829
SLIVEN, Thomas	19	M	Labourer	Ireland	United States	Clothier	22 Nov 1827
SLOAN, B.	26		Farmer	Ireland	United States	Courier	16 May 1825
Charles	35	M	Farmer	Gt. Britain	U. States	Panthia	13 Nov 1824
D.	35		Farmer	Ireland	United States	Courier	16 May 1825
Ellen	45	F	Spinster	Ireland	United States	Trident	17 May 1825
Esther, Child	12 6/12	F		Ireland	New York	Carolina Ann	15 Oct 1824
Geo.	40	M	Farmer	Gt. Britain	United States	Union	9 Jan 1824
J.	26		Farmer	Ireland	United States	Courier	16 May 1825
Jane	27	F	Wife	Ireland	New York	Louisa	20 Jul 1826
John, Mr.	17	M	Gentleman	Ireland	United States	Dublin Packet	22 Aug 1829
Jos.	27	M	None	U. States	U. States	Golden Age	19 Dec 1827
Margaret	4 3/12	F	Daughter	Ireland	New York	Louisa	20 Jul 1826
Mary	30		Farmer	Ireland	United States	Carolina Ann	12 Sep 1823
Philip	30	M	Farmer	Ireland	America	Superior	12 Jun 1824
Robert	3	M	Son	Ireland	New York	Louisa	20 Jul 1826
Susannah	20	F	Spinster	Ireland	United States	Trident	17 May 1825
Thomas	28	M	Shoemaker	Ireland	New York	Louisa	20 Jul 1826
Wm.	35	M	Labourer	Ireland	N. York	Trusty	12 Sep 1828
SLOANE, Joshua	38	M	Merchant			Ann Maria	29 Nov 1821
SLOCAM, Geo. M.	27	M	Mercht.	U. States	U. States	Constitution	17 Mar 1823
SLOCUM, Eduard	6	M		America	America	Soto	1 Aug 1829
Harriet	10	F		America	America	Soto	1 Aug 1829
John D.			Distressed Seaman	Bristol, R.I.	U. States	Mary & Eliza	2 Jul 1829
Jos.	37	M	Merchant	State of Ohio	U. States	Nile	16 Oct 1822
Maria	35	F		America	America	Soto	1 Aug 1829
W. A.	24	M	Merchant	U. States	U. States	Emma	24 Jun 1822
SLOELOMB, Emma	13	F		England	United States	Peru	23 May 1827
Mary	30	F		England	United States	Peru	23 May 1827
Micl.	35	M	Gilder	England	United States	Peru	23 May 1827
SLOMAN, Jno.	21	M	Merchant	England	U. States	Hudson	8 Oct 1827
SLONE, F. S.	20	M	Merchant	America	America	Nancy	18 Aug 1821
SLOON, James	33	M	Gentleman	Ireland	America	Superior	12 Jun 1824
SLOSS, David	2/12		...	Ireland		Westmoreland	1 Aug 1826
Elizh.	36		Spinster	Ireland		Westmoreland	1 Aug 1826
Gordon	1/12		...	Ireland		Westmoreland	1 Aug 1826
Jas.	1		Boy	Ireland		Westmoreland	1 Aug 1826
John	6/12		Boy	Ireland		Westmoreland	1 Aug 1826
Joseph	14		Boy	Ireland		Westmoreland	1 Aug 1826
Peggy	3/12		Spinster	Ireland		Westmoreland	1 Aug 1826
Robert	3/12		Boy	Ireland		Westmoreland	1 Aug 1826
Wm.				Ireland		Westmoreland	1 Aug 1826

*born on board

NAMES OF PASSENGERS	AGE	SEX	OCCUPATIONS	COUNTRY TO WHICH THEY BELONG	COUNTRY THEY INTEND TO INHABIT	SHIPS/DATES OF ARRIVAL	
SLOSSON, John	20	M	Law	America	United States	William Byrnes	15 Aug 1826
William	40	M	Law	America	United States	William Byrnes	15 Aug 1826
SLOTT, Saml.	21	M	Clothier	Great Britain	New York	Superior	5 Sep 1827
SLOTTZ, Joseph, his Wife, his father							
& two Children	38	M	Shoemaker	Swisse	United States	Deux Ernest	29 Dec 1827
*landed at Lewiston, Delw.							
SLOTZ, Christiana	28	F		Germany	U. States	Isabella	10 Aug 1829
Jean	30	M	Manufacturer	Germany	U. States	Isabella	10 Aug 1829
Johannes	30	M	Farmer	Germany	U. States	Isabella	10 Aug 1829
SLOVEN, Michal	28	M	Farmer	Ireland	U. States	Meteor	19 Jul 1828
SLOVERE, Thomas	20 6/12	M	Labourer	Ireland	U. States	Courier	17 Mar 1828
SLOWY, James	21	M	Labourer	Ireland	New York	Atlantic	8 May 1828
SLY, Harriett	16	F		Cincinata	Cincinata	Hudson	20 Nov 1828
Joseph	61	M	Merchant	Cincinata	Cincinata	Hudson	20 Nov 1828
SM..., James	42	M	Farmer	Great Britain	United States	Blakely	29 Sep 1826
SM...TH, Margeret	19	F	Spinster	Ireland	U. States	Courier	17 Mar 1828
SMAILS, Ann	10					Agricola	1 Jul 1820
Elizabeth	14					Agricola	1 Jul 1820
Hannah	1					Agricola	1 Jul 1820
Hannah	40					Agricola	1 Jul 1820
John	8					Agricola	1 Jul 1820
Mary	12					Agricola	1 Jul 1820
Robert	6					Agricola	1 Jul 1820
T.	42	M	Farmer	Great Brittan	U. States	Cadmus	5 Apr 1826
Thos.	3					Agricola	1 Jul 1820
SMALE, Ann	5	F	None	England		Marchioness	13 May 1828
Caroline	3	F	None	England		Marchioness	13 May 1828
Elizabeth	10	F	None	England		Marchioness	13 May 1828
Frances	12	F	None	England		Marchioness	13 May 1828
Harriet	6	F	None	England		Marchioness	13 May 1828
James	13	M	None	England		Marchioness	13 May 1828
James	40	M	Butcher	England		Marchioness	13 May 1828
*Died April 4th							
Maria ...	24	F				Harmony	15 Jul 1820
Mary	18	F	None	England		Marchioness	13 May 1828
Sarah	15	F	None	England		Marchioness	13 May 1828
SMALL, Anne	20	F	Daughter	England	United States	Cambria	8 Oct 1828
Chs. C.	24	M	Gentleman	England	Canada	York	12 Jul 1825
Edward	36	M	...	Gt. Britain	United States	Crisis	13 Nov 1824
Elizth.	26	F	Servt.	England	United States	Bayard	13 Nov 1823
H.	25	M	Seaman	U. States	U. States	Minerva	9 Jan 1827
James	33		Gentleman	Canada	Great Britain	Cincinnatus	17 May 1823
James	40 6/12	M	Dealer	Ireland	United States	Atlantic	21 Jul 1827
James	50	M	Weaver	Great Britain	United States	Courier	26 Jun 1827
Jane	24	F	Lady	U. States Amer		Charlotte Corday	7 Mar 1820
Janet	40	F		Great Britain	United States	Roanoak	19 Sep 1827
John	25	M	Weaver	Great Britain	United States	Roanoak	19 Sep 1827
John	40	M	None	Ireland	America	Hesperus	7 Jul 1820
John	70		Gentleman	England	Great Britain	Cincinnatus	17 May 1823
Joseph	16	M	Son	England	United States	Cambria	8 Oct 1828
Joseph	20	M	Farmer	England	United States	New York Packet	14 Oct 1823
Joseph	51	M	Farmer	England	United States	Cambria	8 Oct 1828
Mary	13	F	Daughter	England	United States	Cambria	8 Oct 1828
Mary	17	F	Wife	England	United States	Cambria	8 Oct 1828
Mary	34	F		U. States	U. States	Minerva	9 Jan 1827
R. H., Mr.	31	M	Merchant	U.S.A.		François I	19 Nov 1828
Samuel	30	M	Farmer	U. Kingdom of Great Britain	United States	Cambria	7 May 1828
William	18					Cincinnatus	17 May 1823
Wm.	2	M	Boy	England	United States	Cambria	8 Oct 1828
Wm.	47	M	Mariner	Providence	U. States	Mona	1 Jul 1823
SMALLER, Ewd.	27	M	Carpenter	England	America	Two Marys	24 Sep 1827
SMART, Abrm.	40	M	Farmer	Great Britain	United States	Ganges	8 Jul 1820
Ann	7	F		G. Britain	United States	Edward	21 Apr 1821
Ann, Mrs.	60	F	None	England	America	Hannibal	4 Oct 1822
Benj.	...	...	...	...	...	Pioneer	21 Jun 1825

NAMES OF PASSENGERS	AGE	SEX	OCCUPATIONS	COUNTRY TO WHICH THEY BELONG	COUNTRY THEY INTEND TO INHABIT	SHIPS/DATES OF ARRIVAL	
SMART (cont'd)							
Caroline	...	...	...	...	...	Pioneer	21 Jun 1825
Chas.	20	M	Shoemaker	England	United States	Cosmo	21 Aug 1828
Clarissa	12	F	Child	U.S. America	U.S. America	Vermont	7 Oct 1828
David	22	M	Weaver	Great Britain	United States	Colossus	5 Jun 1827
Diana	30	F	Labourer	U.S. America	U.S. America	Vermont	7 Oct 1828
Elisha	10	...	...	...	...	Pioneer	21 Jun 1825
Elizabeth	35	F		Great Britain	United States	Ganges	8 Jul 1820
George	5	F		G. Britain	United States	Edward	21 Apr 1821
H. L.	21	F	None	England	America	Hannibal	4 Oct 1822
James	Infant	M		Great Britain	United States	Ganges	8 Jul 1820
Jane	13 6/12	F		G. Britain	United States	Edward	21 Apr 1821
Jno.	21	M	Farmer	Great Britain	United States	Penelope	11 Jun 1827
Jno.	24	M	Labourer	England	U. States	William	28 Nov 1823
John	3	M		G. Britain	United States	Edward	21 Apr 1821
John	34	...	...	...	...	Pioneer	21 Jun 1825
John	35	M	Mercht.	France		Radius	21 Jul 1824
John	40	M	Labourer	U.S. America	U.S. America	Vermont	7 Oct 1828
Jos.	16	M	Merchant	England	America	Hannibal	4 Oct 1822
Joseph	6	M	Child	U.S. America	U.S. America	Vermont	7 Oct 1828
Joseph	6...	...	...	...	...	Pioneer	21 Jun 1825
Joshua	3	M	Child	U.S. America	U.S. America	Vermont	7 Oct 1828
Lucy	27	F	None	England	America	Hannibal	4 Oct 1822
Margaret	9	F	Child	U.S. America	U.S. America	Vermont	7 Oct 1828
Mary	30	F	None	England	America	Hannibal	4 Oct 1822
Mary	44	...	...	...	...	Pioneer	21 Jun 1825
Sarah	1...	...	...	...	...	Pioneer	21 Jun 1825
Sh...	...	...	...	...	...	Pioneer	21 Jun 1825
Thomas	11	M		G. Britain	United States	Edward	21 Apr 1821
Thomas	47	M	Farmer	G. Britain	United States	Edward	21 Apr 1821
Thos. C.	61	M	Merchant	England	America	Hannibal	4 Oct 1822
Thos. C., Jr.	24	M	Merchant	England	America	Hannibal	4 Oct 1822
Violet	12	...	...	...	...	Pioneer	21 Jun 1825
William	1...	...	...	...	...	Pioneer	21 Jun 1825
William	30	M	Joiner	Great Britain	United States	Isaac Hicks	10 Jul 1827
Wm.	9	M		G. Britain	United States	Edward	21 Apr 1821
Wm.	22	M	Gent	England	America	Albion	4 Oct 1820
SMARTE, Richard	33	M	Merchant	England	America	Orbit	1 Sep 1823
SMEATEN, Robert D.	29	M	Gentleman	Great Britain	United States	Isaac Hicks	6 Dec 1827
SMEDEN, Frederic	16	F		Germany	United States	Rent	13 May
SMELLIN, Constine	25		Sugar Baker	Germany		Helen	4 Aug 1829
SMELT, Margaret	41 2/12	F		Scotland	United States	Mobile	21 Aug 1827
SMERITH, John	40	M	Merchant	Spain	Spain	Claudio	16 Oct 1827
SMERT, J. Baptist	45	M	Mercht.	France	U.S.	Cadmus	20 Dec 1824
SMIATON, George	32	M	Manuir	England	United States	Dalhouse Castle	6 Sep 1827
SMID, John	46	M	Farmer	G. Brittain	U. States	Cincinnatus	2 Oct 1822
SMIDDY, Joanne	21	F	None	England	U. States	Montgomery	18 Oct 1828
John	11	M	None	England	U. States	Montgomery	18 Oct 1828
Mary	12	F	None	England	U. States	Montgomery	18 Oct 1828
Mary	50	F	None	England	U. States	Montgomery	18 Oct 1828
SMIDTH, Ann Maria	26	F		Germany	Missouri	Isabella	15 Sep 1828
John	30	M	Shoemaker	Germany	Missouri	Isabella	15 Sep 1828
Saml.	2	M		Germany	Missouri	Isabella	15 Sep 1828
SMILLIE, Alison	29	F	Wife	Scotland	United States	Tom	2 Jul 1827
Eliz.	2	F	Child	Scotland	United States	Tom	2 Jul 1827
Geo.	1/2	M	Child	Scotland	United States	Tom	2 Jul 1827
James	21	M	Farmer	Scotland	United States	Tom	2 Jul 1827
Jane	32	M	Laborer	Scotland	United States	Tom	2 Jul 1827
SMIT (see Messen Smit)							
Athenna	20			France	U. States	Parachute	14 May 1828
Catharine	50			France	U. States	Parachute	14 May 1828
Chatarina, Kinder (his child [Jacob])	18	F			United States	Juffraw Johanna	16 Oct 1821
Chatarina, Zyn Vrouw (his wife [Jacob]	40	F			United States	Juffraw Johanna	16 Oct 1821
Christaan, Kinder (his child [Jacob])	13	M			United States	Juffraw Johanna	16 Oct 1821

NAMES OF PASSENGERS	AGE	SEX	OCCUPATIONS	COUNTRY TO WHICH THEY BELONG	COUNTRY THEY INTEND TO INHABIT	SHIPS/DATES OF ARRIVAL	
SMIT (cont'd)							
Elizabeth, Kinder (his child [Jacob])	2	F			United States	Juffraw Johanna	16 Oct 1821
Frederik, Kinder (his child [Jacob])	14	M			United States	Juffraw Johanna	16 Oct 1821
George	48		Cooper	France	U. States	Parachute	14 May 1828
Jacob	54	M	Boer	Wellisweide	United States	Juffraw Johanna	16 Oct 1821
Louisa, Zyn Vrouw [his wife, Jacob Klein]	34	F		Hasbach	United States	Juffraw Johanna	16 Oct 1821
Margaret	18			France	U. States	Parachute	14 May 1828
Margaretta, Zyn Vrow Zuster [his wife's sister, Jacob Klein]	28	F		Hasbach	United States	Juffraw Johanna	16 Oct 1821
Maria, Kinder (his child [Jacob])	4	F			United States	Juffraw Johanna	16 Oct 1821
Nicholaas	28	M	Bakker	Meringen	United States	Juffraw Johanna	16 Oct 1821
SMITH, —			Mariner	U. States	U. States	Blooming Rose	14 Jul 1821
—, boy	12	M		Scotland	New York	Joseph Hume	26 Oct 1829
—, Miss	33	F	Lady	United States	United States	Don Quixote	18 Aug 1824
—, Mr.	45	M	Merchant	U. States	U. States	Plough Boy	6 May 1823
—, Mr.	50	M	Farmer	Bristol	U. States	Marathon	11 Nov 1824
—, Mrs.	19	F	Merchant	London	U. States	Catharine	19 Jul 1822
—, Mrs.	28	F		Scotland	U.S.	Curler	19 Jul 1828
—, Mrs.	30	F			U. States	Congress	21 Nov 1823
—, Mrs.	30	F		Bristol	U. States	Marathon	11 Nov 1824
...	...1	M	Labourer	Ireland	Unt. St. America	Wilson	21 May 1827
...	4	F		England	U. States	Hudson	21 Aug 1829
...ock	2	M		France	United States	Stephania	6 Dec 1827
— (Infant)	6/12	M			U. States	Congress	21 Nov 1823
A.	18	M		Ireland	U. States	John Dickinson	13 May 1823
A.	27	F	No	Spain	U. States	Dromo	22 May 1826
Aaron	51	M	Merchant	U. States	U. States	York	10 Dec 1825
Ab.	23	M	Servant	N. York	N. York	Director	20 Sep 1824
Abm.	35	M	Mariner	United States	United States	Heroine	7 Jul 1829
Abraham	30	M	Mariner	Connecticutt	U. States	Planter	16 Mar 1824
Abraham Russell	27	M	Merchant	U.S.A.	U.S.A.	General Jackson	27 Mar 1827
Agnes	5	F		Great Britain	U.S. of America	Gratitude	3 Oct 1829
Aleda	25	F	Spinstress	Germany	United States	Two Marys	12 Feb 1820
Alex	20	M	Labourer	St. John	United States	Hannah Eliza	23 Sep 1826
Alexr.	26	M	Shoemaker	Great Britain	United States	Colossus	5 Jun 1827
Alfred	9	M		England	U. States	Hudson	21 Aug 1829
Alice	25	F	Matron	Ireland	U. States	Josephine	23 Jan 1829
Allan	15	M	Clerk	Scotland	U. States	Hector	18 Apr 1825
Alpia	3	M		England	United States	Cosmo	21 Aug 1828
Am Maria	27	F		France	Unknown	Abby Jones	12 Jul 1827
Amos	30	M	Sailor	U. States	U. States	Sophia & Eliza	13 Jun 1828
Andrew	1	M		Scotland	U.S.	Curler	19 Jul 1828
Andrew	20	M		Ireland	U. States	Nancy	10 Jul 1822
Andrew	24	M	Farmer	Ireland	United States	Dublin Packet	13 Oct 1828
Andrew	28		Carpenter	Scotland	U.S.	Curler	19 Jul 1828
Andrew	35	M	...	Ireland	United States	Trident	18 Jul 1827
Andw.	30	M	Labourer	Ireland	United States	Thomas	13 Dec 1827
Andw.	32	M	Servant	England	Baltimore	Brighton	16 Nov 1826
Ann	3	F	None	Ireland	New York	America	1 Aug 1828
Ann	6	F		Ireland	U. States	Nancy	10 Jul 1822
Ann	8	F	Farmer	Great Britain	New York	Eliza Grant	29 Aug 1829
Ann	9	F	Farmer	England	United States	Euphrates	18 Aug 1827
Ann	17	F	Servant	Ireland	United States	Josephine	30 Apr 1828
Ann	17	F		America	America	Brittania	17 Jul 1828
Ann	20	F	Servt.	United States	U. States	Brown	8 Aug 1825
Ann	20	F		Great Britton	U. State	Earl of Liverpool	16 Aug 1826
Ann	20	F			United States	Java	9 Jul 1827
Ann	22	F		Irland	U. States	Nancy	27 Jun 1823
Ann	22	F	Servant	Ireland	New York	Atlantic	8 May 1828
Ann	22	F	None	Great Britain	United States	Isaac Hicks	22 Aug 1828
Ann	24	F	Matron	Ireland	America	Wilson	16 May 1825
Ann	24	F	Clothier	G. Britain	Canada	Cosmo	25 Nov 1826

NAMES OF PASSENGERS	AGE	SEX	OCCUPATIONS	COUNTRY TO WHICH THEY BELONG	COUNTRY THEY INTEND TO INHABIT	SHIPS/DATES OF ARRIVAL	
SMITH (cont'd)							
Ann	24	F		S...off...ton	United States	Java	9 Jul 1827
Ann	26	F		England	America	John Wells	11 Jun 1823
Ann	29	F		England	America	Silas Richard	24 Oct 1829
Ann	30	F	Wife	Scotland	United States	Tom	2 Jul 1827
Ann	38	F	None	Great Britain		Moro Castle	6 Jul 1827
Ann	40	F	Wife of [John]	England	United States	Aurora	21 Jun 1824
Ann M.	35	F	Lady	St. John, N.B.	St. John, N.B.	Nancy	2 May 1823
Ann Maria	3	F		France	Unknown	Abby Jones	12 Jul 1827
Anna	17	F	Spinstress	Germany	United States	Two Marys	12 Feb 1820
Anna	17	F	Spinster	Swtserland	America	Saluda	18 Jun 1825
Anna Maria	20	F	Servant	Germany	Ohio	James Noble	27 Aug 1827
Anna Maria, his daughter [Tobias]	13	F				Martha	30 Jun 1823
Anne	17	F	Farmer	England	England	Criterion	29 May 1822
Anne	25 8/12	F	Farmer	Switzerland	America	Henry	17 May 1828
Anne	26	F		England	United States	Wm. Byrnes	30 Apr 1828
Anne	33	F	Farmer	England	England	Criterion	29 May 1822
Anthony	42	M	Farmer	Germany	United States	Stephania	16 Aug 1827
Arch.	26	M	Servant	Ireland	United States	Carolina Ann	14 May 1827
B.	20	M	Weaver	Gt. Britain		Dalhouse Castle	13 May 1828
B.	20	F		G. Britain	U. States	London	23 Sep 1828
B.	21	M	...	U. States	U. States	Pacific	11 Sep 1824
B., Capt.	29	M	Mariner	U.S.	U.S.	Frances	21 Mar 1827
Barson	40	F		Ireland	U. States	Nancy	10 Jul 1822
Ben	20	M	Farmer	England	U. States	Thomas Ritchie	2 Jul 1827
Benjn.	35	M	Weaver	England	America	Franklin	19 Nov 1828
Betsey	20	F	None	Great Britain	United States	Isaac Hicks	22 Aug 1828
Betsy	30	F	None	Great Britain	United States	Greek	23 Jan 1828
Betty	29	F	None	Great Britain	United States	William Dawson	18 Jun 1827
Biddy	19	F	None	Ireland	United States	Trident	18 Jul 1827
Bridget	15	F		England	United States	Hannibal	25 Sep 1827
Bridget	20	F		London		Catharine	19 Jul 1822
Bridget	24	F	Spinster	Ireland	U. States	Josephine	7 May 1827
Bridget	24	F	None	Great Britain	United States	Penelope	11 Jun 1827
Bridget	26	F	Servant	Ireland	New York	Atlantic	8 May 1828
Bridget	50	F		London		Catharine	19 Jul 1822
Bryan	9	M		Ireland	United States	Carolina Ann	11 Dec 1826
C.	22	M	Merchant	U. States	U. States	Liverpool Trader	20 Feb 1822
C., Mrs.		F		United States	United States	James Cropper	14 Oct 1824
C. Caroloane [?]	1	F	Laborer	Switzerland	U.S.	C. Amelia	30 Jun 1828
Caroline	9		his Daughter [George R.]	England	United States	Cambria	19 Oct 1829
Caroline	10	F	Farmer	Alsace in the Department of Upper and lower Rhine	United States	Carolina Augusta	16 May 1828
Caroline	11	F	his family [Jacob]	Germany	Pensylvania	Isabella	15 Sep 1828
Cath.	8	F		Switzerland	U.S.	C. Amelia	30 Jun 1828
Catharine	11	F		Ireland		Fame	9 Dec 1826
Catharine	18	F	Servant	Ireland	New York	Atlantic	8 May 1828
Catharine, his daughter [Tobias]	20	F				Martha	30 Jun 1823
Catharine, his wife [Tobias]	44	F				Martha	30 Jun 1823
Catharine M.	26	F	Spinster	Ireland	United States	Dublin Packet	22 Oct 1821
Cathe.	3 6/12	F		S...off...ton	United States	Java	9 Jul 1827
Catherina	5	F	Farmer	Alsace in the Department of Upper and lower Rhine	United States	Carolina Augusta	16 May 1828
Catherine	5	F	Shoe Maker	Great Britain	United States	Dapper	21 Aug 1828
Catherine	7	F	None	Gt. Brittain	United States	Balaena	9 Oct 1823
Catherine	16	F	Spinster	Ireland	United States	Dublin Packet	29 Jun 1825
Catherine	19 5/12	F	Farmer	Switzerland	America	Henry	17 May 1828
Catherine	22	F	Spinstress	Germany	United States	Two Marys	12 Feb 1820
Catherine	30	F	None	Ireland	United States	Lord Wellington	28 May 1827

NAMES OF PASSENGERS	AGE	SEX	OCCUPATIONS	COUNTRY TO WHICH THEY BELONG	COUNTRY THEY INTEND TO INHABIT	SHIPS/DATES OF ARRIVAL	
SMITH (cont'd)							
Catherine	58	F	Farmer	Alsace in the Department of Upper and lower Rhine	United States	Carolina Augusta	16 May 1828
Charles	4	F	None	Great Britain	New York	Superior	5 Sep 1827
Charles	11	M		England	U. States	Hudson	21 Aug 1829
Charles	17	M		England	America	Britannia	22 Jul 1829
Charles	23	M	Farmer	United States	United States	Robert Read	19 Oct 1825
Charles	30	M	Nailor	Ireland	Und. Stts of Amer	Alexander Mansfield	18 Aug 1826
Charles	45	F	Merchant	England	America	Britannia	22 Jul 1829
Charles, Mrs.	28	F	Lady	U.S.	U.S.	Edward Bonnaffe	20 Jun 1825
Charles, working Passage	15	M	...	...	United States	Hanford	17 Oct 1828
Charles F.	38	M	Farmer	Germany	Pensylvania	Isabella	15 Sep 1828
Charlotte	25	F		England	Great Britain	New York	22 Jul 1824
Charlotte	28	F		Great Britain	Great Britain	Wyton	12 May 1821
Chas. C.	2 6/12	M	his family [Charles]	Germany	Pensylvania	Isabella	15 Sep 1828
Chas. M.	25	M	Carpenter	U. States	U. States	Almira	18 Sep 1823
Christiana	24	F	Farmer	Alsace in the Department of Upper and lower Rhine	United States	Carolina Augusta	16 May 1828
Christien	10	F		Switzerland	U.S.	C. Amelia	30 Jun 1828
Christopher	27	M	Labourer	Ireland	New York	Curler	7 Jul 1827
Clark	28		Seaman	United States		Cynosure	4 Mar 1828
*Consul's man, put on bord by the american Consil at St. Michal's Belonging to the brig Emeline of Portland Was Rackt on the 25 of Dec 1827 in the Harber of St. Michals							
Colin C.	40	M		England	New York	Lewis	16 Mar 1826
Cristiana, his daughter [Tobias]	3					Martha	30 Jun 1823
D.	20	M	unknown	U. States	U. States	Mary	7 Nov 1822
Daniel	11	M	Farmer	Great Britain	New York	Eliza Grant	29 Aug 1829
Daniel	11	M	Farmer	Great Britain	U. States	Eliza Grant	29 Aug 1829
Daniel	24	M	Merchant	United States	United States	Tampico	27 Jun 1827
David		M		Scotland	United States	Samuel Robertson	5 Oct 1827
David	12	M			United States	Sarah	9 Nov 1820
David	21 4/12	M	Seedsman	England	United States	London	6 Feb 1829
David	23	M	Seaman	U. States	United States	Brilliant	24 Sep 1827
David	25	M	Farmer	Ireland	United States	Romulus	24 Jun 1826
David	30		Farmer			Rufus King	7 Aug 1820
David	40	M	Farmer	Scotland	U. States	Pleiades	9 Oct 1829
Dawnal	30	M	Laborer	England	United States	Danube	13 Jul 1827
Donald	22	M	Laborer	Gt. Britain	U.S. of America	Friends	25 Sep 1823
Donald.	20		Tu...n	Great Britain	United States	Camillus	12 Sep 1827
E.	15	M	None	Germany	United States	Maria Theresa	28 Aug 1821
E.	17	M			United States	Sarah	9 Nov 1820
E.	40	M	Merchant	Scotland	U. States	Cato	12 May 1828
E.	43	F		Great Britain	U. States	United States	8 Sep 1827
E. H.	27	M	Mariner	United States	United States	Louisa	6 Apr 1822
Ed.	39	M	Farmer	England	U. States	Unity	5 Sep 1828
Ed. S.	38	M	Gent.	England	New York	Cortes	23 Nov 1827
Edward	20	M	Labourer	Ireland	United States	Trident	18 Jul 1827
Edward	24	M	Farmer	Ireland	United States	Princess Charlotte	6 Oct 1827
Edward	25	M	Scissors Smith	England	Great Britain	Florida	26 Sep 1826
Edward	26	M	Farmer	G. Britain	United States	Edward	21 Apr 1821
Edward	35	M	Leather Stainer	England	United States should they approve of it	Robert Edwards	20 Jan 1829
Edward	38			Yorkshire	Ohio	Peru	30 May 1828
Edwd.	22	M	Farmer	England	U. States	Severn	12 Oct 1826
Edwin	17	F		England	America	Britannia	22 Jul 1829
Edwith	40	M		New York	United States	William Byrnes	6 Apr 1826
Eleanor	17	F	Farmer	England	United States	Euphrates	18 Aug 1827
Eleanor, Mrs.	43	F		Scotland	U. States	William Thompson	25 Aug 1828

NAMES OF PASSENGERS	AGE	SEX	OCCUPATIONS	COUNTRY TO WHICH THEY BELONG	COUNTRY THEY INTEND TO INHABIT	SHIPS/DATES OF ARRIVAL	
SMITH (cont'd)							
Eli	38	F	Ar...			Hesperus	2 Nov 1820
Elisabeth	9		Girl	Swtserland	America	Saluda	18 Jun 1825
Elisabeth	9	F		England	United States	Cosmo	21 Aug 1828
Elisabeth	20	F	Servant	Ireland	U.States	Nancy	31 May 1823
Eliz.	22	F		England	United States	St. George	25 Aug 1829
Eliz.	43	F	Farmer	England	United States	Euphrates	18 Aug 1827
Eliza	2	F	None	Great Brittan	U. States	Gem	26 Jul 1827
Eliza	5	F		England	United States	Cosmo	21 Aug 1828
Eliza	6	F	Lady	Charleston, S.C.	Charleston, S.C.	Panthea	22 Jul 1826
Eliza	10	F	None	Great Britain	New York	Superior	5 Sep 1827
Eliza	11	F		G. Britain	U. States	Canada	19 Sep 1828
Eliza	18	F		U. States	U. States	South Carolina Packet	28 Apr 1823
Eliza	21	F		Ireland	United States	Aurora	9 Jul 1827
Eliza	21	F		Great Britain	New York, U.S.	Florida	2 Oct 1828
Eliza	24	F	Farmer	England	England	Criterion	29 May 1822
Eliza	25	F		U. States	U. States	Dollar	29 Aug 1825
Eliza	27	F	Tayloress	Halifax	United States	Genl. Marion	4 Jun 1828
Eliza, his daughter [Ed. S.]	6	F		England	New York	Cortes	23 Nov 1827
Eliza Ann	31	F		England	U. States	Hudson	21 Aug 1829
Eliza M.	18	F	Lady	United States		Elias Burger	28 May 1821
Elizabeth	4	F	None	Gt. Brittain	United States	Balaena	9 Oct 1823
Elizabeth	5	F				Hesperus	2 Nov 1820
Elizabeth	9	F	Farmer	Alsace in the Department of Upper and lower Rhine	United States	Carolina Augusta	16 May 1828
Elizabeth	18	F	None	United States	United States	Cortes	5 Aug 1822
Elizabeth	25	F	Wife of [William]	England	United States	Aurora	5 Sep 1826
Elizabeth	25	F	Wife	England	United States should they approve of it	Robert Edwards	20 Jan 1829
Elizabeth	26	F	Farmer	Bavarian	United States	American	27 Aug 1827
Elizabeth	30	F	Spinstress	Germany	United States	Two Marys	12 Feb 1820
Elizabeth	30	F		Argyle (Tedland) Scotland	United States	Jean Hastie	27 Jul 1829
Elizabeth	50	F		Ireland	United States	Alex. Mansfield	17 May 1823
Elizabeth	74	F	Shoe Maker	Great Britain	United States	Dapper	21 Aug 1828
Elizabeth B. W.	17		his Daughter [George R.]	England	United States	Cambria	19 Oct 1829
Elizth.	30	F	None	England	United States	Dalhouse Castle	6 Sep 1827
Ellen	6	F		America	America	Brittania	17 Jul 1828
Ellen	7	F	None	Ireland	New York	America	1 Aug 1828
Ellen	14	F		G. Britain	U. States	Canada	19 Sep 1828
Ellen	16	F	Sevant			James Monroe	8 Aug 1820
Ellen	20	F	Spinster	Ireland	United States	Fabius	4 Jun 1828
Ellen	24	F		U. States	United States	Sarah G.	15 May 1828
Ellen	45	F		America	America	Brittania	17 Jul 1828
Ellen	47	F		Gt. Britain	United States	John & Elizabeth	25 Sep 1827
Elzabeth	34	F	Farmer	Alsace in the Department of Upper and lower Rhine	United States	Carolina Augusta	16 May 1828
Emma	5		his Daughter [George R.]	England	United States	Cambria	19 Oct 1829
Emma	14	F	Farmer	England	England	Criterion	29 May 1822
Enoch	2	M				Sea Serpent	16 Sep 1820
Ephram	28	M	Cloth maker	St. New York	G.B.	Eliza Grant	29 Aug 1829
Ephram	28	M	Cloth Maker	Great Britain		Eliza Grant	29 Aug 1829
Ernest	3	F	his family [Jacob]	Germany	Pensylvania	Isabella	15 Sep 1828
Eryes	6		Boy	Swtserland	America	Saluda	18 Jun 1825
Esther	19	F	Spinster	Ireland	United States	Fabius	4 Jun 1828
F.	14	M		Great Britain	U. States	United States	8 Sep 1827
F.	36	M	Merchant	America	United States	Maria Theresa	28 Aug 1821
F. K.	47	M	Mechanic	America	United States	Two Marys	12 Feb 1820
Fanny	33	F	None	Great Britain	New York	Superior	5 Sep 1827
Filbence	4	M	his family [Jacob]	Germany	Pensylvania	Isabella	15 Sep 1828

NAMES OF PASSENGERS	AGE	SEX	OCCUPATIONS	COUNTRY TO WHICH THEY BELONG	COUNTRY THEY INTEND TO INHABIT	SHIPS/DATES OF ARRIVAL	
SMITH (cont'd)							
Frances	54	F		England	U. States	William Byrnes	17 Jul 1825
Francis	6	M	...	...	...	Antioch	8 Oct 1827
Francis	21	M	Labourer	Ireland	United States	Josephine	30 Apr 1828
Francis	24	M	Farmer	Great Brittain	U. States	Louisa	11 Jun 1824
Francis P.	22	M	Merchant	U.S.A.	U.S.A.	Silas Richards	7 Mar 1825
Frank	1	M		France	Unknown	Abby Jones	12 Jul 1827
Frank	34	M	Farmer	France	Unknown	Abby Jones	12 Jul 1827
Fras. A.	48	M	Planter	U.S.	U.S.	Minerva	3 Dec 1821
Frederica, his daughter [Tobias]	11					Martha	30 Jun 1823
Frederich	21	M	Merchant	Great Britain, Ireland	New York	Britannia	3 Nov 1827
Frederick	19	M	Merchant	U. Kingdom, G. Britain & Ireland	South Carolina	James Cropper	21 Oct 1825
Frederick	30	M	Farmer	England	United States	Cosmo	21 Aug 1828
G. W.	22	M	Merchant	Phila.	United States	Marmione	20 Nov 1821
Garrett	11	M	None	Ireland	New York	America	1 Aug 1828
Gary, Capt.	26	M	Mariner	United States	United States	Hunter	13 Feb 1829
Genuhil	47	M	Merchant	United States	United States	Cortes	5 Aug 1822
Geo.	5/12	M		Germany	America	Saluda	16 Oct 1824
Geo.	1	M	Clothier	G. Britain	Canada	Cosmo	25 Nov 1826
Geo.	6	M	None	Great Brittan	U. States	Gem	26 Jul 1827
Geo., Jr.	39	M	Collier	England	U. States	Czar	29 Aug 1829
Geo., Sr.	68	M	Collier	England	U. States	Czar	29 Aug 1829
Geo. A.	26	M	Devine	U. States	U.S.	Bayard	10 Nov 1824
Geo. R.	36	M	Merchant	England	U. States	Hudson	8 Oct 1827
George	4/12	M		England	U. States	Hudson	21 Aug 1829
George	20	M	Merchant	Great Britain	United States	Friends	13 Jun 1825
George	20 9/12	M	Farmer	Switzerland	America	Henry	17 May 1828
George	21 7/12	M	Farmer	Switzerland	America	Henry	17 May 1828
George	23	M	Grosser	Liverpool	New York	Washington	3 Mar 1828
George	25	M	Merchant	Spain	U. States	Pocahontas	9 Jun 1823
George	27	M	Merchant	Trinidad	United States	Abigail	23 Nov 1820
George	27	M	Gentn.	Great Brittain	United States	Robert Fulton	13 Mar 1827
George	29	M	Spinner	Great Britain	United States	Ganges	26 Oct 1826
George	29	M	Labourer	Hamilton, Hamilton [Parish], Lanark [County]	New York	Hero	19 May 1828
*to look for employment							
George	30	M	Labourer	Dublin	Dublin	Howard Douglass	11 May 1827
George	35	M	Merchant	America	America	Telegraph	18 May 1827
George	35	M	None	Cuba	United States	Ariel	30 Jun 1828
George	40	M	Mercht.	Great Britian	U. States	Hector	17 Aug 1825
George	43 3/12	M	Farmer	Switzerland	America	Henry	17 May 1828
George R.	37		Merchant	England	United States	Cambria	19 Oct 1829
George Robt.	36	M	Merchant	G. Brittan	U. States	Henry	24 Oct 1828
George W.	24	M	Farmer	England	England	Criterion	29 May 1822
Gordon	26	M	Mechanic	Scotland	U. States	Fanny	18 Dec 1826
Greenwood	2	M	None	Great Brittan	U. States	Gem	26 Jul 1827
H.	20	F	Lady	U. States	U. States	Pacific	11 Sep 1824
H.	22	M	Farmer	G. Britain	Upper Canada	Perseverance	9 Jun 1827
H.	22	M		America	America	Paragon	22 Sep 1827
H.	53	M	Mariner	Connecticutt	U. States	Ann	21 May 1824
H., Lieut.	27		U.S. Navy	U. States	United States	Henri IV	14 Sep 1827
H. B.	30	M	Merchant	Great Britain	Canada	Columbia	7 Sep 1827
Hanna	19 8/12	F	Farmer	Switzerland	America	Henry	17 May 1828
Hannah	8	F		Gt. Britain	United States	John & Elizabeth	25 Sep 1827
Hannah	8	F	Farmer	Great Britain	U. States	Eliza Grant	29 Aug 1829
Hannah	25	F		England	U. States	William Byrnes	17 Jul 1825
Hannah	31	F		Great Britain	U. States	Great Britain	18 Mar 1828
Harriet	16	F		Ireland	United States	Concordia	25 Aug 1827
Harriot	24	F	Lady	Great Britain	U. States	Hope & Esther	12 Nov 1825
Harriot	35	F	Tayloress	Halifax	United States	Genl. Marion	4 Jun 1828
Harriotann, Mrs.	21	M	Watchmaker	Boston	Boston	Amazon	30 Jul 1827

NAMES OF PASSENGERS	AGE	SEX	OCCUPATIONS	COUNTRY TO WHICH THEY BELONG	COUNTRY THEY INTEND TO INHABIT	SHIPS/DATES OF ARRIVAL	
SMITH (cont'd)							
Harry	40	M	Farmer	England	U. States	Emulous	22 Aug 1828
Helen	9	F		Scotland	U. States	Pleiades	9 Oct 1829
Henrietta	63	F	Lady	U. States	U. States	Pacific	11 Sep 1824
Henry	5	M		Great Britain	United States	India	5 Sep 1827
Henry	25	M	Merchant	America		Peruvian	28 Jul 1824
Henry	31	M	Farmer	G. Brittain	U. States	Rockingham	17 May 1821
Henry	46 5/12	M	Gentleman	England	United States	France	6 Oct 1828
Henry J.	36	M	Merchant	Columbia	United States	Allen	29 Mar 1824
Henry F.	24	M	Glass cutter			Washington	15 Sep 1821
Hugh	20	M	Farmers and Mechanics	Ireland	America	Constitution	1 Oct 1825
Hugh	30	M	Merchant	England	U. States	Roman	1 Dec 1828
Hugh C.	23	M	Merchant	U. States	Great Britain	Thompson	26 Apr 1828
Hy.	46	M	Farmer	Great Britian	U. States	Pallas	17 Aug 1824
Hy. T.	32	M	Merchant	New York	U. States	Mosquito	5 Dec 1821
Isaac	0 3/12			England	U.S. of America	Illinois	30 Apr 1823
Isaac	20	M	Weaver	Ireland	U. States of Amer.	Courier	17 Mar 1827
Isaac	44	M	Solder	England	United States	Warrior	6 Oct 1828
Isaac	45		Merchant	U. States	U. States	Nile	30 Apr 1827
Isaac	48	M	Merchant	U. States	U. States	Exchange	25 Sep 1826
Isaac, Mr.	16	M	Student	U. States	U. States	Henri IV	7 May 1827
Isaac K.	32	M	Mariner	United States	United States	Concordia	8 Sep 1823
Isabella	1	F	Child	Scotland	United States	Samuel Robertson	5 Oct 1827
Isabella	30	F		G. Britain	U. States	London	23 Sep 1828
Isabella	35	F		Scotland	United States	Samuel Robertson	5 Oct 1827
Ishmael	2	M	None	Great Brittan	U. States	Gem	26 Jul 1827
J.	27	M	Farmer	Germany	United States	Lydia	18 Jun 1828
J.	28	M	Rhode Island	U. States	U. States	Alpha	28 Apr 1828
J.	30		Merchant	U. States		New York	18 Jul 1828
J. M.	20	M	Baker	Germany	United States	Maria Theresa	28 Aug 1821
Jacob	2	M		Germany	America	Saluda	16 Oct 1824
Jacob	12		Boy	Swtserland	America	Saluda	18 Jun 1825
Jacob	35	M	Farmer	Germany	Pensylvania	Isabella	15 Sep 1828
Jacob	37	M	Shoemaker	Switzerland	America	Saluda	16 Oct 1824
James	7/12	M	Child	Ireland	U. States	Josephine	23 Jan 1829
James	3	M	Farmer	England	United States	Euphrates	18 Aug 1827
James	4	M		Scotland	U.S.	Curler	19 Jul 1828
James	7	M		Scotland	U. States	Pleiades	9 Oct 1829
James	12	M	Labourer	Great Britain	United States	Pacific	7 May 1827
James	16	M	Son	C. Darry	Philedelphia	Nile	18 Aug 1829
James	18		Farmer			Orion	21 Aug 1820
James	21	M	Merchant	England	United States	Nestor	20 Nov 1821
James	21	M	Labourer	Ireland	America	Plutarch	18 Jul 1826
James	21	M	Farmer	Ireland	United States	Concordia	25 Aug 1827
James	21	M	Brewer	Ireland	U.S.A.	Dalhouse Castle	21 Aug 1829
James	21	M	Brewer	Ireland	United States	Dalhouse Castle	21 Aug 1829
James	22	M	Cabinet Maker	Great Britain	U.S. of America	Gratitude	3 Oct 1829
James	23	M	Steward	U.S.A.	U.S.A.	Silas Richards	7 Mar 1825
James	23	M	Farmer	Ireland	United States	Henry Kneeland	7 Jun 1828
James	24	M	Farmer	Great Britain	United States	Ganges	8 Jul 1820
James	24	M	Farmers and Mechanics	Ireland	America	Constitution	1 Oct 1825
James	24	M	Shoemaker	Great Britain	U.S. of America	Gratitude	3 Oct 1829
James	25	M	Mercht.	U. States	U. States	America	17 Oct 1825
James	25	M	Labourer	Ireland	United States	Jubilee	13 Jul 1829
James	26	M	Grocer	Alloa	U. States	Sprightly	14 Jun 1822
James	26	M	Chandler	England	United States	Siroc	31 Dec 1829
James	27	M	Servant	England	Province of New Brunswick	Loire	3 Dec 1821
James	28	M	Laborer	Ireland	United States	St. Michaels	18 Jul 1826
James	28	M	Gentleman	C...	U. States	Agness	23 Jun 1827
James	30	M	Gentleman	St. Croix	U. States	Argo	11 Aug 1824
James	30	M	Farmer	England	United States	Manhattan	11 Oct 1824
James	32	M	Tailor	England	U. States	Congress	21 Nov 1823
James	35	M	Labourer	Ireland	United States	Lord Wellington	28 May 1827
James	36	M	Merchant	Gt. Brittain	United States	Balaena	9 Oct 1823

NAMES OF PASSENGERS	AGE	SEX	OCCUPATIONS	COUNTRY TO WHICH THEY BELONG	COUNTRY THEY INTEND TO INHABIT	SHIPS/DATES OF ARRIVAL	
SMITH (cont'd)							
James	36	M	...	England	America	Hercules	2 Nov 1825
James	41	M	Collier	Scotland	U. States	Czar	29 Aug 1829
James	44	M	...	Scotland	America	Nimrod	9 Jul 1827
James	48	M	Farmer		United States	Sarah	9 Nov 1820
James	50	M	Gent.	Scotland	U. States	William Thompson	25 Aug 1828
James	57	M	Cutter	England	United States	Peru	23 May 1827
James	66	M	Farmer	England	U. States	Lewis	1 Jul 1820
James B.	23	M				Amity	11 Sep 1820
James E.	22	M	Merchant	United States	United States	Nestor in Liverpool	29 Jul 1822
James Elnathan	29	M	Merchant	United States	New York, U.S.	Florida	2 Oct 1828
James T.	31	M	Gentleman	New York	New York	Halcyon	18 Apr 1828
Jane	2	F	None	England	U. States	Corinthian	20 Apr 1825
Jane	5	F		Ireland	United States	Clothier	22 Nov 1827
Jane	7	F		England	U. States	Unity	5 Sep 1828
Jane	13	F			United States	Sarah	9 Nov 1820
Jane	13	F		England	America	Britannia	22 Jul 1829
Jane	17	F	Servant	New York	New York	Nancy	16 Aug 1824
Jane	20	F		Ireland	N. Jersey	Potomac	7 Aug 1827
Jane	20	F		G. Britain	U. States	Camillus	8 Sep 1828
Jane	21	F		England	U. States	William Byrnes	17 Jul 1825
Jane	28	F	Servant	Bermuda	New York	Triton	11 Jul 1826
Jane	30	F	Merchant	Great Britain	U. States	Superb	28 May 1821
Jane	34	F	None	England	U. States	Corinthian	20 Apr 1825
Janes	40	M	Wever	Ireland	United States	Fabius	4 Jun 1828
Janett	24	F	Farmer	Scotland	United States	Friends	16 Aug 1824
Jas.	21	M	Plater	U. States	Great Britain	Thompson	26 Apr 1828
Jas.	22	M	M.D.	Gt. B.	Gt. B.	Caledonia	20 Jan 1829
Jas.	23	M	Smith	G. Britain	U. States	Cosmo	15 May 1827
Jas.	24	M		Great Britain	New York	Dublin	21 Dec 1824
Jas.	28	M	Laborer	Ireland	United States	Weser	29 Jul 1823
Jas.	35	M	Merchant			Frances	17 Aug 1820
Jas.	38	M	Merchant	W. Indies	U. States	William Smith	9 May 1822
Jas.	38	M	Weaver	Scotland	New York	Joseph Hume	26 Oct 1829
Jas.	50	M	Watchmaker	G. Britain	U. States	Cosmo	15 May 1827
Jas. B.	22	M	Merchant	U.S.	U.S.	Anita	5 May 1821
Jenny	40	F	Servant	Ireland	U. States	Nancy	25 Nov 1823
Jerh.	11	M	None	Great Brittan	U. States	Gem	26 Jul 1827
Jno.	13		Labourer	G. Britian	G. Britian	Dewitt Clinton	26 Aug 1825
Jno.	20	M	Servant	Curacoa	Curacoa	Hiram	14 Aug 1829
Jno.	21 9/12	M	... Weaver	Great Britain	Long Island	Venus	8 Sep 1820
Jno.	25	M	Gentleman	England	Great Britain	New York	22 Jul 1824
Jno.	27	M	Gent.	England	United States	Suffolk	12 Jan 1826
Jno.	29			England		Anacreon	7 Sep 1827
Jno.	35	M	Merchant	Philada.	U. States	Ganges	23 Oct 1821
Jno.	35	M	Sailor	America	U. States	Hiram	17 Jun 1826
Jno.	35	M	Blacksmith	France	U.S. America	Huntress	6 Sep 1827
Jno.	40	M	Laborer	Great Brittan	U. States	Gem	26 Jul 1827
Jno.	48	M	Weaver	France	United States	Stephania	6 Dec 1827
Jno.	5...	M	...	...	...	Antioch	8 Oct 1827
Jno.	56	M	Mariner	U. States	U. States	Emma	15 Apr 1822
Jno. A.	32	M	Merchant	Bermuda	Haytie	Pacification	31 Aug 1822
Job	18	M	Weaver	Great Britain	U. States	United States	8 Sep 1827
John	1	M		S...off...ton	United States	Java	9 Jul 1827
John	1	M	Farmer	England	America	Silas Richard	24 Oct 1829
John	1 4/12	M	Farmer	Switzerland	America	Henry	17 May 1828
John	2	M		England	U. States	Hudson	21 Aug 1829
John	4	M				Hesperus	2 Nov 1820
John	8	F	None	Great Britain	New York	Superior	5 Sep 1827
John	13	M	...	Scotland	America	Nimrod	9 Jul 1827
John	13	M		Scotland	U. States	Pleiades	9 Oct 1829
John	13 6/12	M	Farmer	Switzerland	America	Henry	17 May 1828
John	16	M	Wever	Ireland	United States	Fabius	4 Jun 1828
John	17	M		England	U. States	William Byrnes	17 Jul 1825
John	18	M		Church	U. States	Manhattan	21 May 1821
John	18	M	Servant	Ireland	United States	Carolina Ann	11 Dec 1826
John	18	M	Labourer	Ireland	America	Josephine	8 Dec 1827

NAMES OF PASSENGERS	AGE	SEX	OCCUPATIONS	COUNTRY TO WHICH THEY BELONG	COUNTRY THEY INTEND TO INHABIT	SHIPS/DATES OF ARRIVAL	
SMITH (cont'd)							
John	19	M	Labourer	Dull...	United States	Solon	21 Jun 1824
John	19	M	Weaver	Ireland	New York	Atlantic	8 May 1828
John	19		Stone Cuter	b. County of Tirone, last of Briming...	N. York	Peru	30 May 1828
John	19 9/12	M		England	U.S. of America	Illinois	30 Apr 1823
John	20	M	Labourer	England	United States	Roman	12 Jun 1826
John	20	F		Ireland	America	Wilson	27 Nov 1826
John	20	M	Tailor	Scotland	United States	Belmont	30 Aug 1828
John	20	M	Farmer	Great Britain	U. States	Eliza Grant	29 Aug 1829
John	21	M	Boot Maker	England	America	Manhattan	20 Mar 1820
John	21		Merchant	Ireland	United States	Robert Burns	18 Jun 1822
John	21	M	Miller	England	U. States	Solon	31 Aug 1822
John	21	M		Great Britain	U. States	Great Britain	18 Mar 1828
John	22	M	Farmer	England	United States	Andes	16 Sep 1820
John	22	M	Labourer	England	United States	Trident	18 Jul 1827
John	23	M	Cordwainer	Great Britain	United States	Birmingham	15 Jun 1827
John	24	M	Labourer	Ireland	United States	Jubilee	13 Jul 1829
John	24	M	Tailer	England	America	Sarah	18 Aug 1829
John	25			Ireland	United States	Trio	13 Jun 1827
John	25	M	Mechanic	G.B.	U.S.A.	Silas Richard	30 Jun 1828
John	26	M	Labourer	G. Britain	U. States	Margaret Bogle	12 Jun 1828
John	26 3/12	M	Farmer	Switzerland	America	Henry	17 May 1828
John	26 6/12	M	Weaver	Ireland	U. States	Josephine	23 Jan 1829
John	27	M	Printer	Great Britain	United States	William Dawson	18 Jun 1827
John	27	M		Great Brittian	United States	Carolina Augusta	2 Dec 1828
John	28	M	Gardner	Younghall, Great Britain	United States	Union	24 Sep 1823
John	28	M	Laborer	Great Britain	United States	Courier	26 Jun 1827
John	28	M	Farmer	Germany	United States	Lydia	18 Jun 1828
John	28	M	Labourer	Scotland	U. States	Czar	29 Aug 1829
John	30	M	Mariner	N. York	N. York	William Bayard	24 Jan 1825
John	30	M	Labourer	Gt. Britain	United States	Eliza Barker	11 Jan 1826
John	30	M	Merchant	U.S.A.	U.S.A.	Silas Richards	7 Mar 1827
John	30	M	Mechanic	England	United States	Wm. Byrnes	30 Apr 1828
John	30	M		Germany	United States	Lydia	18 Jun 1828
John	30	M	Grocer	U. States	U. States	Mary Howland	22 Sep 1828
John	30	M	Labourer	Scotland	U. States	Czar	29 Aug 1829
John	31	M	Cabinet Maker	Great Brittain	United States	United States	16 Feb 1827
John	31	M	Painter	New Castle	United States	Nile	17 May 1827
John	33	M	Ship Master	Great Britan	Great Britan	Columbia	10 Mar 1824
John	33	M	Labourer	Great Britain	United States	Pacific	7 May 1827
John	33	M	Servant	Scotland	United States	Tom	2 Jul 1827
John	34	M	Weaver	Scotland	New York	Joseph Hume	26 Oct 1829
John	35	M	Japanner	England	New York	Curler	7 Jul 1827
John	35	M	Labourer	Scotland	United States	Samuel Robertson	5 Oct 1827
John	35	M	Spinner	G. Brittain	U.S.	Olive Branch	28 Aug 1828
John	35 1/12	M	Millwright	England	United States	London	6 Feb 1829
John	38	M	Engineer	England	Newyork	Cortes	16 Jul 1827
John	38	M	Teacher	Great Britain	United States	Mary Howland	19 Jul 1827
John	40	M	Farmer	Great Britain	United States	Andes	19 Aug 1829
John	42	M	Farmer	Great Britain	New York	Eliza Grant	29 Aug 1829
John	42	M	Farmer	Great Britain	U. States	Eliza Grant	29 Aug 1829
John	45	M	Weaver	England	U. States	Congress	21 Nov 1823
John	45	M	Merchant	Richmond	Richmond	Wm. & Emiline	16 Jan 1827
John	45	M	Black Smith	England		Hudson	23 Jul 1828
John	46	M	Farmer	G. Britain	U.S. America	Cincinnatus	31 Oct 1820
John	46		Farmer	Scotland	United States	Hudson	5 Apr 1826
John	47	M	Farmer	Yorkshire	Yorkshire	Howard Douglass	11 May 1827
John	49	M	Machinist	England	United States	Aurora	21 Jun 1824
John	50	M	Merchant	U.S.	U.S.	Frances	21 Jul 1827
John	55	M	Tailor	U. States	U. States	United States	11 Sep 1828
John	70	M		Great Britain	United States	Mary	11 Jul 1820
John, (Junior)	16	M	Engineer	England	Newyork	Cortes	16 Jul 1827
John, Jr.	15		Farmer	Scotland	United States	Hudson	5 Apr 1826

NAMES OF PASSENGERS	AGE	SEX	OCCUPATIONS	COUNTRY TO WHICH THEY BELONG	COUNTRY THEY INTEND TO INHABIT	SHIPS/DATES OF ARRIVAL	
SMITH (cont'd)							
John E.	44	M	Merchant	United States	United States	James Monroe	25 Apr 1822
John H.	26	M	Carpenter	New Jersey	Boston, Mass.	Rubicon	22 May 1826
John L.	42	M	Taylor	Swtserland	America	Saluda	18 Jun 1825
John Lyon	23	M	Merchant			Frances	17 Aug 1820
John N.	45	M	None	United States	United States	Cuba	3 Jan 1823
John Oldham	22	M	Carpenter	Great Britain	N. York	Josephine	10 Dec 1825
John R.	29	M	Gent.	U. States	U. States	Hope & Esther	27 Sep 1824
John.	20	M	Farmer	Great Britain	New York	Eliza Grant	29 Aug 1829
Jos.	17	M		Bristol, Engd.	U. States	James Lyon	28 Aug 1828
Jos.	21	M	Farmer	Ireland	America	Mary	29 May 1827
Jos.	39			Great Britain	U. States America	Maria	22 May 1822
Jos.	47	M	Merchant	U. States	U. States	Natchez	18 Aug 1828
Jos. B.	26	M	Butcher	New York	N. York	William	14 Dec 1826
Josep	42	M	Gentleman	America	U. States	Sabina	18 Oct 1824
Joseph	4	M		Great Britain	United States	India	5 Sep 1827
Joseph	18	M	Merchant	U. States	U. States	Tally Ho	22 Mar 1825
Joseph	19	M	Clothier	England	U.S. States	Splendid	14 Aug 1829
Joseph	25	M	Laborer	England	United States	Danube	13 Jul 1827
Joseph	26	M	Farmer	Great Britain	United States	Eliza Barker	3 Jul 1826
Joseph	26	M	Farmer	Germany	Ohio	James Noble	27 Aug 1827
Joseph	26	M	Merchant	Great Britain, Ireland	New York	Britannia	3 Nov 1827
Joseph	28	M	Spinner	G. Brittain	U.S.	Olive Branch	28 Aug 1828
Joseph	32 6/12	M	Farmer	England	U.S. of America	Illinois	30 Apr 1823
Joseph	38	M	Shoe Maker	Ireland	United States	Samuel Robertson	9 Apr 1828
Josia	20		Farmer	Ireland		Westmoreland	1 Aug 1826
Josiah	20	M	Farmer	England	Ut. States	Courier	13 Jul 1826
Judeth	6	F	None	Ireland	United States	Lord Wellington	28 May 1827
Julia	5	F		France	Unknown	Abby Jones	12 Jul 1827
Julia	18	M		Albany	U. States	South Carolina	2 Aug 1822
Julius	34	M	Merchant	Connecticut	New Haven	Monroe	13 Feb 1827
L.	9	F	his family [Jacob]	Germany	Pensylvania	Isabella	15 Sep 1828
Laura	23	F		England		Suffolk	12 Jan 1826
Lawrence	40	M	Labourer			Lady of the Lake	23 Aug 1828
Lewis	25	M	Labourer	Ireland	U. States	Belville	5 Jul 1827
Lorenzo	9 2/12	M		England	U.S. of America	Illinois	30 Apr 1823
Louis	3	M	Farmer	Alsace in the Department of Upper and lower Rhine	United States	Carolina Augusta	16 May 1828
Louis	24	M	Farmer	Alsace in the Department of Upper and lower Rhine	United States	Carolina Augusta	16 May 1828
Louisa	3/12	F	his family [Jacob]	Germany	Pensylvania	Isabella	15 Sep 1828
Louisa	2	F	None	Great Britain	New York	Superior	5 Sep 1827
Louise	2	F	Farmer	Alsace in the Department of Upper and lower Rhine	United States	Carolina Augusta	16 May 1828
Lydia	23	F	Lady	England	United States	Florida	7 Feb 1825
M.	2	F		Gt. Britain	United States	John & Elizabeth	25 Sep 1827
M.	26	M	Labourer	Ireland	United States	Jubilee	13 Sep 1827
M.	31	M	Seaman	Ireland	U. States	Criterion	15 Oct 1822
Madaline	8/12	F	Farmer	Switzerland	America	Henry	17 May 1828
Magdelena, his daughter [Tobias]	8					Martha	30 Jun 1823
Marey	20	F	None	America	America	Hannibal	12 Oct 1826
Margaret	7	F	Child	Scotland	United States	Samuel Robertson	5 Oct 1827
Margaret	14	F	Spinster	Swtserland	America	Saluda	18 Jun 1825
Margaret	16	F		Ireland	U. States	Nancy	16 Aug 1822
Margaret	19	F	Servant	Ireland	New York	Atlantic	8 May 1828
Margaret	24	F	None	Great Britain	United States	Eliza Barker	3 Jul 1826
Margaret	29	F	None	Ireland	New York	America	1 Aug 1828

NAMES OF PASSENGERS	AGE	SEX	OCCUPATIONS	COUNTRY TO WHICH THEY BELONG	COUNTRY THEY INTEND TO INHABIT	SHIPS/DATES OF ARRIVAL	
SMITH (cont'd)							
Margaret	40	F	Farmer	Switzerland	America	Henry	17 May 1828
Margaret, Servant to			Servant to				
Edward Steward	17	F	Mr. E. Steward	England	United States	Caspian	12 Jul 1821
Margareta, his daughter							
[Tobias]	16	F				Martha	30 Jun 1823
Margery	18	F	None	Ireland	United States	Jubilee	12 May 1828
Margret	27	F	his family [Jacob]	Germany	Pensylvania	Isabella	15 Sep 1828
Margt.	22	F		U. States	United States	Sarah G.	15 May 1828
Margt.	40	F		U. States	United States	Sarah G.	15 May 1828
Maria	1 6/12	F		Great Britain	U.S. of America	Gratitude	3 Oct 1829
Maria	3	F		England	U. States	Unity	5 Sep 1828
Maria	8	F		Great Britain	U. States	United States	8 Sep 1827
Maria	23	F		U. States	U. States	Exchange	25 Sep 1826
Maria	33	F	None	Connecticut	New Haven	Monroe	13 Feb 1827
Marian	33	F		France	United States	Stephania	6 Dec 1827
Mark P.	3	M	Shoe Maker	Great Britain	United States	Dapper	21 Aug 1828
Martha	13	F	None	England	United States	Dalhouse Castle	6 Sep 1827
Martha	20	F	Servant	U. States	U. States	Carlo	19 Jun 1828
Martha	21	F	Farmer	Great Britain	New York	Eliza Grant	29 Aug 1829
Martha	21	F	Farmer	Great Britain	U. States	Eliza Grant	29 Aug 1829
Martha	22	F		Ireland	United States	Romulus	24 Jun 1826
Martha	28	F	Servant	Great Britain	United States	Sylvester Healy	23 Nov 1825
Martha	32	F	Shoe Maker	Great Britain	United States	Dapper	21 Aug 1828
Martha, his daughter							
[Tobias]						Martha	30 Jun 1823
*Born on board on the 13th of June							
Martin	28	M	None	G. Bt.	G. Bt.	Canada	13 Oct 1825
Mary		F	Chiefly farmers		United States	Factor	8 Jul 1829
Mary	1 3/12	F		Great Britain	U.S. of America	Gratitude	3 Oct 1829
Mary	1 6/12	F	Child of [John]	France		Aurora	21 Jun 1824
Mary	2	F			U. States	Congress	21 Nov 1823
Mary	5	F	Child	Scotland	United States	Samuel Robertson	5 Oct 1827
Mary	6	F		Scotland	U.S.	Curler	19 Jul 1828
Mary	7	F	None	Great Britain	United States	Ganges	26 Oct 1826
Mary	8	F				Sea Serpent	16 Sep 1820
Mary	8	F	Servant	Ireland	New York	Atlantic	8 May 1828
Mary	10	F	...	Scotland	America	Nimrod	9 Jul 1827
Mary	11	F		Scotland	U. States	Pleiades	9 Oct 1829
Mary	12	F	None	England	U. States	Corinthian	20 Apr 1825
Mary	13	F	None	Great Britain		Moro Castle	6 Jul 1827
Mary	14	F		Ireland	United States	John Dickinson	18 Feb 1822
Mary	14	F	None	Ireland	New York	America	1 Aug 1828
Mary	15	F		England	America	Britannia	22 Jul 1829
Mary	17	F	Spinster	Ireland	United States	Fabius	4 Jun 1828
Mary	17	F	Spinster	Ireland	United States	Fabius	4 Jun 1828
Mary	18	F		Ireland	U. States	Nancy	10 Jul 1822
Mary	19	F	Dress Maker	Ireland	United States	Carolina Ann	14 May 1827
Mary	19	F	Lady	New Brunswick	Canada	Belleville	29 Aug 1827
Mary	19	F	Spinster	United States	United States	James Monroe	12 Aug 1828
Mary	20	F		Ireland	U. States	Wanderer	1 Sep 1828
Mary	22	F		Scotland	United States	Indus	5 Sep 1827
Mary	23	F		Ireland	United States	William Byrnes	6 Apr 1826
Mary	23	F	Spinster	Ireland	U. States	Courier	17 Mar 1828
Mary	24	F		London		Catharine	19 Jul 1822
Mary	25	F	...	...	New Brunswick	Hanford	17 Oct 1828
Mary	25	F		Great Britain	U.S. of America	Gratitude	3 Oct 1829
Mary	26	F	Labourer	Gt. Britain	United States	Eliza Barker	11 Jan 1826
Mary	27		Servant	Denmark	U. States	South Carolina Packet	4 Sep 1822
Mary	27	F	None	Great Brit.	U.S.	Silvanus Jenkins	17 Mar 1828
Mary	27	F		England	United States	Cosmo	21 Aug 1828
Mary	28	F	Lady	Charleston, S.C.	Charleston, S.C.	Panthea	22 Jul 1826
Mary	30		Spinster	England	returns home	Mary	21 Sep 1821
Mary	30	F	None	Gt. Brittain	United States	Balaena	9 Oct 1823
Mary	31	M	Servant	Ireland	United States	Carolina Ann	11 Dec 1826
Mary	33	F		Switzerland	America	Saluda	16 Oct 1824
Mary	35	F	None	England	United States	London	21 May 1828

NAMES OF PASSENGERS	AGE	SEX	OCCUPATIONS	COUNTRY TO WHICH THEY BELONG	COUNTRY THEY INTEND TO INHABIT	SHIPS/DATES OF ARRIVAL	
SMITH (cont'd)							
Mary	36	F		England	New York	Hesperus	2 Nov 1820
Mary	40	F		Scotland	U. States	Pleiades	9 Oct 1829
Mary	41	F	Farmer	Great Britain	New York	Eliza Grant	29 Aug 1829
Mary	41	F	Farmer	Great Britain	U. States	Eliza Grant	29 Aug 1829
Mary	45	F	Spinster	Swtserland	America	Saluda	18 Jun 1825
Mary	50	F	...	...	...	Antioch	8 Oct 1827
Mary	60	F		London		Catharine	19 Jul 1822
Mary	60	F		England	United States	Peru	23 May 1827
Mary	60	F		Ireland	New York	York	2 Dec 1828
Mary, Servant to Edward Steward	17	F	Servant to Mr. E. Steward	England	United States	Caspian	12 Jul 1821
Mary Ann	38	F	Spinster	England	U. States	Trident	1 Dec 1824
Mary Ann	38	F		Great Britain		Corinthian	27 Oct 1829
Mary S. B.	33	M	Student	America	America	Lima	11 Dec 1823
Mat	30	M	Farmer	Ireland	United States	Dublin Packet	22 Aug 1829
Mathew	2/12	M	Farmer	Great Britain	New York	Eliza Grant	29 Aug 1829
Mathew	2/12	M	Farmer	Great Britain	U. States	Eliza Grant	29 Aug 1829
Mathew	1	M	None	Great Britain	United States	Eliza Barker	3 Jul 1826
Mathew	5	M		Germany	America	Saluda	16 Oct 1824
Mathew	30	M	Labourer	Ireland	America	Plutarch	18 Jul 1826
Matilda	10	F	Child	England	United States should they approve of it	Robert Edwards	20 Jan 1829
Michael	1	M	Farmer	Alsace in the Department of Upper and lower Rhine	United States	Carolina Augusta	16 May 1828
Michael	6	M	his family [Jacob]	Germany	Pensylvania	Isabella	15 Sep 1828
Michael	17		Labourer	Scotland	United States	Camillus	3 May 1828
Michael	21	M	Tailor	England	United States	India	8 Jun 1827
Michael	26	M	Labourer	Dull...	United States	Solon	21 Jun 1824
Michael	36	M	Farmer	Alsace in the Department of Upper and lower Rhine	United States	Carolina Augusta	16 May 1828
Michel	23		Labourer	County Carvan	N. York	Peru	30 May 1828
Michl.	21	M	Labourer	Ireland	United States	Henry Kneeland	7 Jun 1828
Milford	35	M	Merchant	United States	United States	Sarah G	11 Sep 1827
Moses C.	24	M	Mariner	U. States	U. States	Eliza	20 Aug 1824
Moses R.	54	M	Mariner	U. States	U. States	Patriot	28 Jun 1824
Nancy	14	F		Ireland	U. States	Nancy	10 Jul 1822
Nancy	26	F	None	England and Ireland	United States	Jubilee	12 May 1828
Nancy E.	8	F		England	U. States	Trident	1 Dec 1824
Nathan	43	M	Currier	England	America	John Wells	11 Jun 1823
Nezeor	13	M		England	America	Britannia	22 Jul 1829
Nicholas	22	M	Labourer	Ireland	United States	Jubilee	13 Jul 1829
Niel	50	M	Laborer	Gt. Britain		Dalhouse Castle	13 May 1828
Niles F.	24	M	Merchant	West Chester	U. States	Mary Ann	12 Jul 1824
Owen	32	M	Weaver	Ireland	United States	Atlantic	21 Jul 1827
P.	28	M		Swiss	U. States	Montano	2 Sep 1828
P.	30	F		England	U. States	Comet	24 Dec 1821
Parker	22	M	Butcher	United States	New London	Dime	15 Mar 1820
Pat	20	M		Ireland	United States	Essex	23 May 1828
Pat	30	M	Laborer	Ireland	United States	Carolina Ann	11 Dec 1826
Patrick	13	M	None	Ireland	New York	America	1 Aug 1828
Patrick	20	M	...	...	...	Indian Chief	8 Sep 1824
Patrick	23	M	None	Ireland	U. States	Franklin	7 Jul 1828
Patrick	26	M	Farmer	Ireland	United States	Lord Strangford	20 Jun 1826
Peggy	25	F	...	...	...	Dawn	19 Aug 1825
Perry	45	M	Merchant	Connecticutt	U. States	Alert	27 May 1825
Peter	21	M	Labourer	Ireland	United States	Thompson	12 Sep 1827
Peter	26	M	Labourer	Great Britain	United States	Penelope	11 Jun 1827
Peter	27	M	Mariner	St. Johns, N.B.	England	Peruvian	7 Oct 1825
Phil	30	M	Labourer			Evergreen	28 Jul 1820
Phil, Junr.	20	M	Labourer			Evergreen	28 Jul 1820
Philip	23	M	Labourer	Ireland	United States	Jubilee	13 Jul 1829
Philip	45	M	Farmer	Nova Scotia	U. States	Vermont	3 May 1827
R.	20	F				Hanford	17 Jul 1828

NAMES OF PASSENGERS	AGE	SEX	OCCUPATIONS	COUNTRY TO WHICH THEY BELONG	COUNTRY THEY INTEND TO INHABIT	SHIPS/DATES OF ARRIVAL	
SMITH (cont'd)							
R.	45	M	Ship master	United States	United States	Pagasus	21 Mar 1829
Rachel	20			Longford	Newyork	Peru	30 May 1828
Rachel	46	F	Labourer	Ireland	U. States	Belville	5 Jul 1827
Ragina	29	F	his family [Charles]	Germany	Pensylvania	Isabella	15 Sep 1828
Ralph	30	M	Farmer	England	U. States	Congress	21 Nov 1823
Rebecca	40	F		England	America	Britannia	22 Jul 1829
Reteline	24	M	Merchant	England	England	Eliza	31 Jul 1826
Richard	6	M		England	U. States	Hudson	21 Aug 1829
Richard	22	M	Butcher	Great Briton	United States	Mount Vernon	30 Dec 1828
Richard	23	M	Cabinet Maker	Gt. Britain	U. States	Sarah G.	14 Apr 1828
Richard	29	M	Labourer	England	U. States	Panthea	8 Apr 1826
Richard	37	M	Merchant	U. States	U. States	Stephania	24 Jul 1820
Richd.	13	M		England	U. States	William Byrnes	17 Jul 1825
Richd. G.	25	M	Mercht.	United States	United States	Manchester	6 Dec 1825
Robart	23	M	Labourer	Ireland	New York	Trusty	12 Sep 1828
Robert	1	M		Scotland	U. States	Pleiades	9 Oct 1829
Robert	10		his Son [George R.]	England	United States	Cambria	19 Oct 1829
Robert	17	M	Clerk	Ireland	United States	Carolina Ann	14 May 1827
Robert	22	M	Labourer	Scotland	U. States	Pleiades	9 Oct 1829
Robert	25	M	Taylor	England	United States	Hamlet	25 Aug 1825
Robert	26	M	Farmer	England	United States	Cincinnatus	21 Nov 1821
Robert	30	M	Laborer	Scotland	United States	Tom	2 Jul 1827
Robt.	19	M	Labourer	Ireland	United States	Fabius	31 Jul 1829
Robt.	21	M	Joiner	G. Britain	U. States	Robt. Edwards	4 Sep 1828
Robt.	30	M	Merchant	England	England	Genl. Victoria	7 Apr 1828
Robt.	40	M	Labourer	Great Britain	United States	William Dawson	18 Jun 1827
Robt.	56	M	Planter	G. Britain	U. States	Canada	19 Sep 1828
Robt. E.	30	M	Watchmaker	Gt. Britain	United States	Europa	20 Apr 1825
Roger	45	M	Mariner	Philada.	U. States	John	7 Jan 1825
Rose	8	F		Ireland	U. States	Nancy	10 Jul 1822
Rose	18	F	None	Ireland	United States	Jubilee	13 Jul 1829
Rt. C.	46	M	Farmer	Great Britain	Great Britain	Wyton	12 May 1821
Russell, Mr.	23	M	Watchmaker	Boston	Boston	Amazon	30 Jul 1827
S.	30	M	Mariner	United States		Pacific	24 Oct 1829
S.	35	M	Mechanic	U. States	U. States	Radius	18 Apr 1825
S.	45	M	Merchant	New York	U. States	John London	26 Mar 1822
S. F.	48	M	Mariner	United States	U. States	Harmony	12 Sep 1823
Sally	18	F	Daughter	C. Darry	Philedelphia	Nile	18 Aug 1829
Sally	26	F			Baltimore	Sea Serpent	16 Sep 1820
Sally	50	F	Wife	C. Darry	Philedelphia	Nile	18 Aug 1829
Sam	21	M	Farmer	Ireland	United States	Princess Charlotte	6 Oct 1827
Saml.	26	M	Block Maker	England		Boyer	9 May 1825
Saml.	54	M	Farmer	America	U. States	William Byrnes	17 Jul 1825
Saml., Jr.	19	M		England	U. States	William Byrnes	17 Jul 1825
Saml. H.	21	M	Merchant	London	U. States	Catharine	19 Jul 1822
Saml. K.	23	M	Doctor	London	U.S.	Panthea	13 Nov 1823
Samuel	6	M				Sea Serpent	16 Sep 1820
Samuel	24	M		Great Britain	United States	Ganges	8 Jul 1820
Samuel	25	M	Taylor	England	United States	Aurelia	7 Jun 1826
Samuel	25	M	Mechanic	England	United States	Wm. Byrnes	30 Apr 1828
Samuel	48	M	Merchant	America	America	Brittania	17 Jul 1828
Samuel D.	23	M	Merchant	New York	[Ditto, first in list]	Eliza Ann	12 Mar 1825
Sarah	3	F		Great Britain	U. States	Great Britain	18 Mar 1828
Sarah	5	F	None	England	U. States	Corinthian	20 Apr 1825
Sarah	5	F		England	U. States	Unity	5 Sep 1828
Sarah	20	F	None	Great Britain	N. York	Josephine	10 Dec 1825
Sarah	27	F		Great Britain	U.S. of America	Gratitude	3 Oct 1829
Sarah	30	F	None	Great Brittan	U. States	Gem	26 Jul 1827
Sarah	32	F	Weaver	Great Britain	United States	India	5 Sep 1827
Sarah	33	M		England	U. States	Unity	5 Sep 1828
Sarah	40	F		Great Britian	United States	Andes	19 Aug 1829
Sarah	56	F	None	England	United States	Dalhouse Castle	6 Sep 1827
Sarah, Mrs.	50	F	Carpenter	England	U.S.	Acasta	11 May 1827
Sidney	19	M	Farmer	England	U. States	Severn	12 Oct 1826
Silas		M	Mariner	U. States	U. States	Packet Margaret	19 Sep 1823
Simson	30	M	Labourer	Kings Co.	Kings Co.	Howard Douglass	11 May 1827

NAMES OF PASSENGERS	AGE	SEX	OCCUPATIONS	COUNTRY TO WHICH THEY BELONG	COUNTRY THEY INTEND TO INHABIT	SHIPS/DATES OF ARRIVAL	
SMITH (cont'd)							
Size [?]	6	F		Switzerland	U.S.	C. Amelia	30 Jun 1828
Sophia	7	F	Farmer	Alsace in the Department of Upper and lower Rhine	United States	Carolina Augusta	16 May 1828
Sophia	8	F	None	England	U. States	Corinthian	20 Apr 1825
Sophia	32 4/12	F		England	U.S. of America	Illinois	30 Apr 1823
Stella	13	F	Lady	U. States	U. States	Pacific	11 Sep 1824
Stewart	10	M		U. States	United States	Sarah G.	15 May 1828
Susan N. Y., Mrs.	30 3/12	F		United States, State of New Jersey	United States, ...	Active	8 Apr 1822
Susanna	21	F	Servant	U. States	U. States	Henry	24 Nov 1828
Susannah	34	F		England	United States	Hannibal	6 Sep 1824
Sylvester	21	M	Labourer	Great Britain	United States	Thomas Dickason	14 Sep 1827
T. C.	30	M	Merchant	Boston	U. States	Sarah	1 Aug 1827
Terrence	34	M	B. Smith	Great Britain	United States	Blakely	29 Sep 1826
Th...a...	5	F		France	United States	Stephania	6 Dec 1827
Thomas	6	M		Great Britain	U. States	Great Britain	18 Mar 1828
Thomas	7	M	Shoe Maker	Great Britain	United States	Dapper	21 Aug 1828
Thomas	9	M	Farmer			Manhattan	25 Dec 1820
Thomas	12 3/12	M		England	U.S. of America	Illinois	30 Apr 1823
Thomas	13	M	Farmer	Great Britain	New York	Eliza Grant	29 Aug 1829
Thomas	13	M	Farmer	Great Britain	U. States	Eliza Grant	29 Aug 1829
Thomas	18	M		America	U. States	Hiram	17 Jun 1826
Thomas	21	M	Labourer	Ireland	United States	Jubilee	13 Jul 1829
Thomas	22	M	Servant	Great Britain	Pennsylvania	Thames	16 May 1821
Thomas	22	M	Merchant	Great Britain	United States	Cortes	19 Nov 1821
Thomas	22	M	Baker	Great Britan	United States	Silvanus Jenkins	10 Mar 1827
Thomas	23	M	Farmer	England	England	Criterion	29 May 1822
Thomas	23	M	Weaver	Ireland	N. Jersey	Potomac	7 Aug 1827
Thomas	24	M	Merchant	Coventry	U. States	New York	15 Nov 1823
Thomas	24	M	Weaver	Great Britain	United States	Roman	10 May 1828
Thomas	25	M	Merchant	U. Kingdom, G. Britain & Ireland	South Carolina	James Cropper	21 Oct 1825
Thomas	25	M	Mechanic	United States	United States	Tampico	12 Mar 1827
Thomas	25	M	Labourer	England	United States	Trident	18 Jul 1827
Thomas	25	M		Great Brittain	United States	Active	12 Sep 1828
Thomas	26	M	Labourer			Evergreen	28 Jul 1820
Thomas	26	M	Baker	Great Britain	U.S. of America	Gratitude	3 Oct 1829
Thomas	26 7/12	M	Master	England	United States	Nimrod	28 Apr 1824
Thomas	27	M	Merchant	Charleston	Charleston	New York	14 Nov 1826
Thomas	27	M	Carpenter	England	United States	Siroc	31 Oct 1829
Thomas	28	M	Weaver	Ireland	Ireland	Trident	17 May 1825
Thomas	30	M	Stone Mason	Great Britan	United States	Clematis	8 May 1827
Thomas	30	M	Labourer	Scotland	United States	Concordia	25 Aug 1827
Thomas	31	M	Brick Maker	Great Britain	U. States	Great Britain	18 Mar 1828
Thomas	31	M	Farmer	England	America	Silas Richard	24 Oct 1829
Thomas	34	M	Sawyer	England	United States	Trident	31 Mar 1827
Thomas	36 11/12	M	Sheet Maker	Scotland	United States	Mobile	21 Aug 1827
Thomas	50	M	Gentleman	Great Britain	U. States	Silas Richard	30 Jun 1828
Thomas	50	M	Lawyer	N. York	Inhabitant N. York	Nile	18 Aug 1829
Thomas	52	M	Smith	Great Britain	United States	Freake	11 Dec 1827
Thomas	70	M	on a visit Returning home	Pensylvany	Pensylvany	Nile	18 Aug 1829
Thomas C., Esq.	25	M	Merchant	United States		Romp	12 Sep 1823
Thomas L.	18	M	Student	Bermuda		Lancatter	5 Jul 1820
Thomas T.	22	M	Merchant	U. States	U.S.	Bramin	16 Feb 1824
Thoms. Robt.	36	M		Great Britain		Corinthian	27 Oct 1829
Thos.	8	M	None	Great Brittan	U. States	Gem	26 Jul 1827
Thos.	14	M	...	...	...	Antioch	8 Oct 1827
Thos.	20	M	Doctor	Great Britain	United States	Diana	6 Jul 1829
Thos.	22	M	Gentleman	Great Britain	New York	Superior	5 Sep 1827
Thos.	23	M	Merchant	United States	United States	New York	12 Nov 1822
Thos.	23 8/12	M	... Weaver	Great Britain	Long Island	Venus	8 Sep 1820
Thos.	27	M	Sawmaker	Engd.	United States	Cosmo	21 Aug 1828

NAMES OF PASSENGERS	AGE	SEX	OCCUPATIONS	COUNTRY TO WHICH THEY BELONG	COUNTRY THEY INTEND TO INHABIT	SHIPS/DATES OF ARRIVAL	
SMITH (cont'd)							
Thos.	30	M	Gent.	Great Britain	New York	Dublin	21 Dec 1824
Thos.	30	M	Mechanic	France	U. States	Lewis	6 Jul 1825
Thos.	30	M	Clothier	G. Britain	Canada	Cosmo	25 Nov 1826
Thos.	30		Brick Layer	G. Britain		Casanda	5 Sep 1827
Thos.	42	M	Gentleman	St. Croix	Denmark	Chase	4 Sep 1821
Thos.	50	M	Farmer	England	America	Panthia	17 Sep 1821
Thos.	55	M	Gentleman	England	U.S. America	Criterion	27 Oct 1821
Thos. C.	25	M	Merchant	Boston	U. States	Laura	8 Dec 1821
Thos. L.	24	M	Student	Bermuda	U. States	Superior Hope	27 Oct 1824
Thos. Mitchell	28	M	Merchant	England	New York	Robert Edwards	17 Mar 1828
Timothy	22	M	Baker	England	United States	Essex	23 May 1828
Tobias	53	M	Black Smith	Germany	United States	Martha	30 Jun 1823
W.	26	M	Mechanic	France	U. States	Lewis	6 Jul 1825
W.	45	M	Merchant	America	America	Rubicon	7 Oct 1826
W. J.	23	M	Merchant	United States	Charleston	Cortes	7 Jul 1821
Warren	18	M	Servant	United States	United States	Only Daughter	29 Apr 1825
Wilalmina	7 4/12	F		England	U.S. of America	Illinois	30 Apr 1823
Wilhelmina, his daughter [Tobias]	5					Martha	30 Jun 1823
William	1	M	Shoe Maker	Great Britain	United States	Dapper	21 Aug 1828
William	3	M	Child	Scotland	United States	Samuel Robertson	5 Oct 1827
William	3	M	Farmer	Great Britain	New York	Eliza Grant	29 Aug 1829
William	3	M	Farmer	Great Britain	U. States	Eliza Grant	29 Aug 1829
William	6	M		Ireland	United States	Carolina Ann	11 Dec 1826
William	10	M		England	America	Britannia	22 Jul 1829
William	13	M		Germany	United States	Two Marys	12 Feb 1820
William	16		Farmer	Ireland	United States	Carolina Ann	12 Sep 1823
William	16	M	Boy	Ireland	United States	Dublin Packet	23 May 1828
William	18	M	Farmer	Ireland	United States	Dublin Packet	13 Oct 1828
William	22	M	Brush maker	England	United States	Hamilton	13 Nov 1827
William	23	M	Sawyer	Great Britain	United States	Unity	20 Oct 1829
William	23 6/12	M	Weaver	Great Briton	uncertain	Mount Vernon	29 Aug 1828
William	25	M	Butcher	England	Pennsylvania	Governor Fenner	23 Jul 1829
William	26	M	Optician	Great Britain	United States	Rosina	28 May 1827
William	26	M	Labourer	New Brunswick	Canada	Belleville	29 Aug 1827
William	27	M		Argyle (Tedland) Scotland	United States	Jean Hastie	27 Jul 1829
William	28	M	Farmer	Great Britain	N. York	Josephine	10 Dec 1825
William	29	M	Saw Maker	England	United States	St. George	25 Aug 1829
William	29	M		Ireland	United States	St. George	25 Aug 1829
William	30	M	Carpenter	England	United States	India	8 Jun 1827
William	30		Painter & Glazier	England	United States	Corinthian	7 Jul 1829
William	35	M	Shoe Maker	Great Britain	United States	Dapper	21 Aug 1828
William	35	M	Taylor	Great Britain	United States	Samuel Wright	12 Oct 1829
William	36	M	Merchant	Great Britain	United States	Rosina	12 Aug 1823
William	38	M	Merchant	Great Britain	Great Britain	Eliza Ann	5 Jun 1826
William	38	M	Laborer	Great Brittan	U. States	Gem	26 Jul 1827
William	39	M	Merchant	England	United States	Aurora	5 Sep 1826
William	44	M	E...rr...or	England	America	Mary Lord	26 Oct 1829
William	50	M	Clerk	England	United States	William & Henry	19 Jul 1822
William	50	M	Weaver	C. Darry	Philedelphia	Nile	18 Aug 1829
William	64	M	Farmer	Scotland	Canada	Governor Fenner	23 Jul 1829
William	65		Ladies and Gentlemen	England	United States	Corinthian	7 Jul 1829
William, boy	9	M	Labourer	United States	New York	John London	7 Apr 1824
William [crossed out]	23		Cape May Seaman	U. States		Columbia	17 Apr 1827
*Destitute American Seaman							
William Henry	22	M	Commedian	England		Britannia	20 Jun 1827
William L.	30	M	Wheelwright	Great Britain	New York	Superior	5 Sep 1827
Willm.	25	M	Laboror	Ireland	United States	Wilson	27 Jun 1826
Willm.	28	M	weaver	Ireland	United States	Robert Edwards	3 Oct 1829
Wm.	1	M		England	United States	Cosmo	21 Aug 1828
Wm.	2	M	Clothier	G. Britain	Canada	Cosmo	25 Nov 1826
Wm.	10	M	None	Great Brittan	U. States	Gem	26 Jul 1827

NAMES OF PASSENGERS	AGE	SEX	OCCUPATIONS	COUNTRY TO WHICH THEY BELONG	COUNTRY THEY INTEND TO INHABIT	SHIPS/DATES OF ARRIVAL	
SMITH (cont'd)							
Wm.	12	M	...	...	...	Antioch	8 Oct 1827
Wm.	14	M	Farmer	Ireland		Cuba	24 Jun 1822
Wm.	15	M		Nassau	Nassau	Sarah Delight	20 Jun 1825
Wm.	16	M		England	U. States	William Byrnes	17 Jul 1825
Wm.	18			Great Britain	U. States America	Maria	22 May 1822
Wm.	21	M	Gentleman	England	England	Brittania	17 Jul 1828
Wm.	23	M	Farmer	England	U.S. America	Criterion	27 Oct 1821
Wm.	24	M	Farmer	G. Britain	U. States	Camillus	8 Sep 1828
Wm.	25			b. Ireland, last of Yorkshire	Ohio	Peru	30 May 1828
Wm.	26	M	Merchant	Great Britain	U. States	William Thompson	24 Aug 1827
Wm.	27	M	Weaver	England	United States	Hamlet	25 Aug 1825
Wm.	27	M	Weaver	England	New York	Phoenix	29 Apr 1826
Wm.	28	M	Merchant	England	Canada	Corinthian	20 Apr 1825
Wm.	28	M	Tinnor	S...off...ton	United States	Java	9 Jul 1827
Wm.	30	M	Mechanic	Great Britain	United States	Greek	23 Jan 1828
Wm.	35	M	Bricklayer	Great Britain		Moro Castle	6 Jul 1827
Wm.	35	M	Cotton Spinner	G. Britain	U. States	Mary & Harriot	8 Sep 1828
Wm.	36	M	Merchant	Great Britain	U. States	Superb	28 May 1821
Wm.	49	M	Merchant	England	U. States	Gleaner	4 Oct 1828
Wm.	60	M	Merchant	England	England	Genl. Victoria	7 Apr 1828
Wm. C.	22	M	Merchant	England	United States	Florida	7 Feb 1825
Wm. C.	33	M	Mercht.	England	United States	Hannibal	6 Sep 1824
Wm. H.	35	M	Gentleman	Philadelphia	U. States	Bayard	7 Mar 1825
Wm. R.	27	M	Merchant	New York	U.S.	Montano	24 Jun 1823
Zackariah	20	M	Merchant	New Brunswick	Great Brittain	Nancy	9 Jun 1821
SMITHERS, George	21	M	Coachmaker	England	U. States	Stephania	26 Apr 1824
George	34	M	Miner	England	U. States	Pleiades	9 Oct 1829
John	10	M		England	U. States	Pleiades	9 Oct 1829
W.	45	M	Gentleman	Great Britain	United States	Isaac Hicks	6 Dec 1827
SMITHMAN, Thos.	36	M	Farmer	England	U. States	Bayard	11 Mar 1823
SMITHURST, John, Revd.	31	M	Preacher	Great Britain	United States	Ganges	8 Jul 1820
SMITMAN, Conrite	26	M	Baker	Germany	United States	Quito	16 Jun 1826
SMITON, James	27	M	C... Maker	Scotland	United States	Liverpool Trader	24 Oct 1825
SMOAT, Jacob	21	M	Miller	Switzerland	United States	Elbe	2 Aug 1822
SMOOK, Sarah	9	F	Child	Gt. Britain	U. States	New York Packet	6 Aug 1824
SMYE, Joseph	23	M	Carpenter			Czar	29 Aug 1829
SMYTH, —	35	F		Ireland	United States	Thomas	13 Dec 1827
Alice	18	F	Servant	Ireland	New York	Atlantic	8 May 1828
Andrew	7	M	Child	Ireland	U. States	William & John	10 Jul 1824
Ann	...	F	...	Ireland	United States	Carolina Ann	24 Oct 1825
Archibald	19	M	Clerk	Derry	...	Gleaner	24 May 1823
Bill	9	M	Child	Ireland	U. States	William & John	10 Jul 1824
Catherine	23			Baltimore	U. States	Almira	15 Jul 1822
Charles	25	M	Clerk	England	United States	Dublin Packet	6 Dec 1827
Christina	28	F		Ireland	United States	Clothier	22 Nov 1827
Corn.	20	M	Labourer	Ireland	New York	Atlantic	8 May 1828
Eliza	48	F	Widow	Ireland	U. States	William & John	10 Jul 1824
Eliza Jane	7	F	Child	Ireland	U. States	William & John	10 Jul 1824
Elizabeth	18	F		Ireland	United States	John Dickinson	18 Feb 1822
Elizth.	55		Farmer	Ballymore	Ireland	Carolina Ann	21 May 1823
Esther	11	F	Child	Ireland	U. States	William & John	10 Jul 1824
Geo.	30	M	Doctor	England	China	Venus	4 Oct 1824
Grace	33	F	Wife	Ireland	United States	Louisa	18 Apr 1827
Henry	16	M		Ireland	United States	Gem	16 Jun 1824
Henry	21	M	Labourer	Ireland	United States	Princess Charlotte	26 Apr 1827
Hugh	22	M	Weaver	Ireland	United States	Trident	16 May 1826
Hugh	25	M	Labourer	Ireland	New York	Atlantic	8 May 1828
Hugh	30	M	Merchant	Baltimore	Baltimore	Hesperus	7 Jul 1820
J. S. G., Sir, Brit.	45	M	Colonel	England	England	Florida	17 May 1825
James	11	M	Child	Ireland	U. States	William & John	10 Jul 1824
James	18	M	Labourer	Ireland	United States	Princess Charlotte	26 Apr 1827

NAMES OF PASSENGERS	AGE	SEX	OCCUPATIONS	COUNTRY TO WHICH THEY BELONG	COUNTRY THEY INTEND TO INHABIT	SHIPS/DATES OF ARRIVAL	
SMYTH (cont'd)							
James	28	M	Printer	Ireland	United States	Henry Kneeland	7 Jun 1828
James	30	M	Farmer	Ireland	U. States	William & John	10 Jul 1824
James	40	M	Laborer	Ireland	United States	Mary	1 Jul 1829
James	41	M	...	Ireland	United States	Gem	16 Jun 1824
James	50		Farmer	Ballymore	Ireland	Carolina Ann	21 May 1823
Jane	12	F		Ireland	United States	John Dickinson	18 Feb 1822
Jane	40	F	Widow	Ireland	U. States	William & John	10 Jul 1824
John	12	M	Labourer	Ireland	U. States	William & John	10 Jul 1824
John	23	M	Muslin Manufactor	Ireland	United States	Louisa	18 Apr 1827
John	31	M	Farmer	Ireland	United States	Clothier	22 Nov 1827
Margt.	15	F	Spinster	Ireland	U. States	William & John	10 Jul 1824
Margt.	22	F	Servant	Ireland	United States	Trident	16 May 1826
Martha	23	F	Spinster	Ireland	U. States	William & John	10 Jul 1824
Mary	1	F		Ireland	United States	Clothier	22 Nov 1827
Mary	13	F	Servant	Ireland	New York	Atlantic	8 May 1828
Mary	18	F	Dressmaker	Ireland	U. States	Erin	5 Jul 1820
Mary	18	F	Spinster	Ireland	U. States	William & John	10 Jul 1824
Mary	23	F	Servant	Ireland	New York	Atlantic	8 May 1828
Patrick	14	M	Servant	Ireland	New York	Atlantic	8 May 1828
Patrick	22	M	Weaver	Ireland	U. States	Josephine	7 May 1827
Patrick	22 6/12	M	Labourer	Ireland	U. States	Courier	17 Mar 1828
Paul	22	M	Labourer	Ireland	U. States	Josephine	7 May 1827
Peter	29	M	Planter	Ireland	America	Minerva	31 May 1824
Ralph	30	M	Labourer	Ireland	United States	Clothier	22 Nov 1827
Robert	26	M	Physician	Ireland	England	Josephine	7 May 1827
Saml.	9	M	Child	Ireland	U. States	William & John	10 Jul 1824
Samuel	12		Farmer	Ballymore	Ireland	Carolina Ann	21 May 1823
Terence	20	M	Labourer	Ireland	New York	Atlantic	8 May 1828
Thomas S.	24	M		England	England	Birmingham	16 Jun 1828
Thos.	11	M		Ireland	United States	John Dickinson	18 Feb 1822
W.	1		Farmer	Ireland		Schuylkill	22 Aug 1825
Wm.	21	M	Farier	Ireland	Ut. States	Courier	13 Jul 1826
Wm.	33	M	Merchant	Baltimore	Baltimore	Hesperus	7 Jul 1820
SMYTHEMAN, Thos.	25	M	Farmer	England	United States	Nancy	15 Mar 1820
SNALE, Wm.	28	M	Upolsterer	Lpool.	Lpool.	Howard Douglass	11 May 1827
SNEAD, John	45	M	Merchant	U. States	U. States	Nelson	13 Aug 1821
SNEED, Ann	38	F		England	U. States	Cincinnatus	24 May 1821
Edward	5	M		England	U. States	Cincinnatus	24 May 1821
George	15	M	Butcher	Great Britain	Pennsylvania	Venus	8 Sep 1820
Henry	8	M		England	U. States	Cincinnatus	24 May 1821
John	12	M	Lad	England	U. States	Cincinnatus	24 May 1821
John	43	M	Farmer	Great Britain	Pennsylvania	Venus	8 Sep 1820
Joseph	40	M	Butcher	England	U. States	Cincinnatus	24 May 1821
Mary Ann	1	F		England	U. States	Cincinnatus	24 May 1821
Ruth	46 10/12	F	his wife [John]	Great Britain	Pennsylvania	Venus	8 Sep 1820
SNELL, B.	47	M	Mariner	U. States	U. States	Fly	22 Oct 1823
John	45	M	Joiner	England	United States	Danube	13 Jul 1827
Quin	50	M	Labourer	England	Pittsburgh	Orozimbo	8 Jun 1822
SNELLING, F. H.	21	M	Merchant	Canada	Canada	Lucinda	11 Nov 1824
George H.	21		Gentleman	Boston	United States	London	13 Dec 1822
SNIDER, Adam	3	M	Book Binder	Bavaria	United States	American	27 Aug 1827
Barbara	2 1/12	F	Farmer	Switzerland	United States	France	6 Oct 1828
Daniel	5	M	Book Binder	Bavaria	United States	American	27 Aug 1827
Eliza	7 3/12	F	Farmer	Switzerland	United States	France	6 Oct 1828
Elizabeth	24 2/12	F	Farmer	Switzerland	United States	France	6 Oct 1828
Elizabeth	25	F	Book Binder	Bavaria	United States	American	27 Aug 1827
Henry	28	M	Tailor	United States	United States	Globe	30 Aug 1828
Jacob	7	M	Book Binder	Bavaria	United States	American	27 Aug 1827
Jacob	30 7/12	M	Farmer	Switzerland	United States	France	6 Oct 1828
Jacob	32	M	Book Binder	Bavaria	United States	American	27 Aug 1827
Othello	25	F		Amsterdam	New Jersey	Margaret	18 Aug 1825
Thomas	31	M				Eliza Grant	6 Oct 1828
Valentine	23	M	Merchant	Amsterdam	New Jersey	Margaret	18 Aug 1825
SNIER, Barbary	34	F		Amsterdam	New Jersey	Margaret	18 Aug 1825
Catharine	4	F	Child	Amsterdam	New Jersey	Margaret	18 Aug 1825
Joseph	7	M	Child	Amsterdam	New Jersey	Margaret	18 Aug 1825
Joseph	36	M	Miller	Amsterdam	New Jersey	Margaret	18 Aug 1825

NAMES OF PASSENGERS	AGE	SEX	OCCUPATIONS	COUNTRY TO WHICH THEY BELONG	COUNTRY THEY INTEND TO INHABIT	SHIPS/DATES OF ARRIVAL	
SNIER (cont'd)							
Susannah	2	F	Child	Amsterdam	New Jersey	Margaret	18 Aug 1825
SNOCA, Peter W.	40	M	Merchant	United States	U.S.	Chauncy	14 Mar 1820
SNODGRASS, Hannah	18	F		Ireland	United States	Sarah G.	15 May 1828
SNOLY, —	22	F	Cooper	Switzerland	Swizland	Le Voltaire	19 Jul 1828
SNOOK, Ann	42	F	Wife	Gt. Britain	U. States	New York Packet	6 Aug 1824
Betsey	16	F	Child	Gt. Britain	U. States	New York Packet	6 Aug 1824
Grace	14	F	Child	Gt. Britain	U. States	New York Packet	6 Aug 1824
Harriet	11	F	Child	Gt. Britain	U. States	New York Packet	6 Aug 1824
Isaac	1	M	Child	Gt. Britain	U. States	New York Packet	6 Aug 1824
John	23	M	Child	Gt. Britain	U. States	New York Packet	6 Aug 1824
Mary	16	F	Child	Gt. Britain	U. States	New York Packet	6 Aug 1824
William	3	M	Child	Gt. Britain	U. States	New York Packet	6 Aug 1824
Wm.	42	M	Farmer	Gt. Britain	U. States	New York Packet	6 Aug 1824
SNOW, Benjn.	19	M	Merchant	Great Britain	America	Spartan	5 May 1826
H. R.	40	M	Merchant	Connecticut	U. States	Ann Maria	11 Jun 1828
James	17	M	Merchant	Halifax	U. States	Tiger	21 Jul 1825
John	1	M	Taylor	Great Britain	U. States America	Ann Maria	29 Nov 1821
John	22	M	Taylor	Great Britain	U. States America	Ann Maria	29 Nov 1821
Matilda	3	F	Taylor	Great Britain	U. States America	Ann Maria	29 Nov 1821
Matilda	20	F	Taylor	Great Britain	U. States America	Ann Maria	29 Nov 1821
Reuben	34	M	Mariner	U. States	U. States	Fabius	9 Jul 1824
Wiliam	21	M	Gentleman	United States		Chase	13 Apr 1821
SNOWDEN, C.	30	F		Philada.	U. States	Decatur	3 May 1821
D.	35	M	Mariner	Philada.	U. States	Decatur	3 May 1821
Esther	40	F	None	England	U. St.	Manchester	7 Dec 1826
James	30	M	Farmer	England		Manhattan	22 May 1827
Joseph	27	M	Merchant	Grt. Britain	United States	Cortes	7 Jul 1821
SNOWDON, William	30	M	Smith			Eliza Jane	12 Sep 1820
SNOWDOWN, Jno.	28		Ship Manufacturer	Sunderland, Eng.	United States	Hudson	18 Jun 1825

*Officers, Seamen and Passengers belonging to the Ship Jane of Boston and taken from on board the Schooner Olive of St. Johns , N.B. on the 4th June 1825, Lat. 41.30, Long 53.19, which ship foundered on the 31st ultimo in Lat. 41.44 Long 52.

NAMES OF PASSENGERS	AGE	SEX	OCCUPATIONS	COUNTRY TO WHICH THEY BELONG	COUNTRY THEY INTEND TO INHABIT	SHIPS/DATES OF ARRIVAL	
SNURRY, Eliz.	30			England	United States	Hugh Johnson	11 Jun 1828
Henry	1		Labourer	England	United States	Hugh Johnson	11 Jun 1828
Henry	27		Labourer	England	United States	Hugh Johnson	11 Jun 1828
John	10		Labourer	England	United States	Hugh Johnson	11 Jun 1828
SNYDER, Barbara	1	F		Germany	Pensylvania	Isabella	15 Sep 1828
Benjamin	40	M		Taylor	United States	Spartan	21 Aug 1824
Catherine	24	F		Germany	Pensylvania	Isabella	15 Sep 1828
Joseph	32	M	Butcher	Germany	Pensylvania	Isabella	15 Sep 1828
Margret	3	F		Germany	Pensylvania	Isabella	15 Sep 1828
Martin	17	M	Weaver	Germany	U. States	Rook	25 Jul 1827
SOAN, Henry	40	F	Farmer	Brittian	U. States	Acasta	28 Jan 1823
James	9	M	Child	Brittian	U. States	Acasta	28 Jan 1823
John	4	M	Child	Brittian	U. States	Acasta	28 Jan 1823
Susannah	40	F	Wife	Brittian	U. States	Acasta	28 Jan 1823
William	1	M	Child	Brittian		Acasta	28 Jan 1823
SOAVEY, Ellen	30	F		Ireland	U. States	Fame	15 Nov 1826
SODERMAYER, George	45	M	...	...	...	George	23 Sep 1824
SOFFLE, Joh. George	23	M	Waggon...	Wirtemburg	United States	Wade	29 Aug 1825
SOFTLY, John	23	M	Carpenter	England	America	Morning Star	16 Feb 1824
SOHLEMNAR, J.	20	M	Wheelwright	Germany	U. States	Exchange	28 Aug 1828
SOIER, Joseph	49	M	Farmer			Henri IV	17 May 1828
SOINEST, Jno. S.	28	M	Gentleman	Tangiers	U. States	Montano	2 Sep 1824
SOLA, P.	23	M	Clerk	Italy	U. States	Seneca	7 Nov 1825
SOLELLO, Lewis	20	M	Servant	Panama	Panama	Morhey	3 Mar 1825
SOLER, Eliza	20	F	Servant	Scotland	Columbia	Abigail	25 Feb 1826
SOLETANSTALL, Saml.	55		Merchant	Massachusetts	New York	James Cropper	12 Jul 1822
SOLLESSE, John M.	22	M	Manufacturer	Switzerland		Nimrod	21 Sep 1820

NAMES OF PASSENGERS	AGE	SEX	OCCUPATIONS	COUNTRY TO WHICH THEY BELONG	COUNTRY THEY INTEND TO INHABIT	SHIPS/DATES OF ARRIVAL	
SOLMON, Christopher	21	M	Joiner	England	Philadelphia	Indian Chief	19 Jun 1823
SOLN, Maria	42	F	Servant	Mexico	United States	General Warren	8 Jul 1829
SOLO, C.	14	F	Lady	Mexico	Mexico	Brown	29 Apr 1825
J.	1	M	Servant	Mexico	Mexico	Brown	29 Apr 1825
Jose	55	M		Spain	Spain	Fabius	3 Jun 1825
Juan Mala	28	M	Merchant	Mexico	Mexico	Brown	29 Apr 1825
SOLOMAN, E. J.	45	M	Merchant	G. Britain	U. States	Endeavour	1 May 1826
SOLOMON, A.	19	M	Merchant	U. States	U. States	Genl. Marion	9 Jan 1827
Asher	17	M	Gentleman	U. States	U. States	America	17 Sep 1827
John	36	M	Merchant	Philada.	U. States	Herald	6 Feb 1824
Paul	35	M	Merchant	France	France	Almira	14 Jun 1826
Rosa	18	F	Spinster	U. States	U. States	America	17 Sep 1827
Samah	14	M	None	United States	United States	Agenora	3 Oct 1826
SOLOZER, Ann M.	2	F	Farm	Ireland		Quatre Freres	29 Jul 1828
Joseph	4	M	Farm	Ireland		Quatre Freres	29 Jul 1828
Joseph	38	M	Farm	Ireland		Quatre Freres	29 Jul 1828
Margaret	29	F	Farm	Ireland		Quatre Freres	29 Jul 1828
Maryan	1	F	Farm	Ireland		Quatre Freres	29 Jul 1828
Rob	7	M	Farm	Ireland		Quatre Freres	29 Jul 1828
SOLPHER,							
Anne Maria	4 6/12	F		France	United States	Catharine	10 Sep 1827
Eliza	30 2/12	F		France	United States	Catharine	10 Sep 1827
Geo. A.	6 3/12	M		France	United States	Catharine	10 Sep 1827
Henry	39 7/12	M	Blacksmith	France	United States	Catharine	10 Sep 1827
Peter	1 3/12	M		France	United States	Catharine	10 Sep 1827
SOLTZMON, Valentine	28	M	Weaver	France	U. States	Sully	25 Jun 1828
SOLUMAN, J.	40	M	Merchant	U. States	U. States	Alabama	21 May 1823
SOLVEN, James	5	M	Laborer	Ireland	United States	Ann Maria	18 Dec 1827
James	35	M	Laborer	Ireland	United States	Ann Maria	18 Dec 1827
John	7	M	Laborer	Ireland	United States	Ann Maria	18 Dec 1827
Mary	30	M	Laborer	Ireland	United States	Ann Maria	18 Dec 1827
Peter	2	M	Laborer	Ireland	United States	Ann Maria	18 Dec 1827
SOLZS, Jno. A.	24	M	Clerk	Prusia	U. States	Cumberland	10 Nov 1823
SOMER, Barb	6	F	Farmer	Alsace in the Department of Upper and lower Rhine	United States	Carolina Augusta	16 May 1828
Catherin	11	F	Farmer	Alsace in the Department of Upper and lower Rhine	United States	Carolina Augusta	16 May 1828
Christiana	19	M	Farmer	Alsace in the Department of Upper and lower Rhine	United States	Carolina Augusta	16 May 1828
Elizabeth	8	F	Farmer	Alsace in the Department of Upper and lower Rhine	United States	Carolina Augusta	16 May 1828
John	2	M	Farmer	Alsace in the Department of Upper and lower Rhine	United States	Carolina Augusta	16 May 1828
John	52	M	Farmer	Alsace in the Department of Upper and lower Rhine	United States	Carolina Augusta	16 May 1828
SOMERS, Daniel	38	M		France	U. States	Sabina	18 Oct 1824
Francis	51	M	Gentleman	Denmark	Denmark	Jupiter	29 Aug 1828
Isaac	18	M	None	Great Britain	United States	Hannibal	12 Oct 1829
James	30	M	Labourer	Ireland	U. States	Josephine	27 Jul 1825
May	23	F	...	Ireland	U. States	William	27 Jul 1824
SOMERVILLE, James	28	M	Labourer	Scotland	United States	Mary & Susan	5 Aug 1828
John	20		Clerk	Great Britain	United States	Rufus King	4 Sep 1823
John	23	...	...	Scotland	America	Nimrod	9 Jul 1827
SOMES, Francis	42	M	Merchant	Great Britain	U. States	Columbia	24 Dec 1822
SOMICO, Peter	40	M	Mechanic	Switzerland	U. States	Thomas	3 Sep 1822
SOMMER, Elizabeth	56	F		Germany	United States	Origon	8 Jun 1824
Uriah	34	M	Farmer	Germany	United States	Origon	8 Jun 1824

NAMES OF PASSENGERS	AGE	SEX	OCCUPATIONS	COUNTRY TO WHICH THEY BELONG	COUNTRY THEY INTEND TO INHABIT	SHIPS/DATES OF ARRIVAL	
SOMMERS, Bartholemew	60	M	Farmer	United States	United States	Broke	16 Jul 1829
SOMMERSIDES, Mary	29	F			New York	New York	31 Jul 1829
Mary Ann	2	F			New York	New York	31 Jul 1829
William	10/12	M			New York	New York	31 Jul 1829
William	32	M	Missionary		New York	New York	31 Jul 1829
SOMMERVILLE, ...	...		...	Ireland	United States	Robert Burns	18 Jun 1822
...	20		Coppersmith	Ireland	United States	Robert Burns	18 Jun 1822
Thomas	23	M	Servant	Ireland	United States	Carolina Ann	14 May 1827
SOMMERWELL, Robt.	21	F	Farmer	Scotland	U. States	Roger Stewart	9 Jun 1828
SOMNANFEILIN, Louis	32	M	Farmer	Switzerland		Antioch	18 Aug 1829
SOMNER, Isaac	43 5/12	M	Farmer	Switzerland	United States	France	6 Oct 1828
Philip	27	M	Blockmaker	France	United States	Henri IV	2 Oct 1828
SONBI,							
Buena Bentura, Don	47	M	Mechanick	United States	United States	Centurion	22 Dec 1828
SONBOCHER, Adoph	13	F		Baden	United States	Jason	3 Nov 1828
Anton	40	M	Farmer	Baden	United States	Jason	3 Nov 1828
Cresentia	40	F		Baden	United States	Jason	3 Nov 1828
Jerdmand	5	M		Baden	United States	Jason	3 Nov 1828
Joseph Reichamp	16	M	Taylor	Baden	United States	Jason	3 Nov 1828
SONCOMNON, Julian	29	M	Baker	Germany	United States	Origon	8 Jun 1824
SONDON, —, Monsieur	26	M	Gentleman	France	Nuyork	Louisa	17 Jul 1826
SONEDBURG, C. G.	45	M	Merchant	U. States	U. States	Hudson	13 Jan 1827
SONLIGNE, Auguste	22	F	Taylor	France	United States	Henri IV	2 Oct 1828
SONNETT, Patt	21	M	...ker	..., ..., Ireland	U. States	New Orleans	24 Aug 1827
SONVA, B.	45	M	Merchant	Sardinia	U. States	William Howland	21 Mar 1825
SOPA, Edward	28		Butcher	Devinshire/ Devinshire	New York	Venus	12 Apr 1821
Hannah	21			Devinshire/ Devinshire	New York	Venus	12 Apr 1821
SOPPALE, Augustus	30	M	Miller	France	United States	Virginia	31 May 1828
SORAGAN, Danl.	28	M	Farmer	Ireland	U. States	Hibernia	29 Nov 1821
SORBE, E.	25	M	Merchant	United States	United States	Joseph	11 Jul 1821
Peter O.	27	M	Merchant	U. States	U. States	Montano	2 Sep 1828
SORBETT, Eliza	25	F	Farmer	Ireland	U. States	Dickinson	30 Jul 1825
SORDAN, Edward	22	M	Farmer	...ford, Ireland		Mount Vernon	7 Jun 1824
SOREM, John	20	M	Mason	Scotland	United States	Tom	2 Jul 1827
SOREN, Jos.	19	M	Farmer	Switzerland	U.States	C. Amelia	30 Jun 1828
SORENSON, Sophia	24		Servant	Denmark	U. States	South Carolina Packet	4 Sep 1822
SORGEN, John	30	M	Weaver	England		Fame	9 Dec 1826
SORIBNER, George	29	M	Merchant	St. John, N.B.	St. John, N.B.	Ann Maria	1 Apr 1826
SORONDO, S.	30	M	Merchant	Spain	Spain	Virginia	9 Feb 1829
SORQUI, Sophia	30			France	U. States	Parachute	14 May 1828
SORREL, —, Mrs.	17	F		United States	United States	Paris	10 Sep 1823
Martial	31	M	Merchant	France	U. States	Edward Bonnaffe	4 May 1827
Solange	30	M	Physician	United States	United States	Paris	10 Sep 1823
SORSHIELD, Susana	30	F	None	England	U.S.A.	Lima	6 Dec 1826
SOSS, Mary	24	F		Baden	United States	Jason	3 Nov 1828
SOTO, Felix	14	M	Boy	Teneriffe	Teneriffe	Wanderer	6 Oct 1827
Philipe	18	M		So. America	U. States	Eclipse	10 Jun 1823
SOTRES, Geronimus	33	M	Merchant	Spain	New York	Abeona	20 Dec 1823
SOUBAREUZE, Peter	46	M	Merchant	B..., France	United States	Henri IV	2 Oct 1828
SOUBAT, Alphonse	28	M	Merchant	France	France	Henry	16 May 1827
SOUBERCAZE,							
F., Supercargo	36	M	Merchant	France	France	Elisa	23 May 1821
SOUBERER, —	29	M	Painter	France	America	Saluda	18 Jun 1825
SOUERER, M.	33	M	Merchant	France	Spain	Circassian	13 Jun 1825
SOUILLARD, Bernard	29		Merchant	New York	New York	Don Quixote	19 Aug 1825
SOULBY, Michael	32	M	Merchant	Great Britain	United States	Superior	31 Mar 1828
SOULIER, —, Mrs.	24	F	Artist	France	United States	Bayard	15 Feb 1827
A.	38	M	Artist	France	United States	Bayard	15 Feb 1827
SOULLARD, Matilda	32	F		France	U. States	Damon	18 Nov 1826
SOUNALET, —	34	M	Merchant	U. States	U. States	Imperial	10 Dec 1821
SOUNDINGS, Charles	3	M		England	U.S.A.	Hudson	21 Aug 1829
Harriet	28	F		England	U.S.A.	Hudson	21 Aug 1829
James	5	M		England	U.S.A.	Hudson	21 Aug 1829
Jane	1	F		England	U.S.A.	Hudson	21 Aug 1829

NAMES OF PASSENGERS	AGE	SEX	OCCUPATIONS	COUNTRY TO WHICH THEY BELONG	COUNTRY THEY INTEND TO INHABIT	SHIPS/DATES OF ARRIVAL	
SOUNDLETTE, S.		M	Mercht.	U. States	U. States	David	19 Apr 1824
SOURN,							
Anthony Teron	34 5/12	M	Farmer	Switzerland	U. States	France	26 Jun 1828
Antoin	6 4/12	M	Farmer	Switzerland	U. States	France	26 Jun 1828
Bone	7 4/12	M	Farmer	Switzerland	U. States	France	26 Jun 1828
Catharan	32 4/12	F	Farmer	Switzerland	U. States	France	26 Jun 1828
Charly	14 1/12	F	Farmer	Switzerland	U. States	France	26 Jun 1828
Christian	12 2/12	F	Farmer	Switzerland	U. States	France	26 Jun 1828
Elizabeth	9	F	Farmer	Switzerland	U. States	France	26 Jun 1828
Elizabeth	36 2/12	F	Farmer	Switzerland	U. States	France	26 Jun 1828
Jean	32 5/12	M	Farmer	Switzerland	U. States	France	26 Jun 1828
John	17 5/12	M	Farmer	Switzerland	U. States	France	26 Jun 1828
John	40 3/12	M	Farmer	Switzerland	U. States	France	26 Jun 1828
Madolin	12	F	Farmer	Switzerland	U. States	France	26 Jun 1828
Madolin	28 6/12	F	Farmer	Switzerland	U. States	France	26 Jun 1828
Margaret	4 2/12	F	Farmer	Switzerland	U. States	France	26 Jun 1828
Ronne	7 5/12	M	Farmer	Switzerland	U. States	France	26 Jun 1828
Tome	3 5/12	M	Farmer	Switzerland	U. States	France	26 Jun 1828
SOUSHAM, John	30		Merchant	England	United States	Mary	15 Jul 1822
SOUSHERN, Jno.	30	M	Clerk	Gt. Britain	United States	Baltic	11 Apr 1825
SOUTEBERN, Daniel	18	M	Farmer	Corgernon	U.S. America	Superior	18 Jun 1825
SOUTER, John	15	M	Joiner	Great Britain	United States	Dapper	21 Aug 1828
SOUTERBRIDGE, Eliza	16	F	Lady	Bermuda	U. States	Mary & Elizabeth	10 Jul 1824
SOUTES, Nicholas	22	M	Shoemaker	Switzerland	United States	Aurora	21 Jun 1824
SOUTHARD, H.	31	M	Merchant	United States	United States	Howard	19 May 1826
SOUTHARE, Jno.	21	M	Farmer	England	United States	Mary & Harriet	9 Mar 1829
SOUTHER, Stephen	20		Farmer	Great Britain	U. States	Nile	30 Apr 1827
SOUTHERLAND,							
Alexander	31	M	Baker	Grt. Britain	United States	Henry Kneeland	5 Nov 1828
Mary	19		Wife	Grt. Britain	United States	Henry Kneeland	5 Nov 1828
SOUTHERN, Abm.	20	M	Laborer	England	United States	Peru	23 May 1827
SOUTHERTON, John	20	M	Taylor	Scotland	America	Farmer	4 Aug 1825
SOUTHGATE, John M.	24	M	Merchant	U. States	U. States	Constitution	29 Dec 1821
John M.	26	M	Mercht.	U. States	U. States	Constitution	17 Mar 1823
John M.	32	M	Merchant	Virginia	Virginia	Brighton	21 Jan 1826
SOUTHIR,							
Thos. G. S.	16 1/12	M	Clerk	U. States	U. States	Champion	2 Feb 1829
SOUTHLAND, Rob.	28	M	Planter	Jamaica	Jamaica	McFingal	6 Jun 1825
SOUTHMAYD, L. Cory	23	M	Merchant	U.S.	U.S.	Radius	27 Apr 1824
SOUTHWICK, Sarah	21	F	None	Great Britain		Birmingham	11 Oct 1828
SOUTTZENER, Hugarte	22	M	Merchant	Switzerland		Edward Quesnel	17 Nov 1828
SOVEREIGN, David	22	M	Farmer	United States	New York	Rambler	31 Aug 1829
SOVET, Franck	42	M	Merchant	St. Johns	St. Johns	Nancy	3 Apr 1824
SOWDEN, Ebenezer	6	M		Great Brit.	Ohio	Gov. Griswald	3 Jul 1820
Eliah	11	F		Great Brit.	Ohio	Gov. Griswald	3 Jul 1820
Esther	26	F		Great Brit.	Ohio	Gov. Griswald	3 Jul 1820
John	39	M	Merchant	Ireland	United States	Silas Richards	27 Oct 1825
Samuel	27	M		Great Brit.	Ohio	Gov. Griswald	3 Jul 1820
SOWDER, John	43	M	Farmer	Great Britain	New York	Radius	7 Jul 1821
SOWERS, Danl.	35	M	Mercantile	Alexandria	U. States	Talma	23 Sep 1828
SOWTHER, Ann	5	F	None	Great Britain		Moro Castle	6 Jul 1827
Ann	15	F	None	Great Britain		Moro Castle	6 Jul 1827
Elizabeth	16	F	None	Gr. Britain		Moro Castle	6 Jul 1827
Hannah	38	F	None	Gr. Britain		Moro Castle	6 Jul 1827
James	13	M	None	Great Britain		Moro Castle	6 Jul 1827
Jane	18	F	None	Gr. Britain		Moro Castle	6 Jul 1827
John	6	M	None	Great Britain		Moro Castle	6 Jul 1827
Mary	9	F	None	Great Britain		Moro Castle	6 Jul 1827
Thomas	3	M	None	Great Britain		Moro Castle	6 Jul 1827
SP...WARREN, Elisabeth	25	F	Laundress	Great Britain, Ireland	New York	Britannia	3 Nov 1827
SPAIGHT, Thomas	26	M	Joiner	England	United States	Lunar	5 May 1828
SPAIN, Sarah	18	F	Spinner	Great Britain	United States	Grecian	24 Sep 1828
SPALDING, E. W.	27	M	Mechanic	New York	New York	Dandy	17 May 1825
Ed.	28	M	Merchant	Rhode Island	U. States	Blue Ey'd Man	23 Aug 1823
Ewd.	36	M	Merchant	U. States	U. States	Fabius	30 Aug 1827
F. D.	22	M	Mariner	U. States	U. States	Abigail	24 Mar 1825
Fredk. D.	19	M	Gentleman	Connecticutt	U. States	Albert	2 Oct 1823
J. W.	26	M	Merchant	United States	United States	Tampico	27 Jun 1827

NAMES OF PASSENGERS	AGE	SEX	OCCUPATIONS	COUNTRY TO WHICH THEY BELONG	COUNTRY THEY INTEND TO INHABIT	SHIPS/DATES OF ARRIVAL	
SPALLAN, Patt	28	M	Farmer	Ireland	America	Farmer	4 Aug 1825
SPAM, Bridget	16	F	None	Ireland		Marchioness	13 May 1828
Mary	34	F	None	Ireland		Marchioness	13 May 1828
Phoebe	13	F	None	Ireland		Marchioness	13 May 1828
Thomas	37	M	Labourer	Ireland		Marchioness	13 May 1828
SPANE, E. J.	29	M	Physician	France	U. States	Elizabeth	20 Mar 1824
SPARKMAN, Philip	28	M	Farmer	Great Britain	Upper Canada	Florida	10 Dec 1823
SPARKS, John	20			Ireland	U.S.	Union	20 Aug 1827
John	23	M	Trader	England	United States	Cambria	16 Aug 1827
SPARR, John	33 4/12	M	Farmer	Switzerland	U. States	France	26 Jun 1828
SPARWOOD, John	14	M		G. Britain	U. States	Freak	9 Jun 1828
Mary	12	F		G. Britain	U. States	Freak	9 Jun 1828
SPATCH, —	36	M	Labourer	France	United States	Cavalier	25 Jul 1828
—, Wife	33	F		France	United States	Cavalier	25 Jul 1828
E.	5	F		France	United States	Cavalier	25 Jul 1828
Jacob	9	M		France	United States	Cavalier	25 Jul 1828
M.	7			France	United States	Cavalier	25 Jul 1828
Maria	1	F		France	United States	Cavalier	25 Jul 1828
Michael	2	M		France	United States	Cavalier	25 Jul 1828
SPATLEE, John	23	M	Farmer	United States	United States	Seine	21 Oct 1822
SPAVIN, Ann	51	F		Great Britain	United States	Diana	6 Jul 1829
Charlotte	12	F		Great Britain	United States	Diana	6 Jul 1829
Elizabeth	18	F		Great Britain	United States	Diana	6 Jul 1829
Hannah	13	F		Great Britain	United States	Diana	6 Jul 1829
Jane	20	F		Great Britain	United States	Diana	6 Jul 1829
Robert	11	M		Great Britain	United States	Diana	6 Jul 1829
Thos.	55	M	Farmer	Great Britain	United States	Diana	6 Jul 1829
SPEA..., William	23	M	...	England	America, U.S.	Illinois	3 Jun 1822
SPEAIRGHT, R.	28	M	Merchant	U.S.	U.S.	Athenian	8 Feb 1827
SPEAR, Jas.	34	M	Mariner	U. States	U. States	Adonis	23 Jan 1822
SPEARS, John	4	M	Boy	Great Britian	United States	Columbia	17 Apr 1827
Mary	20	F	his wife [William]	Great Britian	United States	Franklin	15 Apr 1826
Mary	54	F		Scotland	U.S. of America	Friends	10 May 1823
William	23	M	Merchant	Great Britain	United States	Franklin	15 Apr 1826
SPEDDING, James, Capt.	42	M	Royal Navy	Great Britain	Great Britain	Roman	10 May 1828
SPEED, John	21	M	Labourer	Ireland	U. States	Loire	6 Dec 1827
SPEERR, James	38	M	Mechanic	G. Britain	U. States	Hercules	24 Oct 1821
John	36	M	Mechanic	G. Britain	U. States	Hercules	24 Oct 1821
SPEIS, A. W., Mr.	26	M	Merchant	America	New York	Birmingham	16 Oct 1826
SPEN...Y, George	36	M	Printer	England	U. States	Roman	1 Dec 1828
SPENCE, Anne	2	F		Ireland	United States	Essex	23 May 1828
Charlotte	7	F	Child	St. John, N.B.	United States	St. Michaels	25 May 1825
Deborah	38	F	Wife	St. John, N.B.	United States	St. Michaels	25 May 1825
Elizabeth	25	F		Ireland	U.S.	Lady Hunter	10 Jul 1826
Geo.	28	M	Labourer	Ireland	United States	Essex	23 May 1828
Issobel	24	F		Ireland	United States	Essex	23 May 1828
James	40	M	Engineer	G. Britain	U. States	Camillus	8 Sep 1828
John	28	M	Farmer	Gt. Britain	United States	Pacific	22 May 1826
Mary	3	F		Ireland	United States	Essex	23 May 1828
Robert	31	M	Cooper	Ireland	U.S.	Lady Hunter	10 Jul 1826
Samuel	35	M	Merchant	St. John, N.B.	St. John, N.B.	St. Michaels	24 Mar 1825
Samuel	40	M	Carpenter	St. John, N.B.	United States	St. Michaels	25 May 1825
Thomas	18	M	Labourer	Great Britain	United States	Sylvester Healy	23 Nov 1825
William	10	M	Child	St. John, N.B.	United States	St. Michaels	25 May 1825
SPENCER, —	14	F	None	U. States	U. States	Planter	17 Jul 1826
—, Mrs.	34	F		U. States	U. States	Elizabeth	20 Sep 1822
Ann	18	F	...	England	United States	Milton	20 Oct 1827
Ann	20	F	None	England	Philadelphia	Concordia	12 Oct 1826
Betsey	2	F		England	United States	William Byrnes	1 Dec 1824
Christopher	27	M	Doctor	Great Britain	United States	Exertion	17 Jul 1829
David	33	M	Labourer	Scotland	U. States	Czar	29 Aug 1829
Edward	4	M	None	England	Philadelphia	Concordia	12 Oct 1826
Elizh.	33	F	None	Scotland		Czar	29 Aug 1829
Ezecal	31	M	Shoemaker	U. States	U. States	Elizabeth	20 Sep 1822
Francis	11	M	None	England		Manhattan	22 May 1827
George	19	M	Miner	England		Manhattan	22 May 1827
Hannah	56	F	None	England		Manhattan	22 May 1827
James	6	M		England	United States	William Byrnes	1 Dec 1824
James	6 2/12	M	None	England	Philadelphia	Concordia	12 Oct 1826

NAMES OF PASSENGERS	AGE	SEX	OCCUPATIONS	COUNTRY TO WHICH THEY BELONG	COUNTRY THEY INTEND TO INHABIT	SHIPS/DATES OF ARRIVAL	
SPENCER (cont'd)							
James	10	M	None	England		Manhattan	22 May 1827
James	34	M	Filer	G.B.	St. New York	Eliza Grant	29 Aug 1829
Jane	20	F		England	United States	William Byrnes	1 Dec 1824
John	10	M	None	England	Philadelphia	Concordia	12 Oct 1826
John	15	M		England	United States	William Byrnes	1 Dec 1824
John	20	M	Merchant	England	U. States	United States	27 Jul 1824
John	22	M	Miner	England		Manhattan	22 May 1827
John	30 1/12	M	Smith	England	Philadelphia	Concordia	12 Oct 1826
John	32	M	Mariner	U. States	U. States	Sabina	25 Apr 1828
John	42	M	Merchant	Great Britain	America	Lady Gallatin	21 Jun 1820
Margaret	40	F		England	United States	William Byrnes	1 Dec 1824
Margt.	12	F		England	United States	William Byrnes	1 Dec 1824
Martha	39	F	None	England	Philadelphia	Concordia	12 Oct 1826
Mary	17	F	None	England		Manhattan	22 May 1827
Mary Ann	5	F		England	United States	William Byrnes	1 Dec 1824
Nancy	16	F		England	United States	William Byrnes	1 Dec 1824
Rebecca	45	F	None	U. States	U. States	Planter	17 Jul 1826
Robert	8	M		England	United States	William Byrnes	1 Dec 1824
Stephans	3	M	None	England	Philadelphia	Concordia	12 Oct 1826
Thomas	29	M	Shoemaker	England	United States	Nancy Henrietta	3 Nov 1828
William	11 2/12	M	None	England	Philadelphia	Concordia	12 Oct 1826
William	26	M	Labourer	Great Britain	United States	Mary & Harriet	3 Jul 1829
Wm.	6	M		U. States	U. States	Elizabeth	20 Sep 1822
SPENDER, Geo.	25	M	Clothier	G. Braitan	U. States	Cosmo	29 Jun 1826
Job	30	M	Clothier	G. Braitan	U. States	Cosmo	29 Jun 1826
SPENSER, Ann	22	F	Spinster	Ireland	United States	Josephine	24 Jul 1826
Eliza	4	F	Child	Ireland	United States	Josephine	24 Jul 1826
Jane	3	F	Child	Ireland	United States	Josephine	24 Jul 1826
John	8/12	M	Child	Ireland	United States	Josephine	24 Jul 1826
John	32	M	Farmer	Ireland	United States	Josephine	24 Jul 1826
Mary	26	F	Matron	Ireland	United States	Josephine	24 Jul 1826
SPEOULS, William	30	M	Labourer	Ireland	United States	Trident	18 Jul 1827
SPERER, D. H.	27	M	Mariner	U. States	U. States	Rose in Bloom	9 Apr 1827
SPERRY, Dd.	50	M	Mariner	U. States	U. States	Irene	14 Apr 1821
F. W.	34	M	Merchant	United States	United States	Martha	21 Mar 1820
Joseph	25	M	Farmer	England	United States	Trident	31 Mar 1827
SPETZ, Ann	8	F		France	U. States	Leonarde	29 Aug 1828
Francoise J.	12	M		France	U. States	Leonarde	29 Aug 1828
Jean	9	F		France	U. States	Leonarde	29 Aug 1828
Madelaine	11	F		France	U. States	Leonarde	29 Aug 1828
Marianne H.	29	F		France	U. States	Leonarde	29 Aug 1828
Thiebault	4	M		France	U. States	Leonarde	29 Aug 1828
Thiebout	36	M	Farmer	France	U. States	Leonarde	29 Aug 1828
SPEYER,							
Chr. Fredk.	43 1/12	M	Merchant	New York	New York	Thames	16 May 1821
SPICE, Bab	20	F	Seamstress	Native of Switzerland	United States	Canaris	30 Jun 1827
SPICER, ...re	8	F		Germany	Missouri	Isabella	15 Sep 1828
Alfred	7	M		England	United States	Amelia	20 Aug 1829
Charles	6	M		Germany	Missouri	Isabella	15 Sep 1828
Harriet	30	F		England	United States	Amelia	20 Aug 1829
Henry	3	M		England	United States	Amelia	20 Aug 1829
Joseph	38	M	Farmer	Germany	Missouri	Isabella	15 Sep 1828
Magdelene	14	F		Germany	Missouri	Isabella	15 Sep 1828
Magdelene	35	F		Germany	Missouri	Isabella	15 Sep 1828
Marian	11	F		Germany	Missouri	Isabella	15 Sep 1828
Mary	11	F		England	United States	Amelia	20 Aug 1829
Richard	7/12	M		England	United States	Amelia	20 Aug 1829
Richard	33	M	Labourer	England	United States	Amelia	20 Aug 1829
Robert	4	M		Germany	Missouri	Isabella	15 Sep 1828
Rosa	2	F		Germany	Missouri	Isabella	15 Sep 1828
Thomas	5	M		England	United States	Amelia	20 Aug 1829
SPIERS, —, Miss	18	F		England	New York	Joseph Hume	26 Oct 1829
—, Mrs.	45	F		England	New York	Joseph Hume	26 Oct 1829
John	16	M		England	New York	Joseph Hume	26 Oct 1829
SPIERS, P...k.	14	M		England	New York	Joseph Hume	26 Oct 1829
SPILHANE, Thos.	21	M	Labourer	Ireland	United States	Matvina	19 Oct 1826
SPILLER, Henry	30	M	White Smith	Great Brittan	United States	Lewis	13 Jan 1827

NAMES OF PASSENGERS	AGE	SEX	OCCUPATIONS	COUNTRY TO WHICH THEY BELONG	COUNTRY THEY INTEND TO INHABIT	SHIPS/DATES OF ARRIVAL	
SPILLER (cont'd)							
Joseph	24	M	Clerk	Great Brittain	U. States	Hibernia	8 Jul 1823
Robert	49	M		Great Brittan	United States	Lewis	13 Jan 1827
SPILMAN, Wm.	27	M	...	Great Britain	United States	Atlantic	28 May 1827
SPINCER, James	34	M	Filer	Great Britain		Eliza Grant	29 Aug 1829
SPINDER, Maria	30	F	Servant	St. Croix	United States	Carlo	28 Jun 1826
SPINHIRNEY, Anna M.	5	F		France	America, U.N.S.	Great Britain	3 Aug 1829
Blaise	7	M		France	America, U.N.S.	Great Britain	3 Aug 1829
Cecilia	11 9/12	F		France	America, U.N.S.	Great Britain	3 Aug 1829
Madeline	2/12	F		France	America, U.N.S.	Great Britain	3 Aug 1829
Marguerita	1 6/12	F		France	America, U.N.S.	Great Britain	3 Aug 1829
Minerva	40	F		France	America, U.N.S.	Great Britain	3 Aug 1829
Pierce	42	M	Farmer	France	America, U.N.S.	Great Britain	3 Aug 1829
SPINK, Elizth.	9	F	Farmer	England	United States	Florida	1 Sep 1823
George	8	M	Farmer	England	United States	Florida	1 Sep 1823
George	45	M	Farmer	England	United States	Florida	1 Sep 1823
Hannah	6	F	Farmer	England	United States	Florida	1 Sep 1823
Jno. H.	26	M	Farmer	Great Britain	U.S.	Nestor	6 Jul 1821
Joseph	45	M	Merchant	Great Britain	United States	Diana	6 Jul 1829
Mary	11	F	Farmer	England	United States	Florida	1 Sep 1823
Mary	19	F		England	England	Ceres	23 Sep 1826
Thos.	4	M	Farmer	England	United States	Florida	1 Sep 1823
SPINNEY, —, Capt.	22	M	Mariner	U. States	U. States	Alexander Le Grand	9 Sep 1823
SPINOLA, J. L.	40	M	Merchant	Madeira	U. States	Pomona	5 Dec 1821
Jno. L.	38	M	Merchant	Portugal	U. States	Lady Tompkins	10 Nov 1823
SPINOLLA, Jno. L.	38	M	Merchant	Madeira	U. States	Sarah & Louisa	7 Jun 1822
SPIRMAN, Jacob	35	M	Baker	Germany	United States	Martha	30 Jun 1823
SPITTA, C. W.	32	M	Merchant	Jemmny	U. States	Mary Livingston	26 Jul 1824
SPITTLE, Harriet	26	F		England	America	Mary Lord	26 Oct 1829
Henriette	2/12	F		England	America	Mary Lord	26 Oct 1829
Jane	20	F		Gt. Britain	U. States	General Marion	14 Jul 1828
John	58	M	Weaver	Gt. Britain	U. States	General Marion	14 Jul 1828
John, of Baltimore	9	M		England	America	Mary Lord	26 Oct 1829
Mathew	29	M	Smith	England	America	Mary Lord	26 Oct 1829
SPLEEN, Edw.	19	M	Watchmaker	Switzerland	America	Saluda	16 Oct 1824
SPOHN, Justin	18	M	Watchmaker	Swiss	Switzerland	Stephania	13 Sep 1821
SPOHR, Joseph	25	M	Farmer	Germany		Ariel	24 Sep 1827
SPONGLE, Rebecca	22	F	Spinster & Servant	Jamaica	U. States	America	17 Sep 1827
SPOONER, —, Miss	25	F	Spinster	Gt. Britain	New York	Columbia	3 Apr 1826
F., Miss	22	F	Spinster	Gt. Britain	New York	Columbia	3 Apr 1826
H.	27	M	Merchant	England	U. States	Panthea	5 Oct 1822
H.	32	M	Merchant	United States	United States	Silas Richards	9 Mar 1829
H.	84	M	Merchant	America	America	Silas Richard	24 Oct 1829
Harriet	28	F		Liverpool		New York	31 Jul 1829
Maria	22	F		Liverpool		New York	31 Jul 1829
SPOTTSWOOD, Robert B.	18	M	Navy	Richmond	Philadelphia	Independence	25 Oct 1828
SPOTWOOD, Margaret	50	F		Ireland	United States	Princess Charlotte	26 Apr 1827
SPRACKLAN, Alpia	11	M		England	United States	Earl of Liverpool	29 Sep 1823
Ann	18	F		England	United States	Earl of Liverpool	29 Sep 1823
Eliza	22	F		England	United States	Earl of Liverpool	29 Sep 1823
Eliza	51	F		England	United States	Earl of Liverpool	29 Sep 1823
George	9	M		England	United States	Earl of Liverpool	29 Sep 1823
Pamela	20	F		England	United States	Earl of Liverpool	29 Sep 1823
Peter	14	M		England	United States	Earl of Liverpool	29 Sep 1823
Peter	45	M	Farmer	England	United States	Earl of Liverpool	29 Sep 1823
SPRACKLING, Mary	28	F	None	U. States	U. States	Silvia	10 Sep 1827
SPRAGGE, John	36	M	Merchant	Great Britten	United States	Cortes	6 Mar 1827
SPRAGGON, George	24	M	Carpenter	England	United States	Brighton	11 Mar 1825
SPRAGUE, Peleg	30	M	Mariner	U.S.A.	U.S.A.	Noble	2 Nov 1826

NAMES OF PASSENGERS	AGE	SEX	OCCUPATIONS	COUNTRY TO WHICH THEY BELONG	COUNTRY THEY INTEND TO INHABIT	SHIPS/DATES OF ARRIVAL	
SPRAGUE (cont'd)							
W. B.	30	M	Dr. of Divinity	United States	United States	John Jay	8 May 1828
SPRAIGHT, R.	24	M	Merchant	New York	U. States & Spain	Seneca	21 May 1825
SPRATLEY, Geo.	13	M	Shoemaker	Ireland	U. States	Howard Douglass	29 Jan 1828
James	41	M	Shoemaker	Ireland	U. States	Howard Douglass	29 Jan 1828
SPRATT, Judith	24	F		G. Britain	U. States	Margaret Bogle	12 Jun 1828
Mary	25			Ireland	United States	Alexander Mansfield	9 Nov 1822
Thomas	25	M	Hatter	G. Britain	U. States	Margaret Bogle	12 Jun 1828
SPRAUL, Benjamin	18	M				Nancy	12 Aug 1820
Chas.	5	M				James Monroe	8 Aug 1820
Joseph	9	M				James Monroe	8 Aug 1820
Mary	30	F	None			James Monroe	8 Aug 1820
SPRAY, L. M.	20	M	Merchant	U. States		Star	7 Jan 1827
SPRIERT, Jean	26	F	Weaver	Switzerland	Swizland	Le Voltaire	19 Jul 1828
SPRINAN, Henry	30	M	Farmer	Germany	United States	Oxford	14 Aug 1828
SPRING, Christian	10	M	Tailour	Germany	United States	Virginia	31 May 1828
Christian	30	M	Clouthier	Germany	United States	Virginia	31 May 1828
Christian	51	M	Tailour	Germany	United States	Virginia	31 May 1828
Edward	13		Gentleman	Newhaven	United States	London	13 Dec 1822
Edward	23	M	Labourer	Ireland	United States	America	25 Dec 1827
Elisabeth	50	F	Weaver	Germany	United States	Virginia	31 May 1828
Frances	1 1/2	F	Tailour	Germany	United States	Virginia	31 May 1828
Frederick	50	M	Farmer	U. States	U. States	New Packet	20 Sep 1826
Fredrick	8	M	Tailour	Germany	United States	Virginia	31 May 1828
Georg	55	M	Weaver	Germany	United States	Virginia	31 May 1828
J.	40	M	Gardner	Ireland	Upper Canada	Infant	21 Nov 1820
Jacob	4	M	Tailour	Germany	United States	Virginia	31 May 1828
Margret	19	F	Weaver	Germany	United States	Virginia	31 May 1828
Mary	38	F	None	Ireland	Upper Canada	Infant	21 Nov 1820
Materlain	28	F	Clouthier	Germany	United States	Virginia	31 May 1828
Materlane	10	F	Weaver	Germany	United States	Virginia	31 May 1828
Materlane	48	F	Tailour	Germany	United States	Virginia	31 May 1828
Salne	6	M	Tailour	Germany	United States	Virginia	31 May 1828
SPRINGER, B. H.	34	M	Merchant	U. States	U. States	Othello	11 Jul 1825
J. S.	42	M	Merchant	America	U. States	Jason	17 Jul 1821
SPRINGS, Dolly	40	F		United States	United States	Only Daughter	29 Apr 1825
Thomas	45	M	Farmer	United States	United States	Only Daughter	29 Apr 1825
William	16	M	Servant	United States	United States	Only Daughter	29 Apr 1825
SPRINK, Joseph	25	M	Carpenter	Providence	U. States	Betsey	2 May 1825
S.	28	M	Carpenter	Providence	U. States	Betsey	2 May 1825
SPROALES, Jane	18	F		G. Britain	U. States	Nimrod	31 Jul 1828
SPROAT, Margeret	30	F	Merchant	United States	United States	Cyno	8 Dec 1827
SPROOL, Saml.	14	M	Farmer	Ireland	United States	William & George	14 May 1828
SPROUL, Ann	13	F	None	Scotland	U. States	Czar	29 Aug 1829
Elizh.	16	F	None	Scotland	U. States	Czar	29 Aug 1829
George	20	M	Clerk	Ireland	America	Josephine	8 Dec 1827
Helen	40	F	None	Scotland	U. States	Czar	29 Aug 1829
James	20	M	Sailor	Scotland	U. States	Czar	29 Aug 1829
Janet	9	F	None	Scotland	U. States	Czar	29 Aug 1829
John	24	M	Farmer	England	United States	Siroc	31 Oct 1829
Margt.	4	F	None	Scotland	U. States	Czar	29 Aug 1829
Peter	2	M	None	Scotland	U. States	Czar	29 Aug 1829
William	22	M		England	United States	Siroc	31 Oct 1829
SPROULE, Catherine	21	F	Spinster	Ireland	United States	Asia	29 Jul 1829
Robert	26	M	Gentleman	U. Kingdom, G. Britain & Ireland	Ohio	James Cropper	21 Oct 1825
SPROULES, Solomon *Died June 22	28	M	Shop Keeper	G. Britain	U. States	Nimrod	31 Jul 1828
SPROULL, Robert	20	M	Gentleman	Ireland	U. States	William & John	10 Jul 1824
SPROULLES, Samuel E.	17 4/12	M	Clerk	U. States	U. States	Hesper	25 Apr 1828
SPRUELL, Jane	...	...	...	Scotland	America	Nimrod	9 Jul 1827
Mary	...	...	...	Scotland	America	Nimrod	9 Jul 1827
William(see 88 & 89)	22	M	...	Scotland	America	Nimrod	9 Jul 1827
SPRUILL, Maria	4					Harmony	15 Jul 1820

NAMES OF PASSENGERS	AGE	SEX	OCCUPATIONS	COUNTRY TO WHICH THEY BELONG	COUNTRY THEY INTEND TO INHABIT	SHIPS/DATES OF ARRIVAL	
SPUER, Josah	30	M	U. States	U. States	U. States	Columbia	1 Dec 1824
SPUR, James	40	M	Mechanic			Hercules	25 Sep 1820
SPURLING, —, Mrs.		F		Maine	U. States	Four Sisters	11 Aug 1823
SPURR, James	20	M	Labourer	England	U. States	Emulous	22 Aug 1828
SPURRIER, W. J.	35	M	Gentleman	England	England	Pedler	1 Aug 1829
SPURRING, G.		M		England	United States	Earl of Liverpool	28 Apr 1824
Mary	21	F		England	United States	Earl of Liverpool	28 Apr 1824
SQUARE, Jane	18	M	Merchant	Connecticut	United States	St. Michaels	18 Jul 1826
SQUIBB, Wm.	30	M	Servant	England	U.S. America	Leeds	6 Jun 1826
SQUINTS, John	24	M	None	Great Britain	United States	William Dawson	18 Jun 1827
SQUIRE, Elizabeth	20	F	Lady	U. States	U. States	Nancy	19 Oct 1821
Francis	28	M	Moulder	Great Britan	United States	Silvanus Jenkins	10 Mar 1827
Levi	6	M	None	Great Britan	United States	Silvanus Jenkins	10 Mar 1827
Mary	8	F	None	Great Britan	United States	Silvanus Jenkins	10 Mar 1827
Samuel	4	M	None	Great Britan	United States	Silvanus Jenkins	10 Mar 1827
Sarah	28	F	None	Great Britan	United States	Silvanus Jenkins	10 Mar 1827
SQUIRES, Benj.	23		Weaver	England	America	Sarah	18 Aug 1829
D. T.	23	M	Merchant	U. States	U. States	Mary	22 May 1822
Elizabeth	40		Ladies and Gentlemen	England	United States	Corinthian	7 Jul 1829
John	25	M	Farmer	Great Britain	United States	Freake	25 Jun 1827
John Baxter	8		Ladies and Gentlemen	England	United States	Corinthian	7 Jul 1829
John Edward	45		Ladies and Gentlemen	England	United States	Corinthian	7 Jul 1829
Sarah	6	F		St. Johns	St. Johns	St. Michael	26 Oct 1824
Susan	4	F		St. Johns	St. Johns	St. Michael	26 Oct 1824
Susan	26	F		St. Johns	St. Johns	St. Michael	26 Oct 1824
SQULADA, F.	28	M		Spain	Spain	Fabius	3 Jun 1825
SRAYNOR, John	30 5/12	M	Farmer	Great Briton	United States	Mount Vernon	30 Dec 1828
SREEN, —, Miss	15	F		England	U.S.	Henri IV	14 Sep 1827
SROL, John H.	22	M	Merchant	United States	United States	Nancey	8 Jun 1822
SRUMBURG, Charles H.	34	M	None	Germany	America	Braganza	1 Dec 1824
ST...ER, Ulrich	24	M	Farmer	Switzerland	United States	Elbe	2 Aug 1822
STAATS, Frederick	4	M		France	U. States	Edward Quesnel	4 Aug 1828
George	13	M		France	U. States	Edward Quesnel	4 Aug 1828
George	37	M	Baker	France	U. States	Edward Quesnel	4 Aug 1828
Jacob	7	M		France	U. States	Edward Quesnel	4 Aug 1828
Magdalina	2	F		France	U. States	Edward Quesnel	4 Aug 1828
Magdalina	42	F		France	U. States	Edward Quesnel	4 Aug 1828
STAB, Benja.	26	M	Farmer	Great Britian	United States	London	24 Jun 1823
STABLER, James S.	30	M	Merchant	United States	U. States	Pacific	5 Sep 1827
STACE, Sophia	20	F		Rye, England	United States	William	21 May 1828
William	23	M	Farmer	Rye, England	United States	William	21 May 1828
STACHCLIFF, Harriet	20	M		G. Britain	U. States	Mary & Harriot	8 Sep 1828
STACK, —, Mrs.	29	F		Ireland	U.S.	Francois I	8 Aug 1829
P., Mr.	25	M	Merchant	Ireland	U.S.	Francois I	8 Aug 1829
Robt.	3	M		Ireland	U.S.	Francois I	8 Aug 1829
STACKART, Moses	21			G. Britain	America	Magnet	24 Sep 1824
STACKELBERG, —, Barron	42	M	Charge des Affaires from Sweden	Sweden	U. States	Martha	17 Jan 1826
STACKHOUSE, William	34	M	Farmer	England	...	Braganza	8 Aug 1825
STACKPOLE, John	21	M	Farmer	England	U.S.	Pacific	24 Oct 1828
STACY, Davis B.	27	M	Merchant	U. States	U. States	York	10 Dec 1825
Sarah	19	F		U. States	U. States	York	10 Dec 1825
STAELD, Jane	21	M	Farmer	Wirtermberg	United States	Olympia	20 Aug 1829
STAFALES, Richd.	30	M	...	Great Britian	U. States	St. Michael	3 Jan 1825
STAFFER, Christ.	20		Farmer	France	U. States	Elizabeth	9 Jul 1825
STAFFORD, —, Miss	6/12	F		Baltimore, U.S.	U. States	Fortuna	11 Oct 1827
—, Mrs.	22	F		Baltimore, U.S.	U. States	Fortuna	11 Oct 1827
James	12			b. York County, G.B., last of N. York	N. York	Peru	30 May 1828
James	30	M	Weaver	G. Britain	U. States	Nimrod	31 Jul 1828
Jno.	25	M	Physician	Baltimore, U.S.	U. States	Fortuna	11 Oct 1827

NAMES OF PASSENGERS	AGE	SEX	OCCUPATIONS	COUNTRY TO WHICH THEY BELONG	COUNTRY THEY INTEND TO INHABIT	SHIPS/DATES OF ARRIVAL	
STAFFORD (cont'd)							
John		M		Richmond		Antelope	22 Aug 1820
Stephen	30	M	Mason	Great Britain	United States	Mount Vernon	20 May 1822
STAFOUR, Assare	38	M	Merchant	Austria	United States	Ann	11 Sep 1827
STAGEMAN,							
Bernard	24 4/12	M	Merchant	Germany	Traveler	Cadmus	12 Dec 1823
STAGG, Florence	28	M	Carpenter	Ireland	Newyork	Cortes	16 Jul 1827
J.	20	M	Merchant	U. States	U. States	Ardell	7 Jul 1827
Mary	18	F		Ireland	Newyork	Cortes	16 Jul 1827
Philip		M	Merchant	U. States	U. States	Hippomenes	22 Jun 1822
STAHILL, Barbara	6 6/12	F		France	United States	Catharine	10 Sep 1827
D.	31 3/12	M	Miller	France	United States	Catharine	10 Sep 1827
E.	4 1/12			France	United States	Catharine	10 Sep 1827
Fred	10 9/12	M		France	United States	Catharine	10 Sep 1827
M.	32 9/12	F		France	United States	Catharine	10 Sep 1827
STAHL, Catharine L.	38	F		Germany	America	Falcon	28 Aug 1828
Catherina	7 6/12	F		Germany	America	Falcon	28 Aug 1828
Charles	7	M		Bavaria	U. States	Indiana	20 Sep 1828
Christin	12	M		Germany	America	Falcon	28 Aug 1828
H.	28	M	Sugar Baker	Switzerland	U. States	Romulus	24 Sep 1828
J. Fredk.	17	M	Baker	Germany	America	Falcon	28 Aug 1828
J. V.	46	M	Farmer	Bavaria	U. States	Indiana	20 Sep 1828
Jacob	14	M		Germany	America	Falcon	28 Aug 1828
Jacob	40	M	Farmer	Germany	America	Falcon	28 Aug 1828
Joh. Fredk.	6/12	M		Germany	America	Falcon	28 Aug 1828
Joh. George	9 6/12	M		Germany	America	Falcon	28 Aug 1828
Johannis	6 6/12	M		Germany	America	Falcon	28 Aug 1828
John	10	M		Bavaria	U. States	Indiana	20 Sep 1828
Loninel	4	M		Germany	America	Falcon	28 Aug 1828
Margt.	9	F		Bavaria	U. States	Indiana	20 Sep 1828
Maria	2 6/12	F		Germany	America	Falcon	28 Aug 1828
Maria	11	F		Bavaria	U. States	Indiana	20 Sep 1828
S.	36	F		Bavaria	U. States	Indiana	20 Sep 1828
STAHLSCHMIDT, Jacob	21	M	Clerk	Germany	United States	Cadmus	9 Dec 1825
STAIB, Magdelene	18	F	there child [Michael & Magdelene]	Germany	United States	Helen	5 Sep 1828
Magdelene	55	F	his wife [Michael]	Germany	United States	Helen	5 Sep 1828
Michael	62	M	Farmer	Germany	United States	Helen	5 Sep 1828
Theophilus	28	M	there child [Michael & Magdelene]	Germany	United States	Helen	5 Sep 1828
STAIT, John	33	M	Scool Maker	Wurtemburg		Constitution	20 Jun 1828
STAKES, Joseph	24	F	Silk Mercer	England	U.S. States	Splendid	14 Aug 1829
William	18	M	Miller	England	United States	Delta	24 Oct 1829
STALER, Patrick	28			Ireland	Philidelphia	General Marion	21 Nov 1828
STALEY, Abraham	10					William	17 Aug 1820
George	16					William	17 Aug 1820
Hannah	12					William	17 Aug 1820
Priscilla	6					William	17 Aug 1820
Thomas	20					William	17 Aug 1820
Wm.	14					William	17 Aug 1820
Zilpha	8					William	17 Aug 1820
Zilpha	50		Farmer			William	17 Aug 1820
STALIE, Christiaan	60	M	Schoemaker	Alt Thornbach	United States	Juffraw Johanna	16 Oct 1821
Susanna, Zyn Vrouw [his wife, Christiaan]	36	F		Clein Steinhauer	United States	Juffraw Johanna	16 Oct 1821
STALKER, Betty	8	F	None	Scotland	America	Mentor	21 Sep 1824
Catherine	23	F	Spinster	Scotland	America	Mentor	21 Sep 1824
Duncan	52	M	Farmer	Scotland	America	Mentor	21 Sep 1824
Elizabeth	11	F	None	Scotland	America	Mentor	21 Sep 1824
Euphemia	18	F	Spinster	Scotland	America	Mentor	21 Sep 1824
Gilbert	25	M	Farmer	Scotland	America	Mentor	21 Sep 1824
John	7	M	None	Scotland	America	Mentor	21 Sep 1824
Margaret	21	F	Spinster	Scotland	America	Mentor	21 Sep 1824
Mary	15	F	Spinster	Scotland	America	Mentor	21 Sep 1824
Mary	50	F	None	Scotland	America	Mentor	21 Sep 1824
Nancy	13	F	None	Scotland	America	Mentor	21 Sep 1824

NAMES OF PASSENGERS	AGE	SEX	OCCUPATIONS	COUNTRY TO WHICH THEY BELONG	COUNTRY THEY INTEND TO INHABIT	SHIPS/DATES OF ARRIVAL	
STALL, Catharine	20	M		Native of Switzerland	United States	Canaris	30 Jun 1827
Catharine	46 1/12	F		Native of Switzerland	United States	Canaris	30 Jun 1827
George	23	M		Native of Switzerland	United States	Canaris	30 Jun 1827
James	7	M		Native of Switzerland	United States	Canaris	30 Jun 1827
James	56	M	Weaver	Native of Switzerland	United States	Canaris	30 Jun 1827
Margaret	10	M		Native of Switzerland	United States	Canaris	30 Jun 1827
Stan	22	M	Farmer	England	U. States	Canaris	30 Jun 1827
STALLFORTH, F. M.	20	M	Merchant	U. States	U. States	Hercules	6 Jul 1827
STAMFIELD, Abraham	25	M	Merchant	G. Bt.	U. States	Conveyance	15 Jan 1827
Hamer	24	M	Merchant	England	G. Bt.	Canada	13 Feb 1826
STAMMERS, Charlotte	9	F	Merchant		United States	Martha	17 Sep 1821
Charlottee, (his Wife [Josiah])	40	F		England	United States	Acosta	28 Jul 1823
Elizabeth	18	F		England	United States	Hudson	17 Mar 1828
Emily	7	F		England	United States	Acosta	28 Jul 1823
George, (son [of Josiah])	12	M		England	United States	Acosta	28 Jul 1823
Harry	19	M		England	United States	Hudson	17 Mar 1828
J.	16	M	Mechanic	Gt. Britain	U. States	Acosta	28 Jul 1823
Jonathan	11	M		England	United States	Columbia	7 Sep 1827
Joseph	52	M	Farmer	England	United States	Acosta	28 Jul 1823
Josiah	52	M	Miller	England	United States	Acosta	28 Jul 1823
Martha	16	M		England	United States	Hudson	17 Mar 1828
Mary	23	F		England	United States	Acosta	28 Jul 1823
Mary Ann	44	F		England	United States	Acosta	28 Jul 1823
Robt.	14	M	Miller	England	United States	Acosta	28 Jul 1823
Shepherd	13	M		England	United States	Acasta	14 Jun 1824
Thomas	21	M		England	United States	Acosta	28 Jul 1823
Wm.	16	M	Painter	England	United States	Acosta	28 Jul 1823
STAMPER, Maria	27	F		Great Britian	U. States	Hudson	17 Mar 1824
STAMPS, Joseph	22	M	Merchant	England	United States	McDonough	3 Nov 1823
STANBURY, A. O.	42	M	Teacher	England	America	Cincinnatus	19 Oct 1826
STANDEN, Elizabeth	35	F		U. States	U. States	Lima	13 Nov 1822
P...on	1/12	F		England	United States	Danube	22 Aug 1825
STANDING, Richard	40	M	Farmer	England	United States	Danube	22 Aug 1825
STANDISH, Samuel	30	M	Cutler	England	U. States	Cincinnatus	24 May 1821
STANDLEY, A.	1	M	Child	England	America	Britannia	22 Jul 1829
Dan	10	M	Child	G. Brittan	U. States	Henry	24 Oct 1828
F.	13	F	Child	G. Brittan	U. States	Henry	24 Oct 1828
F.	35	F	Wife	G. Brittan	U. States	Henry	24 Oct 1828
G.	6	M	Child	G. Brittan	U. States	Henry	24 Oct 1828
John	12	M	Child	G. Brittan	U. States	Henry	24 Oct 1828
John	41	M	Master	G. Brittan	U. States	Henry	24 Oct 1828
Thos.	4	M	Child	G. Brittan	U. States	Henry	24 Oct 1828
Wm.	8	M	Child	G. Brittan	U. States	Henry	24 Oct 1828
STANDLY, William	33	M	Wheelwright	Great Brittain	United States	Nimrod	9 Jan 1827
STANEN, Murry	18	M	Labourer	Ireland	U. States	Two Marys	20 Apr 1825
Wm.	28	M	Labourer	Ireland	U. States	Two Marys	20 Apr 1825
STANES, Frederick	21	M	Merchant	Scotland	Scotland	Virginia	26 May 1828
STANFIELD, Abrm.	28	M	Merchant	England	U. States	New York	8 Mar 1825
Geo.	24	M		Great Brittain	U. States	Atticus	25 Apr 1822
George	19	M	Farmer	England	America	Manhattan	20 Mar 1820
James	20	M		Great Brittain	U. States	Atticus	25 Apr 1822
Thos.	24	M	Hatter	England	America	Two Marys	24 Sep 1827
STANISLAS, Aimé	28	M	Merchant	France	U.S.	Edward Bonnaffe	20 Jun 1825
STANISLAUS, Louis	27	M	Merchant	Holland	U. States	Emma	25 Feb 1826
STANLEN, Jemy.	20		Laborer	Great Britain	United States	Comet	9 Aug 1822
STANLEY, A.	45	M	Mariner	United States	United States	Daphne	20 May 1823
E. G.	25	M	Gentleman	England	England	New York	22 Jul 1824
Edward	43		Dearbyshire	Dearbyshire	N. York	Peru	30 May 1828
Elizabeth	22	F	None	England	New York	America	1 Aug 1828
G...	32	M	Labourer	Great Britain	United States	Robert	15 Jul 1822

NAMES OF PASSENGERS	AGE	SEX	OCCUPATIONS	COUNTRY TO WHICH THEY BELONG	COUNTRY THEY INTEND TO INHABIT	SHIPS/DATES OF ARRIVAL	
STANLEY (cont'd)							
George	19		Bricklayer	England	United States	Corinthian	7 Jul 1829
Hannah	36	F	...	...	...	Meteor	16 Aug 1824
Lewis	25	M	Merchant	Germany	Kingdom of Holland	Martha	17 Nov 1821
Sarah	43			Dearbyshire	N. York	Peru	30 May 1828
STANLING, Geo.	3	M		America	United States	Ann	22 Dec 1821
Hariot	23	F		America	United States	Ann	22 Dec 1821
Mary Ann	5	F		America	United States	Ann	22 Dec 1821
STANLY (see Slanty)							
Abraham	18	M	Shoemaker	Ireland	U. States	Josephine	30 Aug 1828
Martha	13	F		G. Britain	U. States	Mary & Harriot	8 Sep 1828
Mary	40	F		G. Britain	U. States	Mary & Harriot	8 Sep 1828
Samuel J.	37	M	...	...	...	Meteor	16 Aug 1824
STANMAN, Wm.	25	M	Miller	Great Britten	U. States	Magnet	29 Sep 1823
STANNAR, Rachel	29	F	Commedian	England		Britannia	20 Jun 1827
STANNIS, Jan	40	M	Bl...ker	E...	United States	Juffraw Johanna	16 Oct 1821
STANSBIE, Alexr.	...	M	Merchant	England	New York	Amity	13 Sep 1821
STANSBURY, D.	55	M	Gentleman	U. States	U. States	Martha	20 Jun 1825
Walter G.	20	M	Merchant	U. States	U. States	Emma	15 Dec 1824
STANSFELD, J...ua	44		Merchant	Halifax	Great Britain	William Thompson	13 May 1823
James	30	M	...	England	Canada	William Thompson	10 May 1825
STANSFIELD, Abraham	21	M	Merchant	England	United States	Nestor	20 Nov 1821
Abraham	26	M	Merchant	Great Britain, Ireland	New York	Britannia	3 Nov 1827
Abrm.	23	M	Merchant	Great Britain	United States	Britannia	29 Oct 1829
Ame	28	F		Great Britain	United States	John Jay	8 May 1828
Ann	24	F		England	America	Franklin	3 Dec 1827
Jane	6/12	F		England	America	Manhattan	21 Sep 1822
Jane	37	F	Cotton Spiner	England	America	Manhattan	21 Sep 1822
John	37	M	Merchant	England	Canada	Corinthian	20 Apr 1825
John	42	M	Cotton Spiner	England	America	Manhattan	21 Sep 1822
Joseph	43	M		Great Britain	Canada	James Monroe	25 Apr 1822
Maciah	16	F	Cotton Spiner	England	America	Manhattan	21 Sep 1822
Margary	13	F	Cotton Spiner	England	America	Manhattan	21 Sep 1822
Maria	18	F	Cotton Spiner	England	America	Manhattan	21 Sep 1822
Rosamund	9	F	None	England	America	Manhattan	21 Sep 1822
William	5	M	None	England	America	Manhattan	21 Sep 1822
STANSKURSHT,							
Elizabeth	40	F	One Family [John]	France	United States	Henri IV	2 Oct 1828
John	9	M	One Family [John]	France	United States	Henri IV	2 Oct 1828
John	36	M	Agriculturalist	France	United States	Henri IV	2 Oct 1828
STANTON, ...	22	F		Great Britian	United States	London	24 Jun 1823
...	30	M	Gentl.	Great Britian	United States	London	24 Jun 1823
Frederick	28	M	None	England	United States	Montgomery	6 Mar 1829
J.	21	F	Labourer	Ireland	United States	Combine	4 Jun 1825
Jno.	36	M	Merchant	Massachusetts	U. States	Scio	8 Feb 1825
M.	12	F	Labourer	Ireland	United States	Combine	4 Jun 1825
Michaal	29	M	Labourer	Ireland	United States	Combine	4 Jun 1825
Peter	29	M	Merchant	U. States		Emerald	9 Sep 1820
STANWOOD, Lewis N.	15	M		Boston	U. States	Abeona	2 Sep 1823
W.	21	M	Merchant	America, U.S.A.	United States	Belle	3 Aug 1822
STAPELEY, Ann	30	F	None	England	United States	Trident	18 Jul 1827
Caroline	11	F	None	England	United States	Trident	18 Jul 1827
Eliza	4	F	None	England	United States	Trident	18 Jul 1827
John	8	M	None	England	United States	Trident	18 Jul 1827
Richard	41	M	Labourer	England	United States	Trident	18 Jul 1827
Sarah Ann	1	F	None	England	United States	Trident	18 Jul 1827
Thomas	9	M	None	England	United States	Trident	18 Jul 1827
STAPFORD, Jas.	18	M	Gent.	Gt. Britian	U.S. America	Columbia	3 Apr 1826
STAPLES, B.	33	M		Germany		Apollo	11 Jun 1828
George	21		Stone Mason	England	United States	Corinthian	7 Jul 1829
John	21	M	Cooper	Great Britain	U. States	Hudson	12 Mar 1824
Ruth	40	F		United States	United States	Rambler	31 Aug 1829
STAPLETON, Bridget	23	F	Spinster	Ireland	America	Parrington	9 Jun 1827
Jane	21	F		St. John	Great Britain	General Coffin	9 Mar 1827
Mary	6/12	F		St. John	Great Britain	General Coffin	9 Mar 1827
Mary	21	F		St. John	Great Britain	General Coffin	9 Mar 1827

NAMES OF PASSENGERS	AGE	SEX	OCCUPATIONS	COUNTRY TO WHICH THEY BELONG	COUNTRY THEY INTEND TO INHABIT	SHIPS/DATES OF ARRIVAL	
STAPLETON (cont'd)							
Patt	37	M	Labourer	Great Brittain	United States	Active	12 Sep 1828
Wm.	20	M	Laborer	Ireland	America	Parrington	9 Jun 1827
STAPPIN, James	25	M	Labourer	England	U. States	Ayrshire	12 May 1828
STAPYLTON, Stapylton	29	M	None	U. States	U. States	Sully	25 Jun 1828
STAR, Alfred	28	M	Sailor	United States	United States	Gem	24 Oct 1825
Charles	14	M		U. States	U. States	Edward Bonaffe	23 Jul 1828
Edward	16	M		U. States	U. States	Edward Bonaffe	23 Jul 1828
STARCKE, Chas.	22	M	Mercht.	United States	United States	Bayard	23 Mar 1826
STARK, Andrew	16	M		Scotland	United States	Camillus	9 May 1827
Daniel	45 2/12	M	Tailor	G. Britain	United States	Dutchess of Portland	30 Oct 1826
Daniel, Jr.	12 6/12	M	his child [Margaret]	G. Britain	United States	Dutchess of Portland	30 Oct 1826
Jacob	28	M	Farmer	Germany	United States	Martha	30 Jun 1823
James	3 1/12	M	his child [Margaret]	G. Britain	United States	Dutchess of Portland	30 Oct 1826
Janet	8 3/12	F	his child [Margaret]	G. Britain	United States	Dutchess of Portland	30 Oct 1826
Jos.	26	M	Clerk	G. Britain		Ann Maria	3 Jul 1820
Margaret	35 6/12	F	his wife [Margaret]	G. Britain	United States	Dutchess of Portland	30 Oct 1826
Robert	21	M		Scotland	United States	Camillus	9 May 1827
William	17	M	Clark	Scotland, Great Britain	America	Superb	11 Oct 1821
STARKEY, Ann	37	F		Gt. Britan	U. States	Sarah Skeafe	10 Sep 1827
Chas.	14	M	Nothing	England	England	Britannia	5 Nov 1828
John	30	M		England	U. States	Edward Bonaffe	11 Dec 1827
Martha	20	F	None	England	England	Britannia	23 Mar 1829
Thomas	35 1/12	M	Grocer	Ireland	United States	London	6 Feb 1829
STARKY, Adele	17	F	Watchmaker	Suisse	United States	Montano	5 May 1828
Benj.	21	M	...			Manhattan	25 Dec 1820
STARLING, Wm.	22	M		Scotland	U.S.	Curler	19 Jul 1828
STARR, —, Miss	12	F		Great Britian	United States	Columbia	17 Apr 1827
Peter	20		Weaver		United States	Atlantic	2 Apr 1827
STARRY, Jane	27	F		England	U. States	Howard Douglass	29 Jan 1828
STARS, May	21	F	Servant	Ireland	United States	Josephine	30 Apr 1828
STARSCH, Jacob	26	M	Baker	Netherlands	New York	Louisa	6 Oct 1828
STARSHANSKEE, Mary	17	F	Servant	Philada.	U. States	Elba	21 May 1825
START, Phelim	26	M	Farmer	Ireland	United States	Lima	19 Jun 1824
STARTEAU, Jno.	40	M	Cotton Spinner	Great Britain	United States	India	5 Sep 1827
STATER, Nat	24		Labourer	England	United States	Hugh Johnson	11 Jun 1828
STATES, Jno.	55			England		Anacreon	7 Sep 1827
STATFORD, Hannah	29	F		Bristol	New York	Cosmo	25 Sep 1827
STATTERS, Geo.	10	M		G. Britain	U. States	Freak	9 Jun 1828
John	33	M	Labourer	G. Britain	U. States	Freak	9 Jun 1828
Mark	5	M		G. Britain	U. States	Freak	9 Jun 1828
Mary	0 5/12	F		G. Britain	U. States	Freak	9 Jun 1828
Mary	33	F		G. Britain	U. States	Freak	9 Jun 1828
Robt.	7	M		G. Britain	U. States	Freak	9 Jun 1828
Sarah	0 5/12	F		G. Britain	U. States	Freak	9 Jun 1828
STAUB, Margaret	40	F		Native of Switzerland	United States	Canaris	30 Jun 1827
STAUCH, Johann Conrad	26	M	Clerk	Germany	Philadelphia	Falcon	21 Oct 1826
STAUFFER, Benedict	13	M		Switzerland	America, U.N.S.	Great Britain	3 Aug 1829
Benedict	45	M	Farmer	Switzerland	America, U.N.S.	Great Britain	3 Aug 1829
Doark	6	M		Switzerland	America, U.N.S.	Great Britain	3 Aug 1829
Elizabeth	9	F		Switzerland	America, U.N.S.	Great Britain	3 Aug 1829
Jacob	3	M		Switzerland	America, U.N.S.	Great Britain	3 Aug 1829
John	18	M		Switzerland	America, U.N.S.	Great Britain	3 Aug 1829
Maria	24	F		Switzerland	America, U.N.S.	Great Britain	3 Aug 1829
Maria	46	F		Switzerland	America, U.N.S.	Great Britain	3 Aug 1829
STAUNTON, James	20	M	Mason	England	Upper Canada	Lima	5 Aug 1829
STAVELY, Wm.	27	M	Farmer	Ireland	New York	Carolina Ann	15 Oct 1824
STAYNER, Elizabeth	22	F		France	United States	Elizabeth	13 Nov 1824
STEAD, Alice	47	F		G. Britain	New York	Radius	7 Jul 1821
Carnah	33		Farmer	England	America	Sarah	18 Aug 1829
Daniel	22	M	Flourist	England	U. States	Trident	8 Mar 1824

NAMES OF PASSENGERS	AGE	SEX	OCCUPATIONS	COUNTRY TO WHICH THEY BELONG	COUNTRY THEY INTEND TO INHABIT	SHIPS/DATES OF ARRIVAL	
STEAD (cont'd)							
Daniel	27	M	Merchant			Hercules	25 Sep 1820
Danl.	5	M		England	U. States	Amity	23 Sep 1823
Elias	6		Farmer	England	America	Sarah	18 Aug 1829
Hannah	25	F	None	England	United States	India	8 Jun 1827
Hannah	27	F		England	United States	Yobah	26 Sep 1827
Isabella	1			England	America	Sarah	18 Aug 1829
James	18	M	Farmer	G. Britain	New York	Radius	7 Jul 1821
James	40	M	Weaver	England	United States	India	8 Jun 1827
John	3		Farmer	England	America	Sarah	18 Aug 1829
John	36		Farmer	England	America	Sarah	18 Aug 1829
Joshua	9		Farmer	England	America	Sarah	18 Aug 1829
Mary	11		Farmer	England	America	Sarah	18 Aug 1829
Mary	24	F		England	U. States	Amity	23 Sep 1823
Robert	13	M	Farmer	G. Britain	New York	Radius	7 Jul 1821
Robert	49	M	Farmer	G. Britain	New York	Radius	7 Jul 1821
Sarah	23	F		G. Britain	New York	Radius	7 Jul 1821
T.	25	M	Merchant	England	N. York	James Monroe	29 Apr 1823
Thomas	24	M	Manufacturer	G. Brittain	United States	Hercules	24 Oct 1821
Thomas	25	M	Farmer	G. Britain	New York	Radius	7 Jul 1821
Thos.	27	M	Merchant	U. States	U. States	Pacific	11 Sep 1824
Thos.	30	M		England	United States	Yobah	26 Sep 1827
W.	6/12	M		England	U. States	Amity	23 Sep 1823
William	22	M	Farmer	G. Britain	New York	Radius	7 Jul 1821
STEADDY, Hannah	4	F	Child	G. Brittan	U. States	Henry	24 Oct 1828
John	3 3/12	M	Child	G. Brittan	U. States	Henry	24 Oct 1828
May	29	F	Smith	G. Brittan	U. States	Henry	24 Oct 1828
May	29	F	Child	G. Brittan	U. States	Henry	24 Oct 1828
Thos.	31	M	Smith	G. Brittan	U. States	Henry	24 Oct 1828
STEADLY, Thos.	1	M	Child	G. Brittan	U. States	Henry	24 Oct 1828
STEAL, —, Mrs.	30	F		Scotland	U. States	Majestic	27 Jul 1829
Alexr.	5	M				Majestic	27 Jul 1829
Elizabeth	15/12	F				Majestic	27 Jul 1829
James	7	M				Majestic	27 Jul 1829
John, Mr.	22	M	Labourer	Scotland	U. States	Majestic	27 Jul 1829
Peter	3	M				Majestic	27 Jul 1829
Thomas	21	M	Farmer	England	Hallifax, N.V.	Hercules	10 Apr 1823
STEALES, Charles	45	M	Seaman	America	America	L'Oristelle	15 Dec 1826
STEAN, Margaret	67	F	None	France	U. States	Sully	25 Jun 1828
STEAVENS, John	35	M	Farmer	United States	Ohio	Brighton	19 Aug 1829
STEAWARTSON, James	16	M	Servant	Jamaica	Jamaica	Leo	31 Jul 1826
STEBBINS, ...	3/12		child of the above [...]	U. States	U. States	South Carolina Packet	7 Jul 1821
...	3		child of the above [...]	U. States	U. States	South Carolina Packet	7 Jul 1821
...	5		child of the above [...]	U. States	U. States	South Carolina Packet	7 Jul 1821
...	7		child of the above [...]	U. States	U. States	South Carolina Packet	7 Jul 1821
...	9		child of the above [...]	U. States	U. States	South Carolina Packet	7 Jul 1821
...	27		wife of the above [...]	U. States	U. States	South Carolina Packet	7 Jul 1821
...	35		Merchant	U. States	U. States	South Carolina Packet	7 Jul 1821
Ashael	23	M	Mechanic	United States	United States	Tampico	12 Mar 1827
STEBER, Cathrine	24	F	his wife [David]	Germany	United States	Helen	5 Sep 1828
David	31	M	Farmer	Germany	United States	Helen	5 Sep 1828
Elizabeth	3	F	there child [David & Cathrine]	Germany	United States	Helen	5 Sep 1828
STEBLER, John	26	M	Cultivator	Brattain		L'Esperance	6 Sep 1828
STEBLING, William	30	M	Machine Maker	Great Britain	U. St.	Manchester	7 Dec 1826
STECK, John	28		Farmer	State N. York	...	Oglethorpe	25 Aug 1825
STEDD, Geo.	65	M	Farmer	England	U.S. America	Cortes	19 May 1826
STEDDELFORD, Robert J.	12	M	None	United States	United States	Paez	5 Mar 1827
STEDDIFORD, —, Master	12	M		Curacoa	U. States	Douglass	16 Jul 1824
W. C.	36	M		Curacoa	U. States	Douglass	16 Jul 1824

NAMES OF PASSENGERS	AGE	SEX	OCCUPATIONS	COUNTRY TO WHICH THEY BELONG	COUNTRY THEY INTEND TO INHABIT	SHIPS/DATES OF ARRIVAL	
STEDMAN, —, Miss	27	F		St. Croix	St. Croix	South Carolina Packet	16 Sep 1823
Elizabet	20	F		England	U. States	Hudson	8 Oct 1827
K., Miss	24	F		St. Croix	St. Croix	South Carolina Packet	16 Sep 1823
STEED, John	35	M	Merchant	Scotland	United States	Nestor	20 Nov 1821
Wm.	40		Labourer	England	United States	Hugh Johnson	11 Jun 1828
STEEGEAR, Rodolphe X.	22	M	Gentn.	Switzerland	United States	Stephania	16 Aug 1827
STEEL, —, Mrs.	23	F	None	U. States	U. States	Adze	24 Jul 1820
—, Mrs.	24	F		England	U. States	Elizabeth	20 Sep 1822
—, Mrs.	40	F		Scotland	New York	Broughty Castle	18 Dec 1826
Alexander	47	M	Laborer	G. Britain	United States	Edward	21 Apr 1821
Andrew	26	M	Farmer	Great Britain	United States	Eliza Barker	3 Jul 1826
Ann	30	F	Servant	Ireland	Ireland	Sarah G.	28 Nov 1827
Archabald	4	M	None	Scotland	United States	Mary & Susan	5 Aug 1828
Barbary, Child	3	F		Scotland	New York	Broughty Castle	18 Dec 1826
D.	25	M	Showman	U. States	U. States	Adze	24 Jul 1820
E.	19	M	Labourer	England	America	Two Marys	24 Sep 1827
Elisa	5	F	None	Scotland	United States	Mary & Susan	5 Aug 1828
Eliza	6	F		Scotland	U.S.	Curler	19 Jul 1828
Eliza	8	F	Farmer	Whalton ...ll..., England	Gt. Britain	Orozimbo	19 Oct 1822
Francis	31	F	Farmer	Whalton ...ll..., England	Gt. Britain	Orozimbo	19 Oct 1822
George	27	M	Labourer	Ireland	Ireland	Sarah G.	28 Nov 1827
Henry	30	M	Weaver	Ireland	United States	Princess Charlotte	26 Apr 1827
James	27	M	Gentleman	England	U. States	Elizabeth	20 Sep 1822
Jane	4	F		Scotland	U.S.	Curler	19 Jul 1828
Jane	18	F		G. Britain	United States	Edward	21 Apr 1821
John	11	M		G. Britain	United States	Edward	21 Apr 1821
John	45	M	Gentleman	Great Britain	Great Britain	Agenora	3 Oct 1826
John, Jr.	22	M		Scotland	U.S.	Curler	19 Jul 1828
John F.	30	M	Merchant	U. States	U.S.	Bayard	10 Nov 1824
Joseph	28	M	Labourer	Ireland	Ireland	Sarah G.	28 Nov 1827
Judy	8	M		Scotland	U.S.	Curler	19 Jul 1828
Margaret	6	F	None	Scotland	United States	Mary & Susan	5 Aug 1828
Margaret	9	F		G. Britain	United States	Edward	21 Apr 1821
Margret	29	F	None	Scotland	United States	Mary & Susan	5 Aug 1828
Margt.	13	F		Scotland	U.S.	Curler	19 Jul 1828
Martha	18/12	F	Farmer	Whalton ...ll..., England	Gt. Britain	Orozimbo	19 Oct 1822
Mary	2	F		Scotland	U.S.	Curler	19 Jul 1828
Mary	19	F		Scotland	U.S.	Curler	19 Jul 1828
Mary	22	F	Servant	Ireland	Ireland	Sarah G.	28 Nov 1827
Mary	36	F		Scotland	U.S.	Curler	19 Jul 1828
Mathew	8	M	None	Scotland	United States	Mary & Susan	5 Aug 1828
Mathew	21		Merchant	Gt. Britan	Portauprince	James Monroe	11 Dec 1821
Matilda	15	F		G. Britain	United States	Edward	21 Apr 1821
Nancy	12	F		G. Britain	United States	Edward	21 Apr 1821
Peter	19	M		Scotland	U.S.	Curler	19 Jul 1828
Rebecca	14	F		G. Britain	United States	Edward	21 Apr 1821
Saml.	24	F	Farmer	Whalton ...ll..., England	Gt. Britain	Orozimbo	19 Oct 1822
Samuel	2	M	Child	U. States	U. States	Adze	24 Jul 1820
Sarah	5	F	Farmer	Whalton ...ll..., England	Gt. Britain	Orozimbo	19 Oct 1822
Sarah	7	F	None	Scotland	United States	Mary & Susan	5 Aug 1828
Susan	1	F	None	Scotland	United States	Mary & Susan	5 Aug 1828
Wm.	40	M	Shoe Maker	St. Johns, N.B.	United States	Antioch	21 Sep 1827
STEELE, Catharine	27			Ireland	United States	John Dickinson	28 Jun 1822
Henry	22	M	...	U.S. America	U.S. America	Columbia	26 Nov 1825
James	16	M	Farmer	Great Britain	United States	Grecian	24 Sep 1828
James	38		Shoemaker	Great Brittain	Great Brittain	Commerce	14 Mar 1823
Job	23	M	Seaman	N. York	N. York	St. Helena	18 Feb 1823

*Invalid from the U.S. Ship Cayenne, to be received in the Maine Hospital

John	21	M	Preacher	Great Britain	United States	Grecian	24 Sep 1828
Martha	3			Ireland	United States	John Dickinson	28 Jun 1822

NAMES OF PASSENGERS	AGE	SEX	OCCUPATIONS	COUNTRY TO WHICH THEY BELONG	COUNTRY THEY INTEND TO INHABIT	SHIPS/DATES OF ARRIVAL	
STEELE (cont'd)							
Nancy	40	F	Spinster	St. Johns, N.B.	United States	Antioch	21 Sep 1827
STEELTON, S.	34	M	Farmer	Ireland	U. States	Francis	6 Sep 1827
STEEMSFIELD, George	18	M	Farmer	Great Brit.	Ohio	Gov. Griswald	3 Jul 1820
STEEN, Charles	18	M	Weaver	C. Tirone	Ohione	Nile	18 Aug 1829
Eliza	26	F	Spinster	Bellany Derry	...	Gleaner	24 May 1823
Helen	26	F		Glasgow	U. States	Duchess of Gloucester	1 Dec 1823
Jane	28	F	Wife of J. R. Steen, sent for by him	Ireland	United States	Asia	29 Jul 1829
John	28	M	Farmer	Glasgow	U. States	Duchess of Gloucester	1 Dec 1823
Thomas	3/52	M	their child [J. R. & Jane]	Ireland	United States	Asia	29 Jul 1829
STEENSON, Ann Jane	4	F		Ireland	America	Carolina Ann	7 Apr 1826
James	20			Great Britan	United States	Newry	11 Jul 1827
Mary	20 5/12	F		Ireland	America	Carolina Ann	7 Apr 1826
Nancy	24 10/12	F		Ireland	America	Carolina Ann	7 Apr 1826
STEEP, Johannes	28	M	Weaver	Switzerland	U.S.	Francois I	8 Aug 1829
STEEPHENS, Wm.	25	M	Painter	Ireland	United States	Wilson	6 Jun 1828
STEER, George	24	M	Confectioner	Great Britain	America	Lady Gallatin	21 Jun 1820
Mary	22	F		Great Britain	America	Lady Gallatin	21 Jun 1820
STEFFINGTON, Bernard	20	M	Labourer	Ireland	United States	Lord Wellington	28 May 1827
STEGMAN, Catherine	19	M		Switzerland	U.S.	Francois I	8 Aug 1829
Joha.	25	F		Switzerland	U.S.	Francois I	8 Aug 1829
STEI..., Catherina	28	F		Switzerland	United States	Elbe	2 Aug 1822
Christ.	6	M		Switzerland	United States	Elbe	2 Aug 1822
John	4	M		Switzerland	United States	Elbe	2 Aug 1822
STEILLHUTS, S. W.	14	F	Servant	Germany	U.S.A.	Noble	5 Nov 1828
STEILMAN, —, child *bierth 11 November		F		Germany	New York	Orient	25 Nov 1825
Jane	21	F		Germany	New York	Orient	25 Nov 1825
Shon	3	M		Germany	New York	Orient	25 Nov 1825
STEIN, Ceaule	10	F	Farmer	Germany	United States	Oxford	14 Aug 1828
Christian	26	M	Marner	Germany	U. States	Emma	15 Dec 1824
Christian	28	M	Mercht.	Germany	Mexico	Lewis	29 Oct 1825
Fredk. W.	22	M	Gentleman	Germany	United States	Richmond	4 Aug 1829
Gustavus A.	20	M	Mercht.	Germany	Mexico	Lewis	29 Oct 1825
Madelaine	40	F	Farmer	Germany	United States	Oxford	14 Aug 1828
Philipe	40	M	Farmer	Germany	United States	Oxford	14 Aug 1828
Robert	22	M	Clerk	Great Britain	U. States	Great Britain	18 Mar 1828
STEINARD, Gotlieb	28	M		Selesia		François I	19 Nov 1828
STEINBACH, —	36	M	Architech	France	United States	Cavalier	25 Jul 1828
—, Wife	39	F		France	United States	Cavalier	25 Jul 1828
STEINBIN, Frederick	31	M	Locksmith	Swiss	U. States	Montano	23 Apr 1825
STEINBRENNER, F. W.	35	M	Merchant	U. States	U. States	Quesnel	6 Sep 1824
STEINE, Catherine	50	F		Switzerland	U.S.	Francois I	8 Aug 1829
Maria	70	F		Switzerland	U.S.	Francois I	8 Aug 1829
STEINEN, Anna	50	F	Farmer	France	U. States	Lewis	6 Jul 1825
Barbara	25	F	Farmer	France	U. States	Lewis	6 Jul 1825
Catharine	3	F	Farmer	France	U. States	Lewis	6 Jul 1825
Margt.	1 6/12	F	Farmer	France	U. States	Lewis	6 Jul 1825
Ulrich	30	M	Farmer	France	U. States	Lewis	6 Jul 1825
STEINER, —	57	F		Switzerland	United States	Elbe	2 Aug 1822
Annah	2		Farmer	France	U. States	Elizabeth	9 Jul 1825
Barbara	7		Farmer	France	U. States	Elizabeth	9 Jul 1825
Barbary	6		Farmer	France	U. States	Elizabeth	9 Jul 1825
Christian	36		Farmer	France	U. States	Elizabeth	9 Jul 1825
Christine	32		Farmer	France	U. States	Elizabeth	9 Jul 1825
Daniel	4		Farmer	France	U. States	Elizabeth	9 Jul 1825
Daniel	4		Farmer	France	U. States	Elizabeth	9 Jul 1825
Daniel	38		Farmer	France	U. States	Elizabeth	9 Jul 1825
Elizabeth	2		Farmer	France	U. States	Elizabeth	9 Jul 1825
Elizabeth	9		Farmer	France	U. States	Elizabeth	9 Jul 1825
Frene	30		Farmer	France	U. States	Elizabeth	9 Jul 1825
Jannett	9		Farmer	France	U. States	Elizabeth	9 Jul 1825
John	26		Farmer	France	U. States	Elizabeth	9 Jul 1825
John	30	M	Farmer	Switzerland	United States	Elbe	2 Aug 1822

NAMES OF PASSENGERS	AGE	SEX	OCCUPATIONS	COUNTRY TO WHICH THEY BELONG	COUNTRY THEY INTEND TO INHABIT	SHIPS/DATES OF ARRIVAL
STEINER (cont'd)						
John	30	M	Labourer	Germany	U. States	Edward Bonaffe 11 Dec 1827
Maria	5		Farmer	France	U. States	Elizabeth 9 Jul 1825
Maria	6		Farmer	France	U. States	Elizabeth 9 Jul 1825
Michel	9		Farmer	France	U. States	Elizabeth 9 Jul 1825
STEINERE, John	2/12		Farmer	France	U. States	Elizabeth 9 Jul 1825
John	2/12		Farmer	France	U. States	Elizabeth 9 Jul 1825
STEINH...FER, C. G.	45	M	Doctor	Germany	United States	Elizabeth 27 Jul 1824
Emilia	10	F		Germany	United States	Elizabeth 27 Jul 1824
Lotte	6	F		Germany	United States	Elizabeth 27 Jul 1824
Mina	13	F		Germany	United States	Elizabeth 27 Jul 1824
Mina	58	F		Germany	United States	Elizabeth 27 Jul 1824
Sophia	1	F		Germany	United States	Elizabeth 27 Jul 1824
STEINICK, Michael	30	M	Farmer	Switzerland	United States	Elbe 2 Aug 1822
STEINMEY, —, Mr.	25			G. Britain	America	Magnet 24 Sep 1824
STEINNEZ, Jno. H.	36	M	Merchant	St. Bart	St. Bartholomews	Fair American 7 Feb 1825
STEINSON, Ann	1 6/12		None	Gt. Britan	United States	James Monroe 11 Dec 1821
Margret	25		None	Gt. Britan	United States	James Monroe 11 Dec 1821
Mary	3 2/12		None	Gt. Britan	United States	James Monroe 11 Dec 1821
Robert	31 6/12		Farmer	Gt. Britan	United States	James Monroe 11 Dec 1821
STEKEL, Adam	21	M	Shoemaker	France	United States	Le Voltaire 19 Jul 1828
STELFOX, Peter	25	M	Merchant	England	United States	Minerva 25 Aug 1823
STELLE, Robert	20	M	Merchant	America	United States	Pegasus 17 May 1828
STELTCOCH, Stephen W.	25	M	Merchant	N. York	U. States	Caravan 14 Apr 1824
STENEN, James	32	M	Labourer	Ireland	U. States	Two Marys 20 Apr 1825
STENGES, —, Mr.		M	Merchant	U. States	U. States	Galaxy 9 Sep 1826
—, Mrs.	30	F	None	United States	United States	Galaxy 9 Sep 1826
STENMAN, Cath.	2	F		Germany	United States	Lydia 18 Jun 1828
Jack	9	M		Germany	United States	Lydia 18 Jun 1828
Jacob	46	M	Farmer	Germany	United States	Lydia 18 Jun 1828
Maria	40	F		Germany	United States	Lydia 18 Jun 1828
Mary	6	F		Germany	United States	Lydia 18 Jun 1828
P.	18	M		Germany	United States	Lydia 18 Jun 1828
STENNET, George R.	23	M	Doctor (M.D.)	Jamaica	Jamaica	Peace 27 Dec 1824
STENSON, James	25	M	Mechanic	Scotland	United States	Concordia 25 Aug 1827
Wm.	26	M	Merchant	England	U. States	Cumberland 10 Nov 1823
STENZAR, C. A.	27	M	Merchant	Hamburg	U. States	Minerva 23 May 1825
STEPHAN, Michl.	18	M	Weaver	France	America, U.N.S.	Great Britain 3 Aug 1829
STEPHEN, —	42	M	Shoe Maker	France	United States	Cavalier 25 Jul 1828
—, his wife	40	F		France	United States	Cavalier 25 Jul 1828
Francois	16	M		France	United States	Cavalier 25 Jul 1828
John	21	M		G. Britan	U. States	William Neilson 26 Jul 1828
John	47	M	Baker	New Haven	U. States	Wanderer 1 Sep 1828
Joseph	12	M		France	United States	Cavalier 25 Jul 1828
STEPHENS, —, Mrs.	30			New York	Ireland	Carolina Ann 21 May 1823
—, Mrs.	36	F		Scotland	United States	William 4 Oct 1822
—, their child [James and Mrs.]	6			Scotland	United States	William 4 Oct 1822
—, their child [James and Mrs.]	8			Scotland	United States	William 4 Oct 1822
—, their child [James and Mrs.]	12			Scotland	United States	William 4 Oct 1822
A., Mrs.	30	F	None	England	United States	Manchester 16 Dec 1828
Amelia	28			Ireland	U.S.	Hibernia 27 Jun 1821
Bart	22	M	Shoemaker			Commerce 22 Jun 1825
Charles	31 6/12	M	Planter	U. States	U. States	John Wells 29 Jan 1825
Chas.	24	M	Mechanic	Great Brittan	Great Brittan	Tuscarora 26 Jan 1827
George, Mr.	23	M	Merchant	Ireland	United States	Dublin Packet 6 Dec 1827
Henry	38	M	Miner	Cornwall	Cornwall	Alto 8 Jun 1827
James	18		Labourer	England	United States	Hugh Johnson 11 Jun 1828
James	37	M	Merchant	Scotland	United States	William 4 Oct 1822
Jno.	7	M				Hibernia 15 Aug 1820
Joseph	23	M	spinner	Great Britain		Moro Castle 6 Jul 1827
Martin	24 2/12	M	Distiller	Germany	U.S. American	Criterion 7 Jul 1824
Mary	30	F	None	Grt. Brittain	United States	Euphrates 8 Nov 1821
Michael	22	M	Farmer	Ireland	United States	Dublin Packet 3 Sep 1822
Richard	17	M	Merchant	Sligo	Jamaica	Susquehana 27 Jun 1823
Stephen	44	M	Merchant	Grt. Brittain	United States	Euphrates 8 Nov 1821

NAMES OF PASSENGERS	A G E	S E X	OCCUPATIONS	COUNTRY TO WHICH THEY BELONG	COUNTRY THEY INTEND TO INHABIT	SHIPS/DATES OF ARRIVAL	
STEPHENS (cont'd)							
Thomas	22	M	Labourer	Ireland	United States	Helen	27 Jun 1821
William	13	M	None	England	United States	Jubilee	1 Oct 1828
William	27	M	Merchant	England	Great Brittan	Amity	11 May 1821
Wm.	20	M	Merchant	Great Britain	Canada	James Monroe	25 Apr 1822
Wm.	32	M	Cloathier	G. Britain	America	Spring	12 Oct 1821
Wm.	35	M	Merchant	Great Britain	Canada	Pacific	7 May 1827
STEPHENSON, C.	26	F	Servant	Jamaica	Jamaica	Huntress	15 Oct 1823
E.	30	M	private	U. States	U. States	Enterprize	9 Aug 1825
Eleanor	26	F		G. Britain	U. States	London	23 Sep 1828
Geo.	19	M	Farmer	G. Britain	U. States	Freak	9 Jun 1828
Hannah	6	F		Great Britain	United States	Freake	25 Jun 1827
Hugh	35		Merchant	New York	United States	Carolina Ann	21 May 1823
Isaac	57	M	Miller	Great Britan	Great Britan	Columbia	11 Aug 1823
James		M	Chiefly farmers		United States	Factor	8 Jul 1829
Jane	47	F		Great Britain	United States	Freake	25 Jun 1827
John	13	M		Great Britain	United States	Freake	25 Jun 1827
John	24	M	Doctor	Canada	Canada	Cortes	7 Jul 1821
John	31	M	Mercht.	South America	South America	Tampico	7 Jan 1828
Maria	9	F		Great Britain	United States	Freake	25 Jun 1827
Mary	19	F	Spinster	Lochurnnock	U.S. America	Camillus	10 Sep 1821
Peter	3	M		Great Britain	United States	Freake	25 Jun 1827
Peter	57	M	Farmer	Great Britain	United States	Freake	25 Jun 1827
Robert	40	M	Labourer	England	United States	Jubilee	1 Oct 1828
Robert, Jur.	13	M	None	England	United States	Jubilee	1 Oct 1828
Robt.	22	M	Engineer	England	England	Bunker Hill	20 Sep 1827
Robt.	25	M		G. Britain	U. States	London	23 Sep 1828
William	19	M		Great Britain	United States	Freake	25 Jun 1827
STEPHENSTON, Thos.	28	M	Carpenter	Lochurnnock	U.S. America	Camillus	10 Sep 1821
STEPHINSON, George	41		Mariner	New York	U. States	Lucy	16 Apr 1821
STEPHNSON, An	31	F	Accountant	G. Brittan	U. States	Henry	24 Oct 1828
Sarah	7	F		G. Brittan	U. States	Henry	24 Oct 1828
Thos.	33	F	Accountant	G. Brittan	U. States	Henry	24 Oct 1828
STEPHONS, John	42	M	Miner	G. Brittan	England	Frances	23 Mar 1827
STEPNA..., David	25	M	Farmer	Switzerland	United States	Olympia	12 Aug 1828
STEPPER, Andrew	20	M	Butcher	Germany		Ariel	24 Sep 1827
STERAT, William	21	M	Weaver	Scotland	United States	Mary & Susan	5 Aug 1828
STERBELE, Catherine	6	F	Farmer	Germany	United States	Oxford	14 Aug 1828
*Died on the voyage							
Catherine	20	F	Farmer	Germany	United States	Oxford	14 Aug 1828
Catherine	37	F	Farmer	Germany	United States	Oxford	14 Aug 1828
Frederic	10	M	Farmer	Germany	United States	Oxford	14 Aug 1828
Jean	37	M	Farmer	Germany	United States	Oxford	14 Aug 1828
Marguerite	4	F	Farmer	Germany	United States	Oxford	14 Aug 1828
Maria	6	F	Farmer	Germany	United States	Oxford	14 Aug 1828
STERET, Jean Louis	30	M	Farmer	Germany	United States	Oxford	14 Aug 1828
STERGEON, Catherin	22	F	Wife	Ireland	United States	Champion	3 Nov 1827
Ellen	3	F	Labourer or Spinster	Ireland	United States	Champion	3 Nov 1827
Robert	32	M	Weaver	Ireland	United States	Champion	3 Nov 1827
Wm. James	4	M	Child	Ireland	United States	Champion	3 Nov 1827
STERLING,							
C. M. Bd. D.	21	F		England	nonresident	Hudson	20 Nov 1828
Clara Ann	40	F		England	nonresident	Hudson	20 Nov 1828
Harry G.	27 4/12	M	Lawyer	U.S. America	America	Erie	19 Oct 1829
Henry	30	M	Farmer	Scotland	U. States	Camillus	27 Jun 1826
Robt.	32	M	Accountant	Great Britain	United States	Aurora	5 Sep 1826
Selvanus	35	M	Merchant	U. States	U.S.	Madison	13 May 1822
Wm.	25	M	Labourer	Ireland	United States	Neury	27 Jan 1827
STERMBROOK, Phillip	24	M		Switzerland	U.S.	C. Amelia	30 Jun 1828
STERN, Ann	2	F		G. Britain	U. States	Mary & Harriot	8 Sep 1828
Ann	5	F		G. Britain	U. States	Mary & Harriot	8 Sep 1828
Ann	38	F		G. Britain	U. States	Mary & Harriot	8 Sep 1828
Barbe	8	F	his family [Henry]	Germany	United States	Wm. Osborne	16 Sep 1828
Barbe	40	F	his family [Henry]	Germany	United States	Wm. Osborne	16 Sep 1828
Danl.	13	M		G. Britain	U. States	Mary & Harriot	8 Sep 1828
Elizabeth	4	F		G. Britain	U. States	Mary & Harriot	8 Sep 1828
Helene	6	F	his family [Henry]	Germany	United States	Wm. Osborne	16 Sep 1828
Henry	1	M	his family [Henry]	Germany	United States	Wm. Osborne	16 Sep 1828
Henry	45	M	Shoemaker	Germany	United States	Wm. Osborne	16 Sep 1828

NAMES OF PASSENGERS	AGE	SEX	OCCUPATIONS	COUNTRY TO WHICH THEY BELONG	COUNTRY THEY INTEND TO INHABIT	SHIPS/DATES OF ARRIVAL	
STERN (cont'd)							
Henry C.	27	M	Shoe Maker	Hamburg	U. States	Minerva	13 Sep 1827
John	38	M	Farmer	U. States	U. States	Martha	20 Jun 1825
John	38	M	Labourer	G. Britain	U. States	Mary & Harriot	8 Sep 1828
Joseph	9	M		G. Britain	U. States	Mary & Harriot	8 Sep 1828
Sophia	11	F		G. Britain	U. States	Mary & Harriot	8 Sep 1828
William	7	M		G. Britain	U. States	Mary & Harriot	8 Sep 1828
STERNBACK, Adam	6	M		Switzerland	U.States	C. Amelia	30 Jun 1828
Cath.	10	F		Switzerland	U.States	C. Amelia	30 Jun 1828
Cath.	30	F		Switzerland	U.States	C. Amelia	30 Jun 1828
Geo.	4	F	Tailor	Switzerland	U.States	C. Amelia	30 Jun 1828
Jean	60	M		Switzerland	U.States	C. Amelia	30 Jun 1828
Mary	2	F		Switzerland	U.States	C. Amelia	30 Jun 1828
Sophia	8	F		Switzerland	U.States	C. Amelia	30 Jun 1828
STERNBRICK, Christian	1	F		Switzerland	U.S.	C. Amelia	30 Jun 1828
STERNER, ...n	21 5/12	F	Farmer	Switzerland	U. States	France	26 Jun 1828
Barbara	7	F	None	France	U. States	Sully	25 Jun 1828
Barbara	40	F	None	France	U. States	Sully	25 Jun 1828
Christian	18	M	Weaver	France	U. States	Sully	25 Jun 1828
Elizabeth	64 3/12	F	Farmer	Switzerland	U. States	France	26 Jun 1828
John	20	M	Farmer	France	U. States	Sully	25 Jun 1828
John	66 8/12	M	Farmer	Switzerland	U. States	France	26 Jun 1828
Paul	5	M	None	France	U. States	Sully	25 Jun 1828
Peter	15	M	None	France	U. States	Sully	25 Jun 1828
Peter	50	M	Farmer	France	U. States	Sully	25 Jun 1828
Ulrick	10	M	None	France	U. States	Sully	25 Jun 1828
STERNS, —, Mrs.		F	Lady	France	France	Lincoln	12 Jun 1824
Samuel	19	M	Clerk	United States	United States	John London	13 Dec 1824
STERNTZ, Geo.	57	F		Switzerland	U.States	C. Amelia	30 Jun 1828
STERRETT, Benjn.	25	M	Merchant	America	United States	William Byrnes	15 Aug 1826
John	25	M	Schoolmaster	Great Britain	United States	Ann Maria	17 Apr 1827
STERRILL, Benjn.	55	M	Merchant	Pennsylvania	U. States	Columbia	7 Jul 1824
STERTAR, James	14	M		Stedford	United States	Swift	13 Jan 1827
STERTER, —, Mr.	40	M	Linen Manufactory	Stedford	United States	Swift	13 Jan 1827
Alexander	2	M		Stedford	United States	Swift	13 Jan 1827
Christain	12	M		Stedford	United States	Swift	13 Jan 1827
David	11	M		Stedford	United States	Swift	13 Jan 1827
Elisabeth	9	F		Stedford	United States	Swift	13 Jan 1827
J., Mrs.	40	F		Stedford	United States	Swift	13 Jan 1827
John	6	M		Stedford	United States	Swift	13 Jan 1827
STETSON, C.	24	M	Merchant	U. States	U. States	Topaz	5 Jul 1825
Lemuel	28	M	Mariner	U. States	U.S.	Ceres	16 Jan 1826
STEUBEN, E.	8	M	None	United States	United States	Robert Read	19 Oct 1825
Hannah	6	F	None	United States	United States	Robert Read	19 Oct 1825
Mary	12	F	None	United States	United States	Robert Read	19 Oct 1825
STEVEN, John	26	M	Taylor	Hanover	United States	Robert Edwards	3 Oct 1829
STEVENS, A.	34	M	Farmer	England	U. States	Acasta	12 May 1825
Ann	30	F		G. Brittain	U. States	Wm. Penn	6 Feb 1822
Benj.	13	M	Servant	Gt. Britain	Nova Scotia	Columbia	3 Apr 1826
Benj.	26	M	Merchant	N. York	U. States	Brandt	20 Sep 1822
Catharine S.	24	F		United States	United States	Hercules	16 Mar 1826
Charles	13	M	Boy	England	United States	Robert Edwards	3 Oct 1829
David	26	M	Watchmaker	Engd.	United States	Cosmo	21 Aug 1828
Dorothy	58	F	None			Evergreen	28 Jul 1820
E., Mr.	35			Massachusetts	New York	Felix	10 Sep 1824
Eliza	3/12	F		England	United States	Concordia	25 Aug 1827
Eliza Ann	16	F	None	England	England	John Wells	14 Oct 1823
G.	36	M	Farmer	England	U. States	Acasta	12 May 1825
H. H.	25	M	Mercht.	U. States	New York	Evelina	31 May 1825
Henry	20	M	Merchant	Grat Britan	Great Britan	Columbia	7 Apr 1823
Henry	31	M	Mechanic	England	United States	Concordia	25 Aug 1827
James	29	M	Gentleman	U. States	U. States	John & Robert	4 Sep 1827
Jane	6	F	Farmer	England	U. States	Acasta	12 May 1825
Jane	30	F	None			Evergreen	28 Jul 1820
Jas.	30	M	Weaver	Great Britain	U. States	Ganges	21 Jun 1827
John	3	M	Farmer	England	U. States	Acasta	12 May 1825
John	20	M	Labourer	Ireland	New York	Louisa	18 Apr 1827
John	35	M	Farmer	United States	Ohio	Brighton	19 Aug 1829
John	44	M		England	U. States	Electra	7 Jul 1828

NAMES OF PASSENGERS	AGE	SEX	OCCUPATIONS	COUNTRY TO WHICH THEY BELONG	COUNTRY THEY INTEND TO INHABIT	SHIPS/DATES OF ARRIVAL	
STEVENS (cont'd)							
Margery	26	F	None			Evergreen	28 Jul 1820
Martin H.	24	M	Laborer	Scotland	United States	Camillus	28 Apr 1824
Mary	20	F	Farmer	England	U. States	Acasta	12 May 1825
Mary	28	F	None			Evergreen	28 Jul 1820
Michael	33	M	Merchant	U. States	U. States	Radius	25 Jul 1820
Susannah	31	F		England	United States	Concordia	25 Aug 1827
Thomas	22		...	Co...	...	Hudson	14 Jun 1827
Thomas	30		Smith	County of Kent	N. York	Peru	30 May 1828
Thomas	34	M	Farmer	United States	Indianna	Brighton	19 Aug 1829
William	8	M		England	United States	Concordia	25 Aug 1827
William	16	M	Farmer	England	New York	Chelsea	16 May 1828
William	20	M	...	Ireland	United States	Carolina Ann	24 Oct 1825
William	22	M	Farmer	England	United States	Caspian	12 Jul 1821
Wm.	25		Servant	Denmark	U. States	South Carolina Packet	4 Sep 1822
STEVENSON, —, Mr.	49	M	Mariner	U. States	U. States	Frances Miller	9 Aug 1824
A.	35	M	Manufacture	England	England	James Cropper	10 Feb 1823
Adam	28	M	Merchant	Ireland	U. States	Chase	2 Oct 1826
Adam	28		Planter	Denmark	St. Croix	Eliza Davidson	8 Aug 1829
Andrew	39	M	Merchant	Great Britan	U. States	Columbia	10 Mar 1824
Ann	30	F		U. States	U. States	United States	11 Sep 1828
E.	7	F		England	U. States	Canning	18 Jul 1828
E.	9	M		England	U. States	Canning	18 Jul 1828
E.	36	F		England	U. States	Canning	18 Jul 1828
Edward	2			Ireland	United States	Courier	15 Oct 1827
Elizabeth	33 2/12	F				Cririe	18 Sep 1820
H.	11	M		England	U. States	Canning	18 Jul 1828
Hugh	24		Copper Smith	Ireland	United States	Robert Burns	30 May 1823
J.	13	M		England	U. States	Canning	18 Jul 1828
J.	38	M	Shoe Maker	U. States	U. States	Columbia	7 Sep 1827
J.	40	M	Cooper	England	U. States	Canning	18 Jul 1828
J. G.	26	M	Doctor	Boston	U. States	Desdemona	21 Oct 1825
James	8 1/12	M				Cririe	18 Sep 1820
James	28		Morocco dresser	Ireland	United States	Robert Burns	30 May 1823
James	39	M	Merchant	Great Britten	United States	Cortes	6 Mar 1827
Jno. B.	24	M	Doctor	U. States	U. States	Bayard	11 Jul 1825
John	19		Weaver	Ireland	G. Britain	Robert Burns	14 Jun 1824
John	30	M	Carpenter	G. Britain	U. States	Camillus	8 Sep 1828
John	34	M		Argyle (Tedland) Scotland	United States	Jean Hastie	27 Jul 1829
John G.	3...	M	...	America	United States	London Packet	25 Dec 1820
Leih	1 7/12	M				Cririe	18 Sep 1820
Mary	3	F		England	U. States	Canning	18 Jul 1828
Mary	3 4/12	F				Cririe	18 Sep 1820
Mary	19	F	Spinster	Ireland	United States	Fabius	31 Jul 1829
Mary Ann	21		Spinster	Ireland	United States	Courier	15 Oct 1827
Mathew	14	M	Labourer	Ireland	United States	William & George	14 May 1828
Paul	28	M	Cooper	Isle of Man	United States	Aurora	9 Jul 1827
R.	16	F		England	Canada	Brighton	14 Apr 1828
Rebecca	22	F	Spinster	Ireland	United States	Fabius	31 Jul 1829
Richard	32	M	Farmer	Ireland	America	Minerva	31 May 1824
Robert	25					Zamoa	5 Nov 1828
Samuel	5 1/12	M				Cririe	18 Sep 1820
W.	15	M		England	U. States	Canning	18 Jul 1828
Waller	41 4/12	M	Merchant	Gt. Britain	U. States	Maria	22 May 1822
William	19	M	Farmer	Ireland	United States	Trident	17 May 1825
William	22	M	Labourer	Ireland	United States	Meteor	26 Jun 1827
William	34	M	Merchant	Ireland	St. Croix	Phocian	5 Aug 1826
William	54	M	Gentleman	U. States, N. York	U. States	Jupiter	4 Mar 1828
Wm.	30	M	Merchant	Canada	Canada	William Byrnes	6 Apr 1826
Wm.	30	M	Merchant	G. Britain	United States	United States	11 Sep 1828
Wm. Jas.	3			Ireland	United States	Courier	15 Oct 1827
STEVERDING,							
Rel des ph	58	M	Merchant	Steenfield	U. States	Constitution	10 Jan 1827
STEVESON, Robt.	20	M	Weaver	Ireland	United States	Henry Kneeland	7 Jun 1828

NAMES OF PASSENGERS	AGE	SEX	OCCUPATIONS	COUNTRY TO WHICH THEY BELONG	COUNTRY THEY INTEND TO INHABIT	SHIPS/DATES OF ARRIVAL	
Thos.	25	M	Labourer	Ireland	Und. Stts of Amer	Alexander Mansfield	18 Aug 1826
STEVETY, James	38	M	Merchant	Ireland	United States	Bogota	16 Dec 1826
STEWARD, A.	23	M	Physician	Ireland	United States	Wm. Byrnes	30 Apr 1828
C. C.	16		None	New London	United States	Elizabeth	8 Dec 1821
Charles	44	M	Confectioner	Great Britian	United States	Mount Vernon	19 May 1823
Charles James, Rvd.	50	M	Lord Bishop of Quebec	Gt. Britian	Canada	Pacific	22 May 1826
David	65	M	Taylor	England	United States	Criterion	27 Oct 1820
Edward	46	M	Professor of Music	England	United States	Caspian	12 Jul 1821
Eliza	40			England		Anacreon	7 Sep 1827
Enoch	30	M	Mechanic	U. States	U. States	Acasta	21 Jan 1825
George	30	M	Servant	United States	United States	Only Daughter	29 Apr 1825
Hellen, his Daughter [David]	14	F		England	United States	Criterion	27 Oct 1820
Isabella, his Wife [David]	63	F		England	United States	Criterion	27 Oct 1820
James	2	M	None	England	United States	Hamilton	13 Nov 1827
James	28	M	Spinner	Scotland	America	Josephine	24 Jul 1826
James	35	M	Agent	England	U.S.	Panthea	13 Nov 1823
James, his Son [David]		M		England	United States	Criterion	27 Oct 1820
Jas.	29	M	Farmer	England	U. States	Oglethorpe	9 Nov 1824
Jno.	25	M	Coachmaker	England	United States	Nancy Henrietta	3 Nov 1828
John	4	M		Great Britian	United States	Mount Vernon	19 May 1823
John	25	M		Ireland	U. States	Nancy	16 Aug 1822
Joseph	11	M	None	England	United States	Hamilton	13 Nov 1827
Mary	18	F				Imperial	19 Jul 1820
Mary	27	F	None	England	United States	Hamilton	13 Nov 1827
Mary	35	F	Lady	New Jersey	United States	St. Michael	21 Aug 1824
Michael	57	M	Merchant	G. Britain	U. States	America	17 Oct 1825
Nancy	20	F	Miliner	Ireland	U. States	Beaver	27 Oct 1828
Nancy	45			England	United States	Caspian	12 Jul 1821
Priscilla Ann	18	F	Lady	New Jersey	United States	St. Michael	21 Aug 1824
Rachal	1		Child			Orion	21 Aug 1820
Rosy	18	F	Miliner	Ireland	U. States	Beaver	27 Oct 1828
Sophia Willmot	18	F	Wife	England	England	Virginia	26 May 1828
Thompson	20	M		Ireland	U. States	Nancy	16 Aug 1822
William	10	M	Boy	New Jersey	United States	St. Michael	21 Aug 1824
William	25	M	Labourer	Ireland	United States	Sylvester Healy	19 Aug 1825
Wm.	22	M	Engineer	England	England	Ambuscade	1 Jul 1820
Wm.	30	M		Ireland	U. States	John Dickinson	13 May 1823
Wm.	36	M	Labourer	Ireland	Ohio	Commerce	24 Sep 1823
STEWART, Agness	26	F			United States	Sarah	9 Nov 1820
Alex., Mr.	20	M	Merchant	Ireland	United States	Alex. Mansfield	17 May 1823
Alexander	53	M	Shipmaster	United States	United States	Howard	11 Jun 1824
Alexr.	4			Scotland	United States	Camillus	3 May 1824
Alexr.	29	M	Tanner	Scotland	New York	Joseph Hume	26 Oct 1829
Alexr.	31	M	Farmer	London, Great Britain	United States	Union	24 Sep 1823
Alexr. P.	26	M	Weaver	Ireland	United States	Commerce	13 Jun 1828
Alice	33	F	Wife	Great Britain	United States	Washington	3 Sep 1827
Allen	20	M	Farmer	Scotland	United States	Samuel Robertson	5 Oct 1827
Alxander	22	M	Weaver	Ireland	U. States	Josephine	7 May 1827
Amelia	7	F	None	London, Great Britain	United States	Union	24 Sep 1823
Andrew	26	M	Blacksmith	Great Britain	United States	Rosina	28 May 1827
Ann	2	F			United States	Sarah	9 Nov 1820
Ann	9	F	Child	Scotland	United States	Tom	2 Jul 1827
Ann	17					Amity	11 May 1821
Ann	18	F	None	Ireland	United States	Friends	21 Oct 1825
Ann	20	F	None	Ireland	U.S.A.	Lima	6 Dec 1826
Ann	22	F		Great Britain		Corinthian	27 Oct 1829
Ann	56	F		Ireland	United States	Commerce	13 Jun 1828
Anthony	21	M	Gardner	Ireland	United States	Trident	17 May 1825
Anthony	26	M	Fuller	Ireland	United States	Asia	29 Jul 1829
Barbary	26	F		Ireland	United States	Lincoln	10 Dec 1823

NAMES OF PASSENGERS	AGE	SEX	OCCUPATIONS	COUNTRY TO WHICH THEY BELONG	COUNTRY THEY INTEND TO INHABIT	SHIPS/DATES OF ARRIVAL	
STEWART (cont'd)							
Bridget	30	F	Labourer	Ireland	United States	Hope	12 Jun 1828
C. S.	30	M	Clergyman	United States	United States	Richmond	4 Aug 1826
Carden	16	M		Great Britain		Corinthian	27 Oct 1829
Cat.	25	M	Farm	Ireland	U. States	Meteor	19 Jul 1828
Catharine	4			Scotland	United States	Camillus	3 May 1828
Catharine	12	F		Ireland	United States	Lincoln	10 Dec 1823
Catharine	60	F	None	Ireland	U. States	Josephine	27 Jul 1825
Charles	3	M		United States	United States	Richmond	4 Aug 1826
Charly	9	M	Labourer	Ireland	United States	Hope	12 Jun 1828
Da...	6 6/12	M	Child	Scotland	United States	Samuel Robertson	9 May 1827
Daniel	3	M		Ireland	United States	Lincoln	10 Dec 1823
Daniel	48	M	Weaver	Ireland	United States	Kleber	23 Jul 1827
David	3			Scotland	United States	Camillus	3 May 1828
David	16	M	Clerk	Gt. Britain	U.S. of America	Friends	25 Sep 1823
David	20	M	Weaver	Ireland	United States	Trident	17 May 1825
Donald	22	M	Farmer	Ireland	U. States	Josephine	27 Jul 1825
Elisabeth	23					Zamoa	5 Nov 1828
Eliza	3	F	Child	Scotland	United States	Tom	2 Jul 1823
Eliza Jane	6/12	F	None	Great Britain	United States	Mary & Harriet	3 Jul 1829
Elizabeth	20	F		Scotland	United States	Camillus	9 May 1827
Elizabeth	27	F	None	Montreal, Canada	Great Britain	James Cropper	7 Oct 1823
Elizabeth	30	F	Wife	Scotland	United States	Samuel Robertson	9 May 1827
Elizabeth	45	F		Great Britain		Corinthian	27 Oct 1829
Frances	20	F		Great Britain		Corinthian	27 Oct 1829
Geo. D.	10			Ireland	United States	Jno. Dickinson	21 Sep 1821
Georg	30	M	Labourer	Ireland	United States	Hope	12 Jun 1828
George	20	M	Farmer	Ireland	U. States	Josephine	27 Jul 1825
George	22	M		Scotland	United States	Camillus	9 May 1827
George	26	M	Carpenter	Ireland	United States	Carolina Ann	11 Dec 1826
George	28	M	Cordwaner	England	America	Franklin	13 Aug 1827
H.	38	M	Planter	St. Croix	St. Croix	Chase	29 Apr 1825
Hamilton	22	M	Woolen Manufacturer	Ireland	United States	Kleber	23 Jul 1827
Harriet	1	F		United States	United States	Richmond	4 Aug 1826
Harriet	26	F	Lady	United States	United States	Richmond	4 Aug 1826
Isaac	27	M		Scotland	United States	Camillus	9 May 1827
Isabella	20	F		G. Britain	U. States	Camillus	8 Sep 1828
Isabella	25	F	None	London, Great Britain	United States	Union	24 Sep 1823
J. C.	22	M	Merchant	U. States	U. States	Venus	27 Jun 1821
James	6			Scotland	United States	Camillus	3 May 1828
James	18	M	Labourer	G. Brittian	United States	Louisa	14 Jun 1825
James	23	M	Labourer	Ireland	United States	Hope	12 Jun 1828
James	24	M	Mechanic	Great Britain	United States	Mary & Harriet	3 Jul 1829
James	26		Farmer	Ireland	United States	Carolina Ann	12 Sep 1823
James	28	M		Ireland	U. States	John Dickinson	13 May 1823
James	30	M		Ireland	U. States	John Dickinson	13 May 1823
James	30	M	Merchant	Gt. Britain	U. States	Panthia	13 Nov 1824
James	30	M		G. Britain	U. States	Camillus	8 Sep 1828
James	35	M	Lawyer	Canada	United States	Corinthian	10 Jan 1826
James	35	M	Merchant	Scotland	Scotland	Virginia	26 May 1828
James	38	M	Merchant	N. Carolina	U. States	Maria	30 Jul 1823
James	38	M	Merchant	U. States	U. States	Silas Richards	29 Oct 1828
James	41	M	Advocate	Canada	Canada	William Thompson	18 Jan 1825
James	43	M	Advocate	Montreal, Canada	Great Britain	James Cropper	7 Oct 1823
James	50	M				Acasta	14 Jun 1824
James	60	M		Great Britain		Corinthian	27 Oct 1829
Jane	4	F		Ireland	U. States	John Dickinson	13 May 1823
Jane	22	M	Labourer	Ireland	United States	Hope	12 Jun 1828
Jane	25	F		Scotland	U.S.	Curler	19 Jul 1828
Jane	30	F	Wife	Scotland	United States	Tom	2 Jul 1827
Jane	50	F	Seamstress	Scotland	U. States	Camillus	27 Jun 1826
Janet	1			Scotland	United States	Camillus	3 May 1828

1207

NAMES OF PASSENGERS	AGE	SEX	OCCUPATIONS	COUNTRY TO WHICH THEY BELONG	COUNTRY THEY INTEND TO INHABIT	SHIPS/DATES OF ARRIVAL	
STEWART (cont'd)							
Janet	20			Scotland	United States	Camillus	3 May 1828
Janet	28			Scotland	United States	Camillus	3 May 1828
Janette	17	F	Seamstress	Scotland	U. States	Camillus	27 Jun 1826
Jas.	30	M	Miller	Great Britain	United States	Atlantic	8 Dec 1827
Jas.	32	M	Gentleman	Ireland	America	Alexander	28 Jul 1821
John	1	M			United States	Sarah	9 Nov 1820
John	5	M		Ireland	United States	Lincoln	10 Dec 1823
John	6	M	Labourer	Ireland	United States	Hope	12 Jun 1828
John	16	M	None	England	U. States	Montgomery	18 Oct 1828
John	20	M	Laborer	Ireland	United States	Mary	1 Jul 1829
John	24	F	Merchant	England	England	Venus	15 Apr 1822
John	25	M	Weaver	Ireland	New York	Atlantic	8 May 1828
John	30	M	Servent	England	United States	Nestor	20 Nov 1821
John	32	M	Labourer	Scotland	United States	Samuel Robertson	9 May 1827
John	33	M	Black Smith	Great Britain	United States	Washington	3 Sep 1827
John	34	M	Merchant	Philad.	U. States	Convoy	14 Mar 1823
John	36	M	Gentleman	U. States	U. States	Indus	24 Jul 1827
John	37	M	Farmer	Ireland	United States	Lincoln	10 Dec 1823
John	40	M	Shoemaker	Scotland	United States	Tom	2 Jul 1827
John	40	M	Farmer	Scotland	United States	Tom	2 Jul 1827
Maagy	1	F	Labourer	Ireland	United States	Hope	12 Jun 1828
Margaret	7	F		Ireland	United States	Lincoln	10 Dec 1823
Margaret	25	F	Farmer	Scotland	America	Mentor	21 Sep 1824
Mary	7			Scotland	United States	Camillus	3 May 1828
Mary	10	F	None	Scotland	U. States	Camillus	27 Jun 1826
Mary	10	F		U.S.	N. York	France	29 Nov 1827
Mary	15	F	Seamstress	Scotland	U. States	Camillus	27 Jun 1826
Mary	16	F	Child	Great Britain	United States	Washington	3 Sep 1827
Mary	18	F	Spinster	Ireland	U. States	Lady Hunter	18 Jul 1825
Mary	23	F		Ireland	United States	Alexander Mansfield	16 Sep 1823
Mary	24	F	None	Great Britain	United States	Mary & Harriet	3 Jul 1829
Mary	30		Wife, going to her husband	Scotland	United States	Camillus	3 May 1828
Mary	31	F		Ireland	United States	Aurora	9 Jul 1827
Mary Ann	6/12	F		Ireland	United States	Lincoln	10 Dec 1823
Molly	26	F		Ireland	United States	Carolina Ann	11 Dec 1826
Otty	35	M	Farmer	England	United States	Meteor	16 Aug 1824
Peter	20	M	Labourer	Scotland	United States	Samuel Robertson	5 Oct 1827
Richard	25	M	Weaver	Ireland	New York	Trusty	12 Sep 1828
Robert	28	M	Blacksmith	Great Britain	United States	Mary Howland	19 Jul 1827
Saml.	60	M	Farmer	Pitsburg	United States	Carolina Ann	11 Jun 1824
Sarah	24	F		St. Johns, N.B.	America	Franklin	13 Aug 1827
Sarah	30	F		Scotland	United States	Camillus	9 May 1827
Susan	20	F		U. States	U. States	Carlo	19 Jun 1828
T. W.	32	M	Captain	G. Britain	London	William	31 Aug 1820
Thomas	21	M	Clerk	Ireland	United States	Friends	21 Oct 1825
Thomas	30	M		Ireland	United States	William & George	14 May 1828
Thomas	40	M	Farmer	Ireland	U. States	Josephine	27 Jul 1825
Thos.	23	M	Farmer	Fife, Scotland	N. York	New Orleans	24 Aug 1827
Walter	31	M	Labourer	Scotland	United States	Friends	7 Jul 1827
William	... 6/12	M	Child	Scotland	United States	Samuel Robertson	9 May 1827
William	5	M	None	London, Great Britain	United States	Union	24 Sep 1823
William	15	M	Seamstress	Scotland	U. States	Camillus	27 Jun 1826
William	21	M	Woolen Manufacturer	Ireland	United States	Kleber	23 Jul 1827
William	21	M	Manufacturer	Great Britain	U. States	United States	8 Sep 1827
Wm.	25	M	Baker	G. Britain	U. States	Robt. Edwards	4 Sep 1828
Wm.	27	M	Farmer	Scotland	U.S.	Curler	19 Jul 1828
Wm.	30	M	Farmer	Scotland	United States	Margaret Bogle	11 Jun 1824
Wm.	70	M	Weaver	Ireland	United States	Commerce	13 Jun 1828
STEWINSON, Henry	23	M		England	United States	St. George	25 Aug 1829
STEWITT, Thos.	...	M	...			Rufus King	27 Jun 1821

NAMES OF PASSENGERS	AGE	SEX	OCCUPATIONS	COUNTRY TO WHICH THEY BELONG	COUNTRY THEY INTEND TO INHABIT	SHIPS/DATES OF ARRIVAL	
STEZER, Catharan	54	F	Washerwoman	Ireland		Quatre Freres	29 Jul 1828
STIBBS, Jno.	55	M	Weaver	Great Britain	United States	India	5 Sep 1827
STICKLAND, Ann	8			England	England	Thames	25 Oct 1821
Eliza	5			England	England	Thames	25 Oct 1821
Elizabeth	3/12			England	England	Thames	25 Oct 1821
Emma	28			England	England	Thames	25 Oct 1821
John	10			England	England	Thames	25 Oct 1821
Joseph	33		Black Smith	England	England	Thames	25 Oct 1821
William	3			England	England	Thames	25 Oct 1821
STICKLE, M.	32	M	Farmer	Switzerland	U. States	Romulus	24 Sep 1828
STICKLER, Ann	2	F	Agriculture	Bavaria	United States	Henri IV	14 Oct 1829
Eva	11	F	Agriculture	Bavaria	United States	Henri IV	14 Oct 1829
Eva	35	F	Agriculture	Bavaria	United States	Henri IV	14 Oct 1829
Jas.	41	M	Agriculture	Bavaria	United States	Henri IV	14 Oct 1829
Nicholas	4	M	Agriculture	Bavaria	United States	Henri IV	14 Oct 1829
STICKNEY, Peter	30	M	Mariner	U. States	U. States	Danube	2 Sep 1828
STIEBB, Anthony	3	M		France	U. States	Edward Quesnel	4 Aug 1828
Joseph	7	M		France	U. States	Edward Quesnel	4 Aug 1828
Joseph	27	M	Farmer	France	U. States	Edward Quesnel	4 Aug 1828
Theresa	26	F		France	U. States	Edward Quesnel	4 Aug 1828
STIEST, Catherine	14	F	Farmer	Germany	United States	Oxford	14 Aug 1828
John	46	F	Farmer	Germany	United States	Oxford	14 Aug 1828
Joseph	7	M	Farmer	Germany	United States	Oxford	14 Aug 1828
Marguerite	40	F	Farmer	Germany	United States	Oxford	14 Aug 1828
Pauline	13	F	Farmer	Germany	United States	Oxford	14 Aug 1828
Rosine	10	F	Farmer	Germany	United States	Oxford	14 Aug 1828
STIFFER, Barbara	22	F	None	France	U. States	Sully	25 Jun 1828
Catharan	9	F	None	France	U. States	Sully	25 Jun 1828
David	58	M	Weaver	France	U. States	Sully	25 Jun 1828
Dorra	14	M	None	France	U. States	Sully	25 Jun 1828
Honour	45	M	None	France	U. States	Sully	25 Jun 1828
STIGE, —				Scotland	United States	Camillus	27 Oct 1829
STIGMERE, Godfrey	26	M	Carpenter	Germany	U. States	Isabella	10 Aug 1829
STILELES, —, Miss	18	F		England	U.S. America	Leeds	6 Jun 1826
STILES, G.	22	M	Supercargo	U. States	U. States	Sea Flower	23 May 1826
Jane	26		Joiner	England	U. States	Venus	4 Oct 1821
John	30		Joiner	England	U. States	Venus	4 Oct 1821
STILL, John	20	M	Labourer	Ireland	U.S.	Ann	10 Jan 1825
STILLSON, Edward	18	M	Farmer	England	U.S. America	Cortes	19 May 1826
STILMAN, Jno.	18	M	Carpenter	New York	U. States	Almira	3 Sep 1822
Mary	40	F		New York	U. States	Almira	3 Sep 1822
STIMINS, Jesse	30	M	Merchant	St. John	St. John	St. Michael	27 Mar 1827
STIMPSON, John	24	M	Mercht.	Massachusetts	U. States	Lydia	7 Oct 1823
STINAMON, Harman	30	M	Baker	Germany	U. States America	Electra	17 Nov 1828
STINE, Robt.	35	M	...			Manhattan	25 Dec 1820
STINEMAN, George	35	M	Plater	Prussia	Philadelphia, U.S. of America	Europa	6 Oct 1828
STINER, Anna	30	F	Framer	Switserland	Ohio	Danube	20 Jul 1826
Anna	40	F	Framer	Switserland	Ohio	Danube	20 Jul 1826
Barbara	6	M	Framer	Switserland	Ohio	Danube	20 Jul 1826
Christian	1	M	Framer	Switserland	Ohio	Danube	20 Jul 1826
Christian	4	M	Framer	Switserland	Ohio	Danube	20 Jul 1826
Elizabath	13	F	Framer	Switserland	Ohio	Danube	20 Jul 1826
Elizabath	40	F	Framer	Switserland	Ohio	Danube	20 Jul 1826
John	10	M	Framer	Switserland	Ohio	Danube	20 Jul 1826
John	20	M	Framer	Switserland	Ohio	Danube	20 Jul 1826
John	44	M	Framer	Switserland	Ohio	Danube	20 Jul 1826
Lizabath	18	F	Framer	Switserland	Ohio	Danube	20 Jul 1826
Trena	16	F	Framer	Switserland	Ohio	Danube	20 Jul 1826
STINGEON, Saml.	21	M	Farmer	Great Britain	U. States	Princess Charlotte	6 Sep 1828
STINGER, Saml.	25	M	Merchant	U. States	U. States	General Paez	17 Aug 1825
STINKEN, John	16	M	Sugar baker	Hannover	U. States	Constitution	15 Nov 1822
STINMAN, John, Capt.	46	M	Marner	United States	United States	Commerce	7 Jul 1826
STINMATS, Mary	29	F		Native of Switzerland	United States	Canaris	30 Jun 1827
STINSON, Ann	27	F		Great Brit.	Ohio	Gov. Griswald	3 Jul 1820
David	18	M	Labourer	Great Britain	United States	Atlantic	8 Dec 1827
Eliz.	60	F	Spinner	Great Britain	United States	Atlantic	8 Dec 1827

NAMES OF PASSENGERS	AGE	SEX	OCCUPATIONS	COUNTRY TO WHICH THEY BELONG	COUNTRY THEY INTEND TO INHABIT	SHIPS/DATES OF ARRIVAL	
STINSON (cont'd)							
Eliz., Junr.	16	F	Spinner	Great Britain	United States	Atlantic	8 Dec 1827
Hugh	30	M	Laborer	Ireland	United States	Carolina Ann	11 Dec 1826
James	70	M	Weaver	Great Britain	United States	Atlantic	8 Dec 1827
Jane	1 6/12	F		Ireland	United States	Carolina Ann	11 Dec 1826
John	25	M	Farmer	Great Brit.	Ohio	Gov. Griswald	3 Jul 1820
Mary	5	F		Ireland	United States	Carolina Ann	11 Dec 1826
Mary	23	F		Ireland	United States	Carolina Ann	11 Dec 1826
Robt.	20	M	Weaver	Great Britain	United States	Atlantic	8 Dec 1827
Sally	4	F		Ireland	United States	Carolina Ann	11 Dec 1826
STINSTON, James	20	M	Labourer	Scotland	United States	Samuel Robertson	5 Oct 1827
Jane	22	F		Scotland	United States	Samuel Robertson	5 Oct 1827
STIRLING, Robert	26	M	Mason	Great Britain	United States	Colossus	5 Jun 1827
STIRRAT, Andrew	19		Clerk	Ireland	Great Britain	Robert Burns	14 Jun 1824
STITH, Griffin	32	M	Merchant	United States	U. States	Corinthian	2 Sep 1824
STITS, Richard	30	M	Ship Master	England	U. States	Manchester Packet	30 Nov 1822
STITSON, H.	25	M	Mariner	Baltimore	U. States	George	25 Sep 1820
STITZER, Elizabeth	35	F	Wife of [Jacob]	Switzerland	United States	Aurora	21 Jun 1824
Jacob	36	M	Mason	Switzerland	United States	Aurora	21 Jun 1824
John	8	M	Child of [Jacob]	Switzerland	United States	Aurora	21 Jun 1824
Mary An	...	F	Child of [Jacob]	Switzerland	United States	Aurora	21 Jun 1824
STIYNETS, Jesse	18	M	Clerk	St. John, N.B.	St. John, N.B.	St. Michaels	24 Mar 1825
STO...W, Thos. W.	48	M	Merch.	U. States	United States	Henri IV	14 Oct 1829
STOAKES, John	22	M	Pa...	Ireland	U. States	Howard Douglass	29 Jan 1828
STOB, Charlotte	24	F	Spinster	England	America	Friends	24 Sep 1821
STOBB, T.	26	M	Merchant	Switzerland	U. States	Marmion	29 Sep 1823
STOBE, James	24	M	Farmer	Scotland	America	Friends	24 Sep 1821
STOBLE, B.	30	F		Scotland	U. States	Superior	25 Sep 1828
J.	16	M	Farmer	Scotland	U. States	Superior	25 Sep 1828
Robt.	60	M	Farmer	Scotland	U. States	Superior	25 Sep 1828
STOCK, Dennis	30	M	Servant	England	America	William	21 Sep 1821
STOCKBERGER, Geo.	35	M	Watchmaker	Switzerland	U. States	Hewes	30 Oct 1829
STOCKDALE, John	23	M	Farmer	Great Britain	United States	William Dawson	18 Jun 1827
STOCKDALL, —, Miss	28	F		Bermuda	U. States	Agnes	1 Jul 1825
Ben	25	M	Servant	Bermuda	U. States	Agnes	1 Jul 1825
STOCKER, Leopold	18	M	Servant	Germany	U. States	Hesper	28 Jun 1825
W.	25	M	Mariner	U. States	U. States	Dromo	22 May 1826
STOCKES, Elick	18	M	Seaman	America	America	Peruvian	11 Mar 1822
STOCKING, M.	20	M	Mariner	Middletown	United States	Windham	7 Mar 1823
STOCKOE, John	46	M	Doctor	London	Philadelphia	Falcon	10 Sep 1823
STOCKS, Robert	28	M	Farmer	England	New York	Robert Edwards	17 Mar 1828
STOCKTON, Ann	32	F	Seamstress	St. Johns, N.B.	United States	Henrietta	17 Aug 1825
Betsey	31	F	Nurse	United States	United States	Richmond	4 Aug 1826
Danl.	34	M	Farmer	Great Britain	U.S. of Ama.	Robert Fulton	16 Aug 1824
Elizabeth	6	F		St. Johns, N.B.	United States	Henrietta	17 Aug 1825
Harriet	8	F		St. Johns, N.B.	United States	Henrietta	17 Aug 1825
Nancy	1 2/12	F		St. Johns, N.B.	United States	Henrietta	17 Aug 1825
Tamer	4 6/12	F		St. Johns, N.B.	United States	Henrietta	17 Aug 1825
STOCKWELL, John	27	M	Printer	United States	District Columbia	Atlantic	6 Oct 1828
Josiah	45	M	Chair Maker	U.S.A.	U.S.A.	Enterprize	30 Aug 1821
Leister	13	F	None			Euphrates	8 Aug 1820
STODDARD,							
A. D., & Servant	45	M	Merchant	America	America	Galatea	20 Jul 1829
Asy	29	F	None	United States	United States	Euphrates	15 Jul 1822
Bernard	24	M		Ireland	U. States	Fame	15 Nov 1826
Chs.	26		Ship Master	United States	U. States	Cadet	11 Jan 1826
Jno. B.	23	M	Blacksmith	America	America	Martha Pond	7 Sep 1820
Thomas	32	M	Labourer	England	America	Franklin	19 Nov 1828
William	...	M	...	England	United States	London Packet	25 Dec 1820
STODDART, —, Mr.	30	F	Waiter	Scotland	United States	Camillus	27 Oct 1829
—, Mrs.	28	F		Scotland	United States	Camillus	27 Oct 1829
Bryce	2	M	Gardener	Scotland	U. States	Warrior	16 Mar 1826
David	3	M		Scotland	United States	Camillus	27 Oct 1829
Mergnut	24	F	Gardener	Scotland	U. States	Warrior	16 Mar 1826
Richart	1	M		Scotland	U. States	Warrior	16 Mar 1826

NAMES OF PASSENGERS	AGE	SEX	OCCUPATIONS	COUNTRY TO WHICH THEY BELONG	COUNTRY THEY INTEND TO INHABIT	SHIPS/DATES OF ARRIVAL	
STODDART (cont'd)							
Walter	26	M	Gardener	Scotland	U. States	Warrior	16 Mar 1826
STODDER, Robert H.	21	M	Merchant	United States	U. States	William Byrnes	24 Apr 1827
STODDERD, James	24	M	Farmer	Great Brittain	United States	Robert Fulton	13 Mar 1827
STOECHE, Adam	7	M	Farmer	Switzerland	United States	Olympia	12 Aug 1828
Adams	57	M	Farmer	Switzerland	United States	Olympia	12 Aug 1828
Elizabeth	37	F	Farmer	Switzerland	United States	Olympia	12 Aug 1828
Michel	1	M	Farmer	Switzerland	United States	Olympia	12 Aug 1828
STOEL, Wm.	22 5/12	M		U.S. America	U.S. America	Edward Bonnaffe	20 Jun 1826
STOERY, J.	30	M	Mariner	England	England or Jamaica	Packet	11 Oct 1823
STOFFELD, As.	30	M	Merchant	Switzerland	Uncertain	Ocean	30 Jun 1821
STOFFER, Benj.	24	M	Labourer	Swiss	U. States	Comet	28 Jul 1825
John	26	M	Labourer	Swiss	U. States	Comet	28 Jul 1825
STOFFORD, Cath.	17	F		G. Britain	U. States	St. George	7 Jun 1828
W.	17	F		G. Britain	U. States	St. George	7 Jun 1828
STOGUN, Henry	18	M	Labourer	U. States	U. States	Nancy	19 Oct 1821
STOKE, Alfred	6	M	son of Mr. W. S. [William]	England	United States	Robert Edwards	4 Jun 1824
Ellen	7/12	F	...	England	United States	Robert Edwards	4 Jun 1824
Jane	8	F	...	England	United States	Robert Edwards	4 Jun 1824
M., Mrs.	38	F	wife of Mr. W. S. [William]	England	United States	Robert Edwards	4 Jun 1824
Sydney	10	M	son of Mr. W. S. [William]	England	United States	Robert Edwards	4 Jun 1824
Thomas	14	M	son of Mr. W. S. [William]	England	United States	Robert Edwards	4 Jun 1824
William	12	M	son of Mr. W. S. [William]	England	United States	Robert Edwards	4 Jun 1824
William	40	M	Miller	England	United States	Robert Edwards	4 Jun 1824
STOKER, James	22	M		Great Britten	U. States	Magnet	29 Sep 1823
Richard	38	M	Clerk	France	State of N. York	Danube	20 Jul 1826
STOKES, Betsey	35	F		Curacoa	U. States	Matteawan	6 Apr 1822
Chas. Wm.	34	M	Merchant	Gt. Brittain	United States	York	6 Dec 1826
Eliza	27	F		Ireland	United States	Trio	2 Oct 1828
Frederick	5	M		Ireland	United States	Trio	2 Oct 1828
George	21	M	Preacher	Ireland	United States	Trio	31 Oct 1827
James	18	M	Weaver	England	New York	Cincinnatus	16 Apr 1824
John	12	M	None	England		Manhattan	22 May 1827
Judeth	20	F		Ireland	New York	Eliza Grant	29 Aug 1829
M.	25	M	Merchant	England		Marchioness	13 May 1828
Marianne	34	F		Ireland	United States	Criterion	27 Oct 1820
Pat	27	M	Laborer	Ireland	New York	Eliza Grant	29 Aug 1829
Patk.	26	M	Tailor	Ireland	United States	Wilson	27 Jun 1826
Thomas	24	M	Weaver	England	United States	Brighton	11 Mar 1825
Thomas	45	M	Weaver	England	New York	Cincinnatus	16 Apr 1824
Thos.	24	M	Merchant	Gt. Brittain	United States	York	6 Dec 1826
STOKPOLE, Barney	24	M	Laborer	Ireland	New York	Indian Chief	19 Jun 1823
STOKY, Charles	17	M	Farmer	France		Pallas	14 Jun 1828
Eliz.	33	F		France		Pallas	14 Jun 1828
Frea	21	M	Farmer	France		Pallas	14 Jun 1828
Henry	23	M		France		Pallas	14 Jun 1828
Loasia	3	F	Farmer	France		Pallas	14 Jun 1828
Lyon Ledre	51	M		France		Pallas	14 Jun 1828
Perre	26	M		France		Pallas	14 Jun 1828
STOLL, John	28	M	Shoemaker	England	U. States	Spartan	21 Apr 1826
STOLLES, Ann Maria	1	F		France	Canada	Abby Jones	12 Jul 1827
Antoney	19	M	Wheelwright	France	Canada	Abby Jones	12 Jul 1827
Catharine	10	F		France	Canada	Abby Jones	12 Jul 1827
Frank	7	M	Wheelwright	France	Canada	Abby Jones	12 Jul 1827
John	54	M	Wheelwright	France	Canada	Abby Jones	12 Jul 1827
John, Jr.	26	M	Wheelwright	France	Canada	Abby Jones	12 Jul 1827
Joseph	24	M	Wheelwright	France	Canada	Abby Jones	12 Jul 1827
Maria	6	F		France	Canada	Abby Jones	12 Jul 1827
Mary Ann	41	F		France	Canada	Abby Jones	12 Jul 1827
Nicholas	3	M	Wheelwright	France	Canada	Abby Jones	12 Jul 1827
Thaesey	12	F		France	Canada	Abby Jones	12 Jul 1827
STOLTE, George Fredk.	26	M	Farmer	Hanover	U. States	Minerva	24 Sep 1821
STOLTZ, Johan	46	M	Weaver	Switzerland	U. States	Hewes	30 Oct 1829

NAMES OF PASSENGERS	AGE	SEX	OCCUPATIONS	COUNTRY TO WHICH THEY BELONG	COUNTRY THEY INTEND TO INHABIT	SHIPS/DATES OF ARRIVAL	
STONDER, Henry	45	M	Mercht.	Switzerland	U. States	Brown	8 Aug 1825
STONE, ...	27	M	Farmer	Great Brittain	United States	Sarah Ralston	27 Jan 1827
Aaron	32	M	Mercht.	United States	United States	Importer	21 May 1821
Alexander	21	M	Labourer	England	United States	Comet	6 Mar 1823
Alfred	2	M	None	England		Marchioness	13 May 1828
Ann	6	F	None	England		Marchioness	13 May 1828
Bertha	7/12	F	None	England		Marchioness	13 May 1828
Danl.	21	M	Shoemaker	England		Marchioness	13 May 1828
Eliza	3	F		Ireland	U. States	Ganges	8 May 1823
Eliza	26	F	None	United States	United States	Importer	21 May 1821
Elizabeth	infant	F		Great Britain	United States	Ganges	8 Jul 1820
Fredk. W., Mr.	26	M	Mercht.	United States	United States	Manchester	15 Aug 1826
Geo.	36	M	Farmer	G. Braitan	U. States	Cosmo	29 Jun 1826
George	28	M	Labourer	Ireland		Marchioness	13 May 1828
Hannah	20	F	None	England		Marchioness	13 May 1828
Harriot	2	F	None	United States	United States	Importer	21 May 1821
Isaac	35	M	Mariner	U. States	U. States	Florida	25 Apr 1825
James	7/12	M	None	England		Marchioness	13 May 1828
James	29	M	Shoemaker	England		Marchioness	13 May 1828
Jane	20	F		Great Brittain	United States	Sarah Ralston	27 Jan 1827
Jane	29	F		Great Britain	United States	Ganges	8 Jul 1820
Jason	34	M				Hudson	23 Jul 1828
John	3	M	None	United States	United States	Importer	21 May 1821
John	4	M	None	England		Marchioness	13 May 1828
M.	24	F		Great Brittain	United States	Sarah Ralston	27 Jan 1827
Mary	5	F		Great Britain	United States	Ganges	8 Jul 1820
Mary	16	F	None	England		Marchioness	13 May 1828
Mary	32	F	None	England		Marchioness	13 May 1828
Olive P.	23	M	Merchant	New York	New York, U.S.	New York	14 Mar 1828
Peggy	3	F		Great Britain	United States	Ganges	8 Jul 1820
Saml.	24	M	Shoemaker	England		Marchioness	13 May 1828
Sarah	5	F	None	England		Marchioness	13 May 1828
William	18	M	Labourer	Ireland	U. States	Wanderer	1 Sep 1828
William	20	M	Merchant	St. John, N.B.	St. John, N.B.	Sarah G	19 Jun 1827
William	33	M		Great Britain	United States	Ganges	8 Jul 1820
Wm.	35	M	Farmer	England	United States	Silas Richards	27 Oct 1825
Wm., Junr.	7	M		Great Britain	United States	Ganges	8 Jul 1820
STONEHOUSE, Adam	26	M	Labourer			Lady of the Lake	23 Aug 1828
Agnes	30	M				Lady of the Lake	23 Aug 1828
Phineas	25	M	Labourer			Lady of the Lake	23 Aug 1828
STONES, Michael	21	M	Labourer	Ireland	United States	Trident	18 Jul 1827
Sylvester	23	M	Labourer	Ireland	Baltimore	Lima	5 Aug 1829
STONEY, John	33	M	Dyer	Great Britain	United States	Ganges	26 Oct 1826
P. G.	20	M	Merchant	U. States	U. States	Pacific	19 Oct 1829
STOOB, James	478	M	Merchant	Great Britian	United States	Orbit	31 Dec 1821
STOOKS, James	32	M	Merchant	Ireland		William Tell	24 Oct 1829
STOOPS, Wm.	21	M	Baker	Ireland	United States	Essex	23 May 1828
STOPFORD, Jas.	30	M	Mason	Great Britain	United States	Penelope	11 Jun 1827
STOPLELISH, Jean	18	M	Agriculturist	France	U.S.	Helen	3 May 1828
STOPPANI, Gamdenzo	16	M	Confectioner	St. ...	New York	Young Phenix	17 Jan 1825
STOPPELL, Henry Wm.	29	M	Merchant	Germany	Hambro [?]	Virginia	8 Mar 1828
STOPPLECAMP, John	23	M	Baker	Germany	United States	Francis	12 Jun 1826
Moris	25	M	Baker	Germany	United States	Francis	12 Jun 1826
STORDFALL, Thomas	23	M	Butcher	G. Britain	United States	Edward	21 Apr 1821
STORER, Ebenezer	24		Merchant	United States	United States	Hudson	14 Jun 1827
Susan	9	F	None	United States	U. States	Hercules	24 Oct 1821
Thomas W.	20	M	Merchant	U. States	U. States	Bayard	25 Apr 1828
STOREY, Elizabeth	4	F	None	England	America	Ann	2 Nov 1820
Emma	41	F	None	England	America	Ann	2 Nov 1820
Jane	12	F	None	England	America	Ann	2 Nov 1820
Mary	15	F	None	England	America	Ann	2 Nov 1820
Robert	6	M	None	England	America	Ann	2 Nov 1820
Robert	46	M	Labourer	England	United States	Trident	30 Sep 1826
STORK, —, Mr.	36	M	Coach Maker	England	U.S.	Robert Edwards	11 Nov 1822
—, Mrs.	30	M	Wife	England	U.S.	Robert Edwards	11 Nov 1822
STORKS, Elizabeth	49	F	None	England		Manhattan	22 May 1827

NAMES OF PASSENGERS	AGE	SEX	OCCUPATIONS	COUNTRY TO WHICH THEY BELONG	COUNTRY THEY INTEND TO INHABIT	SHIPS/DATES OF ARRIVAL	
STORKS (cont'd)							
Samuel	50	M	Farmer	England		Manhattan	22 May 1827
STORMONT, Rachael	29	F		United States	United States	Britannia	29 Oct 1829
Wm.	3	M		United States	United States	Britannia	29 Oct 1829
STORMS, Peter	34	M	Ship Master	United States	United States	Ceres	7 Aug 1826
Peter, Jr.	8	M		United States	United States	Ceres	7 Aug 1826
STORROW, Thomas	14	M		Boston	U. States	Nimrod	21 Sep 1820
STORRY, C. W.	38	M	Merchant	U. States	U. States	Circassian	13 Jun 1825
John	4	M		England	U. States	Howard Douglass	29 Jan 1828
Wm.	2	M		England	U. States	Howard Douglass	29 Jan 1828
STORY, Richard	32	M	Servant	St. Martins	St. Martins	Lucy	26 May 1827
Robt.	25	M	Farmer	Ireland	Pittsburg	Triton	12 Jul 1823
T. W.	44	M	Mariner	U. States	U. States	Constitution	29 Dec 1821
Wm.	30	M	Farmer	England	America	Josephine	8 Jan 1827
STOTT,							
Elizabeth, & infant	25	F	None	Great Britain	United States	Nestor in Liverpool	29 Jul 1822
James	21	M	Whitesmith	Yorkshire	Pittsburg	Curler	7 Jul 1827
James	33	M	Farmer	Great Britain	United States	Nestor in Liverpool	29 Jul 1822
Jas.	42	M	Land Surveyor	Great Britain	America	Lady Gallatin	21 Jun 1820
Jonathan	26	M	Farmer	Great Britain	United States	Nestor in Liverpool	29 Jul 1822
STOTZ, Henri	18	M	Farmer	Germany	United States	Oxford	14 Aug 1828
STOUDER, Henry	45	M	Merchant	Matanzas	Matanzas	Romulus	9 Oct 1828
STOUDOR, Henry	46	M	...	Switzerland	Switzerland	Columbia	26 Nov 1825
STOUPER, —	29	F		Switzerland	United States	Elbe	2 Aug 1822
STOURBRIDGE, James	18	M	Labourer	England	U. States	Ayrshire	12 May 1828
STOUT, Betty	24	F		G. Britain	United States	United States	11 Sep 1828
C. R.	22	M	Gentleman	United States	United States	Cortes	7 Dec 1825
Charles	18	M		G. Britain	United States	United States	11 Sep 1828
Hannahy	16	F		G. Britain	United States	United States	11 Sep 1828
James	13	M		G. Britain	United States	United States	11 Sep 1828
James	55	M	Clothier	G. Britain	United States	United States	11 Sep 1828
Mary	21	F		G. Britain	United States	United States	11 Sep 1828
Sally	53	F		G. Britain	United States	United States	11 Sep 1828
Sarah	11	F		G. Britain	United States	United States	11 Sep 1828
Wm.	12	M	Gentleman	U. States	U. States	Abeona	1 Oct 1823
STOUTT, Margret	30	F	Spinster	Ireland		Robert Fulton	4 Jun 1828
STOW, Joshua	56	M	Cotton Spinner	England	Boston	Curler	7 Jul 1827
Thomas	35	M	Merchant	U. States	United States	Fornax	31 Oct 1828
Thomas	43	M	Merchant	U. States	U. States	Orion	15 Apr 1822
STOWELL, Tamsone, Mrs.	24	F	Lady	Ireland	United States	Dublin Packet	22 Aug 1829
STRA..., Jacob	4	M		Switzerland	United States	Elizabeth	27 Jul 1824
Jacob	33	M	Farmer	Switzerland	United States	Elizabeth	27 Jul 1824
Johanes	1	M		Switzerland	United States	Elizabeth	27 Jul 1824
Li...	5	F		Switzerland	United States	Elizabeth	27 Jul 1824
Louisa	6	F		Switzerland	United States	Elizabeth	27 Jul 1824
Rosena	30	F		Switzerland	United States	Elizabeth	27 Jul 1824
STRACHAN, —,							
Arch Deacon	50	M	Clergy	England	Canada	Brighton	24 Aug 1827
—, Mrs.	30	F		Massachusetts	U. States	Dalmarnock	23 May 1823
Charity	45	M	Farmer	Scotland	U. States	Roger Stewart	9 Jun 1828
Robert, Mr.	32		Mercht.	London		Hercules	19 Jun 1821
STRACHER, Jno.	46	M	Merchant	England	U. States	New York	4 Nov 1824
STRACK, Catherine	26	F		Gt. Brittan		L'Esperance	6 Sep 1828
Magdelene	8	F		Gt. Brittan		L'Esperance	6 Sep 1828
P.	32	M	Carpenter	Gt. Brittan		L'Esperance	6 Sep 1828
Pierre	2	M		Gt. Brittan		L'Esperance	6 Sep 1828
STRADELE, Thomas		M	Miner	England	England	Iris	7 Dec 1827
STRADFORD, Caroline	6	F		Bristol	New York	Cosmo	25 Sep 1827
Ellen	28	F	Lady	Ireland	United States	William	20 Jul 1829
Hannah	1	F		Bristol	New York	Cosmo	25 Sep 1827
Jane	3	F		Bristol	New York	Cosmo	25 Sep 1827
Joseph	30	M	Labourer	Ireland	United States	William	20 Jul 1829
Mary	2	F		Ireland	United States	William	20 Jul 1829
Michl.	6	M		Ireland	United States	William	20 Jul 1829

NAMES OF PASSENGERS	AGE	SEX	OCCUPATIONS	COUNTRY TO WHICH THEY BELONG	COUNTRY THEY INTEND TO INHABIT	SHIPS/DATES OF ARRIVAL	
STRAHAN, Peter	30 5/12	M	Farmer	Switzerland	U. States	France	26 Jun 1828
STRAIN, Agnes	3	F	Spinster	Ireland	United States	Fabius	4 Jun 1828
Bryan	17	M	Labourer	Ireland	America	Fairy	8 Aug 1821
M.	28		Farmer	Ireland	United States	Courier	16 May 1825
STRAM, John Jacques	49	M	Farmer	Switzerland	United States	Thetis	5 Jul 1821
Jonas	6/12	M		Switzerland	United States	Thetis	5 Jul 1821
Saml.	43	M	Shoemaker	Switzerland	United States	Thetis	5 Jul 1821
STRANDGARD, S.	32	M	Officer	Denmark	U. States	Chase	2 Oct 1826
STRANG, Bart.	4	M		Great Britain	United States	Rosina	12 Aug 1823
Cathn.	15	F		Great Britain	United States	Rosina	12 Aug 1823
Fancis	28	M		Irland	U. States	Nancy	27 Jun 1823
James	8	M		Great Britain	United States	Rosina	12 Aug 1823
Jenn	10	F		Great Britain	United States	Rosina	12 Aug 1823
John	2	M		Great Britain	United States	Rosina	12 Aug 1823
John	40	M	Carpenter	U. States	U. States	Brothers	7 Aug 1820
Margaret	11	M		Great Britain	United States	Rosina	12 Aug 1823
Martin	30	M	Laborer	Ireland	United States	Sarah G	19 Jun 1827
Mary	6			Great Britain	United States	Rosina	12 Aug 1823
Mary	35	F		Great Britain	United States	Rosina	12 Aug 1823
William	8	M		Great Britain	United States	Rosina	12 Aug 1823
STRATALL, James	43	M		England		Ann	17 May 1822
STRATFORD, John	10	M		Bristol	New York	Cosmo	25 Sep 1827
STRATHERS, Neil	34	M	Mechanic	U. States	U. States	Acasta	21 Jan 1825
STRATTON, Charles	12		Stone Mason	England	United States	Acasta	16 Aug 1826
Francis, Mrs.	38	F	Yeoman	England	U. States	Acasta	11 Dec 1826
John, Master	4	M	Yeoman	England	U. States	Acasta	11 Dec 1826
Joseph	37		Stone Mason	England	United States	Acasta	16 Aug 1826
Joseph, Master	8	M	Yeoman	England	U. States	Acasta	11 Dec 1826
Wm.	11		Stone Mason	England	United States	Acasta	16 Aug 1826
STRAUGHN, Thomas	28	M	Farmer	Great Britain	United States	Eliza	15 Aug 1826
STRAW (see Stram)							
Benjamin	9	M	None	England	U. States	Montgomery	18 Oct 1828
Henry	40	M	Nail Maker	England	U. States	Montgomery	18 Oct 1828
Richard	12	M	None	England	U. States	Montgomery	18 Oct 1828
STRAWBRIDGE, George	39	M	Merchant	U. States	U. States	Moro	26 Aug 1824
STRAY, William	18	M	None	Great Britain	United States	Hannibal	12 Oct 1829
STREAKEN, Eliza	3	F		Scotland	U. States	James & Margaret	28 Jun 1826
Eliza	30	F		Scotland	U. States	James & Margaret	28 Jun 1826
Ellen	5	F		Scotland	U. States	James & Margaret	28 Jun 1826
Hannah	10	F		Scotland	U. States	James & Margaret	28 Jun 1826
James	35	M	Farmer	Scotland	U. States	James & Margaret	28 Jun 1826
STREELING, George A.	20	M	Carpenter	England	U. States	Electra	7 Jul 1828
John H.	5/12	M	Carpenter	England	U. States	Electra	7 Jul 1828
Joseph A.	13	M	Carpenter	England	U. States	Electra	7 Jul 1828
Joseph H.	39	M	Carpenter	England	U. States	Electra	7 Jul 1828
Margaret	37	F	Carpenter	England	U. States	Electra	7 Jul 1828
Robrt. H.	5	M	Carpenter	England	U. States	Electra	7 Jul 1828
Wm. H.	11	M	Carpenter	England	U. States	Electra	7 Jul 1828
STREEN, Hannah	25	F		Ireland	U. States	Calais Packet	7 Jul 1828
STREES, Elizabeth	69	F	None	England	Cincinnati	Concordia	12 Oct 1826
STREET, Benjamin	27	M	Farmer	Great Britain	United States	Dapper	21 Aug 1828
E. L.	17	M	Farmer	U. States	U. States	Hanford	18 Sep 1828
Eliza S.	30 5/12	F		U.S. American	U.S. American	Criterion	7 Jul 1824
Elizabeth	14	F		Great Britain	United States	Dapper	29 Jan 1829
L.	28	F			U. States	Hippomenes	9 Jun 1821
Nancy	27	F		Ireland	U. States	Nancy	1 Sep 1823
Sarah	12	F		Great Britain	United States	Dapper	29 Jan 1829
Thomas	18	M		Great Britain	United States	Dapper	29 Jan 1829
William	25	M	Labourer	Ireland	U. States	Nancy	1 Sep 1823
William	52	M	Farmer	Great Britain	United States	Dapper	29 Jan 1829
STREITER, D.	34	M	Merchant	U. States	U. States	Tryon	25 Apr 1825
STRENTZ, Fredrich	30	M	Sevant	Hamburgh	Mexico	Canada	13 Feb 1826
STRESEL, Andrias	50	M	Farmer	Wortenberg	Lancaster	Louisa	6 Oct 1828
Jacob	25	M	Farmer	Wortenberg	Lancaster	Louisa	6 Oct 1828

NAMES OF PASSENGERS	A G E	S E X	OCCUPATIONS	COUNTRY TO WHICH THEY BELONG	COUNTRY THEY INTEND TO INHABIT	SHIPS/DATES OF ARRIVAL	
STRESEL (cont'd)							
Johann Georg	22	M	Farmer	Wortenberg	Lancaster	Louisa	6 Oct 1828
Rosina	20	F	Farmer	Wortenberg	Lancaster	Louisa	6 Oct 1828
Rosina	31	F	Farmer	Wortenberg	Lancaster	Louisa	6 Oct 1828
STRETCH, Geo.	36	M				Cassack	25 Jul 1820
STRETTON, John	20	M	Taylor	England	United States	Andes	2 Oct 1828
John	47	M	Labourer	England	United States	Maria	12 May 1823
STRICKER, Thos.	36	M	Merchant	England	U. States	Defiance	13 Jul 1824
STRICKLAND, Wm.	36	M	Architect	U. States	U. States	Wm. Penn	6 Feb 1822
STRICKY, Henriech	25	M	Farmer	Switzerland	U. States	Hewes	30 Oct 1829
STRIDIRON, John G.	34		Planter	St. Croix	United States	South Carolina Packet	18 Apr 1826
STRIKY, Catharine	23	F	Wife	Switzerland	U. States	Hewes	30 Oct 1829
John	33	M	Smith	Switzerland	U. States	Hewes	30 Oct 1829
STRINGER, John	26	M	Spinner	England	United States	Jubilee	13 Jul 1829
STRINGFELLOW, John	43	M	Stocking Hosier	England	U. States	Montgomery	18 Oct 1828
STRINGHAM, Henry	10	M	Schollar	Denmark	America	Jupiter	29 Aug 1828
STRITCH, Margt.	19		Spinster	Ireland		Westmoreland	1 Aug 1826
STROB, F.	28	M	Teacher	Germany	United States	Maria Theresa	28 Aug 1821
STROBEL, Joacum	26	M	Butcher	Germany	America	Orozimbo	1 Oct 1827
STROCHAN, Jas.	19	M	Gentleman	Spain	Spain	Bengal	14 Jul 1825
Wm.	47	M	Gentleman	Spain	Spain	Bengal	14 Jul 1825
STROEDEL, F. G.	23	M	Merchant	Saxony	United States	Howard	6 Jul 1829
STROHAN, Edward	7	M	None	Great Britain	New York	Superior	5 Sep 1827
Elenor	2	M	None	Great Britain	New York	Superior	5 Sep 1827
Eleonor	36	F	None	Great Britain	New York	Superior	5 Sep 1827
Jane	3	M	None	Great Britain	New York	Superior	5 Sep 1827
Jane	33	F	None	Great Britain	New York	Superior	5 Sep 1827
Mary Ann	6	F	None	Great Britain	New York	Superior	5 Sep 1827
Thomas	8	M	None	Great Britain	New York	Superior	5 Sep 1827
STROHM, Michael	28	M	Farmer	France	France	Sully	15 Jul 1829
STROME, Catherine	32	F		Germany	Philadelphia	Isabella	15 Sep 1828
Charles	3	M		Germany	Philadelphia	Isabella	15 Sep 1828
Francisca	42	F		Germany	Philadelphia	Isabella	15 Sep 1828
Jacob	37	M	Butcher	Germany	Philadelphia	Isabella	15 Sep 1828
STRONACH, Ann	19	F		G. Britain	U. States	Eliza	31 Jul 1828
Eliza	20	F		G. Britain	U. States	Eliza	31 Jul 1828
Wm.	65	M	Spinner	G. Britain	U. States	Eliza	31 Jul 1828
STRONG, Agnes	6	F	None	Great Britain	United States	Manchester	12 Aug 1829
Catherine	11	F	None	Great Britain	United States	Manchester	12 Aug 1829
E.	46	M	Mariner	U. States	U. States	Florida	25 Apr 1825
Elizabeth	17	F	None	Great Britain	United States	Manchester	12 Aug 1829
Erastus	31			America	U. States	Agricola	1 Jul 1820
John	27	M	...	England	United States	Silas Richards	27 Oct 1825
John	45	M	Farmer	Brittian	U. States	Acasta	28 Jan 1823
Maria	18	F		England	United States	Acasta	28 Jul 1823
Mary	45	F	None	Great Britain	United States	Manchester	12 Aug 1829
Michael	53	M	Tanner	Great Britain	United States	Manchester	12 Aug 1829
Nathl. W.	40	M	Merchant	United States	United States	Eliza Pigott	27 Mar 1820
Robert	36	M	Mariner	England	England or Jamaica	Packet	11 Oct 1823
Sophia	20	F		England	United States	Acasta	28 Jul 1823
Susan	40	F		England	United States	Acasta	28 Jul 1823
Thomas	13	M	Child	Brittian		Acasta	28 Jan 1823
Thomas	15	M	None	Great Britain	United States	Manchester	12 Aug 1829
William	12	M	Child	Brittian		Acasta	28 Jan 1823
William	20	M	Merchant	Scotland	America	John Wells	11 Jun 1823
STROOLHOF,							
Ann Catharine	40			Kingdom of Hanover	U. States	Princess Louise	10 Mar 1825
Ann Margt.	5			Kingdom of Hanover	U. States	Princess Louise	10 Mar 1825
Anton Henry	37		Sailor	Kingdom of Hanover	U. States	Princess Louise	10 Mar 1825
Catharine Adelbert	13			Kingdom of Hanover	U. States	Princess Louise	10 Mar 1825
John D.	11			Kingdom of Hanover	U. States	Princess Louise	10 Mar 1825
John Henry Bernard	16			Kingdom of Hanover	U. States	Princess Louise	10 Mar 1825

NAMES OF PASSENGERS	AGE	SEX	OCCUPATIONS	COUNTRY TO WHICH THEY BELONG	COUNTRY THEY INTEND TO INHABIT	SHIPS/DATES OF ARRIVAL	
STROPSENDORFF, C.	45	M	Merchant	Germany	New York	Brighton	20 Aug 1825
STROSSER, Andrew	30	M	Joiner	Switzerland	United States	Elizabeth	27 Jul 1824
Catherina	30	F		Switzerland	United States	Elizabeth	27 Jul 1824
Elizabeth	5	F		Switzerland	United States	Elizabeth	27 Jul 1824
STROUACH, Ebenezer	27	M	Plasterer	Gt. Britain	U. States	Eldon	21 Aug 1827
STROUD, Daniel	35	M	Shoe Maker	New York	New York	Brighton	29 Aug 1828
STROUDS, John	28	M	Marble cutter	England	United States	Brighton	11 Mar 1825
STROW, Frederick	27	M	Mariner	United States	U. States	Robert Reade	9 Feb 1822
STROWSON, David	22	M	Laborer	Scotland	U. States	Camillus	27 Jun 1826
STRUT, John	30	M	Farmer	Switzerland	United States	Howard	11 Jun 1824
STRUTTON,							
Mary Anne, Miss	22	F		England	Albany	Cortes	23 Nov 1827
STUARD, Meret	20	F		Halifax, N.S.	New York	Citizen	1 Nov 1828
Thomas, Mr.	25		Cotton Spinner	Glasgow		Hercules	19 Jun 1821
STUART, B.	23	M	Merchant	U. States	U. States	New England	11 Sep 1828
Charles	27	M	Marble Cutter	Philadelphia	American	Midas	9 May 1827
Chas.	45		Capt. Madras Army	Ireland	United States	Courier	15 Oct 1827
Hugh	24	M	Labourer	Ireland	United States	Catharine	22 Jul 1825
James	21	M	Merchant	England	America	Silas Richard	24 Oct 1829
James	25	M	Labourer	Ireland	U. States	Sarah G	30 Jun 1828
James	30	M	Merchant	Ireland	United States	Herald	29 Oct 1825
James	34	M	Merchant	Pittsburg	Pittsburg	New York	14 Nov 1826
Jane	21	F	None	New York	U. States	Ann Maria	1 Jun 1824
Jas.	34		Mercht.	United States	U. States	New York	30 Oct 1827
John	22	M	Teacher	England	America	Britannia	22 Jul 1829
John	31	M	Merchant	America		Manhattan	7 Nov 1827
Jos.	3	M	Merchant	U. States	U. States	New England	11 Sep 1828
Joseph	22	M	None	Great Britain		Manhattan	7 Nov 1827
Mary Ann	21	F		Philadelphia	American	Midas	9 May 1827
P.	30	M	Planter	Scotland	Jamaica	Superior	18 Nov 1823
Samson	38	M		G. Britan	U. States	Geo. Canning	2 Sep 1828
Sarah	17	F		Great Britain		Manhattan	7 Nov 1827
William	26	M	Merchant	England	United States	Nestor	20 Nov 1821
William	30	M	Trader	U. States	U. States	Rodney	19 Jun 1827
Willm.	32		Mercht.	England	U. States	New York	30 Oct 1827
Wm.	25	M	Merchant	Scotland	United States	Ann Maria	9 Jun 1824
Wm.	27	M	Merchant	G. Britain	United States	New York	12 Nov 1822
STUBBERT, Ackba	28	F		France	United States	Stephania	6 Dec 1827
Joseph	5	M		France	United States	Stephania	6 Dec 1827
STUBBS, Alfred	14	M		Turks Island		Splendid	1 Jul 1829
Alice	9	F		Great Britain	United States	Mary Howland	19 Jul 1827
Barbara	52	F	None	Great Britain	United States	Mary & Harriet	3 Jul 1829
Elizabeth	1	F	Labourer	England	U. States	Comet	23 Aug 1828
Elizabeth	21	F		Great Britain	United States	Samuel Wright	12 Oct 1829
Fanny	13	F	None	Great Britain	United States	Mary & Harriet	3 Jul 1829
George	11	M	None	Great Britain	United States	Mary & Harriet	3 Jul 1829
H.	11	M		G. Brittain		Planter	17 Sep 1821
Horatio	12	M		Turks Island	U. States	DeWitt Clinton	16 Nov 1824
Joseph	33	M	Weaver	Great Britain	United States	Mary Howland	19 Jul 1827
Martha	32	F		Great Britain	United States	Mary Howland	19 Jul 1827
Mary	22	F	Labourer	England	U. States	Comet	23 Aug 1828
Mary	26	F	None	Great Britain	United States	Mary & Harriet	3 Jul 1829
Richd.	15	M	None	Great Britain	Great Britain	Champion	2 May 1828
Thomas	27	M	Blacksmith	Great Britain	United States	Samuel Wright	12 Oct 1829
William	11	M		Great Britain	United States	Mary Howland	19 Jul 1827
William	19	M	None	Great Britain	United States	Mary & Harriet	3 Jul 1829
STUBER, T.	43	M	Merchant	France	United States	Helen Mar	29 Jun 1827
STUBERS, Mary	32	F	Spinster	United States	United States	Robert Read	19 Oct 1825
STUDER, George	1	M		France	U. States	Edward Quesnel	4 Aug 1828
Margaretta	40	F		France	U. States	Edward Quesnel	4 Aug 1828
Philip	44	M	Taylor	France	U. States	Edward Quesnel	4 Aug 1828
STUERD, William	25	M		Ireland	United States	Nancy R. Crowell	21 Sep 1822
STUGES, Lewis B.	57	M	Merchant	U. States	New York	South Carolina Packet	22 Jul 1820
STUKER, Henry	26	M	Sugar Baker	Ireland	U. States	Frederick	2 Apr 1828
STUKNEY, Thos.	28	M		England	United States	Hercules	25 Jan 1820
STUKY, Robert Sipeore	26	M	Dyer	Switzland	America	Henry	15 Feb 1826
STULTZ, Barbara	40			France	America	La Grange	7 Aug 1828

NAMES OF PASSENGERS	AGE	SEX	OCCUPATIONS	COUNTRY TO WHICH THEY BELONG	COUNTRY THEY INTEND TO INHABIT	SHIPS/DATES OF ARRIVAL	
STULTZ (cont'd)							
Farewell	50			France	America	La Grange	7 Aug 1828
Hannah	16			France	America	La Grange	7 Aug 1828
Henry	10			France	America	La Grange	7 Aug 1828
Michael	6			France	America	La Grange	7 Aug 1828
STULTZBACH, Henry	25	M	...	U. States	U. States	New England	28 Sep 1824
STULTZMANN, Joseph	23	M		France	United States	Henri IV	2 Oct 1828
STUMFIELD, Joseph	21	M		Great Britain	United States	Mary Howland	19 Jul 1827
STUNAM, David	25	M	Farmer	England	United States	Euphrates	18 Aug 1827
STUNT, Joseph	22		Joiner	England	New York	Caroline	10 Mar 1828
STUPPER, Christiana	31	F		Switzerland	U.S.	Francois I	8 Aug 1829
STURBIDE, Jesus	7	F	None	Mexico	U. States	Cincinnatus	9 Jul 1825
Joanna	13	F	None	Mexico	U. States	Cincinnatus	9 Jul 1825
Passa	10	F	None	Mexico	U. States	Cincinnatus	9 Jul 1825
Sabina	14	F	None	Mexico	U. States	Cincinnatus	9 Jul 1825
STURBIND, Angeloe	8	M	None	Mexico	U. States	Cincinnatus	9 Jul 1825
STURDEVANT, Stephen	38	M	Merchant	United States	Pensylvania	Brighton	9 Dec 1828
STURGEON, Ewd.	2/12	M		Ireland	U. States	Calais Packet	7 Jul 1828
Mary Jane	2/12	F		Ireland	U. States	Calais Packet	7 Jul 1828
Oliva	30	F		Ireland	U. States	Calais Packet	7 Jul 1828
Robt.	6	M		Ireland	U. States	Calais Packet	7 Jul 1828
Robt.	24	M	Farmer	Ireland	U. States	Josephine	7 May 1827
Saml.	35	M	Preacher	Ireland	U. States	Calais Packet	7 Jul 1828
Wm.	5	M		Ireland	U. States	Calais Packet	7 Jul 1828
STURGES,							
Seth Morehouse	18 9/12		Cordwander	United States	Conneticut	Swift	9 Jan 1826
STURGINGER, Frederica	11	F	his Sister [Michael]	Germany	United States	Helen	5 Sep 1828
Ivan	23	F	his Sister [Michael]	Germany	United States	Helen	5 Sep 1828
Michael	26	M	Farmer	Germany	United States	Helen	5 Sep 1828
STURGIS, Geo. W.	30	M	Merchant	U. States	U. States	Huntress	6 May 1823
Thomas	32	M	Mariner	U. States	U. States	Rice Plant	22 May 1827
STURM, —, Miss	33	F		Hannover	United States	Constitution	6 Jul 1829
—, Mr.	22	M	Farmer	Hannover	United States	Constitution	6 Jul 1829
STUSACO, William	26	M	Weaver	England	United States	Lord Wellington	14 Nov 1827
STUTLEY, Mary Ann	20	F	Lady	England	U.S. America	Cortes	19 May 1826
STUTTER, Clira	22	F	Servant to Mr. Blakey	England	United States	Robert Edwards	3 Oct 1829
STUWART, Sarah	27	F		Ireland	United States	Clothier	22 Nov 1827
STWART, Alexander	26	M	Labourer	Scotland	United States	Friends	7 Jul 1827
STYGER, Lucas	22	M	Cleermaker	Bleicheim	United States	Juffraw Johanna	16 Oct 1821
STYLES, Ellen	30	F	Spinster	Ireland	United States	Ann Maria	8 Jun 1824
STYMETT, Melcha	64	F		Born in New York		Potomac	7 Aug 1827
STYON, Agnis	10			England	United States	Thomas Dickason	5 Jun 1827
Hannah	13			England	United States	Thomas Dickason	5 Jun 1827
Maria	12			England	United States	Thomas Dickason	5 Jun 1827
Mary	50		Farmer	England	United States	Thomas Dickason	5 Jun 1827
William	10			England	United States	Thomas Dickason	5 Jun 1827
William	50	M	Weaver	England	United States	Thomas Dickason	5 Jun 1827
SUAREZ, C.	26	M	Merchant	Spain	Spain	Richmond Packet	30 Oct 1827
Jos. N.	35	M	Merch.	Spain	U. States	Brown	11 Jan 1825
S.	31	M	Lawyer	Cuba	U.S.	Edward Quesnel	31 Jul 1827
SUBB, Henry	26	M	Bookkeeper	Great Brittain	U. States	William Byrnes	23 Jul 1824
Martha	20	F		G. Britain	U. States	Mary & Harriot	8 Sep 1828
Robt.	63	M	Farmer	G. Britain	U. States	Mary & Harriot	8 Sep 1828
SUCHEVEDA, J.	23	M	Servant	Mexico	Mexico	York	2 Dec 1828
SUCKLEY, John	42	M	Merchant	U. States	U. States	Exchange	25 Sep 1826
John L.	27	M	Physician	U.N. States	U.N. States	Exchange	13 Mar 1827
SUDDIS, James	37	M	Mason	State of Ohio	United States	Nancy	16 Aug 1824
SUDER, Conrad	3	M	...	Wirtemburg	United States	Wade	29 Aug 1825
SUDLIN, William	40	M	Officer	Great Brittain	Canada	Nancy	16 Aug 1822
SUDMAN, Jean	40	M		France	United States	La Flora	30 Jun 1828

NAMES OF PASSENGERS	AGE	SEX	OCCUPATIONS	COUNTRY TO WHICH THEY BELONG	COUNTRY THEY INTEND TO INHABIT	SHIPS/DATES OF ARRIVAL	
SUDMAN (cont'd)							
John	20	M		France	United States	La Flora	30 Jun 1828
M.	18	M		France	United States	La Flora	30 Jun 1828
Nicholas	14 1/12	M		France	United States	La Flora	30 Jun 1828
William	5	M	None	Great Britain	United States	John	6 Oct 1820
SUELL, Isabella	24	F	Servant	Bermuda	New Jersey	Camden	14 May 1825
SUFIELD, Anna	10	F	Farmer	Alsace in the Department of Upper and lower Rhine	United States	Carolina Augusta	16 May 1828
Catherina	24	F	Farmer	Alsace in the Department of Upper and lower Rhine	United States	Carolina Augusta	16 May 1828
Catherina	44	F	Farmer	Alsace in the Department of Upper and lower Rhine	United States	Carolina Augusta	16 May 1828
John	24	M	Farmer	Alsace in the Department of Upper and lower Rhine	United States	Carolina Augusta	16 May 1828
John	48	M	Farmer	Alsace in the Department of Upper and lower Rhine	United States	Carolina Augusta	16 May 1828
Margaritta	8	F	Farmer	Alsace in the Department of Upper and lower Rhine	United States	Carolina Augusta	16 May 1828
Maria	18	F	Farmer	Alsace in the Department of Upper and lower Rhine	United States	Carolina Augusta	16 May 1828
Michael	33	M	Farmer	Alsace in the Department of Upper and lower Rhine	United States	Carolina Augusta	16 May 1828
SUGANSTAIN, Sabastien	32	M	Winedealer	France	U. States	Edward Bopnnaffe	30 Jul 1829
SUGDEN, Abram	39	M	Farmer	Great Brit.	Ohio	Gov. Griswald	3 Jul 1820
John	42	F	Farmer	Great Brit.	Ohio	Gov. Griswald	3 Jul 1820
Maryann	22 1/12	F	Servant	Great Britain		Silas Richards	27 Oct 1826
Sarah	39	F		Great Brit.	Ohio	Gov. Griswald	3 Jul 1820
Susannah	18	F		Great Brit.	Ohio	Gov. Griswald	3 Jul 1820
SUI..., Joseph	15	M	Shoe Maker	Switzerland	United States	Elbe	2 Aug 1822
SUINDER, Joh.	28	M	Agriculture	Wirtemburg	United States	Henri IV	14 Oct 1829
SUISTA, Ann	67	F	None	Lincolnshire	United States	Dalhousie Castle	27 Jul 1826
Charles	34	M	Weaver	Lincolnshire	United States	Dalhousie Castle	27 Jul 1826
Christiana	20	F	None	Breeton	United States	Dalhousie Castle	27 Jul 1826
Elizabeth	28	F	None	Lincolnshire	United States	Dalhousie Castle	27 Jul 1826
James	26	M	Weaver	Lincolnshire	United States	Dalhousie Castle	27 Jul 1826
John	1 1/2	M	None	Breeton	United States	Dalhousie Castle	27 Jul 1826
Thomas	2 1/2	M	None	Breeton	United States	Dalhousie Castle	27 Jul 1826
SULA, —, Mr.	32	M	Merchant	Spain	U. States	Cadmus	12 Apr 1825
SULAIRD, John	32	M	Calico Printer	Great Britain	United States	Thomas Dickason	31 Jul 1829
SULAM, Joseph C.	28	M	Mariner	U. States	U. States	Lion	20 Aug 1821
SULDSTON, Ths.	23	M	Spinster	Great Brittain	United States	Corinthian	9 Jan 1827
SULE, Iffleo	28	M	Merchant	France	U.S. America	Cincinnatus	31 Oct 1820
SULEVAN, E.	21	F		Galway	U. States	Eliza Ann	30 Jul 1823
SULIVAN, Andrew	25 4/12	M	blacksmith	Ireland	America	Enterprize	29 Jun 1827
Catharine	19		Labourer	Ireland	United States	Corinthian	30 May 1828
Ellen	24	F	Labourer	Ireland	U.S.A.	Dalhousie Castle	21 Aug 1829
Frances	1		Labourer	Ireland	United States	Corinthian	30 May 1828
John	21		Labourer	Ireland	United States	Corinthian	30 May 1828
Mary	40	F				Nancy	10 Jul 1820
SULIVEN, Jer.	30	M	Merchant	U. States	U. States	Income	12 Mar 1822
SULL..., John	21	M	Merchant	England	United States	Blakely	29 Sep 1826

NAMES OF PASSENGERS	AGE	SEX	OCCUPATIONS	COUNTRY TO WHICH THEY BELONG	COUNTRY THEY INTEND TO INHABIT	SHIPS/DATES OF ARRIVAL	
SULLAGHAN, Bryan	21	M	Weaver	Ireland	United States	Wilson	27 Jun 1826
Cathn.	21	F	Servant	Ireland	United States	Wilson	27 Jun 1826
SULLIMAN, Josep A.	25	M	Mariner	U. States	U. States	Belvidera	28 Dec 1825
SULLIMAND, Rosalie	23	F	Milliner	France	U. States	Edward Quesnel	16 Nov 1827
SULLINGER, Fran	20	F	Mantumake	France	U. States	Edward Bonaffe	23 Jul 1828
SULLIVAN, —, Childe	2					Trio	5 May 1828
—, Infant	1					Trio	5 May 1828
Abigale	4	F		Ireland	United States	John & Adam	21 Sep 1822
Ann	38	F		Ireland	America	Corinthian	1 Sep 1827
Bridget	13	F	None	Ireland	U.S.A.	Dalhouse Castle	21 Aug 1829
Bridget	28	F	Matron	Ireland	America	Parrington	9 Jun 1827
Bridjet	20	F	None	Ireland	U. States	Henry Kneeland	27 Jul 1825
Briget	22			Ireland	U.S.	Union	20 Aug 1827
Catharine	40			Cork	Philadelphia	Schuylkill	22 Aug 1825
Catherine	3	F		Ireland	United States	Sarah G.	20 Jul 1827
Catherine	24	F	Lady	Ireland	United States	Borneo	9 Jul 1827
Catherine	25					Trio	5 May 1828
Catherine	26	F		Ireland	United States	Trio	2 Oct 1828
Catherine	28	F		Ireland	United States	Sarah G.	20 Jul 1827
Cathr.	30	F		Gt. Britan	U. States	Sarah Skeafe	10 Sep 1827
Cornelius	61	M		Ireland	United States	John & Adam	21 Sep 1822
D.	28	M	Labourer			Hanford	17 Jul 1828
Daniel	4	M		Ireland	United States	Trio	2 Oct 1828
Daniel	24					Trio	5 May 1828
Danl.	25	M	Labourer	G. Britain	U. States	Sarah G	5 Jun 1828
Denis	25	M	Labourer	Ireland	United States	Trio	2 Oct 1828
Dennis	32	M		Ireland	United States	John & Adam	21 Sep 1822
Edwd.	25	M	Farmer	Ireland	America	Mary	29 May 1827
Eliza	28	F	Labourer	Ireland	U. States	Two Marys	20 Apr 1825
Eliza	30	F	Spinster	Ireland	America	William	21 May 1825
Elizabeth	42	F	None	Ireland	U.S.A.	Dalhouse Castle	21 Aug 1829
Ellen	10	F		Ireland	United States	John & Adam	21 Sep 1822
Ellen	21					Trio	5 May 1828
Ellen	24	F	Labourer	Ireland	United States	Dalhouse Castle	21 Aug 1829
Ellen	34	F		Ireland	United States	John & Adam	21 Sep 1822
Eugene	24	M	None	England and Ireland	United States	Jubilee	12 May 1828
Florence	6	F		Ireland	United States	John & Adam	21 Sep 1822
Herbert J.	15	M	None	Ireland	U. States	Union	3 Jun 1822
J. M.						Day	14 Jun 1822
James	17					Trio	5 May 1828
James	21	M	Labourer	Great Britain	U. States	Lady Hunter	26 Nov 1823
James	24		Farmer	Kerry	Philadelphia	Schuylkill	22 Aug 1825
James	26	M	Farmer	Great Briton	Pensylvania	Brighton	12 Jun 1826
Jas.	22	M	Farmer	England	United States	Ganges	10 May 1828
Jeremiah	4	M		Ireland	United States	John & Adam	21 Sep 1822
Jeremiah	22	M	Mason	England	U.S. America	Cortes	19 May 1826
Jeremiah	40	M	Blacksmith	Ireland	U. States	Albion	11 May 1827
Jerh.	28	M	Laborer	Ireland	United States	Trio	13 Jun 1827
Jerimiah	24	M	Labourer	Great Brittan	United States	Hanford	3 Aug 1829
Joanna	16	F		Ireland	United States	Trio	2 Oct 1828
Joanna	30	F		Ireland	United States	Trio	2 Oct 1828
John	25	M	Labourer	Ireland	United States	Trio	2 Oct 1828
John	26	M	Labourer	Ireland	New York	William	26 Apr 1823
John	35	M	Clerk	Ireland	United States	Pallas	28 Oct 1828
John	40	M	Gentn.	England	United States	Columbia	16 Jan 1829
John	42	M	Labourer	Ireland	United States	Trio	2 Oct 1828
Julia	20	F		Ireland	United States	John & Adam	21 Sep 1822
Magee	22	M	Gentleman	United States	United States	Sarah Herrick	24 Oct 1825
Margaret	2			Cork	Philadelphia	Schuylkill	22 Aug 1825
Margaret	6	F	None	Ireland	U.S.A.	Dalhouse Castle	21 Aug 1829
Margaret	18			Cork	Gt. Britain	Enterprize	19 Feb 1822
Margt.	6	F	None	Ireland	United States	Dalhouse Castle	21 Aug 1829
Maria	21	F	None	England and Ireland	United States	Jubilee	12 May 1828
Mary	3	F		Ireland	United States	Trio	2 Oct 1828
Mary	8	F		Ireland	United States	John & Adam	21 Sep 1822
Mary	8	F		Ireland	United States	Sarah G.	20 Jul 1827
Mary	20	F		Ireland	New York	William	26 Apr 1823

NAMES OF PASSENGERS	AGE	SEX	OCCUPATIONS	COUNTRY TO WHICH THEY BELONG	COUNTRY THEY INTEND TO INHABIT	SHIPS/DATES OF ARRIVAL	
SULLIVAN (cont'd)							
Mary	24	F	...	Ireland	U. States	William	27 Jul 1824
Mary	30	M	Labourer	Ireland	United States	Essex	23 May 1828
Mary, Mrs.	26	F	Lady	England	United States	Maria	29 Sep 1823
Mary Ann	2	F		Ireland	New York	William	26 Apr 1823
Mary O.	32	F	None	London	London	New York	14 Nov 1826
Mical	22	M	Labourer	Ireland	Ireland	Sarah G.	28 Nov 1827
Michael	21	M	Carpenter	Great Britain	U. States	Lady Hunter	26 Nov 1823
Michael	22	M	Laborer	Ireland	United States	St. Michaels	12 Jun 1826
Michael	34	M	Clerk	Great Britain	United States	Sylvester Healy	23 Nov 1825
Narned	6			Ireland	United States	Sarah G.	20 Jul 1827
Owen	36	M		Ireland	United States	Sarah G.	20 Jul 1827
Owen	45	M	Seaman	N. York	N. York	St. Helena	18 Feb 1823
*Invalid from the U.S. Ship Cayenne, to be received in the Maine Hospital							
P.	34	M	Farmer	Ireland	United States	Aurora	27 Apr 1825
Pat	30	M	Labourer	Ireland	United States	Essex	23 May 1828
Patrick	26	M	Labourer	Ireland	U. States	Two Marys	20 Apr 1825
Patrick	27	M	Gentleman	U. States	U. States	John & William	20 Aug 1827
Patrick	35	M	Merchant	Ireland	United States	John & Adam	21 Sep 1822
Peter	11	M		Ireland	United States	Trio	2 Oct 1828
Peter	27	M	Weaver	Ireland	U. States	Josephine	27 Jul 1825
R.	1 4/12	M		Gt. Britan	U. States	Sarah Skeafe	10 Sep 1827
R.	30	M	Hatter	Gt. Britan	U. States	Sarah Skeafe	10 Sep 1827
Sarah	13	F		Ireland	U. States	Union	3 Jun 1822
Timothy	8	M		Ireland	United States	Sarah G.	20 Jul 1827
Timothy	19					Trio	5 May 1828
Tom	21	M	Shoemaker	Ireland	U.S.A.	Dalhouse Castle	21 Aug 1829
William	23		Farmer & Labourer	Great Britain & Ireland	United States	Trio	8 Feb 1827
William	40		Weaver	Cork	Philadelphia	Schuylkill	22 Aug 1825
Wm. O.	16	M	Sailor	U. States	U. States	Thacher	23 Sep 1828
SULLIVEN, John	40	M		G. Britain	U. States	Canada	19 Sep 1828
SULLON, George	23	M	Labourer			Splendid	14 Aug 1829
SULLRIFF, Jas.	37	M	Weaver	England	America	John Adams	2 Aug 1827
SULLVN, J.	2		Farmer	Ireland	United States	Courier	16 May 1825
SULOUR, Wm.	28	M	Farmer	Ireland	N. York	Elizabeth	20 Jun 1828
SULVAN, Mary	20	F		Galway	U. States	Eliza Ann	30 Jul 1823
SULY, Ann	22 6/12	F	Wife	Ireland	United States	Louisa	27 Nov 1826
James	37	M	Weaver	Ireland	United States	Louisa	27 Nov 1826
SUM..., ...lezarus	16 1/12	M	Planter	U.S.A.	U. States	Silas Richards	27 Oct 1826
SUMBER,							
Brazillia, Miss	16	F	None	U. States	U. States	John Laird	16 Jun 1827
SUMERVILL, —, Mr.	27		Mason	London		Pomona	28 May 1822
—, Mrs.	23		Wife	London		Pomona	28 May 1822
Eliza	45	F	Servant	Ireland	America	Carolina Ann	7 Aug 1826
Mary	18	F	Servant	Ireland	America	Carolina Ann	7 Aug 1826
SUMMER, John		M	Taylor	Switzerland	United States	Aurora	21 Jun 1824
Wm.	20	M	Farmer			Hercules	25 Sep 1820
SUMMERFIELD,							
J., Revd.	24	M	Clerk	England	United States	Orbit	22 Apr 1824
SUMMERHOUSE, Ann	22		Servant			Helen	4 Aug 1829
SUMMERS, Bastin	30	M	Brewer Cooper	Germany	United States	Ohio	10 Jul 1820
Owen	22	M	Labourer			Plutarch	18 Jul 1826
Rose	20	F		Ireland	America	Plutarch	18 Jul 1826
SUMMERSET,							
Robert	30 9/12	M	Labourer	Ireland	United States	Atlantic	21 Jul 1827
SUMMERVILLE,							
Jane	19 6/12	F	Spinster	Ireland	United States	Robert Fulton	24 Jul 1826
John	20	M	Servant	Ireland	America	Carolina Ann	7 Aug 1826
SUMMIT, Robert	36	M	Merchant	Ireland	United States	Florida	7 Feb 1825
SUMNER, Charles	30	M	Ship Master	U. States	U.S.	Fame	22 Mar 1826
John	23	M	Labourer	England	U. States	Ayrshire	12 May 1828
John	28	M		Scotland	New York	Joseph Hume	26 Oct 1829
Mary	38	F	Merchant	England	U.S.	Panthea	13 Nov 1823
William	24	M	Shais Maker	United States	United States	Pilot	27 Feb 1826
SUMNERS, John	32	M	Laborer	England	United States	Delta	24 Oct 1829
SUMSON, Charles	22	M	Laborer	Ireland	United States	Fabius	4 Jun 1828
Hannah	23	F		Ireland	United States	Fabius	4 Jun 1828
Jane	68	F		Ireland	United States	Fabius	4 Jun 1828

NAMES OF PASSENGERS	AGE	SEX	OCCUPATIONS	COUNTRY TO WHICH THEY BELONG	COUNTRY THEY INTEND TO INHABIT	SHIPS/DATES OF ARRIVAL	
SUMSON (cont'd)							
William	1	M		Ireland	United States	Fabius	4 Jun 1828
SUMTER, Mary, Mrs.	42	F	None	U. States	U. States	John Laird	16 Jun 1827
Sebastian	7	M	None	U. States	U. States	John Laird	16 Jun 1827
SUNDERLAND, A. S.	35		Brick Layer	G. Britain		Casanda	5 Sep 1827
Ann	12	F				Lady of the Lake	23 Aug 1828
B.	50	M	Farmer	Gt. Brittain	United States	Balaena	8 Jan 1825
Hannah	6	F				Lady of the Lake	23 Aug 1828
James	5	M				Lady of the Lake	23 Aug 1828
Sarah	13	F				Lady of the Lake	23 Aug 1828
Sarah	36	F				Lady of the Lake	23 Aug 1828
Thomas	8	M				Lady of the Lake	23 Aug 1828
SUNDERSON, Mary	20		Servant	Ireland	U. States	Xenophon	28 May 1822
SUNNER, Joseph	25	M	Clerk	...	United States	Wade	29 Aug 1825
SUNNEY, Thomas	37		Farmer	Belfast	Ireland	Carolina Ann	21 May 1823
SUNNY, M.	23	M	Labourer	Ireland	U. States	Wanderer	1 Sep 1828
SUPERVEILE,							
John, Servant	23	M	Servant	France	Cuba	James Cropper	2 Aug 1827
SUPPLE, Caroline	21 3/12	F		Ireland	United States	Wilson	27 Jun 1826
Dd.	17	M	Clerk	Ireland	U. States	Alex Mansfield	1 Jun 1822
John	5/12	M		Ireland	United States	Wilson	27 Jun 1826
John Joseph	28	M	Farmer	Ireland	United States	Wilson	27 Jun 1826
Jos.	24	M	Clerk	Ireland	U. States	Alex Mansfield	1 Jun 1822
SURAULET, Jas. F.	28	M	Clergyman	France	U. States	America	22 Sep 1826
SURCAZ, Frs.	25	M	Merchant	Spain	Spain	Weymouth	13 Aug 1822
SURGEON, John	27	M	Labourer	Whittlehills	Lancashire	Howard Douglass	11 May 1827
SURGY, Edmon Neron	21	M	Merchant	Guadeloupe	New York	Notre Dame	6 Oct 1827
SURMAN, Catharen	8	F	Farmer	Ireland		Quatre Freres	29 Jul 1828
Georg	40	M	Farmer	Ireland		Quatre Freres	29 Jul 1828
George	5	M	Farmer	Ireland		Quatre Freres	29 Jul 1828
Haoe	30	M	Farmer	Ireland		Quatre Freres	29 Jul 1828
John	4	M	Farmer	Ireland		Quatre Freres	29 Jul 1828
Margaret	10	F	Farmer	Ireland		Quatre Freres	29 Jul 1828
Margaret	30	F	Farmer	Ireland		Quatre Freres	29 Jul 1828
Mary	3	F	Farmer	Ireland		Quatre Freres	29 Jul 1828
SURNAN, Felix	35	M	Merchant	U. States	U. States	Buck	7 Aug 1822
SURRELLE, Mary	34	F		G. Britain	U. States	St. George	7 Jun 1828
SURTREMUS, Adam	8	F	Broker	Ireland		Quatre Freres	29 Jul 1828
Burac	9	M	Broker	Ireland		Quatre Freres	29 Jul 1828
Catharan	5	F	Broker	Ireland		Quatre Freres	29 Jul 1828
James	36	M	Broker	Ireland		Quatre Freres	29 Jul 1828
John	4	M	Broker	Ireland		Quatre Freres	29 Jul 1828
Margaret	11	F	Broker	Ireland		Quatre Freres	29 Jul 1828
Margaret	28	F	Broker	Ireland		Quatre Freres	29 Jul 1828
SUSSALL, P. M.	20	M	Joiner	France	United States	La Flora	30 Jun 1828
SUSSE, Carlotte	1	F		France	U. States	Edward Bopnnaffe	30 Jul 1829
Carlotte	24	F		France	U. States	Edward Bopnnaffe	30 Jul 1829
Henri	32	M	Mason	France	U. States	Edward Bopnnaffe	30 Jul 1829
SUTCHOLS, Thos.	30	M	Farmer	Ireland	America	Mary	29 May 1827
SUTCLIFF, Ann	8	F	Child	England	U. States	Emulous	22 Aug 1828
Benjamin	24	M	Farmer	Great Brit.	Ohio	Gov. Griswald	3 Jul 1820
Edward	9 5/12	M		England	United States	Alexander Mansfield	9 Jul 1829
Elisabeth	35	F		England	U. States	Emulous	22 Aug 1828
John	4	M		England	United States	Alexander Mansfield	9 Jul 1829
John H.	37	M	Joiner	England	U. States	Emulous	22 Aug 1828
Joseph	2	M	Child	England	U. States	Emulous	22 Aug 1828
Joseph	32	M	Merchant	England	U. States	Radius	16 Mar 1822

NAMES OF PASSENGERS	AGE	SEX	OCCUPATIONS	COUNTRY TO WHICH THEY BELONG	COUNTRY THEY INTEND TO INHABIT	SHIPS/DATES OF ARRIVAL	
SUTCLIFF (cont'd)							
Phineas	...	M	...	...	...	Frances Henrietta	30 Jun 1827
Robt.	21	M	Merchant	England	Quebec	Washington	16 Sep 1820
Sarah	50	M	None			Washington	16 Sep 1820
Sophia	7	F		England	United States	Alexander Mansfield	9 Jul 1829
Susanna	32	F	Weaver	England	United States	Alexander Mansfield	9 Jul 1829
Wm.	50	M	Preacher	England	Quebec	Washington	16 Sep 1820
SUTCLIFFE, J.	24	M	Joiner	Great Britain	United States	Isaac Hicks	6 Dec 1827
SUTER, Margaret	60	F		Gt. Britain	U. States	Sarah G.	14 Apr 1828
SUTERMASTER, —,							
Mrs.	40	F		U. States	U. States	Eliza	31 Jul 1821
Harmonia	17	F		U. States	U. States	Eliza	31 Jul 1821
Henrietta, Child [of T. H.]	4	F		U. States	U. States	Eliza	31 Jul 1821
Mary, Child [of T. H.]	6	F		U. States	U. States	Eliza	31 Jul 1821
T. H.	5...	M	Mercht.	U. States	U. States	Eliza	31 Jul 1821
William, Child [of T. H.]	9	M		U. States	U. States	Eliza	31 Jul 1821
SUTERNO, John	45	M	Mariner	U.S.	U.S.	Toison	21 Nov 1827
SUTHERLAND, —, Mr.			Merchant	England	England	Henrietta	18 Aug 1829
A. D.	36	M	Merchant	Massachusetts	U. States	Tobasco	23 Jul 1827
A. S.	43	M	Mariner	United States	United States	Penobscot Packet	4 May 1826
Anne	9	F		U. States	U. States	Hebe	27 Jan 1827
David	70	M	P.M.G.B.N.A.	G.B.	Canada	George Canning	2 May 1828
James	50	M	Merchant	Great Britain	Unknown	William Thompson	1 May 1827
John	34 1/12	M	...	England	America, U.S.	Illinois	3 Jun 1822
John	42	M	Merchant		U. States	Margaret	3 Jun 1822
Mary	5	F		U. States	U. States	Hebe	27 Jan 1827
Mary	27 5/12	F		England	America, U.S.	Illinois	3 Jun 1822
Susan	19	F	Seamstress	Ireland	United States	Concordia	25 Aug 1827
William	21	M	None	Great Britain	Unknown	William Thompson	1 May 1827
Wm.	7	M		U. States	U. States	Hebe	27 Jan 1827
SUTHERLIN, G.	26	M	Sadler	Bardin	U. States	Bayard	5 Sep 1828
SUTHHILL, Cornelius	25	M	Gentn.	United States	United States	Magnet	28 Jun 1821
SUTLIFF, Alexander	50	M		England	U. States	William Prince	13 Dec 1827
SUTOR, Dionysius	21	M	Musician	U. States	U.S.	Queen Mab	26 Nov 1825
SUTTEN, Danil	18		Farmer	France	U. States	Elizabeth	9 Jul 1825
SUTTER, Carlian	16	F		France	America, U.N.S.	Great Britain	3 Aug 1829
Catharina	20	F		France	America, U.N.S.	Great Britain	3 Aug 1829
Critein	50	M	Weaver	France	America, U.N.S.	Great Britain	3 Aug 1829
Frederick	17	M		France	America, U.N.S.	Great Britain	3 Aug 1829
George	9	M		France	America, U.N.S.	Great Britain	3 Aug 1829
John	32 2/12	M	Watchmaker	Switzerland	U.S. America	Edward	28 Oct 1825
Maria	4 1/12	F		Switzerland	U.S. America	Edward	28 Oct 1825
Nicholas	25	M	Farmer	Switzerland	U. States	Sully	15 Jul 1829
Rosenia	6 2/12	F		Switzerland	U.S. America	Edward	28 Oct 1825
Rosenia	34 3/12	F		Switzerland	U.S. America	Edward	28 Oct 1825
Sophia	50	F		France	America, U.N.S.	Great Britain	3 Aug 1829
SUTTIN, B.	18	F	Gent	French	Switzerland	Charlemagne	19 Sep 1828
M.	36	F	Gent	French	Switzerland	Charlemagne	19 Sep 1828
T.	16	F	Gent	French	Switzerland	Charlemagne	19 Sep 1828
SUTTON, —, Miss	3	F		England	U. States	Perseverance	18 Nov 1824
—, Mr.	25	M	Merch.	England	U. States	Perseverance	18 Nov 1824
—, Mr.	48	M	Farmer	England		Hercules	19 Jun 1821
—, Mrs.	18	F	Mercht.	England	U. States	Perseverance	18 Nov 1824
Ann	8	F	Child	Ireland	United States	Dublin Packet	9 Jul 1827
Charles	11	M	Child	Ireland	United States	Dublin Packet	9 Jul 1827
Christp.	28	M	Farmer	England	England	William Byrnes	14 Apr 1824
Danl.	2...	M	...	...	...	Antioch	8 Oct 1827
David	5/12	M		England	Novascotia	Maria	3 Oct 1823
Edmond	53	M	Farmer	American	U.S. America	Majestic	24 Mar 1828
Edmund	13	M	Agriculture	England	United States	Hercules	24 Oct 1821
Elijah	11	M	Agriculture	England	United States	Hercules	24 Oct 1821
Elisha	11	M	Agriculture	England	United States	Hercules	24 Oct 1821

NAMES OF PASSENGERS	AGE	SEX	OCCUPATIONS	COUNTRY TO WHICH THEY BELONG	COUNTRY THEY INTEND TO INHABIT	SHIPS/DATES OF ARRIVAL	
SUTTON (cont'd)							
Eliza	4	F	Child	Ireland	United States	Dublin Packet	9 Jul 1827
Eliza	7	F		G. Britain	U. States	Armadello	22 Jun 1827
Elizabeth	15	F	Agriculture	England	United States	Hercules	24 Oct 1821
Elizabeth	22	F		England	Novascotia	Maria	3 Oct 1822
Elizabeth	25		Farmer	France	U. States	Elizabeth	9 Jul 1825
George	32	M	Laborer	Ireland	United States	Dublin Packet	9 Jul 1827
H. E.	21	M	Gentleman	England		Hudson	23 Jul 1828
Hannah	22	F	Agriculture	England	United States	Hercules	24 Oct 1821
Henry	2	M		G. Britain	U. States	Armadello	22 Jun 1827
James	28	M	Shoemaker	Ireland	America	Wilson	16 May 1825
Jane	52	F	Agriculture	England	United States	Hercules	24 Oct 1821
Jane, Miss, his							
Daughter [Mr.]	18	F		England		Hercules	19 Jun 1821
Jno.	30	M	Laborer	Ireland	United States	Weser	29 Jul 1823
John	19		Mason	Ireland	United States	Fabius	18 Mar 1829
John	26	M	Carpenter	England	Novascotia	Maria	3 Oct 1822
John	30		Farmer	France	U. States	Elizabeth	9 Jul 1825
John	33	M	Schoolmaster	England	Upper Canada	Comet	6 Mar 1823
Joseph	30	M	Servant	Great Britain	Canada	James Monroe	5 Apr 1820
Margaret	9	F	Agriculture	England	United States	Hercules	24 Oct 1821
Maria	1	F	Child	Ireland	United States	Dublin Packet	9 Jul 1827
Maria	32	F	Wife	Ireland	United States	Dublin Packet	9 Jul 1827
Mary	20	F	Agriculture	England	United States	Hercules	24 Oct 1821
Mary	36	F		G. Britain	U. States	Armadello	22 Jun 1827
Michl.	25	M	Labourer	Great Britain	United States	Mary & Harriet	3 Jul 1829
Richard	50	M		U.S. Citizen	Portsmouth, N.h.	Napoleon	7 Jul 1829
Robert	24	M	Agriculture	England	United States	Hercules	24 Oct 1821
S. C.	40	M	Mariner	U. States	U. States	New Packet	27 Jul 1822
Samuel	40	M	Labourer	G. Britain	U. States	George Clinton	10 Sep 1828
Susanah	27	F	...	Ireland	United States	Wilson	22 Jun 1824
Thomas	24	M	Merchant	England	England	James Cropper	3 Mar 1825
Thos.	23	M	Cord weaver	England	U. States	Electra	7 Jul 1828
Willm.	22	M	Confectioner	England	New York	Brighton	16 Nov 1826
Wm.	5	M		G. Britain	U. States	Armadello	22 Jun 1827
SUTUPHAN, Pat	25	M	Labourer	Ireland	United States	Louisa	18 Apr 1827
SUTZ, Joseph	23	M	Clergyman	Germany	U. States	America	22 Sep 1826
SUWLER, Ellen	20	F		G. Britain	U. States	Dalhouse Castle	12 Sep 1828
SUYBOT, William	32	M	Mariner	U. States	U. States	Savannah	10 Jan 1828
SUYBOWSKIE, Joseph	27	M	Servant	Poland	Poland	Corinthian	2 Sep 1824
SUYDEN, Wm.	30	M	Labourer	Great Britain	United States	Aspasia	16 Jul 1828
SUYRLEE, John	27	M	Mechanic	Philada.	U. States	Douglass	7 Aug 1827
SVENAN, Mary	20	F				Ocean	17 Aug 1820
SVIGADO, Petter	28	M	Officer	Spain	Havana	Alfred	22 May 1824
SWADDLING, James	8	M	None	England	United States	London	21 May 1828
Samuel	6/12	M	None	England	United States	London	21 May 1828
Sarah	32	F	None	England	United States	London	21 May 1828
Solomon	6	M	None	England	United States	London	21 May 1828
Spencer	4	M	None	England	United States	London	21 May 1828
Stephen	9	M	None	England	United States	London	21 May 1828
Stephen	33	M	Laborer	England	United States	London	21 May 1828
SWAIL, William	46	M	Farmer	England	Geneva, U. States	Ann Maria	26 Apr 1822
SWAILRICK, Edward	64	M	Merchant	United States	United States	Aurora	11 Dec 1824
SWAILS, William	...5	M	Farmer	Great Britian	United States	Silvanus Jenkins	6 Apr 1826
SWAIN, Ann	22 6/12	F		United States	United States	Alexander Mansfield	9 Jul 1829
James C.		M	Mariner	Nantucket	Nantucket	Nimrod	21 Sep 1820
Mirbal	40	M	Mariner	U. States	U. States	Prince Edward	29 Jul 1823
Rebecca	35	F		U. States	U. States	Colosso Conti	17 Apr 1822
Thomas	22	M	Merchant	United States	United States	Persia	21 Oct 1824
SWAINE, James	23	M	Farmer	Ireland	United States	Dublin Packet	9 Jul 1827
John	46	M	...	Scotland	U.S. of America	Friends	10 May 1823
SWALE, —, Mrs.	20	F		Great Britian	United States	Isaac Hicks	13 Jan 1826
Thomas	25	M	Merchant	Great Britian	United States	Isaac Hicks	13 Jan 1826
SWAN, —, one Child							
at the Breast	8/12	F	Child	Glenssark	U.S. America	Camillus	10 Sep 1821
Benjamin L.	37		Merchant	...	...	James Cropper	28 Jun 1824
Charles	30	M	Seaman	New York	New York	Mary & Elizabeth	7 Sep 1824

NAMES OF PASSENGERS	AGE	SEX	OCCUPATIONS	COUNTRY TO WHICH THEY BELONG	COUNTRY THEY INTEND TO INHABIT	SHIPS/DATES OF ARRIVAL	
SWAN (cont'd)	Edwd.	30	M	Weaver	Great Britian	U. States Kneedland	Henry 7 Aug 1826
Elisabeth	35	F		Ireland	United States	Nancy R. Crowell	21 Sep 1822
Eliza	23		Servant	England	England	Silvanus Jenkins	30 Nov 1827
Esther	20	...		Ireland	U. States	Nancy	16 Aug 1822
Grace	25	F	Seamstress	Ireland	America	Caroline	25 Jul 1828
James	10	M		Ireland	U. States	Nancy	16 Aug 1822
James	10	M	Boyo	Ireland	United States	Robert Fulton	24 Jul 1826
Jams	51	M	Weaver	Ireland	America	Caroline	25 Jul 1828
Jane	11	F	Seamstress	Ireland	America	Caroline	25 Jul 1828
Jas.	22	M	Hatter	Derbeyshire	U. States	Ann	11 Feb 1822
Jas.	28	M	Hatter	Yorkshire	U. States	Ann	11 Feb 1822
John	60	M	Farmer			John & Edward	25 Aug 1820
Joseph	14	M		Ireland	U. States	Nancy	16 Aug 1822
Margalet	70	F	Seamstress			John & Edward	25 Aug 1820
Margaret	1	...		Ireland	U. States	Nancy	16 Aug 1822
Margaret	22	F	Seamstress	Ireland	America	Caroline	25 Jul 1828
Margret	8	F		Ireland	United States	Nancy R. Crowell	21 Sep 1822
Mary Ann	22	F	Wife	Glenssark	U.S. America	Camillus	10 Sep 1821
Mary C.	24			...	...	James Cropper	28 Jun 1824
Maryan	20	F	Seamstress	Ireland	America	Caroline	25 Jul 1828
Robert	34	M	Trader	...	...	Hunter	19 May 1823
Robt.	18	M	Merchant	Scotland	United States	Favorite	9 Oct 1823
Sarah, wife [of Robert]	39	F		...	...	Hunter	19 May 1823
Susan	47	F	Seamstress	Ireland	America	Caroline	25 Jul 1828
Thomas	30	M		Ireland	U. States	Nancy	16 Aug 1822
Timothy	32 8/12	M	Merchant	United States	United States	James Monroe	27 Jul 1821
Timothy	35		Merchant	...	...	James Cropper	28 Jun 1824
Timothy	38	M	Merchant	New York	New York	New York	31 Jul 1829
William	25	M	Merchant	U. States	U. States	Blooming Rose	14 Jul 1821
Wm.	18	M	Seamstress	Ireland	America	Caroline	25 Jul 1828
SWANDELL, James	22	M			United States	Mary & Harriet	9 Mar 1829
SWANEY, Elenor	25	F	Spinster	Ireland	United States	Robert Fulton	24 Jul 1826
George	5	M		Ireland	U. States	Nancy	2 May 1823
Mary	8	F		Ireland	U. States	Nancy	2 May 1823
Mary	25	F		Ireland	U. States	Nancy	2 May 1823
SWANSON, George	2	M	his child [William]	Great Britain	United States	Elizabeth & Mary	20 Mar 1828
Isabella	4	F	his child [William]	Great Britain	United States	Elizabeth & Mary	20 Mar 1828
Margaret	1	F	his child [William]	Great Britain	United States	Elizabeth & Mary	20 Mar 1828
Margaret	30	F	his Wife [William]	Great Britain	United States	Elizabeth & Mary	20 Mar 1828
William	30	M	Farmer	Great Britain	United States	Elizabeth & Mary	20 Mar 1828
SWANY, Catherin	5	F	Child	Ireland	United States	Robert Fulton	10 Aug 1827
Charles	30	M	Labourer	Ireland	United States	Robert Fulton	10 Aug 1827
SWARES, D. W.	32	M	Merchant	United States	United States	Baltic	24 Nov 1828
SWART, Benja.	17	M	Farmer	Gt. Britain	United States	Importer	21 May 1821
Thos. C.	60	M	Farmer	Gt. Britain	United States	Importer	21 May 1821
SWARTIVONT, Samuel	25	M	U.S. Navy	United States	United States	Chili	9 Jan 1829
SWARTWOUT, Samuel	21 3/12	M	Officer U.S.N.	New York	New York	Potosi	28 May 1825
SWARTZ, Anthony	6	M	Family [of Fitz]	France	America	La Grange	7 Aug 1828
Fitz	40	M	Farmer	France	America	La Grange	7 Aug 1828
Geirre	12	F	Family [of Fitz]	France	America	La Grange	7 Aug 1828
Geirre	38	F	Family [of Fitz]	France	America	La Grange	7 Aug 1828
Joseph	10	M	Family [of Fitz]	France	America	La Grange	7 Aug 1828
SWAYINGBURG, Adaline	47	F		Germany	United States	Samuel Robertson	8 Aug 1828
Conrard	8	M		Germany	United States	Samuel Robertson	8 Aug 1828
Conrard	46	M	Shoemaker	Germany	United States	Samuel Robertson	8 Aug 1828

NAMES OF PASSENGERS	AGE	SEX	OCCUPATIONS	COUNTRY TO WHICH THEY BELONG	COUNTRY THEY INTEND TO INHABIT	SHIPS/DATES OF ARRIVAL	
SWAYINGBURG (cont'd)							
George M.	6	M		Germany	United States	Samuel Robertson	8 Aug 1828
Grater	13	F		Germany	United States	Samuel Robertson	8 Aug 1828
Madaline	17	F		Germany	United States	Samuel Robertson	8 Aug 1828
SWEATON, George	26	F	Spinster	Ireland	United States	Fabius	4 Jun 1828
Mary	20	F	Spinster	Ireland	United States	Fabius	4 Jun 1828
SWEENEY, A.	30	M	Merchant	Great Britain	United States	Isaac Hicks	6 Dec 1827
Betty	...	F	Spinster	Ireland	Unt. St. America	Wilson	21 May 1827
Bridget	60	F	Wife	Ireland	United States	Henry Kneeland	7 Jun 1828
Catharin	27		Wife	Ireland		Westmoreland	1 Aug 1826
Catherine	22	F	Spinster	Ireland	United States	Wilson	6 Jun 1828
Catherine	24					Trio	5 May 1828
Edward	31	M	Dyer	Ireland	America	Liverpool	31 Aug 1827
Edwd.	4		Boy	Ireland		Westmoreland	1 Aug 1826
Ellen	15	F		Ireland	United States	Trio	2 Oct 1828
George	2	F		Ireland	United States	Kleber	23 Jul 1827
Hugh	22		Farmer	Ireland		Westmoreland	1 Aug 1826
James	28					Trio	5 May 1828
James	38		Farmer	Ireland		Westmoreland	1 Aug 1826
Jane	30	F	Lady	England	U. States	Pacific	11 Sep 1824
Pegy D.	22	F		Ireland	United States	Kleber	23 Jul 1827
Susan	5	F		Ireland	United States	Kleber	23 Jul 1827
Thomas	25	M	Mason	Ireland	United States	Kleber	23 Jul 1827
William	25	M	Farmer	Ireland	United States	Sarah G.	11 Jan 1828
Wm.	32	M	Farmer	Ireland	United States	Henry Kneeland	7 Jun 1828
SWEENY, Alexander	3	M	None	Ireland	United States	Catharine	22 Jul 1825
Alexander	22	M		Ireland	United States	William & George	14 May 1828
Andw.	20	M	Servant	Ireland	United States	William	20 Jul 1829
Bridget	15	F	Servant	Ireland	New Jersey	Atlantic	8 May 1828
Catharine	28			Ireland	United States	Robert Burns	30 May 1823
Catherine	20	F	Spinster	Ireland	America	Liverpool	31 Aug 1827
David	37	M	...	Ireland	United States	Carolina Ann	24 Oct 1825
Dennis	32	M		Ireland	U. States	Wanderer	1 Sep 1828
Edward	20	M		Ireland	United States	Alex. Mansfield	17 May 1823
Geo. W.	28	M	Mariner	Baltimore	Baltimore	Francis Jarvis	30 Aug 1826
Hannah	1	F	None	Ireland	United States	Catharine	22 Jul 1825
Hugh J.	20	M	Gentleman	Philadelphia	Jamaica	Emily Cook	10 Apr 1826
James	11	M	Boy	Ireland	United States	Trident	17 May 1825
James	20	M		G. Britan	U. States	Geo. Canning	2 Sep 1828
James	32	M	Doctor	Ireland	U. States	Wanderer	1 Sep 1828
John	14	M	Farmer	Ireland	America	Liverpool	31 Aug 1827
John	19	M	Weaver	Ireland	United States	Trident	17 May 1825
John	20	M	Labourer	Ireland	United States	Asia	29 Jul 1829
John, Junr.	1 2/12	M		Ireland	America	Liverpool	31 Aug 1827
Mary	6	F	None	Ireland	United States	Catharine	22 Jul 1825
Mary	32	F		Ireland	U. States	Wanderer	1 Sep 1828
Nancy	27	F	Spinster	Ireland	United States	Catharine	22 Jul 1825
Patrick	28	M	Shoemaker	Ireland	United States	Catharine	22 Jul 1825
William	19	M		Limerick	N. York	Thomas & William	25 May 1827
SWEERSON, Ewd.	25	M	Labourer	Ireland	U. States	Sarah G	30 Jun 1828
SWEERY, Cathe.	27	F	Spinster	Ireland		Robert Fulton	4 Jun 1828
Morgan	8	M	Labourer	Ireland		Robert Fulton	4 Jun 1828
Robt.	5	M	Labourer	Ireland		Robert Fulton	4 Jun 1828
SWEET, W. S.	28		Merchant			Charlotte Corday	11 Sep 1820
SWEETHARTT, Joseph	20	M	Farmer	England	U. States	Montgomery	18 Oct 1828
SWEETING, Ann	21			England		Anacreon	7 Sep 1827
Elizabeth	15			England		Anacreon	7 Sep 1827
Estha	52			England		Anacreon	7 Sep 1827
George	12			England		Anacreon	7 Sep 1827
Mary	3			England		Anacreon	7 Sep 1827
Richard	51			England		Anacreon	7 Sep 1827
Robt.	13			England		Anacreon	7 Sep 1827
Sidden	18			England		Anacreon	7 Sep 1827

NAMES OF PASSENGERS	AGE	SEX	OCCUPATIONS	COUNTRY TO WHICH THEY BELONG	COUNTRY THEY INTEND TO INHABIT	SHIPS/DATES OF ARRIVAL	
SWEETMAN, Brion	21	M	Servant to Captn. Morgan	Boston		Phoebe Ann	27 Dec 1825
SWEEZEY, Catherine	19	F	None	England	United States	Jubilee	1 Oct 1828
Thomas	18	M	Labourer	England	United States	Jubilee	1 Oct 1828
SWEID, Richard	24	M	Chairmaker	New York	U.S.	McDonough	21 May 1821
SWEING, Felix	18	M	Labourer	Ireland	United States	Fabius	31 Jul 1829
SWELLS, David	40	M	Farmer	England	Nasau	Concordia	12 Oct 1826
SWENEY, Edward	30	M	Dyer	Ireland	United States	John Wells	18 Sep 1826
William	25	M	Dyer	Ireland	United States	Pallas	28 Oct 1828
SWENSON, Jonas	3 6/12	M	Farmer	Norway	United States	Salem	31 Aug 1829
Swen	6	M	Farmer	Norway	United States	Salem	31 Aug 1829
SWEREDGE, Jos.	27	M	Farmer	England	U. States	New England	12 Apr 1825
SWETMAN, Eliza	3	F	None	Great Britain	United States	John	6 Oct 1820
Eliza	30	F	None	Great Britain	United States	John	6 Oct 1820
Wm.	31	M	Currier	Great Britain	United States	John	6 Oct 1820
SWETT, James L.	18	M	Gentleman	America	America	Columbia	22 May 1822
SWIFT, A. B.	49	M	Distiler	U. States	U. States	Catharine	19 Jul 1822
Ann	...			England	United States	Hugh Johnson	11 Jun 1828
Ann	7			Waterford	Gt. Britain	Enterprize	19 Feb 1822
Ann	30			Cork	Gt. Britain	Enterprize	19 Feb 1822
Edwin	21	M	Merchant	U. States	U. States	Robert Y. Haynes	22 Mar 1827
Esther	60	F		England	Great Britain	Manchester Packet	30 Nov 1822
Geo.	7			England	United States	Hugh Johnson	11 Jun 1828
Geo.	34		Farmer	England	United States	Hugh Johnson	11 Jun 1828
James	20	M	Labourer	Ireland		Marchioness	13 May 1828
Jane	20	F		England	Great Britain	Manchester Packet	30 Nov 1822
John	32	M	M...	Great Britain	Albany	Zodiac	14 Jun 1822
Lawrence	28	M	Butcher	Ireland	United States	Meteor	19 Aug 1829
M.	21	M		Ireland	U. States	Howard	25 Jul 1823
Mary	1			England	United States	Hugh Johnson	11 Jun 1828
Mary	22			England	United States	Hugh Johnson	11 Jun 1828
Matthew	40	M	Merchant	England	United States	Cincinnatus	21 Nov 1821
Sarah	3			England	United States	Hugh Johnson	11 Jun 1828
Timothy	46	M	Cloth Dresser	Great Britain	United States	Orozimbo	5 Mar 1827
Wm.	8	M		England	Great Britain	Manchester Packet	30 Nov 1822
Wm.	54	M	Farmer	Great Britain	Albany	Zodiac	14 Jun 1822
SWINDELLS, James	30	M	Bricklayer	Hyde, Stockpin		Colossus	27 Mar 1828
SWINDLEHURST, George	21	M	Taylor	Great Britain	United States	George Clinton	27 Aug 1827
SWINDLES, Samuel	27	M	Mechanic	Great Britain		Birmingham	11 Oct 1828
SWING, Eliza	6	F		G. Britain	U. States	Robt. Edwards	4 Sep 1828
Francis	1	M		G. Britain	U. States	Robt. Edwards	4 Sep 1828
Geo.	37	M		G. Britain	U. States	Robt. Edwards	4 Sep 1828
John	2	M		G. Britain	U. States	Robt. Edwards	4 Sep 1828
Lydia	38	F		G. Britain	U. States	Robt. Edwards	4 Sep 1828
SWINS, Nicolus	19	M	Fer.	Wales	U. States	Franklin	7 Jul 1828
SWINSON, John	23	M	Gentleman	England	England	Leo	30 Apr 1825
SWISTE, L.	33	M	Baker	France	U. States	Montano	2 Sep 1828
SWORDEN, Jane	28	F	Se[r]vant	Ireland	United States	Sylvester Healy	17 Oct 1825
Mary	6	F	Child	Ireland	United States	Sylvester Healy	17 Oct 1825
SWORES, John	23	M	Weaver	Ireland	State of New York	Louisa	18 Apr 1827
SYERS, Alice	3/12	F		Sefton, Great Britain	United States	Robert Fulton	22 Oct 1821
Allan	2	M		Sefton, Great Britain	United States	Robert Fulton	22 Oct 1821
Martha	22	F		Sefton, Great Britain	United States	Robert Fulton	22 Oct 1821
Philip	7	M		Sefton, Great Britain	United States	Robert Fulton	22 Oct 1821
Thomas	...	M	Farmer	Sefton, Great Britain	United States	Robert Fulton	22 Oct 1821
William	32	M	Farmer	Sefton, Great Britain	United States	Robert Fulton	22 Oct 1821
SYKE, Fred.	3	M	Farmer	Hessian-Germany	Canada	Caesar	8 Sep 1828

NAMES OF PASSENGERS	AGE	SEX	OCCUPATIONS	COUNTRY TO WHICH THEY BELONG	COUNTRY THEY INTEND TO INHABIT	SHIPS/DATES OF ARRIVAL	
SYKES, Caroline	6	F	None	England	United States	Jubilee	13 Jul 1829
Catherine	32	F	None	England	United States	Jubilee	13 Jul 1829
Eliza	1	F		G. Britain	U. States	Mary Howland	22 Sep 1828
Elizabeth	20	F		England	United States	Cosmo	21 Aug 1828
Hannah	28	F	None	England	U. States	Birmingham	12 Oct 1827
Hannah	35	F	None	England	Pittsburgh	Orozimbo	8 Jun 1822
Hariot	4	F	None	England	United States	Jubilee	13 Jul 1829
James	6	M	None	England	Pittsburgh	Orozimbo	8 Jun 1822
James	40	M	Woolencloth Dyer	England	United States	Andes	2 Oct 1828
Jno.	36	M	Farmer	England	U.S. America	Cortes	19 May 1826
John	2	M		England	United States	Cosmo	21 Aug 1828
John	4	M	None	England	U. States	Birmingham	12 Oct 1827
John	22	M	Painter	England	United States	Cosmo	21 Aug 1828
John	33	M	Weaver	England	Great Britain	Florida	26 Sep 1826
John	40	M	Farmer	...ddlesworth	...ddlesworth	Howard Douglass	11 May 1827
Jonathan	22	M	Labourer	Ireland	United States	Jubilee	1 Oct 1828
Jos.	2	M	None	England	U. States	Birmingham	12 Oct 1827
Jos.	37	M	Manufacture	U. States	United States	Cortes	18 Oct 1820
Joseph	40	M	Farmer	Great Britain	United States	Mary & Harriet	3 Jul 1829
Joshua	34	M		G. Britain	U. States	Mary Howland	22 Sep 1828
M.	6	F	None	England	U. States	Birmingham	12 Oct 1827
Martha	60	F		G. Britain	U. States	Mary Howland	22 Sep 1828
Mary	10	F	None	England	Pittsburgh	Orozimbo	8 Jun 1822
Mary	12	F	None	England	United States	Jubilee	13 Jul 1829
S.	6	F	None	England	U. States	Birmingham	12 Oct 1827
Saml.	1	M	None	England	U. States	Birmingham	12 Oct 1827
Sarah	28	F		G. Britain	U. States	Mary Howland	22 Sep 1828
Thomas	7	M	None	England	United States	Jubilee	13 Jul 1829
Thomas	26	M	Shoemaker	England	United States	Siroc	31 Oct 1829
William	10	M	None	England	United States	Jubilee	13 Jul 1829
Willm.	8	M	None	England	Pittsburgh	Orozimbo	8 Jun 1822
Wm.	64	M	Manufacturer	G. Britain	U. States	Mary Howland	22 Sep 1828
SYLVA, Abrm.	18 2/12	M	Servant Boy	Bengall	United States	America	18 Jan 1820
SYLVANUS, Elizabeth	50	F	Taylor	England	U. States	Hudson	8 Oct 1827
Hugh	40	M	Taylor	England	U. States	Hudson	8 Oct 1827
SYLVESTER, Fred.	14	M	Gentleman	England	Newyork	Cortes	16 Jul 1827
SYMES, E. B.	38	M	Gentleman	G. Brittain	U. States	Wm. Penn	6 Feb 1822
John	31	M	Cooper	Philadelphia	U.S.	London	19 Dec 1823
SYMONDS, Hannah	20	F		England	United States	Acasta	14 Jun 1824
Lewis	38	M	Merchant	England	United States	Acasta	14 Jun 1824
SYMS, John	5	M	Shoemaker	Great Briton	New York	Brighton	12 Jun 1826
Rebecca	2	F	None	Great Briton	New York	Brighton	12 Jun 1826
Rebecca	24	F	None	Great Briton	New York	Brighton	12 Jun 1826
Samuel	26	M	Shoemaker	Great Briton	New York	Brighton	12 Jun 1826
SYNAR, Richard	28	M	Warehouseman	England	United States	Alexander Mansfield	16 Sep 1823
SYNETH, Bernard	18	M	Labourer	Ireland		Robert Fulton	4 Jun 1828
SYNN, Patrick	22	M	Mariner	Great Britain	State of N. York	Robert Fulton	30 Dec 1824
SYNOD, Jas.	25	M	Laborer	Ireland	U. States	Albion	9 Aug 1826
SYNOTT, ...k	25	M	Labourer	...ford	...	Frances Henrietta	30 Jun 1827
SYPLE, Michael, Mr.	42	M	Gentleman	Nova Scotia	United States	Washington	23 Dec 1828
SYPSON, Francis	24	F	None	Great Brittan	Canada	Electra	28 Apr 1827
Henry	27	M	Accountant	Great Brittan	Canada	Electra	28 Apr 1827
SYRINGTON, Gilbert			Merchant	America	America	Columbus	20 Aug 1828
SYTLE, Estec	57	F	Spinster	Ireland	United States	Wilson	6 Jun 1828
T..., Allexander	29	M	Farmer	Great Brittain	U. States	William Byrnes	23 Jul 1824
Ann Maria	2	M	Joiner	Great Britain		Caravan	8 Sep 1828
C.	30	F		Great Britain		Caravan	8 Sep 1828
Catarina	53		Weaver	Great Britain		Caravan	8 Sep 1828
Cath.	23	M	Weaver	Great Britain		Caravan	8 Sep 1828
Charles	4	M	Joiner	Great Britain		Caravan	8 Sep 1828
Charles	21	M	Labourer	Ireland	America	Plutarch	18 Jul 1826
Douder	21	M	Weaver	Great Britain		Caravan	8 Sep 1828
Eliza	1	F		Great Britain		Caravan	8 Sep 1828
Eliza	33	F		Great Britain		Caravan	8 Sep 1828
Eliza	73	M	Weaver	Great Britain		Caravan	8 Sep 1828

NAMES OF PASSENGERS	AGE	SEX	OCCUPATIONS	COUNTRY TO WHICH THEY BELONG	COUNTRY THEY INTEND TO INHABIT	SHIPS/DATES OF ARRIVAL	
T... (cont'd)							
George	16	M	None	G. Britain	United States	New York	12 Nov 1822
Go.	36	M	Joiner	Great Britain		Caravan	8 Sep 1828
Henry P.	52	M	Weaver	Great Britain		Caravan	8 Sep 1828
James	25	M	Sawyer	Ireland	America	Plutarch	18 Jul 1826
M	6	M		Great Britain		Caravan	8 Sep 1828
William	27	M	Grocer	England	New York	Thames	6 Oct 1820
William	38	M	Merchant	G. Britain	United States	New York	12 Nov 1822
T...D, James	10	M	Weaver	England	United States	Trident	30 Sep 1826
T...ES, —, Doct.	23		Doctor	U.S. America	America	Hesper	9 Jun 1827
T...GER, Henry	25	M	Farmer	Great Britian	United States	London	24 Jun 1823
T...KENEN, Thomas	20	M				Eliza Grant	6 Oct 1828
T...OIS, Phillip	25	M	Farmer	Great Britian	United States	London	24 Jun 1823
T...OUDEANT, Fr...i...	...	M	...	France	United States	Stephania	20 Apr 1827
T...TE, Joseph	14	M	Gentleman	St. Croix	U. States	Jupiter	27 Jun 1828
TA...T, Pierre Denis	23	M	...r...nt	France	United States	Montano	8 May 1827
TABAER, Manuel	17			Mexico	Mexico	Horatio	3 Dec 1827
TABAS, Abraham	17	M		Suisse	United States	Montano	5 May 1828
Anne	28	F		Suisse	United States	Montano	5 May 1828
Anne	54	F		Suisse	United States	Montano	5 May 1828
Charles	23	M		Suisse	United States	Montano	5 May 1828
Emmanuel	20	M		Suisse	United States	Montano	5 May 1828
Guillaume	16	M		Suisse	United States	Montano	5 May 1828
Louis	12	M		Suisse	United States	Montano	5 May 1828
TABER, Wm.		M	Merchant	U. States	U. States	Augustus & John	15 Jun 1822
TABERNER, James	50	M	Weaver	Great Britain	United States	Ganges	26 Oct 1826
TABOR, Juan	35	M	Cook	Spaniard	United States	General Warren	8 Jul 1829
TACELL, Ann	50	F	Wife	Ireland	United States	Ann Maria	21 May 1827
Charles	60	M	Labourer	Ireland	United States	Ann Maria	21 May 1827
Hugh	38	M	Labourer	Ireland	United States	Ann Maria	21 May 1827
TACHE, Morris H.	22	M	Merchant	United States		Andromache	7 Feb 1820
TACKER, Elizabeth	17	F		Switzerland	U.S.	Francois I	8 Aug 1829
Francis	14	F		Switzerland	U.S.	Francois I	8 Aug 1829
Henry	11	M		Switzerland	U.S.	Francois I	8 Aug 1829
Henry	23	M		Switzerland	U.S.	Francois I	8 Aug 1829
Valentine	31	M	Glazier	Switzerland	U.S.	Francois I	8 Aug 1829
Veshis	39	F		Switzerland	U.S.	Francois I	8 Aug 1829
TAFFE, Peter	30	M				Lady of the Lake	23 Aug 1828
*left ship							
TAFFILE, Jno.	53	M		U. States	U. States	William	30 Jul 1824
TAFFY, —, Mr.	22	M	Labourer	England	U. States	Ann Maria	13 Mar 1823
TAFT, Robert	33	M	Carpenter	United States	United States	Good Hope	10 Mar 1828
Robert, Mr.	36		Grocer	England		Hercules	19 Jun 1821
TAGAN, Chrles, his son [John James]	13	M	Farmer	Swissarland	United States	Montano	13 Jan 1826
Eliza, his daughter [John James]	19	F	Farmer	Swissarland	United States	Montano	13 Jan 1826
Frederic, his son [John James]	17	M	Farmer	Swissarland	United States	Montano	13 Jan 1826
John James	49	M	Farmer	Swissarland	United States	Montano	13 Jan 1826
Julia, his daughter [John James]	14	F	Farmer	Swissarland	United States	Montano	13 Jan 1826
Julia, his wife [John James]	46	F	Farmer	Swissarland	United States	Montano	13 Jan 1826
Lewis, his son [John James]	1 10/12	M	Farmer	Swissarland	United States	Montano	13 Jan 1826
Louisa, his daughter [John James]	4	F	Farmer	Swissarland	United States	Montano	13 Jan 1826
Maria Ann, his daughter [John James]	7	F	Farmer	Swissarland	United States	Montano	13 Jan 1826
Rosina, his daughter [John James]	10	F	Farmer	Swissarland	United States	Montano	13 Jan 1826
TAGARTY, Thomas	20	M	Labourer	England	U. States	Hope & Esther	10 Jul 1827
TAGG, Elizabeth	20	F	Brushmaker	Great Britain	United States	Unity	20 Oct 1829
William	39	M	Brushmaker	Great Britain	United States	Unity	20 Oct 1829
TAGGART, Catherine	21	F		Ireland	United States	Meteor	19 Aug 1829
John	21	M	Merchant	Ireland	United States	Meteor	19 Aug 1829

NAMES OF PASSENGERS	AGE	SEX	OCCUPATIONS	COUNTRY TO WHICH THEY BELONG	COUNTRY THEY INTEND TO INHABIT	SHIPS/DATES OF ARRIVAL	
TAGGART (cont'd)							
John, Jr.	2	M		Ireland	United States	Meteor	19 Aug 1829
Wm.	35	M	Mercht.	U. States	U. States	Hiram	4 Sep 1824
TAGGERT, Jelty	20	M	Labourer	Great Britain	United States	Atlantic	28 May 1827
TAGNER, Dorother	50	F	Farmer	Switzerland	United States	Olympia	12 Aug 1828
TAGNO, Jerome	32	M	Merchant	Spanyard	U. States	Romulus	31 Jul 1823
TAGUE, Patrick	26	M		Ireland	America	Carolina Ann	7 Aug 1826
Thomas	32	M		Ireland	America	Carolina Ann	7 Aug 1826
TAHAR, Frederic	35	M	Gentleman	Ireland	United States	Ann Maria	21 May 1827
TAHON, C.	12	M		France	United States	La Flora	30 Jun 1828
Cathr.	17	F		France	United States	La Flora	30 Jun 1828
Emma	5	F		France	United States	La Flora	30 Jun 1828
Jacob	0 3/12	M		France	United States	La Flora	30 Jun 1828
M.	10	F		France	United States	La Flora	30 Jun 1828
N.	35	F		France	United States	La Flora	30 Jun 1828
P.	20	F		France	United States	La Flora	30 Jun 1828
TAIFFE, Catherine	30		Maid Servant	Ireland	America	Sarah	18 Aug 1829
TAILEY, Judith	26	F		Ireland	U. States	Balaena	29 Apr 1825
TAILOR, David	20	M	Taylor	Scotland	U. States	Roger Stewart	9 Jun 1828
Jas.	27	M	Mechanic	Albany	U. States	Martha	28 Jan 1826
John		M	None	Ilan...	U. States	Electra	7 Jul 1828
John	25	M	Labourer	Ireland	America	Wilson	16 May 1825
Mary	18	F		Scotland	U. States	Superior	25 Sep 1828
Theodore, Mr.	15	M	Merchant	Germany	America	Birmingham	16 Oct 1826
Thomas	30	M		U. States	U. States	Dollar	29 Aug 1825
TAINTER, J. A.	23	M	Gentn.	U. States	U. States	Silas Richards	29 Oct 1828
TAIRN, Christophr.	5	M	Weaver	France	U. States	C. Amelia	30 Jun 1828
TAIRNE, Jacqus	28	M	Weaver	France	U. States	C. Amelia	30 Jun 1828
TAIT, John	23	M	Merchant	U.S.	U.S.	Hesperus	13 Mar 1826
John	27	M	Saddler	New York	Boston, Mass.	Rubicon	22 May 1826
Thomas	31	M	Weaver	England	United States	Trident	31 Mar 1827
Wm.	15	M	None	U. States		Ann Maria	3 Jul 1820
TAITE, Robert	40	M	Farmer	Scotland	United States	Friends	16 Aug 1824
Wm.	34	M	Seaman	U. States	U. States	Boston	26 Sep 1820
TAITO, Jno.	20	M	Mercht.	U. States	N. York	Favourite	8 Oct 1823
TAITOR, Marthow	19	F	Farmer	Scotland	U. States	Roger Stewart	9 Jun 1828
TALBERT, Ann, Miss	14	F	Carpenter	England	U.S.	Acasta	11 May 1827
Eliza, Miss	16	F	Carpenter	England	U.S.	Acasta	11 May 1827
TALBOT, John	18	M	Weaver	Ireland	U. States	Ann Maria	6 Jul 1824
Saml. W., Mr.	25	M	Mercht.	United States	United States	Manchester	16 Dec 1828
Seth	47	M	Merchant	U.S.	U.S.	Marcia	5 Jul 1823
Thomas	45	M	Gentleman	Gt. Britain	Canada	Maria	22 May 1822
TALBOTT, John	Prisoner taken by the U.S. Ship Cyane and sent by the Consul at St. Iago					Maria	20 Jul 1820
TALFER, W.	28	M	Joiner	Great Britain	United States	Isaac Hicks	6 Dec 1827
TALLA, —	1	M		Hamburg	U. States	Martha	4 Sep 1828
—	2	M		Hamburg	U. States	Martha	4 Sep 1828
—	30	F		Hamburg	U. States	Martha	4 Sep 1828
Charles A.	35	M	Copper Smith	Hamburg	U. States	Martha	4 Sep 1828
TALLANT, John B.	29 1/12	M	Farmer	France	United States	France	6 Oct 1828
Robert	30	M	Mercantile	England	America	Erin	7 Nov 1824
TALLEL, Susannah	25	F		Ireland	United States	Silas Richards	27 Oct 1825
Wm.	25	M	Labourer	Ireland	United States	Silas Richards	27 Oct 1825
TALLMAN, J. N.	40	M	Merchant	Philad.	U. States	Carlo	6 Oct 1827
TALLON, Bryan	20 6/12	M	Farmer	Ireland	U. States	Virginia	20 Jun 1825
Honour	6	F		Ireland	U. States	Virginia	20 Jun 1825
Terresse	9	F		Ireland	U. States	Virginia	20 Jun 1825
TALLOWS,							
Robert Kirman, Mr.	27		Drugist	England		Hercules	19 Jun 1821
TALLY, Catharine	20	F	Servant	Ireland	New York	Atlantic	8 May 1828
Owen	19	M	Labourer	G. Britain	U. States	St. George	16 Jan 1829
Peter	23	M	Farmer			Orion	21 Aug 1820
Thos.	27	M	None	England	United States	Dalhouse Castle	6 Sep 1827
TALMAN, Jos. V.	38	M	Merchant	U. States	U. States	Lydia Davis	5 Jan 1824
TALRANCE, B., Mrs.	54	F	Sandy	St. Domingo	U. States	Edward Bonaffe	23 Jul 1828
TALT, Margat	18	F	None	England	United States	Aurelia	7 Jun 1826
TAMARAN, —, Child	10	F		I[sland] Cuba	Spain	Abigail	21 Mar 1825
—, Mrs.	55	F		I[sland] Cuba	Spain	Abigail	21 Mar 1825
TAMLIN, Edward	18		Clerk	England	Boston	Xenophon	25 Jul 1826
TAMTSON, Addam	24	M	Miller	Holland	U. States	Edward Bonaffe	23 Jul 1828

NAMES OF PASSENGERS	AGE	SEX	OCCUPATIONS	COUNTRY TO WHICH THEY BELONG	COUNTRY THEY INTEND TO INHABIT	SHIPS/DATES OF ARRIVAL	
TANDELL, John	30	M	Labourer	G. Britain	U. States	Freak	9 Jun 1828
TANG, Louis	29	M	Mercht.	Prussian	America	Protection	5 Nov 1825
TANKERD, Ellen	26	F	None	Great Britain	United States	Mary & Harriet	3 Jul 1829
James	28	M	Farmer	Great Britain	United States	Mary & Harriet	3 Jul 1829
John	4	M	None	Great Britain	United States	Mary & Harriet	3 Jul 1829
TANNAHILL, A.	35	M		G. Britain	U. States	Camillus	8 Sep 1828
Agness	3	F		G. Britain	U. States	Camillus	8 Sep 1828
James	5	M		G. Britain	U. States	Camillus	8 Sep 1828
Janet	0 6/12	F		G. Britain	U. States	Camillus	8 Sep 1828
Margt.	7	F		G. Britain	U. States	Camillus	8 Sep 1828
TANNER, Ann	11	F		Ireland	U. States	Howard Douglass	29 Jan 1828
George, Mr.	19	M	Gentleman	Ireland	United States	Dublin Packet	9 Jul 1827
John	38	M	Butcher	Ireland	U. States	Howard Douglass	29 Jan 1828
Mary	27	F		Ireland	U. States	Howard Douglass	29 Jan 1828
Nancey	20	F	Spinster	Ireland	United States	Wilson	4 Oct 1827
Nathaniel	14	M	Mechanic	U. States	U. States	Acasta	21 Jan 1825
Richard, Mrs.	23	F	Lady	United States	U.S.	Acasta	11 May 1827
TANNEY, Thomas	30	M	Farmer	St. Johns, N.B.	United States	Henrietta	17 Aug 1825
TANNY, Patk.	25	M	Farmers and Mechanics	Ireland	America	Constitution	1 Oct 1825
TAOLIN, Thos.	24	M	Farmer	Great Brittan	United States	America	24 Jul 1827
TAP..., James	14	M		Great Britain	U. States	Hector	11 Oct 1824
TAPART, M.	28	M	Merchant	France	United States	Elizabeth	22 May 1822
P.	36	M	Merchant	France	United States	Elizabeth	22 May 1822
S.	3	M	Merchant	France	United States	Elizabeth	22 May 1822
TAPE, Richard	22	M	Jeweller	United States		Spartan	13 Apr 1826
TAPEN, —, Mrs.	40	M	Planter	Barbadoes	Barbadoes	William & Nancy	5 Jun 1823
TAPHEN, M., Mrs.	19	F				Auritz	20 May 1823
TAPIN, Conceptin	38	F				Apollo	11 Jun 1828
TAPLEY, Solomon	30	M	Mechanic	Switzerland	America	Bayard	15 Dec 1828
TAPLY, Hetty	22	F	Farmer	New Brunswick	Canada	Susan Morton	17 Jun 1823
Jonas	3	M	Farmer	New Brunswick	Canada	Susan Morton	17 Jun 1823
Nathl.	28	M	Farmer	New Brunswick	Canada	Susan Morton	17 Jun 1823
TAPP, William	47	M	Farmer	England	England	Venus	15 Apr 1822
TAPPAN, Elizabeth	24	F		Holland	Holland	Lydia	30 Apr 1821
Lucy			Girl	Holland	Holland	Lydia	30 Apr 1821
T. P.	24	M	Merchant	Holland	Holland	Lydia	30 Apr 1821
T. P., Mr.	27	M	Merchant	U. States	U. St.	Auritz	20 May 1823
TAPPEN, —, Mr.	21	M		N. York	United States	Loire	4 Oct 1824
TAPPENSON, Eliz.	18/12	F	Carpenter	England	U. States	Electra	7 Jul 1828
Eliz.	25	F	Carpenter	England	U. States	Electra	7 Jul 1828
Mary	3/12	F	Carpenter	England	U. States	Electra	7 Jul 1828
Wm.	24	M	Carpenter	England	U. States	Electra	7 Jul 1828
TAPPIN, John	11	M	None	England	New York	Brighton	14 Oct 1824
Samuel	8	M	None	England	New York	Brighton	14 Oct 1824
TARANTALIA, A.	50	M	Mariner	Spain	U. States	Sea Flower	16 Jul 1821
TARBAY, Jos. K.	25	M	Merchant	France	U. States	Sancho Panza	2 Jun 1824
TARBERT, Gilbert	7	M	Child	G. Brittan	U. States	Henry	24 Oct 1828
John	7/12	M			U. States	Henry	24 Oct 1828
John	45	M	Child	G. Brittan	U. States	Henry	24 Oct 1828
Levi	6	M	Child	G. Brittan	U. States	Henry	24 Oct 1828
Saml.	17	M	Sho Maker		U. States	Henry	24 Oct 1828
Sarah	31	F	Child	G. Brittan	U. States	Henry	24 Oct 1828
Thomas	3	M			U. States	Henry	24 Oct 1828
TARBET, James	27	M	Labourer	England	United States	Jubilee	1 Oct 1828
TARBRAY, Jas.	36	M	Merct.	England	U.S.	Stephania	15 Aug 1825
TARDIN, A. Auga.	30	M	Mariner	Portugal	U. States	Edward & Frances	9 May 1823
TARDY, Eli...	...			A...	England	Great Britain	7 May 1827
TARGET, —, Mrs.	29	F	Carpenter	England	U. States	Cowper	8 Jan 1827
Wm.	6	M		England	U. States	Cowper	8 Jan 1827
Wm.	28	M	Cabinet Maker	England	U. States	Cowper	8 Jan 1827
TARIBALDY, Angel			Secretary	Italy	Italy	Dewitt Clinton	26 Aug 1825
TARIM, Margret	5/12	F		France	U. States	C. Amelia	30 Jun 1828
P.	9	M		France	U. States	C. Amelia	30 Jun 1828

NAMES OF PASSENGERS	AGE	SEX	OCCUPATIONS	COUNTRY TO WHICH THEY BELONG	COUNTRY THEY INTEND TO INHABIT	SHIPS/DATES OF ARRIVAL	
TARK, John W.	24	M	U.S. Navy	United States	U. States	Frances	6 Feb 1829
TARKENTONE, Jemmy	58	M	Weaver	Ireland	United States	Danube	13 Jul 1827
TARLEY, Paul	45			England	U. States	Corinthian	8 Oct 1828
TARNAY, Joseph	3	M		G. Britain	U. States	Hanford	18 Sep 1828
Margaret	27	F		G. Britain	U. States	Hanford	18 Sep 1828
TARQUAND, Peter	45	M	Commasory, the British Service	England	Canada	Mentor	24 Mar 1823
TARR, David, Jur.	35	M	Mercher	U.S.	U.S.	Charleston Allen	15 Nov 1826
John	35	M	Planter	Antigua	U. States	Spartan	17 Dec 1823
TARRAK, Jos.	32	M	Merchant	G. Britain	U. States	Canada	19 Sep 1828
TARRINGTON, Elisha	28	M	Chair Maker	U. States		Ambuscade	30 Dec 1820
TARROW, John	27	M	Labourer	G. Briton	United States	James Monroe	14 Dec 1820
TARRVET, Augustus	21	M	Student at Law	France	United States	Howard	11 Jun 1824
TARRY, H. J.	27	M	Merchant	America	U. States	Ladies Delight	9 Aug 1823
TARSDAILE, Thomas	36	M	Joiner	Great Britain	United States	Ganges	26 Oct 1826
TARSFIELD, Easter	30	F	None	Great Britain	United States	Ocean	27 Jul 1825
TART, John, Jr.	24	M	Merchant	U. States	U. States	Exploit	3 Jan 1828
TASENA, Antona	14	M	None	U. States	U. States	Howard	21 May 1827
TASK, An	40	F	...stress	England	U.S. States	Splendid	14 Aug 1829
Josiah	7	M	Miner	England	U.S. States	Splendid	14 Aug 1829
TASKER, Saml.	14	F	None	Great Brittain	U. States	Louisa	11 Jun 1824
TASTUM, Thomas	19		Farmer	England	England	Thames	25 Oct 1821
TAT..., Sil...	...	...	...	...	...	Pioneer	21 Jun 1825
TATE, —, Mr.	42	M	Planter	Barbadoes	Barbadoes	William & Nancy	5 Jun 1823
Alexander	32	M	Merchant	United States	United States	Robert Read	10 Jan 1825
Alexr.	33	M	Merchant	Aux Cayes	U. States	Milo	7 Jul 1823
James	20	M	Labourer	Ireland	United States	Henry Kneeland	7 Jun 1828
James	23	M	Saddler	United States	United States	Atlantic	16 Dec 1825
James	24	M	Farmer	Scotland	United States	Indus	5 Sep 1827
Jno.	34	M	Shoemaker	U. States	U. States	Patty & Sally	29 Apr 1822
John	35	M	Shomaker	U. States	U. States	Francis Jarvis	17 Oct 1822
Mary	21	F	Labourer	Ireland	United States	Hope	12 Jun 1828
Mary	22	F	Farmer	Ireland	U. States	Meteor	19 Jul 1828
Meratt, Servant Coulard Man	30	M				Elias Burger	19 Dec 1820
Thomas	58	M	Grocer	New York	New York	General Jackson	31 Oct 1820
Wm.	23	M	Labourer	Ireland	United States	Hope	12 Jun 1828
TATEM, C.	23	F	None	U. States	U. States	Ice Plant	29 May 1826
TATES, Elizabeth	23	F		Great Britain	U. States	United States	8 Sep 1827
George	21	M	Merchant	England	U. States	Florida	16 May 1827
James	23	M	Mariner	Great Britain	U. States	United States	8 Sep 1827
TATHAM, Margaret	18	F		Great Britain	Jersey	Zodiac	14 Jun 1822
TATHUD, Josiah	30	M	Officer of the Navy	U. States	U. States	Mary	19 May 1823
TATON, Joseph	24	...	...	...	...	Pioneer	21 Jun 1825
TATTERSALL, Chas. G.	25	M	Merchant	Great Britain	United States	James Monroe	5 Apr 1820
TAUBMAN, Joshua	30	M	Miner	G. Britain	G. Britain	Brittania	17 Jul 1828
TAUIEWIEZ, —	27	M	Servant	G. Britain	U. States	Robt. Edwards	4 Sep 1828
TAUNSON, James	29	M	Mariner	Nantucket	U. States	Douglass	7 Aug 1827
TAUNTON, Samuel H.	50	M	Merchant	Great Britain	U. States	Columbia	24 Dec 1822
TAUPET, M.	23	F		England	U. States	Talma	23 Sep 1828
TAUTGEN, Maria	16	F		Altona	U. States	Eagle	18 Jul 1822
TAVIAN, C. A.	30	M	Merchant	France	United States	James Monroe	14 Dec 1820
TAWAY, Neil	22	M		Ireland	United States	Sarah G.	20 Jul 1827
TAWNSEND, S.	27	M		New York	New York	Amity	31 May 1822
TAXON, Richd.	45	M	Merchant	U. States	U. States	Rival	25 May 1826
TAY, Lorenzo	26	M	Merchant	Balboa	Havana	Mary	1 Nov 1824
TAYER, Rebecca	25 3/12	F	Lady	Gt. Britain	U. States	Maria	22 May 1822
TAYLER, Abraham	32	M	Farmer	England	America	Comet	26 Jun 1822
Ann	5	F		England	United States	Comet	6 Mar 1823
Danl.	20	M	Labourer	G. Britain	U. States	London	23 Sep 1828
Edwin	1	M		England	United States	Comet	6 Mar 1823
Eliza	7	F	None	Great Britain	United States	William Dawson	18 Jun 1827
James	3	M		England	United States	Comet	6 Mar 1823
James	27	M	Labourer	Ireland	United States	Kleber	23 Jul 1827
James	35	M	Farmer	England	United States	Comet	6 Mar 1823
Jas.	12	M				John Dickinson	14 Sep 1820
John	8	M	None	Great Britain	United States	William Dawson	18 Jun 1827
John	32	M	...b...	...shire	U. States	Panthea	24 Mar 1825

NAMES OF PASSENGERS	AGE	SEX	OCCUPATIONS	COUNTRY TO WHICH THEY BELONG	COUNTRY THEY INTEND TO INHABIT	SHIPS/DATES OF ARRIVAL	
TAYLER (cont'd)							
John	40	M	Weaver	Great Britain	United States	William Dawson	18 Jun 1827
Leonard A.	3	M		England	America	Comet	26 Jun 1822
Mary	4	F		England	United States	Comet	6 Mar 1823
Mary	30	F		England	United States	Comet	6 Mar 1823
Robert	5	M		England	America	Comet	26 Jun 1822
Sarah	2	F		England	America	Comet	26 Jun 1822
Sarah	24	F		England	America	Comet	26 Jun 1822
Sarah	30	F	None	Great Britain	United States	William Dawson	18 Jun 1827
Thomas	33	...	...	...	United States	Criterion	27 Jun 1827
William	36	M	D...s...	G. Britain	U. States	Armadello	22 Jun 1827
Wm.	24	M	Weaver	Great Britain	United States	William Dawson	18 Jun 1827
TAYLOR, —, Mrs.	30	F		England	U. States	Asia	5 Jul 1823
A. K.	26	M	Mercht.	England	U. States	Pacific	20 Aug 1825
Agness	28	F	Spinster	Ireland	N. York	Volant	29 Dec 1820
Alex	1	M	child	Scotland	America	Camillus	12 Sep 1822
Alexander P., (alias Povis)	29	M	Iron Founder	England	United States	Robert Edwards	3 Oct 1829
Alice	21	F	None	England	United States	Trident	31 Mar 1827
Allice	26	F				Acosta	28 Jul 1823
Andrew, Mr.	28	M	Merchant	America	America	Atlantic	11 Oct 1822
Andw.	24	M	Merchant	G. Britain	U. States	New York	11 Mar 1823
Andw. K.	38	M	Merchant	Great Brittain	Great Brittain	James Cropper	23 Mar 1827
Ann	9	F		England	America	James Cropper	10 Feb 1823
Ann	20	F	None	Ireland		Marchioness	13 May 1828
Ann	38	F		England	America	James Cropper	10 Feb 1823
Ann	39		Servant	England	England	Corinthian	8 Oct 1828
Ann	40	F		Great Britain	United States	Samuel Wright	12 Oct 1829
Anne	16	F		England	United States	Lord Wellington	14 Nov 1827
Anne	30	F		Ireland	United States	Romulus	24 Jun 1826
Archibald	20	M	Planter	G. Britain	U. States	Little Cherub	11 Nov 1826
Betty	31	F	None		C...enham	Governor Clinton	3 Jul 1827
Catharine	20		Niece [of John Lirtch]	Great Britain	United States	Camillus	12 Sep 1827
Catharine	24	F		England	U. States	Cincinnatus	24 May 1821
Catherine	17	F		Gt. Britain		Dalhouse Castle	13 May 1828
Charles	9	M		G. Britain	U. States	Robt. Edwards	4 Sep 1828
Charles	16	M	Dyre	England	U.S.	Maria Caroline	12 Jul 1820
Charles	45	M	Farmer	G. Britain	U. States	Robt. Edwards	4 Sep 1828
Charles	47	M	Farmer	Great Brittan	United States	America	24 Jul 1827
Charlotte	28	F	Spinster	Ireland	N. York	Volant	29 Dec 1820
Christina	23	F	Wife	Scotland	United States	Samuel Robertson	9 May 1827
Clementine	28			England	Jersey	Caroline	10 Mar 1828
David	24	M	Labourer	Abernethy, Abernethy [Parish], Perth [County]	New York	Hero	19 May 1828
*to look for Employment							
David	29	M	Weaver	Great Britain	United States	Ganges	26 Oct 1826
E.	1	F		Great Britain	United States	Isaac Hicks	6 Dec 1827
E.	24	F		Great Britain	United States	Isaac Hicks	6 Dec 1827
E.	25	M	Mariner	U. States	U.S.	Exertion	6 Sep 1828
Edith	12 7/12	F		England	U.S. of America	Illinois	16 Jun 1821
Edw.	8	M				Hector	11 Sep 1820
Edward	22	M	...	...	...	Frances Henrietta	30 Jun 1827
Edward	35	M	Weaver	United States	United States	George Clinton	13 Apr 1826
Elisa	8	F		England	United States	Cosmo	26 Aug 1829
Elisa	22 2/12	F	Mantua Maker	Ireland	New York	Louisa	20 Jul 1826
Eliza	3	F		G. Britain	U. States	St. George	7 Jun 1828
Eliza	5	F		U. States	Great Britain	Thompson	26 Apr 1828
Eliza	14	F		G. Britain	U. States	Robt. Edwards	4 Sep 1828
Eliza	21		None	Great Britain	United States	Roman	10 Sep 1827
Eliza, Miss	7			England	England	Corinthian	8 Oct 1828
Elizabeth	9	F		England	America	James Cropper	10 Feb 1823
Elizabeth	11	F	None	England	Pittsburgh	Orozimbo	8 Jun 1822
Elizabeth	14 4/12	F		England	U.S. of America	Illinois	16 Jun 1821

NAMES OF PASSENGERS	AGE	SEX	OCCUPATIONS	COUNTRY TO WHICH THEY BELONG	COUNTRY THEY INTEND TO INHABIT	SHIPS/DATES OF ARRIVAL	
TAYLOR (cont'd)							
Elizabeth	21	F	Farmer, Labourer or Spinster	Ireland	U. States	Meteor	4 Oct 1827
Elizabeth Ann	21			Stepney, Eng./ Stepney	New York	Venus	12 Apr 1821
Emelia	23		None	Great Britain	United States	Roman	10 Sep 1827
Emna	11	F		G. Britain	U. States	Robt. Edwards	4 Sep 1828
Epsalia	4	F	None	England	Pittsburgh	Orozimbo	8 Jun 1822
Esther	33	F		England	United States	Cosmo	26 Aug 1829
F.	22	M	Wheelwright	N. York	U. States	Chase	29 Apr 1825
Felix	18	M	Merchant	U.S.	U.S.	Stephania	13 Sep 1821
Francis	28	M	Merchant	American	Richmond, Va.	Hesperus	13 Oct 1825
Fredk.	28	M	Tailor	England	America	Josephine	8 Jan 1827
G.	30	F		G. Britain	U. States	St. George	7 Jun 1828
Geo.	60	M	Hatter	Great Britain	United States	Samuel Wright	12 Oct 1829
Geo., Jr.	9	M		Great Britain	United States	Samuel Wright	12 Oct 1829
Geo. R.	42		Mechanic	England	England	Hudson	14 Jun 1827
George	7 3/12	M		England	U.S. of America	Illinois	16 Jun 1821
George	22	M	Moulder	England	Pittsburg	Curler	7 Jul 1827
George	23	M	Mariner	U. States	U. States	Mary Livingston	14 May 1827
George	26	M	Labourer	Airdrie, Airdrie [Parish], Lanark [County]	New York	Hero	19 May 1828
*to look for employment							
George	27	M	Labourer	Great Brittian		Merchant	22 Apr 1822
George	30	M	Miner	England	England	Ranger	15 Jan 1827
George	31	M	Labourer	Ireland	America	Plutarch	18 Jul 1826
George	32	M	Weaver	England	America U. States	La Grange	27 Sep 1826
George	33	M	Farmer	England	U. States	Rover	28 Oct 1825
George	50	M	Farmer	Great Britain	United States	Birmingham	15 Jun 1827
Go	18	M		G. Britain	U. States	Robt. Edwards	4 Sep 1828
Grace P., (alias Povis)	2	F	daughter	England	United States	Robert Edwards	3 Oct 1829
Hannah	23	F		England	United States	Marion	25 Nov 1825
Hannah	43	F		England	United States	Lord Wellington	14 Nov 1827
Harriet	4	F		Gt. Britain		Dalhouse Castle	13 May 1828
Helen	6	F		England	America	James Cropper	10 Feb 1823
Henry	6	M				Hector	11 Sep 1820
Henry	12	M		Gt. Britain		Dalhouse Castle	13 May 1828
Henry	13	M	Servant	Great Britain	United States	Cortes	19 Nov 1821
Henry	19	M	Mechanic	England	United States	Concordia	25 Aug 1827
Henry	23	M		Lancashire	U. States	Atlantic	13 Jul 1824
Henry	31	F	Lady	United	United States	Sarah	31 Oct 1829
Heny	7	M		G. Britain	U. States	Robt. Edwards	4 Sep 1828
Hiram	19	M	Supercargo	U. States	U. States	Abeona	16 Mar 1820
Hy.	44	M	Moulder	England	U. States	Columbia	20 Jul 1825
Isaac	2	M		England	U. States	Asia	5 Jul 1823
Isaiah	6	M	Youth	Ireland	United States	Romulus	24 Jun 1826
J.	3	M	Farmer	Great Britain	United States	Isaac Hicks	6 Dec 1827
J.	3	F		Great Britain	United States	Isaac Hicks	6 Dec 1827
J. P.	25	M	Merchant	Virginia	U. States	William Thompson	6 Sep 1822
Jacob	36	M	Farmer	Great Brittan	U.S.	Emulous	29 Jun 1827
James	10/12	M	None		C...enham	Governor Clinton	3 Jul 1827
James	15	M	Farmer	England	Pittsburgh	Orozimbo	8 Jun 1822
James	21	M	Laborer	Scotland	United States	Tom	2 Jul 1827
James	23	M	Farmer	Scotland	United States	Indus	5 Sep 1827
James	24	M	Farmer	England	Alexandria, U.S.	Roman	17 Oct 1826
James	25	M		G. Britain	U. States	Camillus	8 Sep 1828
James	28	M		Ireland	United States	Thompson	12 Sep 1827
James	31	M	Merchant	England	England	Gulnard	24 Mar 1825
James	35	M	Labourer	Great Britain	U. States	Princess Charlotte	6 Sep 1828
James	35	M	Shoe Maker	Ireland	New Jersey	Atlantic	6 Oct 1828
James	40	M	Shoemaker	Ireland	N. York	Volant	29 Dec 1820
James	50	M	Merchant	England	London	William Byrnes	14 Apr 1824
James	60	M	Music	England	U.S.A.	Hudson	21 Aug 1829
James B.	14	M				Hector	11 Sep 1820
James P., (alias Povis)	16	M		England	United States	Robert Edwards	3 Oct 1829

1233

NAMES OF PASSENGERS	AGE	SEX	OCCUPATIONS	COUNTRY TO WHICH THEY BELONG	COUNTRY THEY INTEND TO INHABIT	SHIPS/DATES OF ARRIVAL	
TAYLOR (cont'd)							
Jane	1	F		England	United States	Lord Wellington	14 Nov 1827
Jane	2	F		Ireland	United States	Thompson	12 Sep 1827
Jane	4	F		England	U. States	Asia	5 Jul 1823
Jane	12	F				Hector	11 Sep 1820
Jane	19	F	going to her husband	Scotland	America	Camillus	12 Sep 1822
Jane	22	F		Ireland	United States	Alex. Mansfield	17 May 1823
Jane	22	M		Bermuda	U. States	Agnes	1 Jul 1825
Jane	25	F		U. States	U. States	Arthenian	28 Apr 1827
Jane	30	F		Ireland	United States	Curler	3 Mar 1828
Jane	30		Farmer	England	Jersey	Caroline	10 Mar 1828
Jane	44	F		England	U. States	Aolus	1 Aug 1823
Jane	52	F		Ireland	United States	Marion	25 Nov 1825
Jas.	28	M	Spinner	England	U. States	Thomas Ritchie	2 Jul 1827
Jas.	28		Joiner	Great Britain	United States	Roman	10 Sep 1827
Jeamette	30	F		U. States	Great Britain	Thompson	26 Apr 1828
Jesse	28	M	Farmer	U. States	U. States	Ariadne	15 Apr 1822
Jno.	22	M	Cotton Spinner	England	United States	Euphrates	18 Aug 1827
Jno. R.	21	M	Seaman	New York	U. States	Martha	28 Jan 1826
Job	5	M	Farmer	Great Britain	United States	Birmingham	15 Jun 1827
John	5	M		England	United States	Lord Wellington	14 Nov 1827
John	5	M		Gt. Britain		Dalhouse Castle	13 May 1828
John	7			England	Jersey	Caroline	10 Mar 1828
John	9	M	Youth	Ireland	United States	Romulus	24 Jun 1826
John	11 2/12	M		England	U.S. of America	Illinois	16 Jun 1821
John	15	M	Clerk	England	U. States	York	4 Apr 1826
John	18	M	Farmer	Steers	Yorkshire	Howard Douglass	11 May 1827
John	20	M	Labourer	Trobotton	U.S. America	Camillus	10 Sep 1821
John	20		Farmer	Scotland	United States	Camillus	3 May 1828
John	21	M		Ireland	U. States	Howard	25 Jul 1823
John	21	M	Gentleman	Ireland	United States	Dublin Packet	24 Sep 1823
John	21	M	Labourer	G.B.	America	Pacific	13 Jan 1827
John	22	M	Labourer	Scotland	United States	Samuel Robertson	9 May 1827
John	22	M	Stone Cutter	Liverpool	United States	Nile	17 May 1827
John	22	M		England	United States	St. George	25 Aug 1829
John	23	M	Labourer	Greenock, Mid [Parish], Renfrew [County]	New York	Hero	19 May 1828
*to look for Employment							
John	24	M	Merchant	England	Canada	Corinthian	20 Apr 1825
John	25	M	Watchman	England	United States	Marion	25 Nov 1825
John	26	M	Servant	Ireland	U. States	Henrietta	7 Jul 1825
John	27	M	Painter	England	United States	Cambria	8 Oct 1828
John	30	M	Shop Keeper	England	United States	Jubilee	4 Mar 1829
John	31	M	...	U. States	U. States	Queen Mab	26 Jul 1824
John	33	M	Farmer	Scotland	U. States	Phocion	8 May 1824
John	34	M	Merchant	England	America	Manhattan	23 May 1822
John	36	M	Shoemaker	Ireland	N. York	Volant	29 Dec 1820
John	36	M	Iron Founder	England	New York	Corinthian	5 May 1827
John	40	M	Carpenter	Holland	America	Friends	28 Sep 1822
John	40	M	Farmer	England	America	James Cropper	10 Feb 1823
John	40	M	Merchant	Great Britain	U.S. of America	Canada	1 Oct 1827
John	40 7/12	M	Farmer	England	U.S. of America	Illinois	16 Jun 1821
John	44	M	Weaver	Ireland	United States	Dalhouse Castle	8 May 1827
John	44	M	Weaver	Ireland	United States	Atlantic	21 Jul 1827
John	50	M	Farmer	C..., ..., England	U. States	New Orleans	24 Aug 1827
John, Capt.	40		Mariner	United States	United States	John Dickinson	5 Apr 1821
John, Mr.	40	M		England	England	Corinthian	8 Oct 1828
John F.	18	M	Farmer	Canada	Canada	Ann	29 Jan 1820
John F., Miss	10			England	England	Corinthian	8 Oct 1828
Jos.	51	M	Farmer	England	U. States	James Cropper	10 Jun 1823
Joseia	36	M	Farmer	Ireland	United States	Curler	3 Mar 1828
Joseph	15	M		Gt. Britain		Dalhouse Castle	13 May 1828
Joseph	24	M	Clothier	England	United States	Trident	31 Mar 1827
Joseph	25	M	Joiner			Acosta	28 Jul 1823
Joseph	54	M	Weaver	England	U. States	Panthea	8 Apr 1826

NAMES OF PASSENGERS	AGE	SEX	OCCUPATIONS	COUNTRY TO WHICH THEY BELONG	COUNTRY THEY INTEND TO INHABIT	SHIPS/DATES OF ARRIVAL	
TAYLOR (cont'd)							
Joseph	56	M	Farmer	England	Pittsburgh	Orozimbo	8 Jun 1822
L.	2	F		G. Britain	U. States	Robt. Edwards	4 Sep 1828
Louisa	6	F	Lady	United	United States	Sarah	31 Oct 1829
Lucey	10	F		England	United States	Cosmo	26 Aug 1829
Luke	7	M		England	United States	Cosmo	26 Aug 1829
M.	24	F	Spinstress	Great Britain	United States	Isaac Hicks	6 Dec 1827
Mahey	16 10/12	F		England	U.S. of America	Illinois	16 Jun 1821
Margaret	23	F		Gt. Britain		Dalhouse Castle	13 May 1828
Margaret	24	F		Scotland	United States	Camillus	9 May 1827
Margaret	30	F	Servant	Ireland	United States	Carolina Ann	14 May 1827
Margret	... 1/12	F		England	U.S. of America	Illinois	16 Jun 1821
Margret	43 2/12	F		England	U.S. of America	Illinois	16 Jun 1821
Maria	1	F		England	United States	Cosmo	26 Aug 1829
Maria, Miss	27			Stepney, Eng./ Stepney	New York	Venus	12 Apr 1821
Martha	34	F		U. States	Great Britain	Thompson	26 Apr 1828
Mary	1	F		Ireland	United States	Thompson	12 Sep 1827
Mary	4	F		England	United States	Cosmo	26 Aug 1829
Mary	6	F		England	U. States	Asia	5 Jul 1823
Mary	7	F		England	United States	Lord Wellington	14 Nov 1827
Mary	16	F		G. Britain	U. States	Robt. Edwards	4 Sep 1828
Mary	19	F		Ireland	United States	Jno. Dickinson	21 Sep 1821
Mary	26	F	Servant to Mr. Butter	Great Britain	United States	Robert Fulton	27 Jun 1822
Mary	31	F		Great Britain	United States	Washington	3 Sep 1827
Mary	32	F	Servant	Ireland	United States	Carolina Ann	14 May 1827
Mary	34	F		U. States	U.S.	Mentor	8 Sep 1821
Mary	40	F		Manchester		Hector	11 Sep 1820
Mary	40	F	None	Great Brittan	United States	America	24 Jul 1827
Mary	40	F		Gt. Britain		Dalhouse Castle	13 May 1828
Mary	40	F	Wife	Ireland	New Jersey	Atlantic	6 Oct 1828
Mary	45	F		Scotland	U. States	Silas Richards	29 Oct 1828
Mary	46			Bermuda		Ocean	28 Jul 1820
Mary, (alias Povis)	30	F	Wife	England	United States	Robert Edwards	3 Oct 1829
Mary, Mrs.	28 5/12	F		United States	United States	Tontine	6 Dec 1827
Mary Ann	6	F		Gt. Britain		Dalhouse Castle	13 May 1828
Mary Ann	8	F	None	England	Pittsburgh	Orozimbo	8 Jun 1822
Mary P., (alias Povis)	7/12	F	daughter	England	United States	Robert Edwards	3 Oct 1829
May	8	F		England	America	James Cropper	10 Feb 1823
May	39	F		G. Britain	U. States	Robt. Edwards	4 Sep 1828
Michael	2			England	Jersey	Caroline	10 Mar 1828
Peter	9	M	School boy	Ireland	United States	Carolina Ann	14 May 1827
Peter	23	M	Farmer	Great Britain	United States	Natchez	17 Aug 1822
Peter	25	M	C. Spinner	G.B.	N. York	Eliza Grant	29 Aug 1829
Peter A.	30	M	Merchant	England	U. States	Cincinnatus	24 May 1821
Phobe	19	F	Music	England	U.S.A.	Hudson	21 Aug 1829
R. B.	32	M	Joiner	United States	United States	John Wells	18 Sep 1826
Rachael	41	F.	None	England	Pittsburgh	Orozimbo	8 Jun 1822
Rachel	25	F	Spinster	Dungiranderry	...	Gleaner	24 May 1823
Rebecca	24	F		Ireland	United States	Thompson	12 Sep 1827
Richard	28	M	Merchant	Virginia	Virginia	Brighton	21 Jan 1826
Richard, Mr.	43	M	Merchant	England	England	Hector	20 Sep 1821
Rob.	28	M	Gardner	England	England	Gulnard	24 Mar 1825
Rob.	30		Joiner	Manchester, England	Great Britain	Franklin	22 Jun 1827
Robert	3	M		Gt. Britain		Dalhouse Castle	13 May 1828
Robert	15	M		Gt. Britain		Dalhouse Castle	13 May 1828
Robert	43	M	Weaver	England	United States	Lord Wellington	14 Nov 1827
Robert	50	M	Farmer	England	United States	Marion	25 Nov 1825
Robt.	24	M	Shoe Maker	Gt. Britain	U. States	Diana	28 Apr 1828
Robt.	43	M	Barber			Manhattan	25 Dec 1820
Robt., Mrs.	35	M		England	England	Corinthian	8 Oct 1828
Saml.	10	M		G. Britain	U. States	George Clinton	10 Sep 1828
Saml.	24	M	Mechanic	Scotland	United States	Concordia	25 Aug 1827
Saml.	25	M		Ireland	United States	Thompson	12 Sep 1827
Saml.	26	M	Shoe Maker	Europe	United States	Aspasia	5 Sep 1827
Samuel	21	M	Merchant	Manchester	U. States	Columbia	7 Jul 1824

NAMES OF PASSENGERS	AGE	SEX	OCCUPATIONS	COUNTRY TO WHICH THEY BELONG	COUNTRY THEY INTEND TO INHABIT	SHIPS/DATES OF ARRIVAL	
TAYLOR (cont'd)							
Samuel	25	M	Merchant	England	England	William Thompson	19 Aug 1829
Samuel, Mr.	24	M	Musician	England	U. States	Emily	25 Aug 1827
Sands	5	F		G. Britain	U. States	Robt. Edwards	4 Sep 1828
Sarah	7	F	None	England	Pittsburgh	Orozimbo	8 Jun 1822
Sarah	9	F		England	United States	Lord Wellington	14 Nov 1827
Sarah	13	F		G. Britain	U. States	Robt. Edwards	4 Sep 1828
Sarah	50	F	Wife	C..., ..., England	U. States	New Orleans	24 Aug 1827
Sybel	24	M	None	...	...	Frances Henrietta	30 Jun 1827
T.	19		Farmer	Ireland	United States	Courier	16 May 1825
T. M.	20	M	Merchant	U. States	U. States	Endymion	22 May 1822
Tere	6	M		England	United States	Cosmo	26 Aug 1829
Thomas	10 3/12	M		England	U.S. of America	Illinois	16 Jun 1821
Thomas	11	M		England	U. States	Aolus	1 Aug 1823
Thomas	14	M	Weaver	England	United States	Lord Wellington	14 Nov 1827
Thomas	20	M	...	Phila.	Philada.	Pacification	28 Jul 1824
Thomas	25	M	None	South Carolina	United States	Amity	11 May 1821
Thomas	26	M	Labourer	Abernethy, Abernethy [Parish], Perth [County]	New York	Hero	19 May 1828
*to look for Employment							
Thomas	28	M	Gardner	England	U.S. America	New Hampshire	28 Sep 1826
Thomas	29	M	Labourer	Ireland	America	Plutarch	18 Jul 1826
Thomas	30	M		Scotland	United States	Camillus	9 May 1827
Thomas	60	M	Labourer	Abernethy, Abernethy [Parish], Perth [County]	New York	Hero	19 May 1828
*to look for Employment							
Thos.	20	M		G. Britain	U. States	Robt. Edwards	4 Sep 1828
Thos.	42	M	Mechanic	U. States	U. States	New York	13 Mar 1824
Thos.	50	M	Farmer	England	U. States	Aolus	1 Aug 1823
Thos., Senr.	25	M	Hudson Bay Co.	Gt. Brittian	North Brittian		6 Apr 1826
W.		M	Mainer	N. York	U. States	Herald	6 Feb 1824
Walker	28	M		Scotland	U.S.	Curler	19 Jul 1828
Weiley	2	M	Farmer, Labourer or Spinster	Ireland	U. States	Meteor	4 Oct 1827
William	1	M		Gt. Britain		Dalhouse Castle	13 May 1828
William	3	M		England	United States	Cosmo	26 Aug 1829
William	10	M	Youth	Ireland	United States	Romulus	24 Jun 1826
William	11	M		Gt. Britain		Dalhouse Castle	13 May 1828
William	15 4/12	M	Farmer	Ireland	Redstone	Triton	12 Jul 1823
William	18	M	Farmer	Scotland	America	Friends	24 Sep 1821
William	24	M	Professor of Music	England	New York	Hercules	11 Feb 1822
William	36	M	Bleacher	G.B.	New York	Eliza Grant	29 Aug 1829
William	52	M	Tinker	Gt. Britain	U.S. of America	Friends	25 Sep 1823
Wm.	1	M		G. Britain	U. States	St. George	7 Jun 1828
Wm.	15	M		Great Brittain	U.S.	Trafalgar	22 Jun 1821
Wm.	21	M	Joiner	Scotland	United States	Tom	2 Jul 1827
Wm.	26	M	Farmer	Great Britain	United States	Ann Maria	12 Jul 1821
Wm.	30	M	Mariner	U. States	U. States	New Packet	27 Apr 1822
Wm.	39	M	Brick Layer	Great Britain	United States	Washington	3 Sep 1827
Wm.	39	M	Weaver	U. States	Great Britain	Thompson	26 Apr 1828
Wm.	55	M	Famer	England	U. States	Asia	5 Jul 1823
TAYLOUR, Wm.	26	M		Great Brittain	U. States	Atticus	25 Apr 1822
TAYNER, Samuel	25	M	Farmer	Switzerland	United States	Olympia	12 Aug 1828
TAZ, Benjamin	24	M	Seaman	U. States	U. States	William	11 Dec 1827
TCHEITLER, John	28	M	Baker	Germany	U. States	Sully	24 Oct 1828
TEADALE, Thomas	24	M	...	G. Britain	U. States	New England	28 Sep 1824
TEADALL, Joseph	22	M	Merchant	Ireland	Philadelphia	Virginia	7 May 1824
TEAL, Christopher	26	M	Sugar Refiner	Bremen	U. States	Acasta	21 Oct 1825
TEALE, David	40	M	Merchant	Gt. Brittain	United States	Cortes	11 Aug 1823
T. F.	24	M		France	America	Saluda	16 Oct 1824
TEANGUIRIEN, Abm.	28	M	Carpenter	Switzerland	United States	Stephania	6 Dec 1827
TEAR, Cathe.	4	F	None	Isle of Man		Ocean	13 Jul 1827
Cathr.	37	F	None	Isle of Man		Ocean	13 Jul 1827

NAMES OF PASSENGERS	AGE	SEX	OCCUPATIONS	COUNTRY TO WHICH THEY BELONG	COUNTRY THEY INTEND TO INHABIT	SHIPS/DATES OF ARRIVAL	
TEAR (cont'd)							
Esther	6	F	None	Isle of Man		Ocean	13 Jul 1827
Jas.	1	M	Joiner	Isle of Man		Ocean	13 Jul 1827
John	10	M	Joiner	Isle of Man		Ocean	13 Jul 1827
John	19		Joiner	Great Britain	United States	Thomas Dickason	29 Aug 1828
John	37	M	Joiner	Isle of Man		Ocean	13 Jul 1827
Lace	2	M	Joiner	Isle of Man		Ocean	13 Jul 1827
Wm.	29	M	Taylor	Isle of Man		Ocean	13 Jul 1827
TEARE, Ann	33	F		Ireland	America	Plutarch	18 Jul 1826
Mary	4	F		Ireland	America	Plutarch	18 Jul 1826
Patrick	36	M	Labourer	Ireland	America	Plutarch	18 Jul 1826
TEARNEY, Barney	20	M	Labourer	Ireland	Ireland	Sarah G.	28 Nov 1827
TEARS, Thos.	26	M	Shoemaker	Isle of Man		Ocean	13 Jul 1827
TEAS, David	6	M	Child	Ireland	United States	St. Michaels	27 Nov 1824
Martha	28	F	Wife	Ireland	United States	St. Michaels	27 Nov 1824
William	30	M	Cooper	Ireland	United States	St. Michaels	27 Nov 1824
TEASE, Wm.	33	M	Farmer	Ireland	U. States	William & John	10 Jul 1824
TEATE, Chas.	34	M	Labourer	Longford	Longford	Howard Douglass	11 May 1827
James	19	M	Lab.	Longford	Longford	Howard Douglass	11 May 1827
Mary	21	M	None	Longford	Longford	Howard Douglass	11 May 1827
TEATES, Willm.	35		Shoe Maker	Manchester, England	Great Britain	Franklin	22 Jun 1827
TEBBALD, Margaret	55	F		Scotland	United States	Acasta	15 Jul 1822
TEBING, D. L. W.	48	F		Germany	U. States	Falcon	11 Jun 1827
TECHER, Cescile	2	F				Henri IV	17 May 1828
Francoise	22	F				Henri IV	17 May 1828
Piere	28	M	Carpenter			Henri IV	17 May 1828
TEDFORD, Robert	20	M	Merchant	Ireland	America	Carolina Ann	7 Aug 1826
TEENY, John	36		Wheelwright	Lastrim	N. York	Peru	30 May 1828
TEER, Ann	32	F		Isle of Man	Ohio	Curler	7 Jul 1827
Jane	6	F		Isle of Man	Ohio	Curler	7 Jul 1827
John	27			Great Britan	United States	Newry	11 Jul 1827
Juddy *died	1	F		Isle of Man		Curler	7 Jul 1827
M.	30	M	Shipmaster	U. States	U. States	Gertrude	13 Nov 1826
Mary	4	F		Isle of Man	Ohio	Curler	7 Jul 1827
Thomas	8	M		Isle of Man	Ohio	Curler	7 Jul 1827
Thomas	34	M	Cooper	Isle of Man	Ohio	Curler	7 Jul 1827
Will	30			Great Britan	United States	Newry	11 Jul 1827
TEGAN, Michael	24	M	Labourer	Great Brittan	United States	America	24 Jul 1827
TEGART, Charles	6	M		Ireland	U.States	Nancy	31 May 1823
Mery	26	F		Ireland	U.States	Nancy	31 May 1823
Peter	24	M	Labourer	Ireland	U.States	Nancy	31 May 1823
William	4	M		Ireland	U.States	Nancy	31 May 1823
TEISSURE, —, Madam	58	F		France	United States	Henry	9 Jun 1826
TELBY, John	28	M	Surgeon	Gt. Britain	U. States	Maria	22 May 1822
TELE, T.	28	M	Merchant	U. States	U. States	Ranger	2 Jul 1827
TELERS, A. G. L.	23	M	Merchant	U. States	U. States	New Packet	20 Sep 1826
TELL, A. W.	30		Mariner	France	United States	General Marion	18 Jul 1829
Mary	25	F		G. Brittain	U. States	Frances Henrietta	19 Feb 1823
Mytella	1	F		G. Brittain	U. States	Frances Henrietta	19 Feb 1823
Nixon	23	M	Painter	France	America	Saluda	16 Oct 1824
Wm.	46	M	Schoolmaster	G. Brittain	U. States	Frances Henrietta	19 Feb 1823
TELLY, Hugh	12	M	Labourer	Ireland	United States	Fabius	31 Jul 1829
TELTER, Catharan	2	F	Weaver	France	U. States	Edward Bonaffe	23 Jul 1828
Catharan	18	F	Manumaker	France	U. States	Edward Bonaffe	23 Jul 1828
Hannah	7	F	Weaver	France	U. States	Edward Bonaffe	23 Jul 1828
Jacob	4	M	Weaver	France	U. States	Edward Bonaffe	23 Jul 1828
Margaret	11	F	Weaver	France	U. States	Edward Bonaffe	23 Jul 1828
Margaret	43	F	Weaver	France	U. States	Edward Bonaffe	23 Jul 1828
Philip	46	M	Weaver	France	U. States	Edward Bonaffe	23 Jul 1828
TEMATRICE, John	36 6/12	M	hairdresser	United States	Philadelphia	Cadmus	19 Aug 1823

NAMES OF PASSENGERS	AGE	SEX	OCCUPATIONS	COUNTRY TO WHICH THEY BELONG	COUNTRY THEY INTEND TO INHABIT	SHIPS/DATES OF ARRIVAL	
TEMMAY, Patrick	26	M	Cabinet Maker	Ireland	U. States	Othello	11 Jul 1825
TEMMINS, Henry	24	M	Merchant	Gt. Britain	Great Britain	Martha	4 Oct 1822
TEMPLE, Charlotte, Miss	26	F	Servant	Pensylvania	Pensylvania	Florida	1 Jun 1827
James	32	M	Farmer	Great Britian	United States	Robert Quayle	29 Jul 1822
TEMPLEMAN, Caroline	17	F	Lady	England	U. States	Radius	16 Mar 1822
Jas.	40	M	Artist	G. Britain	New York	Radius	7 Jul 1821
Mary	38	F		G. Britain	New York	Radius	7 Jul 1821
Thomas	14	M	None	England	U. States	Radius	16 Mar 1822
William	7	M		G. Britain	New York	Radius	7 Jul 1821
TEMPLETON, James	35	M	Merchant	Scotland	U. States	Combine	11 Apr 1823
Jas.	24		Merchant	Scotland	Great Britain	Brown	11 Jun 1827
TEMPSON, Thos.	15	M	None	Great Britain	U.S. America	Mentor	22 Jul 1823
TENANT, John	50	M	Confectioner	Nova Scotia	United States	Sarah Ann	18 Nov 1826
TENEFORT, F.	42	M	Merchant	Mayagues	U. States	Director	14 Apr 1828
TENET, George	35	M	Merchant	France		Traveller	2 Jun 1822
TENG, John	37	M	Weaver	England	New York	Corinthian	5 May 1827
TENGIR, B.	22	M				Hanford	17 Jul 1828
TENN, Henry	26	M		Great Brittian	United States	Carolina Augusta	2 Dec 1828
TENNANT, Anne	45	F		England	United States	Lord Wellington	14 Nov 1827
Hannah	12	F		England	United States	Lord Wellington	14 Nov 1827
J. C.	23	M	Merchant	England	Great Britain	James Barron	26 Jun 1823
John	45	M	Weaver	England	United States	Lord Wellington	14 Nov 1827
S. C.	25	M	Mercht.	Havana	England	Evelina	31 May 1825
William	22	M	Farmer	Scotland	United States	Friends	13 Mar 1824
TENNELY, Jas.	21	M	Labourer	Great Britain	United States	Atlantic	28 May 1827
TENNENT, Catharine	12	F		Irereland	America	Carolina Ann	20 Jun 1825
Catharine	35	F		Irereland	America	Carolina Ann	20 Jun 1825
Christopher	35	M		Irereland	America	Carolina Ann	20 Jun 1825
Eliza	6	F		Irereland	America	Carolina Ann	20 Jun 1825
Isabella	14	F		Irereland	America	Carolina Ann	20 Jun 1825
Jane	4	F		Irereland	America	Carolina Ann	20 Jun 1825
John	10	M		Irereland	America	Carolina Ann	20 Jun 1825
Joseph	8	M		Irereland	America	Carolina Ann	20 Jun 1825
TENNEY, Susan	44	F		U.S.	U.S.	Edward Quesnel	31 Jul 1827
Timothy	23	M	Farmer	Ireland	United States	Aurelia	7 Jun 1826
TEN RYCK,							
Julia Ann	22 3/12	F	None	New York	New York	Monroe	18 May 1827
TENY, Richard	26	M	Labourer	Ireland	United States	Potomac	28 Sep 1827
TEPKA, Jacob D.	44	M	Mariner	U.S. America	U.S. America	Cortes	19 May 1826
TEPPIER, Rooney	30	M	Miner	England	England	Eliza	31 Jul 1826
TERANT, Magoret	17	F	Servant	France	U. States	Sully	25 Jun 1828
TERBBIN, Rose	21	F	Spinster	Ireland	United States	Dublin Packet	29 Jun 1825
TERELINE, Eliza	19	F		G. Britain	U. States	Dalhouse Castle	12 Sep 1828
Mary	20	F		G. Britain	U. States	Dalhouse Castle	12 Sep 1828
TERKELSON, Maria	32	F	Servant	Hamburg	United States	Maria Elizabeth	6 Jan 1823
TERLAND, F.	11	M		France	United States	Le Voltaire	19 Jul 1828
Francoise	50	F		France	United States	Le Voltaire	19 Jul 1828
Jean	40	M	Artichitect	France	United States	Le Voltaire	19 Jul 1828
Louis	7	M		France	United States	Le Voltaire	19 Jul 1828
TERNAN, Chr.	24	M	Farmer	Ireland	United States	Curler	3 Mar 1828
Mary	20	F		Ireland	United States	Curler	3 Mar 1828
TERNBRIDGE, Caleb	15		Painter	England	U.S. America	Constitution	18 Jun 1827
TERNEAUX, Henry	23	M	Gentleman	France	America	Don Quixotte	2 Jun 1828
TERNOG, Martin	21	M	Merchant	G. Britain	U. States	Canada	19 Sep 1828
TEROHY, Margaret	18	F	Farmer	Ireland	U. States	Sabina	29 Apr 1825
TERPERTE, F.	40	M	Merchant	Porto Rico	Spain	New Packet	16 Apr 1822
P.	13	M	Merchant	Porto Rico	Spain	New Packet	16 Apr 1822
TERRELEY, John	12	M	Labourer	Ireland	New York	Bowditch	27 Apr 1826
TERRI...TON, Chs.	46	M	Farmer	England	United States	Trident	30 Sep 1826
TERRIER, Wm.	21	M	Mechanic	England	U. States	Birmingham	23 Feb 1829
TERRIERE, Catherine	16	F	None	Great Britain	U. States	Birmingham	11 Oct 1828
Charles	9	M	None	Great Britain	U. States	Birmingham	11 Oct 1828
Edward	11	M	None	Great Britain	U. States	Birmingham	11 Oct 1828
Penelope	19	F	None	Great Britain	U. States	Birmingham	11 Oct 1828
Penelope	50	F	None	Great Britain	U. States	Birmingham	11 Oct 1828
Susan	22	F	None	Great Britain	U. States	Birmingham	11 Oct 1828
Wm.	45	M	Merchant	Great Britain	U. States	Birmingham	11 Oct 1828
TERRIFORT, Frans.	40	M	Merchant	France	Porto Rico	Francis Jarvis	9 May 1825
TERRILL, Ephraim	28	M	Merchant	U.S. Amer.	U.S.A.	Robert Y. Hayne	21 Aug 1828

NAMES OF PASSENGERS	AGE	SEX	OCCUPATIONS	COUNTRY TO WHICH THEY BELONG	COUNTRY THEY INTEND TO INHABIT	SHIPS/DATES OF ARRIVAL	
TERRY, Charles	24	M	Saddlier	Ireland	United States	Ann Maria	1 Apr 1826
John	28	M	Watch Maker	England	Canada	Brighton	14 Oct 1824
Mary Ann	19	F		England	U.S.	York	1 Dec 1827
Michael	23	M	Labourer	Ireland	United States	Concordia	25 Aug 1827
Mills	27	M	Farmer	Ireland	United States	Clothier	22 Nov 1827
TERSAS, Sinanter	22	M	Servant	Mexico	America	Galatea	20 Jul 1829
TERSEL, Philip							
[crossed out]	50	M	Merchant	Jersey	U. States	Otter	30 Oct 1826
TERTY, Ann	25	F	Servant	Great Britain	Canada	Florida	2 Oct 1828
TESELUBE, Elizabeth	28	F	None	Edinburgh	U. States	Milton	21 May 1827
George	9	M	None	Edinburgh	U. States	Milton	21 May 1827
Isabella	16	F	None	Edinburgh	U. States	Milton	21 May 1827
James	13	M	None	Edinburgh	U. States	Milton	21 May 1827
Jane	20	F	Glass Maker	Edinburgh	U. States	Milton	21 May 1827
John	3	M	None	Edinburgh	U. States	Milton	21 May 1827
John	18	M	Turner	Edinburgh	U. States	Milton	21 May 1827
Robt.	7	M	None	Edinburgh	U. States	Milton	21 May 1827
Ruton	11	M	None	Edinburgh	U. States	Milton	21 May 1827
TESNER, James	19	M	Merchant	Ireland	United States	Curler	3 Mar 1828
TESSARD, Joseph	25	M	Clerk	France	U. States	Hewes	30 Oct 1829
TESSEN, Michiel	40 5/12	M	Weaver	America	America	France	28 Mar 1829
TESSIER, —, Madam	53	F		U. States	U. States	Cadmus	28 May 1821
E., Mrs.	23	F		U. States	U. States	Cadmus	28 May 1821
TESTE, Joseph	22	M	Gilder	Italy	United States	Acasta	15 Jul 1822
TESTER, Agostora	25	M	Servant	Italy	United States	Manchester	15 Aug 1826
TETLOW, Ann	28	F	None	England	United States	Trident	18 Jul 1827
Emmy	10	F	None	England	United States	Trident	18 Jul 1827
Francis	13	M	Printer	England	United States	Trident	18 Jul 1827
Hannah	6	F	None	England	United States	Trident	18 Jul 1827
James	4	M	None	England	United States	Trident	18 Jul 1827
James	12	M	Printer	England	United States	Trident	18 Jul 1827
Martha	32	F	None	England	United States	Trident	18 Jul 1827
TETTAN, Benjamin, Consul's Man			Seaman			Athenian	1 Dec 1827
TEXERO, Lewis	45	M	Merchant	Teneriffe	Spain	Louisiana	20 Sep 1822
TEXIDO, Manuel		M	Merchant	Spain	U. States	Packet	13 Jun 1821
TEYRA, Domonick	22	M	Merchant	Tenerife	New York	Emeline	14 Dec 1827
TH...DRICIN, Johanna Margt.	28	F		Germany	America	Falcon	28 Aug 1828
TH...TON, Stephen	32	M	None	Virginia	United States	Martha	22 Jul 1820
TH...ULE, Joseph	31	M	Labourer	B...lon	Bolton	Howard Douglass	11 May 1827
THA...KER, Wm.	18	M	Labourer	..., ..., England	Sommersworth (N.Y)	New Orleans	24 Aug 1827
THACKER, John	31		Dyer	Dublin		Mount Vernon	18 Oct 1822
THAIN, Alex	26	M		Great Britain	Canada	James Monroe	25 Apr 1822
THAL, John, Sr.	18	M	Sugar baker	Hannover	U. States	Constitution	15 Nov 1822
THANIS, James	30	M	Weaver	Great Britain	United States	Robert Fulton	18 May 1825
THATCHER, —, Mr.	28	M	Mariner	Connecticutt	U. States	Amanda	19 Jan 1824
THAXTER, A. W.	22	M	Merchant	U. States	U. States	Harriet	2 Jan 1829
THAYER, —	2	M		United States	United States	Four Sons	1 Sep 1827
—, Mrs.	22	F		United States	United States	Four Sons	1 Sep 1827
A.	36	M	Mariner	America	U. States	Confiance	26 Apr 1828
William	31	M	Gentleman	U.States	America	Robin Hood	20 Jul 1827
THEALL, William Y.	21	M	Gentleman	St. John, N.B.	St. John, N.B.	Ann Maria	5 Mar 1827
THEBAUD, Eugene	16	M	Farmer	Switzerland	America	Don Quixotte	2 Jun 1828
J. J.	28	M	Merchant	U. States	U. States	Howard	27 Jan 1825
Jno. J.	30	M	Merchant	United States		Montano	3 Jan 1823
John S., Mr.	30	M	Merchant	U.S.	U.S.	Cadmus	11 Jul 1827
THEBURY, Ann	6/52			England		Anacreon	7 Sep 1827
Ann	28			England		Anacreon	7 Sep 1827
Wm.	30			England		Anacreon	7 Sep 1827
THEDERICH, Hy.	34	M	Mason	Switzerland	U. States	La Urania	3 Jul 1828
M. L.	27	M		Switzerland	U. States	La Urania	3 Jul 1828
THEE, T. H.	19	M	Laborer	Hannover	New York	Constitution	12 Jul 1827
THEGORY, Edward	13	M	Boy	Ireland	U. States	Concordia	11 Jun 1823
THEHANZ, Abraham	34	M	Carpenter	Germany	United States	Origon	8 Jun 1824
Anna	24	F		Germany	United States	Origon	8 Jun 1824
Jean	54	M	Carpenter	Germany	United States	Origon	8 Jun 1824

NAMES OF PASSENGERS	AGE	SEX	OCCUPATIONS	COUNTRY TO WHICH THEY BELONG	COUNTRY THEY INTEND TO INHABIT	SHIPS/DATES OF ARRIVAL	
THEHANZ (cont'd)							
Mina	57	F		Germany	United States	Origon	8 Jun 1824
THEIS, John	32	M	Tailor	Hamburgh	United States	Union	9 Jan 1824
THEMANS, Alexer.	18	M	Segar Maker	Island of Cuba	United States	Betsey	28 Oct 1825
THEOBALD, S. R.	26	M	Mariner	Maine	United States	Pamelia	3 Aug 1829
Catherine	30	F	Farmer	United States	United States	Globe	30 Aug 1828
Christian	14	M	Farmer	United States	United States	Globe	30 Aug 1828
Frederic	6	M	Farmer	United States	United States	Globe	30 Aug 1828
Henry	3	M	Farmer	United States	United States	Globe	30 Aug 1828
Petter	35	M	Farmer	United States	United States	Globe	30 Aug 1828
Philip	9	M	Farmer	United States	United States	Globe	30 Aug 1828
THERASSON, Lewis	36	M	Merchant	America	New York	Chauncy	10 Jan 1820
Lewis	38	M	Merchant	United States	United States	General Brown	24 Nov 1820
THERIATS, A. R.	32	M	Merchant	France	France	Bayard	27 Jun 1821
THERNIVAL, Samuel	34		Farmer	England	America	Governor Griswold	6 Jun 1821
THEROUANNE, E.	21	M	Merchant	France	U. States	Stephania	26 Apr 1824
THERY, J.	27	M	Weaver	France		Queen Mab	24 Sep 1827
THEW, Ann	30	F		England	U. States	Commerce	28 May 1824
Betsey	3	F		England	U. States	Commerce	28 May 1824
Henry	8	M		England	U. States	Commerce	28 May 1824
John	10	M		England	U. States	Commerce	28 May 1824
Joseph	5	M		England	U. States	Commerce	28 May 1824
Martha	1	F		England	U. States	Commerce	28 May 1824
Richd.	33	M	Farmer	England	U. States	Commerce	28 May 1824
Wm.	12	M		England	U. States	Commerce	28 May 1824
THIBAUD, Edw.	23	M	Merchant	United States	United States	Joseph	11 Jul 1821
THIBAULT, Jean	67	M	Farmer	Switzerland	U. States	La Urania	3 Jul 1828
THIEL, —, Mrs.	28	F	Merchant	Germany	Philadelphia	Maria Elizabeth	16 Feb 1826
THIFFENEY, Ph.	35	F	Min	France		Antioch	18 Aug 1829
THILL, Francis	26	M	Sadler	Holland	United States	American	27 Aug 1827
THIMMINGS, Jos.	29	M	Farmer	England	U. States	Hercules	6 Jul 1827
THIN, Michael	25	M	Labourer	Ireland	U. States	Borneo	15 Apr 1828
THIOT, Le Chiralier Caravossy			Consul to the States	Italy	Italy	Dewitt Clinton	26 Aug 1825
THIRSTON, Mary	25	F		Halifax	Great Britton	William	11 May 1821
THISTLE, Isabella	18	F		Ireland	U. States	Nancy	16 Aug 1822
THISTLETHWAITE,							
James	35	M	Farmer	G. Britain	U. States	James Monroe	18 Apr 1821
John	28	M	Farmer	G. Britain	U. States	James Monroe	18 Apr 1821
THISTLETON, Ann	6	F		Great Britain	United States	Diana	30 Oct 1827
Eliza	30	F		Great Britain	United States	Diana	30 Oct 1827
Frederick	2	M		Great Britain	United States	Diana	30 Oct 1827
George	34	M	Linen Weaver	Great Britain	United States	Diana	30 Oct 1827
Henry	5	M		Great Britain	United States	Diana	30 Oct 1827
THITLE, N. A.	28	M	Army	Denmark	Denmark	Chase	24 Aug 1822
THO...PSON, John	85	M	Farmer	Ireland		Cuba	24 Jun 1822
THOM, James	26	M	Lapidary	G. Britain	U. States	Camillus	8 Sep 1828
THOMAS, —, Capt.	34	M	Mariner	England	U. States	Union	10 Mar 1823
—, Mrs.	21	F	None	U. States	U. States	Superion	30 Apr 1825
—, Mrs.	35	F		England	United States	Cosmo	26 Aug 1829
—, Mrs.	50	F		New Brunswick	to return	Lady Hunter	10 Jul 1826
—, Mrs., his wife [John]	37	F	None	Great Britain	U.S. Am.	Eliza	12 May 1828
...drew	25	M	Farmer	Gt. Britain	U. States	Maria	22 May 1822
Abm.	21	M	Carpenter	G. Britain	America	Spring	12 Oct 1821
Abraham	3	M		Great Britain	United States	Washington	3 Sep 1827
Agatha	33	F	his wife [Joe]	Germany	United States	Helen	5 Sep 1828
Ann	10	F	Farmer	England	United States	Joseph	13 Oct 1823
Ann	13 9/12	F		England	United States	John Wells	22 May 1826
Ann	15	F	None	Great Britain	U.S. Am.	Eliza	12 May 1828
Ann	18	F		Great Britton	U. State	Earl of Liverpool	16 Aug 1826
Ann	24	F	Seamstress	Great Britain	United States	Henrietta	19 Oct 1825
Ann	25	F		England	U. States	Pacific	5 Sep 1827
Ann	42	F	None	England	United States	Euphrates	12 May 1823
Antony	28	M		France		Pallas	14 Jun 1828
Augustus	40	M	Labourer	U. States	U. States	Robt. Reade	12 Apr 1825

NAMES OF PASSENGERS	AGE	SEX	OCCUPATIONS	COUNTRY TO WHICH THEY BELONG	COUNTRY THEY INTEND TO INHABIT	SHIPS/DATES OF ARRIVAL	
THOMAS (cont'd)							
Bill, (a black boy)	7	M	Mariner	U. States	U. States	New Packet	27 Jul 1822
C.	20	M	Mercht.	England	England	Britannia	5 Nov 1828
C.	25		None	G. Britain	United States	Roman	10 Sep 1827
Catharine	13	F	None	U. States	U. States	Emblem	14 May 1827
Catharine	45	F		Llannstyn	United States	Marquis of Anglesea	8 Jun 1827
Cathe.	23	F		North Wales	United States	Magnet	16 May 1823
Charles, Capt.	35		Mariner	America	America	Edward	24 Oct 1827
Chas.	2	M		England	United States	Cosmo	26 Aug 1829
Chas.	7	M				Harmony	15 Jul 1820
D...	...	M	Smith	England	Pensylvania	Lima	5 Aug 1829
David	17	M		England	United States	William Byrnes	1 Dec 1824
David	26	M	Merchant	Ireland	United States	Silas Richards	27 Oct 1825
David	26	M	Brickmaker	Wales	America	Josephine	24 Jul 1826
David	28	M	Gentleman	U. States	U. States	Genl. A. Jackson	6 Sep 1820
David	37	M	Smith	England	U. States	Lima	5 Aug 1829
David	47	M	Farmer	England	United States	William Byrnes	1 Dec 1824
E.	18	F	Farmer	St. Johns	U. States	Isabella	28 Jun 1825
E.	34	F	Wife	Great Britain	United States	Washington	3 Sep 1827
E. S.	48	M	Gentleman	America	America	London Packet	25 Dec 1820
Eben	24	M	Blacksmith	Great Britain	United States	Asia	14 Jul 1829
Ed.	23	M	Servant	England	on a Visit	Catharine	3 Sep 1821
Edward	11	M	None	Great Britain	United States	Aurora	10 Nov 1827
Edward	23	M	Sevant	Newyork	New York	South Carolina Packet	16 Sep 1820
Edward	36	M	Farmer	England	America	New York Packet	8 May 1823
Edwd.	28	M	Farmer	U. States	U. States	Robt. Reade	12 Apr 1825
Eleonor	61	F		Wales	U. States	Mary Stewart	12 May 1827
Elias	28	M	...	G. Brittain	America	Robin Hood	20 Jul 1827
Eliza	17	F	None	Great Britain	U.S. Am.	Eliza	12 May 1828
Elizabeth	5	F	Farmer	England	United States	Joseph	13 Oct 1823
Elizabeth	37	F	Farmer	England	United States	Joseph	13 Oct 1823
Elizabeth	37	F	None	Great Britain	United States	Aurora	10 Nov 1827
Ellen	23	F	None	Great Brittan	U.S.	Emulous	29 Jun 1827
Elvira	60	F	Seamstress	Great Britain	United States	Henrietta	19 Oct 1825
Emily	3	F		England	United States	Cosmo	26 Aug 1829
Evan	45	M	Gent.	U.S. America	U.S. America	James Cropper	29 Nov 1827
Evan	70	M	Farmer	Wales	United States	Orozimbo	11 Aug 1823
F.	12	M	None	Aux Cayes	United States	Paquet Des Cayes	9 Jul 1827
Frederick	5	M	None	Great Britain	United States	Aurora	10 Nov 1827
G.	45	M	Merchant	U. States	U. States	Prudence	11 Jun 1825
Gardener	45	M	Purser of the U.S. Navy	U.S. of America		Six Brothers	10 Aug 1829
Geo.	30	M	Mechanic	United States	United States	Columbia	16 Jan 1829
Griffith	3	M	Farmer	England	United States	William Byrnes	1 Dec 1824
H.	16	F	Farmer	St. Johns	U. States	Isabella	28 Jun 1825
Hannah	24	F		England	United States	William Byrnes	1 Dec 1824
Hannah	35	F	Servant	U. States	U. States	Cadmus	9 Apr 1825
Hannah	47	F		England	United States	William Byrnes	1 Dec 1824
Howell	39	M	Farmer	Britain	U. States	Fame	3 Jun 1828
Hugh	19	M	Labourer	Lancster County		Aurora	8 Jun 1827
Hugh	27	M	Miller	Wales	U. States	Mary Stewart	12 May 1827
Isabella	23	F				Harmony	15 Jul 1820
J.	6	M	Farmer	St. Johns	U. States	Isabella	28 Jun 1825
J.	8	M	Farmer	St. Johns	U. States	Isabella	28 Jun 1825
J.	30	M	Farmer	U. States	U.S.	Ambuscade	14 Mar 1820
J.	50	M	Farmer	St. Johns	U. States	Isabella	28 Jun 1825
James	7	M		England	United States	Cosmo	26 Aug 1829
James	8	M	Farmer	England	United States	Joseph	13 Oct 1823
James	26	M	Painter	U. States	United States	William Howland	5 Jul 1821
James	32	M	Mariner	Ireland	England	Eliza	22 Dec 1826
James	32	M	Coker			Plato	31 Oct 1829
James	41	M	Coal Miner	Wales	Baltimore	Indian Chief	19 Jun 1823
Jane	2	F				Harmony	15 Jul 1820

1241

NAMES OF PASSENGERS	AGE	SEX	OCCUPATIONS	COUNTRY TO WHICH THEY BELONG	COUNTRY THEY INTEND TO INHABIT	SHIPS/DATES OF ARRIVAL	
THOMAS (cont'd)							
Jane	4	F	Farmer	Britain	U. States	Fame	3 Jun 1828
Jane	13		Farmer	England	United States	Joseph	13 Oct 1823
Jane	20	F		Wales	U. States	Marquis of Anglesea	12 Sep 1828
Jane	25	F	Servant	Great Britain	New York	Corinthian	27 Apr 1824
Janie	25	F		U. States	U. States	Robt. Reade	12 Apr 1825
Jas.	5	M				Harmony	15 Jul 1820
Job B.	32	M	Master	G. Britain		Harmony	15 Jul 1820
Joe	36	M	Shoemaker	Germany	United States	Helen	5 Sep 1828
Joe T.	5	M	there Son [Joe & Agatha]	Germany	United States	Helen	5 Sep 1828
John	8	M	Farmer	Britain	U. States	Fame	3 Jun 1828
John	12	M	Farmer	England	United States	Joseph	13 Oct 1823
John	21	M	Gentleman	Barbados, U.S.	West Indies	Spartan	24 Jul 1826
John	22	M				Belfast	28 Sep 1820
John	23	M	Farmer	North Wales	United States	Magnet	16 May 1823
John	25	M	Farmer	England	United States	John Wells	16 May 1825
John	25	M	Iron Moulder	England	U.N. States	Jane	7 Oct 1826
John	25	M	Farmer	Great Brittan	U.S.	Emulous	29 Jun 1827
John	27	M	Miner	England	England	Eliza	22 Dec 1826
John	28	M	Labourer	England	United States	Orozimbo	11 Aug 1823
John	28 5/12	M	Farmer	England	U.S. of America	Illinois	16 Jun 1821
John	36	M	Baker	England	United States	Euphrates	12 May 1823
John	40	M	Merchant	U. States	U. States	Silvia	10 Sep 1827
John	42	M	Farmer	England	United States	Joseph	13 Oct 1823
John	43	M	Mechanic	Great Britain	U.S. Am.	Eliza	12 May 1828
John	45	M	Labourer	Llannstyn	United States	Marquis of Anglesea	8 Jun 1827
John	46	M	Schoolmaster	Great Britain	United States	Ann Maria	23 Oct 1820
John	50 3/12	M				Cririe	18 Sep 1820
John, Junr.	7 8/12	M				Cririe	18 Sep 1820
Joseph	24	M	Farmer		Perien [?]	Governor Clinton	3 Jul 1827
Joseph	26	M	Carpenter	England	New York	Brighton	19 Aug 1829
Joseph	26	M	Carpenter			Brighton	19 Aug 1829
Justine, Mademoiselle	30	F		France	United States	Henry	9 Jun 1826
Ludlow	5			U. States	U. States	Hudson	4 Sep 1823
Margaret	21	F		Ireland	Canada	Wanderer	31 Aug 1829
Margaret	68	F	None	Wales	United States	Orozimbo	11 Aug 1823
Margt.	20	F	Spinster	Great Britain	United States	Washington	3 Sep 1827
Margt.	22	F		England	United States	William Byrnes	1 Dec 1824
Maria	2	F	Farmer	England	United States	Joseph	13 Oct 1823
Maria	23	F		England	New York	Thames	6 Oct 1820
Maria	24	F	Lady	Great Britten	United States	Cortes	6 Mar 1827
Mary	6/365		Farmer	Britain	U. States	Fame	3 Jun 1828
Mary	8/12	F		England	U.S. of America	Illinois	16 Jun 1821
Mary	2					Agricola	1 Jul 1820
Mary	2	F		Great Britain	United States	Washington	3 Sep 1827
Mary	9			England	United States	Cosmo	26 Aug 1829
Mary	13	F	None	Tobassa	U. States	Morning Star	28 Apr 1824
Mary	16	F		U. States	Great Britain	Thompson	26 Apr 1828
Mary	21					Agricola	1 Jul 1820
Mary	25 5/12	F		England	U.S. of America	Illinois	16 Jun 1821
Mary	36	F	Farmer	Britain	U. States	Fame	3 Jun 1828
Mary	40	F	None	Wales		Aurora	8 Jun 1827
Mary Ann	11	F	Farmer	St. Johns	U. States	Isabella	28 Jun 1825
Mary F.	38			U. States	U. States	Hudson	4 Sep 1823
Mullen	20	M	Joiner	Great Britain	United States	Samuel Wright	12 Oct 1829
R.	13	F	Farmer	St. Johns	U. States	Isabella	28 Jun 1825
R.	39	F	Farmer	St. Johns	U. States	Isabella	28 Jun 1825
Randolph	20	M	Carpenter	Philadelphia	Philadelphia	Gertrude	6 Mar 1827
Rawlins	40	M	Navy	G. Brittain	England	Columbia	12 Apr 1826
Richard	18	M	Weaver	Wales	U. States	Henry Kneeland	27 Jul 1825
Richd.	24	M	Moulder	Great Britain	United States	Washington	3 Sep 1827
Robert	32		Farmer	Wales		Agricola	1 Jul 1820
Robt	54	M	Mariner	Gt. Britain	Ireland	Isaac Hicks	18 Apr 1825
Robt.	30	M	Labourer			Evergreen	28 Jul 1820
Rowland	6/12	M	Farmer	England	United States	Joseph	13 Oct 1823

NAMES OF PASSENGERS	AGE	SEX	OCCUPATIONS	COUNTRY TO WHICH THEY BELONG	COUNTRY THEY INTEND TO INHABIT	SHIPS/DATES OF ARRIVAL	
THOMAS (cont'd)							
S.	4	F	Farmer	St. Johns	U. States	Isabella	28 Jun 1825
Saml.	20	M	Labourer	England	United States	Nimrod	31 Jul 1828
Samuel	29	M	Stone Mason	England	New York	Thames	6 Oct 1820
Sarah	7	F		England	United States	William Byrnes	1 Dec 1824
Sarah	10			England	United States	Cosmo	26 Aug 1829
Sarah	18	F		England	United States	John Wells	22 May 1826
Seragh	27	F	None		Perien [?]	Governor Clinton	3 Jul 1827
Simon	28	M	Farmer	England	United States	John Wells	16 May 1825
Sophia	35 6/12	F	Servant	U. States	U. States	Isabella	31 Oct 1829
Sorris	10	M		U.S. of America		Six Brothers	10 Aug 1829
Stephen	42	M	Labourer	Great Britain	United States	Aurora	10 Nov 1827
Stephen	44	M	Plater	U. States	Great Britain	Thompson	26 Apr 1828
Susan	11			England	United States	Cosmo	26 Aug 1829
Theodore	31	M	Sailor	U. States	U. States	Swift	28 Jan 1828
Thomas	12	M		England	United States	William Byrnes	1 Dec 1824
Thomas	18	M	Servant	England	England	Tontine	1 Jun 1826
William	19	M	Labourer	Great Britain	United States	Fidelity	16 Oct 1820
William	20	M	Miner	England	England	Hiram	14 Aug 1829
William	25	M	Farmer	Great Britan	United States	Clematis	8 May 1827
William	28	M	Surgeon	Ohio, U.S.	United States	Cosmo	21 Aug 1828
William, Mr.	36	M	Merchant	England	England	Governor Fenner	23 Jul 1829
Willm.	13		Carpenter	England	America	Cosmo	17 Mar 1828
Willm.	28	M	Carpenter	G. Britain	America	Spring	12 Oct 1821
Willm.	30	M	Laborer	Liverpool	United States	Nile	17 May 1827
Wm.	22	M	Merchant	United States	United States	Prince Edward	13 Apr 1824
Wm.	25	M	Farmer	Wales	U. States	Mary Stewart	12 May 1827
Wm.	26	M	Farmer	England	U. States	Mary	24 Jun 1824
Wm.	42	M	Gentleman	Tobassa	U. States	Morning Star	28 Apr 1824
Wm.	45	M	Carpenter	Great Britton	U. State	Earl of Liverpool	16 Aug 1826
Wm. G.	19	M	Gent.	U.S. America	U.S. America	James Cropper	29 Nov 1827
THOMASSON, —, Mrs.	28	F	Wife	France	U. States	Sultana	6 Nov 1828
Ann	19	F	Servant	Germany	New York	Elizabeth	5 Jul 1821
Augustus	32	M	Apothecary	France	U. States	Sultana	6 Nov 1828
THOMES,							
William, Captr.	25	M	Ship Master	Portland		Leander	18 May 1827
THOMLINS, Ann	2...			L...	England	Great Britain	7 May 1827
Mary	9			L...	England	Great Britain	7 May 1827
THOMLY, E.	22	F		Great Britain	United States	Isaac Hicks	6 Dec 1827
THOMMASON,							
Augustus	32	M	Blacksmith	United States	United States	Paris	10 Sep 1823
THOMPSEN, James	25	M	Shoolmaster	England	United States	Hamilton	13 Nov 1827
THOMPSON, —, Mr.	25	M	Merchant	Great Britain	Canada	Columbia	7 Sep 1827
—, Mr.	34	M	Farmer	Gt. Britain	U. States	Constitution	19 Jul 1825
—, Mrs.	25	F		N. Jersey	U. States	Romeo	23 Jun 1823
—, Mrs.	26	F	Farmer	Gt. Britain	U. States	Constitution	19 Jul 1825
—, Mrs.	32	F	None	Scotland	United States	Camillus	27 Oct 1829
—, Mrs.	50	F		St. Andrews	U. States	Mary Louisa	6 Mar 1827
...	25	M	Weaver	Scotland	New York	Joseph Hume	26 Oct 1829
...	38	M	Weaver	Scotland	New York	Joseph Hume	26 Oct 1829
... H.	28	F	Lady	U.S.A.	U.S.A.	Bayard	25 Aug 1829
...jamin	49		...	Fairford, E.	United States	Packet	27 Aug 1822
A.	25	F		U. States	U. States	Genl. Victoria	7 Apr 1828
A.	44	M	Mariner	U. States	U. States	Jane	29 Jul 1823
Agnes	1	F	Farmer	Argyle (Tedland) Scotland	United States	Jean Hastie	27 Jul 1829
Agnes	6	F	None	Scotland	United States	Camillus	27 Oct 1829
Alex.	23		Weaver	Ireland	United States	John Dickinson	28 Jun 1822
Alex.	30	F		Scotland	U. States	Roger Stewart	9 Jun 1828
Alexander	20	M	...	Ireland	United States	Carolina Ann	24 Oct 1825
Alexander	30	M	Labourer	Ireland	America	Minerva	15 Nov 1823
Alexander	52	M	Mariner	U. States	United States	Pionier	4 Mar 1828
Alexr.	16	M	Farmer	Glasgow	United States	Dalhousie Castle	27 Jul 1826
Alexr.	42	M	Merchant	United States	U. States	Hercules	24 Oct 1821
Alister	25	F	Lady	St. John, N.B.	United States	Sylvester Healy	19 Aug 1825
Allis	17			Ireland	New York	Lady Hunter	19 Oct 1826

NAMES OF PASSENGERS	AGE	SEX	OCCUPATIONS	COUNTRY TO WHICH THEY BELONG	COUNTRY THEY INTEND TO INHABIT	SHIPS/DATES OF ARRIVAL	
THOMPSON (cont'd)							
Alx.	42	M	Mercht.	Scotland	N. York	Canada	1 Nov 1823
Andrew	12	M	Laborer	Ireland	United States	Sarah G	19 Jun 1827
Andrew	20	M	Joiner	Great Britain	United States	Frances	
						Henrietta	17 Sep 1827
Andrew	29	M	Mason	G. Britain	U. States	Wanderer	23 Jun 1828
Ann	42	F		Ireland	America	Franklin	13 Aug 1827
Anna	3	F	Child	Ireland	United States	Sarah G	19 Jun 1827
Archd.	12			Scotland	United States	Camillus	3 May 1828
Archd.	27	M	...hinemaker	Ayreshire	Ayreshire	Howard	
						Douglass	11 May 1827
B...	34	M	Laborer	Great Britain	United States	Wanderer	11 Jul 1826
Betsey	18	F		Ireland	America	Liverpool	31 Aug 1827
Betsey	30	F		Bermuda	England	Mary &	
						Elizabeth	1 Apr 1824
Bridget	10	F	None	Great Britan	United States	Hamilton	19 Mar 1827
C.	28	M	Merchant	Vera Cruz	U. States	Eliza	11 Apr 1826
Catharine	1_/12	F		Ireland	United States	William &	
						George	14 May 1828
Catharine	54	F	None	Great Britain	United States	Mount Vernon	17 Jun 1825
Catherine	26	F	None	Scotland	United States	Mary & Susan	5 Aug 1828
Charlotte	40	F	Lady	England	United States should		
					they approve of it	Robert Edwards	20 Jan 1829
Chas.	26	M	Gentleman	England	British America	Criterion	27 Oct 1821
Christopher	18	M	Merchant	Gt. Britain	U. States	Canada	4 Oct 1824
D.	23	M	Gentleman	U. States	U. States	Abeona	1 Oct 1823
David	24			Ireland	U.S.	Union	20 Aug 1827
David	29	M	Merchant	U.S.		Bliss	28 Jul 1821
David	32	M	Farmer	Scotland	U.S. States of Am.	Camillus	17 Sep 1823
Dorea	17	F		Ireland	America	Franklin	13 Aug 1827
E., Mrs.		F	Captain's Wife	U.S.	U.S.	Oswego	12 Apr 1824
Edward	16	M	Laborer	Ireland	United States	Sarah G	19 Jun 1827
Edward	26	M	Mariner	America	America	Atlantic	29 Jun 1822
Edward	28	M	Ship Master	United States	U. States	Saml. Smith	24 Jul 1826
Edward	28	M	Merchant	G. Brittane	U. States	Panama	9 Apr 1828
Edward	29	M	Master Mariner	United States	United States	New York	14 Jul 1827
Edward	36		Painter	Great Britain	United States	Camillus	12 Sep 1827
Edwin	11	M	Child	U. States	U. States	Josephine	30 Aug 1828
Elisabeth	1	F	None	Scotland	United States	Mary & Susan	5 Aug 1828
Eliza	2 6/12	F		U. States	U. States	Canada	19 Sep 1828
Eliza	10	F		G. Britain	U. States	St. George	7 Jun 1828
Eliza	25			Ireland	New York	Lady Hunter	19 Oct 1826
Eliza	37	F		G. Britain	U. States	St. George	7 Jun 1828
Eliza	50			Ireland	New York	Lady Hunter	19 Oct 1826
Eliza P.	10	F	Child	Ireland	Pennsylvania	Wilson	28 Aug 1822
Elizabeth	6			Scotland	United States	Camillus	3 May 1828
Elizabeth	10	F	None	Scotland	United States	Camillus	27 Oct 1829
Elizabeth	16	F	None	Great Britan	United States	Hamilton	19 Mar 1827
Elizabeth	38	F	Wife	Ireland	United States	Sarah G	19 Jun 1827
Elizabeth	47	F	None	Great Britan	United States	Hamilton	19 Mar 1827
Ellen	28	F	Spinster	Great Britain	U. States	William	
						Thompson	29 Jan 1823
Esther	48	F		England	U. States	Panthea	22 Nov 1826
Faith	22	F				Eliza Grant	6 Oct 1828
Frances	34 2/12	F		England	United States	Criterion	27 Oct 1820
Francis, Jr.	25	M	Merchant	England	America	William	
						Thompson	29 Jan 1824
Francis, Junr.	29	M	Merchant	U. States	U. States	Canada	12 May 1828
Fras.	23	M	Merchant	Great Britain	United States	James Monroe	25 Apr 1822
Fras.	25	M	Labourer	Limerick	United States	Union	24 Sep 1823
Gaspool							
Diederick	20 5/12	M	Tailor	Denmark	United States	Howard	28 Aug 1828
Geo.	5	M	None	Great Britain	U. States	William	
						Thompson	29 Jan 1823
Geo.	20					Harmony	15 Jul 1820
George	1			Scotland	United States	Camillus	3 May 1828
George	7	M	Ca...ire	Argyle (Tedland)			
				Scotland	United States	Jean Hastie	27 Jul 1829

NAMES OF PASSENGERS	AGE	SEX	OCCUPATIONS	COUNTRY TO WHICH THEY BELONG	COUNTRY THEY INTEND TO INHABIT	SHIPS/DATES OF ARRIVAL	
THOMPSON (cont'd)							
George	24	M	Gentleman	Great Britain	United States	Thomas Dickason	31 Jul 1829
George	30	M	Labourer	Ireland	U.S. of America	Meteor	19 Mar 1828
George	32	M	Merchant	Great Britain	U. States	William Thompson	29 Jan 1823
George	35	M	...	Great Britain	United States	Ann	24 Sep 1822
George	35	M		England	New York	Lima	16 Mar 1829
George C. F.	32	M	Mariner	U. States	United States	Pionier	4 Mar 1828
George W.	26	M	Labourer	Scotland	United States	Mary & Susan	5 Aug 1828
Hannah	5/12	F	None	England	New York	America	1 Aug 1828
Hannah	1	F		G. Britain	U. States	Dalhouse Castle	12 Sep 1828
Hannah	2	F				Eliza Grant	6 Oct 1828
Hannah	8			Ireland	America	Franklin	13 Aug 1827
Hannah	29	F		England	New York	Lima	16 Mar 1829
Hannah	56	F		America	America	James Cropper	14 Oct 1822
Harriet	3	F		England	New York	Lima	16 Mar 1829
Harriet H.	16	F	Child	Saint John	St. John	Nancy	11 Apr 1822
Henry	20	M	Smith	Ireland	United States	Gem	16 Jun 1824
Hugh	2			Ireland	Great Britain	Robert Burns	14 Jun 1824
Hugh	21	M	Dyer	Wales	United States	Orozimbo	11 Aug 1823
Isabella	24	F	Seamstres	Ireland	America	Hesperus	7 Jul 1820
Issabella	19	F		Ireland	America	Franklin	13 Aug 1827
J.	25	M	Planter	U.S.	U.S.	New England	11 Jul 1827
J.	40	M	Merchant	Scotland	Halifax	Mary Ann	24 Feb 1827
James	13	M	None	Great Britan	United States	Hamilton	19 Mar 1827
James	16	M		Great Brittain	United States	Corinthian	9 Jan 1827
James	23	M	Captain, Officers & crew of the Brig George of New York (wrecked at Fayal)	U.S. America	U.S.A.	Gallego	13 Mar 1829
James	25	M	None	Scotland	United States	Mary & Susan	5 Aug 1828
James	25 5/12	M	Weaver	Ireland	U. States	Fabius	22 Sep 1828
James	27	M	Mashian Maker	G.B.	N. York	Eliza Grant	29 Aug 1829
James	27	M	Machine Maker	Ireland		Eliza Grant	29 Aug 1829
James	30	M	Book binder	Great Britain	United States	Birmingham	15 Jun 1827
James	31	M	Mason	Scotland	U. States	Roger Stewart	9 Jun 1828
James	34	M	...	Ireland	United States	Carolina Ann	24 Oct 1825
James	38	M	Farmer	England	Ut. States	Courier	13 Jul 1826
James	40	M	Laborer	Ireland	United States	Sarah G	19 Jun 1827
James	42	M	Farmer	England	England	William Byrnes	14 Apr 1824
James	47	M	Farmer	Scotland	United States	John Dickinson	12 Aug 1824
James S.	28	M	Labourer	England	United States	Jubilee	1 Oct 1828
Jane	2	F	None	Ireland	America	Hesperus	7 Jul 1820
Jane	16	F	None	Scotland	United States	John Dickinson	12 Aug 1824
Jane	16	F		G. Britain	U. States	St. George	7 Jun 1828
Jane	23	F	his wife [John]	Ireland	United States	Asia	29 Jul 1829
Jane	30	F		Scotland	United States	Concordia	25 Aug 1827
Jane	37	F		G. Britain	U. States	St. George	7 Jun 1828
Jane	50	F	None	Scotland	United States	Colossus	26 Aug 1828
Jane, Miss	18	F	Lady	New York	U. States	Circassian	3 Jun 1826
Janet	4			Scotland	United States	Camillus	3 May 1828
Jannet	18	F	Daughter	Ireland	United States	Sarah G	19 Jun 1827
Jas.	7			Ireland	Great Britain	Robert Burns	14 Jun 1824
Jas.	22					Harmony	15 Jul 1820
Jas.	28	M	Weaver	Scotland	New York	Joseph Hume	26 Oct 1829
Jas.	34	M	Marchant	N. York	U. States	Commodore Perry	9 Apr 1821
Jas. C.	22	M	Merchant	U. States		Charleston Packet	4 May 1821
Jere	38	M	Farmer	G. Britain	U. States	St. George	7 Jun 1828
Jno.	6	M	Ca...ire	Argyle (Tedland) Scotland	United States	Jean Hastie	27 Jul 1829
Jno.	22	M	Labourer	England	England	Sir James Kempt	10 Dec 1827
Jno.	30		Grocer	Great Britain	United States	Camillus	12 Sep 1827
Jno.	32	M				Harmony	15 Jul 1820

1245

NAMES OF PASSENGERS	AGE	SEX	OCCUPATIONS	COUNTRY TO WHICH THEY BELONG	COUNTRY THEY INTEND TO INHABIT	SHIPS/DATES OF ARRIVAL	
THOMPSON (cont'd)							
Jno.	32	M	Turner	England	United States	Orozimbo	5 Mar 1827
Jno.	45	M	Merchant	Maine	U. States	Signal	18 Apr 1826
Jno.	55	M	Sadler			Belfast	28 Sep 1820
Jno., Jur.	28					Harmony	15 Jul 1820
Jno. R.	22	M	Merchant	Baltimore	U. States	Vestal	8 May 1822
John	6/12	M		Scotland	United States	Concordia	25 Aug 1827
John	2	M		G. Britain	U. States	Dalhouse Castle	12 Sep 1828
John	3			Ireland	Great Britain	Robert Burns	14 Jun 1824
John	8 6/12	M	Child	Ireland	Pennsylvania	Wilson	28 Aug 1822
John	18	M	Merchant	U. States	U. States	New England	11 Sep 1828
John	20	M	Miller	Ireland	United States	Gem	16 Jun 1824
John	20	M	Farmer			Commerce	22 Jun 1825
John	20	M	...	Ireland	United States	Carolina Ann	24 Oct 1825
John	20	M	Labourer	Scotland	U. States	Czar	29 Aug 1829
John	22		Sailor	England	United States	Mary	15 Jul 1822
John	24	M	Mechanic	New York	United States	Champion	3 Nov 1827
John	24	M	Merchant	Great Britian	United States	Sarah	11 Jul 1829
John	25		Printer	England	England	London	16 Aug 1824
John	25	M	Merchant	Ireland	United States	Sarah Ann	6 Mar 1827
John	25	M	Cabinet Maker	Ireland	United States	Asia	29 Jul 1829
John	28	M	Clothier	Great Britain	United States	Colossus	1 Nov 1826
John	28	M	Ropemaker	Scotland	U. States	Czar	29 Aug 1829
John	30	M	Merchant	Scotland	America	Tontine	25 Jan 1827
John	30	M	Brewer	England	U. States	Robert Edwards	9 May 1827
John	32	M		Great Britain	United States	Mary Howland	19 Jul 1827
John	35	M	Blacksmith	New York	New York	Sarah G.	28 Nov 1827
John	38	M	Plater	Great Britain	United States	Ganges	26 Oct 1826
John	38	M	Mechanic	Scotland	United States	Concordia	25 Aug 1827
John	39	M	Merchant	Great Britain	United States	Freake	25 Aug 1829
John	40	M	Farmer	Scotland	U.S.	Curler	19 Jul 1828
John N.	23	M	Ship Master	United States	United States	Hudson	17 Mar 1828
Jonah	40	M	Merchant	U. States	U. States	France	14 Mar 1828
Jos.	21	M	Labourer	Ireland		Robert Fulton	4 Jun 1828
Joseph	27	M				Eliza Grant	6 Oct 1828
Joseph	29	M	Farmer	C. Armannar [Armagh or Farmanagh?]	Boston	Nile	18 Aug 1829
Joshua L.	2	M	None	U. States	U. States	Canada	12 May 1828
Julia	1					William Thompson	29 Jan 1823
Julia Hannah	10 6/12	F	Child			Criterion	27 Oct 1820
Kille	30	M	Farmer	England	England	Criterion	29 May 1822
Lucy	12	F		Cuba	U. States	Rubicon	2 Jun 1828
Lucy	14	F		G. Britain	U. States	St. George	7 Jun 1828
Lucy	30	F		U. States	U. States	Canada	19 Sep 1828
M.	35	M	Mercht.	Bermuda	Scotland	Mary & Elizabeth	1 Apr 1824
M. D.	30	M	Merchant	U. States	U. States	Neptunes Barge	1 Oct 1822
Margaret	2	F	None	Scotland	United States	Camillus	27 Oct 1829
Margaret	16	F	Wife	St. John, N.B.	United States	St. Michaels	23 Dec 1826
Margaret	26	F		Ireland	United States	William & George	14 May 1828
Margret	24	F	Servant	Ireland	America	Weser	26 Jun 1821
Margt.	10			Scotland	United States	Camillus	3 May 1828
Margt.	22	F	None	England	New York	America	1 Aug 1828
Margt.	28		Wife, Going to her Husband	Scotland	United States	Camillus	3 May 1828
Maria	2	F	Farmer	Argyle (Tedland) Scotland	United States	Jean Hastie	27 Jul 1829
Maria	24	F				Harmony	15 Jul 1820
Maria	27	F	Farmer	Argyle (Tedland) Scotland	United States	Jean Hastie	27 Jul 1829
Maria Ann	9	F		Ireland	America	Carolina Ann	7 Aug 1826
Martha	25	F	Servant to Mr. Froste	Great Britain	United States	Robert Fulton	27 Jun 1822
Martha	26		Wife	Ireland	Great Britain	Robert Burns	14 Jun 1824
Mary	8	F	None	Scotland	United States	Camillus	27 Oct 1829
Mary	11	F		Ireland	America	Franklin	13 Aug 1827

NAMES OF PASSENGERS	AGE	SEX	OCCUPATIONS	COUNTRY TO WHICH THEY BELONG	COUNTRY THEY INTEND TO INHABIT	SHIPS/DATES OF ARRIVAL	
THOMPSON (cont'd)							
Mary	16	F	None	Scotland	U. States	Czar	29 Aug 1829
Mary	21	F		G. Brittain	U. States	Canada	6 Jun 1825
Mary	25	F	None	Ayreshire	Ayreshire	Howard Douglass	11 May 1827
Mary	38	F		G. Britain	U. States	St. George	7 Jun 1828
Mary	42	F	None	Scotland	U. States	Czar	29 Aug 1829
Mary Ann	30	F		Great Britain	United States	Ann	24 Sep 1822
Mason	10	M	Mechanic	New York	United States	Champion	3 Nov 1827
Michael	22	M	Farmer	Ireland	United States	Dublin Packet	9 Jul 1827
Moses	40		Farmer	Ireland	Great Britain	Robert Burns	14 Jun 1824
N.	40	M	Mariner	U. States	U. States	Emma	25 Oct 1825
Nicholas	6	M	None	Great Britan	United States	Hamilton	19 Mar 1827
P.	40	M	Merchant	U. States		Charleston Packet	4 May 1821
P. T.	31	M	Carpenter	Baltimore	U. States	Duly Ann	6 Jul 1825
Ralph	40	M	Merchant	Island Jamaica	U. States	Burdett	7 Dec 1827
Rebecca	1			Ireland	Great Britain	Robert Burns	14 Jun 1824
Richard	20	M	Merchant	Great Britain	United States	James Monroe	25 Apr 1822
Richard	24	M	Labourer	Ireland	United States	Catharine	22 Jul 1825
Richard	24	M	Merchant	G. Britan	U. States	Canada	27 Sep 1826
Richard, Mr.	38	M	Manufacturer	U.K. Gt. Britain	Great Britain	James Cropper	29 Nov 1827
Richd.	24	M	Farmer	Great Brittan	United States	Euphrates	12 Mar 1824
Robert	13	M		Ireland	America	Franklin	13 Aug 1827
Robert	19	M	Spinner	Great Britan	United States	Hamilton	19 Mar 1827
Robert	21	M	Farmer	Great Britan	United States	Hamilton	19 Mar 1827
Robert	23			Ireland	New York	Lady Hunter	19 Oct 1826
Robert	28	M	Weaver	Scotland	America	John Adams	2 Aug 1827
Robert	28	M		Ireland	United States	William & George	14 May 1828
Robert	30	M	Farmer	England	United States	Resign	7 Oct 1822
Robert	38	M	Labourer	G. Britain	U. States	Freak	9 Jun 1828
Robert	44		master	U. States	U. States	Mount Vernon	26 Aug 1820
Robert	50	M	Grocer	Scotland	unknown	Robert Edwards	4 Jun 1824
Robert	52	M	Merchant	America	America	James Cropper	14 Oct 1822
Robt.	12	M	None	Scotland	United States	Camillus	27 Oct 1829
Robt.	26			England		Anacreon	7 Sep 1827
Robt.	38	M	Merchant	United States	United States	John Jay	8 May 1828
Robt.	50	M	Gentleman	Ireland	U. States	Fame	15 Nov 1826
Rose	55	F	...	Ireland	United States	Carolina Ann	24 Oct 1825
Saml.	31	M	Merchant	U. States	U. States	Canada	19 Sep 1828
Samuel	22	M	Merchant	Gt. Britain	U. States	Canada	4 Oct 1824
Samuel	25	M	Merchant	England	United States	Nestor	20 Nov 1821
Samuel	60	M	...	Ireland	United States	Carolina Ann	24 Oct 1825
Sarah	8	F		G. Britain	U. States	St. George	7 Jun 1828
Sarah	22	F		Scotland	United States	Colossus	26 Aug 1828
Sarah	24			England		Anacreon	7 Sep 1827
Sarah A.	35	F		New York	U. States	William Thompson	6 Sep 1822
Sophia	35	F		Jamaica	U. States	Rubicon	2 Jun 1828
Susan M.	25	F	None	U. States	U. States	Canada	12 May 1828
T. M.	25	M	Mariner	Germany	United States	Howard	15 Jun 1825
Thomas	2/12	M		Ireland	United States	William & George	14 May 1828
Thomas	22	M	Blockmaker	United States	United States	St. Michaels	23 Dec 1826
Thomas	24	M		England	New York	Lady Hunter	5 Jun 1826
Thomas	27	M	Farmer	Ireland	America	Minerva	31 May 1824
Thomas	27		Farmer	England	United States	Corinthian	30 May 1828
Thomas	40	M	Porter	C. Dary	N. Jersey	Nile	18 Aug 1829
Thomas	49	M	Spinner	Great Britan	United States	Hamilton	19 Mar 1827
Thomas	65	M	Farmer	Ireland	America	Franklin	13 Aug 1827
Thomas, Jr.	20	M	Spinner	Great Britan	United States	Hamilton	19 Mar 1827
Thomas, Mr.	23		Merchant	England	returns to England	Mary	21 Sep 1821
Thos.	4		Labourer	England	United States	Hugh Johnson	11 Jun 1828
Thos.	25		Merchant	England		Corinthian	11 Mar 1829
Thos.	30	M	Farmer	Ireland	U. States	Dickinson	30 Jul 1825
Thos.	52	M	Merchant	Gt. Britain	United States	Seeds	29 Sep 1824
W.	28	M	Mechanic	American	U. States	Pacification	6 Oct 1823
W.	37	M	Merchant	S. Carolina	U. States	Almira	8 Aug 1822

NAMES OF PASSENGERS	AGE	SEX	OCCUPATIONS	COUNTRY TO WHICH THEY BELONG	COUNTRY THEY INTEND TO INHABIT	SHIPS/DATES OF ARRIVAL	
THOMPSON (cont'd)							
W.	44	M		Ireland	U. States	Fame	15 Nov 1826
Walter	30	M	Weaver	Scotland	New York	Joseph Hume	26 Oct 1829
Walter	36	M	Gentleman	Great Britain	U. States	Importer	21 Feb 1820
William	2	M	None	Great Britan	United States	Hamilton	19 Mar 1827
William	3 6/12	M	Child			Criterion	27 Oct 1820
William	4	M	None	Scotland	United States	Camillus	27 Oct 1829
William	11	M	None	Scotland	U. States	Czar	29 Aug 1829
William	18	M	Stone Mason	Great Britain	United States	Samuel Wright	12 Oct 1829
William	22	M		England	New York	Lady Hunter	5 Jun 1826
William	22	M	Labourer	Ireland	U. States	Wanderer	1 Sep 1828
William	25	M	Farmer	Ireland	United States	Dublin Packet	22 Aug 1829
William	26 10/12	M	Miller	Great Briton	United States	Mount Vernon	30 Dec 1828
William	30	M		Ireland	United States	William & George	14 May 1828
William	31	M	Labourer	G. Britain	U. States	Freak	9 Jun 1828
William	45	M	Weaver	Great Britain	United States	Birmingham	15 Jun 1827
William	57	M	Weaver	England	New York	Lady Hunter	5 Jun 1826
William, Mr.	38	M	Manufacturer	U.K. Gt. Britain	Great Britain	James Cropper	29 Nov 1827
Willm.	29	M	Farmer	England	England	William Byrnes	14 Apr 1824
Wm.	3/12	F				Eliza Grant	6 Oct 1828
Wm.	3	M	None	Great Britain	U. States	William Thompson	29 Jan 1823
Wm.	5	M	Farmer	Argyle (Tedland) Scotland	United States	Jean Hastie	27 Jul 1829
Wm.	21	M	Mason	England	U. States	Shallet	21 Apr 1821
Wm.	22	M	Farmer	Great Britian	United States	Robert Quayle	29 Jul 1822
Wm.	24	M	Blacksmith	Great Britain		Moro Castle	6 Jul 1827
Wm.	25		Farmer	England	United States	Hugh Johnson	11 Jun 1828
Wm.	25	M	Stone Cutter	Scotland	U. States	Loire	18 Jul 1828
Wm.	27	M	Distiller	Ireland	United States	Clothier	22 Nov 1827
Wm.	27	M	Labourer	England	United States	Montgomery	6 Mar 1829
Wm.	35	M	Ca...ire	Argyle (Tedland) Scotland	United States	Jean Hastie	27 Jul 1829
Wm.	37	M	Farmer	Argyle (Tedland) Scotland	United States	Jean Hastie	27 Jul 1829
Wm.	40	M	Farmer	Glasgow	United States	Dalhousie Castle	27 Jul 1826
Wm.	45	M	Merchant	U. States	U. States	Osgood	9 Dec 1826
Wm.	46	M	Brewer	England	U. States	Panthea	22 Nov 1826
Wm., Jur.	16	M		England	U. States	Panthea	22 Nov 1826
Wm. D.	22	M	Gentleman	United States	United States	Elias Burger	25 Feb 1820
THOMS, William	15	M	Farmer	England	New York	Brighton	20 Aug 1825
THOMSON, —,							
Master	10/12	M		N. Jersey	U. States	Romeo	23 Jun 1823
—, Miss	4	F		N. Jersey	U. States	Romeo	23 Jun 1823
—, Mr.	34	M	Mariner	N. Jersey	U. States	Romeo	23 Jun 1823
A., Jr.	21	M	Merchant	United States	United States	New York	12 Nov 1822
Alexander	50	M	Merchant	Scotland	United States	Camillus	27 Oct 1829
Andrew	6	M	Child	Britain	America	Camillus	9 Oct 1820
Andrew	23	M	Farmer	Great Britain	United States	Friends	13 Jun 1825
Andrew	60	M	Farmer	Great Britain	United States	Friends	13 Jun 1825
Andrew, Jr.	50	M	Merchant	Scotland	Gt. Britain	Friends	29 Apr 1822
Ann	4	F	Child	Britain	America	Camillus	9 Oct 1820
Ann	7	F		G. Britain	U. States	Dalhouse Castle	12 Sep 1828
Berthia	5	F		Scotland	United States	Camillus	9 May 1827
Christian	31	F		Edinr., E...pi... [Parish], Edinr. [County]	New York	Hero	19 May 1828
*going with their friends							
Christopher	30	M	Moulder	England	America	Franklin	19 Nov 1828
David	22	M	Farmer	Scotland	United States	Commerce	17 Jul 1823
Edward	20	M	Weaver	Gt. Britain		Dalhouse Castle	13 May 1828
Edward D.	26	M	Gentleman	London	London	New York	14 Nov 1826
Edward H.	8	M	Child	Britain	America	Camillus	9 Oct 1820
Elizabeth	12	F	Child	Britain	America	Camillus	9 Oct 1820
Elizabeth	23	F		Scotland	United States	Commerce	17 Jul 1823
Elizabeth	40	F	Wife of do [James]	Britain	America	Camillus	9 Oct 1820
Francis	20	M	Labourer	Ireland	N. York	Trusty	12 Sep 1828
Francis	25	M		G. Britain	U. States	Dalhouse Castle	12 Sep 1828

NAMES OF PASSENGERS	AGE	SEX	OCCUPATIONS	COUNTRY TO WHICH THEY BELONG	COUNTRY THEY INTEND TO INHABIT	SHIPS/DATES OF ARRIVAL	
THOMSON (cont'd)							
George	27	M	Farmer	Great Britain	United States	Friends	13 Jun 1825
Hellen	19	F		Scotland	United States	Camillus	9 May 1827
Isabella	6	F		G. Britain	U. States	Dalhouse Castle	12 Sep 1828
James		M		Scotland	U.S.	Curler	19 Jul 1828
James	1 1/2	M				Harmony	15 Jul 1820
James	17	M		Scotland	United States	Camillus	9 May 1827
James	20	M	Labourer	Ireland	U. States	Josephine	7 May 1827
James	25	M	Weaver	Irland	United States	Nancy	28 Oct 1822
James	28	M	Clothier	Great Britain	United States	Colossus	1 Nov 1826
James	34	M	Paper Maker	Great Britain	United States	India	5 Sep 1827
James	45	M	Farmer	Britain	America	Camillus	9 Oct 1820
Jane	7	F		Scotland	United States	Camillus	9 May 1827
Jane F.	9	F	Child	Britain	America	Camillus	9 Oct 1820
Janet	4	F				Harmony	15 Jul 1820
Jas.	30	M	Laborer	Ireland	U. States	Albion	9 Aug 1826
Jas.	32	M	Merchant	U. States		Charleston Packet	4 May 1821
John	2	M		Scotland	United States	Commerce	17 Jul 1823
John	21	M	Farmer	Great Britain	United States	Ann	22 Dec 1821
John	26	M	Architect	Scotland	New York	Joseph Hume	26 Oct 1829
John	32	M	...	Scotland	United States	Louisiana	3 Nov 1827
Jos.	22	M	Saddler	U. States	U. States	Emigrant	20 Sep 1823
Joseph	28	M	Labourer	Ireland	United States	Hope	12 Jun 1828
Joseph H.	2	M	Child	Britain	America	Camillus	9 Oct 1820
Lanslot	25			Cumberland	Ohio	Peru	30 May 1828
Margaret	11	F		Scotland	United States	Camillus	9 May 1827
Margaret	44	F		Scotland	America	Eyder	7 Aug 1826
Margaret	57	F	None	Great Britain	United States	Friends	13 Jun 1825
Mary	2	F		Edinr., E...pi... [Parish], Edinr. [County]	New York	Hero	19 May 1828
*going with their friends							
Mary	19	F	None	Great Britain	United States	Friends	13 Jun 1825
N., Mr. of Philia.	38	M	Merchant, Phild.	America	America	Henry	19 Jun 1825
Nancey	22	F		Irland	United States	Nancy	28 Oct 1822
Peter	23	M	Chemist	Great Britain	United States	Elizabeth & Mary	20 Mar 1828
R.	4	M		G. Britain	U. States	Dalhouse Castle	12 Sep 1828
Robert	35	M		Scotland	Uncertain	Britannia	22 Jul 1829
Roderick	25		Spinster	Great Britain	United States	Camillus	12 Sep 1827
Rt.	8/12	M		Edinr., E...pi... [Parish], Edinr. [County]	New York	Hero	19 May 1828
*going with their friends							
Sophia	4	F		Scotland	United States	Camillus	9 May 1827
Sophia	40	F		Scotland	United States	Camillus	9 May 1827
Susan	20	F	Servant	Ireland	United States	Carolina Ann	14 May 1827
Thomas E.	28	M	Mercht.	G.B.	G.B.	George Canning	2 May 1828
William	3	M		Scotland	United States	Camillus	9 May 1827
William	26	M	Farmer	Ireland	United States	Fabius	4 Jun 1828
William	28	M	Farmer	Great Britain	United States	Friends	13 Jun 1825
William	30	M	Mason	Great Britain	United States	Rosina	28 May 1827
Wm.	8	M		Edinr., E...pi... [Parish], Edinr. [County]	New York	Hero	19 May 1828
*going with their friends							
Wm.	28	M	Butcher	G. Britain	U. States	Dalhouse Castle	12 Sep 1828
Wm.	41	M	Labourer	Edinr., E...pi... [Parish], Edinr. [County]	New York	Hero	19 May 1828
*to look for employment							
THOMSTON, John	30		Labourer	Great Britan	United States	Newry	11 Jul 1827
THOMY, John	24	M	Painter	Ireland	America	Parrington	9 Jun 1827
THON, ...	25 4/12	F	Farmer	Switzerland	U. States	France	26 Jun 1828
THONKE, Carl Edw.	26	M	Cloth manufacturer	Germany	New York	Maria Elizabeth	16 Mar 1829
THONN, Ann Maria	4	F		G. Britain	U. States	Wanderer	23 Jun 1828
Robt.	34	M	Farmer	G. Britain	U. States	Wanderer	23 Jun 1828

1249

NAMES OF PASSENGERS	AGE	SEX	OCCUPATIONS	COUNTRY TO WHICH THEY BELONG	COUNTRY THEY INTEND TO INHABIT	SHIPS/DATES OF ARRIVAL	
THONSBIEURG,							
Catherine	9	F	Farmer	Switzerland	United States	Olympia	12 Aug 1828
Frederich	1	M	Farmer	Switzerland	United States	Olympia	12 Aug 1828
George	40	M	Farmer	Switzerland	United States	Olympia	12 Aug 1828
Joannah	4	F	Farmer	Switzerland	United States	Olympia	12 Aug 1828
Marie	7	F	Farmer	Switzerland	United States	Olympia	12 Aug 1828
Marie	52	F	Farmer	Switzerland	United States	Olympia	12 Aug 1828
THORBAM, John	27	M	Merchant	Scotland	U. States	General Graham	9 May 1827
THORBUCK, F. R.	36	M	Merchant	Germany	U. States	John London	1 Sep 1823
THORBURN, A.	29	M	Merchant	Scotland	U. States	Birmingham	12 Oct 1827
Catharine	36	F	...maker	Scotland	U. States	Roger Stewart	9 Jun 1828
Ellen	22	F	None	Scotland	U. States	Camillus	27 Jul 1825
Ellison	10/12			Ireland	U. States	Josephine	27 Jul 1825
George	36	M	...maker	Scotland	U. States	Roger Stewart	9 Jun 1828
Margaret	9	F	...maker	Scotland	U. States	Roger Stewart	9 Jun 1828
Marion	2 1/2	F	None	Ireland	U. States	Josephine	27 Jul 1825
William	28	M	Gardiner	Scotland	U. States	Camillus	27 Jul 1825
THORENCER, A.	22	M	Merchant	France	U. States	Edwd. Quesnel	30 Apr 1825
THORLEY, John	25	M	Machine Maker	Great Britain	United States	Orbit	23 Oct 1826
THORMBALL, John	26	M	Farmer	G. Britain	G. Britain	Brittania	17 Jul 1828
THORN, —, Mr.	36	M	Gent.	England	United States	Warrior	6 Oct 1828
..., Miss	25	F	Lady	United States	United	Greyhound	27 Nov 1820
Catherine	40	F		G. Britain	Canada	Nancy	12 Aug 1820
Edward	40	M	Merchant	New Brunswick	Great Brittain	Nancy	9 Jun 1821
Ewd.	50			Halifax	U. States	Edwin	26 Sep 1828
Jas.	16	M		Ireland	U. States	Greenhow	10 Mar 1823
John	25	M	Carpenter	G. Brittain	U. States	Cincinnatus	2 Oct 1822
Levis S.	7/12	M	Child	United States	United	Greyhound	27 Nov 1820
Mary	26	F		G. Britain	U. States	Wanderer	23 Jun 1828
Mary	27	F		G. Brittain	U. States	Cincinnatus	2 Oct 1822
R.	3	M		G. Britain	U. States	Wanderer	23 Jun 1828
Robert	30	M	Laborer	Great Britian	United States	Columbia	17 Apr 1827
S.	20			Halifax	U. States	Edwin	26 Sep 1828
Saml.	1 8/12	M		G. Britain	U. States	Wanderer	23 Jun 1828
THORNBEE, John	22	M	Pattern Maker	England	U.S. America	Columbia	31 Jul 1826
THORNBY, Margaret	8	M				Splendid	14 Aug 1829
Mary	11	M	Labourer			Splendid	14 Aug 1829
Mary	30	M	Labourer			Splendid	14 Aug 1829
Wm.	1	M				Splendid	14 Aug 1829
THORNCROFT, William	24	M	Farmer			Acosta	28 Jul 1823
THORNDIKE, Andw.	30	M	Merchant	U. States	U. States	Draper	18 Nov 1822
Ano.,	2	M	Merchant	Massachusetts	U. States	Draper	18 Jun 1822
THORNE, Benjamin	33		Merchant	England	Upper Canada	Xenophon	25 Jul 1826
John	30	M	Farmer	England	United States	Cincinnatus	21 Nov 1821
THORNHILL, Emma	1	F	Gent		United States	Cosmo	21 Aug 1828
Lydia	29	F	Gent		United States	Cosmo	21 Aug 1828
THORNLEY, James	48	M	Weaver & Warper	England	United States	Andes	2 Oct 1828
THORNNBY, Wm.	35	M	Labourer			Splendid	14 Aug 1829
THORNTON, Ann	6	F	None	Haddersfield		Aurora	8 Jun 1827
Betty	32	F	None	Haddersfield		Aurora	8 Jun 1827
Eliz.	9	F		England	United States	Curler	3 Mar 1828
Eliza	35	F	None	England	United States	Nestor	20 Nov 1821
Elizabeth	4...	F	...	G. Brittain	America	Robin Hood	20 Jul 1827
Ellen	24	F	None	Ireland		Marchioness	13 May 1828
G.	26	M	Carpenter	U. States	U. States	Signal	3 Jan 1826
Isaac	19	M	Labourer	Ireland		Marchioness	13 May 1828
Jane	17	F	None	Ireland	United States	Mary & Harriet	3 Jul 1829
Jno.	23	M	Grocer	G.B.	G.B.	Cadmus	26 Apr 1824
John	10	M	None	England	United States	Nestor	20 Nov 1821
John	30	M	Labourer	Haddersfield		Aurora	8 Jun 1827
Jonathan	29	M	Labourer	Haddersfield		Aurora	8 Jun 1827
Joseph	6	M	None	England	United States	Nestor	20 Nov 1821
Joseph	48	M	Manufacturer	Great Brittain	America	Pacific	13 Jan 1827
Maria	10	F	...	G. Brittain	America	Robin Hood	20 Jul 1827
Mary	11/12	F	None	Haddersfield		Aurora	8 Jun 1827
Mary	12	F	None	England	United States	Nestor	20 Nov 1821
Mary	17	F	Spinstress			Orion	21 Aug 1820
Mary	18	F	None	England	United States	Nestor	20 Nov 1821
Rebecca	11	F		England	United States	Curler	3 Mar 1828

NAMES OF PASSENGERS	AGE	SEX	OCCUPATIONS	COUNTRY TO WHICH THEY BELONG	COUNTRY THEY INTEND TO INHABIT	SHIPS/DATES OF ARRIVAL	
THORNTON (cont'd)							
Richard	10	M				Orion	21 Aug 1820
Richard	23	M	Farmer	Great Britian	United States	Andes	19 Aug 1829
Sarah	3	F	...	G. Brittain	America	Robin Hood	20 Jul 1827
Sarah	37	F		England	United States	Curler	3 Mar 1828
Thomas	7	M		England	United States	Curler	3 Mar 1828
Thomas	8	M	None	England	United States	Nestor	20 Nov 1821
Thomas	36	M	...	G. Brittain	America	Robin Hood	20 Jul 1827
Wm.	5	M		England	United States	Curler	3 Mar 1828
Wm.	33	M	Farmer	England	U. States	James Cropper	10 Jun 1823
THORNVILLE, G. C.	40	M	Merchant	England	United States	Comet	24 Dec 1821
S.	32	F				Comet	24 Dec 1821
THORP, —, Mrs.	18	F			U. States	Criterion at London	10 May 1821
Daniel	9	M	Farmer	England	New Jersey	Chelsea	16 May 1828
Elizabeth	41	F	Farmer	England	New Jersey	Chelsea	16 May 1828
Elizabeth	50	F		Great Britain	New York	Radius	7 Jul 1821
Francis	1	M	Farmer	England	New Jersey	Chelsea	16 May 1828
Harriet	14	F	Farmer	England	New Jersey	Chelsea	16 May 1828
Issachar	23	M	Gentm.	Manchester	Philadela.	Hector	30 Dec 1820
James	20	M	Farmer	England	New Jersey	Chelsea	16 May 1828
James	25	M	Labourer	Great Britian	United States	William Dawson	18 Jun 1827
Jno.	17	M	Labourer	England	United States	Essex	23 May 1828
John	5	M		Great Britain	New York	Radius	7 Jul 1821
John	23	M	Labourer	Great Britian	United States	William Dawson	18 Jun 1827
John	29	M	Merchant	England	United States	Indian Chief	16 Aug 1822
John	45	M	Bleecher	England	U. States	Camillus	27 Jul 1825
John	52	M	Merchant	Great Britian	Great Britain	Martha	25 Nov 1820
John, & family	53	M	Farmer	England	New Jersey	Chelsea	16 May 1828
Mary	4	F	Farmer	England	New Jersey	Chelsea	16 May 1828
Rebbecca	45	F			U. States	Camillus	27 Jul 1825
Richard	11	M	Farmer	England	New Jersey	Chelsea	16 May 1828
Salena	17	F		Great Britain	New York	Radius	7 Jul 1821
Thirza	11	F			U. States	Criterion at London	10 May 1821
Thomas	16	M	Farmer	England	New Jersey	Chelsea	16 May 1828
THORPE, Abraham	30	M	Taylor	Gt. Britain	United States	Meteor	19 Aug 1829
Isaac	8	M		Gt. Britain	United States	Meteor	19 Aug 1829
Jno.	30	M	Carpenter	Ireland	United States	Margarett Scott	22 Aug 1827
Joseph	5	M		Gt. Britain	United States	Meteor	19 Aug 1829
Sarah	29	F		Gt. Britain	United States	Meteor	19 Aug 1829
William	7	M		Gt. Britain	United States	Meteor	19 Aug 1829
THORSPICKEND, J.	22	M	Merchant	Germany	U. States	Dido	26 Apr 1825
THORTON, Allice	20	F	Spinstress	Ireland		Orion	21 Aug 1820
Jane	13	F		England	United States	Curler	3 Mar 1828
Mary	52	F	Spinstress	Ireland	United States	Orion	21 Aug 1820
THORZ, C.	30	M	Merchant	France	France	Eliza	28 Apr 1827
THOTON, Wm.	40	M	Farmer	England	United States	Curler	3 Mar 1828
THOUET, Annah	62		Farmer	France	U. States	Elizabeth	9 Jul 1825
David	32		Farmer	France	U. States	Elizabeth	9 Jul 1825
John	24		Farmer	France	U. States	Elizabeth	9 Jul 1825
Madeline	22		Farmer	France	U. States	Elizabeth	9 Jul 1825
Peter	56		Farmer	France	U. States	Elizabeth	9 Jul 1825
Peter, Jr.	19		Farmer	France	U. States	Elizabeth	9 Jul 1825
THOUVENIN, A.	24	M	Merchant	U. States	U.S.	Edward Quesnel	21 Apr 1827
THRAITS, Josha.	29	M	Mercht.	England	Buenos Ayres	Perserverance	2 Mar 1822
THRASHER, B.	28	M	Baker	U.S.	U.S.	Mary Ann	1 Jun 1822
THREADWAY,							
David	1 6/12	M	Farmer	Ireland	U. States	Napolean	26 Sep 1828
James	28	M	Farmer	Ireland	U. States	Napolean	26 Sep 1828
Jane	5	M	Farmer	Ireland	U. States	Napolean	26 Sep 1828
John	3	M	Farmer	Ireland	U. States	Napolean	26 Sep 1828
Mary	27	M	Farmer	Ireland	U. States	Napolean	26 Sep 1828
William	0 3/12	M	Farmer	Ireland	U. States	Napolean	26 Sep 1828
THRIM, Edward	32	M	Merchant	Ireland	America	Carolina Ann	7 Aug 1826
Elizabeth	28	F		Ireland	America	Carolina Ann	7 Aug 1826
THROCKMORTON, Jno.	50	M	Merchant	U. States	Canada	Loire	4 Oct 1824
THRUSON, Ann	28	F	Servant	Scotland	United States	Camillus	27 Oct 1829
THRUSTER, Davy	21	M	Weaver	Scotland		France	28 Mar 1829

NAMES OF PASSENGERS	AGE	SEX	OCCUPATIONS	COUNTRY TO WHICH THEY BELONG	COUNTRY THEY INTEND TO INHABIT	SHIPS/DATES OF ARRIVAL	
THUFFEE, F. A.	22	M	Farmer	Switzerland	America	Don Quixotte	2 Jun 1828
THULER, Anne	18	F	Farmer	Biglen	U.S. America	Superior	18 Jun 1825
Benoit	10	M	Farmer	Biglen	U.S. America	Superior	18 Jun 1825
Elizabeth	4	F	Farmer	Biglen	U.S. America	Superior	18 Jun 1825
Elizabeth	41	F	Farmer	Biglen	U.S. America	Superior	18 Jun 1825
Jean	15	M	Farmer	Biglen	U.S. America	Superior	18 Jun 1825
Jean	41	M	Farmer	Biglen	U.S. America	Superior	18 Jun 1825
Margerritte	2	F	Farmer	Biglen	U.S. America	Superior	18 Jun 1825
Nicolas	8	M	Farmer	Biglen	U.S. America	Superior	18 Jun 1825
THULWELL, William	27	M	Mason	England	New York	Lima	5 Aug 1829
William	27	M	Maison	England	U. States	Lima	5 Aug 1829
THURCELIN, Alex M.	22	M	Baker	France	U. States	America	22 Sep 1826
THURLES, Abm.	2	M		York, Great Britain		Casanda	5 Sep 1827
Allen	1	M		York, Great Britain		Casanda	5 Sep 1827
Eliza	4	M		York, Great Britain		Casanda	5 Sep 1827
Geo.	28	F	None	York, Great Britain		Casanda	5 Sep 1827
John	22	M	Gardner	G. Britain		Casanda	5 Sep 1827
Martha	6	F		York, Great Britain		Casanda	5 Sep 1827
Mary	24	F	None	York, Great Britain		Casanda	5 Sep 1827
THURLEY, ...	23	M	Farmer		New York	Hesperus	2 Nov 1820
THURSTON, John	10	M	Farmer	Great Britian	United States	Columbia	17 Apr 1827
THUXTER, J. H.	25	M	Optioner	U. States	U. States	Ann	16 Mar 1826
THWAITE, John	56	M	Labourer	Great Britain	Cannada	Columbia	1 Dec 1823
THWALD, John	20	M	Watchmaker	Switzerland	U.S.	Francois I	8 Aug 1829
THYHURST, Carolin	6	F		England	U. States	Emily	25 Aug 1827
Margaret	18/12	F		England	U. States	Emily	25 Aug 1827
Mary, Mrs.	28	F	Milliner	England	U. States	Emily	25 Aug 1827
Mary A.	8	F		England	U. States	Emily	25 Aug 1827
Richard	4	M		England	U. States	Emily	25 Aug 1827
THYNOR, Owen	28	M	Farmer	Ireland	United States	Concordia	25 Aug 1827
TIAVON, Edward	26	M	Printer	England	U.S.	Pacific	24 Oct 1828
TIBAND, F.	26		Baker	Suisse	New York	Manchester	30 May 1821
TIBBETTS, Jas.	29	M	Mechanic	U. States	U. States	Radius	18 Apr 1825
TIBBITTS, Samuel	23		Farmer	Ma...	...	Hudson	14 Jun 1827
TIBMAN, John	27	M	Watch Maker	Great Britain	United States	Aspasia	16 Jul 1828
TICE, William	40	M	Tailor	United States	United States	Brighton	12 Jun 1826
TICHLING, Philip	60	M	Farmer	Alsace in the Department of Upper and lower Rhine	United States	Carolina Augusta	16 May 1828
TICKER, J.	31	M	Farmer	United States	U. States	Reindeer	29 Jun 1827
TIEBARD, J.	28	M	Merchant	Havre	Havre	Mary Emily	10 Jun 1825
TIEFFENBACH, Theophile Henry	36	M	Cabinet Maker	Switzerland	America	Bolivar	2 Oct 1826
Theophile Henry, Jr.	15	M		Switzerland	America	Bolivar	2 Oct 1826
TIEMAN, Caroline	12	F				Brighton	19 Aug 1829
Margaret	17	F				Brighton	19 Aug 1829
TIEMBERGER, A. W.	35	F		Philada.	U. States	Brandt	11 Oct 1824
TIENMAN, Ferdinans	29	M		Hesse	United States	Constitution	2 Aug 1826
George	52	M	Chirurgical Instrument Maker	Hesse	United States	Constitution	2 Aug 1826
Julius	56	M	Merchant	America	United States	Constitution	2 Aug 1826
Nicolaus	14	M		America	United States	Constitution	2 Aug 1826
TIER, Christie	18	F		England		Anacreon	7 Sep 1827
John	12	M	None	Isle of Man	United States	Aurelia	7 Jun 1826
John	65	M	Labourer	Isle of Man	United States	Aurelia	7 Jun 1826
Judy	16	F	None	Isle of Man	United States	Aurelia	7 Jun 1826
Judy	40	F	None	Isle of Man	United States	Aurelia	7 Jun 1826
Margaret	3	F	None	Isle of Man	United States	Aurelia	7 Jun 1826
Thomas	7	M	None	Isle of Man	United States	Aurelia	7 Jun 1826
Thomas	28	M	Labourer	G. Britain	U. States	Nimrod	31 Jul 1828
William	40	M	Fisherman	Isle of Man	United States	Aurelia	7 Jun 1826
Willm.	13	M	None	Isle of Man	United States	Aurelia	7 Jun 1826

NAMES OF PASSENGERS	AGE	SEX	OCCUPATIONS	COUNTRY TO WHICH THEY BELONG	COUNTRY THEY INTEND TO INHABIT	SHIPS/DATES OF ARRIVAL	
TIER (cont'd)							
Wm.	40	M	Labourer	G. Britain	U. States	Nimrod	31 Jul 1828
TIERNAY, Hugh	...	M	...	Ireland	United States	Carolina Ann	24 Oct 1825
TIERNEY, De.	40	M	Laborer	Ireland	United States	Trio	13 Jun 1827
Jno.	43	M	Laborer	Ireland	United States	Trio	13 Jun 1827
TIERNNEY, Hate	35	F		Ireland	United States	Trio	13 Jun 1827
Jerh.	6	M	Laborer	Ireland	United States	Trio	13 Jun 1827
John	10	M	Laborer	Ireland	United States	Trio	13 Jun 1827
TIESTE, M. J.	19	M	Merchant	Cuba	U. States	Brown	29 Apr 1825
TIETYEN, Martin	20		...	Breman	Germany	Hudson	14 Jun 1827
TIFFENBACK, Suset	14	F	None	Switzerland	America	Bolivar	2 Oct 1826
TIFFETT, Thos.	30	M	Mariner	U. States	U. States	Morning Star	6 Oct 1823
TIFFINY, Eliza	20	F	Taylor	Ireland	U. States	Virginia	20 Jun 1825
TIKLING, Catherine	3	F	Farmer	Alsace in the Department of Upper and lower Rhine	United States	Carolina Augusta	16 May 1828
Christiana	10	F	Farmer	Alsace in the Department of Upper and lower Rhine	United States	Carolina Augusta	16 May 1828
Elza	15	F	Farmer	Alsace in the Department of Upper and lower Rhine	United States	Carolina Augusta	16 May 1828
George	32	M	Farmer	Alsace in the Department of Upper and lower Rhine	United States	Carolina Augusta	16 May 1828
Michael	27	M	Farmer	Alsace in the Department of Upper and lower Rhine	United States	Carolina Augusta	16 May 1828
Salome	18	F	Farmer	Alsace in the Department of Upper and lower Rhine	United States	Carolina Augusta	16 May 1828
Salome	53	F	Farmer	Alsace in the Department of Upper and lower Rhine	United States	Carolina Augusta	16 May 1828
TILBY, Elizabeth	4	F		U. States	United States	Crisis	6 Apr 1825
Elizabeth	30	F		U. States	United States	Crisis	6 Apr 1825
Jno.	30	M	Physician	U. States	United States	Crisis	6 Apr 1825
Jno., Jr.	1 6/12	M		U. States	United States	Crisis	6 Apr 1825
TILDEN, Bryant P.	40 6/12	M	Merchant	United States	Boston, U.S.	Amity	31 Jan 1822
Bryant P.	45	M	Merchant	United States A.	United States	Circassian	27 Dec 1827
T. B.	23	M	Navy	Baltimore	U. States	Romulus	7 Oct 1822
Thos. B.	28	M	U.S. Officer	U. States	U. States	Columbia	1 Dec 1824
TILISTON, Nathaniel	28	M	Boston	Boston	U. States	Paquet Des Cayes	11 Oct 1827
TILL, Eliza	18	F		England	U. States	Nile	15 Aug 1823
TILLER, Lorentz	30	M	Cooper	France	United States	Cavalier	25 Jul 1828
TILLERTON, Agnes	21	F	Farmer	Great Britian	U. States	Henry Kneedland	7 Aug 1826
Saml.	21	M	Farmer	Great Britian	U. States	Henry Kneedland	7 Aug 1826
TILLEY, Amelia		F	None	United States	United States	Hero	5 Jul 1822
Anth., Mr.	69	M	Gent.	Gt. Britain	England	James Cropper	2 Aug 1827
James M.	18		Clerk	United States	United States	South Carolina Packet	18 Apr 1826
James M.	22	M	Gentn.	U.N. States	U.N. States	William Byrnes	13 Aug 1829
Maria, Miss	28	F	None	Gt. Britain	England	James Cropper	2 Aug 1827
William, Mrs.	24	M	Glassblower	England	United States	Maria	29 Sep 1823
TILLING, T.	18	M	Labourer	Ireland	U. States	Loire	6 Dec 1827
TILLMANN, August	2	M		Germany	Jersey	Columbia	5 Oct 1824
Catharine	11	F		Germany	Jersey	Columbia	5 Oct 1824
Christina	3	F		Germany	Jersey	Columbia	5 Oct 1824
Ernest	6	M		Germany	Jersey	Columbia	5 Oct 1824

NAMES OF PASSENGERS	AGE	SEX	OCCUPATIONS	COUNTRY TO WHICH THEY BELONG	COUNTRY THEY INTEND TO INHABIT	SHIPS/DATES OF ARRIVAL	
TILLMANN (cont'd)							
Peter	34	M	...	Germany	Jersey	Columbia	5 Oct 1824
Sophia, Mrs.	34	F		Germany	Jersey	Columbia	5 Oct 1824
TILLOTSON, J., Mr.	33	M	Gentleman			Henri IV	14 Sep 1827
M., Mr.	27	F				Henri IV	14 Sep 1827
Margt.	3 6/12	F				Henri IV	14 Sep 1827
TILLY, James	19	M	Shoemaker	Ireland	United States	Trident	17 May 1825
TILMORE, James	50	M	Farmer	England	U.N. States	Helen	17 Dec 1827
TILSON, Edwin	19	M	Painter	England	New York	Brighton	9 Dec 1828
John	21	M	Farmer	Ireland	U. States	William	27 Jul 1824
TILT, Eliza	26	F	Seamstress	Ireland	U. States	Atlantic	19 Aug 1825
Jane	6	F	Seamstress	Ireland	U. States	Atlantic	19 Aug 1825
Jas.	1 1/2	M	Farmer	Ireland	U. States	Atlantic	19 Aug 1825
TILTON, ...w	24	M	Laborer	Ireland	United States	Trio	13 Jun 1827
Besey	13	F		U. States	U. States	Nimrod	1 Jun 1821
Catherin	11	F		U. States	U. States	Nimrod	1 Jun 1821
Charles	1	F		U. States	U. States	Nimrod	1 Jun 1821
Charles	6	M		U. States	U. States	Nimrod	1 Jun 1821
Debby Ann	3	F		U. States	U. States	Nimrod	1 Jun 1821
E.	22	M	Joiner			Eliza Jane	12 Sep 1820
Elizabeth	16	F	Spinster	Ireland		William Tell	24 Oct 1829
Hannah	6	F		U. States	U. States	Nimrod	1 Jun 1821
Hannah	37	F		U. States	U. States	Nimrod	1 Jun 1821
John	17	M		U. States	U. States	Nimrod	1 Jun 1821
Mary Ann	15	F		U. States	U. States	Nimrod	1 Jun 1821
Samuel	43	M	Farmer	U. States	U. States	Nimrod	1 Jun 1821
William	23	M	Merchant	U. States	U. States	Rodman	22 Mar 1825
TIM..., John	23		Sugar Baker	Germany	Germany	London	16 Aug 1824
TIMAN, Caroline	12	F	None	England	New York	Brighton	19 Aug 1829
James	50	M	Turner	England	New York	Brighton	19 Aug 1829
James	50	M	Farmer			Brighton	19 Aug 1829
John	6	M	None			Brighton	19 Aug 1829
Margaret	17	F	None	England	New York	Brighton	19 Aug 1829
Margaret	42	F	None	England	New York	Brighton	19 Aug 1829
TIMENS, Jno.	22	M	Merchant	Gt. Britain	Great Britain	Martha	4 Oct 1822
TIMKINS, Benj.	30	M	Potter	England	U.N.S.	Helen	16 Mar 1829
Richard	23		Merchant	England	New York	Xenophon	25 Jul 1826
TIMLTY, Elinor	12	F		County of Down, Ireland	U. States	Lady Washington	16 Oct 1821
TIMMERMAN, Henry	24	M	Blacksmith	Germany	U. States	Hudson	10 Nov 1825
TIMMERS, John	27	M	Baker	Ireland	United States	Belleville	13 Oct 1827
TIMMING, Samuel, Mr.	40		Farmer	England		Hercules	19 Jun 1821
TIMMINGS, John	22	M	Farmer	Ireland	United States	Dublin Packet	22 Aug 1829
TIMMINS, Frances	24	F	Wife	United States	United States	Pacific	24 Oct 1828
Frs.	21	M	None	Gt. Britain	Great Britain	Martha	4 Oct 1822
John S.	24	M	Merchant	New York	America	William Thompson	18 Jan 1825
John S.	28	M	Mercht.	United States	United States	Pacific	24 Oct 1828
TIMMONS, Charles	21	M	Farmer	England	United States	Jubilee	1 Oct 1828
G.	38	M	Merchant	U. States	U. States	Emma	24 Jun 1822
John	26		Labourer	Ireland	United States	Geo. Canning	5 Jun 1828
John S.	26	M	Merchant	Great Britain	United States	Pacific	7 May 1827
Philip	41	M	Labourer	G. Britain	U. States	Nimrod	31 Jul 1828
TIMMONY, Patrick	28	M	Merchant	U. States	U. States	Virginia	8 Mar 1828
TIMMORY, John	20	M	...	Ireland	United States	Carolina Ann	24 Oct 1825
TINALE, Claudia	36	M	Painter	Mexico	Germany	Conveyance	15 Jan 1827
TINCH, John	30	M	Gentleman	England	U. States	Acasta	28 Jan 1823
TINCKERLAND, Robt.	23	M	Black Smith	Scotland	United States	Essex	23 May 1828
TINCKSELY, Joh. Georg	18	M	Carpenter	Wirtemburg	United States	Wade	29 Aug 1825
TINDALE, Ruchton	17	M	Farmer	Great Britain	United States	Hamilton	21 Nov 1826
TINDALL, Catharine	64	F	None	Great Britain	United States	Hamilton	21 Nov 1826
Catharine, Junr.	22	F	None	Great Britain	United States	Hamilton	21 Nov 1826
TINDELL, Peter	40			Ireland	United States	Trio	13 Jun 1827
TING, John	23	M	Shoemaker	Ireland	United States	Catharine	22 Jul 1825
TINGHAM, James	35	M	Farmer	England	America	Corinthian	1 Sep 1827
TINGLE, ...	31	F		Great Britian	United States	London	24 Jun 1823
...	33	M	Merchant	Great Britian	United States	London	24 Jun 1823
Ann	35	F		U. States	U. States	Genl. Victoria	7 Apr 1828

NAMES OF PASSENGERS	AGE	SEX	OCCUPATIONS	COUNTRY TO WHICH THEY BELONG	COUNTRY THEY INTEND TO INHABIT	SHIPS/DATES OF ARRIVAL	
TINGLE (cont'd)							
Henry	25	M	Shoemaker	Great Britain	United States	Diana	6 Jul 1829
Thos.	65	M		England	America	Corinthian	1 Sep 1827
TINGLEY, A.	41	M	Merchant	Massachs.	U. States	Pomona	26 Jul 1821
TINKER, Thomas	34	M	Farmer	England	Kentuckey	Indian Chief	16 Aug 1822
TINKHAM, —, Mrs.	28			New York	New York	Orbit	31 Dec 1823
TINNEY, Kitty	20	F	None	Ireland	United States	Jubilee	1 Oct 1828
TIO, James	25	M	Merchant	Spain	Matanzas	Edgar	11 Feb 1824
TIPLADY, Sarah	24	F		Great Britain	United States	Diana	6 Jul 1829
Thos.	18	M	Farmer	Great Britain	United States	Diana	6 Jul 1829
TIPLING, William	31	M	Farrier	England	Canada	Governor Fenner	23 Jul 1829
TIPPING, Catherine	30	F	Lady	Ireland	United States	St. Michael	24 Jun 1824
TIRRENCE, Alex	30	M	Teacher	Scotland	United States	Margaret Bogle	11 Jun 1824
TISDALE, James	22	M	Mason	Ireland	United States	Carolina Ann	14 May 1827
John	28	M	Farmer	England	United States	Jubilee	13 Jul 1829
TISONBERG, Casper	51		Weaver	Germany	United States	Brandt	26 Jun 1826
TITCOMB, Caroline	12		Servant	Denmark	U. States	South Carolina Packet	4 Sep 1822
TITHE, Peter	27	M	Glacksmith	Great Briton	New York	Brighton	12 Jun 1826
TITICER, Henry	36	M	Gent.	France	U. States	Cadmus	28 May 1821
TITLER, Wm. A.	22	M	Book Seller	Germany	U. States	Jane	11 Jul 1828
TITTUS, Edward	24	M	Farmer	Great Britain	United States	Ganges	8 Jul 1820
TITUS, David Marshall	3	M		Ireland	Canada	Wanderer	31 Aug 1829
Deborah Jane	5	F		Ireland	Canada	Wanderer	31 Aug 1829
Elizabeth	38	F	Farmer	Ireland	Canada	Wanderer	31 Aug 1829
Henry Albert	9	M		Ireland	Canada	Wanderer	31 Aug 1829
John	12	M		Ireland	Canada	Wanderer	31 Aug 1829
Jonathan	7	M		Ireland	Canada	Wanderer	31 Aug 1829
Margaret Ann	16	F		Ireland	Canada	Wanderer	31 Aug 1829
Thomas Clark	4/12	M		Ireland	Canada	Wanderer	31 Aug 1829
TIVNIN, Dennis	20	M		Ireland	U.S. of America	Douglass	6 Jul 1829
TLAMMER, Theophilus	21	M	Farmer	Germany	United States	Helen	5 Sep 1828
TO...ER, Pat	26	M	Labourer	Ireland	United States	Aurelia	7 Jun 1826
TO...LER, Ann	19	F	Dress Maker	Ireland	United States	Carolina Ann	14 May 1827
TO...LEY, John	33	M	Labourer	Ireland	United States	Lord Wellington	28 May 1827
TOAFFE, Ann	4			Great Britan	United States	Newry	11 Jul 1827
Ann	30			Great Britan	United States	Newry	11 Jul 1827
Law	35		Farmer	Great Britan	United States	Newry	11 Jul 1827
TOAL, Willm.	27	M	Servt.	Ireland	America	Josephine	8 Dec 1827
TOBAANA, Abraham	27	M		Leohar...r	Jamaica	Little Cherub	11 Aug 1825
TOBAY, Wm.	24	M	Laborer	...	United States	Combine	20 Nov 1824
TOBE, Henry	38	M	Sugar Baker	Prussia	United States	Richmond	4 Aug 1826
TOBELL, Benj.	22	M	Carpenter	Germany	America	Saluda	18 Jun 1825
TOBEN, Edward	30	M	Mariner	Nova Scotia	Nova Scotia	Sarah Ann	18 Nov 1826
TOBIAS, —, child,							
Two Infants (Twins)		F	Farmer	Wales	U. States	Harmony	12 Jul 1821
—, Mrs.	30	F	Farmer	Wales	U. States	Harmony	12 Jul 1821
A.	40	M	Farmer	Wales	U. States	Harmony	12 Jul 1821
Charles	9	M		England	America	Ann	3 Jul 1820
Charles Michael	22	M	Merchant	England	Mexico	Silas Richards	19 Mar 1828
Chs.	17	M	Mercht.	L'pool	L'pool	Wm. Thompson	13 Sep 1823
David, child		M	Farmer	Wales	U. States	Harmony	12 Jul 1821
Enos, child		M	Farmer	Wales	U. States	Harmony	12 Jul 1821
Harriot	7	F		England	America	Ann	3 Jul 1820
Henry	6	M		England	America	Ann	3 Jul 1820
Jenny	11	F		England	America	Ann	3 Jul 1820
John, child		M	Farmer	Wales	U. States	Harmony	12 Jul 1821
M. J.	43	M	Merchant	Gt. Brittain	United States	Leeds	19 May 1823
Rachael, child		F	Farmer	Wales	U. States	Harmony	12 Jul 1821
Rebecca, Mrs.	26	F		England	America	Ann	3 Jul 1820
S. J.	38	M	Merchant	England	England	Albion	4 Oct 1820
Sophia	4	F		England	America	Ann	3 Jul 1820
Willm., child		M	Farmer	Wales	U. States	Harmony	12 Jul 1821
TOBIN, ...	20			Ireland	U.S.	Hibernia	27 Jun 1821
C., Miss	17	F	None	Halifax, N.S.	Nova Scotia	Lewis	25 Jun 1824
Daniel	33		Butcher	Ireland	U.S. of America	Mary	21 Sep 1821
James	16	M	Merchant	Halifax, N.S.	Nova Scotia	Lewis	25 Jun 1824
James	19	M	Labourer	G. Britain	U. States	St. George	7 Jun 1828

NAMES OF PASSENGERS	AGE	SEX	OCCUPATIONS	COUNTRY TO WHICH THEY BELONG	COUNTRY THEY INTEND TO INHABIT	SHIPS/DATES OF ARRIVAL	
TOBIN (cont'd)							
James	25	M	Labourer	Ireland		Marchioness	13 May 1828
Jno.	36	M	Labourer	England	United States	Essex	23 May 1828
John	9/12	M		England	United States	Margaret	5 Sep 1827
John	3	M		New Brunswick	United States	Henrietta	19 Oct 1825
John	27	M	Labourer	Great Britain	United States	Henrietta	19 Oct 1825
John	27	M	Miller	Great Britain	U. States	Hope & Esther	12 Nov 1825
John	28	M	Marble Cutter	England	United States	Margaret	5 Sep 1827
Judy	29	F		Ireland	Upper Canada	Lady Hunter	10 Jul 1826
Margaret	1	F		New Brunswick	United States	Henrietta	19 Oct 1825
Mary Ann	21	F		England	United States	Margaret	5 Sep 1827
Micheal	20	M	Merchant	Halifax, N.S.	Nova Scotia	Lewis	25 Jun 1824
Nicholas	22	M	Clerk	G. Britain	U. States	Margaret Bogle	12 Jun 1828
Norez	26	F		Ireland	Upper Canada	Lady Hunter	10 Jul 1826
Patrick	22	M	Laborer	...	United States	Combine	20 Nov 1824
Peter	6	M		New Brunswick	United States	Henrietta	19 Oct 1825
Richd.	25	M	Labourer	Ireland		Marchioness	13 May 1828
Sarah	25	F	Seamstress	Great Britain	United States	Henrietta	19 Oct 1825
Thomas	14	M	Merchant	Halifax, N.S.	Nova Scotia	Lewis	25 Jun 1824
Thomas	24	M	Farmer	England	United States	Siroc	31 Oct 1829
Thos.	23	M	Labourer	Ireland	United States	Matvina	19 Oct 1826
TOBLER, F. J. F.	28	M	Merchant	Dutch	U. States	Dawn	8 Jun 1827
TOBSER, Lewis	26	M	Merchant	German	U. States	Franklin	6 May 1828
TOBY, —, Mr.	26		Mercht.	America	America	Magnet	24 Sep 1824
TOBZ, Franklin	22	M	Supercargo	U. States	U. States	Eunice	15 May 1827
TODD, Alexander	50	M	Mariner	U. States	United States	Trident	22 Jan 1822
Andrew	5	M		Great Britain	United States	Atlantic	8 Dec 1827
Ann, Mrs.	56	F	None	Scotland	New York	Hector	11 May 1821
Anna Maria	3	F		Great Britain	United States	Atlantic	8 Dec 1827
Elizabeth	23	F	Spinster	Ireland	United States	Trident	17 May 1825
Henry	34	M	Merchant	United States	United States	Martha	17 Sep 1821
Henry	52	M	Merchant	Bermuda	Bermuda	Alpha	15 Jul 1823
Heny	40	M	Merchant	U. States	U. States	Geo. Canning	2 Sep 1828
James	21	M	Weaver	Gt. Britan	America	Braganza	1 Dec 1824
John		M	Chiefly farmers		United States	Factor	8 Jul 1829
John	23	M	Mason	Scotland	United States	Urania	17 May 1828
John	30	M	Joiner	England	United States	Andes	2 Oct 1828
Maria	30	F		Great Britain	United States	Atlantic	8 Dec 1827
Martha	19	F	Spinster	Ireland	United States	Trident	17 May 1825
Richd. J.	30	M	Merchant	Great Britain	United States	Atlantic	8 Dec 1827
Robert	27	M	Merchant	Scotland	Scotland	Virginia	26 May 1828
Robt.	27	M	Cutler	Gt. Britain	U. States	Isaac Hicks	18 Apr 1825
Ths.	25	M	Farmer	Great Brittan	U. States	John & Elizabeth	11 Dec 1826
Wm.	23	M	Mechanic	U. States	U. States	France	5 Dec 1827
Wm.	39	M	Merchant	U. States	U. States	Geo. Canning	2 Sep 1828
TODERHORST, Emma	8	F	None	Hamburg	United States	Maria Elizabeth	2 Sep 1822
John	6	M	None	Hamburg	United States	Maria Elizabeth	2 Sep 1822
John	40	M	Merchant	Hamburg	United States	Maria Elizabeth	2 Sep 1822
Sophia	10	F	None	Hamburg	United States	Maria Elizabeth	2 Sep 1822
TODERHORT, Wm. E.	40	F		Germany	U. States	Lycurgus	3 Dec 1821
TODHUNTER, John	20	M	Carpenter	England		Marchioness	13 May 1828
TODS, Henry	40	M	Merchant	United States	U. States	William Thompson	29 Jan 1823
TOFFEL, Anggelica	31	F		Charleston, S.C.	New York	Hiram	10 Nov 1824
Eliza	19	F		Charleston, S.C.	New York	Hiram	10 Nov 1824
TOGG, Silvester P.	23	M	Seaman	U. States	U. States	William	11 Dec 1827
TOKERMAN, Samuel	31	M	Fur maker	Russia	U.S.A.	Silas Richards	28 Jun 1825
TOLAN, Cathr.	28	F	Seamstress	Great Britain	United States	Grecian	24 Sep 1828
John	22	M	Baker	Great Britain	United States	Grecian	24 Sep 1828
Matilda	3	F		Great Britain	United States	Grecian	24 Sep 1828
TOLAND, G. H.	23	M	Merchant	United States	United States	Helen Mar	29 Jun 1827
TOLBETT, Peter	30	M	Merchant	France	Savannah	Tuscaloosa	31 Oct 1825
TOLD, David	21		Clock Maker	Germany	Germany	London	16 Aug 1824
TOLEMAN, James	55	M	Farmer	Ohio, U.S.	United States	Cosmo	21 Aug 1828
TOLER, —	4	M		Gt. Britain	U. States	Tantiva	7 Jul 1828
—	9	M		Gt. Britain	U. States	Tantiva	7 Jul 1828
—, Mrs.	19	F	Lady	United States	U. States	Gertrude	17 Jul 1827
Charles	30	M	Farmer	Gt. Britain	U. States	Tantiva	7 Jul 1828

NAMES OF PASSENGERS	AGE	SEX	OCCUPATIONS	COUNTRY TO WHICH THEY BELONG	COUNTRY THEY INTEND TO INHABIT	SHIPS/DATES OF ARRIVAL	
TOLER (cont'd)							
Chs.	3/12	M		United States	U. States	Gertrude	17 Jul 1827
Dav. J.	28		Merchant	United States	United States	Horatio	3 Dec 1827
Maria	25	M	Farmer	Gt. Britain	U. States	Tantiva	7 Jul 1828
W. H.	25	M	Merchant	United States	U. States	Gertrude	17 Jul 1827
Wm.	18/12	M		United States	U. States	Gertrude	17 Jul 1827
TOLERTON, John H.	26	M	Farmer	Ireland	United States	Dublin Packet	3 May 1823
TOLFREE,							
James Hurbert	14	M		England	New York	Frances Henrietta	3 Apr 1826
TOLITSON, Joseph	28	M	...	...	...	Laurel	16 Nov 1824
TOLL, Mary	17	F	Servant	Great Britain	United States	John	6 Oct 1820
TOLLE, Thomas	24		Labourer	Great Britan	United States	Newry	11 Jul 1827
TOLLER, Elizabeth	30	F	Lady	England	United States	Cambria	8 Oct 1828
Frank	27	M	Farmer	Holland	U. States	Martha	13 Sep 1827
Mary	25	F	Lady	England	United States	Cambria	8 Oct 1828
Mary	67	F	Lady	England	United States	Cambria	8 Oct 1828
TOLLEREN, Barbara	30	F	...	Baden	United States	Wade	29 Aug 1825
TOLLEY, Henry Stiles	2		Tailor	England	U. States	Venus	4 Oct 1821
John	57		Tailor	England	U. States	Venus	4 Oct 1821
Maria	31		Tailor	England	U. States	Venus	4 Oct 1821
TOLLHURST, Henry	19	M	Labourer	England		Marchioness	13 May 1828
John	21	M	Labourer	England		Marchioness	13 May 1828
TOLLY, Philip	34	M	Labourer	G. Britain	U. States	Margaret Bogle	12 Jun 1828
TOLMAN, W.	21	M	Labourer	England	U. States	William	28 Nov 1823
TOLSA, Manuel	9	M		Mexico	Mexico	Virginia	9 Feb 1829
TOLSON, T. B.	22		Grocer	Great Britain	United States	Roman	10 Sep 1827
TOLTON, Wm.	27	M	Labourer	Ireland	U. States	Atlantic	19 Aug 1825
TOM, J. A.	21	M	Mariner	G. Britian	U. States	Prince Edward	29 Jul 1823
TOMANY, Hannah	22		Farmer	Ireland	United States	Carolina Ann	12 Sep 1823
Patrick	15		Farmer	Ireland	United States	Carolina Ann	12 Sep 1823
TOMASOWITSCH,							
Antony	42	M	Merchant	Teneriffe	Teneriffe	Wanderer	6 Oct 1827
TOMES, Charles	14	M	None	England	United States	William Thompson	19 Aug 1829
Frances	48	M	Merchant	England	U. States	Florida	16 May 1827
Frances, Jr.	15	M	Merchant	U. States	U. States	Florida	16 May 1827
Francis	47	M	Merchant	U. States	U. States	Caledonia	10 Sep 1828
Francis	48	M	Merchant	England	United States	William Thompson	19 Aug 1829
TOMEY, W., Junr.	29	M	Merchant	U. States	United States	Birmingham	12 Oct 1827
TOMKIN, Eliza, Mrs.	40	F	Farming	England	America	Maine	16 Jul 1821
Henry	6	M	Farming	England	America	Maine	16 Jul 1821
James	22	M	Farmer	Rye, England	United States	William	21 May 1828
John	8	M	Farming	England	America	Maine	16 Jul 1821
Thomas, Mr.	38	M	Farming	England	America	Maine	16 Jul 1821
TOMKINS, Ann	24	F		England	U.N.S.	Helen	16 Mar 1829
Belvil	32	M	Merchant	United States	United States	Ardelle	18 Jan 1828
Jane	41	F	Captain's Lady	United States	United States	Ganges	20 Aug 1825
TOMLIN, Mary Ann	30			England	Boston	Xenophon	25 Jul 1826
TOMLINSON, Hill	17	M	Farmer	Great Britain	United States	Ann Maria	12 Jul 1821
Hy.	26	M	Merchant	U. States Amer	U.S. America	George	17 Jul 1823
John	39	M	Manufacturer	Great Britain	United States	Ganges	26 Oct 1826
Saml.	29	M	Blacksmith	England	U. States	Thomas Ritchie	2 Jul 1827
Thomas	22	M	Joiner	Gt. Britain	United States	Meteor	19 Aug 1829
Thomas	40	M	Farmer	England	United States	Panthia	7 Feb 1822
TOMNEY, Mary	24 4/12	F	Servant	Ireland	United States	Atlantic	21 Jul 1827
TOMPKINS, Ann	17			England	United States	Hugh Johnson	11 Jun 1828
Eliz.	7			England	United States	Hugh Johnson	11 Jun 1828
Eliz.	13			England	United States	Hugh Johnson	11 Jun 1828
Eliz.	40			England	United States	Hugh Johnson	11 Jun 1828
Francis	4			England	United States	Hugh Johnson	11 Jun 1828
Francis	18			England	United States	Hugh Johnson	11 Jun 1828
Hannah	26	F				Lady of the Lake	23 Aug 1828
Henry	11			England	United States	Hugh Johnson	11 Jun 1828
Jane	9			England	United States	Hugh Johnson	11 Jun 1828
John	6			England	United States	Hugh Johnson	11 Jun 1828
John	13			England	United States	Hugh Johnson	11 Jun 1828

NAMES OF PASSENGERS	AGE	SEX	OCCUPATIONS	COUNTRY TO WHICH THEY BELONG	COUNTRY THEY INTEND TO INHABIT	SHIPS/DATES OF ARRIVAL
TOMPKINS (cont'd)						
John	15	M				Lady of the Lake 23 Aug 1828
John	40		Farmer	England	United States	Hugh Johnson 11 Jun 1828
Joseph	1			England	United States	Hugh Johnson 11 Jun 1828
Joseph	9			England	United States	Hugh Johnson 11 Jun 1828
Mary	11			England	United States	Hugh Johnson 11 Jun 1828
Mary	35			England	United States	Hugh Johnson 11 Jun 1828
Robt.	37		Shoemaker	England	United States	Hugh Johnson 11 Jun 1828
Sarah	5			England	United States	Hugh Johnson 11 Jun 1828
Thomas	7			England	United States	Hugh Johnson 11 Jun 1828
TOMPKINSON, Beny	13	M		G. Britain	United States	Siroc 13 Sep 1828
Edmund	3	M		G. Britain	United States	Siroc 13 Sep 1828
John	4	M		G. Britain	United States	Siroc 13 Sep 1828
Joseph	15	M		G. Britain	United States	Siroc 13 Sep 1828
Joseph	44	M	Potter	G. Britain	United States	Siroc 13 Sep 1828
Mary Ann	6	F		G. Britain	United States	Siroc 13 Sep 1828
Saml.	9	M		G. Britain	United States	Siroc 13 Sep 1828
Sarah	45	F		G. Britain	United States	Siroc 13 Sep 1828
William	11	M		G. Britain	United States	Siroc 13 Sep 1828
TOMPSEN, John	28	M	Joiner	England	United States	Hamilton 13 Nov 1827
TOMSON, Peter	25	M	Labourer	Great Britain	State of N. York	Robert Fulton 30 Dec 1824
TONER, Biddey	33	F	Spinster	Ireland	U.S. of America	Meteor 19 Mar 1828
John	40	M	Labourer	Ireland	U.S. of America	Meteor 19 Mar 1828
Mary	23 7/12	F		Ireland	U. States	Fabius 22 Sep 1828
TONG, A.	39	M	Plastar	Scotland	U. States	Superior 25 Sep 1828
TONGE, Ann	33	F	None		New York	Governor Clinton 3 Jul 1827
J. R.	22	M	Apothecary	Great Britain	United States	Dapper 24 Aug 1827
James	36	M	Weaver		New York	Governor Clinton 3 Jul 1827
Jane	6	F	None		New York	Governor Clinton 3 Jul 1827
Margret	4	F	None		New York	Governor Clinton 3 Jul 1827
TONLOURN, Daniel	20	M	Cotton Spinner	Ireland	United States	Fabius 4 Jun 1828
TONNANT, Benjamin	47	M	Merchant	Scotland		Reuben & Eliza 21 Aug 1820
TONNILLE, Henry	19	M	Sig. Maker	G. Britain	United States	Louisa 14 Jun 1825
TONOR, M.	27		Labourer	England	United States	Hugh Johnson 11 Jun 1828
TONQUIST, Francis	40	M	Merchant	Germany	America	Saluda 16 Oct 1824
TONTIN, M.	30	M	Duck Dresser	Scotland	United States	Indus 5 Sep 1827
TOOGOOD, Christopher	30	M	Farmer	England	U. States	Criterion at London 10 May 1821
Josephina	2	F		England	U. States	Criterion at London 10 May 1821
Mary Ann	26	F		England	U. States	Criterion at London 10 May 1821
William	1	M		England	U. States	Criterion at London 10 May 1821
TOOL, Ellen	28	F	Spinster	Great Britain	United States	Greek 23 Jan 1828
James	49	M	Mariner/ship master	England	England	Francis Jarvis 10 Jan 1825
John	25	M	Hatter	G. Britain	U. States	Margaret Bogle 12 Jun 1828
Lawrence	20	M		Ireland	New York	Lady Hunter 5 Jun 1826
TOOLE, Ann	55	F	None			Brighton 19 Aug 1829
Bridget	30	F	Servant	Ireland	United States	William 20 Jul 1829
Brighton	3/365	M		England		Brighton 19 Aug 1829
Martin	28	M	Labourer	Ireland	United States	Jubilee 12 May 1828
Michael	25	M	Labourer	Ireland	United States	Jubilee 12 May 1828
Robert	52	M	Farmer			Brighton 19 Aug 1829
Thomas	1	M				Brighton 19 Aug 1829
Thos., Jr.	28	M	Player	United States	U. States	Pacific 5 Sep 1827
William	22	M	Labourer	Ireland	United States	Jubilee 12 May 1828
William	25	M	Weaver	England	United States	Jubilee 12 May 1828
TOOLEY, Ann	22	F	None	Ireland		Marchioness 13 May 1828
James	1	M	None	Ireland		Marchioness 13 May 1828
Patrick	30	M	Labourer	Ireland		Marchioness 13 May 1828
TOOLITE, Dennis	21	M	Weaver	England	U. States	Severn 12 Oct 1826
TOOLS, Francis	25	M		Ireland	U. States	Balaena 29 Apr 1825
TOOMY, Margaret	26	F			New York	Robert Fulton 8 Mar 1823

NAMES OF PASSENGERS	AGE	SEX	OCCUPATIONS	COUNTRY TO WHICH THEY BELONG	COUNTRY THEY INTEND TO INHABIT	SHIPS/DATES OF ARRIVAL	
TOOMY (cont'd)							
Patrick	1 9/12	M			New York	Robert Fulton	8 Mar 1823
Stephen	28	M	Farmer		New York	Robert Fulton	8 Mar 1823
TOOR, J. B.	42	M	Merchant	England	U. States	Dromo	19 Jul 1827
TOOT, Aron	35	M	Merchant	United States	United States	Nancy	8 Mar 1822
TOPAS, M.	18	M	Gentleman	Columbia	Columbia	Gertrude	13 Nov 1826
TOPHY, Jenny	20	F	Labourer	Ireland	United States	Hope & Esther	17 Oct 1827
TOPPA, Charles	26	M	Merch.	America	America	William Thompson	18 Jan 1825
TORANCE, Francis	23	M	Weaver	Great Britain	United States	Courier	26 Jun 1827
TORBORK, Sion	20	F	W. Right	Ireland		Quatre Freres	29 Jul 1828
TORES, Dolores	25	F	Servant	Mexico	Mexico	Virginia	9 Feb 1829
TORFTENSON, Hans	20	M	Shoe Maker	Norway	United States	Salem	31 Aug 1829
TORGE, Francesco A.	56	M	Merchant	Havana	U. States	Hesper	28 Dec 1825
TORILLA, D. J.	43	M	Merchant	Spain	U. States	Frances	7 Aug 1826
Elizabeth	8	F		Spain	U. States	Frances	7 Aug 1826
TORINGER, John	37 1/12	M	...	England	America, U.S.	Illinois	3 Jun 1822
TORNASSO, J.	17	M	Merchant	Spain	U. States	Ranger	2 Jul 1827
TORNEY, Mary	19	F	Servant	Ireland	New York	Atlantic	8 May 1828
TORNHILL, Evans	36	M	Merchant	England	America	Ann	11 Apr 1821
TORNSIDE, Elisabeth	20	F		England	United States	William Byrnes	11 Dec 1827
TORONTO, Antony	23	M	Merchant	Matanzas	Matanzas	William	16 Apr 1823
TORQU, Peater B., Lt. Col.	58	M	Merchant	Havana	U. States	Peter Remsen	30 Jun 1828
TORQUEMAN, T.	21	M	Merchant	France	New York	Nimrod	21 Sep 1820
TORRANCE, John	24	M	Merchant	England	England	Brown	23 Dec 1826
TORRENCE, Catherin	8	F	None	G. Bt.	Canada	Canada	12 May 1828
Elizabeth	33	F	None	G. Bt.	Canada	Canada	12 May 1828
Jane	15	F	None	G. Bt.	Canada	Canada	12 May 1828
John	42	M	Merchant	G. Bt.	Canada	Canada	12 May 1828
Saliena	14	F	None	G. Bt.	Canada	Canada	12 May 1828
TORREY, Micael	25	M	Blacksmith	France	U. States	India	8 Dec 1826
TORRUS, Francis	44	M	Merchant	G. Bt.	U. States	Canada	13 Oct 1825
TORRY, Henry	51	M	Carpenter	England	[Port?]...smith	Thames	6 Oct 1820
TORY, James	45	M	None	Great Britain	United States	John	6 Oct 1820
TOSE, William	30	M	Mercht.	U. States		Hector	17 Aug 1825
TOSINA, Martin Ceho	28	M	Traveller	Mexico	Mexico	Virginia	8 Mar 1828
TOSS, —, Mrs.	35	F	Farmer	Switzerland	U. States	Seine	30 Aug 1824
B.	9	M	Farmer	Switzerland	U. States	Seine	30 Aug 1824
B.	21	M	Farmer	Switzerland	U. States	Seine	30 Aug 1824
Henry	25	M	Labourer	Hamburg	United States	Brilliant	24 Sep 1827
T.	7	M	Farmer	Switzerland	U. States	Seine	30 Aug 1824
T.	14	M	Farmer	Switzerland	U. States	Seine	30 Aug 1824
W.	18	M	Farmer	Switzerland	U. States	Seine	30 Aug 1824
W.	38	M	Farmer	Switzerland	U. States	Seine	30 Aug 1824
TOSTASBAR, Edmund	12	M	None	France	France	Joseph	22 Jan 1822
TOTTEN, C.	17	F		St. Croix	U. States	Elias Burger	21 Aug 1823
Charles G.	22	M	Merchant	U. States	U. States	Mora	30 Apr 1827
E.	13	F		St. Croix	U. States	Elias Burger	21 Aug 1823
J. W.	30	M	Merchant	United States	United States	Andromache	18 May 1825
Rd.	28	M	Servant	St. Croix	U. States	Elias Burger	21 Aug 1823
S., Miss	17	F	Army	St. Croix	U. States	Chase	6 Jun 1822
TOUBACK, Anna	3	F	Daughter	Swiss	United States	Elizabeth	4 Sep 1826
Elizabeth	7 6/12	F	Daughter	Swiss	United States	Elizabeth	4 Sep 1826
James	6/12	M	Son	Swiss	United States	Elizabeth	4 Sep 1826
Johannes	5 6/12	M	Son	Swiss	United States	Elizabeth	4 Sep 1826
Martelena	13	F	Daughter	Swiss	United States	Elizabeth	4 Sep 1826
Martelena	37	F	Wife	Swiss	United States	Elizabeth	4 Sep 1826
Peter	10	M	Son	Swiss	United States	Elizabeth	4 Sep 1826
Peter	37	M	...is...	Swiss	United States	Elizabeth	4 Sep 1826
Rosina	4	F	Daughter	Swiss	United States	Elizabeth	4 Sep 1826
Susana	12	F	Daughter	Swiss	United States	Elizabeth	4 Sep 1826
TOUCHINE, Antonio	25	M	Sailor	Venice	France	Jean Baptiste	11 Aug 1828
TOULENIN, J. B.	37	M	Merchant	U. Kingdom, G. Britain & Ireland	Mobile	James Cropper	21 Oct 1825
TOULMIN, Amy	6	F				Hercules	25 Sep 1820
Amy	30	F				Hercules	25 Sep 1820
Anna	4	F				Hercules	25 Sep 1820

NAMES OF PASSENGERS	AGE	SEX	OCCUPATIONS	COUNTRY TO WHICH THEY BELONG	COUNTRY THEY INTEND TO INHABIT	SHIPS/DATES OF ARRIVAL	
TOULMIN (cont'd)							
J. B.	36	M	Merchant	Gt. Britain	U. States	Canada	4 Oct 1824
John Butler	32	M	Merchant	G. Britain	U. States	Hercules	25 Sep 1820
Joshua	2	M				Hercules	25 Sep 1820
Mary	1	F				Hercules	25 Sep 1820
TOUPET, A. F.	35	M	...	...	United States	Origon	8 Jun 1824
Ch.	20	M	Clerk	France		Montano	3 Jan 1823
F. C.	3	F		...	United States	Origon	8 Jun 1824
M. A.	7	F		...	United States	Origon	8 Jun 1824
P. A.	5	F		...	United States	Origon	8 Jun 1824
R. C.	30	F		...	United States	Origon	8 Jun 1824
TOURANG, Peter	27	M	Keyper & Stoker	Milleb Burchbach	United States	Juffraw Johanna	16 Oct 1821
TOUREN, Rich.	28	M	Miner	G. Britain	G. Britain	Brittania	17 Jul 1828
TOURNALIERRE, Gabriel	25	M	Farmer	France	United States	Montano	8 May 1827
TOURNEIER, Jean François	26	M	Gold Smith	France	United States	Montano	5 May 1828
TOURS, William	21	M	Farmer	Gt. Britain	U. States	Diana	28 Apr 1828
TOUZALINE, Stephen, Jur.	10	M		Jamaica		Midas	9 May 1827
Stephen, Senr.	45	M	Merchant	Jamaica		Midas	9 May 1827
TOVANCE, G.	38	M	Farmer	Great Britain	United States	Isaac Hicks	6 Dec 1827
TOWEL, H.	30	M		Great Britain	United States	Isaac Hicks	6 Dec 1827
M.	30	F		Great Britain	United States	Isaac Hicks	6 Dec 1827
TOWELL, David	20	M				Trio	5 May 1828
TOWERS, Ann	17	F		England	Utica	Cortes	16 Jul 1827
Benjamin	14	M		England	Utica	Cortes	16 Jul 1827
Caroline	30					Hudson	5 Apr 1826
Charles	8/12	M		England	Utica	Cortes	16 Jul 1827
Charles	16		Painter	England	United States	Hudson	5 Apr 1826
Christopher	1 9/12	M		England	Utica	Cortes	16 Jul 1827
Elizabeth	19	F		England	Utica	Cortes	16 Jul 1827
Elizabeth	28	F		England	Utica	Cortes	16 Jul 1827
Margaret	54	F		England	Utica	Cortes	16 Jul 1827
Pat	30	M	Labourer	England	U. States	Thomas Ritchie	2 Jul 1827
Philip	21	M	Farmer	...st...	...	Frances Henrietta	30 Jun 1827
Thomas	28	M	painter & glazier	England	Utica	Cortes	16 Jul 1827
William	28		Painter	England	United States	Hudson	5 Apr 1826
William, Jr.	1					Hudson	5 Apr 1826
TOWLE, John	22	M	Labourer	Ireland	United States	Edwin	29 Nov 1828
Nicholas, Mr.	50	M	Farmer	England	U. States	Acasta	11 Dec 1826
TOWLONG, Jno.	34	M	Labourer	England	United States	Essex	23 May 1828
TOWN, Robt.	28	M	Farmer	G. Brittan	U. States	Henry	24 Oct 1828
TOWNER, E. W.	32	M	Merchant	U. States	U. States	John Wells	22 Sep 1824
Edw.	25	M	Merchant	America	America	Albion	4 Oct 1820
TOWNING, Richard	34	M	Merchant	England	United States	Curlew	30 Oct 1824
TOWNLEY, Hill	15	M	Farmer	Great Britain	United States	Ann Maria	12 Jul 1821
Hill	17	M	Farmer	Great Britain	United States	Ann Maria	12 Jul 1821
James	6	M	None	England	Alexandria, U.S.	Roman	17 Oct 1826
Robert	3	M	None	England	Alexandria, U.S.	Roman	17 Oct 1826
Sarah	4	F	None	England	Alexandria, U.S.	Roman	17 Oct 1826
Sarah	28	F	None	England	Alexandria, U.S.	Roman	17 Oct 1826
Thomas	7	M	None	England	Alexandria, U.S.	Roman	17 Oct 1826
TOWNLY, William	32	M	Cotton Dresser	Great Britain	New York	Hesperus	13 Oct 1825
TOWNS, Peter	42	M	Merchant	U. States	U. States	Queen Mab	16 Mar 1825
TOWNSAND, Charles	34		...er	Edonton	America	Rockingham	23 Aug 1822
TOWNSEND, —, Dr.	20	M	Doctor	N. York	United States	Superior	14 Apr 1825
Daniel	60	M	Farmer	England	United States	Caspian	12 Jul 1821
Isaac	19	M	Seaman	U. States	U. States	Tryon	25 Apr 1825
Jereh. J.	22	M	Merchant	Connecticut	United States	Amity	11 May 1821
Jno. R.	26	M	Gentleman	United States	U. States	York	7 Aug 1828
John	29	M	Tobacconist	England	United States	Caspian	12 Jul 1821
Mary	16			England	United States	Caspian	12 Jul 1821
Mary	31	F	None	England	Boston	Thames	6 Oct 1820
Ruth	60	F	Farmer	England	United States	Caspian	12 Jul 1821
S.	40	M	...	United States	United States	Loire	18 Oct 1820

NAMES OF PASSENGERS	AGE	SEX	OCCUPATIONS	COUNTRY TO WHICH THEY BELONG	COUNTRY THEY INTEND TO INHABIT	SHIPS/DATES OF ARRIVAL	
TOWNSEND (cont'd)							
S.	40	M		U. States	U. States	Admittance	17 May 1826
*Died							
Samuel	22	M	Labourer	Bristole		Aurora	8 Jun 1827
Soln.	44	M	Mariner	U. States	U. States	Ohio	2 May 1821
Solomon	21	M	Merchant	United States	United States	Washington	15 Apr 1826
Thos.	22	M	Farmer	Bristol	United States	Hector	29 Nov 1823
William	23	M	Farmer	Ireland	U.S.A.	Dalhouse Castle	21 Aug 1829
William	35	M	Farmer	Great Britain	Connecticut	Thames	16 May 1821
Wm.	23	M	Farmer	Ireland	United States	Dalhouse Castle	21 Aug 1829
TOWSE, Anthoney	40		Seaman	England	U. States	Hudson	4 Sep 1823
TOWY, Michael	30 8/12	M	Labourer	Ireland	United States	Bethlehem	18 Oct 1828
TOXER, Charles	24	M	Tinman	Great Briton	New York	Brighton	12 Jun 1826
TOYNE, John	13	M	None	England	Canada	Roman	12 Jun 1826
TOYNTON, Thomas	30	M	Labourer	England	U. States America	Columbus	23 Mar 1829
TOYSENT, Hubert	28	M	Basket Maker	France	United States	Montano	29 Apr 1826
TOZER, Sarah	21	F	Tinman	Great Briton	New York	Brighton	12 Jun 1826
TR..., J. W.	38	M	Gentleman	Great Brittain	G. Brittain	Gleaner	31 Jul 1821
TRACEY, Bridget	30	F	Farmer	London	New York	Bowditch	27 Apr 1826
Edwd.	28	M	Farmer	Ireland	United States	Essex	23 May 1828
Henry	26	M	...	Ireland	United States	Carolina Ann	24 Oct 1825
James	35	M	Farmer	London	New York	Bowditch	27 Apr 1826
John	23	M	Farmer	Ireland	U. States	Henry Kneeland	27 Jul 1825
Richd.	26	M	Farmer	Ireland	United States	Curler	3 Mar 1828
TRACY, Bridget	24	F	Spinster	Ireland		Dublin Packet	30 Apr 1821
Catherine	16	F	Spinster	Ireland	United States	Dublin Packet	29 Jun 1825
Francis M.	26	F	Lady	Ireland	United States	Dublin Packet	3 Sep 1822
James F.	54	M	Merchant	Ireland	United States	Dublin Packet	3 Sep 1822
Jereh. L.	32	M	Merchant	Havana	United States	Abeona	26 Jun 1824
Louiza	35	F	None	United States	United States	Isaac Hicks	22 Aug 1829
Margaret	25	F	Spinster	Ireland	U. States	Globe	14 Jul 1821
Mary	26	F	Spinster	Ireland		Dublin Packet	30 Apr 1821
Patrick	25	M	Labourer	Ireland	New York	America	1 Aug 1828
T.	23	M	Labourer	G. Britain	U. States	Hanford	18 Sep 1828
TRADENICK, John	34	M	Miner	England	United States	Jubilee	12 May 1828
TRAELL, —, Mr.	35	M	Shoe Maker	Gt. Britain	U.S.	Robert Edwards	11 Nov 1822
TRAIL, Mary	18	F		Ireland	America	Carolina Ann	7 Apr 1826
Willm.	18 4/12	M		Ireland	America	Carolina Ann	7 Apr 1826
TRAIN, Saml., Mr.	45	M	Merchant	America	America	Birmingham	16 Oct 1826
TRAINER, Agnes	4	F	Child, on a visit	Armar	N. York	Nile	18 Aug 1829
Athy	25	F	on a visit	Armar	N. York	Nile	18 Aug 1829
James	20	M	Labourer	Ireland	United States	Fabius	31 Jul 1829
James	25	M	Labourer	Ireland	United States	Louisa	18 Apr 1827
John	25	M	Brick Layer	Great Britain	United States	Orbit	23 Oct 1826
TRAKHUPE, Heny.	38	M		Great Britain	U. States	Lady Hunter	28 May 1823
TRALET, Catherine	30	F	Farmer	Switzerland		Charlemagne	20 Aug 1829
John	35	M	Farmer	Switzerland		Charlemagne	20 Aug 1829
TRAMBLY, Alexr.	29	M	Gilder	France	U. States	Montano	23 Apr 1825
TRAMOUR, Patk.	14			Great Britan	United States	Newry	11 Jul 1827
TRANCHANT, C.	28	F	Merchant	France	United States	Elizabeth	22 May 1822
G.	35	M	Merchant	France	United States	Elizabeth	22 May 1822
J.	6	F	Merchant	France	United States	Elizabeth	22 May 1822
TRANER, Alexr.	21		Shoemaker			Zamoa	5 Nov 1828
C.	16 2/12	F		France	United States	Catharine	10 Sep 1827
Cathr.	9 4/12	F		France	United States	Catharine	10 Sep 1827
G. A.	30 7/12	M	Tailor	France	United States	Catharine	10 Sep 1827
H.	7 3/12	M		France	United States	Catharine	10 Sep 1827
M.	47 3/12	F		France	United States	Catharine	10 Sep 1827
Philip	11 2/12	M		France	United States	Catharine	10 Sep 1827
TRANY, John	26	M	Tailor	Manchester	United States	Aurelia	7 Jun 1826
TRAPADOUX, John	35	M	Merchant	France	U. States	Marmion	17 Feb 1824
TRAPADOX, Frances	3 1/2	F		France	U. States	Marmion	17 Feb 1824
Jane	21	F		France	U. States	Marmion	17 Feb 1824
John	4/12	M		France	U. States	Marmion	17 Feb 1824
Mark	2	M		France	U. States	Marmion	17 Feb 1824
TRAPINGER, Lewis	40	M	Hamburg	U. States	U. States	Columbia	1 Dec 1824
TRAPMAN, Lewis	40	M	Merchant	U.S. America	U.S. America	Columbia	15 Nov 1826
TRAQUTT, Peter	50	M	Planter	American	U. States	Romulus	31 Jul 1823
TRASK, B. T.	28	M	Mariner	Massachusetts	U. States	General Pike	2 Oct 1826

NAMES OF PASSENGERS	AGE	SEX	OCCUPATIONS	COUNTRY TO WHICH THEY BELONG	COUNTRY THEY INTEND TO INHABIT	SHIPS/DATES OF ARRIVAL	
TRASK (cont'd)							
Thos.	22	M	Mariner	U. States	U. States	Atlas	24 Jun 1828
William	16	M	Cordwainer	Great Britain	United States	Juno	5 Oct 1822
TRATINS, —, Mrs.	36	F		Baltimore	U. States	Emigrant	9 Oct 1826
TRAVASA, John	35	M	Merchant	France	U. States	Purrington	14 May 1827
TRAVELLL, William	34	M	Labourer	England and Ireland	United States	Jubilee	12 May 1828
TRAVERS, Thomas	30	M	Labourer	Ireland	America	Weser	26 Jun 1821
TRAVEY, Elijah	8	M		Great Britain	United States	Diana	6 Jul 1829
Harriette	10	F		Great Britain	United States	Diana	6 Jul 1829
Lucy	30	F		Great Britain	United States	Diana	6 Jul 1829
Matilda	1	F		Great Britain	United States	Diana	6 Jul 1829
Richd.	4	M		Great Britain	United States	Diana	6 Jul 1829
Richd.	23	M	Tailor	Great Britain	United States	Diana	6 Jul 1829
TRAVIS, Eleanor	2	F		Ireland	U. States	Sarah G	7 May 1827
Eleanor	26	F		Ireland	U. States	Sarah G	7 May 1827
James	66		Gentleman	New York	England	London	13 Dec 1822
TRAVISS, Jno.	35	M		Ireland	U. States	St. Michael	27 Mar 1827
TRAWIN, —, Mrs.	31	F		England	United States	Cosmo	26 Aug 1829
Catherine	2	F		England	United States	Cosmo	26 Aug 1829
Samuel	4	M		England	United States	Cosmo	26 Aug 1829
TRAYMOR, Cathrine	20			Great Britan	United States	Newry	11 Jul 1827
James	28			Great Britan	United States	Newry	11 Jul 1827
TRAYMOUR, John	1			Great Britan	United States	Newry	11 Jul 1827
TREADWELL, D. H.	26	M	Gentlemn.	Portsmouth	Portsmouth	Wm. Thompson	13 Sep 1823
H.	28	M	Sailor	America	U. States	Hiram	17 Jun 1826
S.	30 11/12	M	Mercht.	N. York	N. York	Mary	21 May 1821
TREAT, James	29	M	Mercht.	Connecticut	Connt.	Emma	14 Oct 1825
TREBECON, J.	35	M	Miner	New York	New York	Gertrude	6 May 1828
TREBUCHIO, Edwd.	44	M	Merchant	France		Charlemagne	16 Jan 1829
TRECOTA, Barte	31 8/12	M	Farmer	France	America	France	28 Mar 1829
TREDLONE, John	40	M	Merchant	New Brunswick	Great Brittain	Nancy	9 Jun 1821
TREDWELL, C. C.	22	M	Gentleman	America	N. York	Stephania	7 Aug 1824
TREE, Thomas	17	M	Farmer	England	Gallaway, N.Y.	Chelsea	16 May 1828
TREEFE, Lawrence	42	M	Farmer	Great Britain	United States	Ann Maria	9 Mar 1820
TREEN, Geo.	30	M	Merchant	Scotland	United States	Trent	10 Jul 1827
TREGASCAS, John	19	M	Miner	Ireland	United States	Curler	3 Mar 1828
TREGEAR, Fred. A.	28	M	Merchant	Great Britain	Great Britain	John & Edward	7 Nov 1825
TREGEY, James	26	M	Minor	England	America	Minerva	31 May 1824
TREIVICKIN, Richd.	34	M	Miner	U. States	U. States	Martha	20 Jun 1825
TREMAIN, Joseph	40 4/12	M	Merchant	U. States	U. States	Maria	22 May 1822
TRESS, Mary	25	F		Great Britain	United States	India	5 Sep 1827
Richard	27	M	Taylor	Great Britain	United States	India	5 Sep 1827
TRESSER, C.	27	M	Shoe Maker	France	United States	La Flora	30 Jun 1828
P.	33	M	Iron Monger	France	United States	La Flora	30 Jun 1828
TRESTLER, Jno. B. C.	23	M	Prof. of Medicin	England	Montreal	Cadmus	27 Aug 1822
TREVACKISS, John	38	M	Taylor	England	England	Venus	15 Apr 1822
John, Junr.	6 6/12	M		England	England	Venus	15 Apr 1822
TREVEND, Elizabeth	28	F		England	America	Comet	26 Jun 1822
TREVERO, L. T.	40	M		Colombia	Different	Tampico	11 Jul 1826
TREVERRO, Sebastian	18			Mexico	Mexico	Horatio	3 Dec 1827
TREVHY, Judith	22	F	None	Ireland	United States	Jubilee	1 Oct 1828
TREVMEL, J. L.	25	M	Mechanic		U. States	Indiana	20 Sep 1828
TREVOR, Ricd.	42	M	Farmer	Great Britian	U. States	Dalhouse Castle	28 Feb 1826
TREVOTT, John	51	M	Bedstead Maker	England	New York	Brighton	16 Nov 1826
Sarah	64	F	None	England	New York	Brighton	16 Nov 1826
TREWECK, Joseph	30	M	Miner	Great Britain	Great Britain	Sisters	10 Jan 1826
TREWMAN, Ann	28	F		U. States	U. States	Yamacraw	9 Mar 1822
TRIANOR, R.	25		Farmer	Ireland	United States	Courier	16 May 1825
TRIBLE, J.	18	F	Servant	Ireland	N. York	Trusty	12 Sep 1828
TRIBLEY, George	28	M		England	United States	Acosta	28 Jul 1823
TRIEDLE, C.	3 1/2	F		Germany	U. States	Falcon	11 Jun 1827
Catharine	16	F		Germany	U. States	Falcon	11 Jun 1827
Christian	10	M		Germany	U. States	Falcon	11 Jun 1827
Frederick	12	M		Germany	U. States	Falcon	11 Jun 1827
Mathias	45	M	Gardner	Germany	U. States	Falcon	11 Jun 1827
Matthias	7	M		Germany	U. States	Falcon	11 Jun 1827
TRIERBENGER, N.	33	M	Weaver	Switzerland	U. States	La Urania	3 Jul 1828

NAMES OF PASSENGERS	AGE	SEX	OCCUPATIONS	COUNTRY TO WHICH THEY BELONG	COUNTRY THEY INTEND TO INHABIT	SHIPS/DATES OF ARRIVAL	
TRIHON, Margaret	20	F	Labourer or Spinster	Ireland	United States	Champion	3 Nov 1827
Mary Ann	4	F	Labourer or Spinster	Ireland	United States	Champion	3 Nov 1827
TRIM, Elizabeth	2	F	Child	Ireland	United States	Dublin Packet	9 Jul 1827
Georgiana	1	F	Child	Ireland	United States	Dublin Packet	9 Jul 1827
TRIMBALL, Thos.	32			Ireland	Philildelphia	General Marion	21 Nov 1828
TRIMBLE, Authur	35	M	Farmer	Ireland	United States	Dublin Packet	29 Jun 1825
Eliza	24	F	Spinster	Ireland	United States	Dublin Packet	29 Jun 1825
Esther	38	F	Wife	Ireland	United States	Dublin Packet	29 Jun 1825
Geo. T.	28	M	Merchant	United States	U. States	Hercules	24 Oct 1821
Isabella	4	F	Child	Ireland	United States	Dublin Packet	23 May 1828
Peggy J.	21	F	Spinster	Cookstown	N. York	Favourite	8 Oct 1823
Susan	9	F	Spinster	Ireland	United States	Dublin Packet	29 Jun 1825
Thomas	10	M	Boy	Ireland	United States	Dublin Packet	29 Jun 1825
TRIMBY, James	22	M	Merchant	England	America	Courier	24 Jul 1820
TRIMER, Geo.	38	M	Mariner	England	U. States	Greek	17 May 1825
TRIMM, John	56	M	Waggoner	Great Britain	United States	Florida	10 Dec 1823
TRINDER, —, Mr.	31	M	Merchant	G. Britain	Canada	Corinthian	29 Apr 1826
TRINIDAD, Maria	20	F	Servant	Spain	Spain	Paquebot Bordeaux	25 May 1828
TRIP, Carline	11	F		St. Johns, N.B.	United States	Antioch	21 Sep 1827
H.	12	F	Spinster	St. Johns, N.B.	United States	Antioch	21 Sep 1827
John	14	M	Farmer	St. Johns, N.B.	United States	Antioch	21 Sep 1827
Lavina	15	F	Spinster	St. Johns, N.B.	United States	Antioch	21 Sep 1827
Moses	18	M	Farmer	St. Johns, N.B.	United States	Antioch	21 Sep 1827
Rebecca	35	F	Spinster	St. Johns, N.B.	United States	Antioch	21 Sep 1827
Solomon	25	M	Farmer	Ireland	United States	Antioch	21 Sep 1827
TRIPPAL, C. F.	16	F		Bardin	U. States	Bayard	5 Sep 1828
Christian	43	M	Cooper	Bardin	U. States	Bayard	5 Sep 1828
Dorthia	18	F		Bardin	U. States	Bayard	5 Sep 1828
Eliz.	6	F		Bardin	U. States	Bayard	5 Sep 1828
J. A.	13	F		Bardin	U. States	Bayard	5 Sep 1828
J. H.	11	F		Bardin	U. States	Bayard	5 Sep 1828
Johnathan	36	M	Shoe Maker	Bardin	U. States	Bayard	5 Sep 1828
Magdaline	4	F		Bardin	U. States	Bayard	5 Sep 1828
Magdaline	77	F		Bardin	U. States	Bayard	5 Sep 1828
Mariah C.	27	F		Bardin	U. States	Bayard	5 Sep 1828
Phelp	1 1/2	M		Bardin	U. States	Bayard	5 Sep 1828
TRISEVANT, Hayes	30	M	M.D.	U.S.	U. States	Canada	5 Feb 1827
TRISK, Sarah	38	F	Lady	England	New York	Brighton	16 Nov 1826
TRISTAM, Charlotte		F		England		Boyer	9 May 1825
Elizabeth	8	F		England		Boyer	9 May 1825
Elizabeth	31	F		England		Boyer	9 May 1825
Martha	13	F		England		Boyer	9 May 1825
Sarah	14	F		England		Boyer	9 May 1825
Thomas	56	M	Farmer	England		Boyer	9 May 1825
TRITH, James	52	M	Clothier	England	U.S.A.	Lima	6 Dec 1826
TRITON, Ann	11	F		England	U.S. America	Magnet	17 Aug 1825
Ann	41	F		England	U.S. America	Magnet	17 Aug 1825
Caleb	9	M		England	U.S. America	Magnet	17 Aug 1825
Joshua	6	M		England	U.S. America	Magnet	17 Aug 1825
Stephen	12	M		England	U.S. America	Magnet	17 Aug 1825
Stephen	40	M	Farmer	England	U.S. America	Magnet	17 Aug 1825
TRIVAN, Thomas	33	M	Blacksmith	England	England	Virginia	8 Mar 1828
TRIVEY, George	30	M	Mariner	U. States	U. States	Sarah Herrick	15 Apr 1823
TROACEY, Richd.	19	M	Lab.	Rathangar	K. Co.	Howard Douglass	11 May 1827
TROAVES, Ramon	13	M		So. America	U. States	Eclipse	10 Jun 1823
TROBERT, Baptist	39	M	Merchant	France	United States	Charles	18 Aug 1826
TROBILLI, Joshua	45	M	Clothier	G. Britain	U. States	London	23 Sep 1828
TROBRIAND, A.	45	M	Merchant	France	France	Medina	23 Apr 1828
TROBYER, Josh.	32	M	Merchant	United States	United States	Cortes	19 Nov 1821
TROCH, Carl Gofflick	30	M	Saddler	Germany	Philadelphia	Falcon	21 Oct 1826
Gittoeb	28	F		Germany	Philadelphia	Falcon	21 Oct 1826
TRODLE, John	24	M	Farmer	Germany	United States	Elizabeth	4 Sep 1826
TRODLE, Madelena	22	F	Wife	Germany	United States	Elizabeth	4 Sep 1826
Mathew	1 6/12	M	Son	Germany	United States	Elizabeth	4 Sep 1826
TROHEE, Maxwell	44	M	Merchant	Scotland	Gt. Britain	Columbia	31 Jul 1826

NAMES OF PASSENGERS	AGE	SEX	OCCUPATIONS	COUNTRY TO WHICH THEY BELONG	COUNTRY THEY INTEND TO INHABIT	SHIPS/DATES OF ARRIVAL	
TROIG, Margaret	34	F	Farmer	Switzerland	United States	Olympia	12 Aug 1828
Marie	7	F	Farmer	Switzerland	United States	Olympia	12 Aug 1828
Nicolas	4	M	Farmer	Switzerland	United States	Olympia	12 Aug 1828
Nicolas	34	M	Farmer	Switzerland	United States	Olympia	12 Aug 1828
TROLLOP, Thom Adolfis	20			England	U. States	Corinthian	8 Oct 1828
Thomas A.	45			England	U. States	Corinthian	8 Oct 1828
TROMBULL, Wm.	29 5/12	M	Merchant	United States	United States	Minerva	26 May 1821
TRONCHIN, Bernard	30	M	Bookkeeper	Guadaloupe		Tryon	3 Sep 1827
Bernardine	7	F		St. Barts		Tryon	3 Sep 1827
Cleobuline	5	F		St. Barts		Tryon	3 Sep 1827
Emma	10/12	F		St. Thomas		Tryon	3 Sep 1827
Magdelena	22	F		St. Barts		Tryon	3 Sep 1827
TROONT, Jno.	18	M	Shoemaker	England	U. States	Hope & Esther	22 Jul 1825
TROOP, Archibald	8 1/12			Scotland	United States	Mobile	21 Aug 1827
Catherine, Mrs.	36 7/12	F		Scotland	United States	Mobile	21 Aug 1827
James	6 3/12	M		Scotland	United States	Mobile	21 Aug 1827
Malcom	4 8/12	M		Scotland	United States	Mobile	21 Aug 1827
Mary	1 1/12	F		Scotland	United States	Mobile	21 Aug 1827
Mathew	12	M		New York	United States	Andrew Jackson	8 Mar 1820
William	10 4/12	M		Scotland	United States	Mobile	21 Aug 1827
William	36 4/12	M	Cloth...apper	Scotland	United States	Mobile	21 Aug 1827
TROPOLI, John	30	M	Merchant	Spain	Spain	Virginia	26 May 1828
TROSCHER, Joseph	20	M	Blacksmith	Germany	United States	Montano	8 May 1827
TROSSITT, Thos.	30	M	Laborer	Great Britain	United States	Diana	6 Jul 1829
TROTMAN, —, Miss	25	F	Farmer	Barbadoes	U. States	Azores	2 Jun 1824
Charles	30	M	Gentleman	England	New York	Jupiter	19 Oct 1826
TROTT, —, Miss	13	F	Merchant	Bermuda	Bermuda	Improvement	6 Jun 1826
—, Mrs.	38	F	Merchant	Bermuda	Bermuda	Improvement	6 Jun 1826
Anne	28	M		U.S.A.		François I	19 Nov 1828
Sam	20	M	Mercht.	Bermuda	U. States	Susan	2 Aug 1822
TROTTER, —	35	M		...		Amity	11 May 1821
Andrew B.	5	M		Great Britain	United States	Freak	14 oct 1828
Charles	33	M	Merchant	Great Britain	United States	Freak	14 oct 1828
Charles	36	M		Great Britain		Casanda	5 Sep 1827
Christopher	2	M				John Dickinson	14 Sep 1820
Elizabeth	34	F		Great Britain	United States	Freak	14 oct 1828
Hannah	4	F				John Dickinson	14 Sep 1820
Hannah	17	F		Great Britain	United States	Freak	14 oct 1828
Jonathan	7	M		Great Britain	United States	Freak	14 oct 1828
Margaret	25	F				John Dickinson	14 Sep 1820
Mary J.	2	F		Great Britain	United States	Freak	14 oct 1828
Susan	48	F	Servant	U.S.	New York	Brighton	24 Aug 1827
Thomas	18	M	Clerk	Ireland	New York	Brighton	24 Aug 1827
TROUIT, Nathl.	23	M	Merchant	U. States	U. States	Sanford William	14 Dec 1824
TROUT, Jonas	25	M	Blaise Dr...	Great Britain	New York	Zodiac	14 Jun 1822
TROUTMAN, Catharine	5	F		Amsterdam	New Jersey	Margaret	18 Aug 1825
Jacob	39	M	Farmer	Amsterdam	New Jersey	Margaret	18 Aug 1825
Maria	9 6/12	F		Amsterdam	New Jersey	Margaret	18 Aug 1825
Maria	37	F		Amsterdam	New Jersey	Margaret	18 Aug 1825
TROVORT, Joseph	45	M	Merchant	Quebeck	Quebeck	Superior	25 Sep 1828
TROWBRIDGE, S.	42	M	Mariner	Milford	United States	Levant	15 Aug 1823
TROWMAN, Ben	10	M	None	Great Britain	United States	Ann Maria	12 Jul 1821
Hanna	7	F	None	Great Britain	United States	Ann Maria	12 Jul 1821
Joseph	12	M	None	Great Britain	United States	Ann Maria	12 Jul 1821
Mary	38	F	None	Great Britain	United States	Ann Maria	12 Jul 1821
Rachl.	8	F	None	Great Britain	United States	Ann Maria	12 Jul 1821
TRUDDA, Pat	20	M	Gardner	Ireland	United States	Josephine	30 Apr 1828
TRUDEN, Ann	27	F		Irereland	America	Carolina Ann	20 Jun 1825
Patrick	25	M	Labourer	Irereland	America	Carolina Ann	20 Jun 1825
TRUEBA, Pedro José	34	M	Merchant	Spain	U. States	Pomona	4 Apr 1823
TRUEBORN, Margaret	34	F	Farmer	France	United States	Crescent	12 Jul 1827
Ray	32		Farmer	France	United States	Crescent	12 Jul 1827
TRUEDDL, Th.	24	M	Iron Founder	Scotland	United States	Louisiana	3 Nov 1827
TRUEFIL, Wm.	23		Mercht.	U. States		Columbia	7 May 1828
TRUEMAN, Ann	10	F		Great Britain	United States	Freake	25 Aug 1829
Ellen	65	F		Great Britain	United States	Freake	25 Aug 1829
George	49	M	Hatter	New York	New York	Brighton	21 Jan 1826
Harman	48	M		Great Britain	United States	Freake	25 Aug 1829
John	7	M		Great Britain	United States	Freake	25 Aug 1829

NAMES OF PASSENGERS	AGE	SEX	OCCUPATIONS	COUNTRY TO WHICH THEY BELONG	COUNTRY THEY INTEND TO INHABIT	SHIPS/DATES OF ARRIVAL	
TRUEMAN (cont'd)							
Martha	4	F		Great Britain	United States	Freake	25 Aug 1829
Richard	46	M	Farmer	Great Britain	United States	Freake	25 Aug 1829
Sarah	13	F	None	New York	New York	Brighton	21 Jan 1826
William	6	M		England	United States	Cosmo	26 Aug 1829
William	8	M	None	New York	New York	Brighton	21 Jan 1826
Wm.	10	M		Great Britain	United States	Freake	25 Aug 1829
TRUFF, Mary	21	F	Servant	Great Brittain	Savannah	Albion	11 Jun 1821
TRUKY, —, Mrs.	30	F	Lady	Nassau	United States	Superior	14 Apr 1825
TRULL, Mary	21	F		United States	United States	Abigail	23 Nov 1820
TRULOVE, —, Mrs.	36		Wife [of James]	London		Pomona	28 May 1822
Hannah	6/12		Daughter [of James]			Pomona	28 May 1822
James	38		Engineer	London		Pomona	28 May 1822
John	2		Son [of James]			Pomona	28 May 1822
Leo	6		Son [of James]			Pomona	28 May 1822
TRUMAN, Clisa	8	F		England	United States	Cosmo	26 Aug 1829
Emma	1	F		England	United States	Cosmo	26 Aug 1829
Louisa	4	F		England	United States	Cosmo	26 Aug 1829
Rachel	31	F		England	United States	Cosmo	26 Aug 1829
William	32	M	Mason	England	United States	Cosmo	26 Aug 1829
TRUMBETE, W.	26	M	Mariner	G. Brittain	U. States	Jane	13 Dec 1824
TRUMBLE, G.	1	M		England	U. States	Champion	7 Jun 1822
James	35	M	Blacksmith	England	U. States	Champion	7 Jun 1822
Jas., Jr.	4	M		England	U. States	Champion	7 Jun 1822
Jno.	10	M		England	U. States	Champion	7 Jun 1822
Margaret	36	F		England	U. States	Champion	7 Jun 1822
Thos.	8	M		England	U. States	Champion	7 Jun 1822
Wm.	6	M		England	U. States	Champion	7 Jun 1822
TRUMPF, Paul	30	M	Farmer	France	France	Edward Quesnel	3 Jul 1829
TRUSCOTT, Ann	30			Northampton-shire	N. York State	Peru	30 May 1828
James	9			Northampton-shire	N. York State	Peru	30 May 1828
Luke	30		Farmer	Northampton-shire	N. York State	Peru	30 May 1828
Thomas	3			Northampton-shire	N. York State	Peru	30 May 1828
TRUSSON, Edward	28	M	Merchant	U. States	U. States	Bayard	19 Mar 1824
G. E.	29 9/12	M	Merchant	United States	United States	Cadmus	9 Dec 1825
G. E.	30		Merchant	Philadelphia	U. States	Brown	11 Jun 1827
TRYON, Mose	40	M	Merchant	U. States	U. States	Dover	17 Aug 1821
*Landed at Cape May							
Moses	38	M	Merchant	U.S.	U.S.	Radius	10 Aug 1822
Moses	40	M	Merchant	U.S.	U.S.	Radius	29 Jul 1823
TSAR, E.	28	M	Merchant	Spain	Havana	Tarantula	31 Oct 1823
TUCHEY, Charles	21	M	Farmer	G.B.	U.S.	London	19 Dec 1823
John	55	M	Farmer	G.B.	U.S.	London	19 Dec 1823
TUCKER, —	4	M		Bermuda	U. States	Agnes	1 Jul 1825
—	6	F		Bermuda	U. States	Agnes	1 Jul 1825
—, Mrs.	30	F		Bermuda	U. States	Agnes	1 Jul 1825
A., Miss	28	F		Denmark	Denmark	Gleaner	31 Jul 1821
A., Mrs.	60	F		Denmark	Denmark	Gleaner	31 Jul 1821
Adam	6	M	Farmer	Germany	United States	Lydia	18 Jun 1828
B. J.	35	M	Merchant	Barbadoes	Barbadoes	Macdonough	5 Jul 1823
C. C.	22	M		U. States	United States	Florida	14 Sep 1827
Charlotte	35	F	Lady	G. Brittain		Mary & Elizabeth	17 May 1824
D.	26	M	Seaman	U. States	U. States	Atlantic	15 Oct 1821
Daniel	26		Mariner	U. States	U. States	Eliza Pigott	25 Sep 1820
Eliza	8	F	Farmer	Germany	United States	Lydia	18 Jun 1828
Francis	3...	F		Switzerland	U. States	Robert Edward	2 Nov 1827
Frs. G.	29	M	Merchant	Antigua	U. States	Spartan	17 Dec 1823
Geo	38	M	Farmer	Germany	United States	Lydia	18 Jun 1828
Geo.	25	M	Merchant	G. Brittain	U. States	Nestor	3 Apr 1822
Geo. D.	20	M	Merchant	U. States	U. States	Mary Margaret	26 Apr 1823
Geo. D.	23	M	Merchant	Bermuda	Bermuda	Emblem	25 Oct 1825
George D., Sr., Mrs.	25	F	family [of George D.]	Turks Island	U. States	Gold Hunter	24 Oct 1829

NAMES OF PASSENGERS	AGE	SEX	OCCUPATIONS	COUNTRY TO WHICH THEY BELONG	COUNTRY THEY INTEND TO INHABIT	SHIPS/DATES OF ARRIVAL	
TUCKER (cont'd)							
George D., Sr. [Sir]	28	M	Gover. of Turks Island & family	Turks Island	U. States	Gold Hunter	24 Oct 1829
James D.	35	M	Merchant	Bermuda	U. States	Spartan	26 Dec 1826
Jno.	42	M	...	Switzerland	U. States	Robert Edward	2 Nov 1827
John B.	30	M	Joiner	Bermuda	U. States	Agnes	1 Jul 1825
John R.	21	M	Merchant	U. States	U. States	Robert Edwards	25 Apr 1821
Joseph	22	M	Merchant	America	America	Pilgrim	24 Nov 1820
Js. L.	40	M	Merchant	Norfolk		William	23 Jun 1821
Lewis	2	M	family [of George D.]	Turks Island	U. States	Gold Hunter	24 Oct 1829
M.	39	F	Farmer	Germany	United States	Lydia	18 Jun 1828
M., Miss	32	F		Denmark	Denmark	Gleaner	31 Jul 1821
Peter	14	M	Farmer	Germany	United States	Lydia	18 Jun 1828
Richard, Capt.				England	Ut. States	Courier	13 Jul 1826
Saml.	28	M	Mariner	U. States	U. States	Tally Ho	22 Mar 1825
T.	5	M	Farmer	Germany	United States	Lydia	18 Jun 1828
Thomas	22	M	Merchant	Maine	U. States	Orlando	5 May 1826
Thomas W.	20	M	Advocat at Law	New York	New York	Florida	28 Jun 1825
William						Aria	16 Jan 1829
*American Seaman sent home by the U.S. Consul at St. Barts							
William	32	M	Preacher	London	New York	Ann Maria	24 Feb 1824
TUCKEY, Damaris	50	F	None	Ireland	America	Minerva	31 May 1824
Francis	13	M	None	Ireland	America	Minerva	31 May 1824
TUCKS, Emma	24	F	Lady	England	U. States	Bayard	5 Sep 1828
Jacob	21	M	Farmer	Switzerland	America	Don Quixotte	2 Jun 1828
TUDOR, Samuel P.	32	M	Merchant	Barbados	Supposition is he will return	Superb	7 Jul 1823
TUFFERN, George	26	M	Merchant	England	U. States	Florida	16 May 1827
TUGGARD, John	49	M	Tailor	Northwick	Northwick	Howard Douglass	11 May 1827
TUGHES, —, Mrs.	37	F		G. Britain	U. States	St. George	7 Jun 1828
Cathr.	5	F		G. Britain	U. States	St. George	7 Jun 1828
Emily	20	F		G. Britain	U. States	St. George	7 Jun 1828
Henry	37	M	Labourer	G. Britain	U. States	St. George	7 Jun 1828
Heny.	7	M		G. Britain	U. States	St. George	7 Jun 1828
Mary Ann	24	F		G. Britain	U. States	St. George	7 Jun 1828
Sophia	14	F		G. Britain	U. States	St. George	7 Jun 1828
TUINEGAN, Eliz.	22	F		Bavaria	United States	Cavalier	25 Jul 1828
TUINER, Jas.	26	M	None	Gt. Britain	Gt. Britain	Adno	29 Apr 1825
TUIRSE, Perre	31	M	Farmer	France	U. States	C. Amelia	30 Jun 1828
TUIT, Alicia, Miss	25	F	Spinster	G. Britain	U. States	Canada	19 Sep 1828
Aron	2	M		G. Britain	U. States	Canada	19 Sep 1828
Ewd.	32	M		G. Britain	U. States	Canada	19 Sep 1828
James	27	M	Farmer	England	United States	India	8 Jun 1827
Marian	24	F		G. Britain	U. States	Canada	19 Sep 1828
Susan	26	F		G. Britain	U. States	Canada	19 Sep 1828
Thos.	4	M		G. Britain	U. States	Canada	19 Sep 1828
TUITE, B.	34	M	Doctor	St. Croix	U. States	Victory	26 Oct 1824
TUITT, Jno.	9	M		Great Britain	United States	Atlantic	28 May 1827
Margert	56	F		Great Britain	United States	Atlantic	28 May 1827
Walter	57	M	Labourer	Great Britain	United States	Atlantic	28 May 1827
TULL, Samuell T.	35	M	Marener	U.N. States		Orient	9 Dec 1826
*sent Home by the Marican Counsell							
Sarah E., Miss		F	Lady	Barbados	unknown	Superb	23 Apr 1823
TULLER, W. H.	25	M	Merchant	U. States	U. States	Ardell	14 May 1828
TULLEY, J.	2	M	None	Ireland	Upper Canada	Infant	21 Nov 1820
Rosand	4	F	None	Ireland	Upper Canada	Infant	21 Nov 1820
TULLIGAN, Charlotte	15	F		England	United States	William Byrnes	11 Dec 1827
Elisabeth	13	F		England	United States	William Byrnes	11 Dec 1827
Elisabeth	36	F		England	United States	William Byrnes	11 Dec 1827
George	17	M		England	United States	William Byrnes	11 Dec 1827
Henry	6	M		England	United States	William Byrnes	11 Dec 1827
James	3	M		England	United States	William Byrnes	11 Dec 1827
John	5	M		England	United States	William Byrnes	11 Dec 1827
Mary Ann	9	F		England	United States	William Byrnes	11 Dec 1827
Thomas	11	M		England	United States	William Byrnes	11 Dec 1827
Thomas	40	M	Farmer	England	United States	William Byrnes	11 Dec 1827
William	3/12	M		England	United States	William Byrnes	11 Dec 1827

NAMES OF PASSENGERS	AGE	SEX	OCCUPATIONS	COUNTRY TO WHICH THEY BELONG	COUNTRY THEY INTEND TO INHABIT	SHIPS/DATES OF ARRIVAL	
TULLY, Bridget	20	F	Servant	Ireland	United States	William	20 Jul 1829
Eleanor	21	F	Servant	Ireland	United States	Wilson	27 Jun 1826
Jas.	24	M	Laborer	Scotland	U. States	Czar	29 Aug 1829
John	36	M	Dyer	Great Britain	United States	Ganges	26 Oct 1826
Margaret	52	F	Woman	Ireland	U. States	Erin	5 Jul 1820
Mathew	30		Farmer	Great Britan	United States	Newry	11 Jul 1827
Patrick	20	M	Farmer	Ireland	U. States	Erin	5 Jul 1820
Rossey	29	F	None	Ireland	Upper Canada	Infant	21 Nov 1820
TULOOGA, Antoniro	12	M	Merchant	Spain	France	Greek	19 May 1826
J.	43	M	Merchant	Spain	France	Greek	19 May 1826
TULY, Wm.	22	M	Sevt.	England	England	Manhattan	21 Sep 1822
TUMBLE, Anne	24	F	Servant	Ireland	America	Weser	26 Jun 1821
John	25	M	Carpenter	England	United States	Jubilee	1 Oct 1828
TUMBLETY, James	24	M	Baker	Ireland	United States	Carolina Ann	11 Dec 1826
Nichl.	19	M	Baker	Ireland	United States	Carolina Ann	11 Dec 1826
TUMEY, Jeremiah	15	M	Seaman	N. York	N. York	St. Helena	18 Feb 1823
TUMLTY, Catharine	50	F		County of Down, Ireland	U. States	Lady Washington	16 Oct 1821
Magret	18	F		County of Down, Ireland	U. States	Lady Washington	16 Oct 1821
Patrick	22	M		County of Down, Ireland	U. States	Lady Washington	16 Oct 1821
Thomas	10	M	Capt.	Orange County	U. States	Lady Washington	16 Oct 1821
Thomas	54	M	Cooper	County of Down, Ireland	U. States	Lady Washington	16 Oct 1821
TUMMIN, Patrick	24	M	Mason	Ireland	U. States	Courier	17 Mar 1828
TUMPKIN, John	30	M	Farmer	England	United States	Jubilee	1 Oct 1828
TUNCODILLO, M.	55	M	Merchant	Mexico	Mexico	Eunice	17 Jul 1828
TUNCOT, Mary	21	F	Farmer, Labourer or Spinster	Ireland	U. States	Meteor	4 Oct 1827
TUNIRAL, T.	21	M	Merchant	France	America	Don Quixote	2 Jun 1828
TUNIS, Catharine	19	F		Irereland	America	Carolina Ann	20 Jun 1825
John, Jr.	21	M	Mechanic	N. York	U. States	Adams	27 Jun 1825
TUNNCHEAL, Agness	20	F	None	Scotland	United States	Washington	2 Oct 1828
John	25	M	Weaver	Scotland	United States	Washington	2 Oct 1828
Mary	9/12	F	Weaver	Scotland	United States	Washington	2 Oct 1828
*Dide Sept 21 - 1828							
TUNSALL, Josiah	11			Ireland		Anacreon	7 Sep 1827
Reidal	50			Ireland		Anacreon	7 Sep 1827
Wm.	50			Ireland		Anacreon	7 Sep 1827
TUOMY, David	23	M	Farmer	Ireland	America	William	21 May 1825
Jeremiah	28	M	Gardoner	Great Britain	United States	Henrietta	19 Oct 1825
John	30	M	Labourer	Great Britain	United States	Henrietta	19 Oct 1825
TUR, John	23	M	Shoe Maker	G. Britain	U. States	George Clinton	10 Sep 1828
TURBEE, Jas.	27	M	Tailor	Switzerland	U.S. America	Huntress	6 Sep 1827
TURELL, John Emele	13	M		Spain	U. States	Commerce	8 Aug 1821
TURES, J.	13	M	Merchant	Havana	Havana	Crusader	23 Apr 1827
TURFF, Daniel	30	M	Labourer	Scotland	U.S.	Curler	19 Jul 1828
TURGUAND, Alexander	51	M	Gentleman	England	Uncertain	John Wells	22 Sep 1824
TURK, Hannah	19 4/12	F		England	United States	Caspian	12 Jul 1821
John	4/12				United States	Caspian	12 Jul 1821
John W.	20	M	Navy	New York	New York	Betsey	10 Nov 1826
Thomas	20	M		England	United States	William Byrnes	11 Dec 1827
Thos.	3	M	None	Gt. Brittain	United States	Balaena	24 Aug 1825
W. T.	4	M	None	Gt. Brittain	United States	Balaena	24 Aug 1825
TURKE, Bridget	28	F	None	Gt. Brittain	United States	Balaena	24 Aug 1825
Margaret	1	F	None	Gt. Brittain	United States	Balaena	24 Aug 1825
TURKER, Catherine	22	F	Servant	Ireland	United States	St. Michaels	24 Mar 1825
TURKEY, Thos.	19	M	Laborer	England	America	Francis & Henrietta	11 Jul 1823
TURLAR, George	25	M	Merchant	Great Britan	Great Britan	Columbia	11 Aug 1823
TURLEY, Patrick	24 1/12	M	Farmer	Ireland	U.S. America	Illinois	16 Oct 1822
TURMEN, Mary, D...	13		Girl	Ireland	N. Jersey	Potomac	7 Aug 1827
TURNBALL, James	45	M	Merchant	Scotland	U. States	Camillus	27 Jun 1826
Will	40	M	Merchant	Great Britain	United States	James Cropper	14 Oct 1824
TURNBUL, Isabella, Mrs.	22	F		England		Hudson	23 Jul 1828
TURNBULL, —	1	F		Scotland	Scotland	Yamacraw	10 May 1821

NAMES OF PASSENGERS	AGE	SEX	OCCUPATIONS	COUNTRY TO WHICH THEY BELONG	COUNTRY THEY INTEND TO INHABIT	SHIPS/DATES OF ARRIVAL	
TURNBULL (cont'd)							
—, Child	4	M		United States	United States	Langdon Cheeves	19 Mar 1827
—, Mrs.	28	F		United States	United States	Langdon Cheeves	19 Mar 1827
Alaxander	28	M	Weaver	Great Britain	United States	Courier	26 Jun 1827
Alex.	28	M	Merchant	Philada.	U. States	Ardent	2 Nov 1826
Alexr.	30	M	Merchant	United States	United States	Langdon Cheeves	19 Mar 1827
David	28	M	Blacksmith	Scotland	United States	Mary & Susan	5 Aug 1828
Ellen	1 6/12	F	Female	Great Brittain	N. York	Leonidas	24 Jul 1824
Ellen	24	F	Female	Great Brittain	N. York	Leonidas	24 Jul 1824
George	25	M	Baker	Scotland	U. States	Othello	3 Dec 1828
Isabella	28	F		Scotland	Scotland	Yamacraw	10 May 1821
James	21	M	Farmer	England	U. States	Corinthian	2 May 1823
John	45	M	Labourer	Scotland	United States	Samuel Robertson	5 Oct 1827
Rob.	34	M	Weaver	Scotland	Scotland	Yamacraw	10 May 1821
Sandeman	44	M	Merchant	G.B.		Silas Richards	29 Oct 1827
Sandeman	47	M	Merchant	Scotland		Silas Richards	7 Mar 1827
Thos.	30	M	Farmer	Great Britain	America	Samuel Robertson	26 Nov 1825
TURNE, John	45	M	Merchant	U. States	U. States	Ben & James	15 Aug 1820
TURNELL, Mary S.	4	F	Child	G. Brittan	U. States	Henry	24 Oct 1828
TURNER, —, Mrs.	22	F		N. York	U. States	South Carolina	2 Aug 1822
—, Mrs.	35	F	Spinster	France	U. States	Othello	31 Aug 1824
Agnes	53	F		Great Britain	United States	Natchez	17 Aug 1822
Agrs	16	F	Doctor	Scotland	U. States	Roger Stewart	9 Jun 1828
Ann	5	F	None	G. Britain		Ann Maria	3 Jul 1820
Ann	21	F	Doctor	Scotland	U. States	Roger Stewart	9 Jun 1828
Ann	48	F		England	United States	Concordia	25 Aug 1827
Ann Jane	17	F		Ireland	United States	Courier	15 Oct 1827
C. D.	22	F		U. States	U. States	Cannon	25 Apr 1821
Charles	33	M	Merchant	America	U. States	Governor Lincoln	10 Jul 1827
Christiana	53	M	Spinster	Ireland	United States	Courier	15 Oct 1827
Coll	24	M	Labourer	Great Britain	United States	Colossus	5 Jun 1827
David	21	M	Mechanic	England	United States	Concordia	25 Aug 1827
Eliz.	3	F		Great Britain	United States	Atlantic	8 Dec 1827
Elizabeth	6	F		England	United States	Cincinnatus	21 Nov 1821
Ellis	32	F	Servant	Irereland	America	Carolina Ann	20 Jun 1825
Enoch	22	M	Worker at Steam Engines	England	New York	Exertion	3 Dec 1828
Evelina	20	F		U. States	U. States	Brighton	14 Apr 1828
F. H.	29	M	Capt. In the B. Army	England	England	Virginia	8 Mar 1828
Francis	24	M	Laborer	Ireland	United States	Fabius	4 Jun 1828
Francis	25	M	Gentleman	France	U.S.	Helen	3 May 1828
Frederick	20	M	Servant	Creole	don't Know	Industry	31 Jul 1826
Fredrick	15	M	None	U. States	U. States	Roman	1 Dec 1828
Fredrick	20 4/12	M	Merchant	London	New York	Swift	18 Apr 1826
Geo.	13	M	None	Great Britain	United States	Mary & Harriet	3 Jul 1829
Geo. W.	18/12	M		U. States	U. States	Cannon	25 Apr 1821
George	14	M	Mechanic	England	United States	Concordia	25 Aug 1827
George	23	M	Clerk	Great Britain	United States	Hope & Esther	12 Nov 1825
George	25 4/12	M	Farmer	Great Britain	State of N. York	Robert Fulton	30 Dec 1824
Hannah	21	F	None	England	United States	Jubilee	1 Oct 1828
Hannah	29	F	None	Great Britain	United States	William Dawson	18 Jun 1827
Hariet	29			Great Britain	U. States	Nile	30 Apr 1827
Henry	12		Child	England	United States	Cincinnatus	21 Nov 1821
Henry	39	M	Braser	England	United States	Cincinnatus	21 Nov 1821
Henry W.	40	M	Mariner	United States	United States	General Warren	5 May 1828
*Distressd. Seaman from Schnr. Indus							
Isaac	1	M	None	England	U. States	Thomas Ritchie	2 Jul 1827
James	25	M	Baker	England	U. States	Rising Sun	1 May 1823
James	34	M	Shopkeeper	Great Britain	United States	Ann Maria	12 Jul 1821
James	41	M	Indianerr	N. York		Swift	28 Jun 1828
James	46	M	Engineer	England	America	Two Marys	24 Sep 1827
James	55	M		Ireland	United States	Trio	2 Oct 1828

TURNER (cont'd)

NAMES OF PASSENGERS	AGE	SEX	OCCUPATIONS	COUNTRY TO WHICH THEY BELONG	COUNTRY THEY INTEND TO INHABIT	SHIPS/DATES OF ARRIVAL
Jno.	2	M	None	England	U. States	Thomas Ritchie 2 Jul 1827
John	4	M	None	Great Britain	United States	William Dawson 18 Jun 1827
John	20	M	Mechanic	England	United States	Concordia 25 Aug 1827
John	22	M	Shoemaker	Ireland	United States	Trio 2 Oct 1828
John	24	M	Merchant	Great Britain		Birmingham 11 Oct 1828
John	25	M	Farmer	Great Britain	United States	Natchez 17 Aug 1822
John	25	M	Farmer	England	United States	Richmond 4 Aug 1826
John	25	M	Labourer	Ireland	United States	Meteor 26 Jun 1827
John	26	M	Merchant	United States	United States	Baltic 21 Apr 1827
John	26	M	Bricklayer	G. Britain	U. States	Armadello 22 Jun 1827
John	27	M	Farmer	England	Alexandria, U.S.	Roman 17 Oct 1826
John	40	M	Labourer	Great Brittan	U. States	John & Elizabeth 11 Dec 1826
John	46			England	England	London 16 Aug 1824
John	60	M	Doctor	Scotland	U. States	Roger Stewart 9 Jun 1828
John	61	M	School Master	England	United States	Concordia 25 Aug 1827
John M.	45	M		U. States	U. States	Magnet 29 Sep 1823
Joseph	32	M	Weaver	Great Britain	United States	William Dawson 18 Jun 1827
M.	34	M	Farmer	Great Britain	United States	Washington 3 Sep 1827
Margt.	5		Child	England	United States	Cincinnatus 21 Nov 1821
Margt.	22	F	Sempstress	Great Britain	United States	Atlantic 8 Dec 1827
Maria	19	F	...	Great Britain	Taunton, Mass.	Hesperus 13 Oct 1825
Martha	24	F	Housekeeper	Ireland	America	Alexander Mansfield 18 Jun 1821
Mary	1	F		Great Britain	United States	Atlantic 8 Dec 1827
Mary	18	F	Spinner	G. Brittian	United States	Louisa 14 Jun 1825
Mary	24	F	None	G. Britain		Ann Maria 3 Jul 1820
Mary	26	F	None	England	U. States	Thomas Ritchie 2 Jul 1827
Mary	48	F	Doctor	Scotland	U. States	Roger Stewart 9 Jun 1828
Mary	54	F		England	United States	Nancy Henrietta 3 Nov 1828
May	14	F	Doctor	Scotland	U. States	Roger Stewart 9 Jun 1828
Michael	31	M	Silversmith	Great Britain	United States	George Clinton 27 Aug 1827
Michl.	18		Labourer	Ireland	United States	Courier 15 Oct 1827
Peter	20	M	Labourer	Great Britain	U. States	Superb 28 May 1821
Peter	40	M	Carpenter	U. States	U. States	Commodore Perry 9 Apr 1821
Ralph	26	M	...	Great Britain	Taunton, Mass.	Hesperus 13 Oct 1825
Ralph	27	M	Merchant	Great Britain	United States	Dapper 21 Aug 1828
Rebecca	5	F	None	England	U. States	Thomas Ritchie 2 Jul 1827
Rebecca	31	F		Great Britain	United States	George Clinton 27 Aug 1827
Rebecca	35	F		England	United States	Cincinnatus 21 Nov 1821
Richard	23	M	Farmer	England	United States	Jubilee 1 Oct 1828
Richd.	21	M	Carpenter			Hercules 25 Sep 1820
Robert	43	M	Carpenter	New York	New York	Harriot 1 May 1822
S. F.	4	M		U. States	U. States	Cannon 25 Apr 1821
Saml.	32	M	Merchant	U. States	U. States	Cannon 25 Apr 1821
Saml.	33	M	Merchant	N. York	U. States	South Carolina 2 Aug 1822
Samuel *Dead	42	M	Supercargo	U. States	U. States	Mary 12 Aug 1828
Samuel, Capt.	39	M	Mariner	New York	New York	Douglass 8 May 1826
Sarah	2	F		G. Britain	U. States	Armadello 22 Jun 1827
Sarah	19	F	Servant			Hercules 25 Sep 1820
Sarah	24	F	Weaver	Ireland	New York	America 1 Aug 1828
Sarah	33	F	None	Great Britain		Birmingham 11 Oct 1828
Susannah	7/12	F		G. Britain	U. States	Armadello 22 Jun 1827
Susannah	30	F		G. Britain	U. States	Armadello 22 Jun 1827
Thomas	20	M	Joiner	B...lon	Bolton	Howard Douglass 11 May 1827
Thomas	23	M	Servant	England	United States	Nancy Henrietta 3 Nov 1828
Thomas	28		Baker	Great Britain	U. States	Nile 30 Apr 1827
Thos.	16	M		N. York	U. States	Mercator 27 Aug 1821
William	20	M	Merchant	Great Britain	United States	Hannibal 12 Oct 1829
William	48	M	Printer	England	U. States	Roman 1 Dec 1828
William	50	M	Brickmaker	England	United States	Nancy Henrietta 3 Nov 1828
William, Jr.	6	M	None	England	United States	Nancy Henrietta 3 Nov 1828
Wm.	1	M	None	G. Britain		Ann Maria 3 Jul 1820
Wm.	5	M		Great Britain	United States	Atlantic 8 Dec 1827
Wm.	25	M	Surgeon	England	America	James Cropper 10 Feb 1823

NAMES OF PASSENGERS	AGE	SEX	OCCUPATIONS	COUNTRY TO WHICH THEY BELONG	COUNTRY THEY INTEND TO INHABIT	SHIPS/DATES OF ARRIVAL	
TURNER (cont'd)							
Wm.	28	M	Merchant	Scotland	U. States	Ductile	12 Apr 1825
Wm.	30	M	Labourer	England	U. States	Thomas Ritchie	2 Jul 1827
Wm.	34	M	Farmer	Great Britain	United States	Rosina	28 May 1827
TURNESS, Marcella	31	F	None	Great Britain	New York	Superior	5 Sep 1827
TURNEY, Ann	30	F		Great Britain	United States	Mary Howland	19 Jul 1827
TURNIS, Wm.	24	M	Shoemaker	Belfast	United States	Carolina Ann	11 Jun 1824
TURNLY, Joseph	54	M	Merchant	England	United States	Cincinnatus	21 Nov 1821
TURRELL, Jno. Thomas	11	M		N. Orleans	U. States	Commerce	25 Mar 1822
TURRET, Isablla	25	F	Matron	Ireland	United States	Robert Fulton	24 Jul 1826
TURTON, Ferdon	35	M	Shoemaker	Great Britain	United States	Colossus	1 Nov 1826
John	48	M	Linin Draper	England	America	Ann	2 Nov 1820
TURUNQUE, Augustus	20	M	Gentleman	Columbia	U. States	John Marshall	1 Aug 1825
TUSA..., Alphe	12			United States	United States	Britannia	29 Oct 1829
TUSK, Morly	28	M	Merchant	Europe	United States	Braganza	30 Nov 1827
TUSSUM, John P.	47	M	Servant	France	U. States	Lewis	6 Jul 1825
TUTA, Thomas	25	M	Farmer	England	United States	Justina	5 Aug 1823
TUTE, Catherine	24	F		Ireland	United States	Essex	23 May 1828
Peter	30	M	Weaver		uncertain	Mount Vernon	29 Aug 1828
Richd.	26	M	Labourer	Ireland	United States	Essex	23 May 1828
TUTHETT, Henry ...	23 6/12	M	Merchant	Ireland	New York	Wilson	10 Apr 1823
TUTS, Michl.	22	M	Labourer	Ireland	United States	Essex	23 May 1828
TUTTERTON, Wm.	18	M	Farmer	Scotland	U. States	Hannah	16 Sep 1823
TUTTLE, Dl., Jr.	25	M	Merchant	U. States	U. States	Actress	11 Jul 1822
George	18		Merchant	United States	United States	Xenophon	3 Oct 1829
W.	30	M	Gentleman	New York	New York	Carlo	27 Aug 1829
TUTTON, Jane	24	F	Servant	Canada	Canada	Manchester	6 Dec 1825
Joseph	30	M	Servant	Canada	Canada	Manchester	6 Dec 1825
TUYLL, —, Baron	40	M	Gentleman	Russia	Russia	New York	11 Mar 1823
TWAFE, Geo.	39	M	Farmer	Great Britain	United States	William Dawson	18 Jun 1827
TWEED, John	26	M	Royal Navy	England	Canada	Brighton	11 Mar 1825
Richard	35	M	N. Merchant	York	U. States	Douglass	16 Jul 1824
Richard	36		Mechanic	New York	U. States	Pettrell	15 Sep 1826
Richd.	36		Mechanic	U. States		Patriot	31 May 1825
William	32	M	Merchant	United States		Commerce	3 Nov 1820
William	34	M	...	...	U. States	New England	28 Sep 1824
TWEEDLE, Edward	26	M	Labourer	Scotland	United States	Friends	7 Jul 1827
TWEHEY, C.	9	F		Nova Scotia	United States	Superior	14 Apr 1825
P.	14	F		Nova Scotia	United States	Superior	14 Apr 1825
TWELOVE, S.	25	M	Musician	Genoa	U. States	Nimrod	31 Jul 1828
TWIDALE, John	26	M	Farmer	Scotland	United States	Curler	3 Mar 1828
TWIDDLE,							
Robt. Wharton	23	M	Commissary	Great Brittan	Canada	Cambria	3 Jul 1829
TWIG, Agness	65	F		G. Britain	U. States	Camillus	8 Sep 1828
TWIGY, Paul	40	M	G...	...land	U.S.	Chase	26 Jul 1824
TWINING, Ellen	28 5/12	F		Ireland	U. States	Hopes Delight	21 Apr 1828
TWINNER, Geo.	37	M	Farmer	England	U. States	Commerce	2 Oct 1823
TWIS..., James	22		Laboring Class		United States	Atlantic	2 Apr 1827
TWISWELL, Isabella	23	F	None	Scotland	U. States	Czar	29 Aug 1829
Wm.	21	M	Painter	Scotland	U. States	Czar	29 Aug 1829
TWOMEY, Daniel	29	M	Labourer	Ireland	United States	Trio	2 Oct 1828
John	20	M	Farmer	Ireland	America	Liverpool	31 Aug 1827
Patrick	29	M	Farmer	Ireland	America	William	21 May 1825
TWOMGY, Cathr.	25	F		Ireland	America	Liverpool	31 Aug 1827
TWORGACK, Thomas	26	M	Mechanic	Germany	U. States	Caesar	3 Apr 1828
TWYFORD, Ann	7	F		England	U.S.A.	Hudson	21 Aug 1829
Fanny	13	F		England	U.S.A.	Hudson	21 Aug 1829
Fanny	45	F		England	U.S.A.	Hudson	21 Aug 1829
Lucy	10	F		England	U.S.A.	Hudson	21 Aug 1829
W. B.	25	M	Surgeon	England	America	Birmingham	16 Oct 1826
TYACK, W.	30	M	Gentleman	New York	United States	Howard	14 May 1825
TYBOUT, Thomas M.	17	M	Gent.	U.S. America	U. States	William Thompson	25 Aug 1828
TYFE, Thomas	23	M	Clerk	Aberdeen	Canada	Atlantic	19 Mar 1827
TYHERT, Solomon	52	M	Black Smith	U. States	U. States	Acasta	28 Jan 1823
TYLAR, Wm.	25	M		Great Brittian	United States	Carolina Augusta	2 Dec 1828
TYLER, Daniel, Lt.	30	M	U.S. Armey	U.S.A.	America	Helen	4 Aug 1829
Mary Ann	20	F		United States	United States	Columbia	16 Jan 1829

NAMES OF PASSENGERS	AGE	SEX	OCCUPATIONS	COUNTRY TO WHICH THEY BELONG	COUNTRY THEY INTEND TO INHABIT	SHIPS/DATES OF ARRIVAL	
TYLER (cont'd)							
William	27	M	Merchant	U. States	U. States	Bolivar	9 Dec 1826
Willm.	31	M	Art of Milling	New York	New York	St. Michael	28 Feb 1826
TYLNERST, Richd.	30	M	Farmer	Sussex	U. States	New York	15 Nov 1823
TYLTER, Thos.	53	M	Farmer	Switzerland	U. States	Robert Edward	2 Nov 1827
TYNAM, Dennis	16	M	Mechanic	Ireland	United States	Wm. Byrnes	30 Apr 1828
TYNAN, Bridget	20	F		Ireland	New York	Lima	5 Aug 1829
Bridget	20	F		Ireland	New York	Lima	5 Aug 1829
Joseph	20	M	Druggist	Ireland	Great Brittan	Venus	15 Apr 1822
Michl.	30	M	Servant	Ireland	United States	William	20 Jul 1829
TYNING, Alace	9	F		England	U. States	Florida	13 Jan 1827
Ann	36	F		England	U. States	Florida	13 Jan 1827
Michael	36	M	Calico Printer	England	U. States	Florida	13 Jan 1827
TYROSE, Patt.	27	M	Labourer	Ireland	America	Plutarch	18 Jul 1826
TYRREL, Pattinger	18	M	Labourer	England	America	Sarah	18 Aug 1829
TYSARST, Sarah Anne	2	F	Girl	England	United States	Cambria	8 Oct 1828
Thos. Wm.	11/12	M	Boy	England	United States	Cambria	8 Oct 1828
William	27	M	Baker	England	United States	Cambria	8 Oct 1828
TYSON, —, Mr.	22	M	Merchant	Bermuda	Bermuda	Improvement	6 Jun 1826
Allen	13	M		G. Britain	U. States	Freak	9 Jun 1828
Ann	39	F		G. Britain	U. States	Freak	9 Jun 1828
Ann	78	F		G. Britain	U. States	Freak	9 Jun 1828
Anthony	23	M	Bookkeeper	Gt. Britain	United States	Eliza Barker	11 Jan 1826
Geo.	4	M		G. Britain	U. States	Freak	9 Jun 1828
John	4	M		G. Britain	U. States	Freak	9 Jun 1828
Mary	18	F		G. Britain	U. States	Freak	9 Jun 1828
Mary	30	F	Spinster	Great Britain	United States	Superior	31 Mar 1828
W.	31	M	Planter	St. Croix	St. Croix	Betsey	20 Jun 1826
Wm.	16	M		G. Britain	U. States	Freak	9 Jun 1828
Wm.	27	M	Mariner	N. York	United States	Levant	15 Aug 1823
Wm.	78	M	Farmer	G. Britain	U. States	Freak	9 Jun 1828
TYSZKIEWIEZ, —,							
Count	26	M	Military	G. Britain	U. States	Robt. Edwards	4 Sep 1828
TYTLER, Banja.	48	M	Printer	Great Britain	United States	Albion	18 Feb 1823
TZEBIKI, J., Mr.	34		Colonel	Poland	traveling	Romulus	15 May 1828
UBBERSSELL, C.	30	M	Mechanic	Hanover	U. States	Indiana	20 Sep 1828
UGARTE, Geo.	43	M	Merchant	Spain	Mexico	Cato	2 Jan 1824
UHENS, —, Mr.	25	M	Commedian	Great Britain	U.S.	Robert Edwards	11 Nov 1822
ULISE, Savoie	17	M	Watchmaker	Suisse	United States	Montano	5 May 1828
ULLRICH, Mary	7	F	None	Germany	New York	Elizabeth	5 Jul 1821
ULMAN, J.	17	M		India	India	Wm. Henry	25 Sep 1827
ULMER, Michel	27	M	Taylor	France	U. States	Edward Bopnnaffe	30 Jul 1829
ULRICH, —, Mr.	26	M	Merchant	Germany	New York	Elizabeth	5 Jul 1821
—, Mrs.	24	F	None	Germany	New York	Elizabeth	5 Jul 1821
Ann	13	F		Brattain		L'Esperance	6 Sep 1828
Anna	50	F		Brattain		L'Esperance	6 Sep 1828
Cathr.	3	F	None	Germany	New York	Elizabeth	5 Jul 1821
Jane	5	F	None	Germany	New York	Elizabeth	5 Jul 1821
John	16	M		Brattain		L'Esperance	6 Sep 1828
John	50	M	Cultivator	Brattain		L'Esperance	6 Sep 1828
Maria	3	F		Brattain		L'Esperance	6 Sep 1828
Peter	65	M	Commissioner	Germany	Philadelphia	James Noble	27 Aug 1827
ULTA, Denis	20	M	Labourer	Co. M...tt	Co. M...tt	Howard Douglass	11 May 1827
ULTHES, David	25 3/12	M	Farmer	Switzerland	U. States	France	26 Jun 1828
ULTRA, Daniel	20	M	Lab.	Co. M...tt	Co. M...tt	Howard Douglass	11 May 1827
UMBLER, Richd.	28	M	Packer	England	United States	Essex	23 May 1828
UMISIG, Agatha	21	F		Switzerland	U. States	Romulus	24 Sep 1828
Francis	0 3/12	M		Switzerland	U. States	Romulus	24 Sep 1828
Jacob	32	M	Farmer	Switzerland	U. States	Romulus	24 Sep 1828
John	2	M		Switzerland	U. States	Romulus	24 Sep 1828
Mary	3	F		Switzerland	U. States	Romulus	24 Sep 1828
UMPENHAUER, Phillip	21	M	Baker	France	U. States	Edward Quesnel	4 Aug 1828
UMPHREYS, Charles	24	M	Laborer or Spinster	Ireland	United States	Sarah G.	15 Aug 1827
UMPHRY, George	20	M	Merchant	Barbados	Supposition is he will return	Superb	7 Jul 1823

NAMES OF PASSENGERS	AGE	SEX	OCCUPATIONS	COUNTRY TO WHICH THEY BELONG	COUNTRY THEY INTEND TO INHABIT	SHIPS/DATES OF ARRIVAL	
UNBACKER, Christan	29	M	Merchant	Switzerland	United States	Howard	11 Jun 1824
Elizabeth	23	F		Switzerland	United States	Howard	11 Jun 1824
UNDERHILL, Abraham	25	M	Farmer	St. John, N.B.	Canada	St. Michael	21 Aug 1824
Benjamin	26	M	Cordwainer	Great Britian	U. States America	Columbia	15 Nov 1826
Daniel	26	M	Farmer	St. John, N.B.	Canada	St. Michael	21 Aug 1824
Elethim	70	M	Farmer	St. John, N.B.	Canada	St. Michael	21 Aug 1824
George	21	M	Gentleman	West Indies	U. States	American	29 Nov 1823
Hannah	17	F	Daughter	St. John, N.B.	Canada	St. Michael	21 Aug 1824
Hannah	65	F	Wife	St. John, N.B.	Canada	St. Michael	21 Aug 1824
Jane	15	F	Daughter	St. John, N.B.	Canada	St. Michael	21 Aug 1824
Mary	28	F	Wife	St. John, N.B.	Canada	St. Michael	21 Aug 1824
Patty	14	F	Daughter	St. John, N.B.	Canada	St. Michael	21 Aug 1824
Phillis	28	F	Servant	St. John, N.B.	Canada	St. Michael	21 Aug 1824
Polly	12	F	Daughter	St. John, N.B.	Canada	St. Michael	21 Aug 1824
Samuel	30	M	Farmer	St. John, N.B.	Canada	St. Michael	21 Aug 1824
Stebhan	20	M	Farmer	St. John, N.B.	Canada	St. Michael	21 Aug 1824
UNDERWOOD, J.	60	M	Farmer	Ireland	United States	Dublin Packet	22 Apr 1822
Wm.	20	M		Great Britain	U. States	Ann Marria	6 Aug 1823
UNGA, Fred.	43	M	Joiner	Great Britain		Caravan	8 Sep 1828
Jacob	30	M	Optician	Great Britain		Caravan	8 Sep 1828
UNGAR, Christiana	11	F		Switzerland	U.S.	Francois I	8 Aug 1829
Magdalen	1	F		Switzerland	U.S.	Francois I	8 Aug 1829
Magdalen	32	F		Switzerland	U.S.	Francois I	8 Aug 1829
UNGARETTE,							
Geovachino	20	M	Sculptor	Italy		Edward Quesnel	17 Nov 1828
UNGERER, Peter	40	M	Weaver	France	United States	Helen	5 Sep 1828
UNGEWITTER,							
Christian	36	M	Merchant	Sweden	Sweden	James Cropper	14 Oct 1822
UNIS, Thos.	25	M	Labourer	England	U. States	Thomas Ritchie	2 Jul 1827
UNSWORTH, Robert	44	M	Weaver	England	America	Two Marys	24 Sep 1827
UNTHANK, George, Jr.	28	M	Trader	Great Britian	United States	Isaac Hicks	13 Jan 1826
UPJOHN, Charles	20	M		England	U. States	Criterion	20 Nov 1823
Charles	40	M	Taylor	England	U. States	Criterion	20 Nov 1823
Elizabeth	15	F		England	U. States	Criterion	20 Nov 1823
Mary	35	F		England	U. States	Criterion	20 Nov 1823
Phoebe	19	F		England	U. States	Criterion	20 Nov 1823
Richard	12	M		England	U. States	Criterion	20 Nov 1823
Sarah	17	F		England	U. States	Criterion	20 Nov 1823
Sarah	66	F		America	America	Comet	26 Jun 1822
Wm.	18	M		England	U. States	Criterion	20 Nov 1823
UPPS, James	22	M	Farmer	England	England	Criterion	29 May 1822
UPSHAW, Johob	49	M	Farmer	France	United States	Great Britain	18 Sep 1826
URE, Andrew	28	M	Gardner	Great Britain	United States	Courier	13 Mar 1820
UREN, John	49	M	Farmer	U. Canada	U. Canada	Alexander Mansfield	16 Sep 1823
URGHART, F., Mr.	25	M	Clerk	England	U.S. America	Leeds	6 Jun 1826
URGUHART, Daniel	39	M	Moulder	Great Britain	United States	Thomas Dickason	14 Sep 1827
URIOT, Sarah	5	F		England	United States	Ann Maria	27 Aug 1822
Sarah	25	F		England	United States	Ann Maria	27 Aug 1822
Wm.	26	M	Farmer	England	United States	Ann Maria	27 Aug 1822
URK, M.	40	M	Joiner	Great Britain		Caravan	8 Sep 1828
URNINETTA, Heronimus	9	M	a Child	Valparaiso	U.S.	Fame	22 Mar 1826
URQUGA, Leonarda	7	F	None	Spain	U. States	Frances	22 May 1827
URQUHART, George	23	M	Farmer	Scotland	United States	Belmont	30 Aug 1828
URTIQUA, J. G.	36	M	Mercht.	Spain	U. States	Brown	7 Jul 1826
URY, M. W.	28	F		Barbadoes	U. States	Venus	1 Apr 1828
USHER, Francis	25	M	Grocer	Great Britian	United States	Andes	19 Aug 1829
N. L.	40	M	...	England	U.S.	Chase	26 Jul 1824
Patrick	23	M	Merchant	U. States	U. States	Midas	25 Nov 1824
Silas, Mr.	26	M	Carpenter	England	U. States	Acasta	11 Dec 1826
USUNA, B. Jas.	52	M	Gent.	Spain	Spain	Fabius	19 Mar 1825
UTLEY, Jacob	21	M	Joiner	America	America	Pilgrim	24 Nov 1820
UTTEN, —, Mrs.	46	F		Jamaica	Jamaica	Huntress	15 Oct 1823
V..., ...erbeca	8	F		Switzerland	United States	Elbe	2 Aug 1822
Berbeca	8	F		Switzerland	United States	Elbe	2 Aug 1822
V...GE, Frederick	22	M	Farmer	Switzerland	United States	Elbe	2 Aug 1822
VACANO, John	12	M		Spain	U. States	Genl. Victoria	7 Apr 1828

NAMES OF PASSENGERS	AGE	SEX	OCCUPATIONS	COUNTRY TO WHICH THEY BELONG	COUNTRY THEY INTEND TO INHABIT	SHIPS/DATES OF ARRIVAL	
VACAR, John	2		Boy	Ireland	Albany	Potomac	7 Aug 1827
Mary	22	F		Ireland	Albany	Potomac	7 Aug 1827
VACKEVISSER, G.	30	M	Merchant	Holland	Holland	James Cropper	29 Nov 1827
VAGER, Wm.	23	M	Lawer	Spain	Spain	Saluda	15 Jul 1826
VAGG, Ann	19	F	Lady	New York	New York	Brighton	11 Dec 1827
VAIL, —, Mrs.	30	F		N. York	N. York	Hope & Esther	19 Aug 1824
Benjamin	5	M		England	U.S.A.	Hudson	21 Aug 1829
Eliza	4	F		England	U.S.A.	Hudson	21 Aug 1829
Eliza	5	F		N. York	N. York	Hope & Esther	19 Aug 1824
Euphemia	8	F		England	U.S.A.	Hudson	21 Aug 1829
Hepzibah	39	F		England	U.S.A.	Hudson	21 Aug 1829
Mary	45	F	Lady	St. John	St. John	Ann Maria	5 May 1824
Matilda	9	F		England	U.S.A.	Hudson	21 Aug 1829
VAILLARD, Joseph	28	M	Servant	France		Birmingham	11 Oct 1828
VALACTIN, Fred	37 4/12	M	Farmer	Switzerland	U. States	France	26 Jun 1828
VALADE, Jules	25	M	Merchant	Gaudaloupe	Gaudaloupe	Jane	13 Aug 1827
VALADO, Cepreano	36	M	Servant	Spain	S. America	Abeona	12 Oct 1825
VALASCO, Antonio	32	M	Merchant	Spain	U. States	Magnet	3 May 1826
VALCREES, Isabella	26	F	Spinster	Ireland	United States	Trident	16 May 1826
VALDERE, John	45	M	Merchant	America	U. States	Belle Victorie	18 Oct 1827
VALDES, Aug.	20	M	Gent.	Havana	U. States	Silas Richards	29 Oct 1828
VALDORE, Tim.	35	M	Merchant	Spain	U. States	Colonel George Armstead	13 May 1823
VALEE, Philip	26	M	Merchant	Charleston	U. States	Circassian	3 Jun 1826
VALENTINE, Ann	25	F		Gt. Britain	U. States	Camberwell	7 Apr 1828
David	42	M	Gentleman	Jamaica	U. States	Plandome	12 Aug 1826
E. A.	24	M	Merchant	U. States	U. States	Emblem	14 May 1827
Eug.	33	M	Servant	Germany	U. States	Bayard	5 Sep 1828
Gilbert	2 3/12	M		St. Johns, N.B.	United States	Henrietta	17 Aug 1825
James	32	M	Shoe Maker	Gt. Britain	U. States	Camberwell	7 Apr 1828
John James	9	M		St. Johns, N.B.	United States	Henrietta	17 Aug 1825
M. G.	37	M	Farmer	St. Johns	U. States	Isabella	28 Jun 1825
Margaret	14	F		St. Johns, N.B.	United States	Henrietta	17 Aug 1825
Martha	8	F		St. Johns, N.B.	United States	Henrietta	17 Aug 1825
Mary	30	F		United States	New York	Leeds	7 Nov 1828
Mary	33	F	Seamstress	St. Johns, N.B.	United States	Henrietta	17 Aug 1825
VALERE, Paul	38	M	Merchant	St. Domingo	Hayti	Fair Play	22 May 1821
VALET, Mary	24	F	Servant	England	U.S. America	Huntress	6 Sep 1827
VAL FORTH, Ehert	45	M	Weaver	Ireland		Quatre Freres	29 Jul 1828
Joseph	16	M	Weaver	Ireland		Quatre Freres	29 Jul 1828
Maryen	45	F	Weaver	Ireland		Quatre Freres	29 Jul 1828
VALFORTH, Ehert	8	F	Weaver	Ireland		Quatre Freres	29 Jul 1828
Maryan	17	F	Weaver	Ireland		Quatre Freres	29 Jul 1828
Teboth	3	M	Weaver	Ireland		Quatre Freres	29 Jul 1828
VALIANT, Alexander	24	M	Merchant	France	U. States	Edward Bonnaffe	4 May 1827
Cornelia	20	F	Wife	France	U. States	Edward Bonnaffe	4 May 1827
Maria Fraziska	34	F		France	United States	New England	29 Aug 1828
VALLALLY, Mary	19		Spinster	Ireland	United States	Courier	15 Oct 1827
VALLE, Jas. M.	19	M	Merchant	Mexico	U. States	Sarah	26 Jul 1824
VALLENTINE, J.	22	M	Mariner	America	U. States	Ambuscade	11 Jul 1821
VALLER, Elizabeth	5	F		Switzerland	United States	Elizabeth	27 Jul 1824
Elizabeth	29	F		Switzerland	United States	Elizabeth	27 Jul 1824
Johanes	28	M	Farmer	Switzerland	United States	Elizabeth	27 Jul 1824
John, Mr.	31	M	Carpenter	England	U.S.	Acasta	11 May 1827
M. J.	22	M	Doctor	France & Switzerland	U. States	Bayard	14 Jul 1826
Maria	2	F		Switzerland	United States	Elizabeth	27 Jul 1824
Phillip	51	M	Painter	St. Domingo	U. States	Purrington	14 May 1827
VALLERS, Lewis	20	M	Mercht.	Swiss	Swiss	Stephania	13 Sep 1821
VALLET, Christopher	27	M	Weaver	Germany	United States	Helen	5 Sep 1828
VALLIE, G.	28		Merchant	France	New York	James Cropper	12 Jul 1822
VALLOLDS, R.	36	M	Merchant	Havana	United States	James Monroe	3 Jul 1824
VALLS, Jose	25	M	Merchant	Cuba	Cuba	William	18 Oct 1824
VALLUS, Henry, Servant	40	M	Servant	Hamburgh	U.S. of America	Canada	1 Oct 1827
VALLY, Barb	20	F	Weaver	Switzerland	United States	Thetis	5 Jul 1821
VALO, Jean B.	42	M	Farmer	France	U. States	Leonarde	29 Aug 1828
Joseph	6	M		France	U. States	Leonarde	29 Aug 1828

NAMES OF PASSENGERS	AGE	SEX	OCCUPATIONS	COUNTRY TO WHICH THEY BELONG	COUNTRY THEY INTEND TO INHABIT	SHIPS/DATES OF ARRIVAL	
VALO (cont'd)							
Marie J. M.	27	F		France	U. States	Leonarde	29 Aug 1828
VALOIS, Victor	28	M	Clerk	France	U. States	Sully	15 Jul 1829
VALOT, Henry	17	M	Apothicary	Bardin	U. States	Bayard	5 Sep 1828
VALRICK, Chas.	2	M		England	U.S. America	Cortes	19 May 1826
Eliza	25	F		England	U.S. America	Cortes	19 May 1826
Margaret	1	F		England	U.S. America	Cortes	19 May 1826
W., Jr.	4	M		England	U.S. America	Cortes	19 May 1826
William	25	M	Farmer	England	U.S. America	Cortes	19 May 1826
VALSER, Catrina	4	F		Great Britain		Caravan	8 Sep 1828
Geo.	7	M		Great Britain		Caravan	8 Sep 1828
VALTERRE, Henriette	24	F	Servant	France	U. States	Sully	15 Jul 1829
VALVY, Dennis	27	M	Labourer	Ireland	Ireland	Sarah G.	28 Nov 1827
VAMCHEAD, P.	31	M	Baker	France	U. States	Montano	2 Sep 1828
VAN ...ERSEN, Chto.	26	F		France	United States	Britannia	29 Oct 1829
VAN AURTIE, C.	30	M	Mecanick	America	America	Rubicon	7 Oct 1826
VANAY, G. M.	35	M	Commerce		United States	New York	5 Nov 1828
VAN BADLEN, H. G.	22	M	Merchant	Germany	U. States	Endymion	2 Jul 1821
VAN BEOREN,							
Buckman P.	27	M	Mariner	United States	United States	Morkey	18 Aug 1825
VANBER, Joseph	38	M	Mason	Ireland		Quatre Freres	29 Jul 1828
VAN BEURER, E.	50	M	Seaman	North America	Different	Tampico	11 Jul 1826
VAN BLACKLE,							
Mary D., Miss	17	F	Lady	England	St. Croix	Stephania	16 Aug 1827
VAN BOTERDAIL,							
Francois	30	M	Druggist	Flanders	Brazil	Roanoke	21 May 1828
VAN BRACKLE,							
Alfred	11/12		Child	St. Croix	St. Croix	Emelia	26 Jun 1828
Eliza, Mrs.	26		Lady	St. Croix	St. Croix	Emelia	26 Jun 1828
Grace, Miss	9		Lady	St. Croix	St. Croix	Emelia	26 Jun 1828
John	34		Planter	St. Croix	St. Croix	Emelia	26 Jun 1828
Mary Ann, Miss	15		Lady	St. Croix	St. Croix	Emelia	26 Jun 1828
S. H., M.D.	38		Physician	St. Croix	St. Croix	Emelia	26 Jun 1828
VAN BRAKLE,							
Elisa Smith	9	F		Danish	U. States	Mary & Nancy	7 Aug 1824
James	32		Merchant	St. Croix	United States	Emelia	10 Dec 1827
Mary	11	F		Danish	U. States	Mary & Nancy	7 Aug 1824
VAN BRANT, Corns.	30	M	Merchant	U. States	U. States	William Tell	3 Dec 1825
VAN BRUNT, Corns.	27	M	Mercht.	U. States	U. States	Lydia	16 Nov 1822
Corns.	33	M	Merchant	U. States	U. States	Potosi	2 Jun 1828
VANCE, —, Master	2			Ireland	Great Britain	Brown	11 Jun 1827
—, Master	5			Ireland	Great Britain	Brown	11 Jun 1827
—, Master	9			Ireland	Great Britain	Brown	11 Jun 1827
—, Master	16			Ireland	Great Britain	Brown	11 Jun 1827
—, Miss	13			Ireland	Great Britain	Brown	11 Jun 1827
—, Mrs.	35			Ireland	Great Britain	Brown	11 Jun 1827
David H.	25	M	Land Agent & Sur.	Geneva, N.Y.	New York	Ann Maria	24 Feb 1824
James, Miss	25 6/12	M	Merchant	Ireland	United States	Josephine	30 Apr 1828
John, Mr.	60	M	Merchant	France	Curacoa	Douglass	8 May 1826
Rose	21	F	Wife	Ireland	United States	Dublin Packet	22 Apr 1822
Thomas	25	M	Farmer	Ireland	U. States	Erin	5 Jul 1820
William	34	M	Farmer	U. States	U. States	Erin	5 Jul 1820
VANCLOOSTER, Vital	28	M	Student in Bardstown's College	Netherland	America	Henry	17 May 1828
VANCONER, Christiana	28	F		Switzerland	United States	Howard	11 Jun 1824
John	48	M	Carpenter	Switzerland	United States	Howard	11 Jun 1824
Madeline	9	F		Switzerland	United States	Howard	11 Jun 1824
Rodalph	8	M	Boy	Switzerland	United States	Howard	11 Jun 1824
VANCOTT, Joshua	30	M	Hostlier	U. States	U. States	Nassau	30 Mar 1824
VAN DART, Irvin	19	M	Merchant	Great Britain	United States	Pacific	7 May 1827
VANDEGRIFT, Asa	27	M	Blacksmith	U. States	U. States	Virginia	26 May 1828
VANDEN BRACH, J. C.	36	M		Netherlands	New York	Louisa	6 Oct 1828
VANDENDALE,							
Thomas, Mr.	27	M	Farmer	England	U. States	Acasta	3 Apr 1826
VANDEN HEWELL,							
Isaac	38	M	Gentleman	Amsterdam	U. States	Amity	23 Sep 1823
VANDERAN, Amelia	29	F		Holland	America	Albion	4 Oct 1820

NAMES OF PASSENGERS	AGE	SEX	OCCUPATIONS	COUNTRY TO WHICH THEY BELONG	COUNTRY THEY INTEND TO INHABIT	SHIPS/DATES OF ARRIVAL	
V. DE RAYMACKER,							
John B.	32	M	Teacher, Bardstown's College	Nederland	America	Henry	17 May 1828
VANDERBELT, John	60	M	Grocer	New York	U. States	Ann Maria	1 Jun 1824
VANDERBILT, Frans.	50	M	Merchant	Germany	Trinadad in Cuba	Catharine & Jane	15 Nov 1823
VANDER BRACH,							
Cornelis Joh.							
Laurantius Webner	9	M	One Family [J. C.]	Netherlands	New York	Louisa	6 Oct 1828
Johanna Elsabeth	4	F	One Family [J. C.]	Netherlands	New York	Louisa	6 Oct 1828
Johannes Corneilus	2	M	One Family [J. C.]	Netherlands	New York	Louisa	6 Oct 1828
Laurantius, Aderzanier							
Wilhelmes	7	M	One Family [J. C.]	Netherlands	New York	Louisa	6 Oct 1828
VAN DER BROOK, —	33	M	Merchant	Germany	U. States	Caesar	3 Apr 1828
VANDER HORST,							
Thos. Cooper	45	M		Great Britain		Corinthian	27 Oct 1829
VANDERHOVELL, M.	40	M	Gent.	Netherlands	U. States	James Cropper	17 Jun 1825
VAN DER HUYS,							
Helena	4	F	...	Holland	N. York	Albion	11 Jun 1821
Henry	6/12	M	...	Great Brittain	N. York	Albion	11 Jun 1821
Jasher	30	M	...	Holland	N. York	Albion	11 Jun 1821
Maria C.	20	F	...	Holland	N. York	Albion	11 Jun 1821
Matilda	2	F	...	Great Brittain	N. York	Albion	11 Jun 1821
Sarah	7	F	...	Holland	N. York	Albion	11 Jun 1821
VANDERMOOLIN, Israel	17		Merchant	England	England	London	16 Aug 1824
VANDERS, Thomas	25	M	Mariner	U.S.	U.S.	Abigail	21 Mar 1825
VAN DER SMISSER,							
Louis J. D.	36	M	Artillery Officer	New Orlans	New Orlans	Aurora	11 Dec 1824
Louisa C. C.	25	F	Mrs. of [Louis J. D.]	New Orlans	New Orlans	Aurora	11 Dec 1824
William	7	M	child of [Louis J. D.]	New Orlans	New Orlans	Aurora	11 Dec 1824
VANDERVANT, William B.	18	M	Merchant	U.S.	U.S.	Montano	24 Jun 1823
VANDERVOORT, Helen	18	F	Merchant	New York	U. States	Chase	12 May 1826
Polly	22	F		U. States	U. States	Abeona	5 Jul 1822
VANDEVEER, John	38	M		New Jersey	U. States	Nile	15 Aug 1823
VAN DIBBER, Andrew	22	M	Gentleman	United States		Edward Quesnel	17 Nov 1828
VAN DYCK, Antony	22	M	Joiner	Holland	United States	Alexander	2 Oct 1829
VAN DYKE, M.	22	M	Merchant	U. States	United States	Autumn	1 Aug 1828
Sarah	27	F	Captain's Wife	United States	United States	Bayard	13 Nov 1823
VANDYKE, Jane	36			Great Britain	U. States	Columbia	7 May 1828
VANGER, Joseph	5/12	M		Switzerland	United States	Elbe	2 Aug 1822
Joseph	3	M		Switzerland	United States	Elbe	2 Aug 1822
VANGINNER, E.	34	F	Gent	French	Switzerland	Charlemagne	19 Sep 1828
F.	20	M	Gent	French	Switzerland	Charlemagne	19 Sep 1828
M.			Gent	French	Switzerland	Charlemagne	19 Sep 1828
VANGLEN, Jno.	36	M	Gentleman	U. States	U. States	General Marion	1 Sep 1824
VANGUK, M.	19	F	Spinster	Switzerland	U. States	La Urania	3 Jul 1828
M. Loo	50	F	Spinster	Switzerland	U. States	La Urania	3 Jul 1828
VANHALLEN, —		F		Spain	Spain	Fabius	19 Mar 1825
—, Mrs.	22	F		Spain	Spain	Fabius	19 Mar 1825
J.	35	M	Mercht.	Spain	Spain	Fabius	19 Mar 1825
V HOETIN, Jon	27	M		France		Pallas	14 Jun 1828
VANHORN, A. B.	28	M	Merchant	United States	U. States	Betsey	10 Aug 1822
VAN HORNE, Gregory	31	M	Merchant	St. John, N.B.	St. John, N.B.	Loire	3 Dec 1821
VANHORNE, Lawrence	40	M	Farmer	Upper Canada	Upper Canada	Lady Hunter	22 Aug 1825
Wm.	8	M	Son	Upper Canada	Upper Canada	Lady Hunter	22 Aug 1825
VANIGER, Catharen C.	45	F		Ireland		Quatre Freres	29 Jul 1828
Nicolas	60	M	Black Smith	Ireland		Quatre Freres	29 Jul 1828
VAN LALKWYCK, Augt.	25	M	Merchant	Guadeloupe	New York	Notre Dame	6 Oct 1827
Eliza	21	F		Guadeloupe	New York	Notre Dame	6 Oct 1827
VAN LANCKER, Leo	23	M	Student	Flanders	America, U.N.S.	Great Britain	3 Aug 1829
Peter	43	M	Student	Flanders	America, U.N.S.	Great Britain	3 Aug 1829
VANLEE, Barbery	29	F	Farmer	France	United States	Crescent	12 Jul 1827
Jacob	28	M	Farmer	France	United States	Crescent	12 Jul 1827
Kesty	3	F	Farmer	France	United States	Crescent	12 Jul 1827
Mary	8	F	Farmer	France	United States	Crescent	12 Jul 1827
VAN LEELE, Charles	23	M	Engineer	Brussells	Great Britain	Lawson	31 Aug 1825
VAN LENGERKE, H. F.	31	M	Merchant	United States	United States	New York	12 Nov 1822

NAMES OF PASSENGERS	AGE	SEX	OCCUPATIONS	COUNTRY TO WHICH THEY BELONG	COUNTRY THEY INTEND TO INHABIT	SHIPS/DATES OF ARRIVAL	
VAN LOAN, Matthew D.	35	M	Merchant	U. States		Lucy	26 Oct 1829
VAN LOMNEL, John	25	M	Clergeman	Antwerp	U. States	Dawn	9 Dec 1826
VANMAN, Andw.	37	M	Collier	Scotland	U. States	Czar	29 Aug 1829
Barbara	37	F	None	Scotland	U. States	Czar	29 Aug 1829
VANNER, Dennis	34		Laboourer			Helen	4 Aug 1829
VAN NESS, Geo.	28	M	Merchant	U. States	U. States	Morning Star	28 Apr 1824
VAN OOSTERBIN, Lousa	21	F				Auritz	20 May 1823
VANPEL, —	28	M	Attendent on Sheep	Bremen	to return	Louisa	16 May 1826
VAN PELL, Henry, Jr.	30	M	Mechanic	New York	U. States	Eliza	29 Dec 1827
VAN PRAAG, Moses	15	M	Farmer	Holland	U. States	Martha	13 Sep 1827
VAN PRAGG, Ahahan	10 3/12	M		Holland	America	Martha	2 Jul 1828
B.	6 6/12	F		Holland	America	Martha	2 Jul 1828
C.	5/12	M		Holland	America	Martha	2 Jul 1828
Isaac	30	M	Merchant	Amsterdam (Holland)	N. Orleans	Napoleon	7 Jul 1829
Jonias	3 10/12	M		Holland	America	Martha	2 Jul 1828
Judica	43 4/12	F		Holland	America	Martha	2 Jul 1828
L.	13 4/12	M		Holland	America	Martha	2 Jul 1828
M.	2 10/12	M		Holland	America	Martha	2 Jul 1828
N.	15 2/12	M		Holland	America	Martha	2 Jul 1828
Roos	5 2/12	F		Holland	America	Martha	2 Jul 1828
Solomon	44	M	Merchant	Holland	America	Martha	2 Jul 1828
T.	8 8/12	F		Holland	America	Martha	2 Jul 1828
VAN RANSSALAER, H. H.	20	M	U.S. Navy	United States	U. States	Nimrod	24 Jan 1826
VAN REANSELEAR, Jeremiah	26 3/12	M	Gentleman	United States	United States	Hector	8 Jan 1820
VAN RHYER, John	42	M	Merchant	United States	U. States	New York	19 Nov 1828
VAN RHYN, F. H.	30	M	Merchant	St. Martins		Mary Ann	10 Oct 1820
VANSALER, Ann	15 6/12	F		Switzerland	United States	Criterion	13 Oct 1825
Christian	20 4/12	M	Farmer	Switzerland	United States	Criterion	13 Oct 1825
Christian	43 ...	M	...	Switzerland	United States	Criterion	13 Oct 1825
Daniel	6 4/12	M	...	France	United States	Criterion	13 Oct 1825
Elizabeth	14 7/12	F		Switzerland	United States	Criterion	13 Oct 1825
Frederick	18 ...	M		Switzerland	United States	Criterion	13 Oct 1825
John	14 1/12	M	Lad	Switzerland	United States	Criterion	13 Oct 1825
Mactalena	40 ...	F	Spinster	Switzerland	United States	Criterion	13 Oct 1825
Samuel	8 .../12	M	...	Switzerland	United States	Criterion	13 Oct 1825
VAN SALKWYCK, —, Miss	4/12	F		Guadeloupe	New York	Notre Dame	6 Oct 1827
VAN SALZEN, Lurt	20	M	Sugar baker	Hanover	New York	Thames	16 May 1821
VAN SANTINE, R. F.	20	M		Amsterdam	New York	Silvanus Jenkins	24 Jul 1828
VAN SCHAIET, John D.	23	M	Servant	U. States	U.S.	Edward Quesnel	19 Dec 1826
VAN SHELLBERT, Christiana	30	F		U.S.	N. York	France	29 Nov 1827
VAN SLYCK, Andrew	18	M	Mechanic	America	America	Soto	1 Aug 1829
VAN SPANKERN, M.	18	M	Dyer	Prussia	United States	Alexander	2 Oct 1829
VAN STAUTENBURGH, Eliza	12	F		U. States	U. States	Matteawan	6 Apr 1822
VANSTIENBAUGH, C. S.	28	M	Gentleman	America	America	Abeona	17 May 1825
VAN STOUGHTEN- BURGH, P.	25	F		U. States	U. States	Matteawan	6 Apr 1822
VAN TAMBACHT, Antoine	28	M	Watchmaker	Flanders	New York	Sully	4 Mar 1828
VAN TASSEL, James	27	M	Butcher	U.S.		Superb	27 Sep 1820
VANTIGER, Joseph	40	M	None	United States	United States	Annah	21 Jun 1826
VANUCCI, Joseph	28	M	Misionary	Italy	Kentucky	Abigail	9 Aug 1821
VAN VICHTEN, Jacob	35	M	Divine	U.S.	U. States	Edward Quesnel	16 Nov 1827
VAN VLEAK, John	44	M	Mariner	U. States	Resides in New York	Craven	8 Apr 1822
VANWART, Henry, Jr., Mr.	18	M		United States	U.S.	Pacific	22 May 1826
VAN ZANDO, —	40	M	Merchant	Holland	U. States	Emma	25 Feb 1826
VAPER, Agusta	12	M	Farm	Ireland		Quatre Freres	29 Jul 1828
Andrew	8	M	Farm	Ireland		Quatre Freres	29 Jul 1828
Anthony	5	M	Farm	Ireland		Quatre Freres	29 Jul 1828
Eloda	4	F	Farm	Ireland		Quatre Freres	29 Jul 1828
Joseph	7	M	Farm	Ireland		Quatre Freres	29 Jul 1828

NAMES OF PASSENGERS	AGE	SEX	OCCUPATIONS	COUNTRY TO WHICH THEY BELONG	COUNTRY THEY INTEND TO INHABIT	SHIPS/DATES OF ARRIVAL	
VAPER (cont'd)							
Magelen	38	F	Farm	Ireland		Quatre Freres	29 Jul 1828
Marian	2	F	Farm	Ireland		Quatre Freres	29 Jul 1828
Perre	6	M	Farm	Ireland		Quatre Freres	29 Jul 1828
Peter	39	M	Farm	Ireland		Quatre Freres	29 Jul 1828
VARDY, Ann	4	F	Labourer	England	United States	Essex	23 May 1828
Hannah	30	F	Seamstress	England	United States	Essex	23 May 1828
Jno.	1	M	Labourer	England	United States	Essex	23 May 1828
Wm.	8	M	Labourer	England	United States	Essex	23 May 1828
VAREY, Joseph	30	M	Merchant	England	America	Cordelia	21 Feb 1820
VARHAS, H. V. H.	22	M	Merchant	U. States	U. States	Pacific	17 Jun 1828
VARLEY, Elihu	35	M	Merchant	Great Britain	United States	Corinthian	5 Jan 1824
VARLOW, C.	32	M	Farmer	Great Britain	United States	Freake	25 Aug 1829
VARNEN, W.	20	M	Mariner	U. States	U. States	Artibonite	19 Apr 1827
VARNER, Leopold	35	M	Cook	Germany	France	Favorite	27 Dec 1825
VARNET, Joseph	50	M	Planter	France	France	Rover	31 May 1824
VARNICK, Jerry	30	M	Seaman	America	America	Buck	2 Feb 1822
VARNILL, George	22	M	Farmer	Gt. Britain		Corinthian	27 Oct 1829
VARNOCK, Jane	4	F		G. Britain	U. States	London	23 Sep 1828
Wm.	7	M		G. Britain	U. States	London	23 Sep 1828
VARQUIS, Joachimo Bo.	39	M	Gentleman	Portugal	United States	Howard	27 Sep 1824
VARRAN, M.	25	M	Commerce	France	United States	New York	5 Nov 1828
Wm.	32		Miner	Great Britain	United States	Roman	10 Sep 1827
VARRICK, Jerry	30	M	Merchant	U. States	U. States	Buck	7 Aug 1822
VARRON, A.	32	M	Merchant	Italy	U. States	Musidora	20 Feb 1823
VARS, Pardon	27	M	Mariner	U. States	U.S.	Robert Y. Haynes	13 Mar 1826
VASCHTER,							
Madelaine	3 6/12	F	Agriculturist	France	U.S.	Helen	3 May 1828
Madelaine	37	F	Agriculturist	France	U.S.	Helen	3 May 1828
Maria	6	F	Agriculturist	France	U.S.	Helen	3 May 1828
Samuel	27	M	Agriculturist	France	U.S.	Helen	3 May 1828
VASE, Rufus	27	M	Merch.	America	America	William Thompson	18 Jan 1825
VASEY, George	1	M	Farmer	England	United States	Florida	1 Sep 1823
Jane	37	F	Farmer	England	United States	Florida	1 Sep 1823
John	6	M	Farmer	England	United States	Florida	1 Sep 1823
Sam	21	F	Servant	U. States	U. States	Canada	12 May 1828
William	3	M	Farmer	England	United States	Florida	1 Sep 1823
William	40	M	Farmer	England	United States	Florida	1 Sep 1823
VASHIE, V.	40	M	Merchant	France	U. States	Eugene	12 Jul 1822
VASQUER, Francelo	2	M		Spain	U. States	Lucy Ann	6 Sep 1826
VASQUES, J. S.	36	M	Merchant	Portugal	U. States	Canada	12 May 1828
Thos.	40	M	Merchant	Spain	U. States	Pocahontas	9 Jun 1823
Y.	25	M	Mercht.	Spain	N. York	Lyon	6 Feb 1826
VASQUEZ, M. R.	30	M	Gentleman	Havanna	Different	Tampico	11 Jul 1826
VASSE, Victor	38	M	Merchant	France	France	Don Quixote	12 Feb 1829
VASSER, James	60	M	Farmer	America	America	Criterion	27 Oct 1821
VASSIEUR, Francis	25	M	Merchant	Cuba		Radius	9 May 1823
VASSNER, J.	30	M	Planter	Spain	U.S.	Radius	29 Jul 1823
VAUGHAN, Jno. A.	26	M	Planter	Maine	Maine	Lady Tompkins	11 Jul 1826
Patrick	22	M	Labourer	Ireland	United States	Trio	2 Oct 1828
Peter	36	M	Mechanic	Ireland	United States	Wm. Byrnes	30 Apr 1828
Wm.	25 3/12	M	Merchant	England	England	Rising States	16 Jan 1829
VAUGHN, Charles	22	M	Merchant	U. States	U. States	Henry Johnson	29 Apr 1825
Harriet	27	F		Gt. Britain	United States	Robert Edwards	1 Jun 1826
Hugh	24	M	Laborer	Ireland	America	Parrington	9 Jun 1827
Thos.	27	M	Farmer	Gt. Britain	United States	Robert Edwards	1 Jun 1826
VAUGIER, Anthony	38	M	Miner	France	U. States	Sully	24 Oct 1828
Anthony, Jr.	6	M	None	France	U. States	Sully	24 Oct 1828
Jane	40	F	None	France	U. States	Sully	24 Oct 1828
Joseph F.	13	M	None	France	U. States	Sully	24 Oct 1828
Margaret	14	F	None	France	U. States	Sully	24 Oct 1828
Melanie	9	F	None	France	U. States	Sully	24 Oct 1828
Theodore	3	M	None	France	U. States	Sully	24 Oct 1828
VAUHAN, Judith	26			Pitsburg	U. States	Almira	15 Jul 1822
VAURIGAND, Theodore	21	M	Gentleman	Cuba	U. States	Purrington	14 May 1827
VAUTIER, Frances	33	F	his wife [John B.]	France	United States	Helen	5 Sep 1828
John B.	32	M	Tailor	France	United States	Helen	5 Sep 1828

NAMES OF PASSENGERS	AGE	SEX	OCCUPATIONS	COUNTRY TO WHICH THEY BELONG	COUNTRY THEY INTEND TO INHABIT	SHIPS/DATES OF ARRIVAL	
VAUTIER (cont'd)							
Nicol	7	M	there Son [John B. & Frances]	France	United States	Helen	5 Sep 1828
VAUX, Margaret	16	F	None	England	United States	Jubilee	12 May 1828
VAZAVILDAY, P. D. E.	28	M	Merchant	U. States	U. States	Fabius	30 Aug 1827
VAZSER, Peter	20	M	Baker	Scotland	U. States	Othello	3 Dec 1828
VEAIL, Jos.	26	M	Clockmaker	Germany	U. States	Ann	19 Aug 1824
VEALLECHIO, F.	60	M	Servant	Spain	Spain	Savannah	24 Apr 1828
VEAPEN, Jose G.	12	M	Gentleman	Columbia	Columbia	Gertrude	19 May 1826
VECAL, Sabastian	31	M	Servant	Spain	Spain	James Monroe	5 Apr 1820
VEDAEL, Edward, Mr.	25	M	Gentleman	...	United States	Belle	3 Aug 1822
VEGA, —, Mr.	45	M	Merchant	Havana	Havana	Milo	15 May 1824
Carlos	41	M	Mercht.	Tenerief	Spain	Orozimbo	16 Apr 1821
Carlos	50	M	Merchant	Spain	United States	Alfred	3 Jun 1826
Juan	52	M	Merchant	Spain	United States	Alfred	3 Jun 1826
VEGNARDONE,							
Ferdnan	46	M	Merchant			Montano	15 Jan 1829
VEGUUS, Jn. Peter L.	23	M	Mechanic	France	U.S.	Montano	24 Jun 1823
VEH, Jacob	25	M	Meckanic	Hamburg	United States	Maria Elizabeth	2 Sep 1822
VEIL, Ivert Victor	28	M	Merchant	France	France	Nestor	3 Nov 1820
VEINCK, Jos., Jr.	21	M	Merchant	N. York	New York	Agenora	29 Nov 1824
VEINGGAN, A. M.	31	M		G. Britain	United States	Siroc	13 Sep 1828
VEIRL, Barben	23	F	Tailor	Switzerland	U.States	C. Amelia	30 Jun 1828
Michel	1	M	Farmer	Switzerland	U.States	C. Amelia	30 Jun 1828
Michel	24	M	Tailor	Switzerland	U.States	C. Amelia	30 Jun 1828
VEISSE, Catherine	53 1/12	F		Germany	New York, U. States	Cadmus	12 Dec 1823
Isaac	46 2/12	M	Rope Maker	Germany	New York, U. States	Cadmus	12 Dec 1823
VEITCH, James	34	M	Director of Mines	Great Britain	Mexico	Corinthian	27 Apr 1824
VEITE, Felix	21	M	Farmer	England	U. States	Cincinnatus	24 May 1821
VELDEN, John	28	M	Farmer	France	United States	American	27 Aug 1827
VELEZ, D. Turto	52	M	Merchant	Havana	U. States	Peter Remsen	30 Jun 1828
Manuel		M	Merchant	Colombia		William Bayard	14 Jun 1827
VELLINGEN, Francis	29	M	Mariner	France	France	Charlotte Corday	8 Nov 1823
VELLIZ, Alex	32	M		Columbia	America	Pleiades	13 Nov 1826
VELLORA, E. J.	25	M	Merchant	Portugal	U. States	Haxall	21 Oct 1826
VELLOS, Jos. P.	35	M	Merchant	Spain	United States	Neptunes Barge	23 Apr 1821
VELVICK, William	48	M	Farmer	England	U. States	Cincinnatus	24 May 1821
VENA, Manuel Pedro	28	M	Merchant	Portugal	U. States	Dart	2 Dec 1822
Pedro	28	M	Servant	Island of Cuba	Cuba	James Monroe	21 May 1825
VENABLE, J.	30	M	None	U. States	U. States	Golden Age	19 Dec 1827
Sam	24	M	None	U. States	U. States	Golden Age	19 Dec 1827
VENDEVOGHEL, Maria	32	F	Nurse	Holland	U. States	America	22 Sep 1826
VENER, John	24	M	...	Germany	U. States	York	10 Dec 1825
VENICE, Caroline	3	F	Farmer	England	In the Country	Chelsea	16 May 1828
Edward	8/12	M	Farmer	England	In the Country	Chelsea	16 May 1828
*Died Apl. 29							
Harriet	29	F	Farmer	England	In the Country	Chelsea	16 May 1828
John, & family	31	M	Farmer	England	In the Country	Chelsea	16 May 1828
Mary	2	F	Farmer	England	In the Country	Chelsea	16 May 1828
Sarah	4	F	Farmer	England	In the Country	Chelsea	16 May 1828
William	6	M	Farmer	England	In the Country	Chelsea	16 May 1828
*Died May 5th							
VENIS, Harriet	6	F	Farmer	England	In the Country	Chelsea	16 May 1828
John	12	M	Farmer	England	In the Country	Chelsea	16 May 1828
Mary	30	F	Farmer	England	In the Country	Chelsea	16 May 1828
VENT, Alexander	19	M	Engraver	France	U. States	Edward Quesnel	4 Aug 1828
VENUS, John	21					Cincinnatus	29 Apr 1822
Maria	50	F		Guadaloupe	France	Elizabeth	17 Jul 1823
VERANIO, Loreto	30	F	Wife	Spain	Spain	Paquebot Bordeaux	25 May 1828
VERAY, Pierre	22	M	Tailor	France	New York	Sully	4 Mar 1828
VERCASTER, J.	14	M	Merchant	Vera Cruz	U. States	Eliza	11 Apr 1826
VERDIER, Simon	46	M	Planter	U. States	U. States	Brandt	8 Nov 1828
VERDING, George	22	M	Frecher	Ireland		Quatre Freres	29 Jul 1828
VERDONNET,							
Elizabeth	43 3/12	F	Farmer	Switzerland	United States	France	6 Oct 1828
John	46 6/12	M	Farmer	Switzerland	United States	France	6 Oct 1828
VERELA, F., Don	30		Gentleman	Spain	Cuba	Draper	17 Dec 1823

NAMES OF PASSENGERS	AGE	SEX	OCCUPATIONS	COUNTRY TO WHICH THEY BELONG	COUNTRY THEY INTEND TO INHABIT	SHIPS/DATES OF ARRIVAL	
VERER, T.	45	M	Gentleman	Netherlands	Netherlands	Jasper	22 Sep 1827
VERG, James	24	M	Laborer	Scotland	United States	Coquet	6 Jun 1827
VERICON, —, Mrs.		F		France	U. States	Amelia	14 Dec 1827
VERIE, James P.	27	M	Merchant	Native of Switzerland	United States	Canaris	30 Jun 1827
VERJOSSERE, John	32	M	Merchant	St. Domingo	U. States	Topaz	23 Feb 1827
VERKLIN, Benjamin	12	M	his family [Joseph]	Germany	Missouri	Isabella	15 Sep 1828
Caroline	5	F	his family [Joseph]	Germany	Missouri	Isabella	15 Sep 1828
Jacob	3	M	his family [Joseph]	Germany	Missouri	Isabella	15 Sep 1828
Joseph	41	M	Farmer	Germany	Missouri	Isabella	15 Sep 1828
Magdelene	11	F	his family [Joseph]	Germany	Missouri	Isabella	15 Sep 1828
Marian	16	F	his family [Joseph]	Germany	Missouri	Isabella	15 Sep 1828
Tedna	35	F	his family [Joseph]	Germany	Missouri	Isabella	15 Sep 1828
Teresa	7	F	his family [Joseph]	Germany	Missouri	Isabella	15 Sep 1828
VERMÉ, Dal, Count	36	M	Gentleman	Italy	Italy	Britannia	22 Jul 1829
VERMILYE, Thomas P.	45	M	Mariner	U.S.A.	U.S.A.	General Jackson	27 Mar 1827
VERNACCI, Joaquin	26 2/12	M	Merchant	Spain	Spain	Swiftsure	27 Feb 1826
VERNARD, Arthur N.	25	M	Merchant	U. States	U. States	Union	22 Jul 1820
VERNER, George	35		Ladies and Gentlemen	United States	United States	Corinthian	7 Jul 1829
VERNET, P.	20	M	Merchant	United States	United States	Mazzinghi	31 Mar 1826
VERNIER, Catharine	21	F	Farmer	France	France	Sully	15 Jul 1829
Frederick	13	M	Farmer	France	France	Sully	15 Jul 1829
John	18	M	Farmer	France	France	Sully	15 Jul 1829
Marie	16	F	Farmer	France	France	Sully	15 Jul 1829
Susanne	45	F	Farmer	France	France	Sully	15 Jul 1829
VERNOF, Georg	18	M	Farmer	France	United States	Virginia	31 May 1828
VERNON, Edwd.	28	M	Gentleman	France		Ann Maria	3 Jul 1820
Geo.	32	M	Artist	England	Gt. Britain	Electra	4 Sep 1827
William	22	M	Farmer	England	Rhode Island	Governor Fenner	23 Jul 1829
Wm.	21	M	Smith	Ireland	United States	Trio	13 Jun 1827
Wm.	23	M	Merchant	Wales	U. States	Constitution	16 Sep 1823
VERNOT, J.	22	M		France & Switzerland	U. States	Bayard	14 Jul 1826
M.	18	F		France & Switzerland	U. States	Bayard	14 Jul 1826
VERON, Lewis	27	M	Merchant	America	America	Albion	4 Oct 1820
Tim	21	M	Merchant	U. States	U. States	Trimmer	30 Apr 1825
Timothy	24	M	Merchant	U.S. America	U.S. America	Columbia	31 Jul 1826
VEROR, Mary	50	F	None	Great Brittan	United States	America	24 Jul 1827
VERPLANCH, Wm. W.	19	M	Merchant	U. States	U. States	Pacific	17 Jun 1828
VERPLANK, Phillip				St. Croix		Virginia	12 Jul 1820
Samuel	25		Professional	New York	United States	General Marion	18 Jul 1829
VERRICE, Marie	24	F		France	United States	Origon	8 Jun 1824
VERRON, Francisco	24	M	Servant	Island of Cuba	Cuba	James Monroe	21 May 1825
VERRY, George	21		Weaver	Ireland	Great Britain	Robert Burns	14 Jun 1824
Joan	23	F	Farmer	France	United States	Crescent	12 Jul 1827
Joan	55	F	Farmer	France	United States	Crescent	12 Jul 1827
John P.	26	M	Farmer	France	United States	Crescent	12 Jul 1827
VERT, Peter	36	M	Gentleman	France	France	Cadmus	23 Mar 1827
VERVIER, —, Madam	42	F	None	St. Martins	St. Martins	Lucy	26 May 1827
VESTAT, F.	27	M	Merchant	France		Queen Mab	24 Sep 1827
VETLER, —, Miss	13	F		Prussia	United States	Constitution	6 Jul 1829
—, Mrs.	59	F		Prussia	United States	Constitution	6 Jul 1829
VETRY, Antoine	65	M	Merchant	France	United States	Bayard	13 Nov 1823
VETTER, John	35	M	Planter	St. Eustatia	St. Croix	Chase	2 Oct 1823
VEURRI, David	22	M	Gentleman	Swissland	U.S.	Pacific	24 Oct 1828
VIADO, Jose	20	M	Merchant	Guatemala	Guatemala	Stephania	26 Apr 1824
VIANA, J. Xavier	14	M	Merchant	Portugal	U. States	Frederick	27 Jan 1823
VIATCH, James	15	M	Painter	Ireland	Amarica	United States	22 Mar 1824
VIBAL, F.	20		Gentleman	Great Britian	Halifax	America	28 Jul 1826
VIBERT, Louis	35	M	Farmer	France	France	Sully	15 Jul 1829
VICAL, Charles	21	M	Gentleman	Genavia	U. States	Farmers Fancy	7 Mar 1823
VICAS, Joseph	17	M	Labourer	G. Britain	U. States	London	23 Sep 1828
M.	18	M	Labourer	G. Britain	U. States	London	23 Sep 1828
VICAT, Chas.	32	M	Merchant	United States	United States	Betsey	13 Feb 1826
VICE, John	6/12	M		Switzerland	United States	Elbe	2 Aug 1822

NAMES OF PASSENGERS	AGE	SEX	OCCUPATIONS	COUNTRY TO WHICH THEY BELONG	COUNTRY THEY INTEND TO INHABIT	SHIPS/DATES OF ARRIVAL	
VICE (cont'd)							
Madalin	5	F		Switzerland	United States	Elbe	2 Aug 1822
Peter	22	M	Farmer	Switzerland	United States	Elbe	2 Aug 1822
Saml.	55	M	...	Switzerland	United States	Elbe	2 Aug 1822
VICERNAN, Jno.	18	M		Ireland	United States	William Byrnes	6 Apr 1826
VICHERS, Charles	14	M		Great Britain	United States	Wyton	12 May 1821
VICIANI, Johnson	27	M	Miner	England	England	Ranger	15 Jan 1827
VICKARS, R.	28	M	Merchant	England		Aspasia	19 Jul 1823
VICKERS, Ann	11	F		Scotland	United States	Delta	24 Oct 1829
Elizabeth	27	F	his Wife	Scotland	United States	Delta	24 Oct 1829
Hannah	3	F		Scotland	United States	Delta	24 Oct 1829
Jane	5	F		Scotland	United States	Delta	24 Oct 1829
John	9	M		Scotland	United States	Delta	24 Oct 1829
Joseph	39	M	Farmer	Scotland	United States	Delta	24 Oct 1829
Mary	7	F		Scotland	United States	Delta	24 Oct 1829
Samuel	13	M		Scotland	United States	Delta	24 Oct 1829
Samuel	70	M	Farmer	Scotland	United States	Delta	24 Oct 1829
Sarah	19	F	Spinstress	Great Britain	U. States	United States	8 Sep 1827
William	29	M	Farmer	Scotland	U. States	Delta	24 Oct 1829
VICKERY, Jane	4	F	None	England	United States	Jubilee	1 Oct 1828
Joshua	1	M	None	England	United States	Jubilee	1 Oct 1828
Mary	35	F	None	England	United States	Jubilee	1 Oct 1828
William	35	M	Farmer	England	United States	Jubilee	1 Oct 1828
VICTOR, Frd.	22	M	Merchant	Bremen	U. States	Caesar	18 Mar 1829
Gray Charles	23	M	Merchant	France	U. States	Dawn	8 Jun 1827
Theodore Franz	22	M	Merchant	Germany	U. States	Constitution	21 Jun 1824
VICTORIER, A.	25	M	Mariner	St. Domingo	U. States	Sentiment	30 Jul 1827
VICTORY, —, Mrs.	25	F		Savannah	U. States	Moxa	28 Jun 1822
E.	3	F		Savannah	U. States	Moxa	28 Jun 1822
James	29	M	Weaver	Ireland	United States	Elizabeth	8 Jun 1827
Jos.	42	M	Doctor	Savannah	U. States	Moxa	28 Jun 1822
Jos., Jr.	4/12	M		Savannah	U. States	Moxa	28 Jun 1822
Rose Ann	25	F	Servant	Ireland	New York	Atlantic	8 May 1828
VIDELL, L.	19 6/12	M		France		Maria	24 Oct 1829
VIDUA, Chs., Count	38	M	Gentleman	Sardinia	Sardinia	Stephania	11 Apr 1825
VIEL, Just	33	...	M	...	U.S. America	Edward	28 Oct 1825
Just.	35	M	Merchant	U. States	S. Carolina	Sully	30 Oct 1827
VIENEIDA, Cleofide	30	F		Italy	U. States	Pedler	16 May 1825
VIENING, Chatarina, Zyn Moeder (his mother [Joseph])	47	F		Bleicheim	United States	Juffraw Johanna	16 Oct 1821
VIESES, Jos.	17	M	Merchant	Teneriffe	Spain	Louisiana	20 Sep 1822
VIGEL, —, Master	12	M	None	Havana	U. States	Milo	15 May 1824
VIGENEUX, John M.	35	M	Merchant	France	U. States	Mont Parnassus	31 Jan 1828
VIGER, Dennis B.	54	M	Advocate	Canada	Canada	New York	19 Nov 1828
William	44	M	Weaver	England	United States	Cosmo	26 Aug 1829
VIGLIUNES, —, Mrs.	50	F	Widow	France	United States	Bayard	13 Nov 1823
VIGNAN, Jno.	40	M	Merchant	France	U. States	Othello	3 Jun 1823
VIGNARDINO, J.	32	M	Barber	France	United States	Marmione	20 Nov 1821
VIGNARDONNE, John	41	M	Merchant	New York	N. York	Queen Mabb	22 Nov 1824
VIGNASDONNE, John	36	M	Merchant	France	Un. States	Ambuscade	30 Dec 1820
VIGNIO, Conrad	26	M	Watchmaker	Switzerland	United States	Howard	27 Sep 1824
VIGO, Bridget	22	F		Great Britain	U. States	Lady Hunter	28 May 1823
Josep	18/12	M		Great Britain	U. States	Lady Hunter	28 May 1823
Joseph	28	M	Mariner	Great Britain	U. States	Lady Hunter	28 May 1823
VILALBA, Juan	28	M	Gentleman	Spain	Mexico	Pharos	10 Jun 1824
VILAMORE, Jesse	30	M	Mariner	Spain	Havana	Bellona	3 May 1826
VILDEBILLE, Catherine	12	F				Henri IV	17 May 1828
Charles	18	M				Henri IV	17 May 1828
J.	51	M				Henri IV	17 May 1828
Lewis	18	M				Henri IV	17 May 1828
Mary Ann	48	F				Henri IV	17 May 1828
VILDUINN, James	30	M	Mercht.	Haiti	U. States	Moreau	21 Jun 1827
VILETT, Thomas	35	M	Army	England	United States	Manhattan	24 Oct 1825
VILLA, —, Mr.	34	M	Merchant	Spain	U. States	Cadmus	12 Apr 1825
VILLAFUERTE, Jose	29	M	Merchant	Spain	Cuba	Isis	17 Nov 1828
Jose	36	M	Mercht.	Spain	Spain	Angelina	28 May 1827
VILLAFURTE, Jose	30	M	Merchant	Spain	Spain	Angelina	17 Sep 1827

NAMES OF PASSENGERS	AGE	SEX	OCCUPATIONS	COUNTRY TO WHICH THEY BELONG	COUNTRY THEY INTEND TO INHABIT	SHIPS/DATES OF ARRIVAL	
VILLARD, Elizabeth	30	F		Switzerland	United States	Montano	27 Aug 1827
Frederick	5	M		Switzerland	United States	Montano	27 Aug 1827
Frederick	30	M	Wool ...	Switzerland	United States	Montano	27 Aug 1827
VILLE DE FUENTE, Cypriano	27	M	Merchant	Spain	Spain	Richmond Packet	15 Jun 1826
VILLEMAIN, J.	20	M	Merchant	Baden	United States	Cavalier	25 Jul 1828
VILLERS, H.	29	M	Surgeon dentist	England	U. States	Birmingham	12 Oct 1827
VILLIARD, ...derick	26	M	Brewer	Switzerland	United States	Elbe	2 Aug 1822
VILLIER, Adolph	38	M	Merchant	France	United States	Montano	8 May 1827
VILLIERS, Adolph	29 4/12	M	Merchant	France	United States	France	6 Oct 1828
Adolphe	25	M	Merchant	France	France	Rose in Bloom	30 Jul 1823
Adolphe	28	M	Merchant	France	United States	Mazzinghi	31 Mar 1826
Josephine	22 3/12	F		France	United States	France	6 Oct 1828
VILLIFUERTE, Jose	27	M	Merchant	Spain	Cuba	Richmond Packet	23 Feb 1827
VILLINEUE, Alexr.	16	M	Mechanic	France	Hayti	Nelson	18 Apr 1826
Geo.	40	M	Mechanic	France	Hayti	Nelson	18 Apr 1826
VILLOLDO, Ricardo	29	M	Mercht.	Havana		Marcella	15 Mar 1827
VILLOLDT, K.	27	M	Merchant	Spainiar	Havana	Bolivar	10 Aug 1827
VILLOZ, R.	45	M		Spain		Apollo	11 Jun 1828
VILMAN, Agatha	12	F	None	Austria	America	Bayard	15 Dec 1828
Apolloni	41	F	Wife to [Christian]	Austria	America	Bayard	15 Dec 1828
Christian	37	M	Farmer	Austria	America	Bayard	15 Dec 1828
Ferdinand	1	M	None	Austria	America	Bayard	15 Dec 1828
Fredeline	2 6/12	M	None	Austria	America	Bayard	15 Dec 1828
Helena	6	F	None	Austria	America	Bayard	15 Dec 1828
Joseph	14	M	None	Austria	America	Bayard	15 Dec 1828
Maria Beatrix	5	F	None	Austria	America	Bayard	15 Dec 1828
VINCE, Robert	26	M	Smith	England	United States	Siroc	31 Oct 1829
VINCENDA, —, Mr.	25	M	None	France	France	Cornelia	12 Mar 1825
VINCENDEN, C.	43	M	Lawyer	Colombia	Different	Tampico	11 Jul 1826
VINCENT, Alexander	28	M	Weaver	Ireland	New York	Louisa	20 Jul 1826
Carolina	10	F	Farmer	Great Britian	U. States	Pallas	17 Aug 1824
Ebenezer	12	M		England	United States	John Wells	16 May 1825
Edgar	8	M	Farmer	Great Britian	U. States	Pallas	17 Aug 1824
Edwin	26	M	Miller	England	Ut. States	Courier	13 Jul 1826
Eleanor	19	F	None	England	Ut. States	Courier	13 Jul 1826
Elenor	20	F		England	United States	John Wells	16 May 1825
Eliza	17	F	Farmer	Great Britian	U. States	Pallas	17 Aug 1824
Elizabeth	24	F		England	United States	John Wells	16 May 1825
Elizabeth	54	F		England	Ut. States	Courier	13 Jul 1826
Emma	22	F		England	Ut. States	Courier	13 Jul 1826
Isaac	20	M	Miller	England	Ut. States	Courier	13 Jul 1826
J. F. Le Jeuen	23	M	Merchant	France	France	Henry Hill	5 Oct 1824
Jane	10	F		England	United States	John Wells	16 May 1825
Jane	52	F		England	United States	John Wells	16 May 1825
John	24	M	Clerk	Great Britain	U. States	Great Britain	18 Mar 1828
Jonathan	56	M	Farmer	England	Ut. States	Courier	13 Jul 1826
Josiah	11	M		England	Ut. States	Courier	13 Jul 1826
Lewis	14	M		England	United States	John Wells	16 May 1825
Lydia	21	F	Farmer	Great Britian	U. States	Pallas	17 Aug 1824
Mary	21	F		France	U. States	Marmion	17 Feb 1824
Michael	42	M	Merchant	United States	Boston	Halecon	12 Feb 1820
Naomi	5	F	Farmer	Great Britian	U. States	Pallas	17 Aug 1824
Ovid	12	M		England	Ut. States	Courier	13 Jul 1826
Patrick	24	M	Farmer	Ireland	United States	Baltic	21 Apr 1827
Rhodia	14	F	Farmer	Great Britian	U. States	Pallas	17 Aug 1824
Richard	40	M	Farmer	Great Brittan	United States	Euphrates	12 Mar 1824
Samuel	3	M	Farmer	Great Britian	U. States	Pallas	17 Aug 1824
Samuel	45	M	Farmer	Great Britian	U. States	Pallas	17 Aug 1824
Seth	12	M	Farmer	Great Britian	U. States	Pallas	17 Aug 1824
Theodore	24	M	Merchant	France	America	Saluda	18 Jun 1825
Winfred	42	F	Farmer	Great Britian	U. States	Pallas	17 Aug 1824
Wm.	17	M	Mechanic	England	United States	John Wells	16 May 1825
Wm.	45	M	Mechanic	England	United States	John Wells	16 May 1825
VINCENTE, A. A.	12	M	None	France	U. States	Rover	31 May 1824
F. E.	16	M	None	France	U. States	Rover	31 May 1824
VINE, Alfred	12	M	Farmer	England	United States	Cambria	3 Jul 1829

NAMES OF PASSENGERS	AGE	SEX	OCCUPATIONS	COUNTRY TO WHICH THEY BELONG	COUNTRY THEY INTEND TO INHABIT	SHIPS/DATES OF ARRIVAL	
VINE (cont'd)							
Elizabeth	48	F	Wife	England	United States	Cambria	3 Jul 1829
George	20	M	Farmer	England	United States	Cambria	3 Jul 1829
Hetty Ann	1 3/12	F	Child	England	United States	Cambria	3 Jul 1829
James	16	M	Farmer	England	United States	Cambria	3 Jul 1829
Jesse	14	M	Farmer	England	United States	Cambria	3 Jul 1829
John	22	M	Farmer	England	United States	Cambria	3 Jul 1829
Mary Ann	21	F	Wife	England	United States	Cambria	3 Jul 1829
Richard	53	M	Farmer	England	United States	Cambria	3 Jul 1829
Robert	8	M	Farmer	England	United States	Cambria	3 Jul 1829
Sarah	27	F		G. Braitan	U. States	Cosmo	29 Jun 1826
Stephn.	48	M	Farmer	Manchester	United States	Nile	17 May 1827
Thomas	18	M	Farmer	England	United States	Cambria	3 Jul 1829
Wm.	29	M	Merchant	G. Braitan	U. States	Cosmo	29 Jun 1826
VINEINZA, W.	40	M	Merchant	Italy	U. States	Pedler	16 May 1825
VINERRY, —, Mr.	20	M	Mercht.	Virginia	U. States	America	9 May 1822
VINES, John	50	M	Merchant	St. Johns	Great Britain	St. Michael	5 Jan 1826
VINGE, John	54	M	Cotton Spinner	England	United States	Aurora	9 Jul 1827
VINING, Jas.	10	M	Merchant	G. Brittain	U. States	York	10 Dec 1825
VINNE, Peter	20	M	Baker	Germany		Ariel	24 Sep 1827
VINNER, Elizabeth	18	F		St. Johns, N.B.	United States	Henrietta	17 Aug 1825
George	28	M	Farmer	St. Johns, N.B.	United States	Henrietta	17 Aug 1825
VIOLE, J. B.	27	M	Merchant	U.S.	U.S.	Stephania	13 Sep 1821
VIOLENT, Celestine	8	F		France	United States	Le Voltaire	19 Jul 1828
Eliz.	13	F		France	United States	Le Voltaire	19 Jul 1828
Eliz.	40	F		France	United States	Le Voltaire	19 Jul 1828
Jean B.	11	F		France	United States	Le Voltaire	19 Jul 1828
Joseph	10	M		France	United States	Le Voltaire	19 Jul 1828
Joseph	40	M	Farmer	France	United States	Le Voltaire	19 Jul 1828
Marie F.	7	F		France	United States	Le Voltaire	19 Jul 1828
Marie F.	12	F		France	United States	Le Voltaire	19 Jul 1828
Marie R.	9	F		France	United States	Le Voltaire	19 Jul 1828
Marrina	6	F		France	United States	Le Voltaire	19 Jul 1828
VIOLETT, Robt. G.	32	M	Merchant	U. States	U. States	Brazillian	21 May 1827
VIRGA, Corraine	14 2/12	M	...	France	United States	Criterion	13 Oct 1825
VIRTUE, Mitchell	25	F		Scotland	U.N. States	Jane	7 Oct 1826
VISHER, Fredk.	18	M	Merchant	Werternburgh	U. States	Amelia	10 Oct 1820
VISOSE, Caliste	8	M		Mexico	Mexico	Virginia	9 Feb 1829
Lewis	15	M		Mexico	Mexico	Virginia	9 Feb 1829
Petra	15	F		Mexico	Mexico	Virginia	9 Feb 1829
VITAR, R. P. M.	53	M	Minister	Spain	Jacqumel	Orion	30 Mar 1825
VITCH, James	26	M	Farmer	Ireland	N. York	Josephine	10 Dec 1825
VITE, Victor	41	M	Merchant	United States		Edward Quesnel	17 Nov 1828
VITH, Nicolo	40	M	Mechanic	Leghorn	U. States	Pedler	9 Jan 1827
VITI, Joseph	13	M	None	Leghorn	U. States	Pedler	9 Jan 1827
VITON, Jules	23	M	Gentleman	France	Unknown	Birmingham	11 Oct 1828
VIVIAN, Christian	30	M	Servant	Switzarland		Armadillo	13 Aug 1829
VIVIEN, Charles J.	59	M	Mechanic	France	New York	Lewis	29 Oct 1825
Lamontagn	32	M	Mechanic	France	New York	Lewis	29 Oct 1825
Mary	51	F	Wife	France	New York	Lewis	29 Oct 1825
VIZNARDONNE,							
Louisa	28	F	Worker	France	U. States	Stephania	24 Jul 1820
VLEESCHORAVER,							
Martin	21	M	Jeweller	Netherland	U. States	Aurora	22 May 1827
VOGA, Catharine	65 5/12	F	Farmer	Switzerland	America	Henry	17 May 1828
George	5 7/12	M	Farmer	Switzerland	America	Henry	17 May 1828
George	27	M	Farmer	Switzerland	America	Henry	17 May 1828
Jacob	39 8/12	M	Farmer	Switzerland	America	Henry	17 May 1828
Madeline	3 4/12	F	Farmer	Switzerland	America	Henry	17 May 1828
Madeline	24 6/12	F	Farmer	Switzerland	America	Henry	17 May 1828
Margaret	1	F	Farmer	Switzerland	America	Henry	17 May 1828
VOGEL, —	3	F		France	United States	Marmione	20 Nov 1821
—	5	F		France	United States	Marmione	20 Nov 1821
—	9	F		France	United States	Marmione	20 Nov 1821
—, Mrs.	35	F		France	United States	Marmione	20 Nov 1821
C. F.	53	M	Merchant	Phila.	U. States	Elisa Pigott	24 Apr 1822
G.	35	M	Mechanic	France	United States	Marmione	20 Nov 1821
Ladvis	19	M	Baker	Switzerland	U. States	Hewes	30 Oct 1829
VOGELSANG, Gustavas	28	M	Merchant	Germany	U. States	Birmingham	16 Jun 1828

NAMES OF PASSENGERS	AGE	SEX	OCCUPATIONS	COUNTRY TO WHICH THEY BELONG	COUNTRY THEY INTEND TO INHABIT	SHIPS/DATES OF ARRIVAL	
VOGLE, Jean Gaspard	32	M	Merchant	Mulhausen	France	Bayard	30 Oct 1820
VOGLES, William	43	M	...	...	...	Camillus	18 Nov 1824
VOGT, Hovatch	23		Sugar Baker	Germany	U.S. of America	Mary	21 Sep 1821
VOHN, S.	24	M	Sadler	New York	U. States	Abeona	23 May 1823
VOIGHT, Henry	40	M	Pastor	Germany	South Carolina	Arab	10 Nov 1826
VOLANEY, Charles	21	M	Gentleman	Ireland	United States	Dublin Packet	29 Jun 1825
VOLANTI, Sebastiano	19	M	Servant	Italy	United States	Corinthian	10 Jan 1826
VOLARE, Mary	25	F	Spinstress	Great Briton	United States	Erin	26 May 1821
VOLCH, ...	45	M	Weaver	France	United States	Stephania	6 Dec 1827
Jno.	7	M		France	United States	Stephania	6 Dec 1827
Margaret	21	F		France	United States	Stephania	6 Dec 1827
Margaret	40	F		France	United States	Stephania	6 Dec 1827
Planesairs	10	M		France	United States	Stephania	6 Dec 1827
VOLISA, C.	18	M	Merchant	Guadaloupe		Industry	11 Jun 1821
VOLLCHETT, Lawrence	40	M	Gentleman	Nassau	U.States	Venus	28 Jun 1825
VOLMAR,							
John Christian	21	M	Tallow Chandler	Switzerland	United States	Elizabeth	13 Nov 1824
VON, H.	24	F	None	America	U. States	Ambuscade	11 Jul 1821
VON BENRAN, Louis	26	M	Gentleman	Switzarland		Armadillo	13 Aug 1829
VON BRETTON,							
Geo. Barton	14	M	Boy	St. Thomas	St. Thomas	Four Sons	8 Dec 1827
James Thad	12	M	Boy	St. Thomas	St. Thomas	Four Sons	8 Dec 1827
VON BRITTEN, Eliza.	18	F	None	St. Croix	St. Croix	Matteawan	30 Nov 1826
VON BUTSON, C.	16	F		Denmark	Denmark	Agness	23 Jun 1828
G.	9	F		Denmark	Denmark	Agness	23 Jun 1828
H.	12	F		Denmark	Denmark	Agness	23 Jun 1828
J.	38	F		Denmark	Denmark	Agness	23 Jun 1828
VONDERVOORT,							
Peter L.	20	M	Merchant	U. States	U. States	Harriet	3 Mar 1828
VON HARTEN, Wm.	50	M	Merchant	U. States	U. States	Topaz	31 Jul 1827
VONINS, Catherine	4 2/12	F	Mechanic	Switzerland	United States	France	6 Oct 1828
Elizabeth	8 1/12	F	Mechanic	Switzerland	United States	France	6 Oct 1828
Felix	27 6/12	M	Mechanic	Switzerland	United States	France	6 Oct 1828
Jacob	29 3/12	M	Mechanic	Switzerland	United States	France	6 Oct 1828
Mary Ann	2 3/12	F	Mechanic	Switzerland	United States	France	6 Oct 1828
Salime	29 4/12	F	Mechanic	Switzerland	United States	France	6 Oct 1828
VON KENDENE, —, Baron	44	M	Diplomatist	Prussia	N. York	France	29 Nov 1827
VON OTIER, J. F.	27	M	Merchant	France	U.S.	Edward Quesnel	19 Dec 1826
VON POST, L. H.	26	M	Merchant	U. States	U.S.	Edward Quesnel	19 Dec 1826
VONSBLOTH, Fred.	26	M	Farmer	Bardin	U. States	Bayard	5 Sep 1828
VON SCHRADER,							
Amalie	25	F		Prussia	United States	Constitution	6 Jul 1829
Coscilia	14	F		Prussia	United States	Constitution	6 Jul 1829
Maria	10	F		Prussia	United States	Constitution	6 Jul 1829
Otto	11	M		Prussia	United States	Constitution	6 Jul 1829
Thekla	13	F		Prussia	United States	Constitution	6 Jul 1829
Theone	10	F		Prussia	United States	Constitution	6 Jul 1829
VOORHEES, D. B. W.	21	M	Merchant	U. States	U. States	Margaret Mercer	3 May 1826
VOORHIS, Peter	23	M	Merchant	U. States	U. States	Virginia	26 May 1828
VORN, Eliza	...	F	Labourer	Ireland	United States	Meteor	26 Jun 1827
VORRENT, Lousia	8	F	Weaver	France		Pallas	14 Jun 1828
Lousia	64	F		Switzerland		Pallas	14 Jun 1828
Margaret Jos.	10	F		Switzerland		Pallas	14 Jun 1828
Margaret M.	25	F		Switzerland		Pallas	14 Jun 1828
Mariah	6	F	Barber	France		Pallas	14 Jun 1828
Michelinon	3	M		France		Pallas	14 Jun 1828
VOSE, F. L.	35	M	Mechanic	Hamburgh	U. States	Robert Burns	1 Dec 1823
VOUSE, Richd.	32	M	Millwright	York, Great Britain		Casanda	5 Sep 1827
VOYA, Joseph	35 3/12	M	Farmer	Switzerland	U. States	France	26 Jun 1828
VOYART, Wm.	37	M	Mariner	U.S.	U. States	Diana	8 Aug 1822
VOYNE, Jaeguer	60	M	Merchant	France	U. States	Jane Blossom	28 Aug 1826
VRAOUS, Christian	22	M		Farmer	U. States	Bayard	5 Sep 1828
Christoph	57	M	Farmer	Farmer	U. States	Bayard	5 Sep 1828
G. A.	28	M	Farmer	Farmer	U. States	Bayard	5 Sep 1828
J. R.	59	M	Maron	Farmer	U. States	Bayard	5 Sep 1828
John	13	M		Farmer	U. States	Bayard	5 Sep 1828
Magdaline	25	M		Farmer	U. States	Bayard	5 Sep 1828
Phil	19	M		Farmer	U. States	Bayard	5 Sep 1828

NAMES OF PASSENGERS	AGE	SEX	OCCUPATIONS	COUNTRY TO WHICH THEY BELONG	COUNTRY THEY INTEND TO INHABIT	SHIPS/DATES OF ARRIVAL	
VRAOUS (cont'd)							
Sarah	16	M		Farmer	U. States	Bayard	5 Sep 1828
VRIOSTE DE LA							
KERRAN, Manuel	29	M	Merchant	Spain	Spain	Napoleon	26 May 1828
VRQUISE, D.	40	M	Merchant	Havana	United States	James Monroe	3 Jul 1824
VUELLARD, N. B.	15	F		France & Switzerland	U. States	Bayard	14 Jul 1826
VUGLER, Jiaderina	18	F	Spinster	Wirtemburg	United States	Wade	29 Aug 1825
Johanna	30	F	Spinster	Wirtemburg	United States	Wade	29 Aug 1825
VULLEAMAZ, Adeline	3	F	Daughter [of Etienne]	France	United States	Elizabeth	13 Nov 1824
Augusta	5	M	Son [of Etienne]	France	United States	Elizabeth	13 Nov 1824
Constant	10	M	Son [of Etienne]	France	United States	Elizabeth	13 Nov 1824
Etienne	55	M	Blacksmith	France	United States	Elizabeth	13 Nov 1824
Marian	39	F	Wife [of Etienne]	France	United States	Elizabeth	13 Nov 1824
Silvia	8	F	Daughter [of Etienne]	France	United States	Elizabeth	13 Nov 1824
VYER, Minnoa	20	M	Lock Smith	Germany	America	Orozimbo	1 Oct 1827
VYSS, John	24	M	Millwright	France	U. States	Benlomond	20 Sep 1822
W..., ...dm...	...			...	England	Great Britain	7 May 1827
Margret	...	F	Spinster	Ireland	Unt. St. America	Wilson	21 May 1827
Urma	13	F		Switzerland	United States	Elbe	2 Aug 1822
W...MAN, J.	25	M	Mechanic	U. States	U. States	Hannah & Rebecca	12 Jun 1824
W...OR, Clare, Miss	19	F		St. Domingo	United States	John Wells	18 Sep 1826
Robert	15	M	Merchant	St. Domingo	United States	John Wells	18 Sep 1826
WA..., Henry	20	M		Great Britain	United States	Zodiac	29 Oct 1822
WA...TEY, E.	60		Farmer	Ireland	United States	Courier	16 May 1825
WABERTON, Wm.	50	M	Gentn.	Gt. Britain		Silas Richards	20 Jun 1826
WACHTER, John	26	M	Merchants Clerk	Germany	United States	Plato	25 Aug 1829
WACHURST, Eliza	7	F	None	England	Ut. States	Courier	13 Jul 1826
Margt.	6	F		England	Ut. States	Courier	13 Jul 1826
WADAL, Saml.	22	M	Merchant	Ireland	U. States	Concordia	11 Jun 1823
WADBERG, F. S.	27		Merchant	Altona	Uncertain, Denmark	Albion	5 Feb 1822
WADDELL, Harriet	22					Xenophon	25 Jul 1826
James	21	M	Merchant	Great Britain	United States	Jean	17 Aug 1827
John	4/12					Xenophon	25 Jul 1826
John	26		Farmer	England	S. New York	Xenophon	25 Jul 1826
William Robert	20 7/12	M	Gentleman	Ireland	Upper Canada	Nimrod	28 Apr 1824
WADDERBURN, Alexander	34	M		Great Britain	U. States	Great Britain	18 Mar 1828
WADDINGTON, Edwd.	27	M	Merchant	England	England	Acasta	15 Jul 1822
Fellice	20	F		England	United States	Dalhouse Castle	8 May 1827
Henry	24	M	Mason	England	United States	Dalhouse Castle	8 May 1827
Samuel	30	M	Clothier	England	United States	Aurora	9 Jul 1827
W...	43	M	Farmer	England	United States	Magnet	16 May 1823
WADDLE, George	18	M	Labourer	Ireland	United States	Catharine	22 Jul 1825
Hester	24	F		England	U. States	Brighton	14 Apr 1828
WADDLEWORTH, Hezekiah	23		Weaver	Manchester	Utica	Peru	30 May 1828
WADDRON, Benjn.	27	M	Servant	Great Britian	U. States	Pallas	17 Aug 1824
WADDY, Eleanor	27	F	None	Ireland	United States	Jubilee	12 May 1828
Margaret	1 8/12	F	None	Ireland	United States	Jubilee	12 May 1828
WADE, Ann	3/12	F		G. Britain	U. States	George Clinton	10 Sep 1828
Catharine	2	F		G. Britain	U. States	George Clinton	10 Sep 1828
Chs.	30	M	Merchant	St. John	St. John	St. Michael	27 Mar 1827
Eleanor	20	F		G. Britain	U. States	George Clinton	10 Sep 1828
Henry	24 9/12	M	Mariner	America	America	Nimrod	1 Dec 1827
James	35	M	Gentleman	L...	U. States	Panthea	24 Mar 1825
John	23	M	Clothier	Leeds		Colossus	27 Mar 1828
Margt.	22	F		Ireland	U. States	William Byrnes	17 Jul 1825
Mary	28	F		Ireland	U. States	William Byrnes	17 Jul 1825
Thos.	24	M	Shoe Maker	G. Britain	U. States	George Clinton	10 Sep 1828
WADELL, Ann	30	F		Great Britain	United States	Fame	26 May 1828
Thomas	7	M		Great Britain	United States	Fame	26 May 1828
Walter	36	M	Farmer	Great Britain	United States	Fame	26 May 1828
WADIL, Rebecker	22	F		Ireland	United States	Nancy R. Crowell	21 Sep 1822

1284

NAMES OF PASSENGERS	AGE	SEX	OCCUPATIONS	COUNTRY TO WHICH THEY BELONG	COUNTRY THEY INTEND TO INHABIT	SHIPS/DATES OF ARRIVAL	
WADINGHAM,							
Elizabeth	22	F		England	America	John Adams	2 Aug 1827
George	31	M	Sailmaker	England	America	John Adams	2 Aug 1827
WADLE, Thos.	24	M	Merchant	United States	U. States	Pacific	5 Sep 1827
WADOCK, Jno.	16	M	Clerk	United States	New York	Elizabeth	9 Aug 1821
WADSLEY, George	30	M	Labourer	England	New York	Lima	5 Aug 1829
WADSWORTH,							
Ann	6/12	F	None	Great Britain	United States	Orbit	23 Oct 1826
Jno. E.	25	M	Merchant	U. States	U. States	Pacific	28 Mar 1822
Jonn. H.	46	M	Manufacturer	England	United States	Silas Richards	3 Apr 1826
Joseph	29	M	Clothier	Great Britain	United States	Orbit	23 Oct 1826
Lydia	28	F	None	Great Britain	United States	Orbit	23 Oct 1826
Mary	2	F	None	Great Britain	United States	Orbit	23 Oct 1826
T. P.	35	M		G. Britain	U. States	John Jay	17 Sep 1828
W.	25	M		G. Britain	U. States	John Jay	17 Sep 1828
William	26	M	Merchant	Great Britain	Canada	Isaac Hicks	22 Aug 1829
William, Mr.	51	M	Gentn.	U. States	United States	Acasta	21 Oct 1825
WAELL, Charles	24	M	Jeweller	England	U. States	Franklin	7 Jul 1828
WAESSNER, Christian	24	M	Weaver	Germany	United States	Helen	5 Sep 1828
WAGENER, Carl Ch.	24	M	Joiner	Germany	Philadelphia	Falcon	21 Oct 1826
J.	28	M	Labourer	Basen		Constitution	20 Jun 1828
WAGFIELD, Joseph	45	M	Merchant	England	United States	Montgomery	6 Mar 1829
WAGNER, Andrew	22	M	Weaver	Germany	United States	Helen	5 Sep 1828
Anton	36	M	Baker	Hessia	United States	Constitution	6 Jul 1829
Anton	49	M	Weaver	Baden	United States	Jason	3 Nov 1828
B.	40	M	Servt. Genl. La Fayette			Cadmus	17 Aug 1824
Carl Fred.	36	M	Butcher	Baden	United States	Jason	3 Nov 1828
Catherine	24	F	his wife	Germany	United States	Helen	5 Sep 1828
Christian Caroline	12	F		Baden	United States	Jason	3 Nov 1828
Frederick	22	M	Farmer	Switzerland		Antioch	18 Aug 1829
G. L.	27	M	Shoe Maker	Germany	U. States	Wm. Penn	1 Sep 1828
Gaspard	12	M	Doctress	Germany		Charlemagne	16 Jan 1829
Gaspard	42	M	Docter	Germany		Charlemagne	16 Jan 1829
Gezore	6	M		Baden	United States	Jason	3 Nov 1828
Henry	23	M	Farmer	Alsace in the Department of Upper and lower Rhine	United States	Carolina Augusta	16 May 1828
Johan Ernest	34	F		Baden	United States	Jason	3 Nov 1828
Joseph	14	M		Baden	United States	Jason	3 Nov 1828
Magdaline Kerling	48	F		Baden	United States	Jason	3 Nov 1828
Marianne	25	F		Baden	United States	Jason	3 Nov 1828
Mary	30		Doctress	Germany		Charlemagne	16 Jan 1829
Michel	23	M	Weaver	Baden	United States	Jason	3 Nov 1828
Sarah	10	F		Germany		Charlemagne	16 Jan 1829
Valentine	3	M		Baden	United States	Jason	3 Nov 1828
Walboret	18	F		Baden	United States	Jason	3 Nov 1828
WAGNET, George, his boy [Joseph Lang]	15	M		Germany	United States	Rent	13 May
WAGRON, Andres	2	M		Switzerland	U. States	Hewes	30 Oct 1829
E.	38	M	Mason	Switzerland	U. States	Hewes	30 Oct 1829
Frances	34	F	Wife	Switzerland	U. States	Hewes	30 Oct 1829
Sabina	7	F		Switzerland	U. States	Hewes	30 Oct 1829
WAGSTAFF, Alfred	25	M	Gentleman	United States	U. States	York	7 Aug 1828
Edward	14	M	Carpenter	Bristol, Engl.	...	Warrior	19 May 1828
Helly	9	F		Great Brittain	U. States	Atticus	25 Apr 1822
Honora	24	F	None	Ireland	New York	America	1 Aug 1828
Jasper C.	2	M	None	Great Briton	United States	Mount Vernon	29 Aug 1828
Jeremiah	4	M	None	Ireland	New York	America	1 Aug 1828
John	8	M	None	Ireland	New York	America	1 Aug 1828
Martha	22	F	None	Great Briton	United States	Mount Vernon	29 Aug 1828
Mary	35	F		Great Brittain	U. States	Atticus	25 Apr 1822
Maryann	4	F	None	Great Briton	United States	Mount Vernon	29 Aug 1828
Wm.	36	M	Farmer	Great Brittain	U. States	Atticus	25 Apr 1822
WAHDLE, Richard	27	M	Taylor	England	New York	Cortes	23 Nov 1827
WAHL, Magdelen	25	F	Maid Servant	Germany	United States	Helen	5 Sep 1828
WAID, L., Miss	24	F		G. Britain	U. States	Robt. Edwards	4 Sep 1828
WAIDLEY, Margery	21	F	None	England	United States	Dalhouse Castle	6 Sep 1827

NAMES OF PASSENGERS	AGE	SEX	OCCUPATIONS	COUNTRY TO WHICH THEY BELONG	COUNTRY THEY INTEND TO INHABIT	SHIPS/DATES OF ARRIVAL
WAIDLEY (cont'd)						
Wm.	2	M	None	England	United States	Dalhouse Castle 6 Sep 1827
WAIHLER, Thos.	24		Sadler			Agricola 1 Jul 1820
WAILING, Morris	25	M	Yeoman	Ireland	United States	Borneo 9 Jul 1827
WAINE, Emma	26	M		England	England	Criterion 29 May 1822
John	41 8/12	M	Farmer	England	U.S. of America	Illinois 16 Jun 1821
Joseph	21	M	Clergyman	England	England	Criterion 29 May 1822
WAINEWRIGHT,						
Richd. Saml.	42	M	Merchant	England	United States	Acasta 14 Jun 1824
WAINMAN, Ann	70	F	None	Great Britain	United States	Ann Maria 12 Jul 1821
WAINRIGHT, Ishmael	29	M		Great Britain	United States	Active 25 Mar 1828
Silvanus	28	M		Great Britain	United States	Active 25 Mar 1828
WAINWRIGHT,						
Charles S.	18/12	M			U. States	Rockingham 29 Nov 1821
Danl.	36	M	Mechanic	England	U. States	Acasta 21 Jan 1825
Eli	37	M	Merchant	England	U. States	Rockingham 29 Nov 1821
John W.	40	M	Button Maker	England	America	William Byrnes 22 Dec 1828
Mary	31	F			U. States	Rockingham 29 Nov 1821
Wm.	6	M	Merchant	United States	U. States	Pacific 5 Sep 1827
Wm. P.	3	M			U. States	Rockingham 29 Nov 1821
WAIRING, Samuel	24	M	Farmer	Great Britain	United States	Ganges 8 Jul 1820
WAIT, —, Mrs.	40	F		Orange County	Orange County	Cosmo 25 Sep 1827
Wm.	45	M	Tobacconist	England	U. States	Trident 8 Mar 1824
WAITE, —, Mrs.	28	F	Wife	U.S.	U.S.	Robert Edwards 11 Nov 1822
David	18	M	Farmer	England	United States	William Howland 5 Jul 1821
Elizabeth	39	F	None	U. States	U. States	Herald 4 Oct 1824
Emma	4	F		England	United States	William Howland 5 Jul 1821
Flower	8	F		England	United States	William Howland 5 Jul 1821
George N.	50	M	Gentleman	U. States	U. States	Cincinnatus 2 Oct 1822
Isacc	57	M	Ma[r?]iner	U. States	U. States	Herald 4 Oct 1824
Jno. G.	30	M	Mariner	U. States	U. States	Prince Edward 5 Jul 1825
John	13	M		England	United States	William Howland 5 Jul 1821
Margaret	17	F	...	England	United States	Milton 20 Oct 1827
Mary	12	F		England	United States	William Howland 5 Jul 1821
Mary	43	F		England	United States	William Howland 5 Jul 1821
R.	22	M	unknown	U. States	U. States	Mary 7 Nov 1822
Samuel	16	M		England	United States	William Howland 5 Jul 1821
Samuel	23		Gentleman	Great Britain	United States	Thomas Dickason 29 Aug 1828
Sarah	6	F		England	United States	William Howland 5 Jul 1821
William	1 6/12	M		England	United States	William Howland 5 Jul 1821
WAKE, Abraham	20	M		Coullon	U. States	Manhattan 21 May 1821
WAKEFIELD, Chas.	18	M	Mason	England	United States	Cosmo 21 Aug 1828
George	44	M	Mason	England	United States	Cosmo 21 Aug 1828
Jacob G.	2...	M	Gentleman	Ireland	America	Wilson 16 May 1825
WAKELAND, John	28	M	Laborer	Ireland	United States	Nancy 15 Nov 1824
Mary	25	F	Wife	Ireland	United States	Nancy 15 Nov 1824
WAKEMAN, Abner	26	M	Sailor	America	U. States	Hiram 17 Jun 1826
WAKES, Saml.	24	M	Miner	Ireland	United States	Curler 3 Mar 1828
WALBE, James	33	M		France	U. States	Great Britain 6 Sep 1828
WALBEFF, Wm.	33	M	Farmer	Great Britian	United States	Mount Vernon 19 May 1823
WALBER, Chas.	40	M	Mariner	America	U. States	Albany Packet 23 Mar 1827
WALCH, Darby	26	M	Nailor	Ireland	United States	Trio 13 Jun 1827
James	31	M	Merchant	Ireland	United States	Samuel Robertson 9 Apr 1828
Margaret, Mrs.	28	F	Baker	England	U.S.	Acasta 11 May 1827
Mary	16	F	Lady	Ireland	United States	Borneo 9 Jul 1827
Thomas	24	M	Coach Man	G. Britain	U. States	Margaret Bogle 12 Jun 1828
Thos.	20		Labourer	Ireland	United States	Geo. Canning 5 Jun 1828
William	20	M	Bricklayer	Ireland	United States	Cambria 16 Aug 1827

NAMES OF PASSENGERS	AGE	SEX	OCCUPATIONS	COUNTRY TO WHICH THEY BELONG	COUNTRY THEY INTEND TO INHABIT	SHIPS/DATES OF ARRIVAL	
WALDAN, Michal, Mr.	30	M	Farmer	Grate Britain	...	Courier	14 Jun 1825
WALDBURG, G. M.	27	M	None	United States	United States	New York	12 Nov 1822
WALDEN, Betty	40	F	None			James Monroe	8 Aug 1820
Nathan	40	M	...	United States	U. States	Seine	20 Dec 1825
Thomas	24	M	Labourer	England	U. States	Comet	23 Aug 1828
WALDER, Cristene	12		Farmer	Switzerland		Charlemagne	20 Aug 1829
Dorothia	46	F	Farmer	Switzerland		Charlemagne	20 Aug 1829
Eshart	14	M	Farmer	Switzerland		Charlemagne	20 Aug 1829
John	6	M	Farmer	Switzerland		Charlemagne	20 Aug 1829
John	8	M	Farmer	Switzerland		Charlemagne	20 Aug 1829
John	48	M	Farmer	Switzerland		Charlemagne	20 Aug 1829
Joseph W.	21	M	Farmer	Germany	Missouri	Isabella	15 Sep 1828
Mary	3	F	Farmer	Switzerland		Charlemagne	20 Aug 1829
WALDO, Eliza	30	F		United States	United States	Alexander Mansfield	9 Jul 1829
WALDRON, C. J.	37	M	Seaman	America	U. States	Mary Jane	2 Jul 1828
M. H.	25	M	Merchant	Barbadoes	Barbadoes	Rose in Bloom	10 Aug 1824
W. W.	32	M	Farmer	G. Britain	U. States	St. George	7 Jun 1828
WALE, Andrew	29	M	Labourer	Ireland	United States	Hope & Esther	17 Oct 1827
Bridget	21	F	Labourer	Ireland	United States	Hope & Esther	17 Oct 1827
Hosanna	25	F	Labourer	Ireland	United States	Hope & Esther	17 Oct 1827
WALER, Jesse	40	M	Merchant	U. States	United States	Alfred	3 Jun 1826
WALERS, Cathe.	24	F	None	Ireland	United States	Dalhouse Castle	6 Sep 1827
George	2	M	None	Ireland	United States	Dalhouse Castle	6 Sep 1827
Owen	30	M	Labourer	Ireland	United States	Thompson	12 Sep 1827
WALERSON, Ann	23	F	None	Isle of Man		Ocean	13 Jul 1827
Wm.	24	M	Labourer	Isle of Man		Ocean	13 Jul 1827
WALES, T.	24	M	Steward	America	U. States	Ambuscade	11 Jul 1821
WALETHROP, Jos.	25	M	Servant	France	U. States	Trimmer	10 Jul 1824
WALHAVEN, Eliza	25	F	Servant	Ireland	U. States	Henrietta	7 Jul 1825
WALISTON, H.	36	M	Merchant	New York	New York	Paquet des Aux Cayes	3 Feb 1827
WALK, Mary	40	F	Child	Ireland	N. York	Trusty	12 Sep 1828
WALKER, —, 3 children	5, etc.			England	New York	Thames	6 Oct 1820
—, Miss	26	F	Lady	England	U. States	Imperial	10 Dec 1821
A.	32	M	Merchant	England	Great Britain	Ranger	3 May 1828
Abraham	35	M	hairdresser	Great Britain	United States	Orozimbo	5 Mar 1827
Agnes	28		Weaver	Scotland	United States	Camillus	3 May 1828
Alexander	23	M	Blacksmith	Scotland	America	Concord	4 Jun 1821
Ann	28	F		Ireland	U. States	Josephine	27 Jul 1825
Ann	65	F	None	St. Johns	St. Johns	Sarah G	7 May 1827
Ann	66	F		Great Britain	Great Britain	Lady Hunter	28 May 1823
Anna	12		Spinster	Ireland	United States	Courier	15 Oct 1827
Anne, Mrs.	20	F	None	U.S. America	U.S. America	James Cropper	29 Nov 1827
Appleton	35	M	Merchant	New York		Desdemona	11 Mar 1829
Barthma.	24	M	Blacksmith	Great Briton	United States	Mount Vernon	30 Dec 1828
Benjn.	19	M	...er	Great Britain	United States	Atlantic	28 May 1827
Betty	12	F	None			John & Edward	25 Aug 1820
Betty	22	F		England	America	Corinthian	1 Sep 1827
C.	10	F		G. Britain	United States	Sarah G.	15 May 1828
Clementina	4		Family [of Margt.]	Great Britain	United States	Camillus	12 Sep 1827
Daniel	25	M	Musician	G. Brittain	U. States	Cincinnatus	2 Oct 1822
David	18	M		Manchester	United States	Nile	17 May 1827
David	71	M	Merchant	Philadelphia	St. Thomas	Express	25 Sep 1827
Dorcas	22	F	Spinster	Ireland	Unt. St. America	Wilson	21 May 1827
Eliza	17	F	Spinster	Ireland	United States	Dublin Packet	9 Jul 1827
Eliza	35	F		G. Britain	United States	Sarah G.	15 May 1828
Eliza	46	F		England	England	Tontin	13 Jun 1825
Eliza, Mrs.	35	F		United States	New York	Cadmus	27 Aug 1822
Elizabeth	40	F	Servant	England	New York	Brighton	19 Aug 1829
Elizth.	17		Spinster	Ireland	United States	Courier	15 Oct 1827
Ellen	27		None	Great Britain	United States	Roman	10 Sep 1827
Ellen	37		Spinster	Ireland	United States	Courier	15 Oct 1827
Eloiad.	20	M		Manchester	United States	Nile	17 May 1827
Emely	20			United States	United States	London	16 Aug 1824
F. B.	24 10/12		Merchant	U. States	U. States	Jackin	15 May 1828
Francis B.	22	M	Merchant	U. States	U.S.	Exertion	6 Sep 1828
G. H.	32	M	Farmer	England	United States	Nestor	20 Nov 1821

NAMES OF PASSENGERS	AGE	SEX	OCCUPATIONS	COUNTRY TO WHICH THEY BELONG	COUNTRY THEY INTEND TO INHABIT	SHIPS/DATES OF ARRIVAL	
WALKER (cont'd)							
Geo.	46	M		U. States	U. States	Cadmus	4 Aug 1829
George	21	M	Farmer	Scotland	U. States	Camillus	29 Jan 1829
George	29	M	Tinman	G. Brittain	U. States	Cincinnatus	2 Oct 1822
George	50	M	Weaver	England	United States	London	21 May 1828
Hannah	7/12		None	Great Britain	United States	Roman	10 Sep 1827
Harriet	14	F	Spinster	England	America	Josephine	24 Jul 1826
Henny	5	M	None			John & Edward	25 Aug 1820
Henry	15		Boy	Ireland	United States	Courier	15 Oct 1827
Henry	25	M	Labourer	Ireland	America	Wilson	16 May 1825
Henry	28	M	Weaver	Ireland	U. States	Josephine	27 Jul 1825
Henry	38		Gentleman	Belfast	U. States	Carolina Ann	14 Feb 1824
Hugh	18	M	Weaver	England	United States	London	21 May 1828
Isaac	22		Farmer	Great Britain	United States	Thomas Dickason	29 Aug 1828
J.	29	M	Mechanic	England	United States	Hogarth	12 Oct 1829
Jacob	24	M	Farmer	Bristol, Engl.	...	Warrior	19 May 1828
James	5		Boy			Rufus King	7 Aug 1820
James	11		Boy	Ireland	United States	Courier	15 Oct 1827
James	12		Family [of Margt.]	Great Britain	United States	Camillus	12 Sep 1827
James	21		Calico Printer	England	America	Florida	14 Oct 1829
James	24 2/12	M	Mason	England	America	John Dickinson	15 Oct 1826
James	38	M	Merchant			John & Edward	25 Aug 1820
James	40 7/12	M	...	England	America, U.S.	Illinois	3 Jun 1822
James	43		Weaver	Scotland	United States	Camillus	3 May 1828
James	55	M	Cotton	Manchester	United States	Nile	17 May 1827
James	63		Broker	England	England	London	16 Aug 1824
Jane	9	F	None			John & Edward	25 Aug 1820
Jane	28	F	Nurse Maid	England	America	Criterion	27 Oct 1821
Jane	60	F		Manchester	United States	Nile	17 May 1827
Jas.	30	M	Mason	Ireland	United States	Trident	16 May 1826
Jno.	24	M	Labourer	Ireland	U. States	William & John	10 Jul 1824
Jno.	25	M	Weaver	Great Britain	United States	Atlantic	28 May 1827
Jno.	30	M	Spinner	Great Britain	United States	Roman	10 Sep 1827
John	3 9/12	M	Child	Ireland	America	Farmer	3 May 1824
John	20	M	Labourer	Scotland	United States	Mary & Susan	5 Aug 1828
John	23		Farmer	Breman	Germany	Hudson	14 Jun 1827
John	24	M	Farmer	Great Britain	United States	Mary Howland	19 Jul 1827
John	24	M	Farmer	Gt. Britain	U. States	Diana	28 Apr 1828
John	25		Farmer			Rufus King	7 Aug 1820
John	25	M	Seaman	U. States		Agnes	30 Sep 1820
John	25	M	Merchant	N. York	New York	Amity	31 May 1822
John	26	M	Farmer	England	Geneva, U. States	Ann Maria	26 Apr 1822
John	26	M		Scotland	U.S.	Curler	19 Jul 1828
John	30	M	Mariner	U. States	U. States	Pedler	27 May 1825
John	30	M	Merchant	Great Britain	U. States	William Thompson	24 Aug 1827
John	31	M	Teacher	G. Brittain	U. States	Cincinnatus	2 Oct 1822
John	37	M	Farmer	England	U.N.S.	Helen	16 Mar 1829
John	38	M	Merchant	U. States	U. States	New York	14 Feb 1826
John, Jr.	11	M	None	Scotland	United States	Mary & Susan	5 Aug 1828
John, Jr.	20	M	None	England	New York	Thames	6 Oct 1820
John J.	28	M	Mercht.	United States	United States	Pacific	24 Oct 1828
Joseph	23 4/12	M	Merchant	Great Britain	Great Britain	James Monroe	27 Jul 1821
Joseph	26		Gun Maker	Birmingham		Mount Vernon	18 Oct 1822
Joseph	27	M	Merchant	Gt. Britain	U. States	Frances Henrietta	18 Apr 1825
Joseph	27	M	Merchant	U. States	Canada	Canada	5 Feb 1827
Joseph	28	M	Merchant	Great Britain	New York	Auritz	20 May 1823
Joseph	33	M	Farmer	England	America	Thames	27 May 1822
Joseph	60	M	Shoemaker	England	America	Josephine	24 Jul 1826
Joshua	31	M	Merchant	U.S.	U.S.	Radius	8 Feb 1822
Lydia	14		Spinster			Rufus King	7 Aug 1820
Margat.	10		Family [of Margt.]	Great Britain	United States	Camillus	12 Sep 1827
Margt.	30		Weaver	Great Britain	United States	Camillus	12 Sep 1827
Maria	3	F		Great Britain	U. States	William Thompson	24 Aug 1827
Maria	18		Calico Printer	England	America	Florida	14 Oct 1829
Martha	...	...	...	Ireland	United States	General Putnam	20 Jun 1825

NAMES OF PASSENGERS	AGE	SEX	OCCUPATIONS	COUNTRY TO WHICH THEY BELONG	COUNTRY THEY INTEND TO INHABIT	SHIPS/DATES OF ARRIVAL	
WALKER (cont'd)							
Martha	21 4/12	F	Wife	Ireland	America	Farmer	3 May 1824
Mary	6		Family [of Margt.]	Great Britain	United States	Camillus	12 Sep 1827
Mary	14		Spinster	Ireland	United States	Courier	15 Oct 1827
Mary	19	F	Spinster	Ireland	America	Wilson	16 May 1825
Mary	22			England	England	London	16 Aug 1824
Mary	30	F	Wife	Ireland	United States	Trident	16 May 1826
Mary	40		Housewife			Rufus King	7 Aug 1820
Mary	41	F	Seamstress			John & Edward	25 Aug 1820
Mary, Mrs.	23	F		England	New York	Thames	6 Oct 1820
Mary Ane	32	F		Scotland	U.S.	Curler	19 Jul 1828
Mary Ann	22		Labourer	Belfast	U. States	Carolina Ann	14 Feb 1824
Mathias	25	M	Labourer	Ireland	United States	Kleber	23 Jul 1827
Matthew	28	M	Ship Master	Great Britain		Silas Richards	7 Mar 1825
Michiel	22	M	Servant	G. Brittian	U. States	Cambria	3 Jul 1829
N.	28	M	None	Columbia	U. States	Theresa	10 Dec 1825
Peter	18		Engineer	Great Britain	United States	Camillus	12 Sep 1827
R.	20	M	Labourer	G. Britain	U. States	London	23 Sep 1828
R. B.	20	M	Gentleman	Great Britan	Great Britan	Columbia	10 Mar 1824
Robert	...	M	Farmer	Ireland	United States	General Putnam	20 Jun 1825
Robert	14	M		Manchester	United States	Nile	17 May 1827
Robert	17		Labourer			Rufus King	7 Aug 1820
Robert	19	M	Farmer	Great Brittain	New York	Albion	11 Jun 1821
Robert	24 6/12	M	Carpenter	Ireland	America	Farmer	3 May 1824
Robert	75		Weaver	Scotland	United States	Camillus	3 May 1828
Robert B.	23	M	Gentleman	Great Britain, Ireland	New York	Britannia	3 Nov 1827
Robt.	8		None	Great Britain	United States	Roman	10 Sep 1827
Robt.	32	M	Labourer	Great Britian	United States	Princess Charlotte	6 Sep 1828
Saml.	24	M	Labourer	Ireland	U. States	William & John	10 Jul 1824
Solomon						Washington	2 Oct 1828
*Seaman Put on board by the Consul							
Sophia	22			Birmingham		Mount Vernon	18 Oct 1822
Susan	5	F		Great Britain	U. States	William Thompson	24 Aug 1827
Susan	26	F		Great Britain	U. States	William Thompson	24 Aug 1827
T.	17	M	Carpenter	Gt. Britain	United States	Robert Edwards	1 Jun 1826
Thomas	...	...	Merchant	Ireland	U. States of Amer	Courier	17 Mar 1827
Thomas	18	M	Laborer	Ireland	United States	Dublin Packet	9 Jul 1827
Thomas	24		Farmer	Great Britain	United States	Thomas Dickason	29 Aug 1828
Thomas	24	M	Farmer	England	U. States	Montgomery	18 Oct 1828
Thomas	32	M	Carpenter	England	U.S.	Acasta	11 May 1827
Thomas	46		Farmer	England	S. New York	Xenophon	25 Jul 1826
Thomas O.	28	M	Merchant	United States	United States	New York	5 Jul 1826
Thos.	21			Ireland		Anacreon	7 Sep 1827
Thos.	24	M	Manufacturer	G. Britain	U. States	Mary Howland	22 Sep 1828
Thos.	40		Merchant	Ireland	United States	Courier	15 Oct 1827
Thos., Mr.	32	M	Merchant	U.S. America	U.S. America	James Cropper	29 Nov 1827
Thos. E.	...	M	Merchant	New York	New York	Amity	13 Sep 1821
Thos. F.	40	M	Gentleman	U.S.	U.S.	Corinthian	11 Mar 1829
Violet	22	F	Spinster	Gt. Britain	U. States	Frances Henrietta	18 Apr 1825
W.	16	M	Farmer	Ireland	United States	Marmion	17 Jun 1825
William	18	M	Farmer	Scotland	United States	Commerce	17 Jul 1823
William	24	M	Tailor	England	United States	Lord Wellington	14 Nov 1827
William	25	M	Baker	St. John	U.S.	Nancy	1 Sep 1823
William	33	M		Great Britain	United States	Ganges	8 Jul 1820
William	33	M	Merchant	Scotland	America	Camillus	9 Oct 1820
William	34	M	Cloth Manufacturer	Great Britain	United States	Freake	25 Aug 1829
William	48	M	Merchant	Great Britain	Pensylvania	Orozimbo	2 Oct 1824
William H.	26	M	Merchant	England	America	Cincinnatus	22 May 1826
Wm.	4		None	Great Britain	United States	Roman	10 Sep 1827
Wm.	8		Family [of Margt.]	Great Britain	United States	Camillus	12 Sep 1827
Wm.	22		Clerk	Ireland	Great Britain	Robert Burns	14 Jun 1824
Wm.	25	M	Merchant	Jamaica	England	Jay	13 Aug 1823

NAMES OF PASSENGERS	AGE	SEX	OCCUPATIONS	COUNTRY TO WHICH THEY BELONG	COUNTRY THEY INTEND TO INHABIT	SHIPS/DATES OF ARRIVAL	
WALKER (cont'd)							
Wm.	29	M	Cotton Weaver	Great Brittan	U. States	John & Elizabeth	11 Dec 1826
Wm.	30	M				Trio	5 May 1828
Wm.	32		Merchant	Kelso	Great Britain	William Thompson	13 May 1823
Wm.	40	M	Labourer	Halifax	U. States	Loire	17 Aug 1827
Wm. J.	28	M	Farmer	C. Down	Philedelphia	Nile	18 Aug 1829
WALKIN, John	14	M		Great Britain	United States	Robert	15 Jul 1822
WALKINGTYHR,							
Edwd. Alfred	27	M	Gentleman	United States	United States	Unity	20 Oct 1829
WALKINSHARD,							
Elisabeth	1	F	None	Scotland	United States	Mary & Susan	5 Aug 1828
Elisabeth	22	F	None	Scotland	United States	Mary & Susan	5 Aug 1828
John	22	M	Labourer	Scotland	United States	Mary & Susan	5 Aug 1828
WALKLEY, Danl.	25		Labourer	England	United States	Hugh Johnson	11 Jun 1828
WALKUM, John	27	M	Gentleman	Gt. Britain		Corinthian	27 Oct 1829
WALKY, James	45	M	Carpenter	England	U.S. America	Magnet	17 Aug 1825
WALL, ...	22	F	Labourer	Kings County, Ireland	Gt. Britain	Orozimbo	19 Oct 1822
...	30	M	Labourer	Kings County, Ireland	Gt. Britain	Orozimbo	19 Oct 1822
Ann	5	F		England	United States	Margaret	5 Sep 1827
Ann	28	F		England	United States	Margaret	5 Sep 1827
Barbe	34	F		France	U. States	Edward Bonaffe	23 Jul 1828
C.	7	F		France	U. States	Edward Bonaffe	23 Jul 1828
Charles, Child [of Lucy]	6	M	None		United States	London Packet	25 Dec 1820
Charlotte	5	F		France	U. States	Edward Bonaffe	23 Jul 1828
Edmund	11			England		Anacreon	7 Sep 1827
Eliza	34	F				Belfast	28 Sep 1820
Eliza, Child [of Lucy]	1	F	None		United States	London Packet	25 Dec 1820
Elizabeth	5	F				Belfast	28 Sep 1820
Ewd.	10	M				Belfast	28 Sep 1820
Francis	8	M				Belfast	28 Sep 1820
Hen.	23	M	Mechanic	Great Britain	United States	Mary & Harriet	3 Jul 1829
J. R.	23	M	Clerk	Great Britain	New York	Dublin	21 Dec 1824
James	20 10/12	M	...	England	America, U.S.	Illinois	3 Jun 1822
James	30	M	Labourer	Ireland	New York	Lima	5 Aug 1829
James	31	M	Labourer	Great Britain	United States	Orbit	23 Oct 1826
James	35	M	Gentleman	England	U. States	Belfast	28 Sep 1820
James	39 11/12	M	Mason	England	United States	Rising States	16 Jan 1829
Jane	6	F				Belfast	28 Sep 1820
John	11	M	None	Ireland	United States	Diana	1 May 1826
John	18 9/12	M	Mason	England	United States	Rising States	16 Jan 1829
John	29	M		England	U. States	Mary	24 Jun 1824
John	36	M	Sawyer	France	U. States	Edward Bonaffe	23 Jul 1828
L.	3/12	F		France	U. States	Edward Bonaffe	23 Jul 1828
Lucy	28	F	None		United States	London Packet	25 Dec 1820
Mary	1	F		England	United States	Margaret	5 Sep 1827
Mary	27	F		England	U. States	Mary	24 Jun 1824
Michael	30	M	Mason	Great Britain	U. States	Great Britain	18 Mar 1828
Micheal	8	M	None	Ireland	United States	Diana	1 May 1826
Richard, Child [of Lucy]	8	M	None		United States	London Packet	25 Dec 1820
Samuel	26	M	Clothier	Great Britain	United States	Frances Henrietta	17 Sep 1827
Sarah, Child [of Lucy]	...	F	None		United States	London Packet	25 Dec 1820
Thos.	22	M	Weaver	Ireland	United States	Trident	16 May 1826
Thos.	23	M	Farmer	Ireland	United States	Trident	16 May 1826
Thos.	30	M	Teacher	Scotland	U. States	Dalmarnock	23 May 1823
Trudom	2	F		France	U. States	Edward Bonaffe	23 Jul 1828
Wm.	25	M	Farmer	Ireland	New York	General Marion	21 Nov 1828
WALLACE, —, Mr.	35	F		U.S.	U.S.	Frances	21 Jul 1827
—, Mrs.		F		U. States	U. States	Robert Fulton	2 Aug 1824
—, Wm.	45	M	Planter	Denmark	Denmark	Gleaner	31 Jul 1821
...	24	F		England	America	Plutarch	18 Jul 1826
...	28 7/12	M	Planter	Great Britton	Great Britton	Elias Burger	18 Sep 1821

NAMES OF PASSENGERS	AGE	SEX	OCCUPATIONS	COUNTRY TO WHICH THEY BELONG	COUNTRY THEY INTEND TO INHABIT	SHIPS/DATES OF ARRIVAL	
WALLACE (cont'd)							
Alex.	26	M	Labourer	Ireland	United States	Essex	23 May 1828
Alex.	37	M	Mason	Scotland	U. States	Roger Stewart	9 Jun 1828
Andrew	40	M	Labourer	Ireland	United States	Gem	16 Jun 1824
Andrew J.	19 7/12	M	Gentleman	Ireland	America	Wilson	16 Nov 1824
Ann	37	F		Gt. Britain		Dalhouse Castle	13 May 1828
Ann Jane	3 4/12	F		Ireland	U. States	Fabius	22 Sep 1828
Bessey	24	F	None	England	United States	Jubilee	1 Oct 1828
Bodan R., Master	14	M	Farmer	England	U. States	Acasta	3 Apr 1826
Charles	26	M	Stone Cutter	U. States	U. States	Laura Ann	2 Feb 1820
Eliza	13 6/12	F		Ireland	U. States	Fabius	22 Sep 1828
Eliza W.	21			United States	United States	Emily	11 Mar 1826
George	22	M	...	Ireland	United States	Carolina Ann	24 Oct 1825
Gideon	34	M	Farmer	Scotland	U. States	Roger Stewart	9 Jun 1828
Henry	21	M	Servant	Gt. Britan	America	Braganza	1 Dec 1824
J. B.	20	F	None	United States	U. States	Brown	8 Aug 1825
James	20	M	Farmer	Great Brittain	United States	Active	12 Sep 1828
James	24	M	Cooper	Scotland	America	Plutarch	18 Jul 1826
James	29	M	Farmer	Ireland	United States	Dublin Packet	29 Jun 1825
Jane	20	F	wife to Patrick	Ireland	U. States	William & John	10 Jul 1824
Jane	23		Gentn.	G.B.	United States	Cadmus	24 Oct 1827
Jas.	27	M	Labourer	Great Britain	United States	William Dawson	18 Jun 1827
John	1	M	Child	Ireland	U. States	William & John	10 Jul 1824
John	10 5/12	M		Ireland	U. States	Fabius	22 Sep 1828
John	20	M	Weaver	Gt. Britain		Dalhouse Castle	13 May 1828
John	25	M	Clergyman	Ireland	United States	Alex. Mansfield	17 May 1823
John	32		Labourer	Ireland	United States	Geo. Canning	5 Jun 1828
John, Mastr.	4			G.B.	United States	Cadmus	24 Oct 1827
John, Mr.	50	M	Farmer	England	U. States	Acasta	3 Apr 1826
John F.	29	M	Merchant	London	Connecticut	Ann Maria	24 Feb 1824
Jos.	30	M	Weaver	Scotland	Ama.	Expedition	19 May 1828
Joseph	2	M		Gt. Britain		Dalhouse Castle	13 May 1828
Joseph	25	M	Labourer	Ireland	United States	William & George	14 May 1828
Magaret	15	M	Mason	Scotland	U. States	Roger Stewart	9 Jun 1828
Margt.	7	F		G. Britain	U. States	Dalhouse Castle	12 Sep 1828
Mary	17	M	None	Car... Street	W. Mouth	Howard Douglass	11 May 1827
Mary	18	F		St. Johns	U. States	Wanderer	30 Oct 1828
Mary	20	F		Great Brittain	United States	Active	12 Sep 1828
Mary	25	F	Spinster	Ireland	United States	Dublin Packet	29 Jun 1825
Mary	26	M		Brittian	U. States	Acasta	28 Jan 1823
Mary	30			Ireland	United States	Geo. Canning	5 Jun 1828
Mary, Mrs.	40	F	Farmer	England	U. States	Acasta	3 Apr 1826
Mary Ann, Miss	18	F	Farmer	England	U. States	Acasta	3 Apr 1826
Nancy	22	F	Labourer	Ireland	U. States	Marcus	7 Apr 1825
Newton	36	M		Great Britain		Corinthian	27 Oct 1829
Oliver	22	M	Clerk	Ireland	New York	America	1 Aug 1828
Patrick	26	M	Labourer	Ireland	U. States	William & John	10 Jul 1824
Patrick	26	M	Planter	Great Britain	Great Britain	Bucksport	5 Jun 1826
Patrick	33		Gentn.	G.B.	United States	Cadmus	24 Oct 1827
Saml.	12 6/12	M		Ireland	U. States	Fabius	22 Sep 1828
Terrence	24	M	Farmer	Ireland	United States	Dublin Packet	29 Jun 1825
Thomas	20	M	Lab.	Car... Street	W. Mouth	Howard Douglass	11 May 1827
Thomas	22	M	Brickmaker	Ireland	America	Wilson	16 May 1825
Thomas	23	M	Laborer	Gt. Britain		Dalhouse Castle	13 May 1828
Thomas	23	M		Ireland	United States	William & George	14 May 1828
Thomas	30	M	Labourer	Ireland	United States	Princess Charlotte	6 Oct 1827
Thomas	35	M	Labourer	Ireland	United States	Kleber	23 Jul 1827
Thos.	25	M	Farmer	Ireland	Canada	Pilgrim	1 Sep 1828
Walter	19	M	Coach Smith	England	America	Sarah	18 Aug 1829
William	7	M		Gt. Britain		Dalhouse Castle	13 May 1828
William	21 1/12	M	...	England	America, U.S.	Illinois	3 Jun 1822
William	24	M	Goldsmith & Jeweller	England	New York	Thames	6 Oct 1820
William	24	M	Painter	Ireland	New York	Trusty	12 Sep 1828

NAMES OF PASSENGERS	AGE	SEX	OCCUPATIONS	COUNTRY TO WHICH THEY BELONG	COUNTRY THEY INTEND TO INHABIT	SHIPS/DATES OF ARRIVAL	
WALLACE (cont'd)							
William	25	M		Ireland	United States	Marmion	17 Jun 1825
William	30	M	Merchant	Gt. Britain	Halifax, N.S.	Maria	22 May 1822
William	33	M	Attorney	Great Britain		Andromache	7 Feb 1820
Wm.	4 6/12	M		Ireland	U. States	Fabius	22 Sep 1828
Wm.	22	M	Merchant	G.B.	G.B.	Sally	19 Sep 1821
Wm.	22	M	Mercht.	England	United States	Nestor	25 Jul 1823
Wm.	34 9/12	M		Ireland	U. States	Fabius	22 Sep 1828
Wm.	40	M	Lab.	Car... Street	W. Mouth	Howard Douglass	11 May 1827
Wm. B.	26	M	Merchant	France	U. States	Victoria	9 Sep 1828
Wm. B.	33	M	Merchant	United States	United States	Herald	21 Sep 1824
Wm. R.	19	M	Gentleman	England	New York	Phoenix	29 Apr 1826
WALLACH, Jas. W.	34	M	Copmedian	Gt. Britain	Gt. Britain	Caledonia	10 Sep 1828
WALLACK, Frs.	24	F	Comedian	G. Britain	U. States	William	2 May 1821
James W.	27	M	Tragedian	England	England	Nestor	20 Nov 1821
Jas. W.	3	M	Comedian	G. Britain	U. States	William	2 May 1821
Jas. W.	28	M	Comedian	Great Britain	U. States	Columbia	24 Dec 1822
Julia	2	F	Comedian	G. Britain	U. States	William	2 May 1821
Wm. H.	28	M	Comedian	G. Britain	U. States	William	2 May 1821
WALLAD, Martha	7	F				Imperial	19 Jul 1820
Sarah	5	F				Imperial	19 Jul 1820
WALLAN, Wm. P.	37	M	Merchant	Havana	Cuba	Noble	2 Nov 1826
WALLAND, Wm.	24	M				Cassack	25 Jul 1820
WALLAS, —, Mrs.	24	F		Great Britain	United States	Lady Hunter	26 Nov 1823
Elizabeth	3	F		Great Britain	United States	Lady Hunter	26 Nov 1823
George	29	M		Great Britain	United States	Lady Hunter	26 Nov 1823
Patrik	1 6/12	M		Great Britain	United States	Lady Hunter	26 Nov 1823
WALLEN, Henry Z.	18	M	Blacksmith	Switzerland	New York	Frances Henrietta	25 Aug 1825
WALLENSTEIN, J.	32	M	Secretary	Russia	Russia	New York	11 Mar 1823
WALLER, Franz	34	M	Tanner	Switzerland	United States	Howard	6 Jul 1829
P.	18	M	Labourer			Lady of the Lake	23 Aug 1828
Susanah	30	F	Labourer	England	U. States	Comet	23 Aug 1828
Wm.	27	M	Painter	England	United States	Copernicus	3 Aug 1829
Wm.	28 8/12	M	Mercantile	England	Mexico	Combine	1 Aug 1825
WALLEY, Alfred	21	M	Merchant	U. States	U. States	Rising States	12 May 1827
WALLIN, William	28	M	Printer	New York	U.S.A.	Hudson	21 Aug 1829
WALLIS, Alice	6			Liverpool		Mount Vernon	18 Oct 1822
Bartholomew	29	M	Labourer	Ireland	United States	Helen	27 Jun 1821
Benjamin	...6	M	Weaver	Great Britain	United States	Ann Maria	17 Apr 1827
Elizabeth	...3	F	Wife	Great Britain	United States	Ann Maria	17 Apr 1827
Fred	32			...	...	James Cropper	28 Jun 1824
Geo. W.	25	M	Merchant	England	U.N. States	Corinthian	1 Sep 1823
Harriet	4 4/12	F		Great Britain	Cuba	Venus	8 Sep 1820
Henry W. P.	21	M	Merchant	Gt. Britian	United States	Cortes	11 Dec 1822
Hugh	4			Liverpool		Mount Vernon	18 Oct 1822
James	8			Liverpool		Mount Vernon	18 Oct 1822
James	50	M	Brewer	England	U. States	Elizabeth	5 Oct 1822
Jane	2			Liverpool		Mount Vernon	18 Oct 1822
Jane	30			Liverpool		Mount Vernon	18 Oct 1822
Jas.	24	M	Mechanic	U. States	U. States	Susan & Sarah	25 Apr 1825
John	20	M	Farmer	G. Britain	U. States	Mary & Harriot	8 Sep 1828
John	24	M	Labourer	England	U. States	Ayrshire	12 May 1828
John	28	M	Merchant	N. Haven	U. States	Pacific	21 Jun 1826
Judith	24	F	Spinster	Ireland	Unt. St. America	Wilson	21 May 1827
Martin	22	M	Whaler	Great Britain	U. States	Robert Fulton	3 Dec 1827
Ned	22	M	Laborer	Ireland	United States	St. Michael	21 Aug 1824
Robert	34	M		Great Britain	United States	Active	25 Mar 1828
Samuel	1			Liverpool		Mount Vernon	18 Oct 1822
W.	32	M	Merchant	England	U.S.	York	1 Dec 1827
W. E.	15	M	Merchant	United States	United States	Tontine	9 Jun 1827
WALLON, James	24	M	Carpenter	England	New York	Brighton	19 Aug 1829
James	24	M	Carpenter			Brighton	19 Aug 1829
Patrick	24	M	...	...	United States	Minerva	30 Oct 1827
WALLOUGHBY, —, Mrs.	50	F		Halifax	some to return & the others to Canada	Albert	14 May 1822

NAMES OF PASSENGERS	AGE	SEX	OCCUPATIONS	COUNTRY TO WHICH THEY BELONG	COUNTRY THEY INTEND TO INHABIT	SHIPS/DATES OF ARRIVAL	
WALLOWAY, Isaac	31	M				Cassack	25 Jul 1820
WALLY, Jas. M.	28	M	Mechanic	Great Brittain		Star	7 Jan 1827
WALMSLEY, Elisabeth	27	F	None	England	United States	Dalhouse Castle	6 Sep 1827
Eliza	8	F	None	England	United States	Dalhouse Castle	6 Sep 1827
John	24	M	Stone Mason	England	United States	Baltic	21 Apr 1827
Mary Ann	5	F	None	England	United States	Dalhouse Castle	6 Sep 1827
Rachel	29	F	None	England	United States	Dalhouse Castle	6 Sep 1827
WALN, J.	38	M	Merchant	New York	U. States	New York	15 Nov 1823
WALRAKER, Elizabeth	55	F	None	England		Aurora	12 Mar 1827
WALROND, M., Mrs.		F	Lady	Bristol, Engd.	unknown	Superb	23 Apr 1823
Nicholas H.		M	Merchant	Barbados	unknown	Superb	23 Apr 1823
WALSET, Frederick	21	M	Farmer	Switzerland	United States	Olympia	12 Aug 1828
WALSH, Abigail	43	F	None	Ireland	United States	Princess Charlotte	6 Oct 1827
Ann	11	F	None	Ireland	United States	Princess Charlotte	6 Oct 1827
Ann	19	F		England	United States	Lord Wellington	14 Nov 1827
Ann	24	F	None	Ireland	United States	Elizabeth	8 Jun 1827
Augusta	11	F				Reuben & Eliza	21 Aug 1820
Bridget *died	1 1/2	F		Ireland	America	Plutarch	18 Jul 1826
Bridget	23	F	Spinster	Ireland	United States	Dublin Packet	3 May 1823
Bridget	25	F		Ireland	America	Plutarch	18 Jul 1826
Bridget	25	F	Laborer	Ireland	America	Parrington	9 Jun 1827
Catharine	1 6/12		Farmer & Labourer	Great Britain & Ireland	United States	Trio	8 Feb 1827
Catharine	30		Farmer & Labourer	Great Britain & Ireland	United States	Trio	8 Feb 1827
Catherine	...3	F	Servant	Ireland	United States	Trio	31 Oct 1827
Catherine	18	F	Spinster	Ireland	United States	Diana	1 May 1826
Edward	40		Farmer & Labourer	Great Britain & Ireland	United States	Trio	8 Feb 1827
Elen	2/12	F	Infant	Ireland	America	Parrington	9 Jun 1827
Eliz.	1	F	None	Ireland	United States	Princess Charlotte	6 Oct 1827
Ellen	6/12	F	None	Great Britain	United States	Purrington	8 Dec 1827
Ellen	12	F		Ireland	America	William	21 May 1825
Elmond	24	M	Farmer	Ireland	America	William	21 May 1825
Frances	14	F				Reuben & Eliza	21 Aug 1820
Hannah	24	F		Ireland	U. States	Balaena	29 Apr 1825
Hen	20	F	Spinster	Ireland	United States	Thomas	13 Dec 1827
Hugh	25	M	Labourer	Glasgow	U. States	Florenzo	29 Jun 1826
Jacob	13	M	None	Ireland	United States	Princess Charlotte	6 Oct 1827
James	3	M	None	Ireland	United States	Princess Charlotte	6 Oct 1827
James	27	M	Farmer	Ireland	America	William	21 May 1825
James	27	M	Laboror	Ireland	United States	Wilson	27 Jun 1826
James	28	M	Farmer	Ireland	U. States	Orozimbo	7 Jul 1825
James	32	M	Clerk	Ireland	America	Erin	14 Feb 1820
James	38	M	Labourer	Ireland	U. States	Albion	11 May 1827
James	40	M	Labourer	Ireland	United States	Aurelia	7 Jun 1826
Jane	17	F				Reuben & Eliza	21 Aug 1820
Jas.	20	M		Dublin	U. States	Hibernia	26 Oct 1826
Jas.	20	M		Ireland	United States	Margarett Scott	22 Aug 1827
John	9		Farmer & Labourer	Great Britain & Ireland	United States	Trio	8 Feb 1827
John	15	M	Labourer	Ireland	United States	Princess Charlotte	6 Oct 1827
John	21	M	Labourer	Ireland	United States	Sarah Ann	11 Jan 1827
John	23	M	None	York, Great Britain		Casanda	5 Sep 1827
John	28	M	Mechanic			Seine	10 Jun 1822
John	29	M	Shoemaker	Great Britain	United States	Purrington	8 Dec 1827
John	46	M	Labourer	Ireland	United States	Trio	31 Oct 1827
John	69	M	Farmer	Ireland	America	William	21 May 1825
John Robin	21	M	Laborer	Ireland	United States	Trio	13 Jun 1827
Joseph	5	M	None	Ireland	United States	Princess Charlotte	6 Oct 1827

NAMES OF PASSENGERS	AGE	SEX	OCCUPATIONS	COUNTRY TO WHICH THEY BELONG	COUNTRY THEY INTEND TO INHABIT	SHIPS/DATES OF ARRIVAL	
WALSH (cont'd)							
Lawrence	16	M	Farmer	Ireland	America	William	21 May 1825
Margaret	16	F				Reuben & Eliza	21 Aug 1820
Margaret	21	F		Great Britain	United States	Wilson	26 Feb 1824
Margaret	68	F	Wife	Ireland	United States	Dublin Packet	13 Oct 1828
Margt.	20	F		Ireland	United States	Trio	13 Jun 1827
Mark	33	M	Farmer	Ireland	New York	Munroe	27 May 1825
Mary	4	F		Ireland	America	Plutarch	18 Jul 1826
Mary	10		Farmer & r Laboure	Great Britain & Ireland	United States	Trio	8 Feb 1827
Mary	14	F	Spinster	Ireland	America	William	21 May 1825
Mary	21	F	Lady			Seine	10 Jun 1822
Mary	21	F		G. Britain	U. States	London	23 Sep 1828
Mary	29	F	None	Great Britain	United States	Purrington	8 Dec 1827
Mary	52	F	Spinster	Ireland	America	William	21 May 1825
Mary	60	F	Spinster	Ireland	United States	Diana	1 May 1826
Mary Ann	3	F	None	Great Britain	United States	Purrington	8 Dec 1827
Mathew	23		Farmer & Laboure	Great Britain & Ireland	United States	Trio	8 Feb 1827
Michael	23	M		Great Britain	United States	Wilson	26 Feb 1824
Michal	48	M	Farmer	United States	Ohio	Susquehanna	9 Jan 1824
Micheal	25	M	Farmer	Gt. Brittain	United States	Balaena	21 Aug 1824
Michl.	20	M	Labourer	Great Britain	United States	William Dawson	18 Jun 1827
Pat.	35	M	Farmer	England	United States	India	8 Jun 1827
Patrick	20					Trio	5 May 1828
Patrick	22	M	Labourer	Ireland	America	Plutarch	18 Jul 1826
Philip	21	M	Farmer	Ireland	America	William	21 May 1825
R. D.	36	M	Merchant	Hayti	Hayti	Aurora Alcide	8 Jul 1826
Ralph	19	M	Labourer	Ireland	United States	Princess Charlotte	6 Oct 1827
Ralph	53	M	Farmer	Ireland	United States	Princess Charlotte	6 Oct 1827
Richard	18	M	Farmer	Ireland	America	William	21 May 1825
Richard	22		Farmer & Laboure	Great Britain & Ireland	United States	Trio	8 Feb 1827
Richd.	27	M	Gentleman	Ireland	United States	Thomas	13 Dec 1827
Robert	10		Farmer & Laboure	Great Britain & Ireland	United States	Trio	8 Feb 1827
Robt.	35	M	Merchant	St. John	St. John	St. Michael	27 Mar 1827
Roxina	20	F				Reuben & Eliza	21 Aug 1820
S. A.	40		Physician	U. States		New York	18 Jul 1828
Sabrina	12	F				Reuben & Eliza	21 Aug 1820
Thomas	9	M	None	Ireland	United States	Princess Charlotte	6 Oct 1827
Thos.	22	M	Farmer	England	U. States	Orozimbo	7 Jul 1825
Thos.	23	M	Labourer	Ireland	U. States	Balaena	29 Apr 1825
Thos.	24	M	Laborer	Ireland	America	Parrington	9 Jun 1827
William	7	M	None	Ireland	United States	Princess Charlotte	6 Oct 1827
William	14	M		Ireland	America	William	21 May 1825
William	30	M	Labourer	Ireland	America	Plutarch	18 Jul 1826
William	35	M	Mercht.	Ireland	Honduras	Francis Jarvis	10 Jan 1825
Wm.	25	M	Labourer	Ireland	United States	Thomas	13 Dec 1827
WALSTEEN,							
Jas. Westervell	26 6/12	M	Comedian	City New York	United States	Jane	13 Mar 1829
WALT..., Christophor	34	M	Merchant	America	America	Henry	18 Oct 1826
WALTCH, Judy	19			Ireland	United States	Geo. Canning	5 Jun 1828
Richd.	16		Labourer	Ireland	United States	Geo. Canning	5 Jun 1828
WALTER, Ann, Mrs.	25	F	Smith	England	U.S.	Acasta	11 May 1827
B.	29	M	Labourer	France	America, U.N.S.	Great Britain	3 Aug 1829
Benjamin	55	M	Merchant	France	U. States	Nancy	17 Mar 1824
David	24	M	Backer	Prussia	Philadelphia	Maria Elizabeth	18 Jun 1827
Jas.	26	M	Mechanic	England	United States	New Packet	7 Aug 1826
John	25	M		G. Britain	U. States	Leavitts	25 Aug 1828
Patrick	18	M	Child	Great Britain	United States	Wanderer	11 Jul 1826
Robert	20	M	Merchant		New York	Governor Clinton	3 Jul 1827
Robert, Mast.	2	M	Smith	England	U.S.	Acasta	11 May 1827
Rudolph	43	M	Farmer	Swis	United States	Iris	21 Sep 1821

NAMES OF PASSENGERS	AGE	SEX	OCCUPATIONS	COUNTRY TO WHICH THEY BELONG	COUNTRY THEY INTEND TO INHABIT	SHIPS/DATES OF ARRIVAL	
WALTER (cont'd)							
T.	27	M	Merchant	Germany	United States	Plato	25 Aug 1829
WALTERA, Thomas	21	M	Labourer	England	U. States	Brighton	14 Apr 1828
WALTERLING, Jno. G.	60	M	Merchant	Demara	U. States	Sudan	6 Aug 1823
Maria J.	30	F		Demara	U. States	Sudan	6 Aug 1823
WALTERS, Jacob	34		Mariner	Baltimore	New York	Xenophon	25 Jul 1826
James	16	M	Labourer	Sligo	New York	Susquehana	27 Jun 1823
Thomas	33	M	...	England	America, U.S.	Illinois	3 Jun 1822
William	25 11/12	M	...	England	America, U.S.	Illinois	3 Jun 1822
William	40	M	None	Great Britain	United States	Hannibal	12 Oct 1829
Wm.	48	M	Farmer	Yorkshire	Yorkshire	Howard Douglass	11 May 1827
WALTERSON, Wm.	22	M	Engraver	England	America	Hercules	2 Nov 1825
WALTH, James	35	M	...	...	America	Farmer	11 Sep 1824
WALTIN, ...	...	M		England		Anacreon	7 Sep 1827
Mary	56	F		England		Anacreon	7 Sep 1827
Robt.	53	M		England		Anacreon	7 Sep 1827
Walter	16	M		England		Anacreon	7 Sep 1827
WALTON, ...er	30	F	None	Great Britain	United States	Dalhouse Castle	21 Aug 1829
A.	21	M	Merchant	United States	U. States	Mary Levengston,	17 Jun 1826
M			Brewer	Bristol	United States	Hector	29 Nov 1823
Edwd.	7	M	None	England	U. States	Dalhouse	23 Mar 1829
G...	5	F		England	America	Criterion	27 Oct 1821
Hester	30	F	None	Gt. Britain	U.S.A.	Dalhouse Castle	21 Aug 1829
J. J.	26	M	Mechanic	N. York	U. States	Elizabeth	24 Feb 1823
Jacob	7/12	M		England	America	Criterion	27 Oct 1821
Jacob	50	M	Capt. H. R. M. Navy	America	America	Criterion	27 Oct 1821
James	23	M	Farmer	Great Briton	Boston	Brighton	12 Jun 1826
James	26	M	Weaver	Great Britain	United States	Frances Henrietta	17 Sep 1827
Jnh.	28	M	Carder	England	U. States	Dalhouse	23 Mar 1829
Jno.	20	M	Farmer	Gt. Britain	U. States	Superior	20 Aug 1825
John	16	M	Mechanic	G.B.	G.B.	George Canning	26 Aug 1829
John	27	M	Farmer	England	U. States	Panthea	22 Nov 1826
Jos.	9	M		England	America	Criterion	27 Oct 1821
Joseph	7	M		Gt. Britain		Dalhouse Castle	13 May 1828
Joseph	30	M	Farmer	Great Britian	United States	Andes	19 Aug 1829
Mary	2	F	None	England	U. States	Dalhouse	23 Mar 1829
Mary Ann	3	F		England	America	Criterion	27 Oct 1821
Philis	26	F	None	England	U. States	Dalhouse	23 Mar 1829
Richd. F.	25	M	Divinity	England	Barbadoes	Celia	15 Oct 1825
Sarah	7	F		England	America	Criterion	27 Oct 1821
Sarah	30	F		England	America	Criterion	27 Oct 1821
Wm.	11	M		England	America	Criterion	27 Oct 1821
WALWORTH, Jno.	46	M	Spinner	Great Britain	United States	Penelope	11 Jun 1827
Thos.	25	M	Spinner	Great Britain	United States	Penelope	11 Jun 1827
WALY, Valentin	25	M	Labourer	France		Pallas	14 Jun 1828
WALZER, J.	6	M		Switzerland	U.S. America	Huntress	6 Sep 1827
J. J.	40	M	Farmer	Switzerland	U.S. America	Huntress	6 Sep 1827
M. V.	30	F		Switzerland	U.S. America	Huntress	6 Sep 1827
Maria	1	F		Switzerland	U.S. America	Huntress	6 Sep 1827
Maria	3	F		Switzerland	U.S. America	Huntress	6 Sep 1827
WAMBERSIE, —, Mrs.	47	F		U. States	Holland	Abigail	4 Oct 1823
E.	60	M	Gentleman	U. States	Holland	Abigail	4 Oct 1823
Lucien	10	M		U. States	Holland	Abigail	4 Oct 1823
Thomas	7	M		U. States	Holland	Abigail	4 Oct 1823
WANDALY, Mathew	25	M	Taylor	Swiss	U. States	Comet	28 Jul 1825
WANDER, Benjamin	33	M	Farmer	France	France	Sully	15 Jul 1829
Eliza	3	F	Farmer	France	France	Sully	15 Jul 1829
George	4/12	M	Farmer	France	France	Sully	15 Jul 1829
Marguerite	34	F	Farmer	France	France	Sully	15 Jul 1829
WANDLE, C.	30	F	Farmer	Switzerland	U. States	Alfred	8 Jul 1828
Cath.	3	F	Farmer	Switzerland	U. States	Alfred	8 Jul 1828
Cath.	5	F	Farmer	Switzerland	U. States	Alfred	8 Jul 1828
Cathr.	3	F	Farmer	Switzerland	U. States	Alfred	8 Jul 1828
D.	31	F	Farmer	Switzerland	U. States	Alfred	8 Jul 1828
E.	5	F	Farmer	Switzerland	U. States	Alfred	8 Jul 1828

WANDLE (cont'd)

NAMES OF PASSENGERS	AGE	SEX	OCCUPATIONS	COUNTRY TO WHICH THEY BELONG	COUNTRY THEY INTEND TO INHABIT	SHIPS/DATES OF ARRIVAL	
M.	2	F	Farmer	Switzerland	U. States	Alfred	8 Jul 1828
N.	7	F	Farmer	Switzerland	U. States	Alfred	8 Jul 1828
S.	7	F	Farmer	Switzerland	U. States	Alfred	8 Jul 1828
WANE, Thos.	13			England	United States	Hugh Johnson	11 Jun 1828
WANHLER, Joseph	9	M	Agriculturist	France	U.S.	Helen	3 May 1828
Lament	41	M	Agriculturist	France	U.S.	Helen	3 May 1828
Margaret	42	F	Agriculturist	France	U.S.	Helen	3 May 1828
WANNOCK, William	25	M	Manufacturer	Great Britain	United States	Illinois	9 Oct 1820
WANOCK, ...es	29	M	Labourer	Ireland	United States	Henry Kneeland	7 Jun 1828
Lesley	17	M	Cl...	Ireland	United States	Henry Kneeland	7 Jun 1828
WANTING, Jos.	18	M		Ireland	U. States	St. Michael	26 Oct 1824
WANTON, John	24	M	Clerk	Ireland	United States	Sylvester Healy	11 May 1825
Joseph	21	M	Merchant	Canada	Unknown	William Thompson	1 May 1827
WANTYN, Wm.	19	M	Merchant	Ireland	New York	Vigilant	6 May 1822
WARA, Thos.	24	M	Mechanic	England	U. States	James Cropper	10 Jun 1823
WARBURTON, James	27	M	Weaver	England	United States	Trident	18 Jul 1827
WARD, Abel	38		Farmer	England	S. New York	Xenophon	25 Jul 1826
Alexa.	30	M	Labourer	Great Brittan	United States	America	24 Jul 1827
Alexander	6/12	M	None	Great Brittan	United States	America	24 Jul 1827
Alfred	17 4/12	M	Clerk	United States	Amarica	Dawn	31 Mar 1828
Alice	11	F		G. Britain	United States	Siroc	13 Sep 1828
Allis	14	F	Farmer	England	America	Franklin	19 Nov 1828
Ann	1	F	Joiner	Great Brittan	United States	Andes	19 Aug 1829
Ann	21	F	Spinster	Ireland	U. States	Josephine	7 May 1827
Ann	21	F	None	Ireland	United States	Jubilee	12 May 1828
Ann	22	F	Joiner	Great Britian	United States	Andes	19 Aug 1829
* Ann	28	F		G. Britain	U. States	Mary Howland	22 Sep 1828
Ann	29	F	None	Gt. Brittian	Gt. Brittain	Manchester	17 Aug 1825
Betty	22			Longford	Newyork	Peru	30 May 1828
Bridget	20	F		Ireland	United States	Enterprize	23 Jul 1827
Bridget	26	F	None	Great Brittan	United States	America	24 Jul 1827
Bridget	45	F	Wife	Ireland	United States	Dublin Packet	22 Aug 1829
Charles	19	M	Farmer	England	America	Franklin	19 Nov 1828
Charls	30	M	Merchant	St. Johns, N.B.	St. Johns, N.B.	Nancy	9 Oct 1820
David	25	M	Gentleman	Great Britain	United States	Aspasia	16 Jul 1828
Edward	30	M	Servant	Ireland	New York	Amanda	23 May 1827
Edwd. C.	33	M	Merchant	United States	United States	Hannibal	27 May 1822
Eliza	1 6/12	F	Butcher	Great Britain	United States	Thomas Dickason	31 Jul 1829
Eliza	10	F	Farmer	England	America	Franklin	19 Nov 1828
Eliza	15	F		G. Britain	United States	Siroc	13 Sep 1828
Eliza	19	F		G. Britain	U. States	Cosmo	15 May 1827
Elizabeth	4	F	Joiner	Great Britian	United States	Andes	19 Aug 1829
Elizabeth	20	F		England	New York	Lima	5 Aug 1829
Elizabeth	20	F	Butcher	Ireland	U. States	Lima	5 Aug 1829
Elizabeth	50	F	Farmer	England	America	Franklin	19 Nov 1828
Ellen	9/12	F	None	Ireland	New York	Margaret	18 May 1825
Ellen	20	F	Farmer	England	America	Franklin	19 Nov 1828
Estor	29	F	Farmer	Great Britan	United States	Clematis	8 May 1827
Francis	17	M	Labourer	Ireland	United States	Jubilee	12 May 1828
Francis	18 6/12	M	Labourer	Ireland	United States	Robert Fulton	24 Jul 1826
Geo.	24	M	Coach Driver	United States	United States	Brown	30 Nov 1827
Geo.	36	M	Merchant	G. Britain	U. States	Geo. Canning	2 Sep 1828
George	2...	M	Butcher	England	New York	Lima	5 Aug 1829
George	25	M	Butcher	Ireland	U. States	Lima	5 Aug 1829
Godfry	23	M	Labourer	Ireland	United States	Enterprize	23 Jul 1827
H. G.	20	M	Merchant	U. States, N. York	U. States	Angelica	19 Sep 1821
H. G.	26	M	Merchant	U. States	U. States	Tampico	20 Apr 1825
H. G.	28	M	Merchant	United States	United States	Tampico	27 Jun 1827
Hannah	3	F		G. Britain	United States	Siroc	13 Sep 1828
Hannah, Mrs.	26	F		England	New York	Hannibal	28 Apr 1824
Heny	8	M		G. Britain	United States	Siroc	13 Sep 1828
Isabela	13	F		G. Britain	United States	Siroc	13 Sep 1828
J.	45	M	Ship Master	United States	United States	Milton	21 Mar 1828
J. [crossed out]						Enterprize	19 Oct 1826
James	16	M	Farmer	Dublin		Mount Vernon	7 Jun 1824

NAMES OF PASSENGERS	AGE	SEX	OCCUPATIONS	COUNTRY TO WHICH THEY BELONG	COUNTRY THEY INTEND TO INHABIT	SHIPS/DATES OF ARRIVAL
WARD (cont'd)						
James	18	M	Farmer	Ireland	United States	Alex. Mansfield 17 May 1823
James	20	M	Labourer	Ireland	United States	Jubilee 13 Jul 1829
James	22	M	Farmer	England	United States	Peru 23 May 1827
James	23	M	Joiner	England	United States	Dalhouse Castle 6 Sep 1827
James	24	M	Labourer	...th...ck	United States	Solon 21 Jun 1824
James	30	M	Laborer	Gt. Britain		Dalhouse Castle 13 May 1828
James	50	M	Farmer	Great Brittain	United States	Robert Fulton 13 Mar 1827
Jane	21	F	Spinster	Ireland	United States	Dublin Packet 29 Jun 1825
Jas.	27		Labourer	Great Britan	United States	Newry 11 Jul 1827
Jas.	44	M	...	...	United States	Minerva 30 Oct 1827
Jno.	45	M	Farmer	England	America	Franklin 19 Nov 1828
John	0 3/12	M		England	New York	Lima 5 Aug 1829
John	3/12	M		Ireland	U. States	Lima 5 Aug 1829
John	18	M	Labourer	Ireland	America	Weser 26 Jun 1821
John	19	M	Gunsmith	England	United States	Siroc 31 Oct 1829
John	20	M	Shomaker	England	United States	Siroc 31 Oct 1829
John	25	M	Labourer	Ireland	United States	General Marion 6 Oct 1828
John	25	M	Joiner	Great Britian	United States	Andes 19 Aug 1829
John	26		Merchant	America		Margarett 2 Mar 1820
John	30	M	Manufacturer	G. Britain	U. States	Mary Howland 22 Sep 1828
John	33	M	Weaver	Colne	England	Helicon 3 Aug 1826
John	36	M	Merchant	Gt. Britain	Gt. Britain	Canada 4 Oct 1824
John	37	M	Farmer	England	United States	Siroc 31 Oct 1829
Judy	47	F	Labourer	Great Britian	United States	Princess Charlotte 6 Sep 1828
Margaret	1	F	None	Ireland	New York	Margaret 18 May 1825
Margaret	1	F		Ireland	United States	Enterprize 23 Jul 1827
Margrath	18	F		Ireland	U. States	Virginia 20 Jun 1825
Margret	16	F		...	...	Nancey 8 Jun 1822
Maria	19	F	None	Great Britain	United States	William Dawson 18 Jun 1827
Mary	5	F		G. Britain	United States	Siroc 13 Sep 1828
Mary	12	F	Farmer	England	United States	Siroc 31 Oct 1829
Mary	14	F		Gt. Britain		Dalhouse Castle 13 May 1828
Mary	18	F		England	United States	Siroc 31 Oct 1829
Mary	44	F		G. Britain	United States	Siroc 13 Sep 1828
Mary A.	20	F	Butcher	Great Britain	United States	Thomas Dickason 31 Jul 1829
Mary Ann, Miss	5					Hannibal 28 Apr 1824
Mary L.	17	F		Ireland	U. States	Hope 4 Jun 1821
Michael	22	M	Blacksmith	Ireland	U. States	Josephine 7 May 1827
Michael	24	M	Labourer	Ireland	United States	Jubilee 12 May 1828
Michl.	18	M	Farmer	England	United States	Peru 23 May 1827
Nahum	45	M	Farmer	Scotland	United States	Commerce 17 Jul 1823
Oliver D.	44	M	Merchant	United States	United States	John Wells 22 May 1826
Oliver D.	46	M	Gent.	U.S. America	U. States	William Thompson 25 Aug 1828
P. [crossed out]						Enterprize 19 Oct 1826
Pat.	34	M	Farmer	Ireland	United States	Dublin Packet 22 Oct 1821
Patk.	25	M	Labourer	...th...ck	United States	Solon 21 Jun 1824
Patrick	22	M	...	Ireland	United States	Wilson 22 Jun 1824
Patrick	26	M	Labourer	Ireland	United States	Lord Wellington 28 May 1827
Patt	4	M	None	Great Brittan	United States	America 24 Jul 1827
Peter	12	M	Farmer	England	America	Franklin 19 Nov 1828
Peter	31	M	Laborer	Ireland	United States	Weser 29 Jul 1823
Peters	26	M	Labourer	Ireland	United States	Essex 23 May 1828
Phelix	23	M	Taylor	Ireland	U. States	Champion 26 Jul 1827
Philip	30	M	Farmer	Great Britan	United States	Clematis 8 May 1827
Richard	23	M	Plumber & Glazier	Great Britain	United States	Diana 30 Oct 1827
Richard	29	M	Draper	Great Britain	United States	Isaac Hicks 10 Jul 1827
Robt.	20	M	...	Ireland	United States	General Putnam 20 Jun 1825
Sarah	30	M	Labourer	Ireland	Canada	Amelia 20 Aug 1829
Sarah, Miss	7	F		England	New York	Hannibal 28 Apr 1824
Stn. G.	20	M	Mercht.	U.S.	U.S.	George Canning 2 May 1828
Theodore	39	M	Mercht.	Gt. Brittian	Gt. Brittian	Manchester 17 Aug 1825
Tho. W.	42	M	Merchant	United States	U. States	New York 19 Nov 1828
Thomas	48	M		France	U. States	Great Britain 6 Sep 1828
Thos.	30		Labourer	Great Britan	United States	Newry 11 Jul 1827
W.	28	M	Merchant	Philadelphia	Philadelphia	Native 30 Jun 1826

NAMES OF PASSENGERS	AGE	SEX	OCCUPATIONS	COUNTRY TO WHICH THEY BELONG	COUNTRY THEY INTEND TO INHABIT	SHIPS/DATES OF ARRIVAL	
WARD (cont'd)							
William	19	M	Labourer	Ireland	United States	Jubilee	12 May 1828
William	25	M	Carpenter	U. States	U. States	Alert	17 Apr 1824
William, Revnd.	50	M	Missionary	Great Britain		Nestor	3 Nov 1820
William A.	13	M	Gent.	U.S. America	U. States	William Thompson	25 Aug 1828
Wm.	9	M		G. Britain	U. States	Cosmo	15 May 1827
Wm.	39	M	Shoe Maker	G. Britain	United States	Siroc	13 Sep 1828
WARDBURN, John	23	M	Weaver	Scotland	U. States	Superior	25 Sep 1828
WARDE, Her.	26	M	Labourer	Ireland	United States	Thomas	13 Dec 1827
WARDEL, Abraham	26	M	Farmer	England	United States	Albion	7 Feb 1820
WARDELL, Asther	30	F	Farmer	Gt. Brittian	United States	Manchester	16 Dec 1828
Edward	25	M	Farmer	England	New York	Indian Chief	16 Aug 1822
Elisha	18	...	...	...	...	Antioch	8 Oct 1827
James	27	M	Farmer	Gt. Brittian	United States	Manchester	16 Dec 1828
Mary	19	F	None	England	New York	Indian Chief	16 Aug 1822
WARDEN, Ann	4	F	...	...	...	Dawn	19 Aug 1825
Ann	28	F		Great Britain	United States	Meridian	2 Jul 1827
Deborah	30	F	...	...	...	Dawn	19 Aug 1825
Evan	27	M	Plaisterer	Great Britain	United States	Meridian	2 Jul 1827
Israel	37	M	...	...	...	Dawn	19 Aug 1825
John	6	M	...	...	...	Dawn	19 Aug 1825
John	33	M	Labourer	England	England	Virginia	26 May 1828
Joseph	6/12	M	...	...	...	Dawn	19 Aug 1825
Mary	1	F		Great Britain	United States	Meridian	2 Jul 1827
Ninian	40	M	Capn. Sea	Great Britain		Dalmannock	24 Ocg 1826
Sally	2	F	...	...	...	Dawn	19 Aug 1825
WARDER, Elisabeth	13	F	None	England	U.S.A.	Brighton	21 Jan 1826
WARDILOAR, R.	50	M	Hatter	London	U. States	Criterion	15 Oct 1822
WARDLOW, Colre. J.	40	M	Colnl. in the Army	Grt. Britain	Canada	Cortes	7 Jul 1821
WARDMAN, Anne	9	F		Great Britain	United States	Aspasia	16 Jul 1828
E.	12	F		Great Britain	United States	Aspasia	16 Jul 1828
Geo.	6	M		Great Britain	United States	Aspasia	16 Jul 1828
John	16	M		Great Britain	United States	Aspasia	16 Jul 1828
John	45	M	Labourer	Great Britain	United States	Aspasia	16 Jul 1828
Sarah	3	F		Great Britain	United States	Aspasia	16 Jul 1828
Sarah	40	F		Great Britain	United States	Aspasia	16 Jul 1828
Thos.	10	M		Great Britain	United States	Aspasia	16 Jul 1828
Wm.	13	M		Great Britain	United States	Aspasia	16 Jul 1828
WARDNER, Edward	16		Painter	Great Britain	United States	Roman	10 Sep 1827
WARDROF, Agnes	8	F	None	Great Britain	United States	Colossus	5 Jun 1827
Agnes	31	F	None	Great Britain	United States	Colossus	5 Jun 1827
John	33	M	Bleecher	Great Britain	United States	Colossus	5 Jun 1827
Margaret	5	F	None	Great Britain	United States	Colossus	5 Jun 1827
WARDROP, Robert	22	M	Farmer	Britain	America	Camillus	9 Oct 1820
WARDS, John	...	M	Merchant	Ireland	United States	Silas Richards	27 Oct 1825
WARDSWORTH, Edwd.	22	M	Merchant	United States	United States	Climax	24 Oct 1829
John	3	M	None	Great Brittain	U. States	William Byrnes	23 Jul 1824
John	24	M	Merchant	Great Brittain	U. States	William Byrnes	23 Jul 1824
WARDY, Edward	33	M	Merchant	U.S.	U. States	Canada	5 Feb 1827
WARE, Capiah	34	F		Great Brit.	Ohio	Gov. Griswald	3 Jul 1820
Daniel	11	M	Shoe Maker	England	United States	Hannibal	25 Sep 1827
Hannah	5	F		Great Brit.	Ohio	Gov. Griswald	3 Jul 1820
Henry	18	M	Labourer	U. States	U. States	United States	11 Sep 1828
John	24	M	Merchant	U. States	U. States	Mora	30 Apr 1827
John	38	M		Great Brit.	Ohio	Gov. Griswald	3 Jul 1820
Joseph	37	M	Shoe Maker	England	United States	Hannibal	25 Sep 1827
Michael	16	M	Labourer	U. States	U. States	United States	11 Sep 1828
Michael	50	M	Weaver	U. States	U. States	United States	11 Sep 1828
Pat	20	M	Weaver	U. States	U. States	United States	11 Sep 1828
WAREE, Thomas	34	M	Courrier	Leybran	Ohio	Manhattan	20 Sep 1821
WAREHOUSE, Ann	9	F		Gt. Britain	U. States	St. George	20 Sep 1828
Charlotte	Infant	M		Gt. Britain	U. States	St. George	20 Sep 1828
Eliza	11	F		Gt. Britain	U. States	St. George	20 Sep 1828
Eliza	35	F		Gt. Britain	U. States	St. George	20 Sep 1828
Emma	13	F		Gt. Britain	U. States	St. George	20 Sep 1828
Helen	7	F		Gt. Britain	U. States	St. George	20 Sep 1828
Joseph	40	M	Jeweller	Gt. Britain	U. States	St. George	20 Sep 1828
Robt.	20	M		Gt. Britain	U. States	St. George	20 Sep 1828

NAMES OF PASSENGERS	AGE	SEX	OCCUPATIONS	COUNTRY TO WHICH THEY BELONG	COUNTRY THEY INTEND TO INHABIT	SHIPS/DATES OF ARRIVAL	
WAREHOUSE (cont'd)							
William	18	M		Gt. Britain	U. States	St. George	20 Sep 1828
WARENS, Thos.	20	M	Farmer	Gt. Britain	U. States	Superior	20 Aug 1825
WARES, Jas.	18		Labourer	Halifax	U. States	Edwin	26 Sep 1828
Rob.	20		Labourer	Halifax	U. States	Edwin	26 Sep 1828
WARHOPE, D.	19	M	Gentleman	Barbadoes	Intend to return	Chasseur	17 Aug 1824
WARICK, Elizabeth	33	F		England	America	Thames	27 May 1822
Harriet	1	F		England	America	Thames	27 May 1822
John	3	M	Farmer	England	America	Thames	27 May 1822
William	28	M	Farmer	England	America	Thames	27 May 1822
WARING, E. W.		M	Merchant	U. States	U. States	Musidora	4 Sep 1821
E. W.	24	M	Merchant	U. States	U. States	Cannon	10 Dec 1821
Edmond, Mr., his Son [William]	23			England		Hercules	19 Jun 1821
Elisabeth, Miss, his Daughter [William]	17	F		England		Hercules	19 Jun 1821
Elizabeth	7	F	None	England	United States	Dalhouse Castle	6 Sep 1827
Ezra	33	M	Mariner	American	U. States	Factor	10 May 1821
Ezra W.	27	M	Merchant	U. States	U. States	Musidora	7 Jun 1821
Gwen, Mrs., his Wife [William]	46	F		England		Hercules	19 Jun 1821
Haney	5		None	England	United States	Dalhouse Castle	6 Sep 1827
Jacob	33	M	Merchant	United States	United States	William Byrnes	1 Dec 1824
John	3	M	None	England	United States	Dalhouse Castle	6 Sep 1827
Mary, Miss, his Daughter [William]	12			England		Hercules	19 Jun 1821
S.	42	M	Mariner	U. States	U. States	Caseo	26 Apr 1828
Serfanna	20	F	None	England	United States	Dalhouse Castle	6 Sep 1827
Thomas, Mr., his Son [William]	14			England		Hercules	19 Jun 1821
W. R.	30	M	Physican	South Carolina	U. States	New York	15 Nov 1823
William, Mr.	61	M	Farmer	England		Hercules	19 Jun 1821
WARK, James	30	M		Scotland	United States	Camillus	9 May 1827
Robert	22		Smith	Ireland	United States	Robert Burns	30 May 1823
WARKER, Burnet	16	M	Laborer	Great Britain	United States	Hanford	9 Oct 1829
WARLAND, G. F.	35	M	Ship Master	U. States	U. States	Abigail	16 Jul 1824
WARLER, Jacob	26	M	gardner	Germany	United States	Rent	13 May
WARLUND, Charles F.	44	M	Mariner	United States	United States	Salem	31 Aug 1829
WARMER, Herientte	25	F		G. Britain	U. States	Mary & Harriot	8 Sep 1828
James	3	M		G. Britain	U. States	Mary & Harriot	8 Sep 1828
Richd.	1	M		G. Britain	U. States	Mary & Harriot	8 Sep 1828
WARN, John	23	M	Tallow Chandler	England	United States	Richmond	4 Aug 1826
WARNACK, —, Mrs.	31	F		Philada.	New York	Alfred	7 Jun 1824
WARNE, Margaret	18	F	None	Ireland		Marchioness	13 May 1828
Michl.	20	M	Labourer	Ireland		Marchioness	13 May 1828
Silas N.	33	M	Merchant	U. States	U. States	James Monrow	25 Jul 1828
WARNEKIN, John	18	M	Clerk	Bremen	U.N. States	Franklin	20 May 1828
WARNER, Edd.	25	M	Carpenter	England	U. States	Howard Douglass	29 Jan 1828
Elizabeth	3		Child	Halifax, N.S.	United States	Hopes Delight	29 Nov 1827
Fred.	20	M		Hamburg	U. States	Martha	4 Sep 1828
Henry	1		Child	Halifax, N.S.	United States	Hopes Delight	29 Nov 1827
J. A.	23	M	Carpenter	U. States	U. States	Frances	22 May 1827
Jacob S.	19	M	Merchant	American	U. States	Molly	30 Oct 1823
Jane	24	F	None	England	United States	Jubilee	1 Oct 1828
John	22	M	Carpenter	U. States	U. States	Rodman	28 May 1825
Leah	45		Servant	St. Croix	U. States	Jupiter	11 Feb 1829
Lydia	5		Child	Halifax, N.S.	United States	Hopes Delight	29 Nov 1827
Lydia	26	F		Halifax, N.S.	United States	Hopes Delight	29 Nov 1827
Mark, Capt.	42	M	Mariner	Philadelphia	United States	Hope Retrieve	7 Jan 1828
Mary	7		Child	Halifax, N.S.	United States	Hopes Delight	29 Nov 1827
P.	24	F		United States	United States	William	1 Jul 1828
Peter	21	M	Clerk	Ireland		Fame	9 Dec 1826
Thomas	24	M	Clerk	United States	U. States	Great Britain	18 Mar 1828
Thomas	40	M	Farmer	St. John, N.B.	Canada	Hannah Eliza	23 Sep 1826
Thos.	38	M	Revd.	U. States	U. States	Chase	5 Oct 1824
W.	20	M	Carpenter	England		New York Packet	20 Mar 1824
William	20	M	Farmer	St. John, N.B.	Canada	Hannah Eliza	23 Sep 1826

NAMES OF PASSENGERS	AGE	SEX	OCCUPATIONS	COUNTRY TO WHICH THEY BELONG	COUNTRY THEY INTEND TO INHABIT	SHIPS/DATES OF ARRIVAL	
WARNER (cont'd)							
William	25	M	Miner	England	United States	Jubilee	1 Oct 1828
William	35	M	Planter	U. States	U. States	John Marshall	1 Aug 1825
WARNINGTON, Willm.	32	M	Plaster ...	Ireland	United States	America	25 Dec 1827
WARNOCH, Robt.	21	M	Labourer	Ireland	United States	Commerce	13 Jun 1828
WARNOCK, Jane, Mrs.	24	F		Ireland	United States	Alex. Mansfield	17 May 1823
John	19	M	Farmer	Ireland	United States	L. M. Pelham	25 Jun 1822
John, Mr.	24	M	Clergyman	Ireland	United States	Alex. Mansfield	17 May 1823
WARR, Wm.	35	M	Farmer	Scotland	U. States	Remittance	30 Jan 1824
WARREL, James	40	M	Farmer	England	U. States	Milton	3 May 1825
Sarah	31	F		Ireland	United States	Marmion	17 Jun 1825
WARRELL, Chas.	5	M	Farmer	Ireland	United States	Marmion	17 Jun 1825
Elizabeth	3	F	Child			Commerce	22 Jun 1825
Rachel	30	F	Wife			Commerce	22 Jun 1825
Rachell	2	M	Farmer	Ireland	United States	Marmion	17 Jun 1825
Rebbeca	4	F	Child			Commerce	22 Jun 1825
Robt.	25	M	Clerk			Commerce	22 Jun 1825
Thos.	16	M	Child			Commerce	22 Jun 1825
WARREN, Charles	21	M	Glassmaker	Great Britain	United States	Isaac Hicks	27 Sep 1826
Deddemin	30	F	Lady	State New York	United States	Sarah G	19 Jun 1827
E.	17	F	Servant	U.S.	U.S.	Florida	30 Jun 1826
George	1	F	Child	State New York	United States	Sarah G	19 Jun 1827
Hannah	20	F	Lady	State New York	United States	Sarah G	19 Jun 1827
J. J.	24	M	Merchant	Hamburgh	N. York	James Cropper	4 Feb 1824
Jas.	22	M	Miller	England		Marchioness	13 May 1828
Margaret	70	F	None	Ireland		Eliza Grant	29 Aug 1829
Margret	70	F		Ireland	New York	Eliza Grant	29 Aug 1829
Mat	14	M	Labourer	England	U. States	Hope & Esther	10 Jul 1827
Mathew	26	M	Labourer	G. Britain	U. States	St. George	7 Jun 1828
Nathanel	60	M	Farmer	State New York	United States	Sarah G	19 Jun 1827
Noah	23	M	Carpenter	U. States		Cumberland	5 May 1828
Peter	31	M	Warehouse Man	Great Britain	Uncertain	Roman	10 May 1828
Richard	28	M	Miner	England	United States	Jubilee	12 May 1828
Valentine	10	M	Child	State New York	United States	Sarah G	19 Jun 1827
William	70	M	Carder	Ireland	New York	Eliza Grant	29 Aug 1829
Wm.	32	M	Weaver	England	United States	Bolivar	15 Jun 1826
WARREN..., ...y	...	...	...	...	...	Pioneer	21 Jun 1825
John	...5	...	...	...	...	Pioneer	21 Jun 1825
Mary	27	...	...	...	...	Pioneer	21 Jun 1825
WARRENER, John	25	M	Stone Cutter	U. States	U. States	Hope	15 Aug 1820
WARRICK, Henry	35	M	Labourer	England	New York	Frances Henrietta	3 Apr 1826
WARRING, H.	18	M	Sugar baker	Germany	U. States	Jane	26 Jul 1825
WARRONS, Wm. G.	25	M	Merchant	U. States	U. States	Rising States	27 Nov 1826
WARRY, Sane	35	M	Labourer	Ireland	U. States	Meteor	19 Jul 1828
Thes.	30	M	Labourer	Ireland	U. States	Meteor	19 Jul 1828
WART, Richard	10	M		Great Britain	United States	Samuel Wright	12 Oct 1829
WARWICK, Abraham	26	M	Merch.	America	America	William Thompson	18 Jan 1825
Corbin	30		Merchant	Amherst, Virga.	United States	William Thompson	13 May 1823
J.	30	M	merchant	U. States	U. States	Alabama	21 May 1823
WASCHTER, Thienbeau	33	M	Agriculturist	France	U.S.	Helen	3 May 1828
WASH, Remond	40		Shoemaker	Ireland	United States	Geo. Canning	5 Jun 1828
WASHBURN, A. H.	20	M	Mariner	U. States	U. States	Florida	25 Apr 1825
Benj.	30	M	Seaman	U. States	U. States	Edward	29 Aug 1820
Margaret, Mrs.	35	F	Lady	England	England	Dublin Packet	24 Sep 1823
S.	28	M	Merchant	U. States	U. States	Rodman	22 Mar 1825
WASHINGCHERD,							
Alexander	28	M	Merchant	St. John, N.B.	St. John, N.B.	St. Michaels	27 Nov 1824
WASHINGTON, John	48	F	Trader	United States	United States	Mazzinghi	31 Mar 1826
L. W. G.	27	M	U.S. Army	U. States	U. States	Quesnel	6 Sep 1824
WASLEY, Eliza	24	F	Farmer	England	United States	Euphrates	18 Aug 1827
Janes	26	M	Farmer	England	United States	Euphrates	18 Aug 1827
Phoebe	3/12	F	Farmer	England	United States	Euphrates	18 Aug 1827
WASORES, Thomas	20	M	Labourer	Ireland	United States	Wilson	4 Oct 1827
WASSBECK, Adam	6	M	his family [Andre]	Germany	United States	Wm. Osborne	16 Sep 1828
Andre	40	M	Farmer	Germany	United States	Wm. Osborne	16 Sep 1828
Barbe	17	F	his family [Andre]	Germany	United States	Wm. Osborne	16 Sep 1828

NAMES OF PASSENGERS	AGE	SEX	OCCUPATIONS	COUNTRY TO WHICH THEY BELONG	COUNTRY THEY INTEND TO INHABIT	SHIPS/DATES OF ARRIVAL	
WASSBECK (cont'd)							
Catherine	9	F	his family [Andre]	Germany	United States	Wm. Osborne	16 Sep 1828
Catherine	40	F	his family [Andre]	Germany	United States	Wm. Osborne	16 Sep 1828
Jean	2	M	his family [Andre]	Germany	United States	Wm. Osborne	16 Sep 1828
Margret	7	F	his family [Andre]	Germany	United States	Wm. Osborne	16 Sep 1828
Michael	4	M	his family [Andre]	Germany	United States	Wm. Osborne	16 Sep 1828
WASSEM,							
Philip Heinrich	26	M		Uler bach	United States	Juffraw Johanna	16 Oct 1821
WATER, Patrick	21	M	Labourer	Younghall, Great Britain	United States	Union	24 Sep 1823
WATERBERY, David	65	M	Merchant	St. Johns	St. Johns	Nancy	3 Apr 1824
WATERBURG, David	42		Merchant			Charlotte Corday	11 Sep 1820
WATERBURY, David	60	M	Merchant	St. John, N.B.	St. John, N.B.	St. Michael	24 Jun 1824
Henry	27	M	Merchant	U. States	U. States	Champion	1 Sep 1820
R.	50		Merchant	Halifax	U. States	Edwin	26 Sep 1828
Rachel	32	F	Lady	St. Johns, N.B.	St. Johns, N.B.	Sarah G	11 Sep 1827
Rachel	45	F	Lady	St. John	St. John	Nancy	31 May 1823
Rachel	60	F	Lady	St. John, N.B.	St. John, N.B.	St. Michaels	12 Jun 1826
WATERHOUSE, ...hn	2	M				Hesperus	2 Nov 1820
...mes	6/12	M				Hesperus	2 Nov 1820
...nn	26	F				Hesperus	2 Nov 1820
...rry	30	M	Farmer			Hesperus	2 Nov 1820
Martha	28	F	None	Ireland	United States	Mary & Harriet	3 Jul 1829
WATERING, S. M.	25	M	Merchant	Surinam	United States	Catharine Rogers	11 Oct 1821
WATERMAN, Calvin	22	M	Merchant	U. States	U. States	Frances	22 May 1827
Daniel C.	24	M	Merchant	U. States	U. States	Mary Ann	13 Mar 1826
WATERS, Brian	20	M		Ireland	U.S. of America	Douglass	6 Jul 1829
Catharine	28	F	Servant	Ireland	United States	Wanderer	1 Aug 1828
Daniel	23	M				Hudson	23 Jul 1828
Daniel	50 3/12	M	Farmer	Great Briton	uncertain	Mount Vernon	29 Aug 1828
Daniel, Jr.	11	M	None	Great Briton	uncertain	Mount Vernon	29 Aug 1828
E.	25	M	Labourer	England	United States	Alicia	9 May 1827
Edward	16 3/12	M	Farmer	Great Briton	uncertain	Mount Vernon	29 Aug 1828
Edward J.	25	M	Farmer	Wales South	U. States	Oglethorpe	8 Jul 1824
Elizabeth	30	F	None	Great Britain	U. States	Hannibal	12 Oct 1829
Fanny	45	F	Cook	Baltimore	United States	New Packet	16 Aug 1827
James	9 10/12	M	None	Great Briton	uncertain	Mount Vernon	29 Aug 1828
James	19	M	Farmer	Great Britian	United States	Andes	19 Aug 1829
James	21	M	Taylor	Ireland	U. States	Virginia	20 Jun 1825
Jno.	17	M	Carpenter	Ireland	United States	Trio	13 Jun 1827
Jno.	30	M	Labourer	Sligo	U. States	Panthea	8 Apr 1826
John	12	M	Labourer	Ireland	United States	Wanderer	1 Aug 1828
John	13	M	None	Great Briton	uncertain	Mount Vernon	29 Aug 1828
John	24	M	Laborer	Ireland	U. States	Nancy	13 Dec 1822
Joseph	6	M	None	Great Briton	uncertain	Mount Vernon	29 Aug 1828
L.	1	F				Hudson	23 Jul 1828
Mary	7	F	None	Great Britain	U. States	Hannibal	12 Oct 1829
Mary	8	F	Servant	Ireland	United States	Wanderer	1 Aug 1828
Nancy	17	F	Servt. Md.	Sligo	New York	Susquehana	27 Jun 1823
Patrick	27	M	...	Ireland	United States	Borneo	2 Oct 1827
Philip	41	M	Seaman	Baltimore	New York	Washington	19 Jun 1826
Robert	29	M	Mariner	U. States	U. States	Florida	25 Apr 1825
Robt.	23	M	Farmer	England		Hudson	23 Jul 1828
Susanah	22	F		Ireland	U. States	Nancy	13 Dec 1822
William	12	M	Boy	Baltimore	United States	New Packet	16 Aug 1827
William	15	M	None	Great Briton	uncertain	Mount Vernon	29 Aug 1828
William	34	M	Gardner	Great Britain	U. States	Hannibal	12 Oct 1829
Wm. G.	26	M	Merchant	U. States	U. States	Purrington	14 May 1827
WATERSON, A.	21		Farmer	Ireland	United States	Courier	16 May 1825
John	18 3/12	M		Ireland	America	Carolina Ann	7 Apr 1826
WATERTON, Charles	40	M	Merchant	England	England	John Wills	21 May 1824
Elizabeth	27	F	None	England	New York	Brighton	20 Aug 1825
William	1	M	None	England	New York	Brighton	20 Aug 1825
William	28	M	Plummer	England	New York	Brighton	20 Aug 1825
WATHERSPOON, Thos.	25	M	Mercht.	England	England	Pacific	24 Oct 1828
WATKIN, Ann	30	F		Great Britain	United States	Robert	15 Jul 1822
Enoch	16	M		Great Britain	United States	Robert	15 Jul 1822
Evan	48	M	Labourer	Great Britain	United States	Robert	15 Jul 1822

NAMES OF PASSENGERS	AGE	SEX	OCCUPATIONS	COUNTRY TO WHICH THEY BELONG	COUNTRY THEY INTEND TO INHABIT	SHIPS/DATES OF ARRIVAL	
WATKIN (cont'd)							
James	12	M		Great Britain	United States	Robert	15 Jul 1822
Jane	9	F		Great Britain	United States	Robert	15 Jul 1822
Jno.	23	M	Dresser	Great Britain	United States	India	5 Sep 1827
WATKINS, George	22	M	None	U. States	U. States	Manhattan	20 Jun 1825
H. D.	26	M	Merchant	United States	United States	Prince Edward	13 Apr 1824
Jno.	19	M	Gentleman	U. States	U. States	Florida	25 Apr 1825
Jno. S.	29	M	Merchant	W. Indies	U. States	William Smith	9 May 1822
John	25	M	Labourer	England		Marchioness	13 May 1828
P.	40	M	Servant	Great Brittain	Great Brittain	Tontine	25 Jan 1827
Pat	18 6/12	M	Labourer	Ireland	United States	Wilson	6 Jun 1828
Ruth	27	F	Missionary		New York	New York	31 Jul 1829
Thomas	23		Farmer	England	United States	Hugh Johnson	11 Jun 1828
Thomas	26	M	Labourer	England		Marchioness	13 May 1828
Thos.	33	M	Labourer	G. Britain	U. States	St. George	7 Jun 1828
Wm.	34	M	...			Manhattan	25 Dec 1820
WATKINSON, David	49	M	Merchant	United States	New York	Britannia	3 Nov 1827
Olivia	44	F		United States	New York	Britannia	3 Nov 1827
Thos.	40	M	Comedian	Great Britain	United States	Columbia	9 Aug 1822
WATLINGTON, Barnard	23	M	Merchant	St. Croix	St. Croix	Havana Packet	13 May 1824
WATROUS, W. G.	22	M	Merchant	N. York	N. York	Exchange	31 Jan 1825
Wm. G.	25	M	Merchant	America	America	Peach	20 Mar 1826
WATS, Samuel, Mr.	25	M	Farmer	England	U. States	Emily	25 Aug 1827
WATSON, —, Captain	25	M	Navigator	United States	United States	Eugenie	2 Oct 1829
—, Mrs.	26	F				Czar	29 Aug 1829
...	...4	F	...	Scotland	America	Nimrod	9 Jul 1827
...son	...4	M	...	Scotland	America	Nimrod	9 Jul 1827
A...	2	M		Great Britain	New York	Philetus	21 Jul 1827
Albert	16		unknown	Gayton, E.	England	Packet	27 Aug 1822
Alex.	...	...	...	Ireland	U. States of Amer	Courier	17 Mar 1827
Alexr.	2	M		Scotland	United States	Camillus	9 May 1827
Alexr.	50	M		Scotland	United States	Camillus	9 May 1827
Alice	13	F		Great Britain	United States	Diana	6 Jul 1829
Amos	12	M		Great Britain	United States	Freake	11 Dec 1827
Andrew	15	M		England	U. States	Emulous	22 Aug 1828
Ann	4	F	None		United States	Mount Vernon	29 Aug 1828
Ann	5	F		Great Britain	New York	Philetus	21 Jul 1827
Ann	11	F		Great Britain	United States	Diana	6 Jul 1829
Ann	19	F	Wife	Montrose	U.S. America	Camillus	10 Sep 1821
Ann	25			England	United States	Thomas Dickason	5 Jun 1827
Ann Guthrie	6/12	F	Child	Montrose	U.S. America	Camillus	10 Sep 1821
Basol	5			England	England	Hudson	4 Sep 1823
Benj.	11	M				Cassack	25 Jul 1820
Benjamin	3	M	Farmer	Ireland	Canada	Champion	26 Jul 1827
Benjamin	40	M	Farmer	Ireland	Canada	Champion	26 Jul 1827
Charles	4	M		Great Britain		Dalmannock	24 Ocg 1826
Charlotte Mateloa	4	F		England	U.S. America	Cortes	19 May 1826
David	6	M		Great Britain		Dalmannock	24 Ocg 1826
Dunham	34	M	Mariner	United States		Asaph	8 Oct 1825
Eazl.	50	M				Cassack	25 Jul 1820
Edwd.	15	M				Cassack	25 Jul 1820
Eleonor	7			England	England	Hudson	4 Sep 1823
Eliz.	24	F	None	United States	United States	Wyton	12 May 1821
Eliza	8	M				Cassack	25 Jul 1820
Eliza	8	F		England	U.S. America	Cortes	19 May 1826
Eliza	8	F		Great Britain		Dalmannock	24 Ocg 1826
Elizabeth	11	F	Farmer	England	Albany	Chelsea	16 May 1828
Elizabeth	14	F		Great Britain	United States	Freake	25 Jun 1827
Elizabeth	22	F		Ireland	New York	Carolina Ann	15 Oct 1824
Elizabeth	25	F	Farmer	England	Albany	Chelsea	16 May 1828
Elizabeth	33			England	England	Hudson	4 Sep 1823
Elizabeth	35	F		Great Britain	United States	Natchez	17 Aug 1822
Fann	7	F	Farmer	Ireland	Canada	Champion	26 Jul 1827
Formans	23	M	Farmer	Great Brittain	U. States	Atticus	25 Apr 1822
Frans.	27	M	Farmer	England	United States	Florida	1 Sep 1823
G.	30	M	Mariner	U. States	U. States	Greek	8 Mar 1828
George	4	M	None	United States	United States	Wyton	12 May 1821
George	13	M		Great Britain	United States	Natchez	17 Aug 1822

NAMES OF PASSENGERS	AGE	SEX	OCCUPATIONS	COUNTRY TO WHICH THEY BELONG	COUNTRY THEY INTEND TO INHABIT	SHIPS/DATES OF ARRIVAL	
WATSON (cont'd)							
George	27	M	Mariner	Great Britian	U. States	Hudson	12 Mar 1824
George D.	22	M	Gardner	Great Brittan	Great Brittan	Orbit	30 Aug 1824
Georgiana	2	F		Great Britain		Dalmannock	24 Ocg 1826
Georgiana	32	F		Great Britain		Dalmannock	24 Ocg 1826
Granter	48	M	Farmer			Cassack	25 Jul 1820
Hannah	18	F	Farmer	Ireland	Canada	Champion	26 Jul 1827
Hannah	23	F	None	Great Briton	United States	Mount Vernon	29 Aug 1828
Hestor	60	F		Great Britain	New York	Philetus	21 Jul 1827
Hugh	17	M		England	U. States	Emulous	22 Aug 1828
Isabella	20	F	Farmer	Scotland	U. States	Roger Stewart	9 Jun 1828
James	...	M	...	Scotland	America	Nimrod	9 Jul 1827
James	1	M				Hector	11 Sep 1820
James	1	M		England	U.S. America	Cortes	19 May 1826
James	2	M	Farmer	England	Albany	Chelsea	16 May 1828
James	3			England	United States	Thomas Dickason	5 Jun 1827
James	10	M		Great Britain	New York	Philetus	21 Jul 1827
James	18	M	Farmer	Younghall, Great Britain	United States	Union	24 Sep 1823
James	18	M	Farmer	England	America	John Adams	2 Aug 1827
James	25	M	Clerk	Scotland	United States	Camillus	9 May 1827
James	26	M	Labourer	Ireland	U. States	Lady Hunter	9 Oct 1825
James	28	M		Great Britain	U. States America	Maria	22 May 1822
James	28	M	Merchant	England	U. States	Brighton	14 Apr 1828
James	29	M	Farmer			Hector	11 Sep 1820
James	37	M		Great Britain		Dalmannock	24 Ocg 1826
James A.	26	M	Merchant	S. Carolina	U. States	St. George	16 Jan 1829
Jane	32	F		G. Britain	U. States	Great Britain	6 Sep 1828
Janet	17	F		Great Britain	United States	Natchez	17 Aug 1822
Jas.	23	M	Farmer	Scotland	U. States	Roger Stewart	9 Jun 1828
Jno.	30	M				Hibernia	15 Aug 1820
John	...	M	...	Scotland	America	Nimrod	9 Jul 1827
John	...2		Merchant	Preston	England	Great Britain	7 May 1827
John	8	M	None	United States	United States	Wyton	12 May 1821
John	8	M		Great Britain	United States	Diana	20 Nov 1828
John	9	M		England	U. States	Emulous	22 Aug 1828
*Died on the Voyage							
John	12	M	Farmer	Ireland	Canada	Champion	26 Jul 1827
John	20	M	Carpenter	Great Briton	New York	Brighton	12 Jun 1826
John	20		Merchant	Great Britain	United States	Camillus	12 Sep 1827
John	20	M	Weaver	Scotland	United States	Camillus	27 Oct 1829
John	21	M	Labourer	...	United States	Carolina Ann	11 Jun 1824
John	21	M	Stone Cutter	Irereland	America	Carolina Ann	20 Jun 1825
John	25	M	...	England	United States	Danube	1 Nov 1827
John	25	M	Farmer	Great Britain	United States	Freake	11 Dec 1827
John	33	M	Farmer	G. Britain	U. States	Freak	9 Jun 1828
John	41	M	Labourer			Hector	11 Sep 1820
John	42	M	Farmer			Lady of the Lake	23 Aug 1828
John	45	M	Farmer	Great Britain	United States	Freake	25 Jun 1827
John	46	M	Farmer	England	United States	Bolivar	30 Nov 1827
John	50	M	Joiner	..., ..., Ireland	Philadelphia	New Orleans	24 Aug 1827
John	74	M	Farmer	Great Britain	United States	Diana	20 Nov 1828
John, Esqre.	25 2/12	M	Merchant	England	United States	London	6 Feb 1829
Jos., Infant	4/12	M		Ireland	New York	Carolina Ann	15 Oct 1824
Joseph	1	M	Farmer	Ireland	Canada	Champion	26 Jul 1827
Joseph	11	M		...	United States	Carolina Ann	11 Jun 1824
Joseph	28		Clothier	England	United States	Thomas Dickason	5 Jun 1827
Joseph	40	M	Cap maker	...	United States	Carolina Ann	11 Jun 1824
Lousia	33			England		Hudson	23 Jul 1828
Lucy	28	F				Hector	11 Sep 1820
M.	40	F	Farmer	Ireland	Canada	Champion	26 Jul 1827
Malann	11	F		England	U. States	Emulous	22 Aug 1828
*Died on the Voyage							
Margaret	20	F		Scotland	United States	Camillus	9 May 1827
Margaret	50	F		Scotland	United States	Camillus	9 May 1827
Margt.	1	F		England	U. States	Emulous	22 Aug 1828

NAMES OF PASSENGERS	AGE	SEX	OCCUPATIONS	COUNTRY TO WHICH THEY BELONG	COUNTRY THEY INTEND TO INHABIT	SHIPS/DATES OF ARRIVAL	
WATSON (cont'd)							
Margt.	13	F		England	U. States	Emulous	22 Aug 1828
Margt.	26	F		Great Britain	New York	Philetus	21 Jul 1827
Margt.	40	F		England	U. States	Emulous	22 Aug 1828
Mariam	1			England	England	Hudson	4 Sep 1823
Marion	1/2	F		Scotland	United States	Camillus	9 May 1827
Martha	18	F	Servant	Irereland	America	Carolina Ann	20 Jun 1825
Mary	3	F		Great Britain	United States	Diana	6 Jul 1829
Mary	4	F		Great Britain	New York	Philetus	21 Jul 1827
Mary	9	F		Great Britain	United States	Freake	11 Dec 1827
Mary	10	F		Great Britain		Dalmannock	24 Ocg 1826
Mary	10	F	Farmer	Ireland	Canada	Champion	26 Jul 1827
Mary	23	F		Scotland	United States	Camillus	9 May 1827
Mary	25	F	Farmer	Scotland	U. States	Roger Stewart	9 Jun 1828
Mary	25	F		Great Britain	United States	Diana	20 Nov 1828
Mary	26			England	United States	Thomas Dickason	5 Jun 1827
Mary	28	F		England	U.S. America	Cortes	19 May 1826
Mary	30	F		England	U. States	Brighton	14 Apr 1828
Mary	32	F		...	United States	Carolina Ann	11 Jun 1824
Mary Ann	10	F		England	U.S. America	Cortes	19 May 1826
Mary Anne	40	F	Wife	S... County, ..., Ireland	Philadelphia	New Orleans	24 Aug 1827
Mary Jane	14			England	England	Hudson	4 Sep 1823
Matilda	3			England		Hudson	23 Jul 1828
May	5	F		England	U. States	Emulous	22 Aug 1828
Nancy	5	F	Farmer	Ireland	Canada	Champion	26 Jul 1827
Naomi	10			England	England	Hudson	4 Sep 1823
Peter	7	M		England	U. States	Emulous	22 Aug 1828
Richd.	6	M	None	United States	United States	Wyton	12 May 1821
Robert	7	M		...	United States	Carolina Ann	11 Jun 1824
Robert	17	M		Great Britain	United States	Natchez	17 Aug 1822
Robert	24		Miniature Painter	England	United States	Corinthian	7 Jul 1829
Robert	24 6/12	M	Weaver	Ireland	New York	Louisa	20 Jul 1826
Robert	39	M	Farmer	Great Britain	United States	Diana	6 Jul 1829
Robert, Child	3	M		Ireland	New York	Carolina Ann	15 Oct 1824
Robt.	9/12	M		Great Britain	New York	Philetus	21 Jul 1827
Robt.	22	M	W. Right	Scotland	U. States	Superior	25 Sep 1828
Robt.	25	M	Merchant	England	Nova Scotia	Arthenian	28 Apr 1827
Robt.	28	M		Great Britain	New York	Philetus	21 Jul 1827
Robt.	30	M	Labourer	Ireland	New York	Carolina Ann	15 Oct 1824
S.	7	F		G. Britain	U. States	Great Britain	6 Sep 1828
S. T.	12			England	England	Hudson	4 Sep 1823
Sampson	16	M	Servant	England		Exchange	11 Jul 1823
Sander	50	M	Farmer	England	U. States	Emulous	22 Aug 1828
Sarah	13	F		...	United States	Carolina Ann	11 Jun 1824
Sarah	41	F		Great Britain	United States	Diana	6 Jul 1829
Sarah	50	F		Great Britain	United States	Freake	11 Dec 1827
Sophia	3			England	United States	Thomas Dickason	5 Jun 1827
Stephen	20	M	Farmer	Great Britain	U. States	Great Britain	18 Mar 1828
Stephen	32		Farmer	England	England	Hudson	4 Sep 1823
Susan	11			England		Hudson	23 Jul 1828
Terrence	22	M		Ireland	U. States	St. Michael	27 Mar 1827
Tho.	22	F	Stone Mason	England	U. States	Electra	7 Jul 1828
Tho.	31		Tin Plate worker	England		Hudson	23 Jul 1828
Thomas	3	M		England	U.S. America	Cortes	19 May 1826
Thomas	21	M		Scotland	United States	Camillus	9 May 1827
Thomas	23	M	Clerk	Scotland	United States	Camillus	9 May 1827
Thomas	28				U. States	Montgomery	18 Oct 1828
Thomas	31	M	Manufacturer	Great Britain	United States	Ganges	26 Oct 1826
Thomas	38	M	Gentleman	England	Great Britain	Ductile	26 Aug 1822
Thomas	44	M	Shoemaker	England	United States	Jubilee	12 May 1828
Thos.	28	M	Farmer	England	U.S. America	Cortes	19 May 1826
Thos.	38	M	Shoemaker	U. States	U. States	Cobbosse Conte	18 Apr 1823
Thos., Jr.	9			England		Hudson	23 Jul 1828
W. B.	37	M	Accounttant			Hudson	23 Jul 1828
William	...	M	...	Scotland	America	Nimrod	9 Jul 1827

NAMES OF PASSENGERS	AGE	SEX	OCCUPATIONS	COUNTRY TO WHICH THEY BELONG	COUNTRY THEY INTEND TO INHABIT	SHIPS/DATES OF ARRIVAL	
WATSON (cont'd)							
William	1			England	United States	Thomas Dickason	5 Jun 1827
William	9	M		...	United States	Carolina Ann	11 Jun 1824
William	9	M	Farmer	England	Albany	Chelsea	16 May 1828
William	11	M		Great Britain	United States	Natchez	17 Aug 1822
William	16	M		Great Britain	United States	Freake	25 Jun 1827
William	21	M	Farmer	England	United States	Florida	1 Sep 1823
William	22	M	Farmer	England	United States	Bolivar	30 Nov 1827
William	28 6/12	M	Accountant	Great Britain	United States	Amity	1 Dec 1826
William	31	M	Gardner	England	New York	Brighton	19 Aug 1829
William	31	M	Gardner			Brighton	19 Aug 1829
William	40	M	...	Great Britain	United States	Robert Fulton	18 May 1825
William	60		Clothier	England	United States	Thomas Dickason	5 Jun 1827
William, & family	30	M	Farmer	England	Albany	Chelsea	16 May 1828
Wm.	2	M	None	United States	United States	Wyton	12 May 1821
Wm.	19	M	Mechanic	Great Britian	U. States	Hudson	12 Mar 1824
Wm.	28	M	Merchant	England	U. States	Abigail	11 Apr 1823
Wm.	28	M	Farmer	Scotland	United States	Margaret Bogle	11 Jun 1824
Wm.	35	M	Gentleman	U. States	U. States	Bengal	14 Jul 1825
Wm.	36	M	Merchant	England	U. States	New York	4 Nov 1824
Wm., Jur.	17			England	United States	Thomas Dickason	5 Jun 1827
WATSUN, Catherine	58	F	Spinster	Ireland		Robert Fulton	4 Jun 1828
Gabriel	21	M	Labourer	Ireland		Robert Fulton	4 Jun 1828
Margret	19	F	Spinster	Ireland		Robert Fulton	4 Jun 1828
Richd.	68	M	Labourer	Ireland		Robert Fulton	4 Jun 1828
WATT, —, Mrs.	24	F		Scotland	United States	Union	6 May 1824
Agnes	2 6/12	F		Scotland	United States	Union	6 May 1824
Archaball, Mr.	35	M	Merchant	Scotland	Gt. Britain	Pacific	22 May 1826
Catherine	5 4/12	F		Scotland	United States	Union	6 May 1824
Daniel	4 1/12	M		Scotland	United States	Union	6 May 1824
Elisbath	16	F	Spinster	Ireland	United States	Fabius	31 Jul 1829
Eliza	20	F	Labourer	Great Britian	United States	Sarah	11 Jul 1829
Francis	6	F		G. Britain	U. States	Mary Howland	22 Sep 1828
Jacob	45	M	Farmer	G. Britain	U. States	Mary Howland	22 Sep 1828
Jno.	23	M	Labourer	Great Britian	United States	Sarah	11 Jul 1829
John	1	M		G. Britain	U. States	Mary Howland	22 Sep 1828
John	7 6/12	M		Scotland	United States	Union	6 May 1824
John	22	M	Merchant	Great Britain		Robert Fulton	8 Mar 1823
John	40	M	Labourer	England	United States	Florida	14 Sep 1827
Joseph	7 6/12	M	Labourer	Ireland	United States	Fabius	31 Jul 1829
Mary	5	F		G. Britain	U. States	Mary Howland	22 Sep 1828
Mary	40	F		G. Britain	U. States	Mary Howland	22 Sep 1828
Robert	26	M	Laborer	Ireland	United States	Mary	1 Jul 1829
Robert	42		Gardener	Great Britain	United States	Roman	10 Sep 1827
William	24	M	Laborer	Ireland	United States	Mary	1 Jul 1829
William	30	M	Farmer	Great Britain	United States	William Dawson	18 Jun 1827
WATTERMAN, Joseph	20	M	Pedlar	Hungary	U. States	Brandt	8 Nov 1828
Wm.	20	M	Traveller	England	U. States	Severn	12 Oct 1826
WATTERS, Henry	24	M	Merchant	U. States	U. States	Dromo	19 Jul 1827
WATTESON, A.	22		Farmer	Ireland	United States	Courier	16 May 1825
WATTS, Amey	15	F		Great Britain	United States	Spartan	25 Jul 1821
B. J.	35	M	U.S. Charge Affairs	U. States	U. States	Medina	23 Apr 1828
Beaufort T.	38		Gentleman	United States	United States	Cambria	19 Oct 1829
Charles	18 1/12	M	Gentleman	Great Britain	United States	Courier	23 Feb 1824
Charles	22	M	Shoemaker	Great Britain	United States	Citizen	25 Aug 1829
Charles	30		Brewer	England	U. States	Venus	4 Oct 1821
Davd.	27	M	Tailor	England	N. York	Salem	15 Mar 1828
Eliza	9	F		Great Britain	United States	Spartan	25 Jul 1821
Eliza	13	F			U. States America	Cambria	2 Jul 1821
Elizabeth	8	F	...	Great Britain	United States	Baltic	24 Dec 1824
Ellen	7	F			U. States America	Cambria	2 Jul 1821
Emma	4	F			U. States America	Cambria	2 Jul 1821
G. W.	22	M	Merchant	U. States	U. States	William Tell	3 Dec 1825
George	2	M			U. States America	Cambria	2 Jul 1821
George	13	M		Great Britain	United States	Spartan	25 Jul 1821
James	6	M	...	Great Britain	United States	Baltic	24 Dec 1824

NAMES OF PASSENGERS	AGE	SEX	OCCUPATIONS	COUNTRY TO WHICH THEY BELONG	COUNTRY THEY INTEND TO INHABIT	SHIPS/DATES OF ARRIVAL	
WATTS (cont'd)							
John	3	M		Great Britain	United States	Spartan	25 Jul 1821
John	25	M	Labourer	Ireland	United States	Trident	31 Mar 1827
John	41	M	...	Great Britain	United States	Baltic	24 Dec 1824
John	70	M	None	United States	United States	Columbia	11 Aug 1823
John, Junr.	4	M	...	Great Britain	United States	Baltic	24 Dec 1824
Mary	11	F		Great Britain	United States	Spartan	25 Jul 1821
Mary	35	F			U. States America	Cambria	2 Jul 1821
Nathaniel	34	M	Weaver	England	United States	Lord Wellington	14 Nov 1827
Rachael	7	F		Great Britain	United States	Spartan	25 Jul 1821
Robt.	24	M	Labourer	England		Marchioness	13 May 1828
Rose Ann	45	F		Great Britain	United States	Spartan	25 Jul 1821
Sarah	31	F	...	Great Britain	United States	Baltic	24 Dec 1824
Thomas	58 3/12	M	Gentleman	Great Britain	United States	Courier	23 Feb 1824
William	5	M		Great Britain	United States	Spartan	25 Jul 1821
William	20	M	Mariner	England	England	Tampico	13 May 1828
William	22	M	Butler	England	America	Francis & Henrietta	11 Jul 1823
WATTSON, Allis	17					William	17 Aug 1820
James	50					William	17 Aug 1820
WAUGH, Eliza	24			Ireland	United States	Robert Burns	30 May 1823
Margaret	22			Ireland	United States	Robert Burns	30 May 1823
Richd.	40	M	Taylor	Ireland	New York	Carolina Ann	15 Oct 1824
Sally	20			Ireland	United States	Robert Burns	30 May 1823
Wm.	23	M	Labourer	Great Britain		Moro Castle	6 Jul 1827
WAUSHOPE, Robt. *Dead		M	Printer	G. Britain	U. States	St. George	16 Jan 1829
WAVE, —, Mrs.	27	F		G. Britain	U. States	St. George	7 Jun 1828
Andw.	21	M	...	England	Canada	William Thompson	10 May 1825
Eliza	6	F		G. Britain	U. States	St. George	7 Jun 1828
Eliza	9	F		G. Britain	U. States	St. George	7 Jun 1828
Esther	8	F		G. Britain	U. States	St. George	7 Jun 1828
Geo.	36	M	Farmer	G. Britain	U. States	St. George	7 Jun 1828
John	2	M		G. Britain	U. States	St. George	7 Jun 1828
May Ane	4	F		G. Britain	U. States	St. George	7 Jun 1828
Sarah	1	F		G. Britain	U. States	St. George	7 Jun 1828
WAY, Ann	20	F	Wife	Ireland	United States	Dublin Packet	23 May 1828
Heming	24	M	Farmer	Ireland	United States	Dublin Packet	23 May 1828
Shank	24	M	Merchant	New York	New York	Lady Hunter	22 Aug 1825
Wm. *landed at Boston	25	M	Merchant	Newfoundland	Newfoundland	Mack	9 Oct 1823
WAYMAN, John S.	17	M	Merchant	Jamaica	United States	Allen	29 Mar 1824
WAYMATCHET, John	31		Merchant	Jermany		Hudson	23 Jul 1828
WEADEBURNS, Alex	23	M	Merchant	G.		Ann Maria	3 Jul 1820
WEAR, L. L.	35	M	Doctor	Hamburgh	U. States	Robert Burns	1 Dec 1823
Walker	24	M	Weaver	Scotland	U.S.	Curler	19 Jul 1828
WEATHERBEE, John	34 2/12	M	Merchant	United States	United States	Venus	8 Sep 1820
WEATHERHEAD, Alex.	27	M	Merchant	Barbadoes	Great Britain	Only Daughter	26 Apr 1826
WEATHERLY, Peter	28	M	Farmer	Scotland	U. States	Milo	24 Jun 1824
WEATHERSPOON, James D.	24	M	Cooper	Scotland	Unt. States	Robert Fulton	14 Mar 1829
WEATHERSTONE, Henry	26 6/12	M	Royl. Engineer	England	British North America	London	6 Feb 1829
WEATON, Eliza	13	F		U. States		Abigail	26 Sep 1820
William	34	M	Merchant	U. States		Abigail	26 Sep 1820
WEATTY, Andrew	22	M	Farmer	Ireland	United States	Asia	29 Jul 1829
WEAVER, Charlotte [with William]	1	F	Farmer	England	Schenecteda, N.Y.	Chelsea	16 May 1828
Cornelius [with William]	2	M	Farmer	England	Schenecteda, N.Y.	Chelsea	16 May 1828
Elizabeth [with John]	26	F	Farmer	England	In the country	Chelsea	16 May 1828
Francis [with William]	11	M	Farmer	England	Schenecteda, N.Y.	Chelsea	16 May 1828
George E.	25	M	Gentleman	U. States	U. States	Milton	20 Aug 1827
Harriet [with John]	5	F	Farmer	England	In the country	Chelsea	16 May 1828
John	28	M	Farmer	Nova Scotia	U. States	Caroline and Nancy	30 Aug 1821
John, & family	29	M	Farmer	England	In the country	Chelsea	16 May 1828

NAMES OF PASSENGERS	AGE	SEX	OCCUPATIONS	COUNTRY TO WHICH THEY BELONG	COUNTRY THEY INTEND TO INHABIT	SHIPS/DATES OF ARRIVAL	
WEAVER (cont'd)							
John G.	28	M	Gent.	Germany	U. States	Harriet	20 Oct 1824
Mary Ann [with William]	8	F	Farmer	England	Schenecteda, N.Y.	Chelsea	16 May 1828
Richard	38	M	Surgeon	England	England	John Wells	29 Jan 1825
Richard [with William]	14	M	Farmer	England	Schenecteda, N.Y.	Chelsea	16 May 1828
Stephen [with William]	5	M	Farmer	England	Schenecteda, N.Y.	Chelsea	16 May 1828
Susannah [with William]	37	F	Farmer	England	Schenecteda, N.Y.	Chelsea	16 May 1828
Thomas [with John]	1	M	Farmer	England	In the country	Chelsea	16 May 1828
William, & family	35	M	Farmer	England	Schenecteda, N.Y.	Chelsea	16 May 1828
Wm. A.	31	M	N.Y. Navy	N. York	U. States	Franklin	27 Aug 1822
Wm. A.	35	M	Mariner	U. States	U. States	Minerva	8 May 1827
WEBB, —, Mr.	23	M	Mercht.	U. States	U. States	General Paez	21 Jun 1826
—, Mrs.		F		U. States	U. States	Milton	3 May 1825
—, Mrs.	17	F		Ireland	U. States	Grand Turk	16 Aug 1822
—, Mrs.	35	F		England	U. States	Milton	6 Dec 1825
Alexander	13	M	None	England	Maryland	Brighton	29 Aug 1828
Ann	7	F	None	Great Britian	United States	Diamond	8 Nov 1824
Ann	9	F		Great Britian	U. States	Great Britain	18 Mar 1828
Ann	23	F		G. Britain	U. States	St. George	7 Jun 1828
Ann	34	F		Great Britain	U. States	Great Britain	18 Mar 1828
Charles	15	M	...	G. Britain	New York	Brighton	26 Mar 1827
Charles	30	M	Clothier	England	United States	Andes	2 Oct 1828
Edward A.	19	M	Farmer	England	U. States	Acasta	21 Oct 1825
Elizabeth	8	F		Great Britain	U. States	Great Britain	18 Mar 1828
Elizabeth	35	F	Servant	London		Hannibal	28 Jul 1823
Fanny	31	F		Great Britain	Upper Canada	Zodiac	14 Jun 1822
Frederick	42	M	...	American	Philadelphia	Hesperus	13 Oct 1825
Han...h	6/12	F		Great Britain	U. States	Great Britain	18 Mar 1828
Harriet	42	F	None	England	Maryland	Brighton	29 Aug 1828
Henry	23	M	Labourer	G. Britain	U. States	St. George	7 Jun 1828
Jacob	45	M	Farmer	Ireland, G.B.		London	29 Apr 1824
John	27	M	...	Ireland	United States	Colossus	30 May 1825
John	28	M	Labourer	England	United States	Montgomery	6 Mar 1829
John	30	M	Merchant	United States	United States	Delta	24 Oct 1829
John	56	M	Merchant	England		Marchioness	13 May 1828
John D.	40	M	Dyer	Great Britain	U. States	Superior	5 Jun 1826
John N.	24	M	Farmer	England	U. States	Acasta	21 Oct 1825
Joseph	25	M	Glassmaker	Great Britain	United States	Isaac Hicks	27 Sep 1826
Joseph	26	M	Farmer	England	America	Francis & Henrietta	11 Jul 1823
Joseph	37	M	Clothier	England	United States	Cosmo	26 Aug 1829
Louisa	22	F	None	England	Maryland	Brighton	29 Aug 1828
Mary	2	F		Great Britain	U. States	Great Britain	18 Mar 1828
Mary Ann	20	F	his Wife	England	United States	Delta	24 Oct 1829
Peter	30	M	Farmer	Ireland	America	Colossus	22 Aug 1829
Robert	21	M	Labourer	Ireland	New York	Louisa	20 Jul 1826
Saml.	36	M	Mechanic	G. Britain	U. States	Mary Howland	22 Sep 1828
Sarah	19	F	None	England	United States	Jubilee	1 Oct 1828
Sarah	24	F	None	England	America	Francis & Henrietta	11 Jul 1823
Sarah	59	F	None	England	United States	Jubilee	1 Oct 1828
Thomas	35	M	Farmer	Great Britain	U. States	Great Britain	18 Mar 1828
Thomas	36	M	Farmer	Great Britain	Upper Canada	Zodiac	14 Jun 1822
WEBBER, —, Mrs.	22	F	Farmer	Gt. Britain	U. States	Constitution	19 Jul 1825
Annette	20	F	his family [William]	Germany	Loussana	Isabella	15 Sep 1828
Elizabeth	32	F	his family [William]	Germany	Loussana	Isabella	15 Sep 1828
Jacob	27	M	his family [William]	Germany	Loussana	Isabella	15 Sep 1828
Jno.	27	M	Farmer	England	United States	Earl of Liverpool	29 Sep 1823
John	14	M	his family [William]	Germany	Loussana	Isabella	15 Sep 1828

NAMES OF PASSENGERS	AGE	SEX	OCCUPATIONS	COUNTRY TO WHICH THEY BELONG	COUNTRY THEY INTEND TO INHABIT	SHIPS/DATES OF ARRIVAL	
WEBBER (cont'd)							
Marian	23	F	his family [William]	Germany	Loussana	Isabella	15 Sep 1828
William	53	M	Manufacturer	Germany	Loussana	Isabella	15 Sep 1828
WEBEL, Michel	29	M	Weaver	Germany	Pensylvania	James Noble	27 Aug 1827
WEBER, —	25	M	Butcher	France	United States	Cavalier	25 Jul 1828
Barbara	22	F		ober ambt Zelbach	United States	Juffraw Johanna	16 Oct 1821
Cath.	30	F		France	United States	Cavalier	25 Jul 1828
E.	30	M	Merchant	Germany	Liverpool	Native	29 May 1824
Edward	33	M	Gentleman	Germany	U.S. America	Leeds	6 Jun 1826
Gurgin H. J.	27	M	Shoemaker	Hannover	New York	Constitution	12 Jul 1827
Henry	1	M	Weaver	Brustedseul	U.S. America	Superior	18 Jun 1825
Jean H.	40	M	Weaver	Brustedseul	U.S. America	Superior	18 Jun 1825
John J.	6/12	M		Hannover	New York	Constitution	12 Jul 1827
Luise M.	34	F		Hannover	New York	Constitution	12 Jul 1827
Marian	3	F	Weaver	Brustedseul	U.S. America	Superior	18 Jun 1825
Marie	26	F	Weaver	Brustedseul	U.S. America	Superior	18 Jun 1825
Sebastiaan	24	M	Boer	ober ambt Zelbach	United States	Juffraw Johanna	16 Oct 1821
WEBLEY, David	39	M	Cloth Dresser	England	United States	Acasta	14 Jun 1824
WEBON, Edwd.	28	M	Farmer	England	U. States	Hercules	6 Jul 1827
WEBOUR, —, Mrs.	33	M	Mechanic	U. States	U. States	Radius	18 Apr 1825
WEBOURN, John	47			Kent County	Albany	Peru	30 May 1828
WEBRY, James	16		Student	U.S.	United States	Cadmus	24 Oct 1827
WEBSTER, Andrew	32	M	Labourer	Scotland	Philadelpah.	Ariel	22 Feb 1823
Author	46	M	Gentlm.	Canada	Canada	James Cropper	13 Mar 1826
C.	23	M	Merchant	England	Canada	Braganza	20 May 1823
Chas.	28	M	...	U.S. America	U.S. America	Columbia	26 Nov 1825
E. W.	40	M	Planter	U.S.	U.S.	New England	11 Jul 1827
Edward	19	M	Painter	England	America	Braganza	1 Dec 1824
James	28	M	Watchmaker	England	United States	Comet	6 Mar 1823
John	28	M	Joiner	England	United States	Baltic	21 Apr 1827
John	35	M	Farmer	England	U.S. America	Samuel Wright	9 Jan 1829
John, Mr.	22	M	Merchant	U.S. America	U.S. America	James Cropper	14 Mar 1828
Noah	66		Gentleman	United States	United States	Hudson	18 Jun 1825
Richd.	43	M	Mason			Helen	4 Aug 1829
Samuel	29	M	Watchmaker	England	United States	Comet	6 Mar 1823
Thomas	14	M	Farmer	Great Britain	United States	Spartan	25 Jul 1821
W. B.	26	M	Doctor	Newbrunsick	Newbrunsick	Nancy	23 Oct 1823
Wm. B.	22	M	...	St. John	St. John	Nancy	19 Oct 1821
Wm. B.	23	M	S...d...y	Horton, Kings County, Nova Scotia	Ny...	Nancy	26 Nov 1822
Wm. G.	23		Gentleman	United States	United States	Hudson	18 Jun 1825
WEDD, John	30		Farmer	England	United States	Cambria	19 Oct 1829
WEDELL, Charles	24	M	Tailor	Wittenburg	U.S. America	Commodore Preble	17 Dec 1825
WEDEY, Henry	30	M	Seaman	Dartmouth	Dartmouth	Olivebranch	15 Mar 1820
WEDLING, Madalina	25	F	None	France	U. States	Sully	25 Jun 1828
WEDY, Mary	18	F	Servant	Great Britain	United States	Sylvester Healy	23 Nov 1825
WEEDER, —, four sons	56	M		Switzerland	U.S. America	Commodore Preble	17 Dec 1825
—, one daughter	12	F		Switzerland	U.S. America	Commodore Preble	17 Dec 1825
Doras, wife	36	F		Switzerland	U.S. America	Commodore Preble	17 Dec 1825
Eberhard	50	M	Mason	United States	United States	Globe	30 Aug 1828
George	21	M	Mason	United States	United States	Globe	30 Aug 1828
J. B.	41	M	Shoemaker	Switzerland	U.S. America	Commodore Preble	17 Dec 1825
WEEDLAND, Johan	23	M	Servt.	Stockholm	Stockholm	Lewis	29 Oct 1825
WEEDNOR, Frederick	26	M	Taylor	Switzerland	United States	Elizabeth	27 Jul 1824
WEEKES, Elizabeth	24		Cooper	England	United States	Corinthian	30 May 1828
Elizabeth	33		Cooper	England	United States	Corinthian	30 May 1828
Elizabeth, Miss	2		Cooper	England	United States	Corinthian	30 May 1828
William, Mastr.	1		Cooper	England	United States	Corinthian	30 May 1828
WEEKS, —, Major	50	M	Military	Gt. Britain	G. Britain	Electra	4 Sep 1827
—, Miss	45	F	Lady	Nassau	United States	Superior	14 Apr 1825

NAMES OF PASSENGERS	AGE	SEX	OCCUPATIONS	COUNTRY TO WHICH THEY BELONG	COUNTRY THEY INTEND TO INHABIT	SHIPS/DATES OF ARRIVAL	
WEEKS (cont'd)							
Charles	27	M	Gent.	United States	United States	Cambria	16 Aug 1827
Ellen	36	F	None	Great Britain	U. States	Birmingham	11 Oct 1828
Ezra	49	M	None	United States	United States	Nestor	20 Nov 1821
Janes	23	M	Seaman	U. States	U. States	Boston	26 Sep 1820
Samuel	25	M	Farmer	Germany	United States	Oxford	14 Aug 1828
Thos. John	3	M	None	Great Britain	U. States	Birmingham	11 Oct 1828
WEESSE, Gustav	22	M	Gentleman	France	France	York	7 Aug 1828
WEG..., George	18	M	Gentleman	Germany		Courier	29 Jun 1827
WEGGENTON, J.	13	M		Great Brittain	United States	Sarah Ralston	27 Jan 1827
J.	43	F	Farmer	Great Brittain	United States	Sarah Ralston	27 Jan 1827
WEHLEY, Antoinne	6	M		Switzerland	Ohio	Eugenie	20 Aug 1827
Joseph	4	M		Switzerland	Ohio	Eugenie	20 Aug 1827
W.	29	M		Switzerland	Ohio	Eugenie	20 Aug 1827
WEIBEL, —, Miss	15 6/12	F		Swisse	United States	Deux Ernest	29 Dec 1827
*landed in New York							
Jh.	37		Cordonnier [shoemaker]	Suisse		Deux Ernest	29 Dec 1827
*son épouse & 3 enfans [his wife and three children]							
John	33	M	Mechanic	Wertenburg	U. States	Minerva	18 Oct 1828
Joseph, his Wife & Two Children	37	M	Shoemaker	Swisse	United States	Deux Ernest	29 Dec 1827
*landed at Lewiston, Delw.							
WEIBER, John R.	67	M	Farmer	Switzerland	America, U.N.S.	Great Britain	3 Aug 1829
Rudolph	8	F		Switzerland	America, U.N.S.	Great Britain	3 Aug 1829
WEICH, Catherine	4	F		Brattain		L'Esperance	6 Sep 1828
Christine	8	F		Brattain		L'Esperance	6 Sep 1828
Magdeline	9	F		Brattain		L'Esperance	6 Sep 1828
Magdeline	33	F	Labourer	Brattain		L'Esperance	6 Sep 1828
Mathius	36	M	Labourer	Brattain		L'Esperance	6 Sep 1828
Rosine	12	F		Brattain		L'Esperance	6 Sep 1828
WEICKEL, Adolph	26	M	Farmer	Germany	United States	Maria Elizabeth	6 Jan 1823
WEIDINGAR, Emanuel	31	M		Prussia		Leonidas	20 Apr 1826
WEIDLE, Ernest	27	M	Weaver	Wertemberg	Wertemberg	Edward Quesnel	3 Jul 1829
WEIDLER, Joh.	28	M	Agriculture	Wirtemburg	United States	Henri IV	14 Oct 1829
WEIDMANN, Philip	32	M	Farmer	Germany	United States	Helen	5 Sep 1828
WEIGHTMAN, Thomas	27	M	Farmer	Great Britian	United States	Isaac Hicks	22 May 1826
William	14	M	Druggist	Great Britain	United States	Freak	14 oct 1828
WEILAND, Johannes	30	M	Weaver	Germany	U. States	Isabella	10 Aug 1829
WEILL, Elizabeth	28	F		France	U. States	Edward Quesnel	4 Aug 1828
George	20	M	Farmer	Germany	United States	Virginia	31 May 1828
Jacob	1	M		France	U. States	Edward Quesnel	4 Aug 1828
WEILLE, Charles	24	M	Mechanic	France	U. States	Edward Quesnel	4 Aug 1828
WEILLES, André	36	M	Farmer	Germany	United States	Oxford	14 Aug 1828
WEINAN, A.	18	M	Merchant	France	United States	Elizabeth	22 May 1822
WEINE, John	24	M	Labourer	Ireland	U. States	William	27 Jul 1824
WEINGARTHER, —,							
Mrs.	38	F		Bremen	U. States	Franklin	23 Sep 1828
L.	13	M		Bremen	U. States	Franklin	23 Sep 1828
Maria Joze	16	F		Bremen	U. States	Franklin	23 Sep 1828
Michael	47	M	Baker	Bremen	U. States	Franklin	23 Sep 1828
R.	11 6/12	F		Bremen	U. States	Franklin	23 Sep 1828
WEINHAUR, Mary	1 1/2	F	None	England	United States	India	8 Jun 1827
WEINMER,							
Earnest P.	12 6/12	M	Student	Denmark	St. Thomas	Four Sons	31 May 1828
WEINNBREMIS, F. C.	30	M	Merchant	Denmark	Denmark	Boon	26 Feb 1820
WEIR, Andrew	30	M	Merchant	Scotland, G.B.		London	29 Apr 1824
Andw.	28		Merchant	Ayrshire	Great Britain	William Thompson	13 May 1823
Chas.	27	M	Cooper	Great Britain	United States	William Dawson	18 Jun 1827
Edward	35	M	Merchant	Ireland	New York	Vigilant	6 May 1822
Eliza	25	F		Ireland	New York	Vigilant	6 May 1822
Jams	35	M	Weaver	Ireland	New York	Trusty	12 Sep 1828
Jas.	25	M	Farmer	Ireland	U. States	Globe	14 Jul 1821
John	22	M	Mechanic	United States	U. States	Reindeer	29 Jun 1827
Robt.	19	M	Weaver	Scotland	United States	Belmont	30 Aug 1828
Robt.	26	M	Servant	England	U. States	Cincinnatus	24 May 1821
Sarah	7	F		Ireland	New York	Vigilant	6 May 1822
Sarah	25	F	None	Great Britain	United States	William Dawson	18 Jun 1827

NAMES OF PASSENGERS	AGE	SEX	OCCUPATIONS	COUNTRY TO WHICH THEY BELONG	COUNTRY THEY INTEND TO INHABIT	SHIPS/DATES OF ARRIVAL	
WEIR (cont'd)							
Silas E.	45	M	Merchant	U. States	United States	New York	12 Nov 1822
Wm.	5	M		Ireland	New York	Vigilant	6 May 1822
WEIS, J.	32	M	Mercht.	U.S.	U.S.	Jacob	2 May 1825
Jacob	36	M	Merchant	Switzerland	U. States	Kanhawa	16 Apr 1823
WEISMAN, Christian	20	M	Children & family of Jacob Weisman	Switzerland	United States	Aurora	21 Jun 1824
Elizabeth	9	F	Children & family of Jacob Weisman	Switzerland	United States	Aurora	21 Jun 1824
Elizabeth	47	F	Wife of [Jacob]	Switzerland	United States	Aurora	21 Jun 1824
Jacob	15	M	Children & family of Jacob Weisman	Switzerland	United States	Aurora	21 Jun 1824
Jacob	53	M	Teacher	Switzerland	United States	Aurora	21 Jun 1824
John	18	M	Children & family of Jacob Weisman	Switzerland	United States	Aurora	21 Jun 1824
John G.	3 6/12	M	Children & family of Jacob Weisman	Switzerland	United States	Aurora	21 Jun 1824
Saml. G.	5	M	Children & family of Jacob Weisman	Switzerland	United States	Aurora	21 Jun 1824
WEISMILLARD, Ann	78	F		Switzerland	Switzerland	Edward Quesnel	3 Jul 1829
WEISS, Catherine	7	F		France	U. States	Edward Quesnel	4 Aug 1828
Catherine	35	F		France	U. States	Edward Quesnel	4 Aug 1828
Joseph	40	M	Farmer	France	U. States	Edward Quesnel	4 Aug 1828
Maria	37	F	Wife	Germany	United States	Elizabeth	4 Sep 1826
Phillip	3	M		France	U. States	Edward Quesnel	4 Aug 1828
Severin	51	M	Farmer	Germany	United States	Elizabeth	4 Sep 1826
WEISSER, Joseph	40	M		Swisse	United States	Deux Ernest	29 Dec 1827
*landed at Lewiston, Delw.							
WEISSINGER, Elizabeth	32	F	Maid Servant	Germany	United States	Helen	5 Sep 1828
WEITH, Joe	26	M	Farmer	Germany	United States	Helen	5 Sep 1828
WELBASKY, Agnes	9	F	None	Russia	United States	Baltic	17 Aug 1824
Edward	14	M	None	Russia	United States	Baltic	17 Aug 1824
Francis	15	M	None	Russia	United States	Baltic	17 Aug 1824
Kitty	7	F	None	Russia	United States	Baltic	17 Aug 1824
Richard	12	M	None	Russia	United States	Baltic	17 Aug 1824
Wm.	11	M	None	Russia	United States	Baltic	17 Aug 1824
WELBONE, Hannah	54	F		U. States	U. States	General Coffin	9 Mar 1827
WELBORFORD, Thos.	72	M	Farmer	England	U. States	Manchester Packet	30 Nov 1822
WELCH, —, Mr.	48	M	None	Ireland	U. States	Ganges	8 May 1823
A.	40	F		Ireland	U. States	Prince Edward	5 Dec 1821
Alice	10 5/12	F				Cririe	18 Sep 1820
Ann	22	F	None	Ireland	New York	Margaret	18 May 1825
Ann	40	M				Cassack	25 Jul 1820
C.	7	F		Ireland	U. States	Prince Edward	5 Dec 1821
C.	40	M	Labourer	Ireland	Massachusetts	York	8 Aug 1829
Edwd.	31	M		G. Britain	U. States	Mary & Harriot	8 Sep 1828
Elizabeth	5 4/12	F				Cririe	18 Sep 1820
Elizabeth	25			...dlef...	...	Hudson	14 Jun 1827
Henry	2	M		Gt. Britain	United States	Columbia	7 Sep 1827
Heny.	48	M	Currier	France	United States	Stephania	6 Dec 1827
Honora	13	F		Ireland	United States	Trio	2 Oct 1828
Isaac	36	M				Cassack	25 Jul 1820
J.	35	M	Merchant	Scotland	U. States	Superior	25 Sep 1828
J.	39	M	Mariner	U. States	U. States	Artibonite	19 Apr 1827
James	26		Merchant	Great Britain		Ruth	26 May 1824
Jeremiah	15	M	Labourer	Ireland	United States	Trio	2 Oct 1828
John	1	M		Gt. Britain	United States	Columbia	7 Sep 1827
John	20	M	Labourer	Ireland	U. States	Hope & Esther	9 Jun 1827
John	37	M	Farmer	Great Britain	United States	Mount Vernon	17 Jun 1825
John, Mr.	40	M	Labourer	England	U.S.	Acasta	11 May 1827
Laurence	38 3/12	M	Surgeon	Hayti	Hayti	Gleaner	6 Jun 1828
Margaret	42		Farmer	Halifax	West Point	Almira	15 Jul 1822

NAMES OF PASSENGERS	AGE	SEX	OCCUPATIONS	COUNTRY TO WHICH THEY BELONG	COUNTRY THEY INTEND TO INHABIT	SHIPS/DATES OF ARRIVAL	
WELCH (cont'd)							
Mary	6	F		Ireland	U. States	Ganges	8 May 1823
Mary	7 5/12	F				Cririe	18 Sep 1820
Mary	24	F	Labourer	Scotland	U. States	New Packet	16 Apr 1828
Mary	25	F		G. Britain	U. States	Margaret Bogle	12 Jun 1828
Mary	26	F		Ireland	U. States	Emeline	4 Sep 1827
Mary	27 3/12	F				Cririe	18 Sep 1820
Mary T., Miss	29 7/12	F	Maister mother	U. States	U. States	John London	21 Mar 1825
Michal	22 5/12	M	Labourer	Ireland	New York	Concordia	12 Oct 1826
Patrick	24	M	Farmer	Ireland	U. States	Emeline	4 Sep 1827
Patrick	24	M	Labourer	Ireland	Ireland	Sarah G.	28 Nov 1827
Patrick	28	M	Labourer	Ireland	United States	Borneo	14 Aug 1827
Richard	15	F		Ireland	United States	Trio	2 Oct 1828
Richard	24	M	Labourer	Ireland	United States	Hope & Esther	27 Jul 1829
Robert	25	M	Gentleman	Great Britain		Charlotte Corday	7 Mar 1820
Robt.	32 1/12	M	Weaver	England		Cririe	18 Sep 1820
Robt., Junr.	12 7/12	M				Cririe	18 Sep 1820
Sarah	36	F		Gt. Britain	United States	Columbia	7 Sep 1827
Thomas	1 3/12	M				Cririe	18 Sep 1820
Thos.	40		Farmer	Halifax	West Point	Almira	15 Jul 1822
Ths.	24	M	Farmer	Ireland	New York	Margaret	18 May 1825
William	18	M	None	Ireland	U. States	Union	3 Jun 1822
William	25	M	Shoemaker	England	United States	Trident	31 Mar 1827
Wm.	24	M	Farmer	Ireland	United States	Curler	3 Mar 1828
Wm., Mr.	36	M	Baker	England	U.S.	Acasta	11 May 1827
WELD, A.	22	M	Marinor	U. States	New York	London Packet	5 Jan 1829
E. W.	38	M	Merchant	Boston	N. York	Eliza Jane	11 Jul 1822
J. C.	30	M	Gentleman	Germany	Germany	Governor Von Schollen	7 Nov 1827
WELDDEN, George	47	M	Capt. R. N.	England	America	Courier	24 Jul 1820
WELDEN, E. W.	48	M	Mariner	U. States	U. States	Dromo	13 Dec 1826
Jas. Jno.	25	M	Labourer	Gt. Britain	U.S. America	James Cropper	2 Aug 1827
Richard	20	M	Shopemaker	Ireland	United States	Silas Richards	3 Apr 1826
WELDER, S. V. S.	42	M	Merchant	United States	Massachusetts	Stephania	28 Jul 1823
WELDON, Bridget	13	F	None	England		Exchange	11 Jul 1823
Chas.	25	M		Galway	U. States	Eliza Ann	30 Jul 1823
James	11	M		England		Exchange	11 Jul 1823
Margaret	1	F		England		Exchange	11 Jul 1823
Margaret	37	F	None	England		Exchange	11 Jul 1823
Mary	46	F		England	America	Plutarch	18 Jul 1826
Morris	9	M		England		Exchange	11 Jul 1823
Patrick	37	M	Labor	England		Exchange	11 Jul 1823
Patrick, Jr.	3	M		England		Exchange	11 Jul 1823
Rose	7	F		England		Exchange	11 Jul 1823
William	56	M	Turner	England	America	Plutarch	18 Jul 1826
WELDS, James	45	M	Distiller	America	America	Trafalgar	18 Jan 1828
WELELY, Dorother	16	F	Farmer	Germany	United States	Oxford	14 Aug 1828
Dorother	43	F	Farmer	Germany	United States	Oxford	14 Aug 1828
Frederic	7	M	Farmer	Germany	United States	Oxford	14 Aug 1828
Georges	3	M	Farmer	Germany	United States	Oxford	14 Aug 1828
Georges	43	M	Farmer	Germany	United States	Oxford	14 Aug 1828
Henry	14	M	Farmer	Germany	United States	Oxford	14 Aug 1828
John	1	M	Farmer	Germany	United States	Oxford	14 Aug 1828
Magdelaine	5	F	Farmer	Germany	United States	Oxford	14 Aug 1828
WELKER, F., Mrs.	20		Lady	England	United States	Acasta	16 Aug 1826
Francis, Mr.	30		Pianoforte Maker	England	United States	Acasta	16 Aug 1826
WELKS, George	24	M	Merchant	England	U. States	William Thompson	17 Dec 1827
WELL, Jno., Rvd.	40	M	D.D.	Engd.	Engd.	Napoleon	26 May 1828
Thomas	21	M	Farmer	Ireland	United States	Fabius	4 Jun 1828
WELLEN, John	31	M	None	Great Britain	United States	Hannibal	12 Oct 1829
WELLER, Aaron	13	M	Potter	Rye, England	United States	William	21 May 1828
Charlotte	37	F		Rye, England	United States	William	21 May 1828
E#mily	4	F		Rye, England	United States	William	21 May 1828
Harriot	15	F		Gt. Britain	Schenectady, N.Y.	Leeds	7 Nov 1828
John	37	M	Shoemaker	Great Brittain	New York	Albion	11 Jun 1821
Luke	6	M		Rye, England	United States	William	21 May 1828
Mark	2	M		Rye, England	United States	William	21 May 1828

NAMES OF PASSENGERS	AGE	SEX	OCCUPATIONS	COUNTRY TO WHICH THEY BELONG	COUNTRY THEY INTEND TO INHABIT	SHIPS/DATES OF ARRIVAL	
WELLER (cont'd)							
Rhoda	8	F	Potter	Rye, England	United States	William	21 May 1828
Sarah	21	F		Gt. Britain	Schenectady, N.Y.	Leeds	7 Nov 1828
Thomas	49	M	Potter	Rye, England	United States	William	21 May 1828
Thos.	18		Baker	Sussex, England		Cincinnatus	17 May 1823
Wm.	23	M	Potter	Gt. Britain	Schenectady, N.Y.	Leeds	7 Nov 1828
Wm., Junr.	1	M		Gt. Britain	Schenectady, N.Y.	Leeds	7 Nov 1828
WELLERS, Margaret	24	F	Labourer or Spinster	Ireland	United States	Champion	3 Nov 1827
WELLES, B.	45	M	Merchant	United States		Edward Quesnel	17 Nov 1828
James W.	19	M	Merchant	Boston, Mass.	U. St.	Manchester	7 Dec 1826
WELLESFORD, Samuel	34	M	Merchant	England	England	Acasta	15 Jul 1822
WELLIARD, Catherine	50	F	Spinster	Ireland	United States	Gem	16 Jun 1824
David	21	M	Labourer	Ireland	United States	Gem	16 Jun 1824
Peter	63	M	Labourer	Ireland	United States	Gem	16 Jun 1824
WELLIMEL, Alliston	40	F		America	America	Pacific	13 Jan 1827
Herriet	14	F		America	America	Pacific	13 Jan 1827
WELLINK, P.	30	M	Dictor	German	U. States	John London	26 Mar 1822
WELLINTON, Thomes	50	M	Farmer	England	Hallifax, N.V.	Hercules	10 Apr 1823
WELLMOTT, Lydia H.	21	F	None	Great Britain	United States	John	6 Oct 1820
WELLOTT, Susan	25	F		G. Britain	U. States	Mary Howland	22 Sep 1828
WELLS, —, Miss	25	F	None	United States	United States	Manchester	24 Aug 1827
Alexander	30	M	Farmer	England	New York	Brighton	11 Dec 1827
Alfred	3	M	Musician	Great Britain	Canada	Columbia	22 Sep 1828
Arthur	5	M	Musician	Great Britain	Canada	Columbia	22 Sep 1828
Benjamin	32	M	Merchant	St. John, N.B.	St. John, N.B.	St. Michaels	24 Mar 1825
Benjamin	40	M	Merchant	United States	United States	Acasta	15 Jul 1822
Castine	7	F	Musician	Great Britain	Canada	Columbia	22 Sep 1828
Charlotte	35 8/12	F	Wife of Geo. Wells	United States	Maryland	Venus	8 Sep 1820
Charlotte, Jr.	8 1/12	F	Daughter of Geo. Wells	United States	Maryland	Venus	8 Sep 1820
Elisha	45	M	Merchant	Massachusetts	U. States	Morning Star	28 Mar 1822
Elizabeth S.	5	F		United States	United States	Acasta	15 Jul 1822
Enoch	18	M	Farmer	Switzerland	U. States	Robert Edward	2 Nov 1827
Frederick	6	M	Musician	Great Britain	Canada	Columbia	22 Sep 1828
Geo.	25	M	Mechanic	Scotland	U. States	Fanny	18 Dec 1826
George	2 11/12	M	Son of Geo. Wells	United States	Maryland	Venus	8 Sep 1820
George, Servant Coullard Man	20 5/12	M		America	America	Elias Burger	19 Dec 1820
George W.	27	M	None	G. Bt.	G. Bt.	Canada	13 Oct 1825
Harriet	30	F		Great Britain	Canada	Columbia	22 Sep 1828
Henry	25	M	Servant	U. States	U. States	Medina	23 Apr 1828
James	30	M	Merchant	England	Jamaica	Ann Maria	14 Mar 1825
James	30	M	Merchant	England	U. States	Tilton	28 Jun 1826
James	31	M	Merchant	England	Jamaica	Columbia	25 Nov 1824
James	35	M	Gentleman	Great Britain	Great Britain	Visitor	30 Jun 1825
James	37	M	Silkmanufacturer	Gt. Britain	United States	Robert Edwards	1 Jun 1826
James	42	M	Merchant	England	Jamaica	Mary Emily	19 Dec 1825
Jane	20	F		America	America	Britannia	22 Jul 1829
Jane	32	F	None	Gt. Britain	United States	Union	9 Jan 1824
John	26	M	Shoemaker	England	United States	Trident	30 Sep 1826
John	28		Labourer	England	United States	Hugh Johnson	11 Jun 1828
John D.	23		Doctor of Physic	Boston	United States	London	13 Dec 1822
Lewis Edward	28	M	Physician	United States	United States	William	31 Mar 1828
Margaret	6 8/12	F	Daughter of Geo. Wells	United States	Maryland	Venus	8 Sep 1820
Mary	40	F	Commedian	England		Britannia	20 Jun 1827
Mehitebal F.	35	F		United States	United States	Acasta	15 Jul 1822
Norman	29	M		U. States	U. States	Alfred	26 Apr 1828
Philip	30	M	Merchant	St. John, N.B.	United States	Sarah G.	11 Jan 1828
R. W.	28	M	Mercht.	U. States	U. States	Wilhelmina	8 Jan 1824
Rd.	34	M	Mariner	U. States	U. States	Venus	27 Jun 1821
Richard	35	M	Merchant	New York	U. States	Radius	12 Feb 1824
Richard	45	M	Mariner	New York	New York	Milo	8 May 1826
Richd.	34	M	Merchant	U.S.	U.S.	Agenoria	15 Jun 1822
Robt. W.	27	M	Merchant	U. States	U. States	Moro	26 Aug 1824
Samuel	45	M	Labourer	Great Britain	United States	Juno	5 Oct 1822
Sarah	17	F	Comedian	England		Britannia	20 Jun 1827

NAMES OF PASSENGERS	AGE	SEX	OCCUPATIONS	COUNTRY TO WHICH THEY BELONG	COUNTRY THEY INTEND TO INHABIT	SHIPS/DATES OF ARRIVAL	
WELLS (cont'd)							
Sarah	25	F	None	England	United States	Aurora	5 Sep 1826
Sarah	40			Ireland	United States	Jno. Dickinson	21 Sep 1821
Sophia	18	F		Switzerland	U. States	Robert Edward	2 Nov 1827
Susan	5 10/12	F	Daughter of Geo. Wells	United States	Maryland	Venus	8 Sep 1820
Thomas	18	M	Labourer	Ireland	U. States	Ann Maria	13 Dec 1824
Thomas	26	M	Merchant	Great Britain	U.S.A.	Silas Richards	7 Mar 1825
W.	24	M	Mechanic	Connecticutt	U. States	Benjamin	1 Jun 1822
William	21	M	Commedian	England		Britannia	20 Jun 1827
William	26	M	Mariner	America	United States	Two Marys	12 Feb 1820
Wm.	35	M	Gun Smith	Great Britain	United States	Thomas Dickason	31 Jul 1829
Wm.	38	M	Miner	Mexico	England	Brown	23 Dec 1826
Wm., Jr.	18	M	Butcher	Halifax, N.S.	N. York	Resolution	6 Jun 1822
WELLSEY, —, Mrs.	25	F	Lady	Columbia	England	Athenian	1 Dec 1827
WELLSFORD, Fredk. W.	38	M	Merchant	England	England	Acasta	15 Jul 1822
WELLSTOAD, Stephen	11	M		Great Britain		Dalmannock	24 Ocg 1826
WELMORE, Chs.	33	M	Labourer	U. States	U. States	Robt. Reade	12 Apr 1825
WELPLEY, W.	26	M	Merchant	U. States	U. States	St. Michael	26 Oct 1824
WELSBY, John	24	M	Merchant	England	United States	Braganza	5 Dec 1821
WELSEY, John	30	M	Merchant	England		Athenian	3 Sep 1827
WELSH, —	50	M	Weaver	England		Manhattan	22 May 1827
—, Mr.	40	M	Servant	Scotland	Columbia	Abigail	25 Feb 1826
...ne	25	F	None	Ireland	New York	Indian Chief	19 Jun 1823
Alexander	19	F	Farmer	Ireland	New York	Trusty	12 Sep 1828
Andr.	22	M	Bleacher	G. Brittian	U. States	Pacific	19 Oct 1829
Bridget	32	F		Great Britain	United States	Isaac Hicks	10 Jul 1827
Charles	27			Ireland	U.S.	Union	20 Aug 1827
Cornelius	9	M		Great Brittain	United States	United States	16 Feb 1827
Danl.	27	M	Seaman	U. States	U. States	Golden Age	6 Jul 1821
E.	20	F	Spinster	Glasgow	United States	Henry Clay	25 Apr 1822
Ealvard	25	M	Farmer	Ireland	Philadelphia	General Marion	12 Jan 1829
Edwd.	22	M	Clerk	Charleston, So. Ca.	Charleston, So. Ca.	Enterprize	31 Jul 1824
Edwd.	30	M	...	D...gl...	United States	Solon	21 Jun 1824
Eliza	15	M	None	Youghall, Co. Cork	Youghall	Aldebaron	21 Jan 1826
Elizabeth	10	F	None	England		Manhattan	22 May 1827
Ellen	23	F	None	Youghall, Co. Cork	Youghall	Aldebaron	21 Jan 1826
Emanuel G.	73	M		Great Brittain	United States	United States	16 Feb 1827
George	16		None	Gt. Britan	United States	James Monroe	11 Dec 1821
H.	30	M	Mercht.	Ireland	United States	Camillus	27 Oct 1829
Helen	20	F	None	G. Brittian	U. States	Pacific	19 Oct 1829
James	13	M	Spinster	Glasgow	United States	Henry Clay	25 Apr 1822
James	23	M	Labourer	...	...	Frances Henrietta	30 Jun 1827
James	25	M	unknown	Great Britain	United States	Ocean	27 Jul 1825
James	27	M	Taylor	Ireland	New York	Indian Chief	19 Jun 1823
James	28	M	Labourer	Ireland	United States	Jubilee	12 May 1828
James	40	M	Mariner	England	United States	Nancy	15 Mar 1820
James	41	M	Merchant	Philada.	U. States	Francis Henrietta	8 Apr 1822
John	18		Shoemaker	Gt. Britan	United States	James Monroe	11 Dec 1821
John	23	M	Labourer	Ireland	United States	General Marion	6 Oct 1828
John	24	M	Farmer	England	U.S. America	New Hampshire	28 Sep 1826
John	26		Plasterer	England	United States	Hudson	5 Apr 1826
John	30	M	English Consul	G. Britain	G. Britain	Burdett	11 Oct 1827
John, Revd.	26	M	Gentleman	Ireland	United States	Erin	25 Dec 1820
Jos.	30	M	Cooper	Ireland	U. States	Prize	10 Jun 1824
Josiah G.	7	M		Great Brittain	United States	United States	16 Feb 1827
Katherine	8					Henry Clay	25 Apr 1822
Katherine	40	F	Spinster	Glasgow	United States	Henry Clay	25 Apr 1822
Laurence	6	M		Great Britain	United States	Isaac Hicks	10 Jul 1827
Lawrence	27	M	Laborer	Ireland	America	Francis & Henrietta	11 Jul 1823
Margaret	30	F	None	England		Manhattan	22 May 1827
Martin	30	M	Stone Mason	Ireland	United States	Roman	12 Jun 1826
Mary	2	F		Great Britain	United States	Isaac Hicks	10 Jul 1827

NAMES OF PASSENGERS	AGE	SEX	OCCUPATIONS	COUNTRY TO WHICH THEY BELONG	COUNTRY THEY INTEND TO INHABIT	SHIPS/DATES OF ARRIVAL	
WELSH (cont'd)							
Mary	26			Ireland	U.S.	Union	20 Aug 1827
Mary	29			Ireland	U.S.	Union	20 Aug 1827
Mary Ann	3	F	None	England		Manhattan	22 May 1827
Mchs.	13	M	...	D...	United States	Solon	21 Jun 1824
Michael	11	M	None	Youghall, Co. Cork	Youghall	Aldebaron	21 Jan 1826
Michael	23	M	Cabinet Maker	Youghall, Co. Cork	Youghall	Aldebaron	21 Jan 1826
Paser	7	M		Great Britain	United States	Isaac Hicks	10 Jul 1827
Patrick	22	M	Weaver	Ireland	United States	Robert Fulton	10 Aug 1827
Patrick	24	M	...	G. Britain	United States	Louisa	14 Jun 1825
Patrick	25	M	Farmer	Ireland	U. States	Edward	15 Jul 1825
Patrick	28	M	Laborer	Ireland	United States	Nancy	15 Dec 1824
Peter	4	M		Great Britain	United States	Isaac Hicks	10 Jul 1827
Peter	27	M	Labourer	Ireland	United States	Dalhouse Castle	8 May 1827
Pierce	13	M	None	Youghall, Co. Cork	Youghall	Aldebaron	21 Jan 1826
Robert	24	M	Joiner	England	United States	Lord Wellington	14 Nov 1827
Robt.	11	M	Spinster	Glasgow	United States	Henry Clay	25 Apr 1822
Robt.	34	M	Weaver	U.S. America	U.S. America	Mentor	22 Jul 1823
Thomas	27	M	Boot Maker	Ireland	United States	Cambria	8 Oct 1828
Thomas	36	M	Labourer	Great Britain	United States	Isaac Hicks	10 Jul 1827
Thomas	50	M	Farmer	Ireland	United States	Lord Wellington	14 Nov 1827
Thos.	7	M	Baker	Great Britain	New York	Superior	5 Sep 1827
Wm.	26	M	...	D...	United States	Solon	21 Jun 1824
Wm.	32	M	Merchant	New York	New York	St. Michael's	10 Feb 1827
Wm. G.	36	M	Weaver	Great Brittain	United States	United States	16 Feb 1827
Zacharia	6/12	M	None	England		Manhattan	22 May 1827
WELSPIE, James	1			England	United States	Hugh Johnson	11 Jun 1828
Jane	23			England	United States	Hugh Johnson	11 Jun 1828
John	24		Labourer	England	United States	Hugh Johnson	11 Jun 1828
WEMBURG, H.	35	M	Merchant	Turkey	U. States	Angenora	16 Jan 1827
WEMER, Christian N. H.	23	M	Merchant	Hamburg	U. States	Martha	4 Sep 1828
WENBAN, Adron	11		Farmer	England	United States	Corinthian	30 May 1828
Ann	19		Farmer	England	United States	Corinthian	30 May 1828
Hannah	15		Farmer	England	United States	Corinthian	30 May 1828
Hezekiah	8		Farmer	England	United States	Corinthian	30 May 1828
James	21		Farmer	England	United States	Corinthian	30 May 1828
John	50		Farmer	England	United States	Corinthian	30 May 1828
John, Mastr.	18		Farmer	England	United States	Corinthian	30 May 1828
Moses	13		Farmer	England	United States	Corinthian	30 May 1828
Simeon	3		Farmer	England	United States	Corinthian	30 May 1828
Susanna	5		Farmer	England	United States	Corinthian	30 May 1828
WENBON, Jos.	20	M	Farmer	England	U. States	Hercules	6 Jul 1827
WENCKLE, Claus	19	M	Labourer	Germany	United States	Constitution	2 Aug 1826
WENCKLEMAN, John	45	M	Farmer	Warington		Colossus	27 Mar 1828
WENDALL, Wm.	25	M	Merchant	N. York	U.S. America	Leeds	6 Jun 1826
WENDEL, A. G.	40	M	Merchant	Germany	U. States	Louisa	21 Aug 1824
Etienne	27	M	Farmer	Swizerland		Antioch	18 Aug 1829
WENDINS, Jos.	25		Cordwainer			Mount Vernon	26 Aug 1820
WENDREN, Benjeman	17 7/12	M	Labourer	Ireland	United States	Louisa	16 Mar 1826
WENDRIM, John	47	M	Farmer	England	U.S.A.	Lima	6 Dec 1826
WENET, Ann	30	F		England	United States	Cosmo	26 Aug 1829
John	12	M		England	United States	Cosmo	26 Aug 1829
William	37	M	Wheelwright	England	United States	Cosmo	26 Aug 1829
WENG, Christoph	40	M	Baker	Germany	Pensylvania	James Noble	27 Aug 1827
WENHAM, Ann	25	F	None	England	United States	London	21 May 1828
Caroline	1 6/12	F	None	England	United States	London	21 May 1828
Hy.	21	M	Farmer	Gt. Britain	United States	Robert Edwards	1 Jun 1826
John	25	M	Laborer	England	United States	London	21 May 1828
WENHY, Jean	23	M	Baker	Germany	United States	Wm. Osborne	16 Sep 1828
Tonaly	21	M	Merchant	Germany	United States	Wm. Osborne	16 Sep 1828
WENLER, Barbara	44	F	Farmer	Switzerland	United States	Olympia	12 Aug 1828
Elizabeth	0 2/12	F	Farmer	Switzerland	United States	Olympia	12 Aug 1828
George	5	M	Farmer	Switzerland	United States	Olympia	12 Aug 1828
Jean	52	M	Farmer	Switzerland	United States	Olympia	12 Aug 1828
Leon	2	M	Farmer	Switzerland	United States	Olympia	12 Aug 1828

NAMES OF PASSENGERS	AGE	SEX	OCCUPATIONS	COUNTRY TO WHICH THEY BELONG	COUNTRY THEY INTEND TO INHABIT	SHIPS/DATES OF ARRIVAL	
WENLER (cont'd)							
Michel	6	M	Farmer	Switzerland	United States	Olympia	12 Aug 1828
Michel	25	M	Farmer	Switzerland	United States	Olympia	12 Aug 1828
WENNEN, Joseph	26	M	Farmer	Germany	America	Orozimbo	1 Oct 1827
WENNENBERG, T.	25	M	Sadler	N. York	U. States	Perry	13 Jul 1826
WENTLE, M.	11	F		Ireland	U. States	Adno	5 Jul 1828
WENTLING, Abram	40	M	Taylor ...	France	America	La Grange	7 Aug 1828
Gertrude	8	F	Child [of Abram]	France	America	La Grange	7 Aug 1828
Gertrude	38	F	Wife [of John]	France	America	La Grange	7 Aug 1828
John	4	M	Child [of John]	France	America	La Grange	7 Aug 1828
John	40	M	Clerk	France	America	La Grange	7 Aug 1828
Joseph	28	M	Taylor	France	America	La Grange	7 Aug 1828
*Died on the Voyage							
Magdalene	6	F	Child [of John]	France	America	La Grange	7 Aug 1828
Maria	14	F	Child [of John]	France	America	La Grange	7 Aug 1828
Maria	32	F	Wife [of Abram]	France	America	La Grange	7 Aug 1828
Michael	4	M	Child [of Abram]	France	America	La Grange	7 Aug 1828
Rosalia	2	F	Child [of Abram]	France	America	La Grange	7 Aug 1828
Theresa	6	F	Child [of Abram]	France	America	La Grange	7 Aug 1828
WENTWORTH, C.	34	M	Mercht.	England	U. States	Pacific	20 Aug 1825
Isaac D.	19		Seaman	Charleston		Hudson	18 Jun 1825
*Officers, Seamen and Passengers belonging to the Ship Jane of Boston and taken from on board the Schooner Olive of St. Johns , N.B. on the 4th June 1825, Lat. 41.30, Long 53.19, which ship foundered on the 31st ultimo in Lat. 41.44 Long 52.							
Mary	26	F	Lady	U. States	U. States	Edwin	1 Jul 1829
T. H.	45	M	Manufacturer	State New York	United States	Ann Maria	2 Nov 1827
WENWAN, Anne	4	F	None	England	America	London	21 May 1828
Edward	6/12	M	None	England	America	London	21 May 1828
Harriet	9	F	None	England	America	London	21 May 1828
Henrietta	30	F	None	England	America	London	21 May 1828
Henry	11	M	None	England	America	London	21 May 1828
Jasper	14	M	None	England	America	London	21 May 1828
Jasper	32	M	Laborer	England	America	London	21 May 1828
Mary	7	F	None	England	America	London	21 May 1828
WERBEN, Hy.	37	M	Weaver	Switzerland	U.S.	C. Amelia	30 Jun 1828
WERCKMULLER,							
Simon B.	67	M	Merchant	U. States	Virginia	Sully	30 Oct 1827
WEREWMAN, Geo.	22	M	Merchant	N. York		Emily	2 Jun 1824
WERKEL, Charlotte	28		Servant	Germany		Bayard	10 Sep 1827
WERKMULLER,							
Saml. B., Mr.	37	M	Merchant	Virginia	U. States	Lewis	11 Nov 1824
WERMGUSTER,							
Catherine	1	F	Farmer	Switzerland	United States	Olympia	12 Aug 1828
Elizabeth	5	F	Farmer	Switzerland	United States	Olympia	12 Aug 1828
Elizabeth	30	F	Farmer	Switzerland	United States	Olympia	12 Aug 1828
Michel	30	M	Farmer	Switzerland	United States	Olympia	12 Aug 1828
WERNER, George	35	M	Merchant	Germany	United States	Germania	29 Aug 1828
J. J.	23	M	Merchant	Hamburg	United States	Maria Elizabeth	2 Sep 1822
Maia	25	F	Agriculturist	France	U.S.	Helen	3 May 1828
Maria, Zyn Vrow [his wife, Marten Scharpentier]	35	F		Nieder aurburg	United States	Juffraw Johanna	16 Oct 1821
WERNERT, Georg	7/12	M	Weaver	Germany	United States	Virginia	31 May 1828
*the 9 May the child died at 11:30 oclock in the Day							
Henrey	3	M	Weaver	Germany	United States	Virginia	31 May 1828
Jacob	9	M	Weaver	Germany	United States	Virginia	31 May 1828
John	2	M	Weaver	Germany	United States	Virginia	31 May 1828
Materlane	5	F	Weaver	Germany	United States	Virginia	31 May 1828
Materlener	38	F	Weaver	Germany	United States	Virginia	31 May 1828
Phillip	6	M	Weaver	Germany	United States	Virginia	31 May 1828
Phillip	41	M	Weaver	Germany	United States	Virginia	31 May 1828
WERRY, Thomas	30 5/12	M	Gentleman	France	United States	Catharine	10 Sep 1827
WERTMAN, Jane	38	M	Farmer	Switzerland		Charlemagne	20 Aug 1829
John	3	M	Farmer	Switzerland		Charlemagne	20 Aug 1829
WERTS, Catharine	1			France	U. States	Parachute	14 May 1828
Eliza	14			France	U. States	Parachute	14 May 1828
Margaret	7			France	U. States	Parachute	14 May 1828
Nicholas	27		Mechanic	France	U. States	Parachute	14 May 1828
Sophia	20			France	U. States	Parachute	14 May 1828

NAMES OF PASSENGERS	AGE	SEX	OCCUPATIONS	COUNTRY TO WHICH THEY BELONG	COUNTRY THEY INTEND TO INHABIT	SHIPS/DATES OF ARRIVAL	
WERZE, Jacob	27	M	Farmer	France	U. States	Edward Bopnnaffe	30 Jul 1829
WESBEN, Fred.	5	M		Switzerland	U.States	C. Amelia	30 Jun 1828
Go.	1	M		Switzerland	U.States	C. Amelia	30 Jun 1828
Hy.	10	M	Weaver	Switzerland	U.States	C. Amelia	30 Jun 1828
WESHLEN, Hannah	24	F		Sweden	U. States	Hamilton	22 Sep 1828
WESSEFER, A., Mr.	21	M	Musician	Bavaria		François I	19 Nov 1828
WESSELHOOF, W.	27	M	Physician	Germany	U. States	Deux Freres	27 Nov 1824
WEST, —, Mrs.	18	F				Congress	21 Nov 1823
—, Mrs., & 2 sons, being the Capts. Family						Antelope	22 Aug 1820
Alice	51 7/12	F	None	Ireland	U.S. of America	Hamilton	18 Jul 1827
Asa C.	37	M	Mariner	United States	United States	Weser	21 Oct 1823
Beal	12	M				Comet	24 Dec 1821
Benjamin	50		Gentleman	England	United States	Cambria	19 Oct 1829
C.	22	F		U. States	U. States	Altamira	24 Jun 1828
Daniel	14	M				Comet	24 Dec 1821
Easter	6	F				Comet	24 Dec 1821
Edward	2			Kent, England		Cincinnatus	17 May 1823
Edward	20	M	Labourer	Ireland	United States	Meteor	26 Jun 1827
Edward	29			Kent, England		Cincinnatus	17 May 1823
Edward	32	M	Seaman	U.States America		Susan	28 Sep 1826
Eliza	10	F				Comet	24 Dec 1821
Elizabeth	20	F	None	England	Rhode Island	Cincinnatus	16 Apr 1824
G. M., Revd.	29			Dutton	England	Great Britain	7 May 1827
Gaul	11	M	Apprentice	U. States	U. States	Cannon	25 Apr 1821
George	18 4/12	M	None	Ireland	U.S. of America	Hamilton	18 Jul 1827
Harriot	4			Kent, England		Cincinnatus	17 May 1823
J. B.	42	M	Mariner	U. States	U. States	New Packet	27 Jul 1822
James	18	M	Farmer	Rye, England	United States	William	21 May 1828
James	35	M	Mariner	Pennsylvania	U. States	Trimmer	19 Nov 1824
James	42	M	Gentleman	U. States	U. States	Montano	2 Sep 1828
Jane	8			Kent, England		Cincinnatus	17 May 1823
Jas.	24		Seaman	Boston		Hudson	18 Jun 1825

*Officers, Seamen and Passengers belonging to the Ship Jane of Boston and taken from on board the Schooner Olive of St. Johns , N.B. on the 4th June 1825, Lat. 41.30, Long 53.19, which ship foundered on the 31st ultimo in Lat. 41.44 Long 52.

NAMES OF PASSENGERS	AGE	SEX	OCCUPATIONS	COUNTRY TO WHICH THEY BELONG	COUNTRY THEY INTEND TO INHABIT	SHIPS/DATES OF ARRIVAL	
Jemima	31			Kent, England		Cincinnatus	17 May 1823
John	9			Kent, England		Cincinnatus	17 May 1823
John	15			Kent, England		Cincinnatus	17 May 1823
John	21	M	Farmer	Rye, England	United States	William	21 May 1828
John	27	...	...	...	United States	Criterion	27 Jun 1827
John	45	M	Clergyman	England	England	York	12 Jul 1825
John	50					Cincinnatus	29 Apr 1822
John	50	M	Farmer	England	Rhode Island	Cincinnatus	16 Apr 1824
John	51 8/12	M	Gentleman	Ireland	U.S. of America	Hamilton	18 Jul 1827
John M.	16 2/12	M	None	Ireland	U.S. of America	Hamilton	18 Jul 1827
Joseph	11			Kent, England		Cincinnatus	17 May 1823
Lydia	11	F				Comet	24 Dec 1821
Margaret	42	F		England	England	Tontine	1 Jun 1826
Mary	1			Kent, England		Cincinnatus	17 May 1823
Mary	8	F				Comet	24 Dec 1821
Mary	13	F	Apprentice	England	America	Maine	16 Jul 1821
Mary	29	F	Mantua Maker	England	England	William Thompson	19 Aug 1829
Mary	40			Kent, England		Cincinnatus	17 May 1823
Mary	44	F				Comet	24 Dec 1821
Otis	25	M	Merchant	Boston	Boston	Elizabeth	6 Oct 1827
Phoebe	1			Kent, England		Cincinnatus	17 May 1823
*died							
Ross	19	M	Tailor	Scotland	United States	Tom	2 Jul 1827
Sarah	48	F	None	England	Rhode Island	Cincinnatus	16 Apr 1824
Spencer	2	M				Comet	24 Dec 1821
Spencer	35	M	Farmer	England	U. States	Comet	24 Dec 1821
Stephn.	23	M	Mariner	N. York	U. States	Dispatch	22 Mar 1822
Stewart	73	M	Planter	England	England	Tontine	1 Jun 1826
Tarquina, Miss	20	F	None	United States	United States	Sally	26 Jun 1822
Thomas	43		Farmer	Kent, England		Cincinnatus	17 May 1823

NAMES OF PASSENGERS	AGE	SEX	OCCUPATIONS	COUNTRY TO WHICH THEY BELONG	COUNTRY THEY INTEND TO INHABIT	SHIPS/DATES OF ARRIVAL	
WEST (cont'd)							
Thos.	28	M	Merchant	U. States	U. States	South Carolina Packet	28 Apr 1823
William	14 10/12	M	None	Ireland	U.S. of America	Hamilton	18 Jul 1827
William	28	M	Miller	England	England	William Thompson	19 Aug 1829
William	47			Kent, England		Cincinnatus	17 May 1823
Wm.	21	M	Labourer	Bristol	U. States	Latona	7 Jul 1827
Wm.	22	M	Farmer	Rye, England	United States	William	21 May 1828
Wm.	35	M	Merchant	England	United States	Congress	21 Nov 1823
Wm., Junr.	1	M				Congress	21 Nov 1823
WESTALL, Ann	12	F	None	England	United States	Dalhouse Castle	6 Sep 1827
Benjn.	2	M	None	England	United States	Dalhouse Castle	6 Sep 1827
Jno.	14	M	None	England	United States	Dalhouse Castle	6 Sep 1827
Pheebe	35	F	None	England	United States	Dalhouse Castle	6 Sep 1827
Thomas	9	M	None	England	United States	Dalhouse Castle	6 Sep 1827
Wm.	4	M	None	England	United States	Dalhouse Castle	6 Sep 1827
Wm.	40	M	Printer	England	United States	Dalhouse Castle	6 Sep 1827
WESTCOTT, Jas.	22	M	Mechanic	Rhode Island	U. States	Columbia	24 Mar 1823
WESTE..., Alexander	...1	M	Merchant	Great Britain	Great Britain	Ann Maria	17 Apr 1827
Frederick	1...	M	Child	Great Britain	Great Britain	Ann Maria	17 Apr 1827
William	7	M	Child	Great Britain	Great Britain	Ann Maria	17 Apr 1827
WESTELL, James	21	M	None	Great Britain	United States	Hannibal	12 Oct 1829
WESTEN, George	32	M	Ship Master	United States	United States	Maria Theresa	13 Apr 1822
WESTERMAN,							
Elizabeth	5/12	F	his family [Johannus]	Germany	Pensylvania	Isabella	15 Sep 1828
Johannus	48	M	Farmer	Germany	Pensylvania	Isabella	15 Sep 1828
John Heny	31	M	Labourer	Germany	United States	Constitution	2 Aug 1826
Johnnas	10	M	his family [Johannus]	Germany	Pensylvania	Isabella	15 Sep 1828
Magdelene	38	F	his family [Johannus]	Germany	Pensylvania	Isabella	15 Sep 1828
WESTERN, Ann	39	F				Acosta	28 Jul 1823
Caroline	13	F				Acosta	28 Jul 1823
Elinor	7	F				Acosta	28 Jul 1823
Eliza	9	F				Acosta	28 Jul 1823
Frances	17	F				Acosta	28 Jul 1823
Hansley	9/12	M				Acosta	28 Jul 1823
Hy. M.	35	M	Lawyer	U. States	U. States	Indian Queen	11 Mar 1826
Jesse	23	M	Farmer	U. Kingdom of Great Britain	United States	Cambria	7 May 1828
Matilda	5	F				Acosta	28 Jul 1823
Samuel	18	M				Acosta	28 Jul 1823
Samuel	41	M	Farmer			Acosta	28 Jul 1823
T. G., Esqr.	35	M	Gentn.	England	England	Acasta	3 Apr 1826
Thomas	15	M				Acosta	28 Jul 1823
Winifred	3	M				Acosta	28 Jul 1823
WESTERNEN, Amelia	5	F				Splendid	14 Aug 1829
Eliz.	22	M				Splendid	14 Aug 1829
Eliza	20					Splendid	14 Aug 1829
George	3	F				Splendid	14 Aug 1829
Joseph	44		Cotton Spinner			Splendid	14 Aug 1829
Lander	13	F				Splendid	14 Aug 1829
Martha	7	F				Splendid	14 Aug 1829
Sarah	45	F	Wife			Splendid	14 Aug 1829
Susannah	11	F				Splendid	14 Aug 1829
Wm.	25	M				Splendid	14 Aug 1829
WESTFELDT, Charles	35	M	Merchant	Sweden	Charleston, U.S.	Florida	2 Oct 1828
Charles	38	M	Merchant	...adland	...adland	Canada	13 Oct 1825
Charles	38		Merchant	Sweaden	America	Florida	14 Oct 1829
Chas.	27	M	Merchant	...	United States	Cortes	18 Oct 1820
WESTFIELD, Fred.	9	M		England	United States	Acasta	25 Sep 1827
James	10	M	None	Great Brittain	U. States	Florenzo	20 Mar 1827
John	24	M	Piano forte Maker	Gt. Britain		Corinthian	27 Oct 1829
WESTHBERCH,							
Joseph	23 2/12	M	Gentleman	United St. Ama.	Philadelphia	Chelsea	16 May 1828
WESTHOFF,							
Maximilian Henry	25 6/12	M	Mercht.	Holland	Holland	Aurora	19 Mar 1828

NAMES OF PASSENGERS	AGE	SEX	OCCUPATIONS	COUNTRY TO WHICH THEY BELONG	COUNTRY THEY INTEND TO INHABIT	SHIPS/DATES OF ARRIVAL	
WESTON, E.	29	M	Merchant	U. States	U. States	Eliza	14 Mar 1825
Henry	50	M	Merchant	U. States		Antioch	18 Aug 1829
J.	26	F	None	U. States		Queen Mab	24 Sep 1827
Jane	24	F	None	United States	United States	Don Quixote	12 Feb 1829
Jane	28	F	Gent	U. States	U. States	Charlemagne	19 Sep 1828
John	18	M	Farmer	England	U. States	Hercules	6 Jul 1827
Maria	18			U. States	U. States	Silvanus Jenkins	30 Nov 1827
T.	31	M	Gentleman	England	U. States	Milton	6 Dec 1825
W.	23	M	Farmer	Gt. Brittain	U. States	Robert Fulton	1 Nov 1822
Wm.	39	M	Wheelwright	Great Britain	United States	Mount Vernon	20 May 1822
WESTRICK, Peter	37	M	Farmer	Germany	U. States	United States	3 Sep 1828
WESTWARD, Josh.	18	M	Labourer	England	United States	Manhattan	11 Oct 1824
WETHELEN, Sarah	20	F	Servant	England	England	Tontine	1 Jun 1826
Alexr.	1	M	None	England	America	Meteor	21 Aug 1822
Amy	6	F	None	England	America	Meteor	21 Aug 1822
Ann	16	F	None	England	America	Meteor	21 Aug 1822
C.	5	F	None	England	America	Meteor	21 Aug 1822
Emily	3	F	None	England	America	Meteor	21 Aug 1822
Fountain	28	F	None	England	America	Meteor	21 Aug 1822
J.	13	M	None	England	America	Meteor	21 Aug 1822
J. G.	11	M	None	England	America	Meteor	21 Aug 1822
T. P.	14	M	None	England	America	Meteor	21 Aug 1822
W. F.	15	M	None	England	America	Meteor	21 Aug 1822
WETHERBEE, John, Mr.	38	M	Merchant	U. States	U. States	Hudson	10 Nov 1825
WETHERLEY, James D.	23	M	Merchant	United States	U. States	Saml. Smith	24 Jul 1826
WETHERSPOON,							
George	23	M	Merchant	Scotland	Breat Britain	Albion	7 Feb 1820
WETTER, Aug	18	M	Child	Switzerland	U. States	Bayard	5 Sep 1828
WEVER, James	18	M	Curier	England	United States	Jubilee	4 Mar 1829
WEYER, Peter	33		Merchant	Holland	U. States	Alfred	24 Jul 1828
WEYERHOST, Frederich	45	M	Musician	Germany	England	Lady Tompkins	21 May 1827
WEYERNAM, —, Mrs.	44	F		Curacoa	U. States	Hippomenes	29 Nov 1822
WEYMAN,							
Charles	23 10/12	M	Merchant	United States	United States	Manchester	12 Aug 1829
Chs. F.	22	M	Merchant	United States	U. States	York	7 Aug 1828
John	24	M	Merchant	United States	United States	St. Thomas	14 Aug 1828
John S.	23	M	Merchant	New York	New York	Secretary	10 Aug 1829
Robert H.	21	M	Merchant	United States	United States	William Byrnes	1 Dec 1824
WEYMAR, John S.	20	M	Merchant	Rhode Isalnd	U. States	Angenora	16 Jan 1827
WEYR, John	45		Shoemaker	England	United States	Mary	15 Jul 1822
WHADAN, Michael	40	M	Labourer	Great Brittan	U. States	John & Elizabeth	11 Dec 1826
Paterick	25	M	Labourer	Great Brittan	U. States	John & Elizabeth	11 Dec 1826
WHAILIN, John	21	M	Farmer	France	U. States	Great Britain	6 Sep 1828
WHALEN, Patrick	14	M	Boy	Ireland	United States	Dublin Packet	23 May 1828
WHALER, Isaac	30	M	Weaver	England	United States	Peru	23 May 1827
WHALIN, Catherine	18	F	Spinster	Great Britain	U. States	Robert Fulton	3 Dec 1827
WHALING, John	23	M	Labourer	Ireland	United States	General Marion	6 Oct 1828
WHALLEY, Ann	45	F	None	England	Pittsburgh	Orozimbo	8 Jun 1822
WHARF, S.	26	M	Mariner	United States	U. States	Hiram	8 Jul 1828
S.	26	M	Mariner	United States	United States	Hiram	8 Jul 1829
WHARTON, J.	29	F		Barbadoes	Barbadoes	Elias Burger	24 Jul 1820
N.	16	M		New York	New York	Reindeer	1 Nov 1824
WHATKINS, Margaret	28	F	Servant	U. States	United States	Vermont	26 Aug 1824
WHATLAN, Chas.	48	M	B...	Gt. Britain	United States	Crisis	13 Nov 1824
Francis S.	30	F	None	Gt. Britain	United States	Crisis	13 Nov 1824
WHATLEY, Charles	20		...	H...ton..., England	Great Britain	Frances Henrietta	31 May 1824
Ely	2		None	H...ton..., England	Great Britain	Frances Henrietta	31 May 1824
Hannah	4		None	H...ton..., England	Great Britain	Frances Henrietta	31 May 1824
Rebecca	32		None	H...ton..., England	Great Britain	Frances Henrietta	31 May 1824
WHATNEOUGH,							
William	29		Clothier	Great Britain	United States	Roman	10 Sep 1827
WHEALAN, Garrot	23 0/12	M	Labourer	Ireland	America	Enterprize	29 Jun 1827
John	24 1/12	M	Labourer	Ireland	America	Enterprize	29 Jun 1827

NAMES OF PASSENGERS	AGE	SEX	OCCUPATIONS	COUNTRY TO WHICH THEY BELONG	COUNTRY THEY INTEND TO INHABIT	SHIPS/DATES OF ARRIVAL	
WHEALAN (cont'd)							
Mary	24 2/12	F	Labourer	Ireland	America	Enterprize	29 Jun 1827
WHEATCROFT, W.	22	M	Farmer	Great Britain	United States	John	6 Oct 1820
WHEATEN, C., Capt.	23	M	U.S.A.	U.S.	U. States	Athenian	18 Oct 1826
WHEATLY, Margaret	20	F	None	Ireland	United States	Dalhouse Castle	8 May 1827
WHEATON, Alley	24	F	None	Ireland	U. States	Erin	5 Jul 1820
Eliza	30 4/12	F	Lady	U.S. America	U.S. America	Erie	19 Oct 1829
H. S., Revd.	32	M	Clergyman	United States	United States	Euphrates	15 Nov 1824
James	43	M	Sailor	England	America	Manhattan	21 Sep 1822
Michael	24	M	Chandler	Ireland	U. States	Erin	5 Jul 1820
Saml.	30	M	Seaman	United States	United States	Mercator	10 Oct 1823
WHEELAN, Joseph	26	M	Labourer	Ireland	New York	America	1 Aug 1828
Peter	26	M	Farmer	England	U.S.	Pacific	24 Oct 1828
WHEELAR, Ann	28	F		G. Britain	U. States	Nimrod	31 Jul 1828
Cathr.	0 9/12	F		G. Britain	U. States	Nimrod	31 Jul 1828
Charles	30	M	Labourer	G. Britain	U. States	Nimrod	31 Jul 1828
Thomas	5	M	Child	G. Britain	U. States	Nimrod	31 Jul 1828
WHEELE, Mark	11	M		England	United States	St. John	5 Oct 1829
Mark	46	M	Joiner	England	United States	St. John	5 Oct 1829
Martha	13	F		England	United States	St. John	5 Oct 1829
WHEELER, —, Capt.	30	M	Mariner	Phila.	Phila.	Leif	6 Sep 1824
—, Mrs.	58	F			U. States	Congress	21 Nov 1823
...t...	8	F		Ireland	United States	Thompson	12 Sep 1827
Amy	16	F	Lady	North Carolina	United States	St. Michael	21 Aug 1824
Ann	20	F		Ireland	United States	Thompson	12 Sep 1827
Ann	60	F	None	Great Britain	United States	Hannibal	12 Oct 1829
Carolilion	2	F	None	England	U.S.A.	Lima	6 Dec 1826
Catharine	40	F		Ireland	United States	Thompson	12 Sep 1827
Catherine	26	F	None	Great Britan	U. States	Ann Marria	6 Aug 1823
Charles	21	M	Servant	Great Britain	United States	Frances Henrietta	17 Sep 1827
Eli	26	M	Labourer	U. States	U. States	Virginia	26 May 1828
Eliza	12	F	Farmer	England	England	Criterion	29 May 1822
Eliza	36	F	Farmer	England	England	Criterion	29 May 1822
Elizabeth	4	F	None	Great Britan	U. States	Ann Marria	6 Aug 1823
George	12	M		Ireland	United States	Thompson	12 Sep 1827
George	23	M	Glass Blower	England	U.S.A.	Lima	6 Dec 1826
Henry	6	M	Farmer	England	England	Criterion	29 May 1822
Isaac P.	30	M	Mercht.	England	U. States	Brown	8 Aug 1825
Isabella	4	F	None	England	U.S.A.	Lima	6 Dec 1826
James	23	M	Taylor	G. Britain	New York	Brighton	26 Mar 1827
Jane	10	F		Ireland	United States	Thompson	12 Sep 1827
Jane	26	F	None	England	U.S.A.	Lima	6 Dec 1826
John	6	M	None	Great Britan	U. States	Ann Marria	6 Aug 1823
John	14	M	Farmer	England	England	Criterion	29 May 1822
John	28	M	P...ical Inst. Maker, etc.	England	New York	Thames	6 Oct 1820
John	40	M		Ireland	United States	Thompson	12 Sep 1827
Joseph	10					Agricola	1 Jul 1820
Margaret	4	F		Ireland	United States	Thompson	12 Sep 1827
Marry	1 2/12	F	None	Great Britan	U. States	Ann Marria	6 Aug 1823
Mary	14	F	Lady	North Carolina	United States	St. Michael	21 Aug 1824
Mary	39	F	Farmer	England	England	Criterion	29 May 1822
Mathew	2	M		Ireland	United States	Thompson	12 Sep 1827
Michael	32	M	Labourer	Ireland	United States	Jubilee	12 May 1828
Michael F.	35	M	Clergiman	U. States	N. York	Charlemagne	20 Aug 1829
Michl.	33	M	None	Great Britan	U. States	Ann Marria	6 Aug 1823
Rebecca	28	F	None	Great Britan	U. States	Ann Marria	6 Aug 1823
Richard	43					Agricola	1 Jul 1820
Richd.	29	M	None	Great Britan	U. States	Ann Marria	6 Aug 1823
Rose	17	F		Ireland	United States	Thompson	12 Sep 1827
Sarah	18					Agricola	1 Jul 1820
Simeon	6	M		Ireland	United States	Thompson	12 Sep 1827
Steph.	35	M	Mariner	U. States	U. States	Ospray	11 Apr 1825
Thomas	1	M	Farmer	England	England	Criterion	29 May 1822
Thos.	35	M	Mariner	U. States		General Brewer	9 Dec 1825
William	10	M	Farmer	England	England	Criterion	29 May 1822
William	20	M	None	Great Britain	United States	Hannibal	12 Oct 1829
Willm.	8/12	M	None	England	U.S.A.	Lima	6 Dec 1826

NAMES OF PASSENGERS	AGE	SEX	OCCUPATIONS	COUNTRY TO WHICH THEY BELONG	COUNTRY THEY INTEND TO INHABIT	SHIPS/DATES OF ARRIVAL	
WHEELER (cont'd)							
Wm.	56	M	Carpenter	England	U. States	Congress	21 Nov 1823
Wm., Junr.	16	M			U. States	Congress	21 Nov 1823
WHEELEY, John	30	M	Merchant	England	America	Manhattan	23 May 1822
WHEELING, Ann	19	F	Labourer	Ireland	U. States	Marcus	7 Apr 1825
Barney	6	M	Labourer	Ireland	U. States	Marcus	7 Apr 1825
Danel	24	M	Laborer or Spinster	Ireland	United States	Frances Miller	27 Jul 1827
Francis	1	M	Labourer	Ireland	U. States	Marcus	7 Apr 1825
John	28	M	Labourer	Ireland	U. States	Marcus	7 Apr 1825
Mary	24	F	Labourer	Ireland	U. States	Marcus	7 Apr 1825
WHEELOCK, Eliza	27	F	Lady	Boston	St. John, N.B.	Ann Maria	7 Aug 1826
WHEELROLER, Jno. M.	23	M	Labourer	Ge...	U. States	Pizarro	21 Oct 1825
WHELAN, Biddy	28	F		Ireland	America	Plutarch	18 Jul 1826
Honor	3	F		Ireland	America	Plutarch	18 Jul 1826
James	22	M	Farmer	Ireland	United States	Dublin Packet	9 Jul 1827
John	30 10/12	M	Farmer	Ireland	United States	Nimrod	28 Apr 1824
Joseph	20	M	Farmer	...st...	...	Frances Henrietta	30 Jun 1827
Judy	9	F		Ireland	America	Plutarch	18 Jul 1826
Martin	28	M	Labourer	Ireland	America	Plutarch	18 Jul 1826
Mary	1/4	F		Ireland	America	Plutarch	18 Jul 1826
Mary	26	F		Ireland	America	Plutarch	18 Jul 1826
Mick	28	M	Labourer	Ireland	America	Plutarch	18 Jul 1826
Patrick	24	M	Farmer	Ireland	United States	Lord Strangford	20 Jun 1826
WHELLAN, Timothy	20	M	Labourer	Great Britain	United States	William Dawson	18 Jun 1827
Wm.	24	F		Gt. Britain	United States	Penelope	9 Sep 1828
WHELLAR, Biddy	40	F		Ireland	United States	Thompson	12 Sep 1827
Jane	13	F		Ireland	United States	Thompson	12 Sep 1827
Joseph	3	M		Ireland	United States	Thompson	12 Sep 1827
Martin	40	M		Ireland	United States	Thompson	12 Sep 1827
Thomas	1	M		Ireland	United States	Thompson	12 Sep 1827
Wm.	12	M		Ireland	United States	Thompson	12 Sep 1827
WHELMAN, D.	48	M	Farmer	United States	United States	Seine	21 Oct 1822
Elizh.	38	F	Farmer	United States	United States	Seine	21 Oct 1822
Fa.	18	F	Farmer	United States	United States	Seine	21 Oct 1822
WHELON, Dnnis	25	M	Laborer	Ireland	America	Parrington	9 Jun 1827
WHELPLEY, A. C.	25	M	Gentleman	U. States	U. States	St. Michaels	25 Apr 1825
Albert O.	3	F	Child	State New York	United States	Sarah G.	15 Aug 1827
Elizabeth	22	F	Lady	U. States	U. States	St. Michaels	25 Apr 1825
Elizabeth	25	F	Lady	State New York	United States	Sarah G.	15 Aug 1827
WHETE, Smith	17	M	Clerk	England	New York	Ann Eliza Jane	3 Apr 1824
WHETTEN, Wm.	20	M	Merchant	U. States	U. States	William & John	21 Aug 1822
WHETTON, Wm.	21	M	Merchant	N. York	U. States	Bordeaux	9 Dec 1823
WHEUB, Josseff	31	M	Baker	Germany	U.S.A.	Robert Wilson	2 Dec 1828
WHIDDAN, Wm.	22	M	Mariner	U. States	U. States	Sussex	9 Mar 1827
WHILE, Mary	20	F		United States		Britannia	20 Jun 1827
WHILEY, Ann	20	F	None	Great Britain	United States	John	6 Oct 1820
WHILLDIN, W.	20	M	Druggist	U. States	U. States	Jane	13 Dec 1824
WHILSON, John	20	M	Draper	England	America	Farmer	4 Aug 1825
WHIMPLE, Richd. P.	21	M	Labourer	England	United States	Nestor	25 Jul 1823
WHIMS, Martin	17	M	Stonemason	Ireland	U. States	Virginia	20 Jun 1825
Michael	12 3/12	M	Stonemason	Ireland	U. States	Virginia	20 Jun 1825
Patrick	12	M				Superb	18 Jul 1820
Patrick	17	M	Stonemason	Ireland	U. States	Virginia	20 Jun 1825
WHISTLER, Charles	36	M	Coach Proprietor	Gt. Britain		Corinthian	27 Oct 1829
George	26	M	Farmer	Gt. Britain		Corinthian	27 Oct 1829
WHISTON, Joseph	19	M	Farmer	England	Ohio	Governor Fenner	23 Jul 1829
WHITACKER, Robert, Mr.	23		Iron Roler Maker	England		Hercules	19 Jun 1821
WHITACRE, Ths.	42	M	Weaver	England	U. States	Alexander Mansfield	9 Jul 1827
William	44	M	Labourer	England	New York	Lima	5 Aug 1829
WHITAKAR, William	29	M	Weaver	England	New York	Colossus	2 Oct 1827
WHITAKER, Elisabeth	45	F		Great Britain	United States	Mary Howland	19 Jul 1827
Hannah	20	F	None	England	America	Cincinnatus	19 Oct 1826
John	3	M	None	England	America	Cincinnatus	19 Oct 1826
John	15	M		Great Brittian	United States	Carolina Augusta	2 Dec 1828

NAMES OF PASSENGERS	AGE	SEX	OCCUPATIONS	COUNTRY TO WHICH THEY BELONG	COUNTRY THEY INTEND TO INHABIT	SHIPS/DATES OF ARRIVAL
WHITAKER (cont'd)						
John	34	M	Dyer & woollen Manufacturer	England	United States	Robert Edwards 3 Oct 1829
Luke	2	M		Great Britain	United States	Mary Howland 19 Jul 1827
Martha	27 6/12	F	Wife	England	United States	Robert Edwards 3 Oct 1829
Mary	36	F		Great Brittian	United States	Carolina Augusta 2 Dec 1828
Robert	32	M	Farmer	Great Britan	Great Britan	United States 21 May 1827
Thomas	1	M	None	England	America	Cincinnatus 19 Oct 1826
WHITALL, Jos. E.	23	M	Merchant	Philada.	U. States	China 5 Apr 1822
Joseph E.	24	M	Merchant	United States	United States	Superior 21 May 1823
Joseph E.	26	M	Merchant	U. States	U. States	Splendid 30 May 1825
WHITALLS, Jos. E.	26	M	Merchant	United States	U. States	Superior 20 Apr 1824
WHITCROFT, Ann	5/12	F	None	England	Pennsylvania	Indian Chief 16 Aug 1822
Catherine	42	F	None	England	Pennsylvania	Indian Chief 16 Aug 1822
Ellen	3	F	None	England	Pennsylvania	Indian Chief 16 Aug 1822
George	9	M	None	England	Pennsylvania	Indian Chief 16 Aug 1822
John	14	M	None	England	Pennsylvania	Indian Chief 16 Aug 1822
Samuel	12	M	None	England	Pennsylvania	Indian Chief 16 Aug 1822
WHITE, —, Mrs.	21	F		G. Britain	U. States	Dalthousie Castle 2 Jan 1827
...	18	M	Weaver	Ireland	United States	Neury 27 Jan 1827
Achisa	14	F	...	Ireland	United States	Carolina Ann 24 Oct 1825
Alex.	34	M	Tailor	Scotland	United States	Camillus 27 Oct 1829
Alexander	7	M	...	Ireland	United States	Carolina Ann 24 Oct 1825
Alexander	12	M				Imperial 19 Jul 1820
Alexander	25	M	Merchant	Scotland	United States	Friends 7 Jul 1827
Alexr.	39		Weaver	Great Britain	United States	Camillus 12 Sep 1827
Ann	20	F		Ireland	United States	Nancey 8 Jun 1822
Ann	20	F		England	U. States	Emulous 22 Aug 1828
Anna	8	F		Ireland		L. M. Pelham 12 May 1823
Anne	6	F	None	Ireland	New York	America 1 Aug 1828
B.	23	M	Labourer	Ireland	United States	Princess Charlotte 6 Oct 1827
Barbara B.	40	F	Wife	England	United States	Robert Edwards 3 Oct 1829
Bickly	4	F		Ireland		L. M. Pelham 12 May 1823
Bridget	25	F	Wife	Ireland	New York	Louisa 20 Jul 1826
Bridget	36	F		Ireland		L. M. Pelham 12 May 1823
Catharine	13			Ireland	United States	Robert Burns 30 May 1823
Charles	4	M		G. Britain	U. States	Dalthousie Castle 2 Jan 1827
Charles	11	M		Great Britain	United States	Samuel Wright 12 Oct 1829
Charles	12	M		England	U. States	Emulous 22 Aug 1828
Charles	26	M	Clerk	Gt. Britain	United States	Neptune 23 Jan 1826
Charlotte	23	F	Farmer, Labourer or Spinster	Ireland	U. States	Meteor 4 Oct 1827
Charlotte	24	F		Great Britain	U.S. of America	Gratitude 3 Oct 1829
Chas.	30	M	Laborer	Ireland	United States	Trio 13 Jun 1827
David	41	M	Farmer	Balgadia, Cortwick [Parish], Kinross [County]	New York	Hero 19 May 1828
*to follow their occupation						
David	60	M				Imperial 19 Jul 1820
Edward	26	M	Farmer	Ireland		L. M. Pelham 12 May 1823
Edward	32	M	Shoemaker	England	Ohio	Cortes 16 Jul 1827
Elinor	4	F		England	U. States	Emulous 22 Aug 1828
Elisabeth	16	F		England	U. States	Emulous 22 Aug 1828
Eliz.	25	F		Great Britain	United States	Ann 22 Dec 1821
Eliza	37	F	None	England	United States	Hercules 24 Oct 1821
Eliza, Jr.	8	F	None	England	United States	Hercules 24 Oct 1821
Elizabeth	18	F	None	Great Britain	United States	Aurora 5 Sep 1826
Elizth.	21	F	None	England		Marchioness 13 May 1828
Ellen	5	F	None	Scotland	America	Minerva 8 Oct 1824
Ellen	7	F	None	Ireland	U. States	Hector 18 Apr 1825
Ellen	12	F		Ireland		L. M. Pelham 12 May 1823
Ellen	16	F	Spinster	Ireland	United States	Wilson 6 Jun 1828
Ellin	17	F	None	Scotland	America	Minerva 8 Oct 1824
Esther	10	M				Imperial 19 Jul 1820
Francis	30	M	Farmer	Ireland	U. States	Dickinson 30 Jul 1825
Fredrick	49	M	Merchant	Great Britan	Great Britan	Columbia 11 Apr 1822

NAMES OF PASSENGERS	AGE	SEX	OCCUPATIONS	COUNTRY TO WHICH THEY BELONG	COUNTRY THEY INTEND TO INHABIT	SHIPS/DATES OF ARRIVAL
WHITE (cont'd)						
Geo.	26	M		G. Britain	U. States	Dalhouse Castle 12 Sep 1828
George	3	M	None	England	United States	Hercules 24 Oct 1821
George	13	M	Weaver	Ireland	United States	Neury 27 Jan 1827
George	20	M	Writer	Ireland	United States	Asia 29 Jul 1829
George	40		Weaver			Zamoa 5 Nov 1828
George	65		Seaman	Yarmouth, E.	England	Packet 27 Aug 1822
Hannah	26	F		G. Britain	U. States	Dalthousie Castle 2 Jan 1827
Hannah	27	F		United States		London 29 Apr 1824
Henry	10	M		England	U. States	Emulous 22 Aug 1828
Henry	25	M	Farmer	Sea Bridge, Staff.	New York	Ann Maria 24 Feb 1824
Henry	32	M	Farmer	Great Britain	U.S. of America	Gratitude 3 Oct 1829
Jacob	8	M		England	U. States	Emulous 22 Aug 1828
James	5	M	None	England	United States	Hercules 24 Oct 1821
James	8	M				Imperial 19 Jul 1820
James	16	M	Farmer	Ireland		L. M. Pelham 12 May 1823
James	17	M	...	Ireland	United States	Carolina Ann 24 Oct 1825
James	18	M	Labourer	Scotland	America	Concord 4 Jun 1821
James	23	M	Papermaker	Great Britain	United States	Ann 22 Dec 1821
James	26	M	Farmer	Great Brittain	United States	United States 16 Feb 1827
James	29	M	Teacher	Scotland	America	Minerva 8 Oct 1824
James	30	M	Farmer	Great Britain	United States	Grecian 24 Sep 1828
James	32		Merchant	Scotland	Canada	Venus 12 Jul 1824
James	38	M	Weaver	Scotland	New York	Joseph Hume 26 Oct 1829
James, Jr.	30	M	Merchant		U. States	Ductile 23 Nov 1824
James B.	14 11/12	M	Son	England	United States	Robert Edwards 3 Oct 1829
Jane	1	F	None	Scotland	America	Minerva 8 Oct 1824
Jane	11	F	...	Ireland	United States	Lima 19 Jun 1824
Janet	3	F	None	Scotland	America	Minerva 8 Oct 1824
Janet	26	F	None	Scotland	America	Minerva 8 Oct 1824
Jas.	25	M	Weaver	Great Britain	United States	Atlantic 8 Dec 1827
Jas. C.	45	M	Mariner	Great Britain	Great Britain	Nestor 6 Jul 1821
Jno.	12	M	Clerk	Ireland	U. States	Hibernia 29 Nov 1821
John	...	M	...	Ireland	United States	Carolina Ann 24 Oct 1825
John	...	M	...	Ireland	United States	Carolina Ann 24 Oct 1825
John	0	M		America	U. States	Venus 1 Apr 1828
John	1 1/2	M	None	Ireland	New York	America 1 Aug 1828
John	4			Ireland	United States	Geo. Canning 5 Jun 1828
John	14	M	Gentleman	Scotland	U. States	Camillus 29 Jan 1829
John	15	M	None	Ireland	United States	Jubilee 13 Jul 1829
John	18	M	Merchant	N. York	N. York	Remittance 2 Aug 1825
John	19	M		England	U. States	Emulous 22 Aug 1828
John	21	M	Shoemaker			Hector 11 Sep 1820
John	23	M	Carpenter	United States	United States	Henrietta 19 Oct 1825
John	23	M	...	Wexford	...	Frances Henrietta 30 Jun 1827
John	24	M	Shoemaker	England	Ohio	Cortes 16 Jul 1827
John	24	M	Merchant	Great Britain	United States	Jean 17 Aug 1827
John	25	M	Labourer	America	America	Josephine 8 Jan 1827
John	26		Farmer	Ireland		Westmoreland 1 Aug 1826
John	27	M	Merchant	England	England	Hope 15 Oct 1821
John	28	M	None	Ireland	U. States	Criterion 23 May 1826
John	28	M	Shoe Maker	G. Britain	U. States	Dalthousie Castle 2 Jan 1827
John	28	M	Baker	Scotland		Zamoa 5 Nov 1828
John	28	M	School Master	Scotland	New York	Joseph Hume 26 Oct 1829
John	29	M	Clerk	England	United States	Dublin Packet 6 Dec 1827
John	30	M	Labourer	Great Brittain	United States	Active 12 Sep 1828
John	32	M	Merchant	Ireland	United States	Clothier 22 Nov 1827
John	37	M	Mariner	U. States	U. States	Hope 29 Dec 1821
John	45	M	Weaver	Great Britain	New York	Superior 5 Sep 1827
John	45	M	Labourer	Ireland	United States	Wilson 6 Jun 1828
John, Revr.	45	M	Merchant	Barbados	Supposition is he will return	Superb 7 Jul 1823
John B.	10	M	Mariner	Ireland		L. M. Pelham 12 May 1823
Jonathan	24	M	Tailor	United States	United States	Gertrude 19 May 1826
Leah	33			Ireland	United States	Robert Burns 30 May 1823

NAMES OF PASSENGERS	AGE	SEX	OCCUPATIONS	COUNTRY TO WHICH THEY BELONG	COUNTRY THEY INTEND TO INHABIT	SHIPS/DATES OF ARRIVAL	
WHITE (cont'd)							
Leonhard	1	M		England	U. States	Emulous	22 Aug 1828
Louisa	2	F		G. Britain	U. States	Dalthousie Castle	2 Jan 1827
Lucy	28	F	Servant	England	U. States	New York	11 Jul 1823
Luke	17	M	Mariner	America	Camden	Rachel Ann	13 Mar 1829
M.	65	M	Gentleman	England	U. States	Signal	5 Oct 1825
Margaret	17	F		Ireland	Virginia	Carolina Ann	15 Oct 1824
Margaret	40	F				Imperial	19 Jul 1820
Margaret, 2d.	4	F				Imperial	19 Jul 1820
Margt.	14	F		England	U. States	Emulous	22 Aug 1828
Margt.	40	F		England	U. States	Emulous	22 Aug 1828
Maria	27	F	Wife	England	America	Nimrod	1 Dec 1827
Martha	15	F				Imperial	19 Jul 1820
Mary	1			Ireland	United States	Geo. Canning	5 Jun 1828
Mary	4	F	None	England	United States	Jubilee	13 Jul 1829
Mary	20	F		Ireland		L. M. Pelham	12 May 1823
Mary	21	F	Wife	Ireland	United States	Sylvester Healy	11 May 1825
Mary	22	F	None	Wexford	...	Frances Henrietta	30 Jun 1827
Mary	25	F		England	United States	Ganges	10 May 1828
Mary	28	F	Spinster	Ireland	U. States	Columbia	20 Jul 1825
Mary	30	F	None	Ireland	New York	America	1 Aug 1828
Mary	42	F	None	Great Britain	New York	Superior	5 Sep 1827
Mary	60	F		England	United States	Ganges	10 May 1828
Mary Ann	2	F		Ireland		L. M. Pelham	12 May 1823
Mary Ann	4	F		Great Britain	U.S. of America	Gratitude	3 Oct 1829
Mary Ann B.	7 1/12	F	daughter	England	United States	Robert Edwards	3 Oct 1829
Mary J.	19	F	None	England	United States	Silas Richards	3 Apr 1826
Mary Jane	2	F	Farmer, Labourer or Spinster	Ireland	U. States	Meteor	4 Oct 1827
Matilda	1/2	F	Farmer, Labourer or Spinster	Ireland	U. States	Meteor	4 Oct 1827
Mattw.		M	Farmer	Ireland	U. States	Edward	15 Jul 1825
Micael	55	M	Planter	G. Britain		Aurora	15 Sep 1823
Michael	3	M	None	Ireland	New York	America	1 Aug 1828
Michael	47	M	Merchant	St. Thomas	New York	St. Pierre	16 Oct 1827
Michl.	22	M		Great Britain	New York	Philetus	21 Jul 1827
Molly	30	F	None	England	United States	Jubilee	13 Jul 1829
Morris	23	M	Farmer	England	United States	Ganges	10 May 1828
Nancy	6	F				Imperial	19 Jul 1820
Nathanie	37	M	Merchant	Great Britan	United States	Silvanus Jenkins	10 Mar 1827
Ncs.	55			Ireland	United States	Geo. Canning	5 Jun 1828
Pat	14	M	Farmer	Ireland		L. M. Pelham	12 May 1823
Patrick	8			Ireland	United States	Geo. Canning	5 Jun 1828
Patrick	25	M	Weaver	Ireland	New York	Louisa	20 Jul 1826
Patrick	40	M	None	Ireland	New York	America	1 Aug 1828
Perla	30	F	Servant	Denmark	U. States	Catherine	3 Jul 1820
Peter	11	M	None	England	United States	Hercules	24 Oct 1821
Pheebe	2 6/12			United States		London	29 Apr 1824
Philip	1 1/12	M	None	England		Marchioness	13 May 1828
Richard	26	M	Gentn.	G.B.	G.B.	George Canning	20 Jan 1829
Richard	30	M	Carpenter	England	United States	Jubilee	13 Jul 1829
Richard	35	M	Merchant	Gt. Britan	Gt. Britan	Canada	8 Jun 1826
Robert	24	M		Ireland	United States	Nancey	8 Jun 1822
Robert	31	M	Merchant	United States		London	29 Apr 1824
Robt. C.	6/12	M		England		London	29 Apr 1824
Sally	20	F				Imperial	19 Jul 1820
Saml.	25	M	Merchant	England		Marchioness	13 May 1828
Samuel	2	M		Great Brittain	United States	Active	12 Sep 1828
Sarah	14	F	...	Ireland	United States	Carolina Ann	24 Oct 1825
Sarah	20	F	Servant	Ireland	United States	Neury	27 Jan 1827
Sarah	22	F		Great Brittain	United States	Active	12 Sep 1828
*Died on the Passage							
Sarah	24	F	Lady	Great Britian	U. States	Hudson	12 Mar 1824
Sarah	26	F		Ireland	United States	Clothier	22 Nov 1827
Sarah	28	F	None	Great Britain	New York	Superior	5 Sep 1827
Sarah	60	F		Great Britain	United States	Samuel Wright	12 Oct 1829
Sophia	28	F	None	Great Brittan	U. States	Gem	26 Jul 1827

NAMES OF PASSENGERS	AGE	SEX	OCCUPATIONS	COUNTRY TO WHICH THEY BELONG	COUNTRY THEY INTEND TO INHABIT	SHIPS/DATES OF ARRIVAL	
WHITE (cont'd)							
T.	18	M	Labourer	Ireland	United States	Princess Charlotte	6 Oct 1827
T. Warner	35	M	Merchant	U. States	U. States	Tobasco	7 Nov 1827
Thady.	6			Ireland	United States	Geo. Canning	5 Jun 1828
Thomas	17	M		England	U. States	Emulous	22 Aug 1828
Thomas	20	M	Farmer	Britain	America	Camillus	9 Oct 1820
Thomas	23	M	Merchant	Charleston	U. States	Susannah	13 Jul 1824
Thomas	42	M	Captain, Officers & crew of the Brig George of New York (wrecked at Fayal)	U.S. America	U.S.A.	Gallego	13 Mar 1829
Thomas	44	M	Paper Maker	Great Britain	United States	Samuel Wright	12 Oct 1829
Thomas D., Capt.	26	M	Shipmaster	Nova Scotia	Nova Scotia	Hopes Delight	31 May 1828
Thos.	23	M	Farmer	Great Britian	U. States	Pallas	17 Aug 1824
Thos.	30	M	Farmer	Ireland	U. States	Hector	18 Apr 1825
Thos. W.	40	M	Merchant	U. States	U. States	Sea Nymph	7 Jul 1827
William						Baltic	20 Aug 1821
William	7	M	None	England	United States	Jubilee	13 Jul 1829
William	14	M		Great Britain	United States	Samuel Wright	12 Oct 1829
William	20	M	Farmer	England	United States	Concordia	25 Aug 1827
William	20 3/12	M	Gardner	England	United States	Nimrod	28 Apr 1824
William	22	M	Weaver	Ireland	United States	Sylvester Healy	11 May 1825
William	22	M		England	U. States	Emulous	22 Aug 1828
William	25		Farmer			Rufus King	7 Aug 1820
William	30	M	Mariner	Charleston	New York	Baltic	20 Aug 1821
William	58	M	Fisherman	England	U. States	Emulous	22 Aug 1828
Willm. B.	2 10/12	M	Son	England	United States	Robert Edwards	3 Oct 1829
Willm. Boulter	39	M	Weaver	England	United States	Robert Edwards	3 Oct 1829
Wm.	6	M		Ireland		L. M. Pelham	12 May 1823
Wm.	21	M	Shoe Maker			Hanford	17 Jul 1828
Wm.	25	M	Optician	Great Brittan	U. States	Gem	26 Jul 1827
Wm.	30	M	Gent.	Great Brittan	U. States	Hudson	12 Mar 1824
Wm.	30	M	Merchant	Ireland	Virginia	Carolina Ann	15 Oct 1824
Wm.	35		Horticulturist	England		Corinthian	11 Mar 1829
Wm.	45		Weaver	Ireland	United States	Geo. Canning	5 Jun 1828
Wm. S., Jr.	23	M	Merchant	U. States	U. States	Sophia & Eliza	13 Jun 1828
WHITEBREAD, David	18		Stone Mason	England	United States	Corinthian	7 Jul 1829
William	16		Stone Mason	England	United States	Corinthian	7 Jul 1829
WHITEFIELD, J.	27	M	Macanick	England	Cuba	Tontine	9 Jun 1827
James	20	M	Collier	Scotland	United States	Camillus	27 Oct 1829
Joseph	22	M	Collier	Scotland	United States	Camillus	27 Oct 1829
WHITEFORCE, Thos.	22	M		Ireland	U. States	Balaena	29 Apr 1825
WHITEFORDE, John	30	M	Labourer	Antrim	United States	Carolina Ann	11 Jun 1824
WHITEHAM, Joseph	27		Worsted Maker	England		Mount Vernon	26 Aug 1820
WHITEHEAD, A.	28	M	Lawyer	England	America	Corinthian	1 Sep 1827
A.	59	F	Wife	England	America	Corinthian	1 Sep 1827
Andrew	17 8/12	M	None	England	New York	Concordia	12 Oct 1826
Atheo	9 5/12	M	None	England	New York	Concordia	12 Oct 1826
Betty	18	F	None	England	U. States	Thomas Ritchie	2 Jul 1827
Charlotte	3	F		England	U. States	Unity	5 Sep 1828
Charlotte	30	F	Seamstress	England	U. States	Atlantic	26 Aug 1820
Charlotte	30	F		England	U. States	Unity	5 Sep 1828
E.	10	F		England	America	Corinthian	1 Sep 1827
Eliza	2	F		England	U. States	Unity	5 Sep 1828
Elizabeth	11	F	Cotton Spinner	England	America	Manhattan	21 Sep 1822
Elizabeth	14	F		England	America	Mary Lord	26 Oct 1829
Fanny	23	F	Weaver	Great Britain	U.S. of America	Gratitude	3 Oct 1829
H.	50	M	Labourer	G. Britain	U. States	St. George	7 Jun 1828
James	13	M	Cotton Spinner	England	America	Manhattan	21 Sep 1822
James	24	M	Clerk	Great Britain	U.S. of America	Gratitude	3 Oct 1829
James	32	M	Farmer	Ireland	United States	Lord Wellington	14 Nov 1827
Jas.	23	M	Labourer	England	U. States	Thomas Ritchie	2 Jul 1827
Jeremiah	6	M		England	U. States	Unity	5 Sep 1828
Jno.	30	M	Farmer	Great Britain	New York	Superior	5 Sep 1827
John	8	M		England	U. States	Unity	5 Sep 1828
John	13 4/12	M	None	England	New York	Concordia	12 Oct 1826

NAMES OF PASSENGERS	AGE	SEX	OCCUPATIONS	COUNTRY TO WHICH THEY BELONG	COUNTRY THEY INTEND TO INHABIT	SHIPS/DATES OF ARRIVAL	
WHITEHEAD (cont'd)							
John	30	M	Fisherman	England	U. States	Unity	5 Sep 1828
John	36	M	Seaman	U. States	U. States	Cobbosse Conte	18 Apr 1823
John	40	M	Schoolmaster	U. States	U. States	Nancy	19 Oct 1821
John	40	M	Shomaker	Manchester	United States	Nile	17 May 1827
John	42	M	Cotton Spinner	England	America	Manhattan	21 Sep 1822
John	44	M	Weaver	England	New York	Concordia	12 Oct 1826
Richd.	5	M		England	U. States	Unity	5 Sep 1828
Saml.	10 5/12	M	None	England	New York	Concordia	12 Oct 1826
Sarah	5	F	None	England	New York	Concordia	12 Oct 1826
Sarah	40 4/12	F	None	England	New York	Concordia	12 Oct 1826
Susan	7 7/12	F	None	England	New York	Concordia	12 Oct 1826
Thomas	20 2/12	M	None	England	New York	Concordia	12 Oct 1826
Thomas	35	M	Weaver	Great Britain	U.S. of America	Gratitude	3 Oct 1829
Thos.	28	M	Clothier	England	America	Birmingham	16 Oct 1826
W.	35	M	Mariner	Great Britain	United States	Nimrod	5 Apr 1821
William	35	M	Merchant	Scotland	United States	Natchez	22 Apr 1822
William	50	M	Weaver	England	America	Plutarch	18 Jul 1826
William	50 6/12	M	Farmer	Great Briton	United States	Mount Vernon	30 Dec 1828
Wm.	18	M	Labourer	England	U. States	Dalhouse	23 Mar 1829
Wm.	28	M	Merchant	England	United States	Minerva	25 Aug 1823
Wm.	28	M		England	United States	Hannibal	6 Sep 1824
Wm.	35	M	Merchant	U. States	U. States	Bengal	30 Jun 1823
WHITEHEARD, Calb	22	F	None	U. States	U. States	Canada	6 Jun 1825
WHITEHILL, Catharine	5			Scotland	United States	Camillus	3 May 1828
Isabella	35		Wife, Going to her husband	Scotland	United States	Camillus	3 May 1828
Wm.	7			Scotland	United States	Camillus	3 May 1828
WHITEHOUS, John	40	M	Master	U. States	U. States	Prince Leopold	2 Jul 1821
WHITEHOUSE, Thomas	28	M	...b...	...shire	U. States	Panthea	24 Mar 1825
WHITELAW, Mark	25	M	Saddler	Scotland	United States	Samuel Robertson	9 May 1827
WHITELOW, William	21 4/12	M	...	Great Britain	United States	Robert Fulton	18 May 1825
WHITELY, Edward	21	M	Labourer	Great Britain	United States	Ann Maria	9 Mar 1820
WHITEMAN, Alice	18	F	...		America	Ann	11 Apr 1821
Anna	10	F			America	Ann	11 Apr 1821
David	34	M	Engineer	England	England	Edward Quesnel	3 Jul 1829
John	8	M			America	Ann	11 Apr 1821
Mary	12	F			America	Ann	11 Apr 1821
Mary	40	F	...		America	Ann	11 Apr 1821
Rebecca	1	F			America	Ann	11 Apr 1821
Sarah	6	F			America	Ann	11 Apr 1821
Thomas	40	M	Maltster	England	America	Ann	2 Nov 1820
Thos.	4	M			America	Ann	11 Apr 1821
Wm.	22	M	...		America	Ann	11 Apr 1821
WHITEMORE, Wm.	26	M	Clerk	Derby Shire	America, New York	Washington	3 Mar 1828
WHITENCORT, Mathew	28	M	Merchant	U. States	U.S.	Adrianna	8 Aug 1822
WHITESIDE, George	7 6/12	M	Son of Spinster [Margaret]	Ireland	United States	James Monroe	26 Aug 1822
Isabella	22	F		England	United States	John Wells	22 May 1826
Joseph	3	M	Son of Spinster [Margaret]	Ireland	United States	James Monroe	26 Aug 1822
Margaret	40	F	Spinster	Ireland	United States	James Monroe	26 Aug 1822
Margt., Jr.	11 6/12	F	Daughter of Spinster [Margaret]	Ireland	United States	James Monroe	26 Aug 1822
Rebecca	6	F	Daughter of Spinster [Margaret]	Ireland	United States	James Monroe	26 Aug 1822
Robt.	9	M	Son of Spinster [Margaret]	Ireland	United States	James Monroe	26 Aug 1822
Wm.	13	M	Son of Margarett	Ireland	United States	James Monroe	26 Aug 1822
WHITFIELD, Jas.	47	M	Farmer	Great Britain	United States	Asia	14 Jul 1829
John	1	M	None	England	United States	Trident	18 Jul 1827
Margaret	21	F	None	England	United States	Trident	18 Jul 1827
Thomas	30	M	Labourer	England	England	Hudson	13 Jan 1827
William	22	M	Turner	England	America	Josephine	24 Jul 1826

NAMES OF PASSENGERS	AGE	SEX	OCCUPATIONS	COUNTRY TO WHICH THEY BELONG	COUNTRY THEY INTEND TO INHABIT	SHIPS/DATES OF ARRIVAL	
WHITFORD, Christopher	21	M	Miner	Great Britain	United States	Thomas Dickason	31 Jul 1829
David	24	M	Cordwainer	U. States	U. States	Eliza Jane	26 Oct 1829
Harriet	6/12	F		U. States	U. States	Eliza Jane	26 Oct 1829
Jno.	22	M	Miner	U. States	U. States	Martha	20 Jun 1825
Mary	21	F		U. States	U. States	Eliza Jane	26 Oct 1829
WHITHAM, Ann	26	F				Hercules	25 Sep 1820
John	35		Worsted Maker	England		Mount Vernon	26 Aug 1820
Sarah	5	F				Hercules	25 Sep 1820
Sebeca	2	F				Hercules	25 Sep 1820
William	3	M				Hercules	25 Sep 1820
William	25		Worsted Maker			Mount Vernon	26 Aug 1820
WHITHER, James	22	M	Weaver	G.B.	Massachusetts	Eliza Grant	29 Aug 1829
Sarah	22	F		G.B.	Massachusetts	Eliza Grant	29 Aug 1829
WHITHMAN, James	26	M	Labourer	England	America	Ann	2 Nov 1820
John	24	M	Labourer	England	America	Ann	2 Nov 1820
WHITING, Ann	14	F	Bricklayer	England	United States	Maria	12 May 1823
Ebenezer	5	M		England	United States	Maria	12 May 1823
Eward	40	M	Mariner	U. States	U. States	Prudence	8 Apr 1822
Geo.	31		Farmer	United States	United States	Hudson	18 Jun 1825
M. A.	25	F		U. States	U. States	Evelina	31 May 1825
Mary	3	F	Bricklayer	England	United States	Maria	12 May 1823
Mary	16	F	Bricklayer	England	United States	Maria	12 May 1823
P. S.	27	M	Merchant	United States	United States	Bunker Hill	16 Apr 1827
Robert	11	M		England	United States	Maria	12 May 1823
Samuel	13	M		England	United States	Maria	12 May 1823
Samuel	46	M	Bricklayer	England	United States	Maria	12 May 1823
Sarah	42	F	Bricklayer	England	United States	Maria	12 May 1823
W. J.	22	M	Merchant	U. States	U. States	Harriet	3 Mar 1828
WHITLAW, H.	21	M	Surgeon	Ireland	United States	Atlantic	21 Jul 1827
WHITLE, William	33	M	Tanner	York Shire	England	Helicon	3 Aug 1826
WHITLEY, Ann	22	F	Wool Sorter	Great Briton	Boston	Brighton	12 Jun 1826
Garrit	30	M	Labourer	Ireland	America	Erin	7 Nov 1821
John	29	M	Wool Sorter	Great Briton	Boston	Brighton	12 Jun 1826
WHITLOCK, John	27	M	Farmer	England	United States	William Howland	5 Jul 1821
WHITLOW, Grizil	16	F	None	Scotland	U. States	Magnet	22 Aug 1822
Jas.	13	M	None	Scotland	U. States	Magnet	22 Aug 1822
Jas.	52	M	Laborer	Scotland	U. States	Magnet	22 Aug 1822
Jean	16	F	None	Scotland	U. States	Magnet	22 Aug 1822
Jean	41	F	None	Scotland	U. States	Magnet	22 Aug 1822
John	11	M	None	Scotland	U. States	Magnet	22 Aug 1822
Walter	6	M	None	Scotland	U. States	Magnet	22 Aug 1822
Wm.	8	M	None	Scotland	U. States	Magnet	22 Aug 1822
WHITMAN,							
Amy Eleanor, Miss	18			London/ London	Susquehannah P	Venus	12 Apr 1821
Ann, Mrs.	47			London/ London	Susquehannah P	Venus	12 Apr 1821
C..., Master	13			London/ London	Susquehannah P	Venus	12 Apr 1821
Emma, Miss	15			London/ London	Susquehannah P	Venus	12 Apr 1821
Frederick	26	M	Tanner	Werdenburg	United States	Xenophon	2 Jun 1824
George	36	M	Butcher	Werdenburg	United States	Xenophon	2 Jun 1824
John, Jr.	23		Silk Manufacturer	London/ London	Susquehannah P	Venus	12 Apr 1821
John, Mr.	48		Silk Manufacturer	London/ London	Susquehannah P	Venus	12 Apr 1821
Samuel	26	M	Slater	Haddersfield		Aurora	8 Jul 1827
WHITMARSH, Stephen	26	M	Mariner	United States	United States	Jan	3 Nov 1821
WHITMON, Andrew	22	M	None	Scotland	U. States	Dalhouse	23 Mar 1829
WHITMORE, J. C.	34	M	Merchant	U. States	U. States	Agnes	6 Oct 1827
J. E.	33	M	Merchant	Maine	U. States	Apollo	10 Jul 1826
M., Miss	22	F	None	New York	U. States	Apollo	10 Jul 1826
R. T.	20	F		U. States	U. States	Elizabeth	3 Jun 1828
Saml.	23	M	Merchant	United States	United States	Good Hope	10 Mar 1828
WHITNALL, Charles	5 6/12	M	None	Great Briton	New York	Brighton	12 Jun 1826
Frances	32	F	None	Great Briton	New York	Brighton	12 Jun 1826

NAMES OF PASSENGERS	AGE	SEX	OCCUPATIONS	COUNTRY TO WHICH THEY BELONG	COUNTRY THEY INTEND TO INHABIT	SHIPS/DATES OF ARRIVAL	
WHITNALL (cont'd)							
Henry	7	M	None	Great Briton	New York	Brighton	12 Jun 1826
Robert	1	M	None	Great Briton	New York	Brighton	12 Jun 1826
Robt.	50	M	Merchant	G. Brittain	U. States	York	10 Dec 1825
William	2	M	None	Great Briton	New York	Brighton	12 Jun 1826
WHITNEY, —, Mr.	25	M	Merchant	United States	United States	Corinthian	29 Apr 1826
—, Mr.	40	M	Merchant	England	Barbadoes	Celia	15 Oct 1825
A.	32	M	Merchant	U. States		Edward Quesnel	13 Mar 1828
Elizabeth	27	F	None	Connecticut	U. States	Ann Maria	1 Jun 1824
Geo.	4	M	None	Connecticut	U. States	Ann Maria	1 Jun 1824
Henry	...	...	...	...	...	St. Michael	22 Sep 1824
J. H., Mr.	25	M	Mercht.	United States	United States	Manchester	6 Apr 1826
Lemuel	37	M	Merchant	Great Britain	Barbadoes	Spartan	5 May 1826
N.	1	M	None	Connecticut	U. States	Ann Maria	1 Jun 1824
Peter	26	M	Mariner	U. States	U. States	Lewis	17 Sep 1821
Polly	30	F	None	Connecticut	U. States	Ann Maria	1 Jun 1824
Richd. R.	22	M	Gentleman	U. States	U. States	Ambuscade	15 Dec 1824
Samuel	35	M	Merchant	Barbados	Supposition is he will return	Superb	7 Jul 1823
WHITNY, Maria	22 6/12	F		England	New London	Chelsea	16 May 1828
Mary	...	...	...	...	...	St. Michael	22 Sep 1824
WHITROFT, Elizabeth	5	F	None	England	Pennsylvania	Indian Chief	16 Aug 1822
Thomas	47	M	Farmer	England	Pennsylvania	Indian Chief	16 Aug 1822
William	10	M	None	England	Pennsylvania	Indian Chief	16 Aug 1822
WHITSFIELD, Alfred	20	M		Great B.	U. States	William Neilson	26 Jul 1828
WHITTACAR, John	20	M	Stone Mason	England	U.S.A.	Lima	6 Dec 1826
WHITTAKER, Catharine	37	F	None	Great Britain	United States	Hamilton	21 Nov 1826
Ellen	3	F	None	Great Britain	United States	Hamilton	21 Nov 1826
James	32	M	Farmer	Great Britain	United States	Hamilton	21 Nov 1826
John	29	M	Mechanic	Gt. Britain	United States	John & Elizabeth	25 Sep 1827
John	33	M	Labourer	England	U. States	Ayrshire	12 May 1828
Mary	1	F	None	Great Britain	United States	Hamilton	21 Nov 1826
Thos.	38		Stone Mason	Blackburn, England	Great Britain	Franklin	22 Jun 1827
WHITTAL, Thomas	24	M	Machine Maker	England	U.S. America	New Hampshire	28 Sep 1826
WHITTAN, A. E.	21	M	Surgeon	Ireland		Louisa	18 Apr 1827
Peter	30	M	Labourer	Dublin	Dublin	Howard Douglass	11 May 1827
WHITTEN, Jeremiah	20	M	Weaver	Ireland	New Jersey	Curler	7 Jul 1827
WHITTING, Nichs.	25	M	Merchant	Philadelphia	Port au Prince	Dart	15 Jul 1823
S., Jr.	28	M	Merchant	U. States	U. States	General Jackson	5 Feb 1827
WHITTINGHAM,							
Catherine	40	F	Spinster	Ireland	United States	St. Michaels	7 Jun 1827
Charles, Jur.	31	M	Merchant	G. Bt.	U. States	Canada	13 Feb 1826
Chas.	32	M	Manufacturer	England	England	Britannia	5 Nov 1828
Rd.	20	M	Seaman	New York	United States	Venus	8 Sep 1820
WHITTLE, —, Mrs.	64		Lady	England	United States	Acasta	16 Aug 1826
Ann	2	F		England	United States	William Howland	5 Jul 1821
Daniel	35	M	Farmer	England	United States	William Howland	5 Jul 1821
Eliza	8	F		England	United States	William Howland	5 Jul 1821
Elizabeth	30	F		England	United States	William Howland	5 Jul 1821
Hollis	19		Mechanist	England	United States	Acasta	16 Aug 1826
Jane	6	F		England	United States	William Howland	5 Jul 1821
John	24	M	Carpenter	England	U. States	Florida	13 Jan 1827
John	29	M	Cordwainer	England	America	Josephine	8 Jan 1827
Matilda	1 3/12	F		England	United States	William Howland	5 Jul 1821
Wm.	53		Mechanist	England	United States	Acasta	16 Aug 1826
WHITTLESEY, Jno.	14	M	Servant	N. York	U. States	United States	10 Jan 1825
Wm.	28	M	Mariner	U. States	U. States	Francis Jarvis	11 Aug 1825
WHITTOCK, Geo. W.	27	M	Merchant	U. States	U. States	Quill	26 Jun 1827
Samuel M.	38	M	Mariner	U. States	U. States	Quill	26 Jun 1827
WHITTTLELES, Geo.	26	M	Wool Dresser	Great Britain	United States	Samuel Wright	12 Oct 1829

NAMES OF PASSENGERS	AGE	SEX	OCCUPATIONS	COUNTRY TO WHICH THEY BELONG	COUNTRY THEY INTEND TO INHABIT	SHIPS/DATES OF ARRIVAL	
WHITTUM, John	15	M	Boy	America	America	Loire	7 Apr 1821
WHITUM, Jane	32	F	Lady	America	America	Loire	7 Apr 1821
William	10	M	Boy	America	America	Loire	7 Apr 1821
WHITWELL, Wm.	25	M	Merchant	U. States	U. States	Colossus	21 Apr 1827
WHITWORTH, Ann	7	F		Great Britain	United States	Dapper	21 Aug 1828
Ann	36	F		Great Britain	United States	Dapper	21 Aug 1828
David	9	M		Great Britain	United States	Dapper	21 Aug 1828
Isaac	24	M	...	Great Britain	United States	Baltic	24 Dec 1824
Rebecca	11	F		Great Britain	United States	Dapper	21 Aug 1828
Tabitha	2	F		Great Britain	United States	Dapper	21 Aug 1828
Wm.	41	M	Fuller	Great Britain	United States	Penelope	11 Jun 1827
WHOLESOME, David	30	M	Mercht.	Great Britiann	United States	Nestor	13 Mar 1824
WHULDON, —, Mrs.	45		Teacher	England	U. States	Bayard	19 Mar 1824
Wm.	35	M	Teacher	England	U. States	Bayard	19 Mar 1824
WHYERS, Joseph	22	M	Baker	England	United States	Comet	6 Mar 1823
WHYTAL, James	20	M	Shoemaker	Great Britain	U. States	Hope & Esther	12 Nov 1825
WHYTE, Anne	25	F	Wife	Ireland	United States	Trident	16 May 1826
Francis	22	M	Stone cutter	Ireland	United States	Trident	16 May 1826
James, Jr.	30	M	Merchant	Scotland	U. States	Ductile	23 Aug 1824
Thomas	22	M	Joiner	Scotland	United States	Culloden	17 May 1828
WICHELIN, Laur...	30		Boulanger [baker]	Suisse		Deux Ernest	29 Dec 1827
*son épouse & 1 enfant [his wife and one child]							
WICHRLIN, Laurent, his Wife & one child	30	M	Baker	Swisse	United States	Deux Ernest	29 Dec 1827
*landed at Lewiston, Delw.							
WICHT, —, Mr.	40			Germany	United States	Henri IV	14 Sep 1827
WICKEL, John	32		Servant	Germany		Bayard	10 Sep 1827
WICKEN, Caroline	1	M		England	America	Sarah	18 Aug 1829
Charles	4	M		England	America	Sarah	18 Aug 1829
Edward	8	M		England	America	Sarah	18 Aug 1829
Fredk.	9	M		England	America	Sarah	18 Aug 1829
George	11	M		England	America	Sarah	18 Aug 1829
George	37	M	Cooper	England	America	Sarah	18 Aug 1829
Henry	23	M	Baker	Germany	United States	Virginia	31 May 1828
Mary	6	M		England	America	Sarah	18 Aug 1829
Mary	38	M		England	America	Sarah	18 Aug 1829
William	12	M		England	America	Sarah	18 Aug 1829
WICKENS, Charlotte	20	F		Rye, England	United States	William	21 May 1828
John	23	M	Farmer	Rye, England	United States	William	21 May 1828
WICKS, Jane	24	F		G. Britain	U. States	George Clinton	10 Sep 1828
Thos.	24	M	Brick Layer	G. Britain	U. States	George Clinton	10 Sep 1828
WICKSALL, Gilbert	10	M		Scotland		Camillus	29 Jan 1829
Grace	28	F		Scotland		Camillus	29 Jan 1829
WICKSON, George, Mr.	23		Farmer	England		Hercules	19 Jun 1821
Samuel, Mr.	40	M	Farmer	England		Hercules	19 Jun 1821
WICKSTEAD, A. B.	34	M	Merchant	Canada	Canada	Silas Richards	9 Mar 1829
WICTERS, John H.	50	M	Shepherd	Bremen	Bremen	Francis	4 May 1826
WIDDONES, James	24	M	Farmer	Ireland	America	Carolina Ann	14 Feb 1825
Jane	17	F		Ireland	America	Carolina Ann	14 Feb 1825
WIDDOWS, Wm.	25	M		Great Britain	United States	Washington	9 Apr 1821
WIDEMAN, Marie	54	F		Bade	United States	Thetis	5 Jul 1821
WIDENER, C., Dr.	45	M	M.D.	Canada	Canada	Brighton	20 Aug 1825
WIDMER, Dinah	23	F	Servant	Great Britain	U. States	Columbia	22 Sep 1828
Felix	23	M	Butcher	Switzerland	United States	Montano	4 Nov 1823
Victor Joseph	44	M	Priest	Switzerland	United States	Montano	4 Nov 1823
WIDNEY, James, Mr.	44	M	Merchant	U.S.A.	New York	Huntress	11 Dec 1821
WIDOWS, Samuel	20	M	...	Ireland	United States	Carolina Ann	24 Oct 1825
WIDREES, Jacob	24	M	Shoemaker	Swis	United States	Iris	21 Sep 1821
WIDTH, A., Mr.	25	M	Musician	Bavaria		François I	19 Nov 1828
WIEDERHOLDT, Eliza, Miss	27	F		New York		Howard	6 Jul 1829
WIENER, H.	25	M	Farmer	Germany	U. States	Minerva	9 Jan 1827
WIENUS, Conrad	18	M	Labourer	Prussia		Constitution	20 Jun 1828
WIEPEN, Joseph	1	M	his family [Pierce]	Germany	United States	Wm. Osborne	16 Sep 1828
Maria	36	F	his family [Pierce]	Germany	United States	Wm. Osborne	16 Sep 1828
Pierce	8	M	his family [Pierce]	Germany	United States	Wm. Osborne	16 Sep 1828
Pierce	40	M	Joiner	Germany	United States	Wm. Osborne	16 Sep 1828

NAMES OF PASSENGERS	AGE	SEX	OCCUPATIONS	COUNTRY TO WHICH THEY BELONG	COUNTRY THEY INTEND TO INHABIT	SHIPS/DATES OF ARRIVAL	
WIER, H.	14	M	Labourer	Ireland	United States	Princess Charlotte	6 Oct 1827
Robert	32	M	Cork Cutter	Argyle (Tedland) Scotland	United States	Jean Hastie	27 Jul 1829
WIERICH, Charles	30		None	London, France	Great Britain	Frances Henrietta	31 May 1824
WIES, Charles	23	M	Farmer	Switzerland		Antioch	18 Aug 1829
WIESS, Michl.	23	M	Servant	France	America, U.N.S.	Great Britain	3 Aug 1829
WIESSER, Jh.	40			Suisse		Deux Ernest	29 Dec 1827
WIGAND, Charles	23	M	Cabinet Maker	Germany	United States	Francis	12 Jun 1826
WIGGIN, Benjamin	52	M	Merchant	U. States	U. States	Cortes	13 Aug 1825
Charlotte	40	F		U. States	U. States	Cortes	13 Aug 1825
Elen	20	F	Farmer	Ireland		Cuba	24 Jun 1822
Michael	25	M	Farmer	Ireland		Cuba	24 Jun 1822
WIGGINS, Chas.	18	M	Gentleman	St. Johns	St. Johns	Sarah Ann	11 Jan 1827
Elizabeth	49	F		Ireland	United States	Romulus	24 Jun 1826
G. J.	24		Merchant			Charlotte Corday	11 Sep 1820
James	11	M	Youth	Ireland	United States	Romulus	24 Jun 1826
John	31	M	Clerk	G.B.	U.S.	London	19 Dec 1823
Joseph	50	M	Farmer	Ireland	United States	Romulus	24 Jun 1826
WIGGLI, Germain	32	M	Blacksmith	Brattain		L'Esperance	6 Sep 1828
WIGHT, Christophe	50	M	Chandler	Ireland	America	Franklin	19 Nov 1828
David	18	M	Smith	G. Britain	U. States	Mary Howland	22 Sep 1828
Wm.	23	M	Cloth Dresser	Great Britain	United States	Washington	3 Sep 1827
WIGHTMAN, David	2	M	None	Scotland	United States	Mary & Susan	5 Aug 1828
Elisebeth	14	F	None	Scotland	United States	Mary & Susan	5 Aug 1828
James	10	M	None	Scotland	United States	Mary & Susan	5 Aug 1828
Janet	8	F	None	Scotland	United States	Mary & Susan	5 Aug 1828
John	16	M	Farmer	Scotland	United States	Mary & Susan	5 Aug 1828
Margaret	12	F	None	Scotland	United States	Mary & Susan	5 Aug 1828
Mary	5	F	None	Scotland	United States	Mary & Susan	5 Aug 1828
Robert	3	M	None	Scotland	United States	Mary & Susan	5 Aug 1828
Robert	35	M	Millright	Scotland	United States	Mary & Susan	5 Aug 1828
Sarah	42	F	None	Scotland	United States	Mary & Susan	5 Aug 1828
William	18	M	Farmer	Scotland	United States	Mary & Susan	5 Aug 1828
William	45	M	Farmer	Scotland	United States	Mary & Susan	5 Aug 1828
WIGLEY, Elias	21	M		Great Britain	United States	Ganges	8 Jul 1820
Eliza	3	F		Great Britain	United States	Ganges	8 Jul 1820
James	16	M	Dyer	U. States	U. States	United States	11 Sep 1828
James	24	M		Great Brittian	United States	Carolina Augusta	2 Dec 1828
Mary	27	F		Great Britain	United States	Ganges	8 Jul 1820
WIGNALL, H.	16	M	Brass Founder	G. Britain	G. Britain	Brittania	17 Jul 1828
WIGNON, Amazon	40	M	Merchant	U. States	U. States	Pedler	27 May 1825
WIGSZELL, Thos.	23	M	Engineer	With intention to become citizen		New York	18 Jul 1828
WILAR, Andreas	17	M	Agriculture	Wirtemburg	United States	Henri IV	14 Oct 1829
WILBER, N.	32	M	Mariner	U. States	U. States	To Vennier	19 Jul 1828
WILBERG, Jane	35	F		England	United States	John Wells	15 Jan 1827
WILBEY, Samuel	26	M	Farmer	England	Canada	Maria	3 Oct 1822
WILBUR, John W.	42	M	Merchant	United States	United States	Cambria	7 May 1828
John W., Junior	11	M	Son of [John W.]	United States	United States	Cambria	7 May 1828
WILBURG, Caroline	9	F		England	United States	John Wells	15 Jan 1827
WILBURN, J.	29	M	Farmer	England	U.S. States	Splendid	14 Aug 1829
WILCKINS, J. T.	26	M	Doct. Medicine	Bremen		Caesar	24 Aug 1829
WILCOCKS, William	30	M	Farmer	United States	U. States	Baltic	29 Jul 1829
*Died 17th July							
WILCOKS, James S.	40	M	Merchant	United States	United States	Otter	25 Feb 1822
WILCOLEFF, Chrisloff	32 7/12	M	Farmer	Germany	Germany	France	28 Mar 1829
WILCOX, Andrew	25	M	Weaver	Ireland	United States	Trident	30 Sep 1826
Fredk.	18	M	Seaman	England	U. States	Acasta	21 Jan 1825
George	36					Cincinnatus	29 Apr 1822
Rebecca	27					Cincinnatus	29 Apr 1822
William	22					Cincinnatus	29 Apr 1822
William	30	M	Farmer	England	U. States	Acasta	21 Oct 1825
William, Mr.	33	M	Gardner	England	Albany	Cortes	23 Nov 1827
WILCRICK, John	16	M	Farmer	Switzerland	U. States	Seine	30 Aug 1824

NAMES OF PASSENGERS	AGE	SEX	OCCUPATIONS	COUNTRY TO WHICH THEY BELONG	COUNTRY THEY INTEND TO INHABIT	SHIPS/DATES OF ARRIVAL
WILD, Abram	24	M	Farmer	England	United States	Aurelia 7 Jun 1826
Ann	26		None	England	New Jersey	Albion 11 Oct 1821
Gabriel	25	M	...	...	...	Sublime 6 Dec 1824
Geo.	2		None	England	New Jersey	Albion 11 Oct 1821
George	3	M		Yorkshire	Pennsylvania	Curler 7 Jul 1827
George	7	M		Great Britain	U.S. of America	Gratitude 3 Oct 1829
George	29	M	Farmer	Oldham	United States	Dalhousie Castle 27 Jul 1826
George	40	M	Farmer	Yorkshire	Pennsylvania	Curler 7 Jul 1827
Honour	24	F	None	England	U. States	Franklin 7 Jul 1828
James	9	M		Great Britain	U.S. of America	Gratitude 3 Oct 1829
James	58	M	Farmer	Gt. Brittian	Gt. Brittian	Manchester 21 Apr 1827
Jeremiah	11	M		Yorkshire	Pennsylvania	Curler 7 Jul 1827
Jesse	2	M		Yorkshire	Pennsylvania	Curler 7 Jul 1827
John	11	M		Great Britain	U.S. of America	Gratitude 3 Oct 1829
John	12	M		Yorkshire	Pennsylvania	Curler 7 Jul 1827
John	19	M	Carpenter	Great Britian	United States	Isaac Hicks 22 May 1826
John	28		Farmer	England	New Jersey	Albion 11 Oct 1821
John	35	M	wheelwright	Great Britain	U.S. of America	Gratitude 3 Oct 1829
Joseph	3	M		Great Britain	U.S. of America	Gratitude 3 Oct 1829
Joseph	10	M		Yorkshire	Pennsylvania	Curler 7 Jul 1827
Ludwick	32	M	Clothier	Germany	U. States	Wm. Penn 1 Sep 1828
Mary	28	F		Great Britain	U.S. of America	Gratitude 3 Oct 1829
Mary Ann	6	F		Yorkshire	Pennsylvania	Curler 7 Jul 1827
Rebecca	30	F		United States		Corinthian 27 Oct 1829
Sarah	5	F		Great Britain	U.S. of America	Gratitude 3 Oct 1829
Sarah	38	F		Yorkshire	Pennsylvania	Curler 7 Jul 1827
Thomas	2	M	None	England	U. States	Franklin 7 Jul 1828
Thomas	28	M	Tin Plate	England		Fame 9 Dec 1826
W.	6		None	England	New Jersey	Albion 11 Oct 1821
William	1	M		Great Britain	U.S. of America	Gratitude 3 Oct 1829
WILDE, Ann	12	F		England	U. States	Birmingham 16 Jun 1828
Benjamin	12	M	None	England	United States	John Wells 11 May 1827
Billey	8	M		England	U. States	Birmingham 16 Jun 1828
Esther	18	F	None	England	United States	John Wells 11 May 1827
Hannah	16	F	None	England	United States	John Wells 11 May 1827
Henry	20	M	Clothier	England	United States	John Wells 11 May 1827
James	10	M		England	U. States	Birmingham 16 Jun 1828
James	34	M	Manufacturer	England	U. States	Birmingham 16 Jun 1828
John	0 11/12	M		England	U. States	Birmingham 16 Jun 1828
John	21	M	Merchant	Great Britain	United States	Florida 2 Sep 1822
Joseph	6	M		England	U. States	Birmingham 16 Jun 1828
Joseph	28	M	Merchant	England	England	New York 3 Apr 1826
Peggy	14	F	None	England	United States	John Wells 11 May 1827
Sarah	4	F		England	U. States	Birmingham 16 Jun 1828
Sarah	52	F	None	England	United States	John Wells 11 May 1827
William	11	M	None	England	United States	John Wells 11 May 1827
WILDEN, Asa W.	43	M	Mariner	United States	United States	Ductile 26 Aug 1822
WILDER, —, Mrs.	30	F	Lady	Jamaica	U. States	Genl. Marin 25 Jul 1825
Electa, Miss	8	F	Child	United States	Massachusetts	Stephania 28 Jul 1823
Electa, Mrs.	25	F	Md. Woman	United States	Massachusetts	Stephania 28 Jul 1823
Elijah	24	M	Marchant	N. York	U. States	Commodore Perry 9 Apr 1821
Francina, Miss	4 6/12	F	Child	United States	Massachusetts	Stephania 28 Jul 1823
James	14	M		Jamaica	U. States	Genl. Marin 25 Jul 1825
Jno.	13	M		Jamaica	U. States	Genl. Marin 25 Jul 1825
Milas	27 6/12	M	Mariner	Boston	Boston	Florida 2 Oct 1828
Oshra	39		Merchant	U. States	U. States	Hudson 4 Sep 1823
Yrylina, Miss	1 11/12	F	Child	United States	Massachusetts	Stephania 28 Jul 1823
WILDERS, George	30	M	Merchant	Great Britain	Great Britain	Columbia 22 Sep 1828
Thomas	26	M	Farmer	England	U. States	Margarett Scott 22 Aug 1827
WILDES, George	23	M		U. States	U. States	Cincinnatus 2 Oct 1822
WILDING, Ann	19	F	Spinster	England	U.N. States	Earl of Liverpool 20 Aug 1825
Susan	12	F		England	U.N. States	Earl of Liverpool 20 Aug 1825
WILDMAN, James	21	M	Farmer	Ireland	United States	Lord Strangford 20 Jun 1826
Paul	27	M	Agriculture	Wirtemburg	United States	Henri IV 14 Oct 1829
Rose	19	F	Spinster	Ireland	United States	Lord Strangford 20 Jun 1826
WILDON, Bridget	9	F	None	Ireland		Marchioness 13 May 1828

NAMES OF PASSENGERS	AGE	SEX	OCCUPATIONS	COUNTRY TO WHICH THEY BELONG	COUNTRY THEY INTEND TO INHABIT	SHIPS/DATES OF ARRIVAL	
WILDRAM, James	22	M	Labourer	Great Brittan	U. States	John & Elizabeth	11 Dec 1826
WILDWATERS, Joseph	28	M	Joiner	England	United States	Comet	6 Mar 1823
WILE, Wm.	36	M	Gent.	Ireland	U. States	Meteor	19 Jul 1828
WILEBEY, Hanner	40					Nancy	10 Jul 1820
WILES, Richard	28	M	Mariner	U. States	U. States	Purrington	14 May 1827
WILEY, Elijah	23			Great Britain		John Dickinson	5 Apr 1821
Eliza	21	F	Labourer	Great Britian	United States	Sarah	11 Jul 1829
Eliza	23			Great Britan	United States	Newry	11 Jul 1827
Eliza	50			Great Britan	United States	Newry	11 Jul 1827
Elizabeth	24			Ireland	U. States	Robert Burns	18 Jun 1822
Elizabeth	67			Ireland	U. States	Robert Burns	18 Jun 1822
Fanny, & Infant	27	F	None	Great Britain	New York	Superior	5 Sep 1827
Ilene	1...			Cork	Philadelphia	Schuylkill	22 Aug 1825
James	30		Weaver	England	United States	India	8 Jun 1827
Joseph	28			Ireland	U. States	Robert Burns	18 Jun 1822
Joseph	30	M	Farmer	Ireland	United States	Trio	2 Oct 1828
L.	16			Cork	Philadelphia	Schuylkill	22 Aug 1825
Margianna	24			Cork	Philadelphia	Schuylkill	22 Aug 1825
Matilda	22			Ireland	United States	Robert Burns	18 Jun 1822
Mical	14	F		France	U. States	Edward Bonaffe	23 Jul 1828
Nancy	28	F	Servant	Ireland	United States	Carolina Ann	11 Dec 1826
Paul	78		Farmer	Ireland	U. States	Robert Burns	18 Jun 1822
Robert	13		Weaver	Cork	Philadelphia	Schuylkill	22 Aug 1825
Robert	28	M	Labourer	Ireland		Dublin Packet	30 Apr 1821
Sarah	25	F				Euphrates	8 Aug 1820
Sarah	27			Great Britan	United States	Newry	11 Jul 1827
William	66	M	Laborer	Ireland	United States	Carolina Ann	11 Dec 1826
Wm.	30		Farmer	Ireland	U. States	Robert Burns	18 Jun 1822
WILFARD, Rebecca	12	F	Gardner	England	U.S. States	Splendid	14 Aug 1829
Wm.	52	F	Gardner	England	U.S. States	Splendid	14 Aug 1829
WILFINDEN, Robert	21	M	Weaver	England	United States	Delta	24 Oct 1829
WILFUR, Fanny	11	F	Gardner	England	U.S. States	Splendid	14 Aug 1829
Harriet	8	F	Gardner	England	U.S. States	Splendid	14 Aug 1829
WILFURD, Sophia	48	F	Gardner	England	U.S. States	Splendid	14 Aug 1829
WILHELM, Elizabeth	9	F	Farmer	Coburg	Ohio	Caesar	24 Aug 1829
Jacob	12	M	Farmer	Coburg	Ohio	Caesar	24 Aug 1829
Jacob	37	M	Farmer	Coburg	Ohio	Caesar	24 Aug 1829
John Nicolas	10	M	Farmer	Coburg	Ohio	Caesar	24 Aug 1829
Maria Salome	30	F	Farmer	Coburg	Ohio	Caesar	24 Aug 1829
Nicolas	72	M	Farmer	Coburg	Ohio	Caesar	24 Aug 1829
Peter	6/12	M	Farmer	Coburg	Ohio	Caesar	24 Aug 1829
Peter	1 6/12	M	Farmer	Coburg	Ohio	Caesar	24 Aug 1829
Peter	28	M	Farmer	Coburg	Ohio	Caesar	24 Aug 1829
Sophia	42	F	Farmer	Coburg	Ohio	Caesar	24 Aug 1829
Valentine	8	M	Farmer	Coburg	Ohio	Caesar	24 Aug 1829
WILHELME, Nicholas	25	M	Agriculturist	France	U.S.	Helen	3 May 1828
WILHIM, Jno. H.	25	M	Artist	England	U. States	Pacific	20 Aug 1825
WILIE, Elizabeth	25	F				Golden Grove	6 Sep 1820
Louisa	1	F				Golden Grove	6 Sep 1820
WILIMAN, Modane	41	F		Germany	United States	Lydia	18 Jun 1828
WILISON, Jane	27	F	Spinster	Great Britain	America	Samuel Robertson	26 Nov 1825
Matilda	7				Pennsylvania	Lady Hunter	19 Oct 1826
WILKASAN, Methony	24	M	Servant	Ireland	United States	Sylvester Healy	19 Aug 1825
WILKERSON, Walker	24	M	Gentleman	America	America	Ann	23 Jul 1821
WILKES, Am	22	F	None	New York	U. States	New York	15 Nov 1823
Amelia	3	F		England	United States	Cambria	16 Aug 1827
Ann	42	F	Farmer	Great Britain	U.S. of Ama.	Robert Fulton	16 Aug 1824
Anne	10	F	Farmer	Great Britain	U.S. of Ama.	Robert Fulton	16 Aug 1824
Caroline	1	F	Farmer	Great Britain	U.S. of Ama.	Robert Fulton	16 Aug 1824
Charles	59	M	None	New York	U. States	New York	15 Nov 1823
Eliza.	3	F	Farmer	Great Britain	U.S. of Ama.	Robert Fulton	16 Aug 1824
Elizabeth	45	F		England	United States	Cambria	16 Aug 1827
Frances	8	F		England	United States	Cambria	16 Aug 1827
Frederick	8	M		England	United States	Cambria	16 Aug 1827
George	13	M		England	United States	Cambria	16 Aug 1827
George	36	M	Macanek	America	America	Commodore Chauncy	19 Jan 1826

NAMES OF PASSENGERS	AGE	SEX	OCCUPATIONS	COUNTRY TO WHICH THEY BELONG	COUNTRY THEY INTEND TO INHABIT	SHIPS/DATES OF ARRIVAL	
WILKES (cont'd)							
Hamilton	19	M	None	New York	U. States	New York	15 Nov 1823
Harriet	16	F		England	United States	Cambria	16 Aug 1827
James	8	M	Farmer	Great Britain	U.S. of Ama.	Robert Fulton	16 Aug 1824
John	5	M	Farmer	Great Britain	U.S. of Ama.	Robert Fulton	16 Aug 1824
Jos.	44	M	Farmer	Great Britain	U.S. of Ama.	Robert Fulton	16 Aug 1824
Josh.	18	M	Farmer	Great Britain	U.S. of Ama.	Robert Fulton	16 Aug 1824
Maria	15	F		England	United States	Cambria	16 Aug 1827
Mary	14	F	Farmer	Great Britain	U.S. of Ama.	Robert Fulton	16 Aug 1824
Sarah	10	F	Farmer	Great Britain	U.S. of Ama.	Robert Fulton	16 Aug 1824
Thomas	11	M		England	United States	Cambria	16 Aug 1827
William	45	M	Merchant	England	United States	Cambria	16 Aug 1827
WILKI, John	25	M	Labourer	Ireland	U. States	Combine	30 Nov 1825
WILKIE, Robt.	28	M	Weaver	Great Britain	United States	Washington	3 Sep 1827
WILKINGSON, Mary	39	F	None	England	U. States	Franklin	7 Jul 1828
WILKINGTON,							
Marianne	14	F	Lady	England	United States	Montano	5 May 1828
WILKINS, —, Mr.	22			N. York	U. States	Sarah Lee	29 May 1826
A.	23	M	Brewer	Ireland	U. States	Favourite	2 Sep 1822
Annette	8/12			Surinam	U. States	Sarah Lee	29 May 1826
Charles	34	M	W. Wright	England	America	Mary Lord	26 Oct 1829
E. M.	29	M	Gentleman	New York	New York	New York	31 Jul 1829
Eliza	23	F	None	England	United States	Jubilee	1 Oct 1828
Elizabeth	10	F		England	America	Mary Lord	26 Oct 1829
Elizabeth	12	F		England	America	Mary Lord	26 Oct 1829
Emma	6/12	F	None	Great Britan	Great Britan	United States	21 May 1827
Fredrick	3	M		England	America	Mary Lord	26 Oct 1829
Henry	24	M	Sugar Baker	Germany		Boyer	9 May 1825
James	31	M	Shoe Maker	Great Britain	United States	Washington	3 Sep 1827
Mary A.	2 6/12	F	None	Great Britan	Great Britan	United States	21 May 1827
Milicent	1 1/2	F	None	England	United States	Jubilee	1 Oct 1828
N.	30	F	Servant	St. Domingo	St. Domingo	Genl. Warren	10 Jul 1828
Peter	30	M	Gentleman	Surinam	U. States	Sarah Lee	29 May 1826
Robert	1 6/12	M		England	America	Mary Lord	26 Oct 1829
Samuel	32	M	Shopkeeper	Great Britan	Great Britan	United States	21 May 1827
Sarah	14	F		England	America	Mary Lord	26 Oct 1829
Sarah	25	F	None	Great Britan	Great Britan	United States	21 May 1827
Simon	25	M	Servant	W. Indies	U. States	William Smith	9 May 1822
Susannah	38	F		England	America	Mary Lord	26 Oct 1829
Thomas	24	M	Bricklayer	England	United States	Jubilee	1 Oct 1828
W.	46	M	Clothier	Bristol	New York	Cosmo	25 Sep 1827
William S.	33	M	Accountant	U. States	U. States	Frances Henrietta	25 Oct 1824
WILKINSON, —, Mrs.	34	F		U. States	U. States	Triton	4 Oct 1822
A.	27		Merchant	Scotland	Newbern, N.C.	Albion	11 Oct 1821
Ann	7	F				John & Edward	25 Aug 1820
Charles	1	M		Great Britain	United States	Diana	6 Jul 1829
Edward	12	M	...ta...maker	England	United States	Trident	30 Sep 1826
Elizabeth	2	F		U. States	U. States	Triton	4 Oct 1822
Ellen	30	F	Servant	Ireland	United States	Sylvester Healy	19 Aug 1825
Frances	6	F		Great Britain	United States	Diana	6 Jul 1829
Harriet	13	F	None			John & Edward	25 Aug 1820
Henery	26	M	Weaver	England	United States	Jubilee	4 Mar 1829
Herbert	22	M	Merchant	England	U.S. of America	Hannibal	17 Dec 1823
James	8	M	None	England	United States	Trident	18 Jul 1827
James	35	M	Miller	Great Britain	United States	Dapper	29 Jan 1829
James	40	M	Farmer	Great Britain	U. States America	Ann Maria	29 Nov 1821
Jane	21	M	Weaver	England	United States	Trident	30 Sep 1826
Jane	52	F	Wife	England	United States	Trident	30 Sep 1826
Jno.	22	M	Farmer	Ireland	U. States	Frances Henrietta	19 Feb 1823
John	5	M				John & Edward	25 Aug 1820
John	21	M	Spinner	England	United States	New Packet	7 Aug 1826
John	23		Farmer	Liverpool	Great Britain	William Thompson	13 May 1823
John	33	M	Weaver	England	United States	Trident	30 Sep 1826
M.	24	M	Uberralla Maker	Ireland	U. States	Albion	11 May 1827
Martha	28	F		Great Britain	United States	Diana	6 Jul 1829
Mary	22	F		Ireland	U. States	Albion	11 May 1827

NAMES OF PASSENGERS	AGE	SEX	OCCUPATIONS	COUNTRY TO WHICH THEY BELONG	COUNTRY THEY INTEND TO INHABIT	SHIPS/DATES OF ARRIVAL	
WILKINSON (cont'd)							
Mary	27			Philadelphia	U. States	Almira	15 Jul 1822
Mary	30	F	None	Ireland	United States	Trident	18 Jul 1827
Mary	32	F	Seamstress			John & Edward	25 Aug 1820
Richard	33	M	None	England	United States	Trident	18 Jul 1827
Robert	2					John & Edward	25 Aug 1820
Thomas	18	M	Labourer	Ireland	United States	Trident	31 Mar 1827
Thos.	24	M	Shoemaker	Yorkshire		Ocean	13 Jul 1827
Thos.	28	M	Farmer	England	America	Hercules	15 Jul 1822
Wm.	13	M		Ireland	U. States	Frances Henrietta	19 Feb 1823
Wm.	19	M	Farmer	Great Britain	U. States America	Ann Maria	29 Nov 1821
Wm. B.	24	M	Gentleman	Gt. Brittain	United States	Cortes	7 Dec 1825
WILKS, George	58	M	Mechanic	New York	U. States	Eliza	29 Dec 1827
Luke	31	M	Tailor	England	United States	Maria	12 May 1823
WILL, John	32	M	Cloth Dresses	England	America	Josephine	8 Jan 1827
WILLARD, B. F.	25	M	Merchant	U. States	U. States	Emma	24 Jun 1822
Ellen	14	F	Spinster	Ireland	United States	Trident	16 May 1826
Jesse	24	M	Farmer	England	U.S. America	Cortes	19 May 1826
Willm.	24	M	Currier	England	United States	Robert Edwards	3 Oct 1829
WILLAY, John	38	M		Germany	United States	Lydia	18 Jun 1828
WILLCOCK, Geo.	30	M	Farmer	England	United States	Delta	24 Oct 1829
Wm.	33	M	Merchant	U. States	U. States	Amphion	24 Aug 1821
WILLCOCKS, A.	25	F		Ireland	United States	John & Adam	21 Sep 1822
WILLER, E.	4	F	Farmer	Switzerland	U. States	Alfred	8 Jul 1828
F.	2	F	Farmer	Switzerland	U. States	Alfred	8 Jul 1828
M.	3	F	Farmer	Switzerland	U. States	Alfred	8 Jul 1828
M.	33	M	Farmer	Switzerland	U. States	Alfred	8 Jul 1828
Ma.	6	M	Farmer	Switzerland	U. States	Alfred	8 Jul 1828
WILLESEY, A., Mrs.	23	F		England	U. States	Convoy	14 Mar 1823
J., Mr.	27	M	Merchant	Jamaica	U. States	Convoy	14 Mar 1823
WILLET, Conrad	42	M	Gardner	Germany	U. States	Aerial	10 Nov 1825
Jno.	21	M	Lady			Hanford	17 Jul 1828
W.	37	M	Trader			Hanford	17 Jul 1828
WILLEY, ...	21	F	Spinster	Great Britain	United States	Superior	31 Mar 1828
...	27	M	Chair Maker	Great Britain	United States	Superior	31 Mar 1828
Ed.	64	M	Planter	G. Britain	America	Spring	12 Oct 1821
Eliza L.	26	F	None	G. Bt.	G. Bt.	Canada	13 Feb 1826
James	19	M	Shoe Maker	Irereland	America	Carolina Ann	20 Jun 1825
James	23	M	Carpenter	England	America	Franklin	13 Aug 1827
WILLIA, —, Mr.	30	M	Manufacturer	Gt. Britain	U.S.	Robert Edwards	11 Nov 1822
WILLIAM, —, Mr.	25	M	Merchant	Great Britian	Canada	Columbia	17 Apr 1827
Betsy M.	19					Zamoa	5 Nov 1828
Christian			Gentleman			Caledonian	16 Aug 1820
Danl.	30	M	Mariner	Salem	U. States	General Vedaneta	25 Nov 1825
James	37	M	Merchant	Ireland		Eliza Grant	29 Aug 1829
WILLIAMON, James	28	M	Weaver			Lady of the Lake	23 Aug 1828
WILLIAMS, —	35	F		Gt. Britain	U. States	Panthea	21 Jul 1825
—, Mrs.	25	F	None	U. States	U. States	Jannette Josephine	22 Aug 1820
—, Mrs.	32	F		America	America	Albion	4 Oct 1820
—, Mrs.	40	F	Labourer	Ireland	United States	Hope	12 Jun 1828
...	42	M	Miner	Great Britain	U. States	Leontine	10 Jul 1826
...ia	5	F		Great Britain	U. States	Hector	11 Oct 1824
...n	27 4/12	F	Farmer	France	U. States	France	26 Jun 1828
A.	35	M	Merchant	England	England	Florida	28 Apr 1823
A.	40	M	Labourer	G. Britain	U. States	George Clinton	10 Sep 1828
Adeline	2 6/12	F		England	U. States	Foster	28 Aug 1822
Alborough	30	M	Merchant	England	U. States	James Cropper	17 Jun 1825
Aldborough	30		Merchant	England	...	James Cropper	28 Jun 1824
Aldborough	34	M	Merchant	Gt. Britain		Silas Richards	20 Jun 1826
Allex	30	M	Cook	United States	United States	Only Daughter	29 Apr 1825
Ann	9/12	F	None	Ireland	United States	Lord Wellington	28 May 1827
Ann	20	F	Lady	United States	United States	Ann Maria	5 May 1824
Ann	21	F	Wife	Great Britain	United States	Washington	3 Sep 1827
Ann	21	F	None	England	United States	Essex	23 May 1828
Ann	27	F	None	Great Britain	New York	Superior	5 Sep 1827

1333

NAMES OF PASSENGERS	AGE	SEX	OCCUPATIONS	COUNTRY TO WHICH THEY BELONG	COUNTRY THEY INTEND TO INHABIT	SHIPS/DATES OF ARRIVAL	
WILLIAMS (cont'd)							
Ann	33	F	Miner	England	Canada	Bowditch	27 Apr 1826
Anne	4	F	None	Aberdarorgen, Great Britain	United States	Marquis of Anglesea	8 Jun 1827
Anne	18	F	Spinster	Wales		Gomer	22 May 1827
Anthony	22	M	Servant	St. Croix	U. States	Elias Burger	18 Apr 1823
Arn	43	F		G. Britain	U. States	London	23 Sep 1828
Benj.	5	M	Miner	England	Canada	Bowditch	27 Apr 1826
Benjamin	8	M		U. States	U. States	Dromo	28 Feb 1829
Betsey	11	F	Farmer	Ireland	U. States	Francis	6 Sep 1827
Betsey	21	F		G. Britain	U. States	London	23 Sep 1828
C.	2-	M	Lawyer	Sweden	U. States	Mount Hope	23 Jul 1821
C. P.	19	M	Gentleman	U. States	U. States	Hercules	27 Aug 1823
C. S.	25	M	Clerk	England	U. States	Foster	28 Aug 1822
Catharan	42	F		Great B.	U. States	William Neilson	26 Jul 1828
Catharine	20	F		Aberdarorgen, Great Britain	United States	Marquis of Anglesea	8 Jun 1827
Catharine	30	F		Aberdarorgen, Great Britain	United States	Marquis of Anglesea	8 Jun 1827
Cathe.	22	F	Farmer	Britain	U. States	Fame	3 Jun 1828
Cathe.	23	F	Spinster	Carnarvon	U. States	Melantho	26 Mar 1827
Catherine	1	F		Great Britain	United States	Gomer	21 May 1828
Catherine	26	F	None	England	United States	Jubilee	1 Oct 1828
Charles	3	M	None	England	United States	Jubilee	1 Oct 1828
Chas.	30	M	Mason	St. Johns, N.B.	United States	Martha	23 Aug 1825
Christopher	60	M	Carpenter	England	United States	Cambria	16 Aug 1827
Chs.	22	M	Merchant	U. States	U. States	Lucy	25 Aug 1821
D. L.	13		None	United States	New York	Albion	11 Oct 1821
Danl.	12	M	Farmer	Ireland	U. States	Francis	6 Sep 1827
Dav...	9	M	None	Aberdarorgen, Great Britain	United States	Marquis of Anglesea	8 Jun 1827
David	3	M		Dolgelle	United States	Marquis of Anglesea	8 Jun 1827
David	6	M		Gt. Britain	U. States	Panthea	21 Jul 1825
David	9	M	Miner	England	Canada	Bowditch	27 Apr 1826
David	10	M	Farmer	Ireland	United States	Justina	5 Aug 1823
David	24	M	Farmer	Wales	U. States	Loire	28 Aug 1824
David	27	M	Farmer	England	United States	William Byrnes	1 Dec 1824
David	30	M	Labourer	...le Kettle ..., Kettle [Parish], Fife [County]	New York	Hero	19 May 1828
*to look for Employment							
David	31	M	Farmer	Great Britain	United States	Mary Howland	19 Jul 1827
David	32	M	Weaver	G.B.	New York	Eliza Grant	29 Aug 1829
David	39	M	Engineer	England	Pensylvania	Lima	5 Aug 1829
David	42	M	Farmer	Ireland	United States	Justina	5 Aug 1823
David	56	M	Farmer	England	U. States	Commerce	2 Oct 1823
Dorothy	20	F	Spinster	Carnarvon	U. States	Melantho	26 Mar 1827
E.	24	M	Farmer	Wales	U. States	Loire	28 Aug 1824
E.	70		Merchant	Halifax	U. States	Edwin	26 Sep 1828
Edmond	6	M	None	England	U. States	Montgomery	18 Oct 1828
Edward	9					Helen	4 Aug 1829
Edward	30	M	Gentleman	United States	U. States	Debby & Eliza	12 Aug 1822
Edwd.	22	M	Mariner	Liverpool	U. States	Douglass	7 Aug 1827
Edwin	22	M	Farmer	Great Britain	United States	Gomer	21 May 1828
Elijah	1	M	Miner	England	Canada	Bowditch	27 Apr 1826
Elinor	5			Great Britain	United States	Gomer	21 May 1828
Elisa	1	F		Great Britain	United States	Mary Howland	19 Jul 1827
Eliz.	18	F		Great B.	U. States	William Neilson	26 Jul 1828
Eliza	4	F				Hercules	25 Sep 1820
Eliza	12	F		Great Britain	United States	Spartan	25 Jul 1821
Eliza	18	F		England	England	Tontin	13 Jun 1825
Eliza	18	F		Wales	U. States	Marquis of Anglesea	12 Sep 1828
Eliza	21	F	Agriculturist	Great Britain	U. States	Columbia	22 Sep 1828

NAMES OF PASSENGERS	AGE	SEX	OCCUPATIONS	COUNTRY TO WHICH THEY BELONG	COUNTRY THEY INTEND TO INHABIT	SHIPS/DATES OF ARRIVAL	
WILLIAMS (cont'd)							
Eliza	27	F	Servant	England	New York	Brighton	16 Nov 1826
Eliza M.	5	F		England	U.S. American	Criterion	7 Jul 1824
Elizabeth	6/12	F				Hercules	25 Sep 1820
Elizabeth	14	F		Aberdarorgen, Great Britain	United States	Marquis of Anglesea	8 Jun 1827
Elizabeth	25	F	Lady	England	U. States	Meteor	4 Oct 1827
Elizabeth	26	F	None	England	United States	Jubilee	1 Oct 1828
Elizabeth	31	F	No Occupation but chance concerns	England	America	Meteor	22 Apr 1822
Elizabeth	37	F	Farmer	Ireland	United States	Justina	5 Aug 1823
Elizabeth	40 6/12	F		England	U.S. American	Criterion	7 Jul 1824
Elizabeth	50	F		G. Brittain	Quebec	Bordeaux	5 Aug 1824
Elizabeth, Jr.	4	F	Farmer	Ireland	United States	Justina	5 Aug 1823
Elizh.	45	F	None	Wales	United States	Orozimbo	11 Aug 1823
Ellen	3	F	None	England	United States	John Dickinson	30 Sep 1823
Ellen	8	F	None	Aberdarorgen, Great Britain	United States	Marquis of Anglesea	8 Jun 1827
Ellen	8	F				Helen	4 Aug 1829
Ellen	20	F		England	America	Silas Richard	24 Oct 1829
Ellen	25		Baker	Ireland	United States	Geo. Canning	5 Jun 1828
Ellen	27	F	Lady	England		Helen	4 Aug 1829
Ellen	33	F				Hanford	17 Jul 1828
Ellen	40	F	None	Great Britain	United States	Atlantic	28 May 1827
Ellenor	41	F	Grocer	Gt. Britain	U. States	Louisa Matilda	25 May 1825
Ellin	5	F		Dolgelle	United States	Marquis of Anglesea	8 Jun 1827
Ellin	31	F		Aberdaron	United States	Marquis of Anglesea	8 Jun 1827
Emanuel	2	M				Hercules	25 Sep 1820
Emanuel	24	M				Hercules	25 Sep 1820
Emily	5	F				Helen	4 Aug 1829
Emily	21	F		England	U. States	Foster	28 Aug 1822
Emma	10 6/12	F		England	U.S. American	Criterion	7 Jul 1824
Ester	3 7/12	F		England	U.S. American	Criterion	7 Jul 1824
Evan	12	M		Dolgelle	United States	Marquis of Anglesea	8 Jun 1827
Evan	43	M	Labourer	Dolgelle	United States	Marquis of Anglesea	8 Jun 1827
Francis	1	F		England	U. States	Meteor	4 Oct 1827
Francis	22	F		Ireland	America	Carolina Ann	7 Aug 1826
Francis	32	M	Merchant	United States	United States	Benjamin Franklin	10 Apr 1827
Francis	36 5/12	M	Farmer	England	U. States	France	26 Jun 1828
Francis	46	M	Mechanic	Great Britain	United States	Washington	22 Mar 1820
Frans., Mrs.	28	F		N. York	N. York	Margaret	7 Dec 1825
Fred	17	M	Gentleman	American	U. States	Romulus	31 Jul 1823
Fredk.	6	M		Great Britain	New York	Superior	5 Sep 1827
George	2	M	None	England	U. States	Montgomery	18 Oct 1828
George	3	M		U. States	U. States	Sarah G.	14 Apr 1828
George	14	M	Miner	England	Canada	Bowditch	27 Apr 1826
George S.	12 2/12	M		England	U.S. American	Criterion	7 Jul 1824
Griffith	23	F		Aberdarorgen, Great Britain	United States	Marquis of Anglesea	8 Jun 1827
Gwen	18	F		Dolgelle	United States	Marquis of Anglesea	8 Jun 1827
Gwen	20	F	Spinster	Wales		Gomer	22 May 1827
H.	16	M		U. States	U. States	Leander	30 Oct 1826
H.	33	M	Labourer			Hanford	17 Jul 1828
H., Mrs.	30	F	None	U. States	U. States	Bayard	9 Jul 1824
H. A.	22	M	Merchant	Bermuda	N. foundland	Orlando	23 Mar 1826
Hannah	22	F		G.B.	America	Pacific	13 Jan 1827
Hannah	25	F	None	Ireland	United States	Lord Wellington	28 May 1827
Hannah	34	F				Hercules	25 Sep 1820
Harbert	25	M	Farmer	Great Britain	United States	Gomer	21 May 1828

NAMES OF PASSENGERS	AGE	SEX	OCCUPATIONS	COUNTRY TO WHICH THEY BELONG	COUNTRY THEY INTEND TO INHABIT	SHIPS/DATES OF ARRIVAL	
WILLIAMS (cont'd)							
Hellen	24	F	None	England	United States	Brighton	11 Mar 1825
Henery	38	M	Artizan	England	United States	Jubilee	1 Oct 1828
Henry	1	M	None	England	United States	Oscar	24 Jul 1823
Henry	18	M	Farmer	Gt. Britain	United States	Meteor	19 Aug 1829
Henry	26	M	...aller	England	United States	Oscar	24 Jul 1823
Henry	37	M	Labourer	England	U. States	Comet	23 Aug 1828
Hugh	1	M	None	England	United States	John Dickinson	30 Sep 1823
Hugh	15	M	None	Wales	United States	Orozimbo	11 Aug 1823
Hugh	30	M	Grocer	Gt. Britain	U. States	Louisa Matilda	25 May 1825
Humpy	45	M	Farmer	Gt. Britn.	U.S.	Belle Isle	9 Aug 1827
Hy. L.	21	M	None	Baltimore	U. States	New York	15 Nov 1823
Isaac	7	M	Boy	United States	United States	Only Daughter	29 Apr 1825
Isabella	24	F	Lady	United States	United States	Wanderer	31 Aug 1829
James	13	M				Helen	4 Aug 1829
James	19	M	None	Great Britain	United States	Ganges	26 Oct 1826
James	25	M	Wheel Right	Ireland	United States	General Marion	20 Aug 1828
James	26	M	Cowper	Nova Scotia	New York	Hope & Esther	21 Dec 1827
James	27	M	Planter	Great Britain	U. States	Hector	11 Oct 1824
James	30	M	Labourer	Ireland	United States	Lord Wellington	28 May 1827
James	37	M	Merchant	Ireland	N. York	Eliza Grant	29 Aug 1829
James L.	26	M	Shipwright	England	England	Nancy	16 Jul 1824
Jane	5	F		Gt. Britain	U. States	Panthea	21 Jul 1825
Jane	6	F		Aberdarorgen, Great Britain	United States	Marquis of Anglesea	8 Jun 1827
Jane	7	F		England	U. States	Meteor	4 Oct 1827
Jane	11	F				Helen	4 Aug 1829
Jane	20	F		Great Britain	United States	Gomer	21 May 1828
Jane	21	F		Great Britain	United States	Aspasia	16 Jul 1828
Jane	22	F		G. Britain	U. States	London	23 Sep 1828
Jane	23	F	Leteward's Wife	U. States		Emerald	9 Sep 1820
Jane	23	F	None	England	United States	Oscar	24 Jul 1823
Jane	24	F				Plato	31 Oct 1829
Jane	25	F	None	U. States	U. States	Emblem	14 May 1827
Jane	27	F	None	United States	United States	Mary	1 May 1828
Jane	34	F		Great Britain	United States	Mary Howland	19 Jul 1827
Jannet	1	F		Aberdarorgen, Great Britain	United States	Marquis of Anglesea	8 Jun 1827
Jas.	52 6/12	M	Gentleman	England	U. States	Panthea	5 Oct 1822
Jno.		M	Merchant	N. York		Margaret	7 Dec 1825
*Died							
Jno.	23	M	Servant	Spanish America	U. States	Endymion	22 May 1822
Jno.	26	M	Laboror	Great Brittian	United States	Perseverance	7 Aug 1826
Jno.	30	M	Weaver	Ireland	United States	Trident	17 May 1825
Job	28	M	Plasterer & Slater	England	U.S. America	New Hampshire	28 Sep 1826
John	2	M	Laboror	Great Brittian	United States	Perseverance	7 Aug 1826
John	2			Great Britain	United States	Gomer	21 May 1828
John	4	M				Helen	4 Aug 1829
John	5	M	None	England	United States	Jubilee	1 Oct 1828
John	7	M				Hercules	25 Sep 1820
John	16	M	Laborer	Ireland	United States	Mary	1 Jul 1829
John	17	M	None	U.S.A.	U.S.A.	Silas Richards	7 Mar 1825
John	17	M	Farmer	Wales	United States	Euphrates	23 Jun 1826
John	20	M	Farmer	Great Brittan	U.S.	Emulous	29 Jun 1827
John	20	M	Farmer	Ireland	United States	Dublin Packet	23 May 1828
John	21	M		Philadelphia	U. States	Falcon	4 May 1826
John	21	M	Clerk	Ireland		Camillus	29 Jan 1829
John	22	M	Miner	England	United States	Jubilee	12 May 1828
John	22	M				Eliza Grant	6 Oct 1828
John	24	M	pudler		uncertain	Mount Vernon	29 Aug 1828
John	25	M	Spinster	Great Brittain	United States	Corinthian	9 Jan 1827
John	25	M	Gentleman	England	U. States	Meteor	4 Oct 1827
John	26	M	Labourer	Aberdaron	United States	Marquis of Anglesea	8 Jun 1827
John	26			Ireland	United States	Geo. Canning	5 Jun 1828
John	27	M	Labourer	Aberdarorgen, Great Britain	United States	Marquis of Anglesea	8 Jun 1827

NAMES OF PASSENGERS	AGE	SEX	OCCUPATIONS	COUNTRY TO WHICH THEY BELONG	COUNTRY THEY INTEND TO INHABIT	SHIPS/DATES OF ARRIVAL	
WILLIAMS (cont'd)							
John	27	M	Merchant	England	England	Tampico	2 Aug 1828
John	28	M	Carpenter	United States	United States	Huntress	5 Apr 1826
John	29			England	America	Robert Burns	8 Dec 1821
John	30	M	Farmer	Ireland	U. States	Francis	6 Sep 1827
John	32	M	Farmer	Scotland	U. States	Spartan	11 Mar 1823
John	32	M	Cabinet Maker	Scotland	United States	Hope	5 Dec 1827
John	34	M	Miner	England	Canada	Bowditch	27 Apr 1826
John	35	M	Mechanic	United States	United States	Mary	1 May 1828
John	36	M	Farmer	Great Britain	United States	Isaac Hicks	10 Jul 1827
John	36		Mason	Great Britain	United States	Gomer	21 May 1828
John	39	M	Merchant	U. States	U. States	Ann	2 Oct 1826
John	42	M	Weaver	Wales	U. States	Henry Kneeland	27 Jul 1825
John	45	M	Weaver	Great Britain		Manhattan	7 Nov 1827
John	59	M	Carpenter	England	United States	Cambria	16 Aug 1827
John G.	6 1/12	M		England	U.S. American	Criterion	7 Jul 1824
John M.	29	M	Planter	U. States	U. States	Panthea	22 Nov 1826
Jos.	28	M	Farmer	England	United States	Essex	23 May 1828
Jos.	30	M	Mechanic	U. States	U. States	Radius	18 Apr 1825
Jos.	38	M	Merchant	U. States	U. States	Huntress	30 Jun 1824
Jos.	42	M	Merchant	Port au Prince	U. States	Liberty	1 Nov 1823
Jos.	43	M	Barber	N. York	U. States	Atalanta	28 Aug 1822
Joseph	2	M				Plato	31 Oct 1829
Joseph	8	F	None	England	United States	Jubilee	1 Oct 1828
Joseph	11	M				Hercules	25 Sep 1820
Joseph	30	M	Barber	U. States	U. States	Curlew	1 Mar 1823
Joseph	30		Mines	England	England	Triumph	23 Jul 1829
Joseph	35	M		America	America	Buck	2 Feb 1822
Joshua	31	M	Ship Master	G. Britain	U. States	Wanderer	23 Jun 1828
Laura	28	F				Acosta	28 Jul 1823
Lawson	5	M		U. States	U. States	Sarah G.	14 Apr 1828
Louisa	18	F	Servant	Jamaica	U. States	Hal	7 Jun 1824
Lowry	6			Great Britain	United States	Gomer	21 May 1828
Lydia	36	F		England	Pensylvania	Lima	5 Aug 1829
M...	30	F	Servant	England	New York	Brighton	19 Aug 1829
Magaret	44	F		Dolgelle	United States	Marquis of Anglesea	8 Jun 1827
Margaret	6	F		Dolgelle	United States	Marquis of Anglesea	8 Jun 1827
Margaret	19	F		England	U. States	Foster	28 Aug 1822
Margaret	28	F	Grocer	Gt. Britain	U. States	Louisa Matilda	25 May 1825
Margaret	55	F	None	Wales	U. States	Henry Kneeland	27 Jul 1825
Margaret	68	F		Great Britain	United States	Robert	15 Jul 1822
Margret	24	F		Ireland	United States	General Marion	20 Aug 1828
Margret	27	F	Farmer, Labourer or Spinster	Ireland	U. States	Meteor	4 Oct 1827
Margret	42			Great Britain	United States	Gomer	21 May 1828
Margt.	9	F				Hercules	25 Sep 1820
Maria	13	F	Gent		United States	Cosmo	21 Aug 1828
Maria	30	F		Java	Java	Eunore Francis	18 Sep 1820
Marsley	22	M		North Wales	United States	Magnet	16 May 1823
Martha	1	F	None	England	United States	Essex	23 May 1828
Martha	4	F		Great B.	U. States	William Neilson	26 Jul 1828
Mary	1 10/12	F		England	U.S. American	Criterion	7 Jul 1824
Mary	3	F		England	U. States	Meteor	4 Oct 1827
Mary	5	F	Farmer	Ireland	U. States	Francis	6 Sep 1827
Mary	7	F				Plato	31 Oct 1829
Mary	11	F		Aberdarorgen, Great Britain	United States	Marquis of Anglesea	8 Jun 1827
Mary	12	F	None	England	U. States	Montgomery	18 Oct 1828
Mary	15	F	Farmer	Gt. Britn.	U.S.	Belle Isle	9 Aug 1827
Mary	16	F		Dolgelle	United States	Marquis of Anglesea	8 Jun 1827
Mary	20	F		U. States	U. States	Lady Tompkins	13 Apr 1824
Mary	20	F	Spinster	Ireland		Robert Fulton	4 Jun 1828
Mary	20	F		Great B.	U. States	William Neilson	26 Jul 1828
Mary	20	F		G. Britain	U. States	Hanford	18 Sep 1828
Mary	22	F	Spinster	Wales		Gomer	22 May 1827

NAMES OF PASSENGERS	AGE	SEX	OCCUPATIONS	COUNTRY TO WHICH THEY BELONG	COUNTRY THEY INTEND TO INHABIT	SHIPS/DATES OF ARRIVAL	
WILLIAMS (cont'd)							
Mary	25	F		Great Britain	U. States	Hector	11 Oct 1824
Mary	29	F				Hercules	25 Sep 1820
Mary	30	F				Fair American	24 Dec 1821
Mary	30	F				Brighton	19 Aug 1829
Mary	40	F	Farmer	Gt. Britn.	U.S.	Belle Isle	9 Aug 1827
Mary	45	M	Labourer	Aberdarorgen, Great Britain	United States	Marquis of Anglesea	8 Jun 1827
Mary Jane	3	F	None	Ireland	United States	Lord Wellington	28 May 1827
Mat	22	M	Farmer	England	America	Silas Richard	24 Oct 1829
Matthew	30	M	Miner	England	England	Virginia	8 Mar 1828
Nathl.	20	M	Labourer	England	United States	Nimrod	31 Jul 1828
Niles	26	M	Mariner			Ladies Delight	18 Sep 1820
Norcott	24	M		Great B.	U. States	William Neilson	26 Jul 1828
Orlando	25		2 Mate	Boston		Hudson	18 Jun 1825

*Officers, Seamen and Passengers belonging to the Ship Jane of Boston and taken from on board the Schooner Olive of St. Johns , N.B. on the 4th June 1825, Lat. 41.30, Long 53.19, which ship foundered on the 31st ultimo in Lat. 41.44 Long 52.

NAMES OF PASSENGERS	AGE	SEX	OCCUPATIONS	COUNTRY TO WHICH THEY BELONG	COUNTRY THEY INTEND TO INHABIT	SHIPS/DATES OF ARRIVAL	
Owen	25	M	Labourer	Wales		Marchioness	13 May 1828
Paul	24	M	Machine Maker	England	New York	Curler	7 Jul 1827
Penny	46	M	Merchant	England	Vera Cruz	Droma	25 Mar 1826
Peter	41	M	Preacher	U. States	U. States	Robt. Reade	12 Apr 1825
Phebe	13	F	Servant	Jamaica	U. States	Hal	7 Jun 1824
Philip	40	M	Laborer	Great Britain	United States	Comet	9 Aug 1822
R. C., Jr.	13	M	Lad	U. States	U. States	Virginia	30 Oct 1828
Ricd.	20	M	Labourer	Ireland		Robert Fulton	4 Jun 1828
Richard	20	M	Labourer	England and Ireland	United States	Jubilee	12 May 1828
Richard	24	M	Moulder			Plato	31 Oct 1829
Richard	32	M	Ship Builder	U. States	U. States	Dromo	28 Feb 1829
Richard	65	M	Labourer	Wales	United States	Orozimbo	11 Aug 1823
Richd.	8	M		Gt. Britain	U. States	Panthea	21 Jul 1825
Robert	5	M	Labourer	Aberdarorgen, Great Britain	United States	Marquis of Anglesea	8 Jun 1827
Robert	18	M	no occupation	Great Britain	United States	Washington	22 Mar 1820
Robert	28 6/12	M	Farmer	England	United States	London	6 Feb 1829
Robert	48	M	Labourer	Aberdarorgen, Great Britain	United States	Marquis of Anglesea	8 Jun 1827
Robert	50	M	Merchant	Great Britain	United States	Courier	13 Mar 1820
Robt.	2	M	Child	Great Britain	United States	Washington	3 Sep 1827
Robt.	4	M	Farmer	Ireland	U. States	Francis	6 Sep 1827
Robt.	17	M	Officer	England	U. States	Hiram	17 Jun 1826
Robt.	28	M	Joiner	Great Britain	United States	Washington	3 Sep 1827
Robt.	28	M	Labourer	G. Britain	U. States	Mary & Harriot	8 Sep 1828
Robt.	62	M		Great B.	U. States	William Neilson	26 Jul 1828
Rose	6/12	F		England	U. States	Foster	28 Aug 1822
Rowland	20	M	Labourer	Aberdarorgen, Great Britain	United States	Marquis of Anglesea	8 Jun 1827
S.	29	M	Merchant	England	U. States	Ranger	2 Jul 1827
Samuel	4	M	None	England	U. States	Montgomery	18 Oct 1828
Samuel, Mr.	36	M	Gent.	England	U.S.	Acasta	11 May 1827
Sarah	3	F		G.B.	America	Pacific	13 Jan 1827
Sarah	18		None	London, England	Great Britain	Frances Henrietta	31 May 1824
Sarah	28	M		U. States	U. States	Sarah G.	14 Apr 1828
Sarah	30	F	None	England	United States	John Dickinson	30 Sep 1823
Sophia	30	F	Farmer	Ireland	U. States	Francis	6 Sep 1827
Sophia B.	30	F	None	United States	United States	Hannibal	12 Oct 1829
Susan	9	F	None	England	U. States	Montgomery	18 Oct 1828
Susan	32	F	None	England	U. States	Montgomery	18 Oct 1828
Theodore	20	M		Ireland	U.S.A.	Robin Hood	6 May 1828
Thomas	...	M	Farmer	Ireland	United States	Justina	5 Aug 1823
Thomas	1	M				Helen	4 Aug 1829

NAMES OF PASSENGERS	AGE	SEX	OCCUPATIONS	COUNTRY TO WHICH THEY BELONG	COUNTRY THEY INTEND TO INHABIT	SHIPS/DATES OF ARRIVAL	
WILLIAMS (cont'd)							
Thomas	6	M	None	Aberdarorgen, Great Britain	United States	Marquis of Anglesea	8 Jun 1827
Thomas	10	M	Labourer	G. Britain	U. States	London	23 Sep 1828
Thomas	25	M	Labourer	Great Britain	United States	Robert	15 Jul 1822
Thomas	29	M	Sawyer	Cl...	Wales	Howard Douglass	11 May 1827
Thomas	30	M	Farmer	Great Britain	United States	Robert Fulton	1 Apr 1824
Thomas	30	M	Farmer	England	United States	William Byrnes	1 Dec 1824
Thomas	34	M	Labourer	Aberdarorgen, Great Britain	United States	Marquis of Anglesea	8 Jun 1827
Thomas	34	M	Weigher	Gt. Britain	United States	Meteor	19 Aug 1829
Thomas	44 9/12	M	Farmer	England	British North America	London	6 Feb 1829
Thomas C.	13 5/12	M		England	U.S. American	Criterion	7 Jul 1824
Thoms.	34	M	Collier	England	U.S. States	Splendid	14 Aug 1829
Thos.	4	M		Great Britain	New York	Superior	5 Sep 1827
Thos.	19	M	Labourer	Great Britain	United States	Washington	3 Sep 1827
Thos.	25		Seaman	Jersey		Hudson	18 Jun 1825
*Officers, Seamen and Passengers belonging to the Ship Jane of Boston and taken from on board the Schooner Olive of St. Johns , N.B. on the 4th June 1825, Lat. 41.30, Long 53.19, which ship foundered on the 31st ultimo in Lat. 41.44 Long 52.							
Thos.	25	M	Glass Blower	G.B.	America	Pacific	13 Jan 1827
Thos.	30	M	Gentleman	Great Britain	New York	Superior	5 Sep 1827
Thos.	33		Farmer	England	United States	Henri IV	14 Sep 1827
Thos., Jr.	35		Seaman	Botson		Hudson	18 Jun 1825
*Officers, Seamen and Passengers belonging to the Ship Jane of Boston and taken from on board the Schooner Olive of St. Johns , N.B. on the 4th June 1825, Lat. 41.30, Long 53.19, which ship foundered on the 31st ultimo in Lat. 41.44 Long 52.							
Thos. S.	27	M	Law	U. States	U. States	Electra	7 Jul 1828
Timothy D.	36	M	Merchant	America	America	Josephine	24 Jul 1826
Violet	25	F		England	U. States	Martha	1 Feb 1822
W.	7	M		Gt. Britain	U. States	Panthea	21 Jul 1825
W.	24	M	Shoemaker	Great Brittan	U. States	John & Elizabeth	11 Dec 1826
W.	30	M	None	Bristol	U. States	Abeona	4 Oct 1824
W. G.	26	M	Cadet	U. States	U. States	Six Brothers	21 Nov 1822
William	1	M	None	Aberdarorgen, Great Britain	United States	Marquis of Anglesea	8 Jun 1827
William	3	M		Aberdarorgen, Great Britain	United States	Marquis of Anglesea	8 Jun 1827
William	4			Great Britain	United States	Gomer	21 May 1828
William	5	M				Hercules	25 Sep 1820
William	12	M	None	England	U. States	Montgomery	18 Oct 1828
William	14	M		Dolgelle	United States	Marquis of Anglesea	8 Jun 1827
William	15	M	None	England	Canada	Cincinnatus	16 Apr 1824
William	18	M	Carpenter	Wales	New York	Governor Fenner	23 Jul 1829
William	18 2/12	M		England	U.S. American	Criterion	7 Jul 1824
William	19 3/12	M	Merchant	Great Britain	United States	Cambria	26 Dec 1827
William	20	M	Labourer	Ireland	U. States	William & John	10 Jul 1824
William	22	M	Labourer	Aberdarorgen, Great Britain	United States	Marquis of Anglesea	8 Jun 1827
William	22 ...	M	...	...	U.S. American	Edward	28 Oct 1825
William	23	M	Farmer	Wales	Ohio	Indian Chief	19 Jun 1823
William	23	M	Labourer	Llannstyn	United States	Marquis of Anglesea	8 Jun 1827
William	25	M	Mariner	England	England	Enterprize	14 Oct 1828
William	26	M		England	Pensylvania	Lima	5 Aug 1829
William	26	M		England	U. States	Lima	5 Aug 1829
William	28	M	Farmer, Labourer or Spinster	Ireland	U. States	Meteor	4 Oct 1827
William	28 4/12	M	Mechanic	America	America	Venus	15 Apr 1822
William	42 4/12	M	...	England	U.S. American	Criterion	7 Jul 1824
William	64 10/12	M	Farmer	England	U.S. of America	Illinois	16 Jun 1821

NAMES OF PASSENGERS	AGE	SEX	OCCUPATIONS	COUNTRY TO WHICH THEY BELONG	COUNTRY THEY INTEND TO INHABIT	SHIPS/DATES OF ARRIVAL	
WILLIAMS (cont'd)							
William, Jr.	34	M	Merchant	United States	U. States	India	29 Apr 1822
William F.	28	M	Merchant	St. John, N.B.	St. John, N.B.	Nancy	2 May 1823
William R.	23 6/12	M	Attorney	United States of Am.	United States of Amer.	Cambria	7 May 1828
Wm.	2	M		Llannstyn	United States	Marquis of Anglesea	8 Jun 1827
Wm.	20	M	Farmer	Great Britain	U. States	Yamacraw	4 Sep 1822
Wm.	21 7/12	M	Labourer	Ireland	U. States	Fabius	22 Sep 1828
Wm.	22	M	Farmer	England		Marchioness	13 May 1828
Wm.	22	M	Mariner	U. States	U. States	Atlas	24 Jun 1828
Wm.	29	M	upholsterer	Gt. Britain	New York	Leeds	7 Nov 1828
Wm.	43	M	Farmer	Wales	United States	Orozimbo	11 Aug 1823
Wm., Jr.	35	M	Merchant	U. States	U. States	Bayard	9 Jul 1824
Wm., Jr.	39	M	Merchant	Norwich	U. States	Electra	4 Sep 1827
WILLIAMSON, —, Mr.	26	M	Doctor	London	London	Swift	13 Jan 1827
—, Mr.	29	M	Doctor	New York	United States	Polly & Sophia	13 Sep 1821
...an...	23	M	Labourer			Hesperus	2 Nov 1820
Ann	16	F	Merchant	Gt. Britain	U. States	Louisa Matilda	25 May 1825
Ann	24	F		G. Britain	U. States	Leavitts	25 Aug 1828
C. L.	24	M	U.S. Navy	U. States	U. States	L. M. Pelham	3 Jan 1823
Chas. A.	30	M	Merchant	U. States	U.S.	Florida	17 May 1825
David	2	M		Irland	United States	Nancy	2 Jan 1824
David	23	M	Smith	Scotland	United States	Confidence	5 Sep 1828
David	59		Minister of the Sector	England	America	Courier	24 Jul 1820
Elisebeth	12	F		Irland	United States	Nancy	2 Jan 1824
Eliza	10	F	Merchant	Gt. Britain	U. States	Louisa Matilda	25 May 1825
Elizabeth	15	F	None	Great Britain	United States	Colossus	5 Jun 1827
Elizabeth	48	F		England	United States	Dalhouse Castle	26 Dec 1827
Ellis	10	M		Irland	United States	Nancy	2 Jan 1824
G. T.	22	M	Printer	U. States	U. States	Electra	28 Apr 1827
Geo.	27	M	Farmer	Ireland	U. States	William & John	10 Jul 1824
Izabella	22	F		England	America	Courier	24 Jul 1820
Izabella	58	F			America	Courier	24 Jul 1820
James	8	M		Irland	United States	Nancy	2 Jan 1824
James	26	M	Carpenter	London	America	Evelina	10 Nov 1825
James	55	M	Merchant	Great Britain	United States	Colossus	5 Jun 1827
James, Jr.	22	M	Merchant	Great Britain	United States	Colossus	5 Jun 1827
Jane	26	F		G. Britain	U. States	Dalthousie Castle	2 Jan 1827
Jane	44	F	Lady	Ireland	United States	Borneo	14 Aug 1827
Janet	23	F	None	Great Britain	United States	Colossus	5 Jun 1827
Janet	57	F	None	Great Britain	United States	Colossus	5 Jun 1827
Jas.	27	M	Farmer	Great Britain	United States	William Dawson	18 Jun 1827
John	4	M		England	United States	Dalhouse Castle	26 Dec 1827
John	6	M		Irland	United States	Nancy	2 Jan 1824
John	27	M	Stone Cuter	Great Britain	United States	Courier	26 Jun 1827
John	31	M	Servant	Great Britain	Great Britain	Fontine	4 Oct 1824
John	42	M	Blacksmith	Great Britain	U. States	Ganges	21 Jun 1827
Joseph	6	M	Merchant	Gt. Britain	U. States	Louisa Matilda	25 May 1825
Marey Ann	20	F		Irland	United States	Nancy	2 Jan 1824
Margaret	15	F		England	America	Courier	24 Jul 1820
Mary	11	F	Merchant	Gt. Britain	U. States	Louisa Matilda	25 May 1825
Mary	47	F	Merchant	Gt. Britain	U. States	Louisa Matilda	25 May 1825
Nancey	50	F		Irland	United States	Nancy	2 Jan 1824
Rebecca	24	F	None	Great Britain	United States	Colossus	5 Jun 1827
Robert	35	M	Weaver	Manchester, England	N. York	New Orleans	24 Aug 1827
Salley	4	F		Irland	United States	Nancy	2 Jan 1824
Sally	22	F	Lady	St. Johns, N.B.	St. Johns, N.B.	Sarah G	11 Sep 1827
Samuel	25	M	Laborer	Irland	United States	Nancy	2 Jan 1824
Sarah	19	F	Servant	England	United States	Dalhouse Castle	26 Dec 1827
Thomas	22	M		Great Brittain	United States	Sarah Ralston	27 Jan 1827
Thomas	33		Painter	England	United States	Corinthian	7 Jul 1829
Thos.	26		Grocer	Ireland	United States	Fabius	18 Mar 1829
William	19	M	Merchant	Great Britain	United States	Colossus	5 Jun 1827
William	21	M	Weaver	Ireland	America	Josephine	8 Dec 1827
Wm.	8	M	Merchant	Gt. Britain	U. States	Louisa Matilda	25 May 1825

NAMES OF PASSENGERS	AGE	SEX	OCCUPATIONS	COUNTRY TO WHICH THEY BELONG	COUNTRY THEY INTEND TO INHABIT	SHIPS/DATES OF ARRIVAL	
WILLIAMSON (cont'd)							
Wm.	19					Trio	5 May 1828
Wm.	24	M	Black Smith	..., ..., England	U. States	New Orleans	24 Aug 1827
Wm.	25		Farmer	G. Britain	U. States	Hamilton	28 Apr 1828
Wm.	46	M	Merchant	Gt. Britain	U. States	Louisa Matilda	25 May 1825
WILLIE, John	23	M	Labourer	G. Britain	New York	Prince Madore	28 Aug 1820
WILLIG, John	55	M	Mercht.	Germany	Germany	Stephania	13 Sep 1821
WILLIM, Francis	21	M	Copper Smith	United States	United States	Globe	30 Aug 1828
WILLINANN, —, Mr.	23	M	Merchant	Germany	New York	Elizabeth	5 Jul 1821
WILLING, L.	24	M	Shephard	Saxony	U. States	Minerva	23 May 1825
Rob. B.		M	Merchant	Philadelphia	Philada.	William Savery	9 Feb 1825
WILLINK, John A.	50	M	...	...	America	William Thompson	10 May 1825
Joseph	34	M	Gentleman	G. Britain	U. States	Congress	23 Mar 1824
WILLIS, —, Miss	7	F		United States	United States	Robert Edwards	21 Sep 1821
—, Miss	18	F	Daughter	Gt. Britain	U.S.	Robert Edwards	11 Nov 1822
—, Mr.	33	F		United States	United States	Robert Edwards	21 Sep 1821
—, Mr.	52	M	Manufacturer	Gt. Britain	U.S.	Robert Edwards	11 Nov 1822
—, Mrs.	56	F	Wife	Gt. Britain	U.S.	Robert Edwards	11 Nov 1822
—, Mrs., & 5 children	32	F	Wife	Gt. Britain	U.S.	Robert Edwards	11 Nov 1822
Ann	1	F		England	U. States	Robert Edwards	9 May 1827
Ann	30	F		England	U. States	Robert Edwards	9 May 1827
Daniel	31	M	Labourer	Ireland	U.S. of America	Meteor	19 Mar 1828
Danl.	26	M	Labourer	U. States	U. States	Aria	16 Jan 1829
Elizabeth	24	F	Wife	Ireland	U.S. of America	Meteor	19 Mar 1828
H. A.	30	M	Merchant	Spain	Bordeaux	Emelia	21 Sep 1826
Henry	40 2/12	M	Mechanic	America	America	Hiram	2 Apr 1828
Jane	23	F	None	England	U. States	Pacific	5 Sep 1827
John	19	M	Weaver	Great Britain	United States	Atlantic	8 Dec 1827
John	35		Painter	London, England	Great Britain	Franklin	22 Jun 1827
John W.	27	M	Judge	England	U. States	Pacific	5 Sep 1827
Letitia	1	F	Child	Ireland	U.S. of America	Meteor	19 Mar 1828
Mary	24	F	None	England	U. States	Pacific	5 Sep 1827
Mary	56	F	None	England	U. States	Pacific	5 Sep 1827
Mary Jane	3	F	Child	Ireland	U.S. of America	Meteor	19 Mar 1828
Nathaniel	45	M	Mariner	U.S. America	U.S. America	Cincinnatus	31 Oct 1820
Nathl.	55	M	Shipmaster	U.N. States	U. States	Washington	7 Jul 1824
Robert	5	M	Child	Ireland	U.S. of America	Meteor	19 Mar 1828
Robert	30 1/12	M	Farmer	England	United States	London	6 Feb 1829
Robt.	0 8/12	M	None	England	U. States	Pacific	5 Sep 1827
Robt.	28	M	Merchant	London	U. States	Bunker Hill	25 Jun 1827
Sarah	28		None	London		Pomona	28 May 1822
Thomas	43	M	Shoemaker	Ireland	U. States	Robert Edwards	9 May 1827
Thos.	4	M		England	U. States	Robert Edwards	9 May 1827
William	26	M	Miller	England	U. States	Unity	5 Sep 1828
WILLISTON, Jos.	33	M	Sailing Master, U.S.N.	U.N. States		Live Oak	13 Aug 1821
WILLMAL, —, Mr.	32			G. Britain	America	Magnet	24 Sep 1824
WILLMAN, George	16	M	Bootmaker	Ireland	U. States	Josephine	7 May 1827
Mary	18	F	Dressmaker	Ireland	U. States	Josephine	7 May 1827
WILLMUTH, Francis	22	M	Joiner	Germany	United States	Wm. Osborne	16 Sep 1828
John	20	M	Joiner	Germany	United States	Wm. Osborne	16 Sep 1828
WILLON, Elisa J.	3	F		Irland	U. States	Nancy	27 Jun 1823
Jane	28	F		Irland	U. States	Nancy	27 Jun 1823
WILLOT, Francisco	5	M		Germany	Missouri	Isabella	15 Sep 1828
Joseph	7	M		Germany	Missouri	Isabella	15 Sep 1828
Marian	9	F		Germany	Missouri	Isabella	15 Sep 1828
Marian	28	F		Germany	Missouri	Isabella	15 Sep 1828
Michael	3	M		Germany	Missouri	Isabella	15 Sep 1828
Sebastian	30	M	Farmer	Germany	Missouri	Isabella	15 Sep 1828
Vandelenet	1 6/12	F		Germany	Missouri	Isabella	15 Sep 1828
WILLOUGHBY, —, Miss	12	F		Halifax	some to return & the others to Canada	Albert	14 May 1822
Hannah	40	F		New York	U.S.	Nancy	1 Sep 1823
Sam A.	28 6/12	M	Merchant	United States	U. States	York	7 Aug 1828
Saml. A.	20	M		U. States	New York	William	22 Jul 1820
Siraphina	23	F	Lady	Great Britain	U. States	Hope & Esther	12 Nov 1825

NAMES OF PASSENGERS	AGE	SEX	OCCUPATIONS	COUNTRY TO WHICH THEY BELONG	COUNTRY THEY INTEND TO INHABIT	SHIPS/DATES OF ARRIVAL	
WILLOW, Ricd.	21		Labourer	England	United States	Hugh Johnson	11 Jun 1828
WILLOWBY, Thos.	24	M	Painter	British ...	American States	Loyalty	9 Sep 1822
WILLRODE, Ann	25	F		England	United States	Delta	24 Oct 1829
WILLS, ...	35	M	Merchant	Britain	U.S. America	Cincinnatus	31 Oct 1820
An.	30	F	Carpenter	England	United States	Essex	23 May 1828
Ann	20	F		Ireland	United States	Princess Charlotte	26 Apr 1827
George	26	M	Musician	England	United States	Cambria	16 Aug 1827
Hny.	10	M	Carpenter	England	United States	Essex	23 May 1828
Mary	30	F	None	England		Manhattan	22 May 1827
Owen	22	M	Labourer	Ireland	United States	Princess Charlotte	26 Apr 1827
R.	25	M	Comb maker	U. States	U. States	Leopard	15 Aug 1825
Richd.	50	M	Carpenter	England	United States	Essex	23 May 1828
Willm.	25	M	Miner	England		Manhattan	22 May 1827
WILLSHIRE, H.	40	F		St. Kitts	U. States	Hunter	1 Jul 1828
Maria	40	F		U. States	U. States	Ann	16 Mar 1826
R.	40	M	Lawyer	London	U. States	Ann	16 Mar 1826
Saml.	18	M		St. Kitts	U. States	Hunter	1 Jul 1828
Thos.	24	M	Carpenter	St. Kitts	U. States	Hunter	1 Jul 1828
WILLSON, Ann	1 3/12	F		Gt. Britan	U. States	Sarah Skeafe	10 Sep 1827
Ann	11	F	None	England	U. States	Courier	25 Aug 1825
Ann	19	F		Ireland	America	Ann	11 Apr 1821
Ann	23	F	Farmer	Ireland	United States	Justina	5 Aug 1823
Cathr.	20	F		Gt. Britan	U. States	Sarah Skeafe	10 Sep 1827
Daniel, Mr.	30	M	Farmer	England	U.S.	Acasta	11 May 1827
Edwin, Mast.	8	M		England	U.S.	Acasta	11 May 1827
Elizabeth, Mrs.	28	F		England	U.S.	Acasta	11 May 1827
Emma, Miss	1	F		England	U.S.	Acasta	11 May 1827
Francis	16	M	Farmer	England	U. States	Courier	25 Aug 1825
Francis	30	M	Farmer	Gt. Britan	U. States	Sarah Skeafe	10 Sep 1827
George	26	M	Farmer	England	Ut. States	Courier	13 Jul 1826
Hamilton	26	M	Printer & Deyer	Ireland	America	Ann	2 Nov 1820
Isaac						Venus	12 Apr 1821
James	20	M	Smith	Sheffield	U. States	Manhattan	21 May 1821
James	21	M	Clouthier	Ireland	Ut. States	Courier	13 Jul 1826
James	25	M	Farmer	Ireland	United States	Justina	5 Aug 1823
Jane	28	F	None	England	U. States	Courier	25 Aug 1825
Jane	55	F	None	England	U. States	Courier	25 Aug 1825
John	19	M	Farmer	Scotland	United States	Margaret Bogle	11 Jun 1824
John	25	M	Artizan	England	United States	Jubilee	1 Oct 1828
John	26	M	Labourer	Glasgow	Glasgow	Howard Douglass	11 May 1827
John	30	M	Gentleman	U. States	U. States	Chase	22 May 1827
John	35	M	Gentleman	U. States	U. States	Hope & Esther	12 Nov 1825
John, Jr.	6	M		England	United States	Curler	3 Mar 1828
John, Mast.	3	M		England	U.S.	Acasta	11 May 1827
Joseph	21	M	Labourer	Ireland	United States	Jubilee	13 Jul 1829
Joseph	50	M	Farmer	England	U. States	Courier	25 Aug 1825
Joseph, Mast.	2	M		England	U.S.	Acasta	11 May 1827
Margt.	18	F	None	England	U. States	Courier	25 Aug 1825
Mary	45	M	Servant	U. States	U. States	Chase	17 Jan 1825
Robert	13	M	Farmer	England	U. States	Courier	25 Aug 1825
Robert, Mast.	4	M		England	U.S.	Acasta	11 May 1827
Stephen	30	M	U.S. Navy	U. States	U. States	Ardelle	27 Nov 1826
Thomas	9	M	Farmer	Ireland	United States	Justina	5 Aug 1823
Thomas	21	M		Ireland	America	Carolina Ann	7 Aug 1826
Thoms.	18	M	Labourrer	Great Britan	U. States	Ann Marria	6 Aug 1823
Wm., Mast.	6	M		England	U.S.	Acasta	11 May 1827
WILMAR, Maurice	26	M	Mercht.	France	New York	Lewis	29 Oct 1825
WILMERDIN, Theadore C., Jr.	27		Merchant			Weser	24 Jul 1820
WILMORE, Benjamin	10/52	M	None	Great Britan	United States	Silvanus Jenkins	10 Mar 1827
Houson	23	M	Hatter	Great Britan	United States	Silvanus Jenkins	10 Mar 1827
Sarah	19	F	None	Great Britan	United States	Silvanus Jenkins	10 Mar 1827
WILMOT, C.	51	F		Great Britain		Caravan	8 Sep 1828
David	26	M	Nail Maker	Great Britain		Caravan	8 Sep 1828
G.	58	M	Joiner	Great Britain		Caravan	8 Sep 1828
Louiza	28	F		Great Britain		Caravan	8 Sep 1828

NAMES OF PASSENGERS	AGE	SEX	OCCUPATIONS	COUNTRY TO WHICH THEY BELONG	COUNTRY THEY INTEND TO INHABIT	SHIPS/DATES OF ARRIVAL	
WILMOT (cont'd)							
R.	8	F		Great Britain		Caravan	8 Sep 1828
Sophia	25	M		Great Britain		Caravan	8 Sep 1828
W.	17	M		England	U. States	Venus	4 Oct 1824
WILNEY, Ann	21	F		Great Britain	United States	Thomas Dickason	14 Sep 1827
Hannah	19	F		Great Britain	United States	Thomas Dickason	14 Sep 1827
Joseph	17	M	Shoe Maker	Great Britain	United States	Thomas Dickason	14 Sep 1827
Wm.	32	M	Shoe Maker	Great Britain	United States	Thomas Dickason	14 Sep 1827
WILOBY, Francis	27	F	Spinster	Ireland	U. States	Josephine	30 Aug 1828
WILPLEY, Elizabeth	29	F	Spinstress	Great Briton	United States	Erin	26 May 1821
WILSON, —, Mr.	23	M	Merchant	England	U. States	Ann Maria	13 Mar 1823
—, Mrs.	24	F	None	America	America	Bolivar	2 Oct 1826
...	5				Pennsylvania	Lady Hunter	19 Oct 1826
...	12	F	None	Great Britain	United States	Dalhouse Castle	21 Aug 1829
...	14	M	None	Great Britain	United States	Dalhouse Castle	21 Aug 1829
...	18	M	None	Great Britain	United States	Dalhouse Castle	21 Aug 1829
...	18	F	None	Great Britain	United States	Dalhouse Castle	21 Aug 1829
...	35	M	Tailor	Great Britain	United States	Dalhouse Castle	21 Aug 1829
...	35	F	None	Great Britain	United States	Dalhouse Castle	21 Aug 1829
...	50	M	Merchant	Great Britain	United States	Dalhouse Castle	21 Aug 1829
..., Jr.	10	M	None	Great Britain	United States	Dalhouse Castle	21 Aug 1829
...denr.	30	M	Farmer	Great Britain	United States	Penelope	11 Jun 1827
...n...	30	M	Farmer	Gt. Britain	P...	Betsey	18 Apr 1822
A.	18	M	Merchant	U. States	U. States	Astrea	19 Jul 1824
Aaron	14	M	Weaver	C. Anthrem	N. York or Jersey	Nile	18 Aug 1829
Agnes	1			Ireland	America	Ann	11 Apr 1821
Agnes	4	F	None	Ireland	United States	Lord Wellington	28 May 1827
Agnes	30	F	Lady	Scotland	United States	Sarah G.	15 Aug 1827
Agness	28	F			United States	Sarah	9 Nov 1820
Alaxander	6	M	None	Scotland	United States	Washington	2 Oct 1828
Alexander	42	M	Labourer	New York	New York	Wilson	28 Aug 1822
Alexr.	20	M	Servant	Ireland	United States	General Putnam	20 Jun 1825
Allan	21 6/12	M	Weaver	G. Britain	United States	Dutchess of Portland	30 Oct 1826
Amelia	1	F		Ireland	United States	Carolina Ann	11 Dec 1826
Amelia	47	F	Wife	G. Britain	U. States	Hynd	12 Jul 1820
Andrew	3	M		Scotland	United States	Samuel Robertson	5 Oct 1827
Andw.	24	M	Farmer	Ireland	United States	Margarett Scott	22 Aug 1827
Ann	3/12	F	None	England	United States	Roman	12 Jun 1826
Ann	4	F	None	Great Britain	United States	James Monroe	5 Apr 1820
Ann	5	F	None	Great Brittian	United States	Cortes	18 Oct 1820
Ann	5	F	his family [Jonathan]	England	U.N. States	Jane	7 Oct 1826
Ann	6	F	None	Gt. Britain	U.S.A.	Dalhouse Castle	21 Aug 1829
Ann	17	F		Gt. Britain		Dalhouse Castle	13 May 1828
Ann	18	F	Spinster	Ireland	United States	Trident	30 Sep 1826
Ann	19		Spinster	Ireland	U. States	Xenophon	28 May 1822
Ann	19	F		U. States	U. States	Hope & Esther	4 Oct 1825
Ann	25	F	None	Ireland	U. States	Henry Kneeland	27 Jul 1825
Ann	28	F	None	Great Britain	United States	James Monroe	5 Apr 1820
Ann	30				Pennsylvania	Lady Hunter	19 Oct 1826
Ann	35	F	None	Gt. Britain	U.S.A.	Dalhouse Castle	21 Aug 1829
Ann C.	6	F	Child	Ireland	America	Josephine	8 Dec 1827
Ann D.	40	F	Lady	Denmark		Elias Burger	28 May 1821
Ann M.	22	F		Halifax	New York	Hope & Esther	25 Aug 1827
Benjamin	38	M	Seaman	U. States		Thetis	29 Dec 1827
Benjn.	32	M		United States	U. States	Alexander	28 Jul 1821
Catharine	1	F		Halifax	New York	Hope & Esther	25 Aug 1827
Catharine	14	F		Great Britian	United States	London	24 Jan 1823
Cathe.	33	F				James Margaret	17 May 1827
Catherine	20	F	None	Scotland	United States	Washington	2 Oct 1828
Cha.	21	M	Child	Ireland	United States	Marmion	17 Jun 1825
Charles	35	M	Merchant	London	U. States	Aurora	22 May 1827
Charles	50	M	Farmer	Ireland	United States	Marmion	17 Jun 1825

1343

NAMES OF PASSENGERS	A G E	S E X	OCCUPATIONS	COUNTRY TO WHICH THEY BELONG	COUNTRY THEY INTEND TO INHABIT	SHIPS/DATES OF ARRIVAL	
WILSON (cont'd)							
Charlotte	4	F	None	England		Marchioness	13 May 1828
Charlotte	15	F	None	United States	United States	William Thompson	19 Aug 1829
Charlotte	22		Tailor	England	United States	Corinthian	7 Jul 1829
Chas.	22	M	Mechanic	Boston	U. States	St. Michaels	21 Apr 1824
Chas.	24	M	Planter	U. States	U. States	Prize	19 Jun 1823
Chas.	40	M		England	U. States	Charlotte	19 Feb 1822
Chn.	6	F				James Margaret	17 May 1827
Christr.	16	M	son of J. W.	Ireland	United States	Trident	30 Sep 1826
Cornelia	25		Servant	St. Croix	St. Croix	Emelia	26 Jun 1828
D.	16	M		Ireland	U. States	Ann Maria	5 Aug 1824
Darby	30	...	...	Ireland	United States	Carolina Ann	24 Oct 1825
David	2	M	None	Ireland	United States	Lord Wellington	28 May 1827
David	16	M	Farmer	Scotland	U.S.	Curler	19 Jul 1828
David	23	M	Farmer	Scotland	United States	Margaret Bogle	11 Jun 1824
David	24	M	Tailor	Scotland	U.S.A.	Hudson	21 Aug 1829
David S.	25	M	Merchant	U. States	U. States	Pacific	17 Jun 1828
Duncan	7 6/12	M	None	Great Britian	United States	George Clinton	21 Oct 1826
E.	20		Farmer	Ireland	United States	Courier	16 May 1825
Ebenr.	30	M	Doctor	Limerick	N. York	Thomas & William	25 May 1827
Edward	14	M	None	Great Britain	U.S.A.	Dalhouse Castle	21 Aug 1829
Edward	35	M	Tailor	Gt. Britain	U.S.A.	Dalhouse Castle	21 Aug 1829
Edward	4...	M	Merchant	Philad.	Philadelphia	Amity	13 Sep 1821
Edward, Jr.	10	M	None	Gt. Britain	U.S.A.	Dalhouse Castle	21 Aug 1829
Edward, Master	5	M		Denmark		Elias Burger	28 May 1821
Elibeth.	4	F				James Margaret	17 May 1827
Elijah	24	M	Accountant	G. Britian	U. States	Corinthian	4 Jan 1825
Elisebeth	20	F	None	Scotland	United States	Mary & Susan	5 Aug 1828
Eliza	2	F	None	Great Britain	United States	James Monroe	5 Apr 1820
Eliza	8	F	None	Great Brittian	United States	Cortes	18 Oct 1820
Eliza	10	F		Ireland	United States	Carolina Ann	11 Dec 1826
Eliza	10	F				James Margaret	17 May 1827
Eliza	12	F	None	Gt. Britain	U.S.A.	Dalhouse Castle	21 Aug 1829
Eliza	14	F	Spinner	Ireland	Red Stone	Triton	12 Jul 1823
Eliza	26	F		Ireland	United States	Marion	25 Nov 1825
Eliza	30	F		Ireland	United States	Carolina Ann	11 Dec 1826
Eliza Jane	14			Pennsylvania		Lady Hunter	19 Oct 1826
Elizabeth	8/12	F		England	New York	York	2 Dec 1828
Elizabeth	9	F	Farmer	Ireland	United States	Colossus	30 May 1825
Elizabeth	16	F		Great Britain	United States	Diana	6 Jul 1829
Elizabeth	21	F		Halifax	New York	Loire	11 Jun 1824
Elizabeth	21	F	None	London	U. States	Aurora	22 May 1827
Elizabeth	22	F	Servant	Ireland	U. States	Nancy	25 Nov 1823
Elizabeth	30	F	None	England		Marchioness	13 May 1828
Elizabeth	38	F	None	England	America	Colossus	22 Aug 1829
Ellen	12	F		Ireland	United States	Carolina Ann	11 Dec 1826
Emanuel	21	M	Collar Ma...	Great Britain	Wilmington, Del.	Zodiac	14 Jun 1822
F. C. C.	7	M		St. Croix	St. Croix	Jane	14 Jul 1825
Francis	18	M	Weaver	C. Anthrem	N. York or Jersey	Nile	18 Aug 1829
Frans.	8			Ireland	U. States	Xenophon	28 May 1822
Geo.	35	M	Sadler	Barbadoes	United States	Francis	11 Apr 1825
Geo. E.	18	M	Surgeon	Great Britain	U. States	Robert Fulton	7 Nov 1823
Geo. W.	31	M	Merchant	England	Canada	Exchange	20 Nov 1823
George	17	M		Great Britain	United States	Diana	6 Jul 1829
George	26	M	Mariner	Edinr., West Church [Parish], Edinr. [County]	New York	Hero	19 May 1828
George	27	M	None	England	America	William Byrnes	22 Dec 1828
George	27	M	Weaver	C. Down	Philedelphia	Nile	18 Aug 1829
George	28	M	Mariner	England	America	Meteor	22 Apr 1822
George	28	M	Farmer	England		Marchioness	13 May 1828
George	57	M	Gentleman	England	United States	Jubilee	1 Dec 1827
H.	25	M	Planter	St. Croix	St. Croix	Jane	14 Jul 1825
H.	32	M	Officer	N. York	U. States	Ann Maria	6 Jul 1824
H. T.	25	M	Merchant	Ohio		Secretary	10 Aug 1829

NAMES OF PASSENGERS	AGE	SEX	OCCUPATIONS	COUNTRY TO WHICH THEY BELONG	COUNTRY THEY INTEND TO INHABIT	SHIPS/DATES OF ARRIVAL	
WILSON (cont'd)							
Hannah	6	F	None	Great Britain	United States	Penelope	11 Jun 1827
Hannah	20	F	Servant	Great Britan	United States	Dispatch	16 Jul 1827
Hannah	32	F	None	Great Britain	United States	Aurora	10 Nov 1827
Harriet, Miss	14	F		Scotland	United States	Samuel Robertson	5 Oct 1827
Harriot	18	F		U. States	U. States	Criterion	29 May 1822
Henriettia	13	F	None	England	Albany	Indian Chief	19 Jun 1823
Henry	5	M	Boy	Ireland	United States	Borneo	14 Aug 1827
Henry	6	M	None	England		Marchioness	13 May 1828
Henry	22	M	Blacksmith	Scotland	United States	Washington	2 Oct 1828
Henry	35	M	Farmer	Ireland	United States	Colossus	30 May 1825
Henry	35	M	Gent.	England		Stephania	4 Apr 1826
Heny.	11			Ireland	U. States	Xenophon	28 May 1822
Hezekiah	22	M	Mariner	U. States	U. States	Telegraph	14 Jun 1828
Hugh	16	M	Farmer	Ireland	America	Wilson	27 Nov 1826
Hugh	48	M	Gentleman	St. Croix	Denmark	Chase	4 Sep 1821
Hugh, Master	3	M		Denmark		Elias Burger	28 May 1821
Isabel	7	F		Ireland	United States	Carolina Ann	11 Dec 1826
Isabella	3	F	None	Great Brittian	United States	Cortes	18 Oct 1820
Isabella	11	F	Child	Ireland	United States	Trident	30 Sep 1826
Isabella	14	F	None	England	Philada.	Colossus	2 Oct 1827
Isabella	18	F	Spinster	Ireland	Und. Stts of Amer	Alexander Mansfield	18 Aug 1826
Isabella	28	F	None	U. States	United States	Cortes	18 Oct 1820
J.	24	M	Mariner	Scotland	U.S. of America	Camillus	16 Apr 1822
J.	31	M	Engineer	England	U.S.	York	1 Dec 1827
J., Mrs.	22	F		U. States	U. States	Mentor	21 Mar 1825
J. S., Jur.	23	M	Merchant	U. States	U. States	Canada	6 Jun 1825
James	3	M	Farmer	Ireland	United States	Colossus	30 May 1825
James	3	M	Boy	Ireland	United States	Borneo	14 Aug 1827
James	4	M	Laborer or Spinster	Ireland	United States	Sarah G	11 Sep 1827
James	18	M	Farmer	Scotland	United States	Margaret Bogle	11 Jun 1824
James	19	M	Machine Maker	Ireland	New York	Atlantic	6 Oct 1828
James	20	M	Weaver	Great Britain	United States	Colossus	5 Jun 1827
James	22	M	Labourer	Ireland	U. States	Nancy	2 May 1823
James	23	M	...	Scotland	unknown	Robert Edwards	4 Jun 1824
James	23	M	Gentleman	U. States	U. States	William Byrnes	23 Jul 1824
James	24	M	...	...	...	Indian Chief	8 Sep 1824
James	24	M	Farmer	England	Great Britian	Florida	13 Feb 1826
James	24	M	Stone Mason	Great Brittian	United States	George Clinton	21 Oct 1826
James	26	M	Farmer	Ireland	United States	Trident	17 May 1825
James	38	M	Merchant	Great Britian	G.B.	Orozimbo	31 May 1824
James	40		Minister		Pennsylvania	Lady Hunter	19 Oct 1826
James [crossed out]	50	M	Farmer	U. States	United States	Columbia	17 Apr 1827
James A., Mr..	25	M	Merchant	Ireland	United States	Dublin Packet	6 Dec 1827
Jane	1	F	None	England	America	William Thompson	10 May 1825
Jane	2	F		Scotland	United States	Samuel Robertson	5 Oct 1827
Jane	8	F	Farmer	Ireland	United States	Colossus	30 May 1825
Jane	21	F		Great Britain		Manhattan	7 Nov 1827
Jane	22	F	...	...	...	Indian Chief	8 Sep 1824
Jane	25	F	Lady	Ireland	United States	Borneo	14 Aug 1827
Jane	40	F	None	Great Britain	United States	George Clinton	21 Oct 1826
Jane	60	F	Matron	Ireland	U. States	Josephine	7 May 1827
Janet	27	F		Scotland	United States	Samuel Robertson	5 Oct 1827
Jansan	4	F	None	Scotland	United States	Washington	2 Oct 1828
Jas.	4	M		England	New York	York	2 Dec 1828
Jas.	21	M		England		Anacreon	7 Sep 1827
Jas.	23	M	Weaver	Ireland	U. States	Atlantic	7 Aug 1823
Jas., Jr.	24	M	Merchant	U. States	New York	Howard	11 Jan 1827
Jesse	6	F	None	Great Brittian	United States	Cortes	18 Oct 1820
Jno.	17	M	None	Great Britain	U.S. America	Mentor	22 Jul 1823
Jno.	39	M	Mechanic	U. States	United States	John Wells	15 Jan 1827
Jno.	56 2/12	M	Farmer	Ireland	Red Stone	Triton	12 Jul 1823
Jno.	66	M	Painter	U. States	United States	Crisis	6 Apr 1825
Jno., Jr.	21 9/12	M	Farmer	Ireland	Red Stone	Triton	12 Jul 1823

NAMES OF PASSENGERS	AGE	SEX	OCCUPATIONS	COUNTRY TO WHICH THEY BELONG	COUNTRY THEY INTEND TO INHABIT	SHIPS/DATES OF ARRIVAL	
WILSON (cont'd)							
Jno. S.	6	M		U. States	U. States	Prize	19 Jun 1823
John	4/12	M	Child	Ireland	U.S. of America	Meteor	19 Mar 1828
John	1	M	Farmer	Ireland	United States	Marmion	17 Jun 1825
John	1	M	None	England		Marchioness	13 May 1828
John	18/12	M			United States	Sarah	9 Nov 1820
John	2	M	Laborer or Spinster	Ireland	United States	Sarah G	11 Sep 1827
John	3	M		Scotland	U. States	Camillus	17 Sep 1823
John	5	M				James Margaret	17 May 1827
John	13			Ireland	U. States	Xenophon	28 May 1822
John	18	M	None	Great Britain	U.S.A.	Dalhouse Castle	21 Aug 1829
John	19	M	Weaver	Ireland	United States	Henry Kneeland	7 Jun 1828
John	19					Zamoa	5 Nov 1828
John	19	M	Labourer	Ireland	New York	Lima	5 Aug 1829
John	20	M	Merchant	Grat Britan	Great Britan	Columbia	7 Apr 1823
John	20	M	Merchant	England	U. States	New York	15 Nov 1823
John	20	M		England	U. States	Criterion	20 Nov 1823
John	20	M	Pemman	Bardos	United States	McFingal	9 Dec 1826
John	20	M	Spinster	Great Brittain	United States	Corinthian	9 Jan 1827
John	20			England	U.N. States	Helen	17 Dec 1827
John	21	M	Farmer	Great Britain	United States	Aurora	5 Sep 1826
John	22	M	Gentleman	Ireland	America	Superior	12 Jun 1824
John	22	M	Farmer	Ireland	United States	Marion	25 Nov 1825
John	22	M	Merchant			General Marion	10 Dec 1825
John	22		Blacksmith	England	America	Sarah	18 Aug 1829
John	22	M	Weaver	Scotland	United States	Camillus	27 Oct 1829
John	24	M	Labourer	Ireland	United States	Trident	16 May 1826
John	24	M	Labourer	Ireland	United States	William & George	14 May 1828
John	25	M	Merchant	England	U. States	Orozimbo	7 Jul 1825
John	26	M	Farmer	Great Britain	United States	Elizabeth & Mary	20 Mar 1828
John	26	M	Farmer	England	United States	Jubilee	1 Oct 1828
John	27	M	Mechanic	St. John, N.B.	United States	Henrietta	3 Jun 1825
John	28	M	Servant	Ireland	U. States	Sarah G	30 Jun 1828
John	30	M	Labourer			Evergreen	28 Jul 1820
John	30		Tailor	England	United States	Corinthian	7 Jul 1829
John	32	M	Farmer	G. Britain	U. States	Freak	9 Jun 1828
John	33 6/12	M	Gentleman	England	America	Josephine	8 Jan 1827
John	34	M	Labourer	Ireland	United States	Hope	12 Jun 1824
John	36	M	Farmer	England	United States	Curler	3 Mar 1828
John	40	M	Clerk	Great Britian	United States	George Clinton	21 Oct 1826
John	40	M	Labourer	Ireland	United States	Lord Wellington	28 May 1827
John	42	M	Farmer	New York	New York	James Margaret	17 May 1827
John	45	M	Farmer	England	U. States	John Wells	16 May 1825
John	48	M	Farmer	United States	United States	Orozimbo	31 May 1824
John	48	M	Weaver	Ireland	United States	Trident	30 Sep 1826
John	57	M	Labourer	England	United States	Jubilee	12 May 1828
John H.	19	M	Cooper	Bermuda	Montreal	Orlando	1 Aug 1826
John P.	32	M	None	United States	United States	Columbia	9 Aug 1822
Jonathan	32	M	Carpenter	England	U.N. States	Jane	7 Oct 1826
Joseph	22	M	Weaver	G.B.	United States	Corinthian	29 Apr 1826
Josiah	26	M	Accountant	G. Britian	U. States	Corinthian	4 Jan 1825
Julia A.	24	F	Lady	Philadelphia, U.S.	United States	Lucinda	29 Jun 1825
Leonard	16	M	Weaver	Ireland	U. States	Atlantic	7 Aug 1823
Liddy	60	F	Spinner	C. Anthrem	N. York or Jersey	Nile	18 Aug 1829
Louisa, Miss	23	F		U. States	U. States	Hudson	10 Nov 1825
Luke	20	M	Weaver	C. Anthrem	N. York or Jersey	Nile	18 Aug 1829
M.	33	F	None	England	U. States	Birmingham	12 Oct 1827
M. M.	21	M	Super Cargo	Germany	United States	Howard	15 Jun 1825
M. M.	21	M	Merchant	America	New York	Howard	18 Jan 1826
Margaret	6	F	None	Great Britian	United States	George Clinton	21 Oct 1826
Margaret	9				Pennsylvania	Lady Hunter	19 Oct 1826
Margaret	23	F		Scotland	U. States	Camillus	17 Sep 1823
Margaret	25	F	None	England	United States	Roman	12 Jun 1826
Margaret	28	F	Spinster	Ireland	United States	Marmion	17 Jun 1825
Margaret	42	F	Spinster	Ireland	United States	Trident	30 Sep 1826
Margaret	61	F		Scotland	United States	Margaret Bogle	11 Jun 1824

NAMES OF PASSENGERS	AGE	SEX	OCCUPATIONS	COUNTRY TO WHICH THEY BELONG	COUNTRY THEY INTEND TO INHABIT	SHIPS/DATES OF ARRIVAL	
WILSON (cont'd)							
Margery	29	F		Ireland	United States	Marmion	17 Jun 1825
Margt.	1	F				James Margaret	17 May 1827
Margt.	16	F		Ireland	United States	Carolina Ann	11 Dec 1826
Margt.	18	F	Wife	Ireland	United States	Trident	16 May 1826
Margt.	23	F	Spinster	Ireland	United States	Trident	17 May 1825
Maria	12	F	None	England	Philada.	Colossus	2 Oct 1827
Maria	17	F	None	United States	United States	William Thompson	19 Aug 1829
Maria	48	F	None	England	Philada.	Colossus	2 Oct 1827
Marion	2	F	None	Great Brittian	United States	Cortes	18 Oct 1820
Martha	2	F	None	Gt. Britain	U.S.A.	Dalhouse Castle	21 Aug 1829
Martha	5	F	Farmer	Ireland	United States	Colossus	30 May 1825
Martha	25	F	Spinner	Ireland	Red Stone	Triton	12 Jul 1823
Martha	36	F	Farmer	Ireland	United States	Colossus	30 May 1825
Martha	50	F		U. States	United States	Crisis	6 Apr 1825
Martin	24	M	Labourer	Ireland	United States	Hope	12 Jun 1828
Mary	5	F		England	United States	Curler	3 Mar 1828
Mary	16	F	Weaver	C. Anthrem	N. York or Jersey	Nile	18 Aug 1829
Mary	21	F		Great Britain	United States	Diana	6 Jul 1829
Mary	22	F	Lady	England	United States	Jubilee	1 Dec 1827
Mary	25	F	Wife	Ireland	U.S. of America	Meteor	19 Mar 1828
Mary	26	F	None	England		Marchioness	13 May 1828
Mary	30	F	None	Great Britain	United States	Penelope	11 Jun 1827
Mary	30	F	Laborer or Spinster	Ireland	United States	Sarah G	11 Sep 1827
Mary	30	F	Matron	Ireland	America	Josephine	8 Dec 1827
Mary	32	F		England	New York	York	2 Dec 1828
Mary Ann	22	F	None	England	America	William Thompson	10 May 1825
Mary Ann	28	F	his wife [Jonathan]	England	U.N. States	Jane	7 Oct 1826
Mary Ann	54	F	Farmer	Ireland	Red Stone	Triton	12 Jul 1823
Mary Thomspon	5	F		Ireland	United States	Carolina Ann	11 Dec 1826
Moses	26	M	Weaver	C. Anthrem	N. York or Jersey	Nile	18 Aug 1829
Moses	30	M	Tanner & Currier	Ireland	United States	Alex. Mansfield	17 May 1823
Nancy	18	F		Ireland	United States	Marmion	17 Jun 1825
Preeson	2	F	None	Scotland	United States	Washington	2 Oct 1828
R.	36	M	Weaver	Scotland		Eliza Jane	12 Sep 1820
Rebecca	1	F	Child			Commerce	22 Jun 1825
Rebecca	20	F		Ireland	United States	Marmion	17 Jun 1825
Rebecca	50	F		Ireland	United States	Marmion	17 Jun 1825
Richard	2	M	None	England		Marchioness	13 May 1828
Richard	6	M	Farmer	Ireland	United States	Colossus	30 May 1825
Rob.	30	M	Farmer	England	U. States	Charles Hamilton	14 Jun 1823
Robert	13	M	Child	Ireland	United States	Trident	30 Sep 1826
Robert	14	M		Ireland	United States	Carolina Ann	11 Dec 1826
Robert	15	M		Scotland	Great Britain	Camillus	28 Apr 1823
Robert	18	M	Farmer	Ireland	United States	Romulus	24 Jun 1826
Robert	23	M	Farmer	Ireland	United States	Trident	30 Sep 1826
Robert	24	M	Spinner	Scotland	United States	Washington	2 Oct 1828
Robert	25	M	Farmer	England		Marchioness	13 May 1828
Robert	27	M	Merchant	United States	United States	Nimrod	30 Aug 1824
Robert A.	24	M	Farmer	Great Britain	U. States	Robert Fulton	7 Nov 1823
Robt.	17	M	Labourer	Great Britain	United States	Atlantic	8 Dec 1827
Robt.	21	M	Farmer	Straban	Baltimore	Favourite	8 Oct 1823
Robt.	23	M	Farmer	Great Britain	United States	Diana	6 Jul 1829
Robt.	25		Weaver	Great Britain	United States	Camillus	12 Sep 1827
Robt.	26	M	Farmer	Great Britain	United States	Mary & Harriet	3 Jul 1829
Robt.	35	M	Merchant	Gt. Britian	United States	Cortes	11 Dec 1822
Robt.	36	M	Weaver	England	U. States	York	4 Apr 1826
Robt.	38	M	Mercht.	Scotland	Mobile	Canada	1 Nov 1823
S.	26	M	Mariner	U. States	U. States	Hope & Esther	4 Oct 1825
Saml.	29	M	Merchandizing	Ireland	America	Josephine	8 Dec 1827
Samuel	3	M	Boy	Ireland	United States	Trident	17 May 1825
Samuel	40	M	Farmer	Ireland	America	Josephine	8 Dec 1827
Samuel	50	M	Husbandry	England	U. States America	Electra	17 Nov 1828
Sarah	1	F	Farmer	Ireland	United States	Colossus	30 May 1825
Sarah	1	F	Child	Ireland	United States	Marmion	17 Jun 1825
Sarah	12	F	Spinner	Ireland	Red Stone	Triton	12 Jul 1823

NAMES OF PASSENGERS	AGE	SEX	OCCUPATIONS	COUNTRY TO WHICH THEY BELONG	COUNTRY THEY INTEND TO INHABIT	SHIPS/DATES OF ARRIVAL	
WILSON (cont'd)							
Sarah	18	F	None	Gt. Britain	U.S.A.	Dalhouse Castle	21 Aug 1829
Sarah	23	F	Wife	Ireland	United States	Marmion	17 Jun 1825
Sarah	23	F	None	Great Britian	United States	George Clinton	21 Oct 1826
Sarah	26 5/12	F	Matron	England	America	Josephine	8 Jan 1827
Sopha	1	F	Servant	Ireland	U. States	Nancy	25 Nov 1823
Sophia	20	F	None	England	America	William Thompson	10 May 1825
Sophia, Miss	23	F		Scotland	United States	Samuel Robertson	5 Oct 1827
Stafford	27	M	Labourer	New York	New York	Hope & Esther	25 Aug 1827
Stanford	28	M	Mariner	U. States	U. States	Vermont	19 Jun 1827
Thomas	8/12	M	his family [Jonathan]	England	U.N. States	Jane	7 Oct 1826
Thomas	3	M	None	England		Marchioness	13 May 1828
Thomas	10				Pennsylvania	Lady Hunter	19 Oct 1826
Thomas	25	M	Weaver	Ireland	U. States	Courier	17 Mar 1828
Thomas	32	M	Merchant	England	U. States	William Thompson	17 Dec 1827
Thomas	40	M	Farmer	Ireland	United States	Carolina Ann	11 Dec 1826
Thos.	...	M	None	Philadelphia	Philadelphia	Amity	13 Sep 1821
Thos.	15/12	M	None	England	United States	India	8 Jun 1827
Thos.	13	M		Great Britain	United States	Diana	6 Jul 1829
Thos.	18	M	Labourer	Ireland	U. States	Balaena	29 Apr 1825
Thos.	20	M	Farmer	Ireland	United States	Meteor	27 Sep 1826
Thos.	21			England		Anacreon	7 Sep 1827
Thos.	23	M	Gardner	York, Great Britain		Casanda	5 Sep 1827
Thos.	42		Capt. Navy	United States	United States	Courier	15 Oct 1827
Thos., boy	15	M		Ireland	Philadelphia	Carolina Ann	15 Oct 1824
Timothy	31	M	Farmer	England		Marchioness	13 May 1828
Val	40	F	Lady	Bardos	United States	McFingal	9 Dec 1826
W.	21	M	Weaver			Hanford	17 Jul 1828
W. H.	27	M	Merchant	England	U. States	Venus	4 Oct 1824
W. W.	22	M	Merchant	G. Brittain	U. States	Pacific	23 Jan 1826
William	1	M	Boy	Ireland	United States	Trident	17 May 1825
William	5	M	None	England		Marchioness	13 May 1828
William	6			Ireland	U. States	Xenophon	28 May 1822
William	6	M	None	Ireland	United States	Lord Wellington	28 May 1827
William	7	M	Merchant	Great Britain	United States	Ann Maria	9 Mar 1820
William	12	M	Child	Ireland	United States	Trident	30 Sep 1826
William	18 4/12	M	None	United States	United States	Florida	10 Dec 1823
William	21	M	Baker	Ireland	U. States	Atlantic	19 Aug 1825
William	21	M	Weaver	Ireland	U. States	Josephine	7 May 1827
William	24	M	Farmer	England	United States	Roman	12 Jun 1826
William	24	M	Mechanic	America	America	Soto	1 Aug 1829
William	25	M	Farmer	Scotland	U. States	Mentor	21 Mar 1825
William	26	M	Carpenter	Ireland	United States	Borneo	9 Jul 1827
William	26	M	Farmer	Scotland	United States	Broke	16 Jul 1829
William	27	M	Merchant	Great Britain	Great Britain	Nancy	13 Dec 1822
William	27	M	Farmer	Scotland	United States	Samuel Robertson	5 Oct 1827
William	28	M	Spirit Healer	Scotland	United States	Samuel Robertson	5 Oct 1827
William	30	M	Meason	Clossion	Ireland	Carolina Ann	11 Jun 1824
William	34		...ght.	P...well, England	Great Britain	Frances Henrietta	31 May 1824
William	35		Blacksmith	England	United States	Thomas Dickason	5 Jun 1827
William	35	M	Merchant	England		Helen	4 Aug 1829
William	50	M	Merchant	Great Britain	U.S.A.	Dalhouse Castle	21 Aug 1829
William Henry	25		Merchant	Yarmouth	England	London	13 Dec 1822
Wm.	12 9/12	M		Ireland	U. States	Fabius	22 Sep 1828
Wm.	19	M	Farmer	Ireland	Red Stone	Triton	12 Jul 1823
Wm.	24		Farmer	England	United States	Mary	15 Jul 1822
Wm.	25	M	Butcher	Great Britain	United States	Diana	6 Jul 1829
Wm.	26	M	Seaman	Ireland	Unknown	Commerce	24 Sep 1823
Wm.	28	M		Great Britain	America	Lady Gallatin	21 Jun 1820

NAMES OF PASSENGERS	AGE	SEX	OCCUPATIONS	COUNTRY TO WHICH THEY BELONG	COUNTRY THEY INTEND TO INHABIT	SHIPS/DATES OF ARRIVAL	
WILSON (cont'd)							
Wm.	28	M	Labourer	Ireland	United States	Hope	12 Jun 1828
Wm.	30	M	Farmer	England	America	William Thompson	10 May 1825
Wm.	32	M	Mercht.	U. States	U. States	Charlotte	19 Feb 1822
Wm.	35	M	Wheelwright	Great Britain	United States	Diana	6 Jul 1829
Wm.	40			Ireland		Anacreon	7 Sep 1827
Wm.	50	M	Merchant	America	America	Corinthian	1 Sep 1827
Wm.	70	M		U. States	U. States	United States	11 Sep 1828
Wm. Henry	23		Attorney	England	England	Venus	4 Oct 1821
Wm. W.	43	M	Servant	Austria	U. States	New York	11 Mar 1823
WILTON, Bridget	30	F	Servant	Ireland	United States	Sarah G.	15 May 1828
Margt.	10	F		Ireland	United States	Sarah G.	15 May 1828
Thomas	35	M	Black Smith	Ireland	America	Carolina Ann	7 Aug 1826
William	30	M	Labourer	Gt. Britain	U. States	Sarah G.	14 Apr 1828
Wm.	25	M	Shoe Maker	Ireland	United States	Sarah G.	15 May 1828
WILTS, Wilhemina C.	15	F		Prusia	U. States	Harmony	6 Jan 1823
WILTSHIRE, Aaron	45	M	Farmer	Great Britain	United States	Mary Howland	19 Jul 1827
WIMBLE, Benj.	30					Cincinnatus	17 May 1823
WIMINGTON, Peter	36	M	Farmer	U. States		New York	18 Jul 1828
WIMMING, Jams	21	M	W. Right	Scotland	U. States	Superior	25 Sep 1828
John	20	M	W. Right	Scotland	U. States	Superior	25 Sep 1828
WIN, Lewis	22	M	Labourer	Wirtemberg	America, U.N.S.	Great Britain	3 Aug 1829
WINAN, John C.	23	M	Gentleman	U. States	U. States	Chase	22 May 1827
WINANS, W. W.	28	M	Gentleman	U. States		Diana	14 Sep 1820
WINBERGER, Margret	23	F	Servant	Germany	Missouri	Isabella	15 Sep 1828
WINBOLT, Samuel	26	M	Surgeon	England	England	Tampico	13 May 1828
WINCHELL, Lois	22	F		U.S.	U.S.	George Canning	26 Aug 1829
WINCKER, —, Miss	30	F		Germany	U. States	Lycurgus	3 Dec 1821
WIND, Robert	21	M	Baker	Scotland	United States	Camillus	9 May 1827
WINDALL, Adam	0 6/12	M	None	Holland	U. States	United States	7 Jul 1827
Mary	22	F	None	Holland	U. States	United States	7 Jul 1827
Peter	23	M	Carriage Maker	Holland	U. States	United States	7 Jul 1827
WINDEATT, Wm. B.	22	M	Merchant	Plymouth	England	Velocipede	24 May 1824
WINDELL, John	39	M		Great Brittain	United States	Sarah Ralston	27 Jan 1827
WINDHAM, George	28	M	Gentn.	England	Canada	Brighton	16 Nov 1826
WINDHOUR, Joseph, Mr.	20	M	Baker	England	U. States	Acasta	11 Dec 1826
WINDLE, Benny	13	M		Great Britain	New York	Panthea	24 Mar 1825
Mary	12	F		Great Britain	New York	Panthea	24 Mar 1825
Rhoda	34	F		Great Britain	New York	Panthea	24 Mar 1825
Thomas	35	M	...	Great Britain	New York	Panthea	24 Mar 1825
WINDLEY, John	18 5/12	M	Groom	England	United States	London	6 Feb 1829
WINDLING, Barbara	9	F		Switzerland	U. States	Hewes	30 Oct 1829
Joseph	21	M	Agriculturist	France	U.S.	Helen	3 May 1828
Matze	48	M	Weaver	Switzerland	U. States	Hewes	30 Oct 1829
Morgan	3	F		Switzerland	U. States	Hewes	30 Oct 1829
Salomer	47	F	Wife	Switzerland	U. States	Hewes	30 Oct 1829
WINDSOR, Ezekiel	48	M	Servant	U. States	United States	Pionier	4 Mar 1828
Mary Ann	22	F	Servant	...nbu...ge	United States	Carolina Ann	11 Jun 1824
WINDUST, Anne	51	F	...	...	New York	Frances Henrietta	25 Aug 1825
John	52	M	...	...	New York	Frances Henrietta	25 Aug 1825
Mary	13	F	...	...	New York	Frances Henrietta	25 Aug 1825
Mary Ann	16	F	...	...	New York	Frances Henrietta	25 Aug 1825
WINEMORE, Henry	32	M	Mariner	United States	United States	Nimrod	5 Apr 1821
WINFORD, Thos.	40	M	Gentleman	Philadelphia	Philadelphia	Inspector	26 May 1828
WING, Barbara	2	F	Farmer	Swizerland		Antioch	18 Aug 1829
Barbara	36	F	Farmer	Swizerland		Antioch	18 Aug 1829
Catherine	10	F	Farmer	Swizerland		Antioch	18 Aug 1829
Charles	8	M	Farmer	Swizerland		Antioch	18 Aug 1829
Charles	40	M	Farmer	Swizerland		Antioch	18 Aug 1829
Charlotte	6	F	Farmer	Swizerland		Antioch	18 Aug 1829
Elizabeth, Zyn Vrouw (his wife [George])	24	F		Toller	United States	Juffraw Johanna	16 Oct 1821
Frederic	4	M	Farmer	Swizerland		Antioch	18 Aug 1829

NAMES OF PASSENGERS	AGE	SEX	OCCUPATIONS	COUNTRY TO WHICH THEY BELONG	COUNTRY THEY INTEND TO INHABIT	SHIPS/DATES OF ARRIVAL	
WING (cont'd)							
George	23	M	Boer	Homburg	United States	Juffraw Johanna	16 Oct 1821
Joseph	29	M	Merchant	United States	United States	United States	18 Oct 1826
Maria	12	F	Farmer	Swizerland		Antioch	18 Aug 1829
WINGALL, J. P.	21	M	Supercargo	Wilmington	U. States	Margaret's Son	6 Jul 1825
WINGATE, Oliver	23	M	Merchant	Scotland	United States	Commerce	17 Jul 1823
R.	25	M	Merchant	England	England	Medina	23 Apr 1828
WINGER, Margt.	23 3/12	F	Servant	Ireland	United States	Atlantic	21 Jul 1827
WINHAM, Charles	15		Joiner	England	United States	Acasta	16 Aug 1826
Eldridge	34		Joiner	England	United States	Acasta	16 Aug 1826
WINIFRESS, Abraham	20	M	Shomaker	England	United States	Danube	13 Jul 1827
Charlotte	5/12	F		England	United States	Danube	13 Jul 1827
Mary	18	F		England	United States	Danube	13 Jul 1827
WINMAN, Wm.	24	M	None	England	U. States	Hercules	6 Jul 1827
WINN, Ann	29	F				Helen	4 Aug 1829
Benjn.	33		Mason			Helen	4 Aug 1829
Charlotte	20	F	None	Ireland	United States	Mary & Harriet	3 Jul 1829
Jas. R.	36	M	Mariner	Salem	U. States	Virginia	2 Feb 1822
Mary	20	F	Laborer	Ireland	United States	Weser	29 Jul 1823
WINNETT, Wm.	21	M	Merchant	Nova Scotia	St. John, N.B.	Hannah Eliza	6 Jun 1826
WINNIMORE, Isaac	30	M	Carpenter	America	America	Telegraph	18 May 1827
WINNING, Abigail	24	F	Wife of a Machinist	England	U.S. America	Criterion	27 Oct 1821
William	30	M	Labourer	England	United States	Criterion	27 Oct 1820
WINNINGTON, Peter	38	M		Gt. Britain	United States	John & Elizabeth	25 Sep 1827
WINNY, Patrick	21	M	Gentleman	Ireland	United States	Neury	27 Jan 1827
WINPENNY, Saml.	45	M	Farmer	England	U. States	Panthea	8 Apr 1826
WINS, John Lee	55	M		Great Britain	United States	Ganges	8 Jul 1820
WINSLAW, Ann	50	F		G. Britain	U. States	George Clinton	10 Sep 1828
WINSLOW, C. F., Mrs.	19	F		Great Britain	New York	Florida	3 Jun 1824
Emmily	7	F	None	United States	United States	Isaac Hicks	22 Aug 1829
F. D., Mr.	24	M	Merchant	Great Britain	New York	Florida	3 Jun 1824
Forbes	9	M	Child	Britain	America	Camillus	9 Oct 1820
H.	35	M	Merchant	U. States	St. Croix	Ice Plant	29 May 1826
Isaac	23	M	Mercht.	Bermuda	Bermuda	London	19 Dec 1823
Isaac	38 10/12	M	Ship Master	United States	United States	Cadmus	9 Dec 1825
J. D.	21	M	Merchant	Bermuda	Bermuda	Magnet	10 Jul 1820
Jeremiah	47 5/12	M	Merchant	U.S. America	U.S. America	Erie	19 Oct 1829
Josh.	39	M	Merchant	Maine	U.S.	Bayard	30 Oct 1820
Mary	47	F		Bermuda	America	Camillus	9 Oct 1820
Octavius	11	M	Child	Britain	America	Camillus	9 Oct 1820
R. F.	22	M	Merchant	U. States	U. States	Lexington	8 Jul 1828
Robert	12	M	Child	Britain	America	Camillus	9 Oct 1820
Susan	30	F	None	United States	United States	Isaac Hicks	22 Aug 1829
WINSOR, Hy.	14	M		Bermuda	U. States	Agnes	1 Jul 1825
Jane	23	F	Lady	U. States	U. States	Amulet	9 Jan 1829
WINSTANLEY, Thomas	21	M	H...	Lancashire	U. States	Atlantic	13 Jul 1824
WINSTONLY, Edwd.	17	M	Labourer	Ireland	U. States	William Byrnes	17 Jul 1825
Elizabeth	19	F		Ireland	U. States	William Byrnes	17 Jul 1825
WINSTUNLEY, James	18	M	Merchant	England		Reuben & Eliza	21 Aug 1820
WINTER, Catherine	24	F	Spinster	Ireland	United States	Asia	29 Jul 1829
Eliza	63	F		G. Britain	U. States	Robt. Edwards	4 Sep 1828
Geo.	5		Labourer	England	United States	Hugh Johnson	11 Jun 1828
Heniretta M.	46	F		England	U.S.	Maria Caroline	12 Jul 1820
James	47	M	Dyre	England	U.S.	Maria Caroline	12 Jul 1820
Jane	23	F		G. Britain	U. States	Robt. Edwards	4 Sep 1828
Mary	21	F	Spinster	Ireland	United States	Asia	29 Jul 1829
Robert	20	M	Laborer	Ireland	U. States	Howard Douglass	29 Jan 1828
Sidney	30	F	Spinster	Ireland	United States	Asia	29 Jul 1829
William	24	M	Farmer	Ireland	United States	Asia	29 Jul 1829
Wm.	19	M	Laborer	Ireland	U. States	Howard Douglass	29 Jan 1828
Wm.	75	M	Farmer	G. Britain	U. States	Robt. Edwards	4 Sep 1828
WINTERBALLON, John	40	M	Clothier	Great Brittain	United States	Nimrod	9 Jan 1827
WINTERBELLO, Robt.	33	M	Merchant	Gt. Britain	U. States	Cortes	6 Apr 1825
WINTERBOTHAM, Abraham	1	F		U. States	U. States	United States	11 Sep 1828

NAMES OF PASSENGERS	AGE	SEX	OCCUPATIONS	COUNTRY TO WHICH THEY BELONG	COUNTRY THEY INTEND TO INHABIT	SHIPS/DATES OF ARRIVAL	
WINTERBOTHAM (cont'd)							
Ann	20	F		U. States	U. States	United States	11 Sep 1828
C.	45	M	Merchant	England	United States	Abigail	25 Jun 1822
Horatio	20	M	Carpenter	U. States	U. States	United States	11 Sep 1828
WINTERBOTTOM, Ann	21	F		Great Britain	United States	Ganges	8 Jul 1820
Ben.	21	M	Labourer	Great Britain	United States	Atlantic	28 May 1827
John	23	M	Farmer	Great Britain	United States	Ganges	8 Jul 1820
Mary	Infant	F		Great Britain	United States	Ganges	8 Jul 1820
Peggy	2	F		Great Britain	United States	Ganges	8 Jul 1820
Racheal	38	F	None	Gt. Brittain	United States	Balaena	21 Aug 1824
Robt.	30	M	Merchant	England	U.N. States	Corinthian	1 Sep 1823
Saml.	28	M	Merchant	G.B.	U. States	Silas Richard	30 Jun 1828
Samuel	21	M	...	...	...	Meteor	16 Aug 1824
Wm.	24	M	Spinner	Great Britain	United States	Penelope	11 Jun 1827
Wm.	25	M		Great Britain	United States	Ganges	8 Jul 1820
WINTERBOTTON,							
Easter	25	F		England	America	Franklin	3 Dec 1827
WINTERS, Chas. Henry	26	M	Gentleman	England	New York	Hudson	20 Nov 1828
Clarise	28	F				Cassack	25 Jul 1820
Henry	22	M	Labourer	Ireland	United States	Carolina Ann	14 May 1827
Joseph	24	M	Coach Spring Maker	Great Britain	United States	Frances Henrietta	17 Sep 1827
Mary	17					William	17 Aug 1820
Peter	26	M	Shoemaker	Ireland	U. States	Josephine	7 May 1827
WINTHROP, Egerton	35	M	Physician	United States	U. States	Edward Bopnnaffe	30 Jul 1829
Robt. B.	23	M	Merchant	America	America	Peach	20 Mar 1826
Thos.	38	M	Merchant	U. States	U. States	Panthea	8 Apr 1826
WINTINGHAM, B.	34	M	Merchant			Eliza Jane	12 Sep 1820
WINTON, S.	28	M	Mariner	Great Britain		General Brown	17 Oct 1820
WIPPENHEIST, W.	24		Farmer	Breman	Germany	Hudson	14 Jun 1827
WIRE, E.	46	M		U. States	U. States	Julia	18 Apr 1828
William	18	M	Baker	Ireland	U. States	Wanderer	1 Sep 1828
WIRK, Christ	35	M	Farmer	Denmark	United States	Maria Elizabeth	6 Jan 1823
Maria	32	F		Denmark	United States	Maria Elizabeth	6 Jan 1823
WIRT, Robt.	12	M	Founder	Ireland	U. States	Meteor	19 Jul 1828
WIRTZ, Anthony	16	M		France	U. States	Edward Quesnel	4 Aug 1828
John Jacob	27	M	Labourer	Switzerland	United States	Thetis	5 Jul 1821
Mary	37	F	Baker	France	U.S.	Helen	3 May 1828
Phillip	40	M	Baker	France	U.S.	Helen	3 May 1828
WISE, Alfonce	22	M	Gentleman	Genavia	U. States	Farmers Fancy	7 Mar 1823
Arnold	17	M	Farmer	Great Britian	United States	Andes	19 Aug 1829
John	19		White Smith	Rewburyport	United States	Elizabeth	8 Dec 1821
Mary	19	F	None	Canada	Canada	James Cropper	29 Nov 1827
William, Mr.	25	M	Merchant	Great Britain	America	Atlantic	11 Oct 1822
WISEBURGH, Jonas	45	M		American	U. States	Prudence	19 Apr 1826
WISEMAN, Alexander G.	27	M	Chemist	Scotland	Unt. States	Robert Fulton	14 Mar 1829
Isabella G.	19	F		Scotland	Unt. States	Robert Fulton	14 Mar 1829
Mathew	39	M	Farmer	England	U. States	Oglethorpe	9 Nov 1824
WISEMOULD, Benj.	19	M	Farmer	Switzerland	United States	Factor	1 Sep 1823
WISER, Elizabeth	35	F	Servant	U. States	U. States	Alabama	21 May 1823
WISH, James	25	M	Merchant	Scotland	U. States	Nile	11 Jul 1822
WISHAM, Esther	18	F	None	England	New York	Thames	6 Oct 1820
WISHART, Jas.	26	M		Scotland	New York	Joseph Hume	26 Oct 1829
WISHET, James	25	M	Weaver	Ireland	United States	Kleber	23 Jul 1827
WISKER, John	39	M	Baker	England	America	Two Marys	24 Sep 1827
Mary	38	F		England	America	Two Marys	24 Sep 1827
WISS, Jacob	35	M	Merchant	Switzerland	New York	Florida	25 Mar 1824
Jacob	36	M	Merchant	U. States	New York	James Monroe	6 Jan 1825
Lewis M.	27	M	Merchant	United States	New York, U.S.	Florida	2 Oct 1828
WISSMANN, Fritz	20	M	Merchant	Germany	United States	Talma	12 Oct 1826
WISTERTON, Ann, Mrs.	50	F	Lady	G. Britain	U. States	Superb	9 Jul 1821
WISTON, Joshua E.	19	M	Gent.	U. States	U. States	James Monroe	24 Jan 1829
WITCHER, Geo.	28	M	Shoe Maker	Ireland	U. States	Albion	11 May 1827
Joseph	31	M	Dyer	Ireland	U. States	Albion	11 May 1827
WITCHERLY, John	21	M	Carpenter	Ireland	America	Liverpool	31 Aug 1827
WITCHIE, Catharina	12	F	children & family of Jno. Witchie	Switzerland	United States	Aurora	21 Jun 1824

NAMES OF PASSENGERS	A G E	S E X	OCCUPATIONS	COUNTRY TO WHICH THEY BELONG	COUNTRY THEY INTEND TO INHABIT	SHIPS/DATES OF ARRIVAL	
WITCHIE (cont'd)							
Catharine	44	F	Wife of [John]	Switzerland	United States	Aurora	21 Jun 1824
Frederick	8	M	children & family of Jno. Witchie	Switzerland	United States	Aurora	21 Jun 1824
Jacob	10	M	children & family of Jno. Witchie	Switzerland	United States	Aurora	21 Jun 1824
John	48	M	Rope Maker	Switzerland	United States	Aurora	21 Jun 1824
John, Jr.	21	M	Mason	Switzerland	United States	Aurora	21 Jun 1824
Lizette	18	F	children & family of Jno. Witchie	Switzerland	United States	Aurora	21 Jun 1824
Magdalena	6	F	children & family of Jno. Witchie	Switzerland	United States	Aurora	21 Jun 1824
Mary Ann	16	F	children & family of Jno. Witchie	Switzerland	United States	Aurora	21 Jun 1824
WITEKIST, Wm.	27	M	Seaman	England	England	Mentor	9 Apr 1822

*The above names seamen were put onboard the Ship Mentor at sea on her passage from Cadiz from onboard the Britishbrig Steel Capt. Crosworthe for alleged mutinous Conduct

NAMES OF PASSENGERS	A G E	S E X	OCCUPATIONS	COUNTRY TO WHICH THEY BELONG	COUNTRY THEY INTEND TO INHABIT	SHIPS/DATES OF ARRIVAL	
WITHELAM, Margaret	18	F		Germany	United States	Rent	13 May
WITHERFORD, Wm. M.	25	M	Mariner	Gt. Britain	U. States	Fourth of July	13 Jul 1825
WITHERS, Ann	16			England	United States	Thomas Dickason	5 Jun 1827
Eben	13			England	United States	Thomas Dickason	5 Jun 1827
Eliza	7	F		England	U. States	Magnet	6 Feb 1823
Esther	4	F		England	U. States	Magnet	6 Feb 1823
Henry	21	M	Labourer	Ireland	America	Wilson	27 Nov 1826
James	22	M	Weaver	Great Britain		Eliza Grant	29 Aug 1829
Jane	18	F		England	U. States	Magnet	6 Feb 1823
Jno.	13	M	Labourer	Ireland	United States	Thomas	13 Dec 1827
Jno.	21	M		Great Britain	U. States America	Maria	22 May 1822
John	21	M	Farmer	G. Britain	United States	Louisa	14 Jun 1825
John	51		Cord Wainer	England	United States	Thomas Dickason	5 Jun 1827
John, Jr.	25			England	United States	Thomas Dickason	5 Jun 1827
Margaret	50			England	United States	Thomas Dickason	5 Jun 1827
Mary	11	F		England	U. States	Magnet	6 Feb 1823
Mary	40	F		England	U. States	Magnet	6 Feb 1823
Richd.	20	M	Gun Smith	G. Britan	U. States	Geo. Canning	2 Sep 1828
Rob.	14	M		England	U. States	Magnet	6 Feb 1823
Robert	47	M		Great Britain	U. States America	Maria	22 May 1822
Sarah	22	F		Great Britain		Eliza Grant	29 Aug 1829
Thos.	44	M	Labourer	Ireland	United States	Thomas	13 Dec 1827
WITHERSPOON (see Wotherspoon)							
Robt.	30	M	...	...	U.S. America	Columbia	26 Nov 1825
WITHERTON, Chs.	39	M	Merht.	U. States	U. States	Hope	21 Oct 1823
WITHEY, George	58	M	Draper	Great Britain	Great Britain	James Monroe	27 Jul 1821
WITHINGTON, Elizabeth	70	F		America	America	James Cropper	14 Oct 1822
Emma	6	F		Great Britain	U. States	Ganges	21 Jun 1827
Jas.	32	M	Seaman	Monmouth	United States	Venus	8 Sep 1820
Louisa	1	F		Great Britain	U. States	Ganges	21 Jun 1827
Susannah	30	F	Manufacturer	Great Britain	U. States	Ganges	21 Jun 1827
Thomas	10	M	Manufacturer	Great Britain	U. States	Ganges	21 Jun 1827
Thomas	30	M	Manufacturer	Great Britain	U. States	Ganges	21 Jun 1827
WITHROW, Jas.	21	M	Farmer	Ireland	United States	Trident	16 May 1826
WITHWORTH, Samuel	17	M	Weaver	G.B.	Massachusetts	Eliza Grant	29 Aug 1829
Samuel	17	M		Great Britain		Eliza Grant	29 Aug 1829
Samuel	54	M	Weaver	G.B.	Massachusetts	Eliza Grant	29 Aug 1829
Sarah	21	F	None	England	United States	Orozimbo	1 Dec 1823
Sarah	54	F		G.B.	Massachusetts	Eliza Grant	29 Aug 1829
WITLOT, —, Mrs.	52	F	None	Scotland	United States	Camillus	28 Apr 1824
WITLOTT, Ann	26	F	None	United States	United States	Camillus	28 Apr 1824
Robert	23	M	Clerk	United States	United States	Camillus	28 Apr 1824
WITMORE, D.	40	M	Merchant	America	America	Nancy	18 Aug 1821
John	30	M	Shoemaker	Germany	United States	Rent	13 May
WITSON, Thomas	40	M	Manufacturer	Great Britain	United States	Ganges	26 Oct 1826
WITT, Antone	10/12	M		Gt. Brittan		L'Esperance	6 Sep 1828
Cath.	29	F		Gt. Brittan		L'Esperance	6 Sep 1828

NAMES OF PASSENGERS	AGE	SEX	OCCUPATIONS	COUNTRY TO WHICH THEY BELONG	COUNTRY THEY INTEND TO INHABIT	SHIPS/DATES OF ARRIVAL	
WITT (cont'd)							
M., Miss	18	F	Spinster	Germany	Charleston	Orion	24 Mar 1825
Maurice	29	M	Saddler	Gt. Brittan		L'Esperance	6 Sep 1828
WITTA, Christian	20	M	Taylor	Swiss	U. States	Comet	28 Jul 1825
WITTAKER, William	20	M	Weaver	England	United States	Cambria	16 Aug 1827
WITTER, Eliz.	2			England	United States	Hugh Johnson	11 Jun 1828
Geo.	9			England	United States	Hugh Johnson	11 Jun 1828
Mary	15			England	United States	Hugh Johnson	11 Jun 1828
Mary	35			England	United States	Hugh Johnson	11 Jun 1828
Ricd.	6			England	United States	Hugh Johnson	11 Jun 1828
Robt.	16			England	United States	Hugh Johnson	11 Jun 1828
Sarah	4			England	United States	Hugh Johnson	11 Jun 1828
Thomas	11			England	United States	Hugh Johnson	11 Jun 1828
Wm.	13			England	United States	Hugh Johnson	11 Jun 1828
Wm.	40		Farmer	England	United States	Hugh Johnson	11 Jun 1828
WITTMAN, Jacob	24	M	Farmer	Germany	U. States	Isabella	10 Aug 1829
Maria	2 6/12	F		Germany	U. States	Isabella	10 Aug 1829
Maria	22	F		Germany	U. States	Isabella	10 Aug 1829
WITTS, Broom	28	M	Merchant	England	U. States	Hudson	8 Oct 1827
WITWORTH, John	23	M	Manufactorer	England	United States	Orozimbo	1 Dec 1823
WITZ, John	23	M	None	Great Britain	United States	Hannibal	12 Oct 1829
WIZARD, Francois L.	4	M	Farmer	Corselle	U.S. America	Superior	18 Jun 1825
Sarah	39	F	Farmer	Corselle	U.S. America	Superior	18 Jun 1825
Solomon	37	M	Farmer	Corselle	U.S. America	Superior	18 Jun 1825
WMES., Wm.	3/12	M		Great B.	U. States	William Neilson	26 Jul 1828
WMOES., Jane	5	F		Great B.	U. States	William Neilson	26 Jul 1828
Richard	20	M		Great B.	U. States	William Neilson	26 Jul 1828
WO..., John	...	...	...	...	...	Pioneer	21 Jun 1825
WO...TON, John	29	M	Weaver	Ireland	U. States	Josephine	7 May 1827
Mary	29	F	Spinster	Ireland	U. States	Josephine	7 May 1827
WODDELL, Esther	63	F	Matron	Ireland	United States	Robert Fulton	24 Jul 1826
Mary	22	F	Spinster	Ireland	United States	Robert Fulton	24 Jul 1826
WODDLE, John	25	M	Weaver	Ireland	New York	Hope & Esther	21 Dec 1827
WODEHOUSE, P., Col.	32		Army	Norfolk	England	Elizabeth	8 Dec 1821
WOFFENDEN, Ann	0 2/12	F		Gt. Britain	U. States	Henry Kneeland	25 Sep 1827
John	1	M		Gt. Britain	U. States	Henry Kneeland	25 Sep 1827
Mary	35	F		Gt. Britain	U. States	Henry Kneeland	25 Sep 1827
P.	3	F		Gt. Britain	U. States	Henry Kneeland	25 Sep 1827
R.	37	M	Cloth Dresser	Gt. Britain	U. States	Henry Kneeland	25 Sep 1827
William	11	M		Gt. Britain	U. States	Henry Kneeland	25 Sep 1827
WOFSTER, C. E.	51	F		Great Britain		Caravan	8 Sep 1828
France	23	F		Great Britain		Caravan	8 Sep 1828
Geo.	53	M	Weaver	Great Britain		Caravan	8 Sep 1828
Theo.	18	F		Great Britain		Caravan	8 Sep 1828
WOHLER, —, Mrs.	63	F	Wife	Hanover	U. States	Minerva	9 Jan 1827
Charlotte	18	F		Hanover	U. States	Minerva	9 Jan 1827
WOHRA, —, Mrs.	35	F		Switzerland	United States	Eliza Grant	18 Aug 1826
Caroline	4	F		Switzerland	United States	Eliza Grant	18 Aug 1826
Magdene	3	F		Switzerland	United States	Eliza Grant	18 Aug 1826
WOLDMAN, Cresentia	6	F		Baden	United States	Jason	3 Nov 1828
Helena	3/12	F		Baden	United States	Jason	3 Nov 1828
Johannes	28	M	Weaver	Baden	United States	Jason	3 Nov 1828
Maria	3	F		Baden	United States	Jason	3 Nov 1828
Mina Kendle	25	F		Baden	United States	Jason	3 Nov 1828
WOLDROP, John	18	M	Merchant	America	America	Samuel Robertson	26 Nov 1825
WOLF, Ann	28	F		United States	United States	Globe	30 Aug 1828
Blacker	18		Servant	U. States	U. States	Zephyr	2 Oct 1826
Catharine	1	F		United States	United States	Globe	30 Aug 1828
E., Miss	16	F		U. States	U. States	Zephyr	2 Oct 1826
Eliza	20	F		United States	United States	Globe	30 Aug 1828
Geo.	70	M	Doctor	U.N. States of America		Franklin	14 Jan 1828
Geo. D. B.	21	M	Merchant	Bristol, R.I.	United States	Milo	8 May 1826
George	20	M	Tailor	United States	United States	Globe	30 Aug 1828
*landed at this Port, Custom House, Portland, Aug 19, 1828							
Henry	29	M	Brewer & Cooper	United States	United States	Globe	30 Aug 1828
Henry B.	32	M	Mercht.	U. States	U. States	Upton	6 Aug 1822

NAMES OF PASSENGERS	AGE	SEX	OCCUPATIONS	COUNTRY TO WHICH THEY BELONG	COUNTRY THEY INTEND TO INHABIT	SHIPS/DATES OF ARRIVAL	
WOLF (cont'd)							
Herbert	56	M	Mechanic	Hackinsack, N. Jersey	U. States	Ann	11 Sep 1823
John S.	35	M	Printer	Netherlands	United States	Ohio	10 Jul 1820
Lewis	22	M	Farmer	Hamburg	U. States	Martha	4 Sep 1828
Michael	21	M	Black Smith	Switzerland	Swizland	Le Voltaire	19 Jul 1828
Wm.	36	M	Captain	U.S.	U.S.	Porcia	4 Jan 1828
WOLFE, Joseph L.	25	M	Physician	Hamburg	U. States	Minerva	13 Sep 1827
WOLFER, John Ange	32	M	Merchant	Saxony	U. States	Franklin	3 Jul 1820
WOLFF, Eiger	40	M	Pedlar	Hungary	U. States	Brandt	8 Nov 1828
Frederick	22		Gentm.	Prussia	United States	Cadmus	24 Oct 1827
George	39	M	Merchant	Citisen of New York	U. States	Maria Elizabeth	9 Jun 1826
WOLFFAN, Catherine	1 4/12	F	Agriculturist	France	U.S.	Helen	3 May 1828
Christiana	3	F	Agriculturist	France	U.S.	Helen	3 May 1828
Christiana	36	F	Agriculturist	France	U.S.	Helen	3 May 1828
Jacque	10	M	Agriculturist	France	U.S.	Helen	3 May 1828
Jacque	37	M	Agriculturist	France	U.S.	Helen	3 May 1828
Mary	7	F	Agriculturist	France	U.S.	Helen	3 May 1828
WOLFFE, Johanna	25	F			U. States	Maria Elizabeth	9 Jun 1826
WOLFORT, Bernard	13	M		Germany	Pensylvania	James Noble	27 Aug 1827
Elizabeth	17	F		Germany	Pensylvania	James Noble	27 Aug 1827
Johannis	18	M		Germany	Pensylvania	James Noble	27 Aug 1827
WOLFSOHN, Jacob	20	M	Clerk	Bohemia	United States	Howard	6 Jul 1829
WOLGAN, Hannah, Miss	10	F	Carpenter	England	U.S.	Acasta	11 May 1827
Richard, Mast.	11	M	Carpenter	England	U.S.	Acasta	11 May 1827
Ruth, Mrs.	45	F	Carpenter	England	U.S.	Acasta	11 May 1827
WOLGAR, Hannah	18	F	Farmer	England	U. States	Acasta	21 Oct 1825
WOLKER, William, Mr.	24	M	Merchant	Great Britain	America	Atlantic	11 Oct 1822
WOLLANS, Robt.	26	M	Gardner	Great Britain	United States	Aspasia	16 Jul 1828
WOLLERDEN, James	26	M	Cloth Dresses	England	America	Josephine	8 Jan 1827
Robert	35	M	Clog & Last Maker	England	America	Josephine	8 Jan 1827
WOLLEY, Mary	55	F	Spinster	Grt. Britain	United States	Robert Fulton	8 Oct 1828
Mary, Junr.	20 6/12	F	Spinster	Grt. Britain	United States	Robert Fulton	8 Oct 1828
WOLLF, —, Child	2	M			U. States	Maria Elizabeth	9 Jun 1826
A.	40	M	Merch.	U. States		David Moffitt	7 Oct 1822
WOLPE, W.	26	M	Ship Master	United States	United States	Saluda	14 May 1827
WOLRIDGE, Henry	28	M	Merchaner	U. States	U. States	Huntress	30 Jun 1824
WOLTERS, Elisabeth	31	F		England	United States	Cosmo	26 Aug 1829
Mary	1	F		England	United States	Cosmo	26 Aug 1829
William	26	M	Sadler	England	United States	Cosmo	26 Aug 1829
WOMESLY, Jos.	50		Farmer	England	United States	Mary	15 Jul 1822
Mary	8		Farmer	England	United States	Mary	15 Jul 1822
Rachael	48			England	United States	Mary	15 Jul 1822
WONAL, Henry	30	M	Tailor	Great Brittan	U. States	John & Elizabeth	11 Dec 1826
WONDERLY, M.	50	M	Saddler	United States	United States	Seine	21 Oct 1822
WONDROBE, David	2	M		Scotland	United States	Camillus	27 Oct 1829
M.	24	F		Scotland	United States	Camillus	27 Oct 1829
WONLEY, Catherine	18	F	Farmer	Alsace in the Department of Upper and lower Rhine	United States	Carolina Augusta	16 May 1828
George	21	M	Farmer	Alsace in the Department of Upper and lower Rhine	United States	Carolina Augusta	16 May 1828
WOOCK, Adams	7	M	Farmer	Switzerland	United States	Olympia	12 Aug 1828
Barbara	3	F	Farmer	Switzerland	United States	Olympia	12 Aug 1828
Barbara	29	F	Farmer	Switzerland	United States	Olympia	12 Aug 1828
Barbe	6	F	Farmer	Switzerland	United States	Olympia	12 Aug 1828
Jacob	1	M	Farmer	Switzerland	United States	Olympia	12 Aug 1828
Salmé	4	F	Farmer	Switzerland	United States	Olympia	12 Aug 1828
Theboen	38	M	Farmer	Switzerland	United States	Olympia	12 Aug 1828
WOOD, —, Mrs.	27	F		England	U. States	Mogul	20 Jul 1825
—, Mrs.	28		Merchant	U. States	U. States	Edwin	26 Sep 1828
—, Mrs.	40	F		Great Britain	United States	Aspasia	16 Jul 1828
A.	40		None	Scotland	Upper Canada	Albion	11 Oct 1821
Alexr.	3/12	M	None	Great Brittan	United States	America	24 Jul 1827

NAMES OF PASSENGERS	AGE	SEX	OCCUPATIONS	COUNTRY TO WHICH THEY BELONG	COUNTRY THEY INTEND TO INHABIT	SHIPS/DATES OF ARRIVAL	
WOOD (cont'd)							
Alice	7	F		Great Britain	United States	Amelia	20 Aug 1829
Amos	32	M		England	U. States	Manhattan	12 Jun 1824
Ange	21	M	Taylor	England	America	Ann	11 Apr 1821
Ann	40	F		England	United States	Acasta	15 Jul 1822
Ann	45	F	Servant	Great Britain	United States	Nestor	3 Nov 1820
Anna	1	F		England	U. States	Howard Douglass	29 Jan 1828
Anne	6	F	None	England	United States	Jubilee	12 May 1828
Anthony	25	M	Black Smith	U. States	U. States	Washington	13 Jun 1825
Benj.	2	M		Great Britain	United States	Britannia	29 Oct 1829
Benjamin	17	M	Labourer	England	United States	Jubilee	12 May 1828
Benjamin F.	35	M	Merchant	G. Britain	U. States	James Monroe	18 Apr 1821
Betty	24	F	None	Great Britain	United States	Penelope	11 Jun 1827
Charles	5 2/12	M		England	U.S. of America	Illinois	16 Jun 1821
Charles W.	26	M	Mason	Great Britain	U.S. America	Chili	7 Jul 1827
Charlotte, Mrs.	35		Ladies	British Colony		Hesper	9 Jun 1827
Chas., Mr.	27	M	None	G. Britian	Canada	Corinthian	4 Jan 1825
Cs.	27	M	Silk weaver	England	United States	India	8 Jun 1827
Edward	11	M		England	America	Ann	11 Apr 1821
Edward, Mr.	30	M	Merchant	England	England	Florida	26 Sep 1826
Edwd.	3	M		England	U.S. of America	Illinois	16 Jun 1821
Elisabeth	25	F	None	Great Brittan	United States	America	24 Jul 1827
Elisabeth	57	F	None	England	U.N. States	William Byrnes	13 Aug 1829
Eliz.	24	F		England	U. States	Howard Douglass	29 Jan 1828
Eliz.	28	F	None	England	United States	India	8 Jun 1827
Eliza	4	F		England	U. States	John Jay	26 Jan 1829
Eliza	17	F				Cassack	25 Jul 1820
Elizabeth	4	F	Brickmaker	Great Britian	United States	Andes	19 Aug 1829
Elizabeth	6	F		England	U. States	John Jay	26 Jan 1829
Ellen	21	F	None	England	America	Ann	11 Apr 1821
Ellen	27	F	None	England	America	Ann	2 Nov 1820
Emma	26	F		England	U. States	Ann	27 Jul 1825
Esther	50	F	None	England	United States	Jubilee	12 May 1828
Esther, Jr.	13	F	None	England	United States	Jubilee	12 May 1828
Ewd.	24	M	Mercht.	G. Britain		Ann Maria	3 Jul 1820
Francis	16	F		Great Britain	United States	Aspasia	16 Jul 1828
Geo.	26	M	Merchant	England	U. States	Mogul	20 Jul 1825
George	4	M	None	England	United States	Jubilee	12 May 1828
George	21	M	Butcher	England	U. States	Manhattan	12 Jun 1824
George	25	M	Smith	Great Britain	United States	Mary Howland	19 Jul 1827
George	42	M	Farmer	United States	United States	Only Daughter	29 Apr 1825
H. R.	21	M	Merchant	N. York	U. States	Holquin	8 Jun 1825
H. R.	25	M	Merchant	U. States	U. States	Abigail	16 Jul 1824
Hanna	3	F		Great Britain	United States	Britannia	29 Oct 1829
Henry	21		Gentleman	Ireland	United States	Robert Burns	30 May 1823
Henry	22	M	Farmer	England	United States	Cambria	3 Jul 1829
Isaac J.	20	M	Merchant	United States	United States	William	7 Jan 1828
Isabella	21		...	Ireland	United States	Alexander Mansfield	23 Nov 1824
J.	12	M	Farmer	Great Britton	U. State	Earl of Liverpool	16 Aug 1826
J.	18	M	Merchant	U. States	U. States	Rising States	27 Nov 1826
J. F.	42	M	Planter	Barbadoes	Intend to return	Chasseur	17 Aug 1824
James	20	M	Clerk	Newfoundland	Nfoundland.	Combine	22 May 1824
James	20	M		Great Britain	United States	Mary Howland	19 Jul 1827
James	22	M	Labourer	England	U. States	Brighton	14 Apr 1828
James	26	M	Grocer	Gt. Britain	U. States	Maria	22 May 1822
James	27	M	Mechanic	England	United States of Am.	Helen	17 Dec 1827
James	27	M		Great Britain	United States	Aspasia	16 Jul 1828
James	28	M	Engraver	Great Britain	U. States	Ann Maria	26 Apr 1822
James	40	M	Carpenter	U. States	U. States	Commodore Perry	9 Apr 1821
James	55	M	Planter	Porto Rico	Porto Rico	Commerce	16 Oct 1821
James	60		Saw filer	Essex	United States	Elizabeth	8 Dec 1821
James B.	22	M	None	Bermuda	Newfoundland	Combine	13 Jul 1824
Jane	1	F	None	England	United States	Jubilee	12 May 1828
Jane	4	F	None	Great Brittan	United States	America	24 Jul 1827

NAMES OF PASSENGERS	AGE	SEX	OCCUPATIONS	COUNTRY TO WHICH THEY BELONG	COUNTRY THEY INTEND TO INHABIT	SHIPS/DATES OF ARRIVAL	
WOOD (cont'd)							
Jane	7			England	U.S. of America	Mary	21 Sep 1821
Jane	20	F		G. Britain	U. States	Dalhouse Castle	12 Sep 1828
Jane	23			England	U.S. of America	Mary	21 Sep 1821
Jane A.	30	F	None	United States	United States	Mount Vernon	30 Dec 1828
Jas.	23	M	None	Great Britain	United States	Penelope	11 Jun 1827
Jas.	33	M	Weaver	Great Britain	United States	Britannia	29 Oct 1829
Jennet	37	F	None	Great Britain	United States	Courier	26 Jun 1827
Jeremiah	36	M	Brickmaker	Great Britian	United States	Andes	19 Aug 1829
Jesse	4	M	None	England	United States	Jubilee	12 May 1828
Jno.	24			England	U.S. of America	Mary	21 Sep 1821
Jno. E.	30	M	Merchant	England	U. States	Ann	27 Jul 1825
Jno. S.	28	M	Mariner	U. States	U. States	Adonis	23 Jan 1822
John	2	M	None	England	America	Ann	2 Nov 1820
John	7	M	None	United States	United States	Hope	13 Jun 1822
John	7 1/12	M		England	U.S. of America	Illinois	16 Jun 1821
John	16	M	...	...	United States	Hanford	17 Oct 1828
John	18	M	Merchant	Great Britain	United States	Hanford	9 Oct 1829
John	21	M	Farmer	Great Britain	United States	Ganges	8 Jul 1820
John	22	M		Great Britain	United States	Mary Howland	19 Jul 1827
John	22	M				Eliza Grant	6 Oct 1828
John	24	M	Farmer	Ireland	U. States	Hibernia	29 Nov 1821
John	24	M	Weaver	England	U. States	Howard Douglass	29 Jan 1828
John	27	M	Farmer	Great Britian	United States	Andes	19 Aug 1829
John	29	M	White Smith	England	U. States	John Jay	26 Jan 1829
John	31	M	Mariner	America		Fame	9 Dec 1826
John	35	M	Labor	Rhode Island	United States	Jane	17 Jul 1821
John	35	M	Cordwainer	Great Brittain	United States	Nimrod	9 Jan 1827
John	40	M	Merchant	Scotland	Scotland	Albion	4 Oct 1820
John	48	M		England	England	Tontin	13 Jun 1825
John	51	M	Taylor	England	America	Ann	11 Apr 1821
John	57	M	Merchant	United States	United States	Maria	3 Oct 1822
John, Jr.	18	M	Carpenter	Great Britain	United States	Courier	13 Mar 1820
Jos.	40	M	Merchant	U. States	U. States	General Jackson	15 Jan 1829
Joseph	6	M	Brickmaker	Great Britian	United States	Andes	19 Aug 1829
Joseph	20 5/12	M	Hatter	England	Philadelphia	Concordia	12 Oct 1826
Joseph	21	M		Bermuda	Bermuda	Leander	30 Oct 1826
Joseph	30	M	Weaver	Harts	Yorkshire	Howard Douglass	11 May 1827
Joseph	30	M	Farmer	Gt. Brittian	United States	Manchester	16 Dec 1828
Joseph B. W.	23	M	Shoe Maker	England	America	William	21 Sep 1821
Juliann	23	F	Domestic	U. States	U. States	Washington	13 Jun 1825
Lewis	8	M	Brickmaker	Great Britian	United States	Andes	19 Aug 1829
Lucy Ann	13	F	None	United States	United States	Hope	13 Jun 1822
Lydia	16	F	None	England	United States	Jubilee	12 May 1828
Margaret	3	F	None	Great Brittan	United States	America	24 Jul 1827
Margart	19	F	Servant	Ireland	America	Carolina Ann	7 Aug 1826
Margt.	24	F	Spinster	Ireland	United States	Dublin Packet	22 Oct 1821
Martin S.	22 10/12	M	Merchant	U. States	U. States	Florida	18 Aug 1823
Mary	7	F	None	England	United States	Jubilee	12 May 1828
Mary	9	F	None	England	America	Ann	2 Nov 1820
Mary	23	F		Great Britain	United States	Britannia	29 Oct 1829
Mary	30	F		Great Britain	United States	Amelia	20 Aug 1829
Mary	34	F	Brickmaker	Great Britain	United States	Andes	19 Aug 1829
Mary Ann	10	F	Brickmaker	Great Britain	United States	Andes	19 Aug 1829
Matilda	11	F	None	United States	United States	Hope	13 Jun 1822
Moses	28	M	Mariner	United States	United States	Morkey	18 Aug 1825
Moses Q.	30		Merchant	U. States	U. States	Edwin	26 Sep 1828
N. C.	18	M	Servant	Ireland	U. States	Xenophon	13 Jun 1823
Nicholas	20	M	Weaver	Ireland	U. States	Josephine	27 Jul 1825
Patience	52	F	None	England	America	Ann	11 Apr 1821
R.	22	M	Farmer	England	U. States	Orazimbo	7 Jan 1821
Richard L.	42	M	Ship Master	United States	United States	Centurion	22 Dec 1828
Rob.	3	M		England	U. States	Howard Douglass	29 Jan 1828
Robert C.	24	M	Physitian	United States	U.S. States	Thrasher	4 Dec 1822
Robt.	30		Merchant	Quebec	Great Britain	William Thompson	13 May 1823

NAMES OF PASSENGERS	AGE	SEX	OCCUPATIONS	COUNTRY TO WHICH THEY BELONG	COUNTRY THEY INTEND TO INHABIT	SHIPS/DATES OF ARRIVAL	
WOOD (cont'd)							
Rosa	20	F	Spinster	Ireland	U.S. of America	Meteor	19 Mar 1828
Ruth	11	F	None	Great Britain	United States	Ganges	26 Oct 1826
Sam	2	M	None	United States	United States	Hope	13 Jun 1822
Saml.	17	M	Farmer	Lisbein	Baltimore	Favourite	8 Oct 1823
Saml.	17	M	Gentleman	Ireland	United States	Trident	16 May 1826
Saml.	40	M	Clergiman	Great Britain	U. States	Silas Richards	29 Oct 1828
Saml.	43	M	Filer	Great Britain	United States	Baltic	5 Apr 1826
Samuel	21	M	Merchant	England	America	Panthia	17 Sep 1821
Sarah	1	F	Brickmaker	Great Britian	United States	Andes	19 Aug 1829
Sarah	21	F	None	England	Pittsburgh	Orozimbo	8 Jun 1822
Sarah	25	F	None	Great Britain	U. States	Hannibal	12 Oct 1829
Sarah	29 11/12	F		England	U.S. of America	Illinois	16 Jun 1821
Sarah	30	F	None	Great Brittan	United States	America	24 Jul 1827
Sarah	38	F	None	United States	United States	Hope	13 Jun 1822
Sarah	55	F		England	United States	Acasta	15 Jul 1822
Thomas	9	M	None	United States	United States	Hope	13 Jun 1822
Thomas	14	M	None	England	United States	Jubilee	12 May 1828
Thomas	55	M	Carpenter	Great Britain	United States	Courier	13 Mar 1820
Thompson	25	M	Mechanic	Great Britain	U. States	Hannibal	12 Oct 1829
Timothy	22	M	Mechanic	U.S.	U.S.	Abeona	24 May 1822
W.	30	M	Merchant	England	U. States	Falcon	12 Oct 1822
W.	39	M	Farmer	Great Britton	U. State	Earl of Liverpool	16 Aug 1826
William	5	M	None	Great Brittan	United States	America	24 Jul 1827
William	20	M	Merchant	England	England	Britannia	5 Nov 1828
William	23	M	Stationer	England	United States	Acasta	15 Jul 1822
William	24	M	Labourer	England	America	Josephine	8 Jan 1827
William	26		Printer	Scotland	United States	Camillus	3 May 1828
William	29	M	Malstar	Great Britain	United States	Amelia	20 Aug 1829
William	30	M	Wool comber	England	America	Josephine	8 Jan 1827
William	54	M	Labourer	England	United States	Jubilee	12 May 1828
Wm.	5	M	None	United States	United States	Hope	13 Jun 1822
Wm.	28	M	Farmer	Great Brittan	United States	America	24 Jul 1827
Wm.	28	M		Scotland	U.S.	Curler	19 Jul 1828
Wm.	40	M	Labourer	Great Britain	United States	Aspasia	16 Jul 1828
Wm.	45	M	Gardner	Great Britain	United States	Penelope	11 Jun 1827
WOODBANK, Barbara	28	M		Bardin	U. States	Bayard	5 Sep 1828
WOODBARY, Samuel M. [crossed out]	37	M	Mariner			Agness	19 Mar 1827
WOODBINE, Robert	46	M	Wheelwright	Great Britian	United States	Andes	19 Aug 1829
Susan	1	F		Great Britian	United States	Andes	19 Aug 1829
Susan	39	F		Great Britian	United States	Andes	19 Aug 1829
William	2	M		Great Britian	United States	Andes	19 Aug 1829
WOODBRIGE, Wm., Revd.	35 2/12	M	Clergame	U.S. America	America	Erie	19 Oct 1829
WOODBURN, Wm.	2...	M	Labourer	Ireland	United States	Hope	12 Jun 1828
Wm.	21		Farmer	Ireland		Westmoreland	1 Aug 1826
WOODBURY, Geo.	25	M	Farmer	Great Britain	U. States	Gem	26 Jul 1827
Wm.	27	M	Farmer	Great Britain	U. States	Gem	26 Jul 1827
WOODCOCK, John	15	M	...	G. Brittain	America	Robin Hood	20 Jul 1827
WOODFIELD, Daniel	20	M	Farmer	England	United States	Jubilee	13 Jul 1829
WOODHAM, Joseph, Mr.	22	M	Miller	England	U. States	Acasta	11 Dec 1826
WOODHAMS, Elizabeth	53	F	Mother of [William]	U. Kingdom of Great Britain	United States	Cambria	7 May 1828
William	30	M	Farmer	U. States of America	United States of Amer.	Cambria	7 May 1828
WOODHEAD, H.	22	M	Joiner	Great Britain	United States	Isaac Hicks	6 Dec 1827
Mathew, Mr.	28	M	Merchant	England	America	Manhatten	4 Feb 1822
Thomas	26	M	Merchant	New York	New York	New York	14 Nov 1826
WOODHOUSE, Anthony	44	M	Turner	Great Britian	United States	George Clinton	21 Oct 1826
John	25	M	Shoemaker			Lady of the Lake	23 Aug 1828
Thomas	25	M	Merchant	England	U. States	Hiram	17 Jun 1826
WOODHULL, Jas.	23	M	Mechanic	Great Brittan	Great Brittan	Tuscarora	26 Jan 1827
John	45	M	Farmer	Great Britain	New York	Superior	5 Sep 1827
WOODKAM, David	26	M	Carpenter	England	U.S.	Acasta	11 May 1827
WOODLAND, Catherine	10/12	F	None	Great Britain	U. States	Hannibal	12 Oct 1829

NAMES OF PASSENGERS	AGE	SEX	OCCUPATIONS	COUNTRY TO WHICH THEY BELONG	COUNTRY THEY INTEND TO INHABIT	SHIPS/DATES OF ARRIVAL	
WOODLAND (cont'd)							
Hester	3	F	None	Great Britain	U. States	Hannibal	12 Oct 1829
Jane	6	F	None	Great Britain	U. States	Hannibal	12 Oct 1829
John	8	M	None	Great Britain	U. States	Hannibal	12 Oct 1829
Robert	12	M	None	Great Britain	U. States	Hannibal	12 Oct 1829
Susanna	5	F	None	Great Britain	U. States	Hannibal	12 Oct 1829
Susanna	40	F	None	Great Britain	U. States	Hannibal	12 Oct 1829
Thomas	15	M	None	Great Britain	U. States	Hannibal	12 Oct 1829
Thomas	44	M	Mechanic	Great Britain	U. States	Hannibal	12 Oct 1829
WOODLE, William	42	M	Farmer	England	Hallifax, N.V.	Hercules	10 Apr 1823
WOODLESS, W.	29	M	Cooper	Great Britain	U. States	Dominica	4 Jan 1823
Wm.	26	M	Ship Master	United States	U. States	Exchange	26 Jul 1824
WOODLIFE, Thos.	24	M	Clothier	Bristol	New York	Cosmo	25 Sep 1827
WOODMAN, D. H.	18	M	Mariner	U. States	U. States	Florida	25 Apr 1825
John	24	M	Baker	Great Britten	U. States	Magnet	29 Sep 1823
WOODROW, Benjamin	45	M	Tailor	England	Baltimore	Hudson	20 Nov 1828
WOODRUFF,							
Lewis	32 4/12	M	Merchant	U.S.A.	U. States	Silas Richards	27 Oct 1826
S.	65	M	Merchant	U. States	U. States	Factor	9 Mar 1829
WOODRUFFE, H. L.	26		Harnessmaker	Great Britian	Halifax	America	28 Jul 1826
WOODS, Barny	27 3/12	M	Shoe Maker	Ireland	United States	Atlantic	16 Dec 1825
Cathrine	28 9/12	F	Wife	Ireland	United States	Atlantic	16 Dec 1825
Charles	30	M	Farmer	Great Britain	United States	Blakely	29 Sep 1826
Charlotte	13	...	...	...	...	Pioneer	21 Jun 1825
Darriol	2 9/12	M	Child	Ireland	U. States	Josephine	30 Aug 1828
Dennis	14	M	Servant	United States	United States	William Bayard	17 May 1825
Eleanor	19 10/12	F		G. Britain	United States	Louisa	14 Jun 1825
Eliza	7	F		G. Britain	U. States	Nimrod	31 Jul 1828
Elizabeth	55	...	...	...	...	Pioneer	21 Jun 1825
Felix	21	M	Weaver	Ireland	United States	Romulus	24 Jun 1826
Frederick O.	32	M	Mariner	U. States	U. States	Rio	11 Sep 1827
Hugh	20	M	Weaver	Ireland	United States	Princess Charlotte	26 Apr 1827
James	...	...	...	...	...	Pioneer	21 Jun 1825
James	5	M		G. Britain	U. States	Nimrod	31 Jul 1828
James	19	M	Brewer	England	U. States	Panthea	22 Nov 1826
James	24	M	Cooper	Irereland	America	Carolina Ann	20 Jun 1825
James	25	M	Weaver	Ireland	Pensylvania	Atlantic	8 May 1828
James	44	M	Merchant	Ireland	United States	Dublin Packet	29 Jun 1825
James	45	M	Merchant	Ireland	G. Britain	Andrew Jackson	9 Oct 1820
James	57	M	Merchant	Ireland	U. States	Commerce	20 May 1823
Jane	2...	...	...	...	...	Pioneer	21 Jun 1825
Jane	24	F	None	Gt. Britain	United States	Eliza Barker	11 Jan 1826
Jno.			Sailor			Swift	28 Jan 1828
*Consul's man							
John	22	F	Farmer	Great Britain	U. States America	Columbia	15 Nov 1826
John	30	M	Tailor	Ireland	United States	Trio	13 Jun 1827
John	36	M	Ship Carpenter	Halifax	Halifax	Emeline	4 Sep 1827
Mary	19	F	Spinster	Ireland	U. States	Courier	17 Mar 1828
Mary	26	F	Matron	Ireland	U. States	Josephine	30 Aug 1828
Mary	30	F		G. Britain	U. States	Nimrod	31 Jul 1828
Mary, Jur.	4	F	Child	Ireland	U. States	Josephine	30 Aug 1828
Mary Ann	25	F		England	U. States	Panthea	22 Nov 1826
Nancy	20	F	Spinster	Ireland	U. States	Meteor	19 Jul 1828
Patrick	21	M	Baker	Gt. Britain	United States	Eliza Barker	11 Jan 1826
Peter	3	M		G. Britain	U. States	Nimrod	31 Jul 1828
Richard	24	M	Taylor	Ireland	U. States	Frances Henrietta	25 Oct 1824
Rose	20	F	Spinner	G. Britain	United States	Louisa	14 Jun 1825
William	22	M	Labourer	Ireland	United States	Robert Fulton	24 Jul 1826
William	65	...	...	...	...	Pioneer	21 Jun 1825
WOODSIDE, William	22	M	Surgeon	Ireland	United States	Orozimbo	21 May 1821
Wm.	30	M	Merchant	U. States	U. States	Georgetown Packet	6 Nov 1822
Wm. S.	20	M	Doctor	U. States	U. States	Leonora	10 Apr 1827
WOODVILLE, Wm.	28	M	Merchant	United States	United States	Orbit	31 Dec 1821
WOODWARD, Ann, Miss	9	F	Farmer	England	U. States	Acasta	12 May 1825
Benjamin	12	M	Gent.	England	America	Panthea	18 Jul 1823
Benjn., Master	10	M	Farmer	England	U. States	Acasta	12 May 1825

NAMES OF PASSENGERS	AGE	SEX	OCCUPATIONS	COUNTRY TO WHICH THEY BELONG	COUNTRY THEY INTEND TO INHABIT	SHIPS/DATES OF ARRIVAL	
WOODWARD (cont'd)							
Chas, Master	4	M	Farmer	England	U. States	Acasta	12 May 1825
Elisabeth, Mr.	65	F		England	U. States	Acasta	12 May 1825
Elish., Miss	11	F	Farmer	England	U. States	Acasta	12 May 1825
Elizabeth	10	F		England	America	Panthea	18 Jul 1823
Esther	8	F		England	America	Panthea	18 Jul 1823
Geo., Master	1	M	Farmer	England	U. States	Acasta	12 May 1825
George	38	M	Plumin	Manchester	United States	Nile	17 May 1827
George, Mr.	25	M	Surgeon	England	U. States	Acasta	12 May 1825
Henry, Master	6	M	Farmer	England	U. States	Acasta	12 May 1825
Henry Thos.	37	M	Farmer	Ireland	America	Panthea	18 Jul 1823
J.	25	M	Merchant	Halifax	Nova Scotia	Andrew Jackson	29 Aug 1823
Jane	1	F		England	America	Panthea	18 Jul 1823
Jery.	50	M	Gentleman	Nova Scotia	Nova Scotia	John	11 Jun 1825
Jesse	60	M	Merchant	United States	United States	Wanderer	31 Aug 1829
John, Master	12	M	Farmer	England	U. States	Acasta	12 May 1825
John, Mr.	39	M	Farmer	England	U. States	Acasta	12 May 1825
Judith	4	F		England	America	Panthea	18 Jul 1823
Lovedy Sarah Ridoux	37	F	Lady	England	America	Panthea	18 Jul 1823
Lucy, Miss	3	F	Farmer	England	U. States	Acasta	12 May 1825
Mary	35	F	Lady	Brit. Crowin	U. States	Edwin	1 Jul 1829
Sarah, Mrs.	38	F	Farmer	England	U. States	Acasta	12 May 1825
Stephen	17 6/12	M	Farmer	England	United States	Eliza Grant	7 Jun 1827
Wm.	31	M	Manufacturer	England	U. States	Mercator	28 Feb 1823
Wm., Master	8	M	Farmer	England	U. States	Acasta	12 May 1825
WOODWITH, Ann	16	F				Acasta	28 Jul 1823
Harriot	33	F				Acasta	28 Jul 1823
Harriott	6	F				Acasta	28 Jul 1823
James	8/12	M				Acasta	28 Jul 1823
John	3	M				Acasta	28 Jul 1823
William	8	M				Acasta	28 Jul 1823
WOODWORTH, W.	40	M	Doctor	St. Johns	St. Johns	St. Michael	26 Oct 1824
Wm. W.	18	M	Miner	United States	U. States	Saml. Smith	24 Jul 1826
WOOLAT, William	17	M	None	England	United States	Roman	12 Jun 1826
WOOLDRIDGE, John	18	M	Merchant	U. Kingdom Great Britain	United States	Cambria	7 May 1828
William	24	M	Surgeon	U. Kingdom Great Britain	United States	Cambria	7 May 1828
WOOLDRIGE, Geo.	35	M	Merchant	U. States	U. States	Liberty	20 Sep 1826
Stephen	54	M	Baker	New York	U. States	Cambria	3 Jul 1829
WOOLET, Ann	6/12	F	Child			Helen	4 Aug 1829
Ann	25	F	Lady	England		Helen	4 Aug 1829
WOOLEY, John	10		Laboring Class		United States	Atlantic	2 Apr 1827
Joseph	23	M	Worker at Steam Engines	England	New York	Exertion	3 Dec 1828
Josiah	20	M	Founder			Plato	31 Oct 1829
Rosa	12		Laboring Class		United States	Atlantic	2 Apr 1827
William	24	M	Farmer	England	United States	Silas Richards	3 Apr 1826
WOOLF, C. D.	44	M	Boddin	Farmer	U. States	Bayard	5 Sep 1828
Carl	24		Farmer	Bardin	U. States	Bayard	5 Sep 1828
Catharan	2	F		Farmer	U. States	Bayard	5 Sep 1828
Christian	9	M		Farmer	U. States	Bayard	5 Sep 1828
Christian	13	M		Farmer	U. States	Bayard	5 Sep 1828
Christian	46	M	Boddin	Farmer	U. States	Bayard	5 Sep 1828
David	5	M		Farmer	U. States	Bayard	5 Sep 1828
Eliz.	14	F		Farmer	U. States	Bayard	5 Sep 1828
Fredrick	21	M	Boddin	Farmer	U. States	Bayard	5 Sep 1828
Lousia	6	F		Farmer	U. States	Bayard	5 Sep 1828
William	15	M		Farmer	U. States	Bayard	5 Sep 1828
WOOLHIAN, John	21	M	Watch Maker	Ireland	United States	Genl. Marion	4 Jun 1828
WOOLLEY, Joseph		M	a Youth	Jamaica		Antelope	22 Aug 1820
Joseph	22	M	Merchant	Jamaica	U. States	Sanford William	28 Jan 1823
Melling	44	M	Merchant	England	United States	Manhattan	11 Oct 1824
Wm.	26	M				Belfast	28 Sep 1820
WOOLNOUGH, ...	3	M				Helen	4 Aug 1829
Ann	35	F				Helen	4 Aug 1829
Cornelius	40	M	Farmer			Helen	4 Aug 1829
Hamden	7	M				Helen	4 Aug 1829
Mary Ann	9	F				Helen	4 Aug 1829

NAMES OF PASSENGERS	AGE	SEX	OCCUPATIONS	COUNTRY TO WHICH THEY BELONG	COUNTRY THEY INTEND TO INHABIT	SHIPS/DATES OF ARRIVAL	
WOOLNOUGH (cont'd)							
Matilda	17	F		England	America	Silas Richard	24 Oct 1829
Monroe	5	M				Helen	4 Aug 1829
Oliver	1	M				Helen	4 Aug 1829
Priestley	11	M				Helen	4 Aug 1829
WOOLPER, Wm.	24	M	Mariner	Baltimore	U. States	Cannon	29 Dec 1825
*gone to Baltimore							
WOOLRIDGE, Henry	24	M	Merchant	New York	New York	Mazzinghi	27 Feb 1824
Henry	27	M	Stone Cutter	Hayti	U. States	Curlew	16 Jun 1823
WOOLSEY, Benjn.	25	M	Seaman	U. States	United States	Alfred	3 Jun 1826
C. W.	25	M	Merchant	U.S.A.	U.S.A.	Cantor	5 Nov 1825
Chs. Wm.	21	M	Merchant	United States	United States	Leeds	29 Sep 1823
E.	22	M	Merchant	England	U. States	New York	4 Nov 1824
Geo.	27	M	Merchant	America	U. States	Cincinnatus	5 Oct 1824
James	18	M	Laborer	Ireland	United States	St. Michaels	18 Jul 1826
Phoebe	28	F		U. States	U. States	Robert Fulton	1 Nov 1822
William D.	23	M	Merchant	Quebec, Canada	Great Britain	James Cropper	7 Oct 1823
WOON, George	47	M	Clothier	Great Britain	United States	John Wells	18 Sep 1826
WOORHEAD, Benjn.	24	M	Clothier	Huddlespits	Huddlespits	Howard Douglass	11 May 1827
WOOS, Mary	50	M	Planter	England	U. States	Electra	7 Jul 1828
Wm.	40	M	Varnish Maker	England	U. States	Electra	7 Jul 1828
WOOSTER, C.	32	M		U. States	U. States	Geo. Canning	2 Sep 1828
Ebenr.	26	M	Merchant	N. York	U. States	Amity	25 Sep 1822
Ebenzr.	24	M	Merch.	N. York	N. York	Wm. Thompson	13 Sep 1823
Eldad	26	M	Merchant	United States	United States	Baltic	21 Apr 1827
WOOTON, Charles	30	M	pudler		uncertain	Mount Vernon	29 Aug 1828
WORCESTER, John	26	M	Manufacturer	United States	United States	Roman	12 Jun 1826
WORD, John	25	M	Labourer	Ireland	U. States	Marcus	7 Apr 1825
WORDEN, Anna	4	F	Child	Ireland	United States	Sylvester Healy	17 Oct 1825
John	26	M	Gentleman	U. States Amer		Charlotte Corday	7 Mar 1820
WORDSWORTH, Betsey	4		Farmer	U. States	U. States	Venus	4 Oct 1821
Esther	7		Farmer	U. States	U. States	Venus	4 Oct 1821
John	34		Farmer	U. States	U. States	Venus	4 Oct 1821
Mary	34		Farmer	U. States	U. States	Venus	4 Oct 1821
WORIMAN, Wm.	58		Farmer	Kent County	Albany	Peru	30 May 1828
WORK, ...	...	F	C...	Ireland	New York	Wilson	10 Apr 1823
WORKMAN, Gordon		M	Chiefly farmers		United States	Factor	8 Jul 1829
John		M	Chiefly farmers		United States	Factor	8 Jul 1829
Mary		F	Chiefly farmers		United States	Factor	8 Jul 1829
Nancy		F	Chiefly farmers		United States	Factor	8 Jul 1829
Robert		M	Chiefly farmers		United States	Factor	8 Jul 1829
Thos.		M	Chiefly farmers		United States	Factor	8 Jul 1829
Wm.		M	Chiefly farmers		United States	Factor	8 Jul 1829
WORLEY, John	46	M		Great Britain	United States	Aspasia	16 Jul 1828
WORLSEY, James	24		Labourer	England	United States	Hudson	5 Apr 1826
William	23		Labourer	England	United States	Hudson	5 Apr 1826
WORMELEY, —	20/12	F	child of R & C. W.	England	unknown	Robert Edwards	4 Jun 1824
C.	25	F	Wife of the foregoing [R.]	England	unknown	Robert Edwards	4 Jun 1824
R., Esqr.	37	M	Post Captn. British Navy	England	unknown	Robert Edwards	4 Jun 1824
WORMLEY, Ralph R.	40		Captain in R.N.	United States	England	Hudson	14 Jun 1827
WORMSLEY, Hannah	32	F	None	England	United States	Hercules	24 Oct 1821
Thos.	48	M	Tailor	England	U. States	Thomas Ritchie	2 Jul 1827
WORNICK, Donel	31	M	Labourer	Ireland	United States	Hope	12 Jun 1828
WORPE, Ferdinand A.	6	M	Carpenter	Sondeborg	U.S. America	Superior	18 Jun 1825
Fredrick	44	M	Carpenter	Sondeborg	U.S. America	Superior	18 Jun 1825
Harriet	8	F	Carpenter	Sondeborg	U.S. America	Superior	18 Jun 1825
Harriet	36	F	Carpenter	Sondeborg	U.S. America	Superior	18 Jun 1825
WORRALL, Benm.	4	M	None	Great Brittain	U. States	William Byrnes	23 Jul 1824
George	3	M	None	Great Brittain	U. States	William Byrnes	23 Jul 1824
Isaac	1	M	None	Great Brittain	U. States	William Byrnes	23 Jul 1824
John	16	M	None	Great Brittain	U. States	William Byrnes	23 Jul 1824
Joseph	11	M	None	Great Brittain	U. States	William Byrnes	23 Jul 1824
Marry	35	F	None	Great Brittain	U. States	William Byrnes	23 Jul 1824
Robt.	9	M	None	Great Brittain	U. States	William Byrnes	23 Jul 1824
Sarah	6	F	None	Great Brittain	U. States	William Byrnes	23 Jul 1824

NAMES OF PASSENGERS	AGE	SEX	OCCUPATIONS	COUNTRY TO WHICH THEY BELONG	COUNTRY THEY INTEND TO INHABIT	SHIPS/DATES OF ARRIVAL	
WORRALL (cont'd)							
Thos.	12	M	None	Great Brittain	U. States	William Byrnes	23 Jul 1824
WORRELL, Geo. W.	22	M	Merchant	American	U. States	Brutus	13 Oct 1823
Geo. W.	26	M	Merchant	U. States	U. States	Dingleys	12 Aug 1824
Geo. W.	28	M	Merchant	Wilmington	Wilmington, N.C.	Eliza Pigott	29 May 1826
Joseph	22	F	Merchant	America	America	Venus	15 Apr 1822
Wm.	37	M	Gentleman	England	U. States	Elizabeth	20 Sep 1822
WORSEY, Richard	22	M	Labourer	Ireland	United States	General Marion	6 Oct 1828
WORSHEL, Eliza	8	F		G. Britain	U. States	London	23 Sep 1828
James	18	M		G. Britain	U. States	London	23 Sep 1828
John	35	M		G. Britain	U. States	London	23 Sep 1828
Mary	24	F		G. Britain	U. States	London	23 Sep 1828
WORSICK, Benjamin	59	M	Weaver	Great Britain	U.S. of America	Gratitude	3 Oct 1829
Jane	55	F		Great Britain	U.S. of America	Gratitude	3 Oct 1829
WORST, Daniel	32		Mechanic	U.S. America	America	Hesper	9 Jun 1827
Samuel	26		Mechanic	U.S. America	America	Hesper	9 Jun 1827
WORSTER, C.	30	M	Merchant	U. States	U. States	Pacific	11 Sep 1824
John	22	M	Cooper	U. States	U. States	Nancy	26 Apr 1828
WORT, Mary	20	F				Bordeaux	17 Jun 1825
S.	31	M	Physician	U. States		Bordeaux	17 Jun 1825
WORTH, Ann	23	F		Philada.	U. States of A.	William	30 May 1826
Isaac	26	M	Weafer			Commerce	22 Jun 1825
Thos.	29	M	Farmer	Great Brittain	U.S. America	York	4 Aug 1826
WORTHING, J.	25	M	Gentleman	American	U. States	Abeona	1 Apr 1824
WORTHINGTON, Eliza	20	F		G. Britain	U. States	John Jay	17 Sep 1828
Jane	3	F		G. Britain	U. States	John Jay	17 Sep 1828
Mary	1	F		G. Britain	U. States	John Jay	17 Sep 1828
Mary	25	F	None	Great Britain	U. States	Columbia	24 Dec 1822
W.	19	M	Physician	U. States	U. States	Trader	24 Jun 1828
W. T.	20	M	Navy	U. States	U. States	Marmion	29 Sep 1823
William	21	M	Mason	Great Britain	United States	Mary Howland	19 Jul 1827
WORTLE, Abraham	25	M	Baker	Germany	United States	Rent	13 May
Jacob	50	M	Miller	Germany	United States	Rent	13 May
Wm.	24	M	Butcher	Germany	United States	Rent	13 May
WORTLEY, Jno. S.	23	M	Gentleman	England	Great Britain	New York	22 Jul 1824
WOTHERSPOON,							
Abraham	47	M	Bricklayer	Great Britain	United States	Colossus	5 Jun 1827
George	25 3/12	M	Merchant	Great Britain	America	Magnet	13 Nov 1821
George	26	M	Merchant	Great Britain	United States	Meteor	15 Apr 1823
J., Mr.	25	M	Merchant	England	England	Manchester	8 Dec 1827
James	24	M		Great Brittain	Canada	Canada	5 Feb 1827
Thomas	21	M	Merchant	England	World	James Cropper	3 Mar 1825
Thos.	23	M	Merchant	G. Britan	G. Britan	Canada	27 Sep 1826
WOTHINGSON, George	24	M	Merchant	Great Britain	Great Britain	Martha	25 Nov 1820
WOTHY, Mary	30	F		Scotland	United States	Delta	24 Oct 1829
WOTKIN, Anne	18	F	None	Great Brittan	U.S.	Emulous	29 Jun 1827
WOTMAN, James	11	M	Farmer	Switzerland		Charlemagne	20 Aug 1829
WOTMANN, John	38	M	Farmer	Switzerland		Charlemagne	20 Aug 1829
WOUDLE,							
Hiam Thomsa	15	M	Farmer	England	Hallifax, N.V.	Hercules	10 Apr 1823
WRAGG, Job	25	M	Bookeeper	England	U.S. of America	Hannibal	17 Dec 1823
Mathew, Mr.	24	M	Merchant	England	America	Manhatten	4 Feb 1822
Thos. B.	23	M	Merchant	England	Canada	Manhattan	12 May 1823
WRATTON, —, Mrs.	51	F		England	United States	Richmond	4 Aug 1826
George	20	M		England	United States	Richmond	4 Aug 1826
James	22	M		England	United States	Richmond	4 Aug 1826
John	17	M		England	United States	Richmond	4 Aug 1826
William	55	M	Farmer	England	United States	Richmond	4 Aug 1826
WRAY, Elenor	8	F	Farmer	Great Britain	United States	Thomas Dickason	31 Jul 1829
John	24	M	Labourer	Ireland	United States	Robert Fulton	10 Aug 1827
Mary	27	F	Farmer	Great Britain	United States	Thomas Dickason	31 Jul 1829
Mathew	30	M	Farmer	Great Britain	United States	Thomas Dickason	31 Jul 1829
Matilda	2	F	Farmer	Great Britain	United States	Thomas Dickason	31 Jul 1829
Sarah	3	F	Farmer	Great Britain	United States	Thomas Dickason	31 Jul 1829

NAMES OF PASSENGERS	AGE	SEX	OCCUPATIONS	COUNTRY TO WHICH THEY BELONG	COUNTRY THEY INTEND TO INHABIT	SHIPS/DATES OF ARRIVAL	
WREAKS, Charles H.	24	M	Merchant	Great Britain	U. States	New York	19 Nov 1828
H.	25	M	Mercht	G. Britain	U. States	New York	6 Mar 1827
WREN, Frances	7	F				Washington	16 Sep 1820
Geor.	8	M				Washington	16 Sep 1820
Harriet	5	F				Washington	16 Sep 1820
Jane	35	F				Washington	16 Sep 1820
Walter	22	M	Miller	England	America	Criterion	27 Oct 1821
William	1 7/12	M				Washington	16 Sep 1820
WRENCH, Christopher	26	M	Labourer	Germany	U.S.A.	Hudson	21 Aug 1829
WREZER, Saml.	30	M		England	U. States	Hiram	25 Jul 1828
WRIANTE, Joachim	50	M	Merchant	France	U. States	Edward Bopnnaffe	30 Jul 1829
WRIEGLEY, Wm.	32	M	Farmer	Saddelworth		Aurora	8 Jun 1827
WRIGHEY, Edward	19	M	Merchant	England	U. States	York	13 Aug 1827
WRIGHT, —, Mr.	25	M	Mariner	New Jersey	U. States	Amanda	19 Jan 1824
—, Mrs.	40	F				Frances	17 Aug 1820
...	25	M	Labourer	Ireland	United States	Fabius	31 Jul 1829
A.	28	M	Merchant	Great Britain	Canada	Columbia	7 Sep 1827
Abraham	30	M	Confectioner	Liverpool	Liverpool	Howard Douglass	11 May 1827
Albinia	21	F		Great Britain		Corinthian	27 Oct 1829
Alexander	10	M	None	Great Britain	United States	Orozimbo	5 Mar 1827
Alfred	22	M	Merchant	U. States	U. States	Golden Age	6 Jul 1821
Allen	2	M		G. Britain	U. States	Freak	9 Jun 1828
Ann	1/12	F		Great Britain	United States	Freake	25 Aug 1829
Ann	18	F	None	Great Britain	United States	Orozimbo	5 Mar 1827
B.	35	M	Labourer	Great Britain	United States	Frances Henrietta	17 Sep 1827
C.	15	M	boy	Ireland	United States	Abigail	25 Jun 1822
Camilla	25	F		Scotland	U. States	London	13 Sep 1824
Caroline	12	F	None	Great Britain	United States	Orozimbo	5 Mar 1827
Daniel	55	M	Farmer	Scotland	Scotland	Chief	14 Nov 1823
David	61	M	Gentleman	Derby, England	Great Britain	James Cropper	7 Oct 1823
Edd.	23		Black Smith	Rualon, England	Great Britain	Franklin	22 Jun 1827
Edmund	30	M	Planter	G. Britain	America	Spring	12 Oct 1821
Edward	22	M	Merchant	United States	United States	York	31 Mar 1828
Edward	30	M	Labourer	England	United States	Jubilee	12 May 1828
Eleanor	1	M	Labourer	Ireland	U. States	Atlantic	19 Aug 1825
Elizabeth	25	F		U. States		Carrier	31 Aug 1820
Elizabeth	38	F		Great Britain	United States	Freake	25 Aug 1829
Ellington	21	M	Mariner	Great Briton	United States	Brighton	12 Jun 1826
Evander	20	M	Weaver	Great Britain	United States	Orozimbo	5 Mar 1827
Ewd.	35	M	Farmer			Belfast	28 Sep 1820
Felicilus	8	F	None	Great Britain	United States	Orozimbo	5 Mar 1827
Francis	27	F		Scotland	U. States	London	13 Sep 1824
George	1 6/12	M	Child	England	United States	Cambria	3 Jul 1829
George	13	M		Irereland	America	Carolina Ann	20 Jun 1825
George	21	M	Mason	England	United States	Cambria	3 Jul 1829
Gersho	18			Bardin	U. States	Bayard	5 Sep 1828
Hannah	4/12	F	Child	Ireland	U.S. of America	Meteor	19 Mar 1828
Hannah	2	F	None	England	United States	Hercules	24 Oct 1821
Harriett	1	F	None	Liverpool	Liverpool	Howard Douglass	11 May 1827
Henry	23	M	Plater	U. States	Great Britain	Thompson	26 Apr 1828
Isaac M.	14	M		United States		Britannia	20 Jun 1827
Isaih	17 9/12	M	Farmer	Great Briton	Pensylvania	Brighton	12 Jun 1826
J.	27	M	Mechanic	England	U. States	Hanover	12 Oct 1822
James	3	M		Great Britain	United States	Freake	25 Aug 1829
James	22	M	Tailor	Great Brittan	U. States	John & Elizabeth	11 Dec 1826
James	26	M	Weaver	Ireland	U. States	Josephine	7 May 1827
James	31	M	Farmer			Frances	17 Aug 1820
James	36	M	Surgeon	Gt. Britain	U. States	Frances Henrietta	18 Apr 1825
James	40	M		England	United States	William Byrnes	6 Apr 1826
James, Doctor	40	M	Surgeon	Ireland		Carolina Ann	7 Apr 1826
James, Dr.	40	M	Surgeon	Ireland		Meteor	27 Sep 1826
James, Esq., M.D.	36		Physician	Ireland	United States	Fabius	18 Mar 1829
James, Sir	23	M	Gentleman	England	England	Manhattan	21 Sep 1822

NAMES OF PASSENGERS	AGE	SEX	OCCUPATIONS	COUNTRY TO WHICH THEY BELONG	COUNTRY THEY INTEND TO INHABIT	SHIPS/DATES OF ARRIVAL	
WRIGHT (cont'd)							
Jane	21	F				Imperial	19 Jul 1820
Jane	22	F	Labourer	Ireland	U. States	Atlantic	19 Aug 1825
Jane	28	F	None	England	United States	Jubilee	12 May 1828
Janet	20	F	None	Scotland	America	Minerva	8 Oct 1824
Jno.	20	M				Cassack	25 Jul 1820
John	6	M		Great Britain	United States	Freake	25 Aug 1829
John	20	M	Labourer	Ireland	U.S. of America	Meteor	19 Mar 1828
John	23	M	Mason	England	United States	Enterprize	19 Oct 1826
John	24	M	Labourer	Scotland	United States	Friends	7 Jul 1827
John	27	M	Farmer	St. Jno. New Brunswick	St. Jno. N.B.	Loire	9 Aug 1821
John	29 4/12	M	Printer	G. Britain	United States	Dutchess of Portland	30 Oct 1826
John	30	M	Wool ...ter	England	Uncertain	John Wells	22 Sep 1824
John	30	M	Farmer	Shropshire	Liverpool	Aldebaron	21 Jan 1826
John	30	M	Farmer	Scotland	U. States of Amer	Dale	14 Mar 1828
John	31	M	Spinner	Scotland	United States	Orion	15 Jan 1827
John	38	M	Gent.	Liverpool	United States	Dalhousie Castle	27 Jul 1826
John	40 5/12	M	Farmer	Great Britain	United States	Venus	8 Sep 1820
John, Dr., of Boston *Died on the Voyage						Columbia	7 Sep 1827
John Kirlew	22	M	Mariner	England	England or Jamaica	Packet	11 Oct 1823
Jonathan	2	M	None	England	United States	Jubilee	12 May 1828
Jonathan	5	M				Euphrates	8 Aug 1820
Joseph	3	M	None	Liverpool	Liverpool	Howard Douglass	11 May 1827
Joseph	14	M	None	Great Britain	United States	Orozimbo	5 Mar 1827
Joseph	35	M	Clergyman	England	United States	Hercules	21 Nov 1822
Kitty	23	F		G. Britain	U. States	Freak	9 Jun 1828
London	64	M	Gent	U. States	U. States	Charlemagne	19 Sep 1828
M.	3/12	F				Belfast	28 Sep 1820
Malcom	21	M	Farmer			Frances	17 Aug 1820
Margaret	18	F	None	Scotland	America	Minerva	8 Oct 1824
Marshall	20	M	Gentleman	United States	United States	Emulous	25 May 1825
Mary	4	F	None	England	United States	Hercules	24 Oct 1821
Mary	14	F		Ireland	U. States	Nancy	16 Aug 1822
Mary	28	F				Euphrates	8 Aug 1820
Mary	40	F	None	Great Britain	United States	Orozimbo	5 Mar 1827
Mary	41	F	Wife	Ireland	United States	Dublin Packet	13 Oct 1828
Mary, Miss	25	F	Lady	England	U. States	Florida	16 May 1827
Matilda	21	F	Wife	Ireland	U.S. of America	Meteor	19 Mar 1828
Michael	44	M	Weaver	Great Britain	United States	Orozimbo	5 Mar 1827
Olive	30	F	None	Liverpool	Liverpool	Howard Douglass	11 May 1827
Patrick	30	M	Farmer	Scotland	America	Minerva	8 Oct 1824
Peter	18	M	Farmer			Frances	17 Aug 1820
Peter	49		Planter	United States	United States	Roman	10 Sep 1827
Robert	9	M	None	Great Britain		Olive Branch	9 Oct 1829
Saml.	30	M	Merchant	Great Britain	Savannah	James Cropper	14 Oct 1824
Saml.	46	M	Labourer	Ireland	U. States	Atlantic	19 Aug 1825
Saml., Mr.	32	M	Merchant	Savannah	Savannah	Birmingham	16 Oct 1826
Samuel	3	M				Carrier	31 Aug 1820
Samuel	6	M	None	England	United States	Hercules	24 Oct 1821
Samuel	23	M	Umbrella Maker	G. Britain	U. States	America	17 Oct 1825
Samuel	25 8/12	M	Merchant	Great Britain	United States	Hector	8 Jan 1820
Samuel	29	M	Merchant	County Down, Ireland	United States	James Cropper	7 Oct 1823
Samuel	31	M	Merchant	U. States	Georgia	James Cropper	21 Oct 1825
Sarah	27	F	None	England	United States	Hercules	24 Oct 1821
Sarah	30	F	Silk Weaver	Great Britain		Olive Branch	9 Oct 1829
Sarah Anne	6/12	F	None	England	United States	Jubilee	12 May 1828
Sophia	26	F	Spinster	United States	United States	Abaco	20 Oct 1829
Susannah	14	F				Imperial	19 Jul 1820
Susannah	27	F	Wife	England	United States	Cambria	3 Jul 1829
Thomas	19	M	Manufacturer	Scotland	United States	Camillus	9 May 1827
Thomas	25		Surgeon	England	England	Hudson	4 Sep 1823
Thomas	29	M	Taylor			Lady of the Lake	23 Aug 1828

NAMES OF PASSENGERS	AGE	SEX	OCCUPATIONS	COUNTRY TO WHICH THEY BELONG	COUNTRY THEY INTEND TO INHABIT	SHIPS	DATES OF ARRIVAL
WRIGHT (cont'd)							
Thomas	46	M	Merchant	Great Britain	United States	Hannibal	27 May 1822
Thos.	9	M				Belfast	28 Sep 1820
Thos.	30	M	Labourer	Gt. Britain	U. States	St. George	20 Sep 1828
W.	11	F				Belfast	28 Sep 1820
W.	34	F				Belfast	28 Sep 1820
W.	35	M	Servant	Great Britain	United States	Nestor	3 Nov 1820
W. P.	20	M	Accoantant	England	America	Franklin	19 Nov 1828
William	5	M				Carrier	31 Aug 1820
William	14	M	Farmer	England	America	Panthia	17 Sep 1821
William	20	M	Yeoman	England	New York	Hudson	20 Nov 1828
William	21	M	Farmer	Ireland	America	Imperial	19 Jul 1820
William	21	M	Mechanic	Ireland	U.S.A.	Dalhouse Castle	21 Aug 1829
William	38	M	Merchant	United States		Britannia	20 Jun 1827
William	40	M	Farmer	Ireland	America	Farmer	15 Nov 1823
William	45	M	Farmer	Great Briton	Pensylvania	Brighton	12 Jun 1826
Wm.	4	M	Labourer	Ireland	U. States	Atlantic	19 Aug 1825
Wm.	6	M	None	Liverpool	Liverpool	Howard Douglass	11 May 1827
Wm.	7	M				Belfast	28 Sep 1820
Wm.	21	M	Blacksmith	Wales	U.S. States	Splendid	14 Aug 1829
Wm.	21	M	Mechanic	Ireland	United States	Dalhouse Castle	21 Aug 1829
Wm.	24	M	None	Great Britian	U. States	Pallas	17 Aug 1824
Wm.	26	M		G. Britain	U. States	Freak	9 Jun 1828
Wm.	35	M	Wheelwright	Great Britain	United States	Freake	25 Aug 1829
Wm.	40	M	Farmer	St. Johns	U. States	Nancy	10 Jul 1822
Wm. W.	21		Merchant	England		Hudson	5 Apr 1826
Wm. W.	38		Merchant	Scotland		Zamoa	5 Nov 1828
WRIGHTSON, John	33	M	Farmer	Great Britain	United States	Dapper	24 Aug 1827
WRIGLEY, Amelia	3	F	None	England	United States	Ann Maria	23 Oct 1820
Ann	33	F	None	England	United States	Ann Maria	23 Oct 1820
Edwd.	7	M	None	England	United States	Ann Maria	23 Oct 1820
Fras.	30	M	Merchant	England	United States	Ann Maria	23 Oct 1820
Fras., Jr.	9	M	None	England	United States	Ann Maria	23 Oct 1820
Jno. M.	23	M	Merchant	G. Brittain	U. States	Canada	6 Jun 1825
John M.	25	M	Merchant	G. Bt.	U. States	Canada	12 May 1828
Joseph	24	M	Merchant	Great Britain	United States	James Monroe	5 Apr 1820
Joseph	30 3/12	M	Mason	England	New York	Concordia	12 Oct 1826
Mary G.	4	F	None	England	United States	Ann Maria	23 Oct 1820
Sarah A.	6	F	None	England	United States	Ann Maria	23 Oct 1820
William	24	M	Labourer	England	U. States	Ayrshire	12 May 1828
WRILEY, Ellen	24	F	None	Great Britan	U. States	Ann Marria	6 Aug 1823
Michael	35	M	None	Great Britan	U. States	Ann Marria	6 Aug 1823
WRIT, Owen	25	M	Laboror	Ireland	United States	Wilson	27 Jun 1826
WROTCROFT, John	32		Cabinet Maker	Sheffield, England	Great Britain	Franklin	22 Jun 1827
WUNDMAN, Archd.	29	M	Seaman	Great Britain	United States	Minerva	28 Jul 1823
WUNINBURGH, Frans., Jr.		M		New York	New York	Fair Play	8 Jun 1824
WURDEMAN,							
Frederick	17	M	None	America	America	Orozimbo	1 Oct 1827
WURTAGH, Mary	35	F	Sevt.	Sligo	New York	Susquehana	27 Jun 1823
WURTMAN, Mary	6	F	Farmer	Switzerland		Charlemagne	20 Aug 1829
Wm.	8	M	Farmer	Switzerland		Charlemagne	20 Aug 1829
WYATT, Emma	2 6/12	F	None	Gt. Britain	U. Canada	Crisis	13 Nov 1824
Francis	1	M	None	Gt. Britain	U. Canada	Crisis	13 Nov 1824
Francis	28	M	Carpenter	Gt. Britain	U. Canada	Crisis	13 Nov 1824
Geo. L., Mr.	32	M	Mercht.	Gt. Brittian	United States	Manchester	16 Dec 1828
Mary Ann	26	F	None	Gt. Britain	U. Canada	Crisis	13 Nov 1824
WYBOURNE, Charles	4	M	None	England	United States	London	21 May 1828
J. O.	24	F	None	England	United States	London	21 May 1828
James	14	M	None	England	United States	London	21 May 1828
John	12	M	None	England	United States	London	21 May 1828
Martha	48	F	None	England	United States	London	21 May 1828
Robert	10	M	None	England	United States	London	21 May 1828
William	19	M	None	England	United States	London	21 May 1828
WYBOUTT, P. R.	30	M	of Connissary Genl.			Washington	16 Sep 1820
WYCKOFF, H. S.	24	M	Merchant	America	America	Britannia	5 Nov 1828
Peter S.	29	M	Farmer	New York	U.S. America	Lafayette	3 Dec 1827
WYER, —, Mr.	22	M	Merchant	N. York	N. York	Nancy	10 May 1825

NAMES OF PASSENGERS	AGE	SEX	OCCUPATIONS	COUNTRY TO WHICH THEY BELONG	COUNTRY THEY INTEND TO INHABIT	SHIPS/DATES OF ARRIVAL	
WYER (cont'd)							
Ann	9	F		Ireland	United States	Enterprize	23 Jul 1827
B.			Mariner	U. States	U. States	Acosta	28 Jul 1823
Catherine	1	F		Ireland	United States	Enterprize	23 Jul 1827
Ed.		M	Bearer of Dispatches	Spain	Spain	Canton	25 Aug 1823
Edward	25	M	Labourer	Ireland	United States	Enterprize	23 Jul 1827
Edward	45	M	Consul	U. States	U. States	Weymouth	3 Apr 1821
Isabella	45	F		G. Britain	U. States	Hanford	10 Jun 1828
John	51	M	Farmer	G. Britain	U. States	Hanford	10 Jun 1828
Judah	21	F		Ireland	United States	Enterprize	23 Jul 1827
M.	18	F		G. Britain	U. States	Hanford	10 Jun 1828
WYETT, Joseph	19	M	Weaver	Great Britain	United States	William Dawson	18 Jun 1827
WYLE, John	40	M	Mariner	N. York	U. States	Planter	16 Mar 1824
WYLIE, G. A.	35	M	Merchant	Virginia	U. States	Pacific	16 Apr 1825
James	23	M	Weaver	Scotland	United States	Hope	5 Dec 1827
WYLIN, F., Mrs.	20	F		Germany	Pennsylvania	Ocean	23 Oct 1820
Godfrey	8	M		Germany	Pennsylvania	Ocean	23 Oct 1820
WYLLER, Christian	24	M	Framer	Switserland	Ohio	Danube	20 Jul 1826
WYMAN, William	21		Brazier			Caroline	10 Mar 1828
WYMBS, James	9 7/12	M		Ireland	U.S. of America	Douglass	6 Jul 1829
Michl.	20	M		Ireland	U.S. of America	Douglass	6 Jul 1829
Pat	8 2/12	M		Ireland	U.S. of America	Douglass	6 Jul 1829
WYND, Alexander	21	M	Baker	Dundee	Noagards	Robert	28 Aug 1829
WYNN, Catharine	21	F	Servant	Ireland	United States	Carolina Ann	14 May 1827
John	22	M	Farmer	Preston	Preston	Howard Douglass	11 May 1827
Mary	60	F	Farmer	Ireland	United States	Carolina Ann	14 May 1827
WYNNE, Ally	19 10/12	F	Servant	Ireland	U. States	Fabius	22 Sep 1828
John	16 5/12	M	Labourer	Ireland	U. States	Fabius	22 Sep 1828
Pat	23	M	Musician	Sligo	U. States	Panthea	8 Apr 1826
WYSE, James	17	M	Confectioner	Great Britain	United States	Elizabeth & Mary	20 Mar 1828
WYVOCK, Edward	24	M	Merchant	Germany	U. States	Kanhawa	6 May 1828
Johannes	45	M	Merchant	Germany	U. States	Kanhawa	6 May 1828
XAVERA, Francisco	20	M	Clerk	Portugal	U. States	Minos	24 Oct 1828
XAVIER, F.		M	Officer	Portugal	Portugal	Diana	7 Jun 1823
XIGLEY, Thomas	28	M	Labourer	Great Britain	United States	Aspasia	16 Jul 1828
XIGUOS, Joseph	11	M	Merchant	Spain	U. States	Dromo	4 May 1827
Lorenzo	13	M	Merchant	Spain	U. States	Dromo	4 May 1827
Namon	13	M	Merchant	Spain	U. States	Dromo	4 May 1827
XIMENES, Alexis	32	M	Merchant	Havana	U. States	Courier	9 Feb 1829
XOQUES, Francisco	26	M	Merchant	Mexico	Mexico	Eliza	14 Mar 1825
XOUPI, —, Mr.	40	M	Professor	France	Baltimore	Cadmus	16 Aug 1826
Y..., Catherine	18	F		Switzerland	United States	Elbe	2 Aug 1822
YALE, Alexr.	19					Zamoa	5 Nov 1828
YANCY, Elsy	1	F		U. States	U. States	Nassau	13 Aug 1825
James H.	5	M		U. States	U. States	Nassau	13 Aug 1825
John	41	M	Labour	U. States	U. States	Nassau	13 Aug 1825
John James	6	M	Labour	U. States	U. States	Nassau	13 Aug 1825
Lucy	11	F	Labour	U. States	U. States	Nassau	13 Aug 1825
Mary	8	F	Labour	U. States	U. States	Nassau	13 Aug 1825
Salinda	33	F	Labour	U. States	U. States	Nassau	13 Aug 1825
William	3	M		U. States	U. States	Nassau	13 Aug 1825
YANFITT, David	27		Mechanic	England		Zamoa	5 Nov 1828
YARDAN, E. S.	25	M	Merchant	Spain	Spain	Prince Edward	25 Feb 1822
YARDERE, E.	30	M	Merchant	France	U. States	Laveria	23 Jul 1828
YARDLEY, W. W.	21	M	Merchant	U. States	U. States	Worromontogus	23 Jun 1823
W. W.	22	M	Merchant	Pennsylvania	U. States	South Carolina	28 Nov 1823
YARRAYHAM, Bridget	20	M	Baker	...	...	Laurel	16 Nov 1824
YATES, Agness	4	F		G. Britain	U. States	William Thompson	30 Apr 1822
Ann	8			England	U. States	Corinthian	8 Oct 1828
Charlotte	22	F	Wife	U. States	U.S.	Queen Mab	26 Nov 1825
Edward	55			England	U. States	Corinthian	8 Oct 1828
Elisebath	1			England	U. States	Corinthian	8 Oct 1828

NAMES OF PASSENGERS	AGE	SEX	OCCUPATIONS	COUNTRY TO WHICH THEY BELONG	COUNTRY THEY INTEND TO INHABIT	SHIPS/DATES OF ARRIVAL	
YATES (cont'd)							
Emma	5	F		G. Britain	U. States	William Thompson	30 Apr 1822
Geo.	7	M		G. Britain	U. States	William Thompson	30 Apr 1822
Hannah	10	F	Wife	Great Brittain	United States	Corinthian	9 Jan 1827
James	9	M		G. Britain	U. States	William Thompson	30 Apr 1822
James	33	M	Taylor	G. Britain	U. States	William Thompson	30 Apr 1822
Jeremiah	17	M	Merchant	United States	United States	Atlantic	3 Dec 1821
Jno.	2	M		G. Britain	U. States	William Thompson	30 Apr 1822
John	3 6/12	M	Wife	Great Brittain	United States	Corinthian	9 Jan 1827
John	26	M	Spinster	Great Brittain	United States	Corinthian	9 Jan 1827
John	26	M	Mechanic	England	United States	John Wells	15 Jan 1827
John A.	28	M	Theologian	U.S.	U.S.	George Canning	26 Aug 1829
Joseph	45	M	Merchant	United States	United States	Atlantic	3 Dec 1821
Joseph	48	M	Farmer	St. John	U. States	Lady Hunter	5 Jul 1823
Lewin	35		Merchant	U. States	U. States	Jupiter	11 Feb 1829
Lewis	30	M	Mercht.	England	U.S.	Queen Mab	26 Nov 1825
Martha	30	F		G. Britain	U. States	William Thompson	30 Apr 1822
Mary	4/12	F	None	U. States	U.S.	Queen Mab	26 Nov 1825
Mary	25	F	Wife	Great Brittain	United States	Corinthian	9 Jan 1827
Mary	40			England	U. States	Corinthian	8 Oct 1828
R. A.	31	M		England	U. States	Brighton	14 Apr 1828
Robert W.	32		C.M.R.N.	England	Great Britain	Cincinnatus	17 May 1823
T. K.	32	M	...ll...	G. Britain	U. States	America	17 Oct 1825
William	1	M	Wife	Great Brittain	United States	Corinthian	9 Jan 1827
William	34	M	Merchant	United States	Philadelphia	Brighton	9 Dec 1828
Wm.	5			England	U. States	Corinthian	8 Oct 1828
YATS, Mary	10			England	U. States	Corinthian	8 Oct 1828
YEADON, James	36	M	Labourer	England	U. States	Ayrshire	12 May 1828
YEATMAN, John	18	M	Laborer	Ireland	United States	Nancy R. Crowell	21 Sep 1822
YECOMAN, Mary	45	F	None	U. States	U. States	Ann Eliza Jane	10 May 1827
YENRIG, Robt.	20	M	Mercht.	England	England	Mercator	10 Oct 1823
YEO, Sarah	50	F	Coral maker	England	United States	John & Robert	17 Oct 1825
YEODEN...Y, Joshua	34	M	Farmer	Great Britain	United States	Blakely	29 Sep 1826
YEPER, Mauricio	30	M	Servant	Island of Cuba	Cuba	James Monroe	21 May 1825
YEPES, N. A.	39	M	Officer	Columbia	Columbia	Tampico	20 Apr 1825
YERRADAILLE, Anthony	44	M	Merchant	Spain	U. States	Governor Lincoln	10 Jul 1827
Y GOY, Jose	28	M	Mercht.	Spain	U. States	Brown	7 Jul 1826
YNCLAN, Francis	24	M	Merchant	Spain	U. States	Dromo	19 Jul 1827
YNFESTIA, Frans.	25	M	Mercht.	Spain	Spain	Richmond Packet	11 Jul 1827
YOCOMBE, Adam	14	M	Farmer	Bavarian	United States	American	27 Aug 1827
Ann Eliza	10	F	Spinster	Bavarian	United States	American	27 Aug 1827
Ann Maria	7	F	Spinster	Bavarian	United States	American	27 Aug 1827
Catherina	3	F	Spinster	Bavarian	United States	American	27 Aug 1827
Elizabeth	42	F	Farmer	Bavarian	United States	American	27 Aug 1827
Louisa	6	F	Spinster	Bavarian	United States	American	27 Aug 1827
Nicholas	8	M	Farmer	Bavarian	United States	American	27 Aug 1827
Peter	15	M	Farmer	Bavarian	United States	American	27 Aug 1827
Peter	40	M	Farmer	Bavarian	United States	American	27 Aug 1827
YOLA, —, Mr.	26	M	Merchant	Spain	U. States	Cadmus	12 Apr 1825
YON, Noal	41	M	Merchant	Paris	United States	Howard	14 May 1825
YONAN, Agasta	22	M	Merchant	France	U. States	Montano	2 Sep 1828
YONG, A.	2	M		Scotland	U. States	Superior	25 Sep 1828
And.	23	M	Laborer	Scotland	United States	Camillus	27 Oct 1829
J.	3	F		Scotland	U. States	Superior	25 Sep 1828
J.	47	F		Scotland	U. States	Superior	25 Sep 1828
John	11	M		Scotland	U. States	Superior	25 Sep 1828
M.	13	F		Scotland	U. States	Superior	25 Sep 1828
R.	7	M		Scotland	U. States	Superior	25 Sep 1828
YONGE, Jane, Miss	24	F	Lady	England	U. Canada	Corinthian	8 Oct 1828

NAMES OF PASSENGERS	AGE	SEX	OCCUPATIONS	COUNTRY TO WHICH THEY BELONG	COUNTRY THEY INTEND TO INHABIT	SHIPS/DATES OF ARRIVAL	
YORE, Bridget	22	F		Ireland	America	John Adams	2 Aug 1827
Mary	1	F		Ireland	America	John Adams	2 Aug 1827
Michael	26	M	Farmer	Ireland	America	John Adams	2 Aug 1827
Peter	5	M		Ireland	America	John Adams	2 Aug 1827
YOREN, Ann	0 6/12	F		G. Britain	G. Britain	Brittania	17 Jul 1828
Grace	24	F		G. Britain	G. Britain	Brittania	17 Jul 1828
YORGAN, Alexrd. Thaway	21	M	Merchant	Spain	Spain	Nancy	21 Jul 1825
YORK, Angerdon	18	F		Germany	United States	Samuel Robertson	8 Aug 1828
Ann	3	F		England	United States	Danube	13 Jul 1827
Ann	20	F	Housekeeper	England	United States	Andes	2 Oct 1828
Catherine	29	F		Germany	United States	Samuel Robertson	8 Aug 1828
Frane Joseph	18	M		Germany	United States	Samuel Robertson	8 Aug 1828
George	31	M	Farmer	Germany	United States	Samuel Robertson	8 Aug 1828
Hana Sep	3	M		Germany	United States	Samuel Robertson	8 Aug 1828
James	20	M	Labourer	England	United States	Jubilee	12 May 1828
Johnston	23	M	Joiner	Great Britain	U. States	Great Britain	18 Mar 1828
Jonathan	5	M		England	United States	Danube	13 Jul 1827
Jonathan	33	M	Baker	England	United States	Danube	13 Jul 1827
Joseph	22	M	Ropemaker	England	United States	Andes	2 Oct 1828
Less Antony	27	M	Farmer	Germany	United States	Samuel Robertson	8 Aug 1828
Mararet	1	M		Germany	United States	Samuel Robertson	8 Aug 1828
Priscilla	26	F		England	United States	Danube	13 Jul 1827
YORMLY, Barnard	24	M				Nancey	25 Jan 1823
YORNG, James	28	M	Baker			Hudson	23 Jul 1828
YOULE, Jane	25	F	None	Scotland	U. States	Camillus	27 Jun 1826
John	3/12	M	None	Scotland	U. States	Camillus	27 Jun 1826
Robert	19	M	None	Scotland	U. States	Camillus	27 Jun 1826
Thos.			Prisoner taken by the U.S. Ship Cyane and sent by the Consul at St. Iago			Maria	20 Jul 1820
William	2	M	None	Scotland	U. States	Camillus	27 Jun 1826
William	26	M	Farmer	Scotland	U. States	Camillus	27 Jun 1826
YOUNE, —, Mrs.	35		Lady	England	England	London	16 Aug 1824
R.	4		Child of [Mrs. Youne]	England	England	London	16 Aug 1824
YOUNER, J., Leut.						Dromo	14 Aug 1829
YOUNG, —, Mrs.	28	F	None	Great Britain	U. States America	Columbia	15 Nov 1826
—, Mrs.	36	F	Merchant	Madeira	Madeira	Howard	18 Sep 1828
Adam	15	M	...	Ireland	U.S. America	Columbia	26 Nov 1825
Agness	6	F	Farmer	Argyle (Tedland) Scotland	United States	Jean Hastie	27 Jul 1829
Agness	36	F	Farmer	Argyle (Tedland) Scotland	United States	Jean Hastie	27 Jul 1829
Alais	26	F	None			Importer	30 Oct 1820
Alexr.	24	M	Taylor	Gt. Britain	U. States	Frances Henrietta	18 Apr 1825
Alexr.	60		Mercht.	Scotland	United States	Camillus	3 May 1828
Allen	16	M	Farmer	Argyle (Tedland) Scotland	United States	Jean Hastie	27 Jul 1829
Andrew	21	M	Farmer	Scotland	U. States	Camillus	27 Jul 1825
Andw.	5	M	Farmer	Argyle (Tedland) Scotland	United States	Jean Hastie	27 Jul 1829
Andw.	46	M	Farmer	Argyle (Tedland) Scotland	United States	Jean Hastie	27 Jul 1829
Ann	7	F		G. Britain	U. States	Camillus	8 Sep 1828
Ann	22	F	Matron	Ireland	U. States	Josephine	30 Aug 1828
Ann	29	F		Ireland	United States	Onion	1 Nov 1821
Anna	8/12			Great Britian	Halifax	America	28 Jul 1826
Arch.	67	M	Laborer	Ireland	United States	Weser	29 Jul 1823
Barbara	18	F	Spinster	Switzerland	United States	Andes	5 May 1828
Catharin	19	F		U. States	U. States	Native	29 Apr 1825
Catharine	47	F	Spinster	Switzerland	United States	Andes	5 May 1828

NAMES OF PASSENGERS	AGE	SEX	OCCUPATIONS	COUNTRY TO WHICH THEY BELONG	COUNTRY THEY INTEND TO INHABIT	SHIPS/DATES OF ARRIVAL	
YOUNG (cont'd)							
Catherine	12	F	Farmers and Mechanics	Scotland	America	Constitution	1 Oct 1825
Charles	21	M	Upho...ter...	England	U.S. American	Criterion	7 Jul 1824
Charles B.	20		Gentleman	England	England	London	16 Aug 1824
Charlotte	55	F	None	England	United States	London	21 May 1828
Christian	8	F	Farmer	Argyle (Tedland) Scotland	United States	Jean Hastie	27 Jul 1829
Christman	21	M		Native of Switzerland	United States	Canaris	30 Jun 1827
Cormick	37	M	Labourer	Great Britain	United States	Ganges	26 Oct 1826
David	1	M	None	Great Britain	United States	Colossus	5 Jun 1827
David	20		Servant	Scotland	Quebec	Albion	11 Oct 1821
David	22	M	Mason	Scotland	New York	Governor Fenner	23 Jul 1829
Eliza	12	F	Farmer	Argyle (Tedland) Scotland	United States	Jean Hastie	27 Jul 1829
Elizabeth	5	F	Child	Ireland	New York	Wilson	28 Aug 1827
Elizabeth	30	F		Scotland	United States	Camillus	9 May 1827
Ellace	24	M	Milliner	United States	United States	Sarah Ann	18 Nov 1826
Evert B.	22	M	Merchant	New York	New York	Monroe	18 May 1827
Francis	28	M	Laborer	England	United States	London	21 May 1828
Geo. R.	24	M	Gentleman	Nova Scotia	Nova Scotia	Hopes Delight	31 May 1828
Geo. W.	22	M	Gentleman	New York	U. States	Dispatch	12 Aug 1825
George	30	M	Draper			Importer	30 Oct 1820
George	36	M	Merchant	Great Britain	United States	John Wells	18 Sep 1826
George	51	M	Farmer	Alsace in the Department of Upper and lower Rhine	United States	Carolina Augusta	16 May 1828
Gilbert A., Mr.	27	M	None	G. Britian	Canada	Corinthian	4 Jan 1825
Hannah	33	F		Great Britain	Baltimore	Philetus	21 Jul 1827
Harriet	14	F	None	England	United States	London	21 May 1828
Harry	7	M	None	Madeira	Madeira	Howard	18 Sep 1828
Harry	45	M	None	Madeira	Madeira	Howard	18 Sep 1828
Helen	16	F		Scotland	United States	Camillus	9 May 1827
Helen	27	F	None	England	U. States	Bayard	18 Jul 1823
Henry	36	M	Farmer			Seine	10 Jun 1822
Hugh	23	M	Farmer	Scotland	U. States	Camillus	27 Jul 1825
Isabella	10	F	Farmer	Argyle (Tedland) Scotland	United States	Jean Hastie	27 Jul 1829
Jacob	20	M	Farmer	Alsace in the Department of Upper and lower Rhine	United States	Carolina Augusta	16 May 1828
Jacob	20	M	Farmer	Alsace in the Department of Upper and lower Rhine	United States	Carolina Augusta	16 May 1828
Jacob	22	M	Farmer	Switzerland	United States	Andes	5 May 1828
Jacob	53	M	Farmer	Switzerland	United States	Andes	5 May 1828
Jame	27 4/12	M	Female	England	America	Euphrates	26 Jun 1821
James	7	M		Ireland	United States	Onion	1 Nov 1821
James	9	M		G. Britain	U. States	Camillus	8 Sep 1828
James	20	M	Farmer	Ireland	America	Plutarch	18 Jul 1826
James	20	M	Labourer	Scotland	United States	Samuel Robertson	5 Oct 1827
James	30	M	Farmer	Gt. Britain	United States	Penelope	9 Sep 1828
James	32	M	Farmer	Great Britain	United States	Friends	13 Jun 1825
James	35	M	Carpenter	G. Britain	U. States	Camillus	8 Sep 1828
Jane	19	F		Antrim, Ireland	Pennsylvania	Anthusa	24 Aug 1825
Janet	10	F	Farmers and Mechanics	Scotland	America	Constitution	1 Oct 1825
Janet	16			Scotland	United States	Camillus	3 May 1828
Janet	40	F	Farmers and Mechanics	Scotland	America	Constitution	1 Oct 1825
Jannet	22	F	Farmer	Scotland	United States	Essex	23 May 1828
Jas.	25	M	Farmer	Scotland	United States	Essex	23 May 1828
Jean	40	F		G. Britain	U. States	Camillus	8 Sep 1828

NAMES OF PASSENGERS	AGE	SEX	OCCUPATIONS	COUNTRY TO WHICH THEY BELONG	COUNTRY THEY INTEND TO INHABIT	SHIPS/DATES OF ARRIVAL	
YOUNG (cont'd)							
Jeremiah	16	M	Student	Bermuda	U. States	Aurora	9 Aug 1825
Jeremiah	22	M	Farmer	Switzerland	United States	Andes	5 May 1828
Jno.	25	M	Farmer	London	Scotland	Yamacraw	10 May 1821
Jno.	25	M	Weaver	Ireland	United States	Trident	16 May 1826
John	4	M		Ireland	United States	Onion	1 Nov 1821
John	4	M	None	Great Britain	U. States America	Columbia	15 Nov 1826
John	4	M	None	Great Britain	United States	Colossus	5 Jun 1827
John	5			Great Britain	Halifax	America	28 Jul 1826
John	13	M	None	Great Britain	U. States America	Columbia	15 Nov 1826
John	18	M		Scotland	United States	Camillus	9 May 1827
John	19	M	Farmer	Switzerland	United States	Andes	5 May 1828
John	24	M	Dyer	Wales	United States	Orozimbo	11 Aug 1823
John	25	M	Merchant	Massachusetts	U. States	Caravan	14 Apr 1823
John	26	M	Mariner	United States	United States	Ann Maria	24 Oct 1827
John	28	M	Labourer	Sligo	U. States	Panthea	8 Apr 1826
John	30	M	Miner	Great Britain	United States	Colossus	5 Jun 1827
John	34 1/12	M	Schoolmaster	Scotland	United States	Mobile	21 Aug 1827
John	45	M	Mariner	U. States	U. States	Transit	26 Apr 1823
John	45	M	Mechanic	England	U. States	Charles Hamilton Aberdeen	11 Jun 1824
John	55	M	Farmer	England	United States	Cosmo	26 Aug 1829
John	58	M	Merchant	Canada	Canada	New York	5 Jul 1826
John	58	M	Merchant	Canada	Canada	John Wells	11 May 1827
John	66	M	Gentleman	Ireland	United States	Dublin Packet	28 Apr 1824
Jos.	18	M	Farmer	Scotland	United States	Essex	23 May 1828
Joseph	22	M	Servant	United States	United States	Nancy	15 Mar 1820
Joseph W.	21	M	Merchant	U. States	U. States	Isabella	10 Aug 1829
Margaret	6	F	None	Great Britain	United States	Colossus	5 Jun 1827
Margaret	20	F				Ocean	17 Aug 1820
Margaret	22	F		Native of Switzerland	United States	Canaris	30 Jun 1827
Margaret	30	F	Spinster	Ireland	New York	Wilson	28 Aug 1822
Margaretta	17	F	Farmer	Alsace in the Department of Upper and lower Rhine	United States	Carolina Augusta	16 May 1828
Margaretta	35	F	Farmer	Alsace in the Department of Upper and lower Rhine	United States	Carolina Augusta	16 May 1828
Margeret	25	F	None	Great Britan	U. States	Ann Marria	6 Aug 1823
Margret	67	F	Spinster	Scotland	United States	Friends	7 Jul 1827
Margt.	3	F	Farmer	Argyle (Tedland) Scotland	United States	Jean Hastie	27 Jul 1829
Margt.	15	F		G. Britain	U. States	Camillus	8 Sep 1828
Margt.	19	F	Farmer	Ireland	U. States	Dickinson	30 Jul 1825
Margt.	46	F	None	Great Britain	United States	Friends	13 Jun 1825
Maria	15	F	Spinster	Switzerland	United States	Andes	5 May 1828
Maria	18	F	Spinster	Switzerland	United States	Andes	5 May 1828
Marion	21	F		Scotland	United States	Camillus	9 May 1827
Martha	50	F		Scotland	United States	Camillus	9 May 1827
Mary	1 3/12	F	Child	Ireland	U. States	Josephine	30 Aug 1828
Mary	3	F	None	England	United States	Great Britain	5 Sep 1827
Mary	16	F		Switzerland	U. States	Robert Edward	2 Nov 1827
Mary	24	F	None	America	United States	Great Britain	5 Sep 1827
Mary	25			Great Britian	Halifax	America	28 Jul 1826
Mary	29	F	None	Great Britain	United States	Colossus	5 Jun 1827
Mary	30	F		G. Brittain	U. States	York	10 Dec 1825
Nathaniel	35	M	Mercer	Ireland	United States	Onion	1 Nov 1821
Peter	7	M	Farmer	Alsace in the Department of Upper and lower Rhine	United States	Carolina Augusta	16 May 1828
Peter	26	M	Labourer	Great Britain	United States	Ganges	26 Oct 1826
Philip	8/12	M	None	England	United States	Great Britain	5 Sep 1827
R. D.	39		1st Mate	Waterford, Con.		Hudson	18 Jun 1825

*Officers, Seamen and Passengers belonging to the Ship Jane of Boston and taken from on board the Schooner Olive of St. Johns , N.B. on the 4th June 1825, Lat. 41.30, Long 53.19, which ship foundered on the 31st ultimo in Lat. 41.44 Long 52.

NAMES OF PASSENGERS	AGE	SEX	OCCUPATIONS	COUNTRY TO WHICH THEY BELONG	COUNTRY THEY INTEND TO INHABIT	SHIPS/DATES OF ARRIVAL	
YOUNG (cont'd)							
Robert	8	M		Scotland	United States	Camillus	9 May 1827
Robert	8	M	None	Great Britain	United States	Colossus	5 Jun 1827
Robert	24	M	Cabinet Maker	Scotland	America	John Adams	2 Aug 1827
Robert	30	M	Tanner	Ireland	United States	Pallas	28 Oct 1828
Robert	36	M	Farmer	England	U.S. of America	Hannibal	17 Dec 1823
Robrt.	8	M	Child	Ireland	New York	Wilson	28 Aug 1822
Robt.	29		Minister	Great Britian	Halifax	America	28 Jul 1826
Samuel	74	M	Labourer	Scotland	United States	Friends	7 Jul 1827
Sarah	2			Great Britian	Halifax	America	28 Jul 1826
Sarah	5	F		Ireland	United States	Onion	1 Nov 1821
Stephen	16	M	None	England	United States	London	21 May 1828
T.	21	M	Merchant	U. States	U. States	Bayard	25 Apr 1828
Thomas	10	M		Scotland	United States	Camillus	9 May 1827
Thomas	55	M		Scotland	United States	Camillus	9 May 1827
Thoms.	30	M	None	Great Britan	U. States	Ann Marria	6 Aug 1823
Thos.			Prisoner taken by the U.S. Ship Cyane and sent by the Consul at St. Iago			Maria	20 Jul 1820
Thos.	26	M	None	America	United States	Great Britain	5 Sep 1827
William	14	M	...	Ireland	U.S. America	Columbia	26 Nov 1825
William	23	M	Joiner	Scotland	United States	Shakespeare	24 Jul 1828
William	27	M	Farmer	Scotland	U. States	Acasta	28 Jan 1823
William	30	M	Cordwainer	England	United States	Indian Chief	16 Aug 1822
William	32	M	Carpenter	Scotland	Ama.	Expedition	19 May 1828
William	56	M	Laborer	England	United States	London	21 May 1828
Willm.	48	M	Weaver	England		Fame	9 Dec 1826
Wm.	1	M	Farmer	Argyle (Tedland) Scotland	United States	Jean Hastie	27 Jul 1829
Wm.	6	M	None	Great Britain	U. States America	Columbia	15 Nov 1826
Wm.	19	M	Farmer	G. Brittan	U. States	Trafalgar	4 Jun 1822
Wm.	23	M	Laborer	Ireland	United States	Weser	29 Jul 1823
Wm.	24	M	Farmers and Mechanics	Scotland	America	Constitution	1 Oct 1825
Wm.	25		Farmer	Ireland		Westmoreland	1 Aug 1826
Wm.	34	M	Merchant	Ireland	U.S.	Florida	17 May 1825
Wm.	36	M	Mason	Ireland	United States	Francis	11 Apr 1825
YOUNGER, Issabella	25	F	None	Great Britain	United States	Friends	13 Jun 1825
William	23	M	...	Great Britain	United States	Friends	13 Jun 1825
YOUNG HUSBAND,							
Eufenia	39	F	None	St. John, N.B.	United States	Edwin	29 Nov 1828
YOUNGHUSBAND,							
Emma	22	F	Lady	United States	United States	Nancy	20 Sep 1821
Eunice	...	...	...	...	...	St. Michael	22 Sep 1824
YOUNGS, Thomas F.	21	M	Merchant	U. States	U. States	Watson	30 Apr 1827
Thos. F.	22		Merchant	U. States	U. States	Alfred	24 Jul 1828
Wm.	30	M	Mariner	U.S.	U. States	Diana	8 Aug 1822
YOURLE, Eliza	40	F	Farming	England	America	Maine	16 Jul 1821
YOURS, John	24	M	Labourer	England	U. States	Emulous	22 Aug 1828
YRARTE, Juan Jose	45	M	Gentleman	Spain	U. States	Vigilant	14 Apr 1823
YUARTTE, Thos.	25	M	Gentn.	So. America	U. States	Pacific	11 Sep 1824
YUNG, Christina	1 6/12	F	None	Germany	U. States	Sully	24 Oct 1828
Fredk.	8	M	None	Germany	U. States	Sully	24 Oct 1828
Jacob	35	M	Weaver	Germany	U. States	Sully	24 Oct 1828
Jacob, Jr.	5	M	None	Germany	U. States	Sully	24 Oct 1828
John G.	3	M	None	Germany	U. States	Sully	24 Oct 1828
Mary	30	F	None	Germany	U. States	Sully	24 Oct 1828
YZNAGA, Concepcion	28	F		Island of Cuba	Cuba	James Monroe	21 May 1825
Jose Antonio	35	M	Planter	Island of Cuba	Cuba	James Monroe	21 May 1825
Juan	8	M		Island of Cuba	Cuba	James Monroe	21 May 1825
Natividad	8	F		Island of Cuba	Cuba	James Monroe	21 May 1825
Pedro	45	M	Planter	Island of Cuba	Cuba	James Monroe	21 May 1825
ZABATER, J. A.	14	M	Mercht.	Spain	Spain	Richmond Packet	11 Jul 1827
ZABELLA, Lorenzo	13	M	Boy	Mexico	United States	Saluda	14 May 1827
ZABRISKEY, Wm.	32	M	Farmer	N. Orleans	U. States	Burdett	11 Oct 1827
ZACHARA, P. J.	18	M	Merchant	U. States	U. States	Noble	9 Jan 1824
ZACHRISSON, Er.	20	M	Merchant	Sweden	United States	Plato	25 Aug 1829
ZACRIAS, Terone	30	F	Servant	St. Croix	St. Croix	Ludwig	10 Aug 1825
ZAHANDER, F. C.	23 6/12	M	Gentleman	Switzarland		Armadillo	13 Aug 1829

NAMES OF PASSENGERS	AGE	SEX	OCCUPATIONS	COUNTRY TO WHICH THEY BELONG	COUNTRY THEY INTEND TO INHABIT	SHIPS/DATES OF ARRIVAL	
ZAHM, Cathr. S.	22	F		France	United States	La Flora	30 Jun 1828
Jean	32	M	Joiner	France	United States	La Flora	30 Jun 1828
Matthias	1 6/12	M		France	United States	La Flora	30 Jun 1828
Nor	3	F		France	United States	La Flora	30 Jun 1828
ZALLWIGER, John	24	M	Merchant	Switzerland	U. States	Montano	2 Sep 1828
ZALTER, Richd.	21	M	Labourer	Great Britain		Moro Castle	6 Jul 1827
ZANDON, Dominique	28	M	Merchant	Italy	U. States	Musidora	20 Feb 1823
ZANG, —, one child born on the passage		F	Farmer	Hessian-Germany	Canada	Caesar	8 Sep 1828
Cathr.	28	F	Farmer	Hessian-Germany	Canada	Caesar	8 Sep 1828
Eliza	43	F	Farmer	Hessian-Germany	Canada	Caesar	8 Sep 1828
Gatiam	23	F	Farmer	Hessian-Germany	Canada	Caesar	8 Sep 1828
Maria	23	F	Farmer	Hessian-Germany	Canada	Caesar	8 Sep 1828
ZANGRENA, F.	18	M	Gentleman	Spain	U. States for a time	Lucy Ann	17 Apr 1822
ZANONES, Antonio	40	M	Grocer	French	America	Britania	27 Mar 1820
ZANONI, Antonio	28	M	Gardener	Italy	U. States	Sarah Lee	21 Jul 1821
Domingos	26	M	Gardener	Italy	U. States	Sarah Lee	21 Jul 1821
Peter	33	M	Mason	Italy	U. States	Sarah Lee	21 Jul 1821
ZARRILLA, —, Miss	11	F		France	U. States	Centurion	20 Oct 1828
—, Mrs.	25	F		France	U. States	Centurion	20 Oct 1828
ZARTE, Joseph	23	M	...	England	U. States	Margarett Scott	22 Aug 1827
ZATES, James	30	M	Tailor	G. Briton	United States	James Monroe	14 Dec 1820
ZATGING, Christian	16	M	Miller	Germany	Missouri	Isabella	15 Sep 1828
Elizabeth	2	F	Miller	Germany	Missouri	Isabella	15 Sep 1828
Elizabeth	7	F	Miller	Germany	Missouri	Isabella	15 Sep 1828
Elizabeth	49	F	Miller	Germany	Missouri	Isabella	15 Sep 1828
Jacob	29	M	Miller	Germany	Missouri	Isabella	15 Sep 1828
Marian	27	F	Miller	Germany	Missouri	Isabella	15 Sep 1828
Regina	24	F	Miller	Germany	Missouri	Isabella	15 Sep 1828
ZEALAR, Barbara	18	F		Germany	U. States	Isabella	10 Aug 1829
ZEANINO, Jean	56 2/12	M	Farmer	France	U.S. America	Illinois	16 Oct 1822
ZEDHIER, Jacob	22 6/12	M	Farmer	France	United States	William	31 Jul 1826
ZEFPHREW, John	40	M	Cook	Hytia	U. States	Pedlar	17 Sep 1824
ZEIGLER, Christian	13	M	One Family [Michael]	France	United States	Henri IV	2 Oct 1828
Eve	7	F	One Family [Michael]	France	United States	Henri IV	2 Oct 1828
Henry Jack	11	M	One Family [Michael]	France	United States	Henri IV	2 Oct 1828
Iago	2 6/12	M	One Family [Michael]	France	United States	Henri IV	2 Oct 1828
Jacob	30	M	Farmer	France	France	Sully	15 Jul 1829
Louisa	37	F	One Family [Michael]	France	United States	Henri IV	2 Oct 1828
Michael	1/12	M	One Family [Michael]	France	United States	Henri IV	2 Oct 1828
Michael	39	M	Agriculturalist	France	United States	Henri IV	2 Oct 1828
Stephen	9	M	One Family [Michael]	France	United States	Henri IV	2 Oct 1828
ZEILEAN, Abby	11	F		Germany	U. States	Isabella	10 Aug 1829
Antoinette	57	F		Germany	U. States	Isabella	10 Aug 1829
August	7	M		Germany	U. States	Isabella	10 Aug 1829
Henry	4	M		Germany	U. States	Isabella	10 Aug 1829
Jacob	24	M	Weaver	Germany	U. States	Isabella	10 Aug 1829
Jean	22	M	Weaver	Germany	U. States	Isabella	10 Aug 1829
Johannes	17	M	Weaver	Germany	U. States	Isabella	10 Aug 1829
Johannes	58	M	Weaver	Germany	U. States	Isabella	10 Aug 1829
Maria	10	F		Germany	U. States	Isabella	10 Aug 1829
Maria Ann	5	F		Germany	U. States	Isabella	10 Aug 1829
ZEILEDER, Albert, Mr.	21	M	Gent.	Swizerland		Henri IV	7 May 1827
ZEILZ, Augustus	25	M	Chirurgical Instrument Maker	Hesse	United States	Constitution	2 Aug 1826
ZEITLER, Alons	27	M	Physician	Germany	U.S.	Edward Quesnel	17 Jan 1825
ZEITTER, Chas.	25	M	None	Germany	U. States	Louise	28 Jul 1823
ZELL, Cath.	47	F		Switzerland	U.S.	C. Amelia	30 Jun 1828

NAMES OF PASSENGERS	AGE	SEX	OCCUPATIONS	COUNTRY TO WHICH THEY BELONG	COUNTRY THEY INTEND TO INHABIT	SHIPS/DATES OF ARRIVAL	
ZEMSER, ...eder	60	M	Blacksmith	United States	United States	Globe	30 Aug 1828
Barbara	48	F		United States	United States	Globe	30 Aug 1828
ZENGE, Henry	27	M	Wheelwright	Bremen	U. States	Massachusetts	30 Oct 1829
ZENIGER, Anna	45	F	Farmer	...	Ohio	Frances Henrietta	25 Aug 1825
Benedict	16	M	Farmer	...	Ohio	Frances Henrietta	25 Aug 1825
Benedict	43	M	Farmer	...	Ohio	Frances Henrietta	25 Aug 1825
Elizabeth	9	F	Farmer	...	Ohio	Frances Henrietta	25 Aug 1825
John	2	M	Farmer	...	Ohio	Frances Henrietta	25 Aug 1825
Rudolph	11	M	Farmer	...	Ohio	Frances Henrietta	25 Aug 1825
ZENNE, Ippolet	51	M	Merchant	Martinique	Martinique	Samuel	28 Nov 1826
ZEPES, Nazes	40	M	Officer	Columbia		Don Quixote	3 Jan 1826
ZEREGA, F.	7	M		Columbia	Columbia	Republicano	5 Nov 1825
ZERIGA, A.	23	M	Mercht.	Columbia	Columbia	Republicano	5 Nov 1825
ZERRIT, John	24	M	Spinster	Ireland	U. States	Meteor	19 Jul 1828
Margaret	21	F	Spinster	Ireland	U. States	Meteor	19 Jul 1828
Mary	9/12	F	Child	Ireland	U. States	Meteor	19 Jul 1828
ZETHELIUS, L.	36	M	Merchant	Sweden	United States	India	8 Oct 1823
ZEULFEBOFF, L. C.	30	M	Army	Germany	New Orleans	Margaret	10 Oct 1823
ZIEGLER, Peter	24	M	Miller	Bardin	U. States	Bayard	5 Sep 1828
ZIELY, Prescilla	19	F	Farmer	England	United States	Oxford	14 Aug 1828
ZIESFERUNFERVE, Gatfroit	10	M	Farmer	France	United States	Great Britain	18 Sep 1826
Ossri	42	M	Farmer	France	United States	Great Britain	18 Sep 1826
ZIGLER, —, Mrs.	20	F		Germany	U. States	Pocahontas	28 Jun 1824
Hy.	30	M	Merchant	Germany	U. States	Pocahontas	28 Jun 1824
ZIGNAIGO, J. B.	23	M	Mercht.	France	U. States	Charles	11 Jul 1823
ZIMBERLIN, Chas.	26	M	Mercht.	Switzerland	U. States	Edward Bonnaffe	12 Oct 1826
ZIMERMAN, A.	19	M	Mercht.	Germany	U. States	Ohio	16 Feb 1822
Barbara	10	F	Butcher	France	America	La Grange	7 Aug 1828
Barbara	36	F	Butcher	France	America	La Grange	7 Aug 1828
Henry	6	M	Butcher	France	America	La Grange	7 Aug 1828
Martin	40	M	Butcher	France	America	La Grange	7 Aug 1828
ZIMMERLE, Gottlieb	28	M	Cotton Spinner	Germany	America	Falcon	28 Aug 1828
ZIMMERLIN, Charles	24	M	Distiller	Germany	U. States	Hudson	10 Nov 1825
ZIMMERMAN, —, his Wife & five children	35	M	Tailor	Swisse	United States	Deux Ernest	29 Dec 1827
*landed at Lewiston, Delw., one child died on the voyage							
A.	19	M	Merchant	Germany	U. States	Ohio	2 May 1821
David	36	M	Labourer	Switzerland	U.S.	Francois I	8 Aug 1829
Geo.	36	M		France	U. States	Danube	21 Nov 1826
Jona.	50			Switzerland	Interior	Desdemona	12 Jun 1826
M.	33	M	Mechanic	Germany	U. States	Condstitution	21 Mar 1825
Nichs.	23	M	Farmer	Switzerland	U. States	Sully	15 Jul 1829
ZIMMERMANN, —	35		Cuillair [?]	Suisse		Deux Ernest	29 Dec 1827
*son épouse & 5 enfans [his wife and five children]							
ZIMPEL, C. F.	27	M	Inginneer	Prussia	United States	Plato	25 Aug 1829
ZINGNER, Eliza	22	F	Farmer	Switzerland		Antioch	18 Aug 1829
Francis	29	M	Farmer	Switzerland		Antioch	18 Aug 1829
ZINGO, Geo.	50	M	Mariner	England	U. States	Hopes Delight	6 Sep 1824
ZINK, Catherine	4	F	his family [Chas. C.]	Germany	Pensylvania	Isabella	15 Sep 1828
Catherine E.	31	F	his family [Chas. C.]	Germany	Pensylvania	Isabella	15 Sep 1828
Chas. C.	38	M	Farmer	Germany	Pensylvania	Isabella	15 Sep 1828
Christian	6/12	M	his family [Chas. C.]	Germany	Pensylvania	Isabella	15 Sep 1828
Christina	12	F				Golden Grove	6 Sep 1820
Elizabeth	2	F	his family [Chas. C.]	Germany	Pensylvania	Isabella	15 Sep 1828
Elizabeth	18	F				Golden Grove	6 Sep 1820
Jacob	16	M				Golden Grove	6 Sep 1820

NAMES OF PASSENGERS	AGE	SEX	OCCUPATIONS	COUNTRY TO WHICH THEY BELONG	COUNTRY THEY INTEND TO INHABIT	SHIPS/DATES OF ARRIVAL	
ZINK (cont'd)							
Micheal	9	M				Golden Grove	6 Sep 1820
Micheal	56	M				Golden Grove	6 Sep 1820
ZINKENAEUR, Geo.	31	M	Butcher	Holland	U. States	Harmony	6 Jan 1823
ZINSSER, John Z.	45 1/12	M	Butcher	United States	United States	Courier	11 Oct 1827
ZLOTZ, Adams	10	M	Farmer	Germany	United States	Oxford	14 Aug 1828
Adams	40	M	Farmer	Germany	United States	Oxford	14 Aug 1828
Dorothe	1	F	Farmer	Germany	United States	Oxford	14 Aug 1828
Eve	36	F	Farmer	Germany	United States	Oxford	14 Aug 1828
Frederic	4	M	Farmer	Germany	United States	Oxford	14 Aug 1828
Georges	3	M	Farmer	Germany	United States	Oxford	14 Aug 1828
Louis	3	M	Farmer	Germany	United States	Oxford	14 Aug 1828
Metdelaine	7	F	Farmer	Germany	United States	Oxford	14 Aug 1828
ZOART, James	24	M	Merchant	England	England	Lovinia	20 Nov 1828
ZOBAL, Eliza	16	F		Great Britain		Caravan	8 Sep 1828
Jacob	6	M		Great Britain		Caravan	8 Sep 1828
M.	9	F		Great Britain		Caravan	8 Sep 1828
M.	42	M	Mason	Great Britain		Caravan	8 Sep 1828
Philip	3	M	Mason	Great Britain		Caravan	8 Sep 1828
Rosina	8	F	Mason	Great Britain		Caravan	8 Sep 1828
T.	43	M	Mason	Great Britain		Caravan	8 Sep 1828
ZOHRINGER, Mich.	21	M	Agriculture	Wirtemburg	United States	Henri IV	14 Oct 1829
ZOLA, T.	20		Farmer	Ireland	United States	Courier	16 May 1825
ZOLBBRURCER, George	24	M		France	U. States	Danube	21 Nov 1826
ZOLLER, Charlotte,							
Zyn Vrouw (his wife [Frederik])	28	F		Klein Otwilder	United States	Juffraw Johanna	16 Oct 1821
Frederick, Kinder (his child [Frederik])	2	M		Homburg	United States	Juffraw Johanna	16 Oct 1821
Frederik	24	M	Boer	Homburg	United States	Juffraw Johanna	16 Oct 1821
Margaretha, Kinder (his child [Frederik])		F		Homburg	United States	Juffraw Johanna	16 Oct 1821
ZORF, Catharen	4	F	Shoe Maker	Ireland		Quatre Freres	29 Jul 1828
Christian	8	F	Shoe Maker	Ireland		Quatre Freres	29 Jul 1828
Margaret	6	M	Shoe Maker	Ireland		Quatre Freres	29 Jul 1828
Mariah G.	32	F	Shoe Maker	Ireland		Quatre Freres	29 Jul 1828
Perre	34	M	Shoe Maker	Ireland		Quatre Freres	29 Jul 1828
Phillip	2	M	Shoe Maker	Ireland		Quatre Freres	29 Jul 1828
ZORILLA, A.	30	F	Lady	Cuba	U. States	Brown	29 Apr 1825
J.	7	F	Lady	Cuba	U. States	Brown	29 Apr 1825
J.	8	F	Lady	Cuba	U. States	Brown	29 Apr 1825
ZUCKSCHWERDT,							
Theodor	40	M	Merchant	Germany	Pensilvania	Maria Elizabeth	24 Mar 1828
ZUIGGART, Catharine	64	F		Switzerland	America, U.N.S.	Great Britain	3 Aug 1829
Cristian	58	M	Shoemaker	Switzerland	America, U.N.S.	Great Britain	3 Aug 1829
Elizabeth	25	F		Switzerland	America, U.N.S.	Great Britain	3 Aug 1829
Jaques	30	M	Shoemaker	Switzerland	America, U.N.S.	Great Britain	3 Aug 1829
ZUNIGA, John A. Paurat	49	M	Merchant	France	U. States	Pomona	4 Apr 1823
ZUNOE, Catherine	5	F		Italy	U. States	Caroline	20 Aug 1825
Estreger	7	F		Italy	U. States	Caroline	20 Aug 1825
Estreger	30	F		Italy	U. States	Caroline	20 Aug 1825
Joseph	1	M		Italy	U. States	Caroline	20 Aug 1825
Michael	3	M		Italy	U. States	Caroline	20 Aug 1825
Michael	37	M	Butcher	Italy	U. States	Caroline	20 Aug 1825
ZURBRUCH,							
M. A., Miss	26	F	Domestic	Switzerland		François I	19 Nov 1828
ZÜRCHER, Abraham	37	M	Turner	Switzerland	United States	Thetis	5 Jul 1821
David	18	M	Domestic	Switzerland	United States	Thetis	5 Jul 1821
Saml.	19	M	Domestic	Switzerland	United States	Thetis	5 Jul 1821
ZWAHLEN, Ann	35	F	Farmer	Switzerland	Switzerland	Edward Quesnel	3 Jul 1829
Anna	7	F		Switzerland	Switzerland	Edward Quesnel	3 Jul 1829
Cristian	12	M		Switzerland	Switzerland	Edward Quesnel	3 Jul 1829
Henri	14	M		Switzerland	Switzerland	Edward Quesnel	3 Jul 1829
Henry	43	M	Joiner	Switzerland	Switzerland	Edward Quesnel	3 Jul 1829

APPENDIX A
A LIST OF PASSENGERS LACKING
NAMES OR COMPLETE NAMES

NAMES OF PASSENGERS	AGE	SEX	OCCUPATIONS	COUNTRY TO WHICH THEY BELONG	COUNTRY THEY INTEND TO INHABIT	SHIPS/DATES OF ARRIVAL	
—, —						Camillus	17 Sep 1823
*A Seafaring man put on board by the American Consul died on the passage							
—			a child Born on the passage			Income	29 May 1824
—		M		Ireland	America	Carolina Ann	7 Aug 1826
—		F	Servant	St. Croix	U. States	South Carolina Packet	29 Aug 1826
—			Servant	Colombia	U. States	Milton	20 Aug 1827
—			Servant	Buenos Ayez	U. States	Milton	20 Aug 1827
—				...	United States	Stephania	6 Dec 1827
—				...	United States	Stephania	6 Dec 1827
—				...	United States	Stephania	6 Dec 1827
—						Oxford	14 Aug 1828
*there are five Persons on Board that were concealed in the hole When we left Havre						New Orleans	27 Feb 1829
*Eighteen seaman from the U.S. Ship Boston put on board by U. States Consul at Rio de Janeiro							
—	10	M	None	St. Croix		South Carolina Packet	
31 Mar 1824*a Coloured Boy found Secreted On board and will be Carried Back							
—	13	F	Servant	Barbadoes	Barbadoes	Elias Burger	24 Jul 1820
—	22	M	Agriculture	Wirtemburg	United States	Henri IV	14 Oct 1829
—	30	M	Labourer	Great Britain	United States	India	5 Sep 1827
—	50	F	Servant	Barbadoes	Barbadoes	Elias Burger	24 Jul 1820
—, 1 male born on board July 30		M				Elbe	2 Aug 1822
—, 2 children				America	U. States	Ambuscade	11 Jul 1821
—, a Black	18	M	Servant	Portugal	Portugal	Ariosto	12 Apr 1822
—, a child born on passage of ...						William	27 Jul 1824
—, a Child Born at Sea					U. States	Princess Louise	10 Mar 1825
—, a deshiped seaman put aboard by the Am. Consul					U. States	Caroline	17 Apr 1821
—, a Secretary to the above	20	M	officer in the Portuguese Navy	Portugal	Portugal	Ariosto	12 Apr 1822
—, a young Bairn	8/12	M			United States	Cato	8 Aug 1825
—, A Child	1	M				Royal Oak	5 Aug 1820
—, Black Child	3	M	Servant	W. Indies	U. States	Elisa	1 May 1821
—, Child		F				Charleston Packet	4 May 1821
—, Child	9/12		Girl	America	America	Saluda	18 Jun 1825
—, Child	5	F		Gaudaloup	U. States	Orono	5 Jun 1823
—, Eight American Seaman and One Officer worked their passage						Victoria	9 Sep 1828
—, five Seamen, United States Navy						Live Oak	13 Aug 1821
—, four Servants						Howard	17 Oct 1822
—, Four Infants at the Breast				Ireland	America	William	21 May 1825
—, Four Servants						Cannon	18 Aug 1821
—, his Servant [R. Maliss]	29	M	Merchant	England	U. States	Caseo	26 Apr 1828
—, Infant						Apollo	11 Jun 1828
—, Infant	0 6/12	M		Gt. Britain	United States	Columbia	7 Sep 1827
—, Infant	6	F		Gt. Britain	United States	Columbia	7 Sep 1827
—, Infant	8	F		Gt. Britain	United States	Columbia	7 Sep 1827
—, Jno. Greig's Child	3/12	F		Java	Java	Eunore Francis	18 Sep 1820
—, Lady Servant	37	F		Pensylvania	Pensylvania	Florida	1 Jun 1827
—, Mr. Cajiga's Servant Boy	20			Manilla	Spain	Brown	11 Jun 1827
—, Mrs. McRea's Servant, Black	14	F		U. States	U. States	Constitution	17 Mar 1823
—, Mrs. Vance's Maid Servant	25			Ireland	Great Britain	Brown	11 Jun 1827

NAMES OF PASSENGERS	A G E	S E X	OCCUPATIONS	COUNTRY TO WHICH THEY BELONG	COUNTRY THEY INTEND TO INHABIT	SHIPS/DATES OF ARRIVAL	
—, Mrs. Vance's Man Servant	24			Ireland	Great Britain	Brown	11 Jun 1827
—, Name Lost	13	M	None	Great Britain	United States	Aurora	10 Nov 1827
—, Name Lost	15	M	None	Great Britain	United States	Aurora	10 Nov 1827
—, Name Lost	25	M	None	Great Britain	United States	Aurora	10 Nov 1827
—, Nine Seamen		M		U.S.	U.S.	Leo	30 Apr 1825
—, one child	5	F		Antigua	United States	Betsey	18 Aug 1823
—, one Seaman *died on the Passage						Live Oak	13 Aug 1821
—, Servant	11	F	Servant	Brazil	Pensylvania	Florida	1 Jun 1827
—, Servant	12	F	Servant	Pensylvania	Pensylvania	Florida	1 Jun 1827
—, Servant	14			Bermuda		Ocean	28 Jul 1820
—, Servant	21	F		England	New York	Thames	6 Oct 1820
—, Servant	25	F	None	Amsterdam	U. States	Margaret	29 Oct 1822
—, Servant	32	M	Servent	St. Croix	Denmark	Elias Burger	11 Jul 1822
—, Servant	40	F		G. Britain	U. States	Hope Success	16 Jul 1828
—, Servant of Count De Miot [De Millito]	...			France		Cadmus	9 Aug 1825
—, Servant to Geo. D. Tucker		F	family [of George D. Tucker]	Turks Island	U. States	Gold Hunter	24 Oct 1829
—, The Prince of Masignaro	25	M	Gentleman	Ittaly	United States	Manchester	24 Aug 1827
—, two Born on the passage						Olympia	12 Aug 1828
—, Two Infants		F		G. Britain	U. States	Robt. Edwards	4 Sep 1828
...	2					Alfred	8 Jul 1822
...	7					Alfred	8 Jul 1822
..., (Mulatto)	18		servant of the above [... Stebbins]	U. States	St. Croix	South Carolina Packet	7 Jul 1821
...offee	18	F	Servant	France	U. States	Superb	9 Jul 1821
Addalin	5			United States	United States	Planter	26 Jul 1822
Adelaide, Servt.	16	F		France	France	Cadmus	11 Jul 1827
Adola	18	F	Servant	Gaudaloupe	Morristown, N.J.	Horace	31 May 1822
Adolphe	11	M	Chair maker	Gaudaloupe	Morristown, N.J.	Horace	31 May 1822
Agnes	28	F	Servant	U. States	U. States	Orono	5 Jun 1823
Alexandrine	34	F	Servant	Gaudaloupe	Morristown, N.J.	Horace	31 May 1822
Alfred	25	M	Servant	U. States	U. States	Helen	24 Apr 1827
Allen, (a Black)	35	M	Servant	Isld. Cuba	I. Cuba	Blue Ey'd Mary	26 Jun 1823
Alphons	15	M	Servant	U. States	U. States	Orono	5 Jun 1823
Alsander	25	M	Servant	Haiti	U. States	Traveller	2 Jun 1822
Amelia	50	F	Servant	U. States	U. States	Wallace	12 Apr 1824
Amy	50	F	Servant	America	United States	Marmion	13 Jun 1823
Anastine	23	F	Servant	France	U.S.	Queen Mab	26 Nov 1825
André	36	M		France	Ohio	Eugenie	20 Aug 1827
Andrietta	40	F		Aux Cayes	U. States	Marshall	12 Jun 1824
Angeletta	16	F		England	Antigua	Illuminator	26 Jul 1825
Ann	24	F	Servant	Sweeden	Sweeden	Tapperheten	12 Jun 1826
Ann	40	F	Lady		New York	Betsy	4 Sep 1820
Ann Helina	16	F		So. America	U. States	Eclipse	10 Jun 1823
Anna	16	F		So. America	U. States	Eclipse	10 Jun 1823
Annette	11	F	Servant	France	U. States	Superb	9 Jul 1821
Anton...	10					Alfred	8 Jul 1822
Antonia	18	M	Servant	S. America	U. States	Mary	18 Jul 1822
Antonio	4					Apollo	11 Jun 1828
Antonio	18	M	Servant	Spain	U. States	Mary Ann	30 Aug 1824
Antonio	50	M	Mercht.	Spain	U. States	Gleaner	18 Jul 1822
Antonio, Don	26	M	Merchant	Conny Island	U. States	St. Bento Leigeiro	2 Nov 1822
Auguste	23	M		France	France	Cadmus	11 Jul 1827
B...k	28	M	Merchant	Germany		Soldado Espanol	8 Jul 1822
Betsey	25	F	Servant	France	France	Caravan	1 May 1824
Betsy	36	F	Colored Servant	Denmark		Elias Burger	28 May 1821
Brasford	24	M	Merchant	Gaudiloupe	Gaudiloupe	Nancy	29 May 1826
Carlo	52	M	Servant	Curaca	Curacoa	Douglass	27 Apr 1824
Caroline	9	F	Sevant	United States	U. States	Fair Trader	25 Jul 1820
Caroline	17	F		Guadaloupe	U. States	Turner	8 Jun 1824

1378

NAMES OF PASSENGERS	AGE	SEX	OCCUPATIONS	COUNTRY TO WHICH THEY BELONG	COUNTRY THEY INTEND TO INHABIT	SHIPS/DATES OF ARRIVAL	
Catalina	20	F	Servent	Spain	Spain	Circassian	13 Jun 1825
Catharine	14	F	free Black Domestic			Margaret & Sarah	31 Oct 1822
Catherine		F		New York	New York	United States	15 Jul 1824
Cezaire	39	M	free woman of Colour	Guadaloupe	France	Elizabeth	17 Jul 1823
Charles		M	Seaman	Germany		Jane	11 Jul 1828
Charles	15	M	Servant	Cuba	Cuba	Clio	8 Apr 1828
Charles	20	M	Student	Gaudaloupe	Morristown, N.J.	Horace	31 May 1822
Charles	33	M	Gentleman	England	Great Britain	New York	22 Jul 1824
Charlotte	18	F		Guadaloupe	U. States	Mentor	27 Nov 1822
Charlotte, Miss	22	F	Servant	St. Croix	U. States	Agnes	29 Nov 1826
Charlotte, Servant	13	F	Servant	France	France	Clio	7 Aug 1826
Christian	18	F	Servant	St. Croix	U. States	Chase	9 Aug 1827
Christian, Black	70	M	Servant	St. Croix	St. Croix	Commerce	13 Nov 1823
Christoine	20	F	Servant	Guadeloupe	New York	Notre Dame	6 Oct 1827
Clara	14	F	Servant	U. States	U. States	Orono	5 Jun 1823
Collett, Miss	22	M		France	N. York	Queen Mabb	22 Nov 1824
Columb	50	F	Servant	Dominico		Adams	11 Nov 1824
Constantia	45	M	Servant	Curaca	Curacoa	Douglass	27 Apr 1824
Constantin, (free negro,servant)	62	M	Servant	United States	United States	Montano	5 May 1828
Cuzuila	17	F	Servant	St. Croix	U. States	Chase	9 Aug 1827
Diana	45	F		New York	Great Britain	Mary & Elizabeth	7 Sep 1824
Dolores	25	F	Servant	Havana	U. States	Senica	17 Mar 1824
Edward	17	M	Servant	Point Peter	France	Pacific	14 May 1827
Elick	21	M		St. Eustatia	U. States	Henry	26 May 1823
Eliza	6	F		Hamburg	U. States	Hope	18 Jun 1824
Eliza	16	F		Guadaloupe	U. States	Turner	8 Jun 1824
Eliza	19	F	Servant	Gaudiloupe	Gaudiloupe	Nancy	29 May 1826
Eliza	20	F	None	England	United States	Montgomery	6 Mar 1829
Eliza, (black)	15	F	Servant	W. Indies	U. States	Elias Burger	12 Sep 1822
Eliza, Servant	21	F	Servant	U. States	U. States	Imperial	10 Dec 1821
Emanuel	18		...	Curacao	Netherlands	Hippomenes	9 Jun 1821
Emily	12	F	Servant	France	U. States	Superb	9 Jul 1821
Etienne	27	M	Mathematician	France		Nimrod	21 Sep 1820
Fanny	20	F		Nova Scotia	United States	Superior	14 Apr 1825
Feliciene	20	F	Servant	Jamaica		Topaz	14 Aug 1826
Ferdinan, Servant	22	M	Servant	France	France	Clio	7 Aug 1826
Fernando	30	M	Servant	Spain	United States	Juliana	25 Jan 1820
Fortuna	27	F	Servant	Spain	Spain	James Barron	26 Jun 1823
Fra...t	40	M		France	America, U.S.	Soldado Espanol	8 Jul 1822
Francisco	10	M		S. American	S. America	Cleanthes	9 May 1825
Francisco	16	M	Servant	Italy	South America	Louisiana	9 Aug 1826
Francisco	30	M	Servant	Columbia	Columbia	Tampico	20 Apr 1825
Frank	38		Servant	U. States	U. States	Robert Read	30 Jan 1826
Franny, (a black)	14	F		Halifax	some to return & the others to Canada	Albert	14 May 1822
George	24	M	Servant	Bermuda	Bermuda	Emblem	25 Oct 1825
Giton	8					Apollo	11 Jun 1828
Guinea	34	F	Domestic	Point Petre, Guadaloupe	United States	General Macombe	17 Jul 1827
Hannah, Servant Made	25	F		...	...	Hunter	19 May 1823
Henriett	7					Olympia	2 Sep 1823
Henry	8	M	None	France	U. States	Edward Quesnel	15 May 1826
Henry	26	M	Servant	Mexico	England	Brown	23 Dec 1826
Henry	35	M	Servant	Italy	United States	Daphne	20 May 1823
Hinry, Servant man	22	M		...	...	Hunter	19 May 1823
Isaac	30	M	Servant	England	Canada	Mentor	24 Mar 1823
Isabella	20	F	Servant	Havana	U. States	Senica	17 Mar 1824
J. Charlotte	35	F	Servant, Black	St. Croix	New York	Clarice	15 Jun 1825
Ja...	14	F	Servant	Havana	So. America	Hesperion	28 Oct 1823
Jack, Sevant	18	M	Sevant			Diana	14 Sep 1820
James	18	M	Servant	St. Croix	St. Croix	Jupiter	21 Nov 1825
James	20	M	Servant	Jamaica	G. Brittain	Cadmus	7 Jun 1824

NAMES OF PASSENGERS	AGE	SEX	OCCUPATIONS	COUNTRY TO WHICH THEY BELONG	COUNTRY THEY INTEND TO INHABIT	SHIPS/DATES OF ARRIVAL	
James	30	M	Servant	Antigua	U. States	Spartan	17 Dec 1823
James	37	M	Servant	St. Thomas	New York	St. Pierre	16 Oct 1827
Jane	14	F	Servant	Jamaica	Jamaica	Wallace	12 Apr 1824
Jane	24	F	Servant	France	U. States	Othello	3 Jun 1823
Jane	30	F	Servant	France	U. States	Superb	9 Jul 1821
Jane, Negro Woman & Infant	36	F	Servant	Gaudaloupe	U. States	Eliza	3 Jul 1820
Jane, Servant				Danish	U. States	Mary & Nancy	7 Aug 1824
Jennet Sophia	1	M	Children & family of Jacob Weisman	Switzerland	United States	Aurora	21 Jun 1824
Jennett	2	F		France	N. York	Queen Mabb	22 Nov 1824
Jenniss, Mons.	22	M	Sailor	France	Nuyork	Louisa	17 Jul 1826
Jenny	14	F	Servant	Spain	U. States	Emma	25 Oct 1825
Jerome		M	Servant	New York	New York	United States	15 Jul 1824
Jim	20	M	Servant	China	China	Savannah	18 May 1822
Jno.	20	M	Servant	Spain	Spain	Fabius	3 Jun 1825
Joacinth	19	M	Servant	Portugal	U. States	Frederick	27 Jan 1823
Joaquim	24	M	Servant	Spain	Spain	Fabius	3 Jun 1825
Joaquin	22	M	Servent	Fayal	U. States	Albert	2 Oct 1823
Joaquin	30	M	Servant	...	America	Columbia	6 Oct 1825
Joe	33	M	Servant	London	U. States	Mary Jane	23 Mar 1829
Johanna	20	F	Servant	Columbia	Columbia	William Bayard	6 Aug 1825
John	12	M	Merchant	St. Croix	U. States	Chase	12 May 1826
John	14	M	Servent	U. States	U. States	Bunker Hill	25 Jun 1827
John	16	M	Apprentice	U. States	U. States	Rice Plant	20 Sep 1827
John	19	M	Servant	France	U. States	Brunswick	14 Feb 1829
John	20	M	Servant	United States	U. States	Saml. Smith	24 Jul 1826
John	20	M	Servant	Columbia	U. States	Bunker Hill	12 Aug 1828
John	21	M	Servant	Cuba	Spain	Romulus	26 Apr 1822
John	21	M	Servant	England	Columbia	Chapman	21 Apr 1826
John	22	M	Comb Maker	Scotland	U. States	Alert	22 Sep 1821
John	25	M	Servant	Mexico	England	Brown	23 Dec 1826
John	30		Mariner	Great Britain	U.S. of America	Estrella de La Mañana	26 May 1825
*Died							
John	52	M	Joiner	Great Britian	U. States	Dalhouse Castle	28 Feb 1826
John, (a black)	23	M	Servant	S. Carolina	U. States	Almira	8 Aug 1822
John, Chld	15/12	M				Falcon	16 Aug 1826
Jorge	30	M	Merchant	Germany		Soldado Espanol	8 Jul 1822
Jos. Antonio, Servant	20	M	Servant	Columbia	U. States	Bunker Hill	12 Aug 1828
Jose	15	M	Servant	Portugal	U. States	Hopes Delight	6 Aug 1823
Josepe	4	M	Merchant	Spain	U. States	Native	15 Apr 1826
Joseph	18	M	Servant	America	United States	America	16 May 1827
Joseph	25	M		So. America	U. States	Eclipse	10 Jun 1823
Joseph	30	M	Farmer	Gt. Britain	U. States	Margaret	26 Jul 1828
Joseph	37	M	Domestic	Spain	Spain	Hippomenes	9 Jun 1821
Joseph, (black)	17	M	Servant	U. States	U. States	Echo	22 Apr 1823
Joseph, (Boy)	18	M	Servant	Spain	U. States	Protector	2 Jul 1824
Josephus	26	M	Labourer	Italy	U. States	Fortune	31 Jul 1824
Juan	6					Apollo	11 Jun 1828
Juan	25	F	Servant	Havana	U. States	Senica	17 Mar 1824
Juliana, col'd	40	F	Servnat	St. Croix	Ireland	Jupiter	6 Aug 1826
Julio	40	F	Servant	Havana	U. States	Senica	17 Mar 1824
Kate, Servant	20	F		I[sland] Cuba	Spain	Abigail	21 Mar 1825
Laleer	48	M	Servant	America	United States	America	16 May 1827
Lamon	26	M	Tallow Chandler	France	America	Zwey Brieder Johanes & Henerick	20 Mar 1820
Loniz	7	F		Spain	Spain	Circassian	13 Jun 1825
Loolo	7	M		St. Thomas	Havre	Mary Hobin	29 May 1826
Lorenzo	12	M	Servant	Spain	Spain	Tampico	14 Jul 1825
Louisa	20	F	Servant	St. Thomas	Havre	Mary Hobin	29 May 1826
Louisa, Miss	28	M		France	N. York	Queen Mabb	22 Nov 1824
Louise, Mad.	11	F	Gentleman	France	Nuyork	Louisa	17 Jul 1826
Lucien, Servant	25	M	Servant	U.S.	U.S.	Montano	24 Jun 1823
M. Arelia	14	F	Servant, Black	St. Croix	New York	Clarice	15 Jun 1825
Magiel	10		Mines	Columbia	England	Triumph	23 Jul 1829
Malein	14	F	Servant	U. States	U. States	Orono	5 Jun 1823

NAMES OF PASSENGERS	AGE	SEX	OCCUPATIONS	COUNTRY TO WHICH THEY BELONG	COUNTRY THEY INTEND TO INHABIT	SHIPS/DATES OF ARRIVAL	
Manuel	35	M	Domestic	Spanish Maine	U. States	Hippomenes	22 Dec 1821
Manuel	40	M		Porto Rico	U. States	Olympia	19 Jun 1828
Manuell	16	M	Miner	Mexico	Mexico	Eliza	31 Jul 1826
Margaret	23	F		Ireland	St. Johns, N.B.	Borneo	26 Apr 1824
Maria	25	F	Servant	St. Croix	U. States	Chase	9 Aug 1827
Maria	42	F		England	United States	McFingal	9 Dec 1826
Maria, (black)	30	F	Servant	W. Indies	U. States	Elias Burger	12 Sep 1822
Mariah	11	F	None	Spain	U. States	Sarah	1 Aug 1827
Mark	30	M	Bricklayer	Spain	U. States	Sarah	4 Aug 1825
Martha	40	F	Servant	St. Croix	New York	Jupiter	19 Oct 1826
Mary	1	F		Great Britian	United States	London	24 Jun 1823
Mary	12	F	Servant	Havana	So. America	Hesperion	28 Oct 1823
Mary	24	F	Servant	St. Croix	on a Visit	Catharine	3 Sep 1821
Mary	24	F	Servant	England	United States	Marmione	20 Nov 1821
Mary	30	F	Servant	New York	U. States	Romulus	26 Apr 1822
Mary	42	F	Servant	St. Croix	St. Croix	Jupiter	19 Oct 1826
Mary, a servant	18	F		Guadaloupe	U. States	Turner	8 Jun 1824
Mary Elizabeth	36	F		Brunswick	not known	Commodore Preble	17 Dec 1825
Masario		M	Servant	Trinidad in Cuba	Spain	Mechanic	17 Aug 1822
Mascalena	14	M		Colombia	U. States	Julia	18 Apr 1828
Matilda	25	F	Servant	U. States	U. States	John Laird	16 Jun 1827
Matilda	30	F	None	U. States	U. States	Georgiana	12 Nov 1822
Men	18	F	Servant	Holland	Holland	Lydia	30 Apr 1821
Mengy	25	F	Servant	Holland	Holland	Lydia	30 Apr 1821
Mesaire	16	M	Servant	Gaudiloupe	Gaudiloupe	Nancy	29 May 1826
Michael	1	M		Spain	Spain	Circassian	13 Jun 1825
Michael	26	M	Servant	United States	U. States	Saml. Smith	24 Jul 1826
Molly, Servant	13	F	Servant			Congress	21 Nov 1823
Moors						Falcon	1 May 1824

*a Mulatto man who secreted himself on board my vessel and kept so secreted for 3 days until I had gotten so far to the northward it was impossable for me to get back to Martinico without runing into the trade winds

NAMES OF PASSENGERS	AGE	SEX	OCCUPATIONS	COUNTRY TO WHICH THEY BELONG	COUNTRY THEY INTEND TO INHABIT	SHIPS/DATES OF ARRIVAL	
Nancy	19	F	Servant	Bermuda	U. States	Susan	2 Aug 1822
Nancy	25	F	Servant	Bermuda	Bermuda	Industry	26 Jul 1825
Nancy	32	F	Servant	Jamaica	Jamaica	Wallace	12 Apr 1824
Nancy	40	F	Servant	United States	United States	Orris	12 Mar 1825
Neignis	20	F	Servant	Gaudiloupe	Gaudiloupe	Nancy	29 May 1826
Nicholas	22	M	Labourer	Italy	U. States	Fortune	31 Jul 1824
Nortson	18	M	Merchant	Gaudiloupe	Gaudiloupe	Nancy	29 May 1826
Ouster	5	M	Merchant	Spain	U. States	Native	15 Apr 1826
Pedro	14	M	Servant	Spain	Spain	Tampico	14 Jul 1825
Pedro	21	M	Servant	Spain	Spain	Fabius	3 Jun 1825
Pedro	23	M	Servant			Imperial	12 Aug 1825
Penelope	60	F	Seamstress	England	U.N. States	Earl of Liverpool	20 Aug 1825
Peter	14	M	Servant	France	Honduras or South America	Alabama	3 Dec 1823
Peter	14	M	Servant	U. States	U. States	Trimmer	21 Jul 1825
Peter	25	M	Servant	Mexico	England	Brown	23 Dec 1826
Peter	40	M	Servant			Imperial	12 Aug 1825
Peter, negro	15	M	Servant	Mexico		Galatea	20 Jul 1829
Peter Luis	38	M	Servant	Spain	Spain	James Barron	26 Jun 1823
Peto	21	M	Servant	Cuba	England	Rebecca	2 May 1825
Petro	40	M	Servant	St. Croix	Denmark	Chase	4 Sep 1821
Petrone	22	M	Servant	Havana	So. America	Hesperion	28 Oct 1823
Philip	12	M	Servant	Madeira	Madeira	Uniao	19 Aug 1829
Philip	17	M	Servant	Hayti	U. States	Native	29 May 1824
Phillis, (a Black)	20	F		U. States	U. States	Six Brothers	4 Jun 1822
Pierre	9	M	Servant	Point Peter	France	Pacific	14 May 1827
Pierre	50	M	Servant	Curaca	U. States	Douglass	27 Apr 1824
Polly	12		Servent		Cuba	Criterion	9 Aug 1826
Pompey	22	M	Servant	Spain	U. States	Leo	7 Jun 1827
Poto	9					Apollo	11 Jun 1828
Prince, (a black)	21	M	Servant	U. States	U. States	Exchange	29 Apr 1822
Rachael, (Servant)		F		United States		Corinthian	27 Oct 1829
Rafael	13	M	Servant to L. Corning	Brazil	United States	Isabella	1 Aug 1829
Regulas		M	None	U. States	U. States	South Carolina	22 Dec 1824

1381

NAMES OF PASSENGERS	AGE	SEX	OCCUPATIONS	COUNTRY TO WHICH THEY BELONG	COUNTRY THEY INTEND TO INHABIT	SHIPS/DATES OF ARRIVAL	
Richard	35	M	Merchant	England	U. States	New York	4 Nov 1824
Ritta, Sevant	20	F	Servant	Spain	Spain	James Barron	26 Jun 1823
Robert		M	Servant	Prusia	U. States	Ann Maria	11 May 1822
Robert	18	M	Servant	W. Indies	U. States	Ductile	12 Apr 1825
Robt.	45	M	Baker	Scotland	U. States	Othello	3 Dec 1828
Rosa, Black	5	F	Servant	U.S.	U.S.	Frances	21 Jul 1827
Rosannah		F		New York	New York	United States	15 Jul 1824
Rose, Servant	12	F	Servant	France	France	Clio	7 Aug 1826
Rosetta	13	F		Spain	Spain	Circassian	13 Jun 1825
Ruth, a black girl	20	F		U. States	U. States	Eliza	31 Jul 1821
S...las	26	M		Spain	Spain	Soldado Espanol	8 Jul 1822
Sally	3/12	F		Philadelphia	U. States	Jean Baptiste	7 Jan 1828
Sally	23	F	Servant	St. Croix	on a Visit	Catharine	3 Sep 1821
Sally	30	F				Manchester Packet	21 Aug 1823
Sam	40	M	Sevant	G. Britain		Emerald	9 Sep 1820
Saphrino	10	M	Servant	So. America	So. America	Endymeon	20 Aug 1822
Sarah	2	F		Great Britian	United States	London	24 Jun 1823
Sarah	17		Servant			St. Anna	8 Aug 1827
Sarah	20	F	Servant	Great Britain	United States	Washington	22 Mar 1820
Sarah	50	F		England	U. States	Ann Maria	13 Mar 1823
Sarah, Mrs.	20	F		Philadelphia	U. States	Jean Baptiste	7 Jan 1828
Seval, (China)	18	M	Servant	China	U. States	Margaret	11 Mar 1823
Sidney	20	F	Servant	G. Bridain		Trio	27 Jun 1823
Simon, Mons.	23	M	Sailor	France	Nuyork	Louisa	17 Jul 1826
Solomon	25	M	Servant	U. States	U. States	Worromontogus	23 Jun 1823
Sophia, (Servant)	24		Servant	St. Croix	New York	South Carolina Packet	19 Jun 1826
Spartacus	20	M	Servant	St. Croix	on a Visit	Catharine	3 Sep 1821
Susan	22	F	Servant	U. States	U.S.	Queen Mab	26 Nov 1825
Tabitha	35	F	Colored Servant	America		Elias Burger	28 May 1821
Themomino		M	Servant	S. America	U. States	Swan	13 Nov 1821
Theodore	35	M	Domestic	Point Petre, Guadaloupe	United States	General Macombe	17 Jul 1827
Thomas	6/12	M		Baltimore	U. States	Emigrant	9 Oct 1826
Thomas	19		Servant	Great Britain	Great Britain	Pacification	31 Aug 1822
Thomas	21	M	Servant	Porto Rico	U. States	Mentor	26 Jul 1825
Thomas	25		Servant			St. Anna	8 Aug 1827
Thomas	28	M	Servant	Bermuda	Bermuda	Emblem	25 Oct 1825
Thomas	28	M	Farmer	Gt. Britain	U. States	Margaret	26 Jul 1828
Thomas	infant			Great Britain	United States	Ganges	8 Jul 1820
Thomas, a servant	18	M		Guadaloupe	U. States	Turner	8 Jun 1824
Titine	16	F	Servant	Gaudaloupe	Morristown, N.J.	Horace	31 May 1822
Tom	10	M	Servant	Virginia	U. States	Leonora	25 May 1826
Tom	20	M	Servant	St. Thomas	St. Thomas	Venus	12 Oct 1824
Tooto	9	M		St. Thomas	Havre	Mary Hobin	29 May 1826
Unthan			Servant			Weser	24 Jul 1820
Victor	35	M	Servant		U. States	Perseverance	11 Jun 1824
Victoria	11	F		Spain	Havana	Lady Tompkins	10 Nov 1823
Victoriana	9					Imperial	12 Aug 1825
Villard	32	M	Merchant	Hayti	Hayti	Fair Play	5 Nov 1821
Whelmina	28	M		Great Britain	United States	Jupiter	14 Sep 1827
William	8	M	Servant		U. States	Flight	9 Jul 1825
William	20	M	Farmer	Hull	U. States	Charles Hamilton Aberdeen	23 May 1825
William	20	M	Merchant	Matanzas	U. States	New England	23 Apr 1827
William, (negro)	25	M	Servant	W. Indies	U. States	Douglass	22 May 1823
Zebindab	28					Caledonian	16 Aug 1820
..., ...			Farmer	Alderson, E.	England	Packet	27 Aug 1822
...		M		Scotland	U.S.	Curler	19 Jul 1828
...	...	...	...	England	New York	Thames	6 Oct 1820
...	...	F		G. Brittain	U. States	Hope & Esther	26 Nov 1822
...	...	F	...	Great Britain	New York	Dublin	21 Dec 1824
...	...	F	Spinster	Gt. Britain	U. States	Frances Henrietta	18 Apr 1825
...	...	M	Weaver	Ireland	America	Carolina Ann	7 Apr 1826
...	...	F		Ireland	America	Carolina Ann	7 Apr 1826
...	...		...		United States	Atlantic	2 Apr 1827

NAMES OF PASSENGERS	AGE	SEX	OCCUPATIONS	COUNTRY TO WHICH THEY BELONG	COUNTRY THEY INTEND TO INHABIT	SHIPS/DATES OF ARRIVAL
...	...	...			United States	Atlantic 2 Apr 1827
...	...	...			United States	Atlantic 2 Apr 1827
...	...	...			United States	Atlantic 2 Apr 1827
...	...	...			United States	Atlantic 2 Apr 1827
...	...	...			United States	Atlantic 2 Apr 1827
...	...	...			United States	Atlantic 2 Apr 1827
...	...	...			United States	Atlantic 2 Apr 1827
...	...	...			United States	Atlantic 2 Apr 1827
...	...	...			United States	Atlantic 2 Apr 1827
...	...	F	Spinster	Ireland	U. States	Josephine 7 May 1827
...	...	M	Labourer	Ireland	U. States	Josephine 7 May 1827
...	...	M	Labourer	Ireland	United States	Carolina Ann 14 May 1827
...	...	...	...	Ireland	Unt. St. America	Wilson 21 May 1827
...	...	F	Spinster	Ireland	Unt. St. America	Wilson 21 May 1827
...	...	...	...	Ireland	Unt. St. America	Wilson 21 May 1827
...	...	...	...	Ireland	Unt. St. America	Wilson 21 May 1827
...	...	...	...	Ireland	Unt. St. America	Wilson 21 May 1827
...	...	F	Spinster	Ireland	Unt. St. America	Wilson 21 May 1827
...	...	...	...	...	...	Silvanus Jenkins 29 Jun 1827
...	...	...	...	...	...	Silvanus Jenkins 29 Jun 1827
...	...	...	...	...	...	Silvanus Jenkins 29 Jun 1827
...	...	...	...	...	...	Silvanus Jenkins 29 Jun 1827
...	...	...	...	...	...	Silvanus Jenkins 29 Jun 1827
...	...	...	...	...	...	Silvanus Jenkins 29 Jun 1827
...	...	F	...	England	United States	Hannibal 25 Sep 1827
...	...	M	None	France	U. States	Sully 25 Jun 1828
...	...	M		Great B.	U. States	William Neilson 26 Jul 1828
...	...	M	Labourer	G. Britain	U. States	Nimrod 31 Jul 1828
...	...	M	...	France	France	Edward Quesnel 3 Jul 1829
...	...	M	...	England	...	Lima 5 Aug 1829
...	...	M	Farmer	Great Britian	United States	Andes 19 Aug 1829
...	...0		...		United States	Atlantic 2 Apr 1827
...	...0	M	Servant	Ireland	United States	Carolina Ann 14 May 1827
...	...3	M		Switzerland		Pallas 14 Jun 1828
...	...4	M		Switzerland		Pallas 14 Jun 1828
...	...5	M	Clerk	Great Brittian		Merchant 22 Apr 1822
...	1	F	Servant	Ireland	United States	Carolina Ann 14 May 1827
...	2	M		Great Britain	...ca	Zodiac 14 Jun 1822
...	2	F		England	U. States	Acasta 12 May 1825
...	2	F		Newmills, Louden [Parish], Dumbarton [County]	New York	Hero 19 May 1828
*going to her friends	2			Isle of Man	Rochester	Peru 30 May 1828
...	4	F	Servant	Ireland	United States	Carolina Ann 14 May 1827
...	6	F	...	Great Britain	New York	Dublin 21 Dec 1824
...	6	M	Mariner	England	U. States	Acasta 12 May 1825
...	9	M	Laborer			Manhattan 25 Dec 1820
...	9	M	Weaver	Switzerland	United States	Elbe 2 Aug 1822
...	10	F				Manhattan 25 Dec 1820
...	10	M	Labourer	Ireland	United States	Carolina Ann 14 May 1827
...	13			England	United States	Hugh Johnson 11 Jun 1828
...	15	M		Great Britain	...ca	Zodiac 14 Jun 1822
...	15	F		Switzerland		Pallas 14 Jun 1828
...	16	F	Servant	England	U. States	Acasta 12 May 1825
...	16	F		Great Britain	Philadelphia	Philetus 21 Jul 1827
...	17	M	Miller	England	U. States	Acasta 12 May 1825
...	18			Scotland	United States	Minerva 29 Oct 1822
...	18	M	Farmer	Ireland	U. States	William & John 10 Jul 1824
...	18	M		Switzerland		Pallas 14 Jun 1828
...	19	M	Farmer	England	U. States	Acasta 12 May 1825
...	19		Laboring Class		United States	Atlantic 2 Apr 1827
...	19	M	Labourer	Ireland	United States	Carolina Ann 14 May 1827
...	2...	F		United States		Howard 17 Oct 1822
...	2...	F	Spinster	Ireland	Unt. St. America	Wilson 21 May 1827
...	20	M	Farmer	England	U. States	Acasta 12 May 1825
...	20	M	Labourer	Ireland	United States	Carolina Ann 14 May 1827
...	20	F		Switzerland		Pallas 14 Jun 1828
...	22	M	Laborer			Manhattan 25 Dec 1820

NAMES OF PASSENGERS	AGE	SEX	OCCUPATIONS	COUNTRY TO WHICH THEY BELONG	COUNTRY THEY INTEND TO INHABIT	SHIPS/DATES OF ARRIVAL	
...	22	M	Clerk	N. York	U. States	Pauline Julia	13 Aug 1821
...	22	M	Shoemaker	Ireland	U. States	Josephine	7 May 1827
...	23	M	Farmer	Ireland	United States	Louisa	18 Apr 1827
...	24	F	Confectioner	England	U. States	Acasta	12 May 1825
...	25	F	Spinster	Ireland	Unt. St. America	Wilson	21 May 1827
...	26	M	Farmer	England	U. States	Acasta	12 May 1825
...	26		...		United States	Atlantic	2 Apr 1827
...	27	M	Labourer	Great Brittian		Merchant	22 Apr 1822
...	27	M	Farmer	Great Brittian	United States	London	24 Jun 1823
...	28	M	Artist	England	U. States	Acasta	12 May 1825
...	28 4/12	M	Merchant	Great Britain		Silas Richards	27 Oct 1826
...	29		Merchant	Court ..., France	France	Frances Henrietta	31 May 1824
...	29			Longford	N. York	Peru	30 May 1828
...	30	F	None	...ia	United States	Martha	22 Jul 1820
...	30	M	Merchant	G. Britain	G. Britain	Charlotte Corday	16 Aug 1821
...	30	F		Great Brittian		Merchant	22 Apr 1822
...	30	M	Farmer	Great Brittian	United States	London	24 Jun 1823
...	30	M	Confectioner	Ireland	U. States	Acasta	12 May 1825
...	30	F	Servant	Ireland	United States	Carolina Ann	14 May 1827
...	32	M	Farmer	England	U.S. States	Splendid	14 Aug 1829
...	34	M	...	England	New York	America	1 Aug 1828
...	35	M	Farmer	England	U. States	Acasta	12 May 1825
...	35	M	Mariner	U. States	U. States	Indus	24 Jul 1827
...	35			England	United States	Hugh Johnson	11 Jun 1828
...	36	F	S...	Ireland	New York	Wilson	10 Apr 1823
...	36	F	Mariner	England	U. States	Acasta	12 May 1825
...	36	F	Housekeeper	Ireland	United States	Carolina Ann	14 May 1827
...	37			England	United States	Hugh Johnson	11 Jun 1828
...	4...	...	Farmer	Ireland	United States	Carolina Ann	14 May 1827
...	40	F		U. States	U. States	Greek	2 Oct 1826
...	41	M	Grocer	Great Brittian		Merchant	22 Apr 1822
...	41	F		Great Britain	...ca	Zodiac	14 Jun 1822
...	41	M	Labourer	Ireland	United States	Carolina Ann	14 May 1827
...	43	M	...	Ireland	United States	Carolina Ann	14 May 1827
...	47	F	Farmer	Great Brittian		Merchant	22 Apr 1822
...	5...	F	Inn Keeper	Ireland	United States	Carolina Ann	14 May 1827
...	50	M	Labourer	Ireland	United States	Carolina Ann	14 May 1827
...	50	M	Labourer	Ireland	United States	Carolina Ann	14 May 1827
..., & fam.	35, 50, 19, etc.	M	Lamp Oil ...	England	Upper Canada	Thames	6 Oct 1820
...athew	30	M	B...	Germany	United States	Montano	8 May 1827
...ia	9	F		Switzerland	United States	Elbe	2 Aug 1822
...ride	...	M	W...	France	U. States	Sully	25 Jun 1828
...t...h	...	...	...	...	...	William Thompson	30 Sep 1824
...w	11			England	United States	Hugh Johnson	11 Jun 1828
A...	17	...	...	Ireland	United States	Carolina Ann	24 Oct 1825
Abisael	29			Stonebridge	England	Great Britain	7 May 1827
Aime	31	M	Traveler	France	U. States	Stephania	24 Jul 1820
Alexand...	...	M	...	Scotland	United States	Siroc	31 Oct 1829
Alice	26	F		England	United States	Lord Wellington	14 Nov 1827
Amelia	...	...	...		United States	London Packet	25 Dec 1820
Ann	15	F	None	Great Britain	United States	Blakely	29 Sep 1826
Ann	25	F		Great Britian	United States	London	24 Jun 1823
Ann	30		Laboring Class		United States	Atlantic	2 Apr 1827
B...	30	M	Merchant	Ireland	Ireland	Nancy	16 Aug 1822
Barbara	5	F		Switzerland	United States	Elbe	2 Aug 1822
Barbara	5	F		Switzerland	United States	Elbe	2 Aug 1822
Barbara	24	F		Switzerland	United States	Elbe	2 Aug 1822
Benjamin	...	...	...	...	...	Silvanus Jenkins	29 Jun 1827
Bridget	...	F	Spinster	Ireland	Unt. St. America	Wilson	21 May 1827
Bridget	...	F	Spinster	Ireland	Unt. St. America	Wilson	21 May 1827
C...	60	M	...	...	Great Brittan	Amity	11 May 1821
Caroline	9	F		Switzerland		Pallas	14 Jun 1828
Cat...	...	...	...	...	...	Silvanus Jenkins	29 Jun 1827
Cath.		F	Weaver	France	U. States	C. Amelia	30 Jun 1828
Catherine	17	F	Servant	Ireland	United States	Carolina Ann	14 May 1827
Catherine	24		Laboring Class		United States	Atlantic	2 Apr 1827
Catherine	30	F	Spinster	Ireland	Unt. St. America	Wilson	21 May 1827

NAMES OF PASSENGERS	AGE	SEX	OCCUPATIONS	COUNTRY TO WHICH THEY BELONG	COUNTRY THEY INTEND TO INHABIT	SHIPS/DATES OF ARRIVAL	
Charles	18	M	...	Ireland	Unt. St. America	Wilson	21 May 1827
Charles	21	M	...	France	United States	Stephania	20 Apr 1827
Charlotte, Madam	40	...	...	...	...	Seine	29 Jun 1827
Chas.	26	M	Clothier	England	U. States	Unity	27 Mar 1827
Col... ...	28	M	Merchant	Great Britain	Great Britain	Martha	22 Jul 1820
Collan	...	...	...	...	...	Silvanus Jenkins	29 Jun 1827
Da...	20	F	F...	Ireland	United States	Carolina Ann	14 May 1827
David	20	M	Labourer	Ireland	United States	Hope	12 Jun 1828
Dennis	...	...	...	Ireland	Unt. St. America	Wilson	21 May 1827
E. V.	1	M	None	Great Britain	United States	Aurora	10 Nov 1827
E...	3	F		G. Brittain	U. States	Hope & Esther	26 Nov 1822
El...	...	F	Servant	Ireland	United States	Carolina Ann	14 May 1827
Elisa	20	F		U. States	U. States	Nancy	16 Aug 1822
Eliz.		F	Weaver	France	U. States	C. Amelia	30 Jun 1828
Elizabeth	10	...	...	...	...	Pioneer	21 Jun 1825
Elizabeth	21	F		Ireland	New York	William	26 Apr 1823
Elizabeth	32	F		Great Britian	United States	Robert Quayle	29 Jul 1822
Elizabeth	54	F	Gin Smith	Switzerland		Pallas	14 Jun 1828
Frances	2	F		Switzerland	United States	Elbe	2 Aug 1822
Frances	21	F	None	Great Britain	United States	Blakely	29 Sep 1826
Geo...	11	M		Great Britain		Robert Fulton	8 Mar 1823
George	...	...	...	...	United States	London Packet	25 Dec 1820
George	...	M	Labourer	Ireland	Unt. St. America	Wilson	21 May 1827
George	10 6/12	M	Gentleman	Great Britain	United States	Venus	8 Sep 1820
George	20	M	...	France	United States	Stephania	20 Apr 1827
George, Jun.	42	M	Farmer	Great Britian	United States	Robert Quayle	29 Jul 1822
George, Mr.	...	...	...	...	...	Seine	29 Jun 1827
Gorge	9	M	Farmer	France	U. States	C. Amelia	30 Jun 1828
H.	25	...	...	...	...	Cuba	25 Mar 1823
H...	...	...	...		United States	Atlantic	2 Apr 1827
Henriettia	...	F		Switzerland		Pallas	14 Jun 1828
Henry	...	...	...	...	...	Pioneer	21 Jun 1825
Henry	40	M	Shoe maker	Ireland	United States	Lord Wellington	14 Nov 1827
Isabella	24	F	Labourer	Ireland	United States	Hope	12 Jun 1828
Isabella	66	F	Widow	Ireland	U. States	Josephine	7 May 1827
J...	...	...	...	...	...	Silvanus Jenkins	29 Jun 1827
Jam...	5	M	Labourer	England	U. States	Comet	23 Aug 1828
James	...	...	...	...	...	Silvanus Jenkins	29 Jun 1827
James	15	M	Servant	Ireland	United States	Carolina Ann	14 May 1827
James	20	...		Ireland	U. States	Nancy	16 Aug 1822
James	22	M	Spinner	Scotland	America	Nimrod	9 Jul 1827
James	26	F		Great Britian	United States	London	24 Jun 1823
James	29	M	Farmer	Gt. Brittian	Gt. Brittian	Manchester	21 Apr 1827
James	30	M	Labourer	Ireland	Unt. St. America	Wilson	21 May 1827
James	33	M	Painter	Great Brittain	United States	Cortes	18 Oct 1820
James, Jr., Mr.	33	M	Gentleman	England	New York	Thames	6 Oct 1820
James, Mr.	55	M	Gentleman	England	New York	Thames	6 Oct 1820
Jane	19	F		Ireland	United States	Magnet	16 May 1823
Jane	30	...	Labourer	England	U. States	Comet	23 Aug 1828
Jean.	44	F	Weaver	France	U. States	C. Amelia	30 Jun 1828
Job	...	...	...		United States	London Packet	25 Dec 1820
John	...	M	Labourer	Ireland	Unt. St. America	Wilson	21 May 1827
John	...	...	...	...	...	Silvanus Jenkins	29 Jun 1827
John	1 1/12	M	...	Scotland	America	Nimrod	9 Jul 1827
John	20		Laboring Class		United States	Atlantic	2 Apr 1827
John	20	M	Labourer	Ireland	United States	Hope	12 Jun 1828
John	21	M	Labourer	New Brunswick [?]	U. States	St. Michael	5 May 1827
John	24	M	Farmer	England	U. States	Manhattan	20 Jun 1825
John	25	M	Stone Merchant	Germany	U. States	Edward Bonaffe	11 Dec 1827
John	32	M	Farmer	Ireland	United States	Lord Wellington	14 Nov 1827
John	60	M	Joiner	Scotland	United States	Samuel Robertson	5 Oct 1827
John...	19	M	Shoemaker	England	New York	Thames	6 Oct 1820
Joseph	...	M	...	Ireland	United States	Colossus	30 May 1825
Joseph	...4	M	Labourer	Ireland	United States	Hope	12 Jun 1828
Joseph	14	M	Labourer	England	U. States	Hamlet	16 Aug 1820
Josephine	...	...	...	...	...	Seine	29 Jun 1827
Law...ce	...	...	...	...	...	Silvanus Jenkins	29 Jun 1827

NAMES OF PASSENGERS	AGE	SEX	OCCUPATIONS	COUNTRY TO WHICH THEY BELONG	COUNTRY THEY INTEND TO INHABIT	SHIPS/DATES OF ARRIVAL
Lee, Mr.	4...	...	...	...	...	Seine 29 Jun 1827
Louisa ...	18	F		England	U. States	St. Michael 5 May 1827
Lucy	...	...	...	...	...	Silvanus Jenkins 29 Jun 1827
M.	9			England	United States	Hugh Johnson 11 Jun 1828
M...	...	F	Spinster	Ireland	Unt. St. America	Wilson 21 May 1827
M...	19	F	Servant	Ireland	United States	Carolina Ann 14 May 1827
Ma...	...	...	...	...	...	Silvanus Jenkins 29 Jun 1827
Margaret	17	F	Weaver	France	U. States	C. Amelia 30 Jun 1828
Margeret	17	F	Labourer	Ireland	United States	Hope 12 Jun 1828
Maria	9	F	None	France	U. States	Sully 25 Jun 1828
Maria	22	F		Switzerland	United States	Elbe 2 Aug 1822
Mary	4		Laboring Class		United States	Atlantic 2 Apr 1827
Mary	16	F		New Brunswick [?]	U. States	St. Michael 5 May 1827
Mary	30	F	Labourer	England	U. States	Comet 23 Aug 1828
Mary Ann	5	F	None	Great Britain	United States	Blakely 29 Sep 1826
Michael	22	M	Weaver	Limerick	N. York	Thomas & William 25 May 1827
Patr...	12	M		Ireland	United States	Lord Wellington 14 Nov 1827
Patrick	...	...	...	Ireland	Unt. St. America	Wilson 21 May 1827
Peter	...	...	...	...	...	C. Amelia 30 Jun 1828
R...	...	M	Labourer	Ireland	Unt. St. America	Wilson 21 May 1827
R...	17	F		Ireland	New York	William 26 Apr 1823
Rob...	7	F		New Brunswick [?]	U. States	St. Michael 5 May 1827
S. F.	32	M	...	...	Canada	Martha 22 Jul 1820
Saml.	22	M	Labourer	Ireland	United States	Aurelia 7 Jun 1826
Sarah	...	...	...	...	...	Silvanus Jenkins 29 Jun 1827
Sarah	35	F	None	Great Britain	United States	Ann Maria 12 Jul 1821
Scot, Mr.	35	M	Gentleman	England	England	Elizabeth 17 May 1822
Sophia	21	F		New Brunswick [?]	U. States	St. Michael 5 May 1827
Susan C.	12	F		Switzerland		Pallas 14 Jun 1828
Susanner	11	F	Weaver	France	U. States	C. Amelia 30 Jun 1828
T.	14 2/12	M	Farmer	America	U. States	France 26 Jun 1828
Th...s	...	...	...	Ireland	Unt. St. America	Wilson 21 May 1827
Thomas	...	...	...	...	...	Silvanus Jenkins 29 Jun 1827
Thomas ...	40, 42	M	Farmer	England	New York	Thames 6 Oct 1820
Thos.	...	...	...	Ireland	United States	General Putnam 20 Jun 1825
Ulrick	24	M	Farmer	Switzerland	United States	Elbe 2 Aug 1822
W.	24	M	Farmer	Great Britain		Robert Fulton 8 Mar 1823
William	1/12	M		England	United States	Lord Wellington 14 Nov 1827
William	4...	M	Merchant	United States	United States	John Wells 18 Sep 1826
William	55	M	Merchant	United States	United States	John Wells 18 Sep 1826
Wm.	...	M	Gent.	England	U.S. States	Splendid 14 Aug 1829
Wm.	21	M	Merchant	Havannah	U. States	Eliza 20 Aug 1827
...A, Arthur	10	M		Ireland	United States	Lord Wellington 14 Nov 1827
...A..., John	19	M	...	Scotland	America	Nimrod 9 Jul 1827
Mathew	30	M	Labourer	Ireland	Unt. St. America	Wilson 21 May 1827
...A...A..., ...	20	M	Labourer	Ireland	Unt. St. America	Wilson 21 May 1827
...AC...Y, Margaret	20	F	...	Ireland	United States	Carolina Ann 14 May 1827
...ACKE..., Th...	25	M	Labourer	Keeghley	Yorkshire	Howard Douglass 11 May 1827
...AFF, James F.	20	M	Merchant	American	U.S.	Alexander 15 Oct 1827
...AHOO, Ann	21	F		Irereland	America	Carolina Ann 20 Jun 1825
...AILEY, Catherine	18	F		Ireland	America	Wilson 27 Nov 1826
...AIN, James	...6		Laboring Class		United States	Atlantic 2 Apr 1827
...AKON, Betty	20	F	None	Ireland	United States	John Wells 11 May 1827
...AL...Y, Charles B.	30	M	B...	England	U. States	St. Michael 5 May 1827
...ALES, ...	8	M	Laborer			Manhattan 25 Dec 1820
...ALL, Rosanna	10		Laboring Class		United States	Atlantic 2 Apr 1827
...AN, ...	21		Laboring Class		United States	Atlantic 2 Apr 1827
...ANEY, Pat	21	M	Labourer	Ireland	Unt. St. America	Wilson 21 May 1827
...ANGAPIN, Caleb	29		Farmer	U. States	U. States	Nile 30 Apr 1827
...ANN, ...	20	F				Robert Burns 13 Jul 1820
...ANS, ...	2...		Laboring Class		United States	Atlantic 2 Apr 1827
...ANUS, J...es	18	M	Labourer	Ireland	Unt. St. America	Wilson 21 May 1827
...ARD, ...	30	M	Merchant	America		Elias Burger 26 Jul 1821
...ARR, Owen	19		Laboring Class		United States	Atlantic 2 Apr 1827

NAMES OF PASSENGERS	AGE	SEX	OCCUPATIONS	COUNTRY TO WHICH THEY BELONG	COUNTRY THEY INTEND TO INHABIT	SHIPS/DATES OF ARRIVAL	
...ASAL, Juan	23	M	Merchant	Havannah	U. States	Eliza	20 Aug 1827
...ASELLI, Alexander	23	M	Merchant	France	France	Cadmus	9 Dec 1826
...AYLOR, James	...			...der	England	Great Britain	7 May 1827
...BBITS, Robert	...			...thampton	England	Great Britain	7 May 1827
Sarah	4...			...thampton	England	Great Britain	7 May 1827
...BLER, Andrew	25	M	Lin. Weaver	P...elphy	U. States	Sully	25 Jun 1828
...CO..., ...	20	M	Labourer	Ireland	Unt. St. America	Wilson	21 May 1827
...COME, Christian	46	M	Farmer	Switzerland	United States	Elbe	2 Aug 1822
...D..., Henry	6	M		G. Britain	U. States	St. George	7 Jun 1828
...DBEAGH, John	24		Laboring Class		United States	Atlantic	2 Apr 1827
...DDON, Edward	...	M	...	...	United States	Delta	24 Oct 1829
...DISON, —	22	M	Cook	France	United States	Stephania	24 Mar 1828
...DLER, —, Miss	15	F		Great Britian	United States	London	24 Jun 1823
...DOC..., James	40	M	Farmer, Labourer or Spinster	Ireland	U. States	Meteor	4 Oct 1827
...E, Jane	60	F		England	U.S. States	Splendid	14 Aug 1829
...EE, Hugh	22		Laboring Class		United States	Atlantic	2 Apr 1827
...EENEY, ...	28	M	Labourer	Ireland	United States	Henry Kneeland	7 Jun 1828
...EL..., ...b	32	M	Merchant	Ireland	United States	Dublin Packet	23 May 1828
...ELL, Sarris	22	M	Weaver	Switzerland	U.S.	C. Amelia	30 Jun 1828
...ELTDEN, Cathe.	30	F		Great Britian	United States	London	24 Jun 1823
Geo.	48	M		Great Britian	United States	London	24 Jun 1823
...EON..., Mary Jane	...			Bolton	England	Great Britain	7 May 1827
...ER, ...oan	40	M	Spinner	Great Britian	United States	Hamilton	19 Mar 1827
Jane	45	F	Spinster	Ireland	United States	Gem	16 Jun 1824
...ERS, ...	23	M	Farmer	England	U. States	Acasta	12 May 1825
...ES, ...	36	M	Gentleman	U. States	U. States	Liberty	23 Feb 1820
Andrew	27	M	Painter	Colenboro	Colenboro	Howard Douglass	11 May 1827
Robert	...	M	...	Great Britain	Great Britain	Ann Maria	17 Apr 1827
Woodard	...	M	Merchant	Great Britain	Great Britain	Ann Maria	17 Apr 1827
...ETT, Catherin	5	F		Switzerland	United States	Elbe	2 Aug 1822
Maria	3	F		Switzerland	United States	Elbe	2 Aug 1822
...EY, Barnard	20	M	Labourer	Ireland	United States	Meteor	26 Jun 1827
Peater	25	M		Irland	United States	Nancy	28 Oct 1822
Phillip	50 ...	M	...	Switzerland	United States	Criterion	13 Oct 1825
...FORD, ...	23	M	Merchant	Georgia	U. States	Abeona	7 Aug 1821
...GAN, Mary	...	F	Spinster	Ireland	Unt. St. America	Wilson	21 May 1827
...GARS, Edward	26	M	Labourer	Ireland	America	Plutarch	18 Jul 1826
...GHT..., ...	...	F	Spinster	Ireland	Unt. St. America	Wilson	21 May 1827
...GHTY, Judith	22	F	Spinster	Ireland	Unt. St. America	Wilson	21 May 1827
...H...GHT, Finlay	...0	M	...	Scotland	America	Nimrod	9 Jul 1827
...HAM, Wm.	20	M				Betsey	17 Aug 1820
...HAN, Jane	3	F	Labourer	England	U. States	Comet	23 Aug 1828
John	25	M	Labourer	England	U. States	Comet	23 Aug 1828
John	30	M	Labourer	England	U. States	Comet	23 Aug 1828
Mary	26	F	Labourer	England	U. States	Comet	23 Aug 1828
Nelly	10	F	Labourer	England	U. States	Comet	23 Aug 1828
...HEAD, ...	16	M	Sevant			Robert Burns	13 Jul 1820
...HNSTONE, ...ary Ann	11		Child	Smartin, E.	England	Packet	27 Aug 1822
...owe	37			Bethusted, E.	England	Packet	27 Aug 1822
Amey	7		Child	Smartin, E.	England	Packet	27 Aug 1822
Amos	4		Child	Smartin, E.	England	Packet	27 Aug 1822
C...	38		Labourer	Smartin, E.	England	Packet	27 Aug 1822
Harriet	Infant		Child			Packet	27 Aug 1822
James	9		Child	Smartin, E.	England	Packet	27 Aug 1822
...HOLES, John	38	M	Manufacturer	Great Britian	United States	Silvanus Jenkins	6 Apr 1826
...HORNSON, Mary Ann	24					Amphion	31 May 1824
...I...TERS, Margret	19	F	Servant	Ireland	United States	Carolina Ann	14 May 1827
...ICHOLSON, William	32	M	Farmer	England	United States	Trident	30 Sep 1826
...ICK, Alexander	...	...	...	Scotland	America	Nimrod	9 Jul 1827
...IDLER, Eliza, Mrs.	32		Lady	...	U. States	South Carolina Packet	17 May 1827
...IGNE, ...	23	F	Farmer	France	U.S.	C. Amelia	30 Jun 1828
...ILK, Jas.	42	M	Carpenter	Ireland	U. States	Albion	11 May 1827
...ILLIS, ...	57	M	Merchant	United States	United States	London	24 Jun 1823
...IMMS, Mary	26	F	Spinster	Ireland	United States	Dublin Packet	6 Dec 1827
...IN, ...	25	M	Farmer			Robert Burns	13 Jul 1820
...INGS, ...	2	F		Great Britian	United States	London	24 Jun 1823

NAMES OF PASSENGERS	AGE	SEX	OCCUPATIONS	COUNTRY TO WHICH THEY BELONG	COUNTRY THEY INTEND TO INHABIT	SHIPS/DATES OF ARRIVAL	
...	5	M		Great Britian	United States	London	24 Jun 1823
...	7	F		Great Britian	United States	London	24 Jun 1823
...	8	M		Great Britian	United States	London	24 Jun 1823
...	10	F		Great Britian	United States	London	24 Jun 1823
...	25	F		Great Britian	United States	London	24 Jun 1823
Danie...	22		Laboring Class		United States	Atlantic	2 Apr 1827
...IRLY, Margaret	18	F	None	Ireland	United States	John Wells	11 May 1827
...ISBETT, Thomas	29	M	Farmer	Ireland	U. States	Josephine	7 May 1827
...ISH, Sarah	20	F		Switzerland	U. States	Robert Edward	2 Nov 1827
...IVEZ, Francisco, Genl. Don	44	M	Spanish Ambassador	Spain	Spain	James Monroe	5 Apr 1820
...KADT, Lavina	22	F	Lady	U. States	U. States	Marcellus	2 Sep 1820
...LARD, ...	37	M			France	Edward Quesnel	3 Sep 1826
...LDWORTH, Richard	42	M	Cord weaver	England	U. States	Electra	7 Jul 1828
Wm.	12	M		England	U. States	Electra	7 Jul 1828
...LEBEY, John	25		Laboring Class		United States	Atlantic	2 Apr 1827
...LER, Christian	19	M	Farmer	Switzerland	United States	Elbe	2 Aug 1822
...LH...H, Thos.	14		Tailor	Bl...	England	Great Britain	7 May 1827
...LIAS, Joseph	16	M	Merchant	Havannah	U. States	Eliza	20 Aug 1827
...LINGS, Martin	23	M	Labourer	Limerick	Baltimore	Thomas & William	25 May 1827
...LIS, Catherine	22	F	Spinster	Ireland	Unt. St. America	Wilson	21 May 1827
...LLAN, Bridget	22		Laboring Class		United States	Atlantic	2 Apr 1827
...LLET..., ...	33	M	Farmer	Germany	United States	Nestor in Liverpool	29 Jul 1822
...LLEY, ...	22	M	Clerk			Robert Burns	13 Jul 1820
...LLI..., Jas.	...0	M	...	Scotland	America	Nimrod	9 Jul 1827
...LLON, ...	44	M	Labourer	Great Brittian		Merchant	22 Apr 1822
...LLORN, Mathew	...	M	Miller	Ireland	Unt. St. America	Wilson	21 May 1827
...LLS, William	20	M	Labourer	Scotland	United States	Samuel Robertson	9 May 1827
...LLST..., James	33	M	Farmer	Germany	United States	Nestor in Liverpool	29 Jul 1822
...LLY, ...	20	M	Farmer			Robert Burns	13 Jul 1820
...LO, Walter	...	M	Sh...	Great Britain	Great Britain	Ann Maria	17 Apr 1827
...LTERS, Owen	12		Laboring Class		United States	Atlantic	2 Apr 1827
...M, Peter	20		Laboring Class		United States	Atlantic	2 Apr 1827
...MAN, ...	...	M	Farmer	France	U.S.	C. Amelia	30 Jun 1828
S., Mr.	5	F		France	U.S.	C. Amelia	30 Jun 1828
Treogoni	10/12	M		France	U.S.	C. Amelia	30 Jun 1828
...MANE, ...or	21		Laboring Class		United States	Atlantic	2 Apr 1827
...MBER, James	22		Baker	Ireland	United States	Fabius	18 Mar 1829
...MISTON, Alexander	...	M	...	Scotland	America	Nimrod	9 Jul 1827
Alexander	...	M	...	Scotland	America	Nimrod	9 Jul 1827
Isabella	...	F	...	Scotland	America	Nimrod	9 Jul 1827
Sarah	...	F	...	Scotland	America	Nimrod	9 Jul 1827
...MPL..., Edward	...	M	...	Scotland	America	Nimrod	9 Jul 1827
...MS..., A...	21	...	...	Scotland	America	Nimrod	9 Jul 1827
...N, John	22	M	Farmer	England	England	Ohio	18 Jul 1821
Mary	21	F	Spinster	Ireland	U. States	Josephine	7 May 1827
...NAN, Owen	22			Longford	N. York	Peru	30 May 1828
...NASTAFF, Francisco	20	F		Germany	United States	Samuel Robertson	8 Aug 1828
...NE, ...	25	M	Labourer	Scotland	New York	America	1 Aug 1828
...NER, Richard	24	M	Cotton Printer	G. Britain	U. States	America	17 Oct 1825
...NEY, Catherine	21	F	Spinster	Ireland	Unt. St. America	Wilson	21 May 1827
...NGER, ...	22	M	Sugar Refiner	Germany	U. States	Acasta	12 May 1825
...NIS, J...	22	M	Farmer			Robert Burns	13 Jul 1820
...NK...SON, Jos...	...2	M	None	Ireland	United States	Trident	18 Jul 1827
...NON, David	32	M	...er	Steal...	Lancaster	Howard Douglass	11 May 1827
...NT, ..., Mrs.	29	M	Tallow Chandler	France	United States	Henry	10 Feb 1825
Frederick	26	M	Brewer	Switzerland	United States	Elbe	2 Aug 1822
Piere	25	M	Wheel Wright	Switzerland	United States	Elbe	2 Aug 1822
...O, ...	23	F	Farmer	England	U. States	Acasta	12 May 1825
Alexander	81	M	Weaver	Paisley	U.S. America	Camillus	10 Sep 1821
...OAK, ...	43	M	Artist		U. States	Edward Quesnel	3 Sep 1826
...OASTER, E. L.	32	M		U. States	U. States	Edward Quesnel	3 Sep 1826

NAMES OF PASSENGERS	AGE	SEX	OCCUPATIONS	COUNTRY TO WHICH THEY BELONG	COUNTRY THEY INTEND TO INHABIT	SHIPS/DATES OF ARRIVAL	
...OH...AN, Catharine	10	F		New Brunswick [?]	U. States	St. Michael	5 May 1827
...OLA..., Bridget	...	F	Spinster	Ireland	Unt. St. America	Wilson	21 May 1827
...OLL, William	18		Servant	England	New York	James Cropper	12 Jul 1822
...ON, ...	47 3/12	M	Merchant	Canada		Silas Richards	27 Oct 1826
James	59 11/12	M	Merchant	Great Britain		Silas Richards	27 Oct 1826
John	18		Labourer	Ireland	New York	Marcella	18 May 1827
...OR..., ...	...	...	...	Ireland	Unt. St. America	Wilson	21 May 1827
...OSWOOD, A. G.	17 2/12	M	Merchant	U.S. America	America	Erie	19 Oct 1829
...OTTON, William	60	M	Machinemaker	Great Britain, Ireland	New York	Britannia	3 Nov 1827
...OUGIRE, J., Mr.	46	M		France		Henri IV	17 May 1828
...OWAN, Thomas	20	M	Labourer	Isle of Man	Isle of Man	Howard Douglass	11 May 1827
...OWN, Hugh	...1	M	Blacksmith	Great Britain	United States	Ann Maria	17 Apr 1827
...R...WEN, John	17	M	Labourer	Ireland	United States	Wanderer	31 Aug 1829
...RALL, Margaret	20		Laboring Class		United States	Atlantic	2 Apr 1827
...RAZIN, Cathe.	10	F		Great Britian	United States	London	24 Jun 1823
...REHEAD, ...	12	M	Sevant			Robert Burns	13 Jul 1820
...ROY, Joseph	...	...	...	...	...	Silvanus Jenkins	29 Jun 1827
...RR..., Nievlin	42	M	Farm	Switzerland		Pallas	14 Jun 1828
...S, ...	40	M	Marine	England	U. States	Acasta	12 May 1825
...SALL, Alice	20	F				Amity	11 Sep 1820
...SEND, ...	28	F		Philada.	U. States	Pauline Julia	13 Aug 1821
...SH, J...	30	M	Labourer	Ireland	New York	Bowditch	27 Apr 1826
...SHANK, Andrew	22	M	Merchant	St. Johns, N.B.	Great Britain	Sylvester Healy	23 Nov 1825
...SLE, Thos.		M	Merchant	England	Great Brittan	Florida	17 May 1825
...SON, Alexr. M	...	M	Farmer	Great Britain	United States	Colossus	5 Jun 1827
Chas.	18		Laboring Class		United States	Atlantic	2 Apr 1827
J...	24	F	None	England	U. States	Unity	27 Mar 1827
...SSON, ...	40 3/12	M	Merchant	Denmark	Denmark	Elias Burger	18 Sep 1821
...T, ...	16	M	Servant	England	U. States	Acasta	12 May 1825
C...	16	M		Great Brittain	United States	Sarah Ralston	27 Jan 1827
Saml.	20	M	Farmer	Ireland	United States	Trident	17 May 1825
...T..., P.	25	M		Great Brittain	United States	Sarah Ralston	27 Jan 1827
...TE, Frederick	27	M	Merchant	Holland	N. York	France	29 Nov 1827
...TEED, Hann...	37	F	None	Great Britain	United States	Aurora	10 Nov 1827
...TION, J...	31	M	Coo...	Steal...	Lancaster	Howard Douglass	11 May 1827
...TO..., Catherine, Miss	15	F		United States	United States	John Wells	18 Sep 1826
...TON, ...	1	M		England	U. States	Acasta	12 May 1825
...TT, Catharine	12	F		Switzerland	United States	Elbe	2 Aug 1822
...TT...KS, Stephen	25	M	Farmer	Great Britian	United States	London	24 Jun 1823
...UR..., Thomas	20	M	Spinner	Steal...	Lancaster	Howard Douglass	11 May 1827
...US, Mary	21	F	Dress maker	Wales	United States	Lord Wellington	14 Nov 1827
...V..., Catharine	3	F		New Brunswick [?]	U. States	St. Michael	5 May 1827
...VENS, ...	4	F	Mariner	England	U. States	Acasta	12 May 1825
...WEN, Mary	50	F	Wife	Ireland	U. States	Meteor	19 Jul 1828
Robt.	26	M	Farmer	Ireland	U. States	Meteor	19 Jul 1828
...WER, ...	2...	M	Merchant	France	U.S.	Francois I	8 Aug 1829
...WRIGHT, William	...	M	...	Scotland	America	Nimrod	9 Jul 1827
...Y, ...	19	M	Teacher	Ireland	United States	Trio	13 Jun 1827
John	...9	M	...	Scotland	America	Nimrod	9 Jul 1827
...YNE, ...	35	M	Painter	England		Marchioness	13 May 1828
A..., —	34	F		Switzerland	United States	Elbe	2 Aug 1822
Elizabeth	50		Spinster	Ireland		Westmoreland	1 Aug 1826
Mary	43	F		Rye, England	United States	William	21 May 1828
Thos. R., Mr.	...	...	...	...	...	William Thompson	30 Sep 1824
A...ERE, G.	28	M		Great Britian	United States	London	24 Jun 1823
A...N..., Mary	13	M	Labourer	Ireland	United States	Hope	12 Jun 1828
A...Y, Th...	18	M	Farmer	Ireland	United States	Dalhouse Castle	21 Aug 1829

APPENDIX B
A LIST OF SHIPS

LIST OF SHIPS
With Ports of Embarkation and Dates of Arrival

SHIP	DATE OF ARRIVAL	PORT OF EMBARKATION	CAPTAIN	YEAR AND SHIP NUMBER
ABACO	20 Oct 1829	Cape Hayti	St. John, Aaron	29-314
ABALINO	13 Sep 1820	Havana	More, Jere.	20-241
ABBY JONES	21 Oct 1824	Cadiz	Crawford, William	24-619
	12 Jul 1827	Havre	Crawford, William	27-445
ABBY M.	7 Apr 1825	Antwerp	Nichols, W.	25-154
ABEONA	16 Mar 1820	St. Lucie	Dryburgh, James	20-066
	31 Oct 1820	Havanna	Porter, R. King	20-310
	7 Aug 1821	Turks Island	..., ...	21-209
	24 May 1822	Matanzas	Blinn, John M.	22-225
	5 Jul 1822	Havana	O'Bryan, John	22-302
	11 Mar 1823	Havana	Lester, N. R.	23-072
	23 May 1823	Havana	Lester, N. R.	23-224
	2 Sep 1823	St. Thomas	Cook, Benja.	23-437
	1 Oct 1823	Havana	Harper, Thomas P.	23-512
	20 Dec 1823	Havana	Harper, Thomas P.	23-650
	1 Apr 1824	Havana	Harper, Thomas P.	24-123
	26 Jun 1824	Havana	Hazard, Daniel	24-330
	4 Oct 1824	Bordeaux	Usher, G. F.	24-566A
	12 Mar 1825	Matanzas	Granger, Benjamin	25-106
	17 May 1825	Curacoa	Fairchild, H.	25-269
	12 Oct 1825	Gibraltar	Fairchild, H.	25-582
	24 Feb 1827	Gibralter	Fairchild, F.	27-091
	20 Aug 1827	St. Domingo	Spicer, D. H.	27-532
	25 Apr 1828	St. Domingo	Spicer, D. H.	28-145
	11 Sep 1828	St. Domingo	Spicer, D. H.	28-527
ABIGAIL	26 Sep 1820	Fairfields	Elwill, Joshua	20-264
	2 Oct 1820	Curacao	Waegenaar, David	20-274
	23 Nov 1820	St. Johns	Elwell, Joshua	20-328
	10 May 1821	St. Johns	Elwell, Josha.	21-055
	9 Aug 1821	Leghorn	Hitchcox, James	21-216
	25 Mar 1822	Amsterdam	Titcomb, John H.	22-090
	6 May 1822	St. Thomas	Elwell, Josha.	22-174
	29 May 1822	Ragged Island	Driggs, B.	22-237
	25 Jun 1822	Dublin	Martin, C.	22-288
	17 Sep 1822	Gibara	Driggs, B.	22-467
	11 Apr 1823	Gibara	Driggs, B.	23-123
	4 Oct 1823	Rotterdam	thomas, Chas., Jr.	23-519
	18 Mar 1824	Gabara	Driggs, B.	24-088
	16 Jul 1824	Gibara	Driggs, B.	24-379
	16 Nov 1824	Nevitas & Gibara	Driggs, B.	24-668
	21 Mar 1825	Hibara	Driggs, B.	25-123
	24 Mar 1825	Bahia	Thomas, Chas., Jr.	25-139
	25 Feb 1826	Carthagina	Gill, James	26-080
	19 May 1826	Xibara	Hallet, John	26-263
	18 Aug 1826	Xibara	Hallett, Jono.	26-499
ABIGALE	9 Aug 1821	St. Johns	Elwell, Josh	21-215
	17 Jul 1822	St. Andrews	Elwell, Joshua	22-331
	9 Aug 1822	St. Andrews	Elwell, Josha.	22-384
ABRONA	1 Nov 1821	Curacoa	Folger, R. C.	21-353
ACARTA (see Acasta)				
ACASTA	27 Aug 1821	Marseilles	Keen, Elisha L.	21-239
	13 Feb 1822	Liverpool	Allyn, Francis	22-045
	15 Jul 1822	London	Griswald, A. H.	22-320
	28 Jan 1823	London	Griswold, A. H.	23-020
	12 Dec 1823	London	Griswold, A. H.	23-636
	14 Jun 1824	London	Griswold, Aujustus Henry	24-307
	21 Jan 1825	London	Meriman, Saml.	25-032
	12 May 1825	London	Chadwick, Daniel	25-251
	21 Oct 1825	London	Chadwick, Daniel	25-605
	3 Apr 1826	London	Chadwick, Daniel	26-140
	16 Aug 1826	London	Chadwick, Daniel	26-485

SHIP	DATE OF ARRIVAL	PORT OF EMBARKATION	CAPTAIN	YEAR AND SHIP NUMBER
	11 Dec 1826	London	Chadwick, Daniel	26-717
	11 May 1827	London	Chadwick, Daniel	27-237
	25 Sep 1827	London	Perry, James	27-657
ACOSTA	28 Jul 1823	London	Griswold, Augustus H.	23-354
ACTIVE	23 Mar 1820	Magadore	Clark, Arnold	20-079
	29 Nov 1820	Porto Rico	Howland, R.	20-339
	8 Apr 1822	Gibraltar	Noble, Daniel T.	22-112
	11 Mar 1823	Jamaica	Jones, Benjamin P.	23-071
	25 Jun 1823	Jamaica	Jones, Benjamin P.	23-285
	9 Feb 1827	Martinique	Butler, Edwin	27-071
	25 Mar 1828	Liverpool	Walker, Alexander	28-089
	12 Sep 1828	Liverpool	Mackie, Robert	28-529
	28 Aug 1829	St. Andrews	McFarland, John	29-262
ACTRESS	17 Mar 1820	Gibralter	Noyes, Benjamin	20-069
	18 Feb 1825	Gibraltar	Anderson, Peter	25-073
ACTRRESS	11 Jul 1822	Malaga	Anderson, Peter	22-313
ADAMS	21 Jun 1824	Bristol, England	Henderson, William	24-319
	11 Nov 1824	Antigua	Emery, John	24-655
	27 Jun 1825	Rio Grande	Tobey, William J.	25-377
	13 Jan 1827	Cadiz	Ward, Thos.	27-026
	17 Feb 1827	St. Thomas	Lane, David, Jr.	27-085
	23 Jun 1828	St. Thomas	Burroughs, Peleg	28-322
ADELINE	30 Apr 1821	Gibraltar	Atwood, Jesse	21-035
	16 Aug 1827	Papalotea	McRoberts, E.	27-522
	25 Sep 1827	St. Ubes	Richardson, E.	27-662
ADMITTANCE	22 Sep 1823	Havana	Pilsbury, William	23-491
	10 Nov 1825	Antwerp	Drinkwater, R.	25-648
	8 Mar 1826	St. Croix	Drinkwater, R.	26-094
	17 May 1826	St. Croix	Drinkwater, R.	26-257
ADNO	7 Apr 1823	Dominica	Woodsum, Jabez	23-108
	29 Apr 1825	St. Thomas	Spring, Seth	25-222
	21 Apr 1827	Matanzas	Patterson, Robert	27-191
	5 Jul 1828	Halifax	Bearse, P.	28-354
	25 Aug 1828	Halifax, N.S.	Bears, Prince	28-466
ADONIS	23 Jan 1822	Canton	Brumley, Ruben	22-016
	29 Sep 1823	Havre	Richards, Benjn.	23-502
	17 Aug 1824	Antwerp	Richards, Benjn.	24-462
	16 Jun 1825	Pernambuco	Richards, Benjn.	25-349
ADORO	14 Apr 1828	Halifax	Bears, P., Jr.	28-126
ADRIANNA	8 Aug 1822	Port au Platt	Quereau, Phillip J.	22-378
	7 Apr 1823	Demarara	Quereau, Rd. P.	23-109
	5 Sep 1823	Demerara	Pearce, Jno. A.	23-450
ADZE	24 Jul 1820	Havana	Armington, A.	20-141
AERIAL	10 Nov 1825	Antwerp	Gage, Isaac	25-650
AGENORA	19 Mar 1823	Bordeaux	Thornbee, Wm.	23-087
	10 Apr 1823	St. Iago de Cuba	Mitchell, Elisha	23-115
	11 Jun 1824	Havana	Andrews, Seth	24-297
	29 Nov 1824	Turks Island	Allen, Samuel	24-695
	28 Jan 1826	Bahia	Brownell, Mager	26-042
	19 Jun 1826	Montego Bay	Phillips, Thomas	26-343
	18 Aug 1826	Demerara	Webber, Nathaniel	26-496
	3 Oct 1826	Montego Bay, Jamaica	Phillips, Thomas	26-583
	23 Aug 1827	Gibraltar	Martin, John	27-545
	12 Jul 1828	St. Thomas	Lockwood, Edmund	28-373A
AGENORIA	17 Sep 1821	Fayal	Clarke, John	21-274
	7 Jan 1822	Havana	Stanley, Viall	22-005
	15 Jun 1822	Matanzas	Maman, Sacket	22-271
	12 Oct 1822	Honduras	Tyler, Solomon	22-522
	27 Jun 1823	Demerara	Gay, Robert	23-297
AGILA (see Alligator)				
AGINORIA	16 Apr 1821	Matauras	Church, Wm., Jr.	21-018
AGNES	30 Sep 1820	Havana	Furman, Daniel	20-273
	12 Apr 1821	Lisbon	White, Aaron C.	21-012
	1 Jul 1825	Bermuda	Newell, W. J.	25-390
	29 Nov 1826	St. Croix	Johnson, Steven	26-689
	6 Oct 1827	St. Croix	Johnson, S.	27-684
	27 Mar 1828	St. Eloise	Johnson, Stephen	28-091
AGNESS	19 Mar 1827	St. Thomas	Johnson, Stephen	27-124

SHIP	DATE OF ARRIVAL	PORT OF EMBARKATION	CAPTAIN	YEAR AND SHIP NUMBER
	23 Jun 1827	St. Croix	Johnson, S.	27-371
	7 Jan 1828	St. Thomas	Johnson, S.	28-009
	23 Jun 1828	St. Croix	Johnson, Stephen	28-323
	9 Oct 1828	St. Croix	Bennett, James S.	28-601
	20 Jan 1829	St. Thomas	Bennett, Jas. S.	29-031
	30 Jul 1829	St. Croix	Bennett, James S.	29-177
AGRICOLA	1 Jul 1820	Liverpool	Dundee, Justus	20-091
	19 Jul 1824	Havana	Gillender, John E.	24-382
AISTHORPE	22 May 1827	Newport	Renney, Andrew	27-285
AJAX	15 May 1822	Manilla	Hubbell, Ezekiel	22-196
ALABAMA	21 May 1823	Havana	Hall, Isaac	23-219
	3 Dec 1823	Honduras	Hazard, Daniel	23-624
ALBANY PACKET	14 Nov 1826	Xibara	Brown, Jeremiah	26-661
	23 Mar 1827	Xibara	Brown, Jeremiah	27-143
ALBANY PKT.	2 Jun 1828	Gibara	Brown, Jere.	28-264
ALBATROSS	25 Jul 1821	Malaga	Harlow, Ellis J.	21-194
ALBERT	1 Apr 1822	Halifax	Walworth, Walter R.	22-101
	14 May 1822	Halifax	Walworth, Walter R.	22-193
	19 Apr 1823	Jamaica	Walworth, Walter R.	23-143
	2 Oct 1823	St. Michaels	Kidder, John	23-516
	17 Jan 1828	Truxillo	Titcomb, Samuel	28-017
ALBION	7 Feb 1820	Liverpool	Williams, John	20-024
	4 Oct 1820	Liverpool	Williams, John	20-279
	11 Jun 1821	Liverpool	Williams, John	21-109
	11 Oct 1821	Liverpool	Williams, John	21-312
	5 Feb 1822	Liverpool	Williams, Jno.	22-026
	23 Apr 1822	Halifax	Hall, Seth	22-145
	18 Feb 1823	Liverpool	Swainson, William	23-032
	17 Jan 1825	Bermuda	Hinks, Jesse G.	25-022
	9 Aug 1826	St. Johns, N.B.	Whitten, Ferguson	26-470
	11 May 1827	Cork	Mills, John	27-236
	27 Jun 1827	Bremen	Lee, George	27-381
	19 Jun 1828	Omoa	Vennard, M. B.	28-314
	11 Dec 1828	Grand Canary	Waters, Robert	28-700
ALCIOPE	6 Jul 1822	London	Adams, Daniel	22-307
ALDEBARON	21 Jan 1826	Liverpool	Galt, James	26-036
ALERT	22 Sep 1821	Alloa, Scotland	McDougal, James	21-297
	17 Apr 1824	Matanzas	York, Joseph U.	24-153
	9 Jul 1824	Matanzas	York, Joseph H.	24-364
	12 Oct 1824	Matanzas	York, Joseph U.	24-591
	27 May 1825	Rio de la Hatch	Rhodes, Josiah	25-301
ALETTA	12 May 1823	Bermuda	Adams, Thomas	23-180
ALEX MANSFIELD	1 Jun 1822	Dublin	Hamilton, Wm.	22-243
	27 Aug 1825	Liverpool	Baush, John	25-552
ALEX. MANSFIELD	17 May 1823	Belfast	Baush, John	23-206
ALEXANDER	28 Jul 1821	Newry	Taylor, William	21-203
	18 Mar 1822	Lisbon	Taylor, Wm.	22-082
	4 Oct 1822	Gottenburgh	McIntire, Charles	22-504
	6 May 1824	Havana	Baker, Barker	24-195
	1 May 1826	St. Thomas	Lovell, D. E.	26-216
	31 Mar 1827	Lisbon	Candler, Wm. A.	27-158
	15 Oct 1827	Lisbon	Lemon, Neal C.	27-705
	18 Aug 1828	Guadaloupe	Shaw, Jno.	28-444
	20 Aug 1828	Antwerp	Colas, P. T.	28-451
	2 Oct 1829	Antwerp	Colas, P. J.	29-275
ALEXANDER LE GRAND	9 Sep 1823	Port au Prince	Favre, Levi	23-456
ALEXANDER MANSFIELD	18 Jun 1821	Belfast	Hamilton, Wm.	21-117
	16 Nov 1821	Liverpool	Hamilton, Wm.	21-371
	9 Nov 1822	Belfast	Baush, John	22-562
	16 Sep 1823	Liverpool	Baush, John	23-476
	23 Nov 1824	Belfast	Baush, John	24-686
	18 Aug 1826	Belfast in Ireland	Minzies, Jacob A.	26-495
	9 Jul 1827	Liverpool	Minsies, J. A.	27-423

SHIP	DATE OF ARRIVAL	PORT OF EMBARKATION	CAPTAIN	YEAR AND SHIP NUMBER
	9 Jul 1829	Liverpool	Swain, Richd.	29-141
ALFRED	20 Dec 1821	Havana	Salder, William	21-424
	8 Jul 1822	St. Thomas	O'Zuill, John	22-308
	17 Sep 1822	St. Thomas	O'Zuill, John	22-468
	22 May 1824	Cadiz	O'Zuill, John	24-224
	7 Jun 1824	Dublin	Warnack, Jacob W.	24-275
	3 Jun 1826	Havanna	O'Zuill, John	26-299
	23 Oct 1826	Havana	Russell, J. G.	26-623
	12 Oct 1827	Havana	Russell, J. G.	27-699
	1 Dec 1827	Gottenburg	Sweetser, Salathiel	27-777
	26 Apr 1828	Cape Haytien	Rossiter, D.	28-155
	8 Jul 1828	Havre	Soule, H. J.	28-365
	24 Jul 1828	Havana	Russell, J. G.	28-396
ALGERINE	27 Sep 1828	St. Croix	Otis, John, Jr.	28-570
ALICIA	9 May 1827	Bristol	Evins, Joshua	27-230
ALIFAIR	11 Jul 1821	Havana	Hall, J.	21-167
ALLEN	29 Mar 1824	St. Andrews	Dunham, Jacob	24-114
ALLIGATOR	15 Aug 1820	Halifax	Heart, James	20-176
ALMIRA	15 Jul 1822	Halifax	Bears, Richard	22-321
	8 Aug 1822	Bermuda	Immohr, F.	22-379
	3 Sep 1822	Halifax	Bears, Richd.	22-446
	18 Sep 1823	Neuvitas	Doane, Seth	23-482
	6 Feb 1826	St. Domingo	Spicer, D. H.	26-051
	14 Jun 1826	St. Domingo	Spicer, D. H.	26-333
	11 Dec 1826	St. Domingo	Spicer, D. H.	26-718
	5 Nov 1827	Benavista	Thompson, John	27-749
ALONZO	16 Jul 1821	Trinidad in Cuba	Easton, Alexr. C.	21-179B
ALPHA	28 May 1823	Bermuda	Balgate, Willm.	23-230
	15 Jul 1823	Bermuda	Algate, Willm.	23-335
	7 Oct 1823	Bermuda	Algate, Wm. B.	23-524
	27 Jul 1827	St. Pierre, Martinique	Fisher, John W.	27-482
	7 Dec 1827	Xibara	Gardner, F.	27-808
	28 Apr 1828	St. Croix	Pierce, William	28-158
	4 Feb 1829	St. Iago	Gardner, F.	29-046
ALPHEUS	5 May 1828	St. Thomas	Whelden, Isaiah	28-182
ALTAMIRA	16 May 1825	Tampico	Walstrom, Saml.	25-257
	31 Jan 1826	Havana	Clasby, Wm. A.	26-047
	5 Aug 1826	Genoa	Gibson, James, Jr.	26-452
	31 Jan 1828	Tampico	Moore, Samuel	28-033
	24 Jun 1828	Tampico	Moore, Samuel	28-325
	21 Feb 1827	Havanna	Moore, Samuel	27-087
ALTO	8 Jun 1827	Tampico	Miller, Caleb	27-331
ALVAREDO (see Alvarado)				
AMANDA	19 Jan 1824	St. Thomas	Carr, Wm.	24-021
	23 May 1827	Galway	Gibbs, Stephen	27-292
AMAZON	7 Jul 1820	Beunos Ayres	Hatch, Joseph	20-109
	8 Dec 1820	Havanna	Elkins, Daniel	20-341
	28 Nov 1821	Turks Island	Hamer, James	21-382
	29 Aug 1825	Jacmel	Bigbee, Saml.	25-555
	22 Jun 1827	Carthagena	Clark, J. A.	27-368
	30 Jul 1827	St. Thomas	Shaw, Ebenezer A.	27-489
AMBUSCADE	14 Mar 1820	Havana	Skidmore, Herbert	20-060
	1 Jul 1820	Havana	Skidmore, H.	20-092
	30 Dec 1820	Havana	Skidmore, Hubbert	20-361
	11 Jul 1821	Havana	Skidmore, Hubbard	21-168
	6 Oct 1821	Havana	O'Bryan, John	21-308
	12 Jan 1822	Havana	O'Bryan, John	22-007
	5 Jul 1822	Havana	Skidmore, Hubbard	22-303
	12 Nov 1823	Port Maria, Jamaica	Knight, Wm.	23-583
	15 Dec 1824	Havana	Teshew, John	24-719
AMELIA	10 Oct 1820	Amsterdam	Nile, James	20-289
	14 Dec 1827	Bordeaux	Williams, Samuel	27-834
	20 Aug 1829	Liverpool	Post, Ezra D.	29-233
AMELIE (see C. Amelia)				
AMERICA	18 Jan 1820	Calcutta	Rossiter, Edward	20-010
	21 Aug 1820	Liverpool	Rosseter, Edward	20-195
	20 Sep 1821	Liverpool	Wallace, George H.	21-286
	9 May 1822	Liverpool	Wallace, George H.	22-181

SHIP	DATE OF ARRIVAL	PORT OF EMBARKATION	CAPTAIN	YEAR AND SHIP NUMBER
	30 Sep 1822	Liverpool	Wallace, George H.	22-492
	17 Oct 1825	Liverpool	Moran, Nicholas	25-594
	28 Jul 1826	Kingston, Jamaica	Luce, John	26-433
	22 Sep 1826	Havre	Moran, Nicholas	26-548
	16 May 1827	St. Salvador	Crabtree, Lemuel	27-257
	24 Jul 1827	Liverpool	Robinson, William J.	27-476
	17 Sep 1827	Cuba	Crabtree, Joseph	27-635
	25 Dec 1827	London	Placer, John S.	27-850
	7 Apr 1828	Bordeaux	Rickett, R.	28-112
	1 Aug 1828	Liverpool	Evans, Richard	28-416
	1 Aug 1829	St. Andrews, N.B.	Wooster, Joseph	29-188
AMERICAN	28 Sep 1822	Havana	Hillard, John	22-486
	4 Aug 1823	Rio Grande	McDominick, Francis	23-377
	29 Nov 1823	Jamaica	Dominick, Francis W.	23-614
	18 Oct 1824	Rio Grande	Becker, Nichs.	24-615
	27 Aug 1827	Havre	Moran, Nicholas	27-559
AMERICAN FREDERICK	26 Oct 1820	St. Croix	Anner, Charles	20-305
AMERICAN HERO	28 Jul 1824	Port au Plate	Coles, John	24-411
AMIABLE MATILDA	28 Sep 1822	Bordeaux	Meyers, David	22-487
AMITY (see Auritz)				
	11 Sep 1820	Liverpool	Maxwell, George	20-233
	11 May 1821	Liverpool	Maxwell, Geo	21-060
	13 Sep 1821	Liverpool	Maxwell, Geo.	21-268
	31 Jan 1822	Liverpool	Maxwell, George	22-018
	31 May 1822	Liverpool	Maxwell, George	22-241
	25 Sep 1822	Liverpool	Maxwell, Solomon	22-483
	21 Feb 1823	Liverpool	Maxwell, Solomon	23-043
	23 Sep 1823	Liverpool	Maxwell, Sol.	23-493
	1 Dec 1826	Greenock	Macfarlane, Dugald	26-696
AMOS PALMER	17 Aug 1826	Antwerp	Moore, Jacob, Jr.	26-493
	29 Sep 1827	Marseilles	Tilton, Z. A.	27-668
	9 Sep 1828	Vera Cruz	Payne, Jno. (Paine)	28-520
	9 Jan 1829	Tampico	Paine, J.	29-009
AMPHIBIOUS	4 Aug 1827	St. Martins	Major, Heny.	27-500
AMPHION	24 Aug 1821	Havana	Blinn, Henry	21-236
	5 Jul 1822	Monteviedo	Blin, Harvey	22-304
	14 Mar 1823	Monteviedo	Blin, Henry	23-080
	31 May 1824	Belfast	Blin, Harvey	24-256
AMULET	9 Jan 1829	Bristol	Winsor, Gersham	29-011
ANACREON	7 Sep 1827	Liverpool	Clark, William	27-599
ANDES	16 Sep 1820	Liverpool	Seden, Chas.	20-247
	22 Oct 1821	Lisbon	Fleming, Wm.	21-338
	5 May 1828	Havre	Patten, John	28-176
	2 Oct 1828	Liverpool	Kelleran, Edward	28-580
	19 Aug 1829	Liverpool	Tomkins, James	29-228
ANDREAS	20 Aug 1821	St. Domingo, Cape Haytien	Roming, Ands. Os.	21-235
ANDREW JACKSON	8 Mar 1820	Bermuda	Gillet, Nathan	20-052
	9 Oct 1820	Porto Rico	Gillett, Nathn.	20-283
	16 Jun 1821	St. Thomas	Gold, William	21-114
	30 Oct 1821	St. Thomas	Gold, William	21-351
	23 Mar 1822	St. Thomas	Gold, William	22-088
	9 Jul 1822	St. Bartholomew	Gold, William	22-310
	29 Aug 1823	Trinadad	Gold, William	23-427
ANDROMACHE	7 Feb 1820	Leith	Fornham, Elias	20-027
	29 May 1821	St. Thomas	Hillman, Francis	21-094
	13 Nov 1822	Pernambuca	Stillman, Thomas	22-566
	30 Jul 1823	Matanzas	Andrews, John G.	23-369
	18 May 1825	Matanzas	Patterson, B.	25-276
ANDROMACKE	31 Aug 1821	St. Thomas	Stillman, Francis	21-252
ANDW. JACKSON (see Andrew Jackson)				
ANGELICA	19 Sep 1821	St. Pierres Martinique	Harding, N.	21-284
	18 Aug 1823	Liverpool	Harsin, Gerard	23-404
ANGELINA	25 Nov 1822	Havana	Merritt, Nathl.	22-580

SHIP	DATE OF ARRIVAL	PORT OF EMBARKATION	CAPTAIN	YEAR AND SHIP NUMBER
	28 May 1827	Neuvitas	Harris, Thomas N.	27-303
	17 Sep 1827	Neuvitas	Harris, T. M.	27-634
ANGENORA	5 May 1826	Bermuda	Masters, Walter	26-235
	12 May 1826	Para	Foster, R. W.	26-251
	22 Dec 1826	Para	Foster, R. W.	26-731
	16 Jan 1827	Kingston, Jamaica	Webber, Nathl.	27-036
ANITA	5 May 1821	Matanzes	Gossenge, Robt.	21-051
ANN	29 Jan 1820	Liverpool	Crocker, Rowland R.	20-020
	3 Jul 1820	Liverpool	Crocker, Rowland R.	20-094
	2 Nov 1820	Liverpool	Crocker, Rowland R.	20-314
	27 Nov 1820	Portsmouth	Ashford, John	20-337
	11 Apr 1821	Liverpool	Crocker, Rowland R.	21-011
	23 Jul 1821	Liverpool	Crocker, Rowland R.	21-187
	22 Dec 1821	Liverpool	West, Edward D.	21-426
	11 Feb 1822	Glasgow	Ashford, John	22-041
	17 May 1822	Liverpool	Williams, Thomas F.	22-201
	24 Sep 1822	Liverpool	Williams, Thomas F.	22-481
	11 Dec 1822	Leghorn	Ashford, John	22-598
	11 Sep 1823	Rotterdam	Ashford, John	23-466
	21 May 1824	Buenos Ayres	Ashton, John	24-219
	26 May 1824	Porto Rico	Morse, George W.	24-239
	19 Aug 1824	Rotterdam	Snow, Henry	24-471
	10 Jan 1825	Greenock	Barney, Michael	25-012
	26 Feb 1825	Mayagues	Abeille, Ed.	25-080
	31 Mar 1825	Buenos Ayres	Hinman, Munson	25-146
	29 Apr 1825	St. Croix	Thomas, W. C.	25-219
	18 May 1825	Jamaica	Barry, Michael	25-277
	27 Jul 1825	New Port, England	O'Reed, Jos.	25-454
	4 Mar 1826	Gibraltar	Bovee, James	26-091
	16 Mar 1826	London	Heath, Caleb	26-115
	2 Oct 1826	Antigua	Trebbles, George	26-574
	3 Oct 1826	Acquin	Stickney, Albert A.	26-582
	11 Sep 1827	Antwerp	Snow, Henry	27-615
ANN CELIA	29 Aug 1826	St. Thomas	Carpenter, Augustus	26-508
ANN ELIZA	2 May 1828	Bordeaux	Reed, Joseph O.	28-169
ANN ELIZA JANE	6 Sep 1822	Mayguez	Abielle, E.	22-454
	1 May 1823	City of St. Domingo	Abielle, E.	23-162
	24 Sep 1823	City St. Domingo	Labousse, Ml.	23-494
	3 Apr 1824	City of St. Domingo	Labervisse, Ml.	24-130
	7 Feb 1825	City of St. Domingo	Hawkins, William	25-051
	19 Dec 1825	St. Domingo	Fowler, Thos.	25-721
	10 May 1827	St. Domingo	Fowler, Thos.	27-235
	30 Jul 1828	Port au Prince	Nichols, F.	28-410
ANN ELIZABETH	24 Jun 1823	Curacoa	Hamilton, Wm.	23-281
	28 Feb 1824	Curacoa	Hamilton, Wm.	24-064
	6 Oct 1824	Curacoa	Brunow, B. J.	24-576
	13 Jul 1826	Curacoa	Brunow, B. J.	26-402
ANN HOWARD	30 Dec 1828	St. Bartholomews (St. Barts)	Curtis, Charles	28-720
	4 Aug 1829	Eleuthera	Fisher, John	29-196
ANN MARIA (see Anna Maria, Ann Marria)				
	9 Mar 1820	Liverpool	Waite, Isaac	20-053
	3 Jul 1820	Liverpool	Waite, Isaac	20-099
	23 Oct 1820	Liverpool	Waite, Isaac	20-302
	12 Jul 1821	Liverpool	Watkinson, James	21-170
	31 Aug 1821	Havana	Gale, A. R.	21-253
	5 Nov 1821	Port au Prince	Summers, A.	21-357
	29 Nov 1821	Liverpool	Graham, Hugh	21-383
	5 Feb 1822	Campeachy	Summers, Alexr.	22-027
	28 Mar 1822	St. Ubes	Berands, B.	22-098
	26 Apr 1822	Liverpool	Graham, Hugh	22-152
	11 May 1822	Port au Prince	Summers, Alexr.	22-189
	27 Aug 1822	Liverpool	Gale, A. R.	22-422
	13 Mar 1823	Liverpool	Gale, A. R.	23-077
	24 Feb 1824	London	Tarr, David, Junr.	24-056
	5 May 1824	St. Johns, N.B.	Rowell, Reuben	24-194
	1 Jun 1824	St. John	Crowell, Ebenezer	24-256A
	8 Jun 1824	Dublin	Blydenburgh, Lucius B.	24-279

SHIP	DATE OF ARRIVAL	PORT OF EMBARKATION	CAPTAIN	YEAR AND SHIP NUMBER
	6 Jul 1824	St. John	Crowell, Ebenezer	24-352
	9 Jun 1824	Grenada	Shaw, John	24-363
	5 Aug 1824	St. Johns, N.B.	Crowell, Ebenezer, Jr.	24-434
	4 Oct 1824	St. Johns, N.B.	Crowell, Ebenezer, Jr.	24-563
	4 Nov 1834	St. Johns, N.B.	Crowell, Ebenezer	24-638
	13 Dec 1824	St. Johns, N.B.	Crowell, Ebenezer, Jr.	24-712
	14 Mar 1825	Jamaica	Delesdernier, John	25-115
	19 Apr 1825	St. John, N.B.	Crowell, R.	25-188
	18 May 1825	Guadaloupe	Shaw, John	25-275
	23 Jan 1826	St. Johns, N.B.	Crowell, Ebenezer	26-037
	1 Apr 1826	St. Johns, N.B.	Crowell, Ebenezer (Reuben)	26-138
	8 May 1826	St. Johns, N.B.	(Crowell, Ebenezer, Jr.	26-240
	12 Jun 1826	St. Johns, N.B.	Crowell, Ebenezer	26-327
	19 Jul 1826	Guayana	Tracy, Wm. H.	26-413
	7 Aug 1826	St. Johns, N.B.	Crowell, Ebenezer, Jr.	26-456
	7 Nov 1826	Ponce Porto Rico	Tracy, Wm. H.	26-648
	5 Mar 1827	Saint Johns, N.B.	Crowell, Ebenezer, Jr.	27-097
	17 Apr 1827	St. Johns, N.B.	Crowell, Ebenezer	27-179
	21 May 1827	St. Johns, N.B.	Crowell, Ebenezer, Jr.	27-273
	3 Jul 1827	St Johns, N.B.	Crowell, Ebenezer, Jr.	27-406
	4 Aug 1827	St. Johns, N.B.	Crowell, Ebenezer, Jr.	27-501
	7 Sep 1827	St. John, N.B.	Crowell, E., Jr.	27-601
	24 Oct 1827	Ponce, P.Rico	Gorsuch, Robert	27-722
	2 Nov 1827	St. Johns, N.B.	Crowell, Ebenezer	27-741
	18 Dec 1827	St. Johns, N.B.	Crowell, Ebenezer, Jr.	27-841
	28 Jan 1828	St. Johns, N.B.	Crowell, Ebenezer, Jr.	28-026
	11 Jun 1828	Ponce, P.R.	Gorsuch, R.	28-292
	10 Sep 1828	Ponce	Gorsuch, R.	28-524
	22 May 1827	Guayama	Gorsuch, Robt.	27-290
ANN MARRIA	6 Aug 1823	Liverpool	Jarr, David, Junr.	23-383
ANNA	23 May 1822	Curacoa	Domingus, Francis	22-221
	12 May 1823	Bermuda	Darrell, Samuel	23-181
ANNA CHRISTINA	24 Dec 1821	Gottenburgh	Pagander, Lars	21-430
ANNA DOREATHA	5 Mar 1822	Marseilles	Harder, J. C.	22-070
	15 Feb 1823	Curacoa	Hamilton, W.	23-029
	14 Jun 1824	Curacoa	Hamilton, Wm.	24-305
ANNA MARIA	22 Feb 1820	Hamburgh	Barends, Barend	20-042
ANNABAL	15 Nov 1824	Oporto	Bernardes, Joaquim Joze	24-661
ANNAH	17 Dec 1823	Turks Island	Stevens, William	23-642
	7 May 1825	Matanzas	O'Bryan, John	25-237
	21 Jun 1826	Port au Prince	Talbot, Josah R.	26-356
ANNAWAN	26 Apr 1824	Marseilles	Allen, William	24-165
	3 Apr 1826	Port au Platt	Wood, Elihu, Jr.	26-143
	3 Apr 1826	Port au Platt	Wood, Elihu, Jr.	26-143
ANNE	20 Jun 1828	Havana	Gonzoloe, Jos.	28-318
ANTELOPE	21 Aug 1820	St. Thomas	Abeille, E.	20-196
	22 Aug 1820	Bermuda	West, Joshua	20-201
	22 Dec 1820	Mayaquez	Abeille, Edward	20-355
	9 Sep 1822	Curacoa & St. Domingo	Berrian, Richd. P.	22-457
	18 Dec 1822	Havana	Berrian, Richd.	22-607
	17 Nov 1823	Havana	Blauvalt, Abraham	23-599
	23 Mar 1824	Havana	Blauvelt, Abraham	24-103
ANTHUSA	24 Aug 1825	Belfast	Fisher, John	25-540
ANTIOCH	21 Sep 1827	St. Johns, N.B.	Branscomb, Chas.	27-645
	8 Oct 1827	Liverpool	Rich, S., Jr.	27-690
	3 Dec 1827	St. Johns, N.B.	Branscom, Charles	27-788
	18 Aug 1829	Havre	Rich, Sylvanus, Jr.	29-223
ANTOINETTE	25 Jan 1828	Valparaiso	Pinniger, Isaac A.	28-023
AOLUS	1 Aug 1823	Havre	Geer, Joshua	23-375
APOLLO	10 Jul 1826	St. Croix	Simmons, Lemuel B.	26-392
	23 Oct 1826	Turks Island	Simmons, Lemuel B.	26-626
	11 Jun 1828	Tampico	Simmons, L. B.	28-294
ARAB	10 Nov 1826	Bremen	Eames, Samuel	26-656
ARCADIA	5 May 1828	Bristol	Forster, Edward	28-183
ARDELL	7 Jul 1827	Havana	Buell, Ellis H.	27-417

SHIP	DATE OF ARRIVAL	PORT OF EMBARKATION	CAPTAIN	YEAR AND SHIP NUMBER
	14 May 1828	Matanzas	Buell, Ellis H.	28-214
ARDELLE	27 Nov 1826	Matanzas	Buell, Ellis H.	26-683
	18 Jan 1828	Havana	Buill, Ellis H.	28-019
ARDENT	2 Nov 1826	Turks Island	Wood, M. S.	26-641
ARGO	5 Aug 1824	Turks Island	Eskildson, George	24-432
	11 Aug 1824	St. Croix	Hunt, Frederick, Jr.	24-444
ARGUS	3 Oct 1825	Trinadad in Cuba	Skidmore, Solomon	25-564
	26 Dec 1825	Trinadad	Howland, Reuben	25-729
	17 Aug 1826	Trinadad (in Cuba)	Howland, Reuben	26-494
	12 Dec 1826	Turks Island	Baxter, Ira	26-721
ARIA	16 Jan 1829	Turks Island	Pitcher, Abner	29-020
ARIADNE	25 Sep 1820	Gibraltar	Summers, Alexr.	20-258
	7 May 1821	Yarmouth & Plymouth	Sommers, Alexr.	21-052
	15 Apr 1822	Havanna	Swain, Shubael	22-125
	25 Jul 1822	Port au Prince	Stinman, John	22-347
	12 Dec 1822	Demerara	Aymar, Danl.	22-600
	4 Apr 1823	Demerara	Aymar, Daniel	23-103
ARIDNE (see Ariadne)				
ARIEL	20 Jul 1822	Dundee	Ritchie, Duncan	22-343
	22 Feb 1823	Greenock	Boag, Walter	23-045
	21 May 1827	Port Glasgow	Smith, Peter	27-277
	24 Sep 1827	Hamburg	Harman, J., Jr.	27-649
	1 Mar 1828	Matanzas	Coffin, Jas.	28-036
	30 Jun 1828	Matazas	Coffin, Jas.	28-338
	5 Dec 1828	Matanzas	Coffin, James	28-696
	9 Mar 1829	Matanzas	Coffin, James	29-077
ARINTHIA BELL	31 Mar 1824	Jacmel	Fearson, Benj. F.	24-119
ARIODNE	17 Nov 1821	Gibraltar	Copland, James	21-372
ARIOSTA (see Ariosto)				
	4 May 1821	Coast of Africa	Smith, James	21-049
	12 Apr 1822	Coast of Africa	Delfosse, C.	22-122
	4 Jun 1823	Princes Island, Africa	Harris, Emon	23-239
ARISTIDES	7 Mar 1825	Halifax	Greenlaw, A. B.	25-090
ARMADELLO	22 Jun 1827	Bristol	Watson, James	27-367
	15 Oct 1827	Liverpool	Watson, James	27-706
	13 Aug 1829	Antwerp	Robertson, John	29-213
ARRINGDON	8 May 1826	Mayaquez, Porto Rico	Abeille, Edwd.	26-239
ARRINGTON	14 Nov 1825	St. Thomas	Abeille, E.	25-657
	9 Oct 1826	Mayagues	Conklin, Joseph H.	26-588
ARSTHORP (see Aisthorp)				
ARTHENIAN	28 Apr 1827	Carthagena	Shipman, Charles R.	27-201
ARTIBONETT	21 Nov 1826	Port au Prince	Roney, J.	26-673
ARTIBONITE	3 Jul 1826	Port au Prince	Pierson, Gustave	26-374
	9 Sep 1826	Port au Prince	Dawson, Wm. A.	26-526
	31 Jan 1827	Port au Prince	Magnan, C.	27-048
	19 Apr 1827	Port au Prince	Magnan, C.	27-183
	2 Jul 1827	Port au Prince	Magnan, C.	27-401
ASAPH	8 Oct 1825	Turks Island	Parratt, Ebenezer	25-576
	23 Mar 1827	Spanish Maine	Shaw, Ebenezer A.	27-140
	25 Dec 1827	Gibraltar	Shaw, Ebenezer A.	27-851
ASIA	5 Jul 1823	Havre	Minugh, Jno.	23-308
	14 Jul 1829	Bristol	Emerson, Joseph	29-148
	29 Jul 1829	Londonderry	Ward, William	29-176
ASPARIA	1 Sep 1824	Jacmel	Brewer, Nicholas	24-500
ASPASIA	19 Jul 1823	Havana	Everitt, Richd.	23-344
	23 Nov 1825	Carthagena	Brewer, Nicholas	25-668
	5 Sep 1827	Liverpool	Bennett, Martin	27-591
	16 Jul 1828	Liverpool	Bennett, M.	28-378
ASSIDUOUS	30 Jul 1822	Bristol	Loveless, Bassett Jones	22-359
ASTREA	3 Jul 1822	St. Croix	Baker, Seth	22-301
	21 Oct 1823	Kingston, Jamaica	Loring, Davis	23-551
	19 Jul 1824	Porto Cabello	Dockray, James R.	24-383
	20 Aug 1825	St. Andrews	Dockray, James R.	25-529
	16 Nov 1825	Port au Prince	Dorkray, James R.	25-660
ATALANTA	13 Oct 1821	Port au Prince	Goldsmith, Danl.	21-318
	28 Aug 1822	Port au Prince	Wiederholt, H. Ls.	22-428
ATHENIAN	18 Oct 1826	Carthagina	Shipman, Charles R.	26-602
	8 Feb 1827	Carthegena	Shipman, C. R.	27-061

SHIP	DATE OF ARRIVAL	PORT OF EMBARKATION	CAPTAIN	YEAR AND SHIP NUMBER
	3 Sep 1827	Carthagena	Shipman, Charles R.	27-578
	1 Dec 1827	Carthagena	Shipman, Charles R.	27-778
	3 Mar 1828	Carthagenia	Sullivan, Thomas	28-041
	8 Jul 1828	Carthagena	Sullivan, Thomas	28-364
	14 Oct 1828	Carthagena	Sullivan, Thomas V.	28-610
	9 Jan 1829	Carthagena	Treby, Geo.	29-013
	17 Jul 1829	Carthagena	Sullivan, Thomas V.	29-154
ATLANTA	5 Jul 1821	Port au Prince	Goldsmith, Danl.	21-150
	20 May 1822	Leghorn	Davis, Nath	22-206
ATLANTIC	26 Aug 1820	Liverpool	Matlack, Wm., Junr.	20-209
	5 Jul 1821	Liverpool	Matlack, White	21-151
	15 Oct 1821	St. Andrews	Richardson, George, Jr.	21-321
	3 Dec 1821	Liverpool	Taylor, Robert L.	21-388
	29 Jun 1822	Dublin	Taylor, Robt. L.	22-300
	11 Oct 1822	Liverpool	Taylor, Robt. L.	22-519
	7 Aug 1823	St. Andrews	Cousins, John, Jr.	23-386
	13 Jul 1824	Liverpool	Taylor, Rob. L.	24-375A
	13 Aug 1824	Matanzas	Blake, Samuel	24-451
	26 Jul 1825	Gibraltar	Moore, S.	25-445
	19 Aug 1825	Belfast	Taylor, Robt. L.	25-517
	16 Dec 1825	Belfast	Fosdick, Peter G.	25-711
	19 Mar 1827	Dundee	Lawson, Alexr.	27-132
	2 Apr 1827	Belfast	..., ...	27-162
	28 May 1827	Liverpool	Johnson, John	27-307
	21 Jul 1827	Belfast	Fosdick, P. G.	27-468
	27 Aug 1827	Dundee	Lawson, Alexr.	27-563
	8 Dec 1827	Belfast	Fosdick, P. G.	27-818
	31 Jan 1828	St. Barts	Allen, John	28-034
	8 May 1828	Belfast	Reeves, M.	28-196
	17 May 1828	Dundee New Castle	Lawson, Alexr.	28-228
	6 Oct 1828	Belfast	Reeves, Matthew	28-587
	7 Nov 1828	Dundee	Lawson, Alexander	28-658
ATLAS	24 Jun 1828	Rio Janeiro	Townsend, J.	28-327
ATREVIDA	26 Jul 1820	Porto Cavello	Sanches, Cayetano	20-152
ATTICUS	25 Apr 1822	Liverpool	Wescoat, Joseph	22-148
AUGUSTA	8 Dec 1821	Canton	Giles, Daniel	21-407
	27 Aug 1829	Rio de Janeiro	Dunlevie, John C.	29-258
AUGUSTUS & JOHN	15 Jun 1822	Escuma	Britton, Wm.	22-272
	10 Apr 1823	Nassau, N. Providence	Hanscom, Moses	23-116
AURELIA	7 Jun 1826	Liverpool	McTaggart, William	26-338
AURILLA	8 Jul 1823	Curacoa	Hawland, Wing	23-319
	28 Oct 1824	Para	Glover, Russell E.	24-631
AURITZ	20 May 1823	Liverpool	Maxwell, Solomon	23-214
AURORA	21 Dec 1820	Aberdeen	Milne, Peter	20-353
	18 Sep 1821	Aberdeen	Courage, George	21-281
	4 Sep 1823	New Castle upon Tyne	Peacock, George	23-444
	15 Sep 1823	St. Vincents	King, Fredrick	23-474
	21 Jun 1824	Havre de Grace	Taubman, John	24-316
	11 Aug 1824	Jeremia	Dukehart, Thos.	24-445
	14 Oct 1824	Jeremie	Dukehart, Thos.	24-598
	11 Dec 1824	Havre de Grace	Taubman, John	24-707
	27 Apr 1825	Lpool	Tautman, John	25-212
	9 Aug 1825	Turks Island	Teer, Mark	25-490
	1 May 1826	Antwerp	Taubman, John	26-214
	5 Sep 1826	Liverpool	Taubman, John	26-518
	12 Mar 1827	Liverpool	Taulman, John	27-116
	22 May 1827	Antwerp	Harlow, Benjamin	27-287
	8 Jun 1827	Liverpool	Gooday, James	27-329
	9 Jul 1827	Liverpool	Taubman, John	27-425
	10 Nov 1827	Liverpool	Taubman, John	27-755
	19 Mar 1828	Antwerp	Harlow, Benjamin	28-075
	22 Sep 1828	Antwerp	Harlow, Benj.	28-555
AURORA ALCIDE	8 Jul 1826	Aquin	Roberts, J. J.	26-387
AUTUMN	1 Aug 1828	Antwerp	Turner, Eleazer S.	28-415
AYRSHIRE	12 May 1828	Liverpool	Smith, James	28-203
AZORA	22 Oct 1824	Jamaica	Babidge, Calvin	24-621

SHIP	DATE OF ARRIVAL	PORT OF EMBARKATION	CAPTAIN	YEAR AND SHIP NUMBER
	18 Apr 1825	Montego Bay	Babbage, C.	25-187
AZORES	2 Jun 1824	Barbadoes	Nichols, John	24-262
	20 Sep 1824	Jamaica	Dutch, Robert	24-541
BALAENA	9 Oct 1823	Liverpool	Wood, Daniel	23-535
	21 Aug 1824	Liverpool	Wood, Daniel	24-477B
	8 Jan 1825	Liverpool	Howland, George	25-008
	29 Apr 1825	Liverpool	Howland, Geo.	25-220
	24 Aug 1825	Liverpool	Howland, Geo.	25-539
BALANCE	12 Oct 1821	St. Petersburgh	Bennett, Martin	21-316
	28 Sep 1822	St. Petersburgh	Bennett, Martin	22-489
	19 Jun 1824	Liverpool	Bennet, Martin	24-314
BALIZE	29 Aug 1825	Gibraltar	Wildes, Wm.	25-557
BALTIC	20 Aug 1821	Guadaloupe	Bailey, Daniel	21-232
	1 Nov 1823	St. Petersburg	Bunker, Thomas G.	23-567
	19 Mar 1824	Liverpool	Bunker, Thomas G.	24-089
	17 Aug 1824	St. Petersburg	Bunker, Thomas G.	24-461
	24 Dec 1824	Liverpool	Bunker, Thomas G.	24-735
	11 Apr 1825	Liverpool	Bunker, T. G.	25-162
	5 Apr 1826	Liverpool	Bunker, Thomas G.	26-151
	21 Apr 1827	Liverpool	Gurrell, John	27-187
	24 Nov 1828	St. Thomas	Hoyt, James S.	28-680
	29 Jul 1829	St. Thomas	Hoyt, Shadrack	29-174
BALTIMORE	6 Dec 1823	Amsterdam	Hubbard, Alfred	23-626
BANIAN	19 Dec 1823	Campeachy	Barstow, Jas.	23-647
BAYARD	30 Oct 1820	Havre	Van Dyck, D.	20-308
	27 Jun 1821	Bordeaux	Van Dyke, D.	21-137
	11 Mar 1823	Liverpool	Van Dyke, Danl.	23-073
	18 Jul 1823	Havre	Van Dyke, D.	23-340
	13 Nov 1823	Havre	Van Dyke, D.	23-584
	19 Mar 1824	Havre	Naghel, F.	24-090
	9 Jul 1824	Havre	Robinson, Henry	24-365
	10 Nov 1824	Havre	Robinson, Henry	24-650
	7 Mar 1825	Havre	Robinson, Hy.	25-089
	8 Mar 1825	Havre	Skiddy, John R.	25-093
	11 Jul 1825	Havre	Robinson, Hy.	25-412
	9 Nov 1825	Havre	Robinson, Henry	25-644
	23 Mar 1826	Havre	Robinson, Henry	26-126
	14 Jul 1826	Havre	Robinson, H.	26-405
	18 Oct 1826	Havre	Robinson, H.	26-603
	15 Feb 1827	Havre	Everleigh, Nathl. W.	27-080
	16 May 1827	Havre	Robinson, Henry	27-253
	10 Sep 1827	Havre	Robinson, Henry	27-608
	17 Dec 1827	Havre	Robinson, Henry	27-839
	25 Apr 1828	Havre	Robinson, H.	28-151
	5 Sep 1828	Havre	Butman, B.	28-502
	15 Dec 1828	Havre	Butman, B.	28-709
	25 Aug 1829	Havre	Butman, Benjn.	29-247
BEAVER	2 Feb 1822	Canton	Jennings, Abraham G.	22-020
	18 Feb 1823	Canton	Peyster, F. H.	23-033
	16 Mar 1824	Canton	De Peyster, F. A.	24-082
	18 Aug 1827	St. Andrews	Spurling, Robert	27-529
	2 Apr 1828	Jacmel	Hadlock, E.	28-109
	27 Oct 1828	St. Andrews	Higgins, Josiah	28-634
	9 Jul 1829	Canton	Hepburn, David	29-142
	29 Aug 1829	Rochelle	Higgins, Josiah	29-263
BEE	2 Oct 1820	Havana	Gray, William	20-275
	18 Dec 1821	Havana	Wilson, Charles	21-422
	12 Apr 1823	Mancinella	Wilson, Charles	23-127
BELFAST	21 Mar 1820	Antwerp	Bunker, Elijah	20-077
	28 Sep 1820	Liverpool	Thomson, Wm.	20-269
BELLE	13 Jul 1821	Bourdeaux	Huntington, Edward	21-174
	3 Aug 1822	Marseilles	Wibray, James	22-369
	10 Sep 1824	Guadaloupe	Croizet, Jacques	24-528
	28 Dec 1824	Guadaloupe	Croizet, J.	24-739
BELLE ISLE	9 Aug 1827	Carnavon	Price, John	27-505
BELLE SAVAGE	15 Aug 1820	Liverpool	Russell, Henry	20-177
BELLE VICTOIRE	10 Oct 1828	Port au Prince	Harvey, William	28-604
	18 Oct 1827	Port au Prince	Trouillot, A.	27-712

SHIP	DATE OF ARRIVAL	PORT OF EMBARKATION	CAPTAIN	YEAR AND SHIP NUMBER
BELLESARIUS	26 May 1828	Ponce, P.R.	Crawford, George	28-245
BELLEVILLE	29 Aug 1827	St. Andrews	Bray, Nehemiah	27-566
	13 Oct 1827	St. Johns, N.B.	Bray, Nehemiah A.	27-704
	7 Dec 1827	St. Andrews, N.B.	Bray, Nehemiah A.	27-811
BELLONA	1 Oct 1822	Marseilles	Holdridge, John	22-494
	3 May 1826	Havana	Crocket, Richard	26-233
	2 Jul 1828	St. Thomas	Hoyt, Lewis C.	28-348
BELLVILLE	14 May 1827	St. Johns	Bray, N. A.	27-250
BELMONT	30 Aug 1828	Greenock	Paul, Edward	28-488
BELUGA	26 Apr 1825	Porto Rico	Mason, E.	25-210
BELVIDERA	28 Dec 1825	Pernambuca	Hewitt, Thos.	25-735
BELVIDERE	31 Jul 1822	St. Andrews	Hathorn, Alexander, Jr.	22-362
BELVILLE	5 Jul 1827	St. Andrews	Boaz, N. A.	27-410
BEN ALAM	24 Jul 1826	St. Anderas (S.M.)	Reeve, Charles	26-422
	23 Dec 1826	St. Andrews	Reeve, Charles	26-734
	2 Aug 1827	Boca del Tora	Roberts, James L.	27-496
BEN & JAMES	15 Aug 1820	Passamaquody	Barter, James	20-179
BEN LOMOND	3 Apr 1823	Greenock	Rattray, Henry	23-099
BENGAL	30 Jun 1823	Buenos Ayres	Conygham, D.	23-298
	14 Jul 1825	Malaga	Stewart, D. R.	25-419
BENJAMIN	10 Aug 1821	Cadiz	Prince, Chris.	21-220
	1 Jun 1822	Matanzes	Smith, H.	22-244
BENJAMIN FRANKLIN	10 Apr 1827	Matanzas	King, Josiah (Benjamin)	27-171
BENLOMOND	20 Sep 1822	Havre	Rattray, Henry	22-472
BETHLEHEM	18 Oct 1828	Halifax, N.S.	Harden, Gideon	28-619
BETSEY	17 Aug 1820	London	Donkin, William F.	20-185
	18 Apr 1822	London	Donkin, William F.	22-136
	10 Aug 1822	Havana	Wales, John	22-387
	31 Aug 1822	St. Andrews	Simington, Thomas	22-437
	7 Sep 1822	Matanzes	Cunningham, Thomas	22-456
	4 Apr 1823	Havana	Wales, John	23-104
	5 Jul 1823	Port au Prince	Eddy, Sylvester	23-309
	18 Aug 1823	St. Johns, Antigua	Tilton, John	23-405
	1 Apr 1824	Antigua	Frisbie, Stephen D.	24-124
	23 Jul 1824	Rum Key	Hallet, Benjam.	24-391
	2 May 1825	Matanzes	Buell, Ellis (Elias)	25-231
	28 Oct 1825	Matanzes	Buell, Elias H.	25-623
	13 Feb 1826	Matanzes	Buell, Ellis	26-060
	6 May 1826	Matanzes	Buell, Ellis	26-236
	20 Jun 1826	St. Croix	Ryan, Ezra	26-350
	31 Jul 1826	Matanzes	Buell, Ellis H.	26-438
	10 Nov 1826	Matanzes	Gates, Wm. B.	26-654
	15 Jun 1827	Matanzes	Rhodes, B.	27-349
	1 Apr 1828	Matanzes	Mayo, Oliver	28-101
	29 Aug 1829	Turks Island	Brown, Jeremiah	29-264
BETSEY ANN	15 Oct 1821	Gibara	Driggs, B.	21-322
	22 Dec 1821	Gibaira (Cuba)	Fisher, John	21-427
BETSY	4 Sep 1820	St. Johns, N.B.	Davis, William	20-223
BILLOW	1 Jun 1826	Rochell	Springer, Mark	26-295
BIRMINGHAM	16 Oct 1826	Liverpool	Cobb, N.	26-598
	15 Jun 1827	Liverpool	Cobb, Nathan	27-350
	12 Oct 1827	Liverpool	Harris, Isaac	27-702
	16 Jun 1828	Liverpool	Harris, Isaac	28-306
	11 Oct 1828	Liverpool	Harris, Isaac	28-605
	23 Feb 1829	Liverpool	Harris, Isaac	29-067
	12 Oct 1829	Liverpool	Harris, Isaac	29-294
BLACK WARRIOR	1 Nov 1827	Hamburg	Hill, Charles	27-740
BLAKELY	29 Sep 1826	Liverpool	Badger, Joseph	26-569
BLISS	28 Jul 1821	St. Thomas	Dungan, Abel S.	21-202
BLOOMING ROSE	2 Apr 1821	Buenos Aires	Sterling, John W.	21-001
	14 Jul 1821	Havana	Hyatt, Samuel	21-175
BLUE EY'D MAN	23 Aug 1823	Matanzes	Gardner, Daniel	23-414
BLUE EY'D MARY	26 Jun 1823	Matanzas	Gardner, Daniel	23-287

SHIP	DATE OF ARRIVAL	PORT OF EMBARKATION	CAPTAIN	YEAR AND SHIP NUMBER
	23 Oct 1823	Matanzas	Gardner, Daniel	23-557
BOGOTA	16 Dec 1826	Carthagena	Sheffield, James P.	26-726
	28 Mar 1827	Carthagena	Palmer, Nathaniel B.	27-156
	25 Oct 1827	Carthagena	Sheffield, James P.	27-726
	17 Jul 1828	Gibralter	Somers, John	28-382
BOLINA	9 May 1822	St. Thomas	Houston, James	22-182
	16 Mar 1826	Jamaica	Chase, Luke	26-119
BOLIVAR	19 May 1826	Dundee	McDonald, James	26-261
	15 Jun 1826	Liverpool	Wilson, J. L.	26-334
	14 Sep 1826	Bristol	Fenwick, John	26-530
	2 Oct 1826	Havre	Wilson, Josiah L.	26-576
	25 Nov 1826	New Castle	McDonald, James	26-678
	9 Dec 1826	St. Salvador	Hurd, N.	26-709
	21 May 1827	London	Wilson, Josiah L.	27-275
	10 Aug 1827	Havana	Turner, S.	27-509
	30 Nov 1827	Havre	Wilson, Josiah D.	27-775
BOLIVAR LIBERATOR	8 Dec 1826	Amsterdam	Hurd, Benjamin	26-707
	3 Jul 1828	Bahia	Hurd, N.	28-352
BONNAFFE	27 Jan 1827	Havre	Funk, James	27-043
BOOER (see Boon)				
BOON	26 Feb 1820	Havana	Humphries, Thomas	20-046
BORDEAUX	13 Oct 1821	San Salvador	Butman, B.	21-319
	12 Apr 1822	San Salvador	Butman, B.	22-123
	21 Sep 1822	St. Salvador	Butman, Benjm.	22-476
	25 Mar 1823	St. Salvador	Butman, B.	23-095
	9 Dec 1823	La Rochelle	Clark, Wm. S.	23-629
	5 Aug 1824	Gibraltar	Bourne, Lemuel	24-431
	26 Nov 1824	Gibraltar	Bourne, Lemuel	24-692
	17 Jun 1825	Alvarada	Bourne, Lemuel	25-351
BORNEO	26 Apr 1824	St. John, N.B.	Kilborn, Geo.	24-166
	27 Oct 1824	Halifax	Kilborn, Geo.	24-627
	4 Dec 1824	St. Johns, N.B.	Kilborn, Geo.	24-701
	23 Jun 1826	Halifax	Kilborn, George	26-360
	9 Jul 1827	St. Johns, N.B.	Kilborn, George	27-429
	14 Aug 1827	St. Johns, N.B.	Crowell, Zenas	27-516
	2 Oct 1827	St. Johns, N.B.	Crowell, Zenos	27-672
	15 Apr 1828	St. Johns	Crowell, Zenas	28-130
	28 Aug 1828	St. Johns, N.B.	Crowell, Zenas	28-468
BOSTON	26 Sep 1820	Fayal	Knows, Nathl.	20-265
	28 Aug 1821	Fayal	Knowles, Nathaniel	21-244
	7 Nov 1823	St. Croix	Cox, John	23-574
	25 Apr 1825	Marseilles	Finley, O. P.	25-205
BOSTON PACKET	5 Jul 1825	St. Iago de Cuba	Lord, Jno.	25-398
	7 Jul 1825	Honduras	Chapman, J.	25-405
BOWDITCH	27 Apr 1826	Liverpool	Curtis, Caleb	26-205
BOYER	9 May 1825	London	Meany, Cornelius	25-238
BRAGANZA	9 Oct 1820	Liverpool	Allen, James W.	20-284
	5 Dec 1821	Liverpool	Rogers, Richd.	21-400
	20 May 1823	Liverpool	Rogers, Richd.	23-215
	7 Oct 1823	Liverpool	Allen, Francis P.	23-527
	1 Dec 1824	Liverpool	Allen, Francis P.	24-698
	16 Apr 1825	Lpool	Allen, F. P.	25-180
	8 Aug 1825	Liverpool	Allen, Francis P.	25-482
	30 Nov 1827	Liverpool	Sullivin, Nicholas	27-774
BRAMIN	16 Feb 1824	Calcutta	Woodbury, Richd.	24-039
	30 Mar 1825	Calcutta, Madeira	Woodbery, Richard, 2nd	25-144
	20 May 1826	Calcutta	Gould, Warren	26-265
	13 Jun 1828	Calcutta	Leach, A. T.	28-299
BRANDT	21 May 1821	La Rochelle	Steinhauer, Geo. W.	21-074
	7 Feb 1822	Rochelle	Steinhauer, George W.	22-033
	20 Sep 1822	Rochelle	Steinhauer, Geo. W.	22-473
	14 Aug 1823	La Rochelle	Stanhauer, G. N.	23-378
	11 Oct 1824	Rochelle	Steinhaur, Geo. W.	24-584
	26 Jun 1826	Bremen	Meany, Cornelius	26-362
	8 Nov 1828	Rochelle	Steinhauer, Geo. W.	28-659
BRAZILLIAN	15 Mar 1824	Buenos Ayres	Hatch, Anselm	24-080

SHIP	DATE OF ARRIVAL	PORT OF EMBARKATION	CAPTAIN	YEAR AND SHIP NUMBER
	18 Oct 1824	Buenos Ayres	Hatch, Anselm	24-613
	21 May 1827	Pernambuco	Andros, Wm.	27-270
BRIGHTON	14 Oct 1824	London	Sebor, William S.	24-594
	11 Mar 1825	London	Sebor, William S.	25-100
	20 Aug 1825	London	Sebor, William S.	25-526
	21 Jan 1826	London	Sebor, William S.	26-035
	12 Jun 1826	London	Sebor, William S.	26-330
	16 Nov 1826	London	Sebor, William S.	26-666
	26 Mar 1827	London	Sebor, William S.	27-147
	24 Aug 1827	London	Sebon, William S.	27-554
	11 Dec 1827	London	Sebor, William S.	27-827
	14 Apr 1828	London	Sebor, William S.	28-124
	29 Aug 1828	London	Sebor, William S.	28-484
	9 Dec 1828	London	Sebor, William S.	28-698
	19 Aug 1829	London	Sebor, William S.	29-227
BRILLANTE	24 May 1822	Havana	de Begona, José	22-226
BRILLIANT	29 Nov 1826	Havana	Carpenter, Walter	26-691
	24 Sep 1827	London	Morris, Charles G.	27-654
	28 Jan 1828	Rio de Janeiro	Elwell, David, Jr.	28-024
	19 Mar 1828	Port Glasgow	Winsor, Hosea	28-073
BRITANIA	27 Mar 1820	Martinique	Cruther, John	20-086
BRITANNIA	20 Jun 1827	Liverpool	Marshall, Charles H.	27-364
	3 Nov 1827	Liverpool	Marshall, Charles H.	27-748
	14 Mar 1828	Liverpool	Marshall, Charles H.	28-057
	5 Nov 1828	Liverpool	Marshall, Chas. H.	28-649
	23 Mar 1829	Liverpool	Marshall, Chas. H.	29-110
	22 Jul 1829	Liverpool	Marshall, Charles H.	29-165
	29 Oct 1829	Liverpool	Marshall, Charles H.	29-334
BRITISH HIBERNIA	13 Mar 1820	Dublin	Walteling, J. G.	20-056
BRITISH KING	4 Apr 1827	Dundee	Young, Jno.	27-164
BRITTANIA	17 Jul 1828	Liverpool	Marshall, Chas. H.	28-381
BRITTANNIA	28 Feb 1827	Liverpool	Marshall, Chas. H.	27-095
BROK	29 Aug 1823	Greenock	McCullock, John (James)	23-428
BROKE	16 Jul 1829	Greenock	Hardie, Alexander	29-151
BROTHERS	7 Aug 1820	Matanzas	Gardner, Joseph	20-162
	28 Apr 1823	St. Martins	Small, Lovell	23-154
	17 Oct 1823	St Johns, N.B.	Baker, Ezra	23-549
	1 Sep 1824	St. Andrews	Brown, John	24-503
	27 Jun 1828	New Castle	Blackett, John	28-334
BROUGHTY CASTLE	18 Dec 1826	Dundee	Law, And.	26-727
BROWN	12 Oct 1824	Havana	Mayer, Philip S.	24-590
	11 Jan 1825	Havana	Meyer, Philip S.	25-017
	29 Apr 1825	Havana	Meyer, P. S.	25-223
	8 Aug 1825	Havana	Meyer, P. S.	25-484
	15 Nov 1825	Havana	Meyer, P. S.	25-659
	30 Jan 1826	Havana	Meyer, P. S.	26-044
	26 Apr 1826	Havana	Wiley, S. A.	26-204
	7 Jul 1826	Havana	Wiley, S. A.	26-385
	23 Dec 1826	Vera Cruz	Skinner, Joseph	26-735
	11 Jun 1827	Vera Cruz	Skinner, Joseph	27-341
	30 Nov 1827	Vera Cruz	Swain, Shubael	27-773
BRUCE	30 Apr 1827	St. Croix	Wa..., Benjamin	27-207
	5 Jul 1827	Xibara	Driggs, B.	27-411
	21 Nov 1827	Xibara	Cook, Nathan P.	27-764
	6 Aug 1828	Xibara	Cook, Nathan P.	28-422
BRUNSWICK	14 Feb 1829	Bordeaux	Baetjen, Herm	29-063
BRUTUS	13 Oct 1823	Antigua	Bradley, Wm.	23-541
	2 Dec 1823	London	Holdridge, Chas.	23-623
	21 May 1824	Porto Rico	Emery, John	24-220
	1 Feb 1825	Buenos Ayres	Wilson, Charles	25-045
	3 Feb 1827	Rio de Janeiro	Wolfe, W.	27-054
	5 Sep 1827	Dundee	Keibler, John	27-592
	6 May 1828	Dundee	Keiller, John	28-191
BUCK	24 Jul 1821	Cape Haytien	Hutchinson, J. B.	21-189
	2 Feb 1822	Port au Prince	Hutchinson, Joseph B.	22-021
	7 Aug 1822	Port au Prince	Hutchinson, Joseph B.	22-377

SHIP	DATE OF ARRIVAL	PORT OF EMBARKATION	CAPTAIN	YEAR AND SHIP NUMBER
	21 Nov 1822	Port au Prince	Hutchinson, Jos. B.	22-575
BUCKSPORT	5 Jun 1826	St. Croix	French, Josiah	26-302
	8 Dec 1827	Jacmel	Herriman, Hezekiah	27-814
	9 Jul 1828	St. Thomas	Herriman, H.	28-366
BUFFALO	7 Feb 1820	Bermuda	Ham, John	20-025
	27 Mar 1820	Bermuda	Ham, John	20-085
BUFFALOE	14 Sep 1820	Bermuda	Ham, John	20-242
BUNKER HILL	10 Dec 1825	Carthagena	Fanning, Wm. A.	25-702
	11 Mar 1826	Carthagena	Breed, Thomas S.	26-098
	9 Jan 1827	Carthagena	Smith, Nathan	27-016
	16 Apr 1827	Carthagena	Smith, Nathan J.	27-176
	25 Jun 1827	Port au Prince	Smith, N. S.	27-373
	20 Sep 1827	Carthagena	Woolsey, B.	27-644
	12 Aug 1828	Carthagena	Shipman, Charles R.	28-430
BURDETT	11 Oct 1827	Havana	Morgan, J.	27-698
	7 Dec 1827	Havana	Morgan, J.	27-805
	30 Apr 1828	Havanna	Campbell, D. H.	28-166
C. AMELIA	30 Jun 1828	Havre	...ae, J...	28-343
CABBASSO CONTA	23 Aug 1824	Havana	Staples, Isaac	24-482
CADET	5 Dec 1824	Carthagina	Palmer, Nathaniel B.	24-702
	11 Jan 1826	Cadiz	Woodbury, Freeborn	26-019
CADMUS	28 May 1821	Havre	Whitlock, S. B.	21-090
	26 Oct 1821	Liverpool	McLintlock, Sidney W.	21-347
	22 Mar 1822	Liverpool	Whitlack, Sidney B.	22-086
	27 Aug 1822	Havre	Whitlock, Sidney B.	22-423
	17 Apr 1823	Havre de Grace	Richards, Benjn.	23-137
	19 Aug 1823	Havre	Whitlock, S. B.	23-410
	12 Dec 1823	Havre	Whitlock, S. B.	23-637
	26 Apr 1824	Havre	Allyn, Francis	24-163
	7 Jun 1824	Kingston	Placer, John S.	24-273
	17 Aug 1824	Havre	Allyn, Francis	24-464
	14 Oct 1824	Jamaica	Place, Jno. S.	24-601
	20 Dec 1824	Havre	Allyn, Francis	24-727
	9 Apr 1825	Havre	Van Dyke, D.	25-157
	12 Apr 1825	Havana	Smith, B., Jr.	25-167
	27 Jul 1825	Havana	Russell, L.	25-453
	9 Aug 1825	Havre	Allyn, Francis	25-487
	6 Oct 1825	Havana	Brittingham, A. P.	25-570
	9 Dec 1825	Havre	Allyn, Francis	25-699
	5 Apr 1826	Havre	Allyn, Francis	26-150
	14 Apr 1826	Port au Prince	Barstow, Wm. C.	26-176
	16 Aug 1826	Havre	Allyn, Francis	26-488
	9 Dec 1826	Havre	Allyn, Francis	26-713
	23 Mar 1827	Havre	Allyn, Francis	27-142
	11 Jul 1827	Havre	Allyn, Francis	27-441
	3 Sep 1827	Porto Rico	White, John	27-577
	24 Oct 1827	Havre	Allyn, Francis	27-724
	18 Aug 1828	Porto Rico	White, Jno.	28-445
	4 Aug 1829	Malaga	Frisbie, Andrew	29-198
CAESAR	8 Oct 1827	Bremen	Deitjen, T.	27-688
	3 Apr 1828	Bremen	Roper, John	28-110
	8 Sep 1828	Bremen	Deetjeen, T.	28-514
	18 Mar 1829	Bremen	Deetjen, T.	29-103
	24 Aug 1829	Bremen	Deetjen, Tjark	29-245
CAIUS	11 Jun 1824	Sunderland	Ashton, Wm.	24-298
CALAIS PACKET	3 Sep 1827	Carthagena	Harvey, J.	27-580
	7 Jul 1828	St. Andrews	Hinckley, Andrew	28-360
	6 Nov 1828	Omoa	Tolmein, James	28-655
CALEDONIA	10 Sep 1828	Liverpool	Rogers, James	28-523
	20 Jan 1829	Liverpool	Rogers, Jas.	29-030
CALEDONIAN	16 Aug 1820	Hamburg	Taubman, John	20-183
CALLIOPE	20 Mar 1824	Havre	Thittier, David	24-091
	15 Aug 1827	Glasgow	Waters, Wm. C.	27-519
CALYPSO	1 Jun 1821	Pernambuco	Newman, S.	21-098
CAMBERWELL	7 Apr 1828	Hull	Rounding, R.	28-113
	2 Oct 1828	Hull	Rounding, Robert	28-579
CAMBRIA	2 Jul 1821	Bristol, England	Jenkins, William	21-146

SHIP	DATE OF ARRIVAL	PORT OF EMBARKATION	CAPTAIN	YEAR AND SHIP NUMBER
	16 Aug 1827	London	Robinson, Geo.	27-523
	26 Dec 1827	London	Warnack, Jacob A.	27-852
	7 May 1828	London	Griswald, A. H.	28-195
	8 Oct 1828	London	Griswold, A. H.	28-595
	11 Feb 1829	London	Griswold, A. H.	29-057
	3 Jul 1829	London	Griswold, A. H.	29-122
	19 Oct 1829	London	Champlin, Henry L.	29-312
CAMBRIDGE	19 Sep 1828	Genoa	Davis, Tobias	28-546
CAMDEN	14 May 1825	Bermuda	Hiscock, Prince	25-252
	24 Aug 1827	St. Thomas	Hiscock, Prince	27-553
CAMILLE	31 Jul 1826	Port au Prince	Moreaux, Alexander	26-437
	1 Nov 1826	Port au Prince	Movaux, Alexr.	26-638
	1 Feb 1827	Port au Prince	Moreau, Alexr.	27-053
CAMILLUS	9 Oct 1820	Greenock	Boyer, Joseph	20-285
	6 Apr 1821	Greenock	Boyer, Joseph	21-005
	10 Sep 1821	Greenock	Peck, Norman	21-263
	16 Apr 1822	Greenock	Beck, Norman	22-131
	12 Sep 1822	Greenock	Peck, Norman	22-461
	28 Apr 1823	Greenock	Peck, Norman	23-155
	17 Sep 1823	Greenock	Peck, Norman	23-481
	28 Apr 1824	Greenock	Peck, Thomas	24-179
	18 Nov 1824	Greenock	Peck, Norman	24-675
	7 Mar 1825	Greenock	Peck, Norman	25-092
	27 Jul 1825	Greenock	Peck, N.	25-456
	10 Dec 1825	Greenock	Peck, Norman	25-706
	27 Jun 1826	Greenock	Peck, Norman	26-364
	9 May 1827	Greenock	Peck, Norman	27-227
	12 Sep 1827	Greenock	Peck, Norman	27-621
	3 May 1828	Greenock	Peck, Norman	28-175
	8 Sep 1828	Greenock	West, John	28-517
	29 Jan 1829	Greenock	Neven, John	29-040
	27 Oct 1829	Greenock	Peck, Norman	29-332
CAMMILLUS (see Camillus)				
CANADA	20 Jun 1823	Liverpool	Macy, Seth G.	23-273
	1 Nov 1823	Liverpool	Macey, Seth G.	23-568A
	14 Feb 1824	Liverpool	Macy, Seth G.	24-035
	2 Jun 1824	Liverpool	Rogers, Jas.	24-259
	4 Oct 1824	Liverpool	Rogers, James	24-569
	6 Jun 1825	Liverpool	Rogers, James	25-320
	13 Oct 1825	Liverpool	Rogers, Jas.	25-587
	13 Feb 1826	Liverpool	Rogers, Jas.	26-062
	8 Jun 1826	Liverpool	Rogers, James	26-313
	27 Sep 1826	Liverpool	Rogers, Jas.	26-563
	5 Feb 1827	Liverpool	Rodgers, James	27-058
	5 Jun 1827	Liverpool	Rogers, James	27-320
	1 Oct 1827	Liverpool	Rogers, Jas.	27-671
	12 May 1828	Liverpool	Rogers, Jas.	28-205
	19 Sep 1828	Liverpool	Graham, H.	28-545
	30 Jan 1829	Liverpool	Graham, Hugh	29-041
CANARIS	30 Jun 1827	Havre	Handley, Simon	27-398
CANNING	18 Jul 1828	Gibraltar	Warren, B.	28-386
CANNON	12 Sep 1820	St. Thomas	Turner, Samuel	20-238
	19 Dec 1820	St. Thomas	Turner, Samuel	20-350
	25 Apr 1821	St. Thomas	Betts, Thomas	21-032
	18 Aug 1821	St. Thomas	Ryan, Daniel	21-230
	10 Dec 1821	St. Thomas	Ryan, Danl.	21-413
	15 Jul 1822	St. Thomas	Ryan, Danl.	22-322
	21 Jul 1824	St. Croix	Rycroft, John	24-386
	6 Nov 1824	Curacoa	Rycroft, John	24-641
	29 Dec 1825	St. Thomas	Johnson, S.	25-737
CANTON	25 Aug 1823	Cadiz	McCauley, Chas. Stewart	23-422
	6 May 1824	Havre	Butman, B.	24-197
	17 Aug 1824	Havre	Butman, B.	24-465
	13 Oct 1824	Copiapo	Page, Jery. L.	24-592
	13 Dec 1824	Carthagina	Butman, B.	24-715
	7 Feb 1826	Carthagena	Butman, B.	26-055
CANTON PACKET	13 Oct 1829	St. Thomas	Berry, Joseph	29-300

SHIP	DATE OF ARRIVAL	PORT OF EMBARKATION	CAPTAIN	YEAR AND SHIP NUMBER
CANTOR	5 Nov 1825	Gibraltar	Lewis, Robert	25-635
CARAVAN	14 Apr 1823	Cadiz	Dill, James H.	23-129
	14 Apr 1824	Tabasco	Sweetser, Jeremiah	24-141
	1 May 1824	Havana	Whitehead, John	24-190
	8 Sep 1828	Havre	Bening, Abrm. (Thing)	28-518
CARIB	11 Apr 1825	Honduras	Nickerson, D.	25-165
CARLO	16 Oct 1825	Coquimbo	Hall, Wm. G.	25-585
	28 Jun 1826	St. Croix	Clear, Michael	26-366
	10 Nov 1826	St. Croix	Clear, Michael	26-655
	28 Mar 1827	St. Croix	Clear, Michael	27-155
	26 May 1827	St. Croix	Clear, Michael	27-300
	30 Jul 1827	St. Croix	Clear, Michael	27-486
	6 Oct 1827	St. Croix	Clear, Michael	27-683
	19 Apr 1828	St. Croix	Clear, Michael	28-135
	19 Jun 1828	St. Croix	Clear, M.	28-315
	28 Nov 1828	St. Croix	Clear, Michael	28-681
	1 Jul 1829	St. Croix	Clear, Michael	29-117
	27 Aug 1829	St. Croix	Clear, Michael	29-257
CARLOW	20 Apr 1826	St. Croix	Hall, Wm. G.	26-196
CAROLINA ANN	5 Jul 1822	Valparaiso	Coffin, George B.	22-305
	21 May 1823	Belfast	Baush, Jacob	23-220
	12 Sep 1823	Belfast	Baush, Jacob	23-467
	14 Feb 1824	Belfast	Baush, Jacob	24-036
	11 Jun 1824	Belfast	Baush, Jacob	24-290
	15 Oct 1824	Belfast	Baush, Jacob	24-604
	14 Feb 1825	Belfast	Baush, Jacob	25-062
	20 Jun 1825	Belfast	Baush, Jacob	25-359
	24 Oct 1825	Belfast	Baush, Jacob	25-609
	7 Apr 1826	Belfast	Baush, Jacob	26-161
	7 Aug 1826	Belfast	Baush, Jacob	26-464
	11 Dec 1826	Belfast	Baush, Jacob	26-720
	14 May 1827	Belfast	Baush, Jacob	27-247
CAROLINA AUGUSTA	16 May 1828	Havre	Merrill, Nath. W.	28-223
	2 Dec 1828	Liverpool	Merrill, Nathaniel W.	28-691
CAROLINE	17 Apr 1821	Havana	Hubbs, Alexr.	21-023
	9 May 1822	Havana	Hubbs, Alexr.	22-183
	21 Jun 1823	Havana	Kidlin, Walter	23-275
	20 Aug 1825	Leghorn	Farmer, Thos.	25-527
	10 Mar 1828	Bristol	Smith, Oliver	28-051
	25 Jul 1828	Saint Andrew	Card, G.	28-400
CAROLINE AND NANCY	30 Aug 1821	St. Andrews	Foster, Nathaniel	21-251
CARPENTER	3 Sep 1821	Teneriffe	Barnes, William	21-255
	12 Aug 1828	St. Thomas	Carroll, Lambard	28-433
CARRIER	31 Aug 1820	Bermuda	Bates, Thos.	20-217
CARVAN (see Caravan)				
CASANDA	5 Sep 1827	Liverpool	Smith, Samuel	27-593
CASEO	26 Apr 1828	Havanna	Choate, D. L.	28-154
CASLO	8 Sep 1828	St. Croix	Clear, Michael	28-513
CASPIAN	12 Jul 1821	London	Standley, Stephen	21-171
CASSACK	25 Jul 1820	London	McBeth, S.	20-149
CATHARINE	23 Jun 1821	St. Croix	Barnard, Geo. F.	21-130
	3 Sep 1821	St. Croix	Barnard, Geo. F.	21-256
	12 Nov 1821	St. Croix	Clark, N. B.	21-365
	22 Jan 1822	St. Thomas	Clark, Alexr. B.	22-013
	15 May 1822	St. Croix	Black, Alex B.	22-197
	19 Jul 1822	St. Croix	Clark, Alexr. B.	22-340
	22 Jul 1825	Londonderry	Patten, John	25-437
	7 Feb 1826	Liverpool	Campbell, Thomas	26-056
	10 Sep 1827	Havre	Lyon, H.	27-607
CATHARINE & JANE	18 Feb 1823	Tampico	Storey, Wm. W.	23-034
	15 Nov 1823	Trinadad in Cuba	Cruse, Niells Chrish.	23-592
CATHARINE ROGERS	11 Oct 1821	Surinam	Barnard, Benjm.	21-314
	6 Oct 1823	Gibraltar	Andros, Wm.	23-520
CATHERINE	3 Jul 1820	St. Croix	Welden, Asa W.	20-095

SHIP	DATE OF ARRIVAL	PORT OF EMBARKATION	CAPTAIN	YEAR AND SHIP NUMBER
	27 Sep 1820	Guadaloupe	Hepburn, David	20-267
	28 Dec 1820	St. John N.B.	Gould, Stephen	20-358
	4 Sep 1824	Alvarado	Austin, Henry	24-511
	19 Aug 1825	St. Johns, N.B.	Bert, Stephen	25-516
CATHERINE & JANE	4 Nov 1820	Havanna	Morrel, Abraham	20-317
CATO	4 Apr 1823	Buenos Ayres	Rawson, E. B.	23-105
	9 Aug 1823	Vera Cruz	Boyer, Joseph	23-388
	2 Jan 1824	Alvarada	Boyer, Joseph	24-001
	8 Aug 1825	Dundee	Ritchie, David, Junior	25-483
	12 May 1828	Dundee	Ritchie, David, Jr.	28-206
CAURIER (see Courier)				
CAVALIER	25 Jul 1828	Havre	Orne, Richard E.	28-399
CECIRO (see Cicero)				
CELIA	15 Oct 1825	Barbadoes	Fuller, Ebenezer	25-592
CENTINEL	11 Oct 1820	Havana	Wilder, Eri	20-292
CENTURION	2 Jan 1826	Demarara	Brighton, Jacob	26-001
	20 Aug 1828	Havana	Meyer, P. S.	28-452
	20 Oct 1828	Havana	Smith, B., Jr.	28-623
	22 Dec 1828	Havana	Smith, Benjn., Junr.	28-715
CERES	20 Nov 1824	St. Petersburg	Prescott, Royal	24-677
	16 Jan 1826	Cronstadt	Dyer, Benjamin	26-028
	7 Aug 1826	Maracaibo	Miller, David	26-458
	23 Sep 1826	Liverpool	Dyer, Benjamin	26-553
	13 Dec 1827	St. Ubes	Crane, John R.	27-833
CEYLON	14 Sep 1824	Hamburg	Defrees, Henry J.	24-535
CHALCEDONY	24 Oct 1829	Marseilles	King, Orice	29-320
CHAMPION	1 Sep 1820	St. Johns, N.B.	Morse, Elijah	20-220
	7 Jun 1822	St. Andrews	Anderson, Samuel	22-258
	26 Jul 1827	St. Johns	Norton, Enoch	27-478
	3 Nov 1827	St. Andrews	Tuttle, E. B.	27-747
	27 Dec 1827	St. Andrews	Tuttle, E. B.	27-860
	19 Apr 1828	St. Andrews	Tuttle, E. R.	28-137
	2 May 1828	Turks Island	Chase, Judah	28-172
	2 Feb 1829	Halifax	Tuttle, E. B.	29-043
CHAPMAN	21 Apr 1826	Calsorona	Nordenskjold, C. R.	26-199
CHARITY	18 Nov 1823	St. Croix	Goodrich, Jasper	23-600
CHARLEMAGNE	19 Sep 1828	Havre	Robinson, H.	28-544
	16 Jan 1829	Havre	Robinson, Henry	29-022
	20 Aug 1829	Havre	Robinson, Henry	29-232
CHARLES	15 Oct 1822	Rio Dela Hatch	Young, John	22-526
	19 Dec 1822	Matanzas	Coffin, James	22-608
	13 May 1823	Port au Prince	Coffin, J. S.	23-193
	11 Jul 1823	Matanzas	Coffin, James	23-327
	5 Mar 1824	Havana	Anthony, D. B.	24-067
	21 Jul 1825	Trieste	Joy, R. M.	25-435
	18 Aug 1826	Matanzas	Coffin, James	26-497
CHARLES AMBURGER	22 Apr 1822	Cadiz	Haskell, William	22-137
	16 Aug 1826	Gibraltar	Savage, Chas. T.	26-491
	11 Oct 1827	Fayal	Savage, Charles T.	27-693
CHARLES CARROLL	16 Jan 1829	Havre de Grace	Clark, James	29-017
CHARLES HAMILTON	14 Jun 1823	Hull	Kendall, John	23-262
CHARLES HAMILTON ABERDEEN	11 Jun 1824	Hull	Dickinson, Wm.	24-296
	2 Nov 1824	Hull	Dickinson, Wm.	24-636
	23 May 1825	Hull	Dickinson, Wm.	25-288
	24 Oct 1825	Hull	Dickinson, Wm.	25-613
CHARLES HAYS	28 Mar 1825	Martinique	Fisher, John W.	25-142
CHARLES MILLER	31 May 1825	Bordeaux	Davis, Francis	25-311
CHARLES SIDNEY	9 Oct 1829	Maracaibo	Revans, Thomas	29-290
CHARLESTON	10 May 1825	Curacoa	Hitchcock, L. M.	25-247
	1 Aug 1825	Curacoa	Hitchcock, L. M.	25-467

SHIP	DATE OF ARRIVAL	PORT OF EMBARKATION	CAPTAIN	YEAR AND SHIP NUMBER
	23 Oct 1825	Curacoa	Hitchcock, L. M.	25-606
	1 Jun 1826	Curacoa	Hitchcock, L. M.	26-296
CHARLESTON ALLEN	15 Nov 1826	Rio Janeiro	Allen, James, Jr.	26-663
CHARLESTON PACKET	4 May 1821	Havana	Vail, Silas B.	21-050
	25 Jul 1821	Havana	Gill, James	21-196
	3 Jul 1823	Angostura	Mansfield, Rueben S.	23-307
	21 Oct 1823	Angustura	Mansfield, Reuben S.	23-552
	26 May 1824	Angustura	Mansfield, R.	24-235
CHARLOTT CORDAY (see Charlotte Corday)				
CHARLOTTE	19 Feb 1822	London	Appleton, Willm.	22-054
	26 Aug 1825	Bristol	Whitnay, Mark	25-550
CHARLOTTE CORDAY	24 Jan 1820	St. Johns, N.B.	Russell, J. G.	20-014
	7 Mar 1820	St. Johns, N.B.	Russell, J. G.	20-051
	15 Jul 1820	St. Johns, N.B.	Russel, J. G.	20-128
	15 Aug 1820	St. Johns N. B.	Russel, Joseph G.	20-178
	11 Sep 1820	St. Johns, N.B.	Russell, J. G.	20-234
	12 Apr 1821	Teneriffe	Russell, Jos. G.	21-013
	16 Aug 1821	Teneriffe	Kapell, J. G.	21-227
	8 Nov 1823	Aux Cayes	Russel, J. G.	23-577
CHART CORDAY (see Charlotte Corday)				
CHASE	11 Sep 1820	St. Croix	Baxter, James	20-235
	29 Dec 1820	St. Thomas	Baxter, James, Junr.	20-359
	13 Apr 1821	St. Croix	Baxter, James, Junr.	21-016
	29 June 1821	St. Croix	Baxter, James, Jr.	21-144
	4 Sep 1821	St. Croix	Baxter, James	21-258
	18 Dec 1821	St. Croix	Baxter, James, Jr.	21-423
	6 Jun 1822	St. Croix	Baxter, James, Jr.	22-255
	24 Aug 1822	St. Croix	Baxter, James, Jr.	22-417
	30 Dec 1822	St. Croix & St. Thomas	Baxter, James, Jr.	22-614
	9 May 1823	St. Croix	Baxter, James, Jr.	23-176
	24 Jul 1823	St. Croix	Baxter, James	23-349
	19 Sep 1823	Havana	Pinckney, Richd. S.	23-484
	2 Oct 1823	St. Croix	Baxter, James	23-517
	27 Feb 1824	St. Croix	Baxter, James	24-059
	29 Apr 1824	St. Croix	Baxter, James, Jr.	24-184
	26 Jul 1824	St. Croix	Baxter, James	24-394
	5 Oct 1824	St. Croix	Baxter, James, Jr.	24-575
	17 Jan 1825	St. Croix	Baxter, James, Jr.	25-023
	29 Apr 1825	St. Croix	Baxter, J.	25-217
	5 Jul 1825	St. Croix	Baxter, J.	25-395
	11 Mar 1826	St. Croix	Baxter, James	26-100
	12 May 1826	St. Croix	Baxter, James, Jr.	26-246
	20 Jul 1826	St. Croix	Baxter, James, Jr.	26-416
	28 Sep 1826	Hamburg	Robbins, Nathan B.	26-565
	2 Oct 1826	St. Croix	Baxter, James	26-575
	22 May 1827	St. Croix	Baxter, James, Jr.	27-284
	9 Aug 1827	St. Croix	Baxter, James	27-507
CHASSEUR	17 Aug 1824	Barbadoes	Paull, Tisdale	24-463
CHATHAM	8 Aug 1822	Rochelle	Harding, Robert	22-380
CHAUNCY	10 Jan 1820	Aux Cayes	Grice, Geo. W.	20-005
	14 Mar 1820	Canton	MacKay, Donald	20-059
CHELSEA	16 May 1828	London	Barnes, Aeon	28-221
CHERUB	1 Nov 1821	St. Augustine	Mister, Swen	21-354
	20 Sep 1824	Curacoa	Smith, Thos.	24-542
CHIEF	14 Nov 1823	Liverpool	Humphrys, Jabez	23-590
CHILDE HAROLD	21 Feb 1825	Jacqumel	Loring, Davis	25-076
CHILE (see Chili)				
CHILI	7 Jul 1827	Liverpool	Jenkins, Reuben	27-420
	9 Jan 1829	Rio de Janeiro	Drew, James	29-012
CHINA	5 Apr 1822	Canton	Dowdall, George R.	22-107
	17 Feb 1824	Santanller	Whitlebey, Ambrose	24-048
CHINCHILLE	14 Apr 1825	Massina	Turner, Chs.	25-175
CICERO	16 May 1823	Eleuthera	Johnson, Samuel	23-202
	21 Aug 1823	Eleuthera	Johnson, Saml.	23-415

SHIP	DATE OF ARRIVAL	PORT OF EMBARKATION	CAPTAIN	YEAR AND SHIP NUMBER
	24 Oct 1823	Eleuthera	Brown, John	23-559
	9 Nov 1825	St. Petersburg	Morris, Frederick W.	25-646
	19 Nov 1825	Maracaybo	Stormes, Peter	25-663
	26 Sep 1826	St. Petersburg	Swift, Asa A.	26-556
	13 Jan 1827	Marracabo	Nye, E.	27-028
	18 Aug 1829	Havana	Rowland, Lynde	29-221
CINCINNATUS	31 Oct 1820	London to New York	Griswold, A. H.	20-311
	24 May 1821	London	Champlin, Henry L.	21-085
	21 Nov 1821	London	Champlin, Henry L.	21-378
	29 Apr 1822	London	Champlin, Henry L.	22-158
	2 Oct 1822	London	Champlin, Henry L.	22-499
	17 May 1823	London	Sebor, William S.	23-205
	16 Apr 1824	London	Sebor, William S.	24-150
	5 Oct 1824	London	Bliss, Fredk.	24-571
	21 Feb 1825	London	Bliss, Theodore	25-078
	9 Jul 1825	London	Bliss, Theo	25-408
	5 Dec 1825	London	Bliss, Theodore	25-689
	22 May 1826	London	Bliss, Theodore	26-266
	19 Oct 1826	Liverpool	Bliss, Theodore	26-606
	3 Sep 1827	St. Petersburg	Seymour, Saml. D.	27-573
	22 Sep 1828	Cronstadt	Minturn, R. G., Jr.	28-558
CIRCASSIAN	26 Jun 1823	Matanzas	Robinson, W. J.	23-288
	13 Jun 1825	Havana	Davis, Henry	25-338
	3 Jun 1826	Matanzas	Struthers, Neil	26-298
	27 Dec 1827	Trieste	Struthers, Neil	27-859
CITIZEN	7 Jul 1823	Canton	Hughes, Wm.	23-315
	1 Nov 1828	Halifax	Crowell, Nehemiah	28-645
	14 Jul 1829	Halifax, N.S.	Crowell, Nehemiah	29-149
	25 Aug 1829	Halifax, N.S.	Crowell, Nehemiah	29-246
CLARENCE	8 Dec 1821	Bristol, R.I.	Walker, S. S.	21-408
CLARICE	15 Jun 1825	St. Croix	Oxnard, Stephen D.	25-346
	1 Feb 1827	Gibralter	Hatch, H.	27-050
	11 Apr 1827	Havana	Blanchard, Reuben	27-173
	27 Aug 1827	Gibraltar	Hatch, Anselm	27-560
	19 Sep 1828	Yoica	Hatch, Anselm	28-543
CLARISSA	14 Jul 1821	Matanzas	Coffin, Chas.	21-176
	23 May 1822	Matanzas	Coffin, Jas.	22-222
	28 Apr 1824	Matanzas	Farrier, William	24-177
	3 Sep 1824	Matanzas	Farrier, William	24-510
CLAUDIO	21 Aug 1827	Havana	Meyer, P. S.	27-540
	16 Oct 1827	Havana	Smith, B., Jr.	27-710
	29 Dec 1827	Havana	Smith, Benjn., Jr.	27-861
	22 Mar 1828	Havana	Smith, Benjn., Jr.	28-078
CLEANTHES	9 May 1825	Rio de la Hatch	Fornier, Willim, Joseph	25-239
CLEMATIS	8 May 1827	Liverpool	Low, David	27-222
CLEO	22 May 1822	Curacoa	Langdon, John W., Jr.	22-212
CLEVELAND	1 May 1821	Bristol, Eng.	Mackey, James	21-041
CLIMAX	6 Aug 1822	St. Andrews	Prince, William	22-374
	24 Sep 1827	Porto Rico	Clark, C.	27-651
	19 Apr 1828	Porto Rico	Clark, C.	28-134
	24 Oct 1829	Brasoris St. Iago	Parker, Peter	29-322
CLIO	1 Dec 1823	Madeira	Baxter, Alexander	23-618
	7 Aug 1826	Point Petre	Gardner, William C.	26-457
	6 Nov 1826	Bermuda	Browne, Moses	26-645
	8 Apr 1828	Matanzas	Thompson, W.	28-117
CLOTHIER	22 Nov 1827	St. Johns, N.B.	Chandler, Joseph, Junr.	27-766
COBBOSSE CONTE	18 Apr 1823	Havana	Jackson, Joseph	23-138
COLLASAS	21 Ocg 1826	Honduras	Morgan, Benja.	26-616
COLLECTOR	6 Oct 1820	Bordeaux	Wardwell, Allen, Junr.	20-280
	7 Aug 1826	Antigua	Pike, Robert	26-463
COLONEL GEORGE ARMSTEAD	13 May 1823	St. Iago de Cuba	Coleman, Robert	23-194
COLONEL GEORGE ARNESTRAD (see Colonel George Armstead)				
COLOSSO CONTI	17 Apr 1822	Havana	Jackson, Joseph	22-134
COLOSSUS	30 May 1825	Liverpool	Marshall, Robert	25-307
	1 Nov 1826	Liverpool	Marshall, Robert	26-639

SHIP	DATE OF ARRIVAL	PORT OF EMBARKATION	CAPTAIN	YEAR AND SHIP NUMBER
	21 Apr 1827	Havana	Morgan, Benja.	27-189
	5 Jun 1827	Glasgow	Maxwell, Solomon	27-321
	2 Oct 1827	Liverpool	Maxwell, Sol.	27-673
	27 Mar 1828	Liverpool	Jammison, John	28-090
	26 Aug 1828	Liverpool	Mayell, John Charles	28-470
	22 Aug 1829	Liverpool	Mayell, John Charles	29-240
COLUMBIA	30 Jul 1821	Port au Platt	Whitman, Wm.	21-204
	11 Apr 1822	Liverpool	Rogers, James	22-120
	22 May 1822	Malaga in Spain	Loring, Braddock	22-214
	9 Aug 1822	Liverpool	Rogers, James	22-385
	24 Dec 1822	Liverpool	Rogers, James	22-612
	27 Dec 1822	St. Thomas	Bradford, Ebenr.	22-613
	24 Mar 1823	Matanzas	Bradford, Ebenr.	23-090
	7 Apr 1823	Liverpool	Rogers, James	23-110
	11 Aug 1823	Liverpool	Rogers, James	23-391
	1 Dec 1823	Liverpool	Rogers, James	23-619
	10 Mar 1824	Liverpool	Rogers, Jas.	24-073
	10 Mar 1824	Liverpool	Rogers, Jas.	24-073
	14 Apr 1824	Gibraltar	Kurtz, Daniel L.	24-142
	4 Jun 1824	Matanzes	Perkins, Thomas	24-268
	7 Jul 1824	Liverpool	Macy, Seth G.	24-358
	5 Oct 1824	Bremen	Kurtz, David L.	24-574
	14 Oct 1824	Point Petre	Perkins, Thos. G.	24-597
	25 Nov 1824	Jamaica	Bradford, Eben.	24-691
	1 Dec 1824	Liverpool	Lee, Wm., Jr.	24-696
	1 Mar 1825	Rio de Janeiro	Hepburn, David	25-083
	20 Jul 1825	Liverpool	Graham, Hugh	25-429
	24 Aug 1825	Gibraltar	Nesbitt, Edwin	25-544
	6 Oct 1825	Port Crotavo, Teneriffe	Myrick, Isaac	25-571
	26 Nov 1825	Liverpool	Graham, Hugh	25-677
	3 Apr 1826	Liverpoool	Graham, Hugh	26-142
	12 Apr 1826	Carthagina	Bradford, Eben	26-173
	31 Jul 1826	Liverpool	Graham, Hugh	26-441
	15 Nov 1826	Liverpool	Graham, Hugh	26-664
	17 Apr 1827	London	Delano, Joseph C.	27-178
	7 Sep 1827	London	Delano, J. C.	27-600
	12 Sep 1827	St. Andrews	Bradford, E.	27-620
	7 May 1828	London	Delano, H.	28-194
	21 Jan 1828	London	Delano, J. C.	28-020
	30 Jun 1828	Guama, Portorico	Bradford, Eben	28-341
	22 Sep 1828	London	Delano, Joseph C.	28-559
	16 Jan 1829	London	Delano, H.	29-021
COLUMBUS	25 Jun 1825	Antwerp	Nye, Nathaniel	25-375
	2 May 1826	Antwerp	Gert, Martin	26-218
	20 Aug 1828	Port au Prince	Creighton, John T.	28-449
	23 Oct 1828	Matanzas	Dayton, Gilbert	28-627
	23 Mar 1829	Antwerp	Drinkwater, Nicholas	29-108
COMBINE	12 Nov 1821	Jeremie	Durham, Jacob	21-366
	11 Apr 1823	Trinadad	Dunham, Jacob	23-124
	22 May 1824	St. Johns, Nfd.	Ryder, Simeon	24-225
	13 Jul 1824	St. Johns, N.foundland	Ryder, Simeon	24-375
	9 Sep 1824	St. Johns (Newfoundland)	Ryder, Simeon	24-526
	20 Nov 1824	St. Johns, Newfoundland	Ryder, Simeon (Simon)	24-676A
	4 Jun 1825	St. Johns, NfLand	Ryder, Simeon	25-317
	1 Aug 1825	St. Johns, Newfoundland	Ryder, Simeon	25-465
	9 Aug 1825	Jamaica	Hulen, Samuel	25-489
	30 Nov 1825	St. Johns, Newfoundland	Ryder, Simeon	25-685
COMET	21 Aug 1820	Havre	Hall, William	20-197
	24 Dec 1821	London	Griswold, A. H.	21-431
	26 Jun 1822	London & Cows	Moore, George	22-292
	9 Aug 1822	Liverpool	Boag, Thomas	22-386
	6 Mar 1823	London	Moore, George	23-057
	10 Mar 1825	Kingston, Jamaica	Johnson, Joseph	25-097
	28 Jul 1825	Havre	Moore, Geo.	25-461
	1 Jun 1826	Martinique	Carr, Nathan	26-297
	19 Oct 1826	Havre	Macy, Charles	26-612
	6 Dec 1827	Trinadad	Eddy, Sylvester	27-796
	23 Aug 1828	Liverpool	Colburn, Henry	28-462

SHIP	DATE OF ARRIVAL	PORT OF EMBARKATION	CAPTAIN	YEAR AND SHIP NUMBER
COMMERCE	3 Nov 1820	St. Croix	Ansley, Ozeus	20-316
	30 Apr 1821	St. Croix	Ansley, Ozias	21-036
	8 Aug 1821	St. Johns, Porto Rico	Funk, John	21-212
	16 Oct 1821	Porto Rico	Funk, John	21-328
	24 Dec 1821	St. Johns, P.R.	Funk, John	21-432
	25 Mar 1822	Porto Rico	Funk, John	22-091
	27 May 1822	St. Johns, P.R.	Funk, John	22-230
	29 Jul 1822	Stockholm	Apelgren, Claus	22-355
	8 Aug 1822	Porto Rico	Funk, John	22-381
	14 Mar 1823	Liverpool	Gardner, Thos. W.	23-082
	20 May 1823	Porto Rico	Langdon, John W.	23-216
	17 Jul 1823	Greenock	Ritchie, Duncan	23-337
	24 Sep 1823	Liverpool	Whitney, Stephen M.	23-495
	2 Oct 1823	Liverpool	Bates, Andrew	23-515
	10 Nov 1823	London	Hayward, Abraham	23-578
	13 Nov 1823	Porto Rico	Clements, Josh.	23-585
	6 Feb 1824	St. Johns, Porto Rico	Clements, Joseph	24-028
	28 May 1824	Hull	Whitney, Stephen M.	24-243
	29 Jul 1824	Porto Rico	Leeds, Gurdon	24-415
	11 Dec 1824	Porto Rico	Leeds, Guirdon	24-711
	22 Jun 1825	St. Johns, Porto Rico	Johnston, George	25-370
	7 Jul 1826	Antigua	Hosack, Alexander	26-384
	13 Jun 1828	Newry	Burton, William	28-301
COMMET (see Comet)				
COMMODORE CHAUNCY	28 Nov 1825	Cadiz	Eklen, A. J.	25-682
	19 Jan 1826	Havana	Kingsberry, E.	26-032
COMMODORE PERRY	24 Nov 1820	Havana	Forbes, Cleaveland A.	20-331
	9 Apr 1821	Havana	Forbes, C. A.	21-009
COMMODORE PORTER	8 Sep 1823	Ponce	Shurtleff, William	23-457
COMMODORE PREBLE	17 Dec 1825	Hamburg	Walker, Luther	25-713
CONCLUSION	4 Feb 1829	Havana	Preble, Havey	29-048
CONCORD	4 Jun 1821	Greenock	Cozins, Benjamin	21-101
	10 Nov 1824	St. Croix	Thomas, George	24-649
CONCORDIA (see Cordelia)				
	8 Nov 1822	Turks Island	Bailey, Saml. G.	22-561
	11 Jun 1823	Newry	Bailey, Saml.	23-254
	8 Sep 1823	Turks Island	Bailey, Samuel G.	23-455
	12 Oct 1826	Liverpool	Bailey, Saml. G.	26-595
	25 Aug 1827	Liverpool	Bailey, Samuel G.	27-555
	20 Oct 1829	Gefle	Falk, Olaf	29-313
CONDOR	22 Aug 1822	St. Croix	Goodrich, Jasper	22-411
	4 Dec 1828	St. Croix	Goodrich, Jasper	28-694
CONDSTITUTION	21 Mar 1825	Bremen	Klockgater, G.	25-125
CONESTOGA	23 Nov 1825	Turks Island	Willis, Thomas	25-670
CONFIANCE	26 Apr 1828	Port au Prince	Bremont, A.	28-153
CONFIDENCE	5 Sep 1828	Dundee	Wesley, John	28-505
CONGRESS	21 Nov 1823	London	Derby, John	23-605
	23 Mar 1824	Liverpool	Asbridge, Peter Collin	24-104
	9 Mar 1829	S. Juans (St. Juan)	Smith, Daniel	29-076
CONSTITUTION	29 Aug 1821	Bremen	Klockgeter, Gerhd.	21-247
	29 Dec 1821	Montiviedo	McRea, John W.	21-437
	14 May 1822	St. Johns, N.B.	Spurling, Robert	22-194
	6 Jun 1822	Bremen	Klockgeter, Gord.	22-256
	15 Nov 1822	Bremen	Klockgeter, Gerd.	22-570
	17 Mar 1823	Buenos Ayres	McRea, John W.	23-086
	24 Jun 1823	St. Andrews	Standley, Sam.	23-282
	25 Jul 1823	Bremen	Klockgeter, G.	23-351
	8 Sep 1823	Havana	Berrian, Richd. P.	23-454
	16 Sep 1823	Cardiff (Wales)	Ward, Elliott	23-477
	21 Jun 1824	Bremen	Klockgeter, G.	24-317
	9 Dec 1824	Pernambuco	McRea, John W.	24-705
	19 Jul 1825	London	McRea, John M.	25-427
	20 Aug 1825	Bremen	Klockgeter, Gerd.	25-532
	1 Oct 1825	Liverpool	Ward, Elliott	25-561

SHIP	DATE OF ARRIVAL	PORT OF EMBARKATION	CAPTAIN	YEAR AND SHIP NUMBER
	2 Mar 1826	Bremen	Klockgeter, Gerd.	26-090
	2 Aug 1826	Bremen	Meyer, Jurgen	26-445
	10 Jan 1827	Bremen	Meyer, T.	27-018
	18 Jun 1827	London	Towne, Robert, Jr.	27-356
	12 Jul 1827	Bremen	Meyer, Furigin	27-442
	7 Dec 1827	Bremen	Meyer, Jurigens	27-810
	2 Apr 1828	Porto Rico	Robinson, A. W.	28-106
	20 Jun 1828	Bremen	Meyer, T.	28-317
	5 Jan 1829	Bermen	Meyer, Jurgin	29-003
	6 Jul 1829	Bremen	Meyer, Jurgen	29-128
CONTENT	28 Aug 1820	St. Johns, N.B.	Baker, Charles	20-211
CONVEYANCE	9 Feb 1825	Marseilles	Dominick, Francis W.	25-057
	27 Dec 1825	Rio Grande	Becker, Nichs.	25-734
	6 Jun 1826	Bremen	Becker, Nicholas	26-306
	15 Jan 1827	Vera Cruz	Collins, John	27-031
CONVIVIAL	10 Nov 1826	Halifax	Hanton, Willm.	26-658
CONVOY	14 Mar 1823	Jamaica	Chapman, Nathan	23-081
	10 Sep 1823	Havre	Curry, Edward	23-460
COPERNICAN	7 Jan 1823	Havana/Maracaybo	Spear, James	23-008
COPERNICUS	3 Aug 1829	London	May, William A.	29-189
COQUET	6 Jun 1827	Dundee	Cowans, Thos.	27-322
CORDELIA	21 Feb 1820	Curracoa	Auger, Ruben	20-040
	8 Sep 1820	Curacoa	Augur, Reuben	20-228
	23 Apr 1821	Oratava Teneriffe	Moffat, Anthy.	21-029
	16 Apr 1824	St. Thomas	Hinman, Munson	24-149
CORINTHIAN	2 May 1823	Liverpool	Davis, George	23-164
	1 Sep 1823	Liverpool	Davis, Geo.	23-430
	5 Jan 1824	Liverpool	Davis, George	24-004
	27 Apr 1824	Liverpool	Davis, George Washington	24-172
	2 Sep 1824	Liverpool	Davis, George	24-508
	4 Jan 1825	Liverpool	Davis, Geo.	25-004
	20 Apr 1825	Lpool	Davis, Geo.	25-195
	10 Jan 1826	Liverpool	Davis, George	26-018
	29 Apr 1826	Liverpool	Davis, George	26-206
	9 Jan 1827	Liverpool	Davis, George	27-013
	5 May 1827	Liverpool	Davis, George	27-214
	1 Sep 1827	Liverpool	Davis, Geo.	27-570
	30 May 1828	London	Chadwick, Daniel	28-258
	8 Oct 1828	London	Chadwick, Daniel	28-594
	11 Mar 1829	London	Chadwick, Daniel	29-080
	7 Jul 1829	London	Chadwick, Daniel	29-135
	27 Oct 1829	London	Chadwick, Daniel	29-333
CORKS	3 Aug 1824	Liverpool	De Cost, Nash	24-428
CORNELIA	16 Feb 1824	Gibraltar	Johnson, John	24-040
	12 Mar 1825	Maracaibo	Storms, Peter	25-108
	30 Jul 1827	St. Thomas	Drinkwater, Mathew	27-490
CORSAIR	2 Oct 1820	Havana	Robinson, Wm. J.	20-276
	1 Sep 1821	Trieste	Robinson, Wm. J.	21-254
CORTES	18 Oct 1820	Liverpool	De Cost, Nash	20-299
	7 Jul 1821	Liverpool	De Colt, Nash	21-159
	19 Nov 1821	Liverpool	De Cost, Nash	21-374
	10 Apr 1822	Liverpool	De Cost, Nash	22-119
	5 Aug 1822	Liverpool	De Cost, Nash	22-372
	11 Dec 1822	Liverpool	De Cost, Nash	22-599
	11 Aug 1823	Liverpool	De Cost, Nash	23-393
	28 Nov 1823	Liverpool	De Cost, Nash	23-610
	23 Mar 1824	Liverpool	De Cost, Nash	24-105
	6 Apr 1825	Liverpool	DeCost, Nash	25-152
	13 Aug 1825	Liverpool	De Cost, Nash	25-500
	7 Dec 1825	Liverpool	De Cost, Nash	25-696
	19 May 1826	London	Sprague, Benjamin	26-264
	6 Mar 1827	London	Sprague, Benjn.	27-102
	16 Jul 1827	London	Sprague, Benjamin	27-452
	23 Nov 1827	London	Sprague, Benjamin	27-767
CORTEX	7 Mar 1823	Liverpool	Ogden, David S.	23-060
	4 Dec 1824	Liverpool	DeCost, Nash	24-700
COSMO	29 Jun 1826	Bristol	Gillespie, John	26-369

SHIP	DATE OF ARRIVAL	PORT OF EMBARKATION	CAPTAIN	YEAR AND SHIP NUMBER
	25 Nov 1826	Bristol	Gillespie, John	26-679
	15 May 1827	Bristol	Gillespie, John	27-252
	25 Sep 1827	Bristol	Gillespie, John	27-664
	17 Mar 1828	Bristol	Gillespie, John	28-066
	21 Aug 1828	Bristol, Eng.	Gillespie, John	28-454
	26 Aug 1829	Bristol	Gillespie, John	29-256
COTTON PLANT	15 Nov 1823	Hamburgh	Gregory, Thomas H.	23-593
COURIER	13 Mar 1820	Liverpool	Eldridge, Jonathan	20-054
	24 Jul 1820	Liverpool	Eldridge, Jonathan	20-142
	23 Feb 1824	Liverpool	Marshall, Robert	24-055
	16 Aug 1824	Liverpool	Wallace, George H.	24-455
	30 Dec 1824	Liverpool	Wallace, George H.	24-743
	16 May 1825	Newry	Wallace, George H.	25-255
	14 Jun 1825	Liverpool	Hudson, Henry	25-341
	25 Aug 1825	Liverpool	Wallace, George H.	25-546
	13 Jul 1826	Liverpool	Wallace, George H.	26-404
	12 Mar 1827	Liverpool	Benjamin, Pulaski	27-118
	17 Mar 1827	Belfast	Thompson, Wm. C.	27-123
	26 Jun 1827	Glasgow	Benjamin, Pulaski	27-377
	29 Jun 1827	Antwerp	Thompson, Wm. C.	27-391
	11 oct 1827	Hamburg	Benjamin, Pulaski	27-696
	15 Oct 1827	Belfast	Thompson, William Consodder	27-708
	17 Mar 1828	Belfast	Britton, Thomas	28-069
	31 Jul 1828	Rio de Janeiro	Wolfe, Wm.	28-413
	9 Feb 1829	Havana	Willis, John W.	29-054
	22 Aug 1829	Marseilles	Wolfe, William	29-238
COWPER	8 Jan 1827	London	Urann, Richard	27-008
CRAVEN	8 Apr 1822	St. Thomas	Sparrow, William T.	22-113
	9 Jul 1823	Demerara	Sparrow, Wm. T.	23-323
CRAWFORD	4 Jan 1826	Nassau	Barnard, Peter	26-013
CRESCENT	12 Jul 1827	Havre	Haley, John B.	27-446
CRIRIE	18 Sep 1820	Liverpool	Humphries, Thos.	20-251
	2 Jul 1821	Liverpool	Humphrais, Thomas	21-147
CRISIS	10 Nov 1823	Stockholm	Brumley, Reuben	23-580
	26 May 1824	Marseilles	McMannus, Jno.	24-236
	13 Nov 1824	London	Harris, John M.	24-660
	6 Apr 1825	London	McManus, J.	25-151
CRITERION	27 Oct 1820	London	Avery, Samuel	20-306
	27 Oct 1821	London	Avery, Saml.	21-348
	29 May 1822	London	Sebor, William S.	22-238
	15 Oct 1822	London	Sebor, Willima L.	22-527
	12 Jun 1823	London	Day, Wm.	23-258
	20 Nov 1823	London	Day, William	23-603
	7 Jul 1824	London	Paine, Jeda.	24-360
	6 Dec 1824	Havre	Paine, J.	24-703
	16 May 1825	Havre	Paine, J.	25-259
	24 May 1825	Grenada	Crane, Barnabas	25-292
	13 Oct 1825	Havre	Paine, J.	25-583
	23 May 1826	Liverpool	Paine, J.	26-279
	9 Aug 1826	Havana	Taylor, Edwd. E.	26-468
	27 Jun 1827	Liverpool	Paine, J.	27-384
CRITERION AT LONDON	10 May 1821	London	Avery, Saml.	21-054
CRUSADER	23 Apr 1827	Matanzas	Couthouy, Joseph	27-192
CUBA	25 Feb 1822	Havana	Cushing, Loring	22-060
	24 Jun 1822	Galway	Cushing, Loring	22-283
	3 Jan 1823	Demerara	Cushing, Loring	23-001
	25 Mar 1823	Cuba	Cushing, Loring	23-096
CULLODEN	21 Oct 1823	Jeremy	Stinman, John	23-553
	17 May 1828	Alloa	Wallace, Peter	28-231
CUMBERLAND	25 Feb 1826	Amsterdam	Morrill, Charels	26-081
	5 May 1828	Omoa	Wheaton, Amos	28-185
CURLER	7 Jul 1827	Liverpool	Reid, Archibald	27-424
	3 Mar 1828	Liverpool	Jones, Joseph R.	28-037
	19 Jul 1828	Grenock	Jones, J. R.	28-388
CURLEW	1 Mar 1823	Port au Prince	Stinman, John	23-053
	16 Jun 1823	Port au Prince	Stinman, John	23-265

SHIP	DATE OF ARRIVAL	PORT OF EMBARKATION	CAPTAIN	YEAR AND SHIP NUMBER
	3 Nov 1823	Aux Cayes	Keating, James H.	23-569
	1 Mar 1824	Aux Cayes	Carlaw, William B.	24-065
	28 Jun 1824	Aux Cayes	Carlaw, Wm. B.	24-332
	30 Oct 1824	Aux Cayes	Johnson, Robert M.	24-633
CYGNET	23 Sep 1820	Halifax	Kimball, Nathl.	20-256
	22 Jun 1821	Newcastle	Henderson, John	21-126
	17 Jan 1824	Marseilles	Kennedy, Saml.	24-019
CYNO	21 Jul 1824	St. Croix	Disney, Thomas	24-385
	22 Jul 1826	Teneriffe	Baker, Hiram	26-418
	18 Sep 1827	Angostura	Baker, Hiram	27-639
	8 Dec 1827	Halifax	Baker, Hiram	27-812
	1 Apr 1828	Fourterentura	Baker, Hiram	28-102
CYNOSURE	4 Mar 1828	Amsterdam by way of St. Michals one of the westernn Islands	Burgess, Theophilus	28-044
CYNTHIA	16 Feb 1824	Guadaloupe	Gibbs, Henry	24-041
CZAR	29 Aug 1829	Greenock	Russell, Alex.	29-266
DALE	14 Mar 1828	Liverpool	Hobson, W. C.	28-056
DALHOUSE	23 Mar 1829	Liverpool	Walton, Robert	29-111
DALHOUSE CASTLE	28 Feb 1826	Liverpool	Harry, John	26-089
	8 May 1827	Liverpool	Walton, Robert	27-221
	6 Sep 1827	Liverpool	Walton, Robert (Dallon)	27-598
	26 Dec 1827	Liverpool	Walton, Robert	27-854
	13 May 1828	Liverpool	Walton, Robert	28-208
	12 Sep 1828	Liverpool	Walton, Robert	28-531
	21 Aug 1829	Liverpool	Walton, Robert	29-236
DALHOUSIE CASTLE	27 Jul 1826	Liverpool	Walton, Robert	26-431
DALMANNOCK	24 Ocg 1826	Greenock	Kinnenment, John	26-628
DALMARNOCK	17 May 1822	Leith	Cummins, James	22-202
	23 May 1823	Aloa, Leith	Kinniment, John	23-225
	11 Dec 1828	Alloa	Kinnenment, John	28-702
DALTHOUSIE CASTLE	2 Jan 1827	Liverpool	Walton, Robt.	27-001
DAMON	18 Nov 1826	Bordeaux	Potter, Gilbert	26-671
DANDY	15 Apr 1824	Laguira	Boddily, John	24-146
	22 Dec 1824	La Guayra	Boddily, John	24-731
	17 May 1825	La Guayra	Boddily, John	25-267
DANUBE	22 Aug 1825	Liverpool	Huntington, Edward	25-535
	11 Apr 1826	Havre	Huntington, Edward	26-169
	20 Jul 1826	Havre De g	Huntington, Edward	26-415
	21 Nov 1826	Havre	Huntington, Edward	26-675
	13 Jul 1827	Liverpool	Rockett, John	27-448
	1 Nov 1827	Liverpool	Kochett, John	27-739
	2 Sep 1828	Lima	Cook, Samuel	28-496
DAPHNE	31 Aug 1822	St. Ubes	Rohn, A.	22-436
	20 May 1823	Hamburg	Kohler, Adolph	23-217
DAPPER	24 Aug 1827	Hull	Dickinson, William	27-551
	14 Mar 1828	Hull	Dickinson, Wm.	28-058
	21 Aug 1828	Hull	Dickinson, William	28-455
	29 Jan 1829	Hull	Dickinson, Wm.	29-023
DART	8 Oct 1821	Para	Van Dine, Henry	21-309
	5 Apr 1822	Para	Van Dine, Henry	22-108
	3 Aug 1822	Para	Van Dine, Henry	22-370
	2 Dec 1822	Para	Van Dine, Henry	22-592
	15 Jul 1823	Port au Prince	Allen, Ichabod	23-336
	24 Oct 1825	Para	Powers, Nicholas	25-612
DAVID	19 Apr 1824	Havana	Osborn, John	24-155
	5 Oct 1824	Havana	Smith, Benjm.	24-573
	4 May 1825	St. Thomas	Smith, Isaac K.	25-235
DAVID MOFFITT	7 Oct 1822	Gibraltar	Caller, Thomas	22-513
DAWN	19 Aug 1825	St. Andrews	Doane, Joshua	25-520
	12 Jun 1826	Antwerp	Doane, Joshua	26-326
	9 Dec 1826	Antwerp	Doane, Joshua	26-711
	8 Jun 1827	Antwerp	Doane, Joshua	27-332
	15 Oct 1827	Antwerp	Doane, Joshua	27-707
	31 Mar 1828	Antwerp	Doane, Joshua	28-095

SHIP	DATE OF ARRIVAL	PORT OF EMBARKATION	CAPTAIN	YEAR AND SHIP NUMBER
	15 Jul 1828	St. Andrews	Doane, Joshua	28-376
DAY	6 Feb 1822	Malaga	Tucker, Daniel F.	22-030
	14 Jun 1822	Gibraltar	Bovre, James	22-268
	11 Jun 1823	Leghorn	Bovre, James	23-255
	16 Aug 1826	Marseilles	Peirce, Jno. W.	26-490
	24 Apr 1828	Gibralter	Stoddard, Charles	28-141
DEAUX AMIS	29 Oct 1828	Cape Hayten	Praderis, Elie	28-639
DEBBY & ELIZA	20 Nov 1820	Liverpool	Sprague, Benjamin	20-325
	12 Aug 1822	Aporta	Sprague, Benjamin	22-390
	29 Jul 1824	Lisbon	Ewen, Edward	24-416
DEBORAH	11 Jun 1824	St. Christopher	Cruthers, S.	24-294
	3 Jul 1824	Matanzas	Bourne, Elijah	24-351
DECATUR	12 Dec 1820	St. Andrews	Hopkins, John	20-344
	3 May 1821	Matanzes	Brownell, Major	21-047
	5 Jul 1821	St. Andrews	Cushing, Abner	21-152
	2 Jan 1822	Fayal	Brownell, Mager	22-001
	5 May 1825	Para	Woodhouse, P.	25-236
	29 Nov 1825	Nassau, New Providence	Griffing, Jno. D. (H. D.)	25-683
	17 Mar 1820	Matanzas	Brownell, Mayer	20-070
DEFENCE	13 Dec 1827	Leith	Rodger, George	27-829
DEFIANCE	13 Jul 1824	Jamaica	Somers, James C.	24-373
	18 May 1826	St. Michaels	Ely, Samuel	26-258
DELAWARE	20 Aug 1829	Liverpool	Bartleson, Chas. M.	29-234
DELIA	26 Oct 1829	St. Thomas	Hoyt, James S.	29-331
DELIGENCE	21 Mar 1825	River Gambia	Eustis, James	25-130
DELTA	24 Oct 1829	Liverpool	Stone, Gyles P.	29-317
DENNY MCCOBB	26 Jul 1827	St. Andrews	Dyer, Howland	27-480
DESDEMONA	6 Oct 1824	Bordeaux	Morris, Patterson	24-577
	21 Oct 1825	Havre	Neghel, Frs.	25-602
	15 Feb 1826	Havre	Neghel, Frs.	26-068
	12 Jun 1826	Havre	Naghel, Francis	26-331
	24 Feb 1827	Campeachy	Coire, V.	27-093
	15 Jun 1827	Campeachy	Corre, Vincent	27-348
	11 Mar 1829	Campeachy	Naghel, F.	29-083
DESDEMONIA	11 Feb 1825	Havre	Naghel, Francis	25-061
	9 Jun 1825	Havre	Nagle, Frs.	25-326
DEUX ERNEST	29 Dec 1827	Havre	Lebeun, A.	27-865
	29 Dec 1827	Havre	Bawel, A.	27-866
	11 Dec 1828	Havre	Le Bain, A.	28-701
DEUX FRERES	27 Nov 1824	Antwerp	Dike, S. H.	24-694
DEWITT CLINTON	27 Jul 1824	Liverpool	Barstow, William C.	24-407
	26 Aug 1825	Liverpool	Barstow, Wm. C.	25-549
	16 Dec 1825	Bahamas Islands	Barstow, Wm. C.	25-712
	16 Nov 1824	Turks Island	Barstow, Wm. C.	24-667
DIAMOND	13 Nov 1823	Liverpool	Macy, Josiah	23-586
	12 Mar 1824	Liverpool	Macy, Josiah	24-074
	27 Jul 1824	Liverpool	Macy, Josiah	24-408
	8 Nov 1824	Liverpool	Macy, Henry	24-644
DIANA	18 Jul 1820	Bermuda	McPherson, S. W.	20-130
	14 Sep 1820	Bermuda	McPherson, Saml. W.	20-243
	1 May 1821	Aux Cayes	Sheed, Abraham A.	21-042
	17 Jul 1821	Aux Cayes	Sheed, Abraham A.	21-180
	4 Dec 1821	Aux Cayes	Sheed, Abraham A.	21-398
	1 Jun 1822	Aux Cayes	McPherson, Saml. W.	22-245
	8 Aug 1822	Aux Cayes	McPherson, Saml.	22-382
	27 Aug 1822	Gottenburgh	Higgins, David	22-426
	31 Oct 1822	Aux Cayes	Kimball, John	22-551
	7 Jun 1823	Para	Mott, Wm. H.	23-247
	9 Aug 1823	Havana	Higgins, David	23-390
	30 Apr 1824	London	Lord, Robt., Jr.	24-186
	12 Apr 1825	London	Hues, Geo.	25-169
	1 May 1826	Cork	Rice, John, Jr.	26-212
	4 Sep 1827	St. Andrews	Otis, Wm. B.	27-583
	30 Oct 1827	Hull	Sugden, John, Junr.	27-733
	28 Apr 1828	Hull	Sugden, John	28-157
	20 Nov 1828	Hull	Sugden, John, Junr.	28-672
	6 Jul 1829	Hull	Sugden, John, Jr.	29-129

SHIP	DATE OF ARRIVAL	PORT OF EMBARKATION	CAPTAIN	YEAR AND SHIP NUMBER
DICK	4 Sep 1823	Buenos Ayres	Woodhouse, P.	23-445
DICKINSON (see Jno. Dickinson)				
	30 Jul 1825	Belfast	Burras, Samuel	25-462
DIDO	26 Apr 1825	Bremen	Hesklots, J. M.	25-209
DILIGENCE	29 Jul 1823	St. Georges, Grenada	Eustis, James	23-364
DIME	15 Mar 1820	St. George Bermuda	Armsburgh, Oliver	20-064
DINGLEYS	12 Aug 1824	Nevis	Cowing, James	24-448
DIONESIO	28 Jan 1828	Havana	Garene, Osborne	28-028
DIONISIO	30 Oct 1827	Havana	Meyers, P. S.	27-731
DIRECTOR	20 Sep 1824	Para	Woodhouse, P.	24-540
	6 Sep 1826	Port au Prince	Laboursse, Michael	26-521
	11 Dec 1827	Mayagues	Laboursse, M.	27-823
	14 Apr 1828	Mayaguez	Labonise, M.	28-125
DIRIGO	24 Mar 1828	Trinadad in Cuba	Pettingill, Elipht., 2nd	28-087
DISPATCH	22 Mar 1822	Havana	Urann, Richd.	22-087
	25 Apr 1825	Jamaica	Finch, H. T.	25-208
	12 Aug 1825	Curacoa	Terhew, John	25-497
	7 Dec 1825	St. Thomas	Teshew, John	25-695
	16 Jul 1827	New Castle	Hunter, John	27-453
DODGE HEALY	14 Oct 1828	Halifax	Hathorn, Alexr.	28-613
DOLLAR	29 Aug 1825	Gibaira	Hall, Benjamin	25-556
DOLPHIN	15 Apr 1822	Havana	Nichols, John M.	22-126
	7 May 1822	Mayagues	Colly, Joseph L., Junr.	22-177
	6 Sep 1822	Havana	Fossett, John	22-453
	31 May 1824	Maricaibo	Russell, J. G.	24-252
DOMESTIC	31 Aug 1820	Halifax	Barnes, Peleg	20-218
DOMINICA	4 Jan 1823	Liverpool	Johnson, Jno.	23-005
DON QUIXOTE	7 May 1824	Havre	Clark, James (John)	24-203
	18 Aug 1824	Havre	Clark, James	24-469
	15 Apr 1825	Havre	Clark, James	25-176
	19 Aug 1825	Havre	Clark, James	25-524
	3 Jan 1826	Havre	Clark, James	26-005
	14 Aug 1826	Havre	Clark, Jas.	26-477
	20 Mar 1827	Havre	Clark, Jas.	27-134
	9 Oct 1827	Havre	Clark, James	27-691
	25 Oct 1828	Havre	Whitall, D. W. (J. D.)	28-633
	12 Feb 1829	Havre	Whitall, Jas. D. W.	29-059
DON QUIXOTTE	27 Jun 1827	Havre	Clark, James	27-383
	2 Jun 1828	Havre	Whitall, J. W.	28-267
	17 Jan 1825	Havre	Clark, James	25-024
DORIS	21 Jan 1826	Bahia	Beard, James	26-033
	22 May 1826	Campeachy	Oliver, B.	26-273
	2 Jun 1828	Musserada	Mathews, W. P.	28-268
DOUGLASS	22 May 1823	Curacoa	Brown, John	23-222
	4 Aug 1823	Curacoa	Brown, Jno.	23-379
	3 Nov 1823	Curacoa	Bourne, Lemuel	23-570
	13 Feb 1824	Curacoa	Brown, Jno.	24-034
	27 Apr 1824	Curacoa	Brown, John	24-170
	16 Jul 1824	Curacoa	Brown, John	24-378
	15 Oct 1824	Curacoa	Brown, John	24-603
	9 May 1825	Curacoa	Brown, John	25-240
	27 Jul 1825	Curacoa	Brown, Jno.	25-452
	25 Nov 1825	St. Iago de Cuba	Fowler, Oliver	25-673
	8 May 1826	Curacoa	Fowler, River	26-238
	30 Oct 1826	Curacoa	Fowler, Oliver	26-632
	7 Aug 1827	Curacoa	Fowler, River	27-502
	9 Nov 1827	Curacoa	Fowler, Oliver	27-753
	29 Apr 1828	Curacoa	Brown, John	28-162
	14 Jul 1828	Curaco	Brown, John	28-374
	14 Oct 1828	Curacoa	Bourne, Lemuel	28-609
	6 Jul 1829	Sligo	Bourne, Lemuel	29-132
DOVER	17 Aug 1821	Matanza	Ferrier Ro.	21-229
DRAPER	18 Jun 1822	Havre	Cary, Nath. C.	22-276
	18 Nov 1822	Havana	Smith, Moses R.	22-573
	17 Dec 1823	Ivica (via Gibraltar)	Thorndike, Andrew, Junr.	23-643
DRIE GEBRUDERS (see Three Brothers)				
DROMA	25 Mar 1826	Vera Cruz	Morgan, James	26-134
DROMO	22 May 1826	Havana	Morgan, J.	26-274

SHIP	DATE OF ARRIVAL	PORT OF EMBARKATION	CAPTAIN	YEAR AND SHIP NUMBER
	24 Jul 1826	Havana	Morgan, J.	26-420
	27 Sep 1826	Havana	Morgan, Jno.	26-560
	13 Dec 1826	Havana	Morgan, J.	26-722
	22 Feb 1827	Havanna	Morgan, J.	27-088
	4 May 1827	Havana	Morgan, J.	27-211
	19 Jul 1827	Havana	Morgan, J.	27-461
	10 Sep 1827	Stockholm	Blanchard, Andrew G.	27-611
	24 Sep 1827	Havana	Robinson, J. (F.)	27-652
	13 Nov 1827	Havana	Campbell, D. H.	27-758
	9 Oct 1828	Buenos Ayres	Morgan, James	28-599
	28 Feb 1829	Havana	Morgan, James	29-069
	14 Aug 1829	Havana	Morgan, James	29-217
	5 Oct 1829	Havana	Smith, Benjamin, Jr.	29-281
DUBLIN	21 Feb 1824	Dublin	Donal, Alexr.	24-054
	21 Dec 1824	Dublin	Donal, Alex	24-728
	21 Feb 1826	Dublin	McLaren, James	26-076
DUBLIN PACKET	9 Oct 1820	Dublin	Coles, Joseph	20-286
	30 Apr 1821	Dublin	Coles, Joseph	21-037
	22 Oct 1821	Dublin	Newcomb, Wm.	21-339
	22 Apr 1822	Dublin	Newcomb, Willm.	22-138
	3 Sep 1822	Dublin	Newcomb, William	22-447
	3 May 1823	Dublin	Newcomb, William	23-166
	24 Sep 1823	Dublin	Newcomb, Wm.	23-496
	28 Apr 1824	Dublin	Newcomb, William	24-176
	8 Feb 1825	Bordeaux	Newcomb, Wm.	25-055
	29 Jun 1825	Dublin	Newcomb, William	25-388
	9 Jul 1827	Dublin	Newcomb, William	27-426
	6 Dec 1827	Dublin	Newcomb, William	27-800
	23 May 1828	Dublin	Newcomb, William	28-241
	13 Oct 1828	Dublin	Newcomb, William	28-608
	22 Aug 1829	Dublin	Newcomb, William	29-241
DUCHESS OF GLOUCESTER	1 Dec 1823	Glasgow	King, John	23-620
DUCTILE	11 Feb 1822	Port au Prince	Williams, Robert	22-042
	26 Aug 1822	St. Thomas	Williams, Robert	22-419
	30 Nov 1822	Port au Prince, St. Domingo		22-588
	23 Aug 1824	St. Iago	Davis, John F.	24-479
	23 Nov 1824	Porto Cavallo	Davis, John F.	24-682
	23 Nov 1824	Porto Cavallo	Davis, John F.	24-682
	12 Apr 1825	Porto Cabello	Davis, Jno. F.	25-173
	4 Oct 1825	Porto Cabello	Davis, John F.	25-565
	12 May 1826	Havana	Downs, Corns. H.	26-245
DULY ANN	6 Jul 1825	St. Thomas	Jefferson, Wm.	25-400
DUPLICATE	22 May 1827	Aux Cayes	Hippolyte, M.	27-282
DUTCHESS OF GLOUCESTER (see Duchess of Gloucester)				
DUTCHESS OF PORTLAND	30 Oct 1826	Glasgow	Hall, James, Jr.	26-637
E. D. DOUGLASS	12 Apr 1824	Maracaibo	Hallet, Sears	24-135
EAGLE	20 Nov 1820	St. Ubes	Mix, Thomas	20-323
	18 Jul 1822	Hamburgh	Mix, Thomas	22-333
	17 Feb 1823	Hamburgh	Adams, Jos.	23-031
	16 Aug 1823	Bordeaux	Tolles, Danl.	23-403
	20 Mar 1824	Antwerp	Adams, Joseph	24-092
	2 Jul 1825	Matanzas	Brothers, Jas.	25-392
	10 Aug 1825	Glasgow	Cary, Abraham B.	25-492
	17 Jun 1826	Key West	Anderson, Wm. D.	26-340
	26 Jul 1828	St. Croix	Davis, John	28-403
EARL OF LIVERPOOL	29 Sep 1823	Bristol	Holladay, Frans.	23-503
	28 Apr 1824	Bristo	Stone, John	24-180
	12 Apr 1825	Bristol	Stone, Jno.	25-168
	20 Aug 1825	Bristol	Stone, John	25-528
	16 Aug 1826	Bristol	Stone, John	26-486
EASTERN STAR	7 May 1824	Martinique	Houdlett, F.	24-200
	15 Aug 1827	St. Croix	Handlette, Francis	27-518
ECHO	22 Apr 1823	Havana	Blanchard, Solo. L.	23-147
	13 Nov 1824	Stockholm	Blanchard, Samuel	24-656

SHIP	DATE OF ARRIVAL	PORT OF EMBARKATION	CAPTAIN	YEAR AND SHIP NUMBER
ECLIPSE	14 Feb 1820	Campeachy	Price, David	20-035
	10 Jun 1823	La Guayra	Hathaway, Wm.	23-252
	3 Aug 1824	Tampico	Ellison, Benjm.	24-426
	20 Jul 1825	Caracoa	Jones, W.	25-430
	26 Feb 1827	St. Thomas	Lindsey, Wm.	27-094
	26 Jun 1827	La Guayra	Holmes, Saml.	27-376
EDGAR	19 Aug 1820	Trieste	Johnson, Robt.	20-192
	1 Oct 1822	Angustura	Johnson, Robt.	22-495
	1 Aug 1823	Vera Cruz	Johnson, Robt.	23-376
	11 Feb 1824	Matanzas	Johnson, Robt.	24-031
	23 Nov 1824	La Guira	Hathaway, W.	24-685
	4 Jan 1826	St. Iago de Cuba	Johnson, Robert	26-010
	4 Jan 1828	Angostura	Johnson, Robert	28-003
EDWARD	10 Aug 1820	Bermuda	Carlisle, John	20-170
	17 Aug 1820	Cadiz & Madeira	Macy, Josiah	20-186
	29 Aug 1820	Turks Island	Bleecher, William P.	20-213
	21 Apr 1821	Liverpool and Lisbon	Hussey, Francis F.	21-025
	6 May 1822	Pamptico	Wheeler, Samuel	22-175
	15 Jul 1825	Liverpool	Howard, Thos.	25-422
	12 Aug 1825	Bordeaux	Snow, Robt.	25-496
	28 Oct 1825	Havre	Funck, James	25-621
	24 Oct 1827	Guayana, Porto Rico	Stover, Peter	27-725
	26 Jun 1828	Porto Rico	Storer, Peter	28-332
EDWARD & QUESNEL (see Edward Quesnel)				
EDWARD & FRANCES	9 May 1823	Madeira	Megrath, Michael	23-177
EDWARD BONAFFE	11 Dec 1827	Havre	Hathaway, E. (W.)	27-824
	23 Jul 1828	Havre	Hathaway, Wm.	28-393
EDWARD BONNAFFE	1 Mar 1825	Havre	Funck, James	25-084
	20 Jun 1825	Havre	Funck, James	25-368
	13 Mar 1826	Havre de Grace in France	Funck, James	26-107
	20 Jun 1826	Havre de Grace	Funck, James	26-349
	12 Oct 1826	Havre	Funk, James	26-594
	4 May 1827	Havre	Funck, James	27-212
	24 Aug 1827	Havre	Hathaway, William	27-552
	17 Mar 1828	Havre	Hathaway, William	28-065
EDWARD BOPNNAFFE	30 Jul 1829	Havre	Hathaway, William	29-179
EDWARD D. DOUGLASS	6 Jun 1823	St. Croix	Hallet, Sears	23-246B
	16 Jun 1824	St. Croix	Hallet, Sears	24-310
	11 Aug 1824	St. Croix	Hallett, Sears	24-443
EDWARD QUESNEL	17 Jan 1825	Havre	Hawkins, Elnathan	25-019
	11 Jan 1826	Havre	Hawkins, E.	26-020
	15 May 1826	Havre	Hawkins, E.	26-253
	3 Sep 1826	Havre	Hawkins, E.	26-516
	19 Dec 1826	Havre	Hawkins, E.	26-730
	21 Apr 1827	Havre	Hawkins, Elnathan	27-188
	31 Jul 1827	Havre	Hawkins, Elnathan	27-493
	16 Nov 1827	Havre	Hawkins, E.	27-762
	13 Mar 1828	Havre	Hawkins, Elnathan	28-055
	4 Aug 1828	Havre	Hawkins, E.	28-419
	17 Nov 1828	Havre	Hawkins, E.	28-662
	17 Mar 1829	Havre	Hawkins, Elnathan	29-100
	3 Jul 1829	Havre	Hawkins, Elnathen	29-127
	19 Oct 1829	Havre	Hawkins, Elnathan	29-307
EDWD. QUESNEL	30 Apr 1825	Havre	Hawkins, E.	25-226
EDWIN	26 Sep 1828	St. Johns	Crowell, R.	28-567
	27 Oct 1828	St. Johns, N.B.	Crowell, Ruben	28-636
	29 Nov 1828	St. Johns	Crowell, Reuben	28-684
	10 Feb 1829	st. Thomas	Crowell, Reuben	29-055
	1 Jul 1829	St. Johns, N.B.	Crowell, Reuben	29-116

SHIP	DATE OF ARRIVAL	PORT OF EMBARKATION	CAPTAIN	YEAR AND SHIP NUMBER
ELBA	21 May 1825	Bordeaux	Wooster, Joseph	25-284
	9 May 1827	Nantes & Le Rochelle	Wooster, Joseph	27-229
	14 Jun 1828	Canaries	Wooster, Joseph	28-303
	21 Sep 1821	Havre	Aldridge, Geo.	21-290
	2 Aug 1822	Havre	Lyme, W. F.	22-364
	8 Jun 1824	Galway	Warner, Nathaniel	24-280
	19 Apr 1826	Monte Video	Akin, Lemuel S.	26-192
	30 Sep 1826	Pernambuco	Akin, Lemuel S.	26-571
	13 Jun 1827	Pernambuco	Akin, Lemuel S.	27-344
	22 Aug 1828	Stockholm	Jones, Jonas	28-459
	13 Mar 1829	Cette [Ceuta?] & Marseilles	Jones, Jonas	29-088
ELDON	21 Aug 1827	Newcastle & Dundee	Cooper, John	27-541
ELECTRA	28 Apr 1827	London	Harris, Robt. W.	27-199
	4 Sep 1827	London	Coit, E. L.	27-582
	7 Jul 1828	London	Baker, J.	28-357
	17 Nov 1828	London	Baker, Jesse	28-663
ELIAS BURGER	25 Feb 1820	St. Croix	Ansley, Ozias	20-044
	24 Jul 1820	St. Croix	Onsley, Ozias	20-143
	19 Dec 1820	St. Thomas	Parker, Samuel F.	20-351
	28 May 1821	St. Croix	Parker, Samuel F.	21-091
	26 Jul 1821	St. Croix	Parker, Samuel F.	21-200
	18 Sep 1821	St. Croix	Parker, L. S.	21-282
	3 Dec 1821	St. Croix	Jennings, Solomon	21-389
	19 Mar 1822	St. Croix	Disney, Thomas	22-085
	11 Jul 1822	St. Croix	Disney, Thomas	22-314
	12 Sep 1822	St. Croix	Disney, Thomas	22-462
	30 Nov 1822	St. Croix	Disney, Thomas	22-589
	18 Apr 1823	St. Croix	Disney, Thomas	23-139
	21 Jun 1823	St. Croix	Disney, Thomas	23-274
	21 Aug 1823	St. Croix	Disney, Thomas	23-416
ELIONOR	5 Aug 1828	Aux Cayes	Tambeau, O.	28-420
ELISA (see Eliza)				
	1 May 1821	Curacoa	Waring, Saml. J.	21-043
	23 May 1821	Campeachy	Heith, Asa	21-083
ELISA JANE (see Eliza Jane)				
ELISA PIGOTT (see Eliza Pigott)				
	17 Jan 1822	St. Thomas & St. Barts	Waterman, Robt.	22-010
	24 Apr 1822	St. Eustatia	Waterman, Robt.	22-147
ELIZA	3 Jul 1820	Gaudaloupe	Gruely, Edward L.	20-096
	31 Jul 1821	Curacoa	Waring, Saml. G.	21-205
	16 Oct 1821	Curacao	Waring, Saml. J.	21-329
	12 Jul 1822	Curacoa	Folger, R. C.	22-318
	29 Aug 1822	St. Johns, N.B.	Nelson, Nicholas	22-432
	23 Dec 1822	Dundee	Burgess, Theops.	22-611
	12 May 1823	St. Johns, N.B.	Lamb, Thomas	23-182
	20 Mar 1824	Leghorn	Gale, Stephen	24-093
	20 Aug 1824	Havana	Carlisle, James	24-474
	13 Nov 1824	Havana	Carlisle, James	24-657
	14 Mar 1825	Havana	Carlisle, James	25-112
	26 Jul 1825	St. Croix	Simmer, A.	25-444
	24 Aug 1825	Stockholm	Mason, Rishworth	25-543
	3 Jan 1826	Alvarado	Beckup, Barth. H.	26-002
	11 Apr 1826	Vera Cruz	Bukut, B. A.	26-166
	31 Jul 1826	Vera Cruz	Beekeep, B. F.	26-440
	15 Aug 1826	New Castle	Ogle, Thomas	26-482
	22 Dec 1826	Vera Cruz	Beekeep, Barth. A.	26-732
	8 Mar 1827	London	Shuster, Jacob	27-109
	28 Apr 1827	Vera Cruz	Beekeep, Barth. A.	27-200
	9 May 1827	Dundee	Hynd, Geo.	27-226
	10 Jul 1827	Mayaguez	Patrick, William	27-434
	20 Aug 1827	Vera Cruz	Beekeep, Barth. A.	27-536
	29 Dec 1827	Vera Cruz	Bukey, Barth. A.	27-864
	12 May 1828	London	Whelden, Seth T.	28-207
	31 Jul 1828	Dundee	Hyne, Geo. S.	28-412
	22 Oct 1828	Gibraltar	Chew, Samuel	28-625
	20 Nov 1828	St. Thomas	Dyer, Howland	28-670

SHIP	DATE OF ARRIVAL	PORT OF EMBARKATION	CAPTAIN	YEAR AND SHIP NUMBER
ELIZA ALLEN	30 May 1827	Maracaybo	Studley, Allen	27-313
ELIZA & MARY	14 Jan 1824	St. Thomas	Griffin, Nathaniel	24-017
ELIZA ANN	29 Sep 1820	Havana	Smith, Egbert B.	20-271
	30 Jul 1823	Galway	Barstow, Wm. C.	23-373
	16 Apr 1824	City of St. Domingo	Burrell, Charles	24-152
	17 Jul 1824	St. Domingo	Tuttle, Reuben	24-381
	12 Mar 1825	Cape Haytien	Phinney, Abner	25-107
	2 May 1826	Kingston, Jamaica	Baker, Elnathan	26-219
	5 Jun 1826	Nassau, N.P.	Sweeting, Richard	26-305
ELIZA BARKER	9 Jun 1823	Pacific Ocean	Alley, Obed	23-248
	13 May 1824	Liverpool	Rawson, A.	24-213
	25 Dec 1824	Port au Prince	Gage, Lot	24-736
	19 Dec 1825	Bermuda	Russell, Abrm.	25-716
	11 Jan 1826	Liverpool	Rawson, Abel	26-022
	3 Jul 1826	Liverpool	Rawson, Abel	26-376
ELIZA DAVIDSON	28 Jul 1828	Ponce	Ripley, John	28-407
	1 Dec 1828	St. Croix	Cartwright, Alexr. J.	28-687
	12 Feb 1829	st. Croix	Cartwright, Alexr. J.	29-060
	8 Aug 1829	(West End) St. Croix	Cartwright, Alexr. J.	29-203
ELIZA GRANT	18 Aug 1826	Havre	Salter, John	26-498
	7 Jun 1827	London	Tibbits, Hale J.	27-323
	6 Oct 1828	Liverpool	Pray, Samuel	28-588
	29 Aug 1829	Liverpool	McManus, John	29-265
ELIZA JANE	12 Sep 1820	Liverpool	Ferris, John M.	20-239
	29 Oct 1821	Turks Island	Wilden, Asa W.	21-349
	11 Jul 1822	Havana	Burger, Robt.	22-315
	23 Aug 1824	St. Iago de Cuba	Bates, Andrew	24-481
	14 Sep 1826	Havre	Center, Amasa K.	26-531
	14 Jun 1828	La Guira	Arnold, R.	28-302
	26 Oct 1829	Halifax	Bassett, Isaac	29-329
ELIZA PIGOTT	27 Mar 1820	St. Thomas	Waterman, Robert	20-083
	25 Sep 1820	St. Thomas	Waterman, Robt.	20-262
	15 Oct 1821	St. Thomas	Waterman, Robt.	21-323
	23 Mar 1824	Havana	Davis, Collin K.	24-106
	29 May 1826	St. Croix	Davis, C. K.	26-289
ELIZABETH	5 Jul 1821	Hamburg	Sebor, William S.	21-153
	9 Aug 1821	Havana	Thornbee, Wm.	21-217
	8 Dec 1821	London	Sebor, William S.	21-409
	31 Dec 1821	Elizabeth	Clark, Saml.	21-441
	7 Feb 1822	La Guira	Loosemon, Wm.	22-034
	17 May 1822	Bristol	Smails, Wm.	22-203
	22 May 1822	Havana	Smith, John R.	22-213
	28 May 1822	Amsterdam	Williams, William	22-233
	20 Sep 1822	London	Delano, Thomas	22-474
	5 Oct 1822	Bristol	Smailes, Wm.	22-509
	24 Feb 1823	Havana	Ballard, Calvin	23-049
	17 Jul 1823	Point Petre, Guadaloupe	Gardner, Wm. C.	23-338
	29 Sep 1823	Havre	Smith, John R.	23-504
	20 Mar 1824	Havre	Smith, John R.	24-094
	27 Jul 1824	Havre	Bowden, John	24-409
	12 Aug 1824	New Castle	Davis, David	24-449
	13 Nov 1824	Havre	Smith, John R.	24-658
	29 Dec 1824	Jamaica	Delano, Henry D.	24-741
	9 Jul 1825	Havre	Smith, Jno. R.	25-406
	10 Apr 1826	Havre de Grace	Smith, John R.	26-164
	5 May 1826	Kingston	Allen, Joshua (Delano, Henry D.)	26-229
	11 Aug 1826	Carnavon	Langdon, W. C.	26-472
	4 Sep 1826	Havre	Smith, John R.	26-517
	8 Jun 1827	Liverpool	Smith, John R.	27-330
	11 Sep 1827	Gottenburg	Parker, A. T.	27-619
	6 Oct 1827	St. Thomas	Langdon, W. C.	27-682
	3 Jun 1828	Victoria, Mexico	Whitmore, S.	28-270
	20 Jun 1828	Halifax	Snow, Alvan	28-319
	23 Oct 1828	Tobasco	Matthews, Wm. (Mathews)	28-626
	1 Jul 1829	Ragged Island	Newton, Francis A.	29-118

SHIP	DATE OF ARRIVAL	PORT OF EMBARKATION	CAPTAIN	YEAR AND SHIP NUMBER
ELIZABETH & MARY	23 Nov 1820	Matanzas	Sayward, Jas.	20-329
	20 Mar 1828	Port Glasgow	Walker, Henry	28-076
ELIZABETH MALVINA	6 Dec 1827	Aux Cayes	Dumas, P. C.	27-793
ELLEN	2 Aug 1822	Porto Rico	Stanwood, Robert	22-365
	13 May 1824	Havana	Hall, Peleg	24-211
ELOISE	30 Apr 1824	Aquin	Morton, Saml.	24-187
EMBLEM	18 Jun 1825	Glasgow	Henderson, Wm.	25-356
	25 Oct 1825	Turks Island	Higgins, Richard (Rob.)	25-617
	15 Apr 1826	St. Thomas	Griffin, Oliver	26-179
	14 May 1827	Havana	Higgans, Richard	27-246
EMELIA	21 Sep 1826	Havana	Perkins, Luke	26-546
	10 Dec 1827	St. Croix	Hartwright, Alexr.	27-819
	26 Jun 1828	St. Croix (W. End)	Cartright, Alexr. (Cartwright)	28-331
EMELIE	6 Nov 1824	Bahia	Scott, Andw.	24-640
EMELINE	5 Jul 1823	St. Iago de Cuba	Rawlings, Chs. S.	23-310
	12 Sep 1823	St. Iago de Cuba	Noyes, Samuel, Jr.	23-468
	21 Nov 1823	St. Iago de Cuba	Noyes, Samuel, Jr.	23-606
	6 Jul 1824	Eleuthura	Hills, Ashbel	24-355
	4 Sep 1827	Halifax	Davis, Robt.	27-584
	14 Dec 1827	St. Thomas	Damon, John	27-835
	24 Apr 1828	St. Croix	Muttlesey, W.	28-143
EMERALD	9 Sep 1820	Bermuda	Rabson, Ebn.	20-231
	27 Mar 1822	Havana	Bradford, Marlbro	22-096
EMIGRANT	23 Jul 1822	St. Andrews	Baker, Paul	22-344
	20 Sep 1823	Havana	Barney, W. J.	23-489
	15 May 1826	Port au Prince	Whitaker, Geo.	26-254
	9 Oct 1826	La Guira	Whitaker, Geo.	26-589
	10 Feb 1827	Havanna	Voorhis, Samuel	27-073
EMILE MARIE (see L. Emilie Marie)				
EMILIA	30 Jul 1827	Cadiz	Barstow, Hatherly	27-485
	25 Aug 1828	St. Croix	Cartwright, Alexr. J.	28-469
	19 Jan 1829	St. Croix	Whittelsey, Wm.	29-025
EMILY	2 Jun 1824	Aquin, St. Domingo	Wing, Clifton	24-258
	10 Sep 1824	Aquin	Wing, Clifton	24-529
	12 Jan 1825	Aquin	Wing, Clifton	25-018
	19 Apr 1825	Aquin, St. D.	Wing, C.	25-190
	11 Mar 1826	Port au Prince	Crapo, Ansel	26-102
	25 Aug 1827	London	Godfrey, Nathan	27-557
	28 Aug 1829	Liverpool	Thomson, Wm.	29-259
EMILY COOK	29 Aug 1825	Gibraltar	Cook, Lemuel	25-558
	10 Apr 1826	Kingston, Jamaica	Cook, Lemuel	26-165
EMMA	15 Apr 1822	Matanzes	Fosdick, Wm.	22-128
	24 Jun 1822	Matanzes	Fosdick, W.	22-284
	7 Jul 1824	Buenos Ayres	Fosdick, William	24-357
	12 Aug 1824	Alvarado	Boyer, Joseph	24-446
	13 Oct 1824	St. Petersburgh	Meigner, J. M.	24-593
	17 Nov 1824	Bordeaux	Rathbone, John	24-671
	15 Dec 1824	Alvarado	Boyer, Joseph	24-720
	24 Jun 1825	Matanzas	Noyes, Samuel, Jr.	25-373
	14 Oct 1825	Alvarado	Boyer, Joseph	25-589
	25 Oct 1825	Matanzas	Lewis, Timothy	25-615
	25 Feb 1826	Alvarado	Boyer, Joseph	26-079
	12 May 1826	Pernambuco	Noyes, Saml., Jr.	26-248
	26 May 1827	Havana	Noyes, Saml., Jr.	27-299
EMPRESS	7 Jul 1827	Havana	Bates, Franklin	27-421
	12 Jul 1827	Havana	Clough, Moses P.	27-444
	22 Dec 1828	Martinique & St. Thomas	Clough, Moses P.	28-714
EMULATION	21 Sep 1821	Liverpool	Morris, John	21-291
	12 Mar 1825	Alvarado	Sawyer, Lemuel	25-105
	22 Jun 1825	Porto Cabello	Sawyer, S.	25-371
	17 Dec 1825	Tampico	Sawyer, Lemuel	25-715
EMULOUS	26 Jul 1821	London	Selden, Charles	21-199
	19 Feb 1822	Liverpool	Selden, Charles	22-055
	7 Oct 1822	Lisbon & Bordeaux	Selden, Charles	22-514
	25 May 1825	Monte Video	Selden, Charles	25-295

SHIP	DATE OF ARRIVAL	PORT OF EMBARKATION	CAPTAIN	YEAR AND SHIP NUMBER
	29 Jun 1827	Liverpool	Ingersoll, Jos. B.	27-389
	22 Aug 1828	Liverpool	Ingersoll, J. B.	28-460
ENDEAVOR	4 Jun 1823	Nassau	Kemp, Benja.	23-240
ENDEAVOUR	1 May 1826	Nassau	Miller, John	26-215
ENDYMEON	20 Aug 1822	Laguira	Hathaway, Wm.	22-405
ENDYMION	2 Jul 1821	Angustura	Hathaway, William	21-148
	12 Mar 1822	La Guira	Hathaway, Wm.	22-078
	22 May 1822	La Guira	Hathaway, Wm.	22-215
ENGLAND	23 Jun 1828	New Castle	Sears, R.	28-324
ENTERPRISE	18 Sep 1820	Havre	Lines, S.	20-252
ENTERPRIZE	28 May 1821	Canton	Brevort, Wm.	21-092
	30 Aug 1821	Matanzes	Maxwell, William	21-249
	19 Feb 1822	Cork	Shaw, Andrew	22-056
	24 Mar 1823	St. Thomas	Hawley, Abijah	23-089
	14 Jul 1823	Hamburgh	Black, Philip	23-334
	31 Jul 1824	Rio Pongo	Sutton, Benjm.	24-421
	3 Nov 1824	City of St. Domingo	Stickney, Abraham	24-637
	20 Apr 1825	Tampico	Harmons, B.	25-193
	9 Aug 1825	Matanzas	Western, John R.	25-488
	19 Aug 1825	St. Domingo	Barron, Oliver	25-521
	15 Nov 1825	Matanzas	Marschalk, Gerard S.	25-658
	27 Feb 1826	St. Domingo	Sticking, Albert A.	26-084
	19 Oct 1826	Liverpool	King, Elisha	26-614
	11 May 1827	St. Thomas	Downes, Baxter	27-239
	29 Jun 1827	Halifax	Proctor, Saml.	27-388
	23 Jul 1827	St. Johns, N.B.	Fullerton, James	27-472
	2 Jun 1828	Teneriffe	Downs, Baxter	28-266
	28 Aug 1828	Bordeaux	Briggs, Nathaniel	28-473
	14 Oct 1828	Porto Cabello	Watson, Dunhan	28-611
	18 Jul 1829	Pictou	Shephard, Benj. (Shepard)	29-157
ENVOY	4 Jan 1826	Calcutta	Cabot, Edward	26-011
ERIE	19 Oct 1829	Havre	Funck, James	29-311
ERIN	14 Feb 1820	Dublin	Newcomb, Wm.	20-036
	5 Jul 1820	Dublin	Newcomb, Wm.	20-101
	25 Dec 1820	Dublin	Newcomb, William	20-357A
	26 May 1821	Dublin	Newcomb, William	21-087
	7 Nov 1821	Liverpool	Bunker, Thomas G.	21-361
ESCORT	30 Jun 1828	Elethra	Bell, N.	28-342
ESPERANZA	7 Jul 1823	Holiquin (Cuba)	Ferrier, Jose Manuel	23-318A
ESSEX	20 Oct 1820	Allmina	Donaldson, Benjamin	20-301
	20 May 1823	Jamaica	Rogers, Richard	23-218
	8 Oct 1823	Cayenne	Upton, Samuel	23-531
	23 May 1828	Liverpool	Tomkins, Willm. H.	28-240
	6 Jul 1829	St. Andrews	Nickerson, Jonathan	29-130
	24 Aug 1829	Halifax	Nickerson, Jonathan	29-244
ESTHER	9 May 1825	St. Thomas	Bowen, Sylvester	25-242
ESTRELLA DE LA MAÑANA	26 May 1825	Mayaques (Marques), Porto Rico	Gueriro, Josquito	25-297
ETHELDRED	17 Oct 1822	Bristol	Clements, John	22-532
EUGENE	12 Jul 1822	Cape Haytien	Foster, S.	22-317
	15 Dec 1828	Leghorn	Frazier, John	28-707
	25 Aug 1829	Leghorn	Frazier, John	29-249
EUGENIE	29 Jan 1827	Port au Prince	Jolineau, Frs.	27-045
	20 Aug 1827	Havre	Talineau, F.	27-537
	2 Oct 1829	St. Iago de Cuba	Sherman, Nathl.	29-276
EUNICE	8 Jan 1825	New Castle	Bond, Wm.	25-010
	15 May 1827	Marseilles	Wood, Elihu, Jr.	27-251
	13 Dec 1827	Glasgow	Briggs, Silvanus	27-831
	17 Jul 1828	La Guira	Stevenson, Wm.	28-380
	12 Mar 1829	Goaniver	Briggs, S.	29-085
EUNICE & WEALTHY	24 Jan 1829	St. Pierres, Martinique	Lawry, Isaac	29-037
EUNORE FRANCIS	18 Sep 1820	Java	Greig, Jno.	20-253
EUPHRATES	25 Mar 1820	Liverpool	Stoddard, William	20-080
	8 Aug 1820	Liverpool	Stoddard, William	20-167
	26 Jun 1821	Liverpool, England	Stoddard, William	21-135
	8 Nov 1821	Liverpool	Stoddard, William	21-363

SHIP	DATE OF ARRIVAL	PORT OF EMBARKATION	CAPTAIN	YEAR AND SHIP NUMBER
	3 Apr 1822	Liverpool	Stoddard, William	22-103
	15 Jul 1822	Liverpool	Stoddard, Wm.	22-323
	12 May 1823	Liverpool	Sprague, Benjamin	23-183
	2 Sep 1823	Liverpool	Sprague, Benjamin	23-438
	12 Mar 1824	Liverpool	Sprague, Benjamin	24-075
	25 Jun 1824	Liverpool	Sprague, Benjn.	24-327
	15 Nov 1824	Liverpool	Sprague, Benjamin	24-662
	9 Apr 1825	Liverpool	Sprague, B.	25-156
	23 Jun 1826	Carnarvon	Smith, John P.	26-359
	10 Apr 1827	Liverpool	Smith, John P.	27-168
	18 Aug 1827	Liverpool	Smith, John P.	27-528
EUROPA	20 Apr 1825	London	Anthony, C., Jr.	25-196
	27 Dec 1827	Hamburg	Davis, Clark	27-857
	6 Oct 1828	Hamburg	Tapka, Jacob Detleff	28-589
	12 Oct 1829	Hamburg	Trepka, Jacob Dettleff	29-296
EVELINA	31 May 1825	Havana	Stephenson, Stephen	25-313
	10 Nov 1825	Liverpool	Knight, John M.	25-651
EVERGREEN	28 Jul 1820	Liverpool	RathBone, John	20-154
EXCEL	26 Apr 1827	St. Croix	Bell, Thomas	27-197
	21 Apr 1828	St. Thomas	Hilliker, Edward	28-139
EXCHANGE	16 Feb 1822	St. Thomas	White, Asa	22-046
	25 Feb 1822	Leghorn	Jenkins, P. T.	22-061
	29 Apr 1822	St. Thomas	White, Asa	22-159
	19 Aug 1822	St. Thomas	Davis, John F.	22-401
	18 Nov 1822	Liverpool	Brown, William	22-574
	4 Jan 1823	St. Thomas	Davis, John F.	23-004
	11 Jul 1823	Liverpool	Arnold, Jared	23-328
	20 Nov 1823	St. Bartholomews	Davis, John F.	23-604
	1 May 1824	Maracaybo	Scribner, Elijah P.	24-191
	26 Jul 1824	Maracaybo	Scribner, Elijah P.	24-403
	11 Oct 1824	Maracaybo	Scribner, Elijah P.	24-587
	31 Jan 1825	Maracaibo	Scribner, Elijah P.	25-041
	4 May 1826	Maricabos	Scribner, Elijah P.	26-227
	10 Aug 1826	Havre	Barstow, Benjamin	26-471
	25 Sep 1826	Maracaibo	Scribner, Elijah P.	26-555
	13 Mar 1827	Maracaibo	Scribner, Elijah P.	27-121
	19 Sep 1827	Liverpool	Barstow, Benj.	27-642
	28 Aug 1828	Amsterdam	Foster, Freeman, Jr.	28-475
	5 Oct 1829	Liverpool	Foster, Freeman, Jr.	29-282
EXERTION	14 Dec 1822	St. Andrews	Hamar, Jonathan	22-605
	26 Jul 1824	Porto Plate	Homer, Jonathan	24-393
	6 Sep 1828	St. Thomas	Chandler, Enos	28-508
	9 Oct 1828	Pictou	Hamer, Jonathan	28-602
	3 Dec 1828	Pictou, N.S.	Chandler, Enos	28-693
	17 Jul 1829	Bristol	Hopkins, Seth	29-155
EXPEDITION	19 May 1828	Newcastle (New Castle) and Aberdeen	Milne, Peter	28-232
EXPLOIT	18 Jun 1827	Havana	Blanchard, Silvanus, Jr.	27-359
	3 Nov 1827	Havana	Blanchard, Sylvanus	27-746
	3 Jan 1828	Havana	Blanchard, Sylvanus	28-002
	19 Apr 1828	Ponce	Taylor, Paul	28-136
EXPRESS	25 Sep 1827	St. Eustatia	Sadler, Henry	27-660
EYDER	7 Aug 1826	Port Glasgow	Merrill, Benjamin	26-459
FABIUS	9 Jul 1824	Cadiz	Toole, Saml. E.	24-362
	19 Mar 1825	Havana	Forbes, Cleavd. A.	25-121
	3 Jun 1825	Havana	Forbes, Cleavd. A.	25-315
	24 Oct 1825	Cadir	Forbes, Cleaveland A.	25-608
	7 Dec 1825	Havana	Forbes, Cleavd. A.	25-697
	2 Oct 1826	Havana	Forbes, Cleaveland A.	26-580
	30 Aug 1827	Havana	Forbes, Cleavd. A.	27-567
	4 Jun 1828	Belfast	Thompson, W. C. (Thomson)	28-278
	22 Sep 1828	Belfast	Thompson, Wm. C.	28-550
	18 Mar 1829	Belfast	Thompson, Wm. C.	29-102
	31 Jul 1829	Belfast	Britton, Alexander	29-180
	25 Aug 1829	Cadiz	Barstow, H.	29-250

SHIP	DATE OF ARRIVAL	PORT OF EMBARKATION	CAPTAIN	YEAR AND SHIP NUMBER
FACTOR	10 May 1821	St. Thomas	Knight, Isaac	21-056
	28 Sep 1822	Havana	Gray, Wm.	22-491
	1 Sep 1823	Havre	Gray, Wm.	23-431
	2 Apr 1824	Trinadad	Hubbs, William	24-127
	27 Mar 1827	London	Floyd, Hugh	27-149
	9 Mar 1829	Malaga	Floyd, Hugh	29-075
	8 Jul 1829	St. Johns	Corry, E. M.	29-140
FAIR AMERICAN	24 Jul 1821	St. Iago	Center, A. K.	21-190
	24 Dec 1821	Havana	Dugan, Edward W.	21-433
	5 Apr 1822	Havana	Dugan, Edward W.	22-109
	25 Jul 1822	Jacqumel/Jacmel	Manshaem, John	22-348
	16 Oct 1822	Havana	Mansham, John	22-529
	6 Feb 1823	Havana	Manshaem, John	23-026
	7 Feb 1825	St. Bartholomews	Parrish, James	25-054
	9 May 1825	Havana	Loring, Solomon	25-241
	26 Jul 1825	St. Barts	Parish, Jas.	25-451
FAIR PLAY	22 May 1821	Aux Cayes	Kimball, John	21-080
	5 Nov 1821	Aux Cayes	Kimball, John	21-358
	29 Apr 1822	Aux Cayes	Kimball, John	22-160
	22 Feb 1823	Aux Cayes	Kimball, John	23-046
	5 Jun 1823	Aux Cayes	Kimball, John	23-241
	9 Sep 1823	Aux Cayes	Kimball, John	23-458
	16 Dec 1823	Aux Cayes	Kimball, John	23-640
	8 Jun 1824	Aux Cayes	Kimball, John	24-284
FAIR TRADER	25 Jul 1820	St. George Bermuda	Higgins, David	20-150
FAIRY	8 Aug 1821	Londonderry	Allen, James, Jr.	21-213
	18 Feb 1825	Liverpool	Brewis, William	25-071
FALCON	12 Oct 1822	Bermuda	Post, George	22-523
	10 Sep 1823	Antwerp	Eames, Samuel	23-459
	19 Sep 1823	Turks Island	Morrill, Benjm.	23-485
	1 May 1824	St. Pierre Martinico	Morill, Benjamin	24-188
	11 Oct 1824	Western Coast of Africa	Johnston, George	24-585
	4 Jun 1825	Barbadoes	Pierce, Joseph	25-319
	4 May 1826	Aux Cayes	Kilbey, Thomas	26-228
	16 Aug 1826	Aux Cayes	Kelby, Thomas	26-484
	21 Oct 1826	Amsterdam	Barrow, John	26-620
	1 Jun 1827	Smyrna	Somes, Isaac	27-314
	11 Jun 1827	Amsterdam	Barrow, John	27-342
	28 Aug 1828	Amsterdam	Barron, John	28-476
FALRON (see Falcon)				
FAME	20 Feb 1822	St. Thomas	Clarke, Henry	22-057
	26 Jul 1822	Havana	Adams, Thos. L.	22-352
	21 Aug 1822	Curacoa	Boss, P. J.	22-407
	3 Mar 1823	Curacoa	Boss, P. T.	23-056
	3 Sep 1824	St. Croix	Totten, Gilbert	24-509
	22 Mar 1826	Guasco	Brown, Job	26-124
	15 Nov 1826	Liverpool	Lewis, Stiles	26-665
	9 Dec 1826	Liverpool	Holmes, Saml.	26-714
	9 Feb 1827	Maricaibo	Gilbert, Jacob	27-069
	26 May 1828	Rye	Crowhurst, James	28-250
	3 Jun 1828	Barmouth & Polhely	Barrow, H.	28-271
FANCY	1 Apr 1824	La Guira	Skinner, Joseph	24-126
	28 Apr 1824	Port au Prince	Baker, John	24-174
	28 Apr 1825	Alvarado	Skinner, Jos.	25-213
	1 Oct 1825	Aux Cayes	Miner, David	25-562
FANNY	14 Mar 1820	Port au Prince	Davis, Nathaniel	20-058
	20 Mar 1820	Havana	Griffith, Stephen	20-072
	23 Apr 1822	Curacoa	Baker, John	22-146
	24 Oct 1822	Curacoa	Baker, John	22-541
	8 May 1824	Antigua	Lubeck, Frederick	24-205
	31 Mar 1825	Curacoa	Baker, John	25-147
	15 Aug 1826	Maracaibo	Davis, Moses	26-483
	18 Dec 1826	Maracaibo	Davis, Moses	26-728
	17 Sep 1827	Jacmel	Reeves, Thomas	27-637
FARMER	15 Nov 1823	Dublin	Collins, John	23-595
	3 May 1824	Belfast	Collins, John	24-192
	11 Sep 1824	Lisbon	Collins, John	24-533
	16 Feb 1825	Havana	Newcomb, R.	25-068

SHIP	DATE OF ARRIVAL	PORT OF EMBARKATION	CAPTAIN	YEAR AND SHIP NUMBER
	4 Aug 1825	Liverpool	Newcomb, Reuben	25-476
	11 Feb 1826	Manzanella	Wilson, Charles	26-058
FARMERS FANCY	7 Mar 1823	Marseilles	Groves, Charles	23-058
FAVORITE	13 Jun 1821	Carnavon	Fanning, Thomas	21-112
	10 Dec 1822	Liverpool	Gardner, Henry	22-597
	12 May 1823	Greenock	Bearns, Henry	23-184
	9 Oct 1823	Belize, Honduras	Dyer, Ebenezer	23-536
	27 Dec 1825	Rio Grande	Pinel, Philip P.	25-733
FAVOURITE (see Favorite)				
	2 Sep 1822	Liverpool	Beavis, Henry	22-442
	27 Jun 1823	Havre	Bunker, Reuben P.	23-292
	18 Aug 1823	Havana	Lefavour, Peter	23-406
	8 Oct 1823	Belfast	Bearns, Henry	23-532
	25 Mar 1824	Belize, Honduras	Dyer, Ebenezer, Jr.	24-110
FELECITA	11 Apr 1828	Palermo	Sorrello, V.	28-121
FELINA (see Selina)				
FELIX	10 Sep 1824	Havana, Cuba	Ross, James	24-530
FENELON	15 Dec 1823	Barbcoa	Lee, Larkin, S.	23-638
FENWICK	16 Aug 1826	Newcastle	Huntington, George	26-487
FIDELITY	16 Oct 1820	Bristol	Lilburn, William	20-295
FIFESHIRE	25 Sep 1827	Newcastle upon Tyne	Wilson, John F.	27-663
FINCHEL	3 Dec 1821	Liverpool	Webster, James	21-390
FIVE BROTHERS	9 Jul 1822	St. Andrews	Stanley, Sans.	22-311
FLIGHT	9 Jul 1825	Jamaica	Harvey, L.	25-407
	2 Nov 1825	Alvarada	Storer, Isaac	25-631
	12 Dec 1825	Jamaica	Harvey, Lemuel	25-708
	23 Sep 1826	St. Thomas	Prentiss, Lodowictz	26-550
	1 Oct 1829	Porto Alegre	Ashford, John	29-271
FLORA	3 May 1825	Liverpool	Blair, Hugh	25-234
FLORENZO	29 Jun 1826	Greenock	Glover, Russell E.	26-368
	20 Mar 1827	London	Marsden, George	27-133
	23 Aug 1827	St. Ubes	Marsden, George	27-546
FLORIAN	28 Sep 1824	Havre	Packard, Henry	24-557
FLORIDA	11 May 1822	Liverpool	Matlack, White	22-187
	2 Sep 1822	Liverpool	Matlack, W.	22-443
	13 Feb 1823	Bristol	Brown, Jesse	23-028
	28 Apr 1823	Liverpool	Matlack, White	23-156
	18 Aug 1823	Trinadad in Cuba	Woodbury, Thomas	23-407
	1 Sep 1823	Liverpool	Matlack, White	23-432
	10 Dec 1823	Liverpool, Engld.	Wilson, James L.	23-631
	25 Mar 1824	Trinadad in Cuba	Woodbury, Thomas	24-111
	3 Jun 1824	Bermuda	Mathews, Jno.	24-263
	7 Feb 1825	Liverpool	Tinkham, Joseph	25-052
	25 Apr 1825	Bermuda	Mathews, John	25-207
	17 May 1825	Liverpool	Tinkham, Joseph	25-261
	28 Jun 1825	Bermuda	Mathews, Jno.	25-381
	23 Aug 1825	Rio De Janeiro	Price, Simeon	25-538
	27 Aug 1825	St. Georges, Bermuda	Mathews, John	25-551
	3 Jan 1826	Lisbon	Rowland, Peter	26-003
	13 Feb 1826	Liverpool	Tinkham, Joseph	26-061
	22 May 1826	Liverpool	Tinkham, Joseph	26-268
	30 Jun 1826	Xibara	Driggs, B.	26-371
	24 Jul 1826	Barbadoes	Kellogg, David	26-425
	26 Sep 1826	Liverpool	Tinkham, Joseph	26-557
	30 Oct 1826	Xibara	Brown, William S.	26-636
	8 Nov 1826	Gothenburg	Delano, Joseph C.	26-650
	13 Jan 1827	Liverpool	Tinkham, Joseph	27-027
	16 May 1827	Liverpool	Tinkham, Joseph	27-254
	1 Jun 1827	Rio De Janeiro	Howland, William	27-315
	14 Sep 1827	Liverpool	Tinkham, Joseph	27-631
	2 Jun 1828	Liverpool	Tinkham, Joseph	28-263
	2 Oct 1828	Hamburg	Tyler, Warren	28-573
	2 Oct 1828	Liverpool	Tinkham, Joseph	28-576
	1 Dec 1828	Cadiz	Tripp, Leml. C.	28-686
	11 Mar 1829	Liverpool	Tinkham, Joseph	29-084
	14 Oct 1829	Liverpool	Tinkham, Joseph	29-303

SHIP	DATE OF ARRIVAL	PORT OF EMBARKATION	CAPTAIN	YEAR AND SHIP NUMBER
FLOS	7 Apr 1826	Vera Cruz	parsons, James	26-160
FLOYD	31 May 1824	St. Croix	Perkins, Joseph	24-251
FLY	9 Apr 1823	Vera Cruz	Boyer, Joseph	23-114
	22 Oct 1823	Vera Cruz	Huntress, Ivory	23-556
	17 Jan 1824	Alvarado	Van Dine, Henry	24-020
	12 Apr 1824	Alvarado	Van Dine, Henry	24-137
	28 Jun 1824	Alvarado	Van Dine, Henry	24-339
FONTINE	4 Oct 1824	Kingston, Jamaica	Betts, Wm. G.	24-567
FOREST	15 Dec 1827	The Port of Omoa	Carlaw, Wm. B.	27-836
FORNAX	31 Oct 1828	St. Thomas	Nye, Thomas, Jr.	28-644
	14 Mar 1829	Port au Platt	Dodge, John	29-093
FORREST	16 May 1821	City of St. Domingo	Blackiston, John	21-066
FORTUNA	11 Oct 1827	Turks Island	Dinzey, Joseph	27-694
	13 Nov 1827	Port au Prince	Pearson, John	27-759
FORTUNE	23 Nov 1821	Trinidad in Cuba	Clark, Wm. S.	21-379
	31 Jul 1824	Antwerp	Dursez, Jno.	24-420
	28 Jul 1825	Malta & Marsala	Jenney, J.	25-460
FOSTER	12 Dec 1821	Gottenburg	Moran, Nicholas	21-418
	28 Aug 1822	London	Moran, Nicholas	22-429
	23 Mar 1829	Hull	Bennett, Robert	29-109
FOUR BROTHERS	28 Jun 1825	St. Salvador, Bahia	Dixon, William P.	25-383
FOUR SISTERS	11 Aug 1823	St. Andrews	Spurling, Thomas	23-394
	25 Sep 1823	St. Andrews	Spurling, Thomas	23-498
FOUR SONS	31 May 1823	St. Croix	Leavitt, Alexander	23-235
	23 Mar 1825	Samana, Hayti	Leavitt, Alexander	25-136
	4 Jun 1827	St. Johns, P.R. (N.B.)	Deming, Henry.	27-316
	1 Sep 1827	St. Thomas	Deming, Henry	27-571
	8 Dec 1827	St. Thomas	Deming, Henry	27-817
	31 May 1828	St. Thomas	Humphreys, Jabez	28-259
	30 Jul 1829	Trinidad de Cuba	Gillet, John	29-178
FOURTH OF JULY	19 Oct 1824	Bahamas	Judson, Philo G.	24-616
	13 Jul 1825	Elethura	Glander, John H.	25-418
FOX	5 Sep 1821	Bahamas	Wheeler, Enoch	21-260
	21 Dec 1821	Port au Prince	Wheeler, Enoch	21-425
	14 Sep 1822	St. Bartholomew	Moody, J.	22-465
	9 Mar 1829	Havana	Stratton, Samuel	29-073
FRANCE	29 Nov 1827	Havre	Funck, James	27-772
	5 Dec 1827	Vera Cruz	Spear, James	27-792
	14 Mar 1828	Havre	Funck, James	28-059
	26 Jun 1828	Havre	Funck, —	28-333
	6 Oct 1828	Havre	Funck, James	28-583
	6 Feb 1829	Havre	Funck, James	29-050
	28 Mar 1829	Havre de Grass	Funck, James	29-113
FRANCES	17 Aug 1820	Greenock	Forman, Jacob	20-187
	17 Aug 1820	Greenock	Forman, Jacob	20-187
	16 Aug 1822	Rio Janeiro	Boyer, Joseph	22-394
	6 Jan 1824	Havana	Wolfe, Wm.	24-007
	4 Jun 1825	Jamaica	Thomson, Robert	25-316
	15 Jun 1825	Tampico	Russell, J. G.	25-344
	17 Dec 1825	Mexico	Russell, J. G.	25-714
	19 Jun 1826	Tampico	Russell, J. G.	26-344
	7 Aug 1826	Havana	Doughty, Joseph	26-462
	27 Dec 1826	Havana	Doughty, Joseph	26-738
	21 Mar 1827	Havana	Doughty, Joseph	27-135
	23 Mar 1827	Vera Cruz	Spear, James	27-139
	22 May 1827	Havana	Doughty, Joseph	27-288
	26 May 1827	Bristol	Gregory, John	27-301
	21 Jul 1827	Havana	Doughty, Joseph	27-465
	28 Jan 1828	Havana	Doughty, Joseph	28-025
	6 Feb 1829	Cadiz	Spear, James	29-049
	19 Feb 1829	Buenos Ayres	Doughty, Joseph	29-066
FRANCES ANN	27 Aug 1821	Cadiz	Geteman, William	21-240
FRANCES AUGUSTA	19 Aug 1825	Bordeaux	McMannus, Richd.	25-522
FRANCES HENRIETTA	19 Feb 1823	Liverpool	Dickinson, Jeremiah J.	23-037
	9 Dec 1823	London	Dickinson, Jeremiah J.	23-630
	31 May 1824	London	Dickinson, Jeremiah J.	24-249

SHIP	DATE OF ARRIVAL	PORT OF EMBARKATION	CAPTAIN	YEAR AND SHIP NUMBER
	25 Oct 1824	London	Dickinson, Jeremiah J.	24-623
	18 Apr 1825	Belfast	Menjes, Jacob	25-186
	25 Aug 1825	Havre	White, Carleton	25-548
	3 Apr 1826	London	White, Carleton	26-141
	17 Sep 1827	Liverpool	White, C.	27-083
	30 Jun 1827	Liverpool	White, Charleton	27-399
FRANCES JARVIS	11 May 1822	Aux Cayes	Sheed, Abraham A.	22-188
FRANCES MILLER	9 Aug 1824	Turks Island	Berrey, Benjamin, Jr.	24-438
	1 May 1826	Gottenburg	Card, George	26-213
	24 May 1827	St. Iago De Cuba	Adams, Richard	27-295
	27 Jul 1827	St. Johns, N.B.	Adams, Richard	27-483
FRANCIS	17 May 1824	Nassau N. P.	Hall, Samuel	24-217
	16 Sep 1824	Havana	Wolfe, Wm.	24-536
	11 Apr 1825	Barbadoes	Robinson, Wm.	25-164
	4 May 1826	Bremen	Russell, Silvanus	26-226
	12 Jun 1826	Antwerp	Robbinson, William	26-325
	6 Sep 1827	Belfast	Laurence, Benj.	27-595
FRANCIS & HENRIETTA	11 Jul 1823	Liverpool	Dickinson, Jeremiah J.	23-329
FRANCIS HENRIETTA	8 Apr 1822	Rotterdam	Dickinson, Jeremiah J.	22-114
FRANCIS JARVIS	16 Feb 1822	Aux Cayes	Sheed, Abraham A.	22-047
	17 Oct 1822	Port au Prince	Stinman, John	22-533
	10 Jan 1825	Balise/Honduras	Skidmore, S.	25-015
	9 May 1825	Porto Rico	Midmore, S.	25-243
	11 Aug 1825	Porto Rico	Ellis, Barthw.	25-495
	30 Aug 1826	Porto Rico	Ellis, Barthw.	26-511
FRANCIS MILLER	22 May 1822	St. Johns, N.B.	Henderson, Dunbar	22-216
FRANCOIS I	8 Aug 1829	Havre	Skiddy, William	29-205
FRANÇOIS I	19 Nov 1828	Havre	Skiddy, William	28-669
FRANKLIN	3 Jul 1820	Hamburg	Holmes, Bartlett	20-097
	27 Aug 1822	Carthagina	Gorsuch, Rob.	22-427
	2 Feb 1824	Tampico	Meaney, Corns.	24-025
	10 Jan 1825	Leghorn	Delano, Jos. C.	25-014
	31 Jan 1825	Jacqumel	Roberts, David	25-044
	3 Feb 1825	Sumatra	Welsh, John	25-049
	28 Feb 1825	Liverpool	Daine, George	25-082
	24 May 1825	St. Andrews	Pilsbury, Moses	25-291
	26 May 1825	St. Johns (Spanish Maine)	Weeks, Ansel	25-299
	27 May 1825	Carthagena	Parish, Lewis	25-300
	28 Jun 1825	Carnarvon	Howland, Abraham	25-384
	15 Apr 1826	Greenock	Drew, Joshua	26-180
	20 Apr 1826	Sumatra	Hale, Horace	26-194
	18 May 1827	Canton	Tillinghast, Jos. R.	27-267
	8 Jun 1827	Bremen	Klockgeler, G.	27-334
	22 Jun 1827	Liverpool	Taylor, Robt. L.	27-369
	14 Jul 1827	Havana	Drinkwater, Nicholas	27-449
	23 Jul 1827	St. Croix	Norton, Robert	27-469
	13 Aug 1827	St. Johns, N.B.	Doane, Seth	27-512
	18 Aug 1827	Bremen	Howland, Abm. H.	27-527
	11 Oct 1827	Bremen	Klockgeter, G.	27-697
	3 Dec 1827	Liverpool	Taylor, Robt. L.	27-784
	14 Jan 1828	Bremen	Howland, Abm. H.	28-016
	6 May 1828	Antwerp	Treadwell, Chas.	28-192
	20 May 1828	Bremen	Klockgeter, Gerol	28-235
	7 Jul 1828	Liverpool	Taylor, R. L.	28-361
	23 Sep 1828	Bremen	Klockgeter, G.	28-561
	19 Nov 1828	Liverpool	Taylor, Robt. L.	28-666
FREAK	9 Jun 1828	Hull	Bouch, J.	28-287
	14 oct 1828	Hull	Bouch, James	28-612
FREAKE (see Freak)				
	25 Jun 1827	Hull	Taylor, Luke	27-374
	11 Dec 1827	Hull	Taylor, Luke	27-828
	25 Aug 1829	Hull	Bouch, James	29-252

SHIP	DATE OF ARRIVAL	PORT OF EMBARKATION	CAPTAIN	YEAR AND SHIP NUMBER
FREDEN	24 Oct 1820	Gothenburg	Hagberg, Johan	20-304
FREDERICK	25 Jan 1820	St. Thomas	Chant, Samuel	20-017
	18 Feb 1822	Havre	Davis, John S.	22-051
	27 Jan 1823	Pernambuca	Hills, A.	23-017
	28 Jul 1823	Pernambuco	Stillman, Francis	23-355
	26 Apr 1824	Rio de la Hatch	Smith, Perry	24-168
	5 May 1826	Rio Hache	Gillett, Dudley	26-232
	2 Apr 1828	London	Sargent, Moses H.	28-108
FREE OCEAN	14 Feb 1824	Campeachy & Havana	Bukeep, Barth A.	24-037
	10 May 1826	Trinadad de Cuba	Cruse, N. C.	26-243
FRIENDS	24 Sep 1821	Greenock	Choate, Thomas	21-298
	29 Apr 1822	Greenock	Choate, Thomas	22-161
	28 Sep 1822	Greenock	Choate, Thomas	22-490
	10 May 1823	Greenock	Choate, Thos.	23-179
	25 Sep 1823	Greenock	Choate, Thomas	23-499
	13 Mar 1824	Greenock	Choate, Thomas	24-077
	16 Aug 1824	Greenock	Choate, Thoms.	24-457
	31 Jan 1825	Greenock	Wamock, Jacob A.	25-043
	13 Jun 1825	Greenock	Warnack, Jacob A.	25-336
	21 Oct 1825	Greenock	Wamack, Jacob A.	25-601
	12 May 1826	Greenock	Wamack, Jacob A.	26-247
	7 Jul 1827	Greenock	Wamack, Jacob A.	27-419
	9 Aug 1827	Carnarvon	Lewis, David	27-506
FRIENDS DELIGHT	5 Dec 1825	Bermuda	Kelly, Doane	25-688
FRIENDSHIP	26 Feb 1820	Port Plata	Gladding, N.	20-045
FRIKETON	7 Nov 1823	Gelfe (Sweden)	Molander, O.	23-575
GALATA	23 Jun 1823	Hamburgh	Goldswart, John	23-276
GALATEA	20 Jul 1829	Tampico	Bailey, John	29-160
GALAXY	17 Feb 1824	Havre	Moison, William	24-049
	10 Jun 1824	Demerara	Hunter, Jno. S.	24-287
	9 Sep 1826	Liverpool	Gurrell, John	26-524
	31 Jan 1828	La Rochelle	Swift, Asa H.	28-032
GALLEGO	13 Mar 1829	Fayal (Azores)	Savage, Charles T.	29-091
GAMACRAW	28 Sep 1820	St. Ubes	Bates, Andrew	20-270
GANGES	8 Jul 1820	Liverpool	Tomkins, James	20-111
	23 Oct 1821	Hamburgh	Tomkins, James	21-342
	8 May 1823	Liverpool	Tomkins, James	23-172
	23 Jul 1824	St. Petersburg	Tomkins, James	24-390
	20 Aug 1825	Liverpool	Tompkins, James	25-531
	26 Oct 1826	Liverpool	Mount, F. M.	26-629
	15 Dec 1826	London	Young, John	26-724
	21 Jun 1827	Liverpool	Jaques, Huff B.	27-366
	10 May 1828	Kinsale	McPherson, Samuel W.	28-199
GARONNE	24 Jul 1821	Trieste	Whiting, Edwd.	21-191
GAZETTE	27 Jul 1824	Matanzas	Case, Ebenezer, Jr.	24-404
GEM	16 Jun 1824	Londonderry	Harrod, Benjamin	24-309
	28 Dec 1824	Cork	Almy, Peleg	24-740
	24 Oct 1825	Liverpool	Ferrier, John M.	25-607
	26 Jul 1827	Liverpool	Ferrier, John M.	27-479
GENL. A. JACKSON	15 Jul 1820	St. Thomas	Nicholas, J. B.	20-127
	6 Sep 1820	St. Thomas	Nichols, John B.	20-225
	10 Sep 1821	St. Thomas	Nicholas, John B.	21-264
GENERAL A. JACKSON	9 Apr 1822	St. Thomas	Bedell, William	22-118
GENERAL BREWER	9 Dec 1825	Maranham	Gale, Edward	25-698
GENERAL BROOKS	21 May 1824	St. Iago	Dauset, Saml.	24-223
	3 Nov 1825	St. Iago de Cuba	Dowst, Saml.	25-633
GENL. BROOKS	17 Jul 1825	St. Iago de Cuba	Daust, Jno.	25-425
GENERAL BROWN	17 Oct 1820	Havanna	Isaacs, Isaac	20-298
	24 Nov 1820	St. Thomas	Godfrey, Knowles	20-332
	10 Dec 1823	Cadiz	Skiddy, Wm.	23-632
GENL. BROWN	3 Dec 1821	Rio de Janeiro	Skiddy, William	21-391

SHIP	DATE OF ARRIVAL	PORT OF EMBARKATION	CAPTAIN	YEAR AND SHIP NUMBER
GENERAL COFFIN	9 Mar 1827	St. Johns, N.B.	Johnston, Nicholas	27-111
GENERAL GRAHAM	9 May 1827	Alloa	Craeger, James	27-228
GENERAL HAND	27 aug 1827	Bordeaux	Gatchell, Jno. G.	27-558
GENL. IRDELLE	13 Sep 1828	Point Petre	Osgood, John	28-533
GENERAL JACKSON	31 Oct 1820	Belfast	Barnes, Norman	20-312
	25 Jun 1823	Teneriffe	Vermilye, Thos. B.	23-286
	12 Aug 1824	Curacoa	Sheils, Robert	24-447
	22 May 1826	St. Anns, Jamaica	Avery, Peter L.	26-271
	5 Feb 1827	Santa Martha	Govell, Daniel	27-060
	27 Mar 1827	Para	Budd, John	27-154
	24 Mar 1828	Tampico	Budd, John	28-083
	15 Jan 1829	St. Thomas	Snow, Thomas A.	29-016
	14 Jul 1829	St. Croix	Shaw, Thomas	29-147
GENERAL LA FAYETTE	1 Aug 1829	Xibara, Cuba	Osborn, William	29-186
GENERAL MACOMBE	17 Jul 1827	Point Petre, Guadaloupe	Douglass, Samuel	27-456
GENL. MARIN	25 Jul 1825	Jamaica	Chadwick, S.	25-443
GENERAL MARION	12 Jul 1823	St. Thomas	Allen, Pearce	23-333
	1 Sep 1824	Montego Bay, Jamaica	Chadwick, Samuel	24-502
	10 Dec 1825	Montego Bay, Jamaica	Chadwick, Samuel	25-704
	17 Mar 1826	Montego Bay	Chadwick, Samuel	26-122
	20 Jun 1826	Jamaica	Chadwick, Saml.	26-348
	14 Jul 1828	Halifax	Hawes, Jacob	28-375
	20 Aug 1828	Halifax, N.S.	Bears, Isaac, Jr.	28-448
	6 Oct 1828	Halifax, Nova Scotia	Bears, Isaac, Jur.	28-586
	21 Nov 1828	Halifax	Hawes, Jacob	28-676
	12 Jan 1829	Halifax	Hawes, Jacob	29-014
	18 Jul 1829	St. Thomas	Davis, Wm.	29-156
	20 Jul 1829	Halifax	Hawes, Jacob	29-159
GENL. MARION	9 Jan 1827	Jamaica	Chadwick, Saml.	27-015
	4 Jun 1828	Halifax	Bears, Isaac	28-276
GENERAL PAEZ	17 Aug 1825	Porto Cavello	Revans, Thomas	25-505
	9 Dec 1825	Porto Cabello	Rivans, Thos.	25-700
	14 Apr 1826	Curacoa	Clark, Alexr. B.	26-178
	21 Jun 1826	La Guayra & Curacao	Johnson, Chas. H.	26-357
	21 Jun 1826	Curacoa	Clark, Alexander B.	26-358
	28 Nov 1826	Curacoa	Clark, Alex. B.	26-687
	30 Apr 1827	Curacoa	Clark, A. B.	27-203
	30 Jun 1827	Curacao	Clark, A. B.	27-397
	28 May 1828	Curacoa	Clark, A. B.	28-252
	18 Aug 1828	Rio de la Hach	Clark, A. B.	28-443
	22 Nov 1828	Curacoa	Clark, A. B.	28-677
	3 Aug 1829	Curacao	Clark, A. B.	29-192
GENERAL PIKE	2 Oct 1826	Vera Cruz	Pike, Joel	26-573
GENL. PIKE	15 Jan 1827	Havanna	Pike, Joel	27-030
GENERAL PULMAN	3 Jun 1828	Halifax	Follansbee, Robt.	28-272
GENERAL PUTMAN (see General Putnam)				
GENERAL PUTNAM	20 Jun 1825	Londonderry	Allen, William	25-360
GENERAL PUTNAN (see General Putnam)				
GENERAL SAUBLETTE	14 Apr 1823	La Guira	Lawrence, Chas. K.	23-130
GENERAL SCOTT	7 May 1824	Rio Janeiro	Sayre, M. G.	24-201
GENL. SCOTT	19 Apr 1825	Cuba	Armour, W. P.	25-189
GENERAL STARK	12 Jun 1826	Halifax	Baker, Charles	26-323
GENERAL STARKE	17 Jul 1827	Halifax	Baker, Abner	27-455
GENL. URDANETA	19 Apr 1826	Maracaibo	Ker, Thomas G.	26-190
GENERAL VEDANETA	25 November 1825	Maracaibo	Ker, Thos. G.	25-675
GENL. VICTORIA	7 Apr 1828	Havana	Beekeep, B. A.	28-115

SHIP	DATE OF ARRIVAL	PORT OF EMBARKATION	CAPTAIN	YEAR AND SHIP NUMBER
GENERAL WARD	22 Jun 1821	Havana	Barber, Thomas	21-127
GENERAL WARREN	5 May 1828	Havana	Wilbur, Jeremiah (Wilber)	28-180
	19 Jan 1829	Madeira	Dexter, Allen	29-026
	6 Mar 1829	Tampico	Hendrickson, J. S.	29-072
	8 Jul 1829	Tampico	Hendrickson, J. S.	29-138
GENL. WARREN	10 Jul 1828	Jacmel	Church, J. W.	28-369
GEO. CANNING	5 Jun 1828	Cork	Brigham, Wm.	28-280
	2 Sep 1828	Liverpool	Allyn, Francis	28-497
GEORGE	31 Jul 1820	Halifax	Berry, Benjn.	20-158
	25 Sep 1820	St. Iago	Killogg, Wm.	20-259
	12 Jul 1821	St. Eustatia	Smith, H.	21-172
	10 Mar 1823	Havre de Grass	Harris, Tho.	23-065
	17 Jul 1823	Havana	Knight, James	23-339
	6 Aug 1823	St. Johns, Puerto Rico	Allen, Henry H.	23-382
	23 Sep 1824	Amsterdam	B..., Wm.	24-550
	12 Mar 1825	Porto Rico	Stevens, Stanton	25-109
	25 May 1825	Matanzas	Stone, Gyles P.	25-294
	9 Jul 1825	Marseilles	Lewis, W. B.	25-409
	10 Jul 1826	Frederickstaat, St. Croix	Myrick, Saml.	26-388
	6 Oct 1827	Guadaloupe	Lear, John	27-685
GEORGE CANNING	13 Jun 1826	Bristol	McClelland, James	26-332
	2 May 1828	Liverpool	Allyn, Francis	28-171
	20 Jan 1829	Liverpool	Allyn, Francis	29-028
	26 Aug 1829	Liverpool	Allyn, Francis	29-255
GEORGE CLINTON	10 Oct 1825	Liverpool	Rawson, Edward B.	25-578
	13 Apr 1826	Liverpool	Rawson, Edward B.	26-174
	21 Oct 1826	Liverpool	Rawson, Edward B.	26-621
	27 Aug 1827	Liverpool	Rawson, Edward B.	27-562
	10 Sep 1828	Liverpool	Rawson, Edward B.	28-522
GEORGE HENRY	24 Mar 1823	Turks Island	Thatcher, Jona.	23-091
GEORGE PORTER	23 Sep 1826	Hull	Fitzgerald, Wm.	26-551
GEORGETOWN PACKET	6 Nov 1822	La Guira	Rathbone, John	22-559
	24 Feb 1823	La Guira	Rathbone, John	23-050
	15 Nov 1823	Saguira	Rathbone, John	23-594
	6 May 1824	Pernambuca	Rathbone, John	24-196
	27 Oct 1824	Port au Prince	Smith, S. F.	24-626
	12 Mar 1825	Port au Prince	Smith, S. F.	25-102
GEORGIANA	12 Nov 1822	Malaga	Chamberlain, E.	22-564
	25 Jun 1824	St. Iago de Cuba	Noble, Daniel P.	24-329
GERMANIA	15 Jun 1825	Bremen	Gatjen, Joh. H.	25-348
	29 Aug 1828	Bremen	Homann, J. H.	28-483
GERTRUDE	24 Jul 1820	Halifax	West, Francis	20-144
	8 Aug 1821	Port au Prince	McCurdy, John G.	21-214
	19 May 1826	Porto Cabello	Butler, Easton	26-262
	12 Aug 1826	Porto Cabello	Butler, Easton	26-475
	13 Nov 1826	Porto Cabello	Bunker, Easter	26-659
	6 Mar 1827	Porto Cabello	Butler, Gaster	27-103
	16 May 1827	Porto Cabello	Butler, Easton	27-256
	17 Jul 1827	Porto Cabello	Butler, Easton	27-457
	6 May 1828	Porto Cabello	Butler, Easton	28-189
GERVIS	18 Aug 1823	Maranhain	Valuda, John Gomas	23-408
GIBRALTAR	12 Oct 1829	Havre	Baker, Richard	29-291
GIPSEY	5 Sep 1823	Jamaica	Fogler, Charles	23-451
GLEANER	17 Jan 1820	St. Croix	O'Zuille	20-008
	30 Apr 1821	St. Thomas	O'Tull, John	21-038
	31 Jul 1821	St. Thomas	O'Zuil, John	21-206
	22 Apr 1822	St. Thomas	Saunders, Richard	22-140
	18 Jul 1822	Nevitus	Saunders, Richard	22-335
	24 May 1823	Londonderry	Pease, W. G.	23-225A
	6 Dec 1827	Aux Cayes	Harris, Herman	27-795
	6 Jun 1828	Port au Prince	Leonard, E. W.	28-283
	4 Oct 1828	St. Croix	Learned, Elijah W.	28-581

SHIP	DATE OF ARRIVAL	PORT OF EMBARKATION	CAPTAIN	YEAR AND SHIP NUMBER
GLEANOR (see Gleaner)				
GLENTHORN	12 Aug 1822	Gibraltar	Lewis, Robert	22-391
GLENTHORNE	25 Jul 1821	Buenos Ayres	Lewis, Robert	21-197
GLOBE	14 Jul 1821	Dublin & Belfast	Johnson, Isaac	21-177
	3 Dec 1821	Belfast	Britton, Thomas	21-392
	14 May 1822	New Castle	Hill, Walter, Jr.	22-195
	30 Aug 1828	Havre	Saule, David	28-487
GOLCONDA	14 May 1823	Trinadad	Small, Jonathan	23-200
GOLD HUNTER	24 Oct 1829	Turks Island	Curtis, Christopher S.	29-323
GOLDEN AGE	6 Jul 1821	St. Barts	Greene, Wm. C.	21-156
	19 Dec 1827	Porto Cabello	Nones, J. B.	27-845
GOLDEN GROVE	6 Sep 1820	Antwerp	Thomas, Nathaniel	20-226
GOMER	22 May 1827	Reolhely, Wales	Prichard, Richard	27-286
	21 May 1828	Wales	Prichard, Richard	28-236
GOOD FRIENDS	20 May 1825	Havana	Midlen, Walter	25-280
GOOD HOPE	10 Mar 1828	Matanzas	Budington, Ozias	28-050
GOOD RETURN	12 Apr 1827	Port au Prince	Bliss, Calvin	27-175
GOVENOR LINCOLN	15 Feb 1827		Flin, Jas.	27-078
GOVERNOR CLINTON	3 Jul 1827	Liverpool	Griswold, L. B.	27-409
	17 Oct 1828	Guayaquil	Griswald, L. B.	28-614
	3 Feb 1829	Liverpool	Rawson, Edward B.	29-044
GOV. CLINTON	1 Feb 1827	Gibralter	Hepburn, David	27-051
GOVERNOR FENNER	23 Jul 1829	Liverpool	Martin, Stephen	29-167
GOVERNOR GRISWOLD	6 Jun 1821	Liverpool	Meader, Benjamin	21-104
	18 Jun 1821	Havana	Smith, Perry	21-118
	4 Feb 1822	St. Ubes	Snow, James D.	22-024
	15 Jul 1826	Matanzas	Tourtelott, Abraham	26-406
GOV. GRISWALD	3 Jul 1820	Liverpool	Meador, Benjamin	20-098
GOVERNOR HAWKINS	16 Mar 1826	Messina	Dunton, George	26-121
GOVERNOR LINCOLN	10 Jul 1827	Carthagena	Stocking, Francis	27-433
GOVERNOR TOMPKINS	7 Apr 1823	Havana	Brownell, Major	23-111
	26 Jul 1824	Galway	Mauran, Jno.	24-399
GOVERNOR VON SCHOLLEN	7 Nov 1827	Vera Cruz	Waldden, A.	27-750
GOVERNOR VON SCHOLTEN	29 Jun 1827	Marseilles	Scott, Francis	27-393
GOVR. VON SCHOLTEN	23 Apr 1825	St. Thomas	Scott, F.	25-202
GOWAN	28 Aug 1822	New Castle	Mearns, Daniel	22-430
GRAMPUS	14 Apr 1823	Bordeaux	Bangs, Elkanah, Jr.	23-131
GRAND TURK	10 Jul 1820	Liverpool	O'Hara, John	20-112
	3 Dec 1821	Liverpool	O'Hara, John	21-393
	16 Aug 1822	Cork & St. Ubes	O'Hara, John	22-396
	19 Aug 1823	Liverpool	Taber, John R.	23-411
GRATITUDE	25 Jun 1828	Dundee	Young, John	28-328
	3 Oct 1829	Liverpool	Child, Jno. S.	29-279
GREAT BRITAIN	18 Sep 1826	Havre	French, Francis M.	26-536
	7 May 1827	Liverpool	French, Francis M.	27-220
	5 Sep 1827	Liverpool	French, Francis M.	27-590
	18 Mar 1828	Liverpool	French, Francis M.	28-070
	6 Sep 1828	Liverpool	French, Francis M.	28-507
	16 Mar 1829	Havre	French, Francis M.	29-095
	3 Aug 1829	Havre De Grace	French, Francis M.	29-190
GRECIAN	24 Sep 1828	Liverpool & Londonderry	Blanchard, L.	28-564
GREEK	3 Mar 1825	Havana	Rivera, P. A.	25-086
	17 May 1825	Havana	Rivero, Peter A.	25-264
	3 Aug 1825	Havana	Rivero, P. A.	25-470
	1 Oct 1825	Havana	Child, Saml. S.	25-563
	19 May 1826	Vera Cruz	Rivero, P. A.	26-259
	2 Oct 1826	Vera Cruz	Rivero, P. A.	26-579

SHIP	DATE OF ARRIVAL	PORT OF EMBARKATION	CAPTAIN	YEAR AND SHIP NUMBER
	23 Jan 1828	Halifax, N.S.	Jones, William M.	28-022
	8 Mar 1828	Halifax	Jones, Thos. J.	28-049
GREENHOW	10 Mar 1823	Liverpool	Gray, John	23-066
GREYHOUND	10 Jan 1820	Halifax	Bedson, Thos.	20-004
	20 Mar 1820	Halifax	Bedson, Thomas	20-074
	19 Aug 1820	Halifax	Bedsen, Thomas	20-194
	29 Sep 1820	Halifax	Bedson, Thos.	20-272
	27 Nov 1820	Halifax	Bedson, Thomas	20-336
	31 May 1823	St. Lucia	Glaudon, Ls.	23-236
GULNARD	24 Mar 1825	Liverpool	Lunt, Micajah, Jr.	25-138
GUSTAVA	9 Jul 1827	Norrhoping, Sweden	Pettersson, Falek. J.	27-431
GYPSY (see Gipsey)				
HAITIEN	10 Jun 1822	St. Thomas	Smith, Wm.	22-263
HAL	7 Jun 1824	Jamaica	Patterson, Wm.	24-271
HALCEON (see Halecon)				
HALCYON	18 Apr 1828	para	Foster, R. W.	28-132
	26 Sep 1828	Maranham	Foster, R. W.	28-569
HALECON	12 Feb 1820	Havana	Macy, Seth G.	20-031
HALSEY	16 Sep 1823	Gibraltar	Small, Benjamin	23-478
HAMILTON	21 Nov 1826	Liverpool	Bunker, Thomas	26-674
	19 Mar 1827	Liverpool	Bunker, Thomas G.	27-125
	18 Jul 1827	Liverpool	Bunker, Thomas G.	27-458
	13 Nov 1827	Liverpool	Bunker, Thomas G.	27-760
	28 Apr 1828	Liverpool	Bunker, Thomas G.	28-160
	22 Sep 1828	St. Petersburg	Bunker, Thomas G.	28-552
HAMLET	16 Aug 1820	Liverpool	Dickerson, Isaac	20-184
	4 Aug 1823	Nantz	Price, Peter	23-380A
	31 Jan 1825	Rio De Janeiro	Price, Peter	25-040
	25 Aug 1825	Liverpool	Mix, Edward A.	25-545
HAMMOND	9 Feb 1820	St. Thomas	Gifford, James	20-029
HANFORD	10 Nov 1827	St. Andrews	Pearce, Thomas	27-754
	15 May	St. Johns, N.B.	Pearce, Thos.	28-220
	10 Jun 1828	St. Johns	Pearce, Thomas	28-291
	17 Jul 1828	St. Johns, N.B.	Pearce, Thomas	28-379
	19 Aug 1828	St. Johns, N.B.	Pearce, Thos.	28-447
	18 Sep 1828	St. Johns	Pearce, Thos.	28-541
	17 Oct 1828	St. Johns, N.B.	Pearce, Thos.	28-615
	29 Dec 1828	St. Johns, N.B.	Pearce, Thomas	28-719
	3 Jul 1829	St. Johns, N.B.	Pearce, Thomas	29-125
	3 Aug 1829	St. Johns, N.B.	Pearce, Thomas	29-194
	9 Oct 1829	St. Johns, N.B.	Crowell, Reuben	29-288
HANNA	3 Jun 1828	Guyama	Prentiss, Ludwick (Prenetiss)	28-275
HANNAH	8 Nov 1821	Dublin	Cullen, Jno.	21-364
	2 Feb 1822	St. Thomas	Mason, Rishworth	22-022
	19 Jul 1822	St. Thomas	Mason, Reshworth	22-341
	16 Nov 1822	Teneriffe	Mason, Richworth	22-571
	16 Sep 1823	Dundee	Martin, Alexr.	23-479
	27 Dec 1827	River La Plate	Corner, John B.	27-858
HANNAH & ELIZABETH	13 Jun 1825	La Guira	Russell, Sam	25-332
HANNAH & JANE	20 Jun 1825	Surriname/Surinam	Packer, Jno. R.	25-366
HANNAH & REBECCA	12 Jun 1824	Matanzas	Sherman, Wm. E.	24-302
HANNAH ELIZA	6 Jun 1826	St. Johns, N.B.	Holmes, Henry	26-307
	23 Sep 1826	St. Johns, N.B.	Holmes, Henry	26-549
HANNAH ELIZABETH	19 Mar 1827	Tampico	Reling, Charles	27-130
	14 Sep 1827	Tampico	Reling, Charles	27-632
HANNIBAL	27 May 1822	Liverpool	Watkinson, James	22-231
	4 Oct 1822	Liverpool	Watkinson, James	22-506
	4 Apr 1823	Liverpool	Watkinson, James	23-106
	28 Jul 1823	Liverpool	Watkinson, James	23-356
	17 Dec 1823	Liverpool	Watkinson, James	23-646
	28 Apr 1824	Liverpool	Atkinson, James	24-182
	6 Sep 1824	Liverpool	Watkinson, James	24-516
	12 Oct 1826	Liverpool	Watkinson, James	26-592

SHIP	DATE OF ARRIVAL	PORT OF EMBARKATION	CAPTAIN	YEAR AND SHIP NUMBER
	28 May 1827	Liverpool	Watkinson, James	27-304
	25 Sep 1827	Liverpool	Watkinson, James	27-656
	12 Oct 1829	London	Hebard, F. H.	29-297
HANOVER	12 Oct 1822	London	Adamson, James	22-524
HAPPY RETURN	11 Jul 1820	Bermuda	Wheaton, Enoch	20-117
	23 Jul 1821	Havana	Wheaton, Joseph	21-186
HAPY RETURN (see Happy Return)				
HARMONY	15 Jul 1820	Greenock	Spence, Charles	20-129
	20 Nov 1820	Havana	Brown, Gilbert	20-324
	12 Jul 1821	Swansea	Kennan, Robt.	21-173
	16 Oct 1821	Port au Prince	Thomas, Job B.	21-330
	19 Aug 1822	Turks Island	Lewis, S. J.	22-402
	6 Jan 1823	Bermuda	Pratt, Amasa	23-006
	12 Sep 1823	Port au Prince	Starbuck, George	23-469
HARRIET	11 Jan 1820	Turks Island	Little, Charles	20-006
	3 Sep 1823	Havre	Williams, Erastin	23-442
	16 Mar 1824	Berbice	Purrington, Joshua	24-083
	20 Oct 1824	Hamburg	Williams, Erastus	24-617
	3 Mar 1828	Hamel at Smyrna	Glover, Russell E.	28-039
	2 Jan 1829	Cronstandt	Cook, Charles C.	29-002
HARRIET & LUCY	3 Oct 1823	Orotava	Farnsworthy, William	23-518
HARRIET FRANCES	10 May 1827	St. Johns	Cutts, Hiram	27-234
HARRIET SMITH	18 Oct 1821	St. Thomas	Tafts, Francis	21-334
HARRIOT	1 May 1822	Havana	Rogers, Thos.	22-169
HAVANA PACKET	13 May 1824	St. Croix	Hall, Gilbert	24-212
	27 Jul 1827	Havana	Folger, William H.	27-481
HAXALL	21 Oct 1826	Madeira	Ripley, John	26-617
HAYTIE	2 Jul 1827	Cape Haytien	Badger, Nathaniel	27-402
HAZARD	27 Aug 1821	Halifax	Higgins, Zachus	21-241
	17 Jul 1822	St. Andrews	Higgins, Zacheus	22-332
	29 Jul 1829	Leghorn	Trott, Mitchell L.	29-175
HEBE	30 Apr 1821	St. Michaels	Pratt, John V.	21-039
	18 Feb 1825	La Guira	Brownell, Thomas	25-075
	14 Jun 1825	La Guira	Gorton, Charles	25-339
	27 Jan 1827	Honduras	Sutherland, N. S.	27-044
HECTOR	8 Jan 1820	Liverpool	Gillender, James	20-003
	11 Sep 1820	Liverpool	Gillinder, James	20-236
	30 Dec 1820	Liverpool	Bennett, Thomas	20-362
	11 May 1821	Liverpool	Gillender, James	21-061
	16 May 1821	Dundee	Webster, James	21-067
	20 Sep 1821	Liverpool	Gillender, James	21-287
	18 Jul 1822	Dundee (London)	Webster, James	22-336
	11 Oct 1822	Liverpool	Gillender, James	22-520
	29 Nov 1823	Liverpool	Gillender, James	23-615
	11 Oct 1824	Liverpool	Gillender, James	24-586
	18 Apr 1825	Greenock	Ogden, D. S.	25-185
	17 Aug 1825	Greenock	Delano, Joseph C.	25-509
HELECON	3 Dec 1821	Turks Island	Johnson, John	21-394
HELEN	7 Feb 1820	St. Barts via St. Thomas	Gold, William	20-028
	5 Jul 1820	Newry	Patterson, Peter	20-102
	27 Jun 1821	Sligo	Patterson, Peter	21-138
	8 Feb 1822	Belfast (Ireland)	Patterson, Peter	22-036
	13 May 1822	Dundee	Erskine, Thomas	22-190
	20 Jan 1825	Gibraltar	Patterson, Peter	25-029
	24 Apr 1827	Chagres	Howes, Jeremiah	27-194
	17 Dec 1827	Liverpool	Cobb, Nathan	27-838
	3 May 1828	Havre	Cobb, Nathan	28-174
	5 Sep 1828	Havre	Cobb, N.	28-503
	16 Mar 1829	Liverpool	Robinson, George W.	29-098
	4 Aug 1829	London	Robinson, George W.	29-199
HELEN MAR	29 Jun 1827	Havre	Harrison, Thos.	27-395
HELICON	26 Jul 1822	Matanges	Dayton, Rob. W.	22-350
	3 Aug 1826	Liverpool	Barnard, Benjamin	26-447
HELSPERUS (see Hesperus)				

SHIP	DATE OF ARRIVAL	PORT OF EMBARKATION	CAPTAIN	YEAR AND SHIP NUMBER
HENRI IV	7 May 1827	Havre	Skiddy, William	27-216
	14 Sep 1827	Havre	Skiddy, William	27-628
	17 May 1828	Havre	Skiddy, William	28-226
	2 Oct 1828	Havre	Pell, John B.	28-578
	3 Feb 1829	Havre	Pell, Jno. B.	29-045
	14 Oct 1829	Havre	Pell, Jno. B.	29-304
HENRIETTA	13 Nov 1822	Curacoa	Akkerman, P. P.	22-567
	27 Mar 1824	Bordeaux & St. Ubes	Lobbe, Jacob	24-113
	3 Jun 1825	St. John, N.B.	Ferguson, John	25-314
	7 Jul 1825	St. John, N.B.	Ferguson	25-403
	17 Aug 1825	St. Johns, N.B.	Merry, Thomas	25-504
	19 Oct 1825	St. Johns, N.B.	Merry, Thomas	25-597
	26 Nov 1825	St. Johns, N.B.	Pundell, David	25-676
	18 Aug 1829	St. Barts	Walker, John	29-220
HENRY	27 Mar 1820	Gibralter	Devall, Stephen	20-082
	10 Oct 1820	Gaudaloupe	Graves, Richard	20-290
	24 Apr 1821	St. Bartholomews	Davis, Andrew	21-031
	21 Dec 1822	St. Bartholomew	Davis, Andrew	22-610
	11 Apr 1823	St. Bartholomews	Davis, Andrew	23-125
	26 May 1823	St. Bartholomews	Henderson, Wm.	23-226
	8 Jun 1824	Bordeaux	Kemp, Aaron	24-283
	11 Oct 1824	Havre	Kemp, Jason (A.)	24-582
	10 Feb 1825	Havre De Grace	Kemp, Aaron	25-060
	19 Jun 1825	Havre de Grace	Kemp, Aaron	25-358
	11 Oct 1825	Havre	Kemp, Aaron	25-580
	15 Feb 1826	Havre De Grace	Kemp, Aaron	26-067
	9 Jun 1826	Havre	Kemp, Aaron	26-315
	30 Aug 1826	St. Croix	Weeks, Henry	26-510
	18 Oct 1826	Havre	Kemp, Aaron	26-605
	16 May 1827	Bordeaux	Kemp, Aaron	27-259
	17 Sep 1827	St. Croix	Baker, Gorham	27-636
	13 Oct 1827	Hull	Dockray, Jas. R.	27-703
	17 May 1828	Havre	Barker, George	28-224
	29 May 1828	Mayaguez	Davis, Hezekiah	28-253
	3 Jun 1828	Rio Grande	Roberts, N.	28-274
	24 Oct 1828	London	More, —	28-631
	24 Nov 1828	Maracaybo	Howland, W. S.	28-679
HENRY CLAY	25 Apr 1822	Greenock	Fosdick, P. G.	22-149
HENRY HILL	5 Oct 1824	Antwerp	Post, Joseph	24-572
HENRY IV	5 Feb 1827	Havre de Grace	Skiddy, William	27-057
HENRY JOHNSON	29 Apr 1825	Jamaica	Mallett, S.	25-214
HENRY KNEEDLAND	7 Aug 1826	Liverpool	Weeks, Joseph	26-466
HENRY KNEELAND	27 Jul 1825	Liverpool	Weeks, Joseph	25-457
	25 Sep 1827	Liverpool	Barstow, Wm. C.	27-659
	7 Jun 1828	Londonderry	Coffin, —	28-286
	5 Nov 1828	Liverpool	Coffin, Hazad.	28-652
HERALD	6 Feb 1824	St. Thomas	Gibson, James, Jr.	24-029
	21 May 1824	Havana	Prince, Joel	24-221
	7 Jun 1824	Liverpool	Forman, Jacob	24-276
	21 Sep 1824	Havana	Prince, Joel	24-546
	4 Oct 1824	Havre de Grace	Forman, Jacob	24-568
	14 Mar 1825	Havana	Prince, Joel	25-110
	7 Jul 1825	Lpool	Forman, Jacob	25-404
	29 Oct 1825	Liverpool	Myer, John	25-626
	13 Mar 1826	Sumatra	Porter, Jeremiah	26-106
	24 May 1826	Carnarvon	Crowell, Nathan	26-280
	25 Nov 1826	Havana	Jennings, Soleman	26-677
	18 Apr 1827	Porto Rico	Ripley, John	27-181
	23 Jun 1827	Ponce, P.R.	Ripley, John	27-370
	1 Apr 1828	Trieste & Gibralter	Nesbitt, Edwin	28-103
HERCULES	25 Jan 1820	Liverpool	Cobb, Nathan	20-015
	25 Sep 1820	Liverpool	Cobb, Nathan	20-260
	19 Jun 1821	Liverpool	Cobb, N.	21-124
	24 Oct 1821	Liverpool	Cobb, Nathan	21-343
	11 Feb 1822	Liverpool	Gardiner, S. W.	22-043

SHIP	DATE OF ARRIVAL	PORT OF EMBARKATION	CAPTAIN	YEAR AND SHIP NUMBER
	15 Jul 1822	Liverpool	Gardner, Thomas W.	22-324
	21 Nov 1822	Liverpool	Gardiner, Thomas W.	22-576
	10 Apr 1823	Liverpool	Gardiner, Thomas W.	23-117
	27 Aug 1823	St. Ubes	Gardner, T. W.	23-426
	4 Oct 1824	Halifax	Johnson, William	24-570
	2 Nov 1825	Liverpool	Marshall, Fredk. W.	25-632
	16 Mar 1826	Bremen	Stevens, Timothy	26-118
	5 Sep 1826	Marseilles	Lambert, Richard	26-519
	8 Jan 1827	Bangor	Preswick, C.	27-007
	6 Jul 1827	Liverpool	Lambert, Richard	27-413
	6 Oct 1828	Dundee	Birnie, James	28-590
HERO	20 Aug 1821	Port au Platt	Daggett, Leander	21-233
	5 Jul 1822	St. Eustatia	Tilley, Edward	22-306
	3 Sep 1823	Havana	Collins, John	23-443
	11 May 1824	Havana	Rowllings, Thomas	24-209
	21 Jan 1825	Havana	Rawllings, Thomas	25-033
	17 May 1825	Tampico	Rowlings, Thomas	25-266
	19 May 1828	Greenock	Potter, Thomas	28-234
	5 Jul 1828	Jacmel	Thompson, R.	28-355
HEROINE	19 Jun 1828	Antwerp	Storer, S.	28-313
	7 Jul 1829	Elethuera	Rowe, William S.	29-136
HESPER	7 Oct 1823	Port au Prince	Hubbard, Richard S.	23-525
	28 Jun 1825	Cette	Nichols, Saml.	25-382
	6 Oct 1825	Havana	Doughty, Joseph	25-572
	28 Dec 1825	Havana	Doughty, Joseph	25-736
	2 May 1826	Havana	Doughty, Joseph	26-217
	25 Jul 1826	Havana	Campbell, Moses	26-430
	9 Jun 1827	Matanzas	Mays, Oliver	27-337
	21 Sep 1827	Havana	Lane, M.	27-646
	7 Dec 1827	Havana	Lane, Marcus	27-803
	25 Apr 1828	Matanzas	Lane, Marcus	28-146
	16 Jun 1828	Matanzas	Lane, Marcus	28-307
HESPERION	28 Oct 1823	Havana	Brightman, Samuel	23-563
HESPERUS	14 Feb 1820	Belfast	McCorkell, Archibd.	20-033
	7 Jul 1820	Belfast	McCarkell, Archibald	20-110
	2 Nov 1820	Liverpool	McCaskell, Archd.	20-313
	16 Feb 1822	Liverpool	McCorkell, Archd.	22-048
	13 Oct 1825	Liverpool	McCorkell, Archd.	25-584
	13 Mar 1826	Havana	Doughty, Joseph	26-110
	29 Sep 1827	Liverpool	Hinman, Munson	27-669
HETTA	15 Dec 1823	Jamaica	Wright, Orimel B.	23-639
	11 Apr 1826	La Guira	Stinman, John	26-168
HEWES	30 Oct 1829	Havre	Spear, John, Jr.	29-338
HIBERNIA	15 Aug 1820	Dublin	Walteling, Jno. G.	20-181
	24 Aug 1820	Teneriffe	Graham, Hugh	20-206
	27 Jun 1821	Dublin	Wathling, John G.	21-139
	29 Nov 1821	Dublin	Walteling, John G.	21-384
	22 Feb 1823	Dublin	Walteling, John G.	23-047
	8 Jul 1823	Dublin	Walteburg, John G.	23-320
	3 Dec 1823	Dublin	Watteling, John G.	23-625
	26 Oct 1826	Dublin	Carpenter, P.	26-630
HIND (see Hynd)				
	12 Jul 1820	Havana	Prince, Joel	20-120
	28 Jan 1822	Dundee	Boyak, John	22-017
	12 May 1823	Dundee	Mauer, Robt.	23-185
	11 Jun 1820	Havanna	Winslow, A.	26-319
HIPPOMENES	7 Jan 1820	Curacoa	Bourne, Lemuel	20-001
	5 Jul 1820	Curacoa	Bourne, Lemuel	20-103
	4 Nov 1820	Curacao	Bourne, Limuel	20-319
	9 Jun 1821	Curacao	Bourne, Lemuel	21-107
	30 Aug 1821	Curacao	Bourne, Lemuel	21-250
	22 Dec 1821	Curacao	Bourne, Lemuel	21-428
	25 Mar 1822	Curacoa	Bourne, Lemuel	22-092
	22 Jun 1822	Curacoa	Bourne, Lemuel	22-281
	12 Sep 1822	Curacoa	Baurne, Lemuel	22-463
	29 Nov 1822	Curacoa	Bourne, Lemuel	22-587
	1 Mar 1823	Curacoa	Bourne, Lemuel	23-054
	23 Jun 1823	Curacao	Bourne, Lemuel	23-277

SHIP	DATE OF ARRIVAL	PORT OF EMBARKATION	CAPTAIN	YEAR AND SHIP NUMBER
HIRAM	21 Jul 1823	Gibraltar	Mosker, Wm. H.	23-345
	4 Jun 1824	Leghorn	Perkins, Ebenezer	24-267
	4 Sep 1824	La Guira	Graves, John G.	24-512
	10 Nov 1824	Matanzas	Russel, Charles	24-648
	10 Dec 1825	Barbadoes	Pike, Robert	25-705
	17 Jun 1826	Vera Cruz	West, F.	26-339
	17 Feb 1827	G...ina	West, Francis	27-084
	10 Mar 1827	Bermuda	Sweet, Ebr.	27-114
	2 Apr 1828	Porto Cabello	Whittaker, George	28-107
	8 Jul 1828	St. Thomas	Barnes, Zacchius	28-362
	25 Jul 1828	La Gura	Whicaker, Geo. (Whitacer)	28-401
	31 Oct 1828	Porto Cabello	Whitaker, Geo.	28-643
	8 Jul 1829	St. Thomas	Barnes, Zaccheus	29-139
	14 Aug 1829	Laguayra & Porto Cabello	Whitaker, Geo.	29-218
HOGARTH	12 Oct 1829	Liverpool	Berry, Arthur	29-295
HOLLY	8 Feb 1827	Rio Grande	Clark, Jos. W.	27-067
HOLQUIN	8 Jun 1825	Gibaira	Barclay, Hy. A.	25-322
HOMER	28 Aug 1829	Bordeaux	Myers, David (Meyers)	29-260
HONDURAS PACKET	30 Jun 1823	Cape Gracia Dois	Hedgcock, Thos.	23-299
HONOR & AMERY (see Honor & Amey)				
HONOR & AMEY	15 Mar 1823	Mayaguez	Stone, Gyles P.	23-084
HOOK	10 Feb 1827	Messina	Atwood, H.	27-075
HOPE	19 Jan 1820	Havana	Smith, E. B.	20-012
	15 Aug 1820	St. Andrews	Lewis, Elnathan	20-182
	12 Dec 1820	St. John	Lewis, Elnathan	20-346
	4 Jun 1821	St. Johns, N.B.	Lewis, Elnathan	21-102
	27 Aug 1821	St. John	Lewis, Elnathan	21-242
	15 Oct 1821	St. Johns, N.B.	Lewis, Elnathan	21-324
	29 Dec 1821	Havana	Hatch, Anselm	21-438
	28 Feb 1822	Montiviedo	Shippen, Richd.	22-065
	13 Jun 1822	St. Johns	Lewis, Elnathan	22-267
	6 Jun 1823	Nassau, N.P.	Clark, Jas. E.	23-246
	7 Jul 1823	Dominico	Lewis, Elnathan	23-316
	21 Oct 1823	Greenock	Moore, Daniel	23-554
	5 Mar 1824	Maganilla (Cuba)	Haskel, Frank	24-068
	17 Apr 1824	Matanzas	Green, Abraham	24-154
	18 Jun 1824	Hamburgh	Stow, Anthony	24-312
	2 Jul 1824	Matanzas	Green, Abraham	24-349
	9 Nov 1824	St. Johns, N.B.	Lewis, Elnathan	24-646
	7 Oct 1825	Buenos Ayres	Spafford, Jacob	25-573
	2 Apr 1827	Lisbon	Halsey, George	27-160
	5 Dec 1827	Port Glasgow	Tycon, Peter	27-791
	12 Jun 1828	Londonderry	Kyle, Wm.	28-297
HOPE & HANNAH (see Hope Retrieve)				
HOPE & ESTHER	26 Nov 1822	Halifax	Bears, Isaac	22-583
	19 Aug 1824	Halifax	Bears, Isaac, Jr.	24-470
	27 Sep 1824	Halifax	Bean, Israel, Jr.	24-555
	22 Jul 1825	Halifax	Bears, Isaac, Jr.	25-439
	4 Oct 1825	Halifax	Bears, Isaac	25-566
	12 Nov 1825	Halifax	Bears, Isaac, Jr.	25-656
	12 May 1826	Halifax	Bears, Isaac, Jr.	26-250
	30 Apr 1827	Halifax	Bears, Isaac, Jr.	27-202
	9 Jun 1827	Halifax	Bears, Isaac, Jr.	27-335
	10 Jul 1827	Halifax	Bears, Isaac, Jr.	27-435
	25 Aug 1827	Halifax	Bears, Isaac	27-556
	17 Oct 1827	Halifax	Bears, Isaac, Jr.	27-711
	21 Dec 1827	Halifax, N.S.	Bears, Isaac, Jr.	27-849
	27 Jul 1829	Halifax	Bears, William	29-172
	13 Oct 1829	Halifax, N.S.	Bears, William	29-298
HOPE & HANNAH	28 Mar 1827	Port au Prince	Chase, Jonathan	27-157
HOPE & HESTER	27 Jun 1823	Halifax	Bears, Isaac, Jr.	23-293
HOPE & POLLY	17 Aug 1827	St. Thomas	Chase, Theophilus	27-525
HOPE MARY ANN	3 May 1824	St. Croix	Chase, Job, 3rd	24-193
	21 Aug 1824	Maracaibo	Chase, Job, Jr.	24-477

SHIP	DATE OF ARRIVAL	PORT OF EMBARKATION	CAPTAIN	YEAR AND SHIP NUMBER
	19 Jan 1825	Maracaibo	Chase, Job, 3d.	25-028
HOPE RETRIEVE	7 Jan 1828	Matanzas	Chase, Jonathan	28-008
HOPE RETURN	6 Jun 1823	Jacmel, Hayti	Downes, James	23-245
	20 Mar 1824	Halifax	Baker, Josiah	24-095
	6 Oct 1824	Aux Cayes	Baker, Josiah	24-578
	13 Jan 1826	Havana	Russell, Leonr.	26-024
	9 Mar 1827	Nassau, N.P.	Mallett, Jesse	27-112
	9 Oct 1827	Marseilles	Chase, Isaiah	27-692
HOPE SUCCESS	16 Jul 1828	Turks Island	Winslow, E.	28-377
HOPES DELIGHT	6 Aug 1823	Madeira	Baker, Isaiah	23-384
	6 Sep 1824	Maranham	Baker, Isaiah	24-517
	16 Feb 1825	Angostura	Chase, Jona.	25-065
	21 Nov 1825	Oporto & Madeira	Chase, Jona.	25-666
	1 Sep 1827	Tobasco	Crowell, Daniel	27-572
	29 Nov 1827	Halifax, N.S.	Harden, Gideon	27-770
	21 Apr 1828	Halifax	Harden, G.	28-138
	31 May 1828	Halifax, Nova Scotia	Harden, Gideon	28-261
	22 Jul 1829	St. Pierre's, Miquelon (St. Pierris)	Harden, Gideon	29-164
	26 Aug 1829	Halifax	Harder, Gideon	29-253
HOPES RETURN	6 Sep 1823	Jacquemel	Baker, Josiah	23-452
	5 Aug 1825	Aux Cayes	Crocket, Luther	25-478
HORACE	31 May 1822	Pointe a Pitre	Hatch, Joseph	22-242
	23 Jun 1827	Basslarre, Guadaloupe	Fulton (Watson), John	27-372
HORATIO	19 Jul 1823	Rio Jeneiro	Bailey, Joseph A.	23-343
	10 Feb 1827	Rio Jeneiro	Ball, Samuel	27-074
	26 Oct 1827	Rio Janeiro	Howland, George	27-727
	3 Dec 1827	Matanzas	Trowbridge, Stephen	27-787
	9 Jun 1828	Brazoz	Strowbridge, S.	28-289
	25 Jun 1828	Rio Janeiro	Howland, George	28-329
	21 Jan 1829	Matamoras, Mexico	Trowbridge, Stephen	29-032
	14 Mar 1829	Rio de Janeiro	Howland, Geo.	29-092
HORIZON	23 Aug 1822	Christiansand	Finch, John G.	22-433
	8 Aug 1823	Cove of Cork	Clark, Thomas	23-387
	26 Apr 1824	Honduras	Arnold, William	24-164
HORNILLUS	13 Aug 1827	Antwerp	Smith, Isaac	27-514
HORSLEY HILL	17 Jun 1823	New Castle upon Tyne	Hunter, John	23-267
HOWARD	17 Oct 1822	Havre	Holdridge, N. H.	22-534
	11 Mar 1823	Bordeaux	Perkins, Joseph	23-070
	14 Apr 1823	Havre	Holdrige, N. H.	23-132
	25 Jul 1823	Cork	Stocking, Wm.	23-352
	26 Aug 1823	Havre	Holdridge, N. H.	23-424
	27 Feb 1824	Havre	Holdridge, N. H.	24-060
	11 Jun 1824	Havre	Holdrige, N. H.	24-289
	27 Sep 1824	Havre	Holdrige, N. H.	24-554
	27 Jan 1825	Havre	Holdrege, N. H.	25-037
	14 May 1825	Havre	Holdrige, N. H.	25-253
	15 Jun 1825	Bremen	McCurdy, J. G.	25-347
	18 Jan 1826	Bremen	McCurdy, John G.	26-031
	4 Feb 1826	Havre	Holdrige, N. H.	26-050
	11 Apr 1826	Madeira	Bright, Jno.	26-171
	19 May 1826	Havre	Holdrige, Nathan H.	26-260
	21 Aug 1826	Marseilles	Baker, John	26-501
	27 Sep 1826	Havre	Holdrige, N. H.	26-558
	11 Jan 1827	Havre	Holdrige, N. H.	27-020
	4 May 1827	Havre	Holdrege, N. H.	27-210
	21 May 1827	Marseilles	Baker, John	27-269
	20 Aug 1827	Havre	Holdrige, Nathan H.	27-535
	3 Mar 1828	Madeira	Deming, John	28-042
	28 Aug 1828	Hamburg	Wiederholdt, Lewis	28-474
	18 Sep 1828	Madeira	Deming, John	28-542
	22 Sep 1828	Marseilles	Pitman, James D.	28-554
	13 Feb 1829	Hamburg	Wiederholdt, Lewis	29-061
	6 Jul 1829	Hamburg	Wiederholdt, Lewis	29-134
HOWARD DOUGLASS	11 May 1827	Liverpool	Harvey, James	27-240
	29 Jan 1828	Liverpool & Bermuda	Hughes, John	28-031

SHIP	DATE OF ARRIVAL	PORT OF EMBARKATION	CAPTAIN	YEAR AND SHIP NUMBER
HUDSON	4 Sep 1823	London	Champlin, Henry L.	23-446
	12 Mar 1824	London	Chadwick, David	24-076
	26 Jan 1825	London	Champlain, Henry L.	25-036
	18 Jun 1825	London	Champlin, Henry L.	25-354
	10 Nov 1825	London	Champlin, Henry L.	25-653
	5 Apr 1826	London	Champlin, H. L.	26-153
	13 Jan 1827	London	Avery, Samuel	27-024
	14 Jun 1827	London	Champlin, Henry L.	27-345
	8 Oct 1827	London	Chambplin, C. H.	27-689
	17 Mar 1828	London	Champlin, Christopher H.	28-064
	23 Jul 1828	London	Champlin, Henry L. (Chaplin)	28-394
	20 Nov 1828	London	Champlin, Christopher H.	28-675
	21 Aug 1829	London	Champlin, Christopher H.	29-235
HUGH JOHNSON	11 Jun 1828	Liverpool	Brown, John	28-295
HULDAH & JUDAH	21 Jun 1822	St. Andrews	Thomas, Benjamin	22-279
	30 Jul 1822	St. Andrews	Thomas, Benjamin	22-360
HUNTER	24 Jul 1821	Halifax	Sears, Winthrop	21-192
	19 Nov 1821	Halifax	Sears, Winthrop	21-375
	2 Aug 1822	Halifax	Sears, Winthrop	22-366
	19 May 1823	Halifax	Sears, Winthrop	23-209
	25 May 1824	Halifax, N.S.	Sears, Winthrop	24-232
	2 Jul 1824	Halifax	Sears, Winthrop	24-348
	4 Aug 1824	Halifax	Sears, W.	24-430
	1 Sep 1824	Halifax	Sears, W.	24-499
	27 Oct 1824	Halifax	Sears, Winthrop	24-628
	30 May 1827	St Johns, N.B.	Crowell, Zenas	27-312
	1 Jul 1828	St. Berts	Spencer, R.	28-347
	13 Feb 1829	Mayaguez	Bonney, Joel	29-062
HUNTRESS	27 Sep 1821	Port au Prince	Spencer, William	21-302
	11 Dec 1821	Havana	Morgan, James	21-416
	25 Mar 1822	Havana	Morgan, James	22-093
	29 May 1822	Havana	Morgan, James	22-239
	6 May 1823	Canton	Lavender, Thomas	23-169
	15 Oct 1823	Jamaica	Morgan, James	23-546
	30 Jun 1824	Port au Prince	Newcomb, Reuben	24-346
	20 Aug 1824	Havana	Morgan, James	24-473
	5 Apr 1826	Havana	Hart, George P.	26-152
	6 Sep 1827	Havre	Marshall, A. C.	27-597
HURON	30 Jan 1827	Gibralter	Coffin, George B.	27-047
	26 Dec 1827	London last from Cork	Burras, Samuel	27-853
HYND	12 Jul 1820	Dundee	Bayak, John	20-121
HYPERION	7 Aug 1826	Bordeaux	Gray, Adams	26-461
	21 Mar 1827	Hamburg	Gray, Adams	27-136
ICE PLANT	18 Dec 1820	St. Andrews	Bunker, Thomas	20-349
	5 Jun 1823	Turks Island	Bunker, Thomas	23-242
	29 May 1826	St. Croix	Satterlee, Jonas	26-290
IF	12 Oct 1820	Havanna	Brownell, Thos.	20-294
ILLINOIS	9 Oct 1820	Liverpool	Funck, James	20-287
	16 Jun 1821	Liverpool	Funck, James	21-115
	18 Jun 1821	Aux Cayes	Grice, Geo. W.	21-119
	26 Dec 1821	Liverpool	Funck, James	21-434
	3 Jun 1822	Liverpool	Funck, Jas.	22-249
	16 Oct 1822	Liverpool	Funck, James	22-528
	30 Apr 1823	Liverpool	Funck, James	23-161
ILLUMINATOR	26 Jul 1825	Antigua	Cunningham, Thos.	25-450
IMPERIAL	19 Jul 1820	Londonderry	Ellkins, Daniel	20-132
	10 Dec 1821	Havre	Destebeche, Peter, Jr.	21-414
	12 Aug 1825	Sisal	Nabb, Jno.	25-498
	23 Oct 1826	Havre de Grace	Nabb, John	26-624
IMPORTER	21 Feb 1820	Liverpool	Lee, William, Jr.	20-039
	24 Jul 1820	Liverpool	Lee, Wm., Junr.	20-145
	30 Oct 1820	Liverpool	Lee, William, Jr.	20-309
	21 May 1821	Liverpool	Lee, William, Jr.	21-073
	15 Sep 1821	Liverpool	Lee, William, Jr.	21-271
	10 Sep 1823	Canton	Kean, Elisha L.	23-461

SHIP	DATE OF ARRIVAL	PORT OF EMBARKATION	CAPTAIN	YEAR AND SHIP NUMBER
IMPROVEMENT	6 Jun 1826	Bermuda	Prude, Powel M.	26-309
INCOME	12 Mar 1822	Havana	Brown, Wm. J.	22-079
	12 Feb 1824	Havana	Allen, Alexr.	24-032
	29 May 1824	Neuvitas	Allen, Alexr.	24-245
INDEPENDENCE	10 Oct 1821	St. Andrews	Hopkins, Seth	21-311
	2 Sep 1824	Nevitus	Glander, John H.	24-506
	10 May 1825	Curacoa	Bartlett, Truman, Jr.	25-246
	19 Aug 1825	Curacoa	Bartlett, Tinman, Jr.	25-519
	19 Oct 1826	Martinique	Bugbee, Saml.	26-610
	25 Apr 1828	Teneriffe	Hallett, William S.	28-144
	25 Oct 1828	Vera Cruz	Whiting, Henry	28-632
INDIA	29 Apr 1822	Lisbon	Hatch, Joseph	22-162
	8 Oct 1823	Gottenburg	Hatch, Joseph	23-534
	24 Mar 1826	Gibraltar	Hatch, Joseph	26-131
	4 Aug 1826	Havre	Jones, Jonas	26-450
	8 Dec 1826	Havre	Jones, Jonas	26-704
	8 Jun 1827	Liverpool	Jones, Jonas	27-328
	5 Sep 1827	Liverpool	Jones, Jonas	27-594
INDIAN CHIEF	8 Feb 1822	Liverpool	Humphreys, Jabiz	22-037
	16 Aug 1822	Liverpool	Humphreys, Jabez	22-395
	22 Aug 1822	Amsterdam	Nye, Phillip	22-412
	19 Jun 1823	Liverpool	Humphreys, Jabiz	23-271
	8 Sep 1824	Liverpool	Humphreys, Jabez	24-525
INDIAN QUEEN	12 May 1823	St. Croix	Springer, Wm.	23-186
	18 Feb 1825	Carthagina	Gibbs, Stephen	25-074
	10 May 1825	St. Croix	Gibbs, Stephen	25-245
	5 Dec 1825	Matanzas	Western, John R.	25-687
	11 Mar 1826	Matanzas	Hanifen, Thos. S.	26-101
	20 Sep 1826	Bremen	Baker, Jesse	26-541
INDIANA	11 Sep 1827	Liverpool	Parker, Gideon (Tucker)	27-618
	20 Sep 1828	Hamburg	Doane, C. R.	28-549
INDIES	19 May 1823	Liverpool	Brown, Stephen	23-210
INDUS	19 Jun 1822	St. Iago de Cuba	Smith, Edward R.	22-278
	24 Jul 1827	Mancinella	Bovee, J.	27-475
	5 Sep 1827	Liverpool	Reid, P. M.	27-586
INDUSTRIOZA	12 Nov 1827	Madeira	de Souza, Francis W.	27-756
INDUSTRY	11 Jun 1821	Guadaloupe	Jenkins, Thos.	21-110
	30 Jul 1822	St. Martins	Jerkins, Thomas	22-361
	3 May 1823	Cadiz/Gibraltar	Spurling, Wm.	23-167
	28 Jul 1823	Grenada	Jerkins, Thomas	23-357
	5 Jan 1824	Aquin, St. Domingo	Beauvais, Andw.	24-005
	5 Apr 1824	Aquin	Beauvais, Andrew	24-131
	1 Sep 1824	Trinadad	Jerkins, Thomas	24-501
	10 Mar 1825	Fernandina	Paddock, Joseph L.	25-098
	26 Jul 1825	Demarara	Paddock, J. L.	25-449
	15 Oct 1825	Antigua	Snow, Washington	25-591
	14 Feb 1826	Aux Cayes	Snow, Washington	26-065
	31 Jul 1826	Demarara	Paddock, Joseph L.	26-435
	29 Jan 1828	Guadaloupe	Hunter, W. C.	28-029
	20 Oct 1828	Ragged Island	Hildreth, Albert G.	28-624
INFANT	21 Nov 1820	St. Andrews	Anderson, Samuel	20-326
	10 Jul 1821	Halifax	Collier, Isaac	21-165
INSPECTOR	26 May 1828	Cape Haytien	Stover, Wanton	28-246
INTREPID	8 Aug 1822	Greenock	Jason, Peter	22-383
IRENE	14 Apr 1821	Havana	Stephens, Charles	21-017
IRIS	26 Jun 1821	Havanna	Dugan, Edward W.	21-133
	21 Sep 1821	Antwerp	Smith, John R.	21-292
	15 Jun 1822	Greenock	Smith, John R.	22-273
	8 Jan 1824	Isle of Carman	Dulany, Hugh	24-009
	30 Aug 1824	London	Howland, George	24-492
	24 Oct 1827	Liverpool	Harris, Charles	27-723
	7 Dec 1827	Porto Cabello	Leth, Carl	27-804
	3 Jul 1828	Neuvitas	Deming, John	28-353
ISAAC HICKS	18 Apr 1825	Lpool	Macy, J.	25-182
	23 Aug 1825	Liverpool	Macy, Josiah	25-537
	13 Jan 1826	Liverpool	Morson, William	26-025
	22 May 1826	Liverpool	Morson, J. William	26-272
	27 Sep 1826	Liverpool	Maison, William	26-562

SHIP	DATE OF ARRIVAL	PORT OF EMBARKATION	CAPTAIN	YEAR AND SHIP NUMBER
	10 Jul 1827	Liverpool	Woodward, Salem	27-437
	6 Dec 1827	Liverpool	Woodward, Salem	27-802
	22 Aug 1828	Liverpool	Dickinson, Jeremiah J.	28-456
	22 Aug 1829	Havre de Grace	Dickinson, Jeremiah J.	29-237
ISAAC MCKIM	25 Nov 1824	La Guira	Gorsuch, Robt.	24-690
	23 May 1826	Tampico	Davis, E.	26-277
ISABELLA	10 Mar 1825	St. Johns, N.B.	Prindell, David	25-096
	18 Apr 1825	St. John, N.B.	Brindall, David	25-183
	21 May 1825	St. Johns, N.B.	Prendell, David	25-286
	28 Jun 1825	St. Johns	Prindle, David	25-380
	26 Nov 1825	Rum Key	Napier, John	25-680
	5 Jul 1826	Dundee	Fyfe, Thomas	26-379
	15 Sep 1828	Havre	Silby, Cyrus	28-536
	1 Aug 1829	Maranham	Stewart, William G.	29-184
	10 Aug 1829	Havre de Grace	Libby, Cyrus	29-209
	24 Oct 1829	St. Domingo	Heyliger, Abram	29-324
	31 Oct 1829	Cadiz	Meyer, Philip S.	29-339
ISIS	17 Nov 1828	Nuevitas	Deming, John	28-665
IVANHOE	10 Mar 1827	Palermo	Tinkham, Jeremiah	27-113
JACKIN	15 May 1828	St. Thomas	Drew, Wm.	28-218
JACOB	2 May 1825	Trinadad	Eddy, Sylvester	25-230
	23 Mar 1826	Trinadad	Eddy, Sylvester	26-125
JAINE LOUIS	24 Aug 1820	Havre	Le Vapeur	20-207
JAINE LOUISE (see Jaine Louis)				
JAMES	29 Jul 1820	Havana	Blunt, Robert	20-156
	31 Oct 1822	Whitehaven	Garrison, Isaac	22-552
	7 MKay 1823	Curacao	De Boot, John J.	23-171
	28 Jul 1823	Curacoa	Burnoes, B. J.	23-358
	27 May 1824	Matanzas	Cote, Samuel	24-241
	23 Oct 1824	Curacoa	Cohlman, John	24-622
	4 Jun 1825	Curacoa	Rogers, David	25-318
JAMES & CAROLINE	3 May 1826	Campeachy	Eaton, James	26-223
JAMES & MARGARET	15 Jul 1822	New Castle	Milne, Peter	22-325
	4 Aug 1823	Newcastle & Aberdeen	Milne, Peter	23-380
	30 May 1825	New Castle & Aberdeen	Milne, Peter	25-310
	28 Jun 1826	New Castle & Aberdeen	Milne, Peter	26-365
JAMES BARRON	26 Jun 1823	Havana	Fisher, R.	23-289
JAMES CROPPER	27 Sep 1821	Liverpool	Bowne, William	21-303
	26 Mar 1822	Liverpool	Bowne, William	22-094
	12 Jul 1822	Liverpool	Reid, Saml.	22-319
	14 Oct 1822	Liverpool	Marshall, Chas. H.	22-525
	10 Feb 1823	Liverpool	Marshall, Chas. H.	23-027
	10 Jun 1823	Liverpool	Marshall, Chas. H.	23-253
	7 Oct 1823	Liverpool	Marshall, Chas. H.	23-528
	4 Feb 1824	Liverpool	Marshall, Chas. H.	24-027
	28 Jun 1824	Liverpool	Marshall, Charles H.	24-338
	14 Oct 1824	Liverpool	Marshall, Charles H.	24-595
	3 Mar 1825	Liverpool	Marshall, Charles H.	25-085
	17 Jun 1825	Liverpool	Marshall, Chas. H.	25-350
	21 Oct 1825	Liverpool	Marshall, Charles D.	25-603
	13 Mar 1826	Liverpool	Marshall, Chas. H.	26-109
	16 Oct 1826	Liverpool	Marshall, Chas. H.	26-600
	23 Mar 1827	Liverpool	Graham, Hugh	27-141
	2 Aug 1827	Liverpool	Graham, Hugh	27-498
	29 Nov 1827	Liverpool	Graham, Hugh	27-771
	14 Mar 1828	Liverpool	Graham, Hugh	28-061
JAMES LAWRENCE	3 Sep 1821	St. Thomas	Copeland, Geo.	21-257
JAMES LYON	28 Aug 1828	Cardiff	Turner, William	28-472
JAMES M	15 Sep 1828	Antwerp	Cooper, G.	28-537
JAMES MARGARET	17 May 1827	New Castle & Aberdeen	Milne, Peter	27-260
JAMES MONROE	5 Apr 1820	Liverpool	Rogers, James	20-089
	8 Aug 1820	Liverpool	Rogers, James	20-168
	14 Dec 1820	Liverpool	Rogers, James	20-347
	18 Apr 1821	Liverpool	Rogers, James	21-024

SHIP	DATE OF ARRIVAL	PORT OF EMBARKATION	CAPTAIN	YEAR AND SHIP NUMBER
	27 Jul 1821	Liverpool	Rogers, James	21-201
	15 Oct 1821	Guadaloupe	Harker, Willm.	21-325
	11 Dec 1821	Liverpool	Rogers, James	21-417
	25 Apr 1822	Liverpool	Lee, William, Jun.	22-150
	23 Aug 1822	Liverpool	Marshall, Robert	22-415
	26 Aug 1822	St. Andrews	Getz, Martin	22-420
	14 Jan 1823	Liverpool	Marshall, Rob.	23-011
	29 Apr 1823	Liverpool	Marshall, Robert	23-159
	21 Apr 1824	Havana	Luddington, Justin	24-159
	11 May 1824	Matanzas	Hall, Seth	24-208
	3 Jul 1824	Havana	Luddington, Justus	24-350
	8 Sep 1824	Trinidad de Cuba	Kingston, N. S.	24-523
	6 Jan 1825	Trinadad in Cuba	Kempton, N. S.	25-005
	21 May 1825	Trinidad in Cuba	Kempton, Noah S.	25-287
	24 Feb 1826	Trinadad in Cuba	Skidmore, S.	26-078
	20 Sep 1826	Trinadad in Cuba	Skidmore, Solomon	26-543
	12 Aug 1828	Cape Haytie	Higgins, L. M.	28-429
	24 Jan 1829	St. Thomas	Moore, Jacob, Junr.	29-036
JAMES MONROW	25 Jul 1828	St. Cruoix	Anderson, Jams	28-402
JAMES MOROW (see James Monrow)				
JAMES MURDOCK	2 Jan 1822	Montiviedo	Fortescue, Jas.	22-002
JAMES NOBLE	27 Aug 1827	Rotterdam	Lewis, Robert	27-564
	12 Oct 1829	Antwerp	Lewis, Robert	29-293
JAN	3 Nov 1821	Port au Platt, St. Domingo	Thompson, John E.	21-356
JANE	9 Jul 1821	St. Bartholomew (St. Thomas)	Fowler, Pexal	21-164
	17 Jul 1821	Turks Island	Gibbs, Daniel	21-182
	15 Oct 1821	St. Thomas	Fowler, Pixcel	21-326
	16 Oct 1821	Turks Island	Gibbs, Danl.	21-331
	7 Dec 1821	Turks Island	Gibbs, Daniel	21-405
	29 Apr 1822	St. Iago de Cuba	Gibbs, Daniel	22-163
	24 May 1822	St. Iago	Copeland, James	22-227
	29 Aug 1822	St. Thomas	Fowler, Pexcel	22-434
	9 Dec 1822	Turks Island	Gibbs, Daniel	22-595
	13 Dec 1822	Antiqua	Fowler, Pexcel	22-602
	3 Apr 1823	St. Thomas	Fowler, Pexel	23-100
	18 Apr 1823	Trinada de Cuba	Rice, Matthew	23-140
	29 Jul 1823	Trinadad in Cuba	Rice, Matthew	23-365
	10 Jan 1824	Port au Prince	Fortescue, Jos.	24-016
	9 Mar 1824	Demerara	Crocker, Gamaliel, Jr.	24-072
	22 Mar 1824	St. Croix	Fowler, Pexcel	24-100
	15 Jun 1824	St. Croix	Richards, Stephen	24-308
	27 Aug 1824	St. Thomas	Fowler, Pexcel	24-490
	13 Dec 1824	St. Thomas	Fowler, Pexcel	24-713
	17 Jan 1825	Pernambuco	Candler, Saml.	25-021
	18 Feb 1825	Calcutta	Maitland, Charles	25-072
	30 Apr 1825	St. Croix	Fowler, P.	25-228
	14 Jul 1825	St. Croix	Richards, S.	25-421
	26 Jul 1825	Bremen	Webber, B.	25-446
	7 Aug 1825	St. Croix	Fowler, Pexcel, Jr.	25-486
	6 Apr 1826	Havana	Hiter, Francis	26-158
	28 Jul 1826	St. Croix	Fowler, Pexcel	26-432
	7 Oct 1826	Liverpool	Devereaux, John	26-587
	2 Nov 1826	St. Croix	Fowler, Pexcel	26-642
	31 Jan 1827	St. Thomas	Fowler, P.	27-049
	28 May 1827	St. Thomas	Fowler, Pexcel	27-306
	13 Aug 1827	Guadaloupe	Jones, Edwd. R.	27-515
	3 Sep 1827	St. Thomas	Fowler, Pexcil	27-576
	11 Dec 1827	St. Thomas	Fowler, Pexcel, Jr.	27-825
	24 May 1828	Guadaloupe	Jones, Edward R.	28-242
	11 Jul 1828	Hamburg	Child, Luther	28-370
	13 Sep 1828	St. Croix	Fowler, Pexcel, Jr.	28-534
	18 Oct 1828	Rio de Janeiro	Attwater, Naemand M. (Atwater)	28-617
	13 Mar 1829	St. Thomas	Fowler, Pexcel, Jr.	29-089

SHIP	DATE OF ARRIVAL	PORT OF EMBARKATION	CAPTAIN	YEAR AND SHIP NUMBER
JANE ANN	19 Aug 1822	St. Johns, N.B.	Calley, James (Thomas)	22-403
	29 May 1826	St. Johns, N.B.	Colley, Thomas	26-287
JANE BLOSSOM	28 Aug 1826	Havre	Post, Ezra D.	26-503
JANE HASTIE (see Jean Hastie)				
JANE MARIA	12 Aug 1829	Havana	Tetterton, Wm.	29-211
JANNETTE				
JOSEPHINE	22 Aug 1820	Antwerpt	Vanhavabeke, J. B.	20-203
JAS. MONROE	11 Aug 1823	Trinadad in Cuba	Kempton, Noah S.	23-395
	9 Jun 1826	Trinidad in Cuba	Skidmore, Solomon	26-318
JASON	17 Jul 1821	Amsterdam	Cox, Wm.	21-181
	25 May 1822	Fernandina, Cuba	Marshall, Dl.	22-228
	3 Nov 1828	Rotterdam	Howland, Stephen H.	28-647
JASPER	24 Feb 1826	Maranham	Beauvais, Andrew	26-077
	17 Jul 1826	Gibraltar	Beauvais, Andrew	26-410
	22 Sep 1827	Vera Cruz	Beauvis, A.	27-647
	30 May 1828	Maracaibo	Beauvais, Andrew	28-257
JAVA	20 Jun 1825	Liverpool	Rich, Abm.	25-362
	9 Jul 1827	Liverpool	Rich, Abm.	27-427
JAY	28 May 1822	Xebara, Cuba	Smith, Egbert B.	22-234
	18 Apr 1823	Halifax	Page, Jos.	23-141
	13 Aug 1823	Jamaica	Boggs, James C.	23-397
JEAN	17 Aug 1827	Glasgow	Paton, William	27-526
JEAN BAPTIST	5 Mar 1827	Port au Prince	Montel, C.	27-099
JEAN BAPTISTE	2 Dec 1826	Port au Prince	Dumas, P. C.	26-697
	7 Jan 1828	Port au Prince	Gachet, A.	28-006
	11 Aug 1828	Port au Prince, Cape Francois	Trouillot, A.	28-428
JEAN HASTIE	27 Jul 1829	Greenock	Forsyth, James O.	29-169
JEFFERSON	7 Aug 1820	St. Andrews	Strout, Anthony	20-163
	29 Nov 1828	Amsterdam	Lesley, Robert	28-683
JESSE	14 Aug 1826	Cadiz	Nye, Nathan	26-479
JEUNE				
ANTOINETTE	31 Oct 1829	St. Domingo	Garcia, Bernardino	29-340
JHON &				
ELIZABETH (see John & Elizabeth)				
JNO.				
DICKINSON	21 Sep 1821	Belfast	Baush, John	21-293
JOHN	6 Oct 1820	Bristol	Thornhill, Evans	20-281
	16 Oct 1820	Havana	Loveland, John	20-296
	2 Feb 1824	Alvarado	Storer, Isaac	24-026
	18 Sep 1824	St. Iago de Cuba	Diggs, Beverly	24-538
	7 Jan 1825	Porto Cabello	Briggs, Beverley	25-007
	11 Jun 1825	Turks Island	Hamor, David	25-330
	10 Aug 1825	St. Andrews, St. Johns	Harmor, David	25-491
	6 Sep 1826	Liverpool	Brewer, Isaac	26-520
	15 Sep 1827	Trinidad de Cuba	Gillet, John	27-633
JOHN ADAMS	17 Jul 1827	St. Thomas	Brown, Stephen	27-454
	2 Aug 1827	Liverpool	Atwood, Henry	27-497
	27 Sep 1827	St. Croix	Brown, Stephen	27-666
JOHN &				
ADAM	21 Sep 1822	Cork	Taber, John R.	22-477
JOHN &				
EDWARD	25 Aug 1820	Liverpool	Webb, William	20-208
	18 Jul 1822	Bordeaux	Webb, Silas S.	22-337
	6 Jul 1824	Glasgow	Greenleaf, Henry	24-353
	7 Nov 1825	Marseilles	Ropes, Jno. M.	25-638
	8 Feb 1827	St. Iago de Cuba	Choate, C. D. (E. D.)	27-064
	18 Oct 1828	Turks Island	Stevens, Thomas C.	28-621
JOHN AND				
EDWARD	6 Jan 1824	Havana	Higgins, David	24-008
JOHN &				
ELIZABETH	11 Dec 1826	Liverpool	Barstow, John	26-719
	25 Sep 1827	Liverpool	Barstow, John	27-661
JOHN & ROBERT	17 Oct 1825	Bristol	Jones, John	25-593
	4 Sep 1827	Bristol	Jones, John	27-581
JOHN &				
WILLIAM	20 Aug 1827	Bordeaux	Hopkins, John	27-534
	20 Jul 1829	Trinidad de Cuba	Consaloi, Camillo	29-158

SHIP	DATE OF ARRIVAL	PORT OF EMBARKATION	CAPTAIN	YEAR AND SHIP NUMBER
JOHN DICKINSON	14 Sep 1820	Belfast	Baush, John	20-244
	5 Apr 1821	Belfast	Baush, John	21-004
	18 Feb 1822	Belfast	Baush, John	22-052
	28 Jun 1822	Belfast	Baush, John	22-297
	13 May 1823	Belfast	Burras, Saml.	23-195
	30 Sep 1823	Liverpool	Burras, Samuel	23-510
	12 Aug 1824	Greenock	Burras, Samuel	24-450
	16 Feb 1825	Antwerp	Burras, Saml.	25-066
	15 Oct 1826	Liverpool	Hintz, Anthony	26-597
	19 Jun 1827	Antwerp	Hintz, Anthony	27-360
	9 Oct 1828	Antwerp	Hintz, Anthony	28-603
JOHN EDWARD (see John & Edward)				
JOHN JAY	8 May 1828	Liverpool	Holdrege, N. H.	28-197
	17 Sep 1828	Liverpool	Holdrige, N. H.	28-540
	26 Jan 1829	Liverpool	Holdrege, N. H.	29-038
JOHN LAIRD	16 Jun 1827	Madeira	Fletcher, George	27-353
JOHN LONDON	26 Mar 1822	Port au Prince	Barber, Thomas	22-095
	26 Jun 1822	Port au Prince	Barber, Thomas	22-293
	1 Oct 1822	Port au Prince	Barber, Thomas	22-496
	20 Jan 1823	Port au Prince	Barber, Thomas	23-012
	8 May 1823	Port au Prince	Barber, Thomas	23-173
	1 Sep 1823	Port au Prince	Hawland, Reuben	23-433
	8 Dec 1823	Port au Prince	Howland, Reuben	23-627
	7 Apr 1824	Port au Prince	Howland, Reuben	24-133
	3 Aug 1824	Port au Prince	Hawland, Reuben	24-429
	13 Dec 1824	Port au Prince	Howland, Reuben	24-714
	21 Mar 1825	Port au Prince	Howland, Reuben	25-127
	20 Dec 1825	Port au Prince	Mayo, Oliver	25-723
JOHN MARSHALL	1 Aug 1825	Bordeaux	Drummond, J.	25-463
JOHN WELLS	11 Jun 1823	Liverpool	Harris, Isaac	23-256
	14 Oct 1823	Liverpool	Harris, Isaac	23-544
	16 Feb 1824	Liverpool	Harris, Isaac	24-042
	22 Sep 1824	Liverpool	Harris, Isaac	24-548
	29 Jan 1825	Liverpool	Harris, Isaac	25-038
	16 May 1825	Liverpool	Harris, Isaac	25-260
	22 May 1826	Liverpool	Harris, Isaac	26-269
	18 Sep 1826	Liverpool	Harris, Isaac	26-538
	15 Jan 1827	Liverpool	Harris, J.	27-034
	11 May 1827	Liverpool	Harris, Isaac	27-238
	8 Sep 1897	Liverpool	Allen, Francis P.	27-606
JOHN WILLS	21 May 1824	Liverpool	Harris, Isaac	24-222
JONES	13 Mar 1822	Liverpool	Davis, Henry	22-080
	28 Aug 1826	Port of Spain, Trinidad	Winchell, Ebenezer	26-504
JONES & SAMUEL	22 Sep 1826	St. Lucia	Best, James	26-547
JOSEPH	3 Oct 1820	Antwerp	Morris, Patterson	20-278
	11 Jul 1821	Bordeaux	Morris, P.	21-169
	22 Jan 1822	Marseilles	Morris, P.	22-014
	13 Oct 1823	Liverpool	Holdrige, Allen	23-542
	20 Jul 1829	Omoa, Honduras	Hull, John	29-161
JOSEPH EASTBURN	6 Feb 1826	St. Thomas	Donaldson, E. M.	26-054
JOSEPH HUME	26 Oct 1829	Greenock	Rattray, Henry	29-326
JOSEPH L. LEWIS (see Joseph S. Lewis)				
JOSEPH S. LEWIS	6 Dec 1822	Havana	Caldwell, Thomas	22-594
JOSEPHINE	27 Jul 1825	Liverpool	Nicoll, S. C.	25-455
	10 Dec 1825	Liverpool	Nicoll, Samuel C.	25-701
	24 Jul 1826	Liverpool	Coles, Hewlett T.	26-428
	8 Jan 1827	Liverpool	Coles, Hewlet T.	27-005
	7 May 1827	Belfast	Coles, Hewlett T.	27-215
	8 Dec 1827	Belfast	Coles, Hewlett T.	27-816
	30 Apr 1828	Belfast	Wilson, J. L.	28-167
	30 Aug 1828	Belfast	Britton, Thomas	28-489
	23 Jan 1829	Liverpool	Brittan, Thomas	29-035
	22 Aug 1829	Halifax	Crowell, Zenas (Jonas)	29-239
	13 Oct 1829	Halifax	Crowell, Zenas	29-301

SHIP	DATE OF ARRIVAL	PORT OF EMBARKATION	CAPTAIN	YEAR AND SHIP NUMBER
JUANITA	13 Oct 1829	Havana	Porben, Alexander	29-299
JUBILEE	1 Jul 1823	Jamaica, Montego Bay	Waterhouse, John	23-303
	13 Sep 1827	Galaway	Nichols, John	27-625
	1 Dec 1827	Liverpool	Chaddock, Moses G.	27-779
	12 May 1828	Liverpool	Chaddock, Moses G.	28-204
	26 Jul 1828	Gonagiers	Wade, John	28-406
	1 Oct 1828	Liverpool	Chaddock, Moses G.	28-572
	4 Mar 1829	Liverpool	Chaddock, Moses G.	29-070
	13 Jul 1829	Liverpool	Chaddock, Moses G.	29-145
JUFFRAW JOHANNA	16 Oct 1821	Amsterdam	Grill, John	21-332
JULIA	28 Jul 1824	La Guira	Spring, John	24-412
	16 Nov 1824	Marseilles	Briggs, Silvanus	24-665
	9 Jun 1825	Matanzas	Briggs, Silvanis	25-324
	20 Dec 1825	Pernambuca	Briggs, Silvanus	25-722
	1 Feb 1827	Trinadad in Cuba	Gillet, John	27-052
	8 Feb 1827	Alicant	Sears, R.	27-062
	22 May 1827	Trinadad	Gillet, John	27-291
	26 Jun 1827	Gibraltar	Thacher, Josiah	27-378
	9 Aug 1827	Mayaguez	Kimball, Nathl.	27-508
	13 Sep 1827	Montego Bay	Wilson, W.	27-623
	18 Apr 1828	Rio Janeiro	Sears, Richard	28-133
JULIA ANN	24 Jul 1820	St. Andrews	Winott, John, Junr.	20-146
	18 Sep 1826	St. Andrews	Oakes, Eben.	26-535
JULIANA	25 Jan 1820	Madeira	Samson, Elgit	20-016
	2 Sep 1826	Xibara	Mendez, Augustus	26-515
JULIUS CAESAR (see Julius Seesar)				
JULIUS SEASAR (see Julius Seesar)				
JULIUS SEESAR	29 Jul 1820	Liverpool	Marshall, Charles H.	20-157
JUNIUS	5 Jul 1820	Bermuda	Dunton, George	20-104
JUNO	26 Nov 1821	Liverpool	Doak, John	21-380
	5 Oct 1822	Liverpool	Doak, John	22-510
	4 Sep 1824	Port au Platt	Hamlin, Nathw. (D.)	24-515
JUPITER	29 Jun 1825	St. Croix	Clark, James G.	25-386
	21 Nov 1825	St. Thomas	Clark, James G.	25-664
	31 Mar 1826	St. Croix	Clark, James G.	26-137
	27 May 1826	St. Croix	Clark, James G.	26-283
	6 Aug 1826	St. Croix	Clark, James G.	26-455
	19 Oct 1826	St. Croix	Clark, James G.	26-611
	12 May 1827	St. Croix	Clark, James G.	27-241
	14 Sep 1827	St. Croix	Clark, James G.	27-630
	26 Dec 1827	St. Croix	Clark, James G.	27-856
	4 Mar 1828	St. Croix	Clark, James G.	28-046
	8 Apr 1828	St. Croix	Clark, J. G.	28-116
	27 Jun 1828	St. Croix	Clark, James G.	28-335
	29 Aug 1828	St. Croix	Clark, James G.	28-482
	11 Feb 1829	St. Croix	Clark, James Z.	29-058
	4 Aug 1829	St. Croix	Clark, James G.	29-197
JUSTINA	29 Jul 1822	Liverpool	Almy, Peleg	22-356
	7 Mar 1823	Liverpool	Almy, Peleg	23-059
	5 Aug 1823	Liverpool	Almy, Peleg	23-381
KANHAWA	16 Apr 1823	Trinadad in Cuba	Lee, Samuel	23-135
	6 May 1828	Hamburg	Reed, John A.	28-193
KATE	2 Oct 1821	Dundee	Anderson, James	21-305
KATHARINE	25 Aug 1828	Havana	Mayo, Oliver	28-465
KENHAWA	20 Jan 1823	Port au Prince	Lee, Saml.	23-013
KENNEBECK TRADER	16 Jul 1822	Havana	Gale, Lewis H.	22-329
KINGSTON	1 Jul 1829	Montego Bay, Jam.	Jackson, George	29-115
KLEBER	23 Jul 1827	St. Johns, N.B.	Hinckley, Jabez	27-473
L. EMILIE MARIE	12 Jul 1820	Havre	Delamare, J.	20-119
L. M. PELHAM	17 Aug 1820	Lisbon	Schuyler, Rew.	20-188
	18 Jun 1821	Gibraltar	McIntire, Charles	21-122
	7 Mar 1822	Gibraltar	McIntire, Charles	22-071
	25 Jun 1822	Belfast	Hatch, Anselm	22-289
	3 Jan 1823	Malaga	Hatch, Anselm	23-003
	12 May 1823	Limerick	Hatch, Anselm	23-191
	23 Aug 1823	Havre	Hatch, Anselm	23-420

SHIP	DATE OF ARRIVAL	PORT OF EMBARKATION	CAPTAIN	YEAR AND SHIP NUMBER
L'ADELEE	22 Aug 1820	Nantz	Lagree, —	20-200
L'AMITUS	2 Mar 1827	Martinique	Ferrandez, —	27-096
L'EGIDE	8 Jun 1824	Havre	Chambron, Pierre	24-281
L'ESPERANCE	6 Sep 1828	Havre	Jombert, —	28-510
L'ORISTELLE	15 Dec 1826	City St. Domingo	Toublane, Charles	26-725
LABURNUM	12 Dec 1821	New Castle	Taylor, Willm.	21-419
	24 Aug 1822	New Castle	Taylor, Wm.	22-418
	10 Apr 1823	New Castle	Taylor, W.	23-118
LA CORALIE	18 Oct 1824	Port Royal	Trillard, A.	24-614
LADIES DELIGHT (see Lady's Delight)				
	18 Sep 1820	Curacoa	Scribner, Elijah P.	20-254
	7 Jul 1821	Curacoa	Scribner, Elijah P.	21-160
	15 Oct 1821	Curacao	Scribner, Elijah P.	21-327
	9 Aug 1823	Havana	Scribner, Elijah P.	23-389
LADY GALLATIN	21 Jun 1820	Liverpool	Basker, Josiah	20-090
	26 Sep 1823	Liverpool	Britton, Wm., Jr.	23-500
LA GRATITUDE	25 Jan 1820	Martinique	LeDepensier, —	20-018
LA GUADALOUPE	26 May 1823	Nantz	Auger, D.	23-227
LADY HUNTER	12 Apr 1823	St. Johns, N.B.	Desbrow, Noah	23-128
	28 May 1823	St. John	Prindall, David	23-231
	5 Jul 1823	St. Johns, N.B.	Palmeters, William	23-311
	26 Nov 1823	St. Johns, N.B.	Palmeter, William	23-609
	22 Mar 1824	St. Johns, N.B.	Holmes, Henry	24-101
	28 Apr 1824	St. Johns, N.B.	Holmes, Henry	24-178
	26 May 1825	St. Johns, N.B.	Holmes, Henry	25-298
	18 Jul 1825	St. John	Holmes, Hy.	25-426
	22 Aug 1825	St. Johns, N.B	Holmes, Henry	25-534
	9 Oct 1825	St. Johns, N.B.	Holmes, Henry	25-577
	27 Dec 1825	St. Johns, N.B.	Holmes, Henry	25-732
	14 Mar 1826	St. Johns, N.B.	Holmes, Henry	26-113
	29 Apr 1826	St. Johns, N.B.	McLaughlin, James	26-208
	5 Jun 1826	St. Johns, N.B.	Fader, William	26-300
	10 Jul 1826	St. Johns, N.B.	McLaughlin, James	26-389
	8 Aug 1826	St. Johns, N.B.	McLaughlin, James	26-467
	19 Oct 1826	St. Johns, N.B	McLaughlin, James	26-607
LADY OF THE LAKE	11 Apr 1825	St. Lucia	Brooks, D. R.	25-161
	23 Aug 1828	Liverpool	Leitch, James	28-461
LADY TOMPKINS	10 Nov 1823	Havana	Russell, Leond.	23-581
	31 Jan 1824	Havana	Russell, Leond.	24-024
	13 Apr 1824	Havana	Russell, Leond.	24-139
	25 Aug 1824	Jamaica	Buttingham, A. P.	24-487
	9 Feb 1825	Havana	Buttingham, A. P.	25-058
	11 Jul 1826	Montigo Bay	Wiederholt, F. L.	26-396
	21 May 1827	Porto Cabello	Manchester, John	27-278
LADY WASHINGTON	16 Oct 1821	St. Andrews	Ealton, James	21-333
	31 Dec 1827	Tampico	Moore, Samuel	27-868
	9 Jun 1828		Claff, James	28-288
LADY'S DELIGHT	21 Dec 1820	Curacoa	Scribner, Elijah P.	20-354
LAFAYETTE	3 Dec 1827	Liverpool	Fanning, Thomas	27-782
LA FAYETTE	7 Apr 1825	Liverpool	Fanning, Thos.	25-153
LA FLORA	30 Jun 1828	Havre	Recourse, —	28-344
LA GRANGE	19 Apr 1826	Valparaiso	Somes, Saml.	26-193
	27 Sep 1826	Carnavon	Kelley, Anthony	26-561
	7 Aug 1828	Havre	Devereux, John	28-424
LAMA	7 Nov 1825	St. Salvador	Wheatland, Richd. G.	25-642
LA MARIE ADELE	8 Jan 1827	Gaudaloupe	Dupont, L.	27-006
LANCASTER (see Lancatter)				
LANCATTER	5 Jul 1820	Bermuda	Japscott, E. L. B.	20-105
LANGDON CHEEVES	19 Mar 1827	St. Thomas	Baker, John	27-128
LA PLATA	29 Dec 1827	Jacmel	Wing, Clifton	27-862
	6 Jun 1828	Gibralter	Wing, Clifton	28-284

SHIP	DATE OF ARRIVAL	PORT OF EMBARKATION	CAPTAIN	YEAR AND SHIP NUMBER
LAPWING	12 Jul 1828	Teneriffe	Wilcox, Daniel L.	28-372
LARCH	6 Jul 1827	Malaga	Simpson, James, Jr.	27-412
	18 Jul 1828	St. Domingo	Simpson, J.	28-384
LARK	10 Mar 1823	St. Domingo	Noyes, Amos	23-067
	28 Jun 1824	Jamaica	Noyes, Amos	24-334
	11 Jun 1828	St. Domingo	Foy, Moses	28-293
LA SOPHIE	23 Dec 1824	Guadaloupe	Le Roy, Peter	24-732
LATONA	7 Jul 1827	Bristol	Dale, Wm.	27-422
LAURA	8 Dec 1821	Leghorn	Holman, John	21-410
LA URANIA	3 Jul 1828	Havre	Marcuis, E.	28-351
LAURA ANN	2 Feb 1820	Havana	Hubbell, Robert A.	20-022
	10 Sep 1821	St. Bartholomews	Bassett, Freeman C.	21-265
	25 May 1822	Buenos Ayres	Bassett, Freeman C.	22-229
	8 Dec 1823	Rio Janeiro	Huntington, Ewd.	23-628
LAUREL	16 Nov 1824	Dublin	Briant, James	24-669
	26 Jul 1825	Antigua	Ames, A.	25-448
	20 Apr 1826	Matanzas	Kimball, Nathaniel	26-197
	29 Aug 1826	Cadiz	Reed, Charles	26-507
	31 Mar 1828	Sunderland	Baxter, John	28-097
	3 Jun 1828	Fernandina	Joseph, John	28-273
LAVERIA	23 Jul 1828	Vera Cruz	Meany, Corns.	28-392
LA VILLE DE CAYES	5 Dec 1826	Aux Cayes	Bailleo, H.	26-698
LAVINIA	19 Aug 1824	Turks Island	Hubbard, Richard S.	24-472
LA VIRGINIE	21 Sep 1826	Havre	Dauboeuf, J. A.	26-545
	6 Aug 1828	La Rochelle	Le Conte, J. B.	28-423
LA VOLTIQUER	23 Jul 1822	Antwerp	De Ruyter, Wm.	22-349
LAWSON	31 Aug 1825	Tampico	Watts, Samuel	25-560
LEADER	17 Sep 1821	St. Andrews	Cousins, Reuben	21-275
	28 Mar 1822	Havana	Jones, Jonas	22-099
	18 Apr 1823	Rochelle	Jones, Jonas	23-142
	18 Aug 1823	St. Andrews	Cousins, Reuben	23-409
	4 Oct 1824	Carnarvon	Jones, Jonas	24-565
	19 Aug 1825	Gibraltar	Jones, Jonas	25-523
	9 Nov 1825	Havana	Jones, Jonas	25-645
	14 Apr 1826	Bristol	Jones, Jonas	26-177
	2 Aug 1826	Aux Cayes	Kimball, John	26-446
	13 Sep 1826	Malaga	Stoddard, Charles	26-528
	20 Apr 1827	Gibraltar	Stoddard, Charles	27-185
	23 Jul 1827	Siral	Grinnell, Isaac	27-470
	31 Dec 1827	St. I[ago] de Cuba	Grinnell, Isaac	27-869
	7 Aug 1829	Santa Cruz	Grinnell, Isaac	29-201
LEANDER	30 Oct 1826	Bermuda	Darrell, Saml.	26-635
	18 May 1827	Malaga & Gibralter	Gill, Christopher	27-266
LEAVITTS	25 Aug 1828	St. Andrews	Dickinson, Saml. W.	28-464
LEBAGO	30 Jun 1826	Havana	Davis, C. M.	26-372
LEDA	30 Aug 1828	Dundee	Lyell, James	28-486
LEEDS	19 May 1823	Liverpool	Stoddard, William	23-211
	29 Sep 1823	Liverpool	Stoddard, William	23-505
	29 May 1824	Liverpool	Stoddard, William	24-244
	16 Apr 1825	Lpool	Stoddard, W.	25-179
	6 Feb 1826	Liverpool	Stoddard, William	26-052
	6 Jun 1826	Liverpool	Stoddard, William	26-308
	26 Sep 1826	Liverpool	Stoddard, Wm.	26-558
	5 Feb 1827	Liverpool	Stoddard, Wm.	27-059
	4 Jun 1827	Liverpool	Stoddard, William	27-318
	24 Sep 1827	Liverpool	Stoddard, Wm.	27-650
	2 Aug 1828	London	Sprague, Benjn.	28-417
	7 Nov 1828	London	Sprague, Benjamin	28-657
LEIF	6 Sep 1824	Havana	Powell, John	24-518
LENO	21 May 1822	St. Thomas	Slade, Laban	22-209
LEO	2 Oct 1822	Aux Cayes	Knight, John	22-500
	30 Apr 1825	Nassau	Claxton, W. N.	25-224
	9 Jul 1825	Alvarado	Partlow, W.	25-411
	31 Jul 1826	Nassau, W.I.	Claxton, William V.	26-436
	7 Jun 1827	Ponce	Morrill, Samuel J.	27-326
LEONARDAS	30 Oct 1822	Carthagena	Bedford, Benjamin	22-550
LEONARDE	29 Aug 1828	Havre	Le Dilly, M. J.	28-479

SHIP	DATE OF ARRIVAL	PORT OF EMBARKATION	CAPTAIN	YEAR AND SHIP NUMBER
LEONIDAS	1 Aug 1822	Amsterdam	Lord, Clement	22-363
	24 Jul 1824	Liverpool	Stevens, Wm. G.	24-392
	3 Aug 1825	Newry	Stevens, William G.	25-472
	20 Apr 1826	Triest	Stevens, William G.	26-195
	22 Jan 1829	Vera Cruz	Bergnon, George	29-033
LEONORA	25 May 1826	St. Martins	Parish, James	26-281
	30 Sep 1826	Havana	Parish, James	26-570
	29 Nov 1826	St. Barts	Parish, James	26-690
	10 Apr 1827	St. Bartholomews	Parish, James	27-169
	3 Dec 1827	St. Bartholomews	Parrish, James	27-786
	9 May 1828	Ponce, P.R.	Parish, James	28-198
LEONTINE	18 Mar 1825	Alvarado	Hazard, Daniel	25-120
	19 May 1825	Havana	Hazard, Daniel, Jr.	25-279
	13 Mar 1826	Vera Cruz	Hazard, Daniel	26-104
	10 Jul 1826	Vera Cruz	Hazard, Daniel	26-390
LEOPARD	23 Nov 1820	Cuba	Fordham, George	20-330
	31 Jul 1824	Rio Grande	Gray, Robert	24-419
	15 Aug 1825	Rio Grande	Gray, Wm.	25-502
	30 Aug 1826	Rio de Janeiro	Gray, William	26-512
LE PACQUET DES CAYES	6 Nov 1826	Aux Cayes	Beagey, Jean L.	26-647
LEVANT	15 Aug 1823	Madeira	Baker, Seth	23-402
	20 Sep 1824	Havana	Leffingwell, Elisha	24-539
	18 Nov 1824	St. Thomas	Davis, Andw.	24-673
LEVANTINE	7 Nov 1825	Alvarada	Hazard, Daniel	25-640
LEVEL	8 Sep 1827	London	Perkins, B.	27-602
LE VOLTAIRE	19 Jul 1828	Havre	Burnoaf, —	28-389
LEWIS	1 Jul 1820	St. Andrews	Sears, Jonathan	20-093
	7 Aug 1821	St. Johns, N.B.	Sears, Jonathan	21-210
	17 Sep 1821	St. Johns, N.B.	Lewis, Jonathan	21-276
	24 Oct 1821	St. Johns, N.B.	Sears, Jonathan	21-344
	30 May 1823	Havre	Skiddy, John R.	23-233
	10 Sep 1823	Havre	Skiddy, John R.	23-462
	20 Feb 1824	Havre	Skiddy, John R.	24-053
	25 Jun 1824	Havre	Skiddy, John R.	24-328
	11 Nov 1824	Havre	Skiddy, John R.	24-653
	6 Jul 1825	Havre	Lambert, R.	25-401
	29 Oct 1825	Havre	Macy, R. J.	25-625
	16 Mar 1826	Havre	Macy, Robert J.	26-116
	13 Jan 1827	Bristol	Blackmer, S.	27-022
LEXINGTON	8 Jul 1828	Maianham	Brownell, S.	28-363
	14 Aug 1828	Gibraltar	Bradford, Lemuel	28-439
LIBERTY	20 Jun 1821	Halifax	Matthews, Abrah..	21-125
	7 Aug 1821	Havana	Andrews, Seth	21-211
	1 Nov 1823	Port au Prince	Hatch, John	23-568
	31 Jan 1826	Havana	Pereira, Domingos	26-048
	27 Mar 1826	Havana	Pereira, Domingos	26-135
	7 Jun 1826	Havana	Pereira, Domingos	26-310
	20 Sep 1826	Havana	Pereira, Dominges	26-544
	26 Mar 1827	Havana	Nivero, P. A.	27-146
	3 Sep 1827	Havana	Rivero, P. A.	27-574
LIMA	13 Nov 1822	Cronstadt	Rich, Richd.	22-568
	11 Dec 1823	Havre De Grace	O'Hara, John	23-635
	19 Jun 1824	Sligo	O'Hara, John	24-313
	6 Dec 1826	Liverpool	O'Hara, John	26-702
	22 Sep 1828	Liverpool	Wyle, John (Wylee)	28-551
	16 Mar 1829	Liverpool	Wyle, John	29-097
	5 Aug 1829	Liverpool	Wyle, John	29-200
LINCOLN	10 Dec 1823	St. Andrews	Johnson, Herod	23-633
	12 Jun 1824	Matanzes	Lincoln, J. B.	24-300
LINGAN	16 Jul 1822	St. Andrews	Haskett, Benjm. S.	22-330
LION	20 Aug 1821	St. Eustatia	Dubois, Theod.	21-234
	5 Sep 1828	Rio de Janeiro	Chace, C. F.	28-506
LITTLE CHERUB	8 Sep 1824	Kingston	Sands, Hart	24-524
	15 Dec 1824	Jamaica	Sands, Hart	24-723
	12 Apr 1825	Jamaica	Sands, H.	25-171
	11 Aug 1825	Kingston, Jamaica	Lamphear, Nathan	25-494

SHIP	DATE OF ARRIVAL	PORT OF EMBARKATION	CAPTAIN	YEAR AND SHIP NUMBER
	11 Nov 1826	Jamaica & Long Island Bahama	Lamphear, M.	26-657
LITTLE JOHN	4 Nov 1820	Guadaloupe	Fulford, Wm.	20-318
	20 Aug 1822	Martinique	Willis, David W.	22-406
LITTLE WILLIAM	16 Jun 1821	Havre	Carnes, John, Jr.	21-116
	14 Jun 1823	Cadiz	Evins, Luther	23-263
LIVE OAK	13 Aug 1821	St. Bartholomews	Bissell, A.	21-222
	16 Oct 1823	Martinique	Blair, Geo.	23-548
LIVELY	23 Jul 1825	Nassau	Shelleton, C.	25-440
LIVELY HOPE	31 Oct 1822	Port au Platt	Lincoln, Isaac	22-553
LIVERPOOL	31 Aug 1827	Cork	Robinson, Alexander	27-569
	25 Mar 1828	Limerick, Ireland	Phillips, Thomas	28-088
LIVERPOOL PACKET	23 Mar 1822	Havre	Coffin, Abel	22-089
	4 Aug 1825	Rotterdam	Adams, Danl.	25-474
LIVERPOOL TRADER	20 Feb 1822	St. Petersburg	Riding, John, Jr.	22-058
	24 Oct 1825	Greenock	Henry, Robert	25-614
LOGAN	14 Aug 1820	Curacoa	Holmes, Saml.	20-175
	10 May 1821	Curacoa	Holmes, Albert	21-058
	22 May 1823	Curacoa	Denison, J. C.	23-223
LOIRE	22 Jul 1820	St. Johns, N.B.	Basset, Isaac	20-135
	8 Sep 1820	Bermuda	Basset, Isaac	20-229
	18 Oct 1820	St. Johns	Bassett, Isaac.	20-300
	12 Dec 1820	St. Johns	Bassett, Isaac	20-345
	7 Apr 1821	St. Johns, N.B.	Crowell, Asa	21-006
	23 May 1821	St. Johns, New Brunswick	Basset, Isaac	21-081
	6 Jul 1821	St. Johns	Basset, Isaac	21-157
	9 Aug 1821	St. Johns, N.B.	Basset, Isaac	21-218
	3 Dec 1821	St. Johns, N.B.	Bassett, Isaac	21-395
	11 Jun 1824	Halifax	Harden, Gideon, Jur.	24-293
	28 Aug 1824	Halifax	Harden, Gideon	24-491
	4 Oct 1824	Halifax	Harden, Gideon	24-564
	7 Jun 1827	Halifax	Harden, Gideon	27-324
	7 Jul 1827	Halifax	Harden, Naranies	27-416
	17 Aug 1827	Halifax	Harden, Naranies	27-524
	6 Dec 1827	Halifax	Harden, Naranies	27-801
	26 May 1828	Halifax, N.S.	Harden, Varanies	28-247
	18 Jul 1828	Halifax	Crowell, H.	28-385
LONDON	13 Dec 1822	London	Candler, Saml.	22-603
	24 Jun 1823	London	Candler, Samuel	23-283
	19 Dec 1823	London	Allyn, Francis	23-649
	29 Apr 1824	Liverpool	Moran, Nicholas	24-183
	16 Aug 1824	London	Champlin, Henry L.	24-452
	13 Sep 1824	Havre	Moran, Nicholas	24-534
	21 May 1828	Liverpool	Brown, Jesse	28-239
	23 Sep 1828	Liverpool	Brown, Jesse	28-560
	6 Feb 1829	Liverpool	Brown, Jesse	29-051
LONDON PACKET	25 Dec 1820	London	Thomas, Geo.	20-357
	5 Jul 1823	Liverpool	Benedict, Isbon	23-312
	8 Mar 1825	Rio de la Plata	Benedict, Isbon	25-095
	5 Jan 1829	Rio de Janeiro	Robinson, Rowland	29-004
LONDON TRADER	29 Mar 1824	China	Ansley, Ozias	24-116
LOORE	9 Sep 1822	St. John	Bassett, Isaac	22-458
LORD GAMBIER	3 Apr 1827	New Castle	Taylor, Thos.	27-163
	4 Feb 1829	New Castle	Taylor, Thomas	29-047
LORD NELSON	8 Nov 1826	Turks Island	Blathwayt, J. W.	26-651
LORD STRANGFORD	20 Jun 1826	Dublin	Sheal, James	26-353
LORD WELLINGTON	17 Mar 1823	Newry	Pollock, James	23-085
	28 May 1827	Newry	Roche, George	27-309
	14 Nov 1827	Liverpool	Roche, George	27-761
LOUISA	10 May 1821	Trinidad in Cuba	Tate, James, Jr.	21-057
	6 Apr 1822	Amsterdam	Smith, Christopher	22-110

SHIP	DATE OF ARRIVAL	PORT OF EMBARKATION	CAPTAIN	YEAR AND SHIP NUMBER
	7 Jun 1824	Antwerp	Colas, P. J.	24-274
	11 Jun 1824	Liverpool	Fosdick, Peter G.	24-295
	21 Aug 1824	Hamburg	Hopkins, Saml. G.	24-475
	7 Oct 1824	Belfast	Fosdick, Peter G.	24-579
	14 Jun 1825	Belfast	Fosdick, Peter G.	25-342
	10 Nov 1825	Havre	Spring, John	25-649
	16 Mar 1826	Belfast	Reeves, Matthew	26-120
	16 May 1826	Bremen	Baetger, Isaac	26-255
	12 Jun 1826	Amsterdam	Brewer, Nicholas	26-324
	17 Jul 1826	St. Puis, Martinique	De Chatellard, Francis	26-409
	20 Jul 1826	Belfast	Reeves, Matthew	26-414
	27 Nov 1826	Belfast	Reeves, Matthew	26-685
	18 Apr 1827	Belfast	Reeves, Matthew	27-182
	6 Dec 1827	Amsterdam	Kelly, Walter	27-797
	10 May 1828	Amsterdam	Brewer, Nicholas	28-200
	9 Jul 1828	Bremen	Bosse, John	28-367
	6 Oct 1828	Amsterdam	Brewer, Nicholas	28-591
LOUISA MATILDA	4 Dec 1821	Amsterdam	Ferrier, John M.	21-399
	9 Jun 1823	Cadiz	Storry, Thos. W.	23-249
	25 May 1825	Liverpool	Wood, D.	25-296
LOUISE	28 Jul 1823	Antwerp	Colas, P. J.	23-359
	30 Jun 1826	Bremen	Bosse, John	26-370
LOUISIANA	20 Sep 1822	Teneriffe	Rugan, William	22-475
	9 Aug 1826	Leghorn	Whitney, Stephen M.	26-469
	31 Oct 1827	Liverpool	Price, Peter	27-737
	3 Nov 1827	Glasgow	Doan, C. R.	27-745
LOVE	12 Oct 1827	La Guayra	Swift, Asaph	27-701
LOVINIA	20 Nov 1828	Vera Cruz	Meany, Corns.	28-674
LOYALIST	17 Oct 1829	Tobago (Tobasco)	Colledge, Teasdle	29-306
LOYALTY	9 Sep 1822	London	Metcalf, Richd.	22-459
LUCINDA	11 Nov 1824	St. Johns, N.B.	Cleves, Robert, 3rd	24-654
	11 Mar 1825	Alvarado	Hiller, Benjn.	25-101
	29 Jun 1825	Alvarado	Hiller, Benjn.	25-387
LUCY	16 Apr 1821	Gibraltar	Paty, Wm.	21-019
	25 Aug 1821	Liverpool	Elkins, Daniel	21-238
	26 May 1827	St. Martin	Church, James	27-297
	26 Oct 1829	St. Thomas	Tisdale, William	29-328
LUCY ANN	17 Apr 1822	Havana	Davis, Saml.	22-135
	4 Sep 1822	Havana	Davis, Sam	22-450
	5 Oct 1825	Vera Cruz	Arnold, Ardhd.	25-567
	6 Sep 1826	Vera Cruz	Andros, Wm.	26-522
LUDWIG	10 Aug 1825	St. Croix	Beck, A. N.	25-493
LUELLA	15 Jun 1825	Liverpool	Wilson, Jas., Jr.	25-343
LUKEY	12 Jun 1822	St. Andrews	Haskell, John R.	22-266
LUNA	25 Jul 1825	Bordeaux	O'Hara, Jno.	25-442
LUNAR	5 May 1828	Liverpool	Paterson, Albert	28-178
LYCURGUS	3 Dec 1821	Hamburgh	Haley, Jno. B.	21-396
LYDIA	30 Apr 1821	Amsterdam	Higgins, Asa	21-040
	16 Nov 1822	Buenos Ayres	Prince, Christopher	22-572
	7 Oct 1823	Montevideo	Prince, Chris.	23-529
	18 Jun 1828	Havre	Madagan, John (Madegan)	28-310
LYDIA ADAMS	11 Sep 1824	Jamaica	Mosman, Ruben	24-532
LYDIA DAVIS	5 Jan 1824	St. Croix	Couzins, Benjamin	24-006
LYGONIA	13 Aug 1829	Pictou	Harden, Eben	29-215
	12 Oct 1829	Pictou	Harden, Eben	29-292
LYON	5 Jul 1825	Alvarado	Handy, John	25-397
	6 Feb 1826	St. Thomas	Hand, John	26-053
MACDONOUGH	5 Jul 1823	Halifax	Baker, Charles	23-313
	28 Dec 1821	Curacoa	Augur, Reuben	21-435
MACK	9 Oct 1823	St. Johns, Newfoundland	Small, Francis	23-537
MADISON	13 May 1822	St. Iago de Cuba	Jones, Francis	22-191
	22 May 1822	Havana	Norris, John	22-217
MAGNET	10 Jul 1820	Bermuda	Waite, Beriah	20-113
	28 Jun 1821	Liverpool	Ogden, D. S.	21-143
	13 Nov 1821	Liverpool	Ogden, David Layne	21-368
	24 Jun 1822	Rochelle	Thaxter, Geo.	22-285

SHIP	DATE OF ARRIVAL	PORT OF EMBARKATION	CAPTAIN	YEAR AND SHIP NUMBER
	19 Aug 1822	Liverpool	Mount, Forman M.	22-404
	22 Aug 1822	Leith	Mitchell, Thos.	22-413
	22 Aug 1822	Sligo	Stewart, Phinehas	22-414
	6 Feb 1823	Liverpool	Mount, F. M.	23-025
	16 May 1823	Liverpool	Mount, F. M.	23-203
	29 Sep 1823	London	Mount, Fernian Marshall	23-506
	1 Oct 1823	Aquin, St. Domingo	Harriden, Thomas	23-513
	24 Sep 1824	London	Mount, F. M.	24-552
	9 Apr 1825	Liverpool	Mount, F. M.	25-158
	17 Aug 1825	London	Mount, F. M.	25-508
	18 Aug 1825	Matanzas	Damon, John	25-511
	3 May 1826	Nuevetas	Damon, John	26-221
MAGNOLA	7 Mar 1827	Halifax	Hall, Freeman	27-106
MAGNOLIA	29 Apr 1822	Port au Prince	Root, Eliakim F.	22-164
MAINE	16 Jul 1821	London	Townson, Daniel	21-179A
	21 May 1822	Martinique	Oxnard, Stephen D.	22-210
	25 Jan 1823	Port au Platt	Ogier, Joseph W.	23-014
	30 Jun 1823	Martinique	Oxnard, Stephen	23-300
	19 Sep 1823	Port de Plate	Ogier, Joseph W.	23-486
	24 Jun 1824	Jamaica	Waterhouse, Samuel	24-322
	2 Nov 1827	St. Andrews	Hatch, Jeremiah	27-742
MAJESTIC	24 Mar 1828	Liverpool	Page, A. S.	28-079
	27 Jul 1829	Aberdeen & Dundee	Lawson, Alexander	29-171
MALABAR	3 Apr 1823	Havre	Orne, Richd. E.	23-101
MALAGA	10 Jul 1828	Malaga	Simmons, J.	28-368
MALIBAR	18 Nov 1823	New Castle	Orne, Richd. E.	23-601
MANCHESTER	30 May 1821	Bordeaux	Lambert, Richard	21-097
	17 Aug 1825	Liverpool	Lee, William, Jr.	25-507
	6 Dec 1825	Liverpool	Lee, William, Jr.	25-693
	23 Jan 1826	Halifax	Carver, John	26-038
	6 Apr 1826	Liverpool	Lee, William, Jr.	26-154
	15 Aug 1826	Liverpool	Lee, William, Jr.	26-481
	7 Dec 1826	Liverpool	Lee, William, Jr.	26-703
	21 Apr 1827	Liverpool	Lee, William, Jr.	27-190
	24 Aug 1827	Liverpool	Lee, William, Jr.	27-549
	8 Dec 1827	Liverpool	Lee, William, Jr.	27-815
	15 Apr 1828	Liverpool	Lee, William, Jr.	28-129
	29 Aug 1828	Liverpool	Lee, Wm., Jr.	28-480
	16 Dec 1828	Liverpool	Lee, William, Jr.	28-710
	12 Aug 1829	Liverpool	Skitchley, William	29-212
MANCHESTER PACKET	23 May 1822	Rochelle	Lambert, Richard	22-223
	30 Nov 1822	Liverpool	Morris, P.	22-590
	21 Aug 1823	Bordeaux	Meek, James	23-417
	29 Jan 1825	Genoa	Marshall, John	25-039
	9 Mar 1826	Marseilles	Marshall, John	26-095
	5 Dec 1826	Gibraltar	Marshall, D.	26-699
	17 Dec 1827	Gibraltar	Marshall, David	27-840
MANHATTAN	20 Mar 1820	Liverpool	Tarr, David, Jr.	20-071
	8 Aug 1820	Liverpool	Sauck, David	20-169
	25 Dec 1820	Liverpool	Farr, David, Jr.	20-356
	21 May 1821	Liverpool	Samkin, David	21-075
	20 Sep 1821	Liverpool	Tarrhein, David	21-288
	23 May 1822	Liverpool	Crocker, Rowland R.	22-224
	21 Sep 1822	Liverpool	Crocker, Rowland R.	22-478
	12 May 1823	Liverpool	Crocker, Rowland	23-188
	22 Sep 1823	Liverpool	Rickitson, Humphrey	23-492
	18 Feb 1824	Liverpool	Ricketson, H.	24-051
	12 Jun 1824	Liverpool	Ricketson, H.	24-299
	11 Oct 1824	Liverpool	Cockstaff, William G.	24-583
	26 Feb 1825	Liverpool	Hackstaff, Wm.	25-079
	20 Jun 1825	Liverpool	Hackstaff, Wm. G.	25-364
	24 Oct 1825	Liverpool	Hackstaff, William Green	25-610
	20 Feb 1826	Liverpool	Marshall, Fred. W.	26-074
	20 Jun 1826	Liverpool	Marshall, Frederick W.	26-351
	22 May 1827	Liverpool	Marshall, Frederick W.	27-281
	7 Nov 1827	Liverpool	Marshall, F. W.	27-751

SHIP	DATE OF ARRIVAL	PORT OF EMBARKATION	CAPTAIN	YEAR AND SHIP NUMBER
MANHATTEN	4 Feb 1822	Liverpool	Crooker, R. R.	22-025
MAPOCHO	9 Jan 1824	Valparaso	Jenckes, Edward F.	24-011
MARATHON	11 Nov 1824	Liverpool/Newport, Wales	Robinson, Chas. H.	24-652
MARCELLA	15 Mar 1827	Havana	Merrill, Eli	27-122
	18 May 1827	Galway, Irland	Swift, Silas	27-263
MARCELLUS	2 Sep 1820	St. Johns	Little, Archd.	20-222
	26 Feb 1824	Gibraltar	Gillet, Nathn.	24-057
	24 Dec 1824	Malaga	Gillett, Nathan	24-734
MARCHIONESS	13 May 1828	Liverpool	Davis, Thomas	28-209
MARCIA	5 Jul 1823	Havana	Bigley, Joshua C.	23-314
MARCUS	7 Apr 1825	Liverpool	Drew, John (Jos.)	25-155
MARGARET (see Margarett)				
	22 Jun 1821	Lisbon	Harris, Ewan	21-128
	3 Jun 1822	Greenock	Craig, Alexander	22-250
	29 Oct 1822	Amsterdam	Nile, James	22-546
	11 Mar 1823	Amsterdam	West, Job	23-074
	12 May 1823	Havana	Harward, William	23-189
	10 Oct 1823	Amsterdam	West, Job	23-538
	31 Jul 1824	West Port	Johnson, Benjamin	24-422
	19 Mar 1825	Dublin	Johnson, Benjn.	25-122
	16 May 1825	Marseilles	Simmons, Nathl.	25-256
	18 May 1825	Liverpool	McLellan, Thomas	25-271
	18 Aug 1825	Amsterdam	Waldron, James R.	25-513
	29 Oct 1825	Barbadoes	Burt, Joseph B.	25-624
	7 Dec 1825	La Guira	Damon, John	25-694
	13 Mar 1826	Cadiz	Chever, Benjn. H.	26-112
	5 Sep 1827	Bristol & Corke	Carman, Ezekiel	27-585
	20 Dec 1827	Antwerp	Mayo, Simeon	27-847
	26 Jul 1828	London	Patterson, John	28-405
MARGARET & SARAH	31 Oct 1822	Point Petre, Gaudaloupe	Lewis, John L.	22-554
MARGARET ANN	3 Apr 1822	Liverpool	Bowman, John	22-104
MARGARET BOGLE	11 Jun 1824	Greenock	Portess, John	24-303
	11 Sep 1827	Liverpool	Smith, Walter	27-616
	12 Jun 1828	Waterford	Smith, Walter	28-296
MARGARET MERCER	21 Dec 1825	Baracoa	Willet, J.	25-726
	3 May 1826	Baracoa	Willit, J.	26-222
MARGARET WRIGHT	20 May 1825	Campeache	Chamberlain, E.	25-281
MARGARET'S SON	6 Jul 1825	St. Domingo	Smith, Jno. M.	25-399
MARGARETT	2 Mar 1820	Buenos Ayres	Hussey, Andrew	20-049
MARGARETT SCOTT	22 Aug 1827	Liverpool	Kennard, Edward	27-544
MARGARETTA	2 May 1826	La Guira	Alzina, Franco.	26-220
MARIA	7 Feb 1820	Calcutta	Raby, J. C.	20-026
	20 Jul 1820	St. Iago	Martinus, Antonio J.	20-133
	22 May 1822	London	Fowler, Gilbert	22-211
	22 May 1822	Liverpool	Hewett, Rob.	22-218
	3 Oct 1822	London	Fowler, Gilbert	22-502
	19 Feb 1823	Cadiz	Chadwick, Wm.	23-038
	12 May 1823	London	Fowler, Gilbert	23-187
	30 Jul 1823	St. Johns, Antigua	Mather, Ezra	23-371
	4 Sep 1823	St. Johns, N.B.	Richardson, James	23-447
	29 Sep 1823	London	Fowles, Gilbert	23-507
	23 Aug 1824	St. Iago	Stephenson, Stephen	24-484
	2 Apr 1827	Canton	Evans, John	27-161
	25 Mar 1829	St. Croix	Lyle, Thomas	29-112
	19 Oct 1829	St. Johns, N.B.	Snow, Israel	29-309
	24 Oct 1829	Marseilles	Yeaton, N.	29-319
MARIA ANN	11 Aug 1820	Lea	Van Name, Michael	20-172
	7 Apr 1823	Port au Prince	Follansbee, Wm.	23-112
	29 Sep 1823	Tampico	Myrick, Charles	23-508
	18 May 1825	Jacmel	Morecock, Edwd. L.	25-270

SHIP	DATE OF ARRIVAL	PORT OF EMBARKATION	CAPTAIN	YEAR AND SHIP NUMBER
	21 Oct 1826	Aux Cayes	Dunning, Honest S.	26-618
MARIA CAROLINE	12 Jul 1820	Havre	Bishop, Nathl.	20-122
MARIA ELIZABETH	2 Sep 1822	Hamburg	Harms, Hans	22-441
	6 Jan 1823	Hamburgh	Fokkes, J.	23-007
	16 Feb 1826	Hamburgh	Harmes, Hans	26-069
	9 Jun 1826	Hamburgh	Fokkes, J.	26-317
	18 Jun 1827	Hamburg	Fokkes, J.	27-358
	24 Mar 1828	Hamburgh	Fokkes, J.	28-082
	16 Mar 1829	Hamburg	Fokkes, Itje	29-099
MARIA THERESA	16 Nov 1820	Bordeaux	Smith, Andrew	20-322
	28 Aug 1821	Ansterdam	Smith, Andrew	21-245
	13 Apr 1822	Bordeaux	Smith, Andrew	22-124
MARIANA & PAULINA	8 Sep 1827	Hamburg & St. Ubes	Steinhagen, P.	27-604
MARINER	11 Jul 1823	Newfoundland	McAllister, John	23-330
	21 Aug 1827	Gibraltar	Thomas, Oliver	27-542
MARION	25 Nov 1825	Liverpool	Goodwin, Ichabod	25-674
MARK	1 Jun 1824	Halifax	Small, Francis	24-257
	14 Oct 1824	La Guira	Small, Francis	24-596
MARMION	13 Jun 1823	Havre	Hawkins, Elnathan	23-259
	29 Sep 1823	Havre	Hawkins, E.	23-509
	17 Feb 1824	Havre	Hawkins, E.	24-050
	7 Jun 1824	Havre	Hawkins, E.	24-277
	18 Oct 1824	Havre	Maghel, F.	24-608
	17 Jun 1825	Londonderry	Huttleston, Henry, Jr.	25-353
	7 May 1827	Trinadad, Cuba	Hart, J. P.	27-217
	30 Apr 1828	Trinadad de Cuba	Hart, Jarvis P.	28-164
	8 Sep 1828	Trinidad De Cuba	Hart, Jarvis P.	28-511
MARMIONE	20 Nov 1821	Havre	Hawkins, E.	21-376
MARQUIS OF ANGLESEA	8 Jun 1827	Wales	Williams, Hugh	27-327
	12 Sep 1828	Palhely in Wales	Williams, Hugh	28-532
MARSEILLES	14 Jan 1826	Gibraltar	Turner, Charles	26-027
MARSHAL WELLINGTON	3 May 1822	Junderland [Sunderland]	Eyre, James	22-173
MARSHALL	12 Jun 1824	Aux Cayes	Grimes, Richard	24-301
MARTHA (see Martha Pond)				
	21 Mar 1820	Liverpool	Sketchley, William	20-076
	22 Jul 1820	Liverpool	Sketchley, William	20-136
	25 Nov 1820	Liverpool	Skitchley, William	20-335
	3 May 1821	Liverpool	Sketchley, Wm.	21-048
	17 Sep 1821	Liverpool	Sketchly, Wm.	21-277
	17 Nov 1821	Amsterdam	Niles, James	21-373
	15 Jan 1822	Gibara	Driggs, B.	22-009
	1 Feb 1822	Liverpool	Barstow, Hatherly	22-019
	6 Feb 1822	Liverpool	Gifford, James	22-031
	29 May 1822	Liverpool	Sketchley, Wm.	22-240
	24 Jun 1822	Eluthera	Towner, Benjn.	22-286
	25 Sep 1822	San Juan (Cuba)	Carlisle, James	22-484
	4 Oct 1822	Liverpool	Sketchley, Wm.	22-507
	19 May 1823	Antigua	Howland, Rueben	23-212
	30 Jun 1823	Amsterdam	Barnard, Peter	23-301
	26 Dec 1823	Amsterdam	Barber, Thomas	23-653
	25 Mar 1824	Gibraltar & Cadiz	Gifford, James	24-112
	8 Jun 1824	Amsterdam	Barrow, John	24-278
	3 Aug 1824	Port au Prince	Smith, S. F.	24-427
	18 Oct 1824	Havre	Snow, James B.	24-606
	20 May 1825	Marseille	Freeman, Seth	25-282
	20 Jun 1825	Liverpool	Snow, James D.	25-365
	23 Jun 1825	Point Petre, Guadaloupe	Francis, James	25-372
	23 Aug 1825	St. Andrews	Isley, Stephen	25-536
	15 Oct 1825	Amsterdam	Edwards, John	25-590
	7 Nov 1825	London	Snow, James D.	25-637
	26 Nov 1825	Madeira	Isley, Stephen	25-681
	17 Jan 1826	Cork	Freeman, Seth	26-030
	28 Jan 1826	Halifax	Isley, Stephen	26-043

SHIP	DATE OF ARRIVAL	PORT OF EMBARKATION	CAPTAIN	YEAR AND SHIP NUMBER
	7 Jul 1826	Porto Rico	Ilsley, Stephen	26-381
	13 Jul 1826	St. Croix	Brooke, Alex H.	26-400
	5 Sep 1827	Stockholm	Freeman, Seth	27-588
	13 Sep 1827	Amsterdam	Edwards, John	27-626
	2 Jul 1828	Amsterdam	Edwards, John	28-350
	4 Sep 1828	Hamburg	Baker, Richd.	28-499
	13 Oct 1828	Amsterdam	Edwards, John	28-607
	10 Mar 1829	Honduras	Hayden, Luther, Jr.	29-079
	16 Mar 1829	Amsterdam	Edwards, John	29-096
	24 Aug 1829	Amsterdam	Stewart, Chas.	29-242
MARTHA POND	7 Sep 1820	St. Bartholomews	Halsey, David P.	20-227
MARY	7 Jan 1820	Matanzas	Maxwell, William	20-002
	29 Feb 1820	Pard	Geer, Greeman	20-047
	16 Mar 1820	Matanzes	Noyes, J. M.	20-068
	11 Jul 1820	Liverpool	West, R.	20-118
	10 Aug 1820	Matangas	Noyes, J. M.	20-171
	26 Sep 1820	Parrie	Gere, Greenman	20-266
	2 Oct 1820	St. Thomas	Ketcham, Solomon, Jr.	20-277
	20 Dec 1820	Turks Island	Filler, Thomas, Jr.	20-352
	21 May 1821	St. Barts Porto Rico, etc., Bahamas	Bremmer, Daniel	21-077
	7 Jun 1821	Para & Maranham	Merrill, Wiggins	21-105
	21 Sep 1821	London	Boyd, James	21-294
	13 Dec 1821	Liverpool	West, Reuben	21-420
	23 Dec 1821	Matanzas	Noyes, John M.	21-429
	28 Feb 1822	Matanzas	Noyes, Saml., Jr.	22-066
	22 May 1822	Matanzes	Noyes, Saml., Jr.	22-219
	15 Jul 1822	Liverpool	West, Reuben	22-326
	18 Jul 1822	Maranham	Schuyler, Peter	22-338
	23 Jul 1822	Matanzes	Burns, Aaron	22-345
	28 Sep 1822	Halifax	Crowell, Elkanah, Jr.	22-488
	7 Nov 1822	Curacao	Burns, Aaron	22-560
	14 Nov 1822	Guadaloupe	Gardner, Wm. C.	22-569
	24 Feb 1823	Matanzas	Noyes, Samuel	23-051
	7 Apr 1823	Matanzas	Sutton, Benjamin	23-113
	19 May 1823	Matanzas	Noyoes, Samuel, Jr.	23-208
	10 Sep 1823	Grenada	Fuller, David	23-463
	29 Dec 1823	Maragalante	Hurd, Benjn.	23-655
	24 Jun 1824	Bristol	Elsden, Henry	24-326
	12 Jul 1824	Guadaloupe	Willis, David W.	24-371
	1 Nov 1824	Havana	Colliver, Henry	24-634
	3 Aug 1825	Turks Island	Given, Robert	25-471
	10 Mar 1826	Gibraltar	Brown, David	26-097
	8 Feb 1827	Bermuda	Jones, Thomas B.	27-065
	29 May 1827	Dublin	McLaren, James	27-310
	1 May 1828	Havana	Northam, William L.	28-168
	12 Aug 1828	St. Bart & St. Eustatia	Black, Philip	28-432
	1 Jul 1829	Londonderry	Parinton, Ezekiel	29-120
MARY & AGNES	26 Jun 1824	La Guera	Ure, James	24-331
MARY & ELIZA	8 Mar 1823	Trinidad	Ellis, Abner	23-062
	13 Dec 1828	Maracaibo	Holden, Ira	28-704
	2 Jul 1829	Turks Island	Chase, Judah	29-121
MARY & ELIZABETH	1 Apr 1824	Bermuda	Catterall, James	24-125
	17 May 1824	Bermuda	Catarall, James	24-216
	10 Jul 1824	Bermuda	Cotterall, James	24-368
	7 Sep 1824	Bermuda	Catterall, James	24-522
MARY & EMILY	23 Mar 1825	Matanzas	Massor, William	25-135
MARY & HARRIET	9 Mar 1829	Liverpool	Barstow, Wm. C.	29-078
	3 Jul 1829	Liverpool	Barstow, William C.	29-123
MARY & HARRIOT	8 Sep 1828	Liverpool	Barstow, W. C.	28-516
MARY & NANCY	7 Aug 1824	St. croix	Theobold, Charles	24-436
	5 Oct 1829	Gibraltar	Carroll, Lambard	29-283
MARY & SUSAN	27 Aug 1825	Marseilles	Cowthony, Joseph	25-553
	5 Aug 1828	Greenock	Candler, Edward	28-421
	5 Oct 1829	Canton	Candler, Edwd.	29-280

SHIP	DATE OF ARRIVAL	PORT OF EMBARKATION	CAPTAIN	YEAR AND SHIP NUMBER
MARY ANN	10 Oct 1820	St. Martins	Weeks, William	20-291
	13 Jun 1821	Crooked Island	Humphreys, R. W.	21-113
	1 Jun 1822	Havana	Martin, William	22-246
	27 Sep 1822	Tampaco, Mexico	Denis, Thomas, Jr.	22-485
	27 Feb 1824	Havana	McSheafe, Augustus	24-061
	28 Jun 1824	Montego Bay, Jamaica	Jones, David	24-335
	12 Jul 1824	Alvarado	Conklin, Joseph R.	24-372
	30 Aug 1824	Havana	Israel, Israel.	24-495
	13 Mar 1826	Parabia	Coggeshall, Charles	26-108
	13 Jul 1826	St. Croix	Anderson, John	26-399
	9 Jan 1827	Malaga	Whittemon, S.	27-011
	24 Feb 1827	Jamaica	Grierson, James	27-092
	11 Apr 1827	Pernambuco	Coggshall, Charles	27-174
	7 Dec 1827	St. Johns, P.R.	Anderson, John	27-809
	5 May 1828	St. Croix	Smith, Isaac	28-184
	6 May 1828	Zanzabar	Stevens, Wm. G.	28-188
	22 Aug 1828	Sidney, N.S.	Woods, Francis	28-458
	2 Jan 1829	Pictou	Smith, Isaac	29-001
	7 Jan 1829	Rio Grande	Stevens, Wm. G.	29-007
MARY BETSEY	10 Dec 1821	St. Domingo	Hall, Arthur	21-415
MARY ELIZABETH	15 Oct 1829	Madeira	Allen, Samuel	29-305
MARY EMILY	10 Jun 1825	Jacmel	Mason, William	25-327
	19 Dec 1825	Falmouth, Jamaica	Berry, Benjamin	25-720
MARY HOBIN	29 May 1826	St. Thomas	Hamilton, Robert M.	26-286
MARY HOWLAND	19 Jul 1827	Liverpool	Tomkins, James	27-462
	22 Sep 1828	Liverpool	Tomkins, James	28-557
MARY JANE	29 Dec 1821	Marseilles	Barnard, Edwd., Jr.	21-439
	21 Dec 1825	Maracaibo	Groves, Samuel	25-727
	8 Dec 1826	Malaga	Correjia, John	26-705
	21 May 1827	Marseilles	Hopkins, Seth	27-271
	29 Mar 1828	Havana	Correja, John	28-094
	2 Jul 1828	Havanna	Correga, John	28-349
	7 Jan 1829	Havana	Correja, John	29-005
	23 Mar 1829	Havana	Correja, John	29-106
MARY JOAN	2 Dec 1822	Matanzas	Arnold, Danl.	22-591
MARY LEVENGSTON,	17 Jun 1826	St. John, C. A.	Ewen, Edward	26-341
MARY LIVINGSTON	26 Jul 1824	Tampico	Barnard, J.	24-401
	7 Jan 1826	St. Juan	Ewen, Edward	26-015
	2 Nov 1826	St. Juan	Ewen, Edward	26-640
	14 May 1827	St. Johns, S.A. (N.B.)	Ewen, Edward	27-248
	6 Dec 1827	Bahia	Rycroft, John	27-794
MARY LORD	26 Oct 1829	London	Wilson, Josiah L.	29-327
MARY LOUISA	6 Mar 1827	St. Andrews	Paul, Jacob	27-105
MARY MARGARET	26 Apr 1823	Turks Island	Herriman, H.	23-151
MARY OLIVIA	10 Jul 1824	Cabello	Wade, W.	24-367
MARY PALMER	28 August 1821	Gibraltar	Hubbard, Richd. S.	21-246
MARY STEWART	12 May 1827	Carnavan	Marjoribanks, John	27-243
MARY WASHINGTON	14 Jan 1824	Jamaica	Rae, Rob.	24-018
MASSACHU-SETTS	30 Oct 1829	Bremen	Hobart, Samuel B.	29-337
MASSASOIT	3 Jul 1829	Hamburg	Holmes, Bartlett	29-126
MATILDA	10 Sep 1821	St. Martins	McKown, Alexr.	21-266
	27 Apr 1822	St. Martins	McKown, Alexr.	22-155
	16 Aug 1822	St. Martins	McKown, Alexr.	22-397
	1 Sep 1823	St. Martins	McKown, Alexr.	23-434
	11 Oct 1824	St. Martins	McKown, A.	24-588
	31 Jan 1826	Maracaibo	Hawley, Lemuel	26-049
	23 May 1826	Para & St. Martins	McKown, Alexander	26-275
MATTEAWAN	6 Apr 1822	Curacoa	Scribner, Elijah P.	22-111
	30 Nov 1826	St. Croix	Waterman, John	26-692
	1 Aug 1827	St. Croix	Waterman, Jno.	27-494
	2 Feb 1829	St. Barts & St. Thomas	Heald, George	29-042

SHIP	DATE OF ARRIVAL	PORT OF EMBARKATION	CAPTAIN	YEAR AND SHIP NUMBER
MATTEWAN	20 Oct 1827	St. Croix	McKensie, Geo.	27-714
MATTRAWAN	1 Oct 1822	Curacoa	Coffin, Danl.	22-497
	31 Jan 1823	Curacoa	Coffin, Danl.	23-023
	15 Sep 1823	Curacoa	Coffin, Danl.	23-475
	16 Dec 1823	Curacoa	Coffin, Danl.	23-641
	5 Apr 1824	Curacoa	Coffin, D.	24-132
	7 Jul 1824	Curacoa	Coffin, D.	24-356
	4 Jan 1826	St. Croix	Coffin, Danl.	26-012
MATVINA	19 Oct 1826	St. Johns	Edwards, James	26-608
MAY FLOWER	7 Jun 1826	Crooked Island	Welch, Eben	26-312
	11 Oct 1826	Guyama	Welch, Ebenezer	26-590
MAZINGHI	15 Jan 1827	Gibralter	Baker, T.	27-029
MAZZINGHI	19 Feb 1823	Turks Island	Thatcher, Joseph	23-039
	27 Feb 1824	Port au Prince	Glover, Russell	24-062
	3 Jan 1826	London	Carlaw, William B.	26-007
	31 Mar 1826	Port au Prince	Carlaw, William B.	26-136
MCDONOUGH	21 May 1821	Curacao	Auger, Reuben	21-076
	3 Nov 1823	Halifax	Baker, Charles	23-571
	31 Jul 1821	Curacoa	Augur, Reuben	21-207
MCFINGAL	6 Jun 1825	Kingston, Jamaica	Montague, G. H.	25-321
	9 Dec 1826	Barbadoes	Montague, Gurdon H.	26-710
MECHANIC	14 Jul 1821	Trinidad in Cuba	Ray, James O.	21-178
	17 Aug 1822	Trinidad in Cuba	Ray, James E.	22-399
	14 Dec 1822	Trinidad in Cuba	Ray, James E.	22-606
	24 Mar 1823	Trinadad in Cuba	Godfrey, Knowles	23-092
	16 Apr 1824	Matanzas	Corey, Ezra	24-151
	11 Apr 1826	St. Michaels	Lear, John	26-170
MEDINA	23 Apr 1828	Carthagena	Shipman, Charles R.	28-140
	4 Sep 1828	Carthagena	Henderson, J. S.	28-501
	17 Dec 1828	carthagena	Beekman, Henry	28-711
MELANTHO	26 Mar 1827	Carnavan	Lloyd, Wm	27-144
	8 Sep 1827	Liverpool	Lloyd, Wm.	27-605
MENTOR	23 May 1821	Matanzas	Pratt, Noah	21-082
	8 Sep 1821	Matanzas	Pratt, Noah	21-262
	9 Apr 1822	Cadiz	Hart, John E.	22-117
	27 Nov 1822	Guadaloupe	Shackford, C. D.	22-586
	24 Mar 1823	Dominica & Anguilla	Martin, Clement	23-093
	22 Jul 1823	Liverpool	Brown, Jesse E.	23-347
	28 Apr 1824	Liverpool	Wilson, Josiah L.	24-173
	21 Sep 1824	Greenock	Wilson, Josiah L.	24-547
	21 Mar 1825	Greenock	Wilson, Josiah L.	25-126
	5 Jul 1825	Liverpool	Wilson, J. L.	25-393
	26 Jul 1825	Porto Rico	Martin, C.	25-447
	20 Oct 1825	Liverpool	Wilson, James L.	25-600
	26 Dec 1826	Vera Cruz	Schooff, D. F.	26-737
MERCATOR	21 Feb 1820	Port au Prince	Taber, John R.	20-041
	27 Aug 1821	St. Andrews	Parsons, William	21-243
	28 Feb 1823	Bermuda	Allen, Henry	23-052
	10 Apr 1823	St. George, Bermuda	Allen, Henry	23-119
	10 Oct 1823	Nassau, N.P.	Allen, Henry	23-539
	18 Aug 1825	Greenock	Lowrance, George	25-514
	24 Mar 1826	Havana	Hubbs, Danl. G.	26-132
	12 Mar 1829	Santos	Andrews, John F.	29-086
MERCED	23 Mar 1824	Havana	Russell, Henry	24-107
MERCHANT	22 Oct 1821	Liverpool	Aymar, Danl.	21-340
	22 Apr 1822	Liverpool	Aymer, D.	22-139
MERCID	21 Oct 1824	Alvarado	Russell, Henry	24-620
	10 Jul 1826	Cadiz	Russell, Henry	26-391
MERCURY	2 Feb 1825	Marseilles	Nickels, Samuel	25-048
	8 Jun 1825	Havre de Grace	Barnett, John P.	25-323
MERIDIAN	2 Jul 1827	Liverpool	Adams, William	27-404
MERMAID	25 Oct 1822	St. Iago de Cuba	Pointer, Wm.	22-542
MEROPE	6 Dec 1825	Lima	Skiddy, Wm.	25-690
MERURY	14 Dec 1824	Teneriffe	Parsons, S. C.	24-717
MESSENGER	10 Jul 1829	Tampico	Dorr, Ebenezer	29-143
MESSOURI	17 Jun 1824	Carnavon (Wales)	Marshall, D.	24-311
META	5 Jun 1824	La Guira	Meyer, John	24-269
METEOR	22 Apr 1822	Liverpool	Cobb, Nathan	22-141

SHIP	DATE OF ARRIVAL	PORT OF EMBARKATION	CAPTAIN	YEAR AND SHIP NUMBER
	21 Aug 1822	Liverpool	Cobb, Nathan	22-408
	15 Apr 1823	Liverpool	Cobb, Nathan	23-133
	25 Aug 1823	Liverpool	Cobb, N.	23-421
	16 Aug 1824	Liverpool	Gardoner, Thomas W.	24-454
	17 Jan 1825	Liverpool	Gardener, Thomas William	25-025
	11 Apr 1825	Liverpool	Gardner, T. W.	25-160
	19 Aug 1825	Liverpool	Nowland, Edward F.	25-518
	26 Dec 1825	Liverpool	Nowland, Edward F.	25-730
	27 Sep 1826	Belfast	Huttleston, Henry, Jur.	26-564
	26 Jun 1827	Belfast	Huttleston, Henry	27-379
	4 Oct 1827	Belfast	Huttleston, Henry	27-677
	19 Mar 1828	Belfast	Huttleston, Henry, Junr.	28-071
	19 Jul 1828	Belfast	Huttleston, H.	28-390
	19 Aug 1829	Liverpool	Perkins, Luke	29-225
MEXICO	1 Jun 1821	Halifax	Steward, William	21-099
	9 Jul 1827	Liverpool	Fairfield, Asa	27-430
	19 Mar 1828	Greenock	Patten, David	28-072
MIDAS	6 Oct 1823	Carthagena	Bennett, Jno. W.	23-521
	25 Nov 1824	Jamaica	Prince, Thaxter	24-688
	9 May 1827	Savanna La Mar, Jamaica	Putman, John Lewis	27-225
	16 Jun 1827	St. Thomas	Mackay, Jno. R. (by Wm. N. Chadwick)	27-351
MILO	7 Jul 1823	Aux Cayes	Hunter, Jno. S.	23-317
	8 Mar 1824	St. Thomas	Higgins, Jonathan	24-069
	15 May 1824	Havana	Jackson, Lewis	24-214
	24 Jun 1824	Jamaica	Eaton, E. H.	24-325
	23 Dec 1824	Havana	Jasper, Lewis C.	24-733
	20 Feb 1826	Havana	Hatch, William	26-075
	8 May 1826	Havana	Hatch, William	26-242
	4 Jun 1827	St. Thomas	Clark, James	27-317
	8 Sep 1828	Bristol	Stark, Peter	28-515
MILTON	16 Jun 1823	Liverpool	Herring, Joseph	23-266
	3 May 1825	Liverpool	Webb, Silas S.	25-233
	6 Dec 1825	Liverpool	Webb, Silas S.	25-691
	21 May 1827	Liverpool	Webb, William B.	27-268
	20 Aug 1827	Porto Cabello	Fisher, Wm. B.	27-533
	20 Oct 1827	Liverpool	Webb, William B.	27-718
	21 Mar 1828	London	Webb, William B.	28-077
MINERVA	25 Sep 1820	Smyrna & Samos	Meldrum, William	20-261
	26 May 1821	Samos	Meldrum, William	21-089
	24 Sep 1821	Hamburg	Fokkes, J.	21-299
	3 Dec 1821	Antwerp	Eames, Samuel	21-397
	29 Oct 1822	Greenock	Anderson, And.	22-547
	28 Jul 1823	Liverpool	Anderson, Andrew	23-360
	25 Aug 1823	Liverpool	Wilson, James L.	23-423
	15 Nov 1823	Liverpool	Mayell, John Charles	23-596
	31 May 1824	Liverpool	Mayell, John Charles	24-254
	30 Jun 1824	St. Martins	Higgins, Lucius M.	24-344
	23 Aug 1824	Hamburgh	Galles, Jno. G.	24-480
	1 Sep 1824	Trieste	Gifford, Henry B.	24-504
	8 Oct 1824	Greenock	Mayell, John Charles	24-580
	23 May 1825	Hamburg	Galles, John G.	25-290
	15 Jun 1825	Liverpool	Mayell, John Charles	25-345
	9 Jan 1827	Hamburg	Galles, J. P.	27-012
	12 Mar 1827	Glasgow	Wallace, George H.	27-117
	8 May 1827	Rio Janeiro	Hammond, William	27-223
	13 Sep 1827	Amsterdam	Galles, John G.	27-627
	30 Oct 1827	Liverpool	Wallace, George H.	27-734
	17 May 1828	Hamburg	Galles, John G.	28-230
	18 Oct 1828	Hamburg	Gallis, John G.	28-618
	9 Feb 1829	Bristol	Huttleston, Henry, Jur.	29-053
	30 Oct 1829	Belfast	Hussey, Charles J.	29-335
MINOS	24 Oct 1828	Madeira	Dennis, John	28-629
MIROPE	8 Mar 1824	Bordeaux	Frisbee, William	24-070
MISSOURI	10 Apr 1821	Greenock	Baush, Jacob	21-010
	4 Aug 1825	Liverpool	Marshall, D.	25-473

SHIP	DATE OF ARRIVAL	PORT OF EMBARKATION	CAPTAIN	YEAR AND SHIP NUMBER
	21 May 1827	Carnavan	Hiller, Thos., Jr.	27-279
	30 May 1828	Canary	Hiller, Thos., Jr.	28-256
MOBILE	21 Aug 1827	Glasgow	Dickenson, Samuel W.	27-538
MOGUL	20 Jul 1825	Lpool	Brodshaw, E. E.	25-428
MOHAWK	18 Jun 1821	St. Ubes	Trowbridge, Stephen	21-120
	15 Nov 1821	Turks Island	Lawrence, C. K.	21-370
MOLLY	30 Oct 1823	Halifax	Baxter, Elijah	23-564
MONA	1 Jul 1823	Turks Island	West, Asa C.	23-304
MONMOUTH	17 Nov 1826	Leghorn	Atkins, Joshua	26-667
MONROE	13 May 1823	Bordeaux	Handley, Simon	23-196
	29 Nov 1823	Honduras	Webber, Aaron	23-616
	23 Aug 1824	Rochelle	Howland, Wing	24-478
	20 Jan 1825	St. Thomas	Humphreys, Jabez	25-031
	12 Dec 1825	Turks Island	Humphreys, Jabez	25-710
	13 Feb 1827	Santa Cruzz	Humphreys, Jabez	27-078
	18 May 1827	St. Croix & St. Thomas	Humphreys, Jabez	27-264
MONT PARNASSUS	31 Jan 1828	Jeremie	Pradens, E.	28-035
MONTANO	3 Jan 1823	Havre	Burke, Miles R.	23-002
	24 Jun 1823	Havre de Grace	Smith, Andrew	23-284
	4 Nov 1823	Havre	Smith, Andrew	23-572
	19 Feb 1824	Havre	Smith, Andrew	24-052
	31 May 1824	Havre	Smith, Andrew	24-247
	2 Sep 1824	Havre	Smith, Andrew	24-505
	3 Jan 1825	Havre	Smith, Andrew	25-003
	23 Apr 1825	Havre	Smith, A.	25-200
	13 Jan 1826	Havre de Grace	Smith, Andrew	26-026
	29 Apr 1826	Havre de Grace	Smith, Andrew	26-211
	12 Jan 1827	Havre	Smith, Andrew	27-021
	8 May 1827	Havre	Smith, Andrew	27-224
	27 Aug 1827	Havre	Smith, Andrew	27-565
	18 Dec 1827	Havre	Smith, Andrew	27-842
	5 May 1828	Havre	Smith, Andrew	28-179
	2 Sep 1828	Havre	Smith, Andrew	28-495
	15 Jan 1829	Havre	Beekeep, Barth A.	29-015
MONTGOMERY	18 Oct 1828	Liverpool	Lise, John H.	28-622
	6 Mar 1829	Liverpool	Sise, John H.	29-071
MONUMENT	22 Sep 1828	Leghorn	Skaff, Stephen	28-553
MORA	30 Apr 1827	St. Thomas	Ripley, E. M.	27-204
MORDICAE	24 Nov 1828	Omoa	Ficher, John W.	28-678
MOREAU	21 Jun 1827	Jeremie	Rocke, S.	27-365
MORGIANA	24 May 1821	Xibara	Fyfe, Wm.	21-086
	18 Sep 1821	Xibara (Cuba)	Fyfe, Wm.	21-283
MORGIANA	31 Dec 1821	Havana	Fyfe, Wm.	21-440
MORHEY	3 Mar 1825	St. Andrews	Teffts, Thos.	25-087
MORKEY	18 Aug 1825	St. Andrews (Maine)	Tufts, Thos.	25-512
MORNING STAR	28 Mar 1822	St. Thomas	Manta, John	22-100
	25 Jun 1822	Greenock	Stevens, Timothy	22-290
	6 Oct 1823	Curacoa	Waring, Saml. J.	23-522
	16 Feb 1824	St. Johns, Porto Rico	Cook, Joshua	24-043
	28 Apr 1824	St. Thomas	Allen, James, Jr.	24-175
	26 May 1824	Balise (Honduras)	Cook, Joshua	24-234
	9 Nov 1824	St. Johns, N.B.	Fisher, John	24-645
MORO	26 Aug 1824	St. Iago de Cuba	Dunn, E.	24-488
	20 Oct 1826	Kingston	Conell, William	26-615
	19 Dec 1827	Bristol, England	Robinson, Woodbury	27-844
MORO CASTLE	6 Jul 1827	Liverpool	Lenox, John	27-414
MOSQUITO	5 Dec 1821	Salt Creek (St. Martin)	Tefft, Thos.	21-401
MOTION	15 Mar 1825	Campeache	Langdon, John W., Jr.	25-116
	11 Jan 1826	La Guira	Langdon, John W.	26-021
MOUNT PARASSES (see Mount Parnasse)				
MOUNT HOPE	23 Jul 1821	Gottenburg	Allen, Alexr.	21-188
	10 Aug 1822	St. Andrews	Allen, Alexdr.	22-388
	30 Sep 1822	Turks Island	Allen, Alexr.	22-493
MOUNT PARNASSAS	2 Sep 1828	Iremie [Jeremie?]	Merceron, M.	28-494
MOUNT PARNASSE	17 Jul 1829	Jeremie	Petit, A.	29-153

SHIP	DATE OF ARRIVAL	PORT OF EMBARKATION	CAPTAIN	YEAR AND SHIP NUMBER
MOUNT PARNASSUS	13 Nov 1827	Jeremie	Pradere, Edmond	27-757
MOUNT VERNON	26 Aug 1820	Liverpool	Rawson, Able	20-210
	20 May 1822	Liverpool	Rawson, Abel	22-207
	18 Oct 1822	Liverpool	Dawson, Abel	22-535
	19 May 1823	Liverpool	Rawson, Abel	23-213
	9 Jun 1823	Bristol, England	Fulford, Robert	23-250
	7 Jun 1824	Dublin	Rawson, Edward B.	24-270
	18 Dec 1824	Cadiz	Rawson, E. B.	24-725
	17 Jun 1825	Liverpool	Bunker, David M.	25-352
	29 Aug 1828	Liverpool	Snow, Ephraim	28-477
	30 Dec 1828	Liverpool	Snow, Ephraim	28-721
MT. VERNON	1 Apr 1824	Porto Rico	Gaul, James	24-122
MOXA	28 Jun 1822	Martinique	West, Francis	22-298
MUNROE	27 May 1825	Galway	Humphreys, Jabez	25-302
	6 Aug 1825	St. Thomas & Turks Island	Humphreys, Jabez	25-480
MUSIDORA	7 Jun 1821	St. Thomas	Dominick, Francis	21-106
	4 Sep 1821	St. Thomas	Hiller, Thomas, Jr.	21-259
	20 Feb 1823	St. Thomas	Smith, Isaac K.	23-041
NANCEY	13 May 1822	St. Johns, N.B.	Crowell, Ruben	22-192
	8 Jun 1822	St. Johns	Crowell, Ruben	22-261
	25 Jan 1823	St. Johns, N.B.	Crowell, Ruben	23-015
NANCY	28 Jan 1820	St. Johns, N.B.	Crowell, Ruben	20-019
	15 Mar 1820	London	Brooke, Joseph	20-065
	20 Mar 1820	Halifax	Crowell, Ruben	20-075
	10 Jul 1820	St. Johns, N.B.	Crowell, Reuben	20-114
	12 Aug 1820	St. Johns, N.B.	Crowell, Ruben	20-174
	11 Sep 1820	St. Johns, N.B.	Crowell, Reuben	20-237
	9 Oct 1820	St. Johns, N.B.	Crowell, Ruben	20-288
	8 May 1821	St. Johns	Crowell, Ruben	21-053
	9 Jun 1821	St. Johns, N.B.	Crowell, Ruben	21-108
	18 Jul 1821	St. Johns, N.B.	Crowell, Ruben	21-184
	18 Aug 1821	St. Johns, N.Brunswick	Crowell, Ruben	21-231
	5 Sep 1821	Rum Key	Wibray, James	21-261
	20 Sep 1821	St. Johns	Crowell, Ruben	21-289
	19 Oct 1821	St. John, N.B.	Crowell, Ruben	21-336
	29 Nov 1821	St. Johns, N.B.	Crowell, Ruben	21-385
	14 Jan 1822	St. Johns, N.B.	Crowell, Ruben	22-008
	8 Mar 1822	St. Johns, N.B.	Crowell, Ruben	22-073
	11 Apr 1822	St. John, N.B.	Crowell, Ruben	22-121
	10 Jul 1822	St. John	Crowell, Reuben	22-312
	16 Aug 1822	Eastport	Crowell, Ruben	22-398
	28 Oct 1822	St. Johns, N.B.	Crowell, Ruben	22-543
	26 Nov 1822	St. Johns, N.B.	Allen, William	22-584
	13 Dec 1822	St. Johns, N.B.	Crowell, Ruben	22-604
	2 May 1823	St. Johns, N.B.	Crowell, Ruben	23-165
	16 May 1823	Tampico	Matthews, David	23-204
	31 May 1823	St. Johns, N.B.	Crowell, Ruben	23-237
	27 Jun 1823	St. Johns, N.B.	Crowell, Ruben	23-294
	23 Aug 1823	Tampico	Matthews, David	23-419
	1 Sep 1823	St. Johns, N.B.	Crowell, Reuben	23-435
	23 Oct 1823	St. Johns, N.B.	Crowell, Ruben	23-558
	17 Nov 1823	Havana	Naghel, F.	23-598
	25 Nov 1823	St. Johns	Crowell, Ruben	23-608
	2 Jan 1824	St. Johns, N.B.	Crowell, Ruben	24-002
	17 Mar 1824	Havana	Griffing, Moses	24-085
	3 Apr 1824	St. Johns, N.B.	Crowell, Ruben	24-129
	15 Apr 1824	Tampico	Macauley, C. H.	24-145
	4 Jun 1824	St. Johns, N.B.	Delesdeiner, John	24-264
	16 Jul 1824	St. Johns, N.B.	De Lesdernier, John	24-380
	16 Aug 1824	St. Johns, N.B.	Delesdarr, John	24-456
	7 Sep 1824	Port au Prince	Griffing, Moses	24-521
	1 Oct 1824	Havana	McCawley, C. S.	24-560
	18 Oct 1824	St. Johns, N.B.	De Lesdernier, John	24-612
	15 Nov 1824	St. Johns, N.B.	Delesdernier, John	24-664
	15 Dec 1824	St. John, N.B.	Delesdesnier, John	24-722
	7 Feb 1825	Tampico	Nicholas, John S.	25-050

SHIP	DATE OF ARRIVAL	PORT OF EMBARKATION	CAPTAIN	YEAR AND SHIP NUMBER
	10 May 1825	St. Croix	Griffing, Moses	25-244
	21 Jul 1825	St. Iago	Struthers, N.	25-433
	29 May 1826	Point Petre	Morrison, Thos.	26-285
	26 Apr 1828	Porto Rico	Stevens, H.	28-156
NANCY & MARIA	11 Jun 1825	Martinique	Rogers, Richard	25-328
NANCY HENRIETTA	3 Nov 1828	Liverpool	White, Carleton	28-646
NANCY R. CROWELL	21 Sep 1822	St. John	Crowell, Ruben	22-479
NANCY TREAT	6 Aug 1825	Nevis	Varnum, Jeremiah	25-481
NAPOLEAN	2 Sep 1828	Havana	Jennings, S.	28-493
	8 Sep 1828	Curacoa	Budd, John	28-512
	26 Sep 1828	Liverpool	Smith, John P.	28-568
NAPOLEON	10 Jan 1828	Liverpool	Smith, J. P.	28-012
	26 May 1828	Liverpool	Smith, Jno. P.	28-249
	28 Jan 1829	Liverpool	Smith, John P.	29-039
	7 Jul 1829	Curacao	Budd, John	29-137
NAPOLIAN	20 Nov 1828	Havana	Jennings, Solomon	28-673
NASSAU	19 Aug 1823	St. Thomas	Welden, A. W.	23-412
	20 Dec 1823	St. Thomas	Welden, A. W.	23-651
	30 Mar 1824	St. Thomas	Welden, Asa W.	24-117
	30 Jun 1824	St. Thomas	Welden. A. W.	24-343
	6 Sep 1824	St. Thomas	Scott, Francis	24-519
	24 Nov 1824	St. Thomas	Scott, Francis	24-687
	13 Aug 1825	Port au Prince	Quereau, P. J.	25-499
	2 Nov 1825	Port au Prince	Quinan, Ph. S.	25-630
	7 Jun 1826	Antigua	Teer, Mark	26-311
NATCHES	13 Sep 1823	Bordeaux	Cook, Wm. D.	23-471
NATCHEZ	22 Apr 1822	Greenock	Cook, William D.	22-142
	17 Aug 1822	Greenock	Cook, William D.	22-400
	10 Apr 1823	Bordeaux	Barnard, Timothy	23-120
	7 Feb 1825	Buenos Ayres	Cook, Wm. D.	25-053
	18 Aug 1828	Coquimbo Arica & Callio	Hart, Gamaliel	28-442
NATIVE	11 Sep 1821	St. Thomas	Bidell, William, Jr.	21-267
	29 May 1824	Port au Prince	Mayo, Oliver	24-246
	31 Jan 1825	Port au Prince	Mayo, Oliver	25-042
	29 Apr 1825	Port au Prince	Denny, A.	25-221
	24 Aug 1825	Havana	Smith, Benjn.	25-542
	16 Nov 1825	Havana	Smith, Benjn.	25-661
	8 Feb 1826	Havana	Marsham, John	26-057
	15 Apr 1826	Havana	Mansheim, John	26-181
	30 Jun 1826	Havana	Myrick, Isaac	26-373
	19 Sep 1826	Havana	Myrick, Isaac	26-539
	1 Dec 1826	Havana	Myrick, Isaac	26-695
NATURE	17 Aug 1824	Port au Prince	Mayo, Oliver	24-466
	2 Jun 1828	St. Croix	Winebury, J.	28-262
NED	1 Oct 1829	Roco de Toro	Roberts, John	29-272
NELSON	13 Aug 1821	Guadaloupe	Lane, John T.	21-223
	14 Mar 1823	Bermuda	Hanson, Henry	23-083
	18 Apr 1826	Aux Cayes	Kimball, John	26-186
NEPTUNE	5 Jul 1820	Matangas	Dimond, Henry	20-106
	11 Oct 1821	Porto Plato	Arzero, Laes.	21-315
	29 Oct 1821	Genoa	Monro, George	21-350
	30 Nov 1821	St. Domingo	Keating, Richd.	21-387
	11 Jun 1822	Gottenburgh	Hagberg, Henry	22-265
	18 Jul 1822	Porto Plate	Argeno, Lewis	22-339
	22 Oct 1822	Havana	Arzino, Lues	22-540
	25 Jan 1823	Havana	Arzeno, Lewis	23-016
	24 May 1824	Bermuda	Hayward, Benjamin	24-228
	20 Apr 1825	Maria Galanta	Madigan, John	25-192
	23 Jan 1826	Greenock	Miller, William	26-039
	11 Feb 1826	Curacoa	Bailey, Job	26-059
	24 Mar 1826	Portorico	Madegair, John	26-130
	19 Nov 1828	London	Waters, Wm. C.	28-667
NEPTUNES BARGE	23 Apr 1821	Havana	Crane, Jno. R.	21-030

SHIP	DATE OF ARRIVAL	PORT OF EMBARKATION	CAPTAIN	YEAR AND SHIP NUMBER
	1 Oct 1822	Havana	Michaletti, P.	22-498
NEPTUNUS	13 Nov 1820	Havre	Former, Peter O.	20-321
NESTOR	3 Nov 1820	Liverpool	Stanton, John	20-315
	6 Jul 1821	Liverpool	Macy, Seth G.	21-158
	20 Nov 1821	Liverpool	Macy, Seth G.	21-377
	3 Apr 1822	Liverpool	Macy, Seth G.	22-105
	9 Dec 1822	Liverpool	Lee, Wm., Junr.	22-596
	10 Jan 1823	Cronstadt	Whiting, Michl.	23-009
	25 Jul 1823	Liverpool	Lee, William, Jr.	23-353
	14 Nov 1823	Liverpool	Lee, William, Jr.	23-591
	13 Mar 1824	Liverpool	Lee, William, Jr.	24-078
	4 Jun 1824	Rotterdam	Whitney, Michl.	24-266
	16 Aug 1824	Liverpool	Lee, William, Jr.	24-453
	7 Jan 1825	Liverpool	Prase, Wm. G.	25-006
	8 Mar 1827	Rochelle	Spurling, Samuel	27-108
	12 Jul 1827	Aux Cayes	Bibbins, Anson	27-443
	20 Oct 1827	Port au Prince	Sylvester, M.	27-715
	15 Dec 1828	Havana	Bibbins, Anson	28-708
	13 Jul 1829	Pernambuco	Bibbins, Anson	29-146
NESTOR IN LIVERPOOL	29 Jul 1822	Liverpool	Macy, Seth G.	22-357
NEURY	27 Jan 1827	Newry	Adams, John	27-042
NEVA	9 Oct 1824	Cronstadt	Burnham, Asa	24-581
NEW BEEN	18 Jan 1820	Turks Island	Cushing, John	20-009
NEW ENGLAND	28 Sep 1824	Liverpool	Berry, Arthur	24-556
	12 Apr 1825	Liverpool	Berry, A.	25-170
	7 Jul 1826	Matanzas	Mathewson, E.	26-386
	5 Feb 1827	Matanzes	Mathewson, E.	27-056
	23 Apr 1827	Matanzas	Deming, John	27-193
	11 Jul 1827	Matanzas	Deming, John	27-439
	29 Jan 1828	Matanzas	Curtis, Andru	28-030
	4 Jun 1828	Matanzas	Curtis, A.	28-277
	29 Aug 1828	Havre	Snow, Jabez	28-481
	11 Sep 1828	Port au Prince	Curtis, A.	28-528
	27 Jul 1829	Matanzas	Martin, Henry	29-173
NEW HAMPSHIRE	28 Sep 1826	Liverpool	Snow, Michael	26-568
NEW ORLEANS	24 Aug 1827	Liverpool	Cole, Stephen E.	27-548
	27 Feb 1829	Rio de Janeiro	Cole, Stephen E.	29-068
NEW PACKET	16 Apr 1822	Mayagues	Bayley, Robt., Jr.	22-132
	27 Apr 1822	Maranham	Chase, Chas. F.	22-156
	27 Jul 1822	St. Thomas	Chase, Chas. F.	22-353
	29 Aug 1822	Fayal & Flores	D'Avella, Joaquin Severino	22-435
	5 May 1823	Havana	Chase, Chas. F.	23-168
	12 Dec 1825	Havana	Graves, Anthony	25-709
	7 Aug 1826	London	Graves, Antonio	26-465
	20 Sep 1826	St. Domingo	O'Hoyt, John	26-542
	19 Oct 1826	Jamaica	Parker, Josiah C.	26-609
	9 May 1827	St. Domingo City	Noyes, Amos	27-231
	24 Jul 1827	St. Andrews	Harris, Enon	27-474
	16 Aug 1827	the City of St. Domingo	Hoyt, John C.	27-521
	20 Oct 1827	St. Domingo	Hoyt, John O.	27-716
	16 Apr 1828	St. Johns	Adams, R.	28-131
	15 Nov 1828	St. Johns, N.B.	Berry, Benjamin	28-661
NEW PRISCILLA	22 Aug 1823	Malaga & Gibraltar	Crowell, James	23-418
NEW SPECULATION	1 Mar 1823	Havana	Coelho, Antonio Ribro.	23-055
	29 Jun 1824	Rio Grande	Carmacho, Antonio Gonsalaes	24-340
NEW YORK	12 Nov 1822	Liverpool	Maxwell, George	22-565
	11 Mar 1823	Liverpool	Maxwell, George	23-075
	11 Jul 1823	Liverpool	Maxwell, George	23-331
	15 Nov 1823	Liverpool	Maxwell, G.	23-597
	13 Mar 1824	Liverpool	Maxwell, G.	24-079
	22 Jul 1824	Liverpool	Maxwell, Geo.	24-388
	4 Nov 1824	Liverpool	Maxwell, Geo.	24-639
	8 Mar 1825	Liverpool	Bennett, Thos.	25-094

SHIP	DATE OF ARRIVAL	PORT OF EMBARKATION	CAPTAIN	YEAR AND SHIP NUMBER
	20 Jun 1825	Port au Plata	Hatch, John	25-367
	15 Jul 1825	Liverpool	Bennett, Thos.	25-423
	14 Feb 1826	Port au Plate	Hatch, John	26-066
	3 Apr 1826	Liverpool	Bennett, Thomas	26-145
	5 Jul 1826	Liverpool	Bennett, Thomas	26-378
	3 Oct 1826	Port au Plate	Hatch, John	26-581
	14 Nov 1826	Liverpool	Bennett, Thomas	26-662
	6 Mar 1827	Liverpool	Bennett, Thomas	27-104
	19 Mar 1827	Port au Platt	Greenman, Wm.	27-126
	29 Jun 1827	Porto Platt	Thorp, David	27-396
	14 Jul 1827	Liverpool	Bennett, Thomas	27-450
	30 Oct 1827	Liverpool	Bennett, Thomas	27-735
	14 Mar 1828	Liverpool	Bennett, Thomas	28-060
	5 May 1828	Teneriffe	Tucker, Zebediah	28-181
	7 Jul 1828	Port Platt	Thop, David	28-359
	18 Jul 1828	Liverpool	Bennett, Thos.	28-383
	5 Nov 1828	Marseilles	Apthorp, J. T.	28-654
	19 Nov 1828	Liverpool	Bennett, Thomas	28-668
	26 Dec 1828	St. Thomas	Sayward, James	28-718
	6 Jul 1829	Porto Plat (Port au Platt)	Thorp, David	29-131
	31 Jul 1829	Liverpool	Bennet, Thos.	29-181
NEW YORK PACKET	19 Aug 1820	Amsterdam	Weiderholdt, Henry L.	20-193
	8 May 1823	Bristol, Engd.	Stone, John	23-174
	14 Oct 1823	Bristol	Stone, John	23-545
	20 Mar 1824	Bristol	Cock, Henry	24-096
	6 Aug 1824	Bristol	Cock, Henry	24-435
NEWPORT	16 Feb 1824	Campeachy	Burroughs, Jno.	24-044
NEWRY	11 Jul 1827	Newry	Anderson, Chas.	27-440
NIAGARA	4 Sep 1824	Tampicao	Tanner, John	24-513
NIGER	29 Jan 1827	Bordeaux	Luce, Mathew	27-046
NILE	24 Aug 1821	Matanzes	Gossage, Robt.	21-237
	11 Jul 1822	Port au Prince	Aldrich, N.	22-316
	16 Oct 1822	Port au Prince	Aldrich, N.	22-530
	12 May 1823	Havana	Aldrick, N.	23-190
	15 Aug 1823	Jamaica	Aldrich, N.	23-401
	22 Nov 1823	Kingston, Jamaica	Morgan, John	23-607
	30 Apr 1827	London	Obear, Benjamin T.	27-205
	17 May 1827	Liverpool	Huntington, Edward	27-261
	5 Oct 1827	Rochelle	Huntington, Edward	27-678
	13 Aug 1828	Rochelle	Rochett, John	28-435
	18 Oct 1828	Havana	Remington, John	28-620
	18 Aug 1829	Belfast	Brayton, William	29-222
NIMROD	21 Sep 1820	Havre	Center, Joab	20-255
	5 Apr 1821	Liverpool	Lavie, Jas. M.	21-003
	1 Jun 1821	St. Johns, N.B.	Alden, James	21-100
	19 Jan 1822	Buenos Ayres	Sterling, Jno. W.	22-012
	30 Jul 1823	Canton & Beunos Ayres	Sterling, Jno. W.	23-370
	28 Apr 1824	London	Fowler, Gilbert	24-181
	30 Aug 1824	London	Fowler, Gilbert	24-493
	24 Jan 1826	Lima	Fowler, Gilbert	26-041
	9 Jan 1827	Liverpool	Nicholl, Wm.	27-014
	9 Jul 1827	Greenock	Allen, William	27-428
	21 Aug 1827	Gibraltar	Hill, John L.	27-539
	1 Dec 1827	London	Allen, William	27-780
	31 Jul 1828	Liverpool	Allen, Wm.	28-411
NOBLE	9 Jan 1824	Havana	Maxwell, Noble	24-012
	2 Nov 1826	Havana	Maxwell, Noble	26-643
	5 Nov 1828	Bremen	Maxwell, Noble	28-650
NONPAREL	11 Jun 1824	St. Thomas	Furlong, Wm.	24-291
NORTH CAROLINA	22 Oct 1827	St. Barts	Allen, Alexr.	27-719
NORTH STAR	27 Oct 1828	Bordeaux	Hall, Joseph	28-635
NORVAL	12 Jun 1826	St. Johns, N. Foundland	Punton, William	26-322
NOTRE DAME	6 Oct 1827	Guadeloupe	Croizet, J.	27-681
NYMPH	5 Jul 1820	Havre	Green, Joshua	20-107
	17 Jan 1822	St. Iago de Cuba	Smith, John	22-011
OCEAN	28 Jul 1820	Bermuda	White, A. C.	20-155

SHIP	DATE OF ARRIVAL	PORT OF EMBARKATION	CAPTAIN	YEAR AND SHIP NUMBER
	17 Aug 1820	Sligo	Stewart, Phinehas	20-189
	23 Oct 1820	Amsterdam	Bond, Nath. Smith	20-303
	30 Jun 1821	Hamburgh	Bond, Nathl. Smith	21-145
	10 Sep 1823	Amsterdam	Bond, Nathaniel Smith	23-464
	27 Jul 1825	Liverpool	Marshall, J. H.	25-458
	8 Jun 1826	Fayal	Searle, John	26-314
	13 Jul 1827	Liverpool	Gibbs, John	27-447
OCTAVIA	26 Jul 1824	Barbadoes	Seluson, Nathl.	24-395
OCTAVIAN	15 May 1824	Havana & Matanzes	Gordon, Nathl.	24-215
OGLETHORPE	8 Jul 1824	Cardiff	Jayne, Charles	24-361
	9 Nov 1824	Liverpool	Jayne, Charles	24-647
	25 Aug 1825	Liverpool	Tenbner, Charles	25-547
OHIO	10 Jul 1820	Amsterdam	Carman, Ezekiel	20-115
	2 May 1821	Amsterdam	Carman, E.	21-045
	18 Jul 1821	Havre	Lunt, Micajah, Jr.	21-183
	16 Feb 1822	St. Ubes	Carman, Ezekiel	22-049
	21 Mar 1825	Belfast	Mansheim, John (James)	25-128
OLIVE & SARAH	27 Jan 1823	Matanzas	Blackmer, Lewis	23-018
OLIVE BRANCH	12 Aug 1822	St. Thomas	Thing, Abraham	22-392
	30 Oct 1823	St. Johns, N.B.	Chestnut, Robert	23-565
	20 Mar 1824	Havana	Allen, Sylvester	24-097
	16 Aug 1826	Neuvitas	Haskell, David	26-492
	23 Nov 1827	Havana	Smith, Solomon	27-768
	28 Aug 1828	Liverpool	Harding, Robert	28-471
	9 Oct 1829	Liverpool	Harding, Robt.	29-287
OLIVEBRANCH	15 Mar 1820	St. Bartholomews & St. Croix	Hawes, Ebenezer	20-063
OLIVER WOLCOTT	3 Nov 1827	Halifax	Ward, Anthony	27-744
OLYMPIA	16 May 1822	St. Salvador	Weston, Wm.	22-199
	2 Sep 1823	Gibraltar	Souther, John	23-439
	19 Jun 1828	Porto Rico	Brown, Thos.	28-312
	12 Aug 1828	Havre de Grace	Wood, Borden	28-434
	20 Aug 1829	Havre	Wood, B.	29-231
ONION	1 Nov 1821	Liverpool	Davis, George	21-355
ONLY DAUGHTER	29 Apr 1825	Port au Prince	Brown, Nicholas	25-215
	9 Nov 1825	Barbadoes	Burrill, Charles	25-647
	20 Feb 1826	St. Domingo	Israel, Israel	26-071
	26 Apr 1826	Barbadoes	Brown, Jesse	26-203
	24 Oct 1827	St. Pierre	Brown, Jesse	27-721
ONLY SON	14 Jun 1827	St. John, Porto Rico	Bowly, Gideon	27-347
	14 Jan 1828	Omoa	Oldridge, Samuel	28-015
ONTARIO	27 Jun 1821	Leghorn	Aderton, Thomas	21-140
	25 Mar 1823	Leghorn	Collins, Jno.	23-097
ORATOR	1 Oct 1829	Maracaibo via Jamaica and Havanna	McKenzie, Reuben	29-270
ORAZIMBO	7 Jan 1821	Liverpool	Nichols, Saml.	22-006
ORBIT	29 Aug 1821	Liverpool	Macy, Josiah	21-248
	31 Dec 1821	Liverpool	Macy, Josiah	21-442
	29 Apr 1822	Liverpool	Macy, Josiah	22-165
	31 Aug 1822	Liverpool	Macy, Josiah	22-438
	10 mar 1823	Liverpool	Macy, Josiah	23-068
	1 Sep 1823	Liverpool	Tinkham, Joseph	23-436
	31 Dec 1823	Liverpool	Tinkham, Joseph	23-657
	22 Apr 1824	Liverpool	Tinkham, Joseph	24-160
	30 Aug 1824	Liverpool	Tinkham, Joseph	24-494
	23 Oct 1826	Liverpool	Harding, Nehemiah (Nathl.)	26-622
OREGON	15 Nov 1824	St. Iago Cape de Verd Islands	Swift, Asa H.	24-663
ORESTELLE	4 Oct 1828	Port au Prince	McNeill, John J.	28-582
ORIENT	20 May 1822	New Castle	Gallilee, Robert	22-208
	25 Nov 1825	Rotterdam	Vanderford, B.	25-671
	9 Dec 1826	St. Pears, Martinique	Chase, Luke	26-715
	10 Mar 1828	Halifax	Matthews, Samuel, Jr.	28-053
	17 Feb 1829	Rio de Janeiro	Young, John H.	29-065
ORIGON	8 Jun 1824	Havre	Swift, Asa H.	24-285

SHIP	DATE OF ARRIVAL	PORT OF EMBARKATION	CAPTAIN	YEAR AND SHIP NUMBER
ORION	1 Feb 1820	Port au Prince	Wheeler, Enoch	20-021
	21 Aug 1820	Belfast	Burns, John	20-198
	18 Jun 1821	Liverpool	Davis, George	21-121
	15 Apr 1822	Havana	Crawford, William	22-127
	3 Apr 1823	Hamburgh	Abendatt, Ernst	23-102
	8 Oct 1823	Hamburgh	Abendroth, Ernst	23-533
	12 Mar 1825	Jamaica	Snow, Levi	25-104
	24 Mar 1825	Hamburgh	Abendroth, Ernst	25-141
	30 Mar 1825	Jacqumel	Deming, Clement S.	25-143
	23 Apr 1825	Martinique	Atwater, E.	25-199
	19 Jun 1826	Madeira	Davies, Robert	26-346
	15 Jan 1827	Glasgow	Bridges, Thos.	27-033
	27 Jul 1827	Nuevitas	Mendell, Wm. P.	27-484
ORISTELLO	19 Mar 1827	Port au Prince	Joublane, Charles	27-131
ORLANDO	8 May 1824	Porto Rico	Burnham, Joseph	24-206
	23 Mar 1826	Bermuda	Tucker, Zebediah	26-128
	5 May 1826	Bermuda	Tucker, Zebediah	26-231
	1 Aug 1826	Bermuda	Tucker, Zebediah	26-443
	28 Sep 1826	Bermuda	Courtny, Hutson	26-566
	8 Nov 1826	Bermuda	Courtney, Hutson	26-652
ORLEANS	14 Dec 1821	Marseilles	Brown, Thos. E.	21-421
	10 Sep 1822	Montevideo	Brown, Thomas E.	22-460
ORNA (see Asaph)				
ORONO	5 Jun 1823	Point Peter	Gordon, Joshua	23-243
	21 May 1827	Matanzas	Skolfield, Thomas	27-280
OROZIMBO	16 Apr 1821	Havanna	Stow, Thomas	21-020
	21 May 1821	Trinidad, Cuba	Deartle, Golden	21-079
	8 Jun 1822	Liverpool	Mayell, John C.	22-262
	19 Oct 1822	Liverpool	Nichols, Samuel	22-536
	11 Aug 1823	Liverpool	Nichols, Samuel	23-392
	1 Dec 1823	Liverpool	Nichols, Samuel	23-622
	31 May 1824	Liverpool	Thomson, William	24-255
	2 Oct 1824	Liverpool	Thomson, William	24-561
	7 Jul 1825	Liverpool	Thompson, Wm.	25-402
	8 Mar 1826	Liverpool	Thomson, William	26-093
	7 Nov 1826	Liverpool	Thomson, Wm.	26-649
	5 Mar 1827	Liverpool	Mayell, John Charles	27-100
	28 Jun 1827	Hamburg	Mayell, John Charles	27-385
	1 Oct 1827	Havre	Mayell, John Charles	27-670
ORRA MARIA	18 Oct 1823	Guadaloupe	Murch, Ephraim	23-550
ORRIS	12 Mar 1825	Havana	Thomas, Henry	25-103
ORVIS	20 Apr 1824	Havana	Thomas, Henry	24-157
OSCAR	21 Oct 1822	Liverpool	Savage, Avery	22-537
	24 Jul 1823	Liverpool	Morris, John	23-350
	4 Sep 1823	Stockholm	Hockert, E.	23-448
OSGOOD	9 Dec 1826	London	Vanderpool, Benjn.	26-712
OSPRAY	27 Aug 1822	St. Andrews	Rice, William	22-424
	2 Apr 1824	Rochelle	Nye, Philip	24-128
	2 Sep 1824	Amsterdam	Nye, Philip	24-507
	11 Apr 1825	Gibraltar	Dossey, R. A.	25-166
	30 Jul 1827	Santa Marta	Grinnell, Joshua	27-487
	8 Mar 1828	Lisbon	Grinnell, Joshua	28-047
OSPREY	22 Nov 1824	Leghorn	Coombs, John	24-679
OSSIAN	18 Feb 1822	Greenock	Black, John	22-053
OSWEGO	12 Apr 1824	Cape de Verds/Praya	Thompson, John	24-136
OTHELLO	3 Jun 1823	Bordeaux	Lambert, Richard	23-238
	6 Nov 1823	Bordeaux	Lambert, Richard	23-573
	31 Aug 1824	Bordeaux	Lambert, Richard	24-498
	11 Jul 1825	Buenos Ayres	Allen, Jas., Jr.	25-413
	3 Dec 1828	Leith	Knight, John M.	28-692
OTHO	2 Jan 1822	Bordeaux	Gifford, James	22-003
OTTER	25 Feb 1822	Havana	Hopkins, Isaac	22-062
	5 Aug 1822	Mayaguez, Porto Rico	Bayley, Robert, Jr.	22-373
	30 Oct 1826	Antwerp	Waters, William D.	26-634
	17 Mar 1828	Halifax	Hadlock, Epps	28-063
OXFORD	14 Aug 1828	Havre	Prince, Thastis	28-437
PACIFFIC (see Pacific)				
PACIFIC	5 Jul 1820	Gibraltar	Smith, J.	20-108

SHIP	DATE OF ARRIVAL	PORT OF EMBARKATION	CAPTAIN	YEAR AND SHIP NUMBER
	28 Mar 1822	Matanzas	Hood, John	22-097
	15 Apr 1824	Bordeaux	Hodges, Hercules	24-148
	24 May 1824	Liverpool	Maxwell, Sol.	24-230
	11 Sep 1824	Liverpool	Maxwell, Sol.	24-531
	29 Dec 1824	Liverpool	Maxwell, Solomon	24-742
	16 Apr 1825	Lpool	Maxwell, S.	25-178
	20 Aug 1825	Liverpool	Maxwell, Solomon	25-525
	23 Jan 1826	Liverpool	O'Grady, John C.	26-040
	22 May 1826	Liverpool	Crocker, Rowland R.	26-267
	21 Jun 1826	St. Croix	Davis, Frs. B.	26-355
	13 Jan 1827	Liverpool	Crocker, Rowland R.	27-023
	7 May 1827	Liverpool	Crocker, Rowland Robinson	27-218
	14 May 1827	Point Petre, Guadaloupe	Jones, Henry A.	27-249
	5 Sep 1827	Liverpool	Crocker, Rowland R.	27-589
	17 Jun 1828	Liverpool	Crocker, Rowland R.	28-309
	24 Oct 1828	Liverpool	Crocker, Rowland R.	28-628
	11 Mar 1829	Liverpool	Skitchley, William	29-081
	19 Oct 1829	Liverpool	Crocker, Rowland R.	29-308
	24 Oct 1829	Havana	Cartwright, Daavis G. (D.)	29-321
PACIFICATION	31 Aug 1822	Bermuda	Gourgon, Joseph	22-439
	30 Jun 1823	Jacmel	Guigon, Joseph	23-302
	6 Oct 1823	Jacmel	Sheed, Abraham A.	23-523
	27 Apr 1824	Jacmel	Hillard, Rob. B.	24-171
	28 Jul 1824	Jacmel	Sheed, Abraham A.	24-414
PACKET	23 Sep 1820	Liverpool	Weekes, Seaman	20-257
	11 Dec 1820	Havana	Foote, Saml. E.	20-343
	13 Jun 1821	Havana	Foote, Sam. C.	21-111
	6 Aug 1822	Havana	Penn, William	22-375
	27 Aug 1822	London	Boggs, James C.	22-425
	4 Nov 1822	Turks Island	Boggs, James C.	22-558
	20 Feb 1823	Havana	Doughty, Joseph	23-040
	24 Apr 1823	Havana	Doughty, Joseph	23-150
	10 Jul 1823	Havana	Daughty, Joseph	23-326
	11 Oct 1823	Havana	Doughty, Joseph	23-540
	26 Dec 1823	Havana	Doughty, Joseph	23-654
	24 Mar 1824	Havana	Doughty, Joseph	24-109
	25 May 1824	Havana	Doughty, Joseph	24-233
	2 Aug 1824	St. Andrews	Grow, John S.	24-425
	11 Nov 1824	La Rochelle	Youngs, Robert	24-651
	31 May 1826	Rachel	Barber, Thomas	26-292
	18 Sep 1826	Jamaica	Heyer, Andrew	26-534
PACKET ELIZA	1 Jul 1829	Jeremie	Fletcher, Foxwell C.	29-119
PACKET FRANCES	30 Jun 1828	Trinidad	Scott, Francis	28-339
PACKET FRANCIS (see Packet Frances)				
PACKET MARGARET	19 Sep 1823	Antigua	Haiden, Joseph	23-487
	20 Sep 1824	Carthagena	Tuelles, Elijah	24-544
PACTOLUS	19 Aug 1823	Aquin, St. Domingo	Kilby, Thomas	23-413
PAEZ	5 Mar 1827	Curacoa	Clark, Alex B.	27-098
PAGASUS	21 Mar 1829	City of St. Domingo	McNeilledge, Alex	29-105
PALESTINE	1 May 1821	Havana	Lancaster, Jos.	21-044
PALLAS	15 Jul 1822	Amsterdam	Cutler, A. K.	22-327
	17 Aug 1824	Liverpool	Center, A. K.	24-460
	14 Jun 1828	Havre	Brown, Henry	28-305
	28 Oct 1828	Cork	Campion, Gifford	28-637
PAMELIA	3 Aug 1829	St. Thomas	McKown, Alexr.	29-191
PANAMA	9 Apr 1828	Canton	Champman, Israel	28-119
PANTHEA	15 Jun 1822	Liverpool	Burwell, Thomas	22-274
	5 Oct 1822	Liverpool	Bennett, Thomas	22-511
	13 Mar 1823	Liverpool	Bennett, Thos.	23-078
	18 Jul 1823	Liverpool	Bennett, Thos.	23-341
	13 Nov 1823	Liverpool	Bennett, Thomas	23-587
	24 Mar 1825	Liverpool	Hathaway, William	25-137
	21 Jul 1825	Liverpool	Hathaway, W.	25-436
	11 Nov 1825	Liverpool	Hathaway, William	25-654

SHIP	DATE OF ARRIVAL	PORT OF EMBARKATION	CAPTAIN	YEAR AND SHIP NUMBER
	8 Apr 1826	Liverpool	Hathaway, W.	26-163
	22 Jul 1826	Liverpool	Hathaway, William	26-419
	22 Nov 1826	Liverpool	Hathaway, W.	26-676
	12 Feb 1827	Havanna	Brittingham, A. P.	27-076
PANTHER	9 Jul 1825	Aux Cayes	Haskell, J. G.	25-410
	21 Oct 1826	City of St. Domingo	Buttingham, A. P.	26-619
	18 Jun 1828	St. Iago de Cuba	Brittingham, A. P.	28-311
PANTHIA	7 Feb 1822	Liverpool	Eldridge, Jonathan	22-035
	23 Apr 1824	Liverpool	Bennett, Thomas	24-161
	13 Nov 1824	Liverpool	Bennit, Thos.	24-659
PAQUEBOT BORDEAUX	25 May 1828	Vera Cruz bound to Bordeaux, put in in distress	Duprat, John	28-243
PAQUET DES AUX CAYES	3 Feb 1827	Aux Cayes	Beaque, Isaac L.	27-055
PAQUET DES CAYES	25 Apr 1827	Aux Cayes	Gallee, J. N.	27-196
	10 Mar 1828	Aux Cayes	Hornby, J.	28-052
	26 May 1828	Aux Cayes	Hornby, J.	28-248
	16 Aug 1828	Aux Cayes	Desmaratte, Fanfair	28-440
	9 Jul 1827	Aux Cayes	Geller, J. N.	27-432
	11 Oct 1827	Aux Cayes, Hayti	Hornby, J.	27-695
PARACHUTE	14 May 1828	Havre	Nichols, Samuel	28-213
PARAGON	4 Oct 1824	Matanzas	Belany, Anthony	24-562
	22 Sep 1827	Port au Prince	Mosson, W.	27-648
	12 Aug 1828	Guayama, P.R.	Pow, John	28-431
PARIS	10 Sep 1823	Havre	Robinson, Henry	23-465
PARNASSON	1 Mar 1820	Naples	Hitch, Joshua	20-048
PARRINGTON	9 Jun 1827	Limerick	Purrinton, Ezekiel	27-338
PARTHIAN	10 May 1824	Fernandina (Cuba)	Bourne, Allen	24-207
PATRIOT	21 Nov 1820	Havana	Shelman, John	20-327
	23 May 1821	Havana	Berrian, Richd. P.	21-084
	23 May 1821	Havana	Berrian, Richd. P.	21-084
	31 Oct 1822	Lisbon	Fairchild, H.	22-555
	13 Nov 1823	Campeachy	Bailey, John	23-588
	28 Jun 1824	Curacoa	Farichild, Hamlet	24-333
	31 May 1825	Curacoa	Ireland, William	25-312
	13 Aug 1828	Tampico	Story, Amos, Jur.	28-436
PATRIOTS EAGLE	30 Oct 1829	St. Johns, N.B.	Graves, Jehu	29-336
PATTY & SALLY	30 Aug 1820	Bermuda	Fitch, Thos. S.	20-215
	25 Apr 1821	Port au Prince	Stinman, John	21-033
	10 Jul 1821	Port au Prince	Stinman, John	21-166
	8 Dec 1821	Port au Prince	Stinman, John	21-411
	23 Feb 1822	Port au Prince	Stinman, John	22-059
	29 Apr 1822	Port au Prince	Stinman, John	22-166
	26 Aug 1822	La Guira	Rawson, E. B.	22-421
PAUL JONES	14 Oct 1829	New Castle	Williams, William	29-302
PAULINA JULIA	22 Feb 1823	River St. Juan	Tooker, D. A.	23-048
	19 Dec 1823	S. Juan de Nicaragua	Tooker, D. A.	23-648
	15 Apr 1824	Baracoa	Tooker, D. A.	24-147
PAULINE JULIA	13 Aug 1821	St. Johns, N.B.	Smith, Isaac	21-224
PEACE	27 Dec 1824	Jamaica	Mariner, Silas	24-738
PEACH	20 Mar 1826	Angostura	Green, Ashbel	26-123
PEACOCK	26 Jul 1820	Malaga	Hardin, Joseph	20-153
PEDLAR	2 Sep 1823	St. Andrews	Larrabee, Saml.	23-440
	17 Sep 1824	Aux Cayes	Kimball, John	24-537
	18 Nov 1824	Leghorn	Bovee, James	24-672
PEDLER	2 Jul 1823	Aux Cayes	Gerrish, Enoch	23-306
	16 Feb 1824	Malaga	Stewart, Phinehas	24-045
	15 Dec 1824	Aux Cayes	Kimball, John	24-721
	28 Feb 1825	Aux Cayes	Kimball, John	25-081
	16 May 1825	Leghorn	Bray, David	25-258
	27 May 1825	Aux Cayes	Kimball, John	25-303
	18 Nov 1825	Leghorn	Bray, David	25-662
	29 May 1826	Leghorn	Tunis, Benjn.	26-288
	9 Jan 1827	Leghorn	Tunis, R.	27-009
	20 Aug 1827	Leghorn	Tunis, Benj.	27-531
	14 May 1828	Marseilles	Tunis, Benjamin	28-215

SHIP	DATE OF ARRIVAL	PORT OF EMBARKATION	CAPTAIN	YEAR AND SHIP NUMBER
PEGASSUS	1 Aug 1829	Leghorn	Tunis, Benjamin	29-187
PEGASUS	7 Aug 1829	St. Domingo	Taylor, Thomas	29-202
	17 May 1828	Leghorn	Lewis, Stiles	28-227
PEIADES (see Pleiades)				
PENELOPE	11 Jun 1827	Liverpool	Leacock, Thos.	27-340
	9 Sep 1828	Liverpool	Wilson, Joseph	28-521
PENOBSCOT PACKET	4 May 1826	Bay of Honduras	Shaw, John A.	26-225
PENOBSCOTT PACKET	1 Jul 1823	Halifax	Staples, Samuel	23-305
PERCIVAL	16 May 1821	Dundee	Scott, John	21-068
PERRY	16 Aug 1825	Maracabo	Hipkins, Loyd B.	25-503
	13 Jul 1826	Havana	Robinson, Thos.	26-401
	21 Mar 1827	Jacmel	Dunning, Chement, S.	27-137
	3 Jul 1827	Jacmel	Dunning, Clement S.	27-407
	21 Jun 1828	Baracoa	Willett, J.	28-320
PERSERVERANCE	2 Mar 1822	South Hampton	Shaw, Thomas	22-068
	21 Jul 1827	Halifax	Chase, Nathaniel	27-466
PERSEVERANCE	25 Jun 1821	Gibraltar	Bover, James	21-132
	25 Oct 1821	Malaga	Bouer, James	21-345
	18 Mar 1822	Malaga	Bray, David	22-083
	3 Aug 1822	Gibraltar	Bray, David	22-371
	11 Jun 1824	Matanzas	Stanhope, Jno. R.	24-292
	18 Nov 1824	Greenock	Pratt, Allen	24-674
	7 Aug 1826	Carnavon	Prince, Cushing, Jr.	26-460
	26 May 1827	Havana	Cornell, Stephen	27-298
	9 Jun 1827	St. Johns, N.B.	Chase, Nathaniel	27-339
	28 Apr 1828	Matanzas	Tarran, John Smith	28-159
PERSIA	19 Sep 1823	Liverpool	Mencheur, Stephen	23-488
	21 Oct 1824	Lisbon	Cross, Latham	24-618
	24 Mar 1828	Leghorn	Lovett, John	28-086
PERU	24 Mar 1828	Leghorn	Lovett, John	28-086
	23 May 1827	Liverpool	Cole, Jeremiah	27-293
	2 Oct 1827	Liverpool	Cole, Jeremiah	27-674
	30 May 1828	Liverpool	Cole, Jeremiah	28-254
PERUVIAN	11 Mar 1822	Havanna	Hall, James	22-075
	13 May 1823	Bordeaux	Russell, Henry	23-192
	28 Jul 1824	Havana	Hall, James	24-413
	7 Oct 1825	Turks Island	Allen, James, 3d.	25-574
	8 Nov 1826	Turks Island	Churchill, Wm.	26-653
PETER FRANCISCO	7 Jun 1822	St. Thomas	Rierson, John	22-259
PETER REMSEN	30 Jun 1828	Havana	Shaw, Saml. S.	28-340
PETIT ANTOINE	18 Jul 1827	Turks Island, St. Thomas	Samand, —	27-459
PETRIL	14 Mar 1826	Curacoa	Rogers, Danl. A.	26-114
PETTRELL	15 Sep 1826	Porto Cabello	Rogers, Daniel A.	26-532
PHAROS	10 Jun 1824	Gibraltar	Hall, Luther	24-286
PHEBE (see Phoebe)				
PHEBE ANN (see Phoebe Ann)				
PHENIX	11 Oct 1825	Liverpool	Jenkins, Reuben	25-579
PHILETUS	21 Jul 1827	Liverpool	Morrill, Charles	27-467
PHOCIAN	5 Aug 1826	Belfast	Quail, William	26-453
PHOCION	19 Sep 1822	Bordeaux	Duplex, George	22-471
	8 May 1824	Greenock	Duplux, George	24-204
PHOEBE	17 Apr 1821	Havana	Monroe, Thomas B.	21-022
	7 Jun 1824	St. Thomas	Grendell, Joseph	24-272
PHOEBE ANN	23 Nov 1824	Malaga	Barker, George	24-681
	27 Dec 1825	Gibraltar	Barker, George	25-731
	6 Sep 1826	St. Iago De Cuba	Davis, Henry	26-523
PHOENIX	29 Apr 1826	Liverpool	Jenkins, Reuben	26-207
PIERSON	26 Apr 1822	Bristol	Terry, Wm.	22-153
PILGRIM	24 Nov 1820	St. Andrews	Cousins, Reuben	20-333
	16 Aug 1821	St. Andrews	Thompson, Wm.	21-228
	27 Mar 1827	Palermo	King, Dauphin	27-152
	1 Sep 1828	St. Andrews	Hopkins, Seth	28-490
PILOT	27 Feb 1826	Cumana	Downes, Baxter	26-086
	11 Apr 1828	Cardiff	Jones, Jenkins	28-122

SHIP	DATE OF ARRIVAL	PORT OF EMBARKATION	CAPTAIN	YEAR AND SHIP NUMBER
PIONEER (see Pionier)				
	21 Jun 1825	London	Smith, Benj., Junr.	25-369
	28 Jun 1827	Hamburg	Smith, Benj., Jr.	27-386
	6 May 1828	St. Johns, P.R.	Stilphen, James	28-190
PIONIER	4 Mar 1828	Montevideo	Potter, Jesse	28-045
PIZARRO	21 Oct 1825	Hamburgh	Stewart, Hampton	25-604
PLANDOME	12 Aug 1826	Jamaica	Williams, Bart	26-474
PLANET	26 May 1824	St. Iago	Radcliff, Chandler	24-237
PLANT	18 Sep 1827	Rio De Janeiro	Mansfield, Charles	27-638
PLANTER	15 Mar 1820	St. Bartholomews	Sanderson, Saml.	20-061
	17 Sep 1821	Turks Island	Prentiss, Lodowich	21-279
	1 Mar 1822	Matanzas	Pratt, Noah	22-067
	7 May 1822	Lisbon	Edes, Thomas	22-178
	26 Jul 1822	Matanges	Pratt, Noah	22-351
	28 Apr 1823	Matanzas	Pratt, Noah	23-157
	16 Mar 1824	St. Thomas	Fisher, W. B.	24-084
	17 Jul 1826	St. Barts & St. Eustatia	Fisher, Thomas	26-408
	7 Jan 1827	St. Bartholomews	White, John	27-003
PLATO	5 Nov 1821	St. Johns, N.B.	Smith, Isaac K.	21-359
	5 Feb 1822	St. Thomas	Smith, Isaac K.	22-028
	18 Apr 1826	Bordeaux	Birkett, James	26-187
	25 Aug 1829	Hamburg	Tatem, Edmund B.	29-248
	31 Oct 1829	Newport (Wales)	Hills, George T.	29-342
PLEIADES	13 Nov 1826	Jamaica	Reynolds, F. A.	26-660
	5 Nov 1828	St. Ubes	Moody, Samuel	28-651
	9 Oct 1829	Liverpool	Seymour, James M.	29-289
PLOUGH BOY	6 May 1823	Matanzas	Manlove, David	23-170
	16 Oct 1823	Matanzes	Manlove, David	23-547
PLUTARCH	18 Jul 1826	Liverpool	Pike, Edmund	26-412
POCAHONTAS	9 Jun 1823	Havana	Cooke, Daniel S.	23-251
	28 Jun 1824	Amsterdam	Brown, Michael	24-337
	1 Feb 1825	St. Iago de Cuba	Foster, R. W.	25-046
	18 May 1825	La Guira	Johnson, Andrew	25-278
	11 Aug 1829	St. Johns, Porto Rico	Teel, Geo. W.	29-210
POLLY	26 May 1821	Newcastle	Wheatley, Henry	21-088
POLLY & ELIZA	23 Mar 1826	Carthagena	Davis, Job	26-127
POLLY & SOPHIA	13 Sep 1821	Nevitus	Sistari, Leonard	21-269
POMONA	26 Jul 1821	Madura	Bright, Jno.	21-198
	5 Dec 1821	Madina	Bright, John	21-402
	28 May 1822	London	Handyride, Henry	22-235
	4 Apr 1823	Havana	Bright, Jno.	23-107
	26 Oct 1823	Madeira	Bright, John	23-561
	18 Aug 1824	Madeira	Deming, John	24-468
	20 Dec 1825	Maranham	Bogman, William	25-724
	19 Feb 1827	Madeira	Fanning, Thomas	27-086
PORCIA	6 Apr 1826	Huasco	Tripp, Leml. C.	26-155
	28 May 1827	Lima	Tripp, Lemuel	27-305
	4 Jan 1828	Rio de Janeiro	Howland, Wm. S.	28-004
PORT CAPTAIN	26 May 1824	Peres & Guayaquil	Shepard, Bartlett	24-238
	17 May 1825	St. Thomas	Tracy, William H.	25-268
	6 Dec 1825	Havana	Ripley, Burr	25-692
PORTLAND	30 Mar 1820	Point Petre Guardaloupe	Sawyer, John	20-088
POST CAPTAIN	12 Dec 1822	Santa Maria	Baldwin, Russell	22-601
POTOMAC	8 Dec 1826	Rio Janeiro	Dexter, Allen	26-708
	7 Aug 1827	St. Johns, N.B.	Bears, Asa	27-503
	28 Sep 1827	Halifax	Bears, Asa	27-667
	29 Oct 1828	Leghorn	Knapp, Charles W.	28-640
	25 Jul 1829	Leghorn & Gibraltar	Knapp, C. W.	29-168
POTOSI	28 May 1825	Cadiz	Baldwin, Russell	25-304
	30 Nov 1826	Manilla	Aderton, Thomas	26-693
	2 Jun 1828	Pacific Ocean	Hind, Benj.	28-269
PRESIDENT	21 Mar 1825	Jacqumel	Bridges, Thomas	25-129
	25 Jul 1825	Honduras	Bridger, Thos.	25-441
	3 Apr 1826	Turks Island	Ames, Isaac	26-146
PRINCE EDWARD	5 Dec 1821	Halifax	Sears, Prince	21-403
	25 Feb 1822	Havana	Sears, Prince	22-063
	2 Sep 1822	Buenos Ayres	Sears, Prince	22-444

SHIP	DATE OF ARRIVAL	PORT OF EMBARKATION	CAPTAIN	YEAR AND SHIP NUMBER
	29 Jul 1823	La Guira	Sears, Prince	23-366
	23 Dec 1823	La Guira	Russell, Abraham	23-652
	13 Apr 1824	Saguiral	Sears, Prince	24-140
	22 Jul 1824	Alvarado	Sears, Prince	24-387A
	1 Apr 1825	Alvarado	Warner, G.	25-148
	5 Jul 1825	Alvarado	Warner, G.	25-396
	11 Oct 1825	Port au Platt, St. Domingo	Howland, Thomas	25-581
	3 Apr 1826	St. Iago de Cuba	Howland, Thomas	26-144
	18 Dec 1826	Tampico	Thompson, John	26-729
	26 Mar 1827	Tampico	Howland, John, Jur.	27-145
	8 Aug 1829	Tampico	Baker, Michael	29-204
PRINCE LEOPOLD	2 Jul 1821	London	Larmour, Robert	21-149
PRINCE MADOC	24 Sep 1821	Greenock	Sullivan, Nicholas	21-300
PRINCE MADORE	28 Aug 1820	Greenock	Watson, James	20-212
PRINCESS CHARLOTTE	26 Apr 1827	Newry	Glederie, John	27-198
	6 Oct 1827	Liverpool & Meury	Glederie, John	27-687
	6 Sep 1828	Newry	Reid, Hugh (Read)	28-509
PRINCESS LOUISE	10 Mar 1825	Bremen	Dehls, Carston	25-099
PRIZE	15 May 1822	Matanzas	Batt, James	22-198
	23 Sep 1822	Matanzas	Talbot, Josiah R.	22-480
	19 Jun 1823	Matanzas	Talbot, Josiah R.	23-272
	20 Sep 1823	Matanzas	Talbot, Josiah R.	23-490
	23 Mar 1824	Matanzas	Talbot, Josiah R.	24-108
	10 Jun 1824	Matanzes	Talbot, Josiah R.	24-288
PROMETHEUS	30 Aug 1828	Matanzas	Lewis, Timothy	28-485
PROSPECT	4 Apr 1822	Turks Island	Perkins, Enoch	22-106
PROTECTION	5 Feb 1822	Rotterdam	Tyson, Peter	22-029
	23 Nov 1824	Bordeaux	Delano, Richard, Jr.	24-684
	5 Nov 1825	Rotterdam	Hatton, Robert	25-634
	6 Nov 1826	Havana	More, Jere	26-646
	26 Oct 1827	Havana	More, Jere, Jr.	27-728
PROTECTOR	21 Apr 1823	St. Thomas	Wilse, John	23-145
	2 Jul 1824	Kingston	Tyler, Joseph	24-347
PROXY	20 Jul 1826	Point Petre Guadaloupe	Lockey, William	26-417
PRUDENCE	8 Apr 1822	Trieste	Jenkins, Reuben	22-115
	11 Jun 1825	St. Thomas	McPherson, Saml. W.	25-331
	19 Apr 1826	St Thomas	McPherson, Saml.	26-191
	31 Oct 1827	Bahia	Richetson, Barton	27-738
	5 Dec 1828	Tobasco	Hinkson, Elisha	28-697
PSYCHE	16 May 1821	Dundee	McIntosh, Thomas	21-069
PULASKI	19 Oct 1825	Alvarado	Brazur, James	25-596
	12 May 1826	Maraham	Barr, James, Jr.	26-249
PULASKI ANDREWS	13 Sep 1826	St. Andres, Columbia	Van Beuren, B. P.	26-529
PURRINGTON	22 Jan 1825	Demara	Purrington, Isaac	25-034
	14 May 1827	Matanzas	Williams, Wm.	27-245
	8 Dec 1827	London	Rowland, Lynde	27-813
QUATRE FRERES	29 Jul 1828	Havre	Le Bois, L.	28-408
QUEEN MAB	26 Jul 1824	Havre	Richards, Henry	24-397
	16 Mar 1825	Havre	Richards, Henry	25-117
	22 Jul 1825	Havre	Richards, H.	25-438
	26 Nov 1825	Havre	Richards, Henry	25-678
	7 Apr 1826	Havre	Cunningham, Jer. C.	26-162
	31 Jul 1826	Havre	Cunningham, J. C.	26-434
	20 Nov 1826	Havre	Cunningham, J. C.	26-672
	16 Jun 1827	Havre	Butman, Benjn.	27-354
	24 Sep 1827	Havre	Butman, B.	27-655
QUEEN MABB	22 Nov 1824	Havre	Richards, Hy.	24-678
QUESNEL	6 Sep 1824	Havre	Hawkins, Elnathan	24-520
QUILL	11 May 1825	Canary	Cooper, Joseph, Jur.	25-250
	31 Oct 1825	Pernambuca	Hillman, Jonathan	25-627
	5 Jun 1826	Rio de Janeiro	Tomkins, James	26-303
	26 Jun 1827	Rio Janeiro & Rio Grande	Hillman, Jonathan	27-375

SHIP	DATE OF ARRIVAL	PORT OF EMBARKATION	CAPTAIN	YEAR AND SHIP NUMBER
	19 Jun 1828	Rio Grande	Pinell, P. P.	28-316
QUITO	9 Jul 1823	Carthagina	Baldwin, Russell	23-324
	15 Mar 1824	Chagres	Murray, O. C.	24-081
	16 Jun 1826	Hamburg	Wing, Clifton	26-336
QULL (see Quill)				
RACHEL	14 Mar 1825	St. Iago de Cuba	Moody, Samuel	25-111
RACHEL ANN	11 Mar 1826	St. Thomas	Sisson, Roswell	26-103
	13 Jul 1826	St. Thomas & St. Croix	Sisson, R.	26-403
	15 Jan 1827	St. Thomas	Risson, Roswell	27-035
	19 Oct 1827	St. Croix	Sisson, Roswell	27-713
	13 Mar 1829	Port au Prince	Weld, Geo. R. M.	29-090
RADIUS	25 Jul 1820	Bremen	Delino, Thos.	20-151
	22 Aug 1820	Matanzas	Granger, Benjamin	20-204
	7 Jul 1821	London	Delino, Thomas	21-161
	8 Feb 1822	Matanzas	Granger, Benjamin	22-038
	16 Mar 1822	London	Delano, Thomas	22-081
	1 May 1822	Matanzas	Granger, Benjamin	22-170
	10 Aug 1822	Matanzas	Granger, Benjamin	22-389
	12 Sep 1822	Liverpool	Fanning, Thomas	22-464
	18 Feb 1823	Matanzas	Granger, Benjamin	23-036
	9 May 1823	Matanzas	Granger, Benjamin	23-178
	28 May 1823	Liverpool	Fanning, Thomas	23-232
	29 Jul 1823	Matanzas	Granger, Benjamin	23-367
	12 Feb 1824	Matanzas	Granger, Benjamin	24-033
	27 Apr 1824	Matanzas	Granger, Benjamin	24-169
	21 Jul 1824	Matanzas	Granger, Benjamin	24-384
	11 Dec 1824	Kingston	Stanley, Viall	24-708
	18 Apr 1825	Matanzas	Noyes, S.	25-184
	12 Jul 1825	Matanzas	Arnold, W.	25-416
	14 Feb 1826	Matanzas	Mathewson, Ebenezer	26-064
RAMBER (see Rambler)				
RAMBLER	17 Feb 1820	Halifax via Barnstable	Hamilton, Thomas	20-037
	12 Feb 1822	St. Eustatia	Sage, Justus	22-044
	28 Oct 1822	St. Johns	Howard, Stephen	22-544
	8 Jul 1823	Barbadoes	Boordman, Ashbel	23-321
	26 Jul 1824	St. Bartholomews	McKee, William A.	24-398
	14 Oct 1824	Liverpool	North, William	24-602
	16 Jul 1829	St. Barts & Rum Key	Colley, Thomas (Colly)	29-152
	31 Aug 1829	St. Johns, N.B.	Staples, Samuel	29-268
RAMPART	4 Jun 1822	Rio Grande	Gorham, John, Capt.	22-252
	28 Nov 1823	Antwerp	Paine, J.	23-611
	16 Apr 1825	Demarara	Morgan, Jno.	25-177
	31 Aug 1826	St. Croix	Morgan, John	26-514
RANGER	16 May 1822	La Guira	Lawrence, C. K.	22-200
	9 Jan 1824	Nassau, N. Providence	Clements, R. E.	24-013
	29 Jul 1824	Nassau, N.P.	Clements, R. E. G.	24-417
	29 Aug 1826	Aux Cayes	Eldridge, Joseph	26-509
	15 Jan 1827	Vera Cruz	Eldrige, Joseph	27-032
	2 Jul 1827	Vera Cruz	Baker, Thocher	27-400
	3 May 1828	St. Thomas	Baker, Thatcher	28-173
	29 Jul 1828	Port au Prince	Eldrege, Jos.	28-409
	13 Mar 1829	Port au Prince	Crowell, Henry	29-087
RANGERS	2 Oct 1826	Halifax	Downes, John	26-577
RAPID	25 Feb 1822	Havana	Richards, Joseph	22-064
	24 Jun 1822	Havana	Nichols, Wm. H.	22-287
	24 Oct 1823	Havana	Hyer, Andrew	23-560
REAPER	31 May 1824	Glasgow	Knight, J. M.	24-253
	31 Aug 1826	Rochelle	Morris, Charles	26-513
REBECCA	20 Dec 1822	Havana	Parrott, Ebenr.	22-609
	22 Mar 1823	Havana	Morrison, Pierson	23-088
	27 May 1823	Matanzas	Parrot, Eben.	23-228
	20 Mar 1824	Glasgow	Loring, Wadsworth D.	24-098
	1 May 1824	Matanzas	Morrison, Pierson	24-189
	17 Aug 1824	Bordeaux	Bower, Abraham, Jr.	24-467
	25 Aug 1824	Jamaica	Strong, James G.	24-486
	2 May 1825	Havana	Jones, Geo. S.	25-232
	1 Aug 1825	Antwerp	Gates, Wm. B.	25-466
	31 Oct 1825	Havana	Teer, Mark	25-628

SHIP	DATE OF ARRIVAL	PORT OF EMBARKATION	CAPTAIN	YEAR AND SHIP NUMBER
	16 Oct 1826	St. Petersburgh	Saul, John	26-599
	20 Dec 1827	St. Petersburg	Saul, John	27-846
	21 Dec 1827	Hamburg	Dawes, William	27-848
	11 Jan 1828	Manzanilla	Moore, Lewis, Jr.	28-014
	6 Jul 1829	St. Thomas	Moore, Lewis, Jr.	29-133
REBECCA & SALLY	12 Nov 1821	St. Ubes	Scull, Saml.	21-367
	21 Jun 1822	Curacoa	Thacker, Lewis	22-280
	16 Oct 1822	Curacoa	Thacher, Lewis	22-531
	18 Jul 1823	Curacoa	Auger, Reuben	23-342
	7 Oct 1823	Curacoa	Augur, Reuben	23-530
	17 May 1825	Porto Cabello	Graves, Saml.	25-265
REBECCA ANN	22 Jul 1820	Carthagena	Brown, John	20-137
	29 Nov 1820	Port au Prince	Beiker, Nundras	20-338
	13 Aug 1821	Curacao	Bicker, Nwpt.	21-225
	5 Dec 1821	Curacoa	Bicker, Nicholas	21-404
REBECCA GROVES	31 Jul 1829	Madeira via Teneriffe	Groves, Saml.	29-183
REHOBOTH	27 Dec 1826	Vera Cruz	Ellis, Joseph	26-739
	10 Apr 1828	Porto Cabello	Ellis, Joseph	28-120
REINDEER (see Riendeer)				
	16 Mar 1820	Havana	Wibray, James	20-067
	15 Aug 1820	St. Andrews	Crowell, Ezekiel	20-180
	1 Nov 1824	Turks Island	Dayton, R. W.	24-635
	29 Jun 1827	Halifax	Crowell, Ezekiel	27-394
	3 Aug 1827	Halifax	Crowell, Ezekiel	27-499
	22 Aug 1827	St. Ubes	Knight, Joshua	27-543
	10 Dec 1827	Halifax, N.S.	Crowell, Ezekiel	27-821
	20 Aug 1828	Halifax, N.S.	Crowell, Ezekiel	28-450
	18 Oct 1828	Halifax, N.S.	Crowell, Ezekiel	28-616
RELIANCE	17 Jun 1828	St. Thomas	Woolbury, Asa (Woodbury)	28-308
REMITTANCE	30 Jan 1824	Gibraltar	Woodhouse, Saml.	24-023
	14 Oct 1824	Buenos Ayres	Brown, Saml.	24-599
	18 Feb 1825	Aux Cayes	Labousse, Ml.	25-070
	2 Aug 1825	St. Domingo	Laboupe, Ml.	25-469
	24 Aug 1825	Liverpool	Champlin, Joshua	25-541
RENGAL	9 Oct 1822	Liverpool	Pearce, John	22-517
RENT	13 May	Rotterdam	Frazar, Amherst A.	28-210
RENUNIERO	3 Jan 1822	Jacqumel	Douge, Daniel	22-004
REPORTER	27 Sep 1823	St. Andrews	Waite, John, Jr.	23-501
REPUBLICANO	5 Nov 1825	La Guira	Gandolph, Franco S. (Grandolph, F. E.)	25-636
RESIGN	20 Oct 1821	Leghorn	Schuyler, Peter	21-337
	1 May 1822	Greenock	Clements, Joseph	22-171
	7 Oct 1822	Hull, England	Clement, Joseph	22-515
RESOLUTION	6 Jun 1822	Halifax, N.S.	Collier, Isaac	22-257
RETRIEVE	10 Jan 1823	Aux Cayes	Theobald, Francis R.	23-010
REUBEN & ELIZA	21 Aug 1820	Liverpool	Harris, Charles	20-199
REUNION	28 Sep 1821	Jacmel	Douge, Daniel	21-304
REVENUE	7 Oct 1829	Maranham	Foster, Robert W.	29-286
RIBICON	13 Mar 1826	Havana	Bourne, Elisha	26-111
RICE PLANT	22 May 1827	St. Thomas	Foster, Freeman	27-283
	20 Sep 1827	Trinidad De Cuba	Foster, F.	27-643
RICHARD	26 Jun 1823	Havana	Harvey, Samuel	23-290
RICHARD MEAD	26 Jun 1821	Swansa (Wales)	Knapp, Thomas	21-134
RICHARD MEADE	27 Apr 1822	Surinam	Barnard, Benjn.	22-157
RICHMOND	18 Feb 1820	Liverpool via Cork	Rugan, William	20-038
	4 Aug 1826	London	Crabtree, Eleazer	26-451
	2 May 1828	Bordeaux	Peabody, John	28-170
	24 Aug 1829	St. Andrews	Beardsley, Ebenezer	29-243
RICHMOND PACKET	8 Apr 1822	St. Thomas	Boardman, Astbel	22-116
	13 Jun 1825	Neuvitas	Harris, Thomas N.	25-335
	28 Oct 1825	Neuvitas	Harris, Thos. N.	25-622
	25 Feb 1826	Nevitus	Harris, Thomas N.	26-082

SHIP	DATE OF ARRIVAL	PORT OF EMBARKATION	CAPTAIN	YEAR AND SHIP NUMBER
	15 Jun 1826	Nuevitas	Harris, Thomas N.	26-335
	27 Nov 1826	Matanzas	Harris, Thomas N.	26-681
	23 Feb 1827	Neuvitas	Harris, Thomas N.	27-089
	11 Jul 1827	Neuvitas	Cobb, Samuel	27-438
	30 Oct 1827	Neuvitas	Cobb, Samuel	27-732
	29 Mar 1828	Nuevitas	Cobb, Samuel	28-093
	10 Dec 1828	Xibara & Neuvitas	Crane, John R.	28-699
	3 Aug 1829	Nuevitas	Pereira, Domingo (Periva)	29-193
RIENDEER	5 Sep 1820	Bonivesta	Wibray, James	20-224
RIO	11 Sep 1827	Bordeaux	Gerry, Saml. R.	27-617
RISING STATE	15 Dec 1820	Havannah	Lake, John	20-348
RISING STATES	23 Apr 1825	Maricabo	Rivans, Thos.	25-201
	8 Aug 1825	Maracaybo	Hoodless, William R.	25-485
	23 Nov 1825	Maracaibo	Hoodless, Wm. R.	25-669
	27 Nov 1826	Sisal	Groves, Saml.	26-680
	12 May 1827	Porto Cabello	Groves, Saml.	27-242
	7 Jul 1828	Sidney	Snow, Silvanus	28-356
	20 Sep 1828	Sydney	Snow, Silvanus	28-547
	16 Jan 1829	Halifax, N.S.	Snow, Silvanus	29-019
RISING SUN	1 May 1823	St. Johns, N.B.	Hale, J. C.	23-163
	24 May 1824	Bermuda	Lawrence, Elisha	24-231
	19 Sep 1826	Havana	Coit, Christopher	26-540
RIVAL	25 May 1826	Bordeaux	Phillips, Joseph	26-282
ROANOAK	19 Sep 1827	Greenock	Barstow, Wm. P.	27-641
ROANOAKE	12 Oct 1826	Stockholm	Barstow, W. P.	26-593
ROANOKE	21 May 1828	Antwerp	Marshall, Frederick W.	28-237
ROBERT	15 Jul 1822	Liverpool	MacKey, John	22-328
	28 Aug 1829	Dundee	Whilton, John (Whetton)	29-261
ROBERT BURNS	13 Jul 1820	Londonderry	Coffin, H.	20-126
	18 Jun 1821	Londonderry	Coffin, Hazadiah	21-123
	8 Dec 1821	Bristol	Coffin, Hazadiah	21-412
	18 Jun 1822	Londonderry	Coffin, Hazadiah	22-277
	30 May 1823	Londonderry	Coffin, Hazadiah	23-234
	1 Dec 1823	Hamburgh	Coffin, Hazad.	23-621
	14 Jun 1824	Londonderry	Coffin, Hazadiah	24-306
ROBERT COCHRAN	6 Nov 1824	Madeira	Bradford, Benj. W.	24-643
	14 Mar 1825	Matanzas	Gorton, Clarke	25-113
	29 Aug 1825	Jamaica	Jones, Sylvester	25-559
ROBERT EDWARD	2 Nov 1827	London	Sherburne, Saml.	27-743
ROBERT EDWARDS	25 Apr 1821	Canton	Sherburne, Samuel	21-034
	21 Sep 1821	London	Sherburn, Samuel	21-295
	11 Mar 1822	London	Sherburn, Sam.	22-076
	11 Nov 1822	London	Sherburne, Samuel	22-563
	4 Jun 1824	London	Sherburn, Samuel	24-265
	8 Nov 1825	London	Sherburn, Samuel	25-643
	1 Jun 1826	London	Sherburne, Samuel	26-294
	9 May 1827	London	Sherburn, Saml.	27-232
	17 Mar 1828	London	Sherburne, Samuel	28-068
	20 Jan 1829	London	Sherburne, Samuel	29-029
	3 Oct 1829	London	Sherburne, Samuel	29-277
ROBERT FULTON	22 Oct 1821	Liverpool	Haldridge, Henry	21-341
	9 Feb 1822	Liverpool	Holdridge, Henry	22-040
	27 Jun 1822	Liverpool	Holdrige, Henry	22-296
	1 Nov 1822	Liverpool	Holdridge, Henry	22-556
	8 Mar 1823	Liverpool	Holdrige, Henry	23-063
	9 Jul 1823	Liverpool	Graham, Hugh	23-325
	7 Nov 1823	Liverpool	Marshall, Robert	23-576
	1 Apr 1824	Liverpool	Graham, Hugh	24-121
	22 May 1824	Havana	Chase, Paul	24-226
	2 Aug 1824	Havana	Chase, Paul	24-424
	16 Aug 1824	Liverpool	Graham, Hugh	24-458
	30 Dec 1824	Greenock	Britten, Thomas	24-744
	11 Jan 1825	Havana	Chase, Paul	25-016
	18 May 1825	Greenock	Britton, Thomas	25-273
	24 Jul 1826	Londonderry	Britton, Thomas	26-427

SHIP	DATE OF ARRIVAL	PORT OF EMBARKATION	CAPTAIN	YEAR AND SHIP NUMBER
	13 Mar 1827	Liverpool	Britton, Thomas	27-120
	10 Aug 1827	Londonderry	Brittan, Thomas	27-511
	3 Dec 1827	Liverpool	Brittan, Thomas	27-790
	4 Jun 1828	Londonderry	Britton, John	28-279
	8 Oct 1828	Belfast	Britton, John	28-596
	14 Mar 1829	Greenock	Britton, John	29-094
ROBERT LENOX	6 Jun 1821	Guadaloupe	Perham, Ezekel	21-103
ROBERT QUAYLE	29 Jul 1822	Liverpool	Rober, Peter	22-358
ROBERT READ	25 Aug 1824	Jamaica	Smith, Samuel	24-485
	10 Jan 1825	Aux Cayes	Haskell, John G.	25-011
	19 Oct 1825	Port au Parma	Mayo, Oliver	25-598
	30 Jan 1826	Aux Cayes	Nichols, Thos. E.	26-045
	8 Dec 1826	Havana	Nicoll, Thos. E.	26-706
ROBERT READE	9 Feb 1822	Havana	Smith, Samuel	22-039
	23 Jul 1823	St. Croix	Smith, Saml.	23-348
	13 Jul 1825	Port au Prince	Mayo, O.	25-417
ROBERT READS (see Robert Reade)				
ROBERT WILSON	2 Dec 1828	Hamburgh	Arnold, Asahel	28-690
ROBERT Y. HAYNE	21 Aug 1828	St. Blass	Roberts, John	28-453
ROBERT Y. HAYNES	7 Nov 1825	Aquin	Lindsey, Wm.	25-639
	13 Mar 1826	Jacmel	Wells, Theodore	26-105
	22 Mar 1827	La Guira	Johnson, Henry	27-138
	3 Jul 1827	Jacmel	Mix, E. A.	27-408
	2 Oct 1829	Rio Salado	Morgan, Zachariah	29-274
ROBIN HOOD	20 Jul 1827	Liverpool	Medberry, Jacob	27-464
	6 May 1828	Liverpool	Willent, Joseph	28-186
ROBT. EDWARDS	4 Sep 1828	London	Sherburne, Saml.	28-500
ROBT. READE	12 Apr 1825	Port au Prince	Mayer, Oliver	25-172
ROBT. Y. HAYNE	27 Jun 1825	Acquin	Lindsay, Wm.	25-378
ROCKINGHAM	17 May 1821	Liverpool	Holdridge, Allen	21-072
	29 Nov 1821	Liverpool	Holdrige, Allen	21-386
	23 Aug 1822	London	Coffin, Chas. M.	22-416
RODMAN	22 Mar 1825	La Guira	Price, Benjamin	25-131
	4 Apr 1825	Matanzas	Talbot, Z.	25-149
	28 May 1825	Matanzas	Talbot, Zephaniah	25-305
	19 Dec 1825	La Guira	Ricketson, Barton	25-717
	9 Mar 1826	La Guira	Ricketson, Barton	26-096
RODNEY	19 Jun 1827	Havana	Arnold, Elisha	27-362
	6 Oct 1827	St. Iago de Cuba	Lewis, Ansel	27-686
ROGER STEWART	9 Jun 1828	Greenock	Ker, Peter	28-290
ROLLA	8 May 1823	Matanzas	Vaughan, George	23-175
	10 Feb 1824	Havana	Read, Daniel	24-030
	24 Apr 1824	City of St. Domingo	Stickney, Albert A.	24-162
	16 Nov 1824	Montegobay, Jamaica	Dennison, George	24-666
	9 Aug 1828	Cadiz	Ferry, Daniel	28-427
ROMAN	19 Dec 1825	Liverpool	Dickinson, Jeremiah J.	25-718
	12 Jun 1826	Liverpool	Dickinson, Jeremiah J.	26-329
	17 Oct 1826	Liverpool	Dickinson, Jeremiah P.	26-601
	10 Sep 1827	Liverpool	Dickinson, Jeremiah J.	27-610
	10 May 1828	Liverpool	Gurrell, John	28-202
	1 Dec 1828	Liverpool	Gurrell, John	28-685
ROMEO	10 Aug 1821	Halifax	Drinkwater, Reuben	21-221
	23 Jun 1823	Nevitus	Barclay, Hy.	23-279
ROMP	12 Sep 1823	Leghorn	Scudder, Prentiss	23-470
ROMULUS	27 Nov 1821	Samarang	Lovett, Jabish	21-381
	26 Apr 1822	Matanzes	Allen, William	22-154
	7 Oct 1822	Cadiz	Allen, William	22-516
	31 Jul 1823	Havana	Allen, William	23-374
	16 Feb 1824	Rio de Janeiro	Hillard, John	24-046
	26 Dec 1825	Batavia	Roberts, John	25-728
	24 Jun 1826	Liverpool	Roberts, John	26-361
	3 Dec 1827	Bordeaux	Coffin, C. H.	27-783
	15 May 1828	Havre	Lovett, Olney	28-219

SHIP	DATE OF ARRIVAL	PORT OF EMBARKATION	CAPTAIN	YEAR AND SHIP NUMBER
	24 Sep 1828	Havre	Webb, Michael	28-565
	9 Oct 1828	Havana	Woodward, Greenleaf C.	28-597
	13 Aug 1829	Buenos Ayres & Rio de Janeiro	Barker, George	29-214
ROOK	25 Jul 1827	Antwerp	Napier, W. M.	27-477
	2 Oct 1829	Turk Island	Thomas, George	29-273
ROSALIE	22 Aug 1820	Havre	Merry, T. H.	20-205
ROSE IN BLOOM	12 Apr 1821	St. Bartholomew	Auchinluck, Alexr.	21-014
	30 Jul 1823	Port au Prince	Betts, Thomas	23-372
	10 Aug 1824	Barbadoes	Spelman, James	24-440
	4 Apr 1826	Barbadoes	Spilman, James	26-148
	9 Apr 1827	St. Domingo	Everett, A. W.	27-167
ROSEWAY	10 Jul 1820	Antwerpt	Simmons, Geo.	20-116
ROSINA	12 Aug 1823	Greenock	Lothgons, Aaron	23-396
	27 Feb 1824	Greenock	Lithgow, Aaron	24-063
	28 May 1827	Glasgow	Butterworth, Thomas C.	27-308
ROUSSEAU	19 Apr 1825	St. Domingo	Le Bail, A.	25-191
ROVER	11 Jun 1823	Aquin, St. Domingo	Lindsey, William	23-257
	31 May 1824	Mayaguiz	Meille, Edward	24-248
	22 Dec 1824	Mayagues	Berry, Walter	24-730
	28 Oct 1825	St. Thomas	Berry, Walter	25-620
	17 Apr 1827	Bermuda	Brownlowe, James P.	27-180
ROXANA	30 Apr 1823	Grenada	Prout, Thomas L.	23-160
ROYAL OAK	5 Aug 1820	Martinique	Alben, James, 3rd	20-160
	16 Oct 1820	Port Au Prince	Allen, James, 3rd	20-297
RUBICON	22 May 1826	Havana	Bourne, Elisha	26-270
	7 Oct 1826	Tampico	Bourne, Elisha	26-586
	16 Feb 1827	Tampico	Bourne, E.	27-081
	8 Jun 1827	Havana	Bourne, E.	27-333
	19 Dec 1827	Matanzas	Bourne, Elisha	27-843
	2 Jun 1828	Manzanilla	Bourne, E.	28-265
RUBY	10 Apr 1823	Havana	Phillips, Thomas	23-121
RUFUS	15 Dec 1828	Aux Cayes	Clarkson, James	28-706
RUFUS KING	7 Aug 1820	Londonderry	Clark, Charles	20-164
	27 Jun 1821	Liverpool	Bennet, Thomas	21-141
	11 Mar 1822	Liverpool via Halifax	Badger, Joseph	22-077
	3 Sep 1822	Liverpool	Badger, Joseph	22-448
	4 Sep 1823	Liverpool	Badger, Joseph	23-449
RUTH	26 May 1824	St. Iago	Patten, Josep	24-240
	1 Aug 1824	St. Croix	Packer, Jno. R.	24-423
SABBATTUS	3 Mar 1828	Cadiz	Howard, William	28-040
SABINA	18 Oct 1824	Gibraltar	Gardner, Geo. G.	24-610
	29 Apr 1825	Liverpool	Nicoll, E.	25-216
	5 May 1826	Manilla	Hubble, Ezekiel	26-230
	25 Apr 1828	Manilla	Hubbell, E.	28-150
ST. ANNA	8 Aug 1827	St. Johns, Porto Rico	Busch, John	27-504
	1 Apr 1828	Porto Rico	Prentiss, Ludwick	28-100
	16 Aug 1828	Guayama, P.R.	Prentiss, Lodowich	28-441
ST. BENTO LEIGEIRO	2 Nov 1822	Bona Vista	de Bruno, Narazo Xer.	22-557
ST. CLAIR	26 Apr 1826	Trinadad	Guthrie, James	26-202
ST. CROIX	31 Jul 1827	Teneriffe	Bowman, John L.	27-491
	13 Sep 1827	St. John, N.B.	Bowman, John L.	27-624
ST. GEORGE	7 Jun 1828	Liverpool	Taulmar, John	28-285
	20 Sep 1828	Liverpool	Taubman, John	28-548
	16 Jan 1829	Liverpool	Taubman, John	29-018
	25 Aug 1829	Liverpool	Taubman, John	29-251
ST. HELENA	18 May 1823	St. Thomas	Petre, Charles H.	23-035
ST. JOHN	5 Oct 1829	Liverpool	Parker, Gideon	29-284
ST. MARTIN	10 Feb 1820	Havre	De Jolly, C.	20-030
ST. MICHAEL	24 Jun 1824	St. Johns, N.B.	Crowell, Reuben	24-324
	21 Jul 1824	St. Johns	Crowell, Reuben	24-387
	21 Aug 1824	St. Johns, N.B.	Crowell, Ruben	24-477A
	22 Sep 1824	St. Johns, N.B.	Crowell, Reuben	24-549
	26 Oct 1824	St. John	Crowell, Ruben	24-625
	3 Jan 1825	St. Johns	Crowell, Ruben	25-002
	5 Jan 1826	St. Johns	Crowell, Ruben	26-014
	28 Feb 1826	St. John, New Brunswick	Crowell, Reuben	26-087

1475

SHIP	DATE OF ARRIVAL	PORT OF EMBARKATION	CAPTAIN	YEAR AND SHIP NUMBER
	27 Mar 1827	St. Johns	Crowell, Ruben	27-148
	5 May 1827	St. Johns, N.B.	Peirce, Thomas	27-213
ST. MICHAEL'S	10 Feb 1827	St. Johns, N.B.	Crowell, Reuben	27-072
ST. MICHAELS	30 Sep 1823	Bordeaux	Tucker, Zebediah	23-511
	21 Apr 1824	Havana	Tucker, Zebediah	24-158
	27 Nov 1824	St John, N.B.	Crowell, Reuben	24-693
	15 Feb 1825	St. John, N.B.	Crowell, Reuben	25-064
	24 Mar 1825	St. John, N.B.	Crowell, Reuben	25-140
	25 Apr 1825	St. John	Crowell, R.	25-204
	25 May 1825	St. John, N.B.	Crowell, Reuben	25-293
	25 Nov 1825	St. Johns, N.B.	Pellengill, Ebenezer	25-672
	12 Apr 1826	St. John, N.B.	Crowell, Reuben	26-172
	11 May 1826	St. Johns, N.B.	Crowell, Reuben	26-244
	12 Jun 1826	St. Johns, N.B.	Crowell, Reuben	26-328
	18 Jul 1826	St. Johns, N.B.	Crowell, Reuben	26-411
	23 Dec 1826	St. Johns, N.B.	Crowell, Reuben	26-733
	7 Jun 1827	St. Johns, N.B.	Pearce, Thomas	27-325
ST. PIERRE	16 Oct 1827	Martinique & St. Thomas	Foster, R. C.	27-709
ST. THOMAS	24 May 1824	St. Thomas	Lane, Gideon	24-227
	14 Aug 1828	St. Thomas	Bacie, Samuel J.	28-438
SALEM	15 Mar 1828	Liverpool	Richardson, Edwd.	28-062
	31 Aug 1829	Gottenburg	Richardson, Edward	29-267
SALL & HOPE	12 Jul 1820	Matanraw	Blinn, Jas. M.	20-123
SALLY	8 Aug 1820	Havana	Whitehead, John	20-166
	15 Sep 1820	West Indies	Clark, Saml.	20-245
	11 Oct 1820	Havanna	Whitehead, John	20-293
	16 Apr 1821	Havana	Bennet, Joseph	21-021
	14 May 1821	Guadaloupe	McPherson, Saml. W.	21-065
	4 Aug 1821	Havana	Bennet, Joseph H.	21-208
	19 Sep 1821	St. Thomas	McPherson, Saml. W.	21-285
	7 Nov 1821	St. Iago de Cuba	McLaughlan, Donald	21-362
	26 Jun 1822	St. Thomas	Gliddin, Samuel	22-294
	14 Jun 1823	St. Andrews	Liscomb, John	23-264
SALLY ANN	28 Mar 1820	Havana	Roden, Charles	20-087
	29 Mar 1824	Port de Plate	Woglom, A. C.	24-115
	6 Nov 1824	Tampico	McGuire, James	24-642
	11 Dec 1824	Havana	Simpson, Josiah	24-710
	23 May 1825	Cadiz	Van Schayck, Wm	25-289
	27 Oct 1825	Havana	Van Schayck, Wm.	25-618
	11 Dec 1826	Bermuda	Phelan, J. R.	26-716
	9 Oct 1828	Port au Prince	Lindsay, William	28-600
SALTANA	18 Apr 1825	Bordeaux	Winson, Geo.	25-181
SALUDA	16 Oct 1824	Havre	Gyles, Charles	24-605
	18 Jun 1825	Havre de Grace	Gyles, Charles	25-357
	15 Jul 1826	Havana	Hood, J. B.	26-407
	14 May 1827	Havana	Hood, James B.	27-244
SALUMITH	17 Nov 1826	Barbadoes	Norris, Peter	26-668
SAMARITAN	24 Nov 1820	St. Johns Porto Rico	Thacker, Samuel G.	20-334
	30 May 1828	Turks Island	Cushing, John	28-255
SAML. SMITH	8 Jul 1823	Turks Island	Sayward, James	23-322
	24 Jul 1826	Carthagena	Howland, Lloyd	26-423
SAML. WIGHT	6 Sep 1827	Liverpool	Lucker, R. H.	27-596
SAMPSON	5 Oct 1825	Havana	Parkes, Robert	25-568
SAMUEL	23 Aug 1824	Antigua & Bermuda	Phelan, John R.	24-483
	14 Feb 1826	Bremen	Webber, Benjn.	26-063
	28 Nov 1826	St. Domingo	Glandon, Lewis	26-686
	25 Apr 1828	Guadaloupe	Smith, G. C.	28-148
SAMUEL ROBERTSON	26 Nov 1825	Greenock	Choate, Thomas	25-679
	9 May 1827	Greenock	Choate, Thomas	27-233
	5 Oct 1827	Greenock	Choate, Thomas	27-679
	9 Apr 1828	Liverpool	Choate, Thomas	28-118
	8 Aug 1828	Havre	Choate, Thomas	28-426
SAMUEL WRIGHT	9 Jan 1829	Liverpool	Leach, John	29-010
	12 Oct 1829	Liverpool	Allen, Benjamin L.	29-297A
SANCHO PANZA	2 Jun 1824	Tampico	Mitchell, John K.	24-260

SHIP	DATE OF ARRIVAL	PORT OF EMBARKATION	CAPTAIN	YEAR AND SHIP NUMBER
SANFORD				
WILLIAM	16 Feb 1822	Havana	Chase, Nathan W.	22-050
	28 Jan 1823	Jamaica	Sheffield, Ichabod	23-019
	26 Jul 1824	Kingston, Jamaica	Sheffield, Ichabod	24-402
	14 Dec 1824	Jamaica	Fowler, Oliver	24-718
SARAH	9 Nov 1820	Greenock	Badger, Joseph	20-320
	26 Jul 1824	Havana	Dodge, John	24-400
	14 Mar 1825	London	Drummond, Spencer	25-114
	11 Apr 1825	Rio Grande	Ashford, Jno.	25-159
	4 Aug 1825	Curacoa	Bousie, Wm.	25-475
	5 Aug 1825	Maracaybo	Ashvord, John	25-477
	17 Aug 1825	London	Drummond, Spencer	25-510
	25 Oct 1825	St. Croix	Lowel, James	25-616
	23 Sep 1826	Teneriffe	Mayhew, Wm.	26-552
	1 Aug 1827	Rio Grande	Ashford, John	27-495
	26 Dec 1827	Nuevitas	Latham, Elbert	27-855
	16 May 1828	Bordeaux	Ivy, Thomas	28-222
	12 Jul 1828	Saint Andrews	Hutchings, D. H.	28-373
	12 Dec 1828	Nuevitas	Latham, Elbert	28-703
	17 Mar 1829	Havana	Latham, Elbert	29-101
	11 Jul 1829	St. Johns, N.B.	Shackford, Jacob	29-144
	18 Aug 1829	Liverpool	Harding, Henry F.	29-224
	31 Oct 1829	St. Johns, N.B.	Pearce, Thos.	29-341
SARAH &				
LOUISA	7 Dec 1820	Archangel	Colver, Christopher	20-340
	7 Jun 1822	Lisbon	Calver, Christopher	22-260
SARAH &				
LOUISE (see Sarah & Louisa)				
SARAH ANN	5 Aug 1820	Havana	Gerandel, J.	20-161
	8 May 1822	Havana	Girandel, J.	22-179
	25 Jun 1822	Aquin, Hayti	Vinson, Saml. H.	22-291
	18 Nov 1826	St. Johns, N.B.	Cronk, David	26-670
	11 Jan 1827	St. Johns, N. B.	Cronk, David	27-019
	6 Mar 1827	St. Johns, N.B.	Cronk, David	27-101
SARAH				
DELIGHT	20 Jun 1825	Nassau, N.p.	Fisher, Christopher	25-363
SARAH G	7 May 1827	St. Johns, N.B.	Crowell, Ruben	27-219
	19 Jun 1827	St. Johns, N.B.	Crowell, Reuben	27-363
	11 Sep 1827	Saint Johns, N.B.	Crowell, Reuben	27-614
	5 Jun 1828	St. Johns	Crowell, R.	28-281
	30 Jun 1828	St. Johns	Crowell, Reuben	28-345
SARAH G.	20 Jul 1827	St. Johns, N.B.	Crowell, Reuben	27-463
	15 Aug 1827	St. Johns, N.B.	Crowell, Reuben	27-517
	28 Nov 1827	St. John, New Brunswick	Crowell, Reuben	27-769
	11 Jan 1828	St. Johns, N.B.	Crowell, Reuben	28-013
	14 Apr 1828	St. Johns	Crowell, R.	28-128
	15 May 1828	St. Johns	Crowell, Ruben	28-217
SARAH HERRICK	15 Apr 1823	Lisbon	Bourne, Silas J.	23-134
	11 Jun 1825	Port au Plate	Hubbard, R. S.	25-329
	24 Oct 1825	Puerto del Plata	Sanders, Michael	25-611
	13 May 1826	Port au Platt	Sanders, Michael	26-252
	7 Oct 1826	Port au Plate (Prince)	Sanders, Michael	26-585
	10 Aug 1827	Port au Platt	Sanders, M.	27-510
SARAH LEE	21 Jul 1821	Lisbon	Whitney, Henry	21-185
	29 May 1826	Surinam	Perry, John L.	26-284
SARAH LOUISA	10 Oct 1822	Madeira	Colver, Christopher	22-518
SARAH				
RALSTON	20 Feb 1826	Hamburgh	Winslow, Charles	26-072
	27 Jan 1827	Liverpool	Winslow, Chas.	27-041
SARAH SHEAF	13 Jun 1825	Liverpool	Thompson, J. S.	25-337
SARAH SKEAFE	10 Sep 1827	Liverpool	Barnard, P.	27-613
SARAH				
THORNTON	9 Sep 1826	Bremen	Storer, Tristram	26-527
	13 Sep 1828	St. Thomas	Dunlevie, John C.	28-538
SARAHS				
DELIGHT	13 May 1823	Nassau	Fisher, Christopher J.	23-197
SAUNDERS	16 May 1827	St. Croix	McMilledge, Alexr.	27-255
SAVANNAH	18 May 1822	Canton	Hughes, Wm.	22-205

SHIP	DATE OF ARRIVAL	PORT OF EMBARKATION	CAPTAIN	YEAR AND SHIP NUMBER
	22 May 1827	Omoa	Greene, Wm. M.	27-289
	10 Jan 1828	Vera Cruz	Austin, Henry	28-010
	10 Jan 1828	Omoa	Baker, Allen	28-011
	24 Apr 1828	Vera Cruz	Austin, Henry	28-142
SCEPTRE	24 Jul 1822	Leith in Scotland	Smith, Walter	22-346
SCHUYLKILL	22 Aug 1825	Cork	Nichols, Saml.	25-533
SCIENCE	23 Sep 1824	St. Iago de Cuba	West, F.	24-551
	16 Sep 1826	Montego Bay	Mosely, Sevier	26-533
SCIO	8 Feb 1825	Palermo	King, Dauphin	25-056
	24 Jul 1826	Montego Bay, Jamaica	Graves, John C.	26-424
SCIOT	12 Mar 1828	Tampico	Henchman, Lewis	28-054
SCOTSMAN	22 Aug 1828	Dundee	Reid, Henry	28-457
SEA BIRD	8 Feb 1827	St. Thomas	Cair, G. W.	27-066
SEA BYRD (see Sea Bird)				
SEA FLOWER	16 Jul 1821	Gibaira	Crow, Wm. H.	21-179
	24 Jun 1824	nassau, N. Providence	Dupratt, Lawrence	24-323
	23 May 1826	Guyama	Carr, G. W.	26-276
SEA GULL	27 Mar 1827	Lisbon	Blydenburgh, L. B.	27-150
SEA ISLAND	2 Jul 1825	Rotterdam	Atwood, J.	25-391
	3 Jan 1826	Marseilles	Atwood, Isaac	26-008
SEA NYMPH	7 Jul 1827	Tampico	Anderson, James	27-415
	30 Apr 1828	Tampico	Beekman, H.	28-165
	7 Oct 1828	Tampico	Beckman, Henry	28-592
SEA SERPENT	3 Jul 1820	Martinico	Adams, Elisha	20-100
	16 Sep 1820	St. Andrews	Bunker, Thomas	20-248
	21 Apr 1821	Havana	Howland, A.	21-026
	12 Jul 1828	Mayagues	Rodrigues, J.	28-371
SEAMAN	24 Jul 1826	Samos	Dominick, Francis W.	26-426
SECRETARY	10 Aug 1829	The Island of Curacao	Jones, Benjamin P., Sr.	29-207
SEEDS	29 Sep 1824	Liverpool	Stoddard, William	24-558
SEINE	7 Dec 1821	Bordeaux	Williams, William	21-406
	10 Jun 1822	Bristol, England	Williams, Erastus	22-264
	21 Oct 1822	Amsterdam	Williams, Wm.	22-538
	27 Oct 1823	Gibraltar	Williams, Wm.	23-562
	30 Aug 1824	Havre	Williams, Wm.	24-497
	20 Dec 1825	Monteviedo	Shephard, Bartho.	25-725
	16 Jun 1826	Bordeaux	Williams, Wm.	26-337
	16 Jan 1827	Manilla	Tyson, Wm.	27-037
	29 Jun 1827	Bordeaux	Tyson, Wm.	27-392
SELINA	18 Jul 1822	Carthagina & Trinidad	Sistare, Leonard	22-334
SENECA	15 Mar 1820	Canton	Clark, James	20-062
	14 May 1821	Havana	Copeland, James	21-064
	15 Apr 1822	Monteviedo	Dutch, E. J.	22-129
	21 May 1825	Havana	Doughty, Joseph	25-283
	7 Nov 1825	Liverpool	Lovely, H.	25-641
	23 Oct 1826	Vera Cruz	Levely, Hugh	26-625
SENICA	17 Mar 1824	Havana	Boyd, Andrew	24-086
SENTIMENT	30 Jul 1827	St. Domingo	Linberth, L.	27-488
SERAPH	2 Jan 1828	Malaga	Pendleton, Benjamin	28-001
SERENO	31 Jul 1826	Hamburg	Chase, Constant	26-442
	18 Jun 1827	Carnavon, Wales	Chase, Constant	27-357
SERVANT	30 Aug 1820	Greenock	Sanborn, Green	20-214
SEVERN	12 Oct 1826	Liverpool	Heath, Charles	26-596
SHAKESPEARE	24 Jul 1828	Glasgow	Soldie, John	28-398
SHALLET	21 Apr 1821	Bristol	Mason, John	21-027
SHAMROCK	17 Jun 1822	Matanzas	Holmes, John	22-275
SHAW	23 May 1827	Liverpool	Shaw, Thomas M.	27-294
SHEPHERDESS	16 May 1821	Palermo	Storer, Peter	21-070
	9 May 1822	Messina	Stow, P.	22-184
	17 May	Messina	Storm, Peter	23-207
SICILY	15 Jul 1824	St. Croix	Storer, Peter	24-377
	24 Oct 1827	Trinadad in Cuba	Skidmore, S.	27-720
	25 Apr 1828	Fererandence	Wiederholt, H. L.	28-149
	16 Feb 1829	Jacmel	Bridges, Thomas	29-064
	7 Oct 1829	Marseilles	Bridges, Thomas	29-285
SIGNA	9 Dec 1824	Curacoa	Clark, Chas.	24-706
	6 Apr 1827	St. Croix	Shaeffer, F. W. S.	27-165
SIGNAL	12 Jul 1825	St. Croix	Totton, G.	25-415

SHIP	DATE OF ARRIVAL	PORT OF EMBARKATION	CAPTAIN	YEAR AND SHIP NUMBER
	5 Oct 1825	St. Thomas	Totten, Gilbert	25-569
	3 Jan 1826	St. Thomas	Totten, Gilbert	26-004
	18 Apr 1826	Porto Rico	Totten, Gilbert	26-184
	11 Jul 1826	St. Thomas	Totten, Gilbert	26-394
	3 Jan 1827	St. Thomas	Totten, G.	27-002
SILAS RICHARD	30 Jun 1828	Liverpool	Holdrege, Henry	28-337
	24 Oct 1829	Liverpool	Holdrege, Henry	29-316
SILAS RICHARDS	7 Mar 1825	Liverpool	Holdrege, J. Henry	25-091
	28 Jun 1825	Liverpool	Holdridge, Henry	25-379
	27 Oct 1825	Liverpool	Holdridge, Henry	25-619
	3 Apr 1826	Liverpool	Holdrege, Henry	26-139
	20 Jun 1826	Liverpool	Holdrege, Henry	26-352
	27 Oct 1826	Liverpool	Holdrege, Henry	26-631
	7 Mar 1827	Liverpool	Holdrige, Henry	27-107
	27 Jun 1827	Liverpool	Holdrige, Henry	27-380
	29 Oct 1827	Liverpool	Holdrige, Henry	27-729
	19 Mar 1828	Liverpool	Holdredge, Henry	28-074
	29 Oct 1828	Liverpool	Holdrege, Henry	28-638
	9 Mar 1829	Liverpool	Holdrege, Henry (Holdredge)	29-074
SILK WORM	6 Mar 1820	St. Iago de Cuba	Rogers, Nathaniel	20-050
SILVANUS JENKINS	6 Apr 1826	Liverpool	Macy, Josiah	26-156
	16 Aug 1826	Liverpool	Folger, Thomas J.	26-489
	10 Mar 1827	Liverpool	Macy, Josiah	27-115
	29 Jun 1827	Liverpool	Macy, Josiah	27-390
	30 Nov 1827	Liverpool	Macy, Jonah	27-776
	17 Mar 1828	Liverpool	Allen, Francis P.	28-067
	24 Jul 1828	Liverpool	Allen, Francis P.	28-397
	17 Nov 1828	Liverpool	Allen, Francis P.	28-664
	27 Jul 1829	Liverpool	Allen, Francis P.	29-170
SILVIA	10 Sep 1827	Bristol	Paynter, C. T.	27-612
SIR JAMES KEMPT	10 Dec 1827	Bristol	Robinson, John	27-820
SIROC	13 Sep 1828	Liverpool	Lambert, Richard	28-535
	31 Oct 1829	Liverpool	Marshall, Edward G.	29-343
SISTERS	24 Jan 1820	Havana	Winslow, Charles	20-013
	10 Jan 1826	Tampico	hardie, F. A.	26-017
	7 Jul 1826	Tampico	Leary, William H.	26-382
SIX BROTHERS	4 Jun 1822	Havre	Williams, Calvin	22-253
	21 Nov 1822	Havre de Grace	Williams, Calvin	22-577
	6 Jul 1824	Bordeaux	Williams, Calvin	24-354
	10 Aug 1829	Marseilles	Lee, George W.	29-206
SLOOP PACKET	5 Oct 1821	Havana	Russell, Leond.	21-307
SMYRNA	30 Apr 1825	Bordeaux	Crocker, Walter	25-229
SOFIA	17 May 1828	Messina (Nepina)	La Valle, George (La Ville)	28-229
SOLDADO ESPANOL	8 Jul 1822	Havana	Tarquin, J.	22-309
SOLON	7 Aug 1820	St. Petersburg	Smith, Christopher	20-165
	31 Aug 1822	Liverpool	Joy, Levi	22-440
	21 Jun 1824	Liverpool	Joy, Levi	24-315
	25 Nov 1824	Liverpool	Joy, Levi	24-689
	12 Jun 1826	St. Croix	Prince, Silvanus	26-320
SOPHIA	17 Jun 1823	Bremen	Dietjier, Ijark	23-268
SOPHIA & ELIZA	13 Jun 1828	Rio Grande	White, Wm. S.	28-300
SOTO	11 Nov 1828	Gibraltar	Ricketson, Barbara	28-660
	1 Aug 1829	Buenos Ayres	Ricketson, Barton	29-185
SOUTH AMERICA	29 Aug 1826	St. Salvador, Brazil	Coffin, Job	26-505
SOUTH BOSTON	15 Sep 1821	Liverpool	Campbell, Alexander H.	21-272
SOUTH CAROLINA	2 Aug 1822	St. Thomas	Johnson, Stephen	22-367
	27 May 1823	St. Thomas	Johnson, Stephen	23-229
	14 Aug 1823	St. Croix	Johnson, Stephen	23-400
	28 Nov 1823	St. Thomas	Johnson, Stephen	23-612
	30 Jun 1824	St. Croix	Johnson, Stephen	24-345
	22 Dec 1824	St. Thomas	Johnson, Stephen	24-729

SHIP	DATE OF ARRIVAL	PORT OF EMBARKATION	CAPTAIN	YEAR AND SHIP NUMBER
SOUTH CAROLINA PACKET	15 Jan 1820	(West end) St. Croix	Cartwright, Alexr. J.	20-007
	25 Mar 1820	West end/St. Croix	Cartwright, Alexander J.	20-081
	22 Jul 1820	St. Croix	Cartwright, Alexr. J.	20-138
	16 Sep 1820	St. Croix	Cartwright, Alexr.	20-249
	7 Jul 1821	St. Croix	Cartwright, Alexr. S.	21-162
	5 Nov 1821	St. Thomas	O'Zuill, John	21-360
	4 Mar 1822	(West End) St. Croix	Cartwright, Alexr. J.	22-069
	22 Jun 1822	(West End) St. Croix	Cartwright, Alexr.	22-282
	4 Sep 1822	St. Croix	Cartwright, A. J.	22-451
	28 Apr 1823	St. Croix	Cartwright, Alexr. J.	23-158
	16 Sep 1823	St. Croix	Knapp, C. W.	23-480
	31 Mar 1824	St. Croix	Cartwright, Alexr. J.	24-120
	21 May 1824	St. Croix	Cartwright, Alexr. S.	24-218
	26 Jul 1824	St. Croix	Cartwright, Alexr. J.	24-396
	3 Jan 1825	St. Croix	Cartwright, Alexr. J.	25-001
	30 May 1825	(West End) St. Croix	Cartwright, Alexr. B.	25-306
	2 Aug 1825	St. Croix	Cartwright, Alex. J.	25-468
	16 Feb 1826	St. Croix	Cartwright, Alexr. J.	26-070
	18 Apr 1826	St. Croix	Cartwright, Alexr. J.	26-183
	19 Jun 1826	St. Croix	Cartwright, A. J.	26-342
	29 Aug 1826	St. Croix	Cartwright, Alexr. J.	26-506
	17 May 1827	St. Croix	Cartwright, Alexr.	27-262
SOUTHERN TRADER	23 Apr 1823	Arquin, S. Domingo	Kilby, Thomas	23-148
SPARK	17 Sep 1821	Havana	Johnson, Henry	21-280
SPARTAN	25 Jul 1821	Liverpool	Colesworthy, Charles H.	21-195
	11 Mar 1823	Liverpool	Ward, Thomas	23-076
	17 Dec 1823	Antigua	Delano, Edwin	23-644
	21 Aug 1824	Havre	Cadman, Ezekiel	24-476
	16 Feb 1825	Havre	Caiman, Ezekiel	25-067
	14 Oct 1825	Gibraltar	Wilson, Francis	25-588
	20 Feb 1826	St. Barts	Reeve, John	26-073
	13 Apr 1826	Carthagena	Chapman, Israel	26-175
	21 Apr 1826	Liverpool	Carman, Ezekiel	26-198
	5 May 1826	Barbadoes	Reeve, John	26-234
	24 Jul 1826	Barbadoes	Reeve, John	26-421
	26 Dec 1826	Barbadoes	Reeve, John	26-736
	16 Nov 1827	Gibraltar	Chapman, Isaac	27-763
	7 Jan 1829	Malaga	Winson, Benj.	29-006
SPECULATOR	12 Feb 1827	Aux Cayes	Tambour, P.	27-077
SPERMO	18 Sep 1823	Liverpool	Clark, Alexr. B.	23-483
	12 Aug 1826	Pernambuca	Gale, Edwd.	26-476
SPLENDID	30 May 1825	Canton	Sterling, Jno. W.	25-308
	11 Apr 1826	Vera Cruz	Drew, Ezra	26-167
	11 Jul 1826	Vera Cruz	Drew, Ezra	26-398
	31 Aug 1827	Vera Cruz	Conklin, Joseph H.	27-568
	27 Mar 1828	Canton	De Peyster, F. A.	28-092
	8 Jan 1829	Porto Cavello (Cabello)	Clark, H.	29-008
	23 Mar 1829	Porto Cavello (Porto Cabello)	Clarke, H.	29-107
	1 Jul 1829	Guadaloupe & Turks Island	Barstow, Alexander	29-114
	14 Aug 1829	Liverpool	McPherson, Saml. W.	29-219
SPRIGHTLY	14 Jun 1822	Alloa	Carron, Alexr.	22-270
SPRING	12 Oct 1821	Bristol	Pitteson, Geo.	21-317
STANFORD	19 Mar 1829	St. Eustatia	Pearce, Thomas	29-104
STAR	4 Oct 1826	Havana	Meyer, P. S.	26-584
	7 Jan 1827	Meyer, Havanna	Meyer, P. S.	27-004
STATIRD	26 Aug 1823	Glasgow	Patting, Wm.	23-425
STEPHANIA	13 Mar 1820	Havre	Burkee, M. R.	20-055
	24 Jul 1820	Havre	Burke, Miles R.	20-147
	13 Sep 1821	Havre de Grace	Burke, Miles R.	21-270
	22 Apr 1822	Havre de Grace	Burke, Miles R.	22-143
	3 Oct 1822	Havre de Grace	Smyth, Andrew	22-503
	8 Mar 1823	Havre	Smith, Andrew	23-064
	28 Jul 1823	Havre	Macy, Robt. J.	23-361
	2 Jan 1824	Havre	Macy, Robert J.	24-003

SHIP	DATE OF ARRIVAL	PORT OF EMBARKATION	CAPTAIN	YEAR AND SHIP NUMBER
	26 Apr 1824	Havre	Macy, Robt. S.	24-167
	7 Aug 1824	Havre	Macy, R. J.	24-437
	18 Dec 1824	Havre	Macy, R. T.	24-726
	11 Apr 1825	Havre	Macy, R. J.	25-163
	15 Aug 1825	Havre	Pell, John B.	25-501
	29 Nov 1825	Havre	Pell, John B.	25-684
	4 Apr 1826	Havre	Pells, John B.	26-149
	4 Aug 1826	Havre	Pell, John B.	26-448
	27 Nov 1826	Havre	Pell, John B.	26-682
	20 Apr 1827	Havre	Pell, John B.	27-184
	16 Aug 1827	Havre	Pell, John B.	27-520
	6 Dec 1827	Havre	Pell, Jno. B.	27-799
	24 Mar 1828	Havre	Pell, Jno. B.	28-085
STRANGER	13 Jun 1823	Elethura	Rogers, Henry	23-260
	29 Jun 1824	Elethura	Judson, Philo G.	24-342
	10 Aug 1824	Jacquemel	Glenney, William	24-441
SUBLIME	6 Dec 1824	Bristol	Gleason, David	24-704
SUCCESS	25 Jun 1825	Harbour Island	Brown, William P.	25-374
SUDAN	6 Aug 1823	Barbadoes	Ivey, John O.	23-385
SUFFOLK	12 Jan 1826	Bristol	Ray, Gideon	26-023
	29 Apr 1828	Samatra & Gibralter	Endicott, M.	28-161
SULLY	30 Oct 1827	Havre	Macy, Robert J.	27-730
	4 Mar 1828	Havre	Macy, Robert J.	28-043
	25 Jun 1828	Havre	Macy, Hy.	28-330
	24 Oct 1828	Havre	Macy, R. J.	28-630
	11 Mar 1829	Havre	Macy, Robert J.	29-082
	15 Jul 1829	Havre	Macy, R. J.	29-150
	26 Oct 1829	Havre	Macy, Robert J.	29-325
SULTANA	20 Sep 1824	Rio Janerio	Thomas, Brigge	24-545
	6 Nov 1828	Montevideo	Blunt, O. C.	28-656
SUPERB	27 Mar 1820	Bermuda	Aymar, Daniel	20-084
	18 Jul 1820	Sligo	Hamilton, William	20-131
	27 Sep 1820	Bermuda	Cymar, Daniel	20-268
	28 May 1821	Greenock	O'Connor, John	21-093
	9 Jul 1821	Martinique	Ham, John	21-163
	11 Oct 1821	Greencok, Scotland	O'Connor, John	21-313
	18 Oct 1821	St. Thomas	Ham, Jno.	21-335
	23 Apr 1823	Barbados	Burr, Josiah	23-149
	7 Jul 1823	Barbadoes	Burr, Josiah	23-318
SUPERION	30 Apr 1825	Havana	Russell, L.	25-225
SUPERIOR	21 May 1823	Canton	Dowdall, George R.	23-221
	18 Nov 1823	Jamaica	Tilley, Edward	23-602
	20 Apr 1824	Canton	Dowdall, George R.	24-156
	30 Apr 1824	Marseilles	Sweetser, Salathiel	24-185
	12 Jun 1824	Newry	Tyler, Warren	24-304
	25 Sep 1824	Havana	Russell, Leond.	24-553
	17 Jan 1825	Havana	Russell, Leond.	25-020
	14 Apr 1825	Nassau, N.P.	Soule, J. B.	25-174
	9 Jun 1825	Porto Rico	Sweetzer, S.	25-325
	18 Jun 1825	Havre	Harrod, Benjamin	25-355
	27 Jun 1825	Nassau, New Providence	Soule, John B.	25-376
	20 Aug 1825	Liverpool	Tyler, Warren	25-530
	5 Jun 1826	St. Crhistophers	Richardson, Gates	26-301
	16 Apr 1827	Canton	Dowdall, G. R.	27-177
	5 Sep 1827	Liverpool	Waite, Benjamin L.	27-587
	31 Mar 1828	Liverpool	O'Hara, John	28-099
	25 Sep 1828	Greenock	O'Hara, John	28-566
SUPERIOR HOPE	27 Oct 1824	Bermuda	Baker, Richard	24-629
	15 Feb 1825	Jacqumel	Baker, Richard	25-063
SUPERIOUR (see Superior)				
	11 Oct 1828	Port au Prince	Delarue, John Alfred	28-606
SURPRIZE	1 Aug 1825	Eleuthura	Johnson, John W.	25-464
SUSAN	2 Aug 1822	Bermuda	Chase, James	22-368
	28 Sep 1826	Gibraltar	Gardner, Benjamin	26-567
SUSAN & SARAH	25 Apr 1825	St. Iago	Waterhouse, Jno.	25-203
SUSAN MORTON	17 Jun 1823	St. Johns, N.B.	Sutton, Jonas	23-269
SUSANNAH	19 Apr 1823	Jamaica	Stevens, A. H.	23-144
	20 Mar 1824	Trinadad in Cuba	Stevens, A. H.	24-099

SHIP	DATE OF ARRIVAL	PORT OF EMBARKATION	CAPTAIN	YEAR AND SHIP NUMBER
	13 Jul 1824	St. Iago de Cuba	Stevens, A. H.	24-374
SUSQUEHANA	27 Jun 1823	Sligo	Stewart, Phinehas	23-295
SUSQUEHANNA	23 Nov 1822	Gibraltar	Callison, Joseph	22-579
	9 Jan 1824	Waterford	McMannus, Jno.	24-014
	16 May 1827	Marseilles	Brag, David	27-258
SUSSEX	9 Mar 1827	Carthagena	Shephard, Bartlett	27-110
SWAN	29 May 1821	Angustura	Skinner, Jas.	21-095
	13 Nov 1821	Guayna	Skinner, Joseph	21-369
	24 Mar 1823	Monteviedo	Storer, Isaac	23-094
	23 Jun 1823	Havana	Coggshall, George	23-280
SWIFT	11 May 1824	Aux Cayes	Swift, Silas	24-210
	31 Mar 1825	Porto cabello	Swift, Silas	25-145
	9 Jan 1826	Carthagenia	Swift, Selas	26-016
	18 Apr 1826	Trinidad	Swift, Silas	26-185
	13 Jan 1827	La Guayra	Swift, Joseph	27-025
	7 Apr 1827	La Guyra	Swift, Joseph	27-166
	16 Jul 1827	La Guira	Swift, Joseph	27-451
	28 Jan 1828	La Guira	Swift, Joseph	28-027
	25 Apr 1828	Laguira	Swift, Joseph	28-147
	28 Jun 1828	Novascotio	Swift, Joseph	28-336
	19 Aug 1828	Pictou, N.S.	Swift, Joseph	28-446
SWIFTSURE	27 Feb 1826	Vera Cruz	Tilley, James	26-085
	6 Dec 1826	Malaga	Atwood, Amaziah	26-700
	14 Apr 1828	Gibralter	Atwood, A.	28-123
SYLVESTER HEALY	11 May 1825	St. John, N.B.	Gardiner, Stephen H.	25-249
	14 Jun 1825	St. John, N.B.	Gardiner, S. H.	25-340
	19 Aug 1825	St. John, N.B.	Crowell, Reuben	25-515
	17 Oct 1825	St. Johns, N.B.	Crowell, Reuben	25-595
	23 Nov 1825	St. Johns, N.B.	Crowell, Reuben	25-667
TABASCO	6 Apr 1826	Tampico	Anderson, James	26-157
	5 Aug 1826	Tampico	Anderson, James	26-454
TALLY HO	22 Mar 1825	Marinham	Glover, Russell E.	25-132
TALMA	12 Oct 1826	Havre	Rathbone, John	26-591
	23 Sep 1828	Havre	Marshall, A. C.	28-562
	20 Nov 1828	St. Petersburg	Soule, Richard	28-671
TAMPICO	20 Jan 1825	La Guira	Rathbun, Elisha	25-030
	20 Apr 1825	Carthagenia	Palmer, N. B.	25-194
	14 Jul 1825	Carthagenia	Palmer, A. B.	25-420
	13 Oct 1825	Carthagina	Palmer, Nathaniel B.	25-586
	21 Jan 1826	Carthagena	Sheffield, James P.	26-033
	29 Apr 1826	Carthagena	Palmer, Nathaniel B.	26-210
	11 Jul 1826	Carthagena	Palmer, Nathaniel B.	26-397
	19 Oct 1826	Carthagina	Palmer, Nath. B.	26-613
	12 Mar 1827	Carthagena	Palmer, Alexander S.	27-119
	27 Jun 1827	Carthagena	Palmer, Alexander S.	27-382
	7 Jan 1828	Carthagena	Rathbun, Elisha	28-007
	13 May 1828	Carthagena	Rathbun, Elisha	28-211
	2 Aug 1828	Carthagena	Fish, Nathan G.	28-418
	10 Feb 1829	Carthagena	Fish, Nathan G.	29-056
TANDEM	8 Mar 1826	St. Johns, Nicaragua	Tooker, Daniel A.	26-092
	30 Nov 1826	Pernambuco	Adams, Joseph	26-694
TANTAMOUNT	25 Apr 1822	St. Andrews	Allen, John	22-151
TANTIVA	7 Jul 1828	Bristol	Bell, Isaac	28-358
TAPPERHETEN	12 Jun 1826	Calsorona	Gyllengrant, C. A.	26-321
TARANTULA	31 Oct 1823	Havana	Prats, J.	23-566
TARTAR	13 Aug 1823	Marseilles	Rivans, Thomas	23-399
	14 Apr 1824	Porto Cabella	Revans, Thomas	24-144
	23 Jun 1824	Curacoa	Bevans, Thomas	24-321
TEIO	5 Jun 1826	St. John, N.B.	McKenzie, Reuben	26-304
TELEGRAPH	14 Feb 1820	Liverpool	Corrin, Hator	20-034
	5 Aug 1824	St. Croix	Blanchard, Nathanl.	24-433
	18 May 1827	Matanzas	Blanchard, David	27-265
	24 Mar 1828	Mayaguez, Porto Rico	Blanchard, David	28-084
	14 Jun 1828	Matanzas	Blanchard, David	28-304
THACHER	23 Sep 1828	Gibralter	Thatcher, Isaac	28-563
THAMES	6 Oct 1820	London to New York	Peck, Norman	20-282
	16 May 1821	London	Mershew, Chas. H.	21-071

SHIP	DATE OF ARRIVAL	PORT OF EMBARKATION	CAPTAIN	YEAR AND SHIP NUMBER
	25 Oct 1821	London	Marshall, Chas. H.	21-346
	27 May 1822	London	Marshall, Charles H.	22-232
THANKFUL WINSLOW	9 Jun 1826	Demara	Winslow, Thomas	26-316
THANKFULL WINSLOW	23 Aug 1826	Havana	Baker, Thomas W.	26-502
THERESA	10 Dec 1825	Porto Cabello	Baker, Wrothbon	25-707
THETIS	5 Jul 1821	Havre de Grace	Anderson, E.	21-154
	14 Feb 1824	Havana	Edes, Thomas	24-038
	28 Jun 1824	Bayamo (Cuba)	Cotton, S. B.	24-336
	17 Aug 1824	St. Croix	Goodrich, Jason	24-459
	29 Dec 1827	St. Croix	Clark, Asher	27-863
THOMAS	3 Sep 1822	Cadez	Sampson, Garus	22-449
	29 Jun 1824	St. Andrews	Miller, Saml.	24-341
	30 Aug 1824	St. John	Miller, Saml.	24-496
	13 Dec 1827	Dublin	Duncan, James	27-832
THOMAS & ELIZA	29 Jul 1823	Antiqua	Wallace, James	23-362
THOMAS & SARAH	18 Sep 1822	St. Andrews	Gay, Isaac J.	22-470
THOMAS & WILLIAM	25 May 1827	Limerick	Colley, Thomas	27-296
THOMAS DICKASON	5 Jun 1827	Liverpool	Anthony, Caleb	27-319
	14 Sep 1827	Liverpool	Anthony, Caleb, Jr.	27-629
	29 Aug 1828	Liverpool	Anthony, Caleb, Jr.	28-478
	31 Jul 1829	Liverpool	Anthony, Caleb, Jr.	29-182
THOMAS RITCHIE	2 Jul 1827	Liverpool	Alexander, A.	27-405
THOMAS WILSON	16 Sep 1822	Havana	Blunt, O. C.	22-466
THOMPSON	12 Sep 1827	Dublin	Ortt, Richard	27-622
	26 Apr 1828	Liverpool	Maxwell, G.	28-152
THORNY CLOSE	3 May 1826	Sunderland	Ayre, James	26-224
THRASHER	4 Dec 1822	Matanzas	Smith, Perry	22-593
	3 Jul 1826	Raggio Island	Small, Lovell	26-377
THREE BROTHERS	21 Mar 1825	Amsterdam	Oosterbaun, M.	25-133
	22 Mar 1825	Maracaybo	Drew, George	25-134
	27 Apr 1825	St. Thomas	Foss, Thos.	25-211
THULE	29 Apr 1825	Batavia	Foulke, G.	25-218
TIDAL	28 Oct 1824	St. Martins	Dewever, Chas.	24-630
TIGER	21 Jul 1825	Halifax	Hall, E.	25-431
TILTON	28 Jun 1826	Jamaica	Tilton, Saml.	26-367
TIPPORAH	22 Dec 1828	Turks Island	Delesdenier, John	28-716
TO VENNIER	19 Jul 1828	St. Thomas	Anderson, P.	28-387
TOBASCO	17 Aug 1825	Havana	Williams, Erastus	25-506
	23 Jul 1827	Tampico	Sutherland, A. S.	27-471
	7 Nov 1827	Tampico	Marshall, John Henry	27-752
	14 Apr 1828	Tobasco	Crowell, D.	28-127
TOISON	20 Apr 1827	Xibara	Hallet, John	27-186
	21 Nov 1827	Xibara	Driggs, B.	27-765
	6 May 1828	Matanzas	Eddy, Benjn., Jr.	28-187
	15 Dec 1828	Tampico	Eddy, Sylvester	28-705
TOM	2 Jul 1827	Greenock	Emery, Thomas	27-403
TONTIN	13 Jun 1825	Jamaica	Andrews, John	25-333
TONTINE	1 Jun 1826	Kingston, Jamaica	Mason, John R.	26-293
	25 Sep 1826	Kingston, Jamaica	Mason, John R.	26-554
	25 Jan 1827	Jamacia	Mason, J. W.	27-039
	9 Jun 1827	Havana	Jennings, Soleman	27-336
	6 Dec 1827	Havana	Jenninges, Solomen	27-798
TOPAZ	23 Nov 1824	Trinadad in Cuba	Cruse, N. C.	24-683
	5 Jul 1825	Port Cavella	Schuyler, P.	25-394
	25 Mar 1826	Talabacco	Bush, Henry	26-133
	14 Aug 1826	Kingston	Schuyler, Peter	26-478
	23 Feb 1827	Port au Prince	Weiderholt, H. L.	27-090
	28 May 1827	Port au Prince	Wiederholt, H.	27-302
	31 Jul 1827	Cape Hayti	Weiderholdt, H.	27-492

SHIP	DATE OF ARRIVAL	PORT OF EMBARKATION	CAPTAIN	YEAR AND SHIP NUMBER
	7 Apr 1828	Cape Hayti	Dubois, Theodore	28-114
	27 May 1828	Cape Hayti	Dubois, Jhne.	28-251
	23 Jul 1828	Cape Hayti	Dubois, Chas.	28-395
	2 Oct 1828	Cape Hayti	Dubois, Theodore	28-575
	2 Dec 1828	Cape Hayti	Dubois, Chrs.	28-688
TORCH	21 Nov 1825	Xibara	Nelson, Ambrose	25-665
TRADER	24 Jun 1828	St. Thomas	Johnson, Benj.	28-326
TRAFALGAR	22 Jun 1821	Leith	Henderson, James	21-129
	4 Jun 1822	Leith	Henderson, James	22-254
	18 Jan 1828	Port au Prince	Winsor, Isaac	28-018
TRANSIT	21 Apr 1821	Trinidad in Cuba	Gillet, John	21-028
	28 Jun 1828	Trinidad in Cuba	Gillet, John	22-299
	11 Oct 1822	Trinadad	Gillet, John	22-521
	26 Apr 1823	Trinadad in Cuba	Gillet, John	23-152
	13 Nov 1823	Trinadad in Cuba	Gillet, John	23-589
	17 Mar 1824	Trinadad in Cuba	Gillet, John	24-087
TRANSPORT	19 Aug 1829	Jacquemel (Jacmel)	Brown, James	29-230
TRAVELLER	2 Jun 1822	Jacquemel	Frost, Daniel	22-248
	24 Sep 1822	St. Iago de Cuba	Oldridge, Samuel	22-482
	11 Dec 1824	Montego Bay, Jamaica	Woodbury, Samuel M.	24-709
	10 Sep 1827	Cork	Carr, Joseph	27-609
TRENT	1 Oct 1823	Liverpool	Barstow, Edward	23-514
	10 Jul 1827	Greenock	Foster, Benjamin P.	27-436
	23 Jan 1829	Marseilles	Barstow, Nathl.	29-034
TRIDENT	18 Aug 1820	Liverpool	Watkinson, James	20-191
	22 Jan 1822	Havana	Burnham, James	22-015
	13 Aug 1823	Pacific Ocean	Coffin, Reuben	23-398
	8 Mar 1824	Liverpool	Menzies, J. A.	24-071
	1 Dec 1824	London	Menzies, Jacob	24-697
	17 May 1825	Londonderry	Coffin, Hazad.	25-262
	16 May 1826	Londonderry	Coffin, Hazd.	26-256
	30 Sep 1826	Liverpool	Coffin, Hazadiah	26-572
	31 Mar 1827	Liverpool	Swain, Richard	27-159
	18 Jul 1827	Liverpool	Swain, Richard	27-460
TRIMMER	13 Sep 1823	Gibraltar	Naghel, F.	23-473
	12 Apr 1824	Tampico	Shipman, Charles R.	24-138
	10 Jul 1824	Carthagena	Shipman, Chas. R.	24-369
	19 Nov 1824	Garthagena	Shipman, Chas. R.	24-676
	30 Apr 1825	Alvarado	Eveleigh, N. M.	25-227
	21 Jul 1825	Havana	Story, W. W.	25-434
	3 Jan 1826	Carthagena	Evaleigh, Nathl. W.	26-009
	28 Nov 1826	St. Thomas	Fox, Warren	26-688
TRIO	27 Jun 1823	Nassau	Fulford, Wilb. G.	23-296
	8 Feb 1827	Cork	Lislie, Henry	27-063
	13 Jun 1827	Cork	Leslie, Henry	27-343
	31 Oct 1827	Cork	Patterson, Alexander	27-736
	5 May 1828	Cork	Paterson, Alexander (Patterson)	28-177
	2 Oct 1828	Cork	Paterson, Alexander (Patterson)	28-577
TRITON	4 Oct 1822	Liverpool	Wilkinson, Shubael	22-505
	12 Jul 1823	Londonderry	Wilkinson, Shubael	23-332
	11 Jul 1826	Bermuda	Algate, William B.	26-395
	24 Oct 1826	Bermuda	Algate, William B.	26-627
	30 Oct 1826	Marseilles	Howland, Wm., 2nd	26-633
	10 May 1828	Marseilles	Howland, Wm., 2d.	28-201
TRIUMPH	23 Jul 1829	Carthagena	Latham, Elliot	29-166
TRUMBELL	26 Oct 1829	Bordeaux	Dickinson, Daniel	29-330
TRUSTY	12 Sep 1828	Belfast	Mather, J.	28-530
TRYON	25 Apr 1825	Bonair	Cousins, Jas.	25-206
	20 Jun 1826	Havana	Page, Samuel	26-354
	3 Sep 1827	St. Thomas	Smith, Ezra	27-579
TURNER	8 Jun 1824	Guadaloupe	McManers, Richd.	24-282
TUSCALOOSA	31 Oct 1825	Havana	Mott, John	25-629
	8 May 1826	Rio De Janeiro	Pryce, H. P.	26-241
	19 Mar 1827	Rio de Janeiro	Pryce, W. P.	27-127
TUSCARORA	26 Jan 1827	Liverpool	Serril, James	27-040
TWO BROTHERS	6 Sep 1823	Bermuda	Kimble, Henry	23-453

SHIP	DATE OF ARRIVAL	PORT OF EMBARKATION	CAPTAIN	YEAR AND SHIP NUMBER
TWO FRIENDS	22 May 1822	Bristol	Adams, John	22-220
TWO MARYS	12 Feb 1820	Amsterdam	Fring, Elisha	20-032
	20 Apr 1825	Belfast	Telyan, V.	25-197
	24 Sep 1827	Liverpool	Tilyou, Vincent	27-653
ULYSSES	1 May 1822	Bristol	Stone, John	22-172
	29 Oct 1822	Bristol	Aiery, George T.	22-548
UNIAO	19 Aug 1829	Madeira	La Mong, Antonio Estanz	29-229
UNION	22 Jul 1820	Port au Prince	Leech, Wm., Junr.	20-139
	3 Jun 1822	Cork	Patterson, Robert	22-251
	21 Nov 1822	St. Iago de Cuba	Green, Ashbel	22-578
	10 Mar 1823	Londonderry	Cotter, Michl.	23-069
	13 May 1823	Mayagues, Porto Rico	Titcomb, Wm., Jr.	23-199
	24 Sep 1823	Liverpool	French, Francis M.	23-497
	9 Jan 1824	Liverpool	French, Francis M.	24-015
	6 May 1824	Alloa	Craigie, James	24-198
	9 Aug 1824	Havana	Davis, Joshua	24-439
	4 Sep 1824	St. Croix	Smith, Oliver	24-514
	21 Jul 1825	Havana	Gale, L. H.	25-432
	19 Apr 1826	Guyama, Porto Rico	Tobey, John	26-189
	6 Nov 1826	Teneriffe	Allen, Willis W.	26-644
	20 Aug 1827	Cork	Burton, William	27-530
UNION PACKET	9 Feb 1827	Xibera	Grow, John S.	27-068
	10 Aug 1829	Tobasco	Grow, John S.	29-208
UNITED STATES	29 Nov 1823	La Guira	Hipkins, John	23-617
	22 Mar 1824	Galway in Ireland	Downes, James	24-102
	15 Jul 1824	Angustura	Clark, Henry	24-376
	27 Jul 1824	Jamaica	Downs, James	24-405
	13 Dec 1824	Teneriffe	Downs, James	24-716
	10 Jan 1825	Angastura	Clark, H.	25-013
	18 Sep 1826	Matanzas	Clark, H.	26-537
	18 Oct 1826	Havre	Wilson, James L.	26-604
	16 Feb 1827	Liverpool	Wilson, James L.	27-082
	21 May 1827	Liverpool	Wilson, James S.	27-274
	7 Jul 1827	Amsterdam	Knight, Isaac	27-418
	8 Sep 1827	Liverpool	Wilson, James L.	27-603
	7 Dec 1827	Havana	Kennedy, Alexander L.	27-806
	1 Apr 1828	Port au Prince	Hogg, J. W.	28-105
	3 Sep 1828	Amsterdam	Knight, J. (Right)	28-498
	11 Sep 1828	Liverpool	Wilson, Jas. L.	28-526
UNITY	27 Mar 1827	Bristol	Johnson, John	27-153
	5 Sep 1828	Rye	Hicks, Henry	28-504
	20 Oct 1829	Bristol	Johnson, John	29-315
UPTON	6 Aug 1822	Bermuda	Sampson, Enoch M.	22-376
URANIA	17 May 1828	Dundee	Mearns, William	28-225
VALIANT	21 Oct 1822	Acquin	Calvin, Luther	22-539
	30 Jan 1823	Aquin	Hallock, Justus R.	23-022
VELOCIPEDE	26 Jun 1823	St. Thomas	Kirtland, Danil	23-291
	24 May 1824	La Guayra	Kirtland, Daniel	24-229
	20 Sep 1824	La Guira	Kirtland, Daniel	24-543
	16 Dec 1824	La Guira	Kertland, Daniel	24-724
VENUS	11 Aug 1820	Matanzas	Farrier, William	20-173
	8 Sep 1820	London	Candler, Samuel	20-230
	9 Sep 1820	Aux Cayes	Grice, George W.	20-232
	12 Apr 1821	London	Candler, Saml.	21-015
	27 Jun 1821	Matanzas	Ferrier, William	21-142
	4 Oct 1821	London	Candler, Samuel	21-306
	15 Apr 1822	London	Mount, F. M.	22-130
	26 Jun 1822	Havana	Ferrier, William	22-295
	12 Jul 1824	Jamaica	Kelly, James	24-370
	10 Aug 1824	Jamaica	Mason, John R.	24-442
	4 Oct 1824	London	Allen, Ichabod	24-566
	12 Oct 1824	Havana	Grover, Charles	24-589
	27 Dec 1824	Port Maria, Jamaica	Mason, John R.	24-737
	4 Mar 1825	Terceira	Bray, Nehemiah N.	25-088
	28 Jun 1825	New Providence	Ludington, Justin	25-385
	8 May 1826	Gibraltar	Wheeler, Stephen	26-237
	1 Apr 1828	Turks Island	Holland, Stephen	28-104
VERMONT	29 Oct 1822	Liverpool	Curtis, Hy.	22-549

SHIP	DATE OF ARRIVAL	PORT OF EMBARKATION	CAPTAIN	YEAR AND SHIP NUMBER
	26 Aug 1824	Teneriffe	Dickinson, Saml.	24-489
	17 Nov 1826	Bermuda	Tucker, Zebediah	26-669
	10 Jan 1827	Halifax, N.S.	Tucker, Zebedian	27-017
	19 Mar 1827	Halifax	Tucker, Zebediah	27-129
	3 May 1827	Halifax	Tucker, Zebediah	27-209
	19 Jun 1827	Halifax	Tucker, Zebediah	27-361
	7 Oct 1828	Aux Cayes	Prince, Benj., Junr.	28-593
VERNON	17 Dec 1828	Aux Cayes	Brazier, George	28-712
VESTAL	8 May 1822	Curacoa	Jerland, William	22-180
VICTOR	3 Jul 1829	Ponce, P.R.	Gray, John	29-124
VICTORIA	9 Sep 1828	Vera Cruz	Beekeep, B. A.	28-519
VICTORY	12 Jul 1820	Havana	Sands, Hart	20-124
	1 Sep 1820	Bermuda	Prescott, Wm. P.	20-221
	29 May 1821	Havana	Burr, Josiah	21-096
	8 Oct 1821	Havana	Wilson, Nicho.	21-310
	13 Oct 1823	Vera Cruz	Kingsbury, E.	23-543
	21 Jun 1824	La Guayra	Wise, D., Jr.	24-318
	26 Oct 1824	Havana	Kingsbury, E.	24-624
VIGILANCE	26 Aug 1829	Stockholm	Hertzman, John	29-254
VIGILANT	13 Oct 1821	Curacoa	Brown, Benjn.	21-320
	6 May 1822	Sligo	Stewart, Phinehas	22-176
	25 Nov 1822	Havana	Harper, Thomas L.	22-582
	15 Feb 1823	Havana	Harper, Thomas P.	23-030
	14 Apr 1823	Havana	Harper, Thomas L.	23-201
VILLARD DE CAYES	10 Apr 1827	Aux Cayes	Breman, A.	27-170
VIRGINIA	12 Jul 1820	St. Croix	Funk, John	20-125
	9 Apr 1821	Rio Janeiro	Funk, John	21-007
	24 Jul 1821	St. Croix	Johns, Joel	21-193
	2 Feb 1822	Panambuco	Newman, Saml.	22-023
	16 Apr 1822	St. Croix	Reede, Charles	22-133
	25 Nov 1822	Monteviedo	Reeves, Charles	22-581
	7 May 1824	Limerick	Knapp, Thomas	24-202
	1 Feb 1825	Gibraltar	Knapp, Thomas	25-047
	20 Jun 1825	Sligo	Knap, Thos.	25-361
	30 May 1827	St. Iago de Cuba	Russell, Leond.	27-311
	3 Dec 1827	Vera Cruz	Collins, John	27-785
	31 Dec 1827	Port au Platt	Davis, James R.	27-867
	8 Mar 1828	Vera Cruz	Collins, John	28-048
	26 May 1828	Vera Cruz	Collins, John	28-244
	31 May 1828	Havre	Prince, Reuben	28-260
	30 Oct 1828	Bordeaux	Collins, John	28-641
	9 Feb 1829	Vera Cruz	Collins, John	29-052
VIRGINIA PACKET	1 Jun 1822	Havana	Allen, Ichabod	22-247
VISITOR	21 Jul 1823	Demerara	Heddean, Wm. (Gabriel L. Lewis)	23-346
	30 Jun 1825	Jamaica	Merryman, Joseph	25-389
VOLANT	29 Dec 1820	St. Andrews	Card, George	20-360
	30 Oct 1821	Teneriffe	Wiley, David W.	21-352
	30 Mar 1824	Amsterdam	Nichols, Chas.	24-118
	19 Apr 1826	Antigua	Tupper, Peleg	26-188
VOLTIGEUSE	4 Oct 1827	City of St. Domingo	Brown, John	27-675
VORWARTZ	21 Aug 1822	Port au Prince	Jurgensen, L. A.	22-410
VULCAN	22 Nov 1824	Liverpool	Drew, Ezra	24-680
WABASH	9 Feb 1827	Jamaica	Quereau, Ph. J.	27-070
WADE	29 Aug 1825	Rotterdam	Doak, John	25-554
WALDO	19 Aug 1826	Havre	Henderson, Wm. (H.)	26-500
WALLACE	12 Apr 1824	Jamaica	Clark, Wm. L.	24-134
	18 May 1825	Orataro (Teneriffe)	Myrick, James	25-272
WANDERER	11 Jul 1826	Ireland via Canary Isles	Berry, Benjamin	26-393
	6 Oct 1827	Teneriffe	Berry, Benjamin	27-680
	14 May 1828	St. Johns, N.B.	Berry, Benjamin	28-216
	23 Jun 1828	St. Johns, N.B.	Adams, R.	28-321
	1 Aug 1828	St. John, New Brunswick	Adams, Richard	28-414
	1 Sep 1828	St. Johns	Adams, Richard	28-491
	30 Sep 1828	St. Johns, N.B.	Adams, Richard	28-571
	30 Oct 1828	St. John	Adams, Richard	28-642

SHIP	DATE OF ARRIVAL	PORT OF EMBARKATION	CAPTAIN	YEAR AND SHIP NUMBER
	4 Aug 1829	St. Thomas, St. John, N.B.	Adams, Richard	29-195
	31 Aug 1829	St. John, N.B.	Adams, Richard	29-269
WARREN	10 Sep 1824	St. Thomas	Perkins, Joseph	24-527
	7 Jul 1826	Bremen	Snow, Ephraim	26-383
WARRIOR	16 Mar 1826	Greenock	McVicar, Alexr.	26-117
	19 May 1828	Bristol	Stone, John	28-233
	6 Oct 1828	Bristol	Stone, John	28-585
WASHINGTON	22 Mar 1820	London	Mount, Forman M.	20-078
	16 Sep 1820	London	Mount, F. M.	20-250
	9 Apr 1821	London	Mount, F. M.	21-008
	15 Sep 1821	London	Mount, F. M.	21-273
	2 Oct 1822	Porto Rico	Barstow, Alexander	22-501
	7 Jul 1824	London	Smith, Nathl.	24-359
	22 Apr 1825	Martinique	Gaylord, S.	25-198
	13 Jun 1825	Jacmel	Cook, Joshua	25-334
	8 Oct 1825	Halifax	Norris, Peter	25-575
	15 Apr 1826	Canton	Rossiter, Edward	26-182
	29 Apr 1826	Cadiz	Colburn, Oliver	26-209
	19 Jun 1826	Aquin, St. Domingo	Haff, Robert	26-347
	3 Sep 1827	Liverpool	Coffin, H.	27-575
	7 Dec 1827	Martinique	Quarles, Francis, Jr.	27-807
	3 Mar 1828	Liverpool	Robinson, Wm. I.	28-038
	2 Oct 1828	Liverpool	Robinson, Wm. J.	28-574
	23 Dec 1828	Quebec via Pictow	Parsons, Tyler, Jr.	28-717
WATERVILLE	19 Dec 1825	Jamaica	Harding, Neh.	25-719
WATSON	30 Apr 1827	Havana	Prince, Joel	27-206
WAVE	21 May 1821	Havana	Brown, W. G.	21-078
	15 Aug 1821	Havana	Brown, Wm. Y.	21-226
	28 Dec 1821	Havana	Harper, Thomas P.	21-436
	7 Mar 1822	Havana	Harper, Thomas P.	22-072
	29 Apr 1822	Bermuda	Harper, Thomas P.	22-167
	27 Jul 1822	Havana	Harper, Thomas P.	22-354
WAVERLY	5 Dec 1828	St. Eustatia	Smack, Powell	28-695
WEAVER	26 Nov 1822	Jamaica	Owen, Moses	22-585
WESER	24 Jul 1820	Bremen	Pease, Wm. G.	20-148
	26 Jun 1821	Sligo	Pease, Wm. G.	21-136
	9 May 1822	Limerick	Jenkins, Matthew	22-185
	29 Jul 1823	Liverpool	Slidell, Alexander	23-368
	21 Oct 1823	Turks Island	Slidell, Alexander	23-555
	24 Mar 1826	Matanzas	Ferrier, Robt.	26-129
WESSER (see Weser)				
WESTMORE-LAND	1 Aug 1826	Londonderry	Clark, Garland	26-444
WEYMOUTH	3 Apr 1821	Port au Prince	Masson, Thomas	21-002
	13 Aug 1822	Cuba	Genn, William J.	22-393
	16 Feb 1825	Carthagina	Orne, William B.	25-069
WHITE OAK	30 Oct 1820	Liverpool	Fowler, Gilbert	20-307
	24 Apr 1826	Leghorn	Noyes, Benjamin	26-200
	5 Apr 1828	Messina	Noyes, B.	28-111
	9 Oct 1828	Leghorn	Noyes, Benjamin	28-598
WICKER	1 Aug 1820	Cuba	Ward, Richard	20-159
	19 Jun 1826	Matanzas	Ward, Richd.	26-345
	21 May 1827	Matanzas	Ward, Richd.	27-276
WICKES	27 Feb 1826	Matanzas	Ward, Richd.	26-083
WILHELMINA	8 Jan 1824	St. Iago De Cuba	Engel, H.	24-010
	31 May 1824	St. Thomas	Adecoa, Jno. Bta.	24-250
WILLIAM	19 Jan 1820	Halifax/via Barnstable	Hallet, Allen	20-011
	2 Feb 1820	Cape Henry, Hayti	Dexter, Allen	20-023
	22 Jul 1820	Halifax	Hallet, Allen	20-140
	17 Aug 1820	Liverpool	Collins, J.	20-190
	31 Aug 1820	Halifax	Hallet, Allen	20-219
	11 Dec 1820	Halifax	Hallet, Allen	20-342
	2 May 1821	Hull	Williams, T. F.	21-046
	11 May 1821	Halifax	Hallet, A.	21-062
	23 Jun 1821	Bermuda	Fireman, Judah E.	21-131
	9 Aug 1821	Halifax	Hallet, Allen	21-219
	21 Sep 1821	Liverpool	Noyes, Charles W.	21-296

SHIP	DATE OF ARRIVAL	PORT OF EMBARKATION	CAPTAIN	YEAR AND SHIP NUMBER
	25 Sep 1821	Halifax	Hallet, Allen	21-301
	18 Mar 1822	Greenock	Noyes, Chas. W.	22-084
	1 Apr 1822	Havana	Moffat, Anthony	22-102
	2 Sep 1822	Bristol, Eng.	Morrat, Anthony	22-445
	4 Oct 1822	Liverpool	McMannus, John	22-508
	5 Oct 1822	Liverpool	Noyes, Wm.	22-512
	16 Apr 1823	Matanzas	Gardner, Joseph	23-136
	26 Apr 1823	Cork	McMannus, John	23-153
	17 Jun 1823	Bristol	Moffat, Anthy.	23-270
	11 Nov 1823	Bermuda	Dexter, David	23-582
	28 Nov 1823	Bristol	Moffat, Anthy.	23-613
	10 Dec 1823	Liverpool	Eveleigh, Nathl. W.	23-634
	17 Dec 1823	Port au Platt	Price, Oliver, Jr.	23-645
	6 May 1824	Barbadoes	Drinkwater, Sewall	24-199
	27 Jul 1824	Liverpool	Moffat, Anthy.	24-410
	30 Jul 1824	Havana	Gardner, Joseph	24-418
	14 Oct 1824	Matanzas	Tilley, Edward	24-600
	18 Oct 1824	Neuvitas	Horner, Jacob	24-609
	21 May 1825	Cork	Robinson, Alexander	25-285
	28 Jul 1825	Port Cabello	Pope, C. C.	25-459
	11 Nov 1825	Liverpool	Britton, Wm.	25-655
	31 Jan 1826	Vera Cruz	Spear, James	26-046
	28 Feb 1826	Port au Prince	Bartlett, John E.	26-088
	30 May 1826	Fortune Island	Bartlett, John C.	26-291
	31 Jul 1826	Amsterdam	Barnard, Peter	26-439
	12 Aug 1826	Lisbon	Brownell, Thomas	26-473
	14 Dec 1826	Maracaybo	Storms, Peter	26-723
	29 Jun 1827	Jacmel	Thorndike, Joseph	27-387
	27 Aug 1827	St. Johns, N.B.	Chandler, Enos	27-561
	12 Oct 1827	Maracaybo	Warner, Gilbert	27-700
	11 Dec 1827	Antwerp	Gillis, James D.	27-822
	7 Jan 1828	Maracaibo	Warner, Gilbert	28-005
	31 Mar 1828	Maracaybo	Warner, Gilbert (William)	28-096
	21 May 1828	Rye, England	Vidler, Samuel	28-238
	1 Jul 1828	Maracaybo	Warner, G.	28-346
	6 Oct 1828	Maracaibo	Warner, Gilbert	28-584
	5 Nov 1828	Havana	Pereira, Domingos	28-653
	20 Jul 1829	Dublin	Keating, Richard, Jur.	29-163
WILLIAM & EZRA	18 Oct 1824	Bordeaux	Barstow, Alexr.	24-607
WILLIAM & FREDERICK	16 Feb 1824	St. Vincents	Aertsen, William	24-047
	16 Jun 1827	St. Croix	Brite, Charles L.	27-352
WILLIAM & GEORGE	14 May 1828	Londonderry	Bryson, Thomas	28-212
WILLIAM & HENRY	19 Jul 1822	Liverpool	Drew, Ezra	22-342
	17 Sep 1822	Port au Platt	Stow, Anthony	22-469
	13 Mar 1823	Matanzas	Colver, Christopher	23-079
	9 Sep 1826	Angostura	Stow, Anthony	26-525
	27 Mar 1827	Angostura	Stow, Anthony	27-151
WILLIAM & JANE	22 Aug 1820	Liverpool	Gill, James	20-202
	20 Feb 1823	Canton	Bartlin, Chas.	23-042
	4 Apr 1825	Lpool	Bartling, C.	25-150
WILLIAM & JOHN	21 Aug 1822	Canton	Ebberts, John	22-409
	10 Jul 1824	Londonderry	Davis, Stiles	24-366
WILLIAM & MARY	5 Jul 1826	Kingston, Jamaica	Cady, James	26-380
WILLIAM & NANCY	31 Jan 1823	Bermuda	Hardy, Elisha	23-024
	5 Jun 1823	Barbadoes	Handy, Elisha	23-244
WILLIAM BARKER	21 Apr 1823	Demarara	Nickels, Saml.	23-146
	29 Aug 1823	St. Andrews	Nichols, Saml.	23-429

SHIP	DATE OF ARRIVAL	PORT OF EMBARKATION	CAPTAIN	YEAR AND SHIP NUMBER
WILLIAM BAYARD	21 Feb 1823	Campeachy	Curtis, James F.	23-044
	2 Mar 1824	Tampico & Havana	Seaman, Benson	24-066
	24 Jan 1825	Carthagina	Seaman, B.	25-035
	17 May 1825	Carthagina	Nichols, John S.	25-263
	6 Aug 1825	Carthagina	Stewart, Chas.	25-479
	25 Apr 1826	Havana	Betts, Thos.	26-201
	14 Jun 1827	Carthagena	Hamilton, William	27-346
WILLIAM BYRNES	14 Apr 1824	Liverpool	Cobb, Nathan	24-143
	1 Dec 1824	Liverpool	Cobb, Nathan	24-699
	17 Jul 1825	Liverpool	Cobbs, N.	25-424
	6 Apr 1826	Liverpool	Hackstaff, William Green	26-159
	15 Aug 1826	Liverpool	Hackstaff, William G.	26-480
	24 Apr 1827	Liverpool	Hackstaff, William G.	27-195
	23 Aug 1827	Liverpool	Cockstaff, Wm. G.	27-547
	11 Dec 1827	Liverpool	Hackett, Wm.	27-826
	25 Aug 1828	Liverpool	Hackstaff, Wm. G.	28-467
	22 Dec 1828	Liverpool	Patterson, Hugh C.	28-713
	13 Aug 1829	Liverpool	Hackstaff, Wm. G.	29-216
WILLIAM DAWSON	18 Jun 1827	Liverpool	Hutchinson, John	27-355
WILLIAM FREDERICK	17 Mar 1825	Demerara	Butler, Thomas W.	25-119
WILLIAM HENRY	12 Sep 1820	Havana	Dugan, E. W.	20-240
	29 Dec 1823	City St. Domingo	Lister, James	23-656
	24 Mar 1828	Trinidad de Cuba	Brown, Stephen	28-081
WILLIAM HOWLAND	5 Jul 1821	Bristol	Southworth, Andrew	21-155
	27 Jul 1824	Gottenburgh	Southworth, Andrew	24-406
	21 Mar 1825	Marseilles	Stevens, Henry J.	25-124
	10 Nov 1825	Gothenburg	Southworth, Andrew	25-652
	20 Jul 1829	Gottenburg	Lee, William	29-162
WILLIAM NEILSON (see William Nelson)				
	26 Jul 1828	Liverpool	White, John	28-404
WILLIAM PENN	20 Oct 1825	St. Johns, N.B.	Thompson, William	25-599
	20 Jan 1829	Jacmel	Richardson, Joseph (Hamor, David)	29-027
WILLIAM PRINCE	30 May 1825	Curacoa	Turner, Wm.	25-309
	13 Dec 1827	Curacoa	Wattington, Francis, Jr.	27-830
WILLIAM PRINCES (see William Prince)				
WILLIAM SAVERY	9 Feb 1825	Canton	Phillips, John	25-059
WILLIAM SMITH	9 May 1822	St. Croix	McLellan, Saml.	22-186
WILLIAM TELL	3 Dec 1825	Buenos Ayres	Hinman, Munson	25-686
	3 Dec 1827	Rio de Janeiro	Bassett, F. C.	27-789
	24 Oct 1829	Londonderry	Holdrege, John	29-318
WILLIAM THOMPSON	30 Apr 1822	Liverpool	Thomson, Wm.	22-168
	6 Sep 1822	Liverpool	Thomson, Wm.	22-455
	29 Jan 1823	Liverpool	Thomson, William	23-021
	13 May 1823	Liverpool	Thomson, Wm.	23-198
	29 Jan 1824	Liverpool	Crocker, Rowland R.	24-022
	27 May 1824	Liverpool	Crocker, R. R.	24-242
	30 Sep 1824	Liverpool	C..., Rowland	24-559
	18 Jan 1825	Liverpool	Crocker, Rowland R.	25-027
	10 May 1825	Liverpool	Crocker, Rowland R.	25-248
	16 Jan 1826	Liverpool	Crocker, Rawland	26-029
	1 May 1827	Liverpool	Maxwell, George	27-208
	24 Aug 1827	Liverpool	Maxwell, George	27-550
	17 Dec 1827	Liverpool	Maxwell, G.	27-837
	25 Aug 1828	Liverpool	Maxwell, George	28-463
	19 Jan 1829	Liverpool	Maxwell, Geo.	29-024
	19 Aug 1829	Liverpool	Maxwell, Geo.	29-226
WILLMOT	21 Jul 1820	Angurlura	Hathaway, Wm.	20-134
WILMOT (see Willmot)				
	14 Mar 1820	Kotterdam	Hathaway, Wm.	20-057

SHIP	DATE OF ARRIVAL	PORT OF EMBARKATION	CAPTAIN	YEAR AND SHIP NUMBER
WILSON	25 Sep 1820	St. Ubes	Cone, Vincent	20-263
	22 Apr 1822	Dublin	Britton, Thos.	22-144
	28 Aug 1822	Dublin	Britton, Thos.	22-431
	10 Apr 1823	Dublin	Britton, Thomas	23-122
	2 Sep 1823	Dublin	Britton, Thomas	23-441
	26 Feb 1824	Dublin	Britton, Thos.	24-058
	22 Jun 1824	Dublin	Britton, Thomas	24-320
	16 Nov 1824	Dublin	Coles, Hewlett T.	24-670
	8 Jan 1825	Jamaica	King, Thomas	25-009
	16 May 1825	Dublin	Coles, Hewlett S.	25-254
	3 Jan 1826	Curacoa	Coles, Hewlitt T.	26-006
	27 Jun 1826	Dublin	Britton, James	26-363
	27 Nov 1826	Belfast	Britton, John	26-684
	21 May 1827	Sligo	Button, John	27-272
	4 Oct 1827	Sligo	Britton, John	27-676
	6 Jun 1828	Sligo	Deyton, —	28-282
	28 Nov 1828	Belfast	Britton, Alexr.	28-682
WINDHAM	7 Mar 1823	Havana	Brown, Watson	23-061
WM. & EMILINE	16 Jan 1827	Point Petre, Gaudaloupe	Burke, J. D.	27-038
WM. & HENRY	23 May 1826	Canarvon	Bates, Andrew	26-278
WM. BYRNES	30 Apr 1828	Liverpool	Hagstaff, Wm. G.	28-163
WM. HENRY	11 Mar 1826	Havana	Driscoll, James	26-099
	25 Sep 1827	Amsterdam	Atwood, James	27-658
WM. HOWLAND	30 Aug 1820	St. Petersburgh	Southworth, Andrew	20-216
WM. OSBORNE	16 Sep 1828	Havre via Portland	Blanchard, Reuben	28-539
WM. PENN	6 Feb 1822	Liverpool	Hamilton, James	22-032
	18 Sep 1827	St. Andrews	Hamor, David	27-640
	1 Sep 1828	Bremen	Hamor, David	28-492
WM. TELL	9 Jan 1827	St. Petersburg	Holdrege, John	27-010
	22 Jul 1828	Rio Grande	Bassett, T. C.	28-391
	22 Sep 1828	St. Petersburg	Holdrege, John	28-556
WM. THOMPSON	13 Sep 1823	L'pool	Crocker, R. R.	23-472
WOODROOP SIMS	19 Oct 1829	Marseilles	Anfour, James J.	29-310
WORMONTAGUS	11 Apr 1823	Turks Island	Hill, Jno. L.	23-126
WORMONTOGUS	17 May 1822	Bermuda	Hill, Jno. L.	22-204
WORROMON- TOGUS	23 Jun 1823	Bermuda	Hill, Jno. L.	23-278
WYOMING	21 Jan 1828	Antwerp	Coulon, Joseph	28-021
WYTON	12 May 1821	Liverpool	Cullinson, Richard	21-063
XENOPHON	15 Sep 1820	Amsterdam	Lord, Benjamin	20-246
	28 May 1822	Belfast	Akin, Lemuel S.	22-236
	13 Jun 1823	Belfast	Hillman, Jonathan	23-261
	2 Jun 1824	Amsterdam	Akin, Lemuel S.	24-261
	30 Oct 1824	St. Ubes	Akin, Lemuel S.	24-632
	25 Jul 1826	London	Fleming, William	26-429
	3 Oct 1829	Liverpool	Wallace, George H.	29-278
YAMACRAW	10 May 1821	Greenock	Bates, Andrew	21-059
	9 Mar 1822	Liverpool	Bates, Andrew	22-074
	4 Sep 1822	Liverpool	Bates, Andrew	22-452
	28 Jul 1823	St. Ubes	Clark, Saml.	23-363
YOBAH	26 Sep 1827	Liverpool	Walker, B.	27-665
YORK	12 Jul 1825	London	Baker, W.	25-414
	10 Dec 1825	London	Baker, Wm.	25-703
	4 Apr 1826	Liverpool	De Cost, Nash	26-147
	4 Aug 1826	Liverpool	De Cost, Nash	26-449
	6 Dec 1826	Liverpool	De Cost, Nash	26-701
	11 Apr 1827	Liverpool	De Cost, Nash	27-172
	13 Aug 1827	Liverpool	De Cost, Nash	27-513
	1 Dec 1827	Liverpool	De Cost, Nash	27-781
	31 Mar 1828	Liverpool	De Cost, Nash	28-098
	7 Aug 1828	Liverpool	De Cost, Nash	28-425
	2 Dec 1828	Liverpool	De Cost, Nash	28-689
	8 Aug 1829	Liverpool	De Cost, Nash	29-204A
YOUNG PHENIX	17 Jan 1825	London	Dunbar, Joseph	25-026
YOUNG PHOENIX	26 Jul 1824	London	Dunbar, Joseph	24-403A
YSDVA	11 Sep 1828	Havana	Forbes, C. A.	28-525

SHIP	DATE OF ARRIVAL	PORT OF EMBARKATION	CAPTAIN	YEAR AND SHIP NUMBER
ZAMOA	5 Nov 1828	Greenock	Johnson, F.	28-648
ZEPHER	20 Oct 1827	Havana	Pereira, Domingos	27-717
ZEPHYR	18 Oct 1824	Matanzas	Adams, Guy F.	24-611
	21 Feb 1825	Matanzas	Miner, Allen	25-077
	17 Mar 1825	St. Marys (Africa)	Griffon, Peter	25-118
	18 May 1825	Matanzas	Miner, Allen	25-274
	2 Oct 1826	St. Thomas	Dinzy, Joseph	26-578
ZION	7 Oct 1823	Jamaica	Hoodless, Wm.	23-526
ZIPPORAH	13 Jun 1828	St. Croix	Delesdernier, John	28-298
ZODIAC	14 Jun 1822	Liverpool	Burnes, John	22-269
	29 Oct 1822	Liverpool	Burns, John	22-545
ZWEY BRIEDER JOHANES & HENERICK	20 Mar 1820	Hamburgh & Calais	Haims, Christian	20-073

ZWEY GEBREIDER JOHANNES & HENERICH (see Zwey Brieder Johanes & Henerick)

ZWEY GEBRIDER JOHANUS & HENERICH (see Zwey Brieder Johanes & Henerick)